- 1933 - 1934 - 1935 - 1936 - 1937 - 1938 - 1939 - 1940 - 1941 - 1942 - 1943 - 1944 - 1945 - 1946 - 1947 - 1948
- 1950 - 1898 - 1899 - 1900 - 1901 - 1902 - 1903 - 1904 - 1905 - 1906 - 1907 - 1908 - 1909 - 1910 - 1911 - 1912
- 1914 - 1915 - 1916 - 1917 - 1918 - 1919 - 1920 - 1921 - 1922 - 1923 - 1924 - 1925 - 1926 - 1927 - 1928 - 1929
- 1931 - 1932 - 1933 - 1934 - 1935 - 1936 - 1937 - 1938 - 1939 - 1940 - 1941 - 1942 - 1943 - 1944 - 1945 - 1946
- 1948 - 1949 - 1950 - 1898 - 1899 - 1900 - 1901 - 1902 - 1903 - 1904 - 1905 - 1906 - 1907 - 1908 - 1909 - 1910
- 1912 - 1913 - 1914 - 1915 - 1916 - 1917 - 1918 - 1919 - 1920 - 1921 - 1922 - 1923 - 1924 - 1925 - 1926 - 1927
- 1929 - 1930 - 1931 - 1932 - 1933 - 1934 - 1935 - 1936 - 1937 - 1938 - 1939 - 1940 - 1941 - 1942 - 1943 - 1944
- 1946 - 1947 - 1948 - 1949 - 1950 - 1898 - 1899 - 1900 - 1901 - 1902 - 1903 - 1904 - 1905 - 1906 - 1907 - 1908
- 1910 - 1911 - 1912 - 1913 - 1914 - 1915 - 1916 - 1917 - 1918 - 1919 - 1920 - 1921 - 1922 - 1923 - 1924 - 1925
- 1927 - 1928 - 1929 - 1930 - 1931 - 1932 - 1933 - 1934 - 1935 - 1936 - 1937 - 1938 - 1939 - 1940 - 1941 - 1942
- 1944 - 1945 - 1946 - 1947 - 1948 - 1949 - 1950 - 1898 - 1899 - 1900 - 1901 - 1902 - 1903 - 1904 - 1905 - 1906
- 1908 - 1909 - 1910 - 1911 - 1912 - 1913 - 1914 - 1915 - 1916 - 1917 - 1918 - 1919 - 1920 - 1921 - 1922 - 1923
- 1925 - 1926 - 1927 - 1928 - 1929 - 1930 - 1931 - 1932 - 1933 - 1934 - 1935 - 1936 - 1937 - 1938 - 1939 - 1940
- 1942 - 1943 - 1944 - 1945 - 1946 - 1947 - 1948 - 1949 - 1950 - 1898 - 1899 - 1900 - 1901 - 1902 - 1903 - 1904
- 1906 - 1907 - 1908 - 1909 - 1910 - 1911 - 1912 - 1913 - 1914 - 1915 - 1916 - 1917 - 1918 - 1919 - 1920 - 1921
- 1923 - 1924 - 1925 - 1926 - 1927 - 1928 - 1929 - 1930 - 1931 - 1932 - 1933 - 1934 - 1935 - 1936 - 1937 - 1938
- 1940 - 1941 - 1942 - 1943 - 1944 - 1945 - 1946 - 1947 - 1948 - 1949 - 1950 - 1898 - 1899 - 1900 - 1901 - 1902
- 1904 - 1905 - 1906 - 1907 - 1908 - 1909 - 1910 - 1911 - 1912 - 1913 - 1914 - 1915 - 1916 - 1917 - 1918 - 1919
- 1921 - 1922 - 1923 - 1924 - 1925 - 1926 - 1927 - 1928 - 1929 - 1930 - 1931 - 1932 - 1933 - 1934 - 1935 - 1936
- 1938 - 1939 - 1940 - 1941 - 1942 - 1943 - 1944 - 1945 - 1946 - 1947 - 1948 - 1949 - 1950 - 1898 - 1899 - 1900
- 1902 - 1903 - 1904 - 1905 - 1906 - 1907 - 1908 - 1909 - 1910 - 1911 - 1912 - 1913 - 1914 - 1915 - 1916 - 1917
- 1919 - 1920 - 1921 - 1922 - 1923 - 1924 - 1925 - 1926 - 1927 - 1928 - 1929 - 1930 - 1931 - 1932 - 1933 - 1934
- 1936 - 1937 - 1938 - 1939 - 1940 - 1941 - 1942 - 1943 - 1944 - 1945 - 1946 - 1947 - 1948 - 1949 - 1950 - 1898
- 1900 - 1901 - 1902 - 1903 - 1904 - 1905 - 1906 - 1907 - 1908 - 1909 - 1910 - 1911 - 1912 - 1913 - 1914 - 1915
- 1917 - 1918 - 1919 - 1920 - 1921 - 1922 - 1923 - 1924 - 1925 - 1926 - 1927 - 1928 - 1929 - 1930 - 1931 - 1932
- 1934 - 1935 - 1936 - 1937 - 1938 - 1939 - 1940 - 1941 - 1942 - 1943 - 1944 - 1945 - 1946 - 1947 - 1948 - 1949
- 1898 - 1899 - 1900 - 1901 - 1902 - 1903 - 1904 - 1905 - 1906 - 1907 - 1908 - 1909 - 1910 - 1911 - 1912 - 1913
- 1915 - 1916 - 1917 - 1918 - 1919 - 1920 - 1921 - 1922 - 1923 - 1924 - 1925 - 1926 - 1927 - 1928 - 1929 - 1930
- 1932 - 1933 - 1934 - 1935 - 1936 - 1937 - 1938 - 1939 - 1940 - 1941 - 1942 - 1943 - 1944 - 1945 - 1946 - 1947
- 1949 - 1950 - 1898 - 1899 - 1900 - 1901 - 1902 - 1903 - 1904 - 1905 - 1906 - 1907 - 1908 - 1909 - 1910 - 1911
- 1913 - 1914 - 1915 - 1916 - 1917 - 1918 - 1919 - 1920 - 1921 - 1922 - 1923 - 1924 - 1925 - 1926 - 1927 - 1928
- 1930 - 1931 - 1932 - 1933 - 1934 - 1935 - 1936 - 1937 - 1938 - 1939 - 1940 - 1941 - 1942 - 1943 - 1944 - 1945
- 1947 - 1948 - 1949 - 1950 - 1898 - 1899 - 1900 - 1901 - 1902 - 1903 - 1904 - 1905 - 1906 - 1907 - 1908 - 1909
- 1911 - 1912 - 1913 - 1914 - 1915 - 1916 - 1917 - 1918 - 1919 - 1920 - 1921 - 1922 - 1923 - 1924 - 1925 - 1926
- 1928 - 1929 - 1930 - 1931 - 1932 - 1933 - 1934 - 1935 - 1936 - 1937 - 1938 - 1939 - 1940 - 1941 - 1942 - 1943
- 1945 - 1946 - 1947 - 1948 - 1949 - 1950 - 1898 - 1899 - 1900 - 1901 - 1902 - 1903 - 1904 - 1905 - 1906 - 1907
- 1909 - 1910 - 1911 - 1912 - 1913 - 1914 - 1915 - 1916 - 1917 - 1918 - 1919 - 1920 - 1921 - 1922 - 1923 - 1924
- 1926 - 1927 - 1928 - 1929 - 1930 - 1931 - 1932 - 1933 - 1934 - 1935 - 1936 - 1937 - 1938 - 1939 - 1940 - 1941
- 1943 - 1944 - 1945 - 1946 - 1947 - 1948 - 1949 - 1950 - 1898 - 1899 - 1900 - 1901 - 1902 - 1903 - 1904 - 1905
- 1907 - 1908 - 1909 - 1910 - 1911 - 1912 - 1913 - 1914 - 1915 - 1916 - 1917 - 1918 - 1919 - 1920 - 1921 - 1922
- 1924 - 1925 - 1926 - 1927 - 1928 - 1929 - 1930 - 1931 - 1932 - 1933 - 1934 - 1935 - 1936 - 1937 - 1938 - 1939
- 1941 - 1942 - 1943 - 1944 - 1945 - 1946 - 1947 - 1948 - 1949 - 1950 - 1898 - 1899 - 1900 - 1901 - 1902 - 1903
- 1905 - 1906 - 1907 - 1908 - 1909 - 1910 - 1911 - 1912 - 1913 - 1914 - 1915 - 1916 - 1917 - 1918 - 1919 - 1920
- 1922 - 1923 - 1924 - 1925 - 1926 - 1927 - 1928 - 1929 - 1930 - 1931 - 1932 - 1933 - 1934 - 1935 - 1936 - 1937
- 1939 - 1940 - 1941 - 1942 - 1943 - 1944 - 1945 - 1946 - 1947 - 1948 - 1949 - 1950 - 1898 - 1899 - 1900 - 1901
- 1903 - 1904 - 1905 - 1906 - 1907 - 1908 - 1909 - 1910 - 1911 - 1912 - 1913 - 1914 - 1915 - 1916 - 1917 - 1918
- 1920 - 1921 - 1922 - 1923 - 1924 - 1925 - 1926 - 1927 - 1928 - 1929 - 1930 - 1931 - 1932 - 1933 - 1934 - 1935
- 1937 - 1938 - 1939 - 1940 - 1941 - 1942 - 1943 - 1944 - 1945 - 1946 - 1947 - 1948 - 1949 - 1950 - 1898 - 1899
- 1901 - 1902 - 1903 - 1904 - 1905 - 1906 - 1907 - 1908 - 1909 - 1910 - 1911 - 1912 - 1913 - 1914 - 1915 - 1916
- 1918 - 1919 - 1920 - 1921 - 1922 - 1923 - 1924 - 1925 - 1926 - 1927 - 1928 - 1929 - 1930 - 1931 - 1932 - 1933
- 1935 - 1936 - 1937 - 1938 - 1939 - 1940 - 1941 - 1942 - 1943 - 1944 - 1945 - 1946 - 1947 - 1948 - 1949 - 1950
- 1899 - 1900 - 1901 - 1902 - 1903 - 1904 - 1905 - 1906 - 1907 - 1908 - 1909 - 1910 - 1911 - 1912 - 1913 - 1914
- 1916 - 1917 - 1918 - 1919 - 1920 - 1921 - 1922 - 1923 - 1924 - 1925 - 1926 - 1927 - 1928 - 1929 - 1930 - 1931
- 1933 - 1934 - 1935 - 1936 - 1937 - 1938 - 1939 - 1940 - 1941 - 1942 - 1943 - 1944 - 1945 - 1946 - 1947 - 1948
- 1950 - 1898 - 1899 - 1900 - 1901 - 1902 - 1903 - 1904 - 1905 - 1906 - 1907 - 1908 - 1909 - 1910 - 1911 - 1912
- 1914 - 1915 - 1916 - 1917 - 1918 - 1919 - 1920 - 1921 - 1922 - 1923 - 1924 - 1925 - 1926 - 1927 - 1928 - 1929
- 1931 - 1932 - 1933 - 1934 - 1935 - 1936 - 1937 - 1938 - 1939 - 1940 - 1941 - 1942 - 1943 - 1944 - 1945 - 1946
- 1948 - 1949 - 1950 - 1898 - 1899 - 1900 - 1901 - 1902 - 1903 - 1904 - 1905 - 1906 - 1907 - 1908 - 1909 - 1910
- 1912 - 1913 - 1914 - 1915 - 1916 - 1917 - 1918 - 1919 - 1920 - 1921 - 1922 - 1923 - 1924 - 1925 - 1926 - 1927
- 1929 - 1930 - 1931 - 1932 - 1933 - 1934 - 1935 - 1936 - 1937 - 1938 - 1939 - 1940 - 1941 - 1942 - 1943 - 1944
- 1946 - 1947 - 1948 - 1949 - 1950 - 1898 - 1899 - 1900 - 1901 - 1902 - 1903 - 1904 - 1905 - 1906 - 1907 - 1908
- 1910 - 1911 - 1912 - 1913 - 1914 - 1915 - 1916 - 1917 - 1918 - 1919 - 1920 - 1921 - 1922 - 1923 - 1924 - 1925
- 1927 - 1928 - 1929 - 1930 - 1931 - 1932 - 1933 - 1934 - 1935 - 1936 - 1937 - 1941 - 1942
- 1944 - 1945 - 1946 - 1947 - 1948 - 1949 - 1950 - 1898 - 1899 - 1900 - 1905 - 1906
- 1908 - 1909 - 1910 - 1911 - 1912 - 1913 - 1914 - 1915 - 1916 - 1917 - 1922 - 1923
- 1925 - 1926 - 1927 - 1928 - 1929 - 1930 - 1931 - 1932 - 1933 - 1934 - 1939 - 1940
- 1942 - 1943 - 1944 - 1945 - 1946 - 1947 - 1948 - 1949 - 1950 - 1898 - 1903 - 1904
- 1906 - 1907 - 1908 - 1909 - 1910 - 1911 - 1912 - 1913 - 1914 - 1915 - 1920 - 1921
- 1923 - 1924 - 1925 - 1926 - 1927 - 1928 - 1929 - 1930 - 1931 - 1932 - 1937 - 1938
- 1940 - 1941 - 1942 - 1943 - 1944 - 1945 - 1946 - 1947 - 1948 - 1949 - 1901 - 1902
- 1904 - 1905 - 1906 - 1907 - 1908 - 1909 - 1910 - 1911 - 1912 - 1913 - 1914 - 1917 - 1918 - 1919
- 1921 - 1922 - 1923 - 1924 - 1925 - 1926 - 1927 - 1928 - 1929 - 1930 - 1931 - 1932 - 1933 - 1934 - 1935 - 1936
- 1938 - 1939 - 1940 - 1941 - 1942 - 1943 - 1944 - 1945 - 1946 - 1947 - 1948 - 1949 - 1950 - 1898 - 1899

WHO WAS WHO
IN AMERICA

A COMPANION VOLUME TO
WHO'S WHO IN AMERICA

Vol. 1

1897-1942

Biographies of the Non-Living with
Dates of Deaths Appended

A Third Printing

CHICAGO, U. S. A.

THE A. N. MARQUIS COMPANY

1943

THE NEW COMPANION VOLUME TO
WHO'S WHO IN AMERICA

The 25,000 biographies removed, because of deaths of biographees, from the 21 volumes of WHO'S WHO IN AMERICA published since its founding, in 1897, until—and including—the 1940-41 biennial volume, are contained—with dates of deaths appended—in this first issuance of its new companion book, WHO WAS WHO IN AMERICA.

A primary advantage which results is the increased facility with which sketches of deceased biographees can now be located. Unless the year of death happened to be at hand, this has usually required volume-by-volume inspection of back issues of "Who's Who" until the biography last published was located. Now, the biography is ready to hand in WHO WAS WHO IN AMERICA.

Of equal practical value is the saving in space which results, particularly when preferred library shelving, for which there is insistent demand, is involved. WHO WAS WHO IN AMERICA and the volume of WHO'S WHO IN AMERICA current at its initial issuance (Volume 22, 1942-43) are equivalent to 22 volumes, or over six feet of shelving. And thereafter only the volumes of WHO'S WHO IN AMERICA issued biennially until the second issuance of WHO WAS WHO IN AMERICA (probably about a decade hence, in 1953) will be required to maintain this complete Civil-War-to-date coverage of American biography.

Perhaps as important as these purely utilitarian advantages are the unique characteristics which WHO WAS WHO IN AMERICA legitimately inherits from WHO'S WHO IN AMERICA itself, and which therefore will be found in no other biographical dictionary.

The sketches, for example, have not only been prepared from information originally supplied by the biographees themselves, but have been approved personally—and frequently revised—before publication in a "Who's Who" during the subject's lifetime. As a result many contain personal data—in some instances quaint details—not readily available elsewhere. The preface to the first volume of WHO'S WHO IN AMERICA selected this fact as one of that volume's outstanding characteristics, and stated: "The book is autobiographical, the data having been obtained from first hands." It follows that WHO WAS WHO IN AMERICA is uniquely autobiographical, and therefore probably alone among American biographical dictionaries. And although condensed to the concise style which "Who's Who" has made famous, the sketches contain all essential facts.

The result is far more than a biographical dictionary of 25,000 non-living American notables from the Civil War period to today within the covers of a single volume. It is as well a vital portion of American history, written in the lives of those who made this history, as the subjects themselves recorded the details.

It is this distinguishing characteristic which qualifies WHO WAS WHO IN AMERICA as a new and exceptional reference volume, essential to many—students, journalists, business executives, lecturers, public officials, editors, writers, educators—and of daily usefulness in the home, particularly now that war-brought events make a comprehensive but convenient American biographical compilation a "must" in order to keep abreast.

An interesting instance of the timely usefulness of WHO WAS WHO IN AMERICA is to be found in Clare Boothe's vivid introduction to *The Valor of Ignorance* (republished, 1942, Harper & Brothers) by Homer Lea, who 33 years ago warned the United States of Japan's intentions and showed the course her aggression would take. Miss Boothe writes: "I returned to the library. No, there was no biography. No, he was not in the 1941 *Encyclopedia Britannica.* I sought 'Who's Who' for 1912, the year his last book was published. He was there: 'Lea, Homer, author, soldier; b. Denver, Nov. 17, 1876. . . .' And with this as a clue to other clues . . . I finally came upon one of the strangest, most adventurous and significant stories that America ever knew—and had ever forgotten . . ."

Of course, had WHO WAS WHO IN AMERICA already been issued, Miss Boothe's key "clue to other clues" would have been at her finger tips, along with thousands of easy-to-use references to significant non-living Americans whose lives, like Homer Lea's, reflect in today's events. For instance, only two of the ten presidents of the United States whose biographies have been published in "Who's Who" are currently sketched in it. The sketches of the other eight of course appear in WHO WAS WHO IN AMERICA.

That WHO WAS WHO IN AMERICA is to serve an urgent reference need is assured by the many encouraging comments received from those to whom its publication was first announced. The following are typical: A journalist—"Your idea of a WHO WAS WHO IN AMERICA is an excellent one"; an historian—"The idea is fine; the 'WAS' volume will be a great convenience"; an editor—

"This is a fine idea!"; a writer—"This will be a most valuable reference book"; a business executive—"Sounds very practical"; a publisher—"I think it is a very worthwhile undertaking—by all means I want it"; a lecturer—"To my mind this fills a long-felt want"; a librarian—"WHO WAS WHO IN AMERICA is a fine idea"; a public official —"It is worth more than you charge"; a manufacturer—"I have given away many older volumes of 'Who's Who' and several times have been at a loss to get the information that I wanted. Whoever thought of this idea should have a medal."

WHO WAS WHO IN AMERICA is not only a companion volume to WHO'S WHO IN AMERICA, but in reality a supplement.* For supplemented by it, the current editions of WHO'S WHO IN AMERICA provide over 55,000 significant biographies and three-quarters-of-a-century coverage of *both living and deceased* biographees of current and reoccurring general interest. Moreover, the "Monthly Supplement to Who's Who"—*The Current Bio-*

* Except for certain revisions, the biographies in *Who Was Who in America* are purposely exactly as last published in *Who's Who in America*, even in respect to tense.

graphical Reference Service—now amplifies both volumes, and itself offers over 8,000 "in-the-news" names in the course of a typical biennium. The three publications provide a biographical reference service that is unique—reaching back 75 years and up to "last night."

This rounding out, through the publication of WHO WAS WHO IN AMERICA, of the undertaking which the first A. N. Marquis biographical compilations initiated nearly a half-century ago, recalls two sentences from the preface to Volume I of WHO'S WHO IN AMERICA which by direct inheritance become descriptive also of this volume:

"Without claiming infallibility or inerrancy, it is believed that this publication will be a welcome addition to the list of handy helps that make up the library of indispensable books. Certainly nothing has been omitted that painstaking care, persistent effort, or expenditure of money could supply toward making the volume fully fill the purposes of its compilation."

THE EDITORS.

Chicago, February 11, 1943.

PREFACE TO THE LIBRARY EDITION

The first edition of WHO WAS WHO IN AMERICA having been exhausted in a matter of months, a Library Edition was decided upon, to be printed on paper providing the unusual compactness desirable for a reference work, and to be bound in buckram with careful consideration given to obtaining exceptional sturdiness suitable for constant reference usage. This volume is the result of these plans. The paper utilized provides not only the compactness desired because of the technical reasons mentioned, but as well responds to the wartime need for conservation of paper tonnage—not only in this vital respect, but in others less obvious, the wartime obligation to conserve critical materials has been observed.

In order to make them conveniently and permanently available to reference users of the Marquis compilations, indices to non-current WHO'S WHO sketches and to the sketches in the "Monthly Supplement to WHO'S WHO" (through February of 1942) which have not been published elsewhere, are here added to the content of the first edition. Since these indices were still available in type standing from the current volume of WHO'S WHO. no additional metal was, therefore, required, and it was felt that the reference-usefulness involved justified utilizing the opportunity of making them

available in a volume of an exceptionally permanent reference status.

As would naturally be inferred from the urgency of the demand for the first edition of WHO WAS WHO IN AMERICA, the volume has already established itself as an indispensable reference work, and is in fact in that respect, as well as in its publishers' original concept, the companion volume to WHO'S WHO IN AMERICA.

As was also to be expected—in view of the prepublication commendation mentioned above in the original preface—the publishers have since its actual publication received a steady flow of favorable, even enthusiastic, comment regarding WHO WAS WHO IN AMERICA.

Taking space to more than mention these comments is not justified under the wartime obligation to restrict the use of materials to essentialities, although citing only typical ones would demonstrate that WHO WAS WHO IN AMERICA is already serving important reference needs, many of wartime usefulness, in a surprising number of instances. However, a selection has been made from these comments, and a copy will be sent to those interested, on request to the undersigned.

THE EDITORS.

Chicago, November 15, 1943.

CONTENTS

Preface, First Edition iii

Preface, Library Edition iv

Abbreviations vii

Corrigenda x

Biographies 1

NOTICE

The initial compilations for WHO'S WHO IN AMERICA were under way in 1897. Continuously since their first issuance, these compilations have been thoroughly revised and brought down. Issuance is biennially; the latest (Vol. 26) edition of WHO'S WHO IN AMERICA being in the process of publication. The interval separating the biennial volumes is now served by the "Monthly Supplement."

WHO'S WHO IN AMERICA endeavors to supply a brief, crisp personal sketch of every living American whose position or achievements make his personality of general interest; to provide just the facts every intelligent person wants to know about those who are outstanding in every reputable walk of life. Since the selected biographees themselves supply the necessary information and have the opportunity of revising it before publication, these sketches may be considered condensed autobiographies.

Being a compilation of living men and women in whom there is general interest, necessarily each revision of WHO'S WHO IN AMERICA adds biographies of those coming into the public eye and drops the biographies of those who have died. Therefore considerable searching—unless the date of death and all the earlier volumes are at hand—has heretofore been required to locate the last-published sketch of a deceased biographee.

WHO WAS WHO IN AMERICA saves time by obviating the necessity for such a search, for it contains the last-published sketches of biographees who have died previous to its publication, with ascertained dates of death appended. It also saves valuable space, as non-current editions of WHO'S WHO IN AMERICA need not be consulted. Hence its place as an appropriate companion volume to WHO'S WHO IN AMERICA, totally aside from its general usefulness as an unusual biographical—perhaps more accurately, an autobiographical—dictionary of those who have been most outstandingly significant in the making of post-Civil-War America. WHO WAS WHO IN AMERICA is compiled approximately on a "decade issuance" schedule as about ten-year intervals have been found most suitable for providing ready-for-reference sketches of biographees dropped from WHO'S WHO IN AMERICA because of death. Volume II of WHO WAS WHO IN AMERICA is now in compilation.

In no other biographical reference work will there be found the biographies published in the companion volumes, WHO'S WHO IN AMERICA and WHO WAS WHO IN AMERICA.

THE THIRD PRINTING (1950), VOL. 1 (1897-1942)
containing 1408 pages and 27,458 biographies

THE A. N. MARQUIS COMPANY

Marquis Publications Building   Chicago–11 U. S. A.

ABBREVIATIONS

The following abbreviations are frequently used in this book:

A.A.................Degree of Associate of Arts.
A.A.A..............Agricultural Adjustment Administration.
a.a.g..............asst. adjutant general.
A.A.A.S............American Association for the Advancement of Science.
A. and M..........Agricultural and Mechanical.
A.A.O.N.M.S........Ancient Arabic Order of the Nobles of the Mystic Shrine (Masonic).
A.A.S.R............Ancient Accepted Scottish Rite (Masonic).
A.B. (also B.A.)....Bachelor of Arts.
A.B.C.F.M..........American Board of Commissioners for Foreign Missions (Congregational).
abt................about.
A.C................Air Corps.
acad...............academy; academic.
A.C.P..............American College of Physicians.
A.C.S..............American College of Surgeons
actg...............acting.
a.d.c..............aide-de-camp.
add................additional.
adj................adjutant; adjunct.
adj. gen...........adjutant general.
adm................admiral.
adminstr...........administrator.
adminstrn..........administration.
adv................advocate; advisory.
advt...............advertising.
A.E................Agricultural Engineer.
A.E. and P.........Ambassador Extraordinary and Plenipotentiary.
A.E.F..............American Expeditionary Forces.
A.F. and A.M.......Ancient Free and Accepted Masons.
A.F.D..............Doctor of Fine Arts.
A.F. of L..........American Federation of Labor.
agr................agriculture.
agrl...............agricultural.
agt................agent.
a.i................*ad interim.*
A.I.A..............American Institute of Architects.
Ala................Alabama.
A.L.A..............American Library Association.
Am.................American, America.
A.M. (also M.A.)....Master of Arts.
A.M.A..............American Medical Association.
A.M.E..............African Methodist Episcopal.
Am. Inst. E.E......American Institute of Electrical Engineers.
Am. Soc. C.E.......American Society of Civil Engineers.
Am. Soc. M.E.......American Society of Mechanical Engineers.
A.N.A..............Associate National Academician.
anat...............anatomical.
ann................annual.
anthrop............anthropological.
antiq..............antiquarian.
A.O.H..............Ancient Order of Hibernians.
appmnt.............appointment.
apptd..............appointed.
apt................apartment.
a.q.m..............asst. quartermaster.
A.R.C..............Am. Red Cross.
archeol............archeological
archtl.............architectural.
Ariz...............Arizona.
Ark................Arkansas.
arty...............artillery.
A.S................Air Service.
assn...............association.
asso...............associate; associated.
asst...............assistant.

astron.............astronomical.
astrophys..........astrophysical.
atty...............attorney.
Aug................August.
av.................avenue.

b..................born.
B..................Bachelor.
B.A. (also A.B.)....Bachelor of Arts.
B.A.A.S............British Assn. for the Advancement of Science.
B.Agr..............Bachelor of Agriculture.
Bapt...............Baptist.
B.Arch.............Bachelor of Architecture.
batn., batln., batt. or bn........battalion.
B.B.A..............Bachelor of Business Administration.
B.C................British Columbia.
B.C.E..............Bachelor of Civil Engineering.
B.Chir.............Bachelor of Surgery.
B.C.L..............Bachelor of Civil Law.
B.C.S..............Bachelor of Commercial Science.
bd.................board.
B.D................Bachelor of Divinity.
B.Di...............Bachelor of Didactics.
B.E................Bachelor of Education.
B.E.F..............British Expeditionary Force.
bet................between.
B.F.A..............Bachelor of Fine Arts.
bibl...............biblical.
bibliog............bibliographical.
biog...............biographical.
biol...............biological.
B.J................Bachelor of Journalism.
B.L. (or Litt.B.)....Bachelor of Letters.
bldg...............building.
blk................block.
B.L.S..............Bachelor of Library Science.
bn.................battalion.
B.O................Bachelor of Oratory.
bot................botanical.
boul. (also blvd.)....boulevard.
B.P................Bachelor of Painting.
B.P.E..............Bachelor Physical Education.
B.P.O.E............Benevolent and Protective Order of Elks.
B.Pd. (or Pd.B.)....Bachelor of Pedagogy.
B.Py...............Bachelor of Pedagogy.
br.................branch.
brig...............brigadier; brigade.
brig.gen...........brigadier general.
Brit...............British; Britannica.
bro................brother.
B.S. (also S.B. or Sc.B.) Bachelor of Science.
B.S. in Ry. M.E.....Bachelor in Railway Mechanical Engineering.
B.S.A..............Bachelor of Agricultural Science.
B.S.D..............Bachelor of Didactic Science.
B.Th...............Bachelor of Theology.
bull...............bulletin.
bur................bureau.
bus................business.
B.W.I..............British West Indies.

C.A................Central America.
C.A.C..............Coast Artillery Corps.
Cal. (or Calif.)....California.
Can................Canada.
Cantab.............of or pertaining to Cambridge University, Eng.
capt...............captain.
Cath...............Catholic.
cav................cavalry.
C.E................Civil Engineer; Chemical Engineer.
C.E.F..............Canadian Expeditionary Forces.

ch.................church.
Ch.D...............Doctor of Chemistry.
chem...............chemical.
Chem.E.............Chemical Engineer.
Chirurg............Chirurgical.
chmn...............chairman.
C.I.O..............Congress of Industrial Organizations.
civ................civil.
climatol...........climatological.
clin...............clinical.
clk................clerk.
C.L.S.C............Chautauqua Literary and Scientific Circle.
C.M................Master in Surgery.
co.................company; county.
C. of C............Chamber of Commerce.
C.O.F..............Catholic Order of Foresters.
col................colonel.
coll...............college.
Colo...............Colorado.
com................committee.
comd...............commanded.
comdg..............commanding.
comdr..............commander.
comdt..............commandant.
commd..............commissioned.
comml..............commercial.
commn..............commission.
commr..............commissioner.
Com. Sub...........Commissary of Subsistence.
con................consol'dated.
condr..............conductor.
conf...............conference.
Confed.............Confederate.
Congl..............Congregational; Congressional.
Conglist...........Congregationalist.
Conn...............Connecticut.
cons...............consulting.
consol. (or con.)....consolidated.
constl.............constitutional.
constn.............constitution.
constrn............construction.
contbd.............contributed.
contbg.............contributing.
contbns............contributions.
contbr.............contributor.
conv...............convention.
coöp; co-op........coöperative.
corpl..............corporal.
corp...............corporation.
corr...............correspondent; corresponding; correspondence.
cos................companies; counties.
C.P.A..............Certified Public Accountant.
C.P.H..............Certificate of Public Health.
C.S................Christian Science.
C.S. Army..........Confederate States Army.
C.S.B..............Bachelor of Christian Science.
C.S.D..............Doctor of Christian Science.
C.S.N..............Confederate States Navy.
ct.................court.
C.T................Candidate in Theology.
C.W.S..............Chemical Warfare Service.
cyclo..............cyclopedia.

d..................daughter.
D.Agr..............Doctor of Agriculture.
D.A.R..............Daughters of the American Revolution.
D.C................District of Columbia.
D.C.L..............Doctor of Civil Law.
D.C.S..............Doctor of Commercial Science.
D.D................Doctor of Divinity.
D.D.S..............Doctor of Dental Surgery.
dec................deceased.
Dec................December.
deg................degree.

Del.................Delaware; delegate.
Dem.................Democratic.
D.Eng. (also Dr.
  Engring., or E.D.).Doctor of Engineering.
denom..............denominational.
dep................deputy.
dept...............department.
dermatol...........dermatological.
desc...............descendant.
D.H.L..............Doctor of Hebrew Literature.
dir................director.
disch..............discharged.
dist...............district.
distbg.............distributing.
distbn.............distribution.
distbr.............distributor.
div................division; divinity.
D.Litt. (also L.H.D.).Doctor of Literature.
D.M.D..............Doctor of Medical Dentistry.
D.O................Doctor of Osteopathy.
D.P.H. (also Dr.P.H.).Diploma in Public Health or
                   Doctor of Public Health or
                   Doctor of Public Hygiene.
Dr.................Doctor.
D.R................Daughters of the Revolution.
D.R.E..............Doctor of Religious Ed-
                   ucation.
D.Sc. (or Sc.D.)...Doctor of Science.
D.S.C..............Distinguished Service Cross.
D.S.M..............Distinguished Service Medal.
D.S.T..............Doctor of Sacred Theology.
D.T.M..............Doctor of Tropical Medicine.
D.V.M..............Doctor of Veterinary Medi-
                   cine.
D.V.S..............Doctor of Veterinary Surgery

E..................East.
E. and P...........Extraordinary and Pleni-
                   potentiary.
eccles.............ecclesiastical.
ecol...............ecological.
econ...............economic.
ed.................educated.
E.D. (also D.Eng.,
  or Dr. Engring.)..Doctor of Engineering.
Ed.B...............Bachelor of Education.
Ed.D...............Doctor of Education.
edit...............edition.
Ed.M...............Master of Education.
edn................education.
ednl...............educational.
E.E................Electrical Engineer.
E.E. and M.P.......Envoy Extraordinary and
                   Minister Plenipotentiary.
Egyptol............Egyptological.
elec...............electrical.
electrochem........electrochemical.
electrophys........electrophysical.
E.M................Engineer of Mines.
ency...............encyclopedia.
Eng................England.
engr...............engineer.
engring............engineering.
engrs..............engineers.
entomol............entomological.
e.s................eldest son.
ethnol.............ethnological.
evang..............evangelical.
exam...............examination; examining.
exec...............executive.
exhbn..............exhibition.
expdn..............expedition.
expn...............exposition.
expt...............experiment.
exptl..............experimental.

F..................Fellow.
F.A................Field Artillery.
F.A.C.P............Fellow American College of
                   Physicians.
F.A.C.S............Fellow American College of
                   Surgeons.
F.E................Forest Engineer.
Feb................February.
fed................federal.
Fedn...............Federation.
Fgn................Foreign.
Fla................Florida.
frat...............fraternity.
F.R.C.P............Fellow Royal College of Phy-
                   sicians (England).
F.R.C.S............Fellow Royal College of Sur-
                   geons (England).

frt................freight.
Ft.................Fort.

G.-1 (or other number).General Staff Officer No.....
Ga.................Georgia.
G.A.R..............Grand Army of the Republic.
G.D................Graduate in Divinity.
g.d................granddaughter.
gen................general.
geneal.............genealogical.
geod...............geodetic.
geog...............geographical; geographic.
geol...............geological.
geophys............geophysical.
g.g.d..............great granddaughter.
g.g.s..............great grandson.
G.H.Q..............General Headquarters.
gov................governor.
govt...............government.
grad...............graduated; graduate.
g.s................grandson.
Gt.................Great.
gynecol............gynecological.

Hdqrs..............headquarters.
H.G................Home Guard.
H.I................Hawaiian Islands.
hist...............historical.
H.M................Master of Humanics.
homeo..............homeopathic.
homœ...............homœopathic.
hon................honorary; honorable; honor-
                   ably.
Ho. of Reps........House of Representatives.
hort...............horticultural.
hosp...............hospital.
Hts................Heights.
H.Ty. (or H.T.)....Hawaiian Territory,
hydrog.............hydrographic.

Ia.................Iowa.
Ida................Idaho.
Ill................Illinois.
illus..............illustrated.
inc................incorporated.
Ind................Indiana; Independent.
indsl..............industrial.
inf................infantry.
ins................insurance.
insp...............inspector.
insp. gen..........inspector general.
inst...............institute.
instn..............institution.
instr..............instructor.
instrn.............instruction.
internat...........international.
intro..............introduction.
I.O.B.B............Independent Order of B'nai
                   B'rith.
I.O.G.T............Independent Order of Good
                   Templars
I.O.O.F............Independent Order of Odd
                   Fellows.

Jan................January.
J.B................Jurum Baccalaureus.
J.C.B..............Juris Canonici Bachelor.
J.C.L..............Juris Canonici Lector.
J.D................Doctor of Jurisprudence.
j.g. (or jr.g.)....junior grade.
jour...............journal.
jr.................junior.
J.S.D..............Doctor of Juristic Science.
jud................judicial.
J.U.D..............Juris Utriusque Doctor: Doc-
                   tor of Both (Canon and
                   Civil) Laws.

Kan................Kansas.
K.C................Knight of Columbus.
K.C.C.H............Knight Commander of Court
                   of Honor.
K.P................Knight of Pythias.
K.T................Knight Templar.
Ky.................Kentucky.

La.................Louisiana.
lab................laboratory.
lang...............language.
laryngol...........laryngological.
L.H.D..............Doctor of Literature; Doctor
                   of Humanities.

L.I................Long Island.
lieut..............lieutenant.
lit................literary; literature.
Lit.Hum............Literae Humanores (classics
                   Oxford Univ., Eng.).
Litt.B. (or B.L.)....Bachelor of Letters.
Litt. D............Doctor of Letters.
LL.B...............Bachelor of Laws.
LL.D...............Doctor of Laws.
LL.M. (or M.L.)....Master of Laws.
L.O.M..............Loyal Order of Moose.
L.R.C.P............Licentiate Royal Coll. Physi-
                   cians.
L.R.C.S............Licentiate Royal Coll. Sur-
                   geons.
L.S.A..............Licentiate Society of Apothe-
                   caries.
lt.................lieutenant.
lt. col............lieutenant colonel.
lt. gen............lieutenant general.
lt. gov............lieutenant governor.
ltd................limited.
Luth...............Lutheran.

m..................married.
M.A. (or A.M.).....Master of Arts.
mag................magazine.
M.Agr..............Master of Agriculture.
maj................major.
maj. gen...........major general.
Mass...............Massachusetts.
math...............mathematical.
M.B................Bachelor of Medicine.
M.B.A..............Master of Business Adminis-
                   tration.
M.C................Medical Corps.
M.C.S..............Master of Commercial
                   Science.
mcht...............merchant.
Md.................Maryland.
M.D................Doctor of Medicine.
M.Di...............Master of Didactics.
M.Dip..............Master in Diplomacy.
mdse...............merchandise
Me.................Maine.
M.E................Mechanical Engineer; Meth-
                   odist Episcopal.
mech...............mechanical.
M.E. Ch............Methodist Episcopal Church.
med................medical.
Med. O.R.C.........Medical Officers' Reserve
                   Corps.
Med. R.C...........Medical Reserve Corps.
M.E.E..............Master of Electrical Engineer-
                   ing.
mem................member.
merc...............mercantile.
met................metropolitan.
metall.............metallurgical.
meteorol...........meteorological.
Meth...............Methodist.
metrol.............metrological.
M.F................Master of Forestry.
M.F.A..............Master of Fine Arts (carries
                   title of Dr.).
mfg................manufacturing.
mfr................manufacture; manufacturer.
mfrs...............manufacturers.
mgr................manager.
M.I................Military Intelligence.
Mich...............Michigan.
micros.............microscopical.
mil................military.
mineral............mineralogical.
Minn...............Minnesota.
Miss...............Mississippi.
M.L. (or LL.M.)....Master of Laws.
M.Litt.............Master of Literature.
Mlle...............Mademoiselle (Miss).
Mme................Madame.
M.M.E..............Master of Mechanical En-
                   gineering.
mng................managing.
Mo.................Missouri.
Mont...............Montana.
M.P................Member of Parliament;
                   Methodist Protestant.
M.Pd...............Master of Pedagogy.
M.P.E..............Master of Physical Educa-
                   tion.
M.P.L..............Master of Patent Law.

M.R.C.P.............Member Royal College of Physicians.
M.R.C.S............Member Royal Coll. Surgeons.
M.R.E..............Master of Religious Education.
M.S. (or M.Sc.)....Master of Science.
M.S.F..............Master of Science of Forestry.
M.S.T..............Master of Sacred Theology.
Mt.................Mount.
mtn................mountain.
mus................museum; musical.
Mus.B..............Bachelor of Music.
Mus.D. (or Mus.Doc.)..Doctor of Music.
Mus. M.............Master of Music.
mut................mutual.
M.V.M..............Massachusetts Volunteer Militia.
M.W.A..............Modern Woodmen of America.
mycol..............mycological.

N..................North.
N.A................National Academician; North America; National Army.
N.A.D..............National Academy of Design.
nat................national.
nav................navigation.
N.B................New Brunswick.
N.C................North Carolina.
N.Dak. (or N.D.)...North Dakota.
N.E................Northeast; New England.
N.E.A..............National Education Assn.
Neb................Nebraska.
Nev................Nevada.
N.G................National Guard.
N.G.S.N.Y..........National Guard State of New York.
N.H................New Hampshire.
N.J................New Jersey.
N.M................New Mexico.

Nov................November.
N.Ph.D.............Doctor of Natural Philosophy.
nr.................near.
N.R.A..............National Recovery Administration.
N.S................Nova Scotia.
N.T................New Testament.
numis..............numismatic.
N.W................Northwest.
N.Y................New York.

O..................Ohio.
obs................observatory.
obstet.............obstetrical.
Oct................October.
O.E.S..............Order of the Eastern Star.
ofcl...............official.
Okla...............Oklahoma.
Ont................Ontario.
ophthal............ophthalmological.
O.P.M..............Office of Production Management.
O.Q.-M.G...........Office of Quartermaster General.
O.R.C..............Officers' Reserve Corps.
Ore................Oregon.
orgn...............organization.
ornithol...........ornithological.
O S.B..............Order of Saint Benedict.
O.T................Old Testament.
O.T.C..............Officer's Training Camp (or Corps).
otol...............otological.
O.T.S..............Officers' Training School.
O.U.A.M............Order United American Mechanics.
Pa.................Pennsylvania.
pass...............passenger.
path...............pathological.
Pd.B. (or B.Pd.)...Bachelor of Pedagogy.
Pd.D...............Doctor of Pedagogy
Pd.M...............Master of Pedagogy.
P.E................Protestant Episcopal.
Pe.B...............Bachelor of Pediatrics.

P.E.N..............Poets, Playwrights, Editors, Essayists and Novelists (Internat. Assn.).
penol..............penological.
pharm..............pharmaceutical.
Pharm.D............Doctor of Pharmacy.
Pharm.M............Master of Pharmacy.
Ph.B...............Bachelor of Philosophy.
Ph.C...............Pharmaceutical Chemist.
Ph.D...............Doctor of Philosophy; Doctor of Pharmacy.
Ph.G...............Graduate in Pharmacy.
Phila..............Philadelphia.
philol.............philological.
philos.............philosophical.
photog.............photographic.
phys...............physician; physical.
phys. and surg.....physicians and surgeons.
physiol............physiological.
P.I................Philippine Islands.
Pl.................Place.
P.M................Paymaster.
polit..............political.
poly...............polytechnic.
pomol..............pomological.
P.Q................Province of Quebec.
P.R................Puerto Rico.
prep...............preparatory.
pres...............president.
Presb. (also Presbyn.).......Presbyterian.
presdl.............presidential.
prin...............principal.
proc...............proceedings.
prod...............produced (play production).
prodn..............production.
prof...............professor.
prog...............progressive.
propr..............proprietor.
pros. atty.........prosecuting attorney.
pro tem............pro tempore (for the time being).
psychiat...........psychiatrical; psychiatric.
psychol............psychological.
pub................public; publisher; publishing; published.
publ...............publication.
pvt................private.
Py.B...............Bachelor of Pedagogy.

q.m................quartermaster.
Q.M.C..............Quartermaster Corps.
q.m.gen............quartermaster general.
Q.M.O.R.C..........Quartermaster Officers' Reserve Corps.
quar...............quarterly.
Que................Quebec (Province).
q.v................quod vide (which see.)

R.A.M..............Royal Arch Mason.
R.C................Roman Catholic; Reserve Corps.
R.C.S..............Revenue Cutter Service.
rd.................road.
R.D................Rural Delivery.
R.E................Reformed Episcopal.
rec................recording.
ref................reformed.
regt...............regiment.
regtl..............regimental.
Rep................Republican; representative.
Res................Reserve.
ret................retired.
rev................review; revised.
Rev................Reverend.
R.F.C..............Reconstruction Finance Corp.
R.F.D..............Rural Free Delivery.
rhinol.............rhinological.
R.I................Rhode Island.
röntgenol..........röntgenological.
R.O.S.C............Reserve Officers' Sanitary Corps.
R.O.T.C............Reserve Officers' Training Corps.

R.P................Reformed Presbyterian.
R.P.D..............Rerum Politicarum Doctor (Doctor of Political Science).
r.r................railroad.
R.T.C..............Reserve Training Corps.
ry.................railway.

s..................son.
S..................South.
S.A................South America.
san................sanitary.
S.A.R..............Sons of the Am. Revolution.
S.A.T.C............Students' Army Training Corps.
savs...............savings.
S.B. (also B.S. or Sc. B.) Bachelor of Science.
S.C................South Carolina; Sanitary Corps.
Sc.D. (or D.Sc.)...Doctor of Science.
S.C.D..............Doctor of Commercial Science.
sch................school.
sci................science; scientific.
S.C.V..............Sons of Confederate Veterans.
S.Dak. (or S.D.)...South Dakota.
S.E................Southeast.
sec................secretary.
sect...............section.
seismol............seismological.
sem................seminary.
Sept...............September.
sergt..............sergeant.
S.I................Staten Island.
S.J................Society of Jesus (Jesuit)
S.J.D..............Doctor Juristic Science.
S.M................Master of Science.
soc................society.
sociol.............sociological.
S.O.S..............Service of Supply.
S. of V............Sons of Veterans.
spl................special.
splty..............specialty.
sq.................square.
sr.................senior.
S.R................Sons of the Revolution.
S.R.C..............Signal Reserve Corps.
S.S................Sunday School; Steamship.
St.................Saint; street.
sta................station.
statis.............statistical.
S.T.B..............Bachelor of Sacred Theology.
S.T.D..............Doctor of Sacred Theology.
S.T.L..............Licentiate in Sacred Theology; Lector of Sacred Theology.
supt...............superintendent.
surg...............surgical; surgeon.
S.W................Southwest.

T. and S...........Trust and Savings.
tech...............technical; technology.
technol............technological.
temp...............temporary.
Tenn...............Tennessee.
Ter. (or Ty.)......Territory.
Tex................Texas.
T.H. (or H.T.).....Territory of Hawaii.
Th.D...............Doctor of Theology.
theol..............theological.
Th.M...............Master of Theology.
topog..............topographical.
tp. (or twp.)......township.
T.P.A..............Travelers' Protective Association.
trans..............transactions; transferred.
transl.............translation, translations.
treas..............treasurer.
twp. (or tp.)......township.
ty. (or ter.)......territory.
typog..............typographical.

U..................University.
U.B................United Brethren in Christ.
U.C.V..............United Confederate Veterans.
U.D.C..............United Daughters of the Confederacy.

x ABBREVIATIONS

univ. ....university.
U.P. ....United Presbyterian; Union Pacific.
urol. ....urological.
U.S. ....United States.
U.S.A. ....United States of America.
U.S.C.G. ....United States Coast Guard.
U.S.C.T. ................U.S. Colored Troops.
U.S.M.C. ....United States Marine Corps.
U.S.M.H.S. ....United States Marine Hospital Service.
U.S.N. ....United States Navy.
U.S.N.A. ....United States National Army.
U.S.N.G. ....United States National Guard.
U.S.N.R.F. ....United States Naval Reserve Force.
U.S.P.H.S. ....United States Public Health Service.
U.S.R. ................U.S. Reserves.
U.S.R.C.S. ................U.S. Revenue Cutter Service.
U.S.S. ....United States Ship
U.S.S.R. ....Union of Soviet Socialist Republics.
U.S.V. ....United States Volunteers.

v. ....vice.
Va. ....Virginia.
vet. ....veteran; veterinary.
vice-pres. (or v.p.)....vice-president.
vis. ....visiting.
vol. ....volunteer; volume.
vs. ....versus (against)
Vt. ....Vermont.

W. ....West.
Wash. ....Washington (state).
W.C.T.U. ....Women's Christian Temperance Union.
W.I. ....West Indies.
Wis. ....Wisconsin.
W.Va. ....West Virginia.
Wyo. ....Wyoming.

Y.M.C.A. ....Young Men's Christian Assn.
Y.M.H.A. ....Young Men's Hebrew Assn.
Y.M. and Y.W.H.A. ....Young Men's and Young Women's Hebrew Association.
yrs. ....years.
Y.W.C.A. ....Young Women's Christian Association.

zoöl. ....zoölogical.

CORRIGENDA

Dates of death which were not available at the time of the First Printing and corrections of any erroneous dates in that printing.

A

Achorn, Edgar Oakes, Feb. 13, 1931
Adamowski, Joseph, May 8, 1930
Adkins, John Scudder, July 27, 1931
Adler, Herman Morris, Dec. 7, 1935
Adler, Simon Louis, May 23, 1934
Akeley, Carl Ethan; m. Mrs. Delia Denning Reese, 1903 (divorced 1920); m. 2d Mary L. Jobe, Oct. 18, 1924. Died Nov. 17, 1926
Albertson, George Roger, Nov. 3, 1931
Aldrich, Henry Clay, Sept. 29, 1922
Aldrich, Richard, June 2, 1937
Allen, Francis R., Nov. 7, 1931
Allison, William H., Sept. 9, 1941
Ament, James E., July 21, 1936
Amweg, Frederick J., Dec. 28, 1933
Anderson, George L., Mar. 9, 1934
Andrews, Clarence E., Dec. 12, 1932
Andrews, Launcelot, Apr. 14, 1938
Angellotti, Frank M., May 23, 1932
Armstead, Henry H., Oct. 3, 1940
Armstrong, George W., Jr., June 27, 1932
Arndt, Walter T., Jan. 1, 1932
Ashhurst, Astley Paston C., Sept. 9, 1932
Ashmun, Margaret E., Mar. 16, 1940
Ashton, William E., Mar. 30, 1933
Avery, John, Jan. 21, 1914
Avis, Samuel Brashear, June 8, 1924
Axton, John Thomas, July 20, 1934

B

Bailey, Arthur Low, Feb. 17, 1940
Baldy, Edward Vincent, Mar. 1, 1929
Ball, James Moores, Mar. 1, 1929
Bangs, Outram, Sept. 22, 1932
Batchelder, Frank C., Sept. 28, 1931
Bates, Clement, Jan. 16, 1931
Beck, Johann Heinrich, May 26, 1924
Beebe, James Albert, May 7, 1934
Bentley, Henry, Oct. 21, 1938
Best, Nolan Rice, July 20, 1930
Bethea, Jack, July 2, 1928
Bilgram, Hugo, Aug. 27, 1932
Blackwell, Emily; b. 1826 instead of 1926
Bosworth, Edward I., July 1, 1927
Boyd, Thomas M., June 1, 1932
Brandenburg, Edwin C., Oct. 23, 1935
Brickner, Walter M., July 22, 1930
Brockson, Franklin, Mar. 16, 1942
Browne, George W., Aug. 13, 1930
Brumbaugh, Martin G., Mar. 14, 1930
Buchanan, James Isaac, Jan. 2, 1931
Buschemeyer, John H., Oct. 7, 1935
Byerly, William E., Dec. 20, 1935

C

Cajori, Florian, Aug. 14, 1930
Callaway, Fuller E., Feb. 12, 1928
Campbell, Gilbert W., July 8, 1938
Cannon, Annie Jump, Apr. 13, 1941
Carle, Frank Austin, Jan. 22, 1930
Carpenter, Frank P., Apr. 13, 1938
Casey, Francis de S., May 22, 1934
Chestnut, Victor King, Aug. 29, 1938
Chilton, Arthur B., Apr. 21, 1934
Clark, Grover, July 17, 1938
Cobb, John Nathan, Jan. 13, 1930
Cobb, Nathan Augustus, June 4, 1932
Conklin, Charles, May 27, 1930
Cookson, Walter John, June 11, 1936
Cramer, W. Stuart, Nov. 6, 1930
Cromwell, George, Sept. 17, 1934
Crowder, Frank W., Sept. 27, 1932
Culver, Raymond B., June 7, 1938
Cuppy, Hazlitt Alva, Jan. 26, 1934
Cutler, John C., July 30, 1928
Curry, William M., Dec. 19, 1934

D

Dager, Forrest E., Feb. 13, 1936
Davis, Asa Barnes, Aug. 13, 1930
Dawson, George E., Apr. 21, 1936
Delatour, Henry B., Aug. 23, 1930
Dewey, Harry Pinneo, Apr. 26, 1937
Dewey, W. A., Apr. 1, 1938
Dooley, Michael F., Oct. 6, 1937
Dower, Walter H., Mar. 21, 1934
Dowling, Oscar, Jan. 2, 1931
Dressler, Louis R., Nov. 8, 1932
Duke, Victor LeRoy, Mar. 3, 1933

E

Eggert, Charles A., Feb. 2, 1931
Eliot, Walter Graeme, May 3, 1931
Evans, Aurelius A., Nov. 9, 1935

F

Feustel, Robert M., May 8, 1932
Fisher, William C., Oct. 14, 1932
Floridia, Pietro, Aug. 16, 1932
Frye, James Albert, Mar. 8, 1933
Fuertes, James H., Jan. 30, 1932
Fuller, Edward, Apr. 29, 1938
Fulton, William S., May 30, 1938

G

George, Vesper Lincoln, May 9, 1934
Gerdine, Thomas G., Oct. 31, 1930
Goldschmidt, Samuel A., Jan. 28, 1933
Goodwin, William Hall, May 23, 1937
Green, Berryman, Mar. 10, 1933
Greene, James Leon, Apr. 21, 1930
Grubb, Ignatius C., June 20, 1927
Grunert, Francis E., Dec. 27, 1936
Guion, Walter, Feb. 8, 1927
Gustafson, William, Mar. 10, 1931

H

Hadley, Henry H., Mar. 31, 1934
Hahn, Adolf, Mar. 31, 1934
Haines, John Allen, Aug. 10, 1936
Hall, Edward Hagaman, May 4, 1936
Hall, Maurice Crowther, May 1, 1938
Halliburton, Richard, Mar. 23, 1939
Hamilton, John W., July 24, 1934
Hammond, Edwin P., Jan. 27, 1920
Harrington, Charles M., Mar. 27, 1928
Hartmann, F. M., Mar. 28, 1932
Harvey, LeRoy, Feb. 15, 1928
Hatfield, Charles F., June 22, 1939
Hawn, Henry Gaines, Nov. 2, 1930
Hays, George W., Sept. 15, 1927
Heaton, Augustus G., Oct. 11, 1930
Hehir, Martin A., June 10, 1935
Hepburn, Charles McG., July 10, 1929
Herbert, John Warne, Aug. 26, 1934
Hill, Owen Aloysius, Feb. 25, 1930
Hitchcock, Charles A., Nov. 4, 1932
Hoenshel, Eli J., Sept. 28, 1924
Holden, Ward Andrews, Jan. 24, 1937
Holding, Archibald M., Apr. 21, 1935
Hollomon, James A., Jan. 24, 1929
Horton, Kathrine L. P., Aug. 27, 1931
Howard, James E., July 6, 1930
Howse, Hilary Ewing, Jan. 2, 1938
Hudson, Eric, Dec. 22, 1932
Hulings, Garnet, Apr. 27, 1932
Humphrey, Lewis Craig, Feb. 3, 1927
Humphreys, Milton W., Nov. 2, 1928
Hunt, Benjamin Weeks, June 26, 1934
Hurd, George Arthur, Nov. 15, 1929

I

Inman, Edward H., Apr. 15, 1931

J

Jackson, Charles L., Oct. 31, 1935
Jackson, Charles S., Dec. 27, 1924
Jackson, Thomas H., Apr. 8, 1937
Jacoby, Harold, July 20, 1932
Jeffery, Elmore B., Apr. 25, 1929
Jenkinson, Richard C., Aug. 30, 1930
Johnson, Charles W., July 19, 1932
Johnson, Oliver F., Mar. 9, 1936
Jones, Benjamin F., Sept. 26, 1935
Jones, Lake, June 7, 1930

K

Kasebier, Gertrude, Oct. 13, 1934
Kieffer, Henry M., Apr. 21, 1930
Kimball, George Henry, Aug. 8, 1936
Kingsbury, Joseph T., Apr. 10, 1937
Kirby, Edmund Burgis, May 7, 1935
Krumwiede, Charles, Dec. 28, 1930
Kyle, William S., Jan. 4, 1931

L

Ladd, Herbert Warren, Nov. 29, 1913
Lane, Charles S., Feb. 2, 1938
LaRoque, George Paul, May 16, 1934
Larsen, Peter L.; b. 1833 instead of 1883
Lathrop, Henry B., Nov. 6, 1936
Lawrence, James C., Aug. 14, 1932
Laws, Frank Arthur, Nov. 12, 1936
Leavell, William H., Aug. 1, 1930
Lenski, Richard C. H., Aug. 14, 1936
Leonard, Albert, Dec. 5, 1931
Lewis, Henry, Apr. 23, 1932
Littlefield, Eben N., May 26, 1935
Littlefield, Milton S., June 11, 1934
Logan, James A., Jr., Oct. 27, 1930
Loomis, Samuel Lane, Jan. 11, 1938
Lourie, David A., Jan. 18, 1930
Low, Albert Howard, Apr. 9, 1936
Luccock, George N., Feb. 23, 1943
Lunt, Horace Gray, Feb. 15, 1928
Lupton, Charles Thomas, May 8, 1935

M

Manly, George C., Dec. 15, 1936
Manning, Mary M. F., July 19, 1928
Marble, William A., Sept. 12, 1930
Marshall, William A., Sept. 6, 1931
Mason, William Pitt, Jan. 25, 1937
Mattison, Fitch C. E., Sept. 17, 1932
McChord, Charles C., Nov. 24, 1937
McConnell, James Eli, Apr. 17, 1928
McDermott, Frank, Mar. 1, 1930
McGiffin, Malcolm, Mar. 1, 1934
McIntire, Albert W., Jan. 30, 1935
Michelson, Truman, July 26, 1938
Mills, Ogden, Jan. 29, 1929
Miner, Harlan S., Apr. 14, 1938
Mitchell, Charles E., Mar. 29, 1937
Mitchell, Langdon E., Oct. 21, 1935
Monnette, Orra E., Feb. 23, 1936
Moran, James Thomas, Mar. 23, 1936
Morse, Waldo Grant, Sept. 16, 1934
Mosher, George Clark, Jan. 18, 1929

N

Nagler, Floyd August, Nov. 10, 1933
Neff, George N., May 4, 1933
Neff, John Henry, Nov. 9, 1938
Neff, Joseph Seal, Nov. 4, 1930
Nicholls, Rhoda H., Sept. 7, 1930
Nicholson, John Reed, Dec. 7, 1937

O

O'Meara, Mark, Feb. 6, 1937
Oxnard, Robert, Feb. 9, 1930

P

Palmer, A. Emerson, Apr. 24, 1925
Pammel, Louis H., Mar. 24, 1931
Parsons, Frank N., Aug. 9, 1934
Parsons, Payn B., Sept. 19, 1931
Patterson, John L., Feb. 27, 1937
Patterson, Ross Vernet, May 2, 1938
Patton, Cornelius H., Aug. 17, 1939
Paxton, Joseph F., June 12, 1939
Pearson, Arthur E., June 25, 1934
Pence, Edward Hart, Mar. 4, 1936
Pennington, Leigh H., Apr. 23, 1929
Peoples, William T., Mar. 9, 1923
Persons, Warren M., Oct. 11, 1937
Pettengill, Heman J., Jan. 12, 1931
Phenix, George Perley, Oct. 3, 1930
Pierson, Romaine, Apr. 27, 1932
Pirazzini, Agide, Feb. 1, 1934
Plumb, Charles Sumner, Mar. 4, 1939
Powell, John H., Nov. 16, 1935
Powers, Sidney, Nov. 5, 1932
Prentiss, Francis F., Apr. 1, 1937
Price, Charles W., May 11, 1934
Pulsifer, Nathan T., Sept. 9, 1931
Pulsifer, William E., Jan. 4, 1931

Q

Quincy, Charles F., Oct. 1, 1927

R

Randall, Wyatt W., July 22, 1930
Randolph, Joseph F., Feb. 16, 1932
Ranum, Arthur, Feb. 28, 1934
Raynolds, Joshua S., Nov. 2, 1932
Redding, Joseph D., Nov. 21, 1932
Reeves, Francis B., Aug. 14, 1922
Reichert, Edward T., Dec. 25, 1931
Rice, John Andrew, June 29, 1930
Richardson, Clifford, Feb. 28, 1932
Rigby, William Titus; elected sec. (instead of chmn.) Vicksburg Nat. Mil. Park Assn., 1895; apptd. commr., 1899, chmn. of commn. and resident commr. On 87th birthday (Nov. 3, 1928), the citizens of Vicksburg dedicated in his honor his bust, erected by vol. contbrns. on spot where his tent stood during siege of Vicksburg in 1863. Died May 10, 1929; Interment in Nat. Military Park, Vicksburg, Miss.
Robinson, Lucien M., Mar. 13, 1932
Rogers, Arthur K., Nov. 1, 1936
Rose, Landon Cabell, Dec. 20, 1931
Rosenfeld, Maurice, Feb. 25, 1939
Ross, Erskine Mayo, Dec. 10, 1928

S

Sandt, George W., Jan. 9, 1931
Savage, Giles C., Apr. 8, 1930
Savage, Hiram N., June 24, 1934
Schaller, Albert, Nov. 18, 1934
Schlundt, Herman, Dec. 30, 1937
Schneider, Samuel H., Mar. 17, 1939
Schoonhoven, John J., Dec. 27, 1936
Scripps, Robert P., Mar. 2, 1938
Scully, William A., Oct. 20, 1936
Sears, Frederick W., Aug. 31, 1934
Sheehan, Joseph R., Mar. 28, 1940
Shepard, Andrew N., Dec. 23, 1934
Sherwood, Herbert F., Oct. 3, 1930
Slattery, Leroy, John T., Mar. 27, 1938
Smart, Leroy, Oct. 7, 1936
Smith, Ernest E., Dec. 5, 1930
Smith, John Hammond, Apr. 13, 1932
Smith, Julia Holmes, Nov. 10, 1930
Smith, Seymour W., Jan. 4, 1932
Smith, Thomas Berry, May 8, 1933
Snyder, Monroe B., Sept. 27, 1932
Sokolow, Alexander T., July 26, 1934
Spenzer, John George, July 27, 1932
Spreckels, John D., June 7, 1926
Stecher, Henry W., Oct. 16, 1935
Steele, Hiram R., Nov. 21, 1929
Steele, James D., Dec. 6, 1928
Sterling, Thomas, Aug. 26, 1930
Stimson, John Ward, June 13, 1930
Stone, Walter R., Feb. 22, 1937
Stratton, William B., May 13, 1938
Strickler, Givens B., Aug. 4, 1913
Swearingen, Embry L., July 21, 1931
Sweet, Edwin F., Apr. 2, 1935

T

Teeple, John Edgar, Mar. 23, 1931
Tenney, Edward D., Apr. 29, 1934
Thaxter, Roland, Apr. 22, 1932
Thomas, William, Oct. 18, 1936
Thompson, Wallace, Jan. 7, 1936
Thomson, Edgar S., Jan. 12, 1931
Todd, Albert May, Oct. 6, 1931
Torrey, Raymond H., July 15, 1938
Townley, Calvert, Nov. 27, 1933
Troop, J(ared) G., Feb. 5, 1930
Trotter, Alfred W., Oct. 4, 1928
Tully, William John, Aug. 22, 1930

U

Underwood, Loring, Jan. 13, 1930
Utley, Samuel, Nov. 17, 1930

V

Van Fleet, Vernon W., Feb. 18, 1932
Veeder, Albert H.; died July 13, 1914 (not 1944)
Votey, Edwin Scott, Jan. 21, 1931

W

Waddell, Charles C., June 11, 1930
Waite, Herbert H., Apr. 25, 1931
Walcott, Henry Pickering; m. Charlotte Elizabeth Richards, 1865; children—George, Robert. Died Nov. 11, 1932.
Walker, Robert F., Nov. 19, 1930
Wallace, Henry, Feb. 22, 1916
Walsh, Thomas, Oct. 29, 1928
Waterhouse, Frank, Mar. 20, 1930
Waters, Francis E., Jan. 22, 1936
Weeks, Charles P., Mar. 25, 1928
Weitzel, George T., Jan. 1, 1936
Weller, George E., May 17, 1932
Wells, Edgar H., Jan. 8, 1939
Wells, Ira Kent, Apr. 2, 1934
Westley, George H., Sept. 25, 1936
Whitcomb, Selden L., Apr. 22, 1930
Willcox, Julius Abner, July 2, 1932
Wilson, Ernest Henry, Oct. 15, 1930
Wright, Julian May, Oct. 5, 1938

Y

Yandell, Enid, June 13, 1934

WHO WAS WHO
IN AMERICA

A

ABARBANELL, Jacob Ralph, editor; b. New York, N.Y., Dec. 6, 1852; s. Rudolph and Rosalia A.; A.B., B.S., Coll. City of New York, 1872; LL.B., Columbia, 1874; m. Cornelia L. Eaton, June 30, 1892. Practices law, New York, N.Y. Author: Flirtation, 1884; Monte Cristo and His Wife, 1885; Ma, 1888; The Rector's Secret, 1892; The Heart of the People, 1908; also serials pub. under nom de plume "Ralph Royal." Plays: My Father's Will, 1881; A Model Pair, 1882; All on Account of a Bracelet, 1883; Haydee, Countess of Monte Cristo, 1902; Ma, 1902; When the Cannon Roars, 1905; The Heart of the People, 1909. Also numerous translations of novels of Alphonse Daudet, Octave Feuillet, Henri Créville-Boisgobey, and short stories from French and German for mags. Home: Brooklyn, N.Y. Died Nov. 9, 1922.

ABBATT, Agnes Dean, artist; b. New York, N.Y., June 23, 1847; d. William D. and Agnes Alice (Dean) Abbatt; entered Cooper Union Art Sch., 1873; studied at Nat. Acad. Design and under R. Swain Gifford and James D. Smillie. Paints landscapes, coast scenes, flowers; oil and water colors and black and white; also wax modeling, plants and flowers. Medals at Cooper Union Art Sch. and Mass. Charitable Mechanics Assn.; 1st prize in oil painting San Antonio (Tex.) Internat. Fair. Rep. in Botanical Museum, Bronx Park, N.Y. Home: Westchester, N.Y. Died Jan. 1, 1917.

ABBATT, William, author; b. New York, N.Y., Nov. 16, 1851; s. William D. and Agnes Alice (Dean) A.; ed. pvt. schs., N.Y. and Westchester; unmarried. Editor Inter-State, New York, 1890-93; asst. editor New York News Letter, 1890-94. Author: The Crisis of the Revolution, 1899; Battle of Pell's Point, 1901. Editor: General Heath's Memoirs, 1901; Sargent's Life of Major John André, 1902; Winfield's Block-House by Bull's Ferry; Codman's Arnold's Expedition to Quebec; Hopkins' Historical Memoir of the Housatunnuk Indians, 1911. Home: Tarrytown, N.Y. Died Sept. 7, 1935.

ABBE, Cleveland, meteorologist; b. at New York, N.Y., Dec. 3, 1838; s. George Waldo and Charlotte (Colgate) A.; brother of Robert A. (q.v.); A.B., Coll. City of N.Y., 1857, A.M., 1860, Ph.D., 1891; S.B., Harvard, 1864; LL.D., U. of Mich., 1888, U. of Glasgow, 1896; tutor, Trinity Ch. Grammar Sch., New York. 1857-58; studied astronomy with Brünnow of Ann Arbor, Mich., 1858-59, under B.A. Gould, Cambridge, Mass., 1860-64; m. Frances Martha Neal, May 10, 1870 (died July 24, 1908); 2d, Margaret A. Percival, Apr. 12, 1909; children—Cleveland A., Jr., William and Truman A. Asst. prof. Mich. Agrl. Coll., 1859; tutor, U. of Mich., 1859-60; aid in U.S. Coast and Geod. Survey, 1860-64; guest at Nicholas Central Obs., Poulkova, nr. St. Petersburg, Russia, 1864-66; aid U.S. Naval Obs., 1867-68; dir. Cincinnati Obs., 1868-73. On Sept. 1, 1869, inaugurated daily weather report for Cincinnati Chamber of Commerce, which at once led U.S. Govt. to take up similar work; became widely known as "Old Probs"; meteorologist in the U.S. Signal Service, 1871-91; U.S. Weather Bureau 1891—; editor Monthly Weather Review, 1873 and 1892-1915; editor Bulletin Mount Weather Observatory, 1909-13; prof. meteorology. Columbian (now George Washington) U., 1886-1905; lecturer on meteorology, Johns Hopkins, 1896-1914. Mem. Nat. Acad. Sciences. Author: Report on the Total Solar Eclipse of July 29, 1878, 1881; Report on Standard Time, 1879, which started the agitation that resulted in the modern standard hour meridians from Greenwich; Meteorological Apparatus and Methods, 1887; Preliminary Studies in Storm and Weather Prediction, 1889; The Mechanics of the Earth's Atmosphere, Vol. I, 1891, Vol. II, 1909; The Altitude of the Aurora, 1896; Physical Basis of Long-Range Forecasting, 1902. Died Oct. 28, 1916.

ABBE, Cleveland, Jr., geographer; b. Washington, D.C., Mar. 25, 1872; s. Cleveland and Frances Martha (Neal) A.; A.B., Harvard, 1894, A.M., 1896; Ph.D., Johns Hopkins, 1898; student, geography Imperial U., Vienna, 1901-03; m. Frieda Dauer, Apr. 12, 1903; children—Ernest Cleveland, Elfriede Martha. Inst. physiography, Corcoran Scientific Sch., Columbia, 1894-97; asst. Md. Geol. Survey, 1896-1901; prof. geology and biology, Western Md. Coll., 1898-99; acting prof. natural sciences, Winthrop Normal and Industrial Coll., S.C., 1899-1901; aid U.S. Geol. Survey, 1903-06; research observer, U.S. Weather Bureau, 1906-08; asst. editor Monthly Weather Review, 1908-10, and 1914-16, editor, 1916-18; meteorologist, 1914-18; asst. in library U.S. Weather Bur., 1910-13. Asso. editor in charge Scientific Am. Supplement, New York, May-Oct., 1919; asst. editor Engring. and Mining Jour., New York, 1919-21; asst. prof. Coll. of City of N.Y., 1921-25; editor of volumes of Geo. F. Baker Non-resident Lectureship in Chemistry at Cornell U., 1930—. Home: Ithaca, N.Y. Died Apr. 18, 1934.

ABBE, Robert, surgeon; b. New York, N.Y., April 13, 1851; s. George Waldo and Charlotte (Colgate) A.; brother of Cleveland A.; A.B., Coll. City of N.Y., 1870; M.D., College Phys. and Surg. (Columbia), 1874; m. Mrs. Catherine Amory Palmer, Nov. 14, 1891. Instr. English, drawing and geometry, Coll. City of N.Y., 1870-72; attending surgeon out-patient dept., N.Y. Hosp., 1877-84; prof. didactic surgery, Woman's Med. Coll., 2 yrs.; surgeon to St. Luke's Hosp., 1884—; N.Y. Cancer Hosp., 1893—; attending surgeon N.Y. Babies' Hosp., 1892-97; prof. surgery, N.Y. Post-Grad. Med. Sch., 1889-97. Died Mar. 7, 1928.

ABBEY, Edwin Austin, artist; b. Phila., Pa., Apr. 1, 1852; s. William Maxwell and Margery Anne (Kiple) A.; ed. Pa. Acad. of Fine Arts; (hon. A.M., Yale, 1897; LL.D., U. of Pa., 1902); engaged by Harper & Bros., 1871; went to England for them 1878; m. Mary Gertrude Mead, 1890. Exhibited his first picture, A May Day Morning, at Royal Acad., 1890; other notable pictures: Fiammetta's Song, Richard III and Lady Anne, Hamlet, O Mistress Mine, Who is Sylvia?, 1899; The Trial of Queen Katherine, The Penance of Eleanor, Duchess of Gloucester, 1900. Commissioned, 1901, by King Edward VII of England to paint scene of his coronation. Painted: Crusaders Sighting Jerusalem, Royal Acad., 1901; Columbus in the New World, 1906; Reredos, for American Church in Paris, 1907; paintings for dome of Pa. State Capitol, 1908. Has published illustrated edition of Herrick's Poems, She Stoops to Conquer, Old Songs, Quiet Life, (with Alfred Parsons, English artist) Comedies of Shakespeare. N.A., 1902; mem. Royal Acad. of Eng., Am. Acad. Arts and Letters; hon. mem. Am. Inst. Architects; Chevalier Légion d'Honneur, France. Died 1911.

ABBEY, Henry, poet; b. Rondout, N.Y., July 11, 1842; s. Stephen and Caroline (Vail) A.; ed. Kingston (N.Y.) Acad., Hudson River Inst. and under John N. Pomeroy, writer on internat. law; m. Mary Louise Du Bois, Dec. 26, 1865 (died Nov. 3, 1889). Edited Rondout (N.Y.) Courier, 1862, Orange (N.J.) Spectator, 1863. Author: May Dreams, 1862; Ralph and Other Poems, 1866; Stories in Verse, 1869; Ballads of Good Deeds, 1872; Ballads of Good Deeds and Other Poems, 1876; Poems, 1879; The City of Success and Other Poems, 1883. Collected works: The Poems of Henry Abbey, author's edit., 1885, 3d edit. enlarged, 1895, complete edition, 1904; Phaethon, 1901; The Dream of Love, 1909. Home: Rondout, N.Y. Died 1911.

ABBEY, Charles Wheaton, naval officer; b. in R.I., Nov. 18, 1829. Apptd. purser U.S. Navy, Sept. 2, 1856; promoted pay insp., Mar. 3, 1871; pay dir., July 3, 1871; retired, Nov. 18, 1891; advanced to rank of rear adm., June 29, 1906, for services during Civil War. Home: Warren, R.I. Died 1907.

ABBOT, Edwin Hale, ry. official; b. Beverly, Mass., Jan. 26, 1834; s. Joseph Hale and Frances Ellingwood (Larcom) A.; Boston Latin Sch., 1851; A.B., Harvard, 1855, A.M., 1858, LL.B., 1862; m. Martha T. Steele, Sept. 19, 1866; children—Philip Stanley (deceased), Edwin Hale, Constance (adopted; wife of Dr. Herbert M. Rich). Law editor Boston Daily Advertiser, 1862-70; practiced law, Boston, 1862-76, then removed to Milwaukee to become gen. solicitor and dir. Wis. Central R.R., 1873-78, v.p. and trustee, 1878; took possession as active trustee and operated Wis. Central R.R. for bondholders, 1878-89, constructing Wis. Central asso. lines and effecting entrance into Chicago and erecting Grand Central Sta. and terminals, with Charles L. Colby; pres. and treas., Wis. Central R.R., Chicago, Wis. & Minn. R.R. and Milwaukee & Lake Winnebago R.R., 1890-99; retired from business, 1909, after effecting, against strong opposition, amicable union of all Wis. Central roads into one co.; with W.W. Crapo, established the first car-ferry for entire trains, 54 miles, across Lake Michigan bet. Manitowoc and Ludington. Author of Wis. Central plan, 1879, of corporate organization, by which control of corp. was vested in bondholders through reservation to them of voting-power on stock, being the first and original scheme, out of which many other forms of voting trusts have since grown. Was class sec. class of 1855, Harvard; one of founders Union Club, Boston, 1863. Home: Cambridge, Mass. Died May 30, 1927.

ABBOT, Francis Ellingwood, author; b. Boston, Mass., Nov. 6, 1836; s. Joseph Hale and Fanny Ellingwood (Larcom) A.; studied at pub. Latin Sch.; grad. Harvard, 1859 (Ph.D. 1881); Meadville Theol. school, 1863; Unitarian clergyman, 1863-68; m. Katharine Fearing Loring, Aug. 3, 1859 (died 1893); edited The Index, a weekly journal of free religion, Toledo, 1870-73, Boston, 1873-80. Teacher of classical sch. in N.Y., 1880-81; teacher of private Home for Boys, Cambridge, Mass., fitting for Harvard, 1881-92; instr. in philosophy Harvard, 1887-88. Author: Equal Rights in Religion, Rep. Centennial Congress of Liberals, 1876; Scientific Theism, 1885; The Way Out of Agnosticism, 1890; Arethusa Hall: A Memorial, 1892. Home: Cambridge, Mass. Died 1903.

ABBOT, Frederic Vaughan, army officer, b. Cambridge, Mass., Mar. 4, 1858; s. Henry Larcom and Mary Susan (Everett) A.; grad. Flushing (L.I.) Inst. 1873; grad. U.S. Mil. Acad., 1879; m. Sara Julie Dehon, Oct. 15, 1885; children—Marion Beatrice, Elinor Russell, Henry Dehon. Second lt. engr. corps, June 13, 1879; advanced through grades to col., June 24, 1909, brig. gen. N.A., Aug. 5, 1917. Survey of boundary line bet. Md. and Va., 1883-84; asst. to chief of engrs. U.S. Army, Aug. 12, 1900-10; charge defensive works southern and eastern entrances to N.Y. Harbor, and of river and harbor works, 2d N.Y. Dist., Apr. 30, 1915-Oct. 15, 1917; prin. asst. to chief of engrs. U.S. Army and comdg. officer, post of Washington Barracks, 1917; acting chief of engrs., U.S. Army, 1918-19; retired May 10, 1920. Home: Washington, D.C. Died Sept. 26, 1928.

ABBOT, Henry Larcom, soldier, engr.; b. Beverly, Mass., Aug. 13, 1821; s. Joseph Hale and Frances Ellingwood (Larcom) A.; grad. West Point, 1854; LL.D., Harvard, 1886; m. Mary Susan Everett, Apr. 2, 1856. Served in Civil War; mustered out as col.; retired from regular army as col., 1895; advanced to brig.-gen., retired 1904. Home: Cambridge, Mass. Died Oct. 1, 1927.

ABBOT, Willis John, editor; b. New Haven, Conn.; s. Waldo and Julia (Holmes) Abbot (now Julia Holmes Smith); student literary dept., U. of Mich., 1881-83, LL.B., 1884, L.H.D. from same university in 1927; married. Mng. editor Chicago Times, 1892-93; writing editor New York Journal, 1896-98; editor and part owner The Pilgrim, Battle Creek, Mich., 1900-03; chief editorial writer New York American, 1905-07, 1912-16; writing editor New York Sun, 1916-17,

Chicago American, 1917; staff corr. with Collier's Weekly. Writer on political and internat. topics from Washington for interior newspapers; editor Christian Science Monitor, Jan. 30, 1921-27. Chmn. Henry George campaign com., New York, 1898; mgr. Dem. Nat. Press Bur., presdl. campaigns, 1900, 1908. Decorated Order of the Redeemer (Greek), 1925; decorated by Roumanian Govt., 1927. Vice-pres. for U.S. of Pan. Am. Congress of Journalists; trustee World Peace Foundation, Northeastern Uni. (Boston). Mem. Am. Econ. Assn., Foreign Policy Assn., Council on Foreign Relations, Inst. of Pacific Relations, Japan Soc. of Boston (v.p.), Am. Soc. of Newspaper Editors (dir.), International Chamber of Commerce, English-Speaking Union of U.S., Sigma Delta Chi, Chi Psi. Christian Scientist. Author: Blue Jackets of '76; Blue Jackets of 1812; Blue Jackets of 1861; Battle Fields and Camp Fires, 1902; Battle Fields of 1861, 1902; Battle Fields and Victory; Carter Henry Harrison—A Memoir; Blue Jackets of 1898, 1899; Naval History of the United States, 1902; American Ships and Sailors; Story of Our Navy for Young Americans, 1910; Story of Our Army for Young Ameicans; Notable Women in History, 1913; Panama and the Canal in Picture and Prose, 1914; The Nations at War, 1917; Aircraft and Submarines; Soldiers of the Sea; The United States in the World War; Story of Our Merchant Marine; Blue Jackets of 1918, 1921; Philip Derby, Reporter, 1922; Watching the World Go By, 1933. Home: Brookline, Mass. Died May 19, 1934.

ABBOTT, Alexander Crever, M.D.; b. Baltimore, Md., Feb. 26, 1860; s. Alexander and Elizabeth (Beatty) A.; ed. Baltimore City Coll.; M.D., U. of Md., 1884; grad. student Johns Hopkins and univs. of Munich and Berlin; Sc.D., Dr. P.H.; m. Georgina P., d. Justice Osler, late of Ct. of Appeals of Ont., Aug. 30, 1892; children—Britton Vaughan, Katharine Abbott (Mrs. Archibald Malloch), William Osler. Prof. emeritus U. of Pennsylvania. Author: The Principles of Bacteriology, 1892, 1921; The Hygiene of Transmissible Diseases, 1899, 1902. Home: Philadelphia, Pa. Died Sept. 11, 1935.

ABBOTT, Arthur Vaughan, civil mech. and elec. engr., author; b. New York, N.Y., 1854; mem. Am. Inst. Mining Engrs., 1882—; mem. Am. Inst. Elec. Engrs. (v.p., 1902); was chief engr. Chicago Telephone Co., engr. Westinghouse, Church, Kerr & Co., 1902—. Author Electrical Transmission of Energy; The Evolution of a Switchboard; History and Use of Testing Machines; Treatise on Fuel. Home: New York, N.Y. Died 1906.

ABBOTT, Augustus Levi, lawyer; b. Weymouth, Mass., Aug. 6, 1858; s. Rev. Levi Augustus (D.D.) and Mary Abby (Preston) A.; desc. of George Abbott, from Guilford, Eng., 1642, settled at Rowley, Mass.; student U. of Chicago; A.B., Brown U., 1880, A.M., 1883; LL.B., Washington U., St. Louis, Mo., 1885; LL.D., Benton Coll. of Law, St. Louis, 1917; m. Annette Blair, Apr. 20, 1887; children—John Blair, Marjory (Mrs. Arthur Bartlett Hague), Preston Ober. Asso. prof. mathematics, Shurtleff Coll., Alton, Ill., 1881-84; admitted to Mo. bar, 1884; lecturer in law, Benton Coll. Law, St. Louis, 1897-1933; sr. mem. Abbott, Fauntleroy, Cullen & Edwards, 1920-33. Trustee Brown U., 1909—; mem. law com. Northern Bapt. Conv., 1908—, chmn., 1910—. Democrat. Co-Author: Law of Eminent Domain, 1888. Home: St. Louis, Mo. Died Oct. 1934.

ABBOTT, Byrdine Akers, clergyman, editor; born Abbott, Va., Jan. 26, 1866; s. Sinclair Calvin and Lucinda Jane (Williams) A.; student U. of Va.; A.B., Milligan Coll., 1887; D.D., Butler U., 1927; m. Olivia C. Carper (died 1907); children—Frederick, Book (dec.), Crystal Carper, Lyman Sinclair, Thomas Byrdine (dec.), Robert Davis, Richard Ireland (deceased); m. 2d, Helen B. Ireland (A.B., Goucher, 1901), Sept. 12, 1910; 1 dau., Jane Bancroft. Ordained ministry Christian (Disciples) Ch., 1888; pastor Charlottesville, Va., 1888-94, Baltimore, Md., 1894-1910, St. Louis, Mo., 1910-17; editor The Christian-Evangelist, 1917-34. Mem. Fed. Council of Chs.; del. World Conf. on Faith and Order, Lausanne, Switzerland, 1927; fraternal del. to Conf. of Chs. of Christ, Glasgow, Scotland, 1927. Trustee William Woods Coll., Butler University. Democrat. Author: Life of Chapman S. Lucas; The Disciples—An Interpretation, 1924; At the Master's Table, 1925. Home: St. Louis, Mo. Died June 24, 1936.

ABBOTT, Charles Conrad, naturalist; b. Trenton, N.J., June 4, 1843; s. Timothy and Susan (Conrad) A.; M.D., U. of Pa., 1865; m. Julia Boggs Olden, Feb. 13, 1867. Made large collection of archaeol. specimens, now in Peabody Mus., Cambridge, Mass., where he was asst., 1876-89. Demonstrated existence of man in Delaware River Valley during glacial and subsequent prehistoric periods. Made 2d large archaeological collection of Del. Valley for Princeton, 1901-07. Author: The Stone Age in New Jersey, 1876; Primitive Industry, 1881; A Naturalist's Rambles About Home, 1884; Upland and Meadow, 1886; Wasteland Wanderings, 1887; Days Out of Doors, 1889; Outings at Odd Times, 1890; Recent Rambles, 1892; Travels in a Treetop, 1894; The Birds About Us, 1894; Notes of the Night, 1895; A Colonial Wooing (novel), 1895; Birdland Echoes, 1896; When the Century Was New (novel), 1897; The Hermit of Nottingham (novel), 1897; The Freedom of the Fields, 1898; Clear Skies and Cloudy, 1899; In Nature's Realm, 1900; Archaeological Explorations in the Valley of the Delaware, 1894; Rambles of an Idler, 1906; Archaeologia Nova Caesarea, 1907, 1908, 1909; Ten Years' Diggings in Lanâpè Land, 1912. Home: Bristol, Pa. Died July 27, 1919.

ABBOTT, Charles Frederick; b. Concord, N.H., Jan. 24, 1876; s. George W. and Margaret (Weir) A.; high sch. and business coll.; m. Florence J. Smith, June 25, 1901; children—Robert Chester, Charles F. Began as office boy with J.A. & W. Bird & Co., Boston, 1899, and continued as salesman, branch mgr. and gen. sales mgr. until 1909; gen. sales mgr. Flintkote Mfg. Co., Boston, 1910-14; asst. gen. mgr. in charge of sales, Art Metal Constrn. Co., Jamestown, N.Y., 1914-16; dir. Sales Celluloid Co., N.Y. City, 1916-19; dir. publicity and commercial research, Nat. Aniline & Chem. Co. (div. of Allied Dye & Chem. Co.), New York, 1919-21; exec. dir. Am. Inst. Steel Constrn., Inc., 1923—. Republican. Episcopalian. Home: Montclair, N.J. Died Oct. 27, 1933.

ABBOTT, Edville Gerhardt, orthopedic surgeon; b. Hancock, Me., Nov. 6, 1871; s. Alonzo and Maria B. (Mercer) A.; grad. E. Me. Conf. Sem., Bucksports, Me., 1889; M.D., Bowdoin, 1898, A.B., 1906, A.M., 1908, Sc.D., 1914; Sc.D., Colby, 1925; studied Friedrich Wilhelm Universität, Berlin, 1900-01; also in Vienna, Paris, Göttingen and London; m. Sara Sargent, Mar. 14, 1893. Surgeon in chief, Children's Hosp., Portland, Me. Mem. bd. dirs. Nat. Bank of Commerce, Portland. uthor: Treatment of Scoliosis (trans. foreign langs.). Home: Portland, Me. Died Aug. 27, 1938.

ABBOTT, Edward, clergyman; b. Farmington, Me., July 15, 1841; 4th s. Jacob and Harriet (Vaughan) A.; bro. Rev. Lyman Abbott; grad. N.Y. Univ., 1860 (D.D., 1890); studied theology Andover Theol. Sem.; 4 years pastor Pilgrim Congl. Ch., Cambridge. An editor The Congregationalist, 1869-78; editor Literary World, 1877-88, and 1895-1903. Ordained P. E. minister, 1879; rector St. James' Ch., Cambridge, 1879-1906; elected missionary bishop of Japan, 1889, declined. Author: The Baby's Things, a Story in Verse, 1871; Conversations of Jesus, 1875; A Paragraph History of the United States, 1875; A Paragraph History of the American Revolution, 1876; Revolutionary Times, 1876; Long Look Series (juvenile), 1877-80; History of Cambridge (in Drake's History of Middlesex County, Vol. 1), 1880; Memoir of Jacob Abbott (memorial edit. of The Young Christian), 1882; Phillips Brooks, 1900. Home: Cambridge, Mass. Died 1908.

ABBOTT, Edwin Milton, lawyer; b. Phila., Pa., June 4, 1877; s. Theodore and Alvina (Rosewig) A.; LL.B., U. of Pa., 1896, hon. N.Ph.D.; m. Florence H. Wilson, Nov. 9, 1905; children—Emilie Ferry Ella, T. H. Wilson. Admitted to Pa. bar, 1896; chief counsel in fight of commuters in and about Phila. against the railroads; mem. Pa. Ho. of Rep., 1911-12; chmn. Commn. on Revision of Criminal Laws, State of Pa., 1912-15, 1917-25. Apptd. spl. asst. city solicitor, Feb. 1924, and assigned as spl. counsel to Gen. Smedley D. Butler, dir. of Pub. Safety; atty. Dept. of Justice of Pa., assigned to Banking Dept., 1931-35; apptd. spl. counsel Dept. of Pub. Safety, Phila., Feb. 1936; counsel for Director Pub. Safety Elliott; gen. counsel for Sesqui-centennial; counsel for Boys' Week Council; dir. Allied Youth. Presbyn. Mason. Author: The Law and Religion. Wrote words and music of "Alma Mater Red and Blue" (U. of Pa. song). Home: Philadelphia, Pa. Died Nov. 8, 1940.

ABBOTT, Ernest Hamlin, editor; b. Cornwall-on-Hudson, N.Y., Apr. 18, 1870; s. Lyman and Abby Frances (Hamlin) A.; Hill Sch., Pa.; A.B., Harvard, 1893; Union Tehol. Sem., 1893-95; grad. Andover Theol. Sem., 1896; m. May Louise Kleberg, Sept. 28, 1899; children—John Maunder Kleberg (adopted), Alexander Lyman, Lawrence Jacob, Theodore Vaughan, Ernest Hamlin. Ordained Congl. ministry, 1896; pastor 1st Ch., Fryeburg, Me., 1896-1902; became mem. editorial staff of The Outlook, 1902; sec. The Outlook Co., 1913-28, dir., 1913—; editor-in-chief The Outlook, 1923-28; asso. editor Outlook and Independent, 1928—. Dir. Grenfell Assn. America, 1907-12; formerly mem. com. on ch. and social service Federal Council of Chs. of Christ in America; chmn. exec. com. Nat. Service Commn. of Congl. Chs., 1917-19. Editorial corr. of The Outlook, in France, 1918-19, and at Washington Conf., 1921. Author: Religious Life in America, 1902; On the Training of Parents, 1908; What They Did With Themselves, 1909. Home: Cornwall-on-Hudson, N.Y. Died Aug. 8, 1931.

ABBOTT, Frances Matilda, writer; b. Concord, N.H., Aug. 18, 1857; d. John and Matilda (Brooks) Abbott; A.B., Vassar, 1881; unmarried. Press agt. N.H. Equal Suffrage Assn., 1913—. Conglist. Author: Domestic Customs and Social Life in History of Concord, N.H., 1903; Birds and Flowers about Concord, 1906; The Simple Single, 1909. Home: Concord, N.H. Died Sept. 21, 1939.

ABBOTT, Frank Frost, univ. prof.; b. Redding, Conn., Mar. 27, 1860; s. Thaddeus Marvin and Mary Jane (Frost) A.; A.B., Yale, 1882, Ph.D., 1891 (hon. A.M., 1912); universities of Berlin and Bonn, 1888-89; at Rome, 1889; m. Jane Harrison, June 21, 1888. Tutor Latin, Yale, 1884-91; chosen 1st mem. of faculty of U. of Chicago; asso. prof. Latin, 1891-94, prof., 1894-1908, U. of Chicago; Kennedy prof. Latin, Princeton, 1908—. Prof. Latin Am. Sch. Classical Studies, Rome, 1901-02; asso. editor Classical Philology and Studi Storici. Author: Repetition in Latin, 1900; A History and Desciption of Roman Political Institutions, 1901; The Toledo Manuscript of the Germania of Tacitus, 1904; A Short History of Rome, 1906; Handbook for the Study of Roman History, 1906; Society and Politics in Ancient Rome, 1909; The Common People of Ancient Rome, 1911; The Spanish Pleas of Alberico Gentile, Vol. I (Latin Text with Introduction), Vol. II (Translation with Introduction), 1921; Roman Politics, 1923. Trustee Am. Acad. in Rome; ex-pres. Am. Philol. Assn. Home: Princeton, N.J. Died July 27, 1924.

ABBOTT, Frederick H., sec. Bd. Indian Commrs.; b. near Niles, Mich., July 31, 1872; s. Hiram and Frances Edna (Steinbeck) A.; U. of Neb., 1895-98; B.A., State U. of Ia.; m. Anita Muir, June 20, 1900; children—Aubrey Muir, Anita Carter. In newspaper business, 1904-09; asst. commr. of Indian Affairs, 1909-12, acting commr., 1912-13; again asst. commr., June-Oct. 1913; sec. Bd. Indian Commrs., Oct. 11, 1913-July 1, 1915. Mem. bd. of regents, U. of Neb., 1905-09. Exec. sec. Georgia Assn.; editor Georgia Magazine. Republican. Mason. Home: Waycross, Ga. Died Aug. 27, 1932.

ABBOTT, Frederick Wallace, physician; b. Dover, N.H., Mar. 5, 1861; s. Sylvester and Elizabeth Graves (Wortman) A.; A.B., U. of America, 1883; attended Med. Sch. of Me. (mem. dept. Bowdoin Coll.), 1884, 1885; M.D., Eclectic Med. Coll. of Me., 1886; H.F.B.S., 1893; A.M., Taylor U, 1901; Ph.D., Nat. Normal U., 1901; LL.D., Potomac U., 1905; F.S.Sc. (London), 1908; F.S.P. (Eng.), 1914; F.B.P.C. (Eng.), 1915; F.P.C. (London), 1916; D.P.H., Eclectic Med. U., Kansas City, Mo., 1917; m. Sylvina Apphia Emery, Sept. 2, 1886. Practiced in Taunton, Mass., 1886—; lecturer on physiology and hygiene in Merrimack County Acad., 1892; asso. editor Mass. Med. Jour., 1894-1904, Am. Med. Jour., 1906—; senior censor Eclectic Med. Coll. of City of New York; prof. eugenics, Eclectic Med. U., Kansas City, Mo., 1913—; prof. med. history and of med. ethics, Middlesex Coll. Medicine and Surgery, and consulting physician at Middlesex Hosp., 1916—. Pres. Mass. Eclectic Med. Soc., 1894, N.E. Eclectic Med. Assn., 1900, Am. Eclectic Materia Medica Assn., 1905-07, Boston Dist. Eclectic Med. Soc., 1910; v.p. Am. Anti-Tuberculosis League, 1907. Academician of Toulouse, France; life-mem. and medalist of the 1st class (gold) Italian Acad. Physics and Chemistry; chmn. bd. of trustees, and sec.-treas. Alumnal Soc., Potomac U. Democrat. Author: Limitation of the Family, 1891; The Education of Youth Upon Matters Sexual, 1895. Home: Taunton, Mass. Died June 19, 1919.

ABBOTT, George Birch, jurist; b. at Brookfield, Vt., Sept. 27, 1850; s. Benjamin Franklin and Diancy (Pickering) A.; A.B., Williams Coll., 1872, A.M., 1875; LL.B., Columbia Law Sch., 1874; (LL.D., Williams, 1907); m. Eva Topping Reeve, Nov. 20, 1878. Admitted to bar, 1874; pub. administrator, 1881-89, surrogate, 1889-1901, Kings County, N.Y.; justice Supreme Court, N.Y., Jan. 1, 1907-Dec. 31, 1920. Home: Brooklyn, N.Y. Died 1908.

ABBOTT, Gordon, banker; b. Boston, Jan. 18, 1863; s. Jeremiah and Ellen (Bangs) A.; A.B., Harvard, 1884; m. Katherine Tiffany, Nov. 6, 1895. Mem. firm of Abbott, Wheelock & Co., mchts., Boston and New York, 1884-93; v.p., 1893-1900, pres., 1900-10, chmn. bd., 1910—, Old Colony Trust Co., Boston; dir. Gen. Electric Co., N.E. Mut. Life Ins. Co. (bd. of investment), N.Y. Central R.R. Trustee, 1895-1905, treas., 1905-15, mem. exec. com., 1916-31, pres., 1931-35, now mem. bd. mgrs., Children's Hosp., Boston. Home: Manchester, Mass. Died Jan. 24, 1937.

ABBOTT, Grace, social worker; b. Grand Island, Neb., Nov. 17, 1878; d. of Othman A. and Elizabeth M. (Griffin) Abbott; Ph.B., Grand Island Coll., 1898, LL.D., 1931; U. of Neb., 1902-03, LL.D., 1931; Ph.M. in Polit. Science, U. of Chicago, 1909; LL.D., U. of N.H. and U. of Wis., 1932, Mt. Holyoke Coll., 1935, Wilson Coll., 1934; unmarried. Teacher Grand Island High Sch., 1899-1902 and 1903-07; dir. Immigrants' Protective League, 1908-17; resident Hull House, Chicago, 1908-15; mem. faculty Chicago Sch. of Civics and Philanthropy, 1910-17; dir. child labor div. of Children's Bur., Washington, D.C., 1917-19; adviser, War Labor Policies Bd., 1918; exec. sec. Ill. Immigrants' Commn., 1920-21; chief of U.S. Children's Bur., 1921-34; prof. of pub. welfare, and editor Social Service Rev., U. of Chicago. Pres. Nat. Conf. Social Work, 1924; mem. for U.S. of advisory com. on traffic in women and children, League of Nations, 1923—; mem. bd. Internat. Conf. Social Work. Awarded gold medal, Am. Social Science Assn., 1931; Govt. del. 19th and 23d Internat. Labor Confs.,

1933, 37. Author: The Immigrant and the Community; The Immigrant in Massachusetts. Home: Chicago, Ill. Died June 19, 1939.

ABBOTT, Herbert Vaughan, coll. prof.; b. Terre Haute, Ind., Jan. 3, 1865; s. Lyman (q.v.) and Abby Frances (Hamlin) A.; A.B., Amherst Coll., 1885; m. Senda, d. Albert Berenson, June 15, 1911. Lit. critic N.Y. Commercial Advertiser, 1890-91; asst. and instr., English Dept., Harvard, 1894-98; instr. English, Horace Mann Sch. and Teachers Coll., New York, 1898-1905; asso. prof. and prof. English, Smith Coll., 1905—. Editor: Roger de Coverly Papers; Selections from Addison and Steele. Author: English Composition (with Franklin Thomas Baker). Home: Northampton, Mass. Died Mar. 24, 1929.

ABBOTT, Horatio Johnson, pres. The Abbott Gasoline Co.; b. Clayton, Mich., Mar. 26, 1876; s. Aaron and Mabel (Johnson) A.; student U. of Mich., 1899-1900; m. Florence A. Sutton, Nov. 29, 1905; children—Floyd W., Herbert N., Robert S. Pub. Ann Arbor (Mich.) Record, 1902-04; bldg. supt., 1904-15; register of deeds, Washtenaw County, Mich., 1908-13; postmaster, Ann Arbor, 1915-23; pres. The Abbott Gasoline Co., 1923—; pres. Washtenong Assn.; dir. Artificial Ice Co., Farmers & Mechanics Bank, Gill Lumber Co. Collector of internal revenue, Detroit, 1933-34. Mem. Mich. Dem. State Central Com., 1910-24, chmn., 1924-28; mem. Dem. Nat. Com., 1928—. Methodist. Mason. K.P., Odd Fellow. Home: Ann Arbor, Mich. Died Apr. 24, 1936.

ABBOTT, Ira Anson, judge; b. Barnard, Vt., July 20, 1845; s. Daniel and Deborah (DeWolfe) A.; pvt. 9th Vt. Vols., 1864-65; A.B., Dartmouth, 1870; m. Emma Nichols, Apr. 30, 1879 (died 1884). Began practice of law at Haverhill, 1872; city solicitor, 1873-75; mem. law firm of Abbott & Pearl, 1877-98; judge Mass. Central Dist. Ct. of Northern Essex, 1898-1904; asso. justice Supreme Ct. of Ty. of N.M., 1901-12. Republican. Home: Haverhill, Mass. Died Oct. 19, 1921.

ABBOTT, James Francis, Orientalist; b. Greeley, Colo., Sept. 27, 1876; s. Eugene Herbert and Marian Belle (Getty) A.; A.B., Stanford, 1899, A.M., 1905; spl. student U. of Tokyo, 1900, 02; Ph.D., U. of Chicago, 1907; m. Marguerite Zuck, Aug. 21, 1904; children—Dorland, Jean, James Staniford, Andrew Patterson. Instr. Shigaken Commercial Sch., Omi, Japan, 1900-01; prof. English, Imperial Japanese Naval Acad., 1902-03; prof. zoology, Washington U., 1904-17, apptd. commercial attaché Am. Embassy, Tokyo, Jan. 11, 1919; mem. tech. staff, Am. Delegation, Conf. on Limitation of Armament, Washington, D.C., 1921. Capt. Mil. Intelligence Div. Gen. Staff, U.S. Army, Washington, 1918-19. Author: The Elementary Principles of General Biology, 1912, 7th edit., 1916; Japanese Expansion and American Policies, 1915; Nichi-Bei Mondai (Japanese), 1918. Home: San Francisco, Calif. Died July 3, 1926.

ABBOTT, Jo, lawyer, congressman; b. near Decatur, Ala., Jan. 15, 1840; s. William and Mary A.; m. Rowena W. Sturgis, Dec. 15, 1868. Served in C.S. army as 1st lt. 12th Tex. cav.; admitted to Tex. bar; mem. Tex. legislature, 1869-71; judge 28th jud. dist. Tex., 1879-84; mem. Congress, 1887-97. Democrat. Home: Hillsboro, Tex. Died 1908.

ABBOTT, Lawrence Fraser, editor; b. Brooklyn, June 25, 1859; s. Lyman and Abby Fances (Hamlin) A.; A.B., Amherst Coll., 1881, L.H.D., 1931; Litt.D., Bowdoin and U. of Vt., 1923; m. Mary C. Valentine, May 1889 (died, 1899); m. 2d, Winifred Buck, Sept. 7, 1905. Pres. The Outlook Co., 1891-1923. Trustee N.Y. Life Ins. Co., 1918-31, sec., 1931—. Edited (with intro.) Roosevelt's African and European Addresses, 1910; Letters of Archie Butt, with biog. sketch, 1924; author of article on Theodore Roosevelt in Ency. Britannica, 1911. Author: Impressions of Theodore Roosevelt, 1919; Twelve Great Modernists, 1927; The Story of Nylic, 1930. Decorated Officier de l'Instruction Publique (France); Order of Prince Danilo, 3d class (Montenegro). Home: Cornwall, N.Y. Died Feb. 7, 1933.

ABBOTT, Leon Martin, lawyer; b. Richmond, N. H., Aug. 28, 1867; s. Joseph B. and Lydia C. (Martin) A.; Mass. Inst. Tech., 1885-86; Harvard Coll., 1886-87, 1890-91, Harvard Law Sch., 1887-90; m. Florence M. Tallman, Apr. 19, 1894. Began practice in Boston, 1891; mem. Abbott, Dane, Buffum & Howe; trustee Mass. Savings Bank. Republican. Mem. Am. and Mass. bar assns. Past Grand Master Masons in Mass.; Sovereign Grand Comdr. of Supreme Council 33° N.M.J. Home: Brookline, Mass. Died Oct. 10, 1932.

ABBOTT, L(uther) Jewett, author; b. Fremont, Neb., Nov. 8, 1871; s. Luther Jewett and Clara Frances (Culbertson) A.; A.B., U. of Neb., 1896, LL.B., 1900; A.M., Columbia, 1906; m. Lillie Riley, Aug. 27, 1905. With bro., Keene A., established Lawton (Okla.) Lariat, 1901; editor and pub. Progress (monthly ednl. mag.), Oklahoma City, 1911-13; prin. Lawton High Sch., 1903-05; prof. Am history, Central State Normal Sch., Edmond, Okla., 1907—. Sec. Okla. Sch. Land Preservation League, 1908; chmn. exec. com. Okla. Ednl. Assn., 1909-10. Democrat. Presbyterian. Author: Race Question in the 46th State, 1907; The Truth About the School Lands, 1908; Oklahoma School Civics, 1909; History and Civics of Oklahoma, 1910; Story of Oklahoma, 1913; The Tobacco Toboggan. Home: Edmond, Okla. Died Mar. 29, 1914.

ABBOTT, Lyman, editor; b. Roxbury, Mass., Dec. 18, 1835; s. Jacob and Harriet (Vaughan) A.; A.B., New York U., 1853 (D.D., 1876; D.D., Harvard, Yale, 1903; LL.D., Western Reserve, 1900, Amherst, 1908; L.H.D., Miami, 1909); m. Abby Frances Hamlin, Oct. 14, 1857 (died 1907); children—Lawrence F., Harriet F., Herbert V., Ernest H., Theodore J., Beatrice V. Admitted to N.Y. bar, 1856; ordained Congl. ministry, 1860; pastor, Terre Haute, Ind., 1860-65, New England Ch., New York, 1865-69; sec. Am. Union Commn. (Freedman's), 1865-68; in lit. work, 1869-88; pastor Plymouth Ch., Brooklyn (succeeding Henry Ward Beecher), 1888-99; was editor Lit. Record of Harper's Mag. and of Illustrated Christian Weekly; asso. editor, with Henry Ward Beecher, The Christian Union; editor-in-chief The Outlook, 1893—. Author: Jesus of Nazareth; Old Testament Shadows of New Testament Truth; A Layman's Story; How to Study the Bible; Illustrated Commentary on the New Testament, 1875; Dictionary of Religious Knowledge (with late T. J. Conant), 1876; A Study in Human Nature, 1885; In Aid of Faith, 1891; Life of Christ, 1894; Evolution of Christianity, 1896; The Theology of an Evolutionist, 1897; Christianity and Social Problems, 1897; Life and Letters of Paul, 1898; The Life That Really Is, 1899; Problems of Life, 1900; Life and Literature of the Ancient Hebrews, 1900; The Rights of Man, 1901; Henry Ward Beecher, 1903; The Other Room, 1904; The Great Companion, 1904, 1905; Christian Ministry, 1905; Personality of God, 1905; Industrial Problems, 1905; The Home Builder, 1908; The Temple, 1909; The Spirit of Democracy, 1910; My Four Anchors, 1911; America in the Making, 1911; Letters to Unknown Friends, 1913; Reminiscences, 1915; The Twentieth Century Crusade, 1918; What Christianity Means to Me, 1921. Home: Cornwall on Hudson, N.Y. Died Oct. 22, 1922.

ABBOTT, Mary Perkins, author; b. Salem, Mass., Oct. 17, 1857; d. Stephen Bradshaw Ives, jr., long at head of Essex bar; grad. Salem High School, 1873; m. Charles Patterson Abbott, mcht. of Calcutta, E.I., 1874; resided in India five years; book reviewer and spl. writer Chicago Evening Post and Chicago Times-Herald. Author: Alexia (romance); The Beverleys (a sotry of Calcutta life). Died 1904.

ABBOTT, Mather Almon, headmaster; b. Halifax, N.S., Mar. 1, 1874; s. Rev. John and Ella (Almon) A.; B.A., King's Coll., Windsor, N.S., 1893; B.A., Worcester Coll. (Oxford U., Eng.), 1896; M.A., Oxford, 1916; hon. M.A., Yale, 1918; Litt.D., Princeton, 1920; m. Elizabeth Twining, Sept. 1, 1897. Master, Groton (Mass.) Sch., teacher of Latin and Greek, 1897-1916; prof. Latin, Yale, 1916-19; headmaster, Lawrenceville (N.J.) Sch., 1919—. Organized Yale Naval Unit, 1917; commd. lt. U.S.N.R.F., 1918; head coach Univ. Crew (Yale), 1918, 19. Republican. Presbyn. Author: First Latin Writer, 1904; The Boy Today, 1930. Home: Lawrenceville, N.J. Died May 17, 1934.

ABBOTT, Nathan, univ. prof.; b. Norridgewock, Me., July 11, 1854; s. Abiel and Sarah S. (Davis) A.; A.B., Yale, 1877; LL.B., Boston U., 1893; m. Frances Field, Apr. 23, 1884 (dec.); children—Dorothy (Mrs. Richard Ames), Phyllis (Mrs. John T. Burnett). Tappan prof. law, U. of Mich., 1891; prof. law, Northwestern U., 1892-94, Stanford U., 1895-1907, Columbia, 1907-22. Home: Harrison, N.Y. Died Jan. 29, 1941.

ABBOTT, Samuel Appleton Browne, lawyer; b. Lowell, Mass., Mar. 6, 1846; s. Josiah Gardner and Carolina (Livermore) A.; A.B., Harvard, 1866, A.M., 1872; admitted to bar, 1868; m. Mary Goddard, May 21, 1869; m. 2d, Abby Frances Woods, Oct. 15, 1873; children—Helen Frances (Mrs. Maurice K. Washburn), Madeline Livermore (Mrs. John Ormsbee Ames), Anne Francie (Mrs. Charles Kilvert), Caroline Livermore; m. 2d, Maria Elizabeth Dexter, Apr. 16, 1896 (died 1923). Practiced Boston, 1868—; police commr., 1887-89; trustee Boston Pub. Library, 1879-92 (pres., 1889-94); acting librarian, same, 1890-94; dir. Am. Acad. in Rome, 1897-1903. Episcopalian. Home: Villa Lontana, Ponte Miliro, Rome, Italy. Died June 19, 1931.

ABBOTT, Samuel Warren, M.D., sec. Mass. State Bd. of Health, 1886—; b. Woburn, Mass., June 12, 1837; grad. Brown, 1858; Harvard Med. School, 1862; asst. surgeon, U.S. Navy, 1861-64, resigned; asst. surgeon and surgeon 1st Mass. cav., 1864-65; coroner, Middlesex County, Mass., 1872-77; med. examiner, same, 1877-84; practiced medicine at Woburn, 1865-69; later at Wakefield. Author of The Past and Present Condition of Public Hygiene and State Medicine in the United States, 1900 (U.S. Commrs. Paris Expn.). Home: Newton Centre, Mass. Died 1904.

ABBOTT, W. Herbert, leather mcht.; b. Boston, Mass., July 14, 1866; s. William T. and Frances A. (Hoyt) A.; ed. high sch., Boston; m. Fannie E. Whipple, June 8, 1892; m. 2d, Euna M. Lawrence, Jan. 14, 1921. Pres., treas. W. Herbert Abbott, Inc., leather, 1900—; pres. Abbott & Fernald Co.; v.p. Liberty Trust Co.; dir. United Cape Cod Cranberry Co.; trustee Dorchester Savings Bank; dir. N.E. Bond & Mortgage Co.; pres. Beneficial Loan Soc., Inc., of Boston, Personal Finance Co., of Cambridge. Dir. N.E. Evangelistic Assn. Conglist. Clubs: Economic, Longwood Cricket. Home: Newtonville, Mass. Died Oct. 11, 1928.

ABBOTT, Wallace Calvin, physician, editor; b. Bridgewater, Vt., Oct. 12, 1857; s. Luther and Wealtha (Barrows) A.; Randolph (Vt.) State Normal Sch.; St. Johnsbury (Vt.) Coll.; Dartmouth Coll.; M.D., U. of Mich., 1885; m. Clara Ingraham, Aug. 10, 1886. Settled in Chicago, 1886, and engaged in gen. practice; established The Abbott Alkaloidal Co., now The Abbott Laboratories; mng. editor Am. Jour. Clin. Medicine. Republican. Methodist. Clubs: Hamilton, Press, Chicago Advertising, Union League. Author: (with W. F. Waugh) Text-Book of Alkaloidal Therapeutics; Text-Book of Alkaloidal Practice. Home: Chicago, Ill. Died July 4, 1921.

ABBOTT, William Martin, lawyer; b. San Francisco, Calif., Mar. 17, 1872; s. William and Anna Bell (Casselman) A.; LL.B., U. of Calif., 1893; m. Annie Josephine McVean, Aug. 3, 1895. Practiced at San Francisco, 1893—; asst. atty. gen. of Calif., 1898-1902. V.p., gen. counsel, Market St. Ry. Co., S.F.; pres. San Mateo Electric Ry. Co., Sutro Ry. Co., Met. Ry. Co.; gen. atty. United Railroads of San Francisco. Republican. Mason, Elk. Home: San Francisco, Calif. Died Nov. 13, 1941.

ABBOTT, William Tabor, lawyer, banker; b. Wells River, Vt., Feb. 16, 1868; s. Orrin S. and Ella J. (Tabor) A.; A.B., Dartmouth, 1890; m. Elsie Parsons Bourland, June 28, 1905. Admitted to bar, 1893; mem. Stevens, Horton & Abbott, Peoria, Ill., 1893-1904, Ritsher, Montgomery, Hart & Abbott, Chicago, 1904-10; v.p. Central Trust Co. of Ill., Mar. 1910—. Trustee Rufus F. Dawes Hotel Assn. Asst. dir. Bur. of the Budget, to assist Gen. Charles G. Dawes in making up the First nat. budget for U.S. Govt., June-Dec. 1921; mem. Tax Simplification Bd., Dec. 1921—. Republican. Conglist. Mason (32°). Home: Evanston, Ill. Died May 29, 1922.

ABEL, John Jacob, pharmacologist; b. Cleveland, O., May 19, 1857; s. George M. and Mary (Becker) A.; Ph.B., U. of Mich., 1883, A.M., 1903, Sc.D., 1912; Sc.D., U. of Pittsburgh, 1915; LL.D., U. of Cambridge, Eng., 1920; Sc.D., Harvard, 1925, Yale U., 1927; hon. M.D., John Casimir U., Lwow, Poland, 1926; LL.D., U. of Aberdeen, 1932; grad. student Johns Hopkins, 1883-84; student of chemistry and medicine at Leipzig, Strassburg, Heidelberg, Vienna, Berne, Würsburg and Berlin. 1884-91; M.D., Strassburg, 1888; m. Mary W. Hinman, July 10, 1883. Lecturer and prof. materia medica and therapeutics, U. of Mich., 1891-93; prof. pharmacology, Johns Hopkins, 1893-1932; prof. emeritus pharmacology, and dir. of Laboratory for Endocrine Research, 1932—. Editor Jour. of Pharmacology and Exptl. Therapeutics, 1909-32. Awarded Research Corporation prize, 1925; first award of lectureship of Kober Foundation, Am. Assn. Physicians, 1925; Willard Gibbs medal, Chicago sect. Am. Chem. Soc., 1926; gold medal, Soc. of Apothecaries, London, 1928; Philip A. Conné medal, New York Chemists' Club, 1932; Kober medal awarded, 1934. Home: Baltimore, Md. Died May 26, 1938.

ABELES, Edward S., actor; b. St. Louis, Mo., Nov. 4, 1869. Appeared in "Alabama" at Palmer's Theatre, New York, Nov. 2, 1891; played part of Charley Wykeham, in "Chariey's Aunt," Empire Theatre, 1894; appeared in "My Friend from India," Bijou Theatre, 1896; in "Hidenseek," Globe Theatre, London, 1901; as Simpson, the valet, in "The Dictator," Criterion Theatre, New York, 1904, and in same part at Comedy Theatre, London, 1905; toured in "Brewster's Millions," 1906; appeared in "He Tried to Be Nice," in vaudeville theatres, 1911. Died July 10, 1919.

ABELL, Edwin Franklin, newspaper pub.; b. May 15, 1840; s. late Arunah S.A., founder Baltimore Sun.; m. Elizabeth M., d. late Frank Laurenson of Baltimore. Succeeded to the paper with brothers, 1878, and became pres. A.S. Abell Co., pubs., May 1, 1894. Home: Baltimore, Md. Died Feb. 28, 1904.

ABELL, Harry Clinton, pub. utilities; b. of Am. parents, Winnipeg, Manitoba, Can., July 8, 1871; s. Edmund Richard and Nancy (Noel) A.; student St. John's Coll., Winnipeg; B.S. in E.E., Armour Inst. Tech., 1897, E.E., 1906; m. Fannilee Martin, June 25, 1902; 1 dau., Margaret A. Engring. apprentice Canadian Pacific Ry., 1889; with Belding Motor Co., Chicago, and Canadian Gen. Electric Co., 1892, 93; in employ Anchor Line and Internat. Navigation Co., 1898; marine engr. Spanish-Am. War, 1898; with Emerson McMillin & Co., later with Am. Light & Traction Co., operating pub. utilities, 1898-1921; now v.p. Electric Bond & Share Co. Pres. Am. Gas Assn., 1925, 26. Republican. Episcopalian. Mason, Elk. Clubs: Engineers', Bankers. Died Nov. 1938.

ABERCROMBIE, John William, educator; b. St. Clair County, Ala., May 17, 1866; s. Henry M. and Sarah A. (Kendrick) A.; A.B., Oxford Coll., Ala., 1886; LL.B., U. of Ala., 1888, LL.D., 1904; LL.D., U. of S.C., 1905; D.C.L., U. of the South, 1907; m. Rose Merrill, Jan. 8, 1891; children—Myrl (Mrs. Edward J. Thomas), Clare (Mrs. C. H. Barnwell), Ruth (Mrs. J. C. Bondurant), Rose (dec.), Jane (Mrs. Joseph W. Taber). Prin. high schs., supt. city schs., and pres. colleges, 1888-98; state supt. of edn. of Ala., 1898-1902, 1920-27; asst. state supt. of edn. of Ala., 1927-35; state supervisor of teacher certification of Ala., 1935—. Pres. U. of Ala., 1902-11; mem. 63d and 64th Congresses (1913-17), Ala.-at-large; solicitor and acting sec. for U.S. Dept. of Labor, 1918-20. Mem. Ala. Senate, 1896-98, chmn. Com. on Edn.; mem. Ala. Text-Book Commn., 1903-08; became mem. Nat. Council of State Univ. Presidents, 1903—, v.p., 1908-09; chmn. Ala. Commn. for Selection of Rhodes Scholars, 1903-11; pres. Ala. Soc. for Mental Hygiene, 1915-17; mem. Ala. State Bd. of Edn., 1920-27; mem. Ala. Child Welfare Commn., 1920-27; mem. Ala. Interracial Com., 1920—; mem. Ala. Conf. of Social Work, 1920-27; mem. bd. dirs. Nat. Illiteracy Crusade, 1926—; mem. Ala. Edn. Assn., 1892—; pres. Southern Ednl. Assn., 1906-07; organizer, and pres. Ala. Coll. Assn., 1908-12; mem. Nat. Council of Edn., 1908-12, 1926—; mem. Southern Ednl. Council, 1908-14, pres., 1912-14. Mem. bd. dirs. Ala. Bapt. Conv., 1920-37; mem. Edn. Bd. So. Baptist Conv., 1921-28, Nat. Advisory Com. on Illiteracy, 1929-33, Commn. on Interracial Coöperation, 1931—, Advisory Council of Nat. Conf. Jews and Christians, 1933—. Mason (32°). Baptist. Democrat. Author: Repts. State Dept. of Edn., Ala., 1898-1902, 1920-27; Univ. of Ala., 1902-11. Consulting author: Library of Southern Literature. Advisory editor: History of Alabama and Her People. Home: Anniston, Ala. Died July 1940.

ABERNATHY, Alonzo, educator; born Sandusky County, O., Apr. 14, 1836; s. Jehiel and Anna Mary (Ettinger) A.; A.B., U. of Chicago, 1866; Ph.D., Lenox Coll., Ia., 1886; m. Louise E. Eaton, Jan. 21, 1868. Pvt. to col. 9th Ia. Vols., 1861-65; participated in 40 engagements; twice wounded. Mem. Ia. Ho. of Rep., 1866-68; prin. Des Moines Coll., 1870-71, since then on bd. trustees same; supt. pub. instrn., Ia., 1871-76; pres. U. of Chicago, 1876-78; prin. Cedar Valley Sem., 1881-1902; mem. bd. regents, State U. of Ia., 1890-1909. Author: Iowa Under Territorial Government, and the Removal of the Indians, 1906; History of Iowa Baptist Schools, 1907; Glimpses of Abraham Lincoln, 1909. Editor Whitman's Early Life of Jesus, and New Light on Passion Week, 1913. Home: Des Moines, Ia. Died Feb. 1915.

ABERT, Silvanus Thayer, civil engr.; b. Philadelphia, Pa., July 22, 1828; ed. at Princeton; entered service U.S. Govt. in 1848 and was active in canal construction; on staff Gens. Banks and Meade in Civil War; in river surveys for Columbian govt., 1865-66; re-entered U.S. service, and in 1873 took charge of geog. div. from Washington to Wilmington, N.C. Died 1903.

ABERT, William Stone, lawyer; b. Washington, D.C., July 27, 1845; s. Lt.-Col. James William (U.S. Army) and Jane Lenthal (Stone) A.; A.B., Princeton, 1865, later A.M.; LL.B., Cincinnati Law Sch., 1868; m. Nannie S. Hamilton, Oct. 5, 1875. Practiced at Cincinnati, 1868-77; then before Supreme Ct. of U.S. and local courts of D.C. Compiler "Laws of the District of Columbia" by appmt. of Supreme Court of D.C. Home: Washington, D.C. Died 1921.

ABORN, Milton, impresario; b. Marysville, Calif., May 18, 1864; married; children—Fannie, Amie. Theatrical mgr. at 21; appeared in comic opera 2 seasons, then stage dir. and leading comedian with B. F. Keith's Comic Opera Co., Boston, New York, Phila. for 8 yrs.; toured with own company 5 yrs.; asso. with bro., Sargent, in organizing circuit of 12 companies in grand and comic opera, 1902-13; selected by Otto H. Kahn first native Am. dir. of subsidized opera, Century Opera Co., 1913-15; made elaborate revival of "The Mikado" in New York with Messrs. Shubert, 1925; mammoth prodn. of "Pinafore," Century Theatre, New York, 1926. Home: New York, N.Y. Died Nov. 12, 1933.

ABOTT, Bessie Pickens, operatic soprano; b. Riverdale, N.Y.; began with sister Jessie in vaudeville; sang in Empire Theatre, London, 1898; returned to New York, upon advice of Jean de Reszké, and studied under Mme. Freda Ashforth; later studied under Victor Capoul, Paris; made début as Juliette, in "Romeo et Juliette," Paris Opera House; appeared with Met. Opera Co., New York, 1907; sang in De Koven's "Robin Hood," Chicago, 1913; m. T. Walso Story, Sept. 26, 1912. Died Feb. 9, 1919.

ABRAHAM, Abraham, dry goods mcht.; b. New York, Mar. 9, 1843; s. Judah A.; ed. pub. schs. Began as apprentice in dry goods house, Newark, N.J., at age of 14; later with his father in wholesale dry goods store. In 1865 formed partnership with Joseph Wechsler as Wechsler & Abraham in small dry goods store in Brooklyn; firm expanded and changed to Abraham & Straus. Pres. Temple Israel and Jewish Hosp.; v.p. Hebrew Orphan Asylum, Brooklyn; dir. Brooklyn Soc. for Prevention of Cruelty to Children, Kings County Trust Co.; mem. Chamber of Commerce, New York; trustee Baron de Hirsch Fund; dir. Brooklyn Inst. Arts and Sciences, Brooklyn Acad. Music. Home: Brooklyn, N.Y. Died 1911.

ABRAHAMS, Henry, labor advocate; b. Buffalo, N.Y., Sept. 23, 1855; pub. sch. edn.; m. Phoebe Levy, of Brooklyn, N.Y., Feb. 2, 1880 (died June 15, 1913). Sec. Cigarmakers' Union No. 97 (Boston), Boston Central Labor Union, 1893—; mem. Commn. on High Cost of Living, 1910. Trustee Franklin Inst., Boston; sec. Boston United Hand in Hand, largest Jewish organization in Boston. Republican. Jewish religion. Mem. City Planning Bd.; mem. Boston Sch. Com., Dec. 19, 1916—. Home: Boston, Mass. Died Jan. 15, 1923.

ABRAMS, Albert, physician; b. San Francisco, Dec. 8, 1863; s. Marcus and Rachel (Leavey) A.; M.D., U. of Heidelberg, 1882; A.M., Portland U., 1892 (LL.D.); post-grad. courses, London, Berlin, Vienna, Paris; m. Jeanne Roth, Nov. 25, 1897; 2d, Blanche Schwabacher, Sept. 28, 1915. Prof. pathology, Cooper Med. Coll., 1893-98; pres. Emanuel Polyclinic, 1904—. Author: Synopsis of Morbid Renal Secretions, 1892; Manual of Clinical Diagnosis, 1894; Consumption—Its Causes and Prevention, 1895; Scattered Leaves of a Physician's Diary, 1900, Diseases of Heart, 1901; Nervous Breakdown, 1901; Hygiene, in A System of Physiologic Therapeutics, 1901; Diseases of the Lung, 1905; Self-Poisoning; Diagnostic-Therapeutics, 1909; Spinal Therapeutics, 1909; Spondylotherapy, in Reference Handbook Medical Sciences, 1917. Discoverer Abram's Reflexes and Electronic Reactions of Abrams. Home: San Francisco, Calif. Died Jan. 13, 1924.

ACHESON, Albert Robert, mech. and elec. engr.; b. Riverton, New Zealand, Oct. 12, 1882; s. Robert and Annie (Sinclair) A.; B.S.C. in M.E., 1905, B.E., in E.E., 1906, Canterbury Coll. (New Zealand U.); m. Pansy Kate Shaw, July 1, 1909; children—Cedric Robert, Mildred Frances (Mrs. Raymond Ames), Dorothy Violet, Douglas Frank. In employ New Zealand Government railways, summers, 1901-04; with Westinghouse Air Brake Co., Addington, New Zealand, 1904-05; with Wellington & Manawatu Ry. Co., 1905-06; with Westinghouse Electric & Mfg. Co., Pittsburgh, 1906-08; prof. mech. engring. and head of dept. of mech. engring., Coll. of Applied Science, Syracuse U., 1908—; industrial engr. with Westinghouse Electric & Mfg. Co., summer of 1910; operating engr. in charge 6000 h.p. boiler room, Utica & Mohawk Valley Ry. Co., Utica, N.Y., summer of 1911; cons. engr. Bur. of Gas and Electricity, Syracuse, 1914-19; gen. cons. engring. practice, 1919—. Home: Syracuse, N.Y. Died Feb. 25, 1941.

ACHESON, Alexander W. (Sandie), M.D.; born Washington, Pa., Oct. 12, 1842; s. Judge Alexander Wilson and Jane (Wishart) A.; hon. A.B., Washington and Jefferson Coll., 1866; M.D., U. of Pa., 1867; m. Sarah M. Cooke, June 20, 1864 (deceased). 1 dau., Mrs. Alice A. Sproule. Pvt. 13th Pa. Regt., 1861; pvt. 140th Pa. Regt., 1862; sergt., 1862; capt., 1863; a.-d.-c. on staff of Gen. Nelson A. Miles, 1863; was the 1st U.S. Army officer on the captured Confederate breastworks at the "bloody angle," in the charge at Spottsylvania, Va.; shor through the face there. Began practice at Phila.; removed to Denison, Tex., 1872. Was mayor of Denison 4 terms; Rep. candidate for gov. of Tex., 1906, for U.S. senator, 1916, for mem. Congress, 1920; city physician, 1923-29. Hon. life v.p. Red River Flood Control and Navigation Assn.; Tex. dir. Miss. Valley Assn.; del. to rivers convs. at New Orleans, Washington and Chicago. Presbyn. Club: Elks. Home: Denison, Tex. Died Sept. 7, 1934.

ACHESON, Edward Campion, bishop; b. Woolwich, Kent, England, Apr. 7, 1858; s. of Alexander and Mary (Campion) A.; grad. Wycliffe Coll. (U. of Toronto), 1889; M.A., New York U., 1892; S.T.D. Trinity Coll., 1916; D.D., Wesleyan U., 1916, Berkeley, 1916, and Wycliffe Coll., 1917; m. Eleanor G. Gooderham, June 8, 1892; children—Dean Gooderham, Margaret Campion, Edward Campion. Deacon, June 10, 1888, priest, July 14, 1889, Ch. of England in Can.; curate, All Saints Ch., Toronto, 1888-89; asst. minister St. George's Ch., Stuyvesant Sq., N.Y. City, 1889-92; rector Holy Trinity Ch., Middletown, Conn., Apr. 17, 1892-Nov. 4, 1915; suffragan bishop of Conn., 1915—. Trustee Berkeley Div. Sch. (Middletown, Conn.). Served as chaplain with Co. K, Queen's Own Rifles, during rebellion in Canadian Northwest, 1885, and present at Cut Knife Creek fight, hon. mention and medal; Red Cross chaplain and field worker with 26th Div. in France, Nov., 1918-Mar., 1919. Republican. Mason. Home: Middletown, Conn. Died Jan. 28, 1934.

ACHESON, Edward Goodrich, inventor; b. Washington, Pa., Mar. 9, 1856; s. William and Sarah D. (Ruplé) A.; acad. edn. Bellefonte, Pa.; hon. Sc.D., U. of Pittsburgh, 1909; m. Margaret Maher, 1884; children—Veronica Belle, Edward Goodrich, Raymond Maher (dec.), Sarah Ruth, George Wilson, John Huyler, Margaret Irene, Jean Ellen (dec.), Howard Archibald. Asst. to Thomas A. Edison, 1880-81. Inventor of carborundum, siloxicon, Egyptianized clay, Aquadag, Oildag, and a method of making graphite. Awarded Rumford medal of Am. Acad. of Arts and Sciences, 1908; Perkin Research medal, 1910; grand prix, Paris Expn., 1900, St. Louis Expn., 1904. Officer Royal Order of the Polar Star (Sweden). Hon. mem. Russian Imperial Tech. Soc., Swedish Tech. Soc.; was pres. Electrochem soc.; v.p. Am. Inst. Chem. Engrs., E.E. Donor of $25,000, 1928, to Electrochem. Soc., to establish Edward Goodrich Acheson biennial prize; received Acheson medal from Electrochem. Soc., 1929. Died July 6, 1931.

ACHESON, Ernest Francis, congressman; b. Washington, Pa., Sept. 19, 1855; s. Judge Alexander Wilson and Jane (Wishart) A.; grad. Washington and Jefferson Coll., 1875, hon. A.M., 1889; admitted to bar, 1877; m. Jane B. Stewart, Nov. 22, 1882. Owner and editor Washington (Pa.) Daily Observer, from 1879, and of Daily Reporter, 1902-12. Pres. Pa. Editorial Assn., 1893-94; rec. sec. Nat. Editorial Assn., 1893-94. Mem. 54th to 60th Congresses (1895-1909), 24th Pa. Dist.; del. Rep. Nat. convs., 1884, 1906. Trustee Washington and Jefferson Coll. and Washington Sem. Republican. Presbyn. Home: Washington, Pa. Died May 16, 1917.

ACHESON, John Carey, coll. pres.; b. Fairfield, Ia., May 30, 1870; s. David and Jennie (Carey) A.; A.B., Centre Coll., 1898, M.A., 1900; LL.D., Central U. of Ky., 1913; m. Mary Virginia Berry, June 5, 1900. Instr. in Greek, Caldwell Coll., Danville, 1897-1900; asso. prin. Centre Coll. Acad., 1898; prin. Harrodsburg Acad., 1899-1902; pres. Caldwell Coll., 1902-13. Pres. Ky. Coll. for Women, 1913-15, and 1922-24; pres. Pa. Coll. for Women, 1915-22; pres. Macalester Coll., 1924—. Chmn. state exec. com. Ky. Y.M.C.A., 1908-15; v.p. Internat. Conv. Y.M.C.A., 1910-13; apptd. spl. commr. Internat. War Work Council of Y.M.C.A., Europe, 1917; mem. Nat. Bd. of Christian Edn., Presbyn. Ch., U.S.A., 1922-29; mem. Council Synods of Ky., Presbyn. Ch., 1923-25; trustee Pa. Coll. for Women, 1915-23; dir. Western Theol. Sem., 1915-23; pres. Constl. Conv. Y.M. C.A., Cleveland, 1923; mem. State Com., Minn. Y.M.C.A., 1924—; mem. bd. dirs. St. Paul Y.M. C.A., 1925—; pres. Minn. Council of Religious Edn., 1925—; chmn. Nat. Elec. Com. Laymen's Missionary Movement, 1926—; vice-moderator Gen. Assembly Presbyn. Ch., St. Paul, 1929; pres. bd. United Charities of St. Paul, 1930-34. Home: St. Paul, Minn. Died Nov. 24, 1937.

ACHESON, Marcus W., apptd. U.S. circuit judge 3d circuit, 1891; b. Washington, Pa.; admitted to bar and practiced at Pittsburgh; U.S. dist. judge for Western dist. Pa., Jan. 14, 1880, until 1891. Mem. Universal Congress Lawyers and Jurists, St. Louis, 1904. Home: Pittsburgh, Pa. Died 1906.

ACHESON, William McCarthy, civil engr.; born Cohoes, N.Y., July 16, 1878; s. James Francis and Mary (McCarthy) A.; prep. edn., Troy (N.Y.) Acad.; student Rensselaer Poly. Inst., 1895-98, also Union U., Royal Engrs. Sch., Chatham, Eng., 1917; hon. E.D., Syracuse U., 1927; m. Inger Thira Miller, Apr. 25, 1908; children—Margaret Miller, Thomas Temple. Began in water works dept., Troy, N.Y.; in Isthmian Canal Service, Panama, 1904-10; supervising engr. with contractor, later div. engr. N.Y. State Highway Dept., Buffalo, same, Syracuse Div., 1915-16; chief engr. Crescent Portland Cement Co., 1916-17; div. engr. N.Y. State Dept. Highways, Syracuse, 1917, 1919-23; div. engr., Bur. of Highways and Bur. of Canals, N.Y. State Dept. Pub. Works, 1923-27, in charge div. engring., later chief engr., 1927—; lecturer on engring., Syracuse U., 1922—. Served as capt., later maj. engrs. U.S. Army, assigned to staff of chief of roads and railroads, 1917, chief of road service, 1918; maj. Engr. R.C., 1919, lt. col., 1920. Mem. Nat. Research Council. Citation from Gen. Pershing and Maj. Gen. Langfitt, chief of engrs., World War. Repbulican. Catholic. Consultant on pub. works to Republic of Cuba. Home: Syracuse, N.Y. Died Jan. 25, 1930.

ACHORN, Edgar Oakes, lawyer; b. Newcastle, Me., Aug. 20, 1859; s. John Taylor and Clara (Rundlett) A.; A.B., Bowdoin Coll., 1881; (LL.D., Lincoln Memorial U., 1910); m. Sophie Apenes, of Christiania Sept., 1889; 2d, Alice Gorham Morse, Sept. 27, 1906. Instr., 1881-83, supt., 1883-84, Whitman (Mass.) High Sch.; admitted to bar, 1884, and in practice in Boston. Unitarian. Republican. Organized Scandnavian Rep. League; sec. of embassy, St. Petersburg, 1896. Trustee Lincoln Memorial U. (Tenn.), Montclair (N.J.) Mil. Acad.; overseer Bowdoin Coll. Author: The Unknown Quantity, 1919. Decorated Royal Order of Vasa, first class (Swedish). Home: Brunswick, Me. Deceased.

ACKER, Charles Ernest, inventor, mfr.; b. Bourbon, Ind., Mar. 19, 1868; s. William James and Mercia (Grant) A.; Ph.B., Cornell, 1888; m. Alice Reynolds Beal, Apr. 26, 1892. Elec. engr., Chicago, 1888-93; originator of the Acker process of mfr. caustic soda by electrolysis of molten salt, and built works at Niagara Falls; originator chem. and electrochem. processes; granted many patents. Awarded Elliott Cresson gold medal by Franklin Inst.; also awarded other medals. Home: Ossining, N.Y. Died Oct. 18, 1920.

ACKER, George Nicholas, physician; b. Washington, D.C., Oct. 5, 1852; s. Nicholas and Sarah E. (Bisby) A.; A.B., Pa. Coll., 1872, A.M., 1875; M.D., Columbian (now George Washington) U., 1874; M.D., U. of Berlin, 1877. Demonstrator practical physiology, 1880, pathol. histology, 1879-87, prof. physiology, 1880-88, Columbian U.; clin. prof. medicine and diseases of children, George Washington U.; attending phys., Children's Hosp. Home: Washington, D.C. Died July, 1923.

ACKERMAN, Ernest R., congressman; b. New York, N.Y., June 17, 1863; ed. pvt. and pub. schs. Mfr. and banker; mem. Common Council, Plainfield, N.J., 1891, 92; McKinley presdl. elector, 1896; mem. N.J. Senate 2 terms, 1905-11 (pres., 1911); del. Rep. Nat. Conv., Chicago, 1908, 16; mem. 66th to 71st Congresses (1919-31), 5th N.J. Dist. Trustee Rutgers College. Home: Painfield, N.J. Died Oct. 18, 1931.

ACKERMAN, John Henry, normal school pres.; b. Warren, O., Nov. 7, 1854; s. John Philip and Caroline (Hartman) A.; grad. State Normal Sch., Milwaukee, Wis., 1889; (Ph.D., Ore. Agrl. Coll., Corvallis, Ore., 1907); m. Ellen Boorman, Sept., 1875. Began as teacher rural schs., 1875; prin. grammar schs., Portland, Ore., 1889-93; asst. supt. city schs., Portland, 1893-94; county supt. schs., Multnomah County, Ore., 1894-99; state supt. pub. instrn., Ore., 1899-1911; pres. Ore. Normal Sch., Monmouth, Ore., 1911—. Republican. Unitarian. Mason. Home: Monmouth, Ore. Died July 10, 1921.

ACKERSON, James Lee, naval officer; b. Lowell, Mich., Aug. 8, 1881; s. John Elbert and Katherine (Labadie) A.; grad. U.S. Naval Acad., 1901; M.S., Mass. Inst. Tech., 1906; m. Martha Allston Buist, Apr. 21, 1906. Promoted ensign, June 7, 1903; master, Dec. 1, 1903; lt. comdr., Aug. 21, 1916; comdr., Oct. 1, 1917. Naval constr., 1903—; v.p. and trustee U.S. Shipping Bd. Emergency Fleet Corp., 1918. Episcopalian. Died Sept. 13, 1931.

ACKERT, Charles H., ry. official; b. in Dutchess County, N.Y.; Feb. 19, 1856; common sch. edn. Began ry. service as a telegraph operator, 1872, filling various positions until becoming gen. mgr. Iowa Central Ry., 1888-93; gen. mgr. Elgin, Joliet & Eastern Ry., 1893-99; pres. and gen. mgr. same road, and of Chicago, Lake Shore & Eastern Ry., 1899-1901; gen. mgr. Mobile & Ohio R.R., Mar., 1901-Mar., 1902; gen. mgr., Mar., 1902-Apr., 1905, 4th v.p., 1905-10, Southern Ry.; v.p. in charge of operation C. & A., Toledo, St. Louis & Western, Ia. Central, and Minneapolis & St. Louis rys., 1910—. Home: Chicago, Ill. Died June 5, 1927.

ADAIR, John A.M., banker, mfr.; b. Jay Co., Ind.; s. James G. and Sarah A. (Hutson) A.; ed. high sch., Portland, Ind.; m. Grace R. Johnson; 1 son, Herbert J. Entered mercantile business, Portland, 1888; city clk. Portland, 1888-90; clk. Circuit Court, 1891-95; mem. Ind. Legislature, 1902-04; mem. Congress, 8th Ind. Dist., 1907-17; became pres. 1st Nat. Bank of Portland, 1904; pres. Internat. Finance Co., 1918-20; v.p. Southern Dairies, 1924-31; chmn. of bd. Finance Service Co., Baltimore, 1933-35; v.p. Atlas Tack Corp., Fairhaven, Mass., 1935—. Democrat. Methodist. Home: New Bedford, Mass. Died Oct. 5, 1938.

ADAM, James Noble, mayor; b. Peebles, Scotland, Mar. 1, 1842; s. Thomas and Isabella (Borthwick) A.; ed. parochial schs., Scotland; apprenticed to business, Edinburgh, 1854-64; engaged in business there, 1865-72; m. Margaret L. Paterson, of Edinburgh, Jan. 9, 1872 (deceased). Came to U.S., 1872; engaged in business, New Haven, Conn., 1874-81, Buffalo, 1881—. Was alderman and councilman of Buffalo, mayor, 1906-09. Democrat. Presbyterian. Home: Buffalo, N.Y. Died Feb. 9, 1912.

ADAMOWSKI, Joseph, cellist; b. Warsaw, Poland, July 4, 1862; studied at Warsaw Conservatory; diploma, silver medal and A.B., Imperial Conservatory, Moscow; m. Antoinette Szumowska, pianist, 1896; children—Helenka, Tadeusz. Debut as soloist, Warsaw, 1883; prof. cello and ensemble, Cracow Conservatory, 1885-87; traveled as soloist in Russia and Germany, 1888; joined Boston Symphony Orchestra, 1889; mem. Adamowski Quartet and Trio; prof. cello, ensemble and quartet classes, N.E. Conservatory of Music, 1903—. A founder and dir. Boston Symphony Orchestra Pension Instn.; trustee Paderewski Fund. Home: Cambridge, Mass. Died Feb. 1930.

ADAMS, Alva, governor; b. Iowa Co., Wis., May 14, 1850; ed. common schools; went to Colo. and became hardware merchant; mem. 1st Colo. legislature, 1876; gov. of Colo., 1887-89, 1897-99; candidate for gov., 1904, and was declared elected and was seated on Jan. 10, 1904, but on Mar. 20, 1905, was ousted by legislature, which gave the office to James H. Peabody, who served 1 day and resigned in favor of the lt.-gov. Mem. Dem. Nat. Com., 1908—. U.S. commr.-gen. to Australia and N.Z., Java, Siam, Cochin China and China, and at head of commn. to urge co-operation of these govts. in Panama Expn., 1915. Mason (33°). Home: Pueblo, Colo. Died Nov. 1, 1922.

ADAMS, Alva Blanchard, senator; b. Del Norte, Colo., Oct. 29, 1875; s. Alva and Ella (Nye) A.; Ph.B., Yale, 1896; LL.B., Columbia, 1899; m. Elizabeth Matty, Oct. 25, 1909; children—Ella (Mrs. Joseph A. Uhl), Elizabeth (Mrs. James W. Booth), Alva B., William H. Admitted to Colo. bar, 1899; began practice at Pueblo; mem. firm Adams & Gast; county atty. Pueblo County, Colo., 1908-10; city atty., Pueblo, 1911-15; apptd. by gov. of Colo. mem. U.S. Senate, May 17, 1923, to fill vacancy caused by death of Samuel D. Nicholson; elected to Senate, Nov. 1932, for term 1933-39; re-elected Nov. 1938, for term 1939-45; pres. Pueblo Savings & Trust Co.; dir. Standard Fire Brick Co. Maj. J.A. Gen.'s Dept., U.S. Army, 1918-19. Democrat. Mason (33°), Elk. Home: Pueblo, Colo. Died Dec. 1, 1941.

ADAMS, Andrew Addison, lawyer; b. Columbia City, Ind., Jan. 27, 1864; s. John Quincy and Christiana (Elliott) A.; Wabash Coll., 1880-81; A.B., Washington and Jefferson Coll., Pa., 1884; A.M., 1887, LL.D., 1913; m. Lois Andrew, 1890; 1 son, Robert Andrew. Was admitted to federal and state courts, 1887; practiced at Columbia City, Ind., 1888-1910; judge Appellate Ct. of Ind., 1910-13 (resigned); atty. for Arbuckle Bros., New York, 1913—. Mem. Ind. Ho. of Rep., 1888-92; mem. Dem. State Com., 1904. Trustee Purdue U., 1907-12; mem. Uniform State Laws Commn., 1909-13. Mason. Presbyn. Home: New York, N.Y. Died May 5, 1936.

ADAMS, Arthur Lincoln, engineer; b. Greensburg, Ind., Sept. 15, 1864; s. Jacob Clendenin and Nancy (Hamilton) A.; student Hanover (Ind.) Coll., 1882-83, Washburn Coll., Kan., 1883-84; B.S., C.E., Kansas State U., 1886; m. Mary Gemmell, Dec. 18, 1889. Engr. Burlington & Mo. River R.R. in Neb., 1886-87, of Ore. Pacific R.R., and Ore. & Wash. Ty. R.R., 1887-89; in pvt. practice at Pendleton, Ore., 1889-96, during which time prepared plans for city waterworks at Dayton, Waitsburg and Colfax, Wash., La Grand and Astoria, Ore., etc.; practiced as waterworks expert, San Francisco, 1896-97; mgr. West Los Angeles Water Co. and West Side Water Co., also practicing as consulting hydraulic engr., Los Angeles, Calif., 1897-1900; mgr. Contra Costa Water Co., supplying Oakland, Alameda, Berkeley and other Calif. towns, 1901-02; in pvt. practice as consulting hydraulic engr., San Francisco, 1902—. Awarded Thomas Fitch Rowland prize, Am. Soc. Civil Engrs., 1897. Presbyn. Republican. Home: Oakland, Calif. Died Sept. 17, 1913.

ADAMS, Asael Edward, banker; b. Cleveland, O., Oct. 25, 1866; s. Comfort Avery and Katherine (Peticolas) A.; student Case Sch. Applied Science, Cleveland, 1883-87; m. Anna Julia Shook, Oct. 28, 1897. With First Nat. Bank, Youngstown, O., 1907—, pres., 1912—; pres. Dollar Savings & Trust Co. Republican. Unitarian. Home: Youngstown, O. Died Jan. 3, 1930.

ADAMS, Brooks, author; b. Quincy, Mass., June 24, 1848; s. Charles Francis and Abigail Brown (Brooks) A.; A.B., Harvard, 1870; Harvard Law Sch., 1 yr.; went as sec. to his father to Geneva, where latter was arbitrator upon the Alabama claims under "Treaty of Washington." Admitted to bar, 1873; practiced at Boston, 1873-81; m. Evelyn, d. Admiral Charles Henry Davis, Sept. 7, 1889. Lecturer Boston U. Sch. of Law, 1904-11. Member Nat. Inst. Arts and Letters. Author: The Emancipation of Massachusetts, 1887; The Law of Civilization and Decay, 1896 (translated into French and German); America's Economic Supremacy (transl. into German), 1900; The New Empire (transl. into German and Russian), 1902; two chapters in Centralization and the Law, 1905; Railways as Public Agents, 1910; The Theory of Social Revolutions, 1913; Emancipation of Massachusetts—The Dream and the Reality, 1919. Home: Quincy, Mass. Died Feb. 13, 1927.

ADAMS, Charles, surgeon; b. Northamptonshire, Eng., May 29, 1847; s. John and Elizabeth (Clarke) A.; brought to America at 10 yrs. of age; M.D., Hahnemann Med. Coll., Chicago, 1872; M.D., Rush Med. Coll., 1898; m. Mary Curtis, of Wellingborough, Eng., 1875 (died 1888); 2d, Mrs. Elizabeth Mitchell Gaylord, 1889. In gen. practice, Chicago, 1873-95, exclusively in surgery, 1895—; prof. surg. pathology, Hahnemann Med. Coll., 1873-75; prof. principles and practice of surgery, Chicago Homoe. Coll., 1875-84; cons. surgeon, Chicago Nursery, Evanston, Passavant, and St. Joseph's hosps. Surg. maj. 1st Inf., Ill. National Guard, 15 yrs.; maj. and brigade surg., U.S. Volunteers, 1898; surg. gen. I.N.G., 1908-13; apptd. 1st lt. M.R.C., U.S. Army, 1911. Home: Chicago, Ill. Died May 6, 1924.

ADAMS, Charles E., mfr.; b. Cleveland, O., June 8, 1859; s. Edgar and Mary Jane A.; common sch. edn.; m. Jennie M. Bowley, June 11, 1884. With The Chandler & Rudd Co., Cleveland, 1884-91; pres. Cleveland Hardware Co., June 1891—; dir. Cleveland Trust Co. Republican. Presbyn. Home: Cleveland, O. Died Nov. 4, 1933.

ADAMS, Charles Follen, author; b. Dorchester, Mass., Apr. 21, 1842; s. Ira and Mary Elizabeth (Senter) A.; ed. common sch. Was in 13th Mass. Inf. in Civil War, wounded and taken prisoner at Gettysburg; m. Harriet Louise Mills, Oct. 11, 1870. In 1872 began contributing to periodicals humorous poems in German dialect. Author: Leedle Yawcob Strauss, and Other Poems; Dialect Ballads; also booklets—Dot Long-Handled Dipper, Vas Marriage a Failure? and Der Oak und Der Vine; Yawcob Strauss and Other Poems (complete poems), 1910. Home: Boston, Mass. Died Mar. 15, 1918.

ADAMS, Charles Francis, publicist; b. Boston, Mass., May 27, 1835; s. Charles Francis and Abigail Brown (Brooks) A.; A.B., Harvard, 1856 (LL.D. 1895, Princeton, 1909); admitted to bar, 1858; served in Union Army through Civil War; hon. mustered out, Sept. 1, 1864; lt.-col. 5th Mass. Cav., Sept. 8, 1864; col., Mar. 14, 1865; bvtd. brig.-gen. vols., Mar. 13, 1865; resigned Aug. 1, 1865; m. Mary Hone Ogden, Nov. 8, 1865. Identified with ry. interests; mem. Bd. R.R. Commrs. of Mass., 1869-79 (chmn. 7 yrs.); mem. bd. arbitration, Trunk Line R.R. Orgn., 1879-84; govt. dir. U.P. R.R., 1877-90, pres., 1884-90; overseer Harvard, 1882-94 and 1895-1907. Pres. Mass. Hist. Soc., 1895; fellow Am. Acad. Arts and Sciences; mem. Am. Acad. Arts and Letters. Author: Chapters on Erie and Other Essays; Railroads, Their Origin and Problems; Notes on Railway Accidents; Massachusetts, Its Historians and Its History; Three Episodes of Massachusetts History; Life of Charles Francis Adams; Richard Henry Dana, a Biography, and others. Home: South Lincoln, Mass. Died Mar. 20, 1915.

ADAMS, Charles Kendall, univ. pres.; b. Derby, Vt., Jan. 24, 1835; grad. Univ. of Mich. (A.M., LL.D.); studied in Germany, France, Italy. Asst. prof. hist. and Latin, 1863-67; prof. hist., U. of Mich., 1867-85; pres. Cornell U., 1885-92; pres. U. of Wis., 1892—. Author: Democracy and Monarchy in France; Manual of Historical Literature; British Orations; Christopher Columbus, His Life and Work; also many papers in reviews. Editor-in-chief Johnson's Universal Cyclopedia, 1892-95, now the Universal Cyclopedia. Home: Madison, Wis. Died 1902.

ADAMS, Charles Remington, newspaperman; born Maywood, Ill., Dec. 31, 1881; s. Edward Augustus and Margaret Rosalind (Swain) A.; student U. of Mich., 1899-1902; unmarried. Reporter Chicago Evening Post, 1902-04; mng. editor Commercial West, 1904-08, Minneapolis Journal, 1908-12; v.p. Minn. Jour. Co., 1912-19; mng. editor Duluth News-Tribune, 1923-25; business mgr. Syracuse (N.Y.) Herald, 1926. Chmn. Am. Com., an orgn. formed to combat radicalism in Minn., 1918-20; chmn. Minn. Rep. State Central Com., 1920-24. Republican. Quaker. Home: Syracuse, N.Y. Died Dec. 22, 1938.

ADAMS, Clair Stark, clergyman; b. Manteno, Will County, Ill., Oct. 27, 1862; s. Jay and Sophronia (Wright) A.; B.A., Western Reserve U., Cleveland, O., 1888; grad. McCormick Theol. Sem., 1895; m. Nettie Vanderhoef, Nov. 4, 1896; children—Robert Wright, Paul Jay, Jean. Ordained Presbyn. ministry, 1895; pastor various chs., 1894-1912; field asst. and evengelist, Dept. of Town and Country Work, of Bd. of Nat. Missions of the Presbyn. Ch. in U.S.A., until Sept. 1, 1912. Dir. 3d Ann. Rural Life Conf., Ia. State Coll., 1913, 5th Ann. Conf., 1915; lecturer, Rural Pastors Conf., Coe Coll., 1916, Okla. Agrl. Coll., Stillwater, 1920, Athens (Tenn.) Coll., 1920, Wofford Coll., 1922, Trinity Coll., Tex., 1924, Dallas, Tex., 1925, U. of Ill., 1925, Ill. Synodical Conf., 1926; pastor, and dir. religious edn., Alpine Inst., 1927—. Republican. Home: Alpine, Tenn. Died 1940.

ADAMS, Cuyler, mining engr.; b. Canton, Ill., Aug. 20, 1852, but reared in N.Y.; s. Herman Cuyler and Frances M. (Burr) A.; ed. tutors, pvt. schs. and Poughkeepsie Mil. Inst., N.Y.; m. Virginia B., d. Col. J. B. Culver, Oct. 20, 1881; children—Cuyler Culver (dec.), Francis Salisbury (dec.), Robert M. Went to Minn., 1870, for the N.P. Ry. on dock constrn.; lager bonanza farmer in Stutsman County, N.D., and exploring and developing mining properties in western Ont.; discovered by magnetic observation and developed the Cuyuna Iron Range in Minn.; built Cuyuna Iron Range Ry., of which was pres. and gen. mgr.; pres. Biwanago Mining Co., Cuyuna Northern Ry. Co. Republican. Episcopalain. Home: Duluth, Minn. Died Nov. 29, 1932.

ADAMS, Cyrus Cornelius, geographer; b. Naperville, Ill., Jan. 7, 1849; s. Cyrus and Cornelia (Stevens) A.; A.B., U. of Chicago, 1876; m. Mrs. Blanche C. Dodge, Aug. 17, 1877; children—Jessie, Ernest. First pres., dept. of geography, Brooklyn Inst. of Arts and Sciences; journalist, Chicago and New York, 1874-03; geog. writer on New York Sun, 1884-06; editor Bull. Am. Geog. Soc., 1908-15. Pres. Assn. Am. Geographers, 1906. Author: Commercial Geography for High Schools, 1901; Elementary Commercial Geography, 1902. Wrote: David Livingstone, African Development (in Vol. XIV, Beacon Lights of History), 1902. Home: Jewett, N.Y. Died May 4, 1928

ADAMS, Edward Dean, financier; b. Boston, Mass., Apr. 9, 1846; s. Adoniram Judson and Harriet Lincoln (Norton) A.; B.S., Norwich U., 1864, M.S., 1897, LL.D., 1906, M.A., 1908, Sc.D., 1927; Dr., honoris causa, U. of Louvain, 1928; m. Frances Amelia Gutterson, Oct. 10, 1872 (died 1921); children—Ernest Kempton (dec.), Ralph Lanier (dec.), Ruth (Mrs. Leighton Lobdell). Bookkeeper, cashier, 1866-70, mem. 1870-78, Richardson, Hill & Co., bankers, Boston; mem. Winslow, Lanier & Co., bankers, New York, 1878-93; identified with orgn. of numerous ry. cos.; reorganized N.P. R.R. System and chmn. bd., 1896-97; rep. of Deutsche Bank, Berlin, 1893-1914; dir. Western Md. Ry. Co., Clinchfield Coal Corp., N.J. Gen. Security Co., New York & Long Branch R.R. Co., Niagara Falls Power Co., W.Va. Central & Pittsburgh Ry. Co., Passaic Holding Co. Trustee Am. Acad. in Rome, Am. Scenic and Historic Preservation Soc., Grant Monument Assn., Met. Mus. Art; mem. bd. mgrs. New York Bot. Garden; mem. exec. com. Rumson Borough Improvement Assn.; sr. warden, co-trustee Endowment Fund St. George's By-the-River; chmn. Kahn Foundation for Foreign Travel of Am. Teachers; mem. exec. com. Nat. Research Council; mem. advisory bd. Sch. of Business, Columbia U.; mem. com. World Congress of Engrs. in Japan; chmn. and del. to Louvain of War Memorial Com. of United Engring. Soc.; del. of four founder socs. at 500th anniversary of U. of Louvain; mem. bd. dirs. Am. Commn. for Devastated France. Home: Rumson, N.J. Died May 20, 1931.

ADAMS, Edward Francis, editorial writer; b. Augusta, Me., Dec. 30, 1839; s. Thomas (D.D.) and Catherine (Lyman) A.; Western Reserve Coll., 1860; m. Roah Elmira Shattuck, Jan. 30, 1860 (died 1866), 1 son, Edward Thomas; m. 2d, Delia Ray Cooper, Dec. 25, 1868 (died 1918); children—Evangeline (widow of Dr. A. Spozio), Mrs. Katherine Hicks (dec.), Marion, William, Frank. Pvt. 41st Ohio Inf., Civil War. Active for many yrs. in promoting cooperation in econ. and civic lines; editorial writer San Francisco Chronicle on econ., financial and agrl. topics. Pres. or v.p. Commonwealth Club of Calif. for its first 10 yrs. Presbyn. Author: The Modern Farmer, 1899; Critique of Socialism, 1905; Inhumanity of Socialism, 1913. Home: San Francisco, Calif. Died Nov. 19, 1929.

ADAMS, Edward Le Grand, consul; b. Clarence, N.Y., Jan. 3, 1851; s. Benjamin T. and Janet (Gibson) A.; A.B., U. of Rochester, 1875; m. Kate L. Atwater, Jan. 22, 1879. On staff Rochester Democrat and Chronicle, 1873-80; oil producer, Bradford, Pa., 1880-83; editor Elmira Daily Advertiser, 1883-98; deputy collector U.S. Internal Revenue, 28th N.Y. Dist., 1890-94; N.Y. State tax commr., 1895-98; asst. lit. bur., Rep. Nat. hdqrs., New York, campaigns of 1896, 1900; sec. Am. legation, and consul-gen. at Stockholm, Sweden, 1902-09; chargé d'affaires, ad interim, at Am. legation, Stockholm, Dec. 1902-Mar. 1903; consul at Dublin, Ireland, 1909-19; at Sherbrooke, P.Q., Can., 1920—. Home: Elmira, N.Y. Died Oct. 2, 1928.

ADAMS, Edwin Augustus, clergyman; b. Franklin, Mass., Oct. 21, 1837; s. Newell and Abigail Fales (Blake) A.; A.B., Amherst, 1861; Union Theol. Sem., 1864-65; Andover Theol. Sem., 1867-68; (D.D., Ill. Coll., 1891, Knox Coll., 1891); m. Caroline Amelia Plimpton, May 16, 1866. Ordained Congl. ministry, 1868; pastor N. Manchester, Conn., 1868-72; missionary A.B.C.F.M., Prague, Bohemia, 1873-82; pastor Northboro, Mass., 1882-84; head of Bohemian mission Congl. Ch., Chicago, 1884-1907. Home: Chicago, Ill. Died Apr. 10, 1927.

ADAMS, Elmer Bragg, judge; b. Pomfret, Vt., Oct. 27, 1842; s. Jarvis and Eunice (Mitchell) A.; A.B., Yale, 1865; (LL.D., U. of Mo., 1898, also LL.D., Washington U., 1907); m. Emma Richmond, Nov. 10, 1870. Went to Georgia under auspices American Union Commn. and inaugurated system of free schools for white children at Atlanta and Milledgeville; returned to Vt., 1866; studied law there and at Harvard Law Sch.; admitted Vt. bar, 1868; settled in practice, St. Louis, Mo., 1868; judge Circuit Court, St. Louis, 1879-85, declined re-election and resumed practice; U.S. dist. judge, Eastern Dist., Mo., 1895-1905; U.S. circuit judge, 8th Jud. Circuit, 1905—. Spl. lecturer on succession and wills, U. of Mo. Presbyn. Home: St. Louis, Mo. Died Oct. 24, 1916.

ADAMS, Ephraim Douglass, univ. prof.; b. Decorah, Ia., Dec. 18, 1865; s. Ephraim and Elizabeth S. A. (Douglass) A.; A.B., U. of Mich., 1887, Ph.D., 1890; LL.D., Grinnell Coll., 1917; Litt.D., Tufts Coll., 1918; m. May Stevens Breakey, June 8, 1893 (died 1916); children—James Douglass, Sidney Francis, William Forbes; m. 2d, Florence S. Ober, Aug. 11, 1917; children—Elizabeth Douglass, Roberta Ober, Florence Mattle, Sally Ann. Principal high school, McGregor, Ia., 1887-88; special agent in charge of street railways, 11th Census, at Washington, 1890-91; asst. prof. history and sociology, 1891-94, asso. prof., 1894-99, prof. European history, 1899-1902, U. of Kan.; asso. prof. history, 1902-06, prof., 1906—, Leland Stanford, Jr. U. Dir. Hoover War Library, Stanford. Author: The Control of the Purse in the U.S. Government, 1894; The Influence of Grenville on Pitt's Foreign Policy, 1904; British Interests and Activities in Texas (Albert Shaw Lectures, Johns Hopkins U., 1910); The Power of Ideals in American History (Dodge Lectures on Citizenship, Yale U., 1913); Great Britain, America, and Democracy, 1919; Great Britain and The American Civil War (2 vols.), 1925. Editor British Correspondence Concerning Texas (in Southwestern Hist. Quarterly, 1912-17). Home: Stanford University, Calif. Died Sept. 1, 1930.

ADAMS, Franklin George, sec. Kan. State Hist. Soc. from its foundation, Feb., 1876; b. Rodman, Jefferson County, N.Y., May 13, 1824; ed. country schools, N.Y., and Cincinnati law and med. colleges; m. Harriet Elizabeth Clark, Sept. 29, 1855; removed to Kan., 1855; practiced law in Atchison, 1857-61; probate judge Atchison County, 1858-59; register of U.S. Land Office, 1861-64; clerk U.S. dist. court, 1863; U.S. agt., Kickapoo Indians, 1865-69. Home: Topeka, Kan. Died 1899.

ADAMS, Franklin Pierce; b. Napa, Calif., Oct. 9, 1868; s. Henry and Sarah True (Judkins) A.; Stockton (Calif.) High Sch.; elec. lab. of Charles Jenney, Indianapolis, 1888-90; m. Harriet Chalmers, Oct. 5, 1899 (died 1937). Assisted in the construction of engines for Fort Wayne (Ind.) Electric Co., 1890-91; elec. engr. Stockton Gas & Electric Co., 1892-1900; toured and studied conditions in Mexico, 1900; toured Latin America, 1903-05, 1906-07, 1910-12; studied conditions in Spain and Portugal, 1912-13, Orient, 1913-14, England, 1916, S. America, 1918-19, Spain and Portugal, 1926-29, Spain, 1931, Near East, North Africa and Spain, Central Europe, 1934, 36 and 37. Editor Bull. of Pan-Am. Union, Washington, 1908-19; apptd. first counselor Pan-American Union, 1920; retired, Jan. 1, 1934. Decorated Star of Ethiopia, 1932; Order of Cervantes (Cuba), 1933; Star of Chile, 1934. Contributor articles on Latin America to North and South Am. mags.; introduced the music of Latin America, especially of the indigenous races, to the U.S. through a series of broadcast concerts at the Pan Am. Union, and in Spain through 60 concerts by U.S. Army band, at Seville, Madrid and Barcelona, summer of 1929. Died Oct. 10, 1940.

ADAMS, Frederic, judge; b. Amherst, N.H., Oct. 9, 1840; s. Frederic A. and Mary Jane (Means) A.; grad. Phillips Acad., Andover, Mass., 1858; B.A., Yale, 1862, LL.D., 1899; Harvard Law Sch., 1863-64; m. Ella King, Oct. 27, 1870 (died 1896); 2d, Ella King, July 20, 1904. Admitted to N.Y. bar, 1864; in N.J. as atty., Feb., 1868, as counselor, Nov., 1873; practiced at Newark many yrs. Was spl. master in chancery, and clerk and counsel of E. Orange Tp., Essex County, N.J.; judge Ct. of Errors and Appeals of N.J., 1897-1903; judge Circuit Ct., terms 1903-10, 1910-17, 1917-24; resigned, Jan. 30, 1919. Republican. Home: East Orange, N.J. Died July 24, 1923.

ADAMS, Frederick Upham, author; b. Boston, Mass., Dec. 10, 1859; s. John Spencer and Fannie Emeline (Smith) A.; grad. Elgin (Ill.) High Sch., 1876; m. Alice Mary Whitaker, Sept. 24, 1884. Mech. engr. by private instrn. and practice, 1882-90. Invented electric lamp-post (now standard in U.S.) 1886, electric light towers, 1887; chief smoke insp., Chicago, 1894-97; constructed exptl. passenger train for B.&O. Ry., which broke speed records, 1900. Lit. sec. Dem. Nat. Com., 1896; founder and editor The New Time, social reform mag., 1896-98. Author: Atmosphere Resistance and Its Relation to the Speed of Railway Trains, 1893; How Cities Are Governed in Great Britain, 1904; The Bottom of the Well, 1905; The Oil War in Mexico, 1909; The Story of Edward Hines, 1912; Conquest of the Tropics, 1913; Romance of Big Business, 1915; Woodrow Wilson vs. Woodrow Wilson, 1919; The Open Shop, 1919. Home: Larchmont Manor, N.Y. Died Aug. 28, 1921.

ADAMS, George Bethune, jurist; b. Phila., Pa., Apr. 3, 1845; s. Andrew W. and Mary A. A.; ed. public schools, Philadelphia and by private tuition; m. Helen Jean Balfour, July 12, 1904. Served with 3 months vols., May to Aug. 1861; also went to the front at the time of Lee's invasion of Pa.; on receiving discharge entered q.m.'s dept. remaining until 1871, when he engaged in mercantile pursuits. Studied law in office of Frederick S. Dickson. Admitted to practice in lower courts, 1878, in Supreme Court of Pa., 1880; mem. Wilcox, Adams & Green; became judge U.S. Dist. Court, Southern dist. New York, Aug. 30, 1901. Republican. Home: New York, N.Y. Died 1911.

ADAMS, George Burton, univ. prof.; b. Fairfield, Vt., June 3, 1851; s. Rev. Calvin Carlton and Emeline (Nelson) A.; A.B., Beloit College, 1873, A.M., 1876; B.D., Yale, 1877; Ph.D., U. of Leipzig, 1886; Litt. D., Beloit, 1903; m. Ida Clarke, July 1, 1878. Prof. history, Drury Coll., 1877-88, Yale, 1888—. Editor Am. Hist. Review, 1895-1913. Editor: Duruy's Middle Ages, Bémont and Monod's Mediaeval Europe, Select Documents of English Constitutional History. Author: Civilization During the Middle Ages; The Growth of the French Nation; European History; Vol. II in Hunt and Poole's Political History of England; The Origin of the English Constitution; Outline Sketch of English Constitutional History; The British Empire; Constitutional History of England. Home: New Haven, Conn. Died May 26, 1925.

ADAMS, George Everett, ex-congressman; b. Keene, N.H., June 18, 1840; s. Benjamin Franklin and Louise Ruth (Redington) A.; attended sch. at Keene, N.H.; family moved to Chicago, 1853; A.B., Harvard, 1860, LL.B., 1865; during war served a short time as mem. of Battery A, Ill. Arty.; m. Adele Foster, Nov. 30, 1871. Mem. Ill. Senate, 1881, resigned, 1883; mem. 48th to 51st Congresses (1883-91); served on banking, currency, judiciary coms. Republican. Overseer Harvard, 1892-1904; trustee Newberry Library, Field Mus.; mem. Chicago Bd. Edn.; pres. Chicago Orchestral Assn., 6 yrs. Home: Chicago, Ill. Died Oct. 5, 1917.

ADAMS, George Francis, M.D.; b. Theresa, Jefferson County, N.Y., Jan. 28, 1863; s. Elias and Cornelia Elizabeth (Hall) A.; ed. State Normal Sch., Potsdam, N.Y.; M.D., Hahnemann Med. Coll., Chicago, 1888; studied Post-Grad. Med. Sch., New York, 1898; m. Beulah Muzzy, Sept. 9, 1891. Taught sch., 3 yrs.; practiced, Pulaski, N.Y., 1888-95; chief of staff, Westboro (Mass.) State Hosp., 1895-98; chief of staff Gowanda (N.Y.) State Hosp., 1898-1904; sec. and joint mgr. Pennoyer Sanitarium Co., Kenosha, Wis., 1904-15; spl. lecturer and adj. prof., mental diseases, Hahnemann Med. Coll., Chicago, 1904-15. Episcopalian. Mason. Home: Kenosha, Wis. Died Oct. 10, 1937.

ADAMS, George Herbert, lawyer; b. Campton, N.H., May 18, 1851; s. Isaac Lamson and Louisa Cox (Blair) A.; A.B., Dartmouth Coll., 1873; m. Sarah Katherine Smith, June 14, 1877. Began practice at Plymouth, N.H., 1876; mem. Burleigh & Adams, 1879—; pres. Pemigewassett Nat. Bank; trustee Plymouth Guaranty Savings Bank; dir. Pemigewassett Valley R.R., White Mountain Tel. & Tel. Co., Plymouth Elec. Light Co. Mem. N.H. Constl. Conv., 1876, N.H. Ho. of Rep., 1883, 1884, Senate, 1899, 1900, 1905, 1906 (pres. 1905-06); solicitor for Grafton County, 1895-99; judge adv. gen. staff Gov. J. B. Smith, 1893, 1894; ins. commr. N.H., 1905—. Republican. Home: Plymouth, N.H. Died 1911.

ADAMS, Geoge Irving, geologist; b. Lena, Ill., Aug. 17, 1870; s. Howard Brooks and Ruth Ann (Harris) A.; grad. Kan. State Normal Sch., 1889; A.B., U. of Kan., 1893, A.M., 1895; Sc.D., Princeton, 1896; student U. of Munich and Yale U.; m. Bertha Barin, 1914. Instr. natural sciences, Kan. State Normal Sch., 1893-94; asst. geologist Univ. Geol. Survey of Kan., 1894-97; field asst. U.S. Geol. Survey, 1898-99, asst. geologist, 1900-04; chief hydrologist Cuerpo de Ingenieros de Minas del Peru, 1904-06; mine examinations, S. America, 1906-07; geologist Div. of Mines, Bur. of Science, P.I., 1908-10; prof. geology and mining, Pei Yang U., Tientsin, China, 1912-15; with Peking Govt. U., 1915-20; prof. geology and mineralogy, U. of Ala., 1920—; geologist Geol. Survey of Ala., 1927—. Home: Tuscaloosa, Ala. Died Sept. 8, 1932.

ADAMS, George Moulton, clergyman; b. Castine, Me., July 7, 1824; s. Samuel and Lucy Sewall (Moulton) A.; A.B., Bowdoin Coll., 1844, A.M., 1847, D.D., 1884; studied Bangor Theol. Sem., 1844-46, univs. of Halle and Berlin, 1847-49, Andover Theol. Sem., 1849-50, grad., 1850; m. Sarah Hills Crosby, Jan. 22, 1852 (died 1859); m. 2d, Louise Lord Dana, June 4, 1862. Ordained to Congl. ministry, 1851; pastor Congl. Ch., Conway, Mass., 1851-63, North Ch., Portsmouth, N.H., 1863-71; traveled in Europe, Egypt and Palestine, 1871-72; pastor Congl. Ch., Holliston, Mass., 1873-89; then in lit. work. Mem. bd. overseers, Bowdoin Coll. Author: The Biblical Encyclopedia (5 vols.), 1903 B30 (revision of James C. Gray's The Biblical Museum, 8 vols., 1871). Home: Auburndale, Mass. Died 1906.

ADAMS, Granger, army officer; b. Williamson, N.Y., Sept. 28, 1852; s. Orlando and Emily (Granger) A.; grad. U.S. Mil. Acad., 1876, Arty. Sch., 1882; m. Mary Ingham Williams, Sept. 14, 1881 (died 1902). Commd. 2d lt. 5th Arty., June 15, 1879; advanced through grades to brig. gen., July 1, 1916; retired after 44 yrs. service, Sept. 28, 1916. Prof. mil. science and tactics, St. John's Coll., Fordham, N.Y., 1893-95; sr. instr. arty. tactics, U.S. Mil. Acad., 1895-1900; comdg. Morro Castle, Santiago, Cuba, 1903-04; apptd. pres. Field Arty. Bd., 1910. Home: Front Royal, Va. Died Mar. 27, 1928.

ADAMS, Harriet Chalmers, explorer, lecturer; b. Stockton, Calif.; d. Alexander and Frances (Wilkins) Chalmers; ed. pvt. tutors; m. Franklin Pierce Adams, Oct. 5, 1899. Traveled through Mexico and became student of Latin Am. affairs, 1900; began 3 yrs.' journey through Central and S. America, Jan., 1903; lecturing and writing in U.S. upon S.A., Mar. 1906—. Crossed Haiti in saddle, 1910, returning with 8 Solenodon, classed among rarest known animals; followed the trail of Columbus through the Old and the New World, 1912; traveled through Philippines, 1913; from Siberia to Sumatra, studying ancient races allied with earliest American peoples, 1913-14; war corr. at the French front, 1916; visited every Indian tribe in U.S.; in S. America, 1919-20; research work in Spain and Spanish Africa, 1923-24, in Spain and Portugal, 1926-27, in Libya and Near East, 1929, in Ethiopia, Egypt and Palestine, 1930, in Italy and Spain, 1931, in Near East, North Africa, Spain and Portugal, 1933, in the Balkans, 1934-36. Pres. Internat. Soc. of Woman Geographers, 1925-33, hon. pres., 1933—. Died July 17, 1937.

ADAMS, Harry M., ry. official; b. Comanche, Ia., Jan. 3, 1867; s. John C. and Katharine A.; ed. pub. schs.; m. Josephine A. Moore, Oct. 10, 1890. Began as messenger St.L.&S.F. R.R., 1880; in service K.C., Ft. Scott & Gulf Ry. and Southern Kan. Ry. until 1886; with gen. baggage dept., later local frt. office, Southern Kan. Ry., 1886-87; chief clk. gen. baggage dept. Ore. Ry. & Nav. Co., 1887-89; div. baggage agt., later adv. agt., U.P. Ry., Portland, Ore., 1889-90; baggage agent United Carriage & Baggage Transfer Co., Portland, 1890-93; tkt. clk., U.P. Ry., and Ore. Ry. & Nav. Co., Seattle, Mar.-Oct. 1894; clk. gen. frt. office, Ore. Ry. & Nav. Co., Portland, 1894-95; traveling frt. and pass. agt., 1895-97, chief clk. gen. frt. dept., 1897-98, gen. agt., Spokane, 1898-1902, asst. gen. frt. agt., Portland, 1902-05, same co.; asst. traffic mgr. Great Northern Ry., Seattle, 1905-07; gen. frt. and pass. agt., Spokane, Portland & Seattle Ry., Portland, 1907-10; frt. traffic mgr. Western Pac. Ry., 1910-14; gen. traffic mgr., 1914-17, v.p. in charge traffic, 1917-18, Mo. P. Railway; chief of inland traffic service, War Dept., Jan. 10, 1918-Feb. 28, 1919; traffic asst. regional dir. U.S. R.R. Adminstrn., Southwestern Region, Mar. 1-Sept. 30, 1919; v.p. in charge of traffic, U.P. R.R. Co., 1919-27; pres. Western Pacific R.R. Co., 1927-31, later dir. Home: San Francisco, Calif. Died July 30, 1932.

ADAMS, Henry, author; b. Boston, Mass., Feb. 16, 1838; 3d s. Charles Francis and Abigail Brown (Brooks) A.; A.B., Harvard, 1858; LL.D., Western Reserve, 1892; pvt. sec. to his father, who was Am. minister at London, 1861-68; asst. prof. history, Harvard, 1870-77; editor North Am. Review, 1870-76; removed to Washington, 1877. Author: Essays in Anglo-Saxon Law, 1876; Documents Relating to New England Federalism, 1800-15, 1877; Life and Writings of Albert Gallatin, 1879; John Randolph, 1882; History of Jefferson's and Madison's Administrations, 1889, 91; Historical Essays, 1891; Mont Saint Michel and Chartres, 1904; Letter to American Teachers of History, 1910; Life of George Cabot Lodge, 1911, etc. Mem. Am. Acad. Arts and Letters. Home: Washington, D.C. Died Mar. 28, 1918.

ADAMS, Henry Austin, author; b. Santiago, Cuba, Sept. 20, 1861; s. William Newton and Maria del Carmen (Michelena) A.; father citizen of U.S.; prep. edn., Poly. Inst. of Brooklyn, and Stewart Hall, Baltimore; S.T.B., Gen. Theol. Sem., New York, 1882; M.A., Trinity Coll., Conn., 1885; m. Flora C. Butler, 1883; children—Frederick Laud, Margaret (Mrs. Thomas N. Faulconer), Dorothy (Mrs. Jacob German), John Henry Newman; m. 2d, Gertrude Julia Desch, June 1903; 1 son, Percival Henry. Began writing for mags., 1903; contbr. short stories to leading mags.; wrote play, "'Ception Shoals," in which Nazimova starred, also other plays. Author: The Mortgage on the Brain, 1905. Home: Coronado, Calif. Died 1931.

ADAMS, Henry Carter, college prof.; b. Davenport, Ia., Dec. 31, 1851; s. Ephraim and Elizabeth S. A. (Douglass) A.; A.B., Ia. Coll., 1874; fellow polit. economy, Johns Hopkins, 1876-78, Ph.D., 1878; student at Heidelberg, Berlin, Paris, 1878-79, Andover Theol. Sem., 1875; LL.D., Ia. Coll., 1898, U. of Wis., 1903, Johns Hopkins U., 1915; m. Bertha H. Wright, 1890. Lecturer, 1880-83, asso. prof. polit. science, 1883-87, Cornell; lecturer polit. science, 1880-87, prof. polit. economy and finance, 1887—, U. of Mich.; dir. div. transportation, 11th Census; statistician, Interstate Commerce Commn., 1887-1911; in charge div. statistics and accounts of Interstate Commerce Commn., 1906-11; adviser to a commn. of the Chinese Republic on standardization of ry. accounts, 1913-16. Asso. editor International Journal of Ethics. Pres. Am. Econ. Assn., 1895-1927. Author: Outline of Lectures on Political Economy, 1881, 1886; State in Relation to Industrial Action, 1887; Taxation in the United States, 1787-1816, 1884; Public Debts, 1887; The Science of Finance, 1898; Statistics of Railways, 1888-1910; Economics and Jurisprudence, 1897; Chinese Railway Accounting, 1916; Description of Industry, 1918; American Railway Accounting, 1918. Home: Ann Arbor, Mich. Died Aug. 11, 1921.

ADAMS, Henry Cullen, congressman, dairyman; b. Verona, Oneida County, N.Y., Nov. 28, 1850; s. Benjamin Franklin and Caroline Melissa A.; moved to Wis. with parents, 1851; ed. dist. school, 1 yr. Albion Acad., and 3 yrs. U. of Wis.; m. Anna B. Norton, Oct. 15, 1878. Engaged in farming upon property adjoining the city of Madison, and built up profitable dairy and small-fruit business. Was mem. assembly, 1883, 1885; engaged during winters of 1887, 1888 and 1889 in farmers' institute work; pres. State Dairymen's Assn. 3 terms, 2 yrs. sec. State Hort. Soc., and many yrs. mem. State Bd. Agr.; supt. of public property, State of Wis., 1888-90; dairy food commr., 1895-1902; mem. Congress, 2d Wis. dist., 1903-07. Republican. Del. at large to Nat. Rep. Conv., 1888; chmn. Rep. State Conv., 1900. Home: Madison, Wis. Died 1907.

ADAMS, Henry Heberling, army officer; b. Short Creek, Harrison County, O., Sept. 4, 1845; s. Joshua and Jane (Brown) A.; ed. pub. schs. of Ohio; m. Mary Stiles, Oct. 31, 1878. Began mil. career as pvt. Co. F, 78th battalion Ohio Nat. Guard, 1863, in pursuit of command of Gen. John Morgan in his raid through Ohio; joined Co. C, 98th Ohio Vol. Inf., at Rossville, Ga., Mar. 1864; and served in Sherman's army until Mar. 1865; took part in engagements at Tunnel Hill, Rocky Face Ridge, Ga., battles of Resaca, Rome, Dallas, Peach Tree Creek, Kenesaw Mountain, Atlanta and Jonesboro; then with 2d div., 14th A. C., iin pursuit of Gen. Forrest in N. Ga. and Ala.; later to Rome, Ga., and Atlanta, and on the March to the Sea, then on campaign in Carolinas, battle of Avensboro and Bentonville, N.C., where received gun-shot wound in face which caused his discharge, June 26, 1865. Apptd. 2d lt. U.S. Army, Feb. 23, 1866; served in South until 1879, when went to Mont.; took part in campaigns against Sitting Bull and Gall, and other duties until 1884; in 1885 with co. at Ft. Reno, Ind. Ty.; later on recruiting duty at Pittsburgh and after that in Ind. Ty., Texas, etc. Promoted 1st lt., 1885, capt., Oct. 1886, maj., Mar. 1899, col., Feb. 10, 1903; served with regt. at Iloilo, P.I., 1899; afterward comd. various posts; commandant at Plattsburgh Barracks, N.Y., Feb. 1903—. Died 1907.

ADAMS, Henry Herschel, iron mfr.; b. E. Cleveland, O., 1844 (descendant of Henry Adams of Braintree, Mass.); s. Lowell L. and Hepzibah (Chamberlain) A.; ed. dist. school, E. Cleveland, and Shaw Acad.; m. Helen E. Relington, Mar. 26, 1867. Served, 1861-65, in 125th O. vol. inf.; was in battles of Chickamauga, Missionary Ridge and many others; 3 months in Confederate prison, 1864. In pig-iron business at Cleveland after war until 1886; since then at New York. Now pres. Old Sterling Iron and Mining Co., of Antwerp, N.Y., Colonial Iron Co., of Pa., Algonquin Copper Co., of Wyo., Adams Gold and Silver Mining Co., of Colo., Riverside Water Co., of Conn., Adams Crucible Steel Co., etc. Was col. Nat. Guard of Conn.; mem. Nat. Com. to build Univ. of U.S.; trustee State Bd. Y.M.C.A. of Conn.; trustee and treas. Lincoln Memorial U. of Cumberland Gap, Tenn. Past comdr. Lafayette post, G.A.R., etc. Home: Greenwich, Conn. Died 1906.

ADAMS, Henry Martyn, army officer; b. in Mass., May 8, 1844. Grad. U.S. Mil. Acad., 1866. Apptd. 2d lt. U.S. Engrs., June 18, 1866; 1st lt., July 10, 1866; capt., Sept. 2, 1874; maj., Jan. 10, 1887; lt. col., May 2, 1901; col. asst. chief engrs., U.S. Army, June 26, 1905. Died 1909.

ADAMS, Herbert Baxter, educator; b. Shutesbury, Mass., Apr. 16, 1850; grad. Amherst, 1872; Ph.D., Heidelberg U., 1876, LL.D., U. of Ala., 1891; fellow in history, 1876-78, and later prof. history, Johns Hopkins U.; lecturer Smith Coll., 1878-81; sec. Am. Hist.; editor its reports since 1884; trustee Amherst Coll. and of Boys' Country School (Baltimore). Editor "Contributions to American Educational History" for the U.S. Bureau of Edn., 1887—; editor "Johns Hopkins Univ. Studies in Historical and Political Science," now embracing 19 series, with many extra volumes. Author: Life and Writings of Jared Sparks. Home: Baltimore, Md. Died 1901.

ADAMS, James Alonzo, clergyman; b. Ashland County, O., May 21, 1842; s. John and Sarah Deardorff (Funk) A.; served in Co. D, 69th Ill. Vols., 1862; A.B., Knox Coll., 1867, A.M., 1870, D.D., 1899; grad. Union Theol. Sem., 1870; m. Emma A. Maunder, Dec. 24, 1873. Stated supply Marshfield, Mo., 1870-71; prof. Straight U., New Orleans, 1875-77; editor Dallas (Tex.) Daily Commercial, 1877-80; ordained Congl. ministry, 1880; pastor Plymouth Ch., St. Louis, 1880-86, Millard Av. Ch., Chicago, 1887-88, Warren Av. Ch., Chicago, 1889-95; editorial writer, 1887-1903, editor-in-chief, 1903—, The Advance; author of the "Grapho" articles. Del. Internat. Congl. Council, London, 1891, and to several nat. councils. Author: Colonel Hungerford's Daughter (fiction), 1896; Life of Queen Victoria, 1901; also tracts on Christian Science and Divisive Theology. Home: 3316 Calumet Av., Chicago, Ill. Died June 4, 1925.

ADAMS, James Dexter, rear adm. U.S. Navy; b. Catskill, N.Y., May 4, 1848; s. Frederick Chollet and Mary Dexter (Reynolds) A.; grad. U.S. Naval Acad., 1868; m. Margaret J. Phelps, May 6, 1873. Ensign Apr. 17, 1869; advanced through grades to rear admiral, Oct. 25, 1908. Comdt. Navy Yard, Charleston, S.C., Jan. 2, 1909-June 1, 1910; retired, May 4, 1910. Clubs: Army and Navy, Chevy Chase (Washington); New York Yacht. Home: Washington, D.C. Died Feb. 19, 1922.

ADAMS, Jed Cobb, lawyer; b. Kaufman, Tex., Jan. 14, 1876; s. Z. T. and Elizabeth (Ratliff) A.; student Southwestern U., Georgetown, Tex., 1889-91, Bingham Sch., Asheville, N.C., 1892-93; hon. LL.D., Jefferson Sch. of Law, 1931; m. Allie Nash, Dec. 1, 1897; children—Nash Ratliff, Elizabeth Michaux. Admitted to Tex. bar, 1895; state's atty. Kaufman County, Tex., 1898-1902; del. Dem. Nat. Conv., St. Louis, 1904; Dem. presdl. elector at large, 1908; moved to Dallas, Tex., 1909; U.S. atty. Northern Dist. of Tex., Oct. 1919-Jan. 1920 (resigned); mem. U.S. Board of Tax Appeals, May 1933—; mem. Dem. Nat. Exec. Com. from Tex., 1924-34. Maj. J.A.G.'s Dept., U.S. Army, hdqrs. Governor's Island, N.Y., Oct. 1918-Apr. 1919, World War; lt. col. R.C., U.S. Army. Methodist. Home: Dallas, Tex. Died Jan. 29, 1935.

ADAMS, Jewett W., governor; b. S. Hero Island, Grand Isle County, Vt., Aug. 6, 1835; s. William and Nancy A.; ed. dist. sch.; m. Emma Lee, 1878. At 16 went to Cal. via Panama; engaged in mining and other pursuits, 1852-57; conducted gen. store at Baer Valley, Mariposa County, 1857-60; p.-m. Fremont estate, 1860-64; removed to Carson City, Nev., 1864, and engaged in stockraising; lt. gov., 1874-82; gov. of Nev., 1882-86; supt. U.S. Mint at Carson City, 1894-98; Democrat. Home: Carson City, Nev. Died June 18, 1920.

ADAMS, John Coleman, clergyman; b. Malden, Mass., Oct. 25, 1849; s. John Greenleaf and Mary Hall (Barrett) A.; A.B., Tufts, 1870, B.D., 1872, A.M., 1884 (S.T.D., 1888); m. Miriam P. Hovey, July 18, 1883. Ordained Universalist ministry, 1872; pastor Newton, Mass., 1872-80, Lynn, Mass., 1880-84, Chicago, 1884-90, Brooklyn, 1890-1901, Hartford, Conn., 1901—. Trustee Tufts Coll., 1880—. Author: The Fatherhood of God, 1888; Christian Types of Heroism, 1890; The Leisure of God, 1895, Nature Studies in Berkshire, 1899; Life of William Hamilton Gibson, 1901; An Honorable Youth, 1906; Short Studies in the Larger Faith, 1907; Santa Claus' Baby, 1911; Universalism and the Universalist Church, 1915. Home: Hartford, Conn. Died June 22, 1922.

ADAMS, John Gregory Bishop; b. Groveland, Mass., Oct. 6, 1841; enlisted, April 19, 1861, in Maj. Ben Perley Poore's Rifle Battalion (afterward merged in 19th Mass. vols.); served private to capt., 1861-65, in Army of Potomac except during nine months when he was a prisoner of war and when he was in hospital from wounds received at Gettysburg; has held several local offices; was three times post comdr. G.A.R., Lynn, Mass.; comdr.-in-chief, G.A.R., 1893-94. Home: Lynn, Mass. Died 1900.

ADAMS, John Hampton, cotton mfr.; b. Adamsville, S.C., Sept. 10, 1875; s. Jonathan and Martha Jane (Newton) A.; ed. Palmetto High Sch., Adamsville, and Oak Ridge (N.C.) Inst.; m. Elizabeth Barnes, June 14, 1906; children—Martha Ellen (Nell), Elizabeth B. Began as mfr. cotton and hosiery, High Point, N.C., 1900; chmn. bd. Triangle Hosiery Co.; pres. Highland Cotton Mills, Adams-Millis Corp., Textile Mills Corp., Cloverdale Dye Works. Democrat. Methodist. Mason. Home: Sedgefield, High Point, N.C. Deceased.

ADAMS, John Haslup, editor; b. Baltimore, Md., Jan. 31, 1871; s. John Wesley and Ruth (Haslup) A.; m. Lilian Craigen Coyle, Aug. 1, 1911. Mng. editor, The Baltimore News, 1904-06; editor, Evening Sun, Baltimore, 1910-12, Morning Sun, 1912—. Home: Ruxton, Md. Died Oct. 13, 1927.

ADAMS, John Jay, dean law coll.; b. nr. Dresden, Muskingum County, O., Nov. 18, 1860; s. George Willson and Mary Jane (Robinson) A.; A.B., Kenyon Coll., Ohio, 1879, A.M., 1889, LL.D., 1910; m. Dora May. Black, Oct. 26, 1892 (died, 1904). Teacher, Harcourt Acad., Gambier, O., 1879-82; admitted to Ohio bar, Jan. 2, 1883; judge Ohio Circuit Ct., 5th Circuit, 1895-1901; dean Coll. of Law, Ohio State U., Aug. 7, 1909—; mem. com. examiners for Ohio bar, 1905-10. Pres. Kenyon Alumni Assn., 1910-18. Trustee, Kenyon Coll. Republican. Home: Columbus, O. Died July 17, 1926.

ADAMS, J(ohn) Ottis, artist; b. Amity, Ind., July 8, 1851; s. Alban Housley and Elizabeth Strange (Thomas) A.; Wabash Coll., 1869-71, M.A., 1898; studied art under John Parker, London, 1872-74, Royal Acad., Munich, Germany, 1880-87; m. Winifred Brady, Oct. 1, 1898; children—J(ohn) Alban, Edward W(olf), Robert B(rady). Splty., landscape painting; bronze medal, St. Louis Expn., 1904; Fine Arts Bldg. prize ($500), Chicago, 1907; hon. mention, Internat. Exhbn., Buenos Aires, 1910. Pres. Soc. Western Artists, 1907-09. Home: Brookville, Ind. Died Jan. 28, 1927.

ADAMS, John Taylor, chmn. Nat. Rep. Com.; b. Dubuque, Ia., Dec. 22, 1862; s. Shubael P. and Diana R. (Taylor) A.; grad. Dubuque High Sch., 1881; m. Winifred Rose, May 19, 1902; children—Mrs. Elizabeth Burden, Mrs. Susan Bissell, Paul Livermore. In sash and door mfg. business since 1881; pres. Carr, Ryder & Adams Co. Mgr. campaign of U.S. Senator Allison, defeating Senator Cummins in primary, June 1908; mgr. Taft campaign in Ia. primaries, 1912; mem. Rep. Nat. Com. for Ia., 1912-24 (v.chmn. 1917-21); mem. Rep. exec. and campaign coms., 1912-16; in charge western headquarters in 1920 campaigns; chmn. Rep. Nat. Com., June 8, 1921-June 1924. Home: Dubuque, Ia. Died Oct. 28, 1939.

ADAMS, John William, veterinary surgeon; b. Middleton, Miss., Nov. 8, 1862; s. Rev. John Charles and Helen Marr (Doty) A.; grad. U. of Minn., 1886; taught Shattuck Mil. School, Faribault, Minn.; V.M.D., U. of Pa., 1892; m. Mary, d. Dr. O. B. Adams, Dec. 28, 1893; children—Alice Naomi, Helen Janet. Veterinary practitioner, 1892—; asst. prof., 1893-96, prof. veterinary surgery and obstetrics, 1896—, U. of Pa. Republican. Episcopalian. Author: Text-Book on Horse-Shoeing, 1898; Disease of the Horse's Foot, 1903; Horse-Shoeing, 1903; A Movable School of Horse-Shoeing, 1907. Home: Swarthmore, Pa. Died Oct. 22, 1926.

ADAMS, J(ohn) Wolcott, artist; b. Worcester, Mass., Nov. 7, 1874; s. John Francis and Ellen (Wilson) A.; Art Mus., Boston; Art Students' League, N.Y.; m. Frances Sheldon Adams, Nov. 14, 1902. Began as illustrator, 1899. Illustrator: Hoosier Romance (by James Whitcomb Riley), 1910; known for drawings in connection with old songs, Colonial incidents, etc. Home: New York, N.Y. Died June 3, 1925.

ADAMS, Julius Walker, civil engr.; b. Boston, Mass., Oct. 12, 1812; entered U.S. Mil. Acad., 1830, but did not graduate; engaged in engring work, 1832-60; col. 67th N.Y. vols. in Civil war; wounded at Fair Oaks; became chief engr. city works, Brooklyn, N.Y. Has been pres. Am. Soc. Civ. Engrs. Cons. engr. to dept. of pub. works, N.Y. Home: Brooklyn, N.Y. Died 1899.

ADAMS, Mary Mathews, author; b. (Mathews), Ireland, Oct. 23, 1840; came to U.S. in childhood; ed. Packer Inst., Brooklyn; m. Charles Kendall Adams. Author: The Choir Visible (poems); also wrote: The Epithalamium, and other poems. Home: Madison, Wis. Died 1902.

ADAMS, Maxwell, teacher; b. St. George, W.Va., Feb. 28, 1869; s. Daniel Currence and Dorcas Ann (Boonifield) A.; State Normal Sch., Fairmont, W.Va., 1888; U. of W.Va., 1890-91; A.B., Stanford, 1895, A.M., 1896; Ph.D., U. of Chicago, 1904; student Zurich, Switzerland, 1913, U. Göttingen, 1914; m. Elizabeth Quinn, July 27, 1898; children—Lyndel Dorcas, Gregory Randolph. Teacher State Normal Sch., Chico, Calif., 1896-1904, acting v.p., 1901-05; prof. chemistry, 1906—, dean Coll. Arts and Sciences, 1918—, U. of Nev., also v.p., dir. Nev. State Soils Lab., 1915-17. Pres. Nev. State S.S. Assn., 1910-12; exec. com. Internat. S.S. Assn., 1911. Methodist. Home: Reno, Nev. Died Sept. 15, 1939.

ADAMS, Melvin Ohio, lawyer; b. Ashburnham, Mass., Nov. 7, 1850; s. Joseph and Dolly W. (Whitney) A.; A.B., Dartmouth, 1871 (LL.D., 1912); LL.B., Boston U., 1874; m. Mary Colony, Jan. 20, 1874. Practiced, Boston, 1876—; asst. dist. atty., 1876-86; U.S. atty., 1895-1906; pres. Boston, Revere Beach & Lynn R.R. from 1891; v.p. Liberty Trust Co. from 1907; trustee Dartmouth Coll.; pres. trustees, Cushing Acad.; asst. adj. gen. on staff Gov. Brackett, 1890-91, with rank of col. Republican. Home: 36 Beacon St., Boston, Mass. Died Aug. 9, 1920.

ADAMS, Milward, consul; b. Lexington, Ky., Jan. 6, 1857; s. Samuel L. (surgeon U.S.A.) and Mary J. A.; ed. pub. schs.; m. Florence James, Aug. 23, 1883. Home: Chicago, Ill. Died June 18, 1923.

ADAMS, Myron Eugene, social worker; b. Palmyra, N.Y., Feb. 19, 1876; s. Myron H. and Lydia (Brewster) A.; A.B., Syracuse U., 1898; Rochester Theol. Sem., 1901; D.D., Syracuse U., 1920; m. Roma M. Howell, July 7, 1914; children—Brewster Howell, Grant Howell. Dir. 1st playground, Rochester, N.Y., 1899; Cleveland, 1901; resident worker and probation officer, Welcome Hall Settlement, Buffalo, 1901-04; head worker, West Side Neighborhood House, New York, 1904-06; ordained Baptist ministry, 1905; pastor Midland, Mich., 1906-09, Warren Av. Ch., Detroit, 1909-12, 1st Baptist Ch., Chicago, 1912-16. Organized and became 1st dir. dept. of morale (afterwards a dept. under Chief of Staff U.S. Army) R.O.T.C., Ft. Sheridan; capt. administrative staff Adj. Gen. Ill., 1917-21; exec. sec. Nat. Rehabilitation Com., 1922; associated with Marshall Field and Albert A. Sprague in the Public Service Associates, inc., for pub. service purposes, 1922-26; consultant Reorganization Hosp. Service, downtown, N.Y. City, 1924-25; made plans for Chicago Centennial Celebration, 1925; sec. Pub. Health Inst. Mason (32°). Home: Hubbard Woods, Ill. Died Jan. 17, 1930.

ADAMS, Myron Winslow, univ. pres.; b. Gilsum, N.H., Nov. 27, 1860; s. Rev. Ezra and Alice Melissa (Ware) A.; A.B., Dartmouth, 1881 (first honor), A.M., 1886, D.D., 1923; grad. Hartford Theol. Sem., 1884, Ph.D., 1895; LL.D., Wilberforce U., 1927; m. Nellie B. Davis, May 29, 1884 (died 1912); 1 dau., Margaret; m. 2d, Cora Hardy, Nov. 25, 1914. Ordained Congl. ministry, 1885; pastor Middle Haddam, Conn., 1884-86, Hopkinton, N.H., 1886-88; prof. Greek, 1889-1929, dean, 1896-1923, acting pres., 1919-23, pres., 1923-29, Atlanta U., now emeritus. Pres. Assn. of Colleges for Negro Youth, 1917-19. Author: History of Atlanta University, 1930; History of Dartmouth Class of 1881, 1931. Home: West Townsend, Mass. Died May 26, 1939.

ADAMS, Oliver Stephen, editor; b. Gates, N.Y., Feb. 4, 1844; s. Rodney L. and Martha A. (Southworth) A.; musical edn.; spent 18 yrs. as pianist, teacher and composer; m. Mary Nichols, Nov. 27, 1866. Joined staff of Rochester Democrat and Chronicle, Mar. 1886; successively night editor, editorial writer, mus. critic, mng. editor, same; became editor-in-chief June 1, 1910. Home: Rochester, N.Y. Died Apr. 29, 1924.

ADAMS, Oscar Fay, author; b. Worcester, Mass.; s. William Fuller and Amelia (Merrifield) A.; grad. N.J. State Normal Sch.; unmarried. Author: Handbook of English Authors; Hand-Book of American Authors; Through the Year with the Poets (12 vols. edited); Post-Laureate Idyls; Chapters from Jane Austen (edited); Morris's "Atalanta's Race," with notes (edited); Dear Old Story Tellers; The Poet's Year (edited); The Story of Jane Austen's Life; The Presumption of Sex; Dictionary of American Authors (5th edition, enlarged), 1905; The Archbishop's Unguarded Moment, and Other Stories; Some Famous American Schools; Sicut Patribus and Other Verse; A Motley Jest—Shakespearean Diversions; Scotland Since Culloden. Am. editor of The Henry Irving Shakespeare. Home: Boston, Mass. Died Apr. 30, 1919.

ADAMS, Ralph Snyder; b. Jacksonwald, Pa., Mar. 20, 1894; s. Albert Hartman and Deborah Tobias (Snyder) A.; grad. Perkiomen Sem., Pennsburg, Pa., 1916; B.S., Pa. State Coll., 1922; grad. study U. of Wis. and U. of Pa.; m. Louisa Ellison Kriebel, June 30, 1917; children—Corinne Millar, Marilyn Louise, Ralph Ellison. Teacher, rural schs., Exeter Twp., Berks County, Pa., 1912-15; instr. Perkiomen Sch., 1916-17, 19; mgr. St. Lawrence Dairy Co., Reading, Pa., 1918-19; supt. dept. country life, Ref. Ch. in U.S., 1922-29; dir. research and service, Intersem. Commn. for Training for Rural Ministry, also dir. rural dept., Bangor (Me.) Theol. Sem., 1929—. Republican. Editor Rural Church Worker, 1923-29. Wrote: Project and Study Manual for Rural Church Groups Using "Our Templed Hills," 1926; Leader's Manual for Adult Groups Studying Christianity and the Rural Life of the World, 1931. Home: Bangor, Me. Died Aug. 28, 1933.

ADAMS, Robert, Jr., congressman; b. Phila., Pa., Feb. 26, 1849; grad. Univ. of Pa., 1869; studied and practiced law 5 yrs.; mem. U.S. Geol. Survey, 1871-75, on exploration of Yellowstone Park; mem. State senate, 1883-87; grad., 1884, Wharton School of Economy and Finance, U. of Pa.; U.S. minister to Brazil, 1889-90. Mem. Congress, 1893-1907, 2d Pa. dist.; as acting chmn. Foreign Affairs com., 55th Congress, reported and passed Cuban resolutions and declaration of war against Spain. Republican. Home: Philadelphia, Pa. Died 1906.

ADAMS, Samuel, lawyer; b. Syracuse, N.Y., Nov. 12, 1871; s. Charles True and Emma S. A.; A.B., Harvard, 1892; LL.B., Northwestern U. Law Sch., 1893; m. Louise Koerner, May 20, 1899; 1 son, Charles True. Admitted to Ill. bar, 1893; mem. firm Bancroft & Adams, 1899-1904; spl. traction counsel, City of Chicago, 1906-07; mem. firm Adams & Candee, 1908-11; 1st asst. sec. of the Interior, June 1, 1911-Mar. 7, 1913; mem. firm Adams, Hawley, Brown and Adams, 1929—. Prof. law, Northwestern U. Law School, 1901-09. Pres. Municipal Voters' League, 1917-19. Home: Chicago, Ill. Died May 29, 1935.

ADAMS, Samuel, editor, fruit grower; b. Westfield, Mass., May 13, 1876; s. Sherman and Frances Ellen (Selley) A.; Fla. State Coll., Lake City, 1892-94, George Washington U., 1907-08; m. Mary Lee Campbell, Dec. 22, 1903. Formerly business and promotion mgr. daily newspapers; editor, fruit grower and farmer, 1910—; now editor Public Affairs, Washington, D.C.; dir. gen. Nat. Fedn. Uncle Sam's Voters; asso. editor Am. Fruit Grower Mag., Chicago. Candidate for nomination for v.p. of U.S., Rep. Nat. Conv., Chicago, 1920. Ex-pres. Am. Agrl. Editors' Assn. Episcopalian. Mason. Home: Washington, D.C. Died Jan. 3, 1927.

ADAMS, Samuel Barnard, lawyer; b. Savannah, Ga., Sept. 8, 1853; s. William B. and Laleah (Pratt) A.; A.B., U. of Ga., 1872 (LL.D.); m. Annie Wynn, Dec. 19, 1877. Admitted to bar, 1873, and since in practice at Savannah; asso. justice Supreme Court of Ga. for unexpired term; dir. Citizens & Southern Nat. Bank, Bibb Mfg. Co., Southwestern R.R. Co. Trustee U. of Ga. over 20 yrs.; pres. Bd. Edn. City of Savannah and Chatham County, Ga., over 10 yrs. Pres. Ga. State Bar Assn., 1907-08. Democrat. Home: Savannah, Ga. Died Mar. 20, 1938.

ADAMS, Samuel Shugert, physician; b. Washington, D.C., July 12, 1853; s. George Roszel and Mary Ann A.; A.B., W.Va. U., 1875, A.M., 1878; M.D., Georgetown U., 1879; m. Lida W. Hollister, Apr. 30, 1890. Prof. theory and practice of medicine, Georgetown U., 1898—; attending phys. Children's, and Georgetown U. hosps. Sec. Am. Pediatric Soc. many years. Home: Washington, D.C. Died 1928.

ADAMS, Thomas Sewall, univ. prof.; b. Baltimore, Md., Dec. 29, 1873; s. John Wesley and Ruth (Haslup) A.; grad. Baltimore City Coll., 1893; A.B., Johns Hopkins, 1896, Ph.D., 1899; m. Elizabeth Matthews, Sept. 11, 1902; children—Elizabeth Noel, Ruth Haslup. Prof. political economy, Yale, 1916—. Economic advisor, Treasury Dept., 1917—. Pres. Nat. Tax Assn., 1922-23, Am. Economic Assn., 1927; mem. fiscal com., League of Nations, 1929—. Author: Taxation in Maryland, 1900; Labor Problems (with Helen L. Sumner), 1905; Mortgage Taxation in Wisconsin and Neighboring States, 1907; Out-

lines of Economics (with Richard Theodore Ely), 1908. Died Feb. 8, 1933.

ADAMS, Wilbur Louis, congressman; b. Georgetown, Del., Oct. 23, 1884; s. William Dunning and Sarah Lavinia (Thompson) A.; student Delaware Coll., Dickinson Coll. and Law Sch. of U. of Pa.; unmarried. Admitted to Del. bar, 1907. Dem. candidate for atty. gen. of Del., 1924; mem. 73d Congress (1933-35), Del. at large; Dem. candidate for U.S. Senate, 1934. Mason. Home: Georgetown, Del. Died Dec. 4, 1937.

ADAMS, William A., physician, surgeon; b. Hancock County, Ga., Sept. 10, 1853; s. Thomas J. A.; prep. edn. Washington Inst.; grad. Mercer Univ. (A.M., LL.D.); grad. med. dept. Univ. of Ga.; m. Carrie Eaton, 1876. Surgeon of 6 railroads; prof. theory and practice of medicine, med. dept., Fort Worth Univ. Gold Democrat. Home: Fort Worth, Tex. Died 1902.

ADAMS, William Forbes, bishop; b. Enniskillen, Ireland, Jan. 2, 1833; came to U.S., 1841; acad. edn.; D.C.L., U. of the South, 1874; D.D., St. John's Coll., Md.; LL.D., Washington Coll., Md.; admitted to Miss. bar, 1854. Deacon, 1859, priest, 1860, P.E. Ch.; rector St. Paul's, Woodville, Miss., 1860-66, St. Peter's, New Orleans, 1866-67, St. Paul's, New Orleans, 1867-75; consecrated bishop of N.M. and Ariz., 1875; resigned because of failing health, 1877; rector Holy Trinity Ch., Vicksburg, Miss., 1876-87; 2d bishop of Easton, Md., 1887—. Died Mar. 5, 1920.

ADAMS, William Grant, lawyer; b. Rockford, Ill., Feb. 1, 1867; s. Samuel H. and Adelaide (Grinnell) A.; grad. Genesee Wesleyan Sem., Lima, N.Y., 1884; LL.B., U. of Mich., 1889; m. Helen A. Lumbard, June 24, 1896. Practiced at Chicago, 1890—; mem. Knight, Barbour & Adams. Dir. and atty. Chicago & Oak Park Elevated R.R. Co.; atty. Northwestern Elevated R.R. Co., Union Elevated R.R. Co. Republican. Home: Oak Park, Ill. Died 1911.

ADAMS, William Henry, jurist; b. Lyons, N.Y., Mar. 27, 1841; s. John and Rebecca B. A.; ed. pub. schs., and in prep. school at Geneva, N.Y. (LL.D., Hobart Coll., 1899); m. Charlotte L., d. U.S. Senator Elbridge G. Lapham, Sept. 27, 1865. Served in Union army in Civil War as lt. and capt. 98th N.Y. vols. and asst. adj. gen. on staff of Gen. J. J. De Forrest; admitted to bar; elected, 1887, and re-elected 1901, justice Supreme Court, N.Y., renominated on both Republican and Democratic tickets, 1901, and vote practically unanimous (term to expire 1915); now presiding justice Appellate div. Supreme Court, 4th dept. Republican. Home: Canadaigua, N.Y. Died 1903.

ADAMS, William Jackson, judge; b. Rockingham, N.C., Jan. 27, 1860; s. Rev. S. D. and Mary (Jackson) A.; A.B., U. of N.C., 1881, LL.D., 1924; studied law same; m. Florence Wall; 1 son, William. Admitted to N.C. bar, 1883; mem. N.C. Ho. of Rep., 1893, Senate, 1895; mem. Bd. of Internal Improvements, 1899-1901; apptd. judge Superior Court for unexpired term Dec., 1908; elected to same office, 1910-18 and 1918-26, resigned Sept., 1921; apptd. justice Supreme Court of N.C., Sept., 1921, for unexpired term of Justice W. R. Allen, deceased; twice elected to same office, term ends 1934. Democrat. Methodist. Home: Carthage, N.C. Deceased.

ADAMS, Winston Davis; b. Florence County, S.C., Apr. 2, 1883; s. Joseph Quincy and Mamie (Davis) A.; B.A., Wake Forest (N.C.) Coll., 1900, M.A., 1901; unmarried. City editor Charlotte (N.C.) observer, 1905-16; commercial agt. New York office Dept. of Commerce, 1916-17; sec.-treas. in charge of reorganizing Am. Cotton Mfrs.' Assn., 1917—; sec. nat. council Am. Cotton Mfrs., Washington, 1918-19, 1920-26 (charged with securing adequate supply of cotton goods for war purposes), also advisor to price fixing com. of War Industries Bd.; rec. sec. World Cotton Conf., New Orleans, La., Oct., 1919; sec. Am. delegation World Cotton Conf. Liverpool-Manchester, Eng., 1921. Democrat. Baptist. Mason (32°). Home: Charlotte, N.C. Died Aug. 18, 1929.

ADAMSON, Alfred, rear adm.; b. Brownsville, N.Y., Sept. 19, 1836. Apptd. 3d asst. engr. U.S. Navy, May 13, 1861; promoted 2d asst. engr., Dec. 17, 1862; 1st asst. engr., Jan. 1, 1865; chief engr., May 19, 1879; retired on account of age, Sept. 19, 1898; advanced to rank of rear adm. retired, June 29, 1906, in recognition of service during Civil War. Home: Boston, Mass. Died Feb. 22, 1915.

ADAMSON, Charles, lawyer, mfr.; b. Phila., Pa., Mar. 17, 1859; s. Thomas Adamson and Sarah Victorine (Wright) A.; ed. Pernambuco, Brazil, Honolulu and U. of Melbourne, Australia (father being Am. consul gen.); B.S. in M.E., U. of Pa., 1880; LL.B., U. of Pa., 1882; m. Katharine Brand Cook, Oct. 27, 1897; children—Sarah Victorine (Mrs. Donald E. Montgomery), Katherine (Mrs. Thomas Brandon Munroe), Charles. In active practice, Phila., 1883-90; organized Cedartown Land Improvement Co., Ga., 1890, Cedartown Cotton Co., 1896, Southern Extension Cotton Mill Co., 1898, Paragon Mills, 1899; consolidated 3 latter cos. aggregating 25,000 spindles, 1899, as Cedartown Cotton & Export Co., of which was v.p., later pres.; consolidated Cedartown Co. (Land) and Cedartown Cotton & Export Co., now aggregating 47,000 spindles; also organized Cedartown Warehousing Co. Mem. Common Council, Phila., 1889-90; del. Rep. Nat. convs., 1896, 1904, 1908; alternate del. Progressive party conv., 1912; del. at large for Leonard Wood at conv. that nominated Warren G. Harding (delegation not seated); del. at Coolidge conv.; treas. Rep. State Central Com. of Ga. Unitarian. Home: Cedartown, Ga. Died May 26, 1931.

ADAMSON, William Charles, lawyer; b. Bowdon, Ga., Aug. 13, 1854; s. John W. and Mary A. (McDaniel) A.; A.B., Bowdon Coll., 1874, A.M., 1883, LL.D., 1915; m. Minna Reese, Jan. 29, 1885 (died 1912); m. 2d, Mrs. Ellen Zellars Camp, Jan. 1, 1917. Admitted to bar, 1876; judge City Court, Carrollton, 1885-89; atty. city for several yrs.; presdl. elector, 1892; mem. 55th to 65th Congresses (1897-1919), 4th Ga. Dist.; resigned from 65th Congress, Dec. 1917, upon appmt. as mem. Bd. U.S. General Appraisers (Customs Court), retired to resume practice of law, Jan. 1928. Democrat. Mem. Gen. Conf. M.P. Ch., 4 times; del. to Ecumenical Council of Methodism, London, 1901. Home: Carrollton, Ga. Died Jan. 6, 1929.

ADDAMS, Jane, settlement worker, author; b. Cedarville, Ill., Sept. 6, 1860; d. Hon. John H. and Sarah (Weber) A.; A.B., Rockford Coll., 1881; spent 2 yrs. in Europe, 1883-85; studied in Phila., 1888; LL.D., U. of Wis., 1904, Smith Coll., 1910, Tufts, 1923, Northwestern, 1929, U. of Chicago, 1930; A.M., Yale, 1910. With Ellen Gates Starr opened Social Settlement of Hull House, Chicago, 1889, of which became head resident. Insp. of streets and alleys in neighborhood of Hull House, 3 yrs. Pres. Nat. Conf. Charities and Corrections, 1909; pres. Woman's Internat. League for Peace; presided at convs. at The Hague, 1915, Zurich, 1919, Vienna, 1921, The Hague, 1922, Washington, 1924, Dublin, 1926, Prague, 1929. Awarded Gold Medal of Military Merit (Greece); Bryn Mawr achievement award of $5,000, 1931; shared Nobel peace prize with Nicholas Murray Butler, 1931. Author: Democracy and Social Ethics, 1902; Newer Ideals of Peace, 1907; The Spirit of Youth and the City Streets, 1909; Twenty Years at Hull House, 1910; A New Conscience and an Ancient Evil, 1911; The Long Road of Women's Memory, 1916; Peace and Bread in Time of War, 1922; The Second Twenty Years at Hull House, 1930; The Excellent Becomes the Permanent, 1932. Home: Chicago, Ill. Died May 21, 1935.

ADDEMAN, Joshua Melancthon, banker, lawyer; b. New Zealand, Nov. 15, 1840; s. Thomas and Mary (Fligg) A.; brought to U.S., 1843; A.B., Brown U., 1862, A.M., 1865; m. Louise W. Winsor, Oct. 25, 1872. Served in U.S. Vols., 1862-65; mustered out as capt.; admitted to bar, 1866; clk. Common Council, Providence, R.I., 1867-81; sec. of State R.I., 1872-87; commr. to revise the R.I. Public Statutes, 1880; v.p. Industrial Trust Co., 1895—. Mason. Republican. Episcopalian. Home: Providence, R.I. Died Oct. 13, 1930.

ADDICKS, George B., coll. pres.; b. at Hampton, Ill., Sept. 9, 1854; s. Gerhard and Mary Dorothy (Franke) A.; A.B., Central Wesleyan Coll., Mo., 1875, A.M., 1880; Garrett Bibl. Inst., 1876-77; D.D., German Wallace Coll., Berea, O., 1899; m. Mary W. Wellemeyer, June 26, 1884. Taught prep. dept. Central Wesleyan Coll., 1875-76; ordained M.E. ministry, 1878; prof. practical theology and philosophy, 1890-95, pres. and prof. philosophy, 1895—, Central Wesleyan Coll. Del. Gen. Conf. M.E. Ch., 1900, 1904; served on Univ. Senate, 1896-1904. Republican. Home: Warrenton, Mo. Died 1910.

ADDICKS, John Edward, capitalist; b. Phila., Pa., Nov. 21, 1841. Became interested in building of gas plants and later in gas cos.; organized, 1884, and became pres. Bay State Gas Co., Boston; bought majority interest and became pres., 1892, Brooklyn (N.Y.) Gas Co.; also at head of other cos. in Brooklyn and in Wilmington, Del. Received largest vote for U.S. senator from Del. in legislature, 1899, but failed of election; also candidate for U.S. senator, 1901 and 1903. Died Aug. 7, 1919.

ADDICKS, Walter Roberts, pub. utility exec.; b. Philadelphia, Pa., Apr. 14, 1861; s. John Edward Charles O'Sullivan and Margaretta Turner (McLeod) A.; prep. edn., Episcopal Acad., Phila.; grad. U.S. Naval Acad., 1882; m. Margaret Jardine, Jan. 22, 1890. Resigned from U.S. Navy, 1883; draftsman, Pa. R.R., Altoona, Pa., 1883-84, in charge surveys of shops and yards east of Pittsburgh and Erie, 1885-86; chief engr., Brookline Gas Light Co. and cons. engr. Mass. Pipe Line Gas Co. and N.E. Gas and Coke Co., 1887-1903; 1st v.p. and trustee Consol. Gas Co. of N.Y., 1903-25, sr. v.p., 1925—, acting pres., 1904-09; pres. United Electric Light & Power Co., 1904-12; pres. Municipal Lighting Co., 1906-13. Served as lt., sr. grade, U.S. Navy comdg. U.S.S. Eileen and U.S.S. Huntress, Spanish-Am. War. Mem. nat. com. on gas and electric service, Council Nat. Defense, and in charge Govt. plants producing tuluol, carbon and soda lime, World War. Republican. Baptist. Home: Mt. Kisco, N.Y. and New York City. Died Apr. 14, 1931.

ADDINGTON, Keene Harwood, lawyer; b. Baltimore, Md., Mar. 3, 1874; s. James D. and Emma A. (Martin) A.; prep. edn. Norfolk (Va.) Mil. Acad.; removed to Chicago, 1890; studied law in office of John T. Richards and at Chicago Coll. of Law; m. Florence E. La Victoire, June 26, 1901. Admitted to Ill. bar, 1895; now mem. Jones, Addington, Ames and Seibold; an official reporter of Appellate Courts of Ill. for many yrs.; pres. Sprague Canning Machinery Co. and sec. Benjamin Electric Mfg. Co. of Ill., etc. Republican. Mason. Compiler and editor (with W. Clyde Jones) Annotated Statutes of Ill. (6 vols.), also Notes of Ill. and Appellate Court Reports (15 vols.). Home: Lake Forest, Ill. Died Oct. 18, 1922.

ADDINGTON, Sarah (Mrs. Howard Reid), author; b. Cincinnati, O., Apr. 6, 1891; d. Benton C. and Martha (Benham) A.; A.B., Earlham Coll., Richmond, Ind., 1912; studied Columbia; m. Howard (Carl) Reid, Mar. 20, 1917. Author: The Boy Who Lived in Pudding Lane, 1922; The Pied Piper in Pudding Lane, 1923; The Great Adventure of Mrs. Santa Claus, 1923; Round the Year in Pudding Lane, 1924; Pudding Lane People, 1926; Jerry Juddikins, 1926; Tommy Tingle Tangle, 1927; Grammar Town, 1927; Dance Team, 1931; Hound of Heaven, 1935. Home: New York, N.Y. Died Nov. 7, 1940.

ADDISON, Daniel Dulany, clergyman; b. Wheeling, W.Va., Mar. 11, 1863; s. Thomas Grafton and Marie E. (Addison) A.; A.B., Union Coll., 1883, D.D., 1901; grad. Episcopal Theol. Sch., Cambridge, Mass.; LL.D., Liberia Coll., 1926; m. Julia de Wolf Gibbs, Feb. 20, 1889; children—Mariame Bradford (dec.), Julia Dulany. Asst. Christ Ch., Springfield, Mass., 1886-89; rector St. Peter's Ch., Beverly, Mass., 1889-95; All Saints' Ch., Brookline, Mass., 1895—; rector honorarius, 1920—. Pres. Fedn. of Chs. of Greater Boston, 1918-20. Pres. Beverly Hosp., 1892-95; trustee Pub. Library, Brookline; registrar Diocese of Mass.; sec. Cathedral Chapter of Diocese of Mass.; deputy to Gen. Conv.; trustee Coll. of Monrovia, Liberia; dir. Church Temperance Soc., pres. Mass. Clerical Assn.; pres. trustees Donation for Edn. in Liberia; knighted by govt. of Liberia, 1904. Author: Lucy Larcom, Life, Letters and Diary, 1894; Phillips Brooks, 1894; Life and Times of Edward Bass, First Bishop of Massachusetts, 1897; All Saints' Church, Brookline, 1896; The Clergy in American Life and Letters, 1900; The Episcopalians, 1904. Home: Brookline, Mass. Died Mar. 27, 1936.

ADEE, Alvey Augustus, govt. official; b. Astoria, N.Y., Nov. 27, 1842; s. Augustus A. (U.S. Navy) and Amelia Kinnaird (Graham) A.; private edn.; hon. M.A., Yale, 1888; unmarried. Apptd. sec. of legation, Madrid, Sept. 9, 1870; chargé d'affaires at different times; chief of Diplomatic Bur., June 11, 1878; 3d asst. sec. of state, July 18, 1882; 2d asst. sec. of state, 1886—. Was present at signing of Peace Protocols between U.S. and Spain. Apptd. sec. of state ad interim to fill vacancy, Sept. 17-Sept. 29, 1898; acting sec. of state during a critical period of the Chinese troubles in Aug. and Sept. 1900. Home: Washington, D.C. Died July 5, 1924.

ADGATE, Frederick Whitney, consulting engr.; b. Keeseville, N.Y., June 5, 1868; s. George and Martha (Whitney) A.; student Kan. State Agrl. Coll., 3 yrs.; m. Dolly May Triplett, June 21, 1904; children—George, Dorothy. Engr. and supt. various cos. until 1902; with The Foundation Co., Chicago, Ill., since its organization, 1902, successively as engr., supt., asst. western mgr. and mgr.; has built numerous large bridges, power plants, mining shafts, foundations, etc.; v.p. and dir. Money Corp.; dir. Service Oil Co., Chariton Fur Corp. In charge ship building and dry dock during World War. Republican. Episcopalian. Mason. Home: Wheaton, Ill. Died Oct. 23, 1934.

ADKINS, Charles, congressman; b. Pickaway County, O., Feb. 7, 1863; s. Sampson and Eliza Ann (Mintun) A.; ed. common schs.; m. Dora Ellen Farrow, 1888; children—Dora Ellen (widow of Romie Campbell), Charles Otis, Ben. F., Reuben (dec.), Roy, Howard, Ruth (Mrs. Claud Shirey), Grace, Martha, Mary. Farmer till 1918; mem. 69th to 72d Congresses (1925-33), 19th Ill. Dist. Republican. Methodist. Mason. Home: Decatur, Ill. Died Mar. 31, 1941.

ADKINS, John Scudder, architect; b. St. Louis, Mo.; s. Silas and Maria G. (Morgan) A.; ed. tech. div. Washington U. Sch. of Fine Arts; m. Olive Bridgman, Oct. 5, 1898; children—Marcia Lee (Mrs. Ralph Ingalsbe Finn), Eleanor Pelton (Mrs. Stanford Church Richmond). Designer, Barnett, Haynes & Barnett, later with Shepley, Rutan & Coolidge, St. Louis; began practice as architect, 1900. Architect: Clinton County Court House, Wilmington, O.; Scioto County Court House, Portsmouth, O.; City Hall, Norwood, O.; Governor's Mansion, Frankfort, Ky.; Second Nat. Bank, Oakley Bank Bldg., Cincinnati Gymnasium and Athletic Club and Grace Episcopal Ch., Cincinnati; First and Merchants Nat. Bank, Middleton, O.; Kanawha Nat. Bank, Charleston, W.Va.; Audubon Bldg., New Orleans; First Bapt. Ch., Lexington, Ky.; Nurses Home, Muncie, Ind. Mem. City Planning Commn., Cincinnati. Episcopalian. Mason. Home: Vernon Manor, Cincinnati, O. Deceased.

ADLER, Cyrus, college pres.; b. Van Buren, Ark., Sept. 13, 1863; s. Samuel and Sarah (Sulzberger) A.; A.B., U. of Pa., 1883, A.M., 1886, Litt.D., 1930; Ph.D., Johns Hopkins U., 1887; L.H.D., Hebrew Union College, 1925; m. Racie Friedenwald, Sept. 1905. Fellow, instr., and asso., Semitic langs., Johns Hopkins, 1884-93; librarian Smithsonian Instn., 1892-1905, asst. sec. same, 1905-08; curator of historic archæology and historic religions, U.S. Nat. Mus., 1889-1908; pres. Dropsie College for Hebrew and Cognate Learning, Phila., 1908—; acting pres. Jewish Theol. Sem. of America (N.Y. City), 1916-24, pres., 1924—. Mem. Bd. Pub. Edn., Phila., 1921-25; pres. trustees, Free Library of Phila., 1925-39, pres. bd. dirs., 1930; mem. bd. overseers Gratz Coll., Hebrew Edn. Soc., Phila. Special commr. of Chicago Expedition to Turkey, Egypt, Tunis, Algiers, Morocco, 1890-92; U.S. del. to Conf. on an Internat. Catalogue of Scientific Lit., 1898 (internat. council). Mem. Am. Philos. Soc. (v.p.), Am. Oriental Soc. (pres. 1923), Am. Jewish Hist. Soc. (ex-pres.). One of editors Jewish Encyclopedia; editor so-called Jefferson Bible, Am. Jewish Year Book, 1899-1906, and Jewish Quarterly Review (pub. by Dropsie Coll.), 1910—; chmn. bd. editors New Jewish Translation of the Bible; chmn. Jewish Classics Com. of Jewish Publication Soc. America; pres. Am. Jewish Com., 1929—; mem. council of The Jewish Agency for Palestine; mem. bd. govs. Hebrew Univ. in Jerusalem; mem. exec. bd. Boy Scouts of America; chmn. Army and Navy Com., Jewish Welfare Board; mem. bd. dirs. Jewish Joint Distribution Com., Fedn. of Jewish Charities of Phila. Winner of Phi Epsilon Pi Service Award, 1937. Author: Told in the Coffee House—Turkish Tales (with Allan Ramsay), 1898; Jacob H. Schiff, His Life and Letters, 1928; Memorandum on the Western Wall, prepared for the Spl. Commn. of the League of Nations on behalf of the Jewish Agency for Palestine, 1930. Lectures, selected papers, addresses by Cyrus Adler, collected and published by his colleagues and friends on the occasion of his 70th birthday, Sept. 13, 1933, with a bibliography. Home: Philadelphia, Pa. Died Apr. 7, 1940.

ADLER, Dankmar, architect; b. Langsfeld, Saxe Weimar, July 3, 1844; ed. public schools; studied architecture, Detroit and Chicago, 1857-62; m. Dila, d. Abraham Kohn, of Chicago, June 25, 1872. Served, 1862-65, Bat. M, 1st Ill. Artillery. Began practice of architecture in Chicago, 1869; with A. J. Kinney, 1869-71; with Edward Burling, 1871-78; with Louis H. Sullivan, 1881-95; architect of Unity Ch., Grace M.E., and 1st M.E. Chs., Sinai, Zion, Anshe Maariv and Isaiah synagogues, Central Music Hall, McVicker's Theatre, The Auditorium, Stock Exchange bldg., and Schiller bldg., Chicago; Pueblo (Colo.) Opera House; Union Trust, Wainwright and St. Nicholas Hotel bldgs., St. Louis; Guaranty bldg., Buffalo, N.Y.; I.C. R.R. passenger station, New Orleans; asso. architect Carnegie Music Hall, New York, etc. Home: Chicago, Ill. Died 1900.

ADLER, Felix, lecturer; b. Alzey, Germany, Aug. 13, 1851; s. Rabbi Samuel and Henrietta (Frankfurter) A.; A.B., Columbia, 1870; studied at Berlin and U. of Heidelberg, Ph.D., 1873; m. Helen Goldmark, May 24, 1880; children—Waldo, Eleanor, Lawrence, Margaret, Ruth. Prof. Hebrew and Oriental lit., Cornell, 1874-76; established, 1876, New York Soc. for Ethical Culture, to which he gives regular Sunday discourses; prof. polit. and social ethics, Columbia, 1902—; Roosevelt exchange prof., U. of Berlin, 1908-09; Hibbert lecturer, Oxford, Eng., 1923. Mem. editorial bd. Internat. Journal of Ethics; pres. Eastern Div. Am. Philos. Assn., 1928; chmn. Nat. Child Labor Com. Author: Creed and Deed, 1877; The Ethics of the Political Situation, 1884; The Moral Instruction of Children, 1892; Life and Destiny; Marriage and Divorce, 1905; Religion of Duty, 1905; Essentials of Spirituality, 1905; The World Crisis and Its Meaning, 1915; An Ethical Philosophy of Life, 1918; The Reconstruction of the Spiritual Ideal (Hibbert Lectures), 1923. Home: New York, N.Y. Died Apr. 24, 1933.

ADLER, Herman Morris, psychiatrist; b. New York, N.Y., Oct. 10, 1876; s. Isaac and Frieda (Grumbacher) A.; A.B., Harvard, 1897; A.M., M.D., Columbia, 1901; m. Frances Porter, Mar. 17, 1917; 1 dau., Frances Porter. Asst. prof. psychiatry, Harvard Med. Sch., 1912-17; was chief of staff, Boston Psychopathic Hosp.; removed to Chicago, 1916, to make a study of facilities in Cook County for detection and care of mental diseases and mental deficiency, under auspices of Rockefeller Foundation and Nat. Com. Mental Hygiene. Apptd. by Judge Scully, 1917, to make survey of Cook County's psychopathic cases and to act as med. adviser to county bd.; apptd. state criminologist of Ill. by Gov. Lowden, June 30, 1917; dir. Juvenile Psychopathic Inst., Feb. 10, 1917—. Maj. Med. Corps, U.S. Army, July 1918-Mar. 1919; spl. duty in disciplinary psychiatry at mil. prisons; prof. criminology and head of dept. of social hygiene, med. jurisprudence and criminology, Med. Coll. U. of Ill., 1919-28; prof. psychiatry, U. of Calif., 1930—; also advisor Calif. Dept. of Instns.

Dir. Behavior Research Fund, 1926—; mem. Harvard Survey of Crime and Law; consultant to Nat. Commn. on Law Observance and Enforcement. Author of section on Medical Science and Criminal Justice, in Criminal Justice Survey of the Cleveland Foundation, 1921. Home: Berkeley, Calif. Deceased.

ADLER, Simon Louis, judge; b. Seneca Falls, N.Y., Aug. 30, 1867; s. Lewis and Anne (Zalinski) A.; B.L., Cornell U., 1889; law study, Harvard, 1891-92; unmarried. Admitted to N.Y. bar, 1892, and began practice at Rochester. Mem. N.Y. State Assembly, 1911-26 (majority leader 1916-26); apptd. judge U.S. Dist. Court, Western Dist. of N.Y., 1927. Home: Rochester, N.Y. Deceased.

ADOLPHE, Albert Jean, artist; b. Phila., Pa., Feb. 17, 1865; s. Anthony and Mary (Weaver) A.; ed. Central High Sch., Phila.; pupil Pa. Acad. Fine Arts; Sch. of Industrial Art of Pa. Mus.; École des Beaux Arts, Paris; studied with Gérome and Whistler, Paris, de Vriendt in Antwerp. Former instr. in interior decoration, Drexel Inst., also at Sch. Industrial Art, and scenic artist, Acad. of Music, Phila.; instr. at La France Art Inst.; supplied decorations for steamships St. Louis and St. Paul, of the Am. Line. Exhibited at Glass Palais, Munich; Salons des Artists Francais, Paris; Art Inst. Chicago; Chicago Expn. also Acad. Fine Arts, Art Club, Graphic Sketch Club, Phila. Sketch Club, Imps Club—all of Phila. Awarded Charles Toppan Prize, Pa. Acad. Fine Arts, 1891; hon. mention, Chicago Expn., 1893, Paris Salon, 1899, gold medal, Art Club of Phila., 1904, and hon. mention, same, 1921; Stotesbury prize, Phila., 1916, for "Americanization Through Art." Free Thinker. Home: Philadelphia, Pa. Deceased.

AFRICA, John Simpson, banker; b. Huntingdon, Pa., Sept. 15, 1832; academic edn.; brought up as a surveyor and civil engr. and was in active practice for many years; m. Dorothea C. Greenland, Jan. 1, 1856 (died Nov. 15, 1886); surveyor, Huntingdon County, Pa., 1853-57; mem. Pa. legislature, 1860; deputy sec. Internal Affairs of Pa., 1875-79; sec., 1883-87; cashier 1st Nat. Bank of Huntingdon; pres. Union Trust Co. of Phila., 1887—. Grand master Masons of Pa., 1891-92. Home: Huntingdon, Pa. Died 1900.

AGAR, John Giraud, lawyer; b. New Orleans, La., June 3, 1856; s. William and Theresa (Price) A.; A.B., Georgetown U., 1876, A.M., 1888, Ph.D., 1889, LL.D., 1910; LL.B., Columbia, 1880; m. Agnes Louis Macdonough, Feb. 18, 1892; children—Lt. John Giraud (killed in France, Oct. 1918), William Macdonough, Herbert Sebastian, Agnes Dorothea, Philip Sylvester. Asst. U.S. atty., Southern Dist., N.Y., 1881-82; chmn. campaign com. People's Municipal League, 1891; lt. comdr. and p.m. and judge advocate on staff of capt. naval militia, N.Y., 1897-98; mem. New York Bd. Edn., 1896-98. V.p. Nat. Civic Fedn., 1905; pres. Reform Club, 1906-08, Municipal Art Soc., 1908-09, Nat. Arts Club, 1910. Trustee Mut. Life Ins. Co., 1916-31, Farmers Loan & Trust Co., 1919-30. Died Sept. 20, 1935.

AGASSIZ, Alexander (Emmanuel Rodolphe), naturalist; b. Neuchatel, Switzerland, Dec. 17, 1835; s. Professor Jean Louis Rodolphe and Cecile (Braun) A.; came to U.S., 1849; A.B., Harvard, 1855; B.S., Lawrence Scientific Sch., 1857; LL.D., Harvard, 1885, St. Andrew's, 1901; Sc.D., U. of Cambridge, 1887, Bologna, 1888; m. Anna Russell, Nov. 13, 1860. Asst. on U.S. Coast Survey in Calif., 1859; asst. in zoölogy, Mus. Comparative Zoölogy, Harvard, 1860-65; developed and was supt., 1865-69, Calumet & Hecla copper mines, Lake Superior; dir. Anderson Sch. of Natural History on Penikese Island, 1874; mem. expdn. to S. America, 1875, where inspected copper mines of Peru and Chili and made surveys of Lake Titicaca; curator Mus. Comparative Zoölogy, 1874-85, dir. same, 1902—; has made gifts to the museum aggregating over $1,000,000; also valuable W. Indian, Central, S. America and Pacific zoöl. collection, 1898. Assisted Sir Charles Wyville Thomson in classifying the collections of the expdn. of the Challenger in her voyage of 68,900 miles of deep-sea exploration, 1872-76; spent winters 1876-81 in deep-sea dredging in W. Indies on board U.S. Coast Survey steamer Blake; in charge of expdn. to the Sandwich Islands, the West Indies, the Fiji Islands, the Great Basin Reef of Australia; in charge of expdn. of U.S.S. Albatross to the Panamic regions and Galapagos, to the central Pacific and to eastern Pacific. Overseer, 1873-78 and 1885, fellow, 1878-84 and 1886-90, Harvard. Knight Order of Merit (Prussia), 1902; Officer Legion of Honor (France), 1896. Pres. Nat. Acad. of Sciences; pres. Am. Acad. Arts and Sciences, 1898. Author: Seaside Studies in Natural History (with Mrs. Elizabeth Cabot Agassiz), 1865; Marine Animals of Massachusetts Bay, 1871; Explorations of Lake Titicaca; Three Cruises of the Blake; Revision of the Echini; Coral Reefs of Florida, Bahamas, Bermudas, W. Indies, of the Pacific, of the Maldives; Panamic Deep Sea Echini; Hawaiian Echini, Embryological Memoirs on Fishes, Worms, Echinoderms, etc. Home: Cambridge, Mass. Died 1910.

AGASSIZ, Elizabeth Cabot, author; b. Boston, Mass., d. Thomas Greaves Cary; m. late Prof. Louis Agassiz; accompanied her husband to Brazil, 1865-66, and on Hassler expdn., 1871-72; was associated with him in many of his studies and writings; has taken active part in promoting the welfare of Radcliffe Coll., formerly the Harvard "Annex." Author: Seaside Studies in Natural History (with her son, Alexander Agassiz); Life of Louis Agassiz. Home: Cambridge, Mass. Died 1907.

AGASSIZ, Rodolphe Louis; b. Cambridge, Mass., Sept. 3, 1871; s. Alexander and Anna (Russell) A.; A.B., Harvard, 1892; m. Maria Dallas Scott, Mar. 27, 1894. Chairman bd. Calumet & Hecla Consol. Copper Co.; dir. State Street Trust Co., First Nat. Bank of Boston, Old Colony Trust Co., Edison Electric Ill. Co.; v.p. Mass. Hosp. Life Ins. Co. Home: Prides Crossing, Mass. Died July 31, 1933.

AGER, Waldemar (Theodore), editor, author; b. Fredriksstad, Norway, Mar. 23, 1869; s. Martinus M. and Mathea Marie Fredrikke (Johnson) A.; common sch. edn., came to America, 1885; m. Gurolle Johanne Blestren, of Tromsoe, Norway, July 5, 1899; children—Eyvind Blestren, Gudrun Fredrikke, Trygve Martinus, Valborg Hansine, Solveig Camilla, Magne Otterbeck, Roald Sneve, Hildur, Johndine, Borghild Gurolle. Connected with Fremad Pub. Co., Eau Claire, Wis., 1892—; treas. and editor "Reform" (weekly), 1903—. Prohibitionist. Lutheran. Author: Kristus for Pilatus, 1911; Sons of the Old Country, 1926; I Sit Alone, 1931, and many other novels and short stories in Norwegian lang. Knight Order of St. Olaf (conferred by king of Norway), 1923. D.Litt., St. Olaf Coll. Home: Eau Claire, Wis. Died Aug. 1, 1941.

AGGELER, William Tell, judge; b. Downieville, Sierra County, Calif., Aug. 7, 1866; s. John Joseph and Mary Ann (Rinderer) A.; LL.B., U. of Mich., 1893; J.D., Loyola U., Los Angeles, 1925, LL.D., 1930; m. Margaret Ann Ford, Sept. 14, 1897; children—Adele Marguerite, Leo Ignatius, Claire Marie, William Ford, Mervyn Aloysius. Began practice at Eureka, Calif., 1893; chief dep. pub. defender, Los Angeles County, 1914-21, pub. defender, Mar. 7, 1921-Aug. 2, 1927; judge Superior Court, Aug. 3, 1927—; prof. law, Loyola Univ., 1921-34. Democrat. Catholic. Home: Los Angeles, Calif. Died July 15, 1937.

AGNEW, Daniel, jurist; b. Trenton, N.J., Jan. 5, 1809; Irish and Welsh descent; m. 1831, Elizabeth Moore; grad. Western Univ. of Pa., and studied law with Henry Baldwin and W. W. Hetterman; LL.D., Washington and Dickinson Colls. Admitted to bar, 1829; mem. constl. conv. of Pa., 1837-38; president judge 7th jud. dist. Pa., 1851-63; justice Supreme Court Pa., 1863-79, and chief justice, 1874-79. Home: Beaver, Pa. Died 1902.

AGNEW, William Henry, clergyman, educator; b. Westphalia, Kan., Oct. 12, 1881; s. Matthew and Bridget (McManus) A.; A.B., St. Louis U., 1905, A.M., 1907, M.S., 1911; grad. in theology, same univ., 1916. Joined Soc. of Jesus (Jesuits), 1900; ordained priest R.C. Ch., 1915; dean dept. of science and mathematics, Loyola U., Chicago, 4 yrs., St. Louis U., 1 yr.; prof. natural theology, St. Louis U., 1919-20; pres. Loyola U., July 31, 1921-27; rector Sacred Heart Ch., Chicago, 1927-28; pres. Creighton U., Omaha, 1928—. Served as chaplain Cook County (Ill.) Hosp., Met. Hosp. (New York), N.Y. State Psychopathic Hosp., Blackwell's Island Workhouse. Mem. Nat. Catholic Welfare Council, Catholic Students' Mission Crusade (advisory council), K.C. Died Feb. 13, 1931.

AGNUS, Felix, editor; b. Lyons, France, July 4, 1839; ed. Coll. Jolie Clair, near Paris; traveled around the world 4 yrs.; vol. under Napoleon III during Franco-Austrian War; also served under Garibaldi; came to U.S., 1860; m. a d. of Charles C. Fulton, of Baltimore, Dec. 13, 1864. Enlisted as sergt. in Duryea's 5th N.Y. Zouaves, May 9, 1861; 2d lt., Sept. 6, 1861, for saving life of Gen. Judson Kilpatrick at Big Bethel; 1st lt., July 8, 1862; capt. 165th N.Y. Inf., Nov. 6, 1862; maj., Sept. 2, 1863; resigned, July 26, 1865. Bvtd.: lt.-col., Mar. 13, 1865, "for gallant and meritorious services at battle of Gaines' Mill," June 13, 1862 (wounded); col., Mar. 13, 1865, for same at battle of Port Hudson, La. (wounded); brig-gen. vols., Mar. 13, 1865, for same during the war. Apptd. asst. assessor internal revenue, Baltimore, 1865; business mgr., later editor and publisher Baltimore American and Baltimore Star; retired. Home: Stevenson, Md. Died Oct. 31, 1925.

AGRAMONTE, Aristides, bacteriologist; b. Camagüey, Cuba, June 3, 1869; s. Dr. Edward and Mathilde (Simoni) A.; brought to U.S., in infancy; student Coll. City of New York, 1885-87; M.D., Coll. Physicians and Surgeons (Columbia), 1892 (Harsen prize); M.B., Havana U., 1899, M.D., 1900; (Sc.D., Columbia U., New York, 1914); m. Frances Pierra, Apr. 17, 1895. Practiced, New York; asst. surgeon U.S. Army, May, 1898-Oct., 1902; mem. U.S. Army bd. that discovered, 1901, transmission of yellow fever by mosquitoes; chmn. Bd. of Infectious Disease and mem. Nat. Bd. of Health, Republic of Cuba; prof. bacteriology and exptl. pathology, U. of Havana, 1900—. Mem. Am. Acad. Sciences. Home: Havana, Cuba. Died Aug. 19, 1931.

AHERN, Mary Eileen, editor; b. on farm near Indianapolis, Ind.; d. William and Mary (O'Neill) Ahern; grad. Central Normal Coll. of Ind., 1881; Library Sch., Armour Inst. Tech., Chicago, 1895-96. Formerly teacher; asst. state librarian of Ind., 1889-93, state librarian, 1893-95; an organizer, 1896, and then editor, "Public Libraries" (library jour.). Publicity agent in France for Am. Library Assn., Jan.-July, 1919; organized Ind. Library Assn. and its sec., 1889-96; an organizer, 1896, and sec. 1896-1907, library dept. N.E.A. Home: Chicago, Ill. Died May 22, 1938.

AHRENS, Theodore, mfr.; b. Baltimore, Md., Sept. 21, 1859; s. Theodore and Mary (Nebel) A.; ed. pub. schs., Louisville, Ky.; m. Elizabeth Pfeister, Apr. 30, 1885; 1 dau., Elsie. Began, 1880, title of Ahrens, Welker & Ryan, contracting plumbers, Louisville, Ky., elected gen. mgr. The Ahrens & Ott Mfg. Co., 1886; organizer, 1900, and pres. Standard Sanitary Mfg. Co., Pittsburgh, Pa., now chmn. bd.; dir. Am. Radiator Co. Served as alderman and mem. Sewerage Commn. of Louisville; dir. Lincoln Inst. of Ky. Republican. Home: Louisville, Ky. Died June 12, 1938.

AID, George Charles, artist; b. Quincy, Ill., Aug. 26, 1872; s. Francis and Louise (Huber) A.; student Sch. Fine Arts, Washington U., St. Louis, 1890-93; Academie Julian, Paris, France, 1899-1901; m. Mary Orr, 1910; 1 son, George Charles. Painting exhibited at Paris Salon, 1906, purchased by Swedish govt.; etchings purchased by Musee National du Luxembourg (Paris), Royal Gallery of Dresden, N.Y. Pub. Library; historical subject, "Baptism of Virginia Dare," purchased for Mint Mus., of Charlotte, N.C., 1937. Awarded hon. mention Paris Salon; silver medal La. Purchase Expn.; bronze medal San Francisco World's Fair. Home: Tryon, N.C. Died May 12, 1938.

AIKEN, Charles Francis, educator, author; b. Boston, Mass., Apr. 8, 1863; s. of Albert and Maria (Murphy) A.; A.B. summa cum laude, Harvard, 1884; studied philosophy and theology St. John's Eccles. Sem., Brighton, Mass., 1886-90; student Catholic U., 1890-92, S.T.B., 1891 (S.T.L., 1897, S.T.D., 1900). Taught classics, Heathcote Sch., Buffalo, N.Y., 1884-86; ordained priest, R.C. Ch., 1890; curate, St. Patrick's parish, Boston, 1892-95; lecturer apologetics, 1897-1900, prof., 1900—, dean Faculty of Theology, 1909-11, 1913-15, 1921-23, Catholic U. of America. Author: The Dhamma of Gotama the Buddha and the Gospel of Jesus the Christ, 1900. French transl.: Buddhisme et Christianisme (by Abbé L. Collin), 1903. Contbd. to Catholic Encyclopedia articles on Apologetics, Brahmanism, Buddhism, Confucianism, Hinduism, Jainism, The Laws of Manu, Mencius, Monotheism, Felix Nève, Religion. Died July 8, 1925.

AIKEN, Charles Sedgwick, editor; b. Cleveland, O., Feb. 6, 1863; s. Charles Grant and Julia Antoinette (Cleveland) A.; ed. Central High Sch. (Cleveland), Berkeley (Cal.) High Sch., U. of Cal.; m. Ednah Robinson, Aug. 24, 1905. On editorial staff Evening Bulletin, San Francisco, 1885-95, The Call, July-Oct., 1895, Examiner, 1895-1900; editor Sunset Magazine, 1900-06; editor and mgr. Ridgway's Weekly, San Francisco edit., Oct.-Dec., 1906; editor Sunset Mag., 1906—. Corr. New York Post, Phila. Inquirer, Washington Post. Republican. Congregationalist. Home: San Francisco, also Los Altos, Cal. Died 1911.

AIKEN, Frank Eugene, actor; b. Boston, Mass., Aug. 31, 1840; s. Lemuel Gilman and Susan (Wyatt) A.; ed. Mayhew (pub.) Sch., Boston. Began theatrical career in George H. Wyatt's (an uncle) stock co.; later leading man at Barnum's Mus., New York; with E. L. Davenport Co., Boston, 3 seasons; leading man, Boston Theatre, 1 season; Mrs. John Drew's Arch St. Theatre, Phila., 1 season; Wood's Mus., Chicago, 1864; mgr. Wood's Mus., Aiken's Mus., Dearborn Theatre, Hooley's Theatre, Chicago, 1868-71; owner and mgr. Aiken's Theatre, Chicago, 1871-73; starred in own company, 1873-88; under T. Henry French as "The Earl" in Little Lord Fauntleroy, 3 seasons; with Frank Mayo in Pudd'nhead Wilson, 2 seasons; 3 seasons as "Lord Rintoul" in The Little Minister; was prominent mem. Mrs. George H. Gilbert's co. at time of her death in Chicago, 1904; lifelong friend of Edwin Booth and often appeared with him in Shakespearean and romantic plays; under engagement to Charles Frohman in support of John Drew. Address: New York, N.Y. Died 1910.

AIKEN, John Adams, judge; b. Greenfield, Mass., Sept. 16, 1850; s. David and Mary Elizabeth (Adams) A.; A.B., Dartmouth, 1874 (LL.D., 1905); m. Maria Willard Dickinson, Mar. 29, 1895. Admitted to Mass. bar, 1876; practiced with father in Greenfield, Mass., several yrs. and then alone. Mem. Mass. Ho. of Rep., 1883; dist. atty. Northwest Dist., Mass., 1890-97, justice, 1898, chief justice, 1905-23, Superior Ct. of Mass. Home: Greenfield, Mass. Died Jan. 28, 1927.

AIKEN, William Appleton, mfr.; b. Manchester, Vt., Apr. 18, 1833; s. John and Mary Means (Appleton) A.; ed. pub. and pvt. schs., Lowell, Mass., Dummer Acad., Byfield, Mass., Phillips Acad., Andover, Mass., to 1851; m. Eliza Coit, d. Gov. William A. Buckingham of Norwich, Conn., Aug. 28, 1861.

Acting asst. paymaster U.S. Navy, 1861-62; q.-m.-gen. of Conn., 1862-65. Was pres. Norwich Nickel & Brass Co. Republican. Home: Norwich, Conn. Died Nov. 7, 1929.

AIKEN, William Martin, architect; b. Charleston, S.C., April 1, 1855; s. Joseph Daniel and Ellen Daniel (Martin) A.; attended U. of the South, 1872-74; taught in same, 1874; taught in high school, Charleston, 1874-76; spl. course in architecture, Mass. Inst. Tech., 1877-79; student in office of H. H. Richardson, 1880-83 and W. R. Emerson, 1883-85, Boston; in office James W. McLaughlin, Cincinnati, 1885-86; practiced architecture, Cincinnati, 1886-95; taught in Cincinnati Art Acad., 1894-95; supervising architect U.S. Treasury Dept., 1895-97, and designed Govt. expn. bldgs., Atlanta 1895, Nashville 1897, and Omaha 1898, also mint bldgs. at Phila. and Denver, and numerous postoffices and custom-house bldgs.; in practice, New York, with Bruce Price, 1897-1901; taught in Columbia, 1899; cons. architect for Borough of Manhattan, 1901-03. Fellow Am. Inst. Architects. Collaborator with Russell Sturgis: Dictionary of Architecture. Home: New York, N.Y. Died 1908.

AIKENS, Andrew Jackson, journalist; b. Barnard, Vt., Oct. 31, 1830; s. Warren and Lydia A.; m. 1st, 1854, Amanda L. Barnes (died 1893); 2d, 1895, Katherine V. Crehore. Became, 1854, city editor Evening Wisconsin, Milwaukee, then a propr., and from 1857 gen. mgr.; in 1864 firm of Cramer, Aikens & Cramer began printing "patent insides" for country newspapers, being the pioneers in that business. Home: Milwaukee, Wis. Died 1909.

AIKENS, Charles Thomas, univ. pres.; b. Siglerville, Mifflin County, Pa., Dec. 14, 1862; s. Andrew Jackson and Lucinda (Hassenplug) A.; grad. Missionary Inst., Selinsgrove, Pa., 1883; A.B., Pa. Coll., Gettysburg, 1885, A.M., 1888; grad. Theol. Sem., Gettysburg, 1888; D.D., Wittenberg Coll., Springfield, O., 1907; m. Athalia Clara Gitt, Nov. 26, 1889 (died Dec. 3, 1910); m. 2d, Feb. 3, 1915, Mrs. Carrie (Specht) Smith. Ordained Luth. ministry, 1888; pastor, Pine Grove, Pa., 1888-1905; pres. Susquehanna U., Selinsgrove, 1905—. Pres. Selinsgrove Realty Co., Phi Delta Theta Corp. (State Coll., Pa.); v.p., treas. Nittany (Pa.) Real Estate Co. Pres. Synod of Central Pa., 1897-1901; del. Gen. Synod, 1895, 1913, 1917. Pres. Selinsgrove Chamber of Commerce; pres. Susquehanna Trail Assn.; chmn. Eastern State Hosp. Commn. of Pa. Mason (32°). Home: Selinsgrove, Pa. Died June 21, 1927.

AIKMAN, William, clergyman; b. New York, Aug. 12, 1824; grad. New York Univ., 1846 (D.D., 1869); m. Anna M. Burns, 1849. Pastor Presbyn. chs., Newark, N.J., Wilmington, Del., New York, Detroit, Atlantic City, N.J. Moderator Synod Pa., Washington, D.C., 1863. Author: Our Country Strong in Her Isolation; Seductive Power of the Romish Ritual; Future of the Colored Race in America; Government and Administration; Moral Power of the Sea; Life at Home; Talks on Married Life and Things Adjacent; Heavenly Recognitions. Home: Atlantic City, N.J. Died 1909.

AILES, Milton Everett, banker; b. Shelby County, O., Aug. 19, 1867; s. Hezekiah S. and Jane A.; grad. high sch., Sidney, O.; LL.B., Nat. U. Law Sch., Washington, 1889, LL.M., 1890; admitted to D.C. bar, 1890; m. Mary E. Gowans, Nov. 25, 1891. Apptd. minor position Treasury Dept., 1887; served through the various grades of the classified service; apptd. sec. to the sec. of the treasury, Dec. 1, 1897; asst. sec. of the treasury, 1901-03; v.p. 1903-21, pres., 1921—, Riggs Nat. Bank. Republican. Home: Washington, D.C. Died Oct. 30, 1925.

AINEY, William David Blakeslee, chmn. Public Serv. Commn. of Pa.; congressman; b. New Milford, Susquehanna County, Pa., Apr. 8, 1864; s. David C. and Kathleen (Blakeslee) A.; State Normal, Mansfield and Lehigh U.; LL.D., L.H.D.; m. Emma E. Lyons, Oct. 10, 1888. Admitted to Pa. bar, 1887; dist. atty., Susquehanna County, 2 terms; elected Nov. 1911, mem. 62d Congress; re-elected to 63d Congress (1913-15). Republican. Del. to Interparliamentary Conf., Geneva, Switzerland, 1912; del. to The Hague, 1913, and there made sec. Japanese-Am. Groups of Parliamentarians. Visited Japan, 1914, on invitation of members of Imperial Parliament, as del. from U.S.; del. Interparliamentary Union, Paris, France, 1927; apptd. May 26, 1915, mem. Pub. Service Commn. of Pa., chmn., 1915—; apptd. chmn. Pa. Fuel Commn., Aug. 1922. Pres. Nat. Assn. Railroad and Utility Commrs., 1925. Trustee Wilson Coll.; chmn. State Y.M.C.A. Presbyn. Mason. Odd Fellow. Home: Harrisburg, Pa. Died Sept. 4, 1933.

AINSLIE, George, lawyer; b. Boonville, Mo., Oct. 30, 1838; s. John A.; one yr. at St. Louis U.; m. Sallie Owens, Mar. 27, 1866. Admitted to Mo. bar, Apr., and went to Colo. (then known as "Pike's Peak"), 1860; practiced law at Gregory Diggings, 1860-62; with a company of 16 men went to headwaters of Salmon River, in what is now Ida., prospecting for gold, 1862; later mined, and practiced law in Ida. Mem. Territorial legislative council, 1865-66; editor Idaho World, 1869-73; dist. atty. 2d Dist. Ida., 1875-79; del. to 46th and 47th Congresses (1879-83); mem. State Constl. Conv., 1889; chmn. Dem. State Central Com., 1890-91; Ida. mem. Dem. Nat. Com., 1896-1900; well known advocate of free silver. Pres. Boise Rapid Transit Co., 1890-1904. Home: Alameda, Cal. Died May 19, 1913.

AINSLIE, Peter, clergyman; b. Dunnsville, Va., June 3, 1867; s. Peter and Rebecca Etta (Sizer) A.; ed. Transylvania Coll., Lexington, Ky., 1886-89; D.D., Drake U., 1911, Yale U., 1914; LL.D., Bethany Coll., W.Va.; m. Mary Elizabeth Weisel, June 30, 1925; children—Mary Elizabeth, Peter. Temp. supply, Newport News, 1889-91; pastor Baltimore, 1891—; under his administration new building erected known as Christian Temple, and 9 br. chs. established. Editor Christian Union Quarterly, 1911—. Founder 1899, Girls' Club, on self-governing basis for girls from rural dists. Trustee Disciples Div. House (U. of Chicago); trustee Ch. Peace Union, founded by Andrew Carnegie; del. to Ch. Peace Conf., Constance, Germany, 1914, Hague, 1919, Geneva, 1920, Copenhagen, 1922; Life and Work Conf., Stockholm, 1925; mem. internat. com. of World Alliance for Promoting Internat. Friendship Through the Churches; pres. Assn. for Promotion Christian Unity, 1910-25; pres. Christian Unity League for Equality and Brotherhood, 1927, and mem. of its 8 nation-wide conferences; mem. deputation apptd. by P.E. Ch. to visit Great Britain in interest of World Conf. on Faith and Order, 1913-14; member Lausanne Conf., 1927; editorial board Encyclopedia Britannica, 1927. Author: Religion in Daily Doings, 1903; Studies in the Old Testament, 1907; Among the Gospels and the Acts, 1908; God and Me, 1908; My Brother and I, 1911; The Unfinished Task of the Reformation, 1910; Introduction to the Study of the Bible, 1910; The Message of the Disciples for the Union of the Church (Yale Lectures), 1913; Christ or Napoleon—Which? 1915; Working with God, 1917; If Not a United Church—What? 1920; Christian Worship (with H. C. Armstrong), 1923; The Way of Prayer, 1924; The Scandal of Christianity, 1929; Some Experiments in Living, 1933. Home: Baltimore, Md. Died Feb. 23, 1934.

AINSWORTH, Fred Crayton, major-general U.S.A.; b. Woodstock, Vt., Sept. 11, 1852. M.D., Univ. Med. Coll. (New York U.), 1874. Apptd. from Vt. asst. surgeon, Nov. 10, 1874; capt. asst. surgeon, Nov. 10, 1879; maj. surgeon, Feb. 27, 1891; col. and chief of Record and Pension Office, May 27, 1892; brig. gen., Mar. 2, 1899; maj. gen. and mil. sec. U.S.A., Apr. 23, 1904; maj. gen. and the adj. gen. U.S.A., Mar. 5, 1907, with rank from Apr. 23, 1904; retired at own request, Feb. 16, 1912. Home: Washington, D.C. Died June 5, 1934.

AIREY, Charles Theodore, ry. official; b. Perryville, Ala., Aug. 17, 1866; s. Capt. Joseph C. and Emma (Smith) A.; ed. pub. and pvt. schs.; m. Geraldine, d. William E. McAndrew, Dec. 18, 1894; 1 son, Charles Theodore (dec.). Began, 1882, as clk. in shops E. Tenn., Va. & Ga. Ry. (now a part of Southern Ry. System), Selma, Ala.; various clerical positions in shops and local agencies same rd. until 1889; city passenger and ticket agt., at Selma, freight agt., Talladega, and chief clk. to supt., Macon, Ga.—all with same rd., until 1894; gen. agt., Southern Ry., at Macon; gen. agt., Mobile & Ohio R.R., at Atlanta; gen. agt., New York & Tex. Steamship Co., at Atlanta, until 1904; apptd. asst. gen. freight agt., Central of Georgia Ry., at Savannah, 1904, freight traffic mgr., 1907-18; chmn. Southern Export Com., by apptmt. U.S. Railroad Adminstrn.; v.p. and traffic mgr. Central of Georgia Ry. Co. 1919-28, v.p., 1928—. Democrat. Episcopalian. Home: Savannah, Ga. Died March 14, 1930.

AITCHISON, John Young, clergyman; b. Cascade, Ia., May 27, 1868; s. William, Jr., and Harriet Amelia A.; B.A., Des Moines Coll., 1893, M.A., 1894, D.D., 1904; Div. Sch., U. of Chicago, 1893-96; m. Estella Viola Sutton, Aug. 5, 1896. Ordained Bapt. ministry, 1896; pastor 1st Church, Wasco, Ill., 1894-95, 1st Ch., Maywood, 1895-96, Garfield Park Ch., Milwaukee, 1896-98, 1st Ch., Shenandoah, Ia., 1898-1902, 1st Ch., Galesburg, Ill., 1902-09; sec. Am. Bapt. Home Missionary Soc., Chicago, 1909-12; joint dist. sec. Am. Bapt. Home Mission Soc. and Am. Bapt. Foreign Mission Soc., Chicago, 1912-16; home sec. Am. Bapt. Foreign Mission Soc., 1916-19; gen. dir. Gen. Bd. of Promotion of Northern Bapt. Conv., 1919—. Home: Yonkers, N.Y. Died March 15, 1926.

AKED, Charles Frederic, clergyman; b. Nottingham, Eng., Aug. 27, 1864; s. Charles and Ann A.; ed. Midland Baptist Coll. and Univ. Coll., Nottingham; D.D., Temple Coll., 1901, Brown U., 1907; LL.D., U. of Nev., 1913, Drury Coll., 1923; Litt.D., U. of Southern Calif., 1929; m. Anne Hithersay, of Ilkeston, Eng., Nov. 10, 1886. Ordained Baptist ministry, 1886; pastor, Syston, Leicestershire, 1886-88, St. Helens and Earlestown, 1888-90, Pembroke Chapel, Liverpool, 1890-1907, Fifth Av. Baptist Ch., New York, 1907-11, First Congl. Ch. San Francisco, Apr. 16, 1911-15, First Congl. Ch., Kansas City, Mo., 1919-24, All Souls' Ch., Los Angeles, 1925—. Made annual lecture and preaching trips to U.S., 1893-1907. V.p. United Kingdom Alliance; one of the founders Passive Resistance League (England). Author: The Courage of the Coward, 1905; Wells and Palm Trees, 1908; Old Events and Modern Meanings, 1908; The Lord's Prayer, 1910; The Divine Drama of Job, 1913. Home: Los Angeles, Calif. Died Aug. 12, 1941.

AKELEY, Carl Ethan, taxidermist, inventor; b. Orleans Co., N.Y., May 19, 1864; s. Daniel Webster and Julia M. (Glidden) A.; ed. State Normal Sch. Brockport, N.Y.; m. 2d, Mary L. Jobe, Oct. 18, 1924. With Field Mus., Chicago, 1895-1909, Am. Mus. Natural History, New York, 1909—. Served as cons. engr., div. of investigation, research and development, Engr. Dept., U.S. Army, also as spl. asst. concrete dept. Emergency Fleet Corp.; inventor of cement gun, Akeley Camera, etc.; medalist Franklin Inst. Big game hunter; made four trips to Africa for study and collection of big game. Republican. Author: In Brightest Africa, 1923. Died Nov. 17, 1926.

AKELEY, Healy Cady, lumber merchant; b. Stowe, Vt., March 16, 1836; s. George A.; acad. edn. in Vt.; admitted to bar, 1857; engaged in practice at Grand Haven, Mich., 1858; m. Anna Murray, 1859 (dec.); 2d, Hettie E. Smith, 1869. Enlisted, 1863, as pvt. 2d Mich. Cav., mustered out, 1865, as adj. of regt. Resumed practice after war, and engaged in lumber business, 1872-87; mayor Grand Haven 2 terms; collector customs, dist. of Mich., 1866-81; in Minneapolis, 1887—; pres. H. C. Akeley Lumber Co., Itasca Lumber Co., etc. Home: Minneapolis, Minn. Died July 30, 1912.

AKERS, Elizabeth, author; b. (Chase) at Strong, Me., Oct. 9, 1832. Began to write at 15 under pen-name "Florence Percy"; became contbr. to Atlantic Monthly, 1858; wrote her famous poem, "Rock Me to Sleep, Mother," 1859. Was for several years literary editor Portland (Me.) Advertiser; m. Paul Akers, sculptor (died, 1861); 2d, E. M. Allen, 1865. Author: Forest Buds from the Woods of Maine, 1855; Poems by Elizabeth Akers, 1866-68-69; Queen Catharine's Rose, 1885; The Silver Bridge, 1885; The Triangular Society (prose), 1887; Two Saints, 1888; The High-Top Sweeting, 1891; The Proud Lady of Stavoren, 1897; The Ballad of the Bronx, 1901; The Sunset Song, 1903. Home: Tuckahoe, N.Y. Died 1911.

AKERSON, George Edward, sec. to the President; b. Minneapolis, Sept. 5, 1889; s. Charles G. and Mary (Larson) A.; student Allegheny Coll., Meadville, Pa., 1909-10; A.B., cum laude, Harvard, 1912; m. Harriet Blake, June 28, 1915; children—George Edward, Frederick Blake, Charles Baily. With Minneapolis Tribune, 1912-25, Washington corr., 1921-23, 25, asst. mng. editor, 1923-24; sec. Nat. Sesqui-Centennial Expn. Commn., 1925-26; asst. to sec. of commerce, Herbert Hoover, 1925-28; sec. to President Hoover, 1929-31; mem. exec. staff Paramount Publix Corp., 1931-33; exec. sec. Nat. Code Authority of Paper Distributing Trade under NRA, 1934-35. Republican. Presbyn. Mason (Shriner). Home: Bronxville, N.Y. Died Dec. 1937.

AKIN, Theron, congressman; b. Johnstown, Fulton Co., N.Y., 1855; s. Ethan and Susan (St. John) A.; ed. pub. sch. and at home; m. Mrs. Jennie S. Roberts. Engaged in farming at Akin, N.Y., 1859—. Pres. Village of Akin, N.Y., 1909-11; mem. 62d Congress (1911-13), 25th N.Y. Dist.; Progressive Republican. Home: Akin, N.Y. Died March 26, 1933.

ALBAUGH, John W., actor, theatrical mgr.; b. Baltimore, Sept. 30, 1837; s. John W. and Elizabeth (Peters) A.; first stage appearance at Baltimore Museum, Feb. 1, 1855 (Joseph Jefferson being stage mgr.) as Brutus in "Brutus, or the Fall of Tarquin"; afterward in many companies as walking gentleman, heavy man, leading support and star; m. Mary Mitchell; co-mgr. Olympic, St. Louis, 1868-69; mgr. Trimble Opera House, Albany N.Y., 1870; partner of Ben De Bar in St. Charles Theatre, New Orleans, 1870-71; mgr. Leland Opera House, Albany, 1873-81; mgr. and sole lessee Holliday St. Theatre, 1878-90; and sole prop. New Lyceum, Baltimore; built and was half owner, and mgr. for 3 yrs. Lafayette Sq. Opera House, Washington, 1895-98; lessee and mgr. Albaugh's Grand Opera House, Washington, 1884-94; lessee and mgr. National Theatre, Washington, 1879-84. Retired. Last appearance on the stage as Shylock, Lyceum Theatre, Baltimore, Dec. 1899. Home: Long Branch, N.J. Died 1909.

ALBEE, Edward F., theatrical mgr., b. Machias, Me., Oct. 8, 1857; s. Nathan S. and Amanda A.; pub. sch. edn.; m. Laura S. Smith, May 13, 1881; children—Reed A., Mrs. Ethel A. Lauder. Associated with late B. F. Keith from beginning of vaudeville 45 years ago; pres. Keith-Albee Vaudeville Circuit, consisting of about 70 theatres, located in largest cities of Middle West and in East; pres. Keith-Albee Vaudeville Exchange (representing 317 theatres in various cities U.S. and Canada). V.p. Actors' Fund of America; trustee St. Stephen's Coll., Cathedral of St. John the Divine (New York), St. John's Episcopal Ch. (Larchmont, N.Y.). Died March 11, 1930.

ALBEE, Ernest, univ. prof.; b. Langdon, N.H., Aug. 8, 1865; s. Solon and Ellen Lucilia (Eames)

A.; A.B., U. of Vt., 1887; studied at Clark and Cornell, Ph.D., 1894. Fellow psychology, Clark, 1891; fellow philosophy, 1892, instr., 1892-1902, asst. prof., 1902-07, prof. philosophy, 1907—, Cornell; m. Emily Humphreys Manly, Dec. 23, 1911. Mem. Am. Philos. Assn., Phi Beta Kappa. Co-editor The Philosophical Review, 1903-08, and from 1924. Author: A History of English Utilitarianism, 1902. Home: Ithaca, N.Y. Died May 26, 1927.

ALBEE, John, author; b. Bellingham, Mass., Apr. 3, 1833; s. John and Esther (Thayer) A.; grad. Phillips Acad., Andover, Mass., 1854, Harvard Div. Sch., 1858; m. Helen Rickey, Feb. 15, 1894. Author: Literary Art, 1881; Poems, 1883; History of New Castle, N.H., 1884; Prose Idylls, 1892; Biography of Henry Dexter, sculptor, 1898; Remembrances of Emerson, 1900; Lake Chocorua, 1910; Confessions of Boyhood, 1910. Home: Pequaket, N.H. Died Mar. 24, 1915.

ALBERT, Charles Stanley, editor; b. Hanover, Pa., Aug. 17, 1847; s. John Jacob and Juliana (Diehl) A.; A.B., Pa. Coll., 1867, A.M., 1870 (D.D., 1887); grad. Mt. Airy Theol. Sem., 1870; m. Mary W. Baker, July 2, 1872. Ordained Luth. ministry, 1870; asst. pastor, Lancaster, Pa., 1870-72, Carlisle, Pa., 1872-81, St. Mark's English Luth. Ch., Baltimore, 1881-93; editor Augsburg Teacher, 1894—. Pres. Bd. Home Missions, Gen. Synod, 1881-97; pres. Gen. Synod Luth. Ch. in America, 1893-95. Editor Augsburg Quarterlies, Luth. Young People, Lutheran Church Work; lit. editor Luth. Publ. Soc. (Gen. Synod). Home: Philadelphia, Pa. Died Jan. 28, 1912.

ALBERT, Charles Sumner, newspaper corr.; b. Union County, Ind., July 16, 1858; acad. edn., Dublin, Ind.; m. Miss Fletcher, May 22, 1895. Formerly mgr. Press News Assn., Washington, also traveling corr. and night editor United Press; 27 yrs. in Washington newspaper work; Washington corr. New York World. Home: Washington, D.C. Died Mar. 27, 1923.

ALBERT, Henry, pathologist, bacteriologist; b. Wolcott, Scott County, Ia., Oct. 11, 1878; s. Fred and Catharina (Stiefel) A.; B.S., State U. of Ia. 1900, M.S., 1902, M.D., 1902; studied U. of Austria, 1902; m. Edith Whiteis, June 10, 1905. Instr. pathology and bacteriology, 1902-03, prof. and head of dept., 1903-22, State U. of Ia. Dir. labs. Ia. State Bd. of Health, 1903-22; dir. Hygienic Lab., U. of Nev., 1922—; commr. Ia. State Dept. of Health, 1926—. Republican. Lutheran. Home: Des Moines, Ia. Died Apr. 6, 1930.

ALBERTSON, George Roger, M.D., educator; b. Moline, Ill., Dec. 24, 1886; s. Charles Sampson and Sarah Denman (Williams) A.; M.D., State U. of Ia., 1910, M.S., 1912; A.B., U. of S.D., 1916; grad. study U. of Chicago, 1917; m. Maisie Kracke, Sept. 8, 1910; 1 dau., Mary Snell. Asst. demonstrator of anatomy, State U. of Ia., 1910-12; prof. anatomy, U. of S.D., 1912—, dean of Sch. of Medicine, 1926—. Mem. med. advisory bd., Vermilion, S.D., World War. Mason (32°, K.T.). Home: Vermilion, S.D. Deceased.

ALBING, Otto Frederick, an editorial writer on Buffalo Courier, 1875-1901, and editor Buffalo Demokrat, 1885—; b. Hanover, Germany, Mar. 25, 1840; univ. edn. at Göttingen and Heidelberg; engaged in newspaper work; came to U.S., 1866; was connected with German papers in Phila., New York and Buffalo. Address: Buffalo, N.Y. Died 1905.

ALBRIGHT, Edward, foreign service; b. in Sumner County, Tenn., Aug. 18, 1873; B.L., Cumberland U., 1898. Admitted to Tenn. bar; newspaper publisher, 1907-33; apptd. E.E. and M.P. to Finland, July 21, 1933. Pres. Nat. Editorial Assn., 1919-20. Died May 25, 1937.

ALBRIGHT, Edwin, president judge dist. court Lehigh County, Pa., 1878-1908; b. Lehigh County, Pa., Nov. 8, 1838; admitted to bar, 1862; practiced law until 1878; was 3 yrs. dist. atty., and 6 yrs. State senator. Home: Allentown, Pa. Died 1902.

ALBRIGHT, Frank Herman, army officer; b. Putnam County, O., Aug. 2, 1865; s. William L. and Mary (Shierlow) A.; grad. U.S. Mil. Acad., 1887, Army War Coll., 1915; m. Minnie Louise, d. Chaplain Winfield Scott, U.S. Army, Mar. 4, 1891. Commd. 2d lt. 12th Inf., June 12, 1887, and advanced through grades to brig. gen. N.A., Aug. 15, 1917. Service in Cuba and P.R., 1898, in Philippines, 1899-1902, 1907-09; prof. mil. science and tactics, U. of N.D., 1898, Purdue U., 1903-05; comdg. 151st Inf. Brigade, Camp Devens, Ayer, Mass., Aug. 25, 1917, later with A.E.F. in France; hon. disch. as brig. gen., Nov. 27, 1918; retired. Republican. Home: San Diego, Calif. Died Apr. 10, 1940.

ALBRIGHT, John Joseph, art patron; b. Buchanan, Va., Jan. 18, 1848; s. Joseph J. and Elizabeth (Sellers) A.; grad. Williston Sem., East Hampton, Mass., 1864; M.E., Rensselaer Poly. Inst., Troy, N.Y., 1868; m. Harriet Langdon, Dec. 4, 1872; m. 2d, Susan Fuller, Mar. 23, 1897. In wholesale coal business, Pa., till 1873, Washington, D.C., till 1883. Donor Albright Art Gallery, Buffalo; an incorporator Am. Academy in Rome (Italy). Home: Buffalo, New York. Died August 20, 1931.

ALBRIGHT, Percy R., ry. official; b. Greensboro, N.C., June 26, 1866; ed. high sch., Greensboro. Began as clk. with Cape Fear & Yadkin Valley R.R., Aug. 1, 1888, chief clk., 1890-98; mgr. North Carolina Demurrage Bur., 1898-1904; with Atlantic Coast Line, 1904—, successively as asst. to gen. mgr. until 1914, asst. gen. mgr., 1914-16, gen. mgr., 1916-23, v.p. and gen. mgr., 1923-28, v.p. in charge operations, 1928—. Home: Wilmington, N.C. Died Dec. 17, 1936.

ALBRO, Addis, clergyman; b. Middleburgh, N.Y., Feb. 18, 1855; s. William Bliss and Ann Elizabeth (Wood) A.; B.S., Lawrence U., 1880; LL.B., Albany Law Sch., 1886; (D.D., Grant Memorial U., 1886); m. Mary Alice Scribner, Feb. 19, 1878; 2d, Jane Harrison, of Ind., Nov. 7, 1907. Ordained M.E. ministry, 1881; coll. pres. and prof., 1879-86; pastor Moline, Ill., 1887-89, Utica, N.Y., 1890-93; field sec. N.Y. State Sabbath Assn., 1894-98; gen. sec. Am. Reform Assn., 1898—. Chaplain N.Y. Senate, 1893, Mich. Mil. Acad., 1901-03; del. Rep. Nat. convs., 1880, 1900; hon. and corr. mem. World's Congress Auxiliary, Chicago Expn., 1893. On staff United Editors' Encyclopedia; U.S. commr. K.T. Home: Columbus, N.M. Died 1911.

ALDEN, Bertram F., surgeon; b. Vallejo, Calif., Jan. 5, 1873; s. Eugene Beaubarnois and Lydia (Webster) A.; M.D., Cooper Med. Coll., 1894; m. Leonie E. Gless, May 11, 1903; 1 dau., Victoria. House surgeon Lane Hosp., 1895; surgeon French Hosp., 1903-20; mem. attending staff S.P.R.R. Gen. Hosp. Served as capt. Med. R.C., Fort Riley, Kan., 1917; maj., later lt. col. Med. Corps, U.S. Army, chief of surg. service, Base Hosp., Fort Riley, Ft. McArthur, Tex., and Toul, France, World War. Democrat. Mason (Shriner). Home: San Francisco, Calif. Died May 14, 1939.

ALDEN, Charles Henry, brig. gen. U.S. Army; retired; late asst. surgeon gen. U.S. Army; b. Phila., April 28, 1836; grad. Brown, 1856; Pa. Med. Coll., 1858; (hon. M.D., U. of Pa., 1901); m. Katherine Russell, Oct. 25, 1864. Pres. Army Med. School. Deceased.

ALDEN, Mrs. Cynthia May Westover, journalist; b. Afton, Ia., May 31, 1861; d. Oliver S. and Lucinda (Lewis) Westover; grad. Denver Business Coll.; B.A., U. of Colo.; M.Litt., Alfred U., 1905; m. John Alden, of Brooklyn Eagle, 1896. Taught geology, bookkeeping, vocal music; U.S. Insp. of Customs, New York, 1887, at times substituting for the interpreter; sec. for 2 yrs. to commr. of street cleaning (first woman to receive apptmt. to a polit. position in N.Y. State); editor Woman's Dept. New York Recorder; editor Woman's Dept. New York Tribune 3 yrs.; mem. editorial staff Ladies' Home Journal 10 yrs. Founder and pres. gen. Internat. Sunshine Soc. (membership over 300,000); founder Internat. Sunshine Blind Babies' nurseries, homes, hospitals, etc., combined (only instns. of the kind in U.S.). Author: Manhattan, Historic and Artistic; Bushy—Child Life in the Far West; Women's Ways of Earning Money, 1904; The Baby Blind, 1915. Home: Brooklyn, N.Y. Died Jan. 8, 1931.

ALDEN, Henry Mills, editor; b. Mt. Tabor, near Danby, Vt., Nov. 11, 1836; s. Ira and Elizabeth (Moore) A.; desc. of John Alden; A.B., Williams Coll., 1857; grad. Andover Theol. Sem., 1860, but never took orders; (L.H.D., 1890, LL.D., 1907, Williams); m. Susan Frye Foster, July 3, 1861; 2d, Mrs. Ada Foster Murray, Feb. 22, 1900. Mng. editor Harper's Weekly, 1863-69; editor Harper's Mag., 1869—. Mem. Am. Acad. Arts and Letters. Author: God in His World, 1890; A Study of Death, 1895; Magazine Writing and the New Literature, 1908; Harper's Pictorial History of the Civil War (with A. H. Guernsey), etc. Home: Metuchen, N.J. Died Oct. 7, 1919.

ALDEN, Isabella Macdonald ("Pansy"), author; b. Rochester, N.Y., Nov. 3, 1841; d. Isaac and Myra (Spafford) Macdonald; ed. Seneca Collegiate Inst., Ovid, N.Y., and Young Ladies' Inst., Auburn, N.Y.; m. Rev. Gustavus R. Alden, May 30, 1866; 1 son, Raymond Macdonald (dec.). Author of about 75 Sunday Sch. books and of a number of volumes of fiction for older readers; also "The Prince of Peace," a life of Christ. Works translated into Swedish, French, Japanese, Armenian, etc. Edited the juvenile periodical "Pansy," 1873-96. Home: Palo Alto, Calif. Died Aug. 5, 1930.

ALDEN, John, editor; b. Hoosick Falls, N.Y., Aug. 30, 1860; s. Edwin Painter and Martha A. (Andrews) A.; 9th in direct descent from John Alden, of the Mayflower; B.A., Rutgers, 1882, M.A., 1885; m. Cynthia May Westover, founder Internat. Sunshine Soc., Aug. 15, 1896 (died 1931). Reporter, Washington corr., dramatic editor, Brooklyn Times, 1882-86; mng. editor Troy Press, 1887; news editor New York Press, 1888; night editor Morning Advertiser, under John A. Cockerill, 1890-93; editorial writer and Albany corr., New York Recorder, 1893-96; editor "Fame," 1897-1902; editor and editorial writer, Brooklyn Eagle, 1901—. Has written more than 9,000 signed poems. Home: Brooklyn, N.Y. Died Mar. 4, 1934.

ALDEN, John B(erry), editor, pub.; b. Henry County, Ia., Mar. 2, 1847; s. Zephania and Damaris (Thompson) A.; common sch. edn.; m. Ellen Tracy, 1874 (died, 1880); m. 2d, Ada Tracy, 1882. Editor and pub. juvenile mags., "The Bright Side" and "What Next?" Chicago, 1869-73; asst. editor and pub. "Hearth and Home," New York, 1874-75; began, 1879, as pub. classical and standard works, including Chambers's Ency., Library of Universal Knowledge, Cyclo. of Universal Literature, Elzevir Library, etc.; also editor and pub. Library Magazine, Good Literature; retired, 1908. Author: The Book of the Farmers Republic, 1912; Peace and Prosperity via Justice and Practical Sense, 1919; (with U.S. Senator Morris Sheppard) Universal Thrift and Prosperity; (booklet) The National Farmers' Economic Republic. Author Industrial Savings Act, introd. by Senator Morris Sheppard, of Tex. Home: Neshanic, N.J. Died Dec. 4, 1924.

ALDEN, Raymond Macdonald, univ. prof.; b. New Hartford, N.Y., Mar. 30, 1873; s. Rev. Dr. Gustavus R. and Isabella (Macdonald) Alden (q.v.); student at Rollins Coll., Fla.; A.B., U. of Pa., 1894, Ph.D., 1898; A.M., Harvard, 1896; (Litt.D., Rollins, 1910); m. Barbara G. Hitt, May 24, 1904. Instr. English, Columbian (now George Washington) U., 1894-95; asst. in English, Harvard, 1896-97; sr. fellow in English, U. of Pa., 1898-99; instr. 1899-1901; asst. prof. English lit. and rhetoric, 1901-09, asso. prof. English, 1909-11, Stanford U.; prof. English, U. of Ill., 1911-14; same, Stanford, 1914—. Author: Rise of Formal Satire in England, 1899; The Art of Debate, 1900; On Seeing an Elizabethan Play, 1903; English Verse, 1903; Consolatio—an Ode, 1903; Knights of the Silver Shield, 1906; An Introduction to Poetry, 1909; Why the Chimes Rang, 1909; Tennyson, How to Know Him, 1917; Shakespeare (Master Spirits of Literature series), 1921; The Boy Who Found the King, 1922. Contbr. to ednl. journals, and of short stories to various periodicals (won 3d prize of $1,000 in Collier's short-story contest, 1905). Dir. Drama League America from its founding to 1914. Home: Palo Alto, Calif. Died Sept. 27, 1924.

ALDEN, William Livingston, author; b. Williamstown, Mass., Oct. 9, 1837; grad. Jefferson Coll., Pa., 1858; m. Agnes M. McClure, 1865; admitted to N.Y. bar, 1860; practiced until 1865; leader-writer on New York World, Times, Graphic, etc., until 1885; U.S. consul-gen. at Rome, 1885-89; leader-writer on Paris Herald, 1890-1903; then resident in London. Decorated Knight of the Crown of Italy, 1890. Author: Canoe and Flying Proa; Domestic Explosives; Shooting Stars; Life of Columbus; Adventures of Jimmie Brown; Loss of the Swansea; The Moral Pirates; Cruise of the Ghost; Cruise of the Canoe Club; New Robinson Crusoe; Trying to Find Europe; A Lost Soul; Told by the Colonel; Among the Freaks; The Mystery of Elias G. Roebuck; His Daughter; Van Wagener's Ways; Drewitt's Dream, 1902 A2; Cat Tales, 1905; etc. Died 1908.

ALDERMAN, Edwin Anderson, univ. pres.; b. Wilmington, N.C., May 15, 1861; s. James and Susan J. A.; Ph.B., U. of N.C., 1882; D.C.L., U. of the South, 1896; LL.D., Tulane, 1898, Johns Hopkins, 1902, Columbia, 1905, Yale, 1905, U. of N.C., 1906, Williams, 1908, Harvard, 1909, Dartmouth, 1909, U. of Pa., 1911, Coll. of William and Mary, 1922; m. Emma Graves, 1886 (died 1896); m. 2d, Bessie Green Hearn, Feb. 11, 1904; 1 son, Edwin Anderson. Prof. history N.C. State Normal Coll., 1892; prof. edn., 1893-96, pres., 1896-1900, U. of N.C.; pres. Tulane U., 1900-04, U. of Va., June 14, 1904—. Mem. Gen. Edn. Bd., bd. trustees Woodrow Wilson Foundation, also of Inst. of Economics, bd. govs., Thomas Jefferson Memorial Foundation, bd. advisors, Inst. of Politics. Author: A Brief History of North Carolina; Life of William Hooper; Life of J. L. M. Curry; Obligations and Opportunities of Citizenship; Southern Idealism; The Spirit of the South; Sectionalism and Nationality; The Growing South; Can Democracy Be Organized? Causes of the European War; Some Tests of an Educated Man; Function and Needs of Schools of Education in Universities and Colleges; Memorial Address on Woodrow Wilson; The Nation Exalts Jefferson. Editor in Chief Library of Southern Literature. Home: Charlottesville, Va. Died Apr. 29, 1931.

ALDERMAN, Grover Henry, educator; b. Nevada, Ia., June 30, 1886; s. Silas Pritten and Mary Jane (Ellison) A.; B.A., Ia. State Teachers Coll., Cedar Falls, Ia., 1913; M.A., State U. of Ia., 1919, Ph.D., 1920; m. Nell Newton, Aug. 13, 1913; children—Bruce Warren, Robert Newton. Teacher rural sch., 1904-06; supt. schs., Walker, Ia., 1912-15, Lake Park, 1915-18, Newton, 1920-22; asso. prof. edn., Ind. U., 1922-23, prof., 1923-25; dean Sch. of Edn., U. of Pittsburgh, 1925—. Mem. N.E.A., Ednl. Council of Pa. Republican. Presbyn. Home: Pittsburgh, Pa. Died Nov. 28, 1930.

ALDIS, Arthur Taylor; b. St. Albans, Vt., July 7, 1861; s. Judge Asa Owen and Mary T. (Taylor) A.; St. Paul's Sch., Concord, N.H.; student, Harvard Univ., 1880-82; studied, Harvard Law Sch.; m. Mary Reynolds, June 8, 1892; 1 son, Graham. Engaged in ranching in Wyo., 1885-89; in real estate business, and trusteeships, Chicago, as mem. Aldis, Aldis & Northcote and subsequently, Aldis & Co., 1890—. Republican. Episcopalian. Sec. Friends of Am. Art

Assn.; trustee Art Inst., Chicago. Home: Lake Forest, Ill. Died Nov. 23, 1933.

ALDIS, Owen Franklin, lawyer; b. St. Albans, Vt., June 6, 1853; s. Judge Asa Owen and Mary Townsend (Taylor) A.; A.B., Yale, 1874; ed. in law, Columbian Law Sch.; m. Leila Houghteling, 1878 (dec.). Practiced law, 1877-90, when retired from active practice and became trustee of various estates. Republican. Dir. Chicago Expn., 1893. Home: Chicago and Washington. Died Aug. 5, 1925.

ALDREY Y MONTOLIO, Pedro de, judge; b. San Juan, P.R., Dec. 23, 1864; s. Antonio and Mercedes (Montolio) de Aldrey; B.A., Coll. of Jesuit Fathers, San Juan, P.R., 1883; D.C.L., U. of Barcelona, Spain, 1891; m. Rosenda Montilla, Jan. 1, 1899 (dec.); children—Mercedes (dec.), Emilio, Pedro (dec.), Jorge. Practiced in Barcelona, 1891-93, in P.R., 1901-04; apptd. clk. Territorial Court, 1894; municipal judge Dist. of San Francisco, San Juan, 1896; judge of 1st Instance, Guayama, 1898; sec. Territorial Court, 1898, Fiscal Supreme Court, 1899; successively judge Dist. Court of Humacao, 1899, Fiscal Dist. Court of Arecibo, 1904, Dist. Court of Arecibo, 1905, Dist. Court of San Juan, 1906; asso. justice Supreme Court of Puerto Rico, Jan. 16, 1911—. Catholic. Home: San Juan, Puerto Rico. Died July 26, 1936.

ALDRICH, Charles, founder, in 1892, and curator Historical Dept. of Iowa; b. Ellington, N.Y., Oct. 2, 1828; s. Stephen and Eliza (Nichols) A.; ed. pub. schls. and Jamestown, N.Y., Acad. (A.M., Iowa Coll., 1869); m. Matilda Olivia Williams (died 1892); m. 2d, Thirza Louise Briggs, Nov. 12, 1898. Founded "The Freeman," newspaper, Webster City, Ia., June 29, 1857; chief clerk Ia. Ho. of Reps., 1860, 62, 66, 70; mem. house, 1882; 1st lt. and adj. 32d Ia. Vol. Inf., 1862-64; mem. U.S. Geol. Survey, 1875, in Rocky Mountains. A founder Am. Ornithologists' Union. Home: Boone, Ia. Died 1908.

ALDRICH, Charles Henry, lawyer; b. La Grange County, Ind., Aug. 28, 1850; s. Hamilton M. and Harriet (Sherwood) A.; A.B., U. of Mich., 1875 (hon. A.M., 1893); m. Helen Roberts, Oct. 13, 1875. Admitted to bar, 1876; in practice Ft. Wayne, Ind., 1876-86, Chicago, 1886—; solicitor-gen. U.S., 1892-93. Republican. Home: Chicago, Ill. Died Apr. 13, 1929.

ALDRICH, Charles John, physician; b. Spencer, O.; Oct. 13, 1861; s. Charles Wesley and Mary (Reed) A.; ed. pub. schs. and Baldwin Univ.; M.D., Western Reserve Med. Coll., 1882; attended lectures and hosps., London, Berlin, Paris, 1896, 1906; m. Jessie E. Critchfield Hutchinson, May 27, 1883. Elected to staff Cleveland Gen. Hosp. and lecturer on nervous diseases, Univ. of Wooster, 1890; cons. and visiting neurologist to Cleveland City Hosp., 1893—; cons. neurologist and psychiatrist to St. Luke's Hosp., 1907; prof. neurology, Cleveland Coll. Phys. and Surg., 1905; prof. mental and nervous diseases, 1906—. Home: Lakewood, O. Died 1908.

ALDRICH, Chester Hardy, judge; b. Pierpont, O., Nov. 10, 1862; s. George W. and Sophrona E. (Hardy) A.; A.B., Ohio State U., 1888; (LL.D., Neb. Wesleyan U., 1911); m. Sylvia E. Stroman, June 4, 1889. Admitted to bar, 1891, and practiced at David City, Neb.; also stock raiser. Mem. Neb. Senate, 1907; gov. of Neb., term Jan., 1911-Jan., 1913; justice Supreme Court of Neb., 1919-25. Republican. Methodist. Mason (K.T.). Home: Lincoln, Neb. Died March 10, 1924.

ALDRICH, Chester Holmes, architect; b. Providence, R.I., June 4, 1871; s. Elisha S. and Anna E. (Gladding) A.; Ph.B., Columbia, 1893, Litt.D., 1929; Diploma École des Beaux Arts, 1900; unmarried. In practice since 1903; mem. Delano & Aldrich; firm architects of Colony Club Bldg.; Kips Bay Boys' Club, Miss Chapin's School, Child Edn. Foundation, Nightingale School, New York; Smith Coll. Music School; Hotchkiss School Chapel and Dormitory, Lakeville, Conn.; Riggs Foundation, Stockbridge, Mass.; also residences for many noted Americans. Dir. Am. Acad. in Rome since Oct. 1935. A.N.A.; fellow A.I.A.; mem. Nat. Inst. Arts and Letters. Dir.-gen. civil affairs, Am. Red Cross Com. to Italy, 1917-19. Decorated Order of S. Maurizio e Lazzaro, Order of Crown of Italy, medal of honor Italian Red Cross, etc. Democrat. Home: New York, N.Y. Died Dec. 26, 1940.

ALDRICH, Edgar, judge; b. Pittsburg, N.H., Feb. 5, 1848; s. Ephriam C. and Adeline Bedel (Haynes) A.; ed. Colebrook (N.H.) Acad.; LL.B., U. of Mich., 1868; (hon. A.M., 1891, LL.D., 1901, Dartmouth; LL.D., U. of Mich., 1907); m. Louise M. Remick, Oct. 7, 1872. Admitted to N.H. bar, 1868; practiced at Colebrook, N.H., 1868-81, Littleton, N.H., 1881-91; solicitor Coos Co., N.H., 1872-74 and 1876-79; mem. and speaker N.H. Ho. of Rep., 1885; mem. N.H. Constl. Conv., 1902; U.S. dist. judge, Dist. of N.H., since 1891. Republican. Home: Littleton, N.H. Died Sept. 15, 1921.

ALDRICH, George Ames, artist; b. Worcester, Mass., June 3, 1872; s. George Wellington and Caroline Richmond (Ames) A.; student Dean Acad., 1880-89, M. I. T., 1892, Art Students League, N.Y., 1892-94; also studied Acad. Julian and Acad. Colarossi, Paris, 1894; pupil of J. Aman-Jean, Raphael Collin, James McNeill Whistler and Fritz Thaulow, 1900; m. Esta Grantham, Dec. 24, 1922; 1 dau., Elizabeth Grantham. Illustrator for London and N.Y. mags. to 1899 and landscape painter since then; rep. in permanent exhbns. in Sioux City Mus., Decatur (Ill.) Art Mus., Purdue U., U. of Ill. Awarded Robert Rice Jenkins prize (Art Inst. Chicago); Chicago Hoosier Salon prize for best snow painting; Indiana Alumni prize, Lawrence A. Downs prize, Alexander F. Banks prize (all Hoosier Salon awards); etc. Studio: Chicago, Ill. Died Mar. 7, 1941.

ALDRICH, Henry Clay, surgeon; b. Minneapolis, Apr. 13, 1857; s. Cyrus and Clara Adelia (Heaton) A.; U. of Minn., 1873-75; D.D.S., Dental Dept., U. of Pa., 1879; M.D., Hahnemann Med. Coll., Phila., 1881; m. Grace Reade, Sept. 5, 1903. Practiced, Charles City, Ia., 1881-2, Nashua, Ia., 1882-87, Minneapolis, 1887—; prof. diseases of women, Med. Dept., U. of Minn., 1907-10. Republican. Unitarian. Home: Minneapolis, Minn. Deceased.

ALDRICH, John Merton, entomologist; b. Olmsted Co., Minn., Jan. 28, 1866; s. Levi O. and Mary M. (Moore) A.; B.S., S.D. State Coll., 1888, M.S., 1891; studied entomology, etc., U. of Minn., Mich. Agrl. Coll., and U. of Kan., M.S., 1893; Ph.D., Leland Stanford Jr. U., 1906; m. Ellen J. Roe, Jan. 3, 1893 (died 1897); 1 son, Spencer (dec.); m. 2d, Della Smith, June 28, 1905. Prof. zoology and entomologist of Expt. Sta., 1893-1905; prof. biology, 1905-13, U. of Ida.; entomol. asst., U.S. Dept. of Agr., 1913-19; asso. curator of insects, 1919—, U.S. Nat. Museum. Mason. Unitarian. Democrat. Author: Catalogue of North American Diptera, 1905; Sarcophaga and Allies. 1916. Editor, Thomas Say Foundation. Home: Washington, D.C. Died May 27, 1934.

ALDRICH, Mary Jane; b. Sidney Plains, N.Y., March 19, 1833; d. Milton and Delia (Hull) Johnston; m. John Aldrich, 1855; lived in Neb., 1855-66; then Cedar Rapids, Ia.; moved to Mo., 1894. Began temperance work with the Crusade movement; became Nat. v.p. and State pres. W.C.T.U.; joined Non-Partisan W.C.T.U., 1890, becoming sec. of evangelistic work. Home: Springfield, Mo. Died 1909.

ALDRICH, Mildred, author; b. Providence, R.I., Nov. 16, 1853; d. Edwin and Lucy Ayers (Baker) A.; grad. high. sch., Boston, 1872; spl. course in science, Lowell Inst. Author: Hilltop on the Marne, 1915; Told in a French Garden, 1916; On the Edge of the War Zone, 1917; Peak of the Load, 1918; When Johnny Comes Marching Home, 1919. Residence: La Creste, Huiry par Couilly, department Seine et Marne, France. Died Feb. 19, 1928.

ALDRICH, Nelson Wilmarth, senator; b. Foster, R.I., Nov. 6, 1841; acad. edn.; (LL.D., Brown U., 1892). Mem. Providence Common Council, 1869-71, 1872-75 (pres. 1872-73); mem. R.I. Ho. of Rep., 1875-77 (speaker 1876-77); elected to 46th and 47th Congresses (1879-83); elected U.S. Senator, Oct. 5, 1881, to succeed Gen. A. E. Burnside (dec.), and resigned from House; reëlected, 1886, 1892, 1898, 1905; last term expired Mar. 3, 1911; declined nomination for reëlection, 1910. Chmn. Nat. Monetary Commn., 1908—. Republican. Home: Warwick, R.I. Died Apr. 16, 1915.

ALDRICH, Perley Dunn, vocal teacher; b. Blackstone, Mass., Nov. 6, 1863; s. Andrew Jackson and Auretta (Roys) A.; ed. N.E. Conservatory of Music; m. Jennie Lamson, Aug. 19, 1886. Teacher music, Troy Conf. Acad., 1884; prof. music, U. of Kans., 1885-88, Tremont Sch. of Music, Boston, 1899, Utica (N.Y.) Conservatory, 1890-93, Rochester, N.Y., 1893-1905. Was asst. to Mons. Sbriglia, summer sch., Paris, 1904-05. Author: Vocal Economy, 1895; La Belle Dame (male voices), 1895; Book of Songs, 1896; The Sleeping Wood-Nymph, cantata, 1896. Home: Philadelphia, Pa. Died Nov. 20, 1933.

ALDRICH, Richard, music critic; b. Providence, R.I., July 31, 1863; s. Elisha S. and Anna E. (Gladding) A.; A.B., Harvard, 1885; A.M., Brown U., 1935; studied music under Prof. J. K. Paine in regular Harvard course, later in Germany; m. Margaret Livingston Chanler, Oct. 3, 1906; children—Richard Chanler, Margaret Astor Chanler. Reporter, music and dramatic critic and editorial writer, Providence Journal, 1885-89; pvt. sec. Senator Dixon, 1889-91; on staff New York Tribune, 1891-1902; music critic New York Times, 1902—. Author: A Guide to Parsifal, 1904; A Guide to the Nibelungen Ring, 1905; Musical Discourse, 1928. Translator: Lilli Lehmann's "How to Sing," 1902. Mem. Nat. Inst. Arts and Letters. Capt. U.S.A., Mil. Intelligence Div., Gen. Staff, stationed in Washington, Feb. 18, 1918-May 9, 1919. Home: New York, N.Y. Died June 1937.

ALDRICH, Richard S., congressman; b. Washington, D.C., Feb. 29, 1884; s. Nelson W. and Abby (Chapman) A.; B.A., Yale, 1906; LL.B., Harvard, 1909; m. Janet Innis White, Apr. 30, 1921. Lawyer; dir. Providence Jour., Providence Nat. Bank, Providence Washington Ins. Co.; elected mem. R.I. Ho. of Rep., 1914, Senate, 1916, 68th to 72d Congresses (1923-33), 2d R.I. Dist. Republican. Home: Providence, R.I. Died Dec. 25, 1941.

ALRICH, Samuel Nelson, pres. State Nat. Bank of Boston, Dec. 15, 1890—; b. Upton, Mass., Feb. 3, 1839; s. Sylvanus Bucklin and Lucy Jane (Stoddard) A.; ed. Worcester Acad., Brown U., and Harvard Law Sch.; m. Mary J., d. J. T. Macfarland, Sept., 1865. Admitted to bar 1863, practiced Marlborough, Mass., 1863-74, after that in Boston retaining residence in Marlborough; was 9 yrs. mem. Marlborough School Com.; 4 yrs. mem. bd. of selectmen; was pres. old Framingham & Lowell R.R., later pres. Mass. Central R.R. and Central Mass. R.R. Mem. Mass. State senate, 1879, 1880, Ho. of Reps., 1883; Dem. candidate for Congress old 7th dist., Mass., 1880; asst. treas. U.S. in Boston, Mar., 1887-Jan. 15, 1891. Home: Boston, Mass. Died 1908.

ALDRICH, Sherwood, mining; b. Riverhead, L.I., N.Y., Sept. 4, 1868; ed. Riverhead Acad., pub. schs., Brooklyn; LL.B., New York U., 1889; married. Admitted to N.Y. bar, 1889; engaged in mining in Colo., 1890—. Home: Great Neck, N.Y. Died July 3, 1927.

ALDRICH, Thomas Bailey, author; b. Portsmouth, N.H., Nov. 11, 1836; passed part of boyhood in La.; returned to Portsmouth, 1850, and prepared for Harvard (A. M., 1883, 1896; L. H. D., 1901, Yale; L. H. D., Univ. of Pa., 1905). Father died, 1852; employed in an uncle's banking house, New York, 1852-55; m. 1865. Occupied editorial positions on New York Evening Mirror, N. P. Willis's Home Journal, and the Illustrated News until 1865; conducted Every Saturday, Boston, 1865-74; editor The Atlantic Monthly, 1881-90. Author: The Ballad of Baby Bell, and Other Poems; Poems; The Story of a Bad Boy; Cloth of Gold; Flower and Thorn; Mercedes, and Later Lyrics; Marjorie Daw, and Other People; Prudence Palfry; The Queen of Sheba; The Stillwater Tragedy; From Ponkapog to Pesth; Wyndham Towers (poem); The Sisters' Tragedy; An Old Town by the Sea; Two Bites at a Cherry, and Other Tales; Unguarded Gates; Judith and Holofernes; A Sea Turn and Other Matters, 1902; Ponkapog Papers, 1903; Judith of Bethulia (drama), 1905. Died 1907.

ALDRICH, Truman Heminway, mining engr.; b. Palmyra, N.Y., Oct. 17, 1848; ed. in pub. schs., the Mil. Acad., West Chester, Pa.; M.E. Rensselaer Poly. Inst., 1869. Practiced, N.Y. and N.J., 1869-71; in banking business, Selma, Ala., 1871-73; since then in coal mining. Rep. candidate for Congress (indorsed by People's party), 1894; after a contest he was seated near the close of the 1st session 54th Congress; postmaster Birmingham, Ala., Nov., 1911—. Home: Birmingham, Ala. Died Apr. 28, 1932.

ALDRICH William Farrington, congressman; b. Palmyra, N.Y., Mar. 11, 1853; s. William Farrington and Louisa Maria (Klapp) A.; grad. Warren's Mil. Acad., Poughkeepsie, taking course in civil engring.; m. Josephine Cables, Apr. 16, 1889 (died Aug. 12, 1917); m. 2d, Fannie Spire, July 15, 1920. Removed to Alabama, 1874; engaged in mining and mfg.; built up town of Aldrich, postmaster same; del. Rep. nat. convs., 1896, 1900, 1904; mem. Rep. Congressional Com., Ala., 6 yrs., Ala. State Exec. Com. Mem. 54th, 55th and 56th Congresses (1895-1901), 4th Ala. Dist.; engaged in sale of mineral lands. Died Oct. 30, 1925.

ALDUNATE, Don Santiago, A. E. and P. from Chile to U.S., 1917—. Died Apr. 17, 1918.

ALERDING, Herman Joseph, bishop; b. in Westphalia, Germany, Apr. 13, 1845; s. B. Herman and Theresa (Schrameier) A.; ed. Vincennes, Ind., St. Thomas, Ky., and St. Meinrad's Abbey, Spencer Co., Ind. Ordained priest, Sept. 22, 1868, at St. Meinrad; consecrated bishop of Ft. Wayne, Ind., Nov. 30, 1900. Author: History of the Catholic Church in the Diocese of Vincennes, Ind., 1883; History of the Diocese of Fort Wayne, Ind., 1907; Plymouth Rock and Maryland, 1886. Died Dec. 6, 1924.

ALESHIRE, Arthur William, congressman; b. Luray, Va., Feb. 15, 1900; s. James Wm. and Ada (Painter) A.; ed. pub. schs.; m. Myrtle G. Marsh, May 11, 1921; 1 son, Melvin Arthur. Mem. 75th Congress (1937-39), 7th O. Dist. Democrat. K.P. Home: Springfield, O. Died Mar. 11, 1940.

ALESHIRE, James Buchanan, army officer; b. at Gallipolis, O., Oct. 31, 1856; s. Reuben and Margaret (Shepard) A.; ed. Galia Acad., Gallipolis, O.; grad. U.S. Mil. Acad., 1880; m. Harriet A. Dana, Nov. 3, 1886. Commd. 2d lt. U.S. Cav., June 12, 1880; advanced through the ranks to q.m. gen., U.S.A., Apr. 27, 1914. Served in operations against hostile Apache Indians, Oct., 1881-Apr., 1882; Sioux campaign, S.D., Nov., 1890-Feb., 1891; in Cuba, Jan.-July, 1899, and Nov., 1899-Aug., 1900; China Relief Expdn., Sept. 1, 1900-Feb., 1901; Philippines, Feb., 1901-Sept. 1, 1903. Retired for disability in line of duty, Sept. 12, 1916. Home: Sheridan, Wyo. Died June 1, 1925.

ALEXANDER, Charles Beatty, lawyer; b. at N.Y. City, Dec. 6, 1849; s. Henry Martyn and Susan Mary (Brown) A.; g.s. late Rev. Archibald Alexander, D.D., a founder, and first prof. Princeton, Theol. Sem., and on mother's side of Rev. Matthew Brown, D.D., who was pres. Jefferson Coll., Pa.; A.B., Princeton, 1870, A.M., 1873; LL.B., Columbia, 1872;

LL.D., Princeton; 1895, Washington and Jefferson, 1902, N.Y. Univ., 1923; Litt.D., Washington and Lee, 1913; m. Harriet, d. Chas. Crocker, of San Francisco, Apr. 26, 1887. Admitted to bar, N.Y., 1872, Calif., 1888, bar Supreme Court of U.S., 1884; mem. Alexander & Green until close of 1912; counsel, now dir. Equitable Life Assurance Soc. U.S.; dir. Tri-State Land Co.; trustee Equitable Trust Co.; pres. Alexander Estate, Inc. Elected regent Univ. State of N.Y., 1913, term exp. 1925, re-elected 1925, term exp., 1937; chmn. state science work and State mus. and mem. coms. on higher edn., state library and law legislation; trustee Princeton U. many yrs. (Alexander Hall built and presented by wife, 1892). Del. Dem. Nat. Conv., Baltimore, Md., St. Louis, Mo., 1916. San Francisco, Calif., 1920. Trustee N.Y. State Hist. Assn. Decorated Order of White Eagle, 3d class (Comdr.), by Prince Regent Alexander of the Kingdom of the Serbs, Croats and Slovenes, 1919; Crown of Italy by King of Italy, 1920; Officer Legion of Honor by French Govt., 1925. Home: Tuxedo Park, New York. Died Feb. 7, 1927.

ALEXANDER, Charles McCallon, evangelist; b. nr. Maryville, Tenn., Oct. 24, 1867; s. John D. and Martha (McCallon) A.; M.A., Maryville Coll., Tenn.; student Moody Bible Inst., Chicago; m. Helen Cadbury, July 14, 1904. Engaged in evangelistic work, singing, organizing and conducting large chorus choirs 10 yrs.; made an evangelistic tour of the world with Rev. R. A. Torrey, 1902-06; 2d tour of the world with his wife, 1906-07; conducted evangelistic choir of 4,000 members, for two months daily in Royal Albert Hall, London, Eng.; has conducted evangelistic missions, 1908—, with J. Wilbur Chapman, in Australasia (twice), China, Japan, Korea, Can., U.S. and Great Britain. Chmn. Business Men's Council for evangelistic work among the troops in camps during the World War, especially forwarding the work of the Pocket Testament League. Author: Alexander's Revival Songs (Australia, 1902); Alexander's Revival Hymns (England, 1903); Revival Hymns (America, 1905); Song in the Service of Christ, 1906; Soul Winning Around the World, 1907; Alexander's Gospel Songs, I, II, III (America); Alexander's Hymns, I, II, III (Great Britain); Alexander's Songs and Stories. Home: Birmingham, Eng. Died Oct. 13, 1920.

ALEXANDER, Charles Tripler, brig.-gen. U.S.A.; b. Indian Ty., May 3, 1833. Apptd. from Ark., asst. surgeon U.S.A., Oct. 1, 1856; capt. asst. surgeon, Oct. 1, 1861; maj. surgeon, Feb. 9, 1863; lt.-col. surgeon, July 26, 1886; col. chief med. purveyor, Sept. 11, 1891; retired by operation of law, May 3, 1897; advanced to rank of brig. gen. retired, by act of Apr. 23, 1904. Bvtd.: lt. col., Mar. 13, 1865, "for faithful and meritorious services during the war"; col., Feb. 27, 1890, "for gallant services in action at Clearwater, Ida., July 11 and 12, 1877." Died Feb. 28, 1918.

ALEXANDER, Charlton, lawyer; b. Starkville, Miss., Aug. 14, 1884; s. Charlton Henry and Matilda (MacMillan) A.; A.B., Millsaps Coll., Jackson, Miss., 1904; LL.B., U. of Miss., 1906; m. Helen Sherman, June 25, 1908; children—Helen S., Frances M. Admitted to Miss. bar, 1906, and practiced at Jackson, mem. Alexander & Alexander, until 1919; mem. Curlee & Hay, St. Louis, Mo., 1919-23, Cobbs, Logan & Alexander, 1923-27; v.p. and head of trust dept., Liberty Central Trust Co., St. Louis, 1927-28; v.p. Miss. Valley Trust Co., 1928—. Dir. and chmn. Guaranty Fund, St. Louis Municipal Theatre Assn. Democrat. Presbyn. Mason (32°, K.T., Shriner). Home: St. Louis, Mo. Died Dec. 11, 1935.

ALEXANDER, DeAlva Stanwood, congressman; b. Richmond, Me., July 17, 1845; pvt. 128th Ohio Inf., 1862-65; A.B., Bowdoin Coll., 1870, A.M., 1873 (LL.D., 1907); m. Alice Colby, Sept. 14, 1871 (died Feb. 23, 1890); m. 2d, Anne Gerlach Bliss, Dec. 28, 1893. Editor Daily Gazette, Ft. Wayne, Ind., 1871-74; sec. Rep. State Com. of Ind., 1874-78; practiced law at Indianapolis, 1877-81; 5th auditor U.S. Treasury, 1881-85; in law practice at Buffalo, N. Y., 1885—. U.S. atty. Northern Dist. of N.Y., 1889-93; mem. 55th to 61st Congresses (1897-1903), 33d N.Y. Dist. and (1903-11), 36th Dist.; Republican. Pres. bd. overseers Bowdoin Coll.; trustee N.Y. State Hist. Assn. (ex-pres.). Author: Political History of the State of New York (3 vols.), 1906-09; History and Procedure of the House of Representatives, 1916; Four Famous New Yorkers (4th vol. Polit. History of State of N.Y.), 1923. Home: Buffalo, N.Y. Died Jan. 29, 1925.

ALEXANDER, Eben, univ. dean; b. Knoxville, Tenn., Mar. 9, 1851; s. Judge Ebenezer and Margaret White (McClung) A.; A.B., Yale, 1873; (hon. Ph.D., Maryville Coll., 1886; LL.D., U. of N.C., 1893); m. Marion Howard-Smith, Oct. 15, 1874. Instr. and prof. ancient langs., 1873-86, chmn. faculty, 1885-6, U. of Tenn.; prof. Greek, U. of N.C., 1886-93; E.E. and M.P. to Greece, Roumania and Servia, 1893-97; prof. Greek, 1897—, dean, 1900—, U. of N.C. Pres. Tenn. State Teachers' Assn., 1886. Home: Chapel Hill, N.C. Deceased.

ALEXANDER, Edward Porter, engr.; b. Washington, Ga., May 26, 1835; s. Adam Leopold and Sarah Gilbert A.; grad. U.S. Mil. Acad., 1857; m. Bettie Mason, 1860; 2d, Mary L., d. Augustine S. Mason, of Hagerstown, Md., Oct. 1, 1901. Apptd. 2d lt. U.S. engr. corps.; resigned, 1861; entered C.S.A. and served through war; was brig.-gen. and chief of arty., Longstreet's Corps, at Appomattox, 1865; prof. of mathematics and engring., U. of S.C., 1866-70; gen. mgr. and pres. of various railroads (including L.&N., Central of Ga., Ga. R.R. & Bank Co.), 1871-92; capitol commr., State of Ga., 1883-88; mem. bds. on navigation of Columbia River, Ore., and on ship canal between Chesapeake and Delaware bays, 1892-94; govt. dir. U. P. R.R. Co., 1895-97; arbitrator boundary survey between Costa Rica and Nicaragua. Rice planter on South Island, Georgetown, S.C. Author: Railway Practice; Military Memoirs of a Confederate. Home: Savannah, Ga. Died 1910.

ALEXANDER, Francesca, artist, author; b. Boston; d. Francis Alexander, artist; resided in Italy, 1830—. Author: Story of Ida (edited by Ruskin), 1883; Roadside Songs of Tuscany, 1884; Christy Folk in the Apennine, 1888; Tuscan Songs, 1897; The Hidden Servants and Other Very Old Stories, 1900. Home: Florence, Italy. Died Jan. 22, 1917.

ALEXANDER, George, clergyman; b. W. Charlton, N.Y., Oct. 12, 1843; s. Alexander F. and Margaret (Bunyan) A.; A.B., Union Coll., 1866 (D.D., 1884, LL.D., 1916, hon. chancellor, 1923); grad. Princeton Theol. Sem., 1870. Ordained Presbyn. ministry, 1870; pastor East Av. Ch., Schenectady, N.Y., 1870-83, Univ. Pl. Church, New York, 1884-1918, First Presbyterian Ch., New York, 1919—. Prof. rhetoric and logic, Union Coll., 1877-83; became pres. New York Coll. Dentistry, 1897; mem. Council of New York U., 1887— (v.p. 1898-1909, pres., 1909—); pres. Presbyterian Bd. Foreign Missions, 1903-24; pres. Union Coll., 1907-09 (chmn. bd. trustees, 1918—); pres. bd. trustees MacKenzie Coll., São Paulo, Brazil; dir. Princeton Theol. Sem.; pres. Am. and Foreign Christian Union; pres. Council of Ref. Chs. in America holding the Presbyn. System, 1915-16; pres. Leopold Schepp Foundation. Home: New York, N.Y. Died Dec. 12, 1930.

ALEXANDER, Gross, clergyman; b. Scottsville, Ky., June 1, 1852; s. of Dr. Charles Holliday and Eliza A. (Drane) A.; A.B., U. of Louisville, 1871; tutor in same, 1871-73; prof. Latin and Greek Warren Coll., Ky., 1873-75; B.D., Drew Theol. Sem., 1877; (S.T.D., Emory and Henry Coll., 1890; D.D., Emory Coll., 1912); m. Helen M. Watts, Aug. 12, 1875; 2d, Arabel Wilbur, Nov. 30, 1887. Pastor at Lake Mohonk, N.Y., 1875-76, New Brighton, S.I., 1877; joined Louisville Conf. M.E. Ch., S., 1877; was pastor in Ky., 1877-84; prof. N.T. Greek and exegesis, Vanderbilt U., 1885-1902; presiding elder, Louisville, 1902-06; editor Methodist Review and book editor, M.E. Ch., S. Mem. and one of secs. of Gen. Conf., Memphis, 1894, Baltimore, 1898, Dallas, Tex., 1902, Birmingham, Ala., 1906, Asheville, N.C., 1910, Oklahoma City, 1914. Editor: Homilies of Chrysostom on Galatians and Ephesians, 1889. Author: Life of S. P. Holcombe, 1888; History of Methodist Episcopal Church, South (Am. Church History Series), 1894; The Beginnings of Methodism in the South, 1897; The Son of Man—Studies in His Life and Teaching, 1899; Commentary on Colossians and Ephesians, 1909. Died Sept. 6, 1915.

ALEXANDER, Hartley Burr, univ. prof.; b. Lincoln, Neb., Apr. 9, 1873; s. George Sherman and Abby Gifford (Smith) A.; A.B., U. of Neb., 1897; fellow U. of Pa., 1898-1900; fellow Columbia, 1900-01, Ph.D., 1901; m. Nelly King Griggs, July 15, 1908; children—Hubert Griggs, Beatrice Kirk (dec.). Office editor and contbr. to New Internat. Ency., 1903; editor and contbr. to Webster's Dictionaries, 1903-08; prof. philosophy, U. of Neb., 1908-27; on leave as acting prof., U. of Wis., 1927; prof. Scripps Coll., 1927—. Mem. Am. Philos. Assn. (pres. 1919; pres. Pacific Div. 1929), Am. Assn. Univ. Profs., Southwestern Archæol. Fedn. (pres. 1928, 29); hon. mem. A.I.A.; hon. fellow U. of Southern Calif. Sch. of Philosophy; mem. bd. dirs. and lecturer Sch. of Am. Research. Author: The Problem of Metaphysics, 1902; Pilgrim Alden (anonymous), 1903; Poetry and the Individual, 1906; The Mid Earth Life, 1907; Odes on the Generations of Man, 1910; The Religious Spirit of the American Indian, 1910; The Mystery of Life, 1913; Mythology of All Races, Vol. X, North American, 1916, and Vol. XI, Latin American, 1920; Liberty and Democracy, 1918; Letters to Teachers, 1919; Odes and Lyrics, 1922; Nature and Human Nature, 1923; Manito Masks, 1925; L'Art et la Philosophie des Indiens de l'Amérique du Nord, 1926; The Architectural Sculpture of the State Capitol (Lincoln), 1926; God's Drum, 1927; Truth and the Faith, 1929; Pueblo Indian Painting, 1931; Taiwa, 1934; God and Man's Destiny, 1936. Died July 27, 1939.

ALEXANDER, Henry Martyn, lawyer; grad. Princeton; trustee of Princeton; senior of Alexander & Green, counsellors at law. Home: New York, N.Y. Died 1899.

ALEXANDER, Herbert G(eorge) B(arlow), life ins.; b. London, Eng., Dec. 26, 1860; s. Ebenezer and Louisa (Barlow) A.; ed. Romford, Eng.; m. Louisa Denhard, 1883 (dec.); children—Italy (Mrs. Allen C. Southard), Margherita (Mrs. Robert W. Hyman), Dorothy (Mrs. Benj. F. Hitchens), Mrs. Marjorie A. Eaton; m. 2d, Edna Bartholomew Miner, 1917. Came to U.S., 1885, naturalized citizen, 1892. State agt., N.Y., Ry. Officials' and Employes' Assn., 1890-96, gen. supt. of agencies, Indianapolis, Ind., 1896-1900; v.p. and gen. mgr. Continental Casualty Co., and Continental Assurance Co., pres. both cos., 1906—; pres. H.G.B. Alexander & Co. Mason (K.T., Shriner). Clubs: Union League, Chicago Athletic, South Shore Country, Exmoor Country. Home: Chicago. Ill. Died Oct. 5, 1928.

ALEXANDER, Hooper, lawyer; b. Rome, Ga., Oct. 6, 1858; s. Thomas Williamson and Sarah Joyce (Hooper) A.; A.B., U. of Ga., 1879; m. May H. Field, Jan. 28, 1889 (died 1890); m. 2d, Amelia Hutchins, Oct. 17, 1894; children—Mrs. Amelia Greenawalt, Hooper, Mrs. Hallie Turner, Miller. Thomas W., Mrs. Joyce Rhine. President S. Georgia Agr. and Mech. Coll., Thomasville, 1880-84; admitted to Georgia bar, 1884, and since practiced in Atlanta; mem. Ga. Ho. of Reps., 1904-12, and 1928-30; U.S. atty. Northern Dist. of Ga., 1913-21; resumed pvt. practice. 1st lt. Gate City Guards, Atlanta, 1888; trustee Decatur Pub. Schs., 1908-17. Democrat. Presbyn. Home: Decatur, Ga. Deceased.

ALEXANDER, James F., M.D.; b. Greenville Dist., S.C., May 28, 1824; ed. Oglethorpe Univ. and at Lawrenceville, Ga.; grad. Med. Coll. of Ga., Augusta, 1849; located at Atlanta; delegate to secession conv., 1861; surgeon 7th Ga. regt., C. S. A.; m. Georgia Orme, 1855 (died 1876); m. 2d, Ada Reynolds; chmn. Fulton County Dem. Com. during reconstruction times; several yrs. pres. Atlanta Bd. of Health; has been pres. Ga. State Med. Assn. Home: Atlanta, Ga. Died 1901.

ALEXANDER, James Strange, banker; b. Tarrytown, N.Y., Feb. 21, 1865; s. James Strange and Susan M. (Coe) A.; ed. pub. schs.; married; children—Emma Myer (Mrs. Lesley G. Sheafer), James Strange. Clerk, chief clerk, asst. cashier, Nat. Bank of Commerce, N.Y. City, 1885-1907; treas. Am. Express Co., 1907-08; returned to Nat. Bank of Commerce as v.p., 1908, pres., 1911-23, later chmn. bd.; then chmn. bd. Guaranty Trust Co. of N.Y.; retired 1929. Mem. Fed. Reserve Board (advisory com.), 1926-28; dir. Am. Tel. & Tel. Co., Merc. Stores Co., Prudential Ins. Co. of Am., Southern Pacific Co., Winifred Masterson Burke Foundation. Mem. New York Clearing House Com., 1913-16, 1919-21 (chmn. com. on credit and finance; pres. 1923); chmn. exec. com. Nat. Com. on European Finance; mem. N.Y. Liberty Loan Com. from its orgn., and of its subcom. on money rates; mem. advisory com. Am. sect. Internat. Chamber Commerce; mem. com. on finance and currency of C. of C. of State of N.Y. Chevalier Legion of Honor (France); Chevalier Crown of Italy; Knight Comdr. Order of Leopold II (Belgium). Republican. Home: New York, N.Y. Died July 16, 1932.

ALEXANDER, James Waddell; b. Princeton, N.J., July 19, 1839; s. Rev. Dr. James W. A.; A.B., Princeton, 1860, later A.M.; admitted to bar, 1862; m. Elizabeth Beasley, d. Chancellor Benjamin Williamson, of N.J., Nov. 24, 1864. In law practice, New York, 1862-66; entered service Equitable Life Assurance Soc. of U.S., becoming pres. on death of President Hyde; retired, 1905. Trustee Princeton U. Home: Princeton, N.J. Died Sept. 21, 1915.

ALEXANDER, John L., religious edn.; b. Arbroath, Scotland, May 17, 1878; s. Charles and Ann (Davidson) A.; B.A., Ursinus Coll., 1901, D.D., 1926; m. Evalyn E. Kerstetter, July 31, 1903; children—Donald K., Martha Romaine. Gen. sec. Y.M.C.A., Oil City, Pa., 1901-03, Spring Grove, 1903-08; asso. gen. sec., Phila., 1908-10; exec. sec. Boy Scouts of America, 1910-11; boys' work expert, Men and Religion Forward Movement, 1911-12; supt. young people's work, Internat. S.S. Assn., 1912-24; exec. dir. Am. Youth Foundation, 1924—, also trustee. Presbyn. Mason. Club: City. Home: Webster Groves, Mo. Died May 28, 1932.

ALEXANDER, John White, painter; b. Allegheny City, Pa., Oct. 7, 1856; s. John and Fanny (Smith) A.; art edn. Royal. Acad. Fine Arts, Munich; (hon. A.M., Princeton, 1905, Litt.D., 1909); m. Elizabeth Alexander, Nov. 2, 1887. Received Temple gold medal, Pa. Acad. Fine Arts, 1897; gold medal, Paris Expn., 1900, Buffalo Expn., 1901, St. Louis Expn., 1904; Lippincott prize and Gold Medal of Honor, Pa. Acad. Fine Arts; Carnegie prize, Soc. Am. Artists; first prize, Corcoran Gallery; 1st prize gold medal, Carnegie Inst., 1911. Rep. in Luxembourg, Paris, and many Am. and European collections. Chevalier Légion d'Honneur, 1901. Trustee Pub. Library, Met. Mus. Art; mem. council Cooper Inst. Pres. Nat. Acad. Design, Nat. Inst. Arts and Letters, MacDowell Club, School Art League; v.p. Nat. Fedn. Fine Arts, Nat. Soc. Mural Painters; mem. Am. Acad. Arts and Letters, Nat. Acad. Arts and Letters; v.p. Am. Fedn. of Arts; trustee Fine Arts Soc. Home: New York, N.Y. Died June 1, 1915.

ALEXANDER, Joshua W., govt. official; b. Cincinnati, Jan. 22, 1852; s. Thomas W. and Jane (Robinson) A.; A.B., Christian U., Mo., 1872, A.M.,

1907; LL.D., Culver-Stockton Coll., 1923; m. Roe Ann Richardson, Feb. 3, 1876; children—Samuel T. (dec.), Walter R. (dec.), Mrs. Julia J. Jenner, Mrs. Frances Ficklin, George F., Roena, Preston C., Laurence W., and 4 sons who died in infancy. Admitted to bar in 1875, pub. adminstr., Daviess County, Mo., 1876-82; mem. Mo. Ho. of Rep., 1883-87 (speaker, 1887); pres. and sec. bd. edn., Gallatin, Mo., 1882-1903; mayor of Gallatin 2 terms; judge 7th Jud. Circuit, Mo., 1901-07; mem. 60th to 66th Congresses (1907-21), 3d Mo. Dist. (resigned); sec. of Commerce Dec. 11, 1919-Mar. 4, 1921; resumed practice of law. Democrat. Chmn. U.S. Commn. to Internat. Conf. on Safety of Life at Sea, London, 1913-14; del.-at-large, Constl. Conv. of Mo., 1922-23. Home: Gallatin, Mo. Died Feb. 27, 1936.

ALEXANDER, Magnus Washington, engineering; b. New York, Feb. 1870; s. Alexander M. and M. (Jelenkiewicz) A.; studied mech., metall. and elec. engring. at Austrian univers., in Wien, 1889, Leoben, 1891, Gratz, 1892; hon. M.S., Trinity Coll.; married. Began as engineer with largest Austrian iron and steel co.; designer and engr. with Weston Elec. Instrument Co., 1893-94 and with Westinghouse Electric & Mfg. Co., 1894-99; chief designer and engr. Siemens & Halske Electric Co. of America, 1899-1900; engr. in charge of designing, 1900-18, cons. engr. on economic issues, 1918-1922, Gen. Electric Co. Pres. Nat. Indsl. Conf. Bd. from its orgn., May 1916. Home: New York, N.Y. Died Sept. 10, 1932.

ALEXANDER, Maitland, clergyman; b. New York, Apr. 8, 1867; s. Henry M. and Susan M. (Brown) A.; A.B., Princeton, 1889, A.M., 1892; McCormick Theol. Sem., Chicago, 1889-90; grad. Princeton Theol. Sem., 1892; D.D., Lafayette, 1897; LL.D., Worcester U., 1900; m. Madelaine F. Laughlin, Apr. 17, 1906; children—Maitland Alexander, Alexander Laughlin, Madelaine Laughlin, Charles Beatty II. Ordained Presbyn. ministry, 1892; pastor Long Branch, N.J., 1893-97, Harlem, N.Y., 1897-99, 1st Ch., Pittsburgh, 1899-1927 (emeritus). Moderator Presbyn. Gen. Assembly, 1914. Republican. Home: Sewickley, Pa. Died Jan. 3, 1940.

ALEXANDER, Moses, governor; b. Germany, Nov. 13, 1853; s. Nathan and Emma A.; ed. common schs.; m. Helena Keastner, Nov. 4, 1876; children—Nathan, Emma, Leha. Came to America, 1868; in clothing business as mem. Wallbrunn & Alexander, Chillicothe, Mo., 1873-90; moved to Boise, Ida., 1891, and since in business there; pres. Alexander Clothing Co., Alexander Realty Co., Alexander's (Nampa), M. Alexander, Inc., etc. Mem. City Council, 1886, 87, mayor, 1888, Chillicothe; mayor of Boise, 1897-99, 1901-03; gov. of Idaho 2 terms, 1915-19. Democrat. Mason; mem. B'nai B'rith. Home: Boise, Ida. Died Jan. 4, 1932.

ALEXANDER, Robert, army officer; b. Md., Oct. 17, 1863; s. Judge William Alexander, of Baltimore; distinguished grad. Army Sch. of the Line, 1909; grad. Army Staff Coll., 1910; LL.D., St. John's Coll., Annapolis, Md., 1920; LL.D., Coll. of Puget Sound, Tacoma, Wash., 1931; m. Mollie Augur, d. Brig. Gen. Earl D. Thomas, 1892; children—William Denison, Robert. Pvt., sergt. and 1st sergt. Co. G, 4th U.S. Inf., 1886-90; 2d lt. 7th Inf., Dec. 17, 1889; promoted through grades to brig. gen. N.A., Feb. 9, 1918; maj. gen. (temp.), Aug. 26, 1918-Aug. 1, 1919; brig. gen., N. A., Apr. 30, 1921, maj. gen., Aug. 26, 1927; retired Oct. 17, 1927. In Indian campaign 1890-91, Spanish-Am. War, 1898, also in Philippines, Cuba, and Mexico; insp. gen. Line of Communications, A.E.F., in France, Nov. 1917-Feb. 1918. Decorated D.S.C. (U.S.); Croix de Guerre (2 citations), and Comdr. Legion of Honor (France). Apptd. comdr. 3d F.A. Brigade, Aug. 4, 1921. Elected to Wash. State Conv., 1933. Mason (33°). Home: La Jolla, Calif. Died Aug. 26, 1941.

ALEXANDER, Robert C., editor the New York Mail and Express; b. West Charlton, N.Y., July 7, 1857; grad. with first honors, Union Coll., N.Y., 1880 (A.M.); Albany Law School, 1881; m. Annie Clare, Aug. 21, 1884. Practiced law at Elmira, N.Y., 1881-84; removed to New York, 1884; became counsel for Col. Elliott F. Shepard and negotiated for him purchase of Mail and Express from Cyrus W. Field, 1888; sec. and treas. of the corp.; editor-in-chief since March, 1895; in March, 1897, with R. E. A. Dorr, pub., bought Mail and Express of Shepard estate. Organized 1890, and was two years pres. Adirondack League Club. Orgn. Trustee Union Coll. Home: New York, N.Y. Died 1899.

ALEXANDER, Taliaferro, lawyer; b. Catahoula Parish, La., Mar. 17, 1846; s. John Steele (M.D.) and Susan (Taliaferro) A.; student La. State U., 1861-3; LL.B., La. State U. Law Sch., 1869; m. Laura Lister, Oct. 31, 1876. Practiced, Shreveport, La., 1869—; mem. Alexander & Blanchard, 1878-97, Alexander & Wilkinson, 1899—. Democrat. Home: Shreveport, La. Deceased.

ALEXANDER, Wallace McKinney, sugar factor; b. of Am. parents, Island of Maui, Hawaii, Nov. 10, 1869; s. Samuel Thomas and Martha Eliza (Cooke) A.; A.B., Yale, 1892; m. Mary S. Barker, Aug. 16, 1904; 1 dau., Mrs. Martha Gerbode. Chmn. bd. Alexander & Baldwin, Ltd.; v.p. Matson Navigation Co., Honolulu Oil Corp., Ltd.; dir. Home Fire and Marine Ins. Co., Gladding, McBean & Co., Pacific Lighting Corp. Chmn. Commn. from San Francisco to Japan, 1920; chmn. Japanese Relations Com. of Calif. Trustee Stanford U., Carnegie Endowment for Internat. Peace. Republican. Conglist. Home: Piedmont, Calif. Died Nov. 22, 1939.

ALEXANDER, William, clergyman; b. Huntington Co., Pa., Dec. 18, 1831; s. Ranald and Sara Henderson (Carothers) A.; prep. edn. Tuscarora and Juniata Acads., Pa.; studied 3 yrs. Lafayette Coll.; grad. Jefferson Coll.; grad. Princeton Theol. Sem., 1861 (D.D., U. of Wooster, O.; LL.D., Washington and Jefferson Coll., Pa.); m. Miss M. P. Osborne, Dec. 25, 1861. Ordained Presbyn. ministry, June, 1862; pastor Lycoming Church Williamsport, Pa.; pres. Carroll Coll., 1863-65; pastor Beloit, Wis., 1865-69; San José, Calif., 1869-71; pres. City Coll., San Francisco, 1871-74; prin. founder San Francisco Theol. Sem., 1871; prof. New Testament Greek and Exegesis, 1871-76; Ch. history, same, 1876—; traveled in Europe and the East, 1899-1900; Dem. until 1862 then Rep. Mem. com. to revise Westminster Confession of Faith, 1890-93; one of editors Presbyn. and Reformed Reviews. Home: San Anselmo, Calif. Died 1906.

ALEXANDER, William DeWitt, surveyor; b. Honolulu, H.I., Apr. 2, 1833; s. Rev. William Patterson and Mary Ann (McKinley) A. (both Americans); A.B., Yale, 1855, A.M., 1858 (LL.D., 1903); m. Abigail C. Baldwin, July, 1860. Went to Harrisburg, Pa., 1849; tutor Beloit Coll., 1856; taught in acad., Vincennes, Ind., 1857; returned to Hawaii, 1858; prof. Greek, Oahu Coll.; pres. same, 1864-71; mem. privy council, 1884; bd. of edn., 1887-1905; commr. Internat. Meridian Conf., Washington, 1884, and again commr. from provisional govt. to Washington, 1893; surveyor-gen. H.I. since Mar., 1872; asst. U.S. Coast and Geod. Survey, 1901-07; commr. of pub. instrn., H.I., 1887-1905; trustee Honolulu Library Assn. and commr. Govt. Archives; Republican. Author: A Brief History of the Hawaiian People, 1891; History of the Later Years of the Hawaiian Monarchy, and of the Revolution of 1893, 1896; Brief Hawaiian Grammar; Intro. to L. Andrew's Hawaiian Dictionary. Home: Honolulu, T.H. Died Feb. 22, 1913.

ALEXANDER, William Leidy, brig. gen; b. in Iowa, Sept. 9, 1842. Apptd. 1st lt. 30th Ia. Vol. Inf., Sept. 23, 1862; capt., Oct. 1, 1863; hon. mustered out, July 27, 1865; apptd. capt. commissary of subsistence U.S.A., Oct. 4, 1889; advanced through grades to col. asst. commissary-gen., July 27, 1903; brig. gen. and retired at own request, Jan. 19, 1905. Died Dec. 1, 1915.

ALEY, Robert Judson, educator; b. Coal City, Ind., May 11, 1863; s. Jesse J. and Paulina (Moyer) A.; B.S., Valparaiso (Ind.) Coll., 1882; A.B., Indiana U., 1888, A.M., 1890; Stanford U., 1894-95; Ph.D., U. of Pa., 1897; LL.D., Franklin Coll., 1909; LL.D., U. of Pa., 1917, Butler Coll., 1922; m. Nellie Archer, Aug. 28, 1884; children—Bruce (dec.), Maxwell. Taught country schs., 1877-81, Coal City graded sch., 1881-82; prin. Spencer (Ind.) High Sch., 1882-85, 1886-87; instructor mathematics, Indiana Univ., 1887-88; prof. mathematics, Vincennes U., 1888-91, Ind. U., 1891-1909; supt. pub. instrn. of Ind., Mar. 1909-Nov. 12, 1910; pres. U. of Me., 1910-1921; pres. Butler U., 1921-31, emeritus. Acting asst. prof. mathematics, Stanford, 1894-95; was math. editor Inland Educator and Educator-Journal; editor-in-chief and pres. Educator-Journal, Aug. 1, 1903-Aug. 1, 1912. Trustee N.E.A., 1911-17 and pres. 1916-17; sec. Nat. Council Edn., 1911-13 and pres. 1913-16. Member Disciples Ch. Mason (33°). Democrat. Author: The Geometry of the Triangle, 1897; Graphs, 1900; Revision of Cook and Cropsy Arithmetics (with O. L. Kelso), 1904; The Essentials of Algebra (with David Andrew Rothrock), 1904; Supplementary Problems in Algebra (with same); Story of Indiana (with Max Aley), 1912. Home: Indianapolis, Ind. Died Nov. 18, 1935.

ALFANO, Vincenzo, sculptor; b. at Naples, Italy, Nov. 11, 1854; s. Tommaso and Antonietta (Minichini) A.; ed. High Sch., Tarsia Sch., Via Tarsia, Naples; licensed as teacher, tech. schs., 1885; unmarried. Teacher in chiseling, sch. of Industrial Museum, Naples, 1888-96; prin. works; bronze figure of David, bought by Italian Govt., 1887, for Modern Art Gallery, Rome; large figure of Cicero (prize); relief bronze panel, 18 ft. by 6 ft. and bronze sarcophagus, cemetery of Naples; many small figures. Came to America, 1896, and is rep. by interior figures of Pa. Capitol, Harrisburg; bronze bust of Columbus, New Rochelle, N.Y.; pediments of City Investing Bldg., New York; Court House, St. Louis; pediment St. John the Baptist Ch., New York, etc. Home: New York, N.Y. Deceased.

ALFORD, Leon Pratt, engr., editor; b. Simsbury, Conn., Jan. 3, 1877; s. Emerson and Sarah Merriam (Pratt) A.; B.S. in E.E., Worcester Poly. Inst., 1896, M.E., 1905, Dr. of Engring., 1932; m Grace A. Hutchins, Jan. 1, 1900; 1 son, Ralph I. Shop foreman McKay Metallic Fastening Assn., Boston, 1896-97, McKay-Bigelow Heeling Assn., 1897-99; prodn. supt., McKay Shoe Machinery Co., 1899-1902; mech. engr. United Shoe Machinery Co., Boston, 1902-07; engring. editor Am. Machinist, 1907-11, editor in chief, 1911-17; editor Industrial Management, 1917-20, Management Engineering, New York, 1921-23, Mfg. Industries, 1923-28; v.p. Ronald Press Co., 1928-34; asst. engr. in charge mfg. costs, Fed. Communications Commn., 1935-37; prof. administrative engring., N.Y. Univ., 1937—. Past v.p. and mem. research coms. Am. Engring. Council. Melville Gold Medalist, 1927; Gantt Gold Medalist, 1931. Methodist. Author: Bearings and Their Lubrication, 1912; Laws of Management, 1928; Life of Henry Laurence Gantt, 1934. Editor: Artillery and Artillery Ammunition, 1917; Management's Handbook, 1924; Cost and Production Handbook, 1934. Home: Montclair, N.J. Died Jan. 2, 1942.

ALGER, Horatio, Jr., author; b. Revere, Mass., Jan. 13, 1834; grad. Harvard, 1852; ordained pastor Unitarian ch., Brewster, Mass., 1864; lived in New York, 1866-96. Author: Ragged Dick series, Tattered Tom series; Luck and Pluck series; Atlantic and Pacific series, etc., in all about 70 books, mostly juveniles, of which nearly 800,000 have been sold. Home: Natick, Mass. Died 1899.

ALGER, Philip Rounseville, naval officer; b. Boston, Mass., Sept. 29, 1859; s. William Rounseville and Anne Langdon (Lodge) A.; grad. Boston Latin Sch., 1876; grad. U.S. Naval Acad., 1880; m. Louisa Taylor, Apr. 29, 1891. Served on bd. Richmond, China Sta., 1880-82; at Navy Dept., 1882-85; on Pensacola, Mediterranean Sta., 1885-88; at Navy Dept., 1888-91; prof. mathematics, on duty at Navy Dept., Washington, 1881-99; head of Dept. of Mechanics, Naval Acad., 1899-1907 (dept. abolished), rank of capt.; mem. Spl. Naval Bd. of Ordnance. Sec. and treas. U.S. Naval Inst. (editor Proceeding, 1903—). Republican. Unitarian. Author: Exterior Ballistics, 1904; Elastic Strength of Guns, 1906; Hydromechanics, 1902. Died Feb. 23, 1912.

ALGER, Russell Alexander, senator; b. Lafayette Township, Medina County, O., Feb. 27, 1836; orphaned at 12 yrs. of age and for 7 yrs. worked on farm, earning money to defray expenses at Richfield (O.) Acad. during winters. Taught school 2 winters; admitted to bar, 1859; began practice in Cleveland; removed to Mich., Jan. 1, 1860; began lumbering in a small way; enlisted, Sept. 2, 1861, and served as capt. and maj. 2d Mich., lt. col. 6th Mich., col. 5th Mich. cav.; bvtd. brig. gen. and maj. gen. vols. In lumber business after war; head of Alger, Smith & Co., and Manistique Lumbering Co. Was gov. Mich., 1885 and 1886; a leading candidate for pres. in Rep. Nat. Conv., 1888; 1 term comdr.-in-chief G. A. R.; Sec. of War of U.S., 1897-99, resigned; apptd. U.S. senator Sept. 27, 1902, to succeed James McMillan deceased, and elected Feb. 1903, for term expiring 1907. Author: The Spanish-American War, 1901. Home: Detroit, Mich. Died 1907.

ALGER, William Rounseville, Unitarian clergyman; b. Freetown, Mass., Dec. 28, 1822; grad. Harvard Theol. School, 1847 (A.M., Harvard, 1852); m. Anne Langdon Lodge, 1847. Filled pastorates in Roxbury, Mass.; Boston; New York; Denver; Chicago; Portland, Me.; New Orleans; and Newport, R.I., and returned to Boston. Author: Symbolic History of the Cross; The School of Life; History of the Doctrine of a Future Life; The Genius of Solitude, etc. Home: Boston, Mass. Died 1905.

ALLAIRE, William Herbert, army officer; b. Pocahontas, Ark., Jan. 1, 1858; s. William Herbert and Nancy Green (James) A.; grad. U.S. Mil. Acad., 1882; m. Florence Benton Whitehead, May 14, 1902. Served as 2d lt., 1st lt., then capt., 23d Inf., 1898; advanced through grades (in various inf. cos.) to brig. gen., Aug. 15, 1917. Served in the Southwest until 1893; instr. U.S. Mil. Acad., 1893-97; in Philippines during insurrection, 1899-1901; under Gen. Wood in P.I., expdns. against Moros, 1903-05; mil. attaché at Vienna, 1907-11; served under Gen. Pershing in Mexico, 1916-17; with first expdn. to France, June, 1917; apptd. provost marshal gen. A.E.F. in France, Aug. 30, 1917. Died May 1, 1933.

ALLARDICE, Robert Edgar, mathematician; b. Edinburgh, Scotland, Mar. 2, 1862; s. John and Isabella Edgar (Laing) A.; A.M., U. of Edinburgh, 1882, post-grad., 1882-84; unmarried. Asst. prof mathematics, U. of Edinburgh, 1882-92; prof. mathematics, Leland Stanford Jr. U., 1892—. Home: Stanford University, Calif. Died 1928.

ALLEE, James Frank, senator; b. Dover, Del., 1857; ed. pub. schs.; m. Lizzie Stevens, Jan. 18, 1882. Succeeded father in jewelry and watchmaking business; became pres. Bay State Gas Co. of Del., Staten Island Brick Co. Mem. Del. Senate, 1898-1906, as Union Republican; chmn. Union Republican Com.; U.S. senator from Del., 1903-07. Republican. Home: Dover, Del. Died Oct. 13, 1938.

ALLEN, Abel Leighton, author, lawyer; b. Kenton, O., Jan. 25, 1850; s. Abel H. and Rebecca (Mackey) A.; B.A., Ohio Wesleyan U., 1875; LL.B., Cincinnati Law Sch., 1877; m. Emily Bonnell Leigh, Oct. 22, 1884. Gen. practice civ. and corp. law. Republican. Mason. Author: The Message of New Thought, 1914;

also article on New Thought in Hastings' Ency. of Religion and Ethics, 1916. Home: Chicago, Ill. Died Dec. 8, 1927.

ALLEN, Alexander Viets Griswold, prof. ch. history, Episcopal Theol. School, 1867—; b. Otis, Mass., May 4, 1841; s. Rev. Ethan and Lydia Child (Burr) A.; grad. Kenyon, 1862; Andover Theol. Sem., 1865; (D.D., Harvard, 1886, Yale, 1901); m. Elizabeth Kent Stone, 1872 (died 1892); m. 2d, 1907, Paulina Cony Smith. Ordained priest in P. E. Ch., 1865. Author: Continuity of Christian Thought, 1884; Life of Jonathan Edwards, 1889; Religious Progress, 1893; Christian Institutions, 1897; Life and Letters of Phillips Brooks, 1900; Freedom in the Church, 1907. Home: Cambridge, Mass. Died 1908.

ALLEN, Alfred Gaither, congressman; b. on farm near Wilmington, O., July 23, 1867; s. Isaac B. and Eliza W. (Gaither) A.; ed. grammar and high schs., Wilmington; LL.B., Cincinnati Law Sch., 1890; m. Clara B. Forbes, Dec. 10, 1901. Admitted to bar, 1890, and since in practice at Cincinnati; U.S. commr., 1896-1900; councilman-at-large, Cincinnati, 1906-08; mem. Bd. Sinking Fund Trustees of Cincinnati, 1908-10 and 1926—; mem. 62d, 63d, 64th Congresses (1911-17), 2d Ohio Dist. Atty. for Selective Draft Bd., 1917-18. Democrat. Methodist. Mason, Elk. Home: Cincinnati, O. Died Dec. 9, 1932.

ALLEN, Alfred Reginald, neurologist; b. East Greenwich, R.I., May 26, 1876; s. Rev. George Pomeroy (D.D.) and Elizabeth Marshall (Howe) A.; ed. Lehigh U., 1893-94; M.D., U. of Pa., 1898; m. Helen, d. E. Burgess and Emma (Bolton) Warren, Jan. 21, 1904. Practiced in Phila., 1898—; lecturer in neurol. electrotherapeutics, U. of Pa., 1908-11; pathologist, Eastern Pa. State Instn. for Feeble Minded and Epileptic, 1909; asso. in neurology, and in neuropathology, U. of Pa., 1912—. Grad. Inf. Sch. of Arms, Ft. Sill; commd. maj., 314th U.S. Inf.; dir. Sch. of Automatic Arms, in Inf. Sch. of Arms, of 79th Div. and was some time actg. comdt. same. Mem. Am. Psychopathol. Assn. (pres. 1914, 15), Am. Neurol. Assn. (sec. and treas. 1909-17), Phila. Neurol. Soc. (pres. 1910); sec. of U.S. delegation to 16th Internat. Med. Congress, Budapest, 1909; U.S. Govt. del., also sec. of delegation, to 17th Internat. Med. Congress, London, 1913. Republican. Author of various clin. and exptl. works in neurology. Home: Philadelphia, Pa. Died 1918.

ALLEN, Amos Lawrence, congressman; b. Waterborough, Me., Mar. 17, 1837; A.B., Bowdoin, 1860; LL.B., Columbian (now George Washington) U., 1866; admitted to bar, 1866. Clerk U.S. Treasury Dept., 3 yrs.; clerk of courts, York County, Me., 1870-83; clerk judiciary com., U.S. Ho. of Rep., 1883-84; spl. examiner Pension Bur., 1884-85; mem. Me. Ho. of Rep., 1886-87; del.-at-large and mem. com. on resolutions, Rep. Nat. Conv., St. Louis, 1896; pvt. sec. Speaker Thomas B. Reed, 1893-96; elected to 56th Congress, Nov. 6, 1899, to fill unexpired term (1899-1901), of Thomas B. Reed, resigned; reëlected 57th to 61st Congresses (1901-11), 1st Me. Dist. Home: Alfred, Me. Died 1911.

ALLEN, Andrew Hussey, author; b. New York, N.Y., Dec. 6, 1855; s. Julian and Mary Abby (Hussey) A.; A.B., Harvard, 1878; admitted to bar, 1889, but never practiced; unmarried. Disbursing agt. court of commrs. of Alabama Claims, 1882-85; mem. U.S. Bd. on Geographic Names, Sept. 4, 1890-1905 (was sec., chmn. bd.); chief Bur. of Rolls and Library, Dept. of State, 1892-1905. Inaugurated Sept. 1893, and edited, to its conclusion, 1905, Bulletin of Rolls and Library, as a medium for pub. of catalogues, indices and important papers of the Nat. Archives. Author: Official Relations of the United States with the Hawaiian Islands, from the First Appointment of a Consular Office There by the United States Government, 1893; The Historical Archives of the Department of State, 1895; Method of Recognition of Foreign Governments and Foreign States by the Government of the United States, 1897. Editor: Volumes I-V, Documentary History of the Constitution of the United States, 1894-1905. Died Nov. 15, 1921.

ALLEN, Andrews, engr.; b. Madison, Wis., Jan. 11, 1870; s. Prof. William Francis and Margaret Loring (Andrews) A.; B.S. in C.E., U. of Wis., 1891, C.E., 1893; m. Margaret Isabel Thomas, Oct. 9, 1894 (divorced 1915); m. 2d, Elizabeth Emerson Cooke, Jan. 15, 1916; children—Andrews, Katharine Elisabeth, Francis J. and Henry (both adopted). With U.S. Geol. Survey in Upper Mich., 1891; draftsman and asst. engr., Edge Moor Bridge Works, 1891-99; contracting engr., Wis. Bridge & Iron Co., 1899-1911; pres. Allen & Garcia Co., 1911—. Mason (K.T., Shriner). Home: Glencoe, Ill. Died Mar 21, 1931.

ALLEN, Arch Turner, state supt. schs.; b. Hiddenite, N.C., Jan. 10, 1875; s. George James and Mary Elizabeth (Cambell) A.; student Morganton (N.C.) Acad., 1892; Voshti Acad., 1893; Ph.B., U. of N.C., 1897; student summers univs. of N.C. and Tenn., and winter term Columbia, 1922; D.C.L., Elon Coll., 1924; LL.D., U. of N.C., 1927; m. Claribel McDowell, June 19, 1909; children—Arch Turner, Elizabeth McDowell. Prin. high sch., Statesville, N.C., 1897-1904, Washington, 1904-05, Dilworth, 1905-07; supt. schs., Graham, 1907-10, Salisbury, 1910-17; with State Dept. Edn., Raleigh, N.C., 1917-23; state supt. pub. instrn., 1923—. Democrat. Mem. M.E. Ch., S. Home: Raleigh, N.C. Died Oct. 20, 1934.

ALLEN, Benjamin, wholesale jeweler; b. Goderich, Ont., Oct. 7, 1848; s. John and Mary (Braden) A.; ed. grammar and high schs., Can.; m. Mae West Lamos, Aug. 29, 1871. Settled at Chicago, 1865; began with M. T. Quimby & Co., wholesale jewelers, 1865, succeeding to the business in 1870 under name of Stark & Allen, firm becoming Benj. Allen & Co., 1872; then v.p., treas. Spaulding & Co.; dir. First Nat. Bank, First Trust & Savings Bank, Nat. Safe Deposit Co.; owner Silversmiths' Bldg. Republican. Episcopalian. Mason. Home: Winnetka, Ill., and Chicago. Died Aug. 1, 1924.

ALLEN, Benjamin Leach, banker; b. Manchester, Mass., Jan. 3, 1874; s. Capt. John and Eveline Foster (Hooper) A.; ed. pub. schs. and business coll.; m. Louie Sutherland, Oct. 10, 1900; children—Catharine, Evelyn, Benjamin L., Louis S. Became v.p. Irving Trust Co., New York, 1903; retired; pres. Vandewater Paper Co., N.Y. Harbor Realty Co., Brunswick Site Co.; v.p. and dir. Consol. Laundries Co.; dir. De Hanen Razor Co., Inc.; dir. and treas. Am. Defense Soc., Inc. Republican. Episcopalian. Home: Westhampton Beach, L.I., N.Y. Died Nov. 5, 1939.

ALLEN, Beverly Sprague, prof. English; b. San Francisco, Apr. 9, 1881; s. William Henry and Mary (Sprague) A.; B.A., U. of Calif., 1903, M.A., 1905; Ph.D., Harvard, 1913; unmarried. Instr. English, U. of Ida., 1905-07; asst. prof. English, State Coll. of Wash., 1911-13; Sheldon traveling fellow, Harvard, 1913-14; asst. prof. English, New York U., 1914-22, asso. prof., 1922-24, prof., 1924—. Instr. at L'École Militaire d'Artillerie, Fontainebleau, France, 1918. Mem. Modern Lang. Assn. Am., English-Speaking Union. Unitarian. Home: New York, N.Y. Died 1934.

ALLEN, Charles, judge; b. Greenfield, Mass., Apr. 17, 1827; s. Sylvester and Harriet (Ripley) A.; A.B., Harvard, 1847 (LL.D., 1892); admitted to bar, 1850; unmarried. Practiced law in Greenfield until 1862, after that in Boston. Reporter decisions, Supreme Jud. Ct., Mass., 1861-67; atty.-gen. of Mass., 1867-72; chmn. Commn. to Revise Statutes of Mass., 1881; justice Supreme Jud. Ct., 1882-98. Author: Allen's Massachusetts Reports (14 vols.), 1861-69; Telegraph Cases, 1873; Notes on the Bacon-Shakespeare Question, 1900. Died Jan. 13, 1913.

ALLEN, Charles Claflin, lawyer; b. St. Louis, Mo., July 25, 1855; s. John Arthur and Jane Elizabeth (White) A.; student Washington U., St. Louis; A.B., Princeton, 1875, A.M., 1878; LL.B., St. Louis Law Sch., 1877; m. Carrie Louise Richards, Mar. 27, 1890; children—Grace (Mrs. Dudley French), Charles Claflin. Admitted to Mo. bar, 1877; mem. Mo. Ho. of Rep., 1881-82; asso. city counselor, St. Louis, 1895-1901; judge 8th Jud. Circuit of Mo., 1907-13. Republican. An organizer Universal Congress Lawyers and Jurists, St. Louis, 1904 (govt. del. and mem. com. on plan and scope); del. to city and state convs. Wrote words and music of hymn, "The New America," 1918, and other patriotic verse. Home: St. Louis, Mo. Died 1927.

ALLEN, Charles Dexter; b. Windsor Locks, Conn., 1865. Lit. editor Hartford Post, 1895-97; editor of In Lantern Land, 1898. Mem. Internat. Jury of Awards, St. Louis Expn., 1904. Author: American Book-Plates, 1894; A Classified List of Early American Book-Plates (Grolier Club), 1894; Ex-Libris-Essays of a Collector, 1896; A Talk on Book-Plates (Club of Odd Volumes, 1901). Unitarian. Home: Montclair, N.J. Died Sept. 10, 1926.

ALLEN, Charles Edward, consul; b. Foster, Ky., April 13, 1891; A.B., Centre College, 1911; m. Doris Harty, May 2, 1917; children—Charles E. (dec.), Heather, Rosemary. Prin. high sch., Mt. Sterling, Ky., 1911-12; student interpreter, Am. Embassy, Constantinople, 1914-15; consular agt., Adrianople, Turkey, 1915-16; v. consul, Constantinople, 1916-17; attached to Am. Consulate, Algiers, 1917-18; v. consul, Nantes, France, 1918-19; v. consul and consul, Constantinople, 1919-21; consul at Damascus, 1921-23, at Constantinople, 1923—. Home: Maysville, Ky. Died Apr. 8, 1935.

ALLEN, Charles Herbert, banker; b. Lowell, Mass., Apr. 15, 1848; s. Otis and Louise (Bixby) A.; A.B., Amherst, 1869, A.M., 1872 (LL.D., 1900); m. Harriet C. Dean, Nov. 10, 1870. Engaged in lumber business in firm Otis, Allen & Son, Lowell, Mass.; dir. Guaranty Trust Co., Appleton Nat. Bank; trustee Am. Surety Co. Mem. Mass. Ho. of Rep., 1881, 1882, Senate, 1883; on staff Governor Robinson with rank of col., 1884-86; mem. 49th and 50th Congresses (1885-89); mem. State Prison Commn., 1897-98; Rep. nominee for gov. of Mass., 1891; asst. sec. of the Navy, 1898-1900, succeeding Theodore Roosevelt; gov. of Porto Rico, 1900-02. Home: Lowell, Mass. Died Apr. 20, 1934.

ALLEN, Charles Julius, brig. gen. U.S.A.; b. Buffalo, N.Y., Jan. 31, 1840; s. Charles H. and Melissa M. (Kissam) A.; grad. U.S. Mil. Acad., 1864; m. Elizabeth Wallbridge, Jan. 20, 1869. Commd. 1st lt. engrs., June 13, 1864, and advanced through grades to lt. col., Feb. 5, 1897; brig.-gen., Jan. 22, 1904; retired at own request after 40 years service, Jan. 23, 1904. Served in Div. of West Miss. and Dept. of La. during Civil War; in charge of defenses of Natchez; acting chief engr. 16th Army Corps at siege of Spanish Ft., Ala., etc.; chief engr. Army of Observation on Rio Grande, Tex., June-Aug., 1865; in charge defenses of Washington during Spanish-Am. War, 1898. Died June 15, 1915.

ALLEN, Charles Lucius, grinding tools and abrasives; b. Worcester, Mass., Mar. 6, 1858; s. George Lucius and Eliza Jane (Black) A.; grad. high sch., Worcester, 1876; m. Helen Louise Norton, Dec. 23, 1886; 1 dau., Mary Norton. With Norton Co. since 1886, pres., gen. mgr., 1919-33, chmn. bd., 1933—; dir. Bancroft Realty Co., Riley Stoker Co., Liberty Mut. Ins. Co., Worcester Mfrs. Mut. Ins. Co.; trustee Worcester 5 Cent Savings Bank. Chmn. Municipal Auditorium Commn.; mem. St. Lawrence Waterway Commn. Trustee Worcester Poly. Inst., Jr. Achievement Inc. Mason. Home: Worcester, Mass. Died Nov. 4, 1940.

ALLEN, Charles Warrenne, physician; b. Flemington, N.J., Dec. 4, 1854; s. George Anderson and Mary (Bonnell) A.; early edn. Lycée Imperial, Nantes, France; grad. Exeter Acad., 1875, med. dept. Columbia Coll. (Phys. & Surg.), New York, 1878; post-grad. studies univs. of Vienna and Paris; m. Grace Lawrence Boardman (dec.). Prof. dermatology, N.Y. Post-Grad. Med. Sch. and Hosp.; cons. surgeon in various hosps. Author: Practitioners' Manual, 1899; Handy Book of Medical Progress, 1899; Radiotherapy, Photography, Radium and High Frequency Currents, 1904. Home: New York, N.Y. Deceased.

ALLEN, Dudley Peter, surgeon; b. Kinsman, O., Mar. 25, 1852; s. Dudley and Janette (Frame) A.; A.B., Oberlin, 1875, A.M., 1883; M.D., Harvard, 1880; (LL.D., Oberlin, 1908); m. Elizabeth S. Severance, Aug. 4, 1892. Prof. principles and practice of surgery from 1893, then emeritus prof. surgery, Western Reserve U.; trustee Oberlin Coll., 1898—, Western Reserve Hist. Soc., Mus. Art. Home: Cleveland, O. Died Jan. 6, 1915.

ALLEN, Edmund Thompson, lawyer; b. Fairhaven, Mass., Aug. 10, 1836; s. Edmund and Sarah Russell (Freeman) A.; A.B., Yale, 1857, A.M., 1860; m. Sylvia T. Bowen, Jan. 13, 1863 (died 1903). Admitted to bar, 1859; practiced at New Bedford, Mass., 1859-63; shorthand writer in mil. courts, St. Louis, 1863-66; sr. mem. E. T. & C. B. Allen, 1887—. Republican. Home: St. Louis. Died. May 1913.

ALLEN, Edward Patrick, bishop; b. Lowell, Mass., Mar. 17, 1853; s. John and Mary (Egan) A.; A.M., Mount St. Mary's Coll., 1878, followed by course in theology; ordained R.C. priest, Dec. 17, 1881; prof. of English and Greek, Mt. St. Mary's Coll., 1881-82; asst. at Cathedral, Boston, 1882, at Framingham, Mass., 1883-84; pres. Mt. St. Mary's Coll., 1884-97; consecrated 5th bishop of Mobile, May 16, 1897. Home: Mobile, Ala. Died Oct. 21, 1926.

ALLEN, Edwin West, chemist; b. Amherst, Mass., Oct. 28, 1864; s. Lysander H. and Mary M. (Bullard) A.; grad. Mass. Agrl. Coll., 1885; B.S., Boston Univ., 1885; Ph.D., U. of Göttingen, 1890; LL.D., U. of Mo., 1929; m. Estelle Standish Perkins, Apr. 2, 1891; children—Myles Standish (dec.), Dorothy Helen. Entered service of U.S. Dept. of Agr., Aug. 11, 1890; asst. dir., 1893-1915, then chief Office of Expt. Stas.; asso. editor to 1895, editor in chief to 1924, Experiment Station Record, also asst. dir. of scientific work. Exec. sec. of Commn. on Country Life, 1908. Contbr. to The Am. and Internat. Yearbooks; editor agr. and agrl. chemistry of New Internatl Ency. Editor Jour. Agrl. Research, 1926—. Home: Washington, D.C. Died 1929.

ALLEN, Ernest Bourner, clergyman; b. Kalamazoo, Mich.; s. George Ladd and Harriet (Bourner) A.; B.A., Olivet Coll., Mich., 1895; B.D., Oberlin Theol. Sem., 1903; D.D., Olivet, 1907, Oberlin, 1923; m. Mary R. Bryant, June 2, 1897. Ordained Congl. ministry, Sept. 19, 1895; pastor, Lansing, Mich., 1895-1901, Toledo, O., 1901-18, Pilgrim Ch., Oak Park, Ill., 1918—. Trustee Ohio Congl. Conf., 1907-14, moderator, 1910-11. Trustee Olivet Coll., 1897—, Chicago Congl. Missionary and Extension Soc., 1918—; moderator Ill. Congl. Conf., 1926-27; trustee Congl. Foundation for Edn., 1923—. Home: Oak Park, Ill. Died Nov. 16, 1931.

ALLEN, Ethan, lawyer; b. Monmouth Co., N.J., May 12, 1832; s. Samuel Fleming and Phœby (Goble) A.; A.B., Brown U., 1860, A.M., 1870; LL.B., valedictorian, U. City of New York, 1861; recruited a brigade for Civil War, but did not enter service because ordered by Sec. of War to remain in civil service; m. Eliza Clagett, Aug. 20, 1861 (died 1899). Deputy U.S. atty., Southern Dist., N.Y., 1861-69, apptd. by President Lincoln chm. Nat. Com. of Liberal Reps. to make Horace Greeley pres.; pres. Cuban League U.S., 1870-72, 1896-98; retired, 1890. Author: Washington, or the Revolution (history Am. Revolution in dramatic form, blank verse; also in prose); Rozina (drama). Home: New York, N.Y. Died 1911.

ALLEN, Francis Richmond, architect; b. Boston, Mass., Nov. 22, 1843; s. Frederick Deane and Mary Richmond (Baylies) A.; A.B., Amherst, 1865; Mass. Inst. of Tech., 1876-77; M. Vandremer's atelier Ecole des Beaux Arts, Paris, 1877-78; hon. M.A., Williams, 1905; LL.D., Amherst, 1912; m. Elizabeth Bradlee Wood, Jan. 5, 1875. With Allen, Lane & Co., Boston, 1865-77; in practice of architecture, 1879-1924; mem. Allen & Collens, Boston and New York, 1904-26. Principal works: 8 bldgs., Williams Coll.; 12 bldgs., Vassar Coll.; Woman's Hosp., 110th St., New York; Emmanuel Ch., Boston; Memorial Hosp., Canandaigua, N.Y.; Union Theol. Sem. bldgs., New York; Andover Theol. Sem. bldg., Cambridge, Mass.; also hospitals, residences, office bldgs., etc. Fellow A.I.A., 1895. Republican. Episcopalian. Home: Boston, Mass. Deceased.

ALLEN, Fred Hovey, author; b. Lyme, N.H., Oct. 1, 1845; s. Philander and Rhoda (Lord) A.; grad. Hartford Theol. Sem., 1875; studied Boston U., Berlin, Vienna, Paris; LL.D., 1904; m. M. Cora Bumpus, Apr. 26, 1881. A founder, 1867, and editor, 1867-69, Lawrence (Mass.) Eagle; propr. and editor Suffolk Co. Journal, Boston, 1869-70. Ordained Congl. ministry, 1874; acting pastor N. Brookfield, Mass., 1875-76; pastor E. St. and Olivet chs., Boston, 1877-80, Abington, Mass., 1894-95, Rockland, Mass., 1895-1902; became dir. Majestic Art Galleries. Author: Glimpses of Parisian Art, 1882; Masterpieces of Modern German Arts, 1884; Modern German Masters, 1885; Recent German Art, 1885; Great Cathedrals of the World, 1886; Famous Paintings, 1887; Grand Modern Paintings, 1888; Bowdoin Art Collection, 1887; Popular History of the Reformation, 1887. Home: New York, N.Y. Died Dec. 24, 1926.

ALLEN, F(rederic) Sturges, editor; b. at Norwalk, Conn., Oct. 1, 1861; s. Alfred Burr and Caroline (Sturges) A.; A.B., Yale, 1884; Yale Law Sch., 1890-92; m. Annie M. White, Apr. 9, 1895. On staff Webster's Internat. Dictionary, 1884-90; edited or abridged various smaller Webster's dictionaries, 1892-98, practiced law, 1892-1903; chief editor (under late Dr. W. T. Harris), of supplement of Webster's Internat. Dictionary (pub. 1900); contbr. and editor of law articles of Johnson's Universal Ency.; contbr. law dept. Appleton's Universal Ency. Supplement; editor law dept., New Internat. Ency., contbr., dept. of Pronunciation in same; gen. editor (under Dr. Harris), of Webster's New Internat. Dictionary; contbr. to Teacher's Ency., 1911. Awarded gold medal for work in lexicography, San Francisco Expn., 1915; William Pynchon medal, 1916. Author: The Principles of Spelling Reform, 1907; Dictionary of Synonyms and Autonyms, 1920; The Art of Punctuation, 1920. Died Aug. 8, 1920.

ALLEN, Frederic Winthrop, banker; b. Walpole, Mass., May 26, 1877; s. Melzar W. and Martha (Metcalf) A.; B.A., Yale, 1900; m. Irene Catlin, Feb. 4, 1911; children— Justine Catlin, Irene Winthrop, Martha Emily. Entered employ Simmons Hardware Co., St. Louis, 1901, becoming asst. sec. and dir.; elected v.p. Mechanics & Metals Nat. Bank, New York, Nov. 1, 1910; mem. Lee, Higginson & Co., bankers, Jan. 1, 1915—; chmn. bd. North Am. Reassurance Co., Am. Enka Corp., Dunlop Tire & Rubber Co.; dir. Air Reduction Co., Inc., E. G. Budd Mfg. Co., European Mortgage Investment Corp., and numerous other cos.; dir. Chase Nat. Bank. Trustee Johns Hopkins Univ., Barnard Coll., Brook Sch., Miss Chapin's Sch.; dir. Doctors Hosp.; gov. New York Hosp. Home: New York, N.Y. Died Nov. 25, 1933.

ALLEN, Frederick Baylies, clergyman; b. Boston, Mass., Nov. 5, 1840; s. Frederick Dean and Mary Richmond (Bayliss) A.; Harvard, 1859-61; A.B., Amherst Coll., 1863, hon. A.M., 1866; Andover Theol. Sem., 1866; (A.B., Harvard, 1907); m. Louisa Ripley Vose, Apr. 24, 1867 (died 1872); m. 2d, Alberta H. Lewis, June 4, 1884. Ordained Congl. ministry, 1866; pastor, Newport, R.I., 1866-67, Canandaigua, N.Y., 1868-73; entered P.E. ministry, 1879; asst. to Phillips Brooks at Trinity Ch., Boston, 1879-88; supt. Episcopal City Mission, Boston, 1888-1914, financial sec., 1914-23; sec. Gen. Theol. Library, Boston. Republican. Home: Boston, Mass. Deceased.

ALLEN, Frederick Hobbes, lawyer, economist; b. Honolulu, T. H.; s. Elisha H. (mem. Congress, later chief justice of Hawaiian Kingdom, E.E. and M.P. to U.S.) and Mary Harrod (Hobbes) A.; studied in Germany, Switzerland and under tutors; A.M., LL.B., Harvard, 1883; m. Adele Livingston Stevens, 1892; children—Frederic Stevens, Mary Dorothy Adele (dec.), Barbara Frances (Madame Andre Vagliano), Joan Livingston (Mrs. Goodhue Livingston, Jr.), Julian Broome Livingston, Priscilla Alden Sampson. Became sec. of Hawaiian Legation, Washington, D.C., 1882; chargé d'affaires same, 1883; mem. Adams & Allen, New York, 1894-1900, then Allen & Cammann; served as corp. counsel and pres. Pelham Manor, and chmn. Dem. County Com., Westchester Co.; mem. Dem. Nat. Finance Com., 1912, 20, 24, 28, 32; mem. com. sent to Europe to study agrl. production, distribution and rural credits (report of com. was basis for Fed. Farm Loan Act). Rep. of Pan-European Am. Coöp. Com. at Pan-European Congress, Vienna, 1926; observer for Pan-European Council of Economic Conf., Geneva, 1927. Mem. com. of 4 which secured formation of Lafayette Escadrille, 1916; commd. lt. comdr. U.S.N.R. Flying Corps, Aug. 20, 1917, and served as aide to comdr. of U.S. aviation forces in Europe, hdqrs. in Paris. Lt. comdr. U.S.N.R.F. Res. Decorated Officer Legion of Honor (French); Officer Order of Leopold II (Belgian); Star of Order of Polonia Restituta (Polish); Comdr. Order of the White Lion (Czechoslovakia). Home: Newport, R.I. Died Dec. 12, 1937.

ALLEN, Frederick Innes, lawyer; b. at Auburn, N.Y., June 19, 1859; s. William and Sarah Martha (Palmer) A.; Ph.B., Sheffield Scientific Sch., Yale, 1879; m. Cornelia Margaret, d. Gen. William H. Seward, of Auburn, N.Y., June 3, 1884. Admitted to bar, 1882; in practice at Auburn, 1882-1901; U.S. commr. of patents, 1901-07; in practice at New York, 1907—. Lecturer on patent law, George Washington U., 1903-05. Rep. U.S. at Congress Internat. Assn. for Protection of Industrial Property, Berlin, and Berne, Switzerland, 1904. Home: New York, N.Y. Died May 17, 1938.

ALLEN, Frederick James, author; b. Limerick, Me., Feb. 23, 1864; s. Francis Henry and Hannah Maria (Chase) A.; A.B., Dartmouth, 1889, A.M., 1892; post-grad. work, Harvard, 1902-03; m. Maria Porter Hitchcock, Mar. 9, 1893 (died 1895); children—Charles F. A., Marie C.; m. 2d, Wilhelmina Pingree, July 14, 1897; children—Wilhelmina F., Frederick C., Theodora B. Prin. high sch. for 10 yrs.; instr. history and mathematics, Boston U., 1900-03; instr. mathematics, Simmons Coll., 1903-04; dir. Y.M. Civic Club of Boston, 1904—; also investigator of occupations, Vocation Bur., Boston, 1910-17; asst. dir., Bur. of Vocational Guidance of Harvard, 1917—; lecturer in vocational guidance, Boston U. and Harvard. Republican. Conglist. Author: A Topical Outline of English History, 1894; Poems, 1898; The Boston Game, 1905; In Crystal Hills, 1908; Vocations for Boys and Young Men, 1911; The Law as a Vocation, 1913; Business Employments, 1916; The Shoe Industry, 1916; Advertising as a Vocation, 1918; The Shipbuilding Industry, 1918; A Guide to the Study of Occupations and Studies of Occupations in Agriculture, Forestry, and Animal Industry, 1921. Editor Vocational Guidance Mag., 1922—. Home: Arlington, Mass. Died Feb. 17, 1927.

ALLEN, Geo. A., Jr., state supt. public instrn.; b. Rolla, Mo., June 30, 1868; s. George A. and Anna Maria (Ellis) A.; student Campbell (now Kansas City) U., 1891-94; B.S., Kan. State Teachers Coll. of Emporia, 1916; grad. study U. of Kan., summers, 1913-14, Washburn Coll., Topeka; m. Emma Maude McComas, July 3, 1897; children—Anna Martha (Mrs. W. R. Rickert), Charles McComas, Fred Augustus, Paul Johnson. Teacher, schs. of Jackson Co., Kan., 1891-1905; supt. schs., Jackson Co., 1905-09; prin. and supt. city schs., 1909-19; asst. Kan. State supt. pub. instruction, 1919-23; prin. city schs., Topeka, 1923-27; Kan. State supt. pub. instrn., 1927—. Mem. Kan. State Reading-Circle Bd., 1912-19, now ex-officio chmn.; officio mem. Kan. State Bd. Edn. (chmn.), Kan. State School Book Commn., Kan. School-Fund Commn. (sec.), Kans. State Teachers' Assn. (dir.); v.p. N.E.A., 1929. Republican. Methodist. Mason (32°, Shriner). Home: Topeka, Kan. Died Dec. 7, 1932.

ALLEN, George Washington, jurist; b. Warren Co., Pa.; s. Samuel and Mary A.; ed. Randolph Acad., and State Normal Sch.; m. Sarah Orville Allen; children—Orren, Harrison, James Kinnear, George Willis. Admitted to Pa. bar and began practice at Warren; mem. Pa. Ho. of Rep., 1874-76; mem. legislative com. on construction and development of Centennial Expn., Phila., 1876; moved to Denver, 1880; judge Dist. Court, Denver, 1888-1916; Rep. nominee for gov. of Colo., 1896 (defeated); received unanimous vote of Rep. members of legislature for U.S. Senator, session 1896-97 (defeated); justice Supreme Court of Colo., 1916-26, chief justice, 1926—. Mason (32°, Shriner). Home: Denver, Colo. Died Jan. 29, 1928.

ALLEN, George Whiting, banker, lawyer; b. Jacksonville, Fla., Sept. 1, 1854; s. William Smith and Mary Jane (Sprague) A.; ed. pvt. and pub. schs., Jacksonville and Key West, Fla., and Ithaca, N.Y.; m. Leonor X. Browne, May 26, 1880. In active practice of law, 1880—; pres. 1st Nat. Bank, Key West, from its orgn., 1891; pres. Key West Realty Co.; dir. Fla. Nat. Bank, Jacksonville; mem. Porter-Allen Co., real estate and ins. Deputy clk. U.S. Dist. Ct., Southern Dist. Fla., 1873-78; dep. collector internal revenue, 1879-90; treas. city of Key West, 1891; collector of customs, Dist. Key West, 1897-June 30, 1913; mem. Fla. State Senate, 2 terms, 1879-83; alternate del. Rep. Nat. Conv., 1900, del., 1904, 08, 12; Rep. nominee for gov. of Fla., 1896, for Congress, 1908, 12; Rep. and Prog. nominee for governor, 1916. Episcopalian. Home: Key West, Fla. Died May 30, 1922.

ALLEN, Grant, author; b. Kingston, Ont., Feb. 24, 1848; ed. U.S., France and England; grad. Merton Coll., Oxford; is a writer uoon evolution, and also a novelist. Author: Physiological Aesthetics; Charles Darwin; The Evolutionist at Large; The Color Sense; Phillistia; Babylon; Colin Clout's Calendar; The Color of Flowers; Flowers and Their Pedigrees; For Mamie's Sake In All Shades; The Beckoning Hand; The Devil's Die; This Mortal Coil; White Man's Foot; Force and Energy; The Tents of Shem; The Women Who Did; Post-Prandial Philosophy; Strange Stories; Anglo-Saxon Britain; The British Barbarians; Science in Arcady; Historical Guides to Paris, Florence and Belgium; The Evolution of the Idea of God; etc. Died 1899.

ALLEN, Henry Tureman, army officer; b. Sharpsburg, Ky., Apr. 13, 1859; s. Sanford and Susan (Shumate) A.; prep. edn. in Ky., and at Peekskill Mil Acad., and Georgetown Coll., A.M., 1898; grad. U.S. Mil. Acad., 1882; LL.D., Lincoln Memorial U., 1915, Georgetown, 1922; m. Dora Johnston, July 12, 1887. Commd. 2d lt. 2d Cav., June 13, 1882; promoted through grades to lt. col., vols., 1901, and to brig. gen. regular army, 1917; maj. gen. N.A., Aug. 5, 1917; maj. gen., Mar. 6, 1921; retired Apr. 13, 1923. Instr. U.S. Mil. Acad., 1888-90; mil. attaché Russia, 1890-95, Germany, 1897-98; served in Santiago campaign as maj. and adj. gen., in Philippines at lt. col. 43d Regt.; gov. Island of Leyte, Apr.-July, 1901; started orgn. of Philippine constabulary, July 1901, as its chief; brig. gen. and chief of constabulary by act of Congress, Jan. 1903; later lt. col. Gen. Staff in charge of cav. sect.; with Mexican Punitive Expdn., 1916; assigned comdr. 90th Div., Camp Travis, Tex., Sept. 1917; apptd. comdr. 90th Div., A.E.F., Sept. 1917, participating in Toul sector, St. Mihiel and Meuse-Argonne offensives; assigned as comdr. 8th Army Corps, Nov. 24, 1918, 9th A.C., Apr. 20, 1919, 7th A.C., May 5, 1919; apptd. comdr. Am. Forces in Germany, July 2, 1919. Decorated D.S.M.; Croix de Guerre with palm and Comdr. Legion of Honor (France); Comdr. Order of Leopold (Belgium); plaque Order of Prince Danilo; medal de la Solidaridad (Panama); Grand Cordon of Order of the Crown (Italian); Croix de Guerre with palm (Belgian). Author: Reconnaissance of Copper, Tannana and Kuyukuk Rivers, 1886; Military System of Sweden, 1895; My Rhineland Journal, 1923; The Rhineland Occupation, 1926. Home: Washington, D.C. Died Aug. 30, 1930.

ALLEN, Horace Newton, diplomatist; b. Delaware, O., Apr. 23, 1858; s. Horace and Jane M. (Riley) A.; B.S., Ohio Wesleyan, 1881; M.D., Miami Med. Coll., 1883; (LL.D., Ohio Wesleyan, 1911, also from U. of Vermont, 1923); m. Frances Ann Messenger; children—Horace Ethan, Maurice. Medical missionary Presbyterian Ch. in China; went to Korea, 1884; saved life of a prince and others in a revolution; became med. officer to Korean Court; founded a mission hosp. with govt. support; established Protestant missions; resigned to take embassy to Washington and establish a legation; returned to mission, 1889; again resigned to become sec. of U.S. Legation, 1890; promoted minister resident and consul-gen., 1897, E.E. and M.P., 1901-June 10, 1905. Hon. commr. and took Korean Govt. exhibit and a commn. to Chicago Expn., 1893; spl. envoy to Korean coronation, 1902; thrice decorated by Korean Emperor. Author: Korean Tales, 1889; Chronological Index of Foreign Relations of Korea from Beginning of Christian Era to 20th Century, 1900 (Seoul); Supplement to same, 1903; Korea—Fact and Fancy, 1904 (Seoul); Things Korean, 1908. Home: Toledo, O. Died Dec. 11, 1932.

ALLEN, Ira Wilder, clergyman; b. Lafayette, Ind., July 15, 1865; s. Ira Wilder and Lydia Reed (Ford) A.; Allen Acad., Chicago; B.A., Williams Coll., Williamstown, Mass., 1884 (class poet), M.A., 1887; grad. McCormick Theol. Sem., Chicago, 1895; (D.D., Blackburn U., 1911); m. Emily Rose Elmore, June 26, 1889. Teacher Latin, Greek, German and English lit., Allen Acad., 1884-90; ordained Presbyn. ministry, 1895; pastor Central Church, Rock Island, Ill., 1895-1900; asst. in homiletics, McCormick Theol. Sem., 1901-03; prof. English lit. and dean Occidental Coll., Los Angeles, Calif., 1904-06; pastor Paris, Ill., 1906—. Mem. Delta Upsilon. Home: Paris, Ill. Died Nov. 2, 1935.

ALLEN, James, brig. gen. U.S. Army; b. Laporte, Ind., Feb. 13, 1849; s. Mark and Matilda A.; grad. U.S. Mil. Acad., 1872. Commd. 2d lt. 3d U.S. Cav., June 14, 1872; advanced through the grades to brig. gen. chief signal officer U.S. Army, Feb. 10, 1906; retired Feb. 13, 1913. Served in Cuba, Puerto Rico, Philippine Islands and Alaska. Died Feb. 19, 1933.

ALLEN, James Lane, author; b. near Lexington, Ky., 1849; s. Richard and Helen (Foster) A.; A.B., A.M., Transylvania U.; (LL.D., same; Litt.D., Tulane and Ky. univs.). Taught in pub. and pvt. schs. and Kentucky U.; later prof. Latin and higher English, Bethany (W.Va.) Coll.; unmarried. Author: Flute and Violin, 1891; The Blue Grass Region and Other Sketches of Kentucky, 1892; John Gray—a Novel, 1893; The Kentucky Cardinal, 1895; Aftermath, 1896; A Summer in Arcady, 1896; The Choir Invisible, 1897 (dramatized 1899); The Reign of Law, The Mettle of the Pasture; The Bride of the Mistletoe, 1909; The Doctor's Christmas Eve, 1910; The Heroine in Bronze, 1912; The Last Christmas Tree,

1914; Sword of Youth, 1915; The Cathedral Singer, 1916; Kentucky Warbler, 1918; Emblems of Fidelity, 1919; The Alabaster Box, 1923. Home: New York, N.Y. Died Feb. 18, 1925.

ALLEN, Joel Asaph, curator; b. Springfield, Mass., July 19, 1838; s. Joel and Harriet (Trumbull) A.; studied at Wilbraham Acad.; then studied zoölogy under Agassiz, Lawrence Scientific Sch., Harvard; (hon. Ph.D., Ind. U., 1886); m. Mary Manning Cleveland, Oct. 6, 1874 (died Apr. 17, 1879); 2d, Susan A. Taft, of Cornwall-on-Hudson, N.Y., Apr. 27, 1886. Lecturer, 1871-73, asst. in ornithology, Mus. Comparative Zoölogy, 1871-85, Harvard; curator mammalogy and ornithology, Am. Mus. Natural History, New York, 1885—. Editor Bull. Nuttall Ornithol. Club, 1876-83, The Auk (ornithol. quarterly), 1884-1912, Bulletin and Memoirs, Am. Mus. Natural History, 1889-1917. Awarded Walker Grand Prize, 1903. Mem. Nat. Acad. Sciences, Am. Ornithologists Union (1st pres.). Fellow Am. Acad. Arts and Sciences. Author: History of North American Pinnipeds; Monographs of North American Rodentia (with Elliott Coues); Mammals of Patagonia, Belgian Congo, etc. Home: New York, N.Y. Died Aug. 29, 1921.

ALLEN, John Beard, U.S. senator, lawyer; b. Crawfordsville, Ind., May 18, 1845; ed. Wabash Coll.; served private 135th Ind. vols., Civil war; after war in Rochester, Minn., until 1870; admitted to bar; removed to Washington Ty., 1870; U.S. atty. for Washington Ty., 1878-85; was reporter for Territorial and U.S. courts for years; author 1st volume of Washington Territory Reports; elected to Congress for term 1889-91, but resigned on being elected U.S senator on admission of Washington as State; took seat, Dec. 2, 1889. Mem. firm Struve, Allen, Hughes & McMicken. Home: Seattle, Wash. Died 1903.

ALLEN, John Mills, congressman; b. Tishomingo County, Miss., July 8, 1846; s. David M. and Sallie Ann (Spencer) A.; country sch. edn.; pvt. C.S.A. during Civil War; LL.B., U. of Miss., 1870; m. Georgia Taylor, Dec. 24, 1872. In practice at Tupelo, Miss., 1870—; dist. atty. 1st Jud. Dist., 1876-80; mem. 49th to 56th Congresses (1885-1901), 1st Miss. Dist.; declined renomination. Democrat. Mem. Nat. Commn. St. Louis Expn. Dir. 1st Nat. Bank, People's Bank and Trust Co., Tupelo Cotton Mills, Tupelo Fertilizer Factory. Home: Tupelo, Miss. Died Oct. 30, 1917.

ALLEN, J(ohn) Weston, lawyer; b. Newton Highlands, Mass., Apr. 19, 1872; s. Walter and Grace Mason (Weston) A.; desc. Richard Warren and George Soule, of the Mayflower; A.B., Yale, 1893; LL.B., Harvard, 1896, LL.D., 1922; m. Caroline Cheney Hills, June 12, 1901; children—Helen Spencer, Grace Weston (Mrs. William D. Hogarth), Caroline Hills (Mrs. Howard V. H. Inches). Began practice at Boston, 1896; mem. Mass. Ho. of Rep., 1915-18; atty. gen. of Mass., 1920-22. Mem. Atty. Gen. Cummings Com. on Crime Conf., Washington, 1935; later mem. Atty. General's Advisory Com. on Crime; apptd. spl. asst. to atty. gen. of U.S., acting as consultant to Commr. of Immigration and Naturalization on pending legislation in Congress relating to deportation of aliens, 1935-36; official rep. Dept. of Justice at 2d Internat. Congress of Comparative Law, The Hague, 1937 (v.p. of Congress); spl. asst. to Atty. Gen. of U.S. acting as consultant on pending legislation in Congress relating to federal firearms control, 1937-38. Trustee New England Town Hall, Inc. (exec. com.). Trustee Am. Indian Inst., 1915-29. Republican. Conglist. Home: Newton Highlands, Mass. Died Jan. 1, 1942.

ALLEN, Kenneth, civil engr.; b. New Bedford, Mass., Apr. 6, 1857; s. Edward Augustus Holyoke and Eugenia Sophia (Teulon) A.; grad. West Newton (Mass.) English and Classical Sch., 1874; C.E., Rensselaer Poly. Inst., 1879; m. Rose Whitmore Switzer, Sept. 11, 1886; children—Edward Switzer, Harold Ames, Russell (dec.), Frances Eleanor. In ry. engring. work in the West, 1879-83; asst. engr., water dept., Phila., 1883-86; mem. Breithaupt & Allen, cons. engrs., and later supt. of constrn. for City of Kansas City, Mo., 1886-90; engr. in charge topog. survey of Connellsville coke region for H. C. Frick Coke Co., 1890-93; asst. engr. in charge pub. work, Yonkers, 1893-95; prin. asst. engr., Baltimore Sewerage Commn., 1895-99; mem. Hill, Quick & Allen, engrs., Baltimore, 1899-1902; engr. and supt. water dept., Atlantic City, N.J., 1902-06; div. engr., Baltimore Sewerage Commn., 1906-08; engr. Met. Sewerage Commn., New York, 1908-14; engr. Bur. of Sewer Plan, New York, 1915-16; engr. sewage disposal, and then sanitary engr. Bd. Estimate and Apportionment of New York, 1916-30; sanitary engr. Sanitation Commn., New York, 1930—. Dist. engr. U.S. Housing Corp., Washington, until armistice. Pres. N.Y. State Sewage Works Assn. Democrat. Unitarian. Home: White Plains, N.Y. Died Sept. 7, 1930.

ALLEN, Leon Menard, ry. official; b. Davenport, Ia., July 4, 1863; s. Elbridge Gerry and Christina (Hannah) A.; grad. high sch., Davenport, 1879; m. Katherine Augusta Ballord, June 26, 1888. News editor Davenport Gazette, 1880-81; various positions on C.,R.I.&P. Ry. at Davenport, 1881-98; with passenger dept., same rd., 1898—; gen. pass. agt. all Rock Island lines, 1903, passenger traffic mgr., 1909-20, v.p. and passenger traffic mgr., 1920—. Republican. Home: Kenilworth, Ill. Died May 25, 1936.

ALLEN, Louis J., naval officer; b. Md., 1840; apptd. in U.S. Navy as 3d asst. engr., 1859, served on steam sloop Dacotah, 1859-61; promoted 2d asst. engr. 1861, 1st asst. engr. 1863, chief engr. 1871, capt. Mar. 3, 1899, rear adm. and placed on retired list 1902. In Civil war was on steam sloop Adirondack until wrecked, later as sr. engr. of "doubleender" Conemaugh participated in attacks on forts around Charleston, etc.; later in various squadrons and navy yards on engring. duties. Died 1905.

ALLEN, Lyman Whitney, clergyman, author; b. St. Louis, Mo., Nov. 19, 1854; s. George Otis and Julia Olds (Whitney) A.; A.B., Washington U., St. Louis, 1878, later A.M.; Princeton Theol. Sem., 1878-80; post-grad. studies at Princeton; D.D., U. of Wooster, 1897; m. Myra Irwin, Sept. 5, 1880 (died 1900); children—June Thornton (Mrs. William M. Gardiner), Mildred Steele (Mrs. Egbert A. Jurgensen), Thornton Whitney, Marguerite Irwin (Mrs. Nathan Hesslem); m. 2d, Mrs. Phebe L. Le Massena, Sept. 5, 1904 (died 1915); m. 3d, Nellie L. Campbell, Sept. 14, 1921. Ordained Presbyn. ministry, 1882; stated supply Kimmswick, Mo., 1881-83, DeSoto, Mo., 1883-85; pastor elect. Carondelet Ch., St. Louis, 1885-89; pastor S. Park Ch., Newark, N.J., 1889-1916 (resigned to devote entire time to lit. work). Dir. Bd. Home Missions Presbyn. Ch., 1896-1921. Pres. N.J. Soc. S.A.R. (bd. mgrs.), 1920-22; chaplain gen. Nat. Soc. S.A.R., 1921. Author: Abraham Lincoln (New York Herald's $1000 prize poem), 1895; Parable of the Rose and Other Poems, 1908; Triumph of Love, 1910; also many celebration odes, articles, etc. Home: Newark, N.J. Died Jan. 27, 1930.

ALLEN, Martha Meir (Mrs. James E. Allen), temperance advocate; b. Owen Sound, Ont., Can., Mar. 31, 1854; d. John H. Meir; ed. Owen Sound High Sch. and under pvt. tutors, m. Rev. James E. Allen, June 25, 1880; children—Mrs. L. L. Post, J. Roy, Martha. Supt. dept. of med. temperance, for Nat. W.C.T.U., 1895—; for World's W.C.T.U., 1906—; del. from U.S. Govt. to World's Congress on Alcoholism, London, Eng., 1909; also delegate same, Washington, D.C., 1920. Methodist. Author: Alcohol, a Dangerous and Unnecessary Medicine, 1900; also many pamphlets against use of alcohol and patent medicines, which have had wide circulation. Home: Forest Hills Gardens, L.I., N.Y. Died June 19, 1926.

ALLEN, Maryland (Mrs. Edward Tyson Allen), writer, book reviewer; b. Montgomery County, Md.; d. Philander Chase and Virginia Covington (Smith) Riley; ed. principally under pvt. tutors; m. Edward Tyson Allen, Oct. 20, 1902; children—Olmsted Tyson, Barbara. Visited the South Seas with husband; first story appeared in Sunset Magazine, 1909, and since has been writing steadily for mags. and newspapers. Home: Rock Spur, Ore. Died Jan. 31, 1927.

ALLEN, Perry S.; b. nr. Pittsburgh, Pa., July 4, 1854; s. Richard Boyd and Mary Van Derland (Stoops) A.; grad. U. of Wooster, Ohio, 1874, Western Theol. Sem., 1877; D.D., U. of Omaha, 1902; m. Mary T. Kinter, Nov. 8, 1877 (died 1890); m. 2d, Virginia Gertrude Oliver, June 2, 1894. Ordained Presbyn. ministry, 1877; pastor Edenburg, Pa., 1877-78, Sharon, 1878-82, Warren, 1882-87, Saratoga Springs, N.Y., 1887-92; pres. Presbyn. Ministers' Fund for Life Ins., Phila., 1894—. Home: Philadelphia, Pa. Died Nov. 8, 1930.

ALLEN, Philip Loring, journalist; b. Madison, Wis., May 25, 1878; s. William Francis and Margaret (Andrews) A.; ed. Wis. Acad., and Univ. of Wis., B.L., 1899; m. Ferne Ryan, Oct. 10, 1906. Reporter and exchange editor New York Evening Post, 1899-1903; in Washington bureau of same and Boston Transcript, 1903-04; editorial writer New York Evening Post from 1904; sec. and treas. N.Y. Evening Post Co. from 1906. Author: America's Awakening, 1906. Contbr. short stories, etc., to mags. Died 1908.

ALLEN, Philip Schuyler, prof. German; b. Lake Forest, Ill., Aug. 23, 1871; s. Ira W. and Lydia (Ford) A.; A.B., Williams Coll., 1891; U. of Berlin, 1892-94; fellow in German, U. of Chicago, 1895-97, Ph.D., 1897; m. Jessie Acker, Dec. 21, 1894. Instr. German, Allen Acad., Chicago, 1891-92; instr. English, Shattuck Sch., Faribault, Minn., 1894-95; asst., asso. instr. and asst. prof. German, 1903-09, asso. prof. 1909, now prof., U. of Chicago. Mng. editor Modern Philology, 1900-08; directing editor Scott-Foresman Modern Foreign Lang. Program. Author: The Romanesque Lyric, 1927; Medieval Latin Lyrics, 1931. Home: Chicago, Ill. Died Apr. 27, 1937.

ALLEN, Ray, clergyman; b. Pavilion, N.Y., Mar. 22, 1860; s. Daniel and Laverna (Cheney) A.; student Academic Inst., LeRoy, N.Y., 1874-76; D.D., Syracuse U., 1910; m. Bessie J. Bond, Dec. 20, 1885 (died May 25, 1888); m. 2d, Sarah E. Martin, July 2, 1895 (died May 29, 1914); children—Earl, Carl, Ralph; m. 3d, Mabel E. Crabbe, Dec. 20, 1919. Traveling passenger agt. G.T. Ry. and St. Paul, Minneapolis & Manitoba Ry., 1881-86; ordained ministry M.E. Ch., 1886; missionary, Calcutta and Simla, India, 1886-88; pastor successively Alden, Buffalo, Rochester, Springville, Somerset, LeRoy, Rochester, Buffalo and Hornell; supt. Central and Rochester dists., 1914-20; exec. sec. and treas. Genesee Wesleyan Sem., Lima, N.Y., 1920-24; treas. Genesee Conf., 1925—; sec. Genesee Conf., 1898-1911. Mem. Gen. Conf. M.E. Ch., 1908, 16, 20, 24, 28, 32. Republican. Author: History of East Genesee Conference, 1908. Translator: The Gospel of Mark, 1927 (rev. edits. under title That Wonderful Man, by John Mark, over 230,000). Home: Buffalo, N.Y. Died Mar. 4, 1938.

ALLEN, Samuel Edward, army officer; b. New Lebanon, Ind., Aug. 12, 1858; s. Arthur P. and Rachel Josephine (Dodds) A.; grad. U.S. Mil. Acad., 1881, Coast Arty. Sch., Ft. Monroe, Va., 1892; m. Conchita Alvarez de la Mess, Dec. 9, 1885. Commd. 2d lt. 5th Arty., June 11, 1881; advanced through the grades to col., Coast Arty. Corps, Feb. 2, 1911. Instr. philosophy, U.S. Mil. Acad., 1892-96; retired at own request, after 42 yrs. service, July 1, 1919. Died Dec. 11, 1926.

ALLEN, Stephen Haley, lawyer; b. Sinclairville, N.Y., Mar. 19, 1847; s. Caleb Johnson and Emily (Haley) A.; ed. at home; admitted to bar, Buffalo, N.Y., 1869; m. Lucina A. Smith, Dec. 24, 1872. Located in Pleasanton, Kan., Feb. 1, 1870, and began practice; county atty. Linn County, 1874; judge 6th Jud. Dist., 1890-92; asso. justice Supreme Ct., Kan. (by combined vote of Populists and Democrats), 1892-99; resumed practice. Commr. for Kan. on uniform state laws, 1909. Author: The Evolution of Governments and Laws and International Relations. Home: Topeka, Kan. Died Oct. 26, 1931.

ALLEN, Thomas, painter; b. St. Louis, Mo., Oct. 19, 1849; s. Thomas and Anne C. (Russell) A.; ed. Wash. U., St. Louis; grad. Royal Acad., Düsseldorf, 1877; studied 3 yrs. in France; m. Eleanor G. Whitney, 1880; m. 2d, Alice Ranney, 1884. First exhibited at Nat. Acad. Design, 1877; at salons at Paris, 1882, 1887 and 1889; resided in Boston from 1883. Trustee Boston Mus. Fine Arts; chmn. council and the faculty, Sch. of Drawing and Painting, same. Awarded medals, Boston and Buffalo; judge awards, Chicago Expn., 1893; chmn. Internat. Jury of Awards, St. Louis Expn., 1904; chmn. Department Jury Fine Arts, St. Louis, 1904; chmn. Art Commn. City of Boston, May, 1910—; A.N.A., 1884. Pres. The Macallen Co. (Boston), Allen Estate Assn. (St. Louis), Wellesley (Mass.) Knitting Mills. Home: Boston, Mass. Died Aug. 25, 1924.

ALLEN, Timothy Field, M.D.; b. Westminster, Vt., Apr. 24, 1837; grad. Amherst Coll., 1858 (LL.D., Amherst, 1885); M.D., Univ. City of New York, 1861; M.D., Univ. of State of N.Y. and Hahnemann Med. Coll., Phila., 1865; m. Julia Bissell, 1862. Acting asst. surgeon, U.S. Army, 1862-64. Prof. materia medica and dean N.Y. Homœ. Med. Coll.; pres. bd. trustees N.Y. Homœ. Med. Coll.; pres. N.Y. Ophthalmic Hosp. Author of numerous works on med. topics, etc. Home: New York, N.Y. Died 1902.

ALLEN, Walter, journalist, author; b. Boston, Mass., Mar. 21, 1840; s. Josiah W. and Nancy (Hinds) A.; grad. Yale, 1863 (A.M., 1893); actg. asst. paymaster U.S. Navy, 1864-65; m. Grace Mason Weston, Oct. 9, 1866. Employed as corr., writer and editor on Cairo, Ill., Times, New York Herald, Cincinnati Gazette, Boston Advertiser, Portland, Me., Press, New York World, New York Times. Contbr. to other papers and to New England Mag., Atlantic Monthly, etc. Was clerk U.S. senate Com. on Indian Affairs; mem. commn. apptd. by President Hayes to investigate condition of Ponca Indians; editorial writer Boston Herald. Mem. Mil. Order Loyal Legion. Was in spl. service, New York, New Haven & Hartford R.R. Co., 1895-99. Asst. editor Webster's Internat. Dictionary. Author: Governor Chamberlain's Administration in South Carolina; Life of General Ulysses S. Grant (Riverside Biog. Series). Home: Newton Highlands, Mass. Died 1907.

ALLEN, William Frederick, editor; b. Bordentown, N.J., Oct. 9, 1846; s. Col. Joseph Warner and Sarah (Burns) A.; ed. P.E. Acad., Phila.; civ. engr. from practice in the field and private study; (hon. M.S., Princeton, 1906); m. Caroline Perry Yorke, Apr. 20, 1871. V.p., mgr. Nat. Ry. Pub. Co.; editor Official Railway Guide, 1873—; gen. sec. and treas. Am. Ry. Assn., 1875—. Took the leading part in proposing and securing the adoption of the present system of Standard Time, 1883; U.S. del. to Internat. Meridian Conf., 1884, Internat. Ry. Congress, Paris, 1900; del. Am. Ry. Assn. to Internat. Ry. Congresses in U.S. and Europe; mem. Permanent Commn. Internat. Ry. Congress Assn.; del. Rep. Nat. Conv., 1908. Contbr. to mags. and encys., on subjects of rys. and standard time. Home: South Orange, N.J. Died Nov. 9, 1915.

ALLEN, William Joshua, U.S. dist. judge Southern dist. Ill., April 18, 1887—; b. Wilson Co., Tenn., June 9, 1828; removed to Ill., 1829; employed in office of co. clerk, Williamson Co., 1846-47; attended Louisville, Ky., Law School, 1847-48; admitted to bar, 1848; practiced in Metropolis, Massac Co., 1848-53; joined his father, Willis Allen, in law partnership at Marion, Ill., 1853; mem. legislature, 1854; U.S. dist. atty., Southern dist. Ill., 1855-59; circuit judge, 26th Ill. Circuit, 1859-61; member Constl. Conventions, 1861 and 1870; mem. Congress, 1862-65, succeeding law partner, John A. Logan, while latter was in army; practiced at Cairo, Ill., 1865-74; after 1874 at Carbondale, Ill., until apptd. judge. Democrat. Home: Springfield, Ill. Died 1900.

ALLEN, William Orville, coll. prof.; b. Waddington, N.Y., Feb. 26, 1873; s. Henry William Powell and Elizabeth (Carter) A.; A.B., Syracuse U., 1897, A.M., 1899; S.T.B., Boston U., 1902, Ph.D., 1905; fellow Boston U., resident at Leipzig U., 1903-04; m. Eva E. Jackson, June 3, 1902; children—Elizabeth, Addison Jackson, Ruth Constance (dec.), Richard Carleton. Prin. Union Sch., Camillus, N.Y., 1896-98; ordained M.E. ministry, 1898; pastor, Parish, N.Y., 1898-99, Springfield, Vt., 1902-03; joined Congl. ministry, 1909; prof. psychology and edn., Tabor (Ia.) Coll., 1905-07, Cornell Coll., Mt. Vernon, 1907-09, Drury Coll., Springfield, Mo., 1909-14; pres. Doane Coll., Crete, Neb., 1914-18; prof. psychology and edn., Ill. Wesleyan U., Bloomington, 1918-20; prof. philosophy, Lafayette Coll., Easton, Pa., 1920—. Republican. Mason. Home: Easton, Pa. Died July 13, 1929.

ALLEN, William Reynolds, judge; b. at Kenansville, N.C., Mar. 26, 1860; s. William Anderson and Maria Goodwin (Hicks) A.; ed. Trinity Coll., N.C.; m. Mattie M. Moore, Nov. 3, 1886. Admitted to bar, 1881; practiced at Goldsboro, N.C., from 1881. Mem. N.C. Ho. of Rep., 1893, 1899, 1901; judge Superior Ct., N.C., by appmt., July-Dec. 1894, and elected for term, 1902-10; asso. justice Supreme Ct., 2 terms, 1910-27. Democrat. Methodist. Home: Goldsboro, N.C. Died Sept. 8, 1921.

ALLEN, William Vincent, senator; b. at Midway, O., Jan. 28, 1847; s. Rev. Samuel and Phoebe (Pugh) A.; g.g.s. Capt. Ananias A., 2d Sussex, N.J., Regt. in Revolutionary War; removed with family to Ia., 1857; ed. Upper Ia. U.; pvt. 32d Ia. Inf., Civil War; admitted to bar, May 31, 1869; m. Blanche Mott, May 2, 1870. Practiced law in Ia. until 1884, after that in Neb. until 1891; judge 9th Jud. Dist. of Neb., 1891-93; U.S. senator from Neb., 1893-99 and by appmt., Dec. 18, 1899-Mar. 27, 1901; dist. judge by appmt., Mar. 9-Dec. 13, 1899; reëlected dist. judge Nov., 1899, but did not take seat because of appmt. to Senate; again judge 9th Jud. Dist. of Neb., 1917-21. Permanent pres. Populist State Conv., 1892, 1894, 1900, and of Populist Nat. Conv., 1896. Home: Madison, Neb. Died Jan. 12, 1924.

ALLEN, Willis Boyd, author; b. Kittery Point, Me., July 9, 1855; s. Stillman Boyd and Harriet (Seaward) A.; A.B., Harvard, 1878; LL.B., Boston U., 1881; unmarried. Practiced law several years in firm Allen, Long & Savage, Boston. On staff Gov. John D. Long, with rank of lt. col., 1881-82. Republican. Author: Pine Cones, 1885; Silver Rags, 1886; Christmas at Surf Point, 1886; Northern Cross, 1887; Mountaineer Series (5 vols.), 1887; Kelp, 1888; Cloud and Cliff, 1889; The Red Mountain of Alaska, 1889; Forest Home Series (5 vols.), 1889; The Lion City of Africa, 1890; In the Morning (verse), 1890; John Brownlow's Folks, 1891; The Boyhood of John Kent, 1891; Gulf and Glacier, 1892; Lost on Umbagog, 1894; Snowed In, 1894; The Mammoth Hunters, 1895; Son of Liberty, 1896; Called to the Front, 1897; Great Island, 1897; Around the Yule Log, 1898; Cleared for Action, 1898; Navy Blue, 1898; Pineboro Quartette, 1898; The Head of Pasht, 1900; Play Away, 1902; Under the Pine Tree Flag, 1902; Sword and Ploughshare, 1904; The North Pacific, 1905; Gold Hunter of Alaska (2d edit.), 1906; The Violet Book, 1909. Home: Boston, Mass. Died Sept. 9, 1938.

ALLERTON, Samuel Waters, capitalist; b. Amenia Union, Duchess Co., N.Y., May 26, 1828; reared on farm; ed. common schs.; dealer in live stock in N.Y., 1852-56; then in Chicago; has extensive interests in the stock yards at Chicago, Omaha, St. Louis, Pittsburgh, Phila., Jersey City and Baltimore; also owns 40,000 acres of stock farms; dir. Allerton-Clarke Co., Arcade File Works, Chicago City Ry. Co., 1st Nat. Bank, etc. Dir. Chicago Expn., 1893; candidate for mayor of Chicago, 1893. Republican. Home: Chicago, Ill. Died Feb. 22, 1914.

ALLEY, James Pinckney, cartoonist; b. nr. Benton, Ark., Jan. 11, 1885; s. Rev. John Pinckney and Melinda Catherine (Everett) A.; ed. pub. sch. Benton; m. Nona Lane, Dec. 1908; children—Nona Elizabeth, Jessie Kathryn, James Pinckney, Calvin Lane, Richard Wesley (dec.). Cartoonist Commercial Appeal, Memphis, 1916—; known for "Hambone's Meditations" (syndicated), also in book form, 1917, 19; author of most widely published cartoon, presidential campaign of 1924; author of "Distinguished Folks," 1928. Democrat. Methodist. Home: Memphis, Tenn. Died Apr. 16, 1934.

ALLIN, Arthur, psychologist, educator; b. Utica, Ont., Dec. 1, 1869; s. William and Rosamond A.; grad. Victoria Univ., Toronto, 1892; studied psychology, Heidelberg, Berlin, Breslau, Paris, London, and Clark U., Worcester, Mass.; (Ph.D., Berlin, 1895); m. Alberta Mabel Carey, June, 1899. Prof. psychology and edn., Ohio U., 1895-96, U. of Colo., 1897—; editor Investigations of Dept. Psychology and Education 1901—. Pres. Ednl. Council of Colo., 1901-02. Author: Ueber das Grundprincip der Association, 1895 (Berlin). Home: Boulder, Colo. Died 1903.

ALLIN, Cephas Daniel, coll. prof.; b. Clinton, Ont., Can., Aug. 18, 1875; s. Rev. Roger and Jane (Williams) A.; A.B., U. of Toronto, 1897, LL.B., 1899; A.M., Harvard, 1900; U. of Berlin, 1903; U. of Oxford (Oriel Coll.), 1904; m. Martha W. Washburn, July 30, 1913. Instr. polit. science, Leland Stanford Jr. U., 1902-03; instr. history, Queen's U., Can., 1906-07; instr. polit. science, 1907-09; asst. prof., 1910-13, asso. prof., 1913-15, prof., 1915-17, prof. public law, 1917-19, Law Sch., chmn. Dept. Polit. Science, 1920—, U. of Minn. Author: The Early Federation Movement of Australia, 1907; Annexation, Preferential Trade and Reciprocity, 1911; The Tariff Relations of the Australian Colonies, 1917. Home: Minneapolis, Minn. Died Oct. 23, 1927.

ALLING, Asa Alling, lawyer; b. New York, May 4, 1862; grad. Cornell, 1883 (Ph.B.); Columbia Law School, 1885 (LL.B.); m. Louise Floyd-Smith, Jan. 20, 1894. In active practice as corp. lawyer; counsel for trust companies and banks; earlier, lecturer on American statesmen and contbr. to papers and publs.; active as political speaker; gold-standard Democrat. Home: New York, N.Y. Died 1900.

ALLING, John Wesley, lawyer; b. Orange, Conn., Oct. 24, 1841; s. Charles Wyllys and Lucy (Booth) A.; A.B., Yale, 1862, A.M., 1864; m. Constance Adelaide Parker, Oct. 10, 1867 (died Jan. 11, 1903); children— Arnon Augustus, Mrs. Agatha Durland; m. 2d, Margaret Thompson, Jan. 25, 1906. Admitted to bar, 1864; pros. atty. City of New Haven, 1871-73; mem. Alling, Webb & Morehouse 45 yrs. (retired); pres. Security Ins. Co., New Haven, Oct. 1906—; pres., 1908-17, chmn. bd., Jan. 1917—, Southern N.E. Telephone Co.; dir. Merchants Nat. Bank, New Haven, United Illuminating Co., Conn. Ry. & Lighting Co. Republican. Episcopalian. Home: New Haven, Conn. Died Jan. 9, 1927.

ALLING, Joseph Tilden, merchant, mfr.; b. Rochester, N.Y., Jan. 19, 1855; s. William and Clementine Lyman (Tilden) A.; grad. Rochester Free Acad., 1872; A.B., U. of Rochester, 1876, A.M., 1884; m. Rose Lattimore, June 23, 1881; children—Harold Lattimore, Eric Lattimore. Began as partner firm Alling & Cory, paper mchts., Rochester, 1880; pres. Alling & Cory Co., Rochester, 1908-35; chmn. bd. dirs. The Alling & Cory Co., 1935—; dir. Lincoln Alliance Bank, Rochester Capital Corp. Mem. Nat. War Work Council, Y.M.C.A., 1917-19, gen. sec. Camp Dix, N.J., 1917-18, sec. France, 1918, mem. Internat. Com., 1920—; pres. Am. Red Cross, Rochester, 1917. Pres. Nat. Paper Trade Assn., 1914-16; trustee U. of Rochester (treas. 1903-16, 1st v.p., chmn. exec. and finance coms.; chmn. bd. 1932), Rochester Community Chest. Pres. Rochester Y.M.C.A., 1891-97, N.Y. State Y.M.C.A., 1894, Rochester Fedn. of Chs., 1920-21, etc. Decorated Order of St. Sava (Jugoslavia), 1931. Republican. Presbyn. Mason (32°, K.T.). Home: Rochester, N.Y. Died Sept. 20, 1937.

ALLINSON, Anne Crosby Emery (Mrs. Francis Greenleaf Allinson); b. Ellsworth, Me., Jan. 1, 1871; d. Lucilius Alonzo Emery and Anne S. (Crosby) Emery; A.B., Bryn Mawr Coll., 1892, Ph.D., 1896; U. of Leipzig, 1893-94; Litt.D., Bowdoin, 1911, and Brown, 1916; m. Prof. Francis Greenleaf Allinson, Aug. 22, 1905. Dean of women and asst. prof. classical philology, U. of Wis., 1897-1900; dean Women's Coll., Brown U., 1900-05; acting dean Women's College, same, 1920-21, and one semester 1922-23. Author of the daily "Disstaff," Providence Evening Bulletin, 1926—. Alumnæ dir. Bryn Mawr Coll., 1906-08. Author: Greek Lands and Letters (with husband), 1909, 12, and 13; Roads from Rome, 1913, 22; Children of the Way, 1923; Friends with Life, 1925. Home: Providence, R.I. Died Aug. 16, 1932.

ALLINSON, Francis Greenleaf, coll. prof.; b. Burlington, N.J., Dec. 16, 1856; s. William J. and Rebecca W. (Hinchman) A.; A.B. Haverford, 1876, A.M., 1879; A.B., Harvard, 1877; fellow Johns Hopkins, 1877-80, Ph.D., 1880; hon. A.M., Williams, 1895; Litt.D., U. of Wis., 1922, Trinity, 1922; m. Mary Irwin Carey, Sept. 10, 1885; 1 dau., Susanne Carey (Mrs. Henry Crosby Emery); m. 2d, Anne Crosby Emery, Aug. 22, 1905. Asst. prof. Greek and Latin, Haverford Coll., 1880-82; head master classics, Univ. Sch., Baltimore, 1882-91; asst. prof. Greek and Latin, Williams Coll., 1892-95; asso. prof. Greek and classical philology, 1895-98, prof. classical philology, 1898-1915, prof. Greek lit. and history, 1915-28, Brown Univ. Annual prof. Am. Sch. Classical Studies, Athens, Greece, 1910-11, mem. mng. com., 1913—; Sather lecturer on classical lit., U. of Cal., Aug.-Dec. 1917. Trustee Providence Pub. Library, 1904—. Author: Greek Prose Composition, 1895; Lucian (selections), 1905; Greek Lands and Letters (with A. C. E. Allinson), 1909, 12 and 13; Menander (Loeb Classical Library, London), 1921; Lucian—Satirist and Artist, 1926. Home: Providence, R.I. Died June 23, 1931.

ALLIOT, Hector, archeologist; b. Chateau des Forestiers, Gironde, France, Nov. 20, 1862; s. Jehan Hector and Lelia (Boymier) A.; ed. Lycée Bordeaux; Acad. of Medicine, Sch. of Tech., Montpelier (France); A.B., U. of France; D.Sc., U. of Lombardy; m. Laurena Moore, Aug. 20, 1893. Associated with Farah Pasha in explorations at Tyre, Asia Minor, 1891; dir. Cliff Dwellers exploration, Chicago Expn., 1893; prof. art history, U. of Southern Calif., 1908-09; dir. Southwest Mus., Nov. 1, 1909—. Trustee Los Angeles Sch. of Art and Design; v.p. Southern Calif. Acad. Sciences; sec. Los Angeles Soc. Archæol. Inst. America; sec.-treas. Hispanic Soc. of Calif. Officier d'Académie, 1907; Knight Comdr. O. of M. (P.M.), 1910; officer de l'Instruction Publique, 1913. Deviser of Metrical Color Standard, Marine Colormeter, 1910; del. Internat. Congress Geog., Rome, 1911. Author: Bibliography of Arizona. Home: Los Angeles, Calif. Died Feb. 15, 1919.

ALLIS, Oscar Huntington, surgeon; b. Holley, N.Y., Sept. 9, 1836; s. William and Maria (Jones) A.; A.B., Lafayette Coll., Easton, Pa., 1864, A.M., 1866 (LL.D., 1914); m. Julia W. Thompson, 1877 (died 1912). Interne, Blockley Gen. Hosp. Phila., 1866-67; practiced in Phila., 1868—; formerly surgeon to Howard, Jefferson Med. Coll., and Presbyn. hosps.; cons. surgeon to Presbyn. and Roosevelt hosps.; Mütter lecturer, Coll. Physicians of Phila., 1888, 1906; Lane lecturer, Cooper Med. Coll., San Francisco, 1903. Awarded Gross prize ($1,000) for brochure, "Obstacles to the Reduction of Dislocations of the Hip." Republican. Presbyn. Home: Philadelphia, Pa. Died May 16, 1921.

ALLISON, James Nicholls, brig. gen. U.S.A.; b. Catlettsburg, Ky., Sept. 4, 1848; s. James Willetts and Mary McClellan (Boal) A.; ed. pub. schs., Ironton, O., to 1863, and from close of Civ. War to 1867; grad. U.S. Mil. Acad., 1871; m. Susan Whalley, May 12, 1887. Served as pvt. 39th Ky. Inf., Aug. 10, 1863-June 3, 1865; advanced through the grades to col., asst. commissary gen., Oct. 13, 1907; brig. gen., retired after 46 yrs. service, June 7, 1912. Sec. Mil. Service Instn. of U.S., and editor Journal same; sr. v.comdr. N.Y. Commandery Loyal Legion; sr. v.comdr. George Washington Post, G.A.R. (New York). Died May 2, 1918.

ALLISON, Nathaniel, surgeon; b. St. Louis, Mo., May 22, 1876; s. James W. and Addie (Shultz) A.; Harvard Coll., 1900; M.D., Harvard Medical Sch., 1901; m. Marion Aldrich, 1909. Practiced at St. Louis, 1903-23; formerly asso. surgeon St. Louis Children's Hosp. and Barnes Hosp.; dean and prof. orthopedic surgery, Washington U., 1919-23; later prof. orthopedic surgery, Harvard Med. Sch.; became prof. surgery U. of Chicago, in charge Div. Orthopedic Surgery; was chief of orthopedic service, Mass. Gen. Hosp., Boston; chief surgeon N.E. Peabody Home for Crippled Children. Fellow Am. Acad. Arts and Letters. Awarded D.S.M. for services as chief of orthopedic surgery, First Army, A.E.F., 1917-19. Presbyn. Home: Chicago, Ill. Died Aug. 30, 1931.

ALLISON, William Boyd, senator; b. Perry, O., Mar. 2, 1829; s. John and Mary A.; ed. Allegheny Coll., Pa., and Western Reserve Coll., O.; admitted to bar, 1850; m. Anna Carter, Feb., 1854. Practiced in Ohio, 1850-57; removed to Dubuque, Ia., 1857; del. Rep. State Conv., 1859, Nat. Rep. Conv., Chicago, 1860; mem. gov.'s staff and raised troops for Civil War, 1861; mem. Congress, 1863-71; U.S. senator, Ia., 1873-1909. Candidate for presdl. nomination, Nat. Rep. Conv., 1888, 96. Home: Dubuque, Ia. Died 1908.

ALLISON, William Henry, historiographer; b. Somerville, Mass., Aug. 17, 1870; s. George Augustus and Julia Lucinda (Powers) A.; A.B., Harvard, 1893; Newton Theol. Instn., 1896, B.D., 1902; U. of Halle, 1896-97; U. of Chicago, 1902-05, Ph.D., 1905; m. Elizabeth Lincoln Smith, Sept. 6, 1899 (died 1900); m. 2d, Emily Mills, July 31, 1905; 1 dau., Elizabeth Mills (Mrs. Albert E. Bailey, Jr.). Ordained Baptist ministry, 1896; pastor Penacook Ch., Concord, N.H., 1899-1902; acting prof. ch. history, Pacific Theol. Sem., 1904-05; prof. history and polit. science, Franklin (Ind.) Coll., 1905-08; head of dept. of history, Bryn Mawr Coll., Pa., 1908-10; prof. ecclesiastical history and dean Theol. Sem., Aug. 1910-15, prof. ecclesiastical history, 1910-28, Colgate U.; prof. emeritus of ch. history, Colgate-Rochester Div. Sch., 1928—. Consultant in ch. history, Library of Congress, 1930—. Republican. Author: Baptist Councils in America, 1906; Inventory of Unpublished Manuscript Material relating to American Religious History (pub. by Carnegie Inst.), 1911. Home: Washington, D.C. Died Sept. 1941.

ALLPORT, Frank, ophthalmologist, otologist; b. Watertown, N.Y., Feb. 22, 1857; s. Walter Webb and Sarah M. (Haddock) A.; ed. at Chicago U. and Racine Coll.; M.D., Chicago Med. Coll., 1876; U. of Heidelberg, 2 yrs.; LL.D., Notre Dame U.; m. Kate A. Ellwood, Oct. 26, 1880; m. 2d, Susannah Flint, 1926. Practiced medicine, Sycamore, Ill., 5 years; specializing in ophthalmology and otology, Minneapolis, 10 years, then in Chicago. Served as prof. clin. ophthalmology and otology, U. of Minn., several yrs., later at Northwestern U.; was eye and ear surgeon St. Luke's Hosp. Appointed 1st lt. Medical R.C., Feb. 1911. Home: Nice, France. Died Aug. 2, 1935.

ALLWARDT, Henry Augustus, clergyman; b. Mecklenburg, Germany, Mar. 2, 1840; s. John and Elisabeth (Weisshahn) A.; ed. pub. schs. Cattaraugus Co., N.Y.; Practical Theol. Sem. of Evang. Luth. Synod of Mo. and Other States, Ft. Wayne, Ind., 1859-60; grad. Concordia Coll., St. Louis, 1862; Concordia Theol. Sem., St. Louis, 1862-65; (D.D., Capital U., Columbus, O., 1900); m. Katharine Kalbfleisch, Nov. 11, 1866. Pastor in Luth. Ch. from Aug. 5, 1865; mem. Evang. Luth. Synod of Mo., Ohio and Other States, 1865-81; withdrew on account of "Predestination" controversy; mem. Evang. Luth. Joint Synod of Ohio and Adjacent States. Pastor Germania, Marquette Co., Wis., 1865-74; Lebanon, Wis., 1874—. Pres. bd. trustees Practical Theol. Luther Sem., St. Paul, Minn. Democrat. Author: A Testimony Against the False Doctrine of Predestination Recently Introduced by the Missouri Synod (with Henry Ernst), 1883. Home: Watertown, Wis. Died 1910.

ALMON, Edward Berton, congressman; b. Moulton, Ala., Apr. 18, 1860; s. George W. and Nancy (Eubank) A.; grad. State Normal Coll., Florence, Ala.; LL.B., U. of Ala., 1883; m. Luie Clopper, Dec. 13, 1887; children—Mrs. Lottie Ryder, Clopper. Admitted to Ala. bar, 1883, and practiced in Tuscumbia; mem. Ala. Senate, 1892-96, Ho. of Rep., 1911 (speaker of House); Dem. presdl. elector, 1896; judge 11th Jud. Circuit, Ala., 1898-1906; mem. 64th to 72d Congresses (1915-33), 8th Ala. Dist. Methodist. Mason. Home: Tuscumbia, Ala. Died June 22, 1933.

ALMY, Frederic, social worker; b. New Bedford, Mass., Nov. 28, 1858; s. Charles and Mary (Cummings) A.; A.B., Harvard Univ., 1880, A.M., 1883; Harvard U. Law Sch., 1882-84; admitted to bar, 1885, and practiced in Buffalo, N.Y.; unmarried. Secretary Buffalo Civil Service Reform Assn., 1886-1911, Buffalo Charity Orgn. Soc., 1894-1921. Mem. Council Nat. Civil Service Reform League, 1905-17; exec. com. Nat. Municipal League, 1907-10; trustee George Junior Republic, 1898-1914; pres. Nat. Conf. of Social Work, 1916-17. Home: Buffalo, N.Y. Died Aug. 24, 1935.

ALPERS, William Charles, chemist; b. Harburg, Germany, July 7, 1851; s. Julius and Elise (Nonnenkamp) A.; B.Sc., Poly. Inst. Hanover, Germany; studied U. of Göttingen; came to America, 1872; D.Sc., New York U., 1890; m. Bertha Guder, Oct. 29, 1885 (dec.); m. 2d, Miss M. Van Damm, 1910. Pharmacist, Bayonne, N.J., 1879-97; conductor Merck's Chem. and Bacteriol. Lab., 1897-99; pres. Alpers Chem. Co., 1901—, Alpers Pharmacy, 1902. Dean Sch. of Pharmacy, Western Reserve U., 1913—. Mem. N.J. State Bd. Pharmacy, 1893-97. Author: The Pharmacist at Work; The Medicinal Plants of Staten Island. Home: Cleveland, O. Died 1917.

ALSBERG, C(arl) Lucas, biochemist; b. New York, N.Y., Apr. 2, 1877; s. Meinhard and Bertha (Baruch) A.; A.B., Columbia, 1896, A.M., 1900; M.D., Coll. of Phys. and Surg. (Columbia), 1900; univs. of Strassburg and Berlin, Germany, 1900-03; m. Emma B. Peebles. Asst. in physiol. chem., 1902-05, instr. in biol. chem., 1905-08, Harvard; chem. biologist Bur. Plant Industry, 1908-12, chief Bur. Chem., 1912-21, U.S. Dept. Agr.; dir. Stanford Food Research Inst., 1921-37, consultant, 1937—; dean of grad. study, Stanford, 1927-33; dir. Giannini Foundation of Agrl. Economics, U. of California. Investigator U.S. Bureau of Fisheries, 1906-08. Home: Berkeley, Calif. Died Nov. 1, 1940.

ALSCHULER, Alfred S., architect; b. Chicago, Ill., Nov. 2, 1876; s. Samuel and Fannie (Guggenheimer) A.; M.S., Armour Inst. Tech., 1899; studied Art Inst. Chicago, 1899; m. Rose Haas, Dec. 17, 1907; children—Marian, Frances, Alfred S., Jr., Richard H., John. Began architectural work in firm Dankmar Adler, Chicago, 1899; mem. Treat & Alschuler, 1904-07, alone from 1907; designed London Guarantee and Accident, Westminster, Cunard, John R. Thompson, John Sexton, Utilities, Lake Michigan, Mercantile Exchange, Adams Franklin and Garment Center buildings, plants of E. J. Brach & Son, Chicago Mail Order, Sinai Temple, Isaiah Temple—all in Chicago. Trustee Armour Inst.; treas. Hadley Correspondence Sch. for the Blind. Mason. Home: Winnetka, Ill. Died Nov. 6, 1940.

ALSCHULER, Samuel, judge; b. Chicago, Ill., Nov. 20, 1859; s. Jacob and Caroline (Stiefel) A.; family moved to Aurora, Ill., 1861; ed. Aurora High Sch.; m. Ella Kahn, Mar. 5, 1923. Was admitted to bar, 1881; practiced at Aurora, 1881-1901, Chicago, 1901-15; mem. Kraus (Adolf), Alschuler & Holden, 1901-15. Dem. candidate for Congress, 1892; mem. State Commn. of Claims, 1893-96; mem. Ill. Ho. of Rep., 1896-1900; Dem. candidate for gov., Ill., 1900; judge U.S. Circuit Court of Appeals, Aug. 16, 1915-May 15, 1936. Apptd. by President Harding mem. U.S. Coal Commn., 1922; apptd. arbitrator between packers and their employes, Feb. 7, 1918, by U.S. sec. of labor. Home: Chicago, Ill. Died Nov. 9, 1939.

ALSTON, Robert Cotten, lawyer; b. Barbour County, Ala., Apr. 30, 1873; s. Augustus Holmes and Anna (Ott) A.; A.B., U. of Ala., 1890, LL.D., 1928; LL.B., Atlanta Law School, 1893; D.C.L., U. of the South, 1918; LL.D., Atlanta Law School, 1926; m. Caro Lamar du Bignon, Jan. 1, 1900. Practiced, Atlanta, 1893—; was mem. Tompkins & Alston (Judge Henry B. Tompkins) until 1903, then mem. McDaniel, Alston & Black; mem. Robert C. & Philip H. Alston, 1911-21, Alston, Alston, Foster & Moise, 1921—. Democrat. Home: Atlanta, Ga. Died Feb. 4, 1938.

ALSTORK, John Wesley, bishop; b. Talladega, Ala., Sept. 1, 1852; s. Rev. Frank and Mary Jane A.; ed. Talladega Coll.; (D.D., Livingstone [N.C.] Coll., 1892; LL.D., Princeton [Ind.] Coll., 1908); m. Mamie M. Lawson, May 26, 1872. Ordained A.M.E. Zion ministry, 1882; financial sec. Ala. Conf., 1884-92, A.M.E. Zion Connection, 1892-1900; presiding elder, 1889-1900; elected bishop, May 14, 1900. Del. Ecumenical Conf., London, 1901, Toronto, 1911. Mem. Am. Fedn. of Chs., Southern Sociol. Congress. Mason. Home: Montgomery, Ala. Died July 23, 1920.

ALTER, George Elias, lawyer; b. Springdale, Pa., May 8, 1868; s. Elias and Martha (Ferson) A.; ed. pub. schs.; (LL.D., Lafayette, 1921); read law in office of William Yost, Pittsburgh; m. Diana J. Swanton, Sept. 11, 1902; children—Georgia (dec.), Diana (dec.), Kathleen E., Helen Martha (dec.), Frances E., Geo. E., Jr., David S. Admitted to Pa. bar, 1893, and began practice at Pittsburgh; mem. Pa. Ho. of Rep., 1908-14 (speaker 1913-14); atty. gen. of Pa., term Dec. 14, 1920-Jan. 16, 1923; mem. Alter, Wright & Barron. Republican. Methodist. Home: Pittsburgh, Pa. Died Aug. 18, 1940.

ALTGELD, John Peter, gov. Ill.; b. Germany, Dec. 1847; brought to U.S. when 3 months old, his parents settling nr. Mansfield, O.; ed. in public schools; entered Union army as private at 16; fought until close of war; taught school and studied law in Mo.; admitted to Mo. bar, 1869; elected State's atty., Andrew County, Mo., 1874; resigned, 1875, and moved to Chicago; unsuccessful candidate for Congress, 1884; judge superior court, Chicago, 1886-91; gov. Ill., 1893-97; his pardon of Fielden, Schwab and Neebe, known as "the anarchists," excited wide comment. Prominent advocate of free coinage of silver; Democrat; independent candidate for mayor of Chicago, 1899, defeated. Author: Our Penal Machinery and Its Victims; Live Questions, etc. Home: Chicago, Ill. Died 1902.

ALTHOUSE, Harry Witman, mining engr.; b. Pottsville, Pa., June 14, 1867; s. Daniel Seidel and Clara Marstella (Witman) A.; ed. public schs.; unmarried. In employ Phila. & Reading Coal & Iron Co., 1886-90; with Consolidated Coal Co., St. Louis, Mo., 1890-92; later with Collins Colliery Co., Louisville Coal & Coke Co., etc.; in practice as engr. and geologist, 1904—. Home: Pottsville, Pa. Deceased.

ALTSHELER, Joseph Alexander, author; b. Three Springs, Ky., Apr. 29, 1862; s. Joseph and Lucy (Snoddy) A.; student Liberty Coll., and Vanderbilt U.; m. Sarah Boles, May 30, 1888. On staff Louisville Courier-Journal, 1885-92, New York World, 1892—. Author: The Sun of Saratoga, 1897; A Soldier of Manhattan, 1897; A Herald of the West, 1898; The Last Rebel, 1899; In Circling Camps, 1900; In Hostile Red, 1900; The Wilderness Road, 1901; My Captive, 1902; Before the Dawn, 1903; Guthrie of The Times, 1904; The Candidate, 1905; The Young Trailers, 1907; The Forest Runners, 1908; The Recovery, 1909; The Free Rangers, 1909; The Last of the Chiefs, 1909; The Riflemen of the Ohio, 1910; The Horsemen of the Plains, 1910; The Scouts of the Valley, 1911; The Quest of the Four, 1911; The Border Watch, 1912; The Texan Star, 1912; The Texan Scouts, 1913; The Texan Triumph, 1913; Apache Gold, 1913; The Guns of Bull Run, 1914; The Guns of Shiloh, 1914; The Scouts of Stonewall, 1914; The Sword of Antietam, 1914; The Star of Gettysburg, 1915; The Rock of Chickamauga, 1915; The Guns of Europe, 1915; The Forest of Swords, 1915; The Hosts of the Air, 1915; The Shades of the Wilderness, 1916; The Keepers of the Trail, 1916; The Tree of Appomattox, 1916; The Hunters of the Hills, 1916; The Shadow of the North, 1917; The Eyes of the Woods, 1917; The Rulers of the Lakes, 1917. Home: New York, N.Y. Died June 5, 1919.

ALVERSON, Claude B., judge; b. town of Hounsfield, Jefferson County, N.Y., July 19, 1878; s. Samuel and Fannie E. (Phelps) A.; grad. Albany Law Sch., 1905; m. Grace P. Hilliker, Sept. 27, 1907. Began practice at Watertown, N.Y., 1905; dist. atty. Jefferson County, 1911-17; county judge Jefferson County, 1918-20; justice Supreme Court of N.Y., 5th Dist., term, 1921-35. Republican. Mason (32°, K.T.), Shriner, Odd Fellow, Elk. Home: Dexter, N.Y. Died Dec. 23, 1922.

ALVEY, Richard Henry, chief justice court of appeals, D.C., Apr. 1893—; b. southern Md., Mar. 1826; ed. St. Mary's County, Md.; m. Julia Hays, 1862. In clerk's office, Charles County, Md., 1844-50; admitted to bar, 1849; moved to Western Md. and engaged in practice at Hagerstown, 1850; one of Pierce presdl. electors, 1852; mem. Md. State Constl. Conv., 1867. Home: Hagerstown, Md. Died 1906.

ALVORD, Benjamin, army officer; b. Wash., May 15, 1860; s. Brig. Gen. Benjamin A. (U.S. Army); grad. U.S. Mil. Acad., 1882. Inf. and Cav. Sch., Ft. Leavenworth, Kan., 1887. Commd. 2d lt. 20th Inf., June 13, 1882; advanced through the ranks to brig. gen. and adj. gen. A.E.F., France, 1917. Died Apr. 13, 1927.

ALVORD, Clarence Walworth, univ. prof.; b. Greenfield, Mass., May 21, 1868; s. Daniel Wells and Caroline Betts (Dewey) A.; A.B., Williams Coll., 1891; U. of Berlin, 1893-95; U. of Chicago, 2 quarters, 1895; Ph.D., U. of Ill., 1908; m. Jennie Kettell Blanchard (née Parrott), July 25, 1893 (died Sept. 12, 1911); 1 dau., Genevieve; m. 2d, Idress Head, Apr. 10, 1913. Instr. Milton (Mass.) Acad., 1891-93; instr. Prep. Sch., U. of Ill., 1897-1901; instr. in history, 1901-06, asso., 1906-07, asst. prof., 1907-09, asso. prof., 1909-13, prof., 1913-20, U. of Ill.; prof. history U. of Minn., 1920-23. Gen. editor Ill. Hist. Collections, 1906-20; mng. editor Miss. Valley Hist. Review, 1914-23; editor-in-chief Ill. Centennial History. Unitarian. Author: Mississippi Valley in British Politics (2 vols.), 1917 (awarded Loubat prize, 1917); The Illinois Country, 1919. Contbr. to numerous periodicals. Died Jan. 27, 1928.

ALVORD, Henry Elijah, organized 1895, and from then chief Dairy Div., U.S. Dept. of Agr.; b. Greenfield, Mass., Mar. 11, 1844; s. late Hon. Daniel Wells A.; studied at Norwich Univ. (B.S., 1863; C.E., LL.D.); served as private U.S.V., 1862, to maj. 2d Mass. cav., 1865; capt. regular army, 1866-72; m. Martha Scott Swink, Sept. 6, 1866. Farmed and taught agr. in Va., N.Y., Mass., Md. and N.H.; prof. agr. Mass. Agrl. Coll., 1885-87; pres. Md. Agrl. Coll., 1887-92; pres. Assn. of Am. Agrl. colleges and Expt. Stations, 1894-95; mem. Internat. Jury (and v.p. class 40), Universal Expn., Paris, 1900; mem. Standing Commn. for Internat. Agrl. Congress. Author: Am. chapters of "Dairy Farming," 1881. Home: Lewinsville, Fairfax County, Va. Died 1904.

AMBLER, Benjamin Mason, lawyer; b. Winchester, Va., Jan. 14, 1850; s. Rev. John and Anna Maria (Mason) A.; grad. U. of Va. in several schools, 1871; m. Nannie Baker, Nov. 17, 1875; children—Mason Gaither, Mrs. Anna A. Moss, Mrs. Katherine A. Crawford. Admitted to bar, 1874; settled at Parkersburg; formed partnership with W. W. Van Winkle, 1875, as Van Winkle & Ambler; later Ambler, McCluer & Ambler; city atty. Parkersburg, 1879-81; admitted to Supreme Ct., U.S., 1882. Episcopalian. Chancellor of Diocese of W.Va. Democrat. Home: Parkersburg, W.Va. Deceased.

AMBRUSTER, Watson, journalist; b. Phila., Pa., Aug. 19, 1842; ed. Pennington Sem., N.J.; Chester Acad., Pa.; Univ. of Mich., 1859-62, law dept., 1862-64; admitted to bar but never practiced. On staff of Phila. Evening Telegraph, 1866— (city editor, 1866-67; mng. editor, 1868-97; editor-in-chief, Apr. 1897—). Home: Germantown, Pa. Died 1904.

AMEN, Harlan Page, academy prin.; b. Sinking Spring, Highland County, O., Apr. 14, 1853; s. Daniel and Sarah J. (Barber) A.; student Phillips Exeter Acad., 1872-75; A.B., Harvard, 1879; (hon. A.M., Williams, 1886; Litt.D., Dartmouth, 1911). Instr. classics, mathematics and English, 1879-82, instr. Latin and Greek and joint prin. and propr., 1882-95, Riverview Acad., Poughkeepsie, N.Y.; prin., 1895—, prof. Latin, 1895-99, Phillips Exeter Acad., Exeter, N.H. Home: Exeter, N.H. Died Nov. 9, 1913.

AMEND, Edward Bernard, judge; b. New York, N.Y., June 2, 1858; A.B., St. Francis Xavier Coll., 1877, A.M., 1878; LL.B., Columbia, 1879; married. Admitted to bar, 1879; practiced at N.Y. City, 1879-1903, justice Supreme Ct., N.Y., 1st Dist., for term Jan. 1, 1903-Dec. 31, 1916. Democrat. Home: New York, N.Y. Died Oct. 20, 1914.

AMENT, James E., educator, farmer, banker; b. Woodburn, Ill.; s. Rev. James Roe and Emily (Dodson) A.; g.g.s. Thomas Metcalfe, U.S. senator, and 10th gov. of Ky.; grad. Ill. Normal U.; LL.D., Transylvania U.; Ph.D., Oskaloosa Coll.; m. Teresa Catherine Welch, of Canada. Was supt. schs., Carroll, Ia., and Rock Island, Ill.; later pres. state teachers colls., Okla., Mo., Indiana, Pa. Inspected secondary and collegiate schs. in Eng., Scotland, France, Germany and Switzerland, and independent student of univ. adminstrn. in U.S. Elected pres. for life, 1916, National Park Sem., Washington, D.C. Founder and life mem. Congressional Country Club. Knight Order of the Holy Sepulchre (Jerusalem). Mem. Ch. of Disciples. Mason (32°). Home: Forest Glen, Md. Died Aug. 1936.

AMERMAN, Ralph Alonzo, banker; b. Scranton, Pa., May 19, 1884; s. Lemuel and Mary (Van Nort) A.; prep. edn., Hill Sch., Pottstown, Pa., and Worcester (Mass.) Acad.; student Cornell U., 1903-04; m. Ada May Wrightnour, Apr. 13, 1905; children—Jean, Ralph. Began in 1904 with Spring Brook Water Supply Co.; gen. agt. for Buick, northeastern Pa., 1906-18; gen. mgr. Scranton Glass Instrument Co., 1919-23; v.p. Lincoln Trust Co., 1923-26, chmn. bd., 1926-28; pres. Dime Bank-Lincoln Trust Co., 1928-32;

v.p. First Nat. Bank of Scranton, 1932—; pres. Lincoln Realty Co. Business mgr., later divisional sec., Y.M.C.A., A.E.F., France, 1 yr. Trustee Keystone Junior Coll., Bucknell U., Scranton Community Welfare Assn. Republican. Presbyn. Mason. Home: Scranton, Pa. Died June 4, 1941.

AMES, Charles Bismark, lawyer; b. Macon, Miss., Aug. 1, 1870; s. Charles Bingle and Sarah Jane (Longstreet) A.; B.S., Emory and Henry Coll., 1890; LL.B., U. of Miss., 1892; LL.D., Emory and Henry Coll., 1924; m. Elizabeth P. Allen, Feb. 6, 1894; children—Ben Allen, Elizabeth (Mrs. J. L. Cleveland, Jr.), Charles B., Fisher, Longstreet. Practiced law at Macon, 1893-99; settled at Oklahoma City, 1899; presiding judge of Div. No. 1 of Supreme Court Commn. of Okla., Sept. 1, 1911-Mar. 1, 1913, resigned; mem. Okla. State Council Defense, federal food adminstr. for Okla., and chmn. Okla. City Liberty Loan Com. World War; asst. to the atty. gen. U.S., June 1919-Sept. 1920 (resigned); gen. counsel and dir. of The Texas Co., Mar. 1923-Nov. 1925, with offices in New York (resigned); v.p. and dir. The Texas Corp., Jan. 1, 1928-Nov. 1932, chmn. bd.; pres. Am. Petroleum Inst., Nov. 1932-May 1933. Democrat. Home: New York, N.Y. Died July 21, 1935.

AMES, Charles Gordon, clergyman; b. Dorchester, Mass., Oct. 3, 1828; adopted s. Thomas and Lucy (Foster) A.; student Geauga Sem., Ohio, 1847-49; (D.D., Bates Coll., 1896); m. Sarah Jane Daniels, Mar. 28, 1850; m. 2d, Fanny Baker; father of Charles Wilberforce A. Ordained Free Bapt. ministry, 1849, Unitarian ministry, 1859; pastor Minneapolis, 1851-56, Bloomington, Ill., 1859-62, Albany, N.Y., 1863-65, California Missions, 1865-72, Germantown, Pa., 1872-77, Phila., 1880-88, Ch. of the Disciples, Boston, Jan. 1, 1889-1910, pastor emeritus, 1910—. Editor Minn. Republican, 1855-57, Christian Register, Boston, 1877-80. Author: George Eliot's Two Marriages, 1886; As Natural as Life, 1894; Sermons of Sunrise, 1901; Poems, 1898; Five Points of Faith, 1903; Living Largely, 1904. Home: Boston, Mass. Died Apr. 15, 1912.

AMES, Charles Wilberforce, publisher; b. Minneapolis, Minn., June 30, 1855; s. Charles Gordon (q.v.) and Sarah Jane (Daniels) A.; Litt.B., Cornell, 1878; m. Mary Lesley, June 25, 1883. Learned printer's trade in office of San José (Calif.) Mercury, 1869-71; engaged in ry. engring. and on Pa. State Geol. Survey, 1877-79; assisted his father, editing Christian Register, Boston, 1879-80; sec., v.p., pres., and, since 1899, gen. mgr. West Pub. Co. Pres. St. Paul Inst. Science and Letters, 1906-07, St. Paul Inst. Arts and Sciences, 1908-09, St. Paul Inst., 1910-12; pres. bd. trustees St. Paul Acad.; v.p. Am. Unitarian Assn. (Boston); v.p. Am. Fund for French Wounded; trustee Am. Fellowship in French Univs. (visited France in its interest, 1916). Awarded bronze medal of honor, and decorated Chevalier Legion of Honor by French Govt. Unitarian. Home: St. Paul, Minn. Died Apr. 4, 1921.

AMES, Eleanor Kirk (Mrs.), author; b. (Ellen M. Easterbrooks) Warren, R.I., Oct. 7, 1831. Author: Up Broadway; Periodicals That Pay Contributors; Information for Authors; Beecher as a Humorist; Influence of the Zodiac Upon Human Life; Perpetual Youth; Libra, or What the Stars Told Elizabeth; The Bottom Plank of Mental Healing; Where You Are. Publisher and editor Eleanor Kirk's Idea (mag.). Home: Brooklyn, Mass. Died 1908.

AMES, Herman Vandenburg, univ. prof.; b. Lancaster, Mass., Aug. 7, 1865; s. Rev. Marcus and Jane (Vandenburg) A.; A.B., Amherst, 1888; post-grad. student, Columbia, 1888-89; A.M., Harvard, 1890, Ph.D., 1891; Litt.D., Univ. of Pa., 1925; LL.D., La Salle College, Phila., 1927; taught history, Univ. of Mich., 1891-94; post-grad. Leipzig and Heidelberg, 1894-95; unmarried. Asst. prof. history, Ohio State U., 1896-97; instr. Am. constl. history, 1897-1903, asst. prof. Am. history, 1903-08, prof. Am. constl. history, 1908—, dean of Grad. Sch., 1907-28, U. of Pa. Taught Am. history, Columbia, summer session, 1906, 1907, U. of Wis., summer session, 1908, U. of California, summer session, 1927. Editor: State Documents on Federal Relations, The States and the United States. Author: The Proposed Amendments to the Constitution of the United States (awarded, 1897, prize of Am. Hist. Assn.); Outline of Lectures on American Political and Institutional History during the Colonial and Revolutionary Periods, 3d edit., 1908; Syllabus of American Colonial History (with Dr. W. T. Root), 1912. Home: Philadelphia, Pa. Died Feb. 7, 1935.

AMES, James Barr, dean Harvard Law School, 1895—; b. Boston, Mass., June 22, 1846; grad. Harvard, 1868 (A.M., 1871); Harvard Law Sch., 1872 (LL.D., U. City of New York, U. of Wis., 1898, U. of Pa., 1899, Northwestern, 1903, Williams, Harvard, 1904); m. Sarah Russell, June 29, 1880. Taught in pvt. sch., Boston, 1868-69; tutor in French and German, Harvard, 1871-72, instr. in history, 1872-73, asso. prof. of law, 1873-77, prof. law, 1877—, Harvard. Compiled collections of cases on torts, pleading, bills and notes, partnership, trusts, suretyship, admiralty and equity jurisdiction. Home: Cambridge, Mass. Died 1910.

AMES, John Griffith, librarian; b. East Dorset, Vt., Dec. 11, 1834; s. Benjamin and Lydia (Griffith) A.; A.B., Williams, 1858; grad. Theol. Sem., Ohio, 1863; m. Elizabeth, d. Hon. Columbus Delano, of Mt. Vernon, O., Oct. 4, 1864. Deacon, 1863, priest, 1864, P.E. Ch.; rector Ch. of the Redeemer, Morristown, N.J., 1864-66, Christ Ch., Springfield, O., 1867-70; head of House of Evangelists, New York, 1870-73; supt. documents, Dept. of the Interior, 1874-1908; librarian and minor canon Washington Cathedral, 1909—. Author: Report on Mission Indians of California, 1873; Comprehensive Index to Publications of U.S. Govt., 1889-93 and 1881-93; compiled Official Register of the U.S., 1875-93. Home: Mt. St. Alban, Washington. Died 1910.

AMES, John Ormsbee, cotton mfr.; b. Providence, R.I., Jan. 9, 1872; s. William and Harriette Fletcher (Ormsbee) A.; Mass. Inst. Tech., 1889-90; m. Madeleine Livermore Abbott, Nov. 27, 1900. Began 1890, as clk. with Fletcher Mfg. Co., and became sec., 1895, agt., 1902, treas., 1912; elected treas. Internat. Braid Co. 1912 (pres., 1921), Fletcher Mfg. Co. being absorbed by it; mem. firm Goddard Bros. Republican. Episcopalian. Home: Providence, R.I. Died Mar. 30, 1936.

AMES, Joseph Bushnell, author; b. Titusville, Pa., Aug. 9, 1878; s. Elias Hurlbut and Eleanor Gray (Bushnell) A.; student St. Mark's Sch., Southboro, Mass., 1893-95; grad. Stevens Prep. Sch., 1897; M.E., Stevens Inst. Tech., 1901; unmarried. With Lidgerwood Mfg. Co., New York, 1901-03, Public Service Gas Co., Jersey City, N.J., 1904-09. Republican. Episcopalian. Author: The Treasure of the Canyon, 1907; Pete, Cowpuncher, 1908; Under Boy Scout Colors, 1917; The Mystery of Ram Island, 1918; Curly of the Circle Bar, 1919; Curly and the Aztec Gold, 1920; Torrance from Texas, 1921; The Emerald Buddha, 1921; Shoe-Bar Stratton, 1922; The Man From Painted Post, 1923; Loudon From Laramie, 1925; Curly Graham, Cow Puncher, 1924; Clearport Boys, 1925; The Lone Hand, 1926; The Mounted Troop, 1926; The Stranger from Cheyenne, 1927; The Secret of Spirit Lake, 1927; Chaps and Chukkers, 1928; Flame of the Desert, 1928; also Moran of Saddle Butte, 1924, and The Valley of Missing Men, 1925 (under nom de plume of Lynn Gunnison). Home: Morristown, N.J. Died June 20, 1928.

AMES, Knowlton Lyman; pres. Booth Fisheries Co.; A.B., Princeton, 1890; m. Adelaide Schroeder. In investment business, Chicago, title of K. L. Ames & Co.; later pres. Booth Fisheries Co. Home: Chicago, Ill. Died Dec. 23, 1931.

AMES, Mary Lesley (Mrs. Charles W. Ames); b. Philadelphia, Pa.; d. J. Peter and Susan Inches (Lyman) Lesley; ed. pvt. schs.; m. Charles Wilberforce Ames, June 25, 1883. Asst. librarian Am. Philos. Soc., 1873-83. Pres. St. Paul Sch. of Fine Arts, 1907-08. Unitarian. Author: Life and Letters of Peter and Susan Lesley, 1909. Home: St. Paul, Minn. Died Feb. 22, 1929.

AMES, Oliver, mfr.; b. N. Easton, Mass., Oct. 21, 1864; s. Frederick Lothrop and Rebecca C. (Blair) A.; A.B., Harvard, 1886; m. Elise West, Dec. 3, 1890. V.p., treas. Oliver Ames & Sons Corp.; dir. C.&N.W. Ry. Co., U.P. R.R. Co., C.,St.P.,M.&O. R.R., Western Union Telegraph Co., and a number of other large corps. Republican. Unitarian. Home: North Easton, Mass., and Boston. Died June 18, 1929.

AMES, William, soldier, mfr.; b. Providence, R.I., May 15, 1842; s. Hon. Samuel and Mary T. (Dorr) A.; A.B., Brown U., 1863, A.M., by spl. vote, 1891; m. Henriette F. Ormsbee, Nov. 8, 1871 (died 1875); m. 2d, Mrs. Anne Ives Carrington Dwight, Apr. 27, 1882 (died 1904). Entered army as 2d lt. 2d R.I. Inf., June 5, 1861; advanced through grades to col., Oct. 10, 1864; bvtd. brig. gen. vols., Mar. 13, 1865, "for meritorious services during the war"; hon. mustered out, Aug. 27, 1865. Connected with Allen's Print Works, 1865-69; collector U.S. internal revenue, 1st R.I. dist., 1870-75; agt. and mgr. Fletcher Mfg. Co., Providence, 1875-1904, pres. and treas. same, 1904—; pres. Blackstone Canal Nat. Bank, 1877—. Mem. Providence Common Council, 1872-73; mem. R.I. Ho. of Rep., 1898-99; chmn. State House Commn. Republican. Home: Providence, R.I. Died Mar. 8, 1914.

AMES, Winthrop, theatrical producer; b. N. Easton, Mass., 1871; s. Oakes Angier and Catharine (Hobart) A.; A.B., Harvard, 1895; post-grad. work at Harvard, 1895-96; m. Lucy Fuller, 1911; children—Catharine Hobart, Joan. In editorial and gen. pub. work, spl. field of art, architectural books and mags. until 1904; mgr. Castle Square Theatre, Boston, 1904-08, dir. The New Theatre, New York, 1908-11; dir. The Little Theatre and Booth Theatre, both of New York. Mem. Nat. Inst. Arts and Letters. Republican. Unitarian. Home: N. Easton, Mass. Died Nov. 3, 1937.

AMIDON, Charles Fremont, judge; b. Clymer, N.Y., Aug. 17, 1856; s. John Smith and Charlotte A. (Curtis) A.; A.B., Hamilton Coll., 1882; m. Beulah R. McHenry, Nov. 15, 1892. Went to Fargo, N.D., 1882; admitted to bar, 1886; mem. commn. to revise code and statutes of N.D., 1893; U.S. Dist. judge, Dist. of N.D., 1896-1928, retired. Home: Fargo, N.D. Died Dec. 1937.

AMIDON, Samuel Barker, lawyer, banker; b. Perry, Lake Co., O., May 3, 1863; s. Henry Nelson and Marietta (Barker) A.; grad. Geneva (O.) Normal Sch., 1882; student Oberlin Coll. 1 yr., Hiram Coll. 1 yr.; m. Alice N. Noyes, Nov. 15, 1893. Began practice 1886; mem. Amidon & Conly, later mem. Amidon, Buckland, Hart & Porter; pres. First Nat. Bank (Mt. Hope, Kan.), Viola State Bank, Maize State Bank; v.p. Southwest State Bank (Wichita), Valley Center State Bank, etc.; pros. atty. Sedgwick Co., 1896-1900; mem. Dem. State Com., Kan., 1902-04; mem. Dem. Nat. Com., 1917— (vice-chmn. Mar. 1919—); asst. to atty. gen. of U.S. to assist in prosecution of I.W.W. cases in Kan., 1919—. Mem. Christian (Disciples) Ch. Mason. Home: Wichita, Kan. Died May 8, 1925.

AMIGER, William Thomas, clergyman, educator; b. Culpepper, Va., July 16, 1870; s. Rowland and Margaret (Alexander) A.; B.A., Lincoln U., Pa., 1899, A.M., S.T.B., 1902, D.D., 1909; student Newton Theol. Instn., 1902-03; LL.D., Central Law Sch. of Ky., 1912; m. Eleanor Green, Nov. 30, 1892. Ordained Bapt. ministry, 1903; pastor Third Ch. Springfield, Mass., 1903-08; pres. Simmons U., 1908-16; served as chaplain, lt. U.S.A., overseas, World War; supt. missions in Liberia and W. Africa, 1919-22; dean Am. Bapt. Theol. Sem., Nashville, 1924-27, pres., 1927—. Author: Emotion in Religion, 1916. Home: Nashville, Tenn. Died May 26, 1929.

AMMONS, Elias Milton, gov.; b. in Macon, Co., N.C., July 28, 1860; s. Jehu R. and Margaret C. (Brendle) A.; removed to Colo., 1871; grad. E. Denver High School, 1880; m. Elizabeth Fleming, Jan. 29, 1889. Worked as spindle feeder in Denver Woolen Mills at 10; drove team for timber camp at 11; paid expenses in high sch. by working as street lamplighter, and at odd jobs; with Denver Times 4½ yrs.; in ranch business from 1885. Apptd. clk. Dist. Ct., Douglas Co., Colo., 1890; mem. Colo. Ho. of Rep., 1890-94 (last 2 yrs. as speaker), State Senate, 1898-1902; candidate for lt. gov., 1904, 1906 (defeated); gov. of Colo., 1913-15; Democrat. Pres. Farmers' Life Ins. Co., Middle Park Land & Live Stock Co. V.p. State Bd. of Agr. Home: Denver, Colo. Died May 20, 1925.

AMORY, Arthur; b. Boston, Mass., Feb. 6, 1841; s. James Sullivan and Mary Copley (Greene) A.; bro. of Robert A. (q.v.); prep. edn. in sch. of Dr. Epes Dixwell, Boston; A.B., Harvard, 1862; visited Greenland while an undergraduate, with expdn. sent there by Nat. Hist. Soc. of Williams Coll.; m. Elizabeth Ingersoll, June 6, 1866. Clerk in a Boston office, 1862-63; entered employ by Upham, Tucker & Co., 1863, and lived in New York until 1877, when returned to Boston; admitted as partner, 1866, firm name Amory, Brown & Co., 1896—. Republican. Episcopalian. Home: Boston, Mass. Died Aug. 1911.

AMORY, Charles Walter, financier; b. Oct. 16, 1842; s. William and Anna (Sears) A.; A.B., Harard, 1863; m. Elizabeth Gardner, Oct. 23, 1867. Pres. Amoskeag Mfg. Co., Great Falls Mfg. Co., Fifty Associates; v.p. Provident Instn. for Savings. Home: Boston, Mass. Died Nov. 5, 1913.

AMORY, John James, shipbuilder; b. Fond du Lac, Wis., July 15, 1856; s. John and Jane (Smith) A.; ed. Riverview Mil. Acad., Poughkeepsie, N.Y.; m. Mary Shephard Hull, Sept. 1, 1881; children—John Hull (dec.), Eugene Horton, Clement Gould. Began in livery and mining business, Ariz., 1878; with Pacific Express Co. at Texarkana, Ark., 1881-82; hotel business, Billings, Mont., 1883-84; sec. and treas. Armstrong Mfg. Co., Bridgeport, Conn., 1885-86; pres. Gas Engine & Power Co. and Charles L. Seabury & Co., Consolidated, Morris Heights, N.Y. City, after 1886; pres. Consol. Shipbuilding Corp. after 1919. Republican. Episcopalian. Died Feb. 27, 1930.

AMORY, Robert, physician; b. Boston, Mass., May 3, 1842; s. James Sullivan and Mary Copley (Greene) A.; brother of Arthur A. A.B., Harvard, 1863, A.M., M.D., 1866; m. Mary A. Lawrence, 1864 (died 1882); 2d, Katharine Leighton Crehore, 1884. Lecturer on physiol. action of drugs, Harvard, 1870-71; prof. physiology, Bowdoin, 1872-75. Author of volume on Poisons in Wharton and Stille's Medical Jurisprudence, and of works on physiology and therapeutics. Fellow Am. Acad. Arts and Sciences. Home: Boston, Mass. Died Aug. 28, 1910.

AMOS, Thyrsa Wealhtheow, dean; b. Frankfort, Ind., Nov. 20, 1879; d. Joseph Bonaparte and Mary Agness (Grove) A.; Fairmount Coll., Wichita, Kan., 1903; A.B., A.M., U. of Kan., 1917; LL.D., U. of Pittsburgh, 1930. Successively teacher pub. schs., prin. elementary sch. and high sch., dean of girls, high sch., Shawnee, Okla.; instr. in psychology, U. of Kan., 1917-18; also social dir. summer session; dean of women, U. of Pittsburgh, 1919—. Democrat. Episcopalian. Home: Pittsburgh, Pa. Died May 5, 1941.

AMSTER, Nathan Leonard, capitalist; b. Roumania, Apr. 14, 1869; s. Isaac and Miriam (De Stahl) A.;

ed. in Roumania; came to U.S., 1885; m. Estelle Dreyfus, Oct. 30, 1901; children— Nathan Leonard, James Randolph. Dir. and chmn. exec. com. C.R.I.&P. Ry. Co.; pres. Granby Consol. Mining, Smelting & Power Co., Ltd. Died Sept. 22, 1939.

AMWEG, Frederick James, civil engr.; b. Harrisburg, Pa., May 9, 1856; s. John M. and Margaret H. (Fenn) A.; studied civ. engring. and architecture in Phila.; m. Blanche Estelle Parsons, Oct. 10, 1883; children—Blanche Ethel, Fred'k J. Began in engring. dept. Pa. R.R., later asst. engr. bridges and bldgs.; employed by City of Phila. in design and constrn. cantilever bridge over Schuylkill River, in line of Market St.; chief engr. City Av. and Germantown Bridge Co.; chief engr. building and installation of elec. st. ry., Honolulu, H.T., 1899; pvt. practice as cons. engr. and manager of construction, San Francisco, 1903—; chief engr. Mission Rock Terminal Co., in development of pier and terminal bldgs., San Francisco Bay. Chief of engrs. N.G. of Calif. with rank of col. Mason. Home: San Mateo, Calif. Deceased.

ANCENEY, Charles L., cattle raiser; b. Denver, Colo., Apr. 17, 1863; s. Charles and Angelique (Frazie) A.; ed. pub. schs., Gallatin Co., Mont., and Helena Business Coll.; m. Kate R. Allen, Dec. 23, 1897; children—Angelique Rea, Charles L. In charge cattle outfit at age of 14; was with first herd of cattle going into lower Yellowstone ranges, 1879, and first drive to Bismarck, N.D., 1881, swimming Missouri River and loading shipment to Buffalo, N.Y.; fought with Sioux, Blackfeet and Cheyenne Indians; asso. Harry W. Child, as Child & Anceney, 1910, in Flying D Cattle Ranges, covering 500,000 acres and furnishing support for 15,000 to 25,000 head of cattle; pres. Gallatin Gateway State Bank. Promoted Camp Creek Br. of N.P. Ry., terminal at townsite of Anceney, Mont. Mem. Pioneer Soc. of Gallatin County, Mont. Republican. Mason. Home: Bozeman, Mont. Deceased.

ANDEREGG, Frederick, prof. mathematics; b. Meiringen, Switzerland, June 11, 1852; s. Andrew and Magdalena (Otth) A.; brought to America, 1862; A.B., Oberlin Coll., 1885; A.M., 1889; A.M., Harward, 1889; studied U. of Berne, Switzerland, 1903-04; m. Anna E. Krebs (died 1879); m. 2d, Mary Osband Swift. Prof. mathematics, Oberlin Coll., 1890-1920. Conglist. Joint Author: Anderegg and Roe's Trigonometry, 1896, rev. edit., 1913. Home: Oberlin, O. Died Oct. 9, 1922.

ANDERS, James Meschter, M.D.; b. Fairview, Village, Montgomery County, Pa., July 22, 1854; s. Samuel Drescher and Christina (Meschter) A.; ed. acad. dept. of a theol. sem. at Wadsworth, O.; Ph.D., U. of Pa., M.D., 1877; m. Margaret Wunderlich, Apr. 30, 1902. Visiting phys., P.E. Hosp., 1878-92; was mem. visiting med. staff Phila. Hosp., many years, later mem. med. advisory board; prof. medicine, Medico-Chirurg. Coll., 1892-1918; prof. medicine and clin. medicine, Medico-Chirurg. Coll., Grad. Sch. U. of Pa., Phila., 1917-28, emeritus; phys. Medico-Chirurg. Hosp.; cons. mem. Bd. of Health, Phila. Pres. bd. trustees Perkiomen School; mem. bd. dirs. Ursinus College; mem. bd. mgrs. City Parks Assn., Phila. Hosp. (v.p.), Medico-Chirurg. and Graduate hosps.; chmn. Better Homes Committee, Phila. Author: House Plants as Sanitary Agents, 1887; Principles and Practice of Medicine, 14 editions, 1897-1917; Text-Book of Medical Diagnosis (with L. Napoleon Boston), 1909; Meditations in Verse, 1934. Officier de l'Instruction Publique, 1912; Chevalier Legion of Honor (France), 1923. Home: Philadelphia, Pa. Died Aug. 29, 1936.

ANDERS, Thomas Jefferson, judge; b. at Bloomville, O., Apr. 4, 1838; student lit. dept., U. of Mich., and LL.B., 1861; m. Viola Hull, Dec. 10, 1873. Practiced law in Mont. Ter., 1864-71, Walla Walla, Wash., from 1871; asso. justice Supreme Ct. of Wash., 1889-1905. Republican. Home: Olympia, Wash. Died 1910.

ANDERSEN, Christian Schmidt; b. Aarhus, Denmark, Aug. 30, 1879; s. Rasmus Marcus and Anine Margrete (Rasmussen) A.; ed. high sch. and commercial sch.; m. Margareta Lindman, 1913 (died 1924); children—Robert Lindman, Margaret, Christian, Else; m. 2d, Adeline Mildred Waller. Served in Danish Army 1 yr.; employed in mfg. plant, London, Eng., 3½ yrs., later accountant and comptroller in Copenhagen, Johannesburg, S. Africa, Baden Baden, Germany; came to U.S., 1912, naturalized citizen, 1923; with Ritz-Carlton Hotel, New York, 1912-13, Congress Hotel, Chicago, 1913-17; mgr., dir. and sec. Va. Hot Springs Co., 1917—; mgr. Homstead Hotel, Hot Springs. Republican. Evang. Lutheran. Home: Hot Springs, Va. Died Dec. 19, 1931.

ANDERSEN, Hendrik Christian, sculptor; b. Bergen, Norway, Apr. 17, 1872; s. Anders and Helene M. A.; brought to U.S. in infancy, settling at Newport, R.I., 1873; studied art and architecture at Boston, Paris, Naples, Rome. Author of Creation of a World Centre of Communication (2 vols.). Prin. works: Fountain of Life; Fountain of Immortality; Jacob Wrestling with the Angel; Study of an Athlete; busts and medallions and portraits of Pope Benedictus XV, in Rome, etc. Died Dec. 19, 1940.

ANDERSON, Abraham Archibald, artist; b. N.J., 1847; s. William and Sarah Louise (Ryerson) A.; early edn. Columbia Coll. Grammar Sch. and high sch. course, completing gen. studies in Europe under pvt. tutors; painting under Cabanel, Bonnât, Cormon, Godin and Collin; m. Elizabeth Milbank, 1887. Exhibited Paris Salon, Universal Expn., Paris, 1899, etc.; pictures: (portraits) Gen. O. O. Howard, Gov. Morgan, H. B. Claflin, Thomas A. Edison, Bishop Cleveland Coxe, Elihu Root, Charles Stewart Smith, John Wanamaker, etc., also Morning After the Ball, The Convalescent, Neither Do I Condemn Thee, and others. Died Apr. 27, 1940.

ANDERSON, Albert, alienist; b. Eagle Rock, Wake County, N.C., Oct. 18, 1859; s. Jesse and Mary (Tucker) A.; A.M., Trinity Coll., N.C., 1883; M.D., Dept. of Medicine, U. of Va., 1888; post-grad. studies, New York Polyclinic; spl. courses in bacteriology, in Govt. Lab., Washington; m. Pattie Roundtree Woodard, Dec. 12, 1888. Taught sch., Middleburg, N.C., 1883-87; founded Middleburg Acad.; founded (with Dr. C. E. Moore) The Wilson Sanatorium, Wilson, N.C., 1898; mem. State Bd. of Health, N.C., 1896-1900, State Med. Examining Bd., 1898-1902; med. dir. Jefferson Standard Life Ins. Co., Raleigh, 1907-12; supt. State Hosp., N.C., 1913—. Lecturer in psychiatry, Duke University, also trustee. Democrat. Methodist. Home: Raleigh, N.C. Died Oct. 16, 1932.

ANDERSON, Albert Barnes, judge; b. nr. Zionsville, Boone Co., Ind., Feb. 10, 1857; s. Philander and Emma A. (Duzan) A.; A.B., Wabash Coll., 1879, later A.M., LL.D., 1907; m. Rose Campbell, Nov. 14, 1882. Admitted to bar, 1881; pros. atty., Montgomery Co., Ind., 1886-90; U.S. dist. judge, Dist. of Ind., 1902-25; judge U.S. Circuit Court of Appeals, 1925-29, retired. Republican. Died Apr. 27, 1938.

ANDERSON, Amabel A., pres. bd. Chicago Law Sch.; b. of Am. parentage at Chatham, Ont., Can., May 31, 1883; d. William Henry and Annie Mellissa (Brown) A.; grad. normal course, Ferris Inst., Big Rapids, 1907; LL.B., City Coll. of Law and Finance, St. Louis, 1912; LL.M., Benton Coll. of Law, St. Louis, 1912; B.A., Nat. Univ. of Arts and Sciences, 1916; Dr. Jurisprudence, Chicago Law Sch., 1931, D.C.L., 1932; m. W. E. Arnold, M.D., 1906. Teacher pub. schs., Mich., until 1907; prin. Arnold Prep. Sch., St. Louis, 1907-12; prof. med. botany, Am. Med. Coll., 1907-09; dean of women and mem. exec. bd. City Coll. of Law and Finance, St. Louis, 1913-15; pres. Coll. Dept. of Nat. Univ. of Arts and Sciences, St. Louis, 1915-17; practiced law, Little Rock, Ark., 1917-24; sec.-treas. Colo. Coop. Mining & Milling Co., 1919-23; pres. bd. Chicago Law Sch., 1931—, dean faculty, 1932—. Lecturer on suffrage and temperance for 20 yrs. Home: Chicago, Ill. Died Feb. 18, 1936.

ANDERSON, Andrew Freeman, clergyman; b. Volant, Pa., Oct. 15, 1866; s. Barnabas and Margaret Ellen (Fasick) A.; student State Normal Sch., Edinboro, Pa., 1886-87; B.A., Bucknell U., Lewisburg, Pa., 1894, D.D., 1915; student Rochester Theol. Sem., 1899-1900; m. Blanche C. Koones, Nov. 28, 1894; 1 dau., Josephine Margaret; m. 2d, Lulu M. Burket, Mar. 14, 1921; children—Freeman Burket, Charles Truman. Ordained Bapt. ministry, 1894; pastor Grace Ch., Washington, D.C., 1894-99; asst. pastor Calvary Ch., Washington, D.C., 1900-02; pastor First Ch., Harrisburg, Pa., 1904-09, Normal Park, Chicago, 1909-14; asst. Calvary Ch., Washington, D.C., 1914-24; pastor First Ch., East Orange, N.J., 1924-28, First Park Ch., Plainfield, N.J., 1929—. Home: Plainfield, N.J. Died Nov. 13, 1936.

ANDERSON, Asher, editor; b. Flatlands, L.I., N.Y., July 23, 1846; s. John William and Eliza Ann (Duryea) A.; A.B., Rutgers Coll., 1870, A.M., 1873; B.D., New Brunswick Theol. Sem., 1873; (D.D., Iowa Coll., 1904, Rutgers, 1904); m. Mary E. R. Dorrance, Oct. 2, 1873. Ordained Ref. Ch. in America ministry, 1873; pastor Flatbush, N.Y., 1873-75, Fishkill, N.Y., 1875-80, Passaic, N.J., 1880-85; installed Congl. ministry, 1885; pastor Bristol, Conn., 1885-90, Meriden, Conn., 1890-1901; editor Congl. Year Book, 1900-13. Mem. bd. pub. sch. examiners, Passaic, N.J., 1882-85; mem. Meriden bd. of edn., 1892-98; registrar Central Conf., Conn., 1892-1901; chaplain 2d Regt. Conn. N.G., 1895-99; trustee Hartford Theol. Sem., 1895—; moderator Conn. State Assn., 1899; sec. Nat. Council Congl. Chs. in U.S., 1901-13; editor Minutes of Nat. Council, 1901, 04, 07, 10; pastor, Fitchburg, Mass., 1914, Dorchester, 1917-19, Framingham, 1921, Leominster, 1923. Pres. Dewing Memorial, Revere, Mass., 1910. Republican. Mason. Home: Randolph, Mass. Died Feb. 14, 1925.

ANDERSON, Carl C., congressman; b. Bluffton, O., Dec. 2, 1877; s. John J. and Mary L. (Barringer) A.; pub. sch. edn.; m. Helen May Ford, Sept. 17, 1904. Sec. and gen. mgr. C. C. Anderson Mfg. Co.; pres. Metal Reversible Co. (Fremont, O.). Mayor of Fostoria, O., 1905-09; mem. 61st and 62d Congresses (1909-13), 13th Ohio Dist. Democrat. Home: Fostoria, O. Died Oct. 1, 1912.

ANDERSON, Chandler Parsons, lawyer; b. Lakeville, Conn., Sept. 5, 1866; s. Henry Hill and Sarah (Burrall) A.; B.A., Yale, 1887; Harvard Law Sch., 1888-89; m. Harriet S. Ward, May 17, 1899. Admitted to N.Y. bar, 1891. Sec. for U.S. and Great Britain of Bering Sea Claims Commn., 1896-97, U.S. sec. Joint Commn. with Great Britain for settlement of Canadian questions, 1898-99; U.S. asso. counsel Alaska Boundary Arbitration, 1903; U.S. counsel, Passamaquoddy Bay boundary settlement, 1909; spl. counsel for Dept. of State under Sec. Root, 1905-09, and Sec. Knox. 1909-10, in negotiation of treaties with Great Britain concerning British N. America; U.S. agt. N. Atlantic Coast Fisheries Arbitration, The Hague, 1910; U.S. del. Fur Seal Conf., Washington, D.C., 1911; counselor Dept. of State, 1910-13; U.S. arbitrator, British-Am. Pecuniary Claims Arbitration, 1913-23; counsel for Costa Rica in Costa Rica-Panama boundary arbitration, 1913-14, before Chief Justice White; legal adviser for Am. embassies and legations in Europe on questions involving Am. interests growing out of European war, and for Dept. State in Washington, 1914-15; counsel on internat. questions for U.S. War Industries Bd., 1917-18 (mem. spl. mission to London and Paris, summer of 1918); counsel for Internat. Com. Red Cross in the organization of League of Red Cross Socs., France, 1919; counsel for Guatemala in Guatemala-Honduras boundary mediation before Sec. of State of U.S., 1918—; counsel for Nicaragua in Nicaragua-Honduras boundary mediation before Sec. of State of U.S., 1920—; U.S. arbitrator in Am.-Norwegian shipping claims arbitration, 1921-22; U.S. legal expert, Armament Conf., Washington, D.C., 1921-22; counsel for Costa Rica in arbitration with Great Britain before Chief Justice Taft, 1923; U.S. commr. Mixed Claims Commn. between U.S. and Germany, 1923—; sole commr. Tripartite Claims; commr. between U.S., Austria and Hungary, 1933. Home: Washington, D.C. Died Aug. 2, 1936.

ANDERSON, Charles Palmerston, bishop; b. Kemptville, Can., Sept. 8, 1864; s. Henry and Maria R. A.; ed. Trinity Coll. Sch., Port Hope, Ont.; Trinity U., Toronto, D.D., 1900; D.D., Western Theol. Sem., Chicago, 1905; m. Janet Glass, Sept. 4, 1889. Deacon, 1887, priest, 1888, P.E. Ch.; in charge Beachburg, Can., 1889-91, Grace Ch., Oak Park, Ill., 1891-1900; consecrated bishop of Chicago, 1900. Author: Letters to Laymen, 1913; The Religion of Our Lord, 1923; Religion and Morality, 1924. Home: Chicago, Ill. Died Jan. 30, 1930.

ANDERSON, Clifford Le Conte, lawyer; b. Macon, Ga., July 7, 1862; s. Clifford and Anna (Le Conte) A.; A.B., Mercer U., 1880, LL.B., 1883; m. Kitty Van Dyke, Sept. 10, 1884; children—Mrs. John Gelzer, Jr., Clifford V.; m. 2d, Mary Alice Van der Grifft, April 30, 1910; 1 son, Jackson V. Practiced at Macon, Ga., 1883-86, at Atlanta, 1886—; sr. mem. Anderson, Rountree, Crenshaw & Hansell. Commr. roads and revenue, Fulton County, Ga., 1899-1914, inclusive. Brig.-gen. comdg. Ga. N.G. (retired). Home: Atlanta, Ga. Died Sept. 17, 1933.

ANDERSON, Edward, clergyman; b. Boston, Mass., Nov. 19, 1833; s. Rufus (D.D., LL.D.) and Eliza (Hill) A.; ed. in Boston schs.; pvt. instrn.; studied theology with father and pastor; m. Harriet Flora Shumway, July 29, 1857. Ordained Congl. ministry, 1858; pastor, St. Joseph, Mich., 1858-60, Quincy, Ill., 1874-80, Toledo, O., 1880-84, Norwalk, Conn., 1884-89, Danielson, Conn., 1890-95. Served with John Brown in Kansas; chaplain 37th Ill. Vols. till after the Mo. campaign, 1862; col. 12th Ind. Vol. Cav. until close of war. Mason. Home: Quincy, Mass. Died May 21, 1916.

ANDERSON, Edward Lowell, lawyer; b. at Cincinnati, O., Oct. 4, 1842; s. Larz and Catharine (Longworth) A.; ed. pub. schools and tutors to 1861; left school to enter army; LL.B., U. of Cincinnati, 1866; m. Mary Fore, Dec. 5, 1865. Served 1st lt. and capt. 52d Ohio Inf., 1862-65; capt. on staff Gen. William T. Sherman; was in battles of Perryville, Murfreesboro, Chickamauga, Mission Ridge, Kenesaw Mountain, Jonesboro' (wounded), and other engagements; mustered out at close of war; admitted to bar, 1866. Author: Northern Ballads, 1874; Soldier and Pioneer, 1879; Six Weeks in Norway, 1877; Modern Horsemanship, 1884; Curb, Snaffle and Spur, 1894; Riding and Driving (with Price Collier), 1905; Horses and Riding, 1909. Home: Cincinnati, O. Died Mar. 29, 1916.

ANDERSON, Edwin Alexander, naval officer; b. Wilmington, N.C., July 16, 1860; grad. U.S. Naval Acad., 1882. Ensign, July 1, 1884; promoted through the grades to rear adm., Nov. 28, 1918. In service on Marblehead and as comdr. Sandoval, Spanish-Am. War, 1898; advanced 5 numbers in rank "for extraordinary heroism" during Spanish-Am. War; comdr. 2d Regt. of Bluejackets at capture of Vera Cruz, Mexico, 1915; awarded Congressional Medal of Honor "for extraordinary heroism in battle on that occasion"; rear adm. Nov. 28, 1918. D.S.M. for services during World War; vice adm. comdg. European Forces, 1922; comdr. in chief Asiatic Fleet, 1922-23; retired, 1923. Home: Wilmington, N.C. Died Sept. 23, 1933.

ANDERSON, Elbert Ellery, lawyer; b. New York, N.Y., Oct. 31, 1833; ed. Harvard Univ.; traveled abroad, 1843-48; admitted to bar, 1854; prominently identified with reform campaigns in New York politics; rapid transit commr. and commr. in reference to acquiring lands for the Croton aqueduct and the elevated ry.; dir. several ry. cos. and receiver Union Pacific Ry.; sr. mem. Anderson & Warren, lawyers. Democrat. Home: New York, N.Y. Died 1903.

ANDERSON, Frank Bartow, banker; b. Macon, Ga., July 15, 1863; s. George Wayne and Katharine (Berrien) A.; ed. pvt. sch., West Chester, Pa., and Mt. Pleasant Mil. Acad., Ossining, N.Y.; m. Elizabeth May Jadwin, July 27, 1887. With Am. Exchange Nat. Bank, New York, 1880-1902; v.p., 1902-09, pres. 1909-25, chmn. bd., 1925—, Bank of Calif., N.A., San Francisco. Trustee Leland Stanford Jr. U. Served in 1st Naval Batt., New York, 9 yrs.; lt. sr. grade U.S. Navy during Spanish-Am. War, 1898. Episcopalian. Democrat. Home: San Rafael, Calif. Died Sept. 17, 1935.

ANDERSON, Frank Leonard, clergyman; b. Red Wing, Minn., Aug. 7, 1865; s. John and Britta Maria (Gustafsdatter) A.; A.B., U. of Minn., 1896; B.D., U. of Chicago Div. Sch., 1900; post-grad. work, same; D.D., Central U., 1916; m. Linda Williams, Dec. 26, 1896 (died 1919); children—Paul Alexander, Hope Evangeline; m. 2d, Mrs. Mabelle Grant Meeker, June 10, 1922. Ordained Bapt. minister at Maywood, Ill., Nov. 14, 1900; pastor First Ch., Austin, Minn., 1900-05, Normal Park Ch., Chicago, 1905-09; supt. Bapt. Exec. Council of Chicago, 1909-20; pres. Bapt. Young People's Union of America, 1913-16; pres. Internat. Bapt. Sem., East Orange, N.J., 1920—. Republican. Home: East Orange, N.J. Died Aug. 30, 1935.

ANDERSON, F(rederick) Paul, coll. dean; b. South Bend, Ind., Feb. 10, 1867; s. John Wesley and Sarah (Hall) A.; B.M.E., Purdue U., 1890, M.E., 1894; m. Josephine Fisher, June 24, 1891; children—Virginia Frances, Frederick Paul. Dean and dir. Coll. of Engineering, and prof. mech. engring. U. of Ky., 1891—; consulting engr. Queen & Crescent Ry., 1900—; mem. Anderson & Frankel, cons. engrs.; dir. research lab. Am. Soc. Heating and Ventilating Engrs., 1921-25, at U.S. Bur. of Mines, Pittsburgh. Democrat. Episcopalian. Mem. Internat. Jury of Awards, St. Louis Exposition, 1904. F. Paul Anderson Gold Medal established by Am. Soc. Heating and Ventilating Engrs., 1929. Home: Lexington, Ky. Died Apr. 8, 1934.

ANDERSON, Galusha, theologian; b. Clarendon, N.Y., Mar. 7, 1832; s. Seneca and Lucy (Webb) A.; A.B., U. of Rochester, 1854, A.M., 1857; grad. Rochester Theol. Sem., 1856; (S.T.D., Rochester, 1866, LL.D., 1884; LL.D., Madison, now Colgate U., 1884); m. Mary E. Roberts, Apr. 23, 1861; Father of Frederick Lincoln A. Ordained Bapt. ministry, 1856; pastor Janesville, Wis., 1856-58, St. Louis, 1858-66; prof. homiletics, ch. polity and pastoral duties, Newton Theol. Instn., 1866-73; pastor Brooklyn, 1873-76, Second Ch., Chicago, 1876-78; pres. old Chicago Univ., 1878-85; pastor First Ch., Salem, Mass., 1885-87; pres. Denison U., Ohio, 1887-90; prof. in Bapt. Union Theol. Sem., 1890-92; prof. practical theology, Div. Sch., U. of Chicago, 1892-1904, emeritus. Author: Ancient Sermons for Modern Times, translated from Asterius, 1904; The Story of a Border City During the Civil War, 1908; Hitherto Untold, 1910; When Neighbors Were Neighbors, A Story of Love and Life in Olden Days, 1911; Science and Prayer and Other Papers, 1915; The Poems and Biography of Mary Eleanor Anderson, 1917. Home: Newton Centre, Mass. Died July 20, 1918.

ANDERSON, George Everett, consul-gen.; b. Bloomington, Ill., Aug. 20, 1869; s. Orson B. and Harriet V. (Smith) A.; ed. Shurtleff Coll., Ill., 1888-91; LL.B., Ill. Wesleyan U., 1899; m. Mary A., d. John A. Kumler, Oct. 31, 1895; children—George Kumler, Mary Kumler; divorced 1925; m. 2d, Elizabeth H. MacKinnon, Apr. 24, 1928. Newspaper reporter, editor and pub., 1891-94. Consul at Hangchow, China, 1904-05, at Amoy, 1905-06; consul-gen. at Rio de Janeiro, Brazil, 1906-10, at Hongkong, China, May 1910-20, Rotterdam, 1920-24, retired; specializes in study of internat. finance and exchange, gold movements, Am. banking, etc. Home: Washington, D.C. Died Mar. 17, 1940.

ANDERSON, George Lucius, army officer; b. Delafield, Wis., Apr. 9, 1849; s. Archibald A. and Clarissa E. (Clarke) A.; A.B., Lawrence U., 1870, A.M., 1873; grad. West Point, 1874, U.S. Arty. Sch., 1876, Naval War Coll., 1897; unmarried. Apptd. 2d lt., June 17, 1874; promoted through grades to col. and insp. gen., Oct. 1, 1908; retired Apr. 9, 1913. Elec. engr. Calif. Power & Light Transmission Lines, Palo Alto, 1913-17; on duty in office of Board of Ordnance and Fortification, Washington, 1917-18. Asst. prof. mathematics, West Point, 1885-89; instr. electricity and submarine mines, U.S. Arty. Sch., Ft. Monroe, 1889-95; mil. attaché to U.S. Embassy at St. Petersburg, 1897; mem. U.S. Ordnance Bd., New York, 1903-06; insp. gen. Dept. of Calif., 1906-09. Author: Handbook for U.S. Electricians in the Management and Care of the Machinery of Sea Coast Fortifications 1902; Instructions in Electricity for Non-Commissioned Officers, 1894. Home: Washington, D.C. Died 1934.

ANDERSON, George Smith, army officer; b. Bernardsville, N.J., Sept. 30, 1849; s. John Hill and Susan Ogden (Lewis) A.; unmarried. Grad. U.S. Mil. Acad., 1871; commd. 2d lt. 6th Cav., June 12, 1871; advanced through the grades to brig. gen., U.S.A., Mar. 20, 1911; retired Oct. 16, 1912. Home: Bernardsville, N.J. Died Mar. 7, 1915.

ANDERSON, George Weston, judge; b. Acworth, N.H., Sept. 1, 1861; s. David Campbell and Martha Lucinda (Brigham) A.; grad. Cushing Acad., Mass., 1882; A.B., Williams Coll., 1886, LL.D., 1921; LL.B., summa cum laude, Boston U. Law School, 1890; LL.D., Boston U., 1931; m. Minnie E. Mitchell, 1897 (died 1906); m. 2d, Addie Earle Kenerson, Jan. 25, 1908. Practiced, Boston, 1890—; mem. Sch. Com., Boston, 1895-1900; Dem. candidate atty. gen. of Mass., 1911, 1912; apptd. mem. Pub. Service Commn., July 1, 1913, term of 4 yrs. (resigned); U.S. dist. atty., Mass., Nov. 1, 1914-Oct., 1917; mem. Interstate Commerce Commn., Oct. 1917-Nov. 1918; became judge U.S. Circuit Court of Appeals, Boston, 1918 retired. Trustee World Peace Foundation, Cushing Academy. Unitarian. Mason. Home: Wellesley Hills, Mass. Died Feb. 14, 1938.

ANDERSON, Harold MacDonald, journalist; b. Great Barrington, Mass., Aug. 22, 1876; s. Rev. Daniel Goodwin and Martha (MacDonald) A.; ed. pub. schs. Great Barrington; m. Helen De Mott, Oct. 23, 1901; 1 son, Dan Curtis. Joined staff of The Sun, New York, 1894, and continued as reporter, war corr. Spanish-Am. War, polit. reporter and corr., editorial writer and executive until The Sun and New York Herald were consolidated in 1920; editorial writer and exec., New York Herald, 1920-24; editor Yonkers Statesman, 1924-25; editorial writer and exec. The Sun, New York, 1925—. Awarded U. S. Treasury medal for services in Liberty Loan campaigns. Del. 1st Pan Am. Congress of Journalists, 1926. Episcopalian. Home: New York, N.Y. Died Dec. 26, 1940.

ANDERSON, Harry Bennett, judge; b. Van Buren County, Mich., Nov. 5, 1879; s. Seneca Benjamin and Adelaide, (Bennett) A.; Ph.B., U. of Chicago; A.M., Christian Brothers College, Memphis; LL.B., Columbia, 1904; m. Patty C. Crook, Oct. 8, 1908; children —Seneca B., Adelaide, Joseph C., Harry B. Moved to Memphis, 1889; admitted to Tenn. bar, 1904; mem. Brown & Anderson, 1904-18; mem. Rep. State Com., Tenn., 1904-10; presdl. elector on Roosevelt, Taft and Roosevelt (Bull Moose) tickets; referee in bankruptcy, 1919-21; judge U.S. Dist. Court, Western Dist. of Tenn., 1925—. Lt. col., judge adv. 26th Div., A.E.F., World War; col. J.A.G., O.R.C. Episcopalian. Home: Memphis, Tenn. Died Apr. 9, 1935.

ANDERSON, Harry Reuben, army officer; b. Chillicothe, O., Jan. 20, 1844; s. Col. William Marshall and Eliza (McArthur) A.; captain's clerk in U.S. Navy, May 2, 1863-June 30, 1864; cadet U.S. Mil. Acad., July 1, 1864-Jan. 18, 1865; grad. Arty. Sch., 1875; m. Florence Allison, Aug. 26, 1869. Capt. 6th U.S. Vol. Inf., Apr. 28, 1865-June 12, 1866; 2d lt. 6th U.S. Inf., Mar. 7, 1867; advanced through the grades to col., Mar. 26, 1906; brig. gen., retired Apr. 5, 1907. Participated in campaign against Sioux Indians on Powder River, Neb., 1865; apptd. a.-d.-c. to Gen. E. R. S. Camby, 1868; in campaign against Modocs, 1873 (hon. mention); against Sioux Indians, under Gen. Crook, 1876; against Bannocks, in Ore., 1877-78; served in Cuba and P.R. during Spanish-Am. War. Home: Circleville, O. Died Nov. 22, 1918.

ANDERSON, Henry Clay, prof. and dean engring.; b. Morganfield, Ky., Dec. 4, 1872; s. John Gerry and Sophia F. (Cromwell) A.; prep. edn., Morganfield Acad. and Acad. of Ky. State Coll., Lexington, Ky.; B.M.E., U. of Ky., 1897; s. Sara Graham Simrall, Aug. 19, 1903 (died Jan. 1920); children—Henry Clay (dec.), Ellen Harrison, John Gerry. Asst. master mechanic, C., N.O.&T.P. Ry., Chattanooga, Tenn., 1897-1900; with U. of Mich. as instr. in mech. engring., 1900-03, asst. prof., 1903-06, jr. prof. steam power engring, 1912-17, prof. mech engring. and head of dept., 1917-39, dir. student-alumni relations, 1933-39, dean Coll. of Engring, 1937-39, also consulting practice, appraisal of steam and electric rys., etc., and spl. engring. investigations. Democrat. Episcopalian. Mason. Home: Ann Arbor, Mich. Died Oct. 14, 1939.

ANDERSON, Henry William, insurance; b. Cranston, R.I., May 23, 1885; s. Mandus and Hilma Christine (Swenson) A.; ed. pub. schs.; m. Emily Almira Rodman, Nov. 8, 1909 (dec.); 1 son, Henry Rodman; m. 2d, Jane Rewcastle Hindmarsh, Oct. 15, 1931. With Employers Liability Assurance Corp., 1912-18; branch mgr. Am. Mutual Liability Ins. Co., 1918-21; sec. and asst. treas. Automobile Mutual Ins. Co. of America and Factory Mutual Liability Ins. Co. of America, 1921—; pres. both companies since 1933; pres. Amica Credit Corp. Republican. Episcopalian. Mason (32°). Home: Providence, R.I. Died Jan. 30, 1940.

ANDERSON, John, publisher; b. Voss, Norway, 1836; s. Andrew and Laura (Sampson) A.; brought by parents to Chicago, 1844; attended public school 1 yr.; father died, and at 12 he had the support of a mother and a baby sister placed upon him; became apple peddler, worked in butcher shop, carried newspapers; learned typesetting; became printer on Chicago Tribune; m. Maria C. Frank, 1859 (died 1874); 2d, Julia Sampson, 1875. Established "Skandinaven," a Norwegian newspaper, 1866; lost all in great fire, 1871; borrowed money and reestablished paper. The completion of a third of a century by the Skandinaven was celebrated May 2, 1899, at Chicago. Presdl. elector, 1908. Home: Chicago, Ill. Died 1910.

ANDERSON, John Crawford, judge; b. Greene County, Ala., Aug. 5, 1863; s. Dr. John Crawford and Elizabeth (McAlpine) A.; ed. pub. schs., Greene County, Ala.; LL.B., U. of Ala., 1883; m. Mary Bird Martin, Feb. 24, 1897; children—Julia, Elizabeth McAlpine. Engaged in practice of law at Demopolis and Linden, Ala., 1885-95; judge 1st Jud. Circuit, Ala., 1895-1904; asso. justice Supreme Court of Ala., terms 1904-10, 1910-16, chief justice, 1914—. Home: Demopolis, Ala. Deceased.

ANDERSON, John Francis, bridge builder; b. Jemshög, Sweden, Dec. 30, 1848; s. Anders Anderson Thore and Ingar Suneson; self ed.; m. Cecelia Anderson, of Scania, Sweden, May 19, 1880. Came to America as a sailor, 1869; assisted in constrn. of bridge across Mo. River for U.P. Ry., 1870; built river piers for South St. Bridge, Phila., 1872; foundations for Iron Mountain Ry. bridge over Ark. River, at Little Rock, 1873; employed by govt. of Venezuela, 1876; engaged in bridge work in Eng., 1876-79; supt. Hudson River Tunnel, between New York and Jersey City, 1879-82; built bridge over Atchafalaya River, La., for Tex. Pacific Ry., 1882-84; mem. Anderson & Barr, 1884-95. Inventor and owner of patents for aerial bridges and the pilot system of tunneling. Decorated Merit of Military, Spain; Knight Comdr. Order of Vasa, Sweden. Home: San Diego, Calif. Died Jan. 23, 1927.

ANDERSON, John Jacob, author; b. New York, N.Y., Sept. 30, 1821; grad. Normal School, City of New York, 1846 (A. M. Rutgers Coll., 1867; Ph.D., N.Y. Univ., 1876); m. Elizabeth B. Baldwin, Aug. 3, 1848, (died June 17, 1905). Was teacher for 30 years, including 20 years as principal of a large public grammar school in New York. Author: Pictorial School History of the United States; Popular School History of the United States; Manual of General History; Manual of Ancient History; Manual of Mediæval and Modern History; History of France; History of England; The Historical Reader; The United States Reader; Grammar School History of the United States; A Junior Class History of the United States; History of the State of New York, 1902. Home: Brooklyn, N.Y. Died 1906.

ANDERSON, Joseph, clergyman; b. Broomton, Rossshire, Scot., Dec. 16, 1836; s. William and Mary (Rose) A.; came to America, 1842; A.B., Coll. City of New York, 1854, A.M., 1857; grad. Union Theol. Sem., 1857 (D.D. Yale, 1878); m. Anna Sands Gildersleeve, Jan. 24, 1859. Ordained to ministry, 1858; pastor First Ch., Stamford, 1858-61, First Ch., Norwalk, 1861-64, First Ch., Waterbury, 1865-1905, emeritus. Editor of the Waterbury American, 1872-73; moderator Gen. Assn. of Conn., 1877, 1890, Gen. Conf. Congl. Chs. of Conn., 1878; del. Internat. Congl. Council, London, 1891; mem. Corp. of Yale, 1884—. Corporate mem. A.B.C.F.M. Has made spl. study of languages and antiquities of Am. Indians. Died Aug. 18, 1916.

ANDERSON, Joseph Gaudentius, bishop; b. Boston, Mass., Sept. 30, 1865; s. John J. and Ellen (McVay) A.; A.B., Boston Coll., 1887 (D.D., 1909); grad. St. John's Sem., Brighton, Mass., 1892. Ordained priest R.C. Ch., 1892; chaplain Mass. State Prison, 1894-1904; dir. Bur. of Catholic Charities, Boston, 1903-08; diocesan dir. of charities, 1908—; vicar gen. Boston Diocese, Jan. 14, 1909; prothonotary apostolic, Apr. 9, 1909; consecrated auxiliary bishop, of Boston, July 25, 1909; pastor St. Paul's Ch., Dorchester, Mass., 1908-17, St. Peter's Ch., Dorchester, 1917—. Home: Boston, Mass. Died July 2, 1927.

ANDERSON, Larz, diplomat; b. Paris, France, Aug. 15, 1866; s. Gen. Nicholas Longworth and Elizabeth Coles (Kilgour) A.; ed. abroad and at Phillips Exeter Acad.; A.B., Harvard, 1888; spent 2 yrs. in travel around the world; m. Isabel, d. Commodore George Perkins, U.S. Navy, June 10, 1897. Second sec. U.S. Legation and Embassy at London, 1891-93; 1st sec. and chargé d'affaires, U.S. Embassy, Rome, 1893-97; capt. and asst. adj. gen. U.S.V., during Spanish-Am. War, 1898, acting as adj. gen. 2d Div. 2d Army Corps. E.E. and M.P. to Belgium, Aug., 1911-13; apptd. ambassador extraordinary and plenipotentiary to Japan, Nov. 1912, resigned with change of administration, 1913. Comdr. Order of St. Maurice and St. Lazarus (Italy). Grand Officer of Crown of Italy; Grand Cordon, 1st Class, Order of Rising Sun, Japan; Grand Cordon Order of Crown, Belgium. Republican. Episcopalian. Home: Washington, D.C. Died Apr. 13, 1937.

ANDERSON, Lewis Flint, univ. prof.; b. Waterford, Ont., July 18, 1866; s. Samuel Graham and

Julia (Handy) A.; B.A., U. of Toronto, 1893, M.A., 1902; studied U. of Leipzig, 1897-99; Ph.D., Clark U., 1907; m. Harriet Cobb, June 24, 1897; children—Donald Benton, Malcolm Graham, Lewis Gordon. Prin. high sch., Three Rivers, Mich., 1893-94; supt. schs., Three Rivers, 1894-97; head of Dept. of Edn. and Psychology, Northern State Normal Sch., Marquette, Mich., 1899-1909; asst. prof. of edn., U. of Ill., Sept. 1, 1909; then prof. history and philosophy of edn., Ohio State U. Unitarian. Author: Outline Sketch of History of Common School Education, 1909; History of Manual and Industrial School Education, 1926; Pestalozzi on Education, 1931. Home: Columbus, Ohio. Died Nov. 17, 1932.

ANDERSON, Melville Best, univ. prof.; b. Kalamazoo, Mich., Mar. 28, 1851; s. Rev. Edward C. and Helen (Best) A.; student Cornell, 1870-72, U. of Göttingen, 1875-76, and at Paris, 1876-77; A.M., Butler, 1877; (LL.D., Aberdeen, 1906; Dr. U. of Padua, 1922; D.Litt., Mills, 1923); m. Charlena Van Vleck, 1875; children—Balfour (dec.), Malcolm Playfair (dec.), Gertrude (dec.), Robert Van Vleck. Prof. modern langs., Butler U., 1877-80, English lit., Knox Coll., 1881-86, lit. and history, Purdue U., 1886-87; English lang. and lit., State U. of Ia., 1887-91; English literature, Stanford U., 1891-1910, emeritus. Translator in tersa rima of the Divine Comedy of Dante, 1921; Editor Bacon's Essays. Author: The Happy Teacher, 1910; The Great Refusal (war poem), 1916; Study of Dante and His Florence (with new issue of the Divine Comedy, revised version), 1929, new edit., 1 vol. and 3 vols., 1931. Home: La Jolla, Calif. Died June 22, 1933.

ANDERSON, Neal Larkin, clergyman; b. York, S.C., July 15, 1865; s. Rev. John Monroe and Margaret (Neel) A.; prep. edn., Bingham Sch., N.C.; A.B., Davidson Coll., 1885, A.M., 1888, D.D., A.M., Princeton, 1888; grad. Princeton Theol. Sem., 1890; m. Anna Howard Faison, Aug. 14, 1890; children—Lucius Faison (dec.), Margaret Neal (wife of Rev. Legh R. Scott), Neal Larkin (dec.), Ruth (Mrs. Alan S. O'Neal), Monroe (dec.). Prin. Clinton (N.C.) Acad., 1885-87; ordained ministry Presbyn. Ch. of U.S., 1890; pastor successively Marion, Ala., First Central Ch. (now Trinity Ch.), Montgomery, First Ch., Winston-Salem, N.C., until 1916; pres. Austin (Tex.) Theol. Sem., 1916, 17; pastor Independent Presbyn. Ch. (founded 1755), Savannah, Ga., 1917—. Moderator synod of Ala., 1900, Synod of Ga., 1926, 27. A founder Nat. Child Labor Com.; chaplain 2d Ala. N.G., 1898-1905; asst. chaplain Gen. Sons Conf. Vets. Mason. Author: Handbook of Missions, 1898; God's World and Word, 1927; also writer History of the Independent Presbyterian Church; A Woman's Heart, the Gateway of Christ to Europe; The Recoil of Evolution's Assault on Teleology; With Wings—A Bird's Eye View of Western Europe; etc. Inventor of carriage return on Remington electric typewriter. Home: Savannah, Ga. Died May 19, 1931.

ANDERSON, Paul Y., newspaper corr.; b. Knox County, Tenn., Aug. 29, 1893; s. William Holston and Elizabeth Dill (Haynes) A.; ed. pub. schs., Knoxville, Tenn.; special course Washington U., 1920-22. Began as reporter on Knoxville Journal, 1911; reporter St. Louis (Mo.) Times, 1912-13, St. Louis Star, 1913-14; reporter, 1914-21, editorial writer, 1921-23, nat. corr., Washington, D.C., 1923—, St. Louis Post-Dispatch. Commended by congl. com. for work in connection with E. St. Louis race riots, 1917; awarded Pulitzer prize for best example of reporter's work (in reopening Senate oil investigation), 1928; awarded gold medal of Headliners' Club for best series of news stories on subject of great public interest (Senate civil liberties investigation), 1937. Home: Washington, D.C. Died Dec. 6, 1938.

ANDERSON, Peirce, architect; b. Oswego, N.Y., Feb. 20, 1870; s. Hugh and Hannah Louisa (Peirce) A.; A.B., Harvard, 1892; E.E., Johns Hopkins, 1894; post-grad. work École des Beaux Arts, Paris Architecte diplome par le gouvernement, 1900; unmarried. With D. H. Burnham & Co., architects, and their successors, Graham, Burnham & Co., 1900-17, and Graham, Anderson, Probst & White, 1917—. Apptd., July 1912, by President Taft mem. Commn. Fine Arts, in place of D. H. Burnham, deceased. Home: Chicago, Ill. Died Feb. 9, 1924.

ANDERSON, Rasmus Björn, editor; b. Albion, Dane County, Wis., of Norwegian parentage, Jan. 12, 1846; s. Björn and Abel Catherine (von Krogh) A.; A.M., Luther Coll., Ia., 1866; hon. A.B., U. of Wis., 1885, LL.D., 1888; m. Bertha Karina Olson, July 21, 1868; children—Carletta Catherine (Mrs. Vedel, Denmark), George Krogh, Hjalmer Odin, Rolf Bull. Prof. Greek and modern langs., Albion (Wis.) Acad., 1866; instr. langs., 1869-75, prof. Scandinavian langs. and lit., 1875-83, U. of Wis.; U.S. minister to Denmark, 1885-89; editor and pub. Amerika (weekly) Oct. 1898-June 1922. Pres. Wis. Life Insurance Co., 1895-1922, Wis. Rubber Co., 1904—. Author: America Not Discovered by Columbus, 1874; Norse Mythology, 1875; Viking Tales of the North, 1877; The Younger Edda, 1880; First Chapter of Norwegian Immigration, 1821-40, 1895; Life Story of Rasmus B. Anderson, 1915. Translator of numerous works from the Norse and from Danish and Swedish. Home: Madison, Wis. Died Mar. 2, 1936.

ANDERSON, Sherwood, author; b. Camden, O., Sept. 13, 1876; s. Irwin and Emma (Smith) A.; ed. public schools. Wife, Eleanor C. Author: Windy McPherson's Son, 1916; Marching Men, 1917; Mid-American Chants (poems), 1918; Winesburg, Ohio, 1919; Poor White, 1920; The Triumph of the Egg, 1921; Many Marriages, 1922; Horses and Men, 1923; A Story Teller's Story, 1924; Lark Laughter, 1925; Note Book and A New Testament (verse), 1926; Tar, 1927; Hello Towns, 1929; Perhaps Women, 1931; Beyond Desire, 1933; Death in the Woods, 1933; No Swank, 1934; Puzzled America, 1935; Kit Brandon, 1936; Plays, 1937. Home: Marion, Va. Died Mar. 8, 1941.

ANDERSON, Stonewall, minister; b. Helena, Ark., Mar. 7, 1864; s. Rufus Doak and Matha Elizabeth (Peyton) A.; A.B., Hendrix Coll., 1891 (D.D., 1907); m. Mamie C. Bagwell, Oct. 1894. Ordained ministry M.E. Ch., S., 1891; pastor Fayetteville, Ark., 1891-92, Ft. Smith, 1893-94, Conway, 1895, Clarksville, 1896-97; presiding-elder (Ark. Conf.) 1898-1902; pres. Hendrix Coll., 1902-10; sec. of education, M.E. Ch., S., 1910—. Mem. Gen. Conf. M.E. Ch., South, 6 times to 1926. Home: Nashville, Tenn. Died June 8, 1928.

ANDERSON, Thomas Davis, clergyman; b. Roxbury, Mass., Feb. 26, 1853; s. Thomas Davis and Lucy Ann (Spense) A.; A.B., Brown, 1874, D.D., 1894; grad. Newton Theol. Instn., 1877; m. Fanny M. Cross, Nov. 27, 1877 (died 1885); m. 2d, Mrs. Jane A. Hartwell, Dec. 13, 1893. Ordained Bapt. ministry, Nov. 22, 1877; pastor First Ch., Portland, Me., 1877-82, Seventh Ch., Baltimore, 1882-87, Central Ch., Providence, 1887-1902, Emmanuel Ch., Albany, N.Y., 1902-10; then engaged in lit. work. Overseer, Columbian U., Washington, 1883-89; fellow Brown U., 1890—, and sec. Corp., 1890-1924. Pres. R.I. Bapt. State Conv., 1895-1902; trustee Newton Theol. Instn., 1897—, Rochester Theol. Sem., 1903-25. Republican. Author: Memorial of Ezekiel G. Robinson, Pres. of Brown U., 1895. Home: Worcester, Mass. Died Nov. 11, 1928.

ANDERSON, Thomas H., judge; b. Belmont County, O., June 6, 1848; s. John and Amelia (Dallas) A.; ed. pub. schs. and Mt. Union Coll., Ohio; m. Laura B. Augustine, Oct. 1879. Prin. high sch., Cambridge, O., 1871; admitted to bar, 1871; practiced Cambridge, O., 1871-89; U.S. minister to Bolivia, 1889-93; practiced at Washington, 1893-99; U.S. dist. atty., D.C., 1899-1901; asso. justice Supreme Ct., D.C., 1901—. Author of volume on Bolivia, published by the Bur. of Am. Republics, and of numerous valuable reports to the U.S. Govt. on our trade relations with the Spanish-Am. republics. Home: Washington, D.C. Died Oct. 1, 1916.

ANDERSON, Thomas McArthur, army officer; b. Chillicothe, O., Jan. 21, 1836; s. William Marshall and Eliza (McArthur) A.; grad. Mt. St. Mary's Coll., Md., 1855 (LL.D.); grad. Cincinnati Law Sch., 1858; admitted to Ohio bar, 1858, Ky bar, 1859; practiced law, 1858-61; m. Elizabeth Van Winkle, 1869. Pvt. Co. A, 6th Ohio Inf., Apr. 20, 1861; advanced through the grades to brig. gen. U.S. Army, Mar. 31, 1899; retired by operation of law, Jan. 21, 1900. Bvtd.: maj., Aug. 1, 1864, "for gallant services in Battle of Wilderness"; lt. col., Aug. 1, 1864, for same in battle of Spottsylvania. Comd. 1st expdn. to P.I.; occupied Cavite, June 30, 1898; comd. land forces taking Manila, Aug. 13, 1898; comd. 1st div. 8th Army Corps in battles of Santana, San Pedro, Passe and Guadalupe, Feb. 5-Mar. 17, 1899. Mason. Home: Vancouver, Wash. Died May 8, 1917.

ANDERSON, William A., lawyer; b. Botetourt County, Va.; s. Judge Francis T. and Mary Ann (Alexander) A.; ed. Washington Coll. (now Washington and Lee U.); LL.B., U. of Va., 1866; hon. LL.D. from Hampton-Sydney Coll., Virginia; m. Maza Blair, Aug. 9, 1875; children—Ruth Floyd (wife of Dr. Charles McCulloch), Anna Aylette (Mrs. C. S. McNulty), Maj. W. D. A., Judith N., Ellen Graham. Served in 4th Va. Inf., Stonewall Brigade, 1861; wounded, battle Manassas. Admitted to bar, 1866. Mem. Va. Senate, 1869-73; House of Delegates, 3 terms; U.S. commr. Paris Expn., 1878; atty.-gen. of Va., 1902-10. Mem. Va. Consti. Conv., 1901-02. Trustee Washington and Lee U., 1885—, and rector, 1914-23. Home: Lexington, Va. Died June 21, 1930.

ANDERSON, William Brennan, clergyman; b. Monmouth, Ill., Dec. 7, 1868; s. David and Margaret (Nelson) A.; A.B., Westminster Coll., 1894, D.D., 1914; grad. Pittsburgh Theol. Sem., 1897; LL.D., Westminster, 1924; m. Mary Blanche Heidelbaugh, June 30, 1897 (died 1928); children—Gerald Howard (dec.), Lelia Blodwen (dec.), David Dean, Douglas McClure, Harriet Margaret. Ordained U.P. ministry, 1897, and went as missionary to India; pres. Gordon Coll., Rawal Pindi, 1899-1903; asso. sec. Bd. of Foreign Missions U.P. Ch. of N.A., 1909-10, 1914-16; corr. sec. same, 1916—; moderator of Gen. Assembly U.P. Ch., 1933-34. Republican. Author: Bible Lessons for Bible Teachers, 1901; Far North in India (with C. R. Watson), 1909; A Watered Garden, 1919. Home: Philadelphia, Pa. Died Jan. 6, 1940.

ANDERSON, W(illiam) C(larence), chmn. bd. Food Machinery Corp.; b. Worthington, Ind., Jan. 19, 1860; s. John W. and Elisabeth Ann (Stark) A.; ed. in public school, San Joaquin County, Calif.; m. Margaret Melvina Shafer, Sept. 10, 1885; children—Elmer Shafer, Clarence Cecil, Earl Raymond, Marjory Elizabeth, W. Charles, Albert Ardis, Gertrude Evlyn (Mrs. Raymond Lowell). Father moved by covered wagon to Calif., 1863; began to learn blacksmith trade, 1876, later worked on a farm, San Joaquin County, until 1884; began mfr. fruit handling machinery, San Jose, Calif., 1889; organized Anderson Prune Dipper Co., 1898; consol. with similar concerns to form Anderson Barngrover Mfg. Co., mfrs. canning machinery, and served as pres.; sold out to Food Machinery Co., 1927, and then chmn. bd. dirs.; pres. Anderson Barngrover Ranch Co.; pres. Anderson Orchard Co. Trustee Coll. of the Pacific. Republican. Methodist. Home: Los Gatos, Calif. Died Mar. 19, 1940.

ANDERSON, William Henry, pub.; b. Troy, N.Y., Jan. 31, 1862; s. Robert and Honora (Burke) A.; ed. Christian Brothers Acad., pub. schs. and Troy Business Coll.; m. Carolyn L. Poole, Oct. 15, 1890; children—Charles Francis, Robert P., William N., Elizabeth. With Troy (N.Y.) Times, 1878—, mgr., 1897-1916, co-proprietor and pub., 1916—. Republican. Catholic. K.C. Home: Troy, N.Y. Died Oct. 1, 1940.

ANDERSON, William Madison, clergyman; b. Rock Hill, S.C., Sept. 29, 1889; s. William Madison and Sarah Knott (Latta) A.; student Vanderbilt U., 1907-10; A.B., Austin Coll., Sherman, Tex., 1911, D.D., 1924; B.D., Austin Theol. Sem., 1914; m. Nancy Lee Gossett, Oct. 23, 1916; children—Sarah Catherine, Nancy Lee. Ordained ministry Presbyn. Ch. in U.S., 1914; pastor East Dallas (Tex.) Ch., 1914; sec. schs. and colleges of Presbyn. Ch. in Tex., 1915; asso. with father as pastor First Ch., Dallas, until his decease, 1924; pastor same ch., 1924—. An organizer Evangelical Theol. Coll., Dallas, and Presbyn. Clinic ($200,000)—charity clinic for babies—of which was pres. Trustee Austin Coll., Evang. Theol. Coll. Mason. Home: Dallas, Tex. Died Nov. 11, 1935.

ANDERSON, Winslow, surgeon; collegiate edn.; M.D., U. of Calif., 1884; L.R.C.P., M.R.C.P., London, 1891; M.R.C.S., Eng., 1891; L.S.A., London, 1891; m. Bertha Lillian Collins, Mar. 1890. Pres. and prof. gynecology and abdominal surgery, Coll. Phys. and Surg., San Francisco, 1896-1911; emeritus; surgeon-in-chief to St. Winifred's Hosp., San Francisco, 1899—, to Sierra Ry. Co., 1904—; abdominal surgeon and gynecologist to San Francisco Hosp. Mem. State Bd. Health, Calif., 1893-97, 1900-03; ex-mem. Bd. Med. Examiners, State of Calif.; surgeon-gen. N.G. Calif., 1900-04, 1907-11. Editor Pacific Med. Jour., 1890—. Author: Mineral Springs and Health Resorts of California; also articles on diseases of the lungs, in 20th Century Practice of Medicine. Home: San Francisco, Calif. Died May 8, 1917.

ANDRADE, Cipriano, rear adm. U.S. Navy; b. Tampico, Mex., Sept. 1, 1840; s. Cipriano and Elizabeth (Edwards) A.; ed. pub. and pvt. schs., Phila., to 1857; studied engrng. at Franklin Inst., in connection with practical course at Southwark Foundry, Phila., 1858-61; m. Annie A. Berry, June 1, 1870. Apptd. 3d asst. engr., July 1, 1861; advanced through the grades to capt. navy on active list, Mar. 3, 1899; rear adm., retired, July 1, 1901, under naval personnel act. Took part in various engagements in Civil War, and afterward in active service as engr. officer of navy; active service during Spanish War on shore and afloat. Died 1911.

ANDREEN, Gustav Albert, coll. pres.; b. Porter, Ind., Mar. 13, 1864; s. Rev. Andrew and Hilda (Esping) A.; A.B., Augustana Coll., 1881; European univs., 2 yrs.; Ph.D., Yale, 1898; studied law 1½ yrs. in Rock Island, Ill.; m. Mary Strand, Aug. 7, 1890. Instr., Augustana Coll., 1882-84; prof. langs., Bethany Coll., Kan., 1886-93; instr. German, 1894-1900, prof. Scandinavian langs. and lit., 1900-01, Yale; pres. Augustana Coll., 1901-35 (emeritus); serving as gen. alumni sec. of the coll. Author: Det Svenska Språket i Amerika, 1900; Studies in the German Idyl, 1902; History of the Educational Work of the Augustana Synod, 1910; L. P. Esbjorn and The Pioneers of 1849 (75th Anniversary), 1924; The Early Missionary Work of the Augustana Synod in New York City (1865-1866), 1932; History of Augustana College at Its 75th Anniversary, 1935. Home: Moline, Ill. Died Oct. 1, 1940.

ANDRESS, James Mace, psychologist; b. Chesaning, Mich., July 30, 1881; s. James Thomas and Susan (Babion) A.; B.Pd., A.B., Mich. State Normal Coll., 1905, M.Ed., 1923; Ph.M., U. of Chicago, 1906; A.M., Harvard, 1908; Ph.D., Clark U., 1916; m. Annie Laura Turner, June 29, 1910; children—Judith, Charlotte, Philip, Ruth. Instr. history and edn., Manchester (Ind.) Coll., 1906-07; head dept. of psychology and sch. hygiene, State Normal Sch., Worcester, Mass., 1908-15; head dept. of psychology and child study, Boston Normal Sch., 1915-23. Congregationalist. Mason. Author: Johann Gottfried Herder as an Educator, 1916; Teaching Hygiene in the Grades, 1918; Health Education in Rural Schools, 1919; Rosy Cheeks and Strong Heart, 1920; A Journey to Health Land, 1924; The Boys and Girls of Wake-up Town, 1924; Summer Fun, 1931. Collaborator in various works and health series; editor of "Understanding the Child," 1930-35; editor of School and Health Dept., Hygeia (pub. by A.M.A.), 1928—. Home: Newtonville, Mass. Died Feb. 5, 1942.

ANDREW, A(bram) Piatt, congressman; b. La Porte, Ind., Feb. 12, 1873; s. Abram Piatt and Helen (Merrell) A.; B.A., Princeton, 1893, M.A. (hon.), 1923; univs. of Halle, Berlin, Paris, 1897-99; A.M., Ph.D., Harvard, 1900. Instr. and asst. prof., economics, Harvard, 1900-09; expert asst. and editor of publs. of Nat. Monetary Commn., 1908-11; dir. of the mint, Nov. 1909-June 1910; asst. sec. of the Treasury, 1910-12; elected mem. 67th Congress, 6th Mass. Dist., to fill vacancy, Sept. 1921; re-elected 68th to 74th Congresses (1923-37). Republican. Commd. maj. U.S.N.A., Sept. 1917; lt. col. Sept. 1918; served in France, first with the French, later with U.S. Army, Dec. 1914-May 1919; organized and directed Am. Field Service with the French Army (consisting of 44 vol. ambulance and transport sections), 1914-17. Awarded Croix de Guerre and named Chevalier de la Légion d'Honneur, 1917; Officier de la Légion d'Honneur, 1927; D.S.M. (U.S.), 1919; Officer Order of Leopold (Belgium). Treas. Am. Red Cross, 1910-12; del. Internat. Conf. of Red Cross, 1912; del. Rep. Nat. Conv., 1924 and 1928; del. of Am. Legion to Fidac Congress, Rome, 1925. Trustee Princeton U. Home: Gloucester, Mass. Died June 3, 1936.

ANDREW, Harriet White Fisher (Harriet White Fisher), author; b. Pennline, Crawford Co., Pa.; d. Oscar A. and Hannah (Fisher) White; ed. Young Ladies' Classical Sem., Cleveland; finished at Hildesheim, Germany, 1882; m. Clark Fisher (chief engr. U.S.N.), July 20, 1898 (died Dec. 31, 1903); m. 2d, Sylvano Alfredo Andrew (lt. Argentine Navy), Apr. 27, 1912. Owner Eagle Anvil Works, Trenton, N.J., conducting business as Fisher & Norris. Presbyterian. Author: A Woman's World Trip in a Motor Car, 1911. Home: Trenton, N.J. Died Nov. 16, 1939.

ANDREW, Henry Hersey; b. Boston, Mass.; Apr. 26, 1858; s. Gov. John A. (war gov. of Mass.) and Eliza Jones (Hersey) A.; student Harvard, 1880-81; U. of Ga. Law Sch., 1888; 3 yrs. in Europe; married; children—Beatrice, Margaret Forrester; m. 2d, Mary Raymond Garrettson, Jan. 16, 1901; 1 son, John Albion II (dec.). Admitted to W.Va. bar, 1888; Rep. nominee for W.Va. Senate, 1898; founder West Virginia News, Ronceverte, 1898. Commd. capt. W. Va. Militia, Nov. 16, 1887; raised 2d Regt. and commd. col., Mar. 31, 1888; with Am. Red Cross, in France and Eng., May 6-Nov. 7, 1918; rank of capt. U.S.A. (assimilated). Republican. Episcopalian. Mason. Home: New York, N.Y. Died Aug. 9, 1934.

ANDREWS, Addison Fletcher, musical mgr.; b. Cavendish, Vt., Apr. 2, 1857; s. Rufus F. and Mary Cornelia (Fletcher) A.; removed to New York in boyhood; A.M., Dartmouth, 1878; studied law; also studied violin with Godone and vocal art with Tamaro; m. Ella Reed, May 23, 1883. Tenor in ch. choirs 25 yrs., and in Schumann Male Quartet 15 yrs.; in newspaper work on Tribune, Telegram, Commercial Advertiser, Graphic and other New York journals; asst. mgr. Carnegie Hall and the Symphony Orchestra, 1 yr.; then in business as musical mgr. Composer quartets, anthems, piano and violin pieces, "Dartmouth Songs" (16 compositions for male voices), Tiny Tunes for Tiny People, etc. Home: New York, N. Y. Died Oct. 27, 1924.

ANDREWS, Alexander Boyd, railroad official; b. Franklin Co., N.C., July 23, 1841; s. William J. A. Entered C.S.A. as 2d lt. Co. E, 1st N.C. Cav., June 1861; wounded at Jack's Shop, Va., Sept. 1863; m. Julia M. Johnston, Sept. 1, 1869. Supt. Raleigh & Gaston Ry. Co. and Raleigh & Augusta R.R., 1867-75; supt. N.C. div. Richmond & Danville R.R., 1875-83; also supt. Atlantic & N.C. R.R., 1878-80; pres. Western N. C. R.R., 1881; asst. to the pres., 1883-86, 3d v.p., 1886-89, 2d v.p., 1889-94, and gen. agt. of receivers, 1892-94, Richmond & Danville Ry. Co.; 2d v.p., 1894-95, 1st v.p., Oct. 1, 1895—, Southern Ry.; also 1st v.p. M.&O. R.R., Ala., Great Southern R.R.; pres. Danville & Western Ry. Co., Blue Ridge Ry. Co., Augusta Southern R.R. Co., Tallulah Falls Ry. Co., Hartwell Ry. Co. Dir. since 1871, v.p., 1890—, Citizens' Nat. Bank, Raleigh. Trustee U. of N.C. Home: Raleigh, N.C. Died Apr. 19, 1915.

ANDREWS, Arthur Leonard, lawyer; b. Marion, Linn Co., Ia., Apr. 16, 1855; s. George (M.D.) and Julia Ann (Hooker) A.; B.A., Wesleyan U., Conn., 1875, M.A., 1878; m. Alice Anable, Sept. 4, 1879; 1 son, Harold F. Admitted to N.Y. bar, 1877; practiced, Albany; mem. Thompson & Andrews, 1879-85, Stedman, Thompson & Andrews, 1885-96, again Thompson & Andrews, 1896-1902, then alone; corp. counsel, Albany, 1900-20. Apptd. commr. to devise charter for cities of 2d class, N.Y., 1895; commr. Hudson-Fulton Celebration, 1909. Republican. Mason. Home: Albany, N.Y. Died Sept. 15, 1938.

ANDREWS, Charles, judge; b. Whitestown, N.Y., May 27, 1827; acad. edn. at Cazenovia Sem.; (LL.D., Hamilton, 1877, Columbia, 1887, Yale, 1898); admitted to bar, Jan. 1849; m. Marcia A. Shankland, May 17, 1855; father of William Shankland A. Dist. atty., Onondaga Co., 1853-56; mayor Syracuse, 1861, 1862, 1868; del.-at-large N.Y. Constl. Conv., 1867; judge N.Y. Ct. of Appeals, 1870-97 (chief judge, 1881-84, 1893-97). Home: Syracuse, N.Y. Died Oct. 22, 1918.

ANDREWS, Charles Bartlett, chief justice State of Conn.; b. Sunderland, Mass., Nov. 4, 1834; grad. Amherst Coll. (LL.D., Amherst, Wesleyan, Yale); mem. Conn. senate, 1868, and 1869; house, 1878; gov. Conn., 1879-81. Home: Litchfield, Conn. Died 1902.

ANDREWS, Christopher Columbus, soldier, diplomat; b. at Hillsboro, N.H., Oct. 27, 1829; s. Luther and Nabby (Beard) A.; attended Francestown Acad. and Harvard Law Sch.; admitted to Mass. bar, 1850; m. Mary Baxter, Dec. 1868 (died 1893). Went to Kan., 1854, later to St. Cloud, Minn.; served in Union Army as capt. 3d Minn. Inf., Nov. 4, 1861; lt. col., Dec. 1, 1862; col., Aug. 9, 1863; brig. gen. vols., Jan. 5, 1864; bvtd. maj. gen. vols., Mar. 9, 1865; hon. mustered out, Jan. 15, 1866, U.S. minister to Sweden and Norway, 1869-77; supervisor U.S. Census, Minn., 1880; consul gen., Rio de Janeiro, 1882-85; forestry commr. of Minn., 1895-1911; sec. Minn. Forestry Bd., 1899-1923. Author: History of Campaign of Mobile, 1867; Brazil, Its Conditions and Prospects, 1886; Administrative Reform, etc. Furnished report on forestry of Sweden to U.S. Dept. of State, 1872; 16 of his ann. reports on forestry have been published. Home: St. Paul, Minn. Died Sept. 21, 1923.

ANDREWS, Clarence Edward, college prof.; b. N.Y. City, Nov. 25, 1883; s. William Sturgis and Ida Augusta (Clark) A.; B.A., Yale, 1906, M.A., 1908, Ph.D., 1912; unmarried. Instr. English, Yale, 1908-09; Amherst, 1909-11, asst. prof. same coll., 1911-14; asst. prof. and prof. English, Ohio State U., 1915—. Commd. 1st lt., Air Service U.S.A., Oct. 8, 1917, duty at Washington, D.C.; with A.E.F. in France, 1918-19; attached to Balkan Div. of Am. Commn. to Negotiate Peace, Paris, Feb.-May 1919; officer Am. relief adminstrn. in Serbian Macedonia, summer 1919. Awarded Médaille de Miséricorde (Serbia); Chevalier Order of St. Sava (Serbia). Author: Richard Brome, A Study of His Life and Works, 1913; From the Front, 1918; Writing and Reading of Verse, 1918; Old Morocco and the Forbidden Atlas, 1922; The Innocents of Paris, 1928. Compiler and editor; Romantic Poetry (with M. O. Percival), 1924; Victorian Poetry (with same), 1924; The Poetry of Eighteen Nineties (with same), 1926. Home: Columbus, O. Deceased.

ANDREWS, Clement Walker, librarian; b. Salem, Mass., Jan. 13, 1858; s. Joseph and Judith (Walker) A.; A.B., Harvard, 1879, A.M., 1880; (LL.D., Northwestern, 1911); unmarried. Instr. chemistry, 1883-95, librarian, 1889-95, Mass. Inst. Tech.; librarian John Crerar Library, Chicago, 1895-1928. Home: Chicago, Ill. Died Nov. 20, 1930.

ANDREWS, Daniel Marshall, civil engr.; b. Americus, Ga., Oct. 24, 1853; s. Judge Garnett and Annulet (Ball) A.; bro. of Eliza Frances A.; U. of Ga. Sch. of Civ. Engring., 1872-74 inclusive (graduation prevented by illness); m. Adeline Van Court, Apr. 20, 1897. In ry. engring., Ga. and S.C., 1881-84; asst. engr., U.S. Engr. Dept., on river and harbor improvement, Ga., Ala. and Fla., 1884—. Episcopalian. Home: Rome, Ga. Died June 28, 1917.

ANDREWS, Edmund, surgeon; b. Putney, Vt., April 22, 1824; grad. Univ. of Mich., 1849; M.D. and A.M., 1852 (LL.D., 1880); m. E. Eliza Taylor, Apr. 13, 1852; m. 2d, Mrs. Frances M. Barrett, Apr. 25, 1877. Demonstrator and prof. med. dept. same, 1852-56; surgeon 1st Regt. Ill. Light Art.; surgeon-in-chief Camp Douglas, Civil war; since then in practice in Chicago; was instr. in human and comparative anatomy, Rush Med. Coll.; a founder and prof. surgery, Chicago Med. Coll. (now med. dept. Northwestern Univ.); was surgeon-in-chief Mercy Hospital. Home: Chicago, Ill. Died 1904.

ANDREWS, Edward Gayer, M.E. bishop, May 24, 1872—; b. New Hartford, N.Y., Aug. 7, 1825; s. George and Polly A.; grad. Wesleyan Univ., Conn., 1847 (D.D., Genesee Coll.; LL.D., Allegheny Coll., and Wesleyan Univ.). Began M.E. ministry, 1848; pastor in Central N.Y., 6 yrs.; teacher and prin. Cazenovia Sem., 1854-64; pastor in Stamford, Conn., and Brooklyn, N.Y., 1864-72. Visited missions in Europe and India, 1876-77; in Mexico, 1881; in Japan, Korea and China, 1889-90. Home: New York, N.Y. Died 1907.

ANDREWS, E(dward) Wyllys, surgeon; b. Chicago, Ill., Mar. 25, 1856; s. Dr. Edmund and Sarah E. (Taylor) A.; A.B., Northwestern U., 1878, A.M., 1881; M.D., Chicago Med. Coll., 1881; U. of Vienna, 1884-85; m. Alice Scranton, 1890, g.d. of Hon. David Davis, judge and v.p. of U.S., and U.S. senator. Engaged in practice as surgeon in Chicago, 1881—; prof. surgery, Northwestern U. Med. Sch., 1883—; surgeon to Mercy Hosp., 1881—, Michael Reese Hosp., 1891, Wesley Hosp., 1900. Capt.-surgeon, I.N.G., 1884. Home: Chicago, Ill. Died Jan. 21, 1927.

ANDREWS, E(lisha) Benjamin, educator; b. at Hinsdale, N.H., Jan. 10, 1844; s. Erastus and Almira (Bartlett) A.; served pvt. to 2d lt. in Union Army in Civil War; wounded at Petersburg, Aug. 24, 1864, losing an eye; A.B., Brown U., 1870, A.M., 1873; Newton Theol. Inst., 1872-74; matriculated universities of Berlin and Munich, 1882-83 (D.D., Colby, 1884; LL.D., U. of Neb., 1884, Brown, 1900, U. of Chicago, 1901; Ph.D., U. of Neb., 1912); m. Ella Anna Allen, Nov. 25, 1870. Principal of the Conn. Lit. Instn., Suffield, 1870-72; ordained Bapt. ministry, 1874; pastor Beverly, Mass., 1874-75; pres. Denison U., Granville, O., 1875-79; prof. homiletics, Newton Theol. Instn., 1879-82; prof. history and polit. economy, Brown U., 1882-88; prof. polit. economy and finance, Cornell, 1888-89; pres. Brown U., 1889-98; supt. schs., Chicago, 1898-1900; chancellor U. of Neb., 1900-08, emeritus. Author: Institutes of Constitutional History, English and American, 1884; Institutes of General History, 1885, 1895; Institutes of Economics, 1889, 1900; Outlines of the Principles of History (transl. from Droysen), 1890; Eternal Words (sermons), 1893; An Honest Dollar, 1894; Wealth and Moral Law, 1894; History of the United States, 1894, 1902; History of the Last Quarter Century in the United States, 1896; Cosmology, 1900; History of United States in Our Own Times, 1904; The Call of the Land, 1913. Died Oct. 30, 1917.

ANDREWS, Eliza Frances, author; b. Washington, Ga., Aug. 10, 1840; d. Judge Garnett and Annulet (Ball) A.; A.B., La Grange Coll., Ga., 1857; hon. A.M., Wesleyan Coll., Macon, 1882; prof. latter, 1885-97. Author: A Family Secret, 1876; A Mere Adventure, 1878; Prince Hal, or the Romance of a Rich Young Man, 1882; Botany All the Year Round, 1903; The Wartime Journal of a Georgia Girl, 1908; A Practical Course in Botany, 1911. Also serials: How He Was Tempted (Detroit Free Press); The Story of an Ugly Girl; The Mistake of His Life (Chautauquan). Home: Rome, Ga. Deceased.

ANDREWS, Frank, lawyer; b. Fayette County, Tex., June 15, 1864; s. Rev. G. L. and Martha A. (Sellers) A.; B.A., Southwestern U., Georgetown, Tex., 1885; m. Roxalie Smith, Dec. 22, 1891. Began practice, Belton, Tex., 1887; removed to Houston, 1895; mem. Andrews, Kelley, Kurth & Campbell; city atty., Belton, 1887-91; asst. atty. gen. of Tex., 1891-95; chmn. Dem. State Exec. Com., 1904-06; declined apptmts. as dist. judge, 1897, judge Court of Civil Appeals, 1899, and judge Supreme Court of Tex., 1918. Mason. Home: Houston, Tex. Died Dec. 7, 1936.

ANDREWS, Frank Taylor, gynecologist; b. Chicago, Ill., Apr. 10, 1858; s. Edmund (M.D.) and Sarah E. (Taylor) A.; A.B., Northwestern U., 1881, A.M., 1884; M.D., Chicago Med. Coll., 1884; m. Clara M. Gallup, 1893; children—Frank Taylor, Jr., Howard Gallup, Robert Harvey, Susanna Elizabeth (Mrs. Hallett Wilber Thorne). Practiced at Chicago, 1884—; emeritus prof. gynecology, Northwestern U. Med. Sch.; formerly gynecologist to Mercy and Wesley hosps. Commd. 1st lt. M.R.C. U.S. Army, 1911. Republican. Home: Winnetka, Ill. Died Nov. 7, 1940.

ANDREWS, Garnett, lawyer; b. Washington, Ga., May 15, 1837; s. Judge Garnett and Annulet (Ball) A.; ed. Washington Male Acad. and Univ. of Ga.; m. Rosalie Champ Beirne of Va., 1867. Lt.-col. C. S. A., comd. 8th battalion Confed. Inf.; fought last action of any troops attached to Army of Northern Va., at Salisbury, N.C., April 12, 1865, three days after Appomattox, where, with 600 men, resisted Gen. Stoneman's whole div. until trains with officials and treasure from Richmond passed South; desperately wounded there in hand-to-hand combat, shot and sabered. Lawyer Yazoo City, Miss., until 1882; took leading part in overthrow of carpet-bag govt.; mem. Miss. legislature 1879-80; removed to Chattanooga 1882; mayor 1891-92. Author: Andrews' Mississippi Digest, 1881. Home: Chattanooga, Tenn. Died 1903.

ANDREWS, George, army officer; b. Providence, R.I., Aug. 26, 1850; s. George Lippitt and Alice Beverly (Potter) A.; grad. U.S. Mil. Acad., 1876; m. Katherine Brayton Taintor, Dec. 10, 1882. Apptd. 2d lt. 25th U.S. Inf., June 15, 1876; promoted through the ranks to brig.-gen. and adj.-gen. U.S. Army, Aug. 5, 1912; retired, Aug. 26, 1914. Died Sept. 10, 1928.

ANDREWS, George Leonard, col. U.S. Army, retired 1892; b. Bridgewater, Mass., Aug. 31, 1828; grad. West Point, 1851 (A.M., Dartmouth); m. Sara Bridge Fiske, Dec. 21, 1853. Superintended erection of fortifications in Boston harbor; asst. prof. engineering, West Point, 1854-55; civil engr. until 1861; lt. col. and col. 2d Mass. Vols. in Civil war, 1861-65;

brig. gen. and bvt. maj. gen.; U.S. marshal for Mass. in 1867-71; prof. French, 1871-82; prof. modern languages, 1882-92, West Point. Home: Brookline, Mass. Died 1899.

ANDREWS, George Lippitt, brig. gen. U.S. Army; b. Providence, R.I., Apr. 22, 1828; s. George and Cornelia Augusta (Lippitt) A.; ed. in grammar schs., Providence, R.I.; m. Alice Beverly Potter; m. 2d, Emily Kemble (Oliver) Brown, May 13, 1874; father of George A. In business life June, 1841, at Providence, R.I., afterward New York, and St. Louis, 1858. Entered R.I. Militia, 1844, maj., 1848, col., 1853; resigned 1856; 2d lt. 2d Co., Mo. N.G., 1859; advanced through the grades to col. 25th U.S. Inf., Jan. 1, 1871; retired for age, Apr. 22, 1892; advanced to rank of brig. gen. retired, by act of Apr. 23, 1904. Supt. Indian Affairs for Ariz., July 1869-71. Served at beginning of Civil War through campaign under Gen. Nathan Lyon, 1861; wounded and horse killed under him at battle of Wilson's Creek, Mo., Aug. 10, 1861, while comdg. brigade and regt.; with Army of Potomac and engaged in its operations, 1862-63; organized and recruited 17th and 13th Inf., U.S. Army, 1863-66; in Indian Country west of the Mississippi for 25 yrs. Bvtd.: lt. col., Aug. 30, 1862, "for gallant and meritorious services at 2d Bull Run"; col. May 3, 1863, for same at Chancellorsville. Republican. Episcopalian. Home: Washington, D.C. Died July 19, 1920.

ANDREWS, George Pierce, lawyer; b. North Bridgeton, Me., Sept. 29, 1835; s. Solomon and Sibyl Ann A.; ed. Williston Sem., Easthampton, Mass.; grad. Yale, 1858; m. Mrs. Catherine M. Van Auken, 1889. Admitted to bar, 1861; asst. U.S. dist. atty., N.Y., 1859-65; asst. and corporation counsel, N.Y., 1872-84; asso. justice supreme court, N.Y., 1884-1901. Died 1902.

ANDREWS, George Whitfield, musician; b. Wayne, Ashtabula County, O., Jan. 19, 1861; s. Melanchthon Zuinglius and Augusta Caroline (Cathcart) A.; ed. pub. schs., Oberlin; grad. Oberlin Conservatory of Music, 1879, Mus. Bac., 1906; hon. A.M., Oberlin Coll., 1900, Mus. Doc., 1903; studied in Europe, 1884-86, 1898-99; m. Harriet Augusta Clark, July 3, 1888; children—Esther Cathcart, Mildred Clark (dec.), Elizabeth Crosby (dec.), George Whitfield, Eleanor Rice. Teacher organ and composition, Oberlin Conservatory of Music, 1883—; concert organist, 1876— (still active); orchestral and choral conductor, 1892—; organist at Congl. Ch., Oberlin, 1883—. Condr. Oberlin Musical Union until 1929. Conglist. Home: Oberlin, O. Died Aug. 18, 1932.

ANDREWS, Harry Eugene, editor; b. Pittston (now Randolph), Me., Dec. 22, 1861; s. John Albion and Delia (Brookings) A.; pub. sch. edn.; m. Lisbeth Bertrand, Oct. 25, 1900. Entered newspaper business at 17, with Lewiston (Me.) Journal, 1878-98, last 8 yrs. one of proprs.; with Los Angeles Times, 1898—, mng. editor, 1906— (one of owners); was in office when the Times Bldg. was blown up by dynamiters, Oct. 1, 1910, and 20 men killed; dir. The Times-Mirror Co.; pres. Big Conduit Land Co.; v.p. Van Nuys Boul. Land Co. Republican. Episcopalian. K.T. Home: Los Angeles, Calif. Died Sept. 20, 1926.

ANDREWS, Herbert Marston, missionary; b. Enfield, N.H., Sept. 9, 1851; s. Randall and Rhoda Choate (Marston) A.; B.A., Dartmouth, 1876, M.A., 1881; grad. Union Theol. Sem., 1879; m. at Phila., Sara Catherine Hutchinson, Nov. 16, 1887; 1 dau., Helen Ethel (dec.). Deacon, 1879, priest, 1880, P.E. Ch.; pastoral work, New York, 1879-81; rector Littleton, N.H., 1881-83; stated supply Congl. Ch., Bethlehem, N.H., 1883-84; pastor, Franklin, N.H., 1884-85, Enfield, 1885-86, Peacham, Vt., 1887-88, Romeyn Chapel (Presbyn.), New York, 1889-90; missionary Presbyn. Ch. U.S.A. in India, 1890-99; pres. Woodstock Coll., India, 1899-1915; retired. Presbyn. Republican. Home: Bellingham, Wash. Died Mar 16, 1929.

ANDREWS, Horace Ellsworth, capitalist; b. 1863; s. Samuel A.; Ph.B., Yale, 1882. Pres. N.Y. State Rys., Mohawk Valley Co., Rochester Ry. & Light Co. Home: St. James, N.Y. Died Dec. 1, 1918.

ANDREWS, J. Warren, organist; b. Lynn, Mass., Apr. 6, 1860; s. Samuel Herrick and Hannah G. (Kelly) A.; ed. in music principally in Boston; m. Addie M. Breed, Apr. 22, 1880; children—Nellie Edna (wife of Dr. Harry L. Fisher), Willard Elmer, Ralph Warren. Began as organist M.E. Ch., Swampscott, Mass., 1871; later organist 1st Bapt. Ch. and Boston Street M.E. Ch., Lynn, Mass.; organist and choirmaster Trinity Ch., Newport, R.I., 1879-88, also organist Zion Ch. and condr. St. John's Boy Choir; organist Pilgrim Ch., Cambridge, Mass., 1888-91, Plymouth Ch., Minneapolis, 1891-98; organist and choirmaster Ch. of the Divine Paternity, New York, 1898—. Mason. Composer music for organ and ch. services. Home: Grantwood, N.J. Died Jan. 18, 1932.

ANDREWS, James DeWitt, lawyer, author; b. Sterling, Ill., Feb. 22, 1856; s. Robert C. and Rhoda Clark (Kingsbury) A.; grad. Sterling High Sch., 1876, LL.B., Albany Law Sch. (Union U.), 1879; LL.M., Chicago Law Sch., 1897; (LL.D., Ruskin U., 1904); m. Minnie Alice Barrett, June 9, 1880. Admitted to bar, 1879; practiced law, Whiteside County, Ill., 1879-1891, Chicago, 1891-1903, New York, 1903—. City atty., Sterling, Ill., 1880. Became law critic, Callaghan & Co., law pubs., Chicago, 1891; prof. law, Northwestern U., 1895; prof. jurisprudence (post-grad.), Chicago Law Sch., 1897. Presbyn. Republican. Author: Andrews' Stephen's Pleading (2 edits.), 1894, 1902; Wilson's Works (edited), 1896; Illinois Supreme Court Manual, 1898; Cooley's Blackstone (4th edit.), 1899; Andrews' American Law (2 edits.), 1900, 1908. Home: New York, N.Y. Died Apr. 11, 1928.

ANDREWS, John Newman, brig. gen. U.S. Vols., retired April 1, 1899; b. "Andrusia," Wilmington, Del., Sept. 16, 1838; grad. U.S. Mil. Acad., 1860; m. Lucy McEntee. Served through Civil war; bvtd. capt. for gallantry, Cedar Mountain; maj., for same, Franklin, Tenn.; and lt. col. Served in Indian country and Spanish-Am. war. Home: Wilmington, Del. Died 1903.

ANDREWS, Launcelot (Winchester), chemist; b. London, Can., June 13, 1856; s. Alfred A. and Louisa (Jones) A.; Ph.B., Yale, 1875; A.M., Ph.D., Göttingen, 1882; grad. course in philosophy, history, etc., Harvard; m. Anna Ritter Lane, 1883. Taught high sch., Springfield, Mass., 1876-77; practiced as analytical chemist, Springfield, 1878-82; prof. chemistry, Ia. State Coll. of Agr., 1884-85; prof. chemistry, State U. of Ia., 1885-1904; research and cons. chemist to Mallinckrodt Chem. Works, St. Louis, 1904-10; special investigator in canning, U.S. Dept. of Agr., 1913-14; research chemist to Victor Chem. Works, Chicago, 1915-21. Author: An Introduction to the Study of Qualitative Analysis, 1891; etc. Home: Williamstown, Mass. Died 1938.

ANDREWS, Marietta Minnigerode (Mrs. Eliphalet Fraser Andrews), painter, author; b. Richmond, Va., Dec. 11, 1869; d. Charles and Virginia Cuthbert (Powell) Minnigerode; studied art under E. F. Andrews (Washington, D.C.), William M. Chase (New York), Luigi Chialiva (Paris), Ernst Lieberman (Munich); m. Eliphalet Fraser Andrews, dir. Corcoran Sch. of Art, Sept. 24, 1895 (died 1915); children—Mary Lord (dec.), Eliphalet Fraser. Awarded Corcoran gold medal, 1899. Author: Songs of a Mother (verse), 1917; Out of the Dust (verse), 1920; The Darker Drink, 1922; (pageants) The Cross Triumphant; The Master Builders; Voice of the Wild Flowers; Our Common Heritage; That Sweet Story of Old; Thomas Jefferson; Joan of Arc; Memoirs of a Poor Relation, 1927. Home: Washington, D.C. Died Aug. 7, 1931.

ANDREWS, Martin Register, coll. prof.; b. Meigs, O., Apr. 6, 1842; s. Seth and Elvira Thora A.; grad. McConnelsville (O.) High Sch., 1859; pvt. 62d Ohio Inf., 1861; in signal corps U.S. Army, 1863; 2d lt. and adj. 43d Battalion, Ohio Vol. Inf., 1863-64; A.B., Marietta Coll., 1869, A.M., 1872; m. Amanda Laughlin, Aug. 12, 1869; m. 2d, Susan K. Hook, Sept. 1, 1891. Supt. Steubenville (O.) pub. sch., 1870-79; prin. Marietta Acad., 1879-94; prof. history and polit. science, Marietta Coll., 1895-1910; emeritus prof. on Carnegie Foundation, 1910—. Home: Marietta, O. Died Apr. 20, 1913.

ANDREWS, Mary Raymond Shipman, novelist; d. Rt. Rev. Jacob Shaw and Ann Louise Shipman; m. William Shankland Andrews, Dec. 31, 1884. Author: Vive L'Empéreur; A Kidnaped Colony; Bob and the Guides, 1906; A Good Samaritan, 1906; The Perfect Tribute, 1906; The Militants, 1907; Better Treasure, 1908; Enchanted Forest, 1909; Lifted Bandage, 1910; Counsel Assigned, 1912; Marshall, 1912; Eternal Masculine, 1913; (with Roy Irving Murray) August First, 1915; Three Things, 1915; The Eternal Feminine, 1916; Crosses of War, 1918; Joy in the Morning, 1919; His Soul Goes Marching, 1922; Yellow Butterflies, 1922; Lost Commander, 1929. Home: Onondaga, N.Y. Died Aug. 2, 1936.

ANDREWS, Matthew Thomas, clergyman; b. near McComb City, Miss., Apr. 13, 1869; s. Thomas J. and Margarett Ellen (Rollins) A.; prep. edn., Gillsborg (Miss.) Collegiate Inst.; A.B., Mississippi Coll., 1894; D.D., Howard-Payne Coll., 1919, Baylor U., 1920; m. Theodocia Ernest Cook, Dec. 22, 1891 (dec.); children—Mamie (Mrs. B. Y. Daniel), Birdie (Mrs. S. B. Dandridge), Rosamonde, Tommie (Mrs. J. Leighton Beavers), Balla (Mrs. Wallace Wyman), Louis E. (dec.), Edna Hyatt (Mrs. Rufus Hyde); m. 2d, Gertrude Wright, Apr. 6, 1938. Ordained ministry Missionary Bapt. Ch., 1895; pastor successively Amite City, La., First Ch., Marshall, Tex., Marlin, First Ch., Denton, First Ch., Hillsboro, First Ch., Temple, 1924—, First Ch., Texarkana, 1924—. Trustee Southern Baptist Theol. Seminary. Democrat. Mason. Author: Seeing Europe with Dr. Andrews, 1923; Growing a Soul, 1926; Comrades of the Road, 1930; Adults and the Art of Learning, 1936; Seeing Africa through Africans, 1939. Home: Texarkana, Tex. Died 1939.

ANDREWS, Newton Lloyd, coll. prof.; b. Fabius, N.Y., Aug. 14, 1841; s. Nathaniel and Catharine Gertrude (Remsen) A.; A.B., Colgate U., 1862, A.M., 1864; grad. theol. dept. same, 1864; (Ph.D., Hamilton Coll., 1878; LL.D., U. of Chicago, 1883; L.H.D., Colgate U., 1914); m. Cynthia S. Burchard, Sept. 6, 1865 (died 1886); m. 2d, Charlotte P. Harbach, Dec. 27, 1888. Prin. prep. dept. Colgate U., 1864-69; prof. Greek, 1868, dean coll. faculty, 1880-95, acting pres., 1890-95, prof. Greek and lecturer on history of art, 1895—, Colgate U. Home: Hamilton, N.Y. Died Sept. 14, 1918.

ANDREWS, Robert Day, architect; b. Hartford, Conn., Mar. 5, 1857; s. Samuel James and Catharine Augusta (Day) A.; grad. Hartford High Sch., 1874; spl. course architecture Mass. Inst. Tech., 1875-76; traveled abroad as student, 1884; hon. A.M., Colo. Coll., 1901; m. Elisabeth Seaman, Apr. 20, 1887; children—Robert Engs (dec.), Katharine Day (Mrs. Clarence Cook Little), Elisabeth (Mrs. H. E. Bronson), Ellen Putnam (Mrs. William Power Blodget), Tracy Coit. Sr. mem. Andrews & Jaques, 1884-90, Andrews, Jaques & Rantoul, 1890-1917, then Andrews, Jones, Biscoe & Whitmore. Architect for new wings of Bulfinch State House, Boston, and for restoration of Bulfinch State House, Hartford, Conn., 1913-17. Author of inscription, "Obedience to Law Is Liberty," upon court houses of Worcester and Cleveland. Home: Boston, Mass. Deceased.

ANDREWS, Robert Robbins, dental surgeon; b. Boston, Mass., Aug. 7, 1844; s. Thomas Jefferson and Jerusha (Baker) A.; ed. pub. schs.; D.D.S., Boston Dental Coll., 1875; (hon. A.M., Dartmouth, 1892); m. Mary Emily Leseur, Sept. 14, 1870. Served 2 yrs. in Civil War, pvt. to lt. and adj., 47th and 60th M.V.M. Dental surgeon, Cambridge, 1869—; prof. histology, Boston Dental Coll. (trustee); trustee Tufts Coll. Awarded Jarvie gold medal, N.Y. State Dental Soc., May 3, 1911, "for distinguished services to the science and art of dentistry." Author: Embriology of the Dental Tissues, 1900; Kirk's American System of Dentistry, 1900; writer of numerous papers on dental histology. Home: Cambridge, Mass. Died Jan. 1921.

ANDREWS, Roland Franklyn, editor; b. Hartford, Conn.; s. Charles B. and Alice J. (Andrews) A.; ed. Cayuga Lake Mil. Acad.; student Cornell U., 1896-98; m. Florence Benedict, June 17, 1916. Began as reporter, Syracuse Standard, later with Hartford Telegram; mng. editor Waterbury Republican, 1900-02; asso. editor Waterbury American, 1902-12; mng. editor Hartford Times, 1912-20; editor Worcester (Mass.) Telegram-Gazette, 1920—. Pvt., lt. and capt. Conn. N.G., 1910-17; served on Mexican border, 1916; capt. comdg. motor supply train 429, U.S. Army, 1917-18. Mem. U.S. Naval Inst. Unitarian. Mason. Home: Worcester, Mass. Died Dec. 21, 1930.

ANDREWS, Samuel James, clergyman; b. Danbury, Conn., July 31, 1817; s. Rev. William and Sarah (Parkhill) A.; grad. Williams, 1839 (D.D., Union); m. Catherine A. Day, April 15, 1850; admitted to Conn. bar, 1842; Ohio bar, 1844; studied Lane Theol. Sem., Cincinnati; licensed to preach, 1846; ordained pastor Congl. Ch., E. Windsor, Conn., 1848; dismissed because of loss of voice, 1855; entered ministry of Catholic and Apostolic Ch. (Irvingite); then in charge of a congregation in Hartford. Author: Life of Our Lord Upon the Earth, 1862; God's Revelations of Himself to Men, 1885; Christianity and Anti-Christianity in Their Final Conflict, 1898; The Church and Its Organic Ministries, 1899; William Watson Andrews, a Religious Biography, 1900; Man and the Incarnation, 1905. Home: Hartford, Conn. Died 1906.

ANDREWS, Sidney Francis, lawyer; b. Allegheny City, Pa., Mar. 2, 1857; s. James and Maria (Carson) A.; B.S., Western U. of Pa., 1878; post-grad. course, Cornell U., 1878-79, Carlsruhe, Germany, 1879-80; studied law at St. Louis, 1880-82; m. Mary W. Fentress, 1887. Admitted to Mo. bar, 1882, and began practice at St. Louis; with legal dept. I.C.R.R., advancing to gen. atty.; gen. solicitor U.S.R.R. Administration, Washington, D.C. Republican. Home: Washington, D.C. Died Feb. 16, 1933.

ANDREWS, T(homas) Wingate, educator; b. Orange County, N.C., Mar. 22, 1882; s. Wilton Volney and Annie Aiken (Lloyd) A.; A.B., U. of N.C., 1908; student summers, Columbia, 1912-16; Dr. Edn., High Point (N.C.) Coll., 1933; m. Eleanor Watson, June 28, 1922. County supt. schs., Orange County, N.C., 1908-11; supt. schs., Reidsville, 1911-17, Salisbury, 1917-24, High Point, 1924—. Mem. N.C. Textbook Commn., 1922, N.C. Edn. Commn., 1926. Democrat. Baptist. Home: High Point, N.C. Died Feb. 11, 1937.

ANDREWS, Vernon Daniel, Jersey cattle breeder; b. Van Wert, Ia., July 25, 1890; s. William L. and Blanche I. (Hougas) A.; student U. of Neb., 1909-11, Neb. Sch. of Business, 1912; m. Luella Dierks, Oct. 17, 1911; children—Eloise, Doris, Beatrice, Luella Jean; m. 2d, Cecille Parker, Dec. 24, 1933. Head of commercial dept. Beatrice High Sch., 1912-13; Buick automobile distributor, 1913-16; farming and ranching, 1916—; cashier Farmers State Bank, 1919-22, pres., 1922-29; mem. Ho. of Rep., Neb., 1929-31; chief clk. Neb. Ho. of Rep., 1931—; owner Hillcrest Jersey Farm; formerly exec. sec. Cosmopolitan International; sec.-treas. and chmn. exec. com. Nat. Coursing Assn.; organizer, sec.-treas. and chmn. exec. com. Nat. Greyhound Breeders and Racing Assn.

Served as 2d lt. Neb. N.G., 1915. Republican. Mason. Author: Greyhound Stud Book (Vol. 14), 1920. Editor of Coursing News and Greyhound Stud Book. Died Mar. 13, 1937.

ANDREWS, Walter Pemberton, lawyer; b. Montgomery Co., N.C., June 7, 1865; s. Maj. Lorenzo Dow and Martha Ann (Pemberton) A.; A.B., Trinity Coll. (now Duke U.), 1887; LL.D., Washington and Lee U., 1891; m. Leontine Chisholm, July 1, 1899. Teacher, high sch., Monroe, N.C., 1887-90; admitted to Ga. bar, 1891, and practiced at Atlanta. Apptd. U.S. commr. gen. to Mediterranean and Balkan States, by President Wilson, 1913, upon behalf Panama-Pacific Expn., San Francisco, 1915; lt. col., staff of Govs. J. M. Terrell and Hugh M. Dorsey. Mem. Ga. Ho. of Rep., 1915-16, Ga. State Senate, 1917-18. Democrat. Methodist. Mason. Home: Daytona Beach, Fla. Deceased.

ANDREWS, William Given, clergyman; b. Kent, Conn., Oct. 8, 1835; s. Rev. William Watson and Mary Anne (Given) A.; A.B., Marietta (O.) Coll., 1855, A.M., 1858 (D.D., 1885); Princeton Theol. Sem., 1859-61; m. Caroline Caldwell, d. late Rear-Admiral T. A. Jenkins, U.S.N., of Washington, Dec. 11, 1895. Teacher Peekskill, N.Y., Fairfield and Hamden, Conn., 1855-59; tutor Marietta Coll., 1861-62; deacon, 1862, priest, 1864, P.E., Ch.; officiated Princeton and Rocky Hill, N.J., 1862-66; teacher and clerical asst., Hamden, Conn., 1866-67; abroad, 1867; rector, Ch. of Ascension, New Haven, Conn., 1868-79; officiated Trinity Ch., Princeton, N.J., 1880; rector Christ Ch., Guilford, Conn., 1881-1906 (emeritus). Instr. doctrinal theology, Berkeley Div. Sch., 1899. Home: Guilford, Conn. Died Dec. 23, 1912.

ANDREWS, William Loring, author; b. New York, Sept. 9, 1837; s. Loring and Caroline C. (Delemater) A.; ed. in pvt. schs.; (hon. M.A., Yale, 1893); m. Jane Elizabeth Crane, Oct. 17, 1860. Trustee Bank for Savings; dir. Continental Ins. Co.; trustee and hon. librarian Met. Mus. of Art; mem. Council of New York U. Hon. mem. 11th Army Corps Assn.; mem. Nat. Acad. Design, Met. Mus. of Art, St. Nicholas Soc.; founder and pres. Soc. of Iconophiles. Author: New Amsterdam, New Orange, New York, 1898; Fragments of American History, 1898; Old Book Sellers of New York; Prospectus of Colleges in Cambridge; Sexto Decimos et Infra, 1899; A Trio of French Engravers, 1899; Portraiture of the American Revolutionary War; James Lyne's Survey, 1900; Gossip About Book Collecting, 1900; Paul Revere and His Engraving; Iconograph of Battery and Castle Garden, Bibliopegy in the United States 1902; Treatyse of Fysshynge Wyth an Angle (black letter, 1903; New York as Washington Knew It After the Revolution, 1906; An English Bibliopole. Sportsman and Binder of Angling Books, 1907; The Heavenly Jerusalem; Catalogue of Early Printed Books Given to Yale University, 1912. Died Mar. 20, 1920.

ANDREWS, William Page, author; b. at Framingham, Mass., Nov. 22, 1848; s. Samuel Page and Rebecca Bacon (Scudder) A.; ed. pub. schs. of Salem and pvt. tutor; defective eyesight precluded univ. edn., and his health obliged a residence in Italy during greater part of last 10 yrs.; m. Edith H. Weston, Sept. 3, 1889. Unitarian. Republican. Author: Jones Very, a Memoir, 1884; Charles T. Brooks, a Memoir, 1888. Home: Salem, Mass. Died Sept. 22, 1916.

ANDREWS, William Shankland, judge; b. Syracuse, N.Y., Sept. 25, 1858; s. Charles and Marcia A. (Shankland) A.; A.B., Harvard, 1880; LL.B., Columbia, 1882; (LL.D., Syracuse, 1912, L.H.D., 1922; LL.D., Columbia, 1923); m. Mary Raymond Shipman, Dec. 31, 1884. Admitted to bar and practiced at Syracuse; justice Supreme Ct. of N.Y. for terms 1900-14, 1914-28; became judge Court of Appeals, 1917. Republican. Home: Split Rock, N.Y. Died Aug. 5, 1936.

ANDREWS, William Symes, electrical engr.; b. Saltford, Somersetshire, Eng., Sept. 10, 1847; s. Bailey Symes and Selina (Chesterton) A.; ed. pvt. sch., Bath, and bus. coll., Beckington, Eng.; came to America, 1875; m. Emma J. Marden, Jan. 1, 1891. With Edison at Menlo Park, N.J., 1879-81; supt. of testing, Edison Machine Wks. New York, 1881-83; chief elec. engr., Edison Electric Constrn. Co., 1883-86; gen. supt. Marr Constrn. Co., 1886-88; v.p., sec. and treas., Leonard & Izard Co., Chicago, 1888-89; supt. United Edison Mfg. Co., New York, 1889-91; tech. asst. Edison Gen. Electric Co., New York, 1891-92; supt. Peterboro Wks., Canada Gen. Elec. Co., Canada, 1892-93; sec. and gen. mgr. Edison Electric Illuminating Co., Lancaster, Pa., 1893-94; with Gen. Electric Co., in various capacities from 1894, then cons. engineer. Republican. Episcopalian. Home: Schenectady, N.Y. Died July 1, 1929.

ANDRUS, John Emory, congressman, mfr.; b. Pleasantville, N.Y., Feb. 16, 1841; s. Rev. Loyal B. and Ann (Palmer) A.; A.B., Wesleyan U., Conn., 1862 (LL.D., 1911); m. Julia M. Dyckman, June 23, 1869. Taught sch. in N.J. 4 yrs.; engaged as mfr. medicinal preparations; pres. Palisade Mfg. Co.; treas. Arlington Chem. Co. Pres. N.Y. Pharmacal Assn.; treas. N.Y. Conf.; v.p., treas., Ocean Grove Assn.; trustee N.Y. Life Ins. Co., 1906. Elected mayor of Yonkers, N.Y., 1903; mem. 59th to 62d Congresses (1905-13), 19th N.Y. Dist.; Republican. Methodist. Trustee Wesleyan U. Founder, 1917, Surdana Foundation, with endowment of $2,500,000, for orphan homes, nr. Hastings, N.Y. Home: Yonkers, N.Y. Died Dec. 26, 1934.

ANDRUSS, E(lias) Van Arsdale, brig. gen. U.S.A.; b. Newark, N.J., Dec. 18, 1839; s. Isaac Mix and Lydia I. A.; grad. U.S. Mil. Acad., 1864, Arty. Sch., 1876; m. Elizabeth Kinne, 1868. Acting midshipman U.S.N., 1854-56; commd. 2d lt. 1st Arty., June 13, 1864; promoted through grades to col. Arty. Corps, Sept. 23, 1901; retired at own request after 40 yrs. service, Apr. 1, 1902; brig. gen. retired, by act of Apr. 23, 1904. Bvtd.: 1st lt., Apr. 2, 1865, for capture of Petersburg, Va.; capt. Apr. 9, 1865, for campaign ending with surrender of Confederate Army of Northern Va. Comd. defenses of the Delaware during Spanish-Am. War. Home: Brooklyn, N.Y. Died 1910.

ANGELL, Alexis Caswell, judge; b. Providence, R.I., Apr. 26, 1857; s. James Burrill and Sarah Swoope (Caswell) A.; bro. James Rowland A.; A.B., U. of Mich., 1878, LL.B., 1880, LL.D., 1915; m. Fanny C. Cooley, June 6, 1880; children— Sarah C. (dec.), Thomas C. (dec.), Alice (dec.), James B., Elizabeth H. (dec.), Robert C. Began practice at Detroit, 1880, mem. Wells, Angell, Boynton & McMillan, 1892-1902, Angell, Boynton, McMillan & Bodman, 1902-11; U.S. dist. judge Eastern Dist. of Mich., July 1, 1911-June 1, 1912, resigned; mem. Angell, Boynton, McMillan (Philip H., Bodman & Turner, 1912-14, Angell, Bodman & Turner, 1914-19, Angell & Turner, 1919-20, Angell, Turner & Dyer, 1920-30, Angell, Turner, Dyer & Meek, 1930—. Prof. law, U. of Mich., 1893-98. Republican. Home: Detroit, Mich. Died Dec. 23, 1932.

ANGELL, Frank, psychologist; b. S. Scituate, R.I., July 8, 1857; s. Charles and Harriet (King) A., B.S., U. of Vt., 1878, L.H.D., 1892; Ph.D., U. of Leipzig, 1891; m. Louisa Lee Bayard, 1891. Teacher in high sch., Washington, 1880-87; asst. prof. psychology, Cornell, 1891-92; prof. psychology, Stanford, 1892-1923, emeritus. Spl. rep. Commn. for Relief in Belgium, 1916. Chevalier de l'Ordre de la Couronne (Belgium), 1919. Died Nov. 2, 1939.

ANGELL, George Thorndike, founder and pres. Am. Humane Edn. Soc.; b. Southbridge, Mass., June 5, 1823; grad. Dartmouth, 1846; studied at Harvard Law School; m. Mrs. Eliza A. Martin, 1872. Admitted to bar, 1851; one of founders, 1868, and pres. until death, Mass. Soc. for the Prevention of Cruelty to Animals; editor of "Our Dumb Animals," which he founded, 1868; promoted orgns. for protection of animals in England, Chicago, and various States; active also in movements for prevention of crime; for preventing sale of adulterated foods, etc. Home: Boston, Mass. Died 1909.

ANGELL, Henry Clay, M.D.; b. Providence, Jan. 27, 1829; grad. Hahnemann Med. Coll., Phila., 1853; studied 3 yrs. in Vienna Univ., Austria, and has since practiced in Boston; for 20 yrs. prof. of ophthalmology, Boston U.; later pres. Philharmonic Soc., Boston. Author: Diseases of the Eye; also other tech. books, and papers on literary and art subjects. Home: Boston, Mass. Died 1911.

ANGELL, James Burrill, educator, diplomatist; b. Scituate, R.I., Jan. 7, 1829; s. Andrew Aldrich and Amey (Aldrich) A.; A.B., Brown U., 1849, A.M., 1853; (LL.D., Brown, 1868, Columbia, 1887, Rutgers, 1896, Princeton, 1896, Yale, 1901, Johns Hopkins, 1902, U. of Wis., U. of Vt., 1904, Harvard, 1905, Dartmouth, 1909, Miami U., 1911, U. of Mich., 1912, Peking U., 1913); asst. librarian, Brown, 1849-50; studied in Europe, 1850-53; m. Sarah S., d. Dr. Alexis Caswell, pres. Brown U., Nov. 26, 1855; father of Alexis Caswell and James Rowland A. Prof. modern langs. and lit., Brown, 1853-60; editor Providence Journal, 1860-1866; pres. U. of Vt., 1866-71; pres. U. of Mich., 1871-1909, pres. emeritus, 1909—. U.S. minister to China, 1880-81, acting as commr. in negotiating important treaties; mem. Anglo-Am. Internat. Commn. on Canadian Fisheries, 1887; chmn. Canadian-Am. Commn. on Deep Waterways from Lakes to Sea, 1896; appt. minister to Turkey, 1897, but resigned, Aug. 1898. Regent Smithsonian Instn. Author: Progress in International Law, 1875; The Higher Education, 1897; Reminiscences of James B. Angell, 1912; Selected Addresses, 1912; also addresses and articles in leading reviews. Home: Ann Arbor, Mich. Died April 1, 1916.

ANGELL, Martin Fuller, educator; b. Delavan, Wis., Dec. 29, 1878; s. Stephen Francis and Anna A. (Shimmins) A.; B.S., U. of Wis., 1902, M.A., 1905, Ph.D., 1911; m. Mary Alta Gilbert, Dec. 26, 1903; children—Mary Evelyn, Virginia Gilbert, John Robert, Donald Stephen. Prof. physics and mathematics, 1903-04, 1905-06, prof. physics, elec. engring., and dean, 1906-13, U. of N.M.; prof. physics, U. of Ida., 1913-29, also dean Coll. of Letters and Science 1921—, acting exec. dean, Southern Br. U. of Ida., at Pocatello, 1927-29, and July 1929—, dean Coll. Letters and Science and dean Grad. Sch., U. of Ida., Moscow. Home: Moscow, Ida. Died Sept. 2, 1930.

ANGELL, Robert Henderson; b. Franklin Co., Va., Jan. 25, 1868; ed. pub. schs.; m. Mary J. Barlow, 1897. Pres. Shenandoah Life Ins. Co., Liberty Trust Co., Central Mfg. Co., Va. Lumber Mfg. Co., Lynchburg Lumber Mfg. Co., Diamond Orchard Co., Roanoke Auditorium Corp., Covington Home Bldg. Corp.; chmn. bd. Colonial Am. Nat. Bank; v.p. Roanoke Iron & Bridge Works, Roanoke Iron Works, Old Dominion Fire Insurance Co.; treas. MacBain Bldg. Corp. Former mem. Va. Ho. of Rep.; mem. Governor's State Advisory Bd. on Efficiency and Economy; ex-chmn. Va. State Rep. Com. Chmn. bd. trustees Bapt. Orphanage of Va. Home: Roanoke, Va. Died Nov. 12, 1933.

ANGELL, Walter Foster, lawyer; b. Eminence, Ill., Dec. 17, 1858; s. George Manton and Abby Owen (Evans) A.; desc. Thomas Angell, one of the first 5 settlers of Providence, 1636; A.B., Brown U., 1880 (Phi Beta Kappa); m. Annie P. Studley, June 30, 1888 (died 1912). Admitted to R.I. bar, 1883, and since practiced in Providence; counsel in firm of Edwards & Angell; asst. atty. gen., R.I., 1886-87; gen. counsel R.I. Co., 1902-07; pres. Providence & Worcester R.R. Co., 1907-27. Home: Providence, R.I. Died July 7, 1936.

ANGELLOTTI, Frank M., lawyer; b. San Rafael, Calif., Sept. 4, 1861; s. Giuseppe and Frances L. (Osgood) A.; ed. pvt. schs. and Lowell High Sch., San Francisco; LL.B., Hastings Coll. Law (U. of Calif.), 1882; m. Emma C. Cearley, Dec. 27, 1884; 1 dau., Marion Polk. Practiced law, San Rafael, 1883-91. Dist. atty., Marin Co., Calif., 1885-91; judge Superior Ct., 1891-1903; asso. justice Supreme Ct. of Calif., Jan. 1903-15, chief justice, 1915-21; resigned Nov. 15, 1921, to engage in pvt. practice; gen. counsel Western Pacific R.R. Co. Life trustee Hastings Coll. of the Law, U. of Calif. Mason. Republican. Died May 1932.

ANGERT, Eugene Henry, lawyer; b. St. Charles, Mo., Oct. 21, 1877; s. Henry and Adelaide (Mlizko) A.; A.B., St. Louis U., 1896; LL.B., Harvard, 1899; m. Vera Giannini, Dec. 14, 1912; children—Eugene Henry, Vera Virginia, Claire Jane. Admitted to N.Y. bar, 1899; settled in St. Louis, 1900; practiced alone, 1900-12; mem. Jones, Hocker, Sullivan & Angert, 1912—. Trustee John Burroughs Sch., Central Inst. for the Deaf. Democrat. Home: Clayton, Mo. Died May 2, 1929.

ANGIER, Walter Eugene, civil engr.; b. Fitzwilliam, N. H., May 18, 1863; s. Philip Doddridge and Sarah Arabella (Reed) A.; B.S., N.H. Coll. Agr. and Mechanic Arts, 1885; C.E., Dartmouth, 1887; m. Mary Elizabeth Powell, 1889; children—Philip Powell, Mary Estelle, Robert Mitchell. Began practice at Fort Madison, Ia., 1887; moved to Chicago, Ill., 1892; mem. Modjeski & Angier, 1910-27, retired, 1927. Democrat. Baptist. Home: Wheaton, Ill. Died Dec. 29, 1928.

ANGLE, Edward Hartley, orthodontist; b. Herrick, Bradford County, Pa., June 1, 1855; s. Philip Case beer and Isabel (Erskine) A.; ed. high sch., Canton, Pa.; grad. Pa. Coll. Dental Surgery, Phila., 1878; M.D., Marion Sims Coll. of Medicine, St. Louis, 1897; Sc.D., U. of Pa., 1915; m. Anna Hopkins, June 27, 1908; 1 dau., Florence Isabel. Began practice of dentistry at Towanda, Pa., 1878; prof. orthodontia, U. of Minn., 1887-92, Northwestern U., 1892-98, Marion Sims Coll. of Medicine, 1896-99, med. dept. Washington U., 1897-99; founder, 1900, and first pres. Angle Sch. of Orthodontia, St. Louis, also of Angle Coll. of Orthodontia and Infirmary, Pasadena, Calif., 1917. Established orthodontia as a specialty and was the first orthodontic specialist; made 40 orthodontic inventions, granted 43 patents. Presbyn. Author: Malocclusion of the Teeth, 1887 (8 edits.). Home: Pasadena, Calif. Died Aug. 11, 1930.

ANGLE, Edward John, dermatologist; b. Cedarville, Ill., Apr. 1, 1864; s. John Bouslough and Jane (Bell) A.; B.Sc., U. of Wis., 1886; M.D., Med. Coll. of Ohio (U. of Cincinnati), 1887; A.M., U. of Neb., 1898; M.D., U. of Pa., 1895; postgrad work, New York; m. Agnes Lillian Wolf, June 6, 1889; children—Sarah Jane (dec.), Florence Bell (Mrs. Guy E. Reed), Edward Everett Dupuytren, Barbara Josephine (dec.), Agnes Evelyn (Mrs. Harry Stevens). Practiced at Lincoln, Neb., 1895—; now associated in practice with son, Dr. Everett Angle; grad. research student in embryology, U. of Neb., 1896-98; prof. skin and genito-urinary diseases, Neb. Coll. of Medicine, 1905-10; dermatologist St. Elizabeth's and Lincoln Gen. hospitals; cons. dermatologist Bryan Memorial and Lincoln Veterans hospitals. Editor dept. skin and genito-urinary diseases, Western Med. Rev., 1902-07. Republican. Presbyn. Mason. Author: Parents and Their Problems (series of vols. pub. by Nat. Congress of Mothers and Teachers Assn.), 1914; American Medicine—Expert Testimony Out of Court (2 vols. pub. by Am. Foundation); also articles on dermatology, venereal diseases, etc. Home: Lincoln, Neb. Died Apr. 24, 1940.

ANGLE, George Keyser, oculist, aurist; b. Hainesburg, N.J., Oct. 12, 1865; s. Jacob Jay and Elisa Fulmer (Keyser) A.; A.B., Lafayette Coll., 1885, A.M., 1890; M.D., Bellevue Hosp. Med. Coll., 1891;

m. Helen Goldthorpe Williams, Sept. 16, 1896; children—Mary Elisabeth (dec.), Katherine Goldthorpe, Richard Williams. Practiced at Richmond, Ind., Easton, Pa., Silver City, N.M., Albuquerque, N.M., 1916—. Capt. Med. Corps. U.S. Army, 1917; Gen. Hosp., Ft. Des Moines, Ia., June 1918 to close of war; sec. med. sect. N.M. Council Defense. Del. Dem. Nat. Conv., Baltimore, 1912. Wrote 1st state paper on Malta Fever in the Southwest, 1907; and many others on med. subjects. Home: Albuquerque, N.M. Deceased.

ANKENY, Levi, senator; b. nr. St. Joseph, Mo., Aug. 1, 1844; crossed plains to Ore. with parents, 1850; ed. pub. schs., Portland, Ore.; m. Jennie, d. late U.S. Senator James W. Nesmith, of Ore., Oct. 2, 1867. After leaving sch. engaged with his father in transportation business to and from the mines; was agt. for Wells-Fargo Co., and later in merc. business at Lewiston, Ida.; was first mayor of Lewiston; later moved to Walla Walla, Wash., and engaged in banking business, being pres. of 7 banks in Wash. and Ore. Chmn. Wash. delegation Rep. Nat. Conv., 1900; apptd. mem. Pan-Am. Commn. for Wash. and became its chmn.; candidate for U.S. Senate, 1895 and 1899; elected U.S. senator from Wash. for term 1903-09; del. Rep. Nat. Conv., 1904; mem. Rep. Nat. Com., 1904-08. Home: Walla Walla, Wash. Died Mar. 29, 1921.

ANSHUTZ, Edward Pollock, editor, author; b. Clarington, O., Mar. 23, 1846; s. Jacob and Abigail Jane (Pollock) A.; ed. dist. schs., Va., and Heron's Sem., Cincinnati; (hon. M.D., Hering Med. Coll., Chicago). Removed to Phila., 1872; editor New Church Life, 1880-85; editor for Boericke & Tafel, pubs., Phila., 1886—; editor Homœopathic Recorder, Homœopathic Envoy. Author: New and Old Forgotten Remedies, 1900; A Guide to the Twelve Tissue Remedies, 1909; Elements of Homœopathic Theory, Materia Medica, Practice and Pharmacy, 1907; Therapeutic By-Ways, 1916. Home: Philadelphia, Pa. Died Jan. 31, 1918.

ANSHUTZ, Thomas Pollock, artist; b. Newport, Ky., Oct. 5, 1851; s. Jacob and Abigail (Pollock) A.; studied at Nat. Acad. of Design, New York, until 1875, Pa. Acad. Fine Arts, 1875-81, in Paris under Doucet and Bouguereau, 1892-93; m. Effie Shriver Russell, Sept. 1, 1892. Mem. faculty Pa. Acad. Fine Arts, 1882—, and represented in its permanent collection; instr. life and portrait classes. Hon. mention, Art Club of Phila., 1901; silver medal, St. Louis Expn., 1904; Walter Lippincott prize, Phila., 1909; gold medal of honor, Pa. Acad. Fine Arts, 1909; gold medal, S. Am. Expn., Buenos Aires, 1910. A.N.A., 1910. Home: Ft. Washington, Pa. Died June 16, 1912.

ANSLEY, Clarke Fisher, editor; b. Swedona, Ill., Dec. 29, 1869; s. Dr. J. M., and Jennie (Clarke) A.; A.B., U. of Neb., 1890, Litt.D., 1917; grad. study univs. of Leipzig, Heidelberg and Paris, 1892-94; m. Annie Childe, Aug. 9, 1890; children—Arthur Childe, Alice Delight. Instr. in English, U. of Neb., 1894-96, asst. prof., 1897-98, prof., 1898-99; prof. English and head of dept., State U. of Ia., 1899-1917, also dean Coll. of Fine Arts, 1911-15; editor The New State, Lincoln, 1921-22; dir. New Sch. for Social Research, 1922-23; editorial work for Macmillan Co., Ency. Britannica, G. & C. Merriam Co., 1925-27; editor-in-chief Columbia U. Press and Columbia Encyclopedia, 1927—. Unitarian. Home: Solebury, Bucks County, Pa. Died Feb. 14, 1939.

ANSTADT, Henry, clergyman; b. Selinsgrove, Pa., June 18, 1869; s. Peter (D.D.) and Elizabeth Ann (Benson) A.; grad. York (Pa.) Collegiate Inst., 1887; A.B., Pa. Coll., 1890, A.M., 1893, D.D., 1917; grad. Luth. Theol. Sem., Gettysburg, 1894; m. Emma Cavender Jones, Oct. 24, 1906; 1 dau., Mary Elizabeth. Ordained Luth. ministry, 1894; asst. pastor Trinity Ch., Pittsburgh, Pa., 1894-95; editor Internat. S.S. Lesson Publs. (Teachers' Jour., Scholars' Quarterly, Christian's Guide), 1895-1906; pastor Christ's (Coll.) Ch., Gettysburg, Pa., 1906-11, Luther Place Memorial Ch., Washington, D.C., 1912-18, First Luth. Ch., Chambersburg, Pa., 1918—. Mem. bd. dirs. Nat. Luth. Home for the Aged, Tressler Orphans' Home, Grace Coll. for Women; dir. United Luth. Ch. Publ. Bd.; chmn. Com. of Twelve for Redistricting Luth. Synodical Territory in State of Pa. Republican. Apptd. editor Centennial History of W. Pa. Synod of Luth. Ch.; contbg. editor to a N.T. commentary, 1935. Home: Chambersburg, Pa. Deceased.

ANSTICE, Henry, clergyman; b. New York, Oct. 7, 1841; s. Henry and Mary (Saltonstall) A.; A.B., with honors, Williams Coll. 1862, A.M., 1865; grad. Phila. Div. Sch., 1865; (D.D., U. of Rochester, 1875); m.; Flora Fenner, May 30, 1865. Deacon and priest, P.E. Ch., 1865; in charge St. Barnabas, Irvington-on-Hudson, N.Y., 1865-66; rector St. Luke's Ch., Rochester, N.Y., 1866-97, St. Matthias' Ch., Phila., 1897-1903. Sec. Gen. Conv., P.E. Ch.; overseer Phila. Div. Sch.; mem. Bd. of Missions P.E. Ch. Home: Montclair, N.J. Died Dec. 18, 1922.

ANTHONY, Alfred Williams, educator; b. Providence, R.I., Jan. 13, 1860; s. Lewis W. and Brittania F. (Waterman) A.; A.B., Brown U., 1883, A.M., 1886; Cobb Div. Sch., 1883-85; U. of Berlin, 1888-90; D.D. Bates Coll., 1902, Brown U., 1908; LL.D., Colby Coll., 1914, Bates Coll., 1920; L.H.D., Hillsdale Coll., 1937; m. Harriet W. Angell, Sept. 15, 1885 (died Sept. 13, 1899); children—Elisabeth Williams (Mrs. Robert C. Dexter), Margaretha (dec.), Lewis Wilmarth (dec.), Alfred Williams; m. 2d, Gertrude B. Libbey, Feb. 26, 1903; children—Richard Lewis, Warren Shaw, Charles Sheldon. Ordained Free Bapt. ministry, 1885; pastor Essex St. Ch., Bangor, Me., 1885-88; prof. N.T. exegesis Cobb Div. Sch., 1890-1908; prof. Christian lit. and ethics, Bates Coll., 1908-11; corr. sec. and treas. of Gen. Conf. of Free Baptists and spl. joint sec. of Bapt. Foreign Mission, Home Mission and Publn. socs., 1911-15; chmn. of Commn. on State and Local Fedns. of the Fed. Council of Chs., 1912-16; exec. sec. Home Missions Council, 1918-23. Trustee Maine Indsl. Sch. for Girls, 1899-1909; pres. bd. trustees Storer Coll., Harper's Ferry, West Va.; mem. bd. trustees of Bates Coll., Lewiston, Me. Mem. exec. com. and administrative com. Federal Council Chs.; founder Com. on Good Will between Jews and Christians, also chmn. Com. on Financial and Fiduciary Matters; chmn. com. uniting Free Bapts. with Bapts., 1904—; mem. advisory com. uniting Conglists. and Christian Connection, 1929—; mem. bd. mgrs. Am. Bapt. Home Mission Soc., 1923-36; asso. sec. Council of Ch. Bds. of Edn., 1925-33; chmn. Commn. on Permanent and Trust Funds, Assn. Am. Colleges, 1929-33. Author: An Introduction to the life of Jesus, 1896; The Method of Jesus, 1899; The Conscience and Concessions, 1918; A Tale Never Told, 1928; Bates College—a Review of Origins and Causes, 1935. Home: Lewiston, Me. Died Jan. 20, 1939.

ANTHONY, Andrew Varick Stout, artist, engraver, mag. writer; b. New York, 1838. One of foundation members N.Y. Water Color Soc.; one of organizers St. Botolph Club, Boston; had sole charge of illustrated work issued by Ticknor & Fields, and Fields, Osgood & Co., and their successors, 1866-89; projected and superintended publ. of quarto illustrated edition Longfellow's Works; contbr. articles, many illustrated by himself, to several mags.; connected with literary dept. Harper & Bros. Home: New York, N.Y. Died 1906.

ANTHONY, Benjamin Harris, newspaper pub.; b. New Bedford, Mass., Aug. 1, 1863; s. Benjamin and Eliza LeDieu (Coggeshall) A.; A.B., Yale, 1886; m. Harriet Davis Peirce, Sept. 25, 1888; children—Edmund, Margaret (Mrs. Edward Drake), Catharine Chandler (Mrs. Abbott M. Smith). Began with E. Anthony & Sons, pubs. New Bedford Evening Standard, 1886, and also with New Bedford Morning Mercury, 1894; mgr. both newspapers, 1906-31, then pres.; trustee New Bedford Instn. for Savings. Dir. Asso. Press. Republican. Unitarian. Home: New Bedford, Mass. Died Oct. 16, 1932.

ANTHONY, Daniel Read, editor and propr. Leavenworth Times; b. S. Adams, Mass., Aug. 22, 1824 (brother of Susan B. Anthony); ed. in common school Battenville, N.Y.; worked for his father as clerk in store and in a cotton mill; removed to Rochester, N.Y., 1847, and to Kan., July, 1854; was lt. col. in Union army, 1862-63; editor of Daily and Weekly Times for 40 yrs.; mayor of Leavenworth, 1863 and 1872; mem. Kan. legislature, 1873; postmaster Leavenworth, 1874-85; govt. dir. Union Pacific R.R., 1886; m. Annie E. Osborne, Jan. 21, 1864. Home: Leavenworth, Kan. Died 1904.

ANTHONY, Daniel Read, Jr., congressman; b. Leavenworth, Kan., Aug. 22, 1870; s. Daniel Read and Annie (Osborne) A.; ed. pub. schs.; grad. Mich. Mil. Acad., Orchard Lake, 1887; LL.B., U. of Mich., 1891; m. Elizabeth Havens, June 21, 1897; children—Eleanor Havens, Daniel Read. Editor and mgr. Leavenworth Times after death of his father, 1904; postmaster Leavenworth, 1898-1902; mayor, 1903-05; elected 60th Congress, Mar. 29, 1907, and reëlected 61st to 70th Congresses (1909-29), 1st Kan. Dist.; declined renomination to 71st Congress. Republican. Home: Leavenworth, Kan. Died Aug. 4, 1931.

ANTHONY, Gardner Chace, coll. dean; b. Providence, R.I., Apr. 24, 1856; s. David Chace and Sarah Clark (Carpenter) A.; ed. English and Classical Sch., Providence; spl. course in engring. Brown U. and Tufts, 1875-78; hon. A.M., 1889, Sc.D., 1905, Tufts; m. Susan Pearson, June 25, 1879 (died 1917); 1 son, Charles Pearson; m. 2d, Ella M. Taylor, April, 1921. Practiced engineering 1878-85; dir. mech. dept., R.I. School of Design, 1886; founded R.I. Tech. Drawing Sch., 1887; dean Bromfield-Pearson Sch. and prof. drawing, Tufts Coll., 1893-1927; dean Engring. Sch., 1898-1927, Tufts Coll. (emeritus). Author: Elements of Mechanical Drawing, 1893; Machine Drawing, 1893; Essentials of Gearing, 1897; Descriptive Geometry (with G. F. Ashley), 1909; An Introduction to the Graphic Language, 1921. Home: New Rochelle, N.Y. Died Nov. 28, 1937.

ANTHONY, Susan Brownell, reformer; b. Adams, Mass., Feb. 15, 1820; d. Daniel and Lucy (Read) A.; ed. in school maintained by father for his own and neighboring children, Battenville, N.Y., and 1837-38 at Friends' Boarding School, West Phila. Taught school from age of 15 to 30; aided, 1852, in organizing the first State woman's temperance soc.; active in anti-slavery and woman's rights work; organizer and sec. Women's Nat. Loyal League during Civil war. Since war entirely devoted to the woman suffrage movement; founded, 1868, "The Revolution," exclusively woman's rights paper; managed it several yrs.; in 1869 organized, with Mrs. Stanton, Nat. Woman Suffrage Assn. (became hon. pres.); arrested and tried for voting under the Fourteenth Amendment in 1872; has been engaged in 8 different State campaigns for a constl. amendment enfranchising woman; has been granted a hearing before committees of every Congress since 1869. Joint author with Mrs. Elizabeth Cady Stanton and Mrs. Matilda Joslyn Gage of "The History of Woman Suffrage" (3 vols.), and of Vol. IV with Mrs. Ida Husted Harper; has contributed in leading mags. and has lectured in England and throughout the U.S. Home: Rochester, N.Y. Died 1906.

ANTHONY, William Arnold, prof. physics, electrical expert; b. Coventry, R.I., Nov. 17, 1835; s. William H. and Hannah W. (Arnold) A.; grad. Yale Scientific School (Ph.B.); m. Eliza Matilda Girven, 1861. Taught science at Providence Conference Sem., 1859-60; Delaware Lit. Inst., Franklin, N.Y., 1862-67; prof. physics and chemistry, Antioch Coll., 1867-69; prof. physics Iowa Agrl. Coll., 1869-72, Cornell, 1872-87; cons. electrician to Mather Electric Co., Manchester, Conn., 1887-93. From 1893 cons. electrician, New York, and prof. physics, Cooper Union Schs. of Science. Author: (with Prof. Cyrus Fogg Brackett) Manual of Physics; Lecture Notes on the Theory of Electrical Measurements, 1898. Home: New York. Died 1908.

ANTISDALE, Louis Marlin, editor; b. at Marion, N.Y., Oct. 27, 1869; s. Philander and Elizabeth H. (Lyke) A.; A.B., U. of Rochester, 1893; m. Margaret McIntyre, Aug. 15, 1895. Reporter Rochester Herald, 1891-93; deputy collector internal revenue, 1893-94; business mgr., 1894-97, editor-in-chief, 1898—, Rochester Herald, and pres. Rochester Herald Co. Democrat. Home: Rochester, N.Y. Died June 28, 1923.

ANUNDSEN, Brynild, publisher; b. Skien, Norway, Dec. 29, 1844; s. Amund Brynildsen and Maren A.; printing office edn.; came to America, 1864; m. Mathilde Hoffstrom, of Sweden, Oct. 26, 1865 (died 1899); 2d, Helma Hegg, Sept. 10, 1902. Pvt. 22d Wis. Inf., 1865; founded, 1874, and pub. Norwegian semi-weekly, Decorah-Posten. Home: Decorah, Ia. Died Mar. 23, 1913.

APGAR, Austin Craig, educator; b. Peapack, Somerset County, N.J., Aug. 4, 1838; s. David and Hannah (Whitehead) A.; grad. N.J. State Normal School, 1862; m. Maria Elizabeth Whitlock, Dec. 27, 1866. Teacher, 1862—; now at State Normal School. Student at Penikese School, under Louis Agassiz, 1873, under Alexander Agassiz, 1874. Author: Geographical Hand Book, 1865; Geographical Drawing Book, 1866; Plant Analysis, 1874; Mollusks of the Atlantic Coast, 1891; Pocket Key of Trees, 1891; Trees of the Northern United States, 1892; Pocket Key of Birds, 1893; Birds of the United States, 1898. Home: Trenton, N.J. Died 1908.

APPEL, Daniel Frederick, life ins.; b. Cumberland, Md., June 24, 1857; s. John and Fredericka (Hetzel) A.; ed. pub. schs.; m. Mary Horne, 1881; children—Mrs. Robert W. Moore, Jr., Mrs. Leigh B. Liggett. In fire ins. business, 1875-85; gen. agt., Ind., of N.E. Mutual Life Ins. Co., 1885-95, supt. of agts., Boston, Mass., 1895-1905, sec., 1905-08, v.p., 1908-24, pres., 1924—. Republican. Episcopalian. Home: Brookline, Mass. Died Nov. 23, 1929.

APPEL, Theodore, Reformed Ch. clergyman; b. Easton, Pa., April 30, 1823; grad. Marshall Coll., Mercersburg, Pa., 1842, (D.D., U. of Pa.); m. Susan Burton, d. Rev. B. C. Wolff, D.D., 1854. Rector, 1845-50; pastor and prof. mathematics Marshall Coll., 1851-53; prof. mathematics, physics and astronomy, Franklin and Marshall Coll., 1853-77; acting editor, Mercersburg Review, 1851-56; delivered popular lectures on astronomy at many places, 1873-88; gen. supt. home missions Reformed Ch., 1878-86; editor Reformed Missionary Herald, 1880-86; also of Reformed Messenger, in part, 1888-93; retired, 1897. Author: Letters to Boys and Girls About the First Christmas at Bethlehem, 1886; College Recollections, 1886; Beginnings of the Theological Seminary, 1886; Life and Work of Rev. John W. Nevin, D.D., LL.D., 1889. Home: Lancaster, Pa. Died 1907.

APPEL, Theodore Burton, M.D.; b. Lancaster, Pa., Sept. 8, 1871; s. Rev. Theodore (D.D.) and Susan Burton (Wolff) A.; A.B., Franklin and Marshall, 1889, A.M., 1892; Sc.D., 1915; M.D., U. of Pa., 1894; m. Mary Calder, June 18, 1900; children—Mary Calder, Susan Burton, Ellen Ellery, Theodore Burton, James Ziegler. Interne, Presbyn. Hosp., Phila., 1894-96; in practice at Lancaster; med. dir. Lancaster Gen. Hosp., 1906-20; sec. Health Com., Pa., 1927-35. First lt. and asst. surgeon Battery C, N.G. Pa., 1905; commd. capt., Med. R.C., June 6, 1917; maj., Sept. 18, 1917; lt. col. Med. Corps U.S. Army, Nov. 6, 1918; lt. col. Med. O.R.C., 1919;

col., 1924. Home: Lancaster, Pa. Died July 31, 1937.

APPELT, Frank R., textile mfr.; b. Webster, Mass.; s. Joseph and Mary (Quaiser) A.; ed. pub. schs.; m. Orin Emerson, 1906. Began as apprentice in woolen mfg. plant; then pres. Warrenton Woolen Co., Torrington, Conn. Died Feb. 17, 1939.

APPLE, Andrew Thomas Geiger, astronomer; b. Hamburg, Pa., Mar. 5, 1858; s. Rev. Dr. Joseph Henry and Elizabeth Ann (Geiger) A.; A.B., Franklin and Marshall Coll., 1878, A.M., 1881; m. Ada Krebs, Sept. 4, 1884 (died 1910). Prof. natural science, Palatinate Coll., Myerstown, Pa., 1880-83; ordained ministry Ref. Ch. in U.S., 1883; pastor in Bedford County, Pa., Catawissa, Bedford, and Washington, D.C., until 1907; prof. mathematics and astronomy and dir. Daniel Scholl Obs. of Franklin and Marshall Coll., 1907—. Made observations of total eclipse of the sun, in connection with Franklin and Marshall expdn., Centerville, Va., May, 1900. Frequent contbr. to scientific and popular mags. and to encys. Home: Lancaster, Pa. Died Feb. 15, 1918.

APPLEBY, (Theodore) Frank, congressman; b. Old Bridge, N.J., Oct. 10, 1864; s. Theodore Frelinghuysen and Margaret Susanna (Mount) A.; ed. high school and Pennington (N.J.) Sem.; m. Alice C. Hoffman, Apr. 10, 1889. Real Estate and ins. business, Asbury Park, 1885—; mem. T. Frank Appleby Co.; dir. Asbury Park and Ocean Grove Bank. Mem. Bd. of Edn., Asbury Park, 1887-97; mem. N.J. State Bd. of Edn., 1894-1902; del. Rep. Nat. Conv., 1896; mayor of Asbury Park, 1908-12; mem. Monmouth Park Bd. of Taxation, 1917-20; mem. 67th Congress (1921-23), 3d N.J. Dist. Methodist. Mason. Home: Asbury Park, N.J. Died Dec. 15, 1924.

APPELBY, William Remsen, metallurgist; b. Hoboken, N.J., Feb. 11, 1865; s. J. Charles and Julia M. (Curtis) A.; A.B., Williams, 1886, A.M., 1893; student Columbia Sch. of Mines, 1886-87; m. Elizabeth Y., d. Thomas McDonald Waller, Nov. 21, 1889. Asst. analytical and pharm. chemist, N.Y. Coll. of Pharmacy, 1888-89; prof. mining and metallurgy, 1890-91, prof. metallurgy and dean Sch. of Mines, 1891-1935, emeritus, U. of Minn. In charge of party examining coal and iron properties and operations of the South Manchurian Ry., in Manchuria, 1921. Home: Newton Centre (Boston), Mass. Died Apr. 8, 1941.

APPLEGATE, Frank G., artist; b. Atlanta, Ill., Feb. 9, 1882; s. Albert A. and Clara A. (Miller) A.; A.B., U. of Ill., 1906; art edn., Pa. Acad. Fine Arts, Phila., 2 yrs., and Julian Acad., Paris; m. Alta B. Chenoweth, Aug. 25, 1908; 1 dau., Betty. Teacher of sculpture and ceramics, Art Sch., Trenton, N.J., 1908-20; time devoted to painting from 1921. Author: Indian Stories from the Pueblos, 1929. Owner of one of largest Spanish colonial art collections in U.S. Home: Santa Fe, N.M. Died Feb. 13, 1931.

APPLEGATE, H. W., lawyer; b. Union City, Tenn.; s. Samuel E. and Harriett Almyra (Duncan) A.; ed. pub. schs. and Eastman College, N.Y. City; m. Margaret E. Thomas, Nov. 12, 1904 (died 1908); children—Allan W., Margaret E. (dec.). Admitted to Ark. bar, 1898, and began practice at Jonesboro; mayor of Jonesboro, 1899-1903; atty. gen. of Ark. 2 terms, 1924-28. Democrat. Methodist. Mason. Home: Jonesboro, Ark. Died Aug. 12, 1930.

APPLEGATE, John Stilwell, lawyer; b. Middletown, N.J., Aug. 6, 1837; s. Joseph Stilwell and Ann (Bray) A.; ancestors settled in Monmouth Co., N.J., in 17th century; A.B., Colgate, 1858 (LL.D., 1904); studied law with Hon. William L. Dayton; m. Deborah Catharine Allen, Oct. 5, 1865. Admitted to N.J. bar, 1861; partner in practice with Hon. Henry M. Nevius, 1875-79; then mem. John S. Applegate & Son. An incorporator N.Y., Atlantic & Highlands R.R. Co. and pres. of same until its consolidation with Central R.R. of N.J.; pres. 1st bldg. and loan assn. in Red Bank, 1871-75; pres. Red Bank Gas Light Co., 1872—; founder and pres. Second Nat. Bank of Red Bank, 1875-86. Mem. Governor's Light Guard, 1861-65; supt. pub. schs., Shrewsbury Tp., N.J., 1861-66; mem. Rep. State Exec. Com., 1865; Supreme Ct. commr., 1865—; mem. 1st municipal commn. of Red Bank, 1870, pres. 1871; mem. N.J. Senate, 1882-85; spl. master in chancery. Pres. trustees First Bapt. Ch., Red Bank, 1869—. Hon. mem. 157th Regt. N.Y. State Vols. Home: Red Bank, N.J. Died Nov. 10, 1916.

APPLETON, Daniel, publisher; b. New York, Feb. 24, 1852; s. John A. and Serena P. (Dale) A.; g.s. Daniel Appleton (founder of D. Appleton & Co.); ed. New York and Carlsruhe, Germany; unmarried. Entered employ D. Appleton & Co., pub., 1871, becoming mem. firm, 1879, and later v.p. Retired 1913. Mem. 7th Regt. N.G.N.Y., 1871, becoming its col., July 18, 1889; retired Feb. 24, 1916, rank of bvt. maj. gen. N.G.N.Y. Home: North Andover, Mass. Died Mar. 16, 1929.

APPLETON, Francis Henry, agriculturist; b. Boston, June 17, 1847; s. Francis Henry and Georgiana Crowninshield (Silsbee) A.; A.B., Harvard, 1869, A.M., 1872; student Mass. Inst. Tech., 1871; m. Fanny Rollins Tappan, June 2, 1874 (died); m. 2d, Mary Spencer Tappan, Nov. 6, 1907 (died). Pvt. to capt. Mass. Vol. Militia; later commissary gen. of Mass.; then maj. gen., retired. Mem. Mass. Ho. of Rep., 1891, 1892, Senate, 1902, 1903; del. Rep. Nat. Conv., 1892. Curator Bussey Inst., 1873-75; mem. Mass. Bd. Agr., 1891-1907 (elected sec., 1887, but declined); reporter on agr. for Mass. commrs., Vienna Expn., 1873; mem. bd. commrs., Jamestown Expn. mem. bd. control Mass. Agrl. Expt. Sta. Pres. Perkins Instn. and Mass. Sch. for Blind, Watertown, Mass., for 33 years, retiring in 1933; trustee Peabody Mus. (Salem), Mass. Gen. Hosp., Mass. Soc. Promoting Agr. (sec. and ex-pres.). Home: Boston, Mass. Died Apr. 5, 1939.

APPLETON, Francis Randall, lawyer; b. New York, Aug. 5, 1854; s. Daniel F. and Julia (Randall) A.; A.B., Harvard, 1875; LL.B., Columbia, 1877; m. Fanny, d. Charles Lanier, Oct. 7, 1884. Mem. Robbins & Appleton, New York; dir. Waltham Watch Co., Mt. Morris Bank, Nat. Park Bank, etc. Overseer, Harvard U., 1903—. Maj. and insp. rifle practice, 2d Brigade, 1st Div., N.G.S.N.Y. Home: New York, N.Y. Died Jan. 2, 1929.

APPLETON, John Howard, chemist; b. Portland, Me., Feb. 3, 1844; s. Elisha Williams and Martha Wylly (Hyde) A.; Ph.B., Brown, 1863, A.M., 1869, Sc.D., 1900; m. Louise Mumford Day, Feb. 24, 1875; children—Ruth (Mrs. George Albert Goulding), Everard, William Day (dec.), Alice, Paul, Marguerite. Asst. instr. and instr. analytical chemistry, 1863-68, prof. chemistry applied to arts, 1868-72, prof. chemistry, 1872-1914, emeritus, Brown. State sealer weights and measures many yrs.; was chemist R.I. State Bd. Agr., and Providence Water Works; mem. U.S. Mint Commn., 1891. Author: The Young Chemist, 1878; Short Course in Qualitative Analysis, 1878; Quantitative Analysis, 1881; Laboratory Year-Book, 1883-92; Beginner's Hand-Book of Chemistry, 1884; Advanced Quantitative Analysis, 1889; Medical Chemistry, 1889; Lessons in Chemical Philosophy, 1890; Metals of the Chemist, 1891; Report Books for Chemical Work, 1891; Carbon Compounds, 1892; Chemistry of Nonmetals, 1897; Easy Experiments of Organic Chemistry, 1898. Home: Providence, R.I. Died Feb. 18, 1930.

APPLETON, L(illa) Estelle, psychologist; b. Victory, Vt., Nov. 9, 1858; d. George Ashley and Fanny Reed (Wooster) A.; 8th generation from Saml. Appleton, Ipswich, 1636; grad. State Normal Sch., Randolph, Vt., 1879; B.L., Oberlin, 1886, Ph.B., 1890; grad. State Normal Sch., Oswego, N.Y., 1897 and 1898; Ph.D., U. of Chicago, 1909; research student Clark U., 1908-09, Columbia U., 1910-11. Teacher, supervisor, and prin. schs. until 1903; dir. Sch. of Edn., Upper Ia. U., Fayette, 1907-08; actg. head dept. of edn. and supt. training sch., Marshall Coll., Huntington, W.Va., 1909-10; actg. head dept. of philosophy, Milwaukee-Downer Coll., 1911-12; instr. psychology and edn., Kindergarten Training Sch., Grand Rapids, Mich., 1912-16; head dept. psychology and education, Oxford (O.) Coll. for Women, 1919-28; dir. of teacher-training, 1927-28. Conglist. Author: A Comparative Study of Play Activities of Adult Savages and Civilized Children. Home: Oxford, O. Died 1937.

APPLETON, William Henry, mem. of D. Appleton & Co., pubs., 1838—; b. Haverhill, Mass., Jan. 27, 1814 (son of Daniel Appleton, founder D. Appleton & Co.); ed. Andover, Mass.; m. Mary Worthen. Entered business with father in New York about 1830; placed in charge of a book department which had been added to the business; in England, 1835-36, establishing branch there; mem. firm, 1938; sr. active member after 1848; one of earliest and most active advocates of international copyright; first pres. Am. Publishers' Copyright League; trustee N.Y. Life Ins. Co. nearly 50 years; dir. many other large corps. Home: Riverdale, Borough Bronx, N.Y. Died 1899.

APPLETON, William Worthen, pub.; b. Brooklyn, Nov. 29, 1845; s. William Henry and Mary M. (Worthen) A.; fitted for Harvard but did not enter owing to ill health; traveled and studied abroad; m. Anna D. Sargent, Apr. 20, 1881. Became mem. D. Appleton & Co., 1868; now chmn. bd. dirs. same; has spl. charge editorial dept. many yrs.; trustee Bank for Savings. Like his father, he took an active part in securing internat. copyright and aided largely in securing passage of Copyright Act of 1891. Pres. Am. Publishers' Copyright League; trustee and chmn. com. on circulation New York Public Library. Died Jan. 27, 1924.

ARANETA, Gregorio, insular official; b. Iloilo, P.I., Apr. 19, 1869; s. Felix and Paz (Soriano) A.; B.A., Jesuit Coll., Manila, 1884; diploma in law, U. of Santo Tomás, Manilla, 1891; m. Carmen Zaragosa, Mar. 7, 1896. Asst. atty., atty.-gen.'s office, 1895-96; mem. Advisory Assembly of Philippines, 1898; sec. Assembly of Revolutionary Govt., Sept. 1898, and sec. of justice, Oct.-Dec., 1898; justice Supreme Ct. of P.I., 1899-1901; solicitor gen., 1901-06; atty.-gen., 1906-08; commr. and sec. finance and justice, 1908—. Catholic. Home: Manila, P.I. Deceased.

ARANT, Herschel Whitfield, judge; b. Church Hill, Tallapoosa County, Ala., July 18, 1887; s. William Jackson and Villulia (Akin) A.; B.S., U. of Ala., 1910, LL.D., 1938; B.A., Yale, 1911, M.A., 1912, LL.B., 1915; LL.D., Tulane U., 1938; m. Charlotte Marguerite Hein, Aug. 16, 1915; children—Mary Pickett, Frances Elizabeth, Charlotte Marguerite. Practiced law in Atlanta; mem. Arant & Trimble, 1915-20; mem. Ohio bar; served as sec. and prof. law, Lamar Sch. of Law, Emory U., 1916-20; asst. prof. law, Yale U., 1920-22; dean law sch. and prof. law, U. of Kan., 1922-28; dean and prof. of law, Ohio State U., 1928-39; judge U.S. Circuit Ct. of Appeals, 6th Circuit, 1939—. Taught summer sessions law schs., U. of Mich., Cornell, George Washington, Northwestern U., U. of Chicago, U. of Southern Calif. Democrat. Methodist. Author: Cases on Law of Suretyship and Guaranty, 1926; Handbook on Suretyship, 1931; Cases on The American Bar and Its Ethics, 1933. Home: Columbus, O. Died Jan. 14, 1941.

ARBUCKLE, John, businessman; ed. Allegheny, Pa.; in 1871, with brother Charles (dec.), established New York firm of Arbuckle Bros., which introduced on a large scale the roasting of coffees for sale in packages, becoming largest in country in that line; head of firm. Trustee Kings Co. Trust Co.; pres. Royal Horse Assn., owning ranches in Wyoming, etc. Home: Brooklyn, N.Y. Died Mar. 27, 1912.

ARBUCKLE, Maclyn, actor; b. San Antonio, Tex., July 9, 1866; ed. English and Classical Sch., W. Newton, Mass. Admitted to Tex. bar, 1887; joined Pete Baker and made début on stage in "The Emigrant," Shreveport, La., Dec. 25, 1888; later with Frohman's cos., until 1894; appeared as Marc Antony with Louis James in "Julius Cæsar"; subsequently in "Why Smith Left Home," in England and U.S.; created rôle of Hon. Jim Hackler in "The County Chairman," "Slim" Hoover, the sheriff, in "The Round Up," etc. Appeared, 1915-16, as the Rev. Murray Hilton in a re-written revival of "The Henrietta"; created part of "John Tarleton," of Tarleton's Underwear, in William Faversham's production of G. Bernard Shaw's play, "Misalliance," 1917. Appeared in "Lord and Lady Algy" and "Home Again," 1917, "The Better 'Ole," 1918; organized and became president and star of the San Antonio Pictures Corp. producing Maclyn Arbuckle Photo Plays, Mar. 1918. Died Apr. 1, 1931.

ARBUCKLE, Roscoe Conkling, ("Fatty" Arbuckle), motion pictures; b. Smith Center, Kan., Mar. 24, 1887; s. William Goodrich and Mary (Gordon) A.; ed. grammar school, Santa Ana, Calif.; m. Minta Durfee, Aug. 5, 1908. Toured U.S. as actor, later managed own co. 2 yrs.; began screen career as extra man, 1913, later playing leads and became dir.; became v.p. and dir. gen. Comique Film Corp.; has appeared in "His Wife's Mistake," "The Waiter's Ball," "The Butcher Boy," "A Reckless Romeo," "A Rough House," "His Wedding Night," "Fatty in Coney Island," "The Bell Boy," "Moonshine," "Out West," "The Sheriff," etc. Republican. Baptist. Home: Los Angeles, Calif. Died June 29, 1933.

ARBUTHNOT, Wilson S(haw), merchant; b. Pittsburgh, Pa., July 28, 1865; s. Charles and Elizabeth (Shaw) A.; A.B., Princeton, 1887. Pres. Arbuthnot-Stephenson Co., drygoods, Pittsburgh; dir. Mellon Nat. Bank. Dir. and treas. Citizens Com. on City Plan of Pittsburgh, 1918-30. Trustee Carnegie Inst., Carnegie Inst. Tech.; trustee Princeton U., 1920-32; pres. and dir. Western Pa. Hosp. Home: Pittsburgh, Pa. Died Nov. 1, 1938.

ARCHBALD, James, VI; b. Scranton, Pa., Feb. 19, 1866; s. James Archbald, V, and Hannah Maria (Albright) A.; grad. Phillips Acad., Andover, Mass., 1883; A.B., Yale, 1887; m. Margaretta Thompson, Oct. 21, 1897; children—Margaretta Thompson, Sara Thompson, James, Wodrow. Mining engr. and agt. Girard Estate; pres. Miners Nat. Bank, Thompson Realty Co. Dir. Pottsville Chamber Commerce, Schuylkill Regional Clearing House Assn. Pvt. and capt. Pa. N.G. 6 yrs.; lt. col. and a.d.c. staff of gov. of Pa., 1904-11; capt. engineers, Mexican border, 1916-17; mem. Council Nat. Defense and Com. of Pub. Safety, Pa., 1917-18; chmn. Mil. Com., Schuylkill County, 1917-18; chmn. Fed. Labor Bd., same, 1918. Republican. Presbyn. Home: Pottsville, Pa. Died July 24, 1937.

ARCHBALD, Robert Wodrow, judge; b. Carbondale, Pa., Sept. 10, 1848; s. James and Augusta (Frothingham) A.; A.B., Yale, 1871; studied law at Scranton in office of Hand & Post; (LL.D., Dickinson Coll., 1908); m. Elizabeth B. Cannon, Jan. 21, 1875. Admitted to bar, Sept. 1873, and practiced at Scranton; additional law judge, 1885-8, pres. judge, 1888-1901, 45th Jud. Dist. of Pa.; U.S. dist. judge of newly created Middle Dist. of Pa., 1901-1910; apptd. additional U.S. circuit judge by President Taft, Dec. 1910, and assigned to U.S. Commerce Court for 4 yrs. from Feb. 1, 1911. Declined appmt. as U.S. circuit judge, 3d Circuit, 1909. Republican. Home: Scranton, Pa. Died Aug. 19, 1926.

ARCHBOLD, John Dustin, capitalist; b. Leesburg, O., July 26, 1848; went to Pa. oil regions, 1864; spent 11 yrs. in petroleum industry; pres. Acme Oil Co.; officer or dir. in various enterprises; connected with Standard Oil Co., 1875— as dir. v.p. till 1911 and pres. and dir., Standard Oil Co. of N.J., 1911—. Home: Southampton, L.I. Died Dec. 5, 1916.

ARCHER, Belle, actress; b. Easton, Pa., 1860; first appearance National Theatre, Washington, D.C., with W. J. Florence in "The Mighty Dollar;" later as Cousin Hebe in "Pinafore." Went to New York and played in "Sixes and Sevens;" Grace Fleming in "Won at Last," and title role in "Hazel Kirke." Leading lady for Annie Pixley one year and later supported Edward H. Sothern, Alexander Salvini and others. Home: Bayonne, N.J. Died 1900.

ARCHER, Frederic, music dir. Carnegie Music Hall and city organist of Pittsburgh, 1895—; b. Oxford, England, 1838; ed. there; studied organ; organist, 1852, St. Clement's Ch. and Merton Coll. Chapel, Oxford; continued studies and later became organist of Royal Panopticon, London; joint conductor with Sir Julius Benedict of London Vocal Assn., 1863; organist and choirmaster, Christ Ch., Lancaster Gate, London, 1865; later, Ch. of Jesuit Fathers, and, in 1873, organist and orchestral and choral dir. at Alexandra Palace; musical examiner Glasgow Univ., 1879, and condr. Glasgow select choir. In 1880 became organist Plymouth Ch., Brooklyn, N.Y.; later of Ch. of Incarnation, New York. In 1885 founded "The Keynote," of which he was editor. In 1887, condr. Boston Oratorio Soc. and dir. to club. Founded, 1896, Pittsburgh Symphony Orchestra; also, May 1898—, musical examiner U. of Toronto, Canada. Has given many recitals and concerts in U.S. and Canada; organist and choirmaster Ch. of the Ascension, Pittsburgh. Author: Organ School, etc. Home: Pittsburgh, Pa. Died 1901.

ARCHIBALD, Andrew Webster, author; b. New Kingston, N.Y., Apr. 10, 1851; s. Robert and Betsy (Hamilton) A.; A.B., Union Coll., 1872; taught in acad., Pulaski, N.Y., 1872-73; B.D., Yale, 1876; Andover Theol. Sem., 1887-88; D.D., Union, 1891; m. Julia Agnes Warren, May 18, 1876 (died 1921); 1 son, Warren Archibald; m. 2d, Mrs. Rena Bennett Gurley, Jan. 22, 1924. Ordained Congl. ministry, 1876; pastor Nevinville and Fontanelle, Ia., 1876-77, Stuart, Ia., 1877-80, Ottumwa, Ia., 1880-87, Davenport, Ia., 1888-92, Hyde Park, Boston, 1892-97, Brockton, Mass., 1897-1905. Trustee Ia. Coll., 1889-99; ex-pres. Ia. Home Missionary Soc.; moderator Boston Congl. Ministers' Meeting; del. at large from Mass. to Nat. Congl. Council. Served as acting pastor 1st Ch. New Britain, Conn., 1st Ch., Springfield, Mass., Pilgrim and Dorchester 2d, Boston, etc.; organizer of 3 chs., Plymouth, Ottumwa, Ia., and in Cliftondale and Waban, Boston suburbs. Established, 1921, high scholarship prize fund at Yale Div. Sch., also at Union Coll. Author: The Bible Verified (4 edits., besides transls. into Spanish and Japanese), 1890; The Trend of the Centuries, 1901; The Easter Hope, 1909; Biblical Nature Studies, 1915; The Modern Man Facing the Old Problems, 1916; A Cruise to the Orient, 1921; Out of Joint with the Moral Order, 1922. Home: New Haven, Conn. Died Nov. 15, 1926.

ARCHIBALD, Frank C., lawyer; b. Exeter, N.H., 1857; ed. high sch. (Middlebury) and Vt. Acad., Saxtons River. Admitted to Vt. bar, 1886, and began practice at Manchester Center; state's atty. Bennington Co., 1892, 1914, 1916; mem. Vt. Ho. of Rep., 1904, 06, Senate, 1910; elected atty. gen., Vt., 1918, 20, 22 and 24. Republican. Baptist. Home: Manchester Center, Vt. Died Apr. 9, 1935.

ARCHIBALD, Mrs. George, author. See Anna C. Palmer.

ARDEN, Edwin Hunter Pendleton, actor, playwright; b. St. Louis, Feb. 13, 1864; common sch. edn. Went West 1881; successively mine helper, cowboy, railroad brakeman, clerk, reporter and theatrical mgr. Went on stage, Chicago, 1882, with Thomas W. Keene's company; since then with various cos.; 9 yrs. a star, under own management, in Eagle's Nest, Barred Out, and Raglan's Way, of which he was either part or sole author. In 1889, produced his own play "Zorah"; star and co-author of dramatization of Marah Ellis Ryan's book, "Told in the Hills." Home: Forest Hills, L.I., N.Y. Died Oct. 2, 1918.

ARENS, Franz Xavier, conductor; b. Neef, Rhenish Prussia, Oct. 28, 1856; s. Clemens and Maria Anna (Schmitz) A.; emigrated to U.S., 1866; grad. Royal Conservatory of Music, Dresden, 1885; m. Emma L. Huegel, May 18, 1886. Conductor, Cleveland (O.) Philharmonic Orchestra, 1885-88; Am. Composers' Concerts in Europe, 1890-92. Am. Composers' Concerts at Vienna Internat. Mus. and Theatrical Exhbn., Indianapolis May music festivals, 1892-96; pres. Metropolitan Sch. of Music and prin. vocal dept., until 1897, when he removed to New York; condr. N.Y. Manuscript Soc. concerts, 1898; founder and condr. N.Y. People's Symphony concerts, 1900—. Died Jan. 28, 1932.

AREY, Melvin Franklin, college prof.; b. Hampden, Me., Jan. 19, 1844; s. Nathaniel S. and Eliza Ann (Baker) A.; A.B., Bowdoin, 1867, A.M., 1870; m. Louise H. Smith, May 16, 1869. Pvt. and corpl. Co. A, 22d Me. Inf., 1862-63; taught in pub. and pvt. schs. in Me. and N.H.; supt. schs., Cedar Falls, Ia., 1873-77, Ft. Dodge, Ia., 1877-90, prof. natural sciences, 1891-1917, curator of museum, 1917—, Ia. State Teachers' Coll. Sec. Ia. Ednl. Council 25 yrs.; mem. Ia. expdn. to Bahamas, 1893; spl. asst., Ia. Geol. Survey. Councilman, 4th Ward, Cedar Falls, Ia., 1899-1915; trustee City Hosp. Republican. Methodist. Home: Cedar Falls, Ia. Died 1931.

ARGALL, Philip, mining engr.; b. Belfast, Ireland, Aug. 27, 1854; s. Philip and Sarah A.; ed. Wicklow and Dublin schs.; m. Frances Ellen Oates of Ovoca, Ireland, Aug. 31, 1876. Came to America, 1887; practices as cons. mining and metall. engineer. Republican. Presbyterian. Home: Denver, Colo. Died Mar. 18, 1922.

ARKELL, William J., publisher; b. Canajoharie, N.Y., Mar. 26, 1856; s. James and Sarah Hall A.; ed. Hamilton Coll.; married. Pres. Arkell News Corp.; for many years pres. Judge Pub. Co.; pub. of Judge, Leslie's Weekly and Demorest's Family Magazine; also standard subscription books. Chmn. bd. of dirs. Arkell & Smiths; pres. U. S. Light & Heating Co.; v.p. Am. Barrel & Package Corp., Manhattan Transit Co.; sec. and treas. Am. Venture Co. Died Dec. 30, 1930.

ARMOUR, Allison Vincent, plant and archæol. research; b. Chicago, Ill., Mar. 18, 1863; s. George and Barbara (Allison) A.; grad. Harvard Sch., Chicago, 1880; B.A., Yale, 1884; m. Anne Louise Kelley, Dec. 10, 1885 (died 1890). Conducted 8 voyages for plant research, U.S. Dept. Agr., also several voyages in archæol. research. Vol. aid (temp. service) Naval Intelligences, World War. Awarded Meyer medal by Am. Genetic Assn. for plant exploration. Republican. Home: New York, N.Y. Died Mar. 6, 1941.

ARMOUR, Herman Ossian, packer, commission mcht.; resident New York mem. Armour & Co.; b. Stockbridge, N.Y., March 7, 1837; brother of P. D. Armour; in Milwaukee, Wis., 1855-62; grain commn. mcht., Chicago, 1862; in 1865, leaving business in a brother's hands, went to New York to represent Plankington, Armour & Co. Chicago firm of H. O. Armour & Co. began pork-packing, 1868, and in 1870 changed to Armour & Co. Home: New York, N.Y. Died 1901.

ARMOUR, J(onathan) Ogden, capitalist, packer; b. Milwaukee, Wis., Nov. 11, 1863; s. Philip Danforth and Malvina Belle Armour; entered Yale, but did not complete course, yielding to request of father that he should return to Chicago and relieve him of some of his business cares; m. Lolita Sheldon; 1 dau., Lolita Ogden (Mrs. John J. Mitchell, Jr.). Chmn. bd. Armour & Co., 1923—. Trustee Armour Inst. Tech. Republican. Author: The Packers and the People, 1906. Home: Lake Forest, Ill. Died Aug. 16, 1927.

ARMOUR, Philip Danforth, merchant; b. Stockbridge, N.Y.; May 16, 1832; ed. common schools; mined in Calif., 1852-56; in commission business, Milwaukee, 1856-63; member Plankinton, Armour & Co., packers, 1863; later became interested in Chicago grain commission firm of H. O. Armour & Co., which established a pork-packing plant, 1868, and became Armour & Co., 1870; from 1875 in Chicago at head of the firm, conducting the largest pork-packing, dressed-meat and provision business in the world; interested in many important business enterprises; founder of Armour Mission and Armour Inst. of Technology. Home: Chicago, Ill. Died 1901.

ARMSBY, Henry Prentiss, agrl. chemist; b. Northbridge, Mass., Sept. 21, 1853; s. Lewis and Mary A. (Prentiss) A.; B.S., Worcester Poly. Inst., 1871; Ph.B., Yale, 1874, Ph.D., 1879; (LL.D., U. of Wis., 1904); m. Lucy A. Harding, Oct. 15, 1878. Instr. chemistry, Worcester Poly. Inst., 1871-72; teacher, Fitchburg (Mass.) High Sch., 1874-75; asst. in chemistry, Rutgers, 1876-77; chemist to Conn. Agrl. Expt. Sta., 1877-81; v.p. Storrs Agrl. Sch., 1881-83; prof. agrl. chemistry, U. of Wis., 1883-87; dir. Pa. Agrl. Expt. Sta., 1887-1907; dir. Inst. of Animal Nutrition, Pa. State Coll., 1907—. Chmn. com. on expt. sta. exhibit, Chicago Expn., 1893, Paris Expn., 1900; expert in animal nutrition, U.S. Dept. Agr., 1898—; mem. Commn. on Agrl. Research, 1906-08. Mem. agrl. com. Nat. Research Council, 1917; del. Inter-Allied Scientific Food Commn., 1918. Author: Manual of Cattle Feeding, 1880; Principles of Animal Nutrition. 1903; The Nutrition of Farm Animals, 1917; Conservation of Food Energy, 1918. Died Oct. 19, 1921.

ARMSTEAD, Henry Howell, cons. mining engineer; b. Chicago, Ill., Aug. 4, 1872; s. of the late Henry Howell and Alice Mary (McPherson) A.; ed. pvt. schs. and Columbia Sch. of Mines; unmarried. Maj. of Engrs., U.S.A., World War; retired col., Officers Reserve Corps, Apr. 30, 1928. Mason. Home: New York, N.Y. Deceased.

ARMSTRONG, Alexander, atty. gen. of Md.; b. Hagerstown, Md., June 28, 1877; s. Alexander and Elizabeth Key (Scott) A.; A.B., Princeton, 1899, A.M., 1900; LL.B., U. of Pa., 1903; LL.D., U. of Md., 1923; m. Mary Rebekah Woods, Jan. 25, 1911. Began practice at Hagerstown, 1904; mem. Armstrong & Scott, 15 yrs.; practiced at Hagerstown in own name; mem. Armstrong, Machen & Allen, Baltimore; pres. Armstrong Co. of Detroit, Mich. City solicitor, Hagerstown, 1904-06; state's atty., Washington County, Md., 1908-12; pres. Bd. of Supervisors of Election, Washington County, 1912-16; atty. gen. of Md., 1919-23; Rep. candidate for gov. of Md., 1923; del. at large Rep. Nat. Conv., 1924. Pres. Md. State Bd. Law Examiners; mem. Nat. Conf. Uniform State Laws (pres. 1936—). Presbyn. Mason. Home: Boyce Av., Ruxton, Md. Died Nov. 20, 1939.

ARMSTRONG, Andrew Campbell, college prof.; b. New York, N.Y., Aug. 22, 1860; s. Andrew Campbell and Isabella Johnston (Sinclair) A.; B.A., Princeton, 1881, fellow, 1881-82, M.A., 1884; grad. Princeton Theol. Sem., 1885; studied U. of Berlin, Germany, 1885-86; hon. M.A., Wesleyan U., Conn., 1894, L.H.D., 1930; hon. Ph.D., Princeton, 1896; m. Mabel Chester Murray, Sept. 6, 1888; children—Andrew Campbell, III (dec.), James Syng, Sinclair Wallace. Asso. prof. ecclesiastical history, Princeton Theol. Sem., 1886-87; instr. in hist., Princeton Coll., 1887-88; prof. philosophy, Wesleyan U., 1888-1930, emeritus. Associate editor New Princeton Review, 1887-88; coöperating editor Psychol. Review, 1904-09. Mem. Internat. Congress Arts and Sciences, St. Louis, 1904 (chmn. sect. of metaphysics); hon. sec. 6th Internat. Congress of Philosophy, 1926, and mem. Permanent Internat. Com., 1926—. Author: Transitional Eras in Thought, 1904. Translator: History of Modern Philosophy (by Richard Falckenberg), 1893. Home: Middletown, Conn. Died Feb. 22, 1935.

ARMSTRONG, Arthur Henry, clergyman; b. Morris, Ill., Nov. 27, 1866; s. Julius C. and Harriet V. (Goodrich) A.; A.B., Beloit (Wis.) Coll., 1889, B.D., Chicago Theol. Sem., 1894; D.D., Drury Coll., Springfield, Mo., 1915; m. Catherine Cameron Schultz, Mar. 26, 1895; 1 son, Arthur Alexander. Ordained Congl. ministry, 1894; pastor Waveland Av. Ch., Chicago, 1894-1901, 3d Ch., Oak Park, Ill., 1901-10; supt. Mo. Congl. Conf., and supt. Congl. City Missionary Soc. of St. Louis, 1910-17; exec. sec. Ch. Fedn. of Toledo, O., 1917-19; exec. sec. Met. Ch. Fedn. of St. Louis (interdenom. coop. orgn.), 1919-36, retired. Trustee Iberia Academy. Home: Vinita Terrace, Mo. Died June 7, 1938.

ARMSTRONG, Charles Dickey, cork products mfr.; b. Pittsburgh, Pa., Oct. 12, 1861; s. Thomas Morton and Martha Jane (Porter) A.; grad. Central High Sch., Pittsburgh, 1878; m. Gertrude Virginia Ludden, Nov. 19, 1885; children—Charles Dudley, Dwight Ludden, Mary Martha. Began as clk. in father's firm, Armstrong, Brother & Co., mfr. cork stoppers, 1878; v.p. Armstrong Cork Co. (successor), 1891-1908, pres., 1908-29, chmn. of bd., 1929—; also chmn. bd. Union Nat. Bank. Republican. Presbyterian. Home: Pittsburgh, Pa. Died Apr. 2, 1935.

ARMSTRONG, D(avid) Maitland, artist; b. "Danskammer," Newburgh, N.Y., Apr. 15, 1836; s. Edward and Sarah Hartley (Ward) A.; A.B., A.M., Trinity Coll., Conn., 1858; admitted to bar, 1862; studied art in Paris and Rome; m. Helen Neilson, 1866. Practiced law at New York, 1862-69; U.S. consul-gen. at Rome, Italy, 1869-72. Designer and maker of stained glass windows and other decorations for many yrs.; head of Maitland, Armstrong & Co., New York. Executed memorial figure windows in Ascension, St. Michael's, Holy Communion, Holy Trinity and other chs., New York; in Mrs. O. H. P. Belmont's memorial chapel, Woodlawn Cemetery, and in her armory; 15 memorial windows in All Souls' Ch., Biltmore, N.C.; also many hundred works throughout the country. Dir. Am. Art Dept., Paris Expn., 1878; received decoration of Legion of Honor; A.N.A. Home: New York, N.Y. Died May 26, 1918.

ARMSTRONG, DeWitt Clinton, banker; b. Milan, O., Nov. 25, 1868; s. DeWitt Clinton and Frances M. A.; pub. sch. edn.; m. Anna E. Hibbs, 1893. Began as messenger 1st Nat. Bank, Erie, Pa., 1881; teller, later mgr., Freeborn County Bank, Minn., 1883-1902; then cashier, later pres., Albert Lea State Bank. Republican. Presbyn. Home: Albert Lea, Minn. Died Nov. 8, 1914.

ARMSTRONG, Edward Ambler, lawyer; b. Woodstown, Salem County, N.J., Dec. 28, 1858; s. Francis W. and Rebecca Brown (Jess) A.; high sch. edn.; hon. A.M., Bucknell U., Pa.; m. Mellie M. Fortiner, June 15, 1881 (died Mar. 23, 1883); 1 son, Wynn; m. 2d, Carrie W. Morgan, Apr. 30, 1907. Began practice, Camden, 1880, spl. attention to corps.; mem. N.J. Ho. of Rep., 4 terms, 1884-87, inclusive (speaker 1885, 86); judge Camden City Dist. Ct., 1888-91; pres. judge Camden County Ct. of Common Pleas, 1897-1902; mem. State Bd. of Equalization of Taxes, 1906-09; asso. gen. counsel Pub. Service Corp. of N.J., 1911-28, retired; pres. Camden Horse R.R. Co., Camden & Suburban Ry. Co. Judge advocate 2d Brigade, N.G.N.J., with rank of maj., 7 yrs. Home: Princeton, N.J. Died May 1, 1932.

ARMSTRONG, Frank C., mem. Commn. to treat with the Five Tribes in the Indian Territory; b. Choctaw Agency, Ind. Ter., 1835; s. Frank W. and Anne M. (Millard) A.; ed. Holy Cross Coll., Worcester, Mass.; went to Tex., 1854, and made a trip across State from Corpus Christi to El Paso with his stepfather, Gen. Persifer F. Smith, U.S. Army; for bravery in an encounter with Indians on this trip was apptd., June, 1855, lt. 2d U.S. dragoons, serving in Tex., Kan. and Neb. until 1857, then went to Utah with Gen. Albert Sydney Johnston; resigned commn., 1861, and joined C. S. army; apptd. adj. gen. under Gen. McCulloch in Ark., and after McCulloch's death, apptd. maj., and soon after elected col. 3d La. inf. Under orders from Gen. Bragg organized cav. command and engaged in Miss. and Ala.; attacked and captured Federal camp, Courtland, Ala., and afterward was successful in actions at Bolivar and near Denmark; apptd. brig. gen.; assigned to brigade under Van Dorn, and later under Forrest; comd. brigade during campaign in Tenn., and on retreat to Chattanooga, took important part at Chickamauga, comd. cav. div. Moved with Longstreet to E. Tenn., under Gen. Jos. Wheeler, then moved to Ga. and served until after fall of Atlanta; later in Tenn. and Miss.; surrendered to Gen. Canby. Last battle was at Selma, Ala., under Gen. Forrest. After war engaged in Overland mail service in Tex.; U.S. Indian insp. 1885-89; asst. commr. Indian Affairs, 1893-95; became interested in mining, etc., in Mexico. Died 1909.

ARMSTRONG, George Dodd, author; b. Mendham, N.J., Sept. 15, 1813; grad. Princeton, 1832; studied Union Theol. Sem., Va. (S. T. D., William and Mary, 1854); prof. chemistry and mechanics, Washington Coll., Va., 1838-51; pastor of a Presbyn. ch. in Norfolk, Va., 1851-91; pastor emeritus, 1891—. Author: The Christian Doctrine of Slavery; The Summer of the Pestilence; also several theological works. Home: Norfolk, Va. Died 1899.

ARMSTRONG, George William, Jr., piano mfr.; b. Cincinnati, O., Aug. 18, 1857; s. G. W. and Caroline (Secrist) A.; ed. pub. schs. Engaged in piano mfg., 1874-1930, retired; was chmn. The Baldwin Co. Mem. Civil Service Commn. of Cincinnati 5 yrs.; pres. Commn. for new charter for Cincinnati; dir. Rookwood Pottery. Republican. Episcopalian. Home: Cincinnati, O. Deceased.

ARMSTRONG, James, lawyer; b. Candor, N.Y., July 4, 1834; s. Henry and Elizabeth (Cady) A.; A.B., Hobart Coll., 1856, A.M., 1871 (LL.D., 1906); m. Mary E. Baker, Mar. 23, 1859 (dec.); m. 2d, Elizabeth Douglas, July 14, 1903. Admitted to bar, 1858; practiced at Davenport, Ia., 1858-73; collector of internal revenue, 2d Ia. Dist., under Presidents Johnson and Grant; one of incorporators of 1st Nat. Bank of Davenport, the 1st bank to open its doors for business under banking act of 1863; in practice at New York, 1873—; in charge of law and collection business of H. B. Claflin & Co., 1873-76; sr. mem. Armstrong, Brown & Boland; pres. Mortgage Holding Co. Trustee Hobart Coll. Democrat. Episcopalian. Home: New York, N.Y. Died May 18, 1917.

ARMSTRONG, John Irvine, clergyman; b. Salem, Va., July 10, 1872; s. Edward McCarty and Margaret Moore (Logan) A.; A.B., Hampden-Sidney Coll., 1894, A.M., 1895 (D.D., 1915); grad. Union Theol. Sem. in Va., 1902; m. Ollie Walton Connell, Oct. 11, 1904. Prof. moral philosophy and Bible, Hampden-Sidney Coll., 1904-06; ordained ministry Presbyn. Ch. of U.S., 1906; prof. philosophy and Bible, Agnes Scott Coll., and pastor Kirkwood, Ga., 1906-13. Ednl. sec. of foreign missions, Presbyn. Ch. of U.S., 1913-20; pres. Lewisburg (W.Va.) Sem., 1920—. Democrat. Home: Lewisburg, W.Va. Died Mar. 1924.

ARMSTRONG, Leroy, newspaperman; b. Plymouth, Ind., May 13, 1854; s. Augustus G. and Ara (Strong) A.; ed. pub. schs.; studied law at Ind. U. Began newspaper career at 17; long connected with daily papers of Chicago; editor Salt Lake City Herald-Republican, 5 yrs. Author: An Indiana Man, 1891; Washington Brown, Farmer, 1893; The Outlaws, 1902; John Haliday's Work, 1909. Home: Salt Lake City, Utah. Died Mar. 29, 1927.

ARMSTRONG, Paul, playwright; b. Kidder, Mo., Apr. 25, 1869; s. Richard and Harriet (Scott) A.; ed. high sch., Bay City, Mich.; m. Rella Abell, July 24, 1899; 2d, Catharine Calvert, actress, Dec. 18, 1912. Licensed master of steam vessels on the Great Lakes, 1890-95; play-writing, 1904—. Author (plays): The Heir to the Hoorah, 1904; St. Ann, 1904; Salomy Jane, 1905; In a Blaze of Glory, 1906; Via Wireless (with Winchell Smith), 1909; Going Some (with Rex Beach), 1909; Alias Jimmy Valentine, 1909; The Deep Purple (with Wilson Mizner), 1910; A Romance of the Underworld, 1911; The Greyhound (with Wilson Mizner), 1911. Home: New York, N.Y. Died Aug. 29, 1915.

ARMSTRONG, Robert Allen, univ. prof.; b. Frenchton, Va. (now W.Va.), Sept. 23, 1860; s. Jared Morgan and Eliza (Bennett) A.; A.B., W.Va. U., 1886 (awarded Henshaw gold medal for oratory), A.M., 1889; studied U. of Chicago, 1898, Columbian (now George Washington) U., 1900, Harvard, 1902-03, A.M., 1903; L.H.D., Allegheny Coll., 1908; LL.D., W.Va. Wesleyan College, 1927; m. Carrie Louise Dent, Dec. 28, 1900 (died 1903); 1 dau., Virginia Dent; m. 2d, Myra Louise Shank, June 11, 1914; children—Roberta Jean, Barbara Allen, Stuart Keith, Robert Allen. Admitted W.Va. bar, 1890; prin. W. Liberty State Normal Sch., 1886-93; prof. English, 1893-1901, v.p., 1897-99, prof. English lang. and lit., 1901—, head of English dept., 1903-30 and acting pres., 1935, West Va. U.; prof. English, U. of Mo., summer 1921; prof. of English, Boston U., summer 1930. Inst. instr. in W.Va., Md., Pa., Ohio, Ind., and Ill., 1886—; sec. W.Va. State Board School Examiners, 1899-1909; editor of W.Va. School Journal, 1904-21. Maj., W.Va. N.G., 1887-93. Dem. nominee for state supt. pub. schs., W.Va., 1900, 16. Author: Geography of West Virginia—Supplement to The Natural Geography, 1899; Life Out of Death, 1906; The Law of Service, 1907; Historical and Literary Outlines of the Old Testament, 1907; Dramatic Interpretation of Shakespeare's Tragedies, 1907; Mastering the Books of the Bible, 1916, rev. How to Know the Bible, 1921. Home: Morgantown, W.Va. Died Sept. 15, 1936.

ARMSTRONG, Thomas, Jr., lawyer; b. Fox Lake, Wis., July 18, 1857; s. Thomas and Julia A. (Knapp) A.; grad. Ripon (Wis.) Coll., 1879; m. Evelina Ackerman, May 15, 1883 (died 1911); children—Thomas A., Helen A. (Mrs. Austin Morrill), Marion A. (Mrs. A. H. DeRiemer), Margaret A. (Mrs. George W. Heise), Jean A. (Mrs. Malcolm Lowery), Robert H.; m. 2d, Meda A. McNeff, July 11, 1921. Admitted to Wis. bar, 1880, and began practice at Portage; dist. atty., Columbia County, Wis., 1890-91; pres. 1st Nat. Bank of Portage, 1891-92; moved to Phoenix, Ariz., 1892; mem. Armstrong, Kramer, Morrison & Roche; pres. First Nat. Bank of Ariz., Phoenix, 1924-29. Republican. Mason. Donor of Pueblo Grande Ancient Ruins to City of Phoenix. Home: Phoenix, Ariz. Died Nov. 1937.

ARMSTRONG, William C., civil engr.; b. Marietta, Ia., 1859; s. John C. and Elizabeth (Alexander) A.; B.S. in C.E., Ia. State Coll., Ames, Ia., 1881; m. Mrs. Emma Moody, 1889. Engaged in practice, 1881, and 1899—, with C. & N.W. Ry., as resident engr., 1899-1902, bridge engr., 1902-04, terminal engr. in charge of new passenger terminal in Chicago, 1906-11, and then engr. of bridges. Home: Wilmette, Ill. Died June 12, 1923.

ARMSTRONG, William Wright, banker; b. Darlington, Wis., Sept. 18, 1865; s. William H. and Georgia (Wright) A.; B.S., Baker U., Baldwin, Kan., 1885; LL.B., U. of Wis., 1887; m. Eva Lees, 1889. Settled in Utah, 1890; cashier 1st Nat. Bank of Nephi, 1894, later sec. Salt Lake Hardware Co., asst. mgr. Salt Lake & Ogden Gas Co., cashier 1st Nat. Bank, Park City, Utah; moved to Salt Lake City, 1903; then chmn. bd. Nat. Copper Bank; pres. Bankers Trust Co.; v.p. First Nat. Bank (Park City, Utah). Mem. Utah Senate, 1917-19. Democrat. Mason. Home: Salt Lake City, Utah. Died Nov. 1932.

ARNDT, Walter Tallmadge, publicist; b. De Pere, Wis., Oct. 11, 1873; s. Edward Wilcox and Mary Ellen (Delany) A.; student U. of Wis., 1892-95; A.B., Harvard, 1897, A.M., 1899; last 2 yrs. in Harvard Grad. Sch. in grad. work in history; m. 3d, Lola Clarke Rycroft, Aug. 5, 1928; 1 son (by first marriage), Howard Wilcox. On staff of the New York Sun, 1899-1901; asst. editor International Yearbook, 1901-03; on editorial staff of New International Ency., 1902-04, to which contbd. over 1,000 articles on Am. history and biography; asst. editor Historians' History of the World, 1904-05; dramatic editor Current Literature, 1905; editorial staff Ency. Britannica, 1905-08; legislative corr. and polit. editor New York Evening Post, 1906-13; sec. Municipal Govt. Assn., 1913-20. Dir. publicity Nat. Hughes Alliance, 1916; legislature sec. City Club (N.Y.), 1916-17. Editorial ednl. work Com. on Training Camp Activities, War Dept., 1917-18; sec. Citizens' Union of N.Y. City, 1918-26; v.p. and sec. U.S. Shares Corp., 1927-28; v.p. Seneca Nat. Corp, 1928—. Republican. Author: The Emancipation of the American City, 1917; Reading Course for Citizen Soldiers (jointly with W. H. Lough), published by War Dept., 1918. Home: New York, N.Y. Deceased.

ARNETT, Benjamin William, A.M.E. bishop; b. Brownsville, Pa., Mar. 16, 1838; s. Samuel G. and Mary Louisa A.; ed. common school Bridgeport, Pa., and Wilberforce Univ. (D.D., LL.D. Wilberforce); spl. course in divinity, Lane Theol. Sem., Cincinnati; m. Mary L. Gordon, May 25, 1858. Ordained to ministry A.M.E. Ch., 1868; bishop, 1888—. Mem. Ohio legislature from Greene Co., 1886-87; chaplain Nat. Rep. Conv., St. Louis, 1896. Presided over Parliament of Religions, Chicago, Sept. 15, 1893; presided at Ecumenical Conf. of Methodists, London, Sept. 7, 1901. Trustee United Soc. of Christian Endeavor. Home: Wilberforce, O. Died 1906.

ARNETT, Clare Newton, animal husbandman; b. Lafayette, Ind., Nov. 7, 1884; s. Albert Jefferson and Elizabeth (McBroom) A.; B.S. in Agr., Purdue, 1907; m. Ethel Barnes, Dec. 1914. Teacher, Purdue U., 1907-09; asso. prof. and prof. animal husbandry, Ia.. State Coll., 1910-15; head of animal husbandry dept., Mont. State Coll., and Expt. Sta., 1915-27, vice dean of agr., 1921-27; pres. and mgr. The Rambouillet Co., Inc., 1926—; v.p. Am. Rambouillet Sheep Breeders' Assn., 1926-27, pres., 1929—; pres. Intermountain Livestock Marketing Assn. Breeder of pure bred Rambouillet sheep, Manhattan, Mont. With Am. Red. Cross in France 1 yr., World War. Republican. Home: Bozeman, Mont. Died Aug. 5, 1933.

ARNOLD, Abraham Kerns, brig. gen. U.S.V.; b. Bedford, Pa., March 24, 1837; grad. U.S. Mil. Acad., 1859; bvt. 2d lt., 2d cav.; commd. 2d. lt., June 28, 1860; promoted through grades to brig. gen., U.S. Vols., 1898. Bvtd. capt. June 27, 1862, for gallantry at Gaines' Mill, and maj., May 6, 1864, for gallantry at Todd's Tavern; Congressional medal of honor for gallantry in action at Davenport Bridge, N. Anna River, Va., May 18, 1864; comd. cav. div. at Chickamauga; comd. 5th cav. in Civil war; served against Indianas on frontier; served in war with Spain in the field from April 22, 1898; comdg., 1899, 2d div., 7th Army corps, in Cuba. Died 1901.

ARNOLD, Augusta Foote, author; b. Seneca Falls, N.Y., Oct. 24, 1844; d. Elisha and Eunice (Newton) Foote; ed. private schools, Saratoga Springs, N.Y., and New York; m. Francis B. Arnold, Mar. 6, 1869. Trustee Barnard Coll., 1890-1900; dir. Nursery and Child's Hosp. Author: The Century Cook Book (by "Mary Ronald"), 1898; The Sea Beach at Ebb Tide, 1901. Died 1903.

ARNOLD, Bion Joseph, electrical engr.; b. Casnovia, nr. Grand Rapids, Mich., Aug. 14, 1861; s. Joseph and Geraldine (Reynolds) A.; U. of Neb., 1879-80; B.S., Hillsdale (Mich.) Coll., 1884, M.S., 1887; post-grad. course Cornell, 1888-89; E.E., U. of Neb., 1897; hon. M.Ph., Hillsdale, 1889, hon. diploma, 1903; D.Sc., Armour Inst., 1907; D.Eng., U. of Neb., 1911; m. Carrie Estelle Berry, Jan. 14, 1886 (dec.); m. 2d, Mrs. Margaret Latimer Fonda, Dec. 22, 1909. Chief designer, Ia. Iron Works, Dubuque; mech. engr., C.G.W.Ry.; later cons. engr. for Chicago office Gen. Electric Co.; independent cons. engr., 1893—. Designed and built Intramural Ry., Chicago Expn.; cons. elec. engr. Chicago & Milwaukee Elec. Ry., Chicago Bd. of Trade, C.,B.&Q. R.R., Grand Trunk Ry. on electrification of St. Clair tunnel; cons. engr. Wis. State Ry. Commn., 1905-07; devised plan for electrically operating trains of N.Y. Central R.R. in and out of New York, and mem. Electric Traction Commrs. engaged in carrying on the work; mem. electric traction com. Erie R.R., 1900-04; cons. engr. for city of Chicago to revise street ry. systems of city, 1902; chief engr. rebuilding Chicago traction system at cost approx. $140,000,000, and chmn. bd. supervising engrs. same 1907—; cons. engr. Pub. Service Commn., 1st Dist., N.Y., matters connected with subway and st. ry. properties, New York; chief subway engr. city of Chicago and cons. engr. on traction matters for cities of Pittsburgh, 1910, Providence, Los Angeles, San Francisco, 1911, Toronto and Cincinnati, 1912. Mem. of Chicago Ry. Terminal Commn. until 1921; mem. Traction and Subway Commn., 1916-17; retained by Mass. Pub. Service Commn. to report on rys. and by Bay State Ry. Co., Boston, 1916-17; adviser to Des Moines, Omaha, Winnipeg, Sacramento, New Orleans, Detroit, Harrisburg, Rochester, Syracuse, Jersey City, Toronto, etc. Pres. The Arnold Engineering Co. Mem. Naval Consulting Board. Commd. maj. Engr. R.C., Jan. 23, 1917; transferred to regular army, Dec. 14, 1917, with rank lt. col., Aviation Sect. Signal Corps; assigned to equipment div. production sect. of aircraft, Washington, D.C., and continued to act in advisory capacity to Army and Navy; had control for 5 mos. previous to armistice over development and production of aerial torpedoes, hon. discharged Feb. 6, 1919; commd. maj. Aviation Sect., O.R.C., Mar. 28, 1919, col. Air Service U.S.A., Sept. 13, 1919, col. Aux. Corps, Aug. 14, 1925. Trustee Hillsdale College; bd. mgrs. Lewis Institute, Chicago. Received Washington Award from Western Soc. of Engrs., 1929. Home: Chicago, Ill. Died Jan. 29, 1942.

ARNOLD, Conway Hillyer, rear-admiral U.S.N.; b. New York, Nov. 14, 1848; s. Comdr. Henry Nathan Tewkesbury (U.S.N.) and Cornelia Van Vleck (Sleight) A.; ed. pvt. schs.; grad. U.S. Naval Acad., 1867; m. Fanny, d. William W. W. Wood, engr.-in-chief U.S.N., Nov. 17, 1870. Commd. ensign, 1868; master, 1870; lt., 1874; lt. comdr., 1892; comdr., 1898; capt., Sept. 17, 1902; rear-admiral, Jan. 30, 1908. Pres. Naval Examining and Retiring Bds. Home: New York, N.Y. Died July 16, 1917.

ARNOLD, Edmund Samuel Foster, M.D.; b. Bermondsey, London, England, Jan. 30, 1820; ed. private school and at Moravian Inst., Neuwied, on the Rhine; med. edn. as house pupil, Guy's Hosp., London, 1835-44, and U. of Bonn; licensed med. practitioner at Apothecaries' Hall, London, 1842; M.D., Jefferson Med. Coll., Phila., 1848; m. Eliza, d. James R. Whiting, judge Supreme Court of N.Y., 1856 (died 1897). Practiced in New York, 1848-54, and at Yonkers, 1854-1872; retired from practice, 1872; treas. Internat. Med. Congress, Washington, 1887; living at Newport, R.I., until 1898, when he removed to Fla.; cons. phys. and surgeon of Newport Hosp., R.I.; wrote many papers published in med. journals. Home: Pine Hill, Ulster Co., N.Y. and Mandarin, Fla. Deceased.

ARNOLD, Ernst Hermann, M.D.; b. Erfurt, Germany, Feb. 11. 1865; s. Johann Bruno and Ernestine

(Orzakowsky) A.; ed. Realgymnasium, Halle, to 1883; grad. Normal Sch. of Gymnastics, Milwaukee, Wis., 1888; M.D., Yale, 1894; univs. of Halle and Leipzig, 1895, courses in surgery and orthopædics; m. Marie Nagel, Mar. 1889; children—Marie Ernestine, Hermann Bruno. Chief, New Haven Orthopædic Dispensary; orthopædic surgeon to Griffin Hosp., Derby, Conn., and Grace Hosp., New Haven; late instr. orthopædic surgery, Yale; dir. New Haven Normal Sch. of Gymnastics. Pres. Anderson Gymnasium Co.; Arnold Coll. for Hygiene and Phys. Edn.; formerly asso. editor Mind and Body. Author: Elementary Apparatus Work, 1896; Manual of School Gymnastics, 1898; Gymnasium Tactics, 1899; Gymnastic Games, 1900; Tactics of the Rank, 1914; Tactics of the Body of Ranks, 1922. Home: New Haven, Conn. Died Mar. 1929.

ARNOLD, Felix, author; b. New York, June 15, 1879; s. George and Eliza (Schick) A.; A.B., Coll. City of N.Y., 1898; Pd.M., N.Y. University, 1903, Pd.D., 1904; Ph.D., Columbia, 1905; m. Julia V. Resnick, 1924. Public sch. prin., New York, Sept. 1908—. Lecturer, Dept. of Edn., Baltimore, 1906; lecturer in philosophy, U. of Colo., 1907; lecturer on edn., New York U., 1910; lecturer on edn., Coll. City of New York, 1915. Author: The Psychology of Association, 1906; Text-Book of School and Class Management, Vol. I, 1908, Vol. II, 1910; Attention and Interest, 1910; Outline History of Education, 1911; Special Methods of Instruction, 1913; Measurement of Teaching Efficiency, 1915. Mem. Plattsburg O.T.C., summer, 1917. Home: New York, N.Y. Deceased.

ARNOLD, George Stanleigh, lawyer; b. New Haven, Conn., Apr. 3, 1881; s. George Sumner and Evelyn (Thomson) A.; B.A., Yale, 1903; LL.B., Yale, 1906; m. Elizabeth Sherman Kent, Feb. 26, 1915; children—Elizabeth Sherman, Evelyn, George Stanleigh, Kent, Peter, Anthony. Instructor in rhetoric, Sheffield Scientific School (Yale), 1903-06; law examiner, U.S. Forest Service, 1907-09; served as counsel in the Ballinger-Pinchot controversy, 1909, the former associates in forest service; apptd. special asst. to the atty. gen. in oil land litigation, 1913; asso. with William Denman of Denman & Arnold, 1911-18; pres. Pacific States Lumber Co., 1926-27. Calif. rep. of the President's Labor Mediation Commn., 1917, War Labor Policies Bd., 1918-19; spl. asst. to atty. gen. of U.S., 1934-35; chmn. President's Emergency Boards under Ry. Labor Act in controversies between Western Pacific R.R. Co. and certain employees, 1936, and between Southern Pacific Co. and certain employees, 1937. Episcopalian. Home: Kentfield, Calif. Died Jan. 18, 1942.

ARNOLD, Harold DeForest, physicist; b. Woodstock, Conn., Sept. 3, 1883; s. Calvin and Audra Elizabeth (Allen) A.; Ph.B., Wesleyan U., 1906, M.S., 1907, D.Sc., 1930; fellow in physics U. of Chicago, 1907-09, Ph.D., 1911; m. Leila Stone Beeman, Sept. 3, 1908; children—Audra Elizabeth, Dorothy Edith. Asst. in physics, Wesleyan U., 1906-07; prof. physics, Mt. Allison U., Sackville, N.B., Can., 1909-10; research engr., Western Electric Co., N.Y. City, 1911-24; dir. research, Bell Telephone Labs., N.Y. City, 1925—. Capt. Signal Corps, U.S.R., 1917. Received John Scott medal and award, 1928, for development of 3-electrode high vacuum thermionic tube. Methodist. Home: Summit, N.J. Died July 10, 1933.

ARNOLD, Howard Payson, lawyer; b. Boston, Oct. 12, 1831; s. Samuel S. and Sarah Louisa (Payson) A.; A.B., Harvard, 1852; m. Mrs. Caroline M. Crowninshield (widow of Edward A. Crowninshield), Dec. 23, 1869. Admitted to Suffolk bar, Mass., 1856; traveled several yrs. in foreign countries and was corr. and lecturer. Delivered 12 lectures at Lowell Inst., Boston, 1868, on the Great Expn. of 1867. Moved from Boston to Cal., 1900. Author: European Mosaic, 1864; The Great Exhibition, 1868; Gleanings from Pontresina, 1880; Memoir of Dr. John C. Warren, 1882; Memoir of Dr. J. Mason Warren, 1890; Historic Side-Lights, 1899; The Boston Medal, 1901. Home: Pasadena, Calif. Died 1910.

ARNOLD, James Loring, electrical engr.; b. Brooklyn, N.Y., July 14, 1868; s. James and Marie Bourbon (Scott) A.; B.A., Columbia, 1891; Ph.D., U. of Leipzig, Germany, 1897; m. Lydia W. Gelbach, 1901. Asst. prof. physics, New York U., 1906-10, prof. elec. engring., 1910—, also cons. engr. for some time with Gen. Electric Co. Republican. Episcopalian. Author: The Motor and the Dynamo, 1912; Concise Technical Physics, 1916. Home: Hastings-on-Hudson, N.Y. Died 1935.

ARNOLD, John Jacob; b. Wallace, Can., Dec. 29, 1870; s. Adam and Elisabetha (Stricker) A.; ed. business coll., Stratford, Can.; studied law, 1889-90; m. Olga D. Hoehn, June 9, 1896; children—Rhoda Marguerite, Victor Hoehn (dec.), Herta, (Mrs. H. R. Palmer). Began as jr. clk. First Nat. Bank of Chicago, 1891, v.p., 1912-19, also mgr. foreign exchange and foreign trade depts.; supervisor internat. business of Bank of Italy, San Francisco, Calif., and of its branches until Aug. 1920; chmn. North American Trust Co., Chicago. Mem. Nat. Foreign Trade Council and Council on Foreign Relations; mem. 1st Pan-Am. Financial Conf.; spl. del. Am. Bankers Assn. to

1st U.S.-Mexico Trade Conf., Mexico City; mem. World Cotton Conf. and World Trade Conf.; spl. lecturer on foreign trade and internat. relations, U. of Ill. and Schs. of Commerce of Northwestern U. and U. of Chicago. Home: Chicago, Ill. Died Feb. 23, 1933.

ARNOLD, Lynn John, lawyer, editor, pub.; b. Burlington Flats, N.Y., Sept. 28, 1864; s. Joseph Caswell and Mary J. (Mack) A.; ed. N.Y. State Normal Coll., Albany; m. Euretta A. Babcock, Nov. 27, 1889. Admitted to N.Y. bar, 1889; practiced, Cooperstown, N.Y., mem. Arnold & Cooke, 1889— and at Albany, mem. Arnold, Bender & Hinman, 1911—; surrogate Otsego County, 1895-01; pres. The Knickerbocker Press, Albany; pres. 1st Nat. Bank, Cooperstown; v.p. Cooperstown Aqueduct Assn. Republican. Episcopalian. Mason. Home: Albany, N.Y. Died May 27, 1920.

ARNOLD, Newton Darling, mfr.; b. Millville, Mass., Dec. 8, 1843; s. William Buffum and Matilda Webb (Darling) A.; m. Caroline Louise Gee, Mar. 21, 1866. Dir. Rumford Chem. Works, Providence Gas Co., Nat. Exchange Bank. Republican. Mason. Home: Providence, R.I. Died Aug. 13, 1916.

ARNOLD, Olney, diplomatic service; b. Cumberland, R.I., Sept. 8, 1861; s. William G. and Lucy M. (Aldrich) A.; ed. Mowry and Goff's English and Classical Sch., Providence, R.I.; m. Grace Angell, Apr. 10, 1889. Treas. and mgr. Rogers Screw Co., 1899-1913; pres. Angell Land Co.; mem. R.I. Ho. of Rep., 1908; Dem. candidate for gov. of R.I., 1908, 1909; diplomatic agent and consul gen. to Egypt, 1913—. Unitarian. Home: Providence, R.I. Died Mar. 5, 1916.

ARNOLD, Thomas Jackson; b. Beverly, Va. (now W.Va.), Nov. 3, 1845; s. Jonathan and Laura Ann (Jackson) A.; mother was sister of Gen. Stonewall Jackson; LL.B., Washington Coll. (now Washington and Lee U.), 1867; m. Eugenia, d. Gen. D. H. Hill, of Charlotte, N.C., June 1, 1876; children— Isabel, D. H. Hill, Thomas Jackson, Eugene Hill. Pros. atty., Randolph Co., W.Va., 1868-76; removed to San Diego, Calif., 1880, and became mem. Chase, Arnold & Hunsaker; collector of customs for Dist. of San Diego, by appmt. of Pres. Cleveland, 1886-90; returned to W.Va., 1896; pres. Peoples Nat. Bank, Elkins, W.Va., 1906-07; retired. Presbyn. Democrat. Author: Early Life and Letters of Gen. Thomas J. Jackson ("Stonewall" Jackson), 1916. Home: Arnold-Hill Station, W.Va. Died Jan. 10, 1933.

ARNOLD, William Rosenzweig, univ. prof.; b. Beirut, Syria, of German parents, Nov. 14, 1872; A.B., Ohio Wesleyan U., 1892; grad. Union Theol. Sem., 1895; univ. fellow, Columbia, 1895-96, Ph.D., 1896; studied abroad 1899; m. Ada Hinde Hart, Dec. 22, 1898; children—Isabel Hart (Mrs. Geo. R. Blodgett), Alice (Mrs. Francis H. Blaxill), Margaret Holmes. Curator dept. antiquities, Met. Mus. of Art, New York, 1896-98; lecturer O.T., 1902-03, Hitchcock prof. Hebrew lang. and lit., 1903-22, Andover Theol. Sem.; Andover prof. Hebrew lang. and lit., 1908-22, Hancock prof. of Hebrew and other Oriental langs., Harvard, 1922—. Fellow Am. Acad. Arts and Sciences. Author: Ancient Babylonian Temple Records, 1896; The Composition of Nahum, 1901; The Divine Name in Exodus iii 15, 1905; The Rhythms of the Ancient Hebrews, 1908; The Passover Papyrus from Elephantine, 1912; Ephod and Ark, 1917. Home: Cambridge, Mass. Died Dec. 11, 1929.

ARNOUX, William Henry, jurist; b. New York, Sept. 12, 1831. Admitted to bar of N.Y.; practiced at New York until 1882; judge Superior Court N.Y., 1882-95; resumed practice. Home: Vineyard Haven, Mass. Died 1907.

ARNSTEIN, Henry, chem. and mech. engr.; b. N.Y. City, Nov. 10, 1886; s. Adolph and Rose (Markstein) A.; A.M., U. of Budapest, 1906; Sc.D., U. of Berlin, 1908; D.Eng., U. of Heidelberg, 1910; m. Nettie Becker, June 3, 1917; children—Burnerd, Lawrence Hugo, J. Robert. Began with Krupp's Essen, Germany, 1908; chief chemist and plant mgr. Fleischmann Yeast Co. and Am. Diamalt Co., 1913-19; cons. engr., San Francisco, 1919-21; cons. chemist and industrial engr., Philadelphia, 1921—; pres. Farm Products Chem. Co. of America. Special tech. adviser to govts. of Cuba, Argentine, Brazil, Colombia and Peru. With Chem. Warfare Service, World War. Contbr. many papers to trade and tech. publs.; many of his works pub. by Cuban govt. Spl. research on industrial fermentation and distillation, particularly the production of yeast and alcohol; developer of process for production of fuel alcohol from waste products. Received first prizes from Uruguayan govt. in world-wide competition for best and most practical engineering project dealing with utilization of surplus agrl. crops and establishment of industries. Home: Philadelphia, Pa. Died July 24, 1935.

ARONSON, Rudolph, composer; b. New York, Apr. 8, 1856. Was mgr. Bijou Theatre, New York; projector and builder Metropolitan Concert Hall; also projector and builder Casino (with first roof garden in America). Composer of more than 150 pieces for orchestra, including the famous Sweet Sixteen waltz; in 1894 presented, in behalf of Amer-

ican musicians, to Johann Strauss, Vienna, a silver and gold wreath in honor of his golden jubilee celebration. Home: New York, N.Y. Died Feb. 5, 1919.

ARPS, George Frederick, psychologist; b. Cary, Ill., Jan. 23, 1874; s. August H. and Ida (Hansen) A.; A.B., Leland Stanford Jr. U., 1904; A.M., Ind. U., 1905; student Berlin (Germany) Univ., 1905-06; Ph.D., Univ. of Leipzig, 1908; m. Alice Mary Black, Oct. 18, 1905; children—Leslie H., Margaret M. Asso. prof. psychology, Ind. Univ., 1909-10; asst. prof. psychology, U. of Ill., 1910-12; prof. psychology and head of dept., Ohio State U., 1912—, dean Coll. of Edn., 1920-37, dean Grad. School, 1937—. Appointed capt. Sanitary Corps, U.S.A., major, Feb. 9, 1918-Aug. 14, 1919; served as chief psychol. examiner Camp Sherman, O., also as chief camp morale officer; appt. chief ednl. officer U.S.A. Gen. Hosp. 36, Detroit, Dec. 5, 1918, also chief hosp. morale officer; maj. reserve officer, Sanitary Corps, 1920—. Home: Columbus, O. Died Sept. 16, 1939.

ARREL, George F., lawyer; b. Poland, O., Oct. 1, 1840; s. David and Martha (Moore) A.; A.B., Westminster Coll., 1865, LL.D., 1913; m. Grace Tod, Oct. 18, 1876. Admitted to bar, 1867. City solicitor, Youngstown, 1870-78; judge Common Pleas, Ohio, 1880-87; was mem. Arrel, Wilson, Harrington & De Ford until July 1, 1917; when retired. Home: Youngstown, O. Died Apr. 7, 1923.

ARRICK, Clifford; b. St. Clairsville, O.; s. of Clifford and Margaret Josephine Cochran (Templeton) A.; ed. pub. and prep. schs.; m. Florence Gertrude Miller, Feb. 22, 1892. Began as topographer, U.S. Geol. Survey, 1884; pvt. sec. to W. H. H. Miller, atty. gen. U.S., 1892-93; with Union and Marion Trust cos., Indianapolis, 1893-98; broker in investment securities, Indianapolis, 1899-1908; spl. agt. Bell Telephone System, Indianapolis, 1908-12; mgr. publicity Central Group of Bell Telephone cos., Chicago, 1912-20; v.p. Nat. City Bank, 1920—. Maj. and p.-m. U.S. Vols., Spanish-Am. War, 1898; commd. maj. q.-m. O.R.C., Jan. 10, 1917. Republican. Home: Chicago, Ill. Died July 13, 1922.

ARROWSMITH, Robert; b. Brooklyn, N.Y., Nov. 23, 1860; s. Milton and Phebe Wood (Platt) A.; A.B., Columbia, 1882, A.M., 1883, Ph.D., 1884, univ. fellow, 1882-83, 1885-86; U. of Berlin, 1884-85; m. Edith E. Walton, Nov. 14, 1895. Asst. in modern langs., Columbia, 1883-85; instr. Latin and Sanskrit, Racine (Wis.) Coll., 1886; prin. Barnard Sch., St. Paul, Minn., 1887-90; Erasmus Hall Acad., Flatbush, L.I., 1892-93; prof. Greek and Latin, Teachers Coll. (Columbia), 1893-94; classical and modern lang. editor Am. Book Co., 1894-1913. Mem. Commn. for Relief in Belgium, 1915-18; sec. Am. Mil. Mission, Paris, 1917; reconstruction work Am. Red Cross, France, 1917. Later curator of Columbiana, Columbia U. Chevalier Ordre de la Couronne (France). Episcopalian. Author: English edit. Kaegi's Rigveda, 1885; First Latin Readings (Arrowsmith and Wicher), 1894; Roman Life in Latin Prose and Verse (Peck and Arrowsmith), 1894; Viri Romæ (Arrowsmith and Knapp), 1896. Contbr. to Harper's Classical Dictionary, Internat. Cyclo, etc. Home: Orange, N.J. Died June 1, 1928.

ARTHUR, Alfred, musician; b. Pittsburgh, Pa., Oct. 8, 1844; s. Hamilton and Margaret (Hanna) A.; grad. Boston Music Sch., 1868; student of Julius Eichberg, at Boston Conservatory of Music; m. Kate S. Burnham, Dec. 12, 1871. While in Boston sang tenor in a choir of Ch. of the Advent; settled in Cleveland, O., 1871, and taught and directed musical socs.; founded Cleveland Vocal Soc., 1873; founded Bach Choir of Woodland Presbyn. Ch., 1878, Sacred Music Soc. of the Pilgrim Congl. Ch.; became dir. Cleveland Sch. of Music. Composer: (operas) The Water Carrier, 1876; The Roundheads and Cavaliers, 1878; Adaline, 1879; (songs) Memory's Dream, 1868; Tell It, Silver Throat, 1880; Song of the Opal, 1881. Author: Progressive Vocal Studies, 1887; Seventy-nine Studies for Alto or Bass, 1889; Seventy Lessons in Voice Training, 1889; Vocal Technique, Studies in Articulation, 1896; Exercises in Vocal Technique, 1901; Studies in Elementary Theory; The Night Has a Thousand Eyes (song), 1910; Romance for Violin, 1910; Yesterday (song), 1911. Home: Lakewood, O. Died Nov. 20, 1918.

ARTHUR, Alfred Franklin, musical dir.; b. Cleveland, O., Jan. 12, 1876; s. Alfred and Kate Smith (Burnham) A.; grad. Cleveland Sch. of Music; m. Jessie Rae Larkin, Sept. 28, 1904; 1 dau., Elizabeth Burnham. Began as teacher of music, 1896; dir. Cleveland School of Music, 1918—; condr. Madrigal Club. Conglist. Home: Cleveland, Ohio. Died Apr. 21, 1938.

ARTHUR, Peter M., labor organizer; b. Scotland, 1831. Came to U.S. in boyhood; learned trade of blacksmith and machinist; became locomotive engr. N.Y. Central R.R. One of organizers, 1863, grand chief and engr., 1876—, Internat. Brotherhood of Locomotive Engrs. Home: Cleveland, O. Died 1903.

ARTHUR, Thomas, judge; b. Harrison County, Ia., July 12, 1860; s. William and Ellen A.; LL.B., State U. of Ia., 1881; m. H. Ima Stocker, Dec. 14, 1892. Clerk Dist. Court of Harrison County until

1891; practiced at Logan, Ia., 1891-1911; judge Dist. Court of Ia., 15th Dist., 1911-20; apptd., Sept. 15, 1920, and elected Nov. 1920, justice Supreme Court of Ia.; chief justice, 1923—. Republican. Methodist. Mason. Home: Logan, Ia. Died Sept. 15, 1925.

ARTHUR, William Hemple, army officer; b. Philadelphia, Pa., Apr. 1, 1856; s. Robert and Mary (Hemple) A.; M.D., U. of Md., 1877; m. Laura Bouvier, Sept. 26, 1881. Apptd. asst. surgeon U.S. Army, Feb. 18, 1881; capt. asst. surgeon, Feb. 18, 1886; promoted through grades to brig. gen., Oct. 2, 1917. Comd. hosp. ship Spanish-Am. War; with China Relief Expdn., 1900; in Philippines, 1900-02; duty at Soldiers' Home and Walter Reed Hosp., D.C., until 1911; duty in Philippines until 1915; apptd. comdt. Army Med. Sch., Washington, Oct. 1, 1915; retired Dec. 3, 1918. Med. dir. Georgetown Univ. Hosp., Mar. 10, 1919—. Home: Washington, D.C. Died Apr. 19, 1936.

ARVINE, Earliss Porter, lawyer; b. Woonsocket, R.I., Apr. 19, 1846; s. Kazlitt and Mary Ann (Porter) A.; A.B., Yale, 1869; m. Alice J. Stevens, Sept. 2, 1872. Practiced in New Haven, Conn., 1871—; mem. Arvine, Beers & Woodruff; v.p. F. E. Spencer Co., New Haven. Mem. Interstate Commn. on unification of laws of the different states, apptd., 1894. Democrat. Episcopalian. Home: Westville, Conn. Died June 22, 1914.

ASH, Louis Russell, consulting engr.; b. Uniontown, Ky., Sept. 27, 1873; s. Thomas Henry and Martha (Duval) A.; B.C.E., U. of Ark., 1893, B.E.E., 1894, C.E., 1903; post-grad. work, U. of Chicago; m. Hadgie Borker Davies, June 27, 1905; 1 son, Samuel Wilson. Began practice at Kansas City, Mo., 1901; city engr. Kansas City, 1910-13; city mgr. Wichita, Kan., 1917-19; became mem. Harrington, Howard & Ash, Kansas City, 1915; then mem. Ash, Howard, Needles & Tammen; specialized in design and supervision of constrn. bridges and viaducts. Mem. commn. to draft charter for Kansas City, 1925. Trustee Park Coll., Parkville, Mo. Presbyn. Home: Kansas City, Mo. Died Apr. 7, 1930.

ASH, Percy, architect; b. Philadelphia, Pa., Nov. 5, 1865; s. John Dorsey and Caroline Virginia (McGrath) A.; B.S. and C.E., U. of Pa., 1886; m. Josephine Wharton Barrington, June 1, 1901. Designer in supervising architect's office, Washington, D.C., 1900-05; prof. architecture, 1903-08, dean dept. architecture, 1908-10, George Washington U.; prof. architecture, U. of Mich., 1910-12; asst. prof. design and lecturer history of architecture, U. of Ill., 1913-18; mem. Hewitt (William D.) & Ash, Phila., 1918-24, succeeding firm on death of Mr. Hewitt, Apr. 1924; prof. architectural design and history, Pa. State College. Mem. A.I.A. Republican. Episcopalian. Home: State College, Pa. Died July 19, 1933.

ASHBRIDGE, Samuel H., mayor Phila.; b. Phila., Pa., Dec. 5, 1849; ed. pub. schools. Began as clerk in coal office; later in same business for himself; became known as orator on patriotic occasions; chief clerk coroner's office, 1880-86; coroner, 1886-99; elected mayor, Feb. 1899, by 120,000 majority; term expired, 1903; pres. Tradesmen's Trust Co. Home: Philadelphia, Pa. Died 1906.

ASHBROOK, William Albert, congressman; b. Johnstown, O., July 1, 1867; s. William and Lucy (Pratt) A.; pub. sch. edn.; m. 2d, Marie Swank, Nov. 25, 1920; children—William A., Lucy Marie, Leah Abbie, John Milan, James Howard. Publisher and editor Johnstown Independent, 1885—; pres. Johnstown (O.) Bank and Johnstown Building & Loan Assn. Co. Postmaster, Johnstown, O., 1889-93; mem. 77th Gen. Assembly, 1905-06; mem. 60th to 66th Congresses (1907-21), 74th and 75th Congresses (1935-39), 17th Ohio Dist. Democrat. Baptist. Mason. Home: Johnstown, Ohio. Died Jan. 1, 1940.

ASHBURN, Percy Moreau, med. officer, U.S.A.; b. Batavia, O., July 28, 1872; s. Allen W. (M.D.) and Julia M. (Kennedy) A.; grad. Batavia High Sch., 1890; M.D., Jefferson Med. Coll., 1893; m. Agnes Davis, July 6, 1896; children—Allen D. (dec.), Frank D., Ann Virginia. Apptd. contract surgeon U.S.A., May 30, 1898; commd. 1st lt. asst. surgeon, Dec. 12, 1898; promoted through grades to col. M.C., May 15, 1917. Participated in Philippine Campaign, 1899; pres. army bd. for study of tropical diseases in P.I., 1906-07; attached to U.S. Commn. to Republic of Liberia, 1909; again detailed pres. army bd. for study tropical diseases of P.I., and at Ancon, Panama, June 1913; gen. insp. Health Dept., Panama Canal, 1914-15; comdr. Med. Officers' Training Camp, Ft. Benjamin Harrison, Ind., 1917; on duty in A.E.F., July 1918-July 1919; comdt. Med. Field Serv. Sch., Aug. 1, 1920-Aug. 1, 1923; prof. mil. hygiene, U.S. Mil. Acad., 1923-27; librarian Army Med. Library, Washington, D.C., 1927-32 (retired); apptd. supt. Columbia Hosp. for Women, Sept. 20, 1934. Author: The Elements of Military Hygiene, 1909; History of the Medical Department of the United States Army, 1929. Home: Washington, D.C. Died Aug. 20, 1940.

ASHBURN, Thomas Quinn, army officer; b. Batavia, O., Nov. 17, 1874; s. Allen Wright and Julia (Kennedy) A.; grad. U.S. Mil. Acad., 1897, B.Sc., 1937; grad. Sch. of Submarine Defense, Ft. Totten, N.Y., 1907; m. Frances Marshall Fee; 1 son, Thomas Quinn. Commd. add. 2d lt. U.S.A., June 11, 1897; promoted through grades to col. C.A.C., July 1, 1920; twice promoted by act of Congress to brig. gen., June 3, 1924, maj. gen., Feb. 28, 1927; suggested Inland Waterways Corp. and chmn. bd. and pres. until 1939; pres. Warrior River Terminal Co. Served in Spanish-Am. War, Philippine Insurrection and World War; mil. and civ. gov. in P.I.; organizer and comdr. Met. Police, Manila; expert mil. witness before Spanish Claims Commn.; served as chmn. Claims Bd. for Transportation and chief of Inland Coastwise Waterway Service; chmn. American Waterways Assn. Silver star citation (U.S.); Purple Heart (U.S.); Croix de Guerre and Legion of Honor (France); Condecoracion de Merito Militar, primer clase (Mexico); Spanish-American, Cuba Occupation, Philippine and World War medals; wounded in action insignia. Author: History of 324th Field Artillery, 1919; Waterways and Inland Seaports (govt. printing office), 1925; Technical Discussion Concerning Waterways (Internat. Congress of Navigation, Brussels, Belgium), 1926; Annual Reports (govt. printing office), 1923-36; Inland Waterway Transportation—A National Problem, 1933. Home: Washington, D.C. Died May 2, 1941.

ASHE, Samuel A'Court, lawyer; b. near Wilmington, N.C., Sept. 13, 1840; s. William Shepperd and Sarah Ann (Green); ed. Rugby Acad., 1852-54, Oxford (Md.) Mil. Acad., 1854-55, Naval Acad., 1855-58; LL.D., U. of N.C., 1916; m. Hannah Emerson Willard, Aug. 10, 1871 (died 1892). Capt. and asst. adj. gen. Pender's Brigade, 1862; ordnance officer Battery Wagner, 1863; asst. to comdg. officer, Fayetteville Arsenal, 1863-65, C.S.A. Admitted to bar, 1867; practiced, 1867-79; mem. N.C. Assembly, 1870-72; chmn. Dem. State Com., 1877-80; editor Raleigh News and Observer, 1879-94; postmaster Raleigh, 1885-89; pres. Willard Mfg. Co., 1896-1906; v.p. Raleigh Hosiery Co., 1900-07; expert employee, Finance Com. of U.S. Senate, 1912-17; clerk U.S. District Court, Raleigh, N.C., 1918-36. Editor hist. vols. and author articles in mags. Home: Raleigh, N.C. Died Aug. 31, 1938.

ASHFORD, Bailey Kelly, med. officer; b. Washington, D.C., Sept. 18, 1873; s. Francis Asbury (M.D.) and Isabella Walker (Kelly) A.; grad. Washington High Sch., 1891; Columbian (now George Washington) U., 1 yr.; M.D., Georgetown U. Med. Sch., 1896; grad. Army Med. Sch., 1898; Sc.D., Georgetown, 1911, Columbia Univ., 1933, U. of Puerto Rico, 1933; hon. M.D., U. of Egypt, 1932; m. Maria Asuncion Lopez, June 24, 1899; children—Mahlon, Gloria Maria, Margarita. Resident phys. Children's Hosp., Washington, D.C., 1895-96; apptd. 1st lt. U.S. Army, Nov. 6, 1897; promoted through grades to col., May 15, 1917. Served with mil. expdn. to P.R., July 1898, and in Battle of Hormigueros, Aug. 13, 1898; div. surgeon 1st Div., June-Oct. 1917; in charge battle training of med. officers, Zone of Armies, A.E.F., Nov. 1917-Nov. 1918; battle clasps for Aisne-Marne and Argonne-Meuse. In 1899 determined cause of the anemia of agrl. class of Puerto Rico, later popularized as "hookworm disease"; founded, 1904, P.R. Anemia Commn., which began first campaign against disease in Western Hemisphere. Del. from U.S. to Internat. Cong. Indsl. and Alimentary Hygiene, Brussels, 1910; mem. med. commn. to Brazil, Rockefeller Foundation, 1916; del. from U.S. to Internat. Cong. of Tropical Medicine and Hygiene, Cairo, 1928. Prof. tropical medicine and mycology Columbia U., collaborating with Sch. of Tropical Medicine (Puerto Rico). Hon. mem. and pres. Am. Soc. Tropical Medicine, Puerto Rico Med. Assn.; fellow Am. Coll. Physicians, Am. Coll. Surgeons. Awarded D.S.M. (U.S.); Companion of St. Michael and St. George (Eng.); Grand Cordon, officer 1st class, Order of the Nile. Author: Anemia in Porto Rico, 1904; Uncinariasis in Porto Rico (with Gutierrez), 1911; also The Organization and Administration of the Medical Department, in the Zone of the Armies (Keen's Surgery, Vol. VII); Sprue (Tice's Loose-leaf Medicine), 1931; A Soldier in Science, 1934. Home: San Juan, P.R. Died Nov. 1, 1934.

ASHFORD, Emma Louise, composer; b. Newark, Del., Mar. 27, 1850; d. James and Elizabeth (Pickersgille) Hindle; ed. pub. schs.; studied music with father and under pvt. instrs.; m. John Ashford, Dec. 24, 1867. Organist, Episcopal Ch., Kewanee, Ill., at 12, St. Peter's Ch., Seymour, Conn., at 14; solo alto, St. James Ch., Chicago, 1867-68; organist and choir dir. chs. in Nashville, Tenn., many years. Prize winner various internat. song and anthem contests; gold medalist and hon. life mem. Nashville Art Assn. Composer: Favorite Organ Voluntaries; Organ Praise Series; The Diapason; The Organist's Helper; Ashford's Hymn Voluntaries; The Pedal Organ; Vox Celeste; 14 sacred cantatas; over 300 anthems; about 60 sacred songs and duets; song cycles, graded pieces for piano. Home: Nashville, Tenn. Died Sept. 22, 1930.

ASHHURST, Astley Paston Cooper, surgeon; b. Phila., Pa., Aug. 21, 1876; s. John A., Jr. (M.D., LL.D.), and Sarah Stokes (Wayne) A.; A.B., Univ. of Pa., 1896, M.D., 1900; m. Anna P. Campbell, 1930. Surgeon, out-patient dept., 1903-13, asso. surgeon, 1913-15, surgeon, 1915—, Episcopal Hosp.; surgeon to Phila. Orthopedic Hosp.; prosector applied anatomy, 1904-11, instr. surgery, 1911-18, associate in surgery, 1919-23, prof. clin. surgery, 1923—, U. of Pa. Sch. of Medicine. Maj. Med. R.C., 1917, col., 1918; dir. Base Hosp. 34, A.E.F., France. Republican. Episcopalian. Author: Enlargement of the Prostate (with John B. Deaver), 1905; Surgery of the Upper Abdomen (with same), Vol. I, 1909, Vol. II, 1913, 21; An Anatomical and Surgical Study of Fractures of the Lower End of the Humerus, 1910; Surgery, Its Principles and Practice, 4th edit., 1931. Home: Philadelphia, Pa. Died Apr. 1932.

ASHHURST, John, Jr., M.D.; b. Philadelphia, Pa., Aug. 23, 1839; grad. Univ. of Pa., 1857 (A.M., M.D., 1860); LL.D., Lafayette, 1895; m. Sarah Stokes Wayne, Dec. 8, 1864. Acting asst. surgeon U.S. Army, 1862-65; surgeon to numerous Phila. hosps.; prof. clinical surgery, Univ. of Pa., 1877—; Barton prof. surgery, 1888—; pres. Coll. Phys., Philadelphia, 1898—; mgr. Episcopal Hosp., 1880—; v.-p. surg. sect. Internat. Med. Cong., Phila., 1876; v.-p. Am. Surg. Assn., 1896; v.-p. Phila. Acad. Surgery, 1898—; pres. Pathol. Soc., Philadelphia, 1870-71. Fellow Coll. Phys., Phila.; pres. Evang. Alliance, Phila.; mem. standing com., diocese of Pa., since 1887. Editor numerous med. pubs. Author: Injuries of the Spine (1867); Principles and Practice of Surgery (1871, 6th edition, 1893); De La Laparotomie, ou Section Abdominale, Comme Moyen de Traitement de L'Intussusception Traduit par le Dr. Lutaud (Paris, 1875). Home: Philadelphia. Died 1900.

ASHHURST, John, librarian; b. Phila., Pa., Dec. 31, 1865; s. John, Jr. (M.D., LL.D.), and Sarah Stokes (Wayne) A.; A.B., U. of Pa., 1887, hon. Litt.M., 1925; unmarried. Librarian in charge West. Phila. Br., Free Library of Phila., 1895; librarian, Mercantile Library, 1901-03; asst. librarian, 1903-16, librarian and sec., 1916—, Free Library of Phila. Mem. bd. dirs. Am. Soc. for Extension of Univ. Teaching, Lovett Memorial Free Library, Pa. Home Teaching Soc. and Free Circulating Library for Blind, Drexel Inst. Mem. A.L.A., Franklin Inst., etc. Republican. Home: Philadelphia, Pa. Died Apr. 22, 1932.

ASHHURST, Richard Lewis, lawyer; b. Naples, Italy, Feb. 5, 1838; s. John and Harriet (Eyre) A.; grad. U. of Pa., 1856 (A.M., 1859), law dept., 1859; m. Sarah Frazer, May 30, 1861. Admitted to bar, June 1859. Mustered into Union army, 1st lt. and adj. 150th Pa. Vols., Aug. 11, 1862; hon. disch. for wounds received at Gettysburg, Sept. 5, 1863; bvtd. capt. for services at Chancellorsville; bvtd. maj. U.S. Vols., for distinguished gallantry at Gettysburg. Vice dean Shakespeare Soc.; vice-chancellor Phila. Law Assn. Postmaster, Phila., 1906—. Republican. Home: Philadelphia. Died 1911.

ASHLEY, Charles Sumner, mayor; b. New Bedford, Mass., Sept. 5, 1858; s. Joshua B. and Susan (Sanderson) A.; student Friends' Acad., New Bedford; m. Annie B. Luce, Nov. 13, 1879 (died June 6, 1890); children—R. Eugene, Charles S., Hannah B.; m. 2d, Julia A. Purrington, Feb. 17, 1892 (died Apr. 29, 1914). Mem. City Council, New Bedford, 1884-87, alderman, 1887-88, postmaster, 1894-96; mayor of New Bedford, 1891-94, and almost continuously from 1897-1923, then 1927-32, 1935-37; on sch. com., New Bedford, 1923-26; partner Charles S. Ashley & Sons Co., ins.; v.p. Safe Deposit Nat. Bank. Democrat. Mason (K.T.). Home: New Bedford, Mass Died Feb. 6, 1941.

ASHLEY, Clarence Degrand, lawyer; b. Boston, Mass., July 4, 1851; s. Ossian Doolittle and Harriet A. (Nash) A.; A.B., Yale, 1873; LL.B., Columbia, 1880; U. of Berlin, 1875-77; hon. LL.M., New York U., 1895, J.D., 1903; LL.D., Miami U., 1898; m. Isabella Heyward Ripley, Aug. 12, 1880. Admitted to bar, 1880. Organized 1891, and was prof., Metropolis Law Sch., New York, 1891-95; prof. law, 1895—, vice and acting dean, 1895-96, dean, 1896—, New York U. Law Sch. Author: Cases on Contract, 1899, 1912; The Law of Contracts, 1911. Home: New York, N.Y. Died Jan. 26, 1916.

ASHLEY, Edward, clergyman; b. Road Hill, Eng., Dec. 12, 1854; s. William Wheeler and Charlotte (Watts) A.; came to U.S., 1873, naturalized citizen, 1889; grad. Seabury Div. Sch., 1881, D.D., 1916; LL.D., U. of S.D., 1911; m. Elizabeth Ann Martin, Oct. 6, 1877 (died Dec. 28, 1915); children—Mrs. Charlotte Jessie Winona, Edward Athelstan, Martin Anselm, William Cuthbert, Robert Laud; m. 2d, Elizabeth Goodbody, May 15, 1917. Deacon, 1877, priest, 1881, P.E. Ch.; rural dean many yrs.; gen. missionary among Sioux Indians; archdeacon of Niobrara; examining chaplain; mem. Exec. Council, Dist. of S.D. Joint author Dakota Hymnal and Dakota English Service Book. Lime mem. S.D. State Hist. Soc. Republican. Mason (hon. 33°). Home: Aberdeen, S.D. Died Mar. 30, 1931.

ASHLEY, John Pritchard, clergyman, educator; b. Stoke-on-Trent, Eng., Apr. 14, 1862; grad. Ohio Wesleyan U., 1890; post grad. studies, Boston U., Jena.

Berlin and Oxford; (A.M., S.T.B., Ph.D., D.D.); m. Della Gust. Prof. philosophy; author and lecturer; pres. Genesee Wesleyan Sem., 1895-98; Mich. Coll. Assn., 1898-99; pres. Albion Coll., 1899-1902; pastor Ch. of Christ, Saratoga, Calif. Address: Saratoga, Calif. Deceased.

ASHLEY, Ossian D., railway official; b. Townsend, Vt., April 9, 1821. Began as 2d sec. and transfer agt., Wabash, St. Louis & Pacific Ry., mem. purchasing com., 1885-87; pres. Wabash Western R.R., 1887-1901; chmn. bd., 1901-03. Home: 195 Broadway, New York, N.Y. Died 1904.

ASHMEAD, William Harris, asst. curator, div. insects, U.S. Nat. Museum, 1897—; b. Phila., Pa., Sept. 19, 1855; s. Capt. Albert S. and Elizabeth (Graham) A.; A.M., Fla. Agrl. Coll., 1901; D.Sc., Western Univ. of Pa., 1901; m. Harriet Holmes, 1878. Was with J. B. Lippincott Co., Phila.; with brother became pub. agrl. books, agrl. weekly, and daily, Jacksonville, Fla., 1876; edited scientific dept. of weekly, devoting self chiefly to investigation of injurious insects; spl. field entomologist, U.S. Dept. Agr., 1887; entomologist State Agrl. Coll., Lake City, Fla., 1888; asst. entomologist and investigator, U.S. Dept. Agr., 1889; spl. studies in Berlin, winter 1889-90; returned to Dept. Agr. Author: Orange Insects (treatise on beneficial and injurious insects in Fla.), 1880 A7. Wrote: Monograph of the North American Proctotrypidae; also 250 contributions to jours. Home: Washington, D.C. Died 1908.

ASHMORE, Sidney Gillespie, coll. prof.; b. London, Eng., Apr. 15, 1852; s. Sidney and Maria Elsworth (Phelps) A.; A.B., Columbia, 1872, A.M., 1875; L.H.D., Hobart, 1887; m. Fanny Hart Vail, Oct. 31, 1895. Instr. Latin and Greek, Lehigh U., 1873-76; instr. Latin, Columbia, 1876-81; prof. Latin, Union Coll., 1881—. Mem. mng. com. Am. Sch. Classical Studies, Rome. Author: Terence (Adelphoe), 1893, rev., 1896, Macmillan's Classical Series; The Classics and Modern Training, 1905. Editor: with intro. and notes, The (Six) Comedies of Terence, 1908. Home: Schenectady, N.Y. Died 1911.

ASHMUN, George Coates, M.D.; b. Tallmadge, O., Jan. 31, 1841; s. Russell A. and Marcia (Wright) A.; M.D., Western Reserve U., 1873; m. Laura J. Post, May 20, 1880; m. 2d, Alice Ford, Nov. 27, 1888; children—Russell Ford, Louis Henry, George Slaght, Bernice. Served in Civil War, 1861-62 and 1863-65; U.S. examiner for pensions, Cleveland, 1873-86; health officer, Cleveland, 1881-91; lecturer on hygiene, Case Sch. of Applied Science, 1903-07; prof. hygiene and preventive medicine, 1893-1909, registrar and bursar, 1893-1907, then prof. emeritus med. jurisprudence and ethics, Med. Coll., Western Reserve U. Maj. surgeon 5th Regt. Inf., Ohio N.G., 1889-98. Mem. Cleveland City Council, 1898-99 and 1902-03; mem. Bd. of Edn., 1909-1915. Home: Cleveland Heights, O. Died June 25, 1929.

ASHMUN, Margaret Eliza, author; b. Rural Waupaca Co., Wis.; d. Claude Samuel and Rachael Jane (Smith) A.; grad. Stevens Point (Wis.) State Coll.; Ph.B., U. of Wis., 1904, A.M., 1908; further study, 1908-12. Teacher, Stout Inst., Menomonie, Wis., 1904-06, high sch., Helena, Mont., 1907; instr. English, U. of Wis., 1907-12. Mem. D.A.R. Author: The Study and Practice of Writing English (joint author), 1914; Isabel Carleton Series, 5 Vols., 1916-19; Stephen's Last Chance, 1918; Marion Frear's Summer, 1920; Topless Towers, 1921; Support, 1922; Including Mother, 1922; The Lake, 1924; No School To-Morrow, 1925; School Keeps To-Day, 1926; Brenda Stays at Home, 1926; Mother's Away, 1926; Pa—The Head of the Family, 1927; David and the Bear Man, 1929; Susie Sugarbeet, 1930; The Singing Swan, 1931. Compiler and editor: Prose Literature for Secondary Schools, 1910; Modern Short Stories, 1914; Modern Prose and Poetry for Secondary Schools, 1914. Home: R.F.D. 2, Waupaca, Wis. Deceased.

ASHTON, Joseph Hubley, lawyer; b. Phila., Pa., March 11, 1836; s. Daniel R. and Elizabeth Josiah (Marsh) A.; grad. U. of Pa., 1854, A.M., 1858; LL.D., Georgetown Univ., 1872; m. Hannah R. Wakeman, Oct. 11, 1864. Admitted to Phila. bar, Oct. 9, 1858; one of editors The Legal Intelligence, 1860; asst. U.S. dist. atty., Eastern dist. of Pa., 1861-64; asst. atty. gen. of U.S., 1864-67, 1868-69, actg. atty. gen., July 1865, July 1868; agt. and counsel of U.S. before Internat. Commn. under Claims conv. with Mexico of July 4, 1868; prof. pleading, practice and evidence, Georgetown Univ., 1870-74; counsel for Vice-Adm. Porter and Mortar Flotilla in cases of capture by Adm. Farragut's fleet, New Orleans, May 1862; counsel for U.S. under Act of Mar. 3, 1873, in relation to U.P. R.R. Co.; spl. law del. to Internat. Sanitary Conf., Washington, 1880; counsel for govt. before Venezuela Claims Commn., 1885; counsel for Chinese in U.S. Supreme Court in cases under Chinese Exclusion laws, 1890-97. Edited Vols. 9, 10, 11 and 12 of Opinions of Attorneys General of U.S. One of founders Am. Bar Assn., 1878. Home: Washington, D.C. Died 1907.

ASHTON, William Easterly, gynecologist; b. Phila., Pa., June 5, 1859; s. Samuel Keen and Caroline M. (Smiley) A.; M.D., U. of Pa., 1881; M.D., Jefferson Med. Coll., 1884; LL.D., Ursinus, 1904; m. Alice Elizabeth Rosengarten, Oct. 5, 1891; 1 dau., Dorothy (dec.). Mem. faculty of hosp. and Jefferson Med. Coll., 1884-92; gynecologist to hosp. and prof. gynecology, Medico-Chirurg. Coll., 1892-1916; prof. gynecology, Grad. Sch. of Medicine, U. of Pa., 1916—. Enlisted U.S. Army, 1917; commd. maj. and assigned as regtl. surgeon 309th F.A., 78th Div.; served in France 11 mos., St. Mihiel and Meuse-Argonne offensives; commd. lt. col., Feb. 1919; hon. disch., Camp Dix, N.J., Apr. 1919; gassed in Argonne and retired from practice on leaving army; awarded D.S.C., "for extraordinary heroism," 1918. Fellow Am. Coll. Surgeons. Rep. Epis. Author: Essentials of Obstetrics, 1888 (trans. into Chinese); The Practice of Gynecology (textbook), 1905. Contbr. on surg. subjects. Inventor surg. instruments and appliances; first who substituted pads of gauze for marine sponges. Cited by Maj. Gen. Mark L. Hersey, for award of Congressional Medal of Honor, for "Action beyond call of duty." Home: Philadelphia, Pa. Died 1933.

ASPEGREN, John, merchant; b. Sweden, Aug. 31, 1876; s. John and Emmy (Mullern) A.; grad. U. of Lund, 1894; studied business methods in European countries; came to America, 1899; m. Lucille Vantine Bacon, Dec. 6, 1906. Asso. with brother as Aspegren & Co., commission mchts., N.Y. City, 1899, acquired entire interest, 1919; pres. Gulf & Valley Cotton-oil Co., Ltd., Portsmouth Cotton Oil Refining Corp., Scandinavian Pulp Agency, Aspegren Fruit Co., Interstate Tank Car Corp. V.-p. New York Produce Exchange, 1910-12, pres., 1912-14; pres. New York Produce Exchange Clearing Assn., 1915—; dir. The Internat. Vegetable Oil Co.; Pres. The Swedish Chamber of Commerce of U.S.A. Home: New York, N.Y. Died Nov. 8, 1924.

ASPINALL, Joseph, judge; LL.B., Columbia, 1875. Mem. N. Y. Assembly, 1888-89, 1891, Senate, 1892-93; judge Kings Co. Court, 1896-1907; justice Supreme Ct. of N.Y., 2d Dist., Jan. 1, 1907-Dec. 31, 1924. Republican. Home: Brooklyn, N.Y. Died May 7, 1939.

ASPINWALL, Thomas, civil engr.; b. Brookline, Mass., Sept. 5, 1853; s. William and Arixene Southgate (Porter) A.; S.B., Mass. Inst. Tech., 1876; m. Alicia Stuart Towne, Feb. 3, 1887. Practiced since 1877; mem. Aspinwall & Lincoln; consulting engr. various state bds. of Mass. Mem. 1st Corps Cadets, M.V.M., 1878-81; engr. 1st Brigade 3 yrs. Home: Boston, Mass. Died Mar. 2, 1918.

ASTON, Ralph, naval officer; b. Middletown, Conn., Jan. 31, 1841; s. Henry Hungerford and Ann (Shephard) A.; ed. Chase Sem. and pvt. tutors; m. Jennie R. Preswich, Oct. 1869 (died, 1876); 2d, Salena Hinman, Oct. 26, 1882. Apptd. 3rd asst. engr. U.S.N., 1861, and advanced to capt., Mar. 3, 1899; rear-admiral and retired 1902. First service on steam gunboat Cayuga, West Gulf Sta., which first to pass lower forts at capture of New Orleans. Served in Sampson's fleet during Spanish-Am. war, on cruiser Cincinnati, from which transferred to U.S. cruiser Brooklyn, completing sea service April 23, 1899. Home: Brooklyn, N.Y. Died 1904.

ASTOR, John Jacob, capitalist; b. Rhinebeck, N.Y., July 13, 1864; s. William and Caroline Webster (Schermerhorn) A.; g.gs. John Jacob Astor; B.S., Harvard, 1888; traveled abroad, 1888-91; m. Ava Lowle Willing, 1891; 2d, Madeline Talmage Force, Sept. 9, 1911. Mgr. family estates, 1891—; built, 1897, Astoria Hotel, New York, adjoining Waldorf Hotel, which built by Wm. Waldorf Astor, cousin, two now forming one building under name of Waldorf-Astoria Hotel, one of largest and probably most costly hotels in world. Col. staff of Gov. Levi P. Morton, and May, 1898, commd. lt. col. U.S.V.; presented to govt. mountain battery for use in Spanish war, said to cost over $100,000. After assisting Maj. Gen. Breckinridge, insp. gen. U.S.A., in inspection of camp and troops at Chickamauga Park, Ga., assigned to duty on staff of Maj. Gen. Shafter and served in Cuba in operations ending in surrender of Santiago. Has invented bicycle brake, pneumatic road improver, improved turbine engine, vibratory disintegrator, for getting power gas from peat, and steamship chair, held in place by suction cups. Author: A Journey in Other Worlds, 1890, etc. Home: New York, N.Y. Died Apr. 15, 1912.

ASTOR, William Waldorf, capitalist; b. New York, Mar. 31, 1848; s. John Jacob and Charlotte Augusta (Gibbes) A.; g.g.s. John Jacob, founder of Astor fortune; ed. by pvt. tutors, finishing in Europe; LL.B., Columbia, 1875; m. Mary Dahlgren Paul, June 6, 1878. Entered office of Astor Estate, 1871; succeeded father, 1890, as head of Astor family, with personal fortune estimated at about $100,000,000. Mem. New York legislature, 1878-81; U.S. minister to Italy, 1882-5; removed to England, 1890; became owner Pall Mall Gazette and Pall Mall Magazine, 1893. Naturalized British subject; created baron by King George V, 1916, and viscount, 1917. Author: Valentino, a Story of Rome, 1886; Sforza, a Historical Romance of the 16th Century in Italy, 1889. Home: Kent, England. Died Oct. 18, 1919.

ASWELL, James Benjamin, congressman, lecturer; b. Jackson Parish, La., Dec. 23, 1869; s. Benjamin W. and Elizabeth (Lyles) A.; grad. George Peabody Coll. for Teachers, 1892; A.B., U. of Nashville, 1893, A.M., 1898; LL.D., U. of Ark., 1907; m. Ella Foster, Mar. 3, 1901. Prin. sch., Nash, La., 1886-88; prin. Calhoun (La.) High Sch., 1893-96; prof. English, La. Poly. Inst., 1896-97; training teacher, State Normal Coll., Natchitoches, La., and state inst. conductor, 1897-1900; pres. La. Poly. Inst., 1900-04; state supt. pub. edn., 1904-08; pres. La. State Normal Coll., 1908-11; mem. 63d to 71st Congresses (1913-31), 8th La. Dist. Democrat. Reorganized pub. sch. system of La. Baptist. Home: Natchitoches, La. Died Mar. 16, 1931.

ATCHISON, Thomas Cunningham, clergyman; b. Bloomfield, O., Oct. 31, 1855; s. John and Nancy (Cunningham) A.; A.B., Muskingum Coll., 1878, A.M., 1881; grad. Pittsburgh (Pa.) Theol. Sem., 1881; D.D., Westminster Coll., 1896; m. Mary Jane Shepherd, June 15, 1881 (died May 31, 1923); children—Clyde Shepherd, Mabel Vernon (dec.), Thomas Calvin. Pastor First U.P. Ch., Carnegie, Pa., 1881-1901, North Av. U.P. Ch., Baltimore, Md., 1901-08, First U.P. Ch., Lawrence, Mass., 1908-34; pastor emeritus Lawrence (Mass.) Ch., 1934—. Mem. bd. ch. extension, U.P. Ch., 1885-1901, com. on denominational young people's work, 1894-98 (chmn. Saratoga Conv. 1898); moderator Synod of N.Y., 1914, 72d Gen. Assembly, Des Moines, Ia., 1930; pres. bd. dirs. Pittsburgh Theol. Sem., 1916-18, 1920-21; supt. missions Boston Presbytery, 1913-34. Home: Washington, Pa. Died May 24, 1940.

ATHEARN, Walter Scott, educator; b. Marengo, Ia., July 25, 1872; s. Elisha S. and Susan E. A.; ed. Drake U., State U. of Ia., and U. of Chicago; m. Florence Royalty, June 15, 1894 (died June 8, 1917); children—Clarence R., Gertrude E.; m. 2d, Frances Emily Smith, Sept. 14, 1929. Prin. pub. schs., Delta, Ia., 1894-99; asso. prof. pedagogy, Drake U., 1900-04; editor Midland Schs. (monthly mag.), 1902-07; dean, Highland Park Normal Coll., 1906-09; prof. religious edn., Drake U., 1909-16; prof. religious edn., Boston U., 1916-29; dean Sch. of Religious Edn. and Social Service, 1918-29; became pres. Butler U., 1931. Chmn. Commn. on Character, Moral and Religious Edn., World Federation of Edn. Assns., 1927—. Mem. Church of Disciples of Christ. Author: The Church School, 1914; The City Institute for Religious Teachers, 1915; The Organization and Administration of the Church School, 1917; Religious Education and American Democracy, 1917; The Malden Leaflets, 1917; A National System of Education, 1920; An Introduction to the Study of the Mind, 1921; Character Building in a Democracy, 1924; An Adventure in Religious Education, 1930; The Minister and the Teacher, 1932. Editor and joint author numerous religious edn. publs. Home: Indianapolis, Ind. Died Nov. 13, 1934.

ATHERTON, George W., pres. Pa. State Coll., 1882—; b. Boxford, Essex Co., Mass., June 20, 1837; left fatherless at 12; helped support mother and two sisters; worked in cotton mill, then on farm, later as teacher; worked way through Phillips Exeter Acad. and Yale; grad. 1863; LL.D., Franklin and Marshall Coll., 1883; m. Frances D. W. Washburn, Dec. 25, 1863. Served as lt. and capt. 10th Conn. vols., 1861-63; taught in Albany Boys' Acad., 1863-67; prof. St. John's Coll., 1867-68, Univ. of Ill., 1868-69; prof. polit. economy and constl. law, Rutgers, 1869-82; mem. Bd. of Visitors to U.S. Naval Acad., 1873, 1891; on commn. to investigate Red Cloud Indian agency, 1875; chmn. commn. to digest and revise State system of taxation, N.J., 1878; admitted to N.J. bar, 1878; first pres. Am. Assn. of Agrl. Colls. and Expt. Stas. (reëlected for purpose of recognizing his services in drafting and securing passage of act of Congress establishing agrl. expt. stas. in every State and Territory). Author: Magna Charta, a Comparative View of the Barons' Articles and the great Charter. Home: State College, Pa. Died 1906.

ATKESON, Thomas Clark, agriculturist; b. Buffalo, W.Va., Feb. 15, 1852; s. Thomas and Virginia Harris (Brown) A.; ed. W.Va. U., Ky. Agrl. and Mech. Coll.; LL.B., Ky. U., 1874; hon. Ph.D., Barboursville Coll., 1892; M.S., Morris Harvey Coll., 1897; m. Cordelia Meek, July 8, 1878; children—Thomas Zephaniah, Karl Clark, Mary Meek, Leda Cordelia. Farmer and lawyer, 1878-91; prof. agr., W.Va. U., 1891-93; farmer, 1893-96; pres. Barboursville (W.Va.) Coll., 1896-97; dean Coll. of Agr. and prof. agr., 1897-1910, prof. animal husbandry, 1910-14, prof. animal husbandry emeritus, 1914—, W.Va. U. Editor W.Va. Farmer, Charleston, 1909-15. Democrat. Methodist. Overseer Nat. Grange, 1903-11; master W.Va. State Grange, 1896-1920, Washington rep. Nat. Grange, 1919-27. Author: Bookkeeping for Farmers, 1893; A Catechism of Agriculture, 1913; Semi-Centennial History of the Patrons of Husbandry, 1916; Pioneering in Agriculture, 1924; Outlines of Grange History, 1928; also articles and bulls. Home: Buffalo, W.Va., and Washington, D.C. Died 1935.

ATKINS, Edwin F., manufacturer, importer; b. Boston, Mass., 1850; s. Elisha and Mary E. (Freeman) A.; ed. pvt. schs. of Boston; A.M., Harvard, 1903; m. Katharine Wrisley, 1882. Pres. Bay State Sugar Refinery, 1878-88; partner E. Atkins & Co., importers sugars, commn. mchts. and bankers, 1874—;

chmn. bd. dirs. Am. Sugar Refining Co. until July 13, 1915 (resigned), dir., 1915-20; v.p. U.P. Ry. System, 1889-95; pres. Aetna Mills; dir. Westinghouse Electric & Mfg. Co., Westinghouse Electric Internat. Co., Boston Wharf Co., Guarantee Co. of N. America, Second Nat. Bank, Shirreffs Worsted Co., Caledonia Sugar Co. (Cuba), Soledad Sugar Co. (Cuba), Punta Alegre Sugar Co. (Cuba) and subsidiaries, Caracas Sugar Co., E. Atkins Co., Ltd. (Cuba). Home: Boston, Mass. Died May 20, 1926.

ATKINS, Harry T., cotton mfr.; b. Ohio, Mar. 26, 1849; s. Richard and Frances (Jago) A.; ed. Hughes High Sch., Cincinnati; m. Anna Pearce, June 2, 1875. Entered mfg. business, Cincinnati, 1875; pres. The Atkins & Pearce Mfg. Co., The Deer Creek Mfg. Co. Pres. Ohio State Bd. of Commerce, 2 yrs. Pres. Ohio Mechanics' Inst. Republican. Mem. Disciples of Christ. Mason. Home: Cincinnati, O. Died Oct. 16, 1919.

ATKINS, James, bishop; b. Knoxville, Tenn., Apr. 18, 1850; s. James and Mary F. A.; student Emory and Henry Coll., 1866-72, A.M.; D.D., Trinity Coll.; m. Ella M. Branner, Sept. 14, 1876. Ordained M.E. Ch., S. ministry, 1872; pastor, 1872-79; pres. Asheville Female Coll., 1879-89, 1893-96, Emory and Henry Coll., 1889-93; Sunday sch. editor, M.E. Ch., S., 1896-1906; elected bishop, May 1906; bishop in charge of S. Meth. Mission in Belgium, Poland and Czecho-Slovakia, 1918-21. Home: Waynesville, N.C. Died Dec. 5, 1923.

ATKINS, John De Witt Clinton, farmer; b. Henry Co., Tenn., June 4, 1825; s. John and Sarah (Manley) A.; A.B. (with first honors), E. Tenn. U., 1846; m. Elizabeth Bacon Porter, Nov. 23, 1847 (died 1887); m. 2d, Mrs. Flora Crawford, June 24, 1890. Mem. Ho. of Reps., Tenn., 1859-51; elected to state senate, 1855; pres. Dem. State Conv., 1856; mem. Congress, 9th Tenn. dist., 1858-59; del.-at-large Charleston (S.C.) Conv., 1860, withdrawing from conv. with Tenn. delegation; candidate for presdl. elector, Breckenridge and Lane ticket, 1860; elected to Confederate Provisional Congress, Aug. 1861, to Confederate permanent Congress, Nov. 1861, and re-elected 1863; lt. col. 5th Tenn. Regt. C.S.A.; chmn. Dem. State Conv., 1884; presdl. elector, 1884; commr. Indian Affairs, 1885-88; candidate for U.S. senate, 1888. Home: Paris, Tenn. Died 1908.

ATKINS, Smith Dykins, newspaperman; b. Horseheads, N.Y., June 9, 1836; s. Adna Stanley and Sarah (Dykins) A.; ed. Rock River Sem., Mt. Morris, Ill.; m. Eleanor Hope Swain, Aug. 27, 1865. Admitted to bar, 1854; pros. atty. 14th Jud. Dist., Ill., 1860. Enlisted as pvt., 11th Ill. Inf., Apr. 17, 1861; capt. Co. A, Apr. 30, 1861; maj., Mar. 21, 1862; resigned, Apr. 17, 1862; col. 92d Ill. Inf., Sept. 4, 1862; bvtd. brig. gen. vols., Jan. 12, 1865, "for gallant and meritorious services"; hon. mustered out, June 21, 1865. Editor Freeport Daily Journal, 1878—; postmaster of Freeport. Republican. Home: Freeport, Ill. Died Mar. 27, 1913.

ATKINSON, Christoper Joseph, hon. sec. Boys' Clubs of America; b. Granby, Que., Can., Aug. 31, 1858; s. Bagster and Eliza (Taylor) A.; ed. dist. sch. S. Granby; student Granby Acad., 1872-75; unmarried. Came to U.S., 1914, naturalized, 1926. Worked as printer and pub., 1875-82; established several papers and gen. printing business, 1882-92; sold business, removed to Toronto to follow work among boys which had interested him, 1875—; sec. Victoria Indsl. Sch., 1892-95, Broadview Boys' Inst., 1896-1911, Toronto Boys' Dominion (4 brs.), 1911-14; exec. sec. Boys' Clubs of America, Inc., N.Y. City, 1914-31, hon. sec., 1931—. Sec.-treas. Boys' Club Internat. Com. Awarded gold medal on retirement in recognition of 56 yrs. in work for boys. Democrat. Conglist. Home: Highland Mills, N.Y. Died Apr. 4, 1935.

ATKINSON, Edward, economist, underwriter; b. Brookline, Mass., Feb. 10, 1827; s. Amos and Anna G. A.; ed. pvt. schs.; LL.D., U. of S.C.; Ph.D., Dartmouth Coll.; m. Mary C. Heath, Oct. 4, 1855. For 40 yrs. engaged in authorship of papers and pamphlets on banking, competition, railroading, cotton mfr., fire prevention, tariff, money question, imperialism. Invented improved cooking stove, "Aladdin Oven"; pres. Boston Mfrs.' Mut. Fire Ins. Co., 1878—. Author: The Distribution of Property, P2; Industrial Progress of the Nation, P2; The Margin of Profit, P2; Taxation and Work, P2; The Science of Nutrition; The Prevention of Loss by Fire; Facts and Figures, 1904 H5. Home: Boston, Mass. Died 1905.

ATKINSON, George Francis, botanist; b. Raisinville, Monroe Co., Mich., Jan. 26, 1854; s. Joseph and Josephine (Fish) A.; student Olivet Coll., 1878-83; Ph.B., Cornell, 1885; m. Lizzie S. Kerr, Aug., 1888. Asst. prof. entomology and gen. zoölogy, 1885-86, asso. prof., 1886-88, U. of N.C.; prof. botany and zoölogy, U. of S.C., and botanist of exptl. sta., 1888-89; prof. biology, Ala. Poly. Inst. and Agrl. and Mech. Coll. of Ala., and biologist of exptl. sta., 1889-92; asst. prof. cryptogamic botany, 1892-93, asso. prof., 1893-96, prof. botany and head dept. botany, 1896—, Cornell U. Asso. editor The Botanical Gazette, 1896-98. Author: Biology of Ferns, 1894; Elementary Botany, 1898; Lessons in Botany, 1900; Studies of American Fungi, 1900; Mushrooms, Edible, Poisonous, Etc., 1903; First Studies on Plant Life, 1904; College Text-Book of Botany (enlargement of Elementary Botany), 1905. Contbr. to botan. jours. Home: Ithaca, N.Y. Died Nov. 14, 1918.

ATKINSON, George Wesley, governor; b. Charleston, Va. (now W.Va.), June 29, 1845; s. James and Miriam (Rader) A.; A.B., Ohio Wesleyan U., 1870, A.M., 1873; LL.B., Howard U., 1874; Ph.D., Mt. Union Coll., 1885; hon. A.M., DePauw U., 1876; LL.D., U. S. Grant U., 1890, U. of Nashville, 1890, Ohio Wesleyan, 1906; D.C.L., W.Va. U., 1897; m. Ellen Eagan, Dec. 3, 1868 (died 1893); 2d, Mrs. Myra H. Camden, June 24, 1897. Admitted to bar, 1875; mem. Charleston (W.Va.) Bd. Edn., 1869-71; postmaster, 1870-76; U.S. internal revenue agt., 1876-80; U.S. marshal, W.Va., 1881-85; mem. 51st Cong. (1889-91), 1st W.Va. Dist.; gov. of W.Va., 1897-1901; U.S. atty., Southern Dist., W.Va., 1901-05; judge U.S. Ct. of Claims, 1905-16. Republican. K.T.; Grand Master Free Masons, W.Va., 1876-77. Author: History of Kanawha, 1876; West Virginia Pulpit, 1878; After the Moonshiners, 1879; Revenue Digest, 1880; ABC of the Tariff, 1882; Don't, or Negative Chips from Blocks of Living Truths, 1886; Prominent Men of West Virginia, 1895; Psychology Simplified, 1897; also pub. addresses and poems. Home: Charleston, W.Va. Died Apr. 4, 1925.

ATKINSON, Henry Morrell, financier; b. Brookline, Mass., Nov. 13, 1862; s. George and Elizabeth (Staigg) A.; ed. Harvard, class of 1884; m. May Peters, Apr. 1888. In cotton business, Atlanta, 1886-89; pres. and v.p. banking instns. Atlanta, until 1910, resigning as v.p. Third Nat. Bank (now Citizens & Southern Nat. Bank); organized and built first electric lighting system in Atlanta and first pres. Ga. Electric Light Co.; organized and built and first pres. A.B.&A.R.R.Co. (now owned by Atlantic Coast Line); chmn. bd. Ga. Ry. & Electric Co., 1902-12; chmn. bd. Ga. Ry. & Power Co., 1912-27; now chmn. bd. Ga. Power Co. Home: Atlanta, Ga. Died Jan. 21, 1939.

ATKINSON, Isaac Edmondson, physician; b. Baltimore, Jan. 23, 1846; s. James Edmondson and Hannah Ann (Smith) A.; grad. med. dept., U. of Md., 1865; m. Virginia Rebecca Duval, Oct. 17, 1867. Was pres. of Clinical Soc. of Md., Med. and Chirurg. Faculty of Md., Am. Dermatol. Assn.; emeritus prof. therapeutics and clin. medicine U. of Md. Author many articles in med. jours., chiefly relating to dermatology and internal medicine. Home: Baltimore, Md. Deceased.

ATKINSON, Louis Evans, congressman; b. Juniata Co., Pa., Apr. 16, 1841; s. Adam Holliday and Mary Martha (Evans) A.; ed. Airy View and Milnwood acads., med. dept. U. of Pa., 1858-9; M.D., Univ. Med. Coll. (New York U.), 1861; m. Margaret E. Mathers, Apr. 4, 1878. Admitted to bar, 1870, and practiced at Mifflintown, Pa.; pres. Juniata Nat. Bank; 1st v.-p. First Nat. Bank, New Bloomfield, Pa. Mem. 48th to 52d Congresses (1883-93), 18th Pa. Dist.; judge 41st Jud. Dist., Pa., Dec., 1901-Jan., 1902; asst. surgeon, 1st Pa. Reserve Cav., and surgeon, 188th Pa. Inf., 1861-65. Republican. Presbyn. Home: Mifflintown, Pa. Died 1910.

ATKINSON, Thomas Wilson, educator; b. Spalding Co., Ga., Nov. 28, 1867; s. James Archibald and Rebekah Catherine (Wilson) A.; B.S., La. State U., 1891, C.E., 1892; grad. student Johns Hopkins, 1894-95; Cornell U., 1896-97; m. Marie Antoinette Bilger, July 27, 1898. Instr., prep. dept., La. State U., 1891-94, asst. prof. physics and mechanics, 1895-96, prof. mechanics and drawing, 1897-99, prof. physics and mechanics, 1899-1906, prof. physics and elec. engring., 1906-07, prof. elec. engring. and dean Coll. of Engring., 1907-27, dir. Engring. Expt. Sta., 1923-27, acting pres., 1927-29, pres., 1929-31. Dir. vocational training U.S. Soldiers, La. State U., June-Nov. 1918. Democrat. Episcopalian. Home: Baton Rouge, La. Died Dec. 25, 1933.

ATKINSON, William E., motion picture exec.; b. Sandbach, Cheshire, Eng., Mar. 22, 1880; s. William Henry and Eliza (Edmonds) A.; student Royal Inst. Tech., Worcester, Eng., 1894-97; m. Helen Howard Wilson, May 24, 1903; 1 son, Edward Wilson; m. 2d, Ethel M. Carstang, May 8, 1917; children—William Brockliss, Marian Eleanor. Came to U.S., 1901, naturalized, 1918. Began as mech. engr., 1898; mgr. Welsbach Co. of N.E., 1901-06, Pittsfield (Mass.) Electric Co., 1906-10; sales mgr. Kinemacolor Co. of America, 1910-14; v.p. and gen. mgr. Metro-Goldwyn Pictures Corp., 1914-25, Roxy Theatres Corp., 1925-28; became pres. and receiver Fox Theatres Corp., April. 1932, retired. Served with English Army, Boer War, 1899-1900. Episcopalian. Home: University, Va. Died May 18, 1940.

ATKINSON, William Elrie, lawyer; b. Shelby Co., Ala., July 24, 1852; s. William Wiley and Barbara (Wilder) A.; ed. schs. in Ark. and Tex.; studied law, Washington and Lee U.; m. Lidie Powers, Dec. 16, 1890. Admitted to bar, 1874; practiced at Rosston, Ark., 1874-78, Prescott, Ark., 1878-90, Little Rock, 1890-1910, Clarksville, Ark., 1910—; mem. Atkinson & Brock. Atty.-gen. of Ark., 1889-93. Democrat. Trustee Ouachita Bapt. Coll., and State Mission Bd. Mason. Home: Clarksville, Ark. Died Nov. 8, 1935.

ATKINSON, William Sackston, scientific illustrator; b. Cazenovia, N.Y., Sept. 17, 1864; s. James and Mary (Peck) A.; student Cazenovia Sem.; A.B., Stanford U., 1899; unmarried. With Stanford U. since 1896; specializes in zoöl. and bot. drawing, restoration of fossil fishes of Calif. Miocene. Progressive Rep. Conglist. Has illustrated some 200 scientific publs. of Dr. David Starr Jordan and others, also of Carnegie Mus. and Calif. Acad. Science, and 3 vol. work entitled "Illustrated Flora of the Pacific States." Home: Stanford University, Calif. Deceased.

ATKINSON, William Walker, author; b. Baltimore, Md., Dec. 5, 1862; s. William C. and Emma L. (Mittnacht) A.; ed. pub. sch.; m. Margaret Foster Black, Oct. 31, 1889; children—Joseph W. (dec.), William C. In comml. life, 1882-94; admitted to Pa. bar, 1894, to Ill. bar, 1903; asso. editor "Suggestion," Chicago, 1900; editor "New Thought," Chicago, 1901-05; editor "Advanced Thought," Chicago, 1916-19. Author various works on New Thought and psychology. Home: Los Angeles, Calif. Died Nov. 22, 1932.

ATKINSON, William Yates, gov. Ga., 1894-96 and 1896-98; b. Oakland, Meriwether Co., Ga., 1855; grad. U. of Ga., 1877; m. Susie Cobb Milton, 1880. Admitted to Ga. bar, 1878; solicitor of co. court of Coweta Co., Ga., 1879-82; mem., 1886-94, and speaker, 1892-94, Ga. legislature; apptd., 1890, trustee Univ. of Ga.; pres. Democratic State conv., 1890, 1892; chmn. Democratic State Exec. Com., 1890-92, 1892-94; founder and pres. bd. of trustees, 1889—, Ga. Normal and Indsl. Coll. Home: Newnan, Ga. Died 1889.

ATKINSON, Wilmer, journalist; b. Warwick Twp., Bucks Co., Pa., June 13, 1840; s. Thomas and Hannah (Quinby) A.; three ancestors came over in ship "Welcome" with William Penn; grad. Freeland Sem., Montgomery Co., Pa., 1858; m. Anna Allen, Nov. 28, 1866. With Howard M. Jenkins started first daily paper in Del. (Wilmington Daily Commercial), 1866; published it 1866-76; started, 1877, Farm Journal, Phila., editor emeritus. Mem. Soc. of Friends. Home: Philadelphia, Pa. Died May 10, 1920.

ATTERBURY, Anson Phelps, clergyman; b. N.Y. City, June 18, 1854; s. Benjamin Bakewell and Olivia Eggleston (Phelps) A.; student Yale, 1871-73 and 1875-76; Andover Theol. Sem., 1876-78; grad. Union Theol. Sem., 1879; Ph.D., New York U., 1893; D.D., Hamilton, 1893; m. Catharine G. Van Rensselaer, June 11, 1891. Ordained Presbyn. ministry, 1880; pastor Park Ch., New York, 1879-1918, emeritus. Author: Islam in Africa, 1899; A Story of Life, 1920; Song of the Stars, 1928; Translator of Sombart's Socialism, 1898. Home: New York, N.Y. Died Jan. 4, 1931.

ATTERBURY, William Wallace, ry. official; b. New Albany, Ind., Jan. 31, 1866; Ph.B., Yale, 1886; hon. A.M., 1911; LL.D., U. of Pa., 1919, Yale U., 1926, Villa Nova Coll., 1927, Temple U., 1929; E.D., Pa. Mil. Coll., 1932; m. Mrs. A. R. MacLeod. Began as apprentice in Altoona shops, Pa. R.R., 1886, road foreman on various divs., 1889-92; asst. engr. of motive power Pa. Lines (Northwest System), 1892-93; master mechanic Pa. Co., Ft. Wayne, Ind., 1893-96; gen. supt. motive power, lines east of Pittsburgh and Erie, 1896-1903; gen. mgr. same, 1903-09; 5th v.p. in charge transportation Pa. R.R., Mar. 24, 1909-Mar. 3, 1911, and 4th v.p., Mar. 3, 1911-May 8, 1912, v.p. in charge operations, May 8, 1912. Granted leave of absence, Aug. 6, 1917, to direct constrn. and operation U.S. mil. rys. in France; commd. brig. gen. U.S.A., Oct. 5, 1917-May 31, 1919; v.p. in charge operation Pa. R.R. system, Mar. 1, 1920; v.p. without designation, Nov. 15, 1924; elected pres. Pa. R.R. Co., Oct. 1, 1925; dir. Chicago Union Station Co., N.Y. Connecting R.R. Co., Richmond, Fredericksburg & Potomac R.R. Co., Washington Terminal Co., Pennroad Corp., N.&W. Ry. Co., Phil. Nat. Bank, Guaranty Trust Co. of N.Y.; trustee Penn Mut. Life Insurance Co. D.S.M. (U.S.); Comdr. Legion of Honor (France); Companion of Most Honorable Order of Bath (Great Britain); Comdr. Order of Crown (Belgium); Royal Order of White Eagle (Serbia); Grand Officer of Order of Crown (Roumania). Republican. Home: Philadelphia, Pa. Died Sept. 20, 1935.

ATTERIDGE, Harold Richard, playwright; b. Lake Forest, Ill., July 9, 1886; s. Richard H. and Anna T. (O'Neill) A.; Ph.B., U. of Chicago, 1907; m. Mary Teresa Corless, Feb. 1, 1923. Began playwriting in 1905. Author: A Winning Miss; The Girl in the Kimono (prod., Chicago, 1907); Vera Violetta; The Whirl of Society; Broadway to Paris (with George Bronson-Howard); The Honeymoon Express; The Passing Show of 1912 (with George Bronson-Howard); The Passing Show of 1913; Two Little Brides; The Man with Three Wives; The Whirl of the World; The Passing Show of 1914; Dancing Around; Maid in America; The Peasant Girl; The Passing Show of 1915; A World of Pleasure; Passing Show of 1916; Robinson Crusoe, Jr.; Passing Show of 1917; Show of Wonders; Doing Our Bit; Sinbad; Passing Show of 1918; Monte Cristo, Jr.; Passing Show of 1919; The Little Blue Devil; The Passing Show of 1921; The Last Waltz; Bombo; The Rose of Stamboul; Make It Snappy; Passing Show of 1922; Passing Show of 1923; The Dancing Girl; The Passing Show of 1925; Big Boy; Artists and Models, Paris Edition; Gay Paree; Everybody's Welcome; also talking picture scenarios (in collaboration) Artists and Models; The Courtesan; The Dream Girl; Marjorie; The Ritz Revue; Sky High; Princess Flavia; Night in Paris; Night in Spain; Ziegfeld Follies of 1927; Collette; New Gay Paree of 1927; The Greenwich Village Follies; Night in Spain; Night in Venice; Pleasure Bound; Broadway Nights; Duchess of Chicago; New Ziegfeld Follies, 1933; Thumbs Up. Active in radio work. Home: Lynbrook, L.I., N.Y. Died Jan. 16, 1938.

ATTWILL, Henry Converse, lawyer; b. Lynn, Mass., Mar. 11, 1872; s. Isaac M. and Harriet E. (Sanger) A.; grad. Lynn High Sch., 1890; LL.B., Boston U. Law Sch., 1893; m. Augusta Harris, June 30, 1906. Practiced in Lynn and Boston, 1893—; mem. Mass. Ho. of Rep., 1896, 1897, 1898, Senate, 1899, 1900, 1901; asst. dist. atty. Eastern Dist. of Mass., 1904-09, dist. atty., 1910-15; atty. gen. of Mass., 1915-19; became chmn. Pub. Utilities Commn. of Mass., 1919. Mason. Universalist. Home: Lynn, Mass. Died 1936.

ATWATER, Francis; b. Plymouth, Conn., Dec. 3, 1858; s. Henry and Catherine (Fenn) A.; ed. Plymouth pub. schs.; m. Helena J. Sellew, 1879; 1 child, Dorence Keith (dec.). Learned printer's trade, was foreman composing room, Meriden Recorder, at 16; founder and pub., Windermere Weekly Forum, Wallingford, Conn., 1879-80; asst. foreman, Hartford Courant, 1880; later mgr. Red Bluff (Calif.) Sentinel; founder and pub. Meriden Sunday News; founded Meriden Daily Journal, 1886, and retired as pres. Jour. Pub. Co., 1913; founded, 1898, Havana Journal (now Havana Post), first all-Am. jour. in Cuba; bought and sold New Britain Daily News; bought and sold Waterbury Daily Republican; pres. Meriden, Southington & Compounce Tramway; founder, 1912, Puritan Trust Co.; dir. Broadway Bank & Trust Co., New Haven, 1913; organizer, 1914, Am. Bank & Trust Co.; organizer, 1915, East Hampton Bank & Trust Co., Wallingford Trust Co., Torrington Trust Co. Mem. Conn. Senate, 1906; tax collector, 1907. Pres. Meriden Bd. of Trade; mem. exec. com. Am. Nat. Red Cross; founder, 1912, and pres. Clara Barton Memorial Assn. Author: Histories of Plymouth and Kent, Conn., 1896; Atwater History and Genealogy, 1901, Vol. II, 1906, Vol. III, 1919, Vol. IV, 1927; Atwater Memoirs, 1922; History of Southington, Conn., 1924. Home: New Haven, Conn. Died Nov. 25, 1935.

ATWATER, George Parkin, clergyman; b. Lisbon, O., Sept. 8, 1874; s. Thomas Cook and Clara (Parkin) A.; B.A., Kenyon Coll., 1895, M.A., 1899, D.D., 1918; grad. Bexley Theol. Sch. of Kenyon Coll., 1898; D.Litt., U. of Akron, 1924; m. Marie L. Carey, Nov. 19, 1901; children—David Thomas, Mary Frances. Deacon, 1898, priest, 1899, P.E. Ch. Rector Church of Our Saviour, Akron, Ohio, 1897-1926; rector Grace Ch., Brooklyn, N.Y., 1926—. Dep. to Gen. Conv. of P.E. Ch., 4 times; del. Pan-Anglican Cong., London, 1908. Col. Akron Home Guard Regt., 1917; maj. O.R.C., U.S.A. Republican. Mason (32°, K.T.). Author: The Young Crusaders, 1912; Young Crusaders at Washington, 1912; The Episcopal Church—Its Message for Men of Today, 1917; The Card Method for Instruction, 1921; A Word-Map of the Old Testament, 1923; The A-A Method for the Endowment of Churches, 1924; The Continuous Unit Campaign, 1925; Annals of a Parish, 1927. Contbr. to mags. Home: Brooklyn, N.Y. Died Oct. 21, 1932.

ATWATER, Richard Mead, chemist; b. Providence, R.I., Aug. 10, 1844; s. Stephen and Mary W. (Weaver) A.; A.B., Brown U., 1865, A.M., 1868; spl. studies in chemistry; m. Abby Sophia Greene, Sept. 29, 1867. Supt. schs., Millville, N.J., 1874-75; identified with chem. and mfg. interests, especially with coke and glass; in mercantile business, Paris, 1900-06; farmer, Chadds Ford, Pa., 1907—. Trustee, Brown U., 1878—; judge glass exhibits Chicago Expn., 1893. Hon. v.-p. Internat. Chemists' Assn., Berlin, 1903. Contbr. to tech. jours. on glass and coke mfg. Commr. and mayor of Sea Isle City, N.J., 1913-17. Home: Chadds Ford, Pa. Died Oct. 30, 1922.

ATWATER, Wilbur Olin, prof. chemistry Wesleyan Univ., 1873—; b. Johnsburgh, N.Y., May 3, 1844; grad. Wesleyan U., 1865; Ph.D., Sheffield Scientific Sch., Yale, 1869; student univs. of Leipzig and Berlin; m. Marcia Woodard, Aug. 26, 1874. Prof. chemistry East Tenn. Univ., 1871-72, Me. State Coll., 1873; dir. Conn. Agrl. Expt. Sta., 1875-77; dir. Storrs (Conn.) Expt. Sta., 1887-1902; founded, 1888, and until 1891 dir., Office Expt. Stas., U.S. Dept. Agr., 1891—; spl. agt. Dept. Agr., and, 1908—, chief of nutrition investigations. Author over 150 papers on chem. and allied subjects, notably (with F. G. Benedict) An Experimental Inquiry Regarding the Nutritive Value of Alcohol, Vol. VIII, Nat. Acad. Sciences. Home: Middletown, Conn. Died 1907.

ATWATER, William Cutler, coal operator; b. Brooklyn, N.Y., July 4, 1861; s. John Hoadley and Jane Barker (Leonard) A.; prep. edn., Adelphi Acad., Brooklyn, 1872-79; A.B., Amherst, 1884; m. Ida Wilson Hay, May 1, 1889; children—William Cutler, John Jacob, Margaret Hay (Mrs. George Daniel Olds, Jr.), David Hay. Began as coal salesman, Haddock, Shonk & Co., N.Y. City, 1886; chmn. bd. Wm. C. Atwater & Co., N.Y. City, Wm. C. Atwater & Co., Mass., Am. Coal Co., Mill Creek Coal & Coke Co., Elkhorn Coal Co.; v.p. West Bay Co.; dir. Dead River Timberland Co. Mem. Psi Upsilon (pres. of corp.). Episcopalian. Home: New York, N.Y. Died Feb. 22, 1940.

ATWELL, Charles Beach, teacher; b. Theresa, N.Y., Apr. 11, 1855; s. Joseph and Mary (Beach) A.; Ph.B., Syracuse U., 1879, Ph.M., 1882, Sc.D., 1929; summer student Harvard, 1887, U. of Freiburg, 1891; m. Mary Josephine Kellogg, Dec. 27, 1883 (died Oct. 1929); children—Henry Kellogg, Francis Charles (dec.), Ruth Sarah, William Joseph. Instr. Lowville (N.Y.) Academy, 1879-80; instr. mathematics and physics, Northwestern U. Acad., 1880-82; prin. pub. schools, S. Evanston, Ill., 1882-84; instr. natural science Northwestern U. Acad., 1884-88; instr. biology, 1888-91, prof. biology, 1891-94, prof. botany, 1894-1928, Northwestern U., emeritus. City forester, Evanston, 1909-11, 1919-21. Author: Genealogy of the Atwell Family of New London, Conn., 1906; Ancestors and Descendants of Charles Brewster Beach of Barker, N.Y., 1931. Contbr. to bot. and other jours. Home: Swarthmore, Pa. Died Sept. 11, 1937.

ATWILL, Edward Robert, bishop; b. Red Hook, N.Y., Feb. 18, 1840; s. Robert E. and Margaret E. A.; A.B., Columbia, 1862, A.M., 1865; B.D., Gen. Theol. Sem., 1864; S.T.D., U. of Vt., 1883; m. Mary Whiting, Sept. 14, 1864. Deacon, 1864, priest, 1865, P.E. Ch.; curate, New York, 1864-65; rector, Williamsburg, L.I., 1865-67; curate to bishop of Vt., 1867; rector, Burlington, Vt., 1867-82, Toledo, O., 1882-90; consecrated 1st bishop Diocese of Western Mo., Oct. 14, 1890. Home: Kansas City, Mo. Died 1911.

ATWILL, William, ry. official; b. Rockford, Ill., 1883. Began with I.C.R.R. as asst. to telegrapher, Rockford, 1899; advanced as telegrapher, dispatcher, chief dispatcher, trainmaster, supt. and gen. supt. to gen. mgr., 1929, later v.p. and gen. mgr. Home: Chicago, Ill. Deceased.

ATWOOD, Charles Edwin, neurologist; b. Shoreham, Vt., July 21, 1861; s. Edwin Simons and Laura R. (Moore) A.; B.S., Cornell, 1880; M.D., Bellevue Hosp. Med. Coll. (New York U.), 1883; m. Helen Pearce Jarvis, Feb. 5, 1896. Asst. phys. Hudson River State Hosp., 1885-87, Utica State Hosp., 1887-92; 1st asst. phys., Soc. of N.Y. Hosp., Bloomingdale, 1892-1905; asst. neurologist, Vanderbilt Clinic (Columbia), 1892-1914; post-grad. studies, Vienna, London, 1905-06; neurologist to N.Y. City Hosp. and Schs., Randall's Island, 1907-17. Asso. editor Am. Jour. of Insanity, 1887-92; collaborator Jour. of Nervous and Mental Diseases and N.Y. Med. Record and Jour. A.M.A. Home: New York, N.Y. Died Feb. 19, 1930.

ATWOOD, Edwin Byron, soldier; b. Portage Co., O., Sept. 18, 1842; s. Edwin and Eliza (Byron) A.; ed. Farmington Sem., Trumbull Co., O., and Allegheny Coll., Meadville, Pa.; m. Henrietta M. King, Nov. 23, 1878. In 41st Ohio Inf. as sergt. maj., Sept. 19, 1861, 2d lt., Jan. 1, 1862, 1st lt., Sept. 8, 1862, capt., May 1, 1864; bvt. maj. vols., Mar. 13, 1865, for "valuable and conspicuous service during war"; mustered out Nov. 27, 1865; apptd. 2d lt. 16th U.S. Inf., May 11, 1866, and advanced to col. asst. q. m. gen., Nov. 1, 1900. Bvtd. 1st lt. Mar. 2, 1867, for "gallant and meritorious services" in battle of Murfreesboro, Tenn.; capt., Mar. 2, 1867, for same at Chickamauga, and maj., Mar. 2, 1867, for same at Mission Ridge. Brig.-gen. U.S.A., Aug. 2, 1903, retired Aug. 3, 1903, at own request, being senior col. in q.m. dept. U.S.A., and serving as chief q.m., Div. of Philippines, at Manila. Home: Chicago, Ill. Died 1909.

ATWOOD, Harry, author and publicist; b. nr. Morgan Park, Ill., Jan. 1, 1870; s. Orville Elbridge and Martha Elvira (Townsend) A.; Ph.B., U. of Chicago, 1897; LL.B., Chicago Coll. of Law, 1898, Ill. Coll. of Law, 1899; m. Maude Smith, Aug. 23, 1905; 1 dau., Martha Regina. Asst. U.S. atty., 1908-11; atty. for Bd. Local Improvements, Chicago, 1915-18. Sergt. 1st Ill. Cav., Spanish-Am. War. Pres. Constn. Ednl. Assn. Baptist. Author: Back to the Republic, 1918; Keep God in American History, 1919; Safeguarding American Ideals, 1921; The Constitution Explained, 1927. Lecturer on Americanism, etc. Home: Chicago, Ill. Died Dec. 13, 1930.

ATWOOD, Isaac Morgan, clergyman and editor; b. Pembroke, N.Y., Mar. 24, 1838; s. Orsamus Isaac and Nancy (Shearer) A.; ed. Royalton Acad. and Lockport High Sch.; hon. M.A., St. Lawrence, 1871; D.D., Tufts, 1879; LL.D., Buchtel, 1905; m. Almira Church, Oct. 29, 1861; 1 son, John Murray. Ordained Universalist ministry, 1861; pastorates at Churchville, Clifton Springs and Watertown, N.Y., Portland, Me., Chelsea and Cambridge, Mass.; edited Boston Universalist, 1867-72, Christian Leader, N.Y. City, 1873-74; pres. Canton Theol. Sem., 1879-99; gen. supt. Universalist Ch. in U.S. and Can., 1898-06; sec. Universalist Gen. Conv., 1905-12. Asso. editor Universalist Leader, Boston, 1874-1908; prof. theology and philosophy, St. Lawrence U., 1911—. Author: Have We Outgrown Christianity?, 1870; Latest Word of Universalism, 1879; Walks About Zion, 1880; Episcopacy, 1885; Revelation, 1893; Balance Sheet of Biblical Criticism, 1896; A System of Christian Doctrines, 1900. Also many articles in mags. Home: Canton, N.Y. Died Oct. 26, 1917.

ATWOOD, John Harrison, lawyer; b. Phillipston, Mass.; s. Andrew and Mary Emma (Holden) A.; student Harvard, 1880-81, LL.B., 1884; m. Nellie F. Wyman. In practice at Leavenworth, Kan., 1884-1908, Kansas City, Mo., 1908—; mem. Atwood, Wickersham & Chilcott. Counsel various corps. Co. atty. Leavenworth Co., Kan., 1886-92; Dem. candidate for Congress, 1892; del.-at-large Dem. nat. convs., 1896, 1900, 1908-1916; Kan. mem. Dem. Nat. Com., 1904-09, and chmn. of speakers' bur. in charge Western headquarters, Chicago, 1908. Sent on special mission to Europe, summer, 1918; in Eng. and France, Aug.-Dec.; traversed entire Western battlefront; spl. asst. atty. gen. in prosecution of meat packers, 1919. Mason. Home: Kansas City, Mo. Died June 28, 1934.

ATWOOD, Lemuel True, journalist; b. Abington, Mass., Sept. 17, 1852; s. Albert A.; ed. public schools Mass., Ky., Ill. and Ohio, 1858-65; grad. law dept. U. of Mich., 1876; m. Kate Kenton, Sept. 10, 1877. Practiced law 6 yrs.; reporter and city editor Cincinnati Post, 1882-89; editor same, 1889-95; editorial supt. Scripps-McRae League, consisting of Cincinnati Post, Covington, Ky., Post, Cleveland Press, St. Louis Chronicle, and Kansas City World, from 1895 to 1902; then treas. of those papers and The Des Moines Daily News, Los Angeles Record and Tacoma Times. Home: Walnut Hills, Cincinnati, O. Died 1909.

ATWOOD, Millard V., newspaper editor; b. Groton, N.Y., Aug. 6, 1886; s. Frank R. and Minnie A. (Van Marter) A.; A.B., Cornell U., 1910; m. Grace Doughty, Dec. 14, 1911; children—Ruth, Martha, Susan. Began as reporter, 1904; telegraph editor Ithaca (N.Y.) News, 1910-11; publisher weeklies in central N.Y., 1911-24; mem. extension staff, N.Y. State Coll. of Agr., Cornell U., 1918-24, prof. of extension teaching, 1923-24; mng. editor Utica Observer-Dispatch, 1924-27; mng. editor Rochester Times-Union, 1927-29; asso. editor The Gannett Newspapers, 1929—. Presbyn. Mason. Author: The Country Newspaper, 1923; (with Amy H. Croughton) Shepard's Pie, 1933; Grace in Thine Eyes, 1935; Some Other Power, 1937; Sawdust in His Shoes, 1940. Home: Rochester, N.Y. Died Nov. 3, 1941.

ATWOOD, Oscar, educator; b. Cambridge, Vt., Aug. 5, 1842; s. Norman and Mary Ann A.; ed. Johnson, Vt., 1857-58, Underhill, Vt., 1859-60; Univ. of Vt.; m. Mary J. Oertel, Sept. 24, 1900. Pres. Straight Univ., 1890—. Mem. Nat. com. to promote Univ. of U.S. Republican. Home: New Orleans. Died 1909.

AUBREY, William, lawyer; b. Mobile, Ala., July 29, 1853; s. William and Rosa Matilda (Forsyth) A.; ed. Dews Pvt. Sch., Columbus, Ga., Loyola Coll. and Richard Malcolm Johnston Pvt. Sch., Baltimore, Md.; m. Mrs. Sallie E. Weir, Feb. 14, 1883; 1 son, John Forsyth; m. 2d, Eugenia Dearing Speer, Aug. 25, 1892; children—Mrs. Jean Bulkley, Mary (wife of Dr. Peter McCall Keating), William (deceased). Admitted to Tex. bar, 1874, and began practice at Marshall; moved to San Antonio, Tex., 1882; dean of San Antonio Law Sch., 1928; dir. Tex. Law Review. Served as mayor of Marshall. Trustee Carnegie Pub. Library, San Antonio. Democrat. Episcopalian. Home: San Antonio, Tex. Deceased.

AUCHINCLOSS, John Winthrop, capitalist; Ph.B., Yale, 1873. Formerly mem. firm of Auchincloss Bros. and officer or dir. various corps.; retired. Home: New York, N.Y. Died Jan. 24, 1938.

AUCHINCLOSS, William Stuart, author, inventor; b. New York, N.Y., Mar. 19, 1842; s. John A.; C.E., Rensselaer Poly. Inst., 1862. In construction dept. A.&G.W. Ry., and Jersey City Locomotive Wks., 1863-69; mfr. rolling stock and shipbuilder, 1871-79; commission merchant, 1879-95. Invented averaging instrument for rapid calculation of accounts. U.S. commr. Paris Expn., 1867. Author: Link and Valve Motions; Ninety Days in the Tropics; The Book of Daniel Unlocked; Chronology of the Holy Bible. Home: Atlantic Highlands, N.J. Died 1928.

AUER, Leopold, violinist; b. Veszprim, Hungary, June 9, 1845; ed. in music at Conservatory (Budapest), and Vienna Conservatory, later at Hanover, Germany, under Joachim; m. Nadine Pelikan, May 23, 1874; m. 2d, Madame Stein, June 24, 1924. Appointed, 1868, prof. Imperial Conservatory, Petrograd, Russia, and soloist of the Czar, succeeding Henri Wieniawski; conducted concerts of Imperial Musical Soc., Petrograd, 1887-92; in N.Y. City, Feb. 18, 1918—. Became Russian subject, 1883; created hereditary noble, 1895, and state councillor, 1903; presented Grand Cross Order of Stanislaus, by Czar, 1912; Chevalier Légion d'Honneur, France. Most noted pupils, Mischa Elman, Efrem Zimbalist, Kathleen

Parlow, Jascha Heifetz, Eddy Brown, Toscha Seidel, Max Rosen, Francis Macmillen. Composer numerous pieces and transcriptions for violin. Author of Violin Playing as I Teach It, My Long Life in Music, and Violin Masterworks and Their Interpretation. Naturalized citizen of U.S., 1926. Home: New York, N.Y. Died July 15, 1930.

AUGER, Charles L., silk dyer; b. Philadelphia, Pa., Sept. 29, 1860; s. Peter F. and Marie Florine (Clement) A.; ed. high sch. and commercial sch.; m. Emma Chadwick, Apr. 29, 1884; children—Frank C., Mrs. Emma M. C. Powers (dec.), Mrs. Mary Muhs, Charles L., Louis F. Began in silk dyeing and finishing business in 1885; pres. Nat. Dyeing & Printing Co.; also dir. various other cos. Vice chmn. 2d Liberty Loan drive and chmn. 3d and 4th Liberty Loan drives. Decorated Cross Legion of Honor (French), 1924. Home: Ridgewood, N.J. Died Jan. 1939.

AUGHINBAUGH, William Edmund, author; b. Westmoreland Co., Va., Oct. 12, 1871; s. William L. and Anna M. (O'Neill) A.; LL.B., Nat. Law Sch., Washington, D.C., 1892, LL.M., 1896; M.D., Columbian (now George Washington) U., 1897; m. Mary A. Douglas, Oct. 12, 1900. Mem. bar Supreme Court of U.S.; was asso. editor Leslies Mag. and foreign and export editor New York Commercial; then asso. editor New York Daily Investment News; dir. Joint Securities Corp. Former lecturer foreign economics and foreign trade, New York U. and Columbia U. Mem. Manhattan Med. Soc. (pres.). Author: Selling Latin America, 1915; A Port for Bolivia, 1916; Trademark Tragedies, 1916; Advertising for Trade in Latin America, 1922; Advertising for Trade Abroad, 1922; Volcanoes, Rats and Men, 1932; I Swear by Apollo, 1938. Home: New York, N.Y. Died Dec. 18, 1940.

AUGUR, Jacob Arnold, soldier; b. Ft. Niagara, N.Y., Aug. 21, 1849; s. Gen. Christopher C. and Jane Elizabeth (Arnold) A.; grad. U.S. Mil. Acad., 1869; m. Katherine J. Dodge, Nov. 14, 1872. Commd. 2d lt., 5th Cav., June 15, 1869; promoted through grades to col., 10th Cav., June 9, 1902; employed chiefly on frontier service until 1880; served with Republican River Expdn., 1869, and engaged in affair on Prairie Dog Creek, and in Ute Expdn. during fall and winter of 1879; was instr. at U.S. Mil. Acad., 1883-87; on frontier duty Ind. Ty. and Tex., 1887-97; instr. Inf. and Cav. Sch., 1897-99, 1901-02; in Philippines, 1899-1901; on duty in Neb., 1902-07, in Philippines, Apr. 2, 1907—. Died 1909.

AULT, James Percy, magnetician; b. Olathe, Kan., Oct. 29, 1881; s. Addison and Mary Aleja (McElwain) A.; A.B., Baker U., Baldwin, Kan., 1904; A.M., Columbia, 1909; m. Mamie Alice Totten, Mar. 27, 1907; children—Evelyn Geraldine, Ruth Miriam (dec.), Marjorie Pearl. With Dept. Terrestrial Magnetism, Carnegie Instn. of Washington, 1904—, chief observer, 1918. Comd. yacht Carnegie, cruises in Arctic and Subantarctic regions, 1914-17; chief of section ocean work and comdr. of yacht Carnegie, Jan. 1919—. Lt. comdr. U.S.N. Res., 1927. Methodist. Author: (with others) Researches Dept. Terrestrial Magnetism (Carnegie Instn., Washington), 1917, 26. Home: Washington, D.C. Died 1929.

AULTMAN, Dwight Edward, army officer; b. Allegheny, Pa., Feb. 2, 1872; s. Matthias W. and Mary (Beach) A.; grad. U.S. Mil. Acad., 1894; m. Alma Y. Hickok, Jan. 5, 1898; children—Edith H. (Mrs. Mark H. Doty), Dwight E., Anita B. Commd. 2d lt. 4th Cav., June 12, 1894; promoted through grades to col., May 15, 1917; brig. gen. N.A., Apr. 18, 1918; brig. gen. U.S.A., Apr. 27, 1921. Participated in Battle of San Juan Hill, July 1-3, 1898, and siege of Santiago, Cuba; a.d.c. to Gen. Wheaton in Cuba, Dec. 1898-Jan. 1899, later a.d.c. to Gen. Keifer; organized, and comd. Cuban Arty., 1901-02; instr. same, 1903-06; on staff comdg. gen. Army of Cuban Pacification, 1906-07; instr. dept. of langs., Service Schs., 1907-11; spl. mission to Germany, 1914-15; grad. Army War Coll., 1916; instr. same, 1916-17; comdr. 5th F.A., 1st Div., A.E.F., Oct. 1917-May 1918; comdr. 51st Brigade F.A., 26th Div., 1st A.C., A.E.F., May 8-Aug. 15, 1918; apptd. chief of Arty., 5th Corps, Oct. 1918, and of 2d Army, Dec. 1918; participated in battles, Champagne-Marne, Aisne-Marne, St. Mihiel and Meuse-Argonne. Grad. Gen. Staff Coll., 1920. Decorated D.S.M.; Comdr. Legion of Honor, Croix de Guerre (France). Author: Military Strength and Resources of the United States, 1917. Died Dec. 13, 1929.

AUMAN, William, brig. gen. U.S.A.; b. Berks Co., Pa., Oct. 17, 1838; s. Henry and Catherine (Breyman) A.; ed. pub. schs., Pottsville, Pa., to 1852; Wyoming Sem., Kingston, Pa., 1865; m. Emma Eliza Rosengarten, Sept. 27, 1866. Served as pvt. Washington Arty., of Pottsville, 25th Pa. Vols. (1st troops to arrive for defense of Nat. Capitol), Apr. 15-July 29, 1861; corp. to capt. Co. G, 48th Pa. Vols., Sept. 9, 1861-July 17, 1865; commd. 2d lt. 13th Inf., May 11, 1866; promoted through grades to brig. gen., Apr. 16, 1902. Bvtd. capt. vols., Apr. 2, 1865, "for gallant and meritorious services before Petersburg, Va." (wounded). Participated in 17 general engagements and many minor affairs; assisted in mining and blowing up Confederate fort before Petersburg, Va., July 30, 1864. Was in campaigns against Crow Indians in Mont., 1868 (severely wounded); Ute Indians, Southern Utah, 1872; Sioux Indians, Red Cloud, Neb., 1874; comd. 13th Inf., July 1-24, 1898, in Santiago campaign, which regiment captured Spanish block house and flag in the assault on San Juan Hill, July 1, 1898; comd. sta. of Santa Cruz, Laguna, P.I., 1901; obtained surrender of Col. Julio Herrera and his command; pres. exam. bds. and bds. of survey, Northern Luzon, 1901-02; retired at own request, May 10, 1902. Home: Buffalo, N. Y. Died May 21, 1920.

AURINGER, Obadiah Cyrus, clergyman; b. Glens Falls, N.Y., June 4, 1849; s. Francis Strong and Eliza (Denio) A.; ed. pub. schs. and pvt. tutors; served in U.S. Marine Corps, on bd. flagship Worcester, 1871-75; m. Mrs. Eva Hendryx, Nov. 4, 1876; m. 2d, Alice Stark, 1913; 1 son, Francis Stark. Ordained to Presbyn. ministry, 1890; pastor Northwood, N.Y., 1889-92, Troy, N.Y., 1892-1904, First Ch., Forestport, N.Y., 1904-16; retired. Author: (poems) Scythe and Sword, 1887; The Heart of the Golden Roan, 1890; Book of the Hills, 1896; The Christ, 1900; William McKinley (memorial poem), 1906; Friendship's Crown of Verse, 1908; Aboriginal Stone Implements of Queensbury, 1909; Death of Maid McCrea, and The Lover's Tragedy; The Eagle's Bride (poem), 1911; Quest of the Lamp (poem), 1922; In Praise of Books, 1930; The Eye of the Plain, 1931. Home: Glens Falls, N.Y. Died Oct. 2, 1937.

AUSTEN, Peter Townsend, chemist; b. Clifton, S.I., N.Y., Sept. 10, 1852; s. John H. and Elizabeth (Townsend) A.; Ph.B., Columbia Sch. of Mines, 1872; studied chemistry, U. of Berlin, 3 yrs.; (Ph.D., U. of Zurich). Instr. chemistry, Dartmouth, 1876; prof. chemistry, Rutgers Coll. and N.J. Scientific Sch., 1877-87; continued with the coll. as univ. extension lecturer; prof. chemistry, Brooklyn Poly. Inst., 1893-98; has been chemist to Richmond Co. (N.Y.), New Brunswick (N.J.), Newark (N.J.) bds. of health, N.J. State Bd. Agr., etc.; also State chemist, N.J. Author: Kurtze Einleitung zu den Nitro-Verbindungen, 1876; Notes for Chemical Students, 1897. Transl. and revised Pinner's Organic Chemistry, 1893. Home: New York, N.Y. Died 1907.

AUSTIN, Albert E., congressman; b. Medway, Mass., Nov. 15, 1877; A.B., Amherst Coll., 1899, A. M., 1904; M.D., Jefferson Med. Coll., 1905. Consulting internist Greenwich Hosp., Conn.; pres. and mem. of bd., Trust Co. of Old Greenwich, 1925—. Mem. 76th Congress (1939-41), 4th Conn. Dist. Home: Old Greenwich, Conn. Died Jan. 26, 1942.

AUSTIN, Calvin, corp. official. Dir. Eastern S.S. Lines, Inc., Old Colony Ins. Co., Rand Avery Supply Co., Boston Ins. Co. Home: Dunstable, Mass. Died Dec. 2, 1936.

AUSTIN, Cyrus Brooks, univ. dean; b. Clinton Co., O., Aug. 21, 1851; s. David Sharp and Lois (Smith) A.; B.A., Ohio Wesleyan U., 1879, M.A., 1883; (D.D., Miami U., 1907, Ohio Northern U., 1907); m. Mary Pickering McVay, Aug. 28, 1884. Tutor in mathematics, 1879-82, adj. prof., 1882-84, prof., 1884-1906, prof. mathematics and astronomy, 1906-20; prof. mathematics, 1920—, dean, 1883-1920, v.p., 1920—, Ohio Wesleyan U. Mem. West Ohio Conf. M.E. Ch., 1881—. Mason. Pres. Delaware Savings Bank. Republican. Home: Delaware, O. Died Sept. 9, 1924.

AUSTIN, Francis Marion, college prof.; b. Wilmington, O., Jan. 3, 1862; s. David Sharp and Lois (Smith) A.; A.B., Ohio Wesleyan U., 1887, A.M., 1890; studied Johns Hopkins, 1899-1901; m. Grace Merrill Jewett, Mar. 8, 1893. Instr. Greek, Bucksport (Me.) Sem., 1887-89, Latin and Greek, Tilton (N.H.) Sem., 1889-91, Latin, Wilbraham (Mass.) Acad., 1891-99; fellow in Latin, Johns Hopkins, 1901; prof. Latin, 1901, Ill. Wesleyan U. Republican. Mason. Author: Outline Lessons for Study of Ancient Geography, 1895. Home: Bloomington, Ill. Died Feb. 4, 1922.

AUSTIN, Fred Thaddeus, army officer; b. at Hancock, Vt., Dec. 28, 1866; s. Julius Tilden and Manora (Keith) A.; B.S., Norwich U., 1888, M.S., 1894, C.E., 1896; m. Lenore Harrison, Oct. 21, 1909. Practiced architecture Brockton and Boston, Mass., 1889-98; 1st lt. and adj. 5th Mass. Inf. Vols., July 1, 1898; hon. mustered out, Mar. 31, 1899; 1st lt. 46th U.S. Inf., Aug. 17, 1899; hon. mustered out, June 30, 1901; 1st lt. Arty. Corps, Aug. 22, 1901; promoted through grades to col., Sept. 27, 1925; maj. gen. chief of field artillery, Dec. 20, 1927. Col. N.A., Aug. 5, 1917; brig. gen. N.A., Apr. 18, 1918; dir. Arty. Sch., Fort Sill, Okla., 1920; later in insp. gens. department. Died Feb. 26, 1938.

AUSTIN, Frederick Carleton, financier; b. Skaneateles, N.Y., June 2, 1853; s. Dor and Marietta (Hatch) A.; ed. pub. schs., and Skaneateles Acad.; m. Anna Barker Ogden, 1887. Began business in Chicago as resident partner of Goulds & Austin; organizer, 1897, since pres., treas. and owner, F. C. Austin Mfg. Co.; pres., 1904—, and owner F. C. Austin Drainage Excavator Co. Originator of the first all-steel reversible blade road machine. Donor of $3,000,000 F. C. Austin Bldg. to Northwestern U. as endowment for training of spl. students as business executives, 1929. Home: Chicago, Ill. Died June 11, 1931.

AUSTIN, Isabella McHugh, educator; b. Minneapolis, Minn.; d. Samuel Jones and Isabella (McHugh) A.; B.A., U. of Minn., 1895; kindergarten diploma, Minn. State Normal Sch., Winona, 1897; post-grad. Teachers Coll. (Columbia), 1902. Taught Minneapolis pub. schs., Minn. State Normal Sch., Mich. State Normal Coll. (Ypsilanti), Speyer Sch. (Columbia U.); primary supervisor pub. schs., Tacoma, Wash., 1908; dean of women, U. of Wash., 1909—. Episcopalian. D.A.R. (Rainier Chapter, Seattle). Home: Seattle, Wash. Died Aug. 8, 1915.

AUSTIN, John Osborne, author; b. Providence, R.I., Dec. 28, 1849; s. Samuel and Elizabeth Hanson (Osborne) A.; grad. Union Hall Sch., Providence (of which his father was prin.), 1866; m. Helen Augusta, d. William and Emma Louise (Barker) Whitaker, of Providence, June 24, 1878 (died 1916). Engaged in the wool business until 1883; then in geneal. and lit. work. Traveled extensively, including South African diamond fields (1873), in Europe several times, California, Society Islands and New Zealand. Author: The Genealogical Dictionary of Rhode Island, 1887; Ancestry of Thirty-three Rhode Islanders, 1889; The Ancestral Dictionary, 1891; One Hundred and Sixty Allied Families, 1893; The Roger Williams Calendar, 1897; The Journal of William Jefferay, Gentleman, 1899; More Seven Club Tales, 1900; Philip and Philippa, 1901; A Week's Wooing, 1902; American Authors' Ancestry, 1915; a memorial vol. of stories dedicated to his wife, 1916; Impressions and Reflections of Sixty Years, 1917. Home: Providence, R.I. Died Oct. 27, 1918.

AUSTIN, Leonard S., mining engr.; b. Stratford, Conn., Feb. 26, 1846; s. Thomas and Elvira (Reed) A.; Sheffield Scientific Sch. (Yale), Ph.B., 1868; post-grad. work, Yale, Columbia, and Colo. State Sch. of Mines; m. Mary E. Watson, June 7, 1881. Mech. engrng. work, until 1877; chemist, Exploration Co., E. coast of Patagonia, S.A., 1877-79; chemist and foreman, Germania Lead Works, 1880-86; supt. various smelting works in U.S. to 1902; prof. metallurgy and ore dressing, Mich. Coll. of Mines, 1903-09; pvt. practice, 1909—. Episcopalian. Author: Metallurgy of the Common Metals, 1906, 5th edit., 1920; The Fire Assay, 1907. Annual contbr. to Mineral Industry, on "Metallurgy of Copper," 1903—; contbr. to Appleton's Yearbook, 1911-20. Home: Los Angeles, Calif. Died 1929.

AUSTIN, Louis Winslow, physicist; b. Orwell, Vt., Oct. 30, 1867; s. Prof. Lewis Augustine and Mary Louise (Taft) A.; A.B., Middlebury Coll., 1889, hon. D.Sc., 1920; student U. of Strassburg, 1889-90 and 1891-93, Ph.D., 1893; fellow Clark U., 1890-91; m. Laura A. Osborne, Aug. 16, 1898. Instr. and asst. prof. physics, U. of Wis., 1893-1901; in German govt. service (Phys. Tech. Reichsanstalt), 1902-04; with Bur. of Standards, Washington, 1904—; head of U.S. Naval Radiotelegraphic Lab., 1908-23; chief Lab. for Special Radio Transmission Research, Bur. of Standards, 1923—. Fellow Inst. of Radio Engineers (pres. 1914); v.p. Internat. Union for Scientific Radiotelegraphy and chmn. Am. Sect.; mem. tech. advisory com. Conf. on the Limitation of Armament, Washington, 1921. Medal of Inst. of Radio Engrs., 1927. Author: Physical Measurement (with Prof. C. B. Thwing), 1896. Home: Washington, D.C. Died June 27, 1932.

AUSTIN, Mary (Hunter), author; b. Carlinville, Ill., Sept. 9, 1868; d. George and Savilla (Graham) Hunter; B.S., Blackburn U., 1888; m. Stafford W. Austin, May 19, 1891. Lectured before Fabian Soc., London, summer 1921, U. of Calif., summer 1922. Author: The Land of Little Rain, 1903; The Basket Woman, 1904; Isidro, 1905; The Flock, 1906; Santa Lucia, 1908; Lost Borders, 1909; Christ in Italy, 1911; Woman of Genius, 1912; The Arrow Maker, play, produced New Theatre, New York, 1911; The Lovely Lady, 1913; Fire, drama, produced at Forest Theatre, Carmel, Calif.; Love and the Soul-Maker, 1914; The Man Jesus, 1915; The Man Who Didn't Believe in Christmas (prod. Cohan and Harris Theatre, N.Y., 1916); The Ford, 1917; The Young Woman Citizen, 1918; The Trail Book, 1918; Outland, 1919; 26 Jayne Street, 1920; The American Rhythm, 1923; The Land of Journeys' Ending, 1924; A Small Town Man (rev. of The Man Jesus), 1925; Everyman's Genius, 1925; Lands of the Sun (rev. of California), 1927; The Children Sing in the Far West, 1928; Starry Adventure, 1931; Experiences Facing Death, 1931; Earth Horizon (an autobiography), 1932. Died Aug. 14, 1934.

AUSTIN, Oscar Phelps, statistician; b. Newark, Ill.; s. Benjamin and Emeline M. (Phelps) A.; ed. pub. schs.; hon. A.M., George Washington U., 1913; m. Anna M. Richardson; 1 dau., Florence M. Has been a writer during entire business life, reporter, editor, Washington corr. for metropolitan dailies; chief Bur. of Statistics, Treasury Dept., May 1898, to date of its transfer to Bureau of Statistics, Foreign and Domestic Commerce, of which was asst. chief; statistician National City Bank of New York, 1914-25; lecturer on foreign commerce, for the Nat. City Bank Club. Prof. commerce and statistics, George Washington U., 1903-14. Author: Uncle Sam's Secrets; Uncle Sam's Soldiers; Uncle Sam's Children; Uncle Sam's Boy at War, etc. (series of hist. and statis. novels for youth); also brochures and pamphlets on world commerce. Home: New York, N.Y. Died Jan. 6, 1933.

AUSTIN, Richard Wilson, congressman; b. Decatur, Ala., Aug. 26, 1857; s. John Hall and Mary E. (Parker) A.; ed. U. of Tenn., 1877; attended Columbian (now George Washington) U. Law Sch., 1881; m. Margaret Morrison, May 2, 1882. Admitted to bar, 1878; practiced law in Knoxville, Tenn., and Washington; U.S. marshal, 1897-1906; Am. consul at Glasgow, July 1906-Nov. 1907, resigned; member 61st to 65th Congresses (1909-19), 2d Tenn. Dist. Republican. Home: Knoxville, Tenn. Died Apr. 20, 1919.

AUSTIN, Wilbert John, builder; b. Cleveland, O., Nov. 2, 1876; s. Samuel and Sarah Jane (Gynn) A.; B.S., Case Sch. Applied Science, 1899; m. Ida May Stewart, Sept. 16, 1903; children—Allan Stewart, Donald Gynn, Margaret Louise. Began with Austin Co., builders and engrs., Cleveland, 1900, v.p. and gen. mgr., 1904-24, pres., 1924—; pres. Austin Co. of Calif., Austin Securities Co., Austin Realty Co., Surety Investing Co., Austin Co., Ltd.; chmn. Austin Engineers Builders, Ltd. (London). Trustee St. Luke's Hospital, Windermere M.E. Church. Home: Shaker Heights, Cleveland, O. Died Dec. 4, 1940.

AUSTIN, William Liseter, locomotive mfg.; b. Philadelphia, Pa., Sept. 22, 1852; s. Charles Baldrey and Rebecca (Snyder) A.; ed. Central High Sch., Philadelphia; m. Mary Rogers, Sept. 13, 1877; children—Rebecca Jennie, Mabel Henszey (Mrs. Bernard Todd Converse), Helen Mary (Mrs. Harry Pollard Converse), Anna Alcott, Jean Liseter (Mrs. William du Pont, Jr.), William Liseter. Began as draftsman, patent office, Phila., 1868; draftsman, Kensington Steam Engine Works, 1869; with Baldwin Locomotive Works, 1870—, successively designer, engr., v.p., pres., 1910-11, chmn. bd., 1911-12, then dir. Pres. sch. bd., Lower Merion Tp. Mem. Franklin Inst. Republican. Presbyn. Inventor of number of devices for locomotive. Home: Rosemont, Pa. Died Mar. 10, 1932.

AUSTRIAN, Alfred S., lawyer; b. Chicago, June 15, 1870; s. Solomon and Julia R. A.; A.B., Harvard, 1891; m. Mamie Rothschild, Oct. 1, 1901. Admitted to bar, 1893, and in practice at Chicago; mem. Mayer, Meyer, Austrian & Platt. Home: Chicago, Ill. Died Jan. 26, 1932.

AVELLANUS, Arcadius, writer Latin books; b. Esztergom, Hungary, Feb. 6, 1851; made all studies in Latin and completed edn. in an alumnium in Hungary; learned Latin colloquially as a child; (Litt.D., Ph.D.). Since 1894 editor and publisher Præco Latinus (or Latin Herald), only Latin periodical on this continent, for propagation of Latin language as a spoken tongue. Author: Palæstra, a Primer for Spoken Latin, 1893; Arena Palæs tarum, 1893; Robinson Crusœus, 1897; Medulla, 1898; new Latin version of Thomas à Kempis, 1900; The Colloquia of Maturinus Corderius, the Teacher of John Calvin, 1904. Home: Philadelphia, Pa. Died June 16, 1935.

AVERILL, Glenn Mark, banker; b. Cedar Rapids, Ia., July 15, 1868; s. Arthur Tappan and Allie (Doolittle) A.; student Coe Coll., Cedar Rapids, 1884-86, U. of Mich., 1886-88; m. Edith Sherman, Sept. 15, 1892; children—Arthur Tappan II, Worth Sherman. V.p. Cedar Rapids Gas Co., 1888-1910; v.p. Cedar Rapids Nat. Bank, 1910-21, pres., 1921-31; chmn. bd. dirs. Morris Plan Co., Cedar Rapids; v.p. Cedar Rapids Life Ins. Co., Cedar Rapids & Marion City Ry. Co.; treas. Ky. Midland Coal Co. Trustee Coe Coll. Republican. Christian Scientist. Home: Tampa, Fla. Died May 11, 1940.

AVERY, Catherine Hitchcock Tilden, editor; b. Dundee, Mich., Dec. 13, 1844; d. Hon. Junius and Beruah (Rich) Tilden; grad. State Normal Sch., Framingham, Mass., 1867; m. Elroy McKendree Avery, July 2, 1870. Was prin. high sch., Battle Creek, Mich.; instr. high and normal schs., Cleveland, O.; then editor Am. Monthly Magazine, official organ D.A.R. Elected mem. Cleveland City School Bd., 1895 (first woman ever chosen to elective office in Ohio); elected mem. (first woman) Cleveland City Bd. School Examiners, 1900 (pres., 1911-12); elected (only woman) City Library Bd., 1900. D.A.R. Home: Cleveland, O. Deceased.

AVERY, Coleman, lawyer; b. Cincinnati, O., Feb. 22, 1880; s. William Ledyard and Johanna (Ummethun) A.; A.B., U. of Cincinnati, 1902; LL.B., Cincinnati Law Sch., 1905; m. Elinor Coates Baer, June 7, 1904 (died 1929); children—John Coleman, Ledyard, Elinor Louise, Mary Frances, Elizabeth Coates; m. 2d, Sara L. Loving, May 23, 1934. Began law practice, Cincinnati, 1905; asst. prosecuting atty., Hamilton Co., O., 1909-11; asst. solicitor of Cincinnati, 1911-13; spl. counsel representing the state in cases against George B. Cox, for perjury and Jacob Baschang, for bribery, in Supreme Court of Ohio, 1912-13; Dem. candidate for Court of Common Pleas, Hamilton Co., 1914; prof. law, Cincinnati Law Sch., 1916-18; spl. asst. U.S. atty., Southern Dist. of Ohio, 1918-19; asso. justice Supreme Court of Ohio, June-Dec. 1920; Dem. candidate for asso. justice Supreme Court of Ohio, 1920. Maj. 2d Bn., Cincinnati Home Guard, 1917-19; mem. Legal Advisory Bd., etc., World War. Presbyn. Home: Cincinnati, O. Died Mar. 14, 1938.

AVERY, Elroy McKendree, author; b. Erie, Monroe Co., Mich., July 14, 1844; s. Caspar Hugh and Dorothy (Putnam) A.; Ph.B., U. of Mich., 1871, Ph.M., 1874; Ph.D., Hillsdale Coll., 1881, LL.D., 1894; D.C.L., 1911; served in Civil War; mustered out as sergt.-maj., 11th Mich. Cav.; m. Catherine Hitchcock Tilden, July 2, 1870 (died 1911); m. 2d, Ella Alice Wilson, June 15, 1916. Prin. high sch., Battle Creek, Mich., 1869, high and normal schs., Cleveland, O., 1871-79. Mem. Cleveland City Council, 1891-92, Ohio Senate, 1893-97. Author: Elementary Physics, 1876; Elements of Natural Philosophy, 1878; Physical Technics, 1879; Teachers' Hand Book of Natural Philosophy, 1879; Elements of Chemistry, 1881; Teachers' Hand Book of Chemistry, 1882; Complete Chemistry, 1883; First Principles of Natural Philosophy, 1884; Words Correctly Spoken, 1887; Columbus and the Columbia Brigade, 1892; School Physics, 1895; Elementary Physics, 1897; First Lessons in Physical Science, 1897; School Chemistry, 1904; The Town Meeting, 1904; The Groton Avery Clan, 2 vols., 1912; History of the United States and Its People, 12 vols.; John Humfrey, Massachusetts Magistrate, 1913; Cleveland and Its Environs, 3 vols., 1918; Genesis of New Port Richey, 1923. After living at Cleveland for 48 yrs., moved to Fla., 1919. Hon. pres. and chmn. bd. First State Bank of New Port Richey; first mayor of New Port Richey, 1924-25; founder and for 10 yrs. pres. Avery Pub. Library of New Port Richey (hon. life dir.). Home: New Port Richey, Fla. Died Dec. 1, 1935.

AVERY, George C., mfr.; b. Louisville, Ky., Mar. 1, 1852; s. Benjamin F. and Susan (Look) A.; brother of Lydia Avery Coonley Ward; A.B., Mass. Inst. Tech., 1876; m. Kate S. Jewett, Jan. 7, 1891. In plow mfg. business at Louisville, 1874—; pres. B. F. Avery & Sons. Republican. Presbyn. Home: Louisville, Ky. Died 1911.

AVERY, Isaac Wheeler, lawyer-journalist; b. St. Augustine, Fla., May 2, 1837; grad. Oglethorpe Univ., Ga., 1854; admitted to bar at Savannah, Ga., 1860; in Confederate army 1861-65, private to col. of cav.; practiced law at Dalton, Ga., 1866-69, then at Atlanta. Founded Atlanta Constitution, and was several years its editor; propr. Atlanta Herald, 1875-76 and afterward for one year of Atlanta Evening Capitol; del. to Nat. Dem. Conv., 1872; mem. and sec. State Dem. com. same year; chief Public Dept. Div. U.S. Treas., 1887-89; started in 1892 successful movement for direct trade between southern U.S. and foreign ports; m. Emma Bivings, 1868. Author: History of Georgia; Digest of Ga. Supreme Court Reports. Home: Atlanta, Ga. Died 1897.

AVERY, John, congressman; b. Watertown, N.Y., Feb. 29, 1824; s. John and Susan Mitchel (Cooper) A.; ed. Grass Lake Acad., Mich.; M.D., Cleveland Med. Coll., 1849; m. Jane H. Ewell, May 8, 1851. Surgeon 21st Mich. Inf., 3 yrs. in Civil War; in med. practice at Greenville, Mich., 1867-1900. Mem. Mich. Ho. of Rep., 1869-72; mem. and pres. Mich. State Bd. Health, 1880-92; mem. 53d and 54th Congresses (1893-97); Republican. Home: Greenville, Mich. Deceased.

AVERY, Rachel Foster, reformer; b. Pittsburgh, Pa., Dec. 30, 1858; d. J. Heron and Julia (Manuel) Foster; ed. Phila. and Europe; studied polit. economy at U. of Zurich; m. Cyrus Miller Avery, Nov., 1888. Active from girlhood in woman suffrage movement; had charge of numerous convs. and the Neb. campaign; was corr. sec. Nat. Suffrage Assn. over 20 yrs.; assisted Susan B. Anthony in the preparations for the Internat. Council of Women, Washington, 1888, and was corr. sec., 1888-93; corr. sec. Nat. Council of Women of U.S., 1891-94; 1st sec. Internat. Woman Suffrage Alliance, 1904-09; 1st v.p. Nat. Woman Suffrage Assn., 1906-10; pres. Pa. Woman Suffrage Assn., 1908-10. Home: Philadelphia, Pa. Died Oct. 26, 1919.

AVERY, Robert, lawyer; b. Tunkhannock, Pa., Sept. 22, 1839; s. Abel Marcy and Euphemia Pell A.; ed. Wyo. Sem., Kingston, Pa.; admitted to bar, 1870; m. Virginia C. Risley, July 4, 1874. Capt. 102d N.Y. Inf., Dec. 17, 1861; promoted through grades to lt. col. and retired, Dec. 31, 1870; advanced to rank of col. retired, by act of Apr. 23, 1904. Bvtd. lt. col. vols., Mar. 13, 1865, "for gallant and meritorious services at Chancellorsville"; col. and brig. gen., Mar. 13, 1865, for same at Lookout Mountain (lost right leg); maj. gen. vols., Mar. 13, 1865, for same. Pres. Union Loan & Investment Co., Niagara Tin Smelting Co., Argenteau Kennels; v.p. Burlington and S.E. Ry. Co., Della Realty Co. Home: Brooklyn, N.Y. Died Oct. 2, 1912.

AVERY, Samuel, chemist; b. Lamoille, Ill., April 19, 1865; s. Stephen B. and Mary T. Avery; A.B., Doane Coll., 1887; B.Sc., U. of Neb., 1892, A.M., 1894; Ph.D., Heidelberg, 1896; LL.D., Doane and U. of Idaho, 1909; m. May B. Bennett, Aug. 4, 1897. Adj. prof. chemistry, U. of Neb., 1896-99; prof. chemistry and chemist, Agrl. Expt. Sta., U. of Ida., 1899-1901; prof. analytical and organic chemistry, U. of Neb., 1901; prof. agrl. chemistry and chemist, U. of Neb. Expt. Sta., 1902-05; head prof. chemistry, 1905-08, acting chancellor, 1908-09, chancellor, 1909, chancellor emeritus and prof. of research in chemistry, 1927—, U. of Neb. Leave of absence Jan.-Nov. 1918, as mem. and vice chmn. chemistry com. Nat. Research Council, and maj. chem. warfare service U.S.A., chief of univ. relations unit. U.S. mem. Internat. Conciliation Commn. with Sweden, 1914-15. Mason. Received Kiwanis Medal. Home: Lincoln, Neb. Died Jan. 25, 1936.

AVERY, Samuel Putnam, retired mcht.; b. New York, N.Y., March 17, 1822; s. Samuel P. and Hannah Ann (Parke) A.; (hon. A.M., Columbia Coll., 1896, "for services to cause of art and art culture in U.S."). Learned copper-plate engraving; was with a bank note co., later a wood engraver; compiled and illus. several vols. of humorous quality; in 1865 added to his business art publishing and dealing in art works, retiring, 1888. Was commr. Am. Art Dept., Paris Expn., 1867; sec. Art. Com. Union League Club; a founder and long trustee Met. Museum of Art. Mem. Municipal Art Commn. of New York, 1897-1903; trustee N.Y. Public Library. With his wife, Mary Ann (Ogden) Avery, created and endowed, 1891, the Avery Archtl. Library at Columbia Coll. (now 15,000 vols.) in memory of their deceased son, Henry Ogden Avery. Home: New York, N.Y. Died 1904.

AVERY, Susan Look, writer; b. at Conway, Mass., Oct. 27, 1817; d. Samuel and Polly (Loomis) Look; ed. Utica, N.Y.; m. Benjamin F. Avery, Apr. 27, 1844 (died 1885); mother of Lydia Avery Coonley Ward and George C. A. Has written and spoken much in cause of woman suffrage, temperance, single tax, bimetallism and other reforms. Home: Louisville, Ky. Died Feb. 1, 1915.

AVES, Henry Damerel, bishop; b. Huron Co., O., July 10, 1853; s. Frederick William and Frances Elizabeth (Damerel) A.; Ph.B., Kenyon Coll., 1878; student Cincinnati Law Sch., 1879-80; B.D., Theol. Sem., Bexley Hall, Gambier, O., 1883; LL.D., Rutherford Coll., 1901; D.D., Kenyon, 1905; m. Mary Gertrude Smith, Sept. 11, 1883 (died 1918); children—Mrs. Katherine Elizabeth Harbordt (dec.), Delano Richard, William Leonard, Mrs. Mary Damerel Berthier, Henry Damerel. Deacon, 1883, priest, 1884, P.E. Ch.; rector St. Paul's, Mt. Vernon, O., 1883-84, St. John's, Cleveland, 1884-92, Christ Ch., Houston, Tex., 1892-1904; consecrated bishop of Mex., Dec. 14, 1904. Was pvt., 1889-90, chaplain, 1891-92, 1st City Troop, Ohio N.G., Cleveland. Retired, Nov. 15, 1923. Home: Seabrook, Tex. Died Sept. 20, 1936.

AVIS, Samuel Brashear, congressman; b. Harrisonburg, Va., Feb. 19, 1872; s. Braxton D. and Harriet Elizabeth (Wilson) A.; Staunton (Va.) Mil. Acad.; LL.B., Washington and Lee U., 1893; m. Florence Miriam, d. Gov. G. W. Atkinson, of Charleston, W.Va., Dec. 6, 1899. Admitted to W.Va. bar, 1893; practiced, Charleston; sr. member Avis & Kenna; past asst. U.S. atty. for Southern Dist. W.Va.; pros. atty. Kanawha Co., W.Va., 3 terms, 1900-Dec. 31, 1912; mem. 63d Congress (1913-15), 3d Dist. of W.Va. Republican. Episcopalian. Capt. 2d W.Va. Vol. Inf., Spanish-Am. War. Home: Charleston, W.Va. Deceased.

AXLINE, George Andrew, educator; b. Fairfield, Ia., Sept. 22, 1871; s. Andrew and Almira (Stever) A.; A.B., Parsons Coll., Iowa, 1892, A.M., 1895 (LL.D., 1917); student Chicago Normal Sch., 1899; m. Mabel Estella Rea, Oct. 20, 1898. Prin. high school, Cawker City, Kan., 1892-95; supervising prin. pub. schs., Kirwin, Kan., 1895-96, supt. pub. schs., Humeston, Ia., 1896-1903, Corning, Ia., 1903-04; pres. State Normal Sch., Albion, Ida., 1904—, also ranching. Pvt. and corporal, Co. M, 50th Ia. Regt., Spanish-Am. War. Republican. Presbyn. Mason. Mem. State Council of Defense, 1917—. Address: Albion, Ida. Died Oct. 11, 1919.

AXSON, Stockton, univ. prof.; b. Rome, Ga., June 6, 1867; s. Rev. Samuel Edward and Margaret (Hoyt) A.; A.B., Wesleyan U., Conn., 1890, A.M., 1892, L.H.D., 1914; post-grad. Johns Hopkins, 1890-91; Litt.D., U. of Pittsburgh, 1909; LL.D., Knox Coll., 1920; unmarried. Instr. and asst. prof. English, U. of Vt., 1892-94; staff lecturer Am. Soc. for Univ. Extension, 1894-96; asst. prof. and prof. English, Adelphi Coll., Brooklyn, 1896-99; asst. prof. English lit., 1899-1904, prof., 1904-13, Princeton, prof. English, Rice Inst., Houston, Tex., 1913—. Nat. sec. Am. Nat. Red Cross (loaned by Rice Inst. for period of war), 1917-19. Home: Houston, Tex. Died Feb. 26, 1935.

AXTELL, Decatur, ry. official; b. Elyria, O., Feb. 8, 1848; s. Almon and Sophronia (Boynton) A.; ed. Ill. Coll.; m. May Cantrell. Civ. engr. St. Louis, Iron Mountain & Southern Ry., 1868-80; v.p. and receiver Richmond and Allegheny R.R., 1880-90; v.p. Chesapeake & Ohio Ry., 1890-1918; pres. Toledo & Ohio Central Ry., 1899-1903, chmn. bd., 1903-09; v.p. Kanawha & Mich. Ry., 1899-1903, chmn. bd., 1903-10; 1st v.p. Hocking Valley Ry., 1910-12, Chesapeake

& Ohio Ry. of Ind., 1910-18; retired from ry. service Feb 8, 1918; pres. Va. Hot Springs Co., 1891-1912, White Sulphur Springs, Inc., 1912-18. Home: Richmond, Va. Died Oct. 27, 1922.

AXTELL, Edwin Rodarmel, physician; b. Washington, Ind., Feb. 7, 1866; grad. Miami Med. Coll., Cincinnati, 1888; m. Grace Coffin, 1891. In practice in Denver, 1889—; four years pathologist to Araphoe and St. Luke's Hosp.; 18 months supt. of and still asso. with latter; also asso. with Colo. Cottage Home, and State Home for Dependent Children; editor Colo. Med. Jour.; sec. and treas. faculty Med. Dept., U. of Denver. Home: Denver, Colo. Died 1899.

AXTELL, John Thomas, M.D., surgeon; b. Roseville, Ill., Aug. 11, 1856; s. John Milton and Lydia Letitia (Long) A.; student Med. Dept., U. of Mich., 1880-82; M.D., Bellevue Hosp. Med. Coll., 1883; m. Lucena Chase, May 18, 1882; children—Lilian (wife of Dr. John L. Grove), Marguerite (wife of Dr. Harold M. Glover), Mildred (Mrs. Alden E. Branine), Marian (Mrs. George D. Hanna). Teacher, Anderson Co., Kan., 1875-78; prin. city sch., Newton, 1878-80; founder, 1883, Axtell Hosp. (now Axtell Christian Hosp.), Newton, mem. exec. bd.; formerly prof. orthopedic surgery, Coll. Phys. and Surgeons, Kansas City; pres. Axtell Investment Co., 1st Nat. Bldg. & Investment Co.; dir. 1st Nat. Bank; mem. Axtell Clinic. Republican. Conglist. Mason. Home: Newton, Kan. Died Feb. 20, 1937.

AXTON, John Thomas, chief of chaplains, U.S.A.; b. Salt Lake City, July 28, 1870; s. John and Matilda Loretta (Webb) A.; ed. Salt Lake pub. schs.; D.D., Middlebury, Vt., 1919, Ursinus Coll., Pa., and Elon Coll., N.C., 1923; m. Jane Bean, Aug. 28, 1891; children—John T. (U.S.A.), Matilda, Anna (wife of R. D. Daugherity, U.S.A.), Lily Jane (wife of Frederick R. Pitts, U.S.A.). Was general sec. Y.M.C.A., 1893-1902; apptd. chaplain U.S.A., rank of capt., 1902; maj., 1917; apptd. col. and chief of chaplains, July 15, 1920; retired Apr. 6, 1928, on account of disabilities in line of duty; chaplain Rutgers U., 1928-32. Served in P.I. twice, on Mexican border 5 yrs.; duty at Port of Embarkation, Hoboken, N.J., during World War, in gen. charge philanthropic, social and religious orgns. Officiated at interment of America's unknown soldier, Arlington Nat. Cemetery, Nov. 11, 1921. Awarded D.S.M., 1919; Chevalier Legion of Honor (French), 1922; Croce di Guerra (Italian), 1922. Republican. Conglist. Mason. Home: Washington, D.C. Deceased.

AYCOCK, Charles Brantley, governor; b. Fremont, N.C., Nov. 1, 1859; A.B., U. of N.C.; (LL.D., U. of Me., 1905). Engaged in law practice at Goldsboro, N.C.; supt. schs., Wayne Co., N.C.; U.S. dist. atty., 1893-98; gov. of N.C., 1901-05; presdl. elector-at-large, 1902. Democrat. Trustee U. of N.C. Home: Goldsboro, N.C. Died Apr. 4, 1912.

AYDLETT, Edwin Ferebee, lawyer; b. Camden Co., N.C., May 1857; s. Abner and Clotilda A.; A.M., Wake Forest Coll., 1879; m. Ettie Hunter Briggs, 1883; children—Mrs. Henrietta Minor, Mrs. Evelyn Sawyer, Edwin F., Mrs. Helen Kendrick; m. 2d, Kate Wood, May 14, 1925. Admitted to N.C. bar, 1881; practiced at Elizabeth City; then mem. Aydlett & Simpson. Chmn. Dem. exec. com. 1st Jud. Dist. 10 yrs.; del. Dem. Nat. Conv., 1912, 16; U.S. atty., Eastern Dist. of N.C. by appmt. of resident Wilson, 1920-21. Trustee Wake Forest Coll. (pres. bd.), Thomasville Orphanage; chmn. bd. Elizabeth City Graded Sch. 10 yrs. Baptist. Home: Elizabeth City, N.C. Died June 18, 1930.

AYER, Benjamin F., gen. counsel Ill. Central R.R., 1890—; b. Kingston, Rockingham Co., N.H., April 22, 1825; grad. Dartmouth, 1846 (LL.D., 1878); studied Dane Law School, Harvard; m. Janet Hopkins, 1868. Admitted to N.H. bar, 1849; practiced at Manchester, N.H., 1849-57, then in Chicago. Mem. N.H. legislature, 1853; pros. atty. Hillsborough Co., 1854-57; corp. counsel, Chicago, 1861-63; gen. solicitor Ill. Central R.R., 1876-90; dir. same, 1877—. Home: Chicago, Ill. Died 1903.

AYER, Clarence Walter, librarian; b. Haverhill, Mass., May 29, 1862; s. Walter and Abby West (Stevens) A.; A.B., Harvard, 1885, A.M., 1888; m. Grace Stanwood Blackwell, Oct. 1, 1902. Instr. in languages, Dummer Acad., S. Byfield, Mass., 1885-86; pvt. tutor, Cambridge, 1887-92; acting prof. English, Wittenberg Coll., Ohio, 1892-93; instr. English, Coll. for Women, Western Reserve U., 1893-95, Volkmann Sch., Boston, 1895-96; asst. Harvard Coll. Library, 1896-99; librarian, Pub. Library, Brockton, Mass., 1899-1904, Pub. Library, Cambridge, 1904—. Republican. Home: Cambridge, Mass. Died Apr. 11, 1913.

AYER, Edward Everett, capitalist; b. Kenosha, Wis., Nov. 16, 1841; s. Elbridge Gerry and Mary (Titcomb) A.; ed. pub. schs.; m. Emma Augusta Burbank, Sept. 7, 1865; 1 dau., Elizabeth (Mrs. Frank S. Johnson). Crossed the plains to Pacific Coast, 1860, afterwards serving in U.S. Army in wars against Apaches and other Indian tribes, in Calif., Ariz. and N.M.; owned and operated lumbermill at Flagstaff, Ariz., and acquired forests and timberlands in various sections of the country; a pioneer in the business of supplying cross-ties for Am. rys.; organized with John Brackett Lord, 1893, the Ayer & Lord Tie Co., of which became dir. Donated to Newberry Library, Chicago, library on history of the North Am. Indian (one of the most complete collections of the kind in the world); also donated the Ornithol. and Ichthyol. libraries, and great pewter collection and collection of Indian accoutrements to Field Museum of Nat. History. Dir. Field Museum (pres. 1893-98). Art Inst. Chicago. Home: Chicago, Ill. Died May 3, 1927.

AYER, F(rancis) Wayland, advt. agent; b. Lee, Mass., Feb. 4, 1848; s. Nathan W. and Joanna B. A.; ed. schs. of western N.Y.; m. Rhandena Gilman, May 5, 1875. Began advertising business at Phila., 1869, with his father under firm name of N. W. Ayer & Son; pres. Religious Press Assn.; mem. Ayer & McKinney; pres. Camden & Suburban Ry.; v.p. Camden Horse Ry. Home: Camden, N.J. Died Mar. 5, 1923.

AYER, Frederick, mfr.; b. Ledyard, Conn., Dec. 8, 1822; s. Frederick and Persis (Cook) A.; acad. edn.; m. Cornelia Wheaton, 1858 (died 1878); m. 2d, Ellen Banning, 1884. With his brother, James C., organized J. C. Ayer Co., proprietary medicines, becoming 1st treas. until 1893; with brother, James C., purchased controlling interest of Tremont Mills and Suffolk Mfg. Co., Lowell, consolidating both as Tremont & Suffolk Mills, 1871; purchased Washington Mills, Lawrence, Mass., 1885, which he reorganized as Washington Mills Co., of which he was treas.; one of organizers and pres., 1901-05, Am. Woolen Co.; an organizer and pres. Lowell & Andover R.R. Co. Republican. Conglist. Home: Boston, Mass. Died Mar. 14, 1918.

AYER, Frederick Fanning, lawyer; b. Lowell, Mass.; s. James Cook and Josephine Mellen (Southwick) A.; A.B., Harvard, 1873; unmarried. Admitted to Mass. bar, 1875; after his father's death, 1878, managed the properties of the Ayer estate; presented Ayer Memorial Library to town of Ayer, Mass. Pres. J. C. Ayer Co., The Tremont & Suffolk Mills. Author: Bell and Wing (poems). Died June 9, 1924.

AYER, Harriet Hubbard, journalist, author; b. Chicago, Ill., 1854; d. Henry G. and Juliet Elvira Hubbard; grad. Sacred Heart Convent, Chicago, 1869; m. Herbert Copeland Ayer, 1869. Author: Harriet Hubbard Ayer's Book, 1900. Home: New York, N.Y. Died 1903.

AYERS, Howard, educator; b. Olympia, Wash., May 21, 1861; s. William Norton and Sarah Ann (Sanborn) A.; student U. of Mich., 1879-82; S.B., Harvard, 1883; Ph.D., U. of Freiberg, 1885; studied univs. of Strassburg and Heidelberg; LL.D., U. of Mo., 1899; m. Pauline Shafer, July 7, 1886. Dir. Lake Lab., 1889-93; mem. staff of instrn., Marine Biol. Lab., Woods Hole, Mass., 1889-99; instr. in zoölogy, U. of Mich., 1886, Harvard and Radcliffe Coll., 1887-89; prof. biology and curator Biol. Mus., U. of Mo., 1894-99; pres. U. of Cincinnati, 1899-1904. Author: The Vertebrate Ear, 1893; Vertebrate Cephalogenesis, Vols. I to V, and other works. Home: Cincinnati, O. Died 1933.

AYLESWORTH, Barton Orville, coll. pres.; b. Athens, Ill., Sept. 5, 1860; s. Ezra M. and Malinda A.; A.B., Eureka (Ill.) Coll., 1879; (hon. A.M., Bethany Coll.; LL.D., Drake U., Ia.); m. Georgia L. Shores, Dec. 12, 1882. Pres. Drake U., 1889-97; pastor Central Ch. of Christ, Denver, 1897-99; pres. faculty and prof. polit. economy and logic, Colo. State Agrl. Coll., 1899-1909; nat. lecturer and organizer, Nat. Am. Woman Suffrage Assn., New York, Feb. 1910—. Author: Thirteen and Twelve Others; Song and Fable. Home: Fort Collins, Colo. Died July 1, 1933.

AYLSWORTH, William Prince, univ. pres.; b. Cuba, Ill., Dec. 12, 1844; s. John and Ann Frances (Freeman) A.; student U. of Chicago, 1863-65; A.B., Bethany Coll., 1869, A.M., 1883; (LL.D., Cotner U., 1896); m. Mary Doane Stuzaker, Dec. 5, 1871. Taught in common schs.; prin. schs., Waukegan, Ill., 1866-67; ordained Christian (Disciples) ministry, 1869; pastor, Greensburg, Ind., 1870-71, Angola, 1872-80, Ft. Wayne, 1880-82, Columbus, O., 1882-86; prof. sacred lit., 1886-89, pres., 1887-89, Fairfield Coll.; chancellor Cotner U., 1896-1910, emeritus chancellor and head Coll. Sacred Lit., 1910—. Author: Hebrew Prophecy, 1911. Home: Bethany, Neb. Deceased.

AYMÉ, Louis Henri, consul gen.; b. New York, May 29, 1855; s. Henry (surgeon U.S.A.) and Elizabeth Geraldine (Fitzgerald) A.; grad. Columbia Coll., 1874, A.B., 1884; 2 terms at Coll. Phys. and Surg. (Columbia); m. Mary Stuart, Feb. 19, 1890. Scientific asst. U.S. Transit of Venus Expdn., New Zealand Sta., 1874; U.S. consul, Merida, Yucatan, Mex., 1880-84; spl. ethnologist, Smithsonian Instn. in Oaxaca, Mex., 1884-86; staff Chicago Inter Ocean, 1886-91; foreign press editor, Chicago Expn., 1891-93, Chicago Tribune, 1893-97, including secret war correspondence from Cuba, 1896; consul at Guadaloupe, Jan. 6, 1898-June, 1903, at Para, Brazil, 1903-06; consul-gen. at Lisbon, Portugal, 1906—. Was 2d lt. D Co., 9th Regt., N.G.S., N.Y., 1879. In Martinique disaster was first on spot, May 11, 1902, spl. rep. of U.S. Govt. and spl. corr. Asso. Press. Author: Notes on Mitla, 1882. Asso. editor Elliott's Magazine, Chicago, 1896. Home: Chicago, Ill. Died May 16, 1912.

AYRES, Brown, univ. pres.; b. Memphis, Tenn., May 25, 1856; s. Samuel W. and Elizabeth (Cook) A.; early edn. pvt. schs. Memphis and New Orleans; engring. course Washington and Lee U.; B.S., Stevens Inst. Tech., 1878; fellow Johns Hopkins, 1879-80; (Ph.D., Stevens, 1888; LL.D., Washington and Lee U., 1904, S.C. Coll., 1905, Tulane, 1905, U. of Ala., 1906; D.C.L., U. of the South, 1907); m. Katie A. Anderson, July 5, 1881. Prof. physics, 1880-1904, dean Coll. Technology, 1894-1900, v.chmn. faculty, 1900-04, dean acad. coll., 1901-04, acting pres. 1904, Tulane U.; pres. U. of Tenn., 1904—. Home: Knoxville, Tenn. Died Jan. 28, 1919.

AYRES, Edward, coll. prof.; b. Hadley, Mass., Apr. 15, 1857; s. Rowland and Elvira Jane (Webster) A.; A.B., Amherst, 1878, A.M., 1882; spl. courses Clark U., Harvard, U. of Chicago; m. Alice Hanna Wilson, Nov. 29, 1893. Prin. Hopkins Acad., Hadley, Mass., 1878-80, Orange (Mass.) High Sch., 1880-82; instr. Latin and Greek, Lake Forest (Ill.) Acad., 1882-83; instr. Latin, Amherst, 1883-84; supt. schs., Warren, Mass., 1884-89, Lafayette, Ind., 1889-1900; prof. rhetoric, 1900-14, prof. English and head of dept., 1914—, Purdue U. Republican. Presbyn. Home: Lafayette, Ind. Died Dec. 16, 1919.

AYRES, Eugene Edmond, educator; b. Russelville, Ky., Nov. 22, 1859; s. Prof. James E. and Sara (Crucheron) A.; (D.D., Georgetown (Ky.) Coll., 1902, Richmond (Va.) Coll., 1903); m. Ada Marguerite Underwood, 1887. Teacher Latin and Greek, Eminence Sem., Ky., 1879-81, Georgetown Sem., 1881-83; prof. Greek, Judson Coll., Ala., 1883-89; tutor, Hartford (Conn.) Theol. Sem., 1889-92; pastor, Summerton, S.C., 1892-94, Baltimore, 1894-98; prof. philosophy, Georgetown Coll., 1898-1903; prof. N.T. lit. and exegesis, Crozer Theol. Sem., Chester, Pa., 1903—. Lecturer and teacher, Chautauqua (N.Y.) Inst., summers, 1882-1902; lecturer philosophy, U. of Pa., summer, 1894. Editor, the Etude, Phila., 188°-93, Advanced Quarterly, 1906—. Author: Chautauqua Handbook of Musical History, 1882; Counterpoint and Canon, 1886. Asso. Editor: Sursum Corda, 1898. Home: Chester, Pa. Died Aug. 5, 1920.

AYRES, George Frederic, coll. pres.; b. Hannibal, Mo., May 17, 1865; s. Eugene Walter and Kate James (Hays) A.; A.B., Westminster Coll., 1887, A.M., 1890, Ph.D., 1897; grad. McCormick Theol. Sem., 1891; studied U. of Leipzig, 1 yr.; m. Charlia L. Heron, June 21, 1893. Prof. Latin and Greek (old) Washington Coll., Tenn., 1893-96; prof. Synodical Coll. of Tex., 1892-93; prin. Kansas City Ladies' Coll., 1896-98; pastor Poplar Bluff, Mo., 1898-1902; pres. Lindenwood Female Coll., St. Charles, Mo., 1902—. Del. Presbyn. Gen. Assembly, 1902; chmn. com. on edn. St. Louis Presbytery. Mason. Republican. Author: Present-Day Attitudes Toward the Bible, 1900; A Cursory Investigation into the Respective Functions of Religion and Ethics in Education, 1904. Home: St. Charles, Mo. Died Oct. 23, 1913.

AYRES, Joseph Gerrish, rear adm.; b. Canterbury, N.H., Nov. 3, 1839; s. Charles H. and Almira S. (Gerrish) A.; ed. U. of Vt. and Columbia U.; m. Olinda A. Austin, July 11, 1884. Served in 15th N.H. Vols. as 2d and 1st lt., Oct. 1, 1862-Aug. 13, 1863; apptd. acting asst. surgeon U.S.N., Dec. 17, 1864; advanced through grades to med. dir. U.S.N., Dec. 12, 1898; retired with rank of rear adm., Nov. 3, 1901, for services during Civil War. Home: Montclair, N.J. Died Mar. 21, 1922.

AYRES, Milan Church, editor; b. Lewiston, Ill., May 17, 1850; s. Lorenzo Dow and Lucy (Trowbridge) A.; student Kan. State Agrl. Coll., 1864-66; B.D., Yale, 1879; grad. Nat. Sch. Elocution and Oratory, Phila., 1876; post-grad. course Yale Div. Sch., 1880-81; m. Georgiana Gall, Dec. 24, 1871; 2 sons, Leonard Porter, Milan Valentine. Ordained Congl. ministry; home missionary preacher in Kan., 1872-76; pastor Southington, Conn., 1880-84; journalist and stenographic law reporter, Boston, 1884-90; editor Boston Daily Advertiser, 1890-1903, then in journalistic work, lecturing and management real estate investments. Has been editorial writer for the Boston Transcript, New York Press, Christian Union and its successor The Outlook. Author: Phillips Brooks in Boston (with intro. by Pres. Tucker of Dartmouth Coll.), 1893. Home: Washington, D.C. Deceased.

AYRES, Samuel Loring Percival, rear adm.; b. Stamford, Conn., July 29, 1835; s. Dr. Chauncey and Deborah Ann (Percival) A.; high sch. edn.; m. Almira J. Stonaker, Aug. 17, 1867. Apptd. 3d asst. engr. U.S.N., July 21, 1858; promoted through grades to chief engr., Mar. 21, 1870; retired, July 29, 1897; advanced to rank of rear adm., June 29, 1906, for services during Civil War. Home: Philadelphia, Pa. Died Apr. 29, 1917.

AYRES, Stephen Cooper, oculist; b. Troy, O., June 5, 1840; s. Dr. Henry P. and Eliza K. (Rowan) A.; A.B., Miami U., 1861, A.M., 1876; M.D., Med. Coll. of Ohio, 1864; (hon. A.M., U. of Wooster,

1875); pvt. Co. B, 20th Ohio Vol. Inf., Apr., 1861; med. cadet, 1863; acting asst. surgeon U.S.A., 1864; asst. surgeon U.S.V., 1865; bvtd. capt., 1865; m. Louise McLean, Oct. 28, 1873. Lecturer Cincinnati Hosp., 1871, 84, 98, 99; former prof. ophthalmology, Med. Coll. Ohio (U. Cincinnati), 1898-1910. Del. Internat. Ophthal. Congress, 1905. Republican. Home: Cincinnati, O. Died Sept. 2, 1921.

AYRES, Steven Beckwith, congressman; b. Ft. Dodge, Ia., Oct. 27, 1861; s. Stephen and Artemisia (Dunlap) A.; student Syracuse U., class of 1882, A.B., 1903; m. Harriet Margaret Bower, Feb. 6, 1884; 1 son, Malcolm B.; m. 2d Helen Thompson Haseltine, Oct. 7, 1905. Engaged in real estate operations at New York, 1887—; pres. Wheeler Corp. Mem. 62d Congress (1911-13), 18th N.Y. Dist. Democrat. Lecturer N.Y. U. Summer Sch. Author: Genealogy of the Ayres Family, 1901; Bridge, 1909; Building an American Merchant Marine, 1912; Our U.S. Postal Service, 1913. Home: Woodstock, N.Y. Died June 1, 1929.

B

BABASINIAN, V(ahan) S(imon), chemistry; b. Marsovan, Asia Minor, Nov. 28, 1876; s. Simon and Hripsimeh (Mallian) B.; A.B., Anatolia Coll., Asia Minor, 1895; A.M., Brown U., 1903, Ph.D., 1906; unmarried. Came to U.S., 1897, naturalized citizen, 1910. Instr. in chemistry, Brown U., 1903-06; instr. in chemistry, Lehigh, untly 1909, asst. prof., 1909-11, asso. prof., 1911-22, prof. organic chemistry, 1922—. With Chem. Warfare Service (research), Washington, 1918, du Pont Co., Wilmington, Del., 1919. Republican. Conglist. Mason. Editor: Gattermann's Practical Methods of Organic Chemistry, 1914. Home: Bethlehem, Pa. Died May 24, 1939.

BABB, Clement Edwin, clergyman; b. Pittston, Pa., Aug. 19, 1821; s. John P. and Mary (Shriner) B.; grad. Dickinson Coll., 1840; Dickinson Law Sch., 1842 (D.D., Marietta Coll., 1865); m. Lydia F. Hulbert, Sept. 1848. Admitted to bar, 1842; pros. atty., Hillsdale County, Mich., 1844-47; ordained Presbyn. ministry, May 1848; pastor 2d Presbyn. Ch., Indianapolis (in immediate succession to Henry Ward Beecher), 1848-53; editor Christian Herald and its successor The Herald and Presbyter, Cincinnati, 1853-1905; chaplain 22d Ohio vols., 1862-63. Author C. E. B. Selections from Editorial Correspondence, 1880; Senex Smith, his Notes and Notions, 1890. Home: San Jose, Calif. Died 1906.

BABB, Cyrus Cates, civil engr.; b. Portland, Me., June 18, 1867; s. Cyrus K. and Mary Lucretia (Judkins) B.; B.S., Mass. Inst. Tech., 1890; m. Grace Crowther, Mar. 7, 1906; children—Dudley Cyrus, Kathryn. Hydrographer U.S. Geol. Survey, 1890-1902, engr. same, 1902-06; project engr., U.S. Reclamation Service, 1906-09; dist. engr. U.S. Geol. Survey, 1910; chief engr. Me. State Water Storage Commn., July 1, 1911-Dec. 1914; cons. hydraulic engr., 1914-17; supervisor of lands, water power, etc. The Rhodhiss (N.C.) Mfg. Co., and E. A. Smith Mfg. Co., 1917-18; cons. engr., 1919. Home: Granite Falls, N.C. Died 1937.

BABB, James Elisha, lawyer; b. Champaign County, Ill., Jan. 11, 1864; s. Milton and Elizabeth (Littler) B.; B.S., Ill. Coll., 1882; LL.B., Northwestern U., 1884; LL.D., Whitman Coll., Walla Walla, Wash., 1932; m. Daisy Tinkham, Nov. 5, 1888; 1 son, James Tinkham. Practiced law, Chicago, 1884-92, Lewiston Ida., 1892—. Chmn. Rep. State Conv., Ida., 1896. Mem. bd. overseers Whitman Coll. Home: Lewiston, Ida. Died May 26, 1934.

BABB, Washington Irving, lawyer; b. Des Moines County, Ia., Oct. 2, 1844; s. Miles and Mary (Moyer) B.; A.B., Ia. Wesleyan U., 1866, A.M., 1869 (LL.D., 1898, State U. of Ia., 1907); served 8th Ia. Vol. Cav., 1863-65; m. Alice Bird, Oct. 9, 1873. Admitted to bar, 1868; practiced at Mt. Pleasant, Ia., 1868-1906, Chicago, 1906-10; pres. Western Wheeled Scraper Co., Aurora, Ill., and v.p. Austin Mfg. Co., Chicago, 1910—. Mem. Ia. Ho. of Rep., 1884; judge 2d Jud. Dist., 1891-95; Dem. candidate for gov., 1895; received Dem. vote Ia. Legislature, for U.S. senator, 1896; chmn. Sound Money Dem. Conv., Ia., 1896. Regent State U. of Ia.; trustee Ia. Wesleyan U. Home: Aurora, Ill. Died Sept. 9, 1925.

BABBITT, Edwin Burr, army officer; b. N. Y., July 26, 1862; s. Col. Lawrence Sprague (U.S. Army) and Fannie (McDougall) B.; grad. U.S. Mil. Acad., 1884, Arty. Sch., 1889; m. Maud Ainsworth, Feb. 23, 1924. Commd. 2d lt., June 15, 1884; promoted through grades to brig. gen. N.A., Oct. 2, 1917; brig. gen., U.S. Army, Feb. 12, 1918; maj. gen., Apr. 14, 1923; retired Sept. 19, 1924. Commdg. brigade in Marne, St. Mihiel and Argonne offensives; with Army of Occupation. Awarded D.S.M. "for exceptionally meritorious and conspicuous services"; Officer Légion d'Honneur (French); Comendator Order of El Sol del Peru (Peru); Abdon Calderon, first class (Equador). Home: Santa Barbara, Calif. Died Dec. 9, 1939.

BABBITT, Frank Cole, coll. prof.; b. Bridgewater, Conn., June 4, 1867; s. Isaac and Sarah (Cole) B.; A.B., Harvard, 1890, A.M., 1892, Ph.D., 1895; hon. L.H.D. from Trinity College, 1927; m. Ethel Hall, June 28, 1900; children—Lewis Hall, Sarah Frances, Katherine Maida. Taught in common schs., Conn., 1885-87, pvt. sch., Boston, 1890-95; fellow Am. Sch. Classical Studies, Athens, 1895-96; instr. Greek, Harvard, 1896-98; instr. Greek, 1898-99, prof., 1899—, Trinity. Visiting prof. Am. Sch. Classical Studies, Athens, 1931-32. Author: Greek Grammar, 1902. Translator: Plutarch's Moralia (Loeb, Classical Library), 1927—. Home: Hartford, Conn. Died Sept. 19, 1935.

BABBITT, Irving, univ. prof.; b. Dayton, O., Aug. 2, 1865; s. Edwin Dwight and Augusta (Darling) B.; A.B., Harvard, 1889, A.M., 1893; studied Paris, 1891-92; m. Dora May Drew, June 12, 1900; children—Esther, Edward Sturges. Instr. Romance langs., Williams Coll., 1893-94; instr. French, 1894-1902, asst. prof. 1902-12, prof. French lit., 1912—, Harvard. Larwill lecturer Kenyon Coll., Mar. 1920; Harvard lecturer Yale, Oct.-Feb., 1922; West lecturer Stanford U., Apr. 1922; exchange prof. from Harvard to the Sorbonne, Mar.-May 1923; Clyde Fitch lecturer, Amherst, 1930; lecturer on Alexander Foundation, U. of Toronto, 1930. Author: Literature and the American College, 1908; The New Laokoön, 1910; The Masters of Modern French Criticism, 1912; Rousseau and Romanticism, 1919; Democracy and Leadership, 1924. Editor: Taine's Introduction à l'Histoire de la Littérature Anglaise, 1898; Renan's Souvenirs d'Enfance et de Jeunesse, 1902; Voltaire's Zadig, 1905; Racine's Phèdre, 1910. Home: Cambridge, Mass. Died July 15, 1933.

BABBITT, Kurnal R., lawyer; b. Salem, Mich., Jan. 25, 1864; s. Rufus and Ellen (Cady) B.; grad. Mich. State Normal Sch., 1884; LL.B., Columbian (now George Washington) U., 1889; m. Lucie Cullyford, Dec. 4, 1895. Clerk in P.O. Dept., Washington, D.C., until 1891; practiced law at Aspen, Colo., 1891-93, Cripple Creek, 1893-96, Colo. Springs, 1896-1908, N.Y. City since 1908; now gen. counsel and dir. Utah, Chino, and Butte & Superior copper cos., and Alaska Gold Mines Co. Republican. Office: New York, N.Y. Died Feb. 15, 1920.

BABBITT, Lawrence Sprague, army officer; b. Boston, Mass., Feb. 18, 1839; s. Col. Edwin Burr (U.S. Army) and Sarah Stedman (Sprague) B.; grad. West Point, 1861; m. Fannie, d. Surgeon McDougall, U.S. Army, Oct. 22, 1861. Has served in U.S. Army since 1861 as officer, becoming col. Apr. 7, 1899, and on duty in ordnance dept., U.S. Powder Depot, Dover, N.J., until retired Feb. 18, 1903. Home: Dover, N.J. Died 1903.

BABBOTT, Frank Lusk, mfr.; b. Waterville, N.Y., Aug. 14, 1854; s. Miller and Mary Elizabeth (Crandall) B.; A.B., Amherst, 1878, hon. A.M., 1903, LL.D., 1928; LL.B., Columbia, 1880; m. Lydia Richardson Pratt, Feb. 18, 1886 (dec.). Dir. and officer Chelsea Jute Mills, 1883-1901, when retired from business; trustee Brooklyn Trust Co., Brooklyn Savings Bank, Greenwood Cemetery Co. Mem. Brooklyn Bd. Edn., 1895-1902; v.p. New York Bd. Edn., 1902-04; pres. Packer Collegiate Inst.; trustee Brooklyn Pub. Library; trustee Brooklyn Inst. Arts and Sciences (pres. 1920-28), Brooklyn Acad. Music; mem. Bd. Home Missions Presbyn. Ch., 1906-17; v.p. Brooklyn Art Commn., 1920—. Decorated Chevalier de la Légion d'Honneur (France); comdr., 2d degree, Dannebrogordenen (Denmark). Independent Republican. Author: Classic English Odes, 1902; John Donne's Poems, 1905. Home: Glen Cove, L.I., and Brooklyn, N.Y. Died Dec. 7, 1933.

BABCOCK, Birton E.; b. Clyde, O., May 20, 1870; s. Franklin G. and Adeline (Wagner) B.; A.B., A.M., Coll. of Wooster (O.), 1894; student Lane Theol. Sem., 1896-98; m. Edna C. Wilder, Sept. 25, 1896; 4 children, all dec. Teacher pub. schs., Hanoverton, O., 1894-96; farmed and worked in kraut factory, Clyde, 1898-1900; sec. Empire State Pickling Co., Phelps, N.Y., 1901-07, v.p., sec., 1907-18, pres. and treas., 1918—. Trustee Clifton Springs (N.Y.) Sanitarium, Coll. of Wooster, Bd. of Christian Edn. of Presbyn. Ch. of U.S. Republican. Mason. Large donor to Coll. of Wooster and other ednl. and missionary enterprises. Home: Phelps, N.Y. Died Apr. 7, 1941.

BABCOCK, Charles, univ. prof.; b. Ballston Spa, N.Y., Mar. 29, 1829; s. Rev. Deodatus and Mary (Hine) B.; A.B., Union Coll., N.Y., 1847, A.M., 1850; m. Elisabeth A. Upjohn, Apr. 14, 1853. Mem. Richard Upjohn & Co., architects, New York, 1853-58; deacon, 1860, priest, 1864, P.E. Ch.; rector Greenwood Iron Works, N.Y., 1863-71, St. Paul's, Ithaca, N.Y., 1874-92; prof. architecture, Cornell, 1871-97, emeritus. Hon. men. A.I.A. Home: Ithaca, N.Y. Died Aug. 27, 1913.

BABCOCK, Charles Henry, clergyman; b. New Haven, Conn.; s. Henry Chamberlain and Mary (Thompson) B.; ed. Johnstown Acad. and under pvt. tutors; (D.D., Kenyon, 1886); widower. Deacon, 1871, priest, 1873, P.E. Ch.; asst. minister Christ Ch., Brooklyn (North), 1871; rector St. George's, Brooklyn, 1872-75; asst. minister on Green Foundation, Trinity Ch., Boston, 1875-79; rector Trinity Ch., Columbus, O., 1879-88, Grace Ch., Providence, R.I., 1888-94; relinquished parochial work on account of ill health; recovered after travel. Europe and elsewhere; gen. chmn. Ch. Congress in U.S., 1907—. Pres. Conv. of Southern Ohio 3 yrs., during bishop's illness; deputy to Gen. Conv., 1886. Home: New York, N.Y. Deceased.

BABCOCK, Earle Brownell, univ. prof.; b. Saginaw, Mich., Sept. 12, 1881; s. Alfred Jerome and Henrietta (Ripley) B.; Ph.B., U. of Chicago, 1903, Ph.D., 1915; studied Columbia and Sorbonne, and Collège de France, Paris; m. Madeleine Doby, June 21, 1917 (died Apr. 22, 1919); 1 son, Alfred Robert; m. 2d, Marie-Thérèse Peylade, Jan. 30, 1928. Instr. French and history, Ethical Sch., N.Y. City, 1903-05; instr. French, 1906-10, asst. prof., 1910-15, U. of Chicago; prof. Romance langs. and lits., New York U., 1915—, head of dept., 1915-29, and dean of the Grad. Sch., 1922-27. Officier de l'Instruction Publique, France, 1911; Chevalier Légion d'Honneur, France, 1924, Officier, 1928; Commandeur du Phénix (Greece), 1931; Commandeur de la Couronne de Roumanie, 1933. Major Am. Red Cross and dir. school in Paris for Red Cross personnel, Oct. 1918-Jan. 1919. Dir. Am. Univ. Union in Europe (continental div., Paris), 1920-21. Asst. dir. European center of Carnegie Endowment for Internat. Peace (Paris), 1925—. Republican. Home: Paris, France, and New York, N.Y. Died Mar. 1, 1935.

BABCOCK, Earle Jay, univ. dean; b. St. Charles, Minn., June 11, 1865; s. David L. and Lavinia P. (Campbell) B.; B.S., U. of Minn., 1889; (Sc.D., U. of N.D., 1914); m. Lillian G. Cool, Sept. 17, 1889. State geologist N.D., 1897-1902; prof. indsl. chemistry, metallurgy, and mining, dir. N.D. Mining Expt. Sta. and dean Coll. of Mining Engring., 1898—, dean Colleges of Engineering, 1916—, acting pres., 1917-18, U. of N.D. Mem. exec. com. State Council of Defense, 1917, also chmn. Com. on Fuels, Engring. and Research. Author of geol. and indsl. reports, mining and engring. bulls., etc. Home: Grand Forks, N.D. Died Sept. 3, 1925.

BABCOCK, James Woods, alienist; b. Chester, S.C., Aug. 11, 1856; s. Sidney E. (M.D.) and Margaret (Woods) B.; A.B., Harvard, 1882, M.D., 1886; (LL.D., S.C. Coll., 1905); m. Katharine Guion, Aug. 17, 1892. Asst. phys. McLean Hosp., Somerville, Mass., 1885-91; phys. and supt. State Hosp. for Insane, Columbia, S.C., 1891-1914. One of 1st physicians in the South to recognize pellagra (Dec. 1907); pres. Nat. Assn. for the Study of Pellagra, 1909-12 and sec., 1912—; chmn. S.C. State Hosp. Commns., 1910-13; mem. Columbia Bd. Health, 1898-1901; chmn. Columbia Sewerage Commn., 1901-03, Columbia commn. on water and water works, 1903-07; prof. psychiatry. Med. Coll. of S.C., 1915—. Died Mar. 3, 1922.

BABCOCK, John Breckinridge, army officer; b. in La., Feb. 7, 1843. Sergt. Co. G, 37th N.G.S.N.Y., May 29, 1862; disch., Sept. 2, 1862; 2d lt. 174th N.Y. Inf., Nov. 13, 1862; advanced through grades to brig. gen. vols., June 3, 1898; col. asst. adj. gen. U.S. Army, Feb. 21, 1901; brig. gen., Aug. 7, 1903; retired at own request, over 30 yrs. service, Aug. 8, 1903. Bvtd. 1st lt., capt. and maj., Mar. 2, 1867, for battles of Sabine Cross Roads, Pleasant Hill and Cane River Crossing, La.; lt. col., Feb. 27, 1890, for action against Indians at Tonta Creek, Ariz., June 16, 1873, and at Four Peaks, Ariz., Jan. 16, 1874; awarded medal of honor, Mar. 2, 1899, for most distinguished gallantry in action at Spring Creek, Neb., May 16, 1869. Died 1909.

BABCOCK, Joseph Weeks, congressman; b. Swanton, Vt., Mar. 6, 1850; removed to Iowa, 1855; ed. at Mt. Vernon and Cedar Falls, Ia.; removed to Necedah, Wis., 1881; m. Mary A. Finch, 1867. Elected to Wis. assembly, 1888 and 1890; mem. Congress, 3d Wis. dist., 1893-1907; chmn. Com. on D.C.; mem. Com. Ways and Means; chmn. Nat. Rep. Congressional Com., campaigns of 1894, 1896, 1898, 1900, 1902, 1904. Home: Necedah, Wis. Died 1909.

BABCOCK, Kendric Charles, univ. dean; b. S. Brookfield, N.Y., Sept. 8, 1864; s. Gideon Perry and Lydia (Macomber) B.; Litt.B., U. of Minn., 1889; A.M., Harvard, 1895, Ph.D., 1896; LL.D., Roanoke College, 1914, also U. of Western Ontario, 1924; unmarried. Taught country schs., N.Y., 1881-85; instr. history and old English, U. of Minn., 1890-94; asst. prof. Am. history and polit. science, U. of Calif., 1896-1903; pres. and prof. history, U. of Ariz., 1903-10; specialist in higher edn., U.S. Bur. of Edn., 1910-13; dean, Coll. of Liberal Arts and Sciences, U. of Ill., 1913-31, dean emeritus, was provost, 1920-31. Author: Rise of American Nationality, 1906; Scandinavian Element in The United States, 1914. Died Mar. 11, 1932.

BABCOCK, Robert Hall, M.D.; b. Watertown, N.Y., July 26, 1851; s. Robert Stanton and Emily M. (Hall) B.; ed. Inst. for Blind, Phila., 1864-67, prep. dept. Olivet Coll., Mich., 1867-69, Western Reserve Coll., 1869-73, A.B., 1873, A.M., 1887; U. of Mich. (lit. dept.), 1873-74 (med. dept.), 1874-76; M.D., Chicago Med. Coll., 1878, Coll. Phys. and Surg. (Columbia), 1879; continued med. studies Berlin, Munich, Wurzburg, Germany, 1880-83; LL.D., U. of Mich.,

1910; m. Lizzie C. Weston, June 12, 1879; children—Eleanor Clinton (Mrs. A. M. Coit), Robert Weston. In practice, Chicago, 1883—; prof. clin. medicine and physical diagnosis, Chicago Post-Grad. Med. Sch., 1887-92; prof. clin. medicine and diseases of chest, Coll. Phys. and Surg., Chicago, 1891-1905; attending phys., 1891-1907, later cons. phys., Cook County Hosp. Author: Diseases of the Heart and Arterial System, 1903; Diseases of the lungs, 1907. Home: Chicago, Ill. Died June 27, 1930.

BABCOCK, Samuel Denison, capitalist; pres. and dir. Internat. Bell Telephone Co., New York, Central, Colonial and Manhattan Real Estate Assns.; dir. Am. Exchange Nat. Bank, Bank of New Amsterdam, Nat. Union Bank, N.Y.C.&H. R.R. Co., and numerous other corps. Home: New York, N.Y. Died 1902.

BABCOCK, Stephen Moulton, agrl. chemist; b. Bridgewater, N.Y., Oct. 22, 1843; s. Peleg B. and Cornelia B.; A.B., Tufts, 1866; student chemistry, Cornell, 1872-75; Ph.D., U. of Göttingen, 1879; LL.D., Tufts, 1901; m. May Crandall, Oct. 27, 1896. Instr. chemistry, Cornell U., 1875-76; chemist, N.Y. Agrl. Expt. Sta., Geneva, N.Y., 1882-87; prof. agrl. chemistry, U. of Wis., 1887-1913 (emeritus); chief chemist Wis. Agrl. Expt. Sta., 1887-1913, asst. dir., 1901-13. Awarded bronze medal by Wis. legislature, 1899; grand prize, Paris Expn., 1900; mem. Jury of Awards, Buffalo Expn., 1901; grand prize St. Louis Expn., 1904. Inventor of Babcock test for butter. Home: Madison, Wis. Died July 2, 1931.

BABCOCK, Washington Irving, naval architect; b. Stonington, Conn., Sept. 26, 1858; s. Capt. David S. and Charlotte A. (Noyes) B.; B.S., Poly. Inst. of Brooklyn, 1876; C.E., Rensselaer Poly. Inst., 1878; m. Grace W. Kernochan, Jan. 1, 1890. Was at Roach's Ship Yard, Chester, Pa., 1878-85, Providence & Stonington Steamship Co., New York, 1885-87; supt. Union Dry Dock Co., Buffalo, N.Y., 1887-89; mgr. and pres. Chicago Shipbuilding Co., Chicago, 1889-1900. Has published numerous tech. papers in procs. the socs. Home: New York, N.Y. Died Aug. 10, 1917.

BABCOCK, William Henry, lawyer, author; b. St. Louis, Jan. 1, 1849; LL.B., Columbian (now George Washington) U., 1869; m. Anne Johns Earle, June 1874; m. 2d, Mrs. Gertrude Lee Mahood, Aug. 18, 1897. Lawyer and editor, Kansas City, 1869-70; editor St. Paul, Minn., 1872; asst. examiner in Patent Office, 1873-75; in patent practice. Author: Lord Stirling's Stand and Other Poems; Lays from Over Sea; Cypress Beach; The Brides of the Tiger; An Invention of the Enemy; Cian of the Chariots; Two Lost Centuries of Britain; The Tower of Wye, 1901; Kent Fort Manor, 1902; Early Norse Visits to North America, 1913. Home: "Rock Haven," near Georgetown, D.C. Died 1922.

BABSON, Herman, prof. modern langs.; b. Gloucester, Mass., Dec. 19, 1871; s. Horatio and Charlotte Florence (Babson) B.; A.B., Amherst Coll., 1893, A.M., 1896; U. of Berlin, 1903-04, 1906-07; Ph.D., Harvard, 1908; m. Carrie Anna Richardson, June 17, 1897. Asst. prof. English, 1893-1906, instr. German, 1904-06, Mass. Agrl. Coll.; also acting head dept. of rhetoric, Amherst, 1900; prof. German lang. and lit., Coll. of Hawaii, Honolulu, T.H., 1908-09; prof. German and head of dept., 1909-14, head dept. modern langs., 1914-23, prof. modern langs., 1918-Jan. 1923, Purdue Univ.; studied Paris and Grenoble, France, 1920-21. Republican. Congregationalist. Editor: Frenssen's Peter Moors Fahrt nach Südwest, 1914; Science and Industrial French Reader (with E. V. Greenfield), 1923. Home: Peabody, Mass. Died June 25, 1925.

BACHE, Dallas, asst. to surgeon-gen. U.S. Army, with rank of col.; b. in Pa.; apptd. asst. surgeon U.S. Army, May 28, 1861; bvt. capt. and maj., 1865; capt. and asst. surgeon, May 28, 1866; maj. and surgeon, Aug. 5, 1867; lt. col. surgeon, Feb. 9, 1890; col. and asst. surgeon-gen., Apr. 18, 1895. Died 1902.

BACHE, Leopold Semon, broker; b. N.Y. City, Nov. 12, 1865; s. Semon and Elizabeth (Van Praag) B.; ed. Charlier Inst., New York, 1874-80; Athène Royale, Brussels, Belgium, 1880-82; m. Hattie Stein, Feb. 3, 1892; children—Frank Semon, Harold Leopold. Began in brokerage bus., New York, 1901; partner J. S. Bache & Co.; v.p. N.Y. Casualty Co. Mem. Liverpool Cotton Assn., N.Y. Coffee & Sugar Exchange (v.p.), N.Y. Cotton Exchange, N.Y. Produce Exchange, N.Y. Cocoa Exchange, Rubber Exchange of N.Y., Chicago Bd. of Trade, New Orleans Cotton Exchange. Trustee Home for Aged and Infirm Hebrews. Home: New York, N.Y. Died Oct. 10, 1927.

BACHELDER, Nahum Josiah, governor; b. Andover, N.H., Sept. 3, 1854; s. William Adams and Adeline E. (Shaw) B.; ed. Taunton Hill Sch., Andover, Franklin (N.H.) Acad. and New Hampton (N.H.) Lit. Instn.; (hon. A.M., Dartmouth Coll., 1887; A.B., N.H. Coll., 1899); m. Mary A. Putney, June 30, 1887; children—Ruth, Henry Putney. Farmer, 1875—; sec. N.H. Bd. Agr., 1887-1913; gov. of N.H., 1903-05. Republican. Home: East Andover, N.H. Died Apr. 22, 1934.

BACHELLER, Joseph Henry, banker; b. Newark, N.J., Feb. 1, 1869; s. John Collins and Harriet Amelia (Parcells) B.; ed. high sch., Newark; m. Edith Adele Smith, Apr. 30, 1895; children—Muriel (Mrs. Donald C. Swatland), Adele (wife of Dr. Herbert A. Schulte), Joseph Henry, John Smith. Began as clk. N.Y. Life Ins. Co., 1885; in 1890 asso. with Samuel S. Dennis and later managed estate of A. L. Dennis; v.p. Ironbound Trust Co., Newark, 1907-08, pres., 1908-27 (Ironbound Trust merged with Fidelity Trust Co., 1927); v.p. Fidelity Union Trust Co., Newark, 1927-31, pres., 1931—. Alderman, Newark, 1897-1903, chmn. finance com., 1900-03, pres. bd., 1903; mem. State Assembly, 1900-02, State Senate, 1903-05; comptroller City of Newark, 1905-11; mem. State Water Supply Commn., 1907-13, pres., 1913; pres. Bd. Edn., 1922-23; former trustee Newark Free Pub. Library; pres. Children's Aid Soc. of Newark, N.J. Republican. Baptist. Home: Newark, N.J. Died Dec. 12, 1939.

BACHER, Otto Henry, artist; b. Cleveland, O., March 31, 1856; s. Henry and Charlotte B.; pupil of Duveneck, Carolus-Duran, Boulanger and Lefebvre; m. Mary Holland, 1888. Mem. Soc. of Illustrators, Painters, Etchers, London; A.N.A., 1906. Silver medal, La. Purchase Expn., St. Louis, 1904. Home: Bronxville, N.Y. Died 1909.

BACHMAN, Frank Puterbaugh, educator; b. Mackinaw, Ill., Jan. 29, 1871; s. Aaron Goode and Elissa (Newcomb) B.; State Normal Sch., Normal, Ill.; A.B., U. of Chicago, 1896; studied U. of Marburg, Germany; fellow, Teachers Coll. (Columbia), 1900-01; Ph.D., Columbia, 1902; m. Jessie Gertrude Harris, Sept. 3, 1903; children—Elizabeth Gertrude, John Stuart. Teacher and prin., elementary schs., until 1898; teacher State Normal Sch., N.Dak., 1898-1900; prof. of edn., Ohio U., Athens, 1902-08; asst. supt. schs., Cleveland, 1908-11; ednl. expert to Bd. of Estimate and Apportionment, N.Y. City, 1911-14; to Gen. Edn. Bd., John D. Rockefeller Fund, as dir. Div. of Pub. Edn. and exec. officer, 1915-29; dir. Div. of Surveys and Field Studies, George Peabody Coll. for Teachers, 1929—. Republican. Conglist. Author: Problems in Elementary School Administration, 1915; Principles of Elementary Education, 1915; Great Inventors and Their Inventions, 1916; The Training and Certification of High School Teachers, 1930; The Education and Certification of Elementary School Teachers, 1933. Editor: Poems of John Keats, 1925. Joint Author: Public Education in Maryland; The Gary Public Schools. Home: Nashville, Tenn. Died Mar. 1934.

BACHMAN, Jonathan Waverly, clergyman; b. Roseland, Sullivan County, Tenn., Oct. 9, 1837; s. Jonathan and Frances (Rhea) B.; Emory and Henry Coll., Va.; Union Theol. Sem.; (D.D., Central U., Ky., 1880. Washington and Lee U., Va., 1911); m. Eva Dulaney, Oct. 20, 1863. Pvt. C.S.A., May, 1861; became capt. and comd. 60th Regt. Tenn. Vols. at Vicksburg, during siege, 1863; after being exchanged, comd. regt. until ordained Presbyn. ministry, Oct., 1864, then became chaplain same regt. until close of war; pastor First Ch., Chattanooga, 1873-Sept. 30, 1923. Delegate Am. Conf. on Internat. Arbitration, Washington, 1896; moderator Gen. Assembly Presbyn. Ch. in U.S., 1910. Chaplain genl., U.C.V., 1913—. Mason. Home: Chattanooga, Tenn. Died Sept. 26, 1924.

BACHMAN, Nathan, evangelist; b. in Sullivan County, Tenn., Dec. 13, 1832; s. Jonathan and Frances (Rhea) B.; A.B., Emery and Henry Coll., Va., 1857; studied various periods at Princeton, Union (New York), and Union (Va.) Theol. sems.; (D.D., Southwestern Presbyn. U., Tenn.); m. Sarah Jane Cunningham, 1862 (died 1863). Ordained Presbyn. ministry, 1862; pastor 2d Presbyn. Ch., Knoxville, Tenn., 1866-76. In gen. evangelistic work, 1876—. Author: Light in Dark Places, 1910. Home: Sweetwater, Tenn. Died Dec. 3, 1914.

BACHMAN, Nathan Lynn, U.S. senator; b. Chattanooga, Tenn., Aug. 2, 1878; s. Dr. Jonathan Waverly and Eva D. B.; student Southwestern, Central and Washington and Lee univs.; LL.B., U. of Va.; LL.D., U. of Chattanooga; m. Pearl McMannen Duke, Jan. 7, 1904; 1 dau., Mrs. Thomas A. McCoy. City atty. Chattanooga, 1906-08; circuit judge, 1908-12; asso. justice Supreme Court of Tenn., 1918-24; apptd. U.S. senator, Feb. 28, 1933, to fill unexpired term of Cordell Hull, elected, 1935, for term, 1935-37. Democrat. Home: Chattanooga, Tenn. Died Apr. 23, 1937.

BACKES, John H., judge; b. Trenton, N.J., Aug. 18, 1863. Admitted to N.J. bar as atty., 1884; licensed as counsellor, 1888; practiced in Trenton; vice chancellor of N.J., 1913—. Home: Trenton, N.J. Died June 15, 1935.

BACKUS, Edward Wellington, merchant mfr.; b. Jamestown, N.Y., Dec. 1, 1860; s. Abel and Anna (Anderson) B.; ed. pub. schs. and U. of Minn.; m. Elizabeth Horr; children—Edward Raymond (dec.), Seymour Wellington. In lumber business with Lee & McCulloch, 1882; bought out interest of jr. partner, 1883, and continued business under title of Lee & Backus, succeeded by E. W. Backus & Co., in 1885; firm inc. 1894 as E. W. Backus Lumber Co., which was changed to Backus-Brooks Co., 1899, and inc., 1902, as the Backus-Brooks Co. of Me., of which became pres. Also organized and is pres. Minn. & Ont. Paper Co., Ont. & Minn. Power Co., Ltd., Rainy River Inprovement Co., Ft. Francis Pulp & Paper Co., Ltd., Great Lakes Paper Co., Ltd., Minn., Dak. & Western Ry. Co., Internat. Lumber Co., Keewatin Lumber Co., Ltd., Keewatin Power Co., Ltd., Kenora Paper Mills, Ltd., Kenora Development Co., Ltd., Koochiching Realty Co., Internat. Telephone Co., Internat. Improvement Co. Rep. presdl. elector, 1904. Home: Minneapolis, Minn. Died Oct. 29, 1934.

BACKUS, Manson Franklin, banker; b. Livonia, N.Y., May 11, 1853; s. Clinton T. and Harriet N. (Groesbeck) B.; grad. Friends' Acad., Union Springs, N.Y., 1871; grad. Central N.Y. Conf. Sem., Cazenovia, N.Y., 1872; admitted to N.Y. bar, 1889; m. Emma C. Yawger (died 1884); children—Helen Irene (dec.), Le Roy Manson; m. 2d, Lue Adams (died 1901); m. 3d, Elise Piutti, June 19, 1902 (died 1927). Postmaster, Union Springs, N.Y., 1881-85; moved to Seattle, Wash., 1889; with Edward O. Graves founded Washington Nat. Bank, pres., 1900-06, and now chmn. bd. of its successor, Nat. Bank of Commerce; founded banking house of Graves & Backus (succeeded by 1st Nat. Bank), Bellingham, Wash., 1895; one of organizers of Seattle Clearing House, 1889, and pres. Seattle Clearing House Assn., 1902, 14, 21, 23; one of incorporators Fed. Res. Bank, San Francisco; dir. Seattle br. Fed. Reserve Bank, 1917-33. Spl. commr. to China, Japan and P.I. for Alaska-Pacific-Yukon Expn., 1907; chmn. state com. Mil. Tr. Camp Assn., 1917; mem. Dist. Com. on Capital Issues, World War. Regent U. of Wash., 1909. Trustee Seattle Chamber Commerce; dir. Seattle Pub. Library, 1930-32. Republican. Home: Seattle, Wash. Died Feb. 15, 1935.

BACKUS, Truman Jay, pres. Packer Collegiate Inst.; b. Milan, N.Y., Feb. 11, 1842; s. Rev. Jay S. B. (D.D.); grad. U. of Rochester, 1864 (A.M., 1867; LL.D., 1883); m. Sarah C. Glass, Jan. 9, 1866; m. 2d, Helen C. Hiscock, July 16, 1883. Was Brooklyn civil service commr. under Mayors Schieren and Wurster; pres. bd. of mgrs. of State care of the insane. Pres. Headmasters' Assn. Author: Great English Writers; Outlines of English Literature; Reviser of Shaw's "History of English Literature." Home: Brooklyn, N.Y. Died 1908.

BACON, Albert Williamson, rear adm.; b. Philadelphia, Jan. 5, 1841; s. James Ware and Alice Ann (Riggs) B.; ed. pub. and pvt. schs. at Frankfort, Ky., and Phila.; m. Kate S. Stoughton, Jan. 23, 1873. Apptd. captain's clk., U.S.N., 1861; advanced through grades to pay dir., 1900; retired with rank of rear adm., Jan. 5, 1903. Attached to Admiral Farragut's fleet during Civil War; afterwards on N. Atlantic sta.; in charge U.S.N. depots at Rio de Janeiro, Brazil, and Nice, France; on duty Navy Dept., and Mare Island Navy Yard. Republican. Roman Catholic. Home: Santa Barbara, Calif. Died Sept. 23, 1922.

BACON, Albion Fellows, social reformer; b. Evansville, Ind., Apr. 8, 1865; d. Rev. Albion and Mary (Erskine) Fellows; grad. Evansville High Sch., 1883; m. Hilary E. Bacon, Oct. 11, 1888 (died 1933); children—Margaret (dec.), Albion Mary, Hilary Edwin and Joy (twins). Organizer and leader of men's circle of Friendly Visitors, 3 yrs.; organizer and leader of Flower Mission, 5 yrs.; an organizer Anti-Tuberculosis League, Monday Night Club, Working Girls' Assn. (ex-pres.); organized, Oct. 28, 1911, and sec., Ind. Housing Assn.; dir. Nat. Housing Assn.; mem. Public Healtl Nursing Assn., State Fedn. Women's Clubs, etc. Author and leading advocate of state tenement law enacted in 1913; secured passage of housing law applying to all unsafe or unsanitary dwellings in State of Ind., 1917. Lecturer and writer on tenement reform. Methodist. Author: (with Annie Fellows Johnston) Songs Ysame (poems), 1897; booklets, What Bad Housing Means to the Community, and The Awakening of a State, 1911; book, Beauty for Ashes, 1914; Soldier's Book of Worship; State Centennial Pageant, 1917; War and Peace (pageant), prod. 1920, revised and prod. at Washington, D.C., 1925; Consolation (book), 1922; Citizenship Day Program (pageant), 1923, and adopted by Gen. Fedn. Women's Clubs; (book) The Path to God, 1928; The Charm String, 1929. Mem. Pres. Hoover's Conf. on Home Building and Home Ownership, 1931. Home: Evansville, Ind. Died Dec. 10, 1933.

BACON, Alexander Samuel, lawyer; b. Jackson, Mich., Nov. 20, 1853; s. John Arthur and Harriet (Smith) B.; grad. U.S. Mil. Acad., 1876; m. Harriet Whittlesey Schroter, Sept. 1, 1886. Was apptd. 2d lt. 1st U.S. Arty., June 15, 1876; resigned, Mar. 15, 1878; admitted to bar, 1879; practice has extended to many states and Eng., France, Japan and Central America. Was capt., maj. and lt. col. 23d regt., N.G.S. N.Y., and col. 2d Provisional regt., N.G.S. N.Y. Baptist. Democrat. Mem. N.Y. Assembly, 1887. Author: The Woolly Horse; The Illegal Trial of Christ; Masonic Nobility; Mohammed and Islam; Ancient Calendars. Home: Brooklyn, N.Y. Died May 30, 1920.

BACON, Alice Mabel, author; b. New Haven, Conn., Feb. 26, 1858; ed. pvt. schs.; Harvard exams., 1881; taught at Hampton Inst., 1883-88, and 1889, at Tokyo, Japan, 1888-89 and 1900-02; founded Dixie Hosp. for training colored nurses, 1890. Author: Japanese Girls and Women, 1891; Japanese Interior, 1893; In the Land of the Gods, 1905. Died May 2, 1918.

BACON, Augustus Octavius, senator; b. Bryan Co., Ga., Oct. 20, 1839; s. Rev. Augustus Octavius and Mary Louisa (Jones) B.; A.B., U. of Ga., 1859, LL.B., 1860 (LL.D., 1909); m. Virginia Lamar, Apr. 19, 1864. Adj. 9th Ga. Regt., C.S.A., and capt. on gen. staff; in law practice at Macon, Ga., 1866—; presdl. elector, 1868; mem. Ga. Ho. of Rep., 1870-82, 92, 93 (speaker 1873-82, except 1875-76, when was speaker pro tem); frequently del. to Dem. State convs. (pres. 1880); del.-at-large Dem. Nat. Conv., 1884; several times candidate for Democratic nomination for gov. (within 1 vote of nomination, 1883, when equivalent to election); elected U.S. senator, 1894, 1900, 1907; chmn. com. Engrossed Bills; mem. various coms. Regent Smithsonian Instn.; trustee U. of Ga. Home: Macon, Ga. Died Feb. 14, 1914.

BACON, Benjamin Wisner, theologian; b. Litchfield, Conn., Jan. 15, 1860; s. Rev. Leonard Woolsey and Susan (Bacon) B.; brother of Selden B.; B.A., Yale, 1881, B.D., 1884, A.M., 1892; (D.D., Western Reserve, 1893, U. of Breslau, 1911, Harvard, 1914; Litt.D., Syracuse, 1895, Oxford [Eng.], 1920, Yale, 1929; LL.D., Ill. Coll. 1904); m. Eliza Buckingham Aiken, May 27, 1884; children—Dorothy B. (Mrs. H. M. Woolsey), Benjamin S. Ordained Congl. ministry, 1884; pastor Old Lyme, Conn., 1884-89, Oswego, N.Y., 1889-96; instr. N.T. Greek, 1896-97, prof. N.T. criticism and exegesis, 1897—, Yale. Dir. Am. Sch. of Archæology, Jerusalem, Syria, 1905-06; Earl lecturer, U. of Calif, 1911 and 1924. Author: The Genesis of Genesis, 1891. Triple Tradition of the Exodus, 1894; Introduction to the New Testament, 1900; The Sermon on the Mount, 1902; The Story of St. Paul, 1904; Beginnings of Gospel Story, 1909; The Founding of the Church, 1909; Commentary on Galatians, 1909; The Fourth Gospel in Research and Debate, 1909; Jesus the Son of God, 1911; Making of the New Testament, 1912; Theodore Thornton Munger, New England Minister, 1913; Christianity Old and New, 1913; Is Mark a Roman Gospel?, 1919; Jesus and Paul, 1920; The Teaching Ministry for Tomorrow, 1923; He Opened to Us the Scriptures, 1923; The Gospel of Mark, Its Composition and Date, 1925; The Apostolic Message, 1925; The Story of Jesus, 1927; Studies in Matthew, 1930. Home: New Haven, Conn. Died Feb. 1, 1932.

BACON, Edgar Mayhew, author; b. Nassau, New Providence, Bahamas, June 5, 1855, where his father, John R. B., was then U.S. consul; ed. pvt. schs., Tarrytown, N.Y.; m. Anna H. Beard, Nov. 1903. Worked in bookstore, Albany, N.Y.; later adopted art as a profession; later, editorial writer on New York weeklies; lecturer. Author: The New Jamaica, 1891; The Pocket Piece (short stories), 1892; Chronicles of Tarrytown and Sleepy Hollow; The Hudson River—From Ocean to Source, 1902; Narragansett Bay, 1904; Nation Builders, 1906; Henry Hudson, His Times and His Voyages, 1907. Also hist. chapters in Winston's Story of America and other works. Farming, Mar. 1911—. Home: Wingdale, Dutchess Co., New York. Died Dec. 14, 1935.

BACON, Edward Payson, merchant; b. Schuyler Co., N.Y., May 16, 1834; s. Joseph Franklin and Matilda (Cowles) B.; ed. pub. sch., Geneva, N.Y.; m. Ella Dey Baird, Feb. 14, 1895. Began business life in ry. service, 1851-65; grain commn. merchant at Milwaukee, 1865—; pres. E. P. Bacon Co. Chmn. exec. com. Interstate Commerce Law Conv., St. Louis, 1900 and 1904. Was prin. advocate of nat. legislation for regulation of ry. rates in behalf of associated commercial orgns. of U.S., 1900-06. Mem. Chicago Bd. Trade. Home: Milwaukee, Wis. Died Feb. 1916.

BACON, Edward Rathbone; b. N.Y. City, Nov. 22, 1846; ed. Phillips Exeter Acad.; admitted to bar, Buffalo, 1869. Asso. counsel for various ry. cos., 18 yrs.; v.p., 1881-90, pres., 1890-1902, Cincinnati, Washington & Baltimore R.R.; v.p. and dir. B.&O. Southwestern R.R. Co., 1902—. Home: New York, N.Y. Died Dec. 2, 1915.

BACON, Edwin Munroe, editor, author; b. Providence, R.I., Oct. 20, 1844; academical edn.; (hon. A.M., Dartmouth, 1879). At age of 19 became reporter on Boston Advertiser; then editor Illustrated Chicago News; with New York Times, 1868-72; staff of Boston Advertiser again, 1872-73; editor in chief Boston Globe, 1873-78; mng. editor Advertiser, 1878-84, and editor in chief, 1884-86; editor in chief Boston Post, 1886-91; editor Time and the Hour, 1897-1900. Author and editor of various hist. works relating to Boston and N.E. Home: Boston, Mass. Died Feb. 24, 1916.

BACON, Francis, surgeon; b. Conn.; M.D., Yale, 1853; (hon. Sc.D., 1906). Surgeon 7th Conn. Inf., Sept. 13, 1861; surgeon vols., Aug. 8, 1862; resigned, Aug. 25, 1864. Prof. principles and practice of surgery, 1864-77; lecturer med. jurisprudence, Yale, 1899—. Home: New Haven, Conn. Died Apr. 26, 1912.

BACON, Frank, actor; b. Marysville, Calif., Jan. 16, 1864; s. Lyddall and Jane B.; ed. pub. schs., San Jose, Calif.; m. Jennie Weidman, July 25, 1885. Début at San Francisco; wrote "Lightnin'" (with Winchell Smith), prod. at Gaiety Theatre, New York, Aug. 26, 1918, and was played continuously for 3 yrs. and a day; has appeared in "Alabama," "Pudd'n Head Wilson," "Me and Grant," "Cinderella Man," "Fortune Hunter," etc. Republican. Protestant. Mason. Home: Bayside, L.I., N.Y. Died Nov. 19, 1922.

BACON, George Andrew, publisher; b. Webster, Mass., Jan. 17, 1847; s. George Hale and Ann (Bigelow) B.; A.B., Brown U., 1867; post-grad. study, U.S. and Germany, 1869, 70; Ph.D., Hamilton Coll., 1880; m. Susan Lyman Hillman, Aug. 16, 1871; children—George Morgans, Charles Edward, Paul Valentine, Ann. Prin. Academy, Derby, Vt., 1867-68, high sch., Gardner, Mass., 1868-69; teacher Poly. Inst. Brooklyn, 1871-74, Syracuse (N.Y.) High Sch., 1874-77, prin. 1878-88; partner Allyn & Bacon, sch. bk. pubs., Boston, 1888—. Home: Bolton, Mass. Died Jan. 14, 1930.

BACON, George P(reston), coll. dean; b. Charlemont, Mass., Aug. 24, 1866; s. Rev. William F(erdinand) and Mary Welsh (Beal) B.; A.B., Dartmouth, 1887, A.M., 1890; grad. study, U. of Berlin, 1899, 1909, U. of Mich., 1902, 08; m. Hanna Churchill, Dec. 27, 1898; children—Roger Churchill, Dorothy Carolin, Ruth Elizabeth. Instr. in science, Ripon (Wis.) Coll., 1888-89; asso. prof. mathematics, Beloit (Wis.) Coll., 1892-1902; prof. physics, Coll. of Wooster (O.), 1902-08; asst. prof. physics, Simmons Coll., Boston, Mass., 1910-19; prof. physics, Tufts Coll., 1919-36, dean of Engring. Sch., 1929-36; retired. Conglist. Home: Cambridge, Mass. Died Sept. 17, 1941.

BACON, Henry, architect; b. Watseka, Ill., Nov. 28, 1866; s. Henry and Elizabeth (Kelton) B.; U. of Ill., class of 1888; Rotch traveling scholar in Europe 2 yrs.; m. Laura Florence Calvert, Apr. 27, 1893. In office of Chamberlin & Whidden, Boston, 1885-88; with McKim, Mead & White, 1888-89, 1891-97 (Rotch Traveling Scholar, 1889-91); mem. Brite & Bacon, 1897-1903, then practiced alone. Designer of Lincoln Memorial, Washington, to cost $2,500,000. Mem. Nat. Inst. Arts and Letters, Am. Acad. Arts and Letters, Nat. Acad. Design; fellow A.I.A. Home: New York, N.Y. Died Feb. 16, 1924.

BACON, John Mosby, colonel U.S.A.; b. in Ky., Apr. 17, 1844. Enlisted 2d lt. 11th Ky. Cav., Sept. 22, 1862; promoted through grades to col. 8th Cav., June 29, 1897; brig. gen. vols., May 4, 1898; hon. disch. from vol. service, Feb. 24, 1899; retired at own request, over 30 yrs.' service, May 8, 1899. Bvtd.: maj., Mar. 2, 1867, for siege of Resaca, Ga.; lt. col., Feb. 27, 1890, for actions against Indians on the Rio Pecos, Tex., June 7, 1867, and nr. headwaters of Salt Fork of Brazos River, Tex., Oct. 28, 29, 1869. Col. and a.-d.-c. to Gen. Sherman, 1871-84. Died Mar. 19, 1913.

BACON, John Watson, engr., banker; b. Hartford, Conn., June 9, 1827; grad. Trinity, 1846; m. Caroline E. Botsford, Dec. 20, 1852; studied law 2 yrs., then became civil engr.; made first survey New York and New England R.R., and later was its gen. supt. until 1859; gen. supt. Danbury & Norwalk R.R., 1859-77; gen. R.R. commr. of Conn., 1877-87; pres. Savings Bank of Danbury, 1893—; State commr. of topog. survey of Conn. Home: Danbury, Conn. Died 1907.

BACON, Leonard Woolsey, Congl. clergyman; b. New Haven, Conn., Jan. 1, 1830; s. Leonard and Susan (Johnson) B.; grad. Yale, 1850, theol. studies Andover and Yale, and medicine at Yale; M.D., 1855; m. Susan Bacon, 1857; m. 2d, Letitia Jordan, 1890. Ordained, 1856; served in several Congl. and Presbyn. Chs.; was in Europe, 1872-77; then pastor at Norwich, Conn., and Phila. Author: A Life Worth Living—Life of Emily Bliss Gould, 1878; Church Papers, 1876; The Simplicity That Is in Christ, 1885; Irenics and Polemics, 1898; History of American Christianity, 1898; Story of The Congregationalists, 1904. Home: Assonet, Mass. Died 1907.

BACON, Robert, ambassador; b. Boston, July 5, 1860; s. William B. and Emily C. (Low) B.; A.B., Harvard, 1880; m. Martha Waldron Cowdin, Oct. 10, 1883. Entered banking house of Lee, Higginson & Co., Boston, 1881; became mem. E. Rollins Morse & Bro., 1883, until 1894; mem. J. P. Morgan & Co., New York, 1894-1903. Asst. sec. of state, U.S., 1905-09, except from Jan. 27-Mar. 6, 1909, when was Sec. of State, succeeding Elihu Root, elected to Senate; ambassador extraordinary and plenipotentiary to France, Dec., 1909-Jan., 1912. Mem. Bd. Overseers, Harvard U., 1889-1901 and 1902-08; fellow, Harvard, Jan., 1912. Commd. maj., U.S.R., May, 1917; assigned to staff of Gen. Pershing with A.E.F. in France. Home: New York, N.Y. Died May 29, 1919.

BACON, Robert Low, congressman; b. Jamaica Plain, Boston, Mass., July 23, 1884; s. Robert and Martha Waldron (Cowdin) B.; A.B., Harvard, 1907, LL.B., 1910; m. Virginia Murray, Apr. 14, 1913; children—Alexandra Murray, Virginia Murray, Martha. With U.S. Treasury Dept., 1910-11; mem. Kissel, Kinnicutt & Co., banking, 1911-23. Mem. Rep. State Com., N.Y.; formerly mem. Rep. County Com., Nassau Co., N.Y.; del. Rep. State Conv., N.Y., 1915, 19 and 1920-23 inclusive; del. Rep. Nat. Conv., Chicago, 1920; mem. 68th to 75th Congresses (1923-39), 1st N.Y. Dist.; mem. Rep. Congressional Com. Attended original Plattsburg T.C., 1915; enlisted in N.G.N.Y.; lt. 1st N.Y.F.A., Mexican border service, 1916; with Field Arty., U.S.A., Apr. 24, 1917-Jan. 2, 1919; served as asst. to chief of F.A., Washington, D.C., and promoted maj.; grad. sch. of Fire for F.A., Ft. Sill, Okla., Nov. 10, 1918; lt. col. and col. O.R.C., U.S.A.; comdg. officer 304th Cav., 61st Div., Jan. 1923-Jan. 1924; now col. F.A., O.R.C. Awarded D.S.M. Mem. bd. visitors U.S. Naval Acad.; mem. 150th Anniversary Commn. Battle of Bunker Hill. Episcopalian. Mason. Home: Westbury, L.I., N.Y. Died Sept. 12, 1938.

BADE, William Frederic, univ. prof.; b. Carver, Minn., Jan. 22, 1871; s. William Bruns and Anna (Voigt) B.; A.B., Moravian Coll., Pa., 1892, B.D., 1894, Ph.D., 1898; B.D., Yale, 1895; Lehigh U., 1901-02; U. of Berlin, 1905-06; D.D., Pomona Coll., 1922; Litt.D., Mills Coll., 1925; m. Evelyn Marianne Ratcliff, Sept. 26, 1906 (died 1907); 1 dau., Evelyn Mary; m. 2d, Elizabeth Le Breton Marston, d. George W. Marston, of San Diego, Calif., 1917; children—Elizabeth Le Breton, William George. Asso. prof. Greek and German, 1896-98, prof. Hebrew and O.T. lit., 1898-1902, Moravian College, Pa.; prof. O.T. lit. and Semitic languages, Pacific Sch. of Religion, Berkeley, Calif., 1902—, also dir. of Palestine Institute; dean Federate Summer Sch. of Theology, Berkeley, Calif., 1907. Lecturer univs. of Göttingen and Vienna, 1931. Author: The Old Testament in the Light of ToDay, 1915; also monographs. Lit. executor of the late John Muir, and edited his A Thousand-Mile Walk to the Gulf, 1916; The Cruise of the Corwin, 1917; Steep Trails, 1918; Life and Letters of John Muir, 1924; Preliminary Report, Tell en-Nasbeh Excavations, 1928; Some Tombs of the T. N. Necropolis, 1931. Engaged in archeol. excavation in Palestine, 1926—. Home: Berkeley, Calif. Died Mar. 4, 1936.

BADER, Ralph Hedrick, lawyer; b. McGaheysville, Va., June 8, 1888; s. Arthur Samuel and Margaret Elizabeth (Hedrick) B.; A.B., Washington and Lee U., 1909; post-grad. work, George Washington U., 1909-10; m. Pearle Malvina, d. N. O. Bacon, of Baltimore, Md., Oct. 2, 1920 (died 1921); children—John Hedrick and Arthur Samuel (twins). Apptd. student interpreter at Constantinople, Turkey, Apr. 1, 1910; interpreter to Am. Legation, Teheran, Persia, Feb. 8, 1912, and continued there as v. and dep. consul gen., 1912-15, v. consul, 1915-18, consul at Teheran, Feb. 9, 1918-Nov. 2, 1920, Cairo, Egypt, 1920-22; admitted to Va. bar, 1923. Democrat. Mason. Home: McGaheysville, Va. Died June 7, 1939.

BADGER, Charles Johnston, naval officer; b. Rockville, Md., Aug. 6, 1853; s. Commodore Oscar Charles (U.S.N.) and Margaret M. (Johnston) B.; apptd. to U.S. Naval Acad., at-large, by Pres. Grant, 1869, grad. 1873; m. Sophia J. Champlin, Oct. 4, 1882. Promoted capt., July 1, 1907; supt. U.S. Naval Acad., 1907-09; comdg. battleship Kansas, 1909-11; promoted rear adm., Mar. 8, 1911. Retired by operation of law, Aug. 6, 1915, but continued on active duty as mem. Gen. Bd. until Feb. 28, 1921. Home: Cleveland Park, D.C. Died Sept. 7, 1932.

BADGER, Oscar Charles, commodore U.S. Navy retired, 1885; b. Windham, Conn., Aug. 12, 1823; entered Navy from Philadelphia as midshipman, 1841; grad. Naval Acad., 1847; m. Margaret M. Johnston, Rockville, Md., 1852; served through Mexican and Civil wars; took part in many engagements; promoted through grades to commodore and comdt. Boston Navy yard. Died 1899.

BADGER, Walter Irving, lawyer; b. Boston, Jan. 15, 1859; s. Erastus Beethoven and Fanny (Babcock) B.; A.B., Yale, 1882; LL.B., cum laude, Boston U. 1885; m. Elizabeth Hand Wilcox, Oct. 6, 1887 (died 1923); children—Walter Irving, Mrs. Grace Ansley Holden. Practiced in Boston, 1885—. Home: Cambridge, Mass. Died Mar. 17, 1926.

BADGLEY, Sidney Rose, architect; b. Ernestown, Ont., Can., May 28, 1850; s. William Edwin and Nancy (Rose) B.; ed. pub. schs. and acad.; studied architecture in Toronto, Can., later studied at Oxford and Cambridge, and in France, Italy, Greece, etc.; m. Alma A. Clark, 1872 (died 1874); m. 2d, Charlotte J. Gilleland, Sept. 21, 1876. Settled in Cleveland, O., 1887; in gen. practice, specializing in chs. and pub. bldgs. in leading cities of U.S. and Can., also in China and S. America. V.p. Equity Savings & Loan Co. (Cleveland). Methodist. Republican. Home: Wickliffe, O. Deceased.

BAEHR, Max Joseph, consul; b. Zweibrücken, Bavaria, Aug. 2, 1858; s. Blasius and Josephine (Forstmair) B.; ed. parochial and Latin schs., Zweibrücken, Bavaria; came to U.S., 1878; m. Marie A. Zeminek, Feb. 17, 1885. Rep. candidate for city council, Omaha, 1888, for Neb. legislature, 1889; deputy co. clerk, Howard Co., Neb., 1894-95; clerk

Dist. Ct., 1895-98; Am. consul at Kehl, Baden, Germany, 1898-99; apptd. consul at Santos, Oct. 26, 1899, but did not serve; consul at Magdeburg, Germany, 1900-02, Cienfuegos, Cuba, 1902-14; consul at Berne, Switzerland, 1914-15; attending to his business interests in Cuba, 1915-22; became licensed real estate broker, Long Beach, Calif.; pres. bd. trustees, Long Beach Morning Sun Pub. Co. Home: Long Beach, Calif. Died May 6, 1934.

BAER, George Frederick, lawyer; b. Somerset Co., Pa., Sept. 26, 1842; s. Solomon and Anna Maria B.; ed. Somerset Inst., Somerset Acad. and Franklin and Marshall Coll. (hon. A.M., 1875, LL.D., 1886). At 13 entered office of Somerset Democrat; worked at printing trade over 2 yrs. and with his brother became owner of that paper in 1861. Raised vol. co. Aug., 1862; elected capt., joined Army of Potomac at 2d Bull Run and took part in all engagements up to and including Chancellorsville, when he was detailed as adj. gen. 2d brigade. Admitted to bar, 1864; removed to Reading, 1868; counsel for Phila. & Reading R.R., 1870, and later a dir.; for yrs. confidential legal adviser in Pa. of J. Pierpont Morgan; took prominent part in reorganization of Phila. & Reading R.R., 1893; elected, Apr., 1901, pres. Phila. & Reading Ry. Co., Phila. & Reading Coal & Iron Co., and Central R.R. Co. of N.J. Trustee Franklin and Marshall Coll., 1872—, pres. bd., 1894—. Home: Reading, Pa. Died Apr. 26, 1914.

BAER, John Willis, banker; b. on farm nr. Rochester, Minn., Mar. 2, 1861; s. Anthony and Lucy (May) B.; LL.D., Wooster, 1906; Litt.D., Princeton, 1916; m. Lora B. VanDusen, July 22, 1884. Engaged in journalism, Cedar Rapids, Ia., 1879-81; in grain and coal business, Minneapolis, 1881. Sec. World's Young People's Soc. of Christian Endeavor, 1890-1900 (became hon. sec.); asst. sec. Bd. of Home Missions, Presbyn. Ch. in U.S.A., 1900-06; pres. Occidental Coll., 1906-16; v.p. Union Nat. Bank, Pasadena, 1917-20; v.p. Security-First Nat. Bank, 1920—. Vice-moderator 127th Gen. Assembly Presbyn. Ch. in U.S.A. and elected moderator 131st Gen. Assembly, St. Louis, 1919. Home: Pasadena, Calif. Died Feb. 8, 1931.

BAER, William Jacob, artist; b. Cincinnati, Jan. 29, 1860; s. Henry and Barbara B.; m. Laura Schwenk, 1885 (died July 1924); children—Ella Laura (Mrs. Robert S. Mounce), Marian Ethel, Laura (Mrs. John V. Breisky, dec.), Mildred (Mrs. D. Herbert Smith, dec.); m. 2d, Mrs. Henrietta F. Dixon, Aug. 15, 1929. Pupil of Munich Royal Acad., 1880-84, receiving 4 medals and one of his works being purchased by the Directors for the Acad. Painted pictures in genre and portraits in oil and taught, 1885-92; then confined himself to miniature painting. Awarded 1st medal for miniatures and ideal paintings, New York, 1897; 1st class medals Paris Expn., 1900, Buffalo Expn., 1901, Charleston Expn., 1902, for miniatures and ideal works; hors concours, St. Louis Expn., 1904, and mem. internat. jury of awards; gold medal, East Orange, N.J. Died Sept. 21, 1941.

BAETJER, Frederick Henry, roentgenologist; b. Baltimore, Md., Aug. 7, 1874; s. Henry and Fredericka B.; A.B., Johns Hopkins, 1897, M.D., 1901; m. Mary Yarnall Carey, Oct. 14, 1903. Prof. roentgenology and roentgenologist, Johns Hopkins U. and Hosp.; cons. roentgenologist, Union Memorial Hosp., Church Home and Infirmary, Hosp. for the Women of Md., Children's Hosp. Sch. Maj. Med. Corps U.S. Army, May 1917-Feb. 1919. Pres. Am. Roentgen Ray Soc., 1911-12. Home: Catonsville, Md. Died July 17, 1933.

BAGBY, Albert Morris, musician; b. Rushville, Ill., Apr. 29, 1859; studied music many yrs. in Berlin and in Weimar, Germany, under Oscar Raif, Xaver Scharwenka, and Franz Liszt. Originator, 1891, of the "musical mornings" (for subscribers only), of which he has given over 388 and at which the greatest artists of the day have appeared. Author: Miss Träumerei (musical novel), 1895; Mammy Rosie, 1905. Died Feb. 26, 1941.

BAGBY, George Poindexter, lawyer; b. King and Queen County, Va., Aug. 19, 1879; s. Rev. Alfred (D.D.) and Sarah Jane (Pollard) B.; attended U. of Richmond, Va., 1897-98, U. of Va., 1898-1900; m. Hazel King Jones, Dec. 2, 1908; 1 child, Carol Griffith. Admitted to Md. bar, 1900, and began practice at Baltimore; mem. Bagby & Bagby, later Bagby & Baer; apptd. gen. atty. Western Md. Ry. Co., 1917, gen. solicitor, 1921, v.p. and dir., 1926-30, pres. and gen. counsel, 1930-33, chmn. bd., pres. and gen. counsel, 1933—. Democrat. Baptist. Editor: Annotated Code of Public General Laws of Maryland. Home: Roland Park, Baltimore, Md. Died June 3, 1934.

BAGBY, John Hampden Chamberlayne, coll. prof.; b. Middleburg, Va., July 20, 1867; s. George William and Lucy Parke (Chamberlayne) B.; M.A., U. of Va., 1888, M.E., 1891, Ph.D., 1894; LL.D., Hampden-Sidney (Va.) Coll.; unmarried. Began teaching, Wallace's Univ. Sch., Nashville, Tenn., 1888; prof. natural science, Hampden-Sidney Coll., 1892-99, prof. physics and astronomy, 1899—, v.p., 1904-18 (actg. pres. part of 1904). Democrat. Episcopalian. Home: Hampden-Sydney, Va. Died 1934.

BAGG, Lyman Hotchkiss, author; journalist; b. West Springfield, Mass., Dec. 24, 1846; s. Richard and Susan (Atwater) B.; A.B., Yale, 1869; unmarried. Editor Yale Literary Magazine, 1868-69; College Courant, New Haven, 1870-71; wrote weekly College Chronicle, New York World, 1876-82; managed Harvard-Yale boat race, New London, 1878-83; librarian University Club, 1889-1900. Author: Four Years at Yale, by a Graduate of '69, 1871; Ten Thousand Miles on a Bicycle, by Karl Kron, 1887. Wrote History of Yale Boating, in Kingsley's History of Yale, 1879. Home: West Springfield, Mass. Died 1911.

BAGGS, Mae Lacy, author; b. Independence, Mo.; d. Charles Wesley and Rhoda Gibson (Harris) Lacy; ed. pvt. schs., U.S. and France; m. Thomas Alexander Baggs, Jan. 13, 1916. Has traveled widely in Europe, Asia, Africa and South Seas. Was made a fellow of Royal Geo. Soc., London, and mem. Hakluyt Soc., British Museum. Episcopalian. Author: Colorado, Queen Jewel of the Rockies, 1918; The Ruddies in Boston, 1919; The Ruddies in New York, 1921. Home: Toledo, O. Died Sept. 1922.

BAGLEY, Clarence Booth, newspaper pub.; b. Troy Grove, DeKalb County, Ill., Nov. 30, 1843; s. Daniel and Susannah Rogers (Whipple) Bagley; ed. pub. schs. and Allegheny Coll.; m. Alice Mercer, Dec. 24, 1865 (died 1926); children—Rena (Mrs. Frank S. Griffith), Myrta (Mrs. Earle R. Jenner), Ethel Whipple (Mrs. H. Eugene Allen), Alice Claire (Mrs. Frederick Dent Hammons), Cecil Clarence. Crossed the plains with parents to Ore., 1852; house painter, later clk. in office of U.S. Survey, Seattle, until 1868; newspaper work, 1868-87; was editor, owner or pub. The Echo, Territorial Republican, Commercial Age, and Puget Sound Courier (all of Olympia, Wash.), and business mgr. Post-Intelligencer, Seattle; dep. collector internal revenue, 1871-85; territorial printer, 1873-85; in office of city comptroller, Seattle, 1894-99; sec. Bd. Pub. Works, 1899-1929; retired on pension. Mem. City Council, Seattle, 1890-92; alternate commr. World's Fair, Chicago, 1890-93. Author: Beginning and Growth of Organized Government in the Northwest, 1903; In the Beginning, 1905; Charters of the City of Seattle, 1910; Waterways of the Pacific Northwest, 1915; History of the City of Seattle (3 vols.), 1916; The Acquisition and Pioneering of Old Oregon, 1924; Pioneer Seattle and Its Pioneers, 1925; History of King County, Washington (4 vols.), 1929; Indian Myths of the Northwest, 1930; Chief Seattle and His Daughter Angeline, 1931. Home: Seattle, Wash. Died Feb. 17, 1932.

BAHRENBURG, Louis P. H., U.S. Pub. Health Service; b. N.Y. City, Dec. 28, 1873; s. John Henry and Caroline (Timmermann) B.; student Western Reserve Acad., 1892-93; M.D., Western Reserve Med. Sch., 1896; m. Elizabeth McClurkin, Jan. 8, 1901; children—Elizabeth Carolyn, James Henry. Commd. asst. surgeon U.S.P.H.S., 1900, passed asst. surgeon, 1905, surgeon, 1915, med. dir., 1930; served successively at N.Y. City, Liverpool, Honolulu, Chicago, New Orleans, Del. Breakwater Quarantine, Galveston, St. Louis, Cleveland, Copenhagen, Stuttgart, Cleveland; retired Dec. 31, 1937. Presbyterian (elder). Home: Cleveland Heights, O. Died Oct. 14, 1940.

BAIER, Victor, organist; b. New York, July 25, 1861; s. Robert and Louise (Hübner) B.; Trinity Ch. Sch.; (Mus. D., St. Stephens Coll., Annandale, N.Y., 1910); m. Anna M. Schmitt, Sept. 4, 1902. Assistant organist, 1884-97, organist and choirmaster, July 1897—, Trinity Ch., New York. Home: New York, N.Y. Died Aug. 11, 1921.

BAILEY, Arthur Low, librarian; b. Methuen, Mass., June 29, 1867; s. Frederick Henry and Mary (Low) B.; student Tufts Coll., 1894-96; B.L.S., N.Y. State Library Sch., 1898; m. Mabel Calder Dobbin, Sept. 3, 1903; 1 son, Arthur Chaplin (dec.). Reorganized New Milford Pub. Library, 1898; head of order dept., N.Y. State Library, 1898-1904; librarian Wilmington Inst. Free Library, 1904—; also dir. New Castle County Free Library, 1927—. Mem. Del. State Library Commn.; mem. bd. of review, Wilmington Council Boy Scouts America. Republican. Author: Library Bookbinding, 1916. Home: Wilmington, Del. Deceased.

BAILEY, Bert Heald, zoölogist; b. Farley, Ia., May 2, 1875; s. Turner Smith and Helen (MarGee) B.; B.S., Coe College, 1897, M.S., 1900; M.D., Rush Med. Coll., Chicago, 1900; m. Anna Wright Condit, Dec. 26, 1900. Prof. zoölogy and curator of museum, Coe College, Sept. 1900—. Spent summer of 1905 in zoöl. research in British Honduras. Republican. Presbyn. Mason. Author: 200 Wild Birds of Iowa, 1906. Home: Cedar Rapids, Ia. Died June 23, 1917.

BAILEY, Bertha, educator; b. Albany, N.Y.; d. Rev. William and Mary Loomis (Stark) B.; grad. Albany Girls Acad., 1884; B.S., Wellesley, 1888; unmarried. Teacher of science, Science Hall Sch., Shelbyville, Ky., 1888-90, of science and history, Miss Mittleberger's Sch., Cleveland, 1890-93, of history and mathematics, Ruel Sch., New York, 1893-1900; teacher of history, mathematics, and head of Day Sch., Miss Brown's and Miss Boese's Sch., New York, 1900-02, Miss Stuart's Sch., Pittsburgh, 1902-04; prin. Taconic Sch., Lakeville, Conn., 1904-12; prin. Abbot Acad., Andover, Mass., 1912—. Conglist. Alumnæ trustee of Wellesley College. Died Nov. 16, 1935.

BAILEY, Cassius Mercer, cotton mfr.; b. Clinton, S.C., Nov. 22, 1876; s. Mercer Silas and Rosanna Lydia (Abrams) B.; Presbyn. Coll. of S.C.; A.B., Davidson (N.C.) Coll., 1896; m. Eloise Davenport, Jan. 14, 1902; children—Corinne Davenport (Mrs. Brewer Dixon), Lucy Eloise, Florence Jacobs. Cotton mfg. business, 1896—; pres. and treas. Lydia Cotton Mills, Clinton, S.C. Trustee Clinton Pub. Schs., Presby. Coll. of S.C., Thornwell Orphanage, Clinton. Democrat. Presbyn. Mason. Home: Clinton, S.C. Died July 5, 1935.

BAILEY, Charles Olin, lawyer; b. Freeport, Ill., July 2, 1860; s. Joseph M. (late chief justice Supreme Ct., Ill.) and Anna (Olin) B.; A.B., U. of Rochester, 1880; m. Mary Emma Swan, Mar. 28, 1887; children—Theodore Mead, Charles Olin, Anna Elida (Mrs. John B. Gregg), Joseph Mead (dec.). Admitted to bar, 1882; practiced in Ia. and Ill. and later in S.D.; mayor Eagle Grove, Ia., 1885; dist. atty. Minnehaha Co., S.D., 1889-90; receiver M.R.&N.W. Ry. Co., 1907-11. Mem. Dem. State Central Com., Ia., 1884-85. Mason (33°); grand comdr. K.T. of S.D., 1909-10. Home: Sioux Falls, S.D. Died Dec. 20, 1928.

BAILEY, Charles Reuben, clergyman; b. of Am. parentage at Magog, P.Q., Can., Apr. 19, 1863; s. Charles and Helen Marr (Gale) B.; grad. Newbury (Vt.) Sem., 1880; student Tufts College, 1881-84; grad. Newton Theol. Instn., Newton Centre, Mass., 1886; B.D., Episcopal Theol. School, Cambridge, Mass., 1896; Ph.B., Ill. Wesleyan U., 1887, M.A., 1889, Ph.D., 1892; studied summer, Harvard, 1911; m. Etta Amelia Lord, June 11, 1884 (died 1933); children—William Howard, Ernest Glentworth (dec.). Ordained ministry Bapt. Ch., 1886, serving until 1893; deacon, 1894, priest, 1895, P.E. Ch.; in charge of St. Mary's Ch., Penacook, Concord, N.H., 1893-98, first as lay reader and later as deacon and priest; in charge of St. Andrew's Ch., Manchester, N.H., 1898-1911; rector St. John's Ch., Taunton, Mass., 1911-13, St. Ann's Ch., Revere, 1913-35; for many summers to 1911 in charge St. John's Ch. By-the-Sea, Old Orchard Beach, Me.; in charge Trinity Ch., Hoboken, N.J., summers 1920-29, Grace Ch., Manchester, N.H., summers, 1930—. Republican. Mason. Home: Revere, Mass. Deceased.

BAILEY, Clarence Mitchell, brig. gen. U.S.A.; b. New York, Nov. 26, 1841; ed. pvt. and pub. schs. in Ind. and Pa.; married. Apptd. from Ind., 2d lt. 6th U.S. Inf., Aug. 5, 1861; promoted through grades to col. 16th Inf., Nov. 1, 1898; retired for disability in line of duty, May 5, 1899; advanced to rank of brig. gen. retired, by act of Apr. 23, 1904. Home: Ft. Wayne, Ind. Died May 21, 1920.

BAILEY, Edgar Henry Summerfield, chemist; b. Middlefield, Conn., Sept. 17, 1848; s. Russell B. and Hannah (Miller) B.; Ph.B., Yale, 1873; Ph.D., Ill. Wesleyan, 1883; student Strassburg, 1881, Leipzig, 1895; m. Aravesta Trumbauer, July 13, 1876; children—Kenneth Russell (dec.), Herbert Stevens, William Hotchkiss, Edgar Lawrence, Austin. Instr. in chemistry, Yale, 1873-74, Lehigh U., 1874-83; prof. chemistry and metallurgy, 1883, dir. chem. lab., 1900, U. of Kan., emeritus. Chemist, Kan. State Bd. Agr., 1885—, State Bd. Health, 1899. Presbyn. Author: (with H. P. Cady) Laboratory Guide to Study of Qualitative Analysis, 1901; (with W. R. Crane) Gypsum (Vol. V); Mineral Waters (Vol. VII, Geol. Survey, Kan.); Sanitary and Applied Chemistry, 1906; The Source, Chemistry and Use of Food Products, 1914; Laboratory Experiments on Food Products, 1915; Report on the Dietaries of some State Institutions under the care of the Board of Administration, 1921; (with H. S. Bailey) Foods from Afar, 1922. Home: Lawrence, Kan. Died June 1, 1933.

BAILEY, Edward, corp. official; b. Harrisburg, Pa., Oct. 19, 1861; s. Charles Lukens and Emma Harriet (Doll) B.; grad. Phillips Acad., Andover, Mass., 1878; Ph.B., Yale, 1881; m. Elizabeth Hummel Reily, Oct. 2, 1889; children—Elizabeth Reily (Mrs. Henry M. Gross), Martha (Mrs. Powell Crichton), George Reily. Began career with C. L. Bailey & Co.; vice-pres. Harrisburg National Bank, 1891-92, pres. 1892-1927, chmn. bd., 1927—; pres. Harrisburg Trust Co., 1893-1918, v.p., 1918-26; chmn. bd. Harrisburg Rys. Co.; pres. Williamsport & North Branch Ry. Co. to 1937. Treas. Pa. State Capitol Bldg. Commn.; mem. Pa. Forestry Commn.; pres. Harrisburg Home for the Friendless. Republican. Presbyterian. Home: Harrisburg, Pa. Died Oct. 17, 1938.

BAILEY, E(li) Stillman, physician; b. Little Genesee, N.Y., Sept. 2, 1851; s. James and Tacy (Hubbard) B.; grad. Milton (Wis.) Coll., 1873; M.D., Hahnemann Med. Coll., Chicago, 1878. Practiced Chicago, 1878—; ex-dean Hahnemann Med. Coll. Mem. Am. Inst. Homœopathy. Republican. Seventh-day Baptist. Home: Chicago, Ill. Died Apr. 26, 1926.

BAILEY, Elijah Prentiss, editor; b. Manlius, N.Y., Aug. 15, 1834; s. Wesley (editor of the Liberty Press, anti-slavery paper) and Eunice (Kinne) B.; ed. com. and Latin grammar schs., Utica, N.Y.; (hon. A.M., Colgate U., 1880; LL.D., St. John's Coll. [now Fordham U., New York], 1897); m. Julia S. Wetherby, Sept. 25, 1857 (died 1860); m. 2d, Hannah Chapman, June 24, 1868. City editor, 1853-67, mng. editor, 1867-83, editor-in-chief, 1883—, Utica Observer. Commr. on N.P. R.R., 1886; postmaster Utica, 8 yrs.; sch. commr. 6 yrs.; pres. N.Y. State Civil Service Commn., 1892-94. Pres. State Asso. Press of N.Y., 12 yrs. Home: Utica, N.Y. Died Jan. 17, 1913.

BAILEY, Everett Hoskins, banker; b. Jamestown, N.Y., Apr. 10, 1850; s. Francis Parkman and Caroline (Pier) B.; prep. edn., Erie (Pa.) Acad.; student Antioch Coll., Yellow Springs, O., 1867-70; m. Jeanette L. Jones, June 2, 1874; 1 son, Frederick Stanwood. Bank clerk, Clark & Goodwin, Erie, 1870; clk., First Nat. Bank, St. Paul, 1871; clk. and cashier Second Nat. Bank, Winona, 1872; teller, First Nat. Bank, St. Paul, 1873-80, cashier, 1880-97, v.p., 1897-1906, pres., 1906-18, chmn. exec. com. until retired, 1929; pres. Northwestern Trust Co., 1903-13; treas. St. Paul Union Depot Co., Minn. Transfer Ry. Co. Republican. Unitarian. Home: St. Paul, Minn. Died Nov. 10, 1938.

BAILEY, Frank Harvey, naval officer; b. Cranesville, Pa., June 1851; s. James and Sarah Ann (Hurd) B.; B.S., Scio (Ohio) Coll., 1873; grad. U.S. Naval Acad., 1875; m. Anna J. Markham, Dec. 28, 1881. Commd. asst. engr., July 1, 1877; advanced through grades to capt., July 1, 1908; rear admiral, Feb. 13, 1913; retired on account of age, June 29, 1913. Instr. in marine engring. dept., Cornell U., 1882-85. Served on Raleigh, in Philippine Islands, during Spanish-Am. War and was advanced 3 numbers "for eminent and conspicuous conduct in battle." On duty at Bur. of Steam Engring., Navy Dept., during war with Germany. Republican. Methodist. Home: Gowanda, N.Y. Died Apr. 9, 1921.

BAILEY, Frederick Randolph, physician; b. Elizabeth, N.J., Oct. 26, 1871; s. George W. and Emma M. (Blackman) B.; A.B., Princeton, 1892, A.M., 1895; M.D., Coll. Phys. and Surg. (Columbia), 1895; m. Minnie Josephine Wooden, Dec. 17, 1896. Engaged in practice at Elizabeth, N.J., 1896—; asst. and tutor normal histology, 1895-1901, tutor normal and pathol. histology of nervous system, 1901-02, instr., 1902-03, instr. normal histology, 1903-04, adj. prof. histology and embryology, 1904—, Coll. Phys. and Surg. Home: Elizabeth, N.J. Died Sept. 16, 1923.

BAILEY, George Washington; b. Gloucester Co., N.J., Dec. 5, 1840; s. William and Lydia Low (Densten) B.; State Normal School, Trenton, N.J.; M.D., U. of Pa., 1868; m. Rebecca Hurff, Dec. 10, 1869; m. 2d, Annie Knight McGill, June 18, 1891. Sergt. Co. E, 24th N.J. Vols. Civil War; because of ill health, abandoned practice of medicine, 1872; asso. with William T. Bailey & Co., real estate, 1872-82; entered wholesale coal business on own account, 1882; organized 1894, George W. Bailey Coal Co., and was pres. until 1905 (retired); pres. Overlook Cemetery Co. Trustee Presbyn. Hosp. (Phila.); v.p. W. Jersey Orphanage for Destitute Colored Children (Camden, N.J.); charter mem., trustee Sch. for Christian Workers (Phila.); trustee and v.p. Bd. of Edn., Presbyn. Ch. of U.S.A.; ruling elder Tabernacle Presbyn Ch., Phila., etc.; v. moderator Gen. Assembly Presbyn. Ch. in U.S.A. 1914; mem. Bd. Trustees, Presbyn Ch. in U.S.A. Republican. Home: Philadelphia. Died Dec. 19, 1916.

BAILEY, George Wicks, jurist; b. St. Louis, Mar. 8, 1856; s. Isaiah L. and Sarah Jane (Wicks) B.; ed. country schs., Ill.; m. Belle Jarbeau, Apr. 17, 1883. Admitted to bar, 1885; city atty., Ft. Collins, Colo., 8 yrs.; co. atty., Larimer Co., Colo., 5 yrs.; judge co. ct., Larimer Co., Colo., 4 yrs.; deputy dist. atty., Larimer Co., 7 years; asso. justice Sup. Ct., Colo., 1905—. Republican. Mason. Home: Denver, Colo. Died 1909.

BAILEY, Gilbert Ellis, geologist; b. Pekin, Ill., Apr. 27, 1852; s. Rev. Gilbert Stephen (D.D.) and Sarah Eloise (Bunnell) B.; student U. of Chicago, 1868-72, U. of Mich., 1872-73; Ph.D., Franklin (Ind.) Coll., 1881; m. Martha Cobb, 1876 (died 1879); m. 2d, Reba Boston, 1902. Prof. chemistry, U. of Neb., 1874-79; geologist Wyo. Ty., 1883-87; prof. metallurgy, State School of Mines, S.D., 1888-89; asst., Calif. Mining Bur., 1900, 01; Death Valley explorations, 1901, 02, 03; prof. geology, U. of Southern Calif., 1909—. Republican. Episcopalian. Mason. Author: Saline Deposits of California, 1902; Mines and Minerals of San Bernardino County, California, 1902; California Soils, 1913; the Use of Explosives in Agriculture, 1914; Nitrating by Legumes, 1914; Vertical Farming, 1915; California, A Geologic Wonderland, 1924. Home: Los Angeles, Calif. Died Dec. 6, 1924.

BAILEY, Guy Winfred, college pres.; b. Hardwick, Vt., May 7, 1876; s. John Winthrop and Laura (Cahill) B.; A.B., U. of Vt., 1900; LL.D., U. of Vt., Middlebury Coll., Norwich U., 1921; Vt. Alpha of Phi Beta Kappa; m. Mabel Gertrude Brigham, Dec. 22, 1904. Admitted to Vt. bar, 1904, but never practiced; commr. to edit. pub. statutes of Vt., 1906-07; mem. Vt. Ho. of Rep., 1904-08; sec. of state of Vt., 1908-17; pres. U. of Vt., June 1920—, also comptroller, 1917—. Pres. Kurn Hattin Homes, Westminster, Vt.; v.p. Union Mutual Life Ins. Co. V.p., dir. Mary Fletcher Hosp. Mem. commn. to formulate Employers' Liability and Workman's Compensation Law, 1913, to formulate Uniform System of Accounts for Towns and Villages, 1915. Mem. Vt. State Finance Commn., 1936-37. Republican. Conglist. Mason. Home: Burlington, Vt. Died Oct. 22, 1940.

BAILEY, Hannah Johnston; b. Cornwall-on-Hudson, N.Y., July 5, 1839; d. David and Letitia (Clark) Johnston; father a minister of the Friends Ch.; ed. pub. and pvt. schs.; teacher 10 yrs.; m. Moses Bailey, Oct. 13, 1868 (died 1882). Supt. of Dept. of Peace and Internat. Arbitration, W.C.T.U., 1890—; has traveled extensively in prin. countries of the world, in the interest of the work of the organization; pres. Me. Equal Suffrage Assn., 1891-97; treas. Nat. Council of Women, 1895-99; twice apptd. to represent Me. on Nat. Bd. of Charities and Correction. Mem. Friends' Ch. Home: Winthrop Center, Me. Died Oct. 24, 1923.

BAILEY, Henry Turner, art teacher; b. Scituate, Miss., Dec. 9, 1865; s. Charles Edward and Eudora (Turner) B.; grad. State Normal Art Sch., Boston, 1887; studied abroad, 1898; hon. L.H.D., Denison U., 1925; m. Josephine Litchfield, Sept. 5, 1889. Teacher of drawing, night schs., Boston, 1884-85; supervisor of drawing, City of Lowell, 1886-87; agt. Mass. State Bd. Edn. for the promotion of industrial drawing, 1887-1903; dir. Chautauqua Sch. of Arts and Crafts, 1908-17; editor The School Arts Magazine, Boston, 1903-17; dean Cleveland Sch. of Art and advisor in ednl. work, Cleveland Mus. of Art, 1917-18; dir. Cleveland Sch. of Art, and John Huntington Polytechnic Inst., Cleveland. Author: A First Year in Drawing, 1894; The Blackboard in Sunday School, 1899; School Sanitation and Decoration (with Prof. Severance Burrage), 1899; The Great Painters' Gospel, 1900; The City of Refuge, 1902; Nature Drawing, 1910; The Flush of the Dawn, 1910; Booklet Making, 1912; Twelve Great Paintings, 1913; Art Education, 1914; Photography and Fine Art, 1919; Symbolism for Artists (with Ethel Pool), 1923; The Tree Folk, 1925; The Magic Realm of the Arts, 1928; Yankee Notions, 1929. Home: Cleveland, O. Died Nov. 26, 1831.

BAILEY, Hollis Russell, lawyer; b. North Andover, Mass., Feb. 24, 1852; s. Otis and Lucinda Alden (Loring) B.; A.B., Harvard, 1877, A.M., 1879; LL.B., Harvard Law Sch., 1878; m. Mary Persis Bell, Feb. 12, 1885 (died 1930); m. 2d, Eliza Winifred Campbell, Feb. 27, 1931. Admitted to Mass. bar, 1880; chmn. Mass. Bd. of Bar Examiners, 1903-31; chmn. Mass. Bd. of Commrs. on Uniform State Laws. Democrat. Unitarian. Home: Boston, Mass. Died Nov. 29, 1934.

BAILEY, James Anthony, showman; b. Detroit, July 4, 1847; orphaned in childhood; worked on farm summers, attended school winters; became connected with Robinson & Lake show; with the Nashville Tenn., Theater, 1863; later sutler's clerk with 114th Ohio regt. Re-entered show business after war; partner in 1873 in show which became known, 1875, as the Cooper & Bailey circus, which went to Australia, 1876; consolidated with P. T. Barnum, 1881, firm soon after becoming Barnum & Bailey; became sole owner after death of Mr. Barnum; bought the Adam Forepaugh show after Mr. Forepaugh's death, Jan. 1891; has several times taken show to London, and also to Germany, Austria, Hungary, Holland, Belgium, Switzerland, France and nearly all the cities of Continental Europe. Died 1906.

BAILEY, James Garfield, clergyman; b. Scranton, Pa., Feb. 22, 1882; s. John and Harriet Orinda (Armstrong) B.; B.A., Colgate, 1905; B.D., Union Theol. Sem., 1909; m. Katharine M. Brothers, June 15, 1910; 1 dau., Katharine F. Ordained Presbyn. ministry, 1909; asst. pastor, Lafayette Av. Ch., Brooklyn, N.Y., 1909-11; pastor West Side Ch., Englewood, N.J., 1911-19; asso. field dir. New Era Movement, Presbyn. Ch. U.S.A., 1919-23; dir. field activities Gen. Council, Presbyn. Ch. U.S.A., 1924-26; editor Presbyterian Magazine, 1926—; also instr. Union Theol. Sem. Y.M.C.A. hosp. chaplain Camp Merritt, 1918-19. Home: New York, N.Y. Died Jan. 4, 1929.

BAILEY, John Mosher, lawyer; b. Bethlehem, N.Y., Aug. 24, 1838; grad. Union Coll., 1861; m. Dell L. Hooker, Sept. 21, 1864; entered army, 1862; adj. 177th N.Y. vols.; in dept. of Gulf, battle of Amite River, Pouchatula and siege Port Hudson; asst. dist. atty., 1865-67, dist. atty., 1874-77, Albany County, N.Y.; mem. Congress, 1877-81; U.S. consul Hamburg, Germany, 1881-85; del. Nat. Rep. Conv., 1888; surveyor of customs, port of Albany, 1889-94. Home: Albany, N.Y. Died 1902.

BAILEY, Joseph Weldon, senator; b. Copiah County, Miss., Oct. 6, 1863. Admitted to bar, 1883; presdl. elector from Miss., 1884; removed to Gainesville, Tex., 1885; presdl. elector-at-large, 1888; mem. 52d to 56th Congresses (1891-1901); caucus nominee of Dem. party for speaker, 55th Congress; U.S. senator for terms 1901-07 and 1907-13, resigned 1912, and resumed law practice. Home: Dallas, Tex. Died Apr. 13, 1929.

BAILEY, Loring Woart, geologist; b. West Point, N.Y., Sept. 28, 1839; s. Prof. Jacob Whitman and Maria (Slaughter) B.; brother of William Whitman B.; A.B., Harvard, 1859, A.M., 1861; (hon. Ph.D., U. of N.B., Can., 1873; LL.D., Dalhousie, N.S., 1896; m. Laurestine M. d'Avray, Aug. 19, 1863. Prof. chemistry and natural science, 1861-1901, biology and geology, 1901-06, U. of N.B.; retired under Carnegie Foundation. Dir. Marine Biol. Sta. of Can., 1909. Author: Mines and Minerals of New Brunswick, 1864; Geology of Southern New Brunswick, 1870; Elementary Natural History, 1887. Home: Fredericton, N.B. Died 1925.

BAILEY, Mercer Silas, banker, cotton mfr.; b. nr. Clinton, S.C., Nov. 9, 1841; s. Silas M. and Margaret (Beaseley) B.; ed. common schs.; m. Rosanna Lydia Abrams, Nov. 10, 1860 (died 1898); children—Joseph Abrams, Putsy Silas (dec.), William James, Toccoa Mars, Emma Floride, Cassius Mercer, Mary Ellen. Mem. James Battalion, Civil War. Entered mercantile business on own account, at Clinton, 1865, and in 1870, started milling business; founder, 1886, Bailey's Bank of Clinton, later M. S. Bailey & Son, bankers, of which became pres.; founder and pres. Clinton Cotton Mills, and Lydia Cotton Mills. Trustee Thornwell Orphanage, Clinton. Democrat. Presbyn. Home: Clinton, S.C. Died Feb. 19, 1926.

BAILEY, Morton Shelley, judge; b. Wellsboro, Pa., July 3, 1855; s. John W. and Margaret (Lewis) B.; A.B., Lafayette Coll., 1880, A.M., 1883; m. Lutie Wilkin, Sept. 1, 1888. Admitted to Colo. bar, 1882; practiced at Fairplay, Colo., 1882-92; mem. Colo. Senate, 1890-92; judge 11th Jud. Dist., 1892-1908; justice Supreme Ct., 1908-26. Candidate for gov., 1896. Democrat. Home: Denver, Colo. Died May 16, 1922.

BAILEY, Solon Irving, astronomer; b. Lisbon, N.H., Dec. 29, 1854; s. Israel C. and Jane (Sutherland) B.; A.B., Boston U., 1881, A.M., 1884; A.M., Harvard, 1888; (Sc.D. and hon. prof. astronomy, U. of San Agustin, Peru, 1923); m. Ruth Poulter, 1883; 1 son, Irving Widmer. Sent to Peru, S.A., to investigate conditions there in order to determine best location for a southern sta. for Harvard Coll. Obs., 1889; examined west coast from equator to Southern Chili, resulting in selection of Arequipa, Peru; in charge of work there, 1892—; established meteorol. sta. on summit of El Misti, at 19,000 feet elevation, where observations were carried on for 10 yrs., by far the highest scientific sta. in world, 1893; various other meteorol. stas. have been placed in Peru; asst. prof. astronomy, 1893-98, asso. prof., 1898-1913, Phillips prof., 1913-25, acting dir. observatory, 1919-22, Harvard, emeritus. In 1908 visited S. Africa and carried on astron. observations on elevated plateau in northern part of Cape Colony. Home: Cambridge, Mass. Died June 5, 1931.

BAILEY, Warren Worth, congressman; b. Hendricks County, Ind., Jan. 8, 1855; s. Elisha and Elizabeth (Faught) B.; pub. sch. edn.; m. Georgiana Coffin, Aug. 12, 1894; children—Marion Louise, Warren Worth. Learned telegraphy, later printer's trade, in office of Kansas (Ill.) News; editor Carlisle (Ind.) Democrat, 1877-78, Vincennes News, 1879-87; on staff Daily News, Chicago, 1887-93; pub. Johnstown (Pa.) Democrat, 1893—. Candidate for Congress on Dem. ticket, 1906; del. at large, from Pa. to Dem. Nat. Conv., 1912; mem. 63d, 64th and 69th Congresses (1913-17, 1925-27), 19th Pa. Dist. Advocate of single tax; editor first single tax paper—Vincennes News; del. from Ill. to first nat. single tax conf., New York, 1890; pres. Chicago Single Tax Club, 1887-93; pres. Single Tax Club of Cambria County, Pa. Author: Our Manners and Social Customs, 1890. Home: Johnstown, Pa. Died Nov. 9, 1928.

BAILEY, William Whitman, botanist; b. West Point, N.Y., Feb. 22, 1843; s. Prof. Jacob Whitman and Maria (Slaughter) B.; brother of Loring Woart B.; entered Brown U., 1860; pvt. 10th R.I. Vols., 1862; returned to Brown and grad, 1864, Ph.B., 1873 (A.M., 1893; LL.D., U. of N.B., 1900); studied botany, Columbia, 1872, Harvard Summer Sch., 1875, 1876, 1879; m. Eliza R. Simmons, Mar. 14, 1881. Asst. in chemistry, Mass. Inst. Tech., 1866; asst. chemist, Manchester (N.H.) Print Works, 1866; botanist U.S. Geol. Survey of 40th parallel, 1867-68; deputy sec. of State, R.I., 1868; asst. librarian Providence Athenæum, 1869-71; taught botany pvt. schs., Providence; instr. botany, 1877-81, prof., 1881-1906, prof. emeritus, 1906—, Brown U.; spl. beneficiary of Carnegie Foundation, 1906. Sec. bd. visitors, U.S. Mil. Acad., 1896; del. centennial, U. of N.B., 1900, U.S. Mil. Acad. centennial, 1902; dir. Providence Athenæum, 1900-03. Author: Botanical Collector's Handbook, 1881; Among Rhode Island Wild Flowers, 1885; Botanical Note-Book, 1894; New England Wild Flowers, 1897; Botanizing, 1899; Poems, 1910. Home: Providence, R.I. Died Feb. 20, 1914.

BAILEY, Willis J., gov., banker; b. Carroll Co., Ill., Oct. 12, 1854; ed. Mt. Carroll High Sch., and U. of Ill., 1879 (LL.D., 1904); removed to Nemaha Co., Kan., 1879, and engaged in farming and stock raising; m. Mrs. Ida B. Weed, June 9, 1903. Mem. Kan. State Bd. Agr., 1895-99, Kan. Ho. of Rep., 1888; pres. Rep. State League, 1893; mem. 56th Congress (1899-1901), Kan. at-large; gov. of Kan., 1903-05. Governor Fed. Reserve Bank of Kansas City, 1922-32. Home: Kansas City, Mo. Died May 19, 1932.

BAILHACHE, Preston Heath, surgeon; b. Columbus, O., Feb. 21, 1835; s. Judge John and Elizabeth H. (Heath) B.; ed. Shurtleff Coll., Alton, Ill., St. Xavier U., St. Louis; M.D., Pa. Med. Coll., Phila., 1857; m. Mary L. Goodwin, Oct. 5, 1871. Asst. surg. Camp Yates, Springfield, Ill., Apr. 17, 1861; asst. surg. 19th Ill. Vol. Inf., July, 1861; surg. 14th Ill. Cav., Feb. 14, 1863, serving through war; captured on Stoneman's raid, July 31, 1864; exchanged Sept. 3, 1864; practiced medicine in Ill. and later was asso. editor Quincy (Ill.) Whig, until apptd. to U.S. Marine Hosp. Service (which became U.S.P.H.S.), 1873; surgeon, retired, 1909. Assisted in revising regulations of the service, 1873; mem. Nat. Bd. Health, 1879-85, and selected nat. quarantine stas. for the Bd., 1880. Died Oct. 28, 1919.

BAILIE, Earle, investment banking; b. Milwaukee, Wis., Sept. 17, 1890; s. John and Cornelia Purdy (Conklin) B.; A.B., U. of Minn., 1912; LL.B., Harvard, 1915, S.J.D., 1916; m. Margaret Iselin Henderson, June 11, 1923; children—David Henderson, Susanah Conklin, Joanna De Peyster. Admitted to N.Y. bar, 1916; with Cravath & Henderson, 1916-17 and 1919; with J. W. Seligman & Co., 1919—, partner, 1923—; chmn. bd. Tri-Continent Corp., Selected Industries Co., Broad St. Investing Corp., Capital Administrations, General Shareholdings, Union Securities Corp. Spl. fiscal asst. U.S. Treasury Dept., 1933. Served in U.S. Army, 1917-18, retiring as capt. F.A.R.C. Home: Wilton, Conn. Died Nov. 15, 1940.

BAILIE, Virginia, painist and piano teacher; b. Marshall, Mich., Feb. 3, 1867; d. James D. and Emma V. B.; ed. Marshall, Mich.; pupil in music of C. N. Colwell, Marshall; Max. Pinner, New York; William Mason, New York; Georges Mathias, Paris, and Theodore Leschetizky, Vienna. Home: New York, N.Y. Died 1906.

BAILIE, William Lamdin, naval officer; b. Baltimore, Dec. 15, 1843; s. William and Mary B. B.; ed. by pvt. tutelage and spl. studies mech. engring.; m. Harriet K. McCowen, Feb. 16, 1887. Entered engr. corps U.S.N., Jan., 1863; served through Civil War and was in active service until retired for injuries in line of duty, June, 1885. In scientific work, U.S. Fish Commn., 1882-85; dir. depts. Mechanic Arts, Science and Technology; Drexel Inst., Phila., 1892-1904. Gold medal and diploma of honor for work in deep-sea research from Internat. Fisheries Commn., London. For service in U.S.N. during Civil War, advanced to the grade of chief engr. retired, June 29, 1906, by act of Congress. Died Dec. 27, 1912.

BAILLY-BLANCHARD, Arthur, diplomat; b. New Orleans, Oct. 1, 1855; s. T. Jr., and Jeanne Eliza (Field) B.; ed. Lavender's Coll., New Orleans, and in Paris and Dresden; studied law, U. of La. Clerk La. state assessors, 1878-80; asst. editor Le Petit Journal, New Orleans, 1880-81; with Mexican Central Ry., 1882-83; col. and a.-d.-c. to gov. of La., 1885; pvt. sec. to minister to France, 1885-89; asst. to spl. agt. Dept. of State, French Spoliation Claims; sec. U.S. Commn. to Paris Expn., 1889; pvt. sec. to U.S. minister to France, 1890-93; a sec., Behring Sea Tribunal of Arbitration, 1893-95; a sec. bimetallic mission to France, 1896; sec. to Hon. John W. Foster, spl. ambassador to Russia, 1897; attaché, Am. Peace Commn., Paris, 1898; pvt. sec. to ambassador to France, 1899-1900; a sec., Hague Peace Conf., 1907; apptd. 3d sec. of Embassy, at Paris, 1900, 2d sec., 1901, sec. 1909; del. and minister plenipotentiary to Internat. Sanitary Conf., Paris, 1911; apptd. sec. of Embassy, Tokyo, Japan, 1912; E.E. and M.P. to Haiti, May 22, 1914. Democrat. Cathlic. Died Aug. 22, 1925.

BAILY, Elisha Ingram, army officer; b. in Pa., Nov. 14, 1824. Apptd. from Pa., asst. surgeon, Feb. 16, 1847; capt. asst. surgeon, Feb. 16, 1852; maj. surgeon, May 15, 1861; lt. col. surgeon, June 26, 1876; col. surgeon, Jan. 30, 1883; retired, Nov. 14, 1888; advanced to rank of brig. gen. retired, Apr. 23, 1904. Bvtd. lt. col., Mar. 13, 1865, for services during the war. Died 1908.

BAILY, Joshua L., mcht.; b. Philadelphia, June 27, 1826; s. Joshua and Elizabeth (Lloyd) B.; m. Theodate Lang, 1856. Entered dry goods store at 16; became sr. mem. Joshua L. Baily & Co., Phila. and New York. Pres. Phila. Soc. for Employment and Instrn. of the Poor, Phila. Fountain Soc.; original mem. Com. of 100, 1879; mem. Nat. Relief Commn. during Spanish-Am. War. Home: Ardmore, Pa. Died Dec. 7, 1916.

BAIN, Charles Wesley, college prof.; b. Portsmouth, Va., June 24, 1864; s. George M. and Willie Frances (Cherry) B.; ed. U. of Va., and U. of the South, M.A., 1895; (LL.D., U. of South Carolina, 1913); m. Isabel Plummer, Dec. 28, 1891. Teacher Savannah (Ga.) Acad., 1885-87, pvt. sch., Savannah, 1887-89; joint head master, Rugby Sch., Louisville, Ky., 1900-01; first classical master, McCabe's Univ. Sch., Petersburg, Va., 1889-90, 1891-95; head master, Sewanee (Tenn.) Grammar Sch., 1895-98; prof. ancient langs., S.C. Coll., 1898-1910; prof. Greek, U. of N.C., 1910—. Author: Bain's First Latin Book (Gildersleeve-Lodge Series), 1898. Editor: Homer's Odyssey, Book VI, 1895, Book VII, 1898; Select Poems of Ovid, 1902. Home: Chapel Hill, N.C. Died Mar. 15, 1915.

BAIN, George Washington, lecturer; b. Lexington, Ky., Sept. 24, 1840; s. George W. and Jane (West) B.; ed. Hutchison Sch., Bourbon Co., Ky., 1848-58; m. Anna M. Johnson, Aug. 30, 1860. Chautauqua lecturer and lyceum lecturer, 1880—. Grand counselor, Good Templars of Ky., 1870-75, grand chief templar, 1875-80; editor Riverside Weekly, 1873-77. Home: Lexington, Ky. Died Mar. 28, 1927.

BAIN, Robert Edward Mather, photographer; b. Chicago, Aug. 9, 1858; s. George and Clara (Mather) B.; Washington Univ., 1868-75; m. Mary Valle, Nov. 3, 1880; children—Marie Zoé (Mrs. C. B. R. Fitz-William), Mrs. Catherine Bennett, George Vallée, Marguerite Desolge (Mrs. C. Henry Adams), Lucie Clara (Mrs. John B. Furstenberg), dec. Mem. Mo. House of Representatives, 1884-86; gen. passenger mgr. for the Southwest, Internat. Mercantile Marine Co., 1903-25; retired. Well known amateur photographer; traveled through lower Egypt, Palestine, Turkey, Greece and Italy for the purpose of illustrating Earthly Footsteps of the Man of Galilee and the Self-Interpreting Bible, etc. As a means of recreation operates a motor-run shop in which has constructed 9-foot model of Steamship New York (in Chicago Mus. of Science and Industry), 6-foot model of 1890 type locomotive operative under steam, 30-inch model of tugboat Conestoga, fitted with power and lights (both in Smithsonian Instn.). Home: St. Louis, Mo. Died May 22, 1932.

BAINBRIDGE, Alexander Gilbert, mayor; b. Pittsburgh, Pa., Sept. 4, 1885; s. Alexander Gilbert and Ida Prescott (Stewart) B.; student Central High Sch., Pittsburgh; m. Marie Gale, Aug. 27, 1917; children—Alexander Gale, Thomas Roger. Advertising agt. with Forepaugh-Sells Circus, 1903-05, Barnum-Bailey Circus, 1906-08, 101 Ranch (Wild West Show), 1909-10; lessee and mgr. Shubert Theatre, Minneapolis, 1911-33; also mgr. travelling road shows for E. J. Carpenter, Henry W. Savage and Messrs. Shubert, 1903-11; pres. and gen. mgr. Bainbridge Players, Inc. Mayor of Minneapolis, term 1933-35. Lt. field arty., with A.E.F., World War. Republican. Presbyn. Mason. Home: Minneapolis, Minn. Died Mar. 14, 1936.

BAINBRIDGE, Lucy Seaman (Mrs. William Folwell Bainbridge); b Cleveland, Jan. 18, 1842; d. John and Cleora A. (Stevens) Seaman; ed. Cleveland high sch., Cleveland Sem.; grad. Ipswich (Mass.) Sem.; m. Rev. William Folwell Bainbridge, Sept. 5, 1866. During Civil War served with Potomac Div. at the front, helping wounded; active for many years in philanthropic and social work; organized woman's dept. of Brooklyn City Mission Soc.; supt. woman's branch N.Y. City Mission Soc. about 20 yrs., (hon. supt.). Republican. Baptist. Author: Round the World Letters, 1882; Helping the Helpless, 1917; Jewels from the Orient, 1920; Yesterdays, 1924. Home: New York, N.Y. Died Nov. 19, 1928.

BAIRD, Absalom, brig. gen. U.S. Army (retired, 1888); b. Washington, Pa., Aug. 20, 1824; grad. Washington Coll., 1841; studied law; grad. West Point, 1849; m. Cornelia W. Smith, Oct. 17, 1850 (dec.). Served in Florida, 1850-53; asst. prof. mathematics West Point, 1853,59; served during Civil war in Va., Tenn., and in the march to the sea; became bvt. maj. gen.; after war, insp. general. Died 1905.

BAIRD, Andrew D., banker; b. Kelso, Scotland, Oct. 14, 1839; s. Andrew Baird; m. Mary Warner, 1866; m. 2d, Catherine Lamb, 1882. Apprenticed to stone cutter's trade; became mem. Gill & Baird, stone cutters, 1867. Pres. Williamsburg Savings Bank, Andrew D. Baird & Sons. Enlisted in 79th N.Y. Vols., May 13, 1861, serving throughout Civil War; comdr. 79th N.Y. Vols., May 1864. Twice candidate for mayor of Brooklyn. Pres. Industrial Sch. of Brooklyn; dir. Brooklyn Pub. Library. Republican. Home: Brooklyn, N.Y. Died Sept. 4, 1923.

BAIRD, David, senator; b. County Derry, Ireland, Apr. 7, 1839; orphaned in boyhood; came to U.S., 1856; m. Christiana Beatty, Jan. 23, 1868 (dec.); children—Mrs. Mary Fox (dec.), Irvine Beatty, Mrs. Christianna Humphreys, David. Engaged in lumber business, 1873—; pres. David Baird Co.; chmn. bd. First Nat. State Bank, Security Trust Co. Mem. Bd. Chosen Freeholders, Camden Co., 1876-80; sheriff Camden Co., 1887-89 and 1895-97; mem. State Bd. Assessors, 1895, and 1901-09 (ex-pres. bd.); presdl. elector, 1900; candidate for U.S. senator, 1910; apptd. U.S. senator, Feb. 23, 1918, to succeed William Hughes, deceased; elected U.S. senator for short term, Nov. 1918 and served until Mar. 4, 1919. Republican. Home: Camden, N.J. Died Feb. 25, 1927.

BAIRD, Frank Burkett, iron mfr.; b. Marietta, O., Nov. 24, 1852; s. Samuel and Mary (Steece) B.; m. Flora Cameron, Nov. 21, 1900; children—Frank Burkett, Cameron, William Cameron. In coke, pig iron industry, 1876; organized Buffalo Furnace Co., 1892, Union Iron Works, 1898, Buffalo Charcoal Iron Co., 1899, and consolidated same, 1900, as Buffalo Union Furnace Co.; pres. Buffalo & Ft. Erie Public Bridge Co. (builders of "Peace Bridge," completed 1927). Dir. U. of Buffalo, Nichols Sch. Awarded Norton Medal, U. of Buffalo, 1927. Republican. Episcopalian. Mason. Home: Buffalo, N.Y. Died Nov. 15, 1939.

BAIRD, George Washington, rear admiral U.S.N.; b. Washington, Apr. 22, 1843; s. Matthew and Ophelia (Cauthorn) B.; ed. in pub. schs. and acad.; m. Miss L. J. Prather, 1873. Apptd. 3d asst. engr. U.S.N., Sept. 19, 1862; promoted through grades and retired with rank of rear admiral, Apr. 22, 1905. Pres. Bd. of Edn., Washington. Protestant. Mason. Home: Washington, D.C. Died Oct. 4, 1930.

BAIRD, George William, army officer; b. Milford, Conn., Dec. 13, 1839; s. Jonah Newton and Minerva (Gunn) B.; grad. Hopkins Grammar School, New Haven, 1859; entered Yale, 1859 (given diploma with class of 1863); m. Julia C. Rogers, July 31, 1866. Served in Civil War as pvt. Aug. 25, 1862 to Mar. 18, 1864; promoted from pvt. to col. 32d U.S. colored troops; served in S.C., Ga. and Fla., battles St. John's Bluff, Honey Hill, Deveaux' Neck, James Island, Siege of Charleston, Morris Island, S.C. Entered regular army May 11, 1866, as 2d lt. 19th inf., transferred Sept. 21 to 37th inf.; promoted 1st lt. Apr. 27, 1867; transferred to 5th inf. May 19, 1869; served on Western frontier from Tex. to Mont. and in Indian campaigns, Mar. 1867, to July 1878; left field wounded; adj. 5th inf. and adj. gen. of Gen. N. A. Miles's field commands Jan. 1, 1871, to June 23, 1879; twice recommended for bvts. for gallant services in action; received medal of honor "for most distinguished gallantry in action against hostile Nez Percé Indians at Bear Paw Mountain, Mont., Sept. 30, 1877, where he was twice severely wounded"; promoted maj. and paymaster U.S.A., June 23, 1879; lt. col. and deputy paymaster gen., July 12, 1899; brig. gen, U.S.A., Feb. 19, 1903; on duty as chief disbursing officer, paymaster-gen.'s office, Apr. 1899-Feb. 1903. Wrote "Gen. Miles's Indian Campaigns," The Century, July 1901. Home: Milford, Conn. Died 1906.

BAIRD, Henry Carey, publisher; b. Frankford Arsenal, Phila., Sept. 10, 1825; s. Capt. Thomas J. (U.S.A.) and Eliza C. (Carey) B.; acad. edn.; m. Elizabeth D., d. John Penington, Sept. 1850 (died 1901). Actively engaged in pub. business many yrs.; head of Henry Carey Baird & Co., Phila. Disciple of the "Carey Sch." philosophy of statesmanship; in early life a Whig; Republican, 1865; left party after Civil War but supported Blaine as a protectionist, 1884; later no polit. affiliations; was expert witness before 2 coms. of U.S. Ho. of Rep., and before U.S. Monetary Commn., 1876, on silver. Author (pamphlets): John Sherman—A Critical Examination of His Claims to Statesmanship, 1907; American and English Banking Contrasted, 1908; The Supreme Court of the United States on the Law of Association, 1911; Mr. Champ Clark as a Philosopher, 1911, and others. Home: Wayne, Pa. Died Dec. 31, 1912.

BAIRD, Henry Martyn, prof. Greek N.Y. Univ., 1859—; b. Phila., Jan. 17, 1832; grad. N.Y. Univ., 1850; studied U. of Greece, Athens, 1851-52 (Ph.D., 1867; LL.D., 1882, Coll. of N.J.; D.D., 1877, Rutgers; L.H.D., 1896, Princeton); m. Susan E. Baldwin, Aug. 15, 1860. Author: Modern Greece, 1856; Life of Rev. Robert Baird, D.D. (his father), 1866; Rise of the Huguenots of France, 1879; The Huguenots and Henry of Navarre, 1886; The Huguenots and the Revocation of the Edict of Nantes, 1895; Theodore Beza, the Counsellor of the French Reformation, 1899. Home: Yonkers, N.Y. Died 1906.

BAIRD, Jean Katherine, author; b. Renovo, Pa., Mar. 12, 1872; d. William Preston and Mary Tamson (Hughes) B.; grad. Lock Haven State Normal Sch., 1889; spl. studies at State Normal, Ada U., Ohio, and under pvt. instrs.; spl. work U. of Pa., Randolph-Macon Woman's Coll.; A.B., A.M., Pa. State Coll. Taught in pub. and normal schs. Presbyn. Author: Danny, 1905; Cash Three, 1905; The Honor Girl, 1906; Little Rhody, 1907; Elizabeth Hobart at Exeter Hall, 1907; Second 65, On Time, 1909; The Coming of Hester, 1909; The Boy Next Door, 1910; Hester's Counterpart, 1910; The Heir of Baracah, 1911; Hester's Wage-Earning, 1912; That Little Girl of Miss Eliza's, 1915; The Girl Beautiful, 1917. Home: Beaver, Pa. Died Apr. 20, 1918.

BAIRD, John Wallace, psychologist; b. St. Marys, Ont., Can., May 21, 1873; s. Charles and Agnes (Browning) B.; A.B., U. of Toronto, 1897; student, U. of Leipzig, 1898; fellow in psychology, U. of

Wis., 1899-1901, Cornell U., 1901-02, Ph. D., 1902; m. Barbara Morrison Sparks, 1914. Instr. in psychology Cornell U., 1902-1903; research asst. in psychology, Carnegie Foundation, 1903-04; instr. psychology, Johns Hopkins, 1904-06; asst. prof. psychology, U. of Ill., 1906-10; asst. prof. psychology, 1910-13, prof., 1913—, Clark U. Exec. editor Am. Jour. of Psychology; coöperating editor Psychol. Bull., Jour. of Applied Psychology, and Jour. of Ednl. Psychology. Home: Worcester, Mass. Died Feb. 2, 1919.

BAIRD, Julian William, chemist; b. Battle Creek, Mich., Feb. 14, 1859; s. Abram Henry and Sarah Elizabeth (Wagoner) B.; A.B., U. of Mich., 1882, A.M., Ph.C., 1883; M.D., Harvard, 1890; m. Hattie Bell Ellinwood, Oct. 25, 1897. Asst. chem. analysis, U. of Mich., 1882-83; instr. qualitative chem. analysis and assaying, Lehigh U., 1883-86; prof. analytical and organic chemistry, 1886—, and dean, 1895—, Mass. Coll. of Pharmacy. Home: Boston, Mass. Died 1911.

BAIRD, Phil(ander) C(astor), clergyman; b. DeWitt, Ia., May 7, 1863; s. Andrew Henderson and Isabel W. (Castor) B.; Normal Sch., Paola, Kan.; A.B., Amity Coll., College Springs, Ia., 1891, A.M., 1895; B.D., Xenia (O.) Theol. Sem., 1894; Ph.D., U. of Chicago, 1898; (D.D., Amity, 1901); m. Ida May Pollock, 1892. Ordained U.P. ministry, 1898; pastor 1st Ch., Burlington, Ia., 1898-1900, 1st Ch., Ft. Dodge, 1900-07, 1st Presbyn. Ch., Oklahoma City,, 1907—(membership increased from 500 to 2,400 and $150,000 building erected). Republican. Lecturer. Home: Oklahoma City, Okla. Died Feb. 12, 1923.

BAIRD, Raleigh William, M.D.; b. Shreveport, La., Apr. 9, 1870; s. William Leroy and Mary Eleanor (Law) B.; A.B., Southwestern U., Georgetown, Tex., 1893; M.D., Bellevue Med. Coll. (New York U.), 1896; spl. studies St. Bartholomew Hosp., London, Eng., 1898; m. Lavinia Starley Bishop, Nov. 8, 1900; children—Sara Bishop, Mary Eleanor, Raleigh William and Horace Bishop (twins). Physician Bellevue Hosp., 1896-98, practiced at Dallas, Tex., 1900—; pres. Dallas Med. and Surg. Clinic, 1915—; dir. Dallas Surg. Investment Co.; prof. clinic medicine, Med. Dept. Baylor U. Home: Dallas, Tex. Died July 13, 1941.

BAIRD, William Raimond, lawyer; b. Phila., Apr. 24, 1858; s. William J. and Mary Emma (Cornish) B.; M.E., Stevens Inst. Tech., 1878; LL.B., Columbia Coll. Law Sch. and Sch. of Polit. Science, 1882; m. Jennie G. Mansfield, Sept. 29, 1886. Practiced in New York, 1883—; mem. Baird, Cox, Kent & Campbell. Lecturer on patents and patent law, Stevens Inst. Tech. Pres. Coll. Fraternity Pub. Co.; sec. Fraternity Pub. Co., etc. Republican. Methodist. Author: American College Fraternities, 8th edit., 1915; Principles of American Law, 3d edit., 1893; Study of Languages; Fraternity Studies, 1894; Handbook of Beta Theta Pi, 1907, 2d edit., 1912; Betas of Achievement, 1914. Home: New York, N.Y. Died Mar. 15, 1917.

BAKER, Albert C., judge; b. at Girard, Ala., Feb. 15, 1845; s. Benjamin H. and Eliza B.; student E. Ala. Male Coll.; m. Mary Alexander, Feb. 2, 1881. In practice at Phoenix, Ariz., 1879—; was city atty., Phoenix; dist. atty., Maricopia Co.; asst. U.S. atty.; mem. Ariz. Ho. of Rep.; chief justice Ariz., 1893-97. Democrat. Home, Phoenix, Ariz. Died Aug. 31, 1921.

BAKER, Albert Rufus, ophthalmologist; b. Salem, Pa., Mar. 24, 1858; s. Benjamin Franklin and Sabina (Pershing) B.; M.D., Western Reserve U., 1879; post-grad. New York and London, Berlin, Vienna, Paris, 1881-83; m. Emily L. Shackleton, Dec. 16, 1885. Prof. ophthalmology, otology and laryngology, 1888—, chmn. faculty, 1898-1902, Cleveland Coll. Phys. and Surg. Editor Cleveland Med. Gazette, 1885-96. Author: Coughs, Cold and Catarrh, 1904. Home: Cleveland, O. Died 1911.

BAKER, Alfred Brittin, clergyman; b. Matawan, N.J., Aug. 11, 1836; s. Elihu O. and Joanna (Butler) B.; A.B., Princeton, 1861, A.M., 1864; grad. Gen. Theol. Sem., 1864; (D.D., Princeton, 1891); m. Emila J. Stubbs, Apr. 22, 1867 (died 1913). Deacon, 1864, priest, 1865, P.E. Ch.; asst. minister Christ Ch., New Brunswick, 1864-65; rector Trinity Ch., Princeton, 1866-1914. Dean Convocation of New Brunswick, 1888-1910; sec. Diocesan Conv. 20 yrs.; pres. standing com. Diocese of N.J., 1890—; deputy to Gen. Conv., 1889-1907; mem. Archives Commn. and Court of Review; dean of the Cathedral of the Diocese, 1919—. Trustee Burlington Coll. and St. Mary's Hall, Burlington, N.J. Home: Princeton, N.J. Died July 30, 1928.

BAKER, Alfred Landon, broker; b. Nova Scotia, Can., where parents, of Boston, were temporarily visiting, Apr. 30, 1859; s. Addison and Maria (Mudge) B.; grad. Lynn (Mass.) High Sch., 1876; studied law in office of George W. Smith, Boston; admitted to Essex County bar, 1881; m. Mary Corwith, June 5, 1894; children—Isabelle (Mrs. Robert M. Curtis), Mary Landon. Practiced at Lynn, 1881-86 (Baldwin & Baker); was mem. city council, and sch. bd.; removed to Chicago, 1886; mem. Baker & Greely until 1895, retired; then in banking and brokerage business; sr. mem. Alfred L. Baker & Co., 1896—; v.p. Nat. City Bk., 1907-21. Pres. trustees Lake Forest U., 1906, 1907; trustee and treas. Chicago Bur. Public Efficiency. Mem. Chicago Stock Exchange (pres. 1898-1900), Chicago Bd. of Trade, N.Y. Stock Exchange. Died Mar. 23, 1927.

BAKER, Archibald Eachern, M.D., surgeon; b. Red Banks, N.C., Aug. 29, 1862; s. Angus Sellers and Harriet (McEachern) B.; ed. Davidson (N.C.) Coll., 1879-83; M.D., Med. Coll. State of S.C., 1889; m. Adele Jennings, Feb. 22, 1894; children—Archibald E., Barnwell Rhett, Frances Adele (dec.), Angus Sellers, Robert Jennings. Practiced at Charleston, S.C., 1889—; specialized in surgery, 1907—; owner, pres. and surgeon in charge Baker Sanatorium, 1912—; clin. prof. gynecology and abdominal surgery, Med. Coll. State of S.C., 1913—. Democrat. Presbyn. Mason. Home: Charleston, S.C. Died July 31, 1934.

BAKER, Arthur Latham, mathematician; b. Cincinnati, May 7, 1853; s. John G. and Mary A. (Latham) B.; C.E., Rensselaer Poly. Inst., 1873; studied U. of Göttingen, 1896; hon. Ph.D., Lafayette Coll., 1889; m. Elizabeth Coit, d. Rev. Aaron H. Hand, Sept. 26, 1878; 1 dau., Dorothy (Mrs. J. Roy Allen). Adjunct prof. civ. engring., Lafayette Coll., 1873-80; atty. at law, Scranton, Pa., 1880-89; prin. high sch., Scranton, 1882; editor Common Pleas Reporter and Weekly Digest, Scranton, 1885-87; prof. of mathematics, Stevens High Sch., Hoboken, N.J., 1889-91, U. of Rochester, 1891-1901; head of dept. of mathematics, Manual Training High Sch., Brooklyn, 1901-17. Author: Annual Digest Pennsylvania Supreme Court Decisions, 1886-87; Graphic Algebra, 1892; Elliptic Functions, 1890; Solid Geometry, 1893; Conic Sections, 1893; The Art of Geometry, 1905; Quaternions as the Result of Algebraic Operations, 1910; Elementary Thick-lens Optics, 1911; Micrometry for the Amateur Microscopist, etc. Died 1934.

BAKER, Arthur Mulford, clergyman, editor; b. Wapakoneta, O., Oct. 11, 1880; s. John Mulford and Alice Maria (Arthur) B.; A.B., Defiance (O.) Coll., 1906; grad. McCormick Theol. Sem., 1909; studied Columbia U. and Ind. U.; Ph.D., Ind. U., 1928; m. Glenna Maude Helser, June 20, 1907; children—Margaret (Mrs. Arthur M. Adams), Daniel Arthur. Ordained Presbyn. ministry, 1909; pastor various chs., 1908-24; asst. editor Am. S.S. Union Publs., 1924-30, editor, 1930—. Chaplain 120th Inf., U.S. Army, with A.E.F., 1918-19; capt. Co. K, 151st Ind. N.G., 1923-24; chaplain O.R.C. Author: If I Were a Christian, 1930; Hoofbeats in the Wilderness, 1930; The River of God, 1930. Died Sept. 22, 1941.

BAKER, Asa George, publisher; b. Milwaukee, Wis., Sept. 27, 1866; s. Orlando Merriam and Abbie Maria (Walton) B.; A.B., Amherst, 1888, Litt.D., 1935; m. Lucy Cynthia Chamberlain, Sept. 8, 1892; children—Walton Chamberlain, Ingham Chamberlain, Orlando Merriam (dec.), Frederic Allen. Began with G. & C. Merriam Co., pubs. Webster's dictionaries, Springfield, Mass., 1888, successively in charge editorial work, one of managers, vice-pres. and pres., 1922-34, chmn. bd., 1934—. Republican. Conglist. Home: Springfield, Mass. Died Sept. 10, 1940.

BAKER, Asher Carter, naval officer; b. Matawan, N.J., Dec. 18, 1850; s. Elihu and Charlotte (Carter) B.; grad. U.S. Naval Acad., 1871; m. Mary Elizabeth Reese, Feb. 10, 1880. Served on various ships; served 3 yrs. on deep-sea investigations for U.S. Fish Commn.; commr. to Mexico for Chicago Expn. and later supt. marine div., Transportation Dept., same; connected with Transportation Exhibits Dept. of U.S. Commn. to Paris Expn., 1900; decorated Order of Legion of Honor; asst. chief Dept. Transportation, St. Louis Expn., 1904; dir. exhibits and chief, dept. transportation exhibits, Panama-Pacific International Expn., San Francisco, 1915. Capt. U.S.N. and retired, June 30, 1905. Called to active duty, Apr. 3, 1917, and in France to July 1, 1919; dep. dir. gen. of transportation and dir. of ports, on staff Gen. Pershing. Died June 5, 1926.

BAKER, Benjamin Webb; b. Coles Co., Ill., Nov. 25, 1841; on farm until 1861; served through war, 1861-65, was wounded several times; grad. Ill. State Normal Univ., 1870; A.M., Ph.D., Ill. Wesleyan U.; D.D., Chaddock Coll.; m. Miss M. F. Henry, Dec. 14, 1871. Joined Central Ill. Conf., M.E. Ch., 1874; pastor Denver, 1881-83; presiding elder, 1885-89; financial sec. Ill. Wesleyan U., 1889-93; pres. Chaddock Coll., 1893-98; pres. Mo. Wesleyan Coll., 1898-1908. Died June 20, 1909.

BAKER, Bernard Nadal, capitalist; b. Baltimore, May 11, 1854; s. Charles Joseph and Elizabeth B.; ed. Sheffield Scientific Sch. (Yale); m. Elizabeth Elton Livezey, Dec. 27, 1877. President Atlantic Transport Line; pres. Baltimore Trust & Guarantee Co.; pres. Atlantic & Pacific Transport Co.; dir. numerous commercial enterprises. Trustee Johns Hopkins U.; mem. Nat. Joint Com. on Conservation; mem. Moral Edn. Bd. and actively interested in moral edn. Apptd. mem. U.S. Shipping Bd., Dec. 1916 (resigned). Author: Ships (with J. F. Essary), 1916. Home: Catonsville, Md. Died Dec. 20, 1918.

BAKER, Charles Fuller, zoölogist; b. Lansing, Mich., Mar. 22, 1872; s. Maj. Joseph Stannard and Alice (Potter) B.; B.S., Mich. Agrl. Coll., 1892; A.M., Stanford U., 1903; m. Ninette Evans, Aug. 29, 1894. Asst. in zoölogy, Mich. Agrl. Coll., 1891-92; asst. to zoölogist and entomologist, Colo. Agrl. Coll., 1892-97; zoölogist, Ala. Poly., and entomologist, Expt. Sta., 1897-99; teacher biology, Central High Sch., St. Louis, 1899-1901; asst. prof. biology, Pomona Coll., Calif., 1903-04; chief dept. botany, Estacion Agron. de Cuba, 1904-07; curator Bot. Garden and Herbarium, Museu Goeldi, Para, Brazil, 1907-08; dir.-elect Campo de Cultura Experimental Paraense, 1908; asso. prof. biology, 1908-09, prof., Sept. 1908-June 1912, Pomona Coll., Claremont, Calif.; prof. agronomy, U. of the Philippines, July 1912—. In charge Colo. zoöl. and forestry exhibit, Chicago Expn., 1893; zoölogist and asso. botanist, Ala. Biol. Survey, 1897-98; botanist, H. H. Smith exploring expdn. in Santa Marta Mountains, Colombia, S.A., 1898-99; also conducted field explorations in Southern Ill., Wis., Colo., N.M., Nev., Calif., Nicaragua, Cuba and Brazil. Pub. Invertebrata Pacifica. Home: Los Banos, P.I. Died 1927.

BAKER, Charles Hinckley, civil engr.; b. Chicago, Nov. 30, 1864; s. William T. and Eliza A. (Dunster) B.; C.E., Cornell, 1886; m. Gladys France, June 13, 1888. Resident engr. C.,B.&Q. Ry., C.,R.I.&P. Ry., and C.&N.-W. Ry., 1884-87; resident engr. Seattle, Lake Shore & Eastern Ry., 1887-90; civil engr. and contractor, 1890-95; receiver Merchants' Nat. Bank, Seattle, 1895-98. Built 3d St. and Suburban Ry., Seattle; organized and completed Snoqualmie Falls Power Co. (now Seattle-Tacoma Power Co.), transmitting, electrically, 19,000 h.-p. 30 miles to Seattle and 44 miles to Tacoma, 1898, also White River Power Co.; promoter reclamation Fla. Everglades; pres. Westchester—Putnam Co. Life Soc. Del. Dem. Nat. Conv., 1896; bolted and started Gold Dem. movement in State of Wash. Owner Mohegan Holstein and Knickerbocker farms, Moore Haven, Fla. Home: Mohegan Lake, N.Y. Deceased.

BAKER, Charles Whiting, civil engr.; b. Johnson, Vt., Jan. 17, 1865; s. Thomas Jefferson and Mattie (Whiting) B.; ed. Vt. State Normal Sch.; C.E., U. of Vt., 1886; m. Rebekah Wheeler, June 4, 1890. Editor-in-chief The Engineering News, 1895-1917; in real estate brokerage business, 1920-26; mem. Baker, Simonds & Co., investment bankers, 1926—. Commr. Palisades Interstate Park, 1913—. Author: Monopolies and the People, 1889, 99. Home: Montclair, N.J. Died June 5, 1941.

BAKER, Charles William; b. Bedford, O.; Nov. 11, 1862; s. George Allen and Sarah Gertrude (Bartlett) B.; A.B., Harvard, 1884; m. Frances Anne Chandler, Nov. 12, 1895. Admitted to Ohio bar, 1886. Entered employ Carnegie, Phipps & Co., Ltd., 1889, later Carnegie Steel Co., Ltd., of Pittsburgh, of which became jr. partner, 1899; moved to N.Y. City, 1895; mgr. of sales there for Carnegie Steel Co. and later for Ill. Steel Co. and Tenn. Coal, Iron & R.R. Co.; resigned, 1910; became v.p. Am. Zinc, Lead & Smelting Co., 1915, later pres., chmn. bd., 1917-28, retired. Mem. Zinc Com. Nat. Council of Defense, World War. Home: New York, N.Y. Died Aug. 8, 1938.

BAKER, Chauncey Brooke, army officer; b. Lancaster, O., Aug. 26, 1860; s. Emanuel Ruffner Peter and Eliza (Stoneberger) B.; grad. U.S. Mil. Acad., 1886; honor grad. Inf. and Cav. Sch., Ft. Leavenworth, Kan., 1889 (B.S., Ohio State U., 1904); m. Lucy, d. Gen. Alexander McD. McCook, U.S.A., June 19, 1889 (died 1923); m. 2d, Ella Turner, Dec. 1924 (died 1932); m. 3d, Emily Burr, Oct. 3, 1934. Commd. 2d lt. 7th Infantry, July 1, 1886; advanced through grades to col. q.m. dept., U.S.A., May 15, 1917; brig. gen. N.A., Aug. 5, 1917; retired from active service April 21, 1921. Regtl. officer and a.-d.-c. at frontier posts, 1886-98; depot q.m., Havana, 1898-1900; chief, q.m., Havana, Aug. 1900-May 1902; various assignments in q.m. dept. to 1914; duty Office Q.M. Gen., 1914-16; sr. mem. Mil. Commn. to France, May-July 1917; chief embarkation service, Office Chief of Staff, War Dept., Aug. 7, 1917-Feb. 1918. Presbyn. Mason. Author: Notes on Fire Tactics, 1889; Transportation of Troops and Material, 1905; Handbook of Transportation by Rail and Commercial Vessels, 1916; Coordination between the Transportation Companies and the Military Service, 1916. Chairman bd. Market Exchange Bank Co., Columbus; chmn. bd. Am. Nat. Fire Ins. Co. Home: Bexley, O. Died Oct. 18, 1936.

BAKER, Cornelia, author; b. Jackson Co., O., June 16, 1855; d. William and Electa McGhee; M.E.L. (Mistress English Literature), Wesleyan Coll., Cincinnati, 1871; m. Wilson G. Baker, Sept. 15, 1874. Contributor short stories, verse, etc., to mags., 1904—. Author: Coquo and the King's Children, 1902; The Queen's Page, 1905; Young People in Old Places, 1906; The Court Jester, 1906; The Magic Image from India, 1909. Home: Chicago, Ill. Died Mar. 12, 1930.

BAKER, Darius, judge; b. Yarmouth, Mass., Jan. 18, 1845; s. Braddock and Caroline (Crowell) B.; A.B., Wesleyan U., Conn., 1870, A.M., 1873 (LL.D.,

1906); m. Annie Barker, Oct. 30, 1878 (died 1886); children—Hugh Barkly, George Yelverton (dec.); m. 2d, Bertha A. Neales, Oct. 8, 1891; children—Dorothy Neales, Alfred Colebrooke, Margaret Medley. Served in 5th Regt., Mass. Vol. Militia, Civil War, 1862, 63; admitted to bar of State of Conn., 1874; judge of probate, Newport, R.I., 1877-98; municipal justice, 1879-86; justice 1st Dist. Ct., 1886-1905; justice Superior Ct., 1905-13, justice Supreme Ct., Jan. 31, 1913-Mar. 13, 1919, resigned. Was mem. sch. com., 1877-83 (last 2 yrs. chmn.); trustee Newport Hosp., 1884-96, Wesleyan U., 1887-1912; pres. Charity Organization Soc., 1894—. Home: Newport, R.I. Died Mar. 19, 1926.

BAKER, Elbert H., newspaperman; b. Norwalk, O., July 25, 1854; s. Henry and Clara Maria (Hall) B.; ed. pub. schs.; m. Ida A. Smith, June 1, 1876; children—Mrs. Louise Hastings, Frank Smith, Catherine Hovey (dec.), Elbert Hall, Jr., Alton Fletcher. Began work on Cleveland Herald, 1877; advertising mgr. Cleveland Leader, 1882-97; gen. mgr. Cleveland Plain Dealer, 1898-1920, and pres. Plain Dealer Publishing Co., 1913-29, then chmn. bd.; joint owner, with son, Frank S., of the Morning and Sunday Ledger, and the News-Tribune, Tacoma, Wash.; joint owner with son, Alton F., of Register Guard, daily newspaper, Eugene, Ore. Dir. Asso. Press, 1910—; dir. Am. Newspaper Pubs. Assn., 1907-24 (pres. 1912-14). Trustee Euclid Av. Congl. Ch.; trustee Cleveland Y.M.C.A. (treas. since 1925). Home: South Euclid, O. Died Sept. 27, 1933.

BAKER, Elizabeth Gowdy (Mrs. D. B. Baker), portrait painter; b. Xenia, O.; d. George W. and Ellen (Johnson) Gowdy; ed. Monmouth (Ill.) Coll., Cooper Union and Art Students League (New York), Pa. Acad. Fine Arts (Phila.), Cowles Sch. (Boston), Rome, Florence and Paris; m. D(aniel) B. Baker; 1 son, Munford. Exhibited at Boston Art Club, Nat. Arts Club (New York), Nat. Acad. Women Painters, Art Inst. Chicago, etc. Pres. The Aquarellists. Home: Palm Beach, Fla., and Lake Placid, N.Y. Died Oct. 11, 1927.

BAKER, Francis Elisha, judge; b. Goshen, Ind., Oct. 20, 1860; s. John Harris (q.v.) and Harriet (Defrees) B.; student Ind. U., 1876-78; A.B., U. of Mich., 1882 (LL.D., 1914); lit. editor University Chronicle, 1879-82; m. Mary Irwin, Feb. 21, 1888. Admitted to bar, 1885; practiced at Goshen, with father, firm Baker & Baker, 1885-92, Baker & Miller, 1892-99; judge Supreme Ct., Ind., 1899-1902; U.S. Circuit judge, 7th Circuit, Feb. 4, 1902—. Home: Goshen, Ind. Died Mar. 15, 1924.

BAKER, Frank, judge; b. Melmore, O., May 11, 1840; s. Richard and Fanny (Wheeler) B.; A.B., Ohio Wesleyan U., 1861; LL.B., Albany Law Sch., 1863; m. Eliza Warner, Nov. 10, 1870. In practice in Chicago, 1873-87; judge Circuit Ct. of Cook Co., 1887—; assigned to Appellate Ct. of 1st Dist. of Ill., June 1904. Democrat. Home: Chicago, Ill. Died July 9, 1916.

BAKER, Frank, anatomist; b. Pulaski, N.Y., Aug. 22, 1841; s. Thomas C. and Sybil S. (Weed) B.; sergt. 37th N.Y. Vols., 1861-63; M.D., Columbian (now George Washington) U., 1880; A.M., Georgetown U., 1888, Ph.D., 1890 (LL.D., 1914); m. May E. Cole, Sept. 13, 1873. Prof. anatomy, Georgetown, 1883—; supt. Nat. Zoöl. Park, 1890-1916. Asst. supt. U.S. Life Saving Service, 1889-90; editor Am. Anthropologist, 1891-98. Has contributed anat. articles to Wood's Reference Handbook of the Medical Sciences, Standard Dictionary, Internat. Cyclopedia. Home: Washington, D.C. Died Sept. 30, 1918.

BAKER, George Bramwell, banker; b. Warsaw, Ind., Dec. 7, 1866; s. Joseph Schoonover and Angeline Rebecca (Runyan) B.; B.S., De Pauw U., 1887; m. Edith Kelley Thomas, Apr. 27, 1892; children—Eleanor Thomas (Mrs. Warren D. Arnold), Virginia Carol (Mrs. David B. Arnold). Began in State Bank, Warsaw, 1888, later in Chicago, Cleveland, New York, and settled in Boston, 1898; formerly mem. Baker, Young & Co., estab. 1902. Trustee Boston U. Mem. bd. of overseers Boys Club of Boston; dir. Boys Club Fedn. of America, Soc. for Prevention of Cruelty to Children, Met. Red Cross (Boston). Episcopalian. Mason. Home: Chestnut Hill, Mass. Died May 2, 1937.

BAKER, George Danielson, Presbyn. clergyman; b. Watertown, N.Y., Nov. 30, 1840; s. Josiah W. and Abigail B. (Bates) B.; preparatory edn., Mount Washington Collegiate Inst., New York; grad. Univ. City of New York; Princeton Theol. Sem. (D.D., Olivet Coll., Mich.); m. Gertrude F. Magie, Nov. 30, 1864. Consecutively pastor Stone St. Presbyn. Ch., Watertown, N.Y.; Presbyn. Ch., Oneida, N.Y.; 1st Presbyn. Ch., Detroit; 1st Presbyn. Ch., Phila.; pres. Bd. Edn. of Presybn. Ch. in U.S.A.; pres. bd. directors Princeton Theol. Sem.; pres. Christian League of Phila.; pres. Pa. Bible Soc. Home: Philadelphia. Died 1903.

BAKER, George Fisher, banker; b. N.Y. City, Mar. 19, 1878; s. George Fisher and Florence T. (Baker) B.; A.B., Harvard, 1899; m. Edith Brevoort Kane, Oct. 14, 1911; children—Florence T., Edith B., George F., Grenville K. Chmn. bd. 1st Nat. Bank, New York; dir. numerous corps.; trustee Mutual Life Ins. Co., United States Trust Co., The Frick Collection. Trustee New York Pub. Library; trustee Am. Museum Natural History, N.Y. Zoöl. Society, etc. Head of Am. Red Cross Commn. to Italy, with rank of lt. col., 1917. Republican. Unitarian. Home: New York, N.Y. Died May 30, 1937.

BAKER, George Fisher, banker; b. Troy, N.Y., Mar. 27, 1840; s. George E. B.; m. Florence Tucker Baker (dec.). Chmn. bd. First Nat. Bank of New York, Jan. 1909—, (ex-pres.) First Security Co.; pres. N.Y. & Long Branch R.R. Co.; v.p. Jersey City Water Supply Co.; dir. numerous companies; trustee Mut. Life Ins. Co., Consol. Gas Co., and many other corps. Mem. exec. com. N.Y. Chamber of Commerce. Mem. Met. Mus. of Art, Am. Fine Arts Soc., N.E. Soc., etc. Presented Regault's famous painting "Salome," to Met. Mus. Art, 1916. Home: New York, N.Y. Died May 2, 1931.

BAKER, George Hall, librarian; b. Ashfield, Mass., Apr. 23, 1850; s. George and Mary (Grover) Hall; adopted by Mr. Baker and assumed his name; A.B., Amherst, 1874, A.M., 1878; U. of Berlin, 1876-78; m. Ellen E. Adkins, July 14, 1875. Lecturer on bibliography, 1884-89, librarian-in-chief, 1889-99, librarian emeritus, 1899—, Columbia. Writer on art topics. Editor-in-chief of Cosmo Collection, 1908. Home: New York, N.Y. Died 1911.

BAKER, George Pierce, college prof.; b. Providence, R.I., Apr. 4, 1866; s. Dr. George Pierce and Lucy Daily (Cady) B.; A.B., Harvard, 1887; Litt.D., Allegheny Coll., Pa., 1915; hon. A.M., Yale U., 1925; L.H.D., Williams Coll., 1930; LL.D., U. of Del., 1931; m. Christina Hopkinson, Aug. 16, 1893; children—John Hopkinson, Edwin Osborne, Myles Pierce, George Pierce. Instr. English, 1888-89, forensics, 1889-92, instr. English, 1892-95, asst. prof., 1895-1905, prof., 1905-24, Harvard; prof. history and technique of drama, Yale, 1925-33. Hyde lecturer at the Sorbonne, Paris, France, 1907-08. Mem. Am. Acad. Arts and Letters, Nat. Inst. Arts and Letters; fellow Am. Acad. Arts and Sciences. Dir. of The 47 Workshop, Harvard, to 1924, of University Theatre, Yale, 1925—; author and dir. the Pilgrim Spirit, Mass. Tercentenary Pageant, Plymouth, Mass., July-Aug. 1921. Author: The Principles of Argumentation (with H. B. Huntington), 1895, 1905; The Development of Shakespeare as a Dramatist, 1907; Technique of the Drama, 1915. Editor: Specimens of Argumentation, 1893; The Forms of Public Address, 1904; Belles Lettres Series, Section III (The English Drama); Some Unpublished Correspondence of David Garrick, 1907; The Correspondence of Charles Dickens and Maria Beadnell. Also various Elizabethan plays; Plays of the 47 Workshop, series I-IV; Yale One-act Plays, I; Yale Long Plays, 4 vols. Home: Silver Lake, N.H. Died Jan. 6, 1935.

BAKER, George Randolph; b. Randolph, N.B., Can., Dec. 20, 1871; s. Charles Parker and Hannah Amanda (Shaw) B.; A.B., Cornell U., 1896; grad. Rochester Theol. Sem., 1899; D.D., Lake Forest U., 1922, Acadia U., 1925, Denison U., 1934; m. Kate Hopper, Feb. 20, 1895; children—Ruth Ada (dec.), Kathrine (dec.), Charles Parker. Came to U.S., 1891, naturalized citizen, 1910. Ordained Bapt. ministry, 1896; successively pastor Ft. Plain, N.Y., Leominster, Mass., and Ithaca, N.Y., until 1920; asso. sec. Bd. of Edn., Northern Bapt. Conv., 1920-39. Trustee Keystone Junior Coll.; corporator Peddie School. Mem. bd. of mgrs. of Bd. of Edn. of Northern Bapt. Conv. Republican. Home: New York, N.Y. Died summer 1941.

BAKER, George Titus, civ. engr.; b. Iowa Co., Ia., July 9, 1857; s. Albert Watson and Freelove Malicent (Kenyon) B.; prep. edn., Hall's Sch. for Boys, Ellington, Conn., McClain's Acad., Iowa City, Ia.; student State U. of Ia., Cornell U., 1875-79; m. Clara I. Poole, Apr. 1879 (died 1919); children—Ethel (Mrs. L. H. Brandt), Georgia E. (Mrs. R. E. Risley), Sue A. (dec.). Division engr., C.,R.I.&P. Ry., 1879-85; locating and constrn. engr. A.,T.& S.F. Ry., 1886-88; chief engr., Soo & Southwestern Ry., 1888-89; chief engr. Muscatine (Ia.) High Bridge, also Clinton (Ia.) High Bridge, and cons. engr., Winona (Minn.) High Bridge, 1889-91; mgr. and chief engr., Edwards & Walsh Constrn. Co., also Tri-City Constrn. Co., 1892-1912; v.p. Clinton St. Ry. Co., Choctaw Lumber Co. Mem. Ia. Ho. of Rep., 1896-98; mayor of Davenport, 1898-1900; mem. Ia. State Bd. Edn., 1909—; apptd. mem. Ry. Emergency Bd. by President Coolidge, Oct. 1928. Democrat. Episcopalian. Home: Davenport, Ia. Died Dec. 13, 1940.

BAKER, Harvey Humphrey, judge; b. Brookline, Mass., Apr. 11, 1869; s. James and Harriet M. (Humphrey) B.; A.B., Harvard, 1891, A.M., LL.B., 1894; unmarried. Practiced at Boston, 1894—; mem. firm of Hayes, Williams, Baker & Hersey. Justice of Boston Juvenile Ct., July, 1906—. Home: Brookline, Mass. Died Apr. 10, 1915.

BAKER, Henry Dunster, b. Attleboro, Mass., Feb. 26, 1873; s. William T. B.; A.B., Yale, 1896; m. Miss Griffiths, 1 dau., Valerie. Connected with editorial depts. Chicago Tribune, New York Evening Post and Commercial West, Minneapolis, to 1904; in spl. lit. work, 1904-07; consul at Hobart, 1907-10; spl. duty in New Zealand to investigate trade conditions, 1910-11; consul at Nassau, 1912-13; spl. detail to investigate opportunities for extension of commerce of U.S. in India, 1913; consul at Bombay, 1913-14; apptd. commercial attaché, Dept. of Commerce, Oct. 3, 1914, and designated for duty at Am. Embassy, Petrograd; consul at Trinidad, W.I., 1916-27; resigned to become publisher and editor of the Commercial West, Minneapolis. Home: Minneapolis, Minn. Died Sept. 13, 1939.

BAKER, Henry Moore, lawyer; b. Bow, N.H., Jan. 11, 1841; s. Aaron W. and Nancy (Dustin) B.; A.B., Dartmouth, 1863, A.M., 1866; LL.B., Columbian (now George Washington) U., 1866; (LL.D., Howard U., 1911); unmarried. Pvt. U.S. Treasury Guards, 1864-65; admitted to D.C. bar, 1866, Supreme Ct. of U.S., 1882; began practice in Washington, 1874; judge advocate gen. with rank of brig. gen., N.H. N.G., 1886-87; mem. N.H. Senate, 1891-92; mem. 53d and 54th Congresses (1893-97), 2d N.H. Dist.; mem. N.H. Constl. Conv., 1902; mem. N.H. Ho. of Rep., 1905-07, 1907-09. Pres. trustees Pembroke Acad., 1904—; trustee Howard U., 1906-12; pres. trustees of Mary Baker G. Eddy and her executor. Home: Concord, N.H. Died May 30, 1912.

BAKER, Herbert, chmn. bd. Vacuum Oil Co.; b. Brooklyn, N.Y., Sept. 1866; s. Boaz and Sarah L. (Cornell) B.; ed. pub. schs., Brooklyn; unmarried. With Standard Oil Co., 1881-1906; with Vacuum Oil Co., 1906—, asst. comptroller, 1906-12, treas., 1912-28, dir., 1918—, v.p., 1928-30, vice chmn. bd., 1930-31, chmn. bd., 1931-32; vice chmn. bd. Socony-Vacuum Corp., 1931-32. Home: New York, N.Y. Died July 4, 1939.

BAKER, Herbert Abram, pres. Am. Can Co., b. Harmony, Ont., Can., Aug. 27, 1881; s. John Henry and Mary Emma (Pickell) B.; came to U.S., 1906, naturalized, 1934; A.B., U. of Toronto, 1906; hon. D.S., Colgate, 1933; m. Ethel L. Andem, July 5, 1918; children—Janet H., Katherine Eleanor. Chemist, Chem. Reduction Co., Niagara Falls, 1906; with Am. Can Co. successively as chemist, Central dist. sales mgr., v.p. in charge of sales, 1908-36; pres., 1936—. Chemical tin plate apportionment commission, U.S. Food Adminstrn., 1917-18. Republican. Home: Scarsdale, N.Y. Died Nov. 25, 1940.

BAKER, Ira Osborn, civil engr.; b. Linton, Ind., Sept. 23, 1853; s. Hiram Walker and Amanda (Osborn) B.; B.S., U. of Ill., 1874, C.E., 1877 (D. Eng., 1903); m. Emma Burr, Aug. 5, 1877 (died 1911); m. 2d, Angie Ewing Ritter, Aug. 7, 1913. Assistant in civil engineering and physics, 1874-78, instr. civil engineering, 1878-80, asst. prof., 1880-82, prof., 1882—, U. of Illinois. Author: Leveling, 1886; Treatise on Masonry Construction, 1889, 1899, 1909; Engineer's Surveying Instruments, 1891; Treatise on Roads and Pavements, 1903, 13, 18. Home: Urbana, Ill. Died Nov. 8, 1925.

BAKER, Isaac Post; b. Weston, Mo., July 20, 1855; s. John Finley and Malvina (Frayne) B.; ed. Central Coll., Fayette, Mo.; m. Julia Franklin Barnes, Jan. 10, 1889; children—Benton, Frayne, Julia Franklin, Finley, Anne, Weston. Engaged in transportation business on Ohio, Mississippi and Missouri rivers, at St. Louis; moved to Dak. Ty., 1880, and served for many yrs. as supt. Benton Transportation Co., with hdqrs. at Bismarck, also identified with banking, farming and commercial interests of the Northwest. Mayor of Bismarck, 1890-91; mem. Dem. Nat. Com., 1892-96; mem. bd. dirs. Nat. Rivers and Harbors Congress, 1907—; pres. N.D. Agrl. Expn., 1915; fed. fuel administrator of N.D., 1917-19; commr. for N.D. to Sesquicentennial, Phila., 1926. Mem. M.E. Ch., S. Was awarded gold medal for grass seed, alfalfa and hay, St. Louis World's Fair, 1904. Home: Bismarck, N.D. Died Jan. 28, 1938.

BAKER, J. Thompson, congressman; b. Union Co., Pa.; student Bucknell U., Lewisburg, Pa., studied law with Judge Joseph C. Bucher; m. Margaret Elizabeth Bordner. Admitted to Pa. bar, and practiced over 30 yrs.; pres. Union Nat. Bank, Lewisburg, 12 yrs.; now pres. Wildwood Title and Trust Co.; with brothers founded Wildwood and borough of Wildwood Crest, N.J.; chmn. Dem. State Conv., Pa., 1905; 1st mayor consolidated city of Wildwood, 1911-12; del. Dem. Nat. Conv., Baltimore, 1912; mem. 63d Congress (1913-15), 2d N.J. District. Home: Wildwood, N.J. Died Dec. 7, 1919.

BAKER, James Addison, lawyer; b. Huntsville, Tex., Jan. 10, 1857; s. James Addison and Rowena B.; grad. Texas Mil. Inst., Austin; m. Alice Graham, Jan. 10, 1883. Admitted to bar, 1880; since then in practice at Houston; sr. mem. Baker, Botts, Andrews & Wharton. Home: Houston, Tex. Died Aug. 2, 1941.

BAKER, James Barnes, architect; b. Elizabeth, N.J., 1864; s. Henry Martyn and Susan Virginia (Barnes) B.; brother of William Edgar B.; grad. Lafayette Coll., 1884; studied civ. engring.; not married. Has erected Hanover, Johnston, Bank of Commerce, Presbyterian, United Charities, Chamber of

Commerce and other important bldgs. in New York and elsewhere. Mem. Am. Inst. Architects. Died June 3, 1918.

BAKER, James Heaton, soldier; b. Monroe, O., May 6, 1829; s. Henry and Hannah Woodruff (Heaton) B.; A.B., Ohio Wesleyan U., 1852, A.M., 1851; m. Rose Lucia Thurston, 1851 (died 1873); 2d, Zula Bartlett, Dec. 23, 1879. Sec. of State of Ohio, 1854-56; elected sec. State of Minn., 1857; re-elected, 1861 (resigned to enter army, 1861); commd. col. 10th Minn. Vol. Inf., Nov. 16, 1862; served with Gen. H. H. Sibley in Indian War, 1862-63; ordered to Mo., 1862; placed in command of post of City of St. Louis under Gen. Schofield; provost marshal, Dept. of Mo., under Gen. G. M. Dodge; bvtd. brig.-gen. vols., March 13, 1865, "for faithful and meritorious services"; mustered out of service, Oct. 21, 1865. U.S. commr. of pensions under Pres. Grant, 1871-75; surveyor-gen. of Minn., 1875-79; state railroad commr., 1881-86. Purchased, 1879, The Union and Record, Republican newspapers, Mankato, Minn., combined the two and formed the Mankato Free Press, of which was editor and pub. for several yrs. Methodist. Author: The Lives of the Governors of Minnesota, 1908. Home: Mankato, Minn. Died May 27, 1913.

BAKER, James Hutchins, univ. pres.; b. Harmony, Me., Oct. 13, 1848; s. Wesley and Lucy (Hutchins) B.; A.B., Bates Coll., 1873 (LL.D., 1892); m. Jennie V. Hilton, June 20, 1882. Prin. high sch., Denver, 1875-92; pres. U. of Colo., 1892-1914, emeritus. Originated the plan which led to report of "Nat. Com. of Ten" on secondary edn. in the U.S. Pres. Nat. Council of Edn., 1892, Nat. Assn. of State Univs., 1907; chmn. Com. of Nat. Council of Edn. on Economy of Time in Edn.; mem. committees on university standards, etc. Author: Elementary Psychology, 1890; Education and Life, 1900; American Problems, 1907; Educational Aims and Civic Needs, 1913; American University Progress and College Reform Relative to School and Society, 1916; After the War—What?, 1918; Of Himself and Other Things, 1922. Home: Denver, Colo. Died Sept. 10, 1925.

BAKER, James Marion, diplomat; b. Lowndesville, S.C., Aug. 18, 1861; s. Theophilus and Mandeline (Latimer) B.; student Wofford Coll., Spartanburg, S.C., 1879-80; m. Mary Adams, Jan. 26, 1888; children—James Marion, Lawrence Adams, Mac Latimer. Asst. librarian U.S. Senate, Aug. 7, 1893-Apr. 13, 1913, compiler of numerous govt. publs. in Senate Library; elected sec. U.S. Senate, Apr. 13, 1913; dep. commr. Internal Revenue Bur., U.S. Treasury Dept., July 19, 1919-Feb. 28, 1921; connected with law office of Lawrence A. Baker, Washington, D.C., Feb. 28, 1921-Oct. 15, 1931; Am. minister to Siam, by apptmt. of President Roosevelt, Sept. 7, 1933; owing to ill health resigned, Mar. 17, 1937. Mason. Died Nov. 21, 1940.

BAKER, Jehu, congressman; b. Fayette County, Ky., Nov. 4, 1822; ed. common schools and McKendree Coll. (hon. A.M. and LL.D.); studied medicine, then law, and was admitted to the bar; Master in Chancery, St. Clair County, 1861-65; mem. Congress, 1865-69, 1887-89; U.S. minister Venezuela, 1878-81 and 1882-85; elected to Congress for term 1897-99, as nominee of People's party and Democrats. Home: Belleville, Ill. Died 1903.

BAKER, John Harris, judge; b. Parma Twp., Monroe Co., N.Y., Feb. 28, 1832; ed. Ohio Wesleyan U. (A.M., 1879, A.B., 1894); admitted to bar, 1857; m. Harriet Defrees; father of Francis Elisha B. In practice at Goshen, Ind., 1857-92; mem. Ind. Senate, 1862; mem. 44th to 46th Congresses (1875-81); U.S. dist. judge, Dist. of Ind., 1892-1902; resigned. Republican. Address: Goshen, Ind. Died Oct. 21, 1915.

BAKER, Joseph Dill, banker; b. Buckeystown, Md., Apr. 2, 1854; s. Daniel and Ann Catherine (Finger) B.; Calvert Coll., Carroll Co., Md., 1870-71; m. Emma N. Cunningham, Nov. 13, 1877 (died 1883); children—William (dec.), Daniel (dec.), Holmes D.; m. 2d, Virginia Markell, June 12, 1890; 1 dau., Charlotte M. Organized Montgomery Co. (Md.) Nat. Bank, 1883, Citizens Nat. Bank, Frederick, Md., 1886, Peoples Nat. Bank, Leesburg, Va., 1888 (became pres. of each); formerly pres. Citizens Nat. Bank, now chmn. bd.; refunded bonded indebtedness of Frederick, 1888; served as a receiver Chesapeake & Ohio Canal, 1890; leader in erection of Y.M.C.A. Bldg., Frederick, 1906-07. Pres. Frederick County Chapter Am. Red Cross, World War, also chmn. Selective Service bd. of Frederick County and chmn. Liberty Loan Com. Frederick County. Trustee Frederick Female Sem., Frederick Home for the Aged; a founder and dir. Buckingham Sch.; mem. Goodnow Commn., 1915, apptd. to prepare bills for Md. Legislature, among them the budget bill. Democrat. Methodist. Mason. Home: Frederick, Md. Died Oct. 6, 1938.

BAKER, Lawrence Simons, agt. Seaboard Air Line; b. Gatesville, N.C., May 15, 1830; s. Dr. John and Mary (Wynns) B.; grad. West Point, 1851; m. Elizabeth Earl Henderson, March 13, 1855. Apptd. 2d lt. U.S.A., resigned as 1st lt. mounted rifles, U.S.A., 1861. Apptd. col. 1st N.C. cav., May 20, 1861; brig. gen., Aug. 1, 1863; severely wounded—right arm shattered, Aug. 1, 1863, at battle of Brandy Station; in command eastern dept., N.C., from June 1864 until close of Civil War. Home: Suffolk, Va. Died 1907.

BAKER, Lucien, U.S. Senator, lawyer; b. Fulton Co., O., 1846; shortly afterward removed with parents to Mich.; began to practice law at Leavenworth, Kan., 1869; U.S. senator, 1895-1901. Republican. Home: Leavenworth, Kan. Died 1907.

BAKER, Lucius K., lumberman; b. Kelloggsville, Ashtabula Co., O., Aug. 16, 1855; s. Edward P. and Paulina (Bloss) B.; ed. country schs. and Grand River Inst., Austinburg, O.; m. May C. Foster, June 26, 1882 (died 1890); 1 dau., Helen Foster (Mrs. Austin Jenner). Connected with Thomas R. Lyon, agt. lumber mfrs., Ludington, and engaged in various pursuits there, 1874-96; associated with others, 1893, in organizing the J. S. Stearns Lbr. Co., Odanah, Wis., was sec., treas., 1893-1907, then pres.; chmn. bd. Baker, Fentress & Co., Lyon Lbr. Co., Chehalem Lbr. Co., Langlade Lbr. Co., Saginaw & Manistee Lbr. Co., Continental Timber Co., Naval Stores Investment Co., Northern Nat. Bank (Ashland, Wis.); McCarroll Lumber Co., Ltd., Baker Fentress Investment Company; v.p. Saluda Land & Lbr. Co., Scott & Howe Lbr. Co. Mayor of Ludington, Mich., 1892. Republican. Episcopalian. Home: Winnetka, Ill. Died Feb. 5, 1929.

BAKER, Marcus, cartographer; b. Kalamazoo, Mich., Sept. 23, 1849; s. John and Chastina (Fobes) B.; grad. U. of Mich., 1870; LL.B., Columbian Univ., 1896; m. Marian Strong, May 1899. Connected with U.S. Coast and Geodetic Survey, 1873-86; and with U.S. Geol. Survey, 1886—; spent several yrs. in explorations and surveys in Alaska and on Pacific coast; with William H. Dall, prepared the "Alaska Coast Pilot." Sec. U.S. Bd. on Geographic Names; was cartographer Venezuelan Boundary Commn. Asst. sec. Carnegie Instn. of Washington. Author: Dictionary of Alaskan Geographic Names; Northwest Boundary of Texas; Survey of Northwestern Boundary of United States; and other bulletins and geog. and math. papers. Died 1903.

BAKER, Martha Susan, artist; b. Evansville, Ind.; d. Charles E. and Susan (Stevenson) B.; pupil Art Inst., Chicago; unmarried. First prize (miniatures), Archè Salon, Chicago, 1897; exhibited at Paris Expn., 1900, Buffalo Expn., 1901; bronze medal, St. Louis Expn., 1904; hon. mention, Carnegie Inst., Pittsburgh, 1904; silver medal, Chicago Soc. Artists, 1905; purchase prize, Municipal Art League, Chicago, for permanent collection of Art Inst., Chicago, 1905; hon. mention for miniatures, Salon des Artistes Françaises, Paris, 1909. Home: Chicago, Ill. Died 1911.

BAKER, Newman Freese, prof. law; b. Worthington, Ind., Feb. 18, 1898; s. James William and Bertha (Freese) B.; A.B., Southwestern Coll., Winfield, Kan., 1917; A.M., U. of Mo., 1920, LL.B., 1923; J.S.D., U. of Chicago, 1926; m. Lenore Grubbs, May 19, 1923; children—William Spencer, Lenore. Instr. in history, U. of Mo., 1920-23, State Teachers Coll., Kirksville, Mo., summers 1922, 23; prof. polit. science, Oklahoma City (Okla.) U., 1923-25; grad. fellow, U. of Chicago, 1925-26; admitted to Mo. bar, 1926; instr. in law, U. of Wis., 1927; asso. prof. law, La. State U., 1927-28; prof. law, Tulane U., 1928-30; asso. prof. law, Northwestern U., 1930-32, prof. law, 1932—. Pvt. U.S.A., 1918. Sec. Am. Inst. Criminal Law and Criminology; mem. Chicago Crime Commn. Republican. Methodist. Author: Legal Aspects of Zoning, 1927. Mng. dir. Jour. of Criminal Law and Criminology. Home: Wilmette, Ill. Died Sept. 5, 1941.

BAKER, Newton Diehl, secretary of war; b. Martinsburg, W.Va., Dec. 3, 1871; s. Newton Diehl and Mary (Dukehart) B.; B.A., Johns Hopkins, 1892; LL.B., Washington and Lee U., 1894; m. Elizabeth Leopold, July 5, 1902; children—Elizabeth, Newton D., Margaret. Pvt. sec. to Postmaster Gen. Wilson, 1896-97, began practice at Martinsburg, W.Va., 1897; city solicitor of Cleveland, O., 1902-12; mayor of Cleveland, term 1912-14, and 1914-16; apptd. secretary of war by President Wilson, Mar. 7, 1916, and served until Mar. 4, 1921. Apptd. by President Coolidge mem. Permanent Court of Arbitration, The Hague, 1928; former pres. Woodrow Wilson Foundation; apptd. mem. Law Enforcement Commn., by President Hoover, 1929; mem. advisory council Nat. Economy League. Commd. col., O.R.C., Mar. 1921; D.S.M. (U.S.), 1929. Mem. law firm of Baker, Hostetler, Sidlo & Patterson, Cleveland; dir. Cleveland Trust Co., B.&O. R.R. Co., Radio Corp. of America, Goodyear Tire & Rubber Co. Democrat. Pres. Am. Judicature Society. Awarded medal by Nat. Inst. Social Sciences, 1933, "for services to humanity." Home: Cleveland, O. Died Dec. 25, 1937.

BAKER, Orlando Harrison, consul; b. Brownsville, Ind., Sept. 13, 1830; s. Jacob and Mary (Chesney) B.; A.B., Asbury (now De Pauw) U., Ind., 1858, A.M., 1861; (LL.D., Simpson Coll., Ia., 1906); m. Mary C. Ridley, 1858 (dec.); m. 2d, Mrs. R. V. Beach, 1895. Prin. Cherry Grove (Ill.) Sem., 1858-60, 1862-63, Delaney Acad., Ind., 1860-62, Des Moines (Ia.) Conf. Sem., 1863-66, Glenwood Collegiate Inst., 1866-68; prof. ancient langs., Simpson Coll., 1868-71; pres. Algona Coll., 1871-75; editor Indianola Herald, 1880-86; traveled through southern states and Mex. as spl. corr. Chicago Inter Ocean; Am. consul, Copenhagen, Denmark, 1892-94, Sydney, Australia, 1900-08, Sandakan, N. Borneo, June 10, 1908—. Republican. Methodist. Home: Indianola, Ia. Died Aug. 6, 1913.

BAKER, Page M., manager and editor-in-chief Times-Democrat, New Orleans. Home: New Orleans, La. Died 1910.

BAKER, Purley A., clergyman; b. Jackson Co., O., Apr. 10, 1858; s. Albert and Marinda B.; ed. common and normal schs.; m. Lillie I. Greene, Aug. 27, 1884. Ordained M.E. ministry, 1884; pastor Jasper, O., 1883-84, Racine, 1884-88, Gallipolis, 1888-93, Columbus, 1893-95; in charge of Cleveland dist., Ohio Anti-Saloon League, 1896, state supt., 1897-1903; gen. supt. Anti-Saloon League of America 1903—. Ministerial mem. Gen. Conf. M.E. Ch., 1908, 12, 16. Home: Westerville, O. Died Mar. 30, 1924.

BAKER, Raymond T., banking; b. Eureka, Nev.; s. George Washington and Mary Agnes (Hall) B.; m. Margaret (Emerson) Vanderbilt, 1918; 1 dau., Gloria; m. 2d, Delphine (Dodge) Cromwell, Dec. 4, 1928; 1 dau., Anna Ray. Has been prominently identified with the development of mining in State of Nevada; sec. to American ambassador at Petrograd, Russia, 1914-16; dir. of the Mint, 1917-22. Pres. Scheeline Banking & Trust Co., Reno, Nev.; chmn. United Nevada Bank after merger with former; v.p. Anglo and London Paris Nat. Bank, San Francisco. Mem. Gold Commn., apptd. by sec. of the treasury, 1918; Dem. candidate for U.S. Senate, 1926. Home: Reno, Nev. Died Apr. 28, 1935.

BAKER, Robert Homes, business exec.; b. Memphis, Tenn., Sept. 4, 1858; s. Robert and Annie (Miller) B.; student East Tenn. U. 2 yrs.; m. Nellie Faulkner, Oct. 19, 1886; children—Burke, Nelle (wife of Rufus Boylan, U.S.A.), Elizabeth. Baggage master, M. & T. Ry., Memphis, 1876-79; traveling salesman, 1879-82; merchant, Waco, Tex., 1882-96; gen. mgr. in Tex. of Equitable Life Assurance Soc. of N.Y., 1896-1904; promoter and builder, 1904, pres. and gen. mgr., 1904-11, Trinity & Brazos Valley R.R.; bought, 1912, pres., 1912-14, Tex. Central Ry.; bought Wichita Falls Ry., 1914 (both rys. sold to M., K. & T. Ry.); pres. Houston Terminal Warehouse & Cold Storage Co.; chmn. bd. Seaboard Life Ins. Co. Capt. Waco Light Inf., Tex. N.G., 1886-89; col. on staff Gov. Lanham, 1902-06. Chmn. Tex. State Prison Bd., 1927-29. Democrat. Baptist. Home: Houston, Tex. Died Jan. 9, 1935.

BAKER, Sam(uel) A., governor; b. Patterson, Wayne Co., Mo., Nov. 7, 1874; s. Samuel A. and Mary Amanda (McGhee) B.; B.S.D., Cape Girardeau (Mo.) State Teachers Coll., 1897; A.B., Mo. Wesleyan Coll.; spl. student U. of Mo.; LL.D., Mo. Valley Coll.; m. Nell R. Tuckley, June 1, 1904; 1 dau., Mary Elisabeth. Began teaching at Bethel, Mo., 1895; prin. of schs., Mill Spring, Mo., 1896; supt. schs., Piedmont, Mo., 1897-99; prin. Jefferson City High Sch., 1899-1905, Joplin High Sch., 1905-10; supt. schs., Richmond, Mo., 1910-13, Jefferson City, 1913-19; state supt. of schs. of Mo., 1919-23; gov. of Mo., term 1925-28, inclusive. Republican. Presbyn. Mason. Home: Jefferson City, Mo. Died Sept. 16, 1933.

BAKER, Sarah Schoonmaker (Mrs. Woods Baker), author; b. New Haven, Conn., 1824; d. Cornelius and Louisa C. Tuthill; ed. Hartford Female Sem. and Patapsco Female Inst.; m. Woods Baker of U.S. Coast Survey, 1851 (died 1852). Moved, 1876, to Djursholm, Sweden. Author: Timid Lucy; Aunt Friendly Books; The Babes in the Basket; Salt; Our Elder Brother; Pictures of Swedish Life. Some of the works have been translated into French and Swedish. Home: Arlaryd, Djursholm, Sweden. Died 1906.

BAKER, Simon Strousse, educator; b. Washington Co., Pa., July 11, 1866; s. David B. and Sara Anne (Strousse) B.; B.S., Washington and Jefferson Coll., 1892, M.S.; studied law pvtly. 2 yrs.; extension courses, U. of Pittsburgh; LL.D., same U., 1923; m. Grace Little, 1894; 1 son, Edward David (aviator, killed in action nr. Souilly, France, Oct. 24, 1918). Teacher and prin. pub. schs. and acad. 4 yrs.; prin., dist. supt. and asso. supt. Pittsburgh pub. schs. for nearly 25 yrs.; acting pres. Washington and Jefferson Coll., 1921-22, pres., 1922-31, resigned. Republican. Presbyn. Mason. Home: Pittsburgh, Pa. Died Oct. 11, 1932.

BAKER, Smith, clergyman; b. Bowdoin, Me., Feb. 18, 1836; s. Smith and Mary (Smith) B.; 8th in descent from William Brewster of the Mayflower; grad. Bangor Theol. Sem., 1860; (D.D., Dartmouth, 1891); m. Isabella Ditson, Sept. 13, 1860. Ordained minister Congl. Ch., 1860; pastor Veazie and Orono, Me., 1860-70, Lowell, Mass., 1870-90, Minneapolis, Minn., 1890-94, Boston, 1894-98, Portland, Me., 1898-1907, Atlanta, Ga., 1907-08. Corporate mem. A.B.C. F.M.; moderator at different times of Congl. State Confs. of Mass., Minn. and Me.; ex-pres. State S.S. assns. of Mass., Minn. and Me.; has served as mem. 5 Nat. Congl. councils, 6 Internat. S.S. convs., 5 Internat. Christian Endeavor convs. Author of 2 volumes lectures to young people and many pamphlets and published addresses. Home: Lowell, Mass. Died Nov. 10, 1917.

BAKER, Tarkington, editor, author; b. Vincennes, Ind., Aug. 6, 1878; s. Orlan F. and Mary Josephine (Tarkington) B.; ed. pvt. and pub. schs. and De Pauw U.; m. Myla Jo Closser, Oct. 21, 1901. Served in 1st Colo. Inf. in P.I., 1898-99. Mng. editor and editor Indianapolis Sentinel, 1900-06; dramatic and lit. editor Indianapolis News, 1906-12; theatrical producer and dir., New York, 1912-14; mem. editorial staff, Indianapolis News, 1914-17, Indianapolis Star, 1917-18; gen. mgr. Universal Film Co., N.Y. City, 1918-20; pres. Visugraphic Pictures, Inc., 1921—. Author: Yard and Garden, 1907. Home: New York, N.Y. Died Jan. 1, 1924.

BAKER, Thomas Rakestraw, science teacher; b. Chester Co., Pa., Feb. 27, 1837; s. Samuel and Mary (Rakestraw) B.; M.S., First Pa. State Normal Sch., Millersville, 1860; course in chemistry and geology, Pa. State Coll.; Ph.D., U. of Göttingen, 1871; m. Sophia Way, Mar. 25, 1876 (died 1908); m. 2d, Mary Evans Francis, Oct. 12, 1918. Professor mathematics, Agrl. College (now State Coll.) of Pa., 1861-67; prof. natural science, First Pa. State Normal Sch., 1867-69 and 1871-86; identified with phosphate industry of Fla., 1889-92; prof. natural science, Rollins Coll., Fla., 1892-1910; retired on Carnegie allowance, June 1911. Dir. Rollins College Museum, 1909—. Mayor of Winter Park, Fla., 1917-18. Republican. Member Society of Friends. Author: Elements of Physics, 1881; A Short Course in Chemistry, 1883; Questions in Physics and Chemistry, 1884. Home: Winter Park, Fla. Died 1930.

BAKER, Thomas Stockham, educator; b. Aberdeen, Harford Co., Md., Mar. 23, 1871; s. John H. and Cornelia E. (Stockham) B.; A.B., Johns Hopkins, 1891, Ph.D., 1895; U. of Leipzig, 1892; LL.D., U. of Del., 1924; Sc.D., Duquesne, 1928, Lafayette College, 1932; unmarried. Asso. in German, 1895-1900, lecturer on modern German lit., 1900-08, Johns Hopkins; prof. modern langs., 1900-08, dir., 1909-19, The Jacob Tome Inst., Port Deposit, Md.; sec. Carnegie Inst. Tech., 1919-22, pres., 1922-35, pres. emeritus and trustee, 1935—. Director Forbes Nat. Bank. Mus. critic Baltimore Sun, 1895-1905. Author: Lenau and Young Germany. Editor: Hauptmann's The Sunken Bell, 1898. Contbr. lit. and ednl. essays to mags. and newspapers. Organized first, second and third internat. conferences on bituminous coal, held at Carnegie Inst. of Tech., 1926, 28 and 31. Lectured, 1933, at German univs. under auspices of Carl Schurz Memorial Foundation on "The Significance of the United States for Europe in the Twentieth Century." Home: Pittsburgh, Pa. Died April 7, 1939.

BAKER, William B., congressman; b. nr. Aberdeen, Md., July 22, 1840; ed. public and private schools; worked on farm until 1872; since then engaged in fruit packing. Mem. Md. house of delegates, 1882; Md. senate, 1892; mem. Congress, 1895-1901, 2d Md. dist. Republican. Home: Aberdeen, Md. Died 1911.

BAKER, William Edgar, civil engr.; b. Springfield, Mass., Oct. 18, 1856; s. Henry Martyn and Susan Virginia (Barnes) B.; brother of James Barnes B.; C.E., Lafayette Coll., Pa., 1877; m. Harriet E. Griffin, Feb. 20, 1884. With St. Paul & Pacific Ry., 1877-81; reconnaissance Canadian Pacific Ry., 1881-83; chief engr. Internat. & G. N. Ry., 1884-88; chief engr. and gen. mgr. Columbia Intermural Ry., 1893-94; gen. mgr. and chief engr. Met. West Side Elevated Ry., Chicago, 1894-99; gen. supt. Manhattan Ry., New York, 1899-1902; sr. mem. W. E. Baker & Co., cons. engrs., 1902—. Trustee Lafayette Coll. Presbyn. Died Nov. 7, 1921.

BAKER, William Henry, telegraph official; b. Buffalo, N.Y., Apr. 13, 1855; s. Horace G. and Mary Frances (Coner) B.; ed. pub. schs., Brooklyn, N.Y.; m. Emma A., d. of Gen. E. B. Fowler, of Brooklyn, N.Y., Feb. 16, 1877. Clerk, gen. office Western Union Telegraph Co., 1870-75; cashier and sec. Atlantic & Pacific Telegraph Co., 1875-84; sec. Am. Electric Mfg. Co., 1885; mem. N.Y. Stock Exchange, 1885-87; asst. to Pres. Theodore N. Vail, Met. Telephone Co., 1887-89; v.p., 1889-96, v.p. and gen. mgr., 1896-1907, Postal Telegraph-Cable Co.; sec. Western Union Telegraph Co., 1911—; sec. and dir. Am. Telegraph & Cable Co., Empire & Bay State Telegraph Co., and many other cos.; pres. Am. Dist. Telegraph Co. of N.Y.; asst. gen. mgr. and dir. N.Y. Quotation Co. Home: Bayside, N.Y. Died Jan. 17, 1918.

BAKER, William L., banker; b. Nelson, Madison Co., N.Y., Apr. 9, 1860; s. Anson Monroe and Martha Cecelia (Dana) B.; grad. State Normal Sch., Geneseo, N.Y., 1881; A.B., U. of Rochester, 1885 (Phi Beta Kappa); m. Sarah Elizabeth Wiswall, May 13, 1890; children—Florence Wiswall, Martha (dec.), Elizabeth Lovejoy, William Wiswall, Sarah Louise. Sec.-treas. German Am. Loan & Trust Co., Sioux Falls, S.D., 1886-87; cashier First Nat. Bank, Parker, 1887-88; cashier Minnehaha Nat. Bank (now First Nat. Bank and Trust Co. in Sioux Falls), 1889, pres., 1910—; v.p. Queen City Fire Ins. Co. Pres. and treas. Sioux Falls Community Chest; mem. exec. com., treas. Minnehaha Co. Chapter Am. Red Cross since its organization. Republican. Episcopalian. Mason. Home: Sioux Falls, S.D. Died June 19, 1939.

BAKER, William Pimm, editor; b. Skaneateles, N.Y., Jan. 3, 1870; s. Simeon and Elizabeth (Pimm) B.; B.L., Cornell, 1891; Litt.D., Syracuse, 1921; m. Mary Jack, 1898; children—Alice (Mrs. T. J. Maloney), Eleanor (Mrs. E. J. Dillon), Jack Stuart, Mary. Reporter News, Courier, Standard and Herald, 1892-1908; editorial writer and editor Syracuse Post-Standard, 1909—, also dir. and sec. Founder Shelfless Library; dir. N.Y. Hist. Assn.; regent U. of State of N.Y., 1921—. Republican. Episcopalian. Home: Syracuse, N.Y. Died Jan. 8, 1930.

BAKER, William Taylor, merchant; b. West Winfield, N.Y., Sept. 11, 1841; ed. public schools West Winfield until 1857; Groton Acad., 1857-58; m. Anna F. Morgan, Nov. 18, 1879. Long engaged in grain trade in Chicago; retired. Five times pres. Chicago Bd. of Trade; twice elected pres. World's Columbian Expn., twice pres. Civic Federation. Home: Chicago, Ill. Died 1903.

BAKETEL, Oliver Sherman, clergyman, editor; b. Greentown, O., Oct. 18, 1849; s. Moses A. and Lydia M. (Welch) B.; B.S., Mt. Union Coll., Alliance, O., 1871, D.D., 1898; m. Rosie L. Mack, Oct. 25, 1870 (died 1910); children—Harrie Sheridan (M.D.), Roy Vincent (M.D.), Leon Burt; m. 2d, Annie J. McWhorter, 1912. Ordained M.E. ministry, 1870; pastor Pittsburgh Conf., 1870-77, So. Newmarket, N.H., 1877-78, Manchester, N.H., 1879-80, Methuen, Mass., 1881-84, Greenland, N.H., 1884-87, Portsmouth, N.H., 1887-91; presiding elder, 1891-1903; mem. Gen. Conf., 1892-96; S.S. work, 1903-10; editor Methodist Year Book and the Minutes of Annual Conferences M.E. Ch., 1910-30; librarian Methodist Hist. Soc., 1930. Trustee Tilton (N.H.) Sch. Republican. Author: Concordance to the Methodist Hymnal, 1907. Editor: History of the New Hampshire Conf. of the M.E. Church (with Otis Cole), 1929. Home: Maplewood, N.J. Died Feb. 4, 1937.

BAKHMETEFF, George, imperial Russian ambassador to U.S., Nov. 28, 1911-Apr. 17, 1917, resigned; m. Mary, d. late Gen. E. F. Beale, of Washington, D.C. Died Aug. 29, 1928.

BAKLANOFF, Georges, baritone; b. Petrograd, Russia, Jan. 18, 1882; s. Andreas and Anna (Virubova) B.; grad. as B.L. and Jurisprudence, Petrograd U., 1904; studied voice with Vittorio Vanzo; unmarried. Début in Rubinstein's "Demon," 1905, and later appeared in Covent Garden, London, Royal Opera House, Berlin, with Imperial Opera Co., Vienna, Moscow and Petrograd, also in Monte Carlo, Budapest, Stockholm, Munich, etc.; first came to U.S., 1909, and joined Boston Opera Co., later with Metropolitan Opera Co.; became mem. Chicago Opera Assn., 1917. Prin. rôles: Rigoletto, Tonio, Mephistopheles, Scarpia, Iago, Escamillo, Wotan, Guido in "Monna Vanna," Athanael, Boris Godunov, Hamlet, and others. Died Dec. 6, 1938.

BALCH, Edwin Swift, author; b. Phila., 1856; s. Thomas and Emily (Swift) Balch; brother of Thomas Willing B.; A.B., Harvard, 1878; studied law in office of William Henry Rawle; m. Eugenia H. Macfarlane, Oct. 5, 1904; m. 2d, Emily Tapscott Clark, Nov. 1, 1924. Admitted to Phila. bar, 1882. Author: Mountain Exploration, 1893; Glacières or Freezing Caverns, 1900; Antarctica, 1902; Comparative Art, 1906; The North Pole and Bradley Land, 1913; Mount McKinley and Mountain Climbers' Proofs, 1914; Elise Willing Balch in Memoriam, 1917; (with Eugenia Macfarlane Balch) Art and Man, 1918; Arts of the World, 1920. Home: Philadelphia, Pa. Died Mar. 15, 1927.

BALCH, George Beall, naval officer; b. in Tenn., Jan. 3, 1821. Apptd. from Ala., midshipman U.S.N., 1837; promoted through the grades to rear adm., June 5, 1878. Served in Mexican War, 1846-47, participating in attack on Alvarado and in joint bombardment of Vera Cruz, at surrender of that city; on duty Naval Acad., 1860-61; on board Sabine, 1861-62; comd. Pocahontas, 1862, Pawnee, 1862-65, S. Atlantic Blockading Squadron, 1862; engaged with battery at Stono, S.C., Aug., 1862; engagements in Stono River, S.C., July, 1864, bombardment of battery Pringle on James Island, S.C.; on duty Navy Yard, Washington, 1865-68, 1871-72; comd. Albany, flagship, N. Atlantic Squadron, 1868-70; gov. Naval Asylum, 1873-76; mem. Light-House Bd., 1876-77; mem. Exam. Bd., 1878; supt. Naval Acad., 1879-81; comdr.-in-chief Pacific Sta., 1881-82; retired Jan. 3, 1883. Home: Baltimore, Md. Died 1908.

BALCH, Thomas Willing, lawyer; s. Thomas and Emily (Swift) B.; brother of Edwin Swift B.; A.B., Harvard, 1890; LL.B., U. of Pa., 1895; (L.H.D., Trinity Coll., Hartford, 1917); m. Dulany Whiting, May 26, 1923. In practice at Philadelphia since 1895; mgr. The Children's Hosp., 1905-15; Phila. Assemblies, 1909-12; dir. Chesapeake & Delaware Canal Co., 1906-19. Collaborateur of the Revue de Droit International et de Législation Comparée of Brussels. Fellow Am. Acad. Arts and Sciences. Author: Some Facts About Alsace and Lorraine, 1895; The Brooke Family of Whitechurch, Hampshire, England, 1899; The Alabama Arbitration, 1900; Émeric Crucé, 1900; The Alasko-Canadian Frontier, 1902; The Alaska Frontier, 1903; English Ancestors of the Shippen Family and Edward Shippen of Philadelphia, 1904; The Swift Family of Philadelphia, 1906; Balch Genealogica, 1907; L'Évolution de l'Arbitrage International, 1908; La Question des Pêcheries de l'Atlantique: un différend entre les États-Unis et l'Empire Britannique, 1909; The Arctic and Antarctic Regions and the Law of Nations, 1910; Différends Juridiques et Politiques dans les Rapports des Nations, 1914; Arbitration as a Term of International Law, 1915; The United States and the Expansion of the Law Between Nations, 1915; The Philadelphia Assemblies, 1916; A World Court in the Light of the United States Supreme Court, 1917; Legal and Political Questions Between Nations, 1924. Editor of The New Cyneas le Nouveau Cynée of Émeric Crucé, originally published at Paris in 1623, 1909, also International Courts of Arbitration, by Thomas Balch, originally pub., 1874, 1915. Home: Philadelphia, Pa. Died June 9, 1927.

BALDRIDGE, Howard Hammond, lawyer; b. Holidaysburg, Pa., June 26, 1864; s. Howard Malcolm and Laura (Mattern) B.; A.B., Bucknell U., 1884, A.M., 1887; studied law, U. of Pa. and under Benjamin Harris Brewster, atty.-gen. U.S.; m. Letitia B. Coffey, Sept. 26, 1889. Admitted to bar, 1887, and engaged in practice at Omaha, Neb. Asst. U.S. atty., Neb., 1890-94; dist. atty., Douglas Co., 1894-98; mem. Neb. Senate, 1900-01; del. at large Rep. Nat. Conv., 1916. Home: Omaha, Neb. Died May 16, 1928.

BALDWIN, Abram Martin, banker; b. Montgomery, Ala., Oct. 29, 1860; s. William Owen and Mary J. (Martin) B.; prep. edn., pvt. schs.; student Vanderbilt, 1878; m. Elizabeth Ewin, June 8, 1887; children—Abram Martin (dec.), Katharine E., William O., Ewin. Began as cashier, 1st Nat. Bank, Montgomery, 1886, pres., 1898-1929, chmn. bd., 1929—; pres. Montgomery Cotton Mills, 1st Joint Stock Land Bank, 1st Finance Corp. Dir. Carnegie Library, Montgomery. Democrat. Episcopalian. Home: Montgomery, Ala. Died Oct. 10, 1931.

BALDWIN, A(rchibald) Stuart, civil engr.; b. Winchester, Va., Sept. 28, 1861; s. Robert Frederick and Caroline (Barton) B.; ed. Shenandoah Valley Acad., Winchester, Va., and Staunton (Va.) Mil. Acad.; m. Martha Frazier, Dec. 19, 1883. Rodman on Richmond & Allegheny R.R. (now C.&O. Ry.), 1879; asst. engr. and engr., Iron and Steel Works Assn. of Va., 1880-83; draftsman and asst. engr., Phila. extension, B.&O. R.R., 1883-85; prin. asst. engr., Mo. River Bridge, Kansas City, for C.M.& St.P. Ry., 1885-86; resident engr. Louisville, St. Louis & Tex. R.R., 1886-87; asst. engr. and roadmaster, L.&N. R.R., 1887-1901; prin. asst. engr., 1901-03, engr. of constrn., 1903-05, chief engr, Mar. 20, 1905-Aug. 1, 1918, then v.p. I.C. R.R. Co. Home: Chicago, Ill. Died June 26, 1922.

BALDWIN, Arthur J., lawyer; b. Cortland, N.Y., Aug. 26, 1868; s. Eben R. and Caroline (West) B.; A.B., Cornell U., 1892; m. Frances Smiley, June 18, 1892. Began law practice, North Tonawanda, N.Y., 1894; in office of late James B. Dill, New York, 1897; mem. Dill & Baldwin, 1899, later Griggs, Baldwin & Baldwin, 1902—; sec. and dir. Miss. Glass Co., Miss. Wire Glass Co. Democrat. Methodist. Mason. Home: East Orange, N.J. Died July 21, 1939.

BALDWIN, Benjamin James, M.D.; b. Bullock Co., Ala., Nov. 16, 1856; s. Benjamin James and Martha (Barnett) B.; Randolph-Macon Coll., Ashland, Va.; M.D., Bellevue Med. Coll., New York, 1877; m. Hulit Morris, 1884 (died 1894); 1 dau., Mrs. James F. Hill; m. 2d, Kate Sistrunk, July 1896; 1 son, Josiah Morris (dec.). Practiced at Louisville, Ky., 1879-82, in Montgomery, 1883-93. Dir. N. and S. Ala. Div., L.&N. R.R.; pres. Montgomery Gas Co.; pres. Elyton Land Co., Birmingham, Ala. Pres. Bd. of Edn., Montgomery, 1890-1917. Democrat. Episcopalian. Pres. Ala. State Med. Assn.; mem. Ala. State Bd. of Health, 1890—, sec. and v.p. Conf. for Edn. in South, 1906-08. Trustee George Peabody Coll. for Teachers, Nashville. Home: Montgomery, Ala. Deceased.

BALDWIN, Bird Thomas, college prof.; b. Marshalltown, Pa., 1875; s. Bird L. and Sarah R. B.; B.S., Swarthmore (Pa.) Coll., 1900; studied U. of Pa., 1901-02, Harvard, 1902-03, 1904-05, U. of Leipzig, summer, 1906; A.M., 1903, Ph.D., 1905, Harvard; m. Claudia W. Wilbur, Sept. 1904 (died 1925); children—Bird Wilbur, Alan Wilbur and Jervas Wilbur (twins), Patricia. Supervising prin. Friends' schs., Morrestown, Pa., 1900-02; asst. in edn., Harvard Summer Sch., 1903; asst. in psychology and logic, Harvard, 1903-04; prof. psychology, West Chester (Pa.) State Normal Sch., 1905-09; lecturer on psychology and edn., Swarthmore, 1906-10, U. of Chicago, 1909-10; asso. prof. edn. and head Sch. of Art of Teaching, U. of Tex., 1910-12; prof. edn., U. of Tenn., summers, 1912, 1913; prof. psychology and edn., Swarthmore, 1912-16; prof. ednl. psychology, Johns Hopkins, summers, 1915, 16, 17; lecturer in ednl. psychology, Johns Hopkins, 1916-17; research prof. in ednl. psychology and dir. Ia. Child Welfare Research Sta., State U. of Ia., 1917—. Chmn. Child Development Com. of Nat. Research Council, Washington, D.C. Mem. Friends Ch. Writer of numerous published articles, bulls. and reviews on ednl. and psychol. topics; collaborating editor psychol. and ednl. jours. Maj. Sanitary Corps U.S.A., Mar. 1, 1918-Aug. 1, 1919; in office of Surgeon Gen. of the Army, and chief psychologist and dir. rehabilitation of disabled soldiers, Walter Reed General Hosp., Washington, D.C. Author: Physical Growth and School Progress; Physical Growth of Children from Birth to Maturity; The Mental Growth Curve of Normal and Superior Children; The Psychology of the Preschool Child. Home: Iowa City, Ia. Died May 12, 1928.

BALDWIN, Charles Sears, college prof.; b. New York, N.Y., Mar. 21, 1867; s. John S. and Martha J. (Church) B.; A.B., Columbia, 1888, A.M., 1889, Ph.D., 1894; hon. A.M., Yale, 1909; Litt.D., Columbia, 1929; m. Agnes Irwin, Sept. 20, 1894 (died 1897); 1 son, John Sears; m. 2d, Gratia Eaton Whithed, June 4, 1902; children—Marshall Whithed, Catherine Jane (dec.). Asst. tutor and instr. in English, 1891-94, instr. rhetoric, 1895, Columbia; instr. rhetoric, 1895-98, asst. prof., 1898-1909, prof., 1909-11, Yale; prof. rhetoric and English composition, Columbia, July 1, 1911—. Author: The Inflections and Syntax of the Morte d'Arthur of Sir Thomas Malory, 1894; DeQuincey's Revolt of the Tartars, 1896; The Expository Paragraph and Sentence, 1897; A College Manual of Rhetoric, 1902, 4th edit., revised, 1905; The English Bible as a Guide to Writing, 1905; Essays Out of Hours, 1907; Writing and Speaking, 1909; Composition, Oral and Written, 1909; Introduction to English Medieval Literature, 1931; College Composition, 1917, 29; God Unknown, 1920; Ancient Rhetoric and Poetic, 1924; Medieval Rhetoric and Poetic, 1928; Three Medieval Centuries of Literature in England, 1932. Editor: Specimens of Prose Description, 1895; American Short Stories, 1904, German edit., 1911; Bunyan's Pilgrim's Progress, 1905; DeQuincey's Joan of Arc and English Mail Coach, 1906. Died Oct. 23, 1935.

BALDWIN, Daniel Pratt, capitalist; b. Lenox, N.Y., Mar. 22, 1837; g.s. Daniel Pratt, and nephew U.S. Senator Daniel D. Pratt; A.B., Colgate, 1856, A.M., 1859; LL.B., Columbia, 1860; (LL.D., Colgate, 1872, Wabash, 1872, Hamilton, 1901; Litt.D., Wabash, 1903; L.H.D., Syracuse, 1907); unmarried. Judge Circuit Ct., Ind., 1870-72; attry. gen. of Ind., 1880-82; trip around the world, 1899; lecturer on literature, Wabash Coll., 1903. Endowed Baldwin prize in oratory, Cazenovia Sem. and Wabash Coll.; Baldwin Greek prize, Colgate; Baldwin entrance prize, Hamilton. Trustee Wabash, Colgate, 1900-04. Republican. Wrote: A Lawyer's Readings in the Evidences of Christianity, 1875; How States Grow, 1880; Manners, 1880; Personality, 1883; The Wastes of Life, 1885; Christ's Credentials, 1892; Orators and Oratory, 1903. Home: Logansport, Ind. Died 1908.

BALDWIN, Elbert Francis, editor; b. Cleveland, O., Mar. 10, 1857; s. Elbert Irving and Jeannette (Sterling) B.; A.B., Williams Coll., 1884, A.M., 1887, L.H.D., 1893; U. of Berlin, 1884-86; m. Mary, d. U.S. Senator William Drew Washburn, of Minneapolis, Nov. 23, 1892; children—Elbert, Marian, Theodore Washburn, Gertrude, Janet Sterling. On staff The Independent, 1890-92, New York Mail and Express, 1892, The Outlook, 1893—. Republican. Author: The World War, 1914. Home: Lakewood, N.J. Died Sept. 1927.

BALDWIN, Evelyn Briggs, explorer; b. Springfield, Mo., July 22, 1862; s. Col. Elias Briggs (U.S.V.) and Julia Cornelia (Crampton) B.; M.S., Northwestern Coll., Naperville, Ill., 1885; unmarried. Pedestrian and cyclist in Europe, 1885-86; prin. high school and supt. city schools, Kan., 1887-91; observer U.S. Weather Bur., 1892-1900; inspector-at-large, signal corps U.S.A. Accompanied Robert Edwin Peary on N. Greenland expdn., 1893-94, as meteorologist; meteorologist and 2d in command of Walter Wellman's polar expdn. to Franz-Josef Land, 1898-99; built and named Fort McKinley; discovered and explored Graham Bell Land, 1899; organized and comd. Baldwin-Ziegler polar expdn., 1901-02, etc.; established 4 depots of supplies from south to north coast of Franz-Josef Land as basis for proposed dash to the North Pole, and 3 "safety stas." on northeast coast of Greenland for use on return march. Mason. Author: Search for the North Pole; also meteorol. reports; Franz-Josef Land, 1898-99; Auroral Observations Franz-Josef Land, 1898-99; N. Greenland expdn., 1893-94. Died Oct. 25, 1933.

BALDWIN, F(oy) Spencer, economist, insurance; b. at Charlotte, Mich., July 6, 1870; s. Rev. William Wallace and Caroline (Thompson) B.; A.B., Ph.D., Boston U.; Doc. Polit. Science, U. of Munich; m. Cordelia Schultz Losey, Mar. 5, 1896; children—Fredrus Losey, Marcus Decker. Asst. editor Vermont Watchman, Montpelier, 1889; master St. Luke's Sch., Phila., 1890-91; studied economics in Germany, 1892-93; instr. economics, Norwich (Conn.) Free Acad., 1894; prof. economics, 1895-1914, dean dept. of business administration, 1913-14, Boston U. Sec. Mass. Employees' Ins. Assn., 1912-14; mgr. N.Y. State Ins. Fund, 1914-19; pres. Nat. Guaranty Fire Ins. Co. (Newark), 1925-28; editor, 1930, dir. of research, 1931, Nat. Industrial Conf. Bd. Editorial writer Boston Transcript, 1900-14. Lecturer on sociology, Mass. Inst. Tech., 1903; instr. economics, Simmons Coll., 1904-06. Exec. sec. Mass. Commn. on Old Age Pensions, 1909-10; sec. Mass. Commn. on the Tax Laws, 1909; sec. Mass. Commn. on the Cost of Living, 1910; expert of Mass. Commn. on Factory Inspection, 1910; sec. Mass. Commn. on Cold Storage, 1911; chmn. trustees of Statistics Dept. City of Boston, 1909-14; mem. com. on labor, Nat. Council Defense, 1917. Author: History of Mining Legislation in England. Home: East Orange, N.J. Died Mar. 21, 1934.

BALDWIN, Frank Dwight, army officer; b. Manchester, Mich., June 26, 1842; s. Francis Leonard and Betsy Ann (Richards) B.; ed. pub. schs., Constantine, Mich., and Hillsdale Coll.; m. Alice Blackwood, Jan. 10, 1867. Served in Civil War as 2d lt. Mich. Horse Guards, Sept. 19-Nov. 22, 1861; 1st lt. 19th Mich. Inf., Aug. 12, 1862; capt., Jan. 23, 1864; mustered out of vols., June 10, 1865. In regular army as 2d and 1st lt. 19th Inf., Feb. 23, 1866; promoted through grades to brig. gen. U.S.A., June 9, 1902. Bvtd. capt. Feb. 27, 1890, "for gallantry in action against Indians in Texas," and maj., "for gallantry and successful attack on Sitting Bull's camp of Indians on Red Water River, Mont.," Dec. 18, 1876; medal of honor "for distinguished bravery in battle of Peach Tree Creek, Ga., July 20, 1864," while serving as capt. 19th Mich. Inf.; medal of honor "for distinguished gallantry in action against Indians in Texas, Nov. 8, 1874." Comd. first body of civilized troops that ever successfully reached the south shore of Lake Lanao (Island of Mindanao), and after desperate encounter with Moros at battle of Byian, May 2. 1902, completely overcame them, Americans losing 51 killed and wounded out of 471, and the Moros losing over 300, less than 30 escaping; in command S.W. Division. Retired June 26, 1906. Adj. gen. of Colo., Apr. 1, 1917-Apr. 21, 1919. Hon. LL.D. conferred by Hillsdale Coll., Mich., 1904. Died Apr. 22, 1923.

BALDWIN, George Colfax, Baptist clergyman; b. Pompton, N.J., Oct. 21, 1817; grad. Madison (now Colgate) Univ., 1844 (D.D., Union Coll., New York); pastor First Baptist Ch., Troy, N.Y., 1844-85, retired. Author: Representative Men of the New Testament; Representative Women from Eve to Mary; Model Prayer; Notes of a Forty-one Years' Pastorate. Home: Troy, N.Y. Died 1899.

BALDWIN, George Johnson, engr., executive; b. Savannah, Ga., Aug. 18, 1856; s. Daniel Hoard and Kate Alice (Philbrick) B.; spl. course 4 yrs. in mining engring., Mass. Inst. Tech., class 1877; m. Lucy Harvie Hull, June 27, 1882; children—Geo. Hull, Daniel Hoard (dec.), Dorothea Clifford. Chemist, Woodstock Iron Co., Anniston, Ala., 1877-78; supt. Bradley Gold Mine, Nacoochee, Ga., 1878-79; with Baldwin & Co., cotton factors and dealers in fertilizers, Savannah, 1879-91, partner from 1880; organizer, and pres. and gen. mgr., Baldwin Fertilizer Co., 1887-94, became asso. with Stone & Webster, Boston, 1898, organizing many Southern pub. utility electric cos., of which is pres., including Savannah Electric Co. Became pres. 1917, Pacific Mail Steamship Co.; also chmn. bd. N.Y. Shipbuilding Co. and Am. Internat. Shipbuilding Co. (builders of Hog Island Shipyard and ships). Hon. mgr. Union Soc. Bethesda Orphanage; pres. Kate Baldwin Free Kindergarten Assn. Founder mem. Nat. Marine League; mem. and mgr. Am. Bureau of Shipping. Home: Savannah, Ga. Died Mar. 4, 1927.

BALDWIN, Harmon Allen, clergyman, author; b. Pierpont, Ashtabula Co., O., June 3, 1869; s. Jerub Hamlin and Aceneth Catherine (Aldrich) B.; student Mt. Union Coll., Alliance, O., 1889; m. Clara Etta Weatherly, Feb. 6, 1896; children—Leland De Witt, Harmon Wayland, Clara Evelyn. Entered Free Methodist ministry, 1890; evangelist and missionary, 1890-95; ordained, 1896; pastor Brockwayville, Pa., 1895-96, Fairchance, 1896-98, Blairville, 1898-99; dist. elder, W.Va., 1899-1901; evangelist, 1901-02; pastor Atlanta, Ga., 1902-03, Bridgeport, O., 1903-04; dist. elder, W.Va., 1904-06; pastor Rochester, Pa., 1906-08, Wellsburg, W.Va., 1908-09, Pittsburgh, 1909-11, Kittanning, 1912-13, Fairchance, 1913-14, Gerry, N.Y., 1914-17; evangelist, most of time, 1917-32; pastor Cleveland, 1920-23, Pittsburgh, Pa., 1927-29, Coshocton, Ohio, 1932-1934, Fairmont, W.Va., 1934-35. Author: Lessons for Seekers of Holiness, 1907; Objections to Entire Sanctification Considered, 1911; The Indwelling Christ, 1912; Holiness and the Human Element, 1919; The Fishermen of Galilee, 1923; The Carnal Mind, 1926; Spiritual Maxims—On Walking in the Spirit, 1926; The Coming Judgment—General and at the End of Time, 1927. Home: Pittsburgh, Pa. Died Mar. 11, 1936.

BALDWIN, Henry, custodian Am. History; b. New York, Feb. 1, 1832; s. Simeon and Ann Mehetable (de Forest) B.; attended Washington Inst., New York; entered business at 14; m. Cornelia Estelle Hoskins, April 18, 1872. Sec. New York Exchange Co. 6 yrs.; sec. Gallatin Fire Ins. Co. 6 yrs., at same time directing mission work in New York. April 21, 1861, sergt. in command corps engrs., 12th regt., N.Y. State troops; after 4 months' service organized corps of instruction, from which several grad. as officers in vol. service. Feb. 24, 1891, selected by conv. of patriotic organizations at Chicago to verify "all facts of Am. history," and collect a Library Americana to which work he has since devoted his entire time without pay; collection now deposited with N.Y. Public Library. Author: Historical Landmarks of Connecticut, 1897. Home: New Haven, Conn. Died 1905.

BALDWIN, James, author; b. Hamilton Co., Ind., Dec. 15, 1841; s. Isaac and Sarah (Clayton) B.; received some instruction in dist. schools, but was for the most part self-educated; (hon. Ph.D., De Pauw U., 1884); m. Mary S. Taylor, 1864. Teacher in dist. schs. of native co., 1865-68; supt. city graded schools in Ind., 1869-87; in ednl. dept. of Harper & Bros., 1887-90; asst. editor Harper's periodicals, 1890-93; editor of school books for Am. Book Co., 1894-1924. Author: The Story of Siegfried, 1882; The Story of Roland, 1883; The Book Lover, 1884; A Story of the Golden Age, 1886; Harper's Readers (5 vols.), 1887-90; Harper's School Speakers (3 vols.), 1891; Six Centuries of English Poetry, 1892; The Book of Elegies, 1892; The Famous Allegories, 1893; Choice English Lyrics, 1893; Fairy Stories and Fables, 1895; Fifty Famous Stories Retold, 1895; Old Greek Stories, 1895; Old Stories from the East, 1895; Guide to Systematic Readings in the Encyclopædia Britannica, 1895; Four Great Americans, 1896; The Horse Fair, 1895; Baldwin's Readers (8 vols.), 1897; The Discovery of the Old Northwest, 1901; The Conquest of the Old Northwest, 1901; Barnes' Elementary History of the United States, 1903; Hero Tales Told in School, 1904; Abraham Lincoln, a True Life, 1904; The Fairy Reader, 1905; Thirty More Famous Stories, 1905; The Golden Fleece, 1906; An American Book of Golden Deeds, 1907; Stories of the King, 1909; The Expressive Readers (8 vols.), 1911; Fifty Famous People, 1912; The Sampo, 1912; John Bunyan's Dream Story, 1913; Fifty Famous Rides and Riders, 1915; The Story of Liberty, 1919. Home: South Orange, N.J. Died Aug. 30, 1925.

BALDWIN, James Fairchild, surgeon; b. Orangeville, N.Y., Feb. 12, 1850; s. Cyrus H. and Mary P. (Fairchild) B.; A.B., Oberlin Coll., 1870, A.M., 1876; M.D., Jefferson Med. Coll., Phila., 1874; m. Fidelia Finch, 1874; children—Austin Guy, Fredrika Hull (Mrs. Fred. R. Hoover), Hugh A., Helen F. (Mrs. Helen F. Pease); m. 2d, Ida Strickler, 1889; children—Alice G. (Mrs. Harry B. Hall), Josephine F. (Mrs. Harry W. Yoxall). Professor physiology and anatomy, Columbus Medical Coll., 1875-82; prof. surg. gynecology chancellor, Ohio Med. U., 1892-99; formerly prof. clin. surgery, Ohio State U.; surgeon and chief of staff Grant Hosp. Author: Operative Gynecology, 1898. Contbr. on surgery and gynecology to med. jours. Died Jan. 20, 1936.

BALDWIN, James Mark, psychologist; b. Columbia, S.C., Jan. 12, 1861; s. Hon. Cyrus H. and Lydia Eunice (Ford) B.; A.B., Princeton, 1884, A.M., 1887, Ph.D., 1889; hon. D.Sc., Oxford U., Eng., 1900 (first hon. degree in science ever given by Oxford), and U. of Geneva, 1909; LL.D., Glasgow U., 1901, S.C. Coll., 1905; studied Leipzig, Berlin and Tübingen; m. Helen Hayes, d. Prin. W. Henry Green, D.D., LL.D., Nov. 22, 1888; children—Helen Green (Mrs. John A. Sterrett), Elizabeth Ford (wife of Dr. Philip M. Stimson). Instr. French and German, Princeton, 1886; prof. philosophy, Lake Forest (Ill.) U., 1887-89, U. of Toronto, 1889-93; prof. psychology, Princeton, 1893-1903; prof. philosophy and psychology, Johns Hopkins, 1903-09; Nat. U. of Mexico, 1909-13. Hon. pres. Internat. Congress of Criminal Anthropology, Geneva, 1896; pres.-elect Internat. Congress of Psychology, 1909-13; awarded gold medal, Royal Acad. of Denmark, 1897. Author: Handbook of Psychology (2 vols.), 1889-91; Elements of Psychology, 1893; Mental Development in the Child and the Race, 1896; Social and Ethical Interpretations in Mental Development, 1898; Story of the Mind, 1898; Fragments in Philosophy and Science, 1902; Development and Evolution, 1902; Thought and Things, or Genetic Logic (vols. 1-3), 1906-11; Darwin and the Humanities, 1909; The Individual and Society, 1910; History of Psychology (2 vols.), 1913; Genetic Theory of Reality, 1915; France and the War, 1915; American Neutrality, 1916; The Super-State, 1916; Paroles de Guerre, 1919; Between Two Wars—Memories and Opinions (2 vols.), 1926. Joint Author: History of Psychology in Autobiography (volume 1), 1931. Editor of Psychological Review, 1894-1909, Dictionary of Philosophy and Psychology, 1901-06. His various books have been translated into French, German, Italian and Spanish. Decorated by Pres. of France, in person, with Cross Legion of Honor, 1917; Comdr. St. Saba (Serbian), 1918. Died Nov. 8, 1934.

BALDWIN, Jesse A., judge; b. Greenwood, Ill., Aug. 9, 1854; s. Sebrean C. T. and Lavina (Stevens) B.; student U. of Ill., 1872; taught sch. 5 yrs.; studied law under Hon. T. D. Murphy, Woodstock, Ill.; m. Fannie M. Benton, Jan. 29, 1879. Admitted to bar, 1877; asst. U.S. atty., 1877-84; resigned and began pvt. practice; sr. mem. Jesse A. and Henry R. Baldwin, 1884-1909; judge Circuit Ct. of Cook Co., Ill., terms 1909-15, 1915-21 (judge Appellate Ct., 1910-12). Republican. Was pres. of bd. of edn. and trustee Library Inst. of Oak Park, Ill. Trustee U. of Chicago, Rush Med. Coll., Central Free Dispensary. Home: Oak Park, Ill. Died Dec. 8, 1921.

BALDWIN, Joseph Clark, Jr.; b. N.Y. City, Apr. 23, 1871; s. Joseph Clark and Emma Jane (Mood) B.; ed. St. Paul's Sch., Concord, N.H., and 3 yrs. in Europe; m. Fanny Taylor, Apr. 15, 1896; children—Joseph Clark 3d, Fanny Taylor, Cynthia B., Alexander T., Phyllis, Priscilla, Peter, Jane, Ian. Pres. United Dyewood Corp., Am. Dyco Corp.; chmn. bd. Am. Dyewood Co. Home: Mt. Kisco, N.Y. Died Dec. 29, 1937.

BALDWIN, Le Roy Wilbur, banker; b. Rutland, Vt., Oct. 31, 1865; s. Warner H. and Mary Olive (Hatch) B.; ed. pvt. and high schs., Rutland, Vt.; m. Ettie Lucile Field, Oct. 10, 1890. Began business career, 1886; pres. Empire Trust Co., 1902—. Home: New York, N.Y. Died Mar. 6, 1939.

BALDWIN, Neilson Abeel, physician; b. Brooklyn, Feb. 28, 1839; s. Rev. John Abeel and Elizabeth Elmendorf (Van Kleeck) B.; grad. Lafayette Coll., 1858, A.M., 1861; Med. Dept. Yale Univ., 1861; m. Blanche Chandler Ballam, Sept. 1, 1877. Surgeon U.S. vols. in Civil war, 1862-65, then in practice in Brooklyn; surgeon Nat. Guard, S.N.Y., 1866-70; health insp. Brooklyn, 1870-71; police surgeon, Brooklyn, 1872-75. Republican. Med. supt. Sanitarium, 1890-1900; fellow Am. Acad. Medicine, 1878—. Home: Brooklyn, N.Y. Deceased.

BALDWIN, Samuel Prentiss, naturalist; b. Cleveland, O., Oct. 26, 1868; s. Charles Candee and Caroline Sophia (Prestiss) B.; A.B., Dartmouth, 1892, A.M., 1894, D.Sc., 1932; LL.B., Western Reserve U., 1895; m. Lilian Converse Hanna, Feb. 15, 1898. Admitted to Ohio bar, 1894, and began practice at Cleveland; discontinued practice because of ill health, 1902, has since devoted attention to science, principally ornithology; dir. Baldwin Bird Research Lab. for the study of live wild birds; originator of bird-banding method used in U.S. Biol. Survey; chmn. bd. The Williamson Co.; pres. The New Amsterdam Co. Research asso. in biology, Western Reserve U. Trustee Cleveland Mus. Natural History. Republican. Presbyn. Wrote: Bird Banding by Means of Systematic Trapping (Linnean Soc. of N.Y.), 1920; (with F. C. Lincoln) Manual for Bird Banding; Measurements of Birds; Physiology of the Temperature of Birds. Home: Cleveland, O. Died Dec. 31, 1938.

BALDWIN, Simeon Eben, governor; b. New Haven, Conn., Feb. 5, 1840; s. Roger Sherman and Emily (Perkins) B.; A.B., Yale, 1861, A.M., 1864; studied law at Yale and Harvard; (LL.D., Harvard, 1891, Columbia, 1911, Wesleyan, 1912, Yale, 1916); admitted to bar, 1863; m. Susan Winchester, 1865; children—Florence Winchester (dec.), Roger Sherman, Helen Harriet (wife of Dr. Warren Randall Gilman). Instr. law, 1869-72, prof. law, 1872—, Yale; asso. justice, 1893-1907, chief justice, 1907-10, Supreme Court of Errors of Conn.; gov. of Conn., terms 1911-13, 1913-15. Mem. commn. to revise gen. statutes, Conn., 1873, and for simplifying legal procedure, 1879; mem. commn. and drew report for better system of taxation, 1885; chmn. to revise state taxation system, 1915-17. Author: Baldwin's Connecticut Digest; Baldwin's Cases on Railroad Law, 1896; Modern Political Institutions, 1898; (co-author) Two Centuries' Growth of American Law, 1901; American Railroad Law, 1904; American Judiciary, 1905; The Relation of Education to Citizenship, 1912; Life and Letters of Simeon Baldwin, 1919; The Young Man and the Law, 1919; Osborn's History of Connecticut (co-author), 1925. Home: New Haven, Conn. Died Jan. 30, 1927.

BALDWIN, Theodore Anderson, brig. gen.; b. in N.J., Dec. 31, 1839. Served pvt. and q.-m. sergt. 19th Inf., May 3, 1862-May 3, 1865; promoted through grades to brig. gen. vols., Oct. 6, 1898; hon. discharged from vol. service, Jan. 31, 1899; col. 7th Cav., May 6, 1899; brig.-gen., Apr. 19, 1903; retired at own request after 40 yrs.' service. Apr. 20, 1903. Died Sept. 1, 1925.

BALDWIN, Thomas Scott, aeronaut; b. Quincy, Ill., June 30, 1860. Began with a circus at 10 as a gymnast, later becoming a tight rope walker; as a balloonist, 1887; invented and flew dirigible balloon at St. Louis Expn., 1904, also at Portland, Ore., and Buffalo expns. Apptd. by govt. to superintend bldg. of all spherical, dirigible and kite balloons; built first govt. airship, 1908; commd. maj. Aviation Corps, 1917. Died May 17, 1923.

BALDWIN, Wilbur McIntosh, banker; b. Solon, O., Sept. 27, 1875; s. Francis Hart and Elizabeth Thorburn (McIntosh) B.; ed. high sch., Chagrin Falls., O.; m. Florence Adams Shanklin, June 6, 1900; 1 dau., Elizabeth (Mrs. Richard Marion Brett). Office boy Cleveland Chamber of Commerce, 1984-95; became clk., 1895, Park Nat. Bank, later consolidated with Union Trust Co., of which was pres., 1930-33. Trustee Adelbert Coll. of Western Reserve U., Hiram (O.) Coll. Republican. Mem. Disciples of Christ Ch Home: Cleveland, O. Died Nov. 6, 1938

BALDWIN, William Delevan, mfr.; b. Auburn, N.Y., Sept. 5, 1856; ed. pub. schs.; m. Helen R. Sullivan, 1881. Chmn. bd. Otis Elevator Co., Otis-Fensom Elevator Co., Canada; dir. Barnett Nat. Bank, U.S. Life Ins. Co. in City of N.Y., etc.; trustee U.S. Savings Bank. Home: New York, N.Y. Died Sept. 26, 1930.

BALDWIN, William Henry; b. Youngstown, O., July 16, 1851; s. Timothy D. and Lucretia K. (Manning) B.; A.B., Western Reserve Coll., 1871; m. Isabel Cort, Apr. 26, 1893. Cashier First Nat. Bank, Youngstown, 1877-87, v.p., 1889-1900; v.p. and mgr. Arms-Bell Co., 1887-89; sec. Youngstown Iron & Steel Co., 1890-92, Union Iron & Steel Co., 1892-94; sec. and treas. Ohio Steel Co., 1894-99; sec. Nat. Steel Co., 1899-1901; retired, 1901, and has since devoted attention to social work. Dir. Nat. Tuberculosis Assn., 1906— (exec. com., 1906-20, treas., 1912-19); mem. President's Homes Commission, 1907; del. to Internat. Conf. on Tuberculosis, Brussels, Belgium, 1910; official del. of U.S. to Internat. Congress on Tuberculosis, Rome, 1912; mem. Conf. of Commrs. on Uniform State Laws for D.C., 1913-15; chmn. District Council of Defense, 1917-20; trustee Adelbert Coll. (Western Reserve U.), 1888—; chmn. Phi Beta Kappa Assn., D.C., 1919-21. Republican. Presbyn. Author: Family Desertion and Non-Support Laws, 1904; also numerous articles on sociol. topics. Homes: New York, N.Y., and Washington, D.C. Died Sept. 26, 1923.

BALDWIN, William Henry, Jr., pres. Long Island R.R. Co., 1896—; b. Boston, Feb. 5, 1863; s. W. H. B.; preparatory edn., public schools, Boston, and Roxbury Latin School; A.B., Harvard, 1885; m. Ruth Standish Bowles, Oct. 30, 1889. Prior to June 1, 1888, div. freight agt. Union Pacific Ry., Butte, Mont.; asst. gen. freight agt. same, Omaha, 1888-89; mgr. Leavenworth div., same, Leavenworth, Kans., 1889; gen. mgr. Mont. Union Ry., 1889-90; asst. v.p. Union Pacific Ry., Omaha, Neb., 1890-91; gen. mgr. Flint & Pere Marquette R.R., 1891-94; 3d v.p., 1894-95; 2d v.p. 1895-96, Southern Ry. Home: Brooklyn, N.Y. Died 1905.

BALDWIN, William James (St. John), mech. engr.; b. June 14, 1844, on shipboard; birth recorded at Waterford, Ireland; s. Capt. John and Giovanna Caterina (San Giovanni) B.; ed. Boston, and Charlottetown (St. Dunstan's), P.E.I., 2 yrs.; spl. training in naval architecture; studied navigation drawing, engring. and physics; married. Began in mech. engring. and naval architecture, 1863; spl. work in naval constrn. during Civil War; was with Donald McKay, "prince of ship builders," at East Boston, in the construction of 3 monitors and the conversion of several blockade runners into U.S. cruisers; in the Brazilian service, as asst. naval constr., 1866-67. Was the first domestic engr. in the high buildings of New York; cons. engr. and designer for the U.S. War Coll., Washington, D.C., U.S. Immigrant Station, N.Y. Harbor, U.S. Soldiers' Home, Tennessee, etc., and cons. engr. for Dept. Health, City of New York, hosps. and power-plants; over 24 yrs. cons. engr. N.Y. Telephone Co. and Empire City Subway Co. Asso. editor Engring. Record, 1880-89; lecturer and prof. thermal engring., Poly. Inst., Brooklyn. Mem. Commn. of Am. Soc. Mech. Engrs. that formulated the standard pipe threads (known as "the Briggs formul") for U.S.A. and Can., 1886; mem. internat. commn. for the formulation of an internat. standard for pipes and fittings; mem. spl. com. Am. Soc. M.E. for electric screw thread standards. Life mem. A.I.A. Author: Steam Heating for Buildings, 1881; Hot Water Heating and Fitting, 1887; Baldwin on Heating, 1890; Data for Heating and Ventilation, 1897; An Outline of Ventilating and Warming, 1899; The Ventilation of the School-Room, 1901. Home: Brooklyn, N.Y. Died May 7, 1924.

BALDY, Edward Vincent, clergyman, educator; b. Starkville, Lee Co., Ga., Feb. 4, 1861; s. William Hugh and Mary Caroline (Monro) B.; A.B., Mercer U., 1885, A.M., 1886, LL.D., 1925; Th.M., or full graduate, Southern Bapt. Theol. Sem., 1889; grad. study, U. of Chicago and other instns.; D.D., U. of Richmond, 1906; m. Mary Frances Henderson, Apr. 7, 1897. Ordained Bapt. ministry, 1885; asst. pastor 1st Ch., Macon, Ga., 1887-88, pastor 1st Ch., Cuthbert, Ga., 1890-94, 1st Ch., Bowling Green, Ky., 1894-99, Bainbridge St. Ch., Richmond, Va., 1899-1907, 1st Ch., Hartsville, S.C., 1907-23; pres. Coker Coll., 1908-10, also prof. philosophy and Bible, 1908-16; pres. Judson Coll., Marion, Ala., 1923-30. Mason. Home: Birmingham, Ala. Deceased.

BALL, Alice Worthington, painter; b. Boston, Mass.; d. J. Dorsey and Emily A. (Cole) B.; student Boston Mus. Fine Arts; later Acad. Colarossi and Atelier Collin, Paris; pupil of George Hitchcock, in N. Holland. Exhibited in Paris Salon 4 times; Soc. des Dames Americaine, Paris; New York, Pittsburgh, Boston, Phila., Chicago, Indianapolis, St. Louis, New Orleans, etc. Home: Baltimore, Md. Died July 22, 1929.

BALL, A(lonzo) Brayton, physician; b. New York, Feb. 10, 1840; s. Alonzo S. and Eliza W. B.; A.B., Yale, 1860; M.D. Coll. Phys & Surg., New York, 1863; m. Helen S. Stone, Mar. 15, 1866. Mem. house staff New York Hosp., 1863-65; lecturer Coll. Phys. & Surg., 1870-76; visiting physician Bellevue Hosp., 1885-88; attending physician St. Luke's Hosp., 1881-97, New York Hosp. 1888—; prof. clin. medicine, Columbia Univ. Home: New York, N.Y. Died 1908;

BALL, Charles Backus, sanitarian; b. New Haven, Conn., Aug. 31, 1854; s. Charles and Sarah (Backus) B.; Ph.B., Sheffield Scientific Sch. (Yale), 1880; m. Lydia G. Pratt, Jan. 12, 1881; 1 son, Dwight Backus. Began as field insp. Potomac River Improvement, Washington, 1882; insp. plumbing, Washington, 1895-1901; chief insp. Tenement House Dept., New York, 1902-03; chief sanitary insp., Dept. of Health, Chicago, 1904—; dir. Chicago Regional Planning Assn. 1923—. Mem. Hoover Advisory Com. on City Planning, U.S. Dept. Commerce, 1924. Protestant. Home: Chicago, Ill. Died 1928.

BALL, Farlin Q., judge; b. in Ohio, Mar. 28, 1838; s. James M. and Keturah (Ford) B.; Ph.B., U. of Wis., 1861; pvt. to maj. 31st Wis. Inf., 1862-65; m. Elizabeth Hall, June 23, 1868. Admitted to Wis. bar, Nov., 1865; state's atty. of Dane Co., Wis., 2 terms; removed to Chicago, 1869; was especially prominent in the suits arising out of the lake front controversy as atty. for several owners of riparian rights. Judge Superior Ct. of Ct., 1st Dist. Judge-advocate of the 1st Brigade, I.N.G., 6 yrs. Served in the Appellate. Home: Oak Park, Ill. Died Aug. 29, 1917.

BALL, George Harvey, clergyman, educator; b. Sherbrooke, P. Q., Can., Dec. 7, 1819; s. Jonathan B. and Marcy (Harvey) B.; moved to Ohio, 1837; ed. Farmington Acad. and Grand River Inst., O., and Cobb Divinity School, Lewiston, Me.; read a course of law; m. Jan. 20, 1848, Maria L. Benchley. Prin. Geauga Sem., O., 1848-50; pastor Hudson St. Bapt. Ch., Buffalo, 1850-55; pastor Roger Williams Ch., Providence, R.I., 1855-57; mem. 1st Rep. Conv., Phila., 1856; pastor of ch. at Buffalo again, 1857-71; editor Baptist Union, New York, 1871-77; pastor Buffalo ch. again, 1877-90; founder and pres., 1892—, Keuka Coll. Invited guest Nat. Rep. Conv., Phila., 1900. Author: Guide to the Lord's Supper, 1852; The Story of Jesus, 1857; Christian Baptism, 1891; Bible Syllabus, 1902. Home: Keuka Park, N.Y. Died 1907.

BALL, James Moores, ophthalmologist; b. W. Union, Ia., Sept. 4, 1863; s. Dr. James Moores and Martha G. (Glover) B.; M.D., State U. of Ia., 1884; several post-grad courses in New York and Europe; m. Naomi Marshall, Oct. 16, 1890; children—Logan Marshall, Mrs. Mary Josephine Lafean. Was prof. diseases of the eye, Nat. Univ.; oculist, Nat. Univ. Hosp. Editor Annals of Ophthalmology. Episcopalian. Author: Ball's Modern Ophthalmology, 1904; Andreas Vesalius, the Reformer of Anatomy, 1910. Home: St. Louis, Mo. Died Mar. 1929.

BALL, L(ewis) Heisler, senator; b. nr. Stanton, Del., Sept. 21, 1861; s. John and Sarah (Baldwin) B.; Ph.B., Delaware Coll., 1882; M.D., U. of Pa., 1885; m. Katherine Springer Justis, Nov. 14, 1893. Began practice of medicine, 1885; state treas., Del., 1898-1900; mem. 57th Congress (1901-03). Del. at large; elected mem. U.S. Senate, Mar. 2, 1903, to fill vacancy for term ending Mar. 3, 1905; resumed practice of medicine at Faulkland, Del.; del. Rep. Nat. Conv., 1896; mem. U.S. Senate, 1919-25. Home: Marshallton, Del. Died Oct. 18, 1933.

BALL, Thomas, sculptor; b. at Charlestown, Mass., June 3, 1819; ed. Mayhew Sch., Boston; (hon. A.M., Dartmouth, 1860); m. Ellen Louisa Wild, Oct. 10, 1854. Practiced painting, 1840-52; adopted sculpture, 1851; designed and made equestrian statue of Washington in Boston; statue of Daniel Webster, Central Park, New York, and many other public statues; devoted yrs. 1891-98 to monument of Washington for Methuen, Mass. Resided in Florence, Italy, 1865-97. Amateur musician and original "Elijah" in America, 1848. Author: My Three Score Years and Ten, an Autobiography; and numerous lyrics and minor poems. Home: Montclair, N.J. Died 1911.

BALLANTINE, William Gay, educator; b. Washington, D.C., Dec. 7, 1848; s. Prof. Elisha and Betsy Ann (Watkins) B.; A.B., Marietta Coll., 1868, D.D., 1885; grad. Union Theol. Sem., New York, 1872; U. of Leipzig, 1872-73; LL.D., Western Reserve, 1891; m. Emma Frances Atwood, Aug. 17, 1875; children—Henry Winthrop, Arthur Atwood, Edward, Mary Frances (Mrs. Horace E. Allen). Asst. Eng. Am. Palestine Exploring Expdn., 1873; prof. chemistry and natural science, Ripon Coll., 1874-76; asst. prof. Greek, Ind. U., 1876-78; prof. Greek and Hebrew, 1878-81, prof. O. T. lang. and lit., Oberlin Theol. Sem., 1881-91; pres. Oberlin Coll., 1891-96; prof. of Bible, Internat. Y.M.C.A. Coll., Springfield, Mass., 1897-1920. Author: Inductive Logic, 1896; The Young Man from Jerusalem, 1921; Understanding the Bible, 1925; Discovering Jesus, 1927; The Logic of Science, 1933; Peggy in the Park, 1933. Translator of the Riverside New Testament, 1923. Home: Springfield, Mass. Died Jan. 10, 1937.

BALLARD, Aaron Edward, clergyman; b. Bloomfield, N.J., Dec. 25, 1820; s. Jeremiah and Hetty

(Brown) B.; self-ed.; (D.D., Taylor U., Ind.); m. Emily Young, 1849; m. 2d, Anna Miller, 1887. Licensed as minister M.E. Ch., 1844; served in many pastorates in N.J., also as presiding elder; state temperance agt. and pres. Evang. Ch. Commn., 1890-92; retired from active pastoral work, 1902. Trustee Pennington Sem. Republican. Mason. Home: Ocean Grove, N.J. Died Nov. 27, 1919.

BALLARD, Addison, clergyman; b. Framingham, Mass., Oct. 18, 1822; s. John and Pamelia (Bennett) B.; A.B., Williams, 1842 (D.D., 1867); m. Julia Perkins Pratt, Aug. 7, 1851; father of Harland Hoge B. Prin. Hopkins Acad., Hadley, Mass., 1842-43; tutor Williams, 1843-44; teacher Grand Rapids, 1845-46; ordained Congl. ministry, 1846; prof. Latin, 1848-52, mathematics, 1852-54, Ohio U.; prof. rhetoric, Williams, 1854-55; prof. mathematics, natural philosophy and astronomy, Marietta Coll., 1855-57; pastor Williamstown, Mass., 1857-65, Detroit, 1866-72; prof. Christian Greek and Latin, 1874-79, moral philosophy and rhetoric, 1879-93, Lafayette Coll.; prof. logic, New York U., 1893-1904. Author: Popular Amusements, 1869; Arrows, or Teaching a Fine Art, 1875; From Talk to Text, 1904; Through the Sieve, 1906-07; From Text to Talk, 1910. Home: Pittsfield, Mass. Died Dec. 2, 1914.

BALLARD, Edward Lathrop, fire insurance; b. Noroton, Conn., June 30, 1870; s. Frank Wade and Anna Judson (Marten) B.; ed. pvt. schs., N.Y. City; m. Elizabeth Gates Biglow, Feb. 8, 1906; 2 daughters. Began in fire ins. business with New York Bowery Ins. Co., 1887; with Continental Fire Ins. Co., 1896-1910, asst. sec., 1897-1903, 2d v.p. and sec., 1909-10, also same for subsidiary co., Fidelity Fire Ins. Co., 1909-10; organizer, 1910, pres. to 1920, chmn. bd. to 1930, Merchants Fire Assurance Corp. of New York, chmn. exec. com., 1930—; chmn. exec. com. Washington Assurance Corp. of New York, 1930—; also chmn. exec. com. Merchants Indemnity Corp. Republican. Home: New York, N.Y. Died Dec. 31, 1937.

BALLARD, Ellis Ames, lawyer; b. Athens, O., May 7. 1861; s. Frederic Lyman and Alice (Walker) B.; A.B., U. of Pa., 1881, LL.B., 1883; LL.D., Dickinson Coll, Carlisle, Pa., 1929; m. Nina Schwefel, Oct. 22, 1884; children—Ernest Schwefel, Frederic Lyman, Mary (Mrs. Samuel S. Duryee). Admitted to Pa. bar, 1883, and began practice at Philadelphia; mem. Ballard, Spahr, Andrews & Ingersoll; gen. counsel Phila. Rapid Transit Co., 1902-30; dir. Electric Storage Battery Co. Republican. Episcopalian. Home: Philadelphia, Pa. Died June 13, 1938.

BALLARD, Harlan Hoge, librarian; b. Athens, O., May 26, 1853; s. Addison and Julia Perkins (Pratt) B.; A.B., Williams, 1874, M.A., 1877; m. Lucy Bishop, d. John Pike, of Newburyport, Mass., and g.d. Judge Henry Walker Bishop, of Lenox, Mass., Aug. 20, 1879; children—Harlan Hoge, Elizabeth Bishop, Lucy Bishop, Margaret (dec.). Prin. Lenox (Mass.) High Sch., 1874-80; prin. Lenox (Mass.) Academy, 1880-86; librarian of Berkshire Athenæum and Museum, 1888—. Organized, 1875, and trustee Agassiz Assn. for Study of Nature, which has had over 1,000 branches. Mason. Author: Three Kingdoms, 1882; World of Matter, 1892; Open Sesame, 1896; Reopen Sesame, 1897; Virgil's Æneid, tr. into English Hexameters, 1902-11, bimillennial edit., 1931; The Tiler's Jewel (a Masonic novel), 1921; Adventures of a Librarian, 1929. Joint Author: American Plant Book, 1879; Barnes' Readers, 1883; One Thousand Blunders in English, 1884. Home: Pittsfield, Mass. Died Feb. 18, 1934.

BALLARD, James Franklin, mfr.; b. Ashtabula, O., July 16, 1851; s. James and Eliza (Heath) B.; ed. pub. schs., Almont, Mich.; m. Emma Hill Hadley, June 24, 1878; children—William J. (dec.), Berenice, Mrs. David B. White. Settled in St. Louis, Mo., 1874; with Richardson & Co., wholesale druggists, until 1882; established bus. under name of James F. Ballard, 1882, inc. Jan. 1923; treas. James F. Ballard, Inc.; dir. First Nat. Bank and Union Trust Co. (St. Louis), Fellows Med. Mfg. Co. (New York); owner of bus. of Henry B. Platt Co., New York. Trustee Mo. Hist. Soc., and mem. exec. com. Archæol. Soc., St. Louis; fellow N.A.D. (life); dir. La. Purchase Expn. Presented Met. Mus. of Art, New York, May 1922, $500,000 collection Oriental rugs, said to be the greatest collection of the kind ever assembled by any museum or individual; 3 times around the World in quest of rugs. Republican. Christian Scientist. Presented City Art Mus., St. Louis, with collection of rare Oriental rugs, valued in excess of $250,000.00, 1929. Home: New York, N.Y. Died Apr. 23, 1931.

BALLARD, Russell Henry, utility operator; b. Hamilton, Ont., Can., July 26, 1875; s. Walter John and Harriet A. (Morphy) B.; ed. pub. and high schs.; m. 2d, Gladys Morphy; 1 dau. by 1st marriage, Harriet. Came to U.S., 1883; began as office boy, Thomson, Houston Electric Co., Chicago, 1890; with treasury dept. Gen. Electric Co., Schenectady, N.Y., 1893; in charge credits and collections for Southern states office Gen. Electric Co., Atlanta, Ga., 1895-97; auditor Edison Electric Co., Los Angeles, Calif., 1897-1900; office mgr. Butte (Mont.) Electric & Power Co., 1900-04; with Southern Calif. Edison Co., 1904—. became pres. and gen. mgr.; pres. Phoenix Machinery & Cold Storage Co., Ballard Bros. Co., Los Angeles Fire Alarm Co., Pacific Light & Power Corp., Calif. Inst. Associates, Shaver Lake Lumber Co.; v.p. Santa Barbara Electric Co. Dir. precinct organization Liberty Loan campaigns; dir. Community Development Assn., Los Angeles Community Chest. Republican. Mason. Home: Los Angeles, Calif. Died Aug. 24, 1932.

BALLARD, S(amuel) Thruston, flour miller; b. Louisville, Ky., Feb. 11, 1855; s. Andrew Jackson and Frances Anne (Thruston) B.; B.S., Cornell U., 1878; m. Sunshine Harris, Jan. 25, 1883. With brother, 1880, in organization of Ballard & Ballard Co., flour mfrs., of which is pres.; also pres. Liberty Coal & Coke Co.; v.p. Louisville Nat. Bank. Elected lt. gov. of Ky., term, 1920-23. Mem. Ky. State Cav., 1881. Mem. Employers' Assn., Louisville (pres., 1904-09), Jefferson Co. Rd. Improvement League (1st pres., 1913); apptd. by President Woodrow Wilson member Nat. Industrial Commn., July 1913; greatly interested in welfare of working men and applies profit-sharing system in his mills. A leader in securing child welfare and labor legislation in Ky. Episcopalian. Chmn. nat. com. on cost of living and domestic economy of Council Nat. Defense; mem. com. of 29 millers apptd. by Herbert C. Hoover, Food Administrator, 1917. Was chmn. War Camp Community Service for Ky.; mem. Am. Com. for Devastated France, Dist. Com. on Capital Issues; Ky. chmn. British and Canadian Recruiting Mission. Home: Glenview, Ky. Died Jan. 18, 1926.

BALLENGER, George Walter, clergyman; b. Monroe, Wis., Apr. 1, 1860; s. Asa A. (mem. 28th Wis. Vols. and killed in battle at Petersburg, Va., 1865) and Rebecca M. (Steckle) B.; entered Soldiers' Orphans' Home, Madison, Wis., at age of 7; started for self at 14; student State Acad., and Winslow High Sch., Madison, Wis.; Ill. Evang. Conf. Sem., 1880-84; grad. Oskaloosa (Ia.) Coll. (D.D., 1911); m. Mary L. Becker, May 16, 1889 (died 1897); 2d, Annie Robinson, 1889. Licensed to preach in Evang. Ch., 1880; ordained elder, 1885; pastor under Evang. Conf., Ill., 1881-86, Fairbury, Ill., 1886-87, 6th Av. Ch., Chicago, 1887-91; lecturer for Nat. Religious Liberty Assn., 1 yr., and city mission work in Chicago. Ordained Bapt. ministry, 1891; pastor Tremont, Ill., 1892-99; missionary evangelist, Ill., 1899-1900; pastor 1st Ch., Clinton, Ill., 1901-03; retired, 1903; elected hon. pastor for life, 1st Ch., Tremont, 1911. Home: Tremont, Ill. Died Jan. 1938.

BALLENGER, William Lincoln, physician; b. Economy, Ind., Apr. 26, 1861; s. William and Lydia Ann (Starbuck) B.; student Earlham Coll., 1881; M.D., Bellevue Hosp. Med. Coll. (New York U.), 1886; m. Ada Poarch, July 15, 1886. Teacher in pub. schs., Ind. 1881-83; in gen. practice of medicine, Richmond, Ind., 1886-93; gen. practice at Evanston, Ill., 1893-95; from 1895, practice limited to otology and laryngology; instr., 1895, lecturer, 1898, asst. prof., 1901, asso, prof., 1902, prof. otology and laryngology, 1903—, Med. Dept. U. of Ill., Chicago; instr. Chicago Polyclinic, 1891; prof. otology, Chicago Eye and Ear Coll. Congregationalist. Republican. Author: Diseases of the Nose, Throat and Ear (textbook), 1900; Otology and Laryngology. Home: Hubbard Woods, Ill. Died Dec. 21, 1915.

BALLIN, Max, surgeon; b. Nordhausen, Germany, Aug. 13, 1869; s. Jacob and Clementina (Heineman) B.; ed. Gymnasium, Nordhausen, and at univs. of Freiburg, Munich and Berlin; M.D., U. of Berlin, 1892; m. Carrie Leppel, July 10, 1901. Began practice in Detroit, 1901; surgeon Harper Hosp. Lt. col. Med. O.R.C. Republican. Home: Detroit, Mich. Died Mar. 3, 1934.

BALLINGER, Richard Achilles, sec. of the interior; b. Boonesboro, Ia., July 9, 1858; s. Col. Richard H. and Mary E. B.; prep. edn. U. of Kan. and Washburn Coll.; A.B., Williams Coll., 1884 (LL.D., 1909); m. Julia A. Bradley, Oct. 26, 1886. Admitted to bar, 1886; practiced and was city atty. of Kankakee, Ill., and New Decatur, Ala.; practiced at Port Townsend, Wash., 1889-97, Seattle, from 1897. U.S. court commr., 1890-92; judge Superior Ct., Jefferson Co., Wash., 1894-97; mayor of Seattle, 1904-06; commr. Gen. Land Office, Washington, 1907-09; sec. of the interior, in the cabinet of President Taft, Mar. 4, 1909-Mar. 6, 1911 (resigned); since engaged in law practice at Seattle, Wash.; sr. mem. Ballinger, Battle, Hulbert & Shorts. Chmn. Wash. delegation, Rep. Nat. Conv., 1908. Author: Ballinger on Community Property, 1895; Ballinger's Annotated Codes and Statutes of Washington, 1897. Home: Seattle, Wash. Died June 6, 1922.

BALLMANN, Martin, orchestra and band leader; b. Dortmund, Westphalia, Germany, Sept. 13, 1863; s. Leonhard and Anna (Ritter) B.; ed. Dortmund, Hamburg and Celle, Germany, and Vienna, Austria; m. Anna Ritter, Apr. 24, 1893. Came to U.S. as solo flutist, Eduard Strauss' Orchestra, 1890; mem. Theodore Thomas Orchestra, Chicago, 1891-1908; founder, 1908, and dir. Ballmann's Orchestra and Ballmann's Band of Chicago; founder and dir. Ballmann's Orchestral Sch. Home: Chicago, Ill. Died June 11, 1931.

BALLOU, Charles Clarendon, army officer; b. Orange Tp., N.Y., June 13, 1862; s. William Hosea and Julia A. (Hendrick) B.; U.S. Mil. Acad., grad., 1886; Inf. and Cav. Sch., 1897-98; Field Officers' Sch., 1916; War Coll., 1916-17. Commd. 2d lt. 16th Inf., July 1, 1886; promoted through grades to col., July 19, 1916; brig. gen. N.A., Aug. 5, 1917; maj. gen. N.A., Nov. 28, 1917; retired June 13, 1926. Served as maj. 7th Ill. Inf. Vols., July 8-Oct.20, 1898; regtl. q.m., P.I., 1899; participated in Battle of Zapote River, June 13, 1899, and minor engagements, also assault on Angeles, Aug. 16, 1899; comdr. 92d Div. (colored), A.E.F., Oct. 27, 1917-Nov. 19, 1918; comdr. 6th Army Corps, Oct. 23-Nov. 11, 1918; comdr. 89th Div., Nov. 19, 1918-Feb. 1, 1919. Participated in Battle of the Argonne, battle of Nov. 10th and 11th, on Moselle River, and various engagements in St. Die sector. Notable achievement was passing safely, with one attendant, through the camp of over 5,000 hostile Sioux Indians, soon after the Battle of Wounded Knee, in 1890. Awarded silver star citation by President Coolidge, Mar. 10, 1927, "for gallantry in action"; decorated Croix de Guerre with Palm and Officer Legion of Honor (French). Home: Spokane, Wash. Died July 23, 1928.

BALLOU, Sidney (Miller), lawyer; b. Providence, R.I., Oct. 24, 1870; s. Oren Aldrich and Charlotte (Miller) B.; A.B., Harvard, 1893, A.M., 1899; m. Thomie Duke, Dec. 21, 1895 (died Mar. 7, 1905); 1 dau., Barbara; m. 2d, Lucia Burnett, July 27, 1907. Admitted to bar, 1895; went to Hawaii, 1895; justice Supreme Ct. of Ty. of Hawaii, Aug. 15, 1907-May 7, 1909. Gen. counsel C. & H. Sugar Refining Corp. Served as lt. Coast Arty., World War; lt. comdr. U.S.N. Reserve. Compiler: Civil Laws and Penal Laws of Hawaii, 1897 (compilation officially adopted in act of Congress organizing Ty. of Hawaii). Writer on mil. and economic subjects. Exec. sec. The Sugar Institute. Died Oct. 29, 1929.

BALMANNO, Charles Gorden, banker; b. Brooklyn, N.Y., June 23, 1864; s. Alexander and Annie (Smith) B.; ed. pub. schs., Brooklyn, and Trinity Ch. Sch., New York; m. Martha N. Manning, Sept. 18, 1889. Engaged in banking business in Brooklyn, 1880—; pres. Mechanics Bank; trustee Greater N.Y. Savings Bank; dir. Bank of Flatbush, Bank of Coney Island, N.Y. Title Ins. Co., Brooklyn Warehouse & Storage Co. Trustee Adelphi Coll., Brooklyn; mem. Brooklyn Inst. Arts and Sciences. Formerly color sergt., 3d Gatling Battery, N.G.N.Y. Republican. Episcopalian. Mason. Home: Brooklyn, N.Y. Died Mar. 7, 1916.

BALTZELL, Winton James, editor; b. Shiremanstown, Pa., Dec. 18, 1864; s. Rev. Isaiah and Cecilia Caroline (James) B.; A.B., Lebanon Valley Coll., Annville, Pa., 1884; Mus. Bac., U. of Pa., 1896; studied at N.E. Conservatory of Music, Boston, 1888-89, and pvtly. in London, Eng., 1889-90; m. Bertha Sweet, June 27, 1900; children—Rolfe Edmunds, Ruth James. Professional musician, teacher of singing, and organist, Reading, Pa., 1890-97; editor The Étude, Phila., 1897-99; teacher of history and theory of music, Ohio Wesleyan U., 1899-1900; editor The Étude, 1900-07; editor The Musician, Boston, 1907-19; sec. Nat. Acad. of Music, New York, 1919—. Republican. Episcopalian. Author: A Complete History of Music, 1905; Baltzell's Dictionary of Musicians, 1911; Noted Names in Music, 1927; also elementary text-books on harmony, theory of music, musical form, history of music, The Master Composers, Music Appreciation, A Piano Primer, and a number of songs and part-songs and anthems, violin pieces and a suite for string quartet. Home: New York, N.Y. Died Jan. 10, 1928.

BALZAR, Fredrick Bennett, governor; b. Virginia City, Nev., June 15, 1880; s. Serafino and Minnie (Bennett) B.; grad. Polytechnic High Sch., San Francisco, Calif.; m. Idelle Edna Sinnamon, Nov. 11, 1907; 1 dau., Phylis Rae. Engaged in mining, 1899—. Mem. Nev. Ho. of Rep., 1905, Senate, 1909-17; sheriff and assessor Mineral Co., Nev., 1917-27; state chmn. Rep. Party, 1924; gov. of Nevada, 2 terms, 1927-34. Chmn. Mineral County Draft Bd., World War; chmn. State Bd. of Edn., Nev., 1927—. Christian Scientist. Mason. Home: Carson City, Nev. Died Mar. 21, 1934.

BAMBERGER, Simon, governor; b. Darmstadt, Germany, Feb. 27, 1847; s. Emanuel and Helen (Fleish) B.; brought to U.S., 1861; ed. pub. schs.; m. Ida Maas, Nov. 23, 1881; children—Sidney (dec.), Mrs. Helen Behal, Julian M., Mrs. Elsa Michael. Resident of Utah since 1869; pres. Bamberger Coal Co.; dir. Salt Lake Valley Loan & Trust Co.; dir. and treas. Bamberger Electric R.R. Mem. Utah Senate, 1903-07; mem. Sch. Bd., Salt Lake City, 1898-1903; gov. of Utah, term 1917-21. Democrat. Mem. B'nai B'rith. Mason. Home: Salt Lake City, Utah. Died Oct. 6, 1926.

BANCROFT, Cecil Franklin Patch, prin. Phillips Acad., Andover, Mass., 1873—; b. of early Puritan stock, New Ipswich, N. H., Nov. 25, 1839; grad.

Dartmouth Coll., 1860; Andover Theol. Sem., 1867; Univ. of Halle, Germany; Ph.D., Univ. of New York, L.H.D., Williams; LL.D., Yale; prin. Mt. Vernon, N.H., 1860-64; prin. Lookout Mt. Ednl. Instns., Tenn., 1867-72; ordained (Congregationalist), May 1, 1867, but has never been a pastor; m. Frances A. Kittredge, May 6, 1867 (died, 1898). Trustee Dartmouth Coll., Andover Theol. Sem., and two of the Mass. public instns. of charity; has been pres. Head Masters' Assn. Home: Andover, Mass. Died 1901.

BANCROFT, Charles Parker, alienist; b. St. Johnsbury, Vt., Jan. 11, 1852; s. Jesse Parker and Elisabeth (Speare) B.; A.B., Harvard, 1874, M.D., 1878; m. Susan C. Wood, 1884. Formerly house officer Boston City Hosp.; asst. phys., 1878-79, supt., 1882-1917, chmn. trustees, 1919—, State Hosp.; phys. Boston City Dispensary, 1880. Contbr. to Wood's Handbook of the Medical Sciences and to medical jours. Chmn. N.H. Bd. Charities and Corrections. Home: Concord, N.H. Died Dec. 14, 1923.

BANCROFT, Edgar Addison, lawyer; b. Galesburg, Ill., Nov. 20, 1857; s. Addison N. and Catharine (Blair) B.; brother of Frederic B.; A.B., Knox Coll., 1878, A.M., 1881; LL.B., Columbia Law School, 1880; (LL.D., Knox College, 1912); m. Margaret Healy, Apr. 18, 1896. In gen. practice, Galesburg, 1884-92, Chicago, 1892—; solicitor for Ill. of A.,T. &S.F. R.R. Co., 1892-95; v.p. and gen. solicitor, Chicago & Western Ind. R.R. Co. and the Belt Ry. Co., 1895-1904; mem. Scott, Bancroft, Martin & MacLeish, 1904—; general counsel Internat. Harvester Co., 1907-20. Rep. presdl. elector, 1888. Author: The Chicago Strike of 1894, 1895; The Moral Sentiment of the People, the Foundation of National Greatness, 1896; Destruction or Regulation of Trusts, 1907. Home: Chicago, Ill. Died July 28, 1925.

BANCROFT, Hubert Howe, historian; b. Granville, O., May 5, 1832; s. Ashley and Lucy (Howe) B.; (hon. A.M., Yale, 1875); m. Matilda Griffing, Oct. 12, 1876 (died 1910). Entered book store, Buffalo, N.Y., 1848; established a pub. house at San Francisco, 1856; began collecting Pacific Coast hist. data, 1858, which when turned over to U. of Calif., 1905, numbered 60,000 vols., including 500 original manuscripts, mostly dictations taken from prominent pioneers. Author: West American Historical Series, 39 vols., 1875-87; comprising: Native Races of the Pacific States, 5 vols.; History of Central America, 3 vols.; History of Mexico, 6 vols.; North Mexican States and Texan, 2 vols.; California, 7 vols.; Arizona and New Mexico, 1 vol.; Colorado and Wyoming, 1 vol.; Utah and Nevada, 1 vol.; Northwest Coast, 2 vols.; Oregon, 2 vols.; Washington, Idaho and Montana, 1 vol.; British Columbia, 1 vol.; Alaska, 1 vol.; California Pastoral, 1 vol.; California Inter Pocula, 1 vol.; Popular Tribunals, 2 vols.; Essays and Miscellany, 1 vol.; Literary Industries, 1 vol. Other works are Chronicles of the Builders of the Commonwealth, 7 vols., 1891-92; Resources of Mexico, 1893; The Book of the Fair, 1894; The New Pacific, 1899; Some Cities and San Francisco, 1907; The Book of Wealth, 1909-10; Retrospection, Personal, and Political, 1912. Home: San Francisco, Calif. Died Mar. 2, 1918.

BANCROFT, Hugh, publisher; b. Cambridge, Mass., Sept. 13, 1879; s. William Amos and Mary (Shaw) B.; A.B., Harvard, 1897, A.M., 1898; LL.B., Harvard Law Sch., 1901; m. Mary A. Cogan (died 1903); 1 dau., Mary (Mrs. Sherwin C. Badger); m. 2d, Jane Wallis Waldron Barron, Jan. 15, 1907; children—Jessie (Mrs. William C. Cox), Hugh, Jr., Jane. Asst. dist. atty., Middlesex Co., 1902-06, dist. atty., 1907; chmn. bd. dirs. Port of Boston, 1911-14; pres. Boston News Bur. Co., Cohasset Nat. Bk.; also pres. Dow, Jones & Co., pubs. Wall St. Journal, pub. Barron's Weekly and Phila. Financial Jour. Mem. Mass. Vol. Militia, pvt. to brig. gen., 1894-1909, retired as maj. gen.; 1st lt. and adj., 5th Mass. Inf., U.S. Vols., Spanish-Am. War. Republican. Episcopalian. Author: Inheritance Taxes for Investors, 1911; Inheritance Taxes (with A. W. Blakemore), 1912. Home: New York, N.Y. Died Oct. 17, 1933.

BANCROFT, J(ohn) Sellers, mech. engr.; b. Providence, R.I., Sept. 12, 1843; s. Edward and Mary (Sellers) B.; grad. Central High Sch., Phila., 1861; m. Beulah Morris Hacker, Oct. 17, 1907. Began as apprentice William Sellers & Co., Phila., 1861; admitted to firm, 1873, gen. mgr., 1886-1902; gen. mgr., v.p. and treas. and mech. engr., Lanston Monotype Machine Co., 1902—. Mem. Soc. of Friends. Has taken out about 100 patents for mech. and elec. inventions. Home: Philadelphia, Pa. Died Jan. 29, 1919.

BANCROFT, Joseph, mfr., eng.; b. Rockford (now in Wilmington), Del., May 18, 1875; s. Samuel, Jr., and Mary Askew (Richardson) B.; B.S., in Chem. Engring., Mass. Inst. Tech., 1898; m. Elizabeth Howard, Oct. 29, 1902; 1 dau., Elizabeth (dec.). With Joseph Bancroft & Sons Co., mfrs., bleachers, dyers and finishers, Wilmington, 1898—, dir. and asst. treas., 1901-11, treas., 1911-17, v.p. in charge finance, 1917-28, chmn. bd., 1928-33; dir. same and subsidiaries; chmn. bd. Huntingdon & Broad Top Mountain R.R., 1934—; pres. and treas. Estate of Samuel Bancroft, Jr., Inc., 1916—. Chmn. Draft Bd. No. 1, Wilmington, and chmn. bituminous coal com., Del. Fuel Administration, World War. Mem. Bd. Harbor Commrs., Wilmington, 1919—. Dem. candidate for gov. of Del., 1924. Dir. Homœpathic Hosp., Wilmington. Quaker. Mason. Home: Wilmington, Del. Died May 6, 1936.

BANCROFT, William Amos, chmn. bd. Boston Elevated Ry. Co.; b. Groton, Mass., Apr. 26, 1855; s. Charles and Lydia Emeline (Spaulding) Bancroft; A.B., Harvard, 1878; Harvard Law Sch., 1879-81; capt. and stroke winning Harvard crews, 1977-79; admitted to bar, 1881; m. Mary Shaw, Jan 18, 1878. Practiced law, 1881-85; supt. Cambridge St. R.R., 1885-88; roadmaster West End St. Ry., Boston, 1888-90; pres., 1899-1916, afterward chmn. bd. dirs. Boston Elevated Ry. Co.; dir. U.S. and Chelsea Trust Co., Private to col. 5th Mass. Vol. Inf., 1875-97; brig. gen., 1897, maj. gen., 1901, Mass. Nat. Guard; brig. gen. U.S.V., May 27, 1898; resigned, Aug. 17, 1898. Mem. Cambridge Common Council, 1882; Mass. Ho. of Rep., 1883-85; pres. of aldermen, 1891-92, mayor, 1893-96, Cambridge; chmn. Rep. State Conv., 1893. Overseer Harvard, 1893-1905; trustee Norwich U., 1904-05, Lawrence Acad., Groton, Mass., 1908, Phillips Acad., Exeter, N.H., 1902—. Home: Cambridge, Mass. Died Mar. 11, 1922.

BANCROFT, William H., ry. official; b. Newburg, O., Oct. 20, 1840; s. Samuel O. and Mary B.; ed. pub. schs., Chagrin Falls, O.; m. Mary I. Baird, June, 1864; m. 2d, Margaret Corliss Moore, 1894. Entered ry. service Apr., 1856, as telegraph operator and ticket clerk, Mich. Southern Ry.; div. operator, clerk and dispatcher, Erie R.R., 1861-69; dispatcher, supt.'s clerk and train dispatcher Kan. Pacific R.R., 1883-86; prof. in tech. studies, Swarthmore Coll., 1886-92, but continued studies irregularly in Pa. Acad. Fine Arts; supt. schs. and instr. in Pa. Acad. Fine Arts, 1892-94; studied in Colorossi, Delachuse and Julien acads., Paris, 1894-99. Exhibited in Société des Artists Français, and in all large exhbns. of New York, Phila., Boston, Washington and Chicago; splty. portraits; executed mural decorations for Court of the Seasons, Panama-Pacific Expn., San Francisco. Instr. Mechanics Inst., New York. Home: New York, N.Y. Died Apr. 22, 1915.

BANCROFT, William Poole; b. nr. Wilmington, Del., July 12, 1835; s. Joseph and Sarah (Poole) B.; ed. family and boarding schs., 3 yrs., and for 2 yrs. under Samuel Alsop, of Wilmington; m. Emma Cooper, Nov. 1, 1876. Employed from boyhood in father's cotton factory; dir. Joseph Bancroft & Sons Co.; pres. Woodlawn Trustees, Inc.; dir. Security Trust & Safe Deposit Co. Trustee Del. Hosp., Wilmington Home for Friendless Children. Mem. Soc. Friends. Home: Wilmington, Del. Died Apr. 20, 1928.

BANDELIER, Adolph Francis Alphonse, archæologist; b. at Berne, Switzerland, Aug. 6, 1840; m. Fanny Ritter, Dec. 30, 1893. Came to U.S. in youth; traveled under auspices of Archæol. Inst. of America among native races of N.M., Ariz., Mexico and Central America, 1880-85; went to Peru and Bolivia, 1892, on scientific expdn. for Henry Villard, and has ever since pursued exhaustive archæol., ethnol. and hist. researches in those countries (for six years for Am. Mus. Natural History, for which he has gathered its extensive collection of Peruvian and Bolivian antiquities). Resided in Santa Fe, N.M., 1885-92; in charge documentary studies for Hemenway Archæol. Expdn., 1886-89. Lecturer Columbia U. on Spanish-Am. Literature in its connection with Ethnology and Archæology, July 1904-11. Author: The Art of War and Mode of Warfare, 1877; Tenure of Land and Inheritances of the Ancient Mexicans, 1878; On the Social Organization and Mode of Government of the Ancient Mexicans; Historical Introduction to Studies Among the Sedentary Indians of New Mexico; An Archæological Reconnoissance into Mexico, 1884; A Report on the Ruins of the Pueblo of Pecos, 1881; Final Report of Investigations Among the Indians of the Southwestern U.S., 1880-85, part 1, 1890, part 2, 1892; The Delight Makers (novel of Pueblo Indian Life); The Gilded Man; An Outline of the Documentary History of the Zuñi Tribe, 1892; The Indians and Aboriginal Ruins of Chachapoyas, Peru, 1907; The Islands of Titicaca and Koati (pub. by Hispanic Soc. of America), 1910; The Ruins of Tiahuanaco in Bolivia, 1912. Home: New York, N.Y. Died Mar. 19, 1914.

BANDHOLTZ, Harry Hill, brig. gen.; b. Constantine, Mich., Dec. 18, 1864; s. Christopher John and Elizabeth Ann (Hill) B.; grad. U.S. Mil. Acad., 1890; m. May Cleveland, July 15, 1890; m. 2d, Inez C. Gorman, Apr. 19, 1922. Commd. 2d lt., June 12, 1890; advanced through grades to maj. gen., Nov. 3, 1923. Prof. military science and tactics, Michigan Agrl. College, 1896. Served with 7th Inf. during Santiago campaign; with 2d Inf. in Philippine insurrection campaigns; gov. of Tayabas Province, Mar. 4, 1902-Apr. 1903; only regular army officer elected to such a position; apptd. col. and asst. chief of Philippine Constabulary, Apr. 1903, in comd. Dist. of Southern Luzon; conducted campaign against Simeon Ola in Albay, resulting in destruction of Ola's forces; transferred to comd. Dist. of Central Luzon, Oct. 1905; forced surrender of outlaws Montalan, Sakay and others and accomplished destruction of Felizardo; brig. gen. and chief Philippines Constabulary, June 30, 1907-Sept. 1, 1913; maj. 30th Inf., 1915; chief of staff N.Y. Div. on Mexican border, 1916; chief of staff 27th Div. (N.Y.) till Feb. 9, 1918; comd. 58th Inf. Brig., Feb. 9-Sept. 27, 1918; provost marshal gen. A.E.F., Sept. 27, 1918-Aug. 5, 1919; Am. rep. on Interallied Mil. Mission to Hungary, Aug. 5, 1919; comd. 13th Inf. Brig., Sept. 1, 1920-Sept. 1, 1921; in command Dist. of Washington, Sept. 1, 1921—; suppressed Miners' Insurrection in W.Va., Sept. 1-12, 1921. Awarded D.S.M.; Comdr. French Legion of Honor; Comdr. Belgian Order of the Crown; Comdr. Italian Order of the Crown; Grand Cross Crown of Roumania; Montenegrin decoration. Mason. Home: Constantine, Mich. Died May 7, 1925.

BANDMANN, Daniel Edward, retired actor, rancher; b. in Hesse Cassel, Germany, Nov. 1, 1840; s. Solomon and Rebecca (Ratz) B.; self-ed. in German, French and English; m. Marie Theresa Kelly, Nov. 1890. Made first appearance in German Theatre, New York, 1858; went to Germany, 1859, played in New Strelitz Court Theatre, Prague, and in Vienna and Budapest as a star; ill health caused return to New York, 1862; starred in German Theatre; appeared in English at Niblo's Garden Theatre, New York, 1863, as Shylock, later as Othello, Iago, Richelieu, Narcisse, for 6 yrs. in U.S., then in England, Ireland and Scotland, and afterward in Australia; played Hamlet in San Francisco, 1880, with Clara Morris as Ophelia, later took 2d tour as star in Australia, and extended it to India, China and the Malay Peninsula. The play "The Rightful Heir" was written for him by Lord Lytton in 1869, Tom Taylor wrote for him "Dead or Alive," and was original in U.S. of Robert Louis Stevenson's "Dr. Jekyll and Mr. Hyde," in which starred until 1890, when left stage to go into business of stock raising and mining in Montana. Mem. Garrick Club, London. Home: Missoula, Mont. Died 1905.

BANGS, Francis Reginald, lawyer, trustee; b. Watertown, Mass., Dec. 24, 1869; s. Edward and Anne Outram (Hodgkinson) B.; descendant of Edward Banges, 1623; A.B., Harvard, 1891, LL.B., 1894; m. Anna Dummer Anderson, Dec. 16, 1897; children—Edward, James Outram, Harriet Amory, David Hinckley. Began practice in Boston, 1894; mem. Bangs & Barlow until 1901, Hill, Bangs, Barlow & Homans, 1901-07, then Williams & Bangs. Mem. Boston Bd. of Aldermen, 1906-07; chmn. commn. apptd. by Gov. Foss on fire hazard. Republican. Episcopalian. Home: Boston, Mass. Died Jan. 23, 1939.

BANGS, Isaac Sparrow, soldier; b. Canaan, Me., March 17, 1831; s. Capt. Isaac Sparrow B.; ed. in Me. and New York; m. Oct. 20, 1857, Hadassah J. Milliken. Left position as cashier Waterville Bank to enter Union service, Aug. 9, 1862, as private; mustered in as capt. Co. A, 20th Me. vol. inf., Aug. 29, 1862; served in Army of Potomac in Md. campaign, Sept. and Oct., 1862, including battle of Antietam, Sept. 17, Shepardstown Ford, Sept. 18 and 19, in Va., Oct., 1862, to Feb., 1863; battle of Fredericksburg; expdn. to Ellis and Richard's fords, Burnside's 2d campaign ("Mud March"), etc.; lt. col. U.S. colored troops, Feb. 26, 1863; comd. 4th regt., Ullman's brigade (later named 81st U.S. colored inf.); served in Dept. of Gulf; took part in siege of Port Hudson, La.; pres. of examining bd., Oct. 3, 1863; col. 10th U.S. colored heavy arty., Nov. 10, 1863; comdg. Forts Jackson, St. Phillip, Livingston and Pike, and defenses of New Orleans until hon. disch. July 19, 1864. Bvtd. brig. gen. U.S. vols. Mar. 13, 1865, for gallant and meritorious service during war. Home: Waterville, Me. Died 1903.

BANGS, John Kendrick, author; b. Yonkers, N.Y., May 27, 1862; s. Francis N. and Amelia Frances (Bull) B.; Ph.B., Columbia, 1883; studied law, 1883-84; m. Agnes Lawson Hyde, Mar. 3, 1886; m. 2d, Mary Blakeney Gray, Apr. 27, 1904. Asso. editor Life, 1884-88; editor Drawer, 1888-99, and Literary Notes, July, 1898-Dec. 1899, Harper's Mag.; editor of Literature, 1898-99, Harper's Weekly, 1898-1900, Metropolitan Mag., Dec., 1902-June, 1903, Puck, 1904-05. Democratic candidate for mayor Yonkers, 1894, defeated; v.p. Yonkers Bd. of Edn., 1897; pres. Halsted Sch., Yonkers, 1896-1904. Author: Roger Camerden, 1886; Katharine, 1887; The Lorgnette, 1887; Mephistopheles, 1888; New Waggings of Old Tales, 1888; Tiddledywinks Tales, 1890; The Tiddledywinks Poetry Book, 1890; In Camp with a Tin Soldier, 1891; Half Hours with Jimmieboy, 1892; Coffee and Repartee, 1893, 1899; The Water Ghost, 1893; Three Weeks in Politics, 1894; The Idiot, 1895, 1899; Mr. Bonaparte, of Corsica, 1895; A House Boat on the Styx, 1895; The Bicyclers and Other Farces, 1896; A Rebellious Heroine, 1896; The Pursuit of the House Boat, 1897; Paste Jewels, 1897; A Prophecy and a Plea, 1897; The Mantel Piece Minstrels, 1897; Ghosts I Have Met, 1898; Peeps at People, 1898; The Dreamers, 1898; The Enchanted Type Writer, 1899; Cobwebs from a Library Corner, 1899; The Booming of Acre Hill, 1900;

Toppleton's Client, 1891; The Idiot at Home, 1900; Mr. Munchausen, 1901; Olympian Nights, 1902; Uncle Sam, Trustee, 1902; Bikey, the Skicycle, 1902; Over the Plum Pudding, 1902; Emblemland, 1902; Mollie and the Unwise Man, 1902; Proposal Under Difficulties (farce), 1905; Worsted Man (musical play), 1905; Mrs. Raffles, 1905; R. Holmes & Co., 1906; Alice in Municipaland, 1907; The Inventions of the Idiot, 1907; Potted-Fiction, 1908; Andiron Tales, 1908; The Genial Idiot, 1908; Autobiography of Methuselah, 1909; The Real Thing, 1909; Mollie and the Unwise Man Abroad, 1910; Songs of Cheer, 1910; Jack and the Check-Book, 1911; Echoes of Cheer, 1912; Little Book of Christmas, 1912; Line o' Cheer for Each Day o' the Year, 1913; The Foothills of Parnassus, 1914; A Quest for Song, 1915; From Pillar to Post, 1916; Half-Hours with the Idiot, 1917; The Cheery Way, 1919. Also Lady Teazle, a musical comedy version of The School for Scandal, and Tomorrowland, a musical fantasy. Home: Ogunquit, Me. Died Jan. 21, 1922.

BANGS, L(emuel) Bolton, surgeon; b. New York, N.Y., Aug. 9, 1842; s. Lemuel and Julia A. B.; M.D., Coll. Phys. and Surg. (Columbia), 1872; m. Isabel Hoyt, Dec. 5, 1894. Consulting surgeon St. Luke's, Bellevue, City, St. Vincent's and M.E. hosps.; prof. genito-urinary diseases, N.Y. Post-Grad. Med. Sch. and Hosp.; prof. genito-urinary surgery, Univ. and Bellevue Hosp. Med. Sch., 1898-1901. Editor: American Text Book of Genito-Urinary Diseases. Home: New York, N.Y. Died Oct. 4, 1914.

BANGS, Outram, zoölogist; b. Watertown, Mass., Jan. 12, 1863; s. Edward and Annie Outram (Hodgkinson) B.; ed. Noble's Sch., Boston, and Lawrence Scientific Sch., Harvard. Curator of mammals, Mus. of Comparative Zoölogy, Harvard, 1900—. Home: Cambridge, Mass. Died 1932.

BANGS, Tracy R., lawyer; b. Le Sueur, Minn., Apr. 29, 1862; s. Alfred W. and Alena F. (Baker) B.; ed. pub. schs.; studied law under father; m. Jessie L. Caughell, June 15, 1887; children—Felix F., Philip R. Admitted to N.Dak. bar, 1885; practiced with Charles J. Fisk (late chief justice Supreme Court of N.Dak.), later with Charles M. Cooley (late dist. judge); mem. Bangs, Hamilton & Bangs; has been identified with much important litigation in the state; atty. for Northwestern Bell Tel. Co., Northern States Power Co., Occidental Life Ins. Co., etc.; city atty. Grand Forks, 1889; state's atty. Grand Forks Co., 1892; U.S. dist. atty. for N.D., 1894-98; pres. Grand Forks Park Board. Democrat. Episcopalian. Mem. bd. trustees Univ. of N.Dak., 5 years (pres. 1914, 15). Devoted the greater portion of the time, 1917-18, in war activities, speaking over a large part of U.S., also in Canada. Home: Grand Forks, N.D. Died Feb. 22, 1936.

BANKHEAD, John Hollis, senator; b. Moscow (now Sulligent), Marion (now Lamar) Co., Ala., Sept. 13, 1842; s. James Greer and Susan (Hollis) B.; ed. common schs.; lt. and capt. 16th Ala. Vols., C.S.A., 1861-65; wounded 3 times; m. Tallulah J., d. James Brockman, Nov. 13, 1866; father-in-law of Thomas McAdory Owen (q.v.). Mem. Ala. Ho. of Rep., 1865-67, 1880-81, Senate, 1876-77; warden Ala. Penitentiary, 1881-85; mem. 50th to 60th Congresses (1887-1907), 6th Ala. Dist.; elected alternate U.S. senator, Aug., 1906; apptd., June 17, 1907, and elected, July, 1907, U.S. senator to succeed the late Senator John T. Morgan, for term expiring, 1913; reëlected, terms, 1913-19 and 1919-25. In Congress has been conspicuous as a leader in the work of the Coms. on Public Bldgs. and Rivers and Harbors; apptd. mem. Inland Waterways Commn., Mar., 1907; author of the law for federal aid to post roads. Mason. Methodist. Democrat. Home: Jasper, Ala. Died Mar. 1, 1920.

BANKHEAD, William Brockman, congressman; b. Moscow, Lamar Co., Ala., Apr. 12, 1874; s. Senator John Hollis and Tallulah James (Brockman) B.; A.B., U. of Ala., 1893, A.M., 1896; LL.B., Georgetown U., 1895; m. Adalaide Eugene Sledge, Jan. 31, 1900; m. 2d, Florence McGuire, Jan. 16, 1915. Mem. 65th to 76th Congresses (1917-41), 7th Ala. Dist.; speaker of the House. Democrat. Home: Jasper, Ala. Died Sept. 15, 1940.

BANKS, Charles Eugene, author; b. Clinton Co., Ia., Apr. 3, 1852; s. Seth Lee and Sarah M. (Hubbell) B.; ed. pub. schs., Clinton Co., and afterward Lyons, Ia., and pvtly.; m. Mrs. Carrie Wyatt Lounsberry, Apr. 3, 1892 (died 1926). Editor and propr. Am. Commercial Traveler, Chicago, 1885-87, later The Weekly Outlook, lit. paper, Davenport, Ia.; lit. editor Chicago Sunday Examiner and American, 3 yrs.; removed to Wash., 1907. Was editor and pub. The Peace Pipe, monthly mag., Seattle; dramatic editor Post-Intelligencer, Seattle, 1918; moved to Hawaii; was editor Tribune-Herald, Hilo; now with editorial dept. of the Honolulu Advertiser. Republican. Author: Quiet Music (poems), 1892; Where Brooks Go Softly (poems), 1896; In Hampton Roads, Novel of the Civil War, 1899; Sword and Cross (poems), 1900; A Child of the Sun (novel), 1900; Theodore Roosevelt, a Typical American, 1902; The Life of De Witt Talmage, 1902; An American Woman, 1905 (dramatized); John Dorn, Promoter (novel), 1907; Heart Beats of Hawaii (poems), 1921; The Trail of Love (poems), 1921. Also plays; The Swami, 1909; Vibration, 1909 (both produced). Contbr. poems and short stories to syndicates and magazines. Home: Honolulu, Hawaii. Died Apr. 29, 1932.

BANKS, Elizabeth, author; b. Taunton, N.J.; d. John and Sarah (Brister) B.; grad. Milwaukee-Downer Coll. Was society reporter on St. Paul and Baltimore papers; later sec. to Am. minister to Peru. Originated in 1914 the Authors' Belgian Fund and Dik's Fund for the Allies. Originated and wrote series of essays known as "The Lady at the Round Table" in London Referee under pen name of "Enid": serials "An Englishwoman in New York" and "The All-British Woman" under pen name "Mary Mortimer Maxwell." Author: Campaigns of Curiosity, 1894; The Autobiography of a Newspaper Girl, 1902; The Mystery of Frances Farrington, 1909; The Luck of the Black Cat (stories), 1912; Dik: A Dog of Belgium, 1914; Sergeant Major, of Canada, 1915; Captain Jinks (of French and Russian Descent), 1915; On the Boat that Uncle Sam Built, 1917; School for John and Mary—A Story of Caste in England, 1925; The Re-Making of an American, 1928. Now engaged in newspaper and magazine writing. Owing to series of articles by her, in 1894, entitled "The Almighty Dollar in London Society," in St. James's Gazette, exposing methods by which rich Americans were introduced at Court by payment of large sums to British aristocrats, Queen Victoria made the rule, still in force, that introductions should be made only through ambassadors. Died July 18, 1938.

BANKS, John Henry, mining engr.; b. New York, N.Y., Nov. 28, 1861; s. Joseph and Ellen (Marsh) B.; E.M. Sch. of Mines, Columbia, 1883; Ph.D., Columbia, 1894; m. Emilie S. Hultsch, June 9, 1886; children—Harold Purdy, Reginald Marsh. Mem. John H. Banks & Son. Republican. Episcopalian. Home: New York, N.Y. Died 1934.

BANKS, Louis Albert, clergyman; b. Corvallis, Ore., Nov. 12, 1855; s. Lebbius Irwin and Mary (Hurlburt) B.; ed. Philomath Coll. and Boston Univ.; (D.D., Mt. Union Coll., Ohio, 1891; LL.D., Philomath Coll., Ore., 1918); m. Mary V. Millhollen, 1877 (died 1882); children—Maud Ethel, Mary Fay; m. 2d, Jessie F. Ainsworth, Jan. 1, 1884 (died 1919); children—Gilbert Haven (dec.), Willard Ainsworth, Helen Lambert, Sherlock Lee, Rene Parkman, Marjorie Sloane; m. 3d, Florence Aiken, July 21, 1920. Entered M.E. ministry, 1879; pastor Independence Av. Ch., Kansas City, 1909-11; evangelist, in union evangelistic campaigns, 1911—; nat. lecturer for the Anti-Saloon League of America, in World Prohibition movement, since 1913; also nat. lecturer for same. Prohibition candidate for gov. of Mass., 1893. Author: The People's Christ, 1891; The White Slaves, 1892; The Revival Quiver, 1893; Anecdotes and Morals, 1894; Common Folks' Religion, 1894; Heavenly Trade Winds, 1895; Christ and His Friends, 1896; Paul and His Friends; The Fisherman and His Friends, 1897; Seven Times Around Jericho, 1897; Hero Tales from Sacred Story, 1897; Live Boys in Oregon, 1897; The Christ Brotherhood, 1897; Heroic Personalities, 1898; The Unexpected Christ, 1898; The Christian Gentleman, 1898; John and His Friends, 1899; My Young Man, 1899; The Great Sinners of the Bible, 1899; Chats with Young Christians, 1900; A Manly Boy, 1900; David and His Friends, 1900; The Lord's Arrows, 1900; Fresh Bait for Fishers of Men, 1900; Poetry and Morals, 1900; Hidden Wells of Comfort, 1901; The Great Saints of the Bible, 1901; The King's Stewards, 1902; Life of Rev. T. DeWitt Talmage, D.D., 1902; Youth of Famous Americans, 1902; The Great Portraits of the Bible, 1903; Soul-Winning Stories, 1903; Thirty-one Revival Sermons, 1904; The Great Promises of the Bible, 1905; Capital Stories of Famous Americans, 1905; Spurgeon's Illustrative Anecdotes, 1906; The Problems of Youth, 1909; The World's Childhood, 1910; The Great Themes of the Bible, 1911; Ammunition for the Final Drive on Booze, 1917; The Winds of God, 1920; The New Ten Commandments, 1922; Wonderful Bible Conversions, 1923; Dramatic Stories of Jesus, 1924; Bible Soul Winners, 1924; Christ's Soul Searching Parables, 1925; Sermons for Reviving, 1928, and others. Home: Roseburg, Ore. Died June 17, 1933.

BANKS, Theodore H., banker; b. N.Y. City, Dec. 23, 1866; s. Edward Merritt and Maria Bonnie (Fleet) B.; ed. pub. and pvt. schs., N.Y. City; m. Maude Bowers, Jan. 23, 1895; children—Theodore H., W. Dinsmore. Vice chmn. bd. Irving Trust Co., pres. Am. Exchange Securities Corp.; dir. numerous corps.; trustee North River Savings Bank. Home: New York, N.Y. Died June 8, 1933.

BANNARD, Otto Tremont, banker; b. Brooklyn, Apr. 28, 1854; s. John W. and Eliza Landon (Stone) B.; B.A., Yale, 1876, hon. M.A., 1908; LL.B., Columbia, 1878; LL.D., Colgate, 1924; unmarried. Practiced in New York until 1889; pres. N.Y. Trust Co.; dir. various cos. Trustee Commonwealth Fund. Mem. Bd. of Edn., of New York, 2 yrs.; Rep. candidate for mayor of New York, 1909. Fellow Corp. of Yale U.; v.p. Charity Orgn. Soc., New York; trustee, Provident Loan Soc.; pres. Nat. Employment Exchange, organized 1909. Apptd. chmn. advisory com. to alien property custodian, July 1918. Republican (ex-pres.), Midday. Home: New York, N.Y. Died Jan. 15, 1929.

BANNING, Ephraim, lawyer; b. McDonough Co., Ill., July 21, 1849; s. Ephraim and Louisa Caroline (Walker) B.; ed. public schools and acad.; m. Lucretia T. Lindsley, Oct. 22, 1878 (died 1887); m. 2d, Emilie B. Jenne, Sept. 5, 1889. Admitted to bar, 1872; Rep. presdl. elector, 1896; apptd. mem. State Bd. of Charities, 1897; delegate to Rep. Nat. Conv., 1900. Home: Chicago, Ill. Died 1907.

BANNING, Pierson Worrall, author; b. Chicago, Ill., Sept. 13, 1879; s. Ephraim and Lucretia Thalia (Lindsley) B.; ed. Lake Forest (Ill.) Acad., Lawrenceville (N.J.) Sch. for Boys; student Kent Coll. of Law, Chicago; m. Lila Banning Watkins, May 16, 1913. Settled in Los Angeles, Calif., 1910; in charge of social survey of Los Angeles for Municipal League, 1914; organizer and dir. vol. corps for Mil. Intelligence Dept. U.S.A., Western Dept., and Dept. of Justice, during World War; became mgr. Nat. Statis. and Efficiency Bur., Los Angeles. Republican. Author: Thread of Life Series—Maker, Man and Matter, 1921; Psychology, Super-Psychology and Higher Phases, 1922; Mental Spiritual Healing, 1922. Received, 1923, the first major award (about $12,000) granted in 165 yrs. by Benjamin Franklin Fund, London, Eng., for last-named vol. Home: Los Angeles, Calif. Died July 7, 1927.

BANTA, N(athaniel) Moore, editor, author, b. Rensselaer, Ind., Dec. 3, 1867; s. Henry and Mary Jane (Robinson) B.; grad. Valparaiso (Ind.) U., 1890, Fenton (Mich.) Nat. Normal Sch., 1897; student U. of Chicago, Berlitz Sch. of Langs., Soper School Oratory; m. Minnie Muller, July 17, 1901; 1 dau., Elizabeth Jane (Mrs. Herbert Mueller). Teacher, pub. schs., Ind. and Ill., 1890-1906; trade agt., Chicago, subscription book pubs., 1906-21; editor and mgr. pub. dept. A. Flanagan & Co., book pubs., Chicago, since 1921. Mem. Ill. Hist. Soc., S.A.R. Republican. Presbyterian. Mason. Author: Brownie Primer, 1905; Brownies and the Goblins, 1914; Ten Little Brownie Men, 1918; Bluebird Book, 1922; Bluest of the Bluebirds, 1922; Chickadee Book, 1922; Fairies of the Nine Hills, 1922; Fairy Primer, 1922; Jenny Wren Book, 1922; Little Brown Man, 1922; Little Brown Pitcher, 1922; Robin Redbreast Book, 1922; Busy Little Brownies, 1923; Four and Forty Fairies, 1923; Once Upon a Time Stories, 1923; Autumn and Winter Festivals, 1924; Kriss Kringle Christmas Book, 1924; Old Tales of the East, 1924; Spring and Summer Festivals, 1924; St. Nicholas Christmas Book, 1925; Brownies at Work and Play, 1926; Brownies in the Greenwood, 1927. Editor: Nature Neighbors (11 vols.), 1914. Home: Arlington Heights, Ill. Died Feb. 5, 1932.

BARBE, Waitman, prof. English; b. Monongalia Co., W.Va., Nov. 19, 1864; s. John and Margaret Esther (Robinson) B.; A.B., W.Va. U., 1884, A.M., 1887, M.S., 1897; grad. student Harvard, 1900-01, Oxford U., Eng., 1908-09; (Litt. D., Denison U., 1904); m. Clara Louise Gould, June 6, 1894. Mng. editor Daily State Journal, Parkersburg, W.Va., 1889-95; asst. to pres. and asso. prof. of English, 1895-1910, prof. English and dir. Univ. Summer Sch., 1910—, W.Va. U. Editor West Virginia School Journal, 1904-1923. Mem. bd. regents W.Va. State Normal Schs., 1895-1902. Author: Ashes and Incense (poems), 1891; In the Virginias (stories), 1896; Going to College, 1899; The Study of Poetry, 1905; Famous Poems Explained, 1909; Great Poems Interpreted, 1913. Home: Morgantown, W.Va. Died Oct. 30, 1925.

BARBER, Amzi Lorenzo, of the Barber Asphalt Paving Co.; b. Saxton's River, Windham Co., Vt., June 22, 1843; moved to Ohio, 1852; grad. Oberlin Coll., 1867 (A.M.); grad. law dept. Columbia Univ., 1876; had charge normal dept.; later of preparatory dept.; afterward prof. natural philosophy Columbian Univ., 1868-72. In real estate business, Washington, 1873-78; became paving contractor; his company has a lease of the great lake of natural pitch on the island of Trinidad; m. Julia Louise Langdon, d. John Le Droict Langdon, Harrisburg, Pa., June 1, 1871. Home: New York, N.Y. Died 1909.

BARBER, Donn, architect; b. Washington, D.C., Oct. 19, 1871; s. Charles Gibbs and Georgiana (Williams) B.; Ph.B., Yale, 1893; spl. course in architecture, Columbia, 1893-94; diploma École des Beaux Arts, Paris, 1898; m. Elsie Yandell, Nov. 22, 1899. Practiced New York, 1900—. Prin. works: N.Y. Cotton Exchange, Nat. Park Bank bldg., Mutual Bank, Lotos Club bldg., Inst. of Musical Art bldg., Nat. Headquarters bldg., Central Branch Bldg. of Y.W.C.A. (all of New York), Travelers' Ins. bldg., Ætna Life Ins. bldg., Hartford Ætna Nat. Bank, Hosp. for Feeble Minded, Randalls Island, N.Y. City, Conn. State Library Dept. of Justice bldg. (winner govt. competition), Washington, D.C., etc. One of originators of the atelier idea in U.S. and head of Atelier Donn Barber. Editor of The New York Architect. Fellow Am. Inst. Architects. Home: New York, N.Y. Died May 29, 1925.

BARBER, Edwin AtLee, director; b. Baltimore, Aug. 13, 1851; s. William Edwin and Anne Eliza (Townsend) B.; grad. Williston Sem., Easthampton, Mass., 1869; studied Lafayette Coll. to sr. yr., A.M., 1880, Ph.D., 1893; m. Nellie Louise, d. Maj. W. H. Parker, U.S. Marine Corps, Feb. 5, 1880. Asst. naturalist on Hayden's U.S. Geol. and Geog. Survey of the territories, 1874-75; postmaster West Phila., 1879-85; curator, 1901-07, dir., 1907—, Pa. Mus. and Sch. of Industrial Art, Phila. Author: Pottery and Porcelain of the United States, 1893, 1902, 1909; Historical Sketch of the Green Point (N.Y.) Porcelain Works, 1895; Anglo-American Pottery, 1899 and 1901; American Glassware, 1900; Tulip Ware of the Pennsylvania-German Potters, 1903; Marks of American Potters, 1904; Tin Enameled Pottery, 1906; Salt Glazed Stoneware, 1906; Artificial Soft Paste Porcelain, 1907; Lead Glazed Pottery, 1907; The Maliolica of Mexico, 1908; Hard Paste Porcelain (Oriental), 1910; The Ceramic Collectors' Glossary, 1914; Hispano-Moresque Pottery, 1915; Spanish Porcelains and Terra Cottas, 1915. Collaborator Century Dictionary, 1909. Also mag. articles on archæology, natural history and ceramics, and genealogies of AtLee and Barber families of Pa. Home: West Chester, Pa. Died Dec. 12, 1916.

BARBER, George Holcomb, naval officer; b. Glastonbury, Conn., Nov. 15, 1864; s. Ralph and Mary Henrietta (Holcomb) B.; S.B., Mass. Agrl. Coll., 1885; S.B., Boston U., 1885; M.D., Coll. Phys. and Surg. (Columbia), 1888; unmarried. Apptd. asst. surgeon U.S.N., May 23, 1889; promoted through grades to med. dir., rank of rear admiral, Oct. 15, 1917. Service at sea, 14 yrs., mostly in foreign waters, comdg. hosp. ship relief as last duty; shore duty 14 yrs., on receiving ships, at U.S. Naval Acad., training sta., at Newport, R.I., and naval hosps., New York, Boston, Phila., Olongapo, P.I., and Ft. Lyon, Colo. Conglist. Has specialized in treatment of tuberculosis. Died Aug. 24, 1926.

BARBER, Milton Augustus, clergyman; b. Hyde Co., N.C., Jan. 25, 1869; s. Rev. Samuel Swann and Adelaide (Watson) B.; B.L. from Hobart College, 1895, S.T.D. from same college, 1929; grad. Gen. Theol. Sem., 1898; m. Harriet Winfield, Oct. 4, 1898; children—Alfred Augustus, Adelaide Watson (dec.), Harriet Atkinson, Howard Winfield, Elizabeth Swann, Milton Augustus, Jr. Deacon, 1898, priest, 1899, P.E. Ch.; rector St. Paul's Ch., Wilmington, N.C., 1898-1900, St. Mark's Ch., San Marcos, Tex., 1900-05, St. Athanasius Ch., Burlington, N.C., 1905-07, Christ Ch., Raleigh, N.C., 1907-35; became rector emeritus Christ Ch. Was mem. standing com. Diocese of W. Tex.; 7 times dep. to Gen. Conv., P.E. Ch.; pres. standing com. Diocese of N.C.; trustee St. Augustine Sch., Olivia Raney Library of Raleigh. Mem. bd. dirs. Y.M.C.A., Thompson Orphanage (Charlotte). Home: Charlotte, N.C. Died Mar. 10, 1938.

BARBER, Ohio Columbus, capitalist; b. Middlebury, O., Apr. 20, 1841; s. George and Eliza (Smith) B.; ed. Akron (O.) common schs. until 15 yrs. of age; m. Laura L. Brown, Oct. 10, 1866 (dec.). Began work in father's match factory, 1856; became partner, 1861, and head of firm when father died. In 1881 he arranged consolidation of a number of leading match mfrs., and formed Diamond Match Co., of which was successively v.p., pres., and chmn. bd. Founded, 1891, and developed Barberton, O. Home: Akron, O. Died Feb. 4, 1920.

BARBER, Orion Metcalf, judge; b. Jamaica, Vt., July 13, 1857; s. Emmons D. and Lucia C. (Pierce) B.; ed. Bernardston (Mass.) Acad., Inst. of South Woodstock, and Leland and Gray Sem., Townshend, Vt.; LL.B., Albany (N.Y.) Law Sch., 1882; m. Alice Norton, June 30, 1898; children—Mab Norton and Lucia Pierce (twins), Norton. State's atty., Bennington Co., 1886-87; mem. Vt. Ho. of Rep., 1892, Senate, 1894; mem. com. apptd. to revise Vt. statues, 1892-94, and chmn. com. to edit and pub. Vt. statutes, 1894; state railroad commr., 1894-96; state auditor, 1898-1902; del. Rep. Nat. Conv., 1896; chmn. Special Tax Com., 1906-08; chmn. spl. com. to prepare and publish Digest of Vt. Reports, 1909; asso. judge U.S. Ct. Customs Appeals, 1910-28. Mason. Home: Bennington, Vt. Died Mar. 28, 1930.

BARBOUR, Anna Maynard, Mrs., author; deaconess House of Mercy, Boston, 1907—. Author: Told in the Rockies, 1897; That Mainwaring Affair, 1900; The Award of Justice, 1901; At the Time Appointed, 1903; Breakers Ahead, 1906. Address: Roxbury, Boston. Died May 10, 1941.

BARBOUR, Clarence Augustus, univ. pres.; b. Hartford, Conn., Apr. 21, 1867; s. Hon. Heman Humphrey and Myra (Barker) B.; A.B., Brown U., 1888; grad. Rochester Theol. Sem., 1891; D.D., U. of Rochester, 1901, Brown U., 1909, Williams, 1920, Colgate, 1922; S.T.D., Syracuse, 1921; LL.D., Denison, 1922, Colby, 1929; m. Florence Isabelle Newell, July 28, 1891. Ordained Bapt. ministry, 1891; pastor Lake Av. Ch., Rochester, N.Y., 1891-1909; asso. sec. Internat. Com. Y.M.C. Assns. of N. America, 1909-15; pres. and prof. homiletics, Rochester Theol. Sem., 1915-29, pres. Brown U., 1929—. Trustee Rochester Theol. Sem., 1896— (pres. bd. 1913-15), Rochester Pub. Library, 1912-29, Rochester Sch. for the Deaf, 1916-29, Brown U., 1926—, Peddie Sch., 1929—, Worcester Acad., 1929—. Pres. Northern Bapt. Conv., 1916-17, and fraternal del. from same to Bapt. Union of Great Britain and Ireland, Cardiff, Wales, 1924. Mem. Laymen's Foreign Missions Inquiry in India, Burma, China and Japan, 1931-32. Mason. Author, editor (or both); Fellowship Hymns, 1910; The Bible in the World of Today, 1911; Principles and Methods of Religious Work for Men and Boys, 1912; Making Religion Efficient, 1912; Service Song Book, 1917. Home: Providence, R.I. Died Jan. 16, 1937.

BARBOUR, George Harrison, mfr.; b. Collinsville, Conn., June 26, 1843; s. Samuel Thompson and Phoebe (Beckwith) B.; ed. common schs. of Conn.; m. Katherine Hawley, June 23, 1869. Went to Detroit, July 1872; sec., 1872-86, 1st v.p. and gen. mgr., 1886—, Mich. Stove Co. Also pres. Mich. Copper & Brass Co., Ireland & Matthews Mfg. Co.; v.p. Dime Savings Bank; dir. Peoples' Savings Bank, Mich. Fire & Marine Ins. Co. Dir. and was 1st pres. Chamber Commerce; pres. Detroit City Council, 1888; nat. commr. Columbian Expn., 1893. Democrat. Home: Grosse Pointe, Mich. Died Dec. 21, 1921.

BARBOUR, John Humphrey, prof. N.T. literature and interpretation, Berkeley Div. Sch., 1889—; b. Torrington, Conn., May 29, 1854; grad. Trinity, 1873 (A.M., 1876); deacon (P.E.), 1876; priest, 1878; minister Grace Chapel, Hartford, Conn., 1876-89; librarian Trinity Coll., 1882-89; m. 1878. Author: Beginnings of the Historic Episcopate; etc. Home: Middletown, Conn. Died 1900.

BARBOUR, Thomas Seymour, clergyman; b. Hartford, Conn., July 28, 1853; s. Hon. Heman Humphrey and Frances E. (Merrill) B.; brother of Henry Merlin B. and half brother of Clarence Augustus B.; A.B., Brown U., 1874, A.M., 1877; B.D., Rochester Theol. Sem., 1877; (D.D., Brown, 1895); m. Emma J. White, Sept. 4, 1877. Ordained Bapt. ministry, 1877; pastor Brockport, N.Y., 1877-81, Orange, N.J., 1881-83, Fall River, Mass., 1883-95, Brookline, Mass., 1896-98; foreign sec. Am. Bapt. Foreign Mission Soc., 1899-1912; in lit. work, 1912—. Trustee Newton Theol. Instn., 1893—, Brown U., 1902—. Home: Wollaston, Mass. Died Sept. 26, 1915.

BARBOUR, William, capitalist, pres. Barbour Brothers Co., The Linen Thread Co., Algonquin Co., Am. Net & Twine Co., Dunbarton Flax Spinning Co., Dundee Water Power & Land Co., Finlayson Flax Spinning Co., Hamilton Trust Co., Passaic Water Co., U.S. Twine & Net Co., W. & J. Knox Net & Twine Co.; v.p. Barbour Flax Spinning Co.; trustee Washington Trust Co. Pres. Am. Protective Tariff League, 1910—. Home: New York, N.Y. Died Mar. 1, 1917.

BARCHFELD, Andrew Jackson, congressman; b. Pittsburgh, Pa., May 18, 1863; s. Henry and Mary (Neuenhagen) B.; M.D., Jefferson Med. Coll., Phila., 1884; m. Anna Peiffer, May, 1885. Began med. practice, Pittsburgh, 1884; city phys. several yrs.; pres. bd. dirs. and mem. staff South Side Hosp. Mem. City Council, 1886-88; chmn. Rep. City convs., 1886, 1894, 1901; mem. Rep. State Com.; nominee for Congress, 1902; mem. 59th to 64th Congresses (1905-17), 32d Pa. Dist. Del. Peace Congress, Brussels, 1905. Home: Pittsburgh, Pa. Died Jan. 28, 1922.

BARCLAY, Charles Frederick, congressman; b. Owego, N.Y., May 9, 1844; pvt. to capt. 149th Pa. Vols., 1862-65; studied law, U. of Mich., 1866-67; m. Margaret A. L. Brooks, Aug. 22, 1872. Mem. Barclay Bros., lumber mfrs.; officer or dir. in other corps. Presdl. elector, 1892; del.-at-large Rep. Nat. Conv., 1900; mem. 60th and 61st Congresses (1907-11), 21st Pa. Dist. Republican. Home: Sinnamahoning, Pa. Died Mar. 9, 1914.

BARCLAY, Charles James, naval officer; b. Phila., Pa., Sept. 8, 1843; s. William J. and Anna (Musgrave) B.; grad. U.S. Naval Acad., 1863; m. Annie T. Tobey, Feb. 1868. Promoted ensign, Oct. 1, 1863; advanced through grades to rear admiral, Sept. 11, 1903. On board Wachusett, Brazilian Squadron, 1863-64; participated in capture of Confederate cruiser Florida in harbor of Bahia, Brazil, Oct. 7, 1864; comd. Raleigh, Jan.-Mar. 1897, Amphitrite, 1897-98; comdt. Naval War Coll., 1900; retired Sept. 8, 1905. Home: Brookline, Mass. Died 1909.

BARCLAY, Shepard, lawyer, judge; b. St. Louis, Nov. 3, 1847; g.s. Capt. Elihu H. Shepard who settled in St. Louis in 1823; s. Britton A. and Mary Melinda (Shepard) Hill; name changed to Barclay on marriage of mother to D. Robert Barclay; A.B., St. Louis U., 1867; LL.B., U. of Va., 1869 (final pres. Jefferson Soc.); studied in Paris and U. of Berlin, 1870-72; LL.D., U. of Mo., 1897, St. Louis U., 1904; m. Katie Anderson, June 11, 1873. Practiced law, St. Louis, 1872-82; judge Circuit Ct., 1883-88; judge Supreme Ct. of Mo., 1889-98 (chief justice, 1897-98); resigned and resumed practice; judge St. Louis Ct. of Appeals, 1901-02; resumed practice, 1903. Sec. conf. of judges of Mo., 1882-98. Lecturer, commercial law for business men, Y.M.C.A., 1898-1918; lecturer on trade marks and unfair competition, Kansas City Law Sch.; on med. jurisprudence, Marion Sims-Beaumont (St. Louis U.) Med. Coll.; on historical jurisprudence, St. Louis U. Capt. Lafayette Guard, Co. A, 1st Regt. N.G. Mo., 1877-82. V.chmn. Selective Service Bd. (5th Dist.), 1917-19. Dem. nominee Circuit Court, St. Louis, 1922. Author: Introduction Del Vecchio's Formal Bases of Law (Modern Legal Philos. Series); American System of Law (56 Am. Law Rev. 641); Election of Judges (7 St. Louis Law Rev. 209). Translator of Tarde's Les Transformations du Droit (Evolution of Law Series). Home: St. Louis, Mo. Deceased.

BARCUS, John M., clergyman; b. Tulip, Dallas Co., Ark., Dec. 23, 1860; s. Rev. Edward Rosman and Mary Frances (Smith) B.; M.A., Southwestern U., Georgetown, Tex., 1882, D.D., 1905; m. Mary T. McCrary, Nov. 5, 1885. Licensed ministry M.E. Ch., S., 1880; pastor, Temple, Taylor, Georgetown, Ft. Worth, Cleburne, Vernon—all in Tex.; served as presiding elder 15 yrs.; sec. Central Tex. Conf. M.E. Ch., S., 21 yrs. and elected to Gen. Conf. 6 times; mem. Gen. Bd. Epworth League 12 yrs.; sec. Com. of Appeals, M.E. Ch., S., 1910-22; mem. Joint Bd. of Publn., Tex. Christian Advocate. Trustee Southwestern U. Democrat. Mason. Home: Cleburne, Tex. Died June 12, 1928.

BARD, Cephas L., M.D.; grad. Jefferson Med. Coll., Phila., 1866; private in Rebellion in 126th Pa. vols., and subsequently asst. surgeon in 210th regt. Pa. vols.; pres. Southern Calif. Med. Soc., 1893; pres. Calif. State Med. Soc., 1897. Home: Ventura, Calif. Died 1902.

BARD, Thomas Robert, senator; b. Chambersburg, Pa., Dec. 8, 1841; s. Robert M. and Elizabeth S. (Little) B.; grad. Chambersburg Acad. at 18, at head of class; studied law; m. Mary B. Gerberding, Apr. 17, 1876. Transportation agt., Cumberland Valley R.R. at Hagerstown, Md., 1861; sent by Col. Thomas A. Scott, 1865, to look after latter's landed interests in Southern Calif., where has since resided. Largely interested in lands and in development of oil industry. U.S. senator, 1900-05. Republican. Presbyn. Home: Hueneme, Ventura Co., California. Died Mar. 6, 1915.

BARDEEN, Charles Russell, anatomist; b. Kalamazoo, Mich., Feb. 8, 1871; s. Charles William and Ellen Palmer (Dickerman) B.; ed. Teichmann Sch., Leipzig, 1888-89; A.B., Harvard, 1893; M.D., Johns Hopkins, 1897; m. Althea Harmer, 1905; children—William, John, Helen, Thomas; m. 2d, Ruth Hames, 1920; 1 dau., Ann. Asst. in anatomy, 1897-99, asso., 1899-1901, asso. prof., 1901-04, Johns Hopkins U.; prof. anatomy, 1904—, dean Med. Sch., 1907—, U. of Wis. Home: Madison, Wis. Died June 12, 1935.

BARDEEN, Charles Valdo, justice Supreme Court, Wis., Jan., 1898—; b. Brookfield, Madison Co., N.Y., Sept. 23, 1850; s. Rasselas B.; grad. Albion (Wis.) Acad., 1869; law dept. Univ. of Wis., 1875; m. Frances H. Miller, June 17, 1876; apptd. justice Supreme Court, Wis., Jan., 1898; elected April, 1898. Home: Madison, Wis. Died 1903.

BARDEEN, Charles William, author; b. Groton, Mass., Aug. 28, 1847; s. William Thomas and Mary Ann (Farnsworth) B.; served in 1st Mass. Vols., 1862-64; A.B., Yale, 1869; m. Ellen Palmer Dickerman, July 15, 1868; father of Charles Russell B. Prin. high sch., Meriden, Conn., 1868, Weston (Conn.) Boarding Sch., 1869; v.prin. Conn. State Normal Sch., 1870; supt. schs., Whitehall, N.Y., 1872; editor and pub. the School Bulletin, 1874—. In charge ednl. publs., Internat. Congress, 1893; dir. N.E.A., 1891-95; pres. Ednl. Press Assn. of Am., 1900-06; mem. Nat. Inst. Social Sciences. Author: Manual of School Law, 1875; Roderick Home, 1875; A System of Rhetoric, 1884, and other text-books; also The Little Old Man, or the School for Illiberal Mothers, 1893; History of Educational Journalism in New York, 1893; Teaching as a Business, 1897; Authors' Birthday Exercises, 1897-99; Dictionary of Educational Biography, 1901; A Manual of Civics, 1902; Fifty-five Years Old and Other Stories, 1904; The Woman Trustee, 1905; The Cloak Room Thief, 1906; Educational Journalism for the Past Fifty Years, 1906; The False Entry, 1907; John Brody's Astral Body, 1909; A Little Fifer's War Dairy, 1862-64, 1909; Fables for Teachers, 1909; Tom and Tom Tit, 1911; A Shattered Halo, 1912; The Yellow Streak, 1912; The Trial Balance, 1913; The Girl from Girton, 1913; The Black Hand, 1914; Geraldine's Saints, 1914; Ruby Floyd's Temptation, 1915; The Stolen Payroll, 1915; A Single Session, 1917; Little Bok, 1917; The Allibone Arithmetics, 1918; The Teacher's Wife, 1918; Coykendall Webb, 1919; The Little Old Woman, 1919; Castiron Culver, 1921. Home: Syracuse, N.Y. Died Aug. 19, 1924.

BARDEL, William, consul; b. Nuremberg, Germany, Sept. 20, 1846; commercial edn.; m. d. of C. Kugler, of Nuremberg, 1873. Came to U.S., 1867; engaged in wholesale jewelry business, New York, until 1900; apptd. Am. consular agt., at Bamberg, Bavaria, Dec. 15, 1900; consul, Bamberg, 1902-08, Rheims, France, 1908-15. Ponta Delgada, Azores, 1915—. Died Dec. 31, 1926.

BARDO, Clinton Lloyd, corp. official; b. Montgomery, Lycoming Co., Pa., Oct. 24, 1867; s. Benjamin Franklin and Jennie Grace (Moore) B.; ed.

pub. schs.; m. Hannah Abigail Hartz, Jan. 19, 1887; children—Edith Jennie, Benjamin Franklin, Mildred Amelia, Vernon Hartz. Began as telegraph operator Pa. R.R., 1885; telegraph operator Phila. & Reading Ry. and supply agt. Tidewater Oil Co., 1886-87; operator and dispatcher Lehigh Valley R.R., 1887-93; trainmaster same rd., 1893-1904; asst. supt. N.Y., N.H.&H. R.R., 1904-07; supt. N.Y.C.&H.R. R.R., 1907-12; asst. gen. mgr. Lehigh Valley R.R., 1912-13; became gen. mgr. N.Y.,N.H.&H. R.R. and Central N.E. Ry., 1913, also president Central N.E. Ry., Mar. 1, 1920-Oct. 1, 1925; became pres. N.Y. Shipbuilding Co., Oct. 1928; v.p. Am. Brown Boveri Electric Corp., Nov. 12, 1925—. Presbyterian. Mason. Home: Pine Valley, N.J. Died Aug. 2, 1937.

BARDON, Thomas; b. Maysville, Ky., Oct. 22, 1848; s. Richard and Mary B.; pub. sch. edn. Pres. Ashland Nat. Bank, 1886—, Shattuck Arizona Copper Co. Denn Arizona Copper Co., Northern Chief Iron Co.; identified with various timber and land cos. in Calif. and Wash. Mayor of Ashland 4 terms. Home: Ashland, Wis. Died Feb. 11, 1923.

BARGER, Milton Sanford, ry. official; b. N.Y. City, Feb. 24, 1875; s. Samuel F. and E. Jennie (Lafavere) B.; A.B., Harvard, 1898; m. Mrs. L. H. Morgan, Feb. 1906 (died 1912). Apptd. asst. treas. N.Y.C.&H.R. R.R. Co., Nov. 5, 1902; treas. New York & Harlem R.R., Feb. 14, 1906; treas. N.Y.C. Lines West of Buffalo, Feb. 23, 1912; treas. all N.Y.C. Lines during federal control; gen. treas. N.Y.C. Lines, Mar. 1, 1920—. Home: New York, N.Y. Died Mar. 5, 1925.

BARKAN, Adolf, ophthalmologist; b. Eperies, Hungary, Jan., 1845; M.D., U. of Vienna, 1866; (LL.D., U. of Glasgow, Scotland, 1901). Prof. ophthalmology and otology, U. of the Pacific, 1872-82, Cooper Med. Coll., San Francisco, 1882—; eye and ear surgeon, Lane Hosp., San Francisco, 1895—; prof. structure and diseases of eye, ear and larynx, Leland Stanford Jr. U., 1909—; emeritus prof. Home: San Francisco, Calif. Died Aug. 28, 1935.

BARKER, Albert Smith, rear adm.; b. Hanson, Mass., Mar. 31, 1843; s. Josiah and Eliza (Cushing) B.; Naval Acad. from Mass., 1859-62; m. Ellen Blackmar Maxwell, 1894. Promoted ensign, Nov. 25, 1862; advanced through grades to rear adm., Oct. 10, 1899. Served Mississippi, W. Gulf Blockading Squadron, 1861-63; participated in bombardment and passage of Fts. Jackson and St. Philip, Chalmette batteries and capture of New Orleans, 1862; in attack on Port Hudson, Mar. 14, 1863, where the Mississippi was destroyed; joined the Monongahela; took part in the siege of Port Hudson; torpedo duty, 1873-74; Naval Acad., 1874-76; comd. Palos, 1876-77; lighthouse insp. 8th dist., 1878-81, 2d dist., 1886-89; comd. iron-clad Montauk, 1882; comd. Enterprise, and ran a line of deep-sea soundings around the world, 1882-86; Bur. of Navigation, 1890-91; comd. Philadelphia, 1892-94; Navy Yard, Mare Island, 1895-97; comd. Oregon, 1897; mem. of Bd. of Strategy at beginning of Spanish War, 1898; comd. Newark, May-Aug., 1898; comd. Oregon and also spl. service squadron to the Pacific, Aug., 1898-May, 1899; relieved Admiral Dewey of command of Asiatic Fleet, May, 1899, temporarily; comdt. Navy Yard, Norfolk, 1899-1900, Navy Yard, New York, 1900-03; comdr.-in-chief, N. Atlantic Fleet, 1903-05; retired, Mar. 31, 1905. Was first one in the U.S. to fire high explosives in shells. Home: Washington, D.C. Died Jan. 29, 1916.

BARKER, Charles Whitney Tillinghast; b. Troy, N.Y., Feb. 1, 1882; s. Stephen Willard and Frances Southwick (Tillinghast) B.; grad. Troy Acad., 1899; C.E., Rensselaer Poly. Inst., 1903; unmarried. Civ. engr. with Louisville & Atlantic R.R., Versailles, Ky., 1904; with filtration bureau, City of Pittsburgh, 1904-07, advancing to 2d asst. engr.; pres. Field, Barker & Underwood, contracting engrs., Phila., 1907-14; with J. M. Warren & Co., hardware mchts., Troy, 1914—. President City Planning Commn.; trustee Rensselaer Poly. Inst., Emma Willard Sch., and Russell Sage Coll., Samaritan Hosp., Troy Pub. Library, St. Paul's Ch., Troy; pres. Troy Boys' Club; hon. pres. Troy Council Boy Scouts of America; mem. Nat. Board Boy's Clubs of America, Inc. Mem. Co. A, 2d Inf., N.G. N.Y., 1901-04; 1st lt. same co., July-Nov. 1917; capt., 1917-19. Republican. Episcopalian. Home: Troy, N.Y. Died Apr. 29, 1938.

BARKER, Franklin Davis, prof. zoölogy; b. Ottawa, Kan., Sept. 16, 1877; s. Albert Wentworth and Martha Ella (Luther) B.; A.B., Ottawa U., 1898, A.M., 1900; grad. study U. of Chicago, 1898-1900; Ph.D., U. of Neb., 1910; fellow Harvard, 1912; m. Lena Lovett, 1905; 1 son, John Franklin. Prof. biology, Ottawa U., 1898-1903; prof. med. zoölogy, U. of Neb., 1903-26; also asso. editor Jour. Parisitology, 1915—; prof. zoölogy, Summer Schs. U. of Ill., 1917, Northwestern U., 1923; head prof. zoölogy, Northwestern, 1926—; investigator, Harpswell Biol. Sta., 1907, 12, 14, Bermuda Biol. Sta., 1912, 15. Research grant, Nat. Acad. Science. Republican. Baptist. Author: Synopsis of the Parasites of Man, 1926; Unit System Laboratory Outlines in General Zoölogy, 1926; Unit System Laboratory Outlines in Parasitology, 1926. Home: Evanston, Ill. Died July 10, 1936.

BARKER, George, jurist; b. Cayuga Co., N.Y., Nov. 6, 1823; s. John A. and Phebe (Ogden) B.; ed. common schs. and Aurora (N.Y.) Acad.; m. Achsah Elizabeth Glisan, Oct. 1857. Admitted to N.Y. bar, 1847; located in practice, Fredonia, N.Y., 1848; village clerk, 1850-52; pres. village, 1853, 1857-58; dist. atty., Chautauqua Co., N.Y., 1854-57 and 1863-66; mem. Constl. Conv., N.Y. State, 1867, and Constl. Commn. of 1890; justice N.Y. Supreme Court, 1868-89; at time of retiring was presiding justice of General Term of 5th Dept. Retired. Home: Fredonia, N.Y. Died 1903.

BARKER, George Frederick, physicist; b. Charlestown, Mass., July 14, 1835; s. George and Lydia Prince (Pollard) B.; Ph.B., Yale, 1858; M.D., Albany Med. Coll., 1863; (Sc.D., U. of Pa., 1898; LL.D., Allegheny, 1898, McGill, 1900); m. Mary M. Treadway, Aug. 15, 1861. Prof. natural sciences, Wheaton Coll., 1861; acting prof. chemistry, Albany Med. Coll., 1863; prof. natural sciences, Western U. of Pa., 1864; asst. chemistry, 1865-67; prof. physiol. chemistry and toxicology, 1867-73, Yale; professor physics, 1873-1900; prof. emeritus, 1900—, U. of Pa. Asst. editor Am. Jour. Science, 1868-1909; editor Jour. of the Franklin Inst., 1874-75. U.S. commr. Paris Elec. Exhbn., 1881; del. elec. congress and v.p. jury of award; received decoration comdr. Legion of Honor of France; U.S. commr. Elec. Exhbn., Phila., 1884; on jury of awards, Chicago Expn., 1893. Expert in poisons, criminal cases and in Edison, Berliner and other patent suits. Author: The Forces of Nature, 1863; Textbook of Elementary Chemistry, 1870; Chemical Discoveries of the Spectroscope, 1873; Conversion of Mechanical Energy into Heat by Dynamo-Electric Machine, 1880; Physics, 1892. Home: Philadelphia. Died 1910.

BARKER, Helen Morton, treas. Nat. W.C.T.U., 1893—; b. Richville, N.Y., Dec. 8, 1834; grad. Gouverneur (N.Y.) Wesleyan Sem.; m. Rev. M. Barker, 1858. Pres. W.C.T.U. of Dak., 8 yrs.; asst. to Mrs. Potter Palmer and mem. bd. of Lady Managers, Chicago Expn.; also supt. industrial dept. same. Died 1910.

BARKER, Henry Ames, corp. mgr., city planner; b. Providence, R.I., Apr. 4, 1868; s. Henry Rodman and Annie Cushman (Tripp) B.; grad. English and Classical Sch., Providence, and R.I. Sch. of Design; Ph.B., Brown U., 1893 (hon. A.M., 1910, as civic worker); m. Sarah Elizabeth Minchin, Sept. 1918. Began as sec., 1893, sec., treas. and gen. mgr., 1897-1921, pres. and gen. mgr., 1921—, also dir., 1901—, R.I. Electric Protective Co. (pub. service electric, fire and burglar alarm office and standard time system). Devised comprehensive plans and started movement, 1901, for present met. park system of greater Providence dist., and from its official beginning, 1905, until Apr. 1920, was sec. and exec. officer of the Met. Park Commn. of Providence Plantations. Chmn. Providence City Plan Commn.; treas. Pub. Park Assn. of R.I.; chmn. publicity and statistics com. of Providence Chamber of Commerce, 1913-18 and 1921—; publisher magazine same; sec. Rhode Island State Reservation Commn., 1910-20. Mem. R.I. Hosp. Corp. Production dir. Talma (dramatic) and "Players," Providence, and many college and other dramatic productions; with A. E. Thomas, wrote and prod. hist. pageant drama "In Colony Times" (for 150th anniversary celebration of Brown U.). Home: Providence, R.I. Died Feb. 27, 1929.

BARKER, Henry Stites, univ. pres.; b. Newstead, Christian Co., Ky., July 23, 1850; s. Richard Henry and Caroline M. (Sharp) B.; ed. pub. schs. of Louisville and Ky. U. (now Transylvania U.); m. Kate Sharp Meriweather, May 22, 1886. Admitted to Ky. bar, 1874, and practiced at Louisville; city atty., Louisville, 1888-96; judge Circuit Ct. of Jefferson Co., Ky., 1896-1902; judge Ct. of Appeals, Ky., 1902-11; pres. State U. of Ky., Jan. 1, 1911-17. Gold Democrat. Mem. Christian (Disciples) Ch. Home: Louisville, Ky. Died Apr. 23, 1928.

BARKER, Howard Hines, physician; b. Washington, Sept. 13, 1848; s. James William and Sarah Ann Rozelle (Hines) B.; ed. Union Acad., Everett Inst., and Columbian (now George Washington) U.; M.D., Georgetown U., 1870; (LL.D., Nat. U., 1890); m. Fannie Rozelle Wilson, Sept. 12, 1872. Began practice, 1870; prof. obstetrics and gynecology, Nat. U., 1884—; demonstrator of anatomy, 1871-73, lecturer on same, 1874-75, Georgetown U.; resident physician Columbian Hosp. for Women, 1871; in charge diseases of women and children, Central Dispensary and Emergency Hosp., 1872-77. Home: Washington, D.C. Died 1910.

BARKER, James Madison, asso. justice Supreme Judicial Court of Mass., 1891—; b. Pittsfield, Mass., Oct. 23, 1839; grad. Williams, 1860; studied law in New York, 1861-62, and in Harvard Law School, 1862-63; admitted to bar, 1863; practiced at Pittsfield until apptd. Superior Court judge, 1882; mem. Mass. Ho. Reps., 1872-73; commr. to inquire into expediency of tax and exemption law revision, 1874-75; commr. to consolidate public statutes, 1881-82; del. to Nat. Rep. Conv., 1880. Home: Pittsfield, Mass. Died 1905.

BARKER, John Marshall, univ. prof.; b. Fredericktown, O., Oct. 1, 1849; s. Joseph N. and Nancy J. (Benedict) B.; A.B., Ohio Wesleyan U., 1874, A.M., 1877; B.D., Boston U., 1877, Ph.D., 1892; m. Alice L. Bixler, July 3, 1877; children—Pearl Marcella (dec.), Raymond Marshall (dec.), Alice Mabelle, Paul Victor. Ordained M.E. ministry, 1876; pastor Charlestown, Mass., 1876-77, Cambridge, Mass., 1877-78; missionary in Pachuca, Mex., 1878-85; pastor Ellington, N.Y., 1885-87, Fredonia, N.Y., 1887-89; prof. economics, Ohio Wesleyan U., 1889-99; prof. sociology, Boston U., 1899, emeritus. Republican. Author: Wealth and Its Uses, 1893; Colleges in America, 1895; History of Ohio Methodism, 1898; The Saloon Problem and Social Reform, 1905; Social Gospel and the New Era, 1919. Home: Newton Centre, Mass. Deceased.

BARKER, Reginald Charles, author; b. Brighton, Sussex, Eng., May 15, 1881; s. Reginald and Mimmie (Magnese) B.; ed. pvt. sch., Eng.; m. Edith Maude Granger, Aug. 11, 1911; children—Rudyard Charles (dec.), Thor, Kenneth. Came to U.S., 1900, naturalized citizen, 1923. Worked as sailor, cowboy, miner, trapper and lumberman. Republican. Author: Grizzly Gallagher, 1927; Wild Horse Ranch, 1927; Gentleman Grizzly, 1928; Hair-Trigger Brand, 1929. Contbr. stories to mags. Home: Hollywood, Calif. Died Oct. 21, 1937.

BARKER, Wendell Phillips, lawyer; b. Rosita, Colo., Sept. 5, 1884; s. Anthony and Maria (Savage) B.; ed. pub. and pvt. schs.; LL.B., New York Law Sch., 1906; m. Augusta Giblyn, June 8, 1909; children—Eleanor Wendell, John Wendell. Practiced in N.Y. state and before U.S. Supreme Court, 1906—, specializing in ins. law; apptd. by Gov. Lehman, chmn. Mortgage Commn. State of N.Y., Feb. 1935, resigned, Jan. 1937; resumed practice of law. Home: New York, N.Y. Died Apr. 7, 1941.

BARKER, Wharton, financier, publicist; b. Phila., May 1, 1846; s. Abraham and Sarah (Wharton) B.; paternal ancestors emigrated from England to Mass. in 1628, maternal to Pa. in 1682—Puritans and Quakers; assisted in organizing 3d U.S. Colored Troops, 1863; A.B., U. of Pa., 1866, A.M., 1869; m. Margaret Corlies Baker, Oct. 16, 1867. Mem. Barker Bros. & Co., bankers, Phila.; apptd., 1878, spl. financial agt. in U.S. of Russian Govt., and intrusted with the building of 4 cruisers for its navy; made Knight of St. Stanislaus by Alexander II of Russia, 1879; was called to Russia to advise on development of coal and iron mines north of the Azof and presented plans which were adopted; had important correspondence with Russians, both of the court adherents and some leaders of the late revolution, 1876-1917. Obtained, 1887, valuable railroad, telegraph and telephone concessions from China, withdrawn, 1888, by pressure upon Chinese Imperial Govt. by British Govt.; maintained correspondence with leading Chinese, some of them leaders in the revolution resulting in the republic, and regarded by them as authority on Far Eastern affairs; advocate of Am. coöperation in the development of China's material resources. Founded Penn Monthly, 1869, and merged it, 1880, into The American, a weekly, devoted to economic, social and polit. questions, and published 1880-1900. Chief organizer of anti 3d term opposition to nomination of Gen. Grant for President and proposer of nomination of Gen. Garfield for President, and mgr. of Garfield pre-nomination campaign, 1880. Earliest proposer of nomination for the presidency of Gen. Benjamin Harrison and mgr. of Harrison nomination campaign, 1884-88. Republican until 1896; Populist nominee for President, 1900. Has traveled extensively in U.S., Europe, China, Japan and South America. Trustee U. of Pa. Home: Philadelphia, Pa. Died Apr. 9, 1921.

BARKER, William Morris, P.E. bishop; b. Towanda, Pa., May 12, 1854; s. George R. and Anna Ellis (Morris) B.; ed. in his father's classical school, Germantown, Pa.; grad. Univ. of Pa., 1873; Berkeley Div. Sch., 1879; ordered deacon, 1879; curate St. John's Ch., Troy, N.Y.; ordained priest, 1880; curate St. John's rector St. Paul's, Washington, 1881-87; St. Luke's, Baltimore, 1887-89; St. Paul's, Duluth, Minn., 1889-93. Consecrated Bishop of Western Colo., Jan. 25, 1893; translated to see of Olympia, Oct. 18, 1894. Home: Tacoma, Wash. Died 1901.

BARKLEY, Henry L., bishop; b. Adams Co., Ind., Mar. 19, 1858; s. Samuel T. and Elizabeth (Snyder) B.; ed. normal and high schs., Ohio; m. Ida B. Masters, Sept. 11, 1878. Ordained U.B. ministry, 1877; presiding-elder, Willamette Dist., 1890-95; consecrated bishop, May 1896. Mem. Ore. Ho. of Rep., 1895-97. Home: Portland, Ore. Died Mar. 7, 1915.

BARKLEY, James Morrison, clergyman; b. nr. Statesville, N.C., Nov. 22, 1846; s. John Cathey and Eliza Julia (Morrison) B.; A.B., Princeton, 1876; grad. Princeton Theol. Sem., 1879; (D.D., 1899, LL.D., 1912, Alma Coll.); m. Mary E. Conwell, May 27, 1879. Served pvt. to lt. Co. F, 73d N.C. Inf. (Jr. Reserves), C.S.A., 1864-65. Ordained Presbyn. ministry, 1879; pastor Wickliffe Ch., Newark, N.J., 1879-82, Hillsdale, Mich., 1882-85; state sec.

Y.M.C.A., Mich., 1885-86; pastor 3d (afterward Forest) Av. Ch., Detroit, 1886-1916, pastor emeritus, 1916—. Moderator Presbyn. Gen. Assembly, Denver, 1909; trustee and chmn. bd. Alma Coll. (acting pres., 1915). Republican. Author various pub. sermons and addresses. Home: Detroit, Mich. Died Aug. 1922.

BARLOW, John Whitney, brig. gen.; b. Perry, Wyoming Co., N.Y., June 26, 1838; s. Nehemiah and Orinda (Steel) B.; grad. U.S. Mil. Acad., 1861; m. Hessie McNaughton Birnie, Dec. 26, 1861; m. 2d, Alice Stanton Turner, Sept. 17, 1902. Apptd. 2d lt., 2d U.S. Arty., May 6, 1861; promoted through grades to col. engrs., May 10, 1895; brig. gen. and chief of engrs., U.S.A., May 2, 1901; retired May 3, 1901, at own request, after 40 yrs.' service. Bvtd.: capt., May 27, 1862, "for gallant and meritorious services in battle of Hanover C.H., Va."; maj., July 22, 1864, for same in Atlanta campaign; lt. col., Mar. 13, 1865, for same in battles before Nashville, Tenn. Was with light battery at first Bull Run; with horse battery M, in Peninsular campaign; at Yorktown, Williamsburg, Hanover C.H. (where recommended for medal of honor for holding in check, with one gun, a div. of the enemy); in 7 days' battles before Richmond, notably Malvern Hill; afterward with engr. battalion, Army of the Potomac, building bridges, making roads, building block houses and erecting defensive works; in Ga. campaign, July 12-Aug. 27, chief engr. 17th Army Corps; in charge defenses of Nashville, Nov. 1864-Oct. 1865, etc. Senior commr. of U.S. in marking boundary between U.S. and Mexico, 1892-96. Episcopalian. Republican. Home: New London, Conn. Died Mar. 1, 1914.

BARLOW, Milton Theodore, banker; b. Greencastle, Ind., Jan. 31, 1844; s. Milton Fry and Angeline (Knight) B.; student Asbury U., Greencastle, 2 yrs.; m. Sarah McClintock, Nov. 1894. Began as messenger for Barrows, Millard & Co., bankers, Omaha, Neb., 1863; teller Millard, Caldwell & Co., 1864, and later partner Caldwell, Hamilton & Co.; served as cashier and v.p. U.S. Nat. Bank, becoming pres., 1897, then chmn. bd. Served as corpl. 133d Ind. Vol. Inf.; mustered out Aug. 1864. Republican. Methodist. Mason. Home: Omaha, Neb. Died July 1, 1930.

BARLOW, W(alter) Jarvis, M.D.; b. Ossining, N.Y., Jan. 22, 1868; s. William Henry and Catherine Stratton (Lent) B.; A.B., Columbia, 1889; M.D., Coll. Phys. and Surg. (Columbia), 1892; M.A., 1919; m. Marion Brooks Patterson, Nov. 8, 1898. In practice at New York, 1892-95; moved to Los Angeles, Calif. Episcopalian. Home: Sierra Madre, Calif. Died Sept. 3, 1937.

BARLOW, William Edward, prof. metallurgy; b. Bury, Lancashire, Eng., May 11, 1870; s. William Smythe and Mary (Yates) B.; B.A., Cambridge, 1895, M.A., 1899; Ph.D., magna cum laude, Göttingen, 1903; m. Bernice Gertrude Whiting, Nov. 4, 1893; children—Helen Gertrude, Wallace Dudley. Came to U.S., 1892; with State U. of Ia., as demonstrator chemistry, etc., 1892-1901, asst. prof. 1903-04; with Va. Poly. Inst., 1904—, prof. metallurgy and metallography, 1906—, dean grad. dept., 1908-19. Episcopalian. Mason. Home: Blacksburg, Va. Died Dec. 22, 1938.

BARNABAS, Brother, boy guidance; b. Ogdensburg, N.Y., Mar. 20, 1865; s. John F. and Mary (Byrnes) McDonald; ed. St. Mary Acad., Ogdensburg, and St. Joseph's Normal Coll., Pocantico Hills, N.Y.; LL.D., Notre Dame, 1924. Joined Order of Brothers of the Christian Schs. (F.S.C.), 1885; teacher St. Patricks Parochial Sch., N.Y. City, 1887-89; asst. dir. of novices, Christian Bros. Novitiate, 1889; vocational dir. Province of N.Y., 1890-95; an organizer of N.Y.C.P. Placing-out Bur. for dependent children, and its dir., 1905-14; founder St. Philip's Home for Industrial Boys; founder Lincoln Agrl. Sch., Lincolndale, N.Y., 1909; exec. sec. Boy Life Bur. (Knights of Columbus), New Haven, Conn. Was mem. President Roosevelt's Spl. Conf. on Standards of Child Welfare, 1909. Died Apr. 22, 1929.

BARNABEE, Henry Clay, operatic comedian; b. Portsmouth, N.H., Nov. 14, 1833; s. Willis B.; pub. sch. edn.; m. Clara, d. Maj. Daniel George, of Warner, N.H., 1859. Clerk in dry goods house, Portsmouth, until 1854, later in wholesale house in Boston. Appeared, beginning Apr. 30, 1854, in entertainments of Mercantile Library Assn., where he developed talents as comedian, vocalist and mimic; sang in ch. choirs in Boston, Jamaica Plain, and Roxbury, and for 19 yrs. mem. Ch. of the Unity Quartet, Boston; gave up mercantile pursuits, 1865. Organized Barnabee Operetta Co., and in 1870, the Barnabee Concert Co.; afterward for several yrs. appeared in lyceum courses in his monologue, "Patchwork, or An Evening with Barnabee"; joined Boston Ideal Opera Co., Apr. 1879, appearing as Sir Joseph Porter, in Pinafore, followed by leading rôles in other operas. In 1887, with Tom Karl and W. H. Macdonald, organized The Bostonians, in which he created leading opera rôles; notably the Sheriff of Nottingham in Robin Hood. Mem. Ancient and Hon. Arty. Co., Boston One of founders of Apollo Club. Author: My Wanderings, 1913. Home: Jamaica Plain, Mass. Died Dec. 16, 1917.

BARNARD, Charles, author; b. Boston, Feb. 13, 1838; s. late Rev. Charles F. and Sarah (Holmes) B.; m. Mary E. Knight, May 17, 1881. Has filled several editorial positions. Author of several books on tech. subjects and a great number juvenile stories. Also the County Fair and other plays, and contbr. to Century Dictionary and to leading mags. upon ednl. and scientific subjects. Home: Pasadena, Calif. Died Apr. 11, 1920.

BARNARD, Edward Chester, U.S. boundary commr.; b. N.Y. City, Nov. 13, 1863; s. Owen Howard and Anne E. B.; E.M., Columbia, 1884; m. Mrs. Juliet Gill Rogers, Dec. 16, 1908. Topographer U.S. Geol. Survey, 1884-1907, geographer, 1907-15; mapped sections of Ky., Tenn., Va. and N.Y., in the East, and Calif., Ida., Mont., Ore. and Wash. in the West; had charge of party sent to Alaska by U.S. Geol. Survey to map Forty-Mile Dist., 1898, and Nome Dist., 1900; chief topographer U.S. and Can. Boundary Survey, 1903-15, surveying and relocating U.S. and Can. boundary line, along 49th parallel from Pacific Coast to the Lake of the Woods and through Lake of the Woods, Rainy River and Rainy Lake; apptd. commr. on the part of the U.S. for defining and marking the boundary between U.S. and Can., except on Great Lakes and St. Lawrence River, and for marking and surveying boundary between Alaska and Can., 1915. Home: Washington, D.C. Died Feb. 6, 1921.

BARNARD, Edward Emerson, astronomer; b. Nashville, Tenn., Dec. 16, 1857; learned photography in a studio as a boy; began astron. studies alone, in boyhood; grad. Vanderbilt U., 1887 (Sc.D., 1893; A.M., U. of the Pacific, San José, 1889; LL.D., Queen's U., 1909); m. Rhoda Calvert, Jan. 27, 1881. In charge Vanderbilt U. Obs., 1883-87; astronomer Lick Obs., Calif., 1887-95; prof. practical astronomy, U. of Chicago and astronomer of the Yerkes Obs., 1895—. Mem. U.S. Naval Obs. Eclipse Expdn. to Sumatra, 1901. Discovered 5th satellite of Jupiter, 1892; also 16 comets and many other discoveries; has done much in celestial photography, making photographs of the Milky Way, comets, nebulæ, etc. Received Lalande gold medal, French Acad. Sciences, 1892; Arago gold medal, same, 1893; gold medal, Royal Astron. Soc. of Great Britain, 1897; Janssen gold medal, French Acad. Sciences, 1900; Janssen prize, French Astron. Soc., 1906; Bruce gold medal, Astron. Soc. of the Pacific, 1917. Mem. Nat. Acad. Sciences; asso. fellow Am. Acad. Arts and Sciences. Died Feb. 6, 1923.

BARNARD, Ernest Sargent, baseball exec.; b. West Columbia, W.Va., July 17, 1874; s. Elias and Mary Dillon (Sargent) B.; Ph.B., Otterbein Coll., Westerville, O., 1895; m. Josephine E. Flick, Dec. 7, 1918. Sec. Columbus (O.) Builders Exchange, 1896-97; sporting editor Columbus Evening Dispatch, 1898-1902; sec. Cleveland Ball Club Co., 1903-10, v.p., 1911-15; business mgr. Cleveland Baseball Co., 1916-21, pres. 1922-27; pres. Am. League of Professional Baseball Clubs, 1927—; v.p. Acetylene Stove Mfg. Co., Cleveland. Republican. Mason. Died Mar. 27, 1931.

BARNARD, George Grey, sculptor; b. Bellefonte, Pa., May 24, 1863; s. Joseph H. and Martha (Grubb) B.; studied 1 yr. at Art Inst. of Chicago; École Nationale des Beaux Arts, 1884, 1885, 1886, 1887; m. Edna Monroe, 1895. Exhibited in Paris Salon, 1894, and was then named Associé Société Nationale des Beaux Arts: awarded gold medal, Paris Expn., 1900; gold medal, Buffalo Expn., 1901; special gold medal, Nat. Assn. of Sculptors, Painters and Artists of France. Prof. of sculptors, Art Students' League of New York, 1900-04. Works include: 2-Natures group, Metropolitan Mus., New York, Indianapolis, Chicago; "Brotherly Love," Marble, Norway; "Boy," private museum, New York; 50 Figures carved in Oak, 12 feet high; The Urn of Life, 19 figures, Carnegie Museum; two groups of 31 statues, Harrisburg (Pa.) Capitol; large fountain, Tampa, Fla.; "Maidenhood," Cemetery, Muscatine, Iowa; "Hewer," bronze, Cairo, Ill.; "God Pan," Columbia Coll. grounds; "Cupid and Venus," private collection, Paris; "Maidenhood," collection Blair Thaw; Marble "Hewer," "Rising Woman," "Adam and Eve," property of John D. Rockefeller, all at Pocantico Hills, N.Y.; Barnard Mus. founded in Madison, Ind., some 50 pieces of work; Barnard Mus. founded at Swarthmore, Pa., containing some 200 pieces of his entire work; "Builder" 9 foot statue, study dedicated to the spirit of labor; fifty odd 9 foot statues for Rainbow Arch; "Mother Earth and her Child," 9 foot statue; Marble "Refugee," property of Stephen Clark; "Prodigal Son" group; Lincoln bust, property of French govt.; Lincoln statues, Manchester, Eng., Cincinnati, O., Louisville, Ky.; marble shrine containing bust of Lincoln, Redlands, Calif.; Lincoln bust, Metropolitan Mus., New York. Mem. Am. Academy Arts and Letters, Nat. Institute of Arts and Letters; corr. mem. Inst. of France. Died Apr. 24, 1938.

BARNARD, Joseph Folger, jurist; b. Poughkeepsie, N.Y., 1823; grad. Yale, 1841, Yale Law Sch., 1844 (LL.D., 1894); m. Emily B. Hasbrouck, Jan. 7, 1862. Admitted to N.Y. bar, 1844; practiced in Poughkeepsie until 1862; elected, 1862, and served Jan. 1, 1863, to Dec. 31, 1893, as judge Supreme Court of N.Y.; retired because of age limit; practiced in Poughkeepsie, 1894; reapptd. under provision of new Constitution and again served, 1895-99, for remainder of term to which he was elected in 1885, in all 36 yrs. on Supreme Court bench. Home: Poughkeepsie, N.Y. Died 1904.

BARNES, Amos, hotel proprietor; b. E. Lebanon, N.H., Aug. 15, 1828; ed. village school; m. Emeline P. Currier, Dec., 1851. In R.R. business nearly 20 yrs.; lessee U.S. Hotel, Boston, 1869-79; acquired interest in Burnet House, Cincinnati, with John W. Dunklee, with whom he leased, 1879, Hotel Brunswick, Boston; built 1883, Hotel Ponemah, Milford Springs, N.H.; also lessee, from 1886, of Hotel Victoria and Hotel Vendome, Boston. Pres. Conn. & Passumpsic Rivers R.R., Newport & Richford Vt. Ry., Mascoma Electric Light & Gas Co., N.H. Home: Boston, Mass. Died 1906.

BARNES, Benjamin F., postmaster of Washington, D.C.; b. Yarmouth, N.S., Dec. 3, 1868; s. Benjamin H. and Orena (Higgins) B.; ed. pub. schs. of N.J., law dept. Georgetown (D.C.) Univ., LL.B., 1895; m. Emily Frech, Oct. 18, 1892. Apptd. clerk in P. O. dept. under competitive exam., Oct., 1887; pvt. sec. to 1st asst. p. m. gen., Sept., 1889; later pvt. sec. to chief P. O. insp., and to 4th asst. p. m. gen.; sec. to Hon. James S. Clarkson several yrs.; apptd. stenographer at White House, Jan., 1898; exec. clerk, July 1, 1898; apptd. by President McKinley asst. sec. to the President, May 1, 1900; reapptd. by President Roosevelt, Apr. 22, 1902; apptd. postmaster, Washington, June 23, 1906—. Died 1909.

BARNES, Charles Reid, prof. of plant physiology, U. of Chicago, July, 1898—; b. Madison, Ind., Sept. 7, 1858; grad. Hanover (Ind.) Coll., 1877, (A.M., 1880; Ph.D., 1886), grad. study at Harvard, 1877, 1878, 1885-86, 1892; m. Mary King Ward, Dec. 25, 1882. Prof. natural history, Purdue Univ., 1880-86; prof. botany, U. of Wis., 1886-98; co-editor Botanical Gazette, 1883—. Author: (with J. C. Arthur and J. M. Coulter) Plant Dissection, 1886; Keys to the Genera and Species of North American Mosses, 1896 (Univ. of Wis.); Plant Life, 1898; Outlines of Plant Life, 1900; and numerous bot. papers. Sec. Bot. Soc. of Am., 1893-98 (pres. 1903); gen. sec. A.A.A.S., 1896 (v.p. 1899). Died 1910.

BARNES, Earl, lecturer, writer; b. Martville, N.Y., July 15, 1861; s. James and Minera (Myres) B.; A.B., Ind. U., 1889; M.S., Cornell U. 1891; m. Anna Kohler, 1900; children—Mary, Howard, Joseph, Bernard. Prof. history, Ind. U., 1889; prof. edn., Stanford, 1891-97; staff lecturer, London Soc. for Extension of Univ. Teaching, 1900-01; engaged since in lecturing and writing. Democrat. Author: Studies in Education (2 vols.), 1897; Where Knowledge Fails, 1907; Women in Modern Society, 1912; Psychology of Childhood and Youth, 1914. Home: New Hartford, Conn. Died May 29, 1935.

BARNES, Francis George, educator; b. London, Eng., Jan. 31, 1866; s. Peter Stephen and Sarah Annie (Spencer) B.; came to America, 1872; A.B., Hamline U., 1897; A.M., Harvard, 1907; (D.D., Upper Ia. U. 1901); m. Harriet Leland Morse, A.B., July 18, 1899. Frontier missionary in Canadian dists., 1885-89; ordained M.E. ministry, 1888; pastor, Inkster, N.D., 1889-91; prin. Epworth (Ia.) Sem., 1897-1901; pres. Onarga (Ill.) Sem., 1901-05, Ill. Wesleyan U., 1905-08; gen. sec. of eastern central office for Univ. Research Extension of Chicago, July 1, 1908—. Explored ruins of Cliff Dwellers, Ariz., 1902; studied Shaliko ceremonies of Zuñi Indians in N.M., 1906. Home: Ann Arbor, Mich. Died 1910.

BARNES, Henry Burr, publisher; b. New York, Dec. 14, 1845; s. Alfred S. and Harriet Elizabeth (Burr) B.; A.B., Yale, 1866, A.M., 1870; m. H. Elizabeth, d. Courtlandt P. Dixon, of Brooklyn, June 16, 1869. Entered publishing house A. S. Barnes & Co., 1866; became partner, 1868, sr. partner, 1896. Editor International Review, 1878-80; pres. Stationers' Bd. of Trade, 1886-88; dir. Am. Book Co., 1891; v.p. Central Real Estate Assn., 1895; pres. Barnes Real Estate Assn., 1905; founder Barnes-Curtiss Co., 1896. Republican. Home: New York, N.Y. Died 1911.

BARNES, Henry Whitmer, clergyman; b. Orwell, Pa., Aug., 1832; s. Horace W. and Polly C. (Woodruff) B.; ed. common sch. and acad.; m. Frances M. Camp, Oct. 24, 1857. Ordained Bapt. ministry, 1856; pastor Warren, Pa., 1856-62, Marathon, N.Y., 1862-66, Niagara Falls, 1866-70, Ogdensburg, 1870-82, Spencer, 1882-86; dist. missionary Central Southern Dist. of N.Y., Jan.-Oct., 1886; sec. Bapt. Mission Conv., 1886-1907; asst. sec., 1907-10. Home: Binghamton, N.Y. Died Sept. 29, 1914.

BARNES, James, author; b. Annapolis, Md., Sept. 19, 1866; s. John S. (U.S.N.) and Susan Bainbridge (Hayes) B.; Princeton U., 1891 (hon. A.M., 1894); m. Brooks Browne, Apr. 26, 1921. On staff Scribner's Magazine, 1891-93; asst. editor Harper's Weekly, 1894-95; war corr. in S. Africa, 1899-1901; lit. editor

D. Appleton & Co., 1905-08. Served in Spanish-Am. War, 1st Battalion N.Y. State Naval Militia, acting lt. junior grade, 1898. Author: For King or Country, 1895; Naval Actions of 1812, 1896; A Princetonian, 1896; Midshipman Farragut, 1896; A Loyal Traitor; 1897; Commodore Bainbridge, 1897; Yankee Ships and Yankee Sailors, 1897; The Hero of Erie, 1898; Ships and Sailors, 1898; David G. Farragut, 1899; Drake and His Yeomen, 1899; The Great War Trek, 1901; With the Flag in the Channel, 1902; The Giant of Three Wars, 1903; The Unpardonable War, 1904; The Son of Light Horse Harry, 1904; The Blockaders, 1905; Outside the Law, 1906; The Clutch of Circumstance, 1908; Commodore Perry, 1912; Rifle and Caravan, 1912; Through Central Africa from Coast to Coast, 1915. Shortly before outbreak of the war, for 3 months was head of Princeton Aviation School, Princeton U., and subsequently commd. major, Aviation Sect., Signal Corps, U.S. Reserve; head of photographic div. of the Army and sent to France to organize the U.S. aviation photographic work at the front; comdg. U.S. School of Aerial Photography, Rochester, N.Y., at end of war; commd. lt. col. Air Corps Reserve, 1924, col., 1930, now col. Auxiliary Reserve. Pres. bd. regents, Mercersburg (Pa.) Acad., 1927, 1933; pres. Naval History Soc. of U.S., 1933. Home: Princeton, N.J. Died Apr. 30, 1936.

BARNES, Jasper Converse, psychologist; b. Meigsville, Morgan Co. O., Aug. 28, 1861; s. Abraham and Margaret (Welch) B.; student Muskingum Valley Normal Sch.; grad. Marietta (O.) Acad., 1886; A.B., Marietta Coll., 1890, A.M., 1893; student, summer session, Cornell; Ph.D., Univ. of Chicago, 1911; LL.D. from Maryville (Tenn.) College, 1928; m. Alice Mary Hopkins, Aug. 13, 1890; 1 son, Mark Hopkins. Teacher pub. schs., Morgan Co., O., 1880-84; supt. schs., Belpre, O., 1890-92; prin, prep. dept. and prof. edn., 1892-1901, actg. prof. psychology and polit. science, 1901-03, prof., 1903—, dean 1914-31, dean emeritus and head Dept. of Psychology and Edn., 1931—, Maryville Coll. Mem. faculty State Insts. for Teachers, Clinton and Athens, Tenn., summers 1913, 14; prof. psychology, Summer Sch. of South, 1915, 18; summer, Asheville (N.C.) Normal Sch., 1921-22; Ohio State U., summer 1920, psychology and edn., U. of Tenn., summers, 1923-27, and 1930, dept. psychology, U. of Wyo., summer 1928. Mem. Rhodes Scholarship Com. for Tenn., 1913-19. Democrat. Presbyn. Mason. Author: (booklet) Development of Personality in the Afro-American, 1900; Voluntary Isolation of Control in a Natural Muscle Group, 1915. Home: Maryville, Tenn. Died Sept. 13, 1931.

BARNES, John, judge; b. Manitowoc Co., Wis., July 26, 1859; s. John and Mary (Butler) B.; ed. Manitowoc High Sch. and Oshkosh Normal Sch.; LL.B., U. of Wis., 1883; m. Julia A. Koelzer, July 26, 1887. Admitted to bar, 1885; practiced at Rhinelander, Wis.; municipal judge Oneida Co., Wis., 1887-91 (declined reëlection); apptd. mem., chmn. bd. R.R. Commn. of Wis., 1905-07, resigned; justice of Supreme Ct. of Wis., 1908-16, resigned; gen. counsel Northwestern Mut. Life Ins. Co., Milwaukee, Feb., 1916—. Also 2d v.p. Central Wis. Trust Co.; dir. Rhinelander Paper Co. Democrat. Catholic. Home: Milwaukee, Wis. Died Jan. 1, 1919.

BARNES, John Beaumont, judge; b. E. Trumbull, Ashtabula Co., O., Aug. 26, 1846; s. A. J. S. and Susan M. (Jeffords) B.; ed. in common schs. and at Grand River Inst., Austinburg, O.; pvt. Battery E, 1st Ohio Light Arty. during Civil War; m. Ida Frances Hannant, Nov. 29, 1874. Admitted to bar, 1872; dist. atty. 6th Jud. Dist., Neb., 1875-79; judge 6th Jud. Dist., 1879-83; commr. Supreme Ct., 1902-04; justice Supreme Ct., Jan. 1, 1904—; reëlected, 1909 (chief justice, 1908-09). Republican. Home: Lincoln, Neb. Deceased.

BARNES, Lemuel Call, clergyman; b. Kirtland, O., Nov. 6, 1854; s. Lemuel Munson and Rachel (Call) B.; A.B., Kalamazoo Coll., 1875; grad. Newton Theol. Instn., 1878 (D.D., Kalamazoo, and Bucknell, 1896); m. Mary Emelia Clark, Jan. 2, 1879. Ordained Bapt. ministry, 1878; pastor First Church, St. Paul, 1878-82, First Church, Pittsburgh, 1882-87, First Church, Newton, Mass., 1887-93, First Church, Pittsburgh, 1893-1902, First Ch., Worcester, Mass., 1902-07; field sec. Am. Bapt. Home Mission Soc., Apr. 1, 1907-17, sec. dept. English-speaking Missions and Indian Work, and sec. dept. of evangelism, 1917, also acting sec. dept. of Latin North America, 1918, and dept. of rural church work, 1922; retired, 1924. Mem. bd. mgrs. Am. Bapt. Missionary Union, 1879-1907 (elected foreign sec., 1891, but declined); pres. Fedn. of Chs., Pittsburgh, 1901-02; drafted constitution of Gen. Conv. of Baptists of N. America, St. Louis, 1905; chmn. com. on home missions, Fed. Council Chs. of Christ in America; chmn. Com. on Comity and Coöperation of Home Missions Council, 1919-24; chmn. Joint Com. Home Missions Council and of Fed. Council on Utilizing Surveys; chmn. Regional Conf. of Missions in Central America, Guatemala City, 1920. Trustee Newton Theol. Instn. Author: (brochure) Shall Islam Rule Africa?, 1891; Two Thousand Years of Missions Before Carey, 1901; Elemental Forces in Home Missions, 1912; The New America (with Mary

Clark Barnes), 1913; Intensive Powers on the Western Slopes, 1921; Pioneers of Light, 100 Years of the American Baptist Publ. Soc. (with Mary Clark Barnes), 1924; (brochure) George Washington and Freedom of Conscience, 1932; Coöperation—The Master Key in Universal Problems; also (pamphlets) Coöperation in Home Missions, 1912; Baptist Work among American Indians, 1920; The Power of the Gospel Through the Ministry of Healing, 1921; The Chaplain Gano Evidence of the Religion of George Washington, 1926. Home: Yonkers, N.Y. Died July 18, 1938.

BARNES, Mortimer Grant, engr.; b. Reedsburg, Sauk Co., Wis., Jan. 17, 1867; s. James Brewster and Alice Jane (Randall) B.; B.S. in C.E., U. of Mich., 1896, C.E., 1900, M.E., 1922; m. Mary Wilhelmina Wood, Aug. 17, 1898; children—Alice Elizabeth, Florence Lillian, James Mathew. Worked on waterway constrn. and hydraulic power projects; in charge parties surveying and estimating of proposed Birmingham-Warrior River (Ala.) Canal, 1897, U.S. Deep Waterway, Gt. Lakes to Sea via N.Y. City, 1898; on design and constrn. Hennepin Canal, connecting Ill. and Miss. rivers, 1899, 1905; U.S. asst. engr. in charge design Moline Locks, Rock Island, Ill., 1905-06; design of locks for Panama Canal, 1906-07; mem. bd. cons. engrs., N.Y. State Barge Canal, 1907-15; also pvt. practice, Albany; apptd. by Gov. Lowden to devise means for utilizing waters of Ill. River for power and navigation, 1917; apptd. chief engr. Ill. Waterway, 1917; cons. engr. Ill. Waterway, June 1, 1928—. Mem. Christian (Disciples) Ch. Home: Oak Park, Ill. Died Oct. 7, 1930.

BARNES, Oliver Weldon, civil engr.; b. Berlin, Hartford Co., Conn., May 15, 1823; s. Henry and Marilla (Weldon) B.; grad. high sch., Burlington, N.J., and priv. sch. in engring., Phila.; also studied in Europe, 1846; apptd. asst. engr. in first corps assembled at Pittsburgh on Pa. R.R., May 1, 1847; prin. asst. engr., 1848; made final location of line of the Pa. R.R. from the Allegheny Mountains to Pittsburgh, and constructed Western div. between same points, 1848-53; chief engr. of Pittsburgh & Connellsville R.R. Co., 1853-57; built Western Div. Pittsburgh, Ft. Wayne & Chicago R.R., Plymouth to Chicago, 1858; commenced construction St. Paul & Pacific R.R. at St. Paul, 1861; built branch lines Pa. R.R., 1862; chief engr. Dutchess & Columbia R.R., 1866-70, of Boston, Hartford & Erie R.R., 1866-70; chief engr. various lines, 1871-81; chief engr. South Pa. R.R., 1881; chief engr. N.Y. & Long Island R.R., 1887; 1892, chief engr. and pres. of the N.Y. Connecting R.R. Co., building from the N.Y. & Harlem R.R. across East River to Brooklyn; m. Elizabeth Denny, d. Maj. Ed. Harding, U.S.A. Republican. Home: New York, N.Y. Died 1908.

BARNES, Ralph W(aldo), newspaper corr.; b. Salem, Ore., June 14, 1899; s. Edward Talbot and Mabel (Baker) B.; A.B., Willamette U., 1922; M.A., Harvard, 1924; m. Esther Barton Parounagian, Oct. 11, 1924; children—Joan, Suzanne. Began as reporter Brooklyn Daily Eagle, 1924; with New York Herald Tribune, 1926; mem. editorial staff, New York Herald, Paris, 1926-29; asst. Paris Bur., New York Herald Tribune, 1929, reporting conf. of financial experts that drafted Young Plan; Rome corr. New York Herald Tribune, 1930, Moscow corr., 1931-Central Inf. O.T.S., Waco, Tex., 1918, World War 35, Berlin corr., 1935-39, London corr., 1939. At Home: Salem, Ore. Died Nov. 18, 1940.

BARNES, Stephen Goodyear, educator, clergyman; b. Perth Amboy, N.J.. Apr. 2, 1853; s. Joshua Edward and Elizabeth (Woodbridge) B.; A.B., Lafayette Coll., 1873; Ph.D., for studies in English philology, 1878; Litt.D., for studies in lit., 1890; Andover Theol. Sem., 1878-79; grad. Hartford Theol. Sem., 1892; D.D., Ia. Coll., 1896; m. Hannah W. Magoun, June 14, 1881. Prof. English lit., Ia. (now Grinnell) Coll., 1873-91; ordained Congl. ministry, 1881; pastor Longmeadow, Mass., 1891-1900; coll. pastor and dean theol. dept., Fisk U., Tenn., 1900-02; pastor South Ch., St. Johnsbury, Vt., 1902-11; supplied First Ch., Burlington, Vt., 1912-13. Dir. religious work, U. of Vt., 1913-17, and prof. Biblical History, 1914-18. Lecturer on theology, Hartford Theol. Sem., 1902, and at Fairfax (Vt.) Conf. 1912; lecturer at Knowlton Conf., Que., 1908, 1919, and other similar confs.; v.p. French Am. Coll., Springfield, Mass., 1897-1901; trustee St. Johnsbury Acad., 1908-11. Author: The Spiritual in Art and Literature, 1891; Voices of Faith and Love (poems), 1908, second series, 1923. Also essays and addresses on lit. and religious subjects in various publs. Editor of French American Citizen, 1894-95. Home: Essex Junction, Vt. Died Jan. 5, 1931.

BARNES, Thomas Robert, mfr.; b. Salem, O., Mar. 21, 1862; s. Robert Amos and Avarilla Ann (Gilbert) B.; ed. country schs.; m. Lida Rebecca Scott, Sept. 30, 1885; 1 dau., Ruth Barnes (Mrs. James C. Gorman). Began as grocery clk., 1879; bill clk. Adams Express Co., 1883-87; sec. Humphreyes Mfg. Co., 1889-95; organizer, 1887, and pres. Barnes Mfg. Co., Mansfield, until retired; v.p. Citizens Savings & Loan Co.; mem. bd. of dirs. various cos. Mem. City Council, Mansfield, 2 terms; pres. Mans-

field Conservancy Dist. Del. to Rep. Nat. Conv., 1932; presdl. elector for Coolidge. Mason. Presbyn. Home: Mansfield, O. Died Jan. 30, 1941.

BARNES, Thurlow Weed, businessman; b. Albany, N.Y., June 28, 1853; s. William and Emily P. (Weed) B.; brother of William Barnes and Catharine Weed Barnes Ward; traveled in Europe, 1871-72; A.B., Harvard, 1876. Made tours around the world, 1884-85, 1891-92, 1905-06; chmn. Albany gen. com.; member state com.; interested chiefly in railways, mining. Negotiated the "Hankow-Canton Contract" with the Chinese Govt., 1898; since then other concessions. Author: Life of Thurlow Weed, 1884. Pres. gen. Union Soc. of Civil War, 1917. Died June 27, 1918.

BARNES, Will Croft, author; b. June 21, 1858 s. Enos Rollin and Elizabeth Ann (Croft) B.; ed pub. schs., Minneapolis, Minn., and La Porte, Ind.; studied piano and voice under masters; m. Edith Talbot, May 4, 1897; 1 son, Talbot Croft (dec.). Served as pvt. and sergt. Signal Corps, U.S.A., 1879-82; awarded Congressional Medal of Honor "for bravery in action with hostile Apache Indians," at Ft. Apache, Ariz., Sept. 1881. Mem. Ariz. legislature from Apache Co., 1891-92; mem. Ariz. Commn. to World's Fair, Chicago, 1893. Chmn. Ariz. Live Stock Board, 1897-1900; mem. N.M. legislature, from Colfax Co., 1901-02; chmn. N.M. Live Stock Bd., 1902-06; in open range cattle business many yrs.; asst. U.S. forester, 1907-28; sec. U.S. Geographic Bd., 1929-30. Republican. Conglist. Mason. Author: Western Grazing Grounds and Forest Ranges, 1913; Tales from the X-bar Horse Camp, 1920; Cattle (with Wm. MacLeod Raine), 1930; Arizona Place Names, 1934. Home: Phoenix, Ariz. Died Dec. 17, 1936.

BARNES, William, lawyer; b. Pompey, N.Y., May 26, 1824; s. Orson and Eliza (Phelps) B.; acad. edn., Manlius (N.Y.) Acad.; studied law, 1840-46; m. Emily Peck Kempshall, d. Thurlow Weed, July 10, 1849 (died 1889); m. 2d, Mrs. Lizzie Balmer Williams, June 1, 1891; children—Thurlow Weed, William B., Jr. and Catharine Weed Barnes Ward. Organized and managed with his father the first teachers' institutes in N.Y., 1843-44; was long special counsel bank dept. State of N.Y.; one of organizers Saratoga Springs Conv., held Aug. 1854 (probably 1st state conv. ever held by Rep. party); organized N.Y. State Kan. Conv., 1856, and 2 Nat. Kan. Aid convs., at Cleveland and Buffalo; 1st supt. of ins. of N.Y., 1860-70; apptd. by Pres. Grant, 1872, U.S. del. to Internat. Statis. Congress at St. Petersburg, Russia; was presented by the Czar, Alexander II, with a diamond ring with the imperial monogram as a souvenir of services at this Congress, and was apptd. mem. of Permanent Commn.; spl. counsel for City of New York in Astor and other cases against city for vacation of assessments, 1874; specialist in ins. law; superintended compilation 16 vols. of ins. statistics and edited 1st N.Y. State life ins. valuation tables and condensed ins. reports. Mem. Internat. Peace Congress, Boston, 1904; del. World's Peace and Arbitration Conv., New York, 1907, Rep. State Conv., Boston, 1908, etc. Home: Nantucket Island, Mass. Died Feb. 23, 1913.

BARNES, William, surgeon, entomologist; b. Decatur, Ill., Sept. 3, 1860; s. William A. and Eleanor (Sawyer) B.; student State Normal Sch., Normal, Ill., 1878, Ill. U., 1879; B.S., Harvard, 1883, M.D., 1886; post-grad. work, Boston City Hosp. and Heidelberg, Munich and Vienna; D.Sc., James Millikin U., Decatur, Ill., 1929; m. Charlotte L. Gillett, June 20, 1890; children—Joan Dean Gillett, William. Practiced at Decatur, 1890—; mem. Drs. Barnes & Tearnan; one of builders of Decatur and Macon County Hosp., of which was pres. Chmn. Med. Advisory Bd., Dist. No. 14, World War; chmn., also inspector Am. Protective League, Decatur Div., World War. Fellow Am. Coll. Surgeons; mem. various entomol. socs. Owner of largest collection of N.Am. Lepidoptera in existence; collection housed in fire-proof mus. and consists of several hundred thousand specimens—over 10,000 species and varieties and over 6,000 types of various kinds. Author: Contributions to the Natural History of Lepidoptera of North America, 23 parts, 1911-24; Check List of the Lepidoptera of Boreal North America, 1917; Illustrated Species of the Genus Catocala, 22 plates, 17 colored, 1918; also 95 articles in entomol. mags. Home: Decatur, Ill. Died May 1, 1930.

BARNES, William, publisher; b. Albany, N.Y., Nov. 17, 1866; s. William and Emily P. (Weed) B.; A.B., Harvard, 1888; m. Grace Davis, June 12, 1888; m. 2d, Maude Fiero, Jan. 17, 1923. Publisher Albany Journal, 1889—. Mem. Rep. State Com., 1892-1914 (chmn., 1911-14), Rep. Nat. Com., 1912-16. Home: Mt. Kisco, N.Y. Died June 25, 1930.

BARNES, William H., jurist; b. Hampton, Conn., 1843; s. William and E. A. (Hubbard) B.; ed. Ill. Coll., and A. B., Univ. of Mich., 1865; m. Belle J. Daly. Admitted to bar, 1866; began practice at Jacksonville, Ill.; mem. Ill. state legislature, 1871-72; del. Dem. Nat. convs., 1876-80-84; mem. of Dem. State convs., Ill., 1865-85; apptd. asso. justice Supreme Court of Ariz., 1885; mem. Constl. Conv., Ariz., 1893. Home: Tucson, Ariz. Died 1904.

BARNES, William Henry, ry. official; b. Phila., July 12, 1829; s. Henry and Marilla (Weldon) B.; private sch. edn.; m. Eva Hampton, Oct. 27, 1857. Served on surveys and construction, western div. Pa. R.R., 1848-56; asst. engr. Memphis & Charleston R.R. in Tenn., 1856-57; asst. supt., sec. and comptroller, Pittsburgh, Ft. Wayne & Chicago Ry., 1856-63; in service Union R.R. & Transportation Co. and Empire Transportation Co., 1863-71; dir. and treas., Pa. Co., 1871-83; receiver 1884-92, pres. 1892-1909, Allegheny Valley Ry.; pres. Western N.Y. & Pa. Ry., 1901-09; dir. Pa. R.R., Pa. Co., Pittsburgh, Cincinnati, Chicago & St. Louis Ry., and allied corps. Home: Philadelphia. Died May 5, 1918.

BARNETT, Evelyn Scott Snead, author; b. Louisville, Ky.; d. Charles Scott and Martha Snead; m. Ira Sayre Barnett, June 8, 1886. Lit. editor Louisville Courier-Journal for 7 yrs. Mem. D.A.R., Colonial Dames. Author: Mrs. Delire's Euchre Party, 1895; Jerry's Reward, 1903; The Dragnet, 1909. Contbr. of short stories to mags. Lecturer; first oral book reviewer in U.S. Home: Louisville, Ky. Died Nov. 10, 1921.

BARNETT, George, officer U.S.M.C.; b. Lancaster, Wis., Dec. 9, 1859; s. James and Eliza (Callis) B.; grad. U.S. Naval Acad., 1881; m. Mrs. Basil Gordon (formerly Lelia Montague), Jan. 11, 1908; children—Basil Gordon, Lelia Gordon (Mrs. Robert Dickey, Jr.), Anne H. Gordon (Mrs. Henry W. Suydam). Spent 2 yrs. at sea as cadet midshipman; commd. 2d lt. U.S.M.C., July 1, 1883; promoted through grades to maj. gen. comdt. U.S.M.C., Feb. 1914-July 1920; promoted to perm. maj. gen., Mar. 5, 1921, and placed in comd. Dept. of Pacific, U.S.M.C., hdqrs. San Francisco, Calif.; retired Dec. 9, 1923. Spent 18 years at sea or on duty naval stations abroad. Episcopalian. Home: Huntley, Va. Died Apr. 27, 1930.

BARNETT, James, soldier, merchant; b. Cherry Valley, N.Y., June 21, 1821; s. Melancthon and Mary B.; ed. pub. schs., Cleveland, O.; m. Maria H., d. Dr. Samuel Underhill, of Granville, Ill., June 12, 1845. Joined co. of arty., 1840, afterwards known as Cleveland Light Arty.; col. same, 1859; one of first to answer call for troops; served in most important engagements of Army of the Ohio; mustered out Oct. 20, 1864; again volunteered, before battle of Nashville, aide to Gen. Thomas; commd. brig. gen. As boy became hardware clerk; later with George Worthington, resumed business with latter firm after war; became its head, 1871; later pres. The George Worthington Co.; pres. First Nat. Bank; dir. in other cos. Is mem. and was active in organization G.A.R. Mem. Congress, 1883-85; Republican; mem. Loyal Legion. Home: Cleveland, O. Died 1911.

BARNETT, Tom P., artist; b. St. Louis, Mo., Feb. 11, 1870; s. George I. and Elizabeth (Armstrong) B.; studied architecture under father and painting under Paul Cornoyer; m. Mary Mitchell, 1914. Awarded gold medal for architecture, St. Louis Expn., 1904; bronze medal for architecture and painting, Portland Expn., 1905; awarded 5 first Ives landscape prizes, St. Louis Artists' Guild, 1914-25; Scott memorial prize, from same, 1918; first architectural prize, Cook County Court House, Chicago; St. Louis Art League group prize, 1921, 25; Town Club purchase prize, St. Louis, 1922; hon. mention Art Inst. Chicago, 1922; St. Louis Chamber Commerce prize, 1922, 24; Mo. State Fair purchase prize, 1925; 1st prize, "St. Louis in Colors," competition given by Post-Dispatch, St. Louis; Art League prize, 1926; 1st prize for best group of pictures, St. Louis Artists' Guild, 1927. Decorations in State Capitol, Jefferson City, Mo.; paintings on permanent exhbn. in St. Louis Mus. Fine Arts, St. Louis Pub. Library, etc. Home: St. Louis, Mo. Died Sept. 23, 1929.

BARNEY, Mrs. Alice Pike, artist; b. Cincinnati, O.; d. Samuel and Ellen Meullion (Miller) Pike; studied art with Carolus Duran and Whistler, Paris; m. Albert Clifford Barney, 1878; children—Natalie Clifford, Laura Clifford (Madame Hippolite Dryfus), Alice. Exhibited in New York, Washington, Paris, London; spl. exhbns. Paris Salon and London Acad.; portrait of Natalie Barney purchased by French Govt.; made notable sketch of Whistler; portraits of Alice Roosevelt, Bernard Shaw, etc. Donor of the "Neighborhood House" (settlement of 4 bldgs.) for settlement work, Washington, D.C.; suggested an outdoor theatre on Monument Grounds, Washington, which was built by U.S. Govt., and she named it "The Sylvan Theatre," writing and giving the first 6 productions. Writer of (plays) "The Lighthouse," winner Drama League of America contest, 1927; "False Values," 1st prize Arts Club, Washington; "The Opium Pipe"; "The Dream of Queen Elizabeth"; "Luna, the Man in the Moon"; "Woman"; "Some Years Hence"; "Call of the Allies"; "War"; "Driven"; "Legitimate Lovers." Home: Hollywood, Calif. and Washington, D.C. Died Oct. 12, 1931.

BARNEY, Charles Tracy, banker; b. Cleveland, Jan. 27, 1851; s. A. H. B. (pres. U.S. Express Co.); grad. Williams Coll., 1870; engaged in banking in New York since; has made large real estate investments in city property; spl. mem. Rogers & Gould, mems. N.Y. Stock Exchange. Pres. and dir. Knickerbocker Trust Co., N.Y. Loan and Improvement Co.; dir. Brooklyn Life Ins. Co., Lawyers' Mortgage Ins. Co.; trustee Bank for Savings. Home: New York, N.Y. Died 1907.

BARNEY, Edgar Starr, educator; b. Worcester, N.Y., Apr. 10, 1861; s. Ansyl and Sarah A. (Starr) B.; A.B., and C.E., Union Coll., Schenectady, N.Y., 1884, A.M., 1887, Sc.D., 1904; m. Clara E. Mills, June 7, 1886. Prin., Hebrew Tech. Inst., New York, 1893—. Life trustee Union Coll.; trustee Albany Med. Coll. Sec., dir. Hudson River Day Line of Steamers. Home: Brooklyn, N.Y. Died Dec. 25, 1938.

BARNEY, Samuel Stebbins, judge; b. Hartford, Wis., Jan. 31, 1846; s. John and Adalina (Knox) B.; ed. Lombard U., Ill.; taught high sch., Hartford, 1867-70; admitted to bar, 1873; m. Ellen S. McHenry, May 18, 1876 (died 1901). In practice at West Bend, 1873-1906; supt. schs., Washington Co., Wis., 1876-80; Rep. candidate for 49th Congress, 1884; del. Rep. Nat. Conv., 1884; mem. 54th to 57th Congresses (1895-1903), 5th Wis. Dist.; asso. justice U.S. Ct. of Claims, 1906—. Home: West Bend, Wis. Died Dec. 31, 1919.

BARNHARDT, George Columbus, army officer; b. Gold Hill, N.C., Dec. 28, 1868; s. Marshal L. and Sarah Pines (Dunlap) B.; grad. U.S. Mil. Acad., 1892, Army Staff Sch., 1920, Army War Coll., 1921; m. Floy Rice, d. of late Col. John B. Rodman, U.S. Army, Dec. 19, 1895. Commd. 2d lt. 6th Cav., June 11, 1892; promoted through grades to col. N.A., Aug. 5, 1917; brig. gen. (temp.), Oct. 1, 1918; brig. gen. regular army, June 23, 1927. Served at Ft. McKinney, Wyo., 1892-94; comd. troop in Santiago Campaign, 1898; duty Ft. Leavenworth, Kan., 1898-1900; with China Relief Expdn., Aug.-Nov., 1900; in Philippines, 1900-01, 1902-03, participating in Lake Lanao Expdn.; regtl. q.-m., at Santa Clara and Cienfuegos, Cuba, 1907; duty with Provisional Govt. of Cuba, 1907-09; adj. 15th Cav., 1909-12; duty Gen. Staff Corps, 1912; on Mexican border, 1913-16; with Q.-M. Corps,1916-17; comdr. 329th Inf. at Camp Sherman and in France, 1917-18; comdr. 28th U.S. Inf., 1st Div., July-Oct. 10, 1918, during St. Mihiel and Argonne-Meuse operations; comdr. 2d Brigade, 1st Div., Oct. 10-24, 1918; assigned to 178th Inf. Brig., Nov. 13, and served with it in France and Germany, returning to the U.S. May 31, 1919; gen. staff, 1921-25; comdg. 6th Cav., Aug. 1925-June 1927; comdg. Dist. of Washington, July-Sept., 1927; 22nd Inf. Brig. (Hawaii), Oct. 1927—. Decorated D.S.M. (U.S.); Officer Legion of Honor, Croix de Guerre with palm (France). Address: Schofield Barracks, T.H. Died Dec. 11, 1930.

BARNHART, Henry A., congressman; b. nr. Twelve Mile, Ind., Sept. 11, 1858; s. Jacob and Mary (Fisher) B.; ed. Amboy Acad. and Wabash Normal Training Sch. Taught sch. several terms; co. surveyor, Fulton Co., 1885-87; editor and pub. Rochester Sentinel, 35 yrs.; pres. Rochester Telephone Co., 1896—; pres. Nat. Telephone Assn., 1901-03. Dir. Northern Ind. Prison, Michigan City, 1893-96; trustee Hosp. for the Insane, Longcliff. Elected to 60th Congress for unexpired term (1908-09); reëlected 61st to 65th Congresses (1909-19), 13th Indiana Dist. Democrat. Home: Rochester, Ind. Died Mar. 26, 1934.

BARNHART, William Gray, lawyer; b. nr. Buffalo, Putnam Co., W.Va., Apr. 15, 1880; s. Lewis and Isabel (Hartley) B.; student W.Va. U., 1899-1902; studied law with father; LL.B., W.Va. U. Coll. of Law, 1902. Began practice in Winfield, W.Va., 1902; mem. W.Va. Ho. of Rep., 1903 and spl. session, 1904; del. Dem. Nat. Conv., St. Louis, 1904; removed to Charleston, W.Va., 1907; Dem. candidate for pros. atty., Kanawha Co., 1908 and 1912 (defeated both times); U.S. dist. atty. Southern Dist. of W.Va., by appmt. of Pres. Wilson, Aug. 18, 1913—. Home: Charleston, W.Va. Died, Dec. 24, 1921.

BARNHORN, Clement J., artist; pupil of Marcié, Puech, Bouguereau, Ferrier and Académie Julian, Paris. Hon. mention, Paris Salon, 1895. Exhibited at Paris Expn., 1900. Mem. Cincinnati Art Club, Nat. Sculptors Soc. (New York). Home: Cincinnati, O. Deceased.

BARNICKEL, William Sidney, mfg. chemist; b. Lagrange, Ky., May 18, 1878; s. John and Mary (Dawkins) B.; Ph.G., St. Louis Coll. Pharmacy, 1902, Ph.C., 1903; m. Olive Edgeworth, June 4, 1904. Began as analyt. chemist with Allen Pfeifer Chem. Co., St. Louis, 1903; chief chemist, Judge & Dolph Drug Co., 1904-10; prof. chemistry, Am. Med. Coll., St. Louis, 1905-10; pres. W. S. Barnickel & Co., 1910—. Served with 1st Inf. Tex. N.G., 3 yrs., 1st Inf., Mo. N.G., 3 yrs., Field Battery A, Mo. N.G., 9 yrs. Republican. Mason (32°). Specialized in chemistry of petroleum; inventor of gasoline process; of chem. process for treating waste oil and petroleum emulsions. Home: St. Louis. Died May 19, 1923.

BARNS, William Eddy, editor; b. Vevay, Ind., Aug. 29, 1853; s. Rezin M. and Susan S. (Smead) B.; B.S., Ill. Wesleyan U., 1872; m. Mattie M. Rowe, Nov. 1, 1875 (died 1877); m. 2d, Louise Goode Gillett, Oct. 26, 1880. City editor Daily Republican, Decatur, Ill., 1872-73; corr. Chicago Inter-Ocean, 1874; asso. editor Central Christian Advocate, St. Louis, 1875-84; editor The Age of Steel, St. Louis, 1886-1902; editor St. Louis Lumberman, 1886—; pres. Journal of Commerce Co., pubs. St. Louis Lumberman. One of founders Concatenated Order of Hoo-Hoo; sec. House of Hoo-Hoo; sec. Fed. Rate Regulation Assn.; mem. Jury of Awards (forestry), World's Fair, St. Louis, 1904. Republican. Author: The Labor Problem, 1888; Nobody Knows, 1889; The Utilization of Wood Waste by Distillation, 1907; "The Lumber Octopus," 1911. Home: St. Louis, Mo. and Northport, Mich. Died 1915.

BARNUM, Charlotte Cynthia, editor and mathematician; b. Phillipston, Mass., May 17, 1860; d. Rev. Samuel Weed and Charlotte (Betts) B.; A.B., Vassar, 1881; studied at Johns Hopkins 2 yrs.; grad. student, Yale, 3 yrs.; Ph.D., in mathematics, Yale, 1895; unmarried. Teacher, Stamford, Conn., New Haven, Conn., and at Smith and Carleton colls. Computer, Yale Obs., Dana's Mineralogy, Mass. Mut. Life Ins. Co., Fidelity Mut. Life Ins. Co., U.S. Naval Obs., and 1901-08, U.S. Coast and Geod. Survey. Editorial asst., Webster's Internat. Dictionary, 1886-90 and 1897, Biological Survey, U.S. Dept. Agr., 1908-1913, Carnegie Instn. of Washington, Yale U., Yale Peruvian expdns., etc. Home: New Haven, Conn. Died 1934.

BARNUM, Hedrick Ware, lawyer; b. Danbury, Conn., Apr. 12, 1879; s. Hendrick and Charlotte Marion (Ware) B.; A.B., St. Lawrence U., Canton, N.Y., 1899, A.M., 1909; A.B., Harvard, 1900, LL.B., cum laude, 1903; m. Margaret Helen Currier, Apr. 28, 1906; children—Margaret Elizabeth, Pamela, Marian Ware. Admitted to Mass. bar, 1903, and began practice at Boston; mem. Elder, Whitman & Barnum, 1909-14; gen. counsel Boston Elevated Ry. Co., 1919—; dir. Transit Mut. Ins. Co. Asst. atty. gen., Mass., 1915-18. Home: Canton, Mass. Died Nov. 22, 1936.

BARNUM, Henry Samuel, missionary; b. Stratford, Conn., Aug. 13, 1837; s. Samuel and Harriet (Curtis) B.; A.B., Yale, 1862; grad. Auburn Theol. Sem., 1867; (D.D., Yale, 1898); m. Lucretia L. Parker, May 22, 1867 (died 1867); m. 2d, Helen Randle, Mar. 10, 1869. Ordained Presbyn. ministry, 1867; missionary A.B.C.F.M. (Congl.), Harpoot, E. Turkey, 1867-72, Van, Turkey, 1872-83; at Constantinople, 1884—, where he edited a weekly paper in Armenian and Turkish, 1884-1907, and 1911, 1912. Has prepared commentaries on portions of the Bible, and some other publications, in the Armenian lang. Residence: Constantinople, Turkey. Died Dec. 10, 1915.

BARNUM, Herman Norton, missionary; b. Auburn, N.Y., Dec. 5, 1826; s. Daniel T. and Mary Ann (Tomlinson) B.; A.B., Amherst Coll., 1852; grad. Andover Theol. Sem., 1855; (D.D., Amherst, and Middlebury, 1873); m. Mary Goodell, July 6, 1860. Ordained Presbyn. ministry, 1855; missionary-at-large, Vt., 1855-56; engaged in foreign travel, 1857-58; joined Turkish mission of A.B.C.F.M., 1858, with which has since been connected; has taught at Harpoot Theol. Sem. and Euphrates Coll. and engaged in gen. missionary work. Republican. Residence: Harpoot, Turkey. Died 1910.

BARNUM, William Milo, lawyer; b. Lime Rock, Conn., Jan. 25, 1856; s. William H. and Charlotte A. (Burrall) B.; A.B., Yale, 1877; LL.B., Columbia, 1879; m. Anne Theresa Phelps, June 2, 1879. Practiced law, New York, until 1904; mem. Harvey Fisk & Sons, bankers, until July 1, 1908; chmn. bd. Pacific Coast Co.; dir. Electric Securities Corp. Pres. St. Andrew's Convalescent Hosp. Home: New York, N.Y. Died Oct. 5, 1926.

BARNWELL, Robert Woodward, bishop coadjutor of Ala.; b. Beaufort, S.C., Dec. 27, 1849; grad. Trinity Coll., Hartford, Conn.; studied at Gen. Theol. Sem., New York; ordained deacon by Bishop Williams, and priest by Bishop Beckwith, at Atlanta, 1875; was missionary 2 yrs. at Griffin, Ga.; rector Trinity Ch., Demopolis, Ga., 1876-80; called to St. Paul's Ch., Selma, Ala., 1880; elected bishop of Ala., May 18, 1900. Home: Selma, Ala. Died 1902.

BARR, Albert J., newspaper mgr.; b. Pittsburgh, Pa., Jan. 12, 1851; s. James P. B.; ed. common schs., Pittsburgh, 1860-68, Western U. of Pa., 1868-71; m. Mary A. McDevitt, July 28, 1884. Prominent in Dem. politics and newspaper circles; pres. and gen. mgr. Post Pub. Co., 1886—, and Sun Pub. Co. Home: Pittsburgh, Pa. Died Feb. 24, 1912.

BARR, Alfred Hamilton, clergyman; b. Geneseo, Ill., Sept. 3, 1868; s. Rev. John Campbell and Jane (Hamilton) B.; B.A., Princeton, 1889, M.A., 1892; taught Greek at Kiskiminetas Spgs. Sch., 1889-92; student Western Theol. Sem., 1893-94; B.D., Princeton Theol. Sem., 1896; D.D., Alma Coll., Mich., 1910; m. Annie Elizabeth Wilson, Feb. 17, 1897; children—Alfred Hamilton, Andrew Wilson. Ordained Presbyn. ministry, 1896; pastor Jefferson Av. Ch., Detroit, 1896-1911 (organizing "open church" work and largely instrumental in organizing work among foreign speaking people), 1st Ch., Baltimore, 1911-23; prof. homiletics, Presbyn. Theol. Sem. of Chicago, 1923—. Mem. Gen. Assembly's com. that organized the Presbyn. Brotherhood; mem. Assembly's com. on Christian Life and Work, 1911-23, Assembly's Gen. Bd. of Edn., Com. on Evangelism, and Nat. Service Commn., Assembly's Special Commn. of 1925. Mem. bd. of dirs. Princeton Theol. Sem., 1911-23. Mem. Archæol. Inst. America, Cliosophic Soc. (Princeton). Democrat. Author: printed addresses, The Great Day of the Preacher, 1925, and Present Tendencies of Protestant Preaching, 1929. Home: Chicago, Ill. Died Sept. 2, 1935.

BARR, Amelia Edith, author; b. (Huddleston) Ulverston, Lancashire, Eng., Mar. 29, 1831; ed. Glasgow (Scotland) High Sch.; m. Robert Barr, 1850. Went to Tex., 1854; husband and three sons died of yellow fever at Galveston, 1867; with three daughters removed to New York, 1869; wrote for Christian Union and other periodicals. Author: Jan Vedder's Wife; A Border Shepherdess; Feet of Clay; Bernicia; Remember the Alamo; She Loved a Sailor; The Lone House; A Sister to Esau; Prisoners of Conscience; The Tioni Whelp; The Black Shilling; The Belle of Bowling Green; The Strawberry Handkerchief, 1908; The Hands of Compulsion, 1909; The House on Cherry Street, 1909; Playing with Fire, 1914; Trinity Bells, 1914; Measure of a Man, 1915; Three Score and Ten, 1915; Winning of Lucia, 1915; Profit and Loss, 1916; Joan, 1916; Christine, 1916; An Orkney Maid, 1917; also other novels, about 75 in all. Home: Richmond Hill, L.I., N.Y. Died Mar. 10, 1918.

BARR, Frank, ry. official; b. Nashua, N.H.; s. John N. and Mary A. (French) B.; pub. sch. edn.; m. Alace J. Cooper, Nov. 11, 1875. In various positions on Worcester & Nashua R.R., 1869-92, supt. Worcester, Nashua & Portland div., 1893-96; asst. gen. mgr., 1896-1903, 3d v.p. and gen. mgr., 1903—, B.&M. R.R. Home: Winchester, Mass. Died Sept. 8, 1914.

BARR, John Henry, mech. engr.; b. Terre Haute, Ind., June 19, 1861; s. John Henry and Eliza T. B.; B.M.E., U. of Minn., 1883, M.S., 1888; M.M.E., Cornell, 1889; m. Katherine L. Kennedy, June 4, 1884; 1 son, John H. Engaged in mech. dept. Calumet & Hecla Copper Mining Co. and Lake Superior Iron Works, 1883-85; instr., asst. prof. and prof. mech. engring., U. of Minn., 1885-91; asst. prof. and asso. prof., 1891-98, prof. machine design, 1898-1903, Sibley Coll., Cornell; factory mgr. Smith-Premier Works, Syracuse, N.Y., Feb. 1903; cons. engr. Union Typewriter Co., New York, Sept. 1909-13, and same, Remington Typewriter Co., May 1913-23; v.p. Barr-Morse Corp., 1923—; trustee of Ithaca (N.Y.) Savings Bank. Chairman N.Y. State Voting Machine Commn., 1903-14, Syracuse Lighting Commn., 1907; mem. Syracuse Intercepting Sewer Commn., 1908-12. Maj. ordnance, U.S.R.C., 1917-19, in office of chief of ordnance, U.S.A. and A.E.F., Aircraft Armament Sect., Paris, France. Trustee Cornell U., 1905-15. Author: Kinematics of Machinery, 1899; Notes on Machine Design; Elements of Machine Design (with D. S. Kimball), 1909. Home: Ithaca, N.Y. Died Mar. 29, 1937.

BARR, John W., lawyer; b. Versailles, Ky., Dec. 17, 1826; s. William and Ann (Watson) B.; grad. law dept., Transylvania Univ., 1847; practiced in Versailles and later in Louisville; organized and was several yrs. pres. bd. of sinking fund of Louisville; U.S. dist. judge for Ky., 1880-99. Home: Louisville, Ky. Died 1907.

BARR, Thomas Francis, brig. gen.; b. W. Cambridge (now Arlington), Mass., Nov. 18, 1837; s. Thomas and Jean B.; ed. Lowell, Mass.; admitted to Mass. bar, 1859; m. Julia Maria Minot Chase, Sept. 9, 1863. In U.S. civil service, Washington, 1861-64; practiced law in D.C.; apptd. maj. and judge advocate vols., Feb. 26, 1865; transferred to regular army, Feb. 25, 1867; lt. col. and deputy judge advocate gen., July 5, 1884; col. and asst. judge advocate gen., Aug. 3, 1895; brig. gen. and judge advocate gen., May 21, 1901; retired May 22, 1901. Commr. U.S. Mil. Prison, Ft. Leavenworth, Kan., 1873-94; mil. sec. to Secs. of War Ramsey, Lincoln, Endicott and Proctor; judge advocate in many important court martial cases, notably those of Gen. Innis N. Palmer, Maj. Marcus A. Reno, Maj. Charles B. Throckmorton and Capt. Oberlin M. Carter. Home: Canaan, N.H. Died Dec. 12, 1916.

BARR, William Alexander, clergyman; b. Danville, Ky., Feb. 28, 1856; s. William V. and Janetta Burch B.; A.B., Dartmouth, 1876; B.D., Union Theol. Sem., 1879; (D.D., Westminster Coll., Mo., 1905); m. Ida Stringfellow, Feb. 1, 1893. Deacon, 1895, priest, 1895, P.E. Ch.; rector Monumental Ch., Richmond, Va., 1897-1900, St. Luke's, Norfolk, Va., 1900-07, St. Paul's Ch., Lynchburg, 1907-09; dean Christ Ch. Cathedral, New Orleans, Nov. 1, 1909—. Democrat. Home: New Orleans, La. Died Nov. 12, 1923.

BARR, William Francis, college dean; b. Newark, O., Mar. 16, 1865; s. James William and Bettie Ann (Bader) B.; student Summer Sch., U. of Chicago, 1896, Harvard, 1903; Ph.B., Drake U., 1903, A.M., 1907; m. Carrie Marie Lockwood, Dec. 29, 1896. Teacher rural schs., Ind., 1883-87; prin. schs., Eaton, Ind., 1887-89, Milroy, 1889-91; supt. schs., Greene, Ia., 1891-96, Parkersburg, 1896-1900; teacher Drake U. Acad., 1900-03; dean Normal Sch., 1903-07, dean Coll. of Edn., 1907-11, dir. Sch. of Edn. and dean of men, 1911-13, and dean Coll. of Education, 1913—, Drake U. Dir. edn. 4th Div., U.S.A., Camp Dodge, Ia., Feb. 1, 1920, until camp was abandoned; organized ednl. work at Fort Des Moines; asst. federal food adminstr. for Ia., 1918. Lecturer on school management, social problems in edn. and relation of pub. school to health. Lecturer U. of New York, summer, 1912, U. of Chicago Summer Sch., 1914. Mem. Ia. State Bd. of Ednl. Examiners, 1923-25. Mem. Ch. of Christ. Mason. Author: Drill Lists in Arithmetic, 1894; Outline of Physics, 1904; Manual for Teachers in the Use and Value of Visual Aids in Teaching. Contbr. on rural school problems; also writer and lecturer on use of visual aids in edn. Dir. of ednl. parties doing laboratory and field work in history and geography, 1930—. Home: Des Moines, Ia. Died Jan. 27, 1937.

BARRAS, Harry Watson, clergyman, educator; b. Croton, N.J., Sept. 10, 1868; s. Edward and Mary Ann (Pittinger) B.; grad. Peddie Inst., Hightstown, N.J., 1892; grad. Crozer Theol. Sem., Chester, Pa., 1895; D.D., Temple U., 1922; m. Fanny Elizabeth Sladden, Sept. 10, 1895. Ordained ministry Bapt. Ch., 1895; prof. of homiletics, Eastern Baptist Theol. Sem., Phila. Chmn. Draft Bd., Phila., Pa., World War. Trustee Am. Bapt. Hist. Soc. (sec.), Eastern Bapt. Theol. Sem., George Nugent Home for Aged Ministers. Republican. Mason. Home: Haddonfield, N.J. Died Dec. 22, 1936.

BARRATT, Norris Stanley, judge; b. Phila., Pa., Aug. 23, 1862; s. James, Jr., and Mary Irvine (Cummings) B.; ed. pvt. and pub. schs.; (LL.D., Temple U., 1909); married. Admitted to Pa. bar, 1883; asst. city solicitor, Phila., 1890-1900; first asst. dist. atty., 1902; judge Court of Common Pleas, 1902, president judge 1913—; elected prothonotary of Common Pleas and Municipal courts of Phila. County, Sept. 26, 1923, and declined renom. for judge by both Rep. and Dem. parties, for an additional term of 10 yrs. Chmn. Com. of Library and Museum. Republican. Episcopalian. Mason. Author: (with Dr. Julius F. Sachse) Freemasonry of Pennsylvania, 1827-1907 (3 vols.), 1908-9; Barratt's Chapel and Methodism; Hist. of St. Paul's Church, Phila.; Colonial Wars in America; The Trained Nurse and the Doctor; Bookkeepers and Commercial Law; memoirs of Joseph S. Miller, Mayer Sulzberger, Henry N. Wessel, John Samuel, Rev. John Chambers. Home: Philadelphia, Pa. Died Apr. 26, 1924.

BARRELL, Joseph, geologist; b. New Providence, N.J., Dec. 15, 1869; s. Henry Ferdinand and Elizabeth (Wisner) B.; B.S., Lehigh U., Pa., 1892, E.M., 1893, M.S., 1897 (Sc.D., 1916); Ph.D., Yale, 1900; m. Lena Hopper Bailey, Dec. 27, 1902. Pub. sch. teacher, 1886-87; instr. in mining and metallurgy, Lehigh U., 1893-97; asst. mining engr., Lehigh Valley Coal Co., 1894, Butte & Boston, and Boston & Montana mining cos., Butte, Mont., 1897-98; field asst., U.S. Geol. Survey, 1899-1901; asst. prof. geology, Lehigh U., and in charge of dept. of natural sciences, 1900-03; asst. prof. geology, 1903-08, prof. structural geology, 1908—, Yale U. Home: New Haven, Conn. Died May 4, 1919.

BARRETT, Albert Moore, psychiatrist; b. Austin, Ill., July 15, 1871; s. Edward Newton and Anna Sarah (Moore) B.; A.B., State U. of Ia., 1893, M.D., 1895; Heidelberg U., Germany, 1901-02; m. Eliza Jane Bowman, July 8, 1905; 1 son, Edward Bowman. Pathologist Independence (Ia.) State Hosp. for Insane, 1895-97, 1898-1901; asst. phys. Worcester (Mass.) Insane Hosp., 1897-98; pathologist Danvers (Mass.) State Hosp. for Insane, 1901-05, also asst. in neurol. pathology, Harvard, 1905-06. Called to U. of Mich., 1906, to organize the first univ. hosp. and clinic in America for mental diseases; apptd. asso. prof. of neuropathology, Med. Faculty, U. of Mich., 1906, also med. dir. State Psychopathic Hosp. of U. of Mich.; prof. psychiatry and nervous diseases, Dept. of Medicine and Surgery, U. of Mich., 1907-20; prof. psychiatry, U. of Mich., Med. Sch., 1920—. Mem. Medical Council of U.S. Veterans Bureau. Republican. Episcopalian. Home: Ann Arbor, Mich. Died Apr. 2, 1936.

BARRETT, Charles Simon, official farm orgns.; b. Pike Co., Ga., Jan. 28, 1866; s. Thomas Jefferson and Minerva (Slade) B.; ed. normal schs., Bowling Green, Ky., Lebanon, O., and Valparaiso, Ind.; m. Alma Rucker, Nov. 5, 1891; children—Paul, Charles Sheldon, Howell Slade, Leland Arleigh, Gaines Rucker, John. Gen. farming and teaching to 37; then began organizing farmers; pres. Georgia Farmers' Union, 1905; elected pres. Nat. Farmers' Union, 1906, unanimously reëlected each yr. for 22 yrs., resigned 1928—over 6,000 business orgns. now operating under authority of Union. Represented Ga. at 1st Governors' Conf. held in Washington, D.C., under call of President Roosevelt; apptd. mem. Country Life Commn. estab. by Roosevelt; declined apptmt. by President Taft on Industrial Relations Commn.; del. Agrl. Inst., at Rome, by apptmt. of Sec. of State Bryan; apptd. by President Wilson mem. Nat. Agrl. Advisory Com., also mem. Price Fixing Com. for wheat crop, 1917; del. to Industrial Conf., 1919; rep. Nat. Bd. Farm Orgns. and Nat. Farmers' Union at Peace Conf., Paris, 1918-19; mem. Advisory Council to Am. delegates, at Internat. Conf. on Limitation of Armament; mem. President's Agrl. Commn., 1924. Home: Union City, Ga. Died Apr. 4, 1935.

BARRETT, Edward Ware, editor; b. Athens, Ga., Sept. 4, 1866; s. of Thomas Glascock and Grace Arrington (Ware) B.; ed. Richmond Acad., Augusta, Ga.; Washington and Lee U., Va., 1882-85 (civil engring. course); m. Miss Lewis Robertson Butt, June 27, 1907. Began on Augusta Chronicle, 1885, and advanced to city editor; Washington corr. Atlanta Constitution, 1888-97, also corr. for many other papers; went to Japan and China in winter of 1895, in closing period of the Chinese-Japanese War, for the Atlanta Constitution and New York World; principal owner and editor Birmingham Age-Herald, 1897—. Polit. sec. Charles F. Crisp, of Ga., while latter was speaker Nat. Ho. of Rep., 1891-95. Del. from Ga. to Dem. Nat. Conv., 1892, and del. from Ala. to every Dem. Nat. Conv., 1897—, except 1898; mem. Dem. Nat. Com. from Ala. Visited Eng. and France Oct. and Nov. 1918 as mem. party of 12 editors, guests of British Govt., observing closing period of the war. Presbyn. Home: Birmingham, Ala. Died July 9, 1922.

BARRETT, George Carter, asso. justice Supreme Court, N.Y., 1871—; b. Dublin, Ireland, July 28, 1838; ed. Columbia and Racine colls. (LL.D., Racine Coll.); married. Judge Court of Common Pleas, N.Y., 1869-70. Home: New York, N.Y. Died 1906.

BARRETT, Harrison D., lecturer; b. Canaan, Me., Apr. 26, 1863; s. Levi P. and Lucetta J. (Merrow) B.; acad. edn.; grad. Meadville Theol. Sem., 1889; m. Marguerite Coffyn, Oct. 13, 1897. Teacher and prin. pub. schs.; editor the Banner of Light, 1897-1904. Lecturer throughout U.S.; chmn. Cassadaga Spiritualist Camp Assn., 7 summers. Pres. Nat. Spiritual Assn., 1893—. Author: Cassadaga, Its History and Teaching; Life of Cora L. V. Richmond. Home: Canaan, Me. Deceased.

BARRETT, Harry McWhirter, educator; b. Holland, Vt., July 24, 1869; s. Charles Samuel and Eleanor (Blake) B.; A.B., Allegheny Coll., Meadville, Pa., 1890, A.M., 1893, hon. Litt.D., U. of Denver, 1914; m. Jessie Davis Edwards, June 10, 1896; children—Hugh Edwards (dec.), Almira (Mrs. W. D. Hardaway), Charles McWhirter. Teacher Titusville, Pa., 1890-91; city editor Erie (Pa.) Despatch, 1892-93; teacher East High Sch., Denver, 1893-1903; prin. Central High Sch., Pueblo, Colo., 1903-12, East High Sch., Denver, 1912-20; dir. Coll. of Edn., U. of Colo., 1920-37, emeritus dir. and prof. of edn. Editor, Colo. School Jour., 1895-1903. Served as 2d lt. N.G. Pa., 1891; comdt. Denver High Sch. Cadets, 1900-03. Trustee Iliff Sch. Theology (Denver U.). Republican. Methodist. Home: Denver, Colo. Died May 16, 1940.

BARRETT, John, retired diplomat and counsellor in Pan.-Am. and other internat. relations, pres. and founder Pan-Am. Foundation; b. Grafton, Vt., Nov. 28, 1866; s. Charles and Caroline (Sanford) B.; attended Vt. Acad.; grad. Worcester (Mass.) Acad., 1884; attended Vanderbilt U., 1888; A.B., Dartmouth, 1889, hon. A.M., 1899; LL.D., Nat. U., Bogota, Colombia, 1906, Tulane, 1910, Panama Nat. U., 1920, U. of Southern Calif., 1922; m. Mary Elizabeth Tanner Cady, Nov. 5, 1934 (died 1937). Editorial staff newspapers of San Francisco, Tacoma, Seattle, Portland, Ore., 1889-94; Am. minister to Siam, 1894-98, settling by arbitration Am. claims involving several million dollars, for which was thanked by President McKinley, and King of Siam; press corr. Spanish-Am. War, and spl. diplomatic adviser to Admiral Dewey in P.I., 1898-99; commercial commr. in China, Japan, P.I., Korea, Siberia, India, Australia and Europe, 1899; U.S. del. 2d Pan Am. Conf., Mexico, 1901-02; commr. gen. to Asia, Australia and Europe for St. Louis Expn., 1902-03; Am. minister to Argentina, 1903-04 (President Roosevelt said, "he began a new Argentina-U.S. era"), minister to Panama, 1904-05, where he adjusted complex relations of Panama-Colombia-U.S.-Canal Zone; minister to Colombia, 1905-06, where he negotiated first protocol for settlement of U.S.-Colombia disputes over Panama Canal, for which was thanked by Presidents Roosevelt and Reyes; dir. gen. Pan Am. Union, Jan. 1, 1907-Sept. 1, 1920, (quoting ex-President Roosevelt, "he [Barrett] reorganized and developed it from an unimportant, dying government bureau, into a powerful world-recognized international organization for peace, friendship and commerce, and increased Pan American trade many fold"), also directed erection of its buildings. Elected 1900, hon. mem. Am. Asiatic Assn. for services in developing Am. prestige and interests in Asia; founder, 1912, and v.p. Pan Am. Soc. of U.S.; del. of U.S. and sec. gen. Pan Am. Scientific Congress, 1916; organizer, and was presiding officer in 1st Pan Am. Commercial Conf., 1911, also of 2d, 1919; pres. Pan Am. Adv. Assn., 1919-20; mem. Gen. Com. on Limitation of Armaments, 1921-22. Decorated Order of Liberator, by Venezuela, 1910, again, 1921, in recognition of services in behalf of Pan Americanism; also by Chinese Govt., 1903, for improving Am.-Chinese relations. Author: Admiral George Dewey, 1899; Pan American Union—Peace, Friendship, Commerce, 1911; Panama Canal—What It Is, What It Means, 1913; Pan American Commerce—Past, Present, Future, 1919; Pan America and Pan Americanism, 1922; The Call of South America, 1924; also magazine articles on Latin Am. and other internat. subjects. Home: Grafton, Vt., New York City, and Coral Gables, Fla. Died Oct. 17, 1938.

BARRETT, Joseph Hartwell, journalist; b. Ludlow, Vt., Apr. 15, 1824; s. Edward and Abi (Bassett) B.; A.B., Middlebury Coll., 1845, A.M., 1848; read law with Horatio Seymour and admitted to Vt. bar, 1851; (LL.D., Howard, 1903); m. Harriet Whiting Lowell, Mar. 31, 1853. Editor Middlebury Galaxy, 1848; mem. Vt. Ho. of Rep., 1851-52; sec. Vt. Senate, 1853-54; removed to Cincinnati, 1857; polit. editor Cincinnati Daily Gazette, 1857-61; U.S. commr. of pensions, 1861-68; editor Cincinnati Daily Chronicle and Times, 1868-79. Del. Rep. Nat. Conv., Chicago, 1860, and mem. of platform com. for Ohio. Author: Life of Abraham Lincoln, 1860, 1864, 1865; Abraham Lincoln and His Presidency, 1904. Home: Loveland, O. Died 1907.

BARRETT, Kate Waller, sociologist; b. "Clifton," Stafford Co., Va., Jan. 24, 1858; d. Withers and Ann Eliza (Stribling) Waller; ed. Arlington Inst., Alexandria, Va.; completed course in nursing at Florence Nightingale Training Sch., and St. Thomas' Hosp., London; M.D., Med. Coll. of Ga., 1892 (hon. Sc.D., 1894); m. Rev. Robert South Barrett, 1876 (died 1896). Early became interested in philanthropic work, and has held many important positions; v.p. and gen. supt. Nat. Florence Crittenton Mission, Washington, from 1897, and pres. from Dec. 16, 1909. Well known as a pub. speaker; del. to Conf. for Care of Delinquent Children, called by President Roosevelt, 1909; pres. Nat. Council of Women; del. Internat. Council of Women, 1900, 03, 09, 13; rep. of State of Va. Nat. Congress of Mothers; v.p. Conf. Charities and Corrections for State of Va.; apptd. spl. rep. U.S. Govt., 1914, to investigate conditions in Europe surrounding alien women; spl. rep. U.S. Govt. to the San Francisco and the San Diego expns., 1915. Only woman apptd. by gov. of Va. mem. Com. on Training Camp Activities; nat. chmn. Nat. Congress of Mothers and Parent-Teacher Assns.; chmn. woman's com. Local Council of Defense. Del. Nat. Peace Conf., Zurich, 1919; spl. rep. Bur. Immigration to Europe, 1919. State regent Va. D.A.R., 1918-22; hon. pres. for life Nat. Council of Women; hon. mem. Nat. Council of Women of the Argentine; state pres. Am. Legion Auxiliary; mem. bd. visitors Coll. William and Mary; mem. Société Académique Histoire Internationale; nat. pres. Am. Legion Auxiliary, 1923. Home: Alexandria, Va. Died Feb. 23, 1925.

BARRETT, Michael Thomas, dentist; b. Huntingdon, Que., Can., July 27, 1881; s. Dennis and Catherine (Timlin) B.; ed. acads., Can., and N.Y.; D.D.S., U. of Pa. Dental Dept., 1903; hon. M.S., Villanova, 1915; m. Della MacDonald, June 29, 1921. Came to U.S., 1900; demonstrator in prosthetic dentistry, U. of Pa., 1904-10; instr. in normal histology, same, 1910-14; instr. in oral pathology, Grad. Sch. of Medicine, U. of Pa. Discoverer of amœbæ in pyorrhea, 1914. Roman Catholic. Wrote: The Protozoa of the Mouth in Relation to Pyorrhea Alveolaris (pub. in Dental Cosmos, Aug., 1914); Clinical Report on Amœbic Pyorrhea (same, Dec., 1914); The Internal Anatomy of the Teeth with Special Reference to the Pulp with its Branches; The Effects of Thymus Extract on the Early Eruption and Growth of the Teeth of White Rats; A Study of the Etiological Factors Governing Dental Caries; etc. Home: Philadelphia. Died Aug. 22, 1940.

BARRETT, Oscar Fitzallen, pres. The Barrett Line; b. Racine, O., Apr. 27, 1860; s. John and Dorothy (Harpold) B.; ed. high sch., Cincinnati, O., and Miss Ryal's Collegiate Sch., Campbell Co., Ky.; m. Mamie E. Slack, Aug. 20, 1890; children—Oscar Slack, Dorothy Marie (Mrs. Patterson Pogue), John Jacob (dec.). Associated with father as John Barrett & Son, operators of tow-boats and barges on Ohio and Miss. rivers, 1882-97; sole owner Barrett Line, 1897-1917; pres. Barrett Line, Inc., 1927—; pres. Campbell County Bank, Bellevue, Ky., since orgn., 1902; pres. The Barrett Line Quarries; v.p. Columbia Life Ins. Co.; pres. Nat. Bd. Steam Navigation, Dec. 1928-Oct. 1930; chmn. bd. trustees Highland Dist., 1896-1902; trustee Georgetown (Ky.) Coll., 1900-10. Republican. Mem. Christian (Disciples) Ch. Mason. Home: Cincinnati, O. Died Aug. 12, 1935.

BARRETT, Reginald, composer; b. London, Eng., Jan. 12, 1861; s. Richard and Rachel (Squire) B.; ed. in Eng. and Germany; mus. edn. at Darmstadt and at Guildhall Sch. of Music, London; m. Lucy E. Wilkes, Sept. 1, 1888. Came to U.S., 1888; organist and choirmaster in various churches; teacher organ and voice. Condr. Mamaroneck Choral Union, Fordham Heights Choral Society. Entered field of motion picture organists, officiating in theatres in N.Y. City and vicinity, 1917-25. Awarded composition prize, Nat. Eisteddfod, Scranton, 1905, prize for best song by Musician Mag., 1898. Episcopalian. Democrat. Composer church music, and many works for organ, piano, songs and part songs. Home: Petersburg, Fla. Died Feb. 7, 1940.

BARRETT, William E., journalist; b. Melrose, Mass., Dec. 29, 1850; grad. Dartmouth Coll., 1880. Asst. editor St. Albans (Vt.) Daily Messenger, 1880; Washington corr. Boston Daily Advertiser, 1882-86; editor-in-chief, 1886-88, and chief propr. and mgr. Boston Daily Advertiser and Boston Evening Record, 1888—. Mem. Mass. legislature, 1887-92; mem. Congress, 1895-99. Home: Boston. Died 1906.

BARRETT, William Hale, judge; b. Augusta, Ga., Sept. 10, 1866; s. William Hale and Susan (Rhind) B.; Ph.B., U. of Ga., 1885; m. Ella C. Barnes, Oct. 19, 1892 (she died Jan. 11, 1935); 1 son, George Barnes. Principal Central Grammar Sch., Augusta, 1885-87; began practice of law in Augusta, 1887; served as city recorder and city attorney; U.S. district judge, by apptmt. of President Harding, July 1, 1922—. Democrat. Episcopalian. Home: Augusta, Ga. Died May 1, 1941.

BARRETT, William M., pres. Adams Express Co.; b. Cincinnati, O., Sept. 11, 1858; ed. pub. schs.; m. Mary A. Earley, 1891. Began with Adams Express Co., 1874, now pres.; also pres. Southern Express Co.; dir. Emigrant Industrial Savings Bank, Irving Trust Co. (New York). Home: New York, N.Y. Died Mar. 25, 1937.

BARRETT, Wilson, actor, mgr., playwright, novelist; b. Essex, England, Feb. 18, 1848. London début, 1876; has visited America 5 times; produced there The Sign of the Cross, etc. Author or part author of two or three dozen plays and books, including Nowadays; Good Old Times; The Golden Ladder; The Peoples' Idol; Jenny, the Barber; Ben, My Chree; The Manxman; Pharaoh; Daughters of Babylon; Our Pleasant Sins; Sign of the Cross; Quo Vadis; Man and His Makers; The Christian King. Has visited Australia twice, also New Zealand and S. Africa, with his company. Author and part author (novels): Sign of the Cross; Daughters of Babylon; In Old New York; Harlequin's Last Leap, and numerous essays and mag. articles. Died 1904.

BARRETTE, John Davenport, army officer; b. in Louisiana, May 14, 1862; s. John Dunsworth and Margaret Elizabeth (Maybanks) B.; grad. U.S. Mil. Acad., 1885; m. Katherine Biddle, June 13, 1894; children—Margaret (Mrs. John Barber Harper), Katharine Biddle (Mrs. Maurice Place Chadwick), Mary Lydia (Mrs. William Taylor Sinclair), Elizabeth Biddle, Louisa Biddle (Mrs. Norman Henry Blanch). Commd. 2d lt. 3d Arty., June 14, 1885; promoted through grades to brig. gen. National Army, Aug. 5, 1917; brig. gen. U.S.A., Feb. 2, 1918; retired May 14, 1926. Instructor of mathematics, U.S. Mil. Acad., 1892-96; instr. Arty. Sch., 1903-07; dir. dept. arty. and gun defense, Coast Arty. Sch., Ft. Monroe, Va., 1907-09; comd. Ft. McKinley, 1910; comdg. arty. dist. of Charleston, lt. col. 1st Provisional Regt., Coast Arty., and coast defense officer Eastern Dept., 1911; comd. coast defenses of Baltimore, 1912, of L.I. Sound, 1913-14; adj. gen. Western Dept., 1915, Philippine Dept., 1916; comd. 152d Brigade, Field Arty., 1917; actg. chief Coast Arty., Dec. 1917-May 1918; comdg. A.E.F. Arty. Sch., Saumur, June-Nov. 1918; comdg. Coast Arty. dists., Jan. 1919-May 1926, Southeastern Dept., July-Oct. 1919, Hawaiian Div., Dec. 1921-Feb. 1922, 1st Corps Area, Nov. 1924-Feb. 1925. Died July 16, 1934.

BARRIGER, John Walker, brig. gen.; retired; b. nr. Shelbyville, Ky., July 9, 1832; s. Josiah and Paulina (Elliott) B.; grad. West Point, 1856; m. Sarah A. F. Wright, Mar. 4, 1863. Promoted 2d lt., July 1, 1856; 1st lt., May 2, 1861 (bvtd. capt., for gallantry, at Bull Run, July 21, 1861); apptd. capt. on staff, com. of subsistence, Aug. 3, 1861; lt. col. staff, U.S. vols., Nov. 17, 1863, to Aug. 1, 1865; bvt. maj., lt. col., col. and brig. gen., Mar. 13, 1865, for faithful and meritorious services during war; apptd. maj. staff, commissary subsistence, Nov. 21, 1875; lt. col., later col. staff, asst. commissary gen., Oct. 8, 1894; retired for age, June 1, 1896; apptd. brig. gen., U.S.A. Apr. 23, 1904. Author: Legislative History of Subsistence Department of the United States Army, 1775-1876. Home: New York, N.Y. Died 1906.

BARRINGER, Paul Brandon, coll. pres.; b. Concord, N.C., Feb. 13, 1857; s. Gen. Rufus and Eugenia (Morrison) B.; ed. U. of Va.; M.D., same, 1877; M.D., med. dept. U. of New York, 1878; studied in Europe, 1880-81; (LL.D., U. of S.C. and Davidson Coll.); m. Nannie I. Hannah, Dec. 27, 1882. In practice Davidson, N.C., 1883-88; prof. physiology and materia medica from 1888; chmn. faculty, 1896-1903, U. of Va.; pres. Va. Poly. Inst., 1907-13. Pres. Med. Soc. of Va.; mem. Va. Bd. of Agr., Va. Bd. of Health; Va. Truck Expt. Bd. (pres.). Wrote: The American Negro, His Past and Future, and other articles on the race problem. Died Jan. 9, 1941.

BARRINGER, Daniel Moreau, mining engr., geologist; b. Raleigh, N.C., May 25, 1860; s. Hon. Daniel Moreau and Elizabeth (Wethered) B.; A.B., Princeton, 1879, A.M., 1882; LL.B., U. of Pa., 1882; spl. course in geology, Harvard, 1889, in chemistry and mineralogy, U. of Va., 1890; m. Margaret Bennett, Oct. 20, 1897; children—Brandon, Daniel Moreau, Sarah Drew, John Paul, Elizabeth Wethered, Lewin Bennitt, Richard Wethered, Philip Ellicott. Practiced law with brother, 1882-89; cons. mining engr. and geologist, 1890—; pres. and dir. of several mining cos. Trustee Jefferson Med. Coll. and Hosp. Republican. Author: The Law of Mines and Mining in the United States, 1907; Minerals of Commercial Value, 1907. Discovered origin of Meteor Crater, 4,200 feet in diameter and 570 feet deep (to visible floor), in Northern Central Ariz., 1905, and "proved that it is due to impact of a meteoric mass, probably a compact cluster of iron meteorites." Home: Haverford, Pa. Died 1929.

BARRON, Clarence Walker, editor; b. Boston, Mass., July 2, 1855; s. Henry and Elana (Noyes) B.; ed. English High Sch., Boston; hon. D.S.C. from Boston U., 1927; m. Mrs. Jessie M. Waldron, June 21, 1900. With Boston Transcript, 1875-84; founder, 1887, and now pres. Boston News Bureau; founder Phila. News Bureau, 1897; editor Barron's Financial Weekly; mgr. Dow, Jones & Co., New York, pubs. The Wall St. Journal, 1901, now pres.; pres. The Wall Street Journal Bldg. Co., Doremus & Co. (adv. agts.), New York, Boston, Chicago, San Francisco. Started Oaks Farm and Creamery for certified milk, 1908; served as chmn. Cohasset Harbor Improvement Com.; chmn. Mass. Inland Waterways Commn., 1911. Republican. Mem. Ch. of New Jerusalem (Swedenborgian). Author: The Federal Reserve Act, 1914; The Audacious War, 1915; The Mexican Problem, 1917; War Finance, 1919; A World Remaking, 1920. Home: Cohasset, Mass. and Boston. Died Oct. 2, 1928.

BARRON, Elwyn Alfred, author, playwright; b. Lima, N.Y., boyhood home, Nashville, Tenn.; s. Alfred Lovejoy and Ellen Elizabeth B.; ed. Robert Coll., Tenn.; m. Hannah Lee Bird, Sept. 9, 1884 (died June 11, 1920); children—Harold (dec.), Elwyn Lee (dec.), Margaret Ellen (Mrs. Howard Nye). For 18 yrs. dramatic critic and editorial writer on Chicago Inter Ocean; resided in London and Paris, 1895-1907. Author: The Viking (blank verse drama), 1888; Manders (novel), 1899; In Old New York (novel), 1900; Marcel Levignet (novel), 1906. Plays: A Moral Crime (with Morgan Bates), prod. 1885; Lady Ashley, prod. 1886; When Bess Was Queen, prod. 1894; Out of the Storm, prod. 1894; Romola, prod. 1896; Punchinello, prod. by E. S. Willard, Boston, 1900; The Ruling Power, prod. New York, 1904; A Prince of the People, prod. in Eng., 1905. Home: Kansas City, Mo. Died Sept. 28, 1929.

BARRON, Leonard, horticulturist; b. Chiswick, Eng., Sept. 29, 1868; s. Archibald Farquharson and Eleanor (Ayres) B.; ed. Belmont House, Chiswick, Eng., Gunnersbury Coll., 1880-84, Birkbeck Inst., spl. courses in botany, vegetable physiology and morphology, chemistry and biology, 1884-92; came to U.S., 1894; m. Effie Maud, g.d. Adm. Charles Jepp Robinson, R.N., of Chiswick, Eng., June 3, 1896; children—Eric Stuart, Dorothy Enid. Asst. editor Gardeners' Chronicle, London, 1885-93; editor Am. Gardening, New York, 1894-1904; mng. editor Garden Mag., 1905-11, editor, 1911-24; editor Garden and Home Builder, 1924-28; hort. editor Am. Home and Country Life, 1928-36; editor The Flower Grower, 1936—; advisory editor Doubleday Doran & Co., pubs. Author: Lawns and How to Make Them, 1906; American Home Book of Gardening, 1931; (chief author) Roses and How to Grow Them, 1905. Editor: The Water Garden; The Garden Library; Flower Growing, 1924; The Pocket Garden Library. Home: Rockville Centre, N.Y. Died Apr. 9, 1938.

BARRON, Robert E., banker; b. St. Paul, Minn., Nov. 19, 1873; s. Patrick D. and Josephine Speed (Morris) B.; ed. pub. schs., St. Paul; m. Sadie L. Thompson, Jan. 12, 1905 (now dec.); children—Meredith, Robert E. (dec.). Receiving teller, Nat. German Am. Bank, St. Paul, 1888-1901; cashier, 1st Nat. Bank, Minot, N.D., 1901-13, pres., 1914—; pres. Minot Ins. Agency; partner Show & Barron; mgr. G.N. Ry. Co. feeding yards for livestock, Minot. Democrat. K.C. Home: Minot, N.D. Died Sept. 23, 1940.

BARROW, David Crenshaw, univ. chancellor; b. Oglethorpe Co., Ga., Oct. 18, 1852; s. David Crenshaw and Sarah Eliza (Pope) B.; B.S., U. of Ga., 1874, C.E., 1874 (LL.D., Emory Coll., 1909); m. Fannie Engle Childs, Feb. 5, 1879. With Ga. Geol. Survey, 1874-78; adj. prof. mathematics, 1878-83, prof. engring., 1883-89, prof. mathematics, 1889-1907, chancellor, 1906-25, U. of Ga., chancellor emeritus. Mem. Bd. of Edn., Athens, 1887-88, 1896-1901. Methodist. Died Jan. 11, 1929.

BARROW, Pope, U.S. senator; b. Oglethorpe Co., Ga., Aug. 1, 1839; A.B., Univ. of Ga., 1859, LL.B., 1860; admitted to bar, 1860. Served as a.-d.-c. to Maj. Gen. Howell Cobb, C.S.A.; mem. Ga. Constl. Conv., 1877; mem. Ga. legislature, 1880-81; U.S. senator to fill vacancy, Nov. 15, 1882-Mar. 3, 1883; judge Superior Ct., Ga., 1900-07. Home: Savannah, Ga. Died 1903.

BARROWS, Charles Clifford, surgeon; b. Jackson, Miss., June 5, 1857; s. David Nye and Caroline Elizabeth (Moseley) B.; M.D., U. of Va., 1879; M.D., Univ. Med. Coll. (New York U.), 1880; m. Hettie Curtis, May 19, 1886. House phys. Bellevue Hosp., 1880-81; asst. surgeon U.S.A., 1882-87, serving in Indian campaigns under Gen. Crook; in practice New York, from 1887, specialty gynecology and obstetrics; clin. prof. gynecology, Cornell U. Med. Coll., from 1909; asst. gynecologist and obstet. phys., Bellevue Hosp.; surgeon New Rochelle, Manhattan, Maternity, and Peekskill hosps. Home: New York, N.Y. Died Jan. 2, 1916.

BARROWS, Charles Henry, lawyer; b. Springfield, Mass., Aug. 4, 1853; s. Charles and Lydia (Smith) B.; A.B., Harvard, 1876, LL.B., 1878; m. Jeanie Elizabeth Rayner, Sept. 19, 1889. Practiced in Springfield, since 1879; asst. atty. gen. Mass., 1881-83. Pres. Springfield Y.M.C.A., 1892-93, Internat. Y.M.C.A. Training Sch. (now college), Springfield, 1893-96, Springfield Home for Aged Men, 1897—, Springfield Improvement Assn., 1904-09, Horace Smith Fund, 1909-17. Conglist. Author: The Personality of Jesus, 1906; The Poets and Poetry of Springfield in Massachusetts, 1907; The History of Springfield in Massachusetts for the Young, 1909. Editorial contbr. to Springfield Republican, 1882—. Home: Springfield, Mass. Died Oct. 13, 1918.

BARROWS, Chester Willard, judge; b. Woonsocket, R.I., July 4, 1872; s. William G. and Lydia S. (Willard) B.; desc. John Barrows, Salem, Mass., 1637; A.B., Brown U., 1895; LL.B., Harvard, 1898; m. Mary Etta Crossley, June 21, 1899; children—Doris (Mrs. Frank D. Kent), Willard C., Lois (Mrs. Philip M. Moore). Admitted to Rhode Island bar, 1898, and since practiced in Providence; instructor in law, Brown U., 1899-1903; U.S. referee in bankruptcy, 1900-13; mem. R.I. State Bd. Bar Examiners, 1900-13; mem. Littlefield & Barrows, 1901-13; asso. justice Superior Court of R.I., 1913-25; asso. justice Supreme Court of R.I. since 1925 for life term. Pres. William H. Hall and Edgewood Free Pub. Library assns., 1907—; mem. Sch. Com. of Cranston, 1911-14. Republican. Unitarian. Mason. Home: Edgewood, R.I. Died Feb. 19, 1931.

BARROWS, (Katharine) Isabel (Hayes) Chapin, editor; b. Irasburg, Vt., Apr. 17, 1845; d. Dr. Henry and Anna (Gibb) Hayes; grad. Adams Acad., Derry, N.H., 1862; M.D., med. coll. in N.Y.; studied 2 yrs. in univs. of Leipzig and Vienna; m. William Wilberforce Chapin, missionary to India, 1863 (died 1865); m. 2d, Rev. Samuel June Barrows, June 28, 1867 (died 1909). Practiced some time as oculist; learned stenography and was first woman stenographer ever employed by the Dept. of State, Washington. Editor Proc. Nat. Conf. Charities and Correction, 20 yrs.; asst. editor Christian Register, 16 yrs.; phonographic sec. Nat. Prison Assn., and 17 yrs. sec. and editor Lake Mohonk Conf., etc. Mem. Ordre des Chevaliers Melusine. Editorial contbr. to various publs. Author: The Shaybacks in Camp (with S. J. Barrows), 1887. Home: Croton-on-Hudson, N.Y. Died Oct. 25, 1913.

BARROWS, John Henry, pres. Oberlin Coll., 1899—; b. Medina, Mich., 1847; s. Rev. John Manning and Catherine Payne (Moore) B.; grad. Olivet Coll., Mich., 1867; studied in Yale, Union and Andover Theol. sems. and at Göttingen, Germany; (D.D., Lake Forest Univ.); m. Sarah Eleanor Mole, Williamstown, Mass. Pastor Lawrence and Boston, Mass., 14 yrs.; pastor First Presbyn. Ch., Chicago; organizer and pres. World's Parliament of Religions, 1893; lecturer in India, 1896-97; lecturer Union Theol. Sem., New York, 1898; lecturer on Comparative Religion, U. of Chicago. Author: History of Parliament of Religions; Life of Henry Ward Beecher; Christianity the World Religion; A World Pilgrimage; The Gospels are True Histories; The Christian Conquest of Asia; I Believe in God; etc. Deceased.

BARROWS, John Otis, clergyman, author; b. Mansfield, Conn., Aug. 4, 1833; s. Andrew and Sarah (Storrs) B.; A.B., Amherst, 1860; student Theol. Inst. of Conn. 1 yr.; grad. Andover Theol. Sem., 1863; m. Clara Storrs Freeman, May 6, 1864. Teacher dist. schs. until 21; ordained Congl. ministry, 1864; pastor North Hampton, N.H., 1863-66, 1st Ch., Exeter, N.H., 1866-69; missionary A.B.C. F.M. to Turkey, 1869-80; pastor Atkinson, N.H., later at Newington and Stonington, Conn., until retirement, 1907. Prog.-Republican. Author: Biographical Sketch of Rev. Jesse Page, 1883; On Horseback in Cappadocia, 1884; A Modern Tragedy, 1890; Boarding Round, 1915; In the Land of Ararat, 1916. Home: Norwich, Conn. Died Jan. 26, 1918.

BARROWS, Samuel June, congressman, clergyman; b. New York, May 26, 1845; grad. Harvard Div. School (B.D.), 1875 (D.D., Howard Univ., 1897); m. Isabel Chapin Hayes, June 28, 1867. Before graduation had been stenographer and journalist; pastor First Ch. (Unitarian) Dorchester, Boston, 1876-80; editor Christian Register, 1881-97; mem. Congress, 10th dist. Mass., 1897-99. Republican. Rep. U.S. on Internat. Prison Commn., 1896; corr. sec. Prison Assn. of New York, 1900. Author: The Shaybacks in Camp; Isles and Shrines of Greece; A Baptist Meeting House; The Doom of the Majority of Mankind; Crimes and Misdemeanors in the U.S.; etc. Pres. Internat. Prison Congress, 1905. Died 1909.

BARROWS, William Stanley, clergyman, educator; b. Rome, N.Y., 1861; s. Rev. Napoleon (S.T.D.) and Isabella (Gibson) B.; B.A., Trinity Coll., Conn., 1884, M.A., 1891, and D.D. from same college in 1929; B.D., Gen. Theol. Sem., 1891; m. Margaret Stuart Sartwelle, June 27, 1906; children—John Chester, Wm. Dinsmore, Stanley, George Sartwelle. Master, Ft. Hill Sch., Canandaigua, N.Y., 1884-85; deacon, 1888, priest, 1889, P.E. Church; Zion Ch., Little Neck, L.I., N.Y., 1888-90; missionary in N.C., 1890-94; Mayo fellow, Gen. Theol. Sem., 1894-97; headmaster De Veaux Sch., Niagara Falls, N.Y., 1897—. Died Jan. 26, 1940.

BARRUS, Clara, M.D., author; b. Port Byron, N.Y., Aug. 8, 1864; d. John William and Sarah (Randall) B.; M.D., Boston U., 1888. Gen. practice of medicine, Utica, N.Y., 1889-93; asst. phys., Middletown (N.Y.) Hosp., 1893-1910, also prof. psychiatry, Women's Coll. of N.Y. City; with pvt. sanitarium, Pelham, N.Y., 1912-14; now retired from practice. Lit. executor and official biographer of John Burroughs. Mem. O.E.S. Author: (brochure) The Retreat of a Poet Naturalist, 1905; Nursing the Insane, 1908; Our Friend John Burroughs, 1914; John Burroughs, Boy and Man, 1920; Life and Letters of John Burroughs, 1925; My Dog Friends, 1928. Editor: Under the Maples (posthumous work by John Burroughs), 1921; The Last Harvest (by John Burroughs), 1922; The Heart of Burroughs' Journals, 1928. Home: Roxbury, N.Y. Died Apr. 4, 1931.

BARRUS, George Hale, steam engr.; b. Goshen, Mass., July 11, 1854; s. Hiram and Augusta (Stone) B.; B.S., Mass. Inst. Tech., 1874; m. Louise C. Williams, Oct. 2, 1897; 1 dau., Bella D. (Mrs. Edwin L. Bowman). Asst. in design and constrn., Steam Engring. Lab., Mass. Inst. Tech., 1874-75; cons. practice, Boston, 1875—. Judge of exhibits, Mass. Charitable Mech. Assn., Franklin Inst. Elec. Exhbn., Phila.; Mass. judge of power exhibits, World's Fair, Chicago, 1893. Mem. Govt. Advisory Bd. on tests of fuels and structural materials. Inventor of several forms of steam calorimeter, coal calorimeter, draft gauge, steam meter and drainage system. Home: Brookline, Mass. Died Apr. 1929.

BARRY, David Sheldon; b. Detroit, Mich., May 25, 1859; s. James Richard and Elizabeth Ann (Cotter) B.; ed. pub. schs., Monroe, Mich.; m. Cora Bonney, Apr. 19, 1883; children—Elizabeth Bonney (Mrs. Sevellon Brown), James Richard, David S., Cora (wife of Wilder D. Baker, U.S.N.). Began as page, U.S. Senate, 1875; then Washington corr. Detroit Post-Tribune and Detroit Evening News, New York Sun, 1889-1904; editor Providence (R.I.) Journal, 1904-06; Washington corr. same, 1907-19; dir. publicity, Rep. Nat. Com., 1912-16; sergt. at arms, U.S. Senate, 1919—. Author: Forty Years in Washington, 1924. Home: Washington, D.C. Died Feb. 10, 1936.

BARRY, Edward Buttevant, rear adm.; b. New York, Oct. 20, 1849; s. Garrett Robert and Sarah Agnes (Glover) B.; grad. U.S. Naval Acad., 1869; m. Mary Wycliff Clitz, Apr. 7, 1875 (died 1906). Promoted ensign, July 12, 1870; advanced through grades to rear adm., Feb. 1, 1909. Served on various vessels to 1875; mem. bd. to organize training service, 1875; on Alaska, 1878-80; admiral's sec., Richmond and Monocacy, 1880-83; at Naval Acad., 1883-86, made 2 practice cruises on sailing frigate Constellation; on Alliance and Lancaster, S. Atlantic sta., 1886-89; with Bur. of Navigation, 1889-91; Asiatic sta., 1891-94; office naval intelligence, 1894-97; S. Atlantic and Cuban blockade, 1897-99, present at attack on Matanzas, Cuba, and Ponce, P.R.; comd. collier Marcellus, 1900; at gun factory, Washington, War Coll. and comdg. Vicksburg, Asiatic sta., 1900-02; comd. Kentucky, 1905-07; recruiting duty, New York, 1907; supervisor naval auxiliary service, 1908-09; comdr. 2d div. Pacific Fleet, 1909. Asso. Soc. Naval Architects. Home: New York, N.Y. Died Nov. 27, 1938.

BARRY, James Henry, editor; b. New York, Feb. 15, 1856; s. William I. (printer and pub.) and Mary Ann (Harris) B.; ed. pub. and night schs., printing office and pvt. study; m. Nellie V. Barnum, Jan. 11, 1883; children—Edith Barnum (Mrs. Earle Walthew), William Henry, James Milne. Family removed to Calif., 1859; began in printing business on own account, 1879; 1st man in Calif. to advocate Australian ballot; founded 1884, editor, pub., until 1921, The Star, one of first papers to advocate public ownership and operation of public functions, Henry George's teachings, equal rights for women, initiative, referendum and recall. Dem. candidate for Congress, 1898. Cited for contempt of court in criticising a decision of one of the judges, 1890, and asked to apologize; refused to do so on the ground that he could not conscientiously apologize for telling the truth; sentenced to jail for 5 days and to pay a fine of $500; served sentence; the night released, all classes of people joined in largest mass meeting ever held in San Francisco, and demanded amendment to law of contempt, resulting in adoption of the "Barry Law," depriving judges of power to punish critics without trial and conviction by jury. Pioneer in introducing 8-hour day in printing office on Pacific Coast. Naval Officer, Port of San Francisco, 1913-21 (resigned). Home: San Francisco, Calif. Died Aug. 20, 1927.

BARRY, Joseph Gayle Hurd, theologian; b. Middle Haddam, Conn., Apr. 19, 1858; s. Nathan Fry and Caroline Lockwood (Hurd) B.; ed. Wesleyan U., Middletown, Conn., 1880-84; grad. Berkeley Divinity Sch., 1886; (D.D., Nashotah House, 1906); unmarried. Deacon, 1886, priest, 1887, P.E. Ch.; asst. rector St. James' Ch., Chicago, 1886-88; rector Calvary Ch., Batavia, Ill., 1888-91; instr. Western Theol. Sem., 1891-1901; canon St. Paul's Cathedral, Fond du Lac, Wis., 1901-06; dean Nashotah House, 1906-09; rector Ch. of St. Mary the Virgin, New York, 1909-29 (emeritus). Author: Meditations on the Office and Work of the Holy Spirit, 1908; The Christian's Day, 1910; Meditations on the Apostles' Creed, 1912; The Self-Revelation of Our Lord, Meditations, 1913; Holiness, 1915; The Invitations of Our Lord, 1918; On Prayers to the Dead, 1919; From a Convent Tower, 1919; The Religion of the Prayer Book (with Dr. Delany), 1919; The Holy Eucharist, 1920; Our Lady, S. Mary, 1922; Meditations on the Communion Office, 1924. Home: Kingston, N.Y. Died May 28, 1931.

BARRY, Patrick, bishop; b. in Ireland, Nov. 15, 1868; s. Michael and Catherine (Dixon) B.; student Mungret Coll., Limerick, Ireland, 1887-90, St. Patrick's Coll., Carlow, Ireland, 1890-95. Ordained priest R.C. Ch., 1895; asst. pastor Immaculate Conception Parish, Jacksonville, Fla., 1895-1903; pastor St. Monica Ch., Palatka, Fla., 1903-13, New Parish of the Assumption, S. Jacksonville, also missions, 1913-17; rector Cathedral of St. Augustine and vicar gen. of St. Augustine, Fla., 1917-21; adminstr. of Diocese, 1921-22; consecrated bishop, May 3, 1922. Died Aug. 12, 1940.

BARRY, Thomas Henry, major gen.; b. New York, Oct. 13, 1855; s. David and Margaret (Dimond) B.; ed. pub. schs. and Coll. City of New York; grad. U.S. Mil. Acad., 1877; m. Ellen Bestor, Jan. 23, 1884. Second lt. 7th Cav., June 15, 1877; promoted through grades to lt. col., asst. adj. gen. U.S.A., Jan. 10, 1900; brig-gen. U.S.V., June 18, 1900, to June 30, 1901, serving with China relief expdn. and in Philippines till July 18, 1901; col. asst. adj.-gen. U.S.A., July 15, 1902; brig-gen., Aug. 18, 1903; maj-gen., Apr. 29, 1908. Adj. gen. 8th Army Corps and dept. of Pacific in P.I., Aug. 1898-Feb. 1900; chief of staff, Div. of the Philippines, Nov. 14, 1900-July 18, 1901; comdg. army of Cuban pacification, 1907-Apr. 1, 1909; comdg. dept. of Cal. to Aug. 1910; apptd. supt. U.S. Mil. Acad., Aug. 31, 1910; comdg. Eastern Department, Governor's Island, New York, 1913, Philippine Dept., until 1915, Central Dept., Chicago, until Aug. 1917; comdr. Camp Grant, Rockford, Ill., and 86th Div., N.A., Aug. 1917-Feb. 1918; again comdg. Central Dept., Chicago, Mar. 1918—. Died Dec. 30, 1919.

BARRYMORE, Maurice (Herbert Blythe), actor, playwright; b. India, 1847; grad. Cambridge Univ., Eng., and studied for Indian Civil Service; admitted to bar, but gave up law for the stage. First engagement in U.S., Fifth Av. Theatre, New York; has been leading man for Modjeska, Mrs. Langtry and others, and also in A. M. Palmer and other cos. Author: Nadjeska (written for Mme. Modjeska); The Robber of the Rhine (libretto); and other plays. Died 1905.

BARSE, George Randolph, Jr., artist; b. Detroit, July 31, 1861; s. George R. and Susan B. (Peironnet) B.; pub. sch. edn., Kansas City, Mo.; studied art at École des Beaux Arts and Académie Julian, Paris, 1879-85; pupil of A. Cabanel, Boulanger and Lefebvre; m. Rosa Ferrara, 1891. Academy prize, Paris, France, 1882; New England prize, Boston, 1885; 1st prize Nat. Acad. Design, 1895; Shaw Fund prize, Soc. Am. Artists, 1898; medal, Buffalo Expn., 1901. Painted 8 panels for Library of Congress, 1896; figure and portrait painter, and character of work tends to the decorative. A.N.A., 1898, N.A., 1899; mem. Archtl. League of New York. Represented in Minneapolis Mus. of Art, Syracuse Mus., H.B. Speed Memorial Mus. (Louisville, Ky.), Kansas City Art Inst., Carnegie Mus. (Pittsburgh); also many private and pub. collections. Home: Katonah, N.Y. Died Feb. 24, 1938.

BARSTOW, Frank Quarles, capitalist; b. Waukesha, Wis., Oct. 24, 1847; s. William A. and Maria (Quarles) B.; ed. Madison, Wis. Dir. Standard Oil Co., Ry. Steel Spring Co., Thompson-Starrett Co., Hegeman Co., Corn Products Refining Co., N.Y. Glucose Co., People's Bank, Savings Investment &

Trust Co., Union Tank Line. Home: E. Orange, N.J. Died 1909.

BARSTOW, George Eames, businessman; b. Providence, R.I., Nov. 19, 1849; s. Amos Chafee and Emeline Mumford (Eames) B.; ed. pub. schs. and Mowry and Goff's English and Classical Sch., Providence; m. Clara Drew Symonds, Oct. 19, 1871. Began business career at 17; founded, organized or financed: Barstow Thread Co., Providence Warehouse Co., Nat. and Providence Worsted Mills, Am. Writing Paper Co., U.S. Envelope Co., Barstow Irrigation Co., Barstow Town Co. (Barstow, Tex.); pres. Barstow Town Co. Mem. Sch. Bd., Providence, 14 yrs. (pres. last yr.); mem. Providence Common Council, 4 yrs., R.I. Ho. of Rep., 3 terms. Pioneer in irrigation of arid lands of Southwest; founder town of Barstow, co. seat of Ward Co., Tex., 1894; built irrigation works capable of irrigating 30,000 acres of land. Pres. Nat. Drainage Assn., 1906-07, Internat. Irrig. Congress, 1908-09, upon invitation of President Roosevelt was mem. Conf. of Governors at White House, May, 1908, and guest of the President on trip down the Mississippi River; v.p. Texas Conservation Commn.; pres. W. Texas Reclamation Assn.; mem. com. on confs. Am. Agrl. Assn.; life dir. Euphrates Coll., Turkey; del. World Court Congress, Cleveland. Republican. Conglist. Author of Good Government Coöperative Societies; Creation of a World Centre of Communication; Shall We Bar the Immigrant? Applied Psychology; Shall Democracy Endure? Shall Democracy Endure in the U.S.? The Chino-Japanese Imbroglio; The Effect of Psychology on Americanism. Home: Barstow, Tex. Died 1924.

BARSTOW, John Lester, governor; b. Shelburne, Vt., Feb. 21, 1832; s. Heman and Laura (Lyon) B.; ed. Shelburne; (LL.D., Norwich U., 1909); m. Laura Maeck, Oct. 28, 1856 (died 1885). Served in Union Army, 1861-64, to rank of maj.; was made brig. gen. state troops at time of St. Albans raid. Mem. Vt. Ho. of Rep., 1864-65, Senate, 1866-68; U.S. pension agt., Burlington, Vt., 1870-78; lt. gov., 1880-82; gov., 1882-85. Dir. Burlington (Vt.) Savings Bank, 1887—. Home: Shelburne, Vt. Died June 28, 1913.

BARTCH, George Washington, judge; b. Dushore, Pa., Mar. 15, 1849; s. John G. and Mary Magdalene B.; M.S., Bloomsburg (Pa.) State Normal Sch., 1871 and 1879; m. Amanda Alice Guild, Feb. 16, 1871. Supt. schs., Shenandoah, Pa., 1874-84; practiced law at Bloomsburg, 1884-86, Cañon City, Colo., 1886-88, Salt Lake City, 1888-89; probate judge, Salt Lake Co., 1889-93; asso. justice Supreme Ct. of Utah Ty., 1893-95, State Supreme Ct., 1895-1906 (chief justice, 1899-1900, 1905-06); resigned Oct. 1, 1906, to resume practice of law, including, also, international law. Republican. Home: Salt Lake City, Utah. Died Mar. 15, 1927.

BARTH, Carl G(eorge Lange), mech. engr.; b. Christiania, Norway, Feb. 28, 1860; s. of Jacob Böckman and Adelaide Magdalene (Lange) B.; grad. High Sch., Lillehammer, Norway, 1875; grad. Tech. Sch., Horten, 1876; m. Hendrikke Jacobine Fredericksen, of Lillehammer, Mar. 4, 1882 (died Feb. 25, 1916); children—J. Christian, Carl G., I. Adelaide (dec.), Elizabeth F.; m. 2d, Sophia E. Roever, Jan. 25, 1919. In machine shops, Norwegian Navy Yards; instr. in mathematics and mech. drawing, Tech. Sch., Horten, to 1880; came to America, 1881; mech. draftsman with Wm. Sellers & Co., Phila., 1881-90, and instr. in mech. drawing, evening schs. of Franklin Inst., 1882-88; engr. and chief draftsman with Arthur Falkenau, Phila., 1890-1901; designer, Wm. Sellers & Co., 1891-95; engr. and chief draftsman, Rankin & Fritch Foundry & Machine Co., St. Louis, 1895-97; designer St. Louis Water Dept., Feb.-June, 1897; with Internat. Corr. Schs., Scranton, Pa., 1897-98; instr. in manual work and mathematics, Ethical Culture Schs., New York, 1898-99; machine shop engr. Bethlehem Steel Co., 1899-1901; there met Frederick W. Taylor, the father of scientific management, and was his prin. associate until Taylor's death in 1915; introducing Taylor system of scientific management, in machine shops, 1901-23; rep. of Tinius Olsen Testing Machine Co. in Japan, 1923-24; retired. Expert in shop management, Ordnance Dept., U.S. Army, 1909-18, and again during World War; lecturer on scientific management Harvard U., 1911-16, and 1919-23, U. of Chicago, 1914-16. Home: Philadelphia, Pa. Died Oct. 28, 1939.

BARTH, Charles H., army officer; b. Ia., Dec. 28, 1858; grad. U.S. Mil. Acad., 1881; honor grad. Inf. and Cav. Sch., Ft. Leavenworth, 1891; grad. Army War Coll., 1909; married; children—George B., Charles H. Commd. 2d lt. 12th Inf., June 11, 1881; promoted through grades to brig. gen. Dec. 2, 1922. Apache Indian campaign, 1881; adj. 12th Inf., 1893-97, 1900-03; asst. instr., Inf. and Cav. Sch., 1891-93; Philippine insurrection, 1899-1902; asst., and later senior instr., Inf. and Cav. Sch. and Staff Coll., 1903-05; act. asst. dir. Army War Coll., 1910-11. Comdr. 156th Depot Brig., and 81st Div., Camp Jackson, S.C., 1917; comdr. 13th Inf. Brig. and 7th (regular) Div., Jan. 1-Oct. 24, 1918, Camp MacArthur, Tex., and in France. Recommended 4 times for brevet commn. for bravery in action, Philippine insurrection; citation and silver star, 1899; recommended twice for D.S.M.; decorated by French Govt. with Legion of Honor (officer grade) and Croix de Guerre with palm. Col. 57th Inf., Aug. 29, 1921; comdg. defenses Manila and Subic bays, Apr. 5-Aug. 13, 1921; comdg. 23d Inf. Brig., Jan. 1-Sept. 15, 1922; retired Dec. 28, 1922; gov. Nat. Military Home, Kan., 1925—. Died Dec. 5, 1926.

BARTHOLDT, Richard, congressman; b. Germany, Nov. 2, 1855; s. Gottlob and Caroline Louise (Wagner) B.; came to U.S. in boyhood; classical edn.; learned printing trade; m. Caecilie Niedner, June 27, 1880. Editor-in-chief St. Louis Tribune, 1885-92. Mem. St. Louis Sch. Bd., 1888-92 (pres., 1891-92); mem. 53d to 63d Congresses (1893-1915), 10th Mo. Dist.; Republican. Retired voluntarily from Congress to devote himself to literature. Pres. Interparliamentary Union for Promotion of Internat. Arbitration, and founder and pres. for 11 yrs. of Am. Group in Congress of that organization. Died March 19, 1932.

BARTHOLOMEW, Abram Glenni, lawyer; b. Buffalo, N.Y., Oct. 16, 1878; s. Abram and Florence (Cutler) B.; A.B., Princeton, 1901; LL.B., U. of Buffalo, 1903; m. Amy Kankelwitz, Apr. 9, 1921; 1 dau., Amy (dec). Began practice at Buffalo, 1903, as member Bartholomew & Bartholomew, of which was senior member; prof. law, U. of Buffalo, 1903-27, prof. med. jurisprudence, Med. Dept., 1927-29, now emeritus prof. law; v.p. Deck Bros. Inc., Automatic Buffing Machine Co.; sec. A. H. Case & Co., Fetter Steel Barrel Corp., Pittsford Lumber Co. Dir. publicity, 3d to 5th Liberty Loan campaigns, Buffalo; same for two $5,000,000 endowment campaigns, U. of Buffalo, 1920, 29, Buffalo Centennial Com., 1932; mem. Buffalo Federal Civil Works Adminstrn. Bd., 1934; mem. exec. com. Am. Red Cross, Buffalo. Dir. Legal Aid Bur. of Buffalo (ex-treas.). Chmn. bd. trustees U. of Buffalo; trustee N.Y. State 8th Jud. Dist. Law Library; sec. bd. mgrs. Buffalo State Teachers Coll. Democrat. Presbyn. Home: Buffalo, N.Y. Died Feb. 11, 1936.

BARTHOLOMEW, Allen R., missionary sec.; b. Dannersville, Pa., Sept. 16, 1855; s. George Henry and Hannah (Danner) B.; grad. Theol. Sem. of Ref. Ch. Lancaster, 1877; hon. A.M., 1890; D.D., Franklin and Marshall, 1898; D.Th., U. of Berne (Switzerland), 1926; LL.D., Ursinus Coll., 1927; m. Maria S. Karch, 1878 (died 1906); children—Ruth Amelia Nuss, Joseph K., Mary Hannah MacDonald, Grace Clayton; m. 2d, Julia Hall, 1908. Ordained ministry Ref. Ch. in U.S., 1877; pastor various chs. in Pa., 1877-1902; mem. Bd. Fgn. Missions, Ref. Ch. in U.S., 1887—, and sec., 1887-90, and 1902—. Del. World Missionary Conf., Edinburgh, 1910; tour of Orient, 1909-10. Pres. Pa. Christian Endeavor Union, 1904-06, Eastern Synod. Ref. Ch., 1919, Fgn. Missions Conf. of N.A., 1923, Gen. Synod of Ref. Ch., 1926-29; also pres. Exec. Com. Gen. Synod of Ref. Ch.; del. Alliance of Ref. Chs., 1924-29. Mem. Reference and Counsel Foreign Miss. Conf., 1925-31. Chaplain Huguenot Soc., 1925-32. Democrat. Mason. Author: Won by Prayer (Life of Oshikawa), 1889; The Apostle of Ryo-U, 1917; The Martyr of Huping, 1924. Home: Philadelphia, Pa. Died Nov. 27, 1933.

BARTHOLOMEW, J. M., chief justice supreme court, N. Dak.; Republican. Home: Bismarck, N. Dak. Died 1901.

BARTHOLOMEW, Pliny Webster, judge; b. Cabotville, Mass., Aug. 4, 1840; s. Harris and Betsey (Moore) B.; A.B., Union Coll., 1864, A.M., 1867; read law with Judge Jesse L. L'Amoraux, Ballston Spa, N.Y.; m. Sarah Belle Smith, Jan. 30, 1873; children—Belle Isadora (Mrs. Allin W. Hewitt), Pliny Webster (dec.), Harris Sherley. Admitted to N.Y. bar, 1865, and began practice with preceptor; removed to Indianapolis, Nov., 1866; was partner with Judge Edward Buskirk and Judge David V. Burns; judge of Superior Ct., Indianapolis, terms 1892-96, and 1908-Dec. 31, 1914; resumed practice of law. Democrat. Presbyn. Past Chancellor Comdr. K. of P. Home: Indianapolis, Ind. Died Jan. 29, 1931.

BARTHOLOW, Roberts, emeritus prof. materia medica, gen. therapeutics and hygiene, Jefferson Med. Coll., 1879—; b. Howard Co., Md., Nov. 28, 1831; grad. in arts, Calvert Coll., Md.; grad. in medicine, Univ. of Md. (M. D., 1852); LL. D., St. Mary's Coll. Entered regular army med. staff at head of his class, 1857-64; prof. theory and practice of medicine and clin. medicine and dean of the faculty Ohio Med. Coll., Cincinnati, 1864-79. Hon. Fellow Royal Med. Soc. of Edinburgh. Author: Qualifications for the Military Service; Hypodermic Medication; Treatise on Materia Medica and Therapeutics; Practice of Medicine; (translated into Japanese at Tokio) Medical Electricity; also many papers, essays, etc. Home: Philadelphia, Pa. Died 1904.

BARTLETT, Adolphus Clay, hardware mcht.; b. Stratford, N.Y., June 22, 1844; s. Aaron and Delia (Dibell) B.; ed. Dansville (N.Y.) Acad., Clinton (N.Y.) Liberal Inst.; m. Mary H. Pitkin, Aug. 27, 1867 (died 1890); m. 2d, Abby L., d. Bailey H. Hitchcock, of Toledo, O., June 15, 1893; father of Frederic Clay B. Entered employ Tuttle, Hibbard & Co., of Chicago, at age of 19; Jan. 1, 1882, when business was incorporated as Hibbard, Spencer Bartlett & Co., made sec., chmn. bd. Trustee U. of Chicago; dir. Art Inst., Chicago; has been mem. Chicago Bd. of Edn.; pres. Home for the Friendless; v.p. Old Peoples Home. Republican. Home: Lake Geneva, Wis. Died May 30, 1922.

BARTLETT, Albert LeRoy, author; b. Haverhill, Mass., June 1, 1852; s. Thomas and Patience (Hawkins) B.; A.B., Dartmouth Coll., 1872, A.M., 1875; unmarried. Master Sherborn (Mass.) Acad., 1872, Bradford, Mass., 1875-82; submaster, Haverhill (Mass.) High Sch., 1882-88; supt. pub. instrn., Haverhill, Mass., 1888-97. Lecturer on English lang. and lit. in N.H. Summer Normal Sch., 1895-97, Martha's Vineyard (Mass.) Summer Normal Sch., 1900-01, Va. Summer Normal Sch., 1901. Commr. of pub. safety, Haverhill, Mass., 1912-14, mayor, 1915-16, exec. sec. Com. on Pub. Safety, 1917, mem. Municipal Council, 1919-23. Author: History of Haverhill Academy and High School, 1890; First Steps in English, 1900; Essentials of Langauge and Grammar, 1900; A Golden Way, 1902; The Construction of English, 1903; The Elements of English Grammar, 1907; Some Memories of Old Haverhill, 1915; Haverhill 1640-1915, an hist. address, 1915. Home: Haverhill, Mass. Died June 1934.

BARTLETT, Charles Lafayette, congressman; b. Monticello, Georgia, Jan. 31, 1853; s. George T. and Virginia L. (Saunders) B.; A.B., U. of Ga., 1870; LL.B., U. of Va., 1872; m. Leila Carlton, Dec. 3, 1874. Admitted to bar, 1872, and practiced at Monticello, and then at Macon, Ga.; solicitor gen. Macon Jud. Circuit, 1877-81; mem. Ga. Ho. of Rep., 1882-86, Senate, 1888-90; judge Superior Ct., Macon Circuit, 1893-94, resigned; mem. 54th to 63d Congresses (1895-1915), 6th Ga. Dist. Democrat. Home: Macon, Ga. Died Apr. 21, 1938.

BARTLETT, Charles Ward, commodore U.S.N.; b. Worcester, Mass., Aug. 11, 1850; s. Theodore H. and Elizabeth W. B.; grad. U.S. Naval Acad., 1871; m. Henrietta F. Williams, Nov. 25, 1879. Promoted ensign, June 14, 1872; master, Mar. 17, 1875; lt., Nov. 4, 1882; lt. comdr., Mar. 3, 1899; comdr., Oct. 9, 1901; capt., June 29, 1906; commodore and retired, June 30, 1908. Astron. work for latitude and longitude in the W.I.; surveying coast of Lower Cal., comd. Piscataqua in cruise to China, U.S.S. Isle de Cuba and Petrel on Asiatic sta., U.S.S. Florida in U.S. Coast Squadron; asst. to chief Bur. of Ordnance; comd. U.S.S. Ohio in cruise of Atlantic Fleet to San Francisco. Home: Worcester, Mass. Died 1910.

BARTLETT, Edgar Elliott, newspaper pub.; b. Kalamazoo, Mich., Nov. 30, 1856; s. Azel E. and Jeannette (Packard) B.; ed. pub. schs.; m. Hattie Leach, Oct. 12, 1882; children—Elliott S., Irene (Mrs. James Carroll King). Began as adv. solicitor, Kalamazoo Telegraph, 1879, later business mgr.; moved to Rockford, 1891; associated with others as pub. Rockford Register-Gazette, until 1901, since chief owner and pub. same paper; pub. Kalamazoo Gazette, 1898-1900. Trustee Rockford City Hosp. Republican. Conglist. Home: Rockford, Ill. Died Nov. 11, 1929.

BARTLETT, Edward Theodore, judge; b. Skaneateles, N.Y., June 14, 1841; s. Dr. Levi and Harriette Elizabeth (Hopkins) B.; classical edn. Admitted to bar, 1862; practiced at Skaneateles and Syracuse, 1862-68, New York, 1868-93; candidate for justice Supreme Ct., 1891; asso. judge N.Y. Ct. of Appeals, 1894-1907 and 1908-12. Republican. Died 1910.

BARTLETT, Edwin Julius, prof. chemistry; b. Hudson, O., Feb. 16, 1851; s. Samuel Colcord and Mary Bacon (Learned) B.; A.B., Dartmouth, 1872; Sc.D., 1918; A.M., M.D., Rush Med. Coll., Chicago, 1879; m. Caroline E. Rice, July 8, 1879; children—Harriette Louise (Mrs. Moses B. Perkins), Edwin Rice, Samuel Colcord, John Foster. Instr. sciences, Monson (Mass.) Acad., 1872-73, high sch., Glencoe, Ill., 1874-75, Lake Forest (Ill.) Acad., 1876-78; asso. prof., 1879-83; prof. chemistry, 1883-1920, Dartmouth, emeritus. Mem. N.H. legislature, 1913 (chmn. com. pub. health). Home: Hanover, N.H. Died 1932.

BARTLETT, Franklin, lawyer, writer; b. Worcester Co., Mass., Sept. 10, 1847; grad. Brooklyn Poly. Inst., 1865; A.B., Harvard, 1869, Ph.D., 1878; LL.B., Columbia Law Sch., 1873; admitted to bar upon exam., 1870; studied Exeter Coll., Oxford Univ., Eng., 1870-71. Mem. constl. commn., N.Y., 1890; del. Nat. Dem. Conv., Chicago, 1892; mem. Congress, 1893-97. Died 1909.

BARTLETT, Frederick Bethune, bishop; b. South Manchester, Conn., Aug. 23, 1882; s. Bethune James and Elizabeth (Johnson) B.; A.B., Trinity Coll., Conn., 1904, D.D., 1932; B.D., Episcopal Theol. Sch., Cambridge, Mass., 1908; M.A., Harvard, 1911; m. Jessie Langelle Hale, Oct. 10, 1911; 1 dau., Elizabeth Alden. Deacon and priest P.E. Ch., 1908; missionary in Ore., 1908-10; vicar Christ Chapel, Brooklyn, N.Y., 1911-16; rector St. John's Ch., West Hoboken, N.J., 1917-18, St. Mark's Ch., Aberdeen, S.D., 1918-23, St. Philip the Apostle, St. Louis, Mo., 1923-25; gen. sec. Nat. Council P.E. Ch., 1925-31; consecrated bishop of N.D., Dec. 16, 1931; transferred to Missionary Dist. of Ida., 1935. Exec.

sec. Dept. of Domestic Missions, Nat. Council of Episcopal Church; mem. exec. bd. Home Missions Council. Republican. Mason. Home: Boise, Ida. Died Dec. 15, 1941.

BARTLETT, John, publisher, author; b. Plymouth, Mass., June 14, 1820; was publisher at Cambridge; vol. paymaster U.S.N., 1862-63; partner, 1865-89, senior mem. 1878-89, Little, Brown & Co., pubs., Boston; retired. Edited several works, of which his Familiar Quotations is best known as a standard reference book. Author: The Shakespeare Phrase Book; The Complete Concordance to Shakespeare's Dramatic Works and Poems. Home: Cambridge, Mass. Died 1905.

BARTLETT, John Russell, rear adm. (retired, 1897); b. New York, Sept. 26, 1843; s. John R. and Eliza A. (Rhodes) B.; ed. Cambridge, Mass., and U.S. Naval Acad. (Sc.D., Brown, 1898); m. Jeanie R. Jenckes, Feb. 6, 1872. Ordered into service May, 1861; served during Civil war at passage of Fts. Jackson and St. Philip and capture of New Orleans; on Admiral Dahlgren's staff off Charleston, 1863-64; comd. co. in naval attack on Ft. Fisher; investigated Gulf Stream, 1877-82, in command U.S. Coast Survey Str. Blake; in charge hydrographic office, 1882-88; last command Monitor Puritan. During war with Spain, 1898, in charge of naval intelligence office, and was supt. U.S. Coast Signal Service and chief U.S. Auxiliary Naval Force. Home: Lonsdale, R.I. Died 1904.

BARTLETT, John S.; b. Marblehead, Mass., June 11, 1845; s. George E. and Hannah H. (Girdler) B.; ed. pub. and high schs. of Marblehead and Lynn, Mass.; m. Ella Doak, June 2, 1869. Shoe mfg. business, Lynn, more than 20 yrs.; now pres. East Middlesex St. Ry. Co., Electrical Assn., Ltd., Lynn Gas & Electric Co.; v.p. Brockton Gas Light Co., Essex Trust Co. Republican. Home: Lynn, Mass. Died Jan. 1925.

BARTLETT, J(oseph) Gardner, genealogist; b. Boston, Mass., Aug. 25, 1872; s. Joseph Elbridge, M.D., and Antoinette Frances (Carpenter) B.; student Mass. Inst. Tech., 1890-92; m. Elizabeth French, Sept. 4, 1917. Practiced as architect in Boston, 1892-1904; geneal. and hist. research and compilation, U.S. and Eng., 1904—. Republican. Unitarian. Author: John Hill, of Dorchester and Descendants, 1904; Belcher Families of New England, 1906; Ancestry and Descendants of Rev. John Wilson of Boston, 1907; Hugh Jones of Salem and Descendants, 1908; Robert Coe, Puritan, His Ancestors and Descendants, 1911; Newberry Genealogy, 1914; English Ancestry of Peter Talbot, 1917; Gregory Stone Genealogy, 1918; English Ancestry of Daniel Shed, 1921; Simon Stone Genealogy, 1926; Henry Adams Genealogy, 1927. Home: Watertown, Mass. Died Nov. 11, 1927.

BARTLETT, Paul Wayland, sculptor; b. New Haven, Conn., 1865; s. Truman Howe and Mary Ann (White) B.; ed. pub. schs., New Haven and Boston; began sculpture while a boy, under the instruction of Frémiet; exhibited in Salon at age of 14 (a bust of his grandmother), and 1880 entered École des Beaux Arts, where he was a pupil of Cavelier. In 1887 received recompense at Salon for the group, The Bear Tamer (now in Met. Mus. of New York); was hors concours, Paris Expn., 1889, and mem. Internat. Jury of Awards; also hors concours and represented U.S. on International Jury of Awards for Sculpture, Paris Exposition, 1900. Chevalier Legion of Honor of France, 1895, officer, 1908. Principal works: Statue of Gen. Joseph Warren, Boston; equestrian statue of Lafayette in the Sq. of the Louvre, Paris (gift to France from the school children of the U.S.); statues of Columbus and Michelangelo, in Congressional Library, Washington; a door for tomb of Senator W. A. Clark, in Woodlawn Cemetery; latest works, six statues on the front of the New York Pub. Library; pediment over House wing of the Capitol, Washington, D.C.; statue of Benjamin Franklin; statue of Patriotism, Duluth, Minn. Represented in Boston Museum, Phila. Acad. Design, Art Inst. Chicago, Luxembourg Gallery, Paris, and Mus. of Decorative Art, Paris. Mem. Am. Acad. Arts and Letters; corr. mem. Inst. of France; assn. mem. Royal Acad., Belgium; N.A., 1917. Died Sept. 20, 1925.

BARTLETT, Willard, judge; b. Uxbridge, Mass., Oct. 14, 1846; s. William O. and Agnes E. H. (Willard) B.; LL.B., New York U., 1868; A.B., Columbia, 1869; (LL.D., Hamilton Coll., 1894, New York U., 1904, Columbia, 1904); m. Mary Fairbanks Buffum, Oct. 26, 1870. Practiced law in association with Elihu Root, 1869-83; justice Supreme Ct. of N.Y., 2d Jud. Dept., 1884-1906; justice gen. term N.Y. City, 1887-89; justice Appellate div. Supreme Ct., Brooklyn, 1896-1906; asso. judge Ct. of Appeals, Jan. 1, 1906-14; chief judge Ct. of Appeals, 1914-16, when retired by age and became official referee in state cases; resumed practice of law as counsel in association with Elihu Root, Jan., 1917. Democrat. Dramatic critic, New York Sun, 1871-73; subsequently contbr. of editorial articles on legal topics, and book reviews; reviser Am. Cyclo., 1873-76. Prof. med. jurisprudence, L.I. Coll. Hosp., 1898-1916. Fellow Am. Acad. Arts and Sciences. Home: Brooklyn, N.Y. Died Jan. 19, 1925.

BARTLETT, William Henry, comdr. G.A.R., dept. of Mass., 1898; prin. Worcester pub. sch. Mem. Am. Inst. of Civics. Author: Facts I Ought to Know About the Government of My Country, 1894; The Parliamentary Pathfinder, 1903. Home: Worcester, Mass. Died 1904.

BARTLEY, Elias Hudson, M.D.; b. Bartley, N.J., Dec. 6, 1849; s. Samuel Potter and Anna (Ewalt) B.; B.S., Cornell, 1873; M.D., L.I. Coll. Hosp., 1879; m. Mary Frances Harloe, Nov. 5, 1888; children—Samuel Potter, Mrs. Mildred Simrel. Taught sciences, Princeton High Sch., 1873-74; instr. chemistry, Cornell, 1874-75; prof. chemistry, Swarthmore Coll., 1875-78; instr. chemistry, 1880-86, prof. chemistry and toxicology, 1886-1901, prof. of chemistry, toxicology and pediatrics, 1901-15, dean and prof. pediatrics, 1915-17, emeritus prof., 1917—, L.I. Coll. Hosp.; chief chemist, Health Dept., Brooklyn, 1882-88; mem. Kings Co. Bd. of Pharmacy, 1892-98; dean and prof. of organic chemistry, Brooklyn Coll. Pharmacy, 1892-1902; consulting pediatrist, L.I. Coll. Hosp., Methodist, Kingston Av. Contagious Diseases, and S. Side hosps.; chief of the dept. of pediatrics, Brownsville and East New York Hospital. Author: Textbook of Medical and Pharmaceutical Chemistry (7th edit.), 1909. Manual of Clinical Chemistry (3d edit.), 1907. Died Jan. 12, 1937.

BARTOL, Cyrus Augustus, Unitarian clergyman; b. Freeport, Me., April 30, 1813; grad. Bowdoin, 1832; Cambridge Divinity School, 1835; asst. pastor, 1837-61; about 30 years pastor West Ch., Boston; now retired. Author: Church and Congregation; Radical Problems; The Rising Faith; Principles and Portraits; etc. Died 1900.

BARTOL, George E., pres. Phila. Bourse; b. Phila., Pa., Jan. 29, 1858; s. Barnabas Henry and Emma Jemima (Welchman) B.; ed. pvt. schs., Phila., Brussels (Belgium), Heidelberg (Germany), and Lauderbach Acad. (Phila.); m. Mary Stone Grier, Oct. 21, 1881; m. 2d, Jane Newman Grier, Jan. 5, 1906. Identified with sugar refining business, later export and import grain, glucose and sugar; organized, 1891, and became pres. Phila. Bourse. Also v.p. C. Howard Hunt Pen Co.; dir. and chmn. investment com. Girard Nat. Bank; dir. Dexter Portland Cement Co., Western N.Y.&Pa. R.R. Co. Mem. Com. on Inland and Water Transportation of Council Nat. Defense. Mem. Soc. Mayflower Descendants in Pa., Hist. socs. of Marblehead, Mass., and Pa. Republican. Unitarian. Home: Philadelphia, Pa. Died 1917.

BARTOL, William Cyrus, prof. mathematics; b. Huntingdon, Pa., Nov. 24, 1847; s. Elias and Seba (Wieland) B.; A.B., U. of Lewisburg, Pa. (now Bucknell U.), 1872, A.M., 1875; hon. Ph.D., Adrian, 1893; m. Martha Belle Africa, 1875. Teacher of mathematics in acad., Salisbury, Conn., 1872-73; prin. pub. schs., Centre Hall, Pa., 1874-75, Union Grove, Wis., 1875-76; prin. Huntingdon (Pa.) Acad., 1876-77; prof. mathematics, Pa. State Normal Sch., Mansfield, Pa., 1877-81; prof. mathematics and astronomy, Bucknell U., 1881-1928, also dir. Observatory (emeritus). Republican. Baptist. Author: Solid Geometry, 1903; also various studies in perspective, differential calculus and astronomy. Home: Lewisburg, Pa. Died Oct. 31, 1940.

BARTON, Charles Harmon, banker; b. Kaysville, Utah, Nov. 12, 1871; s. Joseph and Mary Ann (Allen) B.; ed. common schs.; m. Millie Nelson Bonnemort, June 12, 1894; children—Harmon Bonnemort, Mildred Mary (Mrs. Carlyle C. Eubank), Blanch Dorothy (Mrs. John H. Page). Began in banking business at Ogden, Utah, 1890; pres. Nat. Bank of Commerce, 1920—; pres. Ogden Union Stock Yards; dir. Am. Packing & Provision Co., Salt Lake City Br. Fed. Reserve Bank of San Francisco, Utah Industrial Development Assn., Ogden Clearing House Assn., sec.-treas. Utah Rapid Transit Co.; treas. dir. Aleutian Livestock Co.; pres. Ogden Livestock Show, 1919—; dir. Ogden Chamber Commerce. Capt. 1st Cav., Utah N.G., 1894-96; commd. maj., Home Guard, World War. Republican. Home: Ogden, Utah. Died May 6, 1930.

BARTON, Clara, philanthropist; b. Oxford, Mass., 1821; d. Capt. Stephen and Sally (Stone) B.; grad. Clinton (N.Y.) Liberal Inst. Taught sch. 10 yrs.; organized system of pub. schs., Bordentown, N.J. During Civil War did relief work on battlefields and organized at her own expense the search for missing men (for the carrying on of which work Congress voted $15,000 for reimbursement); laid out grounds national cemetery, Andersonville, 1865; asso. with Internat. Red Cross of Geneva and worked through entire Franco-Prussian war, 1870; distributed relief in Strassburg, Belfort, Montpelier, Paris, 1871; secured adoption of treaty of Geneva, by U.S., 1882; 1st pres. Am. Red Cross, 1881-1904; apptd. to represent U.S. in internat. conferences, Geneva, 1884, Carlsrühe, 1887, Rome, 1892, Vienna, 1897, St. Petersburg, 1903; inaugurated Am. amendment of Red Cross, to provide relief for great calamities; distributed relief, Ohio and Mississippi river floods, 1884; Johnstown (Pa.) flood, 1889, Russian famine, 1892, Sea Islands, S.C., 1893, Armenian massacre, 1896; at request of President McKinley carried relief to Cuba, 1898; did personal field work in Cuba before, during, and after Spanish-Am. War; conducted Red Cross relief at Galveston, Tex., after great disaster, Aug. 1900, and other fields; pres. Nat. First Aid Assn., 1905—, hdqrs. Boston, and Children's Star League; hon. mem. Assn. Mil. Surgeons of U.S., etc. Holds decorations or diplomas of honor from Germany (Iron Cross), Baden, Austria, Servia, Turkey, Armenia, Switzerland, Spain, Russia, Belgium, Cuba; vote of thanks from citizens of Johnstown, Pa., Tex. Legislature, etc.; mentioned in President McKinley's annual message to Congress, Dec. 6, 1898, expressing his own appreciation and that of the Am. people for relief work during Spanish-Am. War; only woman for whom a G.A.R. post has been named. Author: History of Red Cross, 1882 (pub. by Government); America's Relief Expedition to Asia Minor (Armenia), 1896; History of the Red Cross in Peace and War, 1898 (pub. by Internat. Soc., New York); A Story of the Red Cross, 1904; Story of My Childhood, 1907. Died Apr. 12, 1912.

BARTON, Donald Clinton, geologist; b. Stow, Mass., June 29, 1889; s. George Hunt and Eva May (Beede) B.; grad. Cambridge Latin Sch., 1907; Harvard, class of 1911, A.B., 1910, A.M., 1912, Ph.D., 1914; m. Margaret Dunbar Foules, June 26, 1923; 1 dau., Ann Foules. Instr. engring. geology, Washington U., 1914-16; field geologist Empire Gas and Fuel Co., 1916-17; geologist Gulf Coast div. Amerada Petroleum Corp., 1919-23; chief geologist Rycade Oil Corp., 1923-27; chief Torsion Balance and Magnetometer Div., Geophysical Research Corp., 1925-27; cons. geologist and geophysicist, 1927-34; research and consulting geologist and geophysicist Humble Oil and Refining Company, 1935—. Private to Master Signal Electrician (weather forecaster), Meteorological Section Signal Corps, A.E.F., 1917-19. Unitarian. Contbr. many papers on geology and geophysics. Home: Houston, Tex. Died July 8, 1939.

BARTON, Enos M., mfr.; b. Lorraine, N.Y., Dec. 2, 1842; s. Sidney William and Fanny (Bliss) B.; ed. pub. and pvt. schs. and U. of Rochester; m. Katharine S. Richardson, Oct. 28, 1869 (died 1898); 2d, Mary C. Rust, Oct. 6, 1899. Located in Chicago, 1869; became sec. Western Elec. Co., 1872, later v.p. and pres., 1887-Oct. 1908, chmn. bd. of dirs., Oct. 30, 1908—; dir. Merchants Loan & Trust Co. Trustee U. of Chicago. Home: Hinsdale, Ill. Died May 3, 1916.

BARTON, George, author; b. Phila., Pa., Jan. 22, 1866; s. George and Maria (Gormley) B.; pub. sch. edn.; m. Sophia McCauley, June 14, 1893. Began newspaper work with Phila. Inquirer, 1887; sec. to collector of customs, Phila., 1898-1913; editorial writer Phila. Evening Bulletin; now editorial writer Phila. Inquirer. Was sec. of joint legislature com. (Pa.) apptd. to investigate the Soldiers' Orphans' schs. of Pa., 1896. Republican. Catholic. Author: Angels of the Battlefield, 1898; Mystery of Cleverly, 1907; Adventures of the World's Greatest Detectives, 1908; Adventures of Bromley Barnes, 1909; Barry Wynn—A Story of the United States Congress, 1912; Great Cases of Famous Detectives, 1913; Bell Haven Nine, 1914; Bell Haven Five, 1914; Bell Haven Eight, 1915; Bell Haven Eleven, 1915; The World's Greatest Military Spies and Secret Service Agents, 1917; Mystery of the Red Flame, 1918; Strange Adventures of Bromley Barnes, 1919; Celebrated Spies and Strange Mysteries of the Great War, 1919; The Pembroke Mason Affair, 1920; Little Journeys Around Old Philadelphia, 1925; Famous Detective Mysteries, 1926; Great Triumphs of Crime Detection, 1937. Home: Philadelphia, Pa. Died Mar. 16, 1940.

BARTON, George Hunt, geologist; b. Sudbury, Mass., July 8, 1852; s. George Washington and Mary S. (Hunt) B.; lived on a farm there until 21 yrs. old; S.B., Mass. Inst. Tech., 1880; m. Eva May Beede, Sept. 18, 1884; children—Harold Beede (dec.), Donald Clinton, Helen Mary. Asst. in drawing, Mass. Inst. Tech., 1880-81; asst. on Hawaiian govt. survey, Honolulu, 1881-83; asst. in geology, 1883-84, asst. prof. till 1904, Mass. Inst. Tech.; same, Boston U., till 1904; now dir. Teachers' Sch. of Science. Lecturer on geology, Boston U., 1915, Wellesley Coll., 1921-22. Was asst. geologist U.S. Geol. Survey; mem. 6th Peary expdn. to Greenland, 1896. Fellow Am. Acad. Arts and Sciences. Author: Outline of Elementary Lithology, 1900; Outline of Dynamical and Structural Geology; also many geol. papers. Traveled extensively in U.S., British America, Hawaii, and Europe. Home: Cambridge, Mass. Died Nov. 25, 1933.

BARTON, James Levi, clergyman; b. Charlotte, Vt., Sept. 23, 1855; s. Jacob V. and Hannah (Knowles) B.; A.B., Middlebury Coll., 1881, A.M., 1884 (D.D., 1894, LL.D., 1913); grad. Hartford Theol. Sem., 1885; LL.D., Oberlin, 1917; D.D., Dartmouth Coll., 1920; LL.D., Grinnell (Ia.) Coll., 1928; m. Flora E. Holmes, June 3, 1885. Ordained Congl. ministry, 1885; missionary A.B.C.F.M. at Harpoot, Turkey, 1885-92; prof. in Mission Theol. Sem., 1888-92; pres. Euphrates Coll., Harpoot, 1893; became foreign sec. A.B.C.F.M.,

1894, now emeritus secretary. Chmn. Deputation to Japan, 1895, Ceylon and India, 1901, China, 1907; dir. relief expdn. to Near East, 1919; chmn. Near East Relief, Persia, Southern Russia, Turkey, Mesopotamia and Syria; chmn. Corp. Near East Relief, 1914—, also special insp. overseas operations, 1925 and 1931; moderator Internat. Congl. Council, 1920-30; v. chmn. Near East Foundation; rep. of Am. religious, ednl. and philanthropic interests in Near East at Lausanne Peace Conf. Mem. Inst. for Social and Religious Research; trustee Middlebury Coll., Hartford Theol. Sem., Peking Union Med. Coll., Peking U., Am. Coll. (Sofia), Anatolia Coll. (Greece), Internat. Coll. (Smyrna); chmn. Am. gov. bd. Woman's Med. Coll. (India), Madras Woman's Christian Coll., St. Christopher's Training Coll. Author: The Missionary and His Critics, 1906; The Unfinished Task of the Christian Church, 1908; Daybreak in Turkey, 1908; Human Progress Through Missions, 1912; Educational Missions, 1913; Christian Approach to Islam, 1918; Story of Near East Relief, 1930; etc. Has served as lecturer at Bangor, Andover, Chicago, Brunswick and Pacific theol. sems. Home: Brookline, Mass. Died July 21, 1936.

BARTON, James Moore, surgeon; b. Phila., Pa., Oct. 16, 1846; s. James M. and Esther (Rathvon) B.; M.D., Jefferson Med. Coll., 1868; m. Mary E. Craig, Feb. 4, 1908. Resident phys. Episcopal Hos., Phila., 1868-69; asst. to Prof. S. D. Gross, 1869-79; surgeon and prof. clin. surgery, Jefferson Med. Coll., 1879-1900. Surgeon to Charity Hosp., 1869-79; lecturer operative surgery, Phila. Sch. of Anatomy, 1877-82; surgeon to German Hosp., 1879-86; surgeon to Phila. Hosp., 1890-1900. In charge of surg. dept. Phila. Med. Times, 1884-89; asso. editor Sajous' Annual of Universal Med. Sciences, 1889-92; author numerous surg. papers and transl. in various med. jours. Senior fellow Am. Surg. Assn.; fellow Am. Acad. Medicine; mem. Volunteer Med. Service Corps. Cons. surgeon to bd. for examining recruits for World War, 1917-18. Address: Atlantic City, N.J. Died June 28, 1926.

BARTON, John Kennedy, rear adm.; b. Phila., Pa., Apr. 7, 1853; s. Joseph and Margaret B.; grad. U.S. Naval Acad., 1873; m. Mildred S. Scott, 1898. Apptd. cadet engr., Oct. 1, 1871; promoted through grades to capt., July 8, 1907; engr. in chief, rank of rear adm., and retired by reason of physical disability incurred in line of duty, Dec. 22, 1908. Served on Richmond, Spanish-Am. War, 1898; at U.S. Naval Acad., 1902-07; head Dept. Steam Engring., Navy Yard, League Island, Pa., 1907-08; engr. in chief and chief Bur. Steam Engring., Navy Dept., Washington, D.C., 1908; mem. Navy Examining Bd., Washington, 1909-10. Episcopalian. Home: Philadelphia, Pa. Died Dec. 23, 1921.

BARTON, John Wynne, educator; b. Overton, Rusk Co., Tex., Oct. 25, 1892; s. Wm. Henry and Jeffie (Wynne) B.; A.B., Trinity U., Tex., 1913, LL.D., 1927; A.M., Columbia, 1914; studied U. of Chicago; m. Nelle Graham, Nov. 24, 1920; children—Mary Jane, John Wynne. Prof. history and economics, Trinity U., 1914-15; adj. prof., dept. history and economics, Southern Meth. U., Dallas, Tex., 1915-16, asso. prof. and acting dean, 1916-17; asst. dir. Bur. War Risk Ins., 6 mos.; engaged wholesale mercantile business, Dallas, 1919; organizer and 1st dean Dallas Sch. of Commerce; one of publishing agts. M.E. Ch., S., Nashville, 1922-26; became v.p. Ward-Belmont Sch., Nashville, 1926, pres. since Dec. 1933. Pvt., later capt., U.S.A., 1917-18; 1 yr. in France. Trustee Scarritt Coll., Meharry Med. Coll.; mem. bd. dirs. Community Chest (Nashville). Pres. Am. Assn. Jr. Colleges, 1928-29, and mem. exec. com., 1928-36; mem. bd. mgrs. Vanderbilt U. Hosp.; mem. book com. Methodist Pub. House, 1927—. Democrat. Mem. M.E. Ch., S. Home: Nashville, Tenn. Died Sept. 2, 1936.

BARTON, Ralph, artist-caricaturist; b. Kansas City, Mo., Aug. 14, 1891; s. Abraham Pool and Catherine Josephine (Wigginton) B.; ed. pub. schs. and under pvt. tutors, Kansas City; studied art in Paris; m. 4th, Germaine Tailleferre (composer), of Paris. Contbr. since 1910, to mags., including Puck, Life, Judge, Collier's, Cosmopolitan, Woman's Home Companion, Vanity Fair, Harper's Bazar, Liberty, etc.; reported war in pictures for Puck, 1915; assisted in reviving and popularizing caricature with drawings in Vanity Fair, 1921-22, also theatre curtain of caricatures for the Chauve-Souris, 1922, and drawings for spl. edition of Balzac's Droll Stories, 1925. Chevalier Légion d'Honneur, 1927. Author: Science in Rhyme Without Reason, 1924; God's Country, 1929; also illustrations for "Gentlemen Prefer Blondes," 1925. Dramatic editor of Life. Home: New York, N. Y. Died May 20, 1931.

BARTON, Robert McKinney, lawyer; b. Greenville, Tenn., Nov. 26, 1851; s. Robert McFarland and Hannah (McFarland) B.; student U. of Va.; studied law under father and uncle, Judge Robert McFarland; m. Virginia McFarland, Oct. 4, 1876 (died 1925); children—Robert McF., McKinney, Grace (dec.). Admitted to bar, 1874, and practiced at Chattanooga, Tenn.; was mem. Barton & Barton, Memphis, Tenn.; served as U.S. commr.; alderman of Chattanooga, 1889-99; mem. Tenn. Senate, 1892-94; Judge Court of Chancery Appeals, later Court of Civil Appeals, 1895-1910; mem. U.S. Ry. Labor Bd., 1920-24 (elected chmn. bd., Apr. 17, 1920); settled at St. Petersburg, Fla., and practiced with son, McKinney, as Barton & Barton. Democrat. Presbyn. K.P. Home: St. Petersburg, Fla. Died Apr. 5, 1928.

BARTON, Robert T., lawyer; b. Winchester, Va., Nov. 24, 1842; s. David W. and Fanny L. (Jones) B.; brother of Randolph B.; acad. edn., Winchester and Bloomfield, Va.; m. Catherine K. Knight, Feb. 19, 1868 (died June 11, 1887); 2d, Gertrude W. Baker, June 10, 1890. Mem. Rockridge Arty., Stonewall Brigade, 1st Va. Brigade, comd. first by Brig. Gen. T. J. Jackson (Stonewall Jackson); was of six brothers in C.S.A. Admitted to bar, 1865; sr. mem. Barton & Boyd, 1869-1910; pres. Farmers & Merchants Nat. Bank, 1902—. Mem. Va. Ho. of Rep., 1883-85; mayor of Winchester, 1899-1903. Democrat (Anti-Bryan). Episcopalian. Author: Barton's Law Practice, 1878; Barton's Chancery Practice, 1881; Virginia Colonial Decisions, 1909. Home: Winchester, Va. Died Jan. 17, 1917.

BARTON, Samuel Marx, univ. prof.; b. nr. Winchester, Va., May 9, 1859; s. Joseph M. and Mary (Neill) B.; A.B., U. of Va., 1883, Ph.D., 1885; fellow Johns Hopkins, 1893-94; m. Mary Millicent Tidball, Dec. 28, 1897; children—Mary Neill, Helen (Mrs. Edward M. Claytor). Taught in pub. and pvt. schs., 1876-77, 1881-82; prof. mathematics, Emory and Henry Coll., 1885-93; prof. mathematics and civil engring., Va. Agrl. and Mech. Coll., 1894-95; prof. mathematics and acting prof. civil engring., 1895-1907, prof. mathematics, 1907—, U. of the South. Episcopalian. Democrat. Author: Elementary Treatise on the Theory of Equations, 1889; The Elements of Plane Surveying (including leveling), 1904. Home: Sewanee, Tenn. Died Jan. 5, 1926.

BARTON, Silas Reynolds, congressman; b. New London, Ia., May 21, 1872; s. Eli B. and Teressa (Nugen) B.; ed. Aurora (Neb.) High Sch., Peru (Neb.) State Normal Sch.; m. Ellen Metcalfe; apptd. civil gov. Canal Zone, Feb. 20, 1913. Farmer and sch. teacher to 1898; deputy county treas. Hamilton Co., Neb., 1898-1901 (resigned); grand recorder A.O.U.W. of Neb., 1901-08; auditor State of Neb., 1909-13; mem. 63d Congress (1913-15) 5th Neb. Dist.; Republican. Mem. many fraternal orders. Home: Grand Island, Neb. Died 1915.

BARTON, Wilfred Mason, M.D.; b. Washington, D.C., July 16, 1871; s. William Henry and Harriet (Garrison) B.; M.D., Georgetown U., 1892, M.A., 1925; m. Mary A. Quinn, Aug. 12, 1905. Practiced in Washington, D.C., 1896—; prof. medicine, Georgetown U.; attending phys. Georgetown Univ. Hosp., Columbia Hosp., Gallinger Hosp.; mem. Med. Advisory Bd. No. 3, D.C., during the war, F.A.C.P. Republican. Mason. Author: (with W. A. Wells) Thesaurus of Medical Words and Phrases, 1903; Manual of Vital Function Testing Methods, 1916; Therapeutic Index, 1917; The Road to Washington, 1919; Medicine (Vol. X in Popular Science Series), 1922; (with Dr. Yater) Symptom-Diagnosis, Regional and General, 1927; also articles in med. jours. Home: Washington, D.C. Died 1930.

BARTON, William Eleazar, clergyman; b. Sublette, Ill., June 28, 1861; s. Dr. Jacob B. and Helen (Methven) B.; B.S., Berea Coll., 1885, M.S., 1888, A.M., 1890; B.D., Oberlin Theol. Sem., 1890; D.D., Berea, 1895; LL.D., Knox, 1913, Drury, 1923; Litt.D., Carleton, 1924; m. Esther Treat Bushnell, July 23, 1885; (died Nov. 7, 1925); children—Bruce, Charles William, Helen (Mrs. Clyde S. Stilwell), Fred B., Robert S. Ordained Congl. ministry, 1885; pastor Robbins, Tenn., 1885-87, Litchfield, O., 1887-90, Wellington, O., 1890-93, Shawmut Congl. Ch., Boston, 1893-99, First Ch., Oak Park, Ill., Mar. 1, 1899-Aug. 31, 1924. Made tour around the world, 1925. Asso. editor Bibliotheca Sacra; editor pastors' dept. of The Advance, 1904-12, editor-in-chief, same, 1913-17, when it was merged with the Congregationalist, and since corr. editor the Congregationalist and Advance. Lecturer on applied practical theology, Chicago Theol. Sem., 1905-09; on ecclesiastical law, Chicago Theol. Sem., 1911-24; on staff Youth's Companion, 1900-17 and 1925—. Corporate mem. A.B.C.F.M.; v.p. Congl. S.S. and Pub. Soc., 1899-1905, Am. Peace Soc., 1898-1915; dir. Congl. Ednl. Soc., 1894-1915, Ill. Home Missionary Soc., 1900-06 (pres. 1906), Chicago Theol. Sem., 1900-10; trustee Berea Coll., 1896—; v.p. American Missionary Assn., 1913-14; pres. Trustees Union Theol. Coll., 1916—; del. Nat. Congl. Council, 1895, 98, 04, 07, 10, 13, 15, 17, 19, 21, 23, 25, 27, 29; sec. commn. of 19 on polity, and principal author of the Kansas City Creed, 1913; delegate to International Council, 1899-1930, and author of its constitution, 1920; delegate Tri-Ch. Union, 1906-07. Moderator Nat. Council Congl. Chs., 1921-23; del. to World Conf. on Faith and Order (Lausanne), 1927. Author: Life of the Hills of Kentucky, 1889; The Improvement of Perfection, 1900; I Go A-Fishing, 1901; Jesus of Nazareth, His Life and the Scenes of His Ministry, 1904; Four Weeks of Family Worship, 1906; (with Sydney Strong and Theo. G. Soares) His Last Week; His Life; His Friends; His Great Apostle, 1906-07; Pocket Congregational Manual, 1910; The Law of Congregational Usage, 1915; Congregational Creeds and Covenants, 1917; The Parables of Safed the Sage, 1917; The Soul of Abraham Lincoln, 1919; Wit and Wisdom of Safed the Sage, 1919; Abraham Lincoln and His Books, 1920; The Paternity of Abraham Lincoln, 1920; Safed and Keturah, 1921; The Life of Clara Barton, 1921; More Parables of Safed the Sage, 1923; Life of Lincoln (2 vols.), 1925; Fun and Philosophy of Safed the Sage, 1925; My Faith in Immortality, 1926; A Beautiful Blunder—the True Story of Lincoln's Letter to Mrs. Bixby, 1926; The Great Good Man, (Young Folks' Life of Lincoln), 1927; and many others. Editor: The Young Folks' Bible Library (8 vols.), 1911; Zachary Taylor (hitherto unpublished address by Abraham Lincoln); The Influence of Chicago on Abraham Lincoln; Abraham Lincoln and Walt Whitman, 1928; The Father of His Country (Young people's Life of Washington), 1928; Abraham Lincoln and the Hooker Letter, 1928; The Lincoln of the Biographers, with a Bibliography of Lincoln Biographies, 1929; The Lineage of Lincoln, 1929; Lincoln at Gettysburg, 1930. Lecturer on Biographical Leadership and Practical Theology, Vanderbilt U., 1928—; organizer, 1928, and minister Collegeside Ch., Nashville, Tenn. Home: Oak Park, Ill., and Foxboro, Mass. Died Dec. 7, 1930.

BARUCH, Emanuel de Marnay, M.D.; b. San Francisco, Calif., Feb. 22, 1870; s. Myron de M. and Elisabeth (Fourman) B.; M.D., Coll. Phys. and Surg. (Columbia), 1889, U. of Tübingen, Germany, 1891, hon. M.D., 1922; studied at univs. of Munich, Berlin and Paris; hon. mem. U. of Innsbruck; m. Bertha Schuyler Pfister. Began practice in N.Y. City, 1889; prof. bacteriology and pathology, U. State of N.Y., 1892—; prof. bacteriology and therapeutics, Met. Post-Grad. Med. Sch.; consulting phys. to Hosp. for Deformities and Joint Diseases and to Philanthropic Hosp. Mem. Internat. Tuberculosis Cong., Paris and Washington, D.C.; rep. Med. Soc. State of N.Y. at Internat. Med. Congress, London, 1913. Decorated with Grand Cross of the Red Cross (Austria), 1922; Grand Cross of the Red Cross (Germany), 1926; Grand Cordon of Order of the Holy Sepulchre, 1927; Grand gold cross of Austria, 1925; Grand gold medal, U. of Innsbruck, 1929; Medal of Honor of the City of Darmstadt, Germany. Unitarian. Author: Judith and Arropherius, drama produced by Sybil Thorndike, London, 1928, and at State Theatre, Darmstadt, 1929. Home: New York, N.Y. Died 1935.

BARUCH, Simon, physician; b. Schwersen, Germany, July 29, 1840; s. Bernard and Teresa (Green) B.; ed. Royal Gymnasium, Posen, Germany; M.D., Med. Coll. of Va., 1862; m. Isabel Wolfe, Nov. 27, 1867. Surgeon in the field in Gen. R. E. Lee's army, C.S.A., 1862-65; captured in charge of wounded on battlefields of South Mountain, Md., and Gettysburg, Pa.; practiced medicine Camden, S.C., 1865-81; since then in New York; specialist as cons. physician in chronic diseases. Diagnosed first recorded case of perforating appendicitis successfully operated on, reported by Dr. Sands, in N.Y. Medical Journal, 1889; introduced free municipal bathhouses, prof. hydrotherapy, College Phys. and Surg. (Columbia.) Chmn. S.C. State Bd. Health, 1880. Author: Uses of Water in Modern Medicine, 1892; The Principles and Practice of Hydrotherapy, 3 edits.; both books also translated and published in Germany and latter in France. Hosp. erected in his honor at Camden, S.C., 1913; free municipal baths named in his honor, Chicago, 1910, New York, 1917. Home: New York, N.Y. Died June 3, 1921.

BARUS, Carl, physicist; b. Cincinnati, Feb. 19, 1856; s. Prof. Carl and Sophia (Mollman) B.; attended Columbia, 1874-76; U. of Wurzburg, Germany, 1876-80, Ph.D., 1879; (LL.D., Brown, 1907, Clark U., 1909); m. Annie G. Howes, Jan. 20, 1887; children—Maxwell, Deborah Howes. Physicist, U.S. Geol. Survey, 1880-92; prof. Meteorology, U.S. Weather Bur., 1892-93; physicist, Smithsonian Instn., 1893-95; prof. physics, 1895-1926, prof. emeritus, 1926—, dean grad. dept., 1903-26, Brown Univ. Awarded the Rumford Medal of Am. Acad. Arts and Sciences for various researches in heat. Mem. advisory com. Carnegie Instn., 1902; mem. hon. com. of Internat. Congress on Radiology, Brussels, 1905, 1910. Fellow Am. Acad. Arts and Sciences; mem. numerous socs. Speaker for Am. Physics, World's Congress, St. Louis, 1904. Original contributions to science number about 400 titles. Author: The Electrical and Magnetic Properties of the Iron Carburets, 1885; Subsidence of Fine Solid Particles in Liquids, 1886; Physical Properties of the Iron Carburets, 1886; The Measurement of High Temperatures, 1889; Viscosity of Solids, 1891; Die Physikalische Behandlung Hoher Temperaturen, 1892; Compressibility of Liquids, 1892; Mechanism of Solid Viscosity, 1892; Volume Thermodynamics of Liquids, 1892; High Temperature Work in Igneous Fusion, 1893; Condensation of Atmospheric Moisture, 1895; Experiments with Ionized Air, 1901; The Structure of the Nucleus, 1902; Nucleation of the Atmosphere, 1905; Nucleation of the Uncontaminated Air, 1906; Condensation Induced by Nuclei and by Ions, 1907, part II, 1908, part III,

1909, part IV, 1910; Elliptic Interferences, 1911, 2d vol., 1913; 3d vol., 1915; Diffusion of Gases through Liquids, 1913; Interferences of Reversed and Non-reversed Spectra, vol. I, 1916, vol. II, 1917, vols. III and IV, 1919; Interferometer Experiments in Acoustics, vol. I, 1921, vol. II, 1923, vol. III, 1925; Acoustic Experiments with Pin-Hole Probe and the Interferometer, 1927. Edited The Laws of Gases, 1899. Home: Providence, R.I. Died Sept. 20, 1935.

BASCOM, John, educator; b. Genoa, N.Y., May 1, 1827; s. Rev. John and Laura (Woodbridge) B.; A.B., Williams, 1849, A.M., 1852; grad. Andover Theol. Sem., 1855; (LL.D., Amherst, 1873, Williams, 1897, U. of Wis., 1905; D.D., Iowa Coll., 1880); m. Emma Curtiss, Jan. 8, 1856; father of Florence B. Prof. rhetoric, Williams Coll., 1855-74; pres. U. of Wis., 1874-87; lecturer on sociology, 1887-91, 1901-03, prof. polit. science, 1891-1901, Williams Coll. Author: Political Economy, 1859; Æsthetics, 1862; Philosophy of Rhetoric, 1865; Principles of Psychology, 1869; Science, Philosophy and Religion, 1871; Philosophy of English Literature, 1874; Philosophy of Religion, 1876; Growth and Grades of Intelligence, 1878; Ethics, 1879; Natural Theology, 1880: Science of Mind (a recast of Principles of Psychology), 1881; Words of Christ, 1883; Problems in Philosophy, 1885; Sociology, 1887; The New Theology, 1891; Historical Interpretation of Philosophy, 1893; Social Theory, 1895; Evolution and Religion, 1897; Growth of Nationality in U.S., 1899; God and His Goodness, 1901. Home: Williamstown, Mass. Died 1911.

BASE, Daniel, chemist; b. Baltimore, Md., Sept. 6, 1869; grad. Baltimore City Coll., 1888; A.B., Johns Hopkins, 1891, Ph.D., 1895. Prof. chemistry and plant histology, Md. Coll. Pharmacy, 1895-1920; prof. inorganic chemistry, Coll. Phys. and Surg., Baltimore, 1899-1904; prof. inorganic chemistry, Med. Dept., U. of Md., 1904-12; chief chemist Hynson, Westcott & Dunning, Baltimore, 1920—. Author: Elements of Vegetable Histology, 1898; (with Dr. William Simon) Simon-Base Manual of Chemistry, 1923. Home: Baltimore, Md. Died June 17, 1926.

BASHFORD, Herbert, author; b. Sioux City, Ia., Mar. 4, 1871; s. Frank Walker and Alice (Beals) B.; ed. pub. and pvt. schs.; m. Kinnie, d. Senator J. A. Cole, of Tacoma, Wash., 1891; 1 dau., Alice Mary. Librarian, Pub. Library, Tacoma, and state librarian of Washington, 1897-1901; editorial staff San Francisco Bulletin, 1909-19. Author: Northwest Nature Stories, 1897; Songs from Puget Sea, 1898; The Tenting of the Tillicums, 1905; At the Shrine of Song, 1909; Yosemite (poem), 1924; A Man Unafraid—the Story of John Charles Fremont, 1927; Stories of Western Pioneers, 1927. Wrote (dramas): Running for Governor; The Defiance of Doris; The Woman He Married, 1910 (prod. by Virginia Harned); The Voice Within; Taken In, 1920, prod. by Henry B. Walthall; Mona Montez, 1926. Home: Piedmont, Calif. Died July 13, 1928.

BASHFORD, James Whitford, bishop; b. Fayette, Wis., May 29, 1849; s. Rev. Samuel and Mary Ann (McKee) B.; A.B., U. of Wis., 1873, A.M., 1876; S.T.B., Boston U., 1876, Ph.D., 1881; grad. Sch. of Oratory, 1878; (D.D., Northwestern, 1890; LL.D., Wesleyan, 1903, U. of Wis., 1912); m. Jane M., d. Hon. W. W. Field, of Madison, Wis., Sept. 24, 1878. Tutor Greek, U. of Wis., 1874; ordained M.E. ministry, 1878; pastoral supply of Harrison Sq., Boston, 1876-78; pastor Jamaica Plain, Mass., 1878-80, Auburndale, Mass., 1881-04, Portland, Me., 1884-87, Buffalo, N.Y., 1887-89; pres. Ohio Wesleyan U., 1889-1904; elected bishop M.E. Ch., 1904. Held conferences in U.S., 1904 and 1906; organized China Centennial Thank Offering, 1907-08, resulting in spl. contribution of $600,000, toward missionary work in China; assisted in organizing relief measures in China famine dist., 1907; visited India on missionary tour, 1907; del. World's Missionary Conf., Edinburg, 1910. Author: Outline of Science of Religion, 1891; The Awakening of China, 1906; China and Methodism, 1907; God's Missionary Plan for the World, 1907; China—An Interpellation, 1916; Oregon Missions, 1918. Died Mar. 18, 1919.

BASHORE, Harvey Brown, physician; b. W. Fairview, Pa., July 31, 1864; s. Dr. D. W. and Amanda (Brown) B.; A.B., Yale, 1886; M.D., U. of Pa., 1889; unmarried. In med. practice, 1889—. Author: Outlines of Rural Hygiene; Sanitation of a Country House, 1905; Outlines of Practical Sanitation, 1906. Home: W. Fairview, Pa. Died 1934.

BASKERVILL, Charles Read, prof. English lit.; b. Covington, Tenn., Apr. 17, 1872; s. of George Booth and Sallie Lewis (Read) B.; B.A., Vanderbilt U., 1896, M.A., 1898; Ph. D., U. of Chicago, 1911; studied in Europe, 1923-24; m. Catharine Pendleton Quarles, Aug. 19, 1903; 1 dau., Latham. Asst. in English, Vanderbilt U., 1898-99; head of dept. of English, Central State Normal Sch., Okla., 1903-05; instr. English U. of Tex., 1905-11; fellow in English, 1901-02, 1907-08, instr., 1911-12, asst. prof., 1912-15, asso. prof., 1915-19, prof., 1919—, chmn. of dept. of English, 1933—, U. of Chicago. Mem. bd. of editors, 1914—, editor English Sect., 1916-21, and mng. editor, 1918-21, of Modern Philology; research associate Huntington Library, 1929-30. Author: English Elements in Jonson's Early Comedy, 1911; Some Evidence for Early Romantic Plays in England, 1916; Dramatic Aspects of Medieval Folk Festivals in England, 1920; The Elizabethan Jig and Related Song Drama, 1929; also introduction to Plutarch's Quyete of Mynde (transl. by Sir T. Wyatt), 1931, and editor Elizabethan Drama (with V. B. Heltzel and A. H. Nethercot), 1933. Died July 22, 1935.

BASKERVILLE, Charles, chemist; b. Noxubee Co., Miss., June 18, 1870; s. Charles and Augusta Louisa (Johnston) B.; studied U. of Miss., 1886-87; grad. U. of Va., 1890; studied Vanderbilt U., 1891; U. of Berlin, 1893; (Ph.D., U. of N.C., 1894); m. Mary Boylan Snow. Instr., 1891-94, asst. prof. chemistry, 1894-1900, prof. chemistry and dir. chem. lab., 1900-04, U. of N.C.; prof. chemistry and dir., Coll. City of New York, 1904—. Discovered the chem. elements, carolinium and berzelium; investigations on chemistry of anæsthetics. Mason. Author: School Chemistry, 1898; Key to School Chemistry, 1898; Radium and Its Applications in Medicine; General Inorganic Chemistry, 1909; Laboratory Exercises (with R. W. Curtis), 1909; Progressive Problems in Chemistry (with W. L. Estabrooke); Qualitative Analysis (with L. J. Curtman); Municipal Chemistry (and editor with other experts); Anesthesia (with J. T. Gwathmey); also numerous scientific, ednl. and technol. articles. Inventor processes for refining oils, hydrogenation of oils, plastic compositions, reinforced lead, etc. Died Jan. 28, 1922.

BASKETT, James Newton, author; b. in Nicholas Co., Ky., Nov. 1, 1849; s. William B. and Nancy E. (Maffitt) B.; Ph.B., U. of Mo., 1872, A.M., 1893; m. Jeannie Gordon Morrison, Feb. 17, 1874. Student of comparative vertebrate anatomy, with ornithology as a specialty; presented paper at World's Congress of Ornithologists (Chicago, 1893) on Some Hints at the Kinship of Birds as Shown by Their Eggs. Author: The Story of the Birds, 1896; The Story of the Fishes, 1899; The Story of the Amphibians and Reptiles, 1902; also novels—At You-All's House, 1898; As the Light Led, 1900; Sweet Brier and Thistledown, 1902; also papers on the early Spanish Expdn. in the South and Southwest, etc. Home: Mexico, Mo. Died June 14, 1925.

BASSETT, Samuel Eliot, prof. Greek; b. Wilton, Conn., Aug. 11, 1873; s. Benjamin Franklin and Mary Louise (Brush) B.; prep. edn., Wilton (Conn.) Acad. and Hopkins Grammar Sch., New Haven, Conn.; A.B., Yale, 1898, Ph.D., 1905; grad. study U. of Berlin, U. of Freiburg, Am. Sch. Classical Studies at Athens; m. Bertha May Raymond, June 18, 1903; children—Raymond Eliot, Catharine Brewster (Mrs. G. I. Hagar, 2d), Thomas Day Seymour. Instructor in Greek, Yale U., 1902-03, tutor, 1903-05; prof. Greek, Univ. of Vt., 1905—; instr. in Greek and archæology, Columbia, summers 1913-14. Organizer and adminstr. War Service Co., U. of Vt., 1918-19. Mem. mng. com. Am. Sch. Classical Studies at Athens, 1905—, chmn. com. on fellowships, 1919—, visiting prof., 1931-32. Republican. Conglist. Contbr., chiefly on Homeric meter and style, to Am. Jour. Philology, Classical Jour., Classical Rev., Classical Quarterly, Classical Philology, Classical Weekly, Am. Jour. Archæology, Trans. Am. Philol. Assn., etc. Home: Burlington, Vt. Died Dec. 21, 1936.

BASSETT, William Hastings, metallurgist; b. New Bedford, Mass., Mar. 7, 1868; s. William Albert and Almira Durfee (Mayhew) B.; S.B., Mass. Inst. Tech., 1891; m. Sarah H. Whiting, Nov. 3, 1892; children—Alice Whiting, William Hastings, Jr., Edward Whiting (dec.). Chemist with Popes Island Mfg. Co., 1891-93, supt. 1893-95; teacher science, Swain Free Sch., 1895-1900; chemist N.J. Zinc Co., 1900-02; chemist Coe Brass Mfg. Co., 1902-03; chief chemist and metallurgist, 1903-12; tech. supt. and metallurgist Am. Brass Co., 1912-30; metallurgical mgr. of same company, 1930—. Mem. metall. advisory bd. U.S. Bur. Standards and U.S. Army Ordnance Dept. Trustee Pub. Library, Cheshire, Conn. Awarded James Douglas medal by Am. Inst. Mining and Metall. Engrs., 1925. Republican. Conglist. Mason. Home: Cheshire, Conn. Died July 21, 1934.

BASKETTE, Gideon Hicks, newspaper editor; b. Rutherford Co., Tenn., Mar. 11, 1845; s. Dr. William T. and Melissa Ann (Ellis) B.; acad. edn. at Murfreesboro, Tenn.; left coll. 1861, to enter C.S.A.; served through Civil War; m. Anna E. McFadden, Sept. 24, 1867. Editor Murfreesboro News, 1874-82, Nashville American, 1882, Chattanooga Democrat, 1883; on staff Cincinnati News, 1883; editor People's Paper, Chattanooga, 1883-84; mng. editor, 1884-85, editor-in-chief, 1885-1911, Nashville Banner; was pres. Nashville Banner Pub. Co. until 1890; editor The Democrat (daily morning), Nashville, 1911-13. Pres. and librarian Carnegie Pub. Library, 1886-1923. Home: Nashville, Tenn. Died Mar. 27, 1927.

BASS, Edgar Wales, col. U.S.A.; b. Prairie du Chien, Wis., Oct. 30, 1843; s. Jacob Wales and Martha Darrah (Brunson) B.; pvt. and q.m. sergt. 8th Minn. Inf., Aug. 13, 1862-June 30, 1864; grad. West Point, 1868; studied Post-Grad. Sch. for Mil. Engrs., Willets Point, N.Y.; m. Adèle Smith, June 26, 1879. Bvt. 2d lt. U.S. Engrs., June 15, 1868; 2d lt., Feb. 15, 1869; 1st lt., Feb. 14, 1871; prof. mathematics, West Point, Apr. 17, 1878; col. U.S.A.; retired at own request, after 36 yrs. service, Oct. 7, 1898. Asst. astronomer, U.S. Transit of Venus Expdn. to New Zealand, 1874-75; U.S. Expdn. Eclipse of Sun, Colo., 1878. Author: Introduction to the Differential Calculus, 1888; Elements of Trigonometry (Ludlow's), 1888; Elements of Differential Calculus, 1896-1905. Home: Bar Harbor, Me. Died Nov. 6, 1918.

BASS, John Foster, war corr.; b. Chicago, Ill., 1866; s. Perkins and Clara (Foster) B.; A.B., Harvard, 1891, LL.B., 1894; m. Abigail Bailey; 1 son, John F. Admitted to N.Y. bar, 1894. Campaigns: 1895, in Egypt with English and Cretan insurrection; 1896, across Armenia at time of massacre; 1897, Cretan rebellion and Greek War; 1898, Spanish-Am. War; 1899, Philippine insurrection; 1900, Boxer insurrection in China, and march of allies to relief of Pekin; 1903, Bulgarian uprising in Macedonia, 1904, Russo-Japanese War. Corr. with Russian Army, in Poland and Galicia, 1914-15, with armies in France, Italy and Balkans, 1915-17, with Italian Army, Jan. 1918; on govt. mission to Italian front, 1918; Am. and French fronts in France, 1918; Peace Conf., Paris, and official rep. Am. press with mission to Poland, 1919. Chmn. exec. council and treas. Nat. Conservation Assn., 1909—. Chmn. Illinois Progressive State Com., 1913. Author: The Peace Tangle, 1920; America and the Balance Sheet of Europe, 1921. Home: Chicago, Ill. Died Apr. 16, 1931.

BASS, John Meredith, educator; b. Nashville, Tenn., Oct. 23, 1845; s. John M. and Malvina (Grundy) B.; grad. Bethany Coll., W.Va., law dept. Cumberland Univ.; law student, Univ. of Va.; m. Mary Wharton Berry, Dec. 1868. Sec. and treas. U. of Nashville, 1894—; sec. Tenn. Hist. Soc. 12 yrs.; commr. Watkins Inst. 6 yrs., pres. bd. 4 yrs.; co-editor Am. Hist. Mag., Nashville, 2 yrs. Writer of various hist. monographs. Home: Nashville, Tenn. Died 1908.

BASS, Joseph Parker, publisher; b. Randolph, Vt., 1835; s. Samuel and Margaret (Parker) B.; ed. common schs. and acad., Randolph; m. Mary March, 1866 (dec. 1899). Began as clk. in dry goods house of Hocum Hosford, Lowell, Mass., 1854, later engaging in same business for self; removed business to Bangor, Me., 1863, and continued until 1870, after which engaged extensively in buying and selling timber lands and city real estate; has devoted attention, from 1879, chiefly to pub. Bangor Daily and Weekly Commercial; pres. and treas. J. P. Bass Pub. Co.; mayor City of Bangor, 1873; mem. Me. Ho. of Rep., 1876; chmn. exec. com. World's Fair Commrs. from Me. to Columbian Expn., Chicago, 1893; was pres. Eastern Me. State Fair Assn. for 12 yrs.; dir. 2d Nat. Bank of Bangor. Home: Bangor, Me. Died Mar. 26, 1919.

BASSETT, Austin Bradley, clergyman; b. Allegan, Mich., Jan. 23, 1859; s. Col. Chauncey J. and Lydia Frances (Bradley) B.; A.B., Williams Coll., 1881; studied Hartford Theol. Sem.; B.D., Chicago Theol. Sem., 1887; studied U. of Berlin, 1897; (D.D. Williams, 1906); m. Mary Ely, July 30, 1892. Teacher Latin and Greek, Temple Grove Sem. and Saratoga Acad., Saratoga Springs, N.Y., 1881-82; prof. mathematics and physics, Mass. Agrl. Coll., 1882-84; ordained Congl. ministry, 1887; pastor Williamstown, Mass., 1887-91, Ware, Mass., 1891-1905; stated supply Park Ch., Hartford, 1906, 1910; asso. prof. exptl. theology and sec., Hartford Theol. Sem., 1905—. Home: Hartford, Conn. Died Oct. 5, 1916.

BASSETT, Ebenezer Don Carlos, diplomatist; b. Ditchfield, Conn., Oct. 16, 1833; grad. Conn. State Normal Sch., 1853; studied at Yale Coll.; was teacher in New Haven and Phila. for 16 yrs.; U.S. minister to Hayti, 1869-77, and 1879-88; was Haytian consul and consul gen. in New York. Home: New York, N.Y. Died 1908.

BASSETT, John Spencer, college prof.; b. Tarboro, N.C., Sept. 10, 1867; s. Richard Baxter and Mary (Wilson) B.; A.B., Trinity Coll. N.C., 1888; Ph.B., Johns Hopkins, 1894; m. Jessie Lewellin, Aug. 10, 1892; children—Richard Horace, Margaret Byrd. Prof. history, Trinity Coll., N.C., 1893-1906, Smith Coll., 1906—. Editor South Atlantic Quarterly, 1902-05; lecturer, Yale, 1907-08, New York U., 1909. Mem. Nat. Inst. Arts and Letters, Am. Acad. Arts and Sciences, and other socs. Author: Constitutional Beginnings of North Carolina, 1894; Slavery and Servitude in Colony of North Carolina, 1896; The Regulators of North Carolina, 1896; Anti-Slavery Leaders of North Carolina, 1898; Slavery in the State of North Carolina, 1899; The Federalist System, 1905; Life of Andrew Jackson, 1911; A Short History of the United States, 1913; The Plain Story of American History, 1915; The Middle Group of American Historians, 1917; The Lost Fruits of Waterloo, 1918, 2d edit. 1919; Our War with Germany, 1919; Selections from the Federalist, 1921. Editor: The Correspondence of Andrew Jackson (6 vols.), 1925—. Home: Northampton, Mass. Died Jan. 27, 1928.

BASSET, Norman Leslie, jurist; b. Winslow, Me., June 23, 1869; s. Josiah Williams and Ella Susan (Cornish) B.; grad. Coburn Classical Inst., 1887; A.B., Colby Coll., 1891; LL.B., Harvard, 1898; LL.D., U. of Me. and Colby Coll., 1925; m. Lula J. Holden, June 24, 1903. Began at Augusta, Me., 1908; mem. Cornish & Bassett, 1901-07, alone 1907-25; mem. Me. Enforcement Commn., 1905-07; mem. City Council, Augusta, 1911; mem. Bd. of Aldermen, 1912-15; became asso. justice Supreme Court of Me., Mar. 26, 1925, for term ending 1932. Pres. Augusta Savings Bank. Trustee Colby Coll. Republican. Unitarian. Mason. Home: Augusta, Me. Died Sept. 29, 1931.

BASSETT, William Austin, civil engr.; b. Boston, Mass., Sept. 29, 1876; s. Isaac Austin and Annie Mary (Tuson) B.; B.S. in C.E., Harvard, 1901; m. Grace Loring, Mar. 30, 1905. With engr. corps, Pa. R.R., 1901-04; engring. dept., Pittsburgh, Pa., 1905-07; mem. faculty, Carnegie Tech. Sch., Pittsburgh, 1908-10, also cons. practice; asst. chief editor Engineering Record, 1911-12; cons. engr. N.Y. Bur. Municipal Research, 1912—; expert on roads. Mem. Nat. Municipal League, Harvard Assn. Engrs. Unitarian. Author: Problems of Road Administration, 1917. Contbr. to tech. press on municipal and state problems relating to engring. Home: Mt. Vernon, N.Y. Died May 16, 1929.

BASSFORD, Homer S., newspaper writer; b. Mexico, Audrain Co., Mo., July 20, 1870; s. James C. and Catherine (Osborne) B.; ed. pub. schs. and acad.; m. Etta Overman Chase, June 25, 1892; children—James Chase, Wallace O'Neill. Began with Mexico (Mo.) Ledger; Sunday editor, 1889, later city editor, Kansas City Times; dramatic and music critic, 1893-1903, Sunday editor, news editor, 1903-07, European corr., 1906, St. Louis Republic; later editor St. Louis Times; with St. Louis Star-Times, 1932—; sec. St. Louis Newspaper Publishers' Assn., 1916-24. Trustee Mo. Hist. Soc. Democrat. Methodist. Has written many reviews of drama and music, politics, history; also at different times European corr. for Am. newspapers; series of Mississippi river articles on river practice and tradition. Home: St. Louis, Mo. Died Jan. 10, 1938.

BATCHELDER, Frank Charles, ry. official; b. Fall River, Wis., May 27, 1857; s. Sanford L. and Dolly B.; ed. common schs.; m. Ursula G. O'Connell, Apr. 2, 1894; 1 dau., Dorothy. Operator and train dispatcher. C.,M.&St.P.Ry., 1874-88; train dispatcher, 1888-93, asst. supt., 1893-99, supt. Wis. and Peninsula div., Feb.-July 1899, M.,St.P.&S.S.M.Ry.; supt. northwestern div., at Garrett, Ill., 1899-1901, Newark (O.) div., 1901-05, Chicago div., 1905-07, gen. supt. main line system, Baltimore, 1907-10, B.& O.R.R.; 1st v.p., 1910, pres., 1912-29, B.&O. Chicago Terminal R.R.; resident v.p. B.&O.R.R., 1915-29. Home: Chicago, Ill. Deceased.

BATCHELDER, Richard N., brig. gen. (retired, July 27, 1896); b. Lake Village, N. H., July 27, 1832; ed. at Manchester, N.H. Entered volunteer service, 1861; rose through successive ranks until bvtd. brig. gen., March 13, 1865; after war in regular service, and became brig. gen. and q.m., U.S. Army, June 26, 1890. Awarded medal of honor for most distinguished gallantry in action during Civil war. Unmarried. Died 1901.

BATCHELDER, Wallace, lawyer; b. Andover, Vt., June 20, 1875; s. Edmund Abel and Lizzie Emma (Nutting) B.; grad. Chester (Vt.) Acad., 1892; m. Maude Leone Thompson, Oct. 16, 1901. Studied law in office of Waterman & Martin, Brattleboro, Vt., and later in office of Hunton & Stickney, Bethel, Vt.; admitted Vt. bar, May 17, 1904, to practice in U.S. cts., Sept. 11, 1905. Counsel for Roosevelt forces in contests before Rep. Nat. Com., Chicago, June, 1912. Chmn. Vt. Roosevelt Com. presdl. campaign, 1912; was on stump in Vt., N.H. and Mass. Trooper in 1st U.S. Vol. Cav. (Roosevelt's Rough Riders), 1898, Spanish-Am. War; commd. by Pres. McKinley 1st lt. U.S. Vols., Aug. 17, 1899; comdr. Co. B, and later Co. C, of the 46th U.S. Inf., Vols. during campaign in P.I.; hon. disch. May 31, 1901. Mason. Republican. Episcopalian. Home: Bethel, Vt. Died June 19, 1919.

BATCHELLER, George Clinton, mfr.; b. Grafton, Mass.; s. Moses Leland and Sarah Ann (Phillips) B., both of Colonial ancestry; grad. Barre (Vt.) Acad., 1855; (LL.D., Coll. of William and Mary, 1907, L.H.D., Ohio Northern U., 1913); m. Sarah Adaline Cummings, Dec. 26, 1859; m. 2d, Truene Ruth Geddes, Sept. 17, 1913. In dry goods house Turner, Wilson & Co., Boston, 1855-57, then mem. Nichols & Batcheller, mfrs. articles of feminine attire, New York; withdrew, 1865, and founded firm Langdon, Batcheller & Co., in same line, now George C. Batcheller & Co.; established factory at Bridgeport, Conn., now employing about 2,000 persons; pres. George C. Batcheller & Co. (New York and Bridgeport), Crown Corset Co. (New York and Bridgeport), Conn. Clasp Co. and Crown Paper Box Co., Bridgeport. V.p. Internat. Peace Forum; v.p. Galen Hall Co., Atlantic City, N.J., and Wernersville, Pa. Pres. bd. of trustees St. Andrew's M.E. Ch. Mason. Has large library, containing many first edits., and valuable art collection, which includes portraits of George and Martha Washington, painted by Sharpless, at Mt. Vernon, 1796. Author: Batcheller, Batchelder Genealogy, 1898. Home: New York, N.Y. Died Jan. 25, 1915.

BATCHELLER, George Sherman, judge Internat. Tribunal (mixed courts) of Egypt; b. Batchellerville, Saratoga Co., N.Y., July 25, 1837; s. Sherman Batcheller; fitted for coll. Ft. Edward Inst.; grad. law dept., Harvard, 1857; admitted to bar, 1858; practiced at Saratoga Springs; m. Catherine Phillips, d. Gen. James M. Cook, of Saratoga. Elected to N.Y. legislature at 21 yrs. of age, 1858. Entered army as capt. 115th regt., N.Y. vols., 1862; taken prisoner at Harper's Ferry, 1862; exchanged, and was in Va. campaigns; later at Hilton Head, and in siege of Charleston; deputy provost marshal gen., Dept. of South, 1863; lt. col. vols.; Jan. 1, 1865, and insp. gen. vols. and Nat. Guard of State of N.Y. Specially designated by govt. to accompany body of Pres. Lincoln through State of N.Y. Resumed practice at Saratoga; mem. N.Y. legislature, 1873-74 (chmn. ways and means and mem. judiciary com.); apptd. 1875, by Pres. Grant, judge Internat. Tribunal of Egypt; chosen by colleagues of all the powers presiding justice; resigned, 1885; elected N.Y. legislature, 1886, 1888-89; 1st asst. sec. Treasury U.S., 1889-91; U.S. minister to Portugal, Nov., 1891; diplomatic representative in Europe, headquarters, Paris, 1893-95; mgr. of governmental affairs of various Am. cos., 1895-96; apptd. by Pres. McKinley to preside over deliberations (in French language) Universal Postal Congress, Washington, 1897; at request of Egyptian govt. again apptd. to Internat. Tribunal, Nov. 1898; promoted by President Roosevelt to Supreme Court of Appeal, May, 1902; companion Mil. Order Loyal Legion; grand officer (with insignia) Imperial Order of the Medjidieh; grand cordon (with cross and insignia), Order Crown of Italy (King Humbert, 1897). Died 1908.

BATCHELOR, George, editor; b. Southbury, Conn., July 3, 1836; s. Matthew and Mary (Axford) B.; grad. Meadville Theol. Sch., 1863; A.B., Harvard, 1866, A.M., 1870; (D.D., Meadville Theol. Sem., 1911); m. Priscilla C., d. Rev. O. Stearns, of Cambridge, Mass., Sept. 18, 1866. Asst. supt. Sanitary Commn., Dept. of W.Va., 1864-65; ordained Unitarian ministry, 1866; pastor, Salem, Mass., 1866-82, Chicago, 1882-85, Lowell, Mass., 1889-93; sec. Am. Unitarian Assn., 1893-97; editor The Christian Register, 1897-1911. Sec. Nat. Conf., 1870-80; chmn. council, 1893-94, 1904-05. Author: Social Equilibrium, 1887. Contbr. to religious and secular press. Home: Cambridge, Mass. Died June 14, 1923.

BATE, William Brimage, U.S. senator from Tenn., 1887-1905; b. nr. Castilian Spring, Tenn., Oct. 7, 1826; academic edn.; was steamboat clerk on Mississippi; private in Mexican war in La. and Tenn. regts.; on return, mem. Tenn. legislature; grad. Lebanon Law School, 1852; practiced at Gallatin, Tenn.; atty. gen. Nashville dist., 1854-60; presdl. elector, 1860, on Breckinridge-Lane ticket; private to capt., col., brig. gen. and maj. gen. in C.S.A., 1861-65; thrice dangerously wounded. Practiced law at Nashville after war; del. Nat. Dem. Conv., 1868; mem. Nat. Dem. Exec. Com. 12 yrs.; presdl. elector, 1876; gov. Tenn., 1883-86. Home: Nashville, Tenn. Died 1905.

BATEMAN, Charles Heisler, newspaperman; b. Pennington, N.J., July 2, 1861; s. Charles Wesley and Mary (Bunn) B.; grad. Pennington Sem., 1880; studied Princeton 1 yr., class 1885; m. Louise Palmer, June 1896; children—Charles Palmer, Ruth. m. 2d, Agnes Rice Hill, 1928. Began active career as reporter Trenton State Gazette, 1886; became city editor Trenton True American and corr. New York, N.J. and Phila. papers; legislative corr., 1887-1908; editor and chief owner Unionist Gazette, Somerville, N.J., 1891—. Mem. N.J. Civil Service Commn., May 1908-14 (pres., May 1913-14). Trustee Somerville Savings Bank. Mem. bd. mgrs. State Reformatory for Boys, Annandale, N.Y. Republican. Home: Somerville, N.J. Died Mar. 25, 1934.

BATEN, Anderson Edith, clergyman, educator; b. Haw Ridge, Ala., Oct. 5, 1855; s. Thomas James and Katherine Matilda (Lunsford) B.; ed. Baylor U., with spl. training in theology under Dr. Rufus C. Burleson; m. Leta Belle Ely, May 23, 1895. Ordained Bapt. ministry, 1881; pastor Marlin, Brenham, Navasota, Ft. Worth, Brownwood and Amarillo, Tex., 1883-1905; prof. of Bible, Howard Payne Coll., Brownwood, 1907-11; pres. Okla. State Bapt. Coll., Blackwell, 1911-13; prof. Bible, 1914—, acting pres., 1915—, Howard Payne Coll. Recording sec. Bapt. Gen. Conv., 1889-1910; charter mem. Tex. Bapt. Edn. Bd.; trustee Southwestern Bapt. Theol. Sem., Ft. Worth, 1907-11. Chaplain Masonic Grand Lodge of Texas, 1910-11. Democrat. Home: Brownwood, Tex. Deceased.

BATES, Alexander Berry, rear admn.; b. Brooklyn, Nov. 25, 1842; s. John A. and Anna M. (Berry) B.; ed. Milton Acad., Md.; m. Fannie J. Everts. Entered naval service as 3d asst. engr., Jan. 16, 1863; served in navy through to end of Civil War on N. Atlantic Squadron; minor engagements in James River, and Albemarle Sound, N.C., with Confederate ram Albemarle; after end of war sent to European sta. and with Admiral Farragut's fleet until end of 1868; afterward served principally on N. Atlantic and Pacific stas.; in Spanish War with Flying Squadron, and Admiral Sampson's fleet before Santiago, and engagement on July 3, 1898, with Spanish fleet, as chief engr. of U.S. battleship Texas; advanced 3 numbers in grade of chief engr. for action at Santiago; transferred from engr. corps to the line, with rank of comdr. and promoted to capt.; also received advancement of 3 numbers in grade of comdr. for service at Santiago, Cuba; retired at own request, July, 1903, with rank of rear-admiral. Home: Binghamton, N.Y. Died Feb. 19, 1917.

BATES, Alfred Elliott, paymaster gen. U.S.A.; b. Monroe, Mich., July 15, 1840; s. Alfred G. and B. Ann B.; Canandaigua, N.Y., Acad., 1853-54, 1856-57; grad. U.S. Mil. Acad.; m. Caroline McCorkle, Dec. 1, 1875. Served 2d U.S. cav., June 1865, to March 1875; scouting and frontier work, Dept. Mo. and The Platte, ranging through the northern border, Tex. to Mont.; instr. cav., West Point, Sept. 1869, to June 1873; paymaster, Dept. Tex., 5 yrs.; Dak., 2 yrs.; Washington, 4 yrs.; Dak., 4 yrs.; New York, 4 yrs.; San Francisco, 4 yrs.; mil. attaché Court of St. James, 1897-99; at Washington as acting paymaster gen., May, 1899; made paymaster gen., with rank of brig. gen., July 12, 1899; maj. gen. U.S.A., Jan. 12, 1904; retired Jan. 14, 1904. Died 1909.

BATES, Arlo, coll. prof.; b. East Machias, Me., Dec. 16, 1850; s. Dr. Niran and Susan (Thaxter) B.; S.B., Bowdoin, 1876, A.M., 1879 (Litt. D., 1894); m. Harriet L. Vose, Sept. 5, 1882 (died 1886). Editor Boston Sunday Courier, 1880-93; prof. English lit., Mass. Inst. Tech., 1893-1915. Fellow Am. Acad. Arts and Sciences; mem. Nat. Inst. Arts and Letters. Author: Patty's Perversities, 1881; Mr. Jacobs; The Pagans, 1884; A Wheel of Fire, 1885; Berries of the Brier; Sonnets in Shadow; A Lad's Love, 1887; The Philistines, 1889; Albrecht; The Poet and His Self; A Book o' Nine Tales; Told in the Gate; In the Bundle of Time; The Torch Bearers; Talks on Writing English, 1897, 2d series, 1901; Talks on the Study of Literature, 1898; The Puritans, 1899; Under the Beech Tree, 1899; Love in a Cloud, 1900; The Diary of a Saint, 1902; Talks on Teaching Literature, 1906; The Intoxicated Ghost, 1908. Died Aug. 25, 1918.

BATES, Arthur Laban, congressman; b. Meadville, Pa., June 6, 1859; s. Samuel P. and S. Josephine B.; grad. Allegheny Coll., 1880 (valedictorian), A.M., 1883 (LL.D., 1920); studied Oxford U., Eng., 1884; m. Emily, d. Gen. James F. Rusling of Trenton, N.J., 1909; children—Josephine Rusling, Arthur Rusling. Admitted to bar, 1882; city solicitor, Meadville, 4 terms, 1889-96; served 12 yrs. in Congress, 1901-13, 25th Pa. Dist.; was mem. Naval Com., and author of bill which passed Congress making mid-Pacific naval base at Pearl Harbor, Hawaii; introduced first Fed. Employer's Liability Bill, which became a law; chosen Rep. presdl. elector, 1916 (declined); del. to Rep. Nat. Conv., Cleveland, 1924. Vice pres. First Nat. Bank (Meadville). Republican. Am. del. Internat. Peace Conf., Brussels, 1905, Rome, 1911. Trustee Allegheny Coll.; dir. Pa. Coll. Music, Meadville City Hosp.; pres. trustees First Baptist Ch.; pres. Meadville Pub. Library. Mason. Home: Meadville, Pa. Died Aug. 26, 1934.

BATES, Blanche, actress; b. Portland, Ore., 1873; d. F. M. Bates; removed to San Francisco with parents, 1876; ed. San Francisco pub. schs.; m. Lt. Milton F. Davis, U.S.A.; m. 2d, George Creel, Nov. 28, 1912. First appearance on stage, Stockwell's Theatre, San Francisco, 1894; starred as Mrs. Hillary, in "The Senator," 1895; played leading parts in various comedies, 1896-98; appeared in Shakespearean rôles in Augustin Daly's Co., 1898; later starred in "The Great Ruby," "The Musketeers," "Madame Butterfly"; created title rôle of Cigarette in "Under Two Flags," Princess Yo-San, in "The Darling of the Gods," the Girl in "The Girl of the Golden West"; with Henry Miller in "The Changelings." Died Dec. 25, 1941.

BATES, Charlotte Fiske (Mme. Rogé), poet; b. New York, Nov. 30, 1838; d. Hervey and Eliza (Endicott) B.; ed. Cambridge, Mass., where for many yrs. she had pvt. pupils; m. M. Adolphe Rogé, June 4, 1891 (died 1896). Author: Risk, and Other Poems, 1879 (long out of print). Editor: Longfellow Birthday Book, 1881; Seven Voices of Sympathy, 1881; Cambridge Book of Poetry and Song, 1882. Aided Mr. Longfellow in compiling Poems of Places. Home: Cambridge, Mass. Died Sept. 1, 1916.

BATES, Clement, lawyer; b. Cincinnati, O., Apr. 1, 1845; s. Joshua Hall (Brig. Gen.) and Elizabeth Dwight (Hoadly) B.; A.B., Harvard, 1867, LL.B., 1869; Cincinnati Law Sch. 1 yr.; m. Fanny Lear Higbee, June 25, 1872; children—Joshua Hall (dec.), Hugh Higbee; m. 2d, Josephine Mackenzie Holland, Nov. 27, 1909. Began practice with father at Cincinnati, 1869; city solicitor, Cincinnati, 1877-79; judge Court of Common Pleas, 1887-92. Republican. Mason. Editor or author: Littleton and Blackley Insurance Digest (2d edit.); Ohio Digest (several edits.), 1875-1923; Pleadings, Parties and Forms (3 edits.), 1881-1923; Law of Limited Partnership, 1885-88; Walker's American Law (10th and 11th edits.), 1895-1905. Home: Cincinnati, O. Died Jan. 1931.

BATES, Emma Frances Duncan (Mrs. Theodore C. Bates), v.p.-gen. D.A.R.; b. N. Brookfield, Mass., Mar. 11, 1845; d. Charles and Tryphosa (Lakin) Duncan; grad. Oread Inst., Worcester, Mass., 1863; m. Hon. Theodore Cornelius Bates, Dec. 24, 1868; 1 dau., Mrs. Tryphosa Bates Batcheller. Lecturer and essayist upon hist. subjects V.p.-gen. D.A.R., 1906—, elected hon. v.p.-gen. for life at the Nat. D.A.R. Cong., Apr. 1913. Mem. com. State Civil Service Reform Assn., state com. on Conservation, state com. on Child Labor. Episcopalian. Home: Worcester, Mass. Died Oct. 5, 1929.

BATES, Ernest Sutherland, author; b. Gambier, O., Oct. 14, 1879; s. Cyrus Stearns and Laverna (Sutherland) B.; grad. Univ. Sch., Cleveland, O.; A.B., U. of Mich., 1902, A.M., 1903; Ph.D., Columbia, 1908; m. Florence Fisher, 1902 (dec.); m. 2d, Rosalind Boido, 1913 (divorced); m. 3d, Gladys Graham, 1920. Instr. in English, Oberlin Coll., 1903-05; tutor in English, Columbia, 1907-08; prof. English, U. of Ariz., 1908-15; prof. English, U. of Ore., 1915-21, prof. philosophy, 1921-25; literary editor Dictionary of Am. Biography, 1926-29; prof. extension div., U. of Ore., 1930, 1932, 1935, 1936; mem. reviewing staff Saturday Review of Literature, 1930; asso. editor The Modern Monthly, 1933-36; lecturer Federal Forum, Portland, Ore., 1936. Author: Study of Shelley's The Cenci, 1908; The Friend of Jesus (pub. in England under original title The Gospel According to Judas), 1928; This Land of Liberty, 1930; Mary Baker Eddy—The Truth and the Tradition (with J. V. Dittemore), 1932; The Story of Congress, 1936; The Story of the Supreme Court, 1936; Hearst, the Lord of San Simeon (with Oliver Carlson), 1936; American Hurly-Burly (with Alan Williams), 1937; Biography of the Bible, 1937. Editor: The Four Gospels, 1932; The Bible Designed to be Read as Living Literature, 1936. Home: New York, N.Y. Died Dec. 4, 1939.

BATES, George Andrew, coll. prof.; b. Boston, Aug. 5, 1847; s. Andrew and Scyeth Ropes (Ames) B.; D.D.S., Boston Dental Coll., 1889; D.M.D., Tufts Coll. Dental Sch., 1903; M.S., Tufts Coll., 1904; m. Aroline Elizabeth Hodskinson, Dec. 22, 1881. Practiced dentistry in Boston 16 yrs.; prof. histology, Boston Dental Coll., 1891-99, Tufts Coll. Med. and Dental Schs., 1899—. Mem. Boston Soc. Natural History, Naturalists' Club of Boston, Am. Assn. Anatomists. Trustee Harpswell (Me.) Biol. Lab. Methodist. Home: Auburndale, Boston. Died 1925.

BATES, George Dennis, banker; b. Akron, O., Aug. 18, 1866; s. George Dennis and Mary Ann (Mathews) B.; ed. pub. schs., Akron; m. Laura Gaebler, Aug. 26, 1905. Began as messenger, 2d Nat. Bank, Akron, 1885, asst. cashier, 1892, cashier, 1902; v.p. 1st-2d Nat. Bank, 1911—; became pres. 1st Trust & Savings Bank, 1926; chmn. bd. First-City Trust & Savings Bank, 1929-31; vice chmn. First-Central Trust Co., 1931—. Mem. Akron Chamber Commerce (pres.). Republican. Mason. Home: Akron, O. Died Nov. 26, 1932.

BATES, George W., banker; b. Lee County, Ia., 1851; s. Nicholas and Matilda B.; ed. pub. schs.; m. Lizzie May Menzies, 1882. Engaged in banking business at Portland, Ore., since 1893; pres. Lumberman's Nat. Bank, Bates Real Estate & Investment Co.; dir. Ore. Life Assn.; mem. Geo. W. Bates & Co., bankers; etc. Republican. Home: Portland, Ore. Deceased.

BATES, George Williams, lawyer; b. Detroit, Nov. 4, 1848; s. Samuel Gershom and Rebecca (Williams) B.; A.B., U. of Mich., 1870, A.M., 1873; m. Jennie Marie Fowler, Apr. 26, 1887. Admitted to bar, 1874, and since in practice at Detroit. Mem. Mich. Commn. on Uniform State Laws; commr. to Nat. Conf. on Uniform State Laws, 1907, 1908, 1909, 1911. Councillor, Archæol. Inst. of Am.; mem. various socs. Has written various papers. Home: Detroit, Mich. Deceased.

BATES, Henry Clay, judge; b. Derby, Vt., Jan. 29, 1843; ed. Derby Acad.; served in 19th and 4th Mass. Heavy Arty., 1864-65; m. Laura E. Jenness, 1866. Practiced law at St. Johnsbury, Vt.; has held various local offices; lt. gov. of Vt., 1890-1900; del.-at-large Rep. Nat. Conv., 1900; v.p. from Vt., Buffalo Expn., 1901; judge Ct. of First Instance, P.I., Feb. 1901—. Republican. Home: St. Johnsbury, Vt. Died 1909.

BATES, Herbert, author; b. Hyde Park, Mass., June 29, 1868; s. Joseph C. and Harriet A. (Pearson) B.; A.B., Harvard, 1890; m. Edna Tibbles, July 9, 1894. In charge English Dept. Manual Training Sch., Brooklyn, 1897—. Author: Songs of Exile (verse), 1896; English Literature, 1918; King's English (one-act play); also reading list prepared for Nat. Council Teachers of English. Editor sch. edits. various classics. Address: Brooklyn, N.Y. Died Apr. 16, 1929.

BATES, John Coalter, lt. gen. U.S.A.; b. St. Charles Co., Mo., Aug. 26, 1842; s. Edward and Julia Davenport (Coalter) B.; ed. Washington U., St. Louis (LL.D., 1904); unmarried. Apptd. from Mo., 1st lt. 11th U.S. Inf., May 14, 1861; promoted through grades to brig. gen. U.S.V., May 4, 1898, maj. gen., July 8, 1898; hon. disch., Apr. 13, 1899; brig. gen. U.S.V., Apr. 13, 1899; maj. gen., Jan. 2, 1900; hon. disch., Feb. 28, 1901; brig. gen. U.S.A., Feb. 2, 1901; maj. gen., July 15, 1902; lt. gen. and chief of staff of the army, Feb. 1, 1906; retired at own request, over 40 yrs'. service, Apr. 14, 1906. Bvtd.: maj., Aug. 1, 1864, "for faithful and meritorious services in the field"; lt. col., Apr. 9, 1865, "for operations resulting in fall of Richmond." Served in Civil War 2 yrs. with regt. and 2 yrs. as a.-d.-c. to comdg. gen. Army of the Potomac; in Spanish-Am. War comd. Bates' Independent Brigade and later 3d Div., 5th Army Corps; comd. dists. of Mindanao and Jolo and 1st Div., 8th Corps, and Dept. of Southern Luzon, P.I., 1899-1901. Home: St. Louis. Died Feb. 4, 1919.

BATES, Katharine Lee, coll. prof.; b. Falmouth, Mass., Aug. 12, 1859; d. Rev. William and Cornelia Frances (Lee) B.; A.B., Wellesley Coll., 1880, A.M., 1891; LL.D., 1925; Litt.D., Middlebury Coll., 1914, Oberlin, 1916. Taught in Natick High Sch., 1880-81, Dana Hall, 1881-85; instr. English lit., 1885-88, asso. prof., 1888-91, prof. 1891-1925, prof. emeritus, 1925—, Wellesley Coll.; 4 yrs. of travel and study abroad. Author: English Religious Drama (lectures), 1893; In Sunny Spain, 1913; Sigurd, Our Golden Collie and Other Comrades of the Road, 1919; Yellow Clover (in memory of Katharine Coman), 1922; Little Robin Stay-Behind, and Other Plays in Verse for Children, 1923; The Pilgrim Ship, 1926, and many others. Editor numerous works. Wrote nat. hymn, "America the Beautiful." Home: Wellesley, Mass. Died Mar. 28, 1929.

BATES, Lindon, Jr., engr.; b. Portland, Ore., July 17, 1883; s. Lindon Wallace (q.v.) and Josephine (White) B.; prep. edn., Harrow Sch., Eng.; Ph.B., Yale, 1902; unmarried. V.p. Bates Engring. Co.; has done engring. work on Galveston grade raising and N.Y. Barge Canal; cons. engr. Western Engring. Corp., Denver Mining Investment Co. Am. mgr. Laguintos Oil Co., Maikop Areas, and Trinidad Cedrus Oil Co. Traveled in Russia, 1896; on exploring and hunting expdn. to islands N. of Hudson Bay, 1900; visited Panama, 1904; made midwinter sledge journey in Siberia and Mongolia, 1908; to Venezuela and up the Orinoco in 1911. Mem. N.Y. Assembly, 1908, 1909; author of condemnation and civil service reform measures, direct nomination and employers' liability bills; mem. N.Y. County Com., 1908-11; apptd. by Gov. Hughes mem. of Nat. Conservation Congress. Author: The Political Horoscope (with Charles A. Moore, Jr.), 1904; The Loss of Water in New York's Distribution System, 1909; The Russian Road to China, 1910; Path of the Conquistadores, 1912. Home: New York, N.Y. Died May 7, 1915.

BATES, Lindon Wallace, civil engr.; b. Marshfield, Vt., Nov. 19, 1858; s. William W. and Mary C. B.; ed. Yale; studied engring.; m. Josephine White; father of Lindon B., Jr. Asst. engr. N.P. and Oregon Pacific rys.; contractor engr. or mgr. various ry., dock and terminal contracts in Ore., Wash., Mont., Kan., Mo., Ill., La., Calif., etc., for transcontinental railways or their subsidiary cos., on Chicago Drainage Canal, etc.; built mammoth dredge "Beta," for U.S. Govt., earning bonus of $86,200 on test of capacity; retained 1896-1902 by Belgian Govt. to prepare reports and projects for improvement of port of Antwerp; on Suez Canal on the enlargement, etc., of the canal; by Russian Govt. on the rivers Volga, Dnieper and Bug, Azov Sea ports and channels, Black Sea ports, etc.; by the Queensland Govt. designed 8 harbors and regulation of Brisbane, Mary, Fitzroy, Norman and Albert rivers; built large hydraulic dredge for Russian Govt., earning bonus of $75,000 on capacity test. In collaboration with leading engrs. designated by govts. of Russia, Germany, Austria and Belgium prepared scheme for improvement of port of Shanghai, etc.; contracting engr. Galveston grade raising works; designed the "Three Lake" Panama Canal. Has been dir. various works in Korea, Trinidad and Peru. Grand prix and decoration from French Govt., 1900, for "distinguished services to science." Author: Retrieval at Panama; Colloidal Fuel, etc. Chmn. engring. com. Submarine Defense Assn., 1917. Inventor of colloidal fuel. Home: Mt. Lebanon, N.Y. Died Apr. 22, 1924.

BATES, Miner Lee, college pres.; b. Fairfield, Mich., Oct. 9, 1869; s. Talcott Arthur and Elvira Hudson (Sparhawk) B.; Normal Coll., Fayette, O., 1882-87, Angola, Ind., 1889-90; Ky. U., Lexington, 1890-91; A.B., Hiram (O.) Coll., 1895; A.M., 1896; Columbia, 1904-07; LL.D., Transylvania U., 1915; m. Georgia Kinney, Feb. 26, 1896. Teacher pub. schs., 1886-89; ordained Christian (Disciples) ministry, 1895; pastor Central Ch. of Christ, Newark, O., 1895-1901, Central Christian Church, Warren, O., 1901-04, Park Av. Ch., E. Orange, N.J., 1904-06, First Ch. of Disciples, New York, 1906-08; pres. Hiram Coll., Mar. 20, 1908—. Home: Hiram, O. Died Aug. 19, 1930.

BATES, Onward, civil engr.; b. St. Charles Co., Mo., Feb. 24, 1850; s. Barton and Caroline Matilda (Hatcher) B.; student Rensselaer Poly. Inst., class of 1875 (non-grad.); hon. C.E., U. of Wis., 1897; hon. D.Eng., Rensselaer Poly. Inst., 1918; LL.D., U. of Mo., 1924; m. Virginia Castleman Breckinridge, June 23, 1892. Retired from active professional practice. Trustee Chicago Bur. Public Efficiency for 12 yrs. Awarded Chanute medal, Western Soc. Engrs., 1910. Presbyn. Home: Chicago, Ill. Died April 4, 1936.

BATES, Oric, archæologist; b. Boston, Mass., Dec. 5, 1883; s. Arlo and Harriet (Vose) B.; A.B., Harvard, 1905, A.M., 1914; studied U. of Berlin, 1906; m. Natica Y. Inches, June 5, 1913. In service Egyptian Govt. Archæol. Expdn. in Nubia, 1906, 1908; of Palestinian Exploration Soc., in Syria, 1907; in charge Am. Archæol. Soc. Expdn. to Cyrenaica, 1909; of Wellcome Archæol. Expdn. at Gebel Moya, Southern Sudan, 1910; pvt. exploration to Oasis of Siwah, 1911; pvt. archæol. expdn. in Libyan Desert, 1913; Peabody Mus. Sudanese Expdn., 1914-15. Curator African dept., Peabody Mus., 1913—. Author: The Eastern Libyans, 1913. Editor, Harvard African Studies, 1917—. Home: Boston, Mass. Died Oct. 10, 1918.

BATES, Samuel Penniman, LL.D., hist. writer; b. Mendon, Mass., Jan. 29, 1827; grad. Brown, 1851; prin. Meadville, Pa., Acad.; supt. schools, Crawford Co., Pa., 1857-60; deputy State supt. schools, 1860-66; State historian, 1866-73. Author: Lives of the Governors of Pennsylvania; History of Pennsylvania Volunteers (5 vols.); History of Battle of Gettysburg; History of Battle of Chancellorsville; Martial Deeds of Pennsylvania; History of Green County; History of Crawford County. Home: Meadville, Pa. Deceased.

BATES, Theodore Cornelius, mfr.; b. N. Brookfield, Mass., June 4, 1843; s. Elijah and Sarah (Fletcher) B.; acad. edn. Derry, N.H.; m. Emma Frances Duncan, Dec. 24, 1868; father of Tryphosa Bates Batcheller. Became identified with Worcester Corset Co., 1876, of which for many yrs. was sole propr.; was the 1st large mfr. of Mass. to adopt weekly payment system; one of the chief promoters Worcester Electric Light Co., N. Brookfield R.R., N. Brookfield Free Pub. Library, N. Brookfield Water Works System; trustee People's Savings Bank of Worcester, 1876—. Mem. Mass. Ho. of Rep., 1879, Senate, 1883 (declined unanimous renomination to both offices); del. Rep. Nat. Conv., 1884; chmn. exec. com. Rep. State Central Com. 10 yrs.; state dir. Boston & Albany R.R., 5 yrs.; mem. Mass. State Bd. of Health, 1885-90. Congregationalist. Mason. Home: Worcester, Mass. Died Mar. 11, 1912.

BATES, Walter Irving, editor, pub.; b. Meadville, Pa., June 15, 1873; s. of Samuel P. (LL.D.) and S. Josephine (Bates) B.; A.B., Allegheny Coll., 1896; studied Sorbonne, Paris, 1896-97; m. Marion Sackett, Feb. 7, 1901; children—Elizabeth (Mrs. Merwin G. Shryock), Edward Irving, Sarah Josephine (Mrs. Donald W. Gapp), Robert S. Admitted to Pa. bar, 1895; was Paris corr. Philadelphia Press; pres. and editor Meadville Tribune-Republican, 1899—; v.p. McCroskey Tool Corp. Recruited company for Spanish-Am. War, 1898, and chosen capt.; maj. 21st Regt. N.G. Pa., Aug. 15, 1898. Rep. presdl. elector, 25th Pa. Dist., 1916, del. to Rep. Nat Convs., 1928, 32. Pres. Meadville Bd. of Edn.; trustee Pa. State Teachers' College, Edinboro. Baptist. Mason. Home: Meadville, Pa. Died May 5, 1934.

BATES, William Oscar, author; b. Harrisburg, Ind., Sept. 19, 1852; s. John and Angeline W. (Thomas) B.; Ph.B., Cornell U., 1875; m. Clara A. Nixon, Oct. 23, 1893. On staff Indianapolis Journal, 1877-81, Cincinnati News-Journal, 1882-84, St. Paul Pioneer Press, 1884-86, New York World, 1889-94, New York Commercial Advertiser, 1897-99. Author: Recitations and How to Recite, 1896; also, Our Foreign Correspondent, 4-act comedy prod. St. Paul, 1888; Uncle Rodney, 1-act comedy prod. Empire Theatre, New York, 1896; The Black Bokhara, 1-act comedy prod. Indianapolis, 1907, pub. 1917; Jacob Leisler, 5-act play, pub. 1913; Polly of Pogue's Run, 1-act drama prod. Indianapolis, 1916, pub. 1917; Asaph, 1-act comedy, prod. Indianapolis, 1918; Merry Mount, 3-act comedy (Drama League prize), 1919; The Dryad and the Deacon, 1-act fœrie, prod. Indianapolis, 1920. Home: Indianapolis, Ind. Died Oct. 29, 1924.

BATES, William Wallace, shipbuilder; b. Nova Scotia, Feb. 15, 1827; s. Stephen and Elizabeth (Wallace) B.; ed. common schs., Calais, Me., beyond that self-educated; also self-educated in naval architecture; m. Marie Cole, Sept. 11, 1856. Began in shipwright trade, 1839; built 1st clipper schooner, "Challenge," at Manitowoc, on the Great Lakes, 1851; editor Nautical Magazine and Naval Journal, New York, 1854-58; capt. in Union Army, 1861-63; in shipbuilding and drydock business, Chicago, 1866-81; dry-dock building, Portland, Ore., 1881-83; mgr. Inland Lloyds, Buffalo, 1885-88; U.S. commr. navigation, Washington, 1889-92; retired. Republican. Author: Rules for Shipbuilding, 1876, 1894; American

Marine, 1892; American Navigation, 1902. Home: Denver, Colo. Died Nov., 1912.

BATHRICK, Ellsworth R., congressman; b. Oakland Co., Mich., Jan. 6, 1863; s. Sumner and Louisa B.; ed. high sch., Pontiac, Mich.; m. May L. Clark, 1889. Mem. 62d and 63d Congresses (1911-15), 19th Ohio Dist.; Democrat. Home: Akron, O. Died Dec. 24, 1917.

BATTELL, Joseph, author; b. Middlebury, Vt., July 15, 1839; s. Philip and Emma Hart (Seymour) B.; Middlebury Coll., Vt., 1856-59; unmarried. Editor and pub. Middlebury Register, 1896; mgr. Am. Pub. Co., Middlebury; owner of Bread Loaf Inn (nr. Ripton, Vt.), also several farms, and about 20,000 acres of forest land; breeder of Morgan horses. Republican. Author: The Morgan Horse Register, Vol. I, 1894, Vol. II, 1905, Vol. III, 1913; American Stallion Register, Vol. I, 1909, Vol. II, 1911, Vol. III, 1913; Ellen, or Whisperings of an Old Pine, 3 vols., 1901-13; The Home Library, Vol. I, 1904; The New Physics, 1909. Home: Middlebury, Vt. Died Feb. 22, 1915.

BATTELS, Sarah M. E. (Mrs.), philanthropist; b. Hudson, O., Nov. 17, 1839; d. Samuel and Amanda M. (Tripp) Edgerly; moved to Akron, O., in childhood; ed. public schools; taught several yrs.; m. Benjamin F. Battels, 1859. Was active in Christian Sanitary Commn. during war; working mem. Ohio Soldiers' Aid Soc., and continued to devote her life to the welfare of veteran soldiers; was 3 yrs. pres. Akron Woman's Relief Corps; pres., sec. and insp. Woman's Relief Corps, Dept. of Ohio; chmn. War Emergency Commn., Dept. O., W.R.C., Cuban War; hon. mem. 29th regt., Ohio Vol. Vet. Soc., etc. Home: Akron, O. Deceased.

BATTEN, Samuel Zane, clergyman; b. Swedesboro, N.J., Aug. 10, 1859; s. George and Sarah P. (Zane) B.; A.B., Bucknell U., 1885, A.M., 1888; Crozer Theol. Sem., 1885-6; (D.D., Bucknell, 1905); m. Winifred Merriman, Oct. 6, 1886. Ordained Bapt. ministry, 1886; pastor Tioga, Pa., 1886-87, Brookville, Pa., 1888-91, Manayunk Ch., Phila., 1891-93, Amity Ch., New York, 1894-95, Morristown, N.J., 1895-1903, First Ch., Lincoln, Neb., 1903-10; head of dept. social science, Des Moines (Ia.) Coll., 1910-12; sec. Baptist Dept. Social Service and Brotherhood. Editor the Nebraska Issue, 1906-10. President Pa. State Baptist Young People's Union, 1893-94; chmn. Christian Citizenship Com., New York Christian Endeavor Union, 1894-95; a founder Brotherhood of the Kingdom, and editorial sec., 1886-99; pres. Neb. Anti-Saloon League, 1903-08, Neb. Bapt. Edn. Soc., 1907-08; chmn. Social Service Commn. of Northern Bapt. Conv., 1908—; asso. sec. Social Service Commn. of Fedn. Council of the Chs.; sec. Neb. Fedn. Chs., 1909-10; pres. Ia. Constl. Amendment Association; pres. Des Moines Fedn. of Chs.; chmn. exec. com. Social Service Commn. Bapt. World Alliance; del. World's Ch. Peace Conf., Constance, 1914; mem. exec. com. Nat. Temperance Union; commr. of edn., World Brotherhood Fedn. Author: Prophets True and False (booklet), 1897; The New Citizenship ($600 prize book, Am. S.S. Union), 1898; The Christian State, 1909; The Social Task of Christianity, 1911; A Working Temperance Program, 1911; The Social Problem, 1915; Moral Meaning of the War, 1918; New World Order, 1919; Christ and the Nations, 1920; Building a Community, 1921; If America Fail, 1921; Why Not Try Christianity? 1923. Editor Social Service Series. Sec. War Commission of Northern Baptist Conv. Home: Lansdowne, Pa. Died June 5, 1925.

BATTERSHALL, Walton Wesley, clergyman; b. Troy, N.Y., Jan. 8, 1840; s. Ludlow A. and Eustatia (Ward) B.; A.B., Yale, 1864, A.M., 1867; grad. Gen. Theol. Sem., 1866; (D.D., Union, 1878, Hobart, 1888); m. Anna Davidson Williams, Oct. 13, 1864. Deacon, 1865, priest, 1866, P.E. Ch.; rector Ravenswood, N.Y., 1868-69, Christ Ch., Rochester, N.Y., 1869-74, St. Peter's, Albany, N.Y., 1874—, Archdeacon of Albany, 1902—; del. gen. convs., 1875—. Author: Interpretations of Life and Religion, 1897; Albany, in Historic Towns of Middle States, 1899; Introduction to History of St. Peter's Church, Albany, 1900. Home: Albany, N.Y. Died Mar. 19, 1920.

BATTERSON, Hermon Griswold, P.E. clergyman; b. Litchfield Co., Conn., 1827 (D.D., Neb. Coll.); deacon, 1861; priest, 1866; rector St. Andrew's, Seguin, Tex., 1861-62; St. Mark's, San Antonio, Tex., 1862; Grace Ch., Wabasha, Minn., 1862-66; St. Clement's (1869-72) and Annunciation (1880-89), Phila.; rector Ch. of the Redeemer, N.Y., 1891. Author: Missionary Tune Book; Pathway of Faith; Sketch-Book of the American Episcopate; Churchman's Hymn Book; Christmas Carols and Other Verses; Manual of Plain Song; Vesper Bells, etc. Died 1903.

BATTERSON, James Goodwin, pres. Travelers' Ins. Co.; b. Bloomfield, Conn., Feb. 23, 1823; academical edn. (A.M., Yale and Williams); m. Eunice E. Goodwin, Hartford. Established as importer and dealer in granite, Hartford, 1845; pres. New England Granite Works; founded, 1863, Travelers' Ins. Co. and became its head. Home: Hartford, Conn. Died 1901.

BATTLE, Archibald John, educator, clergyman; b. Powelton, Hancock Co., Ga., Sept. 10, 1826; s. Dr. Cullen and Jane Andrews (Lamon) B.; ed. Eufaula (Ala.) Acad., Mercer Univ., 1842, and U. of Ala., A.B., 1846, A.M., 1849; (D.D., Howard Coll., Ala., 1872, Columbian Univ., 1872, U. of Ga., 1873; LL.D., Miss. Coll., 1883); m. Mary Elizabeth Guild, Dec. 7, 1846 (died 1897). Tutor ancient languages, Univ. of Ala., 1848; prof. science and ancient languages, E. Ala. Female Inst., Tuskegee, Ala., 1852; pastor Tuscaloosa Bapt. Ch., 1856-57; elected prof. Greek lang. and lit., U. of Ala., 1857; pres. Ala. Central Female Coll., Tuscaloosa, 1860; pres. E. Ala. Female Coll., 1863-65, Judson Female Coll., Marion, 1865-72, Mercer Univ., Macon, Ga., 1872-89, Shorter Coll. for Young Ladies, 1891-98; founder and pres. Anniston (Ala.) Coll. for Young Ladies, 1898-1902; retired, 1902, and removed to Macon, Ga. Founder Lanier Circle, Rome, Ga. (pres. 1891-98); charter mem. The Atheneum, Macon, Ga. (pres. 8 yrs.). Baptist. Democrat. Author: The Human Will, 1876. Home: Macon, Ga. Deceased.

BATTLE, Burrill Bunn, judge; b. Hinds Co., Miss., July 24, 1838; s. Joseph J. and Nancy (Strickiln) B.; A.B., Ark. Coll., Fayetteville, 1856; LL.B., Cumberland U., Tenn., 1858; m. Mrs. Josephine A. Witherspoon, Nov. 29, 1871 (died 1899). Practiced law, Lewisville, Ark., 1858-61; in C.S. Arty., 1861-65, participating in battles of Shiloh, Perryville, Murfreesboro, Chickamauga, Missionary Ridge, etc. Practiced law at Lewisville again, 1865-69, Washington, Ark., 1869-79, Little Rock, 1879-85; mem. Ho. of Rep., 1871; asso. justice Supreme Ct. of Ark., 1885-1911; retired. Home: Little Rock, Ark. Died Dec. 21, 1917.

BATTLE, Cullen Andrews, lawyer, soldier, journalist; b. Powelton, Ga., June 1, 1829; s. Dr. Cullen and Jane A. B.; preparatory edn. Brownwood Inst., nr. La Grange, Ga., 1846-48; grad. Univ. of Ala.; m. Georgia F. Williams, 1851. Admitted to bar, 1852; practiced law in Ala. until 1860; Breckenridge and Lane elector, 1860, and canvassed Ala. with Hon. William L. Yancey. Entered C. S. army as private; elected maj. 3d Ala. regt., April 1861; lt. col., July 1861; col., June 1862; distinguished in battle; promoted brig. gen. on field at Gettysburg, July 1863; maj. gen., Oct. 1864; wounded 7 times; since the war devoted his time chiefly to journalism. Home: New Bern, N.C. Died 1905.

BATTLE, Herbert Bemerton, chemist; b. Chapel Hill, N.C., May 29, 1862; s. Kemp Plummer and Martha Ann (Battle) B.; brother of Thomas Hall and William James B.; B.Sc., U. of N.C., 1881, Ph.D., 1887; m. Alice M. Wilson, Nov. 25, 1885; children—Nell Lewis, James Wilson. Asst. chemist, N.C. Agrl. Expt. Sta., 1881-87; state chemist and dir. in charge of N.C. Agrl. Expt. Sta., 1887-97; pres. Southern Chem. Co., Winston, N.C., 1897-1901; with Southern Cotton Oil Co., Savannah, Ga., and Montgomery, Ala., 1902-06; pres. The Battle Lab. Corp., 1906—. Chemist N.C. State Bd. Health, 1887-97, N.C. Geol. Survey, 1887-92; prof. chemistry, Leonard Med. Sch., 1886-97. Author: (with F. B. Dancy) Chemical Conversion Tables, 1885; Chemical Conversion Tables (with W. J. Gascoyne), 1909. Home: Montgomery, Ala. Died July 3, 1929.

BATTLE, John Thomas Johnson, M.D.; b. Wake Forest, N.C., Apr. 14, 1859; s. John Applewhite and Anne (Capell) B.; A.M., Wake Forest Coll., 1879; M.D., Coll. Phys. and Surg., Baltimore, 1881; post-grad. courses, Johns Hopkins, N.Y. Polyclinic and Post-Grad. Sch.; m. Dora L. Burns, Oct. 12, 1896. Began practice at Wadesboro, 1884; moved to Greensboro, N.C., 1898; mem. State Bd. Med. Examiners, 1902-08; mem. Guilford Co. Bd. of Health, 1911—; med. dir. Jefferson Standard Life Ins. Co., 1918—. Chmn. Guilford Co. Draft Bd., and 9th Dist. N.C. Selective Service Advisory Bd., World War. Trustee Meredith Coll., Wake Forest Coll. Mason. Democrat. Baptist. Home: Greensboro, N.C. Died Sept. 29, 1940.

BATTLE, Kemp Plummer, univ. pres.; b. nr. Louisburg, N.C., Dec. 19, 1831; s. Judge William Horn B. (LL.D.) and Lucy Martin (Plummer) B.; brother Richard Henry B.; A.B., U. of N.C., 1849, A.M., 1852; (LL.D., Davidson Coll., 1882, U. of N.C., 1910); admitted to bar, 1854; m. Martha Ann Battle, Nov. 28, 1855; children—Kemp Plummer, Jr., Thomas Hall, Herbert Bemerton and William James B. Tutor, U. of N.C., 1849-54; in law practice, 1854-76; mem. secession conv. of N.C., 1861; state treas., 1866-68; pres. U. of N.C., 1876-91, prof. history, 1891-1907, emeritus prof., 1907; retired on Carnegie Foundation. Trustee of the univ., 1862-68 and 1874-1923. Author: History of the University of North Carolina, Vol. I, 1789-1868, Vol. II, 1868-1912; History of Supreme Court of North Carolina; Trials and Judicial Proceedings of the New Testament; History of Raleigh, N.C.; and many hist. monographs. Home: Chapel Hill, N.C. Died Feb. 4, 1919.

BATTLE, Kemp Plummer, oculist, aurist; b. Raleigh, N.C., Mar. 9, 1859; s. Kemp Plummer and Martha Ann (Battle) B.; A.B., U. of N.C., 1879; M.D., U. of Va., 1881; M.D., Bellevue Hosp. Med. Coll. (New York U.), 1882; m. Eliza N. McKee, Feb. 4, 1890; m. 2d, Sally Hall Smith Strong, Oct. 20, 1920. Interne Charity Hosp., Blackwell's Island, New York, 1882-83, Blackwell's Island Insane Asylum, 1884; asst. surgeon U.S. Marine Hosp. Service, 1884-85; prof. physiology, Leonard Med. Sch., Raleigh, N.C., 1885-1913; prof. diseases ear, throat and nose, Med. Dept., U. of N.C., 1903-10; mem. firm of Drs. Lewis, Battle & Wright. Visiting surgeon to local hosps. Mem. State Med. Examining Bd., N.C., 1897-1900. Democrat. Episcopalian. Home: Raleigh, N.C. Died Mar. 23, 1922.

BATTLE, Richard Henry, lawyer; b. Louisburg, N.C., Dec. 3, 1835; s. William Horn (LL.D.) and Lucy Martin (Plummer) B.; brother of Kemp Plummer B.; A.B., U. of N.C., 1854, A.M., 1856; LL.B., 1858 (LL.D., 1895); m. Annie Ruffin Ashe, Nov. 28, 1860 (died 1883). Engaged in practice of law, Dec. 1858; was clerk and master in equity, 1861-62; entered C.S.A. as 1st lt.; apptd. capt. q.m., but resigned, for ill health, before getting commn.; successively pvt. sec. to Gov. Z. B. Vance of N.C., and state auditor, 1862-65. Since war in practice of law at Raleigh, N.C. Pres. and atty. N.C. Home Ins. Co.; dir. and atty. Citizens' Nat. Bank of Raleigh, Raleigh Cotton Mill, Neuse River Mills; pres. trustees of Rex Hosp., Raleigh Cemetery Assn., Rainey Library; trustee, sec. and treas. U. of N.C.; trustee and atty. St. Mary's Sch., Raleigh. Apptd. judge superior courts of N.C., 1886, but declined. Episcopalian; del. and mem. Com. on Canons in all Gen. Convs. P.E. Ch., 1889-1910. Democrat; for many yrs. mem. State Dem. Com. of N.C. (chmn. 1884-88); mem. N.C. Ho. of Rep., 1911 (chmn. judiciary com.). Home: Raleigh, N.C. Died 1912.

BATTLE, S(amuel) Westray, M.D.; b. Westrayville, Nash Co., N.C., Aug. 4, 1854; s. William Smith and Elizabeth Mary (Dancy) B.; U. of Va., 1874; M.D., Bellevue Hosp. Med. Coll., New York U., 1875; m. Alice Maude, d. Rear Adm. George E. Belknap, Nov. 1880 (died 1899); children—Madelon, Maude (dec.), Samuel Westray (dec.), Belknap; m. 2d, Jane Hyde (Hall) Liddell, d. Hon. John G. Hall, of Pa., Feb. 8, 1918. Surgeon U.S.N. 10 yrs., retired on account of injury to hand; pvt. practice many yrs.; med. dir. Clarence Barker Memorial Hosp., Biltmore, N.C., since organization of same. Surgeon gen. Nat. Guard of N.C., many yrs., retiring with rank of brig. gen. Democrat. Episcopalian. Home: Asheville, N.C. Died Apr. 29, 1927.

BATTLE, Thomas Hall, banker; b. Raleigh, N.C., Aug. 2, 1860; s. Kemp Plummer and Martha Ann (Battle) B.; A.B., U. of N.C., 1880; student law dept. U. of N.C.; admitted to bar, 1882; m. Bettie Davis, Nov. 9, 1887 (died 1890); 1 son, Kemp Davis; m. 2d, Sallie Hyman, Oct. 23, 1895 (died 1917); children—Hyman Llewellyn, Ethel Hall, Josephine; m. 3d, Mary Weddell, of Tarboro, N.C., Oct. 6, 1920; 1 dau., Martha Ann. Practiced law, 1882-95; pres. Nat. Bank of Rocky Mount and Rocky Mount Savings & Trust Co. until merger with N.C. Bank & Trust Co., now chmn. local bd. dirs. of latter; pres. Rocky Mount Ins. & Realty Co.; treas. Rocky Mount Cotton Mills. Mayor of Rocky Mount, 1886-96. Democrat. Episcopalian. Home: Rocky Mount, N.C. Died Jan. 23, 1936.

BATTS, Robert Lynn, lawyer; b. Bastrop, Tex., Nov. 1, 1864; s. Andrew Jackson and Julia (Rice) B.; ed. U. of Texas, LL.B., 1886; m. Harriet Fiquet Boak, Nov. 12, 1889; children—Robert E. Lee, Mary, Margaret Lynn. Admitted to Tex. bar, 1886; practiced at Bastrop, 1886-91; prof. of law, U. of Tex., 1893-1900; resumed practice at Austin; asst. atty.-gen. of Tex., 1891-93; rep. State of Tex. in case of State vs. Galveston, Harrisburg & San Antonio Ry Co. (recovered for the State 920,000 acres of land); of counsel for State in case of State of Tex. vs. Waters-Pierce Oil Co. (recovered and collected $1,900,000); spl. asst. atty.-gen. of U.S. to prosecute criminal charges against dirs. of N.Y.,N.H.&H. R.R. Co., 1914. U.S. circuit judge as mem. Circuit Ct. of Appeals, 5th Circuit, Mar. 1, 1917-Aug. 13, 1919, resigned; gen. counsel Gulf Oil Corp., Gulf Refining Co., and other subsidiaries, 1919-23; resumed practice of law at Austin, Tex., Jan. 1, 1924. Chmn. bd. regents U. of Tex., 1930-33. Democrat. Author: Annotated Civil Statutes of Texas, 1895; Corporation Laws of Texas, 1902. Home: Austin, Tex. Died May 19, 1935.

BAUER, L(ouis) A(gricola), magnetician; b. Cincinnati, Jan. 26, 1865; s. Ludwig and Wilhelmina (Buehler) B.; brother of William Charles B.; C.E., U. of Cincinnati, 1888, M.S., 1894; Ph.D., A.M., U. of Berlin, 1895; (D.Sc., U. of Cincinnati, 1913, Brown, 1914); m. Adelia Francis Doolittle, Apr. 15, 1891; 1 dau., Mrs. Dorothea Weeks. Astron. and magnetic computer, U.S. Coast and Geod. Survey, 1887-92; docent in math. physics, U. of Chicago, 1895-96; instr. in geophysics, 1896-97, asst. prof. mathematics and math. physics, 1897-99, U. of Cincinnati; insp. magnetic work and chief Terrestrial Magnetism Div., U.S. Coast and Geod. Survey, 1899-1906; dir. dept. Terrestrial Magnetism, Carnegie Instn., 1904-29, dir. emeritus and research asso.,

1930—. Chief Div. of Terrestrial Magnetism, Md. Geological Survey, 1896-99; astronomer and magnetician, western boundary survey of Md.; lecturer in terrestrial magnetism, Johns Hopkins, 1899—; founder, 1896, editor until 1928, co-editor, 1928—, Terrestrial Magnetism and Atmospheric Electricity (mag.). Mem. permanent com. on terrestrial magnetism and atmospheric electricity of Internat. Meteorol. Conf. and of the Internat. Assn. of Academies; fellow A.A.A.S. (v.p. and chmn. Sect. B, 1909), Am. Acad. Arts and Sciences, Am. Geog. Soc. Received the Charles Lagrange prize (Physique du globe) of Académie Royale des Sciences, des Lettres et des Beaux-Arts de Belgique, 1905, and Georg Neumayer Gold Medal, Berlin, May 1913; Halley lecturer on Terrestrial Magnetism at U. of Oxford, May 1913. Mem. Nat. Research Council, 1917—; chmn. com. navigation and nautical instruments, Council Nat. Defense, 1917-18; U.S. del. Brussels meetings, 1919, Internat. Research Council and Internat. Geodetic and Geophys. Union; U.S. del. Rome meeting of latter, 1922, Madrid, 24, Prague, 27; sec. and dir. central bur. sect. terrestrial magnetism and electricity of Internat. Geodetic and Geophys. Union, 1919-27, pres., 1927-30; v.chmn. Am. Geophysical Union, 1920-22 (chmn. sect. terrestrial magnetism and electricity, 1920-22 and 1924-26); chmn. Am. Geophys. Union, 1922-24. Decorated comdr. 2d class Order of St. Olav (Norway). Frequent contbr. to scientific press on terrestrial magnetism, electricity, physics, etc. Died Apr. 12, 1932.

BAUER, Ralph S., mayor, mcht.; b. Provincetown, Mass., Jan. 31, 1867; s. Thomas Dodson and Hannah (Sherman) B.; ed. Boston Latin Sch., Alfred U., Boston U.; m. Fannie Miller, Feb. 20, 1894; 1 son, Paul Sherman. Began as asst. circulator New York Herald, 1889; circulation mgr. Chicago Herald and Post, 1890-93, business mgr. Chicago Mail, 1893-94; business mgr. St. Louis Star, 1895-98; moved to Lynn, Mass., 1898, and organized the R. S. Bauer Co., of which was pres. and treas.; pres. and treas. North Shore News Co. Mem. Constl. Conv., Mass., 1916-17; mayor of Lynn, 1926-29. Pres. Lynn Men's Fellowship Class, largest Sunday morning men's class in Mass. Republican. Conglist. Died July 13, 1941.

BAUGHMAN, L., Victor, capitalist; b. Frederick, Md.; s. John W. B. (editor Frederick Citizen); ed. Rock Hill and Mt. St. Mary's Colls., Md.; left coll., ran the blockade, joined Md. inf., but later transferred to Co. D, 1st Md. Cav., C.S.A.; captured at Moorfield, and held prisoner 9 months at Camp Chase, O.; exchanged Mar. 1865; m. Helen, d. late A. S. Abell, propr. Baltimore Sun. After war worked on Frederick Citizen; studied law and later was employe of Narragansett Steamship Co., New York; on death of his father, 1872, assumed, with brother, ownership of Frederick Citizen; was chmn. Dem. Co. Com., mem. State Dem. Com. and Nat. Dem. Com.; was State Comptroller 4 yrs., and pres. Chesapeake & Ohio Canal; insp. gen. on staff Gov. Smith of Md. and chmn. of commrs. La. Purchase Expn., St. Louis; owner large estate and stock farm. Home: Frederick, Md. Died 1906.

BAUM, Dwight James, architect; b. Little Falls, N.Y., June 24, 1886; s. Fayette and Alma Elizabeth (Ackerman) B.; B.Arch., Syracuse U., 1909, Dr. of Fine Arts; m. Katharine Crouse, Jan. 3, 1912; children—Dwight Crouse, John Leach, Peter Ackerman. Began practice N.Y. City, 1915; has specialized in country houses and institutional work; designed Hotel El Verona and Court House, Sarasota, Fla.; Memorial Hosp., Syracuse; Hendricks Chapel, School of Citizenship and College of Medicine Syracuse U.; architect for Syracuse U., Clarkson, Hartwick, Middlebury and Wells colleges, Westside Y.M.C.A. and Trade Sch., in New York, Federal Bldg. (Flushing, N.Y. City), Columbus Memorial Monument (Syracuse), Great War Memorial Tower (Riverdale, N.Y. City), Recreational Center and Bottling Plant for Saratoga Springs Authority, Shelter Focal Center, N.Y. World's Fair, 1939. Exhibited in Paris Salon, London, Berlin, S. American cities, etc. Archtl. consultant Good Housekeeping Mag. Fellow Am. Inst. Architects (v.chmn. bldg. com.). Winner of fellowship in architecture, Syracuse U.; gold medal, Archtl. League of N.Y., 1923; bronze medal, Better Homes in America, 1931, 32, 34, gold medal, 1932. Contbr. articles on home building and architecture. A book entitled "The Work of Dwight James Baum," by Matlack Price, was issued in 1927. Home: Riverdale, New York, N.Y. Died Dec. 13, 1939.

BAUM, Frank George, electrical engr.; b. Ste. Genevieve, Mo., July 18, 1870; s. Christian and Caroline (Kline) B.; A.B., Stanford U., Calif., 1898, E.E., 1899; m. Mary Dawson, July 18, 1900; children—Esther F., Helen E., Adah C. Elec. engr. Calif. Gas & Elec. Corp., 1902-07; consulting constrn. engr., 1907—; chief engr. hydro-electric work, Pacific Gas & Electric Co., 1912—. Author: Alternating Currents, 1902; Alternating Current Transformer, 1903; Atlas of U.S.A. Electric Power Industry, 1923. Inventor of constant potential electric transmission system. Home: Cassel via Redding, Calif. Died 1932.

BAUM, L(yman) Frank, author; b. Chittenango, N.Y., May 15, 1856; s. of Benjamin Ward and Cynthia (Stanton) B.; acad. edn., at Syracuse, N.Y.; m. Maud, d. Matilda Joslyn Gage, of Fayetteville, N.Y., Nov. 9, 1882. Began newspaper work, 1880; edited the Dakota Pioneer, Aberdeen, S.D., 1888-90, and the Show Window, Chicago, Ill., 1897-1902. Author: Mother Goose in Prose, 1897, 1902; By the Candelabra's Glare (poems), 1898; Father Goose—His Book, 1899; The Wonderful Wizard of Oz, 1900; A New Wonderland, 1900; The Songs of Father Goose, 1900; The Army Alphabet, 1900; The Navy Alphabet, 1900; American Fairy Tales, 1901; Dot and Tot of Merryland, 1901; The Art of Decorating (technical), 1900; The Master Key, 1901; The Life and Adventures of Santa Claus, 1902; Enchanted Isle of Yew, 1903; The Magical Monarch of Mo, 1903; The Marvelous Land of Oz, 1904; The Woggle-Bug Book, 1905; Queen Zixi of Ix, 1905; Animal Fairy Tales, 1905; John Dough and the Cherub, 1906; Ozma of Oz, 1907; Dorothy and the Wizard, 1907; Baum's Fairy Tales, 1908; The Road to Oz, 1908; The Emerald City of Oz, 1909; Baum's Juvenile Speaker, 1909; The Sea Fairies, 1910; The Daring Twins, 1910; Phoebe Daring, Conspirator, 1911; Sky Island, 1912; Little Wizard Series (6 titles), 1913; Patch-work Girl of Oz, 1913; Tik-Tok Man of Oz, 1914; Scarecrow of Oz, 1915; Rinkitink in Oz, 1916; Babes in Birdland, 1917; The Lost Princess of Oz, 1917; The Tin Woodman of Oz, 1918. Plays: The Maid of Arran, produced New York, 1881; Matches, prod. New York, 1882; Kilmorne, prod. Syracuse, 1884; The Queen of Killarney, prod. Rochester, 1885; The Wizard of Oz (musical extravaganza), prod. Chicago, 1902; The Woggle-Bug (musical extravaganza), prod. Chicago, 1905; The Radio-Play (motion pictures of Baum's Fairy Tales), prod. Chicago and New York, 1908-09; Tik-Tok Man of Oz, prod. Los Angeles, 1913. Creator of "Fairyland of Oz," Home. Hollywood, Calif. Died May 6, 1919.

BAUM, William Miller, Jr., clergyman; b. Winchester, Va., June 30, 1858; s. William Miller and Maria Louisa (Croll) B.; A.B., Pa. Coll., Gettysburg, 1877, A.M., 1880, D.D., 1903; grad. Evang. Luth. Theol Sem., Gettysburg, 1880; unmarried. Ordained ministry Evang. Luth. Ch., 1880; pastor Phoenixville, Pa., 1880-83, Canajoharie, N.Y., 1883—. Trustee Hartwick Sem., 1897-1921, pres. bd. 1917-21; sec. Hartwick Synod, 1884-87, pres. 1888-92; pres. Synod of N.Y., 1910-12; sec. orgn. of United Luth. Ch., 1918; many times del. to Gen. Synod. Home: Canajoharie, N.Y. Deceased.

BAUMGARTEN, Gustav, physician; b. Clausthal (in the Hartz), Germany, June 1, 1837; s. Dr. F. Ernst and Louise (Beckmann) B.; ed. at Clausthal and Northeim (Hanover) till 1849, St. Louis, 1850-54; M.D., St. Louis Med. Coll., 1856; studied in univs. of Göttingen, Berlin, Prague and Vienna, 1856-59; (LL.D., Washington U., 1906); m. Aminda Hillegeist, June 1, 1865. In practice since 1859; asst. and passed asst. surgeon U.S.N., 1861-65; prof. physiology, 1873-87, spl. pathology and therapeutics, 1887-92, practice of medicine, 1892—, St. Louis Med. Coll. (Washington U.) Editor St. Louis Medical and Surg. Jour., 1868-71. Home: St. Louis, Mo. Died 1910.

BAUME, James Simpson, judge; b. Chicago, Apr. 13, 1857; s. James and Marie Antoinette (Hawkins) B.; ed. Northwestern U., 1872-74. Admitted to Ill. bar, 1879; practiced, Galena; elected judge Circuit Ct., 15th Jud. Circuit, 1897, re-elected, 1903, 09; apptd. justice Appellate Ct., 3d Dist., 1903, 06, 09; apptd. justice Appellate Ct., 1st Dist., 1911. Dir. Galena Pub. Library. Republican. Methodist. Mason. Home: Galena, Ill. Died July 20, 1919.

BAUMES, Caleb Howard, lawyer; b. Bethlehem, Albany Co., N.Y., Mar. 31, 1863; s. Peter H. and Mary E. (Wiltsie) B.; grad. Ft. Edward (N.Y.) Collegiate Inst., 1883; m. Carrie S. Ten Eyck, Mar. 17, 1883; children—Walton L., Floyd T. Teacher pub. schs., 1883-90; bookkeeper for wholesale provision house Newburgh, 1890-95; pres. Queen City Provision Co., 1895-98; admitted to N.Y. bar, 1898, and began practice at Newburgh. Mem. Gen. Assembly, N.Y., 1909-13, Senate, 1919—, mem. N.Y. State Constl. Conv., 1915; chmn. N.Y. State Crime Commn., 1926—. Republican. Methodist. Mason. Chmn. of Joint Legislative Com. of the N.Y. legislature which drew up amendments and additions to the Code of Criminal Procedure and the Penal Law, 1926. These amendments known as "The Baumes Laws," relate especially to penalties, procedure, appeals and bail. Home: Newburgh, N.Y. Died Sept. 25, 1937.

BAUMGARDT, B. R., scientist; b. Liverpool, England, May 19, 1862; s. Theodore and Mary (Lathangue) B.; ed. Strengnäs, Sweden; grad. Strengnäs Coll., Sweden, spl. studies in astronomy and mathematics; m. Mary Louise Steinhauer, July 20, 1885; children—Mars Frederick, Howard Oscar. Sec. Ore. Acad. Sciences, 1892; pres. and for 10 yrs. chmn. astron. and math. sect. Southern Calif. Acad. Sciences; staff lecturer The Brooklyn Inst. Arts and Sciences, The Am. Inst. (New York), League for Polit. Edn. (New York), Am. Univ. Extension (Phila.), Nat. Geog. Society (Washington, D.C.), Goodwyn Inst. (Memphis), Acad. Science and Art (Pittsburgh), Phila. Forum; hon. mem. Am. Inst. (New York). Has pvt. astron. obs. with 4½-inch refracting telescope. Mason. Author: Tidal Evolution; The Symbolism of the Universe. Contbr. to scientific publs. and daily press. Died June 19, 1935.

BAUR, Bertha, musical dir.; b. Cleveland, O.; d. Prof. Emil (Ann Arbor, Mich.) and Bertha (Herzer) B.; ed. undergrad. sch., Ann Arbor; hon. M.A., U. of Cincinnati, 1925. Pres. and dir. Cincinnati Conservatory of Music, succeeding Clara Baur in 1912; mem. bd. dirs. and exec. bd. Cincinnati Symphony Orchestra. Mem. Am. Red Cross, Alliance Française, Cincinnati Pub. Recreation Commn. (dir.), Matinee Musicale, Nat. Fedn. of Music Clubs, Cincinnati Art Mus., etc. Episcopalian. Home: Cincinnati, O. Died Sept. 18, 1940.

BAUR, Clara, directress (and founder, 1867) Cincinnati Conservatory of Music; b. Stuttgart, Wurtemberg, Germany; d. Rev. G. and Frederika B.; musical edn., Stuttgart Conservatory under Prof. Dr. Feisst, and also in Paris; unmarried. Home: Cincinnati, O. Deceased.

BAUSCH, John Jacob, mfr.; b. Suessen, Württemberg, Germany, July 25, 1830; s. George and Annie (Schmidt) B.; came to U.S. in 1849; m. Barbara Zimmerman, N.Y., 1853; m. 2d, Caroline Zimmerman, 1902. In optical business, Rochester, N.Y., 1853—; pres. Bausch & Lomb Optical Co., mfrs., scientific and optical instruments, 1853—. Formerly pres. Mechanics Savings Bank, now hon. mem. exec. com. Republican. Home: Rochester, N.Y. Died Feb. 14, 1926.

BAUSLIN, David Henry, theologian; b. Winchester, Va., Jan. 21, 1854; s. Michael and Martha (Bauslin) B.; A.B., Wittenberg Coll., 1876, B.D., 1878 (D.D., 1890); m. Elizabeth Clark, June 5, 1879. Ordained Luth. ministry, 1878; pastor Tippecanoe City, O., 1878-81, Bucyrus, O., 1881-89. Springfield, O., 1889-93, Canton, O., 1893-96; prof. practical theology, Wittenberg, Theol. Sem., 1896—, dean, 1911—. Editor Lutheran World, 1901-12. Pres. Gen. Synod Evang. Luth. Ch. in U.S., 1905-07; pres. bd. dirs. Wittenberg Coll., 1895-96. Author: Is the Ministry an Attractive Vocation? 1901; The Genesis of the "New Measure" Movement in the Lutheran Church in this Country; The Lutheran Movement of the Sixteenth Century, 1919. Home: Springfield, O. Died Mar. 3, 1922.

BAUSMAN, Benjamin, clergyman; b. Lancaster, Pa., Jan. 28, 1824; s. John and Elizabeth B.; grad. Marshall Coll., 1851; Theol. Sem., Mercersburg, Pa., 1852; (A.M., D.D., Franklin and Marshall Coll., Lancaster, Pa.); m. Amelia Bingaman, April 6, 1875. Ordained to ministry, Reformed Ch. in U.S., 1853; pastor Reformed Ch., Lewisburg, Pa., 1853; editor Reformed Messenger, Chambersburg, Pa., 1858; pastor Reformed Ch., Chambersburg, 1861, First Reformed Ch., Reading, 1863; founded St. Paul's Reformed Ch., Reading, 1873, became its pastor; del. German Evang. Ch. Diet, Lübeck, Germany, 1856; council of Alliance of Reformed Chs., Belfast, Ireland, 1884; pres. gen. synod Ref. Ch., Baltimore, 1884. Author: Sinai and Zion, 1860 (8 editions), German translation, 1875 M21; Wayside Gleanings in Europe, 1878 M21; Bible Characters, 1893 M21; Precept and Practice, 1901. Edited The Guardian, 1867-82; founded, 1867, and since then editor Reformirte Hausfreund. Home: Reading, Pa. Died 1909.

BAUSMAN, Frederick, author, lawyer; b. Pittsburgh, Pa., Mar. 23, 1861; s. Henry Andes and Susan (Bryar) B.; A.B., U. of Pittsburgh, 1881, LL.D., 1916; student Harvard Law Sch., 1882-83; spl. lit. research in N.Y. City; extensive travel in Europe and other parts of world; m. Adelaide Holmes, Apr. 11, 1894. Began practice at Olympic, Wash., 1886; settled at Seattle, 1891; mem. Code Com., Ty. of Wash., 1888; mem. Charter Com., Seattle, 1894; asso. justice Supreme Court of Wash., 1915-16 (resigned to resume practice); mem. Bausman, Oldham & Eggerman. Episcopalian. Author: Adventures of a Nice Young Man (under nom de plume of "Aix"), 1908; Let France Explain, 1923; Facing Europe, 1926. Home: Seattle, Wash. Died June 19, 1931.

BAUSMAN, J(ohn) W(atts) B(aer), lawyer, banker; b. Lancaster, Pa., Mar. 12, 1855; s. Jacob and Mary (Baer) B.; A.B., Lafayette Coll., Easton, Pa., 1874, A.M., 1877; m. Annette Franklin, Apr. 28, 1880 (died 1882); m. 2d, Blanche Franklin, 1892. Admitted to Pa. bar, 1877; pres. Farmers Trust Co. Trustee Bethamy Home, Reading, Pa., Franklin and Marshall Coll., and Yeates Sch.; dir. numerous cos. Pres. Pa. Bankers' Assn.; exec. council Am. Bankers' Assn. Home: Lancaster, Pa. Died Apr. 18, 1940.

BAXTER, Clarence Hughson, editor; b. N.Y. City, Oct. 28, 1858; s. Elisha Wesley and Eliza (Hughson) B.; ed. pub. schs.; m. Eliza Smith, July 12, 1892. Learned printer's trade and traveled in Latin America, 1874-77; entered newspaper work, 1885; city editor for Guardian, Paterson, 1902, mng. editor, 1903-14; receiver general Santo Domingo, 1914-21. Started crusade that gave Paterson commn. govt. Home: Paterson, N.J. Deceased.

BAXTER, Edmund Dillabunty, lawyer; b. Nashville, Tenn., Aug. 22, 1838; s. Nathaniel and Martha O. (Hamilton) B.; ed. Nashville; admitted to bar,

1857; m. Eliza J. Perkins, Aug. 9, 1859 (dec.); m. 2d, Mrs. Bettie Baxter. In practice at Nashville, 1857—; sr. mem. firm Baxters, 1895—; spl. counsel for numerous rys. and steamship cos. in matters relating to interstate commerce; prof. law, Vanderbilt U., 1875-1905. Del. Universal Congress of Lawyers and Jurists, St. Louis, 1904. Home: Nashville, Tenn. Died 1910.

BAXTER, George Strong, contractor; b. N.Y. City, Nov. 21, 1845; s. George and Anna Smith (Strong) B.; A.B., Williams Coll., 1865; E.M., Columbia, 1868; m. Emmelin Carnes Weeks, Mar. 5, 1874; children—George S., Wylly, Pomeroy, Emmelin W. Engr. of mines, railroads, etc., 1869-79; cashier, asst. treas. and treas. N.P. R.R., 1879-95; in lumber business and ry. contracting, 1895—. Home: New York, N.Y. Died July 2, 1928.

BAXTER, Irving Franklin, lawyer; b. Liverpool, Onondaga Co., N.Y., Jan. 11, 1863; s. George and Amie C. (Sitts) B.; grad. Liverpool Acad., 1879, Syracuse High Sch., 1883; m. Mary C. Gleason, Sept. 26, 1888 (dec.). Admitted to bar and removed to Omaha, 1887; formerly mem. Brown (Norris), Baxter & Van Dusen. Atty. Omaha Bd. Edn., 1892-93; co. judge Douglas Co., Neb., 1893-99; judge 4th Jud. Dist. Neb., 1899-1904; U.S. atty. for Neb., 1904 and 1905; assisted in investigation of "beef trust," also prosecuted land frauds, and land fencing cases for govt. Retired and moved to Los Angeles, Calif., 1927. Republican. Mason. Home: Los Angeles, Calif. Deceased.

BAXTER, James Phinney, author; b. Gorham, Me., Mar. 23, 1831; s. Elihu and Sarah (Cone) B.; acad. edn.; (hon. A.M., 1881, Litt.D., 1904, Bowdoin); m. Sarah Kimball Lewis, Sept. 18, 1854; m. 2d, Mehetabel Cummings Proctor, Apr. 2, 1873. Pres. Savings Bank. Mayor of Portland, 6 terms, 1893-97, 1904-05; organized Associated Charities and was its first pres.; organized and established Portland Soc. of Art, 1883; built and donated to Portland its pub. library, 1888, and Gorham, 1907; also conveyed to Gorham the family mansion for a museum. Pres. Portland Pub. Library, Baxter Library (Gorham), Portland Benevolent Soc.; overseer of Bowdoin Coll. Pres. Me. Hist. Soc., 1890—, N.E. Historic-Geneal. Soc., 1899—; councillor Am. Antiquarian Soc.; fellow Am. Acad. Arts and Sciences. Republican. Conglist. Mason. Author: The Trelawney Papers, 1884; George Cleve and His Times, 1885; The British Invasion from the North, 1887; Sir Ferdinando Gorges and His Province of Maine, 1890; The Pioneers of New France in New England, 1894; The Voyages of Jacques Cartier, 1906; The Greatest of Literary Problems, 1915; also numerous monographs and papers on early Am. history. Edited 20 vols. of Documentary History of Maine, etc. Home: Portland, Me. Died May 8, 1921.

BAXTER, Jere, lawyer, pres. Tenn. Central Ry.; b. Nashville, Tenn., Feb. 11, 1852; s. Judge Nathaniel and Mary Louise (Jones) B.; ed. Montgomery Bell Acad., Nashville; studied law and became publisher the Legal Reporter, later bound in 9 vols. as Baxter's Reports. Before 30 was pres. Memphis & Charleston R.R.; built Sheffield, Ala., and organized S. Pittsburg Town Co.; was candidate for gov., 1889; of late yrs. devoted to railroad affairs, building the Tenn. Central and becoming its pres. Home: Nashville, Tenn. Died 1904.

BAXTER, Sylvester, publicist; b. W. Yarmouth, Mass., Feb. 6, 1850; s. Sylvester and Rosella (Ford) B.; Pilgrim ancestry on both sides; received academic edn. at Leipzig and Berlin, 1875-77; m. Lucia Allen Millet, Sept. 24, 1893. On staff Boston Daily Advertiser, 1871-75, Boston Herald, 1879-83, 1887-1905; editor Mexican Financier, 1883-84, Outing Mag., 1885-86; spl. corr. Boston Advertiser in Germany, 1875-77, Boston Herald and New York Sun in Mexico, 1883-84, of Outlook at Pan.-Am. Conf., Rio de Janeiro, and in Argentina and Uruguay, 1906. A leading factor in promoting development of Boston's municipal park system; as sec. of preliminary Met. Park Commn. for Greater Boston, 1892-93, secured (in coöp. with Charles Eliot, its landscape architect) realization of the project; sec. Met. Improvements Com., 1907-09; ex-chmn. Malden Park Commn.; sec. Met. Improvement League. Mason. Republican. Author: Cruise of a Land Yacht; Berlin—A Study in Municipal Government, 1890; The Boston Park Guide; The Old New World, statement of the Hemenway Southwestern Archæological Expdn., 1888; Greater Boston, monograph, 1891; Spanish Colonial Architecture in Mexico, 1902; The Quest of the Holy Grail, 1904; Old Marblehead, 1906; The Unseen House (poems), 1917. Home: Malden, Mass. Died Jan. 28, 1927.

BAYLES, George James, author; b. Irvington-on-Hudson, N.Y., Aug. 28, 1869; s. Dr. George and Catherine S. (Johnson) B.; A.B., Columbia, 1891, A.M., 1892, LL.B., 1893, Ph.D., 1895; unmarried. Prize lecturer, Columbia, 1897-1903. Republican. Author: Civil Church Law, New Jersey, 1898, New York, 1898, Massachusetts, 1899; Civil Church Law Cases, 1900; Woman and the Law, 1901. Contbr. to Annals Am. Hist. Assn. on Am. Ecclesiology. Home: Orange, N.J. Died Nov. 20, 1914.

BAYLESS, William Silver, lawyer; b. Silvermount, Harford Co., Md., Nov. 25, 1883; s. William Hanna and Annie Pannell (Silver) B.; Lehigh U., 1902-05; Johns Hopkins U., 1905-06; Law Sch., U. of Md., 1905-08; LL.B., U. of Md., 1908; admitted to bar of Md., 1907; m. Lelia Sinclair Blakistone, Feb. 14, 1911. Removed to Juneau, Alaska, June, 1910; mem. Shackleford & Bayless; mem. Rep. Nat. Com. for Alaska, 1912-16. Presbyn. Home: Juneau, Alaska. Died Mar. 14, 1935.

BAYLEY, Edward Bancroft, merchant, trustee; b. Arlington, Mass., May 11, 1864; s. James Reed and Susanna Hubbard (Bancroft) B.; grad. English High Sch., Boston, 1882, Franklin medalist; m. Mary Richards Clark, June 1, 1893; 1 dau., Harriet (Mrs. William Bowditch Long). Began as jr. clk. in office of Henry W. Peabody & Co., importers of cordage fibres and sugar (Boston), Feb. 12, 1883, admitted to firm, 1898, sr. partner, Apr. 1931—; trustee Park Sq. Trust (Boston). Served as chmn. Hemp Importers Com. under War Trade Bd., World War. Republican. Conglist. Home: Boston, Mass. Died July 26, 1936.

BAYLEY, Frank Tappan, clergyman; b. Boston, Mass., Aug. 19, 1846; s. Christopher Tappan and Livona (Sawyer) B.; student, Bowdoin, 1867-69; grad. Union Theol. Sem., 1873; (D.D., Colo. Coll., 1897; LL.D., U. of Denver, 1914); m. Julia M. Palmer, Oct. 22, 1869. Ordained Congl. ministry, 1873; pastor, Canandaigua, N.Y., 1873-78, Westminster (Presbyn.) Ch., Detroit, Mich., 1878-83, State St. (Congl.) Ch., Portland, Me., 1883-91, Plymouth Ch., Denver, Nov. 28, 1892—. Author: Little Ten Minutes, 1909; The Man in the Crow's Nest, 1913. Home: Denver, Colo. Died Oct. 28, 1917.

BAYLEY, Warner Baldwin, rear adm.; b. Baldwinsville, N.Y., Sept. 9, 1845; m. Annette Williamson, Oct. 1890; 1 son, Warner W. Apptd. from N.Y., acting 3d asst. engr., Aug. 4, 1864; promoted through grades to capt., July 1, 1905; retired with rank of rear adm., Apr. 18, 1906. Advanced 2 numbers in rank for "eminent and conspicuous conduct in battle" while attached to the Massachusetts during the Spanish-Am. War. Died Apr. 22, 1928.

BAYLIES, Edmund Lincoln, lawyer; b. N.Y. City, Dec. 2, 1857; s. Edmund Lincoln and Nathalie Elizabeth (Ray) B.; grad. Phillips Exeter Academy, 1875; A.B., Harvard, 1879, LL.B., 1882; LL.B., Columbia, 1882; m. Louisa Van Rennselaer, Jan. 18, 1887. Began practice in office of Scudder & Carter, N.Y. City, 1883; mem. Carter & Ledyard, 1895, Carter, Ledyard & Milburn, 1904-26; pres. Vanderbilt Hotel Co.; v.p., trustee Greenwood Cemetery; trustee Atlantic Mut. Ins. Co. Mem. bd. dirs. Met Opera Co. Pres. Seamen's Ch. Inst. of New York. Seaman's Ch. Inst. of America; trustee Cathedral of St. John the Divine, St. Luke's Hosp. Mem. Mass. Soc. of the Cincinnati. Republican. Episcopalian. Sec. of spl. embassy to Court of St. James to coronation of King Edward VII, 1902; awarded Coronation Medal. Home: New York, N.Y. Died Apr. 29, 1932.

BAYLIES, Walter Cabot, mcht.; b. Taunton, Mass., Aug. 13, 1862; s. Edmund Lincoln and Nathalie Elizabeth (Ray) B.; A.B., Harvard, 1884; m. Charlotte Upham, Nov. 17, 1888. Former mem. Amory, Browne & Co., agts. for various cotton mills; dir. Second Nat. Bank, Edison Electric Illuminating Co. of Boston, Boston Safe Deposit & Trust Co. Trustee Mass. Hosp. Sch. Episcopalian. Home: Taunton, Mass., and Boston. Died July 1936.

BAYLISS, Alfred, teacher; b. Gloucestershire, Eng., Mar. 22, 1847; s. John and Frances (Blake) B.; corp. 11th Mich. Cav., 1863-65; B.S., Hillsdale (Mich.) Coll., 1870, M.S., 1873; m. Clara M. Kern, June 28, 1871. In pub. sch. work, 1870—; state supt. pub. instrn. of Ill., 1898-1907; prin. Western Ill. State Normal Sch., 1906—. Contbr. to ednl. jours. Home: Macomb, Ill. Died 1911.

BAYLISS, Major William, architect; b. Pictou, N.S., Nov. 8, 1848; s. John and Lillia (McKenzie) B.; pub. sch. edn., Pictou; studied architectural drawing at night schs.; m. Marion Francis, d. William A. Ray, Dec. 18, 1872. Became supt. hosp. constrn., office of surg. gen. U.S. Army, 1882. Invented combination steam and hot water heating system, 1893. Sovereign Grand Comdr., Supreme Council of Sovereign Grand Inspectors-Gen. Mason. Home: Washington, D.C. Died 1919.

BAYLOR, Adelaide Steele, home economist; b. Wabash, Ind.; d. James Craig and Susannah (Steele) B.; student U. of Mich., 1893-95; Ph.B., U. of Chicago, 1897 (hon. mention); scholarship, Columbia, 1908, M.A., same univ., 1918; hon. Sc.D., Stout Inst., Menomonie, Wis., 1928. Teacher pub. schs., Ind.; supt. city schs., Wabash, 1903-10; asst. state supt. pub. instrn., Ind., 1911-14; state superv. home economics, Ind., 1915-17; fed. agt. home economics edn., Washington, D.C., 1918-22; chief home economics edn. service, Washington, D.C., 1923—. Pres. City and Town Supts.' Assn., Ind., 1904 (only woman mem.); pres. elementary sect. N.E.A., 1911; pres. nat. council Administrative Women in Edn., 1916-17; nom. for state supt. pub. instrn., Ind., 1920; mem. Nat. Com. on Rural Schs., 1912-23; mem. Nat. Com. on Standards for Ednl. Tests and Measurements, 1912-14; sec. Nat. Council of Edn., 1917—; mem. governing bd. Nat. Council Parent Edn., 1929-32; nat. chmn. of homemaking in Nat. Congress of Parents and Teachers, 1931—. Author: Adventures of Tabby Gray (children's book), 1913. Joint Author: Young America's First Book (reader), 1919. Home: Washington, D.C. Died Dec. 18, 1935.

BAYLOR, James Bowen, geodesist; b. Mirador, Albemarle Co., Va., May 30, 1849; s. Dr. John Roy and Anne (Bowen) B.; hon. grad. Va. Mil. Inst., 1865; B.S., C.E., U. of Va., 1872; (LL.D., Baylor U., 1903); m. Ellen C. Bruce, Jan. 5, 1881 (dec.). Apptd. aid in U.S. Coast and Geod. Survey, 1874, after competitive exam.; made magnetic survey of N.C.; field officer U.S. Coast and Geod. Survey, 1874—. Has determined the elements of earth's magnetism from Can. to Mex. in almost every state, and has done geod., astron. and hydrographic work for survey in various sections of U.S.; oyster surveys in La.; "Baylor survey" of oyster grounds of Va., 1889-94; commr. Supreme Ct. of U.S. for boundary of Va. and Tenn., 1900-02. Served with corps of cadets, Va. Mil. Inst., in Civil War, 1864-65. Boundary engr. for Va. (Va. and Md.); engr. on Pa.-N.Y. boundary and on U.S. and Can. Boundary Survey. Contbr. various reports of U.S. Coast and Geod. Survey. Home: Newmarket, Milford P.O., Va. Died May 1924.

BAYNE, Howard Randolph, lawyer; b. Winchester, Va., May 11, 1851; s. Charles and Mary Ellen (Ashby) B.; M.A., Richmond Coll., 1872, B.L., 1879; admitted to Va. bar, 1879, N.Y. bar, 1882; m. Lizzie S., d. Samuel Preston Moore, surg.-gen. C.S.A., of Richmond, Va., Apr. 27, 1886; children—Samuel Preston Moore (dec.), Mary Ashby Moore (Mrs. Herbert C. Bugbird), Lloyd Moore. Mem. N.Y. Senate, 1909-12 (chmn. jud. com.). Democrat. Mem. N.Y. State Probation Commn., 1905; N.Y. Employers' Liability Commn., 1909; chmn. Albany Investigation Senate Com., 1911. Mem. Bd. of Contract Adjustment, War Dept. Charter mem. Richmond Co. Red Cross Chapter. Vestryman Christ Ch., New Brighton, N.Y.; N.Y. City Visiting Com., State Charities Aid Assn. Editor: Converse's Indexes (Va. and W.Va. law), 1881; Travels of Ego and Alter (joint), 1879. Home: New Brighton, S.I., N.Y. Died Mar. 13, 1933.

BAYNE, Samuel Gamble, banker; b. Ulster, Ireland, Nov. 11, 1844; s. Peter and Margaret B.; ed. Royal Acad. Sch. and Queen's Coll., Belfast; m. Emily Kelsey, Oct. 1874. Started business in office of Sir James Hamilton, Belfast; later linen mfr. in Belfast until Mar. 1869; came to U.S.; went to oil regions, 1870; drilled many wells there; went around the world, 1874-75; started in banking business in Bradford, Pa., organizing First Nat. Bank and becoming its 1st pres.; afterwards organized nat banks in Tex., Kan., Miss., Minn. and Ohio; organized Seaboard Nat. Bank, 1883, later chmn. bd.; pres. Atlas Improvement Co., Riverside Drive Property Assn., N.Y. Produce Exchange Safe Deposit & Storage Co.; dir. Bankers Trust Co. Author: Pith of Astronomy, 1896; On an Irish Jaunting Car Through Donegal and Connemara, 1902; Fantasy of Mediterranean Travel, 1909. Home: White Plains, N.Y. Died Apr. 20, 1924.

BAYNES, Ernest Harold, writer, lecturer; b. Calcutta, India, May 1, 1868; s. John and Helen Augusta (Nowill) B.; ed. Coll. City of N.Y.; m. Louise Birt O'Connell, Apr. 24, 1901. Reporter on New York Times, 1891-92; asst. to father (inventor of photographic modeling), 1893-1900; writing and lecturing on natural history, 1900—. Wrote series "Wild Life in the Blue Mountain Forest," 1904, and other contributions to newspapers and magazines, etc. Mem. Co. K, 3d Conn. Vols., 1908. Hon. mem. Hobby Post G.A.R., Stamford, Conn. Toured Europe, Egypt and Palestine, 1919, as spl. corr. Harper's Mag. to get the story of the part played by animals in the Great War. Organized Meriden (N.H.) Bird Club (gen. mgr.), and over 200 similar clubs. Meriden Humane Soc. (pres.). Acted the part of "Shy," the naturalist, in the original cast of Percy MacKaye's bird masque, "Sanctuary," written in the interest of American bird protection. Author: Wild Bird Guests (preface by Theodore Roosevelt), 1915; Polaris—The Story of an Eskimo Dog, 1922; Jimmie—The Story of a Black Bear Cub, 1923. Actively in favor of vivisection as a practice necessary to the health and longevity of men and animals. Home: Meriden, N.H. Died Jan. 21, 1925.

BAYNES, John, inventor; b. Westmoreland, England, Aug. 24, 1842; s. Oswald and Agnes B.; took 5 yrs.' course at Ackworth (Soc. of Friends' Coll., England); m. Helen A. Nowill, Apr. 24, 1867; mem. Bengal Chamber of Commerce, 1864; engaged in gen. foreign shipping business until 1875. Came to U.S., 1875; invented celluloid photographic films, 1884; gold etching photo process, 1885, and numerous inventions in arts, including photographic modeling; photographically modeled records of sound vibrations. Invented process for producing musical and other sounds from graphic designs; mem. Asiatic Soc. Wrote Chronicles of Westchester Creek, Universal Review, London, 1891. Home: Stamford, Conn. Died 1903.

BEACH, Albert Isaac, lawyer; b. Olathe, Kan., July 30, 1883; s. George H. and Eva F. (Hull) B.; A.B., U. of Kan., 1905; LL.B., Washington U., 1907; m. Marjorie Marshall, Dec. 21, 1907; children—Eleanor, Marshall. Admitted to Mo. bar, 1907, began practice at Kansas City; mem. Harzfeld, Beach, Steeper & Gordon; dir. Business Men's Assurance Co., Trans-Mississippi Life Ins. Co., Westport Avenue Bank, Success Savings & Loan Assn. Mem. Lower House, Common Council, Kansas City, 1910-14, Upper House, 1916-20; mayor of Kansas City, 1924-26, and reëlected under new managerial charter for term 1926-30 (reduced expenses of city $1,200,000 1st yr.). Republican. Presbyn. Mason. Home: Kansas City, Mo. Died Jan. 21, 1939.

BEACH, Arthur Grandville, coll. prof.; b. Marietta, O., Nov. 29, 1870; s. David Edward and Alice (Allen) B.; A.B., Marietta Coll., 1891; B.D., Yale, 1896; studied U. of Berlin, 1896-97; Ph.D., U. of Mich., 1913; m. Mary Frances Dawes, June 8, 1896. Ordained Congl. ministry, 1896; pastor Ashland, Wis., 1897-1901, Ypsilanti, 1901-12; prof. English lit., Marietta Coll., 1913—. Author: Endeavors After The Spirit of Religion, 1912. Home: Marietta, O. Died Jan. 28, 1934.

BEACH, Charles Fisk, lawyer; b. Ky., Feb. 4, 1854; s. Rev. Charles Fisk and Harriette Adelia (Lockwood) B.; A.B., Centre College, 1877, A.M., 1881; LL.B., Columbia, 1881; LL.D., Mount St. Mary's, 1920. Ancien élève de la Faculté de Droit de l'Université de Paris et de l'École Libre des Sciences Politiques; Chevalier de la Légion d'Honneur, 1913. Admitted to bar, 1881; practiced in New York, 1881-95, London, 1896-1900, Paris, 1900— (except 1902-03 in St. Paul, Minn.). Editor Railway & Corp. Law Journal, New York, 1888-92; lecturer St. Paul Coll. of Law, 1902-03; lecturer on Am. law, univs. of Paris and Lille, 1904-06. Author: The Law of Receivers, 1887; Wills, 1888; Railways, 1890; Private Corporations, 1891; Modern Equity Jurisprudence, 1892; Public Corporations, 1893; Modern Equity Practice, 1894; Injunctions, 1895; Insurance, 1895; Contracts, 1897; Contributory Negligence, 1899. Editor of French titles in 2d edition Ency. Americana, 1920. Home: Cannes, France. Died June 6, 1934.

BEACH, Charles Fisk, clergyman, editor, law author; b. Hunter (now Jewett), N.Y., Sept. 5, 1827; s. Fisk and Panthea Dyer B.; ed. at Del. Literary Inst. and Prattsville Acad.; grad. Auburn Theol. Sem. 1854 (A.M., Knox Coll., 1859); m. 1st, Harriette Adelia Lockwood, June 2, 1851; m. 2d, Ophelia L. Higley, Sept. 16, 1890; m. 3d, Helene Louise Lee, June 21, 1898. Licensed to preach by Presbytery of Ithaca, June 7, 1853; ordained by Presbytery of Otsego, Jan. 10, 1856; in active pastorate of Presbyn. Ch., 1854-73; editor and publisher Nat. Presbyterian and Expositor of Internat. Sunday School Lessons, 1873-95; admitted to bar Feb. 5, 1896. Author: The Muzzled Ox, 1866; The Christian Worker, 1869; Commentaries on The Law of Trusts and Trustees, 1897; Monopolies and Industrial Trusts, 1898; also sermons and tracts. Home: Audubon, N.J. Died 1908.

BEACH, Charles Lewis, college pres.; b. Whitewater, Wis., Apr. 6, 1866; s. Charles R. and Mary Janette (Lewis) B.; B.Agr., B.S., U. of Wis., 1886; hon. D.Sc., from Wesleyan Univ., 1927; m. Louise C. Crombie, 1896; 1 dau., Katharine Cordelia (dec.). Instr. and prof. dairy husbandry, Conn. Agrl. Coll., 1896-1906; prof. dairy husbandry, U. of Vt. and Vt. Expt. Sta., 1906-08; pres. Conn. Agrl. Coll., Sept. 15, 1908—. Home: Storrs, Conn. Died Sept. 15, 1933.

BEACH, Daniel, lawyer; b. Tyrone, N.Y., Aug. 29, 1830; s. Obadiah and Mary (Lang) B.; A.B., Alfred U., 1856, A.M., 1885, Ph.D., 1886; (LL.D., Hamilton Coll., 1888, Alfred, 1902); m. Angelica Church Magee, June 4, 1862. Admitted to bar, 1861; in practice at Corning, N.Y., 1864—. V.p. and gen. counsel Fall Brook Coal Co. and other corps., 1864—. Regent U. State of N.Y., 1885—. Republican. Home: Watkins, N.Y. Died Feb. 22, 1913.

BEACH, David Nelson, theologian; b. S. Orange, N.J., Nov. 30, 1848; s. Joseph Wickliff and Mary Angeline (Walkley) B.; A.B., Yale, 1872; grad. Yale Div. Sch., 1876, B.D., 1881; D.D., Western Reserve, 1896; m. Lilian Tappan, Dec. 31, 1878 (died 1902); m. 2d, Dora Freeman, Dec. 18, 1903 (died 1915); m. 3d, Ellen O. Walkley, Oct. 20, 1916. Ordained Congl. ministry, 1876; pastor Westerly, Rhode Island, 1876-79, Wakefield, Mass., 1879-84, Cambridge, Mass., 1884-96, Minneapolis, Minn., 1896-98, Denver, Colo., 1899-1902; pres. and prof. homiletics, Bangor Theol. Sem., 1903-21; preaching and writing, 1921—. Prominent in permanently ridding Cambridge, Mass., from the saloon; in local option and good civics work in Mass. and elsewhere; agitator for grafting modified Norwegian liquor system on Mass. local option laws; also for ch. unity and a better theology. Author: Plain Words on Our Lord's Work, 1886; The Newer Religious Thinking, 1893; How We Rose (a Resurrection parable), 1895; The Intent of Jesus, 1896; Statement of Belief, 1897; The Annie Laurie Mine, 1903; Meanings of the Battle of Bennington, 1903; A Handbook of Homiletics, 1917. Home: Southington, Conn. Died Oct. 18, 1926.

BEACH, Frederick Converse, editor; b. New York, Mar. 27, 1848; s. Alfred Ely and Harriet Eliza (Holbrook) B.; Ph.B., Sheffield Scientific Sch. (Yale), 1868; m. Margaret A. Gilbert, 1875. In 1864, as pastime, began practice of photography; suggested, 1866, to U.S. commr. of patents, utility and practicability of photo-lithographing U.S. patents, a plan later adopted; patent solicitor at Washington, 1868-69; asst. supt. of construction of Beach pneumatic tunnel under Broadway, New York, 1869; afterward mfr. of elec. instruments; in 1877 entered office of Scientific American, assisting his father, and after latter's death became one of editors. Founded, 1884, Soc. Amateur Photographers of New York (now Camera Club); one of founders of mag., Am. Amateur Photographer (now American Photography); editor-in-chief Ency. Americana, 1902—. Home: Stratford, Conn. Died June 8, 1918.

BEACH, Harlan Page, prof. missions; b. S. Orange, N.J., Apr. 4, 1854; s. Joseph Wickliff and Mary Angeline (Walkley) B.; brother of David Nelson B.; A.B., Yale, 1878, A.M., 1901; grad. Andover Theol. Sem., 1883; (D.D., Amherst Coll., 1913); m. Lucy L. Ward, June 29, 1883. Taught at Phillips Andover Acad., 1878-80; missionary in China, 1883-90; taught and was in charge of Sch. for Christian Workers, Springfield, Mass., 1892-95; ednl. sec. Student Volunteer Movement for Foreign Missions, 1895-1906; prof. theory and practice of missions, Yale, 1906-21; lecturer on missions, Drew Theol. Sem., 1921-28. Author: The Cross in the Land of the Trident, 1895; Knights of the Labarum, 1896; Dawn on the Hills of T'ang, 1898; Geography and Atlas of Protestant Missions (2 vols.), 1901, 1903; Princely Men of the Heavenly Kingdom, 1903; India and Christian Opportunity, 1904; Renaissant Latin America, 1916; Missions as a Cultural Factor in the Pacific, 1927. Coauthor: World Atlas of Christian Missions, 1911; World Statistics of Christian Missions, 1916; World Missionary Atlas, 1925. Died Mar. 4, 1933.

BEACH, Harrison L., newspaperman; b. Dubuque, Ia., Jan. 12, 1863; s. Myron H. and Helen Mary (Hoskins) B.; common sch. edn.; m. Jessie M. Bowen, Sept. 5, 1905. Entered newspaper work in Chicago, 1889; was connected with the Asso. Press, 1892-1911; corr. at Santiago and other points during Spanish-Am. War, and for many yrs. rep. Asso. Press at nat. polit. convs.; supt. central div., comprising 16 states, with headquarters at Chicago, Jan. 1, 1909-Apr. 1, 1911; with Charles S. Diehl, owner and pub. San Antonio (Tex.) Light 1921-May 1924. Home: San Antonio, Tex. Died Feb. 18, 1928.

BEACH, Henry Harris Aubrey, surgeon; b. Middletown, Conn., Dec. 18, 1843; s. Elijah and Lucy S. (Riley) B.; served in hosp. service U.S.A., 1864-66; M.D., Harvard, 1868; m. Alice C. Mandell, June 7, 1871 (died 1880); m. 2d, Amy Marcy Cheney, Dec. 2, 1885. In practice at Boston, 1868—; asst. demonstrator anatomy, 1869-79, demonstrator, 1879-84, instr. clin. surgery, 1898-1900, lecturer, 1900-06, Harvard. Consulting surgeon Mass. Gen. Hosp., 1907—; asst. editor Boston Med. and Surg. Journal, 1868-69. Contbr. articles and papers to med. jours. Home: Boston. Died 1910.

BEACH, John Kimberly, lawyer; b. New Haven, Conn., Oct. 18, 1855; s. John Sheldon and Rebecca (Gibbons) B.; B.A., Yale, 1877, LL.B., 1879; hon. M.A., 1908, LL.D., 1914; m. Mary Roland Sanford, Apr. 15, 1890. Phelps prof. commercial law and admiralty, Yale Law Sch., 1908-23. Asso. justice Conn. Supreme Court of Errors, 1912-25; now state referee. Republican. Episcopalian. Home: New Haven, Conn. Died July 6, 1938.

BEACH, Miles, jurist; b. Saratoga Co., N.Y., 1840; s. William A. B.; grad. Union Coll., Schenectady, N.Y.; read law; admitted to bar of Troy; practiced at Troy; became active in politics; removed to New York, 1867; became mem. Beach, Daly & Brown, then Beach & Brown; judge Court of Common Pleas, 1879-94; justice Supreme Court, 1894—; term expires 1907. Home: New York, N.Y. Died 1902.

BEACH, Spencer Ambrose, horticulturist; b. Sumner Hill, Cayuga Co., N.Y., 1860; s. Isaac Ambrose (M.D.) and Maria North (Wood) B.; B.S.Agr., Ia. State Coll., 1887, M.S., 1892; m. Norma Hainer, July 2, 1890. Prof. horticulture and botany, Tex. A. and M. Coll., 1890-91; horticulturist State Expt. Sta., Geneva, N.Y., 1891-1905; prof. horticulture, Sept., 1905—, vice-dean Coll. of Agr., 1906—, Ia. State Coll. Republican. Author: The Apples of New York (2 Vols.), 1905. Home: Ames, Ia. Died Nov. 2, 1923.

BEACH, Sylvester Woodbridge, clergyman; b. Woodville, Miss., July 24, 1852; s. Rev. Charles and Fannie (Woodbridge) B.; A.B., Princeton, 1876; grad. Princeton Theol. Sem., 1880; D.D., Wooster (O.) College, 1914; m. Eleanor Orbison, Aug. 10, 1882 (died 1927); children—Mary Hollingsworth (Mrs. Frederic J. Dennis), Sylvia Woodbridge, Cyprian Woodbridge. Ordained Presbyn. ministry, 1880; pastor Baltimore, 1880-87, First Ch., Bridgeton, N.J., 1887-1900; in charge Am. students, work in Latin Quarter, Paris, France, 1900-05; co-pastor Am. Ch. in Paris, 1903-05; pastor First Ch., Princeton, N.J., 1905-23 (emeritus). Moderator Synod of N.J. Mason. Pastor to President Woodrow Wilson and officiated at the White House, at marriage of two daughters of the President. Contbr. Princeton Rev. and other periodicals. Toured Near East, 1922, as commr. Alliance of Ref. Chs. Home: Altadena, Calif. Died Nov. 16, 1940.

BEACH, William Dorrance, army officer; b. Brooklyn, N.Y., June 18, 1856; s. Joshua M. and Sarah E. (Ford) B.; grad. U.S. Mil. Acad., 1879; m. Miss Bullens, Apr. 27, 1882. Comd. 2d lt. 3d Cav., June 13, 1879; promoted through grades to brig. gen. N.A., Aug. 5, 1917; brig. gen. regular army, Feb. 28, 1927 (retired). Served at Camp Eagle Pass, Tex., 1888-91; instr. in charge dept. engring., Inf. and Cav. Sch., Ft. Leavenworth, 1892-98; comd. cav. troop, Chickamauga Park, Ga., 1898; engr. cav. div. 5th Army Corps, and mem. Gen. Wheeler's staff at battles of Las Guasimas and San Juan, Cuba, 1898; acting insp. gen. 5th Army Corps, 1898-99; participated in various minor engagements, Philippines, 1899; duty Gen. Staff, 1903-06, 1909-12; gov., Santa Clara Province, Cuba, 1908; chief of staff, Philippine Dept., 1910-12; pres. Bd. on Cav. Drill Regulations, 1916; comdg. 176th Inf. Brigade, Camp Dodge, Des Moines, Ia., Sept. 1917 and 8th Div. there and in France, May-Aug. 1918. Decorated D.S.M. (U.S.); 2 citations "for gallantry in action"; Legion of Honor, Croix de Guerre (France). Republican. Episcopalian. Home: San Diego, Calif. Died June 18, 1932.

BEACH, William Mulholland, surgeon; b. Stoneboro, Pa., Sept. 15, 1859; s. Oliver and Ann Elizabeth (Mulholland) B.; A.B., Waynesburg (Pa.) Coll., 1882, A.M., 1885; M.D., Jefferson Med. Coll., 1889; m. Lucy Lazear Miller, 1882. Prof. Latin and Greek, Ozark (Mo.) Coll., 1882-85; pres. Odessa (Mo.) Coll., 1885-87; an organizer and surgeon Presbyn Hosp., Pittsburgh, 1895-1914; proctologist South Side Hosp., 1906-11. Examining surgeon for pensions, 1893-97; 1st lt. Med. Corps, N.G. Pa., 1894-97. Mem. bd. trustees Waynesburg College. Dem. Presbyn. Mason. Contbr. 2 chapters in Cook's Diseases of the Rectum and Colon. Inventor of proctoscope and colostomy supporter. Home: Pittsburgh, Pa. Died 1930.

BEADLE, William Henry Harrison, educator; b. Howard, Parke Co., Ind., Jan. 1, 1838; s. James Ward and Elizabeth (Bright) B.; A.B., U. of Mich., 1861, A.M., 1864, LL.B., 1867, LL.D., 1902; m. Ellen S. Chapman, May 18, 1863 (died 1897). First lt. Co. A, 31st Ind. Inf., Sept. 5, 1861; col. and brig. gen. vols., Mar. 13, 1865; hon. mustered out, Mar. 26, 1866. Practiced law at Evansville, Ind., and Boscobel, Wis., 1867-69; U.S. surveyor-gen. Dak. Ty., 1869-73; sec. commn. to codify laws of Dak. Ty., 1876; mem. Territorial Ho. of Rep., 1877-78; pvt. sec. Gov. William A. Howard, 1878-79; supt. pub. instrn., Dak. Ty., 1879-85, and founder of its sch. system; leader of statehood movement; pres. Madison (S.D.) State Normal Sch., 1889-1905. Wrote article and secured adoption in S.D. state constitution fixing high limitation on sale of sch. and endowment lands granted by U.S.; same feature inserted by Congress in enabling acts of N.D., Mont., Wyo., Ida., Wash. and Okla. Republican. An organizer State Ednl. Assn. (1st and 2d pres. and pres., 1909). Author: Geography, History and Resources of Dakota Territory, 1888. Joint Author: The Natural System of Teaching Geography, 1899. Home: Madison, S.D. Died Nov. 13, 1915.

BEAHAN, Willard, civil engr.; b. Watkins, N.Y., Jan. 15, 1854; s. James and Harriet (Griswold) B.; grad. Starkey Sem., Eddytown, N.Y., 1873; B.C.E., Cornell U., 1878; m. Bessie Bell De Witt, 1892; 1 son, James De Witt. Began under Jay Gould on his Southwest system of rys., 1880; chief of constrn., Chilean Ry., S.A., 1891; with Anderson & Barr, contractors, 1892-96; supt. constrn. for James J. Hill, at Cascade Tunnel, 1897-98; prin. engr. Lehigh Valley R.R., 1899-1901; div. engr., North Western R.R., 1901-05; 1st asst. engr., N.Y.C. R.R., at Cleveland, O., 1905-24; spl. engr. Nickel Plate R.R., 1924-26. Trustee Cornell U. Mem. Bur. Municipal Research, Cleveland. Democrat. Conglist. Home: Cleveland, O. Died Feb. 5, 1928.

BEAKES, Samuel Willard, congressman; b. Burlingham, N.Y., Jan. 11, 1861; s. Dr. George M. and Elizabeth (Bull) B.; Lit. and Law depts., U. of Mich., LL.B., 1883; m. Annie S. Beakes, July 7, 1886. Practiced short time, Westerville, O.; editor and propr. Westerville Review, 1884, Adrian (Mich.) Daily Record, 1884-86, Ann Arbor Argus, 1886-1905; postmaster, Ann Arbor, under President Cleveland; mayor 2 terms, city treas. 4 terms, city assessor 4 terms; mem. 63d, 64th and 65th Congresses (1913-19), 2d Mich. Dist.; asst. chief industrial coöperation service, Dept. of Commerce, Apr.-July 1919; now staff mem. U.S. Veterans Bur., Washington, D.C. Episcopalian. Democrat. Author: History of Washtenaw County, Mich. Home: Ann Arbor, Mich. Died Feb. 9, 1927.

BEAL, Alvin Casey, prof. floriculture; b. Mt. Vernon, Ill., Nov. 30, 1872; s. Lewis N. and Sarah Melissa (Casey) B.; B.S., U. of Ill., 1897; M.S.A., Cornell U., 1903; Ph.D., 1911; m. Ervilla Belle LeFevre, Dec. 31, 1899. Foreman hort. dept. Ill. Expt. Sta., 1898; instr. floriculture, U. of Ill., 1900-08; with Cornell U., 1909—, prof. floriculture, 1913—. Republican. Conglist. Mason. Author: The Gladiolus, 1927. Writer of numerous research bulls. and articles. Home: Ithaca, N.Y. Died May 6, 1929.

BEAL, Foster Ellenborough Lascelles, naturalist; b. S. Groton (now Ayer), Mass., Jan. 9, 1840; s. Jacob Foster and Sarah Jane (Day) B.; B.S., Mass. Inst. Tech., 1871; m. Mary Louise Barnes, Jan. 9, 1877. Instr. mathematics, M.I.T., 1870-74; asst. prof. mathematics, U.S. Naval Acad., 1874-75; prof. civil engring., 1876-82, acting prof. zoölogy, 1879-82, prof. geology, 1883, Ia. Agrl. Coll.; asst. biologist, 1891-1901, economic ornithologist, 1902—, Biol. survey, U.S. Dept. Agr. Writer on econ. ornithology. Home: Berwyn, Md. Died Oct. 1, 1916.

BEAL, Thomas Prince, banker; b. Charlestown, Mass., Sept. 27, 1849; s. James H. and Judith D. (Beal) B.; A.B., Harvard, 1869, A.M., 1872; m. Ida De Ford, Oct. 27, 1881. Traveled in Europe, 1869-70; entered 2d Nat. Bank of Boston (of which father was pres.), 1871, pres., 1888—; pres. Hamilton Woolen Co.; dir. Fed. Reserve Bank of Boston, Bigelow-Hartford Carpet Co., Proprietors of the Cemetery of Mt. Auburn; trustee Suffolk Savings Bank for Seamen and Others; mem. local bd. Am. Surety Co. of New York. Pres. Boston Clearing House Assn. Home: Boston, Mass. Died May 24, 1923.

BEAL, William James, botanist; b. Adrian, Mich., Mar. 11, 1833; s. William and Rachel S. (Comstock) B.; A.B., U. of Mich., 1859, A.M., 1862; S.B., Harvard, 1865; M.S., U. of Chicago, 1875; (hon. Ph.D., U. of Mich., 1880; D.Sc., Mich. State Agrl. Coll., 1905; D.Agr., Syracuse U., 1916); m. Hannah A. Proud, Sept. 2, 1863. Teacher natural science, Friends' Acad. and Howland Inst., Union Springs, N.Y., 1859-68; prof. botany, U. of Chicago, 1868-70; lecturer on botany, 1871, prof. botany and horticulture, 1871-81, prof. botany and forestry and curator of Bot. Mus., 1882-1903, prof. botany, 1903-10, emeritus prof., Mich. State Agrl. Coll. Dir. State Forestry Commn., 1888-92. Home: Amherst, Mass. Died May 12, 1924.

BEALE, Arthur Stanley, clergyman; b. Rockville Center, L.I., N.Y., Feb. 19, 1881; s. Charles Halleck and Mary Smith (Bell) B.; prep. edn., Roxbury (Mass.) Latin Sch.; A.B., Harvard, 1905; B.D., Union Theol. Sem., New York, 1908; m. Ethel Merrill, Apr. 25, 1912; children—Merrill, Mary, Elizabeth, Margaret Anne. Ordained ministry Congl. Ch., 1908; pastor Stoneham, Mass., 1908-16, Highland Congl. Ch., Lowell, Mass., 1916-21, Laconia, N.H., 1921-23, Grand Av. Congl. Ch., Milwaukee, Wis., 1923-34, Milwaukee City Temple, Milwaukee, Wis., 1935—. Ind. Republican. Mason. Home: Milwaukee, Wis. Died Mar. 9, 1938.

BEALE, Truxtun, diplomat; b. San Francisco, Mar. 6, 1856; s. Edward Fitzgerald and Mary (Edwards) B.; grad. Pa. Mil. Coll., Chester, 1874; LL.B., Columbia, 1878; m. Harriet, d. James G. Blaine; m. 2d, New York, Marie Oge, Apr. 23, 1903. Admitted to bar, 1878; mgr. father's ranch, Kern Co., Calif., 1878-91; U.S. minister to Persia, 1891-92, to Greece, Roumania and Servia, 1892-93, E.E. and M.P., 1893-94; traveled in Siberia, Central Asia and Chinese Turkestan, 1894-96. Died June 3, 1936.

BEALE, William Gerrish, lawyer; b. Winthrop, Me., Sept. 10, 1854; s. William and Lucinda (Bacon) B.; A.B., Bowdoin, 1877 (LL.D., 1912); read law in office Williams & Thompson, Chicago; m. Elizabeth Caruthers, Nov. 2, 1904. Admitted to Ill. bar, 1881, and entered practice at Chicago; head Isham, Lincoln & Beale. Pres. Bd. of Edn., Chicago, 1891-92; corp. counsel, Chicago, 1895-97; one of 3 trustees holding majority of stock of Chicago Tribune under will of Joseph Medill, deceased; trustee Chicago Elevated Rys. (Collateral Trust). Overseer Bowdoin Coll., 1912-18, trustee, 1918—. Republican. Home: Chicago, Ill. Died Mar. 2, 1923.

BEALES, C. William, congressman; b. York Springs, Pa., Dec. 16, 1877; s. C. W. and Sarah C. (Naylor) B.; grad. Northern U. of Ohio Coll. of Pharmacy, 1899; m. E. Mae Sentz, Mar. 21, 1901. Began as pharmacist, York Springs, Pa., 1896; removed to Gettysburg, Pa., 1903; dir. Gettysburg Nat. Bank, Gettysburg Ice & Storage Co., Gettysburg Bldg. & Loan Assn., Star & Sentinel Pub. Co.; postmaster of Gettysburg, 1910-14; mem. 64th Congress (1915-17), 20th Pa. Dist. Democrat. Home: Gettysburg, Pa. Died Nov. 15, 1927.

BEALL, Jack, congressman; b. Ellis Co., Tex., Oct. 25, 1866; s. Richard and Adelaide (Pierce) B.; student U. of Tex., 1886-89, LL.B., 1890; m. Patricia Martin, Jan. 19, 1898; 1 son, Jack Beall. Began practice at Waxahachie, 1890; mem. Tex. Ho. of Rep., 1892-94; Senate, 1894-98; mem. 58th to 63d Congresses (1903-15), 5th Tex. Dist.; moved to Dallas, Tex., 1915; pres. Tex. Electric Ry.; Dallas Union Trust Co. Mem. Beall, Worsham, Rollins, Burford & Ryburn. Democrat. Home: Dallas, Tex. Died Feb. 11, 1929.

BEALL, Mary Stevens, author; b. Phila.; d. James and Georgiana Gill (Haines) Stevens; grad. Girls' High and Normal Sch., Phila.; m. Alexander E. Beal. Sec. and librarian, Columbia Hist. Soc., Washington, 1895—. Author: The Military and Private Secretaries of George Washington; The Washington Coachee and Powel Coach; The Merchant of Venice as Shakespeare Saw It Played; Talks on Early Art of Egypt, Greece and Rome. Also stories, hist. sketches, poems and plays. Home: Washington, D.C. Died May 1917.

BEALS, Charles Edward, clergyman; b. Stoughton, Mass., July 15, 1869; s. Charles Emery and Susan (Fisher) B.; student mech. engring. 4 yrs., Mass. Institute of Technology; grad. Drew Theological Seminary, 1892; m. Nellie Vernon Drake, June 30, 1892 (died 1929); children—Helen Drake (dec.), Charles Edward, Mary Lunn (Mrs. Carroll C. Hubbard), Robert Vernon. Entered M.E. ministry, 1892; pastor Mansfield, Mass., 1892-96; entered Congl. ministry, 1896; asst. pastor E. Boston, Mass., 1896-97; pastor Stoneham, 1897-1900, 2d Ch., Greenfield, 1900-03; Prospect St. Ch., Cambridge, 1903-08; field sec. Am. Peace Soc., 1908-12; dir. Central-West. Dept. Am. Peace Soc., 1912-14; sec. Chicago Peace Soc., 1910-14; sec. Free-Religious Assn. of America, 1914-15; pastor Ch. of the Unity, Worcester, 1915-17, Congl. Ch., Conway, N.H., 1920-22, South Main St. Church, Manchester, N.H., 1922-29, East Congl. Church, Taunton, Mass., 1929—. Contributing editor Unity, 1912-29; with The Nation, 1919. Organized 2d Nat. Peace Congress, Chicago, 1909; reorganized Chicago Peace Society, 1910; mem. peace congresses at Boston, New York, Phila., London, etc.; confs. for the judicial settlement of internat. disputes, Washington and Cincinnati; Lake Mohonk arbitration confs., 1908, 09, 10, 11, 12, 13; sec. Sagamore Sociol. Conf., 1907-09; chmn. Commn. on Social Service, N.H. Congl. Conf., 1921-23; moderator N.H. Congl. Conf., 1928. Was capt. 1st Co. Inf., Mass. Provisional Militia, 1898; chaplain 5th Inf., Mass. Vol. Militia, 1899-1901. Editor: Proceedings of Second National Peace Congress, Chicago, 1909, and various other reports. Home: East Taunton, Mass. Died Oct. 4, 1931.

BEALS, Edward Alden, meteorologist; b. Troy, N.Y., Apr. 23, 1855; s. Alden Porter and Emma Z. (Waite) B.; ed. grade and high schs., Stamford, Conn., and Harvard, 1 yr.; m. Frances E. Middaugh, June 26, 1888; children—Nancy Augusta, Clyde Alden. Practiced dentistry until 1880, then entered U.S. Signal Corps; later transferred to U.S. Weather Bur.; in charge offices at New York, 1883, Atlanta, 1883, Mt. Washington, N.H., 1884-85, Chattanooga, 1886-87, La Crosse, Wis., 1887-90, Minneapolis, 1891-95, Cleveland, 1896-99, Portland, Ore., 1900-17, San Francisco, 1917-24; meteorologist in charge Hawaiian weather service, Honolulu, 1924-26, retired. Unitarian. Contbr. on meteorol. subjects to scientific publs. Home: Alameda, Calif. Died Dec. 26, 1931.

BEAMAN, Charles Cotesworth, lawyer, firm Evarts, Choate & Beaman; b. Houlton, Me., May 7, 1840; grad. Harvard, 1861; m. Hettie Sherman Evarts, Aug. 19, 1874. Was solicitor of U.S. before Arbitration Tribunal, Geneva, Switzerland, 1872; examiner of claims, Dept. of State, Washington. Home: New York, N.Y. Died 1900.

BEAMAN, George William, rear adm.; b. Rutland, Vt., May 7, 1837; s. George Hudson and Eleanor Kettele (Gookin) B.; ed. Rutland High Sch., Troy Conf. Acad.; m. Rebecca Swift Goldsmith, May 2, 1866; 1 son, William Major B. Enlisted as pvt. 3d Regt., Mo. U.S. Reserve Corps, May 1861, and took part in capture of Camp Jackson; was war corr. Missouri Democrat, Aug. 1861-Mar. 1862; was with Fremont in S.W. Mo. campaign, and later with Grant in battles Fts. Henry and Donelson; apptd. acting asst. p.-m. U.S.N., Mar. 1862; asst. p.-m., June 1862; promoted p.-m., 1866; pay insp., 1890; pay dir., Apr. 1899; retired with rank of rear admiral, May 7, 1899. Served in S. Atlantic and Gulf Blockading squadrons, and on Miss. River during Civil War; was in several engagements; subsequently served on various ships and stas. Was general storekeeper at Boston and Mare Island navy yards, 1887-93; made last cruise on flagship New York as fleet-paymaster N. Atlantic Sta. Mem. Loyal Legion (Mass. Commandery). Home: Cambridge, Mass. Died May 3, 1917.

BEAMER, Elmer A(ddison), live stock producer; b. Ogden, Mich., Dec. 1881; s. Daniel and Elanor (Rockwood) B.; student Ferris Inst., Big Rapids, Mich.; spl. student short courses in agr., Mich. State Coll.; m. Edna E. Porter, Nov. 28, 1906; children—Miles Eldean, Margaret H. Live stock producer and feeder, specializing in production of baby beef, 1904—; pres. and treas. Ogden and Riga Fire Ins. Co., 1914-20; v.p. Blissfield State Bank, 1918-33, chmn. bd. dirs., same, 1933—; dir. Detroit Packing Co., 1922-25, mem. com. on reorgn., 1933, and pres., 1934-37; dir. Nat Live Stock Pub. Assn., Nat. Feeder & Finance Co., Nat. Live Stock Marketing Assn., Nat. Credit Corp., Nat. Live Stock and Meat Board. Extension specialist in live stock marketing, Mich. State Coll., Lansing. Mem. orgn. com. of 9 to form New Million Dollar Nat. Live Stock Marketing Orgn. sponsored by Fed. Farm Bd. Dir. Mich. State Farm Bur., 1921-25, Lenawee Co. Farm Bur., 1920-24. Sch. inspector, Odgen, 1906-10; justice of the peace, Ogden, 1912-20; mem. Sch. Bd., Victorsville, Mich., 1910-18. Mem. Mich. Republican State Central Com.; chmn. Lenawee County Rep. Com., 1936-38; apptd. commr. of agr. for State of Mich. by Gov., Apr. 15, 1939. Mason. Contbr. to Mich. Farmer, Mich. Business Farmer, Nat. Live Stock Producer. Home: Blissfield, Mich. Died May 14, 1941.

BEAN, Arthur John, financial writer; b. Candia, N.H., Jan. 29, 1883; s. John Tuttle and Cynthia J. (Beaudry) B.; ed. pub. schs.; m. Mae Chlotilde Cummings, Dec. 24, 1914; 1 dau., Lauraine Estelle. Adv. mgr. and spl. news writer, Boston News Bur., 1905-12; financial editor Boston Post, May 1, 1912—. Mem. Pilgrim Publicity Assn. Episcopalian. Mason. Home: Melrose, Mass. Died Sept. 21, 1931.

BEAN, Henry J., judge; b. Bethel, Me., Nov. 13, 1853; s. Timothy and Elizabeth E. (Swift) Bean; acad. edn. in Me.; read law with Hon. Enoch Foster, Bethel, Me.; m. Mattie E. Magahey, June 8, 1886; children—Grace, Hawley J. Admitted to bar, 1881; city atty., Pendleton, Ore., 1883-84; recorder, 1885-86; mem. Ore. Ho. of Rep., 1889; dist. atty., 6th Dist., Ore., 1896-1900; co. judge, Unadilla Co., 1904-06; judge Circuit Ct., 6th Dist., 1906-10; justice Supreme Ct., Ore., 1911—, for term expiring, 1944, chief justice, 1930-32, and 1937-38. Republican. Mason. Home: Salem, Ore. Died May 9, 1941.

BEAN, Robert Sharp, judge; b. Yamhill Co., Ore., Nov. 28, 1854; s. O. R. and Julia A. (Sharp) B.; grad. Christian Coll., Ore., 1873; B.S., U. of Ore., 1878, LL.D., 1895; LL.D., Willamette U., 1895; m. Ina E. Condon, Sept. 7, 1880; children—Condon R., Ernest G. (dec.), Ormond R., Harold C., Robert D. Admitted to bar, 1878; practiced at Eugene, Ore., 1878-82; judge 2d Jud. Circuit, 1882-90; justice Supreme Ct., 1890-1909 (chief justice 1894-96, 1900-02 and 1905-08); U.S. dist. judge, Dist. of Ore., Apr. 1909—. Republican. Regent U. of Ore., 1882-1920, pres. of bd., 1899-1920. Home: Portland, Ore. Died Jan. 7, 1931.

BEAN, Tarleton Hoffman, zoölogist; b. Bainbridge, Pa., Oct. 8, 1846; s. George and Mary (Smith) B.; M.E., State Normal Sch., Millersville, Pa., 1866; M.D., Columbian (now George Washington) U., 1876; M.S., Ind. U., 1883; m. Laurette H. Van Hook, Jan. 1, 1878. Curator, dept. of fishes, U.S. Nat. Mus., 1880-95; dir. N.Y. Aquarium, 1895-98; state fish culturist of N.Y., 1906—. Editor Proc. and Bulls., U.S. Nat. Mus., 1878-86, Report and Bull., U.S. Fish Commn., 1889-92; asst. in charge div. of fish culture, U.S. Fish Commn., 1892-95; acting curator of fishes, Am. Mus. Natural History, New York, 1897. Rep. U.S. Fish Commn. at Chicago Expn., 1893, Atlanta Expn., 1895; dir. Forestry and Fisheries, U.S., Paris Expn., 1900; chief Depts. Fish and Game, and Forestry, St. Louis Expn., 1902-05. Chevalier Legion of Honor and Officer of Mérite Agricole, France; Knight Imperial Royal Order of Red Eagle (Germany); Order of the Rising Sun (Japan). Author: The Fishes of Pennsylvania, 1893; The Salmon and Salmon Fisheries; Oceanic Ichthyology (with late George Brown Goode), 1896; The Fishes of Long Island, 1902; The White World (part author), 1902; The Food and Game Fishes of New York, 1903; The Basses, Fresh-Water and Marine (part author), 1905; The Fishes of Bermuda, 1906. Died Dec. 28, 1916.

BEANBLOSSOM, Moody Lewis, educator; b. Mauckport, Ind., Mar. 19, 1885; s. John Lewis and Alice Dilia (Moyars) B.; B.Sc., Valparaiso U., 1906; B.A., Ind. U., 1911; M.A., U. of Chicago, 1916; m. Goldie Gladdis Draher, Mar. 26, 1912. Prin. high sch., Herrin, Ill., 1906-09; psychologist Indiana Reformatory, 1912-15; supt. high sch., Herrin, 1916-20, same, Lawrenceville, 1921—. Republican. Presbyn. Mason. Author: Mental Examination of Two Thousand Delinquent Boys and Young Men, 1916. Home: Lawrenceville, Ill. Died Dec. 27, 1923.

BEANE, Fred Emery, judge; b. Readfield, Kennebec Co., Me., May 14, 1853; s. Emery Oliver and Elizabeth Hunton (Craige) B.; ed. Maine Wesleyan Sem., and Westbrook (Me.) Sem. to 1871; Tufts Coll., 1875; law in office of father; m. Orella McGilvery, Sept. 26, 1876. Admitted to Me. bar, 1876, to practice in U.S. cts., 1886; city solicitor, Hallowell, Me., 15 yrs.; mayor, 1891, 1907; county atty., Kennebec Co., 1907-11 (resigned), judge Superior Ct., 1911-18. Pres. Hallowell Trust & Banking Co. Sec. Dem. State Com., 1888-1908, chmn. 1908-11. Mem. Sch. Bd. 10 yrs., supt. schs. 4 yrs. Universalist. Mason. Home: Hallowell, Me. Deceased.

BEARD, Adelia Belle, artist; b. Painesville, O.; d. James Henry and Mary Caroline (Carter) B.; ed. pvt. schs.; studied drawing at Cooper Union and Art Students' League, portrait painting with Wyatt Eaton and William Chase. Taught classes in drawing and painting; first painting exhibited at Nat. Acad. Design; illustrator books and mags. Joint author and illustrator (with sister Lina): American Girls' Handy Book, 1887; What a Girl Can Make and Do, 1902; Handicraft and Recreation for Girls, 1904; Things Worth Doing, 1906; Home Missions Handicraft; Little Folks Handy Book, 1910; On the Trail, 1915. Originated, invented and illus. the Look Alive, Stand-up Beard Birds, and Beard Animals. Corr. sec. Girl Pioneers of America. Home: Flushing, L.I., N.Y. Died Feb. 16, 1920.

BEARD, Augustus Field, clergyman; b. Norwalk, Conn., May 11, 1833; s. Algernon Edwin and Mary E. (Mallory) B.; A.B., Yale, 1857, A.M., 1860; Auburn Theol. Sem., 1857-58; grad. Union Theol. Sem., 1860; (D.D., Syracuse U., 1875); m. Eliza Payson Goddard, Aug. 19, 1861; m. 2d, Annie D. Barker, Jan. 2, 1865. Ordained Congl. ministry, 1860; pastor Cape Elizabeth, Me., 1860-62, Bath, Me., 1862-69, Syracuse, N.Y., 1869-83, Am. Ch., Paris, France, 1883-86; corr. sec. Am. Missionary Assn., 1886—. Foreign sec. Am. and Foreign Christian Union, 1883-86; editor Am. Missionary Mag., 1905—. Home: Norwalk, Conn. Died Dec. 22, 1934.

BEARD, Charles Heady, physician; b. Spencer Co., Ky., Jan. 27, 1855; s. James P. and Emerin (Heady) B.; ed. Transylvania U., Lexington, Ky.; M.D., U. of Louisville, 1877; m. Laura Clark, Sept. 24, 1888. In med. practice at Cannelton, Ind., 1877-83; studied at Post-Grad. Med. School, Polyclinic, Knapp's Inst., New York, and then became house surgeon Manhattan Eye and Ear Hosp.; studied in London, Paris, Zürich and Vienna about 2 yrs. In Chicago, 1887—, making specialty of eye and ear practice; asst. surgeon. 1887-90, surgeon, 1890—, Ill. Charitable Eye and Ear Infirmary; oculist to Cook Co. Hosp., 1 yr.; attending phys., Central Free Dispensary 1 yr.; oculist to Passavant Memorial Hosp. Author: Ophthalmic Surgery, 1910-14; Ophthalmic Diagnosis, 1911-13; Collection of Pictures of the Fundus Oculi. Home: Chicago, Ill. Died June 3, 1916.

BEARD, Cyrus, judge; b. Venango Co., Pa., Aug. 13, 1850; s. Thomas and Mary (McKinly) B.; LL.B., State U. of Ia., 1874; m. Nora E. Wilson, Sept. 25, 1875 (died 1893); m. 2d, Frances B. Birkhead, July 22, 1896. Began practice of law at Washington, Ia., 1874; removed to Harlan, Ia., 1878, and to Evanston, Wyo., 1890, practicing law there, 1890-1904; justice Supreme Ct., Wyo., 1904— (chief justice, 1911-13); reëlected 1912, for term expiring 1921. Republican. Mason. Home: Cheyenne, Wyo. Died Dec. 17, 1920.

BEARD, Daniel Carter ("Dan Beard"), artist, author, editor, nat. commr. Boy Scouts of America; b. Cincinnati, Ohio, June 21, 1850; s. James Henry (N.A.) and Mary Caroline (Carter) Beard; academic education at Covington, Ky.; studied at Art Students' League, New York, 1880-84; m. Beatrice Alice Jackson, Aug. 15, 1894; children—Barbara, Daniel Bartlett. Has done illustrating for all the principal publs. and also for books; originator and instructor of the pioneer class in illustration and teacher of animal drawing, Woman's School of Applied Design, 1893-1900, inaugurating the first organized class in animal drawing in the world; editor of Recreation, 1905-06. Former mem. Flushing Bd. of Edn., Queen's Borough Library; v.p. Mark Twain Library, Redding, Conn. Mem. of several zoöl. socs.; was pres. Soc. of Illustrators and Camp Fire Club of America (awarded gold medal); nat. scout commr. and honorary vice-pres. Boy Scouts of America; awarded golden eagle badge, only one ever awarded, also Roosevelt gold medal for distinguished service, Masonic Grand Masters Medal, Silver Buffalo (U.S.), also Silver Wolf (England); was the originator and founder of the first boy scout society from which the others were modeled; chief scout, dept. of woodcraft, Culver (Ind.) Mil. Acad., organizer, and chief, 1911-15. Mt. Beard, the peak adjoining Mt. McKinley, discovered by Browne and Parker Expdn., named after him; bronze tablet marks his boyhood home. Quaker. Author: Moonlight and Six Feet of Romance, 1890; American Boys' Handy Book, 1882; Outdoor Handy Book, 1900; Jack of All Trades, 1900; Boy Pioneers and Sons of Daniel Boone, 1909; The Buckskin Book and Buckskin Calendar, 1911; Boat Building and Boating, 1911; Shelters, Shacks and Shanties, 1914; Bugs, Butterflies and Beetles, 1915; Signs, Signals and Symbols, 1918; American Boys' Book of Wild Animals, 1921; Field and Forest Handybook; American Boys' Book of Camplore and Woodcraft, 1920; The Black Wolf Pack, 1922; American Boys' Book of Birds and Brownies of the Woods, 1923; Do It Yourself, 1925; Wisdom of the Woods, 1927; Buckskin Book for Buckskin Men and Boys, 1929. Asso. editor Boys' Life. Chief of school of woodcraft known as Dan Beard Camp. Awarded 1st medal for outstanding citizenship, State of Ky.; Hornaday gold medal for conservation; bronze plaque, Boy Scouts of America. Studio: Suffern, N.Y. Died June 11, 1941.

BEARD, Edward E., lawyer; born Princeton, Ky., Aug. 27, 1850; s. Richard (D.D.) and Cynthia E. (Castleman) B.; A.B., Cumberland U., 1870, LL.B., 1871; m. Sarah Livingston, Oct. 12, 1876. Practiced, Lebanon, 1871—; mayor of Lebanon 3 terms, 1877-80; mem. Tenn. Ho. of Rep., 1885. Pres. Am. Nat. Bank, Lebanon. Trustee and treas. Cumberland U., 1872-1920; dean and prof. law same univ., 1920—. Democrat. Presbyn. Home: Lebanon, Tenn. Died June 18, 1924.

BEARD, Gerald Hamilton, clergyman; b. Hammersmith, Eng., Mar. 20, 1862; s. Richard and Anne (Olding) B.; came to America with parents, 1870; B.A., Yale, 1887, Ph.D., 1892; B.D., Yale Div. Sch., 1890; studied in Germany, 1891; m. Mary Keyes, July 27, 1892. Ordained minister Congl. Ch., 1892; pastor 1st Ch., South Norwalk, Conn., 1892-1900, College St. Ch., Burlington, Vt., 1900-04; Park St. Ch., Bridgeport, 1904—. Author: Catholic and Protestant Bibles, 1905; Schopenhauer's Philosophy and Pessimism, 1890. Contbr. to Am. Ency. of Christianity. Home: Bridgeport, Conn. Died Oct. 10, 1921.

BEARD, James Carter, illustrator; b. Cincinnati, June 6, 1837; s. James Henry (N.A.) and Mary Caroline (Carter) B.; brother of Adelia Belle, Daniel Carter and Lina B.; m. Martha J. Bray, Dec. 25, 1862. Admitted to bar, 1861, and practiced short time; does much work as illustrator for high-class books and periodicals, making a specialty of pictures of animals. Author: Little Workers, 1878; Curious Homes and Their Tenants, 1897; Billy Possum, 1909. Home: New Orleans, La. Died Nov. 15, 1913.

BEARD, James Thom, mining engr.; b. Brooklyn, Oct. 19, 1855; s. Ira and Isabella O.B.; grad. Adelphia Acad., Brooklyn, 1874; C.E., E.M., Columbia Sch. of Mines, 1877; m. Amelia E. Lawson, May 9, 1887; children—James Thom, Howard Iranæus, Amelia Elizabeth. Asst. engr., Brooklyn Bridge, 1877-79; resident div. engr., C.,B.&Q. R.R., 1880-83; U.S. dep. mineral surveyor, Colo., 1883-85; mining engr. Ottumwa Fuel Co., 1885-91; propr. Iowa Coal Exchange, 1891-96; asso. editor Mines and Minerals and prin. Sch. of Mines, Internat. Corr. Sch., Scranton, Pa., 1896-1911; sr. asso. editor Coal Age, New York, 1911—. Sec. Ia. State Mine Examining Bd., 1888-94. Inventor: Beard-Mackie Sight Indicator for testing gas; Beard deputy safety lamp; Beard-Stine centrifugal mine fan. Republican. Founder, editor in chief Mine Inspectors' Inst. Author: The Ventilation of Mines, 1894; Design of Centrifugal Ventilators, 1899; Mine Gases and Explosions, 1908; Coal Age Pocket Book, 1916; Mine Gases and Ventilation, 1919. Compiler: Mine Examination Questions and Answers (3 vols.), 1923. Home: Danbury, Conn. Died Dec. 26, 1941.

BEARD, Lina, author, illustrator; b. Cincinnati, O.; d. James Henry (N.A.) and Mary Caroline (Carter) B.; ed. Mrs. Collins' Private Sch. (Covington, Ky.), Wesleyan Acad. (Cincinnati) and Dr. Charles West's Brooklyn Heights Sem.; studied drawing at Cooper Union and the Art Students' League. Founder of Good Citizenship League of Flushing, L.I., and was its del. to the 1st Nat. Arbitration and Peace Congress, New York, 1907. Founder and pres. the Girl Pioneers of America. Mem. Nat. Life Conservation Society, National Conference on Outdoor Recreation, L.I. Fedn. of Woman's Clubs; del. to 1st meeting of Conf. on Big Outdoors, Washington, D.C., 1924. Swedenborgian. Singletaxer. Joint author and illustrator (with sister Adelia Belle) American Girls' Handy Book, 1887; What a Girl Can Make and Do, 1902; Handy Craft and Recreation for Girls, 1904; Things Worth Doing, 1906; Home Mission Handy Craft; Little Folks' Handy Book, 1910; On the Trail; Mother Nature's Toy Shop, 1915; An Outdoor Book for Girls; Girl Pioneers of America Manual. Home: Flushing, L.I., N.Y. Died Aug. 13, 1933.

BEARD, Thomas Francis (known only as "Frank Beard"), artist; b. Cincinnati, Feb. 6, 1842; s. James H. and Mary Caroline B.; ed. Cincinnati and Painesville, O. Served in Civil war in 7th Ohio regt.; furnished pictures for all leading publs. from age of 12 to present time; 17 yrs. lecturer at Chautauqua, N.Y.; has lectured for lyceums for 25 yrs.; first lecture was entitled "Chalk Talk," from which the word originated; prof. aesthetics, Syracuse Univ., 1881. Author: Black Board in the Sunday School; also numerous short stories. Home, Chicago, Ill. Died 1905.

BEARD, W.D., justice Supreme Court of Tenn., formerly chief justice. Democrat. Home: Memphis, Tenn. Died Dec. 7, 1910.

BEARD, William Holbrook, painter; b. Painesville, O., April 13, 1825; studied in Europe; settled in New York, 1861; mem. Nat. Acad., 1862. Specialty is painting of humorous pictures of animals and allegory. Has published collections of his sketches, under title Humor in Animals; also a text-book, Action in Art. Among his more prominent recent pictures are Power of Death, Four Seasons, Overboard, Spirit of the Storm, Coming of Day, Witches' Night, Four Elements, Passing of Ages, Shades of the Druids, Speech of Welcome (bears), etc. Home: New York, N.Y. Died 1900.

BEARDSHEAR, William Miller, pres. Iowa State Coll. Agr. and Mechanic Arts (Ames), 1891—; b. Dayton, O., Nov. 7, 1850; boyhood on farm; ed. Otterbein Univ., Ohio. (A.M. and LL.D.); also studied at Yale. Pres. Western Coll., Toledo, Ia., 1881-89; supt. Des Moines (Ia.) city schools, 1889-91; pres. Iowa State Teachers' Assn., 1894; U.S. Indian commr., 1897—. Died 1902.

BEARDSLEE, Clark Smith, theologian; b. Coventry, N.Y., Feb. 1, 1850; s. Samuel Augustus and Lois Diana (Smith) B.; A.B., Amherst, 1876, A.M., 1878 (D.D., 1910); grad. Hartford Theol. Sem., 1879; m. Emma Gilette Alvord, Dec. 13, 1882. Instr. Hebrew, Hartford Sem., 1879-81; pastor Le Mars, Ia., 1883-85; ordained Congl. ministry, 1885; pastor Prescott, Ariz., 1885-86, W. Springfield, Mass., 1886-88; asso. prof. systematic theology, 1888-90, prof. Bibl. dogmatics and ethics, 1890-1907, Bibl. homiletics, 1907—, Hartford Theol. Sem. Author: Christ's Estimate of Himself, 1899; Teacher-Training with the Master Teacher, 1903; Jesus the King of Truth, 1904. Home: Hartford, Conn. Died 1914.

BEARDSLEE, Lester Anthony, rear adm.; b. Little Falls, N.Y., Feb. 1, 1836; entered Navy March 5, 1850; grad. Naval Acad., June, 1856; promoted regularly through all grades to rear adm. in 1895; comdr.-in-chief of naval forces on the Pacific sta., 1894-97; apptd. naval mem. U.S. bd. for testing and reporting upon Am. metals; participated as exec. officer monitor Nantucket in attack on Charleston, April, 1863; participated in capture of Confederate steam sloop Florida in Bahia, Brazil, Oct., 1864, and as prize master brought her to U.S.; in 1870 took tug Palos to China, carrying on her the first U.S. flag through the Suez Canal; while comdg. the U.S.S. Jamestown, 1879-80, in Alaskan waters, discovered, surveyed and named Glacier Bay. Retired from active service on reaching 62 yrs. of age, Feb. 1, 1898; m. Evelyn, d. Isaac Small, Little Falls, N.Y., Jan. 1863. Was one of the officers serving under Commodore Mathew C. Perry; participated in the landing of the commodore at Kurihama, Japan, July 14, 1853, and the interview with the two princes representing the Emperor, to whom commodore presented President Fillmore's letter. As one of few survivors of that event visited Japan, 1900-01, to advocate the erection of a monument by the Japanese on the site of the historic interview; the monument was unveiled with imposing ceremonies July 14, 1901. Home: Beaufort, S.C. Died 1903.

BEARDSLEY, Henry Mahan, lawyer; b. Knox Co., O., Oct. 20, 1858; s. George Fitch and Martha (Mahan) B.; B.L., U. of Ill., 1879, M.L., 1880, A.M., 1905; LL.D., Knox Coll., Galesburg, Ill., 1916; m. Marietta Davis, Apr. 24, 1883; children—Eleanor M. (Mrs. Charles S. Pillsbury), George D., Henry S. Practiced in Champaign, Ill., 1882-86, Kansas City, Mo., 1886—. Mem. upper house Kansas City Common Council, 1898-1902; pres. same and Bd. Pub. Works, 1902-04; mayor of Kansas City, 1906-08. Pres. Kansas City Y.M.C.A., 1892—; moderator Nat. Council Congl. Chs., 1915-17. Trustee Drury Coll., Springfield, Mo. Republican. Home: Kansas City, Mo. Died Apr. 19, 1938.

BEARDSLEY, Samuel Arthur, lawyer; b. Utica, N.Y., Dec. 1, 1856; s. Arthur Moore and Louise Howland (Adams) B.; ed. Williston Sem.; Hamilton Coll. Law Sch., Clinton, N.Y., 1879; m. Elizabeth Ann Hopper, Sept. 14, 1881; m. 2d, Lillian Valérie Ella Walpole-Moore, Sept. 14, 1927. Practiced at Utica, N.Y., corp. business, 1879-97, except when chmn. State Bd. R.R. Commrs., 1892-96; opened office, New York, 1898; now mem. Beardsley & Taylor. Incorporated N.Y. Gas & Elec. Light, Heat & Power Co., now the N.Y. Edison Co., which took over all electric light cos. of New York City; atty. for N.Y. Edison Co., Consol. Subway Co. and other elec. cos. Dir. Consol. Telegraph & Elec. Subway Co. Spl. city judge and city judge, Utica, 1886-92; chmn. State Bd. Commrs., 1892-96; chmn. Dem. Co. Com., Oneida County, 1886-89; mem. and sec. Dem. State Com., 1889-92; del. Dem. Nat. Convs., 1904, 1908, 1912, and all state convs., 1891-1912; head Dem. orgns. in city of Utica, 1891-1913. Mason. Home: Utica, N.Y. N.Y. City, and Easthampton, L.I. Died Apr. 28, 1932.

BEARDSLEY, William H., ry. pres.; b. Cleveland, O., Apr. 7, 1852; s. I. L. B.; ed. Central High Sch., Cleveland; m. Lillian Sterling, 1874. Stenographer, Richmond & Danville R.R., at N.Y. City, 1881; pvt. sec. to H. M. Flagler, 1882, later his asst.; treas., Fla. East Coast Ry., 1895-1914; v.p., 1910-14, later pres.; pres. Fla. East Coast Car Ferry Co., Fla. East Coast Hotel Co. Republican. Unitarian. Home: New York, N.Y. Died Dec. 13, 1925.

BEARDWOOD, Matthew, M.D., chemist; b. Cape May City, N.J., June 22, 1872; s. Matthew and Jane (Mitchell) B.; A.B., Central High Sch., Phila., 1890, A.M., 1895; M.D., Medico-Chirurg. Coll., Phila., 1894; spl. student, U. of Pa., 1906-08, U. of Edinburgh, 1909; (Sc.D., Ursinus, 1916); unmarried. In gen. med. practice, Phila., 1895—. Instr. chemistry, 1896-99, lecturer on clin. chemistry, 1899-1900, adj. prof. chemistry, 1900-14, prof. gen. chemistry and toxicology, 1914-16, Medico-Chirurg. Coll.; prof. chemistry, Ursinus Coll., 1903—. Republican. Presbyn. Author: Students' Notes on Toxicology, 1904. Home: Philadelphia, Pa. Deceased.

BEASLEY, John (Thomas), lawyer; b. Sullivan, Ind., May 29, 1860; s. Ephraim and Sarah (Williams) B.; ed. pub. schs.; m. Cora E. Hoke, Nov. 5, 1885; 1 son, John H. Admitted to Ind. bar, 1881, and began practice at Sullivan; pres. Ind. Gas Utilities Co.; dir. Terre Haute Savings Bank, Evansville, Indianapolis & Terre Haute Ry. Co. Mem. Ind. Ho. of Rep. (chmn. judiciary com.), 1887-93; counsel Sullivan and Sullivan Co., 1882-85. Pres. Terre Haute Chamber Commerce; pres. Ind. Taxpayers' Assn. Democrat. Baptist. Home: Allendale, Terre Haute, Ind. Deceased.

BEATES, Henry, Jr., M.D.; b. Phila., Dec. 20, 1857; s. Henry and Emily A. B.; grad. West Phila. Acad., 1876; M.D., U. of Pa., 1879; Sc.D., Washington and Jefferson Coll., 1911; m. Agnes T. Barrington, Sept. 3, 1897; 3 children—Henry, and 2 dec. Pres. State Bd. of Med. Examiners, Pa. until 1911; pres. Nat. Confederation of State Med. Examining and Licensing Bds., 2 terms. Mason. Home: Wayne, Pa. Died May 25, 1926.

BEATH, Robert Burns, fire ins.; b. Phila., Jan. 26, 1839; s. David and Robena (Wilson) B.; pub. sch. edn.; m. Margaret E. Blinkhorn, 1863. Pvt. to lt. col., Pa. Vols. in Civil War; wounded at Chapin's Farm, Va., Sept. 29, 1864, requiring amputation of right foot; Surveyor-gen. of Pa., 1872-75; agt., spl. agt., and sec., 1881-92, pres., 1892—, United Firemen's Ins. Co. of Phila. Sec., 1885-1902, pres., 1902—, Nat. Bd. of Fire Underwriters. Republican. Comdr. Dept. of Pa. G.A.R., 1873-74, comdr.-in-chief, 1883-84. Author: History of the Grand Army of the Republic, 1888; Historical Catalogue St. Andrew's Soc. of Pa., 1907, 1913; Grand Army Blue Book, Its Decisions and Laws (last edit.), 1910. Home: Philadelphia, Pa. Died Nov. 25, 1914.

BEATLEY, Clara Bancroft, teacher; b. Shirley, Mass., Jan. 12, 1858; d. Edmund Dana and Mary Park (Morse) Bancroft; grad. Bridgewater (Mass.) State Normal Sch.; m. James A. Beatley, Dec. 27, 1887. Teacher pub. schs., 1878-87; prin. Disciples Sch., Ch. of the Disciples, Boston, 1893-1910; chmn. Com. of Edn. Ch. of Disciples, 1911; chmn. Conf. Com. on Moral Edn., 1904—. Dir. Children's Mission, Boston Equal Suffrage Assn. Unitarian. Author: Joys Beyond Joy, 1902. Compiler: Apples of Gold, 1903; Forget Me Not, 1906; Treasures New and Old, 1912. Home: Roxbury, Mass. Died Oct. 20, 1923.

BEATON, David, clergyman; b. Arbuthnot, Scotland, 1848; A.M., U. of Edinburgh, 1876; B.D., Theol. Hall, Scotland Congl. Ch., 1879. Ordained Congl. ministry, 1877; pres. Redfield (S.D.) Coll., 1881-86; supt. and pastor, St. John's, Newfoundland, 1886-91, pastor Lincoln Park Ch., Chicago, 1891-1907; lecturer in gen. lit., U. of Chicago, 1906-10; pastor First Ch., Janesville, Wis., Mar. 10, 1910.- Pres. Poly. Soc., Chicago, 1903—. Author: Cyrus the Magician, 1898; Selfhood and Service, 1898; A Scientific System of Religious Education. Home: Janesville, Wis. Died Feb. 11, 1920.

BEATTIE, Charlton Reid, lawyer; b. Assumption Parish, La., Apr. 22, 1869; s. Hon. Taylor and Fannie Estelle (Pugh) B.; grad. Kenmore Univ. High Sch., Amherst Co., Va., 1888; grad. U. of Va., 1889, LL.B., 1891; unmarried. Admitted to Va. bar, 1891; in practice at Thibodaux, La., 1892-1913, New Orleans, 1913—. Rep. nominee for 61st Congress, 1908; U.S. atty., Eastern Dist. La., Feb. 1909-13; former mem. faculty Tulane U. Law Sch. Home: Thibodaux, La. Died Aug. 23, 1925.

BEATTIE, Francis Robert, theologian; b. Guelph, Ont., Can., Mar. 31, 1848; s. Robert and Janet (McKinley) B.; grad. Toronto Univ., 1875; A.M., 1876, Knox (Theol.) Coll., 1878; B.D., 1882; Ph.D., Ill. Wesleyan, 1884; D.D., Presbyn. Coll., Montreal, 1887 (hon. LL.D., Central Univ. Ky.); m. Jean G. Galbraith, 1879 (died 1897); m. 2d, Lily R. Satterwhite, 1901. Ordained Presbyn. ministry, 1878, pastor in Canada, 1878-88; in Presbyn. Ch. South, 1888—; prof. Columbia, S.C., Sem., 1888-93; prof. apologetics and systematic theology, Presbyn. Theol. Sem. of Ky., 1893—. Asso. editor Christian Observer, 1893—; asso. editor Presbyn. Quarterly, 1895—. Mem. exec. com. Alliance Reformed Chs. Holding the Presbyn. System (Western Sect.); mem. Scottish Soc. of Louisville. Author: Utilitarian Theory of Morals, 1884; Methods of Theism, 1887; Radical Criticism, 1896; Presbyterian Standards, 1898; Apologetics, 1903; Calvinism and Modern Thought, 1901; Christianity and Modern Evolution, 1903. Home: Louisville, Ky. Died 1906.

BEATTY, Frank Edmund, naval officer; b. Azatlan, Wis., Nov. 26, 1853; s. Edmund and Annette (Brayton) B.; grad. U.S. Naval Acad., 1875; m. Anne Meem, d. William Daingerfield and Lelia Russell (Meem) Peachy, Apr. 29, 1891. Promoted through the various grades to rank of capt., July 1, 1908; rear adm., Apr. 27, 1912. Served on various ships; comd. Battleship Wisconsin on tour of world, 1908; commandant Navy Yard, Washington, and supt. Naval Gun Factory, 1910-13; comdr., 1st div., Atlantic Fleet, on U.S.S. Florida, 1914; apptd. comdr. Navy Yard, Norfolk, Va., Jan. 1915; temporarily detached, May 10, 1915, to take command of the "Red,"

enemy forces in a strategical Navy Dept. problem; was successful and constructively defeated the U.S. Fleet and landed 20,000 men on U.S. shores. Episcopalian. Retired Nov. 26, 1915; ordered to active duty, 1917, and assigned as commandant 6th Naval Dist., Charleston, S.C. Home: Washington, D.C. Died Mar. 16, 1926.

BEATTY, John, soldier; b. Sandusky, O., Dec. 16, 1828; pub. sch. edn. Raised a co. of vols., Apr. 1861; lt. col., 3d Ohio Inf., Apr. 27, 1861; col., Feb. 12, 1862; brig. gen. vols., Nov. 29, 1862; was with McClellan in W.Va. campaign; accompanied O. M. Mitchel in dash through Tenn. to Northern Ala.; apptd. provost marshal Huntsville, Ala.; returned with Buell's army to Louisville in pursuit of Bragg; fought his regt. in battle of Perryville, Ky., Oct. 8, 1862; comd. brigade at Stone River; in Tullahoma campaign, 1863; in battle of Chickamauga, and march to Knoxville for the relief of Burnside; resigned Jan. 28, 1864. Presdl. elector, 1860; mem. 40th Congress to fill unexpired term (1868-69); mem. 41st and 42d Congresses (1869-73), 8th Ohio Dist.; presdl. elector-at-large, 1884. Republican. Pres. Ohio, Chickamauga and Chattanooga Nat. Mil. Park Commn. Author: The Citizen Soldier, 1876; Belle o' Becket's Lane, 1882; High Tariff or Low Tariff, Which?, 1894; Answer to "Coin's Financial School," 1896; The Acolhuans, 1902; McLean, A Romance of the War, 1904. Home: Columbus, O. Died Dec. 21, 1914.

BEATTY, John W(esley), dir. emeritus of fine arts, Carnegie Inst.; b. Pittsburgh, Pa.; s. Richard B.; educated Pittsburgh; student of Munich Acad. Fine Arts; (hon. A.M., Western Univ. of Pa. [now Univ. of Pittsburgh], 1900; hon. A.M., Princeton U., 1914). Dir. fine arts, Carnegie Inst., 1896-1922. Member advisory art com., Chicago Expn., 1893, Buffalo Expn., 1901, St. Louis Expn., 1904, San Francisco Expn., 1915. Represented in National Gallery, Washington, D.C. Decorated with the Cross of Knight of the Legion of Honor, France, 1921. Author: An Appreciation of Augustus Saint-Gaudens, 1909; Art of John Alexander (memorial article); also three brochures on the appreciation of painting, sculpture, and architecture and The Relation of Art to Nature, 1922, The Modern Art Movement, 1923. Home: Pittsburgh, Pa. Died Sept. 29, 1924.

BEATTY, Troy, bishop; b. Tuscaloosa, Ala., Nov. 12, 1866; s. William Henry and Rebecca (Troy) B.; student U. of the South, also of theol. dept., same univ.; (D.D., U. of Ga., 1917; D.D. ad eundem, U. of South, 1921; m. Frederika Priest Mayhew, Nov. 24, 1892. Deacon, 1891, priest, 1892, P.E. Ch.; rector Trinity Ch., Mason, Tenn., 1892, St. Andrew's Ch., Darien, Ga., 1893-97, Emanuel Ch., Athens, Ga., 1897-1916, Grace Ch., Memphis, Tenn., 1916-19; consecrated coadjutor bishop of Tenn., Sept. 18, 1919. Dep. to Pan Anglican Conv., London, Eng., 1898; dep. to Gen. Conv. P.E. Ch., 1901—; mem. Standing Com. Diocese of Atlanta many yrs., and of Tenn., 3 yrs. Mason. Home: Nashville, Tenn. Died Apr. 23, 1922.

BEATTY, William Henry, judge; b. Lucas Co., O., Feb. 18, 1838; s. Henry Oscar and Margaret Boone (Runyan) B.; ed. U. of Va., 1856-58; m. Elizabeth M. Love, June 17, 1874. Went from Cal. to Nev., 1863; dist. judge in Nev., 1864-74; asso. justice Supreme Court, Nev., 1875-78; chief justice Nev., 1879-80; afterward practiced law in Sacramento, Calif.; chief justice Calif., 1889—, term expiring Jan., 1915. Home: San Francisco, Calif. Died Aug. 4, 1914.

BEATY, Amos Leonidas; b. Red River County, Tex., Sept. 1, 1870; s. William A. and Ann (Rogers) B.; ed. pub. schs. and acad., Tex.; m. Swan Donoho, Oct. 25, 1893 (died Aug. 1, 1930); m. 2d, Mrs. Martha W. MacNamara, March 5, 1932. Studied law in office of Chambers & Doak, Clarksville; admitted to bar, 1891; practiced at Sherman, Tex., 1892-1907; moved to Dallas, Tex., 1907, to serve as atty. Texas Co., to Houston, 1910, as asso. gen. atty. same co., and to New York, 1913, becoming gen. counsel, dir., mem. exec. com. and pres. Texas Co., 1920-26, chmn. bd., 1926-27 (resigned); pres. Am. Petroleum Inst., 1931-32; chmn. Petroleum Code Authority, NRA, 1934. Democrat. Methodist. Home: New York, N.Y. Died Apr. 29, 1939.

BEAUCHAMP, Lou Jenks, lecturer; b. Cincinnati, Jan. 14, 1851; s. Harry and Sarah (Godman) B.; self-ed.; m. Mellie Gardner, Mar. 31, 1877. Telegraph editor Cincinnati Star (now Times-Star), and writing sketches and poems for New York papers; later mng. editor Ft. Wayne Gazette; lecturer on humorous topics (has delivered over 10,000). Author of many published poems. Democrat. Presbyn. Home: Hamilton, O. Died June 4, 1920.

BEAUCHAMP, William Benjamin, bishop; b. Farnham, Va., Mar. 16, 1869; s. Dandridge C. and Margaret B.; A.B., Randolph-Macon Coll., 1890, D.D., 1906; A.M., B.D., Vanderbilt U., 1893; LL.D., Southern Univ. Lakeland, Fla., 1926; m. Blanche Whitehurst, 1895; children—Ann Dorothy, Margaret, William B., Luke Granberry, Virginia, Harriet Gaulbert, Elisabeth, Bayard. Ordained ministry M.E. Ch., South, 1893; pastor Broad St. and St. James, Rich-

mond, Va., 1891-1903, Newport News, 1903-07, Fourth Av. Ch., Louisville, Ky., 1907-11, Danville, Va., 1911-15, Monumental Ch., Portsmouth, Va., 1915-17; gen. sec. Laymen's Missionary Movement M.E. Ch., South, 1917-22; elected bishop, May 1922; bishop in charge 12th Episcopal Dist. comprising Missions in Europe, 1922-26, now Ga. and Mexico. Mem. World's Missionary Conf., Edinburg, Scotland, 1906; pres. Bd. Missions Va. Conf., 1911-19; foreign sec. for Europe of M.E. Ch., S., 1919; mem. Bd. Missions M.E. Ch., S. (pres., 1926); bd. trustees Randolph-Macon Coll.; dir. gen. of Missionary Centenary M.E. Ch., S., in 8-day drive May 18-25, 1919, for $35,000,000, in which $50,000,000 was subscribed; mem. 5th Ecumenical Conf., London, 1921; mem. exec. com. Federal Council of Chs. in America; mem. Am. sect. com. on arrangements for Universal Conf. Chs. of Christ on Life and Work. Pres. bd. trustees Scarritt Bible Training Sch., Nashville, Tenn.; pres. emeritus Ferrum Training Sch. Ferrum, Va.; elected pres. of World Brotherhood Fedn., London, 1925; mem. theol. faculty Emory U., 1926—; mem. Am. sect. Internat. Council of Missions, Jerusalem, Mar. 1928. Home: Atlanta, Ga. Died June 28, 1931.

BEAUCHAMP, William Martin, clergyman; b. Coldenham, N.Y., Mar. 25, 1830; s. William and Mary B.; ed. Skaneateles Acad. to 1847; Delancey Div. Sch., Geneva, N.Y., 1862; (S.T.D., Hobart College, N.Y., 1886; LL.D., Syracuse U., 1920); m. Sarah Carter, Nov. 26, 1857. Deacon, 1862, priest, 1863, P.E. Ch.; rector Calvary Ch., Northville, N.Y., 1863-65, Grace Ch., Baldwinsville, N.Y., 1865-1900. Examining chaplain Diocese of Central N.Y., 1884-1921; archæologist of N.Y. State Mus. Author: Iroquois Trail, 1892; Indian Names of New York, 1893; Shells of Onondaga County, N.Y., 1896; History of the New York Iroquois, now Commonly Called the Six Nations, 1905; Past and Present Syracuse and Onondaga County, 1908; Revolutionary Soldiers of Onondaga County, N.Y., 1913; Moravian Journals in Central New York! Iroquois Folk Lore, 1921. Home: Syracuse, N.Y. Died Dec. 13, 1925.

BEAUMONT, Lilian Adele, painter; b. Jamaica Plain, Mass., May 18, 1880; d. Francis Britain and Clarissa Ann (Andrews) B.; pupil Sch. of Drawing and Painting, Mus. of Fine Arts, Boston; grad. Boston Sch. Occupational Therapy, 1918. Exhibited Panama P.I. Expn., 1915, etc. Mem. Fedn. of Arts, Copley Soc. of Boston. Reconstruction aide in occupational therapy, at U.S.A. Gen. Hosp. 10, 1919. Universalist. Home: Jamaica Plain, Mass. Deceased.

BEAUPRÉ, Arthur Matthias, diplomat; b. Oswego, Ill., July 29, 1853; s. Matthias and Sarah J. (Patrick) B.; m. Mary F., d. Hon. C. W. Marsh, of Dekalb, Ill., Oct. 20, 1880. Went to Aurora, Ill., at 21; admitted to Ill. bar; co. clerk Kane Co., Ill., 1886-94; apptd. consul-gen. and sec. legation, Guatemala, Oct. 7, 1897; transferred to Colombia in same capacity, Oct. 27, 1899; E.E. and M.P. to Colombia, Feb. 12, 1903; served there during pendency of Panama Canal Treaty in Colombian Congress; E.E. and M.P. to Argentine Republic, 1904-08, to the Netherlands and Luxemburg, 1908-11, to Cuba, Aug. 1911-June 28, 1913. Mem. Administrative Council, Permanent Court of Arbitration, The Hague. Del. Internat. Exchange Conf., The Hague, 1911; signed treaty with Cuba conveying Guantanamo Naval Sta. to U.S., 1913; E.E. and M.P. on spl. mission to attend inauguration of Pres. Menocal of Cuba, 1913, and was made chief of that mission. Home: Chicago, Ill. Died Sept. 13, 1919.

BEAUREGARD, Marie Antoinette (Nettie) Harney, archivist, curator; b. St. Louis, Mo., Oct. 7, 1868; d. John Mullanphy and Mary (Kimball) Harney; ed. Ursuline Convent, Vannes, Brittany, pvt. schs. in Paris and Loretto Convent, Florissant, Mo.; m. Henry Toutant Beauregard, Dec. 5, 1898 (died 1915). Archivist and curator of Mo. Hist. Soc., Jefferson Memorial, St. Louis, Mo., 1913.—. Originated and installed Lindbergh Trophy Gallery at Jefferson Memorial, 1927. Democrat. Catholic. Wrote booklet, Decorations and Trophies of Col. Charles A. Lindbergh, 1928. Contbr. hist. and geneal. articles and transls. from French. Home: Florissant, Mo. Died Apr. 2, 1940.

BEAVER, James Addams, governor; b. Millerstown, Pa., Oct. 21, 1837; s. Jacob and Ann Eliza (Addams) B.; grad. Jefferson Coll., Canonsburg, Pa., 1856; (LL.D., Dickinson, Pa., and Hanover, Ind., 1889, and U. of Edinburgh, Scotland); m. Mary A., d. Hon. H. N. McAllister, Dec. 26, 1865. Admitted to bar, 1858; practiced Bellefonte, Pa., 1859-61; Served as 2d lt. 2d Pa. Inf., Apr. 21, 1861; lt. col. 45th Pa. Inf., Oct. 21, 1861; col. 148th Pa. Inf., Sept. 8, 1862; bvtd. brig. gen. vols. "for highly meritorious and distinguished conduct throughout the campaign, particularly for valuable services at Cold Harbor while comdg. a brigade;" hon. disch., Dec. 22, 1864; shot through body, Chancellorsville, May 3, 1863; shot in side, Petersburg, Va., June 1864; lost a leg at Ream's Station, Aug. 24, 1864; resumed law practice at Bellefonte; was maj. gen. Pa. N.G., 1870-87; defeated for gov. by Robert E. Pattison, 1882; gov. Pa., 1887-91; judge Superior Ct., Pa., 1896-1906,

1906-16. Pres. bd. trustees Pa. State Coll.; del. Rep. Nat. Conv., 1880; vice-moderator Presbyn. Gen. Assembly, 1888, 1895; mem. President's commn. for investigation of War Dept., 1898; del. to Gen. Missionary Conf., Edinburgh, 1910. Died Jan. 31, 1914.

BEBAN, George, actor, producer; b. San Francisco, 1873; ed. pub. schs.; m. Edith Ethel MacBride (died 1926). Began at 8, singing in Reed and Emerson's minstrels, San Francisco; starred in "The American Idea," and with Weber & Fields and Marie Cahill; with "Sign of the Rose" 6 yrs.; leading character in picture plays—"An Alien," "Pasquale," "His Sweetheart," "Cook of Canyon Camp," "A Roadside Impresario," "Marcellini Millions," "Jules of the Strong Heart," "One More American," "Hearts of Men," "One Man in a Million," "The Sign of the Rose," "The Greatest Love of All," "The Loves of Ricardo." Died Oct. 5, 1928.

BECHT, J(ohn) George, educator; b. Montoursville, Pa., July 17, 1865; s. Jacob and Katherine (Kober) B.; Lycoming Normal Sch.; B.S., Lafayette Coll., Pa., 1890, M.S., 1893, A.M., 1896; post-grad. work, Harvard, 1900; Columbia, 1904; (hon. Sc.D., Lafayette, 1910, Bucknell U., 1906); m. Stella M. Howell, 1895 (died 1902); m. 2d, Laura Hunt Deemer, 1919. Prin Lycoming Normal Sch., 1890-93; county supt. schs., 1893-1903; prof. psychology, Westchester (Pa.) State Normal Sch., 1903-04; pres. State Normal School, Clarion, Pa., 1904-12; exec. sec. State Bd. of Edn., Pa., 1912-19; 1st deputy state supt. of pub. instrn. of Pa., July 1919-23; state supt. of pub. instrn., 1923—. Pres. State Council of Edn. Trustee Lafayette Coll., Oral Sch. for Deaf (Phila.). Elder Presbyn. Ch.; dir. Y.M.C.A. Mason. Lecturer on edn., U. of Pa., 1917-18. Home: Harrisburg, Pa. Died Apr. 26, 1925.

BECK, Adam L., cement mfr.; b. Huntington, Ind., May 9, 1862; s. Adam and Magdalena (Stetzel) B.; student Northwestern Coll., Naperville, Ill., (now North Central), 1880-82; m. Lizzie Purviance, June 23, 1887; children—Marshall (dec.), Magdalena (Mrs. Paul M. Taylor). Built roads, bridges and other pub. works for City of Huntington and Huntington Co., Ind., 1883-87; sec. Huntington White Lime Co., 1887-93; organizer and pres. Mitchell (Ind.) Lime Co., 1893-1906; organizer and pres. Okla. Portland Cement Co., 1906-17; organizer and pres. Ind. Portland Cement Co., 1917-25; organizer and pres. Great Lakes Portland Cement Co., 1925—. Served as chmn. Huntington Co. (Ind.) Rep. Com., 1894-1904, 11th Congl. Dist. Chmn. and mem. Ind. Rep. State Com., 1896-1900. Organized and was first pres. Mfrs. Assn. of Okla., now asso. Industries of Okla. Republican. Protestant. Mason. Home: Buffalo, N.Y. Died Aug. 10, 1939.

BECK, Carl, surgeon; b. at Neckargemuend, Germany, Apr. 4, 1856; s. Wilhelm and Sophia (Hoehler) B.; ed. Gymnasium of Heidelberg, 1869-74; studied at univs. of Heidelberg and Berlin; M.D., U. of Jena, 1879; m. Hedwig, d. Chief Justice Heinrich F. von Loeser, of Saxony, Feb. 16, 1889. Came to U.S., 1882; pres. St. Mark's Hosp., New York; surgeon to St. Mark's, 1886— and German Poliklinik, 1883—; prof. surgery, N.Y. Post-Grad. Med. Sch., 1890—. Officer Med. Reserve Corp U.S.A. Author: Manual on Surgical Asepsis, 1895; Text Book on Fractures, 1900; Die Röntgenstrahlen im Dienste der Chirurgie, 1902; Röntgen-Ray Diagnosis and Therapy, 1904; Röntgenchirurgie, Berlin, 1905; Amerikanische Streiflichter, 1905; Feuchtfroehliches and Feuchtunfroehliches, 1906; Der Schwedenkonrad (novel), 1906; Surgical Diseases of the Chest, 1907 (translated into German, 1909); Glimpses from Latin America, 1908; Röntgenuntersuchung der Leber und Gallenblase, 1909. Died 1911.

BECK, Carol H., artist; b. Phila.; d. James Nathan and Margaretta C. (Darling) B.; ed. Pa. Acad. Fine Arts and schs. of Dresden, Paris and Madrid. Received Mary Smith prize, Pa. Acad. Fine Arts, 1899; represented by portraits at Univ. of Pa., Masonic Temple, Odd Fellows' Temple, Mus. Fund Soc., Penn Charter Sch., Woman's Med. Coll., Phila., Pa. Soc. of N.Y., Wesleyan Coll., Swarthmore Coll.; capitals, Harrisburg and Trenton. Arranged and edited catalogue W. P. Wilstach Collection, Memorial Hall, Fairmount Park, Phila. Home: Philadelphia. Died 1908.

BECK, Edward Adam, city manager; b. Peru, Ind., Jan. 19, 1885; s. John Henry and Catherine Magdelan (Silberman) B.; B.S. in C.E., Purdue, 1913, C.E., 1917; m. Hazel Maude Locke, June 26, 1907. With engrng. corps electric and steam rys., various periods, until 1912; ry. terminal studies, Detroit, Toledo, etc., 1912-14; mgr. Borough of Edgeworth, Pa., 1914-17; mng. engr. Borough of Sewickley, June-Sept. 1917; mgr. Goldsborough, N.C., 1917-18; mgr. City of Auburn, Me., also chief engr. sewerage dist., 1919-20; mgr. Lynchburg, Va., Sept. 1920—. Capt. engr. sect. Sanitary Corps, U.S.A., Camp Shelby, Miss., World War; maj. Engr. O.R.C. Democrat. Episcopalian. Mason. Home: Lynchburg, Va. Died Oct. 18, 1925.

BECK, James Montgomery, lawyer; b. Phila., July 9, 1861; s. James Nathan and Margaretta C. (Darling) B.; grad. Moravian College, Pa., 1880; LL.D., Mühlenberg College and Moravian College, 1902, U. of Pa., 1910, McGill U. and Lafayette Coll., 1917; D.Litt., Franklin and Marshall Coll., 1918; LL.D., Loyola U., 1931, U. of Vt., 1935; m. Lilla, d. James Mitchell of Phila., 1890. Admitted to bar of Phila., 1884, N.Y., 1903, to bar of England, 1922; U.S. atty. Eastern Dist. Pa., 1896-1900; asst. atty. gen. U.S., 1900-03; mem. Shearman & Sterling, New York, 1903-17, Beck, Crawford & Harris, 1917-27; solicitor gen. of U.S., 1921-25 (resigned); resumed practice of law in Washington and New York; mem. 70th Congress (1927-29), 1st Pa. Dist., to fill unexpired term of James M. Hazlett, and reëlected to 71st and 72d Congresses (1929-33), same district, and to 73d Congress (1933-35), 2d Pa. District; resigned from Congress, Oct. 1, 1934. Officer Legion of Honor (French); Comdr. Order of the Crown (Belgian); Comdr. Order of Polonia Restituta (Polish). Republican. Author: The Evidence in the Case, 1914; War and Humanity, 1916; The Reckoning, 1918; The Passing of the New Freedom, 1920; The Constitution of the United States, 1922; The Vanishing Rights of the States, 1926; May It Please the Court, 1930; Our Wonderland of Bureaucracy, 1933. Home: Washington, D.C. Died April 12, 1936.

BECK, Johann Heinrich, composer; b. Cleveland, O., Sept. 12, 1856; s. Charles and Rebecca J. (Butler) B.; grad. Leipzig Conservatory of Music, 1882; spl. studies on string instruments and all branches of musical composition; m. Blandina Fellar, June 19, 1890. Ex-mem. examining bd. of Am. compositions and violin examiner of Am. Coll. of Musicians; dir. Detroit Symphony Orchestra, 1895; dir. Cleveland Symphony Orchestra, 1899-1912, also of Pilgrim Orchestra, Hermits Club Orchestra and Elyria Grand Orchestra. Composer: Overture to "Lara," performed by Boston Symphony Orchestra, 1886; "Skirnismal," performed by Thomas Orchestra, Chicago, 1887; "Sextet," performed at Indianapolis, Ind., 1888; "Moorish Serenade," performed at Phila., 1889; "Scherzo" in A major, performed at Detroit by Thomas Orchestra, 1890; "The Kiss of Jov," performed by Cleveland Symphony Orchestra, 1900, and at St. Louis Expn., 1904, by spl. request of music com.; "Meeresabend," for voice and orchestra, "Liebeslied," for same; Scherzo in F major performed by Theo. Thomas at Cleveland, 1896; "Aus meinen Leben," tone poem for grand orchestra; "As a Tale That Is Told," tone poem. Deceased.

BECK, Joseph David, congressman; b. nr. Bloomingdale, Wis., Mar. 14, 1866; s. Mitchel and Susan A. (Snodgrass) B.; grad. State Normal Sch., Stevens Point, Wis., 1897; A.B., U. of Wis., 1903; m. S. Jane Peavy, Nov. 24, 1888. Teacher Wis. pub. schs., 12 yrs.; clk. Bur. of Statistics, Wis., 1901; dep. commr. statistics, 1902; chief Dept. of Labor Statistics, 1903-13; chmn. Indsl. Commn. of Wis., 6 yrs.; mem. 67th to 70th Congresses (1921-29) 7th Wis. Dist.; commr. Dept. of Agr. and Markets, 1931—. Republican. Pres. Internat. Assn. Labor Bur. Officials, 1911-13. Breeder of pure-bred Guernsey cattle. Home: Viroqua, Wis. Died Nov. 8, 1936.

BECK, William, baritone; b. Budapest, Hungary, 1869; s. Alexander and Katherine (Friedmann) B.; studied at Paris Conservatory; unmarried. Sang in grand opera, Paris, 1906-09; created, in French, leading rôles in the principal Wagner operas; joined Manhattan Opera Co., New York, 1909; later in London, Eng.; first appearance in Chicago, with Chicago Grand Opera Co., 1910, returning each yr.; sang the sheriff, in "The Girl of the Golden West," with Henry W. Savage's English Opera Co., 1912; prin. rôles; Scarpia in "Tosca," title rôle in "Rigoletto," Klingsor in "Parsifal," Valentine in "Faust," Wolfram in "Tannhauser," Woten and Alberich in "Das Rheingold," etc. Home: Paris, France. Died Nov. 30, 1925.

BECK, William Henry, brig. gen.; b. Phila., June 29, 1842; s. John Rogers and Jane Owen (Ward) B.; ed. grammar and high schs., Phila.; m. Rachel Wyatt Elizabeth Tongate, Aug. 21, 1863. Corporal Co. B, 10th Ill. Vol. Inf., Apr. 16-July 29, 1861; promoted through grades to col. 49th U.S. Vol. Inf., Sept. 9, 1899; maj. 6th U.S. Cav., Feb. 2, 1901; hon. disch. vol. service, June 30, 1901; transferred to 8th Cav., Feb. 25, 1903; lt. col. 3d Cav., Apr. 15, 1903; brig. gen. U.S.A., Apr. 7, 1905; retired at own request, Apr. 8, 1905. Died 1911.

BECKER, George Ferdinand, geologist; b. New York, Jan. 5, 1847; s. Alexander Christian Becker (member of a Danish family) and Sarah Cary (Tuckerman) Becker; B.A., Harvard, 1868; Ph.D., Heidelberg, 1869; passed final exam. Royal Sch. of Mines, Berlin, 1871; m. Florence Serpell Deakins, Feb. 11, 1902. Instr. mining and metallurgy, U. of Calif., 1875-79; U.S. geologist-in-charge, 1879-92 and 1894—; spl. agt. 10th Census, 1879-83. Examined gold and diamond mines of S. Africa, 1896. Detailed to serve as geologist with army in P.I., 1898-99; now charge div. chem. and physical research, U.S. Geol. Survey; geophysicist, Carnegie Instn. Mem. com. Nat. Acad. apptd. Jan. 1903, to prepare report at Pres. Roosevelt's request, on desirability of instituting scientific explorations of the P.I. and on the scope proper to such an undertaking. Author: Atomic Weight Determinations, 1880; Geology of the Comstock Lode, 1882; Statistics and Technology of the Precious Metals (with S. F. Emmons), 1885; Geology of Quicksilver Deposits of the Pacific Slope 1888; Gold Fields of Southern Appalachians, 1895; Gold Fields of Alaska, 1898; Gold Fields of South Africa, 1897; Geology of the Philippine Islands, 1901; Experiments on Slaty Cleavage, 1904; Tables of the Hyperbolic Functions (with C. E. Van Orstrand), 1908. Home: Washington, D.C. Died April 20, 1919.

BECKER, Thomas A., R.C. bishop; b. Pittsburgh, Pa., 1832; studied at Propaganda, Rome; ordained priest, 1859; consecrated first bishop of Wilmington, Del., Aug. 16, 1868; transferred, May 1886 to see of Savannah. Home: Savannah, Ga. Died 1899.

BECKER, Washington, banker; b. South Worcester, Otsego Co., N.Y., Feb. 22, 1847; s. Abraham and Marie (Danforth) B.; grad. Phillips Exeter Acad., 1865; matriculated in Harvard; LL.B., Albany Law Sch., 1867; m. Sarah W. Merrill, June 22, 1875. Began practice at Worcester, N.Y., 1867; removed to Milwaukee, Wis., 1874; organizer, and pres. Westside Street Ry. system, Milwaukee, 1880-91; apptd. receiver, 1893, of Wis. Marine Fire & Ins. Co. Bank, and after effecting reorganization was elected pres. same; now pres. Marine Nat. Bank. Home: Milwaukee, Wis. Died Dec. 9, 1929.

BECKETT, Wesley Wilbur, M.D., surgeon; b. Forest Grove, Ore., May 31, 1857; s. Lemuel Daugherty and Sarah Springer (Chew) B.; M.D., U. of Southern Calif., 1888, LL.D., 1927; m. Iowa Archer, Jan. 1, 1882. Teacher pub. schs., San Luis Obispo County, Calif., 6 yrs., asst. supt. schs. 2 yrs.; interne Post-Grad. Med. Sch. and Hosp., N.Y. City, 1888-89; practiced at Los Angeles, 1889—; prof. gynecology and surgery, U. of Southern Calif.; dir., v.p., and med. dir. Pacific Mut. Life Ins. Co., 1909—; dir. Citizens Nat. Trust & Savings Bank, Pioneer Securities Corp., Bouldin Land Co. Apptd. 1st lt. M.R.C., U.S.A., 1911. Republican. Methodist. Mason. Home: Los Angeles, Calif. Died June 3, 1936.

BECKHAM, J. Crepps Wickliffe, senator; b. nr. Bardstown, Ky., Aug. 5, 1869; student Central U. of Ky., 1884-86 (LL.D., 1902); m. Jean Raphael Fuqua, Nov. 21, 1900; children—Eleanor Raphael, J. Crepps Wickliffe. Prin. Bardstown High Sch., 1888-91; admitted to Ky. bar, 1889, but did not begin practice until 1893; mem. Kentucky Ho. of Rep., 1894, 1896-98 (speaker of House, 1898); elected lt.-gov. of Ky., 1899, becoming gov. on death of Gov. Goebel, Feb. 3, 1900, and at spl. election, Nov. 6, 1900, was elected to fill unexpired term of Gov. Goebel, ending Dec. 8, 1903; reëlected for full term, 1903-07; Dem. nominee in State primary for U.S. Senate, 1906, but was defeated in Gen. Assembly, 1908; resumed practice of law at Frankfort, Ky.; mem. U.S. Senate, 1915-21; formerly sr. mem. Beckham, Hamilton & Beckham; apptd., Dec. 1935, chmn. Commn. for Reorganization of Ky. State Govt. and chmn. Pub. Service Commn. of Ky. Del.-at-large and mem. Com. on Resolutions Dem. Nat. Conv., 1904, 08, 12 and 20, also del.-at-large, 1916 and 1920. Presbyn. Home: Louisville, Ky. Died Jan. 9, 1940.

BECKINGTON, Alice, painter; b. St. Louis, July 30, 1868; d. Charles and Adeline (Cheney) B.; studied Art Students' League, New York, Académie Julian, Paris, and with Charles Lazar, Paris. Has exhibited at Paris Salons and Paris Expn., 1900, Soc. of Am. Artists, and N.A.D.; hon. mention, Buffalo Expn., 1901; bronze medal, St. Louis Expn., 1904. Miniature portrait of Mrs. Beckington, bought by the Metropolitan Museum. Awarded Medal of Honor by Brooklyn Soc. of Miniature Painters, 1935. Home: Scituate, Mass. Died Jan. 4, 1942.

BECKWITH, Charles Minnigerode, bishop; b. Prince George Co., Va., June 3, 1851; s. Dr. Thomas Stanley and Agnes (Ruffin) B.; A.B., U. of Ga., 1873; studied Berkeley Div. Sch.; D.D., U. of the South, 1902; S.T.D., Berkeley Div. Sch., 1903; m. Lucy Cocke, 1888 (died 1891); 1 son, Edmund Ruffin; m. 2d, Mary Belle Cameron, May 11, 1897. Asst. prof. mathematics, U. of the South, 1874-76; master of grammar schools, U. of the South, 1876-79; deacon, 1881, priest, 1882, P.E. Ch.; asst. rector, St. Luke's Cathedral, Atlanta, Ga., 1880-86; rector, Houston, Tex., 1886-92; gen. missionary Diocese of Tex., 1892-95; rector, Galveston, Tex., 1895-1901; consecrated bishop of Ala., 1902. Author: The Trinity Course of Church Instruction, 1898; The Teacher's Companion to the Trinity Course, 1901; Rightly Instructed in God's Holy Word, 1902. Home: Montgomery, Ala. Died Apr. 18, 1928.

BECKWITH, Clarence Augustine, theologian; b. Charlemont, Mass., July 21, 1849; s. Justin Williams and Sarah (Upton) B.; A.B., Olivet (Mich.) Coll., 1874, A.M., 1877; studied Yale Divinity Sch., 1874-76; grad. Bangor (Me.) Theol. Sem., 1877; U. of Berlin, 1897-98; S.T.D., Olivet College, 1892; LL.D. from same college, 1927; m. V. Eugénie Loba, Sept. 25, 1878; 1 son, Paul Loba. Ordained Congl. ministry, 1877; pastor Brewer, Me., 1877-82, W. Roxbury (Boston), 1882-92; prof. Christian theology, Bangor Theol. Sem., 1892-1905, and in Chicago Theol. Sem., 1905-26; prof. emeritus, 1927—; mem. Soc. Bibl.

Research. Author: Realities of Christian Theology, 1906; The Idea of God, 1922. Editor dept. theology, philosophy and ethics, in the New Schaff-Herzog Ency. Home: Eggemoggin, Me. Died Apr. 2, 1931.

BECKWITH, J(ames) Carroll, painter; b. Hannibal, Mo., Sept. 23, 1852; s. Charles Henry and Martha Melissa (Owen) B.; studied painting in Chicago, where his father was a mcht.; then in Paris, 1873-78, under Carolus Duran and Yvon, and also at the École des Beaux Arts, Paris; m. Bertha Hall, June 1, 1887. Located in New York, 1878; specialty portraits and genre pictures; received awards in Paris Salon and at Expn. Universelle, 1889 and 1900. N.A., 1894; mem. Nat. Inst. Arts and Letters. Died Oct. 24, 1917.

BECKWITH, Paul Edmond, author, anthropologist; b. St. Louis, Sept. 22, 1848; s. Frederick W. and Tullia Chouteau (Paul) B.; ed. in U.S. and Europe. Officer Pontifical Zouaves, corps of Pius IX, 1867-68; U.S. Indian Agent, 1875-76; mem. scientific staff, 1886—, now asst. curator Dept. Anthropology, U.S. Nat. Mus., Washington, D.C. An authority on coins, medals and arms. Author: The Beckwiths; The Creoles of St. Louis; Military Annals of St. Louis, 1764-1865; Amer. Indian Peace Medals. Died 1907.

BECTON, Joseph D. (Joe Becton), surgeon; b. Kilgore, Tex., Oct. 19, 1865; s. E. P. (M.D.) and Mary (Dixon) B.; grad. Austin Coll., Sherman, Tex., 1887; M.D., U. of Nashville, 1890. Began practice at Quanah, Tex., 1890; moved to Greenville, 1897; owner and head of Dr. Joe Becton's Hosp., 1901—; formerly prof. pathol. surgery, Baylor University. Mem. Tex. State Bd. Med. Examiners. Democrat. Presbyn. Home: Greenville, Tex. Died Oct. 14, 1931.

BEDFORD, Alfred Cotton, chmn. bd. dirs. Standard Oil Co. (N.J.); b. Brooklyn, N.Y., Nov. 5, 1864; s. Alfred B.; ed. Adelphi Acad., Brooklyn, and in Eng., Germany and Switzerland; m. Edith Kinsman Clarke, Jan. 8, 1890. Began as clk. E. S. Jaffray & Co., wholesale dry goods, N.Y. City; entered employ, Apr. 9, 1882, of Bergenport Chem. Co. (subsidiary of Standard Oil Co.) and became gen. mgr. of that company, later gen. rep. Charles Pratt & Co.; was made dir. Standard Oil Co. (N.J.), 1907, treas., 1910, v.p., 1911, pres., 1916, chmn. bd. dirs., Nov. 15, 1917. Chmn. petroleum com. of Council Nat. Defense, 1917; v.p., chmn. exec. com. Chamber Commerce U.S.; v.p. Chamber Commerce State of N.Y., Internat. Chamber of Commerce (chmn. Am. com.). Dir. Brooklyn Y.M.C.A.; mem. council Pratt Inst.; pres. trustee Emmanuel Bapt. Ch., Brooklyn. Home: East Norwich, L.I., N.Y. Died Sept. 21, 1925.

BEDFORD, Edward Thomas, capitalist; b. Brooklyn, Feb. 19, 1849; s. Frederick Thomas and Mary Ann Elizabeth (Pace) B.; ed. Maplegrove Acad., Westport, Conn.; m. Mary Ann Dingee, Dec. 1871. Pres. Corn Products Refining Co., Colonial Oil Co. of N.J.; trustee Title Guarantee & Trust Co.; dir. Thompson-Starrett Co., L.I. Safe Deposit Co., Bush Terminal Co., etc. Mem. advisory com. U.S. Lloyds. Home: Brooklyn, N.Y. Died May 21, 1931.

BEEBE, Brooks Ford, physician; b. Washington Co., O., June 25, 1850; s. William (M.D.) and Elizabeth (Rathbone) B.; A.M., Marietta Coll., 1905; M.D., Med. Coll. of Ohio, Cincinnati, 1880; m. Mrs. Beulah Benton Hissem, Aug. 1898. Interne Good Samaritan Hosp., Cincinnati, 1880-81; asst. acting surgeon U.S. Marine Hosp., Cincinnati, 1881-90; in gen. practice, 1890-1900; med. supt. and propr. Grandview Sanitarium, Price Hill, Cincinnati, 1900—; pres. Ohio Valley Med. Assn., 1907; chmn. Council Ohio State Med. Assn., 1902-09, 1st chmn. sect. mental and nervous diseases, 1909. Home: Cincinnati, O. Deceased.

BEEBE, James Albert, clergyman; b. Mound Valley, Kan., Dec. 8, 1878; s. Joseph Ellis and Mary Jane (Stotts) B.; A.B., Simpson Coll., 1903 (D.D., 1911, LL.D., from same coll., 1922); S.T.B. Boston U. Sch. of Theology, 1909, S.T.D., 1929; m. Laura E. Johnson, May 26, 1905; children—James Merten, Norman Richard, Margaret (dec.), Laura Jane, Robert Johnson. Ordained M.E. ministry, 1903; pastor Des Moines, Ia., 1903-06, Newport, N.H., 1906-08, Manchester, N.H., 1908-09, Englewood, Ill., 1909-15; pres. Iliff Sch. of Theology, Denver, Colo., 1915-20; dean Boston U. Sch. of Theology, 1920-26; pres. Allegheny Coll., 1926-30. Served as 1st sergt. Co. C, 51st Iowa Inf., in Philippine Islands, Spanish-Am. War, 1898. Mason. Author: The Pastoral Office, 1923. Home: Newtonville, Mass. Deceased.

BEEBE, William, coll. prof.; b. Litchfield, Conn., Sept. 4, 1851; s. Philip Schuyler and Lucy (Robbins) B.; B.A., Yale, 1873, M.A., 1899; m. Elizabeth Febiger, June 22, 1881. Tutor mathematics, 1876-82, asst. prof. mathematics and astronomy, 1882-97, prof. mathematics and instr. astronomy, 1897—, Yale University. Died Mar. 11, 1917.

BEEBER, Dimner, lawyer; b. Muncy, Lycoming Co., Pa., Mar. 8, 1854; s. Teter D. and Mary Jane (Artley) B.; desc. John B., Berks Co., Pa., 1768; A.B., Pa. Coll., 1874; LL.D., 1911; hon. A.M., Princeton, 1902; m. Blanche McGovney, June 6, 1906. Admitted to bar, 1876; mem. Jones, Carson & Beeber; has appeared in many of most important causes before Pa. state and federal cts.; judge Superior Court of Pa., 1899-1900. Republican. Dir. Bur. Municipal Research; mem. Bd. Edn., Phila., 1910—. Home: Philadelphia, Pa. Died June 28, 1930.

BEECHER, Charles, Congl. clergyman; b. Litchfield, Conn., Oct. 7, 1815 (son of Lyman Beecher, died Jan. 10, 1863); grad. Bowdoin, 1834; theol. course at Lane Seminary, O. Pastorates: Ft. Wayne, Ind.; Newark, N.J.; Georgetown, Mass.; Wysox, Pa. Author: Redeemer and Redeemed; Patmos. Edited his father's Life and Correspondence; Plymouth Collection of Hymns and Tunes. Home: Georgetown, Mass. Died 1900.

BEECHER, Charles Emerson, prof. paleontology and curator of geol. collections, Yale; b. Dunkirk, N.Y., Oct. 9, 1856; grad. Univ. of Mich., 1878 (Ph.D., Yale, 1889); m. Mary Salome Galligan, Sept. 12, 1894. Author: Studies in Evolution, 1901; and over seventy papers in scientific jours. and proceedings of scientific societies, principally on modern evolution and the classification of Brachiopods and Trilobites, and on the development and detailed structure of Trilobites, etc. Home: New Haven, Conn. Died 1904.

BEECHER, Thomas Kinnicut, Congl. clergyman; b. Litchfield, Conn., Feb. 10, 1824 (6th son of Lyman Beecher; brother of late Henry Ward Beecher); grad. Ill. Coll., 1843; taught in Philadelphia and Hartford, Conn. Founded and was pastor (1852-54) Congl. ch. of Williamsburg, L.I., N.Y., and became (1854) pastor Independent Congl. Ch., Elmira, N.Y. Chaplain 141st N.Y. vols. during Civil war. Author: Our Seven Churches; A Well-Considered Estimate of the Episcopal Church, etc. Home: Elmira, N.Y. Died 1900.

BEECHER, Willis Judson, theologian; b. Hampden, O., Apr. 29, 1838; s. Rev. John W. and Achsa (Judson) B.; A.B., Hamilton Coll., 1858, A.M., 1861; Theol. Sem., Auburn, N.Y., 1864; (D.D., Hamilton, 1875, Princeton, 1896); m. Sara Maria Bolter, June 14, 1865. Teacher Whitestown (N.Y.) Sem., 1858-61; ordained Presbyn. ministry, 1864; pastor Ovid, N.Y., 1864-65; prof. moral science and belles lettres, Knox Coll., Ill., 1865-69; pastor First Ch. of Christ, Galesburg, Ill., 1869-71; prof. Hebrew lang. and lit., Theol. Sem., Auburn, N.Y., 1871-1908. Stone lecturer, Princeton Theol. Sem., 1902. Pres. Soc. Bibl. Lit. and Exegesis, 1904. Author: Farmer Tompkins and His Bibles, 1874; The Prophets and the Promise, 1905; The Teaching of Jesus Concerning the Future Life, 1906; The Dated Events of the Old Testament, 1907; Reasonable Biblical Criticism, 1911. Home: Auburn, N.Y. Died May 10, 1912.

BEECKMAN, R(obert) Livingston, governor; b. N.Y. City, Apr. 15, 1866; s. Gilbert Livingston and Margaret (Foster) B.; ed. pub. and pvt. schs.; m. Eleanor Thomas, Oct. 8, 1902 (died 1920); m. 2d, Edna Marston, Sept. 1, 1923. Member N.Y. Stock Exchange, 1887-1906, now dir. Newport Trust Co., Internat. Silver Co.; mem. R.I. Ho. of Rep., 1909-11, Senate, 1912-14; gov. of R.I., 3 terms, 1915-21. Republican. Episcopalian. Home: Newport, R.I. Died Jan. 21, 1935.

BEEDE, Frank Herbert, supt. schs.; b. Dover, N.H., Feb. 15, 1859; s. Augustus and Abbie Elizabeth (Hopkinson) B.; A.B., Yale, 1883; Ed.D., Rhode Island Coll., Edn., Providence, 1931; m. Carrie May Coan, Oct. 24, 1884. Prin. high sch., Farmington, N.H., 1883-84, Weymouth, Mass., 1884-88, Willimantic, Conn., 1888-95; submaster, English High Sch., Somerville, Mass., 1895-96; prin. high sch., Watertown, 1896-97; Melrose, 1897-99, New Haven, Conn., 1899-1900; supt. schs., New Haven, 1900-31, supt. emeritus, 1931—. Lecturer on school organization and adminstrn., Yale, 1905-07. Conglist. Home: Woodbridge, Conn. Died Mar. 15, 1932.

BEEDE, Joshua William, geologist; b. Raymond, N.H., Sept. 14, 1871; s. Hiram Pratt and Lydia Maria (Brown) B.; B.S., Washburn Coll., Kan., 1896, A.M., 1897; Ph.D., U. of Kan., 1899; m. Clara Frances McKee, Dec. 25, 1899; children—Genevieve (Mrs. G. G. Henderson), Lydia May (Mrs. T. O. Todd), Lucile Prosser, Clara Frances. Student asst. in paleontology, U. of Kan., 1897-99; teacher of science, Atchison Co. High Sch., Effingham, Kan., 1899-1901; instr. geology, 1901-06, asst. prof., 1906-09, asso. prof., 1909-17, Indiana U. geologist, bur. econ. geology and technology, U. of Texas, 1917-22; with Empire Gas and Fuel Co., 1922; with Dixie Oil Co., 1924-28; prof. geology and paleontology, Indiana U., 1928—. Mem. Kan. Geological Survey, 1896, 1898-99, 1903-10. Okla. Geol. Survey, 1911-17; aid, U.S. Geol. Survey, 1901-02. Has made extensive researches in the carboniferous and permian formations and fossils from Neb. to Tex. and W.Va., and author of many papers on these topics and on Origin of Sediments and Coloring Matter of Red Beds, Kan.-Okla. Home: Bloomington, Ind. Died Feb. 26, 1940.

BEEHLER, William Henry, commodore, U.S.N.; b. Baltimore, Apr. 2, 1848; s. Francis and Charlotte Maria (Bowers) B.; Concordia Coll., St. Louis; Baltimore City Coll.; grad. U.S. Naval Acad., 1868; Naval War Coll., Newport, R.I.; m. Leila Potter, June 3, 1886. Served in Union League Co. for 3 weeks in defense of city of Baltimore, June-July, 1863, before battle of Gettysburg; ensign, 1869; master, 1870; lt., 1874; lt. comdr., 1896; comdr., 1899; capt., 1904; commodore, 1907; retired Nov. 12, 1910. Naval attaché, Berlin, Rome, Vienna, 1899-1902. Chmn. World's Congress of Meteorology, Chicago, 1893; v.p. World's Congress of Navigation, Paris, 1900; life mem. U.S. Naval Inst. Awarded 2 medals, Spanish-Am. War service and San Juan. Invented and patented a self recording weighing machine, 1879, but did not market it; patented the solarometer, 1892, an instrument to determine position and compass error at sea (now in use nautical colls. U.S. and Germany). Episcopalian. Author: The Cruise of the Brooklyn, 1884; History of the Italian-Turkish War, 1912, 2d edit., 1913. Home: Annapolis, Md. Died June 23, 1915.

BEEKMAN, Charles K., lawyer; b. Milburn, N.J., Sept. 23, 1868; s. William B. and Alice B.; A.B., Columbia U., 1889, LL.B., 1892. Admitted to N.Y. bar, 1892, and began practice in N.Y. City; dir. Mfrs. Trust Co., Wood Newspaper Machinery Corp.; trustee Beekman Estate; mem. Beekman, Bogue, Stephens & Black. Home: New York, N.Y. Died Mar. 1941.

BEER, George Louis, historian; b. Staten Island, N.Y., July 26, 1872; s. Julius and Sophia (Walter) B.; A.B., Columbia, 1892, A.M., 1893; m. Edith Cecilia Hellman, Nov. 11, 1896. Importer of tobacco from Cuba, 1893-1903 and mem. Weil & Co., 1896-1903; lecturer on European history, Columbia, 1893-97. Chief of Colonial Div. of Am. Commission to Negotiate Peace, Paris, France, 1918-19; apptd. dir. Mandatory Sect. of Secretariat of League of Nations, 1919. Republican. Author: Commercial Policy of England Toward the American Colonies, 1893; Cromwell's Policy in Its Economic Aspects, 1902; British Colonial Policy, 1754-65, 1907; Origins of the British Colonial System, 1578-1660, 1908; The Old Colonial System, 1660-1754, Part I in 2 vols., 1912. These last 4 vols. were awarded in 1913 the first Loubat Prize as the best work published in the English lang. during the preceding 5 years on the history, geography or archeology of America, 1917. Died Mar. 15, 1920.

BEER, Thomas, writer; b. Council Bluffs, Ia., Nov. 22, 1889; s. William Collins and Martha Ann Alice (Baldwin) B.; B.A., Yale, 1911; student law dept. Columbia, 1911-13; unmarried. Contbr. short stories to Century, Saturday Evening Post, Smart Set, etc. Served as pvt., F.A., U.S.A., 1917, 1st lt., on staff 87th Div., 1918; in France 6 mos. Author: Fair Rewards, 1922; Stephen Crane, 1923; Sandoval, 1924; The Mauve Decade, 1926; The Road to Heaven, 1928; Hanna, 1929; Mrs. Egg and Other Barbarians, 1933. Home: Yonkers, N.Y. Died Apr. 18, 1940.

BEER, William, librarian; b. Plymouth, Eng., May 1, 1849; s. Gabriel and Harriet B.; grad. Coll. of Physical Science, Newcastle-on-Tyne, Eng., 1879; studied medicine in Paris, 1872-78; unmarried. In business, Newcastle-on-Tyne, 1879-84; mining engr. in U.S., 1886-90; librarian, Topeka (Kan.) Pub. Library, 1890; librarian, Howard Memorial Library, 1891—, jointly with New Orleans Pub. Library, 1897-1906. Home: New Orleans, La. Died Feb. 1, 1927.

BEERS, Alfred Bishop, lawyer; b. New Rochelle, N.Y., Apr. 23, 1845; s. Alfred and Mary Elizabeth (Bishop) B.; ed. pub. and grammar schs.; m. Callie H. House, Feb. 29, 1872. Served as pvt., corporal, orderly sergt., Co. I, 6th Conn. Vol. Inf.; capt. Co. B, same regt., Civil War; enlisted Aug. 25, 1861, discharged Aug. 21, 1865. Prac. law in Bridgeport, 1871; mem. Beers & Foster, 1900—; clk. City Ct., 1873; asst. city atty., 1875; judge of City Court, 1877-93; city atty., 1897-01; pres. Standard Assn., pubs. Bridgeport Standard; v.p. United Illuminating Co. Republican. Episcopalian. Mason. Comdr. in chief G.A.R., 1912-13. Mem. Soldiers' Hosp. Board of Conn., 1886-1906 (chmn. exec. com.). Home: Bridgeport, Conn. Died Mar. 30, 1920.

BEERS, Edward M., congressman; b. Nossville, Huntingdon Co., Pa., May 27, 1877; s. Anderson and Mary E. B.; grad. high sch., Mt. Union, Pa., 1895; m. Iva Clarissa Ewing, Apr. 27, 1910. Succeeded father in hotel business, 1895; was also identified with agrl. pursuits; del. Rep. State Conv., Pa.; mayor of Mt. Union, 1910-14; dir. First Nat. Bank (Mt. Union), Grange Trust Co. (Huntingdon); asso. judge Huntingdon County, 1914-23; mem. 68th to 72d Congress (1923-33), 18th Pa. Dist. Methodist. Home: Mt. Union, Pa. Died Apr. 21, 1932.

BEERS, Henry Augustin, coll. prof.; b. Buffalo, N.Y., July 2,1847; s. George Webster and Elizabeth Victoria (Clerc) B.; A.B., Yale, 1869, A.M., 1887; m. Mary Heaton, July 7,1873; children—Thomas Heaton, Elizabeth Clerc, Katherine, Frederic, Dorothy, Mary Heaton, Henry Augustin, Donald. Admitted to N.Y. bar, 1870; tutor, 1871-74, asst. prof., 1874-80, prof. English lit., 1880-1916, Yale prof. emeritus since 1916. Author: A Century of American Literature, 1878; Odds and Ends (verse), 1878; Nathaniel Parker Willis, 1885; Prose Writings of N. P. Willis, 1885; The Thankless Muse (verse), 1885; From Chaucer to Tennyson, 1890; Initial Studies in American Letters, 1891; Selections from the Prose Writings of S. T. Coleridge, 1893; A Suburban Pastoral and Other Tales, 1894; The Ways of Yale, 1895; A History of English Romanticism in the Eighteenth Century, 1899; A History of English Romanticism in the Nineteenth Century, 1901; Points at Issue, 1904; Milton's Tercentenary, 1910; The Two Twilights (verse), 1917; Four Americans, 1919; The Connecticut Wits, 1920; Poems, 1921; Original Gum (in Liber Scriptorum), 1921. Home: New Haven, Conn. Died Sept. 7, 1926.

BEGG, Alexander Swanson, M.D., educator; b. Council Bluffs, Ia., May 23, 1881; s. Alexander Swanson and Lauretta (Slotterbeck) B.; grad. Collegiate Inst., Sarnia, Ont., Can., 1899; B.S., Drake U., 1906; M.D., 1907; m. Grace Waers, 1908; children—John, Charles, Barbara. Instr. in pathology, Drake U., 1907-09, asst. prof. pathology, histology and embryology, 1909-10, prof. histology and embryology, 1910-13; teaching fellow, Harvard Med. Sch., 1911-12, instr. in comparative anatomy, 1913-18, dean Grad. Sch. Medicine, 1917-18, demonstrator in anatomy and instr. of histology, 1919-21; research asso., Carnegie Inst., 1915-16; prof. anatomy, Boston U. Sch. of Medicine, 1921—, dean, 1923—. Served as 1st lt. and capt., Med. Res. Corps, 1917, major, 1918, lt. col., 1918, col., 1919—; active duty, office of surgeon gen., A.E.F., 1917-19. Republican. Unitarian. Home: West Roxbury, Mass. Died Sept. 26, 1940.

BEGGS, George Erle, prof. civ. engring.; b. Ashland, Ill., Apr. 23, 1883; s. Edwin and Emma (Beggs) B.; A.B., Northwestern U., 1905; C.E., Columbia, 1910; m. Frances May Ingalls, Sept. 26, 1912; 1 son, George Erle. With Princeton U., 1914—, prof. civ. engring, 1930—. Author: Live Load Stresses in Railway Bridges, 1916. Home: Princeton, N.J. Died Nov. 23, 1939.

BEHAN, William James, sugar planter; b. New Orleans, Sept. 25, 1840; s. John Holland and Katherine (Walker) B.; ed. U. of La., Western Mil. Inst., Nashville, Tenn.; m. Katie Walker, June 7, 1866; children—Mrs. Bessie Lewis and Mrs. Andre Dreux. Was extensively engaged in sugar planting (retired). Enlisted in Washington Artillery, New Orleans, and served through Civ. War in Army of Northern Va. (surrendered at Appomattox); a leader in reconstruction period and commanded, 1874, fight in New Orleans which deposed radical carpet-bag govt.; maj. gen. La. State Nat. Guard, 1874-82; mayor of New Orleans, 1882-84; mem. State Senate, 1888-92. Left Dem. party during Cleveland administration because of efforts to place sugar on free list; chmn. Rep. State Exec. Com., 1900-12; del. to all Rep. nat. convs., 1896—; Rep. candidate for governor of La., 1904. Maj. gen. U.C.V., 1889-91; comdr. Washington Artillery Veterans' Assn., 1905—. Active in war work during World War; visited the Aisne and Somme sectors of the battle front in France, 1917. Home: New Orleans, La. Died May 4, 1928.

BEHN, Hernand, telephone official; b. St. Thomas, V.I., Feb. 19, 1880; s. William and Louise (Monsanto) B.; ed. St. Thomas, Ajaccio (Corsica), and Ste. Barbe, Paris, France; m. Helen Rae; children—Elizabeth, Louise, Sosthenes II, Hernand. Pres. Behn Bros., Inc., 1906—; chmn. bd. internat. Marine Radio Co., Ltd.; pres. Havana Subway Co., Internat. Telephone & Telegraph Corp., Internat. Telephone & Telegraph Corp. (Sud America), Radio Corp. of Cuba, Cuban Telephone Co., Cuban-Am. Telephone & Telegraph Co.; vice chmn. Internat. Standard Electric Corp., Mexican Telephone & Telegraph Co., Porto Rico Telephone Co., and other cos.; v.p. Internat. Telephone & Telegraph Corp. (Espana). Served as lt. U.S.N.R.F., Apr. 15, 1918-Feb. 24, 1919. Decorated Chevalier Legion of Honor (French); Comdr. Order of St. Gregory and Grand Cross of Order of Holy Sepulchre (Papal); Grand Cross of Order of Isabela la Catolica of Spain. Catholic. Died Oct. 7, 1933.

BEHNER, Albert Jacob, prof. theology; b. Hopedale, Ill., Sept. 4, 1888; s. Frederick Charles and Josephine Emma (Crichfield) B.; A.B., U. of Denver, 1917; B.D., Iliff Sch. of Theology, Denver, 1919; M.A., U. of Chicago Div. Sch., 1919; grad. study U. of Chicago; m. Anna Mae Peek, Dec. 22, 1915; children—Genevieve Evelyn, Lois Irene. Pastor in Ia. and Ill. until 1919; instr. in sociology, Chicago Training Sch., 1919; prof. religion, Washburn Coll., Topeka, Kan., 1921-24; prof. systematic theology and ethics, Iliff Sch. of Theology, 1924—. Republican. Methodist. Lecturer on Modern Christianity. Home: Denver, Colo. Died Sept. 23, 1928.

BEHREND, Ernst Richard, paper mfr.; b. Coeslin, Germany, Mar. 29, 1869; s. Moritz and Rebecca (Wolf) B.; ed. in Dresden and Charlottenburg; m. Mary Brownell, June 1, 1907; 1 dau., Harriet Ellen. Came to United States, 1896, naturalized citizen, 1901. Engr. with Pusey & Jones Co., Wilmington, Del., later with Nekoosa Paper Co.; rep. of Am. paper mill machinery mfrs. in Eng., France, Germany and Scandinavia, 1897; founder 1898, and pres. Hammermill Paper Co., Erie, Pa. Home: Erie, Pa., and Newport, R.I. Died Sept. 22, 1940.

BEHRENDS, Adolphus Julius Frederick, Congl. clergyman; b. Holland, 1839; ordained to ministry 1865; pastor Central Congl. Ch., Brooklyn, 1883—. Author: Socialism and Christianity; The Philosophy of Preaching; The World for Christ. Home: Brooklyn, N.Y. Died 1900.

BEHRENS, H. Frederick, pres. Sterling Products, Inc.,; b. Wheeling, W. Va., Aug. 4, 1870; s. Hans F. and Marie (Ulrich) B.; Washington and Jefferson Coll., 1887-91; m. Estella Eckhart, June 23, 1897. Began in retail mercantile business, Wheeling, 1892; became associated, 1901, with Neuralgyline Co., now Sterling Products, Inc., of which is pres.; pres. Bayer Co., Inc., Charles H. Phillips Chem. Co., Trustee Washington and Jefferson Coll. Mem. Rep. State Com., W. Va., since 1912. Presbyn. Mason. Home: Wheeling, W. Va. Died Jan. 17, 1935.

BEHREND, Bernard Arthur, cons. engr.; b. Villeneuve, Switzerland, May 9, 1875; s. Moritz and Rebecca (Wolf) B.; ed. by pvt. tutor; partly educated in England; C.E., Univ. and Poly. Inst., Berlin, 1894; D. Eng., honoris causa, Darmstadt, Germany, 1931; m. Margaret Plumer Chase, 1926. Late ch. engr. Bullock Electric Mfg. Co., Cincinnati; chief elec. engr. and consulting engr. Allis-Chalmers Co. and Allis-Chalmers-Bullock, Ltd., Montreal; advisory engr. Westinghouse Co. Non-resident lecturer McGill U., U. of Wis., Leland Stanford Jr. U. Inventor of numerous elec. devices and machinery; designer of some of the largest elec. machinery mfd. by Bullock, Allis-Chalmers and Westinghouse cos. Gold medal, St. Louis Expn., for design of turbo-generators in modern form, 1904. John Scott medal, Franklin Inst., 1912. Author: The Induction Motor—Its Theory and Design, 1900, in French, 1902, in German, 1903; (issued in new edit., 1922, under title, The Induction Motor and Other Alternating Current Motors); The Debt of Electrical Engineering to C. E. L. Brown, 1901; Engineering Education, 1907; The Work of Oliver Heaviside, 1928. Has obtained over 70 patents on his inventions. Contributor of about 30 monographs to leading Am. and European jours. and trans. on the theory of a.c. motors and generators. Mem. com. on orgn. Internat. Elec. Congress, St. Louis, 1904. Fellow Am. Acad. Arts and Sciences, Am. Inst. E.E. (sr. v.p.). Died March 25, 1932.

BEHRMAN, Martin, mayor; b. New York, Oct. 14, 1864; s. Henry and Frederica B.; pub. sch. edn., New Orleans; m. Julia Collins, of Cincinnati, 1887. Has been member sch. bd., assessor, clerk city council, New Orleans; pres. La. State Bd. Assessors; mem. La. Constl. Conv., 1898 and 1921; state auditor, 1904-05; mayor of New Orleans, 4 terms, 1904-20; dir. Am. Bank & Trust Co. Democrat. Pres. League Am. Municipalities, 1917-18. Home: New Orleans, La. Died Jan. 12, 1926.

BEKKER, Leander J. de, editor, pub.; b. Ky., June 26, 1872; m. Sarah F. Winslow, Mar. 16, 1903. Music and dramatic critic, Carter's Mag., Chicago, 1897; editor Afterthought, Washington, 1898; reporter, Baltimore American, 1899; editor and critic, Brooklyn Standard-Union, 1901-06; copy editor New York Tribune, 1909-12; exchange editor New York Evening Post, 1912-18; rejoined editorial staff New York Tribune, 1918; editorial corr. same in Cuba and Mexico, 1919; led opposition to Mexican intervention. Confidential asst. U.S. War Trade Bd. Cofounder, 1914, and first pres. Am. sect. La Ligue des Pays Neutres (devoted to anti-German propaganda). Became sec. 1915, pres. 1921, Writers Pub. Co., Inc. Author: Stokes Encyclopedia of Music and Musicians, 1908 (also pub. as "University Dictionary of Music and Musicians," 1910, Brit. edits., W. & R. Chambers, 1912); The Serio-Comic Profession, 1915; The Birth of the Waltz (ballet), 1916; The Plot Against Mexico, 1919; Idioms and Idiomatic Phrases (with Frank H. Vizetelly), 1921; Paz Americana, and other articles syndicated to Spanish-American press, 1923; De Bekker's Music and Musicians, 1924; Wisdom and The Frail Lady, 1926; Toussaint Louverture (hist. drama); The Black Liberator (biog. of Toussaint Louverture), 1929. Compiler of A History of the United States by the Presidents, 1899. Office editor Hoyt's New Practical Ency. of Quotations (1922 edit.); Business and the Professions; Installment Sales and Collections; Purchasing Principles and Practice; etc. Organized Com. on Haiti, 1927, to restore independence of that republic, and published in support of it, "Occupied Haiti"—nonpartisan Am. commission's report. Died Jan. 26, 1931.

BELASCO, David, dramatist, producer; b. San Francisco, July 25, 1854; s. Abraham and Reina (Martin) B.; ed. Lincoln Coll., Calif., 1875; m. Cecilia Loverish (dec.). Formerly stage mgr. Baldwin's Theatre, Grand Opera House and Metropolitan Theatre, San Francisco; stage mgr. Madison Sq. Theatre, New York, 1880-87, later of the Lyceum; is now owner and mgr. of the Belasco Theatre, N.Y. City. Presented E. H. Sothern, in Lord Chumley, 1887; Mrs. Leslie Carter, in The Heart of Maryland, 1895; Blanche Bates, in Naughty Anthony, 1899; Henrietta Crosman, in Sweet Kitty Bellairs, 1903; David Warfield, in The Music Master, 1904; Frances Starr, in Tiger! Tiger! 1918; Ina Claire, in The Gold Diggers, 1919; David Warfield, in The Merchant of Venice, 1922; Fay Bainter, in The Other Rose (with William Harris, jr.), 1923; Robert Loraine, in Tiger Cats, 1924; Lenore Ulric, in The Harem, 1924; Holbrook Blinn and Judith Anderson, in The Dove, 1925; Willard Mack, in Canary Dutch, 1925; E. H. Sothern, in Accused, 1925; also prod. Madame Butterfly, 1900; The Girl of the Golden West, 1905; The Wandering Jew, 1921; Ladies of the Evening, 1924; Salvage, 1925; Lenore Ulric as Lulu Belle, 1926; Fannie Brice in Fanny, 1926; Lily Sue, 1926; E. H. Sothern in What Never Dies, 1926; Hidden, 1927; June Walker and C. Aubrey Smith in The Bachelor Father, 1927; Lenore Ulric in Mima, 1928; Mildred McCoy and Minor Watson in It's a Wise Child, season 1929-30; and many others. Author (plays): May Blossom, 1884; La Belle Russe, 1881; Hearts of Oak; Valerie; Lord Chumley, 1887; The Wife (with H. C. De Mille); The Charity Ball (with same); Men and Women; The Girl I left Behind Me (with Franklin Fyles); The Heart of Maryland, 1895, Du Barry; The Darling of the Gods (with John Luther Long); Sweet Kitty Bellairs; Adrea (with John Luther Long); The Girl of the Golden West, 1905; The Lily (adaptation), 1907; The Return of Peter Grimm, 1911; Van der Decken, 1915; The Son-Daughter (with George Scarborough), 1919; Kiki (adaptation), 1921; The Comedian (adaptation), 1923; Laugh, Clown, Laugh (with Tom Cushing, from Italian), 1923; Fanny (with Willard Mack), 1926; also many other adaptations. Address: Belasco Theatre, New York, N.Y. Died May 14, 1931.

BELDEN, Charles Dwight, physician; b. Boonton, N.J., Feb. 16, 1845; s. Rev. Henry and Caroline (Wilcox) B.; ed. Williams Coll., 1861-62; served in Civil War, 1862-65; Coll. Phys. and Surg. (Columbia), 1865-66; M.D., New York Homœ. Med. Coll., 1868; m. Mary E. Noble, Feb. 21, 1866; m. 2d, Katinka, Countess de Rudzinski, of Poland, Apr. 26, 1907. In New York banking firms, 1875-82. Discoverer of therapeutic use of venom of Gila monster for paralysis, locomotor ataxia and kindred disorders. Mem. Mass. Ho. of Rep., 1882, 1883. Republican. Dept. comdr. G.A.R., Ariz., 1894. Author: Orations and Addresses, 1902. Home: Eureka Springs, Ark. Died July 27, 1919.

BELDEN, Charles Francis Dorr, librarian; b. Syracuse, N.Y., Oct. 5, 1870; s. Francis Crapo and Jennie Maude (Wright) B.; LL.B., Harvard Law School, 1898; hon. A.M. from Harvard, 1926; m. Anna Marian Blackwell, May 26, 1908; children—Elizabeth Blackwell, Lawrence Putnam, Alison Blackwell, Charles Hastings. Sec. law faculty Harvard Law Sch., Sept. 1, 1899, to Sept. 1, 1902; asst. librarian Harvard Law Library, 1902-08; librarian Social Law Library, Boston, 1908-09, Mass. State Library, 1909-17; dir. Boston Pub. Library since June 1917. Chmn. Free Pub. Library Commn. Mass. (now Div. Pub. Libraries), 1909—. Home: Jamaica Plain, Mass. Died Oct. 24, 1931.

BELDEN, Ellsworth Burnett, judge; b. Rochester, Wis., May 18, 1866; s. Henry Ward and Emily Frances (Brown) B.; LL.B., U. of Wis., 1886; m. Hattie M. Raymond, June 26, 1890; children—Stanley Raymond, John Ellsworth. County judge, Racine Co., Wis., 1890-1901; judge, First Jud. Circuit, Wis., 1901—. Trustee Racine Coll.; mem. bd. of visitors U. of Wis. Republican. Episcopalian. Mason. Home: Racine, Wis. Died Mar. 11, 1939.

BELDEN, James Jerome, congressman, banker; b. Fabius, N.Y., Sept. 30, 1825; is of Puritan descent and charter mem. Order of Founders and Patriots of America; in business life 40 yrs.; pres. and prin. owner of Robert Gere Bank of Syracuse, which he founded. Mayor of Syracuse, 1877-78; mem. Congress, 1887-95; declined nomination for 54th Congress; elected, 1896, to Congress of 1897-99 as Independent Republican. Home: Syracuse, N.Y. Died 1904.

BELDEN, Jessie Van Zile, author; b. Troy, N.Y., Nov. 13, 1857; d. Oscar E. and Sarah (Perry) Van Zile; ed. Troy Female Sem. and (grad.) St. Agnes Sch., Albany, N.Y.; m. James Mead Belden, Oct. 24, 1878. Apptd. by Gov. Roosevelt, reapptd. by Gov. Odell mem. bd. mgrs. State Reformatory, Hudson, N.Y. Mem. Colonial Dames of State of N.Y.; N.Y. State regent D.A.R., 1898-99. Author: Fate at the Door, 1895; Concerning the Ancestors and Descendants of Royal Denison Belden, 1898; The King's Ward, 1898; Antonia. Home: Syracuse, N.Y. Died 1910.

BELDING, Alvah Norton, silk mfr.; b. Ashfield, Mass., Mar. 27, 1838; s. Hiram and Mary (Wilson) B.; ed. pub. schs.; m. Lizzie S. Merrick, Jan. 6, 1870. Moved with parents to Mich., 1855, and asstd. in clearing wild land for a farm where city of Belding now stands; began selling silk in a small way, 1859; started with brothers, first wholesale silk store, Chicago, 1863, New York, 1864, later Cincinnati, Boston, Phila., etc. (co. now operating 9 mills and 10 wh. silk stores). Sec. Belding Bros. & Co. Republican. Home: Rockville, Conn. Died Dec. 18, 1925.

BELDING, Milo Merrick, Sr., silk mfr.; b. Ashfield, Mass., Apr. 2, 1833; s. Hiram and Mary (Wilson) B.; reared on farm; ed. Shelburne Falls Acad.; m. Emily C. Leonard, Apr. 1,1856. Began to sell sewing silk in small way at 17; afterward in other business until 1863, he established, with brothers, a silk house in Chicago, and, 1864, one in New York; from this grew the silk mfg. enterprise of Belding Bros. & Co., of which he was pres.—now the largest in the world; also dir. in many corps., etc. Home: New York. Died May 23, 1917.

BELDING, Milo Merrick, Jr., silk mfr.; b. Brooklyn, N.Y., Apr. 14, 1865; s. Milo M. and Emily C. (Leonard) B.; ed. Adelphi Acad., Brooklyn, and spent 2 yrs. in travel; m. Annie L. Kirk, Feb. 9, 1887. Formerly pres. Belding Bros. & Co., silk mfrs., also pres. Broadway Trust Co.; vice-pres. Internat. Salt Co. of N.J., Internat. Salt Co. of N.Y., Retsof Mining Co., Avery Rock Salt Co., Detroit Rock Salt Co., Genesee & Wyo. R.R.; treas. Internat. Pulp Co., U.S. Talc Co., Union Talc Co., Oswegatchie Light & Power Co. Republican. Home: New York, N.Y. Died Oct. 31, 1931.

BELFIELD, Henry Holmes, educator; b. Phila., Nov. 17, 1837; s. William and Selener (Marshall) B.; bro. of William Thomas B. (q.v.); A.B., Iowa (now Grinnell) Coll., 1858 (Sargent gold medals for scholarship, 1857-8, valedictorian of class), A.M., 1868, Ph.D., 1878; A.M., Griswold Coll., 1861; m. Anne Wallace Miller, July 27, 1869. Served in Civil War as 1st lt. and adj. 8th Ia. Cav., on staffs of Brig. Gen. J. T. Croxton and Maj. Gen. E. M. McCook; prisoner of war in 1864; mustered out, Aug. 27, 1865. Tutor in Greek, Iowa Coll., 1858; prin. and supt. pub. schs., Dubuque, 1859-60, 1861-63, 1865-66; tutor in Latin, Griswold Coll., 1860-61; prin. grammar sch., Chicago, 1866-76, North Div. High Sch., Chicago, 1876-83; organizer and dir. Chicago Manual Training Sch., 1883-1903; dean. Univ. High Sch., 1903-08, retired. One of the earliest advocates (1872) of manual training. Lecturer on edn.; spl. commr. U.S. Dept. of Labor to inspect and report on tech. schs. in Europe and U.S., 1891-92. Republican. Trustee Presbyn. Home for the Aged. Author of series of arithmetics; editor of English and French classics. Home: Chicago, Ill. Died June 5, 1912.

BELFIELD, William Thomas, M.D.; b. St. Louis, 1856; s. William and Selener (Marshall) B.; student U. of Mich., 1872-73; M.D., Rush Med. Coll., Chicago, 1878; post-grad. work in U. of Vienna; unmarried. Lecturer of Cartwright Fund, New York, 1883; prof. genito-urinary and venereal diseases, Chicago Polyclinic, 1888—; prof. genito-urinary surgery, Rush Med. Coll., 1898—. Home: Chicago, Ill. Died Oct. 14, 1929.

BELFORD, James B., jurist; b. Lewistown, Pa., Sept. 28, 1837; s. Samuel and Eliza B.; ed. Dickinson Coll., Pa.; m. Frances McEwen, 1869. Studied law, and admitted to the bar, 1858; judge Sup. Ct., Colo., 1870-75; mem. Congress, 1877-87. Republican. Home: Denver, Colo. Died 1910.

BELKNAP, Edwin Star, playwright; b. San Francisco; s. David Price and Augusta Walton (Yates) B.; ed. pub. sch., San Francisco; LL.B., New York U., 1883; unmarried. Practiced law, 1883-88; actor, 1888-91; since then playwright and public reader; instr. in pantomime, 1894—; special instr. in tech. branches of dramatic art, Am. Acad. of Dramatic Art, New York, and Sch. of English Speech and Expression, Boston. Author (pantomimes): Put to the Test; The Enchanted Fountain; Love and Witchcraft; In Old New Amsterdam; The Traitor Mandolin (all prod. Empire Theatre, New York—music by Harvey Worthington Loomis). Co-author (plays produced): The Better Part; The Three Miss Biddles; The Glove and the Lion; (sole author) "Philopena." Translated a symbolic play, The Tragedy of Death, from the French of René Peter, prod. Empire Theatre, New York. Deceased.

BELKNAP, George Eugene, rear adm. (retired Jan. 22, 1894); b. Newport, N.H., Jan. 22, 1832; s. Sawyer B. Apptd. midshipman, 1852; promoted through grades to rear admiral, 1889; m. Ellen D. Reed, Dec. 8, 1861; m. 2d, Frances G. Prescott, Calcutta, Ind., Dec. 23, 1866. Fighting service in China, capture of the Barrier Forts, 1856, and through Civil war, participating in bombardment of forts and batteries in Charleston harbor, in both fights at Ft. Fisher, etc. In 1873 ordered to steamer Tuscarora to make deep-sea soundings in North Pacific, with view to submarine cable; discoveries concerning topography of ocean bed recognized by scientists world over; senior officer Honolulu at time of disturbances at election of King Kalakaua; at various times in command navy-yards at Norfolk, Pensacola and Mare Island, and supt. Naval Observatory, Washington; pres. torpedo bd.; pres. Naval Bd. of Inspection and Survey; in command Alaska, South American waters, at time of difficulty between Chile and Peru. Author: Deep Sea Soundings; etc. Honored by leading scientific socs. of Europe and America; LL.D., Dartmouth, 1894. Comd. U.S. fleet in the Asiatic Sta., 1889-92. Chairman Bd. Commrs., Mass. Nautical Training School; mem. Loyal Legion, U.S.; Naval Order of the U.S.; Sons of Am. Revolution, and G.A.R. Home: Brookline, Mass. Died 1903.

BELKNAP, Morris Burke, merchant; b. Louisville, Ky., June 7, 1856; s. William Burke and Mary (Richardson) B.; brother of William Richardson B. (q.v.); Ph. B., Sheffield Scientific Sch. (Yale), 1877; m. Lily, d. Gen. S. B. Buckner, C.S.A., June 14, 1883; m. 2d, Marion S. Dumont, July 16, 1900. Served pvt. to lt. col. Ky. N.G., 1879-98; lt. col. and col., 1st Ky. Vol. Inf., Spanish-Am. War, 1898. Rep. candidate for gov. of Ky., 1903. V.p. Belknap Hardware & Mfg. Co. Pres. Louisville Bd. of Trade; U.S. del. Congrés Internat. of Chambers of Commerce, Liege, 1905; pres. Yale Alumni Assn. of Ky. Republican. Presbyn. Home: Louisville, Ky. Died 1910.

BELKNAP, William Richardson, merchant; b. Louisville, Ky., Mar. 28, 1849; s. William Burke and Mary (Richardson) B.; brother of Morris Burke B. (q.v.); B.S., Sheffield Scientific Sch. (Yale), 1869; m. Alice Trumbull, d. Benjamin Silliman, of New Haven, Conn., Dec. 2, 1874 (died 1890); m. 2d, Juliet Rathbone Davison, Feb., 1894. In hardware and mfg. business since beginning of active career; former pres., chairman bd. dirs., Belknap Hardware & Mfg. Co., one of the largest of the kind in U.S. Trustee Berea Coll., Ky. Republican. Presbyn. Home: Louisville, Ky. Deceased.

BELL, Agrippa Nelson, sanitarian; b. in Northampton Co., Va., Aug. 3, 1820; s. George and Elizabeth (Scott) B.; acad. edn.; studied Tremont Med. Sch., Boston, Harvard Med. Sch.; M.D., Jefferson Med. Coll., Phila., 1842; (hon. A.M., Trinity Coll., Hartford, 1860); m. Julia Ann Hamlin, Nov. 22, 1842. Asst. and passed asst. surgeon U.S.N., 1847-55; resigned. Discovered, 1848, and was first to use steam as disinfectant in yellow fever, nr. Vera Cruz. Located in Brooklyn, 1855, active in quarantine reform movement; mem. Quarantine Convs., 1857, 1858, 1859, 1860; chmn. Com. on External Hygiene of latter, which reported system of quarantine regulations upon which all subsequent regulations have been founded; supt. floating hosp. for yellow fever, New York lower bay, 1861-62; drew substance N.Y. Quarantine Law, passed 1863; supervising commr. quarantine, N.Y., 1870-73; insp. quarantine Nat. Bd. Health, 1879; had charge of yellow fever extermination, New Orleans and Memphis, 1879. Founder, editor and pub. The Sanitarian, 1873-1904, 52 vols. A founder Am. Pub. Health Assn. Author: Knowledge of Living Things, 1860; Records of Daily Practice—Scientific Visiting List, 1860; The Climatology and Mineral Waters of the United States, 1885. Home: Brooklyn, N.Y. Died 1911.

BELL, Alexander Graham, scientist, inventor; b. Edinburgh, Scotland, Mar. 3, 1847; s. Alexander Melville and Eliza Grace (Symonds) B.; ed. at Edinburgh and London U. (hon. Ph.D., Wurzburg, 1882; M.D., Heidelberg, 1886; LL.D., Harvard, 1896, Ill., Coll., 1896, Amherst, 1901, St. Andrews, 1902; Edinburgh, 1902; George Washington, 1913; Sc.D., Oxford, 1907); m. Mabel Gardiner, d. G. G. Hubbard, 1877. Went to Canada, 1870, and to Boston, 1871, becoming prof. of vocal physiology, Boston U. Invented telephone, for which patent was granted Mar. 17, 1876; also invented photophone, induction balance and telephone probe for painless detection of bullets in the human body, for which he was awarded hon. M.D. by U. of Heidelberg, at its 500th anniversary; with C. A. Bell and Sumner Taintor invented the graphophone, 1883. Awarded, 1880, by the French Govt., the Volta Prix; medal, London Soc. of Fine Arts, 1902; Royal Albert medal; Elliott Cresson medal; John Fritz medal, 1907; Hughes medal, Royal Soc. of Arts, London, 1913; Edison medal, 1914. Officer French Legion of Honor. Founded and endowed, 1887, Volta Bureau for increase of knowledge relating to deaf; founder, expres. Am. Assn. to Promote Teaching of Speech to Deaf; regent Smithsonian Instn. Fellow Am. Acad. Arts and Sciences, A.A.A.S., etc. Author of many scientific and ednl. monographs, including Memoir on the Formation of a Deaf Variety of the Human Race. Died Aug. 2, 1922.

BELL, Alexander Melville, educator; b. Edinburgh, Scotland, March 1, 1819; studied under his father, Alexander Bell, inventor of a method for removing impediments of speech; m. Eliza Grace Symonds, 1844; m. 2d, Harriet Guess Shibley, 1898. Lectured at univs. of Edinburgh and London; went to Canada, 1870, and Washington, 1881; invented Visible Speech, a method of instruction in orthoepy, which has also been used in teaching deaf-mutes to speak; has written many works on orthoepy, phonetics, stenography and elocution:—all V4. Father of Alexander Graham Bell. Died 1905.

BELL, Charles James, farmer, gov.; b. Walden, Vt., Mar. 16, 1845; s. James Dean and Caroline (Warner) B.; ed. dist. sch. until 1862; m. M. Louise Perry, 1870. Entered Union Army, 1862, pvt. 15th Vt. Inf., later corporal Co. C. 1st Vt. Cav. Mem. Vt. Ho. Reps., 1882, Senate, 1894; r.r. commr., 1895-96, Bd. of Agr. 1897-1904; sec. of Bd. Agr., 6 yrs.; cattle commr., 1898-1902; gov. Vt., 1904-06. Master State Grange, 1894—; on exec. com. Nat. Grange. Republican. Congregationalist. Home: East Hardwich, Vt. Died 1909.

BELL, Charles James, banker; b. Dublin, Ireland, Apr. 12, 1858; s. David Charles and Ellen Adine (Hyland) B.; ed. Wesleyan Coll., Dublin; m. Grace B. Hubbard, Apr. 23, 1887. Came to U.S., 1873; with Imperial Bank of Can., at Toronto, 1875-80; gen. mgr. Nat. Telephone Co., 1880-81, organizing exchanges in north of Eng.; organized banking house of Bell & Co., Washington, D.C., 1881; chmn. bd. Terminal Cold Storage Co., Washington Market Co.; pres. Am. Security & Trust Co., 1893—. Trustee Carnegie Pub. Library, P.E. Cathedral Foundation, Methodist Univ., George Washington Memorial Assn., Nat. Geog. Soc. Republican. Episcopalian. Mason. Home: Washington, D.C. Died Oct. 2, 1929.

BELL, Clark, lawyer; b. Whitesville, Jefferson Co., N.Y., March 12, 1832; s. Philander F. and Sylvia (Jones) B.; ed. Franklin Acad.; (LL.D., Taylor U., Ind., and Rutherford Coll., N.C.); married. Admitted to bar, Rochester, N.Y., 1853; practiced Hammondsport, N.Y., 1853-61 (was postmaster there); practiced Bath, N.Y., 1861-64; was asst. dist. atty. Steuben Co., N.Y.; in practice at New York, 1864—; editor and publisher of Medico-Legal Journal, 1883—. Atty. U.P. Ry., 1864, drew the act which passed Congress to aid its construction; atty. for Pacific Mail Steamship Co. and other corps. Pres. Medico-Legal Society 16 terms; founder Am. Congress on Tuberculosis. Del. U.S. Govt. to Internat. Med. Congress, Paris, 1900, Lisbon, 1906; hon. pres. Am. Internat. Congress on Tuberculosis. Editor Medico-Legal Papers (3 vols.), Bulletin of American Congress on Tuberculosis (4 vols.) and of Medico-Legal Congresses of 1889 and 1895. Author: Bell's Medico-Legal Studies (11 vols.); Judicial History of the Supreme Court of the States and Provinces of North America; Spiritism, Telepathy and Hypnotism, etc. Home: New York, N.Y. Died Feb. 24, 1918.

BELL, Digby (Valentine), actor; b. Milwaukee, 1849; s. late William J. B. (banker) and Jeanette (Seymour) B.; family removed to New York, 1854; collegiate education. Engaged in stock brokerage business; later passenger agent White Star Line; sang in concerts as amateur, studied singing at Naples, Italy, 1871-76; m. Laura Joyce, actress, 1882 (died 1904). Début on Island of Malta, in "La Sonnambula," 1876; sang leading baritone rôles, in "Faust," "Il Trovatore," "Linda," "Traviata," Naples; concertized in U.S. and Can.; first appeared in comic opera in "Pinafore" at Montreal; toured U.S. and Can. in various comic operas; mem. Augustin Daly Co., New York, for 3 seasons, playing dramatic rôles; later with McCaull Opera Co., Duff Opera Co., and leading comedian with Lillian Russell Opera Co., etc.; starred in "Tar and Tartar," "Jupiter," "A Midnight Bell," "The Hoosier Doctor," "The Education of Mr. Pipp," as the admiral in "Pinafore," also in "Patience," "Pirates of Penzance," "Ruddigod," "Indiana," as Koko in "The Mikado," as Nathaniel Berry in "Shore Acres," etc. Starred in vaudeville, "It Happened in Topeka," for 2 seasons; later starring in motion photo plays. Died June 20, 1917.

BELL, Edward, diplomatic service; b. New York, N.Y., Aug. 9, 1882; s. Edward and Helen Augusta (Wilmerding) B.; A.B., Harvard, 1904; traveled and studied abroad several yrs.; m. Etelka, d. Brig. Gen. Conyers Surtees, of Mainsforth Hall, Durham, Eng., Feb. 16, 1914. V.-consul gen. in Egypt., 1909-11; sec. Am. Legation, Teheran, Persia, 1911-12; 2d sec. Am. Legation, Havana, Cuba, 1912; attached to Div. Latin Am. Affairs, Dept. of State, Washington, 1912-13; sec. spl. mission to attend inauguration of Gen. M.G. Menocal as pres. of Cuba, May 1913; 2d sec. Am. Embassy, London, 1913-17, 1st sec., 1917-19; counsellor of Embassy, Tokyo, Japan, 1920-21, chargé d'affaires, May 15, 1920-Sept. 16, 1921; apptd. an expert asst. and one of the secretaries to the Am. Delegation at the Conf. on the Limitation of Armament, Washington, Nov. 1921, and acted as Am. observer at the conversations between Chinese and Japanese representatives in regard to Shantung question; apptd. chief Div. of Current Information, Dept. of State, Washington, Feb. 15, 1922; counsellor of Embassy at Peking, China, 1922—. Episcopalian. Home: New York, N.Y. Died Oct. 28, 1924.

BELL, Edward Theodore, banker; b. Stanhope, N.J., Mar. 26, 1843; s. Edward Sullivan and Catherine Louisa (Beach) B.; ed. Collegiate Inst., Newton, N.J.; m. Anna D., d. Judge Daniel Stuart Anderson, of Newton, June 9, 1870 (she died). Began as messenger Hackettstown (N.J.) Bank, 1860; cashier 1st Nat. Bank, Paterson, N.J., 1864-74, v.p. 1882, pres., 1894—; v.p. Paterson Savings Instn. Hon. mem. Paterson Gen. Hosp. Assn.; pres. bd. Eye and Ear Infirmary; mem. advisory bds. various charitable instns.; pres. bd. trustees Ch. of the Redeemer. Republican. Presbyn. Home: Paterson, N.J. Died Aug. 12, 1921.

BELL, Frederic Somers, lumberman; b. Webster City, Ia., Mar. 19, 1859; s. Jairus Moffat and Helen Eliza (Somers) B.; Ph.B., U. of Mich., 1879; m. Frances Bradley Laird, June 22, 1882; 1 son, Laird.

Admitted to Minn. bar, 1880; in lumber bus., 1881—; chmn. bd. Weyerhaeuser Timber Co., Tacoma, Wash.; dir. Potlatch Forests, Inc.; pres. Laird, Norton Co., Winona, Minn. Mem. Minn. State Highway Commn., 1912-15; pres. bd. trustees Carleton Coll., Minn. State Hist. Soc. Mason. Republican. Home: Winona, Minn. Deceased.

BELL, George, soldier; b. Hagerstown, Md., 1828; s. William Duffield B.; grad. West Point, 1853; served before Civil War mainly on Tex. Indian frontier and in Seminole Indian disturbances in Fla. During Civil War instructing vol. commissaries and in Army of the Potomac on 1st movement to Richmond, in charge of sub-depots of Washington and Alexandria; chief commissary of various depts. and New York sub-depots. Bvtd. maj., lt. col., col. and bvt. brig. gen. Apr. 9, 1865; col. U.S.A. Died 1907.

BELL, George Jr., army officer; b. Ft. McHenry, Baltimore, Md., Jan. 23, 1859; s. George (brig. gen. U.S.A.) and Isabella (McCormick) B.; grad. U.S. Mil. Acad., 1880; student U. of Minn. Coll. of Law, 1891-92; LL.B., Cornell U. Coll. of Law, 1894; admitted to N.Y. bar; m. Mary Elizabeth Huntt, d. Maj. Gen. Robert Ransom, of Newbern, N.C., Jan. 5, 1885. Commd. 2d lit. 3d Inf., June 12, 1880; advanced through grades to brig. gen. July 17, 1914; maj. gen. N.A., Aug. 5, 1917; maj. gen. regular army, Mar. 22, 1921; retired from active service, Nov. 30, 1922. Prof. mil. science and tactics, Cornell U., 1892-96; participated in Cuba Campaign, before Santiago, 1898, and recommended for bvt. of maj.; in Philippine Insurrection, 1900-03; with his command captured Gen. Vincente Lukban, head of insurrection in Samar and Leyte, ending insurrection in Samar; campaign against Pulajanes, in Leyte, 1907, and captured the leader, who also was high priest, bringing peace to the island; in insp. gen.'s dept., 1907-13; head of mil. mission to Swiss maneuvers, 1911; apptd. comdr. Camp Logan, Houston, Tex., Sept. 1917; apptd. comdr. 33d div. (Prairie), 3d A.C., A.E.F., July 1918; comdr. 6th Corps Area, Chicago, 1921. Pres. Hill State Bank. Decorated D.S.M. (U.S.); Knight Comdr. St. Michael and St. George (British); Comdr. Legion of Honor, Croix de Guerre with palm (French). Home: Chicago, Ill. Died Oct. 30, 1926.

BELL, George Fisher, clergyman; b. Shelbyville, Ky., July 21, 1877; s. William Henderson and Sallie Ann (Fisher) B.; B.A., Centre Coll., Danville, Ky., 1898; student Union Theol. Sem., Richmond, Va., 1899-1900; B.D., Louisville Theol. Sem., 1902; D.D., Davidson (North Carolina) Coll., 1923; m. Carrie A. Savage, Apr. 28, 1910; children—Martha Henderson (wife of Rev. James Brent Wood, Jr.), Locklin Savage, Barbara (dec.), Paul Buckner, Dorothy Amelia. Teacher pub. schs., 1895-96, 1898-99; ordained ministry Presbyn. Ch. in U.S., 1903; pastor Greenville and Central City, Ky., 1902-05, Anchorage, 1905-08; evangelist and S.S. dist. supt., 1908-09; pastor Dothan, Ala., 1909-12, First Ch., Florence, Ala., 1912-17, Caldwell Memorial Ch., Charlotte, N.C., 1917-27, Crescent Hill Ch., Louisville, 1927-36; evangelistic and supply work, 1936—. Mem. exec. com. on foreign missions, Southern Presbyn. Ch. Democrat. Wrote: (brochures) Why I am Not a Christian Scientist, 1913; Religion and Science—a Protest Against Dogmatism, 1925. Home: Montreat, N.C. Died Aug. 11, 1941.

BELL, Harmon, lawyer; b. Oakland, Calif., Mar. 23, 1855; s. Rev. Samuel B. (D.D.) and Sophie B. (Walsworth) B.; ed. Hillsdale (Mich.) Coll. and Washington College, Calif.; studied law in the offices at Mansfield, O., and Kansas City, Mo.; m. Katherine Wilson, Jan. 16, 1880. Admitted to Mo. bar, 1878, and practiced in Kansas City; removed to San Francisco, 1898, later to Oakland. Republican. Presbyn. Mason. Home: Piedmont, Calif. Died Apr. 12, 1929.

BELL, Helene S. (Mrs. Clark Bell), philanthropist; b. Wheeler, N.Y., 1835; d. Edric S. and Alemna (Seaman) Taylor; ed. Franklin Acad., Prattsburg, N.Y.; m. Clark Bell, Sept. 8, 1857 (died 1918). A founder, and for many yrs. mem. exec. bd. Hahnemann Hosp.; a founder and pres. Health Protective Assn. of New York; chmn. for 17 yrs. of woman's com. New York Infant Asylum. Member Broadway Tabernacle, 1866—. Home: New York, N.Y. Deceased.

BELL, Hill McClelland, univ. pres.; b. Licking Co., O., June 19, 1860; s. James H. and Elmy A. (Cooper) B.; A.B., Drake U., 1890, A.M., 1899; at U. of Neb., 1896-97; LL.D., Simpson Coll., 1905; m. Edith Luella Orebaugh, Sept. 2, 1886; children—Jessie (dec.), Hugh Samuel, Ruth, Ralph James, Craig Paul, Ross Mark. Taught in rural schs. in Jasper Co., Ia., 3 yrs., schs. Galesburg, 3 yrs., pres. schs. Lynnville, 1 year, supt. schs. Kellogg, 3 yrs.; prof. mathmetics and dean Normal Coll. of Drake U., 1888-90; prof. English, Highland Park Coll., 1890-94; prof. English, and pres. Lincoln (Neb.) Normal U., 1894-97; dean Normal Coll. of Drake U., 1897-1905; dean Coll. Liberal Arts, same univ., 1902-07, acting chancellor, 1902-03, president, 1903-18; now pres. emeritus. Trustee Carnegie Foundation for the Advancement of Teaching, 1905-18; mem. com. of selection of Rhodes scholars in Ia., 1903-18; pres. Ia. State Teachers' Assn., 1910; pres. Internat. Conv. Disciples of Christ, 1913-14; pres. governing bd. Mo. Valley Athletic Conf., 1917-18; acting pres. Assn. Am. Colls., 1917-18. Mason. Home: Los Angeles, Calif. Died Jan. 9, 1927.

BELL, Hillary, dramatic and music critic; b. nr. Belfast, Ireland, 1857; ed. private tutors; studied art and came to U.S.; m. Miss Ireland, 1888; adopted profession of portrait painter in New York and later took up journalism; now dramatic and music critic New York Press. Writer of essays and sketches for numerous periodicals; editor The Insurance Economist; dir. and officer Mutual Reserve Fund Life Ins. Assn. Best known art work, life-size portrait Ada Rehan as Katherine in The Taming of the Shrew, presented by Augustin Daly to the Shakespeare Memorial, Stratford-on-Avon. Home: New York, N.Y. Died 1903.

BELL, Hiram Parks, congressman; b. Jackson Co., Ga., Jan. 19, 1827; academic edn.; admitted to bar, 1849; has since practiced at Cumming, Ga.; State senator, 1861-62; opposed secession originally, but served in C.S.A., becoming col. 43d Ga.; dangerously wounded Chickasaw Bayou, Dec. 29, 1862; mem. 2d Confederate Congress, 1863-64; U.S. Congress, 1873-75, 1877-79; presdl. elector, 1868; Democrat; mem. gen. conf. M.E. Ch., South, St. Louis, 1890. Mem. Ho. Reps., Ga., 1899-1902; State senator, 1901-02; chmn. Com. on Constitutional Amendments, Trustee Wesleyan Female Coll., Macon, Ga., and Emory Coll. Home: Cumming, Ga. Died 1907.

BELL, J(ames) Franklin, maj. gen. U.S.A.; b. Shelbyville, Ky., Jan. 9, 1856; s. John Wilson and Sarah Margaret Venable (Allen) B.; grad. U.S. Mil. Acad., 1878; m. Sarah Buford, Jan. 5, 1881. Additional 2d lt. 9th Cav., June 14, 1878; promoted through grades to brig. gen. U.S.V., Dec. 5, 1899; brig. gen. U.S.A., Feb. 19, 1901; maj. gen., Jan. 3, 1907. Served on plains in 7th U.S. Cav., 1878-94; captured band of half-breed Cree Indians, near Ft. Buford, S.D., 1883; in Sioux campaign, Pine Ridge, S.D., 1891; adj. of regt. and sec. Cav. and Light Arty. Sch., 1891-94; aid to Gen. J. W. Forsyth, Calif., Ariz., Wash.; awarded Congressional Medal of Honor, Nov. 27, 1899, "for most distinguished gallantry in action, Sept. 9, 1899, nr. Porac, Luzon, P.I."; comd. 4th Brigade, 2d Div., 8th Army Corps, and 3d dist., Dept. N. Luzon, to July, 1900; provost marshal gen. of Manila, P.I., to Feb., 1901; comd. 1st dist., Dept. N. Luzon to Nov., 1901, and 3d Brigade, Dept. of S. Luzon to Dec., 1902; returned to U.S., 1903; comdt. of Inf. and Cav. Sch., Signal Sch. and Staff Coll. to Apr. 1906; chief of staff, U.S.A., Apr. 1906-Apr. 1910; comdr. Philippines Div., Jan. 1911-Apr. 1914, 2d Div., U.S.A., Texas City, Tex., May 1914-Dec. 1915; comdr. Western Dept., San Francisco, Calif., to May 1917, Eastern Dept. to Sept. 1917, 77th Div. N.A., Camp Upton, Sept. 1917. Died Jan. 8, 1919.

BELL, James Montgomery, brig. gen. U.S.A.; b. Williamsburg, Pa., Oct. 1, 1837; s. William B.; grad. Wittenberg Coll., Springfield, O., 1862, A.M.; m. Emily M. Hones, of Pittsburgh, Mar. 2, 1872. Entered Union Army, 1st lt. 86th Ohio Inf., June 10, 1862; promoted through grades to brig. gen. U.S. Vols., 1900-01; brig. gen. U.S.A., Sept. 17, 1901; retired Oct. 1, 1901. Bvtd.: 1st lt. and capt. "for gallant and meritorious services in battle of the Wilderness, Va."; maj. for same at Ream's Station, Va., and lt. col. for same against Indians, Cañon Creek, Mont., Sept. 30, 1877. Participated in 16 engagements in Civil War. Served on frontier of Kan., Tex., Indian Ty., Colo., Neb., N. and S. Dak., Mont., and Wyo., 1866-91; Tex., N.M., and Ariz., 1894-96; Okla. and Kan., 1896-98. Served through Civil War, Cuban war, and in the P.I., Oct. 26, 1899-Apr. 1901. Took part in Cheyenne, Arapahoe, and Kiowa war of 1867-69; Sioux wars of 1876-81; Nez Percés war of 1877. Served as guard to engrs. and construction parties on Kan. Pacific, U.P., N.P. and G.N. Trans-Continental railroads, 1867-87; 3 times wounded; Indian agt. of Ogalla Sioux Indians, Pine Ridge Agency, 1886. Comd. Bell's expeditionary brigade to the Camarines provinces, Southern Luzon, Feb., 1900; comdg. 3d dist., Dept. S. Luzon, Mar. 1900-Mar. 1901; mil. gov. 3d dist., Dept. S. Luzon, Apr. 1900-Mar. 1901, composed of Ambos Camarines, Albay and Sorsogon provinces, and the Island of Catanduanes. Home: Pasadena, Calif. Died Sept. 17, 1919.

BELL, James Munsie, prof. chemistry; b. Chesley, Ont., Can., Apr. 19, 1880; s. John Charlton and Hannah (Munsie) B.; student Parkdale Collegiate Inst., Toronto, 1892-98; A.B., U. of Toronto, 1902, A.M., 1905; Sage fellow in chemistry, Cornell U., 1904-05, Ph.D., 1905; m. Mary E. Brawner, Apr. 2, 1909. Came to U.S., 1902, naturalized citizen, 1908. Chemist, U.S. Bureau of Soils, Washington, D.C., 1905-10; asso. prof. physical chemistry, U. of N.C., 1910-13, prof. 1913-19, Smith prof., since 1919, head of chemistry dept. since 1921, Kenan traveling prof., 1926-27, dean Sch. of Applied Science, 1929—. Was in chem. warfare service, U.S.A., 1918. Democrat. Presbyn. Author: (with Paul M. Gross) Elements of Physical Chemistry, 1929. Home: Chapel Hill, N.C. Died Mar. 3, 1934.

BELL, James S., mcht. miller; b. Phila., June 30, 1847; s. Samuel and Elizabeth (Faust) B.; ed. Central High Sch., Phila.; m. Sallie Montgomery Ford, Jan. 8, 1873. Clerk, Phila., 1863-68; partner Samuel Bell & Sons, 1868-88; Washburn, Martin & Co., 1888-89; pres. Washburn-Crosby Co., flour millers, Minneapolis, Sept., 1889—; pres. Royal Milling Co.; v.p. Barnum Grain Co., St. Anthony and Dakota Elevator Co., St. Anthony Elevator Co., Minneapolis Trust Co. Presbyn. Republican. Home: Minneapolis, Minn. Died Apr. 5, 1915.

BELL, John C., congressman; b. Grundy Co., Tenn., Dec. 11, 1851; s. Harrison and Rachel (Laxson) B.; ed. pvt. schs.; m. Susie Abernathy, Aug. 1881. Admitted to bar, 1874; practiced at Saguache, Colo., 1874-76, Lake City, Colo., 1876-85, Montrose, Colo., 1885—. Co. atty. Saguache Co., 1874-76; judge 7th Jud. Dist., 1888-92; mem. 53d to 57th Congresses (1893-1903), 2d Colo. Dist.; now judge Ct. of Appeals of Colo.; Democrat. Was mem. U. S. Industrial Commn. Home: Denver, Colo. Died Aug. 12, 1933.

BELL, John Cromwell, lawyer; b. Elders Ridge, Ind. Co., Pa., Oct. 3, 1861; s. Alfred M. and Sarah (Risher) B.; A.B., Central High Sch., Phila., 1879, A.M., 1883; LL.B., U. of Pa. Law Sch., 1884; LL.D., Temple U., Phila., 1912, and U. of Pittsburgh, 1918; m. Fleurette de Benneville Myers, Dec. 10, 1890. Admitted to bar, 1884; apptd. by judges dist. atty. of Phila., Apr. 1903; elected same office on Rep. ticket, Nov. 1903, serving to Jan. 1907 (declined renom.); atty. gen. of Pa., 1911-15. Mem. State Council of Edn. by apptmt. of Gov. Pinchot, 1922. Trustee U. of Pa., 1911-28. Author: The Several Modes of Instituting Criminal Proceedings in Pennsylvania, 1904; The Medical Witness, 1905; The Public Service Company Law of Pennsylvania, 1913; various opinions as atty. gen.; and vol. of addresses and papers, "Pennsylvania and Its University, and Other Addresses," 1918. Home: Radnor, Pa., and Phila. Died Dec. 29, 1935.

BELL, Laura Joyce, comic opera singer; b. (Maskell) London, England, 1858; musical edn. at Royal Acad. Music; made début (stage-name, Laura Joyce) Strand Theatre, London, as Gertrude in Loan of a Lover; début in U.S. at Niblo's Garden in Leo and Lotus, 1872, singing Blue Danube Waltz; with McCaull's Duff, Daly and Digby Bell opera cos. Afterward played heroine of Evangeline; Buttercup in Pinafore; Katisha in Mikado, and other leading contralto parts of comic opera; m. Digby Bell, 1882. Home: New York, N.Y. Died 1904.

BELL, Lilian, author; b. Chicago, Ill.; d. Maj. William W. and Nancy C. (Brown) B.; early edn. by governess; childhood was passed in Atlanta, Ga.; widow; 1 dau., Lilian. Began story writing at 8; contbr. to mags.; has given over 500 author's readings in principal cities of U.S. Originator, 1914, of the plan to send a Christmas ship, bearing presents from the children of America to orphans of the European war, the idea being taken up by more than 1,000 newspapers and supported by President Wilson, who assigned the ship Jason to make the trip; naval honors never before accorded an alien vessel by the British Admiralty, were paid the Christmas ship on its arrival at Plymouth Harbor. Under her direction Am. children raised $2,000,000 in ten weeks. Ship carried 7,000,000 presents, which were distributed in warring countries through Red Cross. Thanked by queens of England and Belgium and Tzarina of Russia. Thanked by Sec. of War for her hosp. work. Author: Hope Loring, 1902; Carolina Lee, 1906; Concentrations of Bee, 1909; The Runaway Equator, 1912; The Story of the Christmas Ship, 1915; About Miss Mattie Morningglory, 1916; The Land of Don't-Want-To, 1916, and others. Raised about $35,000 through N.Y. Evening World, 1920, and distributed over half of it to disabled soldiers in hosps., the remainder to be applied similarly. Died July 18, 1929.

BELL, Louis, elec. engr.; b. at Chester, N.H., Dec. 5, 1864; s. Gen. Louis (U.S.A.) and Mary Anne Persis (Bouton) B.; A.B., Dartmouth Coll., 1884; grad. student, 1884, fellow in physics, 1885-88, Ph.D., 1888, Johns Hopkins; m. Sarah G. Hemenway, Dec. 3, 1893. Prof. applied electricity, Purdue U., 1888-89, and organized elec. course there; editor Electrical World, New York, 1890-92; chief engr. newly organized elec. power transmission dept. of the Gen. Electric Co.; designed and installed first polyphase plants used in this country, both for power and lighting and for ry. service; consulting engr. engaged mainly on work in connection with elec. power transmission, 1895—. Has taken out 40 patents relating to power transmission and optical apparatus. Lecturer on power transmission, Mass. Inst. Tech., 1895-1905; lecturer on public lighting, Harvard U., also on illumination, Harvard Med. Sch., 1914—. Tech. officer Vol. Elec. Corps, 1898. Fellow Am. Acad. Arts and Sciences; mem. Am. Inst. Elec. Engrs., Illuminating Engring. Soc. (past pres.), etc. Mem. advisory com. Council of Nat. Defense. Unitarian. Republican. Author: The Electric Railway (with Oscar T. Crosby), 1892; Power Distribution for Electric Railroads, 1896;

Electric Power Transmission, 1897; The Art of Illumination, 1902; Boston Electrical Handbook (as chmn. Publn. Com.), 1904; The Telescope, 1922. Home: West Newton, Mass. Died June 14, 1923.

BELL, Raley Husted, author; b. N.Y. City, Feb. 5, 1869; student Med. Coll. of Me. (Bowdoin Coll.), 1895; M.D., Atlanta Med. Coll., 1896; also studied Dartmouth Coll., and in Paris. Retired from med. practice and devoted to lit. and travel. Author: The Worth of Words, 1902; The Changing Values of English Speech, 1909; Words of the Wood (poems), 1906; The Religion of Beauty, 1911; Art-Talks with Ranger, 1914; Taormina, 1916 The Philosophy of Painting, 1916; Woman from Bondage to Freedom, 1917. Died May 29, 1931.

BELL, Roscoe Rutherford, veterinarian, editor; b. Augusta Co., Va., Sept. 16, 1858; s. William H. and Eveline (Shields) B.; ed. Norwood Coll., Va.; grad. Am. Veterinary Coll., New York, D.V.S., 1887; m. Rebecca Moss, Nov. 29, 1888. Veterinary insp. U.S. Dept. Agr., 1888-91; prof. materia medica and therapeutics, New York-Am. Veterinary Coll., 1888—. Editor Am. Veterinary Review, 1895—. Author: The Veterinarian's Call Book, 1893 J10. Deceased.

BELL, Theodore Arlington, congressman; b. Vallejo, Calif., July 25, 1872; s. Charles Edward and Catherine Jane (Mills) B.; ed. dist. schs., Napa Co., Calif.; m. Annie M. Muller, Apr. 23, 1899. Admitted to bar, 1893. Mem. 58th Congress (1903-05), 2d Calif. Dist. Dem. nominee for gov. Calif., 1906 and 1910; temporary chmn. Dem. Nat. Conv., Denver, 1908. Home: San Francisco, Calif. Died Sept. 4, 1922.

BELL, Thomas Montgomery, congressman; b. Cleveland, Ga., Mar. 17, 1861; s. W. B. and Kate (McAfee) B.; ed. common schools; Moore's Business U., Atlanta, 1879; m. Mary Ellen Winburn, Apr. 2, 1885. Taught in pub. schs., 1878-79; traveling salesman, 1880-98; clerk Superior Ct. of Hall Co., Ga., 1898-1905; mem. 59th to 71st Congresses (1905-31), 9th Ga. Dist. Democrat. Methodist. Home: Gainesville, Ga. Died Mar. 18, 1941.

BELL, Wilbur Cosby, clergyman; b. Augusta Co., Va., Apr. 1, 1881; s. Samuel Hendren and Sallie Ellen (Cosby) B.; B.A., Hampden-Sydney Coll., 1909; B.D., Va. Theol. Sem., 1905; D.D., Washington and Lee U., 1914, Princeton U., 1929, Cambridge Theol. Sch., 1929; m. Anne Lee Laird, June 21, 1905. Deacon, 1905, priest, 1906, P.E. Ch.; rector R. E. Lee Memorial Ch., Lexington, Va., 1906-11, St. Andrew's Ch., Louisville, Ky., 1911-12; prof. systematic divinity and apologetics, P.E. Theol. Sem. in Va., 1912—. Chaplain 117th Engrs., A.E.F., 1917-18. Author: Sharing in Creation, 1925; The Making of Man, 1931. Bohlen lecturer, Phila., 1925; Paddock lecturer, New York, 1929. Died Apr. 6, 1933.

BELL, William Hemphill, brig. gen. U.S.A.; retired Jan. 28, 1898; b. West Chester, Pa., Jan. 28, 1834; s. Hon. Thomas S. B. (jurist); grad. West Point, 1858; bvt. 2d lt., Dec. 6, 1858; promoted through the grades to brig. gen. and commissary gen. U.S.A., Nov. 14, 1897. Served during Civil War in line of the army, in field, and in subsistence dept.; much of service west of the Missouri, in Alaska, and on the frontier. Home: Arvada, Colo. Died 1906.

BELL, William Melvin, bishop; b. Whitley Co., Ind., Nov. 12, 1860; s. Isaac H. and Nancy E. (Ihrig) B.; grad. Roanoke (Ind.) Classical Sem., 1879; D.D., Am. Temperance U., 1895; LL.D., U. of Southern Calif., 1914; m. Irene J. Henney, July 11, 1880; children—Mrs. Altha Turvene, Wayland G. (dec.), Clair Hadyn, Alice Estella, Mrs. Geneva Binkley, Mrs. Edna Parks, William M. Ordained U.B. ministry, 1882; pastor at La Grange, Lafayette, Ligonier and Elkhart, Ind., 1879-92; pres. and supt. Ind. S.S. Assn., 1890-93; gen. sec. Dept. of Home and Foreign Missions, 1893-1905; bishop, May 1905; sr. bishop, 1921; in charge East. Dist., including Atlantic and Gulf states, 1917-29; retired. Author: The Love of God, 1902; The Social Message of Our Lord, 1909; Torches Aloft, 1913; Biography of Bishop Nicholas Castle, 1923. Died Oct. 6, 1933.

BELL, William Roe, Washington corr. Pittsburgh Leader, Harrisburg Star-Independent and Erie Herald, 1890—; b. Indiana Co., Pa., Apr. 6, 1859; common sch. edn.; learned printing trade, later worked in Pittsburgh, and finally engaged in reportorial and editorial work. Home: Washington, D.C. Deceased.

BELLAMY, Charles Joseph, publisher; b. Chicopee Falls, Mass., May 7, 1852; s. Rufus K. and Maria L. (Putnam) B.; brother of late Edward B.; ed. Williston Sem., Easthampton, Mass., and 1 yr. at Harvard; m. Imogen A. Cooper, Oct. 14, 1879. Admitted to bar, 1876, and practiced, 1876-80; founded and published, Springfield Daily News, 1880—. Author: The Breton Mills; An Experiment in Marriage; Were They Sinners? A Moment of Madness; The Way Out (study of social and industrial conditions); Return of the Fairies; The Wonder Children, 1906. Home: Springfield, Mass. Died 1910.

BELLAMY, Elizabeth Whitfield, (Mrs.) ("Kamba Thorpe"), author; b. (Croom) Quincy, Gadsden Co., Fla., April 17, 1837; ed. at Spingler Inst., N.Y.; m. Dr. Charles E. Bellamy, 1858. Author: Four Oaks; Little Joanna; Penny Lancaster, Farmer; Old Man Gilbert; also short stories for magazines, etc. Home: Mobile, Ala. Died 1900.

BELLEW, (Harold) Kyrle (Money), actor; b. Calcutta, 1857; s. Rev. J. C. M. B., chaplain cathedral at Calcutta; was cadet English navy, serving 7 yrs., then went to Australian gold fields; worked on Melbourne newspapers; returned to England; unmarried. Made stage début at Theatre Royal, Brighton; became leading man and star in London; came to U.S. as leading man in Wallack's Theatre, New York, Oct. 1885; subsequently starred jointly with Mrs. James Brown Potter, taking leading rôles with her in legitimate drama in all English-speaking countries. Headed exploration expdn. in Northern Queensland, 1900-2, returning to stage at head of own co. in U.S., Oct., 1902. Author: Yvonne; Iolande; Hero and Leander; Charlotte Corday. Also several adaptations. Home: Thamesfield-Bray, Berkshire, England. Died 1911.

BELLINGER, Charles Byron, jurist; b. Maquon, Ill., Nov. 21, 1839; went with parents to Ore., 1847; ed. in Willamette Univ., but did not graduate; studied law; admitted to bar, 1863. Served in Modoc campaign in the Lava Beds, 1873; clerk and official reporter Supreme Court of Ore., 1874-78; judge State Circuit Court, 1878-80; U.S. dist. judge for dist. of Ore., April, 1893—. Home: Portland, Ore. Died 1905.

BELLINGER, John Bellinger, army officer; b. Charleston, S.C., Apr. 15, 1862; s. Amos Northrop and Maria Louisa (Whaley) B.; ed. pvt. schs. in Charleston; m. Marie Clarisse Coudert, Apr. 19, 1892; children—John Bellinger, Frédéric Coudert, Edmund Bellinger and René Duchamp. Grad. U.S. Mil. Acad., 1884, commd. 2d lt., 7th Cav., June 15, 1884; transferred to 5th Cav., Oct. 13, 1884; apptd. capt. and asst. quartermaster, Aug. 11, 1894; promoted through grades to brig. gen., asst. to quartermaster gen., Dec. 4, 1922; retired from active service by operation of law, Apr. 15, 1926, having served 45 years, 9 mos. and 15 days. Served as maj. and lt. col. of vols. July 16, 1898-May 17, 1901; with cav. regt. in Wyo., Kan. and Indian Ty. (now Okla.), Oct. 1884-Aug. 1888; instr. at U.S. Mil. Acad., Aug. 1888-Aug., 1892; studied law and admitted to bar, 1894; quartermaster and disbursing officer, U.S. Mil. Acad., Sept. 1894-May 1898, and June 1900-July 1903; moved 5th Corps (Shafter's from Tampa to Port Tampa for embarkation to Cuba; moved 7th Corps (Fitzhugh Lee's) by Army transports from Savannah, Ga., to ports in Cuba, Dec. 1898-Jan. 1899; planned and executed return of U.S. troops, due to fear of yellow fever, from Cuba and Puerto Rico through quarantine stations, Fla. and Ga., Feb.-May 1899; depot quartermaster and gen. supt. (Pacific) Army Transport Service, San Francisco, Oct. 1906-June 1909; in charge of preparing plans, constructing buildings, water system, sewage, organizing and equipping shops, railroad system and operating them for building of Ft. Mills on top of Corregidor Island, Manila Bay (city of approximately 5,000 people). 1909-11. Awarded D.S.M. "for exceptionally meritorious and distinguished services," as dept. quartermaster P.I., 1921. Originated and executed the supplying of Siberian A.E.F. at Vladivostok (specifically mentioned therefor in report of comdg. gen. of expdn.) and the purchasing of foods in the Orient and shipping them to U.S. on army transports. Also aided Philippine govt. in its problems. Received thanks of the Philippine Senate by resolution adopted Feb. 4, 1920. Died Sept. 22, 1931.

BELLOWS, George Wesley, artist; b. Columbus, O., Aug. 12, 1882; s. George and Anna W. (Smith) B.; Ohio State U., 1905; studied under Robert Henri; m. Emma L. Story, Sept. 23, 1910. Exhibited Internat. Expn., Venice, Royal Acad., Berlin, Royal Soc., Munich, Internat. Expn., Rome, Kensington Mus., London, and in prin. cities of U.S. Represented in collections of Met. Mus., New York, Pa. Acad., Phila., Toledo (O.) Mus. of Art, Savannah (Ga.) Mus. of Art, Columbus (O.) Art Assn., Nat. Arts Club, New York, Art Inst. Chicago, R.I. Sch. of Design, Los Angeles Mus., N.Y. Pub. Library, Detroit Mus., City Mus. of St. Louis. Second Hallgarten prize, 1908; Sessnan medal, 1913; 1st Hallgarten prize, 1913; honorable mention Carnegie Inst., 1913; bronze medal Carnegie Inst., 1914; Maynard prize, N.A.D., 1914; 2d Harris prize, Art Inst. Chicago, 1915; Isador medal, N.A.D., 1917; Temple medal, Pa. Acad., 1917; 1st Harris prize, Art Inst. Chicago, 1921; Nat. Arts Club 1st prize, 1921; Peck medal, Pa. Acad., 1921. Instr. Art Students' League, 1910, 1918, 1919, Art Inst. Chicago, 1919. N.A., 1913; mem. Nat. Inst. Arts and Letters. Home: Woodstock, N.Y. Died Jan. 8, 1925.

BELLOWS, Henry Adams, publicity director; b. Portland, Me., Sept. 22, 1885; s. John Adams and Isabel (Francis) B.; A.B., Harvard, 1905, Ph.D., 1910; m. Mary Sanger, June 12, 1911 (died Jan. 19, 1935); children—Eleanor, Charles Sanger; m. 2d, Alice Rickey Eells, April 13, 1936. Asst. in English, Harvard, 1906-09; actg. editor, Harvard Graduates' Mag., 1906-07; asst. prof. rhetoric, U. of Minn., 1910-12; mng. editor, The Bellman, Minneapolis, 1912-19, The Northwestern Miller, 1914-25; mgr. Radio Station WCCO, 1925-27 and 1928-29; pres. Northwestern Broadcasting, Inc., 1929-34; v.p. Columbia Broadcasting System, 1930-34; dir. pub. relations Gen. Mills, Inc., 1936—. Mem. Fed. Radio Commn., 1927. Music critic Minneapolis Daily News, 1920-23; writer of program notes for Minneapolis Symphony Orchestra, 1923-26. Dir. and chmn. legislative com. Nat. Assn. of Broadcasters, 1928-35. Was major, lt. col. and col. Minn. Home Guards, and 4th Regt. Minn. Inf., 1917-19. Democrat. Author: Manual for Local Defense, 1918; A Treatise on Riot Duty for the National Guard, 1920; Highland Light, and Other Poems, 1921. Translator of the Historia Calamitatum of Abelard, 1922, and The Poetic Edda (Am.-Scandinavian Foundation), 1923. Home: Minneapolis, Minn. Died Dec. 29, 1939.

BELLOWS, Howard Perry, M.D. (aurist); b. Fall River, Mass., Apr. 30, 1852; s. Albert F. (N.A., New York) and Candace (Brown) B.; B.S., Cornell U., 1875, M.S., 1879; M.D., Boston Univ. Medical Sch., 1877; hon. Sc.D., Boston Univ., 1931; also medical courses at Leipzig, Vienna, and Halle, etc.; m. Mary A. Clarke, June 20, 1880. Gen. practitioner until 1890, since exclusively aural practice; for 7 yrs. actively engaged, by experimentation and writing, in promoting a more scientific investigating of drug action, with particular reference to needs of specialists; prof. physiology, 1877-85, prof. otology, 1886-1929, now prof. emeritus, Boston U. Med. Sch.; consl. aural surgeon, Mass. Homeo. Hosp.; mem. consl. bd. Westborough State Hosp. Republican. Swedenborgian. Home: Cambridge, Mass. Died Oct. 16, 1934.

BELMONT, August, banker; b. N.Y. City, Feb. 18, 1853; s. late August and Caroline Slidell (Perry) B.; A.B., Harvard, 1874; m. Elizabeth Hamilton Morgan, 1881 (died 1898); m. 2d, Eleanor Elise Robson, Feb. 26, 1910. Head of August Belmont & Co., bankers; chmn. bd. Interborough Rapid Transit Co., Rapid Transit Subway Constrn. Co.; pres. Boston, Cape Cod & New York Canal Co.; trustee Bank for Savings. Mem. Met. Mus. of Art, S.R. Home: (country) Hempstead, L.I. Died Dec. 10, 1924.

BELMONT, Mrs. O. H. P. (Alva E. Smith Belmont); b. Mobile, Ala.; d. Murray Forbes and Phœbe Ann Smith; g.d. Gen. Robert Desha, of Tenn.; ed. in France; m. William Kissam Vanderbilt, 1874; children—Mrs. Jacques Balsan, William K., Harold Stirling; m. 2d, Oliver Hazard Perry Belmont, 1896 (died June 10, 1908). Actively interested in architecture, hosps., children's homes, abolition of child labor, better and more sanitary conditions for working women, etc., and woman suffrage movement; gave $100,000 to the Nassau Hosp. at Mineola, L.I., N.Y., etc. Founder and pres. Polit. Equality Assn.; an organizer of Woman's Party Conv., San Francisco, Calif., Sept. 1915, and Washington, D.C., Dec. 1915, composed of delegates from the 12 states in which women had right of suffrage in 1915. Gave to Woman's Party "Alva Belmont House" and grounds valued at over $100,000, Washington, D.C. Home: Paris, France. Died Jan. 26, 1933.

BELMONT, Oliver Hazard Perry, capitalist; b. New York, Nov. 12, 1858; s. late August and Caroline Slidell (Perry) B.; ed. U.S. Naval Acad. and served 2 yrs. U.S.N.; m. 1st, Sarah Swan Whitney; m. 2d, Mrs. Alva (Smith) Vanderbilt, 1896. Was mem. August Belmont & Co., bankers; was publisher The Verdict; del. Dem. Nat. Conv., 1900. Mem. numerous clubs New York, London, Paris. Mem. Congress, 1901-03, 13th N.Y. dist. Democrat. Home: New York, N.Y. Died 1908.

BELO, Alfred H., journalist; b. Galveston, Tex., Aug. 1873; s. late Col. Alfred Horatio and Jeannette (Ennis) B.; prep. edn. The Hill Sch., Pottstown, Pa.; grad. Yale, 1896; m. Helen Ponder, 1900. After graduation entered newspaper work, holding various positions until after his father's death, Apr. 19, 1901, when he was made pres. A. H. Belo & Co., publishers Galveston Daily News and Dallas Morning News. Home: Dallas, Tex. Died 1906.

BELO, Alfred Horatio, pres. A. H. Belo & Co., publishers Galveston News and Dallas News; b. Salem, N.C., May 27, 1839; elected capt. Forsyth Rifles, April 1861; served in army of Northern Va. (Confederate); wounded at Gettysburg and at Cold Harbor; went to Texas at close of war; became mgr. Galveston News; established Dallas News, 1885. Home: Dallas, Tex. Died 1901.

BEMAN, Solon Spencer, architect; b. Brooklyn, Oct. 1, 1853; studied architecture with Richard M. Upjohn, New York; m. Mary H. Miller, Apr. 30, 1888. Designed all buildings in town of Pullman (now part of Chicago); also the town of Ivorydale, with the extensive works, nr. Cincinnati, for the Proctor & Gamble Co., Pullman Bldg., Studebaker Bldg., Fine Arts Bldg. and Grand Central Sta., also T. B. Blackstone Memorial Library, First and Second Christian Science chs., St. Paul's Episcopal Ch., besides clubhouses, churches, business buildings and residences, Chicago; Pioneer Press Bldg., St. Paul; Bee Bldg., Omaha; Mining Bldg. and Merchant Tailors' Bldg., Chicago Expn.; Mines Bldg., Omaha Expn., 1898; Pabst Bldg. and Northwestern Mutual Life Bldg.,

Milwaukee; Michigan Trust Co. Bldg., Grand Rapids; T. B. Blackstone Memorial Library, Branford, Conn.; Union Sta., Peoria, Ill.; C.&A. Sta., Springfield, Ill., etc. Home: Chicago, Ill. Died Apr. 23, 1914.

BEMAN, Wooster Woodruff, univ. prof.; b. Southington, Conn., May 28, 1850; s. Woodruff and Lois Jane (Neal) B.; A.B., U. of Mich., 1870, A.M., 1873; (LL.D., Kalamazoo, 1908); m. Ellen Elizabeth Burton, Sept. 4, 1877. Instr. Greek and mathematics, Kalamazoo Coll., 1870-71; instr., mathematics, 1871-74, asst. prof., 1874-82, asso. prof., 1882-87, prof., 1887—, U. of Michigan. Treas. Mich. Bapt. Conv., 15 years; mem. exec. com. Northern Bapt. Conv., 1910-16; of Fed. Council Chs. of Christ in America, 1916-20. Democrat. Joint author (with David Eugene Smith): Plane and Solid Geometry, 1895; Higher Arithmetic, 1897; Famous Problems of Elementary Geometry (from the German of Klein), 1897; New Plane and Solid Geometry, 1899; Elements of Algebra, 1900; A Brief History of Mathematics (from the German of Fink), 1900; Sundara Row's Geometric Exercises in Paper Folding (revision), 1901; Academic Algebra, 1902. Author: Continuity and Irrational Numbers; Nature and Meaning of Numbers (from the German of Dedekind), 1901. Home: Ann Arbor, Mich. Died Jan. 18, 1922.

BEMENT, Clarence Edwin, mfr.; b. Fostoria, O., Mar. 20, 1856; s. Edwin and Louisa (Roberts) B.; grad. Lansing (Mich.) High Sch., 1874, classical course, 1876; student U. of Mich.; m. Carrie R. Roberts, Nov. 26, 1880; children—Constance, Roberts Edwin. Began with E. Bement's Sons, mfrs. agrl. implements and stoves, Lansing, 1878, made supt., 1884; sec. Novo Engine Co., 1907, v.p. and gen. mgr., 1917—; v.p. Federal Drop Forge Co., Am. State Savings Bank. Apptd. mem. Commn. of Inquiry into County, State and Sch. Dist. Govt., Aug. 24, 1931. Mem. Lansing Bd. of Edn., 1898-1910, pres. 1905-06; dir. Mich. State Sch. of Music. Episcopalian. Home: Lansing, Mich. Died June 9, 1935.

BEMENT, Howard, headmaster; b. Lansing, Mich., Feb. 10, 1875; s. George Willis and Sarah Marilda (Finsthwaite) B.; Ph.B., U. of Mich., 1896; M.A., Olivet Coll., 1906; studied Stanford U. and University of Calif., 1905; Litt. D. from Colgate University, 1929; m. Margaret Alice Douglas, 1897; 1 son, Douglas. Treas. E. Bement's Sons, Lansing, 1896-1904; master in English, The Hill Sch., Pottstown, Pa., 1905-1927, head of dept., 1912-1927; headmaster Ashville School, 1927—. Reader in English Coll. Entrance Exam. Bd., 1913-27, examiner in English, 1917-19. Congregationalist. Author: Notes and Outlines on Books Required for Study in English in Preparation for College, 1912; Old Man Dare's Talks to College Men, 1922; The Story of Zeta Psi, 1927. Editor: Selected Essays of Lamb, 1910; Burke's Speech on Conciliation, 1922; The Sir Roger de Coverly Papers, 1925; Hamlet, 1927; The Hill School Book of Verse, 1927. Home: Ashville School, N.C. Died Feb. 21, 1936.

BEMIS, Albert Farwell, merchant, mfr.; b. Boston, Nov. 11, 1870; s. Judson Moss and Alice (Cogswell) B.; Cutler Acad., Colorado Springs, Colo.; Colo. Coll.; S.B. in C.E., Mass. Inst. Tech., 1893; m. Faith Gregg, Dec. 30, 1899. Engaged in business in Boston, 1893—; chmn. bd. Bemis Bro. Bag Co., 1925-34, now dir.; chmn. bd. Building Products, Inc.; pres. Bemis Industries, Inc.; dir. Boott Mills (Lowell, Mass). Alderman City of Newton, 1911-14. Mem. exec. com. Nat. Industrial Conf. Board. Pvt., 1st Corps Cadets, Boston, 1897-99, now vet. mem. Trustee Colorado Coll. (resigned, 1912); life mem. Corp. Mass. Inst. Tech. Republican. Conglist. Home: Chestnut Hill, Mass. Died Apr. 11, 1936.

BEMIS, Edward Webster, economist; b. Springfield, Mass., Apr. 7, 1860; s. Daniel Webster and Mary Wood (Tinker) B.; A.B., Amherst, 1880, A.M., 1884; Ph.D., Johns Hopkins, 1885; m. Annie Louise Sargent, Oct. 28, 1889; children—Walter Sargent, Alice Louise (Mrs. Frank T. H. Doubler), Lloyd Edward. Prof. history and polit. economy, Vanderbilt U., 1889-92; asso. prof. political economy, U. of Chicago, 1892-95; asst. statistician Ill. Bur. of Labor Statistics, 1896; prof. economics and history, Kan. State Agrl. Coll., 1897-99; later dir. Dept. Municipal Monopolies, Bur. of Economic Research, New York; supt. water dept., Cleveland, O., 1901-09; deputy commr. of water supply, gas, and electricity, of New York, Jan.-Oct. 1910; now consulting engr. for cities, states and other public bodies upon pub. utilities of water, gas, electricity, st. rys., telephones. Author: Municipal Ownership of Gas Works in the United States (monograph), 1891; Municipal Monopolies, 1899; also numerous papers and articles, the latest, on "Going Value," in Columbia Law Rev., May 1927. Mem. Phi Beta Kappa. Home: Chicago, Ill., and New York, N.Y. Died Sept. 25, 1930.

BEMIS, Judson Stephen, industrialist; b. San Francisco, Mar. 26, 1867; s. Stephen Allen and Hannah Jane (Thomas) B.; ed. pub. and pvt. schs. of St. Louis; m. Martha Nelson Sikes, Sept. 8, 1896; children—Jane (Mrs. George R. Hann), Elizabeth (Mrs. Samuel D. Conant), Louise (Mrs. William E. Guy). Began as clk. with Bemis Bro. Bag Co., St. Louis, Mo., 1885, and advanced to chmn., 1934, and so continued. Republican. Episcopalian. Home: St. Louis Mo. Deceased.

BENDELARI, George, editorial writer; b. Naples, Italy, July 25, 1851; s. Augusto and Giuseppa Augusta (Carelli) B.; brought to America, 1855; A.B. Harvard, 1874, Kirkland llo, 1875-78; studied at Leipzig and Jena and at Harvard Law Sch.; (hon. A.M., Yale, 1888); m. Emma Damon Coleman Simms, June 8, 1909. Instr. in modern langs., Harvard, 1878-82; instr. and asst. prof. modern langs., Yale, 1882-88; instr. in history, Harvard, 1888-94; instr. in French, Columbia, 1894-95; editorial writer, The Sun, New York, 1894-1917; in U.S. postal censorship, 1917-19; editorial staff India Rubber World, 1919-20; research dept. Federal Reserve Bank of New York, 1920—. Democrat. Home: Brooklyn, N.Y. Died Aug. 12, 1927.

BENDER, Albert Maurice; b. Dublin, Ireland, June 18, 1866; s. Rev. Dr. Philip and Augusta (Bremer) B.; student Dr. Bender's Sch. for Boys, Dublin, 1875-79, Beaufort Coll., St. Leonards on the Sea, Eng., 1879-81; A.M., Mills Coll., Calif.; LL.D., U. of Calif.; hon. Litt.D., Mills College; unmarried. Came to U.S., 1883, naturalized, 1889. Began as errand boy in ins. office, 1883; gen. ins. agent, 1890—. Decorated Cavalier of Crown of Italy; Chevalier Legion of Honor (France); Moraga Crest (highest award) St. Mary's College. Trustee Mills Coll.; commr. San Francisco Pub. Library; dir. Japan Soc., Home for Aged Disabled, San Francisco Symphony Orchestra, San Francisco Art Assn., San Francisco Opera Assn., San Francisco Opera Guild. Fellow Royal Soc. Antiquaries of Ireland, Royal Geog. Soc.; hon. mem. San Francisco Inst. of Art. Home: San Francisco, Calif. Died Mar 4, 1941.

BENDER, Wilbur H., teacher; b. Williams Center, Williams Co., O., Apr. 15, 1860; s. Daniel and Nancy (Fisher) B.; student, Ohio Wesleyan U. and Northwestern Ohio Normal U., 1881-82; B.Di., Ia. State Normal Sch., 1886, M.Di., 1890; Ph.B., State U. of Ia., 1895; post-grad. student, U. of Chicago, spring quarter, 1895; traveled and studied in Europe 2 summers; B.S., in Agrl. Edn. Ia. State Coll., 1914, M.S., 1924; m. Eva Tomlinson, Aug. 8, 1889. Teacher rural schs., Ohio, 1881-83; prin. and supt. schs. in Ia., 1886-89, 1890-93, 1895-97; dir. dept. of training in teaching, Ia. State Teachers' Coll., Cedar Falls, 1897-Aug. 1, 1913; asst. prof. in Dept. Agrl. Edn. and spl. student of industrial and vocational edn., Ia. State Coll. Agr. and Mechanic Arts, Ames, Ia., 1913-14; asso. prof. agrl. edn., Coll. of Agr. U. of Minn., 1914-18; state dir. vocational edn. and supervisor of vocational agrl. edn. with State Bd., at Des Moines, Ia., Feb. 1918-22; instr. Natural Science Dept. Ia. State Teachers Coll., June-Dec. 1922; asso. prof. in Dept. of Vocational Edn., Ia. State Coll., Ames, Ia., since 1923. Republican. Presbyn. Author: The Teacher at Work, 1902; Geography of Iowa, 1908; Iowa Supplement Human Geography Series, 1923. Home: Ames, Ia. Died Sept. 20, 1927.

BENEDICT, Alfred Barnum, lawyer; b. Rochester, N.Y., Apr. 2, 1856; s. John Barnum and Ann Elizabeth (Brush) B.; A.B., U. of Cincinnati, 1878 (Phi Beta Kappa), LL.D., 1917; LL.B. from Cincinnati Law Sch., 1880; m. Emma A. Lyford, June 3, 1927. Practiced law at Cincinnati, 1880—; prof. law, College of Law, U. of Cincinnati (Cincinnati Law Sch.), 1897—, dean, 1917—. Democrat. Compiler (with Rufus B. Smith) of Statute Law of Ohio, 1890. Home: Cincinnati, O. Died Oct. 16, 1933.

BENEDICT, Frank Lee, author; b. Alexander, N.Y., July 6, 1834; ed. in U.S. and Europe, principally by private tutors. Author: My Daughter Elinor; Miss Van Kortland; John Worthington's Name; Miss Dorothy's Charge; Mr. Vaughan's Heir; St. Simon's Niece; 'Twixt Hammer and Anvil; Her Friend Laurence; Madame; The Price She Paid; A Late Remorse; also The Shadow-Worshipper and Other Poems, and many short stories. Home: St. Albans, W.Va. Died 1910.

BENEDICT, George Grenville, editor Burlington (Vt.) Free Press, 1853—; b. Burling, Vt., Dec. 10, 1826; s. Hon. George Wyllys and Eliza (Dewey) B.; grad. Univ. of Vt., 1847 (A. M.); m. Mary A. Kellogg, Oct. 1853; m. 2d, Katharine A. Pease, Dec., 1864. Served as lt. and A. D. C., 12th Vt. vols., 1862-63; postmaster Burlington, 1861-64 and 1871-74; State senator, 1869-71; sec. Univ. of Vt., 1865—; pres. Vt. Press Assn., 1886-90; State Mil. Hist., 1878-86; collector of customs, Vt., 1889-93; pres. Vt. Soc. S.A.R., 1890, Vt. Hist. Soc., 1896—; Gov. Vt. Soc. Colonial Wars, 1902; comdr. Mil. Order Loyal Legion, Vt., 1903. Author: Vermont at Gettysburg, 1866 O1; Vermont in the Civil War (2 vols.), 1886 L11; Army Life in Virginia, 1895 O1. Edited: Bibliography of Vermont, 1897, published by State. Home: Burlington, Vt. Died 1907.

BENEDICT, Harris Miller, botanist; b. Buda, Ill., Dec. 8, 1873; s. Miller Samuel and Anna Maria (Harris) B.; B.A., Doane Coll., Crete, Neb., 1894; B.S., U. of Neb., 1896, A.M., 1897; Ph.D., Cornell, 1914; m. Florence Stevens McCrea, 1906; children—Harris, Jean, Ann, Martha, McCrea. Head of biol. dept. Lincoln (Neb.) High Sch., 1897-99, Omaha High Sch., 1899-1902; instr. biology, 1902-03, asst. prof. 1904-08, asso. prof., 1908-11, prof. 1911-14, prof. botany, 1914— U. of Cincinnati; organized dept. of botany, U. of Cincinnati, 1914. Originator, 1908, and dir. Emery Bird Reserve (the first city bird reserve), Cincinnati and organized the first sch. garden courses, for teachers of Cincinnati schs., and a pre-agrl. course for univ. students. Democrat. Presbyterian. Contbr. articles concerning researches on senility in perennial woody plants, as well as many minor papers of popular nature on botany, nature study and bird protection. Home: Cincinnati, O. Died Oct. 17, 1928.

BENEDICT, Harry Yandell, college pres.; b. Louisville, Ky., Nov. 14, 1869; s. Joseph and Adele (Peters) B.; B.S., U. of Tex., 1892, M.A., 1893; U. of Va., 1893-95; Harvard, 1895-98, Ph.D., 1898; LL.D., Baylor Univ., 1920, Southwestern U., 1929; m. Ada Stone, June 27, 1900; children—Carl Stone (dec.), Harry Yandell. Fellow in pure mathematics, 1891-92, tutor pure and applied mathematics, 1892-93, U. of Tex.; asst. Leander McCormick Obs., U. of Va., 1893-95; instr., in charge ad interim; mathematics and astronomy, Vanderbilt U., 1899, instr., 1899, adj. prof., 1899-1902, asso. prof., 1902-07, prof. since 1907, dir. dept. of extension, 1909-11, dean Coll. of Arts and Sciences, 1911-27, pres., 1927—, U. of Tex. Democrat. Home: Austin, Tex. Died May 10, 1937.

BENEDICT, Henry Harper, mfr.; b. German Flats, Herkimer Co., N.Y., Oct. 9, 1844; s. Micaiah and Catharine (Harper) B.; A.B., Hamilton College, Clinton, N.Y., 1869, also A.M. and LL.D., 1923; m. Maria Nellis, Oct. 10, 1867 (died Aug. 25, 1915); 1 dau., Mrs. Archibald A. Forrest; m. 2d, Josephine Katharine Magill Geddes, Mar. 5, 1917; 1 dau., Josephine C. Benedict. Confidential position with E. Remington & Sons, 1869-82; member firm Wyckoff, Seamans & Benedict, 1882-95; pres. Wyckoff, Seamans & Benedict Corp., 1895-1914; pres. Remington Typewriter Co., 1902-13. Trustee Hamilton Coll., Brooklyn Inst. Arts and Sciences, Am. Scenic and Historic Preservation Soc. (v.p.); v.p. Nat. Inst. Social Sciences. Home: New York, N.Y. and Southampton, L.I., N.Y. Died June 12, 1935.

BENEDICT, Lorenzo, corp. official; b. South Norwalk, Conn., Dec. 25, 1861; s. James and Therza C. (Dibble) B.; ed. South Norwalk High Sch.; m. Minnie Morehouse, Oct. 5, 1887; children—Mrs. Hazel Dickson, Mrs. Mavis Potter. Began as clk. with Salt Co., 1879; pres. of its successor, the Worcester Salt Co., since 1910. Republican. Baptist. Mason. Home: East Orange, N.J. Died May 16, 1932.

BENEDICT, Robert Dewey, lawyer; b. Burlington, Vt., Oct. 3, 1828; s. George Wyllys and Eliza (Dewey) B.; A.B., U. of Vt., 1848, A.M., 1851 (LL.D., 1891); m. Frances A. Weaver, Mar. 2, 1854. Admitted to bar, 1851; established practice in New York; retired 1906. Republican. Dir. Long Island Hist. Soc.; trustee Adephi Coll., Brooklyn; pres. Brooklyn Soc. of Vermonters; mem. Soc. Colonial Wars, Mil. Order Foreign Wars; 1st v.p. Order Settlers and Defenders of America. Author: Reports of Cases Argued and Determined in the District Courts of the United States Within the Second Circuit (10 vols.), 1869-1882. Also many published addresses. Editor: Benedict's Admiralty (3d edit.), 1900. Home: Burlington, Vermont. Died 1911.

BENEDICT, Russell, judge; b. N.Y. City, Nov. 25, 1859; s. Seth Williston and Anna Elizabeth (Russell) B.; ed. pvt. schs.; LL.B., Columbia, 1880; m. May Gillette Sherwood, Oct. 19, 1892; children—Williston, Russell Sherwood (dec.). Began practice in N.Y. City, 1880; served as atty. in many important causes; active for many yrs. in civic work in Brooklyn; succesful in securing reduction of telephone rates for Brooklyn; justice Supreme Ct. of N.Y., 2d Jud. Dist., term 1911-25; appted. official referee of 2d Jud. Dept. Republican. Ex-pres. Brooklyn League, Prospect Park South Assn., Flatbush Playgrounds Assn.; trustee Hudson-Fulton Celebration Commn. Mem. 13th Regt. N.G.N.Y., 10 yrs., advancing to regtl. adjt. Trustee Green-Wood Cemetery, N.Y. Society Library, L.I. Hist. Soc. Home: Great Neck Estates, L.I. Died No. 29, 1936.

BENEDICT, Samuel Ravaud, surgeon; b. Athens, Ga., July 12, 1882; s. Samuel Caldwell and Anne (Bloomfield) B.; student U. of Ga.; M.D., Med. Coll. of Va., 1908; spl. work, Bellevue Hosp., City Hosp. and Willard Hosp., N.Y. City; grad. St. Vincent's Hosp., N.Y. City; m. Martha Milner, May 21, 1912; children—Samuel Ravaud, Willis Milner, Helen Milner. Began practice at Athens, Ga., 1911; moved to Birmingham, 1916; chief surgeon Ala. Power Co., Allied Engrs., Inc.; dist. surgeon I.C. R.R. Co.; surgeon Mobile & Ohio R.R. Co., Pullman Co., U.S. Employees' Compensation Commn.; attending surgeon St. Vincent's Hosp., Birmingham. Fellow A.C.S. Awarded Insull Medal, 1927. Episcopalian. Home: Birmingham, Ala. Died May 10, 1936.

BENEDICT, Stanley R(ossiter), prof. chemistry; b. Cincinnati, O., Mar. 1884; s. Wayland R. and Anne (Kendrick) B.; B.A., U. of Cincinnati, 1906;

Ph.D., Yale, 1908; m. Ruth Fulton, 1913. Instr. chemistry, Syracuse U., 1908-09; asso. in biol. chemistry, Columbia, 1909-10; asst. prof. chem. pathology, Cornell U. Med. Coll., New York, 1910-11; asst. prof. chemistry, 1911-12, prof. 1913—, Cornell U. Mng. editor Jour. Biol. Chemistry. Home: New York, N.Y. Died Dec. 22, 1936.

BENEDICT, Wayland Richardson, college prof.; b. Rochester, N.Y., Jan. 9, 1848; s. Nehemiah W. and Laura (Tobey) B.; A.B., U. of Rochester, 1865, A.M., 1868; prof. Latin and German, Rochester High Sch., 1865-66; in charge Springside Acad., Pittsfield, Mass., 1866-68; grad. Rochester Theol. Sem., 1870, grad. student same, 1870-71, U. of Giessen, 1872-73; m. Anne Elizabeth Kendrick, Oct. 2, 1873; father of Mary Kendrick B. Ordained Bapt. ministry, 1873; pastor Mt. Auburn, O., 1873-75; exec. officer, 1875-76, prof. philosophy and history, 1875-80, psychology and logic, 1880-90, prof. philosophy and dean, 1890-91, prof. philosophy, 1891-1907, prof. emeritus, 1907, U. of Cincinnati. Author: Nervous System and Consciousness, 1885; Theism and Evolution, 1886; Outlines of the History of Education, 1888; Ethics and Evolution, 1889; New Studies in the Beatitudes, 1890; Psychological Table, 1889, 1900; Bible Lectures, U. of Cincinnati; World Views and Their Ethical Implications, 1903; Religion as an Idea, 1903; Greek Thought Movements and Their Ethical Implication, 1905, etc. Home: Cambridge, Mass. Died July 21, 1915.

BENEDICT, William Leonard, banker; b. Boston, Oct. 14, 1860; s. William Gardner and Frances Otis (Wheeler) B.; ed. English High Sch., Boston; Mass. Inst. Technology, 1880; m. Maud Benson, Apr. 7, 1891. Began with Kidder, Peabody & Co., Boston and New York, 1880; resident partner in New York, 1910-27. Republican. Unitarian. Decorated, 1908, by the Emperor of Japan with fourth degree of Order of the Sacred Treasure, by King of Italy with Chevalier Order of the Crown, 1919. Home: Chestnut Hill, Mass. Died June 6, 1935.

BENEKER, Gerrit Albertus, artist; b. Grand Rapids, Mich., Jan. 26, 1882; s. Bartel Albertus and Pauline (Steketee) B.; grad. Central High Sch., Grand Rapids, 1901; studied Art Inst. Chicago, 1901-03, Art Students' League, New York, 1903-05; pupil of Charles W. Hawthorne, Provincetown, Mass., 3 summers; m. Flora Judd Van Vranken, Sept. 12, 1907; children—Katharine, Benson Van Vranken, Helen Martina, Jean. Began as illustrator for mags., 1905; has specialized in industrial art; exhibited at Nat. Acad. Design, New York; Art. Inst. Chicago; Pa. Acad. Fine Arts, Phila.; Carnegie Inst., Pittsburgh; Corcoran Gallery, Washington, D.C.; etc.; "one man" show of 40 paintings on circuit for 13 yrs. Represented in permanent collection, Butler Art Inst., Youngstown, O.; Grand Rapids Art Assn.; Wichita (Kan.) High Sch.; The Loomis Sch., Windsor, Conn.; Bridgewater (Mass.) State Normal Sch., Grand Rapids High Sch. Expert aid, Bur. Yards and Docks, U.S. Navy, Washington, D.C., June-Oct. 1918; active worker Liberty Loan drive, etc., Provincetown. Widely known for Victory Loan poster, "Sure, We'll Finish the Job!"; contbr. to mags.; contributing editor World Unity; also lecturer. Home: Truro, Mass. Died Oct. 23, 1934.

BENGOUGH, Elisa Armstrong, author; b. Frederick Co., Md.; d. William J. and Ada Mossie Armstrong; ed. at pvt. schs.; m. William Bengough, May, 1901. Author: The Teacup Club, 1897; The Very Young Man and the Angel Child, 1900; The Talk of the Town, 1902. Home: Kiamesha Lake, N.Y. Deceased.

BENHAM, Andrew Ellicott Kennedy, rear admiral U.S.N., retired Apr. 1894; b. New York, Apr. 10, 1832; m. 1863, Emma H. Seaman. Apptd. from N.Y., Nov. 24, 1847; served in East India squadron, 1847-51, and asstd. in capture of piratical Chinese junk; slightly wounded; in home squadron, 1851-52; Naval Acad., 1852-53; promoted passed midshipman, June 10, 1853; promoted through grades to rear admiral, Feb. 1890. During Civil war served in S. Atlantic and Western Gulf blockading squadrons; took part in the battle of Port Royal and other engagements; was in command in one of the divs. in the naval display nr. New York, Apr. 1893; in 1894 comd. squadron at Rio de Janeiro, Brazil; forced comdr. of insurgent squadron to raise blockage of city and to discontinue firing upon Am. mcht. vessels; in 1898, prize commr. at Savannah, Ga. Died 1905.

BENINGTON, Arthur, journalist; b. Stockton-on-Tees, Eng., Aug. 20, 1865; s. George and Mary Hannah (Wilson) B.; ed. York Sch., Eng.; came to America, 1883; m. Elizabeth G. Davidson, Sept. 10, 1890. In father's tea importing house, London, 1881-83; mgr. branch of the business at Toronto, Can., 1883-85; reporter Duluth Tribune, 1887, St. Paul Globe, 1888; city editor Journal, Helena, Mont., 1889; Washington corr. St. Paul Globe, 1889-90; reporter New York World, 1890, New York Journal, 1891-96; mng. editor New York Mercury, 1896-97; foreign editor New York American, 1890-1900; on editorial staff, New York World, 1902-04, asst. Sunday editor, 1904—. First introduced Guglielmo Ferrero, the Italian historian, to Am. pub. and translated his articles on America for New York World, 1908. Has written extensively for European and Am. mags. Delivered course of lectures on Dante at New York Univ., 1914. Rep. of Com. on Pub. Information in Italy, 9 months lecturing in Italian on America's part in the war; after the armistice accompanied Admiral Millo to the occupation of Dalmatia. Republican. Catholic. Knight Comdr. Order of Crown of Italy; Chevalier Order of Sts. Maurice and Lazarus; Knight Comdr. Order of Danilo (Montenegrin). Home: Brooklyn, N.Y. Died Mar. 20, 1923.

BENJAMIN, Anna Northend, magazine writer and lecturer; b. Salem, Mass., Oct. 6, 1874; d. Charles A. and Louisa H. B.; grad. St. Gabriel's School, Peekskill, N.Y., 1893; only woman writer who reached Cuba before the surrender of Santiago; was in Santiago day after surrender, after 2 mos. and a half in Tampa, Key West, Guantanamo and Siboney; left New York for Philippines as war corr., May, 1899; there 6 mos., writing for New York Tribune and San Francisco Chronicle; then went to Japan, 3 mos., and to Korea and Peking. Left Peking a few days before Boxer outbreak and proceeded to Vladivostok, Siberia, thence overland to Moscow and Paris. Engaged on book of her experiences, mag. articles and illustrated lectures. The only woman war corr. serving in both Cuban and Filipino campaigns. Home: New York, N.Y. Died 1902.

BENJAMIN, Charles Henry, engr.; b. Patten, Me., Aug. 29, 1856; s. of Samuel E. and Ellen M. (Fairfield) B.; M.E., U. of Me., 1881; (D.E., Case Sch., 1908); m. Cora L. Benson, Aug. 17, 1879. Instr. and prof. mech. engring., U. of Me., 1880-86; mech. engr. for McKay Machine Co., Boston, 1886-89; prof. mech. engring., Case Sch. Applied Science, 1889-1907; dean Engring. Sch., 1917-21, dir. Engring. Expt. Sta., Purdue U., now emeritus. Author: Modern American Machine Tools, 1906; Machine Design, 1906; Steam Engine, 1909. Home: Lafayette, Ind. Died 1937.

BENJAMIN, Eugene S., mgr. Baron de Hirsch Fund; b. Leavenworth, Kan., Jan. 21, 1862; s. Alfred and Sophia (Woolf) B.; ed. pub. schs.; m. Miriam Gutman, Nov. 28, 1890. Began as clk., 1876; pres. Alfred Benjamin & Co., N.Y. City, 1889-1913; partner I. S. Woolf & Co., 1915-21; mng. dir. Baron de Hirsch Fund, 1922—; pres. Woodbine Land and Improvement Co.; v.p. Jewish Agrl. Soc. Author: Practical Credit Analysis, 1933. Home: New York, N.Y. Died June 21, 1941.

BENJAMIN, George Hilliard, engr.; b. New York, Dec. 25, 1852; s. Park and Mary (Western) B.; Union Coll., class of '72; M.D., Albany Med. Coll., 1874; completed edn. in France and Germany; Ph.D., U. of Freiberg, 1882; m. Jane Seymour, Apr. 1875; children—Mrs. Frances B. Lackland, Mrs. Henry H. Rogers, Rosalie de Villers; m. 2d, Grace Tremaine, June 1901. Practiced medicine at Albany, 4 yrs.; asst. editor Appleton's Cyclo. of Applied Mechanics; editor Nat. Cyclo. of Applied Mechanics; admitted to bar, 1884; has devoted attention to scientific work, 1884—; consulting engr. for many large mfg. and elec. corps. in America and Europe; expert in patent causes. Home: New York, N.Y. Died Nov. 10, 1927.

BENJAMIN, Louis, newspaper pub.; b. London, Eng., Nov. 8, 1883; s. Jacob S. and Leah (Levi) B.; brought to U.S. as a child; ed. high sch.; m. Mary L. Voit, Aug. 13, 1904; children—Edna (Mrs. Joseph Rubin), Samuel, Bernard. Pub. Erie (Pa.) Dispatch Herald, 1925—. Became pres. Benjamin Advertising Corp., 1913; pres. Erie Dispatch-Herald Broadcasting Corp. Dir. Zem Zem Shrine Hosp. for Crippled Children. Mem. bd. govs. B'nai B'rith. Republican. Jewish religion. Mason. Home: Erie, Pa. Deceased.

BENJAMIN, Marcus, editor; b. San Francisco, Calif., Jan. 17, 1857; s. Edmund Burke and Sarah (Mitchell) B.; moved to New York, 1867; Ph.B., Sch. of Mines, Columbia, 1878; A.M., Lafayette Coll., 1888; Ph.D., U. of Nashville, 1889; Sc.D., U. of Pittsburgh, 1905; LL.D., St. John's Coll., Md., 1910; m. Carolyn Gilbert, June 16, 1892. Editor Am. Pharmacist, 1882, and later of its successor, Weekly Drug News; chemist U.S. Appraiser's Store, New York, 1883-85; sanitary engr., New York Bd. of Health, 1885; editor, U.S. Nat. Mus., 1896-1931, retired. Lecturer on chemistry, N.Y. Woman's Med. Coll., 1884-86; mem. U.S. Assay Commn., 1896, 1900, 1904, 1906, 1912, 1917, 1918, 1924; mem. jury awards, Chicago, Tenn. Centennial, Trans-Miss., Buffalo, Charleston, St. Louis, Jamestown and Sesquicentennial (Phila.) expns.; sec. sect. of tech. chemistry, Congress of Arts and Sciences, St. Louis, 1904; commr. Hudson-Fulton Celebration, New York, 1909; mem. Council, Washington (P.E.) Cathedral, 1911—. Vol. aid, office Naval Intelligence, World War; Officier de l'Instruction Publique (France), 1920; Officer dell Ordine della Corona d'Italia, 1927; Kings gold crown (1929) and alumni medal (1930), Columbia U. Contbr. to Appleton's Annual Cyclo., 1883-1902; on staff Appleton's Cyclo. of Am. Biography; editor of various Appleton's guides and hand-books, etc. Translator Bertholet's Explosive Materials, 1883. Contbr. to prin. mags. Gov. Soc. Colonial Wars, D.C., 1905-07, dep. gov. gen., 1920-22; pres. S.R., Washington, 1926-27; chmn. Nat. Com. for Celebration of Bicentennial Anniversary of Birth of George Washington, Soc. of S.R. Pres. Churchmen's League, Washington, 1919-24. Home: Washington, D.C. Died Oct. 22, 1932.

BENJAMIN, Park, patent lawyer; b. New York, N.Y., May 11, 1849; s. Park and Mary (Western) B.; grad. Trinity Sch., N.Y., 1862, U.S. Naval Acad., 1867; LL.B., Albany Law School, 1870; Ph.D., Union Coll., 1877; m. Ida E. Crane, 1891. Ensign U.S.N. to 1869; editor Scientific American to 1878; editor-in-chief Appleton's Cyclo. of Applied Mechanics, 1881 and 1892. Author: Early History of Electricity, 1895; History of U.S. Naval Academy, 1900, and numerous essays in Forum, Independent, and other periodicals. Home: New York, N.Y. Died Aug. 21, 1922.

BENJAMIN, Raphael, rabbi; b. London, England, June 19, 1846; s. Elias and Mary (Lazarus) B.; ed. Jews' Free School, London, 1856-71; won Rothschild Scholarship of £30, and a medal, 1860; grad. B.A., Univ. of London, 1871, and M.A., Univ. of Melbourne (Australia), 1879, by exam., Sch. Natural Science; studied divinity Jews' Free School, examined and ordained rabbi and Beth Din (Doctor of Jewish Law) by Chief Rabbi, Dr. N. M. Adler, 1874. Certificated teacher under British Govt.; mem. Tonic-sol-fa Coll., London, Minister Melbourne Hebrew Congregation, 1874, Mound St. Temple, Cincinnati, 1882-88; 15th St. Temple, New York, 1889-1902; Keap St. Temple, Brooklyn, 1902—. Mem. exec. bd. Central Conf. Am. Rabbis; sec. N.Y. Bd. Jewish Ministers; sec. 9th dist. Charity Organization Soc., New York; fellow A.A.A.S.; mem. Met. Museum of Art, Nat. Geog. Soc.; constant contbr. to press. Died 1906.

BENJAMIN, Reuben Moore, judge; b. Chatham Centre, Columbia Co., N.Y., June 29, 1833; s. Darius and Martha (Rogers) B.; A.B., Amherst, 1853, A.M., 1856; law student Harvard, 1854-55; (LL.D., Ill. Wesleyan, 1880); m. Laura Woodin, Sept. 15, 1856. Prin. Hopkins Acad., Hadley, Mass., 1853-54; tutor Amherst Coll., 1855-56; admitted to bar, 1856, and since in practice at Bloomington, Ill. Mem. Ill. Constl. Conv., 1869-70; drafted Art. II, Bill of Rights, prohibiting irrevocable grant of spl. privileges of immunities, and led debates which resulted in Art. XI, Sect. 12, giving legislature power to establish reasonable maximum freight and passenger rates on Ill. rys.; judge McLean Co., Ill., 1873-86. Republican. Dean, 1874-1891, prof. real property and constl. law, 1891—, Ill. Wesleyan U. Author: Principles of Contract, 1889, 1907; Principles of Sales, 1895, 1901; Benjamin and Messing's Cases on Contracts, 1911. Home: Bloomington, Ill. Died Aug. 4, 1917.

BENJAMIN, Samuel Greene Wheeler, author, artist; b. at Argos, Greece, Feb. 13, 1837; s. Nathan B. (Am. missionary) and Mary Gladding (Wheeler) B. (poetical writer), and g.g.s. Capt. Nathan Benjamin and Capt. Charles Seymour, who served in Am. Revolution; studied at home, and at English Coll., Smyrna, Turkey; A.B., Williams, 1859; m. Clara Stowell, Oct. 20, 1863 (died 1880); 2d, Fanny Nichols Weed (author, Sunny Side of Shadow), Nov. 16, 1882. Asst. librarian N.Y. State Library, 1861-64; sent 2 cos. of cav. to war; served in war hosps.; read law; studied art; at sea several years mastering seamanship; 1st U.S. minister to Persia, 1883-85; pres. Rep. Club, Richmond Co., N.Y., 1892. Art editor, Am. dept., Magazine of Art, also New York Mail. Marine painter and illustrator; sent Crimean War marine drawings to London Illustrated News, 1854; opened studio in Boston as artist in oil and water colors, 1870; hon. mention, 1881, for painting; hon. mention for exhibit of Persian products in State Dept. Group, New Orleans Expn.; exhibited painting, "Porto da Cruz," at the Centennial Expn. at Philadelphia, 1876. Author: Constantinople, Isle of Pearls and Other Poems, 1861; Ode on the Death of Abraham Lincoln, 1865; The Turk and the Greek, 1867; Tom Roper, A Yarn for Boys, 1868; The Choice of Paris, A Romance of the Troad, 1870; Advice of Father to Son (transl. from Latin poem), 1871; Contemporary Art in Europe, 1877; What Is Art? 1877; The Atlantic Islands, 1878; Art in America, 1879; Our American Artists (for youth), 1879, 2d series, 1880; The Multitudinous Seas, 1879; The World's Paradises, 1879; Troy, Its Legend, Literature and Topography, 1881; A Group of Etchers, 1883; Cruise of the Alice May, 1884; Persia and the Persians, 1886; The Story of Persia, 1887; Sea Spray, 1888. Several of these books also pub. in England. Home: Burlington, Vt. Died July 19, 1914.

BENNESON, Cora Agnes, lawyer; b. Quincy, Ill.; d. Robert S. and Electa Ann (Park) B.; A.B., U. of Mich., 1878, LL.B., 1880, A.M., 1883; unmarried. Admitted to bar, Mich. and Ill., 1880, Mass., 1894. Spl. commr. in Mass., 1895, et seq. Trip around the world, 1883-85; lectured on travels, 1885-86; edited law reports for West Pub. Co., St. Paul, 1886; fellow in history, Bryn Mawr Coll., 1887-88. Contbr. to jours. on topics of law, edn., polit. and social science, etc. Mem. Mass. Bar Assn. Home: Cambridge, Mass. Died June 8, 1919.

BENNET, Walter Mills, banker; b. N.Y. City, Nov. 3, 1861; s. Orville G. and Anna Jane (Mills) B.; grad. business course, Coll. City of New York, 1879; m. Sara K. Longacre, Feb. 20, 1894. Began in employ of Kountze Bros., bankers, 1879; with Bank of

America, 1884-88, Chrystie & Janney, 1888-92; again with Bank of America, 1892, v.p., 1900, resigning as 1st v.p., 1926, resigning as director, 1929; v.p. Consol. Copper Mines, 1929-31; trustee Dry Dock Savings Trust. Trustee Y.M.C.A., Greenwich, Conn. Republican. Methodist. Home: Greenwich, Conn. Died Jan. 13, 1938.

BENNETT, Alfred S., judge; b. Dubuque, Ia., June 10, 1854; s. Thomas M. and Zylpha Ann (Finnell) B.; ed. pub. schs.; m. Mary V. McCauley, Nov. 7, 1887. Teacher pub. schs. until 1880; admitted to Ore. bar, 1880, and practiced at The Dalles; associated in defense of U.S. Senator John H. Mitchell, Congressman John N. Williamson, and others, in "land fraud cases"; judge 4th Jud. Circuit, Ore., 1882-84; justice Supreme Court of Ore., Nov. 1918-Nov. 1920, resigned and resumed practice. Democrat. Home: The Dalles, Ore. Died Nov. 28, 1925.

BENNETT, Belle H., church worker; b. Richmond, Ky.; d. Samuel and Elizabeth B.; ed. Richmond, Ky.; unmarried. Early became identified with S.S. work and later with missionary work. Founder of the Scarrett Bible and Training Sch., Kansas City, Mo., and raised $75,000 for the building, and nearly $60,000 for endowment; a leader in establishing schs. for mountaineers, indigent girls, etc., also city missions, known as Wesley Houses, in many industrial centers of the South. Formerly pres. Woman's Bd. of Home Missions of M.E. Ch., South; now pres. Woman's Missionary Council of M.E. Ch., South; mem. Gen. Bd. of Misssions, same ch. Advocate of woman suffrage. Home: Richmond, Ky. Died July 1922.

BENNETT, Burton Ellsworth, lawyer; b. North Brookfield, N.Y., Apr. 17, 1863; s. Samuel Rhoades and Mary Hill (Loomis) B.; grad. Brookfield Acad.; Regents' diploma, Univ. State of N.Y., 1881; B.S., Cornell U., 1885 (class orator; honors for general excellence), also awarded D.Sc. and LL.D. by same univ.; unmarried. Admitted to N.Y. bar, 1887, and began practice at Utica; removed to Seattle, Wash., 1887; mem. Board Park Commrs., Seattle, 1892-95; U.S. dist. atty. for Alaska, 1895-98; on the ground in Alaska gold stampedes—Cook Inlet, 1896, Klondike, 1897, Atlin, 1898, Nome, 1900; secured first convictions in Alaska for murder, adultery and illicit sale of intoxicants; secured 99 convictions out of 101 cases, spring term, in 1898. Commr. from Alaska to Internat. Mining Congress, 1898; mem. commn. from Wash. to Buffalo Expn., 1901. Episcopalian; 1st chancellor Am. (Episcopal) Ch. in Alaska. Democrat; mem. city, county and state convs., 1892—. Mason. Home: Seattle, Wash. Deceased.

BENNETT, Charles Andrew Armstrong, prof. philosophy; b. Shankill, County Dublin, Ireland, June 15, 1885; s. James Cavendish and Susan Elizabeth (Bolger) B.; prep. edn., Trent Coll., Derbyshire, Eng.; B.A., Queen's Coll., Oxford U., 1908; Ph.D., Yale, 1913; m. Annie Ferris, June 18, 1912; children—Charles Cavendish, Michael. Came to U.S., 1909; with Yale, 1910—, prof. philosophy, 1926—. Author: A Philosophical Study of Mysticism, 1923; At a Venture, 1924. Home: New Haven, Conn. Died May 1, 1930.

BENNETT, Charles Edwin, philologist; b. Providence, R.I., Apr. 6, 1858; s. James L. and Lucia E. (Dyer) B.: A.B., Brown U., 1878; grad. student, Harvard, 1881-82, Leipzig, 1882-83, Berlin, 1883-84, Heidelberg, 1884; (Litt.D., Brown, 1904); m. Margaret Gale Hitchcock, June 29, 1886. Taught sch., Milton, Fla., 1878-79, Sing Sing, N.Y., 1879-81; prin. prep. dept., U. of Neb., 1884-89; prof. Latin, U. of Wis., 1889-91; prof. classical philology, Brown U., 1891-92; prof. Latin, Cornell, 1892—. Pres. Am. Philol. Assn., 1907-08. Editor Cornell Studies in Classical Philology, 1892—; Allyn & Bacon's College Latin Series, 1895-1905. Author: A Latin Grammar 1895; Appendix to Bennett's Latin Grammar, 1895; A Latin Composition, 1896; The Foundations of Latin, 1898; Critique of Some Recent Subjunctive Theories, 1898; The Quantitative Reading of Latin Poetry, 1899; The Teaching of Greek and Latin in Secondary Schools (with George P. Bristol), 1900; Latin Lessons, 1901; Cæsar's Gallic War, books I-IV, 1903; Cicero, Selected Orations, 1904; Virgil, Æneid, books I-VI, 1905; Preparatory Latin Writer, 1905; The Latin Language, 1907; First Year Latin, 1909; Syntax of Early Latin, Vol. I, 1910; II, 1914; New Latin Composition, 1912. Home: Ithaca, N.Y. Died May 2, 1921.

BENNETT, Charles Goodwin, sec. U.S. Senate; b. Brooklyn, Dec. 11, 1863; s. George C. B.; pub. sch. edn.; LL.B., New York Law Sch., 1882; widower. Mem. Daniels & Bennett; candidate for 53d Congress, 1892; mem. 54th and 55th Congresses (1895-99), 5th N.Y. Dist.; candidate for 56th Congress, 1899; sec. U.S. senate, Jan. 29, 1900-Mar. 1913. Republican. Dir. Mechanics Bank Kings Co. Savings Instn. (Brooklyn). Home: Brooklyn, N.Y. Died May 25, 1914.

BENNETT, Charles Washington, lawyer; b. Duanesburg, Schenectady Co., N.Y., Oct. 14, 1833; academic edn.; grad. Albany Law School, 1857; admitted to bar at Albany, N.Y.; practiced Racine Co., Wis., 1857-69; Chicago, 1869-71; then at Salt Lake; m. Isabella Eupheania Fisher, Sept. 16, 1858. Home: Salt Lake City, Utah. Died 1906.

BENNETT, Claude Nathaniel, founder and pres. Congressional Information Bur.; b. Thomson, Ga., Nov. 29, 1866; s. Nathaniel J. and Eugenia (Pearce) B.; grad. Emory Coll., 1888; m. Mrs. Harriet Graves, June 30, 1915. Washington corr. and govt. official, 1891-97; lecturer, contbr. to periodicals; established Congressional Information Bur., 1897, that prepares data for congressmen and conducts nat. and internat. business in Congressional, deptl. and all nat. service. Home: Washington, D.C. Died June 13, 1926.

BENNETT, Edward Brown, lawyer; b. Hampton, Conn., Apr. 12, 1842; s. William and Marina (Brown) B.; A.B., Yale, 1870; studied law in offices; m. Alice Howard, Apr. 24, 1877. Began practice at Hampton; removed to Hartford, 1869; pres. Hartford City Gas Light Co., Springfield Waste Co., dir. Travelers Ins. Co., etc.; rep. Conn. Gen. Assembly, 1868; asst. clk. of House, 1869; clk., 1870; sec. Rep. State Central Com., 1870-76; clk. of Senate, 1871; clk. of Police Court, Hartford, 1871-73; mem. Common Council, 1872; judge of City Court, Hartford, 1878-91; postmaster, Hartford, 1891-96, 1900-07. Dir. Am. Sch. for Deaf, Hartford; mem. advisory bd. Hartford Orphan Asylum. Republican. Home: Hartford, Conn. Died Mar. 26, 1927.

BENNETT, Emerson, author; b. Monson, Mass., March 16, 1822; ed. dist. schools and Monson Acad.; m. 1847, Eliza G. Daly. Began writing poetry and prose at 18; has since followed literature and written more than 50 novels and serials, and some hundreds of short stories, published in leading literary periodicals, America and Europe. Author: Prairie Flower, Leni Leoti (sold over 100,000 each), Clara Moreland, Border Rover, Phantom of Forest, Villetta Linden, Forged Will, Traitor, Forest Rose, Mike Fink, Outlaw's Daughter, etc. Has also been editor, publisher, lecturer and elocutionist. Resided Cincinnati, and then Phila., 1850—. Died 1905.

BENNETT, Granville G., judge; b. Butler Co., O., Oct. 9, 1833; s. Peter and Mary B.; ed. Howe's Acad., Mt. Pleasant, and Washington Coll., Ia.; m. Mary Dawson, Oct. 11, 1860. Admitted to bar, 1859; practiced at Washington, Ia., 1859-75; commd. officer U.S.V., 1861-65; mem. Ia. Ho. of Rep., 1866-68, Senate, 1868-72; justice Supreme Ct., Dak. Ty., 1875-78; del. 46th Congress, from Dak. Ty., 1879-81; judge co. ct., Lawrence Co., S.D., 1892-96 and 1904-08. Del. Rep. Nat. Conv., 1900. Republican. Home: Deadwood, S.D. Died 1910.

BENNETT, Henry Holcomb, writer; b. at Chillicothe, O., Dec. 5, 1863; s. John Henry and Eliza (McClintock) B.; bro. of John B.; ed. pub. schs. Chillicothe and Kenyon Coll., Ohio; studied landscape, Art Students' League, New York; unmarried. Lived number of yrs. in West; writer chiefly army stories and ornith. articles, with his own illustrations. Is water colorist in landscape, birds and animals and book illustrator. Wrote series of sketches and articles on National Guard, 1898-99; stories of army life, 1898, 1900, 1901. Home: Chillicothe, Ohio. Died Apr. 30, 1924.

BENNETT, Henry William, stove mfr.; b. Indianapolis, Aug. 26, 1858; s. William H. and Helen (Root) B.; ed. pub. schs., Indianapolis; m. Ariana Holliday, Oct. 8, 1890; children—Edward Jacquelin, Louise (Mrs. Albert C. Lord). Sec. and treas. Indianapolis Stove Co., 1877-93, pres., 1893—; pres. State Life Ins. Co., 1907-29. Postmaster of Indianapolis, 1905-08. Trustee Indianapolis Foundation; pres. William E. English Foundation. Republican. Home: Indianapolis, Ind. Died May 19, 1936.

BENNETT, Ida Dandridge, author; b. at Coldwater, Mich., Jan. 3, 1860; d. William and Elizabeth (Davis) B.; ed. Rockford Coll., 1875-77; Art Inst., Chicago, 1881; unmarried. In lit. work, 1892—. Author: The Flower Garden, 1903; The Vegetable Garden, 1907; A Summer Garden, 1912; The Making of a Flower Garden, 1919; The Busy Woman's Vegetable Garden, 1919. Home: Coldwater, Mich. Died Apr. 4, 1925.

BENNETT, James Gordon, proprietor New York Herald; b. New York, May 10, 1841; s. James Gordon and Henrietta Agnes (Crean) B.; ed. abroad by pvt. tutors; returned to New York, 1866; unmarried. Assumed control of New York Herald on father's death, 1872, of which has since been in active control mostly by cable while residing at Paris; for some time published a London edit.; now also publishes a Paris edit. Inaugurated publication in Eng. of storm warnings transmitted from U.S. At own expense sent Henry M. Stanley to Africa to find Livingstone, 1874-77; fitted out the Jeannette Polar expdn., 1879. With John W. Mackay established the Commercial Cable Co. (Mackay-Bennett Cable), 1883. Won yacht race from Sandy Hook to Isle of Wight, with his yacht, "Henrietta," 1866; participated in race from Queenstown to New York, with yacht "Dauntless," 1870. Died May 14, 1918.

BENNETT, James O'Donnell ("Eye Witness"), journalist; b. Jackson, Mich., May 1, 1870; s. Charles Henry and Mary (O'Donnell) B.; student U. of Mich., 1889-92, hon. A.B., 1909; hon. M.A. from Marquette University, 1927; m. Susan North Hayward, June 5, 1901. Newspaper writer, 1890—, chiefly on Chicago press; connected with the exec. staff of Julia Marlowe, 1900-02; corr. Chicago Journa, Spanish-Am. War; dramatic editor Chicago Record Herald, 1902-14; corr. Chicago Tribune during European War, 1914-18; returned to Chicago and The Tribune after close of war. Episcopalian. Republican. Author: Was ich auf dem Kriegsschauplatz sah; Much Loved Books, 1927; Private Joe Fifer, 1936. Home: Chicago, Ill. Died Feb. 27, 1940.

BENNETT, Jesse Lee, writer; b. Baltimore Co., Md., Sept. 20, 1885; s. Vachel Baizman and Helen Lanahan (Shipley) B; B.A., Johns Hopkins, 1904; unmarried. Contributing editor Baltimore Sun and New York Press, 1914-20, lit. critic with weekly signed article in Baltimore Evening Sun, 1916-22; writer of column in Baltimore Sun entitled "I, Sir, Believe in Everything. I am a Skeptic"; editor of The Modern World, 1926—; founder The Arnold Co., Inc., pubs., 1922, The Readers' Advisory Service, Inc., 1924. Dir. The Adult Edn. Assn.; mem. nat. com., The Vanguard League for Education, National Citizen's Com. on Relations with Latin-America. As officer attached to Morale Br., Gen. Staff, U.S.A., during World War, wrote the first comprehensive manuals of systematic morale work ever prepared for an army. Maj. R.C., U.S.A. Author: On Culture and a Liberal Education, with Lists of Books Which Can Aid in Acquiring Them, 1922; What Books Can Do for You, 1923; The Essential American Tradition, 1925; Frontiers of Knowledge, 1925. Home: Arnold, Md. Died Apr. 21, 1931.

BENNETT, John Foster, merchant; b. Birmingham, Eng., July 11, 1865; s. Richard and Maria (Foster) B.; m. Rosetta Wallace, Nov. 17, 1897; children—Wallace F., Harold H., Elizabeth (Mrs. Elwood Winters), Mary (Mrs. Keneth Smith), Richard S. Brought to U.S., 1868; naturalized citizen, 1889. Pres. Bennett Glass & Paint Co., 1900—; pres. Bluebird Candy Co., Cardon Jewelry Co.; v.p. Deseret Book Co., Logan Hardware Co., Maiben Glass & Paint Co., Jordan Valley Investment Co., Zion's Savings Bank, Utah State Nat. Bank, Zion's Benefit Bldg. Soc., Zion's Cooperative Mercantile Instn. Dir. Deseret Sunday Sch. Union. Mormon. Home: Salt Lake City, Utah. Died Feb. 9, 1938.

BENNETT, Johnstone, actress; b. sea of French and Spanish parentage; left motherless and adopted by a Mrs. Bennett; began stage life when a young girl in a small co.; joined Mansfield and played Sally in Monsieur, subsequently taking parts in Beau Brummel and other plays; joined Charles Frohman's co. and originated titular role in Jane; has since starred in The Amazon and other comedies and in The Female Drummer. Not married. Died 1906.

BENNETT, Robert Root, explorer, lawyer; b. Toledo, O., Dec. 12, 1865; s. William Henry and Helen Louise (Root) B.; LL.B., Columbian (now George Washington) U., 1904; m. Edna M. McCracken, Nov. 6, 1889 (died Jan. 23, 1907); 1 son, Tracy William (dec.); m. 2d, Elsie Havener, Aug. 17, 1917. Admitted to D.C. bar, 1904. Spl. agt. U.S. Dept. Justice, Washington, 1917; served as confidential agt. War Dept., later capt. Intelligence Sect., Gen. Staff, U.S.A., 1917-19; confidential mission to Central America, 1919; conducted expdn. to Yucatan, exploring ancient ruins, for Mus. of Am. Indian, New York, 1930. Republican. Episcopalian. Mason. Donor of Bennett medal to Boatswain Leo H. Luksich, U.S. Coast Guard, for avenging insult to Am. flag, 1917. Home: Washington, D.C. Died Dec. 12, 1933.

BENNETT, Samuel Crocker, lawyer; b. Taunton, Mass., Apr. 19, 1858; s. Edmund H. and Sally (Crocker) B.; A.B., Harvard, 1879; LL.B., Boston U., 1882; m. Amy R. Thomas, Sept. 9, 1885. Prof., 1883-1902, dean, 1893-1902, Boston U. Law Sch. One of editors: Smith's Leading Cases; Benjamin on Sales; Cyclopedia of Law and Procedure. Home: Weston, Mass. Died Nov. 25, 1925.

BENNETT, Thomas Gray, mfr.; b. New Haven, Conn., Mar. 22, 1845; s. Thomas and Mary Ann (Hull) B.; Gen. William H. Russell's Sch. to 1861; Ph.B., Yale, 1870; m. Hannah Jane Winchester, May 9, 1872. Apptd. to drill troops for state of Conn., 1861; commd. 1st lt. and adj., Aug. 28, 1862; 2d lt. 28th Conn. Vols., Nov. 26, 1862; 1st lt. 29th Conn. Vols., Jan. 20, 1864; wounded at Battle of Chapin's Farms, Sept. 27, 1864; promoted to capt. 29th Conn. Vols., Sept. 27, 1864; hon. mustered out Nov. 1865. Entered employ of Winchester Repeating Arm Co., Aug. 1, 1870; sec. same 1871-75; dir., 1875—, treas., 1881-82, v.p., 1882-90, pres., 1890-1911; resigned presidency, Jan. 20, 1911, and elected consulting dir. Mem. Corp. Yale U., 1884-1902; trustee Sheffield Scientific Sch.; mem. bd. mgrs. Observatory, in Yale Coll. Received decoration of the Medjidi, Turkey. Home: New Haven, Conn. Died Aug. 19, 1930.

BENNETT, William Wirt; b. Oregon, Ill., Oct. 10, 1869; s. William Wirt and Catharine (Snyder) B.; ed. U. of Ill. (non-grad.); m. Gertrude M., d. Horace C. Scoville, of Rockford, Ill., 1898; children—William Wirt, Eleanor Gertrude, Catharine Rose, Barbara Scoville. Resided at Rockford, 1877—; admitted to Ill. bar, 1896; pres. W. W. Bennett & Co., Inc., investment securities; mem. Bennett & Lupton, Rockford. Mayor of Rockford, 3 terms, 1911-17; treas. Anti-Saloon League of Ill., 1911-13, pres., 1918-26; lecturer on law enforcement. Moderator Congl. Conf. of Ill., 1923, 1924. Trustee Rockford Coll. Mason. Home: Rockford, Ill. Died Apr. 15, 1932.

BENNETT, William Zebina, chemist; b. Montpelier, Vt., Feb. 25, 1856; s. George Hackett and Emiline (Young) B.; A.B., Harvard, 1878, A.M., 1881; Ph.D., U. of Wooster, 1883; studied twice abroad, first time, 1888, in Lab. of Imperial Bd. of Health, Berlin, last time, 1909-10, in lab. of Emil Fischer, Berlin, and in Sorbonne, Paris; m. Minnie Sinclair Proctor, Aug. 14, 1884. Asst. in chemistry, Harvard, 1878-80; asst. prof. chemistry, 1880-83, Kauke prof., natural sciences, 1883-86, Brown prof. chemistry and physics, 1886-1902, Brown prof. chemistry and dir. chem. lab., U. of Wooster, 1902-24; retired. Presbyn. Has done important research work in organic and physical chemistry and water analysis. Home: Pasadena, Calif. Died 1938.

BENNETTS, James Mitchell, anti-saloon worker; b. Totnes, S. Devon, Eng., Oct. 1, 1860; s. George and Mary Ann (Armstrong) B.; ed. Mansion House Collegiate Sch., Totnes; m. Louisa Shand Powell, Sept. 7, 1887; children—Annie Grace Powell (Mrs. John Smeltz, Jr.), George Emil White, Dorothy Crawford (Mrs. Edward Koehler), Marjorie North (Mrs. D. Roscoe Faunce), Walter Walden. Came to U.S., 1891, naturalized citizen, 1896. Teacher in Eng. 2 yrs.; pub. accountant 8 yrs.; worker in East End Wesleyan Mission, London, 1889-91; entered Ministry M.E. Ch.; pastor Johnsville, N.Y., 1891, Franklin St. Ch., N.Y. City, 1892-96, Pine Hill, N.Y., 1897-99, Golden Bridge, 1900-02, Mahanoy City, Pa., 1903, Prospect Park, 1904-06, Scott Ch., Phila., 1907-08, 12th Street Ch., Phila., 1909-10, Darby, 1911-13; field sec. Pa. Anti-Saloon League, 1913—. Republican. Home: Philadelphia. Died Jan. 1929.

BENNITT, George Stephen, clergyman; b. New Milford, Conn., Aug. 29, 1849; s. Noble Sanford and Sarah Maria (Morehouse) B.; St. Paul's Sch., Brookfield, Conn.; Episcopal Acad., Cheshire, Conn.; B.D., St. Stephen's Coll., N.Y., 1894 (D.D., 1906); m. Thomasetta Butler, Nov. 23, 1871. Deacon, 1873, priest, 1880, P.E. Ch.; asst. St. Peter's Ch., Brooklyn, 1873-75; rector All Saints' Ch., Ashmont, Boston, 1875-87, Grace Ch., Jersey City, N. J., 1887—. Deputy Gen. Conv., P.E. Ch., 1889, 1892, 1895, 1898, 1901, 04, 07, 10, 13; pres. bd. missions Diocese of Newark, 1892—; mem. Fed. Council Chs. of Christ in America; mem. Council Christ Hosp. (pres. 1887-1901). Author: Church Catechism in Short Division, 1901. Home: Jersey City, N.J. Died Mar. 15, 1915.

BENOLIEL, Solomon D., electrochemist; b. New York, June 1, 1874; s. David J. and Pauline (Wasserman) B.; B.S., Coll. City of New York, 1893; E.E. and A.M., Columbia, 1896; m. Therese Lindeman, June 1, 1897; children—D. Jacques, L. Osmond, Jean S. Teacher Adelphi Coll., 1897-1901; electrochemist, and gen. mgr. Roberts Chem. Co. (now Niagara Alkali Co.), 1901-06; gen. mgr. Internat. Chem. Co., Camden, from 1906, now of Phila., Pa. Lecturer Bds. of Edn. New York and Brooklyn, and Brooklyn Inst. Arts and Science, 1899-1901. Has perfected new process for production of caustic potash and chemically pure hydrochloric acid by means of electric current; perfected a number of scientific cleaners, lubricants and burnishing compounds for industrial uses, particularly the metal mfg. trades. Writer on liquid air, photo-therapy and electrochemistry. Home: Merion, Pa. Died Nov. 23, 1932.

BENRIMO, Joseph Henry McAlpin, playwright; b. San Francisco, Calif., June 21, 1871; s. Joseph and Edith Mary (McAlpin) B.; educated St. Ignatius U., San Francisco, and Santa Clara (Calif.) Coll.; studied art Sch. of Design, San Francisco. Debut as actor, San Francisco, 1893. Mem. Japan Society, China Society (London, England). Author: (book) The Yellow Jacket, 1913; (plays, in collaboration) The Yellow Jacket, The Willow Tree, Taking Chances, The Peacock Lady, The Desert, The Link, They Sowed, Stucco, etc. Home: London, England. Died March 26, 1942.

BENSEL, John A., civil engr.; b. New York, 1863; s. Brownlee and Mary Maclay B.; M.E., Stevens Inst. Tech., Hoboken, N.J., 1884; m. Ella Louise Day, 1896. Rodman, New York Aqueduct, 1884, Pa. R.R. Co., 1884-87; asst. engr. and asst. supervisor in charge improvement of dock and freight terminals, Pa. R.R., 1887-89; asst. engr., dept. docks, New York, in charge constrn. work N. River water-front, 1889-95; engr. for water-front improvements, as cons. engr. for Central R.R. of N.J., Girard estate, Phila., and City of Phila. in improvement of a mile of water-front on Del. River, 1895-98; apptd. chief engr., dept. docks, New York, 1898. Maj., Engr. Corps U.S.A., comdg. 125th Engr. Batln., 1917-18. Consulting engr. N.Y. and N.J. Bridge and Terminal Commn. and N.J. Inter State Bridge and Terminal Commn. Home: New York, N.Y. Died June 19, 1922.

BENSINGER, Benjamin Edward, pres. Brunswick-Balke-Collender Co.; b. Louisville, Ky., Jan. 4, 1868; s. Moses and Eleanor (Brunswick) B.; ed. South Div. High Sch., and Bryant & Stratton Business Coll., Chicago; m. Rose Frank, Jan. 20, 1896; children—Robert Frank, Benjamin Edward. With Brunswick-Balke-Collender Co., 1885-88; again with Brunswick-Balke-Collender Co., 1890—; 1st v.p., 1903, and upon the death of father, 1905, succeeded as pres. Pres. Associated Jewish Charities of Chicago, 1917. Home: Glencoe, Ill. Died Nov. 27, 1935.

BENSON, Alfred Washburn, judge; b. Chautauqua, Co., N.Y., July 15, 1843; s. Peleg and Hannah (Washburn) B.; acad. edn., Jamestown and Randolph, N.Y.; pvt. to maj. 154th N.Y. Vols., 1862-65; wounded at Chancellorsville; admitted to N.Y. bar, 1866; removed to Ottawa, Kan., 1869; m. Unettie L. Towsley, May 10, 1870. Mayor of Ottawa, 1878-81; mem. Kan. Senate, 1881-83; judge Dist. Ct., 4th Jud. Dist., 1885-97; mem. Kan. Ho. of Rep., 1905-06; U.S. senator to fill unexpired term (1906-07) of J. R. Burton, resigned; justice Supreme Ct. of Kan., Sept., 1907—. Republican. Home: Ottawa, Kan. Died Jan. 1, 1916.

BENSON, Allan L., author; b. Plainwell, Mich., Nov. 6, 1871; s. Adelbert L. and Rose (Morris) B.; pub. sch. edn.; m. Mary Hugh, Nov. 19, 1899; children—Mary, Welton H., Allan L., James A. On reportorial or editorial staffs of newspapers in Chicago, Salt Lake and San Francisco, 1890-97; asst. mng. editor Detroit Journal, 1897-1901; mng. editor Detroit Times, 1901-06; mng. editor Washington (D.C.) Times, 1906-07; writer polit. and economic subjects, Pearson's Magazine, 1908-16; signed editorials, Appeal to Reason, Girard, Kan., 1914-16. Nominee of Socialist Party for President of U.S., 1916. Resigned from party, 1918, because of its attitude toward the government during the war. Founded, 1918 (with William F. Cochran, of Baltimore), Reconstruction Magazine. Wrote: Socialism Made Plain, 1904; The Usurped Power of the Courts, 1911; The Truth About Socialism (9th edit.), 1913; Our Dishonest Constitution, 1914; A Way to Prevent War, 1915; Inviting War to America, 1916; The New Henry Ford, 1923; The Story of Geology, 1927; Daniel Webster, a biography, 1929. Home: Yonkers, N.Y. Died Aug. 19, 1940.

BENSON, Carville Dickinson, congressman; b. Baltimore Co., Md., Aug. 24, 1872; s. Oregon Randolph and Carvilla (Brian) B.; student Lehigh U., 1889-90; LL.B., Baltimore U., 1893; m. Harriette Cassard Miller, Oct. 18, 1893; children—John Oregon, Carville D., William Howard, Harriette Lippincott, Carvilla Brian, Brian Miller. Practiced at Baltimore, 1893—; mem. Benson, Rowe & Cullen; mem. Md. Ho. of Dels., 1904-10, inclusive, and 1918; (speaker of Ho., 1906); mem. Md. Senate, 1912-14; elected to 65th Congress, Nov. 1918, to fill unexpired term of Joshua Frederick C. Talbot, deceased, and at same time elected to 66th Congress (1919-21), 2d Md. Dist. Introduced first state roads law in U.S., in legislature of Md., 1910; chmn. com. which inquired into value of the holdings of State of Md. in Washington br. of B.&O. R.R., resulting in sale of the State's stock of $2,500,000. Democrat. Episcopalian. Mason. Home: Halethorpe, Baltimore Co., Md. Died Feb. 8, 1929.

BENSON, Frank Williamson, governor; b. San José, Calif., Mar. 20, 1858; s. Henry Clark and Matilda (Williamson) B.; A.B., U. of the Pacific, 1877, A.M., 1886; m. Harriet Rush Benjamin, Nov. 4, 1883. Taught sch., Douglas Co., Ore., 1880-82; co. supt. schs., Douglas Co., 1882-86; deputy co. clerk, Douglas Co., 1888-92, co. clerk, 1892-96; admitted to bar, 1896; practiced law, Roseburg, 1896-1906; sec. of state of Ore., Jan. 1, 1907-Mar. 1, 1909, and ex-officio lt. gov.; became gov. upon resignation of Gov. George E. Chamberlain, Mar., 1909; term expires, Jan., 1911. Republican. Pres. Douglas Nat. Bank. Methodist. Home: Roseburg, Ore. Died 1911.

BENSON, Franklin Thomas, editor; b. Queen Anne Co., Md., Aug. 22, 1862; s. Benjamin Franklin and Maria Elizabeth (Thomas) B.; A.B., Western Md. Coll., 1884, A.M., 1886; B.D., Westminster (Md.) Theol. Sem., 1886; D.D., Kan. City U., 1914; m. Frances E. Murray, Oct. 12, 1892; children—Mrs. Mary Gladys Smith, Franklin Murray, Mrs. Elizabeth Thomas Ruppert, Arthur Emory. Ordained ministry M.P. Ch., 1888, pastor, Washington, 1886-88, Wilmington, 1889-90, West Baltimore, 1891, Elizabeth, N.J., 1892, Centerville, Md., 1898-1901, St. John's Ch., Madison Av., Baltimore, 1902-06, Denton, Md., 1907-10, Rhode Island Av. Ch., Washington, D.C., 1910-12, Crisfield, Md., 1913-16; editor Methodist Protestant, 1916—. Mem. Md. Ann. Conf. M.P. Ch.; 5 times elected as del. to Gen. Conf. M.P. Ch. Trustee Western Md. Coll. Home: Baltimore, Md. Died Apr. 5, 1929.

BENSON, Henry Lamdin, judge; b. Stockton, Calif., July 6, 1854; s. Henry C. and Matilda M. (Williamson) B.; A.B., U. of the Pacific, Santa Clara, Calif., 1873, A.M., 1876; m. Susie E. Dougharty, Sept. 7, 1876. Admitted to Calif. bar, 1878, and practiced at San Jose; removed to Ore.; dist. atty., 1st Ore. Dist., 1892-96; mem. Ore. Ho. of Rep., 1897; judge Circuit Court, 1st Jud. Dist. of Ore. (state court), 1898-1915 (resigned); asso. justice Supreme Court of Ore., Jan. 4, 1915—. Republican. Methodist. Home: Salem, Ore. Died Oct. 16, 1921.

BENSON, Louis FitzGerald, clergyman; b. Phila., July 22, 1855; s. Gustavus Smith and Margaretta FitzGerald (Dale) B.; A.B., U. of Pa., 1874, A.M., 1877; admitted to bar, 1877; practiced law, 1877-84; graduated Princeton Theological Sem., 1887; D.D., U. of Pa., 1896; m. Caroline Perot Warren, June 1, 1887; children—Caroline Warren (Mrs. Geo. Philler, Jr., dec.), Margaretta FitzGerald (Mrs. Geo. T. Purves, Jr.), Barbara English (Mrs. Robert F. Jefferys). Ordained Presbyn. ministry, 1888; pastor Ch. of Redeemer, Germantown, Phila., 1888-94; resigned to edit hymnals of the ch. Editor Journal Presbyn. Hist. Society, 1903-11. Special lecturer in liturgics, Auburn Theol. Sem., 1902; lecturer on Stone Foundation, Princeton Theol. Sem., 1907, 1910-1926. Councilor and hon. librarian Presbyn. Hist. Soc., 1904—. Author: Hymns and Verses, 1897; The Best Church Hymns, 1898; Best Hymns—A Hand-book, 1899; Studies of Familiar Hymns, 1903, 23; The English Hymn—Its Development and Use in Worship, 1915; Hymns Original and Translated, 1925; The Hymnody of the Christian Church, 1927. Editor: The Hymnal, published by authority of Gen. Assembly of Presbyn. Ch., 1895; The Hymnal for Congregational Churches, 1896; The Chapel Hymnal, 1898; The School Hymnal, 1899; The Book of Common Worship of Presbyterian Church (with Henry Van Dyke), 1906; The Hymnal Revised, 1911; A Book of Family Worship, 1916; A Book of Worship for Soldiers and Sailors, 1917; Christian Song, 1926; The Smaller Hymnal, 1928. Contbr. to revs. and to Julian's Dictionary of Hymnology, 2d edit.; also many hymns. Has a hymnol. collection of 9,000 vols. Home: Philadelphia, Pa. Died Oct. 10, 1930.

BENSON, Robert Dix, dir. Tide-Water Oil Co.; b. Brewerton, N.Y., May 14, 1861; s. Byron David and Minerva (Stevens) B.; ed. pub. schs. and spl. studies, U. of Pa.; m. Harriet B. Granger, Oct. 11, 1888; children—Byron David, Robert Granger (killed in World War Oct. 1918), Olive Guthrie (wife of Dr. John H. Carlisle). Began, 1880, as sec. to father, pres. Tide-Water Pipe Co., Ltd.; now chmn. bd., Magor Car Corp.; v.p. Muskogee Electric Traction Co. Mem. City Council, Passaic, N.J., 1908-10; pres. Bd. of Edn., Passaic; pres. trustees First Presbyn. Ch., Passaic Pub. Library. Mem. Nat. Petroleum War Service Com., World War. Republican. Home: Passaic, N.J. Died Sept. 1931.

BENSON, William Shepherd, naval officer; b. Macon, Ga., Sept. 25, 1855; s. Richard Aaron and Catherine Elizabeth (Brewer) B.; grad. U.S. Naval Acad., 1877; LL.D. from Villanova College, also from Loyola College, Md., and Georgetown Univ., D.C.; m. Mary Augusta Wyse, Aug. 6, 1879; children—Mrs. Hermann Krafft, Howard H. J., Francis W. Promoted ensign, July 1881; lt., 1893; lt. comdr., 1900; capt., July 24, 1909; rear adm., Nov. 26, 1915. Has served on various assignments at U.S. Naval Acad. and afloat in all duties as high as div. and squadron comdr.; commandant Phila. Navy Yard, 1913-15; apptd. chief of naval operations, May 11, 1915. Mem. commn. apptd. by Pres. Wilson to confer with Allied Powers in Europe, 1917; mem. spl. mission abroad, Oct. 1918; naval rep. in drawing up naval terms of armistice with Germany and Central Powers; naval adviser to Am. Commn. to Negotiate Peace; returned to U.S., June 20, 1919; continued as chief of naval operations until Sept. 25, 1919, when retired by operation of law, after 47 years' active service; recommended to Congress by the President to be made permanent admiral for life. Apptd. chmn. U.S. Shipping Bd., 1920; apptd. commr. same, by President Harding, 1921. Awarded D.S.M., 1919; Grand Cross Legion of Honor (French); Grand Cross Order St. Michael and St. George (British); Order Rising Sun, 1st class (Japanese); Order St. Gregory Great (mil. class, 1st order), by Pope Benedict XV; gold medal by State of New Mexico, etc. Catholic. Home: Washington, D.C. Died May 20, 1932.

BENT, Myron Hammond, newspaper corr.; b. Antwerp, N.Y., Apr. 22, 1865; s. Alvin Finney and Mary Elizabeth B.; ed. Phillips Exeter Acad., N.H., 1884-85, Williams Coll., 1885-86; m. Susie White Caldwell, Oct. 9, 1912. Began as newspaper reporter, 1886; weekly newspaper publisher 3 yrs., later Albany corr.; Washington corr. Brooklyn Daily Times, 1926—. Identified for 20 yrs. with dairy farming and poultry raising; originator, 1904, of use of waste milk products in poultry-keeping on commercial scale, also of use of artificial light in poultry-keeping, 1908. Ind. Republican. Wrote: Round and Round Coming Out Nowhere. Home: Antwerp, N.Y. Deceased.

BENT, Samuel Arthur, lawyer; b. Boston, July 1, 1841; s. Samuel W. and Mary N. (Barrett) B.; A.B., Yale, 1861, A.M., 1864; LL.B., Harvard, 1865; m. Mary E. Thompson, Aug. 30, 1890. Admitted to

Suffolk bar, 1865; was Am. editor Swiss (Geneva) Times, Galignani's (Paris) Messenger, 1872-74; supt. schs., Nashua, N.H., Clinton, Mass., 1878-86. Author: Familiar Short Sayings of Great Men, 1882; Hints on Language, 1883; Notes to the Golden Legend, 1886. Died Nov. 22, 1912.

BENTE, Frederick, clergyman; b. Wimmer, Hanover, Germany, Jan. 22, 1858; s. Frederick John and Anna Maria (Snyder) B.; came to U.S., 1866; A.B., Concordia Coll., Ft. Wayne, Ind., 1878; grad. Concordia Sem., St. Louis, Mo., 1881, D.D., 1923; m. Josephine C. Haserot, Jan. 28, 1886; children—Paul F., Hugo F., Charlotte J., Frieda J., Oscar F., Rhoda J., Esther J., Lois J. Ordained Evang. Luth. ministry, 1881; pastor at Humberstone, Can., 1882-93; prof. of symbolics, Concordia Sem., 1893-1927; coeditor Lehre und Wehre, 1893—. Author: Gesetz und Evangelium, 1917; Was steht der Vereinigung der Luth. Kirche Amerika's im Wege, 1917; Amerikanisches Luthertum, 1918; American Lutheranism (2 vols.), 1919; (with Dr. W. H. T. Dau) Triglot Concordia, The Symbolical Books of Evangelical Lutheran Church (German-Latin-English), 1921; Concordia or Book of Concord (reprint of the Triglot Concordia, English part), 1922. Home: Redwood City, Calif. Died Dec. 15, 1930.

BENTLEY, Charles Edwin, dentist; b. Cincinnati, O., Feb. 21, 1859; s. Charles E. and Sarah (Watson) B.; D.D.S., Chicago Coll. Dental Surgery, 1887; Sc.D., Howard U., 1921; m. Florence Augusta Lewis, June 2, 1897. In practice at Chicago, 1887—; oral surgery, Rush Med. Coll. Dispensary, 1887-90; prof. oral surgery, Harvey Med. Coll. Author: Care of the Mouth, 1911. Home: Chicago, Ill. Died Oct. 13, 1929.

BENTLEY, Charles Eugene, Presidential candidate "Liberty" party, 1896; b. Warner's, N.Y., April 30, 1841; ed. Monroe Inst. and Oneida Conf. Sem., N.Y.; m. Persis Freeman, Oct. 7, 1863. Lived on farm in N.Y. until 1863; removed, 1866, to Clinton, Ia.; 1878— in Neb.; lived on his farm, Butler Co., 1878-90; also Bapt. minister; 1880—, pastor ch. at Surprise, Neb.; chmn. Prohibition State Conv., 1884; successively candidate for Congress, gov., and U.S. senator; when split came 1896 became Presidential candidate Liberty party; now chmn. of its State Com. for Neb. Home: Lincoln, Neb. Died 1905.

BENTLEY, Charles Harvey, fruit packer; b. San Francisco, Calif. Aug. 28, 1869; s. Robert and Frances Almira (Harvey) B.; A.B., U. of Calif., 1891, A.M., 1914; m. Margaret Stearns Wilder, 1899 (died 1905; m. 2d, Florence Beale Hush, 1908. Became connected, 1892, with Sacramento Packing Co., and later traveled in U.S. and Europe establishing agencies; gen. sales mgr. Calif. Fruit Canners' Assn., 1900-16, and v.p. and sales mgr. of its successor, the Calif. Packing Corp.; dir. Alaska Packers' Assn. Mem. exec. com. Calif. Council of Defense, 1917; exec. staff U.S. Food Adminstrn., 1917-18; subcom. on supplies, Nat. Council of Defense, 1918. Trustee San Francisco Pub. Library, 1906-21, Calif. Sch. Mechanic Arts. As pres. Chamber of Commerce instituted and corrected supervision of insurance settlements by fire ins. cos., immediately following the San Francisco fire of 1906. Home: San Francisco, Calif. Died Dec. 30, 1922.

BENTLEY, Henry, lawyer; b. Ludlow, Ky., July 25, 1880; s. Matthew Henry and Mary Leonide (Magee) B.; A.B., U. of Cincinnati, 1901; LL.B., Cincinnati Law Sch., 1903; LL.D., Marietta Coll., 1931; unmarried. Admitted to Ohio bar, 1903, and practiced since at Cincinnati. Pres. Cincinnati City Charter Com., 1924-35; chmn. of com. which secured adoption of amendment to city charter, 1924, establishing city mgr. proportional representation govt. for Cincinnati, and which elected a majority of city council, 1925, 27, 29, 31, 33; chmn. of Commn., which in 1926 drafted present city charter of Cincinnati. Asso. field dir. American Red Cross, 5th Naval District, World War. Mem. Advisory Board Fed. Emergency Adminstrn. of Pub. Works for Ohio. Dir. Cincinnati Community Chest, Nat. Municipal League, Nat. Proportional Representation League, Cincinnati Anti-Tuberculosis League, Pub. Health Fedn. Republican. Episcopalian (vestryman Christ Ch.; trustee Diocese of Southern Ohio). Mason. Home: Cincinnati, O. Died Oct. 1938.

BENTLEY, Irene (Mrs. Harry B. Smith), actress; b. Baltimore, Md.; m. J. T. Sothoron; m. 2d, Harry B. Smith, librettist. Made début in "Little Christopher," Palmer's Theatre, New York, Apr. 1895; first appearance in London as Gladys Glee, in "The Belle of New York," Apr. 12, 1898; toured in U.S. in "It Happened in Nordland," 1905-06; played in "The Mimic World," 1908, and others. Died June 3, 1940.

BENTLEY, Robert Irving, packer; b. Chicago, Ill., July 25, 1864; s. Robert and Frances Almira (Harvey) B.; U. of the Pacific, San Jose, Calif., 1881-83; m. Georgia Dixon, June 10, 1886; children—Robert Irving, Walter H., Mrs. Esther Powell, Mrs. Katharine Phelps. With San Jose Fruit Packing Co., 1884-90; mgr. Sacramento Packing Co., 1890-99; v.p., gen. mgr. Calif. Fruit Canners' Assn., 1899-1916; v.p. and gen. mgr. Calif. Packing Corp., 1916-20, pres. 1920, now chmn. bd.; also chmn. bd. Alaska Packers' Assn.; pres. San Francisco Opera Assn. Republican. Home: San Francisco, Calif. Died Feb. 22, 1932.

BENTLEY, William Frederick; b. Lenox, O., Sept. 12, 1859; s. Cyrus Augustus and Harriett (Prentice) B.; Geneva (O.) Normal Sch.; grad. Oberlin Conservatory of Music, 1883, Mus.B., 1906; Königliches Conservatorium der Musik, Leipzig, 1887-88; Kullak Sch. of Music, Berlin, 1888-89; studied with Enrico Delle Sedie, Paris, 1897-98; Mus.D., Knox Coll., 1909; m. Julia A. Webster, Nov. 28, 1883; 1 dau., Florence May. Began as teacher of music at New Lyme Inst., Ohio, 1883; in charge of music, Knox Coll., 1885, and since head Knox Conservatory of Music, which he has developed from its inception. Chorister Central Congl. Ch., Galesburg, 1886—; condr. choral concerts and musical festivals. Republican. Conglist. Composer songs and piano pieces. Home: Galesburg, Ill. Died Apr. 12, 1936.

BENTLEY, Wilson Alwyn, meteorologist; b. Jericho, Vt., Feb. 9, 1865; s. Thomas Edwin and Fanny Eliza (Colton) B.; ed. pub. sch. Jericho; unmarried. Taught music, 1885-86; 1882—, a student of snow crystals and other meteorol. studies; has made 5,150 photomicrographs of snow crystals, 600 of frost crystals, 200 of ice and ice crystals, hail, etc., and many hundreds of dew, clouds, raindrops, etc. Has written various monographs relating to these studies, published by U.S. Weather Bur., 1902, 1904, 1905, 1908, and articles "Snow" and "Frost" in Ency. Americana, contbns. to mags. and lectures on similar themes. Home: Jericho, Vt. Died Dec. 23, 1931.

BENTON, Angelo Ames, clergyman; b. Canea, Crete, July 3, 1837; s. Rev. George and Caroline (Spencer) B.; A.B., Trinity Coll., 1856, A.M., 1860 (S.T.D., 1888); grad. Gen. Theol. Sem., New York, 1860; m. Elizabeth H. Hall, 1863. Deacon, 1860, priest, 1863, P.E. Ch.; rector Scotland Neck, N.C., 1860-61, Wilson, N.C., 1861-63, Rockfish, N.C., 1863-65, Wilson, N.C., 1865-72, Edenton, N.C., 1872-78, Rockfish, 1878-83; prof. Latin and Greek, Del. Coll., Newark, Del., 1883-87; prof. dogmatic theology, U. of the South, 1887-94; rector Albion, Ill., 1895. Author: The Church Cyclopædia, 1884; Vergil, Bingham series, 1887; The Tome of St. Leo, 1890. Deceased.

BENTON, Arthur B., architect; b. Peoria, Ill., Apr. 1858; s. Ira Eddy and Caroline Augusta (Chandler) B.; grad. Peoria High Sch., 1877, student Sch. of Art and Design, Topeka, Kan., 1888-90; m. Phillipina Harriet Von Schilling, May 1883; 1 dau., Edith May. Practiced, Los Angeles, Calif., 1891—; architect: Glenwood Mission Inn, Riverside; Hotel Arlington, Santa Barbara; Mary Andrews Clark Memorial, Y.M.C.A. and Y.W.C.A. bldgs., Los Angeles; etc. Fellow A.I.A. Republican. Episcopalian. Mem. bd. govs. Los Angeles County Museum; mem. Municipal Art Commn., City of Los Angeles. Clubs: Landmarks, Old Colony. Home: Los Angeles, Calif. Died Sept. 17, 1927.

BENTON, Charles William, philologist; b. Tolland, Conn., 1852; s. William Austin and Loanza (Goulding) B.; prep. edn. Nat. Coll., Beirut, Syria, 1864-69; A.B., Yale, 1874, A.M., 1897; (Litt.D., Western U. of Pa., 1897); m. Elma C. Hixon, May 29, 1899. Prof. Romance langs., U. of Minn., 1880—. Speaks 6 and reads and writes 15 langs. Editor Easy French Plays for sch. use, 1900. Wrote Golden Ages of Literature, Dante, 1899. Home: Minneapolis, Minn. Died Nov. 11, 1913.

BENTON, George Alden, judge; b. Tolland, Conn., May 7, 1848; s. A. L. and Louise (Alden) B.; student Williams Coll., 2 yrs.; A.B., Cornell, 1871; LL.B., Columbia, 1874; m. Catharine Westerdeck, July 8, 1892. Admitted to bar, 1874, and practiced at Rochester; dist. atty., 1886-92, surrogate, 1895-1905; co. judge, 1906, Monroe Co., N.Y.; justice Supreme Ct. of N.Y., 7th Dist., for term 1907-18; retired by age, Jan. 31, 1918; apptd. official referee, Jan. 1919. Republican. Mason. Home: Spencerport, N.Y. Died Sept. 10, 1921.

BENTON, Guy Potter, univ. pres.; b. Kenton, O., May 26, 1865; s. Daniel Webster and Harriet (Wharton) B.; A.B., Baker U.; A.M., Ohio Wesleyan; also studied U. of Wooster, and in Berlin; D.D., Baker, 1900, Ohio Wesleyan U., 1905; LL.D., Upper Iowa U., 1906, U. of Vt., 1911, Middlebury Coll., 1912, U. of Miss., 1914; Miami U., 1916; L.H.D., Norwich U., 1916; m. Dollar Konantz, Sept. 4, 1889; children—Mrs. Helen Minnich, Pauline. Supt. of schs., Ft. Scott, Kan., 1890-95; asst. state supt. pub. instrn., Kan., 1895-96; prof. history and sociology, Baker U., 1896-99; pres. Upper Iowa U., 1899-1902, Miami U., 1902-11; pres. U. of Vt., 1911-19; chief ednl. consultant, pres. U. of Philippines, 1921-24; retired. With A.E.F., 1917-19; gen. sec. Y.M.C.A. for City of Paris, Sept., Oct. and Nov. 1917; chief organizing sec. for Y.M.C.A. with membership on staff of Brig. Gen. Sample, comdr. in chief of advance sect., A.E.F., Nov. 1917-June 1919; chief sec. 8th Region, A.E.F., 1919; mem. U.S. Army Ednl. Corps and chief ednl. dir. Am. Army of Occupation, with hdqrs. at Coblenz, Germany, to June 30, 1919; hon. disch. from U.S.A., July 24, 1919. Awarded D.S.M. by President of U.S. for war service, Apr. 1920. Author: The Real College, 1909. Home: Minneapolis, Minn. Died June 28, 1927.

BENTON, Joel, author; b. Amenia, N.Y., May 29, 1832; ed. Amenia Sem. Prin. of a classical and grammar school at 18; editor Amenia Times at 19; supervisor of his town and active politically. Author: Emerson as a Poet, 1882, 1899; The Truth About Protection, 1892; Greeley on Lincoln, 1893; In the Poe Circle, 1899; also much work as poet and critic, for periodicals. Home: Poughkeepsie, N.Y. Died 1911.

BENTON, John Robert, educator; b. Concord, N.H., June 6, 1876; s. Robert Agnew and Julia Rosalie (Collins) B.; B.S., Trinity Coll., Hartford, Conn., 1897, B.A., 1898; Ph.D., U. of Göttingen, Germany, 1900; m. Mabelle Williams, Aug. 23, 1914; children—Robert Tyrie, Charles Richard, Hugh Herbert, John Joseph. Prof. physics and elec. engring., 1905—, dean Coll. of Engring., 1910—, U. of Fla. Democrat. Episcopalian. Mason. Home: Gainesville, Fla. Died Jan. 8, 1930.

BENTON, Josiah Henry, lawyer; b. Addison, Vt., Aug. 4, 1843; s. Josiah Henry and Martha Ellen (Danforth) B.; ed. New London (N.H.) Lit. and Scientific Inst.; LL.B., Albany Law Sch., 1866; (hon. A.M., Dartmouth, 1869; LL.D., Norwich U., 1908); m. Josephine E. Aldrich, May 19, 1866; 2d, Mary Elizabeth Abbott, of Concord, N.H., Sept. 31, 1875. Pvt. Co. H, 12th Vt. Vols., Aug. 15, 1862-July 1863. Admitted to bar, 1866; practiced at Lancaster, N.H., 1867-73; asst. clerk and clerk N.H. Ho. of Rep., 1868-71, 1870-72; practiced law, Boston, 1873—. Dir. Northern R.R., 1879—. Lecturer on corps. and railroads, Boston U. Law Sch., 1894—. Trustee Boston Pub. Library, 1894— (now pres. bd.); trustee Boston U. Republican. Author of monographs, addresses, etc., on legal, economic and legislative subjects; also Samuel Slade Benton, His Ancestors and Descendants, 1901; A Notable Libel Suit, 1904; Early Census Making in Massachusetts, 1905; The Story of the Old Boston Town House, 1908; The Book of Common Prayer, 1910; Warning Out in New England, 1911; John Baskerville, Type Founder and Printer, 1914; Voting in the Field, 1915. Home: Boston. Died Feb. 6, 1917.

BENTON, Stephen Olin, clergyman; b. Middletown, Conn., Apr. 30, 1849; s. Rev. Josiah T. and Maria E. (Granniss) B.; ed. pub. schs. and Greenwich Acad., E. Greenwich, R.I., to 1867; (hon. A.M., 1885; D.D., 1896, Wesleyan Univ.); m. Ellen M. Taft, June 22, 1869. Entered M.E. ministry in Providence (now N.E. Southern) Conf., 1870; presiding elder Providence Dist., 1890-96, New Bedford Dist., 1901-02; recording sec. Bd. Foreign Missions, Aug. 12, 1902—. Sec. N.E. Southern Conf., 1884-1903; mem. Gen. Conf. M.E. Ch., 1888, 92, 96, 1900, 04, 08 (asst. sec., 1892-1908); sec. Gen. Book Com. M.E. Ch., 1896-1900. Home: Mount Vernon, N.Y. Died Oct. 1915.

BENYAURD, William H. H., lt. col. corps of engrs. U.S.A., July 2, 1889—; b. Philadelphia, May 17, 1841; grad. West Point, 1863; entered army, 1st lt. corps of engrs., June 11, 1863; bvtd. capt. and maj. for services in Richmond campaign and battle of Five Forks; promoted capt., May 1, 1866; maj., Mar. 4, 1879; received Congressional medal of honor for most distinguished gallantry at battle of Five Forks, Va., Apr. 1, 1864; was in many other battles; after war was asst. prof. engring., West Point, 1866-69; since then largely engaged as supt. of river and harbor improvements in all sections of the country. Died 1900.

BENZE, C(harles) Theodore, theologian; b. Warren, Pa., Sept. 19, 1865; s. Adolph Leopold and Elizabeth C. (Kiehl) B.; grad. Erie (Pa.) High Sch., 1883; Thiel Coll., Greenville, Pa., devoted spl. attention to philology; B.D., Chicago Theol. Sem., 1897; D.D., Muhlenberg Coll., 1909; m. Hermine Elizabeth Ohl, June 9, 1898; 1 son, W(infrid) Theodore. Teacher of German, Erie pub. schs., 1883-88; teacher and chief of modern language dept., Erie High School, 1888-95; ordained Luth. ministry, 1897; pastor, Beaver Falls, Pa., 1897-98, St. Stephen's Ch., Erie, Pa., 1898-1908; commr. of Gen. Council to Missions in India, 1908; pres. Thiel Coll., Pa., 1909-13; Am. prof. in divinity sch., Kropp, Germany, 1913-15; professor O. T. theology, Luth. Theol. Seminary, Philadelphia, Aug. 1915—. Pres. Pittsburgh Synod, Luth. Ch., 1908, 1909; dir., pres. Bd. Foreign Missions, United Luth. Ch., 1918-30; commr. Nat. Luth. Council, doing relief work in Russia and other countries, 1922-24; mem. com. of reference and council Gen. Conf. Foreign Missions, 1929-30; dir. Inner Mission Bd., 1930—. Author: Pilgerlieder für Schule Haus, 1891; The Confessional Principle and the Confessions of the Lutheran Church (with Theodore E. Schmauk), 1908. Regular contbr. to Luth. ch. and secular publs., especially on liturgical and mission problems. Decoration of German Red Cross awarded by President Hindenburg, 1931. Home: Philadelphia, Pa. Died July 3, 1936.

BENZENBERG, George Henry, cons. engr.; b. New York, May 31, 1847; s. Henry B. and Christina

(Rugee) B.; C.E., U. of Mich., 1867; (hon. Dr. Engring., 1912; Sc.D., U. of Wis., 1911); m. Alvina Wolfrum, Dec. 16, 1879. Asst. engr. U.S. Lake Survey, 1867-69; transitman, Ia. div. C.,M.&St.P. Ry., with Bay View Iron Works, and with M.&N. Ry., 1869-74; asst. city engr., 1874-82, city engr. and pres. Bd. of Pub. Works, 1882-99, Milwaukee; cons. engr., 1899—. Built Milwaukee's high service pumping sta., new water works tunnel and intake cribs, re-designed the city's sewer system and designed and built the Milwaukee river flushing tunnel; frequently called as cons. engr. by Chicago, Kansas City, Cleveland, New Orleans, Cincinnati, etc.; recovered and completed water works tunnel under Lake Erie at Cleveland, and completed new water supply and filter system, at Cincinnati; retired. Trustee Northwestern Mut. Life Ins. Co. of Milwaukee. Republican. Mason. Home: Milwaukee, Wis. Died May 31, 1925.

BERG, Charles I., architect; b. Phila., Feb. 1856; s. Leon and Mary (Marion) B.; A.B., Central High Sch., Phila., 1873; studied, École des Beaux Arts. Paris, 1877-79; architects' offices, London, Eng.; m. Ada Van Beil, June 1886; 1 child, Hunter Van B. Erected ambulance sta. and vaccine labs. for Health Dept., New York; the Gillender Bldg., 1897, one of first "skyscrapers," on lot 25x73 ft.; also Hotel Touraine, Windsor Arcade, etc.; cons. architect, Presdl. Palace, Havana, Cuba. Fellow A.I.A. (sec. N.Y. Chapter 3 yrs.). Home: New York, N.Y. Died Oct. 13, 1926.

BERG, Ernst Julius, electrical engr.; b. Ostersund, Sweden, Jan. 9, 1871; s. Ernst Victor Gabriel and Josefina (Hamren) B.; M.E., Royal Polytecknicum, Stockholm, 1892; (Sc.D., Union U., 1910); came to U.S., 1892; m. Gwendoline O'Brien, June 15, 1904 (died June 4, 1937). Engaged as electrical engr., 1892-1904, cons. engr., 1904-09, General Electric Co., Schenectady; prof. elec. engring., U. of Ill., 1910-13; prof. elec. engring., Union U., 1913—, dean of engring., 1932—; consulting prof. elec. engring., Union Univ., 1907-09. Author: Electrical Energy, 1908; First Course in Electrical Engineering (with W. L. Upson), 1916; Advanced Course in Electrical Engineering, 1916; Heavisides Operational Calculus, 1929. Home: Schenectady, N.Y. Died Sept. 9, 1941.

BERG, George Olaf, college prof.; b. Sacred Heart, Minn., Feb. 13, 1875; s. Hans Gudbrandson and Marit (Stavne) B.; A.B., St. Olaf Coll., 1899; Ph.D., Johns Hopkins, 1903; studied U. of Berlin and U. of Chicago; unmarried. Began as instr. in Greek, St. Olaf Coll., 1899; prof. Greek, Wittenberg Coll., Springfield, O., 1906-10; prof. Greek, St. Olaf Coll., 1910—, registrar, 1915—. Lutheran. Home: Northfield, Minn. Died Mar. 15, 1935.

BERG, Irving Husted, educator; b. Rocky Hill, N.J., Mar. 8, 1878; s. Herman C. (D.D.) and Estelle (Campbell) B.; prep. edn., Flushing (N.Y.) Inst., 1888-89, Erasmus Hall Acad., Flatbush, N.Y., 1895, Ellenville (N.Y.) Union Sch., 1896-98; A.B., Lafayette Coll., Easton, Pa., 1901, D.D., 1916; B.D., Hartford Theol. Sem., 1904; m. Bessie Humphrey Arthur, Oct. 25, 1904; children—Arthur Campbell, Frederick Vanderveer (dec.). Ordained ministry Ref. Ch., 1904; stated supply, South Congl. Ch., Granby, Conn., 1902-04; pastor North Ref. Ch., Watervliet, N.Y., 1904-06, 1st Ref. Ch., Catskill, N.Y., 1906-12, South Congl. Ch., Hartford, Conn., 1912-17, Fort Washington Collegiate Ref. Ch., 1917-36; dean Univ. Coll., New York Univ., 1936—; chaplain New York U., 1919. Chaplain 1st Conn. Inf., 1915-17, Mexican border, 1916. Trustee Bd. Domestic Missions, Ref. Ch. in America, 1917-36; trustee Hartford Sem. Foundation, Japanese Christian Assn. (hon. pres.); pres. Gen. Alumni Assn. of Lafayette Coll., 1932-33, also trustee of coll.; mem. council (bd. of trustees) New York Univ., 1931-36; pres. bd. of supts. New Brunswick Theol. Seminary, 1933. Fellow Am. Geog. Society. Home: New Rochelle, N.Y. Died Aug. 29, 1941.

BERG, Walter Gilman, civil engr.; b. New York, Jan. 12, 1858; s. Albert W. and Helen M. (Morse) B.; brother of Louis DeCoppet Bergh; ed. pvt. tutors New York and pub. schs. Stuttgart, Germany; grad. civ. engring., Royal Poly. Inst., Stuttgart, 1878; m. Ruby, d. Samuel and Alice (Moncure) Burke, of Va., Feb. 28, 1893. Engaged, 1878— as bridge engr., and engr. in charge Richmond & Allegheny R.R., prin. asst. engr.; E. Tenn., Va. & Ga. R.R., asst. engr., prin. asst. engr., engr. maintenance of way and now chief engr. Lehigh Valley R.R. Author: Buildings and Structures of American Railroads, 1892; American Railway Bridges and Buildings, 1898; Strength of Timber, 1899; American Railway Shop Systems, 1904. Home: New York, N.Y. Died 1908.

BERG, William Henry, pres. Standard Oil Co. of Calif.; b. Tripoli, Ia., Apr. 8, 1882; s. Jacob and Amelia (Schultz) B.; ed. grade schs., Tripoli, and Highland Park Coll., Des Moines, Ia.; m. Irene L. Stayleigh, Aug. 7, 1915. With Standard Oil Co. of Calif., 1902; succesively stenographer, oil scout, chief clk.; gen. supt., asst. mgr. and mgr. land and leases, Producing Dept.; gen. mgr. Fgn. Producing Dept.; dir., 1924—; v.p., 1927-37; pres., 1937. Dir. Anglo Calif. Nat. Bank (San Francisco), Am. Petroleum Institute. Home: Burlingame, Calif. Died June 26, 1940.

BERGE, Edward, sculptor; b. Baltimore, Jan. 3, 1876; s. Henry and Mary Ann (France) B.; ed. Polytechnic Sch., Md. Inst., Charcoal Club Art Sch., Baltimore; Julian Acad., Paris, France; m. Lillian Y. Stephens, July 27, 1907. Awarded bronze medal, Buffalo Expn., 1901; bronze medal, and gold medal, St. Louis Expn., 1904; bronze medal, Santiago Expn., S.A.; Panama-Pacific Internat. Expn., 1915. Prin. works: Watson Monument, Baltimore; "Pieta," St. Patrick's Ch., Washington; Tattersall Monument, Baltimore; "The Scalp," Museum, Honolulu; Gist Memorial, Charleston, S.C. Home: Baltimore, Md. Died Oct. 12, 1924.

BERGÉ, Irénée, composer, director; b. Paris, France, Feb. 1, 1870; s. Paul and Pierrette (Artigues) B.; conservatories Toulouse and Paris; pupil of Dubois and Massenet; first prize piano, harmony, composition; Grand Prix d'honneur presented by the ministre des Beaux-Arts, Paris; m. Jeanne A. Perriére, Dec. 29, 1898. Came to America, 1902; condr. with Fred Whitney and Henry W. Savage, 1909. Author: Premiere Leçon (comic opera); Notre Dame des Fleurs (lyric drama); Le Roi de Carton (comic opera); Gardeval (conte lyrique); Corsica (lyric drama); Knave of Hearts (comic opera); Nicolette (comic opera). Died July 30, 1926.

BERGEN, James J., judge; b. Somerville, N.J., Oct. 1, 1847; s. John J. and Mary A. (Park) B.; ed. pub. schs. and sem., Somerville; studied law with Hugh M. Gaston; admitted to bar, 1868, and practiced at Somerville; m. Helen Arden Huggins, May 3, 1883. Mem. N.J. Ho. of Rep., 1876, 77, 91, 92 (speaker 1891, 92); prosecutor of pleas, Somerset Co., N.J., 1877-83; del. Dem. Nat. Conv., 1896; vice-chancellor of N.J., 1904-07; asso. justice Supreme Ct. of N.J. for terms 1907-14, 1914-21. Democrat. Home: Somerville, N.J. Died Oct. 20, 1923.

BERGEN, Tunis G., lawyer; b. Brooklyn, N.Y., May 17, 1847, in Bergen homestead, where 7 generations of family had lived, since 1646, in same house; s. Garret G. and Mary (Hubbard) B.; ed. Brooklyn Poly. Inst.; A.B., Rutgers, 1868; degree Dr. of Pub. Law, Heidelberg U., Germany, 1872; studied law and history, univs. of Berlin and Paris; LL.B., Columbia, 1874; m. Caroline McPhail, Jan. 26, 1881. Pres. for many yrs., Bogota City Ry. Co. (Colombia), Chapinero Ry. Co.; pres. College Heights Land Co., Niagara Falls, N.Y., and officer or counsel many corps. Was present as guest at hdqrs. crown prince of Prussia (Frederick) in Franco-Prussian War, 1870, and on many battlefields; holds flag of French Imperial Cuirrassiers he captured. Rep. and Independent Dem. candidate for N.Y. Ho. of Rep., 1875; pres. Brooklyn Bd. of Edn., 6 yrs., 1885-91; commr. of charities, N.Y. state, 1895-1900. Trustee Rutgers Coll.; pres. of trustees Brooklyn Heights Sem.; dir. L.I. Hist. Soc. Envoy of Hudson Celebration to Holland, 1907 and 1908, and secured bldg. of ship Half-Moon. Republican. Home: New York, N.Y. Died Mar. 13, 1929.

BERGEN, Van Brunt, civil engr.; b. Brooklyn, Apr. 29, 1841; s. Tennis G. and Elizabeth (Van Brunt) B.; ed. Brooklyn Collegiate and Poly. Inst.; C.E., Rensselaer Poly. Inst., 1863; m. Elizabeth Vanderveer, Aug. 3, 1871. Employed on Brooklyn water works and in dept. city works, Brooklyn, 1864-96, being chief engr. the last 2 yrs. Home: Brooklyn, N.Y. Died Apr. 27, 1917.

BERGER, Calvin Michael, insurance; b. Bethel, Pa., Aug. 25, 1870; s. John Adam and Cecilia (Batdorff) B.; student Cornell U., Ohio State U.; m. Laura Atkinson, July 3, 1900; children—John Calvin, Patricia (Mrs. H. W. Kelley). With Berger Mfg. Co., Canton, 1893-1902; with London Guarantee and Accident Co. Ltd., 1902—, U.S. mgr., 1923—; dir. United Firemen's Ins. Co. of Phila. Mem. Trinity Ref. Ch. Mason. Home: Flushing, L.I., N.Y. Died July 1929.

BERGER, George Bart, banker; b. New Castle, Pa., May 2, 1869; s. William B. and Margaret (Kountze) B.; Ph.B., Sheffield Scientific Sch. (Yale), 1888; m. Carry A. Merriam, Apr. 5, 1899. In banking business in Denver, 1889—; became pres. Colo. Nat. Bank, 1911, then chmn. bd. Republican. Episcopalian. Home: Denver, Colo. Died Aug. 22, 1939.

BERGER, Victor L., congressman; b. Nieder Rehbach, Austria-Hungary, Feb. 28, 1860; came with family to U.S., 1878; m. Meta Schlichting, Dec. 4, 1897; 2 children—Dr. Doris B. Welles and Dr. Elsa B. Edelman. Editor Milwaukee Daily Vorwaerts, 1892-98, later of Wahrheit, and of Social Democratic Herald, 1900; editor Milwaukee Leader, a Socialist daily, 1911—. A pioneer organizer of socialist; del. People's Party Conv., St. Louis, 1896, and tried to organize the Debs sentiment in that conv.; mem. Nat. Exec. Bd. Socialist Party from organization, 1898, until 1923. Social Dem. candidate for mayor of Milwaukee, and for Congress, 1904; received 5 votes in legislature for U.S. senator, 1904; elected alderman at large, 1910; mem. 62d Congress (1911-13), 5th Wis. Dist. (1st Socialist ever elected to Congress); again elected to Congress, Nov. 1918, but excluded from membership, Nov. 10, 1919, by vote of 309 to 1, on ground of disloyalty to U.S. and giving aid and comfort to the enemy in time of war —having previously been indicted in various places, and sentenced to prison for 20 yrs. by Judge Landis of the Federal Court in Chicago; reëlected to Congress, No. 1919, with an increased majority, but again refused admission; once more reëlected with a much increased majority and finally seated without a dissenting vote, Dec. 3, 1923—the Supreme Court of the U.S. having in 1921 reversed the Landis decision and the Govt. in 1922 having withdrawn all other cases against him; reëlected to 69th and 70th Congresses (1925-29); del. Am. Socialist Party to Internat. Socialist Congress, Marseilles, France, 1925; chmn. Nat. Exec. Com. Am. Socialist Party, Oct. 1927—. Writer many essays and pamphlets on social questions. Home: Milwaukee, Wis. Died Aug. 7, 1929.

BERGER, Vilhelm, author; b. Värmland, Sweden, Oct. 17, 1867; s. Anders Alexander and Marie Charlotte (Löwenhielm) B.; came to America, 1896; ed. High Sch., Sweden; M.A., Upsala Coll., Kenilworth, N.J., 1917; m. Bertha Anderson, Apr. 4, 1906. Traveling agt. for Swedish-Am. publs., 1897-1903; editor Nordstjernan (semi-weekly), New York, 1903-13; office mgr. and dir. Swedish Luth. Immigrant Home, New York, June 17, 1913-July 1, 1915; editor Nordstjernan (semi-weekly), New York, 1915-36, then retired; gen. rep. Swedish Tour. Soc., 1922-29; hon. mem. bd. dirs. Swedish Augustana Home for the Aged, Brooklyn. Author: Rätt och Slätt, 1902; Hvardagshändelser, 1903; Emigrant-Oden, 1904, Hundär och Lyckodagar, 1905; Ungdomskärlek, 1908; Vårt Språk, 1912; Vår Kyrka, 1912; Pytt i Panna, 1912; Svensk-Amerikanska meditationer (Swedish- American Meditations), 1916; Svensk Sång i New York, 1929; Augustanasynodens församlingar i New York, 1931. Knight Royal Order of Vasa, 1st Class (Sweden), 1928; Swedish Tourist Soc. silver medal, 1930. Lutheran. Home: Brooklyn, N.Y. Deceased.

BERGEY, David Hendricks, bacteriologist; b. Montgomery Co., Pa., Dec. 27, 1860; s. G. R. and Susan (Hendricks) B.; M.D., B.S., U. of Pa., 1884; A.M., Ill. Wesleyan, 1894; Dr. of Pub. Hygiene, U. of Pa., 1916; m. Annie S. Hallman, June 5, 1884. First asst. Lab. of Hygiene, U. of Pa., 1896—, asst. prof. bacteriology, 1903-16, and asst. prof. of hygiene and bacteriology, 1916-26, prof. of hygiene and bacteriology, 1926-31, acting prof. hygiene, 1931-32; also dir. Laboratory of Hygiene, 1928-31. Dir. research in biology, Nat. Drug Co., 1931—. Commd. capt. Med. R.C., U.S.A., Apr. 1917; maj. May 1918. At training camp, Ft. Oglethorpe, Ga., Aug. 4, 1917; placed in charge of clin. lab. Gen. Hosp. No. 14, Ft. Oglethorpe, Ga., Aug. 19, 1917; transferred to Gen. Hosp. No. 22, Richmond Coll., Va., Nov. 1918; discharged from service, Jan. 1919. Author: Handbook of Practical Hygiene, 1899; The Principles of Hygiene, 1901, 7th edit., 1921; also chapter on domestic hygiene in Pyle's Personal Hygiene, 1904. Home: Philadelphia, Pa. Died Sept. 5, 1937.

BERGH, Louis De Coppet, architect, civ. engr.; b. New York, Dec. 20, 1856; s. Albert W. and Helen M. (Morse) Berg; brother of Walter Gilman Berg; early edn. New York pub. sch.; studied 8 yrs. in Europe at Mil. Gymnasium, Ostrowo, Prussia; Moravian Inst., Lausanne, Switzerland; Royal Real-Schule and later in Royal Poly., Stuttgart; m. Ivah de Chipenham, d. George Richardson, of New York, June 19, 1904. Was expert architectural and sanitary adviser to Mayor Strong's com.; has been architect for numerous pub. and pvt. bldgs., New York and elsewhere. Fellow Am. Inst. Architects. Veteran 13th Regt. Heavy Arty., N.G.S.N.Y. Mason. Author: Safe Building (2 vols.); Safe Building Construction, 1908. Home: Montclair Heights, N.J. Died Jan. 28, 1913.

BERGQUIST J(ohn) Victor, organist, dir.; b. St. Peter, Minn., May 18, 1877; s. Charles Frederick and Emma (Appelquist) B.; Gustavus Adolphus Coll., St. Peter, Minn., 1892-95, Mus.D., 1932, studied piano with Gustavus Johnson, 4 years; pupil of Grunicke, Berger, and Scharwenka, Berlin, and Guilmant, Paris; m. Emelia Elvira Johnson, June 7, 1905; children—Carl Elvir, Helen Aline, Muriel Jeanette, Donald Restor. Organist Luth. Ch., Bernadotte, Minn., 1895, Augustana Luth. Ch., Minneapolis, 1896-1900, 1903-12; dir. of music, Augustana Coll., Rock Island, Ill., 1912-18; supervisor self expression in music, high schs. of Minneapolis, 1918—; organist Central Luth. Ch., Minneapolis, 1922-29; with MacPhail Sch. of Music, 1918—; guest teacher summer session Northwestern U., 1926—. Republican. Composer: (oratorio) Golgotha (prod. Apr. 6, 1906 by Minneapolis Symphony Orchestra and chorus of 250 voices); Reformation Cantata (prod. Rock Island June 16, 1917 by Tri-City Symphony Orchestra and chorus of 400); Julkantat (Christmas cantata); Körsanger for Gudstjänsten (anthems); From the Nursery (awarded internat. prize in piano composition); Lone Eagle (cantata for boys' voices); The Psalter in Song; also 5 organ sonatas, 2 piano suites, etc. Home: Minneapolis, Minn. Died Feb. 28, 1935.

BERGTOLD, William Harry, M.D.; b. Buffalo, N.Y., Oct. 28, 1865; s. Jacob Edward and Louisa (Hoffer) B.; M.D., U. of Buffalo, 1886; post-grad. student, Columbia, 1888; (hon. M.Sc., Hobart, 1891); m. Adele D. Smith, June 20, 1898; children—Adele (dec.), Mrs. Louise Harriet Woolfenden. Began med. practice at Buffalo, 1886; removed to Denver, Colo., 1894; asst. instr. histology, Coll. Phys. and Surg. (Columbia), 1888; prof. pathology, U. of Buffalo, 1893-94, U. of Denver, 1897-1900. Capt. asst. surgeon 74th Regt., N.G.N.Y., 1890-1904, inclusive; commd. maj. Med. Corps, U.S.A., Sept. 13, 1918; chief of med. service U.S. Gen. Hosp. No. 21, Denver, Sept. 13, 1918-June 17, 1919; was col. O.R.C. Author: A Study of the Incubation Periods of Birds, 1917; A Guide to the Birds of Colorado, 1928. Home: Denver, Colo. Died Mar. 1936.

BERINGER, George M., pharmacist, chemist; b. Phila., Pa., Feb. 3, 1860; s. Levi D. and Rebecca (Reinhart) B.; A.B., A.M., Central High Sch., Phila., 1876; A.M., Ph.G., Phila. Coll. Pharmacy, 1880, Ph.M., 1903; Pharm.D., Univ. State of N.J., 1914; m. Estella F. Wolfe, Oct. 3, 1882; children—George M., Franklin L. (dec.). Practiced as pharmacist, Phila., until 1892; removed to Camden, N.J., 1892; frequently called as expert in state and federal courts; editor Am. Jour. Pharmacy, 1917-21. Chmn. trustees Phila. Coll. Pharmacy, 1910-21; mem. com. of revision U.S. Pharmacopœia, also com. revision Nat. Formulary. Mem. Camden City Plan Commn. Author of numerous brochures, and contbr. articles to pharm. jours. Home: Camden, N.J. Died June 23, 1928.

BERKELEY, William Nathaniel, M.D.; b. Chestertown, Md., Nov. 8, 1868; s. Robert Carter and Fanny Campbell (Minor) B.; A.B., W.Va. U., 1886; Ph.B., U. of Va., 1888, M.D., 1891; post-grad. study U. of Vienna, 1891-92; M.D., Bellevue Hosp. Med. Coll., 1896; m. Clara Helene Barker, 1908; children—Edmund C., Ella K. Began practice at Great Falls, Mont., 1892; moved to New York, 1895; attending physician, Good Samaritan Dispensary, 1896-1922; Dir. Lab. of Exptl. Medicine, Cornell U., 1917-18. Democrat. Author: Principles and Practice of Endocrine Medicine, 1926. Contbr. to Boston Med. and Surg. Jour., N.Y. Med. Jour. and Record, Am. Medicine, etc. Research in parathyroid gland, pineal gland and pancreas. Home: New York, N.Y. Deceased.

BERKLEY, Henry Johns, M.D.; b. Baltimore, July 17, 1860; s. Edris and Virginia (Enders) B.; M.D., U. of Md., 1881 (D.Sc., 1907); post-grad. U. of Vienna, 1884-85; m. Ella Linthicum, July 13, 1886; 1 dau., Margaret H. S.; m. 2d, Mary Miles Jordan. Practicing physician in Baltimore, 1889—; prof. psychiatry, Johns Hopkins U. Home: Baltimore, Md. Deceased.

BERKOWITZ, Henry, rabbi; b. Pittsburgh, Pa., Mar. 18, 1857; s. Louis and Henrietta (Jaroslawski) B.; student Cornell U., 1872-73; studied law in office of Brown & Lambie, Pittsburgh, 1874-77; B.Litt., Cincinnati U., 1881; rabbi, Hebrew Union Coll., Cincinnati, 1883 (D.D., 1887); m. Flora Brunn, of Fraustadt, Germany, Oct. 28, 1883. Rabbi, Shaara-Shamayim Congregation, Mobile, Ala., 1883-88, B'nai Jehuda Congregation, Kansas City, Mo., 1888-92, Rodeph Shalom Congregation, Phila., 1892-1921 (emeritus). Mem. bd. govs. Hebrew Union Coll., 1884—; mem. publ. com. Jewish Publ. Soc. America; a founder and 1st sec. Central Conf. Am. Rabbis; instituted humane movement in Mobile for protection of children and animals; organized 1st bur. of charities in Kansas City; founder, 1893, and chancellor of the Jewish Chautauqua Soc.; instituted corr. schs. for study of Jewish subjects, etc. Apptd., 1912, mem. Vice Commn. by mayor of Phila. to make official visit to leading countries of Europe. Vice-pres. Universal Peace Union. Author: Bible Ethics, 1883; First and Second Union Hebrew Readers, 1883; Judaism and the Social Question, 1887; The Pulpit Message, 1892; The Open Bible, 1895; Sabbath Sentiment in the Home, 1898; The New Education in Religion (2 vols.), 1913; Intimate Glimpses of the Rabbi's Career, 1919. Home: Atlantic City, N.J. Died Feb. 7, 1924.

BERLIN, Alfred Franklin, archæologist; b. Cherryville, Pa., Jan. 12, 1848; academic edn. at Easton, Pa.; m. Mary Ella Reed, June 6, 1871. Devotes himself to archæol. research; clerk of Ct. of Common Pleas, Lehigh Co., Pa., 3 yrs. Corr. mem. Anthropol. Soc. Washington, Univ. Archæological Assn. U. of Pa.; hon. mem. Royal Italian Didactic Soc., Rome; charter mem. Lehigh Co. Hist. Soc.; corr. mem. Wyo. Hist. and Geol. Soc.; hon. mem. Hist. Soc. Ala. Author of Sect. VI, The East Allegheny Section in Prehistoric Implements; Chapter III, The Lenni-Lenapé and Their Implements, in History of Lehigh Co., Pa.; Notes on American Antiquities in the A. F. Berlin Collection, Vol. XVI, Trans. Wyoming Hist. and Geol. Soc., The German Immigrant in Pennsylvania before and during the Revolution. Home: Allentown, Pa. Died Oct. 2, 1925.

BERLINER, Emile, inventor; b. Hanover, Germany, May 20, 1851; s. Samuel and Sarah (Friedman) B.; grad. Samson Sch., Wolfenbuttel, 1865; came to the U.S. in 1870; m. Cora Adler, 1881. Invented loose contact telephone transmitter or microphone, 1877; discovered that a loose contact will act as a telephone receiver (Apr. 1877), and was first to use an induction coil in connection with transmitters (pat. Jan. 1878); patentee of other valuable inventions in telephony; invented, 1887, the Gramophone, the first talking machine which utilizes a groove of even depth and varying direction, and in which the record groove not only vibrates but also propels the stylus across the record (known also as the Victor Talking Machine), for which he was awarded John Scott Medal and Elliot Cresson Gold Medal by Franklin Inst., Phila.; also invented and perfected the present method of duplicating disc records; invented, 1925, the acoustic tile and acoustic cells for insuring good acoustics in halls, etc. Ednl. campaign against dangers of raw milk and other dairy products, 1901—. Author and co-author of pamphlets dealing with the prevention of sickness. Planned and was mem. Washington Milk Conf., 1907. First to have made and used in aeronautical experiments light weight revolving cylinder internal combustion motor, now extensively used on aeroplanes (1908). Under his general directions his son, Henry A., designed first successful helicopter, rising and sustaining himself in it, Nov. 1919. Pres. D.C. Tuberculosis Assn., 1915-21. Author: Health Rhymes. Home: Washington, D.C. Died Aug. 3, 1929.

BERN, Paul, motion picture writer and dir.; b. Wandsbeck, Germany, Dec. 3, 1889; s. Julius Levy and Henrietta (Hirsch) L.; brought to U.S., 1898; ed. pub. schs. N.Y. City and Am. Acad. Dramatic Arts. Stage mgr. and dir. theatrical productions, 1911-15; Metro-Goldwyn-Mayer executive, 1926-27; Pathé producer, 1928; Metro-Goldwyn-Mayer associate producer, 1929. Mem. Authors' League America. Lectured at Columbia, Cornell, etc. Wrote screen versions of Marriage Circle; The Christian; Name the Man; The Beloved Rogue; The Dove, etc.; dir. Open All Night; The Dressmaker from Paris; The Flower of Night. Home: Beverly Hills, Calif. Died 1932.

BERNADOU, John Baptiste, naval officer; b. Phila., Nov. 14, 1858; s. George W. and Helen (Hay) B.; apptd. to U.S. Naval Acad. by the President, at large, 1876, grad. 1882. Promoted to midshipman, June 22, 1882; ensign, jr. grade, Mar. 3, 1883; ensign, June 26, 1884; lt., jr. grade, July 1, 1892; lt., June 21, 1896; lt. comdr., Feb. 9, 1902; comdr., Dec. 11, 1906. Served in Bureau of Navigation, 1882; spl. duty Smithsonian Instn., 1882-83; spl. duty in Korea, under Smithsonian Instn., 1883-84; various assignments to 1897; comd. Winslow during Spanish War, 1898; was advanced ten numbers in rank for eminent and conspicuous conduct in battle during Spanish War; served in Bureau of Ordnance, Navy Dept., 1898-99, Indiana, 1899-1900, Kentucky, 1900, Dixie, 1900-02; office of naval intelligence, 1902-04; exec. officer Kearsarge, 1904-06; Naval War Coll., 1906; naval attaché, Am. Embassy, Rome and Vienna, Dec. 1906—. Author: A Trip Through Northern Korea in 1883-84; Pyro-Collodion Smokeless Powder; Smokeless Powder, Nitro-Cellulose, and Theory of the Cellulose Molecule, 1901 W9. Translated (from the Russian, by Vice Admiral Makaroff) Questions in Naval Tactics, 1898. Home: Winslow, N.J. Died 1908.

BERNARD, Sam (Barnett), actor; b. Birmingham, Eng., June 16, 1863. Début at Henderson's Music Hall, Coney Island, N.Y.; highly successful in German character parts in musical comedy; appeared as Hermann Engel in "The Marquis of Michigan," at Bijou Theatre, New York, 1898; played Herman Scholz, in "The Girl and the Wizard," at The Casino, New York, 1909, Herman von Schellenvien, in "He Came from Milwaukee," 1910; went to London, Eng., with "The Belle of Bond Street," and later toured in U.S. with same; later playing in vaudeville and with Ziegfeld Follies. Home: New York, N.Y. Died May 18, 1927.

BERNAYS, Augustus Charles, M.D.; b. Highland, Ill., Oct. 13, 1854; grad. McKendree Coll., 1872; M.D., Heidelberg, Germany, 1876; mem. Royal Coll. of Surgeons, London, Nov. 27, 1877; settled in practice at St. Louis, 1878; inventor of improved methods in operative surgery; noted as a teacher of anatomy and surg. pathology and did much in introducing antiseptic method of surgery in the U.S. Unmarried. Author: Chips from a Surgeon's Workshop, 1880; Development of Valves of Heart, 1876 F5; Development of Joints in General and of the Human Knee Joint, 1877 F5. Home: St. Louis. Died 1907.

BERNEKER, Louis Frederick, artist; b. Clinton, Mo., Aug. 28, 1876; s. Charles and Rosallie Wilhelmina (Guenther) B.; art edn., St. Louis Sch. Fine Arts, 1892-96; Julian Acad., Paris, 1903-04; m. Maud Marie Fox, Jan. 17, 1900. Free lance illustrator, later painter of murals; head of art dept., Mechanics Inst., N.Y. City, 1909—. Murals in Jr. High Sch., Bronx, N.Y., Belmont Theatre, N.Y. City, Erlanger Theatre, Philadelphia, Chicago Theatre, Dallas (Tex.) Mus. A.N.A., 1931. Catholic. Home and Studio: New York, N.Y. Deceased.

BERNET, John J., ry. official; b. Brant, Erie Co., N.Y., Feb. 9, 1868; ed. pub. schs.; married; children—Anna May (Mrs. W. D. Callaghan), William G., Helen F., Bernard F., Maurice J. Telegraph operator, 1889-95, train dispatcher, 1895-1901, trainmaster, 1901-03, asst. supt., 1903-05, div. supt., 1905, asst. gen. supt. and gen. supt., 1905-11, all L.S.&M.S. Ry.; asst. to v.p. N.Y.C. Lines West of Buffalo, at Chicago, 1911-12; v.p. L.S.&M.S. Ry., 1912-16; pres. N.Y.,C.&St.L. R.R. (Nickel Plate), 1916-26; pres. Erie R.R., 1927-29; now pres. C.&O. Ry., N.Y.C.&St.L. R.R. (Nickel Plate) and Pere Marquette Ry. cos. Home: Cleveland, O. Died July 5, 1935.

BERNHARDT, Sarah, actress; b. Paris, Oct. 22, 1845; ed. Grandchamp Catholic Convent nr. Paris; received prize of the Conservatory of Paris, 1862; widow of M. Jacques Damala. Entered the Comédie Française; left it and went to the Odéon, but returned to Comédie Française, 1872-80; made numerous tours of America and Europe, then returned to Paris to the Théâtre de la Porte St. Martin until becoming, 1893-98, mgr. Théâtre de la Renaissance; established, 1898, and ever since mgr., Théâtre Sarah Bernhardt. Has created and appeared in many leading tragic rôles. Also sculptor of many busts, groups, marbles, bronzes (silver medal, Paris Expn., 1900) and painter of tableaux, some of which were awarded prizes at Paris Salon. Writer of several books and plays. Awarded Grand Cross of Legion of Honor, 1914. Home: Paris, France. Died Mar. 26, 1923.

BERNHARDT, Wilhelm, educator, author; b. Halle a. S., Thuringia; grad. Univ. of Leipzig, 1875, Ph.D., 1877; unmarried. Soldier in Franco-German war, 1870-71; came to U.S., 1881; prof. of German, Latin and Greek in Summer Sch. of Languages, Burlington, Vt., Amherst, Mass., and Oswego, N.Y.; dir. of German in high schs., Washington, 1882-96. Author: German Grammar and Reader (2 vols.), 1884-86; History of German Literature, 1892; German Composition, 1898. Editor numerous works of German masters. Died 1909.

BERNSTEIN, Herman, author, diplomat; b. Neustadt-Scherwindt, the Russo-German frontier, Russia, Sept. 21, 1876; s. David and Maria (Elsohn) B.; with his parents at Mohilev on the Dnieper, Russia, 1886-93; came to U.S., 1893; m. Sophie Friedman, Jan. 1, 1902; children—Hilda, Dorothy, Violet, David. Went as spl. corr. of the New York Times to European countries, 1908, 09, 11, 12; visited Count Leo Tolstoy in Yasnaya Polyana, and interviewed some of the most prominent persons in Europe. Founder and editor The Day (nat. Jewish daily), 1914-16; editor-in-chief American Hebrew, 1916-19. Visited Europe, 1915, to study condition of the Jews in war-stricken countries; went to Russia, 1917, as spl. corr. New York Herald, to describe the revolution; published the "Willy-Nicky" telegrams, the secret correspondence bet. the Kaiser and the Tsar which attracted universal attention; visited Russia under bolshevist rule, spring, 1918; war corr. of New York Herald in Siberia, with A.E.F., and to the Czecho-Slovak front in Ural Mountains; rep. Herald at the Peace Conf., Paris, 1919, and made spl. investigation of the pogroms in Poland; E.E. and M.P. to Albania, Feb. 1930-Sept. 1933; while there negotiated naturalization treaty between U.S. and Albania, signed, Jan. 21, 1931, also negotiated extradition treaty, signed, Mar. 1, 1932. Author: The Flight of Time (poems), 1899; In the Gates of Israel, 1902; Contrite Hearts, 1905; With Master Minds (interviews), 1912; The Willy-Nicky Correspondence (with foreword by the late Theodore Roosevelt), 1918; Celebrities of Our Time (interviews), 1925; The Road to Peace (interviews), 1926; Herbert Hoover, the Man Who Brought America to the World, a study, 1928. As spl. corr. New York American to describe the new states created by the Peace Treaty of Versailles; exposed the so-called "Protocols of the Wise Men of Zion" as a literary forgery, in a volume entitled "The History of a Lie." Died Aug. 21, 1935.

BERNSTEIN, Louis, clergyman; b. New Albany, Ind., Nov. 15, 1882; s. Jacob and Bertha (Cohen) B.; grad. Walnut Hills High Sch., Cincinnati, O., 1901; A.B., U. of Cincinnati, 1905; rabbi, Hebrew Union Coll., Cincinnati, 1906; m. Fannie Steiner, June 4, 1917. Rabbi, Temple Adath Joseph, St. Joseph, Mo., 1906-20; Har Sinai Congregation, Baltimore, Oct. 1, 1920—. Mem. St. Joseph Charity Bd., 1906-08; mem. Mo. State Bd. Charities and Corrections, 1910-12 (resigned); mem. exec. com. Nat. Conf. Social Work, 1914-16; pres. Mo. Conf. Social Welfare, 1916-17, St. Joseph Council Boy Scouts, 1917; v.p. St. Joseph Free Pub. Library; hon. v.p. Mo. Peace Soc.; dir. St. Joseph Chapter Am. Red Cross, 1917-20; exec. com. Mo. Tuberculosis Assn., 1919-20; co. chmn. Four Minute Men, 1918-19. Mem. Central Conf. Am. Rabbis, B'nai B'rith. Dir. Jewish Ednl. Alliance, Baltimore. Mem. exec. com. Hebrew Union Coll. Alumni Assn. Mason. Home: Baltimore, Md. Died Oct. 31, 1922.

BERNSTORFF, Count Johann, diplomat; b. London, Eng., Nov. 14, 1862; s. Count Albrecht and Anna (Baroness Anna Koenneritz) B.; ed. Gymnasium, Dresden, and Ratzeburg; (LL.D., Columbia, 1909, Brown U., Johns Hopkins, U. of Wis., and

Union U., 1910, U. of Pa., and U. of Chicago, 1911, U. of Pittsburgh, and Franklin and Marshall, 1912, Princeton, 1913); m. Jeanne Luckemeyer, of New York, Nov. 14, 1887. Officer 1st Regt. Arty. Guards, Berlin, 1881-89; attaché, German Embassy, Constantinople, 1889-90; in foreign office, Berlin, 1890-92; sec. legations at Belgrade, 1892-94, Dresden, 1894-95, embassy at St. Petersburg, 1895-97; legation at Munich, 1897-1902; councilor of embassy, London, 1902-06; minister at Cairo, 1906-08; ambassador of Germany to U.S., 1908—. Died Oct. 6, 1939.

BERNSTROM, Victor, wood engraver; b. Stockholm, Sweden. Pupil Royal Acad., Sweden. Awarded medal (1st class) World's Columbian Expn.; exhibited at Paris Expn., 1900; silver medal Pan-Am. Expn., 1901, St. Louis Expn., 1904. For a number of yrs. on staff London Graphic and Harper & Bros., New York. Home: Grand View-on-Hudson, N.Y. Died 1907.

BERRESFORD, Arthur William, elec. engr.; b. Brooklyn, July 9, 1872; s. John H. and Rebecca B. (Leach) B.; B.S. in E.E., Poly. Inst. of Brooklyn, 1892; M.E. in E.E., Cornell U., 1893; m. Florence King, Apr. 5, 1898 (died Feb. 10, 1929); children—John King, Arthur Beattys; m. 2d, Mrs. Alice McGrath Hopf, Nov. 3, 1931; adopted dau., Eleanor Rose. General electric work, 1893-96; engr. Ward-Leonard Elec. Co., Bronxville, N.Y., 1896-98; v.p. and mgr. Iron Clad Resistance Co., Westfield, N.J., 1898-1900; engr., 1900-01, supt., 1901-05; made gen. mgr., 1905; v.p. Cutler-Hammer Mfg. Co., Milwaukee, till 1923; v.p. Electric Refrigeration Corp., 1926-27; pres. Am. Engring Council, 1928-30; pres. Travis Holding Corp., July 1935—; mng. dir. Nat. Elec. Mfrs. Assn., 1929-34; nat. councilor Purdue Research Foundation; consultant Elec. Testing Lab., 1937—; gen. consultant. Chmn. Gen. War Service Com. of Elec. Mfg. Industry during World War. Received Phebe Hobson Fowler award from Am. Soc. Civil Engrs., 1930. Republican. Presbyn. Home: New York, N.Y. Died May 30, 1941.

BERRI, Wililam, publisher; b. Brooklyn, N.Y., Sept. 12, 1848; s. William and Amanda B.; ed. pub. schs. and business coll.; widower. Sole owner, 1893-1909, William Berri's Sons (carpet mchts. for 50 yrs.), retiring Jan. 1, 1909; owner Brooklyn Daily Standard Union; also of Carpet Trade Review, Furniture Trade Review. Pres. Review Pub. Co.; pres., treas. Brooklyn Union Pub. Co.; v.p. trustee Hamilton Trust Co. Trustee Hudson-Fulton Celebration Commn., 1909. Del. Rep. Nat. Conv., 1904, 08, del. at large, 1912; del. at large, N.Y. Constl. Conv., 1915. Conglist. Home: Brooklyn, N.Y. Died Apr. 19, 1917.

BERRY, Albert Edgar, telephone official; b. Washington, D.C., Aug. 19, 1878; s. Edgar P. and Margaret (Ryon) B.; student Georgetown U.; m. Florence Dyer, 1903. With Bell Telephone service about 20 yrs.; then pres. Chesapeake & Potomac Telephone Co.; dir. Federal Nat. Bank, Washington. Home: Chevy Chase, Md. Died Aug. 9, 1929.

BERRY, Albert Gleaves, rear adm. U.S.N.; b. Nashville, Tenn., Sept. 16, 1848; s. William Tyler and Mary Margaret (Tannehill) B.; grad. U.S. Naval Acad., 1869; m. Lilliam Reed Merriman, Sept. 28, 1881 (died 1931); children—Mary Lillian, Albert Gleaves. Ensign, 1871; master, 1872; lt., 1875; lt. comdr., 1897; comdr., 1900; capt., June 16, 1905; rear adm., June 18, 1909; retired, 1910. Served at sea in European, S. Atlantic, Asiatic (twice), Pacific and N. Atlantic squadrons; also spl. duty and in spl. service squadron; exec. officer Amphitrite during Spanish-Am. War. Awarded medal for action at San Juan, P.R., May, 1898; clasp for action off Cardenas, Cuba; medal for Spanish-Am. War. Home: Coronado, Calif. Died May 12, 1938.

BERRY, Albert Seaton, congressman, lawyer; b. Campbell Co., Ky.; ed. Miami Univ. and Cincinnati Law School; State senator 2 terms; mayor of Newport 5 terms; mem. Congress, 1893-1901, 6th Ky. dist. Democrat. Home: Newport, Ky. Died 1908.

BERRY, Gilbert Milo, banker; b. Columbia, S.C., Jan. 22, 1862; s. Milo H. and Harriet (Meigs) B.; ed. Columbia Male Acad., and King's Mountain Military Sch., Yorkville, S.C.; m. Katharine Fickling, Nov. 29, 1919; children—Katherine Elizabeth, Gilberta Meigs. In drug business, 1879-92; mem. firm Duffie & Berry, 1886-92; cashier Canal Bank, Columbia, 1892-98, Loan & Exchange Bank, of S.C., 1898-1901, Nat. Loan & Exchange Bank, 1901-23; pres. Columbia Nat. Bank, 1923—; pres. Acme Bldg. & Loan Co.; pres. Capital Trust Co., 1926—; treas. S.C. Ins. Co. Served as pvt., later lt. S.C. N.G., 1883-92; alderman City of Columbia 2 terms; trustee pub. schs. of Columbia 2 terms; mem. agrl. loan agency com. War Finance Corp. Democrat. Episcopalian. Mason. Home: Columbia, S.C. Died Oct. 10, 1931.

BERRY, Gordon Lockwood; b. Plantsville, Conn., Jan. 8, 1884; s. Loren Foster and Louise (Coy) B.; ed. Grinnell (Ia.) Coll. 2 yrs., Coll. City of New York 1 yr.; m. Katharine Wolcott Dwight, May 18, 1911; children—Loren Curtis, Helen McClure, Louise Coy, Marion Dwight. Circulation mgr. Van Norden's Mag., The Winthrop Press, New York, 1907-13; field sec. Nat. Com. for Prevention of Blindness, New York, 1913-18; Y.M.C.A. sec. attached to Les Foyers du Soldat, France, 1918-19; European rep. Near East Relief and an organizer and first exec. sec. Internat. Near East Assn., 1919-29. Mem. advisory com. High Commissariat for Refugees, League of Nations; mem. Armenian sub-com., refugees sect. Internat. Labor Office, 1924-29; mem. Am. Com., Internat. Student Service; advisory ednl. com., Russian Student Fund; mem. Com. on Emergency Relief for Chinese Students, 1929-31; mem. advisory council, Am. Friends of Turkey. An organizer Internat. Assn. for Prevention of Blindness, created at The Hague, 1929; asst. dir. Inst. of Internat. Edn., New York, 1929-31; sec. gen. League of Red Cross Socs., Paris, 1931—. Awarded Médaille Commemorative Française de la Grande Guerre; Officier Ordre Royal du Georges I (Grecian). Republican. Conglist. Author: Trachoma—Its Causes and Means of Prevention, 1915; Industrial Hazards to Eyesight, 1917. Died Jan. 5, 1932.

BERRY, James Henderson, senator; b. Jackson Co., Ala., May 15, 1941; removed to Ark., 1848; ed. pvt. sch.; 2d lt. 16th Ark. Inf., C.S.A., 1861-62; lost a leg at Corinth, Miss., Oct. 4, 1862. Admitted to bar, 1866; and then in practice at Bentonville, Ark. Mem. Ho. of Rep., 1866, 72, 74 (speaker, 1874); pres. Dem State Conv., 1876; elected judge Circuit Ct., 1878, gov. of Ark., 1882; elected to U.S. Senate for unexpired term (1885-89); of A. H. Garland; reelected, 1889, 1895, 1901; defeated, 1907. Home: Bentonville, Ark. Died Jan. 30, 1913.

BERRY, Joseph Flintoft, bishop; b. Aylmer, Can., May 13, 1856; s. Francis and Ann L.B.; ed. Milton Acad., Ont.; (D.D., Lawrence U., 1898; LL.D., Cornell Coll., Ia., 1904, Syracuse U., 1905); m. Olive I. Johnson, Oct. 1876. Ordained M.E. ministry, 1874; pastor in Mich. at Memphis, Algonac, Port Huron, Caro, and Mt. Clemens; asso. editor Michigan Christian Advocate, 1884-90; editor Epworth Herald, 1890-1904; elected bishop, May 18, 1904. Home: Binghamton, N.Y. Died Feb. 11, 1931.

BERRY, Robert Mallory, rear adm. U.S.N.; b. Henry Co., Ky., Jan. 28, 1846; s. Edmond T. and S. F. B.; apptd. from Ky., and grad. U.S. Naval Acad., 1866; m. Mary A. Brady, 1895. Promoted ensign, Mar. 12, 1868; advanced through grades to rear adm., June 29, 1906. On bd. the Macedonian, in summer of 1864, in pursuit of the Confederate steamers Florida and Tallahassee; served in the Sabine and Gettysburg, 1866, Guerriere and Huron, 1867-68, Kansas, 1869, Cyane and Pensacola, 1869-72, Tigress, 1873, Dictator, 1874, Franklin, 1874-77; torpedo duty, 1877; exec. officer Saratoga, 1878-80; Navy Yard, Washington, 1881; comdr. of U.S.S. Rogers in search of the Jeanette, 1881-82; exec. officer St. Mary's, 1882-86, Atlanta, 1886-88; torpedo duty and at Naval War Coll., 1889; light house insp., 16th dist., 1889-92; comd. Michigan, 1893-94; Navy Yard, New York, 1895-96; comd. Castine, 1896-99; Naval Home, Phila., 1899-1901; mem. Naval Examining Bd., Washington, 1901; comd. Dixie, 1901-02; Navy Yard, Norfolk, 1902; comd. Kentucky, 1903-04; comdt., Naval Sta., Charleston and 6th naval dist., 1904-05; comdt., Navy Yard, Pensacola and 8th naval dist., 1905-06; comdt., Navy Yard, Norfolk, and 5th naval dist., 1906-07; retired, Jan. 28, 1908. Comdr. U.S. Naval Unit, U. of Mich., Sept. 23, 1918-Jan. 3, 1919. Home: Detroit, Mich. Died May 19, 1929.

BERRY, Walter Van Rensselaer, lawyer; b. Paris, France, July 29, 1859; s. Nathaniel and Catherine (Van Rensselaer) B.; A.B., Harvard, 1881; studied law at Columbia; unmarried. Admitted to bar, 1885, and practiced at Washington, D.C.; judge Internat. Tribunals of Egypt, 1908-11; pres. Am. Chamber of Commerce, Paris, 1916-23. Decorated Comdr. Legion of Honor (France); Order Crown of Italy, and Order St. Maurice and St. Lazarus (Italy). Home: Paris, France. Died Oct. 12, 1927.

BERRY, William Franklin, ry. official; b. Biddeford, Me., Feb. 2, 1844; s. William and Olivia G. B.; grad. Biddeford High Sch., 1862; m. Belinda Tarbox, 1867. Began ry. service Mar., 1864, freight and ticket clerk, becoming sta. agt., 1866, asst. gen. freight agt., 1873, gen. freight agt., 1874, gen. traffic mgr., May, 1892, 2d v.p., Dec. 1, 1895—, B. & M. system (entire service with what is now B. & M. R.R.). Home: Winchester, Mass. Died Jan. 8, 1914.

BERRYMAN, Jerome Woods, banker; b. Arcadia, Mo., Mar. 12, 1870; s. Gerard Quisenberry and Minerva Anderson (Woods) B.; ed. pub. schs. and Belleview Collegiate Inst., Caledonia, Mo.; m. Nancy Annette McNickle, June 8, 1898; children—Dorothy, Jerome Charles, James Woods, Virginia, George Albert. Began as cashier Elk City (Kan.) Bank, 1888; v.p. Citizens Bank, Medicine Lodge, Kan., 1891-92; pres. Bank of Pond Creek, Okla., 1893-97; pres. Stockgrowers Nat. Bank, Ashland, Kan., 1899—; chmn. bd. Aetna Bldg. & Loan Assn., Topeka; pres. Home Lumber and Supplies Co.; v.p. 1st Nat. Bank, Wichita. Mem. Kan. Ho. of Rep. 8 sessions between 1905-28; mayor of Pond Creek, 1894-97; chmn. bd. edn., Ashland, 17 yrs.; dir. all war activities, Clark Co., Kan., World War. Trustee Wm. Woods Coll., Fulton, Mo., 1916-20, Emporia (Kan.) Coll., 1920—(pres. bd. 1932—); dir. Ashland Hosp. Assn. Mem. advisory bd. Reconstruction Finance Corp. for 10th Federal Dist., 1932—. Republican. Presbyn. Mason. Home: Ashland, Kan. Deceased.

BERTHOLF, Ellsworth Price, officer U.S.C.G.; b. New York, Apr. 7, 1866; s. John Jay and Annie Frances (Price) B.; U.S. Naval Acad., 1 yr.; grad. Sch. of Instrn., U.S. Revenue Cutter Service, 1887; m. Emilie Woodruff Inness, Dec. 6, 1902. Third lt. U.S.C.G., June 12, 1889; 2d lt., Oct. 31, 1892; 1st lt., June 18, 1900; capt., June 23, 1907; capt. commandant, June 11, 1911-June 30, 1918; commodore commandant, July 1, 1918, until retired at own request, June 30, 1919. Now v.p. Am. Bureau of Shipping, New York. Served on various stas.; mem. of expdn. to Pt. Barrow for relief of shipwrecked whalers, 1897-98, for which was awarded gold medal by Congress; went alone through Siberia in winter of 1901 for Dept. of Interior to select herd of reindeer for introduction into Northern Alaska; detailed as insp. life saving stas. on coast of N.J., 1902-05; comd. "Bear" in Bering Sea and Arctic waters, 1908-10, "Morrill" at Detroit, 1911. Mem. Order of Midnight Sun. Mem. Dutch Reformed Ch. Was one of authors of Report of the Overland Expedition to Point Barrow, 1899. Mem. U.S. commn. Internat. Conf. on Safety at Sea, London, 1914. Mem. bd. dirs. U.S. Emergency Fleet Corp., 1917. Home: New York, N.Y. Died Nov. 11, 1921.

BERTRAM, James; b. Edinburgh, Scotland, Mar. 17, 1872; s. William Grey and Agnes (Weir) B.; ed. Daniel Stewart's Coll., Edinburgh; m. Janet Tod Ewing, Apr. 1, 1904; 1 dau., Jean Ewing. Became associated with Andrew Carnegie in his ednl. and library interests, 1897; came to U.S., 1898; sec. and life trustee Carnegie Corp., 1911—. Presbyn. Home: New Rochelle, N.Y. Died Oct. 23, 1934.

BERTRON, Samuel Reading, banker; b. Port Gibson, Miss., Feb. 26, 1865; s. Samuel Reading and Ottilie (Mueller) B.; B.A., Yale, 1885; m. Caroline Harding, Jan. 17, 1888; 1 dau., Mrs. Elizabeth Bouimistrow. Founded banking firm of Bertron & Storrs, 1894, now pres. Bertron, Griscom & Co., Inc., New York and Phila.; dir. Atlantic Safe Deposit Co. Active in peace negotiations between Italy and Turkey, 1912; apptd. by President, mem. Spl. Diplomatic Mission to Russia, May 1917; mem. Presdl. Commn. on Belgian Relief; v.p. War Relief Clearing House for France and Allies; apptd. by Sec. McAdoo adviser on Excess Profit Tax Bd. for 4 yrs. Mem. during the war of Excess Profit Tax Commn., Washington, and Capital Issues Com., New York. Chmn. Am. Russian Chamber Commerce. Decorated Cavalier of Crown of Italy, 1917; received thanks of Swiss Govt. for services rendered, 1917; King Albert medal and Commandeur de l'ordre de Léopold II (Belgian), 1919; Legion of Honor (French); Officer of the Crown of Rumania, 1921. Home: Oyster Bay, L.I. Died June 30, 1938.

BERWIND, Edward Julius, capitalist; b. Phila., June 17, 1848. Chmn. bd. Berwind-White Coal Mining Co.; pres. Wilmore, Ocean coal companies, Kentland Coal & Coke Co., Wilmore S.S. Co.; also officer or director numerous other corps. Home: New York, N.Y. Died Aug. 18, 1936.

BESEMER, Howard Burhans, surgeon; b. Dryden, N.Y., Oct. 19, 1869; s. Martin and Emma (Wolcott) B.; Ph.B., Cornell U., 1889; M.D., U. New York City Med. Coll., 1891; M.D., Cleveland Homœ. Med. Coll., 1892; m. Ida M. Burling, Sept. 20, 1910. Practiced, Ithaca, 1895. Mem. Am. Inst. Homœopathy, Am. Med. Assn., Delta Chi. Socialist. Fellow Am. Coll. Surgeons, 1914. Home: Ithaca, N.Y. Died Feb. 10, 1918.

BESSEY, Charles Edwin, botanist; b. on farm, Milton, Wayne Co., O., May 21, 1845; s. Adnah and Margaret (Ellenberger) B.; B.Sc., Mich., Agrl. Coll., 1869, M.Sc., 1872; studied with Dr. Asa Gray at Harvard, 1872-73 and 1875-76; Ph.D., State U. of Ia., 1879; (LL.D., Ia. Coll., 1898); m. Lucy Athearn, Dec. 25, 1873; father of Ernst Athearn B. Prof. botany, 1870-84, acting pres., 1882, Ia. Agrl. Coll.; prof. botany, 1884—, acting chancellor, 1888-91, 1899-1900, and 1907, head dean, 1909—, U. of Neb. Bot. editor Am. Naturalist, 1880-97, of Science, 1897—, Johnson's Cyclo., 1893—. Mem. Neb. Rural Life Commn., 1911-13. Pres. A.A.A.S., 1910-11, Bot. Soc. America, 1895-96, Soc. Promotion Agrl. Science, 1889-91, dept. natural science N.E.A., 1895-96, Am. Micros. Soc., 1902. Progressive Republican. Conglist. Author: Geography of Iowa, 1876; Botany for High Schools and Colleges, 1880; The Essentials of Botany, 1884; Elementary Botanical Exercises, 1892; The Phylogeny and Taxonomy of Angiosperms, 1897; Elementary Botany, 1904; Plant Migration Studies, 1905; Synopsis of Plant Phyla, 1907; The Phyletic Idea in Taxonomy, 1908; Outlines of Plant Phyla, 1909, 11, 12, 13. Home: Lincoln, Neb. Died Feb. 25, 1915.

BEST, George Newton, M.D., botanist; b. Round Valley, N.J., Oct. 16, 1846; s. Cornelius and Elsie (Alpough) B.; attended Lafayette Coll. (class '73);

M.D., U. of Pa., 1875; m. Hannah W. Wilson, 1877. Pres. Lehigh Valley Med. Assn.; permanent del. Med. Soc. N.J.; mem. Torrey Bot. Club; fellow A.A.A.S.; hon. mem. Phila. Bot. Club. Author of numerous papers and addresses; specialty mosses; bryological contbns. including: Revision of the North American Thuidiums, 1896; Revision of the Claopodiums, 1897; Revision of the North American Pseudoleskeas, 1900; Revision of the North American Heterocladiums, 1901; Revision of the North American Leskeas, 1903. Asso. editor The Bryologist. Home: Rosemont, N.J. Died 1926.

BEST, Henry Riley, clergyman; b. Pineville, Mo., Nov. 5, 1872; s. Samuel David and Sarah Anne (Best) B.; student Baylor U., Waco, Tex., 1893-98; D.D., Sioux Falls U., S.Dak., 1913; m. Louise Kennison, 1892; children—Oren M., Frederick Virgil, Henry Randolph (dec.), Ethel Louise (Mrs. James J. Odell); m. 2d, Aimee A. Perreault, Apr. 10, 1919. Ordained Bapt. ministry, 1898; pastor at Chickasha (Okla.), Nevada (Mo.), Winfield (Kan.), Sioux Falls (S.D.), Des Moines (Ia.), and Fargo (N.D.), 1923-29; pastor First Ch., Billings, Mont., 1929—. Principal Bibl. dept. Sioux Falls U., 1904-18; dean Sch. of Religion, Des Moines, 3 yrs.; active in social service and welfare movements; built and operated the City Temple (an open-all-the-time ch.), at Sioux Falls, 14 yrs. Religious work dir., World War; regional dir. Inter-Ch. World Movement. Mem. exec. com. Northern Bapt. Conv., 1917-20; mem. Bd. of Missionary Coöperation, 1924—; mem. N.Dak. Council Religious Edn., 1925—; chmn. Mont. State Bd. of Religious Edn.; pres. Mont. Bapt. Conv. Progressive Republican. Mason. Traveled in Europe, Asia and Africa; lecturer; writer for religious and secular press. Home: Billings, Mont. Died Aug. 3, 1934.

BEST, Nolan Rice, editor; b. Rich Hill, O., Apr. 9, 1871; s. Rev. James and Narcissa M. (Conner) B.; A.B., Otterbein Coll., Ohio, 1892, Litt.D., 1925; m. Anna Drysdale Fulton, Aug. 31, 1898; children—Evelyn, Miriam, Mildred, James Fulton, Nolan Rice. Proofreader U.B. Pub. House, Dayton, O., 1892-93; entered daily newspaper work, Zanesville, O., 1895; mng. editor Daily Courier, Zanesville, 1898-1901; editor The Interior, Chicago, 1901-10; editor of The Continent (consolidation of The Interior and the Westminster of Phila.), with prin. editorial offices in New York, 1910-24; exec. sec. Baltimore Fedn. of Chs., 1925—. Republican. Presbyn. Author: The College Man in Doubt, 1902; Beyond the Natural Order, 1908; Applied Religion for Everyman, 1916; Inspiration, 1923; Two Y. Men, 1925; Yes, It's the Law and It's a Good Law, 1926. Six months in service of Y.M.C.A., A.E.F., France, 1918. Home: Baltimore, Md. Deceased.

BEST, William Parker, M.D.; b. Fairfield, Franklin Co., Ind., Aug. 3, 1864; s. Francis Perry and Mary Virginia (Ogden) B.; ed. pub. schs., Ind.; teacher several yrs.; M.D., Eclectic Med. Inst., Cincinnati, 1888; New York Post-Grad. Sch., 1899; (hon. Sc.D., Potomac U., 1906); m. Harriet Dennett, June 22, 1887; children—Claus H., Mrs. Marie A. Fatout. Practiced, Mt. Carmel, Ind., 1888-92, Dublin, Ind., 1892-99, Indianapolis, 1900—. Trustee Eclectic Med. College of Cincinnati. Mason. Universalist. Home: Indianapolis, Ind. Died Dec. 12, 1938.

BETHEA, Jack, author; b. Birmingham, Ala., Sept. 19, 1892; s. Augustus Brown and Eugenia (Bethea) B.; ed. pub. schs. of Birmingham; m. Alice Sixbey, Aug. 7, 1912; 1 dau., Jean. Reporter Birmingham Age-Herald, 1909-16; city editor Birmingham Ledger, 1916-20; mng. editor Birmingham Post, 1921—. Episcopalian. Mason. Author: Bed Rock, 1924; The Deep Seam, 1925; Honor Bound, 1926; Silver Fleece, 1927. Home: Birmingham, Ala. Deceased.

BETHEA, Solomon Hicks, jurist; b. Lee Co., Ill.; s. William W. and Emily (Green) B.; ed. country dist. sch., and Dixon (Ill.) Sem. and lit. dept. Univ. of Mich.; studied law in offices, and admitted to bar. Practiced law, Dixon, Ill., 1877-98. Mem. Ill. legislature, 1882-83; mayor Dixon, Ill., 2 terms; U.S. dist. atty., northern dist., Ill., 1899-1905; judge U.S. Dist. Court, northern dist., Ill., Mar. 1905—. Died 1909.

BETHEL, George Emmett, medical educator; b. Garland, Tex., Nov. 2, 1894; s. Simpson and Virginia Marcia (Soule) B.; M.D., U. of Tex., 1923; unmarried. Prin. Lockhart (Tex.) Ward Sch., 1914, High Sch., 1917; instr. in anatomy, U. of Tex., 1920-21, adjunct prof., 1923-24, asso. prof., 1926, dean of Med. Branch and prof. tropical medicine, 1928—; asst. chief resident physician, Phila. Gen. Hosp., 1925-26; physician to men, Univ. Health Service, Austin, Tex., 1926-27, dir. of service, 1927-28. Fellow Am. Coll. Physicians. Democrat. Baptist. Mason. Contbr. to med. jours. Address: Galveston, Tex. Died Apr. 27, 1935.

BETHELL, Union Noble, banker; b. Newburg, Ind., Sept. 12, 1859; s. Union and Eva Maffett (Parrett) B.; ed. Hanover (Ind.) Coll. and Columbian Law Sch., Washington; m. Minnehaha Cox, Oct. 14, 1885 (died July 10, 1886), m. 2d, Donna Isabel Brink, Dec. 5, 1893. Admitted bar, D.C., 1885, Ind., 1887, U.S. Supreme Ct., 1902. Prominently identified with Bell Telephone System, 1889-1919, as 1st v.p. Am. Telephone & Telegraph Co., pres. New York Telephone Co. and as officer or dir. in various other Bell cos. throughout the U.S. Chmn. of operating bd., U.S. Telegraph and Telephone adminstrn., 1918-19; pres. First Nat. Bank of Montclair, N.J. Decorated by the Emperor of Japan with the Imperial Order of the Rising Sun, 1909. Home: Upper Montclair, N.J. Died Jan. 13, 1933.

BETHUNE, Louise, architect; b. at Waterloo, N.Y., July 21, 1856; d. Prof. Dalson W. and Emma M. (Williams) Blanchard; grad. Buffalo High Sch., 1874; studied architecture; m. Robert A. Bethune, Dec. 10, 1881. Was a draughtsman, 1876-81; opened independent office, 1881, becoming the first woman architect in the U.S.; practicing architecture with her husband, 1881—. Home: Buffalo, N.Y. Died Dec. 18, 1913.

BETTENDORF, Joseph William, mfr.; b. Leavenworth, Kan., Oct. 10, 1864; s. Michael and Catherine (Reck) B.; ed. grammar sch., Peru, Ill.; m. Elizabeth Ohl, May 8, 1888; children—Edwin Joseph, William Edwin. Apprentice, Peru Herald, 1880-82; dept. store clk., Peru, 1882-84; machinist, Peru Plow Co., 1885-86; supt. Bettendorf Metal Wheel Co. (organized by brother), 1886-93; organizer with brother Bettendorf Axle Co., 1893; pres. The Bettendorf Co., successor to same, 1910—; pres. Bettendorf Water Co., Bettendorf Light & Power Co., Bettendorf Improvement Co., Bettendorf Mfg. Co., Buddy "L" Mfg. Co., Linograph Finance Corp., Micro Machine Co., Westeo-Chippewa Pump Co., Zimmerman Steel Co.; v.p. MacRoh Sales Co. Mem. Ill. Chamber Commerce. Republican. Catholic. Home: Bettendorf, Ia. Died May 16, 1933.

BETTERIDGE, Walter Robert, theologian; b. Riga, Monroe Co., N.Y., Dec. 16, 1863; s. James and Jane (Johns) B.; grad. State Normal Sch., Brockport, N.Y., 1883; A.B., U. of Rochester, 1888, A.M., 1892; Rochester Theol. Sem., 1891 (no degree); studied univs. of Göttingen and Berlin, 1895-96; studied and traveled in Egypt and Palestine, 1909-10; (D.D., Rochester, 1906); m. Mary Caroline Allen, Nov. 5, 1891. Instr. in Hebrew, 1891-92, asst. prof., 1892-1900, acting prof. Hebrew lang. and lit., 1900-01; Hoyt prof., 1901—, Rochester Theol. Sem.; librarian, Rochester Theol. Sem., 1901-13. Ordained Bapt. ministry, 1892, but never held pastorate. Author: Commentary on Exodus, 1914; Commentary on Deuteronomy, 1915. Home: Rochester, N.Y. Died Mar., 1916.

BETTMANN, Bernhard, collector of internal revenue; b. Weidnitz, Bavaria, Aug. 2, 1834; ed. there; came to Cincinnati, 1850; m. Matilda Wald, Oct. 26, 1859. Pres. bd. of govs. of Hebrew Union Coll., 1875—; pres. United Jewish Charities; pres. Golden Jubilee Saengerfest, 1899, of German Day Assn., etc. U.S. collector of internal revenue at Cincinnati. Dir. First Nat. Bank. Author of many poems, essays and addresses. Home: Cincinnati. Died June 18, 1915.

BETTS, B. Frank, M.D.; b. Warminster, Pa., Dec., 1845; ed. in private schools; grad. Hahnemann Med. Coll. of Phila., 1868; spl. study in Europe, 1868-70; since then in practice in Phila.; m. Lucy C. Corse, Nov. 17, 1871. Prof. physiology and microscopic anatomy, Hahnemann Coll., 1873; organized dept. gynecology, 1876, remaining prof. till 1893; lecturer on hygiene 3 yrs., and diseases of children 5 yrs. Consulting gynecologist to the Hahnemann Med. Coll. Hosp. and the Woman's Homeopathic Hosp. Home: Philadelphia. Died 1909.

BETTS, Charles Henry, editor; b. Red Creek, N.Y., Apr. 14, 1863; s. of Thomas and Mary N. (Tiner) B.; left an orphan at 8; student Adrian (Mich.) Coll., 1891-92; L.H.D., George Washington U., 1921; m. Albertine M. Rogers, Nov. 20, 1901; 1 dau., Isabelle M. Editor and pub. Lyons Republican (weekly newspaper), 1897—; pres., Lyons Republican Co.; dir. Hough Shade Corp., Janesville, Wis. Deputy clk. N.Y. Assembly, 1895-98, inclusive; also served as chief of engrossing dept. and chief of revision dept., various sessions. Mem. Rep. State Com. 6 terms, 1904-16; chmn. Wayne Co. Rep. Com., 1921-22; postmaster town of Lyons. Sec. N.Y. State Food Commn. during the war, also sec. dept. farms and markets; mem. N.Y. Assembly, 1920-22. Elk, Mason. Author: Betts-Roosevelt Letters, 1912; The Naked Truth, 1913. Home: Lyons, N.Y. Died Nov. 24, 1929.

BETTS, Craven Langstroth, author; b. St. John, N.B., Apr. 23, 1853; s. Hiram and Sarah Ann (Purdy) B.; desc. from Old Colonial N.E. stock and of United Empire Loyalists; ed. there; removed to New York, 1879; went into business life and pursued lit. studies; m. Elisabeth Cushing Colby, Feb. 10, 1905; children—Elizabeth Gloriana, Mary Colby. Author: Songs from Beranger (translation of 61 chansons); The Perfume Holder; Tales of a Garrison Town (with Arthur W. H. Eaton); A Garland of Sonnets; The Promise, a blank verse poem, 1910; Collected Poems, 1915; The Two Captains (poems), 1921; also many poems in mags. Home: Santa Cruz, Calif. Died July 30, 1941.

BETTS, Frederic H., lawyer; b. Newburgh, N.Y., Mar. 8, 1843; s. Hon. Frederick J. and Mary Ward (Scoville) B.; (colonial and revolutionary ancestry on both sides); grad. Russell's Mil. Acad., 1860, Yale, A.B., 1864, A.M., 1867, LL.D., 1901; grad. Columbia Law Sch., 1866; m. Louise Holbrook, Oct. 16, 1867. Admitted to N.Y. bar, 1866; has been counsel Edison Electric Light Co., Am. Bell Telephone Co., Westinghouse Air Brake Co., City of New York, Marconi Wireless Telegraph Co., Electric Accumulator Co., Western Union Telegraph Co., and many other important corps. and individuals. Lecturer on patent law in law dept., Yale Univ., 1874-85. Republican. Mem. Rep. Co. Com., City and Co. of New York, 1884-85, Citizens Com. of 50, 1882, Citizens' Com. of 100, 1883, People's Municipal League, 1890-91. Episcopalian. Home: New York, N.Y. Died 1905.

BETTS, Frederick William, clergyman; b. Winnebago Co., Ill., Mar. 6, 1858; s. Andrew Jackson and Phoebe (Nichols) B.; ed. St. Lawrence U., 1884-85, D.D., 1903; m. Mary R. Browning, Oct. 1, 1878; children—Welcome A. (dec.), C. Fred. Ordained Universalist ministry, Plymouth, N.H., 1886; pastor 1st Ch., Syracuse, N.Y., Nov. 1, 1889—. Pres. Asso. Charities of Syracuse, 1906-10; chmn. Com. of 18, having in charge the moral survey of Syracuse; pres. N.Y. State Conv. Universalists, 1910-11; trustee Universalist Gen. Conv., 1905-17; trustee N.Y. State Conv. of Universalist, St. Lawrence U., Syracuse Pub. Library (pres. bd.), Canon Theol. Sch.; chmn. Syracuse chapter, Am. Red Cross, 1922—. Mason. Author: A Philosophy and Faith of Universalism, 1913; Billy Sunday, The Man and His Method, 1916; The Abiding Life, 1926; Forty Fruitful Years, 1929. Home: Syracuse, N.Y. Died 1932.

BETTS, George Herbert, prof. edn.; b. Clarksville, Iowa, April 1, 1868; s. Christopher and Lucinda (Elliott) B.; A.B., Cornell Coll., Ia., 1899; Ph.M., U. of Chicago, 1904; Ph.D., Columbia, 1909; m. Anna M. Freelove, 1893; children—Muriel Marie, Harlan Cedric. Prof psychology, Cornell Coll., 1901-18; prof. religious edn., Boston U., 1918-19, Northwestern U., 1919-21, U. of Southern Calif., 1921-22, Northwestern U., 1922-26; prof. edn. and dir, of research, 1926—. Progressive Republican. Methodist. Author: The Mind and Its Education, 1906; Functions and Distribution of Mental Imagery, 1909; The Recitation, 1911; Social Principles of Education, 1912; New Ideals in Rural Schools, 1913; Better Rural Schools (with O. E. Hall), 1914; Fathers and Mothers, 1915; My Chance to Achieve, 1915; Agriculture (with O. H. Benson), 1915; Class Room Method and Management, 1917; How to Teach Religion, 1919; Physiology and Hygiene (with C. P. Emerson), 1919; The New Program of Religious Education, 1921; The Curriculum of Religious Education, 1921; Laboratory Studies in Educational Psychology (with E. M. Turner), 1924; Method in Teaching Religion (with M. O. Hawthorne), 1925; The Beliefs of 700 Ministers, 1929; The Foreign Language Equipment of 2325 Doctors of Philosophy (with R. A. Kent), 1929; Character Outcome of Present-Day Religion, 1931. Home: Evanston, Ill. Died Dec. 8, 1934.

BETTS, James A., lawyer; b. Broadalbin, Fulton Co., N.Y., Mar. 18, 1853; s. Isaiah and Margaret A. (Hoes) B.; grad. State Normal Sch., Albany, N.Y., 1875; sch. prin., 1875-77; law student, 1877-80; m. Frances M. Hill, Oct. 16, 1884 (died June 15, 1905); 1 son, James Hill; m. 2d, Olivia M. (Mathews) North, Nov. 5, 1908. Admitted to bar, 1880; practiced at Kingston; sec. N.Y. State Civil Service Commn., 1883-84; mem. Kingston Bd. Edn., 1885-98 (pres. 1888-90); clerk Ulster Co. Bd. of Supervisors, 1890-91; surrogate of Ulster Co., 1892-98; justice Supreme Ct. of N.Y., 3d Jud. Dist., 1898-1912 (asso. justice Appellate div. 1910-12). Trustee and atty., Kingston Savings Bank; dir. Pine Hill Water Co.; v.p. and atty., Nat. Ulster County Bank. Pres. The City of Kingston Hosp.; trustee Wiltwyck Rural Cemetery, old Senate-House Assn., Kingston Baptist Church. Democrat. Mason. Home: Kingston, N.Y. Died May 7, 1928.

BEUTENMULLER, William, entomologist; b. Hoboken, N.J., Mar. 31, 1864; s. William and Mathilda (Hauser) B.; ed. pub. and pvt. schs. and business coll., New York; m. Edna L. Hyatt, Apr. 15, 1903. Curator dept. entomology, Am. Mus. Natural History, 1889-1910. Author: Butterflies, Moths, Gall-insects; Forestry Insects. Also numerous articles on entomology in scientific mags. Editor Journal of N.Y. Entomol. Soc., Vols. I-XI. Home: Tenafly, N.J. Died Feb. 24, 1934.

BEVAN, Thomas Horatio, foreign service; b. Baltimore, Md., Jan. 29, 1887; s. Richard Alexander and Cora Dimmock (Johnson) B.; Johns Hopkins 2½ yrs.; m. Macey Nichols, Nov. 11, 1912; children—Corilla Dimmock, Richard Alexander. Pvt. sec. to U.S. Senator I. Rayner, 1908-10; clk. Am. Consulate, Tampico, Mexico, 1910-12; apptd. consular asst., 1912, v. and dep. consul same yr., v. consul, 1915, all at Tampico; v. consul, Berne, Switzerland, 1916-17, Glasgow, Scotland, 1917-19; consul Bahia, Brazil, 1919-23, Montevideo, Uruguay, 1923-25, Hamburg, Germany, 1925-28, apptd. consul gen., May 31, 1928; consul gen., Oslo, Norway, 1928-31; apptd. 1st sec.

in Diplomatic Service, Apr. 24, 1931, and charge d'affaires ad interim of Am. Legation at Oslo, May 1, 1931; reassumed charge of the Consulate General at Oslo, June 11, 1931; reapptd. 1st sec. of Legation at Oslo, July 5, 1935, designated charge d'affaires ad interim, Aug. 3, 1935, in addition to duties as consul gen.; apptd. consul gen., Warsaw, Poland, Oct. 28, 1935. Home: Baltimore, Md. Died July 24, 1938.

BEVAN, W(ilson) Lloyd, educator; b. Baltimore, Md., June 17, 1866; s. George Frazier and Harriet Lucretia (Lloyd) B.; B.A., Johns Hopkins, 1886; M.A., Columbia, 1889; S.T.B., Gen. Theol. Sem., 1891; Ph.D., U. of Munich, 1893. Deacon, 1889, priest, 1891, P.E. Ch.; rector Trinity Ch., Concord, Mass., 1894-96; prof. history, U. of the South, 1898-1903, 1909-12; prof. ch. history, Kenyon Coll., 1918-20; prof. history, U. of Del., 1920-26; prof. Theol. Sch., U. of the South, Sewanee, Tenn., 1926—. Author: Sir William Petty, 1895; The World's Conquerors, 1912; Church History—Medieval and Modern, 1913; Gospel and Government, 1914; History of Delaware, 2 vols., 1928. Home: Sewanee, Tenn. Died Apr. 8, 1935.

BEVERIDGE, Albert Jeremiah, senator; b. on farm on border of Adams and Highland counties, O., Oct. 6, 1862; s. Thomas H. and Frances E. (Parkinson) B.; family moved to Ill. after war; from age of 12 led a life of privations; plowboy at 12, railroad laborer at 14, logger and teamster at 15, then attended high sch.; Ph.B., De Pauw U., 1885, A.M., 1888; LL.D., DePauw, 1902, U. of Pa., 1920, Lafayette Coll., 1921, Brown U., 1921; m. Katherine Langsdale, Nov. 24, 1887 (died June 18, 1900); m 2d, at Berlin, Germany, Catherine Eddy, of Chicago, Aug. 7, 1907; children—Albert J., Abby Spencer. Read law in office of Senator McDonald; admitted to bar, 1887, and was associated with McDonald & Butler until he began practice for himself; identified with many important cases; well known as orator and Republican campaign speaker. U.S. senator from Indiana, 1889-1905, 1905-11. Chmn. Prog. Nat. Conv., Chicago, 1912. Mem Am. Acad. Arts and Letters, Nat. Inst. Arts and Letters. Author: The Russian Advance, 1903; The Young Man and the World, 1905; The Bible as Good Reading, 1906; Americans of Today and Tomorrow, 1908; Work and Habits, 1908; The Meaning of the Times, 1907; (speeches) Pass Prosperity Around, 1912; The Invisible Government, 1912; What Is Back of the War, 1915; Life of John Marshall (2 vols.), 1916, same, last two volumes, 1919; The State and The Nation, 1924; The Art of Public Speaking, 1924. Home: Indianapolis, Ind. Died Apr. 27, 1927.

BEVERIDGE, John Harrie, educator; b. Highland Co., O., Jan. 21, 1869; s. John Thomas and Eliza E. (Steen) B.; B.S., Nat. Normal U., Lebanon, O., 1892; B.Pd., A.M., Ohio U., Athens, O., 1897, D.Pd., 1917; A.M., Columbia, 1912; m. Florence M. Haselton, July 7, 1897; children—Lenore Lodema, Wendell Haselton. Prin. schs., Glidden, Ia., 1897-1902; supt. schs., Missouri Valley, Ia., 1902-08, Council Bluffs, Ia., 1908-17, Omaha, July 1, 1917—. Pres. Ia. State Teachers' Assn., 1913, Neb. State Teachers' Assn., 1921. Pres. Y.M.C.A. (Omaha); mem. nat. ednl. com. Boy Scouts America; mem. bd. dirs. and exec. com. Omaha Chamber Commerce. Presbyn. Mason. Home: Omaha, Neb. Died Oct. 12, 1932.

BEVERIDGE, John Lourie, governor; b. Greenwich, Washington Co., N.Y., July 6, 1824; s. George and Ann (Hoy) B.; went to DeKalb Co., Ill., 1842; ed. Rock River Sem., Mt. Morris, Ill., 1843-45; m. Helen May Judson, Jan. 20, 1848 (died May 8, 1909). In autumn of 1845 went south; taught sch. in Tenn. Read law and licensed there; returned to Ill., 1851; located at Sycamore; removed to Evanston, Ill., 1854, and opened office in Chicago; removed to Calif., 1895; maj. 8th Ill. Cav., Sept. 18, 1861; col. 17th Ill. Cav., Jan. 28, 1864; bvtd. brig. gen. vols., Mar. 7, 1865; was in battle of Fair Oaks, Malvern Hill, Fredericksburg and Gettysburg; mustered out Feb. 7, 1866. Elected sheriff Cook Co., Ill., 1866; state senator, 1870; congressman-at-large to succeed Gen. John A. Logan, who had been elected to U.S. Senate, 1871; elected lt. gov., Ill., on Rep. ticket with Gen. Richard J. Oglesby as gov., 1872; upon Gov. Oglesby's election to the U.S. Senate, Jan. 1873, succeeded to the gubernatorial chair and served full term, 4 yrs., save 10 days; asst. treas. of U.S. at Chicago, 1881-84. Home: Hollywood, Calif. Died 1910.

BEVIER, Louis, college prof.; b. Marbletown, Ulster Co., N.Y., Apr. 22, 1857; s. Louis and Catherine (Van Dyck) B.; A.B., Rutgers Coll., 1878, A.M., 1881; Ph.D., Johns Hopkins, 1881; at univs. of Leipzig and Bonn, 1881-82; traveled in Italy, Greece, France, 1882-83; student Am. Sch. Classical Studies, Athens, Greece, winter of 1883; (Litt.D., Rutgers Coll., 1908); m. May Dealing, June 19, 1884. Instr. French, 1883-85, adj. prof. modern langs., 1885-90, and acting prof. Latin, 1887-89, prof. modern langs., 1890-93, prof. Greek lang. and lit., 1893—, sec. extension dept., 1892-1904, dean, Nov. 1, 1912-21, Rutgers Coll. Lecturer on lit. and ednl. subjects. Mem. N.J. State Bd. of Edn., 1901-04; state insp. of high schs., 1904-09. Author: French Grammar, 1896; Brief Greek Syntax, 1904; also numerous monographs and contbns. to periodicals. Home: New Brunswick, N.J. Died May 5, 1925.

BEYE, Howard Lombard, surgeon; b. Oak Park, Ill., Sept. 24, 1886; s. William and Nellie Cristobel (Lombard) B.; B.S., U. of Wis., 1909; M.D., Rush Med. Sch. (U. of Chicago), 1911; m. Ruth Ketcham, July 30, 1920; children—Helen, Cyrus Lombard, Jane Waters, Barbara, Charles Rowan, Ruth. Interne Cook County Hosp., Chicago, 1911-13; asst. in medicine, Rush Med. Coll., 1913; instr. in surgery, State U. of Ia., 1914-17, asst. prof., 1917-20, asso. prof., 1920-24, prof., 1924—, also head of dept., 1927—. Served as 1st lt., later capt. Med. Corps, U.S.A., 1917-19; wounded in action at Chateau Thierry. Fellow Am. Coll. Surgeons. Republican. Unitarian. Home: Iowa City, Ia. Died Sept. 29, 1936.

BEYE, William, v.p. U.S. Steel Corp. of Del.; b. Chicago, Ill., July 21, 1881; s. William and Nellie C. (Lombard) B.; B.L., U. of Wis., 1902; LL.B., Lake Forest Coll. of Law, 1904; m. Genevieve Ainslie, Oct. 17, 1911; 1 son, William, III. Admitted to Ill. bar, Apr. 1904, and practiced in Chicago as mem. Knapp, Beye, Allen & Cushing and its predecessors, 1904-37; v.p. U.S. Steel Corp. in charge industrial relations, 1937; v.p. and gen. counsel U.S. Steel Corp. of Del., 1938—. Republican. Home: Pittsburgh, Pa. Died Oct. 27, 1941.

BEYER, Henry Gustav, med. dir. U.S.N., retired, 1912; b. Saxony, Oct. 28, 1850; s. Carl and Wilhelmine (Scheibe) B.; ed. pub. schs., Hohenstein Ernstthal to 1864; pvt. instrn. (classical) till 1866, pharmacy till 1869; M.D., Bellevue Hosp. Med. Coll. (New York U.), 1876; M.R.C.S., London, 1881; Ph.D., Johns Hopkins, 1887; m. Harriet W. Wescott, May 6, 1880 (died Jan. 4, 1891). Apptd. from N.Y., asst. surgeon U.S.N., May 19, 1876; passed asst. surgeon, Apr. 30, 1880; surgeon, May 19, 1893; med. insp., 1905; med. dir., 1910. Naval Hosp., Brooklyn, 1876-77; various assignments to 1897; on U.S.S. Amphitrite, 1897-99, and during Spanish-Am. War; Wabash, Boston, 1899-1901; U.S.S. Prairie, 1901-03; fleet surgeon Pacific Fleet, 1905-07. Mem. bd. on barracks, visiting Eng. and Germany (spl. commn.), 1903-04; prof. hygiene, Naval Med. Sch., Washington, from 1904; lecturer on naval hygiene, War Coll., Newport, R.I. Del. Internat. Congress, Stockholm, Amsterdam, Berlin and Rome, 1907; chmn. exhibition, Congress on Tuberculosis, Washington, 1909; del. Internat. Hygiene Expn., Dresden, 1911; pres. sec. mil., naval and tropical hygiene, Internat. Congress Hygiene, Washington, 1912. Died Dec. 9, 1918.

BEYER, Samuel Walker, geologist; b. Clearfield, Pa., May 15, 1865; s. Abraham and Barbara Ann (Keagy) B.; B.S., Ia. State Coll., 1889; Ph.D., Johns Hopkins, 1895; m. Jennie Morrison, June 22, 1893; children—Jeanette, Mary Morrison. Instr., 1891-95, asst. prof., 1895-98, prof. geology and mining engring., 1898—, v.-dean engring. div., 1908-17, dean, 1917-18, dean Industrial Science Division, 1919—, Iowa State Coll. Geologist Iowa Geol. Survey, 1892—. Author: The Sioux Quartzite and Certain Associated Rocks, 1895; Geology of Boone, Marshall, Story and Hardin Counties, Iowa, 1895-99; Clays and Clay Industries of Iowa, 1903; Iowa Quarries and Quarry Products, 1906; Iowa Peat Deposits, 1908; Road and Concrete Materials in Iowa, 1914. Home: Ames, Ia. Died June 2, 1931.

BEYERS, Henry Wendell, ry. official; b. Toledo, O., Mar. 26, 1870; s. Adam and Elizabeth (Cortner) B.; ed. pub. schs. and business coll.; m. Anne C. Brown, Apr. 24, 1924; children—Elizabeth, Anne, Barbara Caroline. With C.&N.W. Ry. Co., 1883—, successively as clk, 1883-92, gen. agt. at Cleveland, O., 1892-97, Phila., 1897-1900, Chicago, 1900-06, asst. gen. freight agt., Chicago, 1906-15, asst. freight traffic mgr., 1915-18, asst. traffic mgr., 1918-20, freight traffic mgr., 1920-29, v.p. in charge of traffic, 1929—. Mason. Home: Winnetka, Ill. Died 1936.

BÉZIAT, Andre, univ. prof.; b. Balansun, Basses-Pyrenées, France, Dec. 30, 1870; s. Jacques Béziat and Laetitia Marcillac B.; ed. Collège de Revel and Lycée de Montauban, France; hon. fellow, U. of Chicago, 1898-99, Ph.D., 1899; post-grad. work at Sorbonne, 1901-02, in École des Hautes Études and École des Chartes; m. Kate Mills Bradley. Served in French Army (arty.), 1888-91, and became "maréchal des logis." Prof. French lang. and lit., Peninsular Coll., Barcelona, Spain, 1891-92; asst., 1895-96, and prof. modern langs., 1896-99, Wesleyan Coll., Macon, Ga.; prof. Romance langs. and lits., Kalamazoo (Mich.) Coll., 1899-1900; lecturer in Romance langs. and lits., Columbia U., 1900-01; instr. French, U. of Mich., 1902-03; prof. Romance langs., W.Va. U., 1903-06; asst. prof. Romance langs., U. of Mich., 1906-08; prof. Romance langs., Tulane Univ., 1908-16, Princeton U., 1916-17; adj. prof. modern langs., U. of S.C., 1917; army Y.M.C.A. dir. of French, and lecturer for Southeastern dept., 1917-19; asso. prof. Romance langs., 1919-22, prof. French and Spanish and chmn. dept. Romance langs., 1922—, Vanderbilt U. Del. Alliance Française; lecturer for Alliance Française, 1905-06; lecturer (in France) for Peabody Bur. Internat. Ednl. Correspondence, 1920. Mem. Reformed Ch. of France. Author: Elements of French, 1899; papers and articles in lit. and pedagog. jours.; "La France et la guerre," series of 20 articles about the war, 1915. Home: Nashville, Tenn. Died Dec. 17, 1924.

BIBLE, Frank William, clergyman; b. Milesburg, Pa.; s. Frank Edward and Alice (Minsker) B.; grad. Park Coll., Parkville, Mo., 1901, LL.D., 1926; grad. Auburn (N.Y.) Theol. Sem., 1904; D.D., Coe Coll., Cedar Rapids, Ia., 1924; m. Henrietta Caskey, 1904; children—Frank William, Alice Frances, Beatrice, Barbara. Missionary, Hangchow, China, 1904-19; sec. Foreign Missions Conf. N.A., 1919-23; dist. sec. Presbyn. Bd. Foreign Missions, 1923-29; dir. field work same, 1929-32, exec. sec., 1932—. Home: Oak Park, Ill. Died Nov. 15, 1937.

BICKET, James Pratt, editor; b. Sibley, Ill., Feb. 15, 1876; s. William A. and Ellen (Pratt) B.; ed. Ill. Wesleyan U., 1893-96; unmarried. Engaged in newspaper work, 1896—; editor Chicago Evening American, 1903—. Home: Chicago, Ill. Died Dec. 9, 1937.

BICKETT, Thomas Walter, governor; b. Monroe, N.C., Feb. 28, 1869; s. Thomas W. and Mary A. (Covington) B.; A.B., Wake Forest Coll., N.C., 1890; law course, U. of N.C., 1892-93; m. Fannie N. Yarborough, Nov. 29, 1898. Began practice at Monroe, 1893, later in Danbury, N.C., 1 yr.; located in Louisburg, 1895; sr. mem. Bickett, White & Malone; mem. N.C. Ho. of Rep., 1907-08; atty. gen. of N.C. 2 terms, 1906-16; gov. of N.C., 1917-21. Democrat. Episcopalian. Mason. Home: Louisburg, N.C. Died Dec. 28, 1921.

BICKFORD, Thomas, clergyman, educator; b. Chelsea, Mass., Dec. 30, 1853; s. Thomas and Temperance Snow (Foster) B.; A.B., Colgate, 1875, A.M., 1890; m. Anna M. Searl, July 23, 1878. Ordained Bapt. ministry, 1875; pastor State Street Ch., Lowville, N.Y., 1876-78, Vail Av. Ch., Troy, 1878-80; entered ministry of Congl. Ch.; pastor World Memorial Congl. Ch., Cambridge, Mass., 1882-87, 1st Ch., Branford, Conn., 1887-92, 1st Ch., Springfield, Vt., 1892-96, 1st Ch., Stoughton, Mass., 1902-06; founder, 1906, and prin. Sea Pines Personality Sch. for Girls. Died July 6, 1917.

BICKFORD, Walter Mansur, lawyer; b. Newburg, Me., Feb. 25, 1852; ed. Me. Central Inst., Pittsfield, Me.; m. Emma W. Woodford, Oct. 16, 1878 (died June 17, 1915); m. 2d, Zelma M. Nash, Sept. 25, 1916 (died July 1, 1917); m. 3d, Katherine Gillevan, Aug. 10, 1921. Admitted to Pa. bar, 1878; moved to Mont., 1884; mem. last Territorial Council; was mem. State Constl. Conv., and of State Capitol Commn.; defeated for justice Supreme Court of Mont., 1st State election; exec. commr. Chicago Expn., 1893. Democrat. Home: Missoula, Mont. Deceased.

BICKHAM, Warren Stone, surgeon; b. Shreveport, La., Aug. 23, 1861; s. Dr. Charles Jasper and Annie Augusta (Gray) B.; ed. U. of the South, 1873-78, Yale, 1881, U. of La. (acad. dept.), 1880-82; Pharm. M., M.D., Tulane U. of La., 1883-86, LL.D., 1925; M.D., Coll. Phys. and Surgeons, 1887; student N.Y. Polyclinic, 1887; m. Flora Sabina Brandon, 1895 (died July 28, 1930); m. 2d, Alice Martin, June 30, 1931. Interne and later visiting surgeon Charity Hosp.; demonstrator operative surgery, Tulane U., and jr. surgeon, Touro Infirmary, New Orleans; instr. in surgery, New York Poly.; late surgeon Manhattan State Hosp., New York; late instr. surgery, N.Y. Post-Grad. Med. Sch. and Hosp.; asst. instr. operative surgery, Columbia, 1900-06. Fellow N.Y. Acad. Medicine, Am. Coll. Surgeons. Episcopalian. Author: Textbook of Operative Surgery, 1903; Operative Surgery, 7th Vol., 1933; also sections on Amputations and Ligations in Keen's System of Surgery, 1906. Home: New York, N.Y. Died Dec. 1, 1936.

BICKLEY, George Harvey, bishop; b. Phila., Pa., Feb. 25, 1868; s. George H. and Hester A. (Tull) B.; A.B., Central High Sch., Phila., 1885, A.M., 1889; spl. student, U. of Pa.; B.D., Drew Theo. Sem., 1890; Ph.D., Taylor U., Upland, Ind., 1901; D.D., Dickinson, 1919; m. Anna M. Felton, Feb. 23, 1893. Began preaching at 18; ordained M.E. ministry, 1890; pastor Pottstown, Pa., 1890, Wayne, 1891-92, Somerton, 1893-95, Media, 1896-98, Christ Ch., Phila., 1899-1902, Coatsville, 1903, Arch St. Ch., Phila., 1904-10; dist. supt. North Dist. of Pa., 1910-16; sec. City Mission Soc., 1916-17; dist. supt. Northwest Dist., 1917-20; bishop M.E. Ch., May 21, 1920—, and assigned to Singapore. Mason. Died Dec. 24, 1924.

BICKMORE, Albert Smith, educator; b. St. George, Me., Mar. 1, 1839; s. John and Jane (Seavey) B.; A.B., Dartmouth, 1860, A.M., 1863; served in 44th Mass. Vols., 1862-63; studied with Prof. Louis Agassiz, 1860-64; B.S., Harvard, 1864; Ph.D., Hamilton, 1869, Dartmouth Coll., 1889 (LL.D., Colgate, 1905); m. Charlotte A. Bruce, Dec. 16, 1873. When studying under Prof. Agassiz became his asst., and went to Bermuda collecting for Cambridge Mus.; traveled in E. Indian Archipelago, China, and Japan, returning via Siberia, Moscow, St. Petersburg, Berlin and London, 1865-68; prof. natural history, Madison (now Colgate) U., 1869; supt. Am. Mus. Natural History, 1869-84; prof. in charge dept. pub. instrn., same, 1882— (now emeritus). Traveled 1895-1904, gathering data and illustrations for lectures on natural history, geography and history; under auspices of state supt. of pub. instrn., has delivered 418 lectures upon 213 different subjects. Life fellow Royal Geog. Soc., London; fellow Am. Geog. Soc., N.Y. Acad. Sciences, A.A.A.S. Trustee Am. Mus. Natural History, Colgate U., Vassar College. Died Aug. 12, 1914.

BICKNELL, Ernest Percy, vice chmn. Am. Nat. Red Cross; b. nr. Vincennes, Ind., Feb. 23, 1862; s. Eli P. and Charlotte A. (Ford) B.; A.B., Ind. Univ., 1887, LL.D., 1925; m. Grace Vawter, 1891; children —Scott C., Mrs. Constance B. Will, Mrs. Alberte B. Wright. In newspaper work, chiefly at Indianapolis, 1887-93; sec. Ind. Bd. of State Charities, 1893-98; gen. supt. Chicago Bur. of Charities, 1898-1908; nat. dir., and dir. gen. Civilian Relief, Am. Nat. Red Cross, Washington, Oct. 1, 1908-May 31, 1917; apptd. deputy commr. Red Cross to France, June 1, 1917; commr. to Belgium, Jan. 1, 1918; spl. commr. to Balkan States, Oct. 1918; dep. commr. to Europe, Apr. 1, 1919; acting commr. to Europe, Sept. 1921; commr. to Europe, Oct. 1921; v.chmn. in charge of foreign operations, Apr. 1923—. Rep. Am. Nat. Red Cross at San Francisco, 1906, in Sicily and Calabria, 1909. Represented U.S. at Internat. Red Cross Congresses, London, Eng., 1907, Washington, D.C., 1912, Geneva, Switzerland, 1921, The Hague, 1928, Brussels, Belgium, 1930; pres. Nat. Conf. Charities and Correction, 1908-09; dir. Nat. Assn. for Study and Prevention of Tuberculosis; mem. commn. sent by U.S. Govt. to assist Americans to return from European war zone, 1914; dir. of Rockefeller Foundation War Relief Commn. to help non-combatant war sufferers in European countries, 1914-15; del. Pan Am. Red Cross Conf., Buenos Aires, 1924; vice chmn. and dir. gen. League of Red Cross Socs., Paris, 1926-27 and 1930-31; chmn. Am. Red Cross Commn. to study famine conditions in China, 1929. Awarded decorations by Belgium, Italy, Serbia, Russia, Montenegro, France (Legion of Honor), Poland, Japan, Greece, Czechoslovakia, Germany and Spain. Author: Pioneering with the Red Cross, 1935. Died Sept. 29, 1935.

BICKNELL, Frank Martin, author; b. Melrose, Mass., Jan. 24, 1854; s. William Martin and Lydia Maria (Tobey) B.; grad. English High Sch., Boston, 1872. In business offices, 1872-88; in lit. work, 1888—. Author: The City of Stories, 1897; The Apprentice Boy, 1897; The Bicycle Highwayman, 1900; The Double Prince, 1901; Amy Dora's Amusing Day, 1904; Blitzen the Conjurer, 1906. Contbr. to mags. Home: Malden, Mass. Died Aug. 21, 1916.

BICKNELL, George Augustus, rear adm.; b. Batsto, N.J., May 15, 1846; s. George A. and Elizabeth Haskins (Richards) B.; Scandinavian lineage; early education in private schools; appointed acting midshipman from Indiana, Dec. 2, 1861; served as 1st lt. U.S. Vol. Inf. during Morgan raid in Ind. until regt. was mustered out; grad. U.S. Naval Acad., 1866; Naval Torpedo Sch., 1874 and 1896, U.S. Naval War Coll., 1896 and 1900; m. Annie Sloan, May 22, 1878. Served on Iroquois, Asiatic Fleet, 1867-70; was at opening of ports of Kobé and Osaka, Japan, to trade, 1868; in landing party repelling attack of Prince Hizen and later 2d in command of marines protecting Yokohama until order was restored. Promoted ensign, Apr. 1868; advanced through grades to rear adm., Feb. 8, 1907. Served on numerous vessels and stas.; navigator of Marion, 1880-82, cruised from Montevideo to Heard's Island, about 7,000 miles; rescued 30 survivors of shipwrecked bark Trinity; comd. U.S.S. Niagara in Spanish-Am. War, and in other service in Puerto Rican and Cuban waters until Sept. 1898; comd. Monocacy at Shanghai, China, Dec. 1899, cruised with Hon. E. H. Conger, Am. minister, and suite to Han Kow and river ports, visiting 2 viceroys of river provinces, etc.; comdt. Naval Sta., Key West, Fla., 1902-04; comdg. flagship Texas, flagship U.S. Coast Squadron, 1904-06; comdt. Pensacola Navy Yard, July 1, 1906-Feb. 13, 1907; comdt. Navy Yard, Portsmouth, N.H., 1907-08; retired, May 15, 1908. Life mem. U.S. Naval Inst. Episcopalian; del. Gen. Convs., 1910, 13; sr. warden same ch. in which father and g.f. held same office. Pres. Sinking Fund Commn., City of New Albany. Democrat. Home: New Albany, Ind. Died Jan. 27, 1925.

BICKNELL, Thomas Williams, teacher, author; b. Barrington, R.I., Sept. 6, 1834; s. Allin and Harriet Byron (Kinnicutt) B.; A.M., Brown, 1860; (hon. A.M., Amherst, 1880; LL.D., Drury Coll., and Straight U., 1882); m. Amelia D. Blanding, Sept. 1860 (died Aug. 1896). Sch. teacher and prin., 1860-69; commr. of edn., R.I., 1869-75; founder new Normal Sch., R.I., 1871; founder, editor and pub. New Eng. Jour. of Education, Education, and Primary Teacher, 1875-87; founder, N.E. Bur. of Edn., 1876; mem. R.I. Ho. of Rep., 1859-60, Mass. Ho. of Rep., 1888-90; cofounder of the town, New England, N.D.; founder and 1st pres. Leader Silk Co., 1903. Pres. R.I. Inst. Instrn., 1867-68; founder (1880) and pres. (1880-84) Nat. Council of Edn.; pres. Am. Inst. Instrn., 1877-78, N.E.A., 1884, Internat. S.S. Assn., 1884; founder and sec. Municipal League, Providence. Progressive. Author: Biography of William L. Noyes, 1867; Reports as School Commr. of R.I., 1869-75; Annals of Barrington, R.I., 1870; The Bicknells (4 vols.), 1880-88; John Myles and Toleration, 1888; The History of Barrington, R.I., 1898; Barrington in the Revolution, 1898; Sowams, 1908; Bicknell Family Genealogy, 1913; History of R.I. Normal School, 1912; The Story of Dr. John Clarke, Founder of Civil and Religious Liberty in Rhode Island, 1638, 1915; History of Rhode Island, 4 vols.; Poems, Love and Life; also many hist. addresses and poems. Founder and editor of The Leader, ednl. mag. Has been pres. of 37 orgns. Home: Providence, R.I. Died Oct. 6, 1925.

BICKNELL, Warren Moses, contractor; b. Morrisville, N.Y., Feb. 19, 1868; s. Charles Thompson and Susan (Payne) B.; A.B., Western Reserve, 1890; m. Anne Guthrie, Feb. 19, 1900. Began as coal dealer; now chmn. bd. Lundoff-Bicknell Co., contractors; dir. Wheeling & Lake Erie Ry. Co., Union Salt Co., etc. Trustee Western Reserve U., Western Reserve Acad., Cleveland Mus. Natural History. Home: Cleveland, O. Died Aug. 6, 1941.

BICKSLER, W. Scott, lawyer; b. Salem, Ia., Mar. 4, 1861; s. John and Sarah Ann (Buffington) B.; ed. Whittier Coll., Salem, Ia.; LL.B., State U. of Iowa, 1883; m. Nettie Hampton, June 9, 1885. Admitted to bar, 1883; now mem. Bicksler, Bennett, Dana & Blount; counsel Am. Surety Co., Armour & Co., in Colo. Del.-at-large Universal Congress Lawyers and Jurists, St. Louis, 1904. Republican. Home: Denver. Deceased.

BIDDLE, Arney Sylvenus, clergyman; b. Mercer, Pa., June 12, 1848; s. Jonathan (M.D.) and Mary Jane (Bruce) B.; brother of Henry Chalmers B.; A.B., Monmouth Coll., Ill., 1872; studied theology at Monmouth, Newburg (N.Y.), and Allegheny (Pa.) sems.; (D.D., Muskingum Coll., 1901; LL.D., Ashland Coll., 1902); m. Anna Jane Fraser, Dec. 28, 1876. Ordained U.P. ministry, 1875; pastor Cabin Hill Ch., Delaware Co., N.Y., 1875-79, First Ch., Jersey City, 1879-82, Summit Av. Ch., Jersey City, 1882—. Stated clerk N.Y. Presbytery, 1879-1906, U.P. Synod of N.Y., 1894—, U.P. Presbytery of N.J., Oct. 18, 1906—. Dir. of Allegheny Theol. Sem., 1890-93. Home: Jersey City, N.J. Died May 21, 1914.

BIDDLE, Edward William; b. Carlisle, Pa., May 3, 1852; s. Edward M. and Juliana (Watts) B.; A.B., Dickinson Coll., Pa., 1870, A.M., 1873; m. Gertrude D. Bosler, Feb. 2, 1882. Admitted to Pa. bar, 1873; practiced at Carlisle, 1873-95; presiding judge 9th Jud. Dist. of Pa., 1895-1905; since given attention to gen. business, lit. and philanthropic pursuits; pres. bd. trustees Dickinson Coll.; president J. Herman Bosler Memorial Library. Republican. Presbyterian. Home: Carlisle, Pa. Died July 4, 1931.

BIDDLE, Henry Chalmers, educator; b. Kirkwood, Ill., Oct. 4, 1869; s. Jonathan and Mary Jane (Bruce) B.; A.B., Monmouth (Ill.) Coll., 1891; grad. McCormick Theol. Sem., Chicago, 1896; fellow U. of Chicago, 1897-99, Ph.D., 1900; m. Margaret McCready Wishart, Dec. 29, 1896; children—Charles Jonathan, William Wishart, Sarah Florence, Mary Gertrude, Margaret Julia. Instr. in chemistry, Monmouth Coll., 1891-92, prof. chemistry and physics, 1892-93; prof. chemistry, Maryville (Tenn.) Coll., 1899-1900; asst. in gen. chemistry, U. of Chicago, 1900-01; instr. in chemistry, U. of Calif., 1901-06, asst. prof., 1906-18; practicing chem. engr., 1918-24; also acting prof. chemistry, Temple U., Phila., 1921-22; lecturer San Francisco State Teachers Coll., 1922-31; prof. chemistry, Coll. of Pharmacy, U. of Calif., Jan. 1, 1925—, acting dean, 1926-27, dean, 1927—. Republican. Presbyn. Translator; The Vegetable Alkalaids (transl. and revision of Les Alkaloides Vegetaux, by Prof. Amé Pictet), 1904. Home: Berkeley, Calif. Died Sept. 1, 1935.

BIDDLE, Horace P., retired lawyer; b. Fairfield Co., O., March 24, 1811; admitted to bar, 1839; settled at Logansport, Ind.; presiding judge 8th judicial circuit, Ind., 1846-52; retired, 1881. Has made several translations from French and German poets. Author: The Musical Scale; Elements of Knowledge; Prose Miscellany; A Few Poems; Biddle's Poems; American Boyhood (poems); Glances at the World (poems); Last Poems. Home: Logansport, Ind. Died 1900.

BIDDLE, James, brig. gen.; b. Phila., Dec. 11, 1832; s. Edward R. and Eliza Terry (Davis) B.; ed. U. of New York; m. Ellen F. McGowan, First lt. 10th N.Y. Inf., May 2, 1861; hon. mustered out of vol. service, Aug. 31, 1861; capt. 15th U.S. Inf., Aug. 5, 1861; col. 6th Ind. Cav., Nov. 11, 1862; bvtd. maj. U.S.A., Sept. 1, 1862, "for gallant and meritorious services at battle of Richmond, Ky."; lt. col. U.S.A., Dec. 16, 1864, for same at battle of Nashville; brig. gen. vols., Mar. 13, 1865, for same during the war; hon. mustered out, June 27, 1865; maj. 6th Cav., Feb. 21, 1873; lt. col. 5th Cav., Oct. 19, 1887; col. 9th Cav., July 1, 1891; retired, Dec. 11, 1896; advanced to rank of brig. gen., retired, by act of Apr. 23, 1904. Mem. Loyal Legion, S.A.R. Home: Berkeley Springs, W.Va. Died 1910.

BIDDLE, James Stokes, railroad pres.; b. Philadelphia, Jan. 15, 1818; apptd. midshipman, U.S. Navy, Oct. 18, 1833; lt., Aug. 20, 1844; served in Florida war; comd. gunboat during Mexican war and was with the naval batteries in siege of Vera Cruz and capture of Tobasco; resigned from navy, 1856; was pres. Shamokin Valley R.R. (retired). Democratic candidate for mayor Philadelphia, 1871 (defeated). Home: Philadelphia. Died 1900.

BIDDLE, John, army officer; b. Detroit, Mich., Feb. 2, 1859; s. William S. and Susan D. (Ogden) B.; grad. West Point, 1881; unmarried. Commd. 2d lt. engrs., June 11, 1881; promoted through grades to col., Feb. 27, 1911; brig. gen. U.S.A., May 15, 1917; maj. gen. N.A., Aug. 5, 1917. In charge of river and harbor work at Nashville, Tenn., 1891-98; lt. col. and chief engr. U.S. vols. during war with Spain; served in expdn. to P.R.; in Cuba, 1898-99, P.I., 1899-1901; commr. D.C., 1901-07; in charge river and harbor work at San Francisco, June 1907-Aug. 1911; on duty War Dept., Gen. Staff, 1911-14; in charge rivers and harbors, Savannah, July-Sept. 1914; observer with Austro-Hungarian Army, in Austria and Poland, Dec. 1914-June 1915; in charge river and harbors, Baltimore, Oct. 1915-July 1916; supt. U.S. Mil. Acad., 1916-17; comdg. 6th U.S. Engrs., June 1917; comdg. U.S. Ry. regts. in France, July-Oct. 1917; asst. chief of staff, Nov. 1917-Mar. 1918; comdg. Am. forces in Eng., Mar. 1918-June 1919; comdg. Camp Travis, Tex., Aug. 1919-20, Camp Custer, Feb.-Sept. 1920; retired Dec. 1, 1920. Died Jan. 18, 1936.

BIDDLE, Nicholas, trustee; b. Prescott, Ariz., Dec. 4, 1879; s. Brig. Gen. James (U.S.A.) and Ellen Fish (McGowen) B.; S.B., Harvard, 1900; m. Elizabeth Emmett, Dec. 12, 1905. In Southwest and Mexico, 1900-02; trustee Estate of William Astor, Atlantic Mut. Ins. Co., Bank of Savings in City of New York, New York Life Ins. & Trust Co. Served as maj. and col. Mil. Intelligence Div., U.S.A., World War. Home: New York, N.Y. Died Feb. 18, 1923.

BIDDLE, William Baxter, ry. official; b. Beloit, Wis., Nov. 12, 1856; s. Charles H. and Alice (Coffman) B.; grad. high sch., Beloit; m. Ella H. Frost, Nov. 22, 1880. Entered service of A.,T.&S.F. R.R., as freight brakeman, 1877, sta. agent, 1879-80, div. freight and pass. agt., 1880-86, asst. gen. freight agt., 1886-89, asst. freight traffic mgr., 1889-93, freight traffic mgr., 1893-1905, same road; 3d v.p. C.R.I.,&P. Ry., S.L.&S.F. R.R. and C.&E.I. R.R., Mar. 1, 1905-Dec. 31, 1909; v.p. Frisco Lines Jan. 1, 1910-Dec. 9, 1912. Was receiver and chief traffic officer to Jan. 10, 1917, and since pres. St.L.&S.F. Ry. Co. Republican. Home: St. Louis, Mo. Died Feb. 19, 1923.

BIDDLE, William Phillips, maj. gen. U.S.M.C.; b. Phila., Dec. 17, 1853; s. John Barclay B. (M.D.) and Caroline (Phillips) B.; ed. pvt. schs. and tutor and U. of Pa.; m. Mrs. Martha Reynolds Adger, Apr. 12, 1908. Commd. 2d lt. U.S.M.C., June, 1875; 1st lt., 1884; capt., 1894; maj., 1899; lt. col., 1903; col., 1905; maj. gen., comdt. Marine Corps, Feb. 3, 1911. Commanded marines, Peking relief expdn., marine barracks, Cavite, P.I., and 1st Regt., 1st Brigade, 1900-03; pres. Marine Exam. Bds., Washington, 1903; comd. 1st Regt. marine expeditionary forces, Isthmus of Panama, 1903-04; comd. marine barracks, Phila., 1904-06; comd. 1st Brigade marines, Manila, P.I., 1906-08; comd. marine barracks, New York, 1908-09; Nicaraguan expeditionary marines, Panama, 1909-10; retired, Feb. 26, 1914. Awarded Dewey medal, for Battle of Manila; Spanish War, Philippine and Peking relief campaign medals. Episcopalian. On active duty during World War at San Diego, Calif. Died Feb. 26, 1823.

BIDWELL, Annie Ellicott Kennedy; b. Meadville, Pa., June 30, 1839; d. Joseph Camp Griffith and Catharine (Morrison) Kennedy; ed. Madame Burr's Schs., Washington, D.C.; m. John Bidwell, Apr. 16, 1868. Vol. nurse Govt. hosps. during Civ. War; active worker W.C.T.U.; pastor Indian ch. on husband's ranch, 1875—. Western v.p. Nat. Indian Assn.; hon. pres. Cal. Indian Assn. Prohibitionist. Presbyn. Home: Rancho Chico, Calif. Deceased.

BIDWELL, Daniel Doane, writer; b. East Hartford, Conn., Aug. 7, 1866; s. Charles Marcus and Emma W. (Brewer) B.; desc. John Bidwell, the immigrant, Hartford, 1636; A.B., Yale, 1886; m. Edith Ross, Apr. 18, 1891; children—Pauline, Joseph Barry. With New York Ledger, 1888-94; made two trips around the world, the second in 47 days; mem. Conn. Ho. of Rep., 1905, 07; founder of East Hartford Trust Co. Newspaper corr. various war fronts, 1914-18; mem. Naval Batt., Conn. N.G., 1900-10; with Conn. troops, Mexican border, 1916. Pres. Bidwell Family Assn., 1911, sec. 1912-19. Represented Hartford, Conn., at exercises at Hertford, Eng., June 16, 1922, and represented Connecticut at laying of cornerstone of memorial on battlefield of Seicheprey, France, Apr. 21, 1923. Military expert of Hartford papers, 1917-1928. Interviewed Mercier, Roosevelt, Foch. Republican. Episcopalian. Author: As Far as the East Is From the West, 1910; (with Herbert Ward) Five Years with the Congo Cannibals, 1893; History of Hartford Naval Militia, 1911; History of Twenty-sixth Division, A.E.F., 1920. Author of various travel and hist. articles; contbr. to mags. Home: East Hartford, Conn. Died Apr. 24, 1937.

BIDWELL, Edwin Curtis, physician; b. Tyringham (now Monterey), Mass., Feb. 20, 1821; s. Barnabas and Betsey (Curtis) B.; grad. Williams Coll., 1841, M.D., Yale, 1844; m. Isabella Calder Gibson, Nov. 24, 1856 (died 1888). Surgeon 31st Mass. vols., 1862-65; examining surgeon for pensions, 1869-81. Trustee Iowa State Univ., 1856-8; mem. Am. Inst. Civics, G.A.R.; corr. mem. N.Y. Hist. Soc.; pres. Vineland Hist. and Antiq. Soc. In 1849 wrote article on the Portability of Cholera Infection, which was at that time an important contribution to med. knowledge; discovered, 1880, fungus of the black rot of the grape, since named for him Laestadia Bidwellii (bulls. Dept. Agr., 1886-87-88); pres. Vineland New England Soc. Home: Vineland, N.J. Died 1905.

BIEDERBICK, Henry, insp. of customs; b. Waldeck, Germany, Jan. 25, 1859; s. Chr. Fr. and Frederike (Pohlmann) B.; grad. Gymnasium, Corbach in Waldeck and studied chemistry and pharmacy; m. Augusta Lehmann, May 20, 1886 (died 1910). Came to U.S., 1879; served on Lady Franklin Bay (Greely Arctic expdn.), 1881-84, as hosp. steward and asst. to naturalist; U.S. insp. of customs, 1887—. Fellow Nat. Geog. Soc. Wrote: "The Musk Ox" in The Big Game of North America, 1890, "Polar Hospitals," in The White World, 1902. Home: Jersey City, N.J. Died Mar. 25, 1916.

BIEDERWOLF, William Edward, evangelist; b. Monticello, Ind., Sept. 29, 1867; s. Michael and Abbie (Schnitzer) B.; student Wabash Coll., Ind., 1889 and 1890; A.B., Princeton, 1892, A.M., 1894; grad. Princeton Theol. Sem., 1895; fellowship in Greek, giving 2 yrs. of study in Erlangen and Berlin univs., Germany; hon. D.D., Northern Baptist Theol. Seminary, 1931; hon. LL.D., Beaver College, 1934; m. Ida Casad, Apr. 16, 1896. Ordained Presbyn. ministry, 1897; pastor Broadway Ch., Logansport, Ind., 1897-1900, except 1 yr., 1898-99, as chaplain 1st Ind. Vol. Inf., Spanish-Am. War, 6 mos. in U.S. and 6 mos. in Cuba. Entered evangelistic work, 1900, and has since conducted meetings in most of large cities of U.S., also world tour of evangelism, 1924. Pres. Winona Coll., 1917-19; became dean Winona Sch. Theology, 1922; pres. Winona Lake Christian Assembly; then minister, Palm Beach, Fla.; dir. Am. Mission to Lepers. Author: A Help to the Study of the Holy Spirit, 1903; The Growing Christian, 1903; Evangelism, 1920; Biederwolf Evangelistic Sermons, 1922; The Millennium Bible, 1924; Illustrations in Mythology, Art Literature, History and Science (7 vols.), 1927; The Great Tribulation, 1929; The Adventure of the Hereafter, 1930; Frozen Assets, 1932; Whipping-Post Theology, 1933; The New Paganism, 1934; The Wonderful Christ, 1937; and others. Home: Monticello, Ind. Died Sept. 10, 1939.

BIEN, Julius, artist, lithographer; b. Hesse-Cassel, Germany, Sept., 1826; m. Miss A. M. Brown. Came to U.S., 1849; began business on small scale (1850) with one lithographic hand-press; filled in spare time painting portraits and banners; became specialist in scientific and artistic lithography; illus., 1852, American Locomotives and Railroads (by Colburn & Holly); later illus. Coast Survey Reports, Pacific Ry. surveys; Hayden's and Powell's expdns.; Atlas of the Records of Rebellion; Statistical Atlas of U.S. Censuses, and many other Govt. and State reports. Then head of Julius Bien & Co., lithographers; pres., 1889-95, Nat. Lithographers' Assn.; mem. many scientific socs. Received medals and diplomas Centennial Expn., Phila., 1876; Paris, 1878; Chicago, 1893; Paris, gold and silver medal, 1898. Home: New York, N.Y. Died 1909.

BIEN, Morris, civil engr., lawyer; b. New York, Apr. 17, 1859; s. Joseph and Theresa (Leipold) B.; Ph.B., U. of Calif., 1879; LL.B., Columbian (now George Washington) U., 1895; LL.M., Nat. U., 1896; m. Lilla Virginia Hart, Mar. 25, 1886; children—Van Tuyl Hart, Corabel. In U.S. Geol. Survey in topog. field work and map-drawing; topographer, 1879-93, in charge of work in various parts of the country, including also irrigation investigations in Rocky Mountain States; in Gen. Land Office, Washington, in charge of rights of way upon public lands of U.S. for irrigation, ry., and other purposes, 1893-1902; in U.S. Reclamation Service, now Bur. of Reclamation, in charge of land and legal matters, July 1902-July 1924, asst. commr. in charge of lands and contracts br., also acting dir. and acting commr.; has prepared important Acts of Congress; examined and reported upon right of way and irrigation legislation considered by Dept. of Interior, 1893-1924; prepared reports on right of way and irrigation in Ann. Reports Comm. Gen. Land Office, 1893-1902, and on irrigation matters in Ann. Reports of the Reclamation Service and other publs., 1902-24. In 1904 prepared draft of a State Irrigation Code which was enacted without material change in 1905 by legislatures of N.D., S.D., and Okla., later in part in Ore., Wash., Ida., Utah, Mont. and other states and territories. Home: Takoma Park, D.C. Died July 28, 1932.

BIERBOWER, Austin, lawyer, author; b. Shelly's Island, Pa.; s. Casper and Lydia (Herman) B.; A.B., Dickinson Coll., 1864, A.M., 1866; student U. of Berlin, 1872; (LL.D., Ia. Wesleyan U., 1902); admitted to bar, 1874; unmarried. Prof. Greek and Latin, Ia. Wesleyan U., 1864-68; foreign corr. Chicago Tribune and Cincinnati Times-Star, 1870-72; editorial writer Chicago Daily News, 1879-83; in law practice, 1883—. Author: Principles of a System of Philosophy; The Morals of Christ, 1885; The Socialism of Christ, 1890; The Virtues and Their Reasons, 1896; From Monkey to Man, 1894; How to Succeed, 1900; On the Training of Lovers, 1900; Thoughts for the Rich, 1905. Home: Chicago. Died Sept. 28, 1913.

BIERSTADT, Albert, landscape painter; b. nr. Düsseldorf, Germany, Jan. 7, 1830; came in infancy to New Bedford, Mass.; showed talent for art; studied 4 yrs. in Europe, 1853-57; made repeated visits to the West and to Europe; specialty is pictures of scenes in Rocky Mountains, Sierras, and Switzerland; mem. of Nat. Acad., 1860—; has been awarded many foreign medals and the crosses of the Legion of Honor and St. Stanislaus. Died 1902.

BIESECKER, Frederick Winters, lawyer; b. Jenner Twp., Somerset Co., Pa., Mar. 10, 1858; s. John and Jonnah (Winters) B.; LL.B., Franklin and Marshall Coll., Lancaster, Pa., 1880, LL.D., 1930; m. Edith K. Linton, Aug. 6, 1921. Admitted to Pa. bar, 1882, and began practice at Somerset; dist. atty. Somerset Co., 1884-88; v.p. First Nat. Bank, Somerset; dir. Somerset Trust Co. Vice-pres. bd. trustees Franklin and Marshall Coll., Theol. Sem. Ref. Ch. of U.S., Lancaster, Pa. Republican. Home: Somerset, Pa. Died July 6, 1936.

BIGELOW, Edward Fuller, lecturer and writer; b. Colchester, Conn., Jan. 14, 1860; s. William S. and Mary J. B.; prep. edn. Bacon Acad., Colchester; spl. student Biol. Lab., Yale University, 1896-97; student Biol. Lab., Cold Spring Harbor, L.I., 1899; Nature Study School, Coll. of Agr., Kingston, R.I., 1899; Nature Study Class, Marine Biol. Lab., Woods Hole, Mass., 1900-01; also studied at Nature Study School, Cornell U.; A.M., Ph.D., Taylor U., 1899; m. Mary Augusta Pelton, July 2, 1882; children—Nellie Pelton, Woodbridge Fuller, Pearl Agnes (dec.). Editor Nature and Science dept., St. Nicholas Magazine, 1900-14; for 25 years, took about 4,500 boys and girls yearly on natural history excursions; editor of Popular Science, New York, 3 yrs.; editor The Observer, 8 years; principal public school, 10 years; editor dailies, 18 years; nature lecturer for N.Y. Bd. of Edn., Marthas Vineyard Inst. for Teachers, Cornell U., Cold Spring Harbor Lab., etc.; dir. Conn. Summer Sch. of Nature Study and Natural Sciences, Conn. Coll. Agr., 1902, and Conn. Chautauqua Assembly Assn., 1903-04; lecturer nature study and astonomy, Castle Boarding Sch. for Young Ladies, Tarrytown, N.Y., 1900-31; lecturer and teacher in Miss Spence's School, N.Y. City, 1900-32; with Camp Kineowatha, Maine, and other camps for girls, 1916; gen. dir. Cornucopia Home-Camp, Sound Beach (now Old Greenwich), Conn., 1925-30. Instr. in nature pedagogy at co. teachers' insts., throughout U.S.; instr. nature study in univ. summer schs., Calif., Ohio, Mich., N.C., Ala., Ind., Iowa, etc.; inventor chem. tablets for artificial nutriment of plants, 1901, an ednl. beehive, 1905. Author: (and designer) Bigelow's Descriptive Plant Analysis; How Nature Study Should Be Taught; The Spirit of Nature Study, 1907. Compiler: Walking, a Fine Art, 1907. Editor of The Guide to Nature, 1908-35. Scout naturalist of Boy Scouts of America, and editor "On Nature's Trail," in Boys' Life, 1916-19. Curator The Bruce Museum, Greenwich, Conn., 1915-37, now curator emeritus. Home: Old Greenwich, Conn. Died July 13, 1938.

BIGELOW, Francis Hill, author, antiquarian; b. Cambridge, Mass., Feb. 24, 1859; s. Marshall T. and Caroline Priscilla (Warland) B.; ed. high sch., Cambridge; unmarried. Began, 1879, in employ of Howe & Goodwin, Calcutta commn. mchts., Boston; retired, 1906. Began search in Mass. for American silver, resulting in exhbns. of Am. silver at Mus. of Fine Arts, Boston, 1906 and 1911; made inventory of the ch. silver of N.E., and researches as to Am. silversmiths, resulting, 1913, in publication by Nat. Soc. Colonial Dames of "The Old Silver of American Churches." Author: Historic Silver of the Colonies and Its Makers, 1917. Home: Cambridge, Mass. Died June 17, 1933.

BIGELOW, Frank Hagar, meteorologist; b. Concord, Mass., Aug. 28, 1851; s. Francis Edwin and Ann (Hagar) B.; A.B., Harvard, 1873, A.M., 1880; B.D., Episcopal Theol. Sch., Cambridge, 1880; (hon. L.H.D., Columbian (now George Washington) U., 1899; m. Mary E. Spalding, Oct. 6, 1881. Astronomer at Cordoba Obs., Argentine Republic, 1873-76 and 1881-83; took part in Dr. B. A. Gould's exploration of the Southern heavens; prof. mathematics, Racine Coll., 1884-89; asst. Nautical Almanac Office, 1889-91, and mem. U.S. Eclipse Expdn. to W. Africa, 1889. Newberry, S.C., 1900, Spain, 1905; prof. meteorology, U.S. Weather Bur., 1891-1910; prof. solar physics, George Washington U., 1894-1910; prof. meteorology, Oficina Meteorologica, Cordoba, Argentina, 1910-21; dir. Pilar Solar and Magnetic Obs., 1915-21. Rector, Natick, Mass., 1880-81; chaplain, Racine, Wis., 1885-89; asst. minister St. John's Ch., Washington, 1891-1910; was chief climatol. div. U.S. Weather Bur.; also in charge of researches into the law of evaporation at the Salton Sea and in U.S. generally; then retired. Author of articles and monographs on meteorology, solar physics, meteorol. treatise on Circulation and Radiation of the Atmospheres of the Earth and Sun; Treatise on the Sun's Radiation and other solar phenomena. Deceased.

BIGELOW, Frank Hoffnagel, clergyman, educator; b. N.Y. City, June 10, 1873; s. Loyal Alpheus and Elizabeth (Hoffnagel) B.; prep. edn., Montgomery Bell Acad. (Nashville, Tenn.) and Beeman Acad.; A.B., Middlebury Coll., 1894; studied Union Theol. Sem., Columbia U. (post-grad.); B.D., Episcopal Theol. Sch., 1899; m. Mabel Augusta Brittain, Apr. 2, 1902; children—Elizabeth (Mrs. Abbott), John Brittain. Ordained deacon, 1899, priest, 1900, Protestant Episcopal Church; was with St. Paul Church, Natick, Mass., 1899-1903; vicar St. Luke's Ch., Stamford, Conn., 1903-11; asst. rector St. John's Ch., Bridgeport, 1915; later rector Trinity Ch., Lime Rock, Conn., and rector Christ Ch., Pomfret, until 1927; headmaster Rectory Sch., Pomfret, 1920—. Democrat. Episcopalian. Mason. Home: Pomfret, Conn. Died Mar. 19, 1937.

BIGELOW, George Hoyt, M.D., health officer, hospital adminstr.; b. Framingham, Mass., Nov. 13, 1890; s. Dr. Enos Hoyt and Agnes Elizabeth (Cutter) B.; A.B., Harvard, 1913, M.D., 1916, D.P.H., 1921; m. Margaret Wesselhoeft, June 10, 1916; children—Margaret, Bradley. Dir. industrial medicine and hygiene, Antioch Coll., Yellow Springs, O., 1921-22; dir. Cornell Clinic, N.Y. City, 1922-24; dir. div. communicable diseases, Mass. Dept. Pub. Health, 1924-25; commr. of pub. health, Mass., 1925-33; dir. Mass. Gen. Hosp. and Mass. Eye and Ear Infirmary, 1934—. Served in lab. div. U.S.A., 1917-19. Home: Milton, Mass. Died Dec. 1934.

BIGELOW, Harriet Williams, astronomer; b. Fayetteville, N.Y., June 7, 1870; d. Rev. Dana W. (D.D.) and Katherine (Huntington) B.; A.B., Smith Coll., 1893; Ph.D., U. of Mich., 1904. Asst. in astronomy, 1896-1901, instr., 1904-06, asso. prof., 1906-11, prof., 1911—, Smith Coll. Presbyn. Home: Northampton, Mass. Died June 27, 1934.

BIGELOW, Henry Forbes, architect; b. Clinton, Mass., May 12, 1867; s. Henry Nelson and Clarissa Nichols (Forbes) B.; prep. edn. St. Mark's Sch., Southboro, Mass., 1880-84; B.S. in Architecture, Mass. Inst. Tech., 1888; m. Eliza Frothingham Davis, Oct. 14, 1896 (died 1907); m. 2d, Susan Thayer, June 1, 1912. Practiced in Boston, 1888—; mem. Bigelow & Wadsworth. Architect: St. Mark's Sch., Southboro, Mass.; Shawmut Nat. Bank Bldg., Tremont Bldg., Hotel Touraine, Boston; residences of Robert Saltonstall, of Milton, Mass., J. J. Storrow, Lincoln, Mass., etc. Trustee Boston Museum of Fine Arts, St. Mark's Sch. Fellow Am. Inst. Architects. Republican. Episcopalian. Home: Boston. Died Aug. 12, 1929.

BIGELOW, John, army officer; b. New York, N.Y., May 12, 1854; s. John and Jane Tunis (Poultney) B.; ed. in Paris, Bonn, Berlin, Freiberg and Providence, R.I.; apptd. from N.Y., and grad. U.S. Mil. Acad., 1877; m. Mary Braxton Dallam, Apr. 28, 1883; children—John (dec.), Gladys (dec.), Braxton (dec.), Jane Poultney. Second lt., June 15, 1877; 1st lt., Sept. 24, 1883; capt., Apr. 15, 1893; maj. 9th Cav., Dec. 8, 1902; adj. gen. D.C. militia, 1887-89; prof. mil. sci., Mass. Inst. Tech., 1894-98; wounded in attack on San Juan, July 1, 1898; retired at own request, over 30 yrs. service, Sept. 15, 1904. Prof. French, M.I.T., 1905-10; on duty with organized militia of Mass., Feb. 10, 1906-Aug. 1, 1910; prof. mil. sci., Rutgers Coll., Oct. 15, 1917-May 18, 1918; on duty in hist. branch Gen. Staff, till July 5, 1919. Author: Mars-la-Tour and Gravelotte, 1884; Principles of Strategy, 1894; Reminiscences of the Santiago Campaign, 1899; The Campaign of Chancellorsville, 1910; American Policy, 1914; World Peace, 1915; Breaches of Anglo-American Treaties, 1917. Home: Washington, D.C. Died Feb. 29, 1936.

BIGELOW, John, author; b. Malden, Ulster Co., N.Y., Nov. 25, 1817; s. Asa and Lucy (Isham) B.; A.B., Union Coll., 1835; (LL.D., Union, and Racine Colls., 1886, New York U., 1889); m. Jane Tunis Poultney (dec.); father of John, Jr., and Poultney B. Admitted to bar, 1839; insp. Sing Sing prison, 1845-46; one of the editors New York Evening Post, 1849-61; consul at Paris, France, 1861-64; U.S. minister to France, 1864-67; chmn. of Gov. Tilden's canal investigating com., 1875; sec. of state, N.Y., 1875-77. Executor and trustee of late Samuel J. Tilden; pres. bd. of trustees New York Pub. Library, Astor, Lenox and Tilden foundations; trustee Met. Mus. of Art; pres. Tilden Trust. Pres. Century Assn.; mem. Am. Acad. Arts and Letters. Author: Writings and Speeches of Samuel J. Tilden (2 vols.), 1885; The Life of Benjamin Franklin, 1868, 5th edit., 1905;

The Complete Works of Benjamin Franklin; France and the Confederate Navy, 1888; The Bible That Was Dead and Is Alive Again, 1893; Life of William Cullen Bryant, 1893; Life of Samuel J. Tilden, 1895; The Mystery of Sleep, 1897; Gladstone Morley and the Confederate Loan of 1863, 1905; The Useful Life, a Crown to the Simple Life, 1906; Peace Given as the World Giveth, or the Portsmouth Treaty and Its First Year's Fruits; Letters and Literary Memorials of Samuel J. Tilden (2 vols.), 1908; Retrospections of an Active Life (3 vols.). Died 1911.

BIGELOW, Marshall Train, printer and proof reader (retired June 17, 1893); b. S. Natick, Mass., Oct. 5, 1822; s. Abraham B.; ed. S. Natick, 6 months in each yr. from 4 to 10 yrs. of age; received hon. deg. from Harvard, 1864; m. Caroline P. Warland, Oct. 21, 1847. Pres. common council, Cambridge, and mem. bd. aldermen, same; treas. First Parish, Cambridge, several yrs.; was Republican, then Cleveland Democrat. Author: Punctuation and Other Typographic Matters, 1881; Mistakes in Writing English and How to Avoid Them, 1886. Home: Cambridge, Mass. Died 1902.

BIGELOW, Melville Madison, lawyer, author; b. Eaton Rapids, Mich., Aug. 2, 1846; s. William Enos and Daphna Florence (Madison) B.; A.B., U. of Mich., 1866; LL.B., 1868, A.M., 1871; A.M., Ph.D., Harvard, 1879; (LL.D., Northwestern U., 1896, LL.D., U. of Mich., 1912); m. Alice Bradford Woodman, Nov. 10, 1898. Lecturer, formerly in law dept., Univ. of Mich., and in Northwestern U. Law Sch.; prof. in and some time dean of Boston U. Law Sch. Fellow Am. Acad. Arts and Sciences. Author: The Law of Estoppel, 1872, sixth edition, 1913; Leading Cases in the Law of Torts, 1875; The Law of Torts, 8th edit., 1907, 3d English edit., U. of Cambridge, 1908; Placita Anglo-Normannica, 1879; History of English Procedure, 1880; The Law of Fraudulent Conveyances, 2d edit., 1911; The Law of Bills, Notes and Cheques, 2d edit., 1900; The Law of Wills, 1898. Joint Author: Centralization and the Law, 1906; A False Equation—The Problem of the Great Trust, 1911. Home: Cambridge, Mass. Died May 4, 1921.

BIGELOW, Prescott; b. Jamaica Plain, Mass., July 7, 1884; s. Prescott and Bessie Paine (Nazro) B.; grad. Noble and Greenough Sch., 1904; student Harvard, 1904-06; m. Marion Burdett, Apr. 30, 1908 (died 1926); children—Prescott, Mary Jane; m. 2d, Mrs. Nina Hopkins Grant, Apr. 27, 1927; 1 stepson, William D. Grant. Began with Burroughs & DeBlois, real estate, Boston, 1906; mem. Poole & Bigelow, 1910-18; with Hayden, Stone & Co., investment bankers, Boston, 1919— (partner, 1926—); officer or dir. numerous corps. Republican. Episcopalian. Home: Chestnut Hill, Mass. Died Oct. 27, 1937.

BIGELOW, Willard Dell, chemist; b. Gardner, Kan., May 31, 1866; s. William I. and Jennie (Lytle) B.; A.B., Amherst 1889; m. Nancy M. Nesbit, Apr. 9, 1896. Asst. prof. chemistry, Ore. State Coll., 1889-90; instr. chemistry, Washington High Sch., 1891-92; chemist, July 1, 1892-June 1, 1913, asst. chief, Bur. of Chemistry, 1903-13, chief Div. of Foods, 1901-13, U.S. Dept. Agr.; mem. bd. of food and drug inspection, U.S. Dept. Agr., Jan. 1-June 1, 1913; chief chemist, 1913-18, dir. research laboratories, 1918, Nat. Canners' Assn. Prof. chemistry, Nat. U., Washington, 1893-98. Author of bulls. on the composition and adulteration of food and on technology of canning. Home: Washington, D.C. Died Mar. 6, 1939.

BIGELOW, William Sturgis, M.D.; b. Boston, Apr. 4, 1850; s. Henry J. and Susan (Sturgis) B.; A.B., Harvard, 1871, M.D., 1874. Began practice at Boston, 1878, now out of practice; surgeon to outpatients Mass. Gen. Hosp., 1879-81; later, trustee Mass. Gen. Hosp.; instr. in surgery, Harvard Med. Sch., 1879-81; lecturer on the Buddhist Doctrine, Harvard, 1908. Trustee Mus. of Fine Arts; dir. New Boston Music Hall. Mem. U.S. Assay Commn. Fellow Am. Acad. Arts and Sciences. Comdr. Imperial Order of the Rising Sun, Japan. Author: Buddhism and Immortality, 1908. Home: Boston, Mass. Died Oct. 6, 1926.

BIGGAR, Hamilton Fisk, surgeon; b. Oakville, Ont., Can., Mar. 15, 1839; s. Rev. Hamilton and Eliza Phelps (Racey) B.; A.B., Victoria U., Toronto, 1863 (LL.D., 1893); M.D., Cleveland U. of Medicine and Surgery, 1866; then practiced at Cleveland; m. Sue Miles Brooks, Feb. 25, 1870. Formerly prof. anatomy and clin. surgery, surg. diseases of women, Homœ. Hosp. Coll.; surgeon-in-chief Surg. Inst.; a founder and dean, Training Sch. for Nurses. Episcopalian. Author: Twelve Months of Surgery; Loiterings in Europe. Home: Cleveland, O. Died Nov. 29, 1926.

BIGGERS, Earl Derr, writer; b. Warren, O., Aug. 26, 1884; s. Robert J. and Emma E. (Derr) B.; A.B., Harvard, 1907; m. Eleanor Ladd, Sept. 14, 1912; 1 son, Robert Ladd. With Boston Traveler, 1908-11, inclusive, first as conductor of a humorous column, later as dramatic critic; wrote play, "If You're Only Human," produced Nov., 1912; contbr. to mags. Author: Seven Keys to Baldpate, 1913; Love Inseurance (novel), 1914; Inside the Lines (play), 1915; The Agony Column (novel), 1916; A Cure for Curables (play, written with William Hodge), 1917; See-Saw (musical comedy), 1919; The House Without a Key (novel), 1925; Fifty Candles (novelette), 1926; The Chinese Parrot (novel), 1926; Behind That Curtain (novel), 1928; The Black Camel (novel), 1929; Charlie Chan Carries On (novel), 1930. Home: Pasadena, Calif. Died Apr. 5, 1933.

BIGGS, Albert Welburne, lawyer; b. Trenton, Tenn., Sept. 8, 1871; s. Zach, Jr., and Julia Elizabeth (Raines) B.; prep. edn., Peabody High Sch., Trenton; LL.B., Law Dept., Vanderbilt U., Nashville, Tenn., 1892; m. Margaret Pharr, June 4, 1903. Began practice, Trenton, 1892, as mem. Walker & Biggs, later Taylor & Biggs; removed to Memphis, 1903, to become mem. Carroll, McKellar, Bullington & Biggs; asst. gen. solicitor I.C. R.R. and Yazoo & Miss. Valley R.R. Co., 1905-07; mem. Fitzhugh & Biggs, 1907-13; then in practice alone; atty. for Tenn. for St.L.&S.F. R.R.; local atty. I.C. R.R., Miss Valley R.R. cos., Mobile & Ohio R.R.; counsel and dir. for Bank of Commerce & Trust Co. Democrat. Mem. M.E. Ch., S. Mason. Home: Memphis, Tenn. Died June 28, 1914.

BIGGS, Benjamin T., farmer, gov.; b. Oct. 1, 1821, Summit Bridge, Del.; became farmer, 1847; mem. State constl. conv., 1852; later officer and pres. ry. corps.; mem. Congress, 1869-71; gov. Del., 1887-91. Democrat. Home: Dover, Del. Deceased.

BIGGS, David Clifton, banker; b. Pike Co., Mo., May 2, 1866; s. William Kernan and Martha Ann (Hawkins) B.; ed. high sch., and Gem City Business Coll., Quincy, Ill.; m. Ethel Hill Goddard, June 4, 1902; 1 son, David C. Became identified with banking business, 1889; settled in St. Louis, 1891; and connected with Merchants Laclede Nat. Bank; became treas. Internat. Shoe Co., 1908, gov. Federal Reserve Bank, St. Louis, 1919. Home: St. Louis, Mo. Died Sept. 28, 1931.

BIGGS, Hermann Michael, physician; b. Trumansburg, N.Y., Sept. 29, 1859; s. Joseph Hunt and Melissa T. (Pratt) B.; A.B., Cornell, 1882; M.D., Bellevue Hospital Med. Coll. (N.Y. U.), 1883; (LL.D., New York U., 1910, Rochester U., 1917; D.Sc., Harvard, 1920); m. Frances M. Richardson, Aug. 18, 1898. Interne Bellevue Hosp., 1883-84; visiting phys. Workhouse and Almshouse hosps., 1885-92; asst. pathologist, 1886-92, pathologist, 1892-99, Bellevue Hosp.; pathologist, City Hosp., 1886-92; lecturer and prof. pathol. anatomy, Bellevue Hosp. Med. Coll., 1885-94; consulting phys. Hosp. for Contagious Diseases, 1889—; prof. therapeutics and clin. medicine, 1897-1907, asso. prof. medicine, 1907-14, and prof. of medicine, 1914—, University and Bellevue Hosp. Medical Coll.; pathologist and dir. Bacteriol. Labs., 1892-1901, gen. med. officer, New York Dept. Health, 1901-14; state pub. health commr., N.Y., 1914—. Dir. Rockefeller Inst. for Med. Research since orgn. in 1901. Pres. Tuberculosis Preventorium for Children (pres.). Home: New York, N.Y. Died June 28, 1923.

BIGLER, William H., M.D.; b. Phila., June 10, 1840; grad. Moravian Coll., Bethlehem, Pa.; m. Mary, d. Dr. Aug. W. Koch, 1865; studied 2 yrs. in Berlin and Erlangen univs.; prof. in Moravian Coll. 8 yrs.; grad. Hahnemann Med. Coll., Phila., 1871; connected with it ever since, becoming prof. physiology, 1891; prof. diseases of children, 1898—; specialty, ophthalmology. Author on Syllabus of Lectures on Physiology, 1898. Co-editor, Hahnemannian Monthly. Home: Philadelphia. Died 1904.

BIJUR, Nathan, judge; b. New York, June 1, 1862; s. Asher and Pauline (Sondheim) B.; Ph.B., Columbia, 1881, LL.B., 1882, Ph.D., 1883; m. Lilly Pronick, Nov. 11, 1886; 1 son, Harry. In law practice at New York from 1882; justice Supreme Ct. of New York, term Jan. 1, 1910-Dec. 31, 1923; renominated by both parties and re-elected, term Jan. 1, 1924-Dec. 31, 1937. Republican. Jewish. Home: New York, N.Y. Died July 8, 1930.

BIKLE, Henry Wolf, lawyer; b. Gettysburg, Pa., Oct. 20, 1877; s. Philip Melanchthon B.; D.D., and Emma J. (Wolf) B.; A.B., Pa. Coll., Gettysburg, 1897, A.M., 1900; LL.B., U. of Pa., 1901; LL.D., Gettysburg College, 1928; LL.D., Franklin and Marshall College, 1937; m. Lucy Leffingwell, d. George W. Cable of Northampton, Mass., Sept. 14, 1910. Began practice in Phila., 1901; asst. gen. solicitor, 1907-16, asst. gen. counsel, 1916-22, gen. atty., 1922-32, gen. counsel, 1932—, Pa. R.R. Lecturer on law, 1901-09, asst. prof. of law, 1909-13, prof. law (courses in constl. law and carriers), 1913-29, Law School U. of Pa.; non-resident lecturer on law, Bryn Mawr Coll., 1902-04; lecturer on constl. law, Gettysburg Coll., 1906-22. Mem. Govs. Advisory Com. on Constl. Revision, Pa., 1935; chmn. advisory com. Lawyers constituted in connection with President's Com. on Civil Service Improvement, 1939. Mem. Bd. Edn. of United Luth. Church, 1930-36. Vice pres. Assn. Practitioners before Interstate Commerce Commn., 1929-30, pres. 1931-32. Fellow Am. Academy of Arts and Sciences. Author: (with late Hon. George M. Dallas) Analytical Tables of the Law of Evidence. Contbr. Am. Law Register, U. of Pa. Law Rev., Harvard Law Rev., etc. Home: Strafford, Pa. Died Jan. 26, 1942.

BIKLE, Philip Melanchthon, college dean; b. Smithsburg, Md., Dec. 1, 1844; s. Christian I. and Barbara (Fichte) B.; A.B., Pa. (now Gettysburg) Coll., 1866, D.D., 1914; Ph.D., Roanoke Coll. Va., 1884; m. Anna M. Wattles, Dec. 28, 1869; 1 son, Horace Wattles; m. 2d, Emma J. Wolf, Jan. 2, 1877; children—Henry Wolf, Paul H., Philip R. Ordained Luth. ministry, 1869; prof. Latin and Greek, N.C. Coll., 1869-70; v. prin. Md. College, Lutherville, 1870-73; Ockershausen prof. physics and astronomy, 1874-81, Pearson prof. Latin, 1881-1924, dean from 1889, Pennsylvania (now Gettysburg) Coll., then emeritus. Editor Gettysburg Coll. Monthly, 1877-94, Lutheran Quarterly, 1880-1907. Pres. Md. Luth. Synod, 1888-89. Author: Faraday, the Scientist and Christian, 1877; Our Present Knowledge of the Sun, 1878; Educating Young Men for the Ministry, 1885; Jesus, the Son of God, 1889; Melanchthon's Apology of the Augsburg Confession (transl. from Latin), 1900. Home: Gettysburg, Pa. Died Jan. 19, 1934.

BILBY, George N., surgeon; b. Ottumwa, Ia., Mar. 6, 1868; s. John Franklin and Minerva (Quigley) B.; M.D., Louisville Med. Coll., 1894; m. Alberta Mae Stockbarger, Dec. 29, 1898; children—Afton Pauline, Paul Mathias, Lee Stockbarger. Began practice at Mineola, Ia., 1894; at Cushing and Stroud, Okla., 1894-99, Alva, Okla., 1899-1931; state health commr., 1931-35. Mem. Okla. State Constl. Conv., 1906-07. Served in U.S. Army, World War, 1918-19. Democrat. Methodist. Mason. Home: Oklahoma City, Okla. Died Nov. 26, 1939.

BILES, George Phineas, ry. official; b. Dorset Co., Eng., July 18, 1857; s. Phineas and Anne Cooper (Orchard) B.; ed. common schools; m. Louise A. Pflume, Sept. 20, 1893. Began as ticket clk., London, Brighton & South Coast Ry. at Victoria Sta., London, 1872; came to U.S., 1883; rate clk., gen. frt. office, Ala. Great South R.R., at Chattanooga, 1883-84; rate clk. and chief rate clk., gen. frt. office, Queen & Crescent System, at Cincinnati, O., 1884-88; asst. gen. frt. agt., 1888-95, same system; gen. frt. agt., Cincinnati, New Orleans & Tex. Pacific Ry., Cincinnati, 1895-1907; frt. traffic mgr., C.,N.O.&T.P. Ry. and Ala. Great Southern R.R., Cincinnati, 1907-09; frt. traffic mgr., C.,N.O.&T.P. Ry., 1909—. Democrat. Home: Cincinnati, O. Died Oct. 1920.

BILGRAM, Hugo, machinist; b. Memmingen, Bavaria, Germany, Jan. 13, 1847; s. G. David and Rosina (Wiedemann) B.; grad. Poly. Sch., Augsburg, Bavaria, 1865; came to U.S., 1869; m. Mary Fischer, Dec. 8, 1872. Worked as machinist, instrument maker, draughtsman, until 1879; entered machinery business, 1879, producing spl. machinery. Author: Slide Valve Gears, 1877; Involuntary Idleness, 1889; The Cause of Business Depression, 1914; The Remedy for Overproduction and Unemployment, 1928. Home: Moylan, Pa. Deceased.

BILL, Edward Lyman, editor, author; b. Lyme, Conn., June 5, 1862; s. Judge John Wight and Prudence (Gallup) B.; desc. of William Bill, first dean of Westminster; ed. Conn. State Normal Coll.; Wesleyan Acad., Conn.; m. Caroline Lee Raymond, Feb. 12, 1889. Engaged in business at Fargo, Dakota Ty., also officer in militia; returned east, 1887, and purchased interest in Music Trade Review; editor and propr. same, 1891—, also of Talking Machine World. Treas. N.Y. State Commn., St. Louis Expn., 1904. Republican. Author: The Last of the Danvers, 1896; The Sword of the Pyramids, 1898; Hitting the Thought Trail, 1909. Home: New Rochelle, N.Y. Died Jan. 1, 1916.

BILL, Ledyard, author, publisher; b. Ledyard, Conn., May 14, 1836; ed. public schools; m. Sophia Earle, June 12, 1872. Publisher, Louisville, Ky., 1859; New York, 1862-70; retired to Paxton, Mass. Has held the offices of selectman, overseer of poor, town treas., school committeeman and town clerk. Mem. Mass. legislature, 1891; State senator, 1894-95, 1895-96. Rep. Early an advocate of "Good Roads." Was chmn. the legislative com. that introduced bill and secured the first appropriation ever made to build State roads in Mass. Author: History of the Bill Family; A Winter in Florida; Climate of Minnesota; History of Paxton. Home: Paxton, Mass. Deceased.

BILLER, George, Jr., bishop; b. London, Eng., Feb. 25, 1874; s. George and Clara E. (Smith) B.; ed. St. Austin's Sch., New York; grad. Berkeley Div. Sch., Middletown, Conn., 1898 (D.D., 1913); m. Edna Peninger, Nov. 14, 1901. Deacon P.E. Ch., 1898, priest, 1898; missionary work, Okla., 1898-1903; vicar Chapel of Incarnation, New York, 1903-08; Calvary Cathedral, Sioux Falls, S.D., 1908-09, dean, 1909-12; elected 3d bishop of S.D., Apr. 12, 1912; consecrated Sept. 18, 1912. Home: Sioux Falls, S.D. Died Oct. 22, 1915.

BILLINGHURST, Benson Dillon, supt. schs.; b. McArthur, O., Aug. 15, 1869; s. Charles James and Martha Jane (Dillon) B.; B.S., Ohio Wesleyan U., 1897; research biology, U. of Calif., summer 1905; LL.B., U. of Wash., 1908; summer session, Teachers Coll. (Columbia), 1916; LL.D., U. of Nev., 1924; m. Carrie Emily Burns, Aug. 25, 1892; children—Ruth Anna, Florence Harriet. Teacher dist. schs.

Ohio and Ill., 1886-88; prin. schs., Stanford, Ill., 1891-95; prin. high sch., Danville, Ill., 1897-1900; supt. schs., Prescot, Ariz., 1900-07, Reno, Nev., 1908—. Democrat. Conglist. Home: Reno, Nev. Died Dec. 3, 1935.

BILLINGS, Cornelius Kingsley Garrison, capitalist; b. Saratoga Springs, N.Y., sept. 17, 1861; s. Albert M. and Augusta S. (Farnsworth) B.; moved to Chicago with parents, 1864; grad Racine (Wis.) Coll., 1879; m. Blanche, d. Andrew MacLeish, 1885. Entered office of Peoples Gas Light & Coke Co., Chicago, 1879, of which his father was pres., and after various promotions, succeeded his father as pres., 1887; became pres. of reorganized Co., 1897-1901, and chmn. bd., 1901-11; now chmn. bd. Union Carbide & Carbon Corp. Was dir. World's Columbian Expn. Republican. Home: Santa Barbara, Calif. Died May 6, 1937.

BILLINGS, Edmund, banker, sociologist; b. St. George, N.B., Can., Jan. 14, 1868; s. Edmund and Elizabeth (Sutherland) B.; ed. pub. schs., Boston, and night sch., Harvard; m. Elizabeth Child, Oct. 1, 1896; children—Edmund, Mrs. Katherine L. Wood. Messenger boy, later clk. in art store until 1887; apptd. supt. Wells Memorial Inst., 1888, and 2 yrs. later apptd. supt. People's Inst., Roxbury, holding both positions; pres. Paul Revere Trust Co., 1911 until sold to State St. Trust Co., of which is director; trustee Home Savings Bank. Served as 2d lt. 5th Provisional Militia, Spanish-Am. War; ex-sec. Boston Pub. Sch. Assn.; was mem. exec. com. Municipal League and on com. which erected first municipal bath in Boston. Apptd. by Gov. Draper as rep. of Mass., in Italy, in charge of distribution of $350,-000 fund raised for Messina earthquake sufferers; first boulevard built after disaster in Messina was named Via Billings in his honor; presented by King of Italy with silver medal and diploma. An organizer and 1st sec. for 10 yrs., of Good Govt. Assn., Boston; a founder and mem. 1st exec. com., Boston City Club; was gen. exec. sec. Chelsea Relief Com. when city was devastated by fire; mem. exec. com. on Salem fire and San Francisco earthquake; formerly chmn. Transit Com. City of Boston. Apptd. collector Port of Boston by President Woodrow Wilson, Oct. 8, 1913; resigned July 1, 1921; now v.p. and treas. of gen. ins. business of John Paulding Meade Co., Inc. Democrat. Home: Boston, Mass. Died Feb. 7, 1929.

BILLINGS, Frank, M.D.; b. Highland, Iowa Co., Wis., Apr. 2, 1854; s. Henry M. and Ann (Bray) B.; M.D., Northwestern U., 1881, M.S., 1890; interne Cook Co. (Ill.) Hosp., 1881-82; studied in Vienna, London and Paris, 1885-86; Sc.D., Harvard, 1915; m. Dane Ford Brawley, May 26, 1887; 1 dau., Margaret (Mrs. Geo. R. Nichols, II). Demonstrator of anatomy, 1882-86, prof. physical diagnosis, 1886-91, prof. medicine, 1891-98, Northwestern U.; prof. medicine, 1898—, dean of faculty, 1900—, Rush Med. Coll. (affiliated with U. of Chicago); professorial lecturer, 1901-05, prof. medicine, 1905-24, U. of Chicago. First lt., 1908, major, 1917, Med. R.C. Presbyterian Hosp., 1898-1920; cons. phys. same; retired. Shattuck lect. (Boston), 1902; Lane med. lecturer (Leland Stanford U.), 1915. Chmn. Am. Red Cross Mission to Russia, 1917. Mem. Ill. State Council Defense; mem. advisory bd. of Am. Red Cross War Council; major Med. R.C. U.S.A. as aide to gov. of Ill. in orgn. advisory med. bds. for army draft; col. Med. Corps U.S.A.; served in A.E.F. and office of provost marshal gen. and office of surgeon gen., Feb. 1, 1918-June 28, 1919. Pres. Ill. State Bd. Charities and of State Charities Commn., 1906-12. Home: Chicago, Ill. Died Sept. 20, 1932.

BILLINGS, Franklin Swift, gov.; b. New Bedford, Mass., May 11, 1862; s. Franklin Noble and Nancy Snow (Swift) B.; prep. edn., Adams Acad., Quincy; A.B., Harvard, 1885; LL.D., Middlebury, 1924, U. of Vt. and Norwich, 1925; m. Bessie Hewitt Vail, July 12, 1892 (died 1917); children——Elizabeth Swift (Mrs. Curtis P. Fields), Franklin Noble (dec.), Nancy (Mrs. Morton Keeney); m. 2d, Gertrude Curtis Todd, July 21, 1919; 1 son, Franklin Swift. Chief of staff to Gov. C. J. Bell of Vt., 1904-06; mem. Ho. of Rep., Vt., 1910, 12; mem. State Bd. of Edn., Vt., 1913; again mem. Ho. of Rep., Vt., 1921-23 (speaker of House same period); lt. gov. of Vt., 1923-25; gov. of Vt., term 1925-27. Trustee Ottanquechee Savings Bank, Woodstock, Vt. Overseer Harvard, 1927-32; dir. Harvard Alumni Assn. 3 yrs. Republican. Episcopalian. Home: Woodstock, Vt. Died Jan. 16, 1935.

BILLINGS, George Herrick, metallurgist; b. Taunton, Mass., Feb. 8, 1845; s. Warren and Mary Frances (Caswell) B.; ed. Pittsburg and Mass. Inst. Tech.; m. Harriet Ann Goodwin, Apr. 24, 1879. Was employed in steel mills as roll turner, heater, roller, and later as chemist, mech. engr. and gen. mgr.; mfr. cold drawn steel, 1889—. Inventor of machines for drawing iron and steel bars for shafting and finishing rods. Contributor to current periodicals. Home: Boston, Mass. Died Dec. 8, 1913.

BILLINGS, John Shaw, surgeon, librarian; b. Switzerland Co., Ind., Apr. 12, 1839; s. James and Abbie (Shaw) B.; A.B., Miami U., 1857, A.M., 1860; M.D., Med. Coll. of Ohio, 1860; (LL.D., U. of Edinburgh, 1884, Harvard, 1886, Buda-Pesth, 1896, Yale, 1901, Johns Hopkins, 1902; M.D., Munich, 1889, Dublin, 1892; D.C.L., Oxford, 1889); m. Kate M. Stevens, Sept. 3, 1862. Demonstrator anatomy, Med. Coll. of Ohio, 1860-61; served in U.S.A., as asst. surgeon, Apr. 16, 1862; maj. surgeon, Dec. 2, 1876; lt. col. deputy surgeon gen., June 6, 1894; bvtd. capt., maj. and lt. col., Mar. 13, 1865, "for faithful and meritorious services during the war"; in hosp. service during Civil War; later med. insp. Army of the Potomac, in charge of library of surgeon-general's office until his appmt., Dec. 28, 1883, as curator Med. Mus. and Library; retired Oct. 1, 1895. In charge vital statistics 10th Census, vital and social statistics, 11th Census. Prof. hygiene, U. of Pa., 1891, and dir., 1893-96; dir. N.Y. Pub. Library, Astor, Lenox and Tilden foundations, 1896—; chmn. bd. Carnegie Instn., 1905—. Fellow Am. Acad. Arts and Sciences; pres. A.L.A., 1901-02. Author: Principles of Ventilation and Heating, 1886; Index Catalogue of the Library of the Surgeon-General's Office U.S.A. (16 vols.), 1880-1894; National Medical Dictionary (2 vols.), 1889. Home: New York. Died March. 11, 1913.

BILLINGS, Luther Guiteau, naval officer; b. in New York, 1842; s. Hon. Andrew and Abbie (Sheldon) B.; apptd. acting asst. p.-m. U.S.S. Water Witch, Oct. 22, 1862; took active part in engagement June 4, 1864, when Water Witch was boarded by Confederates, several of whom, including their comdg. officer, he killed in hand to hand conflict, but was wounded and captured, taken to hosp. and later to prison; escaped from moving train, but was recaptured by aid of bloodhounds; imprisoned in Charleston and later in Libby Prison; exchanged late in 1864; promoted 15 numbers in his grade for "eminent and conspicuous conduct in battle"; afterward served on various stas.; was on the Wateree when it was carried about one mile inland during earthquake, Aug. 14, 1868; commd. p.-m. U.S.N., May 4, 1866; gen. insp. pay corps, Sept., 1897; pay dir. with rank of rear adm., Jan. 9, 1895; retired, Mar. 14, 1898. After retirement, was ordered to duty during the Spanish War, and organized the Coast Signal Service, from Eastport, Me., to the Rio Grande; again ordered to active duty, Mar. 8, 1917, as purchasing officer for Eastern Dist., Baltimore. Home: Chappaqua, New York. Died Dec. 30, 1920.

BILLINGS, W(illiam) Chester, U.S. Pub. Health Service; b. Hartford, Conn., Apr. 15, 1872; s. Capt. Henry Ross and Dolly Ann (Clark) B.; M.D., Harvard, 1894; m. Elizabeth Martin Ingersoll, 1899; m. 2d, Adah Laurissa Merritt, 1910. Pvt. practice of medicine, Springfield, Mass., 1894-98; commd. asst. surgeon U.S. P.H.S., 1898; passed asst. surgeon, 1904, surgeon, 1913, senior surgeon, 1929, med. dir., 1930; retired, 1933; served in 19 different stations, including chief med. officer at Angel Island (Calif.) and Ellis Island, and chief surgeon U.S. Coast Guard; med. adviser to Am. Consulate, Liverpool, 1927-30, Am. Consulate Gen., London, 1930-32; served in 5 epidemics including one at Charlestown, W.Va., 1900, and presented with gold watch by people of city. Mem. S.A.R. Republican. Conglist. Mason. Home: La Cañada, Calif. Died Aug. 16, 1939.

BILLSON, William Weldon, lawyer; b. Springfield, Ill., June 7, 1847; s. Thomas and Hester (Watson) B.; grad. high sch., Springfield, 1864; m. Alice L. Harford, Nov. 20, 1872. Admitted to Minn. bar, 1868; practiced, Winona, 1868-70, removed to Duluth, 1870; mem. firm of Billson, Congdon & Dickinson, 1892-02, Billson & Congdon, 1902-10 (retired); was for many years identified with much important litigation in state and federal courts. Mem. Minn. State Senate, 1872, and 1883-85; U.S. atty., Dist. of Minn., 1873-81. Republican. Baptist. Author: Equity in its Relations to Common Law, 1917. Home: Duluth, Minn. Died Sept. 2, 1923.

BINGHAM, Amelia, actress; b. Hicksville, O.; d. John B. and Marie (Hoffman) Smilley; ed. pub. schs. and Ohio Wesleyan U.; m. Lloyd M. Bingham (died 1915). Dêbut "Power of Gold." People's Theatre, New York; various melodramas in other New York theatres; with Augustus Pitou, 1 yr., Charles Frohman, 5 yrs.; was leading lady in "His Excellency, the Governor," "White Heather," "The Cuckoo," and "Hearts Are Trumps"; organized, 1901, The Amelia Bingham Company and produced her own plays, "The Climbers," "A Modern Magdalen," "The Frisky Mrs. Johnson," etc.; appeared in "Big Moments from Great Plays"; starred, 1913, with William Crane and Douglas Fairbanks. Died Sept. 1, 1927.

BINGHAM, David Judson, army officer; b. Massena, N.Y., May 16, 1831; s. Alfred Sidney and Mary (Purcell) B.; grad. U.S. Mil. Acad., 1854, Arty. Sch., Ft. Monroe, Va., 1860; m. Marguerite Gonzalez, Nov. 20, 1856. Apptd. 2d lt. 2d Arty., July 1, 1854; advanced through the grades to maj. q.-m. U.S.A., July 29, 1866; lt. col. deputy q.-m. gen., Mar. 3, 1875; col. asst. q.-m. gen., July 2, 1883; retired by operation of law, May 16, 1895; advanced to rank of brig. gen. retired by act of Apr. 23, 1904; bvtd. maj., lt. col. and col., Mar. 13, 1865, for faithful and meritorious services during the war; bvtd. brig. gen., Apr. 9, 1865, for faithful and meritorious services in the field during the war. Died 1909.

BINGHAM, Henry Harrison, congressman; b. Phila., Dec. 4, 1841; s. James and Ann (Sheller) B.; A.B., Jefferson Coll., Pa., 1862, A.M., 1866; (LL.D., Washington and Jefferson, 1906). First lt. 140th Pa. Inf., Aug. 22, 1862; capt. Sept. 9, 1862; maj. judge advocate vols., Sept. 20, 1864; bvtd. maj. vols. Aug. 1, 1864, "for good conduct and conspicuous gallantry, especially at the Wilderness, Spottsylvania and Gettysburg"; lt. col. vols., Apr. 9, 1865, "for highly meritorious services during campaign terminating with surrender of Gen. R. E. Lee"; col. and brig. gen. vols. Apr. 9, 1865, "for conspicuous gallantry and meritorious services during the war"; awarded medal of honor, Aug. 26, 1893, for Battle of Wilderness; hon. mustered out, July 2, 1866; thrice wounded. Read law with Atty.-Gen. Benjamin H. Brewster; m. Mary H. Alexander, Feb. 4, 1874. Postmaster of Phila., 1867-72; clerk courts of oyer and terminer and quarter sessions of the peace, Phila., 1872-78; mem. 46th to 62d Congresses (1879-1913), 1st Pa. Dist. (longest continuous service of any mem. now in House). Del. Rep. Nat. convs., 1872 (at-large), 1876, 1884, 1888, 1892, 1896, 1900, 1904. Home: Philadelphia. Died Mar. 23, 1912.

BINGHAM, Hiram, congl. missionary; b. Honolulu, H.I., Aug. 16, 1831; s. Hiram and Sybil Moseley B. (pioneer missionaries to Hawaii, 1820); prep. edn. Williston Sem., E. Hampton, Mass.; grad. Yale, 1853; studied divinity at Andover Theol. Sem., 1854-55; (D. D., Yale, 1893; Western Reserve, 1893; Oahu Coll., 1897); m. M. Clarissa Brewster, Nov. 18, 1856. Prin. Northampton High School, 1853-54; in service Am. Bd. Commrs. for Foreign Missions, 1856—; sailed as missionary from Boston, 1856; began pioneer work in Gilbert Islands, Nov., 1857; reduced language to writing; published first portion of Gilbertese Scriptures, 1860; in command missionary brig., Morning Star, 1866-68; corr. sec. Bd. of Hawaiian Evang. Assn., 1877-80; Hawaiian govt. protector of South Sea Immigrants, 1880-82; completed translation of Gilbertese Bible, April 11, 1890; then engaged in preparing a Gilbertese Commentary on the New Testament. Author: Gilbertese Grammar in English (in manuscript), 1861; Story of the Morning Star, 1866; Gilbertese Bible, 1893; Gilbertese Bible Dictionary, Honolulu, 1895; Gilbertese Hymn and Tune Book, 1897; Gilbertese Commentary on Matthew, 1904; Gilbertese Commentary on the Four Gospels, 1905; Gilbertese Commentary of Acts (in manuscript), 1906; Gilbertese-English Dictionary (in manuscript), 1907. Home: Honolulu, H.T. Died 1908.

BINGHAM, Joel Foote, clergyman; b. Andover, Conn., Oct. 11, 1827; s. Cyrus and Abigail (Foote) B.; A.B., valedictorian, Yale, 1852, A.M., 1855; student Union Theol. Sem., (D.D., Western Reserve U., 1869; Litt.D., Trinity Coll., Conn., 1898); m. Susan Grew, July 14, 1857; father of Theodore Alfred B. (q.v.) Head Master, Classical Sch., Bible House, New York, 1852-58; pastor Congl. chs., Cleveland, 1860-61, Buffalo, 1861-67, Augusta, Me., 1867-71; ordained priest P.E. Ch., 1871; rector New Haven, 1871, Portsmouth, N.H., 1872-75, Waterbury, Conn., 1875-79; in lit. work, 1879-88; rector New London, Conn., 1888-90; retired to engage in lit. work, 1890. Lecturer on Italian lit., Trinity Coll., 10 yrs. Author: Our Father's House, 1865; History of Sunday Schools, 1867; Christian Marriage Ceremony, 1871; Francesca da Rimini (translation in verse), 6 edits., 1897, 1904; Twin Sisters of Martigny, 1899; Christian Marriage, 1900; Gemme della Letteratura Italiana (in Italian), 1903, 10; Sacred Hymns and Napoleonic Ode of Alexander Manzoni (transl. in rhyme), 1904. Home: Hartford, Conn. Died Oct. 18, 1914.

BINGHAM, Ralph, humorist; b. Richmond, Va., Aug. 2, 1870; s. Hamilton and Jane E. (McClintock) B.; ed. pub. schs. and pvt. tutelage; (hon. A.B., Villanova Coll., Pa., 1906) m. Christine L. Giles, Oct. 14, 1908. Began on platform as a child in Richmond, Va., and first toured U.S. and Can. under management of father. Founder and pres. Internat. lyceum Assn. America; v.p. Boy Council of Phila. Episcopalian. Home: Philadelphia, Pa. Died Dec. 27, 1925.

BINGHAM, Robert, educator; b. Hillsboro, N.C., Sept. 5, 1838; s. William James and Eliza A. (Norwood) B.; prep. edn. Bingham Sch., 1849-53; A.B., U. of N.C., 1857, A.M., 1860 (LL.D., 1890); married. Capt. Co. G, 44th N.C. troops, Army of Northern Va., C.S.A.; surrendered with Gen. Lee, 1865; col. N.C. N.G.; supt. The Bingham Sch. (founded 1793 by his grandfather), 1873-1920. Dir. Am. Nat. Bank, Wachovia Loan & Trust Co. Life mem. N.E.A.; pres. N.C. Hist. and Lit. Soc. Mason, Grand Master, N.C., 1883-85. Author of various articles, etc. Home: Asheville, N.C. Died May 18, 1927.

BINGHAM, Robert Worth, ambassador; b. Orange Co., N.C., Nov. 8, 1871; s. Col. Robert and Delphine Louise (Worth) B.; grad. Bingham Sch., Asheville, N.C., 1888; U. of N.C.; U. of Va.; LL.B., U. of Louisville, Ky., 1897; LL.D., U. of Ky., University of London and Cambridge U.; m. Eleanor E. Miller, May 20, 1896; children—Robert Worth, Henrietta

Worth, George Barry; m. 2d, Mrs. Mary Lily Flagler, Nov. 15, 1916; m. 3d, Mrs. James Byron Hilliard, Aug. 20, 1924. Pres. Louisville Courier-Journal Co. and Louisville Times Co., pub. of both papers; dir. Am. Creosoting Co. and various other corps. Co. atty. Jefferson Co., Ky., 1904-07; mayor Louisville, 1907; chancellor Jefferson Circuit Court, 1911; A.E. and P. from U.S. to Great Britain, 1933—. Trustee Berea Coll., Centre Coll., Danville, Ky.; regent Smithsonian Instn. Episcopalian. Home: Glenview, Ky. Died Dec. 18, 1937.

BINGHAM, Stillman, newspaper editor; b. Sparta, Wis., May 3, 1873; s. Henry Smith and Sarah Alice (Smith) B.; ed. high sch., Huron, S.D.; m. Alice M. Carroll, Nov. 28, 1895. Began as reporter Duluth Herald, 1892, editor, 1908—; vice pres. Duluth News-Tribune. Republican. Christian Scientist. Home: Duluth, Minn. Died July 22, 1933.

BINGHAM, Theodore Alfred, brig. gen. U.S.A.; b. Andover, Tolland Co., Conn., May 14, 1858; s. Joel Foote and Susan (Grew) B.; grad. West Point, 1879; hon. A.M., Yale, 1896; m. Lucile Rutherfurd, Dec. 15, 1881 (died 1920); m. 2d, Addison Mitchell, Oct. 2, 1926. Commissioned 2d lt., June 13, 1879; promoted through grades to brig. gen., July 11, 1904; retired July 12, 1904. Served in various duties as engineer officer, 1879-90; military attaché, U.S. Legation, Berlin, 1890-92, Rome, 1892-94; in charge Pub. Bldgs. and Grounds, Washington, with rank of col., Mar. 9, 1897-May 17, 1903; in charge of engring. dist., Lake Ontario and Lake Erie, light engr. 10th light house dist., 1903-04. Police commr., New York, Jan. 1, 1906-July 1, 1909; chief engr. highways, New York, May 10th-July 10, 1911; consulting engr., dept. of bridges, N.Y. City, 1911-15 (resigned); recalled to active service in U.S.A., Oct. 11, 1917; in command of 2d engring. dist., N.Y. City; chief engr. on staff of comdg. gen. Dept. of the East, Governor's Island, N.Y. City; discharged from active service and returned to retired list, June 10, 1919. Died Sept. 6, 1934.

BINGHAM, William Theodore, newspaperman; b. nr. Binghamton, N.Y., Aug. 24, 1861, s. William E. and Anna Elizabeth (Gilbert) B.; high sch. edn. Pvt. sec. to vice pres. Levi P. Morton, 1893; actively engaged in journalism, 1894—; Washington staff New York Sun, 1897-1912. Held championship of American Whist League, 1892-93. Home: Washington, D.C. Died Feb. 5, 1929.

BINKLEY, Robert Cedric, prof. history; b. Mannheim, Pa., Dec. 10, 1897; s. Christian Kreider and Mary Engle (Barr) B.; A.B., Stanford U., 1922, Ph.D., 1927; student Universite de Lyon, 1919; m. Frances Harriet Williams, Sept. 13, 1924; children—Robert Williams, Thomas Eden. Reference librarian, Hoover War Library, 1922-27; instr. in history, New York U., 1927-29; asso. prof. history, Smith Coll., 1929-30; actg. prof. history, Western Reserve U., 1930-32; lecturer Harvard, 1932-33; prof. history, Flora Stone Mather Coll., Western Reserve U., 1932—; visting prof., Columbia Univ., 1937-38. Served U.S. Army Ambulance Service, 1917-19. Cited for distinguished service at Fleville, France, Oct. 16, 1918. Chmn. Joint Com. on Materials for Research of Am. Council of Learned Societies and Social Science Research Council, 1932—. Mem. Am. Soc. Archivists (chmn. com. on equipment and mech. techniques), Am. Library Assn. (chmn. com. on photographic reproduction of library materials, 1938-39), Am. Hist. Assn.; Advisory Com. to the Franklin D. Roosevelt Library, Nat. Committee on Intellectual Cooperation of the League of Nations, U.S.A. V.p. Am. Documentation Inst., 1937-39. Author: New Governments of Central Europe (with M. W. Graham), 1924; What Is Right with Marriage (with Frances W. Binkley), 1929; Responsible Drinking, 1930; Methods of Reproducing Research Materials, 1931; Realism and Nationalism, 1935; Manual on Methods of Reproducing Research Materials, 1936. Editor Ronald Series in history, 1937—, asso. editor Jour. of Documentary Reproduction, 1939. Mem. editorial board Jour. of Modern History, 1934-36, Ohio Archeol. and Hist. Quarterly, Paris Peace Conf. History and Documents. Home: Cleveland, O. Died Apr. 11, 1940.

BINNEY, Arthur, naval architect, yacht broker; b. Boston, Dec. 2, 1865; s. Henry P. and Josephine (Hayward) B.; ed. pub. schs., Boston, and course in Mass. Inst. Tech.; m. Daisy Harvey, Dec. 2, 1896. Began as apprentice with Whittier Machine Co., Boston, later employed by Hook & Hastings Organ Co.; associated, 1888, with Edward Burgess, naval architect, who designed yachts Puritan, Mayflower and Volunteer, defenders of the international prize trophy; succeeded to business, upon death of partner, 1891; dir. Rockport Granite Co. Republican. Unitarian. Home: Brookline, Mass. Died Aug. 28, 1924.

BINNEY, Charles Chauncey, lawyer; b. Phila., Oct. 20, 1855; s. Horace (Jr.) and Eliza Frances (Johnson) B.; brother of John B.; A.B., Harvard, 1878; studied law in office William Henry Rawle, Phila., and at U. of Pa.; admitted to bar, 1881; m. Sarah Cooke Dawes, June 24, 1885 (died 1900); 2d, Isabelle Nichols, Nov. 29, 1904. Practiced law Phila., 1881—; asst. atty. U.S. Dept. Justice, 1893-97; spl. atty., same dept., 1897-1901. Independent Democrat. Author: Restrictions Upon Local and Special Legislation in State Constitutions, 1894; Life of Horace Binney, 1903. Home: Philadelphia. Died July 10, 1913.

BINNEY, Edwin; b. Shrub Oak, Westchester Co., N.Y., Nov. 24, 1866; s. Joseph Walker and Anne Eliza (Conklin) B.; ed. N.Y., pub. schs.; m. Alice Stead, Oct. 26, 1886; children—Dorothy (Mrs. Frank M. Upton), Helen (Mrs. Allan F. Kitchel), Mary (Mrs. James A. G. Davey), Edwin (dec.). Began in carbon black factory, 1880; entered firm of Binney & Smith, 1885, pres., 1930—; co-organizer Columbian Carbon Co., 1913, v.p., 1920—; pres. Fort Pierce (Fla.) Financing & Constrn. Co., Sebs Chem. Co., Teton Gas Products Co.; v.p. Miss. River Fuel Corp., Coltexo Corp., Peerless Carbon Black Co., Columbian Gasoline Corp., Southern Carbon Co., Piney Oil & Gas Co., St. Lucie County Bank, Western Carbon Co., Southern Gas Lines. Episcopalian. Home: Old Greenwich, Conn. Died Dec. 17, 1934.

BINNEY, John, theologian; b. Phila., Feb. 23, 1844; s. Horace (Jr.) and Eliza Frances (Johnson) B.; brother of Charles Chauncey B.; A.B., Harvard, 1864, A.M., 1867; grad. Berkeley Div. Sch., Conn., 1868; (S.T.D., Hobart, 1892, Wesleyan U., Conn., 1903); m. Charlotte B. Bush, May 20, 1869. Deacon 1868, priest, 1869, P.E. Ch.; prof. Hebrew, 1874—, O.T. lit. and interpretation, 1882—, dean, 1899-1908, Berkeley Div. Sch. Home: Middletown, Conn. Died June 12, 1913.

BINNION, Randolph (R. B. Binnion), provost Peabody Coll.; b. Biardstown, Tex., Aug. 4, 1878; s. Isaac Jason and Ella (Oliver) B.; prep. edn., Sam Houston Normal Sch., Huntsville, Tex., 1896-99; student at U. of Texas, 1912; B.S., George Peabody College for Teachers, 1923; M.A., New York Univ., 1933; Litt.D., Austin Coll., Sherman, Tex., 1923; m. Emma Shanklin, June 12, 1907. Teacher country schs., Tex., 1897-1902; prin. grammar sch., Paris, Tex., 1902-04; supt. schs., Roxton, Tex., 1904-07; supt. schs., Lamar County, Tex., 1907-11; chmn. Tex. State Bd. of Examiners, 1911-13; first asst. to Tex. State supt. pub. instrn., 1913-17; pres. East Tex. State Teachers Coll., Commerce, Tex., 1917-24; provost George Peabody Coll. for Teachers, 1924—. Democrat. Presbyn. Mason. Home: Nashville, Tenn. Deceased.

BINNS, Charles Fergus, ceramic educator; b. Worcester, Eng., Oct. 4, 1857; s. Richard William B. (F.S.A.), dir. Royal Porcelain Works, Eng.; D.Sc., Alfred (N.Y.) Univ., 1925; m. Mary Howard Ferrar, June 7, 1882 (died 1925); children—Mary Elizabeth, William Hugh Ferrar (dec.), Annie Howard (Mrs. F. Bonnet, Jr.), Dorothy Neville (Mrs. A. H. Remsen), Norah Winifred (Mrs. A. D. Fraser). Was connected with the Royal Porcelain Works, Worcester, Eng., 1872-96; prin. Tech. School of Science and Art, Trenton, N.J., 1897-1900; dir. N.Y. State Coll. of Ceramics, 1900-31. Pres. Am. Ceramic Soc., 1901, sec., 1918-22. Ordained priest P.E. Ch., 1923. Author: Ceramic Technology, 1896; The Story of the Potter, 1897; The Potter's Craft, 1909, 2d edit., 1922. Home: Alfred, N.Y. Died Dec. 4, 1934.

BIRCH, Stephen, corp. official; b. N.Y. City, Mar. 24, 1872; s. Stephen and Emily (Marshall) B.; M.E., Sch. of Mines (Columbia), 1898; m. Mary C. Rand, June 24, 1916 (died 1930); children—Mary M. R., Stephen. Now chmn. bd. Kennecott Copper Corp., Braden Copper Co.; pres. Alaska Steamship Co., Copper River & N.W. Railway Co.; dir. Alaska Development & Mineral Co., Bankers Trust Co., Utah Copper Co., Chicago, Burlington & Quincy Ry. Co., C.&S. Ry. Co., Northern Pacific Ry. Co., Nevada Northern Ry. Co. Home: Mahwah, N.J. Died Dec. 29, 1940.

BIRCH, T(homas) Bruce, prof. philosophy; b. Bloomsburg, Pa., Sept. 11, 1866; s. Richard and Ruth B.; M.E., Bloomsburg State Normal Sch., 1885; A.B., Gettysburg Coll., 1891, A.M., 1894, LL.D., 1936; grad. Gettysburg Theol. Sem., 1894; A.M., Univ. of Pa., 1906, Ph.D., 1908; D.D., Gettysburg Coll., 1926; m. Sarah C. Himmelreich, Sept. 15, 1894; children—George Henry, Edwin Richard, Mrs. Ruth Elizabeth Pontius, James Bruce. Teacher, acad. Gettysburg Coll.; prof., Irving Coll., Mechanicsburg, 1896-1902, Susquehanna U., 1902-05; Harrison Foundation scholar, 1905-06, fellow, 1906-08, U. of Pa.; John W. Bookwalter prof. philosophy, Wittenberg Coll., 1908—, also dir. summer sch. Trustee Irving Coll. Fellow A.A.A.S., Am. Geog. Soc., Royal Soc. of Arts (England). Pres. of Miami Synod of United Lutheran Church. Republican. Mason. Contributor Psychological Clinic (U. of Pa.), to Biblical World (U. of Chicago), Biblical Review, etc. Edited and published manuscripts of William of Ockham's De Sacramento Altaris, Latin-English edit., and English translation of same. Home: Springfield, O. Died Dec. 20, 1937.

BIRCH, Thomas Howard, diplomatic service; b. Burlington, N.J., Sept. 5, 1875; ed. pvt. schs. and business coll.; m. Helen L., d. Dr. Benjamin Barr, Nov. 5, 1903. In carriage mfg. business, Burlington, 1893-1913; col. N.J.N.G.; personal aide to Gov. Woodrow Wilson of N.J., 1912-13; apptd. E.E. and M.P. to Portugal, Sept. 10, 1913. Home: Burlington, N.J. Died Feb. 1, 1929.

BIRCKHEAD, Hugh, clergyman; b. Newport, R.I., Sept. 7, 1876; s. William Hunter (M.D.) and Sarah (King) B.; B.A., Columbia, 1899, M.A., 1906; B.D., Episcopal Theol. Sch., Cambridge, Mass., 1902 (D.D., 1910); m. Caroline Minturn Hall, June 9, 1909; children—Christopher, Hugh. Deacon, 1902, priest, 1903, P.E. Church; asst. St. George Ch., New York, 1902-06, rector, 1906-12; rector Emmanuel Ch., Baltimore, Md., Oct. 1912—. Sent abroad by Am. Red Cross, June 1917, as spl. investigator; at request of Am. ambassador spoke on America in Eng., under auspices of Foreign Office; speaker in various sections of U.S. on behalf of Red Cross, Liberty Loan campaigns and Com. on Pub. Information. Home: Baltimore, Md. Died July 9, 1929.

BIRD, Charles, brig. gen.; b. Wilmington, Del., June 17, 1838; s. James T. and Elizabeth (Kettle) B.; grad. Lawrenceville (N.J.) Sch.; m. Mary C. Bowman, Nov. 15, 1866. First lt. 1st Del. Inf., May 20, 1861; hon. mustered out, Aug. 16, 1861; 2d lt. 2d Del. Inf., Apr. 11, 1862; advanced through the grades to col., May 30, 1865; bvtd. 1st lt. and capt., Mar. 2, 1867, "for gallant and meritorious services in battle of Fredericksburg, Va."; maj., Mar. 2, 1867, for same in battle of Spottsylvania, Va.; various assignments to 1882; capt. asst. q.m., Mar. 14, 1882; maj. q.m., Jan. 14, 1895; lt. col. chief q.m. vols., May 9, 1898; col. q.m. vols., July 10, 1898; brig. gen. vols., Jan. 3, 1901; hon. disch. from vol. service, June 20, 1901; lt. col. deputy q.m. gen., Feb. 2, 1901; brig. gen., Apr. 16, 1902; retired by operation of law, June 17, 1902. Home: Wilmington, Del. Died Mar. 22, 1920.

BIRD, Charles Sumner, paper mfr.; b. Walpole, Mass., 1855; s. Francis William and Abby Frances (Newell) B.; A.B., Harvard, 1877; m. Anna J. Child, of Worcester, Mass., Oct. 19, 1880; children—Charles Sumner, Francis William (dec.), Edith Harlan, Jeanne Child. Engaged in paper making and allied products (paper boxes, roofings, floor coverings) since beginning of business career; pres. Bird & Son., Inc., mills at Walpole and Norwood, Mass., Phillipsdale, R.I., and Chicago, Ill. Prog. candidate for gov. of Mass., 1912, 13. Home: East Walpole, Mass. Died Oct. 9, 1927.

BIRD, Frederic Mayer, clergyman, editor; b. Phila., June 28, 1838; s. Robert Montgomery and Mary E. (Mayer) B.; grad. Univ. of Pa., 1857; Union Theol. Sem., 1860; m. Frances P. Snowhill, April 26, 1877. Rector Spotswood, N.J., 1870-74; chaplain and prof. psychology, Christian evidences and rhetoric, Lehigh Univ., 1881-86; acting chaplain there, 1896-98. Editor Lippincott's Mag., 1893-98. Author: The Story of Our Christianity, 1893. Editor of several collections of hymns and writer on hymnology. Asso. editor of Chandler's Encyclopedia, 1898. Home: S. Bethlehem, Pa. Died 1908.

BIRD, George Emerson, judge; b. Portland, Me., Sept. 1, 1847; s. Robert Alexander and Sarah (Emerson) B.; A.B., Harvard, 1869, A.M., 1872; (LL.D., Bowdoin, 1909); m. Harriet Leonard Williams, July 8, 1890. Admitted to bar, 1872, and practiced at Portland; mem. Thomas & Bird, 1878-83, Bird & Bradley, 1896-1908. U.S. dist. atty. of Me., 1885-90; mem. Me. Ho. of Rep., 1893-95; asso. justice Supreme Jud. Ct. of Me. for terms, 1908-15, 1915-22 (resigned Aug. 29, 1919); apptd. active retired justice Supreme Ct. of Me., term 7 yrs., Oct. 1923. Corporator Portland Savings Bank. Democrat. Unitarian. Home: Portland, Me. Died Jan. 19, 1926.

BIRD, John E., justice Supreme Ct. of Mich. Republican. Home: Lansing, Mich. Died Feb. 9, 1928.

BIRD, Robert Montgomery, prof. chemistry; b. Petersburg, Va., June 13, 1867; s. Henry van Leuvenigh and Margaret (Randolph) B.; B.A., B.S., Hampden-Sidney Coll., Va., 1897; Ph.D., Johns Hopkins, 1901; m. Caroline Reid, June 11, 1902; children—Caroline Page, Robert Montgomery. Clk. mercantile, railroad and mfg. office 10 yrs.; prof. science and mathematics, Frederick (Md.) Coll., 1898-99; acting prof. chemistry, Miss. Agrl. and Mech. Coll., 1901-02; same, U. of Mo., 1902-04; instr., later prof. chemistry, same Univ., 1904-07; prof. chemistry, U. of Va., 1907—. Served in C.W.S., U.S.A., 1917-18; chem. expert to Com. on Spl. Training, Gen. Staff, U.S.A., 1918-19. Trustee Blue Ridge (Va.) Industrial Sch. Democrat. Episcopalian. Author: Chemical Science Reader, 1911; Laboratory Course in General Chemistry, 1911; Typical Reactions of General Chemistry, 1912; Notes on Organic Chemistry, 1923; Typical Reactions of Organic Compounds. Home: University, Va. Died June 4, 1938.

BIRDSALL, Benjamin P., congressman; b. Weyauwega, Wis., Oct. 26, 1858; s. Benjamin and Ann (Hyde) B.; student State U. of Ia., 1874-77; m. Bertha H. Schultz, Dec. 25, 1877 (died 1886); 2d, Belle Johnston, June 9, 1888. Admitted to bar, 1878; dist. judge, 11th Jud. Dist., 1893-1900; mem. 58th to 60th Congresses (1903-09), 3d Ia. Dist. Republican. Home: Clarion, Ia. Died May 16, 1917.

BIRDSALL, William W., pres. Swarthmore Coll., 1898—; b. Richmond, Ind., 1854; grad. Earlham Coll., Richmond, Ind., 1873; teacher mathematics, Richmond High School, 1877-82; prin. Boys' High School, Wilmington, Del., 1882-85; instr. mathematics, Friends' Central School, Phila., 1885-93; prin. boys' dept., 1893-98. Home: Swarthmore, Pa. Died 1909.

BIRDSEYE, Claude Hale, topographic engr.; b. Syracuse, N.Y., Feb. 13, 1878; s. George Frederick Hurd and Katharine Lamb (Hale) B.; A.B., Oberlin, 1901, Sc.D., 1931; post-grad. work, U. of Cincinnati and Ohio State U.; m. Grace Gardner Whitney, Nov. 23, 1904; children—Charles W., Frederick H., Florence W. Instr. in physics, U. of Cincinnati, 1901; field asst., later topographer U.S. Geol. Survey, 1901-06; surveyor Gen. Land Office, 1907-08; with U.S. Geol. Survey, 1909-29 (except when in war service), as topographer, geographer, and from Oct. 1919 to Sept. 1929, as chief topographic engr.; pres. Aerotopograph Corp. of America, 1929-32; asst. to dir. U.S. Geol. Survey, 1932; chief, division of engraving and printing, U.S. Geol. Survey, 1932—. Captain Corps of Engineers, U.S.A., Mar.-July 1917; maj. July 1917-Aug. 1918; lt. col. C.A.C., Aug. 1918-June 1919; served in France, on staff of chief of army arty., Aug. 1917-Jan. 1919. rThen col. engr., O.R.C. Decorated Officier de l'Instruction Publique (French), 1919; Daly medal (American Geog. Soc.), 1924. Author of engring. and tech. repts. Home: Chevy Chase, Md. Died May 30, 1941.

BIRKHIMER, William Edward, brig. gen.; b. Somerset, O., Mar. 1, 1848; s. Nathan and Temperance (Hood) B.; ed. Denmark (Ia.) Acad.; grad. U.S. Mil. Acad., 1870 (LL.D., Univ. of Oregon, 1889); m. Geraldine, d. late R. V. W. Howard, U.S. Army, Sept. 22, 1876. Served as pvt., Co. M, 4th Ia. Vol. Cav., Mar. 21, 1864-Aug. 8, 1865; commd. 2d lt. 3d U.S. Arty., June 15, 1870; hon. grad. Arty. Sch., 1873; 1st lt., Apr. 10, 1879; promoted through grades to maj. arty. corps, U.S.A., Aug. 1, 1901; lt. col., May 20, 1905; brig. gen., Feb. 15, 1906; retired at own request, over 40 yrs.' service, Feb. 16, 1906. Asst. prof. natural and experimental philosophy, U.S. Mil. Acad., 1874-76; judge advocate Dept. of the Columbia, 1886-90; asso. justice Supreme Ct. (the Audiencia), Manila, 1899. Awarded medal of honor "for most distinguished gallantry at San Miguel de Mayumo, Luzon, May 13, 1899." Author: Law of Appointment and Promotion in the Army of the United States, 1880; Historical Sketch of the Organization, Administration, Material and Tactics of the Artillery, United States Army, 1884; Military Government and Martial Law, 2d edit., 1904. Home: Washington, D.C. Died June 10, 1914.

BIRKINBINE, John, cons. engr.; b. nr. Reading, Pa., Nov. 16, 1844; attended Poly. College of Pa. Served in U.S.A. in Civil War; became asst. to his father as engr. of Phila. water supply; has designed and constructed important water supplies, water power and blast furnace plants; examined and reported upon many mines and industries, in U.S., Can. and Mexico; spl. agt. 11th and 12th censuses; expert on iron and manganese ores for U.S. Geol. Survey for 17 yrs.; chmn. Water Supply Commn., Pa., 1905—. Pres. Am. Inst. Mining Engrs., 1891-93, Engrs.' Club, Phila., 1893, Franklin Inst., 1897-1907, Pa. Forestry Assn., 1897—. Editor for 9 yrs. Journal of Charcoal Iron Workers; now editor Forest Leaves. Home: Cynwyd, Pa. Died May 14, 1915.

BIRKMIRE, William Harvey, engr.; b. Falls of Schuylkill, Phila., June 25, 1860; s. John Harvey and Mary A. B.; ed. pub. and pvt. schs.; grad. Phila. Acad. of Music, 1883; studied architecture 4 yrs. with Samuel Sloan; m. Louisa A. Meny, July 12, 1888. Removed to New York, 1885, to take charge construction dept. Jackson Architectural Iron Works, and, 1892, of J. B. & J. M. Cornell Iron Works; made practical steel details for large bldgs. and the Astor hotels; etc. Author: Construction of High Office Buildings, 1898; Skeleton Construction in Buildings, 1893; Architectural Iron and Steel, 1891; The Planning and Construction of American Theatres, 1896; Compound Riveted Girders, 1893. Home: New York, N.Y. Died Feb. 9, 1924.

BIRMINGHAM, Henry Patrick, surgeon U.S.A.; b. in N.Y., Mar. 15, 1854; M.D., U. of Mich., 1876. Apptd. asst. surgeon U.S.A., Feb. 18, 1881; capt. asst. surgeon, Feb. 18, 1886; maj. brigade surgeon vols., June 4, 1898; hon. discharged vols., Feb. 20, 1899; maj. surgeon U.S. Army, Dec. 15, 1898; maj. Med. Corps, Dec. 15, 1898; lt. col., Apr. 23, 1908; col., June 7, 1911; brig. gen., Oct. 2, 1917. Died May 4, 1932.

BIRNEY, Arthur Alexis, lawyer; b. Paris, France, May 28, 1852; s. Gen. William and Catherine (Hoffman) B.; brother of William Verplanck B.; public school edn., Cleveland, O.; LL.B., U. of Mich., 1873; m. Helen Conway, Nov. 3, 1875. Began law practice as jr. mem. Birney & Birney, Washington, 1873; apptd. asst. U.S. atty., 1875; resigned, 1877, to become asst. corp. atty.; U.S. atty. for D.C., 1893-97; prof. Howard U. law dept., 1878—. Episcopalian. Republican. Home: Washington, D.C. Died Sept. 4, 1916.

BIRNEY, Lauress J., bishop; b. Dennison, O., Sept. 11, 1871; s. Nelson L. and Harriet (Haverfield) B.; A.B., Scio Coll., 1895, D.D., 1910; S.T.B., Boston U. Sch. of Theology, 1899; D.D., Wesleyan Coll., 1913; D.D., Yale, 1915; LL.D., Chattanooga U., 1919; m. Laura Close, Sept. 8, 1895; 1 dau., Dorothy Gene. Preached, 1895-96, at Plainfield, O., S. Walpole, Mass., 1899-1901, Park Av. M.E. Church, Worcester, Mass., 1901-02, Hyde Park, Mass., 1902-05; traveled in Europe, 1905-06; pastor Newton Centre, Mass., 1906-08, Malden Center, 1908-11; dean Boston U. Sch. of Theology, Mar. 1911-May 1920; bishop M.E. Ch., May 1920—; trustee Boston U., 1909-11. Home: New York, N.Y. Died May 10, 1937.

BIRNEY, William, lawyer; b. Madison Co., Ala., May 28, 1819; s. James Gillespie B.; m. Catherine Hoffman, 1845. While pursuing studies in Paris took part in the revolution of 1848; was apptd., on public competition, prof. English literature in the coll. at Bourges, France; enlisted in U.S. vols. as private, 1861; rose through all the grades to bvt. maj. gen.; comd. div., 1863-65; practiced law in Washington, 1874-1900, counsel for D.C., 1874-77. Author: Life and Times of James G. Birney; Plea for Civil and Religious Liberty; etc. Died 1907.

BIRNEY, William Verplanck, artist-genre painter and painter of portraits; b. Cincinnati, 1858; s. Gen. William B., now of Washington; g.s. of James G. Birney, the abolitionist (Free-Soil candidate for President of the U.S., 1840, 1844); studied in Boston under Walter Smith at Mass. Normal Art School; in Phila., under Thomas Eakins, at Pa. Acad., and at Royal Acad., Munich, under Julius Benzur and Wilhelm Lindenschmidt. Established in New York, 1884; instr. Cooper Inst. 3 yrs.; exhibited at Paris Expn., 1889, World's Columbian Expn., 1893; bronze medal, Buffalo Expn., 1901; constant exhibitor at standard exhbns. throughout U.S.; del. to Fine Arts Federation; asso. Nat. Acad.; bronze medal La. Purchase Expn., St. Louis, 1904. Died 1909.

BIRREN, Joseph P., painter, lecturer; b. Chicago, Ill., May 14, 1864; s. Henry and Catherine B.; ed. private schs., Art Inst. Chicago, 1883-1900; studied in Philadelphia, New York, Munich, Paris; m. Crescentia Lang, Apr. 11, 1894; children—Jeanette (Mrs. Vincent M. Quinn), William Bryan, Faber. Noted for his tactile quality in landscaping painting. Has exhibited at Art Institute of Chicago, 1917—, also at Pa. Academy, Corcoran Gallery, Washington, D.C., Albright Art Gallery, Buffalo, N.Y., Cincinnati (O.) Art Museum, Providence, R.I., Hartford, Conn., etc. Represented in Chicago Art Commn. collection, Union League Club, Ill. Women's Athletic Club, Chicago Coll. Club, Rockford Art Club, Ill. State Mus., Los Angeles Mus., Washington U. Mus., Lauren Rogers Mus., Pasadena Art Inst., National Mus. (Luxembourg), etc. Decorated Knight of the Oak Leaf Crown (Luxembourg). Mem. Art Inst. Chicago Alumni Assn. (founder-pres. 1911-15, then hon. pres.). Catholic. Home: Chicago, Ill. Died Aug. 4, 1933.

BIRTWELL, Charles Wesley, exec. sec. Stable Money Assn.; b. Lawrence, Mass., Nov. 23, 1860; s. Tempest and Sarah (Pickels) B.; A.B., Harvard, 1885; m. Helen Dow, Oct. 16, 1894; 1 son, Roger. Gen. sec. Boston Children's Aid Soc., 1885-1911; gen. sec. Am. Federation for Sex Hygiene, 1911-12, Mass. Soc. for Sex Edn., 1912-16; mem. bd. dirs. Nat. City Bank, Chelsea, Mass., 1919-21; with Sable Money Assn., 1927—, v.p. and exec. sec., 1931—. Home: Hampton Falls, N.H. Died May 18, 1932.

BISBEE, Frederick Adelbert, clergyman editor; b. Nunda, N.Y., Feb. 28, 1855; s. Hiram Alonzo and Mary Jane (Hand) B.; ed. pub. B.D., Tufts College, 1877, S.T.D. from same, 1897; m. Hannah T. Bradley, Jan. 1, 1880 (died 1886); m. 2d, Matty Gally, June 28, 1891 (died 1921). Ordained Universalist ministry, 1877; pastor Ch. of Our Father, Spencer, Mass., 1877-83, Ch. of Restoration, Phila., 1883-98; editor-in-chief Universalist Leader, Boston, 1898—; editor and pub. monthly review, To-Day, Phila., 1895; sec. Pa. Universalist State Conv., 1885-98. Author: A Summer Flight, 1911; History of Young People's Christian Union, 1914; A California Pilgrimage, 1915; From Good Luck to Gloucester, 1921. Non-resident lecturer Tufts Coll. and St. Lawrence U. Mem. Internat. Peace Union. Home: Arlington Heights, Mass. Died Nov. 15, 1923.

BISBEE, Marvin Davis, educator; b. Chester, Vt., June 21, 1845; s. Abner and Cynthia (Rolph) B.; A.B., Dartmouth, 1871 (hon. A.M., 1908); Andover Theol. Sem., 1871-73; B.D., Chicago Theol. Sem., 1874; m. Susan Augusta Silsby, Aug. 27, 1873. Ordained Congl. ministry, 1874; pastor Fishville (now Penacook), N.H., 1874-77, Cambridge, Mass., 1877-81; asso. editor Boston Congregationalist, 1881-86; prof. divinity and librarian, 1886-93, prof. bibliography and librarian, 1893-1910, Dartmouth; retired on Carnegie Fund, 1910; dir. extension courses and library, Chicago Theol. Sem., 1910—. Republican. Died Aug. 28, 1913.

BISBING, Henry Singlewood, artist; b. Phila., Jan. 31, 1849; student Phila. Acad. Fine Arts, and under F. de Vuillefroy, Paris, and J. H. L. de Haas, Brussels. Awarded 3d class medal Paris Salon, 1891, Temple Gold Medal, Phila. Acad. Fine Arts, 1892; medal, World's Fair, Chicago, 1893; silver medal, Paris Expn., 1900; hors concours, Paris Salon, 1896; medals, Dresden, London, Vienna, Antwerp, etc. Pictures in permanent collections of Pa. Acad. Fine Arts, Berlin Nat. Gallery, Mus. of Nantes, France, etc. Chevalier Legion d'Honneur, France, 1902. Home: Paris, France. Died Nov. 18, 1933.

BISCHOFF, Henry, Jr., judge; b. New York, Aug. 16, 1852; s. Henry and Amalie B.; ed. Bloomfield (N.J.) Acad.; LL.B., Columbia, 1871; m. Annie Louise Moshier, Oct. 26, 1873 (died 1897); m. 2d, Elizabeth, widow of Gilman Collamore, Apr. 1902. Admitted to bar, 1873; atty. for the collection of arrears of personal taxes, 1889-90; judge Court of Common Pleas, N.Y., 1890-95; justice Supreme Ct. of N.Y., 1st Dist., 1896-1917. Democrat. Sr. mem. firm Henry Bischoff & Co., bankers, New York. Home: New York, N.Y. Died Mar. 28, 1913.

BISEY, Sunker Abaji, inventor; b. Bombay, India, Apr. 29, 1867; s. Abaji Balvant and Nanibai (Durvey) B.; ed. high sch., Bombay; passed matriculation exam., 1888; m. Sushila Karnik, Feb. 22, 1893; children—Sonubai (Mrs. Narayan Laxuman Pradhan), Madhu, Reginald, Pramila. Came to U.S., 1916, 1st naturalization papers obtained. In govt. service, India, 1889-98; as the "pioneer Hindu inventor," worked upon inventions in England, 1899-1915, later gen. mgr. Tata-Bisey Invention Syndicate, London; organized Am. Beslin Co., New York, 1918; established, 1920, Bisey Ideal Typecaster Corp., of which is dir. and tech. expert; dir. Am. Beslin Corp. Known as "The Edison of India," for invention of single and multiple typecasting machines, and in chemistry for water soluble non-irritating and nonpoisonous iodine, known as Atomidine and Beslin. Hon. fellow Soc. Science, Letters and Arts, London, and Inst. of Inventors, New York. Awarded gold medal, Earls Court Exhibition, London, 1901; presented with congratulatory address on 60th birthday by various scientific socs. of India and U.S., also conferring hon. degrees of D.Sc. and Ph.D. Home: Mt. Vernon, N.Y. Died Apr. 7, 1935.

BISHOP, Avard Longley, college prof.; b. Wiliamston, N.S., Can., Mar. 4, 1875; s. William and Mary Ann (Morse) B.; B.A., Acadia Coll., Wolfville, N.S., 1901; B.A., Yale, 1903, M.A., 1904, Ph.D., 1906; D.C.L., honoris causa, Acadia College, 1931; m. Rita Lilian Marshall, Sept. 12, 1908; children—Avard Longley, William Marshall. With Yale U., 1904—; instr. in commercial geography, 1904-08, asst. prof., 1908-11; asst. prof. geography and commerce Sheffield Scientific Sch. (Yale), 1911-14; prof. geography and commerce, 1914-18; prof. business administration, Feb. 1918—. Author: The State Works of Pennsylvania, 1907; Physical and Commercial Geography (with H. E. Gregory and A. G. Keller), 1910; Commercial and Industrial Geography (with A. G. Keller), 1912; Industry and Trade (with A. G. Keller). 1918; Outlines of American Foreign Commerce, 1923; The Financing of Business Enterprises, 1929. Home: New Haven, Conn. Died May 8, 1932.

BISHOP, Charles Alvord, jurist; b. Waukesha Co., Wis., May 22, 1854; s. Mathew Patrick and Roxana (Alvord) B.; ed. pub. schs., La Grange and Palmyra, Wis.; studied law privately; m. Della M. Dow, Nov. 2, 1873; m. 2d, Alice S. Lyman, June 24, 1902. Admitted to bar, Waupaca, Wis., 1875; located La Porte City, Black Hawk Co., Ia., 1876; mem. legislature from Black Hawk Co., 1882; moved to Des Moines, 1886; dist. judge 9th dist. Iowa, 1889-90, and 1895-1902; apptd to fill vacancy, 1902, and elected Nov., 1902, as Supreme judge; was chief justice Supreme Court, Iowa; now justice same. Republican. Home: Des Moines, Ia. Died 1908.

BISHOP, Elias B(ullard), judge; b. Newton, Mass., Aug. 2, 1869; s. Robert R. and Mary Helen (Bullard) B.; grad. Phillips Acad., Andover, 1889; A.B., Harvard, 1894, LL.B., 1897; m. Emilie Fanning Hunter, June 28, 1894 (now dec.); children—Robert R., Eleanor, Stephen H.; m. 2d, Della M. Cleaves, Oct. 14, 1914; 1 son, John H. Admitted to Mass. bar, 1897, and began practice at Boston; then judge, Superior Court. Alderman, Newton, 1904-06; mem. Mass. Ho. of Rep., 1907-09. Republican. Conglist. Home: Newton Center, Mass. Died Dec. 30, 1934.

BISHOP, Emily Montague, lecturer; b. Forestville, N.Y., Nov. 3, 1858; d. Asa L. and Ann E. (De Witt) Mulkin; high sch. edn.; m. Coleman E. Bishop. Lecturer, reader and teacher at Chautauqua Instn., Chautauqua Lake, N.Y., 1889—; orginator and interpreter of polit. readings "Dramatic Scenes from the United States Senate." Author: Health and Self-Expression, 1891; Interpretative Forms of Literature, 1903; Seventy Years Young, 1907; Daily Ways to Health, 1910. Home: New York, N.Y. Deceased.

BISHOP, Ernest Simons, M.D.; b. Pawtucket, R.I., Nov. 29, 1876; s. Phanuel Euclid (M.D.) and Louise (Simons) B.; A.B., Brown, 1899; M.D., Cornell Med. Sch., New York, 1908; m. Helen Earle, Jan. 20, 1912; children—Helen Kingsley, Amy. Interne and res. phys. Bellevue Hosp., 1908-12; clin. prof. medicine

New York Polyclinic Med. Sch. Was mem. Med. Advisory Bd. of U.S. Army Draft. Frequently called upon as expert witness in courts, and in advisory capacity has modified and interpreted med. legislation, especially narcotic laws; originator and elaborator of modern conception of narcotic drug addiction as a definite and curable phys. disease. Fellow Am. Coll. Physicians, also of Acad. Medicine (New York). Episcopalian, Mason. Author: The Narcotic Drug Problem; also the Chronic Drug Intoxications and Addictions in George Blumer edit. of Billings-Forchheimer's Therapeusis of Internal Diseases, 1925. Home: New York, N.Y. Died Nov. 16, 1927.

BISHOP, Farnham, author; b. N.Y. City, Jan. 17, 1886; s. Joseph Bucklin and Harriet (Hartwell) B.; B.A., Harvard, 1908, M.A., 1910; grad. student in English, U. of Calif.; m. Miriam Suplee, Feb. 19, 1918; children—William Brewster, Joseph Bucklin. Teacher English composition, Modesto (Calif.) Jr. Coll., 1923-24; teacher of English and history, San Rafael (Calif.) Mil. Acad., 1927—; lecturer on fiction writing. Enlisted in regular army Feb. 1, 1918; hon. disch. as 2d lt. Q.M.C., Dec. 10, 1918. Republican, Unitarian. Author: Panama Past and Present, 1912; The Story of the Submarine, 1916; Our First War in Mexico, 1916; (with Arthur Gilchrist Brodeur) The Altar of the Legion, 1926; The Black Bloodhound, 1927; also one act play, "The Scales and the Sword," 1919. Home: San Rafael, Calif. Died Feb. 16, 1930.

BISHOP, George Sayles, clergyman; b. Rochester, N.Y., June 28, 1836; s. Hon. William S. and Mary (Sayles) B.; student, U. of Rochester, 1854-55; A.B., Amherst, 1858; instr. classics, Williston Sem., 1858-61; student Andover Theol. Sem., 1862-63; grad. Princeton Theol. Sem., 1864; (D.D., Rutgers, 1877); m. Hannah, d. John Payson Williston, of Northampton, Mass., Aug. 11, 1864. Ordained Presbyn. ministry, June 16, 1864; pastor Second Ch., Trenton, N.J., 1864-66, Calvary Ch., Newburgh, N.Y., 1866-72. Second (Brick) Ch., Orange, N.J., 1872-75, First Reformed Ch., Orange, 1875-1906, pastor emeritus, 1906—. Del. of Ref. Ch. to 5 councils in Europe, and interdenominational convs., Phila., Chicago, Baltimore; pres. Gen. Synod Ref. Ch. in America, 1899-1900. Vedder lecturer, Rutgers Coll. and Theol. Sem. Mem. S.A.R., Order Descendants Colonial Govs. Editor The Sower and Gospel Field, organ Ref. Ch., 1877-78. Author: Person and Work of the Holy Spirit, 1897; The Sweep of Time, 1909; The Doctrines of Grace, 1910; Commentary on Galatians, 1912; booklet on Revision, 1912. Contbr. to Christian Intelligencer, Independent, Presbyn. Quarterly, The Fundamentals, etc. Died Mar. 12, 1914.

BISHOP, George Taylor, financier; b. Ravenna, O., Oct. 11, 1864; s. Clark B. and Arvilla A. (Taylor) B.; ed. pub. schs.; m. Anna L. Swearer. Dir. Goodyear Tire & Rubber Co., Sherwin-Williams Co., Youngstown Sheet & Tube Co. Mem. S.A.R., Ohio Soc. of New York, Ohio Soc. of Mayflower Desc. Republican, Mason. Home: Northfield Center, O. Died Aug. 24, 1940.

BISHOP, Heber Reginald, retired merchant, banker; b. Medford, Mass., March 11, 1840; first business training at Boston. In Dec., 1859, settled at Remedios, Cuba; established house of Bishop & Co., March 4, 1861; retired at age of 36 (1876) to Irvington-on-Hudson, where he had summer residence. Since 1880 financially interested in railroad, gas, iron and other properties; dir. New York Elevated Ry. Co., Manhattan Elevated Ry. Co., St. Paul, Minneapolis & Omaha R.R. Co., Chicago, Rock Island & Pacific R.R. Co., Duluth & Iron Range R.R. Co., Minn. Iron Co., Chandler Iron Co., Metropolitan Trust Co., and other corporations; also interested in management of hosps., Am. Museum of Natural History, Metropolitan Museum of Art, etc. Home: New York, N.Y. Died 1902.

BISHOP, Harry Gore, army officer; b. Grand Rapids, Mich., Nov. 22, 1874; s. Louis H. and Jeanette (Atwater) B.; grad. U.S. Mil. Acad., 1897, Sch. Submarine Defense, 1906; distinguished grad. Army Sch. of the Line, 1911; grad. Army Staff Coll., 1912, Sch. of Fire for F.A., 1914, Mounted Service Sch., 1915, Signal Corps Aviation Sch., 1917, Army Center Arty. Studies, Trier, Germany, 1919. Commd. add. 2d lt. 19th Inf., June 11, 1897; 2d lit. 6th Arty., Mar. 8, 1898; advanced through grades to col. 11th F.A., May 15, 1917; maj. gen., chief of F.A. for 4 years from Feb. 16, 1930. Served at Ft. Wayne, Mich., Ft. McHenry, Md., Washington Barracks, D.C., and Ft. Caswell, N.C., until May 1899; in Philippines, May 1899-Sept. 1901, was with troops during Insurrection and as chief of the Dept. of Licenses and Municipal Revenue of City of Manila during mil. govt.; served at Ft. Adams, R.I., 1901-03; adj. Sch. Submarine Defense and sec. Torpedo Bd., Ft. Totten, N.Y., 1903-05; arty. engr. of Arty. Dist. of Columbia, 1906-07; comdr. troops at Ft. Sam Houston, Tex., 1907-10; instr. Army Service Schs., Ft. Leavenworth, Kan., 1912-14; comdr. 1st Bn. 5th F.A., Ft. Sill, Okla., 1915; comdr. arty. on Mexican border, 1916-17; comdr. 11th F.A., on border patrol, Sept. 1917-May 1918; chief of War Plans Div. of Gen. Staff, Washington, D.C., May-June 1918; comdr. 159th F.A. Brig., and 3d F.A. Brig., 3d

Div., Meuse-Argonne Campaign; with Army of Occupation, Germany, Oct. 1918-May 1919; dir. Training Sect., Army Gen. Staff Coll., Washington, D.C., Sept. 1919-20; chief of staff, 4th Corps Area, and chief of staff Philippine Dept., 1920-24; comdr. 15th F.A., Ft. Sam Houston, Tex., 1925-27, 6th F.A., Ft. Hoyle, Md., 1927-28, 8th F.A., Hawaiian Dept., 1928-29; chief of F.A., 1930-1934. Awarded D.S.M. (U.S.); Officer Legion of Honor (France). Home: Washington, D.C. Died Aug. 31, 1934.

BISHOP, Henry Alfred, business man; b. Bridgeport, Conn., Dec. 4, 1860; s. William D. and Julia Ann (Tomlinson) B.; entered Yale with class of 1884, but did not graduate; m. Jessie Alvord Trubee, Feb. 6, 1883; children—William Alfred (dec.), Marguerite Alvord, Henrietta, Henry Alfred. Gen. ticket agt., 1881-83, purchasing agt., 1883-85, asst. supt., 1885-86, Naugatuck R.R.; served as supt. Housatonic Rd. and gen. supt. same, and its branches; purchasing agt., N.Y.,N.H.&H. R.R., 1887-1902; acting v.p. and v.p. W. V. Central and Pittsburgh & Western Md. rds., 1902-03 (resigned); vice pres. Clapp Fire Resisting Paint Co. (exec. com.), 1st Nat. Bank, Pacific Iron Works, Inc. Mem. Conn. Ho. of Rep., 1886; pres. Bd. Police Commrs., Bridgeport, 1888-90; Dem. candidate for sec. of state, Conn., 1888, and for lt. gov., 1904; pres. Bridgeport Pub. Library, Bridgeport Boy's Club; dir. Bridgeport Hosp., St. Vincent's Hosp., Conn. Humane Soc.; trustee Bridgeport Orphan Asylum. Episcopalian, Mason. Home: Bridgeport, Conn. Died Oct. 22, 1934.

BISHOP, James, physician; b. New Brunswick, N.J., Jan. 6, 1870; s. James and Mary Faugeres (Ellis) B.; A.B. Rutgers, 1891; M.D., Columbia, 1895; m. Margaret McGregor Donald, Apr. 20, 1900. Practiced in N.Y. City, 1895—; asst. surgeon, Manhattan Eye and Ear Hosp. Republican. Home: New York, N.Y. Died Oct. 15, 1924.

BISHOP, Joseph Bucklin, journalist, author, govt. official; b. Seekonk, Mass. (now E. Providence, R.I.), Sept. 5, 1847; s. James Madison and Elzada (Balcom) B.; A.B., Brown, 1870, hon. Litt.D., 1923; m. Harriet Hartwell, Dec. 14, 1872 (died 1917); children—Alice (dec.), Hartwell (dec.), Farnham. Editorial staff New York Tribune, 1870-83; editorial writer New York Evening Post, 1883-1900; chief editorial staff New York Globe, 1900-05; sec. Isthmian Canal Commn.,1905-14; mem. Nat. Inst. Arts and Letters. Author: Cheap Money Experiments, 1892; Our Political Drama, 1904; Issues of a New Epoch, 1904; The Panama Gateway, 1913; A Chronicle of One Hundred and Fifty Years, 1918; Theodore Roosevelt and His Time, Shown in His Letters, 2 vols., 1920; Life of Charles J. Bonaparte, 1922; Life of A. Barton Hepburn, 1923; Notes and Anecdotes of Many Years, 1925. Editor: Theodore Roosevelt's Letters to His Children, 1919. Died Dec. 13, 1928.

BISHOP, Louis Faugères, M.D.; b. New Brunswick, N.J., Mar. 14, 1864; s. James and Mary Faugères (Ellis) B.; A.B., Rutgers Coll., 1885, A.M., 1889, Sc.D., 1919; M.D., Coll. Phys. and Surg. (Columbia), 1889; m. Charlotte D. Gruner, Nov. 14, 1899; 1 son, Louis Faugères. Resident phys. St. Luke's Hosp., New York, 1889-92; prof. diseases of the heart and circulation, Fordham U.; heart specialist to Lincoln Hosp.; consultant in cardiovascular diseases, Sea View Hosp. Author: Heart Troubles, Their Prevention and Relief; Heart Disease, Blood Pressure and the Nauheim Treatment; Arteriosclerosis; A Key to the Electrocardiograms; History of Cardiology. Home: New York, N.Y. Died Oct. 6, 1941.

BISHOP, Samuel Henry, clergyman; b. Jericho, Vt., May 1, 1864; s. Leet Asa and Aurill (Clark) B.; A.B., U. of Vt., 1886; grad. Union Theol. Sem., New York, 1891, post-grad., 1893-94; also studied, Columbia U., and univs. of Berlin and Oxford; m. Rosilla Bertha Darrow, Sept. 13, 1897. Deacon and priest, P.E. Ch., 1891; asst., Ch. of the Incarnation, New York, 1891-92; in charge, All Souls', New York, 1892-93; rector, St. Andrew's, S. Orange, N.J., 1893-97, St. Stephen's, Colorado Springs, Colo., 1898-99; gen. agt., Am. Ch. Inst. for Negroes, New York, 1906—. Author: The Words of the Christ; Recent Changes in Theology in the Episcopal Church; The Bible as History; The Virgin Birth, an Irenicon; A Study in Religion; The Religion of the Typal Life; The Church and Charity; English and German Universities. Home: New York, N.Y. Died May 27, 1914.

BISHOP, Sereno Edwards, clergyman; b. Kaawaloa, H.I., Feb. 7, 1827; s. Rev. Artemas (missionary) and Elizabeth (Edwards) B.; grad. Amherst Coll., A.B., 1846 (D.D., 1896), Auburn Theol. Sem., 1851; m. Cornelia A. Sessions, May 31, 1852. Ordained to Presbyn. ministry June 2, 1852; chaplain Am. Seaman's Friends Soc. at Lahaina, Island of Maui, 1853-62; missionary A.B.C.F.M., Hana, Maui, 1862-65; prin. Lahainaluna Sem., 1865-77; editor The Friend, Honolulu, H.I., 1887-1902. In Sept. 1883, discovered Corona caused by Krakatoa Eruption, and since known in Europe as "Cercle de Bishop," or Bishop's Ring; received 3d Warner prize ($50), 1884, for essay on Cause of Red Glows (Krakatoa). Died 1909.

BISHOP, Seth Scott, surgeon; b. Fond du Lac, Wis., Feb. 7, 1852; s. Lyman and Maria (Probart) B.; grad. Pooler Inst., Fond du Lac, Wis.; studied

at Beloit (Wis.) Coll.; New York Univ.; M.D., Northwestern U., 1876 (D.C.L., LL.D.); learned printers' trade; m. Jessie A. Button, Mar. 23, 1885. Formerly prof. diseases of the nose, throat and ear, Loyola U. Med. Sch.; surgeon to Jefferson Park Hosp.; formerly surgeon to Ill. Charitable Eye and Ear Infirmary, etc.; cons. surgeon to Mary Thompson Hosp., Ill. Masonic Orphans' Home (LaGrange, Ill.) and Silver Cross Hosp. (Joliet, Ill.). Mason. Author: Diseases of the Nose, Throat and Ear; The Ear and Its Diseases. Home: Evanston, Ill. Died Sept. 6, 1923.

BISHOP, William Darius, R.R. official; b. Bloomfield, N.J., Sept. 14, 1827; grad. Yale, 1849; was R.R. contractor, 1850-54; pres. Naugatuck R.R. Co., 1854—; congressman from Conn., 1857-59; U.S. commr. of patents, 1859-60; pres. N.Y., New Haven & Hartford R.R., 1867-69; pres. exec. com. Eastern R.R. Assn., 1884—. Home: Bridgeport, Conn. Died 1904.

BISHOP, William Henry, author; b. Hartford, Conn., Jan. 7, 1847; s. Elias and Catherine (Kelly) B.; A.B., Yale, 1867; studied architecture; m. Mary Dearborn Jackson, July 28, 1886; children—Duquesne (dec.), Julian B. (dec.). Editor and propr. Milwaukee Commercial Times till 1877; instr. modern languages, Yale, 1893-1902; United States consul at Genoa, Italy, 1903-04, at Palermo, Italy, Jan. 1, 1905-July 1, 1910, resigned. Republican. Agnostic Mem. Soc. Colonial Wars. Author: Detmold, 1879; The House of a Merchant Prince, 1882; Choy Susan and Other Stories, 1884; Old Mexico and Her Lost Provinces, 1884; Fish and Men in the Maine Islands, 1885; The Golden Justice, 1887; A House Hunter in Europe, 1893; The Brown Stone Boy and Other Queer People (re-issued as Queer People), 1902; Sergeant Von (anonymously), 1889; The Yellow Snake (re-issued as Tons of Treasure), 1902; A Pound of Cure, 1894; Writing to Rosina, 1894; The Faïence Violin (transl. from French of Champfleury), 1893; Anti-Babel, 1919. Mem. Nat. Inst. Arts and Letters. Home: Brooklyn, Conn. Died Sept. 26, 1928.

BISPHAM, David Scull, opera singer; b. Phila., Jan. 5, 1857; s. William D. and Jane L. (Scull) B.; A.B., Haverford (Pa.) Coll., 1876 (LL.D., 1914; Mus.Doc., Hillsdale Coll., 1919); m. Caroline, d. late Gen. Charles S. Russell, U.S.A., Apr. 28, 1885. Made début as the Duc de Longueville in The Basoche, Royal English Opera, Nov. 1891; then with the Royal Opera, Covent Garden, and Met. Opera Co., New York, singing prin. rôles in German, French, Italian, and English. One of founders Soc. Am. Singers, producing classic opera comique in English; entered upon dramatic career, 1915. Author: A Quaker Singer's Recollections. Editor: Song Book for High Schools and Community Singing, and three Bispham Albums of Solos. Died Oct. 2, 1921.

BISPHAM, George Tucker, lawyer, author; b. Phila., May 24, 1838; grad. Univ. of Pa., 1858; law dept. same, 1862; m. June 5, 1872, Nancy d. E. L. Brinley, Phila.; admitted to bar, 1861; has practiced in Phila. ever since; later admitted to bar U.S. Supreme Court. One of solicitors of Pa. R.R. Co.; solicitor Phila. Saving Fund Soc., Girard Trust Co., etc.; prof. equity jurisprudence, law dept., Univ. of Pa.; chancellor Law Assn. of Phila., 1897-99. Author: Principles of Equity, 1905 B10. Home: Philadelphia. Died 1906.

BISSELL, Arthur Douglas, banker; b. New London, N.Y., Jan. 10, 1844; s. John and Isabella Jeannette (Hally) B.; B.A., Yale, 1867; m. Fanny Castle, June 16, 1874; children—Thomas (dec.), Howard, Mrs. Eleanor Warren. Raymond, Arthur D., Mrs. Jeanette Goodyear, Lloyd. Transportation business, Buffalo, N.Y., 1867-85; U.S. collector of customs for dist. of Buffalo, 1885-89; v.p., 1889, then chmn. bd., Peoples Bank of Buffalo. Home: Buffalo, N.Y. Died Nov. 13, 1926.

BISSELL, Dougal, gynecologist; b. Summerville, S.C., July 5, 1864; s. Titus Lucretius and Anna Threadcraft (Thompson) B.; B.S., U. of S.C., 1885; M.D., U. of Md., 1888; grad. Woman's Hosp. State of N.Y., New York, 1893; m. Helen Nutting, Nov. 21, 1906; children—Bradford, Whitner Nutting, Ruth, Cleveland and Nicol (twins). Began practice at Mars Bluff, S.C., 1888; settled at N.Y. City, 1891; surgeon Woman's Hosp., 1910-29; consulting gynecologist to Central Islip Hosp., L.I. Fellow Am. Coll. Surgeons (a founder). Contbr. numerous articles on professional topics. Home: New York, N.Y. Died Dec. 3, 1935.

BISSELL, French Rayburn, corp. official; b. St. Louis, Mo., Mar. 30, 1861; s. James R. and Anna Haight (Christopher) B.; Central Coll., Fayette, Mo., 1875-78; m. Emily F. Watson, Feb. 6, 1907; 1 dau. Janet Watson. In real estate business until 1903; pres. St. Louis Portland Cement Co., 1904-07; then chmn. bd. Internat. Cement Corp., Texas Portland Cement Co., Knickerbocker Portland Cement Co., Kansas Portland Cement Co., Va. Portland Cement Corp., Ind. Portland Cement Co., Ala. Portland Cement Co., La. Portland Cement Co., La Compania Cubana de Cemento Portland. Republican, Mason. Home: New York, N.Y. Died Sept. 25, 1933.

BISSELL, George Edwin, sculptor; b. New Preston, Litchfield Co., Conn., Feb. 16, 1839; s. Hiram and Isabella (Jones) B.; ed. Northville (Conn.) Acad., and the Gunnery, Washington, Conn.; pvt. 23d Conn. Vols., 1862-63; acting asst. p.-m. U.S.N., 1863-65; m. Mary E. Welton, Aug. 16, 1865; father of George Welton B. In marble business with father and brother at Poughkeepsie, N.Y., 1866; studied art, Paris, Rome and Florence, 1875-76; had studio in Paris at different times, for about 6 yrs., between 1884-96; studio in Florence, Italy, 1903-05 and 1907-09. Public monuments and statues: Soldiers' and Sailors' Monument, and statue Col. Chatfield, Waterbury, Conn.; portrait statue Gen. Horatio Gates on Saratoga Battle Monument; Chancellor John Watts and Col. Abraham de Peyster, New York; Abraham Lincoln, Edinburgh, Scotland; relief, Burns and Highland Mary, Ayr, Scotland; Chancellor James Kent, Congressional Library; President Arthur, New York; Lycurgus, Appellate Court, New York; group "The Navy," Colonnade Navy Arch, New York; statue "Hospitality," Buffalo Expn., 1901; bronze statues Admiral Farragut and Gen. Sherman, groups, Science and Music, St. Louis Expn., 1904; statue of Lincoln, Clermont, Ia.; marble bust and bronze statuette in Met. Mus., New York; marble bust Archbishop Corrigan, N.Y. City; bronze statue Hon. John H. Starin, Fultonville, N.Y.; bronze statue Samuel Sloan, pres. D.&L. R.R.; colossal bronze bust of Admiral John A. Dahlgren in Prospect Park, Phila. Hon. mention, Paris Expn., 1900; silver medal, St. Louis Expn., 1904; Elton Memorial Vase, Waterbury, Conn., 1905. Home: Mt. Vernon, N.Y. Died Aug. 30, 1920.

BISSELL, Herbert Porter, judge; b. New London, Oneida Co., N.Y., Aug. 30, 1856; s. Amos Alanson and Amelia Susan (Wilsey) B.; ed. De Veaux Coll., Suspension Bridge, N.Y., 1869-73; Gymnasium, Braunschweig, Germany, 1873-75; A.B., Harvard, 1880; m. Lucy Agnes Coffey, Oct. 30, 1883. Admitted to N.Y. bar, 1883, and practiced in Buffalo; apptd. justice Supreme Court of N.Y. to fill vacancy, 1912; elected to same office, 1913, for term of 14 yrs. Mem. State Hosp. Commn., N.Y., 1911, 1912; pres. Bd. of Edn., East Aurora, N.Y., 1905-12; formerly judge-advocate and maj. 4th Brigade, N.G.N.Y. Trustee DeVeaux Coll., 1887-99. Democrat. Episcopalian. Mason. Home: East Aurora, N.Y. Died Apr. 30, 1919.

BISSELL, Hezekiah, civil engr.; b. Windsor, Conn.; Ph.B., Sheffield Scientific Sch. (Yale), 1861; m. Alice Hughes; children—John H., Paul A., William N. Enlisted as pvt. 1st Regt. Conn. Vols., Civil War; commd. 1st lt. 25th Regt. Civil engr. U.P. R.R. during constrn., 1864-69, Puno & Cuzco R.R., Peru, S.A., 1872-74, C.,C.,C.&St.L. Ry., 1875-78, Eastern R.R., 1878-88; chief engr. B.&M. R.R., 1888-1909; later consulting engr. Home: Wellesley, Mass. Died June 23, 1928.

BISSELL, Howard, banker; b. Buffalo, N.Y., Sept. 30, 1878; s. Arthur Douglas and Fanny (Castle) B.; A.B., Yale, 1900; m. Dorothy Carroll Trego, Oct. 5, 1910; children—Katharine T., Howard. Identified with banking business in Buffalo, 1900—; became pres. Peoples Bank of Buffalo, 1920; chmn. bd. M & T Trust Co. until 1933; pres. Niagara Nat. Bank, 1933—. Apptd., 1929, by Governor Roosevelt, mem. com. to revise banking laws of N.Y.; apptd. by President to Veterans Review Board and to Deposit Liquidation Board for sect. of State of N.Y., 1933. Dem. candidate at large for presdl. elector, 1924; trustee City and County Hall, Buffalo. Presbyn. Home: Buffalo, N.Y. Died Oct. 24, 1937.

BISSELL, John Henry, lawyer; b. Lyons, N.Y., Feb. 22, 1846; s. Rt. Rev. William Henry Augustus and Martha Cotton (Moulton) B.; ed. Hobart Coll. class of 1867 (hon. M.A., 1879); m. Annie A. Soverhill, June 30, 1869. Admitted to Vt. bar, 1870; in practice at Detroit, 1872—; dir. Ideal Mfg. Co. (treas.), Edison Illuminating Co. (Detroit), Peninsular Elec. Light Co. Mem. Mich. Fish Commn., 1883-89. Home: Detroit, Mich. Deceased.

BISSELL, Richard Mervin, insurance pres.; b. Chicago, Ill., June 8, 1862; s. George Francis and Jerusha (Woodbridge) B.; B.A., Yale, 1883; m. Marie Truesdale, June 25, 1901; children—William Truesdale, Anne Carolyn, Richard Mervin. Began with western dept. of Hartford Fire Ins. Co., at Chicago, 1883; asst. gen. agt. same dept., 1895-96; asso. gen. agt., title of Cofran & Bissell, 1896-1902, v.p. of co. at Hartford, 1903-13, pres., Aug. 5, 1913—; pres. Citizens Ins. Co. of N.J., Twin City Fire Ins. Co.; trustee Horace Bushnell Hall Corp., Hartford, Conn., Trust Co. Chmn. Conn. State Council of Defense. Lecturer on ins., Yale U. Dir. Neuro-Psychiatric Inst. of the Hartford Retreat. Pres. Nat. Bd. Fire Underwriters, 1917-18. Home: Farmington, Conn. Died July 18, 1941.

BISSELL, Walter Henry, lumberman; b. Fond du Lac, Wis., July 28, 1858; s. Leonard Charles and Cornelia Bradley (Kenney) Bissell; educated grammar and high schools, Fond du Lac, until 1872; m. Elizabeth May Boardman, Mar. 12, 1880 (dec.); children—May Clara (Mrs. William W. Gamble), Kate Boardman (dec.), Frank Kenney, John Murray, Katharine Ross (Mrs. Winfield S. Thom, dec.), Margaret Boardman (Mrs. Benjamin D. Stone); m. 2d, Grace May Gamble, Apr. 30, 1898; 1 son, Walter Henry. Began as errand boy, later bookkeeper, lumber office, Fond du Lac, 1872; bookeeper, 1877-83; a sawmill mgr. and sec., Schofield, Harrison, and Arbor Vitae, Wis., 1883-1905; pres. various lumber corps., 1902—, and interested in various other enterprises. Presbyn. Mason. Home: Wausau, Wis. Died Dec. 11, 1933.

BISSELL, William Grosvenor, sanitary expert; b. Lockport, N.Y., Jan. 30, 1870; s. Hon. Amos Anson and Amelia Susan (Willse) B.; M.D., Med. Dept. Univ. of Buffalo, 1892; spl. courses in many labs.; Army Med. Sch., 1912, 1915; m. Clara Elizabeth Cronin, Apr. 24, 1912. Began practice in Buffalo, 1892; chief of Bur. and bacteriologist, Dept. of Health, Buffalo, 1894—; lecturer mil. hygiene, Long Island Coll. Hosp., Brooklyn; examiner in preventive medicine and hygiene, N.Y. State Bd. of Med. Examiners; sanitary expert Northern S.S. Co.; health expert Chautauqua Instn., N.Y. Surgeon with rank of maj., 74th Inc., N.G.N.Y. (retired, 1913); now lt. Med. Reserve Corps, U.S. Army. Episcopalian. Home: Buffalo, N.Y. Died Nov. 14, 1919.

BISSELL, Wilson Shannon, postmaster-gen. U.S.; b. New London, N.Y., Dec. 31, 1847; removed to Buffalo in childhood; grad. Yale, 1869 (LL.D., 1893); formed law partnership with Lyman K. Bass, 1872, Grover Cleveland being admitted to the firm a year later, name changed to Bass, Cleveland & Bissell; firm reorganized and is now Bissell, Carey & Cooke. Has been delegate several convs.; Presidential elector 1888; mem. commn. to propose amendment to the judiciary articles constitution of N.Y., 1890; apptd. postmaster-gen. of U.S., Mar. 6, 1893, by President Cleveland; resigned, 1895. Democrat. Chancellor Univ. of Buffalo, 1902. Home: Buffalo, N.Y. Died 1903.

BISSETT, Clark Prescott, prof. law; b. Alameda, Calif., Jan. 11, 1875; s. James M. and Harriet (Prescott) B.; A.B., Hobart Coll., Geneva, N.Y., 1896; LL.B., U. of Minn., 1909; Litt.D., Lincoln Memorial U., Harrogate, Tenn., 1926; LL.D., Jesuit Coll., 1928; m. Edith D. Evelyn, Apr. 12, 1899; children—Mrs. Irene Miller, Clark Prescott. Prof. law, U. of Wash., 1912-29, then emeritus. Knight Comdr. Crown of Italy, 1927. Owner of library of 30,000 vols., including one of largest collections of books and pamphlets on Abraham Lincoln in the world. Republican. Episcopalian. Author: Abraham Lincoln, 1916; Abraham Lincoln, A Universal Man, 1923; Mussolini and Fascismo, 1928; Community Property; also numerous essays on Lincoln. Home: Seattle, Wash. Died Jan. 9, 1932.

BITTER, Karl Theodore Francis, sculptor; b. Vienna, Austria, Dec. 6, 1867; ed. in gymnasium there; studied art in Vienna Acad. Fine Arts. Came to U.S., 1889; was employed in architectural sculpture; won prize in competition for Astor memorial gates, Trinity Ch., New York; executed sculpture on Administration and Manufactures Bldgs., Chicago Expn.; residences of C. P. Huntington and Cornelius Vanderbilt, etc.; dir. of sculpture, Buffalo Expn., 1901; chief dept. sculpture, St. Louis Expn., 1904, Panama-Pacific Internat. Exposition, San Francisco, 1915. Silver medal Paris Expn., 1900; gold medal, Buffalo Expn., 1901, Phila., 1902, St. Louis Expn., 1904. N.A., 1902; mem. Nat. Inst. Arts and Letters. Home: New York, N.Y. Died Apr. 10, 1915.

BITTING, William Coleman, clergyman; b. in Hanover Co., Va., Feb. 5, 1857; s. Charles Carroll (D.D.) and Caroline (Shadinger) B.; ed. Classical and Commercial Sch., Lynchburg, Va., 1869-70; M.A., Richmond (Va.) Coll., 1877; grad. Crozer Theol. Sem., Pa., 1880; D.D., Richmond Coll., 1889, Howard Coll., Ala., 1887, Brown U., 1910; S.T.D., U. of Chicago, 1916; m. Anna Mary Biedler, Nov. 17, 1886; children—William C., Frank Milton, Bitting (dec.), Kenneth Hills. Ordained Bapt. ministry, 1881; supply Lee St. Ch., Baltimore, 1880-81; pastor Luray, Va., 1881-83, Mt. Morris Ch., New York, 1884-1905, Second Ch., St. Louis, Nov. 1, 1905-Dec. 31, 1924. Corr. sec. Northern Bapt. Conv., May, 1907—. Author: Earthly Blooms from Heavenly Stems, 1900; Foundation Truths, 1902; The Teaching Pastor, 1923. Home: St. Louis, Mo. Died Jan. 11, 1931.

BITTINGER, John Lawrence, retired; b. nr. Chambersburg, Pa., Nov. 28, 1833; common sch. edn. in Ashland Co., O.; m. Annie M. Smith, June 10, 1862. Moved to Green Co., Wis.; worked on farm 3 yrs.; office of Freeport (Ill.) Journal, 1852-55; foreman on several papers in St. Louis, 1855-60; represented St. Louis Typographical Union in nat. conv., 1858, Chicago, and 1859, Boston; removed to St. Joseph, 1860; postmaster, 1861-65; maj. and a.-d.-c. on staff Gen. Willard P. Hall, 1861-62; mem. Mo. Gen. Assembly 7 terms; del. Rep. Nat. convs., 1872, 1896; mng. editor St. Joseph Herald, 27 yrs., Kansas City Journal, 5 yrs.; Am. consul-gen. at Montreal, 1897-1903; retired 1903. Home: St. Joseph, Mo. Died 1911.

BIXBY, Ammi Leander, newspaperman; b. Potsdam, N.Y., Apr. 21, 1856; s. Alfred and Catharine (Willson) B.; ed. common schs. and 1 term Rush Med. Coll., Chicago, spring of 1882; m. Mary A. Bates, May 14, 1878; children—Alfred Leroy, Anna Catherine, Florence Lillian (dec.), Bessie May, Alice Lorena. Began newspaper work, Fullerton, Neb., 1881; bought half interest in Nance County Jour., Fullerton, 1883; sold out, 1886, and rented plant for a yr.; went to Denver, 1887, and purchased a half interest in Castle Rock (Colo.) Jour.; sold out in few mos. and returned to Fullerton, purchasing Fullerton Telescope; sold plant in 1889 and engaged in pub. Platte County Sentinel, Columbus, Neb.; with Neb. State Jour., Aug. 24, 1892—, conducting spl. column, "Daily Drift." Republican. Methodist. Mem. Bd. of Edn. 5 yrs. Mason. Author: Driftwood, 1895; Memories and Other Poems, 1900; Bix Abroad, 1907; Bix in America, 1913. Presented with medal by Kiwanis Club of Lincoln, 1928, as "oldest columnist in U.S." Reader and lecturer; spent 2 mos. in Europe, 1907. Home: Lincoln, Neb. Died Dec. 24, 1934.

BIXBY, Edson Kingman, newspaper pub.; b. Red Wing, Minn., Apr. 7, 1887; s. Tams and Clara (Mues) B.; grad. Shattuck Sch., Faribault, Minn., 1904; student U. of Minn., 1904-06; m. Martha Elise Barnes, Feb. 9, 1916. Editor Bixby newspapers—Muskogee Daily Phoenix, Muskogee Times Democrats; editor and gen. mgr. The Springfield (Mo.) Leader and Press, Springfield (Mo.) Daily News; v.p. Oklahoma Press Pub. Co., Phoenix Improvement Co., Springfield Newspapers, Inc. Enlisted U.S. Cav., 1917; commd. 1st lt. arty.; served as comdr. Bat. A, 1st Regt., F.A.R.D., Camp Zachary Taylor, Louisville, Ky.; hon. disch., 1918. Republican. Episcopalian. Home: Springfield, Mo. Died Mar. 17, 1940.

BIXBY, James Thompson, author, clergyman; b. Barre, Mass., July 30, 1843; s. Clark S. and Elizabeth (Clark) B.; brother of William Herbert B.; A.B., Harvard, 1864, A.M., 1867, S.T.B., 1870; Ph. D., Leipzig, 1885; m. Emma A. J. Gibson, Sept. 1, 1870 (died 1902); 2d, Clara Webster Parker, Feb. 24, 1906. Ordained Unitarian ministry, 1870; pastor Watertown, Mass., 1870-74. Belfast, Me., 1875-79, Meadville, Pa., 1879-83, Yonkers, N.Y., 1887-1903; prof. religious philosophy, Meadville Theol. Sch., 1879-83. Lecturer on philosophy of religion, Lowell Inst., 1876, 1883. Author: Religion and Science as Allies, 1895; The Ethics of Evolution, 1900; The New World and the New Thought, 1902; The Open Secret, or Life's Deeper Forces, 1912; What Is Behaism?, 1912; Between the Testaments, 1913; After Death What? (article), 1914. Home: Yonkers, N.Y. Died Dec. 26, 1921.

BIXBY, Tams, newspaperman; b. Staunton, Va., Dec. 12, 1855; s. Bradford W. and Susan (Clarke) B.; ed. pub. schls., Red Wing, Minn.; m. Clara Mues, Apr. 27, 1886. Editor and pub. Red Wing (daily) Republican, 1896-1912; sec. R.R. and Warehouse Commn. of Minn., 1888-89; pvt. sec. to Govs. Wm. R. Merriam, 1889-92, Knute Nelson, 1892-96, David M. Clough, 1896-97; chmn. Commn. to Five Civilized Tribes, Indian Ty., 1897-1905, commr., 1905-07; pres. Muskogee (Okla.) Daily Phoenix Co., 1906—; gen. mgr. Pioneer Press Co., St. Paul, 1907-09; then editor and pub. Daily Phoenix, Muskogee, Okla. Long active in politics, first as chmn. Rep. Co. Com., later sec. State Rep. League, sec. and chmn. Rep. State Central Com. of Minn. Home: Muskogee, Okla. Died Jan. 17, 1922.

BIXBY, William Herbert, army officer; b. Charlestown, Mass., Dec. 27, 1849; s. Clark Smith and Elizabeth (Clark) B.; brother of James Thompson B.; student Mass. Inst. Tech., 1866-67; apptd. from Mass., and grad. U.S. Mil. Acad., 1873; grad. French Govt. Sch. of Bridges and Highways, 1881; m. Lidey H. Rogers Jones, Dec. 27, 1893. Second lt. engrs., June 13, 1873; promoted through grades to brig. gen., June 12, 1910; retired Aug. 11, 1913. Asst. prof. engring., West Point, 1875-79; sent by U.S. Govt. to attend French Army manœuvers, 1880, to examine and report upon iron fortifications in Europe, 1881-82, to inspect buildings Charleston, S.C., earthquake, 1887; lecturer on coast defenses, U.S. Naval War Coll., 1887; with Nat. Waterways Commn. to inspect rivers and harbors in Europe, 1909; in charge removal wreck of the Maine from Havana Harbor, 1912; in charge, at different times, of U.S. river and harbor improvements in N.C., S.C., Va., 1884-91, in Conn., R.I., Mass., 1891-95, in the Ohio River basin, 1897-1901, on ship channel of Great Lakes, 1902-04, in Ill. and Ind., 1905-07; also of lighthouse constrn. in N.J., Pa., Del., Md., Va. and of the Ohio and tributaries, 1884-1905; div. engr. of Northwestern and Western U.S., 1905-08; pres. Miss. River Commn., 1908-10; chief of engrs. U.S.A., June 10, 1910-Aug. 11, 1913; returned to active service May 1917-Apr. 1919; again pres. Miss. River Commn., and div. engr. Western Div. River and Harbor Improvements, and insp. 15th Lighthouse Dist. Home: Washington, D.C. Died Sept. 29, 1928.

BIXBY, William Keeney, mfr.; b. Adrian, Mich., Jan. 2, 1857; s. Alonzo Foster and Emma Louisa (Keeney) B.; grad. Adrian High Sch.; M.A., Amherst, 1913; (LL.D., U. of Mo., 1907); m. Lillian Tuttle, June 13, 1881; children—Sidney Tuttle, Mrs. Emma Stewart Jordan, Wm. Hoxie, Harold McMillan, Mrs. Ruth Stevens, Ralph Foster, Donald Church. Was first pres. Am. Car & Foundry Co. and later chmn. of board; pres. Laclede Gas Co.; one of receivers Wabash R.R., 1909-14; dir. St. Louis Union Trust Co. (exec. com.), First Nat. Bank, St. Louis, Charter Mem. Incorpn. of Am. Red Cross, Washington. Hon. pres. Provident Assn. and Archæol. Soc. (both of St. Louis); pres. City Art Mus., St. Louis; pres. Washington U., Am. Fedn. Art, Washington, D.C.; trustee Y.W.C.A. Endowment Fund, Girls' Industrial Home; dir. Nat. Gallery of Art, Washington, D.C., St. Luke's Hosp., St. Louis. Mem. First Congregational Ch. Mason. Home: St. Louis, Mo. Died Oct. 29, 1931.

BJERREGAARD, Carl Henry Andrew, librarian; b. Fredericia, Denmark, May 24, 1845; s. Janus Bagge Friis and Louise (Bagge-Nielsen) B.; studied Fredericia Coll.; grad. Copenhagen U., 1863; grad. as officer from Mil. Acad. of Denmark, 1866; served as lt. 5 yrs.; m. Matilda J. Thompson, 1868. Prof. botany, Fredericia Coll., 2 yrs.; resigned to join Danish Legation to Court of Russia, served 2 yrs.; came to U. S. for political reasons, 1873; librarian 1879—, Astor Library, then Astor branch New York Pub. Library—Astor, Lenox and Tilden Foundations. Author: Mysticism and Nature Worship (2 vols); Being, and the Philosophical History of the Subject; Sufi Interpretation of Omar Khayyám and Fitzgerald, 1902; History and Doctrine of Mysticism, 16 vols. still in preparation; Jesus, a poet, a prophet, a mystic and a man of freedom, 1912; The Inner Life and The Tao-Teh-King, 1912; The Great Mother, 1913; Sufism, Omar Khayyám and Fitzgerald, 1915. Also a collaborator on Standard Dictionary, Jewish Ency. Internat. Ency. and Ency. Americana; an authority on orientalia and mysticism. Died Jan. 28, 1922.

BJORNSTAD, Alfred William, army officer; b. St. Paul, Minn., Oct. 13, 1874; s. Julius B.; preliminary edn. Luther Coll.; student U. of Minn., 1893-96; honor grad. Army Sch. of the Line, 1909; grad. Army Staff Coll., 1910; m. Pearl Ladd Sabin, Oct. 3, 1905. Commd. 1st lt. 13th Minn. Inf., May 7, 1898; capt., May 16, 1898; hon. mustered out, Oct. 3, 1899; capt. 42d U.S. Inf., Aug. 17, 1899; hon. mustered out vols., June 24, 1901; 1st lt. 29th Inf., U.S.A., Feb. 2, 1901; promoted through grades to rank of brig. gen., Jan. 17, 1925. Engaged in 34 battles and actions in Philippines, 1898-1904; duty Gen. Staff, 1911-12; mil. attaché to Germany, 1912-13; instr. mil. art, Army Staff Coll., 1915-16; duty Gen. Staff, 1917; organized, and directed, 1917, the 16 training camps for officers which produced the original 25,341 officers of the N.A. in the World War; first chief of staff, 30th Div., 1917; organized and directed Army Gen. Staff Coll. in France, 1917-18; brig. gen. N.A., July 12, 1918-July 31, 1919; chief of staff 3d Army Corps, A.E.F., 1918; comdr. 13th Brigade, 1918-19; participated in all major engagements in France; duty Gen. Staff Coll., 1919; comdg. officer, Ft. Snelling, Minn., 1920-23; asst. comdt. Inf. Sch., Ft. Benning, Ga., 1923-25; retired Aug. 31, 1928. Decorated D.S.C., D.S.M., Purple Heart (Oak Leaf Cluster); Companion St. Michael and St. George (British); Legion of Honor, Croix de Guerre (French). Mason. Home: San Francisco, Calif. Died Nov. 4, 1934.

BLABON, Joseph Ward, ry. official; b. Farmington, Franklin Co., Me., Apr. 27, 1858; s. Joseph Eaton and Martha Ward (Smith) B.; ed. pub. schs., Portland, Me.; unmarried. Began as clerk at New York, 1876; in business on own account, St. Paul, Minn., 1883-89; entered ry. service on G.N. R.R., 1890, with which remained until 1905, as purchasing agt., 1890-99, western traffic mgr., at Seattle, 1899-1902, 4th v.p., 1902-05; was also pres. G.N. Express Co. and Northern Steamship Co.; traffic mgr. C.&A. R.R., Jan. 1, 1905-Dec. 31, 1908; v.p. C.G.W. R.R., Chicago, Sept. 1, 1909—. Died Jan. 10, 1933.

BLACK, Alexander, author, editor; b. New York, Feb. 7, 1859; s. Peter and Sarah (MacCrae) B.; ed. grammar schs. Brooklyn; hon. M.A., St. Lawrence U., 1908; m. Elizabeth Helmle, Oct. 4, 1881; children—Mabel Hawthorne (Mrs. Cleland Ruthven Austin), Carlyle Helmle, Malcolm Stuart; m. 2d, Edith O'Dell, Jan. 25, 1935. Became reporter on Brooklyn Times at age of 16; official stenographer in Brooklyn courts, 1882-86; lit. editor Brooklyn Times, 1885-95; art director of New York Sunday World, 1900-05; Sunday editor of the New York World, 1905-10; managing editor "Frank Seaman, Inc.," 1910-13; editor Newspaper Feature Service, 1913-26; art editor King Features Syndicate, 1926-1935. Originated prefilm "picture plays," 1893; brought out first screen drama, in slow motion, 1894. First pres. dept. of photography, Brooklyn Inst. Author: Story of Ohio, 1888; Photography Indoors and Out, 1894; Miss Jerry, 1895; A Capital Courtship, 1897; Miss America, 1898; Modern Daughters, 1899; Captain Kodak, 1899; The Girl and the Guardsman, 1900; Richard Gordon, 1902; Thorney, 1913; The Great Desire, 1919; The Seventh Angel, 1920; The Latest Thing, 1922; Jo Ellen, 1923; Stacey, 1925; American Husbands, 1926; Time and Chance (reminiscence), 1937. Editor: Ostrander's History of the City of Brooklyn and Kings County. Home: New York, N.Y. Died May 8, 1940.

BLACK, Alfred Lawrence, lawyer; b. Springfield Tp., Burlington Co., N.J., Nov. 16, 1858; s. Alfred Lawrence and Margaret Hendrickson (Bunting) B.; A.B., Princeton, 1878, A.M., 1881; studied law in office of James Wilson, Trenton, N.J.; m. Ada Frances Abbott, May 7, 1883. Admitted to bar, N.J., Nov. 2, 1881, counsellor, Nov., 1884, Wash., 1889, Calif., 1897, Supreme Ct. of U.S., 1893. Practiced law, Camden, N.J., 1881-89, Whatcom, Wash., 1889-96, San Francisco, 1896-1902; then in Bellingham, Wash., firm Black & Black. Pres. Bellingham Bay Land Co., Fairhaven Land Co. Mayor of Whatcom, 1894; mayor of Bellingham, 1903-04, 1906-08. Republican. Mem. and official Trans-Mississippi Commercial Congress; was pres. Whatcom Bd. Trade several yrs.; v.p. Wash. State Bar Assn. Home: Bellingham, Wash. Died 1927.

BLACK, Arthur Davenport, dental surgean; b. Jacksonville, Ill., Nov. 15, 1870; s. Dr. Greene V. and Elizabeth (Davenport) B.; B.S., Ill. Coll., 1892; D.D.S., Northwestern U., Dental Sch., 1900; M.D., Northwestern U. Med. Sch., 1901; M.A., Northwestern U.; Sc.D., Illinois College, Jacksonville, Ill.; m. Lenore Bronaugh, Oct. 19, 1897; children—Gilmer Vardiman, Mary Barbara, Jane. Formerly engaged in mfg. business in Indianapolis and Chicago; practiced in Chicago, 1900—; formerly prof. operative dentistry, and asst. oral surgeon, Northwestern U. Dental Sch.; dean and prof. dental pathology, same, 1917—. Editor Index English Dental Literature. Fellow Am. Coll. Surgeons. Republican. Home: Evanston, Ill. Died Dec. 7, 1937.

BLACK, Chauncey Forward, lawyer; b. Somerset, Pa.; s. Jeremiah S. B., atty. gen. and Sec. State, U.S.; lt. gov. Pa., 1882-86; Dem. candidate for gov., 1886; pres. Nat. Assn. Dem. Clubs. Home: York, Pa. Died 1904.

BLACK, E(benezer) Charlton, univ. prof.; b. the Manse, Liddesdale, Scotland, June 18, 1861; s. Rev. John and Mary (Beattie) B.; ed. Edinburgh U., 1875-82, highest honors in rhetoric, Anglo-Saxon, English lit. and poetry; Queen's Coll., London, Westminster Coll., Cambridge, 1882-84; Liddelbank, Liddesdale, 1884-91; LL.D., Glasgow U., 1902; m. Agnes Knox, of Edinburgh, July 26, 1893; children—Margaret Charlton (Mrs. Terrell Moore Ragan), John Gavin (Dec.), Knox Charlton. Lecturer English lit., Harvard, 1891-93; prin. lang. and lit. dept., N.E. Conservatory of Music, 1893-1900; prof. English lit., Boston U., 1900—. Lecturer on English lit., Emerson Coll. of Oratory; Univ. Extension Commn., etc.; hon. librarian, Boston U.; pres. New England Assn. of Teachers of English, and the Boston Drama League; fellow and mem. hon. council N. British Acad. Author: Early Songs and Lyrics, 1886; Shakespeare Manual for Teachers, 1915; University Addresses, 1916; From a Professor's Notebook (series), 1922. Contbr. to Edinburgh Review, International Quarterly, etc. Home: Cambridge, Mass. Died July 11, 1927.

BLACK, Eugene Robert, banker; b. Atlanta, Ga.; s. Eugene Pinckard and Zac (Harman) B.; grad. Boys High Sch., Atlanta, 1889; student U. of Ga.; m. Gussie Grady, May 5, 1897; children—Eugene Robert, H. G., Julia. Admitted to Ga. bar and practiced at Atlanta; later gov. Federal Reserve Bank of Atlanta; gov. Federal Reserve Bd., Washington, D.C., 1933—. Democrat. Baptist. Home: Atlanta, Ga. Died Dec. 19, 1934.

BLACK, Frank B., mfr.; b. Mansfield, O., June 10, 1865; s. Moses and Elizabeth (Blymyer) B.; ed. high sch.; m. Jessie Baxter, Oct. 5, 1892; children—John B. (dec.), Robert B., Donald S., Roger A. Chmn. bd. Ohio Brass Co., Mansfield, 1930—; dir. Citizens Nat. Bank & Trust Co., Mansfield Savings Bank, Perfect Rubber Co., Ohio Insulator Co., Mansfield Telephone Co. Republican. Conglist. Home: Mansfield, O. Died Dec. 19, 1937.

BLACK, Frank Swett, governor; b. Limington, Me., Mar. 8, 1853; s. Jacob and Charlotte B. B.; A.B., Dartmouth Coll., 1875 (LL.D., 1898); m. Lois Hamilton. Editor Johnstown (N.Y.) Journal short time, and read law; later reporter Troy (N.Y.) Whig; admitted to bar, 1879; in practice at Troy till 1898 and since then in New York. Mem. 54th Congress (1895-97); gov. of N.Y., 1897-99. Republican. Home: New York, N.Y. Died Mar. 21, 1913.

BLACK, Greene Vardiman, dentist; b. Scott Co., Ill.; Aug. 3, 1836; D.D.S., Mo. Dental Coll., St. Louis, 1877; M.D., Chicago Medical Coll., 1884; (Sc.D., Ill. Coll., 1892; LL.D., Northwestern, 1898). Prof. operative dentistry, pathology and bacteriology and dean Northwestern U. Dental Sch. Author: Formation of Poisons by Micro-Organisms; Periosteum and Peridental Membrane; Anatomy of the Human Teeth; Operative Dentistry (2 vols.); also many soc. papers and journal articles. Home: Chicago, Ill. Died Aug. 31, 1915.

BLACK, Harry Alfred, hardware mcht.; b. Aug. 22, 1866; s. John Henry and Julia Emma (Bunce) B.; educated in public schools; m. Ella Maud Smith, Oct. 19, 1887. Began in business at Chicago, 1876; pres. Black Hardware Co., 1910—; dir. Hutchins Sealy Nat. Bank, Am. Indemnity Co., Am. Fire & Marine Ins. Co., Galveston Fig Co., etc. Trustee Seamens Bethel. Former v.p. Chamber Commerce of U.S.; mem. Galveston Chamber of Commerce (chmn. traffic com.). Episcopalian. Home: Galveston, Tex. Died Sept. 9, 1935.

BLACK, Harry S(t. Francis), real estate; b. Cobourg, Can., Aug. 27, 1863; s. Maj. Thomas (British Army) and Elizabeth (Wickens) B.; ed. high sch., Cobourg; m. Allon Mae, d. George A. Fuller, 1895 (died 1915); m. 2d, Isabelle, d. Col. Henry, May 1922. Studied engring. and in 1882 joined surveying expdn. operating in the Northwest to Pac. coast; banking business in State of Wash., 1886; entered the George A. Fuller Co. as v.p. in 1896; was projector of enlarged corp. of same name ($20,000,000 capital), of which was pres. (now dir.) and since its consolidation with the U.S. Realty & Improvement Co., has been chmn. bd. Democrat. Mason. Died July 19, 1929.

BLACK, Henry Campbell, law author, editor; b. Ossining, N.Y., Oct. 17, 1860; s. Rev. John Henry and Caroline (Campbell) B.; A.B., 1880, A.M., 1887, Trinity Coll., LL.D., 1916; ed. for bar in Lycoming Co., Pa.; m. Bertha A. Brown, 1910. Admitted to bar, 1883; practiced at Williamsport, Pa., and St. Paul, Minn.; removed to Washington, 1888, and has since followed legal literature as a profession. Editor The Constitutional Review. Lecturer constl. govt., Trinity, 1917. Author: Constitutional Prohibitions, 1887; Law of Tax Titles, 1888, 1893; Dictionary of Law, 1891-1910; Law of Judgments, 1891, 1903; Law of Intoxicating Liquors, 1892; American Constitutional Law, 1895, 1897, 1909, 1926; Construction and Interpretation of Laws, 1896-1911; Handbook of Bankruptcy Law, 1898; Law of Mortgages in Illinois, 1903; Law of Judicial Precedents, 1912; Income Taxation, 1913; Treatise on Bankruptcy, 1914, 1925; Rescission of Contracts, 1916; Income and Other Federal Taxes, 1917, 1919; Relation of Executive Power to Legislation, 1919. Home: Washington, D.C. Died Mar. 19, 1927.

BLACK, James C(onquest) C(ross), lawyer; b. Stamping Ground, Scott Co., Ky., May 9, 1842; A.B., Georgetown (Ky.) Coll. Admitted to Ga. bar, 1866, and practiced at Augusta; was mem. Ga. Ho. of Rep.; elected to 53d and 54th Congresses (1893-97) and served 1893-95 (resigned); subsequently elected to fill vacancy caused by own resignation and served Dec. 1895-Mar. 3, 1897; resumed practice at Augusta. Democrat. Home: Augusta, Ga. Died Oct. 1, 1928.

BLACK, James Dixon, lawyer; b. Knox Co., Ky., Sept. 24, 1849; s. John C. and Clarissa (Jones) B.; A.B., Tusculum Coll., Greeneville, Tenn., 1872, LL.D., m. Mary Jeanett Pitzer, 1875. Mem. Black, Black & Owens, Barbourville, Ky.; pres. Nat. Bank of John A. Black, Barbourville. Mem. Ky. Ho. of Rep., 1876-77; supt. pub. schs., Knox Co., Ky., 1884; commr. from Ky. to World's Fair, Chicago, 1893; 1st asst. atty. gen. of Ky., 1912; elected lt. gov. of Ky., Nov. 1915, for term 1916-19 inclusive; succeeded Gov. A. Owsley Stanley, upon resignation of latter, and served as gov., May-Dec. 1919. Pres. Union Coll., Barbourville, 1910-12 inclusive. Mem. Ky. State Bar Assn. Democrat. Methodist. Mason. Home: Barbourville, Ky. Died Aug. 5, 1938.

BLACK, James William, prof. history; b. Baltimore, Jan. 31, 1866; s. James and Mary Ellen (Fairbank) B.; A.B., Baltimore City Coll.; A.B., Johns Hopkins, 1888, Ph.D., 1891 (Univ. scholarship); m. Jennie Haven Dix, Dec. 26, 1889. Acting prof. history and polit. science, Georgetown (Ky.) Coll., 1891-92; asso. prof. economics, Oberlin Coll., 1892-94; prof. history and political economy, 1894-1912, prof. history and polit. science, 1912, Colby Coll. Republican. Baptist. Author various monographs on hist. topics. Home: Waterville, Me. Died Sept. 3, 1934.

BLACK, John Charles, lawyer; b. Lexington, Miss., Jan. 27, 1839; s. Rev. John and Josephine (Culbertson) B.; ed. Wabash Coll.; (A.M., LL.D., Knox Coll.); m. Adaline L. Griggs, Sept. 28, 1867. Pvt. and sergt. maj. 11th Ind. Inf., Apr. 25-Aug. 4, 1861; maj. 37th Ill. Inf., Sept. 5, 1861; lt. col., July 12, 1862; col., Dec. 31, 1862; bvtd. brig. gen. vols., Apr. 9, 1865, "for gallant services in assault on Ft. Blakely, Ala."; awarded medal of honor, Oct. 31, 1893, for Battle of Prairie Grove, Ark., Dec. 7, 1862 (severely wounded); resigned, Aug. 15, 1865. Admitted to bar, 1867; practiced at Danville, Ill., 1867—; candidate for Congress, 1866, 1880, 1884, for lt. gov., 1872; del.-at-large Dem. Nat. Conv., 1884; Dem. nominee for U.S. senator, 1879; U.S. commr. of pensions, 1885-89; mem. 53d Congress (1893-95), Ill. at-large; U.S. atty. for Northern Dist. of Ill., 1895-99; mem. U.S. Civil Service Commn., Dec. 1903-13, and pres., Jan. 1904-June 10, 1913. Comdr.-in-chief G.A.R., 1903-04 (comdr. Ill. dept., 1903-04). Home: Chicago, Ill. Died Aug. 17, 1915.

BLACK, John Clarke, banker; b. Middlebury, Vt., July 3, 1837; s. Daniel and Jean (Lawrence) B.; pub. sch. edn.; m. Nellie A. Clarke, Sept. 22, 1875. Removed to Chicago, 1856; employed as bookkeeper and cashier for Ross & Ramber, dry goods, and later with Armour & Co. until 1881; one of the organizers and incorporators, 1883, of the Continental Nat. Bank, of which was many yrs. pres.

and later chmn. bd. dirs.; mem. western bd. control Audit Co. of New York; trustee Prussian Nat. Ins. Co. of Stettin, Germany; dir. Continental & Commercial Nat. Bank, Northwestern Safe & Trust Co. Trustee Art Inst. of Chicago, Armour Mission. Mem. Chicago Bd. of Trade. Home: Chicago, Ill. Died June 1, 1917.

BLACK, John Janvier, physician; b. Delaware City, Del., Nov. 6, 1837; s. Dr. Charles Henry and Ann (Janvier) B.; grad. Princeton, 1858 (hon. A.M., 1907); M.D., U. of Pa., 1862; m. Jeanie S. Groome, Jan. 1872. Asst. surgeon U.S.A., 1862-64. Mem. Coll. of Physicians, Phila.; mem. State Med. Soc., Newcastle Co. Med. Soc. Democrat. Presbyterian. Author: Cultivation of the Peach, Pear and Quince, 1886; Forty Years in the Medical Profession, 1900; Eating to Live. Home: Newcastle, Del. Deceased.

BLACK, Samuel Charles, clergyman; b. Monticello, Ia., Sept. 6, 1869; s. William Irvin and Flora A. (Johnson) B.; A.B., Parsons Coll., Ia., 1892, A.M., 1898; grad. McCormick Theol. Sem., Chicago, 1898; (D.D., Blackburn University, 1907, LL.D., Univ. of Pittsburgh, 1919); m. Grace Westcott, Dec. 6, 1892. Telegraph operator, 1884-88; in banking business at Fairfield and Des Moines, Ia., 1892-95; ordained Presbyn. ministry, 1897; pastor, Kewanee, Ill., 1895-97, South Chicago, Ill., 1897-1900, Clinton, Ill., 1900-08, Boulder, Colo., 1908-10; Collingwood Av. Ch., Toledo, O., 1910-19; pres. Washington and Jefferson Coll., June 1, 1919. Instr. Hebrew, U. of Colo., 1908-10; lecturer. Maj. and morale officer, Camp Gordon, Ga., 1918-19. Author: Plain Answers to Religious Questions Modern Men Are Asking, 1907, 1910; Building a Working Church, 1911; Progress in Christian Culture, 1912. Home: Washington, Pa. Died July 25, 1921.

BLACK, Van-Lear, capitalist; b. Cumberland, Md., Dec. 18, 1875; s. H. Crawford and Ida (Perry) B.; ed. pub. schs.; m. Jessie A. Gary, Nov. 3, 1899; children—H. Crawford, James Gary, Van-Lear, Jessie G., Ida Perry, Gar, Madeliene. Began as clk., Fidelity & Deposit Co. of Md., Baltimore, 1894, dir., 1908-20, chmn. bd., 1920—; became pres. Fidelity Trust Co., 1920, now chmn. bd.; chmn. bd. A. S. Abell Co., pubs. Baltimore Sun; Q.M. gen., staff of Gov. Edwin Warfield, of Md., 1904-08. Chmn. publicity com., Liberty Loan drives, World War; del. to Md. State Conv. for League of Nations, 1920; mem. B.&O. R.R. Centennial Com. Mem. Md. State Bd. of Edn., 1920; one of organizers Md. State Police. Export and Import Bd. of Trade. Democrat. Episcopalian. Has flown nearly 200,000 miles by airplane since 1926. Home: Baltimore, Md. Died Aug. 18, 1930.

BLACK, William, mfr.; b. Bordentown, N.J., Sept. 3, 1876; s. Franklin and Mary Tallman (Biddle) B.; ed. high sch., Bordentown; m. Florence Miller, July 17, 1912; children—Florence Miller, William. Pres. B. F. Avery & Sons, mfrs. agrl. implements, 1920—; dir. Louisville Branch Federal Reserve Bank, Louisville Trust Company, Inter-Southern Life Ins. Co. Mem. Chamber Commerce, U.S.A. (dir., exec. com.), Louisville Bd. of Trade (v.p.); chmn. Louisville Bridge Commn. Republican. Mem. Christian (Disciples) Ch. Home: Louisville, Ky. Died Apr. 19, 1930.

BLACK, William Henry, college pres.; b. Centreville, Ind., Mar. 19, 1854; s. Rev. Felix G. and Lydia K. (Frederick) B.; A.B., Waynesburg Coll., Pa., 1876, A.M., 1879; grad. Western Theol. Sem., 1878; spent 1 yr. in post-grad. study; D.D., Cumberland U., 1888; LL.D., Westminster Coll., 1903; Litt.D., Waynesburg Coll., 1915; m. Mary Ella Henderson, Apr. 3, 1879. Ordained Presbyn. ministry, 1876; served as pastor Pittsburgh, 1877-81, St. Louis, 1881-90; pres. Mo. Valley Coll., 1890—. Moderator Gen. Assembly Cumberland Presbyn. Ch., Waco, Tex., 1888; chmn. Cumberland Presbyn. Com. on Fraternity and Union; pres. Mo. State Teachers' Assn., 1900; mem. Nat. Council Edn.; mem. World Conf. of Edn. Assns., Edinburgh, Scotland, 1925. Author: Sermons for the Sabbath School, 1886; God Our Father, 1889; Womanhood, 1890; Outline Life of Paul, 1894, 1904; The Life and Times of Moses, 1901; The Hebrew Monarchy—A Harmony, 1902; The Life of Jesus; Tripaschal, 1906; The Division and Fall of the Hebrew Monarchy—A Harmony, 1910. Home: Marshall, Mo. Died June 22, 1930.

BLACK, William Murray, army officer; b. Lancaster, Pa., Dec. 8, 1855; s. James and Eliza (Murray) B.; ed. Franklin and Marshall Coll., Pa., 1870-73; grad. U.S. Mil. Acad., 1877; Sc.D., Franklin and Marshall Coll., 1912; Dr. Engring., Pa. Mil. Coll., 1920; m. Daisy Peyton, d. Capt. George H. Derby, U.S.A. ("John Phoenix"), 1877; m. 2d, Gertrude Totten, d. Comdr. William M. Gamble, U.S.N. Commd. through all grades to col. corps engrs., U.S.A.; apptd. lt. col. and chief engr. U.S.V., May 25, 1898; hon. dis. from vol. service June 13, 1899. Long engaged on works of river and harbor improvement; also asst. instr. practical mil. engring., U.S. Mil. Acad. and instr. civil engring., U.S. Engr. Sch., Willets Point, N.Y.; asst. in charge works of fortification, office of chief engrs., Washington, 1895-97; commr. of D.C., 1897-98; chief engr. in campaign in P.R., 1898; chief engr. Dept. of Havana, staff Gen. Ludlow, Jan. 2, 1899-Apr. 30, 1900; chief engr. Div. of Cuba, Jan. 1900-Apr. 1901, staff of Gen. Leonard Wood; charge of engr. work, Havana, and supervision of work in Cuba; comdg. Engr. Sch. Application and 3d batn. engrs., 1901-03, and post of Washington Barracks, D.C., 1901-03; observing work of new Panama Canal Co. under orders of Isthmian Canal Commn., Apr. 1903-July 1904; in charge river and harbor improvements and fortifications, Me., 1904-06; adviser, dept. pub. works, Provisional Govt. of Cuba, 1906-09; in charge river and harbor improvements, Dist. No. 1, New York, Feb. 1909-Mar. 1916; brig. gen. chief of engrs. U.S.A., Mar. 7, 1916; promoted to maj. gen., Oct. 8, 1917. Sr. mem. of bd. charged with raising wreck of U.S.S. Maine from Havana Harbor, 1910-13; chief engr. officer Eastern Dept. U.S.A.; div. engr. Eastern Division River and Harbor Improvements, 1909-16; sr. officer bd. of engrs. for Rivers and Harbors, 1912-16; chmn. Inland Waterway Transportation Com. of Council Nat. Defense, 1917; member Nat. Research Council; chmn. port and harbors facilities commn. of U.S. Shipping Bd., Feb. 1919; retired from active Service Oct. 31, 1919. Awarded D.S.M., Dec. 1918, for especially meritorious and conspicuous service in planning and administering the engring. and mil. ry. services during the war. Episcopalian. Author: Improvement of Harbors; South Atlantic Coast; Waterway and Railway Equivalents (prize essays, Trans. Am. Society C.E., 1893-1925); Public Works of United States. Collaborated with Prof. E. B. Phelps in Report on Discharge of Sewage into New York Harbor. Inventor method of purifying sewage by aeration. Died Sept. 24, 1933.

BLACK, Winifred ("Annie Laurie"); journalist; b. Chilton, Wis., Oct. 14, 1869; d. Gen. Benjamin Jeffery and Lovisa (Denslow) Sweet; ed. Sacred Heart Convent, Chicago, Lake Forest (Ill.) Sem., Miss Burnham's Prep. Sch., Northampton, Mass.; m. Orlow Black, June 1892; m. 2d, Charles A. Bonfils, Feb. 7, 1901. Entered journalism, 1890; has been reporter, telegraph editor, Sunday editor, asst. city editor, spl. writer; investigated leper settlement, Molakai, Hawaii, 1892; raised funds for founding several charities; investigated pub. hosps., San Francisco, inaugurating many reforms; helped found Junior Republic for Boys, New York; conducted Calif. Children's Excursion to World's Fair; had for 6 yrs. charge of large charities of San Francisco Examiner and New York Journal; managed hosps. and relief ward for Galveston flood victims. Then on staff of San Francisco Examiner, fighting for better crime control and Americanism. Author: The Little Boy Who Lived on the Hill; Sink or Swim. Organized and managed nat. and internat. fight on the narcotic evil. Home: San Francisco, Calif. Died May 25, 1936.

BLACKALL, Christopher Rubey, editor; b. Albany, N.Y., Sept. 18, 1830; s. Benjamin and Sarah B.; ed. pub. schs.; M.D., Hygieo Therapeutic Med. Coll., New York, 1856, and Rush Med. Coll., Chicago, 1865; (D.D., Carson and Newman Coll., 1890, Temple Coll., 1906); m. Eliza Davis, 1852; m. 2d, Mrs. Emily Lucas Bryant, 1873; m. 3d, Mrs. Eugenie Hitchcock McLure, 1900; father of Clarence Howard B. Asst. surgeon 33d Wis. Vols., early part Civil War; abandoned medicine, 1864. Gen. supt. and editor, Chicago Sunday School Union, 1864-65; sec. and mgr. northwestern dist. Am. Bapt. Pub. Soc., 1865-79; connected with New York and Phila. branch houses, 1869-80; editor of periodicals, 1880-1916, editor emeritus, Dec. 1, 1916, of the Am. Bapt. Pub. Soc., Phila. Ordained to Christian ministry, 1880. Author: Our Sunday School Work and How to Do It, 1877; Story of Six Decades, 1885; Belshazzar (cantata), 1890; Stories About Jesus, 1897; The Son of Timeus, 1914; A Daughter of Naien, 1915; Beautiful Magdalene, 1916; Days of '63, 1919. Home: Philadelphia. Died Jan. 25, 1924.

BLACKALL, Clarence Howard, architect; b. N.Y. City, Feb. 3, 1857; s. Rev. Christopher Rubey and Eliza (Davis) B.; B.S., U. of Ill., 1877; A.M., École des Beaux Arts, Paris, 1878-80; m. Emma Murray, Dec. 5, 1883; children—Marian (Mrs. H. W. Miller), R. M. Practiced, New York, 1880-82, Colorado Springs, Colo., 1882, Boston, 1882; designed and erected 1st steel frame bldg. at Boston, 1892; architect for Tremont Temple, Colonial Theatre, etc., Boston, and other notable structures; mem. Boston and Cambridge bldg. law commns. First holder Rotch Traveling Scholarship, Boston, 1884-86 (sec., 1891). Fellow A.I.A.; mem. Archtl. League America. Trustee Charlestown Five Cents Savings Bank; pres. 245 Tremont St. Inc., 50 Stuart St. Inc. Sch. house commr., Boston, 1923-26. Author: Builders' Hardware, 1890. Editorial writer, The Brickbuilder, Boston, Jan. 1895—. Home: Concord, Mass. Died Apr. 1941.

BLACKALL, Frederick Steele, mech. engr., mfr.; b. Brooklyn, N.Y., July 23, 1865; s. Thomas Edwin and Sarah (Steele) B.; ed. pub. schs., Brooklyn and N.Y. City and Gymnasium, Berlin, Germany; m. Bertha Gates Brown, Dec. 31, 1890; children, George Beach (dec.), Frederick Steele. Pres. Blackall & Baldwin Co., contractors in machinery, New York, 1888-1903, also dir. Central Electric Heater Co.; pres. R. Hoe & Co., 1911-14; pres. Interchangeable Parts Co.; v.p., gen. mgr. Taft Pierce Mfg. Co., 1903—; v.p., mng. dir. Ottoman Am. Development Co.; v.p., gen. mgr. The Mott Haven Co.; dir. Parks & Parks, Inc. Mem. 7th Regt., N.G.S.N.Y., 7 yrs.; spl. intelligence service in Europe, World War, 1915-18. Republican. Presbyn. Home: New York, N.Y. Died Oct. 6, 1928.

BLACKARD, James Washington, clergyman, educator; b. Madison Co., Tenn., Feb. 8, 1857; s. Wiley Freeman and Matilda (Wilie) B.; A.B., Union U., Jackson, Tenn., 1882; D.D., Young Harris (Ga.) Coll., 1900; m. Louiza White, Dec. 27, 1883; children—Wiley W. (dec.), Warner M. (dec.), Mrs. Lucile Hofstead, William F., James R. (dec.), Charles G., Embree H. Ordained ministry M.E. Ch., S., 1885; successively, pastor Big Sandy (Tenn.), Henderson, Dresden, Somerville, McKenzie, Hickman (Ky.), Trenton, St. John's Ch., Memphis; presiding elder Jackson, Tenn., 1901-05, Paducah, Ky., 1905-09, Brownsville, 1909-13; pastor Union Av. Ch., Memphis, 1913-14, 1st Ch., Fulton, Ky., 1914-16, 1st Ch., Dyersburg, 1916-20, Hays Av. Ch., Jackson, 1920-22; pres. Lambuth Coll., 1920-24, became pres. bd. of trustees, 1919, then emeritus. Trustee McFerrin Sch., McTyeire Inst. Del. Ecumenical Conf., London, 1901; mem. Gen. Conf. M.E. Ch., S., 1910 and 1930; mem. Gen. Bd. Edn., M.E. Ch., S., 1910-14; mem. Gen. Bd. Ch. Extension, 1930—; pres. Conf. Bd. Edn., 1918-22, sec., 1924—; presiding elder Jackson Dist., 1926-30; formerly endowment sec. Lambuth Coll.; mem. 6th Ecumenical Conf., Atlanta, Ga., 1931. Democrat. Mason. Home: Jackson, Tenn. Died Mar. 29, 1938.

BLACKBURN, Alexander, clergyman; b. Laporte Co., Ind., Nov. 5, 1844; s. Alexander and Delilah (Polk) B.; ed. Erie Acad., Pa., 1 yr.; Hanover Coll., Ind., 1865, 66; B.S., Monmouth Coll., Ill., 1868; B.D., Div. Sch., U. of Chicago, 1873; (D.D., Franklin Coll., Ind., 1893); m. Margaret E. Hail, Sept. 11, 1868; 2d, Virginia Watson, Apr. 21, 1903. Enlisted as pvt. Co. C, 84th Regt. Ill. Inf., June 14, 1862; promoted to hosp. steward of regt., 1864; severely wounded in Battle of Chickamauga, Sept. 20, 1863; hon. discharged, June 1865. Ordained Bapt. ministry, 1871; pastor Austin Ch., Chicago, 1872-76, Oak Park, Ill., 1876-78, 1st Ch., Lafayette, Ind., 1878-87, Lowell, Mass., 1887-93, 1st Ch., Cambridge, Mass., 1893-98, 1st Ch., Portland, Ore., 1898-1903, 1st Ch., Salem, Mass., 1903-08, 1st Ch., Baker, Ore., 1908-10, South Boston, 1910-12, Southbridge, Mass., 1913-17; then supply pastor. Del. World Bapt. Conf., London, 1905, World Interdenominational Missionary Conf., Edinburgh, 1910. Mason. Mem. G.A.R. Home: Belmont, Mass. Died Sept. 9, 1921.

BLACKBURN, George Andrew, clergyman; b. Green Co., Tenn., Oct. 16, 1861; s. John Nelson and Eliza Jane (Armbrister) B.; grad. Southwestern Presbyn. U., 1883, Columbia (S.C.) Theol. Sem., 1886; (D.D., Presbyterian Coll. of S.C., 1910); m. Annie Williams, d. Dr. J. L. Girardeau, 1886. Pastor of Olivet Ch., McConnellsville, S.C., 1886-87, Arsenal Hill Ch., Columbia, S.C., 1887—. Representative of Charleston Presbytery in Sabbath case before Southern Gen. Assembly, 1894. Editor: Girardeau's Discussions of Philosophical Questions, 1900; Discussions of Theological Questions, 1905; Sermons, 1907; The Life Work of John L. Girardeau, D.D., LL.D., 1916. Died May 1918.

BLACKBURN, Joseph Clay Styles, senator; b. Woodford Co., Ky., Oct. 1, 1838; s. Edward M. and Lavinia S. B.; A.B., Centre Coll., Ky., 1857 (LL.D.); m. Therese Graham, Feb. 10, 1858 (died 1899); m. 2d, Mrs. Mary E. Blackburn, Dec. 11, 1901. Admitted to bar, 1858; practiced at Chicago, 1858-60; served throughout Civil War in C.S.A.; resumed practice in Ky.; mem. Ky. Ho. of Rep., 1871-75; mem. 44th to 48th Congresses (1875-85); U.S. senator, 1885-97 and 1901-07; mem. Isthmian Canal Commn. and head dept. civil administration, Canal Zone, Apr. 1, 1907-Dec. 4, 1909. Del. Dem. nat. convs., 1896, 1900, 1904, a leader in the free-coinage movement; chmn. Dem. caucus, U.S. Senate, 1906, 1907. Home: Versailles, Ky. Died Sept. 12, 1918.

BLACKBURN, Robert, congressman; b. Estell Co., Ky., Apr. 9, 1870; s. James B. and Sarah (Hardwick) B.; ed. pub. schs.; m. Annie Conlee, Jan. 17, 1900; 1 son, Donald Carlson. Traveling salesman, 1891-1900; merchant, 1900-07; engaged in ins. and stock brokerage business, Stanton, Ky., 1910, later at Lexington, Ky. Served as lt., U.S. Vols., Spanish-Am. War, 1898-99. Mem. Ky. Ho. of Rep., 1904, 05; county clk., Powell Co., Ky., 1906-10; mem. 71st Congress (1929-31), 7th Ky. Dist. Mem. Jr. Order Am. Mechanics, Spanish War Vets. Republican. Mem. Christian (Disciples) Ch. Mason. Home: Lexington, Ky. Died Sept. 20, 1935.

BLACKBURN, William Jasper, journalist; b. Randolph Co., Ark., July 24, 1820; ed. common schools; m. Myra Waggoner, 1849. Learned printer's trade at Batesville, Ark.; settled in Homer, La., establishing the Iliad, the only loyal paper in the Gulf States published during the war; mem. of the La. constl. convention, 1867; Congressman from La., July 1868-

Mar. 3, 1869; mem. La. State senate, 1872-76. Republican; later owner of Little Rock Republican. Home: Little Rock, Ark. Died 1899.

BLACKBURN, William Maxwell, pres. emeritus Huron Coll., 1898—; b. Carlyle, Ind., Dec. 30, 1828; grad. Hanover Coll., Ind., 1850; Princeton Theol. Sem., 1854 (D.D., Princeton, 1870; LL.D., Univ. of Wooster, 1894); m. Elizabeth Powell, 1854. Filled several pastorates and professorships until 1886; pres. Pierre Univ. (S.Dak.), 1886-98 (now Huron Coll.). Author: A History of the Christian Church; Geneva's Shield; Exiles of Maderia; Judas the Maccabee; St. Patrick; William Farel; Admiral Coligny and the Rise of the Huguenots; Uncle Alick series of juvenile stories, etc. Home: East Pierre, S.Dak. Died 1900.

BLACKFAN, Kenneth D., prof. pediatrics; b. Cambridge, N.Y., Sept. 9, 1883; s. Harry Smith and Estella (Chase) Blackfan; M.D., Albany (N.Y.) Medical College (Union U.), 1905; m. Lulie Anderson Bridges, Aug. 15, 1920; 1 son, Turner Anderson Bridges. Pathologist Albany Hosp., and bacteriologist Bender Lab., 1905-06; instr. in pediatrics, Polyclinic Hosp., Phila., 1910-11; asst. Washington U., St. Louis, 1911-12; instr. in pediatrics, Johns Hopkins, 1912-17, asso., 1917-19, asso. prof., 1919-20; prof. pediatrics, Coll. of Medicine, U. of Cincinnati, 1920-23; prof. pediatrics, Harvard Med. Sch., Boston, 1923—. Del. White House Conf. on Child Health and Protection, 1930 (chmn. com. on growth and development); chmn. gen. advisory com. on maternal and child welfare under Social Security Act, 1935-37; consultant Children's Bureau, 1935—; mem. Commn. on Grad. Medical Education, 1937—. General sec. 5th Internat. Congress on Pediatrics; del. Internat. Commn. on Nutrition, sponsored by Health sect. League of Nations, Berlin, 1932. Mem. bd. dirs. Infants' Hosp., Boston. Republican. Presbyn. Editor: Report of White House Conference on Child Health and Protection, 1932. Home: Brookline, Mass. Died Nov. 29, 1941.

BLACKFORD, Eugene Gilbert, fish mcht., icthyologist; b. Morristown, N.J., Aug. 8, 1839; common school edn.; m. Frances L. Green, May 16, 1860. Became fish dealer in Fulton Market, New York; was leader in introducing there red snapper, whitebait, pompano and other fine fish; commr. of fish and fisheries, N.Y., 1879; caused establishing of hatching sta. for fish at Cold Spring Harbor; has published many papers on fish. Pres. Bedford Bank, Brooklyn; Am. Writing Machine Co., N.Y.; Biol. School, Cold Spring, N.Y.; v.p. Union Typewriter Co., and v.p. Brooklyn Inst. of Arts and Sciences. Home: Brooklyn, N.Y. Died 1904.

BLACKFORD, Launcelot Minor, educator; b. Fredericksburg, Va., Feb. 23, 1837; s. William M. and Mary (Berkeley) B.; M.A., U. of Va., 1860; (LL.D., Washington and Lee U., 1904); m. Eliza Chew Ambler, Aug. 5, 1884. Was mem. Rockbridge Arty., clerk of Mil. Court, Longstreet's corps, and adj. 24th Va. Inf. in Gen. Lee's army. Asso. prin. Norwood Sch., Nelson Co., Va., 1865-70; prin. Episcopal High Sch. for Boys, Sept. 1870-June 1913, then emeritus prin. Democrat. Home: Alexandria, Va. Died May 1914.

BLACKHAM, George Edmund, M.D.; b. Jersey City, N.J., Aug. 28, 1846; s. David and Susan (Nolan) B.; M.D., U. of Buffalo, 1870; post-grad. work N.Y. Eye and Ear Infirmary and New York Post-Grad. Sch. of Medicine; m. Edith M. Annas, Nov. 11, 1885 (died 1904); children—William C., Edith M. Practiced at Niagara Falls, 1871, 1872, Perth Amboy, N.J., 1873; chief clerk, western div. Erie R.R., at Dunkirk, N.Y., 1873-82; resumed practice at Dunkirk, 1882, giving attention to diseases of the eye and ear; served as dir., surgeon eye and ear dept., president medical and surgical staff for 17 years, and cons. surgeon, Brooks Memorial Hosp. (retired 1927). Pres. Am. Society of Microscopists, 1882; fellow A.A.A.S. Pvt. 187th Regt. N.Y. Vol. Inf., Sept. 23, 1864; promoted regtl. hosp. steward, Oct. 11, 1864; hon. disch. July 1, 1865. Republican. Episcopalian. Died Dec. 28, 1928.

BLACKMAN, William Fremont, educator; b. North Pitcher, N.Y., Sept. 26, 1855; s. John Smith and Orpah (Freeman) B.; A.B., Oberlin, 1877; B.D., Yale, 1880; Ph.D., Cornell, 1893; U. of Berlin, 1893-94; LL.D., U. of Fla., 1910; m. Effleda Veronica Thomson, July 1880; m. 2d, Lucy Worthington, July 1, 1884; children—Berkeley, Worthington, Marjorie. Pastor of Congl. chs. at Steubenville, O., Naugatuck, Conn., and Ithaca, N.Y., 1880-93; prof. Christian ethics, 1893-1901, lecturer social philosophy and ethics, 1901-02, Yale; pres. Rollins Coll., 1902-15. Editor The Yale Review, 1893-1901. Pres. Fla. Conf. Charities and Correction, 1911, Fla. Audubon Soc., 1910—. Pres. Bank of Winter Park, 1911-18; pres. The Wekiwa Ranch, 1915. Author: The Making of Hawaii—a Study in Social Evolution, 1899; A History of Orange County, Florida, 1927. Home: Winter Park, Fla. Died Aug. 9, 1932.

BLACKMAR, Abel Edward, judge; b. Newark, N.Y., Aug. 21, 1852; s. Orrin and Harriet C. (Hurd) B.; A.B., Hamilton Coll., 1874, A.M., 1878, LL.D., 1909; LL.B., Columbia, 1878; m. Adele Mars, June 25, 1885; 1 son, Abel E. Practiced at New York; was counsel New York Produce Exchange, etc.; justice Supreme Ct. of N.Y., 2d Dist., term 1908-22; apptd. Appellate Div., Mar. 1, 1917; apptd. presiding justice Appellate Div., 1921; in practice of law, Jan. 1923—. Republican. Home: Brooklyn, N.Y. Died Feb. 14, 1931.

BLACKMAR, Frank Wilson, univ. prof.; b. W. Springfield, Pa., Nov. 3, 1854; s. John S. and Rebecca (Mershon) B.; Ph.B., U. of the Pacific, 1881, A.M., 1884; prof. mathematics, U. of the Pacific, 1882-86; grad. student and fellow, Johns Hopkins, 1886-89, Ph.D., 1889; LL.D., U. of Southern Calif., 1921, Coll. of Pacific, 1924, Baker Univ., Baldwin, Kan., 1929; m. Mary S. Bowman, June 25, 1885 (died Mar. 4, 1892); m. 2d, Kate Nicholson, July 26, 1900; children—Winifred Margaret, Mrs. Cora Gertrude Geisler, Howard Bowman, Dorothy Leoti. Prof. history and sociology, 1889-99, sociology and economics, 1899-1912, sociology, 1912—; dean Grad. Sch., 1896-1922, U. of Kan. Pres. Kan. Conf. Social Work, 1900-02. Elector Hall of Fame. Author: Federal and State Aid to Higher Education in the United States, 1890; Spanish Colonization, 1890; Spanish Institutions in the Southwest, 1891; The Study of History and Sociology, 1890; The Story of Human Progress, 1896; Economics, 1907; History of Higher Education in Kansas, 1900; Charles Robinson, The Free State Governor of Kansas, 1900; Life of Charles Robinson, The First Governor of Kansas, 1902; The Elements of Sociology, 1905; Economics for High Schools, 1907; Editor Cyclopedia of History of Kansas, 1912; Outlines of Sociology, 1914, 23; History of Kansas State Council of Defense, 1921; Justifiable Individualism, 1922. History of Human Society, 1926. Home: Lawrence, Kan. Died Mar. 30, 1931.

BLACKMON, Frederick Leonard, congressman; b. Lime Branch, Polk Co., Ga., Sept. 15, 1873; s. Augustus Young and Sarah Ann (Ross) B.; ed. State Normal Coll., Jacksonville, Ala., and Douglasville (Ga.) Coll.; LL.B., U. of Ala., 1894; married, Dec. 31, 1908. Admitted to bar, 1894, and then in practice at Anniston, Ala. City atty., 1898-1902; mem. Ala. Senate, 1900-10; mem. 62d to 66th Congresses (1911-21), 4th Ala. Dist. Democrat. Home: Anniston, Ala. Died Feb. 8, 1921.

BLACKMORE, Simon Augustine, educator, author; b. Milwaukee, Wis., Feb. 24, 1849; s. John and Mary B.; studied classics in St. Ignatius Coll., Chicago; entered Soc. of Jesus, studying in Florissant (Mo.) Sem., 1871-75; took the advanced course in philosophy and science at Woodstock (Md.) Coll., 1875-78; studied divinity at Woodstock Coll., 1882-86; ordained priest R.C. Ch., 1885; M.A., Woodstock Coll.; Litt.D., St. Louis U. Prof. langs., Creighton and St. Louis univs., 1878-82; prof. humanities and rheotoric, Marquette Coll., Milwaukee, and St. Xavier Coll., Cincinnati, 1886-88; of Latin and Greek, St. Louis U., 1889-92; of philosophy and lit., St. Mary's (Kan.) Coll., Marquette Coll., and St. Ignatius Coll., 1892-96; Sunday evening lecturer in St. Xavier's Ch., Cincinnati, 1896-97; in Holy Family Ch., Chicago, 1897-98. Prof. lit. and oratory in Creighton U., 1899-1903. Pub. lecturer in prin. cities of the middle west on Shakespeare's religion and his tragedies, 1904-06; prof. of philosophy and lit., Campion Coll., Prairie du Chien, Wis., 1907-17; prof. lit., St. Ignatius Coll., Cleveland, 1917—. Author: A Great Soul in Conflict— a New Commentary on Shakespeare's Master Work, 1914; The Riddles of Hamlet and the Newest Answers, 1917; Shakespeare's Dual Personality, 1923; Spiritism—Facts and Frauds, 1924. Died Sept. 5, 1926.

BLACKSTOCK, Ira Burton; b. nr. Paxton, Ill., Apr. 3, 1866; s. Robert and Emily (Meharry) B.; B.S. and A.M., DePauw U., 1886; m. Mary J. Hardtner, June 16, 1897. Gen. mgr. Blackstock Farms; pres. Kiowa, Hardtner & Pacific R.R. Co.; mgr. Pure Ice & Cold Storage Co.; dir. Springfield Finance & Thrift Co., etc. Joint donor with wife of Blackstock Swimming Pool, Ill. Woman's Coll., Jacksonville, and of Blackstock Athletic Field, DePauw U. Trustee DePauw U.; mem. Book Com. M.E. Ch. Del. Gen. Conf. M.E. Ch., Des Moines, Ia., 1920, Springfield, Mass., 1924, Kansas City, Mo., 1928; also Ecumenical Conf., London, 1921, Atlanta, Ga., 1931; mem. 6th Internat. Art Congress, Prague. Fellow Am. Geog. Soc., Royal Soc. of Arts (London). Mason. Republican. Formerly resided at Springfield, Ill. Died July 24, 1931.

BLACKSTONE, Richard, engineer; b. Connellsville, Pa., Oct. 16, 1843; s. James and Nancy Campbell (Johnston) B.; studied Pa. Mil. Acad., Rensselaer Poly. Inst., Troy, N.Y.; m. Mabel R. Noble, Dec. 28, 1871. Enlisted as pvt. in Co. C, 32d Ohio Vols., July 30, 1861; served in W.Va.; taken prisoner at Harper's Ferry Sept. 12, 1862; exchanged, and assigned to Army of Tenn., under Gen. Grant; participated in many battles, siege of Vicksburg, March to the Sea, Grand Review at Washington; mustered out as capt., July 27, 1865. Placer miner, 2 seasons, Breckenridge, Colo., 1868 and 1869; draftsman in office U.S. surveyor gen., Denver, 1869-70, Cheyenne, Wyo., 1870-78; went to Black Hills, 1878, and engaged in mining and mine surveying; asst. supt., chief engr., 1883-1914, gen. mgr. and supt., Sept. 1914-18. Homestake Mining Co., Lead, S.D. Built Black Hills & Ft. Pierre R.R.; water system for Homestake; hydro-electric sta. at Englewood; electric light and power plant, and hydro-electric power plant, Spearfish, including 5-mile concrete-lined, diverting dam tunnel; complete elec. equipment of Homestead Mine; etc. Mem. Am. Inst. Mining Engrs., Ohio Commandery Loyal Legion. Republican. Home: Lead, S.D. Died Dec. 21, 1922.

BLACKSTONE, Timothy B., ry. exec.; b. Branford, Conn., March 28, 1829; entered railway service Oct., 1847, as rodman on survey of New York & New Haven R.R.; later asst. engr. on survey location and construction of Stockbridge & Pittsfield R.R., 1848-49; Vermont Valley R.R., 1849-51; div. engr. Ill. Central R.R., 1851-55; chief engr. Joliet & Chicago R.R., 1856-61; pres. Joliet & Chicago R.R., 1861-64; Jan., 1864, director, and April, 1864 to April 1, 1899, pres. Chicago & Alton R.R. Home: Chicago. Died 1900.

BLACKTON, J(ames) Stuart, motion pictures; b. Sheffield, Eng., Jan. 5, 1875; s. Henry and Jessie (Stuart) B.; ed. Eton House Collegiate Sch. and Coll. City of N.Y.; m. Paula Hillburn, 1908; children—James Stuart, Marian Constance, Violet Virginia, Charles Stuart. Came to U.S., 1886, later newspaper writer and artist; entered motion picture industry, 1896; asso. with Albert E. Smith, 1900, in organizing Vitagraph Co. (1st co. to make screen plays), of which was v.p.; founder, 1910, Motion Picture Mag.; organizer, 1915, and 1st pres. Motion Picture Bd. of Trade of America; produced The Christian; Island of Regeneration; Battle Cry of Peace; The Glorious Adventure (in natural colors); The Clean Heart; The Happy Warrior; Bride of the Storm. Home: Los Angeles, Calif. Died Aug. 1941.

BLACKWELL, Antoinette Louisa Brown, Unitarian minister; b. Henrietta, N.Y., May 20, 1825; d. Joseph and Abby (Morse) Brown; grad. Oberlin Coll., 1847, Oberlin Theol. Sem., 1850; (hon. A.M., Oberlin, 1878, D.D., 1908); m. Samuel C. Blackwell, Jan. 24, 1856. Began platform speaking, 1846; preaching, 1848; settled as orthodox Congl. pastor, 1852; ordained, 1853; later became Unitarian; prominent in woman suffrage and other movements. Author: Studies in General Science, 1869; The Island Neighbors, 1871; The Sexes Throughout Nature, 1875; The Physical Basis of Immortality, 1876; The Philosophy of Individuality, 1893; Sea Drift or Tribute to the Ocean, 1903; The Making of the Universe, 1914; The Social Side of Mind and Action, 1915. Home: Elizabeth, N.J. Died Nov. 5, 1921.

BLACKWELL, Elizabeth, M.D.; b. Bristol, England, Feb. 3, 1821; emigrated to U.S., 1832; ed. in private schools in Bristol and New York; taught school in Ky., and the Carolinas; sought admission to several med. colls., but was refused until she entered the med. school at Geneva, N.Y., 1847; later studied in La Maternité and Hotel Dieu, Paris, and St. Bartholomew's, London. Established practice in New York, 1851; founded a hosp., and, in 1867, in conjunction with her sister, Dr. Emily Blackwell, organized Woman's Med. Coll. of New York Infirmary; lectured in England, 1858-59; registered as a physician in England, 1859, and, 1869— has practiced in London and Hastings; founded Nat. Health Soc. of London; aided in founding London School of Medicine for Women. Author: Physical Education of Girls; Religion of Health; Counsel to Parents on Moral Education; Pioneer Work in Opening the Medical Profession to Women; The Human Element in Sex; Decay of Municipal Representative Institutions. Died 1910.

BLACKWELL, Emily, formerly dean Woman's Med. Coll., New York Infirmary; b. Bristol, Eng., 1926; M.D., Western Reserve U., Cleveland, O., 1854. One of the founders (1853), with Elizabeth Blackwell, M.D., and then connected with New York Infirmary for Women and Children, 1st woman's hosp. in the country. Home: Montclair, N.J. Died 1910.

BLACKWELL, Robert Emory, coll. pres.; b. Warrenton, Va., Nov. 14, 1854; s. Rev. Dr. John Davenport and Julia Anna (Butts) B.; A.M., Randolph-Macon Coll., 1874; U. of Leipzig, 1875-76; LL.D., Duke Univ., 1936; LL.D., Washington and Lee Univ., Wofford Coll. and Wesleyan U. (Conn.); m. Theela Epia Duncan, Aug. 28, 1877; 1 dau., Epie Duncan (Mrs. J. F. Messick). Prof., 1876—, v.p. and acting pres., 1900-02, pres., 1902—, Randolph-Macon Coll. Author: (with James A. Harrison) Easy French Lessons; (with William W. Smith) Parallel Syntax Chart. Mem. from M.E. Ch. S. of Joint Commn. on Unification, Inter-racial Commn., and state chmn. Va. Inter-Racial Commn. Home: Ashland, Va. Died July 17, 1938.

BLACKWOOD, Alexander Leslie, surgeon; b. Huntingdon Co., Que., Can., July 28, 1862; s. John and Ann (Steell) B.; ed. Huntingdon (Can.) Acad. and McGill U., Montreal; M.D., Hahnemann Med. Coll., Chicago, 1888, N.Y. Post-Grad. Med. Sch. and Hosp., 1889, Johns Hopkins Med. Sch., 1902; m. Helen A. Winslow, Aug. 16, 1891 (died 1903). Sr. prof. materia medica and prof. clin. medicine, Hahnemann Med. Coll., Chicago, 1899—. V.p. Chicago Bd. of

Education, Chicago. Fellow Am. College Physicians. Author: Diseases of the Heart, 1901; Diseases of the Lungs, 1902; A Manual of Materia Media, Therapeutics and Pharmacology, 1906; Pancreas and Ductless Glands, 1907; Diseases of the Food Tract. Home: Chicago, Ill. Deceased.

BLACKWOOD, Ibra C(harles), governor; b. Blackwood, P.O., S.C., Nov. 21, 1878; s. Charles and Luvina (Burns) B.; Furman U., 1893-95; Wofford Coll., Spartanburg, S.C., 1897-98; studied law in office Wilson & Hydrick, Spartanburg; m. Margaret Hodges, Oct. 4, 1915. Admitted to S.C. bar, 1902, and began practice at Spartanburg; mem. S.C. Ho. of Rep., 1903-05; solicitor 7th Jud. Circuit, 1916-31; governor of S.C., 1931— for term 1931-35. Mem. Dem. Nat. Com., 1932—. Baptist. Mason. Died Feb. 12, 1936.

BLACKWOOD, Norman Jerome, rear adm.; b. Philadelphia, Pa., Jan. 3, 1866; s. William and Emma Jerome (Smith) B.; student Franklin and Marshall Coll., 1882-83, U.S. Naval Acad., Annapolis, Md., 1883-86; M.D., Jefferson Med. Coll., Phila., 1888; m. Rebecca Barnes Wilkinson, Nov. 29, 1892. Commd. ensign, U.S.N., July 17, 1890, and advanced through grades to rear adm., Oct. 10, 1929, retired. Comdr. U.S. naval hosps. at Canacao, P.I., 1911-13, Boston, Mass., 1918-23, New York, N.Y., 1923-27, Puget Sound, Wash., 1927-29; comdr. U.S.S. Solace, 1916-17, U.S.S. Mercy, Mar.-Sept. 1918; retired from active service, Jan. 3, 1930; then med. dir. Provident Hosp., Chicago. Served in Spanish-American War, Cuban Insurrection, World War. Fellow Am. Coll. Surgeons. Awarded Navy Cross. Republican. Episcopalian. Mason. Home: Syracuse, N.Y. Died Apr. 1, 1938.

BLAHD, Mose Emmett, surgeon; b. Cleveland, O., Mar. 28, 1883; s. Henry and Emma (Scheuer) B.; student Cornell U., 1902-04; M.D., Western Reserve U. Sch. of Medicine, 1906; grad. study U. of Strasbourg and U. of Vienna; m. Rae Lichtenstader, Nov. 16, 1911; children—Margery, William Henry. In practice at Cleveland, 1906—; then surgeon in charge Mount Sinai Hosp. Served as capt. Med. Corps, U.S.A., World. Fellow Am. Coll. Surgeons. Jewish religion. Contbr. to med. jours. Home: Cleveland, O. Died Feb. 27, 1940.

BLAIKIE, William, lawyer, author, athlete; b. York, N.Y., May 24, 1843; s. Rev. Dr. Alexander and Nancy (King) B.; grad. Boston Latin Sch., 1862 (capt. of its winning football team); grad. Harvard, 1866 (stroke oar Harvard Univ. crew, 1866, defeating Yale); grad. (one of two honor men) Harvard Law Sch., 1868; m. Isabella Stuart Briggs, July 3, 1872; 2d, Rebecca Wynne Scott, Oct. 6, 1891. At 17 (weighing 133 lbs.) lifted 1,019 lbs. with hands alone; walked Boston to New York, 225 miles, in 4½ days, which was, for 10 yrs., amateur long distance outdoor walking record; as sec.-treas. accompanied Harvard crew to England; founded Intercollegiate Athletic Games of America, 1873. Pardon clerk U.S. Atty.-Gen.'s office, 1869-70; asst. office U.S. Dist. Atty., New York, 1870-72; established practice New York. Author: How to Get Strong and How to Stay So; Sound Bodies for Our Boys and Girls. Died 1904.

BLAINE, John J.; b. Grant Co., Wis., May 4, 1875; s. James F. and Elizabeth B.; preparatory education high school; LL.B., Valparaiso (Ind.) U., 1896; m. Anna C. McSpaden, Aug. 23, 1904. Began practice at Boscobel, 1897; partner Austin-Blaine Farm Co.; mayor of Boscobel 3 terms; mem. county bd. Grant Co., Wis., 4 yrs.; mem. Wis. Senate, 1909-13; atty. gen. of Wis., 1919-21; gov. of Wis. 3 terms, 1921-26 inclusive; mem. U.S. Senate, 1927-33; author of Workmen's Compensation Act for Wis. and D.C., and Act for Repeal of 18th Amendment; co-author of Anti-Injunction Act; apptd. mem. bd. of Reconstruction Finance Corp., 1933, for unexpired term ending Jan. 1934. Republican. Home: Boscobel, Wis. Died Apr. 16, 1934.

BLAIR, Andrew Alexander, chemist; b. Woodford Co., Ky., Sept. 20, 1848; s. Gen. Francis Preston and Apolline (Alexander) B.; grad. U.S. Naval Acad., 1866; midshipman, 1862-68, ensign, 1868-69, U.S.N.; m. Anna S. Biddle, Oct. 24, 1872. Chief chemist to U.S. Commn. to test iron, steel and other metals, Watertown Arsenal, N.Y., 1875-78; chief chemist U.S. Geol. Survey and 10th Census, Newport, R.I., 1879-81; in gen. practice, 1882—. Author: The Chemical Analysis of Iron, 1888, 7th edit., 1909. Contbr. article on assaying in Ency. Britannica, 1900. Home: Chestnut Hill, Pa. Died 1932.

BLAIR, Charles Austin, judge; b. Jackson, Mich., Apr. 10, 1854; s. Austin (gov. Mich., 1860-65) and Sarah Louise (Horton) B.; A.B., U. of Mich., 1876 (LL.D., 1909); m. Effie Caroline North, Oct. 8, 1879. Admitted to bar, 1878; city atty. of Jackson, 1882; pros. atty., Jackson Co., 1895-96; mem. sch. bd., City of Jackson, 1902-04; atty-gen. of Mich., 1903-04; asso. justice Supreme Ct. of Mich., 1904—. Home: Lansing, Mich. Died Aug. 30, 1912.

BLAIR, Chauncey J., banker; b. Michigan City, Ind., Apr. 6, 1845; s. Chauncey Buckley and Caroline O. (De Groff) B.; brother of Henry Augustus B.; ed. pvt. schs. in Chicago; m. Mary A. I. Mitchell, Oct. 26, 1882. Entered Merchants Nat. Bank (founded by father), 1879, of which was pres., 1881-03, when it was consolidated with Corn Exchange Nat. Bank, of which is v.p.; pres. The Kennicott Co. V.p. Chicago Home for the Friendless. Republican. Home: Chicago, Ill. Died May 10, 1916.

BLAIR, Eliza Nelson; b. Plymouth, N. H.; d. Rev. William and Dolly Sumner (Elliott) Nelson; m. Henry William Blair, Dec. 20, 1859. Pres. N. H. Daughters of Boston; mem. Nat. Fedn. of Woman's Clubs (has been pres. N. H. Federation); was one of founders Garfield Nat. Hosp. Lecturer on lit., econ., humanitarian and ethnol. subjects. Author: Lisbeth Wilson—A Daughter of New Hampshire Hills (novel of New England life in the early part of XIXth century), 1895. Home: Manchester, N.H. Died 1907.

BLAIR, Emma Helen, editor; b. Menasha, Wis.; d. William Ellsworth and Lucy (Bartlett) B.; B.S., Ripon Coll., A.M., 1902; post-grad., U. of Wis., in economics and history, 1892-94 (hon. A.M., 1909); unmarried. Library asst. State Hist. Library of Wis., 1893-1904; hist. editor, 1893—. Editor of The Philippine Islands, 1493-1898, 1903-07. Asst. editor The Jesuit Relations and Allied Documents, 1896-1902. Home: Madison, Wis. Died 1911.

BLAIR, Francis Grant, supt. public instruction; b. Nashville, Ill., Oct. 30, 1864; s. William and Mary J. (Crane) B.; grad. Ill. State Normal Univ., 1892; B.S., Swarthmore Coll., Pa., 1897; fellow, Columbia, 1899; LL.D., Colgate, 1913, Ill. Wesleyan, 1916; Dr. of Edn., Rhode Island State College, 1926; m. Lillian Caton, 1898. Taught country schs., 1884-86; prin. schs., Malden, Ill., 1886-89, Leroy, Ill., 1892-95, Franklin Sch., Buffalo, N.Y., 1897-99; supt. training dept. Eastern Ill. Normal Sch., 1899-1906; state supt. pub. instrn., Ill., 1906-35. President N.E.A., 1926-27. Author: Schuylkill River Anthology; Song Bird Pageant; Wreath of Wild Flowers; Liberty Bell Pageant; Light Bearers' Pageant; also vol. of ednl. addresses. Home: Springfield, Ill. Died Jan. 26, 1942.

BLAIR, Henry Augustus, financier; b. Michigan City, Ind., July 1852; s. Chauncey Buckley and Caroline O. (De Groff) B.; ed. Williston Sem., Easthampton, Mass.; m. Grace E. Pearce, Feb. 19, 1878; children—Natalie, Anita Carolyn. Began in Merchants Nat. Bank, Chicago, of which his father was founder, and became v.p., continuing until 1902, when the bank consolidated with Corn Exchange Nat. Bank; instrumental in consolidating elevated roads of Chicago in 1911 under Chicago Elevated Railways Collateral Trust, of which was a trustee until 1916; pres. Chicago Rys. Co.. also pres. Chicago Surface Lines. Republican. Home: Chicago, Ill. Died Feb. 15, 1932.

BLAIR, Henry William, senator; b. Campton, N.H., Dec. 6, 1834; s. William Henry and Lois (Baker) B.; acad. edn. in N.H.; (hon. A.M., Dartmouth, 1873); admitted to N.H. bar, 1859; m. Eliza Ann Nelson, Dec. 20, 1859 (died 1907); father of Henry P. B. Served capt. and lt. col. 15th N.H. Vols., Civil War; twice wounded. Solicitor Grafton Co., 1860, for term of 5 yrs.; mem. N.H. Ho. of Rep., 1866, Senate, 1867-68; mem. 44th, 45th and 53d Congresses (1875-79, 1903-05); U.S. senator, 1879-91; declined office judge U.S. Dist. Ct.; apptd. and confirmed U.S. minister to China, 1891, but resigned when Chinese Govt. objected to him because of his opposition to Chinese immigration. Republican. Author Blair bill to extend federal aid to edn. in the states, which 3 times passed Senate; also bills establishing U.S. Labor Dept., the Sunday Rest bill, temperance, financial and other legislation; originator of bills under which about half of the soldiers' pensions are paid; practicing law, 1895—. Author: The Temperance Movement—or the Conflict of Man with Alcohol. Home: Manchester, N.H. Died Mar. 14, 1920.

BLAIR, Hugh McLeod, clergyman, editor; b. in Caldwell Co., N.C., Sept. 9, 1853; s. Morgan and Elizabeth (McLeod) B.; B.S., Rutherford Coll., N.C., 1875, A.M., 1888; m. Effie Bell, Nov. 7, 1878; m. 2d, Laura Ramsaur, Aug. 18, 1903. Ordained ministry M.E. Ch., S., 1883; pastor, 1883-94; asso. editor N.C. Christian Advocate, 1894-95; presiding elder, 1895-99; pastor, 1900-02; editor and bus. mgr. N.C. Christian Advocate, 1902—. Organized, 1909, Bd. of Publ. of Western N.C. Conf., of which is agt. and treas. Trustee Rutherford and Davenport colls. Democrat. Home: Greensboro, N.C. Died 1923.

BLAIR, James A(lonzo), Jr., corp. official; b. Ohio, July 19, 1880; s. James A. and Isabelle B. (Meyers) B.; A.B., Princeton, 1903; unmarried. Chairman of exec. com. Kingsport Press, Inc.; pres. Kingsport Sales Agency; dir. The Securities Co., Clinchfield Securities Co., Macon, Dublin & Savannah R.R., Securities Investment Fund, Kingsport Improvement Co., Continental Trust Co. (Baltimore). Served as 2d lt., capt. and maj. N.Y.N.G.; commd. maj. N.A., U.S.A., 1917, and assigned to hdqrs. Eastern Dept.; lt. col., Mar. 10, 1918, duty with Emergency Fleet Corp., later Gen. Staff; commd. col. G.S., overseas; twice apptd. Army mem. Am. Aviation Mission, Apr. 1919, to study future aviation policy of Eng., France and Italy; hon. disch., Dec. 20, 1919; col. on G.S. eligible list Jan. 10, 1920. Mem. Met. Mus. Art, Mus. Natural History. Decorated by France, Italy, Belgium and Servia. Republican. Home: New York, N.Y. Died Aug. 15, 1934.

BLAIR, James Lawrence, lawyer; b. St. Louis, Apr. 2, 1854; s. Gen. Francis Preston and Apolline (Alexander) B.; grad. Princeton, 1875 (A.M.); studied law Washington Univ. Law Sch., 1877-78; m. Apolline Madison Alexander, Feb. 21, 1883. Admitted to bar, 1879; then practiced in St. Louis; pres. bd. police commrs., St. Louis, 1884-88; apptd. gen. counsel La. Purchase Expn., 1901. Several of his addresses on econ. and legal subjects have been published in pamphlet form. Home: Kirkwood, Mo. Died 1904.

BLAIR, John Halsey, banker; b. Belvidere, N.J., July 6, 1865; s. William and Henrietta (Halsey) B.; B.Ph., Cornell Coll., Mt. Vernon, Ia., 1886, M.Ph., 1889; m. Frances Mullan, Apr. 26, 1905; children—John Mullan, Frances Elizabeth. Admitted to Ia. bar, 1889, and began practice at Des Moines; sec. and atty. Ia. Loan & Trust Co., 1893-1903; v.p. Des Moines Nat. Bank, 1903-17; v.p. Ia. Nat. Bank, 1917-21; dep. gov. Federal Reserve Bank of Chicago, July 1, 1921-33; v.p. Central Ia. Fuel Co. Trustee Cornell Coll., 1901—. Republican. Presbyn. Mason. Home: Chicago, Ill. Died June 20, 1934.

BLAIR, John Insley, retired capitalist; b. on banks of Delaware, about 2 miles S. of Belvidere, N.J., Aug. 22, 1802; m. Nancy Locke, 1826 (died 1888). Started as a merchant at his present place of residence, 1821; at one time had charge of six stores in that section of N.J.; a founder of Belvidere Nat. Bank; now oldest bank pres., in length of service, in U.S. Largely interested in railroads and before the consolidation era owned more miles of railroad than any other individual, being pres., or large stockholder, in 20 railroads; loaned the Govt. over $1,000,000 early in Civil War period. Republican. Home: Blairstown, N.J. Died 1899.

BLAIR, Joseph Cullen, horticulturist; b. Truro, N.S., Apr. 26, 1871; s. Col. William M. and Harriet (Blair) B.; grad. Provincial Coll. of Agr., Truro, 1892; Cornell, 1892-96; hon. M.S.A., Ia. Agrl. Coll., 1906; D.Sc. Coll. of Wooster, 1920; m. Sada Van Horne, June 16, 1898; children—Josephine Van Horne, Robert Collyer, Richard Gordon, Joseph Cullen. Instr. in chemistry, agr. and botany, Provincial Coll. of Agr., 1890-91; instructor in horticulture and horticulturist, Agrl. Expt. Sta., 1896-1901; prof. pomology and chief in horticulture, Coll. of Agr. and Expt. Sta., U. of Ill., 1901-12, prof. and chief in horticulture, 1912—; dean of Coll. of Agr., dir. Agrl. Expt. Sta. and dir. of extension service in agr. and home economics, 1938-39. Republican. Methodist. Prepared plans and directed work for restoration of Ft. Massac State Park, Urbana City Parks, University Heights Addition, Urbana. Home: Urbana, Ill. Died April 2, 1940.

BLAIR, Watson Franklin, capitalist; b. Michigan City, Ind., Jan. 29, 1854; s. Chauncey Buckley and Caroline O. (De Graff) B.; ed. Williston Sem., Easthampton, Mass.; m. Alice Keep, Nov. 15, 1883. With pork and beef packing firm of Culbertson, Blair & Co. until 1877; engaged in the grain commn. business on the Chicago Bd. of Trade, as Blair & Co., until 1890 (retired); was for several yrs. dir. Merchants' Nat. Bank (founded by father) prior to 1902, at which time the bank was consolidated with the Corn Exchange Nat. Bank, a gift of $100,000 being distributed among employes. V.p. and chmn. finance com. Field Mus. Natural History; mem. Chicago Orchestral Assn.; governing mem. Art Inst. Chicago; v.p. Children's Mem. Hosp. Republican. Episcopalian. Home: Chicago, Ill. Died Feb. 7, 1928.

BLAISDELL, Albert Franklin, author; b. S. Hampton, N.H., Aug. 31, 1847; s. John Harper and Lydia (Tuxbury) B.; A.B., Dartmouth, 1869, A.M., 1872; M.D., Harvard, 1879; m. Mary Atwood Emery, Dec. 17, 1879 (died 1919). Physician and surgeon, Providence, R.I.; retired from practice. Author: (sch. books) First Steps with American and British Authors, 1879; Our Bodies and How We Live, 1884; How to Keep Well, 1885; Child's Book of Health, 1886; Readings from the Waverly Novels, 1888; Stories of the Civil War, 1890; Stories from English History, 1897; Practical Physiology, 1897; The Story of American History, 1900; Life and Health, 1902; Hero Stories from American History, 1902; Short Stories from American History, 1905; English History Story Book, 1910; American History Story-Book, 1911; Child's Book of American History, 1913; Heroic Deeds of American Sailors, 1915; American History for Little Folks, 1917; Pioneers of America, 1919; Log Cabin Days, 1921. Home: Winchester, Mass. Died Mar. 17, 1927.

BLAISDELL, Anthony Houghtaling, civ. engr.; b. Coeymans, N.Y., Dec. 23, 1848; grad. Rensselaer Poly. Inst., C.E., 1870; m. Mary McConnell, Aug. 6, 1878. Expert constructor of light draft steamboats in steel and wood; then in pvt. practice, civ. and mech. engr.; most of professional work connected with improvement of Western rivers, as asst. and exec. engr. under Congressional appropriations. Co-propr. Western Iron Boat Building Co., St. Louis, 1880-86; mem. Am. Soc. Civ. Engrs.; mem. of Bd. of St. Louis Public Schools, 1882-85. Died 1905.

BLAKE, Charles S., insurance; b. Windsor Locks, Conn., Oct. 25, 1860; s. John W. and Lucy Chapin (Hitchcock) B.; ed. pub. schs.; m. Elizabeth Reeves, Dec. 25, 1882; children—Charles Edgar, Stanley Reeves. Began in ins. business N.Y. City, 1884; pres., 1916-27, chmn. bd., 1927—, The Hartford Steam Boiler Inspection & Ins. Co. Republican. Conglist. Home: Hartford, Conn. Died Mar. 31, 1931.

BLAKE, Clarence John, physician; b. Boston, Feb. 23, 1843; s. John Harrison and Sarah Anna (Howe) B.; student Roxbury Latin Sch., and Lawrence Scientific Sch. (Harvard); M.D., Harvard, 1865; studied abroad, 1865-69; O.M., U. of Vienna, 1868; m. Miss Hughes, 1874; m. 2d, Mary A. Houghton, Sept. 8, 1907. Lecturer, 1870-75, instr., 1875-88, prof. otology, 1888-1913, resigned; then prof. emeritus, Harvard College; aural surgeon, Mass. Charitable Eye and Ear Infirmary, 1871—; pres. Infants' Hosp.; mgr. Children's Hosp. Trustee Vincent Hosp., Boston, Howe (Ind.) Sch. Editor Am. Jour. of Otology, 1879-82. Fellow Am. Acad. Arts and Sciences, A.A.A.S. Author: Operative Otology. Frequent contbr. to med. text-books and jours. Home: Boston. Died Jan. 29, 1919.

BLAKE, Francis, inventor; b. Needham, Mass., Dec. 25, 1850; s. Francis and Caroline (Trumbull) B.; high sch. edn., Brookline, Mass.; (hon. A.M., Harvard, 1902); m. Elizabeth L., d. Charles T. Hubbard, of Weston, June 24, 1873. Served on U.S. Coast Survey 13 yrs., resigned; during last 2 or 3 yrs. was engaged in field work and its reduction to determine differences of longitude between observatories at Greenwich, Paris, Cambridge and Washington; devoted leisure to experimental physics, and in 1878 invented "Blake Transmitter," which has played important part in development of telephony throughout the world; has patented many other elec. devices. Fellow A.A.A.S., Am. Acad. Arts and Sciences. Home: Keewaydin, Weston (Auburndale P.O.), Mass. Died Jan. 1913.

BLAKE, Henry Nichols, lawyer; b. Boston, June 5, 1838; s. James Howe and Mary (Nichols) B.; grad. Dorchester High Sch., 1856; LL.B., Harvard, 1858; m. Clara J. Clark, Jan. 27, 1870. Began practice at Boston, 1859; sergt. to capt., Co. K, 11th Mass. Vols., 1861-64; promoted 2d lt. for brave conduct at Williamsburg, Va., May 5, 1862; twice wounded. U.S. atty. Mont. Ty., 1869-71; reporter Supreme Ct., Mont. Ty., 1869-75; dist. atty. 1st Dist. Mont. Ty., 1871-73, 1884-86; asso. justice Mont. Ty., 1875-80; mem. Mont. Territorial Legislature, 1881, 1883, 1887; chief justice of territory, 1889, and state of Mont., 1889-93. Republican. Unitarian. Author: Three Years in the Army, 1865. Home: Boston, Mass. Died Nov. 29, 1933.

BLAKE, Henry William, editor; b. New Haven, Conn., Dec. 7, 1865; s. Henry Taylor and Elizabeth Coit (Kingsley) B.; Ph.B., Yale, 1886; spl. course in elec. engring., Mass. Inst. Tech., 1887-88; m. Ida Jewett, June 1, 1891; children—Henry Kingsley, James Pierrepont (dec.), Mary Adelaide. In employ of Sprague Electric Ry. & Motor Co., and its successor, the Edison Gen. Electric Co., 1888-90; connected with Electric Ry. Jour. (formerly St. Ry. Jour.), 1891—, editor in chief, 1894-1922, co-editor, 1923-24, then sr. editor. Mem. Am. Inst. Elec. Engrs. Republican. Presbyn. Author: (with Walter Jackson) Electric Railway Transportation, 1917, 2d edit., 1924. Home: Englewood, N.J. Died May 20, 1929.

BLAKE, James Vila, clergyman; b. Brooklyn, Jan. 21, 1842; s. Hamlin and Elizabeth (Dexter) B.; A.B., Harvard, 1862, B.D., 1866; m. Abbie Frances Hovey, 1869. Ordained Unitarian ministry, 1867; pastor Haverhill, Mass., 1867-69, 28th Congl. Soc., Boston, 1869-72. Second Congl. Ch., Quincy, Ill., 1878-83, Third Unitarian Ch., Chicago, 1883-97, Ch. of All Souls, Evanston, Ill., 1892-1916. Author: Manual Training in Education, 1886; Essays, 1887; Poems, 1887; Legends from Story-Land; A Grateful Spirit, and Other Sermons, 1890; Happiness from Thoughts, and Other Sermons, 1891; Natural Religion in Sermons, 1892; St. Solifer and Other Worthies and Unworthies; More than Kin, 1893; An Anchor of the Soul, 1894; Sonnets, 1902; Songs, 1902; Discoveries, 1904; Church Worship in Readings, Songs and Prayers; Unity Services and Songs; Unity Festivals; The Months, 1907; So Like Her Father (drama), 1909; A Merry-go-Round (comedy), 1910; The Lady Bertha's Honey-Broth (drama), 1911; Love and Law, a Poem, 1920. Compiler: (with Rev. W. C. Gannett and Rev. F. L. Hosmer) Unity Hymns and Chorals, 1907; Sonnets from Marcus Aurelius, 1920. Died Apr. 28, 1925.

BLAKE, John George, physician; b. West Meath, Ireland, Aug. 8, 1837; s. John and Catherine B.; came to America, 1849; ed. pvt. tuition and home study; M.D., Harvard Med. Sch., 1861; m. Mary Elizabeth McGrath, June 19, 1865. Visiting physician, Boston City Hosp., consulting physician, Carney and St. Elizabeth's hosps. Dir. South End Nat. Bank; trustee Union Instn. for Savings. Democrat. Catholic. Home: Boston. Died Mar. 4, 1918.

BLAKE, Joseph Augustus, surgeon; b. San Francisco, Calif., Aug. 31, 1864; s. William Phipps and Charlotte Haven Lord (Hayes) B.; A.B., Yale, 1885, Ph.B., 1886 (M.A., 1909); M.D., Coll. Phys. and Surg. (Columbia), 1889; m. Catherine Ketchum, Dec. 17, 1890; children—Joseph A., Francis Hayes II; m. 2d, Katherine Alexander Duer, Nov. 1914; (divorced 1929); children—Katherine, Joan, William Alexander Duer, Mary; m. 3d, Florence Drake, July 16, 1929; children—Theodore Whitney, Edwin Thorne. Assistant demonstrator in anatomy, 1891, instr. in surgery, 1900, prof., 1903-13, Coll. Physicians and Surgeons; was cons. surgeon, Orthopedic, Presbyterian, St. Luke's and Roosevelt hosps. (New York), St. John's, Dobbs Ferry and Tarrytown hosps. Surgeon Am. Ambulance, Neuilly, France, Aug. 1914-Oct. 1915; médecin chef, Johnstone-Reckitt Hosp., at Ris Orangis, Oct. 1915-Mar. 1917, Am. Red Cross Hosp., Paris, Apr.-Oct. 31, 1917; apptd. comdg. officer and surgeon-in-chief, Am. Red Cross Mil. Hosp. No. 2, Paris; commd. maj. Med. R.C., Aug. 5, 1917; col. M.C., U.S.A., Nov. 1918. Decorated Légion d'Honneur, France, 1917, Officer, 1922; D.S.M. (U.S.), 1919. Fellow Acad. Medicine (New York), N.Y. Acad. Sciences. Home: Eastbrook, Me. Died Aug. 12, 1937.

BLAKE, Katherine Alexander Duer (Mrs. Duer Blake); b. New York City, May 9, 1879; d. William Alexander and Ellin (Travers) Duer; ed. at home; m. Clarence Hungerford Mackay, May 17, 1898; children—Katherine (Mrs. Kenneth O'Brien), Ellin (Mrs. Irving Berlin), John William; m. 2d, Joseph Augustus Blake, M.D., Nov. 1914 (divorced 1929); children—Katherine, Joan, William Alexander Duer, Mary. Episcopalian. Author: Stone of Destiny, 1903; Some Letters, 1917. 1918. Contbr. to N. Am. Review, Harper's Mag., etc. Home: New York, N.Y. Died Apr. 20, 1930.

BLAKE, Lillie Devereux, lecturer, author; b. Raleigh, N.C., Aug. 12, 1835; d. George Pollock and Sarah Elizabeth (Johnson) Devereux; ed. at Miss Apthorp's Sch., New Haven; afterward took Yale course with tutors at home; m. Frank G. Q. Umsted, 1855 (died 1859); m. 2d, Grenfill Blake, 1866 (died 1896). Active in woman suffrage movement, 1869—; pres. N.Y. State Woman Suffrage Assn., 11 yrs.; founded, 1900, and then pres. Nat. Legislative League; has worked for legislation in favor of women, securing statutes enabling women to obtain sch. suffrage, making mother and father joint guardians of the children, etc. Author: Southwold, 1859; Rockford, 1862; Fettered for Life, 1872; Woman's Place To-day, 1883; A Daring Experiment, 1898. Home: New York, N.Y. Died Dec. 30, 1913.

BLAKE, Lucien Ira, elec. engr.; b. Mansfield, Mass., Sept. 12, 1854; s. Mortimer (D.D.) and Harriet Louisa (Daniels) B.; A.B., Amherst, 1877, A.M., 1880; Ph.D., U. of Berlin, 1883; m. Mary Beroset (Nieten), Apr. 18, 1911. Prof. physics and elec. engring., Rose Poly. Inst., Terre Haute, Ind., 1884-87, U. of Kan., 1887-1906; constructing elec. engr., U.S. Light House Bd., 1893-94; chief engr., Submarine Signal Co., Boston, 1906-07; cons. engr., same, 1907—. Dir. and engr., Blake-Morscher Electro-Static Ore Separating Co. Conglist. Home: Newtonville, Mass. Died May 4, 1916.

BLAKE, Mary Elizabeth, author; b. Dungarven, Ireland, 1840; d. Patrick and Mary (Murphy) McGrath; ed. Quincy High School, 1855-59; Mr. Emerson's Private School, in Boston, 1859-61; Acad. Sacred Heart, Manhattanville, 1861-63; m. Dr. John G. Blake, 1865. Mother 5 sons (Harvard men); daughter (ed. Sacred Heart and Radcliffe). Contributor to N. Am. Review; Lippincott; Catholic World; Ave Maria, Independent; Outing; Scribner; Peace Journal; Providence Journal; Congregationalist; The Pilot; Donahue's Mag., and for many yrs., the Boston Journal (Rambling Talks), under initials M. E. B. Author: Poems, 1884, 2d edit., 1890; On the Wing (Western travel), 1885; Mexico, Picturesque and Political (with Margaret Sullivan), 1887; A Summer Holiday in Europe, 1889; Verses Along the Way, 1890; A Memoir, 1895; The Merry Months All (verses), 1885; Youth in Twelve Centuries (verses), 1886; In the Harbor of Hope (verses), 1901. Wrote: A Tilt at a Black Monster, N. Am. Rev.; Muscle and Morals, Lippincott; A Plea for Patriotism, same; Essays, Historic, Critical and Biographical, Catholic World. Home: Boston. Died 1907.

BLAKE, William Phipps, mineralogist; b. New York, June 1, 1826; s. Elihu and Adeline N. (Mix) B.; Ph.B., Yale, 1852; (hon. A.M., Dartmouth, 1863; Sc.D., U. of Pa., 1906); m. Charlotte Haven Lord Hayes, of S. Berwick, Me., Dec. 25, 1885; father of Joseph Augustus B. Officially identified with great expositions, 1853—; geologist and mineralogist for U.S. Pacific R.R. expdn., 1853; edited Mining Magazine, 1859-60; mining engr. in service of Japanese Govt., 1862; explored the Stickeen River, Alaska, 1863, and made report to Sec. of State Seward; prof. mineralogy and geology Coll. of Calif., 1864; geologist and mineralogist U.S. Commn. to Santo Domingo, 1871; exec. commr. Centennial Expn., 1876; prof. geology and dir. Sch. of Mines, U. of Ariz., 1894-1905, emeritus, 1905—; territorial geologist, 1898—. Chevalier Legion of Honor, France, 1878. Author: Geological Reconnaissance, California, 1855; Silver Ores and Silver Mines; Tombstone and Its Mines; Ceramic Art and Glass; Life of Capt. Jonathan Mix. Home: Tucson, Ariz. Deceased.

BLAKELOCK, Ralph Albert, artist; b. N.Y. City, Oct. 15, 1847; s. Ralph (M.D.) and Caroline (Carey) B.; A.B., Coll. City of New York, 1867; m. Cora R. Bailey, Feb. 22, 1876. Mostly self-ed. in painting; visited the West and studied the Indians in their native regions, painting many scenes of striking beauty. Prin. works: Moonlight (purchased for $20,000 in 1916), in Toledo Mus. of Art; Entrance to the Forest; Evening at the Spring; Sunrise (Donner Lake); The Pipe Dance; Early Evening; Indian Encampment; Wayfarers at Eventide; etc. Hon. mention Paris Expn., 1900. A.N.A., 1913, N.A., 1916. Died Aug. 9, 1919.

BLAKENEY, Albert Alexander, congressman; b. Baltimore Co., Md., Sept. 28, 1850; s. John D. and Sarah B.; ed. pub. schs.; unmarried. Elected county commr., Baltimore Co., 1895, term of 6 yrs. and served as pres. of bd.; resigned after serving 4 yrs.; mem. 57th Congress (1901-03), 2d Md. Dist., 67th Congress (1921-23), same dist. Republican. Home: Ten Hills, Md. Died Oct. 15, 1924.

BLAKESLEE, Dennis A., contractor; b. New Haven, Conn., Mar., 1856; s. Charles Wells and Martha (Waters) B.; ed. pub. schs.; m. Lizzie Finette Law, Dec. 4, 1878; children—Harriet Finette, Martha Law, Albert Dennis, Harold Law, Miles Grant, Dorothy. Began as timekeeper, C. W. Blakeslee & Sons, New Haven, 1872, then partner; pres. New Haven Trap Rock Co., Dwight Bldg. Co.; chmn. bd. Mechanics Bank; treas. Seymour Water Co. Maj., Governors Guards, 10 yrs. Mem. Conn. State Senate, 1907-09; lt. gov. of Conn., 1911-12. S.A.R. (pres. Conn. soc.). Republican. Conglist. Home: New Haven, Conn. Died Apr. 3, 1933.

BLAKESLEE, Erastus, soldier, minister, author, editor; b. Plymouth, Litchfield Co., Conn., Sept. 2, 1838; s. Joel and Sarah Maria (Mansfield) B.; grad. Williston Sem., 1859, Yale, 1863, B.A., 1864, M.A., 1866, Andover Theol. Sem., 1879; m. Mary Goodrich North, Mar. 30, 1865. Enlisted Co. A, 1st Conn. Cav., Oct. 9, 1861, commd. 2d lt., Oct. 18, 1861; promoted 1st lt. and adj., Nov. 26, 1861, capt., Co. A, Feb. 28, 1862, maj., July 14, 1863 (for gallantry near Harper's Ferry, Va.), lt. col., May 23, 1864, col., May 27, 1864; mustered out, Oct. 26, 1864; commd. bvt. brig. gen. U.S.V. (for gallant conduct at Ashland, Va., June 1, 1864), Mar. 13, 1865. Engaged in business 1865-75. Student at Andover Theol. Sem., 1876-79; pastor 2d Congl. Ch., Greenfield, Mass., 1880-83, 2d Congl. Ch., Fair Haven, Conn., 1883-87; elected pres. Atlanta Univ., Ga., 1887, but declined; pastor 1st Congl. Ch., Spencer, Mass., 1887-92; organized in Conn. 1st State Christion Endeavor Union, and was its pres. until left state. Began preparation of graded Sunday Sch. Lessons, 1888; removed to Boston, 1892, and then devoted whole time to writing, editing and publishing Bible Study Union Lessons, in 7 grades. Pres. Bible Study Pub. Co. Asso. Victoria Inst., London; mem. Soc. Bibl. Literature and Exegesis, Mass. Commandery and commander in chief, Loyal Legion. Conglist. Republican. Author: Brief History 1st Connecticut Cavalry Vols., 1889; also author or editor of over 100 vols. of the Bible Study Union Lessons. Home: Brookline, Mass. Died 1908.

BLAKESLEE, Raymond Ives, patent law; b. Bridgeport, Conn., Sept. 17, 1875; s. Cornelius and Mary (Sanford) B.; grad. high sch., Brooklyn, N.Y., 1893; acad. equivalent certificate, U. of State of N.Y., 1897; studied in law offices, N.Y. City, and N.Y. Law Sch., 1897-1903; m. Helene M. Beers, Dec. 22, 1906; children—Loren Ray, Anita Dawn. Admitted to N.Y. bar, 1907; patent solicitor, 1899-1907; in practice, specializing in patent law, at Los Angeles, Calif., 1907—. Was of counsel in famous Wright Bros. vs. Glenn Curtiss flying machine patent case, Carson smelting patent litigation and others of note. Republican. Home: Pasadena, Calif. Died Jan. 8, 1941.

BLANCHARD, Amy Ella, author; b. Baltimore; d. Daniel Harris and Sarah (Reynolds) B.; ed. there; taught sch.; studied art. Writer of short stories and numerous books, principally for young people,1881—. Author: An Independent Daughter, 1898; Kittyboys' Christmas, 1898; A Girl of '76, 1898; Miss Vanity, 1899; A Daughter of Freedom, 1900; Little Miss Oddity, 1902; A Loyal Lass, 1902; A Little Tomboy, 1903; Bonny Lesley of the Border, 1904; A Frontier Knight, 1904; Little Grandmother Jo, 1905; The Four Corners, 1906; The Four Corners in California, 1907; A Journey of Joy, 1908; The Four Corners Abroad, 1909; Wits End, 1909; Talbot's Angles, 1911; Four Corners in Japan, 1912; Four Corners in Egypt, 1913; Elizabeth, Betsy and Bess,

1913; Elizabeth, Betsy and Bess, Schoolmates, 1914; The Camp Fire Girls of Brightwood, 1915; Fagots and Flames, 1916; Nancy First and Last, 1917; A Girl Scout of Red Rose Troop, 1918; Lucky Penny of Thistle Troop, 1920; From Tenderfoot to Golden Eaglet, 1921; Becky, 1922; The Awakening of Martha, 1923; An Everyday Girl, 1924; The House That Jack Built, 1925. Home: Washington, D.C. Died July 5, 1926.

BLANCHARD, Charles Albert, coll. pres.; b. Galesburg, Ill., Nov. 8, 1848; s. Jonathan and Mary Avery (Bent) B.; A.B., Wheaton Coll., 1870; student Chicago Theol. Sem., 1875; (D.D., Monmouth Coll., 1896); m. Ella Milligan, Oct. 16, 1873 (died 1884); 2d, Jeannie Carothers, June 30, 1886 (died 1894); 3d, Dr. Frances Carothers, Feb. 18, 1896. Agt. and lecturer Nat. Christian Assn., 1870-72; prin. prep. dept., Wheaton Coll., 1872-74; prof. English lit. and lang., 1874-82, v.p., 1878-82, prof. mental and moral science and pres., 1882—, Wheaton Coll. Pres. Sabbath Assn. of Ill.; pres. coll. sect., Ill. State Teachers' Assn., 1894; pres. Nat. Christian Assn., 1903, 1904. Author: Educational Papers, 1883; Modern Secret Societies, 1903; Light on the Last Days, 1913; Getting Things from God, 1915; Visions and Voices, 1916. Home: Wheaton, Ill. Died Dec. 20, 1925.

BLANCHARD, Frank LeRoy, editor and advertising manager; b. Lewiston, Me., June 12, 1858; s. Joseph Knapp and Elizabeth (Truworthy) B.; ed. Bates College, 1878-82; m. Susie I. Butler, 1884 (died 1885); m. 2d, Louise M. Bricker, Mar. 9, 1887. Reporter New York Tribune, 1882-84, City Press Assn., 1885-86; telegraph editor, Commercial Advertiser, 1886-87; editor and pub., New Britain (Conn.) Herald, 1887-89; bus. mgr. Electric Power, 1889-90; asst. city editor Evening Telegram, 1891-93; with Fourth Estate and Evening World till 1899; editor The Editor and Publisher, 1901-02; editorial staff Daily News, 1902-04; connected with various advertising agencies till 1911; again editor The Editor and Publisher, 1911-16, 1921; editorial staff Printers' Ink, 1916-Mar. 1919; became dir. advt. and news dept., Henry L. Doherty & Co., and Cities Service Co., New York, Mar. 1922; then retired. Lecturer Board of Education, New York, 1902-23; dir. 23d St. Y.M.C.A. Course in Advertising, 1905-25. Mem. Adv. Club of New York (pres.), Pub. Utility Adv. Assn., Financial Adv. Assn., Am. Gas Assn. (chmn. adv. com., 1925-26). Author: Essentials of Advertising, 1921. Home: Brooklyn, N.Y. Died May 30, 1936.

BLANCHARD, George Roberts, commr. Joint Traffic Assn., Jan. 1, 1896—; b. Rochester, N.Y., June 15, 1841; clerk Cincinnati & Chicago R.R., Richmond, Ind., 1858-60; clerk at Cincinnati, 1860-61; chief freight clerk, St. Louis, 1861-62; gen. freight agt., 1862-64, Ohio & Miss. Ry.; gen. freight agt. Central Ohio R.R., 1864-67; same, Baltimore & Ohio R.R., 1867-72; same, Erie Ry., 1872-74; v.p. Erie Ry., 1874-84; commr. Central Traffic Assn., 1886-87; chmn. same 1887-96. Died 1900.

BLANCHARD, Henry, clergyman; b. Phila., Aug. 13, 1833; s. of Gen. Albert Gallatin and Susan (Thompson) B.; A.B., Tufts Coll., 1859, A.M., 1862 (D.D., 1890); m. Anne Eliza Chandler, Dec. 23, 1857. Ordained Universalist ministry, 1857; pastor, Brooklyn, 1857-68, Unitarian Soc., Indianapolis, 1868-69, Unitarian Soc., Lowell, Mass., 1870-73, Ch. of Unity, Worcester, as second successor to Dr. Edward Everett Hale, 1873-80, Shawmut Universalist Soc., Boston, 1880-82, 1st Universalist Soc., Portland, Me., 1882-1903; actg. pastor, Lynn, Mass., 1903-05, Farmington, 1908-11. Trustee Westbrook Sem., Portland, 1882—. Chmn. Me. Child Labor Com.; charter mem. Me. Prison Assn.; dir. Universalist Hist. Soc. Mason. Pres. Single Tax League, Portland. Pres. Me. Woman's Assn., 1886-92; mem. American Free Trade League, Nat. Econ. League (nat. council), League to Enforce Peace. Home: Portland, Me. Died Jan. 9, 1918.

BLANCHARD, James Armstrong, judge; b. Jefferson Co., N.Y., Aug. 16, 1845; s. Philip and Catharine (Drummond) B.; A.B., Ripon (Wis.) Coll., 1871, A.M., 1874; LL.B., Columbia, 1873; (LL.D., Ripon, 1902); m. Sallie Medbery, 1881. Admitted to bar, 1873; in practice, New York, 1873-99; judge Ct. of Gen. Sessions, 1899-1900; apptd., 1900, elected, 1901, justice Supreme Ct. N.Y.; term expired Dec. 31, 1915. N.Y. State v.p. Rep. League of U.S., 1888-89; pres. Rep. Club, 1892; mem. of com. of 30 that reorganized the Republican party in New York Co., and a mem. com. of 70, in 1894; commr. of Grand Boulevard and Concourse, 1895-1900. Home: New York, N.Y. Died July 9, 1916.

BLANCHARD, Lucy Mansfield, author; b. Boston, Mass., Mar. 6, 1869; d. George Samuel and Lucy Mansfield (Chamberlin) B.; B.A., Belmont Coll., College Hill, Cincinnati, 1888, M.A., 1891; studied Harvard, U. of Chicago, and in Europe; traveled in America, Can., Europe and Mexico; m. Charles Harvey Blanchard, July 14, 1904. Prof. Latin and Greek, Belmont Coll., 1888-94; later prof. Latin, history and history of art, Bartholomew Sch. for Girls, Cincinnati. Republican. Presbyn. Author: Joan's California Summer, 1917; Carita and How She Became a Patriotic American, 1918; Carita's New World, 1919; Chico, The Story of a Homing Pigeon, 1922; A Little Singing Bird, 1923; (serials): Berkeley Bells, 1925, Bede—The Story of a Canny Dog, 1925, Grimsel—The Performing Bear, 1926; also short stories. Home: Salt Lake City, Utah. Died April 23, 1927.

BLANCHARD, Nathan Weston, fruit grower; b. Madison, Me., July 24, 1831; s. Merrill and Eunice (Weston) B.; ed. Colby Coll., Me., 2 yrs., class of 1855 (hon. A.M., 1877); m. Ann Elizabeth Hobbs, Dec. 21, 1864. Went to Calif., 1854; engaged in mining and various lines of business; one founders of Santa Paula, 1872; a pioneer in orange and lemon growing in Ventura Co., Calif., and part owner largest lemon orchard in the state; pres. Nathan W. Blanchard Investment Co., Limonicra Co., Thermal Belt Water Co., Santa Paula Water Works, Santa Paula Land Co., Ventura Co. Mutual Fire Ins. Co., 1st Nat. Bank (Corcoran); v.p. 1st Nat. Bank (Santa Paula); officer or dir. many other corps. Mem. Calif. Ho. of Rep., 1862-63. Trustee Pomona Coll. from its incorporation, 1887. Republican. Conglist. Mason. Home: Santa Paula, Calif. Died Oct. 22, 1917.

BLANCHARD, Newton Crain, governor, b. Rapides Parish, La., Jan. 29, 1849; s. Carey H. and Frances Amelia (Crain) B.; reared on cotton plantation; ed. in pvt. schs. and at La. State U.; LL.B., Tulane U., 1870; m. Emily Barret, Dec. 16, 1873; m. 2d, Charlotte Tracy, of Baton Rouge, La., Jan. 25, 1909. Admitted to bar, 1871, and then in practice at Shreveport; then sr. mem. Blanchard, Goldstein & Walker. Mem. La. Constl. Conv., 1879, and pres. conv., 1913; mem. 47th to 53d Congresses (1881-93); apptd., 1893, elected 1894, U.S. senator for unexpired term (1893-97) of Hon. E. D. White; asso. justice Supreme Ct. La., 1897-1904; gov. of La., 1904-08; then in law practice. Democrat. Home: Shreveport, La. Died June 22, 1922.

BLANCHARD, Rufus, cartographer, author; b. Lyndeboro, N.H., 1821; ed. common school and private tutors; pursued various occupations; farmed in Ohio, became an expert in woodcraft on the frontier; taught school in log cabins, etc.; maker and publisher of maps and writer of historical books, 1854—. Author: History of Illinois; Political History of the United States; History of the Northwest and the City of Chicago. Home: Wheaton, Ill. Died 1904.

BLAND, Henry Meade, poet, educator; b. Fairfield, Calif., Apr. 21, 1863; s. Henry James and Annot Lyle (Steele) B.; A.B., U. of Pacific, 1887, A.M., 1889, Ph.D., 1890; A.M. in English philology, Stanford, 1895; grad. study U. of Calif., 1898-99; m. Annie Mabel Haskell, July 25, 1888 (died 1927); children—Henry Morton, Annot Mildred (Mrs. Aloysius L. MacCormack), Harold (dec.). Prin. elementary and high schs., Calif., 1883-94; part-time prof. edn., U. of Pacific, 1898-99; prof. English lit., San Jose State Teachers Coll., 1899—; prof. same, Summer Sessions, U. of Calif., 2 yrs. Mem. Com. of 70 for revision of Calif. sch. law, 1900; mem. Bd. of Edn., Santa Clara Co., 12 yrs.; trustee U. of Pacific 4 yrs.; pres. Edwin Markham Home Assn. Given title of Laurel Crowned Poet by Calif. Assembly, 1929. Republican. Methodist. Author: Studies in Entomology, 1899; A Song of Autumn and Other Poems, 1908; Sierran Pan and Other Poems, 1922; Stevenson's California, 1924; California and Other Poems, 1926; The Search and Other Poems, 1928; Forty-seven Poems, 1928. Home: San Jose, Calif. Deceased.

BLAND, John Randolph, insurance pres.; b. Bridgeton, St. Louis Co., Mo., Mar. 24, 1851; s. Richard Edward and Henrietta (Williams) B.; ed. Washington U., St. Louis; m. Maria Harden, Jan. 13, 1876. With Old Bay Line, Baltimore, until 1880; sec. Mchts.' and Mfrs.' Assn. of Baltimore, 1880-96; organizer, 1896, and then pres. U.S. Fidelity & Guaranty Co. Mem. St. George's Soc. (Baltimore). Mason. Episcopalian. Home: Baltimore, Md. Died Jan. 6, 1923.

BLAND, Pascal Brooke, M.D., prof. obstetrics; b. Monocacy, Pa., May 9, 1875; s. Caleb Harrison and Harriet Amelia B.; M.D., Jefferson Med. Coll., Phila., 1901; m. Susan Montgomery, Dec. 27, 1906; children—Helen Buckley (Mrs. J. Hamilton Coulter), Harriet Harrison, Edward Montgomery. Interne Jefferson Med. Coll. Hosp., 1901-02, asst. gynecologist, 1902-15; asst. prof. gynecology, Jefferson Med. Coll., 1915-25, prof. obstetrics, 1925—; chief obstetrician Jefferson Med. Coll. Hosp.; cons. obstetrician various hosps. Fellow Coll. Phys. of Phila., Am. Assn. Obstetricians, Gynecologists and Abdominal Surgeons, Royal Soc. Medicine (London), Am. Coll. Surgeons. Mason. Author: Text-book on Gynecology, Medical and Surgical, 1934; Text-book on Obstetrics for Students and Practitioners, 1935. Home: Bala-Cynwyd, Pa. Died Oct. 31, 1940.

BLAND, Richard Parks, congressman-lawyer; b. nr. Hartford, Ky., Aug. 19, 1835; acad. edn.; m. Virginia Elizabeth Mitchell, Dec. 17, 1873. Removed to Mo., 1855; thence to Calif., and from there to that part of Utah now Nevada; practiced law at Virginia City; was interested in mining in Calif. and Nev.; treas. Carson Co., Utah, until organization of State govt. of Nev.; returned to Mo., 1865; practiced law at Rolla, Mo., until Aug. 1869; then at Lebanon, Mo. Member of Congress, 1873-95 and 1897—. A leader in the free silver movement; author of the Bland bill for the coinage of not less than $2,000,000 or more than $4,000,000 worth of silver bullion per month, passed in 1878 and repealed by Sherman Act of 1891; received many votes for President of the U.S. in Nat. Democratic Convention, 1896. Home: Lebanon, Mo. Died 1899.

BLAND, William Thomas, congressman; b. Weston, Va. (now W.Va.), Jan. 21, 1861; s. William John and Columbia Madison (Jackson) B.; B.S., U. of W.Va., 1883, LL.B., 1884; spl. course in law, U. of Va., 1884-85; m. Bertha Helen McPike, Aug. 19, 1891. Began practice at Weston, 1885; removed to Atchison, Kan., 1887; county atty., Atchison Co., 1890-92; mayor, Atchison, 1894; judge 2d Jud. Dist. of Kan., 1896-1900, reëlected for term, 1900-04; resigned, 1901, to engage in wholesale drug business; v.p., later pres., McPike Drug Co., Kansas City, Mo., 1901-17 (retired); pres. 1st Nat. Bank, Orlando, Fla. Mem. 66th Congress (1919-21), 5th Mo. Dist.; pres. Board of Education, Kansas City; chmn. 1st Liberty Bond and Red Cross campaigns and mem. exec. com. in subsequent Liberty Bond campaigns. Pres. Mfrs.' and Mchts.' Assn., Kansas City, 1907-08; pres. Commercial Club (now Chamber of Commerce), 1909-10. Democrat. Episcopalian. Mason. Home: Kansas City, Mo. Died Jan. 16, 1928.

BLANDEN, Charles Granger, author; b. Marengo, Ill., Jan. 19, 1857; s. Granger W. and Anna Louise (Tiffany) B.; ed. pub. schs. and Park Av. Inst., Bridgeport, Conn.; m. Elizabeth Mills, Sept. 17, 1884. Teller, asst. cashier and cashier 1st Nat. Bank, Ft. Dodge, Ia., 1875-90; mayor of Ft. Dodge, 1888-89; moved to Chicago, 1890; sec. Rialto Trust, 1891-1923. Mem. Soc. Midland Authors, Poetry Society America, Ill. Society Sons of Revolution. Author: Tancred's Daughter, 1889; A Valley Muse, 1900; A Drift of Song, 1902; An Unremembered God, 1904; A Chorus of Leaves, 1905; The Upper Trail, 1911; A Wilding Bough, 1915; Lyrics, 1920; A Bale of Gossamer, 1927; Lincoln and Other Poems, 1931. Home: San Diego, Calif. Died Dec. 20, 1933.

BLANEY, Isabella Williams (Mrs. Charles D. Blaney); b. Chicago, Ill.; d. John Marshall and Elizabeth Caroline (Smith) Williams; grad. Ogontz Sch., Pa.; post-grad. study, Northwestern U., 1872; m. Charles Duchesne Blaney, Sept. 6, 1877. Mem. legislative com., and chmn. Santa Clara Co. Assembly Dists., Calif. Polit. Equality Assn., 1910-11; del. to Rep. Nat. Conv., June 1912, and to Progressive Nat. Conv., August, same year; mem. Progressive Party Nat. Com., 1912-13 (resigned); mem. Progressive State Central Com. of Calif., 1914-15; mem. Calif. State Rep. Central Com., 1930. Mem. Nat. Child Labor Com., Am. Council Inst. Pacific Relations, A.A.A.S., Soc. of Pacific, Astron. Soc. of Pacific, etc. Home: Saratoga, Calif. Died Mar. 9, 1933.

BLANEY, William Osgood, banker; b. Bristol, Me., July 16, 1841; s. Judge Arnold and Nancy (Hunter) B.; ed. Lincoln Acad., Me.; m. Loella E. Huston, May 16, 1867. Clk. in mercantile houses, Boston, 1864-69; partner, Crosby & Blaney, flour and grain mchts., Boston, 1869-79, Blaney, Brown & Co., 1879-1905; dir., 1892-1900, pres. 1900—, Commercial Nat. Bank, Boston; v.p. John Hancock Mut. Life Ins. Co.; pres. Boston Commercial Exchange, 1883-84; chmn. various coms., Boston Chamber of Commerce; v.p. Asso. Bd. of Trade, Boston, 1891-93; pres. Am. Congl. Assn. Home: Boston, Mass. Died 1910.

BLANKENBURG, Rudolph, mayor, mfr.; b. Lippe Detmold, Germany, Feb. 16, 1843; s. Ludwig and Sophie (Goede) B.; ed. pvt. tutelage and Real Gymnasium; came to America, 1865; m. Lucretia M. Longshore, Apr. 18, 1867. Clerk, traveling salesman and buyer for a mfg. house, Phila., 1865-75; started on own account, as R. Blankenburg & Co., 1875; retired from active management, July 1909, after incorporating as R. Blankenburg Co., of which is dir. Active in reform politics and civic improvements, 1877—; one of seven Philadelphians in charity orgn. movement, 1877; one of originators Citizens Permanent Relief Com., 1878, and visited as its representative the famine regions of Russia, 1892, distributed ship's cargo of flour, etc., and large funds in cash; elected co. commr. by nearly 50,000 majority in great reform movement, 1905, and gave 3 yrs.' salary ($15,000) to police, firemen's and teachers' pension funds; elected mayor of Philadelphia for term, 1912-16. Republican in nat., independent in state and local affairs. Quaker and Unitarian. Contbr. numerous articles to mags. and newspapers, on polit., social and religious subjects; LL.D., Lafayette, Ursinus and Dartmouth. Home: Germantown, Philadelphia, Pa. Died Apr. 12, 1918.

BLANTON, John Diell, educator; b. Cumberland Co., Va., Mar. 26, 1859; s. Francis Baker and Eliza Gilman (Diell) B.; A.B., Hampden-Sydney Coll., 1879; (LL.D., Southwestern Presbyn. Univ., 1903); m. Anna Hawes Miller, May 3, 1883. Teacher, dist. schs., Audrain Co., Mo., 1879-80; prin. public schs., Keytesville, 1880-81; prin. Watson Sem., Ashley, Mo.,

1881-85, Kahoka Coll., Kahoka, Mo., 1885-86, Elizabeth Aull Sem., Lexington, Mo., 1886-92; v.p., 1892-93, pres., 1893-13, Ward Sem.; v.p., June 1913-15, pres., 1915—, Ward-Belmont Sch., Nashville, Tenn. Presbyn. Elder. Democrat. Mason. Home: Nashville, Tenn. Died Oct. 6, 1933.

BLANTON, Lindsay Hughes, educator; b. Cumberland Co., Va., Jan. 29, 1832; s. Joseph and Susan (Walker) B.; A.B., Hampden-Sidney Coll., 1853; student Union, and grad. Danville Theol. Sem., 1857; (D.D., Hampden-Sidney, 1880, LL.D., 1900); m. Elizabeth Irvine, Oct. 6, 1857; 2d, Mrs. Myra Bracken, of Lebanon, Ky., Aug. 17, 1904. Ordained Presbyn. ministry, 1858; pastor Versailles, Va., 1857-61, Salem, Va., 1861-68, Paris, Ky., 1868-80; chaplain 54th and 26th Va. Inf., C.S.A., 1861-65; chancellor Central U. of Ky., 1880-1901 (added $300,000 to endowment and equipment—increased attendance from 120 to 978; v.p. Central U. of Ky., 1901-13. Stated clerk Synod of Ky., 1874-1909. Trustee Confed. Home, Central U.; founder of Lees Collegiate Inst., Jackson, Ky.; five times mem. Gen. Assembly of Presbyn. Ch. Home: Danille, Ky. Died Sept. 17, 1914.

BLASHFIELD, Albert Dodd, Illustrator; b. New York, July 31, 1860; s. William Henry and Eliza (Dodd) B.; brother of Edwin Howland B.; ed. Brooklyn Collegiate and Poly. Inst. and Alexander Mil. Inst.; studied art at Art Students' League, New York. His specialty is illustration of periodicals. Home: Brooklyn, N.Y. Died Feb. 8, 1920.

BLASHFIELD, Edwin Howland, artist; b. New York, Dec. 15, 1848; s. William Henry and Eliza (Dodd) B.; ed. Boston Latin Sch.; studied Paris, 1867, under Léon Bonnât, also receiving advice from Gérôme and Chapu; m. Evangeline Wilbour, July 5, 1881 (died 1918); m. 2d, Grace Hall, Feb. 28, 1928. Exhibited at Paris Salon, yearly, 1874-79, 1881, 1891, 1892; also several yrs. at Royal Acad., London; returned to U.S., 1881; has exhibited genre pictures, portraits and decorations; among his paintings are Christmas Bells and Angel with the Flaming Sword. Decorated one of domes of Mfrs. Bldg., Chicago Expn.; Collis P. Huntington's drawing room; great Central Dome, Library of Congress; decorative panel Bank of Pittsburgh; Lawyers' Club, New York; Astoria Ball-room ceiling; library of town house of G. W. C. Drexel, Phila.; supper-room, New York house of W. K. Vanderbilt; a decoration for the high Appellate Ct. of New York; ceiling and 3 lunettes in bd. room, Prudential Life Ins. Co., Newark, N.J.; decorated room in house of Adolf Lewisohn, New York; court-room in Ct. House, Baltimore; 2 lunettes in senate chamber State Capitol, Minn.; large panel, State Capitol, Ia.; decoration of entire chancel, Ch. of the Saviour, Phila.; decoration of 4 main pendentives dome of new Ct. House, Newark; decoration in Great Hall, Coll. of City of New York; State Capitol, Madison, Wis.; Ct. House, Federal Bldg., Cleveland; decoration in State Capitol of S.D., Pierre; decoration of 4 main pendentives, Ct. House, Youngstown, O. (received for these two latter the gold medal of honor in painting, of the Archtl. League of New York, 1911); decoration of 4 main pendentives, Hudson Co. Ct. House, Jersey City; dome crown, State Capitol, Wis.; mosaic, Ch. of St. Matthew, Washington, D.C., etc. Awarded medal by Nat. Acad. of Design, 1934, "for distinguished service to fine arts." N.A., 1888; mem. Soc. Mural Painters, Archtl. League, Am. Acad. Arts and Letters; pres. Nat. Inst. of Arts and Letters, 1915-16 (gold medal in painting, 1923); v.p. Am. Fedn. of Arts; pres. Nat. Acad. Design, Fedn. of Fine Arts of New York. Pres. Soc. of Am. Artists; hon. mem. A.I.A. Apptd. by Pres. Taft as mem. Nat. Commn. Fine Arts, June 1912. Author (with Mrs. Blashfield): Italian Cities, 1900. Co-editor (with Mrs. Blashfield and A. A. Hopkins): Vasari's Lives of the Painters, 1897. Home: New York, N.Y. Died Oct. 12, 1936.

BLATCHFORD, Eliphalet Wickes, mfr.; b. Stillwater, N.Y., May 31, 1826; s. Dr. John and Frances (Wickes) B.; grad. Ill. Coll., Jacksonville, 1845 (LL.D.); m. Mary Emily Williams, Oct. 7, 1858. Engaged in business at St. Louis, 1850; went to Chicago, 1854; mem. and treas. Northwestern branch U.S. Sanitary Commn., 1861-65; long dir. and over 30 yrs. pres. bd. of trustees, Chicago Theol. Sem.; one of the two original executors and trustees of Walter L. Newberry's estate, charged with duty of creating the Newberry Library, of which he was pres.; trustee John Crerar Library; pres. bd. of trustees, Chicago Manual Training Sch., from its foundation till its absorption by the U. of Chicago, and connected with many other ednl. and religious orgns.; corporate mem. (v.p. 1885-98) A.B.C.F.M. (Congl.). Retired. Home: Chicago. Died Jan. 25, 1914.

BLATCH, Harriot Stanton, lecturer; b. Seneca Falls, N.Y., Jan. 20, 1856; d. Henry Brewster and Elizabeth (Cady) Stanton; A.B., Vassar Coll., 1878, A.M., 1894; m. William Henry Blatch, 1882; children—Nora Stanton, Helen Stanton (dec.). Pres. Women's Polit. Union, 1907-15; head of speakers' bur. of Food Adminstrn., 1917. Author: Mobilizing Woman Power, 1918; A Woman's Point of View, 1919; Elizabeth Cady Stanton as Revealed in Her Reminiscences, Letters and Diary, 1921. Home: New York, N.Y. Died Nov. 20, 1940.

BLATCHFORD, Richard Milford, army officer; b. N.Y., Aug. 17, 1859; m. Elinor Hall, Jan. 1921. Apptd. from civil life, 2d lt. 11th Inf., Oct. 10, 1883; advanced through grades to rank of brig. gen., May 15, 1917; maj. gen. N.A., Aug. 5, 1917, and assigned as comdr. at Panama, C.Z.; disch. from commn. in N.A., Mar. 1918, and continued in command at Panama, as brig. gen. U.S.A., retired Dec. 1, 1922; maj. gen. retired, June 21, 1930. Home: San Francisco, Calif. Died Aug. 31, 1934.

BLATCHLEY, Willis Stanley, naturalist; b. N. Madison, Conn., Oct. 6, 1859; s. Hiram S. and Sarah J. B.; A.B., Indiana Univ., 1887, A.M., 1891, LL.D., 1921; m. Clara A. Fordice, May 2, 1882; children—Raymond S., Ralph F. Assistant Arkansas Geological Survey, 1889-90; mem. Scoville's scientific expdn. to Old Mexico, 1891; asst. on U.S. Fish Commission, 1893; was state geologist of Ind., 1894-1911. Author: Gleanings from Nature, 1899; A Nature Wooing, 1902; Orthoptera of Indiana, 1903; Boulder Reveries, 1906; Coleoptera of Indiana, 1910; Woodland Idyls, 1912; The Indiana Weed Book, 1912; Rhynchophora or Weevils of Northeastern America (with Charles W. Leng), 1916; Orthoptera of Northeastern America, 1920; Heteroptera of Eastern North America, 1926; My Nature Nook, 1931; In Days Agone—Notes on the Fauna and Flora of Subtropical Florida When most of Its Area Was a Primeval Wilderness, 1932; South America as I Saw It, 1934; The Fishes of Indiana, 1938. Editor and part author Vols. XX-XXXV, Annual Repts. Dept. Geology and Natural Resources of Ind. Home: Indianapolis, Ind. Died May 28, 1940.

BLAU, Max Friedrich, college prof.; b. Goerlitz, Germany, Apr. 9, 1864; s. Friedrich Liborius and Malwine (Reiche) B.; grad. Realgymnasium, Goerlitz, 1882; grad. Gymnasium, Goerlitz, 1884; Ph.D., Leipzig, 1888; Berlin U., winter semester, 1909-10; m. Julia Ellsworth, June 24, 1899. Came to U.S., 1890; master of French and German, Thayer Acad., Braintree, Mass., 1892-96; asso. in German, Bryn Mawr, 1896-98; prof. German, Adelphi Coll., Brooklyn, N.Y., 1898-1903; asst. prof. German, 1903-12, prof. German langs. and lits., 1912—, Princeton U. Grad. lecturer, U. of Pa., 1914-15. Became naturalized citizen of U.S., 1900. Author: Zur Alexiuslegende, 1888; Carl Schurz, 1912. Home: Princeton, N.J. Died Nov. 25, 1923.

BLAUSTEIN, Louis, corp. exec.; b. Prussia, Jan. 20, 1869; s. Hyman and Sarah (Sachs) B.; ed. in Prussia; m. Henrietta Gittelsohn, Dec. 19, 1891; children—Jacob, Fanny (wife of Dr. Alvin Thalheimer), Ruth (Mrs. Henry A. Rosenberg). Came to U.S., 1888, naturalized citizen, 1891. Manager for Standard Oil Co., of N.J., 1892-1910; founded Am. Oil Co., 1910, inc., 1922, also incorporated Lord Baltimore Filling Stations; merged with Pan Am. Petroleum & Transport Co. and subsidiaries, 1933, pres. merged cos., 1933—; chmn. bd. Am. Oil Co., Mexican Petroleum Corp. (Me.), Lord Baltimore Filling Stas., Inc.; pres. Pan-Am. Refining Corp., Pan-Am. Pipe Line Co., Mexican Petroleum Corp. (Ga.), Pan-Am. Production Co., Am. Trading Corp. Home: Baltimore, Md. Died July 27, 1937.

BLAUVELT, Charles F., artist; b. New York, 1824; pupil Nat. Acad. and of Charles L. Elliot; had studio in New York and later in Philadelphia; asst. prof. drawing, U.S. Naval Acad., Annapolis, 1878; genre painter. Member Nat. Acad. Design, 1859—; member Pa. Acad. Fine Arts, 1864. Died 1900.

BLAUVELT, Martin Post, ry. official; b. Suffern, N.Y., Feb. 25, 1865; s. Cornelius Aaron and Arminda (Post) B.; ed. Goshen (N.Y.) Collegiate Inst.; m. Mary Fraser, Jan. 20, 1892. Began as clk. D.,L.&W. R.R., Hoboken, N.J., 1885; with Erie R.R. New York, 1887, comptroller, 1904, resigned, 1910; comptroller I.C. R.R., 1910-17; comptroller, July 1917-Jan. 1918, v.p., Jan. 1918-1919, Lehigh Valley R.R.; asst. regional dir. Allegheny region, U.S.R. Administration, Phila., June 1918-Nov. 1919; v.p., I.C. R.R. and the Yazoo & Miss. Valley R.R., Chicago, Nov. 1919—. Republican. Mem. Dutch Ref. Ch. Died Feb. 19, 1923.

BLAYLOCK, Louis, publisher; b. Sevier County, Ark., Oct. 21, 1849; s. Willis and Irene (Gibbs) B.; ed. pvt. sch.; LL.D., Southern Meth. U., 1927; m. Georgia Darton, June 1, 1871 (died 1929); children—Bettie (Mrs. L. B. Torrey), dec., Carrie Irene (Mrs. W. D. Jones), Georgia (widow of King V. Bunting), Louis Watts, Willis Darton. Rode Pony Express, between Brenham and Austin, Tex., at age of 14, in Civil War; learned printer's trade; began as printer in office of State Gazette, Austin, Tex., 1863; became connected with Tex. Christian Advocate, Galveston, 1866, later publisher of the paper, continuing until 1924; settled in Dallas, Tex., 1887, and established the Blaylock Pub. Co.; treas. Praetorians (fraternal ins.); dir. First Nat. Bank in Dallas. Police commr., Dallas, 6 yrs., finance commr. 3 yrs.; mayor of Dallas, 1923-27. Democrat. Methodist. Mason. Home: Dallas, Tex. Died Dec. 4, 1932.

BLAYNEY, John McClusky, clergyman; b. Ohio Co., Va., Feb. 21, 1841; s. Charles and Nancy (Faris) B.; A.B., Washington Coll., Pa., 1860, A.M., 1863; grad. Western Theol. Sem., Allegheny, Pa., 1863; (D.D., Union Coll., 1874); m. Lucy W. Lindsey, Nov. 3, 1870. Ordained to Presbyn. ministry, 1864; pastor Ontario, O., 1862-63, Charleston, W.Va., 1863-66, Frankfort, Ky., 1867-68, 1st Presbyn. Ch., Albany, N.Y., 1868-79, Frankfort, Ky., 1884-1906. Trustee (chmn. exec. com.) Central Univ., Ky.; pres. bd. dirs. Presbyn. Theol. Sem. of Ky. Home: Danville, Ky. Died 1909.

BLEASE, Coleman Livingston, senator; b. Newberry County, S.C., Oct. 8, 1868; s. Henry Horatio and Mary A. (Livingston) B.; LL.B., Georgetown U., 1889; m. Lillie B. Summers, Feb. 1890 (died 1934). Admitted to bar, 1889, and began practice with brother, Harry H., at Newberry; was sr. mem. Blease & Dominick (Hon. Fred H.), and sr. mem. Blease & Blease (with brother, Eugene S., chief justice Supreme Court of S.C.). Mem. S.C. Ho. of Rep., 1890-98 (speaker pro tem. 1891-92); Dem. presdl. elector, 1896, 1900; city atty., Newberry, 1901-02; mem. S.C. Senate, 1904-08 (pres. pro tem. 1907-08); mayor of Newberry, 1910; gov. of S.C., terms 1911-13, 1913-15 (resigned, Jan. 1915, and resumed practice in Columbia, S.C.); mem. U.S. Senate, term 1925-31. Served as chmn. Dem. party, Newberry Co.; del. to state convs. of Dem. party many yrs. and mem. Dem. state exec. com., S.C., 18 yrs.; pres. of State Democratic Conv., 1926; del. to Dem. Nat. Conv., 1928 (com. on platform). Methodist. The only South Carolinian who has been mayor of his city, senator from his county, speaker of the House, pres. of the State Senate, gov. of the State and U.S. senator. Home: Columbia, S.C. Died Jan. 19, 1942.

BLECKLEY, Logan E., jurist; b. Rabun Co., Ga., July 3, 1827; s. James and Catharine B.; ed. the county acad.; m. Caroline Haralson, May 1857; m. 2d, Chloe Herring, Aug. 1893. Admitted to bar, 1846; apptd. Supreme Court reporter, 1864; asso. justice Supreme Court, Ga., 1875; chief justice, 1887; retired, 1894. Home: Atlanta, Ga. Died 1907.

BLEDSOE, Benjamin Franklin, judge; b. San Bernardino, Calif., Feb. 8, 1874; s. Robert Emmett and Althea (Bottoms) B.; A.B., Stanford, 1896; LL.D., U. of Southern Calif., 1920; m. Katharine Marvin Shepler, Dec. 25, 1899; children—Barbara Shepler (Mrs. Glenn E. Pollard), Frances Priscilla. Admitted to Calif. bar, 1896; engaged in gen. practice at San Bernardino in partnership with father; elected judge of Superior Ct. of San Bernardino Co., 1900, for term of 6 yrs., reëlected, 1906, and 1912, both times without opposition; resigned, Oct. 23, 1914, to accept apptmt. by Pres. Wilson as U.S. dist. judge, Southern Dist. of Calif., resigned Mar. 24, 1925; tried litigation between U.S. Govt. and S.P. Ry. in which oil lands valued at more than $500,000,000 were in issue, no appeal taken from judgment rendered; in gen. practice of law as mem. Hill, Morgan and Bledsoe; mem. bar Supreme Court of U.S.; pres. Sunset Ry. Co. Mem. bd. of trustees City Pub. Library, San Bernardino, 1899-1913 (pres. 1905-13); pres. San Bernardino Y.M.C.A., 1911-14; mem. state exec. com. Y.M.C.A. of Calif., 1912—; pres. Los Angeles Grand Opera Assn., 1924-26; v.p. Community Welfare Fed. (operating Los Angeles community chest), 1924-27; pres. Stanford Univ. Alumni Assn., 1915; mem. Stanford Univ. Nat. Board; pres. Los Angeles Oratorio Assn., 1932; chmn. Personnel Commn. of Los Angeles City Sch. Dist. Mason. Democrat. Conglist. Wrote article on "Constitutional Law" in Calif. Jurisprudence. Home: Los Angeles, Calif. Died Oct. 30, 1938.

BLEDSOE, Samuel Thomas, ry. pres.; b. Clinton Co., Ky., May 12, 1868; s. Elijah and Ottilla G. (Snow) B.; studied law U. of Tex., 1888-89; m. Elder Atkinson, May 14, 1890 (died 1897); children—Roy Eugene (dec.), Virgil Thomas; m. 2d, Talitha Bernhard, Dec. 28, 1898; 1 dau., Adelaide Maurine (Mrs. Bartlett Cormack). Admitted to practice law at Sherman, Tex., 1890, and practiced at Ardmore, Indian Territory (Okla.), 1890-1908, Guthrie, Okla., 1908-11, Oklahoma City, 1911-15; local atty. and atty., Gulf, Colo. & S.F. Ry., 1895-1908; solicitor for Okla. of A.,T.&S.F. Ry., 1908, and gen. atty., 1912; asst. gen. solicitor at Chicago, 1915, gen. counsel and dir., also gen. counsel of affiliated carrier companies, 1918-30; chmn. exec. com. and gen. counsel A.,T.&S.F. Ry. Co., Dec. 1930-May 1933, pres. and chmn. exec. com., 1933—; also pres. affiliated cos.; dir. Ry. Express Agency, Inc., Continental Ill. Nat. Bank & Trust Company. Democrat. Mason. Author: Indian Land Laws, 1909, 14. Home: Chicago, Ill. Died Mar. 8, 1939.

BLEECKER, John Van Benthuysen, rear adm.; b. Glen Cove, N.Y., Aug. 16, 1847; s. John V. B. (paymaster U.S.N.) and S. Rosalie (Lynch) B.; grad. U.S. Naval Acad., 1867; promoted ensign, 1868; master, 1870; lt., 1871; lt. comdr., June 30, 1891; comdr., Dec. 8, 1897; capt., June 3, 1902; rear adm. and retired, June 27, 1905. Served 19 yrs. on sea duty at various stas.; shore service at torpedo sta., 1873-74, Navy Yard, Washington, 1877-78; Naval

Acad., 1878-81; insp. of steel, new cruisers, 1887-88; torpedo sta., 1889-90; Navy Yard, Boston, 1893-96; Naval War Coll., 1894; comd. U.S.S. Bancroft, 1898, Isla de Luzon, 1899, Marietta, 1901; Naval War Coll., Navy Yard, Puget Sound; comdg. U.S.S. Columbia, until retired. Home: Jamestown, R.I. Died Feb. 20, 1922.

BLENDINGER, Fred L., ry. official; b. Little Valley, N.Y.; ed. pub. schs. Began as messenger Erie R.R., 1878, and continued as telegraph operator and clk., at Cleveland and New York, until 1898; chief clk. to 2d v.p. in charge of operation, same rd., 1898-1900; supt. telegraph, same rd., and 7th Dist. W.U. Telegraph Co., 1900-02; with Lehigh Valley R.R., 1902—, successively purchasing agt. and supt. telegraph, 1907-11, asst. to v.p. in charge operation, 1911-16, v.p. in charge operation, 1916-18, federal mgr., also of Buffalo Creek R.R. and Susquehanna & N.Y. R.R., 1918-20, v.p. in charge operation Lehigh Valley R.R. and gen. mgr. Buffalo Creek R.R., Mar. 1, 1920—. Died June 2, 1929.

BLENK, James Hubert, archbishop; b. Edenkoben, Bavaria, July 28, 1856; s. James and Catherine (Wiedemann) B.; ed. St. James' Coll., Baltimore; Jefferson Coll. Convent, La.; entered Soc. of Mary, 1874; theol. course at Marist Houses of Studies in France and Ireland; course at Catholic Univ., Dublin. Ordained priest, R.C. Ch., 1885; prof., 1885-90, pres., 1890-96, Jefferson College Convent, La.; rector Holy Name of Mary Ch., Algiers, La., 1897-98; auditor Apostolic Delegation to Cuba and Puerto Rico, 1898; consecrated bishop of Puerto Rico, July 2, 1899; archbishop of New Orleans, July 2, 1906—; received pallium, Apr. 24, 1907. Home: New Orleans, La. Died Apr. 20, 1917.

BLESH, Abraham Lincoln, surgeon; b. Lock Haven, Pa., Jan. 6, 1866; s. Rudolph and Sarah Frances (Bartholomew) B.; Campbell Normal Sch., Holton, Kan.; M.D., Northwestern U. Med. Sch., 1889; U. of Vienna, 1910-11; m. 2d, Beatrice Rogers, Jan. 22, 1921. Practiced at Rio, Wis., 1889-90, Hope, Kan., 1890-91, Lost Springs, Kan., 1891-93, Guthrie, Okla., 1893-1908, Oklahoma City, Okla., 1908—. Practiced surgery exclusively, 1902—; prof. clin. surgery, Univ. Med. Sch., Oklahoma City; chief of staff, chief surgeon, Wesley Hosp.; pres. and chief of staff, Oklahoma City Clinic, 1919—. Fellow and gov. Am. Coll. Surgeons. Mason. Commd. 1st lt. M.R.C., and chief surgeon Base Hosp. No. 1, Ft. Sam Houston, Tex., May 27, 1917; promoted maj., Aug. 23, 1917; detached duty Phila.; chief surgeon, Base Hosp., Camp Sheridan, Montgomery, Ala., June 19-Dec. 29, 1918. Home: Oklahoma City, Okla. Died Feb. 20, 1934.

BLESSING, George Frederick, mech. engr.; b. Carrollton, Ky., July 2, 1875; s. John Jacob and Anna Elizabeth (Leesé) B.; B.M.E., State U. of Ky., 1897, M.E., 1905; Ph.D., Hanover Coll., Ind., 1906; studied and taught at Cornell U., 1906-08; m. Martha Ripperdan White, Dec. 26, 1908. Draftsman various cos. to 1899; asso. prof., mech. engring., 1899-1900, prof., 1900-05, Nev. State U.; asst. engr. of tests, S.P. Co., Sacramento, Calif., summer, 1902; in charge design and research work, Eureka Oil Burning Co., San Francisco, summer, 1903; designer Pacific Foundry, San Francisco, summer, 1904; design and research work in turbine pumps, Platt Iron Works, Dayton, O., 1905-06; designer in steam turbine dept., Gen. Electric Co., Lynn, Mass., 1906; asst. prof. machine design, Sibley Coll. Engring., Cornell U., 1906-08; lecturer Cornell U. Summer Sch., 1907-08; prof. mech. engring. and in charge engring. dept., Swarthmore coll., 1908—. Plant facilities engr., U.S. Ordnance Dept., Phila. dist., 1918. Author: Elements of Drawing, 1912; Elements of Descriptive Geometry, 1913; The Small College and Technical Education, 1917. Home: Swarthmore, Pa. Died June 25, 1921.

BLETHEN, Alden Joseph, editor and publisher; b. Knox, Me., Dec. 27, 1846; s. Alden and Abbie L. B.; grad. Me. Wesleyan Sem. and Coll., 1868; (hon. A.M., Bowdoin, 1872); m. Rose A. Hunter, Mar. 12. 1869. Lessee and prin. Abbott Family Sch., 1869-73; admitted to bar, 1873; practiced at Portland, Me., 1874-80; mgr. Kansas City Journal, 1880-84, half owner, editor and mgr. Minneapolis Tribune and Minneapolis Journal, 1884-88; sold his interest, repurchased Tribune in summer of 1889; fire destroyed Tribune Bldg., Nov., 1889, with net loss of $100,000 to owners of paper; built new Tribune Bldg., 1890, at a cost of $100,000, but lost all in the panic of 1893-95; began life again in 1896 with Seattle Times, of which was editor and pub. Was col. on staff of Govs. Nelson and Clough of Minn. Home: Seattle, Wash. Died July 12, 1915.

BLEWETT, Ben, supt. of pub. instrn.; b. Russellville, Ky., Feb. 25, 1856; s. Benjamin T. and Avis Williams (Hedge) B.; A.B., Washington U., 1876 (A.M., 1879; LL.D., 1914); m. Jessie Hastings Parsons, Aug. 8, 1907. Teacher Cote Brilliante Sch., St. Louis, 1876-77, Eleardville School, 1877-78; prin. various pub. schs., St. Louis, 1878-97; asst. supt. instrn., 1897-1908, supt. pub. instrn., June, 1908—, St. Louis. During 1883-84, as corr. sec., Soc. of Pedagogy, conducted correspondence leading to movement for compulsory sch. attendance. Dir. for Mo., N.E.A., 1904, 1905; pres. Mo. State Teachers' Assn., 1904. Many years mem. of Dist. Sch. Bd. in St. Louis Co.; pres. bd. of dirs., Mo. Sch. for the Blind, 1889-97. Home: St. Louis, Mo. Died Jan. 26, 1917.

BLEYER, Willard Grosvenor, univ. prof.; b. Milwaukee, Wis., Aug. 27, 1873; s. Albert J. and Elizabeth (Groshans) B.; B.L., U. of Wis., 1896, fellow in English, 1896-98, M.L., 1898, Ph.D., 1904; m. Alice Haskell, 1911. In newspaper work, 1892-98; instr. in English, 1900-05, asst. prof., 1905-09, asst. prof. journalism, 1909-11, asso. prof., 1911-16, prof. journalism, 1916—, chmn. course in journalism, 1906-19, dir. same, 1919-27; dir. School of Journalism, 1927—, U. of Wis.; spl. lecturer, Am. Library Assn., 1922, Wis. Library Sch., 1915—. Editor Press Bulletin, U. of Wis., 1904-13. Chmn. Nat. Council on Education for Journalism, 1923—; chmn. Council on Research in Journalism, 1924-29. Conglist. Author: Newspaper Writing and Editing, 1913, 23, 32; Types of News Writing, 1916; How to Write Special Feature Articles, 1919; Main Currents in the History of American Journalism, 1927; Journalism, 1929. Editor: The Profession of Journalism, 1918. Home: Madison, Wis. Died Oct. 31, 1935.

BLINN, Holbrook, actor; b. San Francisco, Calif., Jan. 23, 1872; s. Col. Charles H. and Nellie (Holbrook) B.; ed. Stanford U., Calif.; m. Ruth Benson, actress. First appeared on stage as a child in "The Streets of New York," 1878; played Corporal Ferry in "The New South," at Broadway Theatre, New York, 1893; two seasons with same play, then leading man with Effie Ellsler and Roland Reed; début on London stage as Wing Shee, in "The Cat and the Cherub," at Lyric Theatre, Oct. 30, 1897; in America in "To Have and To Hold" and "The Battle of the Strong"; played for 3 seasons as leading man with Mrs. Fiske in "Salvation Nell," "Becky Sharpe," "Hannele," and a number of other plays. Organized the Princess Theatre, New York, and prod. 30 one-act plays, also toured the country with same; starred with Blanche Bates in a recruiting propaganda play called "Getting Together"; starred in "The Challenge," season 1919-20; joint star with Mary Nash in "Man and Woman," 1920; starred in "The Bad Man," 1920-23; moving pictures, 1923-24; starred in "The Dove," 1925-26; produced, also starred in Molnar's "The Play's the Thing," 1926, and toured with same play, 1927-28. Home: Croton-on-Hudson, N.Y. Died June 24, 1928.

BLISS, Aaron Thomas, gov. of Mich. for 1900-04; b. Smithfield, Madison Co., N.Y., May 22, 1837; s. Lyman and Anna (Chaffee) B.; ed. country schs.; employed in store, 1854-61; enlisted pvt. Co. D., 10th N.Y. cav., Oct. 1, 1961; elected 1st lt.; promoted capt., 1862; in service 3 yrs. 5 months; captured on field, Ream's Sta., Va.; 6 months in prisons at Salisbury, N.C., Andersonville, and Macon, Ga., Charleston and Columbia, S.C.; escaped from Columbia prison Nov. 29, 1864, and reached Union lines Dec. 16, nearly starved; m. Allaseba M., March 31, 1868, d. Ambrose Phelps of Solsville, Madison Co., N.Y. Lumberman in Saginaw, 1865—, large mfr. of lumber and salt, and interested in banking, mercantile and farm enterprises. Has been alderman, supervisor and mem. bd. edn., Saginaw; State senator, 1882; mem. bd. to locate Mich. Soldiers' Home; mem. Congress from 8th Mich. dist., 1889-91; aide on staff Gov. Alger, 1885; dept. comdr. G.A.R., 1897; lay del. Gen. Conf. M.E. Ch., 1900; elected gov. Mich., 1900; re-elected, 1902. Republican. Home: Saginaw, Mich. Died 1906.

BLISS, A(ndrew) Richard, Jr., pharmacologist; b. New York, N.Y., Nov. 10, 1889; s. Andrew Richard and Frances Revue (Sutton) B.; Ph.Ch., Columbia, 1908, Ph.D., 1909; B.S., Howard College, Ala., 1910, A.M., 1912, LL.D., 1932; M.D., U. of Ala., 1913; m. Loretta Ann Deering, Aug. 20, 1918. Adjunct prof. chemistry and pharmacology, Sch. of Medicine, U. of Ala., later dean of college of pharmacy and prof. biochemistry and pharmacology, 1910-15; prof. pharmacology, Emory U. Med. Sch., Atlanta, Ga., 1915-23; chief of division of physiology and pharmacology, U. of Tenn. Coll. of Medicine, 1923-33, and dean of Sch. of Pharmacy, 1925-33; director Reelfoot Lake Biological Station, 1931-36; head of dept. of pharmacology, and dean of pharmacy of Howard College, 1934—. Served as lt. M.C. under Adj. Gen. U.S. Army, World War; then passed asst. surgeon, U.S. Pub. Health Service Res. Awarded Conspicuous Service Medal Columbia U., 1932. Mem. Com. of Revision of U.S. Pharmacopœia, 1930-40; dir. pharmacol. and physiol. studies for Edn. Research Com. of Commonwealth Fund of Pa., 1923-26; dir. health programs, Station WSGN, Birmingham. Fellow Am. Inst. Chemists, A.A.A.S., Am. Acad. Polit. and Social Science, Am. Geog. Soc. Episcopalian (mem. Bishop and Council, Diocese of Tenn.). Mason. Author: Essentials of Physiology (with G. Bachmann), 1939; Physics and Chemistry for Nurses (with A. H. Olive), 1926; Qualitative Analysis (with H. H. Schaefer), 1929; Properties and Uses of Drugs (with H. H. Rusby and C. W. Ballard), 1930; Experimental Pharmacodynamics, 1939. Mem. board editors Chemical Formulary; contbg. editor The Chemist; mem. editorial bd. Am. Professional Pharmacist; contbr. over 200 to scientific educational lit. Home: Birmingham, Ala. Died Aug. 12, 1941.

BLISS, Cornelius Newton, sec. of the Interior; b. Fall River, Mass., Jan. 26, 1833; s. Asahel and Irene Borden (Luther) B.; ed. pub. and high schs.; m. Elizabeth M. Plumer, Mar. 30, 1859. Engaged in his stepfather's counting-room, New Orleans, 1 yr.; clerk in commn. house, Boston; mem. 1866, J. S. & E. Wright & Co., Boston; later moved to New York to take charge there, firm finally becoming Bliss, Fabyan & Co., dry goods commn. mchts., 1881—; trustee Am. Surety Co., Central Trust Co.; dir. Home Ins. Co., Fouth Nat. Bank, Am. Cotton Co. Was mem. Pan-Am. Conf.; was pres. protective Tariff League; chmn. N.Y. Rep. State Com., 1887-88; treas. Rep. Nat. Com., 1892-1908; declined to be a candidate for gov. N.Y., 1885, 1891; Sec. of the Interior, in cabinet of Pres. McKinley, 1897-99, resigned, Feb., 1899. Pres. N.Y. Hosp., N.E. Soc.; v.p. Chamber of Commerce; mem. exec. com. Nat. Civic Fedn. Home: New York, N.Y. Died 1911.

BLISS, Daniel, missionary; b. Georgia, Vt., Aug. 17, 1823; s. Loomis and Susan (Farwell) B.; A.B., Amherst, 1852, A.M., 1855; grad. Andover Theol. Sem., 1855; (D.D., Amherst, 1864); m. Abby M. Wood, Nov. 23, 1855; father of Frederick Jones and Howard Sweetser B. Ordained Congl. ministry, 1855; missionary at Mt. Lebanon, Syria, 1856-62; acting sec. A.B.C.F.M., New York, 1862-64; pres., 1864-1902, pres. emeritus, 1902, Syrian Protestant Coll., Beirut. Author: Mental Philosophy; Natural Philosophy (both in Arabic). Died July 28, 1916.

BLISS, Edwin Munsell, author, editor; b. Erzrum, Turkey, Sept. 12, 1848; s. Rev. Isaac G. (agt. Am. Bible Soc. for the Levant at Constantinople) and Eunice (Day) B.; ed. high sch., Springfield, Mass., 1866-67, Robert Coll., Constantinople, 1862-63; A.B., Amherst Coll., 1871; studied Yale Div. Sch., 1871-72 and 1875-77; (D.D., Amherst, 1896, for spl. work on Encyclopedia of Missions); m. Marie Louise Henderson, June 5, 1885 (died 1887); 2d, E. Theodora Crosby, Nov. 8, 1900. Apptd. asst. agt. Am. Bible Soc. for The Levant, at Constantinople, 1872; traveled extensively in Turkey and Persia; returned to U.S., 1888; edited Ency. of Missions, 1889-91; asso. editor The Independent, 1891-1901; also editorial writer Harper's Weekly and New York Times, 1901-02; field sec. Am. Tract Soc. for N.E.; spl. agt. Bur. of the Census, Apr. 1, 1907. Gen. sec. Foreign Missions Industrial Assn., 1905. Congregationalist. Author: Encyclopedia of Missions, 1891; Turk in Armenia, Crete and Greece, 1896; Concise History of Missions, 1897; The Missionary Enterprise. Editor Census Report on Religious Bodies, 1906, 16; Census Report on Benevolent Institutions, 1913; summary of State Laws relating to Dependent Classes, 1913. Died Aug. 6, 1919.

BLISS, Eliakim Raymond, lawyer; b. New Brunswick, N.J., Sept. 3, 1846; s. George Ripley (D.D., LL.D.) and Mary A. (Raymond) B.; brother of Tasker Howard and Robert Pratt Bliss; educated at the U. of Lewisburg, Pa., and old U. of Chicago, A.M.; LL.B., Columbian (now George Washington) U., 1873; m. Margaret Holmes, 1880. Has lived in Chicago, 1863—; admitted to bar, 1873, but did not begin practice until 1876; co. atty. Cook Co., Ill., 1882-84, 1886-89, in 1889 as co. atty., established validity of law permitting annexation of Hyde Park, Lake View and other suburbs. Mason, 33°; was one of the three Masons apptd. to carry out plan of erecting Masonic Temple in Chicago; recently identified with negotiations relating to Chicago traction problem; spl. counsel and dir. Chicago City Ry. Co.; dir. Calumet & S. Chicago Ry. Co., Southern St. Ry. Co., Hammond, Whiting & E. Chicago Ry. Co. Judge advocate gen. Ill. N.G., retired. Republican. Home: Chicago. Died 1923.

BLISS, Eliphalet, Williams, mfr.; b. Cooperstown, N.Y., Apr. 12, 1836; ed. pub. schs.; apprenticed at 16 to Metcalf & Livington, machinists, Cooperstown; m. Anna E. Metcalf, June 15, 1866. Worked as machinist until 1861; enlisted in 3d Conn. regt. on Lincoln's call and completed his term of service. Supt. Parker Gun Co., Meriden, Conn.; later worked for Campbell Printing Press Co. Started mfr. of spl. machinery for sheet metal goods with capital of $1,250, employing 6 men; then pres. E. W. Bliss Co., capital $2,500,000, employing 1,000 mechanics. Was also pres. U.S. Projectile Co., mfg. Whitehead torpedoes for U.S.N. Was one of com. of 100 apptd. to meet Prince Henry of Prussia, 1902. Home: New York, N.Y. Died 1903.

BLISS, George Yemens, bishop; b. Shelburne, Vt., Mar. 12, 1864; s. George and Mary Adelaide (Stevens) B.; A.B., U. of Vt., 1889 (D.D., 1904); S.T.B., Gen. Theol. Sem., New York, 1892 (S.T.D., 1916); m. Katherine L. Shattuck, Nov. 15, 1893. Deacon, 1892, priest, 1893, P.E. Ch.; curate St. Paul's Ch., Burlington, Vt., 1892-99, rector, 1899-1915; consecrated bishop coadjutor of Vt., Apr. 21, 1915. Home: Burlington, Vt. Died July 10, 1924.

BLISS, Harry Hayner, newspaper pub.; b. Janesville, Wis., June 30, 1871; s. Howard Festes and Caroline (Hayner) B.; educated pub. schs.; m. Clare Smith, May 28, 1896; children—Josephine (Mrs. Fergus Mead), Sidney Howard, Robert Wilmarth. Was owner and publisher Janesville Daily Gazette,

1919—; pres. and prin. owner WCLO Radio Sta.; dir. Rock County Nat. Bank, Rock County Savings and Trust Co. Mem. Wis. N.G., 1886-89; Wis. Home Guard, World War. Mem. Wis. Hist. Soc., Wis. Daily Newspaper League (one of founders; sec. and treas., 1908-27), Inland Daily Press Assn. (pres.). Republican. Conglist. Home: Janesville, Wis. Died Sept. 21, 1937.

BLISS, Howard Sweetser, educator; b. Mt. Lebanon, Syria, Dec. 6, 1860; s. Daniel and Abby M. (Wood) Bliss; brother of Frederick Jones B.; A.B., Amherst, 1882; taught in Washburn Coll., Kan., 1882-84; grad. Union Theol. Sem., New York, 1887, fellow, 1887-89; Oxford U. and Mansfield Coll., Oxford, 1887-88; univs. of Göttingen and Berlin, 1888-89; (D.D., New York U., Amherst, 1902, Princeton U., 1913; LL.D., Amherst, 1919); m. Amy, d. of Eliphalet Wickes Blatchford, Nov. 7, 1889. Ordained Congl. ministry, 1890; asst. pastor Plymouth Ch., Brooklyn, 1889-94; pastor Christian Union Congl. Ch., Upper Montclair, N.J., 1894-1902; pres. Syrian Protestant Coll., Beirût, Syria, in succession to his father, Nov. 1902—. Died May 2, 1920.

BLISS, Malcolm Andrews, M.D.; b. Warsaw, Ill., July 2, 1863; s. Neziah Wright and Amanda Jessie (Andrews) B.; D.D.S., Mo. Dental Coll., Washington U., 1884; M.D., Chicago Med. Coll., 1890; m. Clemmie Chilton Carter, Apr. 29, 1891 (died 1927); children—William Carter, Wyllys King, Helen (dec.). Began practice at Bonne Terre, Mo., 1890; moved to St. Louis, 1892; lecturer in clin. neuro-psychiatry, med. dept., Washington U., 1895-1912. Contract surgeon in neuro-psychiatry, World War. Chmn. bd. Psychiatric Clinic. Republican. Mason. Home: St. Louis, Mo. Died Sept. 4, 1934.

BLISS, Paul Southworth, govt. service; b. Rice Lake, Wis., Apr. 12, 1889; s. Alden Southworth and Olive Irene (Hills) B.; student Hamline Coll., 1907-10; A.B., Harvard, 1913, post-grad. work in drama, 1913-14; unmarried. Wrote for various newspapers, including theatrical and musical criticism, 1913-23; on staff Minneapolis Community Fund, 1923-26; publicity dir. St. Louis Community Fund, 1926-32; exec. sec. St. Louis Chapter Am. Red Cross, 1932-33; field rep. Federal Emergency Relief Adminstrn. of N.D., 1933-35; dir. dept. of intake and certification, Works Progress Adminstrn. of N.Dak., 1935-37; with Social Security Board, 1937—. Served as captain and later maj., U.S. Army, with A.E.F. in France, World War; now col. O.R.C. commanding 406th Inf. Regt., St. Louis. Author: (poetry) Songs for Seven Moods, 1926; After Supper Poems, 1927; Rough Edges and All, 1928; How Pan Shaped the Leaves and Other Poems, 1930; Arch of Spring, 1932; Spin Dance, 1934; Cirrus from the West, 1935; The Rye is the Sea, 1936; Poems of Places, 1937; The Lord Made Kansas for Wheat. Home: Hettinger, North Dakota. Died Dec. 31, 1940.

BLISS, Philip Elijah, pres. The Warner & Swasey Co.; b. Cleveland, O., Dec. 14, 1885; s. Julius E. and Arabel (Hauxhurst) B.; student Ohio Wesleyan U.; m. Loretta E. Crane; children—Mary A. (Mrs. Edgar B. Gausby), Charles William. Pres. The Warner & Swasey Co., machine tools, Cleveland, O., 1928—; vice-pres. Caxton Bldg. Co. Republican. Episcopalian. Home: Cleveland Heights, O. Died Apr. 11, 1939.

BLISS, Tasker Howard, army officer; b. Lewisburg, Pa., Dec. 31, 1853; s. George Ripley (D.D., LL.D.) and Mary Ann (Raymond) B.; ed. Lewisburg Acad., 1867-69, entered Univ. at Lewisburg (now Bucknell U.), 1869 and finished sophomore yr.; grad. U.S. Mil. Acad., 1875; honor grad. U.S. Artillery School, 1884; LL.D. from Bucknell Univ., 1916, Western Reserve U., 1923; Harvard Univ., 1927; m. Eleanora E. Anderson, May 24, 1882. Second lt. 1st Arty., June 16, 1875; commd. 1st lt., July 1, 1880; promoted through grades to brig. gen. vols., Apr. 26, 1901; brig. gen., U.S.A., July 21, 1902. Served 1st U.S. Arty., 1875-92; adj. Arty. Sch., 1884-85; recorder of bd. apptd. by the President, 1884, to report on mil. value of Interior Waterways of the U.S.; prof. mil. science, U.S. Naval War Coll., 1885-88; a.d.c. to Lt. Gen. Schofield comdg. U.S.A., and insp. rifle practice, 1888-95; on spl. duty with Sec. of War, 1895-97; mil. attaché at U.S. Legation, Madrid, 1897-98; served through Puerto Rican campaign, 1898, chief of staff to Maj. Gen. James H. Wilson, comdg. 1st Div. 1st Army Corps; mem. bd. officers to select camp sites for U.S. troops in Cuba, Oct.-Nov. 1898; collector customs, port of Havana, and chief Cuban Customs Service, Dec. 1898-May 20, 1902. Apptd. mem. Army War Coll. Bd., July 21, 1902; apptd. spl. envoy to Cuba to negotiate treaty of reciprocity bet. Cuba and the U.S., Nov. 13, 1902; comdt. Army War Coll., 1903; mem. Joint Army and Navy Bd. and Gen. Staff U.S.A., 1903-05; comdg. Dept. of Luzon, P.I., 1905-06, Dept. of Mindanao, 1906-09, Div. of the Philippines, Dec. 1908-Apr. 1909; mem. Army Gen. Staff and pres. Army War Coll., June-Dec. 1909; asst. chief of staff, Dec. 1909; mem. Joint Army and Navy Bd., 1909-10; acting chief of staff, May-Aug. 1910; comdg. Dept. of Calif., Aug. 1910-June 30, 1911; comdg. provisional brigade on Mexican border, Southern Calif., during Mexican insurrection, Mar.-June 15, 1911; comdg. Western div., July 1-July 30, 1911; comdg. Dept. of the East, Aug. 12, 1911-Feb. 14, 1913; comdg. Eastern Div., Jan. 29-Aug. 31, 1912; comdg. Southern Dept. and the Cav. Div., Feb. 15, 1913-Feb. 15, 1915; apptd. mem. Gen. Staff, U.S. Army, and asst. chief of staff, Feb. 15, 1915; mem. Joint Army and Navy Bd., Sept. 23, 1915, maj. gen. U.S.A., Nov. 20, 1915; chief of staff, Sept. 23, 1917; chief of staff with rank of general, U.S.A., Oct. 6, 1917; retired by operation of law, Dec. 31, 1917; continued on active duty by order of the President. Mem. of the Allied Conf., 1917; mem. Supreme War Council in France; mem. Am. Commn. to Negotiate Peace, Paris, 1918-19; detailed by President as Gov. of U.S. Soldiers' Home, May 1, 1920-May 1, 1927. Apptd. brevet gen. by Act of Congress, May 20, 1918. Awarded D.S.M. (U.S.). Home: Washington, D.C. Died Nov. 9, 1930.

BLISS, Walter Phelps, capitalist; b. New York, Mar. 10, 1870; s. George and Augusta H. (Smith) B.; A.B., Yale, 1892; LL.B., New York Law Sch., 1896; m. Katharine Baldwin, Apr. 29, 1897. Trustee Atlas Assurance Co., Caledonian Ins. Co., Central Union Trust Co. of N.Y., Union Assurance Co., Ltd.; dir. C.,C.,C.&St.L. Ry. Co., N.Y.C. R.R. Co., N.Y. & Harlem Ry. Co., Southern Pacific Co., Commercial Union Assurance Co., Commercial Union Fire Ins. Co., Continental Ins. Co., Quincy Mining Co., Gauley Mountain Coal Co., Fire Cos. Building Corp., Union Assurance Co., Greenwich Savings Bank (New York). Vestryman and treas. Grace Ch.; trustee St. Luke's Hosp. (treas.), N.Y. Soc. for Relief of Ruptured and Crippled. Home: Bernardsville, N.J. Died Jan. 10, 1924.

BLISS, William, ry. official; b. Springfield, Mass., Dec. 11, 1834. Entered ry. service Oct. 1865; asst. to pres., 1865-66, gen. freight agt., 1866-72, Western R.R. of Mass.; gen. mgr., 1872-80, pres., 1880—, Boston & Albany R.R. Also dir. N.Y. Central & Hudson River R.R. Home: Boston, Mass. Died 1907.

BLISS, William Dwight Porter, sociologist; b. Constantinople, Turkey, 1856; s. Edwin Elisha and Isabella Holmes (Porter) B.; early edn. in Robert Coll., Constantinople, and Phillips Acad., Mass.; A.B., Amherst, 1878; grad. Hartford Theol. Sem., 1882, D.D., 1913; m. Mary Pangalo, June 30, 1884; children—Zoe (dec.), Enid (dec.). Congl. clergyman, Denver, Colo., and S. Natick, Mass.; deacon, 1886, priest, 1887, P.E. Ch.; rector, Lee, Mass., 1885, Grace Ch., S. Boston, 1887-90, Linden, Mass., 1890, Ch. of the Carpenter, Boston, 1890-94; San Gabriel, Calif., 1898, Amityville, L.I., 1902-06, West Orange, N.J., 1910-14, St. Martha's Church, N.Y. City, 1921-25. Investigator for U.S. Bur. of Labor, 1907-09. Edited The Dawn, 1889-96, The American Fabian, 1895-96. Nominee of Labor Party for lt.-gov., Mass., 1887; organized 1st Christian Socialist Soc. in U.S., 1889; lecturer for Christian Social Union, 1894; pres. Nat. Social Reform Union, 1899; sec. Garden Cities Assn. of America, 1907. Connected with Am. Inst. of Social Service, 1909-14. Author: Hand Book of Socialism, 1895; Studies in the Gospel of the Kingdom (with Dr. Josiah Strong). Editor: Encyclopedia of Social Reform, 1898, 1907. In charge ednl. work Y.M.C.A. among interned French and Belgian soldiers in Switzerland, 1918-19. Died Oct. 8, 1926.

BLISS, William Henry, lawyer; b. Cuyahoga Falls, O., Oct. 27, 1844; s. Philemon and Martha W. (Tharp) B.; ed. pub. schs.; admitted to bar, 1871; m. Annie Louise Woods, Apr. 6, 1874; children—Robert Woods, Mrs. Annie Louise Warren; m. 2d, Mrs. Anna Blaksley Barnes, Apr. 14, 1894. Asst. and later U.S. dist. atty. at St. Louis, 1872-88; later v.p. and gen. solicitor St. Paul & Duluth R.R. Co. and later asso. counsel N.P. R.R. Co. Home: Santa Barbara, Calif. Died May 5, 1932.

BLISS, William Julian Albert, physicist; b. Washington, Jan. 22, 1867; s. Alexander and Ellen Taylor (Albert) B.; A.B., Harvard, 1888; certificate in elec. engring., Johns Hopkins, 1890, Ph.D., 1894; m. Edith Grantham West, Nov. 19, 1896; children—Eleanor Albert, Frances McDowell. Asst. in elec. engring., 1890-91, lecturer in physics, 1894-95, asst., 1895-98, asso., 1898-1901, collegiate prof. physics, 1901-28, Johns Hopkins, now emeritus. Fellow Am. Phys. Soc. Episcopalian. Author: Manual of Experiments in Physics (with J. S. Ames), 1897. Home: Baltimore, Md. Died Dec. 27, 1940.

BLISS, William Root, author; b. 1825; s. Rev. Seth and Jeanette Root B.; ed. in Boston schs.; grad. Yale, 1850; m. Elizabeth Fearing. Author: Quaint Nantucket; September Days on Nantucket; Side Glimpses from the Colonial Meeting-House; The Old Colony Town and Other Sketches; Colonial Times on Buzzard's Bay; Paradise in the Pacific. Home: Short Hills, N.J. Died 1906.

BLISS, Zenas Randall, maj. gen. U.S. Army (retired); b. Johnston, R.I., April 17, 1835; apptd. cadet, 1850; grad. West Point, 1854; bvt. 2d lt., 1854; 2d lt., 1885; 1st lt., 1860; capt., 1861; maj. inf., Aug. 6, 1867; transferred to 25th inf., 1869; lt. col., 1879; col., 1886; brig. gen., 1895; command of Dept. of Texas, 1895-97; maj. gen., May 14, 1897; retired at his own request after more than 40 years' service, May 22, 1897. Served in Texas until May 9, 1861, when he was captured with the command of Col. I. V. D. Reeve, 8th inf., by a Confederate force under Gen. Earl Van Dorn, and held prisoner of war at San Antonio, Tex., and Richmond, Va., until exchanged April 5, 1862; apptd. col. 10th R.I. vols., May 26, 1862; transferred to 7th R.I. vols., Aug., 1862; mustered out of service, June 9, 1865. In command of northern defenses of Washington, May to Aug. 1862; in Fredericksburg campaign and battle of Fredericksburg, Dec. 1862; then in Div. of Ohio in Ky., to May 1863; transferred with 2d div., 9th corps, and with 2d div., 9th corps, took part in siege of Vicksburg and march to and capture of Jackson, Miss.; then transferred to Ky.; commanded military dist. Middle Tennessee to spring of 1864; commanded 1st brigade, 2d div., 9th corps, in Wilderness campaign and battles of Wilderness, Spottsylvania, Petersburg Mine, etc.; after war commanded military dist. of Chester, S.C., and was asst. commr. of Freedmen and Abandoned Lands, and various branches of military and civil duty; m. Martha N. Work, Oct. 21, 1863. Died 1900.

BLOCH, Alexander, violinist; b. Selma, Ala., July 11, 1881; s. Edward and Elizabeth L. (Long) Bloch; student at Columbia U., 1897-98; studied violin with Edward Herrmann (New York City), O. Sevcik (Vienna, Austria), Leopold Auer (Petrograd); m. Blanche Bloch (cousin), Nov. 1, 1914; children—Alan, Janet. After completing studies under Auer took position as concert master and soloist with symphony orchestra, at Tiflis, in the Caucasus, 1912; returned to New York, 1913; asst. to Prof. Auer since his arrival in America; formerly head of violin dept., Washington, D.C., Coll. of Music; has appeared as soloist in leading cities of the East; conductor of The Alliance Symphony Orchestra. Author: Principles and Practice of Bowing, 1916; Scale Studies in Double-Stops, 1918; Finger-Strengthening Exercises, 1919; How to Practice, 1923. Home: New York, N.Y. Deceased.

BLOCK, Louis James, author; b. Austria, Sept. 10, 1851; s. Lazarus and Fanny (Gostorf) B.; A.B., A.M., Ph.D., Washington U., St. Louis, Mo. Lectured on Platonism at Concord Sch. of Philosophy, 1878, on philosophy of literature, Glenmore, Adirondacks, N.Y., 1885. Author: Dramatic Sketches and Poems, 1891; The New World and Other Verse, 1895; Capriccios, 1898; Many Moods and Many Minds, 1906; The World's Triumph (play), 1909; The Judge (play), 1915. Home: Oak Park, Ill. Died Dec. 8, 1927.

BLOCK, Paul, newspaper pub.; b. Elmira, N.Y., 1877; s. John and Mary B.; student Cornell U. Pres. and pub. Pittsburgh Post-Gazette, Toledo Blade, Toledo Times. Mem. Am. Soc. Newspaper Editors. Home: Greenwich, Conn. Died June 22, 1941.

BLOCK, Rudolph ("Bruno Lessing"), journalist; b. New York, Dec. 6, 1870; ed. Coll. City of New York; m. Emma Hannon; children—Rudolph, Alfred Leavitt. Began newspaper work, 1888; reporter New York Sun, 6 yrs., afterwards Sunday editor New York Recorder and reporter on World; with W. R. Hearst's newspapers, 1896—; editor comic supplement of Hearst newspapers 28 years and originator of many popular "strips" and "series"; columnist of Vagabondia from Foreign Countries, 1928—. Owner of scientific collection of canes of 1400 different woods exhibited in Smithsonian Inst. and New York Bot. Gardens. Author: Children of Men, 1903; With the Best Intentions, 1914; Lapidowitz, 1915. Died Apr. 29, 1940.

BLOCKLINGER, Gottfried, rear adm. U.S.N.; b. Dubuque, Ia., Oct. 23, 1847. Apptd. from Ia., and grad. U.S. Naval Acad., 1868; promoted ensign, Apr. 19, 1868; master, July 12, 1870; lt., Apr. 2, 1874; lt. comdr., May 21, 1895; comdr., Mar. 3, 1899; capt., June 1, 1904; rear adm., Oct. 30, 1908; retired, 1909. Was in active service during Civil War; in summer of 1864 on bd. the Marion, in pursuit of the Confederate cruisers Florida and Tallahassee; served successively in the Pacific squadron, Kearsarge, Enterprise, and Adams, 1868-82; various assignments to 1895; exec. officer, Boston, 1895-96, Navy Yard, Mare Island, Calif., 1897; exec. officer, Charleston, 1898-99; in charge recruiting sta., Chicago, 1899-1901; comd. Alert and Concord, 1901, Wheeling, 1902, Vicksburg, 1902, New Orleans, 1903; Navy Yard, Norfolk, Va., 1904; Navy Yard, New York, 1904-06; comdg. Illinois, 1906-08; mem. Naval Examining and Retiring Bds., 1908-09. Died May 18, 1930.

BLOCKSOM, Augustus Perry, army officer; b. Ohio, Nov. 7, 1854; grad. U.S. Mil. Acad., 1877. Commd. 2d lt. cav., June 15, 1877; maj. insp. gen., Apr. 20, 1905; col. of cav., Jan. 1, 1913; brig. gen., 1917; maj. gen., Aug. 5, 1917. Served on frontier in Ariz. in many campaigns against Apache Indians; operations against Sioux in S.D., 1890, 91; campaign against Santiago de Cuba, 1898; wounded in assault on San Juan Hill, July 1, 1898 (cited by War Dept. in gen. orders for "gallantry in action" and awarded silver citation star); participated in China Expdn.

(Boxer campaign), comdg. charge of 6th Cav. Squadron against Boxers (cited by War Dept. in gen. orders for "gallantry in action" and awarded silver citation star); Philippine Insurrection, 1900-02; comdr. Camp Cody, Deming, N.M., Sept. 1917-Apr. 18, 1918; hon. discharged as maj. gen. N.A., Apr. 18, 1918; brig. gen., comdr. Hawaiian Dept., Apr. 18-Nov. 7, 1918; retired Nov. 7, 1918. Bvtd. 1st lt., July 27, 1890, "for gallant services against Indians at Ash Creek, Ariz., May 7, 1880." Home: Miami, Fla. Died July 26, 1931.

BLODGET, Lorin, statistician-physicist; b. nr. Jamestown, Chautauqua Co., N.Y., May 25, 1823; ed. Jamestown Acad. and Geneva (now Hobart Coll.); asst. Smithsonian Instn., in charge of researches on climatology, 1851-52; on Pacific R.R. survey, 1852-56, for War Dept.; with Treas. Dept., 1863-77. Author: The Climatology of the United States; Commercial and Financial Resources of the United States, and about 150 volumes of financial and industrial reports and statistics. Died 1901.

BLODGETT, Henry Williams, jurist; b. Amherst, Mass., July 21, 1821; ed. at common schools and Amherst Acad.; m. Alathea Crocker, Apr. 1850. Studied land surveying and engring.; began law study at Chicago, 1842; admitted to bar, Dec. 1844; located at Waukegan, Ill., Feb. 1845; mem. Ill. legislature, 1852-54; State senator, 1859-63; U.S. dist. judge, northern dist. Ill., 1869-93 (retired); apptd. 1892, one of counsel of U.S. before arbitration tribunal U.S. and Great Britain in regard to fur seals in Bering Sea. Home: Waukegan, Ill. Died 1905.

BLODGETT, Isaac N., jurist; b. Canaan, N.H., Mar. 6, 1838; academic edn.; (LL.D.); m. Sarah A. Gerould, May 1861. Practiced law in Canaan, 1860-67; in Franklin, N.H., 1867-80; mem. N.H. legislature, 1871, 1873-74 and 1878; N.H. senate, 1879-80; constitutional conv., 1876 and 1889; judge Supreme Court, N.H., 1880-98; chief justice, 1898-1902; mayor, Franklin, N.H., 1903, 1904. Home: Franklin, N.H. Died 1905.

BLODGETT, John Taggard, judge; b. Belmont, Mass., May 16, 1859; s. William Alfred and Anna Maria (Taggard) B.; A.B., Brown U., 1880, A.M., 1883; m. Amelia Wilson Torrey, Mar. 28, 1883 (died); m. 2d, Amy de Lacy Bemiss, Aug. 15, 1900. Admitted R.I. bar, 1883, U.S. Circuit Ct., 1885, U.S. Circuit Ct. of Appeals, 1895; U.S. commr. dist. of R.I., 1890; U.S. chief supervisor elections, dist. R.I., 1892; mem. and chmn. bd. canvassers and registration, Providence, 1895-1900; mem. R.I. Gen. Assembly, 1898-1900; chmn. commn. to readjust ward lines, Providence, 1900; asso. justice Supreme Ct., R.I., 1900—. Republican. Pres. R.I. commn. to Jamestown Expn., 1907. Home: Providence. Died Mar. 4, 1912.

BLODGETT, Rufus, senator; b. Dorchester, N.H., Oct. 9, 1834; common sch. edn.; learned trade of machinist; engaged in R.R. business in N.J., 1866; supt. N.J. Southern R.R., 1874-84, N.Y. & Long Branch R.R., 1884—; organized and is pres. Citizen's Bank of Long Branch. Mayor Long Branch 5 consecutive terms; mem. N.J. legislature, 1878-80; del. Dem. Nat. convs., 1880, 1896; U.S. senator, 1887-93. Democrat. Home: Long Branch, N.J. Died 1910.

BLODGETT, Wells Howard, lawyer; b. Downer's Grove, Ill., Jan. 29, 1839; s. Israel P. and Avis (Dodge) B.; ed. Ill. Inst. (now Wheaton Coll.); admitted to bar, 1861. First lt. 37th Ill. Inf., Aug. 1, 1861; capt., Jan. 1, 1863; judge-advocate Army Frontier, with rank maj. of cav., Mar. 10, 1863; lt. col. 48th Mo. Inf., Sept. 14, 1864; col., Nov. 22, 1864; awarded Congressional Medal of Honor, "for most distinguished gallantry at Newtonia, Mo., Sept. 30, 1862"; hon. mustered out June 29, 1865; m. Emma Dickson, of Waukegan, Ill., July 20, 1865. Mem. Mo. Ho. of Rep., 1866-68, Senate, 1868-72; asst. atty., 1873-74; gen. atty., 1874-79, St. Louis, Kansas City & Northern R.R.; gen. solicitor, Wabash, St. Louis & Pacific Ry., 1879-84; gen. counsel for receiver, Wabash lines, 1884-89; gen. solicitor, Wabash R.R., 1889-1900, and v.p. and gen. counsel, 1900-09, and counsel for receivers, same corp., Dec. 1911-Nov. 1915. Home: St. Louis, Mo. Died May 8, 1929.

BLOEDE, Gertrude ("Stuart Sterne"), author; b. Dresden, Saxony, Aug. 10, 1845; then lived in U.S., 1850—; in Brooklyn, 1861—; parents were refugees of revolution of 1848. Author: Angelo; Giorgio and Other Poems; Beyond the Shadow; Piero da Castiglione (all vols. of verse); also, The Story of Two Lives (a novel). Home: Brooklyn, N.Y. Died 1905.

BLOEDE, Victor Gustave, mfg. chemist; b. Dresden, Saxony, Germany, Mar. 14, 1849; s. Dr. Gustave and Marie Franziska (Jungnitz) B.; grad. in natural science, Cooper Inst., New York, 1867, hon. Chem.E., 1920, also Peter Cooper medal; m. Elise Sehon, June 4, 1883; children—Mrs. Marie Woollcott, Carl S., Ilse, Mrs. Vida Kelly, Victor G. (dec.). Began as mfg. chemist, Brooklyn, about 1865; moved to Parkersburg, W.Va., 1873, to Baltimore, 1883; pres. Victor G. Bloede Co.; dir. W. Baltimore Bank. Prominent in philanthropic and humanitarian work; donor to State of its first hosp. for advanced consumptives, known as Marie Bloede Memorial Hosp., in honor of his mother; dir. Hosp. for Consumptives of Md.; mem. bd. dirs. Brooklyn Bur. Charities. Donor of Marie Bloede Workshop for Blind Women, operated by Brooklyn (N.Y.) Bur. of Charities; founder Summer Home for Blind Women, Suffern, N.Y.; founder of a scholarship in chemistry under control of Chemists' Club of N.Y.; donor of Physical Chemical Lab. of Cooper Union; 1st pres. West Baltimore Gen. Hosp.; apptd. (as a personal tribute) distributor of legacy of $40,000 to Hosp. for Consumptives, Md., by the late Herman B. L. Everding; a founder and pres. The Blind Players Club, Inc., of Suffern, N.Y. Financing biol. research on thyroid gland, 1929. Home: Catonsville, Baltimore Co., Md. Died Mar. 27, 1937.

BLOOD, Henry Ames, poet; b. Temple, N.H., June 7, 1838; s. Ephraim Whiting and Lavinia (Ames) B.; m. Mary E., d. Col. Ephraim F. Miller of Salem, Mass., and g.d. Gen. James Miller, U.S.A., Oct. 19, 1880. Author: History of Temple, New Hampshire; How Much I Loved Thee (drama in verse), under the anagram "Raymond Eshobel." Contributed poems to Century Mag., Jan. and Aug., 1883; Feb. and Dec., 1887; Dec., 1888; May, 1890; July, 1891; Scribner's June, 1875, and other mags. Deceased.

BLOOD, William Henry, Jr., elec. engr.; b. Charlestown, Mass., Mar. 29, 1866; s. of William Henry and Marianna (Williamson) B.; E.E., Mass. Inst. Tech., 1888; m. Grace Marie Nathan, Nov. 6, 1890. With Thomson-Houston Elec. Co., Lynn, Mass., in charge of mfg. elec. motors, etc., 1888-89; with the N. W. Thomson-Houston Co., St. Paul, Minn., 1889-90; partner Franklin Elec. Co., Kansas City, Mo., constructing elec. light and st. ry. plants and waterworks, 1890-96; superintendent Chase-Shawmut Company, mfg. electricians, Boston, 1896-97; vice-pres. Stone & Webster Engineering Corp., Boston, examination and report, construction, expert court work, 1897—. Asst. to pres. Am. Internat. Shipbuilding Corp., Phila., 1917-18. Lecturer on pub. utilities, Harvard U. Grad. Sch. of Business Admn. Republican. Conglist. Fellow Am. Inst. E.E. Home: Wellesley, Mass. Died Feb 13, 1933.

BLOODGOOD, Clare Sutton, actress; b. Long Branch, N.J., 1870; d. Edward and Annie (Sutton) Stephens (Mrs. Ann S. Stephens, author); ed. St. Johns School, Brighton, England; m. William Moller Havemeyer, 1886; 2d, John Bloodgood, Jr. (dec.), 1889; went on the stage as result of financial reverses, Jan., 1898; has played with Miss Annie Russell in Catherine and Miss Hobbs; then in Miss Amelia Bingham's co. in the Climbers. Died 1907.

BLOODGOOD, Delavan, med. dir. U.S.N., retired 1893; b. Springville, N.Y., 1831; grad. Colgate Univ., Hamilton, N.Y., 1852 (A.M.); M.D., Jefferson Med. Coll., Phila.; entered U.S.N.; asst. surgeon, 1857; med. dir., 1884. Served throughout Civil war; on active duty throughout Spanish war; mem. Loyal Legion; Holland Soc.; Order Colonial Wars; Order Foreign Wars. Home: Brooklyn, N.Y. Died 1902.

BLOODGOOD, Joseph Colt, surgeon, cancer research; b. Milwaukee, Wis., Nov. 1, 1867; s. Francis and Josephine (Colt) B.; B.S., U. of Wis., 1888; M.D., U. of Pa., 1891; m. Edith, d. Henry Holt, Sept. 1, 1908. Resident phys. Children's Hosp., Phila., 1891-92; asst. resident surgeon, Johns Hopkins Hosp., Baltimore, June-Nov., 1892; attended foreign clinics and hospitals, 1892-93; resident surgeon, Johns Hopkins Hospital, 1893-97; associate in surgery, Johns Hopkins U. and Hospital, 1897-1903; then adjunct prof. surgery, Johns Hopkins University; chief surgeon, St. Agnes' Hosp. Major Medical R.C., 1917. Mem. gen. med. com. Am. Nat. Red Cross; mem. editorial bd., in charge surgical pathology, Am. Jour. of Cancer; mem. advisory bd. Radiol. Research Inst. Fellow Am. College Surgeons, A.A.A.S. Episcopalian. Died Oct. 22, 1935.

BLOODGOOD, Wheeler Peckham, lawyer; b. Milwaukee, Nov. 4, 1871; s. Francis and Josephine M. (Colt) B.; grad. St. John's Mil. Acad., Delafield, Wis., 1887; studied law in the office of father; m. Elizabeth Twombly Farrand, Sept. 14, 1896. Admitted to Wis. bar, 1894, later to bar Supreme Ct. of Wis. and Sup. Ct. of U.S.; mem. Bloodgood, Kemper & Bloodgood; has been identified with many causes involving principles of corp. ins., bankruptcy and commercial law; gen. counsel U.S. Fidelity and Guaranty Co.; gen. counsel for Wis. of Met. Life Ins. Co., etc. Mem. Prog. Nat. Com., 1912; chmn. Wis. Defense League; mem. exec. com. Nat. Civic Fedn. (chmn. com. on study of anti-trust legislation); commd. civilian aide to Sec. of War for the State of Wis., Mar. 1, 1923. Episcopalian. Mem. Am. and Milwaukee bar assns., Am. Acad. Polit. and Social Science. Mason. Home: Milwaukee, Wis. Died Dec. 17, 1930.

BLOOM, W(illiam) Knighton, clergyman; b. Doncaster, Yorkshire, Eng., Feb. 1, 1866; s. William Knighton and Caroline (Twigg) B.; student Charterhouse Sch., London, 1883, Birkbeck Scientific and Literary Inst., London, 1884, City of London Coll., 1885, Chicago Theol. Sem., 1892-95, U. of Chicago, 1902-05; D.D., Fargo (N.D.) Coll., 1920; m. Emma Mills, July 23, 1890; 1 son, William Knighton. Came to U.S., 1890, naturalized, 1900. Ordained ministry Congl. Ch., 1898; pastor Creal Springs, Ill., 1898-1901, Sandoval, Ill., 1901-06, Oneida, Ill., 1906-09, Williston, N.D., 1909-12, asso. supt. Congl. Conf. of N.D., 1912-19; extension sec. Congl. S.S. Extension Soc., N.Y. City, 1919-26; sec. missions, Congl. Ch. Extension Bds., Washington, D.C., 1926—. Dir. of student service activities Southern Sem. Foundation, Vanderbilt U. Sch. of Religion; mem. bd. mgrs. Missionary Edn. Movement (Washington, D.C.); mem. com. Federal Council of Chs. Home: Washington, D.C. Died Mar. 14, 1934.

BLOOMFIELD, Maurice, Orientalist, philologist; b. Bielitz, Austria, Feb. 23, 1855; student U. of Chicago, 1871-74, Furman U., 1876-77, M.A., 1877; fellow Johns Hopkins, 1878-79, Ph.D., 1879; Berlin, Leipzig, 1879-81 (LL.D., Princeton, 1896; Furman, 1908; L.H.D., U. of Chicago, 1916); honoris causa Dr., U. of Padua, 1922; m. Rosa Zeisler, June 20, 1885 (died 1920); children—Elinor Marie (wife of Dr. A. S. De Witt), Arthur Leonard; m. 2d, Helen Townsend Scott, July 9, 1921. Professor Sanskrit and comparative philology, Johns Hopkins U., 1881—. Fellow Am. Acad. of Arts and Sciences. Hardy prize Royal Acad. Sciences, Munich, 1908. Author: The Atharva-Veda, 1899; Cerberus, the Dog of Hades, 1905; A Concordance of the Vedas, 1907; The Religion of the Veda, 1908; Rig-Veda Repetitions (2 vols.), 1916; Life and Stories of the Jaina Savior Pārçvanātha. Edited for 1st time from original Sanskrit manuscript the Grihyasamgraha of Gobhilaputra, and the Sutra of Kauçika; translated the Atharva-Veda in the Sacred Books of the East (edited by Max Muller); edited, with Prof. Richard Garbe, of U. of Tübingen, the Kashmirian, or Paippalâda-Veda, 1901. Home: Baltimore, Md. Died June 13, 1928.

BLOOMFIELD, Meyer, lawyer; b. Feb. 11, 1878; s. Morris and Bertha B.; B.A., College of the City of New York, 1899; B.A., Harvard Univ., 1901; student Boston Univ. Law Sch., 1903-05; m. Sylvia Palmer, June 20, 1902; children—Catherine Pauline, Joyce Thérèse, Lincoln. Admitted to Mass. bar, 1905; founder and dir. Civic Service House, Boston, 1901-10; dir. Vocation Bur. of Boston, 1909-17. Spl. commr. to Porto Rico for the War Dept., 1911; vocational expert for Bur. of Indian Affairs, 1912; labor arbitrator in garment strikes, 1912; lecturer on vocational guidance at Harvard, Columbia, Brown, U. of Calif., State Teachers' Coll., Colo., etc.; spl. prof. Boston U. Chief industrial service dept., U.S. Shipping Bd. Emergency Fleet Corp., 1918; European labor expert for Saturday Evening Post, 1918-19; founder and pub. Industrial Relations; Bloomfield's Labor Digest. Made trip to Russia as confidential observer for President Harding, 1922; consultant on orgn. problems for R. H. Macy Co., Elec. Research Corp., etc. Apptd. adviser to seniors and prof. of vocational guidance, Coll. of the City of New York, 1929; also appointed to Hunter College, New York, N.Y., 1935. Author: Vocational Guidance of Youth, 1912; The School and the Start in Life (U.S. Bur. Edn.), 1914; Youth, School and Vocation, 1915. Editor: Readings in Vocational Guidance, 1915. Author of "Labor and Compensation," 1918; "Management and Men," 1919; Preventive Management, 1930. Admitted to New York bar, 1925, Federal bar, 1934. Home: New York, N.Y. Died Mar. 1938.

BLOOMINGDALE, Emanuel Watson, lawyer; b. Rome, N.Y., Nov. 25, 1852; s. Benjamin and Hannah (Weil) B.; ed. in New York city schs.; LL.B., Columbia, 1877; m. Adèle Bernheimer, Jan. 3, 1887; 1 dau., Marion H. (wife of Dr. Herman Schwarz). Identified with large dept. store, 1883-1905; acted as receiver of many corps. and firms; pres. Pavonia Trading Co.; pres. bd. mgrs. Soc. for Reformation of Juvenile Delinquents. Mem. N.Y. and N.J. Interstate Bridge Commn., Hudson Ter-Centenary Com., Com. of Seventy, 1894; treas. Election Laws Improvement Assn.; Rep. presdl. elector, 1900; trustee Nat. McKinley Memorial Assn. Clubs: Lotos, Republican. Home: New York, N.Y. Died Feb. 6, 1928.

BLOOR, Alfred Janson; s. John and Sarah Salina (Vidler) B. Studied under a leading architect of America 3 yrs., subsequently his chief asst.; practiced architecture 31 years except during Civil War and when abroad. Fellow Am. Inst. Architects, 1861, and trustee, sec. and editor of its publs. about 10 yrs.; held various offices, also treas. New York chapter same for more than 30 consecutive yrs.; retired from personal practice, 1884, in order to devote exclusive attention to business of the Inst. and Chapter. A founder (1870) and life mem. Met. Mus. Art, and of Willard Architectural Commn. (1886); life mem. Am. Numismatic Soc. (1883); hon. and corr. mem. Royal Soc. Portuguese Architects and Archæologists (1867); mem. Am. Federation Arts, asst. sec. during Civil War of U.S. Sanitary Commn. Author: Architectural and Other Art Societies of Europe, with Suggestions for an Architectural Art Society and Branches in America, 1868; Woman's Work in the Civil War, 1866. Home: New York, N.Y. Died Nov. 19, 1917.

BLOSSOM, Harold Hill, landscape architect; b. Brooklyn, N.Y., Oct. 6, 1879; s. Frederick Augustus and Sarah Carson (Hill) B.; prep. edn., Poly. Inst., Brooklyn, and Pratt Inst. High Sch.; B.S. Amherst, 1902; M.A., Harvard, 1906, Master in Landscape Architecture, 1907; m. Minnie Motley Dawson, Sept. 23, 1908 (died Oct. 19, 1922); children—Elizabeth Thornton, Thomas, Eleanor, Margaret Blackwell; m. 2d, Louise Barnes Thompson, Feb. 16, 1926; 1 dau., Deborah. With Olmstead Bros., landscape architects, Brooklyn, 1907-19, working on Atlantic Coast from Maine to Cuba, and from Seattle to San Diego, on Pacific Coast; practiced on own account in Boston, 1919—, specializing in gardens and country estates, also real estate developments; mem. faculty Lowthorpe Sch. of Landscape Architecture, 1926-27; lecturer to Cambridge Sch. Domestic Architecture and Landscape Architecture; instr. landscape architecture, Harvard, summer 1932. Landscape engr. Conn. Valley Park Commn., 1923; apptd. by gov. mem. Conn. Valley Regional Planning Bd., 1924. Awarded Medal of Honor in landscape architecture by Architectural League of New York, 1923. Fellow Am. Soc. Landscape Architects, Boston Soc. Landscape Architects (pres. 1930-31), Archtl. League of N.Y. Republican. Unitarian. Home: West Roxbury, Mass. Died Dec. 3, 1935.

BLOSSOM, Henry Martyn, Jr., author; b. St. Louis, May 10, 1866; s. Henry Martyn and Susan S. (Brigham) B.; ed. Stoddard Sch., St. Louis; afterward engaged in insurance business at St. Louis; removed to N.Y. City; m. Marjorie Seely. Author: The Documents in Evidence; Checkers—A Hard Luck Story; The Brother of Chuck McGann. Plays: Checkers (prod. by Kirke La Shelle); The Yankee Consul (prod. by H. W. Savage); Mlle. Modiste, a comic opera (prod. by Charles Dillingham); The Prima Donna, an opera (prod. by Charles Dillingham); The Red Mill, a musical comedy (prod. by Charles Dillingham); Miss Philura (prod. by Liebler & Co.); The Slim Princess, comic opera (prod. by Charles Dillingham); Baron Trenck (English version, prod. by F. C. Whitney); The Man From Cooks, musical comedy (prod. by Klaw & Erlanger); also A Trip to Washington, The Only Girl, The Princess Pat, Eileen, etc. Home: New York, N.Y. Died Mar. 23, 1919.

BLOUNT, James Henderson, lawyer; b. Clinton, Ga., Mar. 3, 1869; s. Hon. James Henderson (M.C. from Ga. and Pres. Cleveland's spl. commr. to Hawaii, 1893) and Eugenia (Wiley) B.; A.B., U. of Ga., 1887; Columbia Univ. Law School, New York, 1890-91; Admitted to bar, 1888; practiced at Macon, Ga.; 1st lt. 3d U.S. Vol. Inf., Spanish-Am. War, 1898; 1st lt. 29th Vol. Inf., 1899-1901; U.S. dist. judge (Ct. of First Instance) in Philippines, 1901-05 (resigned on account of ill health). Special rep. U.S. State Dept. in Santo Domingo during revolution of 1914. Democrat. Mason. Author: Georgia Forms and Practice, 1898; American Occupation of the Philippines, 1912. Contbd. to Green Bag a series of articles, beginning Nov. 1907, describing incidents in circuit riding in Philippines in pioneer days; also articles on P.I. and other pub. questions, in N. Am. Review, Review of Reviews, etc. Died Oct. 7, 1918.

BLOUNT, William Alexander, lawyer; b. in Clarke Co., Ala., Oct. 25, 1851; s. Alexander Clement and Julia Elizabeth (Washington) B.; A.B., with first honors, U. of Ga., 1872 (Univ. Essay Medal, 1871), LL.B., 1873; (LL.D., U. of Fla., 1902); m. Cora N. Moreno, June 19, 1878. Began practice, Pensacola, Fla., 1873; mem. Blount & Blount, 1886-1906, Blount & Blount & Carter, 1906—; president J. A. Chaffin & Co.; City attorney, Pensacola, 1884-94; mem. Fla. Constl. Conv., 1885; chmn. commn. to revise statutes of Fla., 1892; mem. State Senate, 1903-05; mem. Capitol Reconstruction Com., 1904, 1905; mem. commn. apptd. by gov. of Fla. to simplify system of pleading and practice; mem. com. 5th Circuit U.S. to assist Sup. Ct. in revising rules in equity for U.S. circuit cts.; mem. from Fla. of Commn. on Uniform State Laws. Order of Cincinnati. Democrat. Episcopalian. Gen. counsel Florida East Coast Ry. Co. Home: Pensacola, Fla. Died June 15, 1921.

BLOXHAM, William D., governor; b. in Leon Co., Fla., July 9, 1835; A.B., William and Mary Coll., Va., 1855; m. Mary C. Davis, Nov. 28, 1856. Mem. Fla. Ho. of Rep., 1860; capt. C.S.A., 1863; presdl. elector, 1868; lt.-gov. of Fla., 1870; mem. Dem. State Exec. Com., 1876; sec. of state, Fla., 1877-81; gov., 1881-85 and 1897-1901. Apptd. minister to Bolivia, 1885, but declined; U.S. serveyor-gen., Fla., 1885-89; comptroller, 1890-96. Died 1911.

BLUE, Victor, naval officer; b. Richmond Co., N.C., Dec. 6, 1865; s. John G. and Annie M. (Evans) B.; grad. U.S. Naval Acad., 1887; m. Eleanor Foote Stuart, Oct. 17, 1899. Promoted asst. engr., July 1, 1889; advanced through grades to rear adm., Apr. 1, 1919; retired July 11, 1919. Served in Quinnebaug, 1887-89, Pensacola, 1889-91; duty Union Iron Works, San Francisco, 1891-92; served in Charleston, 1892; Navy Yard, Norfolk, 1892-93, Alliance, 1893-94, Charleston, 1894, Thetis, 1894-95, Bennington, 1895-96, Naval Acad., 1896-98, Suwanee during Spanish War, 1898, was advanced 5 numbers in rank "for extraordinary heroism" during war, and awarded medal for specially meritorious service; various assignments to 1909; comd. Yorktown, Pacific Sta., 1910; chief of staff, Pacific Fleet, 1910-11; duty, Gen. Bd., Navy Dept., May 25, 1911; chief Bur. of Navigation, Navy Dept., with rank of rear adm., Mar. 26, 1913-Aug. 10, 1916; comd. Battleship Texas, operating with British Grand Fleet under Admiral Beatty in the North Sea, 1917-18; took part in receiving the surrender of German fleet, Nov. 21, 1918; reappointed chief of Bur. of Navigation, Dec. 16, 1918, with rank of rear adm. Awarded D.S.M. "for exceptionally meritorious service" in North Sea; decorated Comdr. Order of Leopold, by King of Belgium. Home: Ft. George, Fla. Died Jan. 22, 1928.

BLUM, Robert Frederick, painter; b. Cincinnati, July 9, 1857; apprenticed in a lithographing establishment in 1871 and attended night clases at McMicken Art School of Design, Cincinnati; studied 9 months Acad. Fine Arts, Phila.; went to New York, 1879; made trips to Europe, 1880 to 1889; visited Japan, 1890-93, illustrating Sir Edwin Arnold's articles for Scribner's Mag. and executing several pictures; then devoted time mostly to mural decoration, Mendelssohn Hall, New York, being his principal work. Awards: Am. Art Assn.; Pa. Acad. Fine Arts; World's Columbian Expn.; Paris Expn., 1900. Unmarried. Home: New York, N.Y. Died 1903.

BLUMENBERG, Marc A., musical critic; b. Baltimore, May 21, 1851; ed. Loyola Coll., Baltimore. Editor Musical Courier (weekly musical jour. devoted to classical music), 1880—; pres. Blumenberg Press Corp. Expert in acoustics and musical instruments. Died Mar. 27, 1913.

BLUMENSCHEIN, William Leonard, musician; b. Brensbach, Germany, Dec. 16, 1849; s. George and Catharine B.; ed. Pittsburgh schs.; studied music at Conservatory, Leipzig, 1869-72. Teacher piano and singing, Pittsburgh, 1872-76; dir. Portsmouth (O.) Harmonic Soc. and Ironton Choral Union, 1876-78, of Philharmonic Soc., Dayton, O., 1878—; organist and choirmaster 3d St. Presbyn. Ch., Dayton, O., 1878—. Was dir. Lyra Society (male chorus and orchestra), Indianapolis, Orpheus Chorus, Springfield, O., Ohio Saengerfests at Dayton and Springfield, and of Cincinnati May Festival Chorus, 1891-96. Composer about 150 pieces for piano and voice. Home: Dayton, O. Died Mar. 27, 1916.

BLUMENTHAL, George, banker; b. Frankfort on Main, Germany; pub. sch. edn.; m. Florence Blumenthal, 1898; m. 2d. Mrs. Mary Payne Clews, 1935. Dir. Continental Fire Ins. Co., Fifth Avenue Bank, Niagara Fire Insurance Co. Grand Officer Legion of Honor (France); Grand Officer order of the Crown (Belgium). Pres. emeritus and trustee Mount Sinai Hosp.; pres. Met. Mus. Art, Am. Hosp. (Paris). Home: New York, and Paris. Died June 26, 1941.

BLUMENTHAL, Gustave Adolph, vocational analyst; b. Mulhouse, Alsace, Oct. 12, 1867; s. Joseph and Theresa (Haas) B.; ed. Mittelschule, Mulhausen, and Inst. Glay, France; grad. Inst. Schiers, Switzerland, 1888; unmarried. Came to U.S., 1910, naturalized citizen, 1916. In missionary work, Australia, 1887-89; official visitor pub. and pvt. schs., Australia, 1889-1909; anthrop. research work, China, Japan, Africa, 3 times around world; organized vocation bureau for Y.M.C.A., Buffalo and New York, N.Y., 1912; dir. U.S. Vocation Bureau, Washington, D.C., 1912-14; in French diplomatic service, 1916-18; mem. French mission to America on question of Alsace-Lorraine. Mem. advisory bd. Central Com. Vocational Guidance, 1912; vocational expert to Nat. Com. on Prisons and Prison Labor, Columbia, 1912; cons. psychologist Ferris Inst. (Big Rapids, Mich.), Grand Rapids and Flint police depts., etc. Fellow Am. Geog. Soc.; mem. French Inst. (New York). Made psychol. survey of Mich. State Prison for the Mich. Prison Commn., 1934. Home: Grand Rapids, Mich. Deceased.

BLUMER, G(eorge) Alder, physician; b. Sunderland, Eng., May 25, 1857; s. Dr. Luke and Mary Jane (Bone) B.; ed. at Newcastle-on-Tyne, Eng.; at Moravian Sch., Neuwied-on-Rhine, Germany; Lycée Corneille de Rouen, France; U. of Durham, Eng., and U. of Edinburgh; M.D., University of Pa., 1879; L.R.C.S. and L.R.C.P., Edinburgh, 1884; Litt.D., Brown U., 1905; L.H.D., Hamilton, 1921; m. Helen Antoinette Spriggs, June 23, 1886 (died 1937); children—Thomas Spriggs, Mrs. Helen Henderson Howe, Mary May, Mrs. Esther Breakenridge Marshall. Resident phys. Lankenau Hosp., Phila., 1879-80; asst. phys., 1880-86, supt., 1886-99, Utica State Hosp.; phys.-in-chief and supt. Butler Hosp., Providence, 1899-1921, supt. emeritus, 1922; editor emeritus Am. Jour. Psychiatry; lecturer on mental diseases, Albany Med. Coll., 1893-99. Pres. Am. Psychiatric Assn., 1903, Boston Society psychiatry and Neurology, 1904, N.E. Soc. Psychiatry, 1917-20. Sec. R.I. Sch. of Design, 1914-31; pres. Providence Athenæum, 1923-28; pres. R.I. Hist. Soc., 1926-27; fellow A.M.A., R.I. Med. Soc. Contbr. to Dictionary of Am. Biography. Home: Providence, R.I. Died Apr. 25, 1940.

BLUN, Henry, banker; b. Savannah, Ga., June 16, 1873; s. Henry and Catherine Ann (Savage) B.; grad. high sch., Savannah; matriculated in Lehigh U., 1890, but left coll. same yr. on account of ill health; traveled in Europe; m. Louise Elizabeth Baker, June 9, 1896; 1 son, William A. Cashier Savannah Gas Co., 1891-92; clk. U.S. custom house, 1893; salesman H. T. Moore & Co., 1894; bookkeeper, A. Ehrlich & Bro. Grocery Co., 1894-98; sec.-treas. Neal-Blun Co., 1899-1928; pres. Liberty Bank & Trust Co. (formerly Germania Bank), 1912-29, chmn. bd., 1929-33. Pres. Ga. State Sav. Assn., 1920—. Mem. Ga. N.G., 15 yrs., retiring with rank of maj.; 2d lt. 2d Ga. Vol. Inf., Spanish-Am. War, May-Dec. 1898; mem. Ga. State Mil. Rifle Team which won nearly all nat. team and individual prizes, at Seagirt, N.J., 1899; maj. 2d Batn. Ga. State Guard, Sept. 1918—. Postmaster Savannah, 1902-12; pres. Savannah Bd. of Edn.; mem. Rep. Nat. Com., 1908-12. Roman Catholic. Home: Savannah, Ga. Died Nov. 3, 1939.

BLUNT, John Ellsworth, civil engr.; b. Brainard, Tenn., Dec. 25, 1828; s. Ainsworth E. and Harriet (Ellsworth) B.; ed. Phillips Acad., Andover, Mass.; m. Augusta E. Wood, Oct. 11, 1853 (died 1911). Engr. on various rys., Ga. and Ala., until 1862; constructing engr. Chicago & Galena Union R.R., 1862-64; div. engr., 1864-88, chief engr., Nov. 1, 1888-Dec. 3, 1899, cons. engr., Dec. 3, 1899—, C.&N.W. Ry. Home: Evanston, Ill. Died Feb. 20, 1923.

BLUNT, Matthew M., soldier; b. New York, Aug. 13, 1830; entered, 1849, grad., 1853, from U.S. Mil. Acad. (A.M., Columbia Coll., 1856). Bvtd. 2d lt., 2d Arty., July 1, and commd. Sept. 30, 1853; promoted 1st lt., 2d Arty., Mar. 31, 1855; capt. 12th Inf., May 14, 1861; maj. 7th Inf., July 30, 1865; transferred to 14th Inf., Mar. 15, 1869; lt. col. 25th Inf., Oct. 7, 1874; col. 16th Inf., July 3, 1883; retired for age, Aug. 13, 1894; advanced in grade to brig. gen., U.S.A., retired, Apr. 23, 1904. In active service during Civ. War in Army of the Potomac and thrice bvtd. for gallant and meritorious services—maj., July 1, 1862 (Malvern Hill), lt. col., Dec. 13, 1862 (Fredericksburg), col., June 19, 1864 (Petersburg). Much of service after war was on frontier in Wyo., Utah and Texas. Died 1907.

BLUNT, Stanhope English, army officer; b. Boston, Sept. 29, 1850; s. Charles E. and Penelope Bethune (English) B.; grad. Oswego (N.Y.) High Sch., 1868, U.S. Mil. Acad., 1872; m. Fanny Smith, Nov. 18, 1873; children—Katharine, Evelyn B., Frances S. Apptd. 2d lt. 13th Inf., June 14, 1872; promoted through grades to col., June 25, 1906; retired from active service at own request, Sept. 1, 1912; recalled to active duty, Apr. 7, 1917; in Ordnance Office, Washington, D.C., till Aug. 4, 1918. Servide in Utah, Wyo. and Colo. with 13th Inf., 1872-74; lt. col. and col. a.d.c. to Gen. P. H. Sheridan, 1885-88; insp. small arms practice, 1885-89; instr. mathematics and in science of ordnance and gunnery, U.S. Mil. Acad., 1876-80; comdg. Rock Island (Ill.) Arsenal, 1897-1907, Springfield (Mass.) Armory, 1907-12. Chmn. Transportation Commn., Springfield, 1912-15; pres. Park Commn., Springfield Planning Commn., Springfield Hosp., 1913-17. Author: Rifle and Carbine Firing, 1885; Firing Regulations for Small Arms, 1889. Home: Springfield, Mass. Died Mar. 22, 1926.

BLYDENBURGH, Charles Edward, judge; b. Brooklyn, N.Y., Mar. 19, 1854; s. Benjamin Brewster and Mary (Brower) B.; A.B., Princeton, 1874, A.M., 1877; E.M., Sch. of Mines (Columbia), 1878; m. Isabel Cannon, June 21, 1894. In charge Wyo. territorial assay office, 1878-80; pres. Rawlins Pub. Co., 1879-98; supt. schs., Carbon Co., Wyo., 1882; admitted to Wyo. bar, 1889; mem. McMicken & Blydenburgh, 1889-1917; sec. and treas. Jack Creek Land & Cattle Co., 1884—; sec. and treas. Wyo. Mines Development Co. Mem. Territorial Legislature, 1886-88; pres. City Council, Rawlins, 1892-94; city atty., 1895-1901; chmn. Dem. State Central Com., 1896-97; del. Dem. Nat. Conv., 1900; candidate for asso. justice Supreme Court of Wyo., 1898, 1914; pres. Bd. of Edn., Rawlins, 1912-17; commr. from Wyo. to Conf. on Uniform State Laws, 1915, 16, 17, 18, 19; apptd. asso. justice Supreme Court of Wyo., Oct. 4, 1917, for term ending Jan. 6, 1919, and elected for term ending Jan. 1, 1923. Presbyn. Was mem. Internat. Rifle Team, 1877. Home: Rawlins, Wyo. Died Apr. 20, 1921.

BLYTHE, Joseph William, lawyer; b. Cransbury, N.J., Jan. 16, 1850; s. Joseph William and Ellen Henrietta (Green) B.; ed. Princeton Coll. (hon. A.B., A.M.,), Hanover (Ind.) Coll. (hon. LL.D.; also LL.D., Bethany Coll., Kan.); m. Margaret E. Gear, Oct. 15, 1877. Admitted to bar, 1876, and engaged in practice in Iowa; now gen. counsel C.,B. &Q. Ry Co. Republican. Home: Burlington, Ia. Died 1909.

BOARDMAN, Albert Barnes, lawyer; b. New York, Feb. 26, 1853; s. Norman and Annie Y. (Williams) B.; A.B., Yale, 1873; LL.B., Columbia, 1875; m. Louise Suydam. Admitted to bar, 1875, and then in practice at New York; then mem. O'Brien (Morgan J.), Boardman, Conboy, Memhard & Early. Was chmn. bd. Thompson-Starrett Co., then dir.; v.p. Lock Joint

Pipe Co.; dir. N.Y. Title & Mortgage Co., Corn Products Refining Co. Home: New York, N.Y. Died Sept. 15, 1933.

BOARDMAN, George Dana, Bapt. clergyman; b. Tavoy, Burmah, Aug. 18, 1838; s. Bapt. missionary, same name; grad. Brown Univ., 1852 (D.D.); Newton Theol. Instn., 1855 (LL.D., Univ. of Pa.); m. Ella W. Covell, Aug. 14, 1855. Entered ministry, 1855; pastor First Ch., Phila., 1864-94; pres. Christian Arbitration and Peace Soc.; pres. Am. Bapt. Missionary Union; univ. lecturer, Chicago and Bucknell. In June 1899, founded perpetual lectureship in Univ. of Pa., called the Boardman Foundation in Christian Ethics; in Nov. 1900 delivered the inaugural lecture on this foundation on the Golden Rule. Author: The Creative Work, 1878; The Model Prayer, 1879; The Epiphanies of the Risen Lord, 1879; The Divine Man, 1880; The Problem of Jesus; The Ten Commandments, 1889; Disarmament of Nations, 1890; The Coronation of Love; The Two Bibles; The Kingdom, 1899; The Church, 1901; The Golden Rule, 1901. Has delivered many addresses which have been published. Home: Philadelphia. Died 1903.

BOARDMAN, George Nye, theologian; b. Pittsford, Vt., Dec. 23, 1825; s. Deacon Samuel Ward and Ann (Gilbert) B.; brother of Samuel Ward B.; A.B., Middlebury Coll., Vt., 1847, A.M., 1850; grad. Andover Theol. Sem., 1852; (D.D., U. of Vt., 1867; LL.D., Lafayette Coll., 1889; Litt.D., Middlebury Coll., 1910); m. Anne Ambrose Walker, Aug. 15, 1854. Ordained Congl. ministry, 1854; prof. rhetoric, English literature and psychology, Middlebury Coll., 1853-59; pastor First Presbyn. Church, Binghamton, N.Y., 1859-71; prof. systematic theol., 1871-93, emeritus prof., 1893—, Chicago Theol. Sem. Pres. Monticello Female Sem., Godfrey, Ill., 1887-93; corporate mem. A.B.C.F.M., 40 yrs., resigned, 1909. Author: Lectures on Natural Theology, 1874; The Will and Virtue; Congregationalism, A History of New England Theology, 1899; etc. Home: New York, N.Y. Died Nov. 9, 1915.

BOARDMAN, Henry Bradford, banker; b. Lynnfield Center, Mass., Aug. 7, 1869; s. Rev. M. Bradford and Ellen (Barbour) B.; ed. high sch., New Britain, Conn., and prepared for Yale at New Haven; m. Carolyn Peck, Apr. 25, 1895; children—Ronald Peck, William Edward Bradford. Began in employ Mechanics Nat. Bank, New Britain, 1887, and advanced to cashier, and was sec. New Britain Trust Co. after consolidation of bank with latter co., 1907; elected treas. Schenectady Trust Co., Nov. 1907, v.p. and pres., 1918-35, retired. Republican. Mem. First Ref. Ch. Home: Schenectady, N.Y. Deceased.

BOARDMAN, Samuel Lane, journalist; b. Bloomfield (now a part of Skowhegan), Me., Mar. 30, 1836; s. Charles Franklin and Philena (Russell) B.; (hon. M.S., U. of Me., 1899); m. Ann Bates, June 12, 1860 (died 1894); m. 2d, Alma Staples, Apr. 19, 1900. Asst. editor Country Gentleman, Albany, N.Y., 1859; editor Maine Farmer, Augusta, 1861-78, American Cultivator, Boston, 1878-79; editor and pub. The Home Farm, Augusta, 1880-88; editor Kennebec Journal, 1889-92, Bangor Daily Commercial, 1895—. Mem. Me. State Bd. of Agr., 1872-74, sec. same, and trustee of State Coll., 1874-79; mem. bd. of mgrs., Me. Expt. Sta., 1885-87; sec. Me. State Agrl. Soc., 1865-74, Me. State Pomol. Soc., 1885-86. Author: Agricultural Bibliography of Maine; Handbook of the Turf; Memoir of Peter Edes, Pioneer Printer of Maine; The Naturalist of the St. Croix; Year Book of The De Burians. Edited 7 vols. on the agr. and pomology of Me. Home: Bangor, Me. Died Oct. 15, 1914.

BOARDMAN, Samuel Ward, prof. emeritus; b. Pittsford, Vt., Aug. 31, 1830; s. Deacon Samuel Ward and Ann (Gilbert) B.; brother of George Nye B.; A.B., Middlebury Coll., Vt., 1851, A.M., 1854; grad. Andover Theol. Sem., 1855; (hon. A.M., Dartmouth, 1859; D.D., Hamilton Coll., 1870; LL.D., Middlebury, 1890); m. Jane Elizabeth Haskell, Sept. 10, 1857 (died 1859); m. 2d, Sarah Elizabeth, d. Rev. David Greene, of Westboro, Mass., May 2, 1861. Ordained Congl. ministry, 1857; pastor, Norwich, Vt., 1857-59; prof. rhetoric, English lit. and psychology Middlebury Coll., 1859-61; pastor Second Presbyn. Ch., Auburn, N.Y., 1862-77. Congl. Ch., Sterling, Ill., 1879-82, Presbyn. Ch., Stanhope, N.J., 1883-89; pres., 1889-1901, prof. emeritus mental and moral science, 1901—, Maryville (Tenn.) Coll. V.p. Evang. Union, N.J.; trustee Danville Theol. Sem., Ky.; moderator synods of Onondaga and Tenn. Home: Bloomfield, N.J. Died Aug. 30, 1917.

BOARDMAN, Waldo Elias, dentist; b. Saco, Me., Sept. 1, 1851; s. Elias and Sarah Hartshorn (Hopkins) B.; D.M.D., Harvard, 1886; m. Margaret Elizabeth Brown, June 15, 1882 (died 1917); m. 2d, Mary Ellen Townsend, Feb. 14, 1921. Engaged in business, 1869-83; began practice of dentistry, Boston, 1885; instr. operative dentistry, Harvard, 1890-1900; curator Dental Mus., Harvard, 1891—; librarian, Dental Library, Harvard, 1897—; editor Quinquesimal Catalogue, Dental Dept., Harvard, 1896—; mem. administrative bd., Dental Dept., Harvard, 1899-1914. Justice of the peace, 1874—. Mem. numerous dental societies. Died Aug. 14, 1922.

BOARDMAN, William Henry, publisher, editor; b. Dixon, Ill., Aug. 3, 1846; s. Isaac S. and Mary L. (Dixon) B.; A.B., U. of Mich., 1868, C.E., 1869; m. Henrietta Frances Hall, Nov. 5, 1874. In U.S. Coast Survey, 1868; editor Dixon Telegraph, 1869-70; asst. editor Railroad Gazette, 1870; pres. Railroad Gazette, 1886—; was for yrs. editor and pres. Railroad Age Gazette and editor of Railway Gazette, London (Eng.); was chmn. bd. dirs. Railroad Age Gazette. Author: Lovers of the Woods, 1901; also stories of life in woods and fish culture in mags. Home: New York, N.Y. Died Feb. 16, 1914.

BOAS, Emil Leopold, resident dir. and gen. mgr. Hamburg-Am. Line; b. Goerlitz Germany, Nov. 15, 1854; s. Louis and Minna B.; ed. Royal Frederick William Gymnasium, Breslau, and Sophia Gymnasium, Berlin, grad., 1872; came to U.S., 1873; m. Harriet B. Sternfeld, Mar. 20, 1888. Gen. mgr. Hamburg-Am. Line, 1892—; pres. Atlas Steamship Co. Decorations: by Emperor of Germany—Knight Royal Prussian Order of the Crown, also Order of the Red Eagle; by Emperor of Austria—officer of Order of Francis Joseph; by King of Italy—chevalier Order of St. Mauritius and St. Lazarus; by King of Sweden and Norway—knight, 1st class, Order of St. Olaf; by Sultan of Turkey—comdr. Order of Osmanieh, also comdr. Order of Medjidié; by King of Greece—officer Order of the Redeemer; by president of Venezuela—comdr. Order of Bolivar. Mem. N.Y. Chamber of Commerce, Maritime Assn., Produce Exchange, German Soc., Charity Organization Soc.; dir. N.Y. Civic Fedn.; dir. Bd. of Trade and Transportation; treas. Greater New York Canal Assn., Germanistic Soc. of America. Home: New York, N.Y. Died May 3, 1912.

BOATRIGHT, William Louis, lawyer; b. Gentry Co., Mo., June 14, 1876; s. James B. and Hettie A. (Christian) B.; ed. pvt. normal sch., Stanberry, Mo.; spl. law courses, Stanford U. and U. of Denver; m. Minnie E. Stump, Feb. 7, 1898; children—Gladys A. (dec.), Byron B., Arlene M., Leland S., Virginia L. Admitted to Colo. bar, 1899, and began practice at Colorado Springs; dist. atty. First Jud. Dist. of Colo., 1920-24; atty. gen. of Colo., 1925-28 inclusive; Rep. nominee for gov. of Colo., 1928. Baptist. Mason. Home: Golden, Colo. Died Nov. 22, 1938.

BOBBS, William Conrad, publisher; b. Montgomery Co., O., Jan. 25, 1861; s. John Antrim and Joan (Crawford) B.; ed. pub. schs., Indianapolis; m. Julia Minich, June 28, 1888 (died 1894); m. 2d, Ruth Pratt, Apr. 17, 1912. Entered employ Merrill, Meigs & Co., booksellers, Indianapolis (est. 1838), 1879, becoming dir., 1890, and pres., of its successor, The Bobbs-Merrill Co., pubs., 1895—; dir. Indiana Nat. Bank, Enterprise Iron Works; chmn. exec. com. State Life Ins. Co. Mem. Merchants' Assn., Chamber of Commerce, Bd. Trade. Home: Indianapolis, Ind. Died Feb. 11, 1926.

BOCHER, Maxime, univ. prof.; b. Boston, Aug. 28, 1867; s. Prof. Ferdinand and Caroline (Little) B.; A.B., Harvard, 1888; Ph.D., Göttingen, 1891; m. Marie Niemann, of Göttingen, July 21, 1891. Instr. mathematics, 1891-94, asst. prof., 1894-1904, prof., 1904—, Harvard. One of Editors of Annals of Mathematics, 1896-1900, 1901-1907 and 1911-1914. Trans. Am. Math. Society, 1907-09, 1910-13. Author: Über die Reihenentwicklungen der Potentialtheorie, 1894; Introduction to Higher Algebra, 1907; Introduction to the Study of Integral Equations, 1909. Contbr. to math. jours.; collaborator Encyclopäie der mathematischen Wissenschaften. Exchange prof. to U. of Paris, 1913-14. Home: Cambridge, Mass. Died Sept. 12, 1918.

BOCKUS, Charles E., coal operator; b. Dorchester, Mass., July 10, 1868; s. Charles E. and Ellen C. (Dolan) B.; ed. Sch. of Mechanic Arts, Boston; m. Mary Clark Hall, Feb. 20, 1900. Reporter and editorial writer Boston Herald, 1890-1906; v.p. and receiver Helena (Mont.) Water Works, 1906-11; asst. sec. Old Colony Trust Co., Boston, 1911-13; with Clinchfield Coal Corp., 1913—, pres. and chmn. bd.; also chmn. bd. Clinchfield New York Corp.; chmn. bd. Port of Asuncion Concession Corp.; pres. Am. Woman's Realty Corp., Pacific Coast Co. Unitarian. Home: East Port Chester, Conn., and New York, N.Y. Died June 29, 1940.

BOCOCK, Clarence Edgar, normal sch. prin.; b. Castleton, Ill., Dec. 14, 1876; s. Cyrus and Eleanor Marie (Fouts) B.; A.B., U. of Ill., 1899; grad. study U. of Chicago, summers 1905, 07, winter 1929; m. Lillian Rodda Normington, Nov. 26, 1907; 1 son, Oscar Lafayette. Teacher, rural schs., 1899-1901; instr. in science, high sch., Corning, Ia., 1901-04; dean and head of science dept., State Normal Sch., Albion, Ida., 1904-20, pres., 1920—. Republican. Mason. Home: Albion, Ida. Died Oct. 1932.

BODANSKY, Meyer, biochemist, pathologist; b. Elizabetgrad, Russia, Aug. 30, 1896; s. Phineas and Eva (Geiro) B.; brought to U.S., 1907; A.B., Cornell U., 1918, Ph.D., 1923; M.A., U. of Tex., 1922; M.D., U. of Chicago, 1935; m. Eleanore Abbott, June 15, 1925; children—Samona, Eleanore Ruth. In Ordnance Dept., U.S.A., later in lab. div. of Med. Corps, 1918-19; instr. in biol. chemistry, U. of Tex. Med. Sch., 1919-23, adj. prof., 1923-25; acting asst. prof., Stanford, 1925-26; asso. prof., U. of Tex., 1926-30, prof. pathol. chemistry, 1930—; dir. labs. John Sealy Hosp., John Sealy Memorial Research Lab.; visiting prof. of physiol. chemistry, Am. Univ. of Beirut, Syria, 1932-33. Certificate Am. Bd. of Pathology. Author: Introduction to Physiological Chemistry, 1927, 30, 34, 38; Laboratory Manual of Physiological Chemistry (with M. Fay), 1928, 31, 35, 38; Biochemistry of Disease (with O. Bodansky), 1940. Contbr. to Jour. Biol. Chemistry, Am. Jour. Clin. Pathology (mem. editorial bd.), etc. Home: Galveston, Tex. Died June 14, 1941.

BODANZKY, Artur, conductor; b. Vienna, Austria, Dec. 16, 1877; s. Carl and Hanna (Feuchtwang) B.; ed. High Sch. and Conservatory, Vienna; m. Ada Elisa Perutz, June 1, 1909; children—Elizabeth Maria, Carl Arthur. Began as conductor at Budveis, Bohemia, 1900; came to America, 1915, as conductor Met. Opera Co., New York, continuing in that capacity until Apr. 1929; conductor Society of Friends of Music, 1916—. Composer: Oberon (by Von Weber) new version, 1917; also recitatives for performance of Weber's "Der Freischütz" at Metropolitan Opera House, 1923. Translator of Don Giovanni (by Mozart) into German, 1911, also of Beethoven's "Fidelio." Died Nov. 23, 1939.

BODDY, William Henry, clergyman; b. Berkeley, Calif., Jan. 5, 1886; s. William and Ruth (Woodcock) B.; prep. edn., Seattle (Wash.) Sem.; B.A., Reed Coll., Portland, Ore., 1914; D.D., Whitman Coll., Walla Walla, 1923; m. Elsa C. Coder, Dec. 25, 1907; children—Helen Louise, William Coder (dec.). Ordained ministry Presbyterian Ch., 1908; pastor Spokane, Wash., 1908-12, Portland, Ore., 1912-15, Hood River, Ore., 1918-23, Woodlawn Presbyn. Ch., Chicago, 1923-25, First Presbyn. Ch., Chicago, 1925-32, Westminster Ch., Minneapolis, 1932—. Mem. faculty Reed Coll., 1915-16; regent Whitman Coll., 1923-24; trustee Albany Coll., Ore., 1922-24, Macalester Coll., 1932— (chmn. instrn. com.); mem. Presbyn. Ch. Extension Bd., Bd. of Nat. Missions of Presbyn. Ch. of U.S.A.; dir. Minneapolis Ch. Fedn.; dir. Minneapolis Y.M.C.A. Home: Minneapolis, Minn. Deceased.

BODE, Frederick, merchant; b. Exkwarden, Germany, Aug. 20, 1856; s. Frederick and Sophia (Kimmann) B.; ed. Hanover Realschule; m. Augusta Ebeling, June 19, 1880 (died 1907); m. 2d, Esther Ellen Simpson, June 19, 1909. Came to America, 1870, and entered employ of D. B. Fisk & Co., wholesale millinery, Chicago, as errand boy, 1871; advanced to city buyer; with Gage Bros. & Co., 1874-76; with Edson, Keith & Co. as buyer and mgr. of hat dept., 1876-92; with others, 1892, purchased the business of Gage Bros. & Co., and became its pres. Pres. The Millinery Jobbers' Assn., 1902-11; mem. exec. com. Chamber of Commerce of U.S. Republican. Home: Chicago, Ill. Died Dec. 23, 1934.

BODENHAMER, Osee Lee, nat. comdr. Am. Legion; b. Goldthwaite, Tex., June 27, 1892; s. John Richard and Anna Lee (Hopkins) B.; grad. Howard Payne Coll., 1912; A.B., Baylor U., 1914, LL.D., 1930; m. Irene Richardson, Oct. 13, 1930. Teacher San Marcos Academy, Tex., 1914-17; real estate and ins. business, 1920—; chmn. bd. Ark. Finance Co. Enlisted in U.S. Army, 1917; hon. disch. as maj. inf., Apr. 1919. Mem. Ark. Honorary Tax and Business Law Commn.; pres. Ark. Real Estate Assn., Baylor Alumni Assn.; also Parks & Playgrounds Assn., Bd. of Pub. Affairs, and DeSoto Boy Scout Council—all of El Dorado, Ark. Served as dept. comdr. Am. Legion of Ark.; nat. comdr. Am. Legion, 1929-30; mem. Forty and Eight. Democrat. Baptist. Home: El Dorado, Ark. Died June 19, 1933.

BODENWEIN, Theodore, newspaper pub.; b. Dusseldorf, Germany, Jan. 25, 1864; brought to U.S., 1869; ed. pub. schs.; twice married. Began as apprentice New London (Conn.) Day, 1881, owner, 1891—; sec. of state of Conn., 1905-09. Republican. Mason. Home: New London, Conn. Died Jan. 12, 1939.

BODINE, James Morrison, physician; b. Fairfield, Ky., Oct. 2, 1831; s. Alfred and Fanny Maria (Ray) B.; ed. St. Joseph's Coll., Ky., and Hanover Coll., Ind.; M.D., Ky. Sch. of Medicine, 1854; (LL.D., Hanover Coll., 1903); m. Mary Elizabeth Crow, Dec. 25, 1855. Practiced in Austin, Tex., Leavenworth, Kan., Louisville, Ky.; demonstrator of anatomy, 1856-57; prof., 1864-66, Ky. Sch. Medicine; prof. anatomy, 1866-1911, dean, 1867-1907, pres. of faculty, 1907—, U. of Louisville. Home: Louisville, Ky. Died Jan. 1915.

BODINE, Samuel Taylor, business man; b. Phila., Pa., Aug. 23, 1854; s. Samuel Tucker and Louisa Wylie (Millikin) B.; g.g.s. Capt. John Bodine, of Revolutionary Army; A.B., U. of Pa., 1873, A.M., 1876, LL.D., 1928; m. Eleanor G. Warden, Nov. 15, 1883; children—Louise W. (Mrs. Harold W. How), Eleanor G. (Mrs. William G. Perry), William W. Began as shipping clk. Royersford (Pa.) Iron Foundry Co., later with Cohansey Glass Co., Bridgeton, N.J.; with Peter Wright & Sons, 1876-82; began as sec. and treas. United Gas Improvement Co., Phila., 1882, then chmn. board; dir. Fidelity-Phila. Trust Co., Pa. Co. for Ins. on Lives & Granting Annuities. Vice-chmn. Appeal Bd. No. 1, Eastern Dist. of Pa. under Selective Service Act, 1917. Home: Villanova, Pa. Died Aug. 19, 1932.

BODLEY, Temple, author; b. Louisville, Ky., Aug. 5, 1852; s. William Stewart and Ellen (Pearce) B.; LL.B., U. of Louisville, 1875; m. Edith Fosdick, Nov. 22, 1892; children—Ellen (Mrs. Wm. Alexander Stuart), Edith (Mrs. James Walker Stites), Temple. Practiced law at Louisville, 1875-1910; park commr., Louisville, 1893-97. First pres. Louisville Art Assn., Bd. of Tuberculosis Hosp. of Louisville. Author: Richard A. Robinson, A Memoir, 1903; Littell's Political Transactions—Introduction, 1926; George Rogers Clark, His Life and Public Services, 1926; History of Kentucky before Louisiana Purchase in 1803, 1928; Our First Great West in War, Diplomacy and Politics, 1937. Home: Louisville, Ky. Died Nov. 23, 1940.

BODY, Charles William Edmund, theologian; b. Clapham, Eng., Oct. 4, 1851; s. Rev. E. E. B.; ed. St. John's Coll., Cambridge, Eng., 1871-76, fellow, 1877-81; B.A., U. of Cambridge, Eng., 1875, Tyrrwhit Hebrew scholar, M.A., 1878; (D.C.L., Trinity U., Toronto, 1883; S.T.D., Hobart, 1887; D.D., Bishop's Coll., Can.); m. Frances Mary Perry, Chesterton, Cambridgeshire, Eng., 1881. Deacon, 1876, priest, 1877, P.E. Ch.; curate Chesterton, 1876-81; provost and vice-chancellor, Trinity U., Toronto, 1881-94; prof. O.T. lit. and interpretation, Gen. Theol. Sem., 1894—. Author: The Permanent Value of Genesis (Paddock lectures for 1894), 1894. Died Sept. 20, 1912.

BOEHMER, Max, mining engr.; b. Lüneburg, Germany, Feb. 27, 1847; s. Louis (privy councilor) and Marie (Wahlstab) B.; ed. Poly. Inst., Hanover, Germany, 1867-69; m. Isabelle C. Canterbury, June 1880. Asst. U.S. engr. on improvements of Miss. and Mo. rivers, 1872-79; consulting mining engr., Leadville, Colo., 1879-98; then in Denver; made specialty of exam. of mines in Western states. Home: Denver, Colo. Died 1913.

BOGAN, William Joseph, supt. schools; b. Mackinac Island, Mich., Oct. 26, 1870; s. Francis and Celia (McCarthy) B.; Ph.B., U. of Chicago, 1909; many post-grad. courses, including tech. course Armour Inst. Tech., Chicago; studied music at Chicago Conservatory of Music and under pvt. teachers; m. Elizabeth Shelley, June 30, 1906; children—Marcella, Katherine, William Shelley. Teacher and prin. elementary sch. and high sch. in Mich.; teacher grades one to eight, Washington Elementary Sch., Chicago, 1893-1900; prin. Washington Elementary Sch., 1900-04, Lane Tech. High Sch., 1905-24; asst. supt. schs., Chicago, 1924-28, supt. schs., 1928—. Chmn. State Com. on Illiteracy, Ill., 1930—. Catholic. Home: Chicago, Ill. Died Mar. 24, 1936.

BOGART, John, engr.; b. Albany, N.Y., Feb. 8, 1836; s. John Henry and Eliza (Hermans) B.; B.A., Rutgers, 1853, M.A., 1856; (Sc.D. 1912); m. Emma Cherington Jefferis, Nov. 2, 1870. In engr. corps N.Y.C. R.R., state canals of N.Y.; U.S. engr. Ft. Monroe, Va., and other points during the war, 1861-66; chief engr. park commn., Brooklyn; engaged on many important works for govt. and pvt. corps., including pub. and municipal works at Albany, New Orleans, Chicago, Nashville, Baltimore, Buffalo, Norfolk, Kansas City, Toronto, Keene, Rochester, etc., 1877—; 6 yrs. chief engr. dept. public parks, N.Y.; 4 yrs. state engr. N.Y.; engr. State Bd. of Health, N.Y.; constructing engr. of Washington Bridge, New York; Harbors of Venezuela; engr. hydraulic and electric development of power at Niagara Falls, Sault Ste. Marie, Massena, St. Lawrence River, Cascade, Brit. Columbia, Knoxville, Atlanta, Chattanooga, Verde, Ariz., and Southern Va., Neb., and Youghiogheny Power companies; cons. engr. several railways, Rapid Transit Commn., New York, Essex Commn. (N.J.), Southern Colo. Power & Rys.; advisory and expert engr. in many cases; chief engr. Chattanooga & Tenn. River Power Co.; mem. various bds. Lt. col. and chief engr. N.G.S.N.Y. Del. for U.S. Govt. at Internat. Congress of Navigation, Düsseldorf, Germany, 1902, Milan, Italy, 1905, St. Petersburg, Russia, 1908, pres. inland navigation sect., Phila., 1912; mem. Permanent Bd. of Internat. Navigation Congresses; only civilian mem. U.S. Govt. Bd. on the Lakes to the Gulf Waterway; mem. Municipal Art Commn. of New York. Hon. mem. A.I.A. Author: Engineering Feats; Papers and Discussions. Home: New York, N.Y. Died Apr. 25, 1920.

BOGARTE, Martin Eugene, college prof.; b. Republic, O., May 3, 1855; s. Martin V. and Nancy (Stewart) B.; student, Northwestern Normal Sch., Republic, O., 1870-72, Valparaiso (Ind.) Coll., 1873-78, Boston U., and Mass. Inst. Tech., 1878-80; (hon. A.M., Valparaiso U., 1885); m. Lillian A. Chamberlin, 1879 (died 1904); m. 2d, Lida M. Homfeld, Aug. 1, 1908. Prof. mathematics, 1880—, sec. bd. trustees, 1909—, Valparaiso U. Pres. M. E. Bogarte Book Co., 1904—, Security State Bank, Gary, Ind., 1910—. Alderman, Valparaiso, 1896-98. Republican. Mem. Disciples of Christ. Mason. Author: Manual of Elocution, 1888; Manual of Orthoepy, 1890. Home: Valparaiso, Ind. Deceased.

BOGERT, Edward Strong, rear adm.; b. Geneva, N.Y., May 7, 1836; s. Stephen Van Rensselaer and Amanda (Strong) B.; ed. Dwight's High Sch., Brooklyn; m. Helen Hart, June 6, 1866. Apptd. asst. surgeon U.S.N., June 10, 1861; promoted passed asst. surgeon, June 22, 1864; surgeon, Apr. 6, 1866; med. insp., Sept. 10, 1882; med. dir., Nov. 28, 1889; retired, May 7, 1898; advanced to rank of rear adm., June 29, 1906, for services during Civil War. Served on various vessels and at various stas. during Civil War; fleet surgeon, Aug. 1, 1884-Sept. 9, 1886; pres. Naval Examining Bd., New York, Oct. 1-Nov. 28, 1889; in charge Naval Hosp., New York, 1892-95. Died 1911.

BOGGS, Carroll Curtis, judge; b. Fairfield, Ill., Oct. 19, 1843; s. Richard L. and Sarah A. (Wright) B.; student lit. dept., U. of Mich., 1862-63, law dept., 1863-64; m. Sarah A. Shaeffer, Oct. 31, 1870. Admitted to bar, 1866, and practiced at Fairfield; state's atty. Wayne Co., 1873-77; judge Co. Ct., 1877-83; judge Circuit Ct., 1885-97 (Appellate Div., 1891-97); asso. justice Supreme Ct., Ill., 1897-1906 (chief justice, 1900-01). Dem. nominee in Ill. Ho. of Rep. for U.S. senator, 1907; del.-at-large Dem. Nat. Conv., 1908, 4th Am. Peace Congress, 1913. Chmn. local chapter Am. Red Cross; chmn. Wayne Co., Ill., Liberty Loan League. Home: Fairfield, Ill. Deceased.

BOGGS, Frank M., artist; b. Springfield, O., Dec. 6, 1855; s. W. G. B.; studied art at École des Beaux Arts, Paris, and under Gérôme; has exhibited in leading cities of France and Germany; silver medal, Salon Exhbn., 1889; 1st prize, Am. Art Gallery, New York. Picture, "Place de la Bastille," Paris, purchased by French Government for Luxemburg Mus., and "Isigny," for Mus. of Niort; has pictures many pvt. galleries in France. Died Aug. 11, 1926.

BOGGS, Gilbert Hillhouse, prof. chemistry; b. Memphis, Tenn., Oct. 2, 1875; s. William Ellison and Marion Brackett (Alexander) B.; B.S., U. of Ga., 1896; Ph.D., U. of Pa., 1901; m. Emily Boulton Newbold, Aug. 24, 1904; 1 son, Gilbert Hillhouse. Instr. chemistry, U. of Me., 1901-03; successively instr., asst. prof., asso. prof. and prof. of chemistry, Ga. Sch. of Tech., 1903-25, head dept. of chemistry, 1925-35, dir. of dept. of chemistry and chem. engring., 1935—, dean graduate courses, 1935-40. Fellow A.A.A.S., Am. Inst. of Chemists. Presbyn. Home: Atlanta, Ga. Died May 14, 1941.

BOGGS, Thomas Richmond, M.D.; b. Memphis, Tenn., Oct. 2, 1875; s. William Ellison and Marion Brackett (Alexander) B.; B.Sc., U. of Ga., 1896, grad. student same, 1896-97; Med. Dept. U. of Pa., 1897-98; Med. Dept. Johns Hopkins, 1898-1901, M.D., 1901; studied U. of Tübingen, Germany, 1903; m. Kate Newell Doggett, Nov. 1928. House officer, 1901-02, asst. resident phys., 1902-03 and 1904-08, resident phys., 1908-11, and students' med. adviser, Johns Hopkins Hosp.; instr. and asso. in medicine, 1904-11, asso. prof. medicine, 1911-15, asso. prof. clin. medicine, 1915-31, asso. prof. of medicine, 1931—, Johns Hopkins U.; physician-in-chief, Baltimore City Hosp. at Bay View, 1911—; asst. visiting phys., Johns Hopkins Hosp., 1915-28, visiting phys., 1928—. Consultant U.S. Vet. Bur., Washington. Democrat. Presbyn. Maj., Med. R.C., 1917; apptd. chief med. officer Base Hosp. No. 18 (Johns Hopkins Unit), with A.E.F. in France, June 1917; col. Med. Corps U.S.A. and med. consultant, Air Service, A.E.F.; hon. disch., Apr. 30, 1919. Officer Order SS. Maurizio e Lazzaro (Italian); Order of the Purple Heart (U.S.), 1932. Home: Baltimore, Md. Died Sept. 2, 1938.

BOGGS, William Ellison, clergyman; b. Ahmednuggar, British India, May 12, 1838; s. Rev. George W. and Isabella Williamson (Ellison) B.; brought to America early in childhood; A.B.; S.C. Coll., 1859, A.M., 1862; grad. Columbia (S.C.) Theol. Sem., 1862; (D.D., Southwestern Presbyn. U., 1873; LL.D., Central U. of Ky., 1899); m. Marion B. Alexander, Nov. 2, 1970. Ordained Presbyn. ministry, 1862; chaplain 6th S.C. Regt., C.S.A., 1862-65; pastor First Ch., Columbia, S.C., 1866-71, Second Ch., Memphis, Tenn., 1871-79, Central Ch., Atlanta, 1879-82; prof. ecclesiastical history and ch. govt., Columbia Theol. Sem., 1882-85; pastor Second Ch., Memphis, 1885-89; chancellor U. of Ga., 1889-99; pastor First Ch. Jacksonville, Fla., 1900-08; Gen. Assembly's sec. of Christian Edn. and Ministers' Relief, with special charge of sch. and coll. work. Presbyn. Ch. U.S., 1909-12; retired. Home: Waynesville, N.C. Died Aug. 1920.

BOGGS, William Robertson, soldier; b. Augusta, Ga., Mar. 18, 1829; s. Archibald and Mary Ann (Robertson) B.; grad. U.S. Mil. Acad., 1853; m. Mary Sophia, d. Col. John Symington, U.S.A., Dec. 19, 1855. Mentioned in general orders by Lt. Gen. Scott during winter of 1859-60; resigned from U.S.A., 1861; served in C.S.A. from organization until disbanded in 1865; attained the rank of brig. gen.; served as chief of staff Trans.-Mississippi dept., Jan., 1863, until close of war; has followed occupations of architect, civ. engr., 1865—, and was for 5 yrs. prof. mechanics, Va. Mech. Coll. Home: Winston, N.C. Died 1911.

BOGLE, Robert Boyd, dentist; b. Midland, Tenn., Mar. 22, 1875; s. Robert Caldwell and Mattie (Boyd) B.; ed. Winchester Normal Coll., 1889-92; M.D., Vanderbilt, 1894; D.D.S., Northwestern U. Dental Sch., 1895; m. Clara Louise Jungerman, June 14, 1905; children—Robert Boyd, Martha Elisabeth. Practiced at Nashville, 1895-1933; prof. exodontia, roentgenology and mouth surgery, Sch. of Dentistry, Vanderbilt U., 1905-26, dean of Sch. of Dentistry, 1919-26, prof. clin. dental surgery and chief dental clinic, Sch. of Medicine, 1931-33, emeritus, 1933—. Mem. Med. Advisory Bd., Nashville, World War. Fellow A.M.A., Am. Coll. Dentists. Presbyn. Mason. Home: Nashville, Tenn. Died May 25, 1941.

BOGLE, Sarah Comly Norris, librarian; b. Milton, Pa.; d. John Armstrong and Emma Ridgway (Norris) B.; ed. Miss Stevens' Sch., Germantown, Pa.; certificate, Drexel Inst. Library Sch., 1904; (A.M., Juniata Coll., 1917). Librarian Juniata Coll., 1904-07; branch librarian Queens Borough (N.Y.) Pub. Library, 1909; librarian East Liberty Br. Carnegie Library, Pittsburgh, 1909-11; head of children's dept., Carnegie Library, Pittsburgh, 1911-17; prin. Carnegie Library School, 1911-20; asst. sec. A.L.A., 1920—; sec. Temporary Library Training Bd. of A.L.A., 1923-24, sec. Bd. of Edn. for Librarianship of A.L.A., 1924; dir. summer library course, Paris Am. Com. for Work in Devastated France, 1923; dir. of Paris Library Sch., under auspices of A.L.A., 1924—. Mem. A.L.A. (council 1917-20). Republican. Episcopalian. Home: Bellefonte, Pa. Died Jan. 11, 1932.

BOGLE, Thomas Ashford, lawyer; b. Guernsey Co., O., May 14, 1852; s. Samuel and Margaret (Gist) B.; ed. State Normal Sch., Leavenworth, Kan., 1875; LL.B., U. of Mich., 1888; m. Alice Burgard, Aug. 27, 1878. Was teacher of dist. schs., prin. city schs.; co. supt. pub. instrn., Marion Co., Kan.; admitted to bar, 1879, and engaged in practice at Marion, Kan.; co. atty., Marion Co.; removed to Mich. and then practicing at Ann Arbor; city atty., Ann Arbor; prof. law, U. of Mich., 1894-1917, prof. emeritus; was judge of the practice court, U. of Michigan. Presbyn. Democrat; has been Dem. nominee for judge Supreme Ct. of Mich. Editor 4th edit. Pomeroy's Code Remedies. Home: Ann Arbor, Mich. Died June 17, 1921.

BOGLE, Walter Scott, coal mcht.; b. Dover, N.H., Apr. 3, 1852; s. Daniel and Mary (Boyd) B.; moved to Chicago with parents at 9; grad. Chicago High Sch., 1868; m. Delia E. Stearns, Mar. 1872. Entered father's coal business; was mgr. Del. & Hudson Canal Co.; pres. Crescent Coal & Mining Co. until 1914; pres. W. S. Bogle & Co., Retlaw Mines Co., Essanbee Mines Co. Mem. West Park Bd., Chicago, 3 yrs. Democrat. Mason. Pres. Iroquois Club. Home: Chicago, Ill. Died May 25, 1922.

BOGUE, Virgil Gay, engr.; b. at Norfolk, N.Y., July 20, 1846; s. George Chase and Mary (Perry) B.; C.E., Rensselaer Poly. Inst., Troy, N.Y., 1868; m. Sybil Russell Bogue, Mar. 2, 1872. Asst. engr., Prospect Park, Brooklyn, 1868-69; asst. engr. Oroya Ry. and mgr. Trajille Ry., Peru, S.A., 1869-79; asst. engr. N.P. R.R. (discovered Stampede Pass), supervised constrn. across Ida. and Wash., 1880-86; chief engr. U.P. R.R., 1886-91; consulting engr., New York, 1891—. Mem. commn. apptd. by President Harrison to investigate methods for improving navigation of Columbia River; consulting engr. for Govt. of New Zealand on proposed ry. across South Island; cons. engr. Dept. Pub. Works, New York, Western Md. R.R., 1903-06; chief engr. and v.p. Western Pacific Ry., 1905-09. Prepared the plan and report for Greater Seattle, Wash.; for harbor of Tacoma and for Grays Harbor, Wash., etc. Fellow Am. Geog. Soc. Office: 15 William St., New York. Died Oct. 14, 1916.

BOHANNON, William Everette, prof. edn.; b. Beech Grove, Ky., Mar. 6, 1882; s. Nathaniel Brown and Tommie (Robertson) B.; B.S., Southern Normal Coll., Bowling Green, Ky., 1904, A.B., 1906; A.B., Ind. U., 1915, A.M., 1916; studied U. of Chicago; m. Ora Ella Daniel, July 31, 1908; 1 dau., Ora Frances. Teacher rural schs., Ky., 2 yrs.; supt. city schs., Ky., La. and Tenn., 1908-14; prof. edn. and psychology, Howard Coll., Birmingham, Ala., 1918—; dean School of Education same coll., 1926—, also dir. Summer Sch., Extension Dept., and Bur. Cooperative Research. Democrat. Baptist. Author: A Philosophy of Education; Hypnotism. Home: Birmingham, Ala. Died Oct. 26, 1940.

BOHM, Max, painter; b. Cleveland, O., Jan. 21, 1868; s. H. E. B.; pupil of Jean Paul Laurens, Lefebvre and Benjamin Constant, Paris; m. Zella Newcomb, 1898. First went to Europe, 1887; first picture exposed in Paris Salon, 1889. Awarded many acad. prizes and gold medal, Paris Salon, 1898; silver medal, Paris Expn., 1900; bronze medal, Buffalo Expn., 1901; silver medal, St. Louis Expn., 1904; gold medal, Panama P.I. Expn., San Francisco, 1915;

Thomas B. Clarke prize, N.A.D., 1917, A.N.A., 1917, N.A., 1920. Mem. Archtl. League of N.Y. Home: Bronxville, N.Y. Died Sept. 19, 1923.

BOIES, Henry Martyn, pres. Moosic Powder Co., the Enterprise Powder Co.; trustee Scranton City Guard; b. Lee, Mass., Aug. 18, 1837; grad. Yale, 1859 (A.M.); m. Emma G., 1861, d. Rev. Thomas C. Brainerd, D.D., Phila.; 2d, Elizabeth, 1870, d. Thomas Dickson, Scranton. Inventor of cartridge-package for blasting powder and a new and improved steel-tired car wheel. Pres. Dickson Mfg. Co., Boies Steel Wheel Co., Scranton Bd. of Trade; mem. Bd. Public Charities, Pa., and com. on lunacy of Pa.; col. 13th regt., Nat. Guard of Pa. Delegate to Nat. Rep. conv., 1884, and to Internat. Conf. on Arbitration, Washington, 1896; pres. Scranton City Club. Author: Prisoners and Paupers, 1893; The Science of Penology, etc. Home: Scranton, Pa. Died 1903.

BOIES, Horace, governor; b. Aurora, Erie Co., N.Y., Dec. 7, 1827; attended dist. school; went to Wis. Ty., 1844, landing at Racine, after voyage around the lakes, with 75 cents in his pocket; worked on farm 6 yrs., attending school winters during the last 4 yrs., of these; studied law in Erie Co., N.Y.; admitted to bar, 1849; practiced at and nr. Buffalo, 1849-67; elected to N.Y. Gen. Assembly, 1858, as Whig; became Republican; moved to Waterloo, Ia., 1867, and began practice there; left Rep. party because of opposition to its tariff and prohibition policy; then acted with Democratic party; gov. of Iowa, 2 terms, 1890-94; only Dem. gov. of Ia. since Rep. party was organized; defeated for 3d term, 1893; stood 2d in balloting for President by Dem. Nat. Conv., 1896; Dem. candidate for Congress, 3d Ia. Dist., 1902. Home: Waterloo, Ia. Died Apr. 5, 1923.

BOIES, William Dayton, congressman; b. Boone Co., Ill., Jan. 3, 1857; s. Wm. Dayton and Sarah C. (Bugbee) B.; ed. pub. schs.; LL.B., State U. of Ia., 1880; m. Lillian E. Bidinger, Nov. 24, 1881; children—Leon Luis, Russell Lowell. Began practice at Sheldon, Ia., 1881; judge 21st Jud. Dist. of Ia., 1913-18 (resigned); mem. 66th to 70th Congresses (1919-29), 11th Ia. Dist. Trustee Morningside Coll., Sioux City, Ia. Mason. Home: Sheldon, Ia. Died May 31, 1932.

BOIFEUILLET, John Theodore, journalist; b. Macon, Ga., Aug. 3, 1859; s. John T. and Anne Lydia (McKinnon) B.; A.B., Mercer U., Macon, 1876, A.M., 1880, LL.D., 1922; m. Clara Augusta Nutting, July 5, 1882; children—Mrs. John A. Crawford, Mrs. Frederick R. Jones. Formerly editor Macon Evening News; also mng. editor and asst. editor Macon Telegraph; now special writer Atlanta (Ga.) Journal; mem. Ga. Ho. of Rep., 1890-98 (speaker pro tem, 1892-93); clk. same, 1898-1917 (longest service in Ga. legislative annals); attached to Am. Embassy, London, Eng., 1915-16; apptd. mem. Railroad Commn. of Ga., by Gov. Harris, 1916, and elected without opposition, 1918, for unexpired term of 1 yr. and full term of 6 yrs., vice chmn. same; state fuel distributor, 1922-23; apptd. by Gov. Northern life trustee Ga. Sch. for the Deaf; apptd. pub. service commr. by Gov. Walker, 1926; unanimously elected sec. of Ga. Senate, 2 terms, 1931-35. Col. on staff of Gov. Atkinson. Private sec. to U.S. Senator A. O. Bacon, and sec. Senate Foreign Relations Com.; frequent del. to Dem. convs.; offered place in European consular service by President Cleveland, 1893, but declined. Presbyn. Democrat. Home: Macon, Ga. Deceased.

BOILEAU, Philip, artist; b. Quebec, Can., June, 1863; s. Baron Charles and Susan Taylor (Benton) B.; ed. in Eng.; studied art in Italy; m. Emily Gilbert, Oct., 1907. Home: New York, N.Y. Died Jan. 18, 1917.

BOISE, Otis Bardwell, music teacher; b. Oberlin, O., Aug. 13, 1844; s. Dr. Otis and Elvira B.; ed. Cleveland pub. schs.; studied music in Leipzig; m. Annie V. Stockly, Jan. 12, 1869. Settled in New York as teacher of composition, New York Conservatory, and organist of John Hall's Ch. In Europe composing, 1876-77, and had the benefit of Liszt's advice and criticism; resumed teaching in New York, 1878-81; in business in New York, 1881-88; in professional work. Author: Harmony Made Practical, 1900; Music and Its Masters, 1901. Died Dec. 2, 1912.

BOISOT, Louis, law author; b. Dubuque, Ia., May 23, 1856; s. Louis and Albertina (Bush) B.; A.B., Hamilton Coll., 1877; A.M., 1898; LL.B., Columbia, 1879; m. Mary Spencer, May 13, 1887; children—Elizabeth (dec.), Pauline. Admitted to bar, 1880; practiced at Chicago, 1880-1903; trust officer First Trust & Savings Bank, Chicago, 1904-12, v.p. 1912-21; dir. West Side Trust and Savings Bank, Liberty Trust and Savings Bank, Community State Bank. Trustee Rollins Coll., Presbyterian Home; commr. to Presbyn. Gen. Assembly, 1884, 1922. Author: By-Laws of Private Corporations, 1892, 1902; Treatise on the Law of Mechanics' Liens, 1897. Home: La Grange, Ill. Died July 21, 1933.

BOISSEVAIN, Inez Milholland; b. New York, Aug. 6, 1886; d. John W. and Jean (Torrey) Milholland; ed. Comstock Sch., New York; Kensington High Sch., London, Eng.; Willard Sch., Berlin, Germany; A.B., Vassar Coll., 1909; LL.B., New York U. Law Sch., 1912; married. Prominent in shirt waist and laundry strikes, New York, 1912; active advocate of woman suffrage. Socialist. Mem. Polit. Equality League, Women's Polit. Union, Nat. Child Labor Com., Women's Social and Polit. Union, England, Fabian Soc., England. Died Nov. 25, 1916.

BOK, Edward William, editor; b. Helder, Netherlands, Oct. 9, 1863; s. William J. H. and Sieke Gertrude (van Herwerden) B.; came to U.S. at age of 6; ed. pub. schs., Brooklyn, N.Y.; LL.D., conferred by Pope Pius, 1907, Rutgers, 1923, Tufts, 1923, Williams, 1926; m. Mary Louisa, d. Cyrus H. K. Curtis, Oct. 22, 1896. Stenographer, 1884-88; edited Brooklyn Magazine at 19; conducted The Bok Syndicate Press, 1886-91; editor in chief The Ladies' Home Journal, 1889-1919. Created $100,000 Am. Peace Award, 1923, Harvard Advertising Awards, 1923. Author: The Young Man in Business; Successward, 1895; Why I Believe in Poverty, 1915; The Americanization of Edward Bok, 1920; Two Persons, 1922; A Man from Maine, 1923; Twice Thirty, 1924; Dollars Only, 1926; Perhaps I Am, 1928. Home: Merion, Pa. Died Jan. 9, 1930.

BOLDT, George C., hotel propr. Pres. Waldorf-Astoria Hotel Co., Waldorf-Astoria Segar Co., Waldorf Importation Co., Apollinaris Agency Co.; propr. Bellevue-Stratford Hotel, Phila.; dir. Commonwealth Trust Co., Lincoln Trust Co., N. British & Mercantile Ins. Co. of London and Edinburgh, N. British & Mercantile Ins. Co. of New York. Trustee Cornell U.; pres. Holland Library of Alexandria Bay, N.Y. Dir. Hotel Assn. of New York City, New York Bd. Trade & Transportation. Mem. Met. Mus. of Art, Am. Fine Arts Soc.; trustee Sat. and Sunday Hosp. Assn., etc. Died Dec. 5, 1916.

BOLE, Benjamin Patterson, publishing; b. Allegheny, Pa., Oct. 23, 1873; s. Joseph Kirkpatrick and Melinda Eliza (Patterson) B.; Ph.B., Western Reserve, 1896, LL.B., 1899; m. Roberta Holden, Sept. 2, 1907; 1 son, Benjamin Patterson. Admitted to Ohio bar, 1899, and practiced at Cleveland until 1913; pres. Hollenden Hotel Co., The Forest City Pub. Co., The Plain Dealer Pub. Co.; mng. dir. Boston-Panama Coconut Co.; dir. The Cleveland Trust Co., The Island Creek Coal Co., Pond Creek Pocahontas Co. Served with Ohio N.G., 1896-98; sergt. and sergt. maj. U.S. Vols., Spanish-Am. War; capt. cavalry, U.S.A., later maj. field arty., World War; then col., Inactive Res., U.S.A. Trustee Western Reserve U. and Adelbert Coll. of Western Reserve U. Home: Cleveland, O. Died Nov. 27, 1941.

BOLE, William McLure, newspaper pub.; b. South Ryegate, Vt., May 30, 1858; s. Rev. John and Marion (Brown) B.; ed. pub. and pvt. schs. and Peacham (Vt.) Acad.; m. Elizabeth S. Dow, Aug. 20, 1881; 1 son, William S., M.D. Settled in Mont. 1891; pub. Great Falls (Mont.) Daily Tribune, Great Falls Daily Leader, Bozeman (Mont.) Daily Chronicle. Dem. presdl. elector, Mont., 1916. Mem. Mont. State Bd. Edn., 1916-20; trustee Mont. State Hist. Soc. Mason. Home: Bozeman, Mont. Died Oct. 10, 1932.

BOLEND, Floyd Jackson; b. Hot Springs, Ark., Aug. 1, 1877; s. George C. and Ethel (McCormick) B.; A.B., Kingfisher Coll., 1899; Ph.C., U. of Okla., 1901; M.D., Coll. Phys. and Surg. (St. Louis), 1906; m. Mary M. Rickey, Mar. 1, 1903; 1 dau., Ethel Rickey. Practiced at Oklahoma City, 1910—; asso. prof. medicine, U. of Okla. Sch. of Medicine, 1911—; prof. of anæsthesia, U. of Okla.; mem. clin. staff Univ. Hosp.; staff St. Anthony and Okla. Gen. hosps. Served as maj. comdg. Okla. F. H., 1916-17; instr. M.O.T.C., Ft. Riley, Kan., 1917; successively div. sanitary insp., comdr. 111th San. Train, and div. surgeon 36th Div., 1917-18; dep. chief surgeon A.E.F. for Italy, 1919; col. U.S.A. (retired). Awarded decoration of Purple Heart by U.S., 1936. Republican. Mason. Home: Oklahoma City, Okla. Died June 22, 1939.

BOLLER, Alfred Pancoast, engr.; b. Phila., Feb. 23, 1840; s. Henry J. and Anna M. (Pancoast) B.; A.M. U. of Pa., 1858; C.E., Rensselaer Poly. Inst., 1861; m. Katherine Newbold, Apr., 1864. Was engr. with ry. and other corps., 1862-85; has for yrs. been cons. engr. or contractor for bridge constrn.; was engr. Albany and Greenbush bridge over Hudson at Albany; the Thames River Shore Line Bridge, New London, Conn.; the Central Bridge and viaducts over Harlem River, N.Y.; the 4-track, Duluth and Superior Interstate Bridge; etc.; cons. engr. Park Dept. and Public Works Dept., New York, under old charter; extension of Wabash lines into Pittsburgh, 1901-04, Brooklyn Rapid Transit Elevated R.R., etc.; senior mem. Boller & Hodges. Author: Treatise on the Construction of Iron Highway Bridges, etc. Home: E. Orange, N.J. Died Dec. 9, 1912.

BOLLES Albert Sidney, author; b. Montville, Conn., Mar. 8, 1846; Ph.D., Middlebury College, Middlebury, Vt., 1881; LL.D., Fafayette College, Easton, Pa., 1890; m. Annette Quackenbush McCandless, July 19, 1917; admitted to Conn. bar and engaged in practice. Elected judge Probate Court for Dist. of Norwich, Conn., 1870; editor Norwich (Conn.) Bulletin, and later editor Bankers' Magazine; prof. mercantile law and banking, Wharton Sch. of Finance and Economy (U. of Pa.), 4½ yrs.; chief Bureau Industrial Statistics, Pa., 8 yrs.; was prof., U. of Pa.; lecturer, Haverford Coll. Author: Financial History of the United States; Practical Banking; Bank Officers; Bank Collections; The Judicial Interpretation of the National Bank Act; Industrial History of the United States; The Conflict Between Labor and Capital; The History of Pennsylvania; Money, Banking and Finance; The Modern Law of Banking, 2 vols.; The Business Man's Legal Adviser, 6 vols.; Putnam's Handy Law Book for the Layman, 1921, new edit., 1925. Home: Williamstown, Mass. Died May 8, 1939.

BOLLES, Edwin Cortlandt, college prof.; b. Hartford, Conn., Sept. 19, 1836; A.B., Trinity Coll., Hartford, 1855, later A.M.; (hon. Ph.D., St. Lawrence U., 1860; S.T.D., Tufts, 1880; LL.D., Trinity, 1905). Ordained Universalist ministry; pastor Portland, Me., 1861, Salem, Mass., 1871; prof. microscopy, St. Lawrence U., 1870-73; pastor New York, 1887; Dickson prof. English and Am. history, Tufts Coll., 1899—. Died Jan. 11, 1920.

BOLLES, Stephen, congressman, editor; b. Springboro, Pa.; s. Nelson Richard and Malvina Belle (Whitford) B.; grad. State Normal Sch. of Pa., 1888; LL.B., from Milton College, Milton, Wis. Reporter Toledo Blade, 1890; mng. editor, same, 1893-94; pub. Erie (Pa.) Dispatch, 1894-96; mng. editor Buffalo Times, 1896-97; Sunday editor Buffalo News, 1897-98; pub. Rochester Daily Times, 1899-1900; pres. dir. Pan-Am. Expn., Buffalo, 1901; sec. McKinley Nat. Memorial Assn., Cleveland, O., 1901-02; mng. editor Buffalo Enquirer, 1902-03; supt. of graphic arts, St. Louis Expn., 1903-05, also dir. and editor of expn. catalog; dir. publicity, Jamestown Expn., 1907; editor Janesville (Wis.) Daily Gazette, 1920—; reported 15 nat. polit. conventions; alternate del. Rep. Nat. Conv., 1928. Mem. 76th Congress (1939-41), 1st Wis. Dist., 1938. Trustee Milton Coll., Janesville Public Library. Decorated Officier d'Académie (France). Republican. Conglist. Home: Janesville, Wis. Died July 8, 1941.

BOLLING, Raynal Cawthorne, lawyer; b. in Ark., 1877; A.B., Harvard, 1900, LL.B., 1902; m. Anna T. Phillips, 1907. Admitted to bar, 1902; then gen. solicitor U.S. Steel Corp.; dir. Tenn. Coal, Iron & R.R. Co.; pres. Ark. Farms Co. Apptd. head of the Aeroplane Bd., 1917; commd. maj., Aviation Sect. Signal Corps, and later col. same; with A.E.F. in France. Home: N.Y. City. Died May 1918.

BOLTON, Benjamin Meade, bacteriologist; b. Richmond, Va., Apr. 7, 1857; s. James (M.D.) and Anna Maria (Harrison) B.; student Charlottesville (Va.) Inst., 1871-75; M.D., U. of Va., 1879; studied S.C. Coll., 1882-83, U. of Heidelberg, 1883-84, U. of Göttingen, 1884-86, U. of Berlin, 1886; m. Johanna Heriette Louise Liebau, Brunswick, Germany, 1886; children—Meade, Theodore; m. 2d, Laetitia Todd, 1898; 1 dau., Laetitia Todd. Asst., 1886-88, asso., 1892-95, Johns Hopkins; prof. hygiene and bacteriology, S.C. Coll., 1888-89; dir. bacteriol. dept., Hoagland Lab., 1889-92; dir. of lab., Bd. of Health, Phila., 1895-96; prof. pathology and bacteriology, U. of Mo., 1896-97; prof. pathology and bacteriology, U. of St. Louis, 1901-04; dir. of Lab., State Bd. of Health, N.J., 1907-08; expert in exptl. therapeutics Bur. of Animal Industry, Washington, D.C.; biologist, Md. Agrl. Expt. Sta., 1912-14; expert in diseases of animals, Cuban Agrl. Expt. Sta., 1914-15; dir. Virchow Lab., St. Louis, 1917-19; pathologist New Samaritan Hosp., Sioux City, Ia., 1920-21; pathologist St. Joseph's Hosp., Paterson, N.J., 1921—; bacteriologist Rhode Island State Bd. of Health. Home: New York, N.Y. Died Aug. 12, 1929.

BOLTON, Charles Edward, lecturer, real estate; b. South Hadley Falls, Mass., May 16, 1841, of New England revolutionary ancestry; A.M., Amherst, 1865; m. Sarah Knowles. Engaged in merc. pursuits at Cleveland, O., later v.p. and mgr. Cleveland Machine Co.; patented several inventions; traveled extensively in Europe; corr. for several newspapers; inaugurated the Cleveland Ednl. Bureau. Has lectured on his travels in all parts of the U.S. and Canada; active in Republican campaigns; mayor E. Cleveland, O. Author: A Few Civic Problems. Wrote: A Model Village, Review of Reviews, Nov., 1899. Home: E. Cleveland, O. Died 1901.

BOLTON, Chester Castle, congressman; b. Cleveland, O., Sept. 5, 1882; s. Charles C. and Julia (Castle) B.; A.B., Harvard, 1905; m. Frances Payne Bingham, Sept. 14, 1907; children—Charles B., Kenyon C., Oliver P. Identified with steel industry, 1905-17; mem. Ohio Senate, 1923-28; del. Rep. Nat. Conv., 1928; mem. 71st to 74th Congresses (1929-37), 22d Ohio Dist. Mem. Ohio N.G., 1905-15; at Plattsburg Mil. Training Camp, 1916; capt. O.R.C., U.S.A., ordered to active service, Mar. 1917; with first War Industries Bd., later aide to asst. sec. of war; trans. to Gen. Staff, 1917, and took course of instrn. in officers' field training, 1918; promoted to lt. col. and apptd. asst. chief of staff, 101st Div.; hon. disch. Dec. 1918. Republican. Episcopalian. Home: Cleveland, O. Died Oct. 29, 1939.

BOLTON, Henry Carrington, chemist; b. N.Y., Jan. 28, 1843; s. Jackson (M.D.) and Anna H. (North) B.; grad. Columbia, 1862; studied chemistry in Europe (Ph.D., Göttingen); m. Henrietta Irving, Oct. 10, 1893. Asst. in quantitative analysis, Columbia Sch. of Mines, 1872-77; prof. chemistry, Woman's Med. Coll. of N.Y. Infirmary; prof. chemistry and natural science, Trinity Coll., 1877-87. Fellow A.A.A.S. (gen. sec., 1878-79, and v.p., 1882); mem. (pres. 1898-99) Library Assn. of D.C.; mem. (pres. 1893) N.Y. Acad. Sciences; one of incorporators, 1888, Am. Folk Lore Soc.; mem. (pres. 1900) Washington Chem. Soc. Author: The Student's Guide in Quantitative Analysis, 1885; The Counting Out Rhymes of Children, 1888; Scientific Correspondence of Joseph Priestly, 1892; A Select Bibliography of Chemistry 1492-1892, 1893, supplements, 1899, 1900; The Family of Bolton in England and America 1100-1894, 1895; A Catalogue of Scientific and Technical Periodicals, 1897; Evolution of the Thermometer 1592-1743, 1900; The Follies of Science at the Court of Rudolph II, 1903. Died 1903.

BOLTON, J(ames) Gray, clergyman; b. Lismoyle, Co. Derry, Ireland, Mar. 17, 1847; s. Samuel and Mary (Gray) B.; A.B., Lafayette Coll., 1871, later A.M.; grad. Union Theol. Sem., 1875; D.D., Lafayette, 1895; m. S. Josephine Townsend, Jan. 11, 1883 (died 1928). Ordained Presbyn. ministry, 1875; founder, 1875, and pastor Hope Ch., Phila., until 1928, now pastor emeritus. Has received nearly 5,000 communicants and erected ch. properties costing $200,000, closing each yr. without debt. Twice moderator Presbytery of Phila.; del. Gen. Assembly 10 times; twice apptd. to defend action of Synod of Pa. in appeal cases to Gen. Assembly. Made opening prayer at Rep. Nat. Conv., 1900. Mason. Home: Philadelphia, Pa. Died Feb. 22, 1931.

BOLTON, Sarah Knowles, author; b. Farmington, Conn., Sept. 15, 1841; d. John Segar and Mary Elizabeth (Miller) Knowles; 2 yrs. in Europe studying lit. and ednl. matters, and what employers are doing to help their workmen; m. Charles Edward Bolton, Oct. 16, 1866 (died 1901); mother of Charles Knowles B. Was for 3 yrs. asso. editor The Congregationalist; also asst. corr. sec. N.W.C.T.U. and v.p. Am. Humane Edn. Soc. Author: How Success Is Won, 1884; Poor Boys Who Became Famous, 1885; Girls Who Became Famous, 1886; Famous American Authors, 1887; Famous American Statesmen, 1888; Famous Men of Science, 1889; Famous English Statesmen, 1891; Famous American Authors, 1905. Home: Cleveland, O. Died Feb. 21, 1916.

BOLTON, William Jordan, U.S. storekeeper, Nov. 16, 1882—; b. Norristown, Pa., Oct. 1833; s. James and Mary Ann B.; ed. Norristown public schools and Tremont Sem.; became machinist and engr.; m. Emma Rupert, Frankford, Pa., Feb. 28, 1868, now deceased. Was burgess and councilman of Norristown, Pa.; sheriff Montgomery Co.; in uniformed militia of Pa., 1855-61; pvt. to maj., capt., maj. and col. Pa. vol. inf., 1861-65; bvt. brig. gen. U.S.V., 1865; capt., col., maj. gen. Nat. Guard of Pa., 1868-78. In Civil War served in depts. of Annapolis, Md., Northeastern Va., N.C., Army of Va., Army of Potomac, 1862; dept. of Va., Army of Ohio, Mil. div. of the Mississippi, Sherman's Expeditionary Army, Mil. divs. of the Tenn. and of the Cumberland, Army of Potomac, 1864-65; Middle Mil. div., dist. of Alexandria, Va.; was mil. gov. of Alexandria, Va. In 23 battles ending at Appomattox C. H., and 25 skirmishes. Republican. Home: Philadelphia. Died 1906.

BOLTWOOD, Bertram Borden, chemist; b. Amherst, Mass., July 27, 1870; s. Thomas Kast and Matilda (Van Hoesen) B.; Ph.B., Sheffield Scientific Sch. (Yale), 1892, Ph.D., 1897; post-grad. studies Munich, Leipzig and Yale; John Harling fellowship, U. of Manchester, 1909-10; unmarried. Asst. analytical chemistry, 1894-96; instr., 1896-1900, asst. prof. physics, 1906-10, prof. radio-chemistry, 1910—, acting prof. chemistry, Yale, and dir. Kent Chem. Lab., 1918-22. Fellow Am. Acad. Arts and Sciences. Translator: Quantitative Analysis by Electrolysis (A. Classen), 1898; Physical Chemistry for Beginners (C. H. Van Deventer), 1899. Died Aug. 15, 1927.

BOLTWOOD, Edward, writer; b. Pittsfield, Mass., Mar. 25, 1870; s. Edward and Sarah Eliza (Plunkett) B.; A.B., Yale, 1892, LL.B., 1894; unmarried. Asst. editor Harper's Mag., 1897-1901; New York lit. corr. Pittsburgh Dispatch, 1898-1903. Democrat. Episcopalian. Author: History of Pittsfield, Mass. (1876-1916), 1918. Contbr. fiction and verse to Century, Harper's Weekly, N.Y. Sun, etc. Has specialized in history and antiquarianism of Am. stage. Home: Pittsfield, Mass. Died 1924.

BOMAR, Paul Vernon, clergyman, educator; b. Spartanburg, S.C., Sept. 9, 1863; s. John Earle and Louise (Nancy) B.; A.B., Wofford Coll., Spartanburg, 1882; Th.M., Southern Bapt. Theol. Sem., Louisville, Ky., 1888; studied U. of Chicago; m. Nannie Elizabeth Earle, Sept. 6, 1888; children—Harriet Eliza (Mrs. Macon C. Ellis), Mary Earle (Mrs. D. W. Wallace), John Earle, Nancy Louisa (Mrs. Geo. W. Greene), Paul Vernon. Ordained ministry Southern Bapt. Ch., 1888; pastor successively, Camden, S.C., Versailles, Ky., Marion, Ala., to 1913; pres. Judson Coll., Marion, 1913-23; traveled in the Orient, 1923-24; pastor Tuskegee, Ala., 1924-31. Trustee Southern Bapt. Theol. Sem. Democrat. Mason. Home: Auburn, Ala. Died Feb. 1932.

BONACUM, Thomas, bishop; b. County Tipperary, Ireland, Jan. 29, 1847; came to U.S. in infancy; studied at St. Francis Sem., Milwaukee, at Cape Girardeau, Mo., and U. of Würzburg, Bavaria. Ordained priest in 1870; served as missionary priest; pastor Ch. of the Holy Name, St. Louis, 1881-87; theologian to the Third Plenary Council of the U.S., Baltimore, 1884; named by Plenary Council 1st bishop of proposed new diocese of Belleville, Ill., but as bishopric was not created for some yrs. afterward, was consecrated 1st bishop of Lincoln, Neb., Nov. 30, 1887. Home: Lincoln, Neb. Died 1911.

BONAPARTE, Charles Joseph, atty.-gen. of U.S.; b. Baltimore, June 9, 1851; s. Jerome Napoleon and Susan May (Williams) B.; g.s. Jerome B., King of Westphalia; A.B., Harvard, 1871, LL.B., 1874; (LL.D., Mt. St. Marys, 1882; LL.D., Catholic University of America, 1915); m. Ellen Channing Day, Sept. 1, 1875. Admitted to bar, 1874, and practiced at Baltimore. Mem. U.S. Bd. Indian Commrs., 1902-04; presdl. elector, 1904; Sec. of the Navy, July 1, 1905-Dec. 17, 1906; atty.-gen., Dec. 17, 1906-Mar. 5, 1909, in cabinet of President Roosevelt. Progressive. Mem. council, Nat. Civ. Service Reform League; pres. Nat. Municipal League; overseer Harvard, 1891-1903; trustee Catholic U. of America, 1904—; pres. Enoch Pratt Free Library, Md. Bd. State Aid and Charities, etc. Awarded Lætare Medal by U. of Notre Dame, 1903. Mem. Advisory Bd. of Council Nat. Defense, 1917. Home: Glen Arm, Md., and Baltimore. Died June 28, 1921.

BONBRIGHT, Daniel, univ. dean; b. Youngstown, Pa., 1831; s. Daniel B. and Mary (Smith) B.; Dickinson Coll., 1846-48; A.B., Yale, 1850, A.M., 1853; tutor, Yale, 1854-56; student univs. of Berlin, Bonn, Göttingen, 1856-58; (LL.D., Lawrence, 1873, Northwestern U., 1908); m. Alice D. Cummings, 1890. Prof. Latin lang. and lit., 1858—, dean Faculty of Liberal Arts, 1899-1902, acting pres., 1900-02, Northwestern U. Home: Evanston, Ill. Died Nov. 28, 1912.

BOND, A(lexander) Russell, editor and patent solicitor; b. of Am. parents, Stara Zagora, Bulgaria, June 12, 1876; s. Lewis and Fannie Grier (Russell) B.; came to U.S., 1890; A.B., Princeton, 1898; m. Edith Louise Pruden, Oct. 22, 1901; 1 son, Gordon Van Der Veer. Asso. editor Scientific American, 1902-15; mng. editor same, 1915-19; editor Scientific American Monthly, 1919-21; mgr. patent dept. Federated Engrs. Development Corp., 1921-26, also sec. and dir.; registered patent atty., 1908. Presbyn. Author: Scientific American Boy, 1905; Scientific American Boy at School, 1909; With Men Who Do Things, 1913; Pick, Shovel and Pluck, 1914; On the Battlefront of Engineering, 1915; American Boys' Engineering Book, 1918; Inventions of the Great War, 1919; Mechanics, 1922. Compiler and Editor: Handy Man's Workshop and Laboratory, 1909. Collaborator with A. A. Hopkins on Scientific American Reference Book, 1904 and 1912; editor Century Books of Useful Science. Home: Plainfield, N.J. Died June 3, 1937.

BOND, Bernard Q(uincy), banker; b. Dalton, N.H., Dec. 19, 1879; s. Frank P. and Emma L. (Cushman) B.; B.L., Dartmouth Coll., 1901; m. Jessica Edwards, Apr. 23, 1908; children—Marguerite, Franklin, Cynthia. Began as clerk, Littleton Nat. Bank, 1902; clerk Rochester (N.H.) Nat. Bank, 1905-08, cashier, 1908-17; treas. Norway Plains Savings Bank, 1908-17; vice-pres. and treas. Rochester (N.H.) Trust Co., 1917-30, now chmn. bd.; dir. Wolfboro (N.H.) Nat. Bank, Provident Ins. Co.; pres. Third Nat. Bank & Trust Co. (Springfield, Mass.), 1930-32. Republican. Conglist. Mason. Home: Rochester, N.H. Died Nov. 25, 1934.

BOND, Edward Austin, civil engr.; b. Dexter, Mich., Apr. 22, 1849; s. Hollis and Emily (Faxon) B.; ed. pub. schs. of Mich., and bus. coll., Utica, N.Y.; m. Gertrude Hollenbeck, Nov. 11, 1873; m. 2d, Clara E. Ellis, Nov. 10, 1904; mem. corps engrs. on construction of D.,L.&W. R.R., between Utica and Binghamton, N.Y., 1868-70; resident engr. Utica & Black River R.R., assisting in constrn. of road, 1870-71; chief engr. Clayton & Theresa R.R., 1871-75, Utica & Black River R.R., 1875-89; chf. engr., gen. supt., location, constrn., operation, Carthage & Adirondack R.R.; mem. Hines & Bond, cons. and advisory engrs. in promotion and constrn. of water works throughout U.S. and Can. State engr. and surveyor of N.Y., 1898-1904; apptd. by Gov., chmn. advisory bd. engrs., and during 1900 as state engr. had full charge surveys, plans and estimates for a barge canal across state, for which legislature appropriated $101,000,000, and which was ratified by people at polls; chmn. advisory bd. of cons. engrs. for constrn. of Barge Canal, 1904-July 21, 1911. Pres. Barrie (Ont.) Water Works Co., Chatham (Ont.) Water Works Co., Napenee (Ont.) Water Works Co. Mason. Home: New York, N.Y. Died Dec. 10, 1929.

BOND, Edward Johnson, insurance; b. Petersburg, Va., Oct. 18, 1888; s. Edward Johnson and Lelia (Seabury) B.; prep. edn., Boys' Latin Sch., Baltimore, Md., 1898-1903; B.S., Va. Mil. Inst., Lexington, Va., 1908; m. Mabel Holle, Oct. 20, 1921; 1 son, Edward Johnson III. Began in insurance business with Md. Casualty Co., Baltimore, 1908, first v.p., 1920-37, pres., 1937—. Fellow Casualty Actuarial & Statis. Soc. Democrat. Home: Baltimore, Md. Died Nov. 1941.

BOND, Frank, chief clerk Gen. Land Office; b. Johnson County, Ia., June 30, 1856; s. Avery John and Sabra Adaline (Dennis) B.; B.S., State U. of Ia., 1880, A.M., 1884; m. Henrietta Ingalls Wallace, Oct. 2, 1883. Removed to Wyo., 1882; mem. City Council, Cheyenne, 1890-96; mem. Ho. of Rep., 1st state legislature, Wyo., 1890-92; mem. Cheyenne Board of Edn., Wyo., 1896-1902; chief clk. Gen. Land Office, Washington, Apr. 1, 1907—. Treas. Soc. of Mayflower Descendants, D.C. Chmn. exec. com. U.S. Geographic Bd., Washington. Episcopalian. Home: Washington, D.C. Died July 21, 1940.

BOND, Frank Stuart, ry. official; b. Sturbridge, Mass., Feb. 1, 1830; s. Rev. Alvan and Sarah (Richardson) B.; ed. Norwich Acad. and Hopkinton High Sch.; not married. Entered ry. service, 1849, clerk N.&W. R.R. Co.; sec. C.,H.&D. Ry. Co., 1850-56; v.p. M.,K.&T. R.R, 1868-73, Texas & Pacific R.R., 1873-81; pres. Phila. & Reading Rd., 1882-83; pres. 5 asso. rys., 1884-86; v.p. C.,M.&St.P. Ry., 1886-1900; dir. New Orleans & Northwestern R.R., Vicksburg, Shreveport & Pacific R.R. Home: New London, Conn. Died Feb. 26, 1912.

BOND, George Meade, mech. engr.; b. Newburyport, Mass., July 17, 1852; s. Daniel George and Wilhelmina (Kruger) B.; M.E., Stevens Inst. Tech., Hoboken, N.J., 1880, E.D., 1921; M.Sc., Trinity College, Hartford, Conn., 1927; unmarried. Mgr. standards and gauge dept., Pratt & Whitney Co., Hartford, Conn., 1880-1902; mech. engr. in standards of length, 1902—. Fellow A.A.A.S. Republican. Episcopalian. Home: Hartford, Conn. Died Jan. 6, 1935.

BOND, Henry, retired; b. Ware, Mass., July 7, 1856; s. Benjamin and Louisa (Eaton) B.; grad. Mass. Agrl. Coll., 1876; m. Emma A. Hardy, Oct. 5, 1881; 2d, Alison E. Cant, Feb. 22, 1900. Purchasing agt., Am. Waltham Watch Co., Waltham, Mass., 1881-91; asst. mgr. Pierce Plant, Am. Radiator Co., Buffalo, N.Y., 1891-1900; chmn. operating bd., Am. Radiator Co., Chicago, 1901-05; retired from active business, 1905, but continued as dir. Am. Radiator Co. Mem. Mass. Legislature, 1910; Republican. Baptist; pres. Chicago Baptist Social Union, Mass. Bapt. Missionary Soc.; pres. Northern Bapt. Conv., 1912-1914, Vt. Bapt. State Conv., 1913-15, 1917; chmn. bd. mgrs. Am. Bapt. Foreign Missionary Soc., 1914-15; chmn. Gen. Bd. of Promotion, Northern Bapt. Conv., 1919-21. Home: Brattleboro, Vt. Died Aug. 9, 1925.

BOND, Henry Whitelaw, judge; b. near Brownsville, Tenn., Jan. 27, 1848; s. Thomas and Ellen Owen (Whitelaw) B.; ed. Harvard; m. Mary D. Miller, Nov. 18, 1880. Admitted to Tenn. bar; removed to St. Louis; elected judge St. Louis Ct. of Appeals for term of 12 yrs. from Jan. 1, 1893; resigned Oct. 7, 1901, to reënter practice of law; mem. Bond, Marshall & Bond, 1906-10, Bond & Bond until Apr. 11, 1911, when was apptd. Supreme Ct. commr. of Mo.; elected judge of Supreme Court of Mo., term, 1913-23. Home: Jefferson City, Mo. Died Sept. 28, 1919.

BOND, Hugh Lennox, Jr., lawyer; b. Baltimore, Dec. 23, 1858; s. Hugh Lennox and Annie Griffith (Penniman) B.; A.B., Harvard, 1880; m. Jessie Van Rensselaer Beale, June 4, 1884. Admitted to bar, 1882, and entered law dept. B.&O. R.R. Co. as asst. in office of gen. counsel; became gen. atty., 1895, 2d v.p. and gen. atty., 1903, 2d v.p. and gen. counsel, 1907-10, and gen. counsel, June 9, 1910—. Home: Baltimore, Md. Died Apr. 1922.

BOND, Lester L., lawyer; b. Ravenna, O., Oct. 27, 1829; ed. common and select schools and Ellsworth Acad.; worked at various occupations; studied law; admitted to bar, 1853; went to Chicago, 1854; specialist in patents and trade-marks; mem. city council, Chicago, 1862-66; acting mayor, 1872; presidential elector, 1868; mem. Ill. legislature, 1866-70; one of founders of West Park system; long mem. Chicago bd. of edn.; m. Amy S. Aspinwall, Oct. 12, 1856. Died 1903.

BOND, Oliver James, educator; b. Marion, S.C., May 11, 1865; s. Oliver James and Sarah Ann (Wayne) B.; B.S., The Citadel, Charleston, S.C., 1886; Ph.D., Ill. Wesleyan U., 1895; LL.D., U. of S.C., 1912; m. Mary Fishburne Roach, July 9, 1889; 1 son, Oliver J. Asst. prof. mathematics, 1886, later prof. mech. drawing and astronomy, pres., 1908-31, dean, 1931—, The Citadel (The Military College of S.C.). Democrat. Episcopalian. Past grand chancellor (S.C.), Knights of Pythias. Author: Amzi (novel), 1904. Home: The Citadel, Charleston, S.C. Died Oct. 1, 1933.

BONDURANT, Alexander Lee, univ. prof.; b. Colalto Plantation, Buckingham Co., Va., June 22, 1865; s. Alexander J. and Emily (Morrison) B.; A.B., Hampden-Sydney Coll., 1884, A.M., 1892; instr. Latin and Greek, Round Rock Inst., Tex., 1885-87; grad. student (Latin and Greek), U. of Tex., 1886-87; U. of Va., 1887-89 (Carey scholarship); Harvard, 1892-93, A.M., 1893 (Morgan fellowship); U. of Berlin, 1910-11; studied Munich, Rome; LL.D., from Mississippi Coll., 1921; hon. Litt.D., Hampden-Sydney College, 1926; m. Gabriella McPheeters Means, June 11, 1907. Asst. prof., 1889, asso. prof., 1890-94, prof. Latin and Greek, 1894-95, prof. Latin, 1895—, U. of Miss., dean of Grad. School, 1927-30, 1932—. Division supt. of edn., advanced sect. Y.M. C.A.; transferred to Army Edn. Corps; dean Am. students, U. of Dijon, France, 1918-19; exchange prof. lecturing on Roman archæology. Prof. of Latin, George Peabody Coll., summers 1922, 23, U. of Ia., 1924; U. of Ill., 1925 (acting head dept. classics), U. of Va., 1926. Sec. Commn. on Instns. Higher Edn. of Southern States, 1923-28. Presbyn. Contbr. to Classical Journal, Nation, Dial, publs. Miss. Hist. Soc., Library of Southern Lit., Sewanee Rev., Proc. Am. Philol. Assn., Classical Weekly, Classical Bull., Latin Notes. Edited The Classics in Mississippi Today (vols. 1 and 2). Decorated Order of the Crown of Italy, 1930. Died Jan. 12, 1937.

BONE, Scott Cardelle, editor, governor; b. Shelby Co., Ind., Feb. 15, 1860; s. Alfred P. and Louisa (Deacon) B.; ed. pub. schs. and high schs.; m. Mary Worth, June 15, 1887; children—Paul Myers, Roger Morse, Mildred (Mrs. John Ford Starr), Scott Worth, Carroll Alfred, Robert Douglas, Marguerite (Mrs. Alfred B. Wilcox). With Indianapolis newspapers, 1881-88; then with the Washington (D.C.) Post, first as news editor and then mng. editor, for 17 yrs.; editor and prin. owner of The Washington Herald, Oct. 8, 1906-Jan. 17, 1911; editor-in-chief Seattle Post-Intelligencer, 1911-18. Chmn. Alaska Bur. Seattle Chamber of Commerce, 1914-15. Del. at large, Rep. Nat. Conv., 1916. Dir. publicity Rep. Nat. Com., 1919-20; Governor of Alaska, 1921-25. Life mem. Am. Red Cross. Decorated Order of Sacred Treasure (Japan). Mem. Disciples of Christ. Author: Alaska, Its Past, Present, Future; Chechahco and Sourdough, a Story of Alaska, 1926; Sketches of Statesmen, and Political Reminiscences. Home: Santa Barbara, Calif. Died Jan. 27, 1936.

BONEHILL, (Capt.) Ralph. See Edward Stratemeyer.

BONER, John Henry, editor; b. Salem, N.C., Jan. 31, 1845; s. Thomas Jacob and Phoebe Elizabeth B.; academic edn.; learned printer's trade; m. Lottie Smith, 1870. Edited papers in Salem and Asheville, N.C.; reading-clerk N.C. constitutional conv., 1868; chief clerk N.C. Ho. Reps., 1869-70; in civil service, Washington, 1871-87; removed to New York, 1887; became mem. of staffs of Century Dictionary, Library of Am. Literature, and Standard Dictionary; literary editor New York World, and Literary Digest, and was on staff Appleton's Cyclopedia; is now again in civil service at Washington. Author: Whispering Pines (1883); etc. Has written (poetry) almost exclusively for the Century Mag., "Poe's Cottage at Fordham," Nov. 1889, being notable. Deceased.

BONHAM, Milledge Louis, Jr., teacher; b. Barnwell, S.C., Feb. 21, 1880; s. Judge Milledge Lipscomb and Martha (Aldrich) B.; prep. edn. Patrick Mil. Inst., Anderson, S.C., and The Citadel, Charleston; B.Litt., Furman U., 1900; studied U. of Va., summer 1903, U. of London, 1929, U. of Paris, 1930; A.M., Columbia, 1910, Ph.D., 1911; m. Odelle Austin Warren, Dec. 22, 1904; 1 son, Luke Warren. Comdt. Univ. Sch., New Orleans, La., 1900-01; comdt. and teacher English and history, Ky. Mil. Inst., 1901-03, Wilmington (Del.) Mil. Acad., 1903-05; teacher and prin. pub. schs., Richmond, Va., 1905-09; headmaster Kohut Sch., N.Y. City, 1909-10; instr. history, Tufts Coll. and Simmons Coll., Mass., 1911-12; asso. prof. history and polit. science, 1912-15, prof., 1915-17; head Dept. of History, La. State U., 1917-19; head of dept. of history, Hamilton Coll., Sept. 1919—. Lecturer summers, Peabody Coll., 1919, U. of Vt., 1920-22, State U. of Ia., 1923, N.C. Coll. for Women, 1927, U. of Rochester, 1928, W.Va. U., 1931, Duke University, 1934, Syracuse U., 1937; prof. ch. history, Utica Sch. for Religious Edn., 1922-23. Served as batt. sergt. maj. 1st S.C. Vol. Inf., Spanish-Am. War; dist. dir. War Aims Course, and War Issues Course, S.A.T.C., 1918. Chmn. Oneida Co. Mental Hygiene Com., 1927-29, 1930—; trustee N.Y. State Hist. Assn., 1934—; mem. Anglo-Am. Hist. Conf., N.Y. State Mental Hygiene Com.; mem. Oneida County Public Welfare Com. Del. Congress on Canadian-American Relations, 1935, 37, 39. Democrat. Unitarian. Author: The British Consuls in the Confederacy, 1911; Robert R. Livingston (in American Secretaries of State, Vol. I), 1927. Editor: Proceedings of the Historical Society of East and West Baton Rouge (2 vols.), 1917, 1918. Home: Clinton, N.Y. Died Jan. 22, 1941.

BONIFIELD, Charles Lybrand, gynecologist; b. Ohio, 1863; M.D., Med. Coll. of Ohio (now Ohio-Miami Med. Coll. of U. of Cincinnati), 1886. Prof. gynecology, U. of Cincinnati, 1910—, also head of Dept. Fellow A.M.A., Cincinnati Obstet. Soc. Home: Cincinnati, O. Died May 1932.

BONNAR, John Duncan, M.D., surgeon; b. King, Ont., Can., nr. Toronto, May 7, 1852; s. James Turnbull and Mary (Kennedy) B.; ed. as teacher, Coll. of Technology, Toronto; M.B., Faculty of Medicine (U. of Toronto), 1878; C.M., M.D., Trinity U., Toronto, 1879; m. Caroline Estella, d. Hon. Marvin Harris, June 24, 1885; children—Benjamin H., M. Clarine (Mrs. Norman T. Avard, Amherst, Nova Scotia), H. Otis, Mrs. Sybil Lyell MacMillan. Began practice at Streetsville, Ont., 1878; surgeon to Credit Valley Ry. when in Canada; practiced in Buffalo, 1880—. Mem. N.Y. State House of Delegates, 6 years; del. Atlantic League to Enforce Peace; delegated 6 times to represent Med. Soc. of Erie County before coms. of State Legislature, also chmn. com. of the society, culminating in building of Buffalo City Hosp.; chmn. com. whose efforts, with the Hamlin orgn., resulted in the building of the Buffalo Mus. of Natural Science, and was a speaker at laying of its corner stone; apptd. del. by Gov. Whitman to Atlantic League to Enforce Peace. Republican. Presbyn. Speaker for League of Nations; Roosevelt Memorial speaker, the address on Theodore Roosevelt now in book form in the archives of the Roosevelt Memorial Assn. Elected hon. pres. U. of Toronto Alumni Assn. of Buffalo and Niagara Falls, 1921; represented U. of Toronto Alumni at reception given Premier Ramsey MacDonald, in Buffalo, 1929; letter of welcome given Premier pub. in Toronto Alumni Journal. Home: Buffalo, N.Y. Died June 24, 1936.

BONNELL, Henry Houston, author; b. Phila., July 14, 1859; s. George Bringhurst and Elizabeth (Dobleman) B.; A.B., U. of Pa., 1880; m. Ethel Hill Chase, Jan. 16, 1901 (died 1904); 1 dau., Mariana; m. 2d, Helen Safford Knowles, June 17, 1915; 1 dau., Helen Safford. Dir. University Settlement. Author: Charlotte Brontë, George Eliot, Jane Austen, Studies in Their Works, 1902; Gloria (25 hymns, music by Sydney Thomson), 1903; Via Crucis cantata, music by Geo. Alex. A. West, 1913. Home: Chestnut Hill. Died Nov. 7, 1926.

BONNER, Geraldine, author; b. Staten Island, N.Y., 1870; d. John and Mary (Sewell) B.; educated by father; unmarried. Went West in 1880; lived in mining camps in Colorado 2 yrs.; went to Calif. and settled in San Francisco. Began writing for San Francisco Argonaut, 1887; dramatic critic, same, 4 years, also foreign corr. same. Author: Hard Pan, 1900; Tomorrow's Tangle, 1902; The Pioneer, 1905; The Castlecourt Diamond Case, 1906; Rich Men's Children, 1906; The Emigrant Trail, 1909. Wrote plays: "Sham" (with Elmer B. Harris), 1908; "Sauce for the Goose" (with Hutcheson Boyd), 1909; The Book of Evelyn, 1913; The Girl at Central, 1914; The Black Eagle Mystery, 1916; Treasure and Trouble Therewith, 1917; Miss Maitland, Private Secretary, 1919; The Leading Lady, 1925; Taken at the Flood, 1927. Home: New York, N.Y. Died July 17, 1930.

BONNER, Griffith, writer; b. N.Y. City, Nov. 4, 1885; s. Robert Edwin and Kate Helena (Griffith) B.; ed. Hill Sch., Pottstown, Pa., Lawrenceville (N.J.) Sch.; A.B., New York U., 1915. Reporter under Calvin Coolidge on Northampton (Mass.) Gazette, 1911; sporting editor Poughkeepsie (N.Y.) Star, 1911-12; on various eastern newspapers, 1918-20; with Capper Publications, Topeka, Kan., 1920-26; special writer on golf subjects for golf magazines, 1926-27; feature and sports writer, Topeka State Jour., 1928. Served with U.S.A. on Mexican border, 1916; with Canadian Expeditionary Force, 1917-18; instr. S.A.T.C., Purdue U., 1918. Historian Kan. dept. S.A.R.; rep. U.S. Golf Assn.; Western alumni sec. New York U., 1920-28. Episcopalian. Republican. Mason. Home: Monrovia, Calif. Died Feb. 26, 1936.

BONNER, Hugh, chief New York Fire Dept.; mem. of the fire dept., 1860-99; began as lad with Lady Washington Engine Co., No. 40; foreman of that co., 1861-65. When paid dept. was organized, 1865, he became foreman attached to Engine No. 20, and operated 1st self-propelling fire engine and chem. engine used by the dept.; chief of battalion, 2d dist., 1873-83; 2d asst. chief, 1883-84; 1st asst. chief, 1884-89; chief, 1889-99; retired May 1, 1899. Home: New York, N.Y. Died 1908.

BONNER, James Bernard; b. Phila., Pa.; s. Patrick and Catharine (Bonner) B.; ed. pub. and pvt. schs.; m. Anne Agnes McConnell, Sept. 2, 1891; children—Marie (wife of C. G. Gilliland, U.S. Navy), Leonard Anthony. Began as clerk with Carnegie, Phipps & Co., Ltd., 1890, and continued with that company and its successors the Carnegie Steel Co., and affiliated organizations, of which was manager of sales. Served at Washington, D.C., during war period as v.chmn. committee on steel distribution American Iron and Steel Inst.; commended by Gen. Pershing for important work during that time. Home: Germantown, Phila. Died Apr. 8, 1931.

BONNER, Robert, prop. The Ledger Monthly; b. Londonderry, Ireland, Apr. 28, 1824; came with parents to U.S., 1839; learned printer's trade in office of Hartford, Conn., Courant; worked in New York, 1845-50. Purchased, 1850, for $900, The Merchant's Ledger, a decadent commercial paper, which he gradually changed into a story paper; published as the New York Ledger, 1855—, until re-named The Ledger Monthly; with Ledger accumulated a large fortune; his sons then managed it as Robert Bonner's Sons. Home: New York, N.Y. Died 1899.

BONNEY, Charles Carroll, lawyer; b. Hamilton, N.Y., Sept. 4, 1831; ed. public schools, Hamilton Acad. and private study, with many advantages from Madison (now Colgate) Univ. (LL.D., same); m. Lydia A. Pratt, Aug. 16, 1855. Taught in public schools and Hamilton Acad., 1848-50; conducted academic school, Peoria, Ill., 1850-52; lecturer on edn., Peoria Co., 1852-53; took leading part in establishing ednl. system of Ill. Admitted to Ill. bar, 1852; U.S. Supreme Court, 1866; practiced Peoria until 1860; then Chicago. Former pres. Ill. State Bar Assn.; v.p. Am. Bar Assn.; had strong press endorsement for U.S. supreme bench, 1887. One of originators law and order movement, which became nat. organization and Internat. Law and Order League at Toronto, 1890; was its pres., 1885-93. Mem. New Jerusalem Ch. Originator, organizer and gen. pres. World's Congresses (over 200 in all), including Parliament of Religions; then pres. The World's Religious Parliament Extension; had deposited in Chicago Public Library a collection of World's Congress publications and papers. Author: Handbook of the Law of Railway Carriers, 1864; Summary of the Law of Insurance, 1865; The World's Parliament of Religions, 1899 (reprint from The Monist, April, 1895); World's Congress Addresses, 1899. Home: Chicago. Died 1903.

BONNHEIM, Albert, humanitarian; b. Hildesheim, Germany, Nov. 12, 1854; s. Joseph and Jenny (Oppenheimer) B.; ed. Hildesheim Gymnasium, Hildesheim Coll.; m. Fannie Weinstock, July 4, 1878. Came to America, 1872; began business, Sacramento, 1876; pres. Sacramento Valley Bank & Trust Co.; v.p. Weinstock, Lubin & Co.; dir. Alta Valley Farm Lands Co.; chmn. Reclamation Dist. 803. Pres. Soc. for Prevention of Cruelty to Children (Sacramento); chmn. probation com. Juvenile Ct. of Sacramento Co.; founder and sec. Joseph Bonnheim Memorial Fund, maintaining about 32 scholarships at univs. and other ednl. instns.; v.p. White Crusaders' Sanatorium; treas. Nat. Red Cross of Sacramento; chmn. lit. com. Temple Circle; mem. Calif. Minimum Wage Commission. Republican. Jewish. Home: Sacramento, Calif. Died Dec. 24, 1916.

BONSALL, Amos, farmer; b. Delaware Co., Pa., Jan. 20, 1830; s. Benjamin and Anne (Heacock) B.; ed. Bolmar Acad., West Chester, Pa., and, 1847-48, med. dept. U. of Pa. (A.M., Lafayette, 1860); m. Anna W. Wagner. In May 1853, accompanied Dr. Kane as master's mate, U.S.N., to Arctic regions, in a search for relics of Sir John Franklin, returning Oct. 1855. Was 32 years on board of mgrs. Pa. Training School for Feeble-Minded Children, Elwyn, Delaware Co., Pa., and 22 yrs. a mgr. of Phila. House of Refuge, now at Glen Mills, Delaware Co. Home: Philadelphia. Died Jan. 31, 1915.

BONSALL, Edward Horne; b. Philadelphia, Nov 19, 1859; s. Jeremiah and Margaret Fimister (Hutchinson) B.; pub. sch. edn.; studied law in office of Richard L. Ashhurst; m. Hannah Rodney Tunnelle, Oct. 4, 1887; children—Edward Horne, Rodney Tunnelle. Admitted to Pa. bar, 1880; title and trust officer and 2d v.p. Commonwealth Title Ins. & Trust Co., Phila., 1887-98; 2d v.p., dir. Land Title & Trust Co., 1899, v.p., dir., 1917, also gen. counsel, 1926; v.p. Real Estate Land Title & Trust Co., 1927; v.p. and dir. Phila. Co. for Guaranteeing Mortgages. Pres. Brotherhood of St. Andrew, 1910-18; pres. Y.M.C.A. of Phila.; chmn. Phila. com. Men and Religion Forward Movement; treas. Phila. Co. S.S. Assn., Bd. of Missions, Diocese Pa., etc. Republican. Episcopalian. Home: Glenolden, Pa. Died Dec. 31, 1933.

BONSALL, Elizabeth Hubbard (Mrs. Edward H. Bonsall, Jr.); b. Cambridge, Mass., Mar. 17, 1890; d. Phineas and Lucinda Ann (Reed) Hubbard; grad. Cambridge Latin Sch., 1907; A.B., Wellesley, 1911; M.A., U. of Pa., 1914; m. Edward H. Bonsall, Jr., Dec. 4, 1912. Editor Union Primary Quarterly. Episcopalian. Author: Famous Hymns, with Stories and Pictures, 1923; Goodwill Lessons (pamphlet), 1926; Famous Bible Pictures and Stories They Tell, 1928; World Friendship Lessons, 1929, 2d series, 1935. Home: Swarthmore, Pa. Died Feb. 14, 1937.

BONSALL, William Hartshorn, manager Soldiers' Homes; b. Cincinnati, Feb. 10, 1846; s. Samuel and Mary (Mills) Bonsall; ed. Cincinnati and Ironton, O.; m. Ella Doddridge McFarland, Oct. 2, 1871. Entered Union army, Aug. 1862, pvt. 1st O. vol. heavy inf.; later regimental commissary sergt. and lt.; at close of war recommended by examining bd. for position of maj. After war fire ins. mgr., excepting 6 yrs. business mgr. of The Spectator Co., New York; then moving to Los Angeles was pres. city council 4 yrs.; Republican. Owned and edited Portsmouth (O.) Tribune, 1877-81. Home: Los Angeles, Calif. Died 1905.

BONSER, Frederick Gordon, prof. edn.; b. Tower Hill, Illinois, June 14, 1875; s. Aaron and Eliza

(Stevens) B.; B.S., U. of Ill., 1901, M.S., 1902; Ph.D., Columbia, 1910; m. Edna Madison MacDonald, Aug. 17, 1902; children—Virginia Madison, Wendel (dec.). Dir. Training Sch. of State Normal Sch., Cheney, Wash., 1902-05, State Normal Sch., Macomb, Ill., 1906-10; prof. edn., Teachers' Coll. (Columbia), 1910—. Mem. Columbia U. Com. on Work on Rehabilitation of Disabled Soldiers, 1918-19; mem. Philippine Ednl. Survey Commn., 1925, Virginia State Ednl. Survey Commn., 1927, and N.J. Ednl. Survey Staff, 1929. Democrat. Universalist. Author: The Reasoning Ability of Children, 1911; Industrial Education, 1914; Educational Use of Recreation Activities of Children, 1918; The Elementary School Curriculum, 1920; Industrial Arts for Elementary Schools, 1923. Home: Leonia, N.J. Died June 8, 1931.

BONSER, Thomas A., Spokane Museum curator; b. Dayton, O., Sept. 21, 1860; s. Thomas and Louisa (Gutbrod) B.; Ph.B., Otterbein Coll., Westerville, O., 1899; M.Sc., U. of Chicago, 1903; m. Edna Flory, 1886 (died 1904); m. 2d, Ethel F. Wilcox, June 15, 1906; children—Mildred Elizabeth, Donald Charles. Head of biol. dept., Spokane High Sch., 1903-07; head of scientific dept. Spokane Coll., 1907-12; head of biol. dept. N. Central High Sch., Spokane, 1912-33; curator Spokane Mus., 1918—; curator Mus. Eastern Washington State Hist. Soc.; cons. botanist Spokane Clin. Lab. Mem. health and sanitation com. Spokane Chamber Commerce. Mem. Spokane Council Boy Scouts. Republican. Conglist. Mason. Discoverer of cause of irregular tides on The Great Lakes, 1895. Author: Ecological Study of Big Spring Prairie, Ohio, 1903. Contbr. papers, repts. and articles on hay fever plants in the Northwest. Home: Spokane, Wash. Died Aug. 4, 1935.

BONTECOU, Daniel, civil engr.; b. Springfield, Mass., Sept. 14, 1851; s. William Ely and Caroline (Thayer) B.; B.S., Coll. City of N.Y., 1871 (Phi Beta Kappa); m. Nathalie Holdrege, Oct. 7, 1885. Civ. engr. on pub. works, N.Y., 1871-81; pvt. practice, Kansas City, Mo., 1881-90; chief engr. Kansas City, Fort Scott & Memphis R.R. and asso. cos., 1890-1901; cons. engr., 1901-18; engaged in govt. work, 1918 (retired). Principal works: Cable rys. of Washington, D.C., and Kansas City, Mo., also various bridges and industrial plants. Mem. Mo. Bd. Industrial Preparedness, 1916. Democrat. Unitarian. Home: Mamaroneck, N.Y. Deceased.

BONTECOU, Reed Brockway, M.D.; b. Troy, N.Y., Apr. 22, 1824; s. Peter and Semantha (Brockway) B.; grad. Rensselaer Poly. Inst. (B.N.S.), 1842; studied in med. dept., Univ. City of New York, 1844-45; M.D., Castleton (Vt.) Med. Coll., 1847; made trip Amazon river, 1846; m. Susan Northrup, New Haven, Conn., 1849. Served through cholera epidemics at Troy, 1848 and 1858; surgeon 24th regt., N.Y. State militia, 1849; surgeon U.S.A., 1861-66; bvt. lt. col. and col. vols.; resumed practice in Troy, 1866; officer sect. on mil. and naval surgery and medicine, 9th Internat. Med. Congress, 1887; del. to 10th Internat. Med. Congress, Berlin, 1900; was the first to operate for repair of perforating typhoid ulcers of the intestines. Home: Troy, N.Y. Died 1907.

BONVIN, Ludwig, clergyman, composer; b. Siders, Switzerland, Feb. 17, 1850; s. John Baptist and Maria (Raimer) B.; grad. Coll. of Sion, Switzerland, 1870; studied medicine, U. of Vienna, 1870-71; studied philosophy in Holland, theology in England; chiefly self-taught in music. Joined Soc. of Jesus, 1874; ordained priest R.C. Ch., 1885; choirmaster and organist, Wynandsrade, Holland, 1876-77, Ditton Hall and Portico, Eng., 1882-87; dir. of chorus, 1888-1905, dir. orchestra, 1888-1907, Canisius Coll., Buffalo, N.Y. Compositions: (orchestra) Symphony in G Minor (op. 67) and 5 other works, op. 12, 25, 27, 31, 71; (organ) Op. 8, 12b, 77a, 95, 110; (violin and orchestra), Op. 19 (romanza); (violin and piano) Op. 56 (melodie). Vocal compositions: 6 masses and much other sacred music;—secular compositions for solo (soli), mixed choir and orchestra op. 20, 39, 50, 60—for soli, male choir and orchestra, op. 28; for female choir and orchestra, op. 73; many songs, op. 13, 14, 23, etc. Died Feb. 18, 1939.

BONWILL, William Gibson Arlington, surgeon and dentist; b. Camden, Del., Oct. 4, 1833; ed. country school; worked, 1847-53, as carpenter, cabinet-maker and school teacher; studied dentistry (hon. degree Dental Coll., 1865, Jefferson Med. Coll., 1865); practiced dentistry, Dover, Del., 1854-71, then in Philadelphia; m. Abagail Elizabeth Warren, June 13, 1891. Invented first dental and surgical engine, 1869; first electrical mallet, 1869; mechanical mallet, 1878; the all-porcelain tooth-crown, 1879; first removable bridge, 1889; also numerous other dental appliances. Invented also first injector for boilers, 1856; first binder to a wheat reaper, 1856; the safety-pointed pin, 1863; the first machine to carve marble and rock by power, 1869, and many others. Author: Geometry and Mechanics Deny Evolution; also, 1888—, of 140 poems; many papers on dental and aural surgery in journals, etc. Home: Philadelphia, Pa. Died 1899.

BONYNGE, Robert William, congressman; b. New York, Sept. 8, 1863; s. Robert and Susan (Burchell) B.; A.B., Coll. City of N.Y., 1882, A.M., 1885; LL.B., Columbia, 1885; m. M. Alida Riblet, Jan. 20, 1886. In practice at New York, 1885-88, Denver, 1888-1912, N.Y., 1912. Mem. Colo. Ho. Rep., 1893-94; Rep. candidate for Congress, 1900, 1902; gross frauds being discovered, the election was contested, and on Feb. 16, 1904, was unanimously awarded the seat; re-elected to 59th and 60th Congresses (1905-09), 1st Colo. Dist.; mem. Nat. Monetary Commn., 1908-12. Delivered addresses throughout U.S. in behalf of monetary reform under auspices Nat. Citizens' League, Chicago, 1912. Chief counsel N.Y. State Industrial Commn., 1916-18. Mason. Apptd. 1923, by President Harding, agt. of U.S. before Mixed Claims Commn., U.S. and Germany; apptd., 1925, by President Coolidge, agt. of U.S. before Tripartite Claims Commn., U.S. Austria and Hungary. Home: New York, N.Y. Died Sept. 22, 1939.

BONZANO, John, apostolic del. to U.S.; b. Casteletto, Italy, 1867; ordained in Rome, 1890; vicar-gen. Diocese of Vigevano, Italy; rector Pontifical Urban Coll., Rome; apostolic del. to U.S., Feb. 1, 1912—; consecrated archbishop of Militene, Mar. 3, 1912. Home: Washington, D.C. Died Nov. 26, 1927.

BOODY, David Augustus; b. Jackson, Me., Aug. 13, 1837; s. David and Lucretia B.; ed. Phillips Acad., Andover, Mass.; m. Abby H. Treat; children—Henry L. (dec.), Mrs. Maude Carey, Charles A., Alvin, Edgar. Mem. Boody, McLellan & Co., bankers and brokers, New York; dir. People's Trust Co., U.S. Title Guaranty Co. Mem. Congress, 1889-92; mayor of Brooklyn, N.Y., 1892-94; pres. bd. trustees of Brooklyn Pub. Library. Home: Brooklyn, N.Y. Died Jan. 20, 1930.

BOOHER, Charles F., congressman; b. E. Groveland, N.Y., Jan. 31, 1848; s. Henry and Catharine B.; ed. dist. schs.; m. Sallie D. Shanks, Jan. 11, 1877. Admitted to bar, 1871, then in practice at Savannah, Mo. Pros. atty., 6 yrs.; presdl. elector, 1880; mayor of Savannah 6 yrs.; mem. 50th Congress for an unexpired term, and 60th to 66th Congresses (1907-21), 4th Mo. Dist. Democrat. Home: Savannah, Mo. Died Jan. 21, 1921.

BOOK, George Milton, rear adm. U.S.N.; b. New Castle, Pa., May 25, 1845; s. Col. William and Ann (Emery) B.; apptd. from Pa., and grad. U.S. Naval Acad., 1865; m. Mary Sippy, May 7, 1867. Promoted ensign, Dec. 1, 1866; master, Mar. 12, 1868; lt. Mar. 26, 1869; lt. comdr., May 28, 1881; comdr., Dec. 16, 1891; capt., Mar. 29, 1899; retired for incapacity resulting from an incident of service, with rank of rear adm., Mar. 8, 1900. In summer of 1864, on board the Marblehead, in pursuit of the Confederate steamers Florida and Tallahassee; served Dakotah, 1865, Rhode Island, 1866, Mackinaw, 1866-67; Portsmouth, 1867-68, receiving-ship at Norfolk, 1868-69, Seminole and Benicia, 1869, Swatara, 1870; retired, 1871, but restored to active list, 1875; various assignments to 1896; comd. Marion, 1897; Navy Yard, Mare Island, 1897; comd. Mohican, 1898; Adams, 1898-99. Died Jan. 22, 1921.

BOOK, William Frederick, psychologist; b. Princeton, Ind., June 10, 1873; s. Christian Henry and Mary Elizabeth (Bussdicker) B.; A.B., Indiana University, 1900; fellow Clark U., Mass., 1903-06, Ph.D., 1906; studied U. of Chicago and Columbia; m. Mary Roach Cougle, Sept. 3, 1907 (deceased); m. 2d, Clara D. King, June 3, 1926. Prof. psychology, Univ. of Mont., 1906-12; prof. ednl. psychology, Ind. U., 1912-13; dir. vocational edn. Ind., 1913-17; prof. psychology and dir. Psychol. Lab. Ind. U., 1917—. Instr. psychology, summer sessions, Ind. U., 1907, 09; instr. and lecturer, summer sessions, Columbia, 1911-12; spl. lecturer, summer session, U. of Wis., 1928, summer session, U. of Hawaii, 1929. Fellow A.A.A.S. Author: The Psychology of Skill, 1908; The Intelligence of High School Seniors, 1921; The Psychology and Pedagogy of Skill, 1925; Learning to Typewrite—with a Discussion of the Psychology and Pedagogy of Skill, 1925; Learning How to Study and Work Effectively, 1926; How to Succeed in College, 1927; Economy and Techinque of Learning, 1931; Experimental Workbook on Psychology of Learning (with Merrill T. Eaton). Editor Jour. Applied Psychology. Home: Bloomington, Ind. Died May 22, 1940.

BOOKER, Joseph Albert, college pres.; b. Portland, Ashley Co., Ark., Dec. 26, 1859; s. Albert and Mary (Punchardt) B.; Branch Normal Coll. (colored), Pine Bluff, Ark., 1878-81; B.A., Roger Williams U., Nashville, Tenn., 1886 M.A., 1889; studied architecture; traveled in Europe, 1913; D.D., State U., Louisville, Ky., 1912, Shaw U., Raleigh, N.C., 1915; m. Mary J. Caver, June 28, 1887. Pres. Ark. Bapt. Coll., 1887—; also prof. logic, psychology and sociology. Editor Baptist Vanguard, 1887—; sec. Home Mission Bd. Nat. Bapt. Conv.; chmn. Little Rock Colored Vice Commn.; mem. Inter-Racial Commn. under Gov. Charles H. Brough; assisted in peaceable settlement of Elaine riots. Mason. Home: Little Rock, Ark. Died Sept. 9, 1926.

BOOKER, William David, M.D.; b. Prince Edward Co., Va., Nov. 11, 1844; s. James Madison and Lucy Ann B.; ed. Hampden-Sidney Coll., 1860-62; pvt. 3d Va. Cav., C.S.A., 1863-65; M.D., U. of Va., 1867; m. Julia T. Manning. Clin. prof. pediatrics, 1897-1909, prof. emeritus, 1909—, Johns Hopkins U. Mem. Am. Pediatric Soc. (pres. 1901), A.M.A., etc. Author med. articles on diseases of children. Home: Baltimore, Md. Died Mar. 15, 1921.

BOOKSTAVER, Henry Weller, lawyer; b. Montgomery, Orange Co., N.Y., Sept. 17, 1835; s. Daniel B.; grad. Rutgers Coll., 1859 (A.M., 1862; LL.D., 1888); admitted to bar, 1861; elected judge court of common pleas, 1885; transferred to Supreme Court, 1895; term expired in 1900; resumed practice, 1900; had large business as counsel and referee in important litigations; m. Mary Bailey Young, Sept. 6, 1865. Home: New York, N.Y. Died 1907.

BOOKWALTER, Alfed Guitner; b. Cedar Rapids, Iowa, Oct. 26, 1873; s. Lewis (LL.D.; retired clergyman) and Emma (Guitner) B.; A.B., Yale, 1897, A.M., 1901; m. Amy Mitchell Shuey, April 21, 1908; children—Alfred Shuey (dec.), Emily Guitner, Effie Mitchell (dec.), Edwina, Lewis. Master St. Paul's Sch., Concord, N.H., 1898-1903; in local, state and overseas service and on Nat. Council of Y.M.C.A.; instr. Yale Univ., 2 years; then pres. Willadean Nurseries, Inc., Sparta, Ky., and Berry Hill Nursery Co., Springfield, O. Rural rehabilitation work for U.S. Govt. at Washington, 1934-35; with cooperation of Ohio State U. and Antioch Coll. has conducted successful experiments on his Guernsey dairy farms in Ohio, in preserving green alfalfa as winter feed for dairy cattle, through packing with dry ice, in metal silos. Trustee Antioch Coll. Episcopalian. Died Apr. 2, 1939.

BOONE, Charles Theodore, lawyer, author; b. Chester Co., Pa., Apr. 11, 1838; s. William and Louisa (Smith) B.; ed. pub. schs., Plainfield and Parkesburg acads., Pa.; grad. law dept. Univ. of Albany, 1871; m. Helen L. Browne, Sept., 1873. Postmaster in Lincoln's first term, 1861; in Union Army, summer of 1863; admitted to N.Y. bar, 1871; removed to San Francisco. Life-long Republican. Mem. G.A.R. Author: Law of Corporations, 1881 B15; Law of Real Property, 1883 B15; Law of Mortgages, 1885; Code Pleading (2 vols.), 1885; Banks and Banking, 1892; Test Book of Law and Practice, 1894; Supplemental vol. (8) Wait's Actions and Defences, 1894. Home: San Francisco. Deceased.

BOONE, John Lee, lawyer; b. Mt. Pleasant, Ia., Aug. 5, 1843; s. John Daniel and Martha Jane B.; ed. Willamette Univ., Salem, Ore., and Ohio Wesleyan Univ.; enlisted in 20th Ohio vols. in junior yr.; studied law while in army and afterward at Salem, Ore.; m. Annie Lawson, July 3, 1863. Admitted to bar, 1867; has made patent law a specialty in practice. Mem. Calif. senate from San Francisco, 1884; was tendered, but refused, congressional nomination from 5th Calif. dist., 1886. Republican. Home: San Francisco, Calif. Deceased.

BOONE, Richard Gause, educator; b. Spiceland, Ind., Sept. 9, 1849; s. Driver and Elizabeth (Cooper) B.; grad. Spiceland Acad., 1871; (hon. A.M., DePauw U., 1883; Ph.D., Ohio U., 1889); m. Mary E. Stanley, July 24, 1874. Supt. schs., Frankfort, Ind., 1876; prof. pedagogy, Ind. U., 1886-93; pres. Mich. Normal Coll., 1893-99; supt. schs., Cincinnati, 1899-1903; editor, Education, Boston, 1901-07; lecturer on edn., 1909-13, prof. edn., 1913—, U. of Calif. Author: Education in the United States, 1888; History of Education in Indiana, 1890; Science of Education, 1904. Home: Berkeley, Calif. Died Apr. 8, 1923.

BOONE, William Judson, college pres.; b. Canonsburg, Washington Co., Pa., Nov. 5, 1860; grad. Elder's Ridge Acad., 1880; B.A., Wooster (O.) Coll., 1884, M.A., 1887, D.D., 1903; S.T.B., Western Theol. Sem., 1887, LL.D., 1934; m. Annie E. Jamison, Nov. 1, 1887; children—Marie (dec.), James Louden, Sarah (Mrs. J. O. Carter), Margaret. Ordained Presbyn. ministry, 1887; founder, and pres. Coll. of Ida., Oct. 7, 1891—. Mason. Home: Caldwell, Ida. Died July 8, 1936.

BOORAEM, John Van Vorst, engr.; b. Jersey City, N.J., Oct. 30, 1838; s. Henry Augustus and Cornelia (Van Vorst) B.; studied mathematics and languages, Hamburg, Germany, 1854-56; M.E., Poly. Sch., Carlsrühe, Baden, 1859; m. Elizabeth Wreaks, Nov. 7, 1867. Followed general machinery and marine engring., 1860-72; designing building and running sugar refineries from 1872—; consulting engr. Am. Sugar Refining Co., 1882-98; retired; v.p. Am. Enamel Brick and Tile Co. Author of monograph, "Internal Energy," 1906. Home: Brooklyn, N.Y. Died 1923.

BOORAEM, Robert Elmer, mining engr.; b. Jersey City, N.J., Mar. 28, 1856; early edn., Germany and New York; E.M., Columbia School of Mines, 1878; unmarried. Mining engr. in practical field work in Colo. and Mont., 1879-91; cons. engr. for western mining cos., New York, 1891-1911; resumed mining work in Colo. and oil business in Calif., 1911. Gold mining in Arizona and Nev., 1915; working oil wells in Wyo., precious metal mining, Nev., 1917. Home: Denver, Colo. Died Sept. 21, 1918.

BOOTH, Agnes, actress; b. (Marion Agnes Land Rookes) Sydney, Australia, Oct. 4, 1846; d. Capt.

Land and Sara Rookes; made début as a dancer when a child, and later was with cos. playing in Calif.; m. at 16, Harry Perry, Am. actor (died 1863); 2d, Junius Booth, 1867 (died 1883); 3d, John B. Shoeffel, 1885. First appearance in New York, 1865; soon after became leading lady with Edwin Forrest; has taken leading rôles in drama with numerous companies. Died 1910.

BOOTH, Ballington, reformer; b. Brighouse, Eng., July 28, 1859; s. Rev. William (founder Salvation Army) and Catherine B.; m. Maud Charlesworth, Sept. 16, 1886; formerly comdr. Salvation Army in Australia and U.S.; founded Vols. of America (inc. Nov. 6, 1896), a religious reform and benevolent orgn., of which became gen. in chief and pres. Ordained presbyter, Chicago, Aug. 1896. Home: Blue Point, N.Y. Died Oct. 5, 1940.

BOOTH, Christopher Henry Hudson, organist, composer; b. Accrington, Lancastershire, Eng., Sept. 5, 1865; s. Charles Hudson and Bathsheba (Whittaker) B.; ed. pub. sch.; studied organ, harmony and orchestration under pvt. teachers; m. 2d, Fannie Marie Baust, Dec. 16, 1908; children—James Charles Hudson, Charles Christopher Hudson (dec.). Came to U.S., 1895, naturalized citizen, 1905. Organist and conductor in England; organist First Ref. Ch., Brooklyn, then organist St. Paul's Luth. Ch., New York, 1899-1905; with Victor Talking Machine Co., 1900-05, playing for Red Seal artists; organist and choirmaster Ch. of the Advent, 1909—. Republican. Composer: Mass in E Flat (Latin), 1892; Second Mass in G, 1893; Divine Tragedy, 1929 (all for soli, chorus and orchestra); Symphony in F Minor (full orchestra), 1933; The Resurrection and Ascension, 1935; Second Symphony in C Major (full orchestra), 1936; also songs, anthems, piano music, etc. Home: New York, N.Y. Died Apr. 19, 1939.

BOOTH, Henry Matthias, pres. and prof. practical theology, Auburn Theol. Sem., 1893—; b. New York, Oct. 3, 1843; grad. Williams, 1864 (A.M., 1867; D.D., 1879; LL.D., 1894); pastor Presbyn. Church, Englewood, N.J., 1867-91; mem. bd. of Home Missions Presbyn. Church, 1881-91; bd. of Church Erection, 1874-79; trustee Princeton Theol. Sem., 1890-92. Author: The Heavenly Vision, and other sermons; Sunrise, Noonday and Sunset of the Day of Grace; First Communion, etc. Home: Auburn, N.Y. Died 1899.

BOOTH, Hiram Evans, lawyer; b. on farm, nr. Postville, Ia., Oct. 25, 1860; s. Joseph and Caroline (Bishop) B.; ed. pub. schs. of Ia. and by pvt. tutors; read law with Hon. Frank Shinn, Carson, Ia.; admitted to bar, 1885; m. Lillian B. Redhead, May 29, 1889. Editor and mgr. Carson (Ia.) Critic, 1885-87; mem. Shinn & Booth, Carson, 1887-88; in practice at Salt Lake City, 1889—; formerly sr. mem. Booth, Lee, Badger & Rich. Mem. Territorial Senate of Utah, 1894-96, State Senate, 1896-97; mem. Rep. Exec. Com., 1904-06; U.S. atty., Dist. of Utah, June 26, 1906-Dec. 20, 1913. Judge advocate-gen. with rank of col., Jan. 30, 1909-Jan. 1, 1917. Home: Los Angeles, Calif. Died July 10, 1940.

BOOTH, Mary Ann Allard, microscopist; b. Longmeadow, Mass., Sept. 8, 1843; d. Samuel Colton and Rhoda (Colton) B.; ed. Wilbraham (Mass.) Acad., and under pvt. teachers. Devoted many yrs. to research with the microscope; traveled widely in U.S., Can. and Alaska and lectured before many scientific socs.; made photomicrographs of germ-bearing fleas of rats, for stereopticon slides, during campaign against bubonic plague in San Francisco, 1907-09; has large pvt. collection of parasites and photomicrographs of same. Editor of Practical Microscopy, 1900-07. Medals and diplomas, New Orleans Expn., 1885, St. Louis Expn., 1904, San Francisco Expn., 1915. Conglist. Home: Springfield, Mass. Died Sept. 15, 1922.

BOOTH, Ralph Harman, publisher, editor; b. Toronto, Can., Sept. 29, 1873; s. Henry Wood and Clara L. (Gagnier) B.; pub. sch. edn.; m. M. Mary Batterman, May 23, 1906; children—John Lord, Virginia Kingswood. Removed with parents to Detroit, 1881; began with Detroit National Bank, 1888; with the Detroit Tribune as cashier and later business mgr., 1892-95; with Chicago Journal, as sec. and mgr., later editor and pub., 1895-1904; returned to Detroit as editor and pub. The Detroit Tribune; pres. and pub. The Grand Rapids Herald, 1905; pres. Booth Newspapers, Inc., Grand Rapids Press, Flint Daily Journal, Saginaw Daily News, Kalamazoo Gazette, Jackson Citizen Patriot, Bay City Daily Times, Muskegon Chronicle, Ann Arbor Daily News; dir. Guardian-Detroit Bank, Detroit Security Trust Co., Union Joint Stock Land Bank, Selected Securities Corp. Apptd. U.S. Minister to Denmark, Jan. 22, 1930. V.p. Associated Press, 1917-18; pres. Detroit Inst. of Art, City Art Commn.; dir. Detroit Symphony Soc.; v.chmn. Detroit Chap. Red Cross. Republican. Episcopalian. Home: Grosse Pointe, Mich. Office: Buhl Bldg., Detroit, Mich. Address: American Legation, Copenhagen, Denmark. Died June 20, 1931.

BOOTH, Robert Russell, clergyman; b. N.Y., May 16, 1830; s. William A. and Alida (Russell) B.; prep. edn. N.Y. Univ., grad. Williams, 1849, A.M., 1852; studied theology Auburn Theol. Sem. and Univ. of Halle, Germany (D.D., Univ. of N.Y., 1864, LL.D., Lafayette Univ., 1895); m. Emma Louise Lathrop, Oct. 26, 1853. Ordained, 1853; pastor 1st Ch., Troy, N.Y., 1853-57; 1st Ch., Stamford, Conn., 1857-60; Mercer St. Ch., N.Y., 1861-70; University Pl. Ch., N.Y., 1870-83; Rutgers' Riverside Ch., N.Y., 1886— (then emeritus). Chaplain 22d regt. Nat. Guard State of N.Y., 1863-69; moderator Synod of N.Y., at Boston, 1871; moderator Gen. Assembly Presbyn. Ch., 1895, Pittsburgh, Pa. Trustee Williams Col., 1866—; dir. Princeton Theol. Sem., 1880—; mem. Presbyn. Bd. For. Missions, 1870—. Author: The Place of Missions in Modern Christianity, 1865; Christian Union and Denominational Loyalty, 1896. Home: 277 West End Av., New York. Died 1905.

BOOTH, Samuel Babcock, bishop; b. Phila., Pa., Oct. 29, 1883; s. Henry Driver and Mary Bourne (Babcock) B.; grad. William Penn Charter Sch., Phila., 1902; A.B., Harvard, 1908 as of 1906; D.D., Va. Theol. Sem., 1925; D.D., Middlebury College and Norwich U.; D.C.L., Bishop's College, Quebec; m. Anna Peck, Sept. 6, 1910; children—Robert Grosvenor, Katherine, Mary Anna (dec.), Ellen Bourne, Anne Curtis, Madelein Tasker Polk, Samuel Babcock. Deacon, 1910, priest, 1911, P.E. Ch.; missionary in Ida., 1910-14; rector St. Luke's Ch., Kensington, Phila., 1914-18; chaplain Am. Red Cross at Evacuation Hosp. No. 9, in France, 1918; asst. at St. Mary's Pro-Cathedral, Phila., 1919; in charge of missions, Bucks Co., Pa., 1920-25; consecrated bishop coadjutor of Vt., Feb. 17, 1925, bishop of Vt., Feb. 26, 1930. Home: Burlington, Vt. Died June 17, 1935.

BOOTH, Thomas Butler, patent lawyer; b. Danbury, Conn., Feb. 12, 1872; s. David B. and Julia A. (Richards) B.; S.B., Mass. Inst. Tech., 1895; student Columbian U. Law Sch., 1889-90, Georgetown U. Law Sch., 1900-01; m. Annie L. Ives, Sept. 17, 1901; children—Edward C., Helen (Mrs. Hans K. Fischer), John W. Electrical engr. with Long Distance Telephone Co., New York, 1895, with Pope Mfg. Co., Hartford, Conn., 1895-99; asst. examiner, U.S. Patent Office, Washington, D.C., 1899-1902; admitted to D.C. bar, 1901; began practice with F. L. Emery at Boston, 1902, then mem. Emery, Booth, Townsend, Miller & Weidner. Republican. Conglist. Home: Newton Center, Mass. Died Oct. 13, 1940.

BOOTH, William Stone, author; b. Gloucester, Eng., Jan. 20, 1864; s. Abraham and Elizabeth Ann (Watts) B.; ed. Cathedral Coll. Sch., Gloucester; m. Mary M. Brewster, 1897 (died 1901); m. 2d, Leonora Howe, Nov. 29, 1904; children—Elizabeth McPherson, Robert Howe, Emily Lampard. In lumber business in Eng., 1880-85, in Australia, 1885; in Brazil investigating the fibre industry for Star Brush Co. of London and Kew Bulletin, 1887-88, Mex. and U.S., 1888-89, Bahamas, 1889-90; in lumber business, at London, 1890-93, in Calif., 1893-94; engaged as librarian at New York, 1894-97; with G. P. Putnam's Sons, pubs., New York, 1897, The Macmillan Co., 1898-1903, Houghton, Mifflin & Co., Boston, 1904-08. Author: A Practical Guide for Authors, 1907; Some Acrostic Signatures of Francis Bacon, 1909; The Hidden Signatures of Francesco Colonna and Francis Bacon, 1910; The Droeshout Portrait of William Shakespeare, an Experiment in Identification, 1911; Marginal Acrostics and Other Alphabetical Devices, a Catalogue, 1920; Subtle Shining Secrecies Writ in the Margents of Books; etc., 1925. Editor: On Many Seas; Wonderful Escapes by Americans. Home: Cambridge, Mass. Died Oct. 14, 1926.

BOOTH TUCKER, Emma Moss, Salvation Army officer; b. Gateshead, England, Jan. 8, 1860; 2d d. Gen. Wm. Booth, comdr.-in-chief Salvation Army; in charge internat. training homes, Salvation Army, 1880-88; m. Comdr. Booth Tucker, 1888; went with him to India, afterward to London, and (1896), to U.S.; held rank of consul in Salvation Army, and had joint and equal authority with her husband in the direction of the Army in the U.S.; prominent as an orator. Died 1903.

BORAH, William Edgar, senator; b. Fairfield, Ill., June 29, 1865; s. William N. and Eliza B.; ed. Southern Ill. Acad., Enfield, and U. of Kan.; m. Mamie McConnell, Apr. 21, 1895. Admitted to bar, 1889; practiced at Lyons, Kan., 1890-91, Boise, Ida., 1891—. Received 22 votes (necessary to choice 26) for U.S. senator from Ida., Jan. 14, 1903; elected U.S. senator, 6 terms, 1907-43; served as chmn. Senate Foreign Relations Com., 1924—, and was mem. Judiciary Com. and the Education and Labor Com.; was chmn. of the Indian Depredations Com., the Expenditures in Department of Justice Com., Interoceanic Canals Com., and Education and Labor Com.; outstanding advocate of Hiram Johnson for president in 1920, and of Herbert Hoover for president in 1928; opposed entrance of U.S. to League of Nations, and "World Court." Mem. Rep. Nat. Com., 1908-12. Home: Boise, Ida. Died Jan. 19, 1940.

BORDEN, George Pennington, brig. gen.; b. Ft. Wayne, Ind., Apr. 24, 1844; s. James W. and Emeline (Griswold) B.; ed. pub. schs. and Fairfield Acad., N.Y., to 1862; m. Elizabeth Reynold, May 25, 1869. Enlisted as pvt. Co. C, 121st N.Y. Vol. Inf., July 23, 1862; disch. Oct. 12, 1863; cadet U.S. Mil. Acad., Sept. 16, 1863-Jan. 23, 1864; apptd. from Ind., 2d lt., 5th U.S. Inf., Oct. 1, 1866; 1st lt., Sept. 4, 1878; capt., Feb. 20, 1891; maj. 3d Inf., Sept. 8, 1899; transferred to 5th Inf., Nov. 3, 1899; lt. col. 2d Inf., Nov. 28, 1902; transferred to 5th Inf., Dec. 24, 1902; col. 24th Inf., Apr. 14, 1905; brig. gen. and retired, Jan. 1, 1907. Home: New York, N.Y. Died Apr. 26, 1925.

BORDEN, William Alanson; b. New Bedford, Mass., Apr. 24, 1853; s. Alanson and Mary (Topham) B.; student Cornell, 1870-73; m. Hope Lewis, June 21, 1892; children—Beulah Byrd (Mrs. Earle Seymour Durham), Lewis Alanson. Began library work, Boston Athenæum, 1883; organized Reynolds Library, Rochester, N.Y., 1886; organized the Young Men's Inst. (library), New Haven, Conn., 1887, and in charge same until 1910; went to India, 1910, upon invitation of the Gaekwar of Baroda, and organized a system of over 400 state-controlled, free pub. libraries in State of Baroda, also founded a library sch. and a library periodical; returned to U.S., 1913; library engr., 1915—; inventor of the Borden cantilever bookstack (steel), and the removable card catalog drawer, now in general use in pub. libraries. Mem. A.L.A. Democrat. Unitarian. Wrote: Scheme of Classification for the Libraries of Baroda State; Alternate Classification for Libraries—a modification of the Decimal Classification. Home: New Haven, Conn. Died Nov. 16, 1931.

BORDEWICH, Henry, consul gen.; b. Vaagan, Norway, Jan. 19, 1844; s. John P. and Leonharde (Linkhausen) B.; ed. high sch. and commercial coll., Bergen, Norway; came to U.S., 1864; m. Bergithe Severinson, 1869. Served in Miss. squadron, U.S.N., during latter part of Civil War; co. auditor Yellow Medicine Co., Minn., 1874-88; postmaster Granite Falls, Minn., 1889-93; candidate for state treas., 1884; consul, 1897-1900, consul gen., 1900—, at Christiania, Norway. Republican. Mason. Home: Granite Falls, Minn. Died Mar. 1912.

BORDWELL, Walter, judge; b. Calhoun Co., Mich., Feb. 26, 1855; s. Charles M. and Eliza (Ingersoll) B.; student Olivet (Mich.) Coll.; m. Mary E. Willits, July 18, 1883. Admitted to Mich. bar, 1888; moved to Los Angeles, Calif., 1889; elected judge Los Angeles County Superior Court, 1905; presided at trial of Title Land cases, involving water front rights in Los Angeles harbor, trial of McNamara brothers for dynamiting Los Angeles Times Bldg. Home: Los Angeles, Calif. Died Sept. 23, 1926.

BOREING, Vincent, congressman, banker; b. Washington Co., Tenn., Nov. 24, 1839; removed to Ky., 1847; ed. Laurel Sem., London, Ky., and Tusculum Coll., Greenville, Tenn.; Nov. 1, 1861, vol. in Union army, Co. A, 24th Ky. Inf.; promoted 1st lt. for meritorious conduct; wounded battle of Resaca, Ga., May 14, 1863. County supt. schools, 1868-70. Founded Mountain Echo, London, Ky., 1875. Elected co. judge, 1886; pres. Cumberland Valley Land Co., 1887—; pres. 1st Nat. Bank of London, Ky., 1888—; lay del. from Ky., Gen. Conf. M.E. Ch., 1880 and 1896; comdr. dept. Ky., G.A.R., 1889; mem. Congress, 1899-1903, 11th Ky. dist. Republican. Home: London, Ky. Died 1903.

BORGLUM, Gutzon (John Gutzon de la Mothe Borglum), sculptor, painter, author; b. Idaho, Mar. 25, 1871; s. Dr. James de la Mothe and Ida (Michelson) de la Mothe B.; ed. in pub. schs. of Fremont and Omaha, Neb.; studied art in San Francisco; went to Paris in 1890, studying in Julian Acad. and École des Beaux Arts; awarded hon. M.A. by Princeton University, and LL.D. by Oglethorpe U.; Dr. of Letters, Dakota Wesleyan U., 1939; aerodynamic engr.; m. Mary Montgomery, 1909; children—James Lincoln, Mary-Ellis. Exhibited as painter and sculptor in Paris Salon and made associate Salon, 1891. Spent year in Spain; in Calif., 1893-94; returned to Europe and located in London and Paris until 1901, then settled in New York; held successful exhibitions abroad. Gold Medallist La. Purchase Expn. Sculptor St. John's Cathedral; produced Sheridan Equestrian, Washington, D.C.; Sheridan Equestrian, Sheridan Road, Chicago; colossal marble head of Lincoln in rotunda, Capitol Bldg., Washington; large bronze group, Mares of Diomedes, Metropolitan Museum; Ruskin (bronze); statue of Lincoln, Newark, N.J.; Trudeau memorial, Saranac Lake; Trail Drivers memorial, Tex.; statues—Mackay, Beecher, Altgeld, Vance, Huntington, Aycock, Alexander H. Stephens, John C. Greenway; O'Connell memorial, University of Virginia; Hoard memorial, Madison, Wis.; Wheeler memorial fountain, Bridgeport, Conn.; Bryan (Wm. Jennings) memorial, Washington, D.C.; Ffoulke memorial, Rock Creek Cemetery, Washington, D.C.; marbles—Wonderment of Motherhood, Modern Atlas (a woman), Conception, Martyr, The Centaurs; colossal monument 42 figures in bronze, Wars of America, Newark, N.J.; North Carolina memorial, battlefield of Gettysburg; memorial to Woodrow Wilson, Posnan, Poland; Northwest Territory memorial at Marietta, Ohio; Thomas Paine memorial, Paris

France; designed and began carving Confederate memorial on face of Stone Mountain, Ga., but a controversy arose with the Stone Mountain Memorial Assn., and all plans and models and work were destroyed; author and designer Confederate half dollar, struck in honor of the Confederate soldiers by nat. govt.; designer and sculptor of first nat. memorial federally authorized, on Mount Rushmore in Black Hills, S.D.; dedicated and officially begun by President Coolidge, Aug. 10, 1927—money appropriated by Congress and commn. apptd. by President in 1929; head of Washington unveiled, 1930, Jefferson unveiled by President Roosevelt in 1936, Lincoln in 1937, Theodore Roosevelt in 1939, work still in progress. Non-Partisan leader in politics, identified with the agrarian revolt in the Northwest; investigated for President Wilson and exposed the colossal aircraft failure. Progressive Republican. Mason. Decorated Order of Knights of Dannebrog (Denmark), 1931; Order of "Reconstructed Poland," 1931. Home: Stamford, Conn. Died Mar. 6, 1941.

BORGLUM, Solon Hannibal, sculptor; b. Ogden, Utah, Dec. 22, 1868; s. Dr. James de la Mothe and Cristine (Michelson) B.; brother of Gutzon B.; pupil Cincinnati Art Sch. and under Louis Rebisso and Frémiet, Paris; m. Emma Vignal, Dec. 10, 1898. Had made spl. study of Western life, living among cowboys and Indians. Had executed portrait equestrian statue of Gen. J. B. Gordon, at Atlanta, Ga., equestrian statue of Capt. O'Neil, at Prescott, Ariz., portrait busts of Mayor C. A. Schieren, of Brooklyn, and late Simon Newcomb; also Backus Memorial, Packer Inst., Brooklyn; portrait relief of Brig. Gen. Joseph A. Mower, placed on the Vicksburg battlefield; soldiers' monument, Danbury, Conn.; portrait statue of Private Jones of the Confederate Army, Lynchburg, Va.; portrait relief of James Edwin Hurley, gen. mgr. A.,T.&S.F. Ry., and many others; represented in Brooklyn Inst. Arts and Sciences, Met. Mus. of Art, New York, Cincinnati Mus. of Art. Spl. prize and home scholarship, Cincinnati Art Sch., 1897; hon. mention, Paris Salon, 1899; silver medal, Paris Expn., 1900, Buffalo Expn., 1901; gold medal, St. Louis Expn., 1904. Mem. Nat. Sculpture Soc. Executed equestrian statue, "The Pioneer," San Francisco Expn., 1915; 5 colossal portrait busts of generals of Civ. War, in Vicksburg Nat. Park. Hon. mem. Soc. Beaux Arts Architects. Y.M.C.A. sec. with French Army, 1918 (Croix de Guerre for courage under fire); later in ednl. work with A.E.F. in France; teacher sculpture, Art Training Center, Bellevue, nr. Paris. Home: Norwalk, Conn. Died Jan. 31, 1922.

BORIE, Adolphe, artist; b. Phila., Pa., Jan. 5, 1877; s. Beauvean and Patty (Neill) B.; grad. Lawrenceville Sch., 1895; A.B., U. of Pa., 1899; studied Pa. Acad. Fine Arts, Royal Acad., Munich, Bavaria; m. Edith Pettit, Apr. 8, 1907. Awarded Carol Beck gold medal, Pa. Acad. Fine Arts, 1910; silver medal, San Francisco Expn., 1915; Isaac N. Maynard prize, N.A.D., 1917; silver medal, Sesquicentennial Internat. Exhbn., Phila., 1926; Third Wm. A. Clark prize and Corcoran medal, Corcoran Gallery of Art, 1926; Norman Walt Harris bronze medal Art Inst. Chicago, 1928. A.N.A., 1917; fellow Pa. Acad. Fine Arts; mem. Nat. Soc. Portrait Painters. Home: Philadelphia, Pa. Died May 14, 1934.

BORING, William Alciphron, architect; b. Carlinville, Ill., Sept. 9, 1859; s. John Melvin and Mary Adeline (Bailey) B.; ed. Blackburn Coll., Carlinville, U. of Illinois, 1881-83, Columbia U., 1886-87, École des Beaux Arts, Paris, France, 1887-90; Litt.D. from Columbia Univ.; m. Florence, d. Henry M. Kimball, Oct. 23, 1894. Practiced as architect in Los Angeles, Calif., 1883-86; built U. of Southern Calif., hotels and schs.; in practice in New York, 1890—; mem. Boring & Tilton. Architect of U.S. Immigrant Sta., Ellis Island, Jacob Tome Institute, Port Deposit, Md., and many other public bldgs. in various parts of U.S. Gold medal, Paris Expn., 1900; medal, Buffalo Expn., 1901; St. Louis Expn., 1904. Mem. Municipal Art Commn., New York; was prof. of architecture and dean of School of Architecture, Columbia U., then dean emeritus. Fellow A.I.A. (2d v.p.; mem. and vice-pres. N.Y. Chapter); pres. Archtl. League of New York; charter mem. and first pres. Soc. Beaux Arts Architects; charter mem. and treas. Am. Acad. in Rome; mem. first U.S. Council of Fine Arts; corr. mem. Society S.A.D.G. A.N.A. Episcopalian. Received medal of honor, N.Y. Chapter, A.I.A. Home: New York, N.Y. Died May 5, 1937.

BORLAND, William Patterson, congressman; b. Leavenworth, Kan., Oct. 14, 1867; s. William Patterson and Elizabeth (Hassan) B.; ed. pub. and high schs., Kansas City, Mo.; LL.B., U. of Mich., 1892; m. Ona Winants, Apr. 27, 1904. In practice at Kansas City, Mo., 1892—. Mem. Bd. of Freeholders to draft charter for Kansas City, 1908; mem. 61st to 65th Congresses (1909-19), 5th Mo. Dist. Mem. faculty Kansas City Sch. of Law (dean 1895-1909). Democrat. Presbyn. Author: Notes on Law of Wills and Administration, 1907; Enlarged edition Kelley's Probate Guide; Borland on Wills, 1914. Home: Kansas City, Mo. Died Feb. 21, 1919.

BORNE, John E., banker; b. New York, Dec. 1, 1852; s. John and Monika (Pfaff) B.; ed. New York schs.; m. Nellie M. Lawrens, Oct. 3, 1877. Pres. Borne, Scrymser & Co., Colonial Safe Deposit Co., Nassau Electric R.R. Co.; chmn. exec. com. Trust Co. of America; dir. Nat. Park Bank, Plaza Bank, Mutual Bank, Mt. Morris Bank, Home Life Ins. Co., Citizens' Water Supply Co. of L.I., Griswold Worsted Co., Phila., Lanyon Zinc Co., Cord Meyer Development Co., Ry. Electric Power Co., Traction, Gas & Electric Finance Co., The Audit Co. Home: New York, N.Y. Died 1910.

BORST, Henry Vroman, judge; b. Cobleskill, Schoharie Co., N.Y., July 6, 1857; s. Isaac and Susan (Vroman) B.; student Cornell U., 1873-75; LL.B., Albany Law Sch., 1877; unmarried. Admitted to N.Y. bar, 1877; served as dist. atty. and county judge and surrogate, Montgomery Co., N.Y.; apptd. justice Supreme Court of N.Y., 4th Dist., 1913, and elected to same office Nov. following for term ending Dec. 31, 1927. Dir. Ft. Plain (N.Y.) Nat. Bank, First Nat. Bank (Johnsville, N.Y.). Democrat. Methodist. Mason. Home: Amsterdam, N.Y. Died Nov. 26, 1925.

BOSE (Diedrich Albert) Emil (Wilhelm), geologist; b. Hamburg, Germany, June 8, 1868; s. Johann Heinrich and Johanna (Karutz) B.; student U. of Berlin, 1888-89; U. of Munich, 1889-93, Ph.D., 1893; m. Helene Miller, Oct. 2, 1900; children—Helen, Emmi, Erna, Arthur, Paul. Scientific travels and pvt. scientific work in Germany, Austria, Switzerland and Italy, 1893-96; asst. at Polytechnicum, Karlsruhe, Germany, 1896-97; geologist Geol. Inst., Mexico, 1898-1903, chief geologist, 1903-15; geologist, Bur. of Econ. Geology and Technology, U. of Tex., 1915-17; cons. geologist, San Antonio, Tex., 1917-23; geologist Richmond Petroleum Co. of Mexico, 1923—. Mem. Internat. Com. for Publ. Palæontologia Universalis, Wiener geologische Gesellschaft (Vienna), Geologische Vereinigung (Berlin); corr. mem. Münchner Geographische Gesellschaft. Author: Die Erdbeben, 1909; (with E. Fraas) La evolucion de la Tierra y de sus Habitantes (enlarged Spanish edit.), 1910; also about 80 different works on geology and paleontology. Home: Mexico D.F., Mexico. Died Nov. 1927.

BOSHER, Kate Lee Langley ("Kate Cairns"), author; b. Norfolk, Va., Feb. 1, 1865; d. Charles Henry and Portia (Deming) Langley; B.A., Norfolk Coll. for Young Ladies, 1882; m. Charles Gideon Bosher, Oct. 12, 1887. Author: Mary Cary, 1910; Miss Gibbie Gault, 1911; The House of Happiness, 1912; The Man in Lonely Land, 1913; How It Happened, 1914; People Like That, 1915; Kitty Canary, 1917; His Friend, Miss McFarlane, 1918. Home: Richmond, Va. Died July 27, 1932.

BOSHER, Lewis Crenshaw, surgeon; b. Richmond, Va., Feb. 17, 1860; s. Robert H. and Elizabeth (Eubank) B.; ed. Richmond Coll.; M.D., Med. Coll. of Va., 1883; post-grad. studies, New York; unmarried. Emeritus prof. practice of surgery and genito-urinary surgery, Med. Coll. of Va.; visiting surgeon Stuart Circle and Memorial hosps. Fellow Am. Surg. Assn. Democrat. Baptist. Home: Richmond, Va. Died Sept. 12, 1920.

BOSKOWITZ, George W., physician; b. New York, 1856; s. Dr. Herman B.; ed. Poly. Inst. of Brooklyn, Cooper Union and pvt. tutors; M.D., Eclectic Med. Coll., New York, 1877; (hon. A.M., Waynesburg, 1892); m. Lena Toms, Apr. 10, 1891. Has practiced in New York, 1877—; dean and prof. surgery, Eclectic Med. Coll., 1884—. Editor Eclectic Review (med. monthly), 1890—. Pres. Nat. Eclectic Med. Soc., 1900-01, N.Y. State Eclectic Med. Soc., 1884-85. Died Mar. 15, 1917.

BOSMAN, David, ry. official; b. Brooklyn, N.Y., Dec. 18, 1864; s. David B.; ed. pub. grammar and high schs.; m. Emily Sloane, 1892. Clerk in law office, 1885-87; with Erie R.R., Co., 1887—, successively as clk., asst. sec., sec., and v.p. and sec.; also v.p. and sec. N.Y., Susquehanna & Western R.R. Co.; N.J.&N.Y. R.R. Co. Trustee Rutherford Trust Co., N.J. Mayor, Rutherford, N.J., 1910-11. Republican. Conglist. Home: Rutherford, N.J. Died Oct. 24, 1919.

BOSS, Lewis, astronomer; b. Providence, R.I., Oct. 26, 1846; s. Samuel P. and Lucinda (Joslin) B.; A.B., Dartmouth Coll., 1870; (LL.D., Union Univ., 1902); m. Helen M. Hutchinson, Dec. 30, 1871. Civilian asst. U.S. Northern Boundary Commn., 1872-76; dir. Dudley Obs., 1876—, and prof. astronomy, Union U. Mem. govt. expdn. to observe total eclipse in Colo., 1878; chief govt. expdn. to observe transit of Venus, Santiago, Chili, 1882; state supt. weights and measures, N.Y., 1883-1906; editor and mgr. Albany Express, 1885; dir. Dept. of Meridian Astronomy, Carnegie Instn., Washington, 1906; editor of Astron. Journal, 1909. Gold medal, Royal Astron. Soc., London, 1905; Lalande prize, Acad. Sciences, Paris, 1911. Mem. Nat. Acad. Sciences. Author: Declinations of Fixed Stars, 1878; Catalogue of 8,241 Stars, Leipzig, 1890 (Astronomische Gesellschaft). Monographs: The Solar Motion, and related papers, 1888; Prize Essay on the Physical Nature of Comets, 1881; Division Correction of the Olcott Meridian Circle, 1896; 179 Southern Stars, 1898; Solar Motion and Related Researches, 1901; Positions and Motions of 627 Standard Stars, 1903; Preliminary General Catalogue of 6,188 Stars, 1910; Catalogue of 1,059 Standard Stars, 1910, etc. Home: Albany, N.Y. Died Oct. 5, 1912.

BOSSARD, Guido, clergyman; b. Sheboygan Falls, Wis., Sept. 2, 1860; s. John James (Ph.D.) and Catherine (Blomker) B.; A.B., Lawrence Coll., Appleton, Wis., 1882, A.M., 1885, D.D., 1904; student univs. of Göttingen and Bonn, 1882-84, Union Theol. Sem., New York, 1884-86; Litt.D., U. of Dubuque, 1933; m. Marie M. Carver, Nov. 10, 1886; children—Jay Carver, Irene (Mrs. Justin R. Peters). Ordained to ministry Presbyn. Ch., 1887; pastor Manitowoc, Wis., 1887-90, Oconto, Wis., 1890-97, La Crosse, Wis., 1897-1903, Overbrook Ch., Phila., 1903-20; prof. New Testament lit. and interpretation, Div. Sch. U. of Dubuque, 1920—. Republican. Home: Dubuque, Ia. Died Nov. 6, 1936.

BOSSIDY, John Collins, oculist; b. Monterey, Mass., June 17, 1860; s. Edmond and Bridget B.; A.B., Holy Cross Coll., Worcester, Mass., 1881; A.M., M.D., Georgetown U., 1885; unmarried. With Interior Dept., Washington, until 1886; chief of pension office, St. Paul, Minn., 1886-91; student London eye hosps., 1891-92; settled in practice at Boston; surgeon in chief, eye dept., Boston City Hosp.; served as visiting surgeon Boston Insane, St. Elizabeths, Mt. Sinai, Sims Arlington hosps. and pub. instns. Republican. Catholic. Author of the noted quatrain beginning "And this is good old Boston, The home of the bean and the cod." Died 1928.

BOSTON, Charles Anderson, lawyer; b. Baltimore, Aug. 31, 1863; s. of John Edwin Hines and Cecilia (Guyton) B.; Baltimore City Coll.; Johns Hopkins U.; LL.B., U. of Md., 1886; m. Ethel G. Lyon, Sept. 29, 1900; children—Mrs. Katharine Daly, Lyon. Moved to New York, 1888; formerly mem. Baldwin & Boston; then mem. Hornblower, Miller, Miller & Boston. One of the 3 permanent members of Legal Advisory Bd. for the City of New York under the Selective Service Law and Regulations. Writer and speaker on legal, constl., medico-legal and ethical subjects. Home: New York, N.Y. Died Mar. 8, 1935.

BOSTON, L(eonard) Napoleon, M.D.; b. Town Hill, Pa., Mar. 18, 1871; s. Alfred H. and Bethiah (Bacon) B.; grad. with highest honors, Phila. Sch. Anatomy, 1895; M.D., Medico-Chirurg. College, Phila., 1896; hon. A.M., Ursinus Coll., Pa., 1902; m. Caroline Crandall, Oct. 28, 1905; children—Barbara C., La Barre (dec.). Bacteriologist Phila. Hosp., 1898-1901, Ayer Clin. Lab., Pa. Hosp., 1901; instr. in obstetrics, 1897-99, medicine, 1899-1901, dir. clin. labs., 1901-05, asso. in medicine, 1904, adj. prof. medicine, 1905, Medico-Chirurg. Coll.; phys. to Phila. Hosp. (Blockley), 1905; dir. Clin. Labs. of Research, Am. Hosp. for Diseases of the Stomach, Phila., 1906; pathologist, Frankford Hosp., 1909; prof. physical diagnosis, Medico-Chirurg. Coll., Phila., 1912-16; same, University of Pa., 1916-17; asso. prof. medicine, Post-Grad. Sch. of U. of Pa., 1919-26; prof. physical diagnosis of Grad. Sch., same univ., 1927 (Sept.)—; also prof. principles and practice of medicine and clin. medicine, Woman's Med. Coll. of Pa., 1928—. Methodist. Republican. Author: Text Book of Clinical Diagnosis by Laboratory Methods, 1904; Text Book of Medical Diagnosis (with James M. Anders), 1911, 3d edit., 1925. Home: Philadelphia, Pa. Died July 4, 1931.

BOSTWICK, Charles Dibble, comptroller Cornell U.; b. Ithaca, N.Y., Apr. 30, 1870; s. Hermon Van Vechten and Emily (Dibble) B.; A.B., Cornell U., 1892, LL.B., 1894; m. Lera Lawrence Cobb, Aug. 12, 1903; children—Charles Lee, Emily. Mem. firm of Newman, Blood, Banks & Bostwick, Ithaca, 1895-98; legal asst. to treas. of Cornell U., 1898-1903; asst. treas. Cornell U., 1903-14, treas., 1914-19, comptroller, 1919—; sec. bd. of trustees, same univ., 1914—; v.p. Ithaca Savings Bank; dir. Tompkins County Trust Co. Trustee Ithaca Children's Home. Sinking Fund commr. City of Ithaca, 1925—. Republican. Episcopalian. Home: Ithaca, N.Y. Died Dec. 16, 1937.

BOSTWICK, Charles Francis, lawyer; b. Tuckahoe, N.Y., Oct. 10, 1866; s. Charles Coffin and Mary Frances (Goodwin) B.; Ph.B., Columbia U., 1886, LL.B. (cum laude), 1886; LL.M., New York U., 1894, J.D., 1915; m. Laura, d. Col. Charles B. Bostwick, of New York, Jan. 20, 1898. Admitted to N.Y. bar, 1887, and since engaged in practice; prof. law, New York U., 1893-1900. Rep. candidate for Senate, 17th Dist., 1900; mem. Gen. Assembly, 1903-04; introduced $101,000,000 barge canal bill, known as Bostwick-Davis bill; asst. dist. atty. County of N.Y., 1910-16. Was mem. 2d co., 7th Regt., N.G.S.N.Y., 13 yrs.; now mem. exempt members 7th Regt. Episcopalian. Author of numerous legal pamphlets, and Bostwick's Lawyers' Manual, 1907. Home: New York, N.Y. Died June 28, 1923.

BOSTWICK, Harry Rice, capitalist; b. Detroit, Oct. 7, 1870; s. Henry Egbert and Sophia (Ashley) B.; ed. pvt. and pub. schs.; m. Emma Lake Hunt, Nov. 21, 1900; children—Florence Emma, Dorothy

Ashley. In conjunction with H. Collbran, constructed the Seoul Chemulpo Ry., the first steam ry. in Korea, 1898; also first electric st. ry., first electric lighting plant, first telephone service and first system of pub. water supply; established first Am. bank in Seoul; took a prominent part in reconstruction of San Francisco after earthquake and fire, 1906. Officer or dir. various corps. Decorated by emperor of Korea with 3d Order of Pal Kwai. Republican. Presbyn. Home: San Francisco, Calif. Died Jan. 1, 1931.

BOSTWICK, Lucius Allyn, naval officer; b. Providence, R.I., Feb. 21, 1869; s. David S. and J. Anna (Tripp) B.; grad. U.S. Naval Acad., 1890; m. Mary S. Wolfer, Sept. 27, 1897. Promoted ensign, July 1, 1892, and advanced through grades to comdr., Mar. 4, 1911; capt., Aug. 29, 1916; rear admiral, June 8, 1923; vice admiral, May 21, 1929; returned to rank of rear admiral, May 21, 1930. Served on Oregon, Spanish-American War, 1898; various assignments to 1914; mem. Gen. Bd., Navy Dept., 1914-17; comdg. South Dakota, Apr. 5, 1917-Sept. 17, 1918, New Mexico, Sept. 27, 1918-May 10, 1919; sr. mem. Naval Overseas Transportation Service Demobilization Bd., New York, May 10-Sept. 19, 1919; duty with office chief of naval operations, Navy Dept., 1919; comdr. U.S.S. California, 1922-23; chief of staff, Battle Fleet, 1923-25; chief of staff, U.S. Fleet, 1925-26; pres. Bd. of Inspection and Survey, Navy Dept. 1926-28; comdr. battleship divs., Battle Fleet, 1929-30; comdt. U.S. Navy Yard, Phila., and 4th Naval Dist., 1930—. Episcopalian. Died Jan. 14, 1940.

BOSWELL, Charles Martin, clergyman; b. Toms River, N.J., Dec. 26, 1859; s. Charles A. and Catharine A. (Wainwright) B.; ed. Pennington (N.J.) Seminary; D.D., Taylor U., Upland, Ind.; m. Florence E. Dobson, May 23, 1888 (died 1923) children —Kathryn Evelyn (Mrs. Frank E. Schofield), Dorothy Florence (Mrs. Thomas J. McKeone), Charles Martin, Samuel Shaw. Ordained ministry M.E. Ch., 1880; pastor, Stony Bank, 1880-81, Clifton and Mt. Pleasant, 1882, Bethany Ch., Phila., 1883-86, Columbia Av. Ch., Phila., 1886-91, Central Ch., Frankford, Phila., 1891-93; corr. sec. Phila. M.E. Soc., 1894-1906; corr. sec. M.E. Bd. Ch. Extension and Bd. Home Missions and Ch. Extensions, 1906-17; corr. sec. M.E. Hosp., Phila., 1917—; pres. Ocean Grove Camp Meeting Assn.; v.p. Chester Heights Camp Meeting Assn.; denominational rep. Federal Council of Chs.; trustee Pennington Sem., Phila. Conf. Tract Bd., Hist. Soc. Phila. Conf. Republican. Mason. Author: Home Missions; Rescue Missions. Contbr. to Christian Advocate, Phila. Methodist. Home: Philadelphia, Pa. Deceased.

BOSWORTH, Benjamin Miller, justice supreme court of R.I., June 2, 1897—; b. Warren, R.I., Jan. 17, 1848; ed. at high school and by private tutors; m. Mary M. Cole, Mar. 17, 1875. Engaged in practice of law; asst. atty. gen. R.I.; del. from R.I. to Republican Nat. Convention, 1888; mem. R.I. legislature, 1880-82, and 1885-86. Justice 5th judicial dist. court, R.I., 1886-97. Home: Warren, R.I. Died 1899.

BOSWORTH, Edward Increase, theologian; b. Dundee, Ill., Jan. 10, 1861; s. Frank S. and Sarah (Hunt) B.; student Oberlin Coll., 1879-81; A.B., Yale, 1883; B.D., Oberlin, 1886; U. of Leipzig, 1890-91, Athens, Greece, winter 1891-92; A.M., 1893, D.D., 1901, Oberlin; m. Bertha McClure, Oct. 1, 1891; children—Lawrence McClure (dec.), Edward Franklin, Richard Wilder, Sarah Frances. Ordained Congl. ministry, 1886; pastor Mt. Vernon, O., 1886-87; prof. English Bible, 1887-90, prof. N.T. langs. and lit., 1892—, dean, and sr. dean, 1903-21, dean, 1921-23, Oberlin Grad. Sch. of Theology. Acting pres. of Oberlin College, 1918-19. Lectured in Japan, 1907, in Turkey, 1911. Author: Studies in the Acts and Epistles, 1898. Studies in the Teaching of Jesus and His Apostles, 1901; Studies in the Life of Jesus Christ, 1904; New Studies in Acts, 1908; Christ in Everyday Life, 1910; Thirty Studies about Jesus, 1917; Commentary on Romans, 1919; What It Means to Be a Christian, 1922; Life and Teaching of Jesus According to the First Three Gospels, 1924. Home: Oberlin, O. Died July 1926.

BOTHNE, Gisle (Christian Johnson), univ. prof.; b. Fredrikshald, Norway, Sept. 7, 1860; s. Thrond J. and Johanne (Okland) B.; came to America, 1876; A.B., Luther Coll., Decorah, Ia., 1878; Northwestern U., Wis., 1878-79; Johns Hopkins U., 1879-80, 1883-84; studied Greece and univs. Christiania and Berlin, 1903-04; m. Kathrine Elise Brandt, June 27, 1895; children—Dikka J., Agnes M. Instructor Greek, 1881-83, prof. Greek and Scandinavian (Norwegian), 1884-1907, prin. Prep. Dept., 1889-96, Luther Coll.; head dept. Scandinavian langs. and lit., Univ. of Minn., 1907-29, retired. Pres. Norse-American Centennial, 1925; hon. mem. Norwegian-Danish Press Assn. of America. Knight Order of St. Olaf, conferred by King of Norway, 1911, Commander, 1925. Home: Minneapolis, Minn. Died Dec. 8, 1934.

BOTKIN, Alexander Campbell, lawyer; b. Madison, Wis., Oct. 13, 1842; grad. Univ. of Wis. (A.B.) and Albany Law School; m. June 11, 1872, Harriet E. Sherman. U.S. marshal, Mont. Ty., 1878-85; lt. gov. Mont., 1893-97; defeated for gov. Mont., 1896;

Republican; apptd., 1897, mem. commn. to revise and codify the criminal and penal laws of U.S.; elected chmn. same, 1898; LL.D., Univ. of Wis., 1904. Home: Helena, Mont. Died 1905.

BOTKIN, Jeremiah Dunham, clergyman; b. Logan Co., Ill., Apr. 24, 1849; s. Richard and Nancy (Barr) B.; county schs. and 1 yr. at DePauw U. Ordained M.E. ministry; presiding elder, 1886-92. Del. Gen. Conf. M.E. Ch., 1888, Ecumenical Conf., Washington, 1891. Was long a Republican; was the Prohibition candidate for gov. Kan., 1888; early espoused the Populist cause; defeated for Congress from 3d Kan. Dist., 1894; mem. 55th Congress (1897-99), Kan.-at-large; renominated by acclamation, 1898, 1900 and 1902; Dem. nominee for gov. of Kan., 1908; warden state penitentiary, Lansing, Kan., 1913-15. Home: Baldwin, Kan. Died Dec. 29, 1921.

BOTSFORD, Elmer Francis, lawyer; b. Burke, Franklin Co., New York, Nov. 24, 1861; s. Henry and Jennie (Bromley) B.; A.B., Dartmouth, 1886, A.M. 1889; m. Katherine L. Lyon, June 29, 1892; 1 son, Benedict Lyon. Admitted to N.Y. Bar, 1899, common counsel, City of Plattsburg; acting mayor, 1904-05; mem. Bd. of Public Works, 1907-08; corp. counsel; as atty. for Joseph Ladue, founder of Dawson City, made seven trips to Alaska and Klondike; interested in N.Y. City real estate and development of suburban property on L.I.; pres. Valley Stream Realty Co., St. Albans Terrace Co.; v.p. Plattsburg-Floral Park Realty Co. Mason. Home: Plattsburg, N.Y. Died July 8, 1930.

BOTSFORD, George Willis, coll. prof.; b. West Union, Ia., May 9, 1862; s. William Hiram and Margaret (Johnson) B.; A.B., U. of Neb., 1884, A.M., 1889; Ph.D., Cornell, 1891; m. Lillie M. Shaw, Aug. 30, 1891. Instr. history of Greece and Rome, Harvard, 1895-1901; lecturer, 1902-03, instr., 1903-05, adj. prof. ancient history, 1905, then prof. same, Columbia. Mem. bd. of editors of Political Science Quarterly; engaged in hist. research in Italy, 1909-10, 13. Author: The Development of the Athenian Constitution, 1893; A History of Greece for High Schools and Academies, 1899; A History of Rome for High Schools and Academies, 1900; An Ancient History, 1901; The Story of Rome, 1902; The Roman Assemblies, 1909; History of the Ancient World, 1911; A Source-Book of Ancient History, 1912; Hellenic Civilization, 1915. Home: Mt. Vernon, N.Y. Died Dec. 13, 1917.

BOTTOME, Margaret, writer, author, pres. Internat. Order of the King's Daughters and Sons, and of the women's branch of Internat. Medical Mission; b. New York, Dec. 29, 1827; ed. Prof. Greenleaf School, Brooklyn Heights, N.Y. Widow of Rev. F. Bottome, D.D. Has given Bible Talks in New York homes for more than 25 yrs.; was one of asso. editors The Ladies' Home Journal, regularly contributing dept. article, entitled "Mrs. Bottome's Heart to Heart Talks with the King's Daughters," 16 yrs.; writes for religious papers and mags. on subjects affecting the lives of women. Author: Crumbs from the King's Table; A Sunshine Trip to the Orient; Death and Life; Seven Questions After Easter. Home: New York, N.Y. Died 1906.

BOTTOMLEY, Allen W. T., banker; b. Glasgow, Scotland, June 15, 1873; s. James Thomson and Frances (Heep) B.; student Glasgow U., 1891-92; m. Lily Grace Jordan, Mar. 17, 1903; 1 son, Francis Kelvin. Settled at Honolulu, 1900; founded the Audit Co. of Hawaii; partner, later mgr. Bank of Bishop & Co., Ltd.; then pres. Bishop First Nat. Bank, formed by merger of First Nat. Bank and Bank of Bishop & Co., Ltd.; pres. Am. Factors, Ltd., Pioneer Mill Co., Ltd., Koloa Sugar Co. Home: Honolulu, T.H. Died Sept. 2, 1933.

BOTTOMLEY, John Taylor, surgeon; b. Lee, Mass., Sept. 24, 1869; s. John and Ellen (Ryan) B.; A.B., Holy Cross Coll., Worcester, Mass., 1889 (LL.D., 1916); M.D., Harvard, 1894; m. Mary Agnes Kenney, June 3, 1908; children—John Kenney, James William, George Taylor, Ellen Mary, Robert McCormack (dec.), May Kenney. Practiced in Boston, 1897—; 1st asst. surgeon Mass. hosp. ship Bay State, Spanish-Am. War, 1898; asst. visiting surgeon, Boston City Hosp., 1899-1903; asst. in surgery, Harvard Med. Sch., 1901-03; supervising surgeon, Boston City Hosp. Relief Sta., 1901-03; surgeon, 1903-10, surgeon in chief, Dec. 1910—, Carney Hosp.; lecturer on surgery, Harvard Grad. Sch. of Medicine. Capt. Med. R.C., 1917. Fellow Am. Coll. Surgeons. Catholic. Home: Boston, Mass. Died Dec. 17, 1925.

BOUCHER, Chauncey Watson, educator; b. Tiffin, O., July 18, 1851; s. Chauncey and Charlotte (Watson) B.; student Nat. Normal Sch., Lebanon, O., 3 years; B.S., Valparaiso U., 1877; m. Celista E. Van Loon, 1879; children—Hattie, Chauncey S., Martha. Teacher, Napoleon, O., 1871-74; Valparaiso Normal, 1876-84; business mgr. Chicago Times, 1887-90; part owner and teacher Dixon (Ill.) Normal Sch. and Business Coll., 1891-97; pres. Marion (Ind.) Normal Coll., 1897-1912; dean Muncie (Ind.) Normal, 1912-15; supt. schs., Valparaiso, 1915-30. Pres. Indiana State Teachers' Assn., 1927. Republican. Presbyn. Mason. Home: Valparaiso, Ind. Died Jan. 6, 1934.

BOUCICAULT, Dion G., actor, director; b. N.Y. City, May 23, 1859; s. Dion (dramatist and actor) and Agnes (Robertson) B.; mother an actress; m. Irene Vanbrugh, of Exeter, Devon, Eng., 1901. Debut as The Dauphin in Louis XI, at Booth's Theatre, New York, Oct. 11, 1879; has appeared principally in London, 1896—. Died June 25, 1929.

BOUCK, Francis Eugene, judge; b. New York, Nov. 25, 1873; s. Dr. Francis Anthony and Pauline Emilie (Raefle) B.; Ph.B., Columbia, 1895, studied law Columbia; LL.B., U. of Denver, 1896; m. Mabel Frankland Worcester, Nov. 29, 1900 (died); children—Constance Worcester, Polly; m. 2d, Harriet Wolcott Vaille, Aug. 20, 1917; 1 dau., Harriet Wolcott. Admitted to Colo. bar, 1896, and practiced in Leadville; city atty., 1900-03; dep. dist. atty. 5th Jud. Dist., 1905-09; county atty. Lake Co., 1909-13; dep. atty. gen. Colo., 1913-18; judge 5th Jud. Dist. Colo., 1918-33; elected justice Supreme Court of Colo. for term 1933-43 (chief justice, 1941-43). Mem. Colo. State Bd. Library Commrs., 1899-1903; former dir. Leadville Pub. Library. Awarded Columbia Alumni medal, 1938. Democrat. Presbyn. Mason. Mem. Royal Arcanum (grand regent Colo., 1911-12). Democratic, Columbia U. Club of Colo. (pres. 3 terms), Colo. Mountain, Denver Country. Home: Leadville, Colo., and Denver. Died Nov. 24, 1941.

BOUCKE, O(swald) Fred, teacher; b. Bremerhaven, Germany, June 1881; s. Friedrich Wilhelm and Bertha (Geburk) B.; B.A., U. of Mich., 1905, M.A., 1906; Ph.D., U. of Pa., 1916; m. Ruth Young. Came to the U.S., 1900, naturalized citizen, 1926. With Pa. State Coll., 1908—, prof. economics, 1920—. Author: Limits of Socialism, 1920; Development of Economics, 1921; Critique of Economics, 1922; Principles of Economics (2 vols.), 1925; Laissez Faire and After, 1932; Europe and the American Tariff, 1933. Home: State College, Pa. Died Mar. 12, 1935.

BOUGHTON, George Henry, artist; b. nr. Norwich, England, 1834, came with family to Albany, N.Y., 1839; ed. in public and high schools there. Began painting in boyhood; went to London to study, 1853; had studio in New York, 1858-61; studied in Paris, 1861-62; settled in London, 1862; famous as a genre and landscape artist. Became Nat. Academician (New York Acad. Design), 1871; asso. of Royal Acad. (London), 1879; Royal Academician, 1896; regular exhibitor in U.S. and England; many of his pictures are owned in this country. Author: (with E. A. Abbey, A.R.A.), Sketching Rambles in Holland. Died 1905.

BOUGHTON, Martha Arnold, author; b. Corunna, Mich.; d. J. M. (D.D.) and Hannah (Redway) Arnold; Ph.B., U. of Mich., 1880; m. Willis Boughton, July 8, 1884; children—Willis Arnold, Paul N. Teacher public and high schs., St. Clair, Mich., and Detroit, 1880-84; abroad summers, 1895 (del. World's W.C.T.U., London) and 1906. Author: Memoir of J. M. Arnold, D.D., 1885; The Quest of a Soul and Other Verse, 1911; Mystery and Other Poems, 1926. Home: Brooklyn, N.Y. Died May 18, 1928.

BOUQUILLON, Thomas, R. C. clergyman, prof. moral theology, Catholic Univ. of America. S.T.B., Gregorian Univ., Rome, 1865; S.T.L., same, 1866; S.T.D., same, 1867; prof. moral theol. in the Seminarium Magnum of Bruges, Belgium, 1867; same in Catholic Univ. of Lille, France, 1877. Died 1902.

BOURGADE, Peter, R. C. archbishop of Santa Fe, N.M., Jan. 7, 1899—; b. France, 1845; ed. Coll. of Billom and Grand Sem. of Mont-Ferrand Puy-de-Dome; went to Ariz. as missionary, 1869; ordained, Santa Fe, Nov. 30, 1869, and began work at Yuma, 1870; consecrated, May 1, 1885, at Santa Fe, Vicar Apostolic of Arizona, with titular rank of Bishop of Taumaco, and resided at Tucson until promoted archbishop. Died 1908.

BOURLAND, Albert Pike; b. Falcon, Ark., Nov. 14, 1861; s. Bayless W. and Frances (Boswell) B.; undergrad. Falcon and Arkadelphia classical acads., Union U. (Jackson, Tenn.), Vanderbilt U. (scholarship in mod. langs., 1882; M.A., Union, 1883; grad. student Columbia, summers 1903-05; U. of Munich, 1906-07, U. of Leipzig, 1907-10; spl. investigations European cultural development; m. Noble, d. of George W. Jarman, of Jackson, Tenn., 1886 (died 1890); m. 2d, Kathleen Graham, d. Col. Archer Anderson, of Richmond, Va., 1915. Prof. English and mod. langs., Union U. Jackson, Tenn., 1883-90, courses in English lit. among first in the South, also organized building and endowment campaign; instructor Monteagle Summer Schs., 1885-91; supt. same, 1890-91; gen. mgr. Monteagle Assembly and Summer Schs., 1891-99; prof. English lit., Peabody Coll. for Teachers, Nashville, Tenn., 1890-1910; chmn. Endowment Com., 1903-06, result nearly $2,000,000 and permanent establishment of the coll.; field agt. Peabody Edn. Fund and Southern Education Bd., 1910-13; exec. sec. Southern Edn. Bd., and Conf. for Edn. in the South, Washington, D.C., 1912-15; coöperated with state depts. of edn. in movement to build up effective systems of rural schs. in 12 Southern States, 1910-15; organized and coöperated in Experimental Rural Sch., Winthrop Coll., 1911-15. Lecture series in colls. and univs., on fundamental educative processes, 1915-22; dir. extension div., Winthrop Coll., S.C., 1922—. Home: Rock Hill, S.C. Died Oct. 30, 1927.

BOURN, Augustus Osborn, governor; b. Providence, R.I., Oct. 1, 1834; s. George O. and Huldah B. (Eddy) B.; A.M., Brown U., 1855; m. Elizabeth R., d. David C. Morrill, of Providence, Feb. 24, 1863. Engaged as mfr. rubber goods in Providence; founded, 1867, and became pres. Nat. Rubber Co., of Bristol, R.I.; removed to Bristol, 1873. Mem. R.I. Senate, 1876-83, 1886-88; gov. of R.I., 1883-85; consul-gen. at Rome, Italy, 1889-93. Served pvt. to lt. col. R.I. militia (cav.). Author: Bourn Amendment to Constitution of Rhode Island extending to foreign-born citizens same rights of voting as enjoyed by native-born. Home: Bristol, R.I. Died Jan. 28, 1925.

BOURNE, Edward Gaylord, prof. history, Yale, 1895—; b. Strykersville, N.Y., June 24, 1860; grad. Yale, 1883 (Ph.D., 1892); m. Annie Nettleton Bourne, July 17, 1895. Instr. history and lecturer on polit. science, Yale, 1886-88; instr. history, Adelbert Coll., 1888-90; prof. history same, 1890-95. Author: The History of the Surplus Revenue of 1837, 1885; Essays in Historical Criticism, 1901; Historical Introduction to the Philippine Islands, 1903; Spain in America, 1904. Editor: Wolley's A Two Years' Journal in New York, 1902; Fournier's Napoleon I, 1903; Roscher's Spanish Colonial System, 1904; The Chase Papers, 1903; editor and translator: The Narrative of De Soto, 1904; The Voyages of Champlain, 1905; Narratives of Columbus and Cabot, 1906. Co-editor Yale Review. Home: New Haven, Conn. Died 1908.

BOURNE, Frank Augustus, architect; b. Bangor, Me., Jan. 14, 1871; s. Augustus L. and M. Antoinette (Stevens) B.; student U. of Me., 1889-91; B.S., Mass. Inst. Tech., 1895, M.S., 1896; Harvard, 1898-99; m. Gertrude Beals, June 15, 1904; 1 son, Philip Walley. Gen. archtl. practice, Boston, 1899—. Principal works: Winchester (Mass.) Congl. Ch., Bangor (Me.) Congl. Ch., St. Lukes Ch., Chelsea, Mass., St. Johns Ch., Franklin, Mass., Mission of the Epiphany, Dorchester, Mass., Ch. of All Nations, Boston, Our Lady of the Snows Ch., Dublin, N.H., Ray Memorial Sch. and Dean Acad. Science Bldg., Franklin, Mass., 21 houses in Charles River Sq., Boston, etc. Mem. Am. Inst. Architects. Republican. Conglist. Author: Study of the Orders of Architecture, 1906; Architectural Drawing (with H. V. von Holst and F. C. Brown), 1914. Compiler of bibliographies of City Planning, 1914, Housing, 1920. Home: Boston, Mass. Died Feb. 15, 1936.

BOURNE, Frederick Gilbert, capitalist. Dir. Singer Mfg. Co.; dir. Knickerbocker Safe Deposit Co., L.I. R.R. Co., Manhattan Co., Bourne & Co., Ltd., of N.J., City & Suburban Homes Co., Babcock & Wilcox Co., Long Island Motor Parkway, Atlas Portland Cement Co., Æolian Co., Æolian, Weber Piano & Pianola Co., Safe Deposit Co., Singer Sewing Machine Co.; trustee New Theatre. Home: Oakdale, L.I. Died Mar. 9, 1919.

BOURNE, Jonathan, Jr., senator; b. New Bedford, Mass., Feb. 23, 1855; s. Hon. Jonathan B.; ed. Harvard, class of 1877; left coll. to go to sea; was shipwrecked off Formosa, picked up and taken to Portland, Ore.; m. Frances Barker Turner, 1925. Admitted to bar, 1881; practiced, 1881-82; engaged in mining, farming and commercial enterprises, 1882; pres. various corps. in Ore. Mem. Ore. Ho. of Rep., 1885, 86, 92; mem. Rep. Nat. Com., 1888-92; del. nat. convs, 1888, 92; U.S. senator, 1907-13. Served as pres. Nat. Progressive Rep. League, and Rep. Publicity Assn. Author of Parcel Post Law. Home: Washington, D.C. Died Sept. 2, 1940.

BOURNE, Randolph (Silliman), author; b. Bloomfield, N.J., May 30, 1886; s. Charles and Sara Randolph (Barrett) B.; M.A., Columbia, 1913 (Gilder fellowship); studied in London and Paris, 1913-14; unmarried. Contbr. to Atlantic Monthly and other mags., 1911—; on staff of New Republic since its inception; contbg. editor The Seven Arts, 1917, also contbg. editor The Dial. Author: Youth and Life, 1913; The Gary Schools, 1916; Education and Living, 1917. Compiler: Towards an Enduring Peace, 1916. Died Dec. 22, 1918.

BOUSCAREN, Louis Frederic Gustave, civ. engr.; b. Pointe-à-Pitre, W.I., Aug. 25, 1840; s. P. G. and E. C. (Segond) B.; prep. edn. St. Xavier Coll., Cincinnati, and Georgetown, Ky., Coll.; entered Lysée St. Louis, in Paris, France, 1853; grad. 1859; studied mech. and civil engring., École Centrale des Arts et Manufactures; m. Helen Seymour Lincoln, Apr. 18, 1876. Mech. and archtl. draftsman, Cincinnati, 1862-65; asst. engr. Ohio and Mississippi R.R., 1865-67; engr. in charge construction, Vandalia R.R.; Cairo & Vincennes R.R.; St. Louis & Southeastern R.R., 1867-73; chief asst. and chief engr., Cincinnati Southern R.R., 1873-84; cons. engr., 1884—. Mem. Am. Soc. Civ. Engrs.; Instn. of Civ. Engrs.; Société des Ingénieurs Civils. Home: Cincinnati, O. Died 1904.

BOUSH, Clifford Joseph, naval officer; b. Portsmouth, Va., Aug. 13, 1854; grad. U.S. Naval Acad., 1876. Promoted ensign, Dec. 1, 1877; lt., jr. grade, Nov. 3, 1884; lt., July 31, 1890; lt. comdr., Mar. 25, 1899; comdr., Jan. 12, 1905; capt., July 20, 1908; rear adm., Mar. 26, 1913. Served in Annapolis during Spanish-Am. War; at Naval War Coll., 1904-05; in Concord, 1905-07; insp. 2d Lighthouse Dist., 1907-08; at Navy Yard, Portsmouth, N.H., 1908-09; comd. Ohio, 1909, North Carolina, 1909-11; mem. Examining and Retiring bds., Washington, D.C., 1911-13; comd. 3d Div., Atlantic Fleet, 1913-15; comdt. Naval Sta., Hawaii, July 17, 1915-Aug. 13, 1917; retired, Aug. 13, 1917. Died July 24, 1936.

BOUTELL, Henry Sherman, diplomatist; b. Boston, Mar. 14, 1856; s. Lewis Henry and Anna (Greene) B.; A.B., Northwestern U., 1874, A.M., 1879; A.B., Harvard, 1876, A.M., 1877; (LL.D., Northwestern, 1904); admitted to bar, 1879; m. Euphemia Lucia Clara Gates, Dec. 29, 1880. In practice, Chicago, 1879-1911; mem. Ill. Ho. of Rep., 1884; mem. 55th, 56th and 57th Congresses, 6th Ill. Dist., and 58th to 61st Congresses (1897-1911), 9th Dist.; apptd. E.E. and M.P. to Portugal, Mar. 2, 1911, to Switzerland, Apr. 24, 1911; resigned, 1913. Offered chief justiceship U.S. Ct. of Claims, Jan. 2, 1913, by President Taft, apptd., Nov. 1913, one of six members of bd. of arbitration that settled the dispute between the operatives and officers of the C.,B.&Q. Ry. Co., and was elected chmn. bd.; prof. constl. law and internat. law, Law Dept. Georgetown U., 1914-23. Republican. Trustee Northwestern U., 1899-1911. Died Mar. 11, 1926.

BOUTELLE, Charles Addison, congressman-journalist; b. Damariscotta, Lincoln Co., Me., Feb. 9, 1839; ed. Yarmouth Acad.; m. Elizabeth, d. Adj. Gen. John L. Hodson, May 16, 1866 (died 1892). Adopted his father's profession of shipmaster; apptd. acting master, U.S. Navy, 1862; took part in blockade of Charleston and Wilmington, promoted lt. for gallantry in engagement with rebel ironclad Albemarle, afterward, in command of U.S.S. Nyanza, participated in capture of Mobile; hon. disch. (at his own request), Jan. 14, 1866; in business, New York, 1866-70; mng. editor, 1870, and proprietor, 1874—, Bangor Whig and Courier; mem. Congress, 4th Me. dist., continuously 48th to 56th Congresses, inclusive. Republican. Chairman Com. on Naval Affairs, 51st, 54th and 55th Congresses. Home: Bangor, Me. Died 1901.

BOUTON, Charles Leonard, mathematician; b. St. Louis, Apr. 25, 1869; s. William and Mary R. (Conklin) B.; M.Sc., Washington U., 1891; A.M., Harvard, 1896; Ph.D., Leipzig, 1898; m. Mary G. Spencer, June 15, 1907. Instr. Smith Acad., St. Louis, 1891-94, Washington U., 1893-94; instr. mathematics, 1898-1904, asst. and asso. prof, 1904—, Harvard. An editor Bulletin of Am. Math. Soc., 1900-02; asso. editor Transactions Am. Math. Soc., 1902-11. Mem. Am. Math. Soc., Deutsche Mathematiker Vereinigung, Berliner Math. Gesellschaft, Circolo Matematico di Palermo; fellow Am. Acad. Arts and Sciences, A.A.A.S. Home: Cambridge, Mass. Died Feb. 20, 1922.

BOUTWELL, George Sewall, sec. of treasury; b. Brookline, Mass., Jan. 28, 1818; admitted to bar, 1862; mem. Mass. legislature 7 terms, between 1842 and 1851; became Democratic leader; gov. of Mass., 1851-52; helped organize Republican party, 1855; apptd. by Pres. Lincoln 1st commr. of new dept. of Internal Revenue, 1862-63; mem. Congress from Mass., 1863-69; one of 7 mgrs. of Johnson impeachment trial; sec. of the Treasury, 1869-73; senator from Mass., 1873-77; afterward practiced law. Pres. Am. Anti-Imperialist League, 1900—. Author: Educational Topics and Institutions, 1859; Manual of Direct and Excise Tax Laws, 1863; Manual of Mass. School Laws, 1861; Volume of Speeches on the Rebellion, 1869; Revision of Statutes of the United States, 1878, as commr.; Why I Am a Republican, 1884; Report on French and American Claims Under the Treaty Between France and the United States of 1880-1884; The Lawyer, the Statesman and the Soldier, 1887; Constitution of the United States at the End of the First Century, 1895; The Crisis of the Republic, 1900; Sixty Years in Public Affairs (2 vols.), 1902. Home: Groton, Mass. Died 1905.

BOUVÉ, Pauline Carrington, author; b. Little Rock, Ark.; d. Gen. Albert Rust, C.S.A., and Anne Cabell (both parents Virginians); reared at Luray, Va.; ed. under pvt. governesses and tutors in Va.; m. Thomas Tracy Bouvé, July 14, 1898. In newspaper work at Boston, 1894—; spl. writer to Boston Transcript and Boston Globe; contbr. to New England Magazine, Donahoe's Youth's Companion, Churchman, Criterion, etc. Author: The Legend of the Luray Caverns (a poem), Phila., 1887; Their Shadows Before (novel), 1900. Translator: La Toison D'Or (The Golden Fleece), from French of Amedée Achard, 1900. Serials: "Ole Miss," Sunday Mercury, Phila., 1890; Stories of American Heroes for Boys and Girls, Brown Book, 1902; Miracle Stories of Science, 1903; Brunetière versus Realism, 1904; Pilate's Wife, Congregationalist, 1907. Wrote History of Pottery, Porcelain and Glass, in History of American Manufactures. Died 1928.

BOUVET, Marie Marguerite, author; b. New Orleans, Feb. 14, 1865; d. Jean François and Adelphine (Bertrand) B.; grad. St. Mary Coll., Knoxville, Ill., 1885; extensive traveler. Author: Sweet William, 1890; Little Marjorie's Love Story, 1891; Prince Tip Top, 1892; My Lady, 1894; A Child of Tuscany, 1895; Pierètte, 1896; A Little House in Pimlico, 1898; Tales of an Old Château, 1900; Bernardo and Laurette, 1902; The Fortunes of Clothilde, 1908; The Smile of the Sphinx, 1911. Home: Reading, Pa. Died June 1, 1915.

BOVARD, Charles Lincoln, clergyman, educator; b. Alpha, Scott Co., Ind., Oct. 10, 1860; s. James and Sarah (Young) B.; bro. of Freeman Daily and George Finley B.; Hanover (Ind.) Coll.; grad. Normal Collegiate Inst., Lexington, Ind., 1879; Ph.B., Ill. Wesleyan U., 1882; D.D., Moores Hill Coll., Ind., 1908; m. Clamenta Smith, Jan. 30, 1883. Licensed to preach, M.E. Ch., 1882; entered S.E. Ind. Conf., 1884; deacon, 1886, elder, 1888; pastor, Holman, Ind., 1884-86, N. Vernon, Ind., 1886-89; missionary in Ariz., 1889-90; supt. N.M. (English) missions, 1889-96; pastor, La Porte, Ind., 1897-99, St. Paul's Ch., Helena, Mont., 1899-1903, Mt. View Ch., Butte, Mont., 1903-06, Oxford, O., 1906-10, Minot, N.D., 1910; dist. supt. Butte Dist., 1910-11; pres. Mont. Wesleyan U., Helena, 1911-16; later dist. supt., Butte Dist.; del. to Gen. Conf., 1916, Bd. Home Missions, 1924; area sec. M.E. Ch., 1922-25; retired, 1926. Trustee Mont. Wesleyan U.; chmn. exec. com. Mont. Wesleyan Coll.; mem. Bd. Foreign Missions, M.E. Ch. Republican. Home: Helena, Mont. Died Mar. 13, 1930.

BOVARD, Freeman Daily, editor; b. Alpha, Ind., Jan. 9, 1851; s. James and Sarah (Young) B.; bro. of George Finley and Charles Lincoln B.; A.B., DePauw Univ., 1875, A.M., 1878 (D.D., 1890; Ph.D., Ill. Wesleyan, 1891); m. Sarah North, June 28, 1875. Ordained M.E. ministry, 1875; pastor Riverside, 1875-76, Orange, 1877-78, Santa Barbara, Calif., 1879-80; v.p. and prof. mathematics, U. of Southern Calif., 1880-85; presiding elder San Francisco Dist., 1887-93; editor Calif. Christian Advocate, San Francisco, 1900-13; corr. sec. Bd. Home Missions and Ch. Extension, M.E. Ch., 1913-16, and office sec. same bd., 1916—. Secretary of movement for the exemption of chs. in Calif. from taxation, 1899-1900; supt. Chinese M.E. Missions, Calif., 1900-13; del. Gen. Conf., 1900, 04, 08, 12, 16; fraternal del. to Meth. Ch. of Can., 1910; del. to Ecumenical Conf., Toronto, 1911. Died Feb. 6, 1920.

BOVARD, George Finley, univ. pres.; b. Alpha, Ind., Aug. 8, 1856; s. James and Sarah (Young) B.; student De Pauw U., 1877-79; A.B., U. of Southern Calif., 1884, A.M., 1887; D.D., Willamette U., 1895; LL.D., Syracuse U., 1910; m. Emma J. Bradley, Oct. 1, 1884; children—Warren Bradley, Edna Georgina, Gladys Freeman. Ordained M.E. ministry, 1883; pastor Orange, Calif., 1884-87; presiding elder, 1887-90; supt. Ariz. missions, 1890-97, presiding elder, 1897-1903; pres. U. of Southern Calif., 1903-21, pres. emeritus. Del. Gen. Conf., M.E. Church, 1900, 04, 16. Mem. Los Angeles City Park Commn., Los Angeles County Bd. of Govs. of Mus. of History, Science and Art. Mem. "The Book Committee," 1900-04; mem. University Senate, 1904-21; fellow Soc. of Philology (England), 1913. Republican. Home: Los Angeles, Calif. Died Sept. 24, 1932.

BOVARD, Warren Bradley, v.p. U. of Southern Calif.; b. Los Angeles, Calif., July 4, 1885; s. George Finley and Emma Josephine (Bradley) B.; student U. of Southern Calif., 1901-05; m. Hazel Berdine, d. Wilson Wayne Jackman, of El Reno, Okla., Mar. 6, 1923. Asst. treas. U. of Southern Calif., 1905-17, comptroller, 1920—, and v.p., 1927—; dir. Calif. Bank. Maj. Air Service U.S.A., Sept.-Dec. 1917; with Gen. Staff Corps, Washington, D.C., Dec. 1917-Jan. 16, 1919; exec. sec. to Gov. William D. Stephens, State of Calif., May 1919-June 1920; lt. col. A.S.O.R.C. Mem. Bd. Park Commrs., Los Angeles. Republican. Methodist. Home: Los Angeles, Calif. Died Dec. 18, 1930.

BOVARD, William Sherman, clergyman; b. Alpha, Ind., Aug. 29, 1864; s. James and Sarah (Young) B.; A.B., U. of Southern Calif., 1888, A.M., 1891; S.T.B., Boston U., 1898; (D.D., Ohio Wesleyan U., 1904; LL.D., U. of Southern Calif., 1921); m. Philena Tufts, Dec. 10, 1889; children—Gilbert S., Burton C., Alice May. Ordained Methodist Episcopal ministry, 1888; pastor San Francisco, College Park, California, York, Me., Portland, Me.; exec. sec. Methodist Brotherhood, 1913-14; supt. adult dept. Bd. of Sunday Schs. of M.E. Ch., 1915-20; corr. sec. Bd. of Sunday Schools of M.E. Ch., 1920-24; corr. sec. Bd. of Edn. M.E. Ch., 1924-32, asst. sec., 1932—. Mason. Republican. Author: Adults in Sunday School, 1918. Home: Evanston, Ill. Died Sept. 6, 1936.

BOVEE, Christian Nestell, author; b. New York, Feb. 22, 1820; ed. pvt. schs.; studied law; m. Mary M. Doubleday, 1849. About 1847 admitted to bar, practiced in New York; one of founders Athenæum Club, and was regent Long Island Coll. Hosp.; at one time edited a periodical called Thoughts and Events. Author: Thoughts, Feelings and Fancies,

1857; Intuitions and Summaries of Thought, 1862. Home: Philadelphia. Died 1904.

BOVEE, J(ohn) Wesley, gynecologist; b. Clayton, N.Y., Dec. 31, 1861; s. William H. and Sarah E. (Roat) B.; prep. edn. high schs. Dexter and Chaumont, N.Y.; M.D., Columbian (now George Washington) U., 1885. Gynecologist, Columbia Hosp. for Women, 1890—, Providence Hospital, 1891-1908, George Washington U. Hosp., 1899—; prof. gynecology, George Washington U., 1903—. Fellow Am. Gynecol. Soc. (pres.), Am. Coll. Surgeons (a founder and mem. bd. govs.), A.M.A. (chmn. sect. diseases of women, 1907), Med. Soc. D.C. Chmn. com. on Am. membership of the Internat. Congress on Gynecology and Obstetrics. Editor: Bovée's Practice of Gynecology. Home: Washington, D.C. Died 1927.

BOWDITCH, Charles Pickering, trustee, archeol. student; b. Boston, Sept. 30, 1842; s. Jonathan Ingersoll and Lucy O. (Nichols) B.; A.B., Harvard, 1863, A.M., 1866; m. Cornelia L. Rockwell, June 7, 1866. President Pepperell Mfg. Co. and Mass. Hosp. Life Ins. Co.; dir. Boston & Providence R.R. Corp. Served as 2d lt., 1st lt., and capt., 55th Mass. Vol. Inf., May 1863-Feb. 1864; capt. 5th Mass. Vol. Cav., Feb.-Aug. 1864. Fellow Am. Acad. Arts and Sciences, A.A.A.S., Archæol. Inst. of America. Republican. Author: Maya Numeration, Calendar and Astronomy; Bacon's Connection with the First Folio of Shakespeare; Pickering Genealogy; also 10 pamphlets on Central Am. archeology, and of History of the Trustees of the Charity of Edward Hopkins. Home: Jamaica Plain, Mass. Died June 1, 1921.

BOWDITCH, Henry Pickering, physiologist; b. Boston, Apr. 4, 1840; s. Jonathan Ingersoll and Lucy Orne (Nichols) B.; brother of Charles Pickering B.; A.B., Harvard, 1861, A.M., 1866, M.D., 1868; (D.Sc., Cambridge, Eng., 1898; LL.D., Edinburgh, 1898, Toronto, 1903, U. of Pa., 1904); lt., capt. and maj. U.S. Vol. Cav., 1861-65; studied physiology in France and Germany, 1868-71; m. Selma Knauth, of Leipzig, Sept. 9, 1871. Asst. prof., 1871-76, prof. physiology, 1876-1903, George Higginson prof. physiology, 1903-06, dean Med. Sch., 1883-93, Harvard. Trustee Boston Pub. Library, 1895-1902. Fellow Am. Acad. Arts and Sciences, A.A.A.S. (v.p., 1886, 1900); mem. Nat. Acad. Sciences. Author: Growth of Children, 1877; Hints for Teachers of Physiology, 1889; Is Harvard a University?, 1890; Are Composite Photographs Typical Pictures?, 1894; Advancement of Medicine by Research, 1896. Home: Jamaica Plain, Mass. Died 1911.

BOWDITCH, Vincent Yardley, M.D.; b. Weston, Mass., July 7, 1852; s. Dr. Henry I. and Olivia (Yardley) B.; A.B., Harvard, 1875, M.D., 1879. House officer, Mass. Gen. Hosp., 1878-79; asst., and instr. clin. medicine, Harvard Medical School, 1892-99; attending physician, Carney Hosp. (South Boston), State Sanatorium (Rutland, Mass.), 1898-1906; med. dir. Sharon (Mass.) Sanatorium; pres. Corp. Central N.E. Sanatorium, Rutland; consulting phys., N.E. Hosp. for Women and Children, Boston City Hosp., St. Luke's Home for Convalescents. Author: Life and Correspondence of Henry I. Bowditch, M.D.; also various monographs and articles in leading med. jours. Home: Boston, Mass. Died Dec. 20, 1929.

BOWDOIN, George Sullivan, banker; b. New York. Mem. J. P. Morgan & Co.; treas. and dir. Met. Opera and Real Estate Co., trustee Bank for Savings, New York Life Ins. & Trust Co.; dir. N.Y.C.&H.R. R.R. Co., Commercial Union Assurance Co., Ltd., of London, Commercial Union Fire Ins. Co. of New York, Mohawk & Malone Ry. Co., N.Y. & Putnam R.R., West Shore R.R. Co. Trustee Am. Mus. Natural History; mem. Am. Fine Arts Soc., N.E. Soc., S.A.R., Met. Mus. of Art. Home: New York, N.Y. Died Dec. 16, 1913.

BOWEN, Benjamin Lester, univ. prof.; b. Chili, N.Y., July 5, 1860; s. Benjamin Franklin and Mary Frances (Bangs) B.; A.B., U. of Rochester, 1881, grad. student, 1881-82; student Paris, Bonn, Rome, Madrid, 1885, 1886-87; Ph.D., Johns Hopkins, 1888; (Litt.D., U. of Rochester, 1912); m. Grace Bowen King, June 21, 1894. Prof. langs., New Windsor Coll., 1882-83; asst. in French, Johns Hopkins, 1884-88; prof. French and Latin, Bowdoin Coll., 1888-89; prof. French lang. and lit., 1889-90, Romance langs., 1890—; chmn. Grad. Sch., 1909-10, Ohio State Univ. Conglist. Author: Introduction to Modern French Lyrics, 1891; First Italian Readings, 1897; Chateaubriand's Atala and René, 1901; First Scientific French Reader, 1902. Died June 28, 1920.

BOWEN, Clarence Winthrop, publisher; b. Brooklyn, May 22, 1852; s. Henry Chandler and Lucy M. (Tappan) B.; brother of Herbert Wolcott B.; A.B., Yale, 1873, A.M., 1876, Ph.D., 1882, LL.D., William and Mary Coll., Va., 1918; m. Roxana, d. of Hon. John Wentworth, of Chicago, Jan. 28, 1892. Corr. for The Independent in Europe in 1875; interviewed Thomas Carlyle, and in 1883 interviewed King Alphonso XII, of Spain, the Duke of Veragua (a desc. of Columbus), and others, with reference to the 400th anniversary of the Discovery of America, which he was the first to agitate, resulting in the Chicago Expn., 1893. Pub. and propr. The Independent (after his father's death), 1896-1912; was sec. com. of arrangements for centennial of Washington's Inauguration, 1889. A founder of Yale Univ. Club, New Haven, 1880; of Wolf's Head Soc., Yale, 1883; of Manhattan Congl. Ch., New York, 1896. Author: Boundary Disputes of Connecticut, 1882; Woodstock, an Historical Sketch, 1887; Memorial of Centennial of Washington's Inauguration, 1892; History of Woodstock, Conn., 1926; Genealogies of Woodstock Families (6 vols.), 1930-34. Home: New York, N.Y., and Woodstock, Conn. Died Nov. 2, 1935.

BOWEN, Clayton Raymond, theol. prof.; b. Wellsboro, Pa., Nov. 25, 1877; s. Benjamin Franklin and Mary (Forsythe) B.; A.B., Franklin Coll., New Athens, O., 1898; U. of Chicago, 1 quarter, 1900; grad. Meadville Theol. Sch., 1901, B.D., 1903, and Th.D. from same, 1920; U. of Berlin, 1 semester, 1901-02; U. of Marburg, 1 semester, 1902; Harvard, 1902-03; m. Margaret Browning Barber, Sept. 12, 1905. Ordained Unitarian ministry, 1903; pastor South Parish, Charlestown, N.H., 1903-05; instr. N.T., 1905-07, asst. prof. N.T. interpretation, 1907-11, prof., 1911—, librarian, 1926—, Meadville Theol. Sch. Mem. Soc. Bibl. Lit. and Exegesis. Author: The Resurrection in the New Testament, 1911; The Gospel of Jesus, 1916. Home: Chicago, Ill. Died Oct. 17, 1934.

BOWEN, Herbert Wolcott, diplomat; b. Brooklyn, Feb. 29, 1856; s. Henry Chandler and Lucy M. (Tappan) B.; brother of Clarence Winthrop B.; studied at Brooklyn Poly. and in Europe; mem. class 1878, Yale, hon. M.A., 1903; LL.B., cum laude, Columbia, 1881; admitted to bar, 1881; m. Carolyn Mae Clegg, Jan. 25, 1902. In practice, New York, 1884-90; consul, 1890-95, consul gen. 1895-99, Barcelona, Spain; minister and consul gen., Teheran, Persia, 1899-1901; E.E. and M.P. to Venezuela, 1901-05, Counsel of U.S. and Venezuela at The Hague Court, in Venezuelan case, 1903; dist. chmn. Conn. State Council of Defense, 1917—. Author: Verses, 1884; Losing Ground, 1889; In Divers Tones, 1890; De Genere Humano, 1893; International Law, 1895. Home: Woodstock, Conn. Died May 29, 1927.

BOWEN, John Templeton, dermatologist; b. Boston, July 8, 1857; s. James and Eliza Matilda (Alline) B.; A.B., Harvard, 1879, M.D., 1884; unmarried. Asst. phys. for skin diseases, 1894-95, phys. 1895-1914, cons. phys., 1914—, Mass. General Hosp.; instr. in dermatology, 1896-1902; asst. prof., 1902-07, Edward Wigglesworth prof., 1907-12, Edward Wigglesworth prof. emeritus, 1912, Harvard. Cont. to Morrow System of Genito-Urinary Diseases, Syphilology and Dermatology, 3 vols., 1893; Bang's-Hardaway's American text-book of Genito-Urinary Diseases, Syphilology and Diseases of the Skin; Twentieth Century Practice of Medicine, New York, 1896. Died Dec. 3, 1940.

BOWEN, Lem Warner, business man; b. Green Bay, Wis., July 12, 1857; s. Charles Clark and Julia M. (Hard) B.; ed. Kalamazoo (Mich.) Coll., Freshman yr.; A.B., U. of Rochester, 1879; m. Grace M. Woodbury, May 10, 1881. Entered employ of D. M. Ferry & Co., seedsmen, Detroit, 1879; elected treas. of co., 1887, gen. mgr., 1900, pres., 1907. V.p., 1900, pres., 1906, Standard Accident Ins. Co.; dir. Detroit Edison Co., Security Trust Co. of Detroit, Wayne County & Home Savings Bank. Home: Detroit, Mich. Deceased.

BOWEN, Marcellus, clergyman; b. Marion, O., Apr. 6, 1846; s. Ozias and Lydia (Baker) B.; A.B., Yale, 1866; grad. Union Theol. Sem., 1872; (D.D., U. of Wooster, 1904); m. Flora Pierpoint Stearns, Aug. 29, 1871. Ordained Presbyn. ministry, 1872; pastor Springfield, N.J., 1872-74; missionary A.B.C. F.M., at Smyrna, Turkey, 1874-84; prin. pvt. sch. for boys, Hartford, Conn., 1885-88; agt. Am. Bible Soc. at Constantinople, 1888—. Died Oct. 5, 1916.

BOWEN, Reuben Dean, planter; b. Montgomery Co., Tex., Dec. 18, 1859; s. William Abraham and Clementine Dalmatia (Richards) B.; ed. St. Mary's Coll., Galveston, Tex.; Agrl. and Mech. Coll. of Tex., 1877-78; m. Bonnybel, d. Capt. Sam J. Wright, of Paris, Tex., May 15, 1890. Bookkeeper, Galveston and New Orleans; traveling salesman for G. R. Finlay, wholesale druggist, New Orleans, 1879-84; became connected with E. J. Hart & Co., New Orleans, 1884, advancing to partnership and gen. mgr., closed out wholesale bus., returned to Texas, 1895; active in promoting investments in Southwest and owner and mgr. of large farming interests in Tex.; pres. Kiomatia Planters' Co., Red River Co., Tex. Originator of movement to popularize use of cotton in U.S. and for many mfg. purposes; chmn. of com. of Farmers' Union on Greater Consumption of Cotton; largely instrumental in securing competition from other states in bidding for cotton-seed in Tex.; also in application of business methods to the farm; engaged largely in stock raising. Apptd. by gov. of Tex. as chmn. com. to receive delegation from Chicago on its visit to Tex., 1902, out of which originated Miss. Valley Assn., of which he was an organizer, and elected as dir. representing agriculture; del. from Tex. in orgn. Am. Farm Bur. Fedn. in Chicago, 1919; one of organizers Farmers-Mfrs. Assn. Movement launched 1924; mem. permanent exec. com. Nat. Flood Control of Miss. River, mem. Farmers Union, Tex. Farm Bur., Tex. Hist. Soc., Southern Sociol. Assn., Improved Order of Red Men. Home: Paris, Texas. Died 1939.

BOWEN, Thomas M., lawyer; b. near Burlington, Ia., Oct. 26, 1835; ed. public schools; admitted to the bar at age of 18; mem. Ia. legislature, 1856; removed to Kan., 1858; enlisted as capt. Union army; raised 13th Kan. inf. and commanded it until end of war; bvt. brig. gen.; comd. brigade, 1863-65, on frontier and with 7th Army Corps; delegate from Kan. to Nat. Rep. conv., 1864. After war settled in Ark.; pres. constl. convs. of 1866 and 1868; justice Supreme Court, Ark., 1867-71; apptd. gov. Idaho, 1871; resigned and returned to Ark.; was defeated as candidate for U.S. senator; removed to Colo.; was 4 yrs. judge Dist. Court; mem. State legislature, 1882; U.S. senator from Colo., 1883-89. Republican. Has been identified with large mining interests since living in Colo. Home: Pueblo, Colo. Died 1906.

BOWEN, Wilbur Pardon, college prof.; b. Lima, Mich., July 28, 1864; s. Charles Marshall and Julia (Peirce) B.; B.Pd., Mich. Normal Coll., 1897; B.S., U. of Mich., 1900, M.S., 1901; student med. dept. same, 1900-02; married; 1 son, Stirling; m. 2d, Lois E. Knapp, Aug. 1898; children—Ruth C., Claribel, Marjory, Eleanor. Teacher, 1884—; taught mathematics, Mich. Normal Coll., 1886-91; dir. gymnasium, U. of Neb., 1891-94, Mich. Normal Coll., 1894-1900; instr. physiology, Univ. of Mich., 1901-02; prof. physical edn., Mich. Normal Coll., 1903—. Author: A Teacher's Course in Physical Training, 1898; Mechanics of Bodily Exercise, 1909; The Teaching of School Gymnastics, 1909; The Teaching of Gymnastic Games, 1909; Action of Muscles, 1912; The Teaching of Play, 1913; The Mechanism of Muscular Movement, 1917; Applied Anatomy and Kinesiology, 1919; The Theory and Practice of Organized Play (with Elmer D. Mitchell), 1923; The Conduct of Physical Activities in Schools, 1927. Editor of Michigan Course in Physical Training for City Schools, 1914. Home: Ypsilanti, Mich. Died Sept. 5, 1928.

BOWEN, William (Alvin), author; b. Baltimore, Md., May 15, 1877; s. Jesse N. and Mary Amanda (Hall) B.; LL.B., U. of Md., 1898; m. Grace Lee Dunan, July 31, 1902; children—Dorothy, William, John, Margery Ann. Began practice of law in Baltimore, 1898; moved to Los Angeles, Calif., 1904, and continued in practice. Republican. Home: Los Angeles, Calif. Died Sept. 18, 1937.

BOWEN, William Abraham, editor, pub.; b. Bagdad, Santa Rosa, Fla., Apr. 14, 1856; s. William Abraham and Clementine Dalmatia (Richards) B.; mainly self-ed.; student Southwestern U., Georgetown, Tex., 1875-77 inclusive; m. Ada, d. Dr. John F. and Mary C. (Murchison) DeBardeleben, of Bastrop, Tex., Dec. 12, 1877. Owner and editor of the Advance Guard, Decatur, Tex., 1873-74; founder Montague News, 1874; staff corr. Houston Daily Post, at Austin, Tex., 1880-81; polit. editor San Antonio Daily Express, at Austin, 1881-86; editorial staff Chicago Times, 1886-90; organizer 1st adv. ry. train, and toured U.S.; sec. Chamber of Commerce, San Antonio, 1891-93; chautauqua lecturer and writer until 1901; field editor Texas Christian Advocate, 1901-04; editorial staff Houston Post, 1904-05, St. Louis Republic, 1905-07; founder, 1908, and pres., Arlington Printing Co.; editor and owner, Farmers' Fireside Bulletin (official paper Farmers' Union for Tex., La. and Okla.), and Arlington Journal. Democrat. Mem. M.E. Ch., South. Author: Chained Lightning, 1883; Why Two M.E. Churches in the United States, 1901; Uncle Zeke's Speculation, 1910. Has made large collection of data on Tex. for Practical History of Texas. Died Apr. 15, 1921.

BOWEN, William Miller, lawyer; b. Lowell, Ind., Jan. 16, 1862; s. Peter M. and Chloe (Miller) B.; student Washington Coll., nr. Niles, Calif., and Meth. Coll., Napa, Calif.; LL.B., Drake U., Des Moines, Ia., 1890; m. Louise A. Martin, Aug. 16, 1892; children—Mary Louise, Wilda Louise (Mrs. Ralph O. Chick, dec.). Admitted to Calif. bar, 1890, and began practice at Napa; removed to Los Angeles, 1894; mem. City Council, Los Angeles, 2 terms (pres. 1 term); served as chief counsel to prohibition enforcement commr.; now counsel for U. of Southern Calif. at Los Angeles; had charge of proceedings in the courts and state legislature to clear title and secure appropriations for Exposition Park, at Los Angeles; mem. Scarborough & Bowen. Pres. 6th Dist. Agrl. Assn.; pres. bd. dirs. Mus. of History, Science and Art, Los Angeles. Mem. Rep. County Central Com., Los Angeles Co., 1898—. Methodist. Mason. Home: Los Angeles, Calif. Died Dec. 22, 1937.

BOWER, Bertha Muzzy (B. M. Bower); author; b. Cleveland, Minn., Nov. 15, 1871; d. Washington and Eunice A. (Miner) Muzzy; ed. pub. sch. and under pvt. teachers; m. Clayton J. Bower, Dec. 20, 1890; children—Bertha Grace, Harold Clayton, Roy

Noel; m. 2d, Bertrand W. Sinclair, of Edinburgh, Scotland, Aug. 14, 1906; 1 dau., Dele Frances; m. 3d, Robert Ellsworth Cowan. Began writing western fiction, 1904. Democrat. Author: Chip of the Flying U, 1906; The Lure of the Dim Trails, 1907; Her Prairie Knight and Rowdy of the "Cross L," 1908; The Lonesome Trail, 1909; The Long Shadow, 1909; The Happy Family, 1910; The Range Dwellers, 1910; Good Indian, 1912; Lonesome Land, 1912; The Uphill Climb, 1913; The Gringos, 1913; Ranch at the Wolverine, 1914; Flying U Ranch, 1914; Flying U's Last Stand, 1915; Jean of the Lazy A, 1915; The Phantom Herd, 1916; Heritage of the Sioux, 1916; The Lookout Man, 1917; Starr of the Desert, 1917; Cabin Fever, 1918; Skyrider, 1918; The Thunder Bird, 1919; Rim o' the World, 1920; The Quirt, 1920; Cow Country, 1921; Casey Ryan, 1921; Trail of the White Mule, 1922; The Voice at Johnnywater, 1923; The Parowan Bonanza, 1923; The Bellehelen Mine, 1924; Desert Brew, 1924; Meadowlark Basin, 1925; Black Thunder, 1925; White Wolves, 1926; Van Patten, 1926; The Adam Chasers, 1927; Points West, 1928; The Swallowfork Bulls, 1928; Rodeo, 1929; Fool's Goal, 1930; Tiger Eye, 1930; The Long Loop, 1931; Dark Horse, 1931; Laughing Water, 1932; Rocking Arrow, 1932; Trails Meet, 1933; Open Land, 1933; The Flying U Strikes, 1934; The Haunted Hills, 1934; The Dry Ridge Gang, 1935; Trouble Rides the Wind, 1935; The Five Furies of Leaning Ladder, 1935; Shadow Mountain, 1936; The North Wind Do Blow, 1936; Pirates of the Range, 1937; The Wind Blows West, Starry Night, 1938; The Singing Hill, 1939. Home: Los Angeles, Calif. Died July 23, 1940.

BOWER, Lucy Scott, artist; b. Rochester, Ia., Jan. 18, 1864; d. James Yelverton and Hannah (Haight) Scott; studied art at Phila. Acad. Fine Arts, New York Sch. of Art, under Chase, and later in Paris at Acad. Julian, under Fleury and Lefebvre, and afterwards at Académie de la Grande Chaumiere, under Menard and Simon; m. John Munroe Bower, Apr. 1890 (died 1912). Exhibited Acad. of Design, New York, and Salon des Artistes Française, Salon d'Autumn, and Arc-en-Ciel, Paris; Royal Acad., London; Museum, Brooklyn; Albright Gallery, Buffalo; Salon, Chicago. Awarded gold prize Arc-en-Ciel, 1917; 1st prize ($100) Nat. Assn. Am. Pen Women, 1929. Works: "The Knitters," Mus. of Vitré, France; "Fishermen Mending Nets," Long Branch (N.J.) club house of Fedn. Women's Clubs; "The Old Street" and "Red Sails," Pen and Brush Club, New York; also picture in Richmond Hill (New York) High Sch. Spent 20 yrs. in France and England. Author: In a Minor Vein (verse), 1913; also contbr. verse in mags. Died Nov. 15, 1934.

BOWERS, Alphonzo Benjamin, inventor and civ., mech., hydraulic engr.; b. W. Baldwin, Me., Sept. 25, 1830; s. Wilder and Sarah Hay (Thompson) B.; desc. from George B., Scituate, Mass., 1637, and through mother from James T., Charleston, Mass., 1630, and Dr. William Hay, Reading, Mass., about 1717; ed. Bridgton Acad., Maine Wesleyan Sem., Bridgewater State Normal Sch., Phillips Acad., Andover, Mass., and by pvt. study. Built 1st dam at 16; went to Calif., 1853; engaged in mining, teaching, writing and lecturing; invented, 1853, method of cheap transportation of earth by stream of water on down grade in open flume for building of dams and embankments; flexibly connected floating pipes, and method of building levees from old style dredges; hydraulic dredging, transportation, filling, and hydraulic dredge, with rotary excavator. Studied law, became his own atty. and obtained over 400 claims, engaging in more than 60 suits against infringers of his patents, costing over $250,000. Del. Rep. State convs., 1861, 1863; offered nomination surveyor gen. (declined); chief clerk office surveyor gen., 1863, deputy surveyor gen., 1864; in charge of sales of state lands, 1863-67. Mem. Internat. Congress of Commerce and Navigation, Brussels, 1898, and entertained by Leopold II; mem. Permanent Internat. Assn. of Navigation Congresses; del. from Calif. to Am. Civic Alliance, New York, 1909. Died Jan. 24, 1926.

BOWERS, George Meade, congressman; b. Gerrardstown, W.Va., Sept. 13, 1863; s. John S. and Mary E. (Stump) B.; ed. high sch., Martinsburg, W.Va., and pvt. tutor 2 yrs.; m. Bessie C. Gray, Nov. 18, 1884. Mem. W.Va. Legislature, 1887; supervisor of U.S. census for W.Va., 1890; del. to Rep. Nat. Conv., Minneapolis, 1892; mem. and treas. Bd. of World's Fair Commrs. for W.Va.; U.S. commr. of fish and fisheries, 1898-1913; elected to 64th Congress, May 9, 1916, for unexpired term (1916-17) of William G. Brown (dec.); reëlected to 65th to 67th Congresses (1917-23), 2d W.Va. Dist. Republican. Home: Martinsburg, W.Va. Died Dec. 7, 1925.

BOWERS, Henry Francis, founder of the "A.P.A."; b. Baltimore, Aug. 12, 1837; ed. at home; removed to Iowa; m. Eliza H., d. Judge Thomas H. Wilson, of Ia. Deputy clerk of cts., 1863; deputy recorder, 1869; co. recorder, 1870-74; admitted to bar, Oct. 1870; practiced in U.S. cts. Spl a.-d.-c., with rank of lt. col., staff of Gov. John H. Gear, 1878-82. Founded, 1887, the Am. Protective Assn.; was its supreme pres. 6 yrs. and was reëlected 1898. Home: Clinton, Ia. Died 1911.

BOWERS, Herbert Edmund, clergyman; b. Southampton, Eng., May 2, 1868; s. John and Elizabeth (Savage) B.; B.A., 1887, M.A., 1889, Hertford Coll., Oxford, Eng.; (LL.D., Chaddock Coll., Ill., 1897; D.D., Rutherford Coll., N.C., 1902); came to America, 1889; m. Emilie Blundell-Blake, July 15, 1892. Tutor St. John's Coll., Qu'Appelle, Can., 1892; ordained P.E. ministry, 1893; rector, St. Paul's, Vancouver, B.C., 1895-96; gen. missionary, diocese of Spokane, Wash., 1896-97; rector, Marshall, Tex., 1901-06, Grace Ch., Galveston, Tex., 1906—. Deputy to Gen. Conv. P.E. Ch., 1904. Republican. Home: Galveston, Tex. Died 1910.

BOWERS, John Hugh, educator; b. near Franklin, W.Va., Aug. 10, 1875; s. Josephus and Emily (Bond) B.; grad. Fairmont (W.Va.) State Normal Sch., 1896; A.B., W.Va. U., 1903, LL.B., 1897; A.M., Ill. Wesleyan U., 1906, Ph.D., 1909; studied Ohio Wesleyan U., U. of Chicago (honor scholarship); m. Pearl Elizabeth Copeland, Apr. 28, 1902. Began teaching at 16; supt. schs. Elizabeth, Pa., Waukon, Ia., and Covington, Tenn.; teacher state normal schs., Fairmont, W.Va., West Liberty, W.Va., Springfield, S.D., and Oshkosh, Wis.; dean and prof. edn. and social science, Okla. Agrl. and Mech. Coll., also dir. summer sch., 1909-19; prof. social sciences, Normal Coll., Pittsburg, Kan., 1919—. Admitted to W.Va. bar, 1897; was nominated for state supt. edn. of W.Va. Commencement speaker and lecturer at teachers' institutes. Prohibitionist. Methodist. Mason. Author: College Teaching; The Kansas Court of Industrial Relations, 1922. Home: Pittsburg, Kan. Died Apr. 6, 1923.

BOWERS, LaMont Montgomery, business man; b. Maine, N.Y., Mar. 7, 1847; s. Gardner Sawin and Achsah (Taylor) Bowers; ed. pub. and select schs. and by pvt. study; m. Fanny A. Gray, 1872 (died 1909); children—Franck Taylor, Clement Gray. Was partner in wholesale grocery house, Binghamton, N.Y., 1868-78; in real estate bus., later in warehouse for machinery and implements, Omaha, 1878-83; engaged in bus. Binghamton and in the West, 1883-94; confidential rep. of John D. Rockefeller, 1896-1921; had charge of constrn. and managed Rockefeller Fleet of 58 ships on the Great Lakes, 1895-1901, together with iron ore docks and transportation; directed several other personal interests of Mr. Rockefeller, management Colo. Fuel & Iron Co., chmn. bd., v.p. and treas.; also v.p. and treas. Colo. & Wyo. R.R. Was an organizer and dir. Superior Savings and Trust Co., of Cleveland, dir. Central Nat. Bank, also pres. Cleveland Steel Co., mem. exec. bd., Am. Shipbuilding Co., Great Lakes Towing Co., etc.; now retired from active business but retained in several corps. in advisory capacity. Inventor and mfr. Nat. Anchor and devices for ships extensively used by Am. shipbuilders and the U.S. Navy, 1900-25. Presbyn. Mason. Home: Binghamton, N.Y. Died June 2, 1941.

BOWERS, Larkin Bruce, clergyman, educator; b. Upper Tract, W.Va., Oct. 16, 1877; s. Josephus and Emily (Bond) B.; teacher's course, State Normal Sch., Fairmont, W.Va.; B.L., Ohio Wesleyan U., 1905; studied W.Va. U. and 2 years' residence Columbia U. and Union Theol. Sem.; D.D., W.Va. Wesleyan U., 1918; D.D., Ohio Wesleyan U., 1924; LL.D., Oklahoma City U., 1935; m. Virginia Smith, Feb. 26, 1908; 1 son, Robert Scott. Teacher pub. schs. of W.Va., 4 yrs.; licensed to preach in M.E. Ch., 1896; jr. pastor Pendleton Circuit, W.Va., 1897-99; pastor S. Charleston Circuit, 1899, Wyatt Charge, 1900, Buena Vista, Colo., 1902; student pastor Zanesville (O.) Circuit, 1904; pastor 1st Ch., Salem, W.Va., 1905-06; asst. to religious work dir. 23rd St. Y.M.C.A., New York, 1907; dir. Speakers' Bur. N.Y. Anti-Saloon League, 1908; pastor Ronceverte, W.Va., 1908-10, Diamond St. Ch., Fairmont, W.Va., 1910-14; dist. supt. Parkersburg Dist., W.Va. Conf., 1914-18; mem. Nat. Campaign Com. of Missionary Centenary, M.E. Ch., 1918-19; pres. Kan. Wesleyan U., July 31, 1919—. Mem. Gen. Conf. M.E. Ch., 1916, 24, 32; mem. 5th Ecumenical Conf. M.E. Ch., London, Eng., 1921, 6th Ecumenical Conf., Atlanta, Ga., 1931. Mason. Rotarian. Home: Salina, Kan. Deceased.

BOWERS, Lloyd Wheaton, solicitor gen.; b. Springfield, Mass., Mar. 9, 1859; s. Samuel Dwight and Martha (Wheaton) B.; A.B., Yale, 1879; LL.B., Columbia, 1882; admitted to bar, 1882; m. Louise Bennett Wilson, Sept. 7, 1887 (died 1897). Gen. counsel C.&N.W. Ry. Co., Chicago, 1893-1909; solicitor gen. of U.S., Mar. 1909—. Republican. Home: Chicago, Ill. Died 1910.

BOWERS, Robert Hood, composer; b. Chambersburg, Pa., May 24, 1877; s. Oliver Cromwell and Ellen Graham (Heyser) B.; A.B., Franklin and Marshall Coll., 1896, A.M., 1899; studied music with Thomas Whitney Surette, the late Frederic Grant Gleason, Constantin Von Sternberg, in Baltimore, Phila. and Chicago; m. Virginia Belvin, Sept. 16, 1905 (dec.); 1 son, Robert Hood; m. 2d, Catherine Meredith Abrams, June 9, 1936. Won gold medal of Chicago Auditorium Conservatory, 1902. Conductor, Columbia Phonograph Co., 1916-20; mus. dir. Aeolian Phonograph Co., 1921, Columbia, 1922-32, comdr. electrical transcription dept. Nat. Broadcasting Co., 1935—; musical dir. Sch. of Radio Technique, Radio City, N.Y., 1935—. Condr. Open Air Theater, Memphis, Tenn., summers. Awarded Alumni Gold Medal by Franklin and Marshall Coll. for distinguished service. Composer: Rubes and Roses, 1903; The Paraders, 1903; The Maid and the Mummy, 1904; The Vanderbilt Cup, 1906; The Hoyden, 1907; A Grecian Garden, 1908; The Anniversary, 1908; The Silver Star, 1909; The Wife Tamers, 1910; A Certain Party, 1911; The Scare Crow, 1911; The Red Rose, 1911; The Antique Girl, 1911; California, 1911; In the Barracks, 1912; The Little Parisienne, 1912; The Red Heads, 1913; The Water Cure, 1913; Omika, 1913; The Hasty Wedding, 1914; The Lasky Beauties, 1914; Garden of Peaches, 1914; Models Abroad, 1915; A Daughter of the Gods, 1916; East Is West, 1918; A Lonely Romeo, 1919; East of Suez, 1922; Hail and Farewell, 1923; The Open Road, 1923; Old English, 1924; Aloma of the South Seas, 1925; Oh, Ernest, 1927; Listen In, 1929; The Legionnaires, 1935; also incidental music for dramatic plays and motion pictures. Radio condr. WEAF and WOR, 1928—; station condr. Station WMCA, 1933-34. Home: New York, N.Y. Died Dec. 29, 1941.

BOWERSOCK, Justin DeWitt, congressman; b. Columbiana, Co., O., Sept. 19, 1842; s. I. and Adaline (McDonald) B.; ed. common schs.; m. Mary C. Gower, Sept. 5, 1866. Settled Lawrence, Kan., 1877; built dam across Kansas River and began mfg.; organized Douglass Co. Bank, 1878 (Lawrence Nat. Bank), pres., 1888—; pres. Bowersock Mills & Power Co., Kan., Water Power Co., Lawrence Ice Co., Lawrence Iron Works, Lawrence Paper Mfg. Co., etc. President of the Lawrence Clearing House Assn. Mayor, Lawrence, 1881-85; mem. Kan. Ho. of Rep., 1887, Senate, 1895; mem. 56th to 59th Congresses (1899-1907), 2d Kan. Dist.; candidate for U.S. senator, 1903. Republican. Pres. trustees Plymouth Congl. Ch. Pres. Lawrence Commercial Club, 1885-90, Merchants' Athletic Assn., 1890-95; pres. Lawrence Chamber of Commerce many yrs.; chmn. War Loan Com., World War. Home: Lawrence, Kan. Died Oct. 27, 1922.

BOWES, Frank B., ry. official; b. Chicago, Jan. 29, 1862. Began ry. service with I.C. R.R., 1876, with which has since been identified; clk. in auditor's, gen. frt. and gen. pass. offices, 1876-87; gen. northern pass. agt., 1886-94; asst. gen. pass. agt., 1894-95; gen. freight agt. southern lines and Yazoo & Miss. Valley R.R., 1895-1903; asst. traffic mgr. same lines, 1903-05, freight traffic mgr. same, 1905-08, and gen. traffic mgr. I.C., Yazoo & Miss. Valley rys., 1909-11; v.p. same rys., in charge of traffic, May 1, 1911—. Home: Chicago, Ill. Died Feb. 15, 1939.

BOWIE, Sydney Johnston, congressman, b. Talladega, Ala., July 26, 1865; s. Andrew W. and Nannie McHenry (Bowdon) B.; ed. in pvt. schs.; LL.B., U. of Ala., 1885; admitted to bar, 1885; m. Annie Foster Etheridge, Apr. 29, 1891; children—Elizabeth, Alice T. In practice, Talladega and Anniston, Ala., 1885-1906; practiced in Birmingham as mem. Cabaniss & Bowie, 1906-19; pres. Crawford's Auto Shop, 1919—. City clerk, 1885-86, alderman, 1891, Talladega; mem. Dem. State Exec. Com., 1894-1900; chmn. Dem. Co. Exec. Com., Talladega Co., 1896-99; mem. 57th to 59th Congresses (1901-07), 4th Ala. Dist.; declined renomination; del. at large Dem. Nat. Conv., San Francisco, 1920, also chmn. delegation. Mem. Bd. of Edn. Birmingham, 1915-19; chmn. Ala. Edn. Commn., 1919. Home: Birmingham, Ala. Died May 7, 1928.

BOWIE, William, engr., geodesist; b. Annapolis Junction, Md., May 6, 1872; s. Thomas John and Susanna A(nderson) B.; St. John's Coll., Annapolis, Md.; B.Sc., Trinity Coll., Conn., 1893; C.E., Lehigh U., Pa., 1895, Sc.D., 1922; M.A., Trinity, 1907, Sc.D., 1919; LL.D., Univ. of Edinburgh (Scotland), 1936; Sc.D., George Washington Univ., 1937; m. Elizabeth Taylor Wattles, June 28, 1899; children—William Bladen (dec.), Clagett. Mem. field force, U.S. Coast and Geod. Surveys, 1895-1937, retired; engaged in field on coast or geod. surveys in many states of U.S. in P.R., P.I., and Alaska, 1895-1909; in charge Div. of Geodesy, 1909-36; commd. hydrographic and geodetic engr., 1917. Maj. engrs. U.S.A., Aug. 1918-Feb. 1919. In charge summer course in practical astronomy and geodesy, Columbia U., 1912-17. Del. from U.S. to number internat. scientific confs. Pres. Internat. Geod. Assn., 1919-33; pres. Internat. Geod. and Geophys. Union, 1933-36; chmn. bd. Surveys and Maps of Federal Govt.; 1922-24. Special lecturer at Lehigh, 1922-36. Author of a number of publs. of the Coast and Geodetic Survey on the various branches of geodesy, including measurement of base lines, triangulation, gravity, isostasy, etc.; also geodetic and engring. articles in scientific and engring. mags. Author of book "Isostasy," 1927. Awarded Cresson medal, Franklin Inst., 1937, William Bowie medal, Am. Geophysical Union, 1939; Officer Order of Orange-Nassau, Holland; comdr. Order St. Sava, Yugoslavia. Home: Washington, D.C. Deceased.

BOWKER, Richard Rogers, editor, publisher and industrial director; b. Salem, Mass., Sept. 4, 1848; s. Daniel R. and Theresa M. (Savory) B.; A.B., Coll. City of New York, 1868; m. Alice Mitchell, Jan. 1, 1902. Lit. editor New York Evening Mail, 1869-75; with lit. dept. New York Tribune, 1875; London rep. of Harper & Bros., 1880-82; 1st v.p. New York Edison Co., 1890-99; pres. R. R. Bowker Co., pubs.; v.p. DeLaval Turbine Co. and DeLaval Separator Co., 1901-31. Trustee Brooklyn Pub. library and Brooklyn Inst. Arts and Sciences; pres. Stockbridge (Mass.) Library Assn., 1904-28; hon. pres. Laurel Hill Assn. Active in independent politics; originated independent Republican movement, 1879, called "original mugwump"; later affiliated with Nat. (gold standard) Dem. party; founder Soc. for Polit. Edn., 1880. V.p. Am. Copyright League, City Club (chmn. council); mem. Council A.L.A. (hon. pres. 1926); fellow Am. Library Inst.; 1st pres. N.Y. Library Club; mem. N.Y. Chamber Commerce, N.Y. Merchants' Assn.; past pres. Assn. of Edison Illuminating Cos., Asso. Alumni Coll. City of N.Y.; v.p. Edison Pioneers. Author: Work and Wealth, 1883; Economics for the People, 1886; Copyright—Its Law and Its Literature, 1886; Primer for Political Education, 1886; Civil Service Examinations, 1886; Electoral Reform, 1889; The Arts of Life, 1900, Of Business, 1901, Of Politics, 1901, Of Education, 1903, Of Religion, 1903; Problems of the Infinitely Little, 1910; Copyright—Its History and Its Law, 1912; From the Pen of R.R.B. (verse), 1916; From Years that Are Past (verse), 1923; Economic Peace, 1923. Editor The Library Journal, 1876—, Publisher's Weekly, 1884—, Am. Catalogue, 1884-1910, The Economic Fact-Book, 1885; The Reader's Guide in Economics, Social and Political Science (with George Iles), 1891; The Campaign Text-Book, Nat. Democratic Party, 1896; Society Publications; State Publications; Am. Library Directory. Home: New York and Stockbridge, Mass. Died Nov. 12, 1933.

BOWLER, John William, physical dir.; b. Boston, Mass., Feb. 25, 1865; s. Edward William and Catherine (Sullivan) B.; M.D., Dartmouth Med. Sch., 1906; hon. A.M., Dartmouth, 1910; m. Ellen C. Pollard, Nov. 24, 1891 (dec.); children—Edmund William, John Pollard, Richard; m. 2d, Mary Duffy Leonard, June 25, 1932. Amateur (later professional) athlete and gymnast, 1879-89; asst. to Dr. Dudley A. Sargent, Harvard U. Gymnasium, 1889-93; dir. Charlesbank Gymnasium, Boston, 1893-1901; gen. supt. Pub. Gymnasia, Boston, 1899-1901; dir. Gymnasium, and athletic coach and trainer, 1901-05, asst. prof., 1905-07, prof. physical edn. and hygiene, and dir. Gymnasium, 1907-36, prof. emeritus, 1936—, all of Dartmouth College. Independent Democrat. Catholic. Died Dec. 27, 1938.

BOWLES, Francis Tiffany, shipbuilder; b. Springfield, Mass., Oct. 7, 1858; s. Benjamin F. and Mary E. (Bailey) B.; grad. U.S. Naval Acad., 1879; (postgrad. degree of Naval Architect from Royal Naval Coll., Greenwich, Eng.); m. Adelaide Hay Savage, Nov. 17, 1886; children— Thomas Savage (dec.), Mrs. Catherine Lowell. In U.S.N. until 1903, serving as constructor at navy yards, etc.; chief constructor U.S.N., with rank of rear adm., 1901-03; pres. Fore River Shipbuilding Corp., Quincy, Mass.; mgr. div. of constrn., afterwards asst. gen. mgr., U.S. Shipping Bd. of Emergency Fleet Corp., Washington, D.C., 1917-19. Mem. Inst. Naval Architects, London; past pres. Soc. Naval Architects and Marine Engrs.; fellow Am. Acad. Arts and Sciences. Home: Boston, Mass. Died Aug. 3, 1927.

BOWLES, Henry Leland, congressman; b. Athens, Vt., Jan. 6, 1866; s. Lyman E. and Julia (Leland) B.; ed. Vt. Acad., Saxtons River (non-grad.); m. Edna Howard, Dec. 1909. Began in lunch business with $1,000 borrowed capital, 1897, and extended business to ten cities in U.S. and Can.; pres.-treas. East Springfield Home Builders Co., Bowles Lunch, Inc., Bowles Lunch, Ltd., dir. Bowles Lunch Co. of Detroit, Union Trust Co. of Springfield, Mass.; elected to 69th Congress, Sept. 29, 1925, to fill unexpired term of George B. Churchill, ending Mar. 3, 1927, and reëlected to 70th Congress (1927-29), 2d Mass. Dist. Republican. Universalist. Mason. Home: Springfield, Mass. Died May 17, 1932.

BOWLES, Phillip Ernest, banker; b. Arcata, Humboldt Co., Calif., 1859; s. Joseph S. and Sara H. (Harding) B.; Ph.B., U. of Calif., 1882; m. Mae A. McNear, 1884. Became identified with banking business, Oakland, Calif., 1893; then pres. American Bank, San Francisco; dir. East Bay Water Co., Key System Transit Co. Mem. bd. regents U. of Calif. Republican. Episcopalian. Home: Oakland, Calif. Died Jan. 20, 1926.

BOWLES, Pinckney Downie, lawyer; b. Edgefield, S.C., July 7, 1835; s. Isaac and Emily Holloway B.; ed. in acad. and law depts. U. of Va.; studied in law offices of Judge Samuel McGowan, Abbeville C.H., S.C.; m. Alice Irene Stearns, Feb. 24, 1863. Located in Sparta (then C.H.), Conecuh Co., Ala., Apr. 15, 1859; elected lt. Conecuh Guard, part of Ala. vol. corps, July 4, 1860; elected capt., April 1, 1861; reëlected capt. at York Town, Va., May 1, 1862; maj., Aug. 22, 1862; lt. col., Sept. 30, 1862; col., Oct 3, 1862; brig. gen., Apr. 2, 1865. Opened law office, Evergreen, Ala., 1866; State's pros. atty., 10 yrs.; apptd. postmaster, Evergreen, Ala., spring of 1887; was probate judge, July 1, 1887-Nov. 3, 1898. Democrat. Home: Evergreen, Conecuh Co., Ala. Died 1910.

BOWLES, Samuel, editor; b. Springfield, Mass., Oct. 15, 1851; s. Samuel and Mary Dwight (Schermerhorn) B.; ed. pub. and pvt. schs., and in Europe; spl. course, Yale, 2 yrs.; (hon. M.A., Amherst, 1879; L.H.D., Olivet Coll., 1913); m. Elizabeth, d. Ebenezer Rockwood Hoar, of Concord, Mass., June 12, 1884. Asst. in editorial dept., 1873-75, business mgr., 1875-78, editor-in-chief and pub., 1878—, Springfield Republican. Home: Springfield, Mass. Died Mar. 14, 1915.

BOWMAN, Albert Chase, mfr.; b. North Andover, Mass., Dec. 2, 1875; s. Joseph A. and Abbie (Chase) B.; ed. Eaton Sch., Middleboro, Mass.; m. May Dascombe, June 30, 1904; 1 son, Lee Dascombe. Vice pres. John T. Slack Corp., Springfield, Vt., 1911-22, pres., 1922—; pres. Keene Silk Fibre Mills, Keene, N.H. Republican. Conglist. Home: Springfield, Vt. Died Sept. 17, 1937.

BOWMAN, Alpheus Henry, brig. gen. U.S.A.; b. Loudon Co., Va., Feb. 28, 1842; s. Henry A. and Martha K. (Polk) B.; ed. Newark (Del.) Acad., Del. Coll., and Chester (Pa.) Mil. Acad., 1855-61; m. Lillie J. Bartlett, Jan. 12, 1898. Entered mil. service in Pa. vols., Dec. 3, 1861; apptd. capt. 9th Inf., 1866; maj. 2d Inf., lt. col. 5th Inf., col. 25th Inf., and brig. gen. U.S.A., retiring Aug. 13, 1903, after more than 40 yrs.' service. Served in command of Co. of Pa. Vols. in Army of the Potomac in Civil War, and from 1866 in regular army, serving in Indian wars, Spanish War, and in the Philippine Islands. Mem. Loyal Legion, S.A.R., Soc. Colonial Wars, Mil. Service Instn. of U.S., Nat. Geog. Soc. Episcopalian. Home: Washington, D.C. Died Nov. 10, 1926.

BOWMAN, Charles Calvin, congressman; b. Troy, N.Y., Nov. 14, 1852; s. Charles and Emilia Strong (Beebe) B.; acad. edn., Lansingburg, N.Y.; C.E., Union Coll., 1875; m. Elizabeth Law, July 20, 1880. In wholesale coal business, 1876—; then pres. Avoca Coal Co.; sec. and treas. Franklin Coal Co.; v.p. Roden Coal Co. (Marvel, Ala.); dir. Raub Coal Co. Mayor of Pittston, Pa., 1886; mem. select and common council 6 terms; mem. 62d Congress (1911-13), 11th Pa. Dist. Del. Independent Rep. and regular Rep. State convs.; mem. local armory bd.; trustee Pittston Hosp.; sec. Soldiers' Relief Assn., Twin Shaft Relief Assn.; pres. Tax Payers' Assn., etc. Mason. Home: Pittston, Pa. Died July 3, 1941.

BOWMAN, Charles Grimes, commodore U.S.N.; b. Delphi, Ind., Oct. 15, 1848; s. John Milton and Elizabeth (Barnett) B.; apptd. from Ind., and grad. U.S. Naval Acad., 1869; m. Josephine McFarlane, Feb. 24, 1876. Promoted ensign, July 12, 1870; master, July 12, 1871; lt., Aug. 9, 1874; lt. comdr., May 4, 1896; comdr., July 8, 1899; capt., Nov. 8, 1904; retired at own request as commodore, June 30, 1907. Served successively on the Sabine, Richmond, Constellation, Yantic, and Hartford, 1869-76; Naval Acad., 1876-79; Adams, 1879-82; Naval Obs., 1882-86; Atlanta, 1886-87; Boston, 1887-89; Naval Acad., 1889-93, head dept. astronomy, navigation and surveying, 1890-93; exec. officer Marblehead, 1894-97; equipment officer Navy Yard, Mare Island, 1897-1900; comd. Castine, 1900-01, Don Juan de Austria, 1901-02; insp. 6th light house dist., 1902-03, Navy Yard, League Island, Pa., 1903-04; equipment officer Navy Yard, New York, 1904-05; capt. of yard, Navy Yard, Pensacola, Fla., 1905-06; comd. Rhode Island, 1906-07. Ordered to active duty, Apr. 7, 1917. Home: Delphi, Ind. Died Oct. 5, 1918.

BOWMAN, Clellan Asbury, coll. pres.; b. Dauphin, Pa., Aug. 29, 1861; s. William and Mary Elizabeth (Brua) B.; grad. Berrysburg (Pa.) Sem., 1879; B.E., M.E., Millersville (Pa.) Normal Sch., 1883; A.M., Central Pa. Coll., 1892; Ph.D., U. of Richmond, 1896; studied Harvard, 1898, U. of Berlin, 1905-06; LL.D., Lebanon Valley Coll., 1927; m. Caroline B. Krimmel, June 25, 1902; children—Pearl Katherine (Mrs. Joseph Milton Gantz), Miriam Gensemer. Formerly ednl. missionary to Oregon of Evang. Ch.; chief work, 1895— has been development of Albright Coll., Myerstown, Pa. and its consolidation with Central Pa. Coll., 1902; has served as pres., dean and acting pres., and again as pres., 1923-29. Republican. Mason (32°, K.T.), Odd Fellow. Home: Coral Gables, Fla. Died Jan. 6, 1937.

BOWMAN, Edward J(onathan), lawyer; b. Oakfield, Kent Co., Mich., Nov. 30, 1871; s. Nelson Bowers and Nancy (Bowman) B.; grad. high sch., Greenville, Mich., 1888; m. Alice Cowin, Oct. 19, 1898. City atty., Greenville, 1898-1905; mem. Sch. Bd., Greenville, 9 yrs.; asst. U.S. atty. Western Dist. of Mich., 1910-13; U.S. atty., same dist., 1922-30. Republican. Methodist. Home: Grand Rapids, Mich. Died Sept. 18, 1935.

BOWMAN, Edward Morris, musician; b. Barnard, Vt., July 18, 1848; s. Joseph and Asenath (Burroughs) B.; grad. St. Lawrence U., Canton, N.Y., 1856; studied music from childhood; later pupil Dr. William Mason, New York, and Franz Bendel, Berlin, in piano; in organ, of John P. Morgan, New York, Eduard Rohde and August Haupt, Berlin, Edouard Batiste and Alexandre Guilmant, Paris, and Sir Frederick Bridge, London; theory of music with Carl Friedrich Weitzmann, Berlin, Sir G. A. Macfarren and Dr. E. H. Turpin, London; m. Mary Elizabeth Jones, June 23, 1870. Organist Old Trinity Ch., New York, 1866-67; teacher and condr. St. Louis, 1867-87; organist and dir. music Peddie Memorial Ch., Newark, N.J., 1887-94; prof. and dir. of music, Vassar Coll., 1891-95; founder, and dir. of The Temple Choir and Temple Orchestra, 200 members, Bapt. Temple, Brooklyn, 1895-1906; founder, and dir. Calvary Bapt. Choir, New York, 1906—. Pres. Virgil Practice Clavier Mfg. Co., New York. Author: Bowman's Weitzmann's Manual of Musical Theory, 1876; Master Lessons in Piano Playing, 1911. Contbr. to mus. jours. Home: Brooklyn, N.Y. Died Aug. 27, 1913.

BOWMAN, Frank Llewellyn, congressman; b. Masontown, Pa., Jan. 21, 1879; s. J. A. and Sue (Llewellyn) B.; A.B., W.Va. U., 1902; m. Pearl Silveus, June 3, 1903; children—Marjorie Virginia, Frank Llewellyn. Admitted to W.Va. bar 1905, and began practice at Morgantown. Postmaster, Morgantown, 1911-15; mayor, 1916-17; mem. 69th to 72d Congresses (1925-33), 2d W.Va. Dist.; apptd. by President Roosevelt to Board of Veterans' Appeals, Oct. 1, 1935. Republican. Presbyn. Mason. Home: Morgantown, W.Va. Died Sept. 15, 1936.

BOWMAN, George Ernest, historian; b. Manchester, N.H., Jan. 5, 1860; s. Rev. George Augustus and Ernestine (Lord) B.; descendant of Nathaniel Bowman, who settled at Watertown, Mass., 1630, and of Elder William Brewster, of the Mayflower, 1620, also Thomas Prence, 18 times gov. of Plymouth Colony, and Thomas Hinckley, 9 times gov. of same; A.B. from Yale U., 1883; unmarried. Devoted 44 yrs. to study of history of the Mayflower passengers and to compilation of the Mayflower genealogies, planned to include every descendant of the passengers. Founder, 1896, and then sec. Mass. Soc. of Mayflower Descendants; founder, 1899, and then editor The Mayflower Descendant (quarterly mag.); founder, 1913, and editor Pilgrim Notes and Queries (monthly mag., 1913-17). Founder, 1895, Boston Chapter, S.A.R., its first sec. and 2d pres.; deputy governor-general of the Society of Mayflower Descendants, 1927-36; hon. life mem., 1915, Mass. Soc. Mayflower Descendants, and 1920, Calif. Soc. Mayflower Descendants. Republican Conglist. Mason. Died Sept. 5, 1941.

BOWMAN, John Brady, educator; b. Robertsville, Stark Co., O., Oct. 5, 1865; s. Jonathan and Eliza (Kelley, daughter Col. Richard Kelley), B.; A.B., Mt. Union Coll., Alliance, O., 1892, A.M., 1903, Ped.D., 1920; m. Hattie May Wert, Aug. 10, 1892 (died 1899); 1 son, Blaine Everett; m. 2d, Nellie Mae Whitney, June 26, 1901; 1 son, Donald Whitney. Teacher pub. schs.; prof. Latin and mathematics, Volant (Pa.) Coll., 1892-98; prof. mathematics, Northeastern Ohio Normal Coll., Canfield, O., 1898-1902, pres., 1899-1902; prof. edn., Mt. Union Coll., 1902—, also sec. and dean, acting pres., 1935. V.p. Midland Savings and Loan Co. Editor The Magnet (ednl. jour.), 1899-1902. Sec. and treas. Ohio Assn. of Coll. Presidents and Deans, 1934—. An organizer and many years director Alliance Y.M.C.A. Teacher large Sunday School classes and S.S. supt. Sec. Selective Service Bd., Dist. No. 2, Stark Co., O., World War; chmn. Alliance Dry Fedn., 1914-17. Mem. survey com. Wilberforce U., 1929; mem. advisory bd. Ohio State Dept. Edn., 1930, 31. Republican. Methodist. Home: Alliance, Ohio. Died Jan. 4, 1936.

BOWMAN, John Calvin, clergyman; b. Chambersburg, Pa., Aug. 15, 1849; s. John and Elizabeth (Nicklas) B.; A.B., Franklin and Marshall Coll., 1871, A.M., 1875; grad. Theol. Sem., Lancaster, Pa., 1875; D.D., Franklin and Marshall, 1883; m. Amelia Davis, Jan. 8, 1878; children—Margaret Angela, Mary Elizabeth, John Davis, William Boone. Ordained Reformed Ch. ministry, 1875; pastor Shepherdstown, W.Va., 1875-82, Hanover, Pa., 1882-90; prof. N.T. exegesis, 1891-1904, practical theology, 1904-20, pres. Theol. Sem. of Ref. Ch. in U.S., Lancaster, Pa., 1906-20, emeritus, 1920—. Home: Honeybrook, Pa. Deceased.

BOWMAN, John McEntee, pres. Bowman Biltmore Hotels Corp.; b. Toronto, Can., July 20, 1875; s. John and Anne (McEntee) B.; ed. pub. schs.; m. Clarice Paterson, June 28, 1919; children—Clarissa Anne, John McEntee. President of the Bowman Biltmore Hotels Corp.; also pres. Bowman Management, Inc., operating another chain of hotels; pres. The Cuban Nat. Syndicate. Home: New York, N.Y. Died Oct. 28, 1931.

BOWMAN, Robert A., dairy business; b. Allegheny (now in Pittsburgh), Pa., Dec. 23, 1855; s. Robert and Jane Maria (Davis) B.; grad. high sch., Centralia, Ill., 1875, and Jones Commercial Sch., St. Louis, Mo., 1879; m. Louise Cruikshank, Oct. 8, 1883 (died 1931); children—Grace Davis (Mrs. Guy Lincoln Jones), Johnston Alexander. Taught country sch., Tonti, Ill., 1875-76; entered milk and ice cream business, St. Louis, 1876; newspaper work, Mo. Republican, 1879-80; Post Dispatch, St. Louis.

1880-81; in dairy business, Chicago, Ill., 1885—; treas. Bowman Dairy Co., 1886-1920, pres., 1920—. Home: Chicago, Ill. Died Mar. 12, 1935.

BOWMAN, Roland Claude, cartoonist, author; b. Mich., 1870; s. Dr. J. D. and Mary E. (Tabor) B.; ed. Benton Harbor, Mich., pub. schs.; m. Byrtha Louise Ryckman, Aug. 1897. Cartoonist on Minneapolis Tribune, 1897—. Author: Freckles and Tan, illustrated verse, 1900. Home: Minneapolis, Minn. Deceased.

BOWMAN, Samuel Henry, Jr., lumber; b. Cleveland, O., July 24, 1887; s. Samuel Henry and Anne Louise (Stevens) B.; prep. edn., Hill Sch., Pottstown, Pa.; LL.B., Yale, 1910; m. Jessie Vincent Stevenson, Apr. 28, 1920; children—Samuel Henry III, Jessie William Stevenson, Anne Louise. President S. H. Bowman Lumber Co., Atlas Lubber Co., Revelstoke Sawmill Co., Builders Hardware Stores, Ltd., Standard Finance Co.; v.p. Bowman-Hicks Lumber Co., Alberta Lumber Co. Republican. Presbyterian. Home: Wayzata, Minn., and Miami Beach, Fla. Died Mar. 30, 1941.

BOWMAN, Thomas, bishop; b. Berwick, Pa., July 15, 1817; s. John and Sarah (Brittain) B.; A.B., Dickinson Coll. (valedictorian), 1837, A.M., 1840; read law 1 yr.; (S.T.D., Ohio Wesleyan, 1853; LL.D., Dickinson, 1872); m. Matilda Hartman, 1842. Entered M.E. ministry in Baltimore conf., 1939; teacher Dickinson Grammar Sch., 1840-43; organized, 1848, pres., 1848-58, Dickinson Sem., Williamsport, Pa.; pres. and prof. mental and moral philosophy, 1858-72, Hannon prof. Bibl. lit., 1867-72, chancellor, 1884-99, chancellor emeritus, 1899, Asbury (now DePauw) U. (trustee same, 1875-95, pres. trustees, 1887-95); chaplain U.S. Senate, 1864-65; elected bishop M.E. Ch., May 1872; became sr. bishop; retired 1896. Has visited all the confs. in Europe, India, China, Japan, Mexico. Home: Orange, N.J. Died Mar. 3, 1914.

BOWMAN, Thomas, bishop; b. Lehigh Gap, Northampton Co., Pa., May 28, 1836; s. Jacob and Elizabeth (Weiss) B.; ed. Vanderveer Sem., Easton, Pa.; (D.D., North Western Coll.); m. Dianna Young, Apr. 26, 1856. Ordained ministry of Evang. Assn., 1859; pastor Lehigh and Northampton circuits, Pa., later Allentown, Reading, Pine Grove, Pa., Phila. and Schuylkill Haven, Pa.; presiding elder, 1870-75; bishop Evang. Assn. 40 yrs.—1875-1915 (retired). Prin. Union Bibl. Inst., Naperville, Ill., 1891-1911; pres. trustees North Western Coll., Naperville, 20 yrs., and twice served as acting pres. of the coll.; trustee Bd. of Publ. of Evang. Assn. 40 yrs., pres. 20 yrs.; treas. Bd. of Ch. Extension, also of Charitable Soc., Evang. Assn.; trustee Schuylkill Sem., Reading, Pa. Republican. Author: Historical Review, 1890; Review Catechism, 1904; The Great Salvation, 1909. Recognized for more than 50 yrs. as one of the foremost pulpeteers of America. Presided at world's conferences of Evang. Assn. in U.S., Japan, China, Germany and Switzerland; del. to the 1st Ecumenical Conf. of Methodism, London, Eng., 1881. Home: Allentown, Pa. Died Mar. 19, 1923.

BOWNE, Borden Parker, univ. dean; b. Leonardville, N.J., Jan. 14, 1847; s. Joseph and Margaret (Parker) B.; A.B., New York U., 1871, A.M., 1876; univs. of Halle, Paris and Göttingen, 1873-75; (LL.D., Ohio Wesleyan, 1881, New York U., 1909); married. Asst. prof. modern langs., New York U., 1875-76; on staff The Independent, 1875-76; prof. philosophy and dean Graduate Sch. Arts and Sciences, Boston U., 1876. Made a tour of the world, 1905-06, and lectured before the Imperial U. of Japan and other ednl. bodies in Japan, China and India; hon. mem. Imperial Edn. Soc. of Japan. Author: The Philosophy of Herbert Spencer, 1874; Studies in Theism, 1879; Metaphysics, 1882, revised edit., 1898; Introduction to Psychological Theory, 1887; Philosophy of Theism, 1888, revised edit., 1902; The Principles of Ethics, 1892; Theory of Thought and Knowledge, 1897; The Christian Revelation, 1898; The Christian Life, 1899; The Atonement, 1900; The Immanence of God, 1905; Personalism, 1907; Studies in Christianity, 1909. Died 1910.

BOWNOCKER, John Adams, geologist; b. nr. St. Paul, O., Mar. 11, 1865; s. Michael and Eliza (Adams) B.; B.Sc., Ohio State U., 1889, D.Sc., 1897; fellow U. of Chicago, 1892-94; grad. scholar, Yale, 1894-95; m. Anna K. Flint, June 12, 1911. Prin. high sch., Martins Ferry, O., 1889-92; asst. Geol. Survey of Ohio, 1892, of N.J., 1893; asst. in geology, 1895-98, asst. prof., 1898-99, asso. prof. inorganic geology, 1899-1901, prof., 1901-17, prof. geology, 1917—, curator of mus., 1899-1917, Ohio State U. Asst. geologist, 1900-06, State geologist of Ohio, 1906—. Fellow Geological Soc. America. Republican. Author of various reports of Geol. Survey of Ohio and numerous papers on geol. subjects. Home: Columbus, O. Died Oct. 20, 1928.

BOWRON, James, steel mfr.; b. Stockton-on-Tees, Durham Co., Eng., Nov. 16, 1844; s. James and Mary Hannah (Moss) B.; ed. spl. schs. and Quaker grammar sch., Eng.; m. Ada Louisa Barrett, of Stockton-on-Tees, June 23, 1870 (died Jan. 10, 1883); children—Charles Edward, Kathleen Mary (dec.), Francis James (dec.), Frederick William, Arthur John, Thomas Whitwell, Edith Ellen (dec.), Ada Mary (wife of Dr. J. S. McLester); m. 2d, Adah S. Cunningham, June 14, 1887; children—Edith Josephine (Mrs. G. C. Davis) (dec.), Richard Louis, James Edgar, Harold Alfred, Robert Henry, Paul Joseph. Began in glass trade, later mining, ry., mercantile and ins. bus. in Eng.; came to U.S., 1877, naturalized citizen, 1885; gen. mgr. Southern States Coal, Iron & Land Co., 1877-82; company merged with Tenn. Coal, Iron & R.R. Co. of which was gen. mgr. and later v.p. and treas. to 1901; pres. Gulf States Steel Co., 1913-21, now chmn. bd.; also served as officer or dir. of many other cos. Built town of South Pittsburgh, Tenn., which was started by his father. Active for many yrs. in athletics, ch. and Y.M.C.A. work. Mem. Am. Iron and Steel Inst. Republican. Presbyn. Mason. Accredited with having brought Ala. to the front as an active factor in the production of steel. Home: Birmingham, Ala. Died Aug. 25, 1928.

BOWSER, Edward Albert, college prof.; b. Sackville, N.B., Can., June 18, 1837; B.S., Rutgers, 1868, also M.S. and C.E.; (LL.D., Lafayette, 1881). Prof. mathematics, Rutgers Coll., 1870—. In charge U.S. Geod. Survey of N.J., 1875—. Author: Academic Algebra; College Algebra; Plane and Solid Geometry; Elements of Plane and Spherical Trigonometry; Treatise on Plane and Spherical Trigonometry; Analytical Geometry; Differential and Integral Calculus; Analytic Mechanics; Hydro-mechanics; Logarithmic Tables; Roofs and Bridges, etc. Home: New Brunswick, N.J. Died 1910.

BOWSFIELD, Colvin C., author; b. Orangeville, Ont.; s. Walter and Ann (Colvin) B.; ed. pub. schs.; m. Inez Pierson, Nov. 1899; 1 dau., Martha Pierson. Became a newspaper reporter in early life and has held responsible places in Washington, D.C., Buffalo, N.Y., and Chicago; edited papers in N.D. and was 1st sec. of senate in that state. Author: Making the Farm Pay, 1913, revised, 1919; Wealth From the Soil, 1914; How Boys and Girls Can Earn Money, 1916. Long an advocate of smaller farms. Died Jan. 28, 1940.

BOWYER, John Marshall, naval officer; b. Cass Co., Ind., June 19, 1853; s. Lewis Franklin and Naomi Emeline (Pugh) B.; apptd. from Ia., and grad. U.S. Naval Acad., 1874; m. Cora McCarter, Oct. 29, 1879. Promoted ensign, July 17, 1875; master, May 28, 1881; lt. jr. grade, Mar. 3, 1883; lt., May 26, 1887; lt. comdr., Mar. 3, 1899; comdr., Mar. 21, 1903; capt., Nov. 8, 1907. Served at various stas. and on various vessels until beginning of war with Spain; apptd. exec. officer, Princeton, May 2, 1898, patrol duty about west end of Cuba; to Philippines, Jan. 11, 1899; detached to Yorktown, Jan. 1, 1900; participated in suppression of Philippine insurrection and the Boxer troubles in N. China; exec. officer, flagship Brooklyn, Sept. 3, 1900; asst. supt. gun factory, Navy Yard, Washington, and head dept. yards and docks, 1901-05; comd. U.S.S. Columbia, July 10, 1905; sr. officer in comd. Columbia at Colon, Marblehead at Panama and 600 marines ashore Isthmus of Panama, during elections, June 1906; aid to asst. sec. navy, Mar. 1907; comd. battleship Illinois, Nov. 25, 1907, and made cruise to Pacific and around the world with Atlantic Fleet; supt. Naval Acad., 1909-11; retired on account of illness contracted in line of duty, Sept. 14, 1911, and commd. rear-admiral, retired. Medals: West India campaign; Spanish-Am. War; Philippines campaign; China campaign. Home: Washington, D.C. Died Mar. 15, 1912.

BOYCE, James, coll. pres.; b. Gaston Co., N.C., Jan. 25, 1860; s. E. E. (D.D.) and Rachel Elizabeth (McElwee) B.; A.B., Erskine Coll., S.C., 1878; grad. Erskine Theol. Sem., 1881; m. Jennie Isabella Thompson, Oct. 17, 1883. Taught at Woodward, S.C., 1879; clergyman Associate Reformed Presbyn. Ch., 1881—; pastor Louisville, Ky., 1882-97, Huntersville, N.C., 1897-99; pres. Due West Female Coll., 1899—. Asso. editor Asso. Reformed Presbyterian, 1890; asst. clerk First Presbytery, 1897—. Prin. clerk Asso. Reformed Presbyn. Synod of the South, 1890—. Home: Due West, S.C. Died 1910.

BOYCE, William H., congressman; b. Sussex Co., Del., Nov. 28, 1855; s. James H. and Sarah J. (Otwell) B.; m. Emma E. Valliant, Oct. 25, 1882; children—Valliant (dec.), James I. (dec.). Practiced law, Georgetown, Del., 1887-97; pres. bd. edn., 1883-86, town commrs., 1895-97, Georgetown; prin. pub. schs., Laurel, Del., 1875-80, high schs., Oxford, Md., 1880-81; recorder deeds Sussex Co., Del., 1881-86; chmn. Sussex Co. Dem. Com., 1893-97; sec. of state, of Del., 1897, resigned; del. Dem. Nat. Conv., 1896, 1924; asso. justice Supreme Court of Del., 1897-1909, resident in Sussex Co.; reappointed 1909, resident in Kent Co., and state judicial reporter, 1909-21; retired, June 15, 1921; mem. 68th Congress (1923-25), at large Del.; mem. Com. on Rivers and Harbors. Former pres. Del. Citizens' Assn.; pres. Elizabeth W. Murphey Sch. for indigent white children in Kent and Sussex counties; dep. P.E. Gen. Conv., 1904, 28. Former capt. Del. N.G. Episcopalian. Home: Dover, Del. Died Feb. 6, 1942.

BOYD, A(ndrew) Hunter, judge; b. Winchester, Va., July 15, 1849; s. Rev. A. H. H. and Eleanor F. (Williams) B.; attended Washington and Lee U., 1866-68, and U. of Va., 1868-69; B.L., Washington and Lee U. Law Sch., 1871; (LL.D., U. of Md., 1909); m. Bessie M. Thruston, Dec. 17, 1874. Began practice at Cumberland, Md., Aug., 1871; state's atty., 1876-80; apptd., May 1, 1893, by Gov. Brown, and elected Nov. 1893, for term of 15 yrs., 1893-1908, chief judge, 4th Jud. Circuit of Md., and ex-officio asso. judge, Ct. of Appeals of Md.; served, 1908-09, under appmt. of gov.; designated as chief judge, Ct. of Appeals, by Gov. Warfield, Nov. 12, 1907, and by Gov. Crothers, 1908; reëlected, 1909, for 15 yrs. and again designated as chief judge of the Ct. of Appeals. Home: Cumberland, Md. Died Aug. 2, 1925.

BOYD, David Ross, educator; b. Coshocton, O., July 31, 1853; s. James and Mary A. (Ross) B.; A.B., U. of Wooster, 1878, A.M., 1881, hon. Ph.D., 1900; LL.D., U. of New Mexico, 1927; m. Jennie Thompson, Sept. 6, 1882; 1 dau., Mary Alice. Pres. U. of Okla., 1892-1908, pres. emeritus, 1929—; supt. edn. Presbyn. Bd. of Home Missions, at head of ednl. work among Alaskans, Indians, Mormons, Southern mountaineers, Cubans and Puerto Ricans, 1908-12; pres. U. of N.M., 1912-19. Pres. Board of Edn., Okla., 14 yrs. Mason. Home: Glendale, Calif. Died Nov. 17, 1936.

BOYD, George Washington, ry. official; b. Indianapolis, Ind., Aug. 1, 1848; s. David Milton and Elizabeth Ann (Brown) B.; ed. Northwestern U., Indianapolis; m. Lydia Paxton Tousey, Dec. 5, 1877; 2d, Miranda C. Noyes, Jan. 29, 1899. Began ry. service as clerk, 1863; held various positions Pa. R.R., 1872-82; asst. gen. pass. agt., 1882-1903, gen. pass. agt., June 1, 1903—, Pa. R.R. Mason. Decorated with Order of the Crown, 2d class, by Emperor of Germany, 1904. Home: Philadelphia, Pa. Died Sept. 22, 1917.

BOYD, James; b. Boston, Mass., Feb. 1, 1858; s. Alexander and Harriet Fay (Wheeler) B.; ed. pub. schs.; m. Elizabeth J. Longstreth, Nov. 8, 1882 (died 1908); children—Fisher Longstreth, Helen Longstreth (Mrs. Albert F. M. Chandler), Harriet Wheeler (Mrs. G. Abbott Hunt), Alexander. Organizer, 1903, pres. until 1915, Electric Hose and Rubber Co., Wilmington, Del.; pres. James Boyd & Bro. Inc., Phila., 1908-17. Mem. exec. council Phila. Bd. of Trade, 1903-17. Awarded Schaffer gold medal, 1924; Centenary gold medal, 1927, Pa. Hort. Soc. Republican. Unitarian. Editor of Peony Manual, 1928, for which received Farr gold medal from Am. Peony Soc., Washington, D.C., 1929. Home: Haverford, Pa. Died Dec. 2, 1929.

BOYD, James E., gov. Neb.; b. County Tyrone, Ireland, Sept. 9, 1834; self-ed.; came to U.S., 1844; settled in Ohio; went to Neb., 1856; mem. 1st State legislature, 1866; mem. constl. convs. of 1871 and 1875; mayor Omaha, 1881-83 and 1885-87; gov. Neb., 1891; removed from office on alleged ground of non-citizenship, May 5, 1891. Declared a citizen of the U.S. by U.S. Supreme Court, and reinstated as gov., Feb. 8, 1892; Democrat. Is a grain commn. mcht. Home: Omaha, Neb. Died 1906.

BOYD, James Edmund, judge; b. Alamance Co., N.C., Feb. 14, 1845; s. A. H. and Margaret B.; ed. Graham Acad. and Davidson Coll., N.C.; served as pvt. 13th N.C. Inf. and 1st N.C. Cav., C.S.A.; admitted to N.C. bar, 1868; m. Sallie Holt, Sept. 12, 1868. Mem. N.C. Legislature, 1874-75; del. State Constl. Conv., 1875; U.S. dist. atty. Western Dist. N.C., 1880-85; asst. atty. gen. of U.S., 1897-1900; U.S. dist. judge, Western Dist. of N.C., July 11, 1900—. Home: Greensboro, N.C. Deceased.

BOYD, James P., author; b. Lancaster Co., Pa., Dec. 20, 1836; A.B., Lafayette Coll., 1859; admitted to bar, 1863; mng. editor Philadelphia Press, 1868-72; editor People's Journal, 1872-85. Author: Lalecca, 1872; Envious Merchant, 1874; Building and Ruling the Republic, 1884; History of the Crusades, 1890; Lives of Grant, Sherman, Sheridan, Blaine, Harrison, McKinley, Emperor William 1; Men and Issues of 1892, 1896, 1900; Bible Dictionary, 1896; Interlinear Edition of Bible, 1898; Paris Exposition, 1900. Home: Philadelphia, Pa. Died 1910.

BOYD, John Hardgrove, clergyman; b. Jackson, Miss., Jan. 19, 1861; s. James Hervey and Eliza (Morehead) B.; A.B., Southwestern Presbyn. U., Clarksville, Tenn., 1883; grad. Princeton Theol. Sem., 1886, spl. student in philosophy under Pres. McCosh; (D.D., Davidson, 1894); m. Ellen Morris Henry, Nov. 13, 1889. Ordained Presbyn. ministry, 1886; pastor Durant and Winona, Miss., 1886-89, Lauderdale St. Ch., Memphis, Tenn., 1889-93, Second Ch., Charlotte, N.C., 1893-95, First Ch., Evanston, Ill., 1895-1908, First Ch., Detroit, 1908-11, First Ch., Portland, Ore., 1911-19; prof. homiletics, McCormick Theol. Sem., Chicago. Died Jan. 12, 1922.

BOYD, Thomas (Alexander), author; b. Defiance, O., July 3, 1898; s. Thomas Alexander and Alice (Dunbar) B.; ed. pub. schs.; m. Margaret Woodward Smith, Oct. 15, 1920; 1 dau., Elizabeth Grace; m. 2d, Ruth Fitch Bartlett, Dec. 30, 1929. Served in U.S.M.C., May 14, 1917-July 10, 1919, World War. Awarded Croix de Guerre (France). Author:

Through the Wheat, 1923; The Dark Cloud, 1924; Points of Honor, 1925; Samuel Drummond, 1925; Simon Girty, the White Savage, 1928; Shadow of the Long Knives, 1928; Mad Anthony Wayne, 1929; Lighthorse Harry Lee, 1931; also short stories and articles in various mags. Home: Woodstock, Vt. Died Jan. 27, 1935.

BOYD, Thomas M., mfr.; b. Monroe, O., July 22, 1860; s. David Bartley and Ellen Eliza B.; ed. pub. schs.; m. Ida Charlotte Kramp, Danzig Free State, Europe, Nov. 1903. Organizer, 1899, and pres. Am. Seating Co., Chicago; pres. Grand Rapids (Mich.) Warehouse Corp.; dir. Am. Finance & Security Corp. Formerly treas. Butler County and Hamilton, O. Conglist. K.P. Home: Chicago, Ill. Deceased.

BOYD, William Kenneth, prof. history; b. Curryville, Mo., Jan. 10, 1879; s. Rev. Harvey Marshall and Mary Elizabeth (Black) B.; Weaver Coll., Weaverville, N.C.; A.B., Trinity Coll., Durham, N.C., 1897, A.M., 1898; scholar and fellow, Columbia University, Ph.D., 1906; m. Pat LeGrand, Dec. 22, 1908; 1 dau., Mary Elizabeth; m. 2d, Marion Colley, Aug. 11, 1931. Served as assistant in history, Trinity College, 1897-98; master in history, Trinity Park Sch., 1898-1900; adj. prof. history, Trinity Coll., 1901-02; staff Ency. Britannica, 1904-05; instr. in history, Dartmouth, 1905-06; prof. history, Trinity Coll. (now Duke U.), Sept. 1906—, also dir. libraries. Mem. M.E. Ch., S. Author: Ecclesiastical Edicts of the Theodosian Code, 1906; History of North Carolina (1783-1860), 1919; Story of Durham, City of the New South, 1925; North Carolina Tracts of the Eighteenth Century, 1927. Joint Author: A Syllabus of North Carolina History, 1913; Syllabus and Bibliography of Southern History, 1918; A School History of the United States. Editor: William Byrd's Dividing Line Histories, 1929. Home: Durham, N.C. Died Jan. 19, 1938.

BOYD, William Young, lawyer, publicist; b. Auburn, N.Y., Feb. 18, 1884; s. David and Mary (Young) B.; B.S., Syracuse U., 1906; m. Katharine Endsley, Oct. 6, 1910; traveled in West Indies and Central and S. America, 1907-16, representing Am. corps. and studying trade and polit. conditions. Commd. lt. U.S.N., 1917; lt. comdr., 1918; assigned to Dept. Naval Communications, Washington, D.C., selected to coördinate and establish censorship between U.S. and its European allies in Brazil; attaché Am. Embassy, Rio de Janeiro, 1917-19; organized system of Brazilian censorship; served as U.S. del. Internat. Cable Censorship Commn., Brazil; U.S. rep. Com. on Pub. Information in Brazil, 1918; invited by French Govt. to reorganize at Brest, France, the S. Am. cable censorship; apptd. mem. commn. to accompany President Pessoa of Brazil on trip to U.S. and Can., 1919. Hon. discharged from Navy, 1919, and with Gen. George W. Goethals and others organized firm of Goethals, Wilford & Boyd, Inc., to develop port of Colon and Republic of Panama, also exploring various dists. of Panama; rep. various Am. bondholders in Mexico, 1922-23; negotiated $4,500,000 loan for Republic of Panama in New York, 1923; by apptmt. of President Chiari of Panama, went to Germany, Holland and Denmark, 1924, to make survey and investigation of the Free Ports of those countries; adminstr. for govt. of Panama in orgn. and operation of Govt. bonded warehouses; spl. envoy to Germany from Panama, 1925, to adjust questions arising from German emigration to Panama; adviser to government of Panama in negotiating treaty with U.S., 1926. Mem. Council of the "Living Age," 1928—; mem. first Nat. Aviation Commn. of Panama, 1928-29; del. of Republic of Panama to Internat. Civil Aeronautic Conf. called by President Coolidge in Washington, D.C., Dec. 1928; established first pvt. commercial air service between Canal Zone and S. America, 1929; organized Panama Chapter of Nat. Aeronautic Assn. of U.S.A., 1929; mem. Free Port Commn. of Panama, 1929-30. Decorated Cross Legion of Honor (French); Cross of Saints Maurizio and Lazzaro (Italian). Compiled survey of compensation insurance and casualty laws of Brazil, Argentina, Venezuela and Colombia for Am. casualty insurance companies. Died Aug. 8, 1932.

BOYDEN, Albert Augustus, editor; b. Sheffield, Ill., Apr. 10, 1875; s. Albert Woodbury and Ellen Rebecca (Webb) B.; A.B., Harvard, 1898; unmarried. Became connected with McClure's Magazine, 1899, mng. editor, 1903-06; mng. editor The American Magazine, 1906-17; Y.M.C.A. service in France, 1918; commr. to Poland League of Red Cross Societies, 1920; sec. Am. Del. Austrian Sect. of Reparations Commn., 1921. Home: New York, N.Y. Died May 2, 1925.

BOYDEN, Albert Gardner, educator; b. S. Walpole, Mass., Feb. 5, 1827; s. Phineas and Harriet (Carroll) B.; grad. Bridgewater (Mass.) State Normal Sch., 1849; studied under pvt. tutors several yrs.; (hon. A.M., Amherst, 1861); m. Isabella Whitten Clarke (died 1895); m. 2d, Clara Adelia Armes, N.H. (died 1906). Asst. teacher Bridgewater State Normal School, 1850-53; principal English High School for Boys, Salem, Mass., 1853-56; sub-master Chapman Grammar Sch., Boston, 1856-57; 1st asst., 1857-60, prin., 1860-1906, principal emeritus, August 1906—, Bridgewater State Normal School. Home: Bridgewater, Mass. Died May 30, 1915.

BOYDEN, Arthur Clarke, educator; b. Bridgewater, Mass., Sept. 27, 1852; s. Albert Gardner and Isabella Whitten (Clarke) B.; student, Bridgewater Normal Sch., 1869-71; A.B., Amherst College, 1876, A.M., 1881; L.H.D. from same college, 1927; Ed.D., Rhode Island College of Education, 1928; studied Teachers' School of Science, Boston, and under spl. instrs.; m. Katharine Chipman Allen, Oct. 11, 1877. Prin. high sch., Medway, Mass., 1871-72; teacher mathematics, Chauncy Hall Sch., Boston, 1876-79; instr., 1879-96, v.prin., 1896, prin., 1906— (succeeding his father), Bridgewater State Normal Sch. Instr. Mass. Teachers' Insts., 1884—, Martha's Vineyard Summer Inst., 1889-97 (clerk 10 yrs.). Mem. ednl. commn. to Jamaica, 1890; pres. library trustees 15 yrs. Mason. Republican. Conglist. Author: Nature Study by Months, 1898; History of Bridgewater Normal School, 1919. Home: Bridgewater, Mass. Died Mar. 15, 1933.

BOYDEN, Roland William, lawyer; b. Beverly, Mass., Oct. 18, 1863; s. William Cowper and Amy Lydia (Hoag) B.; A.B., Harvard, 1885, LL.B., 1888; m. Kate Foster Whitney, July 23, 1895 (dec.). Admitted to bar, 1888; mem. firm Ropes, Gray, Boyden & Perkins, Boston; dir. First Nat. Bank of Boston, Quincy Market Cold Storage & Warehouse Co., Boston & Providence R.R. Corp. Mem. bd. of overseers, Harvard. Formerly unofficial rep. of U.S. with Reparations Commn. Unitarian. Home: Beverly, Mass. Died Oct. 25, 1931.

BOYDEN, William Cowper, lawyer; b. Sheffield, Ill., Apr. 6, 1864; s. Albert W. and Ellen R. (Webb) B.; grad. Phillips Exeter Acad., 1882; A.B., Harvard, 1886, LL.B., 1889; m. Mabel G. Burlingham, Apr. 13, 1893; children—William C., Jr., Preston, Margaret, Elizabeth. In practice at Chicago, 1889; mem. firm Fisher, Boyden, Kales and Bell. Dir. Central Trust Co. of Ill., Sullivan Machinery Co., Liquid Carbonic Co., commr. gen. to Poland of League of Red Cross Socs., 1920. Overseer, Harvard U., 1911-17, 1919-21, 1923—. Decorated Comdr., Order Polonia Restituta (Polish). Republican. Home: Winnetka, Ill. Died May 30, 1929.

BOYÈ, Martin H. (baptized Hans Martin Boyè), chemist and geologist; b. Copenhagen, Denmark, Dec. 6, 1812; ed. Borgerdyskolen, Copenhagen; grad. U. of Copenhagen, 1832; Polytechnic School, Copenhagen, 1835; Univ. of Pa., med. dept., 1844; spl. studies in analytical chemistry and physics (hon. A.M., Univ. of Pa., 1844). Came to U.S., 1836; assisted Dr. Robert Hare in chem. investigations, 1837-38; asst. geologist and chemist first geol. survey of Pa., 1838-43; jointly discovered new compound, chloride of platinum with binoxide of nitrogen, 1839; jointly discovered perchloric ether, the most explosive of all substances, 1841; conducted laboratory for analysis and instruction in analytical and practical chemistry, 1842-45; discovered, and with others applied the first process of refining cotton seed oil, 1845; specimens exhibited at Centennial Expn., Phila., 1876, received 1st premium; prof. chemistry and natural philosophy, Central High Sch., Phila., 1845-59; delivered many lectures; retired, 1859. Author: Pneumatics, or the Physics of Gases, 1856; Chemistry, or the Physics of Atoms, 1857. Wrote also, Explosive Power Perchloric Ether Proc. Am. Philos. Soc., vol. ii, p. 203; Perchloric Ether, Transactions, Am. Philos. Soc., vol. viii, art vi.; "Analysis" in Booth's Chemical Ency.; Analysis of the Bittern of a Saline on the Kiskeminetas; of Magnetic Iron Pyrites Containing Nickel; of Schuylkill, Croton and Rock Creek Waters, etc., in Silliman's and Franklin Inst. Journals, 1842-45. Home: Coopersburg, Pa. Died 1909.

BOYER, Emanuel Roth, asst. to supt. schools, Chicago; b. York, Pa., Apr. 15, 1857; grad. Ill. State Normal Univ., 1879; Harvard, A.B., 1890; m. Emily S. Sherman; engaged in educational-scientific work, 1879—; supt. schools, Fulton Co., Ill., 1882-86; instr. biology and prin. Chicago high schools, 1890—. Contributor to ednl. and scientific journals. Author: A Text Book on Elementary Biology. Home: Chicago, Ill. Died 1900.

BOYER, Joseph, mfr.; b. Can., 1848; m. Clara A. Libby; children—George W. (dec.), Frank H., C. Pearl (Mrs. H. E. Candler), Myrion L., Ruby C. (Mrs. W. A. C. Miller), Lotta E. (Mrs. Standish Backus), Gertrude (Mrs. Harold S. Chase), Joseph. Followed machinists' trade in St. Louis for 31 yrs.; inventor of the first successful pneumatic hammer; associated with William S. Burroughs in construction of the first Burroughs adding machine; formerly pres., now chmn. bd. Burroughs Adding Machine Co.; plant moved from St. Louis to Detroit, 1904. Died Oct. 24, 1930.

BOYKIN, James Chambers, editor; b. Russell Co., Ala., Jan. 11, 1866; s. Thomas Cooper and Belle (Alexander) B.; Agrl. and Mech. Coll., Auburn, Ala., 1879-81; Law Sch. Columbian (now George Washington) U., Washington, 1891-93; m. Eva Paxton, Mar. 16, 1887 (died 1899); children—Irma (Mrs. O. H. P. Clark), Basil Paxton; m. 2d, Margaret Stevenson Getty, Jan. 25, 1905. Apptd. to U.S. Bur. of Edn., Apr. 27, 1887; in charge sect. relating to city sch. systems and mem. editorial com., until Aug. 31, 1903; spl. agt. Bur. of Edn. for Atlanta (Ga.) Expn., 1895; chief spl. agt. Interior Dept. for expns. at Nashville, Tenn., 1897, Omaha, 1898, Buffalo, 1901, Charleston, S.C., 1902, St. Louis, 1904, Portland, Ore., 1905; chief clk. Truckee-Carson project, U.S. Reclamation Service, 1906; asst. rep. Interior Dept., Jamestown Expn., 1907; asst. to chmn. Govt. Bd. and acting rep. Interior Dept., Alaska-Yukon-Pacific Expn., Seattle, 1909; rep. Interior Dept. for expns. at Quito, Ecuador, 1909, and Turin, Italy, 1911; exec. officer U.S. Govt. Exhibit Bd. and rep. Interior Dept., San Francisco Expn., 1915, San Diego Expn., 1916; dir. Am. exhibits, Panama Nat. Expn., Panama City, 1916; mem. com. publs., Interior Dept., 1923. Editor, Bur. of Education, Washington, D.C., 1911—; also editor of School Life. Author: Class Intervals, 1891; History of Physical Training, 1892; Laws Governing City School Boards, 1896; Truant Schools, 1900; Instruction by Correspondence, 1902; Educational Legislation (co-author), 1913; The Tangible Rewards of Teaching, 1914; The Story of the Declaration of Independence, 1926. Home: Washington, D.C. Died July 29, 1929.

BOYLAN, Grace Duffie (Mrs. Louis Napoleon Geldert), author; b. Kalamazoo, Mich.; d. Capt. Phelix and Juliette (Smith) Duffie; ed. under pvt. tutors, also Radcliffe Coll., N.E. Conservatory of Music; m. 2d, Louis Napoleon Geldert, Feb. 27, 1909; children (by 1st marriage) Mrs. Clover Roscoe, (by 2d marriage) Malcolm Stuart Boylan. Began as newspaper writer in Chicago, 1903. Charter mem. Southern States Rep. League, 1925; Memphis chmn. Tenn. League of Rep. Women, 1925-28. Author: The Old House, 1898; Hosanna and Huzza, 1899; Kids of Many Colors, 1900; The Kiss of Glory, 1902; Yama Yama Land, 1909; Steps to Nowhere, 1911; The Supplanter, 1913; The Pipes of Clovis, 1913; Love Finds a Way (one act play), 1913; (collaborated with Mrs. Forrestine C. Hooker in her hist. novel) When Geronimo Rode, 1924; John of Joy, 1926; Conquerors, 1928; also verses, essays, short stories and published lectures. Home: Memphis, Tenn. Died Mar. 24, 1935.

BOYLAN, John J., congressman; b. N.Y. City; ed. De La Salle Inst. Engaged in real estate business; mem. N.Y. Assembly, 1910-12, Senate, 1913-22; mem. 68th to 75th Congresses (1923-39), 15th N.Y. Dist. Democrat. Home: New York, N.Y. Died Oct. 5, 1938.

BOYLAN, William A(loysius), coll. pres.; b. New York, N.Y., Jan. 6, 1869; s. Arthur and Ann (McKenna) B.; A.B., St. Francis Xavier Coll., N.Y. City, 1887, A.M., 1892; Pd.M., New York U., 1898; Ph.D., Fordham U., 1930. Prin. sch., N.Y. City, 1901-13; dist. supt. pub. schs., N.Y. City, 1913-27; asso. supt. schs., N.Y. City, 1927-30; pres. Brooklyn Coll., 1930—. Catholic. Co-author: City Arithmetic (with Floyd R. Smith), 1916; Corrective Exercises in English (with Albert S. Taylor), 1923; Required Spelling (with same), 1925; New Method in Composition (with same and Constance Fuller Simmons), 1926. Home: Brooklyn, N.Y. Died July 8, 1940.

BOYLE, Emmet D(erby), governor; b. Virginia City, Nev., July 26, 1879; s. Edward Dougherty and Sarah (Donoghue) B.; B.Sc., U. of Nev., 1899, E.M., 1903; m. Vida Margaret McClure, Sept. 28, 1903. Mining engr. with Brit. Am. Corp., B.C., 1899-1900; engr. and mine supt. Compania La Esperanza y Anexas, El Oro, Mexico, 1900-01; mgr. North Rapidan Mines, Como, Nev., 1901-07; cons. practice, 1907—; mem. Himdry & Boyle, cons. engrs.; pub. Nevada State Journal, Reno. Pres. Security Finance Co., Reno. State Engr., Nev., 1909-10; mem. State Tax Commn., Nev., 1913-14; gov. of Nev., 2 terms, 1915-23. Mem. U.S. Treas. Dept. Commn. on Gold Production, 1918-19; pres. Reno Chamber of Commerce. Catholic. Home: Reno, Nev. Died Jan. 3, 1926.

BOYLE, James, newspaper writer; b. Essex Co., Eng., Nov. 28, 1853; s. James and Mary (Bowen) B.; came to America, 1870; largely self-ed.; m. Theodora Jessie Farquhar, Nov. 14, 1888. Began newspaper work at Toronto, Can., 1870; was with old Cincinnati Gazette, and polit. corr. and editorial writer Cincinnati Commercial Gazette, 1878-91; mem. non-partisan Bd. Police Commrs. of Cincinnati, under appmt. of Gov. Foraker, to reorganize police force, 1887-90; pvt. sec. William McKinley during his 2 terms as gov. of Ohio, 1892-96; Am. consul at Liverpool, Eng., 1897-1905. A founder of Blaine Club of Cincinnati; known as "Father of the Republican League," from fact that he conceived the idea and was founder of Ohio Rep. League of Clubs, which developed into Nat. Rep. League, of which was chmn. Com. on Constn.; one of 1st presidents Ohio Rep. League. Chmn. Liverpool Barge & Coaling Co., Ltd.; sec. Southern Slate Co. Episcopalian. Author: Life of William McKinley (with Robert P. Porter, 1896. A compiler of Speeches of William McKinley and of Police Manual, Cincinnati. Has made spl. study of socialism, econ. and labor questions. Home: Columbus, O. Died June 11, 1939.

BOYLE, James Ernest, economist; b. Boyle, Kan., Nov. 22, 1873; s. John and Mary Ann (Searle) B.;

A.B., U. of Neb., 1900; A.M., U. of Kan., 1901; Ph.D., U. of Wis., 1904; m. Effie Lytle, Sept. 13, 1902; children—Elizabeth, Louise. Head dept. of economics, U. of N.D., 1904-16; field agt. in marketing, U.S. Dept. of Agr., 1916-17; prof. rural economy, Cornell U., 1917—. A founder and first pres., U. of N.D. Co-operative Store; an organizer and first pres., N.D. State Tax Assn.; was state dir. for N.D. of Nat. Conf. on Marketing and Farm Credits. Republican. Presbyn. Author: Financial History of Kansas, 1904; Government of North Dakota, 1910; Beginner's Civics for North Dakota, 1912; Speculation and the Chicago Board of Trade, 1920; Rural Problems in the United States, 1921; Agricultural Economics, 1921; Marketing of Agricultural Products, 1925; Coöperation in the United States, 1925; Brief on Farm Relief, 1927; Cotton and the New Orleans Cotton Exchange, 1934. Home: Ithaca, N.Y. Died Sept. 18, 1938.

BOYLE, John, newspaperman; b. Washington, D.C., Feb. 25, 1855; s. Cornelius and Fannie (Greene) B.; ed. Gonzaga College, Washington, 1874-76, Georgetown Univ., 1877-78; unmarried. Began as reporter with Charlotte (N.C.) Observer, 1876; Washington corr. Exchange Telegraph Co., Ltd., London, 1898—, Wall Street Journal, 1901—. Democrat. Catholic. Died Dec. 25, 1936.

BOYLE, John J., sculptor; b. New York, 1851; s. Samuel and Catharine (McAuley) B.; pub. sch. edn., Phila.; studied at Pa. Acad. of Fine Arts, Phila., and École des Beaux Arts, Paris; m. Elizabeth Carroll, 1882. Received honors Paris Salon, École des Beaux Arts, Paris, Chicago Expn., 1893, Buffalo Expn., 1901, St. Louis, 1904, Panama P.I. Expn., 1915. Mem. Fine Arts Commn. for Greater New York under Mayor McClellan. A.N.A., 1910; mem. Nat. Sculpture Soc. (exec. council), Architectural League. Died Feb. 10, 1917.

BOYLE, Murat, lawyer; b. Agency, Mo., May 26, 1883; s. Harvey Alexander and Alice (Myers) B.; ed. country schs., Ward Sch., Guthrie, Okla., and 3 mos. in Central High Sch., Kansas City, Mo.; LL.B. cum laude, Kansas City Sch. of Law, 1905; m. Claudine Hancock, June 14, 1910; children—James Hancock, Murat. Admitted to Mo. bar, 1905, and began practice at Kansas City; associated with Harkless & Histed, 1905-07; mem. Hogsett & Boyle, 1907—; has specialized in trial work and insurance law. Democrat. Home: Kansas City, Mo. Died July 10, 1930.

BOYLE, Thomas Newton, clergyman; b. Blairville, Pa., Apr. 26, 1839; s. Thomas and Maria (Adair) B.; ed. Bellefonte (Pa.) Acad., 1856-57; (D.D., Mt. Union Coll., 1884; LL.D., Western U. of Pa., 1894); m. Sarah E. Weatherwax, Mar. 11, 1863. Ordained M.E. ministry, 1859; capt. Co. H, 140th Pa. Vols., Civil War; del. to Gen. Conf. M.E. Ch. 5 times; presiding elder 20 yrs. Chaplain-in-chief, G.A.R., 1901; grand prelate, Grand Commandery K.T. of Pa., 1895—. Trustee Mt. Union Coll., Allegheny Coll., Am. U., Beaver Coll.; mem. bd. of mgrs., Dixmont and West Pa. hosps., Pittsburgh. Home: Crafton, Pa. Died 1911.

BOYLE, Virginia Frazer, author; b. nr. Chattanooga, Tenn.; d. Charles Wesley and Letitia S. (Austin) Frazer; grad. Higsbee School, Memphis, Tenn.; Litt.D. from Southwestern Univ., 1933; m. Thomas R. Boyle. Office of Poet Laureate created for her by change in constn. of U.C.V., May 1910; Poet Laureate. S.C.V., and C.S.M.A. Author: The Other Side (poem), 1893; Brokenburne, 1897; Devil Tales, 1900; Serena (novel), 1905; Love Songs and Bugle Calls, 1906; Union, 1917; Christ in the Argonne, 1918; Song of Memphis, 1919. Wrote Prize Centennial Ode, Tennessee, 1896; series of negro folklore tales in Harper's Magazine, 1900; Jefferson Davis, Centennial Ode, 1908; Abraham Lincoln, for the Centenary celebration of the Phila. Brigade Assn., 1909; The Dream of the Alabama, centenary of Admiral Semmes, C.S.N., for the Confed. Memorial Assn., 1909. Home: Memphis, Tenn. Died Dec. 13, 1938.

BOYLE, Wilbur Fisk, lawyer; b. Brooke Co., W.Va., Aug. 20, 1840; s. Rev. Dr. Joseph and Emeline (Gist) B.; ed. Masonic Coll., Lexington, Mo., 1852-54, Central Coll., Fayette, Mo., 1854-56, Asbury U., Greencastle, Ind., 1856-58; m. Fannie L. Brother, Oct. 6, 1864. Mem. Boyle & Priest; dir. Miss. Valley Trust Co., etc. Home: St. Louis, Mo. Died 1911.

BOYNTON, Arthur Jerome, prof. economics; b. Janesville, Wis., Dec. 11, 1870; s. Jerome Thomas and Catherine Adela (Scott) B.; Ph.B., Beloit (Wis.) Coll., 1896; A.B., Harvard, 1901; A.M., Columbia, 1902; m. Flora Marie Shanklin, June 12, 1920. Asst. prof. economics, U. of Kan., 1903-10, asso. prof., 1910-15, prof., 1915—, also chmn. of dept., 1916-24. Mem. Bd. of Economic Advisers to dir. of the census of 1910. Republican. Conglist. Contbr. to Jour. Polit. Economy, Am. Economic Rev., etc. Home: Lawrence, Kan. Died Mar. 17, 1928.

BOYNTON, Charles Augustus, newspaperman; b. W. Stockbridge, Mass., Sept. 30, 1836; s. Rev. Charles B and Maria (Van Buskirk) B.; removed to Cincinnati in boyhood; ed. Woodward Coll., Cincinnati, and Knox Coll., Ill.; m. Maretta Hudson, Oct. 25, 1866; father of Charles Hudson B. First newspaper work was for the Christian Nation, edited by his father; entered services of Western Asso. Press, 1870, as New York agent; apptd. supt. Southern div. Associated Press, 1894. Charter mem. Gridiron Club; mem. Loyal Legion, S.A.R. Home: Washington, D.C. Died Sept. 5, 1915.

BOYNTON, Charles Hudson; b. Cincinnati, O., May 19, 1868; s. Charles Augustus and Maretta (Hudson) B.; B.S., Lehigh U., 1889; m. Florence Gaines, 1897 (died 1900); 1 son, Henry Gaines; m. 2d, Marie Dmitrenko, 1901; 1 son, Charles Dmitrenko. After graduation engaged in newspaper work in Washington, D.C., and joined the Washington Bur. of Associated Press, 1893; occupied various exec. positions in that orgn., and apptd. gen. supt., 1904; resigned, 1907, to become asso. with Eugene Meyer, Jr., & Co.; sr. partner C. H. Boynton & Co., 1910; mem. N.Y. Stock Exchange until 1921; asst. to pres. Atlas Portland Cement Co. until 1930. Ex-pres. Consol. Copper Mines Co., Am.-Russian Chamber Commerce, Assn. of Stock Exchange Firms. Home: New York, N.Y. Died Feb. 11, 1935.

BOYNTON, Charles Theodore, mfr.; b. West Stockbridge, Mass., Dec. 5, 1858; s. Charles Sumner and Elizabeth (Thompson) B.; ed. pub. schs., Catskill, N.Y.; m. Anna E. Bell, June 17, 1880. Settled at Chicago, 1879; entered employ of the Washburn & Moen Mfg. Co., as office boy, advancing to gen. western mgr.; gen. sales agt. its successor Am. Steel & Wire Co., 1898-1900; pres. Shelby Steel Tube Co., 1900-02; v.p. Pickands, Brown & Co., 1902—; v.p. By-Products Coke Corp.; dir. Continental & Commercial Nat. Bank, Continental & Commercial Trust & Savings Bank, Dearborn Co., Buck & Rayner Drug Co., Smet-Solvay Co., Consumers Co. Republican. Home: Highland Park, Ill. Died July 27, 1923.

BOYNTON, Frank David, supt. schools; b. Potsdam, N.Y., Apr. 29, 1863; s. Franklin and Julina (Hayes) B.; grad. Potsdam State Normal Sch., 1887; A.B., Middlebury Coll., 1891; A.M., Hamilton Coll., 1893; D.Pd., Syracuse U., 1903; m. Flora E. White, June 23, 1887; m. 2d, Jane E. Williams, Nov. 29, 1906. Prin. Union Sch. and Acad., Webster, N.Y., 1891-93, Ithaca (N.Y.) High Sch., 1893-1900; supt. schs., Ithaca, June 1900—; dir. Ithaca Conservatory of Music, Ithaca Savings & Loan Assn., Y.M.C.A. Chmn. com. from assn. of acad. prins. having in charge revision of the regents' acad. syllabus for 1900; re-elected by acclamation for 1905 revision; chmn. com. apptd. by U. State of N.Y. to arrange courses of study for secondary schools of state; chmn. Legislature Com. of Council of School Supts., 1908-1923. Editor New York State Teacher, Vols. 1, 2, 3. Trustee First M.E. Ch., Ithaca. Mason. Lecturer. Author: Plane and Solid Geometry, 1900; Syllabus of Civics, 1901; Manual of Civics, 1902; School Civics, Civics of N.Y. State, 1904; Actual Government of N.Y. State, 1911; Civics for First Voters, 1922. Editorial writer. Home: Ithaca, N.Y. Died June 17, 1930.

BOYNTON, George Mills, clergyman; b. Brooklyn, May 13, 1837; s. John and Louisa (Boutelle) B.; grad. Yale, 1858, Union Theol. Sem., 1863 (D.D., Middlebury Coll., Vt.); m. Julia Holmes, June 1, 1864. Ordained to Presbyn. ministry, 1864; pastor Presbyn. Ch., Riverdale, N.Y.; Congl. chs., Guilford, Conn., Newark, N.J., and Boston; sec. Congl. Sunday Sch. and Publ. Soc., 1888—. Author: The Pilgrim Church Register of Boston, 1891; The Model Sunday School, 1892; The Pilgrim Pastors' Manual, 1894; The Congregational Way, 1904. Died 1908.

BOYNTON, Henry Van Ness, soldier, journalist; b. West Stockbridge, Mass., July 22, 1835; s. Rev. Charles B. and Maria (Van Buskirk) B.; removed to Ohio in boyhood; grad. Woodward Coll., Cincinnati, 1854; Ky. Mil. Inst., 1858 (A.M., 1859; C.E., 1860); m. Helen Augusta Mason, 1871. Maj. and lt. col. 35th Ohio vol. inf., 1861-65; comd. regt. in battles of Chickamauga and storming of Missionary Ridge; bvtd. brig. gen. for gallantry at Chickamauga and Chattanooga; awarded Congressional medal of honor for Missionary Ridge. Newspaper corr. in Washington from 1865. Chmn. Chickamauga and Chattanooga Nat. Mil. Park; brig. gen. vols., war with Spain, June 17, 1898. Pres. Bd. of Edn., D.C. Mem. Soc. Army of the Cumberland. Author: Sherman's Historical Raid, 1875; The Chickamauga National Military Park. Died 1905.

BOYNTON, James Stoddard, lawyer; b. Henry Co., Ga., May 7, 1833; ed. in various schools and acads. of Ga.; m. Fannie Loyal, Dec. 2, 1852; 2d, Susie T. Harris, April 30, 1883. Elected ordinary of Butts Co., Ga., 1860; served in C.S.A., 1861-65, private to col.; judge of Spalding Co. court, 1866-68; mayor of Griffin, 1869-72; pres. State senate, 1880-84, and on death Gov. Alexander H. Stevens was gov. of Ga. until his successor was elected; judge Flint circuit, Jan., 1886, to April, 1893; resigned to accept position as div. counsel, Central of Ga. Ry. Home: Griffin, Ga. Died 1902.

BOYNTON, Nathan Smith, founder Order of Knights of the Maccabees; b. Port Huron, Mich., June 23, 1837; s. Granville F. and Frances B.; ed. dist. schs. and Waukegan (Ill.) High Sch.; m. Annie Fields, June 20, 1859. In mercantile business, Port Huron, Mich., 1856; later in Cincinnati, New Orleans, St. Louis. Served pvt. to maj. 8th Mich. Cav., 1862-65; when lt., cut off retreat of Gen. John Morgan, whom he finally captured. Elected to Mich. Legislature, 1868; mayor Port Huron, 1874-75, again, 2 terms, 1894-98. Was mem. Mich. Constl. Conv., 1907. Was owner and editor Port Huron Press. From 1881 devoted his attention to Order of Knights of the Maccabees, of which he was Supreme and Great Record Keeper, Past Supreme Comdr., Supreme Advisor and was then Great Comdr. of Modern Maccabees. Author: Boynton's Parliamentary Rules; The History of the Maccabees; The Dependency Plan; Fraternal Co-operation. Home: Port Huron, Mich. Deceased.

BOYNTON, Nehemiah, clergyman; b. Medford, Mass., Nov. 21, 1856; s. Eleazar and Mary (Chadbourne) B.; A.B., Amherst, 1879, D.D., 1894; graduate Andover Theol. Sem., 1882; LL.D. from Amherst College, 1929; m. Mary Ella Wilcox, July 5, 1882; children—Daniel Wilcox, Edward Chadbourne, Morrison Russell, Grace Morrison, Mrs. Elizabeth Patton, Mrs. Marjory Rugg, Nehemiah. Ordained Congl. ministry, 1882; pastor Littleton, Mass., 1882-84, Haverhill, 1884-88, Union Ch., Boston, 1888-96; First Ch., Detroit, 1896-1906, Clinton Av. Ch., Brooklyn, 1906-21, became minister emeritus. Lecturer Oberlin Theol. Sem., 1897. Moderator Nat. Council Congl. Chs. of U.S., 1910-13; exec. chmn. World Alliance for Promotion Internat. Friendship Through the Chs. Chaplain 13th Coast Defense Co. N.G.N.Y., 1912-17; in federal service, 1917. Author: Real Preaching, 1897. Home: Medford, Mass. Died Nov. 8, 1933.

BRACE, Charles Loring, sec. Children's Aid Soc.; b. Dobbs Ferry, N.Y., June 2, 1855; s. Charles Loring and Letitia (Neill) B.; Ph.B., Sheffield Scientific Sch. (Yale), 1876; m. Louise Warner, Jan. 14, 1885; children—Dorothy (wife of Dr. John C. Donaldson), Eleanor, Charles Loring (dec.), Betty (Mrs. Huntington Gilchrist), Gerald Warner. Began as rodman in engring. dept. L.S.Ry., and became constrn. engr. on various rys. of middle west; upon death of father, founder of Children's Aid Soc., became sec., 1890, retired, 1927. Episcopalian. Home: Santa Barbara, Calif. Died May 24, 1938.

BRACE, DeWitt Bristol, educator; b. Wilson, N.Y., Jan. 5, 1859; s. Lusk and Emily C. B.; A.M., Boston U., 1882; spl. student Mass. Inst. Tech., 2 yrs.; student physics, Johns Hopkins, 1881-83; U. of Berlin, 1883-85, under von Helmholz and Kirchhoff, Ph.D., 1885; m. Elizabeth Russell Wing, Oct. 16, 1901. Acting asst. prof. physics, U. of Mich., 1887; prof. physics, U. of Neb., 1888—. Fellow and v.p. A.A.A.S. Author: Laws of Radiation and Absorption, 1901 H1. Home: Lincoln, Neb. Died 1905.

BRACKEN, Clio Hirton, sculptor; b. Rhinebeck, N.Y.; d. Howard and Lucy (Bronson) Hinton; studied at Art Students League, N.Y., and with St. Gaudens and MacMonnies, Paris, France; m. James Huneker, Jan. 20, 1892; m. 2d, William Barrie Bracken, May 16, 1900. Exhibited at Paris Salon, Academy of Design (New York), Panama P.I. Expn., San Francisco, 1915. Prin. works: Rubaiat Punch Bowl; portrait of Ignace Jan Paderewski, etc. Home: New York, N.Y. Died Feb. 12, 1925.

BRACKEN, Edward P., railway official. Began as gang foreman, C.,B.&Q.R.R. Co., Aug. 1887, and continued with same rd.; successively in various positions gen. supt. Wyo. div., 1909-10; asst. gen. mgr. lines east, at Chicago, 1910-12; gen. mgr. lines east, 1912-17; v.p. in charge operation, 1917-18; again gen. mgr., 1918-19; federal mgr., 1919-20; v.p. in charge operation entire C.,B.&Q.R.R. System, 1920-31, exec. v.p., 1931-32, retired. Home: Evanston, Ill. Died Dec. 31, 1937.

BRACKEN, Henry Martyn, M.D.; b. Pa., Feb. 27, 1854; s. Dr. William C. and Electa (Alvord) B.; classical edn. Eldersridge Acad.; M.D., Coll. Phys. and Surg. (Columbia), 1877; L.R.C.S., Edinburgh, 1879; m. Emily M. L. Robinson, Feb. 13, 1884. Prof. materia medica and therapeutics, U. of Minn., 1888-1908, prof. preventive medicine, 1908-09; sec. and exec. officer Minn. State Bd. of Health, 1897-1919; surgeon (reserve) U.S.P.H. Service, on active duty, 1919-23, on inactive list with rank senior surgeon (reserve), Sept. 1923. Hon. v.p. 4th Internat. Congress on School Hygiene; sec.-treas. Conf. of State and Provincial Bds. of Health, 1906-13. Presbyn. Republican. Home: Claremont, Calif. Died Sept. 25, 1938.

BRACKENRIDGE, William Algernon, engineer. Engr. on constrn. New York elevated rys., 1876-80, D.L.&W.Ry., 1880-82, Brooklyn Elevated Ry., 1883-85, L.I. R.R., 1885-89; railroad commr. of Conn., 1890-91; cons. engr., Niagara Falls, N.Y., 1891-1904; became mem. advisory bd. of cons. engrs. of N.Y. State Canals, 1904; v.p. and gen. mgr. Southern Calif. Edison Co., Los Angeles, until 1928. Home: S. Pasadena, Calif. Died Nov. 29, 1929.

BRACKETT, Anna Callender, author; b. Boston, May 21, 1836; d. Samuel E. and Caroline S. B.; grad. State Normal Sch., Framingham, Mass., 1856;

unmarried. Teacher graded sch., E. Brookfield, Mass., and Framingham Normal Sch., 3 yrs.; v.prin. Girls' High and Normal Sch., Charleston, S.C., 2 yrs.; asst. high sch., Cambridge, Mass., 1 yr.; prin. Normal Sch., St. Louis, 9 yrs.; prin. girls' pvt. sch., New York, 20 yrs. Author: Education of American Girls, 1874; Poetry for Home and School (collection), 1876; Philosophy of Education (translated from German), 1886; Technique of Rest, 1892; Woman and the Higher Education, 1893. Address: New York, N.Y. Died 1911.

BRACKETT, Byron Briggs, dir. radio engring.; b. Ira, N.Y., Aug. 13, 1865; s. James Henry and Helen Maria (Pierce) B.; A.B., Syracuse U., 1890, A.M., 1893; B.C., Johns Hopkins, Ph.D., 1897; m. Tilla Wilson, 1900; 1 son, Richard Thomas. Inst. in charge elec. engring., Union Coll., Schenectady, N.Y., 1897-98; teacher of physics, Washington, D.C., 1898-1900; engr. for Rowland Telegraph Co., Baltimore, Md., 1900-01; with Inst. Elec. Engring. and Mathematics, Rutgers Coll., 1901-03; prof. elec. engring., Clarkson Coll., Potsdam, N.Y., 1903-09, S. Dak. State Coll., Brookings, 1909-23, U. of S.Dak., 1923-1931; dir. radio, U. of S.D., 1931—. Insp. torpedo cable for U.S. Army Engr. Corps, Spanish-Am. War; mem. S.Dak. Bd. Industrial Preparedness and dir. training of radio operators and electricians in S.A.T.C. work, S.Dak. State College, World War. Republican. Episcopalian. Home: Vermillion, S.D. Died Dec. 12, 1937.

BRACKETT, Charles Albert, dentist; b. Lampster, N.H., Jan. 2, 1850; s. Joseph and Lydia Lucretia (Hunt) B.; ed. pub. schs. and under tutelage of parents; D.M.D., Harvard, 1873; m. Mary Irish Spencer, Feb. 3, 1886. Practiced at Newport about fifty years, retiring June 1923. Inst. dental therapeutics, Harvard Dental sch., 1874-80, asst. prof., 1880-83, prof. dental pathology and therapeutics, 1883-90, dental pathology, 1890-1920, prof. oral pathology, 1920-23, emeritus, 1923—. Pres. R.I. State Bd. of Registration in Dentisty, 1888-97; del. Internat. Med. Congress, London, 1881, 9th Internat. Med. Congress, Washington, 1887, World's Columbian Dental Congress, Chicago, 1893. Trustee and consulting dental surgeon, Newport Hospital; chmn. com. for drafting new city charter, Newport, 1906; pres., trustee People's Library; mem. City Council, 1907—. V.p., dir. Aquidneck Nat. Bank; dir. Newport Trust Co. Unitarian. Home: Newport, R.I. Died Mar. 20, 1927.

BRACKETT, Cyrus Fogg, physicist; b. Parsonfield, Me., June 25, 1833; s. John and Jemime (Lord) B.; A.B., Bowdoin Coll., 1859, M.D., 1863; LL.D., Lafayette Coll., 1883, Bowdoin, 1892, Princeton, 1909; A.M., Princeton, 1896; m. Alice A. Briggs, Dec. 29, 1864. Instr., Bowdoin Coll., 1863, prof. chemistry, 1864-73; prof. physics, Princeton U., 1873-1908, prof. emeritus, 1908. Home: Princeton, N.J. Died Jan. 29, 1915.

BRACKETT, Dexter, civil engr.; b. Newton, Mass., Nov. 30, 1851; s. Cephas Henry and Louisa Thwing (Pierce) B.; grad. High Sch., Brighton, Mass., 1868; Bryant & Stratton Bus. Coll., fall and winter, 1868-69; m. Josephine Dame, Sept. 21, 1875. Asst. engr. in charge of work in connection with Boston Water Works, 1872-88; supt. of distribution, Boston Water Works, 1888-91, and asst. engr., in charge of spl. investigations, 1891-95; dept. engr. Met. Water Works during constrn. of works, 1895-1907, chief engr., 1907—. Has served as consulting engr. or given advice as expert for many municipalities. Home: Brighton, Mass. Died Aug. 26, 1915.

BRACKETT, Gustavus Benson, pomologist; b. Unity, Me., Mar. 24, 1827; s. Reuben and Elizabeth S. B.; ed. pub. schs., Cincinnati, 1838-41; acad. at Denmark, Ia., 1841-47; m. Anna Houston, Nov. 14, 1849. Served 3 yrs. in Civil War as capt. engrs.; after war lt. col. Ia. Militia; commr. in charge Iowa exhibits, Centennial Expn., Phila., 1876; U.S. commr. to Paris Expn., 1878; del.-at-large from Ia., Nat. Cotton Expn., New Orleans, 1885; represented pomol. div. Dept. of Agr. at Chicago Expn., 1893; was on jury of awards, Hort. Dept.; practical nurseryman and horticulturist; was 2 yrs. sec. and 4 yrs. pres. Ia. State Hort. Soc.; hort. expert of U.S. Commn. to Paris Expn., 1900; 2 yrs. sec. Am. Pomol. Soc. Was chief of div. of pomology, U.S. Dept. of Agr. Home: Denmark, Ia. Died Aug. 2, 1915.

BRACKETT, J(ames) Raymond, college prof.; b. Raymond, Me., Apr. 1, 1854; s. Levi and Nancy Jane (Cram) B.; B.A., Bates Coll., Lewiston, Me., 1875, M.A., 1878; Ph.D., Yale, 1880; student of Sanskrit and comparative philology, with W. D. Whitney, of Anglo-Saxon and Early English, with T. R. Lounsberry, and of English lit., with Henry Beers; m. Lottie Small Rolfe, Aug. 29, 1882. Prin. Foxcroft (Me.) Acad., 1875-78, Montpelier (Vt.) High Sch., 1880-83, Drury High Sch., North Adams, Mass., 1883-84; prof. comparative and English lit., 1884-1919, and dean Graduate Sch., 1909-19, also curator Phillips Art Collection, U. of Colo.; then dean emeritus and prof. emeritus. Conglist. Mason. Home: Boulder, Colo. Died July 9, 1922.

BRACKETT, John Quincy Adams, gov.; b. Bradford, N.H., June 8, 1842; s. Ambrose S. and Nancy (Brown) B.; A.B., Harvard, 1865, LL.B., 1868; m. Angie M. Peck, June 20, 1878. In practice at Boston, 1868—. Mem. Boston Common Council, 1873-77 (pres. 1876-77); Mass. Ho. of Rep., 1877-82, 1884-87 (speaker 1885-87); lt. gov. of Mass., 1887-90; gov., 1890-91. Pres. Mercantile Library Assn., Boston, 1871, 1882; judge advocate 1st Brigade, Mass. Militia, 1874-76; del.-at-large and mem. com. on resolutions, Rep. Nat. Conv., 1892. Home: Arlington, Mass. Died Apr. 6, 1918.

BRACKETT, Walter M., painter; b. Unity, Me., June 14, 1823; s. Reuben and Elisabeth (Starkey) B.; self-taught; m. Maria Louise Loring, Jan. 15, 1850. Began painting, 1843, first portraits, but later took to the painting of game fish, especially of salmon and trout; for 50 yrs. exhibitor in Boston, New York, Phila., Vienna, London, etc.; medals from Universal Expn., Vienna, Centennial Expn., Phila.; medal and diploma, Fishery Expn., London, etc.; works hung in Crystal Palace, London, Queen's Corridor, Buckingham Palace, War Dept., Washington, and in collections of Lord Dufferin, Sir Richard Potter, Liverpool Art Assn., etc. Home: Boston, Mass. Died Mar. 4, 1919.

BRACQ, Jean Charlemagne, college prof.; b. Cambrai, France, May 3, 1853; s. Hégesippe B. and Aurore (Louvet) B.; early edn., Rheims, France; came to U.S., 1871; grad. McGill U., Can., 1881; studied Newton Theol. Instn., 1881-83, Edinburgh, 1883-84, Paris, 1884-85; Litt.D., Colgate, 1904; LL.D., McGill, 1911; m. Emma M. Woods, 1883; 1 dau., Florence Beard (Mrs. Robert S. Moulton). Sec. Am. McAll Assn., Phila., 1885-91; asso. prof., 1891-92, prof. Romance langs., 1892-1918, then prof. emeritus, Vassar Coll. Decorated Officier d'Instruction Publique; Laureate of the French Acad.; Laureate of Acad. Moral and Polit. Sciences; Knight of Legion of Honor (France). Delegate Internat. Peace Congress, Rouen, France, 1903, The Hague, 1913, National Peace Congress, Nimes, 1904. Read paper, French Rights in Newfoundland, before Academy of Moral and Political Sciences, Paris, which was used as hist. basis for the settlement of the Newfoundland question. Has written on French Protestantism, Anglo-French relations, colonial expansion of France; took prominent part in defending the French Govt. at the time of the separation of church and state. Lecturer on contemporary French lit., Lowell Inst., Boston, 1898. Hon. mem. Nat. Inst. Social Sciences. Author: France Under the Republic, 1910; The Provocation of France, 1916; The Evolution of French Canada, 1924; L'Evolution du Canada français, 1927. Home: Keene, N.H. Died Dec. 18, 1934.

BRADBURY, Albert Williams, lawyer; b. Calais, Me., 1840; grad. Bowdoin, 1860; served 1st lt. to maj. and bvt. lt. col. 1st Me. mounted arty., 1861; served in dept. Gulf in 19th army corps, of which he became chief of arty., Sept. 1864; chief of arty., Army of the Shenandoah, under Sheridan, Dec. 1864; took part in many battles until mustered out, July 24, 1865. Admitted to bar, 1867; and practiced in Portland; was city solicitor of Portland and, 1894-98, U.S. dist. atty. for Me. Democrat. Home: Portland, Me. Deceased.

BRADBURY, Joseph P., jurist; judge court common pleas, Ohio, 1875-85, resigned; asso. justice Supreme Court, Ohio, Feb. 9, 1889-Feb. 8, 1893, and Feb. 9, 1894-Feb. 8, 1899; chief justice, Feb. 9, 1893-Feb. 8, 1904, and Feb. 9, 1899-Jan. 10, 1900. Republican. Home: Pomeroy, O. Died July 18, 1915.

BRADBURY, William Frothingham, head master; b. Westminster, Mass., May 17, 1829; s. William S. and Elizabeth (Emerson) B.; A.B., Amherst, 1856, A.M., 1859 (L.H.D., 1900); m. Margaret Jones, Aug. 27, 1857. Teacher, 1856-81, head master, 1881-86, Cambridge High Sch.; head master Cambridge Latin Sch., 1886-10, emeritus. Sec. Handel and Haydn Soc., 1899-1909 (pres., 1909—). Has pub. 24 math. text-books, arithmetic, algebra, geometry, trigonometry, logarithms, and other works. Home: Cambridge, Mass. Died Oct. 22, 1914.

BRADBURY, Woodman, clergyman; b. Bangor, Me., Apr. 9, 1866; s. Benjamin F. and Sarah Horton (Woodman) B.; A.B., Colby Coll., 1887; D.D., 1907; grad. Newton Theol. Instn., 1891; m. Mary E. Farr, July 9, 1895; 1 dau., Elizabeth F. (wife of Rev. C. L. Seasholes). Ordained Bapt. ministry, 1891; pastor various chs., 1891-1918; prof. homiletics and pastoral duties, Newton Theol. Instn. (now Andover Newton Theol. Sch.), 1918—. Trustee Colby Coll. Wrote chapters in Heroines of Modern Religion, 1913, and The Newton Chapel, 1920. Home: Newton Center, Mass. Died Feb. 26, 1935.

BRADEN, John, pres. Central Tenn. Coll., 1869—; b. New York, Aug. 18, 1826; grad. Ohio Wesleyan U., 1853 (A.M., 1859; D.D., Iowa Univ., 1873). Home: Nashville, Tenn. Died 1900.

BRADFORD, Amory Howe, clergyman; b. Granby, Oswego Co., N.Y., Apr. 14, 1846; s. Rev. Benjamin Franklin and Mary A. (Howe) B.; A.B., Hamilton Coll., 1867; grad. Andover Theol. Sem., 1870; post-grad. Oxford U., Eng., 1884; (D.D., Hamilton, 1884); m. Julia S. Stevens, Sept. 22, 1870. Ordained Congl. ministry, 1870; pastor First Ch., Montclair, N.J., 1870—. Asso. editor The Outlook, 1892-99; lecturer, Andover Theol. Sem., 1892-93. First sec., 1892, and 2d pres. Am. Inst. Christian Philosophy; mem. deputation sent by A.B.C.F.M. to inspect missions in Japan, 1895; moderator Nat. Council Congl. Chs., 1901; pres. Am. Missionary Assn., 1904. Author: Spirit and Life, 1888; Old Wine, New Bottles, 1892; The Pilgrim in Old England, 1893; Heredity and Christian Problems, 1895; The Growing Revelation, 1897; The Sistine Madonna, 1897; The Holy Family, 1899; The Art of Living Alone, 1899; The Return to Christ, 1900; The Age of Faith, 1900; Spiritual Lessons from the Brownings, 1900; Messages of the Masters, 1902; The Ascent of the Soul, 1902; The Inward Light. Home: Montclair, N.J. Died 1911.

BRADFORD, Charles, author; b. Detroit, Feb. 1862; s. Charles William and Maria (Barker) B.; ed. pub. sch. Detroit; m. Mary Georgina Jackson, Nov. 28, 1889. Served from printer's devil to mng. editor, 1873-83; after that printer and editor in Detroit, Chicago and New York; editor of Outing, 1890, Angler's Journal, Gameland, etc., 1891-98; newspaper reporter in New York 12 yrs. and at same time wrote Rod and Gun column New York Herald. Author: The Brook Trout and the Determined Angler, 1900; The Wild-Fowlers, 1902; The Angler's Secret, 1904; The Angler's Guide, 1908. Home: Richmond Hill, L.I., N.Y. Died Nov. 12, 1917.

BRADFORD, Edward Anthony, newspaper man; b. New York, Nov. 5, 1851; s. George Partridge and Angelina Statira (Oakes) B.; A.B., Yale, 1873; student Harvard Law Sch., 1873-74; LL.B., New York U., 1876; admitted to N.Y. bar, 1876, but never practiced; m. Susan C. Packer, Dec. 29, 1890 (died 1920); m. 2d, Edith H. Myers, Oct. 20, 1926. On staff New York Times, Sept. 1874—, was editorial writer, financial and economic topics; regular corr. London Standard, 1881-1907; founded and edited Yale Record (undergraduate publication). Home: Brooklyn, N.Y. Died May 4, 1928.

BRADFORD, Edward Green, judge; b. Wilmington, Del., Mar. 12, 1848; s. Hon. Edward G. and Mary Alicia (Heyward) B.; A.B., Yale, 1868; admitted to bar, 1870; U.S. dist. judge, Dist. of Del., 1897-1920. Home: Wilmington, Del. Died Mar. 30, 1928.

BRADFORD, Edward Hickling, surgeon; b. Boston, June 9, 1848; s. Charles F. and Eliza E. (Hickling) B.; A.B., Harvard, 1869, A.M., 1872, M.D., 1873; m. Edith Fiske, June 20, 1900. Clin. instr. orthopedic surgery, 1881-82, asst. clin. surgery, 1881-86, instr. surgery, 1886-93, instr. orthopedics, 1889-93, prof. orthopedic surgery, 1903—, dean, June 1912—, Harvard Med. Sch.; surgeon Children's Hosp., 1878-1909, Boston City Hosp., 1880-94. Fellow Am. Acad. Arts and Sciences. Author: Treatise on Orthopedic Surgery, 1895. Home: Boston, Mass. Died May 7, 1926.

BRADFORD, Gamaliel, author; b. Boston, Mass., Oct. 9, 1863; s. Gamaliel and Clara Crowninshield (Kinsman) B.; entered Harvard Coll., 1882, but obliged to leave almost immediately on account of ill health; m. Helen Hubbard Ford, Oct. 30, 1886; children—Gamaliel (dec.), Sarah R. Elected mem. Am. Acad. Arts and Letters, 1931. Republican. Author: Types of American Character (essays), 1895; A Pageant of Life, 1904; The Private Tutor, 1904; Between Two Masters, 1906; Matthew Porter, 1908; Lee, the American, 1912; Confederate Portraits, 1914; Union Portraits, 1916; Portraits of Women, 1916; A Naturalist of Souls, 1917; Portraits of American Women, 1919; A Prophet of Joy (poem), 1920; Shadow Verses (poems), 1920; American Portraits, 1875-1900, 1922; Damaged Souls, 1923; The Soul of Samuel Pepys, 1924; Bare Souls, 1924; Wives, 1925; Darwin, 1926; D. L. Moody—A Worker in Souls, 1927; Life and I, 1928; As God Made Them, 1929; Daughters of Eve, 1930; The Quick and the Dead, 1931. Died Apr. 11, 1932.

BRADFORD, Gamaliel, banker; b. Boston, Jan. 15, 1831; s. Gamaliel B.; A.B., Harvard, 1849; m. Clara Crowninshield Kinsman, Oct. 30, 1861 (died 1866); father of Gamaliel, Jr. Asso. with banking firm Blake Bros. & Co., Boston, 1858-68. First gov. Mass. Soc. of Mayflower Descendants. Author: Lesson of Popular Government, 2 vols., 1898. Home: Boston, Mass. Died 1911.

BRADFORD, John Ewing, church official; b. Bellbrook, O., Dec. 5, 1866; s. James Hervey and Martha (Bradford) B.; A.B., Monmouth (Ill.) Coll., 1889, A.M., 1892, D.D., 1920; post-grad. study Xenia Theol. Sem., U. of Chicago and Harvard Univ.; LL.D., Tarkio Coll., 1931; m. Mary Ella McClellan, Oct. 11, 1894; children—Margaret (Mrs. Jacob L. Sheets), Isabel, James McClellan, Martha Agnes. Ordained ministry U.P. Ch., July 1, 1892; pastor various chs., 1892-1905; prin. Wever-Media Acad., 1900-05; prof history, Miami U., Oxford, O., 1905-19; gen. sec. Bd of Edn., United Presbyn. Ch. of N.A., 1919—. Republican. Author: History of the Miami Valley, 1919. Home: Chicago, Ill. Died July 30, 1936.

BRADFORD, Royal Bird, naval officer; b. Turner, Me., July 22, 1844; s. Phillips and Mary Brett (Bird) B.; grad. U.S. Naval Acad., 1865; m. Harriet Stanhope Engs, May 26, 1875. Commd. ensign, Dec. 4, 1866; promoted through grades to rear-admiral, Nov.

23, 1904. Naval attaché Paris Peace Commn., 1898; mem. many tech. bds.; chief Bur. of Equipment, 1897-1903; retired July 22, 1906. Home: Washington, D.C. Died Aug. 4, 1914.

BRADFORD, Thomas Lindsley, physician, author; b. Francestown, N.H., June 6, 1847; s. Thomas Bixby and Emily Hutchinson (Brown) B.; student Phillips Acad., Andover, Mass., 1864; Harvard Med. Sch., 1866-67; grad. Homœ. Med. Coll. of Pa., 1869; post-grad. work hosps. of Europe, 1872; m. Eliza Virginia Hough, June 15, 1887. Practiced at Skowhegan, Me., 1869-77, then in Phila. Librarian Hahnemann Med. Coll., Phila. Republican. Mason, Odd Fellow. Author: Homœpathic Bibliography of the United States (1825-91), 1892; The Life and Letters of Samuel Hahnemann, 1895; Pioneers of Homœopathy, 1897; History of The Homœopathic Medical College of Pennsylvania; The Hahnemann Medical College and Hospital of Philadelphia, Pa., 1898; Quiz Questions on the History of Medicine, 1898; The Logic of Figures or Comparative Results of Homœopathic and other Treatments, 1900; Index of Provings, 1901; History of Homœopathy and Its Institutions in America, 1905; Autobiography of a Baby, revised edition, 1912. Compiled: Bibliographer's Manual of American History, 5 vols., 1907-10; The Lesser Writings of C. M. F. von Boenninghausen, 1908; Alumni Book of Hahnemann Medical College of Phila. Home: Philadelphia, Pa. Died Dec. 3, 1918.

BRADFUTE, Oscar Edwin, cattle breeder; b. nr. Cedarville, O., Jan. 21, 1862; s. David and Martha E. (Collins) B.; B.A., Ind. U., 1884; m. Jennie M. Collins, Apr. 10, 1890; children—David Collins, Helen Elizabeth, John Edwin. Breeder of Aberdeen-Angus cattle, 1887—; head of firm O. E. Bradfute & Sons; an organizer Internat. Live Stock Expn., at Chicago, 1899, and mem. bd. dirs.; mem. White House Industrial Conf., Oct. 1919; lecturer at agrl. colls. and state farmers' meetings. Trustee Ohio Agrl. Expmt. Sta., 1900-05. Mem. Bd. of Control, Ohio Agrl. Experiment Sta., also chmn. exec. com., 1920-25. Mem. President Coolidge's Agrl. Conf. Com., 1924. Trustee Ohio State U., 1905-25, Cedarville Coll., 1917-23, Greene County Children's Home, 1910-21. Democrat. Mem. and elder U.P. Ch. Home: Xenia, O. Died Mar. 25, 1929.

BRADLEE, Arthur Tisdale, merchant; b. Boston, Dec. 23, 1867; s. John Tisdale and Sarah E. (Goddard) B.; B.S., Mass. Inst. Tech., 1888; m. Gertrude Bemis, 1896. In dry goods commn. business, Boston, 1888—; pres. The William Whitman Co., Inc.; dir. various corps.; mem. corp. Franklin Savings Bank City of Boston. Republican. Unitarian. Home: Chestnut Hill, Mass. Died Aug. 31, 1925.

BRADLEY, Alfred Eugene, army officer; b. Jamestown, N.Y., Nov. 25, 1864; s. Arthur A. and Jane (Parsons) B.; M.D., Jefferson Med. Coll., Phila., 1887; m. Letitia M. Follett, Oct. 4, 1887. Apptd. asst. surgeon, Oct. 29, 1888; capt. asst. surgeon, Oct. 29, 1893; maj. brigade surgeon vols., June 4, 1898; hon. discharged vol. service, Nov. 10, 1899; maj. surgeon U.S.A., Jan. 1, 1902; maj. Med. Corps, Jan. 1, 1902; lt. col., Jan. 28, 1910; col., July 1, 1916; brig. gen. N.A., Aug. 5, 1917; hon. discharged, as brig. gen. N.A., June 20, 1918; retired with rank of col. Mil. observer with British, on duty at Am. Embassy, London, May 20, 1916, June 1917; apptd. chief surgeon A.E.F. in France, June 8, 1917, organizing med. services of Am. forces abroad. Home: Highland Park, Ill. Died Dec. 17, 1922.

BRADLEY, Andrew Coyle, asso. justice Supreme Court, D.C.; b. Washington, Feb. 12, 1844; ed. private schools and Columbian U., Washington, 1859-61; LL.B., Harvard, 1867; m. Sue H. Young, 1872. Prof. law of commercial paper, and criminal law and procedure. Columbian U. Law School. Home: 2013 Q St. N.W., Washington, D.C. Died 1902.

BRADLEY, Bernard James, coll. pres.; b. E. Braintree, Mass., Feb. 19, 1867; s. James and Mary (Allen) B.; A.B., Mt. St. Mary's Coll., Emmitsburg, Md., 1888, A.M., 1890; LL.D., Georgetown U., 1912. Ordained R.C. priest, 1892; asst. Ch. of the Transfiguration, Brooklyn, 1892, prof. liturgy, logic, Latin and Greek, Mt. St. Mary's Coll., 1892-97, treas., 1897-1915, v.p., 1901-11, pres., 1911—. Made domestic prelate by Pope Benedict XV, 1913. Home: Emmitsburg, Md. Died Sept. 21, 1936.

BRADLEY, Charles, real estate; b. Newark, N.J., Aug. 31, 1857; s. Joseph P. and Mary (Hornblower) B.; A.M., Rutgers U., 1876; studied Columbian Law Sch., Washington, D.C., 1877-78; m. Julie E. Ballantine, Apr. 12, 1882; children—Charles Burnet, Robert Ballantine, Anne Brown (Mrs. Samuel Eliot), Francis Barlow (dec.). Began as clk. and bookkeeper, 1878; sec. P. Ballantine & Sons, real estate and insurance, Newark, 1883, advancing to pres., 1927; pres. Saranac Realty Co., Alliance Investment Co., Murphy Varnish Co. Apptd. col. on staff Gov. of Ky., 1930. Dir. Newark Mus., Newark Eye & Ear Infirmary. Republican. Home: Convent Station, N.J. Died Sept. 4, 1938.

BRADLEY, Charles Clark, judge; b. Exira, Ia., May 30, 1879; s. Franklin Pierce and Fannie (Atkinson) B.; B.A., U. of Ia., 1899, LL.B., 1901; unmarried. Admitted to Ia. bar, 1901, and began law practice at Council Bluffs; practiced at Le Mars, Ia., 1902-18; judge Dist. Court, 21st Dist., Mar. 1918-Dec. 31, 1933; trustee under federal court for Royal Union Fund of Lincoln Nat. Life Ins. Co. Chmn. adv. bd. Plymouth County, Ia., World War. Mason, Elk. Home: Le Mars, Ia. Died July 26, 1939.

BRADLEY, Charles Henry, educator; b. Johnson, Vt., Feb. 13, 1860; s. Harmon H. and Sarah G. (Ferguson) B.; ed. State Normal School, Johnson; m. Mary Chilton Brewster, June 7, 1883. Supt. The Farm and Trades Sch., Thompson's Island, Mass., 1888—. Trustee Norwich U. Republican. Baptist. Mason. Home: Boston, Mass. Died Jan. 30, 1921.

BRADLEY, Charles Schenck, inventor; b. Victor, N.Y., Apr. 12, 1853; s. Alonzo and Sarah (Schenck) B.; prep. edn. De Graff Mil. Inst., Rochester, N.Y., 1868-71; student U. of Rochester, 1872; m. Emmaretta Orcutt Brackett, Feb. 16, 1876. Began with Edison Illuminating Co., New York, 1881; successively in employ various elec. cos., 1883-1914; with U.S. Reduction Co., 1916—. Has taken out many patents, including patent for process for production of aluminum, patent for three phase transmission of power, rotary convertor, fixation of atmospheric nitrogen, etc. Home: New York, N.Y. Died 1929.

BRADLEY, Dan Freeman, clergyman; b. Bangkok, Siam, Mar. 17, 1857; s. Dan Beach and Sarah (Blachly) B.; A.B., Oberlin, 1882; grad. theol. sch., same, 1885; D.D., Yankton Coll., 1892, Cornell Coll., 1904, Oberlin, 1908; m. Lillian J. Jacques, July 9, 1883 (dec.); children—Dwight J., Robert G., Theodore Dan. Ordained Congl. ministry, 1885; acting pres. Yankton Coll., 1889-92; pastor First Congl. Ch., Grand Rapids, Mich., 1892-1902; pres. Grinnell Coll., 1902-05; pastor Pilgrim Congl. Ch., Cleveland, 1905-37. Trustee Oberlin Coll. Home: Birmingham, Mich. Died Nov. 11, 1939.

BRADLEY, Denis M., bishop; b. in Ireland, Feb. 25, 1846; ed. in parochial school, Manchester, N.H., and Holy Cross Coll., Worcester, Mass. (grad. 1867); theol. studies at St. Joseph's Sem., Troy, N.Y.; ordained priest there June 3, 1871; exercised the sacred ministry at Portland, Me., and at St. Joseph's Ch., Manchester, N.H.; consecrated bishop, R.C. Ch., 1884. Home: Manchester, N.H. Died 1903.

BRADLEY, Edward Elias, mfr.; b. New Haven, Conn., Jan. 5, 1845; s. Isaac and Abigail Knowles (Hervey) B.; academic and commercial edn.; m. Mary Elizabeth Kimberly, Apr. 26, 1871. Began as shipping clk., New Haven Wheel Co., 1860, pres., 1887—; officer or dir. various corps. Apptd. capt. Co. F, 2d Regt. C.N.G., 1865, col. 2d Regt., 1869, paymaster-gen. of Conn., 1877, adj. gen. Conn., 1893. Mem. Conn. Ho. of Rep., 1882-83, Senate, 1886; pres. Conn. State Park Commn. Episcopalian. Home: New Haven, Conn. Died Sept. 20, 1938.

BRADLEY, Edward Lounsberry, educator; b. Germantown, Phila., Pa., Sept. 14, 1861; s. Joseph William and Clara Amelia (Morse) B.; student Cheltenham Acad., Jenkintown, Pa., 1873-75, Peekskill (N.Y.) Mil. Acad., 1876-78, Germantown (Pa.) Acad., 1878-81, Princeton U., 1881-84; hon. A.M., Princeton, 1884; m. Maud Menefee, July 14, 1906. Began as junior member of pub. firm of Wm. M. Bradley & Bro., 1884; organist and choirmaster, St. Paul's Episcopal Ch., Riverside, Ill., 1890-1900; inaugurated a summer camp for boys at Fox Lake, Ill., 1894, which developed into permanent work for underprivileged boys as Allendale Farm at Lake Villa, 1897, dir. same, 1897—. Episcopalian. Home: Lake Ville, Ill. Deceased.

BRADLEY, Frederick Worthen, mining man; b. Nevada Co., Calif., Feb. 21, 1863; s. Henry Sewall and Virginia (Shearer) B.; student Coll. of Mining, U. of Calif., 1882-84; m. Mary Parks, Sept. 26, 1901; children—Frederick Worthen, James Parks, Henry Sewall, John Davis. Began mining in Calif., 1884; pres. Alaska Juneau Gold Mining Co., Alaska Mexican Gold Mining Co., Alaska Treadwell Gold Mining Co., Alaska United Gold Mining Co., Bunker Hill & Sullivan Mining & Concentrating Co., Ocean Shore R.R. Co., Registration & Securities Co., Treadwell Yukon Co.; v.p. Atolia Mining Co.; also dir. many corps. Republican. Presbyn. Home: San Francisco, Calif. Died July 6, 1933.

BRADLEY, George Beckwith, judge; b. Town of Greene, Chenango County, N.Y., Feb. 5, 1825; s. Orlo F. and Julia A. (Carter) B.; acad. edn., Ithaca, N.Y.; m. Hannah E. Lattimer, July 11, 1850. Admitted to bar, 1848, practiced at Corning, N.Y. Mem. N.Y. Constl. Conv., 1872-73; state senator, 1874-77; justice Supreme Ct., N.Y., 1884-97; during that time judge Ct. Appeals, 2d div., about 4 yrs.; retired. Home: Corning, N.Y. Died Jan. 9, 1916.

BRADLEY, Glenn Danford, prof. history; b. Kinderhook, Mich., Apr. 12, 1884; s. Albert Cooper and Ada (Smith) B.; A.B., U. of Mich., 1907, A.M., 1913, Ph.D., 1915; m. Florence M. Moore, Aug. 6, 1921. With Santa Fe Ry. Co., Topeka, Kan., 1907-09; teacher history Leavenworth (Kan.) High Sch., 1909-10; prin. Newton (Kan.) High Sch., 1910-12; instr. in English, U. of Mich., 1912-16; asst. prof. history and actg. prof. English, U. of Toledo, 1916-17, asso. prof. history and head of history dept., 1917—, prof. history, 1921—, also dir. of evening sessions, 1927—. Mason. Republican. Presbyn. Author: Winning the Southwest, 1912; The Story of the Pony Express, 1913; The Story of the Santa Fe, 1920. Home: Toledo, O. Died Jan. 4, 1930.

BRADLEY, John Edwin, educator; b. Lee, Mass., Aug. 8, 1839; s. Stephen and Hannah (Austin) B.; A.B., Williams Coll., 1865, A.M., 1868, LL.D., 1893; Ph.D., U. of N.Y., 1879; m. Martha J. Gould, July 7, 1870. Prin. high sch., Pittsfield, Mass., 1865-68, Albany, N.Y., 1868-86; supt. city schs., Minneapolis, 1886-92; pres. Ill. Coll., 1892-1900. Commr. state of N.Y. to Paris Expn., 1878; mem. Nat. Council of Edn., 1889—, corporate mem. A.B.C.F.M.; mem. Nat. Congl. Council, Chicago, 1886, Des Moines, Ia., 1904, Boston, 1910; mem. Internat. Congl. Council, Boston, 1899, Edinburgh, 1908; v.p. Ecumenical Internat. Council, New York, 1900. Author: Science and Industry; School Incentives; Healthfulness of Intellectual Pursuits; Unconscious Education; Work and Play; Talks with Students. Home: Randolph, Mass. Died Oct. 7, 1912.

BRADLEY, Luther Prentice, army officer; b. New Haven, Conn., Dec. 8, 1822; ed. common schs. Lt. col. 51st Ill. Inf., Nov. 6, 1861; col., Oct. 5, 1862; brig. gen., July 20, 1864; resigned, June 30, 1865; apptd. from Ill., lt. col. 27th Inf., July 28, 1866; transferred to 9th Inf., Mar. 15, 1869; col. 3d Inf., Mar. 20, 1879; transferred to 13th Inf., June 14, 1879; retired, Dec. 8, 1886; advanced to rank of brig. gen. retired, by act of Apr. 23, 1904. Bvtd. col., Mar. 2, 1867, for battle of Chickamauga; brig. gen., Mar. 2, 1867, for battle of Resaca, Ga. Home: Tacoma, Wash. Died 1910.

BRADLEY, Lydia Moss; b. Switzerland County, Ind., July 31, 1816; d. Capt. Zealy Moss and Jeanette (Glasscock) Moss; ed. in schs. of Switzerland County, Ind.; m. Tobias S. Bradley, May 11, 1837 (dec.). Has given to Peoria Bradley Park, Bradley Home for Aged Women, and founded Bradley Poly. Inst. Home: Peoria, Ill. Died 1908.

BRADLEY, MILTON, mfr.; b. Vienna, Me., Nov. 8, 1836; s. Lewis B.; ed. grammar and high schs., Lowell, Mass., and Lawrence Scientific Sch. (Harvard), 1854-55; spl. studies in engring. Began active life as civil and mech. engr. Became interested in lithography and through that in the publishing of home amusements. Organized the Milton Bradley Co. at Springfield, Mass., for the manufacture and publication of kindergarten and school material, 1863; developed the Bradley system of color instruction, based on spectrum standard colors with a complete and definite color nomenclature; publisher The Kindergarten Review. Author and publisher: Color in the School Room, 1890; Color in the Kindergarten, 1893; Elementary Color, 1895; Water Colors in the Schoolroom, 1900. Home: Springfield, Mass. Died 1911.

BRADLEY, Peter Butler, mfr.; sr. mem. firm Peter B. & Robert S. Bradley (Boston); pres. Bradley Lumber & Mfg. Co.; treas. Bradley Pulverizer Co. Home: Hingham, Mass. Died Aug. 26, 1933.

BRADLEY, Theodore James, educator, chemist; b. Albany, N.Y., Aug. 8, 1874; s. Theodore Frelinghuysen and Elizabeth (Houghkirk) B.; Ph.G., Union U., 1895, hon. A.M., 1912; B.S., Rensselaer Poly. Inst., 1904; hon. Pharm.D., Mass. Coll. of Pharmacy, 1927; hon. Pharm.M., Philadelphia College of Pharmacy, 1933; m. Anna Raymond Peck, Apr. 22, 1896; children—Grace H., Will T. Theodore. Chemist, lab. of N.Y. depts. of health and agr., 1895-1905; instr., asso. prof., sec., Albany Coll. Pharmacy, 1895-1912; master of science and mathematics, Albany Acad., 1896-1912; instructor and lecturer on chemistry, Albany Med. Coll., 1897-1907; dean and prof. chemistry, Mass. Coll. Pharmacy, June 1912—. Mem. revision com., U.S. Pharmacopœia. Republican. Conglist. Home: Brookline, Mass. Died Dec. 12, 1936.

BRADLEY, Thomas W., congressman; b. Apr. 6, 1844. Pvt. to capt. 124th N.Y. Vols.; a.-d.-c. to Maj. Gen. Mott, 3d Div., 2d Army Corps; wounded at Gettysburg, Wilderness and Petersburg; awarded Congressional Medal of Honor; bvtd. maj. vols. Mem. N.Y. Assembly, 1876; was asst. insp.-gen. Nat. Guard; del. Rep. nat. convs., 1892, 1896, 1900, 1908; mem. 58th to 62d Congresses (1903-13), 20th N.Y. Dist. Home: Walden, N.Y. Died May 30, 1920.

BRADLEY, William Aspenwall, author, editor, literary adviser; b. Hartford, Conn., Feb. 8, 1878; s. William Edward Cleveland and Anna Maria (Aspenwall) B.; A.B., Columbia, 1899, A.M., 1900; m. Jenny Serruys, 1921. Editor and pub. East and West Mag. (with G. S. Hellman), 1899-1900; art dir. and lit. adviser, McClure, Phillips & Co., and The McClure Co., 1900-08. Asso. with Boston Herald, American Mag., Delineator, Yale U. Press, The Macmillan Co., Les Editions George Crès at Cie, etc. First lt., Sanitary Corps U.S.A. (A.E.F.), 1918-19. Field sec. for France, Am. Social Hygiene Assn., 1919. Author: William Cullen Bryant (English Men of Letters Series), 1905; Introduction to Correspondence of Sir Philip Sidney and Hubert Languet (in the Humanist Library), 1912; Meryon and Baudelaire in Prints and Their Makers, 1912; Maxime Lalanne in Print Collectors' Booklets (Mus. Fine Arts, Boston), 1914; The Etching of Figures, 1915; French Etchers of the Second Empire, 1916; Garlands and Wayfarings, 1917; Old Christmas and other Kentucky Tales in Verse, 1917; Singing Carr and Other Song-Ballets of the Cumberlands, 1918; Dutch Landscape Etchers of the Seventeenth Century, 1919. Translator: Introduction to Decadence, and Other Essays on the Culture of Ideas (by Remy de Gourmont); The Story of Flamenca (arranged from Provençal original of 13th century), 1922; The Journal of Marie Lenéru, 1923. Editor of The Garden Muse, 1910, and other vols. Contributing editor The Dial, 1917-18. Asso. editor Ex-Libris, 1923-25; Department of Lettres Anglo-Américaines in Vient de Paraitre, 1924-26. Chevalier Legion of Honor (France). Home: New Canaan, Conn. Died Jan. 9, 1939.

BRADLEY, William Harrison, consul gen.; b. Galena, Ill., June 3, 1848; s. William Henry and S.S.B.; A.B., Yale U., 1872; student, Columbia, 1879-80; m. Mary Capen Gray, Sept. 24, 1873 (died 1878); children—William Henry (dec.), Bryson Delavan (dec.); m. 2d, Carolina Lawson, Nov. 13, 1883 (died 1916); children—Marion Kari, Mary Linda. Am. consul, Nice, France, 1889-93, Tunstall, 1897-1903, Manchester, Eng., 1903-05, consul gen., same, 1905-06, consul, same, 1906-07; consul gen. at Montreal, Can., Aug. 15, 1907-Mar. 1917; retired. Home: Ridgefield, Conn. Died Sept. 17, 1929.

BRADLEY, William O'Connell, senator; b. nr. Lancaster, Garrard County, Ky., Mar. 18, 1847; s. Robert M. and Nancy E. (Totten) B.; pvt. in U.S. Vols. short time; admitted to bar by spl. act of legislature, 1865, being only 18 yrs. of age; m. Margaret R. Duncan, July 11, 1867. Elected pros. atty., Garrard County, Ky., 1870; Rep. presdl. elector, 1872; candidate for Congress, 1872 and 1876; nominee for U.S. senator, 5 times; del.-at-large Rep. Nat. convs., 1880, 1884, 1888, 1892, 1900, 04, 08; made speech seconding nomination of Grant, 1880 and Theodore Roosevelt, 1904; mem. Rep. Nat. Com., 12 yrs.; candidate for gov. of Ky., 1887; apptd. E.E. and M.P. to Korea, 1889, but declined; gov. of Ky., 1895-99 (1st Rep. gov. in state); U.S. senator, 1909-15. Home: Louisville, Ky. Died May 23, 1914.

BRADNER, Lester, clergyman; b. Chicago, Ill., Mar. 9, 1867; s. Lester and Lucy A. (Charnley) B.; Ph. D., Yale, 1889; studied U. of Berlin, 1891; grad. Gen. Theol. Sem., 1894; D.D., U. of the South, 1921; m. Edith M. Murray, 1895; children—Leicester, William Murray, John, Edith. Deacon and priest P.E. Ch., 1894; asst. minister Ch. of the Ascension, New York, 8 yrs.; rector St. John's Ch., Providence, R.I., 1902-13; sec. Dept. of Religious Edn., P.E. Ch., New York, 1913-23; sec. for Christian Edn., Diocese of R.I., 1925—. In charge nat. teacher-training work for P.E. Ch., 1913-23. Author: Organizing the Smaller Sunday School, 1917. Home: Saunderstown, R.I. Died Sept. 21, 1929.

BRADSHAW, Sidney Ernest, college prof.; b. nr. Covington, Tenn., Aug. 10, 1869; s. Sidney John and Mollie (Hambleton) B.; B.A., Bethel Coll., Russellville, Ky., 1891, hon. M.A., 1899; Ph.D., U. of Va., 1900; LL.D., Furman U., 1934; studied univs. of Chicago, Leipzig, Berlin and in Paris. Instr. English, Bardstown (Ky.) Male and Female Inst., 1891-92; prof. English. Bethel Coll., 1894-95, 1897-99, 1900-02; prof. English and German, Manual Training High Sch., Louisville, Ky., 1902-03; prof. modern langs., Furman U., 1904—, chmn. faculty, 1912—, acting pres., 1918-19. Baptist; deacon First Baptist Church, Greenville (chmn. bd., 1932); chmn. exec. com. bd. trustees Bapt. Courier. Author: On Southern Poetry Prior to 1860, 1900. Home: Greenville, S.C. Died Aug. 31, 1938.

BRADSHAW, William Francis, banker, lawyer; b. Paducah, Ky., Sept. 17, 1878; s. William Francis and Virginia (Wheeler) B.; B.S., Vanderbilt, 1899; student law dept. Columbia U., 1899-1900; m. Rosena Ashton White, June 21, 1905; 1 dau., Julia Ashton. Began practice at Paducah, as Broadshaw & Bradshaw, 1900; mem. Bradshaw, MacDonald & McMurray; pres. Mechanics Trust & Savings Bank, First Natl. Bank, Paducah; officer or dir. other cos. Democrat. Episcopalian. Home: Paducah, Ky. Died 1930.

BRADT, Charles Edwin, clergyman; b. Laporte, Ind., Nov. 7, 1863; s. Isaac Henry and Ann Elizabeth (Bastow) B.; A.B., U. of Wooster, 1886 A.M., 1889, Ph.D., 1897, D.D., 1905; m. Nellie Acken, June 11, 1889. Ordained Presbyn. ministry, 1889; pastor 2d Ch., Lincoln, Neb., 1889-96, 1st Ch., Wichita, Kan., 1896-1905; sec. Presbyn. Bd. of Foreign Missions at Chicago. Mason. Author: Key to the Kingdom, 1904; Capturing a Community for Christ, 1900; A Working Church, 1903; Problems of Pin-Hole Parish, 1912; Around the World Studies and Stories, 1912; Edwin: Adventures in the Universe, 1922. Home: Evanston, Ill. Died Sept. 5, 1922.

BRADWELL, James B., jurist; b. Loughborough, Eng., Apr. 16, 1828; s. Thomas and Elizabeth (Gutteridge) B.; came with parents to U.S. when 16 months old; reared on farm; ed. in log sch. houses, at Wilson's Acad., Chicago, and at Knox Coll.; m. Myra Colby, 1852 (died Feb. 1894). Admitted to bar, 1852; elected, 1861, and re-elected, 1865, judge of the Cook County Court; mem. Ill. legislature, 1873-75. Prominently identified with the movement for equal rights to women. Invented a process for making halftones. Was chmn. com. World's Congress Auxiliary on Congress of Photographers; del. Universal Congress of Lawyers and Jurists, St. Louis, 1904. Republican. Mason. Home: Chicago, Ill. Died 1907.

BRADY, Alice, actress; b. N.Y. City; d. William A.B.; ed. in convent. First appeared in the "Balkan Princess," later in Gilbert and Sullivan's light operas; achieved signal success in leading feminine rôle in "Forever After," screen début in father's film productions; star in "The Fear Market," "Sinners," etc. Died Oct. 28, 1939.

BRADY, Anthony Nicholas, capitalist; b. Lille, France, Aug. 22, 1843; came to U.S. with parents when a child; did not attend school after age of 13; married. Opened a tea store in Albany, 1864, and others successively till he monopolized tea trade in Albany and Troy; became owner of large granite quarries; purchased, with others, gas plants of Albany, Troy and Chicago, and street car lines of Albany and Troy; rebuilt "Huckleberry" ry. system in New York; planned consolidation of New York surface lines, and promoted similar combinations in Washington, Phila. and other cities. Pres. New York Edison Co., Municipal Gas Co. (Albany), Edison Electric Illuminating Co. (Brooklyn), Memphis Consolidated Gas & Electric Co., Kings Co. (N.Y.) Electric Light & Power Co., Utica Gas & Electric Co.; chmn. of bd. Brooklyn Heights R.R. Co., Brooklyn, Queens County & Suburban R.R. Co., Brooklyn Rapid Transit Co., Brooklyn Union Elevated R.R. Co., Nassau Electric R.R. Co., Peoples Gas Light & Coke Co. (Chicago); dir. Westinghouse Electric & Mfg. Co., Am. Tobacco Co., U.S. Rubber Co., U.S. Cast Iron Pipe & Foundry Co., and about 30 other corps. Home: Albany, N.Y. Died July 23, 1913.

BRADY, Cyrus Townsend, clergyman; b. Allegheny, Pa., Dec. 20, 1861; s. Jasper Ewing and Harriet Cora (Townsend) B.; grad. U.S. Naval Acad., 1883; LL.D., St. John's Coll., Md. 1902; m. Clarissa Sidney Guthrie (died 1890); 2d, Mary Barrett. R.R. service with the Mo. P. and U.P. roads several yrs.; studied theology under Bishop Worthington, Neb.; deacon, 1889, priest, 1890, P.E. Ch.; rector P.E. chs. in Mo. and Colo. and archdeacon of Kan. until 1895, and archdeacon of Pa. till 1899; rector of St. Paul's Ch., Overbrook, Phila., 1899-1902; in lit. work, 1902-05; rector various chs., 1905-14; asst. minister St. Stephen's Ch., New York, 1914—. Chaplain 1st Pa. Vol. Inf. Spanish-Am. War. Author: Commodore Paul Jones, 1900; Under Tops'ls and Tents, 1901; Woven With the Ship, 1902; In the Wasp's Nest, 1902; Border Fights and Fighters, 1902; In the War with Mexico, 1903; Conquest of the Southwest, 1905; The True Andrew Jackson, 1906; On the Old Kearsarge, 1909; The Better Man, 1910; Bob Dashaway, Privateersman, 1911; Bob Dashaway, Treasure Hunter, 1912; Bob Dashaway in Frozen Seas, 1913; And Thus He Came, 1916; also many other books out of print. Home: Yonkers, N.Y. Died Jan. 24, 1920.

BRADY, Francis X., college pres.; b. nr. Gettysburg, Pa., Mar. 29, 1857; s. Samuel J. and Margaret (Goy) B.; entered Society of Jesus, 1873; studied philosophy and science, Woodstock Coll., Md., 1876-79, theology, 1884-86. Prof. Gonzaga Coll., Washington, 1879-81, St. Peter's Coll., Jersey City, N.J., 1881-84; ordained priest R.C. Ch., 1886; editor Messenger of the Sacred Heart, Little Messenger of the Sacred Heart, Pilgrim of Our Lady of Martyrs, and dir. Sacred Heart League of U.S., 1886-92; v.p. Loyola Coll., Baltimore, 1892-95, pastor St. Ignatius' Ch., Baltimore, 1895-1908; pres. Loyola Coll., 1908—. Author: Life of St. Aloysius, 1887; The Holy Hour, 1890; Manual of Bona Mors, 1890; The Great Supper of God, 1901. Address: Baltimore, Md. Died 1911.

BRADY, James Boyd, clergyman; b. County Antrim, Ireland, Sept. 7, 1845; s. James and Isabella (Boyd) B.; Belfast Model Sch. and Ballymena Classical, Ireland; came to U.S., 1867; B.D., Drew Theol. Sem., 1869; Ph.D., New York U., 1892; m. Josephine Louise Wood, June 9, 1877. Entered Newark (N.J.) Conf. M.E. Ch., 1869; pastor various chs. in N.J., N.Y. and Mass., 1869-1903; financial agt. for Conf. Claimants of N.E. Conf., Boston, 1904; later in lit. work. Author: Sermon in Memory of Ellen Leal Osborn, 1883; Sängerfest Sermons, 1892; Missionary Dynamics, 1903; People's Temple Keepsakes, 1898; Divine Immanence, 1903; Beacon Searchlights on Millionaires and Pioneers, 1904; The Human Phronis, and Divine Drama (in preparation). Home: Boston, Mass. Deceased.

BRADY, James Cox, financier; b. Albany, N.Y., Sept. 23, 1882; s. Anthony N. and Marcia (Myers) B.; B.A., Yale, 1904; m. Helen McMahon, Oct. 2, 1920. In banking and commercial business, N.Y. City, 1904—; trustee Central Union Trust Co.; dir. Chrysler Motor Corp., Brooklyn Edison Co., Prudential Oil Corp., Union Oil Co. of Calif., etc. Mem. bd. dirs. New York Post-Grad. Med. Sch. and Hosp. Catholic. Home: Albany, N.Y., and New York, N.Y. Died Nov. 10, 1927.

BRADY, James H., senator; b. Indiana County, Pa., June 12, 1862; s. John and Katherine (Lee) B.; grad. Olathe (Kan.) High School; student State Normal School, Leavenworth, Kan. Removed to Idaho, 1894; pres. Jas. H. Brady Investment Co. Del. Rep. Nat. Conv., 1900, 1908 (chmn. Ida. delegation); chmn. Ida. Rep. State Central Com., 1904-08; gov. of Idaho, 1909-11. Elected U.S. senator, Jan. 24, 1913, for unexpired term (1913-15), Weldon B. Heyburn, deceased; reëlected, Nov. 3, 1914. Home: Pocatello, Idaho. Died Jan. 13, 1918.

BRADY, John, bishop; b. County Cavan, Ireland, 1842; studied at All Hallows Coll., Ireland; ordained priest, 1864; asst. pastor Newburyport, Mass., 1864-68; pastor St. Joseph's Ch., Amesbury, 1868—; apptd., 1891, auxiliary bishop of Boston and consecrated titular bishop of Alabanda, but continued parochial work. Home: South Boston, Mass. Died 1910.

BRADY, John Green, gov.; b. New York, June 15, 1848; early edn. from Judge John Green, Tipton, Ind., 1859; A.B., Yale, 1874; grad. Union Theol. Sem., 1877. Ordained Presbyn. ministry, 1878; engaged 1,700 acres of land in Texas, where he proposed to establish an industrial reform colony for New York slum boys, but on account of the lack of funds it was abandoned; missionary, Sitka, Alaska, with late Dr. Sheldon Jackson, 1877-79; independent missionary and mgr. Sitka Trading Co., 1879-97; gov of Alaska, 1897-1909. Republican. Address: Sitka Alaska. Died Dec. 17, 1918.

BRADY, John J., judge; b. New York, Aug. 30 1853; A.B., Fordham U., 1872, LL.D., 1906; admitted to bar, 1876. Justice Supreme Ct. of N.Y., 1st Dist., 1907-20. Democrat. Roman Catholic. Home: New York, N.Y. Died Jan. 7, 1916.

BRADY, John Leeford, editor; b. Johnson County, Kan., Aug. 18, 1866; s. John and Catherine (Lee) B.; ed. Baker U., 1880-84; m. Lee Crittenden, June 9, 1910; children—Mrs. Vera Shipman (by 1st marriage), Betty Lee (dec., by 2d marriage). With Baldwin (Kan.) Ledger, 1885-87, Salina Journal, 1887-90, Lawrence Journal-World, 1890-1914, Ft. Smith (Ark.) Times Record, 1914-17, Salina (Kan.) Union, 1917-23; editor Oregon Statesman, 1923-25, Idaho State Jour., Pocatello, Ida.; co-publisher of Ida. Blackfoot Daily Bulletin. Dep. oil insp., Kan., 1895-97; mem. Kan. Ho. of Rep., 1905-07, Senate, 1909-13; author first juvenile court law, and city commn. govt. in Kan.; chmn. City Rep. Central Com., Lawrence, 6 yrs. Methodist. Kiwanian. Home: Blackfoot, Ida. Died Mar. 26, 1933.

BRADY, Nicholas Frederic, capitalist; b. Albany, N.Y., Oct. 25, 1878; s. Anthony N. and Marcia A. (Myers) B.; B.A., Yale, 1899; m. Genevieve Garvan, Aug. 11, 1906. Chmn. bd. New York Edison Co., Brooklyn Edison Co.; officer or dir. many corps. Home: New York, N.Y. Died Mar. 27, 1930.

BRADY, Thomas Jefferson, soldier; b. Muncie, Ind., Feb. 12, 1839; s. John and Mary (Wright) B.; ed. Asbury Coll. (De Pauw U.); studied law, but did not practice; m. Emmeline Wolfe, 1864. Supt. Muncie schools, 1860-61; capt. and maj. 8th Ind. inf., 1861-63; col. 117th Ind. inf., 1863-64; col. 140th Ind. inf., 1864-65; bvt. brig. gen. Mar. 13, 1865; U.S. consul, St. Thomas, West Indies, 1870-75; supervisor Internal Revenue, 1875-76; 2d asst. postmaster-gen., 1876-81. Home: Colonial Beach, Va. Died 1904.

BRAGDON, Charles Cushman, educator; b. Auburn, N.Y., Sept. 6, 1847; s. Charles P. and Sarah (Cushman) B.; A.B., Northwestern U., 1865, A.M., 1868, LL.D., 1900; U. of Tübingen, 1872-73; m. Kate E. Ransom, of Williamsport, Pa., June 30, 1869. Taught in Elgin (Ill.) Acad., 1862-63; served in Co. F, 134th Ill. Inf. Vols., as pvt. and co. clerk; taught in Dickinson Sem., 1865-67; asst. editor Little Corporal, Chicago, 1867-68; prof. Latin and Greek, Wesleyan Coll. for Women, Cincinnati, 1868-72, Jennings Sem., Aurora, Ill., 1873-74; prin. Lasell Sem. for Young Women, Auburndale, Mass., 1874-1908 (1st sch. in U.S. to teach domestic science on scientific basis). Methodist Episcopalian; dir Wesleyan Assn., Boston; trustee Boston U.; v.p. N.E. Deaconess Assn. Home: Pasadena, Calif. Died June 21, 1932.

BRAGDON, Olive Hurd, author; b. Limington, York Co., Me., July 13, 1858; d. Andrew Jackson and Hannah Catherine (Bangs) Hurd; ed. Westbrook (Me.) Sem., and under pvt. teachers; m. Frank Adelbert Bragdon, June 14, 1879. Taught in grammar and high schools 3 yrs. Author: The Moon Party, 1904; Pup, an Autobiography of a Greyhound, 1905. Home: Boston, Mass. Died Mar. 14, 1915.

BRAGG, Edward Stuyvesant, congressman; b. Unadilla, N.Y., Feb. 20, 1827; s. Joel and Margaretha (Kohl) B.; student Geneva and Hobart colls.; LL.D., Hobart, 1898, Appleton, 1902; m. Cornelia Colman, Jan. 2, 1854. Dist. atty., Fond du Lac County, 1854-56; mem. Charleston Conv., 1860. Capt. 6th Wis. Inf., July 16, 1861; maj., Sept. 17, 1861; lt. col., June 21, 1862; col., Mar. 24, 1863; brig. gen. vols., June 25, 1864; hon. mustered out, Oct. 9, 1865. Del. Dem. Nat. convs., 1861, 1872, 1884, 1892, 1896, Union Conv., Phila., 1866; mem. 45th,

46th. 47th Congresses (1877-83), 49th Congress (1885-87); E.E. and M.P. to Mexico, 1888-89; prominent gold Democrat, 1896; supported McKinley, 1900; consul-gen. at Havana, May 19-Sept. 15, 1902, at Hongkong, China, 1902-06. Home: Fond du Lac, Wis. Died June 20, 1912.

BRAIN, Belle Marvel, author; b. Springfield, O., Aug. 4, 1859; d. William Grey and Mary (Dyer) B.; grad. Springfield High Sch., 1878; unmarried. Supervisor of drawing, Springfield pub. schs., 1878-95; prominent in ednl. and religious socs.; asso. editor, Missionary Rev. of World, 1914-17. Author: Fuel for Missionary Fires, 1895; Weapons for Temperance Warfare, 1897; The Morning Watch, 1897; Quaint Thoughts of an Old-Time Army Chaplain, 1898; The Transformation of Hawaii, 1898; Fifty Missionary Programmes, 1901; Missionary Readings for Missionary Programmes, 1901; Fifty Missionary Stories, 1903; Holding the Ropes, 1904; Redemption of the Red Men, 1904; All About Japan, 1905; Adventures with Four-Footed Folk, 1908; Love Stories of Great Missionaries, 1913; From Every Tribe and Nation, 1927. Home: Schenectady, N.Y. Died May 25, 1933.

BRAINARD, Clinton Tyler, publisher; b. Denver, Colo., Apr. 3, 1865; s. Thomas Corwin and Anne Mary (McCleery) B.; A.B., Harvard, 1890; m. Lucile Heloise Huyck, Dec. 5, 1896. Practiced law at Omaha, Neb., and at Creede and Cripple Creek, Colo., until 1895; in pub. business with C. T. Brainard Co., New York, later with H. L. Chapman, in the Mountford Press, Boston; in business as C. T. Brainard, Publisher, and as Harcourt Bindery, 1904-09; became identified with Pearson's Pub. Co., 1909; pres. and treas. The McClure Newspaper Syndicate, 1911—; editor Washington (D.C.) Herald and pres. Herald Pub. Co., 1915-19; pres. and treas. Harper & Brothers, 1915-24; pres. The Wheeler Newspaper Syndicate, 1916—. Home: New York, N.Y. Died Sept. 3, 1935.

BRAINARD, Owen, civil engr.; b. Haddam, Conn., Mar. 10, 1865; s. Hubert and Cynthia V. (Brainerd) B.; ed. pub. and pvt. schs.; m. Jean Sawyer, Mar. 10, 1909. Began as chief engr. Carrere & Hastings, architects, New York, 1893, admitted to partnership, 1901. Architect or builder: New York Pub. Library; Yale bi-centennial bldgs.; Goldwin Smith Hall, Cornell U.; Senate and House office bldg., Washington; alterations to U.S. Capitol; etc. Fellow A.I.A. Republican. Conglist. Home: New York, N.Y. Died Apr. 2, 1919.

BRAINERD, Cephas, lawyer; b. Haddam, Conn., Sept. 8, 1831; s. Cephas and Cynthia (Spencer) B.; ed. Brainerd Acad.; farmer until 1849; admitted to N.Y. bar, 1855; m. Eveline Hutchinson, Jan. 12, 1859. Managing clk., then partner, with Truman Smith and Ebenezer Seeley until 1860; then in practice alone. Lecturer on internat. law, New York U., 1885-97. Active in legal, polit. and prison reforms. Republican. Home: New York, N.Y. Died 1910.

BRAINERD, Chauncey Corey, newspaperman; b. New York, N.Y., Apr. 16, 1874; s. Alanson Post and Adelia (Corey) B.; ed. pub. schs., and business coll.; m. Edith Rathbone Jacobs, June 4, 1903. Began as sec. to Dr. St. Clair McKelway, editor Brooklyn Daily Eagle, 1889; became reporter, on the Eagle, city editor, 1899-1909, asst. mng. editor, 1909-11, Washington corr. Daily Eagle, 1911—. Mem. 23d Regt. N.G.N.Y., 1897-1903. Republican. Universalist. Mason. Home: Washington, D.C. Died Jan. 28, 1922.

BRAINERD, Erastus, editor, publicist; b. Middletown, Conn., Feb. 25, 1855; s. Norman Leslie and Leora (Campbell) B.; A.B., Harvard, 1874; m. Mary Bella Beale, May 30, 1882. Curator of engravings, Boston Museum Fine Arts, 1876-77; traveled in Europe, 1878-79; editorial staffs S.S. Times, New York World, Phila. Press, Atlanta Constitution; editor in chief Atlanta Star, Phila. News, Seattle Press-Times, Seattle Post Intelligencer, San Francisco Call; pres. Bd. of Park Commrs., Seattle, 1914-16. Declined appmt. as gov. of Idaho under Pres. Arthur; served as state land commr. of Wash. under Gov. McGraw, 1893-97; representative of Wash. at Conf. of Governors, in Washington, D.C., 1908; rep. of Wash. at National Convention American Academy Political and Social Science, at Philadelphia, 1912. Has served as mem. exec. com. Nat. Municipal League and advisory com. Am. Civic Assn.; mem. Nat. Conf. Charities and Correction, 1909; etc. Consul for Paraguay, 1919—. Republican. Episcopalian. Author: (series of 5 vols.) Life of Titian, Life of J. E. Millais, Great Artists, Gems of the Dresden Gallery, The Gray Collection of Engravings, 1876-77; Alaska and the Klondike. Home: Richmond Beach, Wash. Died Dec. 25, 1922.

BRAINERD, Ezra, college pres.; b. St. Albans, Vt., Dec. 17, 1844; s. Lawrence Robbins and Catherine (Wood) B.; A.B., Middlebury Coll., 1864, A.M., 1867; grad. Andover Theol. Sem., 1868; LL.D., U. of Vt., 1888, Ripon Coll., 1888; D.D., Howard, 1900; m. Frances Viola Rockwell, Dec. 1, 1868; m. 2d, Mary Wright, Dec. 25, 1897. Prof. rhetoric and English lit., Middlebury Coll., 1868-80, physics and applied mathematics, 1880-86, pres., 1885-1908. One of 3 commrs. apptd., 1887, to revise sch. laws of Vt. Home: Middlebury, Vt. Died Dec. 8, 1924.

BRAINERD, Frank; b. Portland, Conn., Oct. 23, 1854; s. Benjamin Franklin and Amelia Ann (Davis) B.; Episcopal Acad., Conn., 1868-70; grad. Phillips Exeter Acad., N.H., 1873; A.B., Harvard, 1877; m. Ida Gillum, Oct. 8, 1879. Engaged in quarrying, 1877—; pres. and treas. Brainerd, Shaler & Hall Quarry Co.; dir. 1st Nat. Bank, Freestone Savings Bank, Portland. Vestryman and treas. Parish of Trinity Ch., Portland. Republican. Home: Portland, Conn. Died Mar. 6, 1916.

BRAINERD, Henry Green, neuropsychiatrist; b. Londonderry, N.H., May 23, 1852; s. Timothy G. and Lucinda R. (Dewey) B.; A.B., Dartmouth, 1874; student Med. Dept. State U. of Ia.; M.D., Rush Med. Coll., Chicago, 1878; post-grad. work in New York and London, Eng.; m. Alma Loomis, 1879 (died 1882); m. 2d, Fannie Howard, 1887 (died 1919); children—Henry Howard, Fred Lindley. Asst. supt. Ia. Hosp. for Insane, 1878-86; prof. mental and nervous diseases, Med. Dept. U. of Southern Calif., 1886-1911, dean of faculty, 1889-1902; organized dental dept. same univ., 1896, and was dean until 1899; supt. Los Angeles General Hosp., 1888-92; chmn. of state commn., Calif., to locate and build hosp. for insane, at Norwalk, and was mem. bd. mgrs.; mem. bd. dirs. Pacific Mut. Life Ins. Co.; v.p. Southern Calif. Sanitarium for Nervous Diseases. Republican. Conglist. Home: Los Angeles, Calif. Died July 22, 1928.

BRAISLIN, Edward, clergyman; b. Burlington, N.J., Nov. 20, 1846; s. Patrick and Tamar B.; ed. Burlington, N.J.; grad. Crozer Theol. Sem., Pa., 1873; D.D., Richmond (Va.) Coll., 1887; m. Margaret M. Kenyon, Mar. 2, 1893. Ordained Bapt. ministry, 1874; pastor various chs., 1874-1905, Dorchester Temple Baptist Church, Boston, 1906-12; retired. Mem. of bd. of mgrs. Am. Bapt. Missionary Union; trustee Colorado Coll. Home: Burlington, N.J. Died July 22, 1915.

BRAISTED, William Clarence, navy surgeon; b. Toledo, O., Oct. 9, 1864; s. Frank and Helen Maria (Fiske) B.; Ph.B., U. of Mich., 1883; M.D., with honors, Med. Dept., Columbia U., 1886; LL.D., U. of Mich., 1917, Jefferson Med. Coll., Phila., 1918; D.Sc., Northwestern U., 1918; m. Lillian Mulford Phipps, Apr. 2, 1886. Served Bellevue Hosp., New York, 2½ yrs.; practiced, Detroit, 1888-90; entered Navy as asst. surgeon, Sept. 26, 1890; promoted passed asst. surgeon, Sept. 26, 1893; surgeon, Mar. 3, med. insp., Oct. 20, 1913; twice instr. in surgery Naval Medical Sch.; fitted out and equipped the hosp. ship Relief, 1904. Represented Med. Dept. in Japan during Russo-Japanese War; asst. chief Bur. of Medicine and Surgery, 6 yrs., 1906-12, and assisted in reorganization of same and of med. service of the Navy; served with Dr. Rixey as attending phys. at White House, President Theodore Roosevelt's administration, 1906-07; fleet surgeon, Atlantic fleet, July 1, 1912-14; surgeon-gen. and chief Bur. of Medicine and Surgery, Feb. 1914-21, rank of rear admiral. Pres. Coll. of Pharmacy and Science, Phila., 1921—; dir. Union Trust Co., Washington, D.C. Mem. bd. dirs. Columbia Hosp. for Women; pres. bd. visitors Govt. Hosp. for Insane, Washington, D.C. Mem. exec. com. central com. and war relief bd., Am. Red Cross, 1914-20. Retired from Navy after 30 yrs.' service, Nov. 1920, with rank of rear admiral. Awarded D.S.M.; decorated by Emperor of Japan, and with Order of Bolivar by pres. of Venezuela. Home: West Chester, Pa. Died Jan. 17, 1941.

BRAITMAYER, Otto Ernest, corp. official; b. Washington, D.C., July 8, 1873; s. John Ernest and Josephine (Tanner) B.; LL.B., Nat. U. Sch. of Law, 1895, LL.M., 1896; m. Kathleen Ketcham, Apr. 21, 1897; children—Margaret Esther (Mrs. Charles K. West, dec.), Kathleen (Mrs. Alexander D. Shaw), Josephine (Mrs. John M. Demarest), Jane; m. 2d, Marian Winifred Schoeffel, Feb. 14, 1929; children—Anne, John Watson. Sec. and office asst. to Herman Hollerith, inventor of punched card method of electric tabulation, Washington, D.C., 1889-1911; asst. gen. mgr. Tabulating Machine Co., N.Y. City, 1911-21, v.p., 1921-25; v.p. Internat. Business Machines Corp., 1925-39, retired Apr. 1, 1939; dir. Weston Elec. Instrument Corp. (Newark, N.J.), Internat. Business Machines Corp. Mason. Home: Point Road, Marion, Mass. Died Feb. 29, 1940.

BRALEY, Henry King, judge; b. Rochester, Mass., Mar. 17, 1850; s. Samuel Tripp and Mary A. (King) B.; ed. Rochester (Mass.) Acad., Pierce Acad., Middleboro, Mass.; hon. A.M., Dartmouth, 1902; LL.D., Tufts, 1922; m. Caroline Ward Leach, Apr. 26, 1875; 1 son, Abner L. In practice of law, Fall River, Mass., 1873-91; city solicitor, 1874, mayor, 1882-83, Fall River; bar examiner Bristol County, by appmt. of Supreme Jud. Ct., 1890-91; asso. justice Superior Ct., 1891-1902; asso. justice Supreme Jud. Ct. of Mass., 1902—. Mem. Am. Acad. Polit. and Social Science. Conglist. Democrat. Home: Boston, Mass. Died Jan. 17, 1929.

BRALLEY, Francis Marion, college pres.; b. Honey Grove, Fannin County, Tex., Mar. 6. 1867; s. John and Katharine Louise (White) B.; grad. Walcott Inst., Honey Grove, 1885; grad. Methodist Coll., Honey Grove, 1887; LL.D., Baylor U., 1920; m. Mary Melzina Meade, Mar. 17, 1892. Teacher pub. schs. until 1892; county supt. schs., Fanning County, 1892-98; supt. schs., Honey Grove, 1898-1905; asst. state supt. pub. instrn., Tex., 1905-08; gen. agt. Conf. for Edn. in Tex., 1908-09; supt. State Sch. for the Blind, Austin, Tex., 1909-10; state supt. pub. instrn., 1910-13; dir. Dept. of Extension, U. of Tex., 1913-14; pres. Coll. Industrial Arts, Denton, Tex., 1914—. Pres. Bd. of Regents, State Normal Coll., 1911-13; exec. sec. Organization for Enlargement by the State of Its Institutions for Higher Edn., 1912-14. Democrat. Mem. Christian (Campbellite) Ch. Mason (32°), K.P. Home: Denton, Tex. Died Aug. 23, 1924.

BRAMAN, Dwight; b. Boston, Mass., Mar. 6, 1861; s. Jarvis Dwight and Amelia (Coverley) B.; ed. pvt. and pub. schs., Boston, and under tutor; m. Helen Stuyvesant Dudley, Jan. 17, 1904. Ex-mem. N.Y. Stock Exchange; was pres. San Diego Land & Town Co., Nat. City & Otay R.R. Co.; trustee Brookline (Mass.) Land Co.; dir. Boston Water Power Co.; was receiver St.L., K.C. & S.W. R.R. Co., also receiver in 6 states for Bay State Gas Co. of Delaware; etc. Vet. mem. 1st Corps Cadets, Mass.; offered gov. of Mass. to raise and equip a cav. regt. for Spanish-Am. War; gave yacht Fredonia to U.S. Govt. as lighthouse tender; was instrumental in securing armistice, at request of Baron Fava of Italy, with President McKinley which resulted in declaration of peace between U.S. and Spain; proposed plan for Govt. Control Bank, with regional bankers, before Com. on Banking Currency, 59th Congress, 1907, which was the genesis of the Federal Reserve System. Republican. Episcopalian. Home: New York, N.Y. Died June 11, 1929.

BRANCH, Anna Hempstead, author; b. New London, Conn.; d. John L. and Mary Lydia (Bolles) B.; grad. Adelphi Acad., Brooklyn, 1893, Smith Coll., 1897, Am. Acad. Dramatic Art, New York, 1900; unmarried. Won the first of the Century prizes awarded to coll. graduates for the best poem with "The Road 'Twixt Heaven and Hell." Contbr. verse and prose to leading mags. Author: The Heart of the Road, 1901; The Shoes That Danced, 1905; Rose of the Wind, Nimrod, and Other Poems, 1910; (play) "Rose of the Wind." Home: New London, Conn. Died Sept. 8, 1937.

BRANCH, Charles Henry Hardin, clergyman; b. Loudoun Co., Va., Aug. 6, 1875; s. Henry and Melissa Maurice (Jarvis) B.; A.B., Johns Hopkins, 1895; student Princeton Theol. Sem., 1895-98; A.M., Princeton, 1898; D.D., Austin Coll., Sherman, Tex., 1917; m. Elisabeth Hertzog Reed, June 1, 1904; children—Charles Henry Hardin, Elisabeth Hertzog. Ordained ministry Presbyn. Ch. in U.S., 1899; pastor various chs., Ky. and Ark., 1902-23, Hyde Park Presbyn. Ch., Tampa, Fla., 1923—. Democrat. Home: Tampa, Fla. Deceased.

BRANCH, Ernest William, civil engr.; b. Smithfield, Me., May 26, 1863; s. William David and Ann Eliza (Newcomb) B.; grad. Williston Sem., Easthampton, Mass., 1883; A.B., Boston U., 1888; LL.B., Suffolk Law Sch., 1918; m. Fairvilla Ardell Gould, Mar. 18, 1890. Civ. engr. and surveyor in employ H. T. Whitman, Boston, 1888-95; mem. firm Whitman & Branch, 1896; chief engr. sewer dept., Quincy, Mass., 1896-1905; then practiced in own name; project engr. for U.S. Housing Corp., on Quincy Project, 1918-19. Republican. Conglist. Home. Quincy, Mass. Died Mar. 1936.

BRANCH, John B., insurance official; b. Brooklyn, N.Y., Feb. 18, 1851; s. William L. and Catharine T. B.; ed. pub. and high schs., Providence, R.I.; m. Fannie W. Mowry, 1879; children—Claude R., Mrs. Beatrice B. Spicer. In employ Am. Ins. Co. until 1871, with Newport Fire & Marine Ins. Co., successor to Am. Ins. Co., 1871-75; asst. sec. Providence Washington Ins. Co. (which absorbed Newport Fire & Marine Ins. Co.), 1875-81, sec., 1881-89, v.p., 1889-1904, pres., 1904-22, chmn. bd.; v.p. Peoples Savings Bank in Providence, Blackstone Canal Nat. Bank. Home: Providence, R.I. Died Mar. 6, 1933.

BRANCH, John Patteson, banker; b. Petersburg, Va., Oct. 9, 1830; s. Thomas and Sarah Pride (Read) B.; ed. pub. schs.; LL.D., Randolph Macon Coll., 1913; m. Mary Louisa Merritt Kerr, May 12, 1863 (dec.). Served as lt., 44th Va. Battalion, C.S.A., Civil War; surrendered at Appomattox C.H., Va., with Gen. Lee, Apr. 9, 1865. Pres. Merchants' Nat. Bank, Petersburg; sr. partner Thomas Branch & Co. Trustee Randolph Macon College. Democrat. Methodist. Home: Richmond, Va. Died Feb. 2, 1915.

BRANCH, Mary Lydia Bolles, author; b. New London, Conn., June 13, 1840; d. John Rogers and Mary (Hempstead) Bolles; ed. common and high schs. and sch. of Lincoln F. Emerson, Boston; m. John L. Branch, 1870; 1 dau., Ann Hempstead. Writer of stories for children. Author: The Kantor Girls, 1895; The Old Hempstead House, the Home of Eight Generations, 1896; A Visit to Newfoundland, 1901; The Manner of Life of Nancy Hempstead, 1902; Guld, the Cavern King, 1917; The Golden Cells of Heaven, 1922. Home: New London, Conn. Died Apr. 17, 1922.

BRANCH, Oliver Ernesto, lawyer; b. Madison, O., July 19, 1847; s. William Witter and Lucy J. (Bartram) B.; A.B. (with highest honors), Hamilton Coll., N.Y., 1873, A.M., 1876; LL.B., Columbia, 1877; hon. A.M., Dartmouth, 1895; LL.D., Hamilton, 1908; m. Sarah M. Chase, Oct. 17, 1878. Admitted to bar in New York, 1877, and practiced with brother, John L.; removed to Weare, 1883, and to Manchester, N.H., 1894; gen. counsel B. & M. R.R. Mem. N.H. Ho. of Rep., 1887, 1889; chmn. Dem. state convs., 1892, 1902; U.S. dist. atty. for N.H., 1894-98. Home: Manchester, N.H. Died June 22, 1916.

BRAND, Charles Hillyer, congressman; b. Loganville, Ga., Apr. 20, 1861; s. Egbert M. and Julia (Cooper) B.; B.S., U. of Ga., 1881; m. Estelle Winn, June 30, 1886 (died July 31, 1889); children—Luelle (Mrs. M. M. Rolleston), Julia (Mrs. B. H. Sasnett); m. 2d, Mary Dixon Hutchins, June 6, 1901 (died Jan. 25, 1913); 1 dau., Mary Caroline (Mrs. P. H. Mell). Admitted to Ga. bar, 1882, and began practice at Lawrenceville; solicitor general for Western Judicial Circuit, 1896-1904; mem. Ga. Senate, 1894-95 (pres. pro tem.); apptd. judge Superior Court of Ga., 1906, to fill unexpired term, and 3 times elected, serving until 1917 (resigned); mem. 65th to 72d Congresses (1917-33), 8th Ga. Dist. Democrat. Presbyn. Grand Master I.O.O.F. of State of Ga., 1906-07. Established the Charles Hillyer Brand Scholarship Fund (2 scholarships, in U. of Ga. and State Normal Sch., Ga.). Home: Athens, Ga. Died May 17, 1933.

BRAND, Edward Parish, clergyman; b. Laurel Point, nr. Morgantown, W.Va., Aug. 9, 1854; s. Alexander W. and Sarah (Bussey) B.; grad. W.Va. State Normal Sch., Fairmont, W.Va., 1878; studied W.Va. State U., 1882, 83; studied Newton Theol. Instn., Newton Centre, Mass., 1884, 85; D.D., Ewing Coll., 1906, Shurtleff Coll., 1916; m. Vienna L. Moore, Sept. 10, 1885. Ordained Bapt. ministry, 1878; pastor various chs., Pa., O., Kan., and Ill., 1885-98; supt. Ill. Bapt. State Conv., 1898-1921. Trustee Shurtleff Coll., Alton, Ill. Independent Republican. Editor and pub. Ill. Baptist Annual, 1898-1921, Ill. Baptist Bulletin, 1909-21; sec. Ill. Bapt. Conv. Moneys and Properties. Home: Normal, Ill. Died July 30, 1924.

BRAND, John W. B., pres. Springfield Instn. for Savings; dir. many other companies. Trustee Horace Smith Fund, Springfield Hosp. Home: Springfield, Mass. Died Feb. 14, 1939.

BRANDEGEE, Frank Bosworth, senator; b. New London, Conn., July 8, 1864; s. Augustus and Nancy Christina (Bosworth) B.; A.B., Yale, 1885; unmarried. Admitted to bar, 1888; mem. Conn. Ho. of Rep., 1888, 99 (speaker, 1899); del. Rep. nat. convs., 1888, 92, 1900, 04; elected to 57th Congress, unexpired term, 1902-03; reëlected to 58th and 59th Congresses (1903-07); elected U.S. senator, May 9, 1905, for unexpired term (1905-09); reelected U.S. senator, 3 terms, 1909-27. Home: New London, Conn. Died Oct. 14, 1924.

BRANDEIS, Frederick, musician; b. Vienna, Austria, July 5, 1835; grad. gymnasium, Vienna, 1848; studied piano and composition under Fischof and Czerny. Arrived in U.S., July 5, 1849. Traveled through U.S. with William Vincent Wallace, as pianist, and later with various organizations; settled in New York as pianist, organist, composer and teacher. Has been organist at St. John's R.C., St. James' R.C., then St. Peter and St. Paul's R.C. Ch., Brooklyn; also 12 years at Synagogue Schaare Tephila. Composer of much instrumental, vocal and chamber music. Home: New York, N.Y. Died 1899.

BRANDEIS, Louis Dembitz, jurist; b. Louisville, Ky., Nov. 13, 1856; s. Adolph and Fredericka (Dembitz) B.; ed. pvt. and high schools, Louisville; Annen Realschule, Dresden, 1873-75; LL.B., Harvard, 1877, hon. A.M., 1891; m. Alice Goldmark, Mar. 23, 1891; children—Susan (Mrs. Jacob H. Gilbert), Elizabeth (Mrs. Paul A. Raushenbush). Admitted to bar, St. Louis, Mo., 1878; practice, Boston, 1879-1916; mem. Warren & Brandeis, 1879-97, Brandeis, Dunbar & Nutter, 1897-1916. Counsel in many frt. rate, wage-hour, pub. utility and other cases. Chmn. of Provisional Com. for General Zionist Affairs, 1914-16. Apptd. asso. justice Supreme Court of U.S., Jan. 28, 1916, and assumed office June 5, 1916; retired Feb. 13, 1939. Author: Other People's Money, 1914; Business, a Profession, 1914; The Curse of Bigness. Home: Washington, D.C. Died Oct. 5, 1941.

BRANDELLE, Gustaf Albert, clergyman; b. Andover, Ill., Mar. 19, 1861; s. Gustaf Johnson and Emma Maria Christina (Nilson) B.; A.B., Augustana Coll., Ill., 1882, A.M., 1896; grad. Augustana Theol. Sem., 1884; D.D., Bethany Coll., Lindsborg, Kan., 1900; LL.D., Augustana Coll., St. Olaf Coll., 1925; m. Lydia Appell, Mar. 18, 1886; children—Ruth Dorothy, Edith Rosalia (wife of Rev. W. C. Ekeberg). Ordained Luth. ministry, 1884; pastor Denver, Colo., 1884-1918, Grace Ch., Rock Island, Ill., 1918-23. Pres. Evang. Lutheran Augustana Synod, 1918—; pres. Nat. Lutheran Council, 8 years; mem. Bd. of Missions Evangelical Luth. Augustana Synod. Comdr. Northern Star, 1st class (Sweden), 1926. Republican. Editor Augustana Journal, 1897-1906; contbr. to ch. publs. Del. to Lutheran World Conv., Eisenach, Germany, 1923, Copenhagen, 1929, Internat. Conv. Life and Work, Stockholm, 1925; 1100th anniversary celebration of introduction of Christianity into Sweden, 1930. Home: Rock Island, Ill. Died Jan. 16, 1936.

BRANDENBURG, Edwin Charles, lawyer; b. Washington, D.C., May 19, 1865; s. Frederick W. and Gertrude E. (Seibel) B.; LL.B., Columbian (now George Washington) U., 1890, LL.M., 1891; m. Emma I. Goodacre, June 19, 1891; children—Millson F., Dorothy I. (wife of Dr. Alfred L. Bou), Ruth G. (Mrs. Jeremiah W. McCarty). Began practice of law at Washington, D.C., 1891; mem. Brandenburg & Brandenburg; was spl. defense atty. for U.S. in Court of Claims; prof. George Washington U. Law Sch., 1901—; v.p. and gen. counsel Norfolk & Washington Steamboat Co.; dir. and gen. counsel Nat. Bank of Washington, Washington Bd. of Trade; dir. many other companies. Presbyn. Mason. Author: Brandenburg on Bankruptcy, 1899; Digest of Bankruptcy Decisions, 1899. Reviser (with others) of Bouviers Law Dictionary, 1894. Home: Montrose, Md. Deceased.

BRANDENBURG, Frederick Harmon, meteorologist; b. Washington, D.C., Aug. 23, 1854; s. Frederick William and Martha Bolling (Sims) B.; ed. pvt. schs. and under pvt. tutors; m. Virginia Pauline Zeh, Nov. 29, 1881. Mem. Signal Corps, U.S.A., 1877-1901, when the dept. was transferred to Weather Bur.; with U.S. Weather Bur., 1901—; served various cities, 1878-94; in charge at Denver, 1894—, apptd. local forecaster, 1895, dist. forecaster, 1901; section dir. Climatol. Service of Colo., 1894—; dist. editor Monthly Weather Review, Colo. River Valley, 1909-13; collected data regarding snowfall and published bulls. giving estimates of water available for irrigation, 1895; organized river and flood service of Colo. River, 1907. Republican. Mason. Home: Denver, Colo. Deceased.

BRANDENBURG, George Clinton, prof. ednl. psychology; b. Volga, Clayton County, Ia., Dec. 2, 1878; s. F. M. and Enfield (Maxwell) B.; Ph.B., Drake U., 1910; A.M., U. of Colo., 1914; Ph.D., U. of Wis., 1915; m. Julia E. Swanson, Aug. 31, 1909; children—Gladys Ethel, Marie Frances (dec.), Ruth Carolyn. Teacher pub. schs., Ia., 1898-1902; prin. high sch., Humboldt, Ia., 1906-09; supt. schs., Brighton, Colo., 1910-13; fellow U. of Wis., 1914-15; instr. in ednl. psychology, Purdue U., 1916-17, asst. prof., 1917-18, asso. prof., 1920, prof., 1920—; also dir. summer session, 1930, head of dept. edn., 1931—; dir. Summer Sch., Winona Lake, Ind., 1920-28; student at Columbia, and visited European schs., 1924-25. Home: West Lafayette, Ind. Died Sept. 3, 1934.

BRANDENBURG, William A., educator, lecturer; b. Clayton County, Iowa, Oct. 10, 1869; s. F. M. and Enfield B.; Ph.B., M.A., Drake U., Des Moines, Ia.; LL.D., Monmouth (Ill.) Coll.; m. Alta Penfield, June 22, 1893. Supt. City Schs., Capitol Park (Des Moines), 1900-05; instr. dept. edn. Drake U., 1904-06; supt. city schs., Mason City, Ia., 1905-10, Oklahoma City, Okla., 1910-13; pres. Kansas State Teachers Coll., Pittsburg, Kan., 1913—. Mem. Okla. State Bd. of Edn., 1911-13; mem. Kan. State Bd. of Edn., 1920—. Mem. Christian Church. Mason. Home: Pittsburg, Kan. Died Oct. 29, 1940.

BRANDON, Morris, lawyer; b. Dover, Tenn., Apr. 13, 1862; s. Nathan and Minerva Elizabeth (Morris) B.; ed. Vanderbilt U., 1880-82; LL.B., Yale Law Sch., 1884; LL.D., Oglethorpe U., 1927; m. Harriet Inman, June 1, 1892; children—Morris, W. P. Inman, Nathan Christopher. Began practice at Dover, 1885; removed to Atlanta, Ga., 1886; mem. Brandon, Hynds & Tindall; gen. counsel Atlanta, Birmingham & Coast Railway Co., First Nat. Bank; and other corps.; chmn. bd. Exposition Cotton Mills. Mem. Ga. House of Rep., 1898; mem. Atlanta Police Commn., 1904-07 (chmn. bd., 1907). Mem. bd. of trustees Vanderbilt U. Democrat. Mason (Shrine). Home: Glenwoods, Atlanta, Ga. Died Feb. 13, 1940.

BRANDON, William Woodward, gov.; b. Talladega, Ala., June 5, 1868; s. Rev. Franklin Thomas Jefferson and Caroline (Woodward) B.; ed. Cedar Bluff Inst., and high sch., Tuscaloosa; studied law, U. of Ala.; m. Mrs. Lizzie Andrews Nabors, June 27, 1900 (died 1933). Admitted to Ala. bar, 1892, and began practice at Tuscaloosa; city clk., 1891-94; mem. Ala. Ho. of Rep. 3 terms, 1894-98; clk. Ala. Constl. Conv., 1901; state auditor of Ala., 1897-1911; probate judge, Tuscaloosa County, 1911-23; gov. of Ala., term 1923-27; again probate judge, Tuscaloosa County. Capt. Co. F, 2d Ala. N.G., 1895-98; capt. and maj. same regt., Spanish-Am. War; brig. gen. and adj. gen. Ala. N.G., 1898-1907. Democrat. Methodist. Mason. Home: Tuscaloosa, Ala. Died Dec. 7, 1934.

BRANDT, Herman Carl George, college prof.; b. Vilsen, Germany, Dec. 15, 1850; s. Frederick and Stine B.; came to U.S., 1867; A.B., Hamilton College, Clinton, N.Y., 1872, A.M., 1875, Ph.D., 1896, L.H.D., 1910; studied at univs. of Göttingen, Freiburg and Strassburg; m. Margaret S. Catlin, Dec. 15, 1875. Instr. Hamilton Coll., 1874-76; asso. prof. German, Johns Hopkins, 1876-82; prof. German, Hamilton, 1883—. Author: German Grammar for Schools and Colleges, 1884; German Reader, 1892; Lessing's Nathan der Weise (edited), 1895; German Science Reader, 1897. Mem. Advisory Council, Simplified Spelling Bd. Home: Clinton, N.Y. Died Dec. 20, 1920.

BRANDT, Joseph Granger, educator; b. Allen Grove, Wis., Dec. 30, 1880; s. Joseph Henry and Mary (McCaughen) B.; Ph.B., Lawrence Coll., Appleton, Wis., 1903; scholar in Latin, U. of Wis., 1905-06, Ph.D., 1911; studied Am. Sch. Classical Studies in Rome, 1911-12; m. Frances Reynolds Irving, Dec. 23, 1908; children—Mary Elizabeth, Helen Charis, Miriam Frances, Joseph Granger. Asst. instr. and instr. Latin, U. of Wis., 1906-11; Carnegie research asso., Rome, 1911-12; instr. Latin, U. of Wis., 1912-13, asst. prof., 1913-14, asst. prof. Latin and Greek, 1914-15; asst. prof. Greek, U. of Kan., 1915-16, asso. prof., 1916-21, prof. Greek and Latin, 1921—, acting dean Coll. Liberal Arts and Sciences, 1920-21, dean, 1921—. Conglist. Home: Lawrence, Kan. Died Oct. 28, 1933.

BRANDT, Olaf Elias, theologian; b. nr. Oconomowoc, Wis., Feb. 19, 1862; s. Rev. Nils and Diderikke (Ottesen) B.; A.B., Luther Coll., Decorah, Ia., 1879; post-grad. study Northwestern Coll., Watertown, Wis., 1879-80, D.D., 1915; post-grad. study Concordia Theol. Sem., St. Louis, 1880-83; U. of Leipzig, 1897; travel and study, Europe, 1923-24; D.S.T., Luther College, 1934; m. Emma Louise Galby, July 12, 1899; children—Margrethe (dec.), Rolf, Kathrine (dec.), Immanuel (dec.), Olaf Ulric Ottesen. Ordained ministry Synod of Norwegian Luth. Ch. America, 1883; pastor Cleveland, O., 1883-92, Chicago, 1892-96; prof. O. T., encyclopedia and homiletics, Luther Theol. Sem., St. Paul, Minn., 1897-1917, v.p., 1917-30, chair of practical theology, also Old Testament exegesis and encyclopedia, 1917-30, chair of New Testament, 1930-36, prof. emeritus, 1936; pastor Hope Ch., Minneapolis, 1905-11. Lecturer on ednl. and religious subjects; active in promotion of ch. work among students of secular schs. Wrote "Friendship" (many edits.). Decorated Comdr. Order of St. Olav by King Haakon of Norway, 1924. Republican. Home: St. Paul, Minn. Deceased.

BRANHAM, William Charles, educator; b. Gallatin, Sumner County, Tenn., June 4, 1867; s. Albert Gallatin and Elizabeth (Ferguson) B.; B.A., Vanderbilt U., 1887, M.A., 1889; m. Willie Hume, Aug. 25, 1890. Fellow and asst. in history and moral philosophy, Vanderbilt U., 1887-88; teacher Greek and English, University Sch., Nashville, 1888-94; instr. in English and history, Vanderbilt U., 1894-97; founder, 1897, and co-principal Branham and Hughes Sch., 1897-1917, and pres. of its successor, Branham & Hughes Mil. Acad., 1917—. Col. Tenn. State Guard. Democrat. Presbyn. Home: Spring Hill, Tenn. Died Oct. 6, 1920.

BRANN, Henry Athanasius, clergyman; b. Parkstown, County Meath, Ireland, Aug. 15, 1837; s. James and Margaret (McGrath) B.; came to U.S., 1849; classical edn., St. Mary's Coll., Wilmington, Del., and St. Francis Xavier's, New York; studied for priesthood at St. Sulpice, Paris, and Am. Coll., Rome; ordained R.C. priest, 1862. V.p. Seton Hall Coll., 1862-64; dir. Sem., Wheeling, W.Va., 1868-97, rector St. Elizabeth's Ch., New York, 1870-90, St. Agnes' Ch., New York, 1890—. Archdiocesan censor of books. Author: Curious Questions, 1867; Truth and Error, 1871; Essay on the Popes, 1875; The Age of Unreason, 1881; Immortality of the Soul, 1882; Life of Archbishop Hughes; Waifs and Strays, 2 vols., 1909; History of the American College, Rome, Italy, 1910. Address: New York, N.Y. Died Dec. 28, 1921.

BRANNAN, John Winters, M.D.; b. Cincinnati, Feb. 14, 1853; s. Benjamin Franklin and Mary (Doddridge) B.; A.B., Harvard, 1874, M.D., 1878; phys. Mass. Gen. Hosp., 1877-78; studied Paris, Vienna, Strassburg, 1879; m. Eunice Dana, Nov. 9, 1882; children—Dana, Eleanor Doddridge. Consulting phys., Bellevue Hosp., hosps. of Health Dept., Italian Hosp., and Hosp. for Ruptured and Crippled; ex-pres. bd. trustees, Bellevue and Allied hosps.; trustee N.Y. Infirmary for Women and Children. Home: New York, N.Y. Died Aug. 30, 1936.

BRANNAN, Joseph Doddridge, prof. law; b. Circleville, O., Jan. 6, 1848; s. Benjamin Franklin and Mary (Doddridge) B.; A.B., Harvard, 1869, A.M. and LL.B., 1872; student U. of Munich, Germany, 1869-70; admitted to Ohio bar, 1873; m. Julia Gardiner Gorham, Sept. 18, 1875. Tutor in German, Harvard, 1871-72, Roman law, 1872-73; practiced at Cincinnati, 1873-98; prof. law, U. of Cincinnati, 1896-98; prof. law, Harvard Law Sch., 1898-1916, prof. emeritus, 1916—. Mem. Ohio State Bd. of Examiners for admission to bar; trustee Cincinnati Hosp., 1885-93. Home: Cambridge, Mass. Died July 26, 1930.

BRANNER, John Casper, geologist; b. New Market, Tenn., July 4, 1850; s. Michael T. and Elsie (Baker) B.; B.S., Cornell, 1874; Ph.D., Ind. U., 1885; LL.D., U. of Ark., 1897, Maryville Coll., 1909, U. of Calif., 1915; Sc.D., U. of Chicago, 1916; m. Susan D. Kennedy, June 22, 1883. Geologist Imperial Geol. Commn., Brazil, 1875-77; asst. engr. and interpreter S. Cyriaco Mining Co., Minas Geraes, Brazil, 1878-79; spl. botanist in S. America, 1880-81; agt. U.S. Dept. Agr. in Brazil, 1882-83; topog. geologist, Geol. Survey of Pa., 1883-85; prof. geology, Ind. U., 1885-92; state geologist of Ark., 1887-93; prof. geology, Leland Stanford Jr. U., 1892-1915, acting pres., 1898-99, v.p., 1899-1913, pres., 1913-15, emeritus. Dir. Branner-Agassiz expdn. to Brazil, 1899; mem. Calif. Earthquake Commn., 1906-07; spl. asst. Geol. Survey of Brazil, 1907-08; dir. scientific expdns. to Brazil, 1899, 1911. Mem. Nat. Acad. Sciences. Asso. editor Journal of Geology. Address: Stanford University, Calif. Died Mar. 1, 1922.

BRANNON, Henry, judge; b. Winchester, Va., Nov. 26, 1837; s. Robert and Catharine (Copenhaver) B.; reared on farm; A.B., U. of Va., 1857; m. Hetta J. Arnold, Dec. 28, 1858. Admitted to bar, 1859; in practice, 1859-81; pros. atty., Louis County, W.Va., 1860-64; mem. W.Va. Ho. of Rep., 1870-71; judge Circuit Ct., 1880-88; asso. justice W.Va. Supreme Ct. of Appeals, 1888-1913. Republican. Author: Treatise on Rights and Privileges Under 14th Amendment to U.S. Constitution. Home: Weston, W.Va. Died Nov. 24, 1914.

BRANSBY, Carlos, educator; b. Bogotá, Colombia, S.A., Aug. 7, 1848; s. John B. and Ana Gòmez de B.; ed. Coll. of Rosario; Coll. of San Bartolomé; came to U.S., 1870; A.B., Lafayette Coll., Pa., 1875, Litt.D., 1903; grad. Union Theol. Sem., 1877; m. Mary Creighton Burns, May 17, 1918. Began teaching in Bogotá, Colombia, 1864; ordained Presbyterian ministry, 1879; pastor in Mo., Kan. and Calif., 1878-88; teacher Occidental Coll., Calif., 1889-92, Los Angeles High Sch., 1892-1901; instr. and later prof., U. of Calif., 1901-21, prof. emeritus. Translator (into Spanish): Ryles' Expository Thoughts on the Gospels, 3 vols., 1877; The Bible Text Book, 1890; Van Dyke's Story of the Other Wise Man, 1905. Editor: Segundo Libro de Español, 1888; Progressive Spanish Reader, 1907; Avellaneda's Baltasar, 1908; Fernán Caballero's Un Servilón y un Liberalito, 1909; etc. Home: Berkeley, Calif. Died Sept. 28, 1923.

BRANSCOMB, Lewis Capers, clergyman; b. Union Springs, Ala., Aug. 27, 1865; s. Richard Edwin and Elizabeth (Murrell) B.; A.B., Southern U., Greensboro, Ala., 1885, A.M., 1886; D.D., Emory Coll., Oxford, Ga., 1909; m. Nannie McAdory, July 1, 1891 (died 1897); children—Louis McAdory (dec.), Bennett Harvie; m. 2d, Minnie McGehee, 1900; children—Louise Hortense, Richard Edwin, Elizabeth, Lamar, Alline, Lewis Capers, Emily (dec.). Ordained ministry, M.E. Ch., S., 1886; pastor various chs. until Dec. 1912; presiding elder Birmingham Dist., 1912-16; editor Alabama Christian Advocate, 1916-22; pastor First Church, Anniston, Ala., 1922-27, First Church, Gadsden, 1928; presiding elder Bessemer District, 1928—. Mem. bd. trustees Woman's College (Montgomery); mem. exec. com. bd. trustees Birmingham-Southern Coll.; commr. for unification Meth. male edn. in Ala.; mem. Gen. Conf. M.E. Ch., S., 1914, 18, 22, 24; chmn. North Ala. Conf. Com. for unification Am. Methodism; mem. exec. com. Fed. Chs. of Christ America; mem. exec. com. bd. dirs. Anti-Saloon League of America; pres. Ala. Anti-Saloon League; mem. Publishing Com. M.E. Ch., S. Democrat. Mason. Home: 1630 Bush Blvd., Birmingham, Ala. Died Oct. 30, 1930.

BRANSFORD, Clifton Wood, banker, miller; b. Owensboro, Ky., Jan. 24, 1858; s. Benjamin and Mary Eleanor (Athy) B.; ed. Bransford Inst., Owensboro; B.A., Cumberland U., 1877; Law Dept., U. of Louisville, 1878 (class honor); m. Virgie Lee Finley, Dec. 21, 1882; children—Mary Boyd (Mrs. Sherwood H. Standish), Virginia Lee (Mrs. Thos. K. Givens, dec.), Benjamin Ammonet (dec.). Pres. Bransford Mills, 1887-1921; organized, 1890, pres. to 1917, Owensboro Banking Co.; reorganized, 1891, Owensboro Wagon Co., v.p. until 1905, when disposed of interest; pres. Florence Wagon Co., Florence, Ala., 1914-21, chmn. bd., 1921—. Identified with Owensboro Messenger as half owner and editor, 1878-87. Dem. elector 2d Congressional Dist. of Ky., 1896; del. at large Dem. Nat. Conv., 1900. Vice chmn. Dem. State Platform Conv. of Ky., 1915. Del. Congress of Constructive Patriotism, 1917; pres. Sr. Service Corps of Owensboro, and "four-minute man," 1917-18. Mem. Millers' Advisory Com. to U.S. Wheat Dir. Barnes, 1919-20. Field rep. Am. Miller, Elevator and Grain Trade, 1923-26, National Miller, 1926-30. Vice chmn. Ky. div., Assn. Against the Prohibition Amendment, 1931-32. Presbyn. Home: Owensboro, Ky. Died Apr. 18, 1933.

BRANSON, Eugene Cunningham, educator; b. Morehead City, N.C., Aug. 6, 1861; s. Rev. L. and Edith (Cunningham) B.; A.M., Trinity Coll., N.C.; A.M., Peabody Normal Coll., Nashville; Litt.D., U. of Ga., 1919; m. Lottie Lanier, Sept. 27, 1889; children—Frank Lanier, Edith Lanier (Mrs. Young B. Smith), Phil Lanier, Elizabeth Lanier. Was prin. high sch., Raleigh, N.C.; supt. pub. schs., Wilson, N.C., and Athens, Ga.; prof. pedagogy, Ga. Normal and Industrial Sch.; pres. State Normal Sch. of Ga., 1900-12, and head of dept. rural economics and sociology, same, 1912-14; Kenan prof., U. of N.C., 1919—, head of dept. rural economics and sociology, 1914—. Editor Home and Farmstead, Athens. Author: Methods of Teaching Arithmetic, 1896; Methods of Teaching Reading and Spelling, 1896; Revised Page's Theory and Practice of Teaching, 1899. Home: Chapel Hill, N.C. Died Mar. 13, 1933.

BRANTLY, Theodore, judge; b. nr. Lebanon, Tenn., Feb. 12, 1851; A.B., South West Presbyn. U., Clarksville, Tenn., 1874; LL.B., Cumberland U., 1881; m. Lois Reat, June 9, 1891. Went to Mont., Sept. 5, 1887; admitted to bar, 1888; taught langs., Coll. of Mont., until 1889; dist. judge 3d dist. Mont., 1892-98; chief justice Supreme Ct., Mont., 1899—. Republican. Address: Helena, Mont. Died Sept. 17, 1922.

BRANTLEY, William Gordon, congressman; b. Blackshear, Pierce Co., Ga., Sept. 18, 1860; s. Benjamin D. and Janet (McRae) B.; ed. common schs. and (2 yrs.) U. of Ga.; m. Jessie Kate Westbrook, June 6, 1883 (died 1895); children—Irene Jeannette (dec.), William Gordon, Jessie Kate, Marguerite, Benjamin Daniel (dec.); m. 2d, Mary George Linn, Jan. 8, 1901; children—Linn McRae, George Daniel, Mary Elizabeth. Admitted to bar, 1881; mem. Ga. Ho. of Rep., 1884-85, Senate, 1886-87; solicitor gen. (pros. atty.), Brunswick Circuit, 1888-96; mem. 55th to 62d Congresses (1897-1913), 11th Ga. Dist. (declined renomination); in law practice as special counsel for railways in federal valuation, Washington, 1913—; v.p. and gen. counsel Fruit Growers Express Co., Western Fruit Express Co., Burlington Refrigerator Express. Democrat. Home: Brunswick, Ga. Died Sept. 12, 1934.

BRAS, Harry Leonard, editor; b. Toolsboro, Ia., Oct. 16, 1862; s. Charles W. and Hannah M. (DeMotte) B.; parents moved to New Boston, Ill., 1868; attended State Normal Sch.; taught sch. in Mercer County, Ill., 2 yrs.; emigrated to Dak. Territory, 1883; grad. U. of S.D., 1890; m. Hattie Betts, Sept. 2, 1885 (dec.); children—Elsie Louise, Lilian Eugenia, Florence, Sara; m. 2d, Pearl Phillips; children—Frank P., Mary Emma. County supt. schs., Davison County, S.D., 1886-92; asst. editor Mitchell (S.D.) Daily Republican, 1892-94; editor S.D. Educator, 1890-1908; postmaster of Mitchell, S.D., 1902-08, Centralia, Wash., 1922-27; moved to Wash., 1909; editor Centralia (Wash.) Daily Chronicle, 1916—. Mem. S.D. Ho of Rep., 1897-1901. Pres. bd. trustees Madison (S.D.) State Normal Sch., 1892-96, Centralia Carnegie Library Bd., 1918-26, Centralia State Normal Sch., 1921-27. Prepared state course of study for common schs., also system of registers and records for pub. schs., S.D., 1890. Home: Centralia, Wash. Died July 3, 1940.

BRASHEAR, John Alfred, mfr.; b. Brownsville, Pa., 1840; s. B. B. and Julia B.; ed. pub. schs.; Sc.D., Western U. of Pa., also Princeton U., 1911; LL.D., U. of Wooster, 1896, and Washington and Jefferson; D.Eng., Stevens Inst. Tech., 1912; m. Phoebe Stewart, Sept. 25, 1862. Learned machinist's trade; mech. engr., 1860-70; began constrn. of astron. and physical instruments, 1870; actively engaged in mfg. same, 1880—. Acting dir. Allegheny Obs., 1898-1900; acting chancellor, Western U. of Pa. Home: Pittsburgh, Pa. Died Apr. 8, 1920.

BRASLAU, Sophie, contralto; b. N.Y. City, Aug. 16, 1892; of Russian parentage; d. Abel (M.D.) and Alexandra (Goodelman) B.; ed. high sch. and under pvt. tutors. Singer with Metropolitan Opera Co. Died Dec. 22, 1935.

BRASTED, Fred, lawyer; b. Findley Lake, Chautauqua Co., N.Y.; s. Nathan Russell and Adaline (More) B.; B.S., State U. of Ia., 1893; studied law at Drake U., Des Moines; m. Estella M. Gleason; children—Nathan Russell, Helene Estella (Mrs. Russell W. Godwin), Fred Brasted. Reporter 16th Judicial Dist. of Ia., 1895-98; sec. to Leslie M. Shaw, gov. of Ia., 1898-99; admitted to Ia. bar, 1899; settled in Oklahoma City, 1903. Republican. Mason. Author: The Gang, 1910; sketches, law articles. Home: Ft. Worth, Tex. Died May 18, 1937.

BRASTOW, Lewis Orsmond, theologian; b. Brewer, Me., Mar. 23, 1834; s. Deodat and Eliza (Blake) B.; A.B., Bowdoin Coll., 1857; studied div., Bangor Theol. Sem.; hon. M.A., 1885; D.D., Bowdoin, 1880; m. Martha Brewster Ladd, May 15, 1872. Ordained Congl. ministry, 1861; chaplain 12th Regt. Vt. Vol. Inf.; mem. Vt. Constitutional Conv., 1870; pastor St. Johnsbury, Vt., 1861-73, Burlington, Vt., 1873-84; prof. practical theology, Yale Div. Sch., 1885-1907. Author: Representative Modern Preachers, 1904; The Modern Pulpit, 1906. Home: New Haven, Conn. Died Aug. 10, 1912.

BRATENAHL, George Carl Fitch, clergyman; b. Cleveland, O., May 4, 1862; s. Charles George and Mary Grant (Fitch) B.; B.A., Williams Coll., 1883 (D.D., 1908); m. Louisa Hall, Aug. 28, 1889 (died 1912); m. 2d, Florence Brown, June 16, 1915; children—Charles, Alexander. Clerk in wholesale warehouse, New York, 1883-86; rep. of New York mfg. corp. in London, 1888-93. Deacon, 1896, priest, 1898, P.E. Ch.; rector St. Alban's Parish, Washington, 1898-1912; canon Washington Cathedral, 1903-16, dean, 1916—. Sec. 3d Dept. of P.E. Ch., 1912-14; sec. Province of Washington, 1914-15. Home: Washington, D.C. Died Feb. 28, 1939.

BRATTON, Samuel Tilden, geographer; b. Johnson County, Mo., Dec. 16, 1878; s. Henry Allen and Nancy (Taylor-Graham) B.; B.S.D., Warrensburg (Mo.) State Teachers Coll., 1905; B.S. in edn., U. of Mo., 1916, A.M., 1917; Ph.D., U. of Chicago, 1925; m. Harriet Elizabeth Thurber, Nov. 9, 1907; 1 son, Samuel Thurber (dec.). Teacher rural sch., 1905-09; prin. high sch., 1909-15; instr. geography, U. of Mo., 1918-20, asst. prof., 1920-21, asso. prof., 1921-30, prof., 1930—. Author: Pupil's Work Book in Geography of Missouri, 1922; Missouri—A Geographical Reader, 1926; Geography of the St. Francis Basin, 1926; State Courses of Study for Junior and Senior High School Geography, 1928; Geography Through People (with A. M. Olson), 1930; Geography of Missouri, 1937. Home: Columbia, Mo. Died Oct. 18, 1940.

BRAUER, George R., clergyman; b. Newark, N.J., Feb. 20, 1871; s. Jacob and Carolyn (Rutger) B.; student Columbia, 1895-96, Union Theol. Sem., 1893-96, U. of Berlin, 1896-98; m. Eugenia Lathrop, Nov. 22, 1903; children—George Robert; m. 2d, Cecelia Bell Russum, Apr. 18, 1931. Ordained to ministry Presbyn. Ch., 1896; asst. pastor Memorial Ch., Newark, N.J., 1894-96; missionary Adirondack Mission, 1898-99; asst. pastor Rutgers Riverside Ch., New York, 1901-02; pastor Setauket and Stony Brook chs., Long Island, 1903-10; office sec. and treas. Coll. Bd. of Presbyn. Ch., 1910-15; pres. Ch. Erection Fund Bd. of Presbyn. Ch., 1915—; custodian mission property, Bd. of Nat. Missions, 1924—; treas. Gospel Mission to the Tombs, New York, 1916—; sec. and treas. Apostolic Inst. of Near East, 1918—. Republican. Home: Summit, N.J. Died May 1935.

BRAUN, John F., mfr.; b. Phila., Pa.; s. John and Christine (Lorey) B.; ed. pub. and pvt. schs. and business coll.; m. Edith Evans, Dec. 11, 1918. V.p. Pa. Lawn Mower Works; dir. Keystone Leather Co. and other corps. Musician and art connoisseur; owner of collection of works of Am. painters. Mem. bd. dirs. Presser Foundation, Pa. Museum Art Alliance Phila. Republican. Home: Merion, Pa. Died Nov. 18, 1939.

BRAUNE, Gustave Maurice, educator; b. Eutaw, Ala., Mar. 3, 1872; s. Gustave and Honoria (Rooney) B.; B.S., Spring Hill, Coll., Mobile, Ala., 1888; grad. in civ. engring., Royal Polytechnic, Dresden, Saxony, 1895; m. Mary Ida Stoelker, Feb. 8, 1899; 1 dau., Anna Parker. Bridge engr. Southern Bridge Co., Birmingham, Ala., 1897-1903; bridge designer New York State Barge Canal, 1904-05; chief engr. for B. H. Hardaway (Hardaway Contracting Co.), 1906-07; bridge designer and asst. chief bridge designer, New York State Barge Canal, 1908-11; pres. Braune Contracting Co., 1912; asst. prof. civil engring., U. of Cincinnati, 1912-13, asso. prof., 1914-17, prof. and head of dept., 1918-21; prof. civ. engring, U. of N.C., 1921-22, dean of engring., 1922—. Home: Chapel Hill, N.C. Died Nov. 26, 1931.

BRAWLEY, Benjamin (Griffith), clergyman, author; b. Columbia, S.C., Apr. 22, 1882; s. Edward MacKnight and Margaret Sophronia (Dickerson) B.; A.B., Atlanta Bapt. Coll. (now Morehouse Coll.), 1901; A.B., U. of Chicago, 1906; A.M., Harvard, 1908; Litt.D., Shaw U., 1927, Morehouse, 1937; m. Hilda Damaris Prowd, July 20, 1912. Instr. in English, Atlanta Bapt. Coll., 1902-06, prof. English, 1906-10; prof. English, Howard U., Washington, D.C., 1910-12; dean and prof. English, Morehouse Coll., 1912-20; prof. English, Shaw U., Raleigh, N.C., 1923-31, Howard U., 1931—. In Africa, 1920; pastor Messiah Bapt. Ch., Brockton, Mass., 1921-22; pres. Assn. of Colleges for Negro Youth, 1919-20. Author: A Short History of the American Negro, 1913; The Negro in Literature and Art, 1918; A Social History of the American Negro, 1921; A Short History of the English Drama, 1921; A New Survey of English Literature, 1925; Freshman Year English, 1929; Doctor Dillard of the Jeanes Fund, 1930; History of the English Hymn, 1932; Early Negro American Writers, 1935; Paul Laurence Dunbar, 1936; The Negro Genius, 1937; Negro Builders and Heroes, 1937. Address: Washington, D.C. Died Feb. 1, 1939.

BRAXTON, A(llen) Caperton, lawyer; b. Union, Monroe County, W.Va., Feb. 6, 1862; s. Dr. Tomlin and Mary (Caperton) B.; ed. Pampatike Academy, King William County, Va.; read law in office and took pvt. course; admitted to bar, 1883; unmarried. Commonwealth's atty. and city atty., Staunton, Va., 1885-89; sr. mem. law firm Braxton & Eggleston. Mem. Va. Constl. Conv. and chmn. com. on corps., 1901-02; also mem. coms. on judiciary and on final revision. Author of provisions creating Va. State Corp. Commn.; of Essays on Legitimate Powers and Functions of Constl. Convs., on History of Enactment of XVth Amendment, and on enactment of XIth Amendment. Home: Richmond, Va. Died Mar. 1914.

BRAY, (Thomas) Henry Truro, author; b. nr. Truro, Eng., Dec. 16, 1846; s. Richard and Lavinia Howe (Truro) B.; came to America at 16; matriculated and did first year's work in Northwestern U., 1871; B.A., Victoria Coll. (U. of Toronto), 1875, M.A., 1878, LL.B., 1883; B.D., Drew Theol. Sem., Madison, N.J., 1876; LL.B., U. of Mich., 1883; M.D., Hahnemann Med. Coll., Chicago, 1902; passed the ten yrs.' post-grad. course for LL.D., Victoria U., Cobourg, Can., 1885; m. Agnes Lawarne, 1875 (died 1877); m. 2d, Mabel Summy, Aug. 17, 1878 (died 1885); m. 3d, Mary Wormald, Oct. 1888. Deacon, 1877; priest, 1879, P.E. Ch.; first charge in Canton, Miss.; rector various chs.; was deposed at own request in St. Louis, Mo., 1889, by the bishop of Mo.; later in practice of medicine, Chicago. Author: The Knowability of God, 1887; God and Man, 1888, 3d edit., 1917; The Evolution of a Life, 1890; Reason and Dogma, 1894; The Living Universe, 1910, 3d edit., 1917; The Voice of the Universe. Address: Chicago, Ill. Died. Oct. 23, 1922.

BRAY, John P., consul gen.; b. Henderson, Minn., Feb. 14, 1859; grad. commercial dept. St. Cloud (Minn.) Coll. Was in mercantile business, Grand Forks; made 1st county auditor Grand Forks County, on organization of county, serving 6 yrs.; 1st state auditor N.D., 1889-92; postmaster Grand Forks, 1892; chmn. commn. apptd. by N.D. Legislature to divide public assets between N.D. and S.D.; Am. consul gen. at Melbourne, Australia, 1897, at Sydney, N.S.W., 1908-15, Singapore, Feb. 22, 1915; later consul at Johannesburg, Transvaal. Died Dec. 20, 1917.

BRAY, Thomas Joseph, mfr.; b. Pittsburgh, Pa., May 1, 1867; s. Thomas Joseph and Anna Jacova (Collins) B.; M.E., Lehigh U., 1894; m. Isabel Matthews, Oct. 7, 1896; children—Thomas J., Theodore M., Charles W. With Lewis Foundry & Machine Co., Pittsburgh, advancing to chief draughtsman, 1883-90, with Ohio Steel Co., Youngstown, O., and McGill & Co., Pittsburgh, 1894-1901; chief engr. United Engring. & Foundry Co., 1901-06; connected with Republic Iron & Steel Co., Youngstown, 1906-28, beginning as asst. to pres., later v.p. in charge operating dept., and pres., 1911-28; dir. Youngstown Sheet & Tube Co. Mem. Am. Iron and Steel Inst., British Iron and Steel Inst. Republican. Unitarian. Home: Youngstown, O. Died Dec. 11, 1933.

BRAYMER, Daniel Harvey, electrical engr., editor; b. Hebron, N.Y., Nov. 29, 1883; s. George W. and Jennie Cordelia (Smith) B.; A.B., Cornell U., 1906, E.E., 1908; m. Ruth McGuire, 1925. Began practice as elec. engr., New York, 1908; editor Electrical Engineering (formerly Southern Electrician), Atlanta, Ga., 1910-15; engring. editor Electrical World, New York, 1915-17; editor Electrical Record, 1917-19; returned to Electrical World as mng. editor, 1919, editor, 1921-22; editorial dir. Industrial Engr., 1922-25; consulting engr., Omaha, Neb., 1925—. Author: American Hydroelectric Practice, 1917; Armature Winding and Motor Repair, 1920; Rewinding Small Motors, 1925; Repair Shop Diagrams and Connecting Tables, 1927; Rewinding and Connecting A.C. Motors, 1931. Died Oct. 29, 1932.

BRAYTON, Alembert Winthrop, M.D.; b. Avon, N.Y., Mar. 4, 1848; s. Elijah F. and Helen (Parker) B.; reared on Ill. farm; grad. Chicago Normal Sch., 1869; attended Cornell, 1871-72; B.S., Butler U., 1878, M.S., 1880; M.D., Ind. Med. Coll., 1879; M.S., Ind. U., 1882; Ph.D., Purdue, 1885; m. Jessie May Dewey, June 29, 1875 (died 1925). On staff Indianapolis Journal, 1880-86; prof. chemistry, physiology, pathology, clin. medicine, syphilology and dermatology, Ind. Med. Coll., 1882—. Editor Indiana Med. Jour., 1892-1911. Author: Birds of Indiana, 1885; Mammals of Ohio, 1886; Fishes of the Southern Allegheny Region, with 20 Species New to Science (with David Starr Jordan). Home: Indianapolis, Ind. Died Sept. 23, 1926.

BRAYTON, Charles Ray, lawyer; b. Warwick, R.I., Aug. 16, 1840; s. William Daniel and Anna Ward (Clarke) B.; ed. Brown U., 1859-61; m. Antoinette Percival Belden, Mar. 13, 1865. Enlisted as 1st lt., 3d R.I. Vols., subsequently heavy arty., Aug. 27, 1861; capt., Nov. 28, 1862; lt. col., Nov. 17, 1863; col., Apr. 1, 1864; hon. mustered out of vol. service, Oct. 5, 1864; bvtd. brig. gen., U.S.V., Mar. 13, 1865; apptd. capt. 17th U.S. Inf., Mar. 7, 1867; resigned, July 6, 1867. Admitted to bar, 1891; U.S. pension agt., R.I., 1870-74; postmaster, Providence, 1874-80; chmn. Rep. State Central Com., 1876-77; chief R.I. State Police, 1886-87; mem. Rep. Nat. Com., 1896-1912. Home: Warwick, R.I. Died 1910.

BRAZELTON, William Buchanan, lumber dealer; b. Winchester, Tenn., Jan. 26, 1857; s. William Wilson and Mary (Buchanan) B.; ed. pub. schs.; m. Alice Berry, Sept. 10, 1890. Began as clk. in gen. store, 1871; entered lumber business in Tex., 1875; partner firm of William Cameron & Co., Waco, Tex., 1882-97; sr. partner Brazelton Lumber Co., Waco, 1906—; chmn. bd. First Nat. Bank; pres. Behrens Drug Co., Wood County Oil Co. Democrat. Presbyn. Home: Waco, Tex. Died June 16, 1934.

BRAZIER, Miss Marion Howard, journalist; b. Boston, Sept. 6, 1850; d. William Henry and Sarah Jane (Sargent) Brazier; ed. Boston pub. schs.; unmarried. Society editor Boston Post, 1890-98; publisher and editor The Patriotic Review, 1898-1904; society editor Boston Journal, 1903-11. Lecturer. Author: Perpetrations; Stage and Screen. Home: Boston, Mass. Deceased.

BREARLEY, William Henry, author, journalist; b. Plymouth, Mich., July 18, 1846; s. Joseph B.; ed. Normal School, Ypsilanti, Mich.; m. Lina De Land, Aug. 27, 1868. Served in Civil War, 17th Mich. vol. inf., 1862-65. Advertising mgr. Detroit Tribune, 1870-73, Detroit News, 1873-87; prop. Detroit Journal, 1887-92; corr. sec. New York City Baptist Mission Soc., 1899-1901. Founded Detroit Museum of Art, 1883; Detroit Chamber Commerce, 1892. Author: Recollections of the East Tennessee Campaign; Wanted, A Copyist; Leading Events of the American Revolution; King Washington (with Adelaide Skeel of Newburgh, N.Y.). Home: New York, N.Y. Died 1909.

BREASTED, James Henry, Orientalist, historian; b. Rockford, Ill., Aug. 27, 1865; s. Charles and Harriet N. (Garrison) B.; A.B., N. Central Coll., Naperville, Ill., 1888; studied Chicago Theol. Sem., 1888-90, hon. B.D., 1898; A.M., Yale, 1892; A.M., Ph.D., U. of Berlin, 1894; LL.D., U. of Calif., 1918, Princeton, 1929; hon. Litt.D., Oxford, 1922; m. Frances Hart, Oct. 22, 1894; children—Charles, James Henry, Astrid. Became asso. with U. of Chicago, 1894, asst. in Egyptology, 1894-96, asst. dir. Haskell Oriental Museum, 1895-1901, dir., 1901-31, instr. Egyptology and Semitic langs., 1896-98, asst. prof., 1898-1902, asso. prof., 1902-05, dir. Egyptian expdn., 1905-07, prof. Egyptology and Oriental history, 1905-33, collecting for the univ. in Egypt, 1894-95, chmn. dept. Oriental langs. and lits., 1915-33, first expdn. of Oriental Inst. in Egypt and Western Asia, 1919-20; relieved of all responsibility for instruction after Aug. 1925, in order to take full charge of work in Oriental Inst. in the Near East and related research projects; dir. Oriental Inst., 1919—. Collaborator on Egyptian Dictionary at Berlin, 1899-1900; apptd. 1900, on mission to museums of Europe by commn. of Royal Acads. of Germany (Berlin, Leipzig, Munich and Göttingen), to copy and arrange Egyptian inscriptions in those museums for the Berlin Egyptian Dictionary (mission completed 1901). Awarded gold medal, Geog. Soc. of Chicago, 1929; Rosenberger gold medal, for contribution to history of civilization, 1929; gold medal, Holland Soc. of New York, 1930. Pres. Am. Oriental Soc., 1918, History of Science Soc., 1926, Am. Hist. Assn., 1928; mem. Nat. Acad. Science. Author: De Hymnis in Solem sub Rege Amenophide IV Conceptis, 1894; Erman's Egyptian Grammar (English edit.), 1894; A New Chapter in the Life of Thutmose III, 1900; The Battle of Kadesh, 1903; Egypt Through the Stereoscope, 1905; A History of Egypt, 1905, 2d edit., 1909 (German edit. 1911; edit. for the blind, London, 1911; Russian edit. 1917; French edit. 1925; Arabic edit. 1929); Ancient Records of Egypt, Historical Documents (5 vols.), 1906; The Temples of Lower Nubia, 1906; A History of the Ancient Egyptians, 1908; The Monuments of Sudanese Nubia, 1908; Development of Religion and Thought in Ancient Egypt, 1912; Outlines of European History (with J. H. Robinson), 1914; Short Ancient History, 1914-15; Ancient Times—A History of the Early World, 1916 (also Swedish and Arabic edits.), revised edit., 1934; Survey of the Ancient World, 1919 (Japanese edit., 1933); History of Europe, Ancient and Medieval (with J. H. Robinson), 1920; General History of Europe (with Robinson and Smith), 1921; The Oriental Institute—A Beginning and a Programme, 1922; Oriental Forerunners of Byzantine Painting, 1924; Conquest of Civilization, 1926; Edwin Smith Surgical Papyrus (2 vols.), 1930; The Oriental Institute (vol. XII of U. of Chicago Survey), 1933; The Dawn of Conscience, 1933. Asso. editor Am. Jourfl of Semitic Langs. Home: Chicago, Ill. Died Dec. 2, 1935.

BREAUX, Joseph A., judge; b. in La., 1838; ed. U. of La. and Georgetown (Ky.) Coll.; admitted to bar, 1859; m. Eugenia Mille, of Iberville, La., 1861. Served in C.S.A., 1861-65; in practice in La., 1865-90; asso. justice, Supreme Court of La., 1890-1904, chief justice, 1904-14. Democrat. Home: Iberia, La. Died July 23, 1926.

BRECK, Edward, author, lecturer; b. San Francisco, July 31, 1861; s. Lt. Comdr. Joseph Berry and Ellen Frances (Newell) B.; ed. Oberlin Coll., Amherst, univs. of Cambridge, Munich, and Leipsic; M.A. and Ph.D., U. of Leipsic, 1887; diploma U.S. Naval War Coll. (corr. course); m. Miss A. Wagner von Kleeblatt, 1889; children—Ellen Frances (Mrs. F. F. Macnee), Margaret Adele (Mrs. H. F. Miller), Josephine Leslie; m. 2d, Mary Louise Stanley, 1923. Was editor and lit. adviser Estes & Lauriat, pubs., Boston; editor in chief of Life, London, 1890-92; Berlin corr. New York Herald and New York Times; vice consul gen., Berlin, 1895-96; asst. to U.S. naval attaché Berlin, during war with Spain; volunteered to go to Spain as secret agent, and operated there till close of war, status of U.S. officer. Lecturer on naval subjects, 1914-16. Lt. comdr. U.S.N.R.F., Feb. 13, 1917; in secret service until Mar. 1918; then apptd. U.S. naval attaché to Portugal; executive of hist. sect. Navy Dept., 1919-22; officially retired from U.S.N.R.F., on account of age, as hon. lt. comdr., July 31, 1925. Temporary editor Living Age, 1923. Awarded Navy Cross for distinguished and dangerous service; Chevalier Legion of Honor (French); Comdr. Order of Aviz, Order of Christ and D.S.M. (Portuguese); Italian War Cross. Deist. Author: De Consuetudine Monachorum, 1887; Art of Fencing, 1894; Way of the Woods, 1908; Wilderness Pets, 1910; Sporting Guide, 1909; The American Naval Railway Batteries in France, 1920; Armed Guards on American Merchant Ships, 1921; The Steel-Trap, 1925; The Lady and the Trapper, 1927. Naval contbr. Dictionary of American Biography, 1926—. Address: Washington, D.C. Died May 14, 1929.

BRECK, George William, artist; b. Washington, D.C., Sept. 1, 1863; s. John and Annie (Auer) B.; studied Art Students' League, New York; first winner Lazarus Scholarship for study of mural painting (offered through Met. Museum), and thereby became student Am. Acad. Fine Arts, Rome, Italy, 1897-1902; m. Katharine Head, June 10, 1903. Dir. Acad. Fine Arts, Rome, 1904-09; removed to New York, 1910. Mural decorations, U. of Va.; Watertown (N.Y.) Pub. Library; mosaics St. Paul's (P.E.) Ch., Rome, Italy; decorations, house of late Whitelaw Reid, New York, etc. Silver medal, St. Louis Expn., 1904. Home: Flushing, L.I., N.Y. Died Nov. 22, 1920.

BRECK, Joseph, art dir.; b. Allston, Mass., Feb. 3, 1885; s. Joseph Francis and Anne Hayes (Wilde) B.; A.B., Harvard, 1907; studied art in Europe, 1907-08; post-grad. work, Harvard, 1908-09. Asst. curator, Dept. of Decorative Arts, Met. Museum of Art, N.Y. City, 1909-14; dir. Minneapolis Soc. of Fine Arts, May 1, 1914-Oct. 15, 1917; asst. dir. and curator Dept. Decorative Arts, Met. Museum of Art, 1917—. Officer of Royal Order of North Star, 1927. Author: Catalogue of Romanesque, Gothic and Renaissance Sculpture, Metropolitan Mus. of Art, 1913. Co-author: The Ballard Collection of Oriental Rugs, 1923; The Pierpont Morgan Wing, 1925; The Cloisters, 1926. Address: New York, N.Y. Died Aug. 2, 1933.

BRECK, Samuel, army officer; b. Middleborough, Mass., Feb. 25, 1834; s. Samuel and Sarah Amelia (Eddy) B.; grad. U.S. Mil. Acad., 1855; m. Caroline J. Barrett, Sept. 23, 1857 (died 1900). Commd. 2d lt. 1st Arty., July 1, 1855; promoted through grades to brig. gen., Sept. 11, 1897; retired Feb. 25, 1898. Author: Genealogy of the Breck Family, 1887; Magoun Memorial, 1891. Home: Brookline, Mass. Died Feb. 23, 1918.

BRECKENRIDGE, Hugh Henry, artist; b. Leesburg, Va., Oct. 6, 1870; s. Alexander P. and Susan B. B.; pupil Pa. Acad. Fine Arts and awarded the European scholarship, 1892; studied in Paris with Bouguereau, Ferrier and Doucet; m. Roxanna Grace Holme, June 15, 1895; children—Grace (dec.), Margaret H. (Mrs. Leslie A. Skinner). Inst., Pa. Acad. of Fine Arts, 1894—; dir. Breckenridge Sch. of Painting, East Gloucester, Mass. Awarded 1st Toppan prize, Pa. Acad. Fine Arts, 1891; medal, Atlanta Expn., 1895; hon. mention, Expn. Universelle, Paris, 1900; medal, Buffalo Expn., 1901; Corcoran prize, Washington, 1903; gold medal, Art Club of Phila., 1907; 1st prize, Washington Color Club, 1908; silver medal, International Expn., Buenos Aires, 1910; gold medal, Panama P.I. Expn., 1915; 3d William A. Clark prize, Corcoran Gallery, Washington, 1916; Stotesbury prize, Pa. Acad. Fine Arts, 1917; Academy gold medal of honor, 1919, Jennie Sesnau gold medal, 1920, gold medal of the Fellowship, 1920—all Pa. Acad. Fine Arts; Locust Club gold medal and purchase prize, 1926; medal for Still Life, Washington, D.C., 1927. Represented in collections of Art Club of Phila.; Delgado Mus. of Art, New Orleans; St. Louis (Mo.); Pa. Acad. Fine Arts; San Francisco Mus. of Art; Los Angeles Mus.; University Club, Indianapolis; U. of Va.; Conn. State Library; U. of Pa.; Jefferson Med. Coll.; etc. Mem. Municipal Art Jury, Phila.; mem. Jury of Selection Buffalo Expn., 1901; Internat. Jury of Awards, St. Louis Expn., 1904; Jury of Selection San Francisco Expn., 1915. A.N.A. Home: Philadelphia, Pa. Died Nov. 4, 1937.

BRECKENRIDGE, Ralph W., lawyer; b. Carlisle, O., Mar. 14, 1860; s. Charles F. and Mary Jane (Foster) B.; ed. pub. schs., Iowa; m. Harriet A. Allen, Sept. 19, 1888. Admitted to bar, 1881; mem. law firm Greene, Breckenridge, Gurley & Woodrough. Delivered numerous addresses and lectures and has written many articles on ins. law and law reform; commr. for Neb. on Uniform State Laws. Republican. Methodist. Home: Omaha, Neb. Died Aug. 8, 1913.

BRECKENRIDGE, Clifton Rodes, diplomatist; b. Lexington, Ky., Nov. 22, 1846; s. Gen. John Cabell (V.p. of U.S.) and Mary C. Burch B.; ed. Washington Coll., Va.; served pvt. C.S.A., and as midshipman in C.S.N.; m. Catherine B. Carson, Nov. 21, 1876 (died 1921); children—James Carson, Mary, Lees Preston, Clifton Rhodes. Cotton planter in

Ark., 1870-83. Mem. 48th to 51st Congresses (1883-91); unseated in 1st session 51st Congress, Sept. 5, 1890; reëlected 2d session, 51st Congress and to 52d and 53d Congresses (1891-95); resigned, Aug. 14, 1894; U.S. minister to Russia, 1894-97. Democrat. Mem. State Constl. Conv., 1917. Pvt. Ark. Home Guard, 1917. Home: Ft. Smith, Ark. Died Dec. 3, 1932.

BRECKINRIDGE, Desha, newspaper man; b. Lexington, Ky., Aug. 5, 1867; s. Hon. William Campbell Preston and Issa (Desha) B.; ed. under James Lane Allen, Lexington, Lawrenceville, N.J., Princeton U., and U. of Va.; m. Madeline McDowell, Nov. 17, 1898 (died 1920); m. 2d, Mrs. Mary Frazer Lebus, July 1929. Admitted to Ky. bar, 1893; jr. mem. Breckinridge & Shelby, 1893-1900; pub. Lexington Herald, 1897—, editor, 1904—. Pres. Lexington Herald Co. Lt. 3d Vol. Engrs. and a. d. c. to Maj. Gen. J. C. Breckinridge during Spanish-Am. War. Democrat. Presbyn. Home: Lexington, Ky. Died Feb. 18, 1935.

BRECKINRIDGE, Joseph Cabell, army officer; b. Baltimore, Jan. 14, 1842; s. Rev. Robert Jefferson B.; attended Centre Coll., Ky., and U. of Va.; m. Louise Ludlow Dudley, July 20, 1868. Entered army, 1861, Gen. Nelson's and Gen. Thomas' staffs; commanded light battery F, 2d Arty., at Atlanta; apptd. 2d lt. 2d Arty., Apr. 14, 1862, "for gallantry at Mill Springs, Ky."; promoted through grades to maj. gen., U.S. Army, Apr. 11, 1903. Bvtd.: capt., July 22, 1864, "for gallant and meritorious services in battle before Atlanta, Ga."; maj., Mar. 13, 1865, for same during the war. Maj. gen. vols., 1898, in Santiago campaign; horse shot under him July 2, 1898; comd. separate army of 44,000 men at Chickamauga, Ga., Aug., 1898; insp. gen. U.S.A., 1889-1904; retired at own request after 40 yrs.' service, Apr. 12, 1903. Traveled throughout Europe and southeastern and western Asia and all over U.S. Del. of Gen. Assembly Presbyn. Ch. in America to Pan Presbyn. Alliance Conf., Liverpool, 1904. Pres. Gen. Nat. Soc. S.A.R., 1900-01; v.p. Soc. Army of the Cumberland, and Soc. of Army of the Tennessee. Home: Washington, D.C. Died Aug. 18, 1920.

BRECKINRIDGE, Madeline McDowell (Mrs. Desha Breckinridge); b. Woodlake, Franklin County, Ky., May 20, 1872; d. Henry Clay and Anne (Clay) McDowell; ed. State Coll., Lexington, Ky.; Miss Porter's Sch., Farmington, Conn.; m. Desha Breckinridge, Nov. 17, 1898. Pres. Ky. Equal Rights Assn., 1912-15, 1919; v.p. State Tuberculosis Commn., 1913-17; v.p. of Ky. Child Labor Com.; mem. bd. trustees Fayette County Tuberculosis Sanatorium; dir. Fayette Co. Pub. Health Nursing Assn., Fayette County Associated Charities, Lexington Civic League (exec. com.); active in securing legislation in interest of rural and city schs., and for the protection of women and children, including the sch. suffrage for women, in Ky., also tuberculosis legislation, etc. Home: Lexington, Ky. Died Nov. 25, 1920.

BRECKINRIDGE, William Campbell Preston, congressman; b. Baltimore, Aug. 28, 1837; s. Rev. Robert Jefferson B.; grad. Centre Coll., Danville, Ky., April 26, 1855; A.M., LL.D.; also LL.B., U. of Louisville, 1857; LL.D., Central U. Richmond, Ky., and Cumberland U., Tenn. Entered C.S.A., as capt.; became col. of 9th Ky cav. and comd. Ky. cav. brigade when it surrendered; afterward prof. of equity jurisprudence in Ky. U. Mem. Congress, 7th Ky. dist., 1884-95. Nat. (gold) Democrat. Home: Lexington, Ky. Died 1904.

BRECKINRIDGE, William Lewis, civil engr.; b. Louisville, Ky., June 29, 1857; s. Marcus P. and Lucy (Long) B.; C.E., Washington U., St. Louis, 1879, hon. M.A., 1906; m. Irene Waples, Oct. 15, 1891. Began in engring. dept. C.,B.&Q. R.R., 1879, and became engr. of maintenance of way, 1900. Republican. Home: Chicago, Ill. Died July 11, 1929.

BRECKONS, Robert W., lawyer; b. Kewanee, Ill., Dec. 16, 1866; s. Edward R. and Mary (Allison) B.; LL.B., Georgetown U., 1890; m. Frances E. Harrison, Aug. 5, 1893. Admitted to bar, 1890; county atty., Laramie County, Wyo., 1896-98; mem. Wyo. Legislature, 1901; U.S. atty. Dist. Hawaii, 1902-13. Del. Universal Congress Lawyers and Jurists, St. Louis, 1904. Republican. Home: Honolulu, H.T. Died Nov. 27, 1918.

BREDIN, R. Sloan, artist; b. Butler, Pa., Sept. 9, 1881; s. Stephen Collins (M.D.) and Catherine (Sloan) B.; grad. Pratt Inst. High Sch., Brooklyn, N.Y., 1899; studied drawing and painting at New York Sch. of Fine Arts, under Chase, Beckwith and Du Mond; m. Alice Price, May 14, 1914; children—Jean Elizabeth, Barbara Alice, Stephen Price. Landscape, figure and portrait painter. Exhibited at important centres in U.S.; awarded bronze medal, San Francisco Expn., 1915; 2d Hallgarten prize, Nat. Acad. Design, New York, 1914; Maynard portrait prize, same, 1921; Vezin prize, Salmagundi Club, New York; bronze medal, Sesquicentennial, Phila.; hon. mention Phila. Art Club, Art Inst. Chicago. Works on permanent exhbn. at Minneapolis Museum, Salmagundi Club, Nat. Arts Club, and Democratic Club, New York; rep. by 5 murals in New Jersey State Museum, Trenton. Foyer du Soldat hosp. work with French Army, 1918-19. A.N.A., 1921. Democrat. Episcopalian. Home: New Hope, Pa. Died July 17, 1933.

BREED, David Riddle, clergyman; b. Pittsburgh, June 10, 1848; s. George and Rhoda Ogden (Edwards) B.; A.B., Hamilton Coll., 1867; grad. Auburn Theol. Sem., 1870; D.D., Hamilton Coll., 1882, LL.D., 1914; m. Mary Elizabeth Kendall, June 16, 1870; children—Esther Kendall, Mary Elizabeth, Maurice Edwards, David Riddle (dec.), Allen. Ordained Presbyn. ministry, 1870; pastor House of Hope Ch., St. Paul, 1870-85; organizer and pastor Ch. of the Covenant, Chicago, 1885-94; pastor First Ch., Pittsburgh, 1894-98; prof. practical theology, Western Theol. Sem., Pittsburgh, Pa., 1898—. Author: Abraham, the Typical Life of Faith, 1886; History of the Preparation of the World for Christ (4 edits.), 1891; Heresy and Heresy, 1891; The History and Use of Hymns and Hymn Tunes, 3 edits.; Preparing to Preach, 1911. Home: Pittsburgh, Pa. Died Dec. 11, 1931.

BREED, Dwight Payson, clergyman; b. Chelsea, Mich., June 10, 1851; s. Samuel Dwight and Amelia Eliza (Bosworth) B.; Oberlin Coll.; Ph. B., Ill. Wesleyan U., 1888, Ph.D., 1892; studied Oberlin Theol. Sem.; m. Delina M. Briggs, Apr. 9, 1873. Ordained Congl. ministry, 1872; pastor various chs., 1872-1901; field sec. Ia. Home Missionary Soc., 1901-08; field sec. Grinnell Coll., Ia., 1908-16; pastor Summerdale Congregational Ch., Chicago, 1916-20, emeritus. Professorial lecturer, Tabor Coll., Ia. Has served as moderator state Congl. bodies. Progressive. Mason (K.T.). Home: Chicago, Ill. Died Oct. 7, 1925.

BREED, R(ichard) E(dwards), pub. utilities; b. Pittsburgh, Pa., Mar. 17, 1866; s. Richard E. and Martha Olivia (Lyon) B.; ed. U. of Ky.; m. Julia Porter, Mar. 7, 1904; children—(by 1st marriage) Mrs. Lucy Tucker, (by 2d marriage) Richard Edwards, Jane Porter, George. Organizer, pres., chmn. bd. Am. Gas & Electric Co.; dir., exec. com. Am. Power & Light Co., Electric Power and Light Corp., Carolina Power & Light Co.; dir. many corps. Served as mem. mil. staffs of Govs. Durbin, Hanly and Goodrich, of Ind., advancing to brig. gen. Republican. Presbyn. Mason. Home: New York, N.Y. Died Oct. 14, 1926.

BREEN, William P., banker; b. Terre Haute, Ind., Feb. 13, 1859; s. James and Margaret (Dunne) B.; A.B., U. of Notre Dame, 1877, A.M., 1879, LL.D., 1902; m. Odelia Phillips, May 28, 1884. Admitted to Ind. bar, 1879, and practiced at Ft. Wayne; mem. firm Breen & Newkirk; pres. Peoples Trust & Savings Co. Catholic. Democrat. Address: Ft. Wayne, Ind. Died Apr. 22, 1930.

BREENE, Frank Thomas, dental surgeon; b. Durant, Ia., Nov. 4, 1866; s. George T. and Harriet H.B.; D.D.S., State U. of Ia., 1888, M.D., 1893; m. Bessie P. Millard. Practiced at Iowa City, Ia., 1896—; prof. Coll. of Dentistry, State U. of Ia., 1888—; dean Coll. of Dentistry, 1914—. Maj., Dental Res. Corps, 1918. Republican. Home: Iowa City, Ia. Died Oct. 15, 1931.

BREESE, Burtis Burr, psychologist; b. Horseheads, N.Y., May 17, 1867; s. Corydon Benton and Ann Elizabeth (Tanner) B.; A.B., U. of Kan., 1896; A.B., Harvard, 1897, A.M., 1898; fellow in psychology and edn., Columbia, 1898-99, Ph.D., 1899, grad. student, 1899-1901; studied in Europe, 1901-02; m. Lillian M. Burnett, Apr. 14, 1903. Asst. in psychology, Harvard, 1897-98; prof. psychology and ethics, U. of Tenn., 1902-04; prof. psychology, U. of Cincinnati, 1904—. Home: Cincinnati, O. Died July 31, 1939.

BREESE, Edmund, actor; b. Brooklyn, June 18, 1871; s. Renshaw and Josephine (Busby) B.; ed. pub. and pvt. schs.; m. Genevieve Landry, Aug. 30, 1899. Supported Madame Rhea, 1896-98, in Nell Gwynn, Marie Stuart and Frou Frou; with James O'Neil in Merchant of Venice, 1898; all star cast of Monte Cristo, 1899; all star cast of Romeo and Juliet, New York, Mar., 1899; with Ada Rehan, 1903, playing classic rôles; with Robert Edeson, in Ransom's Folly, 1904; in Strongheart, 1905. Originated "John Burkett Ryder," in The Lion and the Mouse, Lyceum Theatre, New York, Nov. 20, 1905; appeared in Duke of York's Theatre, London, in same rôle, May 22, 1906; later played "Richard Brewster" in The Third Degree; star in The Earth, beginning Oct. 1909. Died Apr. 6, 1936.

BRÉGY, Francis Amédée, judge; b. Centreville, Pa., Sept. 7, 1846; s. Francis Amédée and Phoebe C. (Anderson) B.; matriculated in U. of Pa., Sept. 1862, but left coll. to join Union Army; B.A., U. of Pa., 1863, LL.B.; m. Katherine S. Maurice, Aug. 5, 1869. Served as pvt. 1st Phila. Battery Light Arty., June-Sept., 1863 (hon. discharged); commd. lt. Co. B, 215th Pa. Inf., 1865. Admitted to Pa. bar, 1867; 1st asst. dist. atty., Phila., Pa., 1881-87; apptd. judge Court of Common Pleas No. 1, Phila., Apr. 1887; elected to same office Nov. 1887, for term of 10 yrs. and reëlected 1897 and 1907 and 1917 without opposition. Republican. Episcopalian. Home: Philadelphia, Pa. Died Jan. 15, 1922.

BREHM, Marie Caroline, lecturer; b. Sandusky, O., June 30, 1859; d. William Henry and Elizabeth (Rhode) Brehm; ed. Sandusky pub. sch., 1866-77; illness prevented coll. course and she studied German, French and civics at home with her father; unmarried. Lecturer W.C.T.U., 1891—; platform lecturer on temperance and woman suffrage; was supt. franchise dept. Nat. W.C.T.U.; pres. Ill. W.C.T.U., 1902-06; elected mem. General Assembly's permanent com. on temperance of Presbyn. Ch. in U.S.A., June 14, 1906, now Bd. of Temperance and Moral Welfare. Candidate on Prohibition ticket, 1902, 1904, 1908, for trustee, U. of Ill.; U.S. del. 12th Internat. Congress on Alcoholism, London, 1909. Inter-ch. Temperance Federation del. to 13th World's Congress on Alcoholism, The Hague, Holland, 1911; chmn. Nat. Com. Prohibition Party, Lincoln, Neb., 1920; mem. Nat. Com. Prohibition Party from Calif.; 1st v.p. Calif. State Woman's Legislative Council, Oct. 4, 1921—. Prohibition Party candidate for v.p. of U.S., 1924; deacon 2d Presbyn. Ch., 1924-25. Home: Long Beach, Calif Died Jan. 26, 1926.

BREIDENBAUGH, Edward Swoyer, chemist; b. Newville, Pa., Jan. 13, 1849; s. Rev. E. and Catherine Elizabeth (Swoyer) B.; grad. Pa. Coll., Gettysburg, 1868; studied chemistry, Sheffield Scientific Sch. (Yale), 1871-73; hon. Sc.D., Pa. Coll., 1883; m. Ida Kitzmiller, Nov. 20, 1873; children—Edna, Ida May. Instr. analytical chemistry, Sheffield Sch., 1872-73; prof. chemistry and mineralogy, Pa. Coll., 1874-1924; emeritus prof., 1925. Was mineralogist to State Bd. of Agr.; practiced as chemist. Author: Pennsylvania College Book; Lecture Notes on Inorganic Chemistry; Mineralogy on the Farm; Directory in Elementary Chemistry; Course in Qualitative Analysis; Syllabus of Lectures on Geology. Home: Gettysburg, Pa. Died Sept. 5, 1926.

BREIDENTHAL, John W., banker; b. Sibley County, Minn., June 22, 1857; s. Matthew and Henrietta E. B.; ed. Terre Haute, Ind., common school; m. Julia Slaughter, 1882. Candidate for lt. gov. of Kan., 1884, on Greenback ticket; assisted in forming the Union Labor party at Cincinnati, 1887; voted for in Kan. legislature for U.S. senator, 1891 and 1897; State bank commr., Kan., 1893-1901; Democratic, Free Silver and Populist candidate for gov. Kan., 1900; chmn. People's Party State Com. of Kan., 6 yrs.; conducted 2 successful campaigns. V.p. and mgr. The Banking Trust Co. of Kan. Author of Kan. banking and trust co. laws. Home: Kansas City, Kan. Died 1910.

BREIL, Joseph Carl, composer; b. Pittsburgh, Pa., June 29, 1870; s. Joseph and Margaret A. (Frohnhoefer) B.; ed. Pittsburgh Coll., St. Fidelis Coll. (Butler, Pa.), Curry U. (Pittsburgh), U. of Leipzig; studied music under pvt. teachers, Conservatory, Leipzig; voice at Milan, Italy; m. Jean F. Stevenson, Feb. 21, 1910. At 17 had written opera, "Orlando of Milan," prod. by amateurs, at Pittsburgh; prin. tenor, Emma Juch Opera Co., 1891-92; tenor soloist and choir dir. St. Paul's Cathedral, Pittsburgh, 1892-97; theatrical music dir., and toured country, 1897-1903; reviser and editor mus. publs., 1903-10; gen. music dir. Am. Grand Opera Assn., season 1919-20. Composer of the music to "The Climax" (play), first prod. at Weber's Theatre, New York, Apr. 1909; "Love Laughs at Locksmiths" (opera), prod., Portland, Me., Oct. 27, 1910; Sarah Bernhardt's "Queen Elizabeth," a musical score to moving picture play film (first ever attempted), prod. at Powers' Theatre, Chicago, 1912, and which has given him sobriquet "father of motion picture music"; also many other film scores, most notable. Wrote grand opera, "The Legend," prod. Metropolitan Opera House, New York. Wrote music of "The Seventh Chord," play prod. Illinois Theatre, Chicago, Apr. 1913; book and music of "Professor Tattle," New York, 1913; music of "The Phantom Legion," New York, 1919. Motion picture music. Died Jan. 23, 1926.

BREITUNG, Edward Nicklas, mining engr.; b. Negaunee, Mich., Nov. 1, 1871; s. Edward and Marie Josephine (Pulan) B.; ed. under pvt. tutelage; m. Charlotte Graveraet Kaufman, Nov. 4, 1892. Began as mining engr., Negaunee, Mich., 1888; owner and operator Mary Charlotte Mining Co., Breitung Hematite and Lucky Star mines (all at Negaunee), and many other mines; pres. Negaunee Nat. Bank, Munising State Bank; officer or dir. many other cos. Republican. Catholic. Home: Marquette, Mich. Died Oct. 2, 1924.

BREM, Walter Vernon, M.D.; b. Charlotte, N.C., Nov. 5, 1875; s. Walter Vernon and Hannie (Caldwell) B.; student Va. A. and M. Coll., Blacksburg, 1889-90, Trinity Coll., Durham, N.C., 1890-92; B.S., U. of N.C., 1896; student Union Theol. Sem., New York, 1897-98, U. of N.C. Sch. of Medicine, 1898-1900; M.D., Johns Hopkins, 1904; m. Marion Wolcott Winkler, Aug. 5, 1905; children—Phyllis (dec.), Lorna, Gwendolyn, Thomas Hamilton, Frederick Winkler, Walter Vernon. Med. house officer Johns Hopkins Hosp., 1904-05; physician and acting pathologist, Ancon Hosp., Canal Zone, 1905-07; chief of med. clinic, Colon Hosp., Canal Zone, 1907-11; prof. pathology and bacteriology, Los Angeles dept. U. of

Calif. Sch. of Medicine, 1911-14; mem. Brem, Zeiler & Hammack, lab. of clin. pathology, Los Angeles, 1911—. Served as 1st sergt. Co. G, 2d N.C. Vol. Inf., Spanish-Am. War; maj. Med. Corps, U.S.A., World War. Dir. southern div. Calif. State Hygienic Lab., 1913-16; mem. Calif. State Bd. Med. Examiners, 1923-25; cons. epidemiologist Calif. State Bd. of Health, 1924-1932. Pres. bd. trustees The Trailfinders (boys' orgn.), 1927-32. Home: Los Angeles, Calif. Died Nov. 18, 1937.

BREMER, Adolf; b. in Germany, July 24, 1869; s. Edward and Matilda (Maeder) B.; ed. gymnasium; m. Mary Schmidt, 1896; children—Edward G., Louise, Adolf, Mrs. V. P. Reim, Mrs. F. H. Matson. Formerly in sporting goods business, St. Paul, and for many yrs. v.p. Jacob Schmidt Brewing Co., later pres.; officer or dir. various corps. Democrat. Lutheran. Home: St. Paul, Minn. Died Oct. 9, 1939.

BREMNER, George Hampton, civil engr.; b. Marshalltown, Ia., Dec. 17, 1861; s. William and Catherine C. (Hampton) B.; C.E., State U. of Ia., 1883; m. Louie A. Stephenson, Sept. 5, 1888. Began in engring. work with C.G.W. Ry., 1883, and C.&N.W. Ry., 1884; with the C.,B.&Q. Ry. in various positions, 1884—, engr. of the Ill. dist., 1902—. Home: LaGrange, Ill. Died Apr. 2, 1927.

BREMNER, William Hepburn, ry. official; b. Marshalltown, Ia., Oct. 24, 1869; s. William and Catherine C. (Hampton) B.; C.E., State U. of Ia., 1891, LL.B., 1895; m. Emily C. McKell, June 17, 1903. Gen. practice Des Moines, Ia., 1895-1909; city solicitor, Des Moines, 1902-08; gen. atty., M.&St.L. R.R., 1909-13, gen. solicitor, 1913-16, gen. counsel, 1916-17, pres., 1917-18, federal mgr., 1918-20, pres., 1920-23, receiver, 1923—. Republican. Presbyn. K. of P. Home: Minneapolis, Minn. Died Dec. 12, 1934.

BRENEMAN, Abram Adam, chemist; b. Lancaster, Pa., Apr. 28, 1847; s. Dr. Abraham and Anna B.; B.S., Pa. State Coll., 1866, M.Sc., 1871; unmarried. Instr. chemistry, Pa. State Coll., 1867-68, prof., 1869-72; asst. prof. industrial chemistry, Cornell U., 1875-79, prof. 1879-82; analyst, chem. expert, writer and lecturer, 1882—; also in consulting practice. Inventor Breneman process of rendering iron non-corrodible. Editor Journal, Am. Chem. Soc., 1884-93. Chmn. internat. jury on mineral waters, Chicago Expn., 1893, St. Louis Expn., 1904; expert mem. municipal explosives commn., New York, 1906-09. Author: (with Prof. G. C. Caldwell) A Manual of Introductory Laboratory Practice, 1875; Report on the Fixation of Atmospheric Nitrogen, 1889; Report on Sewer and Conduit Explosions in New York, 1909, 1910. Address: New York, N.Y. Died May 10, 1928.

BRENNAN, George E.; b. N.Y. State; ed. pub. schs.; married; 1 dau., Mary. Began as coal mine worker, Braidwood, Ill., alternately working and studying; taught sch. for awhile; served in office of W. H. Hinrichsen, sec. of state, Springfield, Ill., 1893-97; later settled in Chicago; in casualty ins. and surety bonds business, 1905—; mgr. Chicago office U.S. Fidelity & Guaranty Co., of Baltimore, Md., 1906—. Chmn. Ill. delegation to Dem. Nat. Conv., N.Y. City, 1924; defeated for U.S. Senate, 1926; mem. Dem. Nat. Com., 1924—. Catholic. Home: Chicago, Ill. Died Aug. 8, 1928.

BRENNAN, James Dowd, banker; b. Huntington, Vt., Apr. 20, 1881; s. Martin Doyle and Margaret (Dowd) B.; U. of Vt., 1899-1900, LL.D., 1931; m. Edith Poor, May 12, 1906. Began as bank clk., 1906; state bank examiner, Mass., 1910-13; nat. bank examiner and chief nat. bank examiner Boston Federal Res. Dist., 1913-18; v.p. First Nat. Bank of Boston, 1918—; pres. Federal Cranberry Co. Pres. Alumni Council U. of Vt., 1926—. Episcopalian. Mason (K.T.). Home: Swampscott, Mass. Died Apr. 1932.

BRENNAN, Martin Adlai, congressman; b. Bloomington, Ill., Sept. 21, 1879; s. Dominick and Bridget (Cunningham) B.; LL.B., Wesleyan Coll. of Law, Bloomington, 1902; unmarried. Admitted to Ill. bar, 1902; in practice, Bloomington, 1903—. Presiding judge Ill. Court of Claims, 1913-17; rep. Ill. Gen. Assembly, 1921-23; mem. 73d and 74th Congresses (1933-37), Ill. at large. Democrat. Catholic. Elk, Woodman, K.C. Home: Bloomington, Ill. Died July 3, 1941.

BRENNER, Victor David, medalist, sculptor; b. Shavly, Russia, June 12, 1871; s. George and Sarah (Margolis) B.; came to U.S., 1890. Started business as die cutter, 1893; went to Paris, 1898, and became pupil Louis Oscar Roty; exhibited Paris Expn. and Salon, 1900, Buffalo, 1901, St. Louis, 1904, receiving awards from each. Works in Paris Mint, Munich Glyptothek, Vienna Numismatic Soc., Met. Mus. of Art, New York, and Numismatic Soc., New York, Luxembourg Museum, Museum Fine Arts, Boston. Gold medal, Internat. Expn., Brussels, 1910. Address: New York, N.Y. Died Apr. 5, 1924.

BRENT, Charles Henry, bishop; b. Newcastle, Ont., Apr. 9, 1862; s. Rev. Canon Henry and Sophia Frances (Cummings) B.; A.B., U. of Trinity Coll., Toronto (with classical honors), 1884, A.M., 1889; D.D., Toronto, 1901, King's Coll., 1910, Yale, 1919, Glasgow, Trinity and Hartford, 1920; S.T.D., Harvard, 1913, Columbia, 1917, LL.D., 1920; LL.D., Hobart, 1919, Rochester U., 1922, Union Coll., 1924, Toronto U., 1924, New York U., 1925. Deacon, 1886, priest, 1887, P.E. Ch.; undermaster at Trinity Coll. Sch., 1885-87; curate St. Paul's Cathedral, Buffalo, 1887, St. John the Evangelist, Boston, 1888-91; asst. minister, St. Stephen's, Boston, 1891-1901; elected bishop of the P.I., 1901, consecrated, 1901, served until 1918; Paddock lecturer Gen. Theol. Sem., New York, 1904; William Belden Noble lecturer Harvard, 1907; Duff lecturer Edinburgh, Glasgow and Aberdeen, 1921. Mem. of com. appointed by Philippine Govt. for investigation of opium question in the Orient, 1903-04; declined bishopric of Washington, D.C., 1908, of N.J., 1914; accepted bishopric of Western N.Y., 1918; bishop in charge Am. P.E. chs. in Europe, 1926-28. Sr. mem. Am. delegation to Internat. Opium Commn., Shanghai, and pres. same, 1909; chmn. Am. delegation and pres. Opium Conf., the Hague, 1911. Chief of chaplain service, G.H.Q., A.E.F., France, 1918-19. Awarded D.S.M.; Comdr. Order of Leopold; Companion of the Bath. Author: With God in the World, 1899; The Consolations of the Cross, 1902; The Splendour of the Human Body, 1904; Liberty and Other Sermons, 1906; Adventure for God, 1904; Leadership; With God in Prayer, 1907; The Revelation of Discovery, 1908; The Sixth Sense, 1911; Presence, 1914; Prisoners of Hope, 1915; A Master Builder (life and letters of Henry Yates Satterlee), 1916. Address: Buffalo, N.Y. Died Mar. 27, 1929.

BRENT, Joseph Lancaster, lawyer, sugar planter, soldier; b. Charles County, Md., Nov. 20, 1826; s. William Leigh B. and Maria (Fenwick) B.; ed. Georgetown Coll., D.C.; m. Rosella Kenner, Apr. 23, 1870. Served in arty. and cav., C.S.A.; chief of ordnance under Gen. John B. Magruder in Va., chief of arty. and ordnance under Gen. Richard Taylor in La., 1862-64; col. arty., Apr. 17, 1864; brig. gen. C.S.A., Oct. 1864; comd. "Brent's Cav. Brigade" (2d, 5th, 7th and 8th La.) cav.; comd. front lines extending from Arkansas line to Gulf (including forts on Red river) at time of Gen. E. Kirby Smith's surrender; comd. wooden gunboats which captured U.S. ironclad Indianola on Mississippi river in Feb. 1863. After war practiced law in Baltimore until 1870, then engaged in farming and sugar planting until 1889, retired. Mem. Calif. legislature, 2 terms; first pres. La. State Agrl. Soc. until 1889; mem. La. legislature 2 terms. Author: Mobilizable Batteries (advocating arming of railways). Home: Baltimore, Md. Died 1905.

BRENTANO, Theodore, judge; b. Kalamazoo, Mich., Mar. 29, 1854; s. Lorenzo and Caroline B.; ed. pub. schs. and in Germany and Switzerland; LL.B., LL.M., Nat. U., 1881; m. Minnie Claussenius, May 17, 1887; children—Mrs. Johanna von Tilly Bersbach, Mrs. Carola Anderson, Mrs. Dorothy Tieken. Admitted to bar by Supreme Ct., D.C., 1882; atty. in office of corp. counsel, Chicago, 1887; asst. city atty. Chicago, 1888; judge Superior Ct., Cook County, Ill., 1890-1921 (served as chief justice); E.E. and M.P. to Hungary, 1922-27. Republican. Home: Geneva, Ill. Died July 2, 1940.

BRENTON, Charles Richmond, banker; b. Dallas Center, Ia.; s. William Henry and Mary Elizabeth (Burton) B.; ed. pub. schs.; m. Carrie Woodward, 1894 (died 1920). Associated in business with brother, Clyde E., Des Moines, Ia.; pres. Farmers Bank of Woodward, Ia., Bank of Granger, Ia., Bank of La Porte, Tex.; v.p. Bank of Dallas Center, Ia., Bank of Waukee, Bank of Dana, also pres. various elevator, lumber and other cos., and owner or mgr. extensive farming interests in Ia. Mem. Ia. State Bd. of Edn., 1906—; pres. Dallas Center Bd. of Edn. Methodist. Mason. Home: Dallas Center, Ia. Died Sept. 1, 1924.

BRENTON, Clyde Edward, banking; b. Dallas Center, Ia., Apr. 20, 1868; s. William Henry and Mary Elizabeth (Richmond) B.; grad. high sch., Dallas Center; student Des Moines U.; m. Alice Gibson Givin, Oct. 10, 1894; 1 son, Woodward Harold. Began in banking business with the Bank of Dallas Center, 1888; chmn. exec. com. Ia.-Des Moines Nat. Bank & Trust Co.; chmn. bd. Poweshiek County Nat. Bank. Republican. Presbyn. Mason. Home: Dallas Center, Ia. Died Sept. 19, 1938.

BRENTON, Cranston, clergyman; b. Jamaica, N.Y., Nov. 20, 1874; s. Benjamin Jahleel and Orvetta (Hall) B.; B.S., Trinity Coll., Conn., 1899, M.S., 1902; grad. Berkeley Div. Sch., Conn., 1901; m. Elizabeth Alden Curtis, June 19, 1901; 1 son, William. Supt. mfg. business, N.Y. City, 1891-96; deacon, 1901, priest, 1902, P.E. Ch.; rector All Saints Memorial Ch., New Milford, Conn., 1901-04; asst. prof. English, Trinity Coll., 1904-06, prof. English lang. and lit., 1906-14; exec. sec. Social Service Commn., Diocese of New York, Feb.-Oct. 1914; New York war relief dir., Am. Red Cross, Oct. 1914-Nov. 1915; chmn. Nat. Bd. of Review of Motion Pictures, July 1915-May 1918. With Y.M.C.A. in charge personnel div. of the United Kingdom, hdqrs. London, May 1918-May 1919; sacrist and comptroller, Cathedral of St. John the Divine, N.Y. City, 1926-31. Home: Brooklyn, N.Y. Died Dec. 21, 1937.

BRESLICH, Arthur Louis, college pres.; b. Insterburg, E. Prussia, Germany, May 8, 1873; s. Louis and Hermine (Kummer) B.; Gymnasium, Insterburg; A.B., Baldwin-Wallace Coll., Berea, O., 1898; B.D., Nast Theol. Sem., Berea, 1898; Ph.D., U. of Wis., 1904; m. Lydia E. Filter, Oct. 11, 1904. Came to America, 1891; in employ Elgin Watch factory, 1891-95; ordained German M.E. ministry, 1898; pastor, Madison, Wis., 1898-1908; instr. Hebrew and Hellenistic Greek, U. of Wis., 1905-08; prof. exegesis, 1908-10, acting pres., 1910-11, pres., June 7, 1911-13, German Wallace Coll. and Nast Theol. Sem.; pres. Baldwin-Wallace Coll. and Nast Theol. Sem., 1913-18; sec. The Biblical Alliance, Madison, Wis., 1919—. Del. Gen. Conf. M.E. Ch., 1911. Author: Poetical Structure of Isaiah, Chapter 53, 1904; Bible Study—Romans, 1909; Bible Study—Matthew, 1909; The Epistle of Paul to the Romans, chapter 1-8, 1910; Problems of Religious Education, 1923. Home: Milwaukee, Wis. Died June 17, 1924.

BRESLIN, James H., capitalist. Pres. Brooklyn Heights Realty Co.; officer or dir. many cos. Address: New York, N.Y. Died 1906.

BRETHERTON, Sidney Elliott, mining engr.; b. Gloucester, England, Apr. 16, 1854; s. George and Elvira (Legg) B.; brought to U.S., 1859; ed. pub. schs., Flinton, Ont., Can., and night sch., Oswego, N.Y.; m. Belle Wright, Sept. 1, 1886. Began as asst. assayer Morgan Smelter, Salt Lake City, Utah, 1877; assayer, Stockton Smelter, Utah, 1878; assayer and chemist, La Plata Smelter, Leadville, Colo., 1879-81; supt. and metallurgist, Bonanza Smelter, Colo., 1882, Ark. Valley Smelter, Leadville, 1882-83; gen. supt. and metallurgist, Am. Smelting Works, Leadville, 1883-93; in consulting practice, 1893-1905; consulting engr., Afterthought Copper Co., 1905-16; consulting practice, 1916; retired, 1926. Mason (K.T.). Home: Berkeley, Calif. Died Oct. 4, 1929.

BRETT, George Platt, publisher; b. London, Eng., 1858; s. George E. and Elizabeth (Platt) B.; ed. at London and at Coll. City of New York; m. Marie Louise Tostevin, 1891. With The Macmillan Company, pubs., 1874—, pres. many yrs., later chmn. bd. Home: Fairfield, Conn. Died Sept. 19, 1936.

BRETT, Lloyd M., army officer; b. Dead River, Me., Feb. 22, 1856; s. John and Elizabeth (Brown) B.; grad. U.S. Mil. Acad., 1879; m. Elma Wallace, Feb. 7, 1887. Commd. 2d lt. 2d Cav., June 13, 1879; promoted through grades to brig. gen., Nat. Army, Aug. 5, 1917. Adj. gen. D.C. Militia, 1903-08; supt. Yellowstone Nat. Park, 1910-16; comdg. 160th Inf. Brigade, Camp Lee, Petersburg, Va., Sept. 1917, and overseas, May 1918-June 1919; col. 3d U.S. Cav., Aug. 1, 1919—. Awarded Medal of Honor "for most distinguished gallantry," in action against hostile Sioux Indians, while 2d lt. 2d Cav., Apr. 1, 1880; D.S.M.; Officer of the Legion of Honor; Croix de Guerre. Died Sept. 23, 1927.

BRETT, William Howard, librarian; b. Braceville, O., July 1, 1846; s. Morgan Lewis and Jane (Brokaw) B.; student Med. Dept. U. of Mich., 1868-69, Western Reserve, 1874-75; hon. A.M., Hiram Coll., 1894; m. Alice L. Allen, May 1, 1879. Librarian, Cleveland Pub. Library, 1884—; dean, Western Reserve Library Sch., 1903—. Pres. A.L.A., 1897, Ohio Library Assn., 1895-96; chmn. Trans-Mississippi Library Congress, 1898. Editor: Cumulative Index, 1896-97. Home: Cleveland, O. Died 1918.

BREVOORT, James Renwick, artist; b. Westchester County, N.Y., July 20, 1832; studied in U.S. and Europe; spent several yrs. sketching scenes in England, Holland and Italy; prof. perspective, Nat. Acad. Design, 1872-75. Specialty was landscape work. A.N.A., 1861, N.A., 1863. Home: Yonkers, N.Y. Died Dec. 15, 1918.

BREWER, Abraham T., lawyer; b. Monroe County, O., Sept. 20, 1841; s. Abraham and Mary (Mitchell) B.; ed. Indiana County, Pa., and Harlem Springs Coll., 1865-66; LL.B., Ohio State Law Coll.; LL.D., Harlem Springs; m. Clara Genella Tagg, Nov. 21, 1900. Served over 3 yrs. in 61st Pa. Vols. in Civil War; seriously wounded at battle of Fair Oaks. Admitted to bar, 1869. Author: Ohio Corporations, 5 editions, 1884-1903; How to Make the Sunday School Go, 1897; True War Stories, 1907; History of Sixty-First Pennsylvania Volunteers, 1911; Fond Retrospect, 1916; Busy Decades, 1923. Home: Cleveland, O. Died Apr. 17, 1933.

BREWER, Charles S(now), corp. official; b. Canton, N.Y., July 30, 1870; s. Sheldon and Emily B.; B.A., St. Lawrence U., 1891, LL.D.; m. Helen J. Marsh, Nov. 5, 1902; children—Sheldon M., Margaret S. (Mrs. Keith C. Spears), Emily S. Began as salesman, Standard Furniture Co., 1893, sec., 1895-1921, also treas., 1910-21, pres., 1921—; chmn. bd. Mohawk Hudson Power Corp., 1924-29; pres. Bond Foley Lumber Co.; dir. Utica Gas & Electric Co. Episcopalian. Home: Utica, N.Y. Died Jan. 9, 1934.

BREWER, Clara Tagg, educator, editor; b. Greenville, Pa.; d. Rev. John Heighton and Laura Ann (Lillie) Tagg; grad. Cleveland Normal Sch., 1878; m. Abraham T. Brewer, Nov. 21, 1900. Prin. South Case Sch., Cleveland, 1890-1900; inst. lecturer, 1895-1900; editor The Epworth Outlook, 1908—. Mem.

Bd. of Edn., City of Cleveland, 1917-34. Republican. Methodist. Home: Cleveland, O. Died Jan. 1934.

BREWER, D(aniel) Chauncey, lawyer; b. Boston, Sept. 14, 1861; s. Daniel Chauncey and Mary Ada (Turpin) B.; A.B., Williams, 1886, LL.B., Boston U., 1883; post-grad. Princeton, 1887; m. Genevieve Withrow, Oct. 18, 1888; children—Daniel Chauncey (dec.), Katherine Chauncey (dec.), John Withrow, Genevieve Eunice. Admitted to bar, 1888, and practiced at Boston. Trustee, dir. or officer, in public service, religious (and ednl.) corps.; pres. N. Am. Civic League for Immigrants; mem. immigration com. Nat. Civic Federation; temp. chmn. N.E. Tercentenary Com. Mem. Mass. Com. on Pub. Safety, World War; exec. com. Citizens of Foreign Birth Liberty Loan Com. of N.E.; mem. Mass. Constabulary Commn., 1916; chief, foreign-speaking soldier sect. of Gen. Staff, U.S.A., 1917-18; pres. Order and Liberty Alliance; mem. exec. com. Mass. br. League for Preservation of Am. Independence; mem. Com. Mass. Tercentenary. Author: Rights and Duties of Neutrals, 1916; The Peril of the Republic, 1922; Conquest of New England by the Immigrant, 1926. Home: Boston, Mass. Died July 30, 1932.

BREWER, David Josiah, jurist; b. Smyrna, Asia Minor, June 20, 1837; s. Rev. Josiah and Emilia (Field) B.; nephew late Justice Stephen J. Field; A.B., Yale, 1856, A.M., 1859; LL.B., Albany Law Sch., 1858; LL.D., U. of Ia., 1884, Washburn Coll., 1888, Yale, 1891, U. of Wis., 1900. Wesleyan, 1901, U. of Vt., 1904, Bowdoin, 1905; m. Louise R. Landon, Oct. 3, 1861 (died 1898); 2d, Emma Miner Mott, June 5, 1901. Began practice, Leavenworth, Kan., 1859; U.S. commr., 1861-62; judge probate and criminal courts, Leavenworth Co., 1863-64; judge Dist. Ct., 1865-69; co. atty., 1869-70; justice Supreme Ct. Kan., 1870-84, U.S. circuit judge, 1884-89; asso. justice Supreme Court of U.S., 1889—. Mem. Venezuelan Boundary Commn., 1896; mem. British-Venezuelan Arbitration Tribunal, 1899. Prof. corp. law, George Washington U. Pres. Universal Congress of Lawyers and Jurists, La. Purchase Expn., St. Louis, 1904. Author: The Pew to the Pulpit, 1897; The Twentieth Century from Another View Point, 1899; American Citizenship, 1902; The United States a Christian Nation, 1905. Address: Washington, D.C. Died 1910.

BREWER, Franklin Nourse, gen. mgr. The John Wanamaker Store; b. Holliston, Mass., May 11, 1864; s. Rufus Franklin and Charlotte Maria (Clisby) B.; ed. pub. schs. and Bordentown (N.J.) Mil. Inst.; m. Julia Billings Root, Jan. 25, 1905; children—Franklin N., Rosemary Payne, Julia Root, Eugene Clisby. Began with John Wanamaker Store, 1876, gen. mgr., 1896—. Dir. Pa. Com. on Penal Affairs. Republican. Presbyn. Home: Moylan, Delaware County, Pa. Died Dec. 16, 1935.

BREWER, George (Allen), clergyman; b. Kingston, Ont., Can.; s. George Clark and Frances Elizabeth (Guess) B.; came to U.S., 1890; student Calif. Coll., 1898, Wooster U., 1902, McCormick Theol. Sem., 1903; grad. Princeton Theol. Sem., 1905; D.D., Alma Coll. (Mich.), 1920; LL.D., Washington College (Tenn.), 1935; m. Frances Alice Glenn, May 27, 1905. Ordained Presbyn. ministry, 1905; pastor First Ch., Columbus, O., 1905-09, First Ch., Coshocton, O., 1909-13, Holland Memorial Ch., Phila., Pa., 1914-15, First Ch., Duluth, Minn., 1915-20, Grosse Pointe Memorial (Presbyn.) Ch., Detroit, Mich., 1921-28, 1st Ch., Piqua, O., 1928—. Lecturer to college students under direction Presbyn. Bd. of Edn.; lecturer under Minn. Commn., World War. Trustee Cedarville College. Author: Daily Devotion, 1919, 1920; The Unfinished Task (patriotic), 1922; Living Messages, 1926; Preachers and Preaching in Detroit, 1926; also (pamphlets) Jesus Christ and the Teachings of Christian Science, 1916; Robert Burns, 1918; Christ's Supremacy, 1926. Home: Piqua, O. Died Feb. 3, 1939.

BREWER, George Emerson, surgeon; b. Westfield, N.Y., July 28, 1861; s. Francis B. and Susan H. (Rood) B.; A.B., Hamilton Coll., 1881, A.M., 1884, LL.D., 1916; M.D., Harvard U., 1885; hon. D.Sc., Columbia U., 1929; m. Effie Leighton Brown, June 29, 1893. Consulting surgeon to Muhlenberg Hosp., Plainfield, N.J., Perth Amboy (N.J.) Hosp., Presbyn., Roosevelt, Woman's St. Vincent's, St. Bartholomay's, City hosps., Ophthalmic and Aural Inst., House of the Holy Comforter, all of New York; asst. demonstrator anatomy, Coll. Phys. and Surg. (Columbia U.), 1892-1900, instr. surgery, 1900-03, clinical lecturer, 1903-04, prof. clinical surgery, 1904-13, prof. surgery, 1913-17, emeritus. Col. Med. Corps U.S.A.; dir. U.S.A. Base Hosp. No. 2 (No. 1 Gen. Hosp. B.E.F.), Etretat, France; later chief surg. consultant, 1st Corps, 1st Army, A.E.F.; officier de l'Ordre de la Couronne (Belgium). Research asso. Somatic anthropology, Am. Mus. Natural History, N.Y. City. Home: New York, N.Y. Died Dec. 24, 1939.

BREWER, John Hyatt, organist; b. Brooklyn, Jan. 18, 1856; s. William and Annie E. B.; vocal pupil of Walter, Cutler and Wilder; learned pianoforte and harmony of Rafael Navarro, organ of Diller, Whiteley, Caulfield; organ harmony, composition, 10 yrs. under Dudley Buck; hon. Doctor of Music, New York U., 1916; m. Emma A. Thayer, June 27, 1888; m. 2d, Cornelia K. Kouwenhoven, July 9, 1921. Organist City Park Chapel, 1871-73, Ch. of the Messiah, 1873-77, Clinton Av. Congl. Ch., 1877-81, Lafayette Av. Presbyn. Ch., 1881—. Has conducted Brooklyn Hill, Orpheus, Damrosch and Boylston glee clubs, Brooklyn Apollo Club, etc. Co-founder, fellow and warden, 1905-08, Am. Guild Organists. Republican. Presbyn. Home: Brooklyn, N.Y. Died Nov. 30, 1931.

BREWER, Leigh Richmond, bishop; b. Berkshire, Vt., Jan. 20, 1839; s. Sheldon S. and Lura (Cramton) B.; A.B., Hobart Coll., 1863, A.M., 1866; grad. Gen. Theol. Sem., 1866; S.T.D., Hobart, 1881, Racine, 1881; m. Henrietta W. Foote, July 10, 1866. Deacon, 1866, priest, 1867, P.E. Ch.; rector Grace Ch., Carthage, N.Y., 1866-72, Trinity Ch., Watertown, N.Y., 1872-80; consecrated missionary bishop of Mont., 1880. Address: Helena, Mont. Died Aug. 28, 1916.

BREWER, Luther Albertus, publisher; b. Welsh Run, Pa., Dec. 17, 1858; s. Jacob and Kate (Brewer) B.; A.B., Pa. Coll., Gettysburg, 1883, A.M., 1886; m. Elinore Taylor, Feb. 3, 1898. Settled in Cedar Rapids, July 1884; entered newspaper work, 1887, with Republican Printing Co., eventually acquiring the property, and selling it 1922; dir. Am. Trust & Savings Bank. State oil insp. of Ia., 1893-97; del. Rep. State Convs.; del. at large Rep. Nat. Conv., Chicago, 1912, 1916. Mem. bd. dirs. Cedar Rapids Auditorium Co., Cedar Rapids Art Assn., Free Pub. Library. Author: History of Linn County, Iowa, 1910. Home: Cedar Rapids, Ia. Died May 6, 1933.

BREWER, Mark Spencer, U.S. civil service commr.; b. Addison Tp., Oakland County, Mich., Oct. 22, 1837; lived on father's farm until 20 years of age; academic edn.; began study of law, 1861; admitted to bar, 1864; practiced at Pontiac, Mich.; circuit court commr. and city atty. of Pontiac, 1866-70; State senator, 1873-74; mem. Congress, 1877-81, and 1887-91, declining renomination; consul general, Berlin, Germany, 1881-85; U.S. civil service commr., 1898—. Address: Washington, D.C. Died 1901.

BREWER, Robert Paine, banker; b. Muskogee, Okla., Dec. 3, 1876; s. Theodore F. and Mary W. B.; A.B., Southwestern U., 1896; m. Lucile Barnett, Jan. 23, 1901; children—Elizabeth, Robert P. Organized First Nat. Bank of Checotah, Okla., 1898, and served as pres.; cashier and pres. First Nat. Bank, Quinton, 1902-08; pres. First Nat. Bank, McAlester, 1908-16; sr. v.p. Commerce Trust Co., Kansas City, Mo., 1916-21; pres. and chmn. bd. Exchange Nat. Bank, Tulsa, Okla., 1921-24; pres. First Nat. Bank, Tulsa, 1924-29; v.p. and dir. Chatham Phenix Nat. Bank & Trust Co., New York, 1929—; dir. Kans., Okla. & Gulf Ry., Kansas City Life Ins. Co. Democrat. Methodist. Mason (32°, Shriner). Address: New York, N.Y. Died June 14, 1933.

BREWER, William Henry, univ. prof.; b. Poughkeepsie, N.Y., Sept. 14, 1828; s. Henry B.; Ph.B., Yale, 1852, A.M., 1859; student Heidelberg, Munich, Paris; Ph.D., Washington and Jefferson, 1880; LL.D., Yale, 1903; m. Angelina Jameson, Aug. 15, 1858 (died 1860); m. 2d, Georgiana Robinson, Sept. 1, 1868 (died 1889). Prof. chemistry and geology, Washington Coll., Pa., 1858-60; 1st asst. on Geol. Survey of Calif., 1860-64; prof. chemistry, U. of Calif., 1863-64; prof. agr. Sheffield Scientific Sch. (Yale), 1864-1903, emeritus. Pres. Conn. Bd. of Health, 1892-1909; has served important govt. commns., such as topog. survey of Conn., on cereal production in U.S. (10th Census); U.S. Forestry Commn., 1896; Scientific Survey of the P.I., 1903, etc. Mem. Nat. Acad. Sciences. Author: Botany of California, 1875, etc. Home: New Haven, Conn. Died 1910.

BREWSTER, Benjamin, bishop; b. New Haven, Conn., Nov. 25, 1860; s. Rev. Joseph and Sarah Jane (Bunce) B.; A.B., Yale, 1882; B.D., Gen. Theol. Sem., New York, 1886; S.T.D., 1909; D.D., Bowdoin Coll., 1929; L.H.D., U. of Me., 1937; m. Stella Yates, June 10, 1891 (died 1929); children—Katrina Mynderse (Mrs. Edgar W. Anderson), Benjamin Yates, Josephine Stella (dec.), William, Stella Frances (Mrs. Arthur P. Spear, Jr.); m. 2d, Mrs. Mary Phillips Hay, Aug. 25, 1937. Deacon, 1886, priest, 1887, P.E. Ch.; asst. minister, Calvary Parish, New York, 1886-91; vicar Calvary Chapel, 1887-91; rector Ch. of Holy Communion, S. Orange, N.J., 1891-95, Grace Ch., Colorado Springs, Colo., 1895-1906; dean St. Mark's Cathedral, Salt Lake City, Utah, 1906-09; consecrated missionary bishop of Western Colo., June 17, 1909; bishop of Me., 1916—. Life mem. B.P.O.E. Address: Portland, Me. Died Feb. 2, 1941.

BREWSTER, Benjamin Harris, Jr., corp. official; b. Phila., Pa., Oct. 22, 1872; s. Benjamin Harris and Mary (Walker) B.; student Brown's Sch., Phila., Columbia Prep. Sch., Washington, D.C., William Penn Charter Sch., Phila., U. of Pa., 1891; m. Elizabeth Baugh, Oct. 22, 1894; children—Daniel Baugh (dec.), Nancy (Mrs. Francis White), Benjamin Harris, 3d. Entered employ of Baugh & Sons Co., Phila., 1892, sec. 1892-1901, v.p. 1901-28, pres. 1928—; pres. Baugh & Sons Co. (Baltimore), Baugh Chemical Co. (Baltimore), Baugh & Sons Co. of Ohio; chmn. exec. com. Union Trust Co. of Md.; dir. Davis Coal and Coke Co., Eutaw Savings Bank, Baltimore. Served as col. on staff of Gov. Goldsborough of Md. Vice-pres. bd. of trustees Sheppard & Enoch Pratt Hosp.; mem. advisory bd. Womens Hosp. of Md. Democrat. Episcopalian. Home: Stevenson, Md. Died Jan. 28, 1941.

BREWSTER, Chauncey Bunce, bishop; b. Windham, Conn., Sept. 5, 1848; s. Rev. Joseph and Sarah Jane (Bunce) B.; A.B., Yale U., 1868, A.M., 1871; D.D., Trinity, 1897, Yale U., 1898, Wesleyan, 1903; m. Susan Huntington Whitney, Oct. 15, 1873 (died 1885); m. 2d, Alice Tucker Stephenson, June 20, 1893 (died 1932); 1 dau., Eleanor Longfellow. Ordained deacon, 1872, priest, 1873, Protestant Episcopal Church; rector of Christ Church, Rye, N.Y., 1873-81, Christ Ch., Detroit, 1881-85, Grace Ch., Baltimore, 1885-88, Grace Ch., Brooklyn, 1888-97; consecrated coadjutor bishop, Conn., 1897, bishop, 1899, resigned, 1928. Author: Key of Life—Good Friday Addresses, 1894; Aspects of Revelation, 1901; The Catholic Ideal of the Church, 1905; The Kingdom of God and American Life, 1912. Home: Hartford, Conn. Died Apr. 9, 1941.

BREWSTER, Edward Lester, broker; b. Brockport, N.Y., 1842; s. Frederick W. and Jeannette (Downs) B.; ed. Brockport Collegiate Inst.; m. Mary Niles. Left school at 15, became clerk in dry goods store, Brockport, 1 yr.; then in ins. office, Buffalo, attending night course in commercial coll.; located at Chicago, 1860; employe banking house, 1860-68; wholesale grocer, 1868-72; mem. Wrenn & Brewster, bankers and brokers, 1872-76; sr. mem. firm of Edward L. Brewster & Co., 1876-1904; spl. partner Russell, Brewster & Co., 1904—. Home: Chicago, Ill. Died 1911.

BREWSTER, Eugene Valentine, author, editor, author's representative; b. Bay Shore, N.Y., Sept. 7, 1871; s. Henry D. and Clotilda T. (Smith) B.; collegiate edn.; m. Emilie C. Churbuck, May 10, 1893; m. 2d, Eleanor V. V. Cator, Dec. 27, 1916; m. 3d, Corliss Palmer, Oct. 27, 1926; m. 4th, Liane Hill, Mar. 22, 1935. Practiced law, Brooklyn, 1894-1910; Dem. campaign speaker and writer; lecturer; editor of The Caldron, 1908-13; legal editor of daily column in Brooklyn Eagle, 1 yr.; editor Motion Picture Mag., 1911-26, also Motion Picture Classic, Movie Monthly, Beauty, and Shadowland; editor and pub. Screen Tattler until 1927; later pres. Brewster Labs. Painter for exhbn., 1919-22, 1922-24; wrote and directed various motion pictures, including Love's Redemption, The Eternal Two, In the Blood, Rose and Thistle. Author: Success Secrets; 100 Helps to Live 100 Years; What to do with the Trusts, 1906; What's What in America, 1920; The Passing of Woodrow Wilson, 1924; Napoleon, 1925; Tons of Gold, 1931; Jesus Comes to Hollywood, 1932; The Wisdom of the Ages, 1932; The Art of Judging a Play, 1933; The Ten Essentials for Successful Pictures, 1933; Surprise Party Murder, 1936; The Devil is Dead, 1937; also stage plays, Cobwebs, Peddlers Lane, The Devil's Playmate, White Lies, Now and Then. Home: Brooklyn, N.Y. Died Jan. 1, 1939.

BREWSTER, George Washington Wales, surgeon; b. Boston, Mar. 26, 1866; s. Benjamin and Annie W. (Emmons) B.; A.B., Harvard, 1889, M.D., 1893; m. Ellen M. Hodge, Nov. 11, 1902; children—Wm. Ledyard, George Washington Wales, Henry Hodge. Practiced in Boston, 1893; hon. surgeon, Mass. Gen. Hosp. Episcopalian. Address: Boston, Mass. Died 1939.

BREWSTER, Henry Colvin, banker; b. Rochester, N.Y., Sept. 7, 1845; s. Simon L. and Editha (Colvin) B.; pub. sch. edn.; m. Alice Chapin, Oct. 5, 1876. Clerk, Traders Nat. Bank, 1863-68, cashier, 1868-1894, pres., 1898—. Mem. 54th and 55th Congresses (1895-99), 31st N.Y. Dist. Address: Rochester, New York. Died Jan. 29, 1928.

BREWSTER, James Henry, lawyer; b. New Haven, Conn., Apr. 6, 1856; s. Rev. Joseph and Sarah Jane (Bunce) B.; Ph.B., Sheffield Scientific Sch. (Yale), 1877; LL.B., Yale, 1879; m. Frances Stanton, June 28, 1888. Practiced law, Detroit, 1883-97; prof. conveyancing, law dept., U. of Mich., 1897— (leave of absence, 1910—). Mem. Detroit Board of Edn., 1888-96; editor Michigan Law Review, 1903-12. Traveled through South America, 1907; lectured on S. American institutions and peoples before geog. socs. and at univs. Episcopalian. Democrat. Author: The Conveyance of Estates in Fee by Deed, 1904. Home: Denver, Colo. Died Oct. 7, 1920.

BREWSTER, Sardius Mason, lawyer; b. Brown County, Kan., June 19, 1870; s. Arthur S. and Anna H. (Byard) B.; student Highland (Kan.) Coll. 2 yrs.; A.B., Washburn Coll., Topeka, 1902, also LL.D.; m. Caroline Brown, Feb. 1, 1899 (dec.); children—Carol V. (Mrs. Fred Flecker), Arthur S., Madge (Mrs. Evan Morgan), G. M., Anna (Mrs. James Dolman); m. 2d, Elizabeth Noyes, May 2, 1921. Admitted to Kan. bar, 1896, and began practice at Troy; county atty. Doniphan County, Kan., 1899-1909; mem. Kan. Senate, 1909-13, Ho. of Rep., 1913-15; asst. atty. gen. of Kan., 1911-15, atty. gen., 1915-19; mem. firm Wheeler, Brewster & Hunt; U.S. dist. atty., Kan. Dist., 1930—. Republican. Presbyn. Home: Topeka, Kan. Died Mar. 5, 1936.

BREWSTER, William, ornithologist; b. Wakefield, Mass., July 5, 1851; grad. Cambridge High School, 1869; hon. A.M., Amherst, 1880, Harvard, 1899; m. Caroline F. Kettell, Feb. 9, 1878. Asst. in charge of collection birds and mammals, Boston Soc. Natural History, 1880-87; in charge dept. of mammals and birds, Cambridge Museum Comparative Zoölogy, 1885-1900, curator, dept. of birds, 1900—; most of his time devoted to managing private museum of ornithology at his place in Cambridge. Trustee Brewster Free Acad. Address: Cambridge, Mass. Died July 11, 1919.

BREWSTER, William Nesbitt, missionary; b. Highland, O., Dec. 5, 1862; s. Samuel A. and Rebecca (Nesbitt) B.; ed. Wittenberg College, Springfield, O., to end of sophomore yr.; B.A., Ohio Wesleyan U., 1883, D.D., 1908; B.D., Boston U. Sch. of Theology, 1886; m. Elizabeth Fisher, Oct. 28, 1890. Ordained M.E. ministry, 1888; went as missionary to Singapore, India, 1888; transferred to Hinghwa, China, 1890; instrumental in founding Hinghwa Annual Conf., with over 100 Chinese evangelists and pastors, and over 20,000 constituency. On furlough, 1913-14. Delivered course of lectures on missions, Boston U. Sch. of Theology, 1904. Acting prof. Chair of Missions, Boston U. Sch. of Theology, scholastic year, 1913-14. Author: The Evolution of New China, 1907; The Cost of Christian Conquest, 1908; The Methodist Man's Burden (pamphlet), 1913; The Dollar Against the Cross (pamphlet), 1914. Assisted in transl. of entire Bible into Hinghwa colloquial dialect, pub. in one volume, 1912. Home: Springfield, O. Died Nov. 22, 1916.

BREYFOGEL, Sylvanus Charles, bishop; b. Reading, Pa., July 20, 1851; s. Seneca and Sarah (Ely) B.; Ph.B., Ill. Wesleyan U.; D.D., Otterbein U., 1901; LL.D., Ohio Northern U., 1909; m. Kate Boas, May 8, 1877; children—Frank Ely, Mrs. G. B. Kimmel, Emily B., Mrs. R. K. Bowman, Mrs. G. E. Schnabel, Charles F. Ordained in ministry of Evangelical Ch., 1873; elected presiding elder, 1886; bishop, 1891—. Has preached in official Episcopal tours throughout U.S., Can., and Europe, and made tours of inspection of missionary fields of ch. in China, Japan and Russia; spoke frequently at summer assemblies, including Ocean Grove, Winona (Indiana) Assembly, chautauquas, etc. Pres. Commn. on Nat. Service; mem. Nat. Commn. Famine Relief; pres. Evang. Sch. of Theology; pres. bd. trustees Albright Coll., Reading, Pa.; gen. sec. Ministerial Pension Fund, Evang. Ch.; mem. exec. com. and administrative council, Federal Council Chs. of Christ in America. Republican. Author: Evangelical Landmarks; Digest of Laws of the Evangelical Church; Great Sermons by Great Preachers. Home: Reading, Pa. Died Nov. 24, 1934.

BRICK, Abraham Lincoln, congressman, lawyer; b. Warren Twp., St. Joseph's Co., Ind., May 27, 1860; ed. common schools, South Bend, Ind., and Cornell, Yale and U. of Mich., where he grad., 1883; mem. faculty law dept., U. of Notre Dame, Ind. (LL.B., M.L.); practiced law South Bend; pros. atty. St. Joseph's and La Porte Cos., Ind., 1886; mem. Rep. State Central Com., 1890; del. Rep. Nat. Conv., St. Louis, 1896; mem. Congress, 13th Ind. dist., 1899-1909. Home: South Bend, Ind. Died 1908.

BRICK, Nicholas William, educator; b. Ontario, Can., Aug. 8, 1861; s. Nicholas and Catherine (Miller) B.; grad. Hamilton Collegiate Inst., 1884; Normal Sch., Toronto, 1882; B.A., Queens U., Kingston, 1896; m. Helen O'Connell, July 24, 1894. Prin. grammar schs., Peterboro and Kingston, Can., until 1895; prof. Normal Sch., Ottawa, 1896, 1897; prin. Regiopolis Coll., Kingston, 1897-1906; came to U.S., 1906; propr. and prin. Calif. Mil. Acad., 1906—. Roman Catholic. Home: Los Angeles, Calif. Died Feb. 28, 1934.

BRICKELL, Robert Coman, judge; b. Tuscumbia, Ala., Apr. 4, 1824; ed. in common schools Athens, Ala.; studied law, admitted to bar, 1844; apptd. asso. justice supreme court of Ala., 1873, elected, Nov. 1874, and became chief justice; reëlected, Aug. 1880; resigned, Oct. 25, 1884, and engaged in practice until 1894, when he was again apptd. chief justice. Address: Montgomery, Ala. Died 1900.

BRICKNER, Walter M., surgeon; b. N.Y. City, Aug. 28, 1875; s. David and Sara M. (Ritterband) B.; B.S., Coll. City of N.Y., 1893; M.D., Coll. Phys. and Surg. (Columbia), 1896; m. Perla S. Abrahams, Apr. 28, 1903. Attending surgeon, Morrisania City Hosp., Hosp. for Joint Diseases; asso. surgeon, Mt. Sinai Hosp. Formerly lt. col. Med. Reserve Corps; chief of surg. service, 1918, Base Hosp. 3 and consultant in neurosurgery, Base Sect. 2, A.E.F. Author: The Surgical Assistant, 1905; 1000 Surgical Suggestions, 1911. Editor in chief Am. Jour. Surgery, 1905-28. Home: New York, N.Y. Died 1930.

BRIDE, William Witthaft, lawyer; b. Washington, D.C., Sept. 9, 1881; s. Cotter T. and Louise Henrietta (Witthaft) B.; LL.B., Georgetown U., 1904; studied Columbian Coll. (now George Washington U.) and U. of Neb.; m. Lula Mae Fairbanks, Mar. 14, 1905; children—Mrs. Dorothy Fairbanks Felix, Mrs. Adelaide Witthaft Kenny, William Witthaft, Noel Crawford. Practiced in Washington, D.C., 1905—; counsel in charge pecuniary claims arbitration between Great Britain and U.S., 1914-15; counsel to foreign trade adviser Dept. of State, 1915 (resigned June 1915); went to England, June 1915, and procured concession from British and allied powers permitting passage through blockade of all goods of German and Austrian origin which were purchased or ordered prior to Mar. 1, 1915; corporation counsel of D.C. and gen. counsel Pub. Utilities Commn. of D.C. Served as col., staff of gov. of Neb.; mem. Inaugural Com. of President Wilson, 1913 and 1917; of President Hoover, 1929; of President Roosevelt, 1933; mem. Com. of 100 for Development of Washington, D.C.; former consul of Rumania. Decorated by King Ferdinand with the Order of the Star of Rumania, by King Mihai with Order of Crown of Rumania, rank of commander, and by President Masaryk of Czechoslovakia with Comdr. Order of the White Lion. Capt. U.S.A. Mil. Intelligence Div., Gen. Staff. Home: Washington, D.C. Died Feb. 26, 1935.

BRIDGE, James Howard, author; b. Manchester, Eng., May 8, 1856; s. Richard and Margaret (Bibby) B.; ed. Grand Lycée, Marseilles (Université de France), 1877; married; 1 dau., Margery (Mrs. John Denison Champlin, III); m. 2d, Clara Blake, June 2, 1913; 1 dau., Cornelia. Engaged in newspaper work in Eng.; pvt. sec. to Herbert Spencer, 1879-84; came to U.S., 1884; literary asst. to Andrew Carnegie, 1884-89; editor Overland Monthly, 1896-1900; editor Commerce and Industry, New York, N.Y., 1902-03. Curator of Frick Art Collection, 1914-1928. Inventor, patentee Howard Bridge system of water purification by electricity. Author: A Fortnight in Heaven, 1886; Uncle Sam at Home, 1888; The Trust—Its Book, 1902; History of Carnegie Steel Co., 1903; Ozone Treatment of Public Water Supplies, 1905; Ozone—Its Nature, Production and Uses, 1907; Purification of Public Water Supplies, 1908; Portraits and Personalities in the Frick Galleries, 1929; Millionaires and Grub Street—Comrades and Contacts in the Last Half Century, 1931. Co-editor of Liber Scriptorum, Second, 1919-21. Home: Scarsdale, N.Y. Died May 28, 1939.

BRIDGE, Norman, physician; b. Windsor, Vt., Dec. 30, 1844; s. James Madison and Nancy Ann (Bagley) B.; M.D., Chicago Med. Coll. (now med. dept. Northwestern U.), 1868, Rush Med. Coll., Chicago, 1878; hon. A.M., Lake Forest U., 1889; LL.D., Occidental, 1920, U. of Calif., 1922; ScD., Northwestern U., 1923; m. Mae Manford, May 21, 1874. Prof. clinical medicine, Rush Med. Coll. (U. of Chicago), 1887-98, prof. medicine, 1898-1901, emeritus prof., 1901—. Mem. Chicago Bd. Edn., 1881-84 (pres., 1882-83); mem. bd. election commrs., 1886-90. Republican. Author: The Penalties of Taste and Other Essays, 1898; The Rewards of Taste and Other Essays, 1902; Lectures on Tuberculosis, 1903; House Health, 1907; Fragments and Addresses, 1915; The Marching Years (autobiographical), 1920; Mental Therapeutics and Other Papers, 1922; also 46 papers on med. and cognate subjects in med. jours. and books. For several years retired from practice and engaged in petroleum business as v.p. Pan Am. Petroleum & Transport Co. and allied cos. Chmn. Nat. Alien Enemy Relief Com., Washington, during World War. Home: Chicago, Ill.; and Los Angeles, Calif. Died Jan. 10, 1925.

BRIDGES, Calvin Blackman, geneticist; b. Schuyler Falls, N.Y., Jan. 11, 1889; s. Leonard Victor and Amelia C. (Blackman) B.; B.S., Columbia, 1912, Ph.D., 1916; m. Gertrude Frances Ives, Sept. 7, 1912; children—Philip Newell, Norman Ives (dec.), Betsy Blackman, Nathan Ives. Research work in heredity under grants from Carnegie Instn., 1915-19; mem. staff, Carnegie Instn., 1919—. Mem. Nat. Acad. Sciences. Atheist. Author: The Mechanism of Mendelian Heredity, 1915; Sex-linked Inheritance in Drosophila (with T. H. Morgan), 1916; Contributions to the Genetics of Drosophila Melanogaster (with same), 1919, 23; Genetics of Drosophila, 1925. Home: Leonia, N.J. Died Dec. 27, 1938.

BRIDGES, Edson Lowell, educator; b. 1874; M.D., U. of Neb., 1896. Practiced at Omaha, Neb., 1897—; was prof. medicine, U. of Neb., also chmn. dept. Home: Omaha, Neb. Died Dec. 4, 1934.

BRIDGES, Fidelia, artist; b. Salem, Mass., May 19, 1835; d. Henry Gardner and Eliza (Chadwick) Bridges; removed to Brooklyn, 1854, and to Phila., 1859, where studied art under William T. Richards; unmarried. Has painted and exhibited many noteworthy landscapes; earlier work principally in oil, later work mostly in water colors. A.N.A., 1869. Home: Canaan, Conn. Died May 1923.

BRIDGES, James Robertson, clergyman, editor; b. St. Louis, Mo., Sept. 29, 1852; s. James Robertson and Mary (Dandridge) B.; A.B., Hampden-Sidney Coll., Va. (D.D.); grad. Union Theol. Sem. in Va., 1880; m. Ann MacGill Bridges, Sept. 17, 1885; children—Helen Venable, James Robertson, Robert Armstrong, Edwin Breathed, Mary Dandridge. Ordained Presbyn. ministry, 1880; evangelist in Ky. and Tex. until 1883; stated supply, Mission Chapel, Baltimore, Md., 1883-85; pastor Leesburg, Va., 1885-89, Salem, Va., 1889-95, Columbia, Mo., 1895-98, Orlando, Fla., 1898-99; pres. Presbyn. Coll. for Women, Charlotte, N.C., 1899-1911; editor Presbyn. Standard, 1911—. Democrat. Home: Charlotte, N.C. Died July 19, 1930.

BRIDGES, Jesse B., judge; b. Putnam County, Ind., Nov. 10, 1862; s. James and Mary (Darnell) B.; A.B., DePauw U., 1885; m. Mary L. Smith, June 26, 1895. Practiced law at Indianapolis, Ind., 1887-90; moved to Aberdeen, Wash., 1891; pros. atty., Grays Harbor Co., Wash.; justice Supreme Court of Wash., 1919—. Republican. Universalist. Home: Olympia, Wash. Died Apr. 14, 1927.

BRIDGES, Milton Arlanden, M.D.; b. New York, N.Y., May 20, 1894; s. Arlanden Clay and Emily Madelaine (Lawler) B.; B.S., Columbia, 1915, M.D., 1919; m. Marie Cecelia Trautwine, Dec. 15, 1927; children—Robert Arlanden, Milton Doane. Practiced medicine in N.Y. City, 1918—; interne N.Y. Post-Grad. Hosp., 1918-20, resident phys., 1920-22; chief of med. clinic, Ruptured and Crippled Hosp., 1922-25; chief of metabolic clinic, N.Y. Post-Grad. Hosp., 1922-26, of diagnostic clinic, 1926—; asst. prof. medicine, 1935—, and lecturer in therapeutics, 1922—, N.Y. Post-Grad. Med. Sch. (Columbia), asst. attending phys., 1934-37, asso. attending physician, 1937—; dir. of medicine, Dept. of Correction Hospitals (sec. med. bd.); cons. phys. Sea View Hospital, Staten Island, N.Y.; practice limited to internal medicine. Republican. Episcopalian. Mason. Author: Dietetics for the Clinician, 3d edit., 1937; Food and Beverage Analysis, 1935. Home: New York, N.Y. Died Aug. 19, 1939.

BRIDGES, Robert ("Droch"), editor, author; b. Shippensburg, Pa., July 13, 1858; s. John and Mary B.; A.B., Princeton, 1879, A.M., 1882, Litt.D., 1919; hon. Litt.D., Columbia, 1924. Reporter Rochester Democrat and Chronicle, 1880; asst. news editor New York Evening Post, 1881-87; asst. editor Scribner's Mag., 1887-1914, editor same, 1914-30; lit. adviser, dir. Charles Scribner's Sons to 1939. Lit. critic, Life, 1883-1900. Mem. Nat. Inst. Arts and Letters. Author: Overheard in Arcady, 1894; Suppressed Chapters, 1895; Bramble Brae (collected poems), 1902. Edited, with introduction, The Roosevelt Book, 1904. Home: Shippensburg, Pa. Died Sept. 2, 1941.

BRIDGMAN, Frederic Arthur, artist; b. Tuskegee, Ala., Nov. 10, 1847; apprentice in engraving dept. Am. Bank Note Co., New York, 1864-65; meanwhile studied in Brooklyn Art. Sch. and Nat. Acad. Design; pupil under J. L. Gérôme at the École des Beaux Arts, Paris, 1866-71; had studio in Paris, occasionally visiting New York. Painter of figure and of oriental and archæol. pictures; 1st and 2d class medals, Paris and Continental Exhibits, hors concours; Officier Légion d'Honneur, France; Officer Order St. Michael of Bavaria. N.A., 1881. Author: Winters in Algeria; and, in French, Anarchy in Art; Vers l'Idéal. Composer of orchestral music. Address: Lyons-la-Forêt, Eure, France. Died Jan. 13, 1928.

BRIDGMAN, Herbert Lawrence, journalist; b. Amherst, Mass., May 30, 1844; s. Richard Baxter and Mary (Nutting) B.; A.B., Amherst Coll., 1866, A.M., 1869, hon. LL.D., 1920; m. Helen Bartlett, Sept. 7, 1887. In journalism, 1864—. Historian Peary Auxiliary Expdn., 1894; asst. to Prof. Libbey in scaling Mesa Encantada, N.M., 1897; in command Peary auxiliary expdns., S.S. Diana, 1899, and S.S. Erik, 1901; del. of U.S., Nat. Geog. Soc., Peary Arctic, Explorers and Arctic clubs, to Internat. Congress for Study of Polar Regions, Brussels, Belgium, Sept. 1906; U.S. del. Internat. Polar Commn., Brussels, 1908, Rome, 1913; lecturer, New York Bd. Edn., 1895—. Chevalier Order of Leopold II, 1908; Officer Order of St. Alexander (Bulgaria). Author: The Sudan-Africa from Sea to Center, 1905. Home: Brooklyn, N.Y. Died Sept. 24, 1924.

BRIDGMAN, Howard Allen, educator; b. Northampton, Mass., Aug. 20, 1860; s. Sidney E. and Harriet (Phelps) B.; A.B., Amherst, 1883; student Hartford Theol. Sem., 1884-85; B.D., Yale Div. Sch., 1887; D.D., Oberlin, 1908; m. Helen North Bryant, July 27, 1898; children—Harriet, Edwin, Marion, Howard Allen. Prin. high sch., Granby, Mass., 1883-84; asso. editor, The Congregationalist, 1887-89, mng. editor, 1889-1911, editor in chief, 1911-21; prin. Lawrence Acad., Groton, Mass., 1922-25; headmaster Bridgman Sch., Shirley Center, Mass., 1925—. Am. corr. Toronto New Outlook. Ordained Congl. ministry, Nov. 19, 1890. Republican. Author: Steps Christward, 1903; Real Religion, 1910; New England in the Life of the World, 1920. Home: Shirley Center, Mass. Died Mar. 16, 1929.

BRIDGMAN, Lewis Jesse, author; b. Lawrence, Mass., Nov. 17, 1857; s. William Hall and Martha Hannah (Neal) B.; A.B., Harvard, 1881; m. Lucy Stanwood Blanchard, Nov. 8, 1883 (died 1892); children—Blanchard (dec.), Neal; m. 2d, Annie Page Campbell, June 7, 1893; children—Marjorie (Mrs. J. H. Capps, dec.), Hugh. Pres. First Nationalist Club, of Boston, 1892-93; del. People's Party Nat.

Conv., Omaha, 1892; now Republican. Was mem. sch. bd. of Salem 16 yrs. (v.p., 1920-21). Author: (and illustrator) Odd Business, 1893; Mother Wild Goose, 1900; Guess, 1901; Gulliver's Bird Book, 1902; Guess Again, 1902; Bridgman's Kewts, 1902; Lawsonized Lyrics, 1905; Seem-So's, 1906; The Santa Claus Club, 1907; 'Fraid Cat., 1909; The Guess Book of Riddles, 1929. Home: Salem, Mass. Died May 2, 1931.

BRIDGMAN, Raymond Landon, author; b. Amherst, Mass., Sept. 26, 1848; s. Richard Baxter and Mary (Nutting) B.; A.B., Amherst, 1871; grad. course Yale, 2 yrs.; m. Mary A. M. Williams, Jan. 6, 1880. Newspaper corr., 1871—; lecturer. Author: Ten Years of Massachusetts, 1888; Biennial Elections, 1896; The Master Idea, 1899; Loyal Traitors, 1903; World Organization, 1905; The Passing of the Tariff, 1909; The First Book of World Law, 1911. History of the Massachusetts Constitutional Convention of 1917, 1923. First series lecturer on "world politics," Mass. Agrl. Coll. Home: Auburndale, Mass. Died Feb. 20, 1925.

BRIER, Warren Judson, author; b. Baraboo, Wis., Nov. 22, 1850; s. Burgess Buell and Rachel (Clark) B.; attended Baraboo high sch. and Collegiate Inst.; U. of Wis., 1874-75; m. Pamelia E. Crawford, 1872 (died 1884); children—May Belle (dec.), Bessie Buell (dec.); m. 2d, Marion L. Royce, 1886; children—Warren Royce, Howard Maxwell. Prin. Plymouth high sch., 1875-86; city supt. Baraboo, 1886-89; pres. Wis. Teachers' Assn., 1895; inst. conductor, State Normal Sch., River Falls, Wis., 1889-98, pres., 1898-1909; head of English dept., Everett (Wash.) High Sch., 1912-24. Author: Mr. Maple and Mr. Pine; (dramas) A Soldier of Fortune; Jedediah Judkins; (with D. L. Hennessey) Twenty-Five Lessons in Citizenship. Home: Seattle, Wash. Died Mar. 26, 1929.

BRIESEN, Arthur von, lawyer; b. Borkendorf, Germany, July 11, 1843; s. Richard and Adeline (Bandtke) von B.; ed. Prussian Gymnasium, Hohenstein, 1852-54, Braunsberg, 1855-56, by pvt. tutor, 1856-58; came to New York, 1858; LL.B., New York U., 1868, LL.D., 1913; m. Anna Goepel, Oct. 22, 1873. Sergt. Co. B, 1st N.Y. Vol. Engrs., 1861-64; on staff Scientific American, 1864-72; admitted to bar, 1868; mem. firm Briesen & Schrenk. Pres. Legal Aid Soc., 1890-1916, Nat. Alliance of Legal Aid Socs. of U.S., 1912—; mem. Com. of Seventy, 1894; pres. Citizens' Union, 1896, German-Am. McKinley and Roosevelt League, 1900; chmn. New York Roosevelt League, 1904, Ellis Island investigating com., 1903. Mentioned in President's annual message to Congress, 1903. Del. Universal Congress Lawyers and Jurists, St. Louis, 1904. Decorated with Cross Legion of Honor by French Govt., 1905; Order of the Crown, Germany, 1907. Home: New York, N.Y. Died May 13, 1920.

BRIGGS, Arthur Hyslop, supt. anti-saloon league; b. San Francisco, Calif., 1858; s. Martin Clock and Ellen (Green) B.; A.B., Northwestern U., 1881, A.M., 1883; S.T.B., Boston U. Sch. of Theology, 1887; studied U. of Berlin and London Library; D.D., Northwestern U., 1899; m. Edna Iliff, June 26, 1897. Ordained M.E. ministry, 1887; pastorates at San Francisco, Vallejo, San Jose, Grace Ch., Denver; pres. Iliff Sch. of Theology, Denver, 1897-1900; pastor Central Ch., San Francisco, 1901-04; state supt. for Calif. of Anti-Saloon League, 1921—; editor California Liberator, 1919—; mem. Nat. Board of Strategy, 1931. Trustee Coll. of the Pacific. Republican. Home: Los Gatos, Calif. Died Oct. 29, 1934.

BRIGGS, Charles, mining man; b. Cincinnatus, N.Y., Nov. 12, 1837; s. Isaac Samson and Mary (Smith) B.; ed. pub. and pvt. schs. and Homer (N.Y.) Acad.; m. Sarah E. Hanna, July 26, 1865. Mem. firm North & Briggs, Calumet and Hancock, Mich., 1868-76; propr. Calumet store, 1876-1908; pres. Merchants & Miners Bank, 1873-1923; pres. 20 yrs., Calumet & Ariz. Mining Co., New Cornelia Mining Co. (retired). Mem. Mich. Ho. of Rep., 1879-80; mem. bd. dirs. pub. schs. of Calumet, 1879-1909, sec. 5 yrs., pres. 10 yrs. Republican. Conglist. Home: Cleveland, O. Died Jan. 18, 1923.

BRIGGS, Charles Augustus, theologian; b. New York, Jan. 15, 1841; s. Alanson and Sarah Mead (Berrian) B.; studied U. of Va., 1857-60, Union Theol. Sem., 1861-63, U. of Berlin, 1866-69; D.D., Princeton, 1875, Edinburgh, 1884, Williams, 1894, Glasgow, 1901; D.Litt., Oxford, 1901; m. Julia Valentine Dobbs, Oct. 19, 1865. Ordained Presbyn. ministry, 1870; pastor Roselle, N.J., 1870-74; prof. Hebrew and cognate langs., Union Theol. Sem., 1875-1900. Bibl. theology, 1890-1904, theol. ency. and symbolics, 1904—. Tried for heresy, 1892, and acquitted by Presbytery of New York, but suspended by Gen. Assembly, 1893; became deacon, 1899, priest, 1900, P.E. Ch. Editor Presbyterian Review, 1880-90. Author: Biblical Study; American Presbyterianism; Messianic Prophecy; Whither? A Theological Question for the Times; The Authority of Holy Scripture; The Higher Criticism of the Hexateuch; The Bible, the Church and the Reason; The Messiah of the Apostles; The Messiah of the Gospels; The Case of Dr. Briggs, 3 parts; General Introduction to the Study of Holy Scripture; The Incarnation of the Lord; New Light on the Life of Jesus; Ethical Teachings of Jesus; Commentary on the Psalms; Church Unity; New Hebrew Lexicon (with Francis Brown and S. R. Driver); The Papal Commission and the Pentateuch (joint author), 1906. Editor: International Theological Library; International Critical Commentary. Address: New York, N.Y. Died June 8, 1913.

BRIGGS, Clare A., cartoonist; b. Reedsburg, Wis., Aug. 5, 1875; s. William Pardee and Ella (Stewart) B.; U. of Neb., 1894-96; m. Ruth Owen, July 18, 1900; children—Sarah Stewart (Mrs. R. A. Lewis, jr.), John Owen, Ruth Clare. Began as newspaper artist with St. Louis Globe Democrat, 1896; with St. Louis Chronicle, 1898, N.Y. World, 1898-99, N.Y. Journal, 1900, Chicago American and Examiner until 1907, Chicago Tribune, 1907-14, New York Tribune Syndicate, 1914—. Creator of "Skin-nay," "The Days of Real Sport," "When a Feller Needs a Friend," "Ain't It a Grand and Glorious Feeling," "Mr. and Mrs.," "Somebody is Always Taking the Joy Out of Life," "How to Start the Day Wrong," "There's at Least One in Every Office," "A Handy Man Around the House," "That Guiltiest Feeling," etc.; (books) The Days of Real Sport; When a Feller Needs a Friend (verse by W. D. Nesbit); Golf; Oh Man. Home: New York, N.Y. Died Jan. 3, 1930.

BRIGGS, Clay Stone, congressman; b. Galveston, Tex., Jan. 8, 1876; s. George Dempster and Olive (Branch) B.; student U. of Tex., 1894-95, Harvard, 1895-96; LL.B., Yale, 1899; m. Mrs. Lois Slayton Woodworth, Aug. 17, 1927. Began practice at Galveston, 1899; mem. Tex. Ho. of Rep., 1906-08; judge 10th Jud. Dist. of Texas, 3 terms, 1909-19; mem. 66th to 72d Congresses (1919-33), 7th Tex. Dist. Democrat. Episcopalian. Home: Galveston, Tex. Died Apr. 29, 1933.

BRIGGS, Edward Cornelius, M.D.; b. Lawrence, Mass., Sept. 6, 1856; s. Caleb Tucker and Emily Gray (Poore) B.; D.M.D., Harvard, 1878, M.D., 1880; m. Louise Lord, Nov. 17, 1885; children—Templeton, Dorothy (Mrs. Charles Wells Hubbard, Jr.); m. 2d, Ethel McClure, July 26, 1905. Practiced dentistry in Boston, 1878—; clin. instr., Harvard Dental Sch., 1880-83, instr. dental materia medica and therapeutics, 1883-89, asst. prof., 1889-95, prof., 1895-1915, prof. emeritus, 1915. Home: Chestnut Hill, Mass. Died Nov. 6, 1926.

BRIGGS, Frank Obadiah, senator; b. Concord, N.H., Aug. 12, 1851; s. James F. and Roxanna (Smith) B.; grad. U.S. Mil. Acad., 1872; m. Emily A. Allison, Sept. 23, 1874. Second lt. 2d U.S. Inf., 1872-77; resigned from army, Dec. 16, 1877. Began service with John A. Roebling's Sons Co., 1877, asst. treas., 1883—; mem. Trenton Sch. Bd., 1884-92; mayor Trenton, 1899-1902; mem. State Bd. Edn., 1901-02; state treas. N.J., 1902-07; elected U.S. senator, Feb. 5, 1907, for term 1907-13; chmn. Rep. State Com., 1904—. Sec. N.J. Wire Cloth Co. and official of other Roebling allied cos.; 1st v.p. Norfolk & Portsmouth Traction Co.; dir. Trenton Savings Fund Soc. Address: Trenton, N.J. Died May 8, 1913.

BRIGGS, Henry Birdice-Richmond, editor, pub.; b. Kalamazoo, Mich., Aug. 18, 1881; s. Henry Clay and Amanda Richmond (Hebard) B.; ed. pub. schs.; m. Mary Florence Dennis, Aug. 15, 1907; children—Reid Richmond, Colver Richmond, Deane Allerton, Alan Crawford. Successively with Kalamazoo Gazette, Saginaw News, Kalamazoo Telegraph, Detroit Tribune, Detroit News, Cleveland News and New York Journal, 1899-1908; editor Kalamazoo Telegraph, 1908-09; European corr. Newspaper Enterprise Assn., 1910, mng. editor, 1910-12; editor St. Paul Daily News, 1913-20, Denver Express, 1921-22, Cleveland Press, 1922-24; editor and pub. Los Angeles Record, 1925-32; asst. chmn. bd. Scripps-Canfield Newspapers, 1928-32; postmaster of Los Angeles, 1934—. Served as pvt. 33d Mich. Vol. Inf., Spanish-Am. War; invasion and occupation of Cuba, 1898. Author of "Brass Tacks," 1932; also various polit. and social essays, 1933-35. Editor The Postmaster's Gazette, official magazine of Nat. Assn. of Postmasters, 1934-35. Home: Los Angeles, Calif. Died Sept. 28, 1936.

BRIGGS, Henry Harrison, M.D.; b. Flag Pond, Tenn., Feb. 20, 1871; s. Adolphus Ervin and Margaret Matilda (Moore) B.; B.A., Tusculum Coll., Greeneville, Tenn., 1893, M.A., 1897; M.D., Yale, 1897; m. A. Lillian Briggs, 1900. Practiced at Asheville, N.C.; specialized in treatment of eye, ear, nose and throat. Trustee Tusculum Coll. Home: Asheville, N.C. Died Feb. 2, 1931.

BRIGGS, J(oseph) Emmons, surgeon; b. Dighton, Mass., Mar. 13, 1869; s. Albert and Sarah Jane (Simmons) B.; Bristol Academy, Taunton, Mass.; M.D., Boston U., 1890; post-grad. work U. of Vienna; m. Carrie A. Moore, Sept. 20, 1893 (died 1900); m. 2d, Flora A. Toulmin, Sept. 10, 1903. Began practice at Boston, 1890; prof. surgery, Boston U. Sch. of Medicine, 1918, emeritus; cons. surgeon Mass. Memorial Hosp. Trustee Mass. Memorial Hosps. Republican. Conglist. Mason. Trustee Boston Univ., Mass. Memorial Hosp. Home: North Dighton, Mass. Died Jan. 3, 1942.

BRIGGS, Le Baron Russell, educator; b. Salem, Mass., Dec. 11, 1855; s. Rev. George Ware and Lucia (Russell) B.; A.B., Harvard, 1875, A.M., 1882; LL.D., 1900, Harvard, Western Reserve, 1906, Yale, 1917; Litt.D., Lafayette, 1906; m. Mary Frances De Quedville, Sept. 5, 1883; children—John De Quedville, Lucia Russell, Le Baron Russell. Asst. prof. English, Harvard U., 1885-90, prof. English, 1890, dean of the coll., 1891-1902, dean faculty of arts and sciences, 1902-25, Boylston prof. rhetoric and oratory, 1904-25, emeritus; pres. Radcliffe Coll., 1903-23. Home: Cambridge, Mass. Died Apr. 24, 1934.

BRIGGS, L(loyd) Vernon, psychiatrist; b. Boston, Aug. 13, 1863; s. Lloyd and Sarah Elizabeth E. (Kent) B.; prep. edn. Boston Latin Sch., Chauncy Hall Sch.; student Harvard Med. Sch., Tufts Med. Coll., Dartmouth Med. Coll.; M.D. Med. Coll. of Va., Richmond, 1899; m. Mary T. Cabot, June 1905; 1 son, Lloyd Cabot. Practiced in Boston, 1899—; visited hosps. for insane in Eng. and Scotland, 1905, Germany, Austria, Holland, Switzerland, 1907; formerly dir. N.E. Hosp. for Women and Children; commr. alien insane for Mass., 1912-16; mem. and sec. Mass. State Bd. of Insanity, 1913-16; pres. of staff, and phys. to mental dept., Boston Dispensary; mem. Commn. for The Reorganization of The Dept. of Mental Diseases of Mass., 1937-38; chief of neuropsychiatric service, Base Hospital, Camp Devens, Ayer, Mass. Mem. 1st Corps Cadets, M.V.M., 6 yrs.; maj. Med. R.C., 1917; div. psychiatrist, 76th Div., A.E.F. in France; chief consultant Hosp. Centre, Commercy, France; later lt. col. and assigned to 2d Div.; mem. war work com. Nat. Com. for Mental Hygiene; rep. of phys. of Mass. in Pub. Safety Com. of 100, apptd. by gov. of Mass.; mem. Mass. Com. for War Work in Neurology and Psychology; formerly mem. Old Colony Commn.; col. Aux. Medical Corps, U.S. Army, and consultant U.S. Veterans' Bureau. Episcopalian. Mason (32°). Author: The Manner of Man that Kills; History of the Boston Psychopathic Hospital; Around Cape Horn in the Bark Amy Turner, 1926; Kent Genealogy; Genealogy of the Cabot Family in America; Experience of a Medical Student in Honolulu, 1926; California and the West, 1931; Arizona and Mexico, 1932; History and Genealogy of the Briggs Family, 1937. Author of "Briggs Law" of Mass. requiring mental examination before trial of all persons indicted for felony in Mass. Home: Boston, Mass. Died Feb. 28, 1941.

BRIGHAM, Albert Perry, geologist; b. Perry, N.Y., June 12, 1855; s. Horace A. and Julia (Perry) B.; A.B., Colgate, 1879, A.M., 1882, LL.D., 1925; student Hamilton Theol. Sem., 1879-82; A.M., Harvard, 1892; Sc.D., Syracuse, 1918; L.H.D., Franklin, 1921; m. Flora Winegar, June 27, 1882; children—Charles Winegar (dec.), Elizabeth (Mrs. Lawrence V. Roth). Ordained Bapt. ministry, 1882; pastor Stillwater, N.Y., 1882-85, Utica, 1885-91; became prof. geology, Colgate, 1892, emeritus prof. Instr. Harvard Summer Sch. of Geology, 4 summers; prof. Cornell Summer Sch., 1901-04, U. of Wis., 1906; lecturer, Oxford U. Sch. of Geography, 4 summers and Hilary term, 1924, also at U. of London, 1924. Chief examiner geography, Coll. Entrance Exam. Bd., 1902-13; examiner in geography, N.Y. State Edn. Dept., 1911-13, 1917-19; vice chmn. div. geol. geography Nat. Research Council; mem. gen. geog. com. U.S. Commn. Washington Bicentenary. Author: A Text-Book of Geology, 1900; Introduction to Physical Geography (with G. K. Gilbert), 1902; Geographic Influences in American History, 1903; Students' Laboratory Manual of Physical Geography, 1904; From Trail to Railway Through the Appalachians, 1907; Commercial Geography, 1911; Essentials of Geography (with C. T. McFarlane), 1916; Cape Cod and the Old Colony, 1920; Manual for Teachers of Geography (with C. T. McFarlane), 1921; The United States of America (U. of London Press), 1927; Glacial Geology and Geographic Conditions of Lower Mohawk Valley, 1929. Collaborator, N.Y. State Museum; consultant in geography, Library of Congress. Contbg. editor Geog. Rev. Died Mar. 31, 1932.

BRIGHAM, Johnson, librarian; b. Cherry Valley, N.Y., Mar. 11, 1846; s. Phineas and Eliza (Johnson) B.; ed. Hamilton Coll. and Cornell U., class 1870; Litt.D., Drake U., 1923; m. Nettie Gano, Sept. 1, 1875; 1 dau., Mrs. Anna Gano Hartley; m. 2d, Lucy Hitchcock Walker, Dec. 20, 1892; children—Mrs. Ida Brigham Storms, Mrs. Mary Brigham Johnson. Editor and half owner Cedar Rapids (Ia.) Daily Republican, 1882-93; Am. consul at Aix-la-Chapelle, Germany, 1893; editor and publ. Midland Monthly mag., 1894-99; state librarian of Ia., 1898—. Pres. Ia. State Rep. League, 1892, Ia. Library Commn., 1900—; v.p. Farm Property Mut. Ins. Assn. Pres. Ia. Library Assn., 1903 and 1927, Nat. Assn. State Libraries, 1904; mem. council A.L.A., 1902-07, 1910-15, and 1927-28; Ia. dir. war service commn. A.L.A., 1917-18; pres. Ia. Soc. of Archæol. Inst. America, 1914-26; mem. advisory council Yenching U., Peiping, China. Republican. Author: An Old Man's Idyl, 1905; The Banker in Literature, 1910; History of Des Moines, 1911; A Library in the Making, 1912; Life of James Harlan, 1913; Iowa, Its History and Its Foremost Citizens, 1915-18; The Many-sided

Omar, 1925; The Sinclairs of Old Ft. Des Moines, 1927; Individuality in Letters—from Queen Elizabeth to Queen Anne, 1932; The Youth of Our Age, 1935 (prize awarded by Iowa Authors' Club, 1935). Home: Des Moines, Ia. Died Oct. 8, 1936.

BRIGHAM, Joseph Henry, asst. sec. of Agr.; b. Lodi, O., Dec. 12, 1838; ed. common schools and 1 term each at Berea U., nr. Cleveland, and Normal School, Lebanon, O.; m. Edna Allman, Dec. 1, 1863. Served through Civil War, private to col. in 12th and 69th Ohio regts.; war farmer in Ohio; has held several county offices; served in State senate; master Nat. Grange 5 successive terms; mem. 6 yrs. and pres. 1 yr. Ohio State bd. of agr.; asst. sec. U.S. Dept. Agr., 1897—. Address: Washington, D.C. Died 1904.

BRIGHAM, Nat Maynard, lecturer; b. South Framingham, Mass., Mar. 8, 1856; s. Alfred Milo and Caroline (Damon) B.; A.B., Harvard, 1880; m. Luella Cobb, Jan. 12, 1894. U.S. marshal Ty. of Utah under President Cleveland, 1893-97, and reappointed when Utah became a state. Illustrated lectures: From Coronado to Kit Carson; The Apache Warpath; The Men Who Won the West; The Grand Canyon of Arizona; The Trail of the Padres, etc. Progressive Democrat. Unitarian. Address: Wheaton, Ill. Died Aug. 9, 1915.

BRIGHAM, Sarah Jeannette, author; b. Manchester, N.Y., Mar. 5, 1835; d. John and Betsy (Jones) Lathbury; m. J. R. Brigham, 1854; 1 dau., Lilian Imogen. For many yrs. contbr. to juvenile publs.; as artist has illus. in color. Author: Under Blue Skies (color book), 1886; Leopold and His Wheel, 1896; In Daisy Time, 1896; The Pleasant Land of Play, 1898. Home: Ocean Grove, N.J. Died Oct. 18, 1929.

BRIGHAM, William Erastus, journalist; b. Boston, Mass., Feb. 16, 1865; s. Moses Bartlett and Almira Elizabeth (Fillebrown) B.; grad. Somerville (Mass.) High Sch., 1884; m. Lettie Jane Mitchell, Sept. 10, 1888 (died 1891); 1 dau., Editha (dec.); m. 2d, Carrie Emerson Brown, Jan. 21, 1899. Founder Somerville High Radiator, 1882; mem. editorial staff Boston Globe, 1884-91; mng. editor Lynn (Mass.) Daily Press, 1891-94; mgr. Somerville Citizen, 1894-98; political writer, Boston Evening Transcript, 1898-1902; pvt. sec. to Hon. Eugene N. Foss, 1902-07; Washington corr. Boston Evening Transcript, 1907-25; editorial writer same, 1925—; mng. dir. Animal Rescue League of Boston, 1930-31; editor Our Four-footed Friends, 1931—. Republican. Mason. Home: Newtonville, Mass. Deceased.

BRIGHAM, William Tufts, museum dir.; b. Boston, Mass., May 24, 1841; s. William and Margaret (Brooks) B.; A.B., Harvard, 1862, A.M., 1865; hon. Sc.D., Columbia, 1905. Explored botany and geology of Hawaiian Islands, 1864-65; admitted to Mass. bar, 1867; instr. botany, Harvard, 1868-69; as. mem. Boston Sch. Bd. inaugurated system of art instruction in pub. schs., also the Sargent method of anthropometry now in gen. use in colls.; dir. Bishop Museum of Ethnology, Honolulu, 1888-1918, emeritus and curator anthropology. Author: Cast Catalogue of Antique Sculpture; Guatemala, the Land of the Quetzal; Volcanic Manifestations in New England; Hawaiian Feather-work; Index to the Islands of the Pacific Ocean; Stone Implements of Ancient Hawaiians; Mats and Baskets of Hawaiians; Ancient Hawaiian House; History of Kilauea and Mauna Loa Hawaiian Volcanoes; Ka Hana Kapa (Bark-cloth Making); A Journey Around the World to Study Museums, 1912; Feather-work, Supplement, 1917. Address: Honolulu, H.T. Died Jan. 29, 1926.

BRIGHT, Alfred Harris, lawyer; b. Jefferson County, N.Y., Oct. 29, 1850; s. Thomas and Jane (Crittenden) B.; A.B., U. of Wis., 1874, LL.B., 1876; m. Emily Haskell, Sept. 15, 1887. Located in Minneapolis, 1891; gen. solicitor Milwaukee & Northern R.R., 1888-91; gen. solicitor, 1891-1908, gen. counsel, 1908—, Minneapolis, St. Paul & Sault Ste. Marie Ry.; v.p. Wis. Central R.R. Co. Home: Minneapolis, Minn. Deceased.

BRIGHT, James Wilson, philologist; b. Aaronsburg, Pa., Oct. 2, 1852; A.B., Lafayette Coll., 1877, A.M., 1880; fellow, 1880-82, Ph.D., 1882, Johns Hopkins; Litt.D., Lafayette, 1907; LL.D., Lake Forest, 1907. Asso. prof. English philology, Johns Hopkins U., 1891-93, prof., 1893-1905, Caroline Donovan prof. English lit., 1905-25. Editor-in-chief Modern Language Notes; hon. sec. for America (South and West) of Early English Text Soc. and of Chaucer Soc. (London); mem. advisory bd. Modern Philology; sec. 1893-1901, pres. 1902-03, mem. editorial com., 1904-14, Modern Lang. Assn. America; mem. Simplified Spelling Bd. until 1918; v.p. Simplified Spelling Soc. (London). Editor-in-chief Albion series of Anglo-Saxon and Middle English Poetry; editor of Hesperia (Supplementary Series). Author and Editor: Anglo-Saxon Reader, and Outlines of Anglo-Saxon Grammar, 1891; Gospel of St. Luke in Anglo-Saxon, 1893; Gospel of St. Matthew in West-Saxon, 1904; Gospel of St. John in West-Saxon, 1904; Gospel of St. Mark in West-Saxon, 1905; Gospel of St. Luke in West-Saxon, 1906. Joint Author and Editor: West-Saxon Psalms, 1907; Elements of English Versification, 1910. Address: Baltimore, Md. Deceased.

BRIGHT, Louis Victor, lawyer, banker; b. Mobile, Ala., Oct. 12, 1863; s. Michael and Adele (George) B.; LL.B., Harvard, 1885; m. Bertha Ralston, June 12, 1895; children—Mrs. Mildred Mailliard, Henry R. Admitted to Pa. bar, 1885, to N.Y. bar, 1886; in office of Shearman & Sterling, New York, 1885-87; became connected with Title Guarantee & Trust Co. as clk., 1887, later sec.; v.p. Lawyers Title Ins. Co. of N.Y., 1901, afterwards Lawyers Title & Trust Co., of which was pres. 1912-25; company divided into Lawyers Trust Co. and Lawyers Title and Guaranty Co., later pres. both cos.; officer or dir. various cos. Mem. Mayor's Com. on Nat. Defense, New York, 1917, also mem. com. to receive missions of allied countries and Com. on City Planning and Survey. Republican. Home: Cold Spring, N.Y. Died Oct. 23, 1933.

BRIGHT, Marshal Huntington, journalist; b. Hudson, N.Y., Aug. 18, 1834; academic edn. and course at Lawrence Scientific School, Harvard, 1852-53; hon. A.M., Rutgers Coll.; became asst. editor Albany Argus, 1854; officer during Civil War, bvtd. maj.; after war supt. silver mine in Nev.; became editor The Christian Work, New York, 1873. Author: (with Hamilton W. Mabie) The Story of America; etc. Home: Tarrytown-on-Hudson, N.Y. Died 1907.

BRIGHTMAN, Alvin Collins, prof. law; b. Norwalk, O., Sept. 29, 1878; s. Daniel Alfred and Ellen (Collins) B.; A.B., Oberlin, 1900; LL.B., Western Reserve U., 1909; m. Esther Waite, Sept. 8, 1917; children—Katherine Waite, Alvin III, Margaret Ellen. Prof. law, Western Reserve U., 1909—. Republican. Presbyn. Asso. editor Throckmorton's Ohio Code; 4th edit. Clark on Contracts (with A. H. Throckmorton), 1931. Home: Cleveland, O. Died May 8, 1932.

BRIGHTMAN, Horace Irving, lawyer; b. N.Y. City, Jan. 29, 1872; s. Horace and Julie (Willson) B.; A.B., Columbia, 1892; LL.B., New York Law Sch., 1893; m. Florence Church Mead, Nov. 10, 1904 (dec.). Admitted to N.Y. bar, 1894, and practiced at N.Y. City. Republican. Home: Lake Waccabuc, N.Y. Died Apr. 3, 1940.

BRIGMAN, Bennett Mattingly, univ. dean; b. Louisville, Ky., Feb. 25, 1881; s. William Frederick and Margaret (Lehman) B.; student U. of Ky., 1901-03; B.S., U. of Louisville, 1908, M.Sc., 1912; post-grad. work, U. of Wis., 1911-15; m. Alice Jessel, Sept. 3, 1904. Instr. manual arts, Univ. Sch. (prep.), 1904-07, Du Pont Manual Training High Sch., 1907-16; asst. prof. physics, U. of Louisville, 1916-19, prof. engring. and drawing, 1919-23; organized Sch. of Engring., 1923-25; dean, Speed Scientific Sch., U. of Louisville, 1924—. Advisory engr. Reconstruction Finance Corp., 1932—. In charge Speakers' Bur. Council Nat. Defense, and Bur. War Savings Stamps, in Ky., World War. Presbyn. Mason, Moose. Home: Louisville, Ky. Died Feb. 8, 1938.

BRILL, George Reiter, author, illustrator; b. Allegheny City, Pa., Aug. 27, 1867; s. William H. and Elizabeth S. (Holstein) B.; high sch. edn.; student Pa. Acad. Fine Arts; m. Susannah J. Brown, 1899. Fellowship of the Acad. Fine Arts. Author: Andy and the Ignoramus, 1902; Bobby Bumpkin, 1903; Rhymes of the Golden Age, 1909. Home: Monument Beach, Mass. Died Mar. 6, 1918.

BRILL, Nathan Edwin, physician; b. New York, Jan. 13, 1860; s. Simon and Adelheit (Frankenthal) B.; A.B., Coll. City of New York, 1877, A.M., 1883; M.D., Univ. Med. Coll. (New York U.), 1880; m. Elsa M. Josephthal, June 8, 1899; children—Elisabeth Joyce, John Lewis. Interne Bellevue Hosp., 1879-81, attending phys. 1st med. div., Mt. Sinai Hosp., 1893—; prof. clin. medicine, Coll. Phys. and Surg. (Columbia), 1910—; consulting phys. Mt. Sinai Hosp. Discoverer, 1910, of previously unrecognized form of typhus fever known as Brill's disease. Major Med. O.R.C., 1917, and dir. Base Hospital No. 3. Trustee N.Y. Acad. Medicine; mem. Pub. Health Com.; fellow New York Acad. Medicine. Translator: Klemperer Clinical Diagnosis, 1898. Home: New York, N.Y. Died Dec. 13, 1925.

BRILL, William Hascal, journalist; b. Litchfield, Minn., Apr. 16, 1871; s. William S. and Annie (Sheldon) B.; A.B., U. of Minn., 1890; attended Coll. of Law, U. of Minn.; unmarried. Abandoned law for journalism; joined St. Paul Pioneer Press; covered campaign against Chippewa Indians, 1898, including battle of Leech Lake, Minn. (last clash between U.S. troops and Indians); city editor St. Paul Daily News, 1900-02; on staff Newspaper Enterprise Assn., Cleveland, O., 1902-04, with 6 months spl. assignment in Alaska; went to Japan for Reuter's Telegram Co., London, and The Associated Press of America, 1904; served 14 months with 2d Imperial Japanese Army in the field; also contbr. articles and photographs to Leslie's Weekly; military editor Ridgeway's Weekly, Washington, 1906; has traveled extensively in the East, Europe, etc. Home: St. Paul, Minn. Died Nov. 30, 1923.

BRIMHALL, George Henry, univ. pres.; b. Salt Lake City, Utah, Dec. 9, 1852; s. George Washington and Rachel Ann (Mayer) B.; B.P.D., Brigham Young Acad., 1893; D.Sc.D., Latter Day Saints Gen. Bd. of Edn., 1898; m. Alsina Elizabeth Wilkins, Dec. 28, 1875 (dec.); children—Lucy Jane, Alsina Elisabeth, George Washington, Mark Henry, Wells Lovill, Milton H. (dec.); m. 2d, Flora Robertson, Sept. 11, 1885; children—Dean Robertson, Fawn Robertson and Fay Robertson (twins). Burns Robertson, Ruth Afton, Paul Robertson, Alta Robertson (dec.), Golden Henry, Areo Robertson. Worked way through sch. from janitor up; served successively as supt. schs., Spanish Fork, Utah County schs., Provo schs.; prin. Normal Sch., Brigham Young Acad.; pres. Brigham Young U., 1903-21, emeritus; prof. theology, Brigham Young U.; supt. Latter Day Saint Seminaries. Republican. Lecturer teachers' insts. Mem. Latter Day Saints' Gen. Bd. Edn., Gen. Bd. Examiners, Gen. Bd. Young Men's Mut. Improvement Assn. Home: Provo, Utah. Died July 29, 1932.

BRIMSON, William George, ry. pres.; b. Tiverton, Eng., Apr. 27, 1845; s. Elias and Mary (Thorne) B.; ed. Norwalk (O.) High Sch., Bryant & Stratton Bus. Coll.; m. Susan H. Smith, Aug. 28, 1873 (died 1910); children—Mary Hunt (Mrs. F. A. Grow), Charles Tamlin, Alice Worthington Smith. Tel. operator, 1868-71, train dispatcher, 1871-75, L.S.&M.S. Ry.; supt. Logansport, Crawfordsville & S.W. Ry., 1875-80; trainmaster, 1880-81, supt., 1881-88, L.E.& W. Ry.; trainmaster, C.&E.I. R.R., 1888-90; supt., 1890-91, pres., 1891-96, Calumet & Blue Island Ry.; pres. and gen. mgr., Chicago, Lake Shore & Eastern Ry., 1896-99; gen. mgr., 1899-1907, v.p., 1907-10, Q.,O.&K.C. Ry.; pres. Tex. City Transportation Co. and Tex. City Ry. Co., Apr. 1, 1910-12. First v.p. Northern Bapt. Conv., Am. Bapt. Home Missionary Soc.; pres. Am. Bapt. Publ. Soc., 1918-20, Ill. Bapt. State Conv., 1913-16, Chicago Bapt. Social Union, 1914-15, Nat. Bapt. Brotherhood, 1916-17, Chicago Bapt. Exec. Council, 1919-27; treas, Nat. Bapt. Slavic Training Sch., 1917-19; mgr. transportation, Northern Bapt. Conv., 1916—; vice-chmn. Northern Bapt. Theol. Sem., 1920—. Home: Chicago, Ill. Died June 30, 1930.

BRINGHURST, Robert Porter, artist; b. Jerseyville, Ill., Mar. 22, 1855; s. Dr. James and Mary (Ryan) B.; ed. in art, St. Louis Sch. of Fine Arts, and at École des Beaux Arts, Paris; m. Mary F. Coolidge, Nov. 8, 1877. Prizes: first class medal, World's Fair, Chicago, 1893; silver medal, St. Louis Expn., 1904; first money prize, Tennessee Centennial. Principal works: Awakening Spring, Art Inst., Chicago; Kiss of Immortality, destroyed at Portland fair; statue of General Grant, City Hall Park, St. Louis; Minnesota's monument at Gettysburg, Pennsylvania's monument at Shiloh. Address: St. Louis, Mo. Died Mar. 22, 1925.

BRINK, Gilbert Nicholas, educator; b. Painesville, O., Sept. 3, 1872; s. Edwin Thomas and Eulalia Alice (Bailey) B.; A.B., Pomona Coll., 1898, A.M., 1905, D.D., 1923; B.D., Pacific Theol. Sem., 1901, D.D., 1917; D.D., Georgetown (Ky.) Coll., 1917; post-grad. work U. of Calif.; m. Nellie Mae Bennett, June 14, 1900. Supt. schs., Philippine Islands, 1901-04; asst. dir. edn., P.I., 1904-09; prin. Berkeley (Calif.) High Sch., 1910-12; asst. head master Belmont (Calif.) Sch. for Boys, 1912-14; supt. edn. Am. Bapt. Home Mission Soc., 1915-18; gen. sec. Am. Bapt. Publication Soc., 1919-25; mem. administration staff, Pomona Coll., 1925. Home: Pomona, Calif. Died May 27, 1936.

BRINKER, Josiah Henry; b. Houston, Miss., Oct. 2, 1851; s. Henry Harrison and Kezziah A. (Kilgore) B.; grad. Oak Grove Acad., Sparta, Miss., 1870; course in bookkeeping, Eastman Business Coll., Poughkeepsie, N.Y.; m. Mary L. Montgomery, Dec. 8, 1870 (died 1892); m. 2d, Henrietta T. Greenwood (nee Thomas), July 17, 1911. Engaged in gen. mercantile business at Sparta and West Point, Miss., 1874-90, also dealt extensively in cotton, 1880-93; postmaster, Sparta, Miss., 1874-79, West Point, 1884-90; an organizer, cashier and dir. First Nat. Bank, West Point, 1880-84; del. to Dem. Nat. Conv., Chicago, 1892; del. Anti-Trust Conv., Chicago, 1893 (sec. com. on platform); supt. documents, Govt. Printing Office, Washington, D.C., 1913—. Served as maj. staff of Gov. Lowry, of Miss., 1886-88; brig. gen. 1st Brigade, Mississippi N.G., 1888-94 (resigned). Commr. from Miss. to World's Fair, Chicago, 1892-93. Baptist. Home: Washington, D.C. Died 1920.

BRINKERHOFF, Roeliff, banker; b. Owasco, N.Y., June 28, 1828; ed. common schs. and Auburn and Homer acads.; taught in common schs. at 16 and 17, went South at 18 and was for 3 yrs. tutor in Hermitage, home of Gen. Jackson; returned North at 21; studied law with Judge Jacob Brinkerhoff, Mansfield, O.; began practice, 1852; editor and propr. Mansfield Herald, 1855-59; m. Mary Bentley. Entered army 1st lt. and q.m. 64th Ohio Vol. Inf.; served 5 yrs. and attained rank of col. in q.m.'s dept. and was bvtd. brig. gen. "for meritorious service." Resumed law practice until 1873, when became cashier Mansfield Savings Bank, later becoming pres. Mem. Ohio State

Bd. of Charities, 1878— (chmn. several yrs. past); pres. Nat. Conf. of Charities and Correction, 1880; v.p. Internat. Prison Congress, Paris, 1895, and pres. Am. delegation; v.p. Am. Nat. Prison Congress, 1884-94, with Gen. R. B. Hayes as pres., becoming pres. at latter's death. Organized, 1875, and 1st pres. and pres., 1893—, succeeding Gen. Hayes, Ohio Archæol. and Hist. Soc. Author: The Volunteer Quartermaster; Recollections of a Lifetime, 1900. Address: Mansfield, O. Died 1911.

BRINKMAN, William Augustus, merchant; b. Lancaster, Pa., Nov. 18, 1868; s. Frank and Fanny (Rinehart) B.; ed. pub. schs.; m. Mary Catharine Krauskop, Sept. 18, 1890; 1 son, Franklin Krauskop. Paper hanger apprentice, 1884-87; with father's firm, Brinkman & Newell, wall paper and interior decorations, 1887-90; mem. firm after father's death, 1890; in business in own name, 1897-1930; pres. Brusstar Co., clothiers, Reading, 1916-22; mem. Groff & Wolf Co. until 1930; partner William A. Brinkman Co., 1930—; dir. and mem. finance com. Northern Trust & Savings Co.; dir. Industrial Building & Loan Assn., Community Discount Co., First Title Insurance Co., Real Estate Inc. Mem. Pa. Home Defense Police, World War, and active in all drives. Dem. presdl. elector for Pa., 1920; mem. City Council, Lancaster, 1922-24. Pres. bd. trustees Memorial Presbyn. Ch. Mason (32°, K.T., Shriner; Most Puissant Grand Master, Grand Council R.&S.M. of Pa., 1928), Elk; mem. Tall Cedars of Lebanon (Supreme Tall Cedar of U.S., 1930). Pub. of Descendants of Otto Henrich Wilhelm Brinkman, 1925. Home: Lancaster, Pa. Died Nov. 5, 1936.

BRINSMADE, John Chapin, educator; b. Springfield, Mass., Apr. 24, 1852; s. William Bartlett and Charlotte Blake (Chapin) B.; A.B., Harvard, 1874; m. Mary Gold Gunn, Oct. 4, 1876; children—Frederick Gunn, William Bartlett (dec.), Chapin (dec.), Eleanor Gold, Mary, John Chapin, Charlotte Blake, Abigail Irene (dec.). Teacher, 1874-81, prin., 1881-1922, Gunnery School. Mem. Conn. Ho. of Rep., 1893, 1909, 23, 25, Conn. Senate, 1911 (chmn. joint legislative com. on edn.); mem. Conn. Constl. Conv., 1902; pres. Conn. State Civil Service Commn. Conglist. Home: Washington, Conn. Died Aug. 21, 1930.

BRINSMADE, Robert Bruce, mining engr.; b. Elmira, N.Y., Aug. 27, 1873; s. Hobart and Ella Mary (Lyon) B.; B.S. in Mining, Washington U., 1894; E.M., Lehigh U., 1895; m. Helen Christine Steenbock, July 24, 1909; children—Virginia Skidmore, Robert Turgot, Harold Steenbock, Akbar Fairchild, Lyon Rufus, Alan Bruce, Christine. Mining engr., various mining cos. of Mont., 1896-99, War Eagle Mine, Rossland, B.C., 1899-1900; metallurgist, Columbia and other mining cos., Mo., 1900-01; mine and smelter supt. at Cordoba, Argentina, S.A., 1901-02; designing engr., Ordnance Bur. U.S.A., Rock Island, Ill., 1902-03, Solvay Coke Co., Syracuse, N.Y., 1903-04; supt. Rossie Iron Mines, St. Lawrence Co., N.Y., 1904-05; prof. mining engring., State Mining Coll., Socorro, N.M., 1905-06; consulting engr., St. Louis, 1906-07; organizer and dir. State Mining Sch., Platteville, Wis., 1907-08; mining exploration, San Domingo, W.I., 1908-09; prof. mining engring., U. of W.Va., 1909-11; consulting practice, 1911—; economist Mexican Ministry of Finance, 1920-24. Unitarian. Author: Mining Without Timber, 1911; Latifundismo Mexicano, 1916; Catastro Democratico, 1926; Exploring Spanish America, 1927; Mexican Religious Crisis, 1928; What's the Use of Working?, 1931; Silver Cure for Uncle Sam, 1933; Engineer's Cure for Plutocracy, 1936. Address: San Luis Potosi City, Mexico. Died Sept. 28, 1936.

BRINSON, Samuel Mitchell, congressman; b. New Bern, N.C., Mar. 20, 1870; s. William George and Kittie Elizabeth (Chestnut) B.; A.B., Wake Forest (N.C.) Coll., 1891; student law dept. U. of N.C.; m. Ruth Martin Scales, Jan. 16, 1901 (died Jan. 19, 1919). Admitted to N.C. bar, 1896, and practiced at New Bern until 1902; supt. schs. of Craven County, N.C., 1902-19; mem. 66th and 67th Congresses (1919-23), 3d N.C. Dist. Democrat. Baptist. Trustee Meredith Coll. (Raleigh, N.C.), East Carolina Teachers' Training Sch. (Greenville, N.C.). Mason (K.T., Shriner). Home: New Bern, N.C. Died Apr. 13, 1922.

BRINTON, Daniel Garrison, univ. prof.; b. Chester County, Pa., May 13, 1837; grad. Yale, 1858 (A.M.; LL.D.); grad. Jefferson Med. Coll., 1861; Sc.D., Univ. of Pa. Asst. surgeon, surgeon and med. director 11th Army Corps, 1862-65; editor Medical and Surgical Reporter, 1867-87; prof. Am. archæology and linguistics, U. of Pa. Author: The Myths of the New World; The Religious Sentiment; American Hero-Myths; Chronicles of the Mayas; The Lenâpé and Their Legends; Races and Peoples; The American Race; The Pursuit of Happiness; Nagualism; Lectures on the Religions of Primitive Peoples; etc. Address: Media, Pa. Died 1899.

BRINTON, John Hill, surgeon; b. Phila., 1832; grad. U. of Pa., 1850, A.M., 1853, LL.D., 1901; grad. Jefferson Med. Coll., Phila., 1852. Brigade surgeon and surgeon vols., U.S. Army, 1861-65; prof. practice of surgery and clinical surgery, Jefferson Med. Coll., 1882. Mütter lecturer on surg. pathology (gunshot injuries), 1869; surgeon to St. Joseph's Hosp., Phila., 1859; Phila. Hosp., 1867-82; Jefferson Coll. Hosp., Phila., 1877; consulting surgeon Phila. Hosp., 1904. Address: Philadelphia, Pa. Died 1907.

BRISBANE, Arthur, newspaper editor; b. Buffalo, N.Y., Dec. 12, 1864; s. Albert and Sarah (White) B.; ed. Am. pub. schs., and 5 yrs. in France and Germany; m. Phoebe Cary, July 30, 1912. Began newspaper work, Dec. 12, 1883, as reporter on New York Sun, later London corr. Sun, and editor Evening Sun; on New York World as mng. editor of different editions 7 yrs.; editor New York Evening Journal, 1897-1921; purchased Washington Times, June 1917, Evening Wisconsin, Milwaukee, Oct. 1918; sold both papers to William Randolph Hearst, 1919. Editorial writer. Address: New York, N.Y. Died Dec. 25, 1936.

BRISCOE, John Parran, judge; b. Calvert County, Md., Aug. 24, 1853; s. James T. and Annie M. (Parran) B.; A.B., St. John's Coll., Annapolis, 1874; m. Kate M. Bowen, 1879. Admitted to bar, 1875, and practiced at Prince Frederick, Md. State's atty., Calvert County, Md., 1879-90; asso. judge 7th Jud. Circuit of Md. and judge Ct. of Appeals, 1890—. Democrat. Home: Prince Frederick, Md. Died Apr. 14, 1925.

BRISTER, John Willard, educator; b. Petersburg, Va., Dec. 28, 1867; s. Samuel George and Mary (Prosise) B.; grad. Petersburg Pub. High Sch., 1885; A.B., Peabody Coll. (U. of Nashville), 1892, A.M., 1893; grad. student U. of Chicago, 1896-97; m. Frances May Taylor. Instr. in Montgomery Bell Acad., Nashville, 1892-96, 1897-1902; prof., mathematics Peabody Coll., 1902-11; state supt. public instrn., Tenn., 1911-13; pres. West Tenn. Normal School, 1913-18; Y.M.C.A. ednl. work over-seas, and mem. army Ednl. Corps, 1918-19; State high sch. inspector, Tenn., 1919-24; pres. State Teachers Coll., Memphis, 1924—. Democrat. Methodist. Address: Memphis, Tenn. Died Sept. 10, 1939.

BRISTOL, Augusta Cooper, author, lecturer; b. Croydon, N.H., Apr. 17, 1835; d. Otis and Hannah Cooper; ed. Kimball Union Acad.; became teacher, 1850; m. Louis Bristol, 1866 (died 1882). Writer and lecturer on moral and social subjects; went, 1880, to study equitable assn. of labor and capital at Guise, France, residing in The Social Palace there 3 months; state lecturer Patrons of Husbandry of N.J., 1881-84; teacher of French, 1899—. Author: Poems, 1868; The Relation of the Maternal Function to the Woman Intellect, 1876; The Philosophy of Art, 1880; The President Phase of Woman's Advancement, 1880; Science as the Basis of Morality, 1880 (French edit., 1882); The Web of Life (poems), 1895; A Spray of Cosmos, 1904. Address: Vineland, N.J. Died 1910.

BRISTOL, Charles Lawrence, biologist; b. Ballston Spa, N.Y., Sept. 29, 1859; s. Lawrence W. and Caroline (Hawkins) B.; B.S., New York U., 1883, M.S., 1888; teacher sciences, Riverview Acad., Poughkeepsie, N.Y., 1884-87; m. Ellen Gallup, Jan. 28, 1890; children—Lawrence, Elisabeth (Mrs. W. E. Greenleaf). Prof. zoölogy, U. of S.D., 1887-91; fellow Clark U., 1891-92, U. of Chicago, 1892-93, Ph.D., 1895; prof. biology, New York U., 1894-1925 (emeritus); prof. biology on University World Cruise, 1926-27. Directed zoöl. expdns. to Bermuda and made successful expts. in transporting tropical marine animals alive to New York Aquarium. Address: New York, N.Y. Died Aug. 27, 1931.

BRISTOL, Frank Milton, bishop; b. Orleans County, N.Y., Jan. 4, 1851; Ph.B., Northwestern U., 1877, hon. A.M., 1883, D.D., 1888; m. Nellie Frisbie, 1878. Ordained M.E. ministry, 1877; pastor Trinity, Grace and Wabash Av. M.E. chs., Chicago, First Ch., Evanston, Ill., and Metropolitan Ch., Washington, until 1908; bishop M.E. Ch., 1908-24; retired 1924. Author: Providential Epochs; The Ministry of Art; Shakespeare and America, etc. Home: Upper Montclair, N.J. Died Apr. 24, 1932.

BRISTOL, George Prentiss, college prof.; b. Clinton, N.Y., June 21, 1856; s. Henry Platt and Martha (Fake) B.; A.B., Hamilton Coll., 1876, A.M., 1883; student Johns Hopkins and Heidelberg; m. Lucia Raymond, July 16, 1880. Asst. prof. Greek and German, Hamilton Coll., 1882-83, Greek, 1883-88; assistant professor Greek, Cornell University, 1888-90, asso. prof., 1890-98, prof., 1898—, dir. summer session, 1906-17, dir. Sch. of Edn., 1910-16. Pres. N.Y. State Teachers Retirement Bd., 1911—. Editor Cornell Studies in Classical Philology, 1891—. Author: Selected Orations of Lysias, 1892; The Teaching of Greek and Latin in Secondary Schools (with Charles E. Bennett), 1900. Home: Ithaca, N.Y. Died May 16, 1927.

BRISTOL, John Bunyan, landscape painter; b. Hillsdale, N.Y., Mar. 14, 1826; early efforts in art were under great difficulties and without instruction or aid; began as a painter of figures and portraits, later becoming a landscape painter; medal Centennial Expn., Phila., 1876; hon. mention Paris Expn., 1878; mem. Nat. Acad., 1875—, and regular exhibitor in its annual exhns. Address: New York, N.Y. Died 1909.

BRISTOL, John Isaac Devoe, life insurance expert; b. Springwells, Mich., Mar. 16, 1845; s. Charles L. and Mary A. (Brevoort) B.; m. Effie A. Roberts, Apr. 18, 1872. At an early age became interested in general science and inventions; later in the lecture field; in life ins., 1868—; represented Conn. Mutual Life in Detroit and later in western states; afterward with Northwestern Mutual in West, gen. agt. at N.Y. City, 1883-1931; engaged in inventions and writing, 1931—. Home: Chappaqua, N.Y. Died Apr. 1932.

BRISTOL, Mark Lambert, naval officer; b. Glassboro, N.J., Apr. 17, 1868; s. Mark Lambert and Rachel Elizabeth (Bush) B.; grad. U.S. Naval Acad., 1887; m. Helen Beverly Moore, June 1, 1908. Ensign U.S.N., May 19, 1889; advanced through grades to capt., July 1, 1913; commd. temporary rear admiral, July 1918; commd. rear admiral, July 1921. Served on board battleship Texas at Battle of Santiago and throughout Spanish-Am. War; closely connected with the development of modern gunnery in the Navy, and of torpedoes and aircraft. In charge aeronautical development of Navy, 1913-16; comdg. North Carolina, Apr. 16, 1917, convoying troops to Europe; comdg. Oklahoma Battleship Div. 6, in European waters, July 1918; comd. U.S. Naval Base, Plymouth, Eng., Oct. 1918-Jan. 1919; mem. Internat. Armistice Commn. in Belgium, Nov. 1918; comd. U.S. Naval Detachment Eastern Mediterranean, 1919; apptd. U.S. high commr. to Turkey, Aug. 12, 1919; mem. internat. com. of inquiry into Greek occupation of Smyrna, Sept.-Oct. 1919; U.S. high commr. to Turkey, 1919-27; comdr. in chief Asiatic Fleet, rank of admiral, 1927-29; became chmn. Gen. Bd., Mar. 1930; retired, May 1, 1932. One of Am. delegates to Lausanne Conf., Nov. 23, 1922-Feb. 5, 1923. Address: Washington, D.C. Died May 13, 1939.

BRISTOL, William Henry, mathematician; b. Waterbury, Conn., July 5, 1859; s. Benjamin Hiel and Pauline (Phelps) B.; M.E., Stevens Inst. Tech., 1884; m. J. Louise Wright, Sept. 8, 1885 (died 1888); m. 2d, Elise H. Myers, June 28, 1899. Organized, 1882, manual training dept. of Workingman's Sch., New York, and teacher same, 1882-86; instr. mathematics, Stevens Inst. Tech., 1886-88, asst. prof., 1888-99, prof., 1899-1906. Organized, 1889, and pres. The Bristol Co. (mfg. his inventions). Inventor of numerous recording instruments for pressure, temperature and electricity, steel belt-lacing, sound amplifying and talking motion picture apparatus, etc.; awarded John Scott Legacy medal, Franklin Inst., Phila., 1890; medal and diploma, Chicago Expn., 1893; silver medal, Paris Expn., 1900; gold medal, St. Louis Expn., 1904; grand prize, Panama P.I. Expn., 1915. Home: Waterbury, Conn. Died June 18, 1930.

BRISTOW, Algernon Thomas, physician; b. Richmond, Eng., Nov. 29, 1851; s. Isaac and Charlotte (Andrews) B.; grad. Brooklyn Poly. Inst., 1869; A.B., Yale, 1873; M.D., Coll. Phys. and Surg. (Columbia), 1876; m. Emeline Ashmead, June 17, 1891. Surgeon L.I. Coll., Kings County, and St. John's hosps.; consulting surgeon to Bushwick Central and L.I. State hosps.; clin. prof. surgery, L.I. Coll. Hosp. Wrote chapter on post-mortem examinations in Hamilton's Legal Medicine; chapter on bacteriology Fowler's Surgery. Home: Brooklyn, N.Y. Died Mar. 26, 1913.

BRITT, James J., congressman; b. nr. Johnson City, Tenn., Mar. 4, 1861; attended pub. schs.; studied law in office, and U. of N.C.; widower. Practiced law at Asheville, N.C.; spl. atty., Dept. Justice, 1906-09; spl. counsel, Post Office Dept., 1909-10; spl. asst. to the atty. gen. U.S. for prosecution of civil cases for Post Office Dept., 1910; 3d asst. postmaster gen., Dec. 1, 1910-Mar. 17, 1913; sr. mem law firm of Britt & Kitchin, Asheville, 1913-19. Del. Rep. Nat. Conv., 1904; Rep. nominee for Congress, 10th N.C. Dist., 1906; mem. N.C. Senate, 1909 (minority leader); mem. 64th and 65th Congresses (1915-19), 10th N.C. Dist.; chief counsel, Bur. of Industrial Alcohol, of Treasury Dept., Washington, D.C., 1922-33; Rep. candidate for chief justice Supreme Court, N.C., 1926. Baptist. Mason, Kiwanian. Home: Asheville, N.C. Died Dec. 26, 1939.

BRITT, Walter Stratton, surgeon; b. Midway, Ala., Sept. 2, 1877; s. Moses Wiley and Mary Hill (Roberts) B.; A.B., Howard Coll., Birmingham, Ala., 1895; M.D., Bellevue Hosp. Med. Coll., New York, 1898; m. Katherine Drewry Comer, Nov. 30, 1899; children—Mrs. Carry Elizabeth Moore, Walter Stratton. Began practice at Midway, 1898; surgeon Central of Ga. Ry, 1900—; also surgeon for Ala. Power Co., Cowikee Cotton Mills (Eufaula, Ala.); v.p. Ala. Power Co.; mem. State Board of Health and Censors, Ala., 1920-22; chmn. board of dirs. Bank of Eufaula, Ala.; propr. Britt Infirmary; dir. Eufaula Ice and Cold Storage Co., Eufaula Building & Loan Assn. Maj. surgeon 4th Regt., Ala. N.G., 1915-16; vol. surgeon World War (not called). Trustee Carnegie Library, Eufaula; pres. bd. trustees Eufaula city schs.; mem. State Board of Health and Censors, 1924-29; mem. Barbour County Bd. of Edn. Democrat. Baptist. Mason; Exalted Ruler B.P.O. Elks for 12 yrs. Home: Eufaula, Ala. Died May 27, 1938.

BRITTAIN, Carlo Bonaparte, naval officer; b. Pineville, Ky., Jan. 16, 1867; s. Carlo Bonaparte and Lydia Susan (Burch) B.; student Cumberland Coll., Barbourville, Ky.; grad. U.S. Naval Acad., 1888; m. Mary Elizabeth Baldwin, June 29, 1897. Commd. ensign, July 1, 1890; promoted through grades to rear adm. (temp.), Sept. 21, 1918. Comd. forces afloat, 5th Naval Dist., June-Oct. 1918; comd. Battleship Div. One, U.S. Fleet, Nov. 1918-June 1919; chief of staff U.S. Atlantic Fleet, attached to fleet flagship U.S.S. Pennsylvania, June 30, 1919. Mem. U.S. Naval Inst. Awarded Sampson medal for engagement at Santiago, Cuba, U.S.S. Newark, July 2, 1898; also West Indian campaign badge, Philippine campaign badge. Mem. Christian (Campbellite) Ch. Author: Elements of Naval Warfare, 1909. Home: Richmond, Ky. Died Apr. 22, 1920.

BRITTAIN, Frank Smith, lawyer; b. Phila., Pa., Nov. 23, 1862; s. Daniel and Eliza (Hart) B.; ed. pub. schs. Phila.; m. Mary Foltz Walshe, Oct. 13, 1898; 1 son, Frank Walshe. Admitted to Tex. bar, 1893, and practiced in Abilene; removed to San Francisco, Calif., 1894; gen. atty. Panama P.I. Expn., 1912-19; asso. justice Dist. Court of Appeal, Calif., 1919-20; gen. atty. Calif. Farm Bur. Federation, 1921-22; mem. Brittain & Weise, 1923—. Served as 1st lt. 2d Regt., U.S. Vol. Engrs., with 3d Battalion, Honolulu, H.T., Spanish-Am. War. Republican. Mason (33°). Home: San Francisco, Calif. Died Feb. 24, 1929.

BRITTAIN, Joseph I., foreign service officer; b. New Britain, Pa., 1858; s. Joseph and Belinda B.; ed. high school, New Brighton, Pa., and Beaver (Pa.) Sem.; m. Martha Louise Clark, Aug. 2, 1894. For some years was engaged in newspaper business at E. Palestine, O.; solicitor for E. Palestine; spl. census agt. in Ohio, 1890; mem. Ohio House of Rep., 2 terms, 1892-95; U.S. consul at Nantes, France, 1897-1902, Kehl, Germany, 1902-07, Prague, Czechoslovakia, 1907-13; consul-gen. Coburg, Germany, 1913-14, Auckland, New Zealand, 1914-15, Sydney, Australia, 1915-19, Winnipeg, Can., 1919-24, retired from service, 1924. Republican. Presbyterian. Lecturer on the Foreign Service of United States. Address: St. Petersburg, Fla. Died Oct. 22, 1930.

BRITTINGHAM, Thomas Evans, lumberman; b. Hannibal, Mo., May 18, 1860; s. Dr. Irvin Baird and Mary (League) B.; ed. pvt. schs. and Hannibal Coll. (now defunct); m. Mary Clark, Dec. 5, 1889. Began in lumber business at MacFarland, Wis., 1885; pres. of number of lumber cos. Chmn. Forest Hill Cemetery Commn., 1907-10; chmn. bd. of visitors U. of Wis., 1907-09. Republican. Home: Madison, Wis. Died May 2, 1924.

BRITTON, Alexander Thompson, lawyer; b. New York, Dec. 29, 1835; served in Civil War, enlisting, 1861, in Nat. Rifles of Washington. Began practice law in Washington, 1865; mem., 1877, of commn. apptd. by President Hayes to codify public land laws; dir. several banks, railroads, etc. Address: Washington, D.C. Died 1899.

BRITTON, Edward Elms, editor; b. Charlotte, N.C., Dec. 19, 1864; s. James Evans and Margaret Elizabeth (Elms) B.; ed. College of Charleston, S.C.; Sauveur College of Langs., Oswego, N.Y.; m. Norma Safford Hardy, Sept. 17, 1906. Served as prin., supt. or pres. various schs. and colls., N.C., S.C., and Ga., 1884-98; editor Wilson Daily News, 1899-1901; began as reporter on News and Observer, Raleigh, Feb. 1901, becoming editor Mar. 4, 1913; resigned Sept. 1, 1917; pvt. sec. to Josephus Daniels, U.S. Sec. of Navy, 1917-21; Washington corr. Raleigh (N.C.) News and Observer, 1921—. Prominent in politics for many yrs.; permanent sec. Dem. Nat. Conv., Baltimore, 1912; del. and asso. sec. Dem. Nat. Conv., St. Louis, 1916; asso. sec. Dem. Nat. Conv., San Francisco, 1920. Past Regent Royal Arcanum; Mason (K.T., 32°, Shriner), pres. Ashlar Club of Master Masons (Washington, D.C.), K.P. Episcopalian. Home: Raleigh, N.C. Died Nov. 9, 1925.

BRITTON, Elizabeth Gertrude, bryologist; b. New York, Jan. 9, 1858; d. James and Sophie A. (Compton) Knight; girlhood spent in Cuba; grad. Normal Coll., 1875, taught in training dept., 1875-82, asst. botany, 1882-85; m. Nathaniel Lord Britton, Aug. 27, 1885. Edited Bulletin of Torrey Bot. Club, 1885-88; studied mosses, 1880—; devoted prin. part of time gratuitously to the collections of Columbia U. and New York Bot. Garden (hon. curator of mosses). Home: New York, N.Y. Died Jan. 1934.

BRITTON, Frank Hamilton, ry. official; b. Ovid, N.Y., Nov. 29, 1850; s. Robert and Mary C. (Hamilton) B.; common sch. edn.; m. Ida F. Freeman, Mar. 1873. Entered ry. service Aug. 1868; telegraph operator, Mich. Southern & Northern Ind. R.R., 1868-71; asst. and chief train dispatcher and master trains various divs. L.&N. R.R., 1871-82; supt. transportation Chesapeake, Ohio & Northwestern Ry., Louisville, 1882-83; supt. transportation, 1883-86, supt., 1886-92, Chicago div. B.&O. R.R.; gen. supt. Minn. & Wis. Ry., 1893-94; div. supt., 1894-98, asst. gen. supt., 1898-99, G.N. Ry.; gen. supt., 1899-1900, v.p. and gen. mgr., 1900-13, pres., 1913—, St. Louis Southwestern Ry. and pres. St. Louis Southwestern Ry. of Texas. Address: St. Louis, Mo. Died July 26, 1916.

BRITTON, John Alexander; b. Boston, Mass., Oct. 9, 1855; ed. pub. schs.; removed to Calif., 1868; m. Florence Eastland, 1879. Began, 1869, as clk. in law office of Charles A. Lowe, of San Francisco, later law clk. under Judge John Curry and Judge O. P. Evans; with Oakland Gas Co. and its successors, 1874—, clk. and collector, 1874-83, sec., 1883-1901, pres., 1901-03, v.p. and gen. mgr. Calif. Gas & Electric Corp., 1903—; also v.p. and gen. mgr. Pacific Gas & Electric Co., 1905—, chief engr., 1908—; mem. bd. dirs. Panama P.I. Expn. Apptd. regent U. of Calif., 1903, and reappointed by Gov. Johnson, 1915, for term of 16 yrs. Mason (33°); Odd Fellow (past grand); Elk. Chmn. San Francisco Chapter Am. Red Cross; chmn. publicity com. 12th Federal Reserve Dist. for all Liberty Loan drives. Address: San Francisco, Calif. Died June 29, 1923.

BRITTON, Nathaniel Lord, botanist; b. New Dorp, S.I., N.Y., Jan. 15, 1859; E.M., Columbia, 1879, Ph.D., 1879, hon. Sc.D., 1904; LL.D., U. of Pittsburgh, 1912; m. Elizabeth Gertrude Knight, Aug. 27, 1885. Asst. in geology, Columbia U., 1879-86, instr. in geology and botany, 1886-90, also instr. in zoölogy, 1887-88, adj. prof. botany, 1891-96, prof. emeritus, 1896—; dir.-in-chief New York Bot. Garden, 1896-1929; dir. emeritus, 1929—. On N.J. Geol. Survey, 5 yrs.; field asst. U.S. Geol. Survey, 1882; editor Bulletin Torrey Bot. Club, 1888-98. Pres. Bot. Soc. America, 1896-98 and 1921, N.Y. Acad. Science, 1905-07, N.Y. State Forestry Assn., 1913. Author: The Flora of New Jersey; Illustrated Flora of Northern United States and Canada, 3 vols., 1896-98, 2d edit., 1913 (with Addison Brown); Manual of the Flora of the Northern States and Canada; Flora of Bermuda, 1918; The Bahama Flora (with C. F. Millspaugh), 1920; monograph of the Cactus Family (with J. N. Rose), 1919-20. Home: Bronx, New York, N.Y. Died June 25, 1934.

BRITTON, Wilton Everett, entomologist; b. Marlboro, Mass., Sept. 18, 1868; s. Benjamin Howard and Emily Eliza (Wright) B.; B.S., U. of N.H., 1893, D.Sc., 1930; grad. study Cornell U., 1893-94; Ph.D., Yale, 1903; m. Bertha Madeline Perkins, Apr. 30, 1895. Horticulturist, Conn. Agrl. Expt. Sta., 1894-1901, entomologist, 1901—, also Conn. state entomologist, 1901—; lecturer, Yale Sch. Forestry, 1901-05; supt. Conn. Geol. and Natural History Survey, 1925—; asso. editor Jour. Econ. Entomology, 1909-28. Pvt., Governors Foot Guard, 1917-20. Chmn. Conn. Tree Protection Examining Bd.; pres. Donald G. Mitchell Library; dir. New Haven Pub. Library, 1926-32, Young Men's Inst., Westville Cemetery. Republican. Conglist. Author: Check-List of the Insects of Conn., 1920. Home: New Haven, Conn. Died Feb. 15, 1939.

BROADHEAD, Garland Carr, geologist; b. Albemarle County, Va., Oct. 30, 1827; s. Achilles and Mary Winston (Carr) B.; attended U. of Mo., 1850-51; M.S., 1873; Western Mil. Inst., Ky., 1851-52; m. Marion Wallace Wright, Dec., 1864 (died 1883); 2d, Victoria Regina Royall, June 1890. Civ. engr. Pacific R.R. of Mo., 1852-57; asst. geologist of Mo., 1857-61; U.S. deputy collector internal revenue, Mo., 1862-64; asst. engr. Mo. Pacific R.R., 1864-66; U.S. assessor 5th Dist., Mo., 1866; asst. geologist of Ill., 1868, of Mo., 1871-73; state geologist of Mo., 1873-75; on surveys and constrn. of rys. in Kan., 1879-80; prof. geology, U. of Mo., 1887-97. Mem. bd. of jurors, Centennial Expn., Phila., 1876; spl. agt. 10th Census, on quarry industry, for Mo. and Kan.; mem. Mo. River Commn., 1884-1902. Author of several geol. reports of Mo. and Ill. and other geol. publs. Address: Columbia, Mo. Died Dec. 1912.

BROCK, Charles Robert, lawyer; b. near London, Ky., May 9, 1865; s. Daniel R. and Mary (Lucas) B.; B.S., Ky. State Coll., 1890; LL.D., Ky. U., 1916; m. Katherine P. Brown, June 1, 1893. Admitted to Ky. bar, 1892, and practiced at London; moved to Denver, Colo., 1901; asst. city atty., Denver, 1903-04; mem. law firms Smith & Brock, 1904-12, Smith, Brock & Ferguson, 1912-22, Smith & Brock, 1922—. Prof., equity pleading, 1904—, and pub. service cos., 1912-20, U. of Denver Law Sch. Mem. 1st Civil Service Commn. of Colo., 1907-11. Pres. Am. Bapt. Home Mission Soc., 1919-22; trustee U. of Denver, Northern Bapt. Theol. Sem. Ind. Democrat. Home: Denver, Colo. Died July 2, 1928.

BROCK, Charles William Penn, physician, surgeon; b. Augusta County, Va., June 1, 1836; s. Ansalem and Elizabeth Beverly (Buckner) B.; ed. pvt. schs. and U. of Va.; M.D., Med. Coll. of Va., Richmond, 1859; m. Elizabeth Tyler, Oct. 1, 1863. Served in Civil War in C.S. Army as pvt. surgeon, and chief surgeon, staff Maj. Gen. James L. Kemper; surgeon police dept., Richmond, 1868-1913; chief surgeon C.&O. R.R., 1882-1913. Democrat. Episcopalian. Mason, K.T. Home: Richmond, Va. Died Oct. 19, 1916.

BROCK, Robert Alonzo, historian; b. Richmond, Va., Mar. 9, 1839; s. Robert King and Elizabeth Mildred (Ragland) B.; acad. edn. Corr. sec. Va. Hist. Soc., 1875-93; edited its 11 vols. of Collections; sec. Southern Hist. Soc., 1887—, editor of 23 vols. of its papers; asso. editor Richmond Standard, 1879-83. Registrar and historian. Va. Soc. S.A.R., 1880—, later sec. Home: Richmond, Va. Died July 12, 1914.

BROCKWAY, Albert Leverett, architect; b. Utica, N.Y., Dec. 28, 1864; s. Leverett E. and Clara (Kingsley) B.; grad. scientific course, Brooklyn Poly. Inst., 1883, followed by 2 yrs.' course in architecture, École des Beaux Arts; m. Frances Hart Dunn, Oct. 31, 1893. Prof. architecture, Syracuse U., 1893-95, completely remodeling course after methods of the École des Beaux Arts. Home: Syracuse, N.Y. Died June 26, 1933.

BROCKWAY, Fred John, anatomist; b. S. Sutton, N.H., Feb. 24, 1860; s. John G. and Amanda C. B.; grad. Yale, 1882; M.D., Coll. Phys. & Surg., New York, 1887; m. Marion L. Turner, Nov. 25, 1891. Asst. demonstrator anatomy, Columbia U. Med. Dept. Author: Essentials Medical Physics, S15; Anatomy, L12. Home: Contoocook, N.H. Died 1901.

BROCKWAY, Zebulon Reed, penologist; b. Lyme, Conn., Apr. 28, 1827; ed. E. Haddam, Conn.; m. Jane Woodhouse, Apr. 13, 1853. Clerk Conn. State Prison, 1848; deputy supt. Albany Penitentiary, 1851; supt. Monroe Co. Penitentiary, 1854, Detroit House of Correction, 1861, N.Y. State Reformatory, Elmira, 1876-1900; retired. Mayor Elmira, 1906-07. Spl. U.S. commr. to establish a U.S. Mil. Prison, 1873. Non-resident spl. lecturer on penology, Cornell U., 1901. Charter mem. Nat. Prison Assn. U.S.A. (pres. 1898). Author: Fifty Years of Prison Service (autobiography). Address: Elmira, N.Y. Died Oct. 21, 1920.

BRODBECK, Andrew R., congressman; b. Jefferson, Pa., Apr. 11, 1860; ed. pub. schs. and acad.; LL.D., Ursinus Coll., Collegeville, Pa., 1920; m. Ellen R. Thoman; children—Estelle, Wilson (dec.), Mary Ellen, Viola. Teacher pub. schs., 1878-80; entered fertilizing business at 19, and later in various industrial enterprises; sheriff of York County, Pa., 1896-99; was mem. Dem. State Central Com.; alternate del. Dem. Nat. Conv., Kansas City, Mo., 1900; del. at large Dem. Nat. Conv., San Francisco, 1920; candidate on Dem. ticket for Congress, 1912; mem. 63d (1913-15) and 65th (1917-19) Congresses, 20th Pa. Dist. Dir. Hanover Saving Fund Soc. Mem. bd. dirs. Ursinus Coll. (Collegeville, Pa.); pres. bd. Hood Coll. (Frederick, Md.). Home: Hanover, Pa. Died Feb. 1937.

BRODEUR, Clarence Arthur, educator; b. Colchester, Vt., Sept. 25, 1865; s. Charles and Priscilla (Marsh) B.; A.B., Harvard, 1887; student law dept. Boston U., 1890-92; m. Mary Cornelia Latta, June 24, 1887. Teacher. Wellesley, Mass., 1887-88, Franklin, Mass., 1888-90, Tacoma, Wash., 1892-93; supt. schs., Warren-Wales, Mass., 1893-96, Chicopee, 1896-1901; prin. State Normal Sch., Westfield, Mass., 1901—. Republican. Congregationalist. Mason. Home: Westfield, Mass. Died Oct. 21, 1923.

BRODHEAD, J(oseph) Davis; b. Easton, Pa., Jan. 12, 1859; s. Richard and Mary (Bradford) B.; student Georgetown Coll., D.C., 1871-73, Seton Hall Coll., South Orange, N.J., 1876-78; LL.M., Catholic U. America, 1909; m. Cecile Harvier, Oct. 18, 1883. Admitted to Pa. bar, 1881, U.S. Supreme Court, 1907; dist. atty. Northampton County, Pa., 1889-92; del. Dem. Nat. Conv., 1892, 1904; mem. 60th Congress (1907-09), 26th Pa. Dist.; resumed practice of law at South Bethlehem, Pa.; judge 3d Jud. Dist., Pa., 1914-15; dir. Federal Reserve Bank, Phila., 1916-17; chief dept. of corp. management under "Trading with the Enemy Act," Nov. 1917-18. Roman Catholic. Home: South Bethlehem, Pa. Died Apr. 23, 1920.

BRODIE, Alexander Oswald, army officer; b. Edwards, N.Y., Nov. 13, 1849; s. Joseph and Margaret (Brown) B.; grad. U.S. Mil. Acad., 1865; m. Louise Hanlon, Dec. 15, 1892. Apptd. 2d lt. 1st Cav., June 15, 1870; 1st lt., May 25, 1875; resigned Sept. 30, 1877; pvt. 6th Cav., Aug. 6, 1883-Feb. 4, 1884; served against Apaches in Ariz. and Nez Percé campaign in Idaho. In cattle trade, Kan., 1878-82; mining in Dak. and Ariz., 1882-87; chief engr. Walter Storage Commn., Walnut Grove, Ariz., 1887-90; civ. and mining engr., Prescott, Ariz., 1893-94; county recorder, Yavapai County, Ariz., 1893-94. Maj. 1st U.S. Cav. ("Rough Riders"), May 17, 1898; lt. col., Aug. 11, 1898; served in Tampa and Cuba; in command left flank action at Las Guasimas, June 24, 1898, wounded. Rep. candidate for del. in Congress from Ariz., 1898; apptd. gov. of Ariz., July 1, 1902. Maj. asst. chief Record and Pension Office, Feb. 15, 1905; lt. col. mil. sec., June 10, 1905; lt. col. adj. gen., Mar. 5, 1907; col., Aug. 24, 1912, retired by operation of law, Mar. 13, 1913. Address: Haddonfield, N.J. Died May 10, 1918.

BRODIE, Edward Everett, diplomat; b. Fort Stevens, Ore., Mar. 12, 1876; s. Elias Henry and

Julia Matilda (Goff) B.; ed. U. of Ore.; m. Imogen Harding, July 12, 1905; children—George Harding, Madelon Jane. Began with Morning Enterprise, Oregon City, 1901, owner and pub. until 1935; v.p. Bowman, Deute, Cummings, Inc., San Francisco. Chmn. Rep. County Central Com., Clackamas County, Ore., 1916-21; mem. Ore. State Prison Commn., 1917; E.E. and M.P. to Siam, 1921-25, resigned; editor and pub. Morning Enterprise, Oregon City, 1908-30; E.E. and M.P. to Finland, 1930-33. Pres. Ore. State Editorial Assn., 1914-17, Nat. Editorial Assn., 1921-22; mem. Ore. State Property Tax Relief Commn., 1927-29; chmn. Ore. Liquor Control Commn., 1934; mem. Republican State Central Com., 1928-30. Mason (32°, Shriner), Woodman. Episcopalian. Home: San Francisco, Calif. Died June 27, 1939.

BRODRICK, Richard Godfrey, M.D.; b. San Francisco, Calif., Apr. 14, 1871; s. Richard and Margaret (Sheridian) B.; M.D., Cooper Med. Coll., San Francisco, 1892; grad. study N.Y. City and U. of Vienna, 1900-03; m. Florence Nightengale Boyd, Feb. 28, 1903; children—Richard Boyd, Sheridian Boyd, Barbara. Began practice at San Francisco, 1892; asst. surgeon, U.S.N., 1893-96, passed asst. surgeon, 1896-99, on retired list, 1899; health officer, San Francisco, 1908-15; supt. San Francisco Hosp., 1915-19; dir. hosps. of Alameda County, Calif., 1919-27; prof. hosp. administration, Stanford, 1927; supt. Stanford U. Hosps.; consultant in planning hosps., including San Francisco Hosp., Highland Hosp., etc.; cons. editor Modern Hospital. Awarded Congressional Medal of Honor, 1898, for services with Dewey in Battle of Manila Bay. Republican. Episcopalian. Home: Piedmont, Calif. Died May 2, 1929.

BROEDEL, Max, educator; b. Leipzig, Germany, June 8, 1870; s. Louis and Henrietta (Frenzel) B.; ed. Acad. Fine Arts, Leipzig; U. of Leipzig, 1886-90; came to U.S., 1894; m. Ruth Marian Huntington, Dec. 31, 1902; children—Elizabeth, Ruth (dec.), Carl, Elsa. Med. illustrator, anatomy and physiology, Leipzig, until 1893; Johns Hopkins Hosp., Baltimore, Md., until 1911; instr., Johns Hopkins, 1907-11, asso. prof. of art as applied to medicine, 1911—, also head of dept. Evang. Lutheran. Home: Baltimore, Md. Died Oct. 26, 1941.

BROGDEN, Willis James, judge; b. nr. Goldsboro, N.C., Oct. 18, 1877; s. Willis Hall and Virginia (Robinson) B.; Ph.B., U. of N.C., 1898; studied law at U. of N.C. and Duke U.; m. Lila Bingham Markham, Jan. 9, 1917; children—Willis James, Blackwell Markham. Admitted to N.C. bar, 1907, and began practice at Durham; v.p. 1st Nat. Bank of Durham, 1922-26. Mayor of Durham, 1911-15; asso. justice, Supreme Court of N.C., 1926—. Trustee U. of N.C., 1923-26, N.C. Coll. for Negroes (chmn. bd.). Democrat. Baptist. Mason. Kiwanian. Home: Durham, N.C. Died Oct. 29, 1935.

BROKAW, Charles Livingston, banker; b. Middlebush, N.J., May 22, 1866; s. Peter Stryker and Adaline B.; ed. common schs. and Chautauqua course 4 yrs.; m. 3d, Inez Eaton, July 28, 1919; children—Mrs. Dorothy Freer, Mrs. Margaret McCann (both by 2d marriage). Began in bank of Louisburg, Kan., 1884; became connected with Wyandotte County Nat. Bank, Kansas City, Kan., 1890; organized Commercial State Bank, Kansas City, Kan., 1897; pres. Commercial Nat. Bank, 1902—; v.p. Kan. Trust Co., Kan. Bankers Surety Co.; treas. Inter-State Bldg. & Loan Assn.; dir. Central Surety and Ins. Corp., Kansas City, Mo. Pres. Kan. State Y. P. Soc. of C. E., 1891, Kan. State S. S. Union, 1914; trustee U. of Kansas City (Kansas City, Mo.), Park Coll., Parkville, Mo. Republican. Presbyn. Woodman, Elk. Home: Kansas City, Kan. Died Oct. 14, 1936.

BROMBERG, Frederick George, lawyer; b. New York, June 19, 1837; s. Frederick and Lisette C. D. (Beetz) B.; A.B., Harvard, 1858; studied chemistry Lawrence Scientific Sch. (Harvard), 1861-63; unmarried. Tutor mathematics, Harvard, 1863-65; city treas., Mobile, 1867-69, postmaster, 1869-71; mem. Ala. Senate, 1868-72; mem. 43d Congress (1873-75), 1st Ala. Dist. as Liberal Republican. Was author of resolution of inquiry which closed the Freedman's Savings & Trust Co. and of first Nat. Quarantine bill; with Philetus A. Sawyer and Edwin O. Stanard, drafted the bill authorizing Capt. Eads to jetty the mouth of the Miss. River; originated idea of the Uniform Negotiable Instruments Law, 1886; mem. Ala. Conf. Commn. on Uniform State Laws. Pres. Mobile Bar Assn., 1900-03, Ala. Harvard Assn., Ala. State Bar Assn., 1906. Polit. and lit. editor "Unionist" (Progressive Republican), Mobile, until Nov. 1912. Home: Mobile, Ala. Died Sept. 4, 1930.

BROMWELL, Charles Summers, mil. engr.; b. Newport, Ky., May 1, 1869; s. Hon. Jacob Henry and Elizabeth (Summers) B.; high sch. edn., Cincinnati; grad. U.S. Mil. Acad., 1890, U.S. Engr. Sch. of Application, Willets Point, N.Y., 1893; m. Letitia G. Scott, June 11, 1896. Apptd. additional 2d lt. engrs., June 12, 1890; 2d lt., May 18, 1893; promoted through grades to maj., June 7, 1907; supt. pub. bldgs. and grounds, Washington, and mil. aid to the President, with temporary rank of col., 1904-09; in charge Milwaukee engring. dist., 1909-12; in charge Cleveland engring. dist., Aug. 1912—. Address: Cleveland, O. Died Dec. 10, 1915.

BRONDEL, John B., bishop; b. Bruges, Belgium, 1842; studied in Am. Coll. of U. of Louvain; ordained priest, Mechlin, 1864; rector at Steilacoom, Wash., 1867-77; of Walla Walla, 1877-78; consecrated bishop of Vancouver Island, 1879; apptd. administrator apostolic of Mont., 1883; bishop of Mont., 1884; was very successful in civilizing the Indians in his diocese. Address: Helena, Mont. Died 1903.

BRONNER, Edmond D., ry. official; b. Buffalo, N.Y., Feb. 19, 1859; s. Charles and Sophia (Devening) B.; ed. grammar and high schs., Buffalo, and U.S. Naval Acad.; m. Hattie M. Bailey, June 16, 1885 (died 1921); m. 2d, Frances Marsh McMicken, Aug. 16, 1923. Began as draftsman in car dept. of Can. Southern Ry., at St. Thomas, Ont., July 1880; draftsman, gen. foreman car shops, 1883-90, master car builder, 1890-96, asst. supt. motive power and equipment, 1896-1900, supt. motive power, 1900-12, gen. mgr., 1912-17, v.p. and gen. mgr., Mar. 15, 1917-June 10, 1918, federal mgr., June 10, 1918-Mar. 1, 1920, v.p., 1920—, M.C. R.R. Co.; pres. Detroit Terminal R.R., Detroit Mfrs. R.R.; v.p. Mackinaw Transportation Co.; dir. Detroit Brass Works, Detroit Valve & Fittings Co., Peoples State Bank. Home: Detroit, Mich. Died Sept. 1, 1930.

BRONNER, Harry, capitalist; b. N.Y. City, Nov. 19, 1868; ed. Coll. City of New York. Elected pres. M.P. R.R. Co., 1918, later chmn. bd.; dir. Chrysler Corp., Internat. Mercantile Marine Co., U.S. Realty & Improvement Co., B.&O. R.R. Co., American Lines Co., U.S. Lines Operations, Inc., U.S. Lines Co. Home: New York, N.Y. Died Dec. 21, 1940.

BRONSON, Samuel Lathrop, lawyer; b. Waterbury, Conn., Jan. 12, 1834; s. Dr. Henry and Sarah M. B.; A.B., Yale, 1855; m. Frances E. Stoddard, Nov. 30, 1861. Admitted to bar, 1857; practiced at Seymour, Conn., 1857-60, New Haven, 1860—; mem. Conn. Ho. of Rep., 1859, 1869, 1876, 1877; recorder City Ct., 1866-69; 1st judge Ct. Common Pleas, 1 yr.; corp. counsel, 1873-78; retired and managed his father's large interests until latter's death, 1893, when he succeeded to family estates. Dem. nominee for gov. of Conn., 1900. Home: New Haven, Conn. Deceased.

BRONSON, Solon Cary, theologian; b. W. Union, Ia., July 26, 1855; s. Harvey S. and Jane (McCool) B.; A.B., Upper Ia. U., 1875, A.M., 1879, LL.D., 1928; B.D., Garrett Bibl. Inst., Chicago, 1878, D.D., 1894; D.D., Cornell Coll., 1902; m. Frances Avann, July 2, 1879. Entered M.E. ministry, 1878; pastor various chs. in Ia., 1878-96; Cornelia Miller prof. practical theology, 1896-1913, prof. practical theology and social relations, 1913-26, emeritus, acting pres., 1908-09, Garrett Bibl. Inst.; also sec. of the faculty, same. Author: Religious Delusions, 1895. Home: Evanston, Ill. Died Mar. 26, 1931.

BRONSON, Walter Cochrane, univ. prof.; b. Roxbury, Mass., Aug. 17, 1862; s. Rev. Benjamin F. and Annie (Chaplin) B.; A.B., Brown U., 1887; Harvard Div. Sch., 1887-88; A.M., Cornell, 1890; Litt.D., Colby, 1904, Brown, 1915; m. Elsie M. Straffin, 1905. Prof. English, DePauw, 1890-92; asso. prof. English lit., 1892-95, prof., 1895-1927, prof. emeritus, 1927, Brown U. Author: Short History of American Literature, 1900; The History of Brown University, 1914. Editor: Poems of William Collins, 1898; English Essays, 1905; English Poems, 1907-10; American Poems, 1912; American Prose, 1916. Home: Providence, R.I. Died June 2, 1928.

BROOKE, Flavius Lionel, judge; b. Simcoe, Ont., Oct. 7, 1858; s. John and Sarah (Mann) B.; ed. Albert Coll., Belleville, Ont., 1877-79, and Osgood Hall, Toronto, 1880-1904; m. Miss B. Reidy, Nov. 27, 1884. Admitted to bar, Toronto, 1884; removed to Detroit, 1885; mem. firm Atkinson, Carpenter & Brooke, 1887-91, Brooke & Spalding, 1892-96. Supervisor of census, 1st Dist., Mich., 1900; judge Circuit Ct., 1900-08; justice Supreme Ct. of Mich., 1908—. Republican. Home: Detroit, Mich. Died Jan. 21, 1912.

BROOKE, Francis Key, bishop; b. Gambier, O., Nov. 2, 1852; s. Rev. John T. and Louisa R. B.; A.B., Kenyon Coll., 1874, A.M., 1881; S.T.D., Kan. Theol. Sch., 1892; D.D., U. of the South, Tenn., 1911, Kenyon, 1912; m. Mildred R. Baldwin, Jan. 5, 1881. Deacon, 1875, priest, 1877, P.E. Ch.; rector College Hill, O., 1875-77, Portsmouth, O., 1877-80, Piqua, O., 1880-84, Grace Ch., Sandusky, O., 1884-86, St. Peter's, St. Louis, 1886-88, Trinity Ch., Atchison, Kan., 1888-93; consecrated 1st bishop of Okla. and Indian Ty., 1893. Address: Oklahoma City, Okla. Died Oct. 22, 1918.

BROOKE, John Mercer, prof. physics; b. Tampa, Fla., Dec. 18, 1826; s. Maj. Gen. George Mercer, and Lucy (Thomas) B.; ed. prep. school, Burlington, N.J., and Kenyon Coll., O.; entered U.S.N. as midshipman, Mar. 3, 1841; grad. Naval Acad., 1847, with 1st class grad. from Annapolis; on duty Naval Observatory, Washington, 1851-53; while there invented deep-sea sounding apparatus; was in N. Pacific surveying and exploring expdn. in sloop-of-war Vincennes, under Commodore John Rogers, having charge of astron. dept.; comd. "Fennimore Cooper" in survey of route between San Francisco, Sandwich Islands, Japan and China; resigned from U.S.N. on secession of Va., 1861; entered C.S. service; made chief of bureau of ordnance and hydrography under Sec. Stephen Mallory; prof. physics, Va. Mil. Inst., 1866-99, emeritus, 1899. Invented Brooke gun; discovered the utility of the air-space in cannon; designed plans for iron-clad vessel with submerged ends—this plan being used in reconstruction of the Merrimac; drew directions for cruise of Shenandoah for destruction of whaling fleet; received from King William of Prussia (Emperor William I.) gold medal of science awarded by Acad. of Berlin. Home: Lexington, Va. Died 1906.

BROOKE, John Rutter, army officer; b. Montgomery County, Pa., July 21, 1838; s. William and Martha (Rutter) B.; ed. Freeland Sem. (now Ursinus Coll.), Pa., and Bolmars Sch., W. Chester, Pa.; m. Louisa Roberts, Dec. 24, 1863 (died 1867); m. 2d, Mary L. Stearns, Sept. 19, 1877. Capt. 4th Pa. Inf., Apr. 20, 1861; hon. mustered out, July 26, 1861; col. 53d Pa. Inf., Nov. 7, 1861; brig. gen. vols., May 12, 1864, "for distinguished services during battles of the Old Wilderness and Spottsylvania C.H., Va.;" resigned from vol. service, Feb. 1, 1866; lt. col. 37th U.S. Inf., July 28, 1866; transferred to 3d Inf., Mar. 15, 1869; col. 13th Inf., Mar. 20, 1879; transferred to 3d Inf., June 14, 1879; brig. gen., Apr. 6, 1888; maj. gen., May 22, 1897. Was head of mil. commn. and gov. gen. P.R.; gov. gen. of Cuba and comdg. Div. of Cuba; later comdg. Dept. of the East; retired by operation of law, July 21, 1902. Address: Washington, D.C. Died Sept. 5, 1926.

BROOKE, Richard Norris, artist; b. Warrenton, Va., Oct. 20, 1847; s. James Vass and Mary E. (Norris) B.; studied Pa. Acad. Fine Arts and under Bonnât and Constant, Paris, France; unmarried. Vice-prin. Corcoran Sch. of Art. Pres. Soc. Washington Artists. Home: Warrenton, Va. Died Apr. 1920.

BROOKE, St. George Tucker, educator, lawyer; b. at U. of Va., July 22, 1844; s. Henry Laurens and Virginia (Tucker) B.; ed. Richmond, Winchester and Ashland, Va.; studied law, U. of Va., 1867-69; hon. A.M., W.Va. U.; LL.D., Wake Forest Coll.; m. Mary Harrison Brown, Aug. 15, 1882. Midshipman C.S.N., 1861-62; pvt. Co. B, 2d Va. Cav., Fitz Lee's Brigade, 1862-65; thrice wounded. Taught school, 1866-67; practiced law, Craig County, Va., 1869-70, Charles Town, W.Va., 1870-78; apptd. to 1st professorship of law in newly established Coll. of Law of W.Va. U., 1878; retired under Carnegie Foundation, 1909. Democrat. Author: Common Law Practice and Pleading for W.Va., 1896. Home: Charles Town, W.Va. Died May 16, 1914.

BROOKE-RAWLE, William, lawyer; b. Phila., Aug. 29, 1843; s. C. Wallace and Elizabeth Tilghman (Rawle) B.; A.B., U. of Pa., 1863; m. Elizabeth Norris Pepper, Feb. 7, 1872. Served in Civil War, lt. and capt. 3d Pa. Cav.; bvtd. maj. and lt. col. Agt. Penn. estates in Pa. Author: The Right Flank at Gettysburg; With Gregg in the Gettysburg Campaign; Gregg's Cavalry Fight at Gettysburg; The General Title of the Penn Family to Pennsylvania. Home: Philadelphia, Pa. Died Dec. 1, 1915.

BROOKER, Charles Frederick; b. Litchfield, Conn., Mar. 4, 1847; s. Martin Cook and Sarah Maria (Seymour) B.; ed. Litchfield, and Torrington, Conn.; hon. A.M., Yale, 1911; m. Julia E. Clarke Farrel, Oct. 30, 1894. Pres. Am. Brass Co., 1900-20, chmn. bd., 1920—; pres. Ansonia Nat. Bank, Ansonia Land & Water Power Co.; dir. U.S. Smelting, Refining & Mining Co., Anaconda Copper Mining Co., Chili Copper Co., Chili Exploration Co., Mines Investment Co. Mem. Com. Ho. of Rep., 1875, Senate, 1893; Conn. commr. Chicago Expn., 1893; mem. Rep. State Central Com.; mem. Rep. Nat. Com., 1900-16 (exec. com. 1904, 08); del. at large Rep. Nat. Conv., 1900, 04, 08, 12, 20. Vestryman Christ Ch. (Ansonia). Home: Ansonia, Conn. Died Dec. 20, 1926.

BROOKINGS, Robert Somers, mcht. and mfr., philanthropist; b. Cecil County, Md., Jan. 22, 1850; s. Dr. Richard and Mary (Carter) B.; ed. West Nottingham Acad., Cecil Co.; hon. A.M., Yale, 1899; LL.D., U. of Mo., 1902, Harvard, 1920; LL.D. and M.D. (hon.), Washington U., 1929; m. Isabel Vallé January, June 19, 1927. Admitted to partnership, Cupples Co., St. Louis, 1872; retired from business, 1896; remainder of life was devoted to philanthropy. Vice-pres. St. Louis Union Trust Co.; president St. Louis Choral Symphony Soc., 1882-97; pres. Mercantile Library, St. Louis; pres. corp. Washington U., St. Louis, 1897-1928; erected and equipped, 1913-14, all the bldgs. of the reorganized Med. Sch. of Washington U.; trustee, Carnegie Instn., Washington, and Carnegie Endowment for Internat. Peace; regent Smithsonian Instn.; founder and chmn. bd. Brookings Instn., Washington; was mem. War Industries Bd. and chmn. Price Fixing Com., also commr. of Finished Products, and mem. Purchasing Commn. during World War; mem. Capital and Labor Commn. apptd. by the President, 1919. Awarded D.S.M. (U.S.); Legion of Honour (French); Comdr. of Crown (Italian); made hon. adviser U.S. Army Industrial Coll. 1925. Author: Industrial Ownership, 1925; Economic Democracy, 1929; A Suggested Evolution of Capitalism, 1930. Home: Washington, D.C. Died Nov. 15, 1932.

BROOKS, Alfred Hulse, geologist; b. Ann Arbor, Mich., July 18, 1871; s. Maj. Thomas Benton and Hannah (Hulse) B.; studied in Germany, 1890-91; B.S., Harvard, 1894; post-grad. study at Paris; hon. D.Sc., Colgate U., 1920; m. Mabel W. Baker, Feb. 23, 1903. Asst. geologist U.S. Geol. Survey, working in various states, and 1898-1923 engaged in geol. and exploratory work in Alaska; chief Alaskan geologist. Vice-chmn. Alaska R.R. Commn., 1911-12. Received gold medals, Am. Geog. Soc. and Geog. Soc. of Paris, 1913. Wrote The Geography and Geology of Alaska, and other papers on Alaska, and on military subjects. Commd. capt. of engrs., Apr. 1917, maj., July 1917, lt. col., Oct. 1918; was chief geologist, A.E.F.; served in France, Aug. 1917-Apr. 1919. With Am. Peace Commn., Feb.-Apr. 1919. Home: Washington, D.C. Died Nov. 22, 1924.

BROOKS, Anson Strong, mfr.; b. Oswego County, N.Y., Sept. 6, 1852; s. Sheldon and Jeannette (Ranney) B.; ed. pub. schs.; m. Georgie L. Andros, July 24, 1876; children—Paul Andros, Stanley (dec.). Began as asst. to father in grain business, 1868; jr. mem. firm Brooks Bros., Minneapolis, 1873-1933, pres., 1930—; lumber mfg., 1901—; mfr. newsprint, 1911—; chmn. bd. Powell River Co., Ltd.; chmn. Brooks-Scanlon Lumber Co., Inc.; pres. Central Fla. Lumber Co.; dir. First Nat. Bank, Minneapolis. Republican. Mason. Home: Minneapolis, Minn. Died Aug. 3, 1937.

BROOKS, Charles Alvin, clergyman; b. Watkins, N.Y., Jan. 7, 1871; s. Charles Wesley and Elsie (Green) B.; Rochester U., 1898-1900; grad. Newton Theol. Instn., 1896; D.D., Bucknell, 1921; m. Ellen Keith, Jan. 7, 1897; children—Majelk, Gladys D., Frances O. Ordained Bapt. ministry, 1896; pastor Waterloo, N.Y., 1896-98, Knowlesville, 1898-1900, Pittsford, 1900-03, 3d St. Ch., Dayton, O., 1903-07; exec. sec. Cleveland Bapt. Assn., 1907-14; sec. City and Foreign Speaking Missions, also sec. social service of Am. Bapt. Home Mission Soc., 1914-24; pastor Englewood Baptist Ch., Chicago, 1924—; mem. bd. mgrs. Am. Bapt. Foreign Missions Soc.; mem. Social Service Commn. of Northern Bapt. Conv. Extended trip through Europe, 1913, to study immigration; European commr. Northern Bapt. Conv., and Bapt. World Alliance, 1919-20; trustee Bapt. Theol. Union, Chicago, Ill. Author: Christian Americanization, 1919; Through the Second Gate. Home: Chicago, Ill. Died Jan. 11, 1931.

BROOKS, Charles Edward, actuary; b. Baltimore, Md., Aug. 26, 1879; s. William Keith and Amelia (Schultz) B.; A.B., Johns Hopkins, 1900, Ph.D., 1904; grad. student Harvard, 1913-14; m. Troy Jackson, June 14, 1913; children—Charles Ernest, Mary Elizabeth. Actuarial clk. Prudential Ins. Co. of America, 1904-06; actuary Southern Life Ins. Co., 1906-09; lecturer Johns Hopkins, 1909; instr. mathematics, Northwestern, 1910-13; asst. prof. mathematics and ins., U. of Calif., 1914-18; actuary or cons. actuary, 1918—, for life ins. orgns. and pub. bodies, including: Carnegie Foundation for Advancement of Teaching, Bur. of War Risks Ins., Teachers Ins. and Annuity Assn. of America, Wis. Joint Legislative Com. on Teachers' Pensions, Lutheran Brotherhood, Wis. State Retirement System, Minneapolis Teachers Retirement Fund Assn., Nat. Ry. Employees Pension Assn. Democrat. Episcopalian. Home: Madison, Wis. Died Dec. 15, 1936.

BROOKS, Charles Stephen, author; b. Cleveland, O., June 25, 1878; s. Stephen Edmund and Mary Elizabeth (Coffinberry) B.; A.B., Yale, 1900; Litt.D., Allegheny Coll., 1928; m. Minerva Cozens Kline, Oct. 12, 1907; m. 2d, Mary Seymour Curtis-Brown, Sept. 4, 1929. With The Brooks Co., printers, Cleveland, 1900-15, advancing to v.p., later dir.; pres. Play House Foundation. With Emergency Fleet Corp., Washington, D.C., World War, subsequently with the House Commn., N.Y. City, under Dept. of State. Lecturer on English lit., Coll. for Women, Western Reserve U., 1922-24. Episcopalian. Author: Journeys to Bagdad, 1915; There's Pippins and Cheese to Come, 1917; Chimney-Pot Papers, 1919; Luca Sarto, 1920; Hints to Pilgrims, 1921; Frightful Plays, 1922; A Thread of English Road, 1924; plays, "Wappin' Wharf," prod. in Cleveland, Mar. 1921, "Luca Sarto," Oct. 1922; (books) Luca Sarto, 1924; Like Summer's Cloud, 1925; Roundabout to Canterbury, 1926; Roads to the North, 1928; Prologue, 1931; The Tragedy of Josephine Maria (1-act plays), 1931; Wappin' Wharf, 1932; English Spring, 1932; An Italian Winter, 1933; A Window at the Inn (play), 1934. Home: Cleveland, O. Died June 29, 1934.

BROOKS, Christopher Parkinson, prof. textile mfg.; b. Blackburn, England, Apr. 17, 1866; s. Thomas and Frances (Parkinson) B.; ed. Queen Elizabeth Sch., Blackburn; m. Emma Higson, Sept. 1888. Organized textile dept., Blackburn, science and technical schools, 1884; supt. and mng. dir. English cotton mills, 1886-95; examiner in cotton mfg. all English Tech. Schools, 1890-95; organized and was dir. Lowell (Mass.) Textile School, 1896-98; organized, 1898, and until 1904 was mng. dir. New Bedford (Mass.) Textile School; prin. Textile dept., Internat. Correspondence Sch.; established Am. Correspondence Sch. of Textiles, 1898; lectured in course of municipal lectures, City of Boston, 1899; honor medallist City and Guilds of London Inst., London. Author: Cotton Manufacturing, 1888 S16; Weaving Calculations, 1889 S16; Cotton, Its Uses, Varieties, Fibre Structure and Cultivation, 1898 S16; Instruction Papers of the American Correspondence School of Textiles, 1898-1901; Textile text-books of Internat. Correspondence Schools, 1902-05; and several smaller publs. Home: New Bedford, Mass. Died 1909.

BROOKS, Edward, educator; b. Stony Point, N.Y., Jan. 16, 1831; removed to Sullivan County, 1846; ed. 1 yr. Normal Inst., Liberty, N.Y.; studied and taught in U. of Northern Pa., 1851-54; prof. mathematics in acad., Monticello, N.Y., 1854-55; hon. A.M., Union, N.Y., Ph.D., Lafayette, and Washington and Jefferson, 1876; m. H. Marie Dean, 1855. Prof. Mathematics, 1855-66, prin., 1866-83, State Normal Sch., Millersville, Pa.; supt. pub. schs., Phila., 1891-1906; reorganized Girls' High Sch. and Girls' Normal Sch., 1903; established Commercial High Sch. for Girls, 1896, and dept. of commerce in Boys' High Sch., 1898; reorganized instrn. in elementary schs., 1892-97; introduced observance of Flag Day, 1893; organized Dept. of Compulsory Education, 1897; reorganized Dept. Superintendence under new state law, 1906. Pres. Pa. State Teachers' Assn., 1868. Author: The Philosophy of Arithmetic, 1876; Normal Methods of Teaching, 1880; Mental Science and Culture, 1883; Reading and Elocution, 1878; The Story of the Iliad, 1889; The Story of the Odyssey, 1891; The Story of the Æneid, 1898; The Story of King Arthur, 1899; The Story of Tristram, 1901; The Story of the Faerie Queene, 1902; The Story of Siegfried, 1903; Wonder Stories from the Mabinogion, 1907; Normal Series of Mathematics (about 20 books), 1858-96. Home: Philadelphia, Pa. Died June 29, 1912.

BROOKS, Elbridge Streeter, author, editor; b. Lowell, Mass., Apr. 14, 1846; s. Elbridge Gerry B.; entered Free Acad., now Coll. City of New York, but left in jr. year, 1864; A.M., Tufts Coll., 1887; m. Hannah Melissa Debaun, Oct. 19, 1870. Connected with book and publishing trade, 1865—; asso. editor St. Nicholas, 1884-87; editor Wide Awake, 1891-93; then literary editor Lothrop Pub. Co., Boston. Author: Historic Boys, 1885; in Leisler's Times, 1886; Chivalric Days, 1886; Storied Holidays, 1887; Historic Girls, 1887; The Story of the American Indian, 1887; The Story of the American Sailor, 1888; The Story of the American Soldier, 1889; The True Story of the United States of America, 1891; The True Story of Christopher Columbus, 1892; The Century Book for Young Americans: the Story of the Government, 1894; The True Story of George Washington, 1895; A Boy of the First Empire, 1895; Great Men's Sons, 1895; Under the Tamaracks—a story of the Thousand Islands, 1896; The True Story of Abraham Lincoln, 1896; The Century Book of Famous Americans, 1896; The True Story of U. S. Grant, 1897; The True Story of Benjamin Franklin, 1898; The Master of the Strong Hearts, 1898; The True Story of Lafayette, 1899; Historic Americans, 1899; Stories of the Old Bay State, 1899; On Woodcone Island, 1899; In Blue and White, 1899; The Story of the Nineteenth Century, 1900; With Lawton and Roberts, 1900; The Century Book of the American Colonies, 1900; also many other books. Home: Somerville, Mass. Died 1902.

BROOKS, Frank Hilliard, mfr.; b. St. Johnsbury, Vt., Nov. 24, 1868; s. Samuel Towle and Lucy Clark (Mills) B.; ed. graded schs. and acad., St. Johnsbury; m. Ellen H. Fairbanks, Jan. 29, 1897; children—Margaret Fairbanks, Priscilla Fairbanks, Frances Clapp. Began as bookkeeper with E. & T. Fairbanks Co., 1886, dir. 1897, chmn. exec. com. of bd., 1910, pres. and mgr., 1912-17. Organized Brooks-Tyler Dry Goods Co. (now Berry-Ball Dry Goods Co.), 1899. Apptd., 1913, by Gov. Fletcher, mem. Bd. of Commrs. to investigate ednl. system of Vt.; ex-mem. of State Bd. of Edn. (examiner 10 yrs.). Pres. and chmn. Vt. Y.M.C.A. State Com. 15 yrs., also of World Y.M.C.A. Council and Personnel, World War; mem. Internat. Y.M.C.A. Com. 15 yrs.; mem. Nat. Congl. Council many yrs. and presided at noted Men's League Dinner, at New Haven, 1915. Was federal food administrator for Vt., World War, also mem. exec. coms. of Vt. and N.E. of U.S. Fuel Administration. Republican. Conglist. Home: Newton Highlands, Mass. Died Feb. 7, 1931.

BROOKS, Franklin Eli, congressman; b. Sturbridge, Mass., Nov. 19, 1860; s. E. T. and Anna E. B.; A.B., Brown U., 1883, A.M., 1886; law student Boston U., 1887-88; m. Sara Brainerd Coolidge, June 3, 1891. Admitted to bar, 1888; practiced at Boston, 1888-91, Colorado Springs, Colo., 1892—; pres. Costilla Estates Development Co. and San Luis Southern Ry. Co. Mem. 58th and 59th Congresses (1903-07), Colo. at-large. Republican. Trustee Brown U., Colo. State Agrl. Coll. Address: Colorado Springs, Colo. Died Feb. 7, 1916.

BROOKS, Fred Emerson, author; b. Waverley, N.Y., Dec. 5, 1850; s. William and Matilda C. (Stone) B.; A.B., Madison (now Colgate) U., 1873; m. Mary Emma Tregidgo, Dec. 1, 1884 (died Jan. 18, 1907); m. 2d, Emma Jahn Holmes, Mar. 28, 1913. Lived in San Francisco, 1873-91, New York, 1891, San Francisco, 1910—. Well known as reader of his own poems on lyceum platform. Author: Battle Ballads, 1886; Old Ace and Other Poems, 1899; Pickett's Charge and Other Poems, 1903; Buttered Toasts, 1911; Cream Toasts, 1915; The Gravedigger, 1916; Patriotic Toasts, 1917; also Christmas Cantatas, Jonnie Doubter, 1900; Santa Claus' Minstrels, 1901; comic opera, The Missing Link, 1917; The Land of Arcadie, 1917; Father Goose Melodies, 1920; California and Other Poems, 1921; (moving picture plays) John Cardon—the Cattle King, Zargo, The Prospector, The Sultan and the Brigand, Yankee Doodledum, Crazy Phil, The Alconda, The Vapor Bath (all 1921). Home: Berkeley, Calif. Died June 1, 1923.

BROOKS, (Henry) Harlow, physician; b. Medo, Minn., Mar. 31, 1871; s. Daniel Walker and Katherine (Riley) B.; High Sch. Minn.; U. of Ore.; M.D., Dept. Medicine and Surgery, U. of Mich., 1895; post-grad. work, U. of Freiburg, Polyclinic, Munich, Bavaria; hon. M.S., U. of Mich., 1929; m. Louise Dudley Davis, June 14, 1899. Asst. demonstrator anatomy, U. of Mich., 1894; instr. histology and embryology, Bellevue Hosp. Med. Coll., 1895-98; instr. and asst. prof. pathology and spl. pathology, 1898-1900, New York U., asst. prof. clin. medicine, 1904-11, prof. clin. medicine, 1912—; visiting phys. Bellevue Hosp.; cons. phys. City Hosp., Montefiore Hosp., Ossining Hosp., Union Hosp., Beth Israel Hospital, Greenwich Hospital; consulting pathologist, Hackensack Hospital. Civilian physician, U.S. Army, 1898-99; mem. 7th Regt. N.G. N.Y., 1896-1915; capt. Med. Corps, 1899, retired; returned to active list as lt. col., chief surgeon 2d Div., July 1916; placed on nat. guard reserve, Jan. 1917; commd. maj., Med. R.C., Aug. 21, 1917; active service, Sept. 7, 1917, med. chief Base Hosp., Camp Upton, Yaphank, L.I.; promoted lt. col., Med. Corps, U.S.A., Aug. 1918; chief consultant in medicine, 1st Army A.E.F., later transferred to 2d Army A.E.F., Nov. 1, 1918; transferred to staff, chief surgeon, 2d Army, A.E.F., Jan. 1, 1919; discharged, Apr. 22, 1919; commissioned col, U.S.R.C., Oct. 14, 1919. Trustee N.Y. Pathol. Soc. Awarded D.S.M. (U.S.). Address: New York, N.Y. Died Apr. 13, 1936.

BROOKS, Henry S., author; b. London, Eng.; ed. San Domingo House, Everton, and U. of London, prep.; student Royal British Sch. of Design, Somerset House; gold medalist, 1849. Calif. pioneer, 1850; editor California Mountaineer, monthly mag., 1861; asso. editor The Pacific, 1862-65; founder and editor the Triunfo Mining Co., mgr., 1862-82. Removed to New York, 1886. Author: Doña Paula's Treasure; A Catastrophe in Bohemia; Progression to Immortality, 1902; also other stories. Home: Dobbs Ferry, N.Y. Died 1910.

BROOKS, Jabez, univ. prof.; b. Stockport, Cheshire, Eng., Sept. 18, 1823; s. David and Ann B.; came to U.S., 1840; A.B., Wesleyan U., 1850, A.M., 1853; D.D., Lawrence U., 1864; m. Ruby B. Pease, Sept. 6, 1851. Prin. Watertown Sem., 1850; prin. prep. dept., Hamline U., 1854-57, pres., 1861-69; prof. Greek, U. of Minn., 1869—. Mem. Normal and Agrl. State bds., Minn., 2 terms each; del. Meth. Gen. Conf., 1864; pres. Minn. Ednl. Assn., 1868. Methodist. Author: Attic Greek, a Book for Beginners, 1891. Home: Minneapolis, Minn. Died 1910.

BROOKS, James Byron, lawyer; b. Rockingham, Vt., June 27, 1839; s. Nathaniel and Emily (Cutler) B.; A.B., Dartmouth, 1869, A.M., 1886; LL.B., Albany Law Sch., 1871; D.C.L., Syracuse U., 1895; m. Caroline Lucelia Jewell, Sept. 7, 1873. Pvt. 1st Vt. Inf., 3 mos.' service, 1861; 2d lt., Co. H., 1st lt., Co. I, 4th Vt. Inf., and capt. Co. H, same regt., but discharged before mustered as capt.; on detached service as signal officer, 1861-63; wounded at Battle of the Wilderness, May 6, 1864; discharged on account of wound, Aug. 5, 1864. In practice at Syracuse, 1872—; sr. mem. firm of Brooks, Gere & Church; dean Coll. of Law, Syracuse U., 1895—. Alderman of Syracuse, 1884; sch. commr., 1886, 1887; mem. water bd., 1888-1901. Republican. Methodist. Trustee Syracuse U. Home: Syracuse, N.Y. Died June 17, 1914.

BROOKS, J(ames) Wilton, lawyer; b. New York, N.Y., Apr. 19, 1854; s. Hon. James and Mary Louisa (Randolph) B.; A.B., Yale, 1875; student, Columbia Law Sch.; LL.D., St. John's Coll., Md., 1890; m. Mrs. Frances Beadel, née Reese, Apr. 2, 1912. Admitted to bar, 1882, and practiced at New York. Mem. N.Y. Assembly, 1882-83. Author: The History of the Court of Common Pleas, 1896. Address: New York, N.Y. Died July 6, 1916.

BROOKS, Jesse Wendell, clergyman; b. Cheshire, Conn., Sept. 26, 1858; s. Jesse R. and Louise A. (Smith) B.; A.B., Rutgers, 1881; grad. Union Theol. Seminary, 1884; Ph.D., New York Univ., 1889; m.

Louise Bissell Upham, 1884. Ordained Congregational ministry, 1884; pastor Bay Shore, L.I., N.Y., 1884-87; in Europe, 1887, Stuyvesant Avenue Church, Brooklyn, 1887-88, East New York Dutch Reformed Church, Brooklyn, 1888-94, Irving Park Ch., Chicago, 1894-98; sec. and supt. Chicago Tract Soc., 1898-1914, and 1916—; sec. Northwestern Agency of American Tract Soc., 1898-1902 and 1910-14; pres. Union Missionary Training Inst. of New York, 1914-16. N.Y. State supt. Christian Endeavor, 1887-88; an organizer and 3 yrs. v.p. Am. Soc. Comparative Religion; mem. Bd. Domestic Missions Reformed Ch. in America and chmn. Gen. Synod's Sabbath Observance Com. several yrs. and addressed Congressional Com. regarding Sunday closing of Chicago World's Fair, 1893. Mem. council Hope Coll., 1898-1904; mem. bd. mgrs. Am. Sabbath Union and of Lord's Day Alliance of U.S., 1892-1914, v.p., 1914—; mem. exec. com. Federal Council Churches of Christ in America, 1912—; chmn. First Gen. Conf. for Evangelization of Russia, Chicago, 1918; editor "Good News for Russia," Chicago, 1918—. Home: Wheaton, Ill. Died July 1920.

BROOKS, John Graham, author, lecturer; b. Acworth, N.H., July 19, 1846; s. Chapin Kidder and Parmelia (Graham) B.; S.T.B., Harvard Divinity Sch., 1875; studied 3 yrs. at univs. of Berlin, Jena and Freiburg. Became lecturer on econ. subjects; 2 yrs. instr. Harvard U.; several yrs. lecturer, extension dept., U. of Chicago; 2 yrs. expert U.S. Dept. Labor at Washington, making report of 1893 upon Workingmen's Insurance in Germany; lecturer, U. of Calif. Author: The Social Unrest, 1903; As Others See Us, 1908; An American Citizen, 1910; American Syndicalism, 1913; Labor's Challenge to the Social Order, 1920. Home: Cambridge, Mass. Died Feb. 8, 1938.

BROOKS, Noah, author, journalist; b. Castine, Me., Oct. 24, 1830; began newspaper career, Boston, 1850; went to Calif., 1859, and with Benjamin P. Avery established the Marysville Appeal; war corr. Sacramento Union, 1862-65; naval officer, port of San Francisco, 1865-66; mng. editor Alta, California, 1866-71; on staff New York Tribune, 1871-75; New York Times, 1875-84; editor Newark (N.J.) Advertiser, 1884-94; m. 1856, Caroline Fellows, 1856 (died 1862). Author: The Boy Emigrants; The Fairport Nine; Our Baseball Club; Abraham Lincoln; The Boy Settlers; American Statesmen; Tales of the Maine Coast; Abraham Lincoln and the Downfall of American Slavery; How the Republic is Governed; Short Studies in American Party Politics; Washington in Lincoln's Time; The Mediterranean Trip; The Story of Marco Polo; The Boys of Fairport; Scribner's History of the United States (2 vols.); General Henry Knox, A Revolutionary Soldier; First Across the Continent, 1901 S 3; Lem—a New England Village Boy, 1901 S 3. Address: Castine, Me. Died 1903.

BROOKS, Richard E., artist; b. Braintree, Mass.; pupil T. H. Bartlett, Boston, and Jean Paul Aubé, and Injalbert, Paris. Hon. mention Paris Salon, 1895; 3d class medal, Paris Salon, 1899; exhibited at Paris Expn., 1900. Mem. Nat. Inst. Arts and Letters. Died May 2, 1919.

BROOKS, Robert Clarkson, college prof.; b. Piqua, O., Feb. 7, 1874; s. James Eugene and Jennie Margaret (Kiser) B.; A.B., Ind. U., 1896; President White fellow, Cornell U., 1897-98; traveling fellow, univs. of Halle and Berlin, 1898-99; Ph.D., Cornell, 1903; Dr. rer. pol. honoris causa, U. of Berne, 1935; m. Elizabeth Hewson, Sept. 4, 1900; 1 son, Robert Clarkson. Instr., Cornell U., 1899-1904; Joseph Wharton prof. economics, Swarthmore Coll., 1904-08; prof. polit. science, U. of Cincinnati, 1908-12, Swarthmore (Pa.) Coll., Sept. 1912—; summer schools, U. of Calif., 1916; Cornell U., 1921. Field dir. Am. Red Cross, League Island Navy Yard, 1918-19. Pres. Am. Polit. Sci. Assn., 1940. Democrat. Author: Corruption in American Politics and Life, 1910; Teachers' Salaries and Cost of Living, 1913; Government and Politics of Switzerland, 1918; Political Parties and Electoral Problems, 1923; Reading for Honors at Swarthmore, 1927; Civic Training in Switzerland, 1930; Deliver Us from Dictators!, 1935. Editor, Bryce's American Commonwealth, Fiftieth Anniversary, 1939. Home: Swarthmore, Pa. Died Feb. 2, 1941.

BROOKS, Samuel Palmer, univ. pres.; b. Milledgeville, Ga., Dec. 4, 1863; s. Samuel Erskine and Aurelia E. (Palmer) B.; A.B., Baylor U., 1893; A.B., Yale, 1894, A.M., 1902; grad. work (history), U. of Chicago; LL.D., Richmond Coll., Va., 1903, Mercer U., 1922, Austin (Tex.) College, 1924, Georgetown Coll., 1929; m. Mattie Sims, Dec. 24, 1895; children—Aurelia Emma, Sims Palmer. Pres. Baylor U., 1902—. Lecturer on ednl. subjects. Corr. sec. Tex. Bapt. Edn. Commn., 1905. Pres. Coll. Sect., Tex. State Teachers' Assn., 1901, 19, Tex. State Y.M.C.A., 1907. Organized Tex. State Peace Congress, the first state organization of its kind in U.S., 1907. Contbr. to "The South in the Building of the Nation," 1908. Grand orator, N.W. Masonic Grand Lodge of Tex., 1908, 22. V.p. Southern Bapt. Conv., Baltimore, 1910, New Orleans, 1917; pres. Bapt. Gen. Conv. of Tex., 1914-17; pres. Southern Sociol. Congress, 1915. Home: Waco, Tex. Died May 14, 1931.

BROOKS, Sarah Warner (Mrs.). Author: English poetry and Poets; My Fire Opal; Poverty Knob, 1900; The Search for Ceres, 1900. Address: Medford, Mass. Died 1906.

BROOKS, Thomas Benton, engr.; b. Monroe, N. Y., June 15, 1836; grad. Union Coll., C.E., 1857 (A.M.); m. Hannah Hulse, 1868 (died 1883); m. 2d, Martha Giesler, 1887. Practiced as civil and mining engr.; in Civil war, lt. 1st N.Y. vol. engrs., serving as engr. officer on staff Gen. Gilmore; bvtd. lt. col. and col.; later State geologist, Mich. and Wis.; published reports on Lake Superior iron regions, 1872-76; later farming; owned live-stock and tobacco plantations in S.W. Ga., spending winters at Bainbridge, Decatur County, Ga. Home: Newburgh, N. Y. Died 1900.

BROOKS, Victor Lee, lawyer; b. Rutledge, Ala., Sept. 25, 1870; s. Lawrence David and Beatrice (Houghton) B.; LL.B., U. of Tex., 1892; m. Grace Harrison, Aug. 16, 1904. Practiced at Austin, 1892—; instr. law dept. U. of Tex., 1892-93; mem. firm Brooks, Hart & Woodward; city atty., Austin, 1894-1901; dist. judge 26th Jud. Dist., 1903-08; mem. Civic Draft Bd., Travis Co., Tex., 1917-18; mem. County Council Defense, 1917-18; chmn. Austin City Charter Commn., 1922. Democrat. K.P., Elk. Home: Austin, Texas. Died Sept. 1, 1925.

BROOKS, William Benthall, naval officer; b. Portsmouth, Va., Nov. 27, 1832; s. William and Mary Elizabeth (Benthall) B.; ed. pvt. schs. and by pvt. tutor; m. Amelia Wright, Sept. 23, 1858. Apptd. from Va., 3d asst. engr. U.S.N., Feb. 1852; promoted 2d asst. engr., Sept., 1855; 1st asst. engr., 1858; lt. chief engr., 1861; retired with rank of capt., Mar., 1892; promoted to chief engr. with rank of rear adm. retired, by act of Congress, June 1896. Episcopalian. Home: Erie, Pa. Died 1910.

BROOKS, William Keith, naturalist; b. Cleveland, O., Mar. 25, 1848; grad. Williams, 1870, Harvard, Ph.D., 1875; LL.D., Williams, 1893, also Hobart and U. of Pa.; m. Amelia Schultz, June 1878 (died 1901). Asst. Boston Soc. Natural History, 1875-76; asso. prof. and prof. zoölogy, Johns Hopkins, 1876. Mem. Nat. Acad. Sciences. Awarded medal, Soc. d'Acclamitation, Paris; challenger medal, Edinburgh; medal, St. Louis Expn., 1904. Author: Handbook of Invertebrate Zoölogy; The Stomatopoda of H. M. S. Challenger, A. Monograph of the Genus Salpa; The Foundations of Zoölogy; The Oyster; Rep. Md. Oyster Commn., etc. Address: Baltimore, Md. Died 1908.

BROOKS, William Myron, educator; b. Laporte, O., Mar. 5, 1835; s. Samuel and Sophia (Johnson) B.; A.B., Oberlin Coll., 1857, A.M., 1861, D.D., 1893; m. Adelia Sophia Jones, Jan. 17, 1860. Prin. Tabor Lit. Inst., 1857-66; pres. Tabor Coll., 1866-96. Supt. schs., Fremont County, Ia., 1860-65; mem. Ia. Ho. of Rep., 1876-78. Republican. Pres. Tabor & Northern Ry., 1891-98. Congl. clergyman; moderator Iowa State Congl. Assn. twice; pres. Iowa State Teachers' Assn., 1868; trustee Nat. Council Congl. Chs., 1895-98. Chaplain of Cumnock Sch., Los Angeles, 1916—. Author: The Story of Tabor College, 1886; Glimpses of Four Score Years, 1915; Chapel Talks, 1921; Golden Keys to the Morning, 1922. Home: Los Angeles, Calif. Died Nov. 23, 1924.

BROOKS, William Penn, agriculturist; b. S. Scituate, Mass., Nov. 19, 1851; s. Nathaniel and Rebecca Partridge (Cushing) B.; B.S. (valedictorian), Mass. Agrl. Coll., 1875, grad. student chemistry and botany, 1876; Ph.D., Halle, 1897; hon. degree Nogaku Hakushi, Japanese Dept. Edn., 1919; m. Eva Bancroft Hall, Mar. 29, 1882; children—Rachel Bancroft, Sumner Cushing. Prof. agr., Imperial Coll. of Agr., Japan, 1877-88, prof. botany, 1880-88, pres. ad interim, 1880-83 and 1886-87; prof. agr., Mass. Agrl. Coll., 1889-1908, lecturer on agr., 1908-18, pres. ad interim, Jan.-Apr., 1903, and 1905-06; agriculturist, Mass. Agrl. Exptl. Station, 1889-1921, dir., 1906-18; consulting agriculturist, 1918-21. Decorated 4th Order of the Rising Sun, Japan, 1888. Contbr. to 2d, 3d and 4th and editor 5th and 6th ann. reports, Imperial Coll. Agr. of Japan. Author: Agriculture (3 vols.), 1901; General Agriculture, Dairying and Poultry Farming. Home: Amherst, Mass. Died 1938.

BROOKS, William Robert, astronomer; b. Maidstone, Kent, Eng., June 11, 1844; s. Rev. William and Caroline (Wickings) B.; came to U.S., 1857; acad. edn., Marion, N.Y.; hon. A.M., Hobart, 1891; D.Sc., Hamilton, 1898; m. Mary E. Smith, Oct. 15, 1868. Founded Red House Observation, Phelps, N.Y., 1874, where he discovered 11 comets; in charge Smith Observation, Geneva, N.Y., 1888—; prof. astronomy, Hobart Coll.; lecturer. Has discovered 16 additional comets, making 27 in all (many of these discoveries made with telescope of his own construction); early worker in photography and later in its application to astronomy. Winner of over $1,000 in Warner gold prizes for astron. discoveries; 10 medals from Astron. Soc. Pacific; Lalande medal, Paris Acad. Sciences; spl. gold medal for list and photographs of cometary discoveries, St. Louis Expn., 1904; spl. gold medal and diploma, Astron. Soc. of Mexico, for discoveries of 25 comets. Address: Geneva, N.Y. Died May 3, 1921.

BROOKSHIRE, Elijah Voorhees, congressman; b. Montgomery County, Ind., Aug. 15, 1856; s. Drake and Sarah (Graves) B.; grad. Ind. Central Normal Sch. (then defunct), Ladoga, Ind., 1878; m. Amanda A. Harshbarger, Feb. 19, 1883. Admitted to Ind. bar, 1883, and practiced at Crawfordsville; mem. 51st, 52d and 53d Congresses (1889-95), 8th Ind. Dist.; practiced in Washington, D.C., 1897—. Democrat. Author: The Law of Human Life, 1916. Address: Washington, D.C. Died Apr. 17, 1936.

BROOME, Isaac, sculptor; b. Valcartier, Lower Can., May 16, 1835; s. Isaac and Annie B.; ed. Phila. until 1850; art at Pa. Acad. Fine Arts, Phila., and pvt. tutors; m. Victoria Myers, Feb. 9, 1856. Worked on Crawford statues for pediment of U.S. Capital, 1855-56; executed statue for W. W. Corcoran's Mausoleum, Georgetown, D.C., 1857; established studio at Rome, Italy, 1858; executed many works in sculpture; mfd. art tiles extensively; devoted to ideal sculpture. Elected academician Pa. Acad. Fine Arts, 1860; dir. life and antique dept., 1860-63. Medals for ceramic arts, Centennial Expn., 1876, Paris Expn., 1878; spl. commr. on ceramics, Paris Expn., 1878, by U.S. Govt. and State of N.J.; dir. many schs. for teaching fine and industrial arts and the sciences. Active in ednl. polit. and industrial reforms; lectured extensively on these subjects; was mem. Ruskin Industrial Coöperative Assn. Chautauqua lecturer on ceramic arts, etc. Invented the Perfected Rotary Press, 1906-07, safety auto wheel, 1909. Author: The Brother, 1890; Last Days of the Ruskin Coöperative Association, 1902. Inventor Broome Safety Wheel for Automobiles. Scientific and tech. expert, Lenox, Inc. (ceramic art), Trenton, N.J. Home: Trenton, N.J. Died May 4, 1922.

BROOMELL I(saac) Norman; b. Chester Co., Pa., Nov. 25, 1858; s. Isaac and Rachel B.; ed. Friends' Central Sch., Phila., 1875-78, A.M., 1878; D.D.S., Pa. Coll. Dental Surgery, 1879; LL.D., 1939; m. Lidia T. Seabury, 1884 (dec.); 1 son, Willard Seabury (dec.). Began Phila., 1881; was prof. dental anatomy and histology, Pa. Coll. Dental Surg., and dean dental dept. Medico-Chirurg. Coll., Phila.; prof. dental anatomy and histology, and dean Phila. Dental Coll., 1918—; also dean Temple U. Dental Sch. (Phila. Dental Coll.). Mem. bd. dirs. Nat. Research Inst. Republican. Author: Anatomy and Histology of the Mouth and Teeth (with Philipp Fischelis), 1898. Compiler and Editor: Practical Dentistry by Practical Dentists, 1908. Home: Philadelphia, Pa. Died Mar. 23, 1941.

BROPHY, Ellen Amelia; b. Waukegan, Ill., Jan. 12, 1871; d. Francis Alexander and Catherine Jane (Delahaunty) Goodbody; ed. private tutors; m. William Henry Brophy, Nov. 17, 1891; children—Mary Columba (dec.), Frank Cullen, Ellenita Amelia (dec.). Engaged in pvt. investments, 1922—. Donor of Mary Columba Brophy Memorial Bldg., Sisters of St. Joseph Home for Children, Tucson, Ariz., 1924; Ellenita Brophy Memorial Convent, Douglas, Ariz., 1925; foundation group of bldgs. for William Henry Brophy Coll., Phoenix, Ariz., 1928. Catholic. Decorated by Pope Pius XI, Pro Ecclesia et Pontifice, 1931. Home: Phoenix, Ariz., and Los Angeles, Calif. Deceased.

BROPHY, Truman William, oral surgeon; b. Will County, Ill., Apr. 12, 1848; s. William and Amelia (Cleveland) B.; D.D.S., Pa. Coll. Dental Surgery, 1872; M.D., Rush Med. Coll., Chicago, 1880; LL.D., Lake Forest U., 1889, Loyola U., 1924; Sc.D., U. of Pa., 1914; m. Emma Jean Mason, May 8, 1873 (died 1899); children—Mrs. Jean Mason Barnes, Mrs. Florence Logan, Truman W., Mrs. Alberta L. Holloway; m. 2d, E. W. Strawbridge, Mar. 31, 1908. Pres. and prof. oral surgery, Chicago Coll. of Dental Surgery; oral surgeon Michael Reese and Frances Willard hosps. Pres. for the U.S. of the 13th Internat. Med. Congress, Madrid, Spain, 1903; was also pres. Internat. Commn. of Edn.; del. 4th Internat. Dental Federation, etc. Officer Pub. Instrn., France, 1913; officer Legion of Honor, France, 1924; Internat. Miller Memorial prize, from Internat. Dental Federation, 1925. Author: Oral Surgery, 1915; Cleft Palate and Cleft Lip, 1923. Home: Chicago, Ill. Died Feb. 4, 1928.

BROPHY, William Henry, banker; b. Ireland, Oct. 12, 1863; s. Michael and Mathilda (Lawlor) B.; ed. common schs. in Ireland; m. Ellen Goodbody, Nov. 17, 1891. Came to U.S., 1881, naturalized citizen, 1888; mgr. Copper Queen Stores, Bisbee, Ariz., 1886-1912; gen. mgr. Phelps Dodge Mercantile Co., 1912-17 (resigned to go to France); pres. Bank of Bisbee, 1900—; v.p. Bank of Douglas, Ariz.; dir. Los Angeles Trust & Savings Bank. Vol. Am. Red Cross, Paris, Oct. 1917-Dec. 1918, as asst. chief, later chief of stores. Del. Rep. Nat. Conv., 1904. Elk, K.C. Home: Phoenix, Ariz., and Los Angeles, Calif. Died Nov. 13, 1922.

BROREIN, William G., telephone official; b. nr. Marion, O., Oct. 30, 1861; s. Gebhard and Sophia B.; student Northwestern Ohio Normal U., 1879-82; m. Sarah E. Butcher, Oct. 29, 1883; 1 dau., Edna (Mrs. W. T. White). Was teacher and supt. schs.,

Ohio, until 1886; mem. firm Brorein Bros., Buckland, O., 1886—, same firm, at Parma, Mo., lumber, farming, etc., 1902; organized, 1901, and pres. and gen. mgr. Peninsular Telephone Co.; dir. Morris Plan Bank of Tampa. Mem. Ohio Ho. of Rep., 1893-97, Senate, 1897-1901; mem. Ohio Commn. to Trans-Miss. Expn., Omaha; mem. commn. apptd. by Gov. Trammell of Fla., 1917, to report on establishment of State Instn. for Feeble Minded; mem. Fla. Purchase Centennial Commn, 1919; mem. Charter Bd., City of Tampa, 1921. Pres. S. Fla. Fair Assn., 1916-27; pres. Tampa Y.M.C.A., 1920-27. Democrat. Mem. Christian (Disciples) Ch., K. of P. Home: Tampa, Fla. Died Dec. 12, 1937.

BROSE, Louis D., physician; b. Evansville, Ind., Apr. 20, 1859; s. Daniel G. and Christine F. (Jenner) B.; M.D., and Ph.D., U. of Pa., 1881; Friedrich Wilhelm U., Berlin, 1891-92; Kaiserlich Koeniglich U., Vienna, spring semester, 1890, fall semester, 1896; m. Mary P. Munger, Dec. 22, 1891 (died 1909). Resident phys. German Hosp., Phila., 1881-82; practiced, Evansville, 1882—; demonstrator and prof. anatomy, Evansville Med. Coll., until it dissolved, 1885; phys. and obstetrician Evansville Home for Friendless, 1883-84, and phys. Evansville Orphans' Home, 2 yrs.; surgeon Peoria, Decatur & Evansville Ry. (now Ill. Central Ry.), 1886; for many yrs. oculist and aurist St. Mary's Hosp.; specialized, 1891—, in diseases of eye, ear, nose and throat. Episcopalian. Del. Pan-Am. Med. Congress, Washington, D.C., 1893; Internat. Med. Congress, Berlin, 1900; Internat. Otol. Congress, Boston, 1912. Home: Evansville, Ind. Died Nov. 15, 1931.

BROSIUS, Marriott, congressman; b. Colerain Tp., Pa., Mar. 7, 1843; academic edn.; m. Elizabeth J. Coates, Mar. 19, 1869. Private, sergt., and 2d lt. U.S. vols., 1861-65; severely wounded in charge at Green Plains in the Bermuda Hundred; after war finished edn. at Millersville Normal School; law course, U. of Mich.; admitted to bar, 1868. Defeated as candidate for Congressman-at-large, 1882; member of Congress, 1889-1901. Republican. Home: Lancaster, Pa. Died 1901.

BROSMITH, William, insurance law; b. N.Y. City, Nov. 8, 1854; LL.D., Holy Cross College, Worcester, Mass. Admitted to New York bar, 1876, and began practice in N.Y. City; atty. Travelers Ins. Co., 1895-99, gen. counsel, 1899—, also v.p. and gen. counsel Travelers Indemnity Co. and Travelers Fire Ins. Co.; dir. Travelers Companies, The Charter Oak Fire Ins. Co., Travelers Bank & Trust Co., Conn. River Banking Co., Dime Savings Bank. Mem. Conn. Civil Service Commn., Conn. Commn. of Pub. Welfare, Conn. State Council of Defense, Bd. of Charity Commrs. of Hartford, etc. Trustee St. Joseph's Cathedral Corp., St. Francis Hosp. Democrat. Catholic. Knight of St. Gregory. Home: Hartford, Conn. Died Aug. 22, 1937.

BROSNAHAN, Timothy, educator; b. Alexandria, Va., Jan. 8, 1856; entered Society of Jesus, 1872; ed. at novitiate, Frederick, Md., to 1876; studied philosophy, science and mathematics, Woodstock Coll., Md., 1876-79, theology, 1884-88. Ordained priest R.C. Ch., 1889; prof. in Boston Coll. and Georgetown Coll., D.C., 1879-84; prof. and prefect of studies, Woodstock Coll., 1898-1908; lecturer in ethics and polit. economy, Loyola Coll., 1908—. Trustee Boston Coll. (pres. bd., 1894-98). Mem. Corp. R.C. Clergymen, Md. Address: Baltimore, Md. Died June 4, 1915.

BROSS, Ernest, editor; b. Newaygo, Mich., Sept. 1, 1860; s. Harmon (D.D.) and Lydia A. Kingsbury B.; A.B., Doane Coll., Neb., 1881, A.M., 1896; m. Caroline Marsh Sheffield; m. 2d, Anne Dickson Parker. In journalism at Omaha, Neb., 1882-86; asso. editor, 1887-97, mng. editor, 1897-1904, Portland Oregonian; editor-in-chief Indianapolis Star, 1904—. Home: Indianapolis, Ind. Died Jan. 31, 1923.

BROSSEAU, Alfred J., corp. official; pres. Mack Trucks, Inc., Mack Bros. Motor Car Co., Internat. Motor Co., Internat. Brunswick Motor Co., and officer or dir. other corps. Address: New York, N.Y. Died Sept. 24, 1936.

BROTHERTON, Alice Williams, author; b. Cambridge, Ind.; d. Alfred Baldwin and Ruth Hoge (Johnson) Williams; m. William Ernest Brotherton, Oct. 18, 1876; children—Frederick W. (dec.), John Williams, Isabel Ruth. Lecturer on Shakespeare. Was Cincinnati's mem. The Vigilantes (for patriotic service), contributing several poems. Charter mem. Cincinnati Woman's Club, McDowell Soc., and Ohio Valley Poetry Soc. Author: Beyond the Veil, 1886; The Sailing of King Olaf, 1887; What the Wind Told to the Treetops, 1888; The Orchard Path and Other Poems, 1917; also 8 poems in Ohio Valley Verse Collections, I and II. Home: Cincinnati, O. Died Feb. 9, 1930.

BROUGHTON, Leonard Gaston, clergyman; b. Wake County, N.C., 1864; s. Gaston H. and Louisa Hawkins (Franks) B.; student Wake Forest Coll., N.C., lacking 6 mos. of graduating on account of illness; M.D., Ky. Sch. of Medicine (U. of Ky.); D.D., Wake Forest; m. Roxana Barnes. Practiced at Reedsville, N.C.; ordained Bapt. ministry, 1893; founder and pastor Atlanta Baptist Tabernacle; also founder of Tabernacle Infirmary, Tabernacle Dormitory for Young Ladies; pastor Christ Ch., London, Eng., First Bapt. Ch., Knoxville, Tenn., Grove Av. Bapt. Ch., Richmond, Va., First Bapt. Ch., Jacksonville, Fla., Bapt. Tabernacle, Atlanta; later engaged in gen. Bible conf. and evangelistic work. Author: Old Wine and New Bottles, 1904; Salvation and the Old Theology, 1908; The Plain Man and His Bible, 1909; Kingdom Parables and Their Teaching, 1910; Where Are the Dead?, 1914; Christianity and the Common Place, 1914; The Prodigal and Others, 1914; Is Preparation for War Unchristian?, 1916; Soul Consciousness After Death, 1924; In His Way, 1925; Spirit-Lit Eyes, 1933. Home: Atlanta, Ga. Died Feb. 22, 1936.

BROUN, Heywood (Campbell), newspaper man; b. Brooklyn, N.Y., Dec. 7, 1888; s. Heywood Cox and Henriette (Brose) Broun; student Harvard U., 1906-10; m. Ruth Hale, June 6, 1917 (divorced 1933); 1 son, Heywood Hale; m. 2d, Mrs. Johnny Dooley (Connie Madison), Jan. 9, 1935. Was a reporter on the Morning Telegraph, New York, 1908-09, 1910-12; then with New York Tribune, 1912-21, and New York World, 1921-28, Scripps-Howard Newspapers, 1928—. Sent to France as corr. with A.E.F., July 1917. Author: A.E.F.—With General Pershing and American Forces, 1918; Seeing Things at Night, 1921; Pieces of Hate, 1922; The Boy Grew Older, 1922; The Sun Field, 1923; Sitting on the World, 1924; Gandle Follows His Nose, 1926; Anthony Comstock, and Roundsman of the Lord (with Margaret Leech), 1927; Christians Only (with George Britt), 1931. Lecturer on the drama, Columbia U., 1920, Rand School, 1921. Address: New York, N.Y. Died Dec. 18, 1939.

BROUN, William Le Roy, educator; b. Loudoun County, Va., 1827; A.M., U. of Va., 1850; LL.D., St. John's Coll., Md., 1874, U. of Ga., 1892; m. Sallie J. Fleming, Nov. 1, 1859. Prof. in a coll. in Miss., 1852-54; prof. mathematics, U. of Ga., 1854-56; in C. S. A. as lt. of arty., 1861, and later as commandant of the Richmond arsenal, with rank of lt. col. in ordnance dept.; at close of war became prof. natural philosophy, U. of Ga.; pres. Ga. Agrl. and Mech. Coll., 1872-75; prof. mathematics, Vanderbilt U., 1875-82; pres. Agrl. and Mech. Coll., Ala., 1882-83; prof. mathematics, U. of Texas, 1883-84; pres. Ala. Poly. Inst., 1884—. Home: Auburn, Ala. Died 1902.

BROUNOFF, Platon, musician; b. Elizabethgrad, S. Russia, May 1863; s. Gregory and Pauline B.; at age of 15 entered musical inst. Warsaw; received scholarship Imperial Conservatory, St. Petersburg; grad. under Anton Rubinstein and Rimsky-Korsakoff. Came to U.S., 1891; went first to La Porte, Ind., and to New Haven, where he gave his first concerts; soon after settled in New York; conductor, teacher, pianist, singer and lecturer. Brought out his cantata, Angel; The Russian Village and other compositions; his overture, "Russia," at a public concert of the New York Manuscript Soc. in Chickering Hall, Dec. 15, 1897, and in Carnegie Hall, New York, May 20, 1896. Composer: The Ten Commandments of Piano Practice, 1913; Palestine (symphony), played by Statium Symphony Orchestra; The Glory of God (oratorio); Ramona (Am. Indian opera); America, My Glorious Land (anthem); etc. Organized Harlem Choral Union. Teacher of Alma Gluck, Herbert Witherspoon, etc. Home: New York, N.Y. Died July 11, 1924.

BROUSSARD, Edwin Sidney, senator; b. Iberia Parish, La., Dec. 4, 1874; s. John D. and Anastazie (Gousoulin) B.; B.S., La. State U., 1896; studied law Tulane U.; m. Marie Patout, 1905. Teacher pub. schs., 1897-98; capt. 2d U.S. Vol. Inf., Spanish Am. War, 1898; served in Santiago Province, and in Cuba 1 yr.; asst. sec. Taft Commn. to Philippines, 1900; admitted to La. bar; apptd. dist. atty., 1903, and twice elected to the office, once as a Democrat and once as a Progressive; candidate of Progressive Party for lt. gov. of La., 1916; mem. U.S. Senate, 2 terms, 1921-33. Democrat. Home: New Iberia, La. Died Nov. 19, 1934.

BROUSSARD, Robert F., senator; b. on Marie Louise plantation, nr. New Iberia, La., Aug. 17, 1864; s. J. D. and A. E. (Gonsoulin) B.; ed. Georgetown U., 3 yrs.; insp. customs, New Orleans, 1885-87; asst. weigher and expert statistician, 1889; LL.B., Tulane U., 1889; m. Marrette Applegate, Jan. 12, 1898. In practice, New Iberia, La., 1889—; prominent in agitation which destroyed the La. State Lottery Co.; dist. atty. 19th Jud. Dist. of La., 1892-97; mem. 55th to 63d Congresses (1897-1915), 3d La. Dist.; elected U.S. senator, May 1912, for term, 1915-21. Democrat. Address: New Iberia, La. Died Apr. 2, 1918.

BROUSSEAU, Kate, psychologist; b. Ypsilanti, Mich.; d. Julius and Caroline (Yakeley) B.; Los Angeles High Sch., and State Normal Sch.; studied in Germany, U. of Paris, Collège de France, École d'Anthropologie, Paris, U. of Minn., U. of Chicago Law Sch.; Docteur de L'Université de Paris, 1904. Teacher Los Angeles High Sch.; teacher psychology and pedagogy, Los Angeles State Normal Sch.; prof. psychology, Mills Coll., 1907-28; dir. psychol. service, Inst. Family Relations, Los Angeles, 1929—. Made psychol. survey of Sonoma State Home for Feeble Minded, 1914-16, giving tests to about 1,200 children; served in French Army, World War, dir. Foyers du Soldat, on Lorraine Front; with French Army of Occupation in Germany and in devastated dists. of northern France; awarded commemorative medal by French Govt., 1920. Democrat. Conglist. Author: L'Éducation des Nègres aux États-Unis; Mongolism, Mental and Physical Characteristics of Mongolian Imbeciles. Home: Los Angeles, Calif. Died July 8, 1938.

BROWARD, Napoleon Bonaparte, gov.; b. on farm in Duval County, Fla., Apr. 19, 1857; s. Napoleon Bonaparte and Mary Dorcas (Parsons) B.; lost both parents when 12 yrs. old; attended country sch.; m. Caroline Georgia Kemps, Jan. 10, 1883 (died 1883); 2d, Annie I. Douglas, May 5, 1887. At 14 worked in a log camp for an uncle; later farm hand, steamboat roustabout, cod fisherman on Grand Banks, and seaman on sailing vessels and fishing boats, steamboat hand and 1 yr. bar pilot on St. Johns' Bar, Fla., then joint owner of steamboat plying between Mayport and Palatka, Fla., until 1887; then propr. of a wood yard in Jacksonville, Fla.; engaged in phosphate mining, 1890-92; again in steamboat business, 1895, as owner of the steam-tug, which in 1896-98 comd. on 8 trips conveying war material to the Cubans; in towing and wrecking business at Jacksonville, Key West and Tampa, 1902—. Mem. Fla. Ho. of Rep., 1900; mem. State Bd. Health, 1900-04; gov. of Fla., 1904-09. Democrat. Address: Jacksonville, Fla. Died 1910.

BROWER, Daniel Roberts, M.D.; b. Phila., 1839; M.S., Polytechnic Coll., Phila., 1860; M.D., U. of Georgetown, 1864; A.M., Wabash Coll.; LL.D., Georgetown, Kenyon Coll. and St. Ignatius Coll., Ill. Asst. surgeon, U.S.V., 1864; later prof. nervous and mental diseases, Rush Med. Coll.; also prof. nervous diseases, Post-Graduate Sch., Chicago. Home: Chicago, Ill. Died 1908.

BROWER, Harriette Moore, musician, author; b. Albany, N.Y., 1869; d. Walter Scott and Harriet A. (Moore) B.; ed. Albany Girls' Acad.; studied music in New York, also in Germany for several yrs.; unmarried. Concert pianist and teacher. Piano editor of The Musician. Author: Art of the Pianist, 1911; Piano Mastery, 1915; Vocal Mastery, 1920; Story—Lives of Master Musicians, 1922; Self Help in Music Study; What to Play—What to Teach, 1925; Modern Masters of the Keyboard, 1926. Home: New York, N.Y. Died Mar. 10, 1928.

BROWER, Jacob Vradenberg, archæologist, explorer, author; b. on farm at York, Mich., Jan. 21, 1844; s. Abraham Duryea and Mary R. B.; ed. pub. schs.; enlisted in vol. cav., 1862; in U.S. vol. navy, 1864; auditor Todd Co., Minn., 1867-73; mem. Minn. legislature, 1873; register U.S. land office, St. Cloud, Minn., 1874-79; Itasca State Park Commr., Minn., 1891-95; charted source of Miss. river, 1889, and source of Mo. river, 1896; discovered mounds and ancient village site at Itasca Lake, 1894-95; rediscovered site of Quivira, 1897-98; discovered 1,125 ancient mounds at Mille Lac, Minn., 1900. Pres. Quivira Hist. Soc. (assn. of explorers, authors and ethnol. students); well known as explorer and archæologist. Author: The Mississippi River and Its Source, 1893; Prehistoric Man at the Head Waters of the Mississippi, 1895 01; The Missouri River and Its Utmost Source, 1896 A7; Quivira, 1898 A7; Harahey, 1899 A7; Mille Lac, 1900 A7; Kathio, 1901 A7; Kakabikansing, 1902 S30; Minnesota—Discovery of Its Area, 1541-1665, 1903 S30; Kansas—Monumental Perpetuation of Its Earliest History, 1541-1896, 1903 S30. Home: St. Paul, Minn. Died 1905.

BROWER, William Leverich, pres. bd. direction Corp. Ref. Ch. in America; b. N.Y. City, Aug. 5, 1846; s. John I. and Sophia Wyckoff (Olcott) B.; ed. pvt. schs.; LL.D., Hope Coll., Holland, Mich., 1929; unmarried. Began business career with Schieffelin & Co., mchts., N.Y. City, 1863, partner, 1880-1903, dir., 1903-11, 1st v.p., 1911-29; retired. Pres. bd. of direction Corp. of Ref. Ch. in America, 1918—; chmn. finance com. Corp. Collegiate Ref. Protestant Dutch Ch., 1918—. Mem. Soc. N.Y. Hosp., 1932; mem. Hudson-Fulton Celebration Com., 1904. Decorated Officer Order Orange-Nassau, 1928. Democrat. Author: History of the Collegiate Reformed Protestant Dutch Church, 1628-1928, 1928. Engaged in social and religious work of Middle Collegiate Dutch Ref. Ch. lower East Side, N.Y. City, 1873—. Home: New York, N.Y. Died May 9, 1940.

BROWN, Abbie Farwell, author; b. Boston; d. Benjamin F. and Clara (Neal) B.; ed. Girls' Latin Sch. and Radcliffe Coll.; traveled abroad, 1899, 1906, 10, 13; unmarried. An editor Young Folks' Library, 1902. Author: The Book of Saints and Friendly Beasts, 1900; The Lonesomest Doll, 1901; In the Days of Giants, 1902; A Pocketful of Posies (verse),

1902; The Curious Book of Birds, 1903; The Flower Princess, 1904; The Star Jewels, and other Wonders, 1905; The Story of St. Christopher, 1905; Brothers and Sisters, 1906; Friends and Cousins, 1907; Fresh Posies (verse), 1908; John of the Woods, 1909; Tales of the Red Children (with J. M. Bell), 1909; The Christmas Angel, 1910; Their City Christmas, 1912; Swapping Day (play), 1912; The Lucky Stone, 1914; Songs of Sixpence (verse), 1914; Kisington Town, 1915; Surprise House, 1917; Heart of New England (poems), 1920; Round Robin, 1921; The Lights of Beacon Hill, 1922; Gigi (motion picture), 1923; The Boyhood of Edward MacDowell, 1924; Our Christmas Tree, 1925. Winner of two prizes for short stories. Author of cantatas: "Rock of Liberty," "The Guardian Angel," and many song-texts and choruses. Home: Boston, Mass. Died Mar. 4, 1927.

BROWN, Abram English, author; b. Bedford, Mass., Jan. 21, 1849; s. Moses Fitch and Elizabeth (Smith) B.; ed. Cambridge and private study; m. Sarah J. Flint, 1877. Mem. Mass. Ho. of Reps., 1902-03. Author: Beneath Old Roof Trees, 1896; Beside Old Hearthstones, 1897; History of Bedford, 1892; Bedford Old Families, 1893; Glimpses of New England, 1894 L3; Flag of the Minute Men, 1894; John Hancock, His Book, 1898; Faneuil Hall and Market, or, Peter Faneuil and His Gift, 1900. Address: Bedford, Mass. Died 1909.

BROWN, Addison, judge; b. W. Newbury, Mass., Feb. 21, 1830; s. Addison and Catharine Babson (Griffin) B.; A.B., Harvard, 1852, LL.B., 1854; LL.D., 1902; m. Mary C. Barrett, Jan. 1, 1856 (died 1887); 2d, Helen C. Gaskin, July 20, 1893. Practiced law, New York, 1855-81; U.S. dist. judge Southern Dist. N.Y., 1881-1901 (resigned). Pres. Torrey Bot. Club, 1890-1900; one of originators and a scientific dir. New York Bot. Garden, whose charter he prepared (1891). Author: Illustrated Flora of the Northern United States and Canada, 3 vols., 1896-98 (with Nathaniel L. Britton); The Elgin Botanical Garden and Its Relation to Columbia College and the New Hampshire Grants, 1908. Address: New York, N.Y. Died Apr. 9, 1913.

BROWN, Alanson David, mfr.; b. Granville, N.Y., Mar. 21, 1847; s. David and Malinda O. B.; ed. dist. sch., and 3 months at Lansley's Commercial Coll., Rutland, Vt., 1864; m. Ella G. Bliss, Jan. 17, 1877. Went to St. Louis, 1872; with James M. Hamilton, established firm of Hamilton & Brown; firm became Hamilton, Brown & Co., 1875, incorporated as Hamilton, Brown Shoe Co., 1883, of which was pres.; pres. Pitchfork Land & Cattle Co.; dir. Commonwealth Trust Co.; pres. Mo. Bapt. Sanitarium. Home: St. Louis, Mo. Died May 10, 1913.

BROWN, Albert Oscar, gov., lawyer; b. Northwood, N.H., July 18, 1852; s. Charles Osgood and Elizabeth (Langmaid) B.; A.B., Dartmouth Coll., 1878, A.M., 1911; LL.B., Boston U. Law School, 1884; LL.D., U. of N.H., 1922; m. Susie J. Clarke, Dec. 20, 1888. Admitted to N.H. bar, 1884; practiced Manchester, 1884-1912; mem. successively, Burnham & Brown, Burnham, Brown & Warren, and Burnham, Brown, Jones & Warren; spl. counsel for N.H. in r.r. tax appeals in Sup. Court, 1910-11; pres. Amoskeag Savings Bank, 1905-12 and 1931—, treas. and sec., 1912-31; dir. Amoskeag Nat. Bank, Pub. Service Co. of N.H., N.H. Fire Ins. Co.; clk. John B. Varick Co. Chmn. N.H. Tax Commn., 1911-21; pres. N.H. Constl. Conv., 1918-21; gov. of N.H., term, 1921-23; mem. N.H. Gen. Court, 1925-26; mem. N.H. Com. of 100 on Pub. Safety; v. chmn. Manchester War Savings Com.; pres. N.H. Bankers' Assn., 1922. Del. at large Rep. Nat. Conv., 1924. Trustee Dartmouth Coll., 1911-31; trustee Coe's Northwood Acad. (pres. bd.). Republican. Conglist. Home: Manchester, N.H. Died Mar. 28, 1937.

BROWN, Alexander, author, farmer; b. Glenmore, Nelson County, Va., Sept. 5, 1843; s. Robert L. and Sarah Cabell (Callaway) B.; ed. private tutors, private schools and (1860-61) Lynchburg Coll.; D.C.L., U. of South, 1893; LL.D., William and Mary, 1901; left coll. to enter C.S.A., serving 1861-65; in mercantile business, 1865-80; farmer, 1872—; m. Caroline Augusta Cabell, Dec. 27, 1873 (died 1876); m. 2d, Sarah Randolph, Apr. 28, 1886. Author: New Views of Early Virginia History, 1886; The Genesis of the United States, 1890; The Cabells and Their Kin, 1895; The First Republic in America, 1898; The History of Our Earliest History, 1898; English Politics in Early Virginia History, 1901. Address: Norwood, P. O., Va. Died 1906.

BROWN, Alexander Ephraim, engr.; b. Cleveland, May 14, 1852; s. Fayette and Cornelia C. (Curtis) B.; ed. pub. and high schs., Cleveland; spl. course civ. engring. Brooklyn Poly. Inst., 1872; U.S. Geol. Survey, 1 yr.; m. Carrie M. Barnett, Nov. 14, 1877. V.p. and gen. mgr. The Brown Hoisting Machinery Co., 1880—; has secured several hundred patents on hoisting machinery, machines and appliances for iron, steel and coke works, ship building, process and material for reinforcing concrete, known as "Fensinclave." Home: Cleveland, O. Died 1911.

BROWN, Amanda Elizabeth; b. Beacon, N.Y., May 20, 1837; d. Elijah and Eunice (Lockwood) Townsend; ed. common schs., Hammondsport, N.Y.; m. Rev. Stephen Brown, Aug. 25, 1855 (died 1901). Has been connected as clk. with Treasury Dept., Washington, D.C., 1875—; recognized as expert in identifying mutilated money; passed favorably upon many thousands of dollars representing charred and almost unrecognizable packages sent to the Treasury Dept. after the San Francisco disaster, 1906. Home: Washington, D.C. Died Dec. 10, 1918.

BROWN, Amos Peaslee, univ. prof.; b. Germantown, Pa., Dec. 3, 1864; s. Amos P. and Frances (Brown) B.; B.S., U. of Pa., 1886, M.E., 1887, Ph.D., 1892; unmarried. Asst. geol. survey of Pa., 1887-89; instr. mining and metallurgy, U. of Pa., 1889-91, prof. geology and mineralogy, 1892—. Author of various papers on geol., palæontol. and mineral. subjects. Editor Erni's Mineralogy Simplified, 1901. Author: Crystallography of Hemoglobin (with E. T. Reichert), 1909. Home: Philadelphia, Pa. Died Oct. 9, 1917.

BROWN, Archer; b. Otsego County, N.Y., 1857; grad. Mich. U., 1872; removed to Cincinnati; engaged in journalism; mng. editor, Cincinnati Daily Gazette, 1875-80. In 1881, with William A. Rogers, organized Rogers, Brown & Co., with offices in 14 leading Am. and foreign cities; removed to New York 1895, and became resident mem. of firm; dir. of several iron, steel and coal corps., also Empire State Trust Co., Phoenix Nat. Bank, New York; pres. Citizens' Union E. Orange, N.J. Home: E. Orange, N.J. Died 1904.

BROWN, Arthur, lawyer, senator; b. Kalamazoo County, Mich., Mar. 8, 1843; grad. Antioch Coll., O., 1862; post-grad. course U. of Mich. (A.M.); grad. law dept. same, 1864; admitted to bar; practiced, Kalamazoo, 1864-79, Salt Lake City, 1879—. Elected to U.S. Senate, Utah, Jan. 22, 1896; term expired Mar. 4, 1897. Republican. Home: Salt Lake City, Utah. Died 1906.

BROWN, Arthur Edward, educator; b. Union Station, O., May 17, 1876; s. Nicholas Comly and Rachel Ellen (Park) B.; grad. Doane Acad., Granville, O., 1898; student Denison U., Granville, 1898-99; A.B., Ohio Wesleyan U., 1902; Boston U., 1904-05, Harvard, 1905-07; hon. Pd.D., Pa. Coll., Gettysburg, 1918; m. Mabel Warner Stoddard, Oct. 22, 1907; children—Philip Stoddard, Virginia, Alice Park, Arthur Edward, Nicholas Comly, III. Headmaster, Harrisburg (Pa.) Acad., 1912—. Republican. Methodist. Home: Harrisburg, Pa. Died Nov. 27, 1940.

BROWN, Arthur Erwin, naturalist; b. Bucks County, Pa., Aug. 14, 1850; s. Samuel Corbin and Achsah Erwin (Kennedy) B.; ed. chiefly in Europe; hon. Sc.D., U. of Pa., 1907. Mem. bd. mgrs. Wistar Inst. of Anatomy; sec. Zoöl. Soc. of Phila.; v.p. and curator Acad. Natural Sciences of Phila. Home: Philadelphia, Pa. Died 1910.

BROWN, Arthur Lewis, judge; b. Providence, R.I., Nov. 28, 1854; s. Samuel Welch and Mary Elizabeth (Thurber) B.; A.B., Brown U., 1876, hon. A.M., 1894, LL.D., 1907; LL.B., Boston U., 1878; admitted to bar, 1878; m. Cora E. Aylsworth, Feb. 12, 1885. In practice, Providence, 1878-96; U.S. dist. judge, Dist. of R.I., 1896-1927 (resigned). Home: Providence, R.I. Died June 10, 1928.

BROWN, Benjamin Chambers, artist; b. Marion, Ark., July 14, 1865; s. Benjamin Chambers and Mary Elizabeth (Booker) B.; ed. U. of Tenn., and Washington U.; student art, Sch. of Fine Arts, St. Louis, and Julian Acad., Paris, France; unmarried. Silver medal, Seattle Expn., 1909; bronze medal, Portland Expn., 1905; silver medal, Panama-Pacific Expn., 1915; bronze medal, San Francisco Expn., 1915; gold medal, Panama-Calif. Expn., 1916; silver medal Sacramento State Fair, 1918; 1st landscape prize, Calif. Art Club, Los Angeles, 1919; same, Phoenix, Ariz., 1920, Santa Ana Expn., 1922, 23; 1st prize (Harrison Award), Los Angeles Mus., 1924; $1,000 Fed. Women's Club prize, Los Angeles, 1924; 2 prizes, Sacramento State Fair, 1924; 1st prize, Springville, Utah, Art Exhibit, 1925; 1st prize, Los Angeles Co. Fair Art Exhibit, Pomona, Calif., 1925; $1,000 prize Tex. wild flower competition, San Antonio, 1927; 1st prize, Gardena (Calif.) Art Inst., 1932; Newhouse prize for color print (1st prize), Los Angeles, 1933. Mem. Internat. Jury for Art of Olympic Games, Los Angeles. Republican. Home: Pasadena, Calif. Died Jan. 19, 1942.

BROWN, Bolton, artist; b. Dresden, N.Y., Nov. 27, 1864; s. Edmund Woodward and Martha Day (Coit) B.; degree Bach. Painting, Syracuse U., 1885, Master Painting, 1888, hon. D.Litt., 1920; m. Lucy Hines Fletcher, 1895; children—Eleanor, Marian, Robert. Instr. drawing, Cornell U., 1885-88; teacher of art, Buchtel Coll., Akron, O., 1889; prin. Toronto Govt. Art Sch., Toronto, Can., 1890; organizer, 1891, dept. of drawing and painting, Leland Stanford Jr. U., and prof. same, 1894-1902; Scammon lecturer, 1929, teacher of lithography, 1930, Art Inst. of Chicago; lecturer on lithography, Nat. Acad. Design, New York, 1930. Has exhibited paintings, etchings and lithographs throughout U.S. Author: The Painter's Palette, 1915; Lithography, 1924; Lithography for Artists, 1929. Address: New York, N.Y. Died Sept. 15, 1936.

BROWN, Calvin Luther, judge; b. Goshen, N.H., Apr. 26, 1854; s. John H. B.; m. Annette Marlow, Sept. 1, 1879. Practiced law at Morris, Minn., until 1887; dist. judge until 1899; asso. justice Supreme Court of Minn. until 1913, chief justice, 1913—. Conglist. Republican. Home: Morris, Minn. Died Sept. 24, 1923.

BROWN, Carleton, philologist, educator; b. Oberlin, O., July 15, 1869; s. Justus Newton and Hattie Augusta (Sparhawk) B.; A.B., Carleton Coll., 1888; studied Andover Theol. Sem., 1890-93; Grad. Sch., Harvard U., 1900-03, A.M., 1901, Ph.D., 1903; Dr. of Letters, New York U., Lawrence Coll., 1939; m. Emily L. Truesdell, June 7, 1893; children—Margery Lorraine, Wendell Edwards (dec.), Truesdell Sparhawk; m. 2d, Beatrice Daw, Aug. 13, 1918; children—Emily Parker Lawless, Beatrice Carleton (dec.), Carleton Justus. Ordained Unitarian ministry, 1894; pastor Unity Ch., St. Cloud, Minn., 1894-97, Helena, Mont., 1897-1900; instr. in English, Harvard, 1903-05; asso. in English, 1905-07; asso. prof. English, 1907-10, prof. English philology, 1910-17, Bryn Mawr Coll.; prof. English, U. of Minn., 1917-21; prof. English, Bryn Mawr Coll., 1921-27; prof. English, New York U., 1927-39, emeritus. Sec. Modern Lang. Assn. America, 1920-34, pres., 1936; fellow Nat. Acad. Arts and Sciences. Author: A Study of the Miracle of Our Lady Told by Chaucer's Prioress, 1910. Compiler: A Register of Middle English Religious and Didactic Verse, Part I, 1916, Part II, 1920; Religious Lyrics of the XIVth Century, 1924; English Lyrics of the XIIIth Century, 1932; Religious Lyrics of the XVth Century, 1939. Editor: Venus and Adonis and other poems, 1913; Poems by Sir John Salusbury and Robert Chester, 1914; The Stonyhurst Pageants, 1920. Home: Upper Montclair, N.J. Died June 25, 1941.

BROWN, Charles Allen, educator; b. Sumterville, Ala., Jan. 5, 1872; s. William Henry and Katherine Billingsley (Henagan) B.; B.Sc., Ala. Poly. Inst., Auburn, 1892, C.E., 1893; post-grad. work U. of Tenn., U. of Chicago; LL.D., Howard Coll., 1915; m. Edna Earle Moore, July 9, 1912. Teacher of science, Birmingham High Sch., 1893-97; prin. Henley School, Birmingham, 1897-1907, Central High School, Birmingham, 1907-21; asso. supt. schs., Birmingham, 1921—. Mem. State Bd. for Vocational Edn., 1918-19. Baptist. Home: Birmingham, Ala. Died July 27, 1939.

BROWN, Charles Francis, lawyer; b. Newburgh, N.Y., Sept. 12, 1844; s. John W. and Eliza (Reeve) B.; B.A., Yale, 1866, LL.D., 1896; m. Harriet E. Shaffer, June 27, 1876; children—Florence E., Anna Higginson. Admitted to bar, 1868; practiced at Newburgh; county atty., Orange County, N.Y., 1875-77; county judge, 1878-82; justice Supreme Court of N.Y., 1883-96; assigned by gov. as mem. Court of Appeals, 1889-92; presiding judge Appellate Div., 2d Dept., 1893-96; declined renomination and resumed practice of law in New York, retired. Democrat. Presbyn. Home: Newburgh, N.Y. Died June 19, 1929.

BROWN, Charles H., judge; b. W. Winfield, N.Y., July 20, 1858; s. Hiram C. and Alice A. (Stuart) B.; ed. W. Winfield Acad. and Hungerford Collegiate Inst., Adams, N.Y.; admitted to bar 1880; m. Alice C. Smith, Nov. 16, 1881. Dist. atty., Allegany County, N.Y., 1890-97; U.S. dist. atty. Western Dist., N.Y., 1898-1906; justice Supreme Court of N.Y., 8th Dist., for terms, 1907-20, and 1921-28. Republican. Home: Belmont, N.Y. Died Jan. 6, 1933.

BROWN, Charles Ira, newspaper editor; b. Woodbury, Pa., Dec. 11, 1861; s. Abram S. and Mary (Keifer) B.; grad. Dickinson Sem., Williamsport, Pa.; post-grad. work, Findlay (O.) Coll., A.M.; D.D., Lebanon Valley Coll., Annville, Pa.; m. Susie Hoffman, Oct. 17, 1888. Early life spent on farm; entered ministry (Ch. of God) in Pa., 1888; served as member of important bds. and coms. of ch.; asst. editor Church Advocate, 1900-04; filled several pastorates, Pa., 16 yrs.; del. to Gen. Eldership Ch. of God, 1893, 96, 99, 1902, 09; trustee, 1896-1904, pres. bd. trustees, 1904-13; pres. Findlay Coll., 1913-15; became mem. State Civil Service Commn., Ohio, Nov. 1, 1915; editor of Defiance Crescent-News. Democrat. Address: Defiance, O. Died 1917.

BROWN, Charles Irwin, civil engr.; b. Winchester, Ind., Nov. 17, 1853; removed to Mankato, Minn., 1865; attended Minn. State U.; began engrng. work on C.,M.&S.P. R.R.; engr. St.L.&S.F. Ry., 14 yrs., chief engr., 6 yrs.; engr. grades and surveys city of St. Louis, 1 yr.; on Cotton Belt Ry., 1 yr.; m. Blanche Clementine Boulanger, 1895. Home: Mankato, Minn. Died 1899.

BROWN, Charles Rufus, theologian; b. E. Kingston, N.H., Feb. 22, 1849; s. Samuel Emmons and Elvira Latham (Small) B.; grad. U.S. Naval Acad., 1869; ensign U.S.N., 1870-71; master, 1871-75; A.B., Harvard, 1877; student Newton Theol. Instn., 1874-75 and 1877-79, Union Theol. Sem., 1878-79, U. of Berlin, 1879-80, U. of Leipzig, 1880-81; Ph.D., Colby U., 1887; D.D., Colgate U., 1892; m. Clarissa Locke Dodge, Nov. 27, 1884. Ordained Bapt. ministry, 1881; pastor Franklin Falls, 1881-83; asso. prof. Bibl. interpretation, 1883-86; prof. Hebrew and cognate lang., 1886—, Newton Theol. Instn. Supplied First Ch., Salem, Mass., 1885; acting pastor, Main St. Church, Worcester, Mass., 1886-87; prof. Hebrew and cognate langs., U. of Chicago, summer quarter, 1897; acting prof. Hebrew and O.T. exegesis, Boston U. Sch. of Theology, 1905-06; resident dir. Am. Sch. of Oriental Research in Jerusalem (Syria), 1910-11. Author: An Aramaic Method, 1884, 1893; The Book of the Prophet Jeremiah (new transl.), 1906; Commentary on Jeremiah, 1907. Home: Newton Centre, Mass. Died Feb. 2, 1914.

BROWN, Charles Sumner, mech. engr.; b. East Hampton, Conn., Aug. 23, 1860; s. Henry B. and Adeline Strong (Gates) B.; Ph.B., Yale, 1883, M.E., 1888; m. Clara Gold Foskett, June 24, 1891; children—Agatha, Foskett. Mech. engr., 1883-88; prof. steam engring., Rose Poly. Inst., Terre Haute, Ind., 1888-96; prof. mech. engring., Vanderbilt U., 1896—. Fuel administrative engr. and chief of conservation for Tenn., U.S. Fuel Adminstrn., 1918. Home: Nashville, Tenn. Died Aug. 31, 1926.

BROWN, Charles Walter, author; b. St. Louis, June 23, 1866; s. Prof. Isaac Hinton and Esther L. (Quin) B.; grad. Edwardsville (Ill.) High Sch., 1883; studied U. of Mo., 1885-87; (hon. A.M., McKendree Coll., Ill., 1902; m. Mary Nelson Matson, Sept. 14, 1904. Engaged in lit. work, 1887—; spl. writer on St. Louis Republic, 1889-93; lecturer on hist. and ednl. subjects. Author: Nathan Hale, 1898; John Paul Jones, 1901; Ethan Allen, 1902; Lafayette, 1903; Pulaski, 1903; Kosciusko, 1903. Joint Author: Common Schol Elocution, 1893; Rational Elocution, 1896; Common School Question Book; Washington, 1902; Lincoln, 1902; Sherman, 1902; Grant; Standard Elocution, 1907. Address: Chicago, Ill. Died Oct. 9, 1934.

BROWN, Charles William, plate glass mfr.; b. Newburyport, Mass., June 14, 1858; s. Capt. Jacob Bartlett B.; ed. pub. sch.; m. Alice Greenleaf Brown, Oct. 30, 1888; children—Mary Agate, Jacob B., Mrs. Theodore B. Anderson, Alice Greenleaf, Charles William, Harold DeWolf. Master mariner in charge vessel, Chinese and Australian trade, 6 yrs.; identified with plate glass mfg., 1898—; pres. Pittsburgh Plate Glass Co., 1916—; chairman board, Brown Graves Co., Akron, O.; dir. Pittsburgh Br. Federal Reserve Bank of Cleveland, Mellon Nat. Bank, Fidelity Title & Trust Co., Bell Telephone Co. of Pa. Trustee Am. Foundation for the Blind, Pittsburgh Assn. Charities, Sewickley Hosp. Assn. Republican. Unitarian. Mason (K.T.), Elk. Home: Sewickley, Pa. Died Mar. 6, 1928.

BROWN, C(hristian) Henry, oculist; b. Lancaster, Pa., May 8, 1857; s. Edwin H. and Susan A. (Widmyer) B.; student Franklin and Marshall Coll., Pa.; M.D., U. of Pa., 1878. Phys. Phila. Hosp., 1878-80, Lancaster County Hosp., 1881-83; located in Phila., 1887; specializes in diseases of the eye; founder, 1889, and pres. Phila. Optical Coll. Established Bd. of Health, Lancaster, and sec. same until left Lancaster. Mason (32°). Author: Optometric Record Book, 1891; The Optician's Manual, Vol. 1, 1895, Vol. 2, 1901; Clinics in Optometry, 1905; State Board Questions, 1909. Home: Philadelphia, Pa. Deceased.

BROWN, Clyde, lawyer; b. McConnellsville, O., Mar. 17, 1873; Ph.B., Ohio U., 1895. Apptd. asst. to v.p. N.Y.C. Lines, 1906, gen. solicitor, 1908—. Address: New York, N.Y. Died Nov. 30, 1932.

BROWN, Daniel Russell, gov.; b. Bolton, Conn., Mar. 28, 1848; s. Arba Harrison and Harriet M. (Dart) B.; acad. edn.; m. Isabel Barrows, Oct. 14, 1874. Engaged in business, Rockville and Hartford, Conn.; settled in Providence and became mem. firm Butler, Brown & Co., 1870 (later Brown Bros. Co.); also pub. The Evening News. Mem. Common Council, 1880-84; presdl. elector, 1888; gov. of R.I., 1892-95. Address: Providence, R.I. Died Feb. 28, 1919.

BROWN, Demarchus Clariton, librarian; b. Indianapolis, Ind., June 24, 1857; s. Philip and Julia (Tröster) B.; A.B., Butler Coll., Ind., 1879, A.M., 1880; U. of Tübingen, Germany, 1882-83; Am. Sch. Classical Studies, Athens, Greece, 1892-93 and 1897 in part; British Museum, 1883, Munich Museum, 1897, Louvre and British Museum, 1899 (summer); m. Jessie Lanier Christian, Sept. 1, 1897. Prof. Greek and Greek art, Butler Coll., 1882-1906; state librarian of Ind., 1906—. Mem. Bd. of State Charities, Ind., 1893-1921; pres. Ind. Conf. Charities, 1904; pres. Nat. Assn. State Librarians, 1910-11; sec. Ind. Centennial Commn. Mem. Christian (Disciples) Ch. Author: Indiana Legislative and State Manual, 1907-1909. Translator: Selections from Lucian, 1896; American Criminology (Freudenthal), 1907. Home: Indianapolis, Ind. Died Aug. 23, 1926.

BROWN, Donald Lamont, corp. official; b. Berlin, Wis., Nov. 17, 1890; s. David and Catherine (Lamont) B.; grad. Berlin (Wis.) High Sch., 1909; student Northwestern U. Sch. of Commerce, 1913-14; m. Ethyl Davis Broffe, 1918; 1 son, Donald Lamont. With Ill. Steel Co., 1913-14, Simplex Automobile Co., 1915-17; successively with Wright-Martin Co., asst. production mgr. Olds Motor Works, production mgr. Houston-Stanwood & Gamble Co., asst. factory mgr. Wright Aeronautical Corp., 1917-25; factory mgr., later v.p., Pratt & Whitney Aircraft Co., 1925-30, pres., 1930; v.p. and dir. United Aircraft and Transportation Corp., 1930-34; pres. United Aircraft Corp., 1934—; dir. Hartford Nat. Bank & Trust Co. (Hartford, Conn.), Dime Savings Bank (Hartford), Taber Cadillac Corp. Republican. Home: West Hartford, Conn. Died Jan. 29, 1940.

BROWN, Edward Miles, educator; b. Schoolcraft, Mich., July 21, 1854; s. E. Lakin and Mary Ann (Miles) B.; ed. Cedar Park Sem., Schoolcraft (Mich.) High Sch.; Ph.B., U. of Mich., 1880; univs. of Strassburg, Berlin, Halle, Göttingen, 1886-89, A.M., Ph.D., Göttingen, 1890; m. Mary Adkins, Apr. 25, 1883. Taught sch., 1874-75 and 1875-76; prin. high sch., Laporte, Ind., 1880-82 and 1884-86; studied law, 1882; in partnership with brother, A. M. Brown, in farming at Schoolcraft, Mich., 1883-84. Actg. asst. prof. English, Cornell U., 1889-90; prof. modern languages, 1890-92, and of English lang. and lit., 1892—, U. of Cincinnati. Author of work in German and English on the Rushworth Gloss to the Gospel of Matthew (Göttingen, 1891-92); gen. editor Sect. 1 (Anglo-Saxon Texts) of Belles-Lettres Series, 1900—. Home: Mt. Auburn, O. Deceased.

BROWN, Edward Osgood, lawyer; b. Salem, Mass., Aug. 5, 1847; s. Edward and Eliza (Dalton) B.; A.B., Brown U., 1867; law studies, Salem, Mass., and Law Sch., Harvard; admitted to bar, 1870; m. Helen Gertrude Eagle, June 25, 1884. Asst. clerk Supreme Ct., R.I., 1870-71; began practice in firm of Peckham & Brown, Chicago, 1872; candidate for judge Superior Ct., 1893; counsel for Lincoln Pk. Commrs., 1894-97; judge Circuit Ct., Cook County, Ill., 1903-09; apptd. justice Appellate Ct., 1st Dist., 1904; mem. law firm Peckham, Brown, Packard & Walsh, 1909-10; again elected judge Circuit Ct., Cook County, 1910, and again apptd. justice Appellate Ct., 1st Dist., 1910; retired from bench, 1915, and reëntered practice in firm of Miller, Starr, Brown, Packard & Peckham. Democrat. Home: Chicago, Ill. Died Dec. 8, 1923.

BROWN, Edwin Hacker, architect; b. Worcester, Mass., July 29, 1875; s. Edwin and Mariana Mifflin (Earle) B.; A.B., Harvard, 1896; S.B. in M.E., Worcester Poly. Inst., 1898; m. Susan Christian, June 1, 1912. Practiced architecture, Minneapolis, 1910—; mem. Hewitt & Brown. Apptd. field dir. Bur. of Camp Service, Am. Red Cross, Camp Cody, Deming, N.M., Aug. 1917; dir. Bur. of Camp Service, Washington, Dec. 1918-Apr. 1, 1919. Mem. Building Code Com., U.S. Dept. of Commerce, 1921—. Fellow A.I.A. (sec., 1923-26, mem. jury of fellows, 1927—). Pres. Architects' Small House Service Bur. of U.S., Inc. Republican. Episcopalian. Home: Wayzata, Minn. Died Apr. 21, 1930.

BROWN, Edwin Perkins, mfr.; b. St. Albans, Vt., June 25, 1868; s. George Washington and Addie E. (Perkins) B.; ed. English High Sch., Boston; m. Emma J. Todd, Sept. 26, 1894; children—George R., Florence E. Began at Albuquerque, N.M., with A.&P. R.R. Co., 1889; western sales agt. Colo. Fuel & Iron Co., at El Paso, Tex., 1893-99; with Am. Zinc, Lead & Smelting Co., 1899, with U.S. Machinery Co., 1900—, gen. mgr., 1911-17, pres., 1917-27, elected chmn. of bd. June 1927, and chmn. exec. com.; officer or dir. many corps. Pres. bd. trustees N.E. Conservatory of Music; trustee Boston U.; mem. bd. overseers Boys' Club of Boston. Episcopalian. Home: Swampscott, Mass. Died Feb. 8, 1934.

BROWN, Edwin Putnam, educator; b. Beaver Dam, Wis., Nov. 18, 1869; s. John Payne and Laura (Putnam) B.; grad. Wayland Acad., 1890; student Brown U., 1892-94; A.B., U. of Chicago, 1896, post-grad. work, 1897; m. Mabel Vaughan, Aug. 31, 1897. Prin. Farmer City (Ill.) High Sch., 1896; instr. Morgan Park Acad. (Ill.), 1896-97; instr. in English, Wayland Acad., 1897-1901, prin., 1901—. Republican. Baptist. Mason. Rotarian. Home: Beaver Dam, Wis. Died Nov. 26, 1934.

BROWN, Edwy Rolfe, corp. official; b. Little Hocking, O., Dec. 4, 1868; s. John A. and Isabel (Shaw) B.; prep. edn., Marietta (O.) Acad.; A.B., Marietta Coll., 1894; m. Florrie Bess McCrery, Apr. 30, 1913; 1 dau., Isabel (Mrs. George Terry Lee). In oil business, Olean, N.Y., 1894-98; moved to Corsicana, Tex., 1898, Dallas, 1914; chmn. bd. Magnolia Petroleum Co.; v.p. Socony-Vacuum Oil Co., Inc.; dir. Southwestern Life Ins. Co. of Dallas, Gulf Ins. Co. Trustee Marietta Coll. Republican. Presbyn. Mason, Odd Fellow. Home: Dallas, Tex. Died Jan. 25, 1942.

BROWN, Elliott Wilber, clergyman; b. West Brookfield, Mass., Aug. 25, 1859; s. Edwin T. and Elizabeth R. (Marsh) B.; A.B., Wabash Coll., 1885, A.M., 1888, D.D., 1904; grad. McCormick Theol. Sem. (now Presbyterian Theol. Sem. of Chicago), 1888; m. Minnie M. Woollacott, Apr. 24, 1888. Ordained Presbyn. ministry, 1888; pastor 1st Ch., Seattle, Wash., 1888-92, Westminster Ch., Detroit, 1892-94, 2d (now Westminster) Ch., Dubuque, Ia., 1894-99, Congregational Church, Glen Ridge, N.J., 1899-1909, St. Nicholas Av. Ch. (now North Presbyterian Church), New York, 1915-25, 1st Congregational Ch., Holyoke, Mass., 1928-33. Vice-moderator Presbytery of New York, 1923-25, also trustee; mem. Moderators' Council; mem. bd. mgrs. Am. Tract Soc., mem. standing com. N.Y. Federation of Chs.; formerly moderator Presbytery of Puget Sound and of Congl. Assn. of N.J. Republican. Home: Northfield, Mass. Died May 25, 1941.

BROWN, Elmer Ellsworth, educator; b. Kiantone, N.Y., Aug. 28, 1861; s. Russell McCrary and Electa (Sherman) B.; grad. Ill. State Normal U., 1881; A.B., U. of Mich., 1889; Ph.D., U. of Halle-Wittenberg, 1890; LL.D., Columbia, 1907, Wesleyan U., 1909, George Washington U., 1911, Rutgers, 1913, U. of State of N.Y., 1930; m. Fanny F. Eddy, June 20, 1889 (died 1932). Sch. prin. and Y.M.C.A. sec. in Ill. and Mich.; acting asst. prof. science and art of teaching, U. of Mich., 1891-92; asso. prof., U. of Calif., 1892-93, prof., 1893-1906, hon. prof. same, 1906-11; U.S. commr. of edn., 1906-11; chancellor New York U., 1911-33, chancellor emeritus, 1933—. Medallist, Royal Yugo Slav Red Cross; Commendatore Order of Crown of Italy; Comdr. Order of Crown of Belgium; Chevalier Legion of Honor (France). Chmn. Lake Mohonk Conf. Friends of the Indian and Other Dependent Peoples, 5 times, 1907-13. Conglist. Author: The Making of Our Middle Schools, 1903; Origin of American State Universities, 1905; Government by Influence, and Other Addresses, 1909; Victory and Other Verse, 1923; A Few Remarks, 1933. Home: New York, N.Y. Deceased.

BROWN, Ernest William, mathematician; b. Hull, Eng., Nov. 29, 1866; s. William and Emma (Martin) B.; B.A., Christ's Coll., Cambridge, Eng., 1887, fellow, 1889-95, hon. fellow, 1911, M.A., 1891, Sc.D., 1897, Adams prize, 1907; hon. A.M., Yale U., 1907; D.Sc., Adelaide U., 1914, Yale, 1933, Columbia, 1934; LL.D., McGill U., 1935; unmarried. Prof. mathematics, Haverford (Pa.) Coll., 1891-1907, Yale, 1907-32. Awarded Bruce Medal, 1920. Mem. Am. Acad. Arts and Sciences, Nat. Acad. Science (Watson medal 1937), Am. Astron. Soc. (v.p. 1923-25; pres. 1928-31). Author: Treatise on the Lunar Theory, 1896; A New Theory of the Moon's Motion, 1897-1905; Tables of the Motion of the Moon, 1920; Planetary Theory (with C. A. Shook), 1933. Address: New Haven, Conn. Died July 1938.

BROWN, Everett Chase; b. Oneida, Ill., Oct. 14, 1863; s. Thomas and Emily (Ware) B.; ed. pub. schs. and business coll.; LL.B., Chicago Evening Coll. of Law (Lake Forest U.), 1892; m. Minerva M. Miner, Apr. 24, 1889; 1 dau., Mrs. William Westcott Block; m. 2d, Elizabeth Sawyer Dupee, Dec. 1901 (died 1919); m. 3d, Agnes Jones, Oct. 1, 1921; 1 son, Everett Thomas. Began in employ St. John & Brown, live stock commn. mchts., Chicago, 1881; later gen. mgr. Brown-St. John Commn. Co.; apptd. mem. U.S. Live Stock Industry Com., 1917; chmn. Price Control Com. of Live Stock, U.S. Food Adminstrn., 1918-19. Pres. Chicago Live Stock Exchange, 1916-20, 1923-28; pres. Nat. Live Stock Exchange, 1918-23. Mem. Chicago Plan Commn. Pres. Nat. Amateur Athletic Union, 1910-11; mem. exec. com. Am. Olympic Com. in charge of Olympic teams to London, 1908, Stockholm, 1912, Antwerp, 1920, Paris, 1924; pres. Chicago Pub. Schs. Athletic League, 1920-28. Mem. Co. C, 1st Inf., Ill. N.G. Republican. Presbyn. Mason (K.T.). Died Apr. 11, 1937.

BROWN, Fayette, iron mfr.; b. N. Bloomfield, O., Dec. 17, 1823; s. Ephraim and Mary Buckingham (Huntington) B.; ed. irregular course at Gambier, O., and Jefferson Coll., Pa.; m. Cornelia C. Curtis, July 15, 1847; 1 son, Alexander E. B. Clerk in dry goods store of brother at Pittsburgh, 1841-45, mem. of firm, 1845-51; mem. firm of Mygatt & Brown, bankers, Cleveland, 1851-57, alone, 1857-61; paymaster U.S. Army, 1861-62; gen. agt. and mgr. Jackson Iron Co., 1862-87; pres. Brown Hoisting Machinery Co.; chmn. Stewart Iron Co., Ltd.; pres. Nat. Chem. Co.; mem. H. H. Brown & Co. (iron ore). Home: Cleveland, O. Died 1910.

BROWN, Francis, theologian; b. Hanover, N.H., Dec. 26, 1849; s. Prof. Samuel Gilman and Sarah (Van Vechten) B.; A.B., Dartmouth, 1870, A.M., 1873; grad. Union Theol. Sem., New York, 1877; U. of Berlin, 1877-79; Ph.D., Hamilton, 1884; D.D., Dartmouth, 1884, Yale, 1894, Glasgow, 1901, Williams, 1908, Harvard, 1909; D.Litt., Oxford, 1901; LL.D., Dartmouth, 1901; m. Louise Reiss, Aug. 7, 1879. Instr. Union Theol. Sem., 1879-81, asso. prof. Bibl. philology, 1881-90, prof. Hebrew and cognate langs., 1890—, pres. and mem. bd. of dirs., 1908—. Dir. Am. Sch. for Oriental Study and Research in Palestine (Jerusalem), 1907-08; trustee Dartmouth Coll., Syrian Protestant Coll.; dir. and pres. Union Settlement Assn. Author: Assyriology—Its Use and Abuse, 1885; The Teaching of the Twelve Apostles (with Prof. R. D. Hitchcock), 1885; A Hebrew and English Lexicon of the Old Testament (with Profs. S. R. Driver and C. A. Briggs), 1891-1906; The Christian Point of View (with Profs. G. W. Knox and A. C. McGiffert), 1902. Address: New York, N.Y. Died Oct. 15, 1916.

BROWN, Francis Henry, physician; b. Boston, Aug. 8, 1835; s. Francis and Caroline Matilda

(Kuhn) B.; A.B., Harvard, 1857, A.M., M.D., 1861; m. Louisa Beckford Eaton, 1861; m. 2d, Mary Sherwood Wood, 1871. Founder, sec., surgeon, The Children's Hosp., Boston; passed asst. surgeon, U.S. Public Health and Marine Hosp. Service; house physician, Mass. Gen. Hosp.; aural surgeon Boston City Hosp.; asst. in chemistry, Harvard, 1857-59; acting asst. surgeon, U.S. Army, 1862-64; surgeon Boston Dispensary, 1866-72; surgeon St. Joseph's Home, 1869-70; physician St. Elizabeth's Hosp., 1880-82. Editor Boston Medical and Surgical Journal. Pres. Suffolk Dist. Med. Soc.; mem. Obstet. Soc. of Boston. Author: Harvard University in the War of 1861-65, 1886; The Second Church in Boston, 1900. Home: Boston, Mass. Died May 16, 1917.

BROWN, Francis Shunk, lawyer; b. Phila., June 9,1858; s. Charles and Elizabeth (Shunk) B.; grad. Wilmington Conf. Acad., Del.; LL.B., U. of Pa., 1879; LL.D., Lafayette, 1915; m. Lizzie Hamm, Apr. 1883; children—Francis Shunk, Anna Haines. In law practice, Phila., 1879—; mem. firm Brown & Williams; special counsel Tax Commn. of Pa., 1909-11, pres. bd. dirs. City Trusts of Philadelphia; atty. gen. of Pa., 1915-19. Home: Philadelphia, Pa. Died May 6, 1940.

BROWN, Frank, gov.; b. Carroll County, Md., Aug. 8, 1846; acad. edn. Clerk state tobacco warehouse, 1870-76; mem. Md. Ho. of Rep., 1876-78; pres. Md. State Agrl. and Mech. Assn., 1880-92; postmaster, Baltimore, 1886-90; gov. of Md., 1892-96. Democrat. Pres. Baltimore St. R.R. Lines, 1894-97. Home: Baltimore, Md. Died Feb. 3, 1920.

BROWN, Frank Llewellyn, Sunday School specialist; b. Brooklyn, Oct. 16, 1862; s. James Bowen and Emma (Ready) B.; pub. sch. edn.; m. Gertrude Lillian Moadinger, Oct. 14, 1886. Cashier Nat. Bank of Deposit, New York, 1891-93, Sprague Nat. Bank, Brooklyn, 1893-98; mem. firm James N. Brown & Co., 1898-1904, retired. Trustee Bushwick Savings Bank, Brooklyn. Chmn. exec. com. N.Y. State S.S. Assn.; mem. exec. com. Internat. S.S. Assn., World's S.S. Assn.; commr. World's S.S. Assn. to Japan, China, P.I., South America; sec. Commn. to the Orient, 1913; elected joint gen. sec. of World's S.S. Assn., 1914; made organizing tour of South America, 1915; supt. Bushwick Av. M.E. S.S., Brooklyn, 36 yrs. Mem. bd. Brooklyn Ch. Soc., Brooklyn S.S. Union; mem. Bd. Sunday Schs. and Bd. Foreign Missions M.E. Ch.; Joint Centenary Com.; mem. Gen. Conf., 1908, 12, 16, 20, Ecumenical Conf., 1911; mem. commn. on religious edn. and com. on inter-ch. world movement of Federal Council of Churches, also coms. on Internal Justice and Good Will, Relations with the Orient, and on Councils of Chs.; mem. Com. on Coöperation in Latin America; mem. mayor of New York coms. on playgrounds, censorship, motion pictures, reception to distinguished guests; chmn. Pub. Sch. Bd., dist. 36, N.Y. City, 12 yrs. Was mem. Minute Men and Commn. on China Famine Relief. Author: The Sunday School and the Home, 1906; The City Sunday School, 1907; The Superintendent and His Work, 1911; The Sunday School Tour of the Orient, 1914; Sunday School Officers' Manual, 1915; Plans for Sunday School Evangelism, 1919. Home: Brooklyn, N.Y. Died Mar. 23, 1922.

BROWN, Frederic Kenyon ("Al Priddy"), author, clergyman; b. Oldham, Eng., Dec. 5, 1882; s. Samuel and Mary Jane (Kenyon) B.; brought to America, 1892; grad. Bangor Theol. Sem., 1907; A.B., Dartmouth, 1910; m. Ethelind Cortland Knight, Jan. 1, 1908; children—Roland Kenyon, Laurance Cortland, Miriam Dalton, Walter Varian, Kennerley Whitney. Ordained Congl. ministry, 1907; pastor Bucksport, Me., 1907-08, Brookfield, Mass., 1910-12, Southwick, Mass., 1913-15, Worcester, Mass., 1915, Lancaster, Mass., 1926—. Author: Through the Mill, 1912; Through the School, 1913; Man or Machine, Which? 1913; The Playtime Guide Book, 1925. Home: Lancaster, Mass. Died Dec. 7, 1935.

BROWN, Frederick Anson, lawyer; b. Decatur, Ill., Aug. 9, 1867; s. Josiah and Sarah Elvira B.; LL.B., U. of Mich., 1889; m. Mary Lois Roby, Jan. 7, 1891; children—Kilburn Roby, Mary Lois (Mrs. Keehn W. Berry). Admitted to Ill. bar, 1889; practiced at Decatur, 1889-90, Tacoma, Wash., 1890-98, Chicago, 1898—; spl. asst. atty. gen. of Ill., 1923-24. Served as officer U.S. Army, World War. Former mem. Ill. State Bd. Law Examiners. Pres. Chicago br. English-Speaking Union, 1928-30; dir. Central Howard Assn. Republican. Presbyterian. Mason (K.T., Shriner). Home: Chicago, Ill. Died Oct. 16, 1939.

BROWN, Frederick Harvey, inventor; b. at Indiantown (now Tiskaiwah), Ill., May 11, 1843; s. Joseph Mortimer and Louisa M. B.; ed. St. Louis High Sch., Washington U. and by pvt. study of natural sciences; m. Ida Moore, 1861 (dec.); 2d, Catherine F. Norwood, Apr. 29, 1877. Asst. auditor and clerk, for Gen. T. J. Haines, purchasing q.-m. commissary U.S. Army, St. Louis, 1862; v.p. Magneto Telegraph Co., New York, 1885-86, Brown Telegraph Co., Chicago, 1890; pres. Electro Geodetic Co., Los Angeles, 1900, Nat. Electric & Magnetic Co., Chicago. Holder many patents on electric inventions in U.S. and foreign countries. Awarded medal for telephone, Paris Expn. Agnostic. Author: One Dollar's Work, 1893; A Few Wise Things It Were Well for You to Read, 1893. Home: Los Angeles, Calif. Died 1911.

BROWN, George, naval officer; b. Rushville, Ind., June 19, 1835; s. William J. and Susan (Tompkins) B.; apptd. to U.S. Naval Acad. from Ind., 1849; m. Kate Morris, Oct. 4, 1871. Promoted passed midshipman, June 12, 1855; master, Sept. 16, 1855; lt., June 2, 1856; lt. comdr., July 16, 1862; comdr., July 25, 1866; capt., Apr. 25, 1877; commodore, Sept. 4, 1887; rear adm., Sept. 27, 1893; retired, June 19, 1897; performed spl. duty on western coast during Spanish-Am. War. Home: Indianapolis, Ind. Died June 29, 1913.

BROWN, George Francis, corp. official; b. Chicago, Oct. 1, 1843; chief clerk U.S. q.-m. dept., Oct. 1861, to Feb., 1866; entered R.R. service, July, 1867, as sec. and treas., for receiver Memphis, Clarksville & Louisville R.R.; agt. in charge of war claims and agt. frt. dept. Ill. Cent. R.R., 1868-69; sec. Bloomington Fire Ins. Co., 1869-71; with The Pullman Company, 1871—, successively as clerk, asst. to gen. supt., 7 yrs., acting gen. supt. and gen. supt., 1880-85, gen. mgr., 1885—. Address: Chicago, Ill. Died 1910.

BROWN, George H., judge; b. Washington, N.C., May 3, 1850; s. Sylvester T. and Elizabeth (Bonner) B.; ed. Horner Acad., Oxford, N.C.; m. Laura Ellison, Dec. 17, 1874. Engaged in practice of law at Washington, N.C., 1872-89; judge Superior Ct. of N.C., 1889-1904; asso. justice Supreme Ct. of N.C., 1905—. Democrat. Episcopalian. Home: Washington, N.C. Died Apr. 14, 1936.

BROWN, George M., judge; b. Roseburg, Ore., May 5, 1864; s. Thomas and Sarah (Flett) B.; B.S., Willamette U., 1885; m. Bertha A. Bellows, Nov. 8, 1895; children—Thomas Leland, Marjorie W., Elaine. Began practice at Roseburg, 1891; dist. atty. 2d Jud. Dist. of Ore., 1895-1914; atty. gen. of Ore., 1915-20, when resigned to accept appointment as asso. justice Supreme Court of Ore.; elected asso. justice, terms 1921-27 and 1927-33. Republican. Presbyn. Mason, Odd Fellow. Home: Roseburg, Ore. Deceased.

BROWN, George Pliny, educator, publisher; b. Lenox, O., Nov. 10, 1836; s. William Pliny and Rachel Howard (Piper) B.; grad. Grand River Inst., Austinburg, O.; m. Mary Louise Seymour, Oct. 30, 1855. Supt. schs., Richmond, Ind., 1860-71; prin. high sch., Indianapolis, Ind., 1871-74; supt. pub. schs., Indianapolis, 1874-79; pres. State Normal Sch., Terre Haute, Ind., 1879-86; editor and publisher Public School Jour., 1887, changed name to Sch. and Home Education, 1895, and continued as editor; organized, 1889, and pres. Pub. Sch. Publishing Co. Author: Elements of English Grammar, 1899 A1; Story of Our English Grandfathers, 1902; The King and His Wonderful Castle, 1903. Address: Bloomington, Ill. Died 1910.

BROWN, George Stewart, judge; b. Baltimore, Aug. 15, 1871; s. Stewart and Anne (Gill) B.; B.A., Johns Hopkins, 1893; LL.B., U. of Md., 1895; m. Susan Morton, June 1, 1904; 1 son, Stewart. Began practice in Baltimore, 1895; mem. Brown & Brune, 1900-13. Mem. City Council, Baltimore, 1899-1907; judge U.S. Customs Court by apptmt. of President Wilson, 1913—. Democrat. Prsbyn. Home: Brooklyn, N.Y. Died Nov. 11, 1941.

BROWN, George W., lawyer; b. Du Page County, Ill., May 17, 1859; s. James and Rosanna B.; ed. pub. schs. of Wheaton, Ill., and Northwestern Coll., Naperville, Ill.; began study of law in office of Hoyne, Horton & Hoyne, and grad. Union College of Law, Chicago, 1883; engaged in practice at Wheaton, Ill.; county judge, Du Page County, 1890-97; elected judge Circuit Court, Ill., 1897, 1903; was apptd. by the Supreme Court as justice of Appellate Court at Ottawa, in the 2d dist., and later in the Appellate bench of the 3d dist. at Springfield, Ill.; served as chief justice of both courts; was chief justice of the latter court when he resigned to resume the practice of law; mem. law firm of Knight & Brown. V.p. Gary-Wheaton Bank, Wheaton, Ill. Republican. Home: Wheaton, Ill. Died 1906.

BROWN, George Warren, shoe mfr.; b. Granville, N.Y., Mar. 21, 1853; s. David and Melinda (Roblee) B.; ed. pub. schs. and business coll.; m. Bettie Bofinger, Apr. 7, 1885. Began in St. Louis as shipping clk. for wholesale shoe house, 1873, and in 10 months became traveling salesman; organizer, 1878, and pres. Bryan-Brown Shoe Co., now The Brown Shoe Co., of which was pres. until May 1, 1916, chmn. bd., 1916—. Actively identified with many enterprises for advancement of St. Louis. Republican. Methodist. Home: St. Louis, Mo. Died Dec. 13, 1921.

BROWN, George Washington, mfr.; b. Northfield, Vt., Aug. 30, 1841; s. Isaac Washington and Sylvia Elvira (Partridge) B.; ed. Northfield Acad., Orange Co. grammar sch., Randolph, Vt., and Newbury (Vt.) Sem.; m. Addie E. Perkins, May 5, 1863 (died 1900). Timekeeper in machine shops, Vt. Central R.R., 1859-65; mem. firms Hyde & Brown and McGowan & Brown, St. Albans, 1865-69; auditor motive power, Central Pacific R.R., Sacramento, Calif., 1869-70; established agencies for Wheeler & Wilson Mfg. Co., 1871-76; N.E. mgr. Wheeler & Wilson (sewing machine) Mfg. Co., Boston, 1876-92; mgr. and treas., Consolidated Hand Method Lasting Machine Co., Boston, 1892-96; mgr. and treas., Consolidated McKay Lasting Machine Co., Boston, 1896-99; mgr. and treas. United Shoe Machinery Co., 1899-1910, v.p., 1910—; v.p. United Shoe Machinery Corp.; dir. First Nat. Bank, Boston Blacking Co., United Shoe Machinery Co. of Me. V.p. and trustee N.E. Conservatory of Music; v.p. Boston Music Sch. settlement. Episcopalian. Presented pub. library to Northfield, 1906. Home: Newton, Mass. Died No. 16, 1928.

BROWN, Glenn, architect; b. Fauquier County, Va., Sept. 13, 1854; s. Bedford B.; attended Washington and Lee U.; M.A., George Washington U.; spl. architectural course Mass. Inst. Tech.; m. Mary Ella Chapman, Feb. 1, 1876; children— Glenn M., Bedford. In practice as an architect, in Washington, Va. and Md., 1878—. Fellow A.I.A. (sec. and treas., 1899-1913). Mem. purchasing com. Avery Library, Columbia U. With Bedford Brown was architect of Dumbarton bridge and Alfred Noble Memorial; architect, U.S. Marines, Quantico, Va., 1921-26. Author: Water Closets—a Historical Mechanical and Sanitary Treatise, 1884; Healthy Foundations for Houses, 1885; Trap Syphonage, 1886; History of the United States Capitol, 1900; Papers on Improvement of Washington City, 1901; (monograph) The Octagon, 1915; Personal Recollections Charles F. McKim, 1916; Roosevelt and the Fine Arts, 1919; Memories of Washington City, 1860-1930. Editor: European and Japanese Gardens, 1902; Frank D. Millet and Augustus Saint Gaudens, memorial volume, 1913. Editor Proc. Am. Inst. Architects, 1899-1909; contributing editor Architectural Record, New York, 1926-30. A.N.A., 1927. Home: Washington, D.C. Died Apr. 22, 1932.

BROWN, Harold Haven, artist; b. Malden, Mass., June 6, 1869; s. Obadiah B. and Sarah H. (Cox) B.; ed. Lowell Sch. of Design, Mass. Inst. Tech., Cowles Art Sch. (all of Boston); grad. Mass. Normal Art Sch. (4 yrs.' course); studied École des Beaux Arts, Paris, under Gérôme, and Acad. Julian, Paris, under Laurens; m. Florence Bradshaw, Nov. 4, 1897; children—Beatrice Bradshaw, Barbara Haven. Served as teacher of art in De Witt Clinton High Sch., High Sch. of Commerce, and Stuyvesant High Sch. (all of New York), University High Sch. (Chicago); dir. Art Museum and School of Art, The John Herron Art Institute, Indianapolis, 1913-21; dir. Provincetown (Mass.) Art Assn., 1926—. Painter, designer, illustrator; exhibited at Am. Water Color Soc., Archtl. League, Nat. Soc. Craftsmen (New York), Buffalo Expn., Art Inst. Chicago, John Herron Art Inst., Am. Rotary Water Color Exhibit. Awarded bronze medal, Buffalo Expn., 1901. Author: Applied Drawing, 1916. Home: Provincetown, Mass. Died Apr. 7, 1932.

BROWN, Helen Dawes, author; b. Concord, Mass., May 15, 1857; d. William Dawes and Martha (Swan) Brown; A.B., Vassar Coll., 1878, A.M., 1890. Author: Two College Girls, 1886; The Petrie Estate, 1893; Little Miss Phoebe Gay, 1895; A Civilian Attaché, 1899; Her Sixteenth Year, 1901; A Book of Little Boys, 1904; Mr. Tuckerman's Nieces, 1907; Orphans, 1911; How Phoebe Found Herself, 1912; Talks to Freshman Girls, 1914; Little Jean, 1918; Snapshots of Nancy and Brothers, 1939. Home: Montclair, N.J. Died Sept. 5, 1941.

BROWN, Henry B., univ. pres.; b. Mt. Vernon, O., Oct. 6, 1847; s. Thomas and Rachel (Mills) B.; grad. Nat. Normal U., Lebanon, O., 1871; m. Neva Axe, Feb. 16, 1886. Prof. mathematics, Northwestern Normal Sch., Republic, O., 1871-73; founded, Sept. 1873, and pres., Northern Ind. Normal Sch., changed, 1901, to Valparaiso Coll., and, 1904, to Valparaiso U. Home: Valparaiso, Ind. Died Sept. 16, 1917.

BROWN, Henry Bascom, machinery mfr.; b. Middleborough, Mass., July 5, 1833; s. Rev. Thomas Gibson and Caroline Maria (Daniels) B.; ed. Wesleyan Acad., Wilbraham, Mass., and Wesleyan U. (A.B., 1911); m. Adaline S. Gates, May 14, 1854 (died 1875); m. 2d, Genevra Sexton, May 1, 1878. Engaged in journalism, beginning 1857 on Middlesex Republican, Middletown, Conn.; later in St. Louis; local editor, Hartford Evening Press, 1861-62; asst. editor New Haven Daily Palladium, 1862-63; acting asst. p.m. U.S. Navy, 1863-65; hon. discharged, Oct. 1865; on editorial staff Boston Journal short time; later machinery mfr. Sec. Rep. State Central Com., 1869; helped organize Prohibition Party in Conn., 1871; chmn. Prohibition State Central Com., 6 yrs. following; editor and propr. State Temperance Journal, 1871-74; mem., 1866—, and later 6 yrs. Grand treas. Order of Good Templars; candidate for Conn. Senate, 1888; ordained minister Advent denomination and one of the editors The Herald of Life, of Springfield, Mass.; chmn. Prohibition State Central Com., 1896-1903; Prohibition candidate for congressman-at-large, 1904; editor and publisher The Christian Inquirer. Home: East Hampton, Conn. Died June 14, 1916.

BROWN, Henry Billings, jurist; b. S. Lee, Mass., Mar. 2, 1836; s. Billings and Mary (Tyler) B.; A.B., Yale, 1856; studied law in private office; attended lectures at Yale and Harvard law schs.; LL.D., U. of Mich., 1887, Yale, 1891; m. Caroline Pitts, July 13, 1864 (died 1901); m. 2d, Josephine E. Tyler, June 25, 1904. Admitted to bar, 1860; dep. U.S. marshal, 1861-63; asst. U.S. atty. for Eastern Dist. of Mich., 1863-68; judge Circuit Ct., Wayne County, Mich., a few months; in practice at Detroit, until 1875; U.S. dist. judge, Eastern Dist. of Mich., 1875-90; asso. justice Supreme Court of U.S., 1890-1906; retired May 28, 1906. Compiler of Brown's Admiralty Reports. Address: Washington, D.C. Died Sept. 4, 1913.

BROWN, Henry Harrison, lecturer; b. Uxbridge, Mass., June 26, 1840; s. Pemberton and Paulina (Whitmore) B.; ed. Nichols Acad., Dudley, Mass., and 1885-86, at Unitarian Div. Sch., Meadville, Pa.; m. Fannie M. Hancox, Sept. 1873 (divorced). Teacher, 1857-70, except 3 yrs. in war as pvt. 18th Conn. Vols., 1st lt. 29th Conn. Vols. (colored), Jan. 1, 1863; capt. 1st U.S.C.T., Mar. 1864; mustered out Sept. 29, 1865. Preached for Unitarian Soc., Petersham, Mass., 1887-88, Salem, Ore., 1890-92; lecturer on spiritualistic, reformatory and econ. topics, 1870-85; lecturer and soul-culture teacher, 1893-1900; editor, lecturer, etc., 1900—. Pres. "Now" Folk, publishers, San Francisco, and editor "Now" (New-Thought mag.); also author of various pamphlets on Suggestion and the New Thought. Pres. World New Thought Federation, 1905. Established a coöperating community at Glenwood, Calif., 1906. Author: Self-Healing Through Suggestion; How to Control Fate Through Suggestion; Man's Greatest Discovery; Dollars Want Me; Concentration, or, the Road to Success; Success: How Won Through Affirmation. Home: Glenwood, Calif. Died May 8, 1918.

BROWN, H(enry) Martin, banker; b. Bolton, Conn., Apr. 28, 1850; s. Arba Harrison and Harriet (Dart) B.; ed. high sch., Rockville, Conn.; m. Annie Weed North, 1875. Began at 16 as clk. in dry goods store, later partner with E. Stevens Henry. Formed partnership with bro., ex-Gov. D. Russell Brown, and Charles H. Child, as Brown Bros. & Co., mill supplies, inc. as The Brown Bros. Co., of which was sec., 1893-99; organizer, 1899, also treas. and gen. mgr. of the U.S. Bobbin & Shuttle Co., owning many plants in N.E.; pres. Industrial Trust Co., 1912-24, later v.chmn. bd.; officer or dir. many corps. Mem. City Council, Providence, 1890; col. and chief of staff under Gov. Brown, 1892-95; mem. R.I. Ho. of Rep., 1900-02, inclusive; del. Rep. Nat. Conv., 1904, and was mem. com. to notify Theodore Roosevelt of his nomination as pres. of U.S. Mason (K.T.). Home: Providence, R.I. Died June 9, 1926.

BROWN, Horace Manchester, surgeon; b. New Bedford, Mass., Oct. 12, 1857; s. Capt. John Cheney and Jane Elisabeth (Taylor) B.; M.D., Univ. Med. Coll. (New York U.), 1880; post-grad. work London, Paris, Munich, Brussels, Berlin; m. Fanny Louise Eldred, Oct. 25, 1882. Practiced at Milwaukee, Wis., 1880—; surgeon C.,M.&St.P. Ry., 41 yrs.; builder, and owner Lakeside Hosp. 26 yrs. until its closure, 1915; later surgeon Columbia Hosp. Capt. and surgeon Wis. N.G. 12 yrs.; 1st lt. M.R.C., U.S.A., retired; chief surg. sect. Advisory Bd. No. 2, World War, also chmn. and organizer Vol. Med. Service Corps. Pres. and treas. Calumet Zinc Land Co.; v.p. Anson Eldred Co.; dir. Physicians' Radium Assn. Author: The Songs of Bilitis (English version), 1904. Translator of De Venenis of Abonus, Anathomia of Mondinus, etc. An editor Annals of Medical History. Home: Milwaukee, Wis. Died Jan. 18, 1929.

BROWN, Howard Nicholson, clergyman; b. Columbia, N.Y., May 11, 1849; s. Rev. M. C. and Sarah A. (Nicholson) B.; m. Inez A. Wicks, Oct. 25, 1872; children—Mary Louise, Howard Wicks, Sarah Nicholson. Ordained Unitarian ministry, 1872; minister First Parish, Brookline, Mass., 1873-95, King's Chapel, Boston, 1895—. Author: Sunday Stories; Life of Jesus for Young People; Sermons in King's Chapel, 1916. Home: Framingham Center, Mass. Died Dec. 13, 1932.

BROWN, Hugh Henry, lawyer; b. Steubenville, O., May 4, 1872; s. Robert McCutcheon and Louise Christina (Smith) B.; student U. of Wooster, O., 1890-92; A.B., Stanford U., 1896; m. Marjorie Moore, Feb. 17, 1904; children—Hugh Harrison, Marshall Roberts, Marjorie. Practiced, San Francisco, with firm of Reddy, Campbell & Metson, 1897-1902; mem. Campbell, Metson & Brown, offices in Tonopah and Goldfield, Nev., and San Francisco, 1902-10; practiced alone, Tonopah, Jan. 1, 1911-19, Walter Rowson associated, 1919—; resumed practice in San Francisco, 1924. Mem. Nev. State Banking Bd., 1911-14; mem. Commn. on Uniform State Laws (v.p. 1918-19). Del. Rep. Nat. Conv., 1908, 16, alternate, 1912, 20. Mem. Nat. Bd., Stanford U., 1923-27. Mason (32°). Elk. Home: Palo Alto, Calif. Deceased.

BROWN, Isaac Eddy, Y.M.C.A. worker; b. Chautauqua County, N.Y., May 17, 1849; s. Russell McCary and Electa Louisa (Sherman) B.; grad. Ill. State Normal U., 1874; A.B., Knox Coll., Ill., 1892, A.M., 1896; m. Mary Johnson, Dec. 28, 1881. Prin. Decatur High Sch. 1874-80; state sec. Ill. Y.M.C.A., 1880-1909; a founder Western Secretarial Institute Y.M.C.A., 1884, and started Training Sch. Y.M.C.A., 1890, the two being combined, 1896, to form the Inst. and Training Sch. for Y.M.C.A. (now Y.M.C.A. College), dean, 1909—. First pres. of 1st student Y.M.C.A. in Ill., at Ill. State Normal U., 1872; mem. 21 yrs. and pres. 13 yrs. of Bd. of Inst. and Training Sch. Y.M.C.A. Conglist.; del. to Nat. Council Congregational Chs., 1915. Author: Y.M.C.A. Buildings; Fifty-five Years, Y.M.C.A., Chicago. Home: Oak Park, Ill. Died July 8, 1917.

BROWN, J(acob) Hay, judge; b. York, Pa., Sept. 11, 1849; s. Rev. James A. and Mary E. (Hay) B.; A.B., Pa. Coll., 1867; LL.D., Dickinson Coll., 1901, U. of Pa., 1916. Practiced law at Lancaster, Pa.; city solicitor, 1874-76; county solicitor, 1876-79; Justice Supreme Ct. of Pa., 1899; chief justice, 1915-21, retired, 1921. Republican. Address: Lancaster, Pa. Died Oct. 10, 1930.

BROWN, James, banker; b. N.Y. City, Apr. 28, 1863; s. George Hunter and Rachel Blanding (Wheeler) B.; B.S., Columbia, 1883; m. Adele Quartley, June 20, 1888. Sr. partner Brown Bros., Harriman & Co., internat. bankers; v.p. Bangor & Aroostook R.R. Co.; dir. Commercial Pacific Cable Co. (finance com.), J. G. White Engring. Corp. (exec. com.), trustee Central Union Trust Co. (exec. com.), Northern Assurance Co. Ltd. (London), Sun Ins. Co. Ltd. (London). Pres. bd. trustees Sailors' Snug Harbor. Decorated Chevalier Legion of Honor (France); Comdr. Order Crown of Roumania. Home: Locust Valley, L.I., and New York, N.Y. Died June 9, 1935.

BROWN, James, judge; b. Crosshouse, Ayrshire, Scotland, Oct. 12, 1858; s. Matthew and Agnes (Longmuir) B.; ed. day and evening schs., Scotland; LL.B., Ia. State U., 1884; m. Jessie Benton Schuyler, Nov. 10, 1886 (died 1912); children—Matthew A., Jean (Mrs. George Drake, dec.), James A. (dec.), Jessie M. (Mrs. Harry Dungan); m. 2d, Martha Barber, 1915. Came to U.S., 1881, naturalized citizen, 1886. Admitted to Dakota Ter. bar, 1885, and began practice at Kimball; county judge Brule County, S.D., 1897-1901; apptd. by Gov. W. H. Bulow, judge Supreme Court of S.D., Nov. 26, 1927, to fill unexpired term of John H. Gates (dec.), ending 1931; asst. atty. gen. of S.D., 1931—. Trustee Yankton (S.D.) Coll. Democrat. Conglist. Home: Chamberlain, S.D. Died Dec. 19, 1936.

BROWN, James B., banker; b. Lawrenceburg, Ky., Nov. 28, 1872; s. Thornton and Paralee (McKee) B.; ed. pub. schs.; m. Elizabeth Kennedy. Began as office boy with the Southern News Co., Louisville, 1887, later cashier; cashier city tax receiver and was elected tax receiver, term 1902-06; cashier First Nat. Bank, 1906-08, elected pres., 1908; with Nat. Bank of Commerce, as 1st v.p., later pres.; bank consolidated, 1919, with the Louisville Bank, under title of Nat. Bank of Ky., of which was pres.; also pres. Herald Post Co. Home: Louisville, Ky. Died Oct. 24, 1940.

BROWN, J(ames) Stanley, educator; b. Cumberland, O., Sept. 1863; s. George William and Lorinda (Robinson) B.; A.B., Denison U., 1889, LL.D., 1910; m. Elizabeth May Seitz, Dec. 1891. Prof. W. Ky. Coll., 1889-92; prin., State Normal Sch., The Dalles, Ore., 1892-93; prin., Joliet (Ill.) City High Sch., 1893-99; supt. and prin., Joliet Twp. High Sch. and Junior Coll., 1899-1919; pres. Northern Ill. State Teachers Coll., De Kalb, Ill., 1919-27. Republican. Baptist. Home: Joliet, Ill. Died Sept. 6, 1939.

BROWN, James F., lawyer; b. Kanawha County, Va. (now W.Va.), Mar. 7, 1852; s. Judge James H. and Louisa M. (Beuhring) B.; A.B., W.Va. U., 1873, A.M., 1875, LL.D., 1917; studied law under his father; m. Jennie M. Woodbridge, Sept. 13, 1877. Admitted to bar, 1875; sr. mem. Brown, Jackson & Knight. Mem. legislature, 1883-84; mem. bd. regents State U., 1890-1901; v.p. Kanawha Valley Bank, George Washington Life Ins. Co. Trustee City Hosp., Masonic Temple, etc. Democrat. Home: Charleston, W.Va. Died Dec. 5, 1921.

BROWN, James R., lecturer, writer; b. Mount Forest, Ont., Can., Aug. 15, 1863; s. James and Helen (Rodgers) B.; ed. pub. schs.; married; children—William M., Florence May, Jennie Fairbairn. Settled in N.Y. City, 1886; accountant, until 1910; lecturer on polit. economy and sociology; pub. of Taxation (jour.). Pres. Manhattan Single Tax Club, 1915—. Author: The Farmer and the Single Tax, 1915; Plain Talk on Taxation, 1916; Open Letter to Legislators, 1917. Home: New York, N.Y. Died Sept. 20, 1931.

BROWN, J. Appleton, artist; b. Newburyport, Mass., July 24, 1844; studied art in Boston under B. C. Porter, and in Paris under Emile Lambinet; returning to U.S. opened a studio in Boston; landscape painter; later removed to New York. A.N.A. Home: New York. Died 1902.

BROWN, John C., judge; b. Carter Co., Mo., Mar. 22, 1860; ed. in Mo. and Colo.; m. Sarah E. Pool, June 22, 1887. Admitted to bar, Oct. 10, 1888; elected pros. atty., Carter County, Nov. 1888; mayor of Willow Springs, Mo., 1895-98; asso. justice Supreme Ct. of Mo., term 1911-20. Republican. Home: Fredericktown, Mo. Died Sept. 4, 1915.

BROWN, John Crosby, banker; b. New York, May 22, 1838; s. James and Eliza Maria (Coe) B.; grad. Columbia Coll., 1859; m. Mary E. Adams, Nov. 9, 1864. Became connected with banking house of Brown Bros. & Co.; later head of firm. Has been mem. Bd. of Edn., trustee of Columbia Coll., Met. Museum of Art; pres. and trustee Union Theol. Sem., and dir. Presbyn. Hosp. Pres. Newburg, Dutchess & Conn. R.R. Co.; dir. Clove Branch R.R. Co., Bank of New York, U.S. Trust Co., and Liverpool and London and Globe Ins. Co.; trustee Bank for Savings. Home: New York, N.Y. Died 1909.

BROWN, John Franklin, editor ednl. books; b. Springboro, O., May 1, 1865; s. Samuel and Elizabeth Wildman (Hadley) B.; Ph.B., Earlham Coll., Ind., 1889, A.M., 1895; Ph.D., Cornell U., 1896; m. Frances D. Guion, May 26, 1904. Teacher, rural schs., Ind., 3 yrs., high schs. and acads., 5 yrs.; instr. philosophy and psychology, Ind. U., 1896-98; v.p. and prof. philosophy, Earlham Coll., 1898-1901; insp. high schs. and prof. edn., State U. of Ia., 1901-05; prof. edn. and prin. Normal Sch., U. of Wyo., 1905-08; exchange teacher of English, Franckesche Stiftungen, Halle, Prussia, 1909; editor in secondary school dept., The Macmillan Co., New York, 1910—. Spl. interest in problems of secondary edn. Editor Wyoming School Journal, 1905-08. Lecturer in edn., Vassar College, 1910, Teachers College (Columbia), summer session, 1910, Wellesley Coll., 1911-12; in Dept. of Edn., N.Y. City. Quaker. Republican. Author: The American High School, 1909; The Training of Teachers for Secondary Schools in Germany and the United States, 1911; State Publication of Schoolbooks, 1916. Home: New Rochelle, N.Y. Died Feb. 15, 1940.

BROWN, John George, painter; b. Durham, Eng., Nov. 11, 1831; s. John and Ann B.; ed. common schs. and Newcastle-on-Tyne, Eng., studied art in Eng., Scotland and U.S.; m. Mary Owen, Sept. 10, 1856; m. 2d, Emma A. Owen, 1871. Came to America, Nov. 1853; began to paint in Brooklyn, 1856; specially known as a painter of New York street boys. Prin. works: A Merry Air with a Sad Heart; A Thrilling Moment; The Stump Speech; Training the Dog; Heels Over Head; The Passing Show; To Decide the Question; 3 for 5 Cents; Be Mine; etc. Mem. jury of awards, Chicago Expn., 1893. Hon. mention, Paris, 1889; medals from Boston and Calif., and popular prize in Tenn.; silver medal, Buffalo Expn., 1901. Founder of new site for Acad. of Design at 110th St., New York, A.N.A., 1862, N.A., 1863; pres. Am. Water Color Soc., 1887-1904, Artists' Fund Soc., 10 yrs.; v.p. Nat. Acad. Design, 1899-1904, and chmn. Art Schs. Home: New York, N.Y. Died Feb. 8, 1913.

BROWN, John Howard, editor; b. Rhinebeck, N.Y., Nov. 8, 1840; s. William Howard and Elizabeth (Conklin) B.; ed. Rhinebeck Acad., Ft. Edward Inst., and Eastman Coll.; taught sch.; was clk. and student in law office, New York; news corr., Washington, 1864-67; removed South, edited a newspaper and engaged in real estate business, Augusta, Ga.; m. Jeannie Hamilton Derby, 1872. Removed to New York, 1872; engaged in editing and publishing subscription books. Planned and passed through the press, Around the World with General Grant (2 vols.), 1879-80. Editor: (6 vols.) National Cyclopedia American Biography, 1890-95; Lamb's Biographical Dictionary of the United States (7 vols.), 1897-1903; Lamb's Textile Industries of the United States (Vol. I), 1911. Author: American Naval Heroes, 1899; American Families of Historic Lineage (Long Island—2 vols.), 1912; (with Carl W. Schlegel) German-American Families (Am. Hist. Soc.), 1916. Historian and genealogist. Home: Brooklyn, N.Y. Died Apr. 22, 1917.

BROWN, John Marshall, trustee of estates, army officer; b. Portland, Me., Dec. 14, 1838; s. John Bundy and Ann Matilda (Greely) B.; ed. Portland, Gould's, Bethel and Phillips Andover Acads.; grad. Bowdoin Coll., 1860; A.M., 1863. Commd. 1st lt., 20th Me. Vols., Aug. 29, 1862; apptd. by Pres. Lincoln, June 1863, capt. and asst. adj. gen. vols.; later served in S.C. and Fla.; promoted to lt. col. 32d Me. vols., Mar. 26, 1864; comd. regt. at Totopotomy and Cold Harbor and preliminary movements at Petersburg, where was severely wounded; discharged for physical disability from wounds, Sept. 23, 1864; bvtd. col. and brig. gen.; m. Alida Catherine Carroll, Dec. 18, 1866. Became mem. firm J. B. Brown & Son, owners Portland Sugar Co. Mem. common council, Portland, 1865, commr. to Paris Expn., 1867. Served in Me. Militia as a.-d.-c., col. and brig. gen. Mem. Me. legislature, 1899. Republican. Pres. Me. Agrl. Soc., 1878; was 25 yrs. mem. and 6 yrs. pres. bd. of overseers, and later mem. bd. of trustees Bowdoin Coll. Mem. bd. of mgrs. Nat. Home for Disabled Vol. Soldiers, and local mgr. Eastern branch, 1898—. Home: Falmouth Fireside, Me. Died 1907.

BROWN, John Pinkney, arboriculturist; b. Rising Sun, Ind., Jan. 19, 1842; s. Capt. Elbridge G. and Adaline (Style) B.; ed. Hanover Coll., Ind.; studied civ. engring.; m. Mary E. Stephens, 1868. Served 16th Ind. Regt., 1861-63; later Miss. River service in U.S. steamers. Organized and later sec. and treas. Internat. Soc. Arboriculture. Originated system of tree planting by rys. for future timber and tie supply; has established model forest farm of 200 acres on which were planted 200,000 young forest trees. Republican. Editor Arboriculture. Author: Practical Arboriculture, 1906. Home: Connersville, Ind. Died 1915.

BROWN, John Richard, clergyman; b. at Brooklyn, Nov. 25, 1870; s. William and Isabel (Runciman) B.; studied Columbia U.; M.A., U. of Edinburgh, 1892, Ph.D., 1895; Rochester Theol. Sem., 1895; m. Gertrude Marion Rowley, Dec. 22, 1896. Ordained Bapt. ministry, 1895. Pastor various chs., Mo., R.I. and Conn., 1895-1919; prof. O.T., Rochester (N.Y.) Theol. Sem., 1919—. Democrat. Author: The Messianic Prophecies, 1899; Jesus, the Joyous Comrade, 1910; Paul and the Social Order. Home: Rochester, N.Y. Died Oct. 1926.

BROWN, J(ohn) Vallance, prof. Greek; b. Clayton, Ill., Apr. 13, 1868; s. Rev. Dr. John Hervey and Catharine (McClanahan) B.; A.B., Monmouth (Ill.) Coll., 1890, A.M., 1893; grad. student Johns Hopkins, 1893-94; corr. student U. of Chicago, 1898; studied Harvard, 1911-12; m. Ada May Moore, Sept. 7, 1893 (died 1917); children—John Moore Findley, Thomas Arthur, James Isaac; m. 2d, Helen Dale Story, Aug. 15, 1923. Professor Greek, Tarkio (Mo.) Coll., 1890—, v.p., 1899-1906, actg. pres., May-Aug. 1900, and school year, 1901-02. Republican. United Presbyn. Winner Chicago Record-Herald Glacier Park trip prize for best story of adventure, 1916; also winner ednl. essay contest of U.P. Ch., for ministers and laymen, 1903. Home: Tarkio, Mo. Died Dec. 7, 1926.

BROWN, John Young, lawyer, gov.; b. Hardin County, Ky., June 28, 1835; grad. Center Coll., Ky., 1855; elected to Congress, 1859, because of age waited 1 yr. to take seat; elected to 40th Congress, 1868, but was refused seat because of political disabilities; mem. Congress, 1873-77; resumed practice; gov. Ky., 1891-95. Home: Henderson, Ky. Died 1904.

BROWN, John Young, surgeon; b. 1865; M.D., Bellevue Hosp. Med. Coll. (New York U.), 1887. City phys., Henderson, Ky., 1887-91; asst. supt. Central Ky. Asylum for Insane, 1891-94; prof. surgery, St. Louis U. Surgeon in chief, St. John's Hosp. Home: St. Louis, Mo. Died Oct. 30, 1919.

BROWN, Joseph Gill, banker; b. Raleigh, N.C., Nov. 5, 1854; s. Henry J. and Lydia (Lane) B.; ed. pvt. schs., Raleigh and Wake County, N.C., Trinity Coll., 1871-72, half through sophomore yr.; m. Alice Burkhead, Nov. 10, 1881; children—Josephine Lane (Mrs. J. K. Doughton), Robert Anderson, Frank Burkhead. Pres. Citizens' Nat. Bank, Raleigh, Raleigh Savings Bank & Trust Co., Atlantic Fire Ins. Co.; dir. Carolina div. Southern Ry., Atlantic Joint Stock Land Bank. Pres. N.C. State Bankers' Assn., 1899-1900; 3 terms on exec. council, 1898-1901 and 1902-04, and one as v.p. for N.C. Am. Bankers' Assn. Mem. M.E. Ch., S.; mem. Gen. Confs., 1908-25 (inc.); mem. Epworth Bd. M.E. Ch., S; del. to Missionary Ecumenical Conf., New York, 1900 to Ecumenical Meth. Conv., London, 1902. Democrat. Treas. City of Raleigh; mem. bd. aldermen; pres. Bd. Charities, Raleigh; mem. State Bd. Charities; pres. trustees Duke U.; pres. bd. dirs. of State Hosps. for Insane; mem. Federal Advisory Council of U.S. Home: Raleigh, N.C. Died Jan. 30, 1927.

BROWN, Joseph M., gov.; b. Canton, Ga., Dec. 28, 1851; s. Joseph E. and Elizabeth (Grisham) B.; Oglethorpe U.; m. Cora A. McCord, Feb. 12, 1889. Ry. service from clerk to traffic mgr., 1877-98. Mem. R.R. Commn. of Ga., 1904-07; gov. of Ga. 2 terms, 1909-13. Baptist. Author: The Mountain Campaigns in Georgia, 1886; Kennesaw's Bombardment, or How the Sharpshooters Woke Up the Batteries, 1890; Astyanax, 1906. Home: Marietta, Ga. Died Mar. 3, 1931.

BROWN, Julius L., lawyer; b. Canton, Ga., May 31, 1848; s. Gov. Joseph E. B.; in C.S.A., 1864-65; A.B., U. of Ga., 1868, later A.M.; LL.B., Harvard, 1870. Admitted to bar, 1869. Asst. U.S. atty., 1870-72; gen. counsel for original lessee of W.&A. R.R., 20 yrs.; was pres. Ga. Mining, Mfg. & Investment Co.; later master of chancery, U.S. Circuit Ct. Mason, 32°; past grand comdr., Grand Commandery of Ga., Knights Templar; past Grand Master R.&S.M. Grand Council of Ga.; past v.p. Grand High Priesthood of Ga. Home: Atlanta, Ga. Died 1910.

BROWN, Justus Morris, army officer; b. in Ohio, Dec. 8, 1840; M.D., U. of Pa., 1862. Apptd. from Ohio, asst. surgeon U.S. Army, July 11, 1862; capt. asst. surgeon, July 28, 1866; col. asst. surgeon gen., Feb. 2, 1901; retired at own request after 40 yrs.' service, Feb. 13, 1903; advanced to rank of brig. gen.; retired, by act of Apr. 23, 1904. Home: Hackensack, N.J. Died Dec. 21, 1912.

BROWN, Kate Louise, author; b. Adams, Mass., May 9, 1857; d. Edgar M. and Mary T. Brown; ed. at Reading high sch., Bridgewater (Mass.) State Normal Sch. and Kindergarten Training Class of Miss Anne Page; unmarried. Teacher in Reading, Wakefield and Milton, Mass., until 1896; in Boston, 1896—. Author: Little People, 1886; Interstate Second Reader, 1889; Stories in Song (with Elizabeth Usher Emerson), 1890; The Plant Baby and Its Friends, 1897; Alice and Tom, 1899; Second and Third Readers, Heath Series; Metcalf Third Reader. Also cantatas (with Elizabeth Usher Emerson), Santa Claus Discovered, The Tables Turned. Home: Dorchester, Mass. Died Dec. 31, 1921.

BROWN, Katharine Holland, author; b. Alton, Ill.; d. Horace Safford and Elizabeth (Holland) Brown; ed. Washington, and U. of Mich., hon. A.M., 1924; unmarried. Author: Diane, a Romance of the Icarian Community, 1904; Dawn, 1907; Philippa at Halcyon, 1910; The Messenger, 1910; White Roses, 1910; Uncertain Irene, 1911; Hallowell Partnership, 1912; Wages of Honor, 1917; The Touchstone, 1919; Stories from the Bible (series), 1922-23. Winner of John Day prize of $25,000 (Woman's Home Companion), 1927. Home: Orlando, Fla. Died June 2, 1931.

BROWN, Lawrason, M.D.; b. Baltimore, Sept. 29, 1871; s. William Judson and Mary Louise (Lawrason) B.; A.B., Johns Hopkins, 1895, M.D., 1900; Sc.D., Dartmouth, 1931; m. Martha Lewis Harris, Oct. 8, 1914. Asst. resident phys., 1900-01, resident phys., 1901-12, visiting phys., 1912-14, Trudeau Sanatorium, Saranac Lake, N.Y., later consulting phys.; consultant, Waverly Hills Sanatorium, Louisville, Ky. Specialized in diseases of lungs. Instr. Trudeau Sch. of Tuberculosis, 1914—; mem. bd. trustees N.Y. State Hosp. for Incipient Tuberculosis (Ray Brook), Potts Memorial Hosp. (Livingston) and of advisory council Henry Phipps Inst., U. of Pa., Milbank Foundation. First pres. Stevenson Soc. America. Democrat. Author: Rules for Recovery from Tuberculosis; (with H. L. Sampson) Intestinal Tuberculosis; The Lung and Tuberculosis (with Fred H. Heise). Home: Saranac Lake, N.Y. Died Dec. 1937.

BROWN, Lucius, lawyer; b. Griswold, Conn., May 5, 1846; s. Daniel and Mary (Stanton) B.; Ph.B., Brown U., 1866; LL.B., Albany Law Sch., 1868; m. Hannah M. Larrabee, June 11, 1878. Mem. law firm Brown & Perkins, 1878—; judge City Ct. of Norwich, 1894-1913; mem. Conn. Senate, 1872, 77, 78, 97. V.p. Norwich Savings Soc. Trustee Brown U. and Conn. Lit. Instn. Republican. Baptist. Home: Norwich, Conn. Died July 31, 1924.

BROWN, Lucius Polk, chemist; b. Maury County, Tenn., Aug. 1, 1867; s. Campbell and Susan R. (Polk) B.; grad. U. of Va., 1889; post-grad. work in chemistry; m. Susan Catherine Massie, Dec. 12, 1903. Engaged in farming, 1890-93; in pvt. practice as mem. firms of Memminger & Brown and Lucius P. Brown & Co., analyt. chemists, 1894-1908; pres. Brown Labs., Inc., 1908-15. Acting chemist, Tenn. Agrl. Expt. Sta., Knoxville, Tenn., 1889-90; food and drugs commr. of Tenn., 1908-15; dir. Bur. of Food and Drugs, Dept. of Health, City of New York, 1915-20. Capt. Nutrition Div., Sanitary Corps U.S. Army, 1918-19. Episcopalian. Home: Franklin, Tenn. Died 1935.

BROWN, Lucy Hall (Mrs.), physician; d. Don C. and Mary Lock (Bell) Hall; ed. Milton (Wis.) Coll. and Dearborn Sem., Chicago; M.D., U. of Mich., 1878; post-grad. work in hosps. of New York, and clinics in London (first woman entered to clinics of St. Thomas Hosp., London); was med. interne at Royal Lying-in and Gynecol. Hosp. of Prof. Fred Winckel, Dresden; m. R. G. Brown, Dec. 1891. On return to U.S. from Dresden, apptd. by Gov. Talbot physician to Mass. Reformatory for Women, and later supt. same. Prof. physiology and hygiene and resident physician, Vassar Coll., 1884-87. After that in practice in Brooklyn. Mem. Council Nat. Red Cross Soc. and del. Internat. confs. Red Cross at Carlsruhe, 1887, Vienna, 1897. First v.p. Alumni Assn. of Dept. Medicine and Surgery, U. of Mich. Inventor numerous elec. devices. Del. of U.S. Govt. to Internat. Congress Hygiene, Internat. Congress Secondary Edn., and Internat. Congress of Psychology. Address: Los Angeles, Calif. Died 1907.

BROWN, M(artha) McClellan, lecturer, reformer; b. Baltimore, Apr. 16, 1838; d. David and Jane Manypenny (Haight) McClellan; moved to Ohio, 1840; grad. Pittsburgh Female Coll., 1862; hon. Ph.D., 1884; LL.D., 1888; m. W. Kennedy Brown, Nov. 16, 1858; 1 son, Orvon Graff B. Officer Grand Lodge, Ohio Good Templars, 1866; grand vice-templar, 1867; grand counselor, 1871; grand chief templar Ohio, 1872-74; del. Internat. meet, London, 1873; supreme vice-templar, 1874; nat. chancellor Coll. Good Templary, 1909; internat. chancellor ednl. courses, 1911; organized, 1867, and conducted lecture system; lectured abroad, 1873, 1881, 1891, 1911; originated Temperance Cadet movement, 1870; started movement for Bible temperance lessons in Internat. Lesson Leaves, 1875; author of Temperance Questions in M.E. Discipline for quarterly conf., 1880; an organizer of Prohibition party, 1869, securing woman's suffrage plank; organizer and lecturer Nat. Prohibition Alliance, 1877-82; called Nat. Conf. Prohibition and Woman Suffrage Workers, New York, 1881, and Chicago, 1882, leading both to unite the two principles. Organized first Woman's State Temperance Assn., Columbus, Feb. 24, 1874; founded Nat. W.C.T.U., Chautauqua, at N.Y., Aug. 12, 1874; conducted state campaign resulting in defeat of liquor license in Ohio, 1874. First woman editor secular weekly, Alliance, O., 1868-78; v.p. and prof. Cincinnati Wesleyan Coll., 1882-92; started Fresh Air Movement, Cincinnati, 1888; originated monthly mother's meetings in pub. schs., 1895; pres. Study Club. Address: Avondale, Cincinnati. Died Aug. 31, 1916.

BROWN, May Belleville, writer, lecturer; b. Sanfords, Ind., July 2, 1867; d. John Campbell and Sophie Eliot (Sink) Brown; ed. pub. schs. and under pvt. tutors; m. Manuel Jay Brown (M.D.), Apr. 25, 1886; children—Edith May (Mrs. Paul F. Edquist), Jeannette (dec.). Was pres. Kan. Federation Women's Clubs, Kan. 5th Dist. Federation of Clubs, and dir. Gen. Federation Women's Clubs. Founder Scholarship Loan Fund (now $50,000), 1907, 8 yrs. chmn. lit.; founder service bur., Kan. Federation Women's Clubs. Served on Kan. Council of Nat. Defense. Mem. Salina Bd. Pub. Welfare (pres.), Salina Pub. Library Bd. (v.p.). Speaker on polit., literary and club topics. Republican. Presbyn. Home: Salina, Kan. Died Mar. 22, 1936.

BROWN, Moses True, educator; b. Deerfield, N.H., 1827; A.M., Tufts Coll.; prof. oratory, Tufts Coll., 30 yrs.; head dept. of elocution, Boston pub. schs., 4 yrs.; supt. schools, Toledo, O., 5 yrs.; head Boston School of Oratory, 10 yrs.; later removing to Ohio. Author: The Synthetic Philosophy of Expression, as Applied to the Arts of Reading, Oratory and Personation. Home: Sandusky, O. Died 1900.

BROWN, Neal, lawyer; b. Hebron, Wis., 1856; s. Thurlow Weed and Helen (Alward) B.; LL.B., U. of Wis. Coll. of Law, 1880; unmarried. Practiced in Wausau, Wis., 1880—; mem. Wis. Ho. of Rep., 1891, Senate, 1892-96; Dem. candidate for U.S. Senate, 1902, 1908; pres. Wis. Valley Electric Co.; dir. Wausau Sulphate Fibre Co., Marathon Paper Mills Co., Colonial Land Co. (Me.). Author: Critical Confessions (essays), 1899. Died Sept. 19, 1917.

BROWN, Olympia, author. See Olympia Brown Willis.

BROWN, Oswald Eugene, univ. prof.; b. Canton, Mo., Dec. 8, 1861; s. Reuben K. and Phœbe E. (Travis) B.; A.B., Christian U., Canton, Mo., 1882, A.M., 1892; B.D., Vanderbilt U., 1889; D.D., Central Coll., Mo., 1893; LL.D., Culver-Stockton Coll., 1925; m. Miss Anna Muse, Aug. 21, 1890. Admitted to bar, 1884; fellow in Bibl. dept. Vanderbilt U., 1889-90; missionary in China under Bd. of Missions M.E. Ch., S., 1890-92; prof. church history, Vanderbilt U., 1892-1937, prof. emeritus, 1937—; dean Vanderbilt U. Sch. of Religion, 1919-31, dean emeritus. Chmn. state com. Y.M.C.A. of Tenn., 1903-28; camp exec. Army Y.M.C.A., 1917-19; mem. Tenn. Annual Conf. of M.E. Ch., S. Mason. Author: Life and Letters of Laura A. Haygood, 1894; Christianization of American Life (MacDonnell Lectures), 1920; Modernism—A Calm Survey, 1925; God and the New Knowledge, 1926; Church History After Forty-Five Years, 1937. Contbr. "The Story of Methodism" to Vol. 3 of The Outline of Christianity. Home: Nashville, Tenn. Died Oct. 22, 1939.

BROWN, Paul Winthrop, editor; b. Peru, Ind., 1870; s. Henry L. and Mary Osborne (Ballantine) B.; privately educated; m. Alma Johnston, 1894; children—Hugh F., Neil W. Ordained Presbyn. ministry, 1892; editorial contbr. Kansas City Journal while asst. pastor 1st Congl. Ch., Kansas City, 1889-99; resigned pastorate 1st Congl. Ch., Moline, Ill., to become spl. corr. on waterways, Chicago Record-Herald, Jan., 1909. Became editorial writer, St. Louis Republic, Mar., 1909, editor in charge editorial page, May, 1912, editor, 1913-17; founder, 1917, and editor and sole owner America at Work, now Executive's Magazine. Democrat. Home: St. Louis, Mo. Died Apr. 6, 1937.

BROWN, Percy Edgar, educator; b. Woodbridge, N.J., Oct. 9, 1885; s. J. Edgar and Jeannette E. (Walker) B.; B.S., Rutgers U., 1906, A.M., 1909, Ph.D., 1912; unmarried. Asst. soil chemist and bacteriologist, N.J. Agrl. Expt. Sta., 1906-10; prof. soils and chief in soil chemistry and bacteriology, Ia. State Coll. Agr. and Mech. Arts and Ia. Agrl. Expt. Sta., also asso. in charge Ia. Soil Survey, 1910-31; prof. and head dept. agronomy, Ia. Agrl. Expt. Sta., 1931—, dir. Ia. Soil Survey, 1931—; cons. editor Soil Science; editor-in-chief and business mgr. Ia. State Coll. Jour. of Science. Republican. Presbyn. Mason (32°, K.C.C.H., K.T., Shriner). Author: Laboratory Guide in Soil Bacteriology (with J. G. Lipman), 1911. Home: Ames, Ia. Died July 7, 1937.

BROWN, Philip E., judge; b. Lafayette County, Wis., June 19, 1856; s. George O. and Sarah R. B.; student, U. of Wis., class of 1879; LL.B., Albany (N.Y.) Law Sch., 1881; m. Ella Ford, Oct. 8, 1882. Practiced law at Darlington, Wis., 1881-83, Luverne, Minn., 1883-91; dist. judge, 13th Jud. Dist. of Minn., 1891-1910; asso. justice Supreme Ct. of Minn., term 1912-18. Republican. Address: Luverne, Minn. Died Feb. 6, 1915.

BROWN, Philip Greely, banking, real estate; b. Portland, Me., June 24, 1855; s. Philip Henry and Fanny (Clifford) B.; A.B., Bowdoin, 1877, A.M., 1880. Entered banking business at Portland, 1877; pres. First Nat. Bank (Portland), Portland Clearing House; treas. J. B. Brown & Sons; dir. Internat. Telegraph Co., Portland and Ogdensburg R.R. Co.; trustee Portland Savings Bank. Trustee Me. Gen. Hosp., Pub. Library (pres.), Portland. Elk. Republican. Conglist. Home: Portland, Me. Died Dec. 18, 1934.

BROWN, Philip King, M.D.; b. Napa, Calif., June 24, 1869; s. Henry Adams and Charlotte Amanda (Blake) B.; A.B., Harvard, 1890, M.D., 1893; U. of Berlin, 1895-96, Göttingen, 1896; m. Helen Adelaide Hillyer, Mar. 7, 1900; children—Hillyer Blake, Harrison Cabot, Phoebe Hearst, Bruce Worcester. Practiced medicine at San Francisco, 1893—; asst. in nervous diseases, 1894, asso. prof. clin. medicine, 1896-98, instr. animal pathology, 1896-99, U. of Calif., visiting phys., 1896-97, later consulting physician, Mt. Zion Hosp., San Francisco; consulting pathologist French Hosp., 1896-1901; asso. in medicine and instr. clin. pathology, Cooper Med. Coll., 1899-1902; instr. clin. pathology and exptl. medicine, U. of Calif.; med. dir. Southern Pacific Hosp.; attdg. physician City and County Hospital, 1905-17; founder, med. dir. Arequipa Sanatorium (for tubercular wage-earning women), Manor, Calif. One of organizers San Francisco Settlement Assn. and San Francisco Boys' Club. Democrat. Mem. Gov. Olsen's Com. on Health Ins., 1939. Home: San Francisco, Calif. Died Oct. 1940.

BROWN, Rexwald, surgeon; b. Joliet, Ill., May 6, 1878; s. Cyrus W. and Ada (Robinson) B.; M.D., Northwestern U., 1903; m. Elizabeth Murphy, 1905 (died 1922); m. 2d, Mabel Johnson, 1923. Began practice at Chicago, surgeon to Armour & Co., 1903; settled at Santa Barbara, Calif., 1906; dir. surg. div. and chmn. exec. com. of staff, Santa Barbara Cottage Hosp.; organizer Santa Barbara Clinic, pres. emeritus, 1936—. Pres. Bd. of Health, Santa Barbara, 1930-34. Mem. Med. Advisory Bd., Pres. Roosevelt's Economic Security Com. Lt. U.S. M.C., Spanish-Am. War; served in World War as capt. U.S. Med. Corps, at Base Hosp. 33 and in France and Eng. Pres. Santa Barbara City and County Planning Commissions, chmn. Probation Com. of Santa Barbara County. Republican. Home: Santa Barbara, Calif. Died June 21, 1940.

BROWN, Robert Abner; b. Florence County, S.C., Mar. 25, 1868; s. John J. and Mary Elizabeth (Exum) B.; ed. Clinton (S.C.) Coll., 1887-89, U. of S.C., 1890-93; m. Rosabel Drennen, July 19, 1927. Pres. R. A. Brown & Co., real estate and ins., Birmingham, 1905—; pres. Steel Cities Chem. Co.; mem. bd. advisers Inland Waterways Corp. Pres. Jefferson Tuberculosis Sanatorium. Baptist. Home: Birmingham, Ala. Died May 12, 1936.

BROWN, Robert Alexander, army officer; b. Delaware County, Pa., Nov. 7, 1859; s. James and Ann (Stewart) B.; grad. U.S. Mil. Acad., 1885, Inf. and Cav. Sch., 1889, Army War Coll., 1910; m. Virginia Long, Nov. 8, 1893. Commd. 2d lt. 4th Cav., June 14, 1885; promoted through grades to brig. gen. N.A., Aug. 5, 1917. Comd. Indian scouts in Capt. Lawton's command which secured surrender of Geronimo, 1886; participated in Cuban Occupation, 1898-99, in subduing Philippine Insurrection, 1899-1901; instr. Army War Coll., 1910-11, 1912-13; officer of Gen. Staff, and chief of staff, Southern Dept., 1913-14; apptd. comdr. 84th Inf. Brigade, Camp A. L. Mills, L.I., N.Y., Sept. 1, 1917; joined A.E.F. in France, Nov. 14, 1917. Address: Washington, D.C. Died Sept. 30, 1937.

BROWN, Robert Burns, newspaper man; b. New Concord, O., Oct. 2, 1844; s. Alexander and Margaret (Lorimer) B.; ed. pub. schs., New Concord; served in U.S.V., 1861-65; grad. Eastman's Business Coll., Poughkeepsie, N.Y., 1866; studied law 3 yrs., but was not admitted, settling in newspaper business; m. Evaline Waters, May 18, 1887. Editor, Apr. 7, 1873—,and bus. mgr. to Apr. 30, 1913. Zanesville Courier; later sec. Zanesville Chamber of Commerce. Republican nominee for gov. of Ohio, 1912. Commander-in-chief, G.A.R., 1896-97. Home: Zanesville, O. Died July 30, 1916.

BROWN, Robert Elliott, clergyman; b. Middleville, Ont., Can., Dec. 17, 1873; s. Robert and Anna H. (Unsworth) B.; A.B., Oberlin Coll., 1901; B.D., Yale Divinity Sch., 1904; D.D., Carleton Coll., 1921; m. Mabel A. Millikan, June 23, 1904; children—Elizabeth, Edward. Ordained Congl. ministry, 1904; pastor Pilgrim Ch., New Haven, Conn., 1904-11, 2d Congl. Ch., Waterbury, 1911-24, 1st Congl. Ch., Oakland, Calif., 1924-29; prof. practical theology, Oberlin Theol. Sem., 1929—. Trustee Oberlin Coll., Suffield (Conn.) School, Pacific Sch. of Religion, Country Life Acad.; mem. exec. com. Gen. Council (Congl.); dir. Northern Calif. Conf.; chmn. nominating com. Nat. Council, 1919-21; Y.M.C.A. work in France, 1917-18; exec. com. Congl. World Movement; alumni lecturer Yale Div. Sch., 1919; preacher at Stanford U.; mem. Commn. on Missions, New Haven Ministers' Assn. Author: How to Use Wheat. Home: Oberlin, Ohio. Died Nov. 25, 1938.

BROWN, Robert Rankins, surety co. official; b. Lee Co., Ala., Nov. 11, 1869; s. Elijah and Araminta (Mosely) B.; ed. pub. and pvt. schs.; C.P.A., State of N.Y.; m. Elizabeth Turner, Sept. 10, 1895; children—Randolph E., Eleanor E. (Mrs. A. S. Gambee). Sec. and exec. asst. to Maj. John William Johnston, pres. Ga. Pacific Ry., 1886-96; with Am. Surety Co. of New York, 1896—, successively sec. to pres., supt. of agencies, v.p., 1st v.p., and pres.; v.p. Century Broadway Corp.; dir. R. E. Brown & Co., New York Casualty Co. Home: Englewood, N.J. Died June 17, 1937.

BROWN, Rome G., lawyer; b. Montpelier, Vt., June 15, 1862; s. Andrew Chandler and Lucia A. (Green) B.; A.B., magna cum laude, Harvard, 1884; admitted to bar in Vt., 1887; went to Minneapolis, 1887; m. Mary Lee Hollister, May 25, 1888; children—Edwin Chandler, Dorothy Hollister (Mrs. Ernest Blue). Gen. counsel various industrial corps.; sr. mem. law firm of Brown & Guesmer. Chmn. State Board Commrs. Uniform State Laws, 1911—; Nat. Conf. Commrs. on Uniform State Laws (v.p. 1913-14). Mem. Am. Bar Assn. (exec. com., 1906-09, chmn. com. to oppose jud. recall, 1912-19). Republican. Unitarian. Home: Minneapolis, Minn. Died May 22, 1926.

BROWN, Samuel Horton, Jr., M.D.; b. Phila., Nov. 16, 1878; s. Samuel Horton and Cecelia Elizabeth (Greaney) B.; ed. high sch., 1893-94, De Lancey Prep. Sch., 1895; M.D., U. of Pa., 1899; m. Margaret Julia Linnane, June 21, 1916; children—Samuel Horton, III, Mary Elizabeth, James Linnane, Franklin Luburg. Resident phys. Howard Hosp., 1899-1900; asst. dermatologist, Phila. and Univ. Hosps.; was dermatologist, Northern and Southern dispensaries, consulting dermatologist M.E. Orphanage, asst. ophthalmologist, Episcopal Hospital, St. Christopher's Hospital for Children; ophthalmologist, Mt. Sinai Hosp.; asst. ophthalmologist, outpatients department Pa. Hosp.; ophthalmologist 9th and 50th local exemption boards, Phila.; St. Luke's and Children's Hosp., American Hosp. for Diseases of Stomach. Asso. editor Am. Year-Book of Medicine and Surgery, 1904-05, Therapeutic Review, 1904, Annals of Ophthalmology, 1904-06, Am. Medicine, 1906. Editor: Hughes' Practice of Medicine (7th, 8th and 9th edits.), 1904-06. Author: Eczema, Its Causes, Diagnosis and Treatment, 1906; History of Will's Hospital, Philadelphia (with William C. Posey), 1931. Editor: Weekly Roster and Med. Digest. Address: Philadelphia, Pa. Died June 12, 1940.

BROWN, Sanford Miller, clergyman; b. Yadkin County, N.C., July 12, 1855; s. William Greene and Priscilla (Eldridge) B.; ed. pub. and pvt. schs. in N.C.; m. Lulu Everingham, Nov. 7, 1887; children—Joseph Everingham, Sanford Miller (dec.), Edith Mayo (Mrs. Frank O. White). Ordained to ministry Baptist Ch., 1876; various pastorates, 1877-84; editor Central Baptist, St. Louis, 1884-86; sec. of missions in Mo., 1886-92; became supt. of missions and pastor, Kansas City, Mo., 1892; founder and editor Word and Way, 1896—; pres. Western Bapt. Pub. Co. Trustee Kansas City Bapt. Theol. Sem. Democrat. Mason. Home: Kansas City, Mo. Died Sept. 21, 1938.

BROWN, Sanger (Monroe), M.D.; b. Bloomfield, Ont., Feb. 16, 1852; s. Stewart and Catherine (Comer) B.; ed. Albert Coll., Belleville, Ont., 1872-73; M.D., Bellevue Hosp. Med. Coll. (New York U.), 1880; m. Bella Christy, July 9, 1885; 1 child—Christy. Asst. phys. Hosp. for Insane, Ward's Island, N.Y., 1880-81, Danvers (Mass.) State Hosp. for Insane, 1881, Bloomingdale Asylum, N.Y., 1882-85, acting med. supt., 1886; prof. neurology, Post-Grad. Med. Sch., Chicago, 1890—; prof. med. jurisprudence and hygiene, Rush Med. Coll., 1892-97; asso. prof. medicine and clin. medicine, 1901-06, prof. clin. neurology, 1901, Coll. Phys. and Surg. (U. of Ill.). Conducted (with Prof. E. A. Schäfer) series of vivisection expts. on monkeys at Univ. Coll., London, 1886-87. Home: Kenilworth, Ill. Died Apr. 1, 1928.

BROWN, Selden Stanley, lawyer; b. Scottsville, N.Y., Oct. 23, 1855; s. Dyer D. S. and Mary Ann (Ensign) B.; A.B., U. of Rochester, 1879, A.M., 1882; m. L. Adell Franklin, June 26, 1883 (died 1912); m. 2d, Mary Elizabeth Stewart, June 17, 1914 (died 1921); m. 3d, Jessie Edith Franklin, Aug. 4, 1923. Was admitted to the bar, 1882; practiced alone, 1882-96, firm of Brown & Poole, 1896-1906; surrogate of Monroe County, N.Y., 1906-1925; practicing law after retiring from bench. Chancellor (Episcopal) Diocese of Western N.Y., from Nov. 1905 to division of the diocese upon organization of the Episcopal Diocese of Rochester, in 1931, also, during same time, mem. Standing Com. same diocese. Republican. Home: Scottsville, N.Y. Died Mar. 31, 1940.

BROWN, Stimson Joseph, astronomer; b. Penn Yan, N.Y., Sept. 17, 1854; s. John Randolph B.; ed. Cornell, 1871-72; grad. U.S. Naval Acad., 1876, at head of class; m. Alice Graham, Nov. 18, 1878; m. 2d, Elizabeth Sharp Pettit, Nov. 12, 1913. Served in U.S. Coast and Geod. Survey, 1879-81; prof. mathematics U.S. Navy, 1883—; astron. dir. U.S. Naval Obs., 1898-1901; dir. Nautical Almanac, 1900-01; on duty at U.S. Naval Acad., April 4, 1901, and head dept. mathematics and mechanics June 1907, retired. Observed Catalogue of Stars for the "Berliner Jahrbuch," at Annapolis, Md., 1885-87, and at the obs. of U. of Wis., 1887-90. Author of text book on algebra, analytical geometry, trigonometry and The Calculus, for use of midshipmen. Mem. Spl. Bd. on Naval Ordnance, 1912—. Address: Washington, D.C. Deceased.

BROWN, Thaddeus Harold, lawyer; b. Lincoln Tp., O., Jan. 10, 1887; s. William Henry and Ella Dell (Monroe) B.; ed. Ohio Wesleyan U. and Ohio State U.; LL.D., Lincoln Memorial U.; m. Marie Thrailkill, Nov. 10, 1915; 1 son, Thaddeus. Journal clk., Ohio Ho. of Rep., 1909-11; asst. sec. 4th Ohio Constl. Conv., Jan.-June 1912; in practice of law at Columbus, O., 1912-17, 1919-20, 1927-29; mem. Civil Service Commn., O., 1920-22; sec. of state, Ohio, 1923-27; chief counsel Federal Power Commn., Sept.-Dec. 1929; gen. counsel Federal Radio Commn., Dec. 1929-Mar. 1932, mem. same, Mar. 1932-July 1934, vice chmn., Apr. 1933-July 1934; mem. Federal Communications Commn., July 1934—. Del. Rep. Nat. Conv., 1928; Ohio Presidential elector, 1928. Captain inf., U.S. Army, July 1917-Feb. 1919; maj. J.A.G. Reserve Corps, 1919-23; lt. col. Inf. R.C., 1923-24; lt. col. J.A.G. R.C., 1924—. Vice chmn. bd. of trustees Lincoln Memorial U. Republican. Presbyn. Mason (32°, Shriner). Home: Columbus, O. Deceased.

BROWN, Theron, editor; b. Willimantic, Conn., Apr. 29, 1832; s. Eliphalet and Ermina (Preston) B.; A.B., Yale, 1856; grad. Hartford Theol. Sem., 1858, Newton Theol. Instn., 1859; m. Helen M. Preston, Nov. 30, 1859. Ordained Bapt. ministry, 1859; pastor S. Framingham, Mass., 1859-62, Canton, Mass., 1863-70; on staff Youth's Companion, 1870—. Author: The Red Shanty Series, 1875-78; The Blount Family, 1876; Walter Neil's Example, 1876; Stories for Sunday, 1877; Life Songs (poems), 1894; Nameless Women of the Bible, 1904; The Story of the Hymns and Tunes, 1907; Under the Mulberry Trees (a novel), 1909; The Birds of God, 1911. Home: Newtonville, Mass. Died Feb. 14, 1914.

BROWN, Thomas Jefferson, judge; b. Jasper County, Ga., July 24, 1836; s. Ervin and Matilda (Burdett) B.; LL.B., Baylor U., 1858; m. Louisa T. Estes, Aug. 7, 1859. Admitted to Tex. bar, in Dist. Ct., 1857, Supreme Ct., 1859; practiced in McKinney, Collins Co., 1859-72, at Sherman, Tex., 1872-92. Elected mem. Texas legislature, 1888 and 1890; judge Dist. Ct., 1892-93; asso. justice Supreme Ct. of Tex., 1893—(chief justice, Jan. 1911—). Home: Sherman, Tex. Died May 26, 1915.

BROWN, W. Kennedy, clergyman; b. Fayette County, Pa., Aug. 3, 1834; s. Alexander and Ruth Salisbury (Coleman) B.; A.B., Allegheny Coll., 1863, A.M., 1867; D.D., Waynesburg Coll., Pa., 1880; m. Martha McClellan, Nov. 16, 1858; 1 son, Orvon Graff B. Entered M.E. ministry, 1856; 30 appmts. by bishops in the Pittsburgh Conf. and 24 appmts. by bishops in Cincinnati Conf.; pres. Cincinnati Wesleyan Woman's Coll., 188?-92; retired at own request, 1909. Declined call to Denver U., 1868; published the Monitor, Alliance, O., 1869-76; gave name to Prohibition Party, 1869. With son, founded Twin Valley Coll. and Ohio Conservatory of Music, 1886, of which was dean and pres. bd. trustees. Author: Scriptural Status of Woman, 1880; The Ethical Status of Woman, 1887; Four Daughters of Galilee. Address Cincinnati, Ohio. Died October 1915.

BROWN, Waldron Post, banker; b. New York; s. James M. and Julia E. B.; m. Miss Wright, Jan. 1870. Mem. firm Brown Bros. & Co., bankers; trustee Atlantic Mut. Ins. Co. Mem. N.Y. Stock Exchange. Home: New York, N.Y. Died May 15, 1915.

BROWN, Wallace Elias, bishop; b. Chittenango, N.Y., Oct. 30, 1868; s. George Cady and Mary Theressa (Clarke) B.; grad. Cazenovia (N.Y.) Sem., 1893; A.B., Syracuse, 1898, D.D., 1909, L.H.D., 1921; LL.D., Bennett College, Greensboro, N.C., 1936; m. Gertrude Estelle Virgil, Feb. 8, 1899; children—Wendell Virgil, George Carleton, Wallace Elias, Don Hadley, Morris Gillespie. Ordained M.E. ministry, 1894; pastor Olivet M.E. Ch., Syracuse, 1897-99, St. Paul's, Syracuse, 1899-1902, Furman St. Ch., Syracuse, 1902-03, First Ch., Ithaca, N.Y., 1903-14; dist. supt., 1914-15; pastor University Ch., Syracuse, 1915-24; bishop M.E. Ch., 1924—. Dir. Epworth League of M.E. Ch.; mem. Gen. Conf., 1912, 16, 20, 24, Ecumenical Conf., London, 1921. Trustee U. of Chattanooga, Tenn. Wesleyan College, Morristown College (all of Tenn.), Cazenovia Sem., Bennett Coll., Snead Jr. Coll. (Boaz, Ala.). Republican. Mason. Home: Chattanooga, Tenn. Died Nov. 18, 1939.

BROWN, Walter Lewis, librarian; b. Buffalo, N.Y., Jan. 4, 1861; s. James Christian and Margaret Greg

(Bullions) B.; ed. pub. schs.; m. Margaret Bruce McCabe, Sept. 11, 1909. In Buffalo Library, 1876-81; in book business, Buffalo, 1881-97; asst. librarian, 1897-1906, librarian, 1906—, Buffalo Pub. Library. Pres. N.Y. State Library Assn., A.L.A., 1916-17. Home: Buffalo, N.Y. Died Oct. 16, 1931.

BROWN, Wilbur Vincent, prof. mathematics; b. Hope, N.J., Mar. 27, 1860; s. Rev. Albert Halsey and Julia Anna (Crane) B.; B.Sc., Stevens Inst. Tech., Hoboken, N.J., 1880, Ph.D., 1889; m. Addie Edson Fish, Aug. 23, 1883. Mem. staff Harvard Astron. Obs., 1880-83; teacher mathematics, Indianapolis High Sch., 1883-85; asst. prof. mathematics, DePauw U., 1885-94, prof., 1894—, also dir. obs. Methodist. Home: Greencastle, Ind. Died Nov. 1, 1928.

BROWN, William, lawyer; b. Boonville, Mo., Sept. 20, 1840; local atty. at Jacksonville, Ill., 1872-90, gen. solicitor, 1890—, Chicago & Alton R.R. Home: Jacksonville, Ill. Died 1909.

BROWN, William C., ry. official; b. Herkimer County, N.Y., July 29, 1853. Began ry. service wooding engines, 1869, section hand and telegraph operator, 1870-72, C.,M.&St.P. Ry.; train dispatcher, I.C. R.R., 1872-75, C.R.I.&P. Ry., 1875-76; train dispatcher to supt., C.,B.&Q. R.R., 1876-90; gen. mgr. Hannibal & St. Joseph and Kansas City, St. Joseph & Council Bluffs rys., 1890-96; also gen. mgr. Chicago, Burlington & Kansas City Ry., and St. Louis, Keokuk & Northwestern R.R., 1891-96; gen. mgr. C.,B.&Q. R.R., 1896-1901; v.p. and gen. mgr. L.S.&M.S. Ry., 1901-02; sr. v.p., 1902-09, pres., 1909-14, N.Y.C.&H.R. RR., and its subsidiary cos.; dir. C.,C.,C.&St.L. Ry. Co. and Indiana Harbor Belt R.R. Co. Mem. U.S. Assay Commn., 1914. Address: Chicago, Ill. Died Dec. 6, 1924.

BROWN, W(illiam) Cabell, bishop; b. Lynchburg, Va., Nov. 22, 1861; s. Robert Lawrence and Margaret Baldwin (Cabell) B.; student U. of Va., 1888-89; Theol. Sem. of Va., 1889-91; D.D., U. of the South, 1907; m. Ida Mason Dorsey, Aug. 4, 1891. Deacon, 1891, priest, 1891, P.E. Ch.; missionary in Brazil, South America, 1891-1914; consecrated bishop coadjutor of Va., Oct. 28, 1914. Trustee Theol. Sem. of Va., Episcopal High Sch., St. Anne's Sch., Charlottesville, Va. Home: Richmond, Va. Died July 25, 1927.

BROWN, William Carey, army officer; b. Traverse des Sioux, Minn., Dec. 19, 1854; s. Garretson Addison and Sue (Carey) B.; grad. U.S. Mil. Acad., 1877, Infantry and Cavalry Sch., 1883; Army War Coll., 1910. Commd. add. 2d lt. 2d Cav., June 15, 1877; promoted through grades to col. cav., Apr. 26, 1914. Participated in Bannock Indian campaign, 1878, Sheepeater Indian campaign, 1879, Sioux Indian campaign, 1890-91; adj. U.S. Mil. Acad., 1885-90; in Santiago campaign and Battle of San Juan, July 1-2, 1898; Philippine Insurrection, 1900-01; an actg. insp. gen., 1900 and 1912-14; comdg. 10th U.S. Cav. at Siege of Naco, Ariz., Oct.-Dec. 1914, and on Mexican Punitive Expdn., Mar. 16-May 3, 1916. Prepared War Dept. report on mobilization nat. guard, 1916; pres. Cantonment Site Bd., Eastern Dept., 1917; in France with 42d Div., insp. Q.M.C., A.E.F., 1917-18, when retired for age after over 41 years of active commissioned service. Bvtd. 1st lt., Feb. 27, 1890, for gallant service in action against Indians at Big Creek, Ida., Aug. 19, 1879, and reconnaissances, Aug. 17 and Sept. 25, 1879. In action at Santa Cruz, P.I., Oct. 13, 1900, and at Malimba River, P.I., Jan. 25, 1901. Devised automatic correction for "drift" of bullet Springfield rifle; invented asbestos stovepipe shield for tents; performing voluntary service in Q.M.G.O., Oct. 1919-July 1923, in matters pertaining to Emergency Rations, and in development of New Reserve Rations for U.S. Army. Awarded D.S.M. for services in World War and Silver Star Citation "for gallantry in action" at Santiago, Cuba, 1898. Apptd. brig. gen. U.S. Army, retired Feb. 28, 1927. Engaged in historical research pertaining to Indian Wars. Home: Denver, Colo. Died May 8, 1939.

BROWN, William Edward, Christian Science lecturer; b. Rochester, N.Y.; s. William Joseph and Susanna (Vincent) B.; ed. pub. schs. of Rochester, St. Louis and San Francisco, and by pvt. tutors; C.S.B., Mass. Metaphysical Coll., 1903; m. Mary Eleanor Young, Aug. 22, 1896; children—Samuel Vincent, Melville Hale. Christian Science practitioner, 1907—; mem. Bd. of Lectureship; served as reader Third Ch. of Christ Scientist, Los Angeles, and as mem. Com. on Publication, State of Calif., 2 terms. Mem. Calif. Senate, 1913-21; civil service commr. Los Angeles, 1921-23; mem. Calif. Rural Credits Commn. Mem. Nat. Guard of Calif. 7 yrs., retiring as capt.; war relief work, Tours, France, World War. Republican. Essay writer under pen name of Edward Braunwill. Address: Los Angeles, Calif. Died Sept. 26, 1937.

BROWN, William G., Jr., congressman; b. Kingwood, Va. (now W.Va.), Apr. 7, 1856; s. Hon. William G. and Margaret P. B.; A.B., W.Va. U., 1877, later A.M.; m. Jessie Thomas, 1883 (died 1886); m. 2d, Flora B. Martin, 1902 (died 1912). In law practice at Kingwood; also interested in banking and extensively in farming and raising thoroughbred stock. Active in Dem. politics many yrs.; Dem. nominee for Congress, 1896, for presdl. elector, 1908; mem. 62d and 63d Congresses (1911-15), 2d W.Va. Dist. Home: Kingwood, W.Va. Died Mar. 9, 1916.

BROWN, William Garrott, author; b. Marion, Ala., Apr. 24, 1868; s. Wilson Richard and Mary Cogswell (Parish) B.; A.B., Howard Coll., Ala., 1886; A.B., Harvard, 1891, A.M., 1892; unmarried. Asst. in Harvard Library, 1893-1901, lecturer, Am. history, 1901-02. Pres. Harvard Dem. Club, 1892; active in Dem. party, serving on various coms. until 1896; then went into Gold Dem. movement and on state com. Author: Official Guide to Harvard University, 1899; A History of Alabama, 1900; Andrew Jackson, 1900; Stephen Arnold Douglas, 1902; The Lower South in American History, 1902; Golf, 1902; A Gentleman of the South, 1903; The Foe of Compromise and Other Essays, 1903; Life of Oliver Ellsworth, 1905. Regular editorial writer Harper's Weekly, 1908—. Address: Cambridge, Mass. Died Oct. 20, 1913.

BROWN, William George, chemist; b. Newcastle-on-Tyne, Eng., Nov. 5, 1853; s. William Robert and Jane Gillie (Sanderson) B.; Miller scholar, U. of Va., 1875, B.S., 1877; Morgan fellow, Harvard, 1884, U. of Heidelberg, Germany, 1880-81; hon. Ph.D., U. of N.C., 1889; m. Isabelle White, Nov. 14, 1895. Prof. chemistry and instr. in geology and mineralogy, E. Tenn. U., 1877-79; prof. gen. and agrl. chemistry, 1879-80, chemistry and mineralogy, 1880-83, U. of Tenn.; instr. chemistry, U. of Va., 1883-85; prof. chemistry and physics, S.C. Mil. Acad., 1885-86; prof. chemistry, Washington and Lee U., 1886-94; asst. chemist U.S. Dept. of Agr., 1894-96; prof. chemistry, 1896—, and dir. of labs., 1905-10, prof. industrial chemistry, 1910-19, U. of Mo.; editor U. of Mo. Studies, 1904-11. Elected dir. Tech. Sch., Newark, N.J., 1884 (declined); elected adj. prof. agr., U. of S.C., 1885 (declined). Mem. U.S. Assay Commn., 1913. Home: Columbia, Mo. Died Aug. 8, 1920.

BROWN, William Henry, botanist; b. Richmond, Va., Oct. 6, 1884; s. John Henry and Julia (Wright) B.; B.S., Richmond Coll., 1906; Ph.D., Johns Hopkins, 1910; m. Mary Angus Blythe, June 3, 1927. Scientific asst., U.S. Fisheries Lab., Beaufort, N.C., 1908; grad. asst., Johns Hopkins, 1908, fellow, 1909-10, Bruce fellow, 1910; bot. investigation in Jamaica, 1910; asst. Desert Lab. of Carnegie Instn., 1910; scientific asst., Mich. Agrl. Expt. Sta., and instr. plant physiology, Mich. Agrl. Coll., 1910-11; plant physiologist, Bur. of Science, Manila, 1911-23; asso. prof. botany, 1915-18; prof. and head of dept., 1919-24, U. of Philippines; chief division of investigation, Bur. of Forestry, Manila, 1918-20; dir. Bur. of Science, Manila, 1924-33. Mason. Author: Vegetation of Philippine Mountains, 1919; A Textbook of General Botany, 1925; Laboratory Botany, 1925; The Plant Kingdom, 1935. Editor: Minor Products of Philippine Forests, vol. 1, 1920, vols. 2 and 3, 1921. Editor in chief Philippine Journal of Science, Manila, 1924-33. Address: Manila, P.I. Died Nov. 9, 1939.

BROWN, William Henry, civil engr.; b. Little Britain Tp., Lancaster County, Pa., Feb. 29, 1836; s. Levi K. and Hannah C. (Moore) B.; ed. Central High Sch., Phila.; m. Sallie A. Rimmel, Oct. 15, 1863. Asst. engr. survey dept., Phila., 1858; engr. constrn. U.S. mil. rys., 1861-63; asst. engr., 1863-64, prin. asst. engr., Jan.-Oct. 1864, Pan Handle R.R.; asst. engr. Pittsburg div., 1864-65, engr. Oil Creek R.R., Mar. 17-July 1, 1865, prin. asst. engr. Phila. & Erie div., 1865-67; engr. same, 1867-69, engr. in charge constrn. Altoona shops, 1869-70, resident engr. middle div., 1870-71, chief engr. and supt. Lewiston div., 1871-72, supt. Bedford div., 1872-74, engr. maintenance of way, 1874-81, chief engr. July 1, 1881-Feb. 28, 1906, Pa. R.R.; during service made 133 changes and revisions of line, built 14 elevated rys. through cities, 41 tunnels, 163 stone bridges, including Rockville stone bridge (largest in world of stone), Broad St. Sta., Phila., etc. Retired Feb. 29, 1906. Republican. Presbyn. Address: Philadelphia, Pa. Died 1910.

BROWN, William Horace, author; b. near Logansport, Ind., Aug. 7, 1855; s. Josiah and Elizabeth (Thompson) B.; acad. edn. Waukon, Ia.; m. Belle Henderson, June 6, 1893. Sec. Civic Federation of Chicago, 1900-10. Author: The Slaves of Folly, 1889; A Southern Heritage, 1902; The Glory-Seekers, 1906; The Story of a Bank, 1912. Home: Chicago, Ill. Died Mar. 19, 1917.

BROWN, William Lee, journalist; ed. common schools; taught school several yrs. in Ohio and Copiah County, Miss.; served in Civil war in 85th and 115th Ohio vol. inf.; rank of col. as a.d.c. on staff of Gov. William Allen, Ohio. After war, one of a party, made trip across the plains with mule team, settling in Mont.; served as chief clerk territorial legislature and engaged in mining; later settled in Youngstown, O.; founded Youngstown Vindicator; elected State senator, 1875; removed to New York, 1877, and bought interest in the Daily News; del. to Dem. Nat. Convs., 1872, 1876, 1884 and 1888; State senator, 5th dist., N.Y., 2 terms; defeated as candidate for Congress, 14th dist., 1893. Home: New York, N.Y. Died 1906.

BROWN, William Liston, iron mfr.; b. St. Joseph, Mich., Aug. 23, 1842; s. Hiram and Jane Reese Tilton (Liston) B.; ed. pub. schs. and Garden City Acad., Chicago; m. Catharine E. Seymour, Sept. 27, 1871. Began as clk. Bd. of Trade commn. house, Chicago, 1857; enlisted in Chicago Mercantile Battery Light Arty., July 1862, and served actively with command until July 1865; mustered out as q.m. sergeant. Bookkeeper, July 1865, later partner, organizing, 1883, Pickands, Brown & Co., of which was dir.; an organizer, 1890, and pres. Chicago Shipbuilding Co.; an organizer, 1899, and was later pres. Am. Shipbuilding Co.; dir. First Nat. Bank, Chicago, First Trust and Savings Bank, Chicago, and By-Products Coke Corp.; also dir. furnace cos. iron mines. Trustee Chicago Symphony (Thomas) Orchestra. Republican. Swedenborgian. Address: Chicago, Ill. Died Nov. 1, 1929.

BROWN, William Montgomery, bishop; b. near Orrville, O., Sept. 4, 1855; s. Joseph Morrison and Lucina (Cary) B.; ed. Gambier, O.; D.D., Kenyon, 1898, U. of the South, 1899; m. Ella Scranton Bradford, Apr. 9, 1885 (died 1935). Became a deacon, 1883, priest, 1884, Protestant Episcopal Ch., rector Galion, O., 1883-91; gen. missionary and archdeacon, Diocese of Ohio, 1891; consecrated bishop coadjutor of Ark., June 24, 1898, bishop of Ark., Sept. 5, 1900; resigned on account of ill health, Apr. 11, 1912. Charged with "heresy" and deposed from office of bishop by vote of 95 to 11, by House of Bishops, P.E. Ch., New Orleans, La., Oct. 1925; later bishop Old Catholic Ch. in America. Author: The Church for Americans, 1895; The Crucial Race Questions, 1907; The Level Plan for Church Union, 1910; Communism and Christianism, 1920; My Heresy, 1926; The Bankruptcy of Christian Supernaturalism, Vol. I, Trial, 1928, Vol. II, Science, 1929, Vol. III, History, 1930, Vol. IV, Philosophy, 1930, Vol. V, The Bible, 1931, Vol. VI, Sociology, 1931, Vol. VII, Other Heretics in the Episcopal Church, 1934; Science and History for Girls and Boys, 1932; Teachings of Marx for Girls and Boys, 1935. Home: Galion, O. Died Oct. 31, 1937.

BROWN, William Wallace, lawyer; b. Summer Hill, N.Y., Apr. 22, 1836; s. Rasselas W. and Mary P. (Brownell) B.; A.B., Alfred U., 1861; LL.D., 1886; pvt. 23d N.Y. and 1st Pa. Rifles in Civil War; m. Ellen Crandall, Mar. 18, 1862. Admitted to bar, 1867; recorder of deeds, 1864-66, supt. schs., 1866-67, dist. atty., 1867-69, McKean County, Pa.; a.d.c. on staff Gov. Hartranft with rank of col., 1875-89; mem. Pa. Ho. of Rep., 1872-76; mem. 48th and 49th Congresses (1883-87); auditor War Dept., 1897-99, Navy Dept., 1899-1907; asst. atty. gen. of U.S., 1907-10. Sr. mem. law firm of Brown, Schoonmaker & Nash. Republican. Home: Bradford, Pa. Died Nov. 4, 1926.

BROWNE, Aldis Birdsey, lawyer; b. Washington, D.C., Dec. 11, 1857; s. Jerome and Mary Elizabeth (Padgett) B.; LL.B., Columbian (now George Washington) U., 1879; m. Mary Barry Delahay, Dec. 1, 1880. Began practice with firm of Britton & Gray, 1879, later sr. mem. Trustee Woman's Coll. (Goucher), Am. U. and George Washington U. Republican. Methodist. Home: Washington, D.C. Died June 1, 1914.

BROWNE, Bennet Bernard, physician; b. Wheatlands, Md., June 16, 1842; s. Charles Cochrane and Mary Elizabeth (Willson) B.; A.B., Loyola Coll., Baltimore, 1858; served in 7th Va. Cav. (Rosser's Laurel Brig.), C.S.A., 1861-65; M.D., U. of Md., 1867; m. Jennie R. Nicholson, Oct. 15, 1872. Practiced at Bay View Asylum; specialist in gynecology; prof. gynecology, Woman's Med. Coll. of Baltimore, 1882—, and in the Polyclinic and Post-Grad. Med. Sch., 1885—. Home: Baltimore, Md. Died Mar. 10, 1922.

BROWNE, Causten, lawyer, author; b. Washington, D.C., Oct. 9, 1828; ed. Columbian U., Washington; M.A., Trinity Coll., 1856; practiced law in Boston. Author: Treatise on the Construction of the Statute of Frauds. Home: Boston, Mass. Died 1909.

BROWNE, Charles Francis, artist; b. Natick, Mass., May 21, 1859; s. George Warren and Emeline (Wetherbee) B.; studied at Boston Art Museum, 1882-84; Pa. Acad. Fine Arts, 1885-87, and at École des Beaux Arts under Gérôme and other masters, 1887-90; m. Miss Taft, May 21, 1909. For many years instr. and lecturer on history of art, Chicago Art Inst. Edited Brush and Pencil, 1897-1900. Exhibited at Paris expns., 1889, 1900, Chicago Expn., 1893, and the important current exhibitions. Asst. U.S. commr. gen. fine art expns., Buenos Aires, Argentina, and Santiago, Chile, 1910; dir. U.S. sect. fine arts and mem. Internat. Jury Awards Panama-Pacific Expn., 1915. Winner of Fine Arts Building Prize ($500), Chicago, 1908. A.N.A., 1913. Dir. Municipal Art League of Chicago; mem. exhbn. com. Am. Federation Arts; life member Nat. Civic Assn. Home: Chicago, Ill. Died Mar. 30, 1920.

BROWNE, Francis Fisher, editor; b. S. Halifax, Vt., Dec. 1, 1843; s. William Goldsmith and Eunice

(Fisher) B.; learned printer's trade and attended high sch. at Chicopee, Mass., leaving school for service in 46th Mass. Vols., 1862-63; studied law Rochester, N.Y., and U. of Mich., 1866-67; m. Susan Seaman Brooks, June 26, 1867. Editor Lakeside Monthly, Chicago, 1869-74; lit. editor of The Alliance, 1878-79; editor The Dial, 1880—. Author: Every-day life of Abraham Lincoln, 1886; Volunteer Grain (poems), 1896, etc. Editor: Golden Poems by British and American Authors, 1883; The Golden Treasury of Poetry and Prose, 1884; Bugle Echoes, a collection of poems of the Civil War, Northern and Southern, 1886; also the "Laurel Crowned" series of standard poetry, 1890-92. Chmn. Com. on Congress of Authors at World's Congress of Auxiliary of Columbian Expn., 1893. One of founders (1874), and hon. mem. Chicago Literary Club. Address: Chicago, Ill. Died May 11, 1913.

BROWNE, George Henry, teacher; b. Natick, Mass., Oct. 11, 1857; s. George Warren and Emeline (Wetherbee) B.; A.B., Harvard, 1878, A.M., 1879; m. Emily Robbins Webster, Oct. 10, 1889. Asso. with Keene (N.H.) High Sch., 1879-80; pvt. tutor, prep. for Harvard, 1880-81; established sch. for boys at Cambridge, 1882, The Browne & Nichols Sch., 1883. Sec. Cambridge Community Forum. Independent Democrat. Unitarian. Author: Notes on Shakespeare's Versification, 1884; Figure Skating, 1892; Poems of Emerson, ed. w. Intro. and Notes, 1897, 2d edit., 1904; Handbook of Figure Skating, 1900; Supplement, 1904; Memory Test Latin Word-List, 1907; Memory Test Note-Book, 1907; The New Skating, 1910; The Essentials of Figure Skating, on Cards, 1911, 2d edit., 1914; Skating Primer, 1912; Handbook of Figure Skating, 1913; The Esthetics of Motion, the Psychology of Grace, 1917; The Modern School and Present Day Distractions, 1918; Forty Years of American Education and Browne and Nichols School, 1922-23. Home: Cambridge, Mass. Died Jan. 20, 1931.

BROWNE, George Waldo ("Victor St. Clair"), author; b. Deerfield, N.H., Oct. 8, 1851; s. John C. and Martha L. B.; ed. Deerfield High Sch.; m. Nellie M. Barber, Jan. 8, 1891; children—Norman Stanley, Rilma Marion. Was editor of the American Young Folks 5 yrs.; also lecturer and pub. speaker. Pres. and mgr. Standard Book Co., Inc. Mem. Bd. of Edn., Manchester. Author: A Daughter of Maryland, 1895; The Woodranger, 1899; Two American Boys in Hawaii, 1899; The Young Gunbearer, 1900; Paradise of the Pacific, 1900; Pearl of the Orient, 1900; The Far East and the New America, 1900-01; Records of Tyng Township, 1901; The Hero of the Hills, 1901; Life of Hon. Samuel Blodget, 1901; Japan—the Place and the People, 1904; Norman Howard Bartlett, 1904; The St. Lawrence River—Historical, Legendary, Picturesque, 1905; With Rogers' Rangers (in Woodranger Series), 1905; also under pseudonym, "Victor St. Clair," For Home and Honor, 1902; From Switch to Lever, 1902; Zip, the Acrobat, 1902; Cast Away in the Jungle, 1902; Post-Boy of the Kanawha, 1902; The Boy Magician; Comrades Under Castro, 1903; Blue Water Rovers; Forge and Furnace, 1903; Break o' Day Boys, 1903; With Axe and Flintlock, 1907; and following under own name: Ruel Durkee (novel), 1910; History of Amoskeag Manufacturing Company, 1911; History of India, 1911; The Merrimac River in Romance and History, 1912; Early Records of Londonderry, N.H., 3 vols., 1911-12; History of Hudson, N.H., 1912; China, the Country and the People, 1913; Green Mountain Pioneers, Franconian Gateway, both 1914; Waynotes of Manchester, N.H., History of Hillsboro, N.H., Bibliography of Mayor Robert Rogers, Heroic Deeds of Many Lands, all 1915-16; Indian Traditions and Folklore, 1917-18; Legends and Deeds of Yesterday; Romance of Reality; Snow Shoe Scouts, 1919-20; American Army in the World War (with R. W. Pillsbury), 1921; Legends and Deeds, 1922-23; Story of New Hampshire (with Rilma M. Browne), 1924-25; Legends of New England, 1925, revised edit., 1927; Story of the Old Bay State, 1927; Indian Nights Entertainment, 1927. Compiled and edited Early Records of Manchester, N.H. (7 vols.), 1905-11. Home: Manchester, N.H. Deceased.

BROWNE, Jefferson Beale, judge; b. Key West, Fla., June 6, 1857; s. Joseph Beverly and Mary Nieves (Ximenez) B.; LL.B., U. of Ia., 1880; m. Frances Williams Atkinson, June 19, 1889; 1 son, Joseph Emmet. Captain's clerk on U.S.S. Marion, 1876; admitted to bar, 1880; city atty., 1880-85, postmaster, 1886-90, collector customs, 1893-97, Key West; mem. Fla. Senate, 1891-95; pres. Fla. Senate and ex-officio lt.-gov. of Fla., 1891-93; chmn. Fla. R.R. Commn., 1903-07; mem. bd. of pub. works, Key West, 1909-12. Del. at large Dem. Nat. Conv., 1888; mem. Dem. Nat. Com., 1904-08; presdl. elector, 1912, and pres. electoral coll., 1913. Receiver Key West Elec. Light & Street Car Co., 1898. Chief justice Supreme Court of Fla., 1917-23, asso. justice, 1923-June 1, 1925; resigned to become judge of 20th Jud. Circuit of Fla. Conglist. Mason (32°, K.T.); Past Exalted Ruler B.P.O.E.; chief justice Grand Forum same, 1923. Author: Key West, Old and New. Home: Key West, Fla. Died May 4, 1937.

BROWNE, J(ohn) Lewis, organist; b. London, Eng., May 18, 1866; s. William and Mary Anne (Grace) B.; brought to America, 1875; ed. U.S. and Europe; Mus.D., U. State of N.Y., 1902; m. Lottie Grace Gray, Oct. 4, 1891 (died 1914); children—Lewis R., William A.; m. 2d, Hazel Irene Struck, Oct. 17, 1916. Soloist, Royal Acad. of St. Cecilia, Rome, 1901; organist Wanamaker's Egyptian Hall, Phila., 1908-10; World's Fair, St. Louis and Jamestown; Carnegie concerts, Pittsburgh; more than 500 appearances in Phila.; recitals in Chicago, New York, Pittsburgh, St. Paul, Minneapolis, San Francisco, Toronto, Atlanta, Salt Lake City, Savannah, Omaha, etc.; designed great organ in Medinah Temple, Chicago, and conducted symphony concerts there; conducted Atlanta Festival 3 yrs.; organist and choirmaster, St. Patrick's Ch., Chicago, 1912—; head of theory dept. Fine Arts Conservatory of Music; ex-mem. faculty, U. of Notre Dame; dir. of music, pub. schs., Chicago, 1928—. Mason (32°). Composer: (opera) "La Corsicana" (recognition, Sonzogno Concorso, Milan, 1902), prod. Playhouse, Chicago, 1923; Missa Solemnis (I. et II.); "Ecce Sacerdos Magnus," prod. Paulist Choristers, Rome, 1912; Missa Immaculatæ Conceptionis B.V.M. (for 100th anniversary of establishment of Diocese of Cincinnati), 1921; also more than 60 songs (sacred and secular), pieces for organ, orchestra, piano; motettes, part-songs, etc. Awarded Bispham memorial medal, 1925. Address: Chicago, Ill. Died Oct. 23, 1933.

BROWNE, Lewis Allen, author, dramatist; b. North Sandwich, N.H., Jan. 18, 1876; s. Jason John Colby and Julia Annette (Cohaski) B.; ed. high sch. and under pvt. tutors; m. Minnie Mae Breck, Oct. 8, 1898; children—Allen Jason, Lois Annette, Dorothy Julia. Began as reporter Evening Press, Laconia, 1898; city editor Boston Journal, 1901-12; asso. editor New York Sunday American, 1912-14; editor Wildman Magazine Service, New York, 1914-19; asso. editor The Forum, 1918-19; writing picture plays and continuities for Selznick Picture Corp., 1919-24; later scenario editor True Story Films, Inc., was mem. editorial staff of Macfadden Publs., and literary editor, Daily Mirror, New York. Republican. Unitarian. Author: Airship Almanac, 1909; Around the Clock, 1910; Indian Fairy Tales, 1912; Prudence Wentworth, 1914; Just Playing Around, 1930; (plays) The Bigamists; Princess Virtue; Rita; (vaudeville acts) Peach and Plumber; Jolt from Jane; Maid and Maniac; Milk and Melody; Peacock Alley; etc. Co-Author: Foolish Almanac, 1905; Foolish Etiquette, 1906; (plays) Please Get Married; The 100 per cent Girl; While You Wait; Received Payment; Page Miss Venus; The Sizzling Sixties; The Mask-Maker; also contbr. short stories to leading mags. Author of the Americanization picture, "The Land of Opportunity;" also many other photoplays. Address: West Englewood, N.J. Died May 23, 1937.

BROWNE, Porter Emerson, novelist, playwright; b. Beverly, Mass., June 22, 1879; s. Joseph Emerson and Evelyn (Porter) B.; ed. Newton (Mass.) High Sch.; m. Myrtle Suzanne May, Feb. 10, 1907 (died 1922); children—Suzanne Lisbeth, Prudence Emerson. Began writing short stories, verse, essays, etc., 1901. A founder The Vigilantes, 1916. Author: (plays) A Fool There Was, 1906; The Spendthrift, 1908; A Girl of Today, 1915; The Bad Man, 1920; (one-act plays) A Hero; In and Out; Married; etc.; (books) A Fool There Was, 1908; Peace at Any Price, 1916; Scars and Stripes, 1917; Someone and Somebody, 1917; (play prod. in motion picture) The Trumpet Blows (with J. Parker Reid), 1933. Home: Westport, Conn. Died Sept. 20, 1934.

BROWNE, Rhodes; b. Columbus, Ga., Sept. 15, 1865; s. John Rhodes and Roberta Hanson Harrison (Yonge) B.; prep. edn., Glenn's Sch., Columbus, 1875-80; student U. of Ga., 1882-84; m. Nina Young, Oct. 30, 1889; children—Marjorie (Mrs. Charles A. Hunt), Rhodes (dec.). Pres. 1st Nat. Bank, Home Savings Bank, Provident Loan and Investment Co., Bull Creek Farms; chmn. bd. Georgia Home Ins. Co. Mayor of Columbus, 1907-11; chmn. bd. water commrs., Columbus bd. county commrs., Muscogee County; 2d lt. Columbus Guards. Mem. Ga. Assn. County Commrs. (pres.). Democrat. Episcopalian. Mason (K.T., Shriner), Elk, Red Man, Woodman of World. Home: Columbus, Ga. Died Oct. 8, 1936.

BROWNE, William Hand, univ. prof.; b. Baltimore, Dec. 31, 1828; s. William and Patience (Hand) B.; M.D., U. of Md., 1850; m. Mary Catherine Owings, June 3, 1863. Librarian and asso. prof., 1879-81, prof. English lit., 1891-1910, emeritus prof., 1910, Johns Hopkins U. Author: Maryland, the History of a Palatinate; George Calvert and Cecilius Calvert, Barons Baltimore; Life of Alexander H. Stephens (with Col. R. M. Johnston). Compiler: The Clarendon Dictionary of the English Language; Selections from the Early Scottish Poets. Translator: Von Falke's Greece and Rome; also various works from the French and German. Editor: Southern Review, 1867-68; Southern Magazine, 1870-75; Archives of Maryland, and other works. Address: Baltimore, Md. Died Dec. 13, 1912.

BROWNE, William Hardcastle, lawyer; b. Phila., Nov. 14, 1840; s. Rev. Charles and Eliza Ann (Hardcastle) B.; ed. Phila. (LL.D.); m. Alice Beaver, 1869. Admitted to bar 1865; practiced in Phila. Author: Digest of the Law of Divorce and Alimony in the United States, 1890; Famous Women of History, 1897; Bible Heroes, 1888; Abridged Editions of Blackstone's Commentaries, 1894; Kent's Commentaries, 1895; Law of Negligence in Penn., 1896; Law on Decedents' Estates in Penn., 1897; Heart Throbs of Gifted Authors, quotations, 1872; Witty Sayings by Witty People, 1888; Odd Derivations of Words and Phrases, 1900; Proverbs, 1900; Waverley Novels, abridged (6 vols.), 1901. Home: Philadelphia, Pa. Died 1906.

BROWNELL, (Wilmot) Atherton, editor, author; b. Lynn, Mass., June 16, 1866; s. Alexander C. and Emily M. (Irish) B.; student Brown U., 1885-86; m. Elspeth Prichard, Nov. 25, 1915. Newspaper work, Providence, R.I., and with Boston Herald, 1888-91; editor Boston Home Journal, 1891-97; editor Am. Syren and Shipping, 1901-02; founder, 1905, and pres. Century Syndicate (newspaper); asso. editor Phila. Public Ledger, 1914; organizer, 1915, and gen. dir. Nat. Editorial Service, Inc. Chautauqua lecturer on internat. conditions, 1915, Industrial Relations, 1921. Author: The Unseen Empire—A Play of Peace, 1914; The Master of Arms (play), 1917. Editorial dir. Nat. Marine League U.S.A., 1916. Editor The Navy and Merchant Marine, 1917-18. Home: Forest Hills, L.I., N.Y. Died Apr. 22, 1924.

BROWNELL, Clarence Ludlow, journalist; b. Hartford, Conn., June 6, 1864; s. Stephen Church and Martha Nevins (Hyde) B.; prep. edn. Mil. Acad., Stamford, Conn., spl. courses in English, Harvard, 1885-86; studied Stevens Inst. Tech., M.A., B.Sc.; m. Noema Pinkerton, Sept. 27, 1911. Instr. English and mil. drill in govt. and pvt. schs., in Japan, 5 yrs. Newspaper corr.; contbr. Internat. Pub. Bur., London, 1900-02; spl. work on Japanese history and Buddhism, British Museum, 1903; asso. editor "East and West," San Francisco, 1906; on staff The Clarion, 1907; edited "Church Paper," West Haven, Conn.; head master Dayton (O.) Latin Sch., 1909; instr. English and mathematics, Valparaiso (Ind.) U. Social service and community survey work. Author: Tales from Tokio, 1900; Hongwan-ji at Home and Abroad, 1902; The Heart of Japan, 1902; Japanese Wrestling, 1903; Japanese Archery, 1903 (6 edits.); Japanese Swordsmen, 1903; Europe and America in Japan; Japan in California, 1906; A Pacific Pacific, 1914; Educational Reciprocity, 1916; Japan and America's Trade Interests, 1916; Japan's War Fund Limit, 1919. Home: Gary, Ind. Died Feb. 2, 1927.

BROWNELL, George Francis, lawyer; b. Des Moines, Ia., June 5, 1861; s. Samuel Clark and Catherine (Fox) B.; LL.B., Albany Law Sch., 1882, U. of Mich., 1883; m. Anne K. Abbott, June 7, 1897. Admitted to bar, 1882; mem. firm of Moot, Sprague, Brownell & Marcy, 1897—; served as gen. solicitor Erie R.R. Co., with offices in New York City, 1st v.p. and gen. solicitor same co. and of the Chicago & Erie R.R. Co. and various other corps. comprised in and controlled by Erie System; was v.p. and gen. counsel. Home: New York, N.Y. Died Apr. 15, 1934.

BROWNELL, George Griffin, univ. prof.; b. Fairfield, N.Y., July 2, 1869; s. Prof. Walter Abner and Helen M. (Davis) B.; A.B., Syracuse U., 1893, A.M., 1896; student The Sorbonne, Paris, 1893-94, Johns Hopkins, 1894-98, Ph.D., 1904; m. Jennie A. Jones, June 8, 1893; children—Ruth, Walter Thomas, George Griffin. Spent 6 yrs. traveling and residing in Africa and the Latin countries; prof. Romance langs., U. of Ala., 1898-1925; later travel dir. Expert in hardy citrus fruit culture, U.S. Dept. Agr., 1911—. Editor: El Capitán Veneno, 1901; El Pájaro Verde, 1901; La Vida de Vasco Nuñez de Balboa, 1913. Author: Position of the Attributive Adjective in Don Quixote, 1910. Joint Author: The Mediterranean Cruise, 1927. Home: Tuscaloosa, Ala. Died Aug. 31, 1931.

BROWNELL, Harry Franklin; b. Black River Falls, Wis., Nov. 22, 1882; s. Edwin Martin and Henrietta Bryant (Randles) B.; ed. high sch. and under tutors of U. of Wis.; m. Elizabeth Jewett Woodford, Nov. 1, 1911; 1 son, Robert Jewett. Settled at Sioux Falls, S.D., as state agt. for Burroughs Adding Machine Co., 1907; later in oil business; officer and mem. bd. of dirs. various corps.; mem. S.D. Senate, 1923-24. Active in campaigns for highway improvements. Mem. bd. of trustees of Children's Home Soc. of S.D. State dir. Four-Minute Men, World War; mgr. Liberty Loan speaking campaigns and committees. Republican. Episcopalian. Mason (32°, K.T., Past Potentate El Riad Temple Shrine), Elk. Candidate for U.S. Senate, 1932. Home: Sioux Falls, S.D. Died Jan. 7, 1940.

BROWNELL, Walter A., educator; b. Evans Mills, N.Y., Mar. 23, 1838; s. Brisbin A. B.; grad. Genessee Coll., 1865; A.M., 1868; Ph.D., Hamilton Coll., 1876; m. Helen M. Davis, 1865. Prin. Red Creek Sem., 1865-68, Fairfield Sem., 1868-71, Syracuse

High Sch., 1871-72, teacher chemistry and geology, Syracuse High Sch., 1872-1902. Extensive traveler in Europe and America and lecturer upon science and subjects of travel. Address: Syracuse, N.Y. Died 1904.

BROWNELL, William Crary, author; b. New York, Aug. 30, 1851; s. Isaac Wilbour and Lucia Emilie (Brown) B.; A.B., Amherst Coll., 1871, L.H.D., 1896, LL.D., 1916; Litt.D., Columbia, 1910; m. Virginia S. Swinburne, Jan. 3, 1878 (died Apr. 3, 1911); m. 2d, Anna Gertrude Hall, Jan. 19, 1921. On staff The Nation, 1879-81; lit. adviser of Charles Scribner's Sons, 39 yrs. Author: French Traits—An Essay in Comparative Criticism, 1889; French Art, Classic and Contemporary Painting and Sculpture, 1892; Newport, 1896; Victorian Prose Masters—Thackeray, Carlyle, George Eliot, Matthew Arnold, Ruskin, George Meredith, 1901; American Prose Masters—Cooper, Hawthorne, Emerson, Poe, Lowell, Henry James, 1909; Criticism, 1914; Standards, 1917; The Genius of Style, 1924; Democratic Distinction in America, 1927. Home: New York, N.Y. Died July 22, 1928.

BROWNING, Charles Clifton, M.D.; b. Denver, Ill., May 25, 1861; s. Enoch Clifton and Sophia Louisa (Pennock) B.; M.D., U. of Mo., 1883; m. Helen E. Tillapaugh, Aug. 26, 1885; 1 dau., Helen Gilberta. Began practice at Denver, Ill., June 1883; with N.Y. City Asylum for Insane, 1888-91; moved to San Jacinto, Calif., 1891, Los Angeles, 1905; prof. emeritus, Coll. Med. Evangelists and U. of Southern Calif. Coll. of Dentistry. Republican. Deceased.

BROWNING, Charles Henry, genealogist; b. Cincinnati; s. Robert LeWright (lt. U.S.N.) and Eleanor Agnes (Hanlon) B.; ed. Clifton Acad., Cincinnati; Harcourt Sch., Gambier, O., and Kenyon Coll.; m. Katherine Campbell, Jan. 1, 1884 (dec.). Phila. corr. New York Herald, 1876-1921; editor-in-chief Am. Hist. Register, 1894-1900. Founder mem. Baronial Order of Runnymede. Democrat. Author: Americans of Royal Descent, 1883-1924 (9 edits.); Magna Charta Barons and Their American Descendants, 2 vols., 1898, 1915; Colonial Dames of Royal Descent, 1900; From Magna Charta Barons, 1903; Welsh Settlement of Pennsylvania, 1912; The True Shakespeare; Tour of General Lafayette in the United States, 1824-25, as the Nation's Guest, etc. Home: Ardmore, Pa. Died June 1926.

BROWNING, John Hull, mcht.; b. Orange, N.J., Dec. 25, 1842; ed. Coll. City of New York; m. Eva Sisson. Was in wholesale clothing business in New York about 20 yrs. as mem. W. C. Browning & Co.; pres. Northern R.R. of N.J. until sold to Erie R.R. Co.; was treas. N.Y. & Hackensack R.R. Co.; pres. Richmond County Gas Light Co., 1884—. Pres. Bergen Co. League many yrs.; presdl. elector, 1892, 96, 1904, 08, 12. Republican. Treas. Am. Ch. Missionary Soc.; mgr. N.Y. P.E. City Mission. Home: Tenafly, N.J. Died Oct. 26, 1914.

BROWNING, John M., inventor; b. Ogden, Utah, Jan. 21, 1855; s. Jonathan and Elizabeth (Caroline) B. Made first gun at 13, of scrap iron in father's gunshop; patented breech-loading rifle, 1879, repeating rifle, 1884, box magazine, 1895; also numerous other patents on rapid fire guns. Automatic guns adopted by European govts.; automatic pistol adopted by U.S. Govt., 1908, machine guns and machine rifle by U.S. Govt., 1918. Decorated Order of Leopold, of Belgium. Home: Ogden, Utah. Died Nov. 26, 1926.

BROWNING, Matthew Sandefur, corp. official; b. Ogden, Utah, Oct. 27, 1859; s. Jonathan and Elizabeth Caroline (Clark) B.; ed. common schs.; m. Mary Ann Adams, Dec. 17, 1885. Pres. Amalgamated Sugar Co., Burton Implement Co., Lindsay Land & Live Stock Co., Superior Rock Springs Coal Co., Utah Nat. Bank, Utah Ida. Central R.R. Co.; officer or dir. other corps. Mayor of Ogden, 1900-01; mem. bd. of Edn., Ogden, 1908-16 (pres. 1912-16). Democrat. Mormon. Home: Ogden, Utah. Died June 29, 1923.

BROWNING, Philip Embury, chemist; b. Rhinebeck, N.Y., Sept. 9, 1866; s. William Garretson and Susanna Rebecca (Webb) B.; A.B., Yale U., 1889, Ph.D., 1892; U. of Munich, 1893-94, also the Sorbonne (Paris), 1913-14; m. Elizabeth Sophia Bradley, Dec. 12, 1899. Asst. in chemistry, 1889-93, instr., 1894-98, asst. prof., 1898-1929, asso. prof. and curator of chemical exhibit, 1929-32, later curator of chem. exhibit, Yale U. Mem. New Haven City Council, 1900-02, board of park commrs., 1901-02. Treas. First Eccles. Soc. in New Haven (founded 1638), 1916-30 and 1931—. Conglist. Author: Notes on Qualitative Analysis (with prof. F. A. Gooch), 1898; An Introduction to the Rarer Elements, 1903, 08, 12; Outlines of Qualitative Chemical Analysis (with same), 1906. Home: New Haven, Conn. Died Jan. 2, 1937.

BROWNING, William, neurologist; b. New London County, Conn., July 7, 1855; s. Dea. William T. and Nancy Crary (Avery) B.; Ph.B., Sheffield Sci. Sch. (Yale), 1876; diploma in anatomy, U. of Pa., 1878; student univs. of Leipzig and Würzburg, 1878-81; M.D., Leipzig, 1881; unmarried. Intern and house officer German Hosp., New York, 1881-82; state examiner in lunacy, 1893—; lecturer on normal neurology, Long Island College of Medicine, 1887-1901; prof. Neuropsychiatry, 1901-26, emeritus, 1926—; attending or consulting neurologist Kings County, Brooklyn, Brooklyn State, Long Island College, Sea View, Norwegian, St. John's, Jewish, Bushwick, Caledonian, and St. Catherine's hosps. Librarian Medical Society, 1891-1900 directing librarian, 1917—; past editor of Neurographs. Introduced spinal puncture in America, 1894. Author: The Veins of the Brain and Its Envelopes, 1884; The Epileptic Interval, 1893; Circulation in the Central Nervous System, 1897; The Thymus and Stammering, 1915; Medical Heredity, 1925. Extensive contbr. to med. history and literature. Address: Brooklyn, N.Y. Died Jan. 5, 1941.

BROWNING, William J., congressman; b. Camden, N.J., Apr. 11, 1850. Began in mercantile business, 1865; mem. City Council, Camden, 4 yrs.; was mem. Bd. of Edn.; postmaster, Camden, 1889-94; chief clk. Ho. of Rep. of U.S., 1895-11; elected to 62d Congress, Nov. 1911, to fill vacancy caused by death of H. C. Loudenslager; reëlected 63d to 66th Congresses (1913-21), 1st N.J. Dist. Republican. Home: Camden, N.J. Died Mar. 24, 1920.

BROWNLOW, Walter Preston, congressman; b. Abingdon, Va.; ed. pub. schs. until 10 yrs. of age; worked at various trades. Owner and editor Herald and Tribune, Jonesboro, Tenn., 1876—. Postmaster of Jonesboro, Mar.-Dec. 1881; doorkeeper 47th Congress (1881-83); mem. Rep. State Com., 1882-90 (chmn. 2 yrs.); chmn. Rep. State Exec. Com., 1898-99; mem. Rep. Nat. Com., 1884-1907; del. Rep. Nat. convs., 1880, 1896, 1900, del.-at-large, 1884, 1904; mem. 55th to 61st Congresses (1897-1911), 1st Tenn. Dist. Mem. bd. of managers Nat. Soldiers' Homes, 1902-08. Home: Jonesboro, Tenn. Died 1910.

BROWNSCOMBE, Jennie (Augusta), artist; b. Honesdale, Pa., Dec. 10, 1850; d. William and Elvira (Kennedy) Brownscombe; pub. and pvt. schs.; pupil Nat. Acad. Design and Art Students' League, New York, and of Henry Mosler, Paris; unmarried. Painter of figures, genre, and portraits of colonial and early Am. hist. subjects in oil and water colors. First exhibited at Nat. Acad., 1876; exhibited at Water Color Soc. (Rome, Italy), Royal Acad. (London), 1900, and elsewhere. Painting, "The First American Thanksgiving," in permanent collection of Museum of Pilgrim Hall, Plymouth, Mass., "The Peace Ball," in collection of Newark Museum; genre painting, "Children Playing in an Orchard," in school bldg., Honesdale, Pa.; portrait of Wm. H. Leupp, Rutgers U. Collection; portraits of Judge William J. Wallace and Judge W. K. Townsend in court room of Federal Circuit Court of Appeals, New York, of Capt. James Ely Miller, Yale College, etc. Address: Bayside, L.I., N.Y. Died Aug. 5, 1936.

BROWNSON, James Irwin, judge; b. Washington, Pa., Jan. 25, 1856; s. (Rev.) James Irwin and Eleanor McCullough (Acheson) B.; A.B., Washington and Jefferson Coll., 1875, LL.D., 1935; unmarried. Admitted to Pa. bar, 1878; in practice at Washington, Pa., 1878-1918; judge Court of Common Pleas of Pa., 1918—, pres. judge, 1922—. Pres. Community Chest of Washington, Pa.; pres. bd. of trustees Washington and Jefferson Coll.; trustee Pa. Training Sch., 1921-35. Local rep. Nat. Council of Boy Scouts of America. Republican. Presbyn. Home: Washington, Pa. Died Dec. 31, 1938.

BROWNSON, Marcus Acheson, clergyman; b. Washington, Pa., June 24, 1859; s. James Irwin and Eleanor McCullough (Acheson) B.; A.B., Washington and Jefferson Coll., 1878, D.D., 1891; grad. Western Theol. Sem., Pa., 1881; m. Julia Janvier Bush, Apr. 23, 1885 (died 1889); m. 2d, Mary Pruyn Strain, Feb. 20, 1895 (died 1934). Ordained ministry Presbyterian Church, 1883; asst. pastor in charge Hebron Memorial Ch., Phila., 1881-83, Central Ch., Wilmington, Del., 1883-84; pastor First Ch., Camden, N.J., 1884-89, First Ch., Detroit, 1889-97, Tenth Ch., Phila., 1897-1924, pastor emeritus, 1924—. Dir. Princeton Theol. Sem., 1898-1929; trustee Presbyn. Hosp. (Phila.), 1898-1927; mem. Presbyn. Bd. Relief and Sustentation, 1897-1926; mem. Presbyn. Gen. Assemblies, 1891, 99, 1901, 12; del. Pan-Presbyn. Council, Liverpool, Eng., 1904, Calvin Celebration, Geneva, Switzerland, 1909; mem. Presbyn. Nat. Service Commn., 1917. Home: Southern Pines, N.C.; and Center Lovell, Me. Died Dec. 18, 1938.

BROWNSON, Willard Herbert, naval officer; b. Lyons, N.Y., July 8, 1845; s. Morton and Harriet (Taft) B.; grad. U.S. Naval Acad., 1865; m. Isabella King Roberts, July 10, 1872; children—Roswell Roberts, Mrs. Harriet Hussey, Mrs. Caroline Hart. Served in flagship N. Atlantic squadron, 1865-68, Pacific sta., 1868-71, Naval Acad., 1872-75; coast survey, Str. Blake, deep sea investigation, 1882-84; insp. hydrography, 1885-89; comdg. Petrel, 1889-91, Dolphin, 1892, Detroit, at Rio de Janeiro, Brazil, during revolution, 1893-94; comdt. cadets Naval Acad., 1894; bd. of inspection and survey, 1896-98; comdg. Yankee during war with Spain; capt., Mar. 3, 1899; comdg. Alabama, 1900-02; supt. U.S. Naval Acad., Nov. 6, 1902-June 1, 1906; rear admiral, May 6, 1905; comd. 4th div. Atlantic Fleet, July 8-Aug. 15, 1906; comd. spl. service squadron, Aug. 15-Oct. 15, 1906; comdr. in chief Asiatic Fleet, Oct. 15, 1906-Apr. 1, 1907; apptd. chief, Bur. of Navigation, May 20, 1907; retired July 8, 1907, but kept on active duty by order of President. Home: Washington, D.C. Died Mar. 16, 1935.

BRUBACHER, Abram Royer, college pres.; b. Lebanon, Pa., July 27, 1870; s. Daniel and Catherine (Royer) B.; grad. Phillips Acad., Andover, Mass., 1893; A.B., Yale U., 1897, Ph.D., 1902; LL.D., Alfred U., 1934; m. Rosa Haas, Aug. 24, 1897; 1 son, John Seiler. Instr. Williston Sem., Easthampton, Mass., 1897-99; Soldiers' Memorial fellow, Yale, 1899-1900; instr. in Greek, Yale, 1900-02; prin. high sch., Gloversville, N.Y., 1902-05; Schenectady, 1905-08; supt. schs. Schenectady, 1908-14; pres. N.Y. State Coll., 1914—; dir. Albany Savings Bank. Dir. Albany Boys' Acad., Albany Home for Children (bd. mgrs.). Presbyn. elder. Author: (with Dorothy Ermina Snyder) High School English (2 vols.), 1912, 14; Teaching—Profession and Practice, 1927; (with Katherine E. Wheeling) High Sch. Composition and Grammar (2 vols.), 1930; (with C. B. Springsteed) Junior English for Everyday Use, 3 vols., 1934; Senior English for Everyday Use, 1935. Home: Albany, N.Y. Died Aug. 23, 1939.

BRUBACK, Theodore, pres. San Pete Valley Ry.; b. Pittsburgh, Pa., Mar. 7, 1851; ed. there; m. Jan. 26, 1886, Jessie White McLean. Pres. Herschel Gold Mining Co., Bingham Placer Mining Co., Triumph Silver Mining Co., Stirling Coal and Coke Co., Gold Belt Water Co., etc. Home: Salt Lake City, Utah. Died 1904.

BRUCE, Andrew Alexander, judge, prof. law; b. Nunda Drug, Madras Presidency, India, Apr. 15, 1866; s. Gen. Edward Archibald and Anne Young (McMaster) B.; ed. Holmesdale House, Sussex, Eng., 1874-79, Bath Coll., Bath, Eng., 1879-81; A.B., U. of Wis., 1890, LL.B., 1892; m. Elizabeth Bacon Pickett, June 29, 1899; children—Glenn, Edward McMaster. Sec. to justices of Supreme Court of Wis., 1890-92; chief clerk law dept. Wis. Central Ry. Co., 1892-93; atty. for State Bd. Factory Inspectors, Ill., 1893-95; practiced law, Chicago, 1893-98; asst. prof. law, U. of Wis., 1898-1902; prof. law, 1902-11, dean Coll. of Law, 1904-11, U. of N.D.; asso. justice Supreme Court of N.D., 1911-16, and chief justice of N.D., 1916-19; prof. law, U. of Minn., Oct. 1919-22; prof. law, Northwestern U., 1922—. Republican. Pres. State Bd. Bar Examiners, N.D.; del. Universal Congress Lawyers and Jurists, St. Louis, 1904; mem. com. of Am. Bar Assn. to investigate and report on courts martial procedure in U.S. Army, 1919. Episcopalian. Author: Property and Society; The Non-Partisan League; Law of Bailments; The American Judge; Parole and the Indeterminate Sentence in Illinois; Crime in the City of Memphis; The Administration of Criminal Justice in Illinois; Cooley's Principles of Constitutional Law (enlarged and revised edit.). Chmn. Chicago (Ill.) NRA Compliance Board. Home: Oak Park, Ill. Died Dec. 6, 1934.

BRUCE, Charles Morelle, asst. land commissioner; b. Staunton Hill, Va., July 6, 1853; s. Charles and Sally (Seddon) B.; grad. Norwood (Va.) High School; student U. of Berlin, 1870-73; m. Mary E. Haly, Jan. 31, 1914. Removed to Arizona Ty., 1880; sec. Washington Mining Co. of Ariz., 1880-82; mem. Tevis, Perrin, Land & Co., cattle ranch, 1883-92; sec. Ariz. Ty. by appmt. of Pres. Cleveland, 1893-97; gov. pro tem. of Ariz. Ty., Mar. 30-April 18, 1896. Returned to Va., 1901; lessee of Staunton Hill Estate, 1902-09; asst. commr. Gen. Land Office, by appmt. of President Wilson, 1913-21. Democrat. Presbyn. Served as pres. Live Stock Assn. of Ariz. and Live Stock Sanitary Commn. of Ariz., also as v.p. State Agrl. Soc. of Va. Home: Staunton Hill, Va. Died June 8, 1938.

BRUCE, Dwight Hall, postmaster; b. Lenox, N.Y., June 21, 1834; s. Gen. Benjamin Franklin B.; ed. Lenox pub. schs. and Jordan Acad.; m. Emilie Northrup, Oct. 13, 1859. Postmaster Syracuse, N.Y., 1872-77 and 1897—. Republican. Journalist, 16 yrs.; prepared Memorial History of Syracuse, Onondaga County's Centennial, 2 vols.; The Empire State in Three Centuries. Home: Syracuse, N.Y. Died 1908.

BRUCE, Eugene Sewell, expert lumberman; b. Stockholm, N.Y., Aug. 17, 1860; s. Timothy Joshua and Mellissa Vilona (Bruce) B.; largely self-ed.; m. Alida Talbot, Sept. 12, 1894. Began in timber business in boyhood; for many yrs. logging supt. for Santa Clara Timber Co. and Dodge, Meigs & Co., New York; entered U.S. forestry work, July 1, 1900, after competitive civil service exam.; was the first "official" lumberman in U.S. Dept. of Agr., and was for many years adviser to the U.S. forester as to timber sales. Has done extensive work in sales of govt. stumpage and purchase of lands to constitute Appalachian and White Mountain nat. forests. Mason (K.T., Shriner). Home: Washington, D.C. Died June 7, 1920.

BRUCE, Harold Lawton, univ. prof.; b. Belchertown, Mass., Aug. 24, 1887; s. George Herbert and

Leah Maria (Dodge) B.; Williams, 1904-05; A.B., U. of Calif., 1908, M.Litt., 1911; Ph.D., Yale, 1915; m. Dorothy Hart, Aug. 20, 1918; children—Alan, Jean Alison. Instr. in English, Yale, 1915-16; asst. prof. English, U. of Calif., 1916-19, asso. prof., 1919-25, prof., 1925—; dean of summer sessions, Los Angeles, 1924-26, Berkeley, 1926—. Author: Voltaire on the English Stage, 1918; William Blake in This World, 1925; Writing Well (with C. N. Greenough and F. W. A. Hersey), 1932. Editor: (with Guy Montgomery) The New World, 1920, 2d series, 1926. Home: Berkeley, Calif. Died Apr. 6, 1934.

BRUCE, Helm, lawyer; b. Louisville, Ky., Nov. 16, 1860; s. Horatio Washington and Elizabeth Barbour (Helm) B.; A.B., Washington and Lee U., 1880; LL.B., U. of Louisville, 1882; m. Sallie Hare White, Dec. 17, 1884; children—James W., Elizabeth, Helm. Practiced at Louisville, 1882—; mem. Bruce & Bullitt, 1910-21, later Bruce, Bullitt, Gordon & Laurent. Dir. First Nat. Bank, Ky. Title Savings Bank & Trust Co., Fidelity & Columbia Trust Co. Trustee Am. Printing House for the Blind, Louisville Y.M.C.A. Home: Louisville, Ky. Died Aug. 10, 1927.

BRUCE, Horatio Washington, lawyer; b. Lewis County, Ky., Feb. 22, 1830; s. Alexander and Amanda (Bragg) B.; private edn.; m. Elizabeth Barbour Helm, June 12, 1856. Admitted to bar 1851; has been common school trustee; mem. Ky. legislature; Commonwealth's atty.; mem. Congress of C. S.; circuit judge in Ky.; chancellor Louisville chancery court; prof. law dept., U. of Louisville; and later chief atty. of Louisville & Nashville R.R. Co. Address: Louisville, Ky. Died 1903.

BRUCE, James Douglas, college prof.; b. Staunton Hill, Va., Dec. 9, 1862; s. Charles and Sarah (Seddon) B.; A.M., U. of Va., 1883, grad. in chemistry, 1884; univs. of Berlin and Strassburg, 1886-88; Ph.D., Johns Hopkins, 1894; unmarried. Prof. modern langs., Centre Coll., Danville, Ky., 1890-91; asso. in Anglo-Saxon and Middle English, 1891-97, asso. prof. English philology, 1897-1900, Bryn Mawr (Pa.) Coll.; prof. English lang. and lit., U. of Tenn., 1900—. Democrat. Episcopalian. Author: The Anglo-Saxon Version of the Psalms, 1894; Le Morte Arthur, 1903; Mort Artu, 1910; Historia Meriadoci and De Ortu Waluanii, 1913. Home: Knoxville, Tenn. Died Feb. 19, 1923.

BRUCE, John, judge; b. Stirlingshire, Scotland, Feb. 16, 1832; removed to Wayne County, O., 1840; grad. Franklin Coll., Ohio, 1854; removed to Iowa; admitted to bar, 1856; practiced at Keokuk, Ia.; served in Union army, becoming col. and bvt. brig. gen.; after war cotton planter in Ala.; mem. Ala. legislature, 1872-75; U.S. dist. judge, Ala., 1875—. Address: Montgomery, Ala. Died 1901.

BRUCE, John Eldridge, lawyer; b. Cleveland, Oct. 1, 1856; s. Eli and Caroline (Eldridge) B.; A.B., Western Reserve, 1876, A.M., 1884; m. Alice Straight Knowlton, Dec. 12, 1883. Admitted to bar, 1879; mem. Ohio Ho. of Rep., 1884-85; asst. U.S. atty., Southern Dist., Ohio, 1885-89, 1893-97. Democrat. Dir. The J. A. Fay & Egan Co. and other corps. Episcopalian. Home: Cincinnati, O. Died Aug. 17, 1924.

BRUCE, Matthew Linn, judge; b. Mercersburg, Pa., Oct. 1, 1860; s. James (D.D.) and Mary (Linn) B.; A.B., Rutgers Coll., 1884, A.M., 1887; m. Mrs. Lillian B. (Ballantine) Knapp, Apr. 10, 1894. Admitted to bar, 1889, and engaged in practice in New York. Pres. Rep. County Com., N.Y. County, 1903; lt. gov., N.Y., 1904-06; justice Supreme Ct., N.Y., 1906-07; defeated for election, Nov. 1907; apptd. justice Supreme Ct. by Gov. Hughes, 1908. Republican. Presbyterian. Home: New York, N.Y. Died Feb. 26, 1936.

BRUCE, Philip Alexander, author; b. Staunton Hill, Va., Mar. 7, 1856; s. Charles and Sarah (Seddon) B.; grad. U. of Va., 1876; LL.B., Harvard, 1879; LL.D., Washington and Lee, 1908, William and Mary, 1909; m. Betty T. Taylor, Oct. 19, 1896; 1 dau., Philippa Alexander. Author: The Plantation Negro as a Freeman, 1888; Economic History of Virginia in the 17th Century, 1895; Short History of the United States, 1903; Rise of the New South; Social Life of Virginia in Seventeenth Century; Life of General Robert E. Lee; Institutional History of Virginia in the Seventeenth Century; Pocahontas and Other Sonnets, 1912; Brave Deeds of Confederate Soldiers, 1916; History of the University of Virginia, 1920-21; History of Colonial Virginia (1606-1764), 1923; Rebirth of the Old Dominion, 1929; The Virginia Plutarch, 1929. Home: University, Va. Died Aug. 16, 1933.

BRUCE, Saunders Dewees, editor Turf, Field and Farm (which he founded, 1865); b. Lexington, Ky., Aug. 16, 1825; Grad. Transylvania U., 1846. Engaged in business, 1848, to Civil War; apptd. Union army, 1861; recruited and was insp. gen. Union Home Guard of Ky., elected col. 20th Ky. vols.; built fortifications mouth of Cumberland river; in command 22d brigade, and in battle of Shiloh; injured by falling horse; in command provisional brigade, opened Cumberland river below Ft. Donelson; recommended for promotion to brig. gen. by Gen. Sherman and Gen. Grant; resigned, 1864, on account of heart trouble, and went to New York. Authority on pedigree of horses. Author: American Stud Book (6 vols.); Horse Breeders' Guide and Handbook; The Thoroughbred Horse. Address: New York, N.Y. Died 1902.

BRUCE, Wallace, author; b. Hillsdale, N.Y., Nov. 10, 1844; s. Alfred and Mary Ann (MacAlpine) B.; A.B., Yale, 1867; m. Annie Becker, June 29, 1870. Engaged in lit. work, 1868—; U.S. consul at Edinburgh, 1889-93; poet and orator at numerous centennial and memorial occasions in U.S., Scotland and England; delivered Burns anniversary addresses at Ayr, Edinburgh and Kilmarnock, Scotland, and at Boston, Hartford and Chicago; address on Washington Irving at (Shakespeare) Stratford Grammar Sch., etc. Hon. pres. Shakespeare Soc. of Edinburgh. Pres. of the Florida Chautauqua at De Funiak Springs, Fla. Mem. Reformed Ch. Republican. Author: The Land of Burns, 1878; The Yosemite, 1879; The Hudson, 1882; From the Hudson to the Yosemite, 1884; Old Homestead Poems, 1887; The Hudson Panorama, 1888; In Clover and Heather, 1889; Here's a Hand, 1893; Wayside Poems, 1894; Scottish Poems, 1907; Leaves of Gold, 1907; Wanderers, 1907; Centennial edition of The Hudson, 1907. Address: Brooklyn, N.Y. Died Jan. 1914.

BRUCE, William Paterson, clergyman; b. Mercersburg, Pa., Dec. 27, 1858; s. Rev. Dr. James and Mary (Linn) B.; B.A., Rutgers, 1884, M.A., 1887; grad. Union Theol. Sem., 1887; D.D., Hope College, Mich., 1912, Rutgers Coll., 1914; m. Elizabeth E. Gordon, June 23, 1887. Ordained ministry Reformed Ch. in America, 1887; pastor Greenville Ch., Jersey City, N.J., 1887-95, Park Hill Ch., Yonkers, N.Y., 1895-1917; editor-in-chief Christian Intelligencer, 1917—. Pres. bd. of supts. New Brunswick Theol. Sem., 1907; pres. Synod of New York, 1901, Gen. Synod of Reformed Church in America, 1912; mem. bd. mgrs. Am. Tract Soc., 1916—, Am. Bible Soc., 1917; mem. Board of Foreign Missions, 1913—. Republican. Home: Yonkers, N.Y. Died Oct. 5, 1920.

BRUCKNER, Henry, congressman; b. New York, N.Y., June 17, 1871; s. John A. and Katharine (Schmidt) B.; ed. pub. schs. and bus. coll.; m. Helen Zobel, Nov. 17, 1904. Pres. Bruckner Bros., manufacturers; director Milton Realty Co., American Metal Cap Company. Mem. New York Assembly, 1900-01; commissioner of pub. works, N.Y., 1902-06; mem. 63d to 65th Congresses (1913-19), 22d N.Y. District; resigned from 65th Congress, 1918; formerly president Borough of the Bronx, New York City. Democrat. Mason. Died April 14, 1942.

BRUEGGEMAN, Bessie Parker; b. Charleston, Ill., Jan. 6, 1878; d. George Washington and Aranella (Ferguson) Parker; ed. Hosmer Hall (St. Louis) and Bradford (Mass.) Acad.; m. Clark E. Toms, June 1, 1892 (died 1896); 1 son, George Parker; m. 2d, Albert H. Brueggeman, Jan. 29, 1899. Organized Ambulance Div. of St. Louis Red Cross Motor Corps for World War, and was made lt., later capt.; elected com. woman from Mo. on Rep. Nat. Com., 1919; del. at large from Mo. to Rep. Nat. Conv., Chicago, 1920; mem. exec. com. of Rep. State Com. of Mo., 1920, also mem. campaign advisory com.; chmn. U.S. Employees' Compensation Commn., by apptmt. of President Harding, Nov. 1, 1921, for term of 6 yrs., reapptd. by Pres. Coolidge, 1927, resigned 1933. Home: Washington, D.C. Deceased.

BRUESTLE, George Matthew, artist; b. N.Y. City, Dec. 21, 1871; s. George John and Elizabeth Catherine (Ihrig) B.; art edn., Art Students League, N.Y. City, Julian Acad. and Colarossi Acad., Paris, under Aman Jean and Gustave Courtois; m. Emma Thompson, May 8, 1901; 1 son, Bertram George. Exhibited at Salon, Paris, 1895, 1911, Nat. Acad. Design, N.Y. City, Art Inst. Chicago, Pa. Acad. Fine Arts, Corcoran Gallery, Washington, D.C., Carnegie Inst., Pittsburgh, Pa. Represented in Gobbs Memorial Museum, Charleston, S.C., Dayton (O.) Museum, Cleveland (O.) Museum, Reading (Pa.) Museum, Beach Memorial Collection, Storrs Coll., Conn. A.N.A., 1927. Awarded 2 prizes, Salmagundi Club, 1918, 29. Home: Old Lyme, Conn. Died Aug. 14, 1939.

BRUFF, Lawrence Laurenson, army officer; b. in Md., Oct. 14, 1851; grad. West Point, 1876. Commd. 2d lt. 3d arty., June 15, 1876; promoted through grades to lt. col., June 25, 1906. Instr. ordnance and gunnery, West Point, 1891-1900; later asst. Watervliet Arsenal, N.Y. Author: Exterior Ballistics, Niven's Method, 1885; Notes on Machine and Rapid Fire Guns, Small-Arms and Ballistic Machines, 1892; Gunpowder and Interior Ballistics, 1892; Exterior Ballistics, Gun Construction, U.S. Sea Coast Guns, 1892; Ordnance and Gunnery, 1906 (all text books, used at West Point). Died 1911.

BRUMBAUGH, Clement, congressman; b. Greenville, O., Feb. 28, 1863; s. Samuel D. and Elizabeth (Darner) B.; B.S., Nat. Normal U., Lebanon, O., 1887; founder and prin. Van Buren Acad., 1887-91; spl. course in ancient langs., Ohio Wesleyan U., 1891-93; A.B., Harvard, 1894; supt. schs., Greenville, O., 1896-1900. Mem. Ohio Ho. of Rep., 1900-04 (minority leader of House); alternate-at-large from Ohio to Dem. Nat. Conv., Kansas City, Mo., 1900; admitted to Ohio bar, 1900, and engaged in practice at Columbus; deputy state supt. of insurance, Ohio, 1911-12; mem. 63d Congress (1913-15), 12th Ohio Dist.; reëlected 64th to 66th Congresses (1915-21). Methodist. K.P., W.O.W., I.O.O.F., Mason. Home: Columbus, O. Died Sept. 28, 1921.

BRUMBAUGH, I(saac) Harvey, college prof.; b. Penn Twp., Huntingdon County, Pa., Mar. 10, 1870; s. Henry Boyer and Susan Fink (Peightal) B.; A.B., Haverford Coll., Pa., 1892; A.B., Harvard, 1895, A.M., 1899; U. of Jena, summer, 1896; Litt.D., Ursinus Coll., 1920; Columbia U., 1924-25; L.H.D., Juniata Coll., 1930; m. Amelia Henrietta Johnson, Apr. 26, 1900; children—Barbara, Catherine Bulfinch, Marion Johnson, Henry Martin (dec.). Instr. Latin and Greek, 1892-94, prof. Latin, 1895-1911, v.p., 1896-1911, pres., 1911-24, prof. edn., 1925—, Juniata Coll. Trustee J. C. Blair Memorial Hosp. (Huntingdon); Morrison's Cove Home for the Aged (Martinsburg); pres. Huntingdon County Library; dir. Union Nat. Bank, Huntingdon. Republican. Mem. Ch. of Brethren. Home: Huntingdon, Pa. Died Aug. 9, 1937.

BRUMBAUGH, Martin Grove, gov.; b. Huntingdon County, Pa., Apr. 14, 1862; s. George Boyer and Martha (Peightal) B.; B.E., Juniata Coll., Pa., 1881, M.E., 1883, B.S., 1885, M.S., 1887; A.M., U. of Pa., 1894, Ph.D., 1895; LL.D., Mt. Morris, 1901, Franklin and Marshall, 1902, Pa. Coll., 1911, Pittsburgh, 1916, Maine, 1919; Litt.D., Lafayette, 1915; L.H.D., Susquehanna, 1917; m. Anna Konigmacher, 1884 (dec.); m. 2d, Flora Belle Parks, Jan. 29, 1916. Co. supt. schs., Huntingdon County, Pa., 1884-90; pres. Juniata Coll., 1895-1906; supt. pub. schs., Phila., 1906-15. State conductor of teachers' insts., in La., 1886-91; 1st commr. of edn., P.R., 1900-02; prof. pedagogy U. of Pa., 1895-1900 and 1902-06; nominated, May 1914, at first direct primaries, as Rep. candidate for gov. of Pa.; elected Nov. 1914 for term, Jan. 1915-Jan. 1919; pres. Juniata Coll., 1924—. Mem. Pa. State Bd. Edn., 1911-17. Author: History of the Brethren; Juniata Bible Lectures; Standard Readers (5 vols.); also (with J. S. Walton) Stories of Pennsylvania and Liberty Bell Leaflets; The Making of a Teacher, 1905; Life and Works of Christopher Dock; Story of Roosevelt, 1922. Editor Lippincott Educational Series. Home: Huntingdon, Pa. Died May 1930.

BRUMBY, Thomas Mason, lt. U.S.N.; b. Marietta, Ga., 1855; grad. U.S. Naval Acad., June 18, 1879; served on various vessels; promoted ensign; was one of survivors of the hurricane off Samoa, March 1889; promoted lt. (jr. grade), April 21, 1887; lt., Aug. 24, 1892; served on New York and Vermont; at Naval Observatory and War Coll., Sept., 1897 to Jan. 1898; flag lt. on Olympia, Asiatic squadron, Jan. 1898, took part in battle of Manila Bay and at surrender of Manila, Aug. 13, 1898, he raised the American flag over Manila. Died 1899.

BRUMM, George Franklin, congressman; b. Minersville, Pa., Jan. 24, 1878; s. Charles Napoleon and Virginia (James) B.; B.S., U. of Pa., 1901, LL.B., 1907; unmarried. Admitted to Pa. bar, 1908, and began practice at Pottsville; solicitor, Miners State Bank and other corps.; Rep. nominee for Congress, 1918, 20, 22; elected to 68th, 69th, 71st to 73d Congresses (1923-27, 1929-35), 13th Pa. Dist. Corpl. Co. C, Pa. Engrs., Mexican border service, 1916; mem. advisory bd. speakers' bur. of Four Minute Men, World War. Episcopalian. Home: Minersville, Pa. Died May 29, 1934.

BRUMMITT, Dan Brearley, clergyman, editor; b. Batley, Eng., Aug. 13, 1867; s. James and Anne E. (Brearley) B.; came to America, 1882; studied Kan. Agrl. Coll.; A.B., Baker U., 1894, A.M., 1898; B.D., Drew Theol. Sem., 1902; post-grad. work, N.Y. U., D.D., Baker, 1906; L.H.D., Syracuse U., 1922; m. Stella Wyatt, Sept. 12, 1894; 1 son, Wyatt Brearley. Entered M.E. ministry, 1891 (ordained, 1893); pastorates, Lawrence, Kan., 1891; Maple Hill, Kan., 1892; Altamont, Kan., 1894; Fort Smith, Ark., 1895; Little Rock, Ark., 1897. Asst. editor The Epworth Herald, 1901-10; mgr. dept. circulation, Methodist Book Concern, 1910-12; editor The Epworth Herald, 1912-24; editor Northwestern Christian Advocate, 1924-32; editor Christian Advocate (Northwestern and Central editions), 1932—. Mem. Meth. Ecumenical Conf., London, 1921. Author: Epworth League Methods, 1906; The Efficient Epworthian, 1914; War's End and After, 1919; John Wesley, Jr. (novel), 1921; Manuel Davidson (novel), 1925; Shoddy (novel), 1927. Mem. Anglo-Am. newspaper mission to war areas, 1918-19. Home: Kansas City, Mo. Died Apr. 5, 1939.

BRUMMITT, Dennis G., lawyer; b. Granville County, N.C., Feb. 7, 1881; s. Thomas Jefferson and Caroline (Bradford) B.; LL.B., Wake Forest Coll., 1907; m. Kate Hays Fleming, June 25, 1912. Admitted to N.C. bar, 1907, and practiced at Oxford; atty. gen. N.C., 1925—; chmn. Dem. Exec. Com., Granville County, N.C., 1908-14; mem. Dem. State Exec. Com., N.C., 1913-24, chmn. 1927-28; mayor of Oxford, 1909-13; mem. N.C. Ho. of Rep., 1915, 17, 19 (speaker of House, 1919); Dem. presdl. elector, 1920. Trustee Wake Forest Coll., 1925—. Mem. gen. bd. N.C. Bapt. State Conv. Baptist. Mason. Home: Oxford, N.C. Died Jan. 1935.

BRUNDAGE, Albert Harrison, M.D., toxicologist; b. Candor, N.Y., Mar. 3, 1862; s. Amos H. (M.D.) and Sarah M. (Dimmick) B.; M.D., Univ. Med. Coll. (New York U.), 1885; Ph.G., Brooklyn Coll. Pharmacy, 1892, Pharm.D., 1897; hon. A.M., U. Nashville, 1898; M.S., R.I. Coll. Pharmacy and Allied Sciences, 1905; m. S. A. Holt, Sept. 26, 1888. Prof. emeritus toxicology and physiology, depts. medicine, dentistry and pharmacy, Marquette Univ., 1908—; prof. toxicology and physiology, Brooklyn Coll. Pharmacy, 1898-1903 (pres. 1893-94), and R.I. Coll. Pharmacy and Allied Sciences, 1903-07. Toxicologist to Bushwick Hosp., 1904-21; lecturer on tuberculosis, Brooklyn Com. for Prevention of Tuberculosis, from 1908; lecturer for Am. Red Cross from 1918; pres. New York State Bd. of Pharmacy, 1903, and Board examiner in toxicology and posology, 1901-04, chmn. state com. on poisons. Mem. Vol. Med. Service Corps, 1918-19; maj. med. staff, Police Reserve, City of New York; cons. toxicologist Bushwick Hosp.; insp. Bd. of Health; asso. in immuno-therapy Polhemus Clinic, L.I. Coll. Hosp. Founder of first open-air classes in Brooklyn public schools. Grand lecturer Order of Eastern Star, State of New York, 1912, and reviser of its ritual. Commr. of Brooklyn to Tennessee Centennial, 1897. Founder and hon. mem. Brooklyn Med. Soc. (pres. 1895-96). Mason (32°). Author: A Manual of Toxicology, 13th edition, 1921; Practical Points in Physiology, 2 edits., 1904. Address: Woodhaven, N.Y. Died Mar. 12, 1936.

BRUNDAGE, Edward Jackson, lawyer; b. Campbell, N.Y., May 13, 1869; s. Victor and Maria L. (Armstrong) B.; ed. pub. schs. of Campbell and Detroit, Mich.; employed in railroad offices in Detroit and Chicago; admitted to Ill. bar, 1892; LL.B., Chicago Coll. of Law, 1893; m. Germaine Vernier, Dec. 17, 1913; children—Edward J., Margaret G., Robert V., Jacqueline L. Practiced in Chicago, 1893—; mem. Ill. Ho. of Rep., 1899-1903; pres. Bd. of County Commrs. of Cook County, 1905-07; corp. counsel City of Chicago, 1907-11; judge of Court of Claims, Ill., 1915-17; atty. gen. of Ill., term, 1917-21 and 1921-25; receiver C.M.&St.P. Ry., Mar. 18, 1925-Mar. 21, 1928. Republican. V.p. for Ill. of Pan-Am. Expn., Buffalo, N.Y., 1901. Mason (33°, K.T.), K.P. Home: Lake Forest, Ill. Died Jan. 20, 1934.

BRUNDAGE, William Milton, clergyman; b. Stone Ridge, N.Y., Jan. 12, 1857; s. Rev. Abraham and Phœbe Melissa (Royce) B.; grad. Wilbraham (Mass.) Acad., 1875; A.B., Wesleyan U., Conn., 1880, A.M., 1882; Ph.D., Boston U., 1889; m. Charlotte H. Flack, Aug. 3, 1886. Teacher Latin and Greek, Troy Conf. Acad., Poultney, Vt., 1880-82; ordained M.E. ministry, 1882; pastor, Ames, N.Y., 1882-83, Slingerlands, 1883-86, Gloversville, 1886-89, Amsterdam, 1889-93, Trinity Ch., Albany, 1893-95. Withdrew from M.E. Ch. because of change of theol. views and joined Unitarian Ch.; established 1st Unitarian Ch., Albany (pastor, 1895-1905); pastor Unity Ch., Brooklyn, 1905-18, pastor emeritus, 1918. Author: Some Things for Which the Unitarian Church Stands, 1895; Religion as a Personal Experience, 1914. Home: Westfield, N.J. Died Aug. 14, 1921.

BRUNE, Adolf Gerhard, musician, critic; b. Bakkum, Germany, June 21, 1870; s. A. Wilhelm and Anna (Segers) B.; studied harmony, composition, piano, organ and violin under masters in Germany; came to U.S., 1889; m. Mary R. Ramsey, Aug. 7, 1899. Instr. in musical theory and piano, Chicago Musical Coll., 1898—; organist St. Joseph's Ch., and Cathedral, Peoria, Ill.; asso. musical editor, Chicago Inter Ocean. Composer: Das Lied des Singschwans; overture to a drama (Chicago Orchestra); Twilight Picture (Chicago and Cincinnati); 7 symphonies, 6 quartets, 2 quintets, sextet, trio, and more than 70 songs, variations and other pieces for piano. Home: Oak Park, Ill. Died Apr. 21, 1935.

BRUNER, Lawrence, entomologist; b. Catasauqua, Pa., Mar. 2, 1856; s. Uriah and Amelia (Brobst) B.; ed. U. of Neb., hon. B.Sc., 1897; m. Marcia Dewell, Dec. 25, 1881; children—Psyche E., Helen M., Alice (dec.). Asst. U.S. Entom. Commn., 1880; field agt. U.S. Dept. Agr., U. of Neb., 1888; in Argentina, S.A., 1897-98; entomologist, Neb. Agrl. Expt. Sta., 1888-90; instr. entomology, 1890-95, and prof., 1895—, U. of Neb. Author: Introduction to Study of Entomology; Destructive Locust of Argentina, 1st rept., 1898, 2d rept., 1900; Locusts of Paraguay, 1906; Vol. II, Orthopt. Biol. Cent. Americana; Salt Orthopt. of Brazil, Locusts of Peru; Preliminary Catalog of Philippine Orthoptera. Also numerous monographs, reports and papers on insects and birds. Joint Author: New Elementary Agriculture. Named as most distinguished Nebraskan by governor's com. to represent the State at the Panama P.I. Expn., 1915. Address: Lincoln, Neb. Died Jan. 30, 1937.

BRUNNER, Arnold William, architect; b. New York, Sept. 25, 1857; s. William and Isabella B.; ed. pub. schs., New York and Manchester, Eng.; Mass. Inst. Tech., 1877-79; m. Emma Beatrice Kaufman, 1906. Architect of Capitol Park State Bldgs., and Soldiers' and Sailors' Memorial Bridge, Harrisburg, Pa.; U.S. Post Office, Custom House and Court House, Cleveland; Stadium, Coll. City of N.Y.; Students' Bldg., Barnard Coll.; Sch. of Mines (Columbia); Mt. Sinai Hosp., N.Y.; Cadet Hosp., West Point; Monumental Bridge, Toledo, O.; and many other pub. and pvt. bldgs. Designed chapel and general arrangement of bldgs. for Denison U., Granville, O.; won competition for new bldg. for Dept. of State, Washington, D.C. Apptd. by Gov. of Ohio, mem. Bd. of Supervision for Pub. Bldgs. and Grounds, Cleveland (pres.), and mem. similar commns. to prepare city plans for Baltimore, Rochester, Denver and other cities; architect for improvements for city and waterfront, Albany, N.Y. Mem. Bd. of Edn., New York, 1902, Art Commn. City of N.Y., 1908-10. A.N.A., 1910, N.A., 1916. Apptd. by Pres. Roosevelt, mem. Nat. Council of Fine Arts. Fellow A.I.A. (pres. N.Y. Chapter, 1909-10). Home: New York, N.Y. Died Feb. 14, 1925.

BRUNNER, David B., educator, author; b. Amity, Pa., Mar. 7, 1835; s. John and Elizabeth B.; ed. private schools and Dickinson Coll.; m. Amanda L. Rhoads, 1862. County supt. Berks County, Pa., 1869-75; taught private school, 1875-80; propr. and prin. Reading Business Coll., 1880—; also well known as student and investigator in mineralogy and microscopy. Mem. Congress, 1889-93; Democrat. Author: English Grammar and Analysis; The Indians of Berks County, Pennsylvania, 1901. Address: Reading, Pa. Died 1903.

BRUNNER, John, engr.; b. Sweden, Nov. 22, 1866; s. John and Anna (Ericson) B.; grad. Inst. Tech., Stockholm, 1887; m. Miss Mitchell, Nov. 16, 1892. Came to U.S., 1888, naturalized citizen 1893. Asst. engr., bridge dept. B.&M. R.R., 1888-90; chief engr. Mt. Vernon (O.) Bridge Co., 1890-95; asst. chief engr., Carnegie Steel Co., Pittsburgh, 1895-96; bridge engr., City of Pittsburgh, 1896-99; chief of Bur. of Engring. and Constrn., City of Pittsburgh, 1899-1902; with Ill. Steel Co. in various capacities, 1902-36, mgr. dept. of metallurgy and inspection, 1923-36; cons. engr. Carnegie-Ill. Steel Corp., 1936—. Decorated Royal Order of Nordstjernan, by King of Sweden, 1919; awarded John Ericsson medal, 1936. Mason (K.T.). Home: Evanston, Ill. Died June 15, 1936.

BRÜNNOW, Rudolph Ernest, prof. semitics; b. Ann Arbor, Mich., Feb. 7, 1858; s. Francis and Rebecca Lloyd (Tappan) B.; St. Columba's Coll., nr. Dublin, Ireland; Trinity Coll., Dublin; univs. of Basel, Tübingen and Strassburg, Ph.D., U. of Strassburg, 1882; LL.D., U. of Mich., 1914; m. Marguerite Beckwith, June 1, 1894 (died 1907). Prof. Semitics, Princeton, 1910—. Protestant. Author: Die Charidschiten unter den ersten Omayyaden (Doctor's dissertation), 1884; A Classified List of all Simple and Compound Cuneiform Ideographs, etc., 1889; The Twenty-first Volume of Kitab al-Aghani (Part I), 1889; Chrestomathy of Arabic Prose-Pieces, 1895; (with Alfred V. Domaszewski) Die Provincia Arabia, 3 vols., 1904-09. Address: Edgehill, Princeton, N.J. Died Apr. 14, 1917.

BRUNS, Henry Dickson, M.D.; b. Charleston, S.C., 1859; s. Dr. John Dickson and Sarah Dickson B.; U. of Va., 1876-78; med. dept. of U. of La.; resident student Charity Hosp., New Orleans; M.D., Jefferson Med. Coll., 1881; married; children—T. M. Logan, John Dickson, James Henry, Thomas Nelson Carter. Pathologist to Charity Hosp. and visiting oculist to same; surgeon-in-chief, Eye, Ear, Nose and Throat Hosp., New Orleans, and emeritus prof. diseases of eye, New Orleans Polyclinic; editor New Orleans Med. and Surg. Journal. Mem. exec. com. in two great reform polit. movements in New Orleans and chmn. of parish com. in campaign against La. State Lottery; pres. La. Ballot Reform League; mem. La. Constitutional Conv., 1898; mem. advisory council Nat. Com. for Prevention of Blindness. Democrat. Translated "Mind Your Eyes," from French of late Francisque Sarcey (with author's permission), 1886. Home: New Orleans, La. Died May 19, 1933.

BRUNTON, David William, mining engr.; b. Ayr, Can., June 11, 1849; ed. Toronto; course mining engring., U. of Mich.; (D.Sc.). Cons. practice in Colo., 1875—; chmn. bd. of consulting engrs., Moffat Tunnel Commn.; m. Katherine Kemble, Feb. 11, 1885; children—Frederick K., John D., Harold J., Marion (Mrs. N. E. Barker). Was chmn. War Com. of Tech. Societies, mem. inventions sect., Gen. Staff U.S. Army, mem. Naval Consulting Bd., and mem. Nat. Research Council World War. Home: Denver, Colo. Died Dec. 20, 1927.

BRUSH, Charles Francis, scientist; b. Euclid, O., Mar. 17, 1849; s. Col. Isaac Elbert and Delia Williams (Phillips) B.; M.E., U. of Mich., 1869; Ph.D., Western Reserve, 1880; hon. M.S., U. of Mich., 1899; LL.D., Western Reserve U., 1900, Kenyon Coll., 1903; Sc.D., U. of Mich., 1912; m. Mary E. Morris, Oct. 6, 1875; children—Charles Francis, Mrs. Edna Perkins, Helene. Chem. expert, Cleveland, 1870-73; iron and ore commn. mcht., 1873-77; pioneer investigator of electric lighting, and invented the Brush electric arc light, 1878, now in gen. use; also the storage battery (fundamental invention) and other devices essential to modern elec. engring.; founder the Brush Electric Co.; credited with "The Practical Development of Electric Arc Lighting" (Rumford medal). Pres. Cleveland Arcade Co., 1887—; founder The Linde Air Products Co. (1st pres.). Trustee Western Reserve U., Adelbert Coll., Univ. Sch., Cleveland Sch. of Art, Lake View Cemetery; corporator Case Sch. Applied Science; Chevalier of Legion of Honor, France, 1881; Rumford medal, Am. Acad. Arts and Sciences, 1899; Edison medal, 1913. Fellow Am. Acad. Arts and Sciences. Warden Trinity Cathedral. Home: Cleveland, O. Died June 15, 1929.

BRUSH, Daniel Harmon, army officer; b. in Ill., May 9, 1848; s. Daniel Harmon and Julia F. B.; was pvt. Co. F, 145th Ill. Inf., May 22-Sept. 23, 1864; grad. U.S. Mil. Acad., 1871; m. Harriet Rapp, Feb. 18, 1874. Commd. 2d lt. 17th Inf., June 12, 1871; promoted through grades to brig.-gen. U.S. Army, Feb. 17, 1908; retired May 9, 1912. Home: Baltimore, Md. Died Mar. 8, 1920.

BRUSH, Edward Nathaniel, M.D.; b. Glenwood, N.Y., Apr. 23, 1852; s. Nathaniel Howland and Myra Theresa (Warren) B.; ed. at Buffalo, N.Y.; M.D., U. of Buffalo, 1874; m. Delia A. Hawley, Sept. 18, 1879 (died 1911); m. 2d, Marie T. Hartman, Aug. 6, 1914. Practiced medicine and surgery, Buffalo, 1874-78; asst. physician, N.Y. State Lunatic Asylum, Utica, 1878-84; asst. phys., Pa. Hosp. for Insane, Phila., 1884-91; phys.-in-chief and med. supt. Sheppard and Enoch Pratt Hospital, Baltimore, 1891-1920 (emeritus); prof. psychiatry, U. of Md. and Coll. Physicians and Surgeons, Baltimore, 1899-1920 (emeritus). Editor Buffalo Medical Jour., 1874-79; asso. editor Am. Jour. Insanity (now Am. Jour. Psychiatry), 1878-84, 1897-1904, editor, 1904-31, editor emeritus, 1931—. Extensive writer on insanity and other medical subjects. Home: Baltimore, Md. Died Jan. 10, 1933.

BRUSH, Frank Spencer, clergyman; b. Zanesville, O., June 7, 1857; s. Edmund and Alice Sparrow (Cone) B.; A.B., Marietta (O.) Coll., 1878, D.D., 1897; grad. Lane Theol. Sem., Cincinnati, 1881; m. Elizabeth Peters Spencer, Apr. 11, 1886; children—Edmund Spencer, Charlotte Peters, (Frank) Spencer. Ordained Presbyn. ministry, 1881; pastor successively Bloomington, Ill., First Ch., Las Vegas, N.M., Los Gatos, Alameda and Berkeley, Calif., until 1924; lecturer on Washington, Lincoln, Woodrow Wilson, etc. Moderator Synod of Calif., 1905; pres. bd. trustees of San Francisco Theol. Sem., 1909. Asst. in psychol. examinations for aviators, World War. Republican. Mason (K.T., 32°). Author: An American Views Communism; They Knew Lincoln. Home: Berkeley, Calif. Died Mar. 13, 1940.

BRUSH, George de Forest, artist; b. Shelbyville, Tenn., Sept. 28, 1855; s. Alfred Clark and Nancy (Douglas) B.; student Nat. Acad. of Design, N.Y. City, and École des Beaux Arts, Paris, France, under Gérôme; hon. M.A., Yale, 1923; m. Mittie Taylor Whelpley, Jan. 11, 1887; children—Alfred Paine (dec.), Gerome, Nancy Douglas (wife of Dr. Harold Bowditch), Tribbie (dec.), Georgia (dec.), Mary (Mrs. Winslow S. Pierce, Jr.), Jane (Mrs. Winslow S. Coates), Thea (Mrs. Thomas Handesyde Cabot). Works: "In the Garden," Metropolitan Museum, N.Y. City; "Mother and Child," Boston Museum; "Mother and Children," Penn Acad., Phila.; "Mother and Child," Corcoran Art Gallery, Washington; "Portrait of Young Woman," Smith Coll.; "The Young Violinist," Museum, Worcester, Mass.; "Family Group," Art Inst. Chicago. Awarded 1st Hallgarten prize, 1888; medal, Chicago Expn., 1893; Temple gold medal, Pennsylvania Academy Fine Arts, 1897; gold medal, Paris Expn., 1900, where his pictures, "The Artist," and "Mother and Child," were exhibited; gold medal, Buffalo Expn., 1901, St. Louis Expn., 1904, A.N.A., 1902, N.A., 1906. Col. on staff of Gov. of Tenn., 1939. Home: Dublin, N.H. Died Apr. 24, 1941.

BRUSH, George Jarvis, mineralogist; b. Brooklyn, Dec. 15, 1831; s. Jarvis and Sarah (Keeler) B.; pvt. sch. edn.; studied chemistry and mineralogy at New Haven; in Oct. 1850, went to Louisville as asst. to Prof. Silliman in univ. there; Ph.B., Yale, 1852; hon. A.M., 1857; LL.D., Harvard, 1886; m. Harriet Silliman Trumbull, Dec. 23, 1864. Asst. in chemistry, U. of Va., 1852-53; studied in Europe, 1853-56; prof. metallurgy, 1855-71, prof. mineralogy, 1864-98, prof. emeritus, 1898—, dir. 1872-98, Sheffield Scientific Sch. (Yale). Address: New Haven, Conn. Died Feb. 6, 1912.

BRUSH, George Washington, M.D.; b. West Hills, Huntington Tp., L.I., N.Y., Oct. 4, 1842; s. John Rogers and Elizabeth (Carman) B.; acad. edn., L.I., N.Y.; served pvt. to capt. in U.S. Vols., 1861-65; awarded Congressional Medal of Honor, Jan. 21, 1897; studied and practiced dentistry several yrs.; M.D., L.I. Coll. Hosp., 1876; spl. course in biology,

Hoagland Lab., and gynecology, New York Post-Grad. Med. Sch.; m. Alice A. Bowers, Mar. 30, 1865; m. 2d, Maria Annette Bowers, Jan. 21, 1868; 1 son, Herbert Bowers. Was pres. U.S. Med. Examining Bd. for Pensions 4 yrs.; asst. surgeon, 13th Regt. N.G.S.N.Y.; instr. clin. medicine, outdoor dept., L.I. Coll. Hosp. and Dispensary; consulting phys. to Bushwick Hosp. and Dispensary; consulting surgeon to Bedford Hosp. and Dispensary; retired from med. practice 1906; devoted much time to municipal govt. and civic betterment, 1906—. Ex-pres. Brooklyn League, Greater New York Tax Payers Conf. Mem. N.Y. Assembly, 1895, Senate, 1896-98. Congregationalist. Mason. Home: Brooklyn, N.Y. Died Nov. 18, 1927.

BRUSH, Henry Raymond, prof. Romance langs.; b. Herkimer, N.Y., Nov. 17, 1878; s. Abraham Stevens and Mary Elizabeth (Quackenbush) B.; A.B., Adelbert Coll. (Western Reserve U.), 1898; Ph.D., U. of Chicago, 1911; m. Maud Amelia Bowman, June 18, 1902; children—Helen Virginia, Marcella Elizabeth, Henry Chapin. Teacher pub. schs., Cleveland, O., 1898-1900; prin. high sch., Ashland, 1900-05; prof. modern langs., Hope Coll., Holland, Mich., 1905-13; fellow U. of Chicago, 1909-11; prof. of French, U. of N.D., 1913-21; prof. same, U. of Calif. at Los Angeles, 1921—. Mem. exec. com. State Council of Defense, N.Dak., 1917-18; ednl. recruiting sec., Central Mil. Dept. of War Work Council, Y.M.C.A., 1918-19. Decorated Officier d'Académie, France, 1934. Republican. Presbyn. Translator: La Bataille de Trente (Middle-French poem). Home: West Los Angeles, Calif. Died Jan. 31, 1941.

BRUSH, Jacob Henry, banker; b. North Salem, N.Y., July 9, 1833; s. Albert and Julia (Birchard) B.; ed. Amenia Sem., N.Y., 1850; Charlotteville Sem., N.Y., 1851; m. Julia Augusta Buckmaster, May 4, 1862. Entered banking business at Decorah, Ia., 1855, as pres. Brush & Meeker Bank; pres. J. H. Brush & Co. Bank, Osage, Ia., 1856, Osage Nat. Bank, 1865; engaged as Brush Bros. for many yrs. at Osage in land, milling and elevator business; pres. Santa Rosa (Calif.) Nat. Bank, Union Trust Savings Bank, Ukiah Water Co. and Merchants' Lighting Co.; dir. Osage Nat. Bank; treas. Green Valley Canning Co. Dir. Osage (Ia.) Sem., Cornell Coll., Ia., U. of Pacific, San José, Calif. Republican. Methodist. Home: Santa Rosa, Calif. Deceased.

BRUSH, Matthew Chauncey, corp. official; b. Stillwater, Minn., 1877; s. George Moses and Maria Louise (Doud) B.; grad. Armour Inst. Tech., 1897; B.S. in Mech. Engring., Mass. Inst. Tech., 1901; m. Elizabeth R. Hunger, June 17, 1933. Engaged in newspaper work in Minneapolis and Chicago, 1893-95; hotel clerk and clerk Franklin MacVeagh & Co., Chicago, 1896; clerk and purser Great Lakes, summers 1897-1901; apprentice and machinist U.P. R.R. Co., Omaha, Neb.; gen. foreman C.,R.I.&P. Ry. Co., Goodland, Kan., 1903; with Newton St. Ry. System, Newtonville, Mass., 1904-09; gen. mgr. Buffalo & L.E. Traction Co. and L.E. Electric Ry Co., 1900-10; asst. to v.p., Boston Elevated R.R., 1910-11, 2d v.p. 1912-13; v.p., later pres., Boston Elevated R.R., 1914-15; pres. Boston Elevated Railroad, 1916-18, later dir.; pres. Am. Internat. Ship-building Corp., Hog Island, Pa., 1918-21; v.p. Am. Internat. Corp, 1918-21, sr. v.p., 1921-23, became pres., 1923. later mem. exec. com.; v.p. and chmn. exec. com. Equitable Office Bldg. Corp.; dir. various corps. Served as Adj. 101st Regt., Mass. N.G. Republican. Episcopalian. Mason (K.T., 32°, Shriner), Elk. Address: New York, N.Y. Died Oct. 15, 1940.

BRUSHINGHAM, John Patrick, clergyman; b. Cuba, N.Y., Feb. 16, 1855; s. Thomas and Mary (O'Hern) B.; A.B., Northwestern U., 1881, B.D., 1883, A.M., 1884, D.D., 1901; m. Lillia S. Norton, Oct. 12, 1881 (died 1916); children—Nellie (Mrs. E. L. Starr), Robert Milton, John Norton; m. 2d, Edith Williamson, 1917. Began preaching at Chicago, 1875; ordained M.E. ministry, 1885; pastor Ravenswood (Chicago), until 1884, Fulton St. Ch., Chicago, 1884-87, Ada St. Ch., 1887-92, Ravenswood, 1892-94, Fulton St. Ch., 1894-98, First Ch. until 1907, Sycamore, Ill., 1907-11, South Park Av. Ch., 1911-18, Central Park Ch., 1917-20; sec. of Morals Commn. of Chicago, 1917—. Mem. Gen. Conf. M.E. Ch. three times; mem. Methodist Ecumenical Conf., London, Eng.; mem. Chicago Meth. Social Union (ex-pres.). Mem. com. of fifteen to organize Municipal Voters' League of Chicago; mem. advisory bd. Commn. on Morals, 1916-17; mem. advisory bd. Wesley Hosp., 1917-20. Mason (32°, Shriner), Odd Fellow. Author: Catching Men, 1906; Spiritual Electrology, 1911. Home: Chicago, Ill. Died Apr. 7, 1927.

BRYAN, Benjamin Chambers, naval officer; b. Throggs Neck, N.Y., Aug. 16, 1858; s. Timothy Matlack and Mary Duncan (Chambers) B.; grad. U.S. Naval Acad., 1879; married; 1 dau., Anne (wife of R. E. S. Williamson, U.S. Army). Asst. engr. U.S.N., June 10, 1881; passed asst. engr., Oct. 3, 1891; chief engr., Jan. 20, 1899; transferred to line as lt., Mar. 3, 1899; promoted through grades to rear adm.; retired Aug. 16, 1922. Served on Dolphin, Spanish-Am. War, 1898; with Bur. Steam Engring., Navy Dept., 1903-08; head of Dept. Steam Engring., Navy Yard, Phila., 1908-12; dir. navy yards, Navy Dept., 1912-15; apptd. Commandant Naval Sta., Charleston, S.C., July 8, 1915. Mem. Naval Examining and Retiring Bd. Died July 21, 1930.

BRYAN, Charles Page, diplomat; b. Chicago, Oct. 2, 1856; s. Hon. Thomas Barbour and Jane Byrd (Page) B.; ed. U. of Va., 1877-79; LL.B., Columbian (now George Washington) U., 1879; admitted to bar, 1878; unmarried. Resided in Colo., 1879-84; mem. Colo. Ho. of Rep., 1880; col. on staff Governor Eaton of Colo., 1884; made 2 tours of Europe for Chicago Expn., 1891, 1892; mem. Ill. Ho. of Rep., 1888-97; col. on staffs of Govs. Fifer, Oglesby and Altgeld, of Ill., 1887-96. E.E. and M.P. to China, 1897-98, to Brazil, 1898-1902, to Switzerland, 1902-03, to Portugal, 1903-09, to Belgium, 1909-11; A.E and P. to Japan, Aug. 12, 1911-Nov. 1912. Republican. Decorated by Emperor of Japan with Grand Cordon of Rising Sun. Home: Elmhurst, Ill. Died Mar. 13, 1918.

BRYAN, Edward Payson, ry. official; b. Ashtabula County, O., July 2, 1847; s. John Love and Calista (Griswold) B.; ed. pub. schs. and prep. dept. Denison U., Granville, O.; m. Arabella Scott Welch, June 6, 1871. Began as telegraph operator L.&N. R.R., at Lebanon, Ky., 1865; held various positions on same rd. and apptd. supt. at Louisville, 1890, later transferred to St. Louis; v.p. and gen. mgr. Terminal R.R. Assn., St. Louis, 1895-1900; v.p. and gen. mgr., 1900-07 (subway then under constrn.), pres. 1907-09, Interborough Rapid Transit Co. of N.J. (resigned June 30, 1909); v.p. Great Western Power Co., San Francisco, 1909—; dir. Metropolitan Securities Co. (New York), New York City Interborough Ry. Co.; trustee N.Y.&L.I. Ry. Democrat. Episcopalian. Home: Bound Brook, N.J. Died 1910.

BRYAN, Elmer Burritt, univ. pres.; b. Van Wert, O., Apr. 23, 1865; s. Daniel and Mary Elizabeth (Beeler) B.; grad. Ind. State Normal Sch., 1889; A.B., Ind. U., 1893; grad. student Harvard and Clark Univs., 1898-1900; LL.D., Franklin Coll., Ind., 1905, Ind. U., 1933; L.H.D., U. of Me., 1915; m. Margaret L. Scott, June 28, 1889; children—Julian Scott, Mary Helen (Mrs. C. W. Sater), Florence (Mrs. J. G. Belcher). Was teacher in common and high schools in Ind., part of each yr., 1882-92; prin. Kokomo High Sch., 1893-94; teacher Manual Training High Sch., Indianapolis, 1894-96; prof. social and ednl. science, Butler Coll., 1896-97; asst. prof. pedagogy, 1897-99, asso. prof., 1899-1901, Ind. U.; prin. Insular Normal Sch., P.I., 1901-03; gen. supt. edn., P.I., Jan. 1 to Aug. 13, 1903; prof. ednl. and social psychology, Ind. U., 1903-05; pres. Franklin (Ind.) Coll., 1905-09, Colgate U., 1909-21, Ohio U., 1921—. Gold medal and diploma from Expn. for Philippine edn. exhibit. Baptist. Author: The Basis of Practical Teaching, 1905; Fundamental Facts for the Teacher, 1911. Home: Athens, O. Died Oct. 15, 1934.

BRYAN, Enoch Albert, educator; b. Bloomington, Ind., 1855; s. Rev. John and Eliza Jane (Philips) B.; A.B., Ind. U., 1878, A.M., 1885; A.M., Harvard, 1893; LL.D., Monmouth, 1902, Mich. Agricultural Coll., 1907, Ind. U., 1920, Wash. State Coll., 1929; m. Hattie E. Williams, 1881; children—Arthur W., Mrs. Eliza May Kulzer, Mrs. Gertrude Hayes. Supt. pub. schs., Grayville, Ill., 1878-82; pres. Vincennes (Ind.) U., 1882-93, Washington Agrl. Coll., and Sch. of Sciences (now State Coll. of Wash.), 1893-1916; commr. of edn. State of Ida., 1917-23; research prof. economics and economic history, State Coll. of Wash., 1923-39 (pres. emeritus). Author: The Mark in Europe and America; History of State College of Washington, 1928; Orient Meets Occident or The Advent of the Railways into the Pacific Northwest, 1935. Home: Pullman, Wash. Died Nov. 6, 1941.

BRYAN, Frederick Carlos, lawyer; b. Cleveland, July 16, 1858; s. Judge Constant and Susan Louise (Barnum) B.; B.A., Western Reserve Coll., 1878; LL.B., Cincinnati Law Sch., 1881; LL.M., Columbian (now George Washington) U., 1903, D.C.L., 1905; m. Blanche Conger, June 18, 1898; children—Blanche Louise, Frederick Conger, Robert Conger. Began practice at Akron, 1881; mem. law firm of Dick, Doyle & Bryan, 1898-1907; practiced in Washington, D.C., 1898—. Instr. in law, Buchtel Coll., O., 1894-96. Maj. 8th Ohio Inf., Spanish-Am. War; judge advocate and lt. col. Ohio N.G., 1903-13; retired after 30 yrs.' service. Home: Washington, D.C. Deceased.

BRYAN, George, lawyer; b. Allegheny, Pa., Feb. 22, 1860; s. Samuel Smith and Kate (Plumer) B.; student Davidson (N.C.) Coll., 1875-76; LL.B., Richmond (Va.) Coll., 1881; studied Summer Law Sch., U. of Va., 1881; Litt.D., Hampden-Sydney, 1923; LL.D., U. of Richmond, 1926; m. Page Bragg Osborne, Oct. 22, 1902. Admitted to Va. bar, 1881, Pa. bar, 1896; gen. counsel, Va. Bankers Assn. Prof. law of banks and banking, U. of Richmond. Editor Va. Law Register, 1901-05. Democrat. Presbyn. Mason. Author: Law of Petroleum and Natural Gas, 1898; The Imperialism of John Marshall, 1924. Home: Richmond, Va. Died Feb. 26, 1930.

BRYAN, Guy Morrison, banker; b. Galveston, Tex., Dec. 16, 1871; s. Guy M. and Laura Harrison (Jack) B.; ed. pvt. schs.; m. Florence Carter, Nov. 18, 1908; children—Carolyn Laura, Guy Morrison, Florence Carter, Hally Ballinger. Began as clk. in hardware store, Galveston, at age 16, became owner of a store at 23; entered banking business, 1902; moved to Houston, 1907; an organizer, 1907, and pres. 2d Nat. Bank, vice chmn. board until 1932, when resigned; chmn. bd. First Texas Joint Stock Land Bank; pres. Second Nat. Corp.; dir. Houston Br. Federal Reserve Bank of Dallas, Tex. Mem. Houston Cotton Exchange and Bd. of Trade; pres. Houston Clearing House, 1916-17 and 1927-29. Democrat. Home: Houston, Tex. Died Apr. 5, 1935.

BRYAN, Henry Lewis, law editor; b. Washington, D.C., Feb. 25, 1853; s. Samuel Davis and Harriet Miles (Hepburn) B.; ed. prep. dept. Columbian (now George Washington) U.; LL.B., Georgetown U., 1888, LL.M., 1889; m. Marion McClery, Oct. 15, 1878. Began practice at Washington, D.C., 1889; served as clk. various Senate coms.; pvt. sec. to sec. of state; sec. Bur. Am. Republics; sec. bd. trustees Phila. Commercial Mus.; retired. Mem. Columbia Hist. Soc., The Fossils. Episcopalian. Democrat. Editor U.S. Statutes at Large, vols. 24-45 inclusive, except vols. 30 and 31. Home: Washington, D.C. Died Jan. 21, 1934.

BRYAN, John P. Kennedy, lawyer; b. Charleston, S.C., Sept. 10, 1852; s. U.S. Judge, George S. and Rebecca L. (Dwight) B.; A.B., Princeton, 1873, A.M., 1876; Mental Science Fellow and student phil. and law, Berlin U., 1873-74, U. of Leipzig, deg. 1874-75; studied law Charleston; m. Henrietta C. King, Aug. 12, 1880. Admitted to S.C. bar, 1877, and practiced in Charleston; mem. Bryan & Bryan; counsel for defense in political trials in S.C., 1877-83; spl. counsel for U.S. in conspiracy cases, 1898-99, and in prize cases during Spanish-Am. War; argued before Supreme Ct. of U.S. the constl. questions affecting "dispensary law" of S.C.; del. to S.C. Constl. Conv., 1895, and a leader in establishing suffrage in S.C. on a basis of property and ednl. qualifications. Mem. and del. International Law Assn. Trustee U. of South, 1891-94, College of Charleston, High School, and Public Schools. Democrat. Address: Charleston, S.C. Deceased.

BRYAN, Joseph Roberts, physician; b. Beverly, N.J., Nov. 7, 1864; s. Dr. John Wolfe and Maria Adele (Laguerenne) B.; ed. Central High Sch., Phila.; M.D., U. of Pa., 1889; m. Isabella McKinstry, Apr. 20, 1891. Visiting phys. to St. Vincent's Hosp., Apr. 1, 1910—, Misericordia Hosp., Phila., Dec. 1917—. Commr. from Pa. to Trans-Mississippi and Internat. Expn., 1897. Address: Philadelphia, Pa. Died Feb. 14, 1922.

BRYAN, Lewis Randolph, lawyer; b. Brazoria County, Tex., Oct. 2, 1858; s. Moses Austin and Cora (Lewis) B.; grad. Baylor U., 1877, law dept. same, 1880; LL.D., Austin Coll., Sherman, Tex., 1925; m. Martha J. Shepard, Oct. 15, 1891. Admitted to bar, Apr. 9, 1880; elected pres. Texas Bar Assn., July 3, 1902; pres. Houston Bar Assn., 1911; mem. firm Bryan, Suhr, Bering & Bell. Home: Houston, Tex. Died Feb. 11, 1938.

BRYAN, Mary Edwards, editor; b. Florida, Ga., 1844; d. Maj. John D. and Louisa Critchfield (Houghton) Edwards; ed. Fletcher Inst., Thomasville, Ga.; m. I. E. Bryan, at age of 15. After marriage studied privately and received A.M. degree from College Temple, Newman, Ga. Edited Literary Crusader, Atlanta, 1862, and Natchitoches (La.) Tri-Weekly; asso. editor The Sunny South, 1874-84, then editor New York Bazaar (mag.) and afterward of The Half Hour Magazine, New York; returned about 1895 to The Sunny South; later on staff of Uncle Remus' Magazine, into which The Sunny South was merged. Author: Manch; Wild Work; Kildee; Nan Haggard; The Bayou Bride; Uncle Ned's White Child; Stormy Wedding; Ruth—an Outcast; My Sin; The Girl He Bought; His Legal Wife; A Fair Judas; His Wife's Friend. Home: Clarkston, Ga. Died June 16, 1913.

BRYAN, Nathan Philemon, judge; b. Orange (now Lake) County, Fla., Apr. 23, 1872; s. John M. and Louisa M. (Norton) B.; A.B., Emory Coll., Oxford, Ga., 1893; LL.B., Washington and Lee U., 1895; m. Julia Smith, Oct. 26, 1898. Admitted to Fla. bar, 1895. Chmn. Board Control, Fla. State Institutions of Higher Education, 1905-09; U.S. senator Fla., term, 1911-17; judge U.S. Circuit Court of Appeals, 5th Jud. Circuit, 1920—. Democrat. Home: Jacksonville, Fla. Died Aug. 8, 1935.

BRYAN, Oscar Eugene, clergyman; b. in Miss., Aug. 4, 1873; s. Jacob Allen and Mutelle (Armour) B.; student Baylor U., 1900-06; Th.G., Southwestern Bapt. Theol. Sem., Ft. Worth, Tex., 1911; D.D., Baylor U., 1921, Georgetown (Ky.) College, 1921; LL.D., Union U., Jackson, Tenn., 1931; m. Fannie Elizabeth Davidson, Sept. 2, 1903; children—Mary Elizabeth, William Ray, Annie Frances, Oscar Eugene, Harriett Newell. Gen. evangelistic work, 1906-09; evangelist Southwestern Bapt. Theol. Sem., 1911-13; pastor Tabernacle Ch. (Bapt.), Waco, Tex., 1913-16; sec. Ky. Bapt. State Bd., 1916-21; supt. evangelism enlistment, Bapt. Home Mission Bd., Atlanta, Ga., 1921-23; budget dir. $75,000,000 campaign, Southern Bapt. Conv., 1923-24; sec.-treas. Tenn. Bapt. State Conv., 1924-33. Democrat. Mason. Home: Nashville, Tenn. Died Jan. 26, 1933.

BRYAN, Robert Coalter, surgeon; b. 1873; s. Joseph B. and Isobel Lamont (Stewart) B.; M.D., College of Physicians and Surgeons (Columbia U.), 1899; m. Grace Hamilton Bryan. Practiced in Richmond, Va., 1899—; emeritus prof. genito-urinary surgery, Med. Coll. of Va.; surgeon, Stuart Circle Hosp.; visiting surgeon, Memorial Hosp. Mem. commission of Am. Red Cross to Roumania, 1917. Home: Richmond, Va. Died Dec. 24, 1941.

BRYAN, Thomas Barbour, lawyer; b. Alexandria, Va., Dec. 22, 1828; grad. Harvard Law School, 1848; practiced in Cincinnati until 1852, Chicago, 1852—. Pres. Chicago Sanitary Fair, which netted more than $300,000 for the Union soldiers; mem. Union Defense Com.; pres. Chicago Soldiers' Home; was founder and owner of Graceland Cemetery, Bryan Hall, and the Fidelity Safe Depository, in which millions were saved in the Chicago fire of 1871; one of commrs. governing Dist. of Columbia, 1875-78; one of the active promoters and v.p. World's Columbian Expn., 1893. Author of German Grammar, also of Fables, Epigrams and Translations from many tongues. Home: Elmhurst, Ill. Died 1906.

BRYAN, W. S. Plumer, clergyman; b. Allegheny City, Pa., Aug. 30, 1856; s. Samuel S. and Kate (Plumer) B.; A.B., Davidson Coll., N.C., 1875, A.M., 1878; grad. Columbia Theol. Sem., 1878; D.D., Centre Coll., Ky., 1892; m. Alice C. Reid, Dec. 1, 1887. Ordained Presbyn. ministry, 1878; pastor chs. in Randolph County, W.Va., 1878-87, Presbyn. Ch., Asheville, N.C., 1887-92, 2d Ch., Cincinnati, O., 1892-95, Ch. of the Covenant, Chicago, Feb. 1, 1895. Lecturer on the Smyth Foundation, Columbia Theol. Sem., 1917. Pres. Presbyn. Home, Chicago. Home: Chicago, Ill. Died May 28, 1925.

BRYAN, William James, senator; b. Ft. Mason, Fla., Oct. 10, 1876; s. John Milton and Louisa Margaret B.; A.B., Emory Coll., Ga., 1896; B.L., Washington and Lee U., 1899; m. Janet Allan, Sept. 1903. Admitted to bar, 1899, and practiced at Jacksonville, Fla.; mem. firm Bryan & Bryan. County solicitor Criminal Ct. of Record, Duval County, Fla., 1902-7; del.-at-large Nat. Dem. Conv., 1904; apptd. U.S. Senator, Dec. 26, 1907, to fill unexpired term of S. R. Mallory, deceased; term expired 1909; Democrat. Episcopalian. Address: Jacksonville, Fla. Died 1908.

BRYAN, William Jennings, Secretary of State; b. Salem, Ill., Mar. 18, 1860; s. Silas Lilliard and Mariah Elizabeth (Jennings) B.; A.B. (highest honors and valedictorian), Ill. Coll., 1881, A.M., 1884; LL.B., Union Coll. of Law, Chicago, 1883; LL.D., U. of Neb., Md., and U. of Ariz.; m. Mary Elizabeth Baird, Oct. 1, 1884. Admitted to Ill. bar, 1883; practiced at Jacksonville, Ill., 1883-87, then at Lincoln, Neb.; mem. 52d and 53d Congresses (1891-95), 1st Neb. Dist.; received Dem. vote for U.S. senator in Neb. legislature, 1893; nominated in Dem. conv. for U.S. senator, 1894, but was defeated in legislature by John M. Thurston; editor Omaha World-Herald, 1894-96; del. Dem. Nat. Conv., 1896; wrote the "silver plank" in its platform, made a notable speech, and was nominated for President of U.S.; traveled over 18,000 miles during campaign, speaking at almost every stopping place; received 176 electoral votes against 271 for William McKinley; lectured on bimetallism, 1897-98; raised 3d Regt. Neb. Vol. Inf. for Spanish-Am. War, May 1898, becoming its col. Again nominated for President, 1900, by Dem., Populist and Silver Rep. convs.; "imperialism" was declared by the platform to be the paramount issue; he made an active canvass, but was again defeated, receiving in electoral college 155 votes against 292 for William McKinley. After the election established a political mag., The Commoner, at Lincoln. Made tour of the world, 1906, and contributed to newspapers. Nominated for 3d time at Denver, 1908, and received 162 electoral votes against 321 for William Howard Taft. Sec. of State in cabinet of President Wilson, Mar. 4, 1913-June 9, 1915 (resigned), during which time negotiated 30 treaties, with governments, representing three-fourths of world's population, providing for investigation of all disputes. Author: The First Battle, 1897; Under Other Flags, 1904; The Old World and Its Ways, 1907; Heart to Heart Appeals, 1917; The Menace of Darwinism, and The Bible and Its Enemies, 1921; In His Image, 1922. Also many articles in mags. and newspapers. Pres. Nat. Dry Federation, 1918. Home: Miami, Fla. Died July 26, 1925.

BRYAN, Mrs. William Jennings; b. Perry, Ill., June 17, 1861; d. John and Lovina (Dexter) Baird; student Monticello Sem., Godfrey, Ill., 1878-79; grad. Presbyn. Acad. for Young Women, Jacksonville, Ill., 1881 (valedictorian); spl. work Ill. Coll. and U. of Neb.; m. William Jennings Bryan, Neb., Oct. 1, 1884 (died July 26, 1925); children—Mrs. Ruth Owen, William Jennings, Grace (Mrs. R. L. Hargreaves). Studied law after marriage, in order to enter more fully into husband's work, and admitted to practice in Dist. Ct. and Supreme Ct., Neb., but never practiced. Presbyn. Home: Miami, Fla. Died Jan. 21, 1930.

BRYAN, William Shepard, Jr., lawyer; b. Baltimore, Dec. 23, 1859; s. William Shepard and Elizabeth Edmondson (Hayward) B.; ed. Bethel Mil. Acad., 1876-79, U. of Va., 1879-80; admitted to bar, 1882; unmarried. Counsel Bd. Supervisors of Elections, Baltimore, 1890-92; city atty. and city counsellor, 1892; city solicitor, 1892-95; atty.-gen. of Md., 1903-Dec. 1907. Democrat. Mem. Md. State Bar Assn., Bar Assn. of Baltimore. Home: Baltimore, Md. Died Apr. 1914.

BRYAN, Worcester Allen, surgeon; b. Alexandria, Tenn., Sept. 1, 1873; s. Joshua Lester and Elizabeth Jane (Wood) B.; A.B., Cumberland U., 1893, A.M., 1897; M.D., Vanderbilt U., 1899; post-grad. work N.Y. Polyclinic, 1902, U. of Vienna, 1910; m. Emma Horatia Berry, Sept. 7, 1904; children—Anne Smith, Elizabeth Nelson, Worcester Allen, Emma Berry. Asst. to chair practice of medicine, 1899-1900, to chair of surgery and demonstrator of surgery, 1900-07, lecturer on principles of surgery, 1902-06, adj. prof. surgery, 1906-09, prof. principles of surgery, 1909-11, prof. surgery and clinical surgery, 1911-25, prof. clinical surgery, 1925—, Vanderbilt U.; prof. oral surgery, Vanderbilt Dental Dept., 1902-25; surgeon Protestant, Vanderbilt and Nashville gen. hosps.; also surgeon Watauga Sanitarium, Ridgetop, Tenn. Mem. Christian Ch. Author: Principles of Surgery. Home: Nashville, Tenn. Died Apr. 30, 1940.

BRYANT, Arthur Peyton, chemist; b. South New Market, N.H., May 7, 1868; s. George Nelson and Anna Maria (George) B.; B.S., Wesleyan U., Middletown, Conn., 1892, M.S., 1895; m. Fannie Wright Burr, Apr. 4, 1893; 1 son, Harold Burr (dec.). Teacher, English and Classical Sch., Providence, R.I., 1893, Swarthmore Coll., 1894; food and nutrition work with Prof. W. O. Atwater, Middletown, Conn., 1895-1901; chemist with Agrl. Expt. Sta., Storrs, Conn., 1901; research chemist Corn Products Co., Chicago, 1902-06; with Bryant-Miner Labs., 1906; directing chemist Clinton Corn Syrup Refining Co. (now Clinton Co.), 1907—, also v.p. and dir.; v.p. and dir. Clinton Corn Syrup Sales Co., Internat. Wheat Malt Syrup Co.; dir. City Nat. Bank of Clinton; cons. chemist Nat. Candy Co. Mem. and ex-pres. Clinton Bd. of Edn., Y.M.C.A., Clinton br. Boy Scouts of America. Republican. Methodist. York and Scottish Rite Mason. Home: Clinton, Ia. Died Feb. 3, 1935.

BRYANT, David E., judge; b. LaRue County, Ky., Oct. 19, 1849; family removed to Grayson Co., Tex., 1853; A.B., Trinity Coll., N.C., 1871; admitted to bar, 1873, and practiced at Sherman, Tex., 1873-90; U.S. dist. judge, Eastern Dist. of Tex., 1890—. Democrat. Address: Sherman, Tex. Died 1910.

BRYANT, Edgar Reeve, physician, surgeon; b. Gilroy, Calif., May 6, 1866; s. Berryman (M.D.), and Henrietta Frances (Reeve) B.; B.Ph., U. of Pacific, 1885, M.Ph., 1888, M.A., 1903; M.D., Hahnemann Med. Coll., Phila., 1889; post-grad. work in Europe, over 3 yrs.; m. Betty Tisdale, May 3, 1899. Resident phys., Hahnemann Hosp., New York, 1889-90; practiced, San Francisco, 1893—; prof. surgery, Hahnemann Med. Coll. of Pacific, 1898; surgeon City and County Hosp., San Francisco. Ex-pres. bd. dirs. Homœ. Sanatorium; dir. Hahnemann Med. Coll., Hahnemann Hosp.; dir. of Golden Gate Commandery Company; prominent in securing smoke abatement in San Francisco. V.p. Bryant Investment Co. Republican. Mem. bd. dirs. and vestryman St. Luke's P.E. Ch. Mason (32°, K.T.). Home: San Francisco, Calif. Died 1917.

BRYANT, Edwin Eustace, dean; b. Milton, Vt., Jan. 10, 1835; s. John C. and Lovina (Green) B.; ed. New Hampton Inst.; m. Louise S. Boynton, June 29, 1859. Moved to Wis., 1857, and engaged in law practice; volunteered in Union army, 1861; became officer in line, staff and field; private and exec. sec. to gov. of Wis., 1868-72; adj. gen. Wis., 1868-82; elected to Wis. legislature, 1878; declined renomination; asst. atty. gen. U.S. for P.O. dept., 1885-89; dean Coll. of Law, U. of Wis., 1889—; pres. Commrs. of Fisheries of Wis., 1893—; pres. Commn. for Natural History and Geolog. Survey of the State. Author: Wisconsin Justice, 1884; History Third Wisconsin Infantry Veterans, 1891; Code Pleading, 1893; Outlines of Law, 1895; Wisconsin Code Practice, 1898; United States Constitution Annotated, 1901. Home: Madison, Wis. Died 1903.

BRYANT, Ernest Albert, surgeon; b. of Am. parents, Woodstock, Ont., Can., Apr. 8, 1869; s. John Henry and Mary Louise (Dunn) B.; M.D., U. of Pa., 1890; m. Susanna Patterson Bixby, July 12, 1904; children—Susanna Patterson, Ernest Albert. Resident phys., St. Agnes Hosp., Philadelphia, Pa., 1890-91; police surgeon, Los Angeles, 1891-96; chief surgeon and supt. Los Angeles County Hosp., 1897-1901; surgeon in charge Sisters Hosp., Los Angeles, 1902-12, Los Angeles Gen. Hosp., 1912-20; chief surgeon Los Angeles R.R. Corp., Southern Calif. Gas Co., Southern Counties Gas Co.; chief of staff, Good Hope Hosp. Clinic; med. dir. Southern Calif. Edison Co.; surg. dir. southern div. S.P. R.R. Co.; dir. Good Hope Hosp., Farmers & Mchts. Nat. Bank. Trustee M. J. Connell Sanatorium, Good Hope Hosp. Assn. Republican. Home: Los Angeles, Calif. Died Oct. 19, 1933.

BRYANT, Frank Augustus, physician, surgeon; b. North Jackson, Pa., Oct. 18, 1851; s. Chauncey Elliott and Hannah (Corse) B.; Windsor (N.Y.) Acad., 1865-68; M.D., Bellevue Hosp. Med. Coll. (New York U.), 1895; post-grad. work, Post-Grad. Med. Sch. and Hosp., New York; m. Miss Sarah M. Mitchell, Nov. 28, 1871 (died 1888). Practiced in New York, 1895—; prin. of sch. for correction of speech disorders; resident phys., Burke Foundation for Convalescents. Republican. Mason. Author: Causes and Treatment of Stammering, 1907; Speech Disorders and Their Treatment, 1914; Manual of Free Gymnastics, 1884. Home: White Plains, N.Y. Died Apr. 1921.

BRYANT, Henry Grier, explorer; b. Allegheny, Pa., Nov. 7, 1859; s. Walter and Ellen A. (Henderson) B.; attended Phillips Exeter Acad., 1876-79; A.B., Princeton, 1883, A.M., 1886; LL.B., U. of Pa., 1886. Explored Grand Falls of Labrador, 1891; 2d in command Peary relief expdn., 1892; comdr. Peary auxiliary expdn., 1894; comdr. Mt. St. Elias (Alaska) expdn., 1897; explored St. Augustine River, Labrador, 1912; mountain ascents in various parts of the world. Pres. Geog. Soc. of Phila. for various terms bet. 1897 and 1932; pres. Assn. Am. Geographers, 1913, Am. Alpine Club, 1911-13; The Contemporary Club, 1923-24. Home: Philadelphia, Pa. Died Dec. 7, 1932.

BRYANT, John H., capitalist; b. Mar. 17, 1840, on shipboard, his parents being Irish immigrants; went west; worked in store at Ypsilanti, Mich.; was one of the first to reach Pike's Peak, 1859; returned to Mich.; worked as lumberman in Saginaw; served as private in Union army; in business in Richmond, Va., 1865; established three sumac factories and operated coal mines; was member convention which nominated Gilbert C. Walker for gov.; was col. of his staff when gov.; has acquired large coal, railroad, iron and industrial interests; officer in various corporations. Address: New York, N.Y. Died 1906.

BRYANT, John Howard, poet, farmer; b. Cummington, Mass., July 22, 1807; s. Dr. Peter and Sarah (Snell) B.; ed. dist. school, winters, in childhood; "Select School" and acad. at Cummington, 1826-27; taught school winters 1828-29 and 1830-31; attended Rensselaer School (now Polytechnic Inst.), Troy, N.Y.; removed to Ill., 1831; m. Hattie Wiswall, June 7, 1833 (died 1887). Served as recorder of deeds, chmn. bd. supervisors, etc., Bureau County; took govt. census of county, 1840; elected to Ill. legislature, 1842 and 1858; Democrat until 1844; then joined Liberty party; Free-soil candidate for Congress, 1854; del. to conv. for organizing Rep. party, Pittsburgh, 1856; del. Nat. Rep. Conv., 1860; Collector Internal Revenue, 5th dist. Ill., 1862-66. Author: Poems, 1855; Life and Poems, 1894 (Life by E. R. Brown). Home: Princeton, Ill. Died 1902.

BRYANT, Joseph Decatur, surgeon; b. E. Troy, Wis., Mar. 12, 1845; s. Alonzo and Harriet (Adkins) B.; ed. Norwich (N.Y.) Acad.; M.D., Bellevue Hosp. Med. Coll., 1868; LL.D., New York U., 1908; m. Annette Crum, 1874. Interne Bellevue Hosp., 1869-71; asst. to chair of anatomy, 1871, lecturer on surg. anatomy (summer course), 1871-74, asst. demonstrator anatomy, 1875-77, prof. gen. descriptive and surg. anatomy, 1877-83, asso. prof. orthopedic surgery, 1883-95, Bellevue Hospital Med. Coll.; prof. principles and practice of surgery, operative and clin. surgery, Univ. and Bellevue Hosp. Med. Coll., 1898—. Sanitary inspector, N.Y. City Health Dept., 1873-79, commr., 1887-93; commr. N.Y. State Bd. Health, 1887-93; surgeon 71st Regt., N.G.S.N.Y., 1873-82; surgeon gen. N.G.S.N.Y., 1882-94; was on staffs of Governors Cleveland, Hill and Flower. Attending surgeon West Side Dispensary, 1872-75, Bur. for Med. and Surg. Relief, 1874-80 (consulting surgeon, 1882); visiting phys. Charity Hosp., 1881-82; visiting surgeon, Bellevue Hosp., 1882; consulting surgeon, New York City Insane Asylum, 1882—; visiting surgeon, St. Vincent's Hosp., 1887—; consulting surgeon, Northwestern Dispensary, Hosp. for Ruptured and Crippled, Woman's Hosp., St. Joseph's Hosp. (Yonkers), Hackensack Hosp.; was personal friend, and physician to Grover Cleveland and family. Author of med. monographs and of Operative Surgery, 2 vols., 4th edit.; Bryant and Buck's American System of Surgery, 8 vols. Address: New York, N.Y. Died Apr. 7, 1914.

BRYANT, Lorinda Munson, author; b. Granville, O., Mar. 21, 1855; d. Marvin M. and Emma (Culbertson) Munson; grad. Granville (O.) Female Coll., 1875, B.S., 1892; student Chicago Coll. Pharmacy, 1887, Denison U., 1886-89, Cornell U., 1889-90; m. Charles W. Bryant, Sept. 16, 1875; children—Fitch C., Miriam J. (dec.). First woman registered pharmacist in Ohio, 1887; instr. sciences, Ogontz Sch., 1890-99; prin. Montrose Sch., S. Orange, N.J., 1899-1905. Author: Pictures and Their Painters, 1907; The Life of the Bible as a Book, 1908; What Pictures to See in Europe in One Summer, 1910; Famous Pictures of Real Boys and Girls, 1912; What Sculpture to See in Europe, 1914; What Pictures to See in America, 1915; American Pictures and their Painters, 1917; Famous Pictures of Real Animals, 1918; French Pictures and Their Painters, 1922; Children's Book of Celebrated Pictures, 1922; Bible Stories in Bible Language, 1922; Children's Book of Celebrated Sculpture, 1923; Children's Book of Celebrated Buildings, 1924; Children's Book of Celebrated Bridges, 1925; Children's Book of Celebrated Towers, 1926; Children's Book of American Landmarks, 1927; Children's Book of European Landmarks, 1928; Children's Book of Celebrated Legends, 1929; Children's Book of Religious Pictures, 1930; Children's Book of Animal Pictures, 1931. Home: New York, N.Y. Died Dec. 13, 1933.

BRYANT, Ralph Clement, forester; b. Princeton, Ill., Jan. 22, 1877; s. Arthur and Elizabeth (Hughes) B.; student U. of Ill., 1896-97; Cornell U., 1898-1900, F. E., 1900; hon. M.A., Yale, 1911; hon. Sc.D., Middlebury Coll., 1928; m. Alice Joiner, June 1, 1904; children—Bettina Joiner (Mrs. S. O. H. Jones), Ralph Clement. Forester N.Y. State Forest, Fish and Game Commn., 1900-01; forester, 1901-02, asst. chief, 1902-05, Philippine Bur. of Forestry; insp. U.S. Forest Service, Washington, 1905-06; prof. of lumbering, Yale, 1906—. Republican. Unitarian. Author: Logging, 1922; Lumber, 1922. Address: New Haven, Conn. Died Feb. 1, 1939.

BRYANT, Samuel Wood, naval officer; b. Washington, Pa., May 24, 1877; s. William Curry and Sarah (McLean) B.; grad. U.S. Naval Acad., 1900; m. Carolina F. Merry, Dec. 18, 1905; children—Gordon McLean, Samuel Wood. Ensign, May 20, 1902; promoted through grades to read adm., July 1, 1933; retired because of physical disability incurred in line of duty, March 1, 1937. Commander torpedo boat destroyer off coasts of Ireland and France, and on staff commander United States destroyer flotillas, in European waters, during World War; tech. adviser on elec. communications to Am. del., Limitation of Armament Conf., Washington, 1921-22; asst. naval adviser to Am. delegation at Internat. Conf. on Rules of Warfare, The Hague, 1922-23; mem. staff U.S. Naval War Coll., 1925-26 and 1928-30; in comd. U.S.S. Detroit, attached to cruiser divs., U.S. Fleet, 1926-27, and as flagship U.S. Naval Forces to Europe, 1927-28; chief of staff Scouting Fleet, 1930-32; dir. War Plans Div., Navy Dept., 1932-34; comdr. battleship div. U.S. Fleet, 1934-35; chief of staff to comdr. in chief U.S. Fleet, 1935. Presbyn. Home: Asheville, N.C. Died Nov. 4, 1938.

BRYANT, Thomas Wallace, chmn. bd. Union Hardware Co.; b. New Haven, Conn., Aug. 18, 1859; s. Clark Bishop and Josephine (Swift) B.; ed. pub. schs.; art study under Rudolph Christiansen, Meriden, Conn., 1876-79; m. Marie Elise Hooghkirk, Apr. 30, 1907; children—Rebecca Swift, Marie Elise (twins), Lucia Josephine, Jane, Thomas Wallace. Sec. and supt. Electrical Supply Co., Ansonia, Conn., 1880-88; sec. and mgr. Union Hardware Co., Torrington, Conn., 1888-1903, pres. 1903-28, chmn. bd., 1928—; v.p. Torrington Printing Co.; dir. Torrington Electric Light Co., Torrington Water Co., Torrington Nat. Bank. Former mem. Conn. N.G.; chmn. Torrington War Bur., World War; mem. Bd. of Edn., Torrington, 1906—. Rep. presdl. elector, 1916; dep. judge City Court. Gov. Charlotte Hungerford Hosp.; trustee Conn. State Hosp. for Insane (Norwich), Torrington Y.M.C.A.; dir. Maria Seymour Brooker Memorial and Day Nursery. Episcopalian. Mason (32°), Elk. Home: Torrington, Conn. Died Mar. 15, 1934.

BRYANT, Victor Silas, lawyer; b. Providence Twp., Mecklenburg County, N.C., Dec. 10, 1867; s. Henry and Julia Sophia (Parks) B.; Ph.B., U. of N.C., 1890; m. Matilda Dewey Heartt, Dec. 8, 1897. Admitted to N.C. bar, 1891; practiced at Roxboro, 1891-95, Durham, 1895—; mem. firm Bryant, Brogden & Bryant; dir. Fidelity Bank; city atty., Durham, 1897-1901. Mem. N.C. Senate, 1913-15, Ho. of Rep., 1919. Trustee U. of N.C., 1903—. Mem. N.C. State Bar Assn. Democrat. Presbyn. Home: Durham, N.C. Died Sept. 2, 1920.

BRYANT, Waldo Calvin, chmn. bd. Bryant Electric Co.; b. Winchendon, Mass., Dec. 17, 1863; s. Calvin Turner and Almeda (Dexter) B.; B.S., Worcester Poly. Inst., 1884; m. Ida Gerald, Apr. 5, 1887; children—Gerald, Doris. Began as elec. engr. with Thomson-Houston Elec. Co., Lynn, Mass., 1884; asst. supt. Bridgeport (Conn.) Electric Light Co., 1884-85; supt. Waterbury (Conn.) Electric Light Co., 1885-88; founder, 1889, and pres., treas., gen. mgr. Bryant Electric Co., Bridgeport, later chmn. bd.; officer or dir. many corps. Dir. Bridgeport Hosp., Bridgeport Public Library, Bridgeport Boys Club. Republican. Episcopalian. Mason (32°). Home: Bridgeport, Conn. Died July 5, 1930.

BRYANT, William Cullen, publisher; b. New York, Aug. 1, 1849; ed. Brooklyn public schools and Polytechnic Inst.; m. Mary W. Peters. Pub. Brooklyn Times, 1875. Last commr. Fire Dept., Brooklyn, before consolidation with New York; sec. and mgr. Am. Newspaper Pubs. Assn., 1893—; treas. Publishers' Press. Home: Brooklyn, N.Y. Died 1905.

BRYANT, William McKendree, teacher; b. Lake County, Ind., Mar. 31, 1843; s. Eliphalet W. and Esther Eliza (Brown) B.; A.B., Ohio Wesleyan U., 1869, A.M., 1871; LL.D., Mo. State U., 1892; pvt. 3d Ia. Inf., 1861-62; adj. 34th Ia. Inf., 1862-64; asst. adj-gen. of brigade during last months of service (spl. hon. mention in official history); m. Sarah Augusta Shade, Aug. 8, 1867. Supt. schs., New Lisbon, O., 1868-69, Burlington, Ia., 1870-73; teacher St. Louis pub. schs., 1873-12; instr. psychology, ethics and history, St. Louis Normal and High Sch., 1881-1912. Lecturer St. Louis, Kindergarten Normal. Translator: Hegel's Philosophy of Art, with Introduction giving outline of entire Aesthetik, 1879. Author: Philosophy of Landscape Painting; The World-Energy and Its Self-Conservation, 1890; A Syllabus of Psychology, 1892; A Syllabus of Ethics, 1893; Hegel's Educational Ideas, 1896; Life, Death and Immortality, 1898. Retired, 1912, and engaged in lit. work. Address: Waynesville, N.C. Deceased.

BRYCE, James, diplomatist; b. Belfast, May 10, 1838; s. James (LL.D.) and Margaret (Young) B.; ed. U. of Glasgow; B.A., Trinity Coll., Oxford, Eng., 1862; D.C.L., 1870; LL.D., U. of Edinburgh, 1883, U. of Glasgow, 1886, U. of Mich., 1887, St. Andrew's U., 1902, Columbia, 1904, Jena, Harvard, Chicago and St. Louis, 1907, Leipzig, 1909; Dr. Polit. Science, Royal Hungarian U., Buda Pesth, 1896; U. of Buenos Aires, Argentine, 1910; D.C.L., Trinity U., Toronto, 1897; Litt.D., Victoria U., 1897, Cambridge U., Eng., 1898, Harvard, 1909; hon. fellow Trinity and Oriel Colls., Oxford, Eng., 1890—; m. Elizabeth Marion Ashton, July 23, 1889. Called to the bar, Lincoln's Inn, 1867, and practiced until 1882; Regius prof. civ. law, U. of Oxford, Eng., 1870-93; mem. Parliament for Tower Hamlets, 1880, Aberdeen, 1885-1907; apptd. under sec. of state for foreign affairs, 1886; chancellor Duchy of Lancaster (with seat in Cabinet), 1892; mem. Senate, London U., 1893; pres. Bd. of Trade, 1894; chmn. Royal Commn. on secondary edn., 1894; chief sec. for Ireland, 1905-07; A.E. and M.P. of Great Britain to U.S., 1907—. Author: The Flora of the Island of Arran, 1859; The Holy Roman Empire, 1862; The Trade Marks Registration Act, with an Introduction and Notes on Trade Mark Law, 1877; Transcaucasia and Ararat, 1877; The American Commonwealth, 1888; Impressions of South Africa, 1897; Studies in History and Jurisprudence, 1901; Studies in Contemporary Biography, 1903; The Hindrances to Good Citizenship, 1909. Home: Sussex, Eng. Died Jan. 22, 1922.

BRYCE, Lloyd, diplomat; b. Flushing, L.I., N.Y., Sept. 20, 1851; s. Maj. J. S. B.; childhood passed at Georgetown, D.C.; ed. at Jesuit Coll. there and in New York; entered Christ Ch., Oxford, Eng., 1869, B.A. and M.A.; studied law, Columbia; m. Edith Cooper. Apptd. postmaster gen. State N.Y., 1886; mem. 50th Congress (1887-89). Democrat. Gained controlling interest in the North American Review, 1889; purchased other interests and conducted the Review until 1896; U.S. minister to the Netherlands and Luxemburg, Aug. 12, 1911-Sept. 1913. Hon. v.p. Conf. on Bills of Exchange; del. Opium Conf., 1913. Author: Paradise; A Dream of Conquest; The Romance of an Alter Ego; Friends in Exile; Lady Blanche's Salon; The Literary Duet; After Christianity, What? Home: Roslyn, N.Y. Died Apr. 2, 1917.

BRYCE, Ronald, author. See Howard Rockey.

BRYSON, Charles William, surgeon; b. Richmond, Va.; s. Zadoc R. and Margaret (Via) B.; grad. Harris Acad.; M.D., Coll. of Physicians, Keokuk, Ia., 1882; m. Myrtle Traughber, Dec. 25, 1908. Practiced at Falls City, Neb., 1882-86, Los Angeles, Calif., 1886—; prof. gynecology, abdominal and clin. surgery, Coll. Phys. and Surg., U. of Southern Calif., 1904—, dean of faculty, 1906—. Address: Los Angeles, Calif. Deceased.

BRYSON, John Paul, M.D.; b. Macon, Miss., Apr. 16, 1846; s. James and Eliza Banks B.; grad. Humboldt Med. Coll., St. Louis, 1868; m. Mary Stirling Winter, 1873. Consulting surgeon of the St. Louis Hosp.; surgeon to the St. Louis Mullanphy Hosp.; prof. genito-urinary surgery, med. dept. Washington U., 1885—. Home: St. Louis, Mo. Died 1903.

BRYSON, Robert Hassey, architect; b. Newark, N.J., June 3, 1875; s. Robert and Margaret (Hassey) B.; ed. pub. schs., Brooklyn; professional training in atelier and offices; m. Charlotte A. Stoddard, Feb. 19, 1910. Practiced, Brooklyn, 1906—; mem. firm Slee & Bryson. Past pres., Brooklyn Chapter Am. Inst. Architects. Home: Brooklyn, N.Y. Died Sept. 10, 1938.

BUBB, John Wilson, brig. gen.; b. Danville, Pa., Apr. 26, 1843; s. Frederick and Sarah J. (Wilson) B.; ed. pub. schs., Danville, Pa.; m. Frances Helena Steele, Nov. 19, 1867. Served pvt., sergt. and 1st sergt. Co. E, 1st Battalion, 12th Inf., Sept. 13, 1861-Apr. 24, 1866; promoted through grades to brig. gen., U.S.A., Apr. 3, 1906. Participated in many battles and campaigns in Civil War, 1862-64; prisoner in Libby, Bell's Island and Salisbury, Aug. 19, 1864-Apr., 1865; chief commissary, Gen. Crook's campaign against Sioux Indians, May-Oct., 1876; served in P.I., 1899-1902, 1904-06, participating in various engagements; recommended for bvt. of col. in regular service for action nr. Dasmarinas, 1899; comd. Dept. of Visayas, Oct. 29-Dec. 23, 1905, Dept. of Dak., May 21, 1906-Apr. 26, 1907; retired. Home: Wilmington, Del. Died Feb. 23, 1922.

BUCHANAN, Andrew Hays, college prof.; b. Washington Co., Ark., June 28, 1828; s. Isaac and Naomi B.; A.B., Cumberland, 1853, A.M.; spl. studies civ. engring. and mathematics; (LL.D., Lincoln U.); m. Malinda Anna Alexander, July 10, 1855. Taught civ. engring., 1854-61; mil. topog. engr., 1861-65, in C.S.A. under Generals Bragg and Johnston; taught high sch., Washington Co., Ark., 1866-69; prof. mathematics and civ. engring., Cumberland Univ., 1869-1911. Employed during vacation periods, 1876-96, by supt. of U.S. Coast and Geod. Survey in the triangulation of Tenn., having entire charge of that work; established state line between Va. and Tenn., 1902-03. Democrat. Cumberland Presbyn. layman. Author: Advanced Text-Book on Plane and Spherical Trigonometry. Home: Lebanon, Tenn. Died 1914.

BUCHANAN, Arthur Stillingfleet, judge; b. DeSoto Co., Miss., Aug. 14, 1856; s. Benjamin B. and Eliza (Smith) B.; LL.B., U. of Miss., 1879; m. Elizabeth G. Looney, Nov. 10, 1891. Admitted to Miss. bar, 1879; mem. Miss. Ho. of Rep., 1885, 86; removed to Memphis, 1887; apptd. justice Supreme Court of Tenn., Dec., 1910, to fill vacancy caused by death of Justice W.D. Beard; resigned, Jan. 1, 1918, to resume practice at Memphis; atty. for Guaranty Bank & Trust Co., Empire Plantation Co., Delta Farms Co., Delta and Pine Land Co. of Miss. Democrat. Baptist. Home: Memphis, Tenn. Deceased.

BUCHANAN, Benjamin Franklin, lawyer; b. Rich Valley, Smyth Co., Va., Oct. 4, 1859; s. Patrick Campbell and Virginia (Copenhaver) B.; LL.B., U. of Va., 1884; LL.D., Hampden-Sidney Coll., 1922; m. Eleanor Fairman Sheffey, Mar. 3, 1887; children—John Preston, Patrick Campbell (dec.), Frank (dec.), Josephine, Virginia B. (wife of G. B. Denit, U.S.A.), Eleanor Fairman (Mrs. Watson Starcher), David Haytor. Admitted to Va. bar, 1885, and began practice at Marion; mem. Buchanan & Buchanan; gen. counsel comptroller of the currency, Washington, D.C., 1915-21; counsel Norfolk & Western Ry. Co., Mathiesen Alkali Wks., etc.; mem. Va. Senate, 1893-97, 1915-17, 1922-30; lt. gov. of Va., 1917-21; del. Dem. Nat. Conv., Kansas City, Baltimore and San Francisco; mem. State Com. to Revise Tax Laws of Va., 1915; patron of bill providing for segregation system of taxation in Va. Presbyn. Mason. Mem. commn., State of Va., to present replica of Houdon statue of George Washington to United Kingdom of Great Britain and Ireland, Trafalgar Sq., London, June 20, 1921. Home: Marion, Va. Died Feb. 21, 1932.

BUCHANAN, Frank, congressman; b. Jefferson Co., Ind., June 14, 1862; s. Joseph and Emeline (Connor) B.; ed. pub. schs.; m. Minnie Murphy, Mar. 17, 1898. By trade a bridge builder and structural iron worker; pres. Bridge and Structural Iron Workers' Local Union No. 1, Chicago, 1898-1901; pres. Internat. Union, 1901-05. Candidate for Congress, 1906, 08; mem. 62d, 63d and 64th Congresses (1911-17), 7th Ill. Dist. Indicted, Dec., 1915, by Federal Grand Jury of N.Y. City for alleged conspiracy to violate the Sherman Anti-Trust Act, by restraining shipment of munitions of war to foreign nations. Democrat. Home: Chicago, Ill. Died Apr. 18, 1930.

BUCHANAN, George Edward, coal merchant, investment banker; b. nr. Thamesville, Ont., Can., Jan. 29, 1869; s. Henry and Sarah (Bentley) B.; unmarried. Began as farmer and live stock mcht. in coal business, Detroit, Mich., 1892; sr. mem. Buchanan and Huff, 1914—; pres. and gen. mgr. Diamond Coal & Coke Co., Buchanan Fuel & Supply Co., Buchanan Coal & Coke Co., John Kraft Coal Co., George E. Buchanan Investment Co.; v.p. and treas. Union Investment Co. Episcopalian. Mason. Organized, 1922, and since sponsor, "On to Alaska with Buchanan, Inc.," a movement for character building in boys. Home: Detroit, Mich. Died Mar. 23, 1939.

BUCHANAN, James Anderson, brig. gen.; b. Washington Co., Md., Dec. 11, 1843; s. Dr. James A. and Eleanora Elder (Miller) B.; m. Helen Warren Myers, 1885. Apptd. from Md. 2d lt. 14th U.S. Inf., Mar. 7, 1867; promoted through grades to col. 24th U.S. Inf., Aug. 14, 1903; brig. gen., Apr. 14, 1905; retired, at own request, over 30 yrs.' service, May 31, 1906. Served at principal western posts for more than 30 yrs., in P.R., 1898-1903, and later in P.I. Home: Upperville, Va. Died May 18, 1926.

BUCHANAN, James Isaac, business mgr.; b. Hamilton, Ont., Can., Aug. 3, 1853; s. Isaac and Agnes (Jarvie) B.; ed. Collegiate Inst., Galt, Ont.; LL.D.,

Allegheny Coll., 1921; m. Eliza Macfarlane, 1901. Settled in Pa., 1877; with Oil City Trust Co., later at Pittsburgh; ex-pres. Pittsburgh Trust Co., then dir.; pres. Pittsburgh Terminal Warehouse & Transfer Co., River & R.R. Terminal Co.; dir. Terminal Trust Co.; trustee Estate of J. J. Vandergrift, Estate of Kate V. Bingham. Mem. bd. Athalia Daly Home. Fellow Am. Inst. of Banking. Presbyterian; teacher of Bible class, 1883—; pres. Presbyn. Union of Pittsburgh and Allegheny. Mason. Extensive traveler; crossed S. Africa in 1870. Home: Pittsburgh, Pa. Deceased.

BUCHANAN, James P., congressman; elected Apr. 5, 1913, to 63d Congress (1913-15), 10th Tex. Dist., to succeed Albert Sidney Burleson; apptd. postmaster-general by President Wilson; reëlected 64th to 74th Congresses (1915-37), same dist. Democrat. Home: Brenham, Tex. Died Feb. 22, 1937.

BUCHANAN, James Shannon, prof. history; b. Franklin, Tenn., Oct. 14, 1864; s. Thomas and Rebecca Jane (Shannon) B.; B.S., Cumberland U., Lebanon, Tenn., 1885; Vanderbilt U., 1893-94, U. of Chicago, 1896; LL.D., Kingfisher Coll., Okla., 1917; m. Vinnie Galbraith, June 24, 1896; children—Frances, James, William, Mary Margaret; m. 2d, Katharyn Osterhaus, Dec. 23, 1924. Prin. Cornersville (Tenn.) Inst., 1887-91; asst. state supt. schs., Tenn., 1891-93; lecturer Watkins Inst., Nashville, 1891-94; prof. history, Central Normal Sch., Okla., 1894-95; prof. history, 1895—, dean Coll. Arts and Sciences, 1909—, acting pres., 1923-24, v.p., 1925—, also prof. history, U. of Okla. Editor Oklahoma Chronicle. Mem. Constl. Conv., Okla., 1906. Democrat. Presbyn. Mason. Died March 20, 1930.

BUCHANAN, John Alexander, judge; b. in Smyth Co., Va., Oct. 7, 1843; served in Stonewall Brigade, C.S.A., 1861-65; taken prisoner at Gettysburg, and confined, 1863-65; A.B., Emory and Henry Coll., 1870; law student U. of Va., 1870-71. Mem. Va. Ho. of Dels., 1885-87; mem. 51st and 52d Congresses (1889-93), 9th Va. Dist.; asso. justice Supreme Ct. of Appeals, Va. Democrat. Home: Richmond, Va. Died Sept. 2, 1921.

BUCHANAN, John Jenkins, surgeon; b. Wellsville, O., 1855; s. James G. and Amanda F. (Jenkins) B.; A.B., Western U. of Pa. (now U. of Pittsburgh), 1877, A.M., 1880; M.D., Med. Dept., U. of Pa., 1881; hon. Ph.D., Washington and Jefferson Coll., 1904; m. Ellen Grier, 1887. Prof. surgery, U. of Pittsburgh, 1900-15 and 1921—; also chief of staff and chief surgeon, Mercy Hosp. Republican. Presbyn. Fellow Am. Surg. Assn. Home: Pittsburgh, Pa. Died Aug. 24, 1937.

BUCHANAN, Joseph Ray, editor; b. Hannibal, Mo., Dec. 6, 1851; s. Robert Sylvester and Mary Ellen (Holt) B.; pub. sch. edn., Mo. and Ill.; m. Lucy A. Clise, Dec. 16, 1879. Went to Denver, 1878; engaged in publishing business; editor and mgr. Denver papers; active in labor and reform movements; went to Chicago, 1887, New York, 1888; engaged in editorial work on Am. Press Assn.; on staff New York Journal, 1904-15. Assisted in organizing People's Party at Omaha, 1892; elected mem. Nat. Com. for N.J., 1892, 1896 and 1900; twice candidate for Congress, 6th N.J. Dist. Commr. of Conciliation, Dept. of Labor, Feb. 1918-July 1921. Author: Story of a Labor Agitator. Home: Montclair, N.J. Died Sept. 13, 1924.

BUCHANAN, Joseph Rodes, author and medical prof.; b. Frankfort, Ky., Dec. 11, 1814; M.D., Louisville Univ., 1842; m. Anne Rowan, 1841; m. 2d, Cornelia Decker, 1881; m. 3d, Mrs. E. S. Worthington, 1894. Was, 1846-56, prof. physiology and institutes of medicine, Eclectic Med. Inst., Cincinnati, and dean of the faculty; afterward in the Eclectic Med. Coll., New York, and Homeopathic Coll., Boston; is the originator of the science system of anthropology, therapeutic sarcognomy and psychometry. Has written works on these and also on "The New Education," and published 8 vols. of Buchanan's Journal of Man. Home: San Jose, Calif. Died 1899.

BUCHANAN, Malcolm Griswold, vice-chancellor of N.J.; b. Trenton, N.J., Mar. 10, 1881; s. Henry Clay and Mary Elizabeth (Griswold) B.; A.B., Princeton, 1900; LL.B., Harvard, 1903; m. Lily Butler, June 9, 1906; 1 dau., Lily Butler; m. 2d, Lucy Baldwin Walradt Kennedy, July 8, 1931. Admitted to N.J. bar, 1904, and began practice at Trenton; mem. James & Malcolm G. Buchanan, 1904-16; apptd. v.-chancellor Court of Chancery of N.J., 1919, reapptd. 1926 and 1933, for term ending 1940; dir. Real Estate Title Co. of N.J. Republican. Episcopalian. Mason. Home: Princeton, N.J. Died Jan. 12, 1942.

BUCHANAN, Roberdeau, astronomer; b. Phila., Nov. 22, 1839; s. McKean (pay dir. U.S.N.) and F. Selina (Roberdeau) B.; B.S., Lawrence Scientific Sch. (Harvard), 1861; m. Lyla M. Peters, 1888. Mathematician, Nautical Almanac Office, U.S. Naval Obs.; has made calculations for Nautical Almanac, 1879—. Author: Genealogy of the Roberdeau Family, 1876; Genealogy of the Descendants of Dr. William Shippen, the Elder, 1877; Genealogy of the McKean Family, 1890; Life of Gov. Thomas McKean of Pennsylvania, 1890; Observations on the Declaration of Independence, 1890; Treatise on the Projection of the Sphere, 1890; The Mathematical Theory of Eclipses. Died Dec. 18, 1916.

BUCHANAN, T(homas) Drysdale, M.D.; b. N.Y. City, Mar. 9, 1876; s. James Drysdale and Margaret (Leslie) B.; M.D., N.Y. Homœ. Med. Coll., 1897; m. Anna Marie Kuper, Apr. 24, 1901; 1 dau., Anna Marie. Practiced in N.Y. City, 1898—; prof. anæsthesia, New York Homœ. Med. Coll., 1900-12; apptd. anæsthetist, N.Y. Post-Grad. Med. Sch. and Hosp., Columbia U., 1915, then prof. anæsthesia and head of dept.; dir. anæsthesia Presbyterian Hosp., also of Med. Centre of Columbia U.; cons. anæsthetist Dept. Corrections, N.Y. City. Commd. capt. M.C., U.S.A., Sept. 12, 1918; in charge U.S. Army Sch. of Anæsthesia, Gen. Hosp. No. 14, Ft. Oglethorpe, Ga.; chief of anæsthesia service U.S. Gen. Hosp. 9, Lakewood, N.J., and Base Hosp., Camp Upton, L.I., also mem. bd. spl. court martials, etc., Gen. Hosp. 9; hon. disch., May 1919; maj. M.R.C., 1923; assigned to surg.-gen.'s office, Aug. 1925. Pres. Am. Bd. Anæsthesiology (affiliate Am. Bd. Surgery). Home: New York, N.Y. Died Mar. 21, 1940.

BUCHANAN, Thompson, author; b. N.Y. City, June 21, 1877; s. Rev. Anselan and Willia (Thompson) B.; ed. U. of the South, 1895-97; m. Katharine Winterbotham, June 3, 1915 (divorced, 1927); children—Katharine Roberta, Thompson. On staff of Louisville Commercial, 1897-1900, Courier Journal, 1900-02, Louisville Herald (dramatic critic), 1902-03, New York Evening Journal, 1904-07. Pvt. Co. C, 1st Ky. Vol. Inf., 1898, and served in Spanish-Am. War, Miles Campaign, Puerto Rico; lt. Ky. State Guard, 1900; enlisted in 1st Ky. Inf., 1917, World War; transf. to arty. and promoted sergeant; in France with 138th F.A., 1918; hon. disch. as 1st lt. C Battery, 138th F.A., Camp Taylor, 1919. Editor Goldwyn Pictures, Hollywood, Calif., 1919-20; supervisor Famous Players, 1920-22. Hon. v.p. and life mem. Authors' League America; organizer, 1920, and 1st pres. Screen Writers' Guild, Hollywood; organizer and 1st pres. The Writers, Hollywood; mem. Dramatist Guild. Episcopalian. Author: The Castle Comedy, 1904; Judith Triumphant, 1905; (plays) The Intruder, A Woman's Way, The Cub, The Rack, Lulu's Husbands, Our Daily Bread, Life, Civilian Clothes, The Sporting Thing to Do, Pride, Bluffing Bluffers, Sinner, The Bridal Path, Star of Bengal, As Good As New, The Romantic Fool, Washington Square South. Home: New York, N.Y. Died Oct. 15, 1937.

BUCHANAN, Walter Duncan, clergyman; b. Milwaukee, Wis., Apr. 13, 1859; s. John Mars and Jane McElderry (Douglass) B.; A.B., New York U., 1881, A.M., 1884; grad. Union Theol. Sem., 1883; D.D., U. of Omaha, 1896; LL.D., Whitworth Coll., Spokane, Wash.; m. Grace Mortimer, May 16, 1882 (died 1903). Ordained Presbyn. ministry, 1884; pastor 7th Av. Mission of 5th Av. Ch., 1883-89, Chalmers Ch., New York, 1889-92, 13th Street Ch., 1892-99, Broadway Ch. (formerly 4th Av. Ch.), 1899—. Home: New York, N.Y. Died Feb. 19, 1934.

BUCHANAN, William Insco, director gen. Pan-Am. Expn., Buffalo, N.Y., 1901; b. nr. Covington, Miami Co., O., Sept. 10, 1853; lived on farm and ed. country schools; engrossing clerk Ind. Ho. of Reps., 1874-75; removed to Piqua, O., 1876; Sioux City, Ia., 1882; one of organizers and mgrs. of first four corn palaces at Sioux City; apptd. Dem. mem. from Iowa of World's Columbian Commn.; apptd., 1890, as chief dept. agr., and 1891, in charge live stock and forestry depts. of World's Fair; m. Lulu, d. J. Insco Williams, artist, 1878. E.E. and M.P. to Argentine Republic, 1894-1900; designated by Chilean and Argentine govts., with approval of Congress of each country as deciding arbitrator in spl. boundary commn. to fix the boundary in the Puna de Atacama; as such arbitrator fixed boundary line between Chile and Argentine Republic between latitudes 23° and 26° 52′ 45″ North. Dir. gen. Pan-Am. Expn., Buffalo, 1901; U.S. del. 2d Pan-Am. Conf., Mex., 1902; was 1st U.S. minister to Republic of Panama. Home: Buffalo, N.Y. Died 1909.

BUCHER, August Johannes, editor; b. Zurich, Switzerland, Feb. 7, 1862; s. Jacob and Ursula (Reutemann) B.; ed. in Switzerland; D.D., Syracuse U.; m. Marie Gebhardt, June 23, 1885; m. 2d, A. Bertha Wahl, Feb. 23, 1921. Engaged in pastoral work, 1883-93; prof. Meth. Theol. Sem., Frankfort on Main, 1893-1910; rector German Bethesda Deaconess Inst., 1910-12; editor Haus and Herd, 1912-18; editor Der Christliche Apologete, 1918—. Methodist. Republican. Home: Mt. Auburn, O. Died Jan. 25, 1937.

BUCHER, William Henry, M.D., surgeon; b. Sunbury, Pa., Jan. 1, 1874; s. John Weiser and Mary (Faust) B.; student Bucknell Acad., Lewisburg, Pa., 1891-92; M.D., Medico Chirurg. Coll., Philadelphia, Pa., 1896; m. Elizabeth Marie Skelton, Aug. 1, 1916; children—William Faust, John Edward. Asst. surgeon, U.S.N., 1898-1901, passed asst. surgeon, 1901-03, surgeon, 1903-10; retired, 1910; returned to active list, comdr. U.S. Naval Hosp., San Diego, Calif., 1917-19; med. dir. Central Div. Am. Red Cross, Irkutsk, Siberia, 1919-20; supt. Olive View (Calif.) Sanatorium, 1921—. Republican. Episcopalian. Mason. Home: Olive View, Calif. Died Dec. 30, 1934.

BUCHHOLZ, Ludwig Wilhelm, univ. prof.; b. Christfelde, Germany, Mar. 25, 1855; s. Martin and Wilhelmina (Foese) B.; grad. Evang. Teachers' Sem., Pr. Friedland, Germany, 1875; hon. M.A., Fla. State Coll., Tallahassee, 1902; m. Emma Emilie Klein, of Marienburg, Germany, Nov. 16, 1876 (died 1881); 1 dau., Mary Margaret Rhea; m. 2d, Mary Augustine Wallace, Jan. 31, 1883 (died 1929); children—Albert Wallace, Frederick William; m. 3d, Mrs. Beatrice Gillis McGarrah, June 6, 1931. Came to U.S. in 1880, began teaching school in Hillsborough Co., Fla., 1884; supt. public instruction same county, 1887-1901; prof. pedagogy, later dean, Fla. State Coll. for Women, Tallahassee, Fla., 1901-09; supt. schs. Tampa, Fla. and Hillsborough Co., 1909-13; prof. edn. and English Bible, U. of Fla., 1913—; head of Rehabilitation Div. for disabled soldiers, sailors and marines at the U. of Fla., Jan. 1919—. Organized and taught the first county teachers' training sch. in Fla., 1887; later introduced manual training, domestic science, sch. gardening, boys' corn clubs and girls' canning clubs. Democrat. Mason. Presbyn; del. Gen. Assembly Presbyn. Ch. of U.S., Durant, Okla., 1918; commr. Gen. Assembly, 1933. Author: Teachers' Arithmetic, 1898. Died Apr. 23, 1935.

BUCHHOLZ, William, lawyer; b. Kansas City, Mo., Jan. 28, 1877; s. John and Barbara (Fisher) B.; LL.B., U. of Mo., 1896; m. Sophronia C. Muehlebach, Jan. 23, 1907; children—George John, Margaret Barbara, William, Sophronia C., Robert Muehlebach, James Henry. Admitted to Mo. bar, 1896; asst. pros. atty., Jackson Co., Mo., 1901-03; dir. Massman Constrn. Co., Central Bridge & Constrn. Co. Mem. Bd. of Pub. Works, Kansas City, 1910-15, pres., 1910, 11, 12, mem. Park Bd., 1916-20; pres. Fire and Water Bd., 1923-25, pres. Bd. of Election Commrs., Kansas City, 1929-33; mem. Community Chest Com., Kansas City, 1919-37; trustee Art Inst., Catholic Welfare Bur., Liberty Memorial; mem. advisory com. Kansas City U. Republican. Catholic. Home: Kansas City, Mo. Deceased.

BUCHNER, Edward Franklin, univ. prof.; b. Paxton, Ford Co., Ill., Sept. 3, 1868; s. Christian Jacob and Louise Caroline (Lohmann) B.; A.B., Leander Clark Coll., Toledo, Ia., 1889; post-grad. student, 1890-93; Ph. D., Yale, 1893; m. Hannah Louise Cable, June 1, 1898; children—Edward Franklin, Morgan Mallory, Elizabeth Sanford, Margaret Louise. Instr. in Leander Clark Coll., 1889-90; lecturer, 1892-94, instr. philosophy and pedagogy, 1894-97, Yale; prof. psychology, New York U., 1896-1901; docent in philosophy, Clark U., 1901-03; prof. philosophy and edn., Univ. of Ala., 1903-08; prof. edn. and philosophy, 1908-15, prof. edn., 1915—, dir. Coll. for Teachers, 1909—, and summer courses, 1911—, Johns Hopkins. Spl. collaborator U.S. Bur. Edn., 1914-19. Lecturer on psychology, Brooklyn Inst. Arts and Sciences, 1898-1900, on edn., Goucher Coll., 1911-15; departmental editor of Cyclo. of Edn. Mem. Commn. on Instns. of Higher Edn. of Assn. Colls. and Secondary Schs. of Southern States, 1919—; fellow A.A.A.S. (v.p. and chmn. sect. L, 1917), N.Y. Acad. Sciences. Author: A Study of Kant's Psychology, with Reference to the Critical Philosophy, 1897; translated and edited The Educational Theory of Immanuel Kant, 1904. Contbr. to Warner's Library of the World's Best Literature, 1897, to Annual Reports of U.S. Commr. of Edn., 1914—, and to tech. and ednl. jours. Editor: Johns Hopkins Univ. Studies in Education, 1917—. Coöperating editor Psychol. Bulletin, 1904-13; collaborator Jour. of Ednl. Psychology, 1910-20. Address: Johns Hopkins Univ., Baltimore, Md. Died Sept. 22, 1929.

BUCHTEL, Henry Augustus, univ. chancellor; b. nr. Akron, O., Sept. 30, 1847; s. Dr. Jonathan B. B.; A.B., Asbury (now DePauw) U., 1872, A.M., 1875 (D.D., 1884, LL.D., 1900); m. Mary N. Stevenson, Feb. 4, 1873. Ordained M.E. ministry, 1872; missionary in Bulgaria, 1873; pastor Greencastle, Ind., 1873-76, Knightstown, Ind., 1876-79, Richmond, Ind., 1879-82, LaFayette, Ind., 1882-85, Evans Chapel, Denver, 1885-86, Trinity Ch., Denver, 1886-91, Central Av. Ch., Indianapolis, 1891-96, Calvary Ch., E. Orange, N.J., 1897-99; chancellor U. of Denver, 1900-21, emeritus. Gov. of Colo., 1907-09. Republican. Home: Denver, Colo. Died Oct. 22, 1924.

BUCK, Albert Henry, physician; b. New York, Oct. 20, 1842; s. Dr. Gurdon and Henrietta E. (Wolff) B.; A.B., Yale, 1864; M.D., Coll. Phys. and Surg. (Columbia), 1867; m. Laura S., d. Rev. John S. C. Abbott, of New Haven, Conn., 1871; father of Harold Winthrop B. Clin. prof. diseases of the ear, Coll. Phys. and Surgeons, Columbia, 1888-1904. Editor: Hygiene and Public Health, 1879; Reference Handbook of the Medical Sciences, 1887, 1901; American Practice of Surgery (with Dr. Joseph D. Bryant), 1905-11. Author: Diseases of the Ear, 1876; Vestpocket Medical Dictionary, 1896; The Bucks of Wethersfield, Connecticut, 1909. Home: Hewlett, L.I., N.Y. Died Nov. 16, 1922.

BUCK, Alfred Eliab, E.E.&M.P. of U.S. to Japan, 1897—; b. Foxcroft, Me., 1832; collegiate edn.; m.

Ellen B. Boker, 1864. Fought through Civil war in Union army; settled in South; mem. Congress from Ala. during reconstruction period; presdl. elector, 1868; moved to Atlanta, Ga., where he was clerk U.S. court and later U.S. marshal for Ga.; delegate to 5 Rep. convs. Home: Atlanta, Ga. Died 1902.

BUCK, Benjamin F., publisher; b. Lawrence, Kan., Sept. 30, 1865; s. Asahel and Mary A. (Hutchings) B.; ed. pub. schs. and St. Ann's Acad., Osage Mission, Kan.; m. Carmaleta M. Ferguson, Aug. 16, 1899. Founder, 1896, and pres., B. F. Buck & Co., pubs., N.Y. City. Mem. Nat. Liberal Immigration League (advisory bd.), Nat. Soc. for Promotion of Industrial Edn., Colonial Soc. of Am. (treas. and dir., 1906-14), Italian-Am. Agrl. Assn. (v.p.), Met. Mus. Art (New York). Mem. exec. com. League of Rep. Clubs of State of N.Y. Spl. commr., 1906, to investigate causes of emigration from Southern European countries. Awarded medal, Milan Expn., 1906, in recognition of efforts in behalf of immigrants; chevalier Imperial Order of Rising Sun, Japan, 1908. Mason. Home: New York, N.Y. Died Feb. 16, 1922.

BUCK, Charles William, lawyer; b. Vicksburg, Miss., Mar. 17, 1849; s. John W. and Mary (Bell) B.; S.B., Georgetown (Ky.) Coll., 1870; LL.B., Ky. U., 1871; m. Elizabeth Crow Bullitt, Mar. 17, 1875. Admitted to bar, 1871, St. Louis; practiced in Miss., 1871-74; active there in politics as Dem. in overthrowing carpet-bag rule; practiced law in Louisville, 1874-79, Woodford Co., Ky., 1879-85; magistrate on Woodford Co. (Ky.) bench, 1880-84; E.E. and M.P. of U.S. to Peru, 1885-89; Democrat until 1896, then Gold Democrat, and independent; supported Republican ticket and stumped Ky. in state and nat. campaigns, 1900, 04, 08; advocate of Dem. Party, 1908—. Author: Under the Sun, 1902; Colonel Bob and A Double Love, 1922. Home: Louisville, Ky. Died Nov. 30, 1930.

BUCK, Daniel, lawyer; b. Booneville, N.Y., May 15, 1857; studied law; practiced at Mankato, Minn., until 1894; mem. Minn. legislature, 1866; senate, 1879-81; 5 yrs. mem. State Normal School Bd.; pros. atty., Blue Earth Co., 4 yrs.; asso. justice Supreme Court, Minn., 1894-1900. Democrat. Home: Mankato, Minn. Died 1905.

BUCK, Dudley, organist, composer; b. Hartford, Conn., Mar. 10, 1839; studied at Trinity Coll., then Leipzig Conservatory of Music, and at Dresden and Paris; for several yrs. organist, Music Hall, Boston; was organist Holy Trinity Ch., Brooklyn, and dir. and organist Apollo Club, 25 yrs.; retired, 1903. Composer of orchestral, organ and vocal music. Died 1909.

BUCK, Florence, denominational sec.; b. Kalamazoo Co., Mich., July 19, 1860; d. Samuel Pierce and Lucy (Reasoner) (originally Reznor) B.; ed. Bapt. Coll., Kalamazoo; grad. Meadville (Pa.) Theol. Sch., 1894, D.D., 1920; studied Manchester Coll., Oxford U., Eng., with spl. lectures at Oxford, 1892-93; teacher and head of science dept., Kalamazoo High Sch., 1883-90; ordained Unitarian ministry, 1893; minister Unity Ch., Cleveland, O., 1893-99; field supt. Am. Unitarian Assn. in Mich., with pastorate at Manistee, 1900-01; minister, Kenosha, Wis., 1901-10; supply, Palo Alto, Calif., Aug.-Dec. 1910, Alameda, 1911-12; asso. sec. Dept. Religious Edn., Am. Unitarian Assn., 1912—. Editor The Beacon (weekly children's paper); joint editor Beacon Course in Religious Edn.; lecturer at teachers' training institutes. Dir. Tuckerman Sch., Boston. Author: The Story of Jesus (manual for teachers), 1917; Religious Education for Democracy, 1919. Home: Brookline, Mass. Died Oct. 12, 1925.

BUCK, Frank Henry, capitalist; b. New York, June 8, 1859; s. Leonard William and Anna (Bellows) B.; grad. Clinton (Ia.) High Sch.; m. Annie Stevenson, Apr. 29, 1886. Removed to Vacaville, Calif., 1875, and engaged in fruit growing; was organizer, and then pres. Frank H. Buck Fruit & Shipping Co.; pres. Booth-Kelly Lumber Co., Eugene, Ore.; v.p. Associated Oil Co., West Coast Oil Co., Belridge Oil Co., Rodeo Land & Water Co., Lost Hills Investment Co.; 2d v.p. Amalgamated Oil Co.; dir. Asso. Pipe Line Co., Sterling Oil & Development Co., Bakersfield Iron Works. Home: San Francisco, also Vacaville, Calif. Died Mar. 9, 1916.

BUCK, George Machan, lawyer, writer; b. Skaneateles, New York; s. of Minerson and Hannah M. (Pierce) B.; ed. common schs.; served in Union Army, 1862-65; m. Anne Bradford, Apr. 14, 1869. Admitted to bar, 1865; Circuit Ct. commr., Kalamazoo Co., 1866, 68, 70; pros. atty., Kalamazoo Co., 1871-74; judge of probate, Kalamazoo Co., 1876-84; judge 9th Jud. Circuit, Mich., 1887-99. Republican. Mem. bd. edn., Kalamazoo City, 1882-88; trustee Albion Coll., 1894-1900. Author: Through Stress and Storm, 1900. Home: Kalamazoo, Mich. Died Feb. 2, 1919.

BUCK, George Sturges, mayor; b. Chicago, Ill., Feb. 10, 1875; s. Roswell R. and Maria Catherine (Barnes) B.; B.A., Yale, 1896; LL.B., Buffalo Law Sch., 1898; m. Louise Hussey, Oct. 6, 1903; children—Roswell Seymour, Ruth, Oliver Hussey, Catherine. Began practice of law in Buffalo, 1898; mem. Erie Co. Rep. Com., 1899-1903; mem. Bd. Supervisors, Erie Co., 1904-11; auditor of Erie Co., 1912-17; mayor of Buffalo, 1918-22; in law practice. Presbyn. Mason. Home: Buffalo, N.Y. Died July 5, 1931.

BUCK, Gertrude, coll. prof.; b. Kalamazoo, Mich., July 14, 1871; d. George M. and Anne Bradford B.; B.S., U. of Mich., 1894, M.S., 1895, Ph.D., 1898; fellow in English, U. of Chicago, 1895; unmarried. Asst. in English, U. of Mich., 1896-97; teacher English, Indianapolis High Sch., 1897; instr. English, 1897-1901, asso. prof., 1901-07, prof., 1907—, Vassar Coll. Author: Organic Education (with Miss H. M. Scott), 1899; A Course in Argumentative Writing, 1899; A Course in Expository Writing (with Elisabeth Woodbridge), 1899; The Metaphor—A Study in the Psychology of Rhetoric, 1899; A Brief English Grammar (with Prof. F. N. Scott), 1905; Ruskin's Sesame and Lilies, in Longman's English Classics series, 1906; A Course in Narrative Writing (with Elisabeth Woodbridge Morris), 1906; The Social Criticism of Literature, 1916. Home: Poughkeepsie, N.Y. Died Jan. 8, 1922.

BUCK, Jirah Dewey, physician; b. Fredonia, N.Y., Nov. 20, 1838; s. Reuben and Fanny B.; ed. at Belvidere, Ill.; M.D., Cleveland Homœopathic Coll., 1864; m. Melissa M. Clough, Oct. 3, 1865. Prof. physiology, Cleveland Homœ. Coll., 1866-71; prof. therapeutics and dean, Pulte Med. Coll., 1880—. Pres. Theosophical Soc. in America, 1892-94, Am. Inst. Homœopathy, 1890, Ohio State Homœ. Med. Soc., 1875. Author: A Study of Man and the Way to Health, 1888; Mystic Masonry, 1896; The Soul and Sex in Education. Mason. Home: Walnut Hills, Cincinnati. Deceased.

BUCK, Leffert Lefferts, civil and cons. engr.; b. Canton, N.Y., 1837; grad. St. Lawrence Univ., B.S., 1863 (M.S.); Rensselaer Poly. Inst., C.E., 1868; served in Union army, 60th N.Y. vols., 1861-65; chief engr., New East River bridge; designer and engr. of 2 steel arch bridges at Niagara Falls; Driving Park Av. steel arch bridge, over Genesee River, Rochester, N.Y.; Platt St. bridge, Rochester; Columbia River bridge for Northern Pacific R.R., Pasco, Wash.; Verugas bridge, Peru, S.A., etc.; m. Mira Rebecca Gould, June 4, 1902. Mem. Am. Soc. Civ. Engrs., Mil. Service Instn., Loyal Legion, Burns Soc. Home: Hastings-on-Hudson, N.Y. Died 1909.

BUCK, Oscar MacMillan, prof. missions; b. of Am. missionary parents, Cawnpore, India, Feb. 9, 1885; s. Philo M. (D.D.) and Caroline (MacMillan) B., B.A., Ohio Wesleyan U., 1905, M.A., 1908, D.D., 1925; B.D., Drew Theol. Sem., 1908; m. Berenice Marie Baker, June 20, 1908; children—Nancy Randolph (dec.), Jean MacMillan, Sara Louise. Ordained M.E. ministry, 1909; prof. Bible, Bareilly Theol. Sem., India, 1909-13; pastor in Ill., 1913-15; prof. missions and comparative religion, Ohio Wesleyan U., 1915-19; prof. missions and comparative religion, Drew Theol. Sem. (of Drew Univ.), 1920—. Sec. Commn. on Christian Higher Edn. in India, 1930-31. Author: India Beloved of Heaven (with others), 1918; Working with Christ for India (monograph), 1922; Out of Their Own Mouths, 1926; Our Asiatic Christ, 1927; India Looks to Her Future, 1930; Christianity Tested, 1934. Died Feb. 10, 1941.

BUCK, Philo Melvin, missionary; b. Corning, N.Y., May 15, 1846; s. Ethal Curry and Miriam (Underwood) B.; ed. select school, Highland, Kan.; Drew Theol. Sem., 1878; (hon. A.M., Baker U., Kan., 1889; D.D., Ohio Wesleyan U., 1908); m. Caroline Louisa MacMillan, May 22, 1872; father of Philo Melvin B., Jr. Ordained M.E. ministry, 1865; served in various pastorates, Kan.; apptd. missionary to India, July 1870; served Shahjahanpore, 1871-76; furlough, 1876-78; presiding elder, Kumaon, 1879-84; served, Cawnpore, 1885; furlough and home pastorates, 1886-88; prin. Philander Smith Inst., Mussoorie, India, 1889-92; supt. Meerut dist., 1893-1912, except during furlough; pastoral and evangelistic work, 1914—. Author: Christianity in Doctrine and Experience, 1914. Home: Delaware, O. Died Sept. 8, 1924.

BUCK, Samuel Jay, mathematician; b. Russia, Herkimer Co., N.Y., July 4, 1835; s. Samuel and Amity (Millington) B.; A.B., Oberlin Coll., 1858, A.M., 1862; grad. Theol. Sch., Oberlin, 1862; (D.D., Tabor Coll., Ia., 1903); m. Jane Cory (coll. classmate), Nov. 17, 1859. Ordained Congl. ministry, 1863; pastor Orwell, O., 1861-63, and prin. Orwell Acad., 1860-63; prin. prep. dept., 1864-69, prof. mathematics and natural philosophy, 1869-93, acting pres., 1884-87, prof. mathematics and astronomy, 1893-1905, prof. emeritus, July 4, 1905, Grinnell Coll. Preached at various places while teaching; co. supt. schs., 1866-69; pres. Ia. State Teachers' Assn., 1871; co. surveyor Poweshiek Co., Ia., 1890-1913. Republican. Was the guest of Gov. George W. Goethals on trip of U.S.S. Ancon through the Panama Canal, signalizing opening of the canal, Aug. 15, 1914. Home: Grinnell, Ia. Died May 10, 1918.

BUCKALEW, Charles H., U.S. senator; b. Columbia Co., Pa., Dec. 28, 1821; acad. edn.; studied law; admitted to bar, 1843; pros. atty., Columbia Co., 1845-47; State senator, 1850-58; U.S. minister to Ecuador, 1858-61; U.S. senator, 1863-69; Democratic candidate for gov., 1872; member of Congress, 1887-91. Democrat. Author: Proportional Representation; An Examination of the Constitution of Pennsylvania. Home: Bloomsburgh, Pa. Died 1899.

BUCKBEE, John T., congressman; b. Rockford, Ill., Aug. 1, 1871; s. Theodore E. and Catherine B.; ed. pub. schs. and tech. training in agriculture and horticulture in Europe. Pres. H. W. Buckbee Seed Co., Rockford; mem. 70th to 74th Congresses (1927-37), 12th Ill. Dist. Republican. Home: Rockford, Ill. Died Apr. 22, 1936.

BUCKHAM, James, author; b. Burlington, Vt., Nov. 25, 1858; s. M. H. (pres. Univ. of Vt.) and Elizabeth (Wright) B.; grad. Univ. of Vt., 1881, A.M., 1884; spl. courses, English, Johns Hopkins, 1888, religious journalism, Andover Theol. Sem., 1891-92; m. Mary Brigham, Aug. 28, 1895. In lit. work, 1882—. Author: The Heart of Life (poems), 1897; Where Town and Country Meet, 1903; A Wayside Altar (poems), 1905; Afield with the Seasons, 1907; The Heritage of Life, 1907. Home: Melrose, Mass. Died 1908.

BUCKHAM, Matthew Henry, univ. pres.; b. Hinckley, Leicestershire, Eng., July 4, 1832; s. Rev. James and Margaret (Barmby) B.; came to U.S. in infancy; A.B., U. of Vt., 1851, A.M., 1854; traveled and studied in Europe, 1854-56; (D.D., Dartmouth, and Hamilton, 1877; LL.D., Middlebury, 1900, Dartmouth, 1909); m. Elizabeth Wright, Dec. 27, 1857; 2d, Martha Goddard Tyler, Sept. 2, 1897; father of John Wright B. Prin. Lenox (Mass.) Acad., 1852-53; tutor U. of Vt., 1853-54; prof. Greek lang. and lit., 1859-71, also English lit., 1863-71, pres., 1871—, U. of Vt. Mem. Vt. State Bd. Edn., 1867-74. Author numerous ednl. papers, etc. Home: Burlington, Vt. Died 1910.

BUCKINGHAM, Charles Luman, lawyer; b. Berlin Heights, O., Oct. 14, 1852; ed. U. of Mich. and Columbian Univ. Counsel for Gen. Electric Co., Westinghouse Electric & Mfg. Co., Edison Cos., Del. and Atlantic Telegraph & Telephone Co. and many others; made a specialty of patent and corp. law. Mem. Ohio Soc., Univ. of Mich. Alumni Assn. Home: New York, N.Y. Died 1909.

BUCKINGHAM, Edgar, physicist; b. Phila., Pa., July 8, 1867; s. Lucius Henry and Angelina Bradley (Hyde) B.; A.B., Harvard, 1887; post-grad. work same, 1887-89, U. of Strassburg, 1889-90, Ph.D., Leipsic, 1893; m. Elizabeth Branton Holstein, July 15, 1901; children—Katharine, Stephen Alvord. Asst. in physics, Harvard, 1888-89, 1891-92, Strassburg, 1889-90; mem. faculty, Bryn Mawr Coll., 1893-99; instr. physics, U. of Wis., 1901-02; asst. physicist Bur. of Soils, U.S. Dept. Agr., 1902-05; with Bur. of Standards, 1905-37, was physicist same. Lecturer on thermodynamics, Grad. Sch. U.S. Naval Acad., 1910-12; asso. scientific attaché, U.S. Embassy, Rome, Italy, 1918. Author: An Outline of the Theory of Thermodynamics, 1900. Home: Chevy Chase, Md. Died Apr. 29, 1940.

BUCKLEY, Ernest Robertson, mining geologist; b. Milbury, Mass., Sept. 3, 1872; s. Thomas M. and Grace R. B.; B.S., U. of Wis., 1895; Ph.D., 1898; married. Dir. Bur. of Geology and Mines of Mo. and state geologist, 1901-08; mining geologist, Federal Lead Co., 1908—. Author: Building and Ornamental Stones of Wisconsin, 1898; Clays and Clay Industries in Wisconsin, 1900; Highway Construction in Wisconsin, 1902; Quarrying Industry of Missouri, 1904; Public Roads in Missouri; The Geology of the Granby Area; The Geology of the Disseminated Lead Deposits of St. Francois and Madison Counties, Missouri. Home: Rolla, Mo. Died Jan. 19, 1912.

BUCKINGHAM, George Tracy, lawyer; b. Delphi, Ind., Apr. 21, 1864; s. Tracy Wilson and Helen (Clark) B.; desc. Thomas Buckingham, Puritan settler of New Haven and Milford, Conn., 1637-38; removed to Ill., 1870; ed. common sch. to 1880; employed on farm, brickyard and store, 1880-90; student at night, law office, Danville, Ill., 1886-90; m. Victoria Donlon, 1894 (died 1922); 1 son, Tracy Wilson; m. 2d, Carol Allen, Jan. 30, 1926. Admitted to Ill. bar, 1890; spl. agt. U.S. Treasury (New York, Boston, Can. and Europe), 1890-94; practiced at Danville, 1894-1908; asst. state's atty., 1894-98; del. to many convs., including Nat. Rep. Conv., 1904, 08; settled in Chicago, 1908; mem. Defrees, Buckingham, Jones & Hoffman (firm consisting of 10 partners and 20 associate lawyers). Trustee Illinois State Hosp., Kankakee, 1897-1901; pres. bd. trustees Joliet Prison, 1901-05; dir. or trustee numerous civic instns. Mem. Ill. N.G., 1886-1904; lt. col., Spanish-Am. War; pres. Nat. Security League, World War. Republican. Methodist. Mason. Home: Lake Forest, Ill. Died Sept. 9, 1940.

BUCKINGHAM, Norman S., lawyer; b. Milford, Conn., Apr. 30, 1881; s. John W. and Alice M. (Baldwin) B.; grad. high sch., Milford, 1897; m. Anna E. Munson, Oct. 11, 1913; children—Norman S., Philip M., Athala. Began as clk., law dept. N.Y.,N.H.&H. R.R. Co., 1898, successively chief clk., asst. atty., (admitted to Conn. bar 1913), asst. solicitor, counsel for Conn., asst. gen. counsel, gen. counsel and gen.

solicitor. Republican. Conglist. Home: Milford, Conn. Died Nov. 30, 1940.

BUCKLEY, Albert Coulson, neuropsychiatrist; b. Phila., Pa., Aug. 6, 1873; s. William Coulson (M.D.) and Lucy Ann (Davis) B.; A.B., Central High Sch., Phila., 1894; M.D., Medico-Chirurg. Coll., Phila., 1897; m. Harriet Ellis Baily, 1904. Asst. neurologist, Medico-Chirurg. Hosp., 1897-1906; asso. prof. normal histology, Medico-Chirurg. Coll., 1899-1908; asso. prof. psychiatry same, 1908-17; asst. neurologist, Phila. Gen. Hosp., 1906-12; asst. phys. Friends Hospital, 1906-18; med. supt. same, 1918—; alienist Phila. Orthopedic Hosp., 1912-21; prof. psychiatry, Grad. Sch. of Medicine of U. of Pa., 1919—; asso. prof. psychiatry, School of Medicine, same, 1930—; neurologist Frankford Hosp., 1930; hon. cons. psychiatrist, Phila. Gen. Hosp., 1931—. Diplomat Am. Board Psychiatry and Neurology, 1936. Fellow Coll. Physicians of Phila., A.M.A.; Author: The Basis of Psychiatry, 1920; Nursing Mental and Nervous Diseases, 1927. Died Aug. 17, 1939.

BUCKLEY, James Monroe, editor; b. Rahway, N.J., Dec. 16, 1836; s. Rev. John and Abbie L. (Monroe) B.; ed. Pennington (N.J.) Sem., and 1 yr. at Wesleyan U.; studied medicine, 1866-69; studied theology, Exeter, N.H.; (hon. A.M., Wesleyan, 1869, D.D., 1872; LL.D., Emory and Henry Coll., 1882; L.H.D., Syracuse U.). Entered M.E. ministry, 1859; pastor Exeter, Dover and Manchester, N.H., 1858-62; Detroit, 1863-66, Brooklyn, 1866-69, Stamford, Conn., 1869-72, Brooklyn, 1872-75, Stamford, 1875-78, Brooklyn, 1878-80, editor New York Christian Advocate, 1880-1912. Pres. M.E. Hosp., Brooklyn, 1882-1916, pres. emeritus. Del. Gen. Conf., 1872—, Ecumenical Confs., London, 1881, Washington, 1891, Toronto, 1911. Author: Travels in Three Continents—Europe, Asia, Africa; Extemporaneous Oratory for Professional and Amateur Speakers; The Fundamentals and Their Contrasts, 1906; The Wrong and Peril of Woman Suffrage, 1909; Constitutional and Parliamentary History of the Methodist Episcopal Ch., 1912. Home: Morristown, N.J. Died Feb. 8, 1920.

BUCKLIN, Edward C., mfr. cotton goods; vice pres. Interlaken Mills, mfrs. cotton goods and book cover cloths; dir. Firemen's Mut. Ins. Co., Mercantile Mut. Fire Ins. Co., Narragansett Mut. Fire Ins. Co., Providence Mut. Fire Ins. Co. Home: Providence, R.I. Died Apr. 3, 1934.

BUCKLIN, James W., lawyer; b. Big Rock, Kane Co., Ill., Nov. 13, 1856; s. George and Arethusa (Winch) B.; ed. Wheaton (Ill.) Coll., 2 yrs.; LL.B., U. of Mich., 1877; m. Mary Lapham, Jan. 1, 1895. Admitted to bar, 1877; practiced Grand Junction, Colo. One of six original locators and founders of city of Grand Junction, Colo., 1881. Mem. Colo. Ho. of Rep., 1885, 1897, Senate, 1898-1902; mayor Grand Junction, 1886; city atty., 1890-92 and 1909-12; co. atty., Mesa Co., Colo., 1894; chmn. Colo. Revenue Commn. to Australia, 1898-1900; active single taxes. Wrote: Report of the Revenue Commission of Colorado, pamphlet, 1901 (also printed in Congressional Record); also many mag. articles, lectures on municipal and social problems. Pres. Grand Junction Charter Conv., 1909, and "father" of its charter, declared to be "the most democratic municipal charter ever adopted"; author of "Preferential Ballot" system in America, now adopted in a number of cities. Retired from practice of law, 1914, to devote attention to lecturing and writing. Home: Grand Junction, Colo. Died July 14, 1919.

BUCKNAM, Ransford D., naval adviser and a.d.c. to H.I.M. The Sultan; b. Hansport, N.S., 1869; s. Ezra Taylor and Isabella (Roscoe) B.; ed. pub. schs. of Me. and N.Y.; m. Rose Thayer, Jan. 2, 1904. Removed with parents to Me. when an infant; lived nr. Bucksport; went to sea in merchant sailing ships at 14 yrs. of age; comd. merchant steam and sailing ships on both Atlantic and Pacific Coasts and Great Lakes. Was supt. Am. Steel Barge Co. of N.Y., Pacific Mail Steamship Co. at Panama; Cramps' shipyards, Phila.; trial comdr. U.S.S. "Maine," and Imperial Ottoman steamship "Medjidia," comd. latter from Phila. to Turkey and apptd. naval adviser and personal a.d.c. to the Sultan, Constantinople, Apr. 19, 1904. Decorated with Turkish Order of Osmanieh, and distinguished service medal. Republican. Died May 27, 1915.

BUCKNER, Emory Roy, lawyer; b. Pottawatomie Co., Ia., Aug. 7, 1877; s. J. D. M. and Sarah A. (Ellis) B.; A.B., U. of Neb., 1904; LL.B., Harvard, 1907; m Katherine Keach, Apr. 4, 1901; children—Ruth Farlow, Elizabeth, Jean. Admitted to N.Y. bar, 1908, and then practiced at N.Y. City; asst. U.S. atty., Southern Dist. of N.Y., 1908-10; asst. dist. atty. New York County, 1910-12; counsel Aldermanic Police Investigation of N.Y. City, 1912-13; U.S. Dist. atty. Southern Dist. of N.Y., by apptmt. of Pres. Coolidge, 1925-27; mem. Root, Clark, Buckner & Ballantine. Special asst. atty. gen. New York state, to investigate and prosecute city officials, 1927-29. Republican. Home: New York, N.Y. Died Mar. 11, 1941.

BUCKNER, Simon Bolivar, soldier; b. on farm, Hart Co., Ky., Apr. 1, 1823; s. Hon. Aylett Hartswell and Elizabeth Ann (Morehead) B.; grad. U.S. Mil. Acad., 1844; m. Delia Claiborne, 1886. Bvt. 2d lt. 2d U.S. Inf., July 1, 1844; 2d lt. 6th Inf., May 9, 1846; regimental q.m., Aug. 8-Dec. 17, 1847; bvtd. 1st lt., Aug. 20, 1847, for gallant and meritorious conduct at battle of Churubusco, Mex., and capt., Sept. 8, 1847, for same at battle of Moline del Rey, Mex.; asst. instr. ethics, West Point, 1845-46, asst. instr. inf. tactics, 1848-50; 1st lt., Dec. 31, 1851; capt. commissary of subsistance, Nov. 3, 1852; resigned from U.S.A., Mar. 26, 1855. Insp.-gen., Ky., 1860-61; brig. gen. C.S.A., Sept. 1861; prisoner of war, Feb.-Aug. 1862; maj. gen., 1863; lt. gen., Sept. 1864, Gov. Ky., 1887-91; mem. Ky. Constl. Conv., 1891; candidate for V.P. of U.S. on Gold Democrat ticket, 1896. Home: Munfordville, Ky. Died Jan. 8, 1914.

BUCKNER, Walker, life ins. exec.; b. Independence, Mo., Mar. 16, 1871; s. Walker and Margaret Ann (Tully) B.; ed. pub. and pvt. schs.; m. Eva Orton, Dec. 11, 1894; children—Tully Orton, Walker Thornton, John Jay, Lewis Probasco. With N.Y. Life Ins. Co., 1885—, cashier St. Paul office, 1890-92, agency dir., 1892-94, agency dir. and supervisor, St. Louis office, 1894-1902, inspector of agencies, 1902-04, trans. to Paris as supt. of agencies European Dept., later 2d v.p. in charge of company's European affairs, 1904-14, trans. New York office, 1914, promoted to v.p., 1925, exec. v.p., 1936—. Trustee Am. and Foreign Christian Union; pres. Nat. Music League, Inc. Apptd. Comdr. Order of the Crown of Italy, 1913. Ind. Republican. Conglist. Home: New York, N.Y. Died Nov. 12, 1939.

BUDD, Charles Jay, illustrator; b. S. Schodack, Rensselaer Co., N.Y., Feb. 14, 1859; s. John Steves and Rosalind E. (Masten) B.; ed. Troy Conf. Acad., Claverack Coll., Hudson River Inst.; art edn. Pa. Acad. Fine Arts, Phila., and Art Students' League, New York; m. Carrie Louise Tillapaugh, Oct. 27, 1892; 1 son, Wilfred Wells. Began illustrating children's mags. and books in Phila., 1885; removed to New York, 1890; has illustrated for most of leading mags.; supervised and illustrated many ednl. books; regular contbr. to "Life," 1894-1917; cartoonist on Harper's Weekly, 1912-13. Head of C. J. Budd Co., mfrs. artistic gifts, etc. Exhibited paintings Nat. Acad. Design. Republican. Author: Around the World in Eighty Minutes; Old Fables Modernized. Home: East Orange, N.J. Died Mar. 1926.

BUDD, James Herbert, lawyer, gov.; b. Janesville, Wis., May 18, 1853; went to Calif. in boyhood; grad. Univ. of Calif., 1873; m. Inez A. Merrill, 1873; admitted to bar, 1873, settled in practice at Stockton; became trustee Stockton Library; pres. bd. of police and fire commr.; congressman, 1883-85; declined renomination; gov., Calif., 1895-99. Democrat. Home: Stockton, Calif. Died 1908.

BUEHLER, Huber Gray, headmaster; b. Gettysburg, Pa., Dec. 3, 1864; s. David A. and Fannie J. (Guyon) B.; A.B., Pa. Coll., 1883, A.M., 1886; grad. Gettysburg Theol. Sem., 1889; A.M., Yale, 1905; Litt.D., Pa. Coll., 1909; m. Roberta Wolf, June 14, 1893. Ordained Luth. ministry, 1889; Instr. Latin and Greek Coll. of St. James, Md., 1883-85; prof. Pa. Coll., 1885-92; English master, 1892-1904, headmaster, 1904—, Hotchkiss Sch., Lakeville, Conn. Author: Practical Exercises in English, 1895; Modern English Grammar, 1900; Modern English Lessons, 1903; Aldine Third Language Book, and Teachers' Manual, 1917. Editor: Macaulay's Life of Samuel Johnson, 1896. Home: Lakeville, Conn. Died June 20, 1924.

BUEHLER, William Emmett; b. Hatboro, Montgomery Co., Pa., Jan. 27, 1869; s. George Washington and Alice (Lewis) B.; M.D., Coll. of Medicine and Surgery, Chicago, 1904, and Valparaiso (Indiana) Univ., 1905; post-grad. work, Hering Med. Coll., Bennett Med. Coll., Am. Coll. of Medicine and Surgery (all of Chicago), also in Vienna, Austria; m. Ella May Abel, Sept. 5, 1893 (died 1933). In practice of medicine at Chicago, 1904—; prof. obstetrics Hering Med. Coll., 1907-08, prof. anatomy Bennett Med. Coll., 1907, minor surgery, 1908-09. Served as mem. Mayor Dever's Safety Commn. Del. Internat. Congress Physicians and Surgeons, Budapest, 1909; founder, pres. emeritus and trustee Ill. Masonic Hosp. Assn. Supreme dictator Loyal Order of Moose, July 1934-Sept. 1, 1935. Mason. Baptist. Home: Chicago, Ill. Died Sept. 19, 1938.

BUEHLER, William George, rear adm. U.S.N.; b. Phila., Mar. 25, 1837; s. William Olds and Henrietta Ruhamah B.; removed to Harrisburg, Pa., 1844, and was ed. in pvt. schs. there. Entered U.S.N. as 3d asst. engr., in May 1857; 2d asst. engr., Oct. 8, 1861; 1st asst. engr., Oct. 6, 1862; chief engr., Nov. 10, 1863; capt., June 4, 1894; rear adm. and retired, Mar. 25, 1899; officer U.S.S. frigate Niagara when 1st Atlantic telegraph was laid (received gold medal N.Y. Chamber of Commerce); served during Civ. War, chief engr. U.S.S. Aroostook, 1861-62; U.S.S. Galena, 1863-65; participated in attacks on James River and Ft. Darling, at passage of forts at entrance of Mobile Bay under Farragut, etc.; engr. on various ships until 1888; mem. U.S. Naval Bd. Inspection 4 yrs.; twice mem. Examining Bd. Naval Engrs.; in charge dept. steam engring. Navy Yard, Portsmouth, N.H., 1894-99. Home: Philadelphia. Died Aug. 10, 1919.

BUEK, Gustave Herman, lithographer; b. Boston, Aug. 25, 1850; s. Herman and Augusta (Siemers) B.; ed. pub. sch., Brooklyn, and 2 yrs. in pvt. sch., Schmieder & Deghuée, Brooklyn; m. Louisa Valentine, Apr. 30, 1873. Apprenticed to Hatch & Co., lithographers, N.Y., 1866; later took charge of art dept. of newly established firm of Donaldson Bros.; started firm of Buek & Lindner, 1881, which soon after became G. H. Buek & Co.; joined in formation of Am. Lithographic Co., New York, 1891, of which is a v.p.; pres. Alco-Gravure, Inc.; dir. Crowell Pub. Co. Was first to introduce facsimile water-color work into commercial lithography. Republican. Home: Brooklyn, N.Y. Died Feb. 8, 1927.

BUEL, Clarence Clough, editor; b. Laona, Chautauqua Co., N.Y., July 29, 1850; attended U. of Minn., 1870-72, U. of Berlin, 1872-73, Poly. Sch. and U. of Munich, 1873-74; m. Mary Alice Snow, Sept. 12, 1888 (died 1898); 2d, Maria Victoria Torrilhon, Apr. 24, 1903. Asst. editor Minneapolis Tribune, 1874-75; on staff New York Tribune, 1875-81; asso. editor Century Mag. Nov. 1881-1910, asso. editor, 1910-13, advisory editor until May, 1914. Editor (with Robert Underwood Johnson) Battles and Leaders of the Civil War (4 vols.). Died May 22, 1933.

BUEL, James William, author; b. Golconda, Ill., Oct. 22, 1849; s. Alexander H. and Sarah (Jones) B.; ed. U. of Ill., class of 1872; m. Eliza Brawner, 1871 (died 1897); 2d, Annie E. Hill, June 5, 1901. Edited country paper in Kan., 1870-71; reporter on daily papers, Kansas City and St. Louis, 1873-78; traveled through Siberia, 1882, visiting convict camps. Author: The Living World, 1891; The Story of Man, 1891; Columbus and Columbia, 1893; The Magic City, 1893; Buel's Manual of Self Help, 1894; America's Wonderlands, 1894; Beautiful Paris, 1895; Roses and Thorns of Paris and London, 1897; The Great Operas (10 sections), 1899; Great Achievements of the Century, 1900; Hero Tales, 1900; McKinley and His Times, 1900; Library of American History, 1901; The Impending Crisis, 1903; Louisiana and the Fair (10 vols.), 1904 (collaborated with Hon. James G. Blaine, Prof. John Clark Ridpath, and Rev. T. De Witt Talmage). Mng. editor and collaborator (with Prof. Rasmus B. Anderson), Norroena (15 vols.), 1906. Home: San Diego, Calif. Died Nov. 16, 1920.

BUELL, Augustus C., author, civ. engr.; b. Norwich, N.Y., Sept. 4, 1847; s. Simon and Julia B.; ed. pub. schs., Norwich to 1862; served in Army of Potomac, 1863-65; at Cazenovia Sem., 1865, until grad. 1868; studied civ. engring. and surveying; m. Madeleine T. Polk, Mar. 11, 1878; 2d, Gertrude Boyer Wickline, Sept. 4, 1896. In civ. engring., 1868-73; journalism, 1873-83; sec. to Charles H. Cramp, shipbuilder, 1883—. Republican since 1896; previously Democrat. Author: The Cannoneer—Recollections of a Private Soldier, 1890; Life of Paul Jones, 1900; Life of Sir William Johnson, 1903. Died 1904.

BUELL, Caroline Brown, lecturer; b. Marlboro, Mass., Oct. 24, 1843; d. Rev. Thomas Gibson Brown; ed. pub. and pvt. schs.; m. Lt. F. W. H. Buell, Aug. 25, 1862 (died in war). Mem. quorum pub. com. "Our Union," 1876-83; corr. sec. Conn. W.C.T.U., 1875-76 (pres. 1904); asst. recording sec., Nat. W.C.T.U., 1878-80, corr. sec., 1880-93; originated the plan of the Loyal Temperance Legion (children's soc. of W.C.T.U.). Has written extensively for temperance publs. and other papers and mags. Home: E. Hampton, Conn. Died Oct. 13, 1927.

BUELL, Charles Edward, electro. mech. engr.; b. Torrington, Conn., May 4, 1841; s. Joseph Case and Mary (Kellogg) B.; ed. Wesleyan Acad., Wibraham, Mass.; m. Annie F. Cooper. Entered army, Co. E, 10th Mass. vols., April 27, 1861; hon. disch. April 23, 1863 (wounds). Registered patent atty., solicitor of patents. Entered telegraph service, 1864, worked for Am. Tel. Co., Western Union Tel. Co., The Franklin Tel. Co., Bankers and Brokers' Tel. Co., as supt. Bankers and Merchants' Tel. Co., building lines; 3 yrs., 1865-68, ticket agent 4 railroads at Albany, N.Y.; 8 yrs., 1872-80, accountant N.Y.,N.H.& H. R.R., New Haven, Conn.; pres. U.S. Telephone Co.; pres. The Buell Elec. and Hydraulic Mfg. Co., (fire protection); spl. agt. class Telegraph and Telephones, U.S. 10th census, 1880; chief of div., class chs., 11th U.S. census, 1890; sec. U.S. spl. commn. to Puerto Rico, 1898-99. Republican. Seventh-day Sabbath-keeper. Home: Camden, N.J. Died 1903.

BUELL, Marcus Darius, theologian; b. Wayland, N.Y., Jan. 1, 1851; s. Rev. Enoch George and Maria (Brownson) B.; A.B., New York U., 1872, fellow, 1872, A.M., 1873; S.T.B., Boston U., 1875; student, Cambridge, Eng., 1884; Berlin, 1885, Heidelberg, 1892-93; D.D., New York U., 1888; m. Edith V. Houghton, Dec. 13, 1875 (died 1931). Entered M.E. ministry, 1875; pastor at Brooklyn, N.Y., and Hartford, Conn., 1879-84; prof. N.T. Greek and exegesis, 1884-1922, asst. dean., 1885-89, dean, 1889-1904, prof. and dean emeritus, 1922—, Boston U. Sch. of

Theology. Bibl. lecturer in China and Japan, 1916. Mem. Gen. Conf. M.E. Ch., 1908; trustee Bd. of Edn. of M.E. Ch., 1912-24. Author: Studies in the Greek Text of the Gospel of Mark, 1890; Autographs of St. Paul, 1912. Home: Winter Park, Fla. Died Nov. 24, 1933.

BUENTING, Otto Wilhelm, v.p. Westinghouse Air Brake Co.; b. Hanover, Kan., May 28, 1873; s. John Wert and Christiana (Schmidt) B.; M.E., Purdue U., 1901; m. Harriet E. Richards, Aug. 12, 1913; children—Elizabeth, Otto William, Robert Ernst, Harriet Ann. Began as machinist apprentice on C.,B.&Q. Ry. Co., 1889; inspector, foreman, later works mgr., Westinghouse Air Brake Co., 1901-17, gen. works mgr., 1917-26, v.p. in charge of mfr., 1927—; also v.p. in charge of mfr. Union Switch & Signal Co. Presbyn. Mason. Home: Pittsburgh, Pa. Died July 27, 1941.

BUFFALO CHILD LONG LANCE, author; b. Mont.; s. Peetah and Eagle's Woman; honor grad. Carlisle (Pa.) Indian Sch., 1909; student Dickinson Coll., Carlisle, 1912-13; grad. Manlius (N.Y.) Mil. Acad., 1915, grad. study, 1915-16; unmarried. Apptd. to West Point Mil. Acad. by President Wilson, 1916, but relinquished appmt. to enter World War; served 3 yrs. with Canadian Army; wounded twice; investigator, contra-espionage, Gen. Staff Intelligence, London, 1918-19; capt., 50th Bn., Calgary, Alberta, Can. Lecturer on N.A. Indian, Am. Mus. Natural History; engaged in Indian research work in Northwest Tys. for Ont. Archæol. Soc., 1923; lecturer for U.S. Bur. Economics, 1924-25; mem. Burden Expdn. into Far North, Am. Mus. Natural History, 1928-29. Decorated Croix de Guerre (France). Author: Long Lance, 1928. Wrote "When the Crees Moved West." Contbr. to Cosmopolitan, Century, The Mentor, McClure's. Chief of Blood Band of Blackfeet Indians. Licensed as commercial airplane pilot. Died 1932.

BUFFINGTON, Adelbert Rinaldo, army officer; b. Wheeling, Va., Nov. 22, 1837; grad. U.S. Mil. Acad., 1861; m. Eliza Allston White, May 14, 1873. Commd. add. 2d lt. ordnance, May 6, 1861; 2d lt., May 14, 1861; capt., Mar. 3, 1863; maj., June 23, 1874; lt. col., June 1, 1881; col., Feb. 28, 1889; brig. gen. and chief of ordnance U.S.A., Apr. 5, 1899; retired, Nov. 22, 1901. Was bvtd. maj., Mar. 13, 1865, "for faithful and meritorious services" in Ordnance Dept. In command Nat. Armory, 1881-82, Rock Island Arsenal, 1892-97. Originator various improvements in ordnance, also methods of mfg. small arms. Home: Madison, N.J. Died July 10, 1922.

BUFFINGTON, Eugene Jackson, capitalist; b. Guyandotte, W.Va., Mar. 14, 1863; s. James H. and Columbia (Nicholas) B.; student Chickering Inst., Cincinnati, 1879-80, Vanderbilt U., 1881-83; m. Drucilla Nicholas Moore, Nov. 27, 1888. Treas. Am. Wire & Nail Co., Anderson, Ind., 1884-98; sec. and treas. Am. Steel & Wire Co., 1898; pres. Ill. Steel Co., 1899-1932; pres. Ind. Steel Co., Gary Land Co. Trustee Community Trust of Chicago, Y.M.C.A. of Chicago, Vanderbilt U., Chicago Sunday Evening Club. Home: Evanston, Ill. Died Dec. 9, 1937.

BUFFUM, George Tower, author; b. Winchester, N.H., Mar. 16, 1846; s. Sampson Wilder and Mary Eliza (Tower) B.; A.B., Amherst, 1868; m. Ethel E. Brown, Sept. 2, 1873. Began in mercantile business, St. Louis, 1871; traveling salesman in Western U.S., Alaska, Mexico, and South Africa, 1878-1908; lumber business, 1882—. Republican. Conglist. Mason. Author: Smith of Bear City and other Frontier Sketches, 1906; On Two Frontiers, 1918. Home: Winchester, N.H. Died Mar. 9, 1926.

BUFFUM, Robert Earle; b. Keene, N.H., June 16, 1879; s. Charles Cornelius and Sarah L. (Willson) B.; LL.B., Boston U., 1901; m. Myrta E. Smith, Sept. 7, 1909. Admitted to N.H. bar, 1901, Mass. bar same yr. and then practiced in Boston; mem. Abbott, Dane, Buffum & Howe. Town meeting mem. Belmont, Mass., 1927—. Pres. The First Ch. of Christ, Scientist, Boston, 1931-32. Republican. Mason. Home: Belmont, Mass. Died Sept. 26, 1932.

BUGBEE, Lester Gladstone, adjunct prof. history, Univ. of Tex.; b. Woodbury, Tex., May 16, 1869; s. Almon and Fannie (Nunn) B.; ed. Mansfield Coll., Tex., 1883-87, Univ. of Tex., 1887-91, 1890-93; grad. Univ. of Tex., B.Litt., 1892; M.A., 1893; Univ. fellow in history, Columbia Univ., 1893-94, 1894-95; unmarried. Corr. sec. and treas. Tex. State Hist. Assn.; mem. Public Archives Commn., Am. Hist. Assn. Writer of hist. articles in reviews, etc. Home: Austin, Tex. Died 1902.

BUHL, Arthur Hiram, capitalist; b. Detroit, Mich., Feb. 11, 1878; s. Theodore DeLong and Julia Elizabeth (Walker) B.; ed. pub. schs.; m. Clara E. May, 1902; children—C. Henry, Julia Elizabeth (Mrs. Julia E. Kugeman), Arthur H. Pres. Buhl Sons Co., wholesale hardware, 1916—; pres. Buhl Land Co., Land Investment Co.; v.p. Parke, Davis & Co., Buhl Stamping Co., Sattley Co.; dir. James S. Holden Co. Republican. Presbyn. Died Sept. 26, 1935.

BUICK, James McNair, corp. official; b. Detroit, Mich., Nov. 7, 1867; s. James S. and Ellen (McNair) B.; ed. pub. and high schs., Detroit. Began, 1880, in shops of Mich. Car Co., Detroit; asst. supt. Mich. Peninsular Car Co., 1892, later auditor; gen. auditor Am. Car and Foundry Co., St. Louis, 1899, later vice-pres. Died 1929.

BUIST, George Alexander, college prof.; b. Greenville, S.C., Apr. 6, 1877; s. Edward Tongué and Flora Ann (McNeill) B.; B.S., Furman U., Greenville, 1898; M.S., Vanderbilt, 1900; m. Ida Angeline Robbins, Sept. 14, 1911; children—Gertrude Robbins, Flora Laura, Ida Angeline. Instr. chemistry, Vanderbilt, 1899-1900; prof. physical and biol. sciences, Winchester (Tenn.) Normal Coll., 1900-07; asst. in science, 1907-11, acting prof. chemistry and biology, 1911-18, prof., 1918-24, prof. chemistry, 1924—, Furman U., sec. faculty and curator mus., instr. and lecturer on science, Summer Sch., 1929-1933; mgr. and treas. Greenville Artist and Lecture Course Assn.; sec. City Dem. Exec. Com. Fellow S.C. Acad. Science, A.A.A.S. Democrat. Presbyn. Home: Greenville, S.C. Died Feb. 26, 1934.

BUIST, George Lamb, lawyer; b. Charleston, S.C., Sept. 4, 1838; s. George and Mary Edwards (Jones) B.; ed. Charleston schools and Charleston Coll.; admitted to bar, 1860; m. Martha Allston White, 1862. Entered C.S.A., 1861, as lt. Palmetto Guard, participated in bombardment of Ft. Sumter and had command of one of iron guns in iron battery on Morris Island. Served through entire war, becoming maj. of arty. Had practiced in Charleston, 1865—, senior mem. Buist and Buist. Mem. Ho. Reps., S.C., 1877-80, senate, 1882-98. Trustee Charleston Coll.; commr. public schools of Charleston; took prominent position in favor of enlarged edn. facilities for S.C. while in senate. Democrat. Home: Charleston, S.C. Died 1907.

BUIST, John Somers, surgeon; b. Charleston, S.C., Nov. 26, 1839; A.B., Charleston Coll., 1858, later A.M.; M.D., Med. Coll. State of S.C., 1861. Prof. surgery, Med. Coll. State of S.C.; commr. Roper Hosp.; mem. Charleston Bd. Health; pres. Med. Soc. of S.C. Author many scientific and med. articles. Home: Charleston, S.C. Died 1910.

BULKELEY, Morgan Gardner, senator; b. E. Haddam, Conn., Dec. 26, 1837; s. Eliphalet Adams (1st pres. Ætna Life Ins. Co.) and Lydia S. (Morgan) B.; family removed to Hartford, Conn., 1846; ed. high school, Hartford; (hon. A.M., Yale U., 1889; LL.D., Trinity Coll., 1917); was merchant in Brooklyn; served in 13th N.Y. Regt. during Civil War; returned to Hartford, 1872; m. Fannie B. Houghton, Feb. 11, 1885. Organized, 1872, and 1st pres., 1872-79, U.S. Bank of Hartford; pres. Ætna Life Ins. Co., 1879—. Councilman, 1875, alderman, 1876, mayor, 1880-88, of Hartford; elected gov. Conn., for term, 1889-91, and as no candidate for election in 1890 received constl. majority of votes cast, he retained office as gov. for term, 1891-93; candidate for U.S. senator, 1893; elected U.S. senator, 1905, for term 1905-11. Del. Rep. nat. convs., 1888-96. Mem. G.A.R. (dept. comdr. of Conn.). Home: Hartford, Conn. Died Nov. 6, 1922.

BULKLEY, Frank, mining engr.; b. Monroe, Mich., July 10, 1857; s. Gershom Tainter and Fidelia (Groendycke) B.; E.M., Colo. Sch. of Mines, 1897; m. Luella Bergstresser, Jan. 22, 1885. Engaged in mining in Colo., 1879—; pres. Crested Butte Anthracite Mining Co., Crested Butte Coal Co., Baldwin Fuel Co., Erie Coal Co., Walsenburg Fuel Co.; formerly gen. mgr. New Pittsburgh Mining Co. (Leadville, Colo.), Rock Hill Consol. Gold and Silver Mining Co., Robinson Consol. Gold and Silver Mining Co., New Robinson Mining Co., Mollie Gibson Con. Mining Co. (Aspen, Colo.), Bushwhacker Mining Co., Aspen Mining and Smelting Co., Park Regent Mines, Dyer Mine, Morning and Evening Star Mines; mgr Marion Mines & Mill Co. Pres. bd. trustees Colo. Sch. of Mines, 1896-1912; mem. Ho. of Rep., Colo., 1885-89. Democrat. Episcopalian. Home: Denver, Colo. Died Mar. 25, 1928.

BULKLEY, George Grant, pres. Springfield Fire & Marine Ins. Co., Sentinel Fire Ins. Co., New England Fire Ins. Co., Mich. Fire & Marine Ins. Co.; v.p. Holyoke Water Power Co.; v.p. and mem. finance com. Springfield Instn. for Savings; dir. Afia Finance Corp., Eaton Paper Co., Holyoke Power & Electric Co., Holyoke Street Ry. Co., Package Machinery Co., Springfield Street Ry., Third Nat. Bank & Trust Co.; mem. exec. com. Arbitration Com. and Conf. with Insurance Depts. Com., Eastern Underwriters Assn. Mem. Arbitration Com. and Conf. with Insurance Departments Com. Eastern Underwriters Assn.; mem. board of incorporators advisory board trustees corp. com., Community Chest; mem. exec., finance and membership coms., Nat. Bd. of Fire Underwriters; dir. Fire Companies Adjustment Bur., Nat. Bd. of Fire Underwriters Bldg. Corp.; trustee and mem. finance com. Wilbraham Acad.; v.p. and trustee Am Foreign Ins. Assn.; trustee and mem. finance com. Springfield Hosp.; mem. corp. Weston Memorial Hosp., Com. on Referenda from U.S. Chamber of Commerce. Home: Springfield, Mass. Died June 1940.

BULKLEY, L(ucius) Duncan, dermatologist; b. New York, Jan. 12, 1845; s. Henry D. and Juliana (Barnes) B.; A.B., Yale, 1866, A.M., 1869; M.D., Coll. Phys. and Surg. (Columbia), 1869; studied dermatology abroad; m. Katherine La Rue Mellick, May 28, 1872. Attending phys., New York Skin and Cancer Hosp., 1882—; cons. phys., New York Hosp., 1894—; cons. dermatologist, Randall's Island Hosp., Hosp. for Ruptured and Crippled, and Manhattan Eye and Ear Hosp. Author: Manual of Diseases of the Skin, 1898; Eczema and Its Management, 1901; Acne and Its Treatment, 1885; Syphilis in the Innocent, 1894; Compendium of Diseases of the Skin, 1912; Diet and Hygiene in Diseases of the Skin, 1913; Cancer, Its Cause and Treatment, Vol. I, 1915, Vol. II, 1917; The Medical Treatment of Cancer, 1919. Home: New York, N.Y. Died July 20, 1928.

BULL, Carroll Gideon, prof. immunology; b. Knoxville, Tenn., June 22, 1884; s. William G. and Emma (White) B.; B.S., Peabody Coll. (U. of Nashville), 1907; M.D., U. of Nashville, 1910; studied U. of Chicago, U. of Mich., Harvard; m. Zelma Smith, 1914; children—Nancy, Carrollyn. Teacher of bacteriology and pathology, Lincoln Memorial U., 1910-12; fellow Nelson Morris Inst., Chicago, 1912-13; asst. and asso. in pathology, Rockefeller Inst., N.Y. City, 1913-17; maj. Med. Corps, U.S.A., 1917-18; asso. prof. immunology, Sch. of Hygiene and Pub. Health, Johns Hopkins, 1918, prof. same, 1921—. Had specialized in researches in agglutination of bacteria in vivo and toxin and anti-toxin for B. Welchi. Home: Baltimore, Md. Died May 31, 1931.

BULL, Charles Livingston, artist, illustrator of many mag. articles. Illustrated books Kindred of the Wild, 1902; Earth's Enigmas; Watchers of the Trails; Call of the Wild, etc. Painted mural decorations in homes of Isaac N. Seligman, William Gray Purcell, Charles S. Chapman. Mem. div. pictorial publicity Com. Pub. Information, 1917-18. Author: Under the Roof of the Jungle, 1911; also of Asiatic sect., big game honor list of Camp-Fire Club of America. Died Mar. 22, 1932.

BULL, Charles Stedman, ophthalmologist; b. New York; s. Henry King and Eliza A. (Ludlow) B.; A.B., Columbia, 1864, A.M., 1867, M.D., 1868; m. Mary E. Kingsbury, June 10, 1882. House phys. Bellevue Hosp., 1867-68; asst. surgeon Manhattan Eye and Ear Hosp., 1871-73, N.Y. Eye and Ear Infirmary, 1871-76 (surgeon, 1876—); visiting surgeon, Charity Hosp., 1875-80; prof. ophthalmology, Cornell U. Med. Coll., 1898—; cons. ophthal. surgeon St. Luke's, Presbyn. and St. Mary's hosps. Pres. Am. Ophthal. Soc., 1903-07. Home: New York, N.Y. Died Apr. 11, 1912.

BULL, Dorothy, educator; b. New York, N.Y., Dec. 10, 1887; d. Charles Stedman and Mary Eunice (Kingsbury) B.; ed. The Brearley Sch., N.Y. City, 1899-1906. Spl. teacher in English dept. Litchfield (Conn.) High Sch., 1924-26; with Mrs. William Spinney, asso. founder and head of Spring Hill School, 1926—; pres. Spring Hill School, Inc. Home: Litchfield, Conn. Died Sept. 1, 1934.

BULL, Frank Kellogg, mfr.; b. Spring Prairie, Walworth Co., Wis., May 7, 1857; s. Stephen and Ellen (Kellogg) B.; grad. Racine Coll., 1878; m. H. Belle Jones, 1880. Entered service of J. I. Case & Co. (of which his father was one of the founders), 1878, in repair dept., to learn business; became sec., 1881, treas., 1896, pres., 1897, J. I. Case Threshing Machine Co., later chmn. bd. of dirs. same (retired). Home: Racine, Wis. Died Mar. 13, 1927.

BULL, James Henry, commodore U.S.N.; b. West Chester, Pa., June 13, 1852; s. James Hunter and Mary Augusta (Sheaff) B.; grad. U.S. Naval Acad., 1870; Naval War Coll., 1892, 1896, 1906; m. Katherine Whittelsey Tillman, Mar. 5, 1878. Ensign, 1871; promoted through grades to commodore, and retired June 30, 1907. For service record see Vol. 12 (1922-23). Home: San Francisco, Calif. Died July 20, 1932.

BULL, Melville, congressman, farmer; b. Newport, R.I., 1854; prepared at Phillips Acad., Exeter, N.H.; grad. Harvard, 1877; then engaged in farming; mem. State legislature, 1883-85; State senator, 1885-92; lt. gov., 1892-94; mem. Rep. State Central Com., 1885-95; del. to Rep. Nat. Conv., 1888; one of bd. of mgrs., R. I. Coll. Agr. and Mech. Arts, 1888—; mem. Congress, 1st R.I. Dist., 1895-1903; Rep. candidate for Congress, 1902, defeated. Home: Middletown, R.I. Died 1909.

BULL, Sara Chapman; b. Oxford, N.Y., 1850; d. Joseph G. and Amelia (Chapman) Thorp; m. Ole Bull, violinist, 1870 (died 1880). Author: Ole Bull —A Memoir, 1882. Home: Cambridge, Mass. Died 1911.

BULL, Storm, prof. steam engring., U. of Wisconsin, 1884—; b. Bergen, Norway, Oct. 20, 1856; grad. Federal Swiss Polytechnic Inst., Zurich, deg. M.E., 1877; in professional work, 1877-79; then became instr. Univ. of Wis. V.-p. of jury of class 21 (gen. machinery), Paris Expn., 1900; pres. jury steam engines, etc., St. Louis Expn., 1904. Author many scientific papers. Died 1907.

BULL, William Lanman, capitalist; b. New York, Aug. 23, 1844; ed. U. City of New York. Mem. firm

Edward Sweet & Co., brokers; trustee Met. Trust Co., and officer or dir. in ry., financial and industrial corps. Pres. N.Y. Stock Exchange, 1888-90. Home: New York, N.Y. Died Jan. 2, 1914.

BULL, William Tillinghast, physician; b. Newport, R.I., May 18, 1849; s. Henry B.; A.B., Harvard, 1869, A.M.; M.D., Coll. Phys. and Surg., New York, 1872; studied with Dr. Sands and at Bellevue Hosp., and in Europe, 2 yrs.; practicing in New York, 1875—. In charge New York Dispensary, 1875-77, Chambers St. Hosp., 1877-88; visiting surgeon New York Hosp., 1883—, St. Luke's Hosp., 1880-83 (cons. surgeon, 1883—); cons. surgeon Hosp. for Ruptured and Crippled, N.Y., State Emigrants' Hosp.; demonstrator anatomy, 1879-80, prof. practice of surgery, 1889—. Coll. Phys. and Surg. (Columbia). Fellow Am. Surg. Assn., etc. Home: New York, N.Y. Died 1909.

BULLA, Charles Dehaven, clergyman; b. Albany, Mo.; s. Andrew J. (of North Carolina) and Elizabeth (Witten) B. (of Va.); ed. U. of Mo.; D.D., Randolph-Macon Coll., 1912; m. Carrie T. Brown, Feb. 12, 1901; children—Paul S. Ruth, Dorothy Taxis, Emily Granbery, Charles Dehaven, Sidney Chappell. Employed in War Dept., Washington, 1887-95; admitted Baltimore Conf. M.E. Ch., S., Apr. 1895; pastor, Roanoke, Va., 1895-98, Baltimore, 1898-1902, Winchester, Va., 1902-06, Alexandria, 1906-10; editor Baltimore Southern Methodist, 1910; corr. sec. Gen. S.S. Bd., Nashville, Tenn., 1910-22; presiding elder San Francisco Dist., 1921-24; presiding elder Los Angeles Dist., 1924-27; now asso. editor of Sunday sch. publs., M.E. Ch., S.; editor Daily Christian Advocate at gen. conf., 5 times to 1930; chmn. Pacific Conf. delegation to Gen. Conf., 1926. Mem. Internat. S.S. Lesson Com. 7 yrs.; mem. exec. com. Federal Council of Chs.; spl. field commr. Boy Scouts America. Democrat. Mason. Home: Nashville, Tenn. Died Feb. 2, 1932.

BULLA, Robert Nelson, lawyer; b. nr. Richmond, Ind., Sept. 8, 1850; s. Hiram and Elizabeth (Staley) B.; M.A., Nat. U., Lebanon, Ohio, 1876; m. Evangeline Sutton, Aug. 4, 1890 (died 1903). Admitted to Ohio bar, 1881, and began practice in Cincinnati; moved to Los Angeles, Calif., 1883; gave up gen. law practice, 1901; dir. Southern Calif. Loan Assn., Inglewood Park Cemetery Assn.; member advisory bd. Bank of America. Mem. Calif. Ho. of Rep., 2 terms, 1893-94, 1895-96, Senate, 1897-99; mem. commn. to report on Torrens land transfer system, 1895, later adopted in modified form in Calif.; mem. commn. to codify laws Calif., 1898, 1899; secured passage in legislature of law under which the State becomes the purchaser of real property sold for taxes, with redemption at reasonable cost. Mem. Los Angeles Chamber of Commerce (pres., 1915). Republican. Unitarian. Mason. Home: Alhambra, Calif. Died Feb. 28, 1935.

BULLARD, Arthur ("Albert Edwards"), author; b. St. Joseph, Mo., Dec. 8, 1879; s. Rev. Henry and Helen (Nelson) B.; grad. Blair Presbyterial Acad., Blairstown, N.J., 1899; Hamilton Coll., Clinton, N.Y., about 2 yrs.; m. Ethel Mather Bagg, July 30, 1918. Probation officer, Prison Assn. of N.Y., 1903-05, also connected with Univ. Settlement; fgn. corr., 1905—, for Harper's Weekly, Collier's Weekly, The Outlook, etc., traveling in Russia, Central America, French N. Africa; represented Outlook in Balkan War, 1912-13, Outlook, Century, Atlantic Monthly, in Europe, 1914-17; mem. Com. on Pub. Information, Washington, D.C., Apr. 1917-June 1919; apptd. dir. Russian Div., same, Moscow, June 1917; transferred to Siberia, at Vladivostok, Sept. 1918-Jan. 1919; apptd. spl. asst. to Dept. of State, for work in Russian Div., Dec. 1919; apptd. chief of Russian Div., Nov. 1920; resigned, Mar. 1921, and returned to mag. and newspaper work; editor Our World, 1921-24; European rep. League of Nations, Non-Partisan Assn. at Geneva, Switzerland, 1925; mem. secretariat League of Nations, 1926-27; attached to Am. Delegation to Internat. Economic Conf., Geneva, 1927. Author: Panama, 1911, A Man's World, 1912; Comrade Yetta, 1913; The Barbary Coast, 1913; The Diplomacy of the Great War, 1915; Mobilizing America, 1917; The Russian Pendulum, 1919; The Stranger, 1920; A B C's of Disarmament and Pacific Problems, 1921. Home: Washington, D.C. Died Sept. 10, 1929.

BULLARD, Ernest Luther, M.D.; b. Montgomery Co., Va., Apr. 19, 1859; s. Dexter and Mary McFarland (Stone) B.; Carroll Coll., Waukesha, Wis.; U. of Wis.; M.D., Rush Med. Coll., 1883; m. Rosalie Means, Nov. 25, 1896; 1 son, Dexter M. (M.D.). Practiced, Waukesha, 1883-1901; supt. Wis. State Hosp. for Insane, 1901-04; prof. neurology and psychiatry, Milwaukee Med. Coll., 1904-08; propr. Chestnut Lodge Sanitarium for nervous and mental diseases, Rockville, Md., 1910—. Formerly surgeon C.&N.W. R.R., C.,M.&St.P. R.R. and Wis. Central R.R.; mem. Wis. Ho. of Rep., 1891-93. Sec. med. preparedness com. of Montgomery Co., Md.; mem. Vol. Med. Service Corps. Mem. Soc. Colonial Wars, etc. Home: Rockville, Md. Died Jan. 17, 1931.

BULLARD, Frank Dearborn, M.D., surgeon; b. Lincoln Center, Me., Dec. 27, 1860; s. William Bradford and Lydia (Dearborn) B.; A.B., Colby, 1881 (Phi Beta Kappa), A.M., 1884; M.D., U. of Calif. Med. Dept., Los Angeles, 1888; studied in Göttingen, Berlin and Vienna; m. Rose Talbott, M.D., May 3, 1888; 1 dau., Helen; m. 2d, Kathryn Fink, 1917. Engaged in med. practice in Los Angeles, 1888—; specializes in treatment of eye, ear, nose and throat; instr. in ophthalmology, U. of Calif. Med. Dept. Consultant ophthalmologist, U.S. Aviation Bd., Los Angeles. Follower of Herbert Spencer. Author: Cupid's Chalice (poems), 1890; The Apistophilon (poems), 1898. Contbr. numerous papers on anæsthesia. Lecturer on biblical criticism in Unitarian Ch., 1921—. Home: Los Angeles, Calif. Died Sept. 8, 1936.

BULLARD, Frederic Field, composer and organist; b. Boston, Sept. 21, 1864; was spl. student in chemistry, Mass. Inst. of Technology, 1884-86; studied composition and organ, Munich Conservatory, with Josef Rheinberger, 1888-92. Best known through his many compositions for the voice, including all forms of songs and part-songs, notably The Sword of Ferrara; A Stein Song; Beam from Yonder Star; There's a Woman Like a Dewdrop. Home: Boston. Died 1904.

BULLARD, Stanley Hale, mfr.; b. Hoboken, N.J., July 4, 1877; s. Edward Payson and Alice Martha (Camp) B.; grad. New York Mil. Acad., 1895; m. Grace Cleaveland, Apr. 3, 1901; children—Frances, Katherine, Stanley Hale. Has been with The Bullard Machine Tool Company (then The Bullard Co.) of Bridgeport, Conn, 1896—, successively machinist apprentice, journeyman machinist, sales rep., sales mgr., works mgr., and in 1918 became v.p. and chief associate with bro. E. P. Bullard, Jr. Mem. Bd. of Edn., Fairfield, Conn. Conglist. Home: Fairfield, Conn. Died Mar. 1931.

BULLARD, William Hannum Grubb, naval officer; b. Media, Del. Co., Pa., Dec. 6, 1866; s. Orson Flagg and Rebecca Ann (Huston) B.; grad. U.S. Naval Acad., 1886; m. Beirne Saunders, Oct. 30, 1889; 1 son, Beirne Saunders. Ensign, July 1, 1888; lt. jr. grade, Sept. 5, 1896; lt., Mar. 3, 1899; lt. comdr., Jan. 1, 1905; comdr., Feb. 1, 1909; capt., July 1, 1912; rear admiral, temporary, July 1, 1918, permanent rank, Oct. 20, 1919. Served on Columbia, Spanish-Am. War, 1898; navigator, Maine, 1905-06; exec. officer same, 1906-07; at U.S. Naval Acad., 1907-11 (organized dept. elec. engring. there); comd. San Francisco, 1911-12; supt. naval radio service, 1912-16; comdg. Arkansas, 1916-18. Served in Atlantic Fleet and in Am. div. of battleships in British Grand Fleet; mem. Inter-Allied Commn. at Malta; comd. U.S. naval forces in Eastern Mediterranean; mem. Inter-Allied Commn. to put into effect the naval terms of the armistice with Austria-Hungary, and received surrender of Austro-Hungarian fleet; mem. Inter-Allied Conf. on Radio, Paris, Jan. and Aug., 1919; dir. naval communications, Mar. 1919-21; comdr. Yangtze Patrol Force, U.S. Asiatic Fleet, 1921-22; retired, Sept. 30, 1922. Del. Internat. Safety at Sea Conf., London, 1913. Medals and decorations: West Indian and Philippine campaigns; Victory Medal; D.S.M. (Navy Dept.); Comdr. Legion of Honor (French); Order of the Knights of Polonia Restituta (Poland). Home: Media, Pa. Died Nov. 24, 1927.

BULLARD, William Norton, neurologist; b. Newport, R. I., Aug. 23, 1853; s. William Story and Louisa (Norton) B.; A.B., Harvard, 1875, M.D., 1880; m. Mary R. Reynolds, Sept. 25, 1900. Interne, Mass. Gen. Hosp., 1879-80; phys., Dept. Diseases of Nervous System, Boston City Hosp.; phys. and neurologist, Carney Hosp.; neurologist, Children's Hosp. Chmn. bd. trustees Monson State Hosp., Palmer, Mass., from its foundation, 1885, to 1912 (resigned). Episcopalian. Home: Lenox, Mass. Died Apr. 13, 1931.

BULLIS, John Lapham, brig. gen.; b. in N.Y., Apr. 17, 1841; s. Abrah R. and Lydia P. B.; ed. at Macedon Center and Lima, N.Y.; m. Alice Rodriguez; 2d, Josephine Withers. Enlisted as corporal Co. H, 126th N.Y. Vol. Inf., Aug. 8, 1862; disch. Aug. 17, 1864; capt. 118th U.S.C.T., Aug. 18, 1864; hon. mustered out, Feb. 6, 1866; apptd. from Ark., 2d lt. 41st U.S. Inf., Sept. 3, 1867; transferred to 24th Inf., Nov. 11, 1869; 1st lt., June 20, 1873; capt., Apr. 29, 1886; maj. p.-m., Jan. 29, 1897; brig. gen. U.S.A., Apr. 13, 1905; retired at own request, after 40 yrs.' service, Apr. 14, 1905. Bvtd. capt., 1890 "for gallant services in action against Indians at Remolina, Mex., 1873," and on Pecos River, Tex., 1875; maj., 1890, for same in action against Indians nr. Saragossa, Mex., 1876, and action against Indians in the Burro Mountains, Mex., 1881. Home: San Antonio, Texas. Died 1911.

BULLITT, John C., lawyer; b. Jefferson Co., Ky., Feb. 10, 1924; grad. Center Coll., Danville, Ky., 1842, with honors of class; studied law at Univ. of Lexington, Ky.; admitted to Louisville bar, 1845; practiced Clarksville, Ky., a short time; soon removed to Louisville, and, in 1849, to Phila.; was receiver of the Schuylkill Bank, gaining reputation by skillful management and settlement of its affairs; leading counsel for Gen. Fitz John Porter before advisory bd. of officers at West Point, 1878-79; owner of Bullitt Bldg., etc. Died 1902.

BULLITT, (Alexander) Scott, lawyer; b. Louisville, Ky., Jan. 23, 1880; s. Thomas Walker and Annie P. (Logan) B.; m. Dorothy, d. C. D. Stimson, May 16, 1918; children—Charles Stimson, Dorothy Priscilla, Harriet Overton. Country atty. Louisville, 1910-17; maj. Judge Adv. Gen.'s Dept., 1919; mem. Bullitt, Kennedy & Schramm, Seattle, 1929; pres. Stimson Realty Co. Dem. nominee U.S. senate, 1926; mem. platform com. Dem. Nat. Conv., 1928; Dem. nominee for gov. of Washington, 1928; mem. Dem. Nat. Com., 1929—. Trustee Am. Red Cross (Seattle Chapter), Am. White Cross. Episcopalian. Home: Seattle, Wash. Died Apr. 10, 1932.

BULLITT, Thomas W., lawyer; b. Oxmoor, Jefferson Co., Ky., May 17, 1838; s. William Christian and Mildred Ann (Fry) B.; grad. Centre Coll.; A.B., 1858 (A.M.), Univ. of Pa. Law Sch., LL.B., 1861; m. Annie P. Logan, Feb. 21, 1871. Lt. Co. C, 2d Ky. Cav., Gen. Morgan's Div., C.S.A.; captured by Federal troops, July, 1863; confined in Columbus (O.) Penitentiary, Aug., 1863, to Mar., 1864; in Fort Delaware, Mar., 1864, to Mar., 1865; paroled in Mar., 1865, for exchange and sent through to Richmond, but Gen. Lee surrendered before actually exchanged. Admitted to bar in Phila., 1861; settled in Louisville, Ky., 1865, practicing law continuously; mem. Bullitt & Bullitt, 1900—. Presbyn. Democrat until 1896; then independent. Home: Louisville, Ky. Died 1910.

BULLOCK, A(ugustus) George, retired; b. Enfield, Conn., June 2, 1847; s. Governor Alexander Hamilton and Elvira (Hazard) B.; A.B., Harvard, 1868, A.M., 1871; m. Mary, d. George Chandler, of Worcester, Mass., Oct. 4, 1871. Admitted to bar, 1875; practiced law until 1883; chmn. bd. dirs. and v.p. State Mutual Life Assurance Co.; pres. Norwich & Worcester R.R. Co.; trustee Worcester Instn. Savings; dir. Worcester Consol. St. Ry. Co., B.&A R.R. Co., Worcester Gas Light Co., Am. Loan & Trust Co. (Boston), N.E. Investment & Security Co. Commr. Chicago Expn., 1893; trustee Clark U., 1905—. Home: Worcester, Mass. Died June 22, 1926.

BULLOCK, Charles Jesse, economist; b. Boston, May 21, 1869; A.B., Boston U., 1889; Ph.D., U. of Wis., 1895 (LL.D., Williams Coll., 1921); m. Helena M. Smith, June 22, 1895; 1 dau., Grace Helena. Instr. economics, Cornell U., 1895-99; asst. prof. economics, 1899-1902, prof., 1902-03, Williams Coll.; asst. prof. economics, 1903-08, prof., 1908-35 (emeritus) Harvard. Mem. Mass. Taxation Commn., 1907. Fellow Am. Acad. Arts and Sciences; pres. Nat. Tax Assn., 1917-19. Author: The Finances of the United States, 1775-89, 1895; Introduction to the Study of Economics, 1900; Essays on the Monetary Hist. of the U.S., 1900; Finances of Massachusetts, 1780-1905, 1907; Economic Essays, 1936; Politics, Finance and Consequences, 1939. Editor: A Discourse Concerning the Currencies of the British Plantations in North America, by William Douglass, 1897; Selected Readings in Public Finance, 1906; Selected Readings in Economics, 1907. Home: Cambridge, Mass. Died Mar. 17, 1941.

BULLOCK, Motier Acklin, clergyman; b. Lapeer Co., Mich., Apr. 18, 1851; s. Daniel and Harriet N. (Tripp) B.; traces ancestry to Richard Bullock, who was born, 1622, and settled in Rehoboth, Mass., 1644; A.B., Olivet (Mich.) College, 1876, A.M., same, 1879 (D.D., 1891); studied theology with Zachary Eddy, D.D., of Detroit, Mich., 1877-78; B.D., Oberlin, 1882; m. Catherine Tunison, Sept. 19, 1877. Ordained Congl. ministry, Oct. 19, 1876; pastor Oakwood, Mich., 1876-78, Metamora, 1878-83 (including leave of absence at Oberlin), Silverton, Colo., 1883-85, South Haven, Mich., 1885-88, Iowa City, Ia., 1888-99, The Vine Ch., Lincoln, Neb., 1899—. Del. to Nat. Council of Congl. Chs., 1889, 1895, 1904, 17, 19; corporate mem. A.B.C.F.M., 1894—; moderator Congl. Assn. of Ia., 1898-99; mem. exec. com. Ia. Home Missionary Soc. several yrs.; mem. bd. dirs. Neb. Home Missionary Soc., 1900-21 (chmn. bd. 10 yrs.; pres. of soc. 1909-11); moderator Neb. Congl. Conf., 1910-11; supt. Neb. Prison Assn., 1909-14. Prog. Republican. Author: Congregational Nebraska, 1905. Home: Lincoln, Neb. Died Oct. 28, 1924.

BUMP, Charles Weathers, journalist; b. Baltimore, Dec. 13, 1872; s. Orlando Franklin B. (legal author); grad. Johns Hopkins, 1892; grad. studies, 1892-94; m. M. Teresa Milholland, 1898. Reporter, 1890-95, dramatic critic and editor, 1895-1901, Baltimore Sun; resided in Loncoln, 1901, engaged in colonial history research; news editor Baltimore Evening News, 1901—. Author: Down the Historic Susquehanna, 1899; Churches and Religious Institutions of Maryland, 1893; Columbus (with H. B. Adams and Henry Wood), 1892; London Plays of 1901, 1901; The Voyage of the Ark and the Dove; His Baltimore Madonna, (vol. of short stories), 1906; The Mermaid of Druid Lake (short stories), 1906. Died 1908.

BUMP, Milan Raynard, elec. engr.; b. Rock Falls, Wis., Mar. 18, 1881; B.S. in E.E., U. of Wis., 1902; m. Mary Morrison, 1909. Asst. engr. Washington Water Power Co., Spokane, Wash., 1902-03; engr. Denver Gas & Electric Light Co., 1904-06; examining engr., Henry L. Dougherty & Co., 1907-09; gen. mgr. Empire Dist. Electric Co., Joplin, 1909-10; chief engr. Henry L. Dougherty & Co., 1910—; dir. of about 30 corps. controlled by the parent co. Home: Montclair, N.J. Died May 5, 1925.

BUMSTEAD, Henry Andrews, physicist; b. Pekin, Ill., Mar. 12, 1870; s. Samuel Josiah (M.D.) and Sarah Ellen (Seiwell) B.; A.B., Johns Hopkins, 1891; Ph.D., Yale, 1897; m. Luetta Ullrich, Aug. 18, 1896. Asst. in physics, Johns Hopkins, 1891-93; instr. in physics, Sheffield Scientific Sch., Yale., 1893-1900; asst. prof., 1900-06, prof., Yale Coll., and dir. Sloane Physicial Lab., 1906—, Yale U. Scientific attaché, Am. Embassy, London, 1918. Fellow Am. Acad. Arts and Sciences. Home: New Haven, Conn. Died Dec. 31, 1920.

BUMSTEAD, Horace, educator; b. at Boston, Sept. 29, 1841; s. Josiah Freeman and Lucy Douglas (Willis) B.; A.B., Yale, 1863. A.M., 1866; maj. 43d U.S.C.T., 1864-65, serving in siege of Richmond and Petersburg, later in Tex.; grad. Andover Theol. Sem., 1870; studied in Europe, 1870, 1871 (D.D., New York U., 1881); m. Anna M., d. Albert G. Hoit, portrait painter, Jan. 9, 1872. Ordained Congl. ministry, 1872; pastor Second Ch., Minneapolis, 1872-75; prof. natural science, 1875-80, prof. Latin, 1880-97, pres., 1888-1907, Atlanta U. (for colored students); retired on Carnegie Foundation, 1907; then engaged in religious and philanthropic work. Home: Brookline, Mass. Died Oct. 14, 1919.

BUNCE, Francis Marvin, rear adm. U.S.N., retired Dec. 25, 1898; b. Hartford, Conn., Dec. 25, 1836; s. James Marvin B.; grad. U.S. Naval Acad., 1857; lt., 1861; lt. comdr., 1863; comdr., 1871; capt., 1883; commodore, 1895; rear adm., 1898. During Civil war was exec. officer Penobscot, 1862, in blockading service off Wilmington, N.C.; took part in various boat expdns. and skirmishes; served on Pawnee and had charge of naval part in attack and capture of Morris' Island, S.C.; served on monitor Patapsco in siege of Charleston, until wounded by explosion of cartridges, Nov., 1863; afterward on several vessels; in 1865-66 took monitor Monadnock from Phila. to San Francisco—1st extended seavoyage ever made by monitor; comd. Naval Training Sta., Newport, R.I., 1891-94; North Atlantic Sta., 1895-97; navy yard, New York, 1897-99; m. Mary E. Bull, 1864. Home: Hartford, Conn. Died 1901.

BUNCE, W(illiam) Gedney, artist; b. Hartford, Conn., Sept. 19, 1840; s. James M. and Elizabeth (Chester) B.; pupil of Cooper Union and William Hart, New York, and Achenbach; also studied Munich, Düsseldorf, Brussels and later opened studio at Paris, then at Hartford, Conn. Exhibited Paris Salon, 1876, 1888, Soc. Am. Artists, 1878; bronze medal, Paris Expn., 1900; medal St. Louis Expn., 1904. A.N.A., 1902, N.A., 1907; mem. Nat. Inst. Arts and Letters. Home: Hartford, Conn. Died Nov. 5, 1916.

BUNDEL, Charles Michael, army officer; b. Sharon, Pa., June 2, 1875; s. Charles Edward and Sarah Elizabeth (Murphy) B.; grad. U.S. Mil. Acad., 1899, Army Sch. of the Line, 1916, Army Gen. Staff Sch., 1921, Army War Coll., 1925; m. Enid Cal Valentine, June 2, 1913. Commd. 2d lt. U.S.A., Feb. 15, 1899; promoted through grades to col. F.A., Nov. 5, 1921; brig. gen., Mar. 1934. Served in Philippine Insurrection, 1899-1903, Mexican Punitive Expdn., 1916, World War. Episcopalian. Contbr. articles on mil. subjects to mil. jours. and mags. Died Sept. 15, 1941.

BUNDY, John Elwood, landscape painter; b. Guilford Co., N.C., May 1, 1853; s. John and Mary (Moore) B.; ed. dist. sch.; mainly self-taught in art; m. Mary E. Marlett, Sept. 15, 1875; children—Arthur L., Walter E. Moved with parents to Ind. at age of 5; teacher drawing and painting, Earlham Coll., Richmond, Ind., 1880-88; noted as painter of woodland landscapes of Ind. Exhibited at Pa. Acad. Fine Arts, Nat. Acad. Design, Art Inst. Chicago, St. Louis Expn., Corcoran Gallery, Washington, D.C., etc. Represented at City Art Mus., St. Louis; John Herron Art Inst., Indianapolis; Art Assn., Richmond, Ind., etc. Republican. Friends' Ch. Home: Richmond, Ind. Died Jan. 18, 1933.

BUNDY, Omar, army officer; b. New Castle, Ind., June 17, 1861; s. Martin L. and Amanda (Elliott) B.; grad. U.S. Mil. Acad., 1883, Inf. and Cav. Sch., 1887, Army War Coll., 1913; LL.D., DePauw U., 1919; m. Miss Harden, Nov. 27, 1889. Commd. 2d lt. 2d Inf., June 13, 1883; promoted through grades to col. 16th Inf., July 20, 1914; adj. gen., Oct. 2, 1915; brig. gen., May 15, 1917; maj. gen. N.A., Aug. 5, 1917. Served in campaign against Sioux Indians, S.D., 1890-91; participated in Battle of El Caney, Cuba, July 1, 1898, and at siege of Santiago; went to Philippines, 1899; operated against insurgents and ladrones until July, 1900; insp. gen. Dept. of Visayas, 1900-01; provost marshal Iloilo, 1901-02; duty Gen. Service and Staff Coll., 1902-05; in Philippines, 1905-07; comd. one of columns in the assault on Moro stronghold at Mount Dajo, Jolo, Mar. 1906; comdg. 2d Div. A.E.F. in France, Oct. 1917-July 1918, 6th and 7th Army Corps, July-Oct. 1918; major gen. regular army, in comd. Philippine Div., 1922; comdr. 5th Corps Area, 1924-25; retired June 17, 1925. Died Jan. 21, 1940.

BUNDY, William Edgar, U.S. atty. Southern dist. Ohio, 1898—; b. Wellston, Jackson Co., O., Oct. 4, 1866; s. William Sanford and Kate (Thompson) B.; grad. Ohio Univ., 1886 (A.M., 1889); Cincinnati Law School, 1889; m. Eva, d. Hon. John P. Leedom, May 8, 1890. Sec. Hamilton Co. Bd. of Elections, 1889-90; solicitor of Norwood, O., 1891-99; province pres. Phi Delta Theta, 1891; comdr. in chief Sons of Veterans, U.S.A., 1895-96; trustee Ohio Univ., 1896, apptd. for life. Editor Wellston Argus and Ohio Mining Journal, 1886-89. Pres. Ohio Rep. League, 1898. Elected col. 1st regt. inf., Ohio Nat. Guard, Dec. 20, 1901 (for life). Home: Norwood, O. Died 1903.

BUNKER, Alonzo, missionary; b. Atkinson, Me., Jan. 30, 1837; s. John and Roxinda (Chandler) B.; grad. Waterville (now Colby) Coll., 1862; grad. Newton Theol. Instn., Newton Centre, Mass., 1865 (D.D., Colby, 1887); m. Louisa Augusta Bradbury, Sept. 5, 1865. Ordained Bapt. ministry, 1865; missionary Am. Bapt. Missionary Union, Burmah, 1866-1904. Mem. Delta Kappa Epsilon. Translator: Hackett's Life of Christ (into Sgau Karen); Cathechism (into Gai-cho Karen and Karennee); Davies' Euclid (into Sgau Karen); Foster's Story of the Bible. Home: Newton Centre, Mass. Died Mar. 1912.

BUNN, Charles Wilson, lawyer; b. Galesville, Wis., May 21, 1855; s. Hon. Romanzo and Sarah (Purdy) B.; Ph.B., U. of Wis., 1874; m. Mary Anderson, Aug. 9, 1877; children—Helen, Donald Charles, Charles. Began practice of law at La Crosse, 1876; at St. Paul, 1885—; gen. counsel N.P. Ry. Co., 1896-1925, v.p. and spl. counsel, July 1, 1925—. Author: Jurisdiction and Practice of the Courts of the United States, 1st edit., 1914, 3d edit., 1927. Home: St. Paul, Minn. Died Jan. 2, 1941.

BUNN, Clinton Orrin, lawyer; b. Ida Grove, Ia., Aug. 25, 1877; s. Isaac and Caroline Elizabeth (Scott) B.; ed. pub. schs.; student Denver Law Sch. (U. of Denver), 1897; m. Mattie Vineyard Pulliam, Aug. 30, 1899. Official reporter, Colo. Ho. of Rep., 1897; same, U.S. Court, Southern Dist. Ind. Ty., 1898-02; admitted to Ind. Ty. bar, 1898; practiced at Ardmore, 1902-10, and 1915—, Oklahoma City, 1910-15; prominent in organization of Rep. party in Ind. Ty., 1898-1906; asst. U.S. atty., Southern Dist. Ind. Ty., 1902-06; in charge of Indian fraud prosecutions, 1905; mem. 1st bd. commrs. and 1st election bd. of Carter Co., Okla., 1907; drafted and successfully advocated provisions in Okla. Constn. relative to prosecution by information; expert, Okla. Code Commn., 1909; mem. from Okla., Conf. of Commrs. on Uniform State Laws, 1911-1915; represented Okla. at launch of battleship Oklahoma, 1914. Republican. Lay delegate General Conv. P.E. Church, New York, 1913, St. Louis, 1916. Special lecturer, U. of Okla. Law Sch. Maj., judge advocate O.R.C., World War, and organized three companies for the war; Y.M.C.A. sec. in France and Italy, 1918-19. Author: Oklahoma Civil Government, 1907 (adopted text, Okla. pub. schs., 1908-14); Okla. Civics and History, 1913, 2d edit., 1914; Constitution and Enabling Act of Oklahoma (annotated), 1907; Oklahoma Civil and Criminal Procedure, 1910; Common Sense Law Making, 1912; Digest of Okla. School Laws, 1913; Supplement to the Revised Laws of Oklahoma, 1915, revised edit., 1917; With the Americans on the Riviera, 1920; Impressions of an Impresario, 1920. Compiled statutes of Oklahoma, 1921; statutes of Nebraska, by apptmt. of State of Neb., 1921; reviser of U.S. Laws, and Code, 1923, by apptmt. of Hon. E. C. Little, chmn. Commn. on Revision of Laws of Nat. Ho. of Rep.; apptd. by Puerto Rican Govt. to revise codes and laws of Puerto Rico, Jan. 1924. Home: Ardmore, Okla. Died Dec. 3, 1924.

BUNN, George Lincoln, judge; b. Sparta, Wis., June 25, 1865; s. Romanzo and Sarah (Purdy) B.; A.B., U. of Wis., 1885; LL.B., Coll. of Law, U. of Wis., 1888; m. Ella Spaulding, Aug. 19, 1890 (died 1891); m. 2d, Fanny Losey, of LaCrosse, Wis., Apr. 2, 1908. Admitted to Minn. bar, 1888; practiced, St. Paul, 1888-97; judge Dist. Ct., 2d Dist., Minn., 1897-11; asso. justice Sup. Ct., Minn., Mar. 1, 1911—. Dean and trustee St. Paul College of Law, 1904—. Democrat. Home: St. Paul, Minn. Died Oct. 9, 1918.

BUNN, Henry Gaston, chief justice Ark., 1893-1904; b. Nash Co., N.C., June 12, 1838; m. Louisa E. Holmes, Sept. 6, 1865; m. 2d, Arralee Connolly, June 3, 1869. Was student Davidson Coll., N.C., but before graduating joined C.S.A.; served 1861-65; 3d lt., adj., lt. col. and col. under Gens. Ben McCulloch, Van Dorn in Ark. and Mo., and Beauregard, Bragg, E. Kirby Smith and J. E. Johnston; after war practiced law in Camden, Ark.; State senator from Ouachita and Nevada counties, 1873-74; mem. Constl. Conv., 1874. Home: Eldorado, Ark. Died 1908.

BUNN, Jacob, watch mfr.; b. Springfield, Ill., Oct. 21, 1864; s. Jacob and Elizabeth (Ferguson) B.; ed. pub. schs.; m. Mildred Jeffress. Pres. Ill. Watch Co., also Springfield Marine Bank, Sangamo Electric Co. Home: Springfield, Ill. Died May 10, 1926.

BUNN, Romanzo, U.S. dist. judge, western dist. Wis., Oct. 30, 1877-1905; b. S. Hartwick, Otsego Co., N.Y., Sept. 24, 1829; removed to Western, N.Y., 1832; to Wis., 1854; ed. Springville Acad., N.Y.; admitted to bar, 1853; practiced Ellicottville, N.Y., 1853-54; dist. atty. Trempealeau and Monroe counties, Wis.; mem. legislature, 1860; circuit judge, 6th circuit, Wis., 1869-77. Home: Madison, Wis. Died 1909.

BUNTING, Guy J., ry. official; b. Va., July 14, 1881; s. Richard Paul and Emily (Lawrence) Bunting; grad. high sch.; m. Mary Harrison Gregory, Sept. 11, 1902; children—Mary Gregory, Margaret Claiborne. Began as gen. accountant small ry. in Va., 1900; accounting expert in ry. affairs, Interstate Commerce Commn., Washington, D.C., 1909-11; gen. accountant C.,M.&St.P. Ry., Chicago, 1911-13, asst. gen. auditor, 1913-20; asst. dir. Bur. of Finance, Interstate Commerce Commn., 1920-22; comptroller I.C. R.R., 1922-23, v.p., 1923—. Republican. Home: Chicago, Ill. Died Dec. 24, 1937.

BUNTS, Frank Emory, surgeon; b. Youngstown, O., June 3, 1861; s. William C. and Clara E. (Barnhisel) B.; grad. U.S. Naval Acad., 1881; served U.S.N., 1881-83; M.D., Western Reserve Med. Coll., 1886; m. Harriet E. Taylor, of Cleveland, Oct. 29, 1888; children—Clara Louise (Mrs. E. C. Daoust), Virgil Corydon (dec.), Alexander Taylor. Prof. surgery, Western Reserve Med. Coll., 1893—. Dir. Cleveland Clinic Foundation, Cleveland Trust Co. Maj. and surgeon 1st O. Vol. Cav., Spanish-Am. War; lt. col., Med. Corps U.S.A., comdg. Gen. Hosp. No. 9, B.E.F., World War. Fellow Am. College of Surgeons, Am. Surg. Assn. Home: Cleveland, O. Died Nov. 28, 1928.

BURBA, George Francis, editor; b. Hodgenville, Ky., May 4, 1865; s. Benjamin F. and Elizabeth (Rodman) B.; LL.B., Columbian Law Sch. (now George Washington U.), Washington, 1903 (never practiced); m. Rebecca Bruce Hunter, Oct. 31, 1895. Worked on Louisville (Ky.) Courier-Journal as printer; started weekly paper at Hodgenville, 1885; apptd. clerk Interior Dept., Washington, 1890; spl. pension examiner; resigned, 1901; mng. editor The Sun, Springfield, O., 1903-04; editor-in-chief News League of Ohio (Dayton Daily News and Springfield Daily News), 1905-17, with exception 1913-14, when served as sec. to gov. of Ohio; editor Columbus (O.) Dispatch, June 1917—. Methodist. Awarded Carnegie Hero Medal, 1910, for rescuing child from drowning. Author: Our Bird Friends, 1908. Home: Columbus, O. Died Aug. 6, 1920.

BURBANK, James Brattle, brig. gen. U.S.A.; b. Hartford, Conn., Sept. 11, 1838; s. David and Julia (Brattle) B.; ed. Hartford Pub. High Sch.; grad. Arty. Sch., U.S.A., Ft. Monroe, Va.; m. Alice Goodrich White, July 17, 1876. Was asst. q.m. gen., State of Conn., 1861; adj. 20th Conn. Inf., 1862; joined 3d U.S. Arty., May 1864; 2d lt. 3d U.S. Arty., Mar. 12, 1865; 1st lt., July 28, 1866; prof. mil. science, Cornell U., 1877-83; capt., Nov. 3, 1882; maj. 5th U.S. Arty., May 8, 1898; lt. col., Feb. 2, 1901; col., Apr. 1, 1902; retired Sept. 11, 1902; advanced to rank of brig. gen.; retired, by act of Apr. 23, 1904. Bvtd. 1st lt., Mar. 13, 1865; bvtd. maj. for gallant conduct at battle of Gettysburg. Home: New York, N.Y. Died Dec. 30, 1928.

BURBANK, Luther, naturalist; b. Lancaster, Mass., Mar. 7, 1849; s. Samuel Walton and Olive (Ross) B.; boyhood on farm; ed. Lancaster Acad.; Sc.D., Tufts, 1905; m. Elizabeth J. Waters, Dec. 21, 1916. Always devoted to study of nature, especially plant life. Moved to Santa Rosa, Calif., 1875; conducted Burbank's Expt. Farms. Originator Burbank potato, rapid-growing edible thornless opuntias (cactus), Gold, Wickson, Apple, October, Chalco, America, Santa Rosa, Formosa, Beauty, Eldorado, and Climax plums; Giant Splendor, Sugar, Standard and Stoneless prunes; a new fruit, the Plumcot; Burbank and Abundance cherries; Peachblow, Burbank and Santa Rosa roses; gigantic forms of amaryllis, tigridias, the Shasta Daisy, Giant and Fragrance callas; and various new apples, peaches, nuts, berries and other valuable trees, fruits, flowers, grasses, grains and vegetables. Special lecturer on evolution, Leland Stanford Jr. University. Life mem. Red Cross; hon. pres. Chamber of Commerce, Santa Rosa; hon. pres. Sonoma Co. (Calif.) Boy Scouts; hon. mem. Am. Playground Soc. Author: Training of the Human Plant; Methods and Discoveries (12 vols.); How Plants Are Trained to Work for Man (8 vols.), 1921; also numerous mag. articles. Died Apr. 11, 1926.

BURCH, Charles Newell, lawyer; b. Nashville, Tenn., Dec. 27, 1868; s. John Christopher and Lucy Whitman (Newell) B.; B.A., Vanderbilt U., Nashville, 1888, LL.B., 1889; LL.D., Southwestern U.,

1930; m. Floy Cooper, Dec. 29, 1891 (died 1902); children—Lucia Newell (Mrs. Thomas W. Vinton), Charles Newell (dec.), Duncan (dec.); m. 2d, Mrs. Evelyn Peters Estes, Jan. 11, 1916. Practiced Nashville, in partnership with Claude Waller, 1890-95; asst. city atty., Nashville, 1895-96; asst. U.S. dist. atty., 1896-98; asso. with Hon. J. M. Dickinson, 1899, as asst. dist. atty., L.&N. R.R. Co. for Tenn., and succeeded him as dist. atty. for the road, Nov. 1899; apptd. gen. solicitor L.&N. R.R. Co., 1901, and removed to Louisville, Ky.; gen. counsel same road, 1903-05; gen. solicitor Yazoo & Miss. Valley R.R. Co. (I.C. R.R. Co.) at Memphis, 1905—, also I.C. System (Southern Lines), 1928. Also counsel Am. Ry. Express Agency; engaged in gen. practice, firm Burch, Minor & McKay. Apptd. Nov. 1920, by gov. of Tenn., a commr. of Goodwyn Inst., a free lecture and library foundation; apptd., 1930, by U.S. Supreme Court as special master in case of N.J. vs. N.Y. State and N.Y. City and Pa. involving diversion of waters of Delaware river. Trustee Vanderbilt U. Democrat. Episcopalian. Home: Memphis, Tenn. Died Aug. 1938.

BURCH, Charles Sumner, bishop; b. Pinckney, Mich., June 30, 1855; s. Lawrence D. and Emily (Dunning) B.; B.A., U. of Mich., 1875; (D.D., St. John's, Md., 1908; S.T.D., Hobart, 1909, Columbia, 1911; LL.D., U. of Mich., 1912; D.D., U. of the South, 1913); m. Margaret Hadley, Nov. 29, 1876. In publishing business, Chicago, 1876-90; editor and manager Grand Rapids (Mich.) Evening Press, 1897-1905. Deacon, 1895, priest, 1905, P.E. Ch.; rector St. Andrew's Ch., S.I., N.Y., 1905-11; consecrated suffragan bishop of New York, Feb. 24, 1911; elected bishop of New York, Sept. 17, 1919. Died Dec. 20, 1920.

BURCH, Ernest Ward, theologian; b. New London, Conn., Sept. 4, 1875; s. Horace Orrin and Ellen (Melzard) B.; A.B., Boston U., 1911, S.T.B., 1912, Ph.D., 1913; studied univs. of Marburg, Halle-Wittenberg and Berlin, Germany, 1911, 12, 13; m. Harriet A. Squire, Apr. 12, 1900. Ordained ministry M.E. Ch., 1901; pastorates in N.E., 1900-08, last 3 yrs. in Newport, R.I.; v.p. East Greenwich (R.I.) Acad., 1914; prof. Bibl. lit., Dakota Wesleyan U., 1914-18; asst. prof. N.T. Interpretation, Garrett Bibl. Inst., Evanston, Ill., 1918-27, asso. prof., 1927—. Author: Ethical Teaching of the Gospels, 1925; also Commentary on Book of Acts, and article, "The Structure of the Synoptic Gospels," Abingdon Bible Commentary, 1929. Home: Evanston, Ill. Died Nov. 8, 1933.

BURCH, Newton Dexter, judge; b. Stewartsville, Mo., June 16, 1871; s. George Nelson and Ann Elizabeth (Dexter) B.; LL.B., U. of Neb., 1898; m. Sarah Eliza Jarman, Mar. 15, 1899; children—Leonard Nelson, Cecil Jarman, Edith Helen. Admitted to Neb. bar, 1899, and began practice at Lynch; states atty., Boyd Co., Neb., 1903-07; moved to Dallas, S.D., 1907; mayor of Dallas, 1915-17, 1919-21; judge Circuit Court of S.D., 1921-25; mem. Supreme Court Commn., 1925-26; judge Supreme Court of S.D., 1926-28. Republican. Methodist. Mason. Home: Pierre, S.D. Died Mar. 18, 1931.

BURCHARD, Horatio Chapin, lawyer; b. Marshall, N.Y., Sept. 22, 1825; s. Horatio and Frances (Chapin) B.; grad. Hamilton Coll., N.Y., 1850, law course same, 1852; m. Jane Lawver, May 1860. Admitted to bar, 1852; mem. Ill. legislature, 1863-65; mem. Congress, 6th Ill. dist., 1869-79; dir. of the mint, 1879-85; mem. State Revenue Commn., 1886; in charge awards in mines and metallurgy, World's Columbian Expn., 1893; census supervisor, 1900. Author: Production of the Precious Metals in the United States, 1881. Home: Freeport, Ill. Died 1908.

BURCKHALTER, Charles, astronomer; b. Taylorsville, O., Jan. 5, 1849; s. Adam and Elisabeth B.; grad. Ottumwa High Sch., 1866; m. Mary Catherine Nash, Sept. 23, 1878. Astronomer in charge Chabot Obs., Oakland, Calif., 1885—. Mem. eclipse expdn. from Lick Obs. to Japan, 1896; in charge from Chabot Obs. to India, 1898; Calif., 1889, and Ga., 1900. Mem. State Earthquake Investigation Commn., 1906. Fellow Royal Astron. Society. Died Sept. 20, 1923.

BURCKHALTER, Frank Lucien, ry. official; b. Truckee, Calif., July 21, 1879; s. Charles and Mary Catherine (Nash) B.; B.S. in C.E., U. of Calif., 1900; m. Rose Van Namee Brydes, Aug. 10, 1902; 1 dau., Ruth Rose (Mrs. John Thomas Beales, Jr.). Began as rodman, in survey party, S.P. Co., 1900, asst. engr., 1902-06, div. and dist. engr., 1906-14, div. supt., 1914-18, asst. gen. mgr., 1918-28, gen. mgr. 1929-33, v.p. exec. dept., 1933—; dir. Southern Pacific Golden Gate Ferries, Ltd. Republican. Episcopalian. Mason. Died Mar. 3, 1936.

BURD, George Eli, naval officer; b. Belfast, Me., Apr. 27, 1857; s. Samuel F. and Rebecca (Brown) B.; grad. U.S. Naval Acad., 1878; m. Frances A. Goodwin, Aug. 3, 1882. Promoted asst. engr., 1880; passed asst. engr., 1889; chief engr., 1898; trans. to line as lt., 1899; lt. comdr., 1901; comdr., 1906; capt., 1910; rear adm., 1916. Served as chief engr. U.S.S. Badger, West India Campaign, Spanish-Am. War, 1898; engr. officer at sea, and navy yards, San Francisco, Bremerton, Boston, Phila. and New York; in charge industrial activities, construction and engr. work at Navy Yard, New York, 1914—; in charge, 1917, of all alteration, reconstruction, engring. and repair work on 723 vessels assigned to 3d Naval Dist., including all troop transports based on New York (these latter vessels carrying over 40 per cent of U.S. Army forces sent to Europe). Home: Brooklyn, N.Y. Died Feb. 18, 1924.

BURDEN, James Abercrombie, mfr., inventor; b. Troy, N.Y., Jan. 6, 1833; s. Henry B. (inventor); ed. by tutor at New Haven, Conn., supplemented by lectures at Sheffield Scientific Sch., Yale, and Rensselaer Poly. Inst.; m. Miss Irvin. Pres. Burden Iron Co.; dir. (pres.) Hudson River Ore & Iron Co. Has made many inventions. Presdl. elector, 1880, 1888. Home: Troy, N.Y. Died 1906.

BURDEN, James Abercrombie, iron mfr.; b. New York, Jan. 16, 1871; s. James Abercrombie and Mary Proudfit (Irvin) B.; A.B., Harvard, 1893; student Harvard U. Law Sch., 1 yr., 1893-94; m. Florence Adele Sloane, June 6, 1895; children—James Abercrombie, William D., Florence Irvin. Became dir. Burden Iron Co., Troy, N.Y., 1894, pres., 1906—(succeeding father). Mem. cooperative com. on steel and steel products of advisory commn. of Council Nat. Defense, 1917. Presbyn. Republican. Home: Troy, N.Y. Died June 1, 1932.

BURDETT, Everett Watson, lawyer; b. Olive Branch, Miss., Apr. 5, 1854; s. Augustus P. and Marian (Newman) B.; ed. Washington U., St. Louis; LL.B., Boston U., 1877; admitted to bar, 1878; m. Maud Warner. Asst. U.S. atty., dist. of Mass., 2 yrs.; mem. firm Burdett & Wardwell; gen. counsel Nat. Electric Light Assn. many yrs.; counsel for asso. electric lighting cos. of Mass., 1889—; dir., v.p. Champion-Internat. (paper mfg.) Co.; trustee Boston Five Cents Savings Bank. Republican. Homes: Boston and Marion, Mass. Died Jan. 18, 1925.

BURDETT, Fred Hartshorn, business coll. pres.; b. Lynn, Mass., Mar. 12, 1861; s. Dr. James Francis and Caroline (Hartshorn) B.; ed. Waltham (Mass.) New Ch. Sch., Boston Latin Sch. and Hinman's Bus. Coll., Worcester, Mass.; m. Sadie E. Hayward, Feb. 24, 1897; children—Charles Fred, Elaine. Co-founder with brother, 1879, Burdett Coll., business training sch., treas., 1879—, pres., 1922—; pres. Lynn br. Burdett Coll. Trustee Boston Soc. New Jerusalem. Republican. Mem. New Ch. (Swedenborgian). Mason (Shriner). Home: Woburn, Mass. Died Nov. 29, 1935.

BURDETT, Samuel Swinfin, lawyer; b. Leicestershire, Eng., Feb. 21, 1836; s. Rev. Cheney and Elizabeth (Swinfin) B.; student Oberlin Coll., 1853-56; studied law under Hon. Edward Graham, De-Witt, Ia.; m. Nancy Eliza Graham, 1864. Admitted to Ia. bar, 1859; apptd. supt. schs., Clinton Co., Ia., 1860; lt. and capt. Co. B, 1st Ia. Cav., 1861-63; Lincoln presdl. elector, 2d Ia. Dist., 1864; circuit atty., Mo., 1866-67; mem. 41st and 42d Congresses (1869-73), 6th Mo. Dist.; commr. Gen. Land Office, 1874-75; in practice at Washington, 1875—. Comdr.-in-chief G.A.R., 1885-86. Home: Glencarlyn, Va. Died Sept. 24, 1914.

BURDETTE, Robert Jones, humorist, lecturer; b. Greensboro, Pa., July 30, 1844; s. Frederick E. and Sophia Eberhardt (Jones) B.; removed in boyhood to Peoria, Ill.; ed. in pub. schs.; (D.D., Kalamazoo Coll., 1908; LL.D., Occidental Coll., Calif., 1913); m. Clara Bradley Baker, March 25, 1899. Private 47th Ill. Vols., 1862-65; was on several newspapers at Peoria, Ill.; later asso. editor Burlington (Ia.) Hawkeye, where he made reputation as humorist; later on Brooklyn Eagle; editorial contbr. Los Angeles Times, 1900—. Licensed minister Bapt. Ch., 1887, ordained, 1903; pastor Temple Bapt. Ch., Los Angeles, 1903-09, pastor emeritus, July 1909—. Author: Sons of Asaph; Smiles Yoked with Sighs, 1900; The Silver Trumpets (poems), 1911. Home: Pasadena, Calif. Died Nov. 19, 1914.

BURDGE, Franklin, lawyer; b. Phila., Feb. 22, 1835; s. Ira and Harriet (Kane) B.; grad. Brown U., 1856 (A.M., 1898); LL.B., Albany Law Sch., 1859; m. Ella Jackson, Sept. 10, 1891. Practiced law in New York, 1867-87, when he retired. Writer of 4 pamphlets relating to Simon Boerum, John Haring and Henry Wisner, members of the Continental Congress, a life of John Brougham, the actor, and other contbns. to Am. biography. Deceased.

BURDICK, Alfred Stephen, pharm. and chem. mfr.; b. DeRuyter, N.Y., Feb. 15, 1867; s. Rev. Stephen and Susan (Maxson) B.; A.B., Alfred U., 1886; M.D., Rush Med. Coll., Chicago, 1891; m. Ella Grace Brown, July 9, 1891. In gen. practice of medicine, Dunlap, Ill., Tampa, Fla., Hinsdale, Ill., and Chicago; asso. prof. practice of medicine, Ill. Med. Coll., 1899-1904. V.p. and asst. gen. mgr. Abbott Laboratories, 1916-21, pres. and gen. mgr., July 1921—. Mem. Selective Service Bd. No. 59, Chicago, 1917-19. Lt. col. Med. R.C., U.S.A., 1923—. Author: Standard Medical Manual, 1904; The Remedy, 1915; Common Emergencies, 1915. Editor Med. Standard, 1899-1904; editor Am. Jour. of Clinical Medicine (now Clin. Medicine and Surgery), Jan. 1904—. Republican. Home: Highland Park, Ill. Died Feb. 11, 1933.

BURDICK, Charles Kellogg, prof. law; b. Utica, N.Y., Feb. 7, 1883; s. Francis M. and Sarah Underhill (Kellogg) B.; B.A., Princeton, 1904; LL.B., Columbia, 1908; m. Ruth Nutting, May 26, 1909. Practiced with firm Wilmer, Canfield & Stone, New York, 1908-09; prof. law, Tulane U., 1909-12, U. of Mo., 1912-14, Cornell U., 1914—, acting dean, 1923-24, 1925-26, dean, 1926-36. Prof. law, summer sessions, Columbia, 1912, 13, 14, 16, U. of Chicago, 1925, Stanford U., 1928; asso. mem. All Souls Coll., Oxford, Eng., 1930. Asso. dir. Bur. of Information Service, Dept. of Civilian Relief, Am. Red Cross Hdqrs., 1918. Mem. N.Y. State Commn. to Investigate Administration of Justice, 1931-39. Mem. N.Y. State Judicial Council, 1934; chmn. N.Y. State Law Revision Commission, 1934—. Counsel to Gov. Lehman of New York in Geoghan removal proceedings, 1936. Unitarian. Author: The Law of the American Constitution; Burdick's Cases on the Law of Public Service and Carriers (2d edit.); Model Draft of an Extradition Convention, with Comment. Home: Ithaca, N.Y. Died June 22, 1940.

BURDICK, Charles Williams, lawyer; b. Toledo, O., Aug. 15, 1860; s. Leander and Celia (Williams) B.; ed. Friends' Sch., Providence, R.I.; Ohio Wesleyan U.; LL.B., U. of Mich., 1894; m. Harriet Parmalee Fuller, Mar. 3, 1885 (dec.); 1 dau., Margaret Fuller (Mrs. George W. Hewlett). Located in Wyo., 1878; began practice, Cheyenne, 1893. Mem. Wyo. Constl. Conv., 1889; mem. Territorial Council 10th Territorial Assembly, 1890; state auditor, 1890-94; sec. of state, 1894-98; chmn. Rep. State Central Com., 1906-12. Sec. State Bd. Law Examiners, 1900-11. Episcopalian. Home: Cheyenne, Wyo. Died Jan. 8, 1927.

BURDICK, Clinton De Witt, financier; b. Smyrna, N.Y., July 24, 1863; A.B., Wesleyan U., Conn., 1886, M.A., 1889; m. Elizabeth Lapzien, Feb. 18, 1898; children—Howard, Robert Andrew. With Title Guarantee & Trust Co., New York, and Bond & Mortgage Guarantee Co., Brooklyn, 1887—, then pres. of both; also officer or dir. various other cos. Treas. and trustee Wesleyan U.; trustee Brooklyn Pub. Library, Packer Collegiate Inst., Y.M.C.A. Died Apr. 11, 1933.

BURDICK, Francis Marion, univ. prof.; b. De Ruyter, N.Y., Aug. 1, 1845; s. Albert G. and Eunetia (Wheeler) B.; A.B., Hamilton Coll., 1869, LL.B., 1872 (LL.D., 1895); m. Sarah Underhill Kellogg, June 8, 1875. Editor Utica Herald, 1870-71; practiced law, Utica, N.Y., 1872-83; prof. law and history, Hamilton Coll., 1882-87; prof. law, Cornell U., 1887-91; Dwight prof. law and mem. univ. council, 1891-1916, emeritus prof. law, 1916—, Columbia U. Mayor of Utica, 1882-83; mem. U.S. Assay Commission, 1889; pres. Patria Club, New York, 1899, Riverside and Morningside Heights Assn., 1900-07; N.Y. commr. on Uniform State Laws, 1907—. Author: The Essentials of Business Law, 1902, 1919; Cases on Torts (3d edit.), 1905; Cases on Sales (2d edit.), 1901; Law of Sales (3d edit.), 1913; Law of Partnership (3d edit.), 1917; Cases on Partnership, 1898. Editor dept. of law Johnson's Universal Cyclopedia; The Law of Torts (3d edit.), 1913. Home: DeRuyter, N.Y. Died June 3, 1920.

BURDICK, Joel Wakeman, steel mfr.; b. Almond, N.Y., June 20, 1853; s. Russell Maxson and Sarah Elizabeth (Farnsworth) B.; common school edn.; m. Ella Pixley Bartlett, Jan. 1878. Tel. operator to pass. traffic mgr., Del. & Hudson Co., resigned, 1907; organizer and chmn. West Penn Steel Co. (employs 1,800 men and makes 150,000 tons of steel per yr.); dir. Nat. Ry. Publications Co. (Phila.), Bank of Pittsburgh. Chief of hosp. and home service sect. of Am. Red Cross, Eastern Advance Zone, France, 1918. Republican. Episcopalian. Home: Pittsburgh, Pa. Died May 12, 1925.

BURFORD, John Henry, lawyer; b. in Parke Co., Ind., Feb. 29, 1852; s. James and Sarah Ann (Reddish) B.; ed. Waveland Collegiate Inst., 1870-72; LL.B., Ind. U., 1874; m. Mary A. Cheek, Feb. 14, 1876. Pros. atty. 22d Circuit, Ind., 1880; apptd. register U.S. Land Office, Oklahoma City, 1890; asso. justice Supreme Ct., Okla. Ty., 1892-96, chief justice, 1898-1907; mem. Okla. State Senate, 1913-17; Rep. nominee for U.S. Senator, 1914. Then sr. mem. Burford, Miley, Hoffman & Burford. Home: Oklahoma City, Okla. Died Sept. 1, 1922.

BURGE, J. H. Hobart, M.D.; b. Wickford, R.I., Aug. 12, 1823; s. Rev. Lemuel B.; private edn.; M.D., Univ. City of New York, 1848; has since continuously practiced medicine and surgery, New York, Sacramento, Calif., and from 1855 in Brooklyn; cons. surgeon to L.I. and St. John's (Episcopal) hosps. Home: Brooklyn, N.Y. Died 1901.

BURGER, Owen Francis, plant pathologist; b. Freeland, Pa., June 8, 1885; s. Amandus Kresge and Eliza Ann (Barthold) B.; A.B., Ind. U., 1909; M.S.,

U. of Fla., 1911; M.S., Harvard, 1915, D.Sc., Harvard, 1916; m. Helen Sanborn Lothrop, July 22, 1916. Asst. plant pathologist, Fla. Agrl. Expt. Sta., 1911-13; univ. scholar, Harvard, 1913-14, and Priscilla Clark Hodges scholarship, same univ., 1914-16; instr. plant pathology, Citrous Expt. Sta., U. of Calif., 1916-18; pathologist U.S. Dept. Agr., 1918-20; plant pathologist Agrl. Expt. Sta., U. of Fla., Dec. 1920—. Fellow A.A.A.S. Democrat. Episcopalian. Mason. Home: Gainesville, Fla. Died 1928.

BURGESS, Alexander, first P. E. bishop diocese of Quincy, Ill.; b. Providence, R.I., Oct. 31, 1819; s. Thomas and Mary (Mackie) B.; grad. Brown Univ., 1838; Gen. Theol. Sem., New York, 1841; (hon., S.T.D., Brown and Racine; LL.D., Griswold); ordered deacon, 1842; ordained priest, 1843; held several pastorates and was rector of Christ Ch., Springfield, Mass., when consecrated bishop May 15, 1878. Died 1901.

BURGESS, Edward Sandford, botanist; b. Little Valley, N.Y., Jan. 19, 1855; s. Rev. Chalon and Emma (Johnston) B.; A.B., Hamilton Coll., 1879, A.M., 1882, Sc.D., 1904; fellow Johns Hopkins, 1880-81; Ph.D., Columbia, 1899; m. Irene S. Hamilton, Dec. 30, 1884. Taught botany in Washington, 1881-95, Marthas Vineyard Summer Inst., 1880-95, Johns Hopkins U., 1885; prof. natural science, Hunter Coll., 1895—, acting pres., Jan.-May 1908. Pres. Torrey Bot. Club, 1912-13. Author: History of Pre-Clusian Botany, 1902; Species and Variations of Biotian Asters, 1906. Died Feb. 23, 1928.

BURGESS, Frank H(enry), newspaper pub.; b. Liverpool, Eng., Sept. 4, 1875; s. Rev. Wm. and Frances B.; brought by parents to U.S., 1879; student Ill. Coll., Jacksonville, Ill., 1893-95; m. May Thomas, Dec. 24, 1904; children—William, Frances, Thomas, Edward. In circulation dept. Chicago Record, 1895-1904; mgr. Rock Island, Ill., Davenport Daily Times, 1904-07; business mgr. LaCrosse (Wis.) Tribune, 1907; pub. LaCrosse Tribune and LaCrosse Leader-Press, 1917—. Conglist. Home: LaCrosse, Wis. Died July 7, 1939.

BURGESS, Frederick, bishop; b. Providence, R.I., Oct. 6, 1853; s. Frederick and Julia Ann B.; A.B., Brown U., 1873; studied Gen. Theol. Sem., 1874-75; in Oxford, Eng., 1876; (D.D., Brown, 1898; LL.D., Cambridge Univ. [England], 1920); m. Caroline Gamble Bartow, Sept. 13, 1881 (died 1894). Deacon, 1876, priest, 1877, P.E. Ch.; rector Mendham, N.J., 1876-77, Grace Ch., Amherst, Mass., 1878-83, Christ Ch., Pomfret, Conn., 1883-89, St. Asaph, Bala, Pennsylvania, 1889-96, Christ Ch., Detroit, 1896-98, Grace Ch., Brooklyn, 1898-1902; consecrated bishop of L.I., Jan. 15, 1902. Home: Garden City, L.I., N.Y. Died Oct. 15, 1925.

BURGESS, Gaven D., judge; b. in Ky., Nov. 5, 1835; s. Henry D. and Evaline D. B.; ed. in schs. of Fleming County, Ky.; m. Cordelia Trimble. Judge 11th and 12th Jud. Circuits of Mo., 1874-92; asso. justice Supreme Ct., 1892— (chief justice, 1901-03). Democrat. Home: Jefferson City, Mo. Died 1910.

BURGESS, George Farmer, congressman; b. Wharton County, Tex., Sept. 21, 1861; s. Dr. C. H. A. B.; pub. sch. edn.; m. Marie Louise Sims, Dec. 28, 1888. Admitted to bar, 1882, in practice at Gonzales, Tex. County atty. Gonzales County, 1886-89; presdl. elector, 1892; mem. 57th to 63d Congresses (1901-13), 10th Texas Dist. and 63d and 64th Congresses (1913-17), 9th Tex. Dist. Democrat. Home: Gonzales, Tex. Died Dec. 31, 1919.

BURGESS, George Kimball, physicist; b. Newton, Mass., Jan. 4, 1874; s. Charles A. and Addie L. (Kimball) B.; S.B., M.I.T., 1896; D.Sc., Paris, 1901; hon. D. Engr., Case Sch. Applied Science, 1923, Lehigh U., 1925; m. Suzanne Babut, of Paris, Jan. 5, 1901. Taught physics at Mass. Inst. Tech., U. of Mich., 1900-01, and U. of Calif.; asso. physicist, Nat. Bur. of Standards, Washington, D.C., 1903-13; physicist and chief of div. of metallurgy, same, 1913-23; dir. Bureau of Standards and member various coms. connected with it; engaged in pyrometric and metall. researches. U.S. del. 7th Internat. Conf. on Weights and Measures, Paris, 1927; U.S. del. World Engring. Congress, Tokyo, 1929; pres. Annual Conf. on Weights and Measures. Mem. foreign service and engring. coms., Nat. Research Council. Author: Recherches sur la constante de Gravitation, 1901; Experimental Physics—Freshman course, 1902; The Measurement of High Temperatures (with H. Le Châtelier), 1912. Died July 2, 1932.

BURGESS, Harry, army officer; b. Starkville, Miss., Feb. 22, 1872; s. James and Susan Elizabeth (Foster) B.; student Miss. Agrl. and Mech. Coll., 1888-91; grad. U.S. Mil. Acad., 1895; grad. study U.S. Engr. Sch. of Application, 1896-98; m. Mary Lillington McKoy, Feb. 27, 1912. Commd. adj. 2d lt., June 12, 1895, and advanced through grades to col., Corps of Engrs., July 1, 1920. Instr. in engring., U.S. Mil. Acad., 1898-1900; in charge surveys and design, Muscle Shoals power development; mem. Miss. River Commn., 1920-22; engr. of maintenance, Panama Canal, 1924-28, gov. of canal, Oct. 16, 1928—; pres. Panama R.R. Co. Served in France, comdr. 16th and 30th Engrs., A.E.F., 1917-19. Home: Balboa Heights, C.Z. Died Mar. 18, 1933.

BURGESS, Ida Josephine, painter; b. Chicago, Ill.; d. William T. and Ophelia R. (Crosby) Burgess; student, Cooper Inst., and Art Students' League, New York; pupil of Profs. Shirlaw, William M. Chase and L. O. Merson, Paris; made spl. study of stained glass; 1st important commn. won in competition, mural decoration of woman's reception room, Ill. State Bldg., World's Fair, Chicago, 1893; decorated Orrington Lunt Library, Northwestern U., Evanston, Ill., with mural paintings in vestibule, 1894; stained glass designer and painter, New York, 1903—. Exhibited at Paris Salon, 1885, later in New York, Chicago and St. Louis. Episcopalian. Home: Woodstock, N.Y. Deceased.

BURGESS, John William, univ. dean; b. Giles County, Tenn., Aug. 26, 1844; A.B., Amherst, 1867, A.M., 1870; hon. Ph.D., Princeton, 1883; LL.D., Amherst, 1884; Ph.D., U. of Leipzig, 1909; J.U.D., U. of Berlin, Germany, 1910, U. of Göttingen, 1923; LL.D., Columbia, 1912; m. Ruth Payne Jewett, Sept. 2, 1885; 1 son, Elisha Payne Jewett. Served in Union Army for two years, 1862-64; admitted to Mass. bar, 1869. Prof. English lit. and polit. economy, Knox Coll., 1869-71; studied history, pub. law and polit. science, Göttingen, Leipzig, Berlin, 1871-73; prof. history and polit. sci., Amherst, 1873-76, prof. polit. sci. and constl. law, 1876-1912, dean faculty polit. sci., 1890-1912, Columbia; dean faculties of philosophy, pure sci. and fine arts, Columbia; emeritus. Roosevelt prof. Am. history and instns., Friedrich Wilhelm U., Berlin, 1906-07; visiting Am. prof., Austrian univs., 1914-15. Decorated Order of Prussian Crown, by German Emperor, and Order of the Albrechts, by King of Saxony, 1907. Author: Political Science and Comparative Constitutional Law (2 vols.); The Middle Period of United States History; The Civil War and the Constitution (2 vols.); Reconstruction and the Constitution, 1902; The European War of 1914, 1915; The Reconciliation of Government and Liberty, 1915; The Administration of President Rutherford B. Hayes, 1915; America's Relations to the Great War, 1916; Russian Revolution and the Soviet Constitution, 1919; The Transformation of the Constitutional Law of the United States between 1898 and 1920, 1921; The Sanctity of Law—Wherein Does It Consist? 1927. Home: Newport, R.I. Died Jan. 13, 1931.

BURGESS, Ruth Payne Jewett (Mrs. John W. Burgess), artist; b. Montpelier, Vt.; d. Elisha Payne and Julia Kellogg (Field) Jewett; ed. Burnham Sch., Northampton, Mass.; student Art Students' League, New York, and in Germany and Italy; m. Prof. John W. Burgess, Sept. 2, 1885; 1 son, Elisha Payne Jewett. Portrait painter and etcher. Home: Newport, R.I. Died Mar. 11, 1934.

BURGESS, Theodore Chalon, educator; b. Little Valley, N.Y., Apr. 27, 1859; s. Rev. Chalon and Emma (Johnston) B.; bro. of Edward Sandford B.; grad. Fredonia (N.Y.) State Normal Sch., 1879; A.B., Hamilton Coll., 1883, A.M., 1886; Ph.D., U. of Chicago, 1898; LL.D. from Hamilton Coll., 1923; m. Laura May Briggs, Aug. 17, 1887. Head classical dept., Fredonia State Normal Sch., 1883-96; head dept. of ancient langs., Bradley Inst., Peoria, Ill., 1897—, dean, 1899—, acting dir., 1903-04, pres., 1904—. Prof. Greek, U. of Chicago, summers of 1900-09. Presbyn. Author: Epideictic Literature, 1902; Elementary Greek, 1907. Died Feb. 26, 1925.

BURGESS, William, clergyman; b. Norwich, Eng., May 26, 1843; s. William and Elizabeth (Taylor) B.; Dowson Coll., Norwich; m. Frances A. Miles, Aug. 2, 1865. Lecturer, Scotland, 1868-70; lecturer and sec. National Med. Assn., for Repeal of the Contagious Diseases Acts, England, 1872-75; editor Medical Enquirer, 1875-78; ordained Congl. ministry, 1879; pastor Canton, Ill., 1882-85, Mendon, 1885-90, Des Plaines, 1897-1902, Park Manor, Chicago, 1905-08; sec. Am. Vigilance Assn., 1911—; dir. Ill. Vigilance Assn., 1919—. Home: Des Plaines, Ill. Died July 31, 1922.

BURGESS, William, mfr.; b. Brooklyn, N.Y., Jan. 18, 1857; s. John Stewart and Elizabeth (Wilson) B.; B.S., Princeton, 1877, M.S., 1880; Coll. Phys. and Surg., New York; m. Clara Dwight Goodman, Jan. 7, 1879; children—William, Clara Goodman (Mrs. Lauren G. Bennett), John Stewart, Elizabeth (dec.). Asst. prof. chemistry, Princeton, 1877; asst. demonstrator anatomy, Coll. Phys. and Surg., 1877-79; entered importing and jobbing of china and pottery wares under title of William Burgess & Co., New York, in connection with father's firm, Burgess & Goddard, 1879; pres. Internat. Pottery Co., Trenton, N.J., 1879-1904; organizer, 1902, and pres. Hudson Porcelain Co. Spl. rep. U.S. Tariff Bd.; on 6 confidential missions abroad in interest of U.S. Govt.; Am. consul to the great pottery producing dist. of the world, Stoke-on-Trent, Eng., 1890-93; rep. pottery industry of U.S. and customs administrative matters before U.S. appraiser and Bd. of Gen. Appraisers from 1884. Dept. head War Industries Bd., World War; confidential mission to Orient, 1919; mem. U.S. Tariff Commn., June 27, 1921-June 1, 1925 (resigned); now acting advisor on tariff and custom matters. Republican. Presbyn. Home: Morrisville, Pa. Died Nov. 20, 1929.

BURK, Frederic Lister, normal sch. pres.; b. Blenheim, Can., Sept. 1, 1862; s. Erastus and Matilda (Turner) B.; B.L., U. of Calif., 1883; A.M., Leland Stanford Jr. U., 1892; Ph.D., Clark U., 1898; m. Caroline Frear, Sept. 30, 1898. In journalism, San Francisco, 1883-89; teacher in pub. and pvt. schs., Calif., 1889-91; supt. schs., Santa Rosa, 1892-96, Santa Barbara, 1898-99; pres. State Normal Sch., San Francisco, 1899—. Mem. Calif. State Bd. Edn., 1899-1912. Author: A Study of the Kindergarten Problem, 1899; Lockstep Schooling and a Remedy, 1913; Every Child a Minor, versus Lockstep Schooling, 1915. Home: Kentfield, Calif. Died June 12, 1924.

BURK, Henry, congressman, 3d Pa. dist., 1901-05; b. Würtemberg, Germany, Sept. 26, 1850; s. David and Charlotte (Reinmann) B.; ed. Phila. public schools, 1856-59; m. Ellen Carney, Aug. 18, 1873. Leather mfr. Home: Philadelphia, Pa. Died 1905.

BURK, Jesse Young, rector St. Peter's P.E. Ch., Clarksboro, N.J., 1878—, and sec. Univ. of Pa., 1882—; b. Phila., Sept. 15, 1840; s. Isaac and Mary Jean (Briggs) B.; prepared in grammar schools and Episcopal Acad., Phila.; grad. U. of Pa., 1862 (A.M., 1865); m. Gertrude Helé, June 19, 1866. Home: Clarksboro, N.J. Died 1904.

BURK, W(illiam) Herbert, clergyman, curator; b. Phila., Pa., Apr. 23, 1867; s. Jesse Y. and Gertrude (Hele) B.; B.A., U. of Pa., 1890; B.D., Phila. Div. Sch., 1893; D.D., St. John's Mil. Coll., Annapolis, Md., 1918, Pa. Mil. Coll., 1921; m. Abbie J. Reeves, Sept. 25, 1894 (died 1907); m. 2d, Eleanor H. Stroud, Apr. 15, 1912. Deacon, 1893, priest, 1894, P.E. Ch.; minister in charge Ascension Ch., Gloucester City, N.J., 1893, rector, 1894; asst. minister St. John's Ch., Norristown, Pa., 1894-97; rector All Saints Ch., Norristown, 1898-1911; founder Washington Memorial Chapel, Valley Forge, 1903, minister in charge, 1903-11, rector, 1911—; founder Trinity Mission, Gulph Mills, 1913, minister in charge until 1915; dean of convocation, Norristown, 1910-19; instr. religious pedagogy, Ch. Training and Deaconess House, 1916-27. Author: Washington at Valley Forge, 1905; Historical and Topographical Guide to Valley Forge, 1906-29; etc. Awarded "Philadelphia Award" for service advancing best interests of Philadelphia, 1928. Home: Valley Forge, Pa. Died June 30, 1933.

BURKE, Daniel Webster, brig. gen. U.S.A.; b. in Conn., Apr. 22, 1841. Served pvt., corporal and 1st sergt. cos. E and B, 2d Inf., June 10, 1858-Nov. 8, 1862; advanced through grades to brig. gen., Oct. 20, 1899; retired at own request after 40 yrs.' service, Oct. 21, 1899. Bvtd.: capt., July 2, 1863, and maj., Jan. 22, 1867, "for gallant and meritorious services in battle of Gettysburg, Pa.;" lt. col. for same during the war; awarded Congl. Medal of Honor, Apr. 21, 1892, "for distinguished gallantry in action at Shepherdstownford, W.Va. Home: Portland, Ore. Died 1911.

BURKE, Edmund Whitney, lawyer; b. Byron, Ill., Sept. 22, 1850; s. Patrick and Nancy (Whitney) B.; A.M., Northwestern U., 1869; LL.B., U. of Mich., 1871; m. Myra Webster, Dec. 5, 1878. Began practice at Chicago, 1876; judge Circuit Ct. of Cook Co., 1893-1902; judge Appellate Ct., 1st Ill. Dist., 1902-03; mem. Burke, Jackson & Burke; lecturer on equity, jurisprudence and procedure, 1893—, dean, 1904—, Chicago-Kent Coll. of Law. Republican. Methodist. Home: Chicago, Ill. Died Sept. 7, 1918.

BURKE, Edward Timothy, lawyer; b. Minneapolis, Nov. 5, 1870; s. John H. and Bridget (O'Boyle) B.; student U. of N.D.; A.B., National U., Washington, D.C., LL.M., 1931; LL.B., U. of Minn., 1894; m. Florence E. Getchell, Dec. 25, 1900; children—Charles Getchell, John Edward, Robert Eugene. Admitted to bar, 1894, and practiced at Valley City; state's atty., Barnes Co., N.D., 1901-05; judge Dist. Court, 5th Jud. Dist., N.D., 1905-11; justice Supreme Court of N.D., 1911-19; resumed practice at Bismarck, N.D.; chief atty. Land Div. Dept. of Justice, Washington, 1926—. Progressive Republican. Mason. Died Dec. 25, 1935.

BURKE, James Francis, lawyer; b. Petroleum Center, Pa., Oct. 21, 1867; s. Richard J. and Ann (Arnold) B.; LL.B., U. of Mich., 1892; LL.D., Duquesne U.; m. Josephine B. Scott, Apr. 15, 1895; children—Josephine Frances, James Scott. Admitted to Pa. bar, 1893, and practiced since at Pittsburgh. Founder and 1st pres., 1892, Am. Rep. Coll. League; sec. Rep. Nat. Com., 1892; mem. 59th to 63d Congresses (1905-15), 31st Pa. Dist.; govt. dir. War Savings, 1918; gen. counsel Chamber Commerce of U.S., Rep. Nat. Com. Catholic. Home: Pittsburgh, Pa. Died Aug. 8, 1932.

BURKE, Jeremiah Edmund, supt. schs.; b. Frankfort, Me., June 25, 1867; s. Patrick and Mary (Hughes) B.; A.B., Colby Coll., 1890, A.M., 1893, Litt.D., 1915; LL.D., Villanova (Pa.) Coll., 1922, Holy Cross Coll., 1925; m. Matilda Catherine Lynch,

Oct. 2, 1901; children—Margaret, Edmund. Supt. schs., Waterville, Me., 1891-93, Marlboro, 1893-94, Lawrence, 1894-1904; asst. supt. schs., Boston, 1904-21, supt., Nov. 1921—. Mem. Mass. State Bd. of Edn., 1914-17. Ex-officio pres. Teachers Coll. of City of Boston. Democrat. K.C. Home: Dorchester, Mass. Died Oct. 29, 1931.

BURKE, John, judge; b. Sigourney, Ia., Feb. 25, 1859; s. John and Mary (Ryan) B.; ed. common schs. and State U. of Ia.; LL.B., from same; m. Mary E. Kane, Aug. 22, 1891; children—Elizabeth, Thomas J., Marion. Admitted to Ia. bar, 1886, and began practice at Des Moines; moved to Dak. Ty., 1888; elected to N.D. Ho. of Rep., 1890, Senate, 1892; gov. of N.D., 1907-13; treas. of U.S., 1913-21; asso. justice Supreme Court of N.D., 2 terms, 1925-37; chief justice, Jan. 1, 1935—. Democrat. Home: Bismarck, N.D. Died May 14, 1937.

BURKE, John J., church official; b. New York, June 6, 1875; s. Patrick and Mary (Regan) B.; A.B., St. Francis Xavier's Coll., 1896; S.T.B. and S.T.L., Catholic U., 1901; Litt.D., Fordham, 1915. Ordained R.C. priest, 1899; mem. Congregation of St. Paul the Apostle. Editor Catholic World, 1904-22. Former chmn. exec. bd. Catholic Press Assn.; and chmn. com. on spl. activities Nat. Catholic War Council; gen. sec. Nat. Catholic Welfare Conf. D.S.M. (U.S.), 1919; S.T.D. from Pius XI, 1927. Died Oct. 30, 1936.

BURKE, Joseph Henry, clergyman, educator; b. Richwood, Wis., Apr. 10, 1876; s. John and Mary (Nolan) B.; A.B., U. of Notre Dame, 1904; theol. course, Holy Cross Coll., 1905-08; grad. study Cath. U. of America, 1905-09; Ph.D., 1909. Ordained priest R.C. Ch., 1909; prof. history and polit. science, U. of Notre Dame, 1909-10, prefect of discipline, 1910-16, dir. studies, prep. dept., 1916-19, dean of studies, 1916-25; pres. St. Edward's Univ., Austin, Tex., 1925-31; prin. St. Thomas Mil. Acad., 1931-33; rector of Dillon Hall, 1933-34, superior Community Infirmary, 1934-37, U. of Notre Dame; pastor St. Bernard's Ch., Watertown, Wis., July 1937—. Died Dec. 30, 1940.

BURKE, Maurice Francis, bishop; b. in Ireland, May 5, 1845; s. Francis Noonan and Joanna (Casey) B.; ed. at St. Mary's of the Lake, Chicago, and Notre Dame, Ind.; for 9 yrs. student at Am. Coll., Rome, Italy. Ordained priest there, May 22, 1875; asst. priest, St. Mary's Ch., Chicago, Ill., till 1878; rector St. Mary's, Joliet, Ill., 1878-87; consecrated bishop of Cheyenne, Wyo., Oct. 28, 1887; transferred to see of St. Joseph, Mo., June 19, 1893. Hon. pres. Am. Dante Soc. Died Mar. 17, 1923.

BURKE, Robert Emmet, congressman, lawyer; b. Tallapoosa Co., Ala., Aug. 1, 1847; volunteered as private, Co. D, 10th Ga. cav., C.S.A., at age of 16; served until close of war; removed to Jefferson, Tex., 1866; admitted to bar, Nov. 1870; located in Dallas, 1871; county judge, 1878-84; dist. judge, 1888-96; mem. Congress, 1897— (6th Tex. dist.); term expired 1901. Democrat. Home: Dallas, Tex. Died 1901.

BURKE, Stevenson, r.r. pres., lawyer, jurist; b. St. Lawrence Co., N.Y., Nov. 26, 1824; admitted to bar, Elyria, O., 1848; judge common pleas and dist. court, 1862-69; practiced law in Cleveland, 1869—. Gen. counsel and dir. Cleveland & Mahoning Valley R.R., 1872-89, then pres., dir. and gen. counsel; dir. and gen. counsel, C.,C.,C.&I. Ry. Co., 1875-81; then v.p. and pres., 1886; also pres. Columbus, Hocking Valley & Toledo Ry. Co., 1881-86; v.p. Indianapolis & St. Louis Ry. Co., 1882-86; pres. Toledo & Ohio Central, and Kanawha & Mich. Ry. Co., 1886—; pres. Central Ontario Ry. Co., 1894—; also pres. Republic Coal Co., Canadian Copper Co., Anglo-Am. Iron Co. Home: Cleveland, O. Died 1904.

BURKE, Thomas, judge; b. in Clinton Co., N.Y., Dec. 22, 1848; s. James and Bridget Delia B.; grad. Acad. Ypsilanti, Mich., 1870; student lit. dept. U. of Mich., 1870-71, law dept., 1871-72; (LL.D., Whitman Coll., Wash., 1902); m. Caroline E. McGilvra, Oct. 6, 1879. Admitted to bar, 1873; in practice at Seattle, Wash., 1875—. Judge Probate Ct., King Co., Wash., 1876-80; candidate for Congress, 1880; chief justice Supreme Ct., Wash. Ty., Dec. 1888-Apr. 1889; resigned. Republican. Trustee Carnegie Endowment for Internat. Peace, 1910—. Home: Seattle, Wash. Died Dec. 4, 1925.

BURKE, Thomas Martin Aloysius, bishop; b. in Ireland, Jan. 10, 1840; s. Dr. Ulic B.; came in childhood to Utica, N.Y.; studied in St. Michael's Coll., Toronto; grad. classics at St. Charles' Coll., Md., 1861; taught in coll.; studied theology in St. Mary's Sem., Baltimore, A.M. and B.T., 1864. Ordained R.C. priest, June 30, 1864; asst. St. John's, Albany, 1864-65; asst. and rector, 1865-74, pastor 1874-94, St. Joseph's, Albany; vicar gen. diocese of Albany, 1887, adminstr., sede vacante, upon death of Bishop McNeirney; preconized May 18, 1894, consecrated July 1, 1894, bishop of Albany. Created Knight of the Holy Sepulchre, 1890; Knight of the Grand Cross, 1894. Died Jan. 20, 1915.

BURKE, William J., congressman; b. Sept. 25, 1862; ed. pub. schs., Reynoldsville, Pa. Long identified with organized labor; chmn. gen. com. of adjustment, Order of Railroad Conductors of B.&O. R.R. system; elected mem. Pa. Senate, 1914; mem. City Council, Pittsburgh, 1917-18; mem. 66th and 67th Congresses (1919-23), at large Pa. Republican. Home: Pittsburgh, Pa. Died Nov. 7, 1925.

BURKET, Jacob F., judge Supreme Court, Ohio, 1893-1904; b. Perry Co., O., March 25, 1837; grad. Seneca Co. Acad., Republic, O., 1859; studied law; admitted to bar, 1861; practiced at Ottawa, O., 1861-62; at Findlay, O., 1862-93; elector on Garfield and Arthur ticket, 1880; grand master Odd Fellows of Ohio, 1882-83; pres. Am. Nat. Bank, Findlay, 1887—; practiced law, 1904—. Home: Findlay, O. Died 1906.

BURKETT, Elmer Jacob, lawyer; b. Mills Co., Ia., Dec. 1, 1867; s. Henry W. and Catharine (Kearney) B.; B.Sc., Tabor Coll., Ia., 1890; LL.B., U. of Neb., 1893, LL.M., 1895; m. Fannie F. Wright, Sept. 1, 1891. In practice at Lincoln, Neb., June 1, 1893—; then mem. Burkett, Wilson, Brown & Van Kirk. Member Neb. Ho. of Rep., 1896-98; mem. 56th to 59th Congresses (1899-1905), 1st Neb. Dist.; U.S. senator, 1905-11. Republican. Trustee Tabor Coll., 1895-1905. Home: Lincoln, Neb. Died May 23, 1935.

BURKHALTER, Edward Read, clergyman; b. New York, Dec. 21, 1844; s. Stephen and Euphemia (Linen) B.; A.B., Princeton, 1862; univs. of Berlin and Heidelberg, 1864-65, Union Theol. Sem., 1867-70; (D.D., Lenox, 1884, Princeton, 1895; LL.D., Coe, 1906); m. Lucy Anna Denise, July 12, 1870 (died Oct. 1914). Ordained Presbyn. ministry, 1870; pastor New Rochelle, N.Y., 1870-76; instr. Hebrew, Union Theol. Sem., 1873-74; pastor First Ch., Cedar Rapids, Ia., 1876-Dec. 1914; emeritus. Mem. Gen. Assembly's com. (Presbyn Ch.) on revision of Westminster Confession of Faith, 1890-92; pres. bd. trustees, Coe Coll. Home: Cedar Rapids, Ia. Died June 15, 1923.

BURKHARDT, Samuel, Jr., army officer; b. Palos, Cook Co., Ill., Sept. 10, 1865; s. Samuel and Margaret Burkhardt; grad. U.S. Military Acad., 1889. Commd. 2d lt. 25th Inf., June 12, 1889; 1st lt. 10th Inf., Jan. 1, 1897; capt., 19th Inf., Sept. 16, 1899; maj., Mar. 11, 1911; lt. col., July 1, 1916; col., July 29, 1917. Participated in Sioux Indian campaign, 1890-91, Santiago campaign, 1898; at Havana and Matanzas, Cuba, Dec. 1898-Nov. 1899; duty Philippines, 1900-02, 1905-07, 1910-12; at Vera Cruz, Mex., Apr.-Nov. 1914. Died Dec. 29, 1929.

BURKHARDT, Wilbur Neil, newspaper editor; b. Altoona, Ia., Nov. 11, 1889; s. Ferdinand and Mary Estelle (Neil) B.; student U. of Wis., 1911-12; m. Irene Catherine Wilson, June 16, 1914; 1 son, Wilbur Neil. Began newspaper work at Des Moines, 1904; moved to Calif., 1923; editor and v.p. San Francisco News, 1923—. Mem. Christian (Disciples) Ch. Home: San Francisco, Calif. Deceased.

BURKHART, Summers, lawyer; b. Martinsburg, Va. (now W.Va.), June 26, 1859; s. William Davidson and Nannie Forest (Summers) B.; Coll. of St. James, Washington Co., Md.; m. Miriam Parsons, May 8, 1889. Admitted to N.M. bar, 1888; clk. 1st Jud. Dist. Ct. of N.M., 1889; clk. Supreme Ct. of N.M., 1889-91 (resigned); city atty., Albuquerque, 1893-94; asst. U.S. atty. Ct. of Pvt. Land Claims, 1894-96 (resigned); mem. Bd. of Aldermen, Albuquerque, 1899-1900; chmn. Dem. Central Com., Bernalillo Co., 1896-1908 (resigned); sec. Dem. State Com., 1908-11; del. Dem. Nat. Conv., 1908; Dem. candidate for justice Supreme Ct. of N.M., 1st State election, 1911 (defeated); legal adviser to gov. of N.M., 1912-13 (resigned); U.S. atty. for N.M., Aug. 5, 1913-Mar. 3, 1921, resigned. Active in securing passage in Congress of the "Flood Amendment" to N.M. Constn. Episcopalian. Home: Albuquerque, N.M. Died May 14, 1932.

BURKS, Martin Parks, judge, educator; b. Liberty (now Bedford City), Va., Jan. 23, 1851; s. Judge Edward C. and Mildred Elizabeth (Buford) B.; A.B., Washington Coll. (now Washington and Lee U.), 1870; B.L., U. of Va., 1872; LL.D., Roanoke Coll., 1903, Washington and Lee U., 1920; m. Roberta Gamble Bell, Dec. 31, 1874; children—Martin P., Elizabeth Gladding (dec.). Reporter of Supreme Ct. of Appeals of Va., 1895-1917; asso. justice Supreme Ct. Appeals of Va., Mar. 1917—. Prof. law, 1900-14, dean law faculty, 1903-17, Washington and Lee U.; one of revisers of the statute laws of Va., 1914-17. Episcopalian. Democrat. Author: Property Rights of Married Women in Virginia; Burks' Pleading and Practice (Common Law), 1913. Lived at Lexington, Va. Died April 30, 1928.

BURLEIGH, Clarence, lawyer; b. Boston, Dec. 20, 1853; s. Thomas D. and Mary L. (Cook) B.; B.A., Western Univ. of Pa.; m. Ida May Wier, Apr. 11, 1878. Admitted to Pa. bar, 1877; asst. city solicitor, Pittsburgh, 1887-91; dist. atty. of Allegheny Co., 1891-95; city solicitor, Pittsburgh, 1895-1902; gen. counsel Pittsburgh Rys. Co., 1902—; mem. Burleigh & Challener. Republican. Methodist. Mason. Home: Pittsburgh. Died 1923.

BURLEIGH, Clarence Blendon, newspaper editor; b. Linneus, Me., Nov. 1, 1864; s. Edwin Chick and Mary Jane (Bither) B.; A.B., Bowdoin, 1887, A.M., 1890; m. Sarah P. Quimby, Nov. 24, 1887. Editor Kennebec Journal, 1887—. Republican. Author: The Smugglers of Chestnut, 1891; The National Editorial Association in Florida, 1895; "Bowdoin 1887," 1900; The Camp on Letter K, 1906; Raymond Benson at Krampton, 1907; The Kenton Pines, 1907; All Among the Loggers, 1908; With Pickpole and Peavey, 1909. Home: Augusta, Me. Died 1910.

BURLEIGH, Edwin Chick, U.S. senator; b. at Linneus, Me., Nov. 27, 1843; s. Hon. Parker Prescott and Caroline Peabody (Chick) B.; ed. common schs. and Houlton Acad.; taught sch. and was land surveyor; m. Mary Jane Bither, June 28, 1863; 1 son, Clarence Blendon. Publisher Kennebec Journal, 1887—. Enlisted in D.C. cav., but illness prevented his passing med. exam.; served in office of state adj. gen.; clk. state land office, 1870-76, state land agt., 1876-78; asst. clerk, Me. Ho. of Rep., 1876-78; clerk in office state treas., 1880-84; state treas., 1885-88; gov. of Me., 1889-92; mem. 55th to 61st Congresses (1897-1911), 3d Me. Dist.; mem. U.S. Senate for term 1913-19. Del.-at-large Rep. Nat. Conv., 1896. Address: Augusta, Me. Died June 16, 1916.

BURLEIGH, George Shepard, author; b. Plainfield, Conn., March 26, 1821; s. Rinaldo and Lydia (Bradford) B.; common school education; reared on farm; m. Ruth Burgess, March 17, 1849. Author: The Maniac, and Other Poems; Signal Fires on the Trail of the Pathfinder (vol. of Fremont campaign poetry). Edited Charter Oak, an anti-slavery paper, in Hartford, Conn. Translated Victor Hugo's The Legend of the Centuries, 1874 XI. Home: Providence, R.I. Died 1903.

BURLEIGH, George William, lawyer; b. Great Falls, N.H., Apr. 18, 1870; s. George William and Louise Hannah (Bryant) B.; prep. edn., St. Paul's Sch., Concord, N.H.; B.A., Princeton, 1892; M.A., 1895; studied law New York Law Sch.; m. Isis Yturbide Potter, d. late Gen. Robert F. Stockton, Nov. 21, 1894. Admitted to N.Y. bar, 1894; dir. Cayuga & Susquehanna R.R. Co., Church Properties Fire Ins. Corp. Private Vet. Corps Arty., N.Y., 1915, advancing to col. C.A.C.; comdr. 9th C.D.C., Sept. 1918-Oct. 1919; judge adv. gen. State of N.Y., 1921-24; col. J.A.G. Insp. Gen. (Res.). U.S.A.; then col. inactive reserve, U.S.A. Commander Legion of Honor (France); Comdr. Order of the Crown (Italy); Order of the Rising Sun, 3d class (Japan), Cross of Independence, Poland, Conspicuous Service Cross of State of N.Y. Mem. bd. mgrs. and treas. Seamen's Church Inst. of America. Episcopalian; vestryman and clk. of vestry, Trinity Parish, New York. Home: New York, N.Y. Died Mar. 15, 1940.

BURLEIGH, Sydney Richmond, artist; b. Little Compton, R.I., July 7, 1853; s. George Shepard and Ruth (Burgess) B.; ed. pub. schs.; hon. A.M., Brown U., 1912; m. Sarah Drew Wilkinson, June 3, 1875. Awarded bronze medal, St. Louis Expn., 1904; open prize, Buffalo (N.Y.) Soc. Artists, 1913. Home: Providence, R.I. Died Feb. 25, 1931.

BURLESON, Albert Sidney, postmaster gen.; b. San Marcos, Tex., June 7, 1863; s. Edward and Emma (Kyle) B.; A.B., Baylor U., 1881; B.L., U. of Tex., 1884; m. Adele Steiner, 1889; children—Laura (Mrs. Richard Van Wyck Negley), Lucy Kyle (Mrs. Charles Greene Grimes), Adele Sidney. Admitted to bar, 1885; asst. city atty., Austin, 1885-90; atty. 26th Jud. Dist., Texas, 1891-98; mem. 56th to 62d Congress, 1899-1903, 9th Tex. Dist., and 1903-13, 10th Dist.; re-elected to 63d Congress, but resigned; postmaster gen. in cabinet of President Wilson, Mar. 5, 1913-Mar. 4, 1921. Apptd. chmn. U.S. Telegraph and Telephone Adminstrn., July 31, 1918; chmn. U.S. commn. to Internat. Wire Communication Conf., 1920. Home: Austin, Tex. Died Nov. 24, 1937.

BURLESON, Hugh Latimer, bishop; b. Northfield, Minn., Apr. 25, 1865; s. Solomon Stevens and Abigail (Pomeroy) B.; B.A., Racine Coll., Wis., 1887; B.D., Gen. Theol. Sem., New York, 1893; S.T.D., Hobart Coll., Geneva, N.Y., 1913; D.D., Gen. Theol. Sem., 1919; m Helen S. Ely, Apr. 4, 1894, 1 son, John Ely. Deacon, 1893, priest, 1894, P.E. Ch.; curate Ch. of Holy Communion, New York, 1893-94; rector Waupaca, Wis., 1894-98; asst. St. Luke's Ch., Rochester, N.Y., 1898-1900; dean Cathedral of Dist. of N.D., 1900-07; sec. Bd. of Missions P.E. Ch. in U.S., 1909-16; editor Spirit of Missions, 1913-16; elected bishop of S.D., Oct. 25, 1916, consecrated Dec. 14, 1916; became asst. to presiding bishop of P.E. Ch. Mem. Nat. Council Episcopal Ch. (1st v.p.). Author: The Conquest of the Continent, 1911; Our Church and Our Country, 1918. Home: New York, N.Y. Died Aug. 1, 1933.

BURLESON, Rufus Columbus, clergyman, educator; b. near Decatur, Ala., Aug. 7, 1823; s. Jonathan and Elizabeth B.; ed. Nashville Univ.; grad. Western

Bapt. Theol. Sem., 1847; ordained to ministry, Starkville, Miss., 1845; m. Georgiana Jenkins, Jan. 3, 1853. Pastor First Baptist Ch., Houston, 1848-51; pres. Baylor Univ., 1851-97; has preached in every town in Tex. except new towns and railroad stations; baptized Gen. Sam Houston, the hero of San Jacinto, and Mrs. Dickinson, the heroine of the Alamo. Has been co-laborer of Sam Houston, Gen. Rush, Gov. Pease, and other distinguished Texans in establishing a grand system of railroads in Tex.; pioneer of co-education in the South. Home: Waco, Tex. Died 1901.

BURLEY, Clarence Augustus, lawyer; b. Chicago, Ill., Oct. 10, 1849; s. Augustus H. and Anna Maria (Force) B.; student Amherst Coll., 1868 (now grad.); LL.B., Union Coll. of Law, Chicago, 1876; m. Avis H. Blodgett, Nov. 11, 1880; m. 2d, Mary E. Blodgett, Mar. 17, 1913. Admitted to Ill. bar, 1876; associated with William H. McSurely, 1897, and established firm of Burley & McSurely, which was dissolved on election of Mr. McSurely as judge of the Superior Court. Republican. Unitarian. Home: Winnetka, Ill. Died Feb. 23, 1928.

BURLIN, Natalie Curtis (Mrs. Paul Burlin), musician; b. N.Y. City; d. late Edward and Augusta Lawler (Stacey) Curtis; studied music, France and Germany; m. Paul Burlin, artist, July 25, 1917. Has made spl. study of musical lore, song-poetry and decorative art of N. Am. Indians; also folklore and music of Africans and Am. Negroes; lecturer before ednl. instns. and scientific bodies. Author: Songs of Ancient America, 1905; The Indians' Book, 1907; Negro Folk-Songs, 1918. Home: New York, N.Y. Died Oct. 23, 1921.

BURLINGAME, Edward Livermore, editor; b. Boston, Mass., May 30, 1848; s. Hon. Anson B. and Jane C. (Livermore) B.; entered Harvard, but left before graduation; private sec. to his father while Am. minister to China; studied in Europe; Ph.D., University of Heidelberg, 1869; (hon. A.M., Harvard U., 1901; Litt.D., Columbia, 1914); m. Ella F. Badger, 1871. On staff New York Tribune, 1871; asst. in revision of Am. Cyclopedia, 1872-76; editorially connected with Charles Scribner's Sons, 1879—, and mem. bd. dirs., 1904—; editor Scribner's Mag., 1886-1914. Home: New York, N.Y. Died Nov. 15, 1922.

BURLINGAME, Eugene Watson, philologist; b. Albany, N.Y., Aug. 5, 1876; s. Eugene and Emma Patton (Watson) B.; B.A., Yale, 1898, M.A., 1902; Ph.D., U. of Pa., 1910; studied Harvard U., 1909-10, Johns Hopkins, 1914-16; unmarried. Served as classical master, St. Luke's and Haverford schs., near Philadelphia, 1902-07, and 1910-13; Harrison fellow and fellow for research in Sanskrit, U. of Pa., 1908-11; Johnston Scholar in Sanskrit and comparative philology, Johns Hopkins, 1914-16; engaged in original investigations and publs. in Indic philology and Hindu fiction, at Yale, 1917—. Fellow Am. Acad. Arts and Sciences. Democrat. Episcopalian. Author: (dissertation) Buddhaghosa's Dhammapada Commentary, 1910; Act of Truth, 1917. Translator: Buddhist Legends, 3 vols. (Harvard Oriental Series, 28-30), 1921; Buddhist Parables, 1922; The Grateful Elephant and Other Stories (illustrated), 1923; Parabole Buddhiste, 1926. Home: Albany, N.Y. Died Aug. 3, 1932.

BURLINGAME, Luther D., mech. engr.; b. Whitesboro, N.Y., Jan. 12, 1865; s. Luther R. and Emeline S. (Aldrich) B.; ed. pub. schs.; m. Christine Ward; children—Mrs. Grace C. Lockwood, Harold L., Mrs. Ethel R. Spooner, Stanley W. With Brown & Sharpe Mfg. Co. since beginning of active career, industrial supt., 1914—, also patent expert. Mem. Nat. Screw Thread Commn.; mem. Joint Com. Am. Soc. Mech. Engrs. and Soc. Am. Engrs. as sponsors of Engring. Standards Com. Republican. Baptist. Home: Providence, R.I. Died June 2, 1932.

BURLINGHAM, Aaron Hale, Bapt. clergyman; b. Castile, N.Y., Feb. 18, 1822; s. Charles and Hannah (Hale) B.; grad. Colgate (formerly Madison) Univ., A.M.; studied divinity, Hamilton Theol. Sem. (D.D., Shurtliff Coll.); m. Emma Starr, Nov. 11, 1851. Pastor: Pittsburgh, Pa.; Owego, Boston, New York, Am. Chapel, Paris; St. Louis. Dist. sec. N.Y. City of Am. Bapt. Missionary Union. Home: Mt. Vernon, N.Y. Died 1905.

BURMA, John Harmon, clergyman, educator; b. Ackley, Ia., Feb. 8, 1874; s. Harmon F. and Anna (Nutbrook) B.; A.B., U. of Dubuque, Ia., 1896; grad. theol. dept., same, 1899; D.D., Trinity U., Waxahachie, Tex., 1917; LL.D., Austin Coll., Sherman, Tex., 1924; m. Manetta Knock, 1899. Ordained Presbyn. ministry, 1899; pastor Hanover, Ill., 1899-1903, Knoxville, Ia., 1903-08, Dallas, Tex., 1908-16; v.p. U. of Dubuque, 1916-20; pres. Trinity Univ., Waxahachie, Tex., from 1920-33; pastor Central Ch., Sherman, 1933—. Mason. Home: Sherman, Tex. Died Mar. 16, 1938.

BURNAM, Anthony Rollins, judge; b. Richmond, Ky., Oct. 10, 1846; s. Curtis F. and Sarah H. (Rollins) B.; ed. Richmond, Ky., and Asbury (now De Pauw) Univ.; m. Margaret A. Summers, Nov. 5, 1874. Admitted to bar, 1869; U.S. collector internal revenue 4 yrs.; asso. justice, 1897-1903, chief justice, 1903-04, Ct. of Appeals of Ky.; mem. Ky. Senate, 1907-11; mem. Rep. Nat. Com. for Ky. Home: Richmond, Ky. Died Sept. 9, 1919.

BURNAM, John Miller, univ. prof.; b. Irvine, Ky., Apr. 9, 1864; s. Rev. Edmund Hall and Margaret Shackelford (Miller) B.; student Central U., Richmond, Ky., 1877-78, Washington U., St. Louis, 1878-80; A.B., Yale, 1884, Ph.D., 1886; in Europe, 1886-89, summers of 1890, 1896-97, 1899-1900, 1903-04, 07, 10-11; unmarried. Prof. Latin and French, Georgetown (Ky.) Coll., 1889-91; asst. prof. Latin, U. of Mo., 1891-99; prof. Latin, U. of Cincinnati, Sept., 1900—. Contbr. American Journal of Archæology, etc. Home: Cincinnati, O. Deceased.

BURNETT, Charles, army officer; b. Knoxville, Tenn., Oct. 28, 1877; s. Jackson G. and Nancy (Smith) B.; student Blackburn Coll., Ill., 1894-95; B.S., U.S. Mil. Acad., 1901; m. Frances Hawks Cameron, Mar. 15, 1905. Commd. 2d lt. U.S. Army, 1901, and advanced through grades to brig. gen., 1937; chief Bur. Insular Affairs, War Dept., Washington, D.C., 1937—. Awarded D.S.M., Victory, and Philippine, Spanish-Am., Mexican Campaign medals (all U.S.); decorated by Japanese, French, Italian, Mexican, Swedish and Ecuador govts. Episcopalian. Died Nov. 28, 1939.

BURNETT, Edgar Albert, educator; b. Hartland, Mich., Oct. 17, 1865; s. Ellsworth S. and Eliza Mary (Crane) B.; B.S., Mich. State Agrl. College, 1887, D.Sc., 1917; LL.D., Nebraska Wesleyan U., 1933; m. Nellie E. Folsom, June 22, 1899; 1 son, Knox Folsom. Asst. in Mich. State Agrl. Coll., 1889-93; prof. animal husbandry, S.D. State Coll., 1896-99; prof. animal husbandry, U. of Neb., 1899-1907, asso. dean in charge of agrl. instrn., 1901-09, dean of Agrl. College, 1909-28, chancellor, 1928-38, U. of Neb. (emeritus). Dir. Neb. Agrl. Expt. Sta., 1901-28. Mem. Am. Ednl. Corps, A.E.F. Univ. Beaune, France. Author of various bulls. of Neb. Agrl. Expt. Sta. Home: Lincoln, Neb. Died June 28, 1941.

BURNETT, Edwin Clark, surgeon; b. Mansfield, O., Jan. 19, 1854; s. Dwight and Mary Ann (Bristol) B.; ed. pvt. and pub. schs., Olney, Ill., and pvt. tutors; M.D., St. Louis Med. Coll. (now med. dept. Washington U.), 1883; unmarried. Practiced medicine, Olney, Ill., 1883-84; returned to St. Louis and began spl. study of genito-urinary diseases in clinics for those diseases at St. Louis Med. Coll.; chief of this clinic, 1890, lecturer on syphilis, 1893; clin. prof. genito-urinary diseases, Washington U., 1904-11. Republican. Deceased.

BURNETT, Frances Hodgson (Mrs. Stephen Townsend), author; b. (Frances Eliza Hodgson), Manchester, Eng., Nov. 24, 1849; family moved to Knoxville, Tenn., 1865; began writing for magazines in 1867; m. Dr. Swan Moses Burnett, 1873; settled in Washington, D.C., 1875; obtained divorce, 1898; m. 2d, Stephen Townsend, 1900 (died 1914). Author: (novels) That Lass o' Lowrie's, 1877; Dolly, a Love Story; Kathleen; Surly Tim and Other Stories, 1877; Haworth's, 1879; Louisiana, 1880; A Fair Barbarian, 1881; Through One Administration, 1883; Little Lord Fauntleroy, 1886; Sara Crewe, 1888; Two Little Pilgrims' Progress: The Pretty Sister of José, 1896; A Lady of Quality, 1896; His Grace of Ormonde, 1897; A Little Princess, 1905; The Shuttle, 1907; The Cozy Lion, 1907; Good Wolf, 1908; Spring Cleaning, 1908; The Dawn of Tomorrow, 1909; The Secret Garden, 1909; My Robin, 1912; T. Tembarom, 1913; Barty Crusoe and His Man Saturday, 1914; One I Knew the Best of All, 1915; The Lost Prince, 1915; Land of the Blue Flower, 1916; Head of the House of Coombe, 1922. Plays: Little Lord Fauntleroy; Phyllis, the Showman's Daughter; Esmeralda; The First Gentleman of Europe; Nixie (with Stephen Townsend); A Lady of Quality (with same). Home: Plandome, L.I., N.Y. Died Oct. 29, 1924.

BURNETT, George Henry, judge; b. Yamhill Co., Ore., May 9, 1853; s. George William and Sidney Ann (Younger) B.; A.B., Christian Coll., Monmouth, Ore., 1873; m. Miriam Belt, Dec. 31, 1879. Practiced law at Salem, 1876-92; dist. atty., 3d Jud. Dist., Ore., 1876-78; reporter, Supreme Ct., Ore., 1890-92; judge Circuit Ct., 3d Dist., 1892-1911, justice Supreme Court of Ore., 3 terms, 1911-29. Republican. Mason. Home: Salem, Ore. Died Sept. 10, 1927.

BURNETT, Henry Lawrence, lawyer; b. Youngstown, O., Dec. 26, 1838; attended Chester Acad.; LL.B., Ohio State Nat. Law Sch., 1859; admitted to bar; married. Capt. 2d Ohio Cav., Aug. 23, 1861; maj. judge adj. vols., Aug. 10, 1863; bvtd. col. vols., Mar. 8, 1865, "for diligent and efficient services," and brig. gen. vols., Mar. 13, 1865, "for meritorious services" in Bur. of Justice; hon. mustered out, Dec. 1, 1865; with General Holt and John A. Bingham was engaged in prosecution of the assassins of Lincoln. In practice, Cincinnati, 1865-72, New York, 1872—; U.S. dist. atty., Southern Dist. of N.Y. Republican. Home: New York, N.Y. Died Jan. 4, 1916.

BURNETT, John Lawson, congressman; b. Cedar Bluff, Ala., Jan. 20, 1854; s. William E. J. and Mary N. (Brandon) B.; father died, 1858; mother supported him and his brothers by teaching until they were old enough to work; worked on farm and in mines, going to school between crops; studied law at Vanderbilt U.; m. Bettie Reader, Dec. 13, 1886. Was admitted to bar, 1876; practiced in Gadsden, Ala.; mem. Ala. Ho. of Rep., 1884, Senate, 1886; mem. 56th to 65th Congresses (1899-1919), 7th Ala. Dist.; chmn. com. on Immigration and Naturalization. Mem. U.S. Immigration Commn., 1907—. Democrat. Home: Gadsden, Ala. Died May 13, 1919.

BURNETT, John Torrey, mfg. chemist; b. Southboro, Mass., Apr. 23, 1868; s. Joseph and Josephine (Cutter) B.; student Harvard, 1891; m. Phyllis Abbot, Nov. 13, 1909; children—Frances, Joseph. Pres. Joseph Burnett Co., Boston, Mass., 1906—; v.p. North End Savings Bank; sec. and treas. Mass. Bonding and Ins. Co.; treas. Big Sandy Co., City Central Corp. of America. Democrat. Episcopalian. Home: Southboro, Mass. Deceased.

BURNETT, Robert M., treas. and dir. Deerfoot Farm Co.; dir. Boston Herald, Inc., Boston R.R. Holding Co., Boston & Me. R.R., Eastern Adv. Agency. Home: Southboro, Mass. Died Apr. 28, 1929.

BURNETT, Swan Moses, M.D.; b. New Market, Tenn., March 16, 1847; grad. Bellevue Hosp. Med. Coll., 1870; began practice in Knoxville, Tenn.; removed to Washington, 1876; prof. ophthalmology and otology, Georgetown Univ., 1879—, and in Washington Post Grad. Med. Sch. Pres. attending staff Central Dispensary and Emergency Hosp.; mem. staffs Children's and Providence hosps. Died 1906.

BURNHAM, Clara Louise, author; b. Newton, Mass.; d. late Dr. George F. Root, composer; moved to Chicago in childhood; married when very young. Has written poems and stories for many mags., and the text for many of her father's cantatas. Author: No Gentlemen, 1881; A Sane Lunatic, 1882; Dearly Bought, 1884; Next Door, 1886; Young Maids and Old, 1888; The Mistress of Beech Knoll, 1890; Miss Bagg's Secretary, 1892; Dr. Latimer, 1893; Sweet Clover, 1894; The Wise Woman, 1895; Miss Archer Archer, 1897; A Great Love, 1898; A West Point Wooing, 1899; Miss Pritchard's Wedding Trip, 1901; The Right Princess, 1902; Jewel, 1903; Jewel's Story Book, 1904; The Opened Shutters, 1906; The Leaven of Love, 1908; Clever Betsy, 1910; The Inner Flame, 1912; The Right Track, 1914; Instead of the Thorn, 1916; Hearts Haven, 1918; In Apple Blossom Time, 1919; The Keynote, 1921; The Queen of Farrandale, 1923; The Lavarous, 1925. Home: Chicago, Ill. Died June 21, 1927.

BURNHAM, Claude George, ry. official; b. Peterboro, Eng., June 20, 1879; s. Harry and Fanny (Brawn) B.; ed. pub. schools of St. Paul; m. Mary Gillis, Sept. 6, 1904. Began ry. service with G.N. R.R., St. Paul, 1895, with which remained in various capacities, 7 yrs.; entered foreign traffic dept. of C.,B.&Q. R.R., 1902, becoming foreign traffic agt., 1904; asst. to the 1st v.p., 1906; v.p. in charge of traffic C.,B.&Q. and C.&S. railroads, 1910-17; exec. v.p. C.,B.&Q. and C.&S. railroads, Oct. 1, 1917-June 21, 1918; federal mgr., C.,B.&Q. and Q.,O.&K.C. rys., June 21, 1918-Nov. 6, 1919; exec. v.p. C.,B.&Q. and C.&S. lines, 1919—. Democrat. Home: Kenilworth, Ill. Died June 22, 1928.

BURNHAM, Daniel Hudson, architect; b. Henderson, N.Y., Sept. 4, 1846; s. Edwin and Elizabeth B.; removed to Chicago, 1856; ed. there and in Mass.; studied architecture at Chicago; (hon. A.M., Harvard and Yale, 1893; Sc.D., Northwestern, 1895; LL.D., U. of Ill., 1905); m. Margaret S. Sherman, Jan. 20, 1876. Sr. mem. firm Burnham & Root, 1872-91, D. H. Burnham & Co., 1891—. Architect of the Rookery, The Temple, Masonic Temple, Ill. Trust Bank, Great Northern Hotel, First National Bank, Ry. Exchange, Field's retail store and many other bldgs. in Chicago and elsewhere, including the Mills Bldg. (San Francisco), Ellicott Sq. (Buffalo), Soc. for Savings and First, Third and Fourth National banks (Cleveland), Land Title Bldg. (Phila.), and new Wanamaker stores, Phila. and New York; Union Sta., Washington; Flatiron Bldg., New York; Selfridge's Store, London, Eng.; Pacific Union Club, San Francisco; Continental-Commercial Bank, Ins. Exchange and Ry. Exchange, Chicago; Filene's, Boston. Chief architect and dir. of works, Chicago Expn., 1890-93; chmn. Nat. Commn. of Fine Arts, and of commn. for beautifying Cleveland, O.; planned cities of Manila, Bagnio, San Francisco, Chicago, Fellow A.I.A. (pres., 1894); mem. Nat. Inst. Arts and Letters. Home: Evanston, Ill. Died June 1, 1912.

BURNHAM, Frederic Lynden, art educator; b. Taunton, Mass., 1871; s. Arunah A. L. and Alice B.; ed. pub. and pvt. schs., Mass. Normal Art Sch., Boston, and Grad. Dept., Yale; m. Elizabeth J. Hinckley, June 28, 1900. Began as teacher of drawing, Taunton night schs.; supervisor of drawing, N. Adams, Mass., 1896-99, New Haven, Conn., 1899-1903, Providence, R.I., 1903-05; agt. for promotion of manual arts in State of Mass, 1906—. Lecturer Mass. Normal Art Sch., 1906—; mem. faculty and instr. in summer courses, Hyannis Normal Sch., Mass. Republican. Baptist. Home: Cambridge, Mass. Died 1911.

BURNHAM, George, congressman; b. London, Eng., Dec. 28, 1868; s. James and Maria Ann Drucilla (Steele) B.; ed. pub. schs.; m. Neva May Ashley, Oct. 1, 1890 (died 1927); children—Beth Marie (dec.), Harold Ashley, Percy Edmund, Helen Estella (wife of Jefferson D. Beard, U.S.N.), Laurence Malin, Virginia Jean (wife of Robt. F. Hickey, U.S.N.), Ben Ashley; m. 2d, Florence Kennett, Dec. 25, 1932. Came to U.S., 1881, naturalized, 1890. Began as clerk in store, 1884; opened shoe store, Jackson, Minn., 1887; organizer Ashley-Burnham Land Co., Spokane, Wash., 1901; engaged in ranching and real estate business, Calif., 1903-17; became v.p. Southern Trust & Commerce Bank, 1917; v.p. Bank of Italy, 1927-30; v.p. its successor Bank of America, 1930-32; mem. 73d and 74th Congresses (1933-37), 20th Calif. Dist. An organizer Panama-Calif. Expn., 1909, v.p., 1909-16; hon. commercial commr. to China, 1910; pres. San Diego Chamber of Commerce, 1910-11; an organizer San Diego Area Council of Boy Scouts of America, pres., 1921; v.p. Calif.-Pacific Internat. Expn., 1935-36. Republican. Mason. Home: Coronado, Calif. Died June 1939.

BURNHAM, George, Jr., retired; b. Philadelphia, Pa., Nov. 30, 1849; s. George and Anna (Hemple) B.; C.E., Rensselaer Poly. Inst., 1872; m. Anna G. Lewis, Apr. 14, 1881. Dir. Central Nat. Bank and the Integrity Trust Co., of Phila.; mem. Burnham, Williams & Co. until 1907, when retired. Mem. Phila. Common Council, 1907. Mem. council Nat. Civ. Service Reform League; pres. Pa. Civ. Service Reform Assn. Home: Philadelphia, Pa. Died Nov. 22, 1924.

BURNHAM, Henry Eben, senator; b. Dunbarton, N.H., Nov. 8, 1844; s. Henry L. and Maria A. (Bailey) B.; A.B., Dartmouth, 1865; studied law in offices and admitted to bar, 1868; m. Elizabeth H. Patterson, Oct. 22, 1874. Dir. Amoskeag National Bank, N.H. Fire Ins. Co. Mem. N.H. Ho. of Rep., 1873-74; treas. Hillsborough County, 1875-77; judge of probate, 1876-79; chmn. Rep. State Conv., 1888; del. N.H. Constl. Conv., 1889; ballot law commr., 1893; U.S. senator, 1901-07, 1907-13. Del. Rep. Nat. Conv., 1904. Home: Manchester, N.H. Died Feb. 8, 1917.

BURNHAM, John Bird; b. New Castle, Del., Mar. 16, 1869; s. John and Elizabeth von Leuveneigh (Bird) B.; B.A., Trinity Coll., Conn., 1891; m. Henrietta Heathcote DuBois, June 15, 1892. Mgr. Forest and Stream, 1891-97; prop. Crater Club; owner Highlands Game Preserve, Willsboro, N.Y. Supervisor Town of Essex, 1902-08; chief game protector and dep. commr. State Forest Fish and Game Commn. of N.Y., 1905-11. Pres. Am. Game Protective Assn., 1911-28; chmn. advisory com. to U.S. Dept. Agr. on migratory bird law, 1913-31, resigned; chmn. U.S. Forest Service Com. on game in nat. forests, resigned 1931. Awarded gold medal Camp Fire Club of America, 1926. Republican. Episcopalian. Mason. Author: The Rim of Mystery, 1929. Home: Keeseville, N.Y. Died Sept. 24, 1939.

BURNHAM, Michael, Congl. clergyman; b. Essex, Mass.; s. Michael and Patience (Andrews) B.; grad. Phillips Acad., Andover, Mass., July, 1863; Amherst Coll., 1867 (A.M., 1877); grad. Andover Theol. Sem., 1870 (D.D., Beloit, 1887); m. Cassandra V. Washburn, February 8, 1871. Ordained October 25, 1870, pastor Central Congregationalist Church, Fall River, Massachusetts; remained until May 1882; pastor Immanuel Congl. Church, Boston Highlands, 1882-85; 1st Ch., Springfield, Mass., 1885-94; Pilgrim Ch., St. Louis, 1894-1905. Trustee Wheaton Female Sem., 1874, Hartford Theol. Sem., 1886—, Amherst Coll., 1888—, School for Christian Workers, Springfield, Mass., 1891—, Drury Coll., 1894—; dir. Chicago Theol. Sem., 1895-1903; corporate mem. A.B.C.F.M., Oct. 28, 1885—; chaplain Mo. Soc. Sons Revolution, 1897, 1899; preached annual sermon for same, 1899, 1901, 1903. Died 1905.

BURNHAM, Ralph W(arren), antiques; b. Ipswich, Mass.; s. Joseph Howard and Sarah Thomas (Trott) B.; grad. Manning High Sch., Ipswich, 1895; m. Nellie Mae Dow, Dec. 25, 1900. Bookkeeper shoe machinery co., Boston, 1896-99; partner Globe Shoe Tool Co., 1899-1900; traveling salesman, United Shoe Machinery Co., 1900-06; dealer in antiques, 1906—; propr. of The Burnham House, 1906-12, Burnham's Antique Trading Post, 1912—. Mem. Sch. Bd., Ipswich, 1918-24, chmn. bd., 1924. Republican. Conglist. Restorer of many historic bldgs.; originator of Burnham system of bldg. constrn. Deceased.

BURNHAM, Sherburne Wesley, astronomer; b. Thetford, Vt., Dec. 12, 1838; (hon. A.M., Yale, 1878). Took up study of astronomy as an amateur, and made many discoveries, especially of double stars, with a 6-inch refractor; observer in pvt. obs., Chicago, 1870-77, Dearborn Obs., Chicago, 1877-81 and 1882-84, Washburn Obs., Madison, Wis., 1881-82; astronomer Lick Obs., 1888-92; prof. practical astronomy and astronomer Yerkes Obs., U. of Chicago, 1893—. Has discovered 1,274 new double stars; expert commr. to test the seeing on Mt. Hamilton, Cal., resulting in locating the Lick Obs. there, 1879. Gold medal, Royal Astron. Soc. (for discovery and measurement of double stars), 1894; Lalande prize in astronomy, Paris Acad. Sciences, 1904. Fellow, 1874, asso. 1898, Royal Astron. Soc.; asso. fellow Am. Acad. Arts and Sciences, etc. Author of Vol. I, publs. of Yerkes Obs. (gen. catalogue of stars discovered by him), 1900; also a gen. catalogue of all known double stars visible in Northern Hemisphere, for Carnegie Instn., Washington, 1907; Measures of Proper-Motion Stars, 1912. (hon. Sc.D., Northwestern U., 1915.) Died Mar. 11, 1921.

BURNHAM, Silas Henry, banker; b. Harrison, Me., Apr. 12, 1848; s. Sumner and Christiana (Washburn) B.; A.B., Dartmouth, 1874; studied law in office of Charles F. Libby, Portland, Me.; m. Eliza Lewis, Oct. 24, 1876. Practiced law in Norway, Me., 1876-80; moved to Lincoln, Neb., 1880; organizer, 1888, and cashier and gen. mgr. Am. Exchange Nat. Bank; bought State Nat. Bank, Lincoln, 1892, and merged same with Am. Exchange Nat. Bank, of which was pres.; bought 1st Nat. Bank of Lincoln, 1899, and merged same with Am. Exchange Nat. Bank under name of 1st Nat. Bank of Lincoln; bought Columbia Nat. Bank, 1907, and merged same with 1st Nat. Bank of Lincoln; organized 1st Savings Bank of Lincoln, 1907, 1st Trust Co., 1912; now chmn. bd. First Nat. Bank and First Trust Co. of Lincoln; v.p. Lincoln Telephone & Telegraph Co. Republican. Congregationalist. Home: Lincoln, Neb. Died Sept. 2, 1933.

BURNHAM, Sylvester, theologian; b. Exeter, N.H., Feb. 1, 1842; s. Edwin and Alice (Dennett) B.; A.B., Bowdoin, 1862, A.M., 1865, D.D., 1885; S.T.D., Colgate, 1918; grad. Newton Theol. Instn., 1873; student univs. of Heidelberg, Göttingen, Leipzig, at various times; m. Miriam M. Tucker, June 28, 1876; 1 dau., Alice Miriam (Mrs. William A. Meyers). Ordained Bapt. ministry, 1873; pastor Amherst, Mass., 1873-74; teacher Greek and German, Worcester (Mass.) Acad., 1874-75; prof. Semitic langs. and O.T. interpretation, 1875-1918, dean, 1893-1910, Theol. Sem. of Colgate U.; retired 1918. Mem. Soc. Bibl. Lit. and Exegesis, Am. Philol. Assn., Council of 70 of Am. Inst. Sacred Lit. Author: Manual of Old Testament Interpretation, 1882; Elements of Syriac Grammar, 1884; Elements of Biblical Hermaneutics, 1916. Home: Newburyport, Mass. Died Sept. 23, 1935.

BURNHAM, William Henry, univ. prof.; b. Dunbarton, N.H., Dec. 3, 1855; s. Samuel and Hannah (Dane) B.; A.B., Harvard, 1882; Ph.D., Johns Hopkins, 1888; unmarried. Instr. Wittenberg Coll., 1882-83, State Normal Sch., Potsdam, N.Y., 1883-85, Johns Hopkins, 1888-89; docent in pedagogy, 1890-92, instr., 1892-1900, asst. prof., 1900-06, prof. pedagogy and sch. hygiene, 1906-26, Clark U. (emeritus). Fellow A.A.A.S. Asst. editor Pedagogical Seminary; departmental editor (hygiene) Cyclo. of Edn. Author: The Normal Mind; Great Teachers and Mental Health. Home: Dunbarton, N.H. Died June 25, 1941.

BURNHAM, William Power, army officer; b. Scranton, Pa., Jan. 10, 1860; s. Maj. David Roe (U.S. Army) and Olive E. (Power) B.; ed. Kan. State Agrl. Coll.; at West Point, 1877-80; grad. U.S. Inf. and Cav. Sch., 1889; m. Grace F. Meacham, Feb. 18, 1890; 1 son, Edward Meacham. Was enlisted man 14th U.S. Inf., 1881-83; promoted from ranks July 1883; served lt. col. 4th Mo. Vols., Spanish-Am. War, and in Philippine Insurrection, 1900-02; maj. U.S. Army, Aug. 20, 1906; mem. gen. staff, 1907-11; lt. col. and comdt. Army Service Schs., Ft. Leavenworth, 1912-14; col. inf., May 1, 1916; comdr. Puerto Rico Regt. of Inf. and Dist. of P.R., 1914-17; served in Canal Zone, May-July 1917; comd. 56th Inf., July-Aug. 1917; brig. gen. N.A., Aug. 5, 1917; assigned to command 164th Inf. Brigade, 82d Div., Camp Gordon, Atlanta, Ga.; maj. gen., Apr. 12, 1918; comd. 82d Div., Dec. 1917-Oct. 5, 1918; in front line sectors (Toul and Moselle River), June-Sept. 1918, St. Mihiel offensive, Sept. 12-16, and Battle of Meuse-Argonne, Sept. 26-Oct. 5, 1918; mil. attaché and Am. del. Inter-Allied Mil. Commn., Athens, Greece, Oct. 20, 1918-June 9, 1919; hon. disch. as temp. maj. gen., July 1919, and reverted to rank of col., regular army; comdr. Ft. McDowell, Angel Island, and Presidio, San Francisco, Aug. 1919-Jan. 1924; brig. gen. Jan. 1, 1924, retired Jan. 10, 1924. Companion of the Bath (English); Croix de Guerre and Officer Legion of Honor (French); Medal of Military Merit, 1st class (Greek). Author: Three Roads to a Commission in the United States Army, 1892; Duties of Outposts, Advance Guards, etc., 1893. Died Sept. 27, 1930.

BURNS, Charles Wesley, bishop; b. Willow Grove, Pa., May 28, 1874; s. George Harrison and Elisabeth Virginia (Bickley) B.; grad. Central High Sch., Phila., 1894; A.B., Dickinson Coll., 1896, A.M., 1899, D.D., 1906, LL.D., 1920; S.T.B., Boston U. Sch. of Theology, 1899; S.T.D., Wesleyan U., Conn., 1920; LL.D., Hamline, 1920, U. of Southern Calif., 1925, Coll. of Pacific, 1932; m. Laura P. Carson, June 11, 1901; children—George Robert, Charles Wesley, Elisabeth Virginia, Barbara. Ordained M.E. ministry, 1899; city missionary, Worcester, Mass., 1899; pastor Lansdowne, Pa., 1899-1904, Coatesville, Pa., 1904-05, Spring Garden Ch., Phila., 1905-06, 1st Ch., Phila., 1906-16, Hennepin Av. Ch., Minneapolis, 1916-20; bishop M.E. Ch., May 1920—. Resident bishop Helena Area, 1920-24, San Francisco Area, 1924-32, Boston Area, 1932—. Trustee Boston Univ., Wilbraham Acad., East Greenwich Acad., N.E. Deaconess Hosp. Mem. Bd. of Hosps. and Homes of M.E. Ch.; pres. Mass. Council of Chs., 1933—. Republican. Home: Boston, Mass. Died Jan. 19, 1938.

BURNS, Cornelius F., mayor; b. Troy, N.Y.; s. John W. and Ellen (Gorman) B.; ed. pub. schs., St. Peter's Acad., La Salle Inst.—all Troy; unmarried. Mem. J. W. Burns' Sons, etc.; has served many terms as mayor of Troy; ex-pres. N.Y. State Conference of Mayors; v.p. Nat. Rivers and Harbors Congress; v. chmn. Deeper Hudson, and officer or dir. various other water organizations; actively interested in water-power development. Mem. Troy Chamber of Commerce (ex-pres.); chmn. Rensselaer County Red Cross Soc. Democrat. Address: Troy, N.Y. Died May 23, 1938.

BURNS, Francis Highlands, insurance pres.; b. Baltimore, Md., May 14, 1873; s. Findley Highlands and Elizabeth Dixon (Brown) B.; student Mass. Inst. Tech.; m. Mary LeGrand Slingluff, Apr. 6, 1899; children—Elizabeth LeGrand, Mary Slingluff (Mrs. J. Albert Owens). Steamship business, 1892-98; an organizer Md. Casualty Co., 1898, 3d v.p., 1905, later 2d and 1st v.p., pres., 1920—; v.p. Western Nat. Bank. Democrat. Episcopalian. Home: Baltimore, Md. Died Mar. 30, 1935.

BURNS, James Aloysius, clergyman, author; b. Michigan City, Ind., Feb. 13, 1867; s. Patrick and Bridget (Connolly) B.; A.B., U. of Notre Dame, Ind., 1888, A.M., 1894; studied theology, same, 1890-93, Ph.D., Catholic U. of America, 1907. Teacher, Sacred Heart Coll., Watertown, Wis., 1888-90; ordained R.C. priest, 1893; prof. sciences, U. of Notre Dame, 1893-1900; became pres. and prof. of moral theology, Holy Cross College, Washington, D.C., July 1900; pres. U. of Notre Dame, 1919-22; provincial superior Congregation of Holy Cross in U.S., 1927-38; asst. to the Superior General, 1938—. Author: Principles, Origin and Establishment of the Catholic School System, 1908; Growth and Development of the Catholic School System, 1912; Catholic Education—A Study of Conditions, 1917. Home: Notre Dame, Ind. Died Sept. 9, 1940.

BURNS, James Austin, educator, lawyer; b. Oxford, Me., Jan. 25, 1840; grad. Bowdoin, 1862 (Ph.D., 1885); admitted to bar, New Haven, Conn., 1861; m. 1864, Mary J. Granniss; m. 2d, Mrs. Lucie E. McClurkan. Served through war as lt. and capt., 7th Conn. inf.; later on staff duty; after war settled at Atlanta, Ga.; prof. chemistry, Southern Med. Coll., 1882-92. Has published a series of Juxtalinear Translations of Greek and Latin classics. Engaged in practice of law. Home: Atlanta, Ga. Died 1902.

BURNS, James J., author; b. Brownsville, O., Oct. 26, 1838; s. Rev. John and Mary Jewett (Pearson) B.; ed. in pub. schs. of several Ohio towns and by pvt. study; read law 3 yrs. at Natchez, Miss., and Washington, O.; (hon. A.M., Washington and Jefferson Coll., 1882; Ph.D., Ohio State U.); m. Kate E. Lyle, July 1860. Began as teacher in 1858; state commr. of common schs., Ohio, 1877-80. Author: Eclectic Geometry, 1884; Story of Shakespeare's English Kings, 1899; How to Teach Reading and Composition, 1900; Some Unsetting Lights of English Literature, 1902; The Educational History of Ohio, 1905. Home: Defiance, O. Died 1911.

BURNS, Louis Henry, judge; b. New Orleans, May 11, 1878; s. Louis and Emily Nebraska (Brockett) B.; LL.B., Tulane, 1904; m. Julia W. Schillinger, Nov. 28, 1896; 1 dau., Louise Hazel (Mrs. George S. Graham). Admitted to the La. bar, 1904; asst. U.S. atty., Eastern Dist. of La., 1911-13; U.S. atty., same dist., 1921-25; U.S. dist. judge, Eastern Dist., La., by appmt. of President Coolidge, Oct. 3, 1925. Mem. Prog. State Central Com., 1912-16; del. Prog. Conv., 1912, 16; candidate for Congress, 1st Dist. of La., 1914; chmn. law com. Prog. Party, 1912-16. Civilian aide to adj. gen. U.S.A., 1917-18; mem. bd. of govs. Mil. Training Camps Assn. U.S., 1917-22. Presbyn. Mason. Home: New Orleans, La. Died June 9, 1928.

BURNS, Melvin P., clergyman; b. Canada, Sept. 14, 1866; s. Bernard and Julia Ann (Baker) B.; ed. Valparaiso (Ind.) Normal U., 1888-90, Little Rock U., 1890-94; D.D., Hamline, 1912, Wesley Coll., N.D., 1912; Ph.D., Ill. Wesleyan U., 1912; m. Jennie B. Tipton, May 10, 1893; children—Wendell T., Russell W., Mildred E. Came to U.S., 1880, naturalized citizen, 1886. Ordained M.E. ministry, 1890; pastor Stuttgart, Ark., 1893-96, Casselton, N.D., 1896-99; supt. Jamestown (N.D.) Conf., 1899-1902, Fargo Dist., N.D., 1922-24, Grand Forks Dist., 1904-07, Minneapolis Dist., Northern Minn.

Conf., 1907-12, Duluth Dist., 1912-16; supt. Dept. of City Work, Bd. of Home Missions, M.E. Ch., 1916—. Republican. Mason. Home: Philadelphia, Pa. Died Sept. 21, 1930.

BURNS, Michael Anthony, neuropsychiatrist; b. Phila., Pa., May 24, 1884; s. James M. and Mary A. (Rowen) B.; M.D., Jefferson Med. Coll., 1907; m. Margaret Agnes Keenan, Oct. 11, 1910; children—Paul Valentine, John Anthony. Asst. visiting neurologist, Phila. Gen. Hosp., 1912-20, visiting neurologist, 1920—; asst. prof. nervous and mental diseases, Jefferson Med. Coll., 1927, prof. neurology, 1934—; cons. neurologist, St. Joseph's Hosp.; neuropsychiatrist, St. Mary's Hosp., Phila. Served with A.E.F., Base Hosp. No. 38; apptd. consultant to dist. of Paris, Dec. 1918, disch. June 1919. Fellow Am. Coll. of Phys., Coll. of Phys. of Phila. Democrat. Catholic. Home: Bala-Cynwyd, Pa. Died Mar. 7, 1938.

BURNS, Walter Noble, author, newspaperman; b. Lebanon, Ky., Oct. 24, 1872; s. Col. Thomas Edgar and Chris Ella (Noble) B.; ed. pub. and high schs., Louisville, Ky.; m. Rose Marie Hoke, Nov. 10, 1902. Began newspaper work on Louisville Evening Post, 1890; later connected with St. Louis Post Dispatch, Kansas City Times, Denver Republican, and San Francisco Examiner; was Sunday editor Chicago Inter-Ocean, 1910-14, Chicago Examiner, 1915, Chicago Tribune, 1918. Made a whaling voyage in the brigantine Alexander, out of San Francisco, in the 90's, to the South Seas, Behring Sea and Arctic Ocean. Served in 1st Ky. Inf., Spanish-Am. War, 1898, taking part in Porto Rico campaign. Republican. Presbyn. Author: A Year With a Whaler, 1913; The Saga of Billy the Kid, 1926; Tombstone, 1927; The One Way Ride, 1931; The Robin Hood of El Dorado, 1932. Died April 15, 1932.

BURNS, William Henry, clergyman; b. New Glasgow, N.S., Can., Sept. 11, 1840; s. Mitchell and Mary Ann (Morrow) B.; A.B., Wesleyan U., Conn., 1867; A.M., 1869 (D.D., 1892); m. Anna P. Foster, May 1, 1872. Ordained M.E. ministry, 1872; pastor in Ill. at St. Paul's Ch., Chicago, 1869-72, Warren, 1872-73, Evanston, 1873-74, Rockford, 1874-77, Elgin, 1877-80, Joliet, 1880-83, Western Av. Ch., Chicago, 1883-86, Wesley Ch., Chicago, 1886-90; presiding elder Joliet Dist., 1890-91, Chicago Dist., 1891-97; pastor, Oak Park, 1897-99; traveled in Europe, and the East, 1899-1900; pastor, Woodlawn, Avondale, Wicker Park and Fowler chs., Chicago, 1900-09; Rock Conf. evangelist, 1909—. Del. Gen. Conf., Omaha, 1891. Author: The Higher Critics' Bible or God's Bible, 1904; Crisis in Methodism, 1909; Answer to Criticisms of Crisis in Methodism, 1910. Home: Evanston, Ill. Died Apr. 4, 1916.

BURNS, William John, detective; b. Baltimore, Oct. 19, 1861; s. Michael and Bridget (Trahey) B.; ed. parochial and pub. schs. and bus. coll.; m. Annie M. Ressler, July 5, 1880; children—George Edward (dec.), Charles Edwin (dec.), Mrs. Florence Borough, Raymond Joseph, William Sherman, Mrs. Kathleen King. Founder and for many years pres. The William J. Burns Internat. Detective Agency; dir. Bur. of Investigation of U.S. Dept. of Justice, 1921-24, resigned. Col. Res. Corps, U.S.A. Republican. Catholic. Died April 14, 1932.

BURPEE, Lucien Francis, judge; b. Rockville, Conn., Oct. 12, 1855; s. Col. Thomas F. and Adeline M. (Harwood) B.; brother of Charles Winslow B.; A.B., Yale U., 1879; LL.B., Hamilton, 1880; admitted to bar, 1881; m. Lida Wood, Sept. 26, 1882 (died 1889); m. 2d, Ina A. Fitch, Apr. 28, 1904. Pros. atty. 1883-90, corp. counsel, 1890-96, Waterbury, Conn.; judge Waterbury City Ct., 1897-1909; judge Superior Court of Conn., 1909-17; justice Supreme Court of Errors of Conn., 1921—. Col. 2d Regt. Conn. N.G., 1895-99; lt. col. U.S. Vols., 1898; on staff Gen. N. A. Miles and Gen. J. H. Wilson in P.R. in Spanish War; hon. mention for distinguished services; resigned and hon. disch., 1899. Was made pres. Mil. Emergency Bd. of Conn., Mar. 9, 1917; commd. maj. gen. comdg. Conn. state troops, Nov. 14, 1917; chmn. com. on state protection Conn. Council of Defense, 1917; del. Nat. Council of Defense, 1917. Home: West Hartford, Conn. Died May 9, 1924.

BURPEE, W(ashington) Atlee, seedsman; b. Sheffield, N.B., Can., Apr. 5, 1858; s. David (M.D.) and Ann Catherine (Atlee) B.; ed. Friends' Central Sch., Phila.; studied 2 yrs., U. of Pa., class of 1878; m. Blanche Simons, Apr. 30, 1892. Started in seed business with two partners, 1876; 2 yrs. later began alone, adopting name of W. Atlee Burpee & Co., now the largest exclusive mail order seed house in the world; owns 3 large seed farms in Bucks Co., Pa., Gloucester Co., N.J., and Santa Barbara Co., Calif. Mem. exec. bd. Nat. Farm Sch. Republican. Home: Doylestown, Pa. Died Nov. 26, 1915.

BURR, Anna Robeson, author; b. Philadelphia, Pa., May 26, 1873; d. Henry Armitt and Josephine Lea (Baker) Brown; ed. pvt. schs.; m. Charles H. Burr, May 27, 1899. Author: The Autobiography—A Study, 1909; Religious Confessions, 1914; The House on Charles Street, 1923; The Great House in the Park, 1924; St. Helios, 1925; The Portrait of a Banker, 1927; Palludia, 1928; Weir Mitchell, 1929; The Same Person, 1931; Wind in the East, 1933; Alice James—Her Journal, 1934; Golden Quicksand (novel), 1936. Home: Bryn Mawr, Pa. Died Sept. 10, 1941.

BURR, C(olonel) B(ell), M.D.; b. Lansing, Mich., Nov. 3, 1856; s. Allen R. and Catharine (Foote) B.; acad. edn., Lansing; M.D., Coll. Phys. and Surg. (Columbia), 1878. Specialist in nervous and mental diseases; asst. phys., 1878-85, asst. med. supt., 1885-89, med. supt., 1889-94, Eastern Mich. Asylum at Pontiac; med. dir. Oak Grove Hosp. for nervous and mental diseases, Flint, Mich., 1894-1920. Fellow Am. Coll. Physicians. Mason. Author: Practical Psychology and Psychiatry, 1921. Compiler, for Mich. State Med. Soc., of Medical History of Michigan, 1929. Home: Flint, Mich. Died Apr. 11, 1931.

BURR, Enoch Fitch, author; b. Westport, Conn., Oct. 21, 1818; grad. Yale, 1839; (D.D., Amherst; LL.D., London). Spent several yrs. in New Haven in theol. and scientific studies, then traveled abroad; became Congl. pastor at Lyme, Conn., 1850. Author: Facts in Aid of Faith; Celestial Empires; Universal Beliefs; Long Ago as Interpreted by the 19th Century; Tempted to Unbelief; The Stars of God and many others. Home: Lyme, Conn. Died 1907.

BURR, George Elbert, artist; b. Monroe Falls, Ohio, Apr. 15, 1859; s. Linus E. and Lucy Ellen (Gaylord) B.; ed. Art Institute, Chicago, and studied five years in France and Italy; m. Elizabeth Rogers, 1884. Paints in oil and water colors. Awarded gold, silver, and bronze medals; made 1,000 pen drawings of bronzes, jades, lacquers, porcelains, etc., for catalogs of Heber R. Bishop collection, N.Y. City (a task of 4 yrs.); set of 35 etchings of Am. desert. Works in perm. collections of Luxembourg, Paris; Met. Mus. and Pub. Library, New York; Carnegie Inst., Pittsburgh; Congressional Library, Washington, D.C.; Art Inst. Chicago; U. of Colo.; Calif. State Library; Brit. Mus., Victoria and Albert Mus., London; Bibliothèque Nationale, Paris; Berlin Museum; Boston Mus.; Cincinnati Art Mus.; Fogg Mus., Cambridge, Mass.; Phoenix Art Museum, and in other museums. Unitarian. Home: Phoenix, Ariz. Died Nov. 17, 1939.

BURR, George Howard, investment banker; b. Florence, Mass.; s. George Ames and Sarah M. (Ely) B.; prep. edn., Friends Sch., Providence, R.I.; B.S., Worcester Poly. Inst., 1886; m. Cecilie de Wasilowska, of Poland, Jan. 7, 1925. Chmn. bd. of Burr & Co., Inc., successor to Geo. H. Burr & Co. Served as Am. Red Cross commr. to France. Officer Legion of Honor (France). Republican. Home: New York, N.Y. Died Dec. 18, 1939.

BURR, George Lincoln, librarian; b. Oramel, N.Y., Jan. 30, 1857; s. William Josiah and Jane (Lincoln) B.; A.B., Cornell U., 1881; student Leipzig, Sorbonne and École des Chartes, Paris, and Zurich, 1884-86, 1887-88; LL.D., U. of Wis., 1904; Litt.D., Western Reserve, 1905; m. Martha Martin, Aug. 20, 1907 (died 1909). Librarian The President White Library, 1878—; mem. Cornell faculty, 1888—; prof. mediæval history, 1892-1919, and John Stambaugh prof. history, 1919-1922. Hist. expert Venezuelan Boundary Commn. Author: The Literature of Witchcraft, 1890; The Fate of Dietrich Flade, 1891; Narratives of the Witchcraft Cases (1648-1706), 1913. Home: Ithaca, N.Y. Died June 27, 1938.

BURR, George Washington, army officer; b. Tolono, Ill., Dec. 3, 1865; s. George W. and Nancy (Scott) B.; grad. U.S. Mil. Acad., 1888; m. Lydia Kent. Commd. 2d lt. 1st Arty., June 11, 1888; promoted through grades to col., July 1, 1916; brig. gen. (temp.), Aug. 6, 1918; maj. gen. (temp.), Mar. 5, 1919; brig. gen., ordnance dept., July 2, 1920. At Presidio, San Francisco, 1890; duty Ft. Hamilton, N.Y., 1891-93; prof. mil. science and tactics, A. and M. Coll. of Miss., 1893-94; various duties to 1907; in Philippines, 1907-10; chief ordnance officer Philippines Div., mem. Fortification Bd., etc.; comdr. Augusta Arsenal, Ga., 1910-11, Rock Island Arsenal, chief ordnance officer, Central Dept., 1911-18; chief ordnance officer, Am. Forces in Eng., and representing U.S. Ordnance Dept. in Eng., 1918; apptd. chief of engring. div. Ordnance Dept., Oct. 1918; apptd. asst. dir. purchase, storage and traffic Gen. Staff, Washington, D.C., Nov. 29, 1918; apptd. asst. chief of staff and dir. of purchase, storage and traffic, Gen. Staff, Mar. 1, 1919. Mem. War Dept. Claims Bd., settling Govt. war business, 1919; spl. rep. Sec. of War in Europe settling war business with English and other govts., Sept.-Dec. 1920; asst. to chief of ordnance, Washington, D.C., Jan. 1921—. Awarded D.S.M.; Companion Order of the Bath (British). Died Mar. 4, 1923.

BURR, Joseph Arthur, judge; b. Brooklyn, N.Y., Sept. 11, 1850; s. Joseph Arthur and Harriet (Nash) B.; A.B., Yale, 1871; LL.B., Columbia, 1873; m. Ella A. Dawson, Oct. 22, 1874. Admitted to bar, 1874. Corp. counsel of City of Brooklyn from Jan. 1, 1896, until Brooklyn was consolidated with New York; justice Supreme Ct. of N.Y., Dec. 1904—; judge Appellate Div., Jan. 1909—; term expires Dec. 31, 1918. Presbyn. Home: Brooklyn, N.Y. Died Apr. 18, 1915.

BURR, Nelson Beardsley, ry. official; b. Auburn, N.Y., Feb. 3, 1871; s. Charles Porter and Frances (Powers) B.; B.S., Yale, 1893; LL.B., Harvard, 1895; m. Helen Van Courtland Morris, June 29, 1904. Practiced law at N.Y. City, 1895-1910; v.p. St.L.& S.W. Ry. Co., 1910—; dir. Am. Writing Paper Co. Trustee Post-Grad. Hosp., Kingsland Av. Children's Home (N.Y.). First lt. Co. B, 12th N.Y. Inf., Spanish-Am. War; lt. col. and col. 12th N.Y. Inf.; col. 212th Arty. (antiaircraft), World War. Republican. Episcopalian. Home: Oyster Bay, L.I., and New York. Died Feb. 11, 1928.

BURR, William Henry, reporter, author; b. Stump City (now Gloversville), N.Y., Apr. 15, 1819; s. James B.; grad. Union Coll., 1838; learned shorthand; became reporter of official record, U.S. Senate; later court reporter, New York; official reporter on Congressional Globe, Washington, D.C., 1865-69; m. Julia A. Simonton, 1850 (died 1867); 2d, Victoria A. Osborn, 1869. Author: Self-Contradictions of the Bible, 1860; Revelations of Antichrist, 1879; both published anonymously. Died 1908.

BURR, William Hubert, civil engr.; b. Watertown, Conn., July 14, 1851; s. George William and Marion Foote (Scovill) B.; C.E., Rensselaer Poly. Inst., 1872; m. Caroline Kent Seelye, 1876 (died 1894); children—Mrs. Marion Elisabeth Mars, William Fairfield, George Lindsley; m. 2d, Gertrude Gold Shipman, 1900; 1 dau., Mrs. Anne Louisa Colgate. Began practice as civ. engr., 1872; prof. rational and tech. mechanics, Rensselaer Poly. Inst., 1876-84; asst. to chief engr., and later gen. mgr., Phœnix Bridge Co., 1884-91; prof. engring. Harvard, 1892-93; prof. civil engring., 1893-1916, prof. emeritus, Columbia U.; civil engr. and consulting engr., N.Y. City, 1916—. Consulting engr. to dept. pub. works, 1893-95, parks, 1895-97, of docks, 1895-97, and then dept. of bridges and bd. of water supply, New York. Mem. bd. of engrs. to investigate feasibility of proposed bridge across North River, 1894; mem. bd. to locate deep water harbor on coast of Southern Calif., 1896; mem. Isthmian Canal Commn. to examine and report upon most feasible and practicable route for an interoceanic canal across the Central American Isthmus, 1902; mem. and chmn. Commn. on Additional Water Supply of City of New York; mem. Isthmian Canal Commn. and mem. bd. consulting engrs., 1905—; cons. engr. to bd. of water supply, New York; mem. advisory bd. of engrs. for constrn. of Barge Canal by State of N.Y., 1911; mem. bd. cons. engrs. by commns. states of N.Y. and N.J. for constructing vehicular tunnel under Hudson river at N.Y City, 1919; cons. engr. N.Y. State Transit Commn., 1923-24, for Port of New York. Authority, 1925—, for constrn. of Ft. Washington Suspension Bridge across Hudson River, and for other bridges being built for the Port. Awarded 1st place in national competition, 1900, for proposed memorial bridge across Potomac at Washington. Decorated Order of Sacred Treasure, 2d degree (Japan). Fellow Am. Acad. Arts and Sciences. Trustee Cathedral of St. John the Divine. Author: The Stresses in Bridge and Roof Trusses, 1881; Elasticity and Resistance of the Materials of Engineering, 1883; Ancient and Modern Engineering and the Isthmian Canal, 1902; The Graphic Method by Influence Lines for Bridge and Roof Computation (with M. S. Falk), 1905; The Design and Construction of Metallic Bridges (with M. S. Falk), 1912; Suspension Bridges, Arch Ribs and Cantilevers, 1913. Home: New Canaan, Conn. Died Dec. 13, 1934.

BURR, William P., judge; b. Dublin, Ireland, Mar. 30, 1856; s. John Archbold and Anne (Lovely) B.; St. James Coll., Baltimore, 1871-73; LL.B., Columbia Coll. of Law, New York, 1879; m. Jennie Philomene Lynch, Aug. 25, 1884 (died 1918); children—Mrs. Natalie Coleman, William Archbold (dec.), Mrs. Constance Trivanovitch, Mrs. Jennie P. Dailey, Mrs. Annette Ross, John Lovely. Began practice, N.Y. City, 1879; del. Constl. Conv., 1894; asst. corp. counsel, City of New York, 1904-14; apptd. corp. counsel, 1918; apptd. justice Supreme Court of N.Y., Apr. 1920, and elected for term expiring Dec. 31, 1926; asso. justice Appellate Div., 1924-27; official referee of the Supreme Court of N.Y., 1927—. Democrat. Catholic. Home: New York, N.Y. Died Nov. 13, 1930.

BURRAGE, Albert Cameron, lawyer; b. Ashburnham, Mass., Nov. 21, 1859; s. George S. and Aurelia (Chamberlin) B.; A.B., Harvard, 1883; m. Alice Hathaway Haskell, Nov. 10, 1885; children—Albert Cameron, Francis H. (dec.), Elizabeth A. (Mrs. Harold L. Chalifoux), Russell. Admitted to Mass. bar, 1884; became counsel Brookline Gas Light Co., 1892, later pres. of the Boston, South Boston, Roxbury and Dorchester gas light cos., and the Bay State Gas Co. Resigned, 1898, to enter copper mining on a large scale; an organizer Amalgamated Copper Co. and a dir. until its dissolution. Mem. Boston Common Council, 1892; mem. Boston Transit Commn. that built the Boston Subway. Republican. Awards: Geo. R. White gold medal; Lindley medal, Royal Hort. Soc., Great Britain. Home: Boston, Mass. Died June 28, 1931.

BURRAGE, Charles Dana, lawyer; b. Ashburnham, Mass., Feb. 20, 1857; s. George S. and Aurelia (Chamberlin) B.; bro. of Albert Cameron B.; A.B., U. of Calif., 1878; m. Martha W. Heywood, June 30, 1884 (died Feb. 17, 1923); m. 2d, Mrs. Irene P. Clapp, Mar. 25, 1925. Admitted to bar, 1882; practiced at Gardner, 1883-97, Boston, 1897—; v.p. and counsel, Boston Gas cos., 1897-1902; founder Rosemary Press; officer many business and mining corps.; resident v.p. Am. Surety Co., of New York. Republican. Mason. Wrote: The Message of Omar Khayyam; Sky Lines of Great Cities, 1923. Has collected notable private library of books pertaining to Omar Khayyam and Edward Fitzgerald. Home: Needham, Mass. Died Jan. 5, 1926.

BURRAGE, Henry Sweetser, clergyman; b. Fitchburg, Mass., Jan. 7, 1837; s. Jonathan and Mary Thurston (Upton) B.; A.M., Brown U., 1861; grad. Newton Theol. Instn., 1867; U. of Halle, Germany, 1868-69; D.D., Brown, 1883; LL.D., U. of Me., 1922; m. Caroline Champlin, May 19, 1873 (died 1875); children—Champlin, Thomas Jayne; m. 2d, Ernestine Mai Giddings, Nov. 8, 1881; children—Margaret Ernestine (dec.), Mildred Giddings, Madeleine. Served in 36th Mass. Vol., 1862-65, as sergt. maj., 2d lt., 1st lt., capt. and bvt. maj.; also acting asst. adj. gen. on staff 1st Brigade, 2d Div., 9th Army Corps. Ordained Bapt. ministry, 1869; pastor Waterville, Me., 1870-73; editor Zion's Advocate, 1873-1905; chaplain Nat. Home for Disabled Vol. Soldiers, 1905-12; state historian of Me., 1907—. Recording sec. Me. Bapt. Missionary Conv., 1875-1905, Am. Bapt. Missionary Union, 1876-1904; pres. Me. Bapt. Edn. Soc., 1893-98. Trustee Colby Coll., 1881-1905, Newton Theol. Instn., 1889-1906, Brown U., 1889-1901 (bd. fellows). Author: The Act of Baptism in the History of the Christian Church, 1879; History of the Baptists in New England, 1894; Gettysburg and Lincoln, 1906; Early English and French Voyages, 1906; Gorges and the Grant of the Province of Maine, 1622, 1923; Thomas Hamlin Hubbard, Bvt. Brig. Gen. U.S. Vols., 1923. Editor: History of the Thirty-sixth Massachusetts Volunteers, 1884; Rosier's Relation of Waymouth's Voyage to the Coast of Maine, 1605, 1887; etc. Home: Kennebunkport, Me. Died Mar. 9, 1926.

BURRAGE, Walter Lincoln, M.D.; b. Boston, Oct. 21, 1860; s. Alvah Augustus and Elizabeth Amelia (Smith) B.; A.B., Harvard, 1883, A.M., 1888; M.D., Harvard Med. Sch., 1888; m. Sally Swan, Oct. 3, 1894. House phys., Boston City Hosp., 1886-88, Woman's Hosp., New York, 1888-90; visiting gynecologist Carney and St. Elizabeth hosps., Boston, 1890-1903; surgeon to out-patients Free Hosp. for Women, 1890-1901; clin. instr. in gynecology, Harvard, 1893-95. Democrat. Unitarian. Hon. fellow Am. Gynecol. Soc. Author: Gynecological Diagnosis, 1910; A History of the Massachusetts Medical Society, 1781-1922, 1923. Collaborator: Dr. Howard A. Kelly's Am. Medical Biography, 2 vols., 1912; rewrote the same author's "Appendicitis," and assisted with the same author's "Medical Gynecology," 1910; (with Dr. Kelly) Am. Med. Biographies, 1920; (with Dr. H. A. Kelly) Dictionary of Am. Medical Biography (2049 biographies), 1928; chapter on "Medicine in Massachusetts," Vol. 5, Commonwealth History of Massachusetts, 1930; Catalogue of Honorary, Past and present fellows, Massachusetts Med. Society, 1781-1931 (11,126 names), 1931. Address: Brookline, Mass. Died Jan. 26, 1935.

BURRELL, David James, clergyman; b. Mt. Pleasant, Pa., Aug. 1, 1844; s. David and Elizabeth (Felgar) B.; A.B., Yale, 1867; grad. Union Theol. Sem., N.Y. City, 1870; D.D., Parsons Coll., 1883, and Rutgers Coll., 1916; LL.D., Hope Coll., 1900; m. Clara De Forest, Oct. 18, 1871. Ordained Presbyn. ministry, 1872; missionary, Chicago, 1872-76; pastor 2d Ch., Dubuque, Ia., 1876-87, Westminster Ch., Minneapolis, 1887-91, Marble Collegiate Ch., New York, 1891— (ch. founded 1628). Author: The Religions of the World; A Quiver of Arrows, 1902; The Lure of the City, 1908; The Sermon; Its Construction and Delivery, 1913; The Church in the Upper Room, 1913; Why I Believe the Bible, 1917; The Laughter of God, 1918. Home: Madison, N.J. Died Dec. 5, 1926.

BURRELL, Edward Parker, mech. engr.; b. Hall, N.Y., Feb. 11, 1871; s. Edward and Elizabeth (Parker) B.; M.E., Cornell U., 1898, M.M.E., 1899; m. Katharine Ward, Dec. 8, 1904. Successively designing engr., works engr., works mgr., Warner and Swasey Co., 1900-24, dir. of engring., 1924—; directed design of all large telescopes built by this co. in past 20 years, including 72-inch reflecting telescope for Dominion Astrophys. Obs., Victoria, B.C.; 69-inch reflecting telescope for Ohio Wesleyan U.; 20-inch refractor for Chabot Obs., Oakland, Calif. Designed and constructed model of proposed 200-inch telescope for Mt. Wilson Obs. Inventor and is holder of many patents in his field. Home: Shaker Heights, O. Died Mar. 21, 1937.

BURRELL, Frederick Augustus Muhlenberg, financier; b. Aaronsburg, Pa., Mar. 13, 1858; s. John Ilgen and Susan Elizabeth (Schwartz) B.; student, Columbia, but withdrew in sophomore yr. on account of death of father; m. Alice Maud Thackeray, 1888; children—Mrs. E. W. Walker, Harold A., Mrs. W. C. Duckham, Frederick D. Early learned telegraphy; served as train dispatcher and agt. 9th Av. Elevated R.R. Co., N.Y. City; entered employ of Charles A. Schieren, leather tanner and mcht., 1878, v.p. Charles A. Schieren Co., 1908-13; an organizer Flatbush Trust Co.; pres. Central Hardy Co.; trustee Brooklyn Savings Bank; treas. Quiogue Homestead Co. Republican. Conglist. Home: Brooklyn, N.Y. Died Nov. 13, 1931.

BURRELL, Herbert Leslie, surgeon; b. Boston, Apr. 27, 1856; s. Randall Gardner and Elizabeth Madeline (Ayer) B.; prep. edn. English High Sch., Boston; M.D., Harvard, 1879; m. Miss C. W. Cayford, Apr. 17, 1899. Surgeon gen. of Mass., 1894; surgeon supt., Mass. Vol. Aid Hosp. Ship, Spanish-Am. War, 1898; surgeon-in-chief, Boston City Hosp., 1907—; surgeon Children's Hosp., 1893—; John Homans prof. surgery, Harvard, 1903—. Fellow Am. Surg. Assn. Author: Case Teaching in Surgery (with John B. Blake), 1904. Home: Boston, Mass. Died 1910.

BURRELL, Joseph Dunn, clergyman; b. Freeport, Ill., Dec. 22, 1858; s. David and Elizabeth (Felgar) B.; B.A., Yale, 1881, M.A., 1893; grad. Union Theol. Sem., 1884; D.D., Park Coll., 1906; m. Caroline Frances Benedict, Oct. 18, 1888; children—Katharine Benedict (Mrs. George H. Sicard), Monica (Mrs. Roberts B. Owen). Ordained Presbyn. ministry, 1884; pastor Clinton, Ia., 1884-92, Classon Av. Ch., Brooklyn, 1892-1919. Am. Red Cross sec. Camp Devens, May-Oct. 1918, at Pontanazen, Brest, France, and at Berlin, Germany, 1918-19; sec. Met. Dist. New Era Movement Presbyn. Ch., U.S.A., 1920-22; exec. sec. Brooklyn Nassau Presbytery, 1922-29. Pres. Brooklyn Fedn. of Churches, 1928; dir. Union Theol. Sem. Republican. Author: The Singular Death of Christ, 1900; A New Appraisal of Christian Science, 1906; (co-author) Hints and Helps, 1892, 93, 94; The Early Church, 1894. Died Apr. 13, 1930.

BURRETT, Claude Adelbert, M.D.; b. Monroe Co., N.Y., July 13, 1878; s. Cyrus A. and Ida I. (Sage) B.; Ph.B., Syracuse U., 1902; student Med. Dept., Syracuse U., 1901-02, 1902-03; M.D., Cleveland Homœ. Med. Coll., 1905; m. Clara Virginia Partridge, July 13, 1905; children—Adelbert Partridge, Helen Louise, John Barton, Virginia. Dir. pathogenic lab. and instr. in toxicology, 1905-08, asst. prof. genito-urinary surgery, dermatology and electrotherapeutics, 1908-13, prof. surgery and genito-urinary surgery, 1913-14, U. of Mich.; prof. surgery and acting dean, Coll. of Homœ. Medicine, Ohio State U., 1914-15, dean same coll., 1915-22; dean and med. dir. N.Y. Medical Coll., Flower and Fifth Av. hosps., 1925—, pres., 1939—. Fellow Am. Coll. Surgeons. Methodist. Home: New York, N.Y. Died Mar. 3, 1941.

BURRILL, Harvey D., editor; b. Syracuse, N.Y., Dec. 20, 1868; s. William H. and Sarah E. (Bonter) B.; ed. pub. schs.; m. Mary L. Dudley, 1891; children—Louis Dudley, Mrs. Esther Picou, Harvey Dudley (dec.). Pres. and editor Syracuse Journal, 1904—. Republican. Episcopalian. Home: Syracuse, N.Y. Died Dec. 24, 1938.

BURRILL, Thomas Jonathan, botanist; b. Pittsfield, Mass., Apr. 25, 1839; s. John and Mary (Francis) B.; grad. Ill. State Normal U., 1865; (hon. A.M., Northwestern, 1876, LL.D., 1893; Ph.D., U. of Chicago, 1881, LL.D., U. of Illinois, 1912); m. Sarah H. Alexander, July 22, 1868. Superintendent Urbana (Ill.) public schools, 1865-68; asst. prof. natural history, U. of Ill., 1868-70; prof. botany and horticulture, 1870-1903, prof. botany, 1903-12 (emeritus), v.p., 1879-1912, dean Coll. Science, 1878-84, dean gen. faculty, 1894-1901, dean Grad. Sch., 1894-1905, acting pres., 1891-94 and 1904, U. of Ill.; botanist, U.S. Agrl. Expt. Sta., 1888-1912. Fellow Am. Micros. Soc. (pres. 1885-86, sec. 1886-89); mem. Am. Acad. Arts and Sciences. Home: Urbana, Ill. Died Apr. 14, 1916.

BURRIS, Benjamin J., educator; b. Daviess Co., Ind., Mar. 19, 1882; s. Tobias and Flora B. (Cole) B.; student Central Normal Coll., Danville, Ind., 1902-06, also at times until 1912; grad. teachers' course, same coll., 1904, scientific course, 1906, classic and law courses, LL.B., 1911, A.B., 1919; M.A., Ind. U., 1924; student Ben Harrison Law Sch., Indianapolis, 1 term; m. Ethel Pearl Little, Oct. 15, 1905; 1 son, Horace Conrad. Pvt. and non-com. officer, U.S.A., in Philippines, Sept. 1899-Sept. 1902. Teacher, Daviess Co., later high sch. prin., Plainville, 1904-07, county supt. Daviess Co., 1907-11; county atty., 1912, 13; practiced law at Washington, Ind., 1913-16; asst. supt. pub. instrn., Ind., 1917-21; apptd. supt. pub. instrn., Oct. 1, 1921, and elected to same office, 1922; resigned Dec. 1, 1924, to become pres. Eastern Div. Ind. State Normal Sch. Made state-wide survey of pub. sch. system, leading to reorganization of method of certificating teachers. Mem. State Bd. of Edn. of Ind. Republican. Methodist. Mason. Home: Muncie, Ind. Died Apr. 26, 1927.

BURRITT, Eldon Grant, college pres.; b. Hilton, N.Y., Sept. 9, 1868; s. Beverly W. and Amelia M. (Bass) B.; A.B., U. of Rochester, 1891, A.M., 1894; post-grad. work, U. of Chicago, 1899-1900; m. Carrie A. Turrell, Aug. 21, 1895. Prin. Bradstreet and Burritt's College Prep. Sch. for Boys, Rochester, N.Y., 1891-93; prof. Greek, Greenville (Ill.) Coll., 1893-99 (v.p., 1897-99); prin. Wessington Springs (S.D.) Sem., 1900-02, Evansville (Wis.) Sem., 1902-05; v.p., 1905-08, pres., 1908—, Greenville (Ill.) Coll. Author: The Pupil and How to Teach Him, 1911. Home: Greenville, Ill. Deceased.

BURROUGHS, Bryson, artist; b. Hyde Park, Mass., Sept. 8, 1869; s. Maj. George (U.S.A.) and Carrie (Bryson) B.; after gen. edn. studied at Art Students' League, New York, and won Chanler Scholarship, 1891; studied in Paris and Florence; m. Edith Woodman, Sept. 5, 1893; m. 2d, Louise Guerber, Oct. 5, 1928. Engaged professionally as artist, 1889—; silver medal, Buffalo Expn., 1901, Pittsburgh Expn., 1903; 3d prize, Worcester Expn., 1904. Curator of paintings, Met. Mus. Art, New York. N.A., 1930. Home: New York, N.Y. Died Nov. 16, 1934.

BURROUGHS, Edith Woodman, sculptor; b. Riverdale-on-the-Hudson, N.Y., Oct. 20, 1871; d. Webster and Mary M. Woodman; ed. Art Students' League, New York, under St. Gaudens; in Paris under Inglebert, and 2 yrs. in Luc Oliver Meeson's Sch.; m. Bryson Burroughs, Sept. 5, 1893. Executed statuettes, portraits in low relief, busts of children in marble and decorative sculpture. Exhibited at Champs de Mars, Paris, and in America; Shaw memorial prize, A.N.A.; silver medal for fountain at Panama P.I. Expn., 1915. Home: Flushing, L.I. Died Jan. 6, 1916.

BURROUGHS, George Stockton, prof. O.T. lang. and lit., Oberlin Theol. Sem., 1899—; b. Waterloo, N.Y., Jan. 6, 1855; s. Rev. G. W. and Olivia C. (Stockton) B.; grad. Princeton, 1873 (Ph.D., 1884; D.D., 1887); Princeton Theol. Sem., 1877; (LL.D., Marietta Coll., 1895); m. Emma Frances Plumley, May 30, 1877. Was 3 yrs. in ministry of Presbyn. ch.; in 1880 removed to New England; successively pastor 1st Ch. of Christ, Fairfield, Conn., 1st Ch. of Christ, New Britain, Conn., and Ch. of Christ in Amherst Coll.; prof. Biblical literature, Amherst Coll., 1886-92; pres. Wabash Coll., Crawfordsville, Ind., 1892-99. Died 1901.

BURROUGHS, John, naturalist; b. Roxbury, N.Y., Apr. 3, 1837; s. Chauncey A. and Amy (Kelly) B.; acad. edn.; (Litt.D., Yale, 1910; Doctor Humane Letters, Colgate, 1911); m. Ursula North, Sept. 13, 1857. Taught school about 8 yrs.; treasury clerk, 1864-73; nat. bank examiner, 1873-84; has lived on a farm, devoting his time to literature and fruit culture, 1874—. Mem. Am. Acad. Arts and Letters. Author: Notes on Walt Whitman as Poet and Person, 1867; Wake Robin, 1871; Winter Sunshine, 1875; Birds and Poets, 1877; Locusts and Wild Honey, 1879; Pepacton, 1881; Fresh Fields, 1884; Signs and Seasons, 1886; Indoor Studies, 1889; Riverby, 1894; Whitman, a Study, 1896; The Light of Day, 1900; Squirrels and Other Fur Bearers, 1900; Literary Values, 1904; Far and Near, 1904; Ways of Nature, 1905; Bird and Bough (poems), 1906; Camping and Tramping With Roosevelt, 1907; Leaf and Tendril, 1908; Time and Change, 1912; The Summit of the Years, 1913; The Breath of Life, 1915; Under the Apple Trees, 1916; Field and Study, 1919. Home: West Park, N.Y. Died Mar. 29, 1921.

BURROUGHS, Sherman Everett, congressman; b. Dunbarton, N.H., Feb. 6, 1870; s. John H. and Helen M. (Baker) B.; A.B., Dartmouth, 1894; LL.B., Columbian U., Washington, D.C., 1896, LL.M., 1897; m. Helen S. Phillips, Apr. 21, 1898. Began practice at Manchester, N.H., 1897; mem. N.H. Ho. of Rep., 1901-02; elected May 1917, mem. 65th Congress (1917-19), to succeed Cyrus A. Sulloway, deceased, 1st N.H. Dist.; reelected to 66th and 67th Congresses (1919-23). Republican. Episcopalian. Mem. N.H. State Board of Charities, 1900-17; mem. State Conf. Charities and Corrections. Mason. Home: Manchester, N.H. Died Jan. 27, 1923.

BURROW, James Randall, banker; b. Smith Center, Kan., Nov. 22, 1894; s. Joel Randall and Hilda Eliza (Ingalls) B.; student U. of Kan., 1914-15, Harvard, 1915-17; m. Mary Edith Cole, Sept. 2, 1916; children—Hilda Mary (dec.), Jane Katherine, James Randall. Engaged in banking, 1917—; successively treas., v.p., and trust officer, Central Trust Co., Topeka, 1918-29, pres., 1929—; v.p. Central Nat. Bank, 1921-29, pres., 1929—; pres. and dir. Central Mortgage Co.; treas. and dir. Kan. Bankers Surety Co. Trustee Washburn Coll. (Topeka). Republican. Episcopalian. Home: Topeka, Kan. Died Mar. 10, 1941.

BURROW, Joel Randall, banker; b. Marion Co., Ill., July 21, 1853; s. Henry G. and Elizabeth A. (Adams) B.; ed. pub. schs.; m. Almina D. Mossman, May 4, 1876 (died 1880); children—Minnie A. (dec.), Francis Henry (dec.); m. 2d, Almeda E.

Buck, Mar. 30, 1882 (died 1886); children—McDowell Parliament (dec.), Joe Warren (dec.); m. 3d, Hilda Elizabeth Ingalls, Aug. 24, 1889 (died 1908); children—Hilda Ingalls (dec.), James Randall. Began in banking business in Smith Co., Kan., 1881; moved to Topeka, 1903; pres. Central Nat. Bank, Topeka, 1908—; pres. Central Trust Co., First State Bank (Agra), First State Bank (Bellaire), First State Bank (Athol), First Nat. Bank (Smith Center), Osage County Bank (Osage City, Kan.); sec. of State of Kan., 1903-07; chmn. Shawnee County Liberty Loan Com., World War. Trustee Christ's Hosp. and Washburn Coll., Topeka. Republican. Episcopalian. Mason. Home: Topeka, Kan. Died Sept. 30, 1931.

BURROWES, Alexander J., coll. pres.; b. St. Louis, Oct. 14, 1853; s. Michael and Mary (Quirk) B.; ed. Christian Brothers' Sch., St. Louis, 6 yrs., Niagara U., 1 yr., Woodstock Coll., Md., 7 yrs. (mental and moral philosophy, theology, science and mathematics). Ordained priest, R.C. Ch., 1886; v.p. Detroit (Mich.) Coll., 1889-90; pres. St. Xavier's Coll., Cincinnati, 1893-97, Marquette Coll. (chartered as univ. during term of office), 1900-08, St. Ignatius Coll., Chicago, 1908-12 (Loyola U., established 1909, with depts. of Law, Medicine and Coll. of Arts and Sciences, is an expansion of St. Ignatius); pres. St. Louis U., 1912-13. Died Jan. 19, 1927.

BURROWES, Edward Thomas, mfr.; b. Sherbrooke, Can., July 25, 1852; s. Ambrose and Jane (Hall) B.; resident of Portland, Me., 1867—; ed. Me. Wesleyan Sem., and Wesleyan U.; m. Frances E. Norcross, Oct. 4, 1880. Began mfr. of wire screens in 1873; founder of The E. T. Burrowes Co., Portland; also pres. of Curtain Supply Co., Chicago. Trustee Boston U. Home: Portland, Me. Died Mar. 19, 1918.

BURROWES, Katharine, music educator; b. Kingston, Ont.; d. Edwin Annesley and Florinda Anne (Radcliffe) B.; ed. by pvt. teachers at home and in Europe; settled in Detroit; specialized in piano under Prof. J. C. Batchelder, Detroit, and Prof. Karl Klindworth, Berlin, Germany; unmarried. Mem. Faculty Detroit Conservatory of Music several yrs.; organized Burrowes Piano Sch., 1895-1903. Author: Burrowes Course of Music Study for Beginners, 1895 (2 U.S. patents and 26 copyrights); Manual for Teachers, 1901; Kindergarten Class Songs, 1901; Modern Music Methods (read before Music Teachers' Nat. Assn.), 1902; Theory Course for Students, 1906; New Manual for Teachers, 1910; Tales of the Great Composers, 1911; New Musical Note Gatherers, 1915; The New Success Music Method, 1917, and others. Home: Detroit, Mich. Died Nov. 5, 1939.

BURROWES, Peter Edward, editor; b. Dublin, Ireland, May 16, 1844; s. Peter and Susan (Hendstock) B.; had few ednl. advantages in youth; widower; spent 18 mos. on N. Coast of Africa; became worker in the London City Mission; came to U.S., 1885, as lit. asso. of Frank Smith in reorganization of the Salvation Army; after some years in that work left it to devote himself as lecturer and essayist in the Socialist propaganda. Inventor, and mfr. the games, Am. Chess and Strategy, 1909—. Author: The Crime of Ruby Rochford; Revolutionary Essays, 1903. Home: Stapleton, S.I., N.Y. Deceased.

BURROWS, Charles William, publisher; b. Hollis, York Co., Me., Dec. 21, 1849; s. Joseph W. and Mary Elizabeth (Atkinson) B.; grad. U.S. Mil. Acad., 1870; served as 2d lt. 3d Light Arty., 1870-72; m. Lottie Thomas Mott, Feb. 26, 1884; children—Lorna Dorothea, Gladys Elgin (Mrs. Jess Taylor Boyd). Started Nov. 1873, firm of Burrows Bros. (the Burrows Brothers Co.), publishers and booksellers, Cleveland, of which was pres. to Jan. 1, 1913; also pres. The Burrows Publishing Co., Cleveland, until Jan. 1, 1912. Republican. Home: Cleveland. Died Apr. 2, 1932.

BURROWS, Julius C., senator; b. Northeast, Pa., Jan. 9, 1837; s. William and Maria B.; academic edn.; (LL.D., Kalamazoo Coll.); officer in Union Army, 1862-64; m. Jennie S. Hibbard, Jan. 29, 1856; 2d, Frances S. Peck, Dec. 25, 1867. Admitted to bar, 1861, and began practice at Kalamazoo, Mich. Pros. atty. Kalamazoo Co., 1865-67; was apptd., 1867, supervisor internal revenue for Mich. and Wis., declined; tendered office of solicitor of the treasury and declined; del.-at-large Rep. Nat. Conv., Chicago, 1884; mem. 43d (1873-75), 46th, 47th (1879-83), 49th to 54th (1885-95) Congresses; twice elected speaker pro-tem. 51st Congress; elected U.S. senator, 1894, for unexpired term (1895-99), of Francis B. Stockbridge, dec.; resigned from Ho. of Rep., 54th Congress, Jan. 23, 1895; reëlected to the Senate for terms 1899-1905, 1905-11. Temporary chmn. Rep. Nat. Conv., Chicago, 1908; mem. Nat. Monetary Commn. Home: Kalamazoo, Mich. Died Nov. 16, 1915.

BURROWS, Lansing, clergyman; b. Phila., Apr. 10, 1843; s. of John Lansing (D.D.) and Adelaide (Van Benthuysen) B., both of Knickerbocker descent; ed. Richmond Coll., Va.; Wake Forest Coll., N.C., class of 1861; A.M., Princeton, 1871, Madison U., 1871; (D.D., Bethel Coll., Russellville, Ky., 1882; LL.D., Union U., Tenn., 1896); m. Lulie Rochester (died 1901). Enlisted C.S.A., Apr. 25, 1861; sergt. Richmond Fayette Arty.; 1st sergt. Sands Battery; arty. instr. W.Va. campaign, 1861-62; spl. duty Naval Ordnance Bur.; reënlisted, 1863, Co. E, 6th Ala. (Battle's Brigade), Rhodes' Div.; captured, Winchester, Va., Sept. 19, 1864; at Ft. Delaware until near close of the war; out of hosp. to volunteer on retreat to Appomattox. Ordained Bapt. ministry, 1867; pastor, Stanford, Ky., 1867, Lexington, Mo., 1868-69, Bordentown, N.J., 1870-76, Newark, N.J., 1876-79, Lexington, Ky., 1879-83, Augusta, Ga., 1883-99, Nashville, Tenn., 1899-1909, Americus, Ga., 1909-16. Sec. Southern Bapt. Conv. and denominational statistician, 1881-1914; pres. Southern Bapt. Conv., 1914-16. Mason. Home: Americus, Ga. Died Oct. 17, 1919.

BURRUS, John Perry, mfr.; b. Bunceton, Mo., Mar. 10, 1872; s. William Carroll and Kathryne (Guyer) B.; ed. high sch.; m. Edna Earle Clardy, Apr. 6, 1897; children—Mrs. Kathryne Eudora Caldwell, Jack Perry. Pres. Tex-O-Kan Flour Mills Co. (Dallas), Waxahachie Cotton Mills Co., Brazos Valley Cotton Mills (West); chmn. bd. Mercantile Bank & Trust Co. of Texas. Dir. Dallas Vocational Sch.; mem. Tex. Industrial Commn. Baptist. Home: Dallas, Tex. Died Jan. 26, 1933.

BURRUS, John T., surgeon; b. Surry Co., N.C., July 13, 1876; s. John G. and Bettie (Reece) B.; M.D., Davidson (N.C.) Coll., 1899, Baltimore Med. Coll., 1900, Grant U., 1901; grad. N.Y. Skin and Cancer Hosp.; post-grad. work, N.Y. Polyclinic, N.Y. Post-Grad. and Univ. Coll. of Medicine, also abroad; m. Mary B. Atkins, Apr. 2, 1899; 1 dau., Iris. Began practice at Jonesville, 1899; moved to High Point, 1904; owner and surgeon High Point Hosp.; visiting surgeon Western N.C. Hosp.; chief surgeon Carolina & Yadkin River R.R.; surgeon Thomasville Bapt. Orphanage; visiting lecturer in clin. surgery, Duke U. Commd. 1st lt. Med. R.C., 1908; maj., 1917; lt. col. N.A., 1918-Jan. 1, 1919; served as chief of surg. service and comdg. officer Base Hosp. at Camp Beauregard, 1918. Pres. N.C. State Bd. Health. Fellow Am. College Surgeons. Baptist. Mason. Home: High Point, N.C. Died June 8, 1938.

BURRY, William, lawyer; b. Montreal, Can., Jan. 10, 1851; s. William and Mary (Bryson) B.; A.B., Harvard, 1874; m. Jane R. King, June 3, 1896; 1 son, William. Admitted to Ill. bar, 1875, and began practice at Chicago; mem. Runnells & Burry, 1887-1905, later Runnells, Burry & Johnstone, and Burry, Johnstone & Peters, then Burry, Johnstone, Peters and Dixon; counsel for French Govt. and for French consul in Chicago. Vice pres. Home for Destitute Crippled Children. Officer Legion of Honor (France). Democrat. Presbyn. Home: Chicago, Ill. Died Dec. 27, 1935.

BURT, Alonzo, telephone official; b. nr. Cambridge, O., Dec. 6, 1849; ed. pub. schs., Cambridge; m. Virginia Clark, 1873. In employ mdse. concern, Cambridge, O., 1864-73; postal service at Cincinnati, 1873-92, as clk. and chief clk., 1873-79, supt. Cincinnati Post Office, 1879-84, and supt. ry. mail service at Cincinnati, 1884-92; represented Bell Telephone Co. as mem. bd. dirs. of all its asso. companies west of Chicago except Pacific Coast, from 1892; gen. mgr. Mo. & Kan. Telephone Co., comprising Mo., Kan., Okla. and Ind. Ty., 1893-1900, and pres. same, 1900-05; pres. Wis. Telephone Co., 1903-11; 1st v.p. and treas. Chicago Telephone Co., Cleveland Telephone Co., Mich. State Telephone Co. and Wis. Telephone Co., 1911-20. Mason. Presbyn. Home: Pasadena, Calif. Died Oct. 1929.

BURT, Andrew Sheridan, brig. gen.; b. Cincinnati, Nov. 21, 1839; s. Andrew Gano and Anna (Thompson) B.; m. Elizabeth Johnstone Reynolds, Sept. 13, 1862. Enlisted as pvt. Co. A, 6th Ohio Inf., Apr. 20, 1861; disch., July 15, 1861; apptd. from Ohio, 1st lt. 18th U.S. Inf., May 14, 1861; promoted through grades to brig. gen. vols., May 4, 1898; hon. disch. from vol. service, Dec. 31, 1898; brig. gen. U.S.A., Apr. 1, 1902; retired at his own request, Apr. 15, 1902. Bvtd. capt., June 19, 1862, "for conspicuous gallantry in battle of Mill Spring, Ky." (wounded); maj., Sept. 1, 1864, for Atlanta campaign and battle of Jonesboro, Ga. Author: May Cody, or Lost and Won (W. F. Cody's most successful play). Died Jan. 12, 1915.

BURT, Edward Angus, botanist; b. Athens, Pa., Apr. 9, 1859; s. Howard Fuller and Miranda (Forsyth) B.; grad. N.Y. State Normal Sch., Albany, 1881; A.B., Harvard, 1893, A.M., 1894, Ph.D., 1895; m. Clara M. Briggs, Aug. 21, 1884; children—Angus Edward (dec.), Albert Forsyth, Farlow, Howard. Teacher, Albany Boys' Acad., 1880-85; prof. natural sci., State Normal Sch., Albany, 1885-91; prof. botany, Middlebury (Vt.) Coll., 1895-1913; asso. prof. botany, 1913-18, prof., 1918-25, Washington U., and librarian and mycologist, Mo. Bot. Garden, 1913-25. Home: Middle Grove, N.Y. Died Apr. 27, 1939.

BURT, Henry Jackson, civil engr.; b. Urbana, Ill., Feb. 6, 1873; s. Henry Jackson and Isabelle (Dunlap) B.; B.S. in C.E., U. of Ill., 1896, C.E., 1914; m. Edith Fleming, July 2, 1901; children—Henry Jackson, Luella, Jesse Fleming, Morris Nathan, Helen Edith. Draftsman, 1896-99; railroad surveys and construction, 1900; asst. prof. civ. engring., Ia. State Coll., 1901; designer, estimator and office mgr., Am. Bridge Co., Salt Lake City, and Denver, 1901-11; cons. structural engr. for Holabird & Roche, architects, Chicago, 1911—, also gen. practice as consultant, 1921—. Maj. Q.M.C., Construction Div., U.S.A., Feb. 1918-May 1919; lt. col. O.R.C., 1919—. Republican. Mason. Home: Wheaton, Ill. Died July 28, 1928.

BURT, Horace, Greeley, engr.; b. Jan. 1849; C.E., Univ. of Mich., 1872. Began ry. service, 1868; resident engr., Mar., 1873-81, div. supt., 1881-87, chief engr., Aug., 1887-Nov., 1888, C.&N.W. Ry. Co.; gen. mgr. Fremont, Elkhorn & Mo. Valley and Sioux R.R. cos., 1888-96; gen. mgr. C.,St.P.,M.&O. Ry., July-Oct., 1896; 3d v.p. C.&N.W. Ry. Co., 1896-97; pres. U.P. R.R., 1898-1904; traveled around world, 1904-05; cons. engr., 1905-09; receiver C.G.W. Ry., Jan.-Sept., 1909; cons. engr., Sept., 1909-11; chief engr. of com. of investigation smoke abatement and electrification of ry. terminals, Chicago, 1911—. Home: Oak Park, Ill. Died May 19, 1913.

BURT, Mary Elizabeth, author; b. Lake Geneva, Wis.; ed. Lake Geneva pub. schs., Anna Moody's Acad., and student at Oberlin Coll., 1 yr.; unmarried. Teacher River Falls (Wis.) Normal Sch., 1870-71; teacher in Chicago schs. 22 yrs., Cook Co. Normal Sch., Chicago, 3 yrs., pvt. sch., New York, 1893-1905; editor Scribner School Reading Series, 1893—. Mem. Chicago Bd. Edn., 3 yrs.; edited sch. dept. Home, School and Nation (with Bishop Fallows), 1891-92. Editor: Poems Every Child Should Know, 1904—. Joint editor (for sch. reading): Fanciful Tales, 1893; Eugene Field Book, 1895; Cable Story Book, 1896; Prose Every Child Should Know, 1904, etc. Pub. Bird Song Phonetic Charts, No. I, 1913. Address: Englewood Cliffs-on-Palisade, N.J. Died Oct. 17, 1918.

BURT, Silas Wright, civil service reformer; b. Albany, N.Y., Apr. 25, 1830; s. Thomas M. and Lydia (Butts) B.; A.B., C.E., Union Coll., 1849; m. Jeanette S. Ferrell, Sept. 25, 1855. Civ. engr., 1849-54; in Pike's Peak region, 1860; col. and asst. insp. gen. N.Y. State, 1861-68; engaged in raising, organizing and equipping vols. for Civil War, and subsequently in same for N.G.S.N.Y., and adjustment of war claims. Spl. deputy naval officer port of New York, 1869-78; naval officer, 1878-83; chief examiner state civ. service, 1883-85; naval officer port of New York, 1885-89; civ. service commr. State of N.Y., 1895-1900 (pres. 1900). Made 1st civ. service examiner in U.S. service, Mar. 1, 1871; chmn. supervisory Civ. Service Bd., New York, 1872-75. A founder, 1880, and pres. 1907, Civ. Service Reform Assn. of New York. Died Dec. 1, 1912.

BURT, Stephen Smith, M.D.; b. Oneida, N.Y., Nov. 1, 1850; s. Oliver T. and Rebecca (Johnston) B., student, Cornell U., 1869-70; grad. Coll. Phys. and Surg. (Columbia), M.D., 1875, and Roosevelt Hosp., 1877; hon. A.M., Yale, 1890; unmarried. Instr. medicine and phys. diagnosis, 1882-84, prof. medicine, 1884-1908, and mem. corp., New York Post-Grad. Med. Sch. and Hosp. (emeritus); prof. thoracic diseases, U. of Vt., 1884-85; attending phys. New York Post-Grad. Hosp. Author: Exploration of the Chest in Health and Disease, 1889. Died Mar. 26, 1932.

BURT, Thomas Gregory, educator; b. Wittersham, County Kent, Eng., Aug. 1, 1867; s. Thomas and Caroline (Standen) B.; brought to U.S., 1870; A.B., Hamilton Coll., Clinton, N.Y., 1895, A.M., 1898; Ph.D., Kansas City U., 1901; studied U. of Leipzig, Germany; m. Mary Hubbard Vail, July 19, 1899. Prof. history and German, 1895-1906, chaplain and head dept. Bibl. lit., 1906-09, Park Coll., Parkville, Mo.; acting dean and prof. Bibl. lit., 1909-10, prof. philosophy, 1910—, acting pres., 1916-17, 1920-21, Occidental Coll., Los Angeles, also dean from 1910 (dean emeritus). Republican. Presbyn. Home: San Marino, Calif. Died June 1941.

BURT, William, bishop; b. Padstow, Cornwall, Eng., Oct. 23, 1852; s. William and Mary Ann (Hellyar) B.; A.B., Wesleyan U., 1879; grad. Drew Theol. Sem., Madison, N.J., 1881; D.D., Grant U., 1888, Wesleyan, 1902, LL.D., 1909; S.T.D., Dickinson, 1913; L.H.D., Syracuse, 1913; m. Helen B. Graves, Apr. 14, 1881; children—Edith H., Mrs. F. Otto Schroedter, William W., V. Romana, Paul. Entered New York East Conf., Meth. Episcopal Ch., 1881, pastor St. Paul's Ch., Brooklyn, 1881-83, De Kalb Av. Ch., Brooklyn, 1883-86; transferred to Italy Conf., 1886, and made presiding elder Milan Dist.; moved to Florence, 1888, and to Rome, 1890, remaining there 14 yrs. in charge of chs. and schs. of Italy; built several chs., founded a pub. house, organized a boys' coll., a young ladies' coll. and other schs.; elected bishop of M.E. Ch. by Gen. Conf. at Los Angeles, 1904, and consecrated, 1904; resident bishop M.E. Ch. in Europe, 1904-12; resident bishop at Buffalo, N.Y., 1912-24 (retired). Republican.

Received Order of Cavaliere di SS. Maurizio e Lazzaro from King of Italy, 1903. Died Apr. 9, 1936.

BURTIS, Arthur, naval officer; b. New York, June 29, 1841; s. Rev. Arthur (D. D.) and Grace Ewing (Phillips) B.; ed. pvt. schs. in Buffalo, Union Coll., and Hobart Coll. (A.M.); m. Ida Thomas, 1884. Entered U.S.N., asst. paymaster, July 14, 1862; promoted through all grades to pay dir. with rank of captain, 1899; served on U.S.S. Connecticut, 1862-64, Muscoota, 1865-66, N. Atlantic Squadron; various duties to 1897; on flagship, New York, 1897-99, as fleet paymaster under Rear Admiral W. T. Sampson, off Santiago, Cuba, at destruction of Spanish fleet, July 3, 1898; afterward in navy pay offices in Boston and New York until 1903; retired with rank of rear adm., Nov. 21, 1902. Home: Buffalo, N.Y. Died 1908.

BURTON, Alfred Edgar, coll. dean; b. Portland, Me., Mar. 24, 1857; s. Alfred Merrill and Martha J. (Larrabee) B.; S.B., Bowdoin, 1878, C.E., 1881 (Sc.D., 1913); m. Gertrude Hitz, June 16, 1884 (died 1896); 2d, Lena Yates, of Donisthorpe, Eng., July 19, 1906. Draftsman and topographer U.S. Coast and Geod. Survey, 1879-82; instr., 1882-84, asst. and asso. prof., 1884-96, prof. topog. engring., 1896—, dean, 1902—, Mass. Inst. Tech. Mem. Mass. Topog. Survey Commn., 1895-1900; in charge scientific expdn. to Umanak, N. Greenland, 1896, eclipse expdn. to Washington, Ga., May, 1900, to Sumatra, May, 1901. Overseer, Bowdoin Coll., 1905—. Fellow Am. Acad. Arts and Sciences. In charge instrn. in Free Navigation Schs. of U.S. Shipping Bd. Recruiting Service, 1917-19. Died May 11, 1935.

BURTON, Charles Emerson, clergyman; b. Poweshiek Co., Ia., Mar. 19, 1869; s. Ira J. H. and Jane A. (Simmons) B.; A.B., Carleton Coll., Northfield, Minn., 1895, M.A., 1898, D.D., 1911; B.D., Chicago Theol. Sem., 1898; LL.D., Beloit Coll.; m. Cora V. King, Oct. 17, 1898; children—Dorothy Viola, Lyndon David, Malcolm King, Myron Simmons. Lay pastor various chs. until 1898; ordained Congl. ministry 1898; pastor Puritan Ch., Chicago, 1898-99, Lyndale Ch., Minneapolis, 1899-1909; asso. pastor with Washington Gladden, First Ch., Columbus, Ohio, 1909-11; pastor Euclid Avenue Ch., Cleveland, 1911-14; gen. sec. Congl. Home Missionary Soc., 1914-21. Gen. sec. Congl. Ch. Bldg. Soc., 1916-21, and Congl. S.S. Extension Soc., 1917-21; sec. Nat. Council Congl. Chs. (then Gen. Council of Congl. and Christian chs.), 1921-38, sec. emeritus. Author: Finding a Religion to Live By; Manual of Congregational and Christian Churches; National Council Digest. Died Aug. 27, 1940.

BURTON, Charles Germman, lawyer; b. Cleveland, Apr. 4, 1846; s. Leonard and Laura B.; ed. pub. schs., Warren, O.; enlisted as pvt. Co. C, 19th Ohio Inf., Sept. 7, 1861; hon. disch., Oct. 29, 1862; corporal Co. A, 171st Ohio N.G. in 100 days' campaign, 1864; admitted to bar, 1867; m. Elsie W. Meyers, 1870 (died 1870); 2d, Alice A. Rogers, Jan. 1, 1874. Located at Nevada, Mo., 1871; circuit atty., 1872; judge 25th Jud. Circuit, Mo., 1881-87; mem. 54th Congress (1895-97), 15th Mo. Dist.; del. Rep. Nat. convs., 1884, 1906; collector of internal revenue for 6th (western) Dist. of Mo., 1907-15 (resigned). Comdr.-in-chief G.A.R., 1907-08. Home: Nevada, Mo. Died Feb. 25, 1926.

BURTON, Clarence Monroe, lawyer; b. Calif., Nov. 18, 1853; s. Charles S. B.; B.S., U. of Mich., 1873, LL.B., 1874, hon. A.M., 1905; m. Harriet J. Nye, Dec. 25, 1872 (died 1896); children—M. Agnes, Charles W., Clarence H., Louise, Fred, Frank, Harriet B. (Mrs. Roland Reed), Ralph; m. 2d, Lina Grant, Dec. 27, 1897 (died 1898); m. 3d, Anna M. Knox, June 20, 1900 (died 1925); 1 dau., Elizabeth. Was admitted to the bar at the age of 21; devoted spare time to study of history of Detroit and the Northwest, and collection of one of largest libraries of Americana in West, including many unpublished documents, copies of archives in France, Canada and U.S. Proprietor Wayne Co. Abstract of Land Titles. Mem. Mich. Hist. Commn.; city historiographer of Detroit. Author: Sketch of the Life of Antoine de la Mothe Cadillac, founder of Detroit; Cadillac's Village, or Detroit, 1701-11; In the Footsteps of Cadillac—a Chapter in the History of Cleveland; The Building of Detroit; Early Detroit; Detroit, Financial and Commercial, 1780-1850, etc. Presented his library, library bldgs. and home to Pub. Library Commn. of Detroit, 1914; then open in the pub. library under title Burton Hist. Collection. Home: Detroit, Mich. Died Oct. 28, 1932.

BURTON, Ernest DeWitt, theologian; b. Granville, O., Feb. 4, 1856; s. Nathan Smith and Sarah J. (Fairfield) B.; brother of Henry Fairfield B.; A.B., Denison U., 1876; grad. Rochester Theol. Sem., 1882; student U. of Leipzig, 1887, U. of Berlin, 1894; (D.D., Denison Univ., 1897, Oberlin, 1912, Harvard, 1920); m. Frances Mary Townson, Dec. 28, 1883. Taught in acad. and pub. sch., 1876-79; instr. N.T. Greek, Rochester Theol. Sem., 1882-83; asso. prof. N.T. interpretation, 1883-86, prof., 1886-92, Newton Theol. Instn.; prof. and head of dept. N.T. lit. and interpretation, U. of Chicago, 1892—. Asso. editor, 1892-1906, 1913-20, editor-in-chief, 1906-13, Biblical World; mng. editor Am. Jour. of Theology, 1907-15; chmn. China Ednl. Commn., 1921—; Oriental ednl. commr., U. of Chicago, 1908-09; dir. U. Libraries, U. of Chicago, 1910—; pres., U. of Chicago, 1923—. Author: Syntax of the Moods and Tenses in New Testament Greek, 1893; Harmony of the Gospels for Historical Study (with the late W. A. Stevens), 1894, 1904; Records and Letters of the Apostolic Age, 1895; Handbook of the Life of Paul, 1899; Constructive Studies in the Life of Christ (with Shailer Mathews), 1901; Principles and Ideals of the Sunday School (with Shailer Mathews), 1903; Short Introduction to the Gospels, 1904; Studies in the Gospel of Mark, 1904; Principles of Literary Criticism and Their Application to the Synoptic Problem, 1904; Biblical Ideas of Atonement (with J. M. P. and G. B. Smith), 1909; Harmony of the Synoptic Gospels in English (with Edgar J. Goodspeed), 1917; Spirit, Soul, and Flesh, in Greek writings from the Earliest Period to 180 A.D., 1918; Harmony of the Synoptic Gospels in Greek (with Edgar J. Goodspeed), 1920; Commentary on Paul's Epistle to the Galatians, in International Crit. Com., 1920; Source Book for the Study of the Teaching of Jesus, 1923. Home: Chicago, Ill. Died May 26, 1925.

BURTON, Frederick Russell, author, composer; b. Jonesville, Mich., Feb. 23, 1861; grad. (with highest honors in music and other honors) Harvard, 1882; resident Yonkers, 1895—, engaged in music and lit. composition; organized Yonkers Choral Soc. Author: Shifting Sands, 1898; Her Wedding Interlude, 1902; The Song and the Singer; also musical essays, short stories, etc. Composer: Hiawatha, 1898; The Legend of Sleepy Hollow, 1900, dramatic cantatas; Inauguration Ode (composed for 2d inauguration President McKinley), 1901; Songs of the Ojibway Indians, 1903; An Indian Campfire, 1907; songs, anthems, etc. Died 1909.

BURTON, George Dexter, inventor; b. Temple, N.H., Oct. 26, 1855; s. Dexter L. and Emily F. B.; ed. Appleton Acad. and Comer's Commercial Coll., Boston; m. Frances C. Jones, Jan. 1894. Editor and pub. New England Star, New Ipswich, N.H., 1873-77. Inventor of the Burton stock car, and especially well known for his inventions of a liquid process of heating and welding metals by an electric current; pres. Am. Electric Forge Co.; invented process of unhairing and tanning animal skins and hides by electricity; also process of degumming and separating vegetable fibres by electricity, etc. Pres. Electrochem. Pulp and Paper Co., Reno (Nev.) Reduction Works; pres. The Burton Co., mills at Clinton and Holliston, Mass. Lecturer on heating and working metals by electricity before Harvard Lecture Club of Jefferson Physical Lab., Harvard Coll., before Soc. of Arts of M.I.T., Franklin Inst., etc. Had received over 500 U.S. and foreign patents; awarded more than a dozen gold and silver medals from scientific and corporate instns. for various discoveries and inventions. Home: New Ipswich, N.H. Died Jan. 7, 1918.

BURTON, George Hall, brig. gen.; b. Millsboro, Del., Jan. 12, 1843; s. Benjamin and Catherine R. (Green) B.; grad. U.S. Mil. Acad., 1865; m. Minnie Larrabee, Nov. 24, 1870. Promoted 2d lt. and 1st lt. 12th Inf., June 23, 1865; promoted through grades to brig. gen. insp. gen. U.S.A., Apr. 12, 1903; retired at own request, over 40 yrs.' service, Sept. 30, 1906. Bvtd. maj., Feb. 27, 1890, "for gallant services" in action against Indians in the Lava Beds, Calif., Jan. 27, 1873, and at the Clearwater, Ida., July 11 and 12, 1877. Served in Modoc Indian War, in northern Calif. and Ore.; Nez Perce War in Idaho, and across the Continent to the Mo. River; Bannock War in Ore.; served on frontier and in the Indian country, 1869-78 and 1880-84. Home: Los Angeles, Calif. Died Oct. 20, 1917.

BURTON, Hazen James, clothing mfr.; b. Boston, Mass., July 14, 1847; s. Hazen James and Harriet Lincoln (Smith) B.; ed. English High Sch., Boston, 1860-63; Mass. Inst. Tech., 1863-67; m. Alice G. Cotton Whitney, 1870; children—Hazel Burton (dec.), Ralph Walter (dec.), Ward Cotton, Ariel, Hazen James (dec.). Began with C. W. Freeland & Co., clothing mfrs., Boston, 1867; moved to Minneapolis, 1880, and established the Plymouth Clothing House, of which is pres. Republican. Unitarian. Home: Deephaven, Minn. Died Sept. 21, 1934.

BURTON, Henry Fairfield, univ. prof.; b. Elyria, Ohio, July 17, 1851; s. Nathan Smith and Sarah J. (Fairfield) B.; bro. of Ernest DeWitt B.; A.B., U. of Mich., 1872, A.M., 1875; (LL.D., Denison U., 1909); m. Anna Cushing McKay, June 28, 1883; m. 2d, Marian Williams Perrin, June 14, 1898. Instr. Latin and Greek, Denison U., 1872-74; instr. Latin, U. of Mich., 1874-75; studied philology, U. of Leipzig, 1875-77; asst. prof. Latin, 1877-83, prof., 1883—, acting pres., 1898-1900 and 1903-99, U. of Rochester. Home: Rochester, N.Y. Died Aug. 27, 1918.

BURTON, James, photographic illustrator; b. London, Eng., Jan. 1, 1871; common sch. edn.; came to U.S., 1894; m. Miss E. H. F. McMillan, Oct. 21, 1897. Illustrator for New York Herald, Harper's, Leslie's and other New York and London papers; represented Harper's Weekly as photographer in Spanish-Am. War, 1898, Santiago campaign; also Paris Expn., 1900; Mt. Pelee eruption for Collier's Weekly, 1902. Home: Lynbrook, L.I. Deceased.

BURTON, Joseph Ralph, U.S. senator; b. nr. Mitchell, Ind., Nov. 16, 1851; s. Allen C. and Elizabeth (Holmes) B.; lived on farm during boyhood; ed. Franklin Coll., Ind., 3 yrs., DePauw Univ., 1 yr., left in senior yr.; m. Mrs. Carrie (Mitchell) Webster, 1875. Admitted to bar, 1875; mem. Kan. legislature 3 terms; mem. World's Columbian Commn. from Kan.; has spoken in every political campaign, 1876—, and has campaigned from Me. to Colo.; U.S. senator, Kan., 1901-07. Republican. Home: Abilene, Kan. Died Feb. 28, 1923.

BURTON, Lewis William, bishop; b. Cleveland, O., Nov. 9, 1852; s. Rev. Lewis and Agnes Jane (Wallace) B.; A.B., Kenyon, 1st honors, 1873, A.M., 1886; grad. Phila. Div. Sch., 1877; D.D., Kenyon, 1896, Univ. of South, 1896; LL.D., St. John's College, Annapolis, 1917, Transylvania College, 1930; m. Georgie Hendree Ball, Jan. 15, 1883 (died 1931); children—Lewis James Hendree (dec.), Sarah Louise (Mrs. Henry Kavanaugh Milward), Cornelia Paine Wallace (Mrs. Thomas Gresham Machen). Deacon, 1877, priest, 1878, P.E. Ch.; asst. and rector All Saints', 1877-80, St. Mark's, 1881-84, Cleveland; rector St. John's, Richmond, Va., 1884-93, St. Andrew's, Louisville, Ky., 1893-96; consecrated bishop of Lexington, Ky., Jan. 30, 1896; resigned jurisdiction over Diocese of Lexington, Oct. 16, 1928. Past pres. Fourth Province P.E. Ch. Died Oct. 17, 1940.

BURTON, Marion LeRoy, univ. pres.; b. Brooklyn, Iowa, Aug. 30, 1874; s. Ira John Henry and Jane Adeliza (Simmons) B.; A.B., from Carleton Coll., Minn., 1900; B.D. (summa cum laude), Yale, 1906, Ph.D., 1907; (D.D., Carleton, 1909; LL.D., Tufts Coll., 1911, Western Reserve U., 1911, Amherst Coll., 1913, Hobart, 1913, U. of Mich., 1920); m. Nina Leona Moses, June 14, 1900. Teacher Greek, Carleton Acad., 1899-1900; prin. Windom Inst., Minn., 1900-03; asst. prof. Yale, 1907-08; pastor Ch. of the Pilgrims, Brooklyn, 1908-09; traveled in Europe as pres.-elect of Smith Coll., 1909-10; pres. Smith Coll., 1910-17; pres. U. of Minn., 1917-20; pres. U. of Mich., July 1920—. Trustee Carnegie Foundation for Advancement of Teaching, New York. Mem. advisory council Inst. Internat. Edn.; mem. administrative bd., Inst. of Internat. Edn. Corporate mem. A.B.C.F.M. Republican. Died Feb. 18, 1925.

BURTON, Myron Garfield, educator; b. Joliet, Hamilton Co., Ind., Sept. 13, 1880; s. Allden Morris and Martha Jane (Ramsey) B.; student Indiana U., 1901-05; A.B., Ind. State Normal Sch., Muncie, Ind., 1913; M.Sc., Kan. State Agrl. Coll., 1918; m. Ida Robinson, June 27, 1915. Teacher elementary schs. 4 yrs. and prin. high sch. 6 yrs., Ind.; supt. schs. Plano, Ill., 1909-12; editor for Nat. Manual Training Co., 1911-13; v.p. and dir. of extension, Muncie (Ind.) Normal Inst., 1913-15; dir. home study service, Kan. State Agrl. Coll., 1915-18; dir. vocational and manual training Instrn., Kansas City (Mo.) pub. schs., 1918-21; asst. supt. schs., Kansas City, July 1921—. Republican. Methodist. Author: Shop Projects Based on Community Problems, 1915. Exec. sec. for State Food Adminstr. of Kan., World War. Home: Kansas City, Mo. Died Feb. 20, 1923.

BURTON, Richard (Eugene), poet, lecturer; b. Hartford, Conn., Mar. 14, 1861; s. Rev. Nathaniel Judson and Rachel (Chase) B.; A.B., Trinity Coll., 1883; Ph.D., Johns Hopkins, 1888; L.H.D., Trinity and U. of Southern Calif.; m. 2d, Mrs. Ruth Guthrie Harding, Aug. 24, 1931. Taught Old English, Johns Hopkins, 1888; mng. editor Churchman, New York, 1888-89; traveled in Europe, 1889-90; lit. editor Hartford Courant, 1890-97; asso. editor Warner's Library of the World's Best Literature, 1897-99; head English dept., U. of Minn., 1898-1902; editor Lothrop Pub. Co., 1902-04; professorial lecturer on English lit., U. of Chicago, 1902-06; head English dept., U. of Minn., 1906-25; resigned to devote attention to lit. work; lecturer on lit., Columbia, 1921-33, Sarah Lawrence Coll., 1928-31; pres. Richard Burton Schools, Inc., 1925—. Mem. Nat. Inst. Arts and Letters; mem. Pulitzer Coms. on Drama, Poetry, Fiction, Biography, 1920-40; also mem. other coms. Author: Dumb in June (poems), 1895, 10th edition, 1927; Memorial Day (poems), 1897; Lyrics of Brotherhood (poems), 1899; Life of Whittier, 1900; Message and Melody—A Book of Verse, 1903; Rahab—a poetic drama, 1906; From the Book of Life (verse), 1909; Masters of the English Novel, 1909; How to See a Play, 1914; Bernard Shaw—The Man and the Mask, 1916; Poems of Earth's Meaning, 1917. Mem. bd. editors Book League America; editor Dept. of Literature for the Screen, Warner Brothers Pictures, Inc., 1930-34. Prof. of lit., Rollins Coll., Fla., 1933—. Died Apr. 8, 1940.

BURTON, Robert Mitchell, mfr.; b. Cincinnati, O., July 7, 1864; s. Stephen Remington and Jane E. (Mitchell) B.; ed. Harcourt Acad., Gambier, O., St. Paul's Sch., Concord, N.H.; m. Mary Tylor, Oct. 24,

1889. With stove foundry 10 yrs., hotel kitchen outfitting, 4 yrs.; in laundry machinery business, 1896—; pres. The Am. Laundry Machinery Co.; sec. and treas. Avon Hills Realty Co. Republican. Episcopalian. Home: Cincinnati, O. Died Aug. 10, 1925.

BURTON, Theodore Elijah, congressman, former senator; b. Jefferson, O., Dec. 20, 1851; s. Rev. William and Elizabeth (Grant) B.; A.B., Oberlin Coll., 1872, A.M., 1875; LL.D., Oberlin, 1900, Dartmouth, 1907, Ohio U., 1907; St. John's, Md., 1913, New York U., 1919; unmarried. Admitted to bar, 1875, practiced at Cleveland. Mem. 51st Congress (1889-91), and 54th to 60th Congresses (1895-1909), 21st Ohio Dist.; elected to 61st Congress but resigned upon election to U.S. Senate for term 1909-15; mem. 67th to 70th Congresses (1921-29), 22d Ohio Dist. Chmn. Inland Waterways Commn., 1907-09; chmn. Nat. Waterways Commn., created by Congress, 1909-12; mem. Nat. Monetary Commn., 1908-12; mem. Interparliamentary Union (exec. council 1904-14 and 1921—, executive com. 1921); mem. Foreign Debt Commn., 1922-27; chmn. U.S. delegation to Conf. for Control of Traffic in Arms, at Geneva, May and June 1925; pres. Am. Peace Soc., 1911-15 and 1925—. Del. Rep. Nat. convs., 1904, 08, 12 and 24; received unanimous support of Ohio delegation for presdl. nomination in Rep. Nat. Conv., 1916. Pres. Merchants Nat. Bank, N.Y. City, 1917-19. Stafford Little lecturer at Princeton, 1919, Cutler lecturer, Rochester U., 1922. Author: Financial Crises and Periods of Industrial and Commercial Depression, 1902; Life of John Sherman, 1906; Corporations and the State, 1911; Some Political Tendencies of the Times and the Effect of the War Thereon, 1919; The Constitution, Its Origin and Distinctive Features, 1923. Home: Cleveland, O. Died Oct. 28, 1929.

BURTS, Charles Elford, clergyman; b. Abbeville Co., S.C., Dec. 5, 1867; s. Rev. Richard Ward and Amanda (Latimer) B.; B.A., Furman U., Greenville, S.C., 1893, D.D., 1906; M.Th., Southern Bapt. Sem., 1898; m. Sarah Watson, June 28, 1905; 1 son, Charles Watson. Teacher pub. schs. 5 yrs.; ordained ministry Southern Bapt. Ch., 1898; pastor successively Gallatin, Tenn., Blackville, Edgefield, First Ch., Columbia—all S.C.—until 1920; gen. sec. Bapt. Gen. Bd. of S.C., Columbia, 1920-24; gen. dir. Coöperation Commn. Southern Bapt. Conv., Nashville, Tenn., 1924-26; pastor First Ch., Newberry, S.C., 1926-27, Macon, Ga., 1927-33, St. Matthews, S.C., 1933—. Chmn. State Illiteracy Commn.; mem. Gov.'s Staff; pres. State Bapt. Conv. of S.C. (mem. Social Service Commn.). Del. Bapt. World Alliance, Stockholm, Sweden, 1923. Democrat. Mason. Home: St. Matthews, S.C. Deceased.

BURWELL, Armistead, judge; b. Hillsboro, N.C., Oct. 22, 1839; s. Rev. Robert and Margaret Anna (Robertson) B.; A.B., Davidson Coll., 1859; m. Ella M. Jenkins, Dec. 14, 1869. Capt. C.S.A. during Civil War; admitted to bar, 1869; mem. N.C. Senate, 1881; justice Supreme Ct. of N.C., 1892-95; sr. mem. Burwell & Cansler, 1895—. Home: Charlotte, N.C. Died May 1913.

BURWELL, Benjamin Franklin, judge; b. Armstrong Co., Pa., Apr. 15, 1866; s. Joseph Yarenton and Maxia (Lanham) B.; ed. pub. and normal schs., W.Va.; m. Agnes Jane Carnahan, Dec. 25, 1888. Admitted to bar, 1890; practiced at Gypsum City, Kan., 1890-91, Oklahoma City, 1891—. Candidate for probate judge, Oklahoma Co., 1892; asso. justice Supreme Ct. of Okla., 1898-1908; resumed practice, 1908. Republican. Home: Oklahoma City, Okla. Died Apr. 2, 1916.

BURWELL, William Turnbull, naval officer; b. Vicksburg, Miss., July 19, 1846; s. Armistead B. and Priscilla Withers (Manlove) B.; grad. U.S. Naval Acad., 1866; m. Miss Bradford. Promoted ensign, Apr. 1868, master, Mar. 26, 1869, lt., Mar. 21, 1870, lt. comdr., Sept. 1885, comdr., July 3, 1894, capt., Nov. 29, 1900, rear admiral, June 6, 1906; served in various stas. and commands; comd. Wheeling, May 31, 1898, to May 1900, Puget Sound Naval Sta., 1900-02; comdg. Oregon, 1902-04, Independence, Nov. 1904; comdt. Navy Yard, Puget Sound, 1905. Died 1910.

BUSBEE, Charles Manly, lawyer; b. Raleigh, N.C., Oct. 23, 1845; s. Perrin and Anne (Taylor) B.; prep. edn. Raleigh; at Hampden-Sidney Coll., 1862-63, to end of sophomore yr.; left to enter army Northern Va.; studied law, Univ. of N.C., 1866-67; m. Lydia L. Littlejohn, July 30, 1868; 2d, Florence E. Cooper, Jan. 21, 1891. Served in Civil War as sergt. maj. 5th N.C. inf., army Northern Va.; captured battle Spottsylvania, May 12, 1864; in prison Fort Delaware, Morris Island (under fire), and Fort Pulaski. Admitted to N.C. bar, 1867; State senator, 1875-76; mem. Ho. Reps., 1885-86. Democrat. Home: Raleigh, N.C. Died 1909.

BUSBEE, Fabius Haywood, lawyer; b. Raleigh, N.C., Mar. 4, 1848; s. Perrin and Anne (Taylor) B.; ed. Lovejoy's Acad., Raleigh, N.C., 1859-63; grad. Univ. of N.C., A.B., 1868, later A.M. (A.M., Princeton Univ., Trinity Coll., 1871); m. Annie McKesson, Nov. 1870; 2d, Sallie H. Smith, June 5, 1877. Admitted to bar, 1869; sr. mem. F. H. Busbee & Son. Lt. 71st N.C. troops, 1865; presdl. elector, 1876, at large, 1880; U.S. dist. atty., 1885-89; del. to Nat. Dem. convs. Trustee Univ. of N.C. over 25 yrs. Mason. Author: Busbee's Criminal Digest. Home: Raleigh, N.C. Died 1908.

BUSBEY, Hamilton, editor; b. Clark Co., O., Apr. 1, 1840; s. Thomas Carlton and Ann (Botkin) B.; bro. of L. White B.; m. Emily, d. Gov. James F. Robinson, of Ky., Dec. 20, 1871. On staff Louisville Journal, 1863-65; one of founders, 1865, editor, 1865-1903, Turf, Field and Farm, New York. First advocate of Nat. Trotting Assn., the New York speedway, and of field trials and bench shows in America; officiated as judge in nearly all prin. trotting tracks and horse shows in U.S.; awarded medal as internat. juror of awards, St. Louis Expn., 1904. Trustee Am. Vet. Coll., 1882-96; v.p. N.Y. State Agrl. Soc., 1892-1900. Author: The Trotting and Pacing Horse in America, 1904; History of the Horse in America, 1906; Recollections of Men and Horses, 1907. Rep. State of Ky. at funeral of President Lincoln, Springfield, Ill., May, 1865. Address: South Vienna, O. Died Aug. 1, 1924.

BUSBEY, L. White, newspaperman; b. Vienna, O., Nov. 22, 1852; s. Thomas Carlton and Ann (Botkin) B.; bro. of Hamilton B.; pub. sch. edn.; m. Katherine Graves, 1896. Spl. and Washington corr. Chicago Inter-Ocean, 1879-1905; sec. to the speaker, Ho. of Rep., Washington, 1904-11; sec. Am. sect. of Internat. Joint Commn. (created by treaty with Great Britain for settlement of water boundary questions between U.S. and Can.), 1911-15. Author of Republican side of "The Battle of 1900," a general discussion of political issues before the country; Willis J. Abbott, author of Democratic side of controversy. Died Oct. 1925.

BUSBY, Leonard Asbury, lawyer; b. Jewett, Harrison Co., O., May 22, 1869; s. Sheridan and Margaret (Quigley) B.; A.B., Ohio Wesleyan, 1894; LL.B., Northwestern U. Law Sch., 1895; m. Esther C. Boardman, 1912; children—Janet and Jack. Began practice at Chicago, 1895; gen. counsel various south side street ry. cos., 1906-11; pres., 1911— of Chicago City Ry. Co., Calumet and South Chicago Ry. Co. and The Southern Street Ry. Co.; pres. Chicago Surface Lines, 1914-20; mem. Bd. of Operation and Exec. Com., Chicago Surface Lines, 1914—; mem. governing Com. Chicago City and Connecting Rys. Collateral Trust; Pres. Iron Mountain Co., Am. X-Ray Corp. Pres. bd. trustees John Crerar Library; trustee Lincoln Monument Fund. Home: Chicago, Ill. Died Sept. 9, 1930.

BUSCH, Adolphus, brewer; b. Mayence-on-the-Rhine, Germany, July 10, 1839; s. Ulrich and Barbara (Pfeifer) B.; ed. gymnasium at Mayence, Acad. at Darmstadt, and high schs. at Brussels; came to U.S., 1857; m. Lilly Anheuser, Mar. 7, 1861. Served 4 months in Union Army, 1861, under Gen. Lyon; became asso. with E. Anheuser in brewing business, and in 1865 became partner in E. Anheuser Brewing Co., which later became the Anheuser-Busch Brewing Assn., of which was pres.; pres. South Side Bank, Mfrs. Ry. Co., Busch-Sulzer Bros., Diesel Engine Co., Geyser Ice Co., Waco, Tex. Decorated by Emperor of Germany. Republican. Unitarian. Home: St. Louis. Died Oct. 10, 1913.

BUSCHEMEYER, John Henry, mayor; b. Louisville, Ky., Feb. 24, 1869; s. Henry and Helen (Bollinger) B.; Ph.G., Louisville Coll. Pharmacy, 1889; M.D., Med. Dept., U. of Louisville, 1892; post-grad. work, N.Y. Polyclinic, 1892-93; m. Florence Byrne, Dec. 30, 1903. Prison physician, for U.S. Govt., Louisville, 1893-97, surgeon Louisville Ry. Co.; med. examiner, Mass. Mut. Life Ins. Co., Louisville. Pres. Bd. Aldermen, Louisville, 1909-13; mayor of Louisville, 1913-17. Democrat. Pres. Louisville Pub. Library. Mem. German Evang. Ch. Home: Louisville, Ky. Deceased.

BUSEY, Samuel Clagett, M.D.; b. on farm in Montgomery Co., Md., July 23, 1828; attended Rockville Acad.; M.D., Univ. of Pa., 1848 (LL.D., St. Mary's Univ., Baltimore). In practice, Washington. Pres. Med. Soc. of D.C., 1877, 1894-98; prof. materia medica, diseases of infancy and childhood, and theory and practice of medicine at different periods, and became emeritus prof. theory and practice of medicine, med. dept., Georgetown Univ., Washington, D.C. Author: Occlusion and Dilatation of Lymph Channels, Acquired Forms; Lymph Channels. Died 1901.

BUSH, Albert Peyton, financier; b. Mobile, Ala., Nov. 21, 1876; s. Thomas Greene and Alberta (Williams) B.; prep. edn., Marion (Ala.) Mil. Inst.; A.B., Howard Coll., Birmingham; student Eastman Bus. Coll., Poughkeepsie, N.Y.; m. Marcia Burgess, Dec. 21, 1905; children—Albert Peyton, Isabelle Burgess. Former pres. Imperial Coal & Coke Co., Majestic Coal Co.; pres. Highland Lake Land Co.; dep. chmn. bd. Federal Reserve Bank of New Orleans; v.p. Ala. By-Products Corp.; dep. chmn. of bd. and dir. Fed. Reserve Bank (New Orleans); pres. Highland Lake Land Co.; v.p. Shelby Iron Co. Mem. Ala. Ho. of Rep., 1910; rep. of govt. in distribution of funds lent on cotton. Democrat. Home: Mobile, Ala. Died Apr. 8, 1938.

BUSH, Asahel, banker; b. Westfield, Mass., June 4, 1824; s. Asahel and Sally (Noble) B.; ed. Westfield Acad.; began learning printer's trade at 15; m. Eugenia Zieber, Oct. 12, 1854 (died 1863). Removed to Ore. via Panama, 1850; actively identified with pub. affairs until 1859, when Ore. became a state; was editor of The Oregon Statesman, the prin. Ore. paper, and 1st state printer; retired from newspaper business, 1862. Associated with W. S. Ladd and established banking house of Ladd & Bush, 1868. Trustee U. of Ore., 1882-92. Democrat. Unitarian. Home: Salem, Ore. Died Dec. 23, 1913.

BUSH, Benjamin Franklin, ry. pres.; b. Wellsboro, Pa., July 5, 1860; s. James and Rosella (Henry) B.; ed. pub. schs. and State Normal Sch., Mansfield, Pa.; m. Catherine Idelia Hawkins, May 30, 1883. Began ry. service as rodman on N.P. R.R., 1882; div. engr. U.P. R.R., in Ida. and Ore., 1887-89; chief engr. and gen. supt. Ore. Improvement Co., Seattle, Wash., 1889-96; gen. mgr., Northwestern Improvement Co., Roslyn, Wash., 1896-1903; fuel agent, Mo. P. R.R., St. Louis, 1903-07; pres. 1907-08, receiver, 1908-10, again pres., 1910-11, Western Md. R.R.; pres. 1911-15, receiver, 1915-17, again pres., 1917—, Mo. Pacific R.R. Co. Pres. D.&R.G. R.R., 1912-15, Western Pacific Ry., 1913. Cons. engr., U.S. Geol. Survey, 1900; mem. advisory bd. on fuels and structural materials, 1907. Regional dir. Southwestern Dist., U.S. R.R. Administration. Home: St. Louis, Mo. Died July 29, 1927.

BUSH, Charles G., cartoonist; b. Boston, Sept. 1842; spent first few yrs. of his life in China where his father was 1st Am. consul apptd. to Hong Kong; ed. Boston Latin Sch., and partly at U.S. Naval Acad. After few yrs. work for Harper & Bros., studied in Paris; was cartoonist for N.Y. Herald several yrs., then for N.Y. World. Died 1909.

BUSH, Ira Benton, supt. schools; b. Cox's Mills, W.Va., Feb. 14, 1876; s. Carr Bailey and Virginia (Woodford) B.; Glenville (W.Va.) Normal, 1893-97; B.A., W.Va. U., 1900; Vanderbilt, 1900-01; extension course, U. of Pittsburgh, 1915-17; m. Effie Sweeney, Dec. 24, 1902; children—Ira Benton, Virginia Elizabeth (Mrs. Geo. L. Cole), Robert Edwin, Anne Margaret. Teacher, Concord State Normal Sch., Athens, W.Va., 1901-04; supt. schs., Hinton, W.Va., 1904-10, Parkersburg, W.Va., 1910-14, Erie, Pa., 1914-22; sec.-treas. Midland Investment Corp., 1922-28; mgr. Fidelity Mut. Life Ins. Co., 1928-31; supt. schs., Loudon Dist., S. Charleston, W.Va., 1931-32; pres. Armstrong Jr. Coll., Alderson, W.Va., 1932—. Mem. W.Va. State Bd. of Edn., 1908-14. Democrat. Baptist. Mason. Home: Alderson, W.Va. Deceased.

BUSH, Katharine Jeannette, zoölogist; b. Scranton, Pa., Dec. 30, 1855; d. William Henry and Eliza Ann (Clark) B.; ed. New Haven pvt. and pub. schs. and New Haven High Sch.; studied many yrs. under Prof. A. E. Verrill; Ph.D., Yale, 1901; unmarried. Asst. zoöl. dept. Yale U. Mus., 1879—; on U.S. Fish Commn. several yrs.; assisted in revision of Webster's Dictionary, resulting in Webster's Internat. Dictionary, edit. of 1890. Author: The Tubicolous Annelids of the Tribes Sabellides and Serpulides—Harriman Alaska Expedition, Vol. XII, 1905. Home: New Haven, Conn. Died 1937.

BUSH, Lincoln, civil engr.; b. Cook Co., Ill., Dec. 14, 1860; s. Lewis and Mary (Ritchie) B.; M.S., Cook County Normal School, 1880; B.S., U. of Ill., 1888, hon. D.Engring., 1904; m. Alma R. Green, 1890; children—Cedric Lincoln, Denzil Sidney. Asst. engr. U.P. R.R. and Pacific Short Line, 1888-90; asst. engr. with E. L. Corthell, 1890-92; chief draftsman, West Office Pittsburgh Bridge Co., 1892-96; asst. bridge engr. and acting div. engr. C.&N.W. R.R., 1896-99; bridge engr., 1899-1900, prin. asst. engr., 1900-03, chief engr., D.,L.&W. Railroad, 1903-08; then retired. Inventor of a new method of constructing concrete and pile footings; also the Bush train shed, Bush track constrn. Col. Q.M.C., U.S.A., World War. Home: Kansas City, Mo. Died Dec. 10, 1940.

BUSH, Thomas Greene; b. Pickensville, Ala., 1847. In 1861, at age of 13, organized 2 mil. cos., one of which was accepted temporarily by gov. of Ala.; cadet, U. of Ala., 1861-64; resigned and entered C.S.A. as adj., 62d Ala. Regt.; was captured by federal troops, 1865; prisoner at Ship Island and New Orleans until surrender of Gen. Dick Taylor, when he was exchanged at Vicksburg, Miss. Grad. U. of Miss., 1867; engaged in business pursuits; pres. Mobile & Birmingham Ry. Co., 1886—; pres. Shelby Iron Co., of Shelby, Ala. Mem. Ala. Legislature, 1886; mem. Monetary Commn. created by Indianapolis Monetary Conf., 1897; trustee The Foundation for the Promotion of Industrial Peace. Address: Birmingham, Ala. Deceased.

BUSH, Wendell T., college prof.; b. Ridgeway, Mich., Sept. 25, 1866; s. Rufus T. and Sarah M. (Hall) B.; Poly. Inst., Brooklyn; A.M., Harvard, 1898; U. of Berlin, 1900-01; Ph.D., Columbia, 1905; m. Mary L. Potter, Sept. 28, 1896. Lecturer, 1905-08, asso. in philosophy, 1908-12, asso. prof., 1912-28.

prof., 1928—, Columbia. Co-editor Journal of Philosophy. Home: New York, N.Y. Died Feb. 10, 1941.

BUSH-BROWN, Henry Kirke, sculptor; b. Ogdensburg, N.Y., Apr. 21, 1857; s. Robert W. and Caroline (Udall) B.; ed. Siglar's Sch., Newburgh, N.Y.; studied art at Nat. Acad. Design, pupil of Henry Kirke Brown; studied in Paris and Italy, 1886-89; m. Margaret W. Lesley, Apr. 7, 1886; children—Lydia, Harold, Malcolm (dec.), James. Prin. works: Equestrian statues Gen. G. G. Meade, Gen. John F. Reynolds, and Gen. John Sedgwick, Gettysburg, Pa.; statues Justinian, Appellate Court, New York; Indian Buffalo Hunt, Chicago Expn., 1893; group representing Truth, Buffalo Expn., 1901; decorative figures, Hall Records, New York; equestrian statue Gen. Anthony Wayne for Valley Forge, Pa.; memorial arch, Stony Point, N.Y.; The Lincoln Memorial, Gettysburg, 1911; portrait bust of Henry Kirke Brown, sculptor, for Hall of Fame, U. of New York; historical panels, U.S. Post Office, Wellsville, N.Y., etc. Died Mar. 1, 1935.

BUSHNELL, Asa Smith, gov. Ohio; b. Rome, N.Y., Sept. 16, 1834; moved to Cincinnati, 1845; common school edn.; from 1851 at Springfield, O.; was dry goods clerk, then bookkeeper, then mfr., then pres. Warder, Bushnell & Glessner Co., mower and reaper mfrs.; comd. a company in 152d Ohio vol. inf. in war; mem. G.A.R.; 33° Mason; chmn. Rep. State Exec. Com., 1885; elected gov. Ohio, 2 terms, 1895-99. Republican. Died 1904.

BUSHNELL, George Ensign, surgeon U.S.A.; b. Worcester, Mass., Sept. 10, 1853; s. George and Mary Elizabeth (Blake) B.; A.B., Yale, 1876, M.D., 1880; m. Adra Holmes, 1881 (died 1896); 2d, Ethel M. Barnard, Dec. 24, 1902. Apptd. asst. surgeon, Feb. 18, 1881; capt. asst. surgeon, Feb. 18, 1886; maj. chief surgeon vols., June 4, 1898; maj. surgeon U.S.A., Dec. 10, 1898; maj. Med. Corps, Dec. 10, 1898; hon. disch. from vol. service, Jan. 23, 1899; lt. col. U.S.A., Apr. 23, 1908; col. May 1, 1911. Comd. U.S.A. Gen. Hosp., Ft. Bayard, N.M., about 14 yrs. Retired by operation of law, Sept. 10, 1917. Republican. Author: A Study in the Epidemiology of Tuberculosis, 1920. Deceased.

BUSHNELL, Winthrop Grant, elec. engr.; b. New Haven, Conn., Mar. 20, 1864; s. Cornelius S. and Emilie Fowler (Clark) B.; B.A., Yale, 1888; m. Harriet Elizabeth Scofield, June 7, 1911. Night editor New Haven Journal and Courier, 1889; commercial elec. engr. with Edison Electric Co. and Gen. Electric Co., 1890-1906; owner and mgr. various pub. utilities, water powers, etc.; v.p. Conn. Power Co. State chmn. Y.M.C.A. and chmn. exec. com. New Haven Chapter Am. Red Cross, 1917; Conn. state chmn. United War Work Campaign, 1918. Republican. Conglist. Home: New Haven, Conn. Died Oct. 23, 1921.

BUSIEL, Charles Albert, gov. N.H.; b. Meredith, N.H.; academic edn. at Gilford, Belknap Co., N.H.; m. Eunice Elizabeth Preston, Nov. 21, 1864. Is a mfr.; pres. Laconia Nat. Bank and City Savings Bank; has been pres. Lake Shore, and dir. Concord & Montreal R.R.; etc.; formerly a Democrat, but Republican for yrs.; chief engr. fire dept., 1872-85; mem. N.H. legislature, 1878-79; del. Dem. Nat. Conv., 1880. Was 1st mayor of Laconia, 1893-94; gov. N.H., 1895-96; candidate U.S. senate, 1896. Home: Laconia, N.H. Died 1901.

BUSSEY, Cyrus, asst. sec. interior; b. Hubbard, O., Oct. 5, 1833; s. Rev. Amos and Hannah (Tylee) B.; m. Ellen Kiser, May 15, 1855. Engaged in mercantile pursuits; mem. Ia. Senate, as Democrat; del. Baltimore conv., 1860, that nominated Stephen A. Douglas for president; raised 3d Ia. Vol. Cav., Aug., 1861, becoming its col., later brig. gen. and bvt. maj. gen.; comd. a brigade in battle of Pea Ridge, Mar. 7, 1862; comd. 2d Cav. Div., Army of the Tenn.; chief of cav. Grant's army, siege of Vicksburg; led advance Sherman's army against Gen. Johnston's army to Jackson, Miss.; defeated Jackson at Canton, July 18, 1863; comd. 1st Div. 7th Army Corps, at Little Rock, and the last yr. of war comd. 3d Div. 7th Army Corps, Western Ark. and Indian Ty. After war commn. mcht. in St. Louis and New Orleans; pres. New Orleans Chamber of Commerce 6 yrs.; moved to New York, 1881; del. Rep. Nat. Conv., 1868, 1880; del. Meth. Ecumenical Conf., London, 1881. Asst. sec. of the interior, 1889-93; then in law practice. Home: Washington, D.C. Died Mar. 2, 1915.

BUSTARD, William Walter, clergyman; b. Paterson, N.J., Aug. 21, 1871; s. Robert and Sarah Frances (Matthews) B.; A.B., Brown U., 1895; grad. Newton Theol. Institution, 1898; (D.D., Brown U., 1921); m. 2d, Helen N. McCurdy, June 2, 1928. Ordained Bapt. ministry, 1898; pastor Amesbury, Mass., 1898-99, Dudley St. Ch., Boston, 1900-09, Euclid Av. Ch., Cleveland, 1909-25; then pastor 10th Ch., Oakland, Calif. Independent Republican. Died June 25, 1935.

BUSWELL, Henry Foster, lawyer; b. Bradford, N.H., Mar. 1, 1842; s. Martin R. and Phebe W. (Upton) B.; A.B., Harvard, 1866; student Harvard Law Sch., 1869-70; unmarried. Asst. prof. ethics and internat. law, U.S. Naval Acad., 1868-69; began practice, 1872; spl. justice Dist. Ct. of Southern Norfolk, Mass., 1891—. Republican. Author: Pleading and Practice in Personal Actions in Courts of Massachusetts, 1875; Law Insanity, 1885; Limitations and Adverse Possession, 1889; Civil Liability for Personal Injuries, 1893. Home: Canton, Mass. Died Sept. 13, 1919.

BUTCHER, William Lewis, social worker, boy specialist; b. Holyoke, Mass., Oct. 1, 1886; s. Samuel and Emily (Lewis) B.; ed. Wilbraham Acad.; m. May E. Lewis, Oct. 3, 1906; children—William L., Ruth L. Advertising business until 1910; dir. West Side Boys' House, N.Y. City, 1910-13; dir. Brace Memorial Newsboys' House till 1922; dir. Boys' Welfare (New York), Children's Aid Soc. Founder and sec. Internat. Boy's Week, held in 4,000 cities around the world; sec. Internat. Boys' Work Council; spl. field commr. Boy Scouts of America; dir. Boys' Club Fedn.; chmn. exec. com. Big Brother and Big Sister Fedn.; formerly advisor on boys' work to Rotary Internat.; mem. N.Y. State Crime Commn.; chmn. Sub-Commn. on Causes of Crime, which made studies of crime areas, relation of press to crime, case studies of major offenders and study of 201 truants; vice chmn. N.Y. City Advisory Crime Prevention Commn.; mem. exec. com. N.Y. State Conf. on Social Work, N.Y. City Conf. on Social Worw; vice chmn. boys' work sect., Welfare Council of N.Y. City; mem. teach advisory com., Brooklyn Boy Life Council. Conglist. Home: Brooklyn, N.Y. Died Jan. 15, 1931.

BUTIN, Romain Francois, prof. Oriental langs.; b. Saint-Romain-d'Urfé, Loire, France, Dec. 3, 1871; s. Antoine and Jeanne-Marie (Poyet) B.; ed. St. Pierre des Salles and Petit Séminaire de St. Jodard, France; student in divinity, Marist Coll., Washington, D.C., 1890-97; S.T.B., Catholic U. of America, 1898, S.T.L., 1900, Ph.D., 1904. Came to U.S., 1890, naturalized citizen, 1908. Joined Soc. of Mary (Marist Fathers), 1893; prof. apologetics, Marist Coll., 1900-04; prof. Hebrew and Sacred Scripture, same, 1900-08; prof. philosophy, Jefferson Coll., St. James, La., 1908-12; instr. Semitic langs. and lit., Catholic U. of America, 1912-16, asso. prof., 1916-23, prof., 1923—; also curator Museum of Catholic U.; annual prof. and acting dir. of the Am. Sch. of Oriental Research, Jerusalem, 1926-27. Provincial of Washington Province Marist Fathers, 1930—. Author: The Ten Nequdoth of the Torah, 1906, Progressive Lessons in Hebrew, 1915; Key to the Progressive Lessons in Hebrew, 1915. Died Dec. 8, 1937.

BUTLER, Alford Augustus, theologian; b. Portland, Me., Sept. 23, 1845; s. Alford and Caroline Ilsley (Partridge) B.; M.A., Griswold Coll., Ia., and theol. grad., same, 1873; (D.D., Seabury Div. Sch., Minn., 1902); unmarried. Deacon, 1873, priest, 1874; P.E. Ch.; asst. Grace Cathedral, Davenport, Ia., 1873; rector Grace Ch., Cedar Rapids, Ia., 1873-77, Trinity Ch., Bay City, Mich., 1877-84, Ch. of the Epiphany, New York, 1884-91. Christ Ch., Red Wing, Minn., 1891-94; warden and prof. homiletics, liturgics and religious pedagogy, Seabury Div. Sch., 1894-1905. Author: How to Study the Life of Christ, 1902; How Shall We Worship God?, 1904; The Churchman's Manual of Sunday School Methods, 1906; How to Understand the Words of Christ, 1909. Address: Redlands, Calif. Deceased.

BUTLER, Amos William, zoölogist; b. Brookville, Ind., Oct. 1, 1860; s. William Wallace and Hannah (Wright) B.; A.B., Indiana U., 1894, A.M., 1900, LL.D., 1922; LL.D., Hanover Coll., 1915; m. Mary I. Reynolds, June 2, 1880; children—Mrs. Carrie Hannah Watts, Mrs. Alice Kaylor (dec.), Wm. Reynolds, Gwyn Foster, Mrs. Anne Harrison, Hadley Butler (dec.). Ornithologist, dept. of geology and resources of Ind., 1896-97; sec. Ind. Bd. State Charities, 1897-1923. Mem. White House Children's Conf., 1909. Lecturer on economics, Purdue U., 1905. Pres. Nat. Conf. Charities and Corrections, 1906-07; chmn. Am. com. on Internat. Prison Congress, Washington, 1910; mem. Am. Prison Assn.; v.p. Internat. Prison Congress; del. from U.S. to Internat. Prison Congress, London (v.p. sect. 2), 1925, Prague, 1930; pres. Ind. Conf. Charities and Correction, 1915; fellow A.A.A.S.; chmn. exec. com. Ind. Soc. for Mental Hygiene, 1918-25, pres., 1925-30, emeritus; sec. Ind. Com. on Mental Defectives, 1915; senior sociologist U.S. Bureau of Efficiency, 1928-29; founder Internat. Com. on Mental Hygiene, Washington, 1930; mem. advisory com. to Nat. Commn. on Law Observance and Enforcement, 1929-31; sec. Ind. Com. on Observance and Enforcement of Law, 1929-31; mem. exec. bd. Am. Inst. of Criminal Law and Criminology, 1935—. Author: Birds of Indiana; Also Indiana—A Century of Progress, The Development of Public Charities and Corrections. Home: Indianapolis, Ind. Died Aug. 5, 1937.

BUTLER, Charles Henry, lawyer; b. New York, June 18, 1859; s. William Allen and Mary R. (Marshall) B.; g.s. Benjamin F. B. (atty. gen. of U.S.) and of Capt. Chas. H. Marshall, of the Black Ball Clipper Ship Line; ed. Princeton U., non grad. class of 1881, hon. M.A., 1912; m. Marcia, d. Ethan Flagg, Nov. 21, 1882 (died 1928); children—Ethan Flagg, Marcia Flagg (dec.), Charles Marshall, Henry Franklin. In the practice of law 20 years in New York; became legal expert Anglo-American Canadian Commission, 1898; reporter of Decisions, Supreme Court of U.S., 1902-16, and edited Vols. 187-242 of U.S. Reports; law practice at Washington, D.C., with John A. Kratz, 1916-33; in practice with his son, Henry F., 1933—. Republican. Presbyn. Tech. del. Am. delegation to The Hague Peace Conf., 1907. Author: Cuba Must Be Free, 1898; The Voice of the Nation, 1898; Our Relations with Spain, 1898; Our Treaty with Spain, 1899; Freedom of Private Property on the Sea, 1899; Treaty-Making Power of the United States (2 vols.), 1902. Home: Woolwich, Me. Died Feb. 9, 1940.

BUTLER, Edward Burgess, merchant; b. Lewiston, Me., Dec. 16, 1853; s. Manly Orville and Elizabeth (Howe) B.; ed. Boston pub. schs.; m. Jane, d. William Henry Holly, of Norwalk, Conn., 1880. With bro., George H., founded ho. of Butler Bros., at Boston, 1877; then at N.Y., Chicago, St. Louis, Minneapolis and Dallas, Tex.; dir. Ill. Merchants Trust Co., Chicago. Chmn. ways and means com., and chmn. of dept. admissions and collections, Chicago Expn., 1893. Pres. for thirty years Glenwood (Ill.) Manual Training Sch.; trustee Hull House, Art Inst. Chicago. Home: Chicago, Ill. Died Feb. 20, 1928.

BUTLER, Edward H., banker; b. Detroit, Aug. 1841; s. William A. and Mary A. (Harter) B.; student U. of Mich., 1857-60; m. Julia E. Smith, Dec. 1868 (died 1869); m. 2d, Harriette P. Stryker, Oct. 1874 (died 1898); m. 3d, Lillie Garth Burbridge, 1901. In banking business in Detroit, 1860—; pres. Detroit Fire & Marine Ins. Co. Presdl. elector, 1880; state treas. of Mich., 1883-87. Chmn. Detroit Clearing House, 1893-1901. Home: Grosse Pointe Farms, Mich. Died Dec. 29, 1928.

BUTLER, Edward Hubert, newspaper editor; b. Le Roy, N.Y., Sept. 5, 1850; ed. pub. and pvt. schs.; m. Mary Elizabeth Barber, 1872 (died 1892). Established the Buffalo Sunday News in 1873, and on Oct. 11, 1880, started the Evening News, of which he is sole propr. Rep. presdl. elector-at-large, N.Y., 1896, 1900; pres. State Editorial Assn., 1891; pres. Rep. State Editorial Assn., 1898; mem. Grade Crossings Commn.; chmn. bd. of trustees Grosvenor Library; pres. bd. of mgrs. State Normal Sch.; dir. Rivers and Harbors Congress. Home: Buffalo, N.Y. Died Mar. 9, 1914.

BUTLER, Ellis Parker, author; b. Muscatine, Ia., Dec. 5, 1869; s. Audley Gazzam and Adella (Vesey) B.; high sch. edn.; m. Ida Anna Zipser, June 27, 1899; children—Elsie McColm, Jean, Marjorie, Ellis Olmsted. Pres. Flushing Federated Savings & Loan Assn. Mem., pres. of Authors' League of America. Author: French Decorative Styles; Pigs is Pigs, 1906; The Incubator Baby, 1906; Perkins of Portland, 1906; Great American Pie Co., 1907; Confessions of a Daddy, 1907; Kilo, 1907; That Pup, 1908; Cheerful Smugglers, 1908; Mike Flannery, 1909; Thin Santa Claus, 1909; Water Goats, 1910; Adventures of a Suburbanite, 1911; Jack-Knife Man, 1913; Red Head, 1916; Dominie Dean, 1917; Goat's Feathers, 1919; Philo Gubb, 1919; Swatty, 1920; How It Feels to be Fifty, 1920; In Pawn, 1921; Ghosts What Ain't, 1923; Jibby Jones, 1923; Jibby Jones and the Alligator, 1924; Many Happy Returns of the Day, 1925; Butler Readings, 1926; The Behind Legs of the 'Orse, 1927; Pigs, Pets and Pies, 1927; Dorna, 1929; Dollarature, 1930; Jo Ann (with Louise Andrews Kent), 1933; The Young Stamp Collectors' Own Book, 1933; Hunting the Wow, 1934. Home: Flushing, N.Y. Died Sept. 13, 1937.

BUTLER, Fred Mason, judge; b. Jamaica, Vt., May 28, 1854; s. Aaron Mason and Emeline (Muzzy) B.; ed. Leland and Gray Sem., Townsend, Vt.; m. Lillian H. Holton, Nov. 24, 1875; children—Anza L. (Mrs. Wallace W. Nichols), Helen M. (Mrs. John A. Barney), Florence M. (Mrs. Leon E. Ellsworth). Admitted to Vt. bar, 1877; mem. Butler & Maloney many years; judge City Court, Rutland, 1889-95; mem. State Senate, 1908; judge Superior Court, 1909-23 (chief of Superior judges, 1922); elected by legislature justice Supreme Court of Vt., 1923, to succeed Justice Willard W. Miles (resigned), reëlected, 1925, retired, 1926. Republican. Baptist. Home: Rutland, Vt. Died Dec. 24, 1932.

BUTLER, George Bernard, artist; b. New York, Feb. 8, 1838; studied painting under Thomas Hicks, also Thomas Couture, Paris; served in Union army in Civil war, losing an arm at Gettysburg; studied and painted animals and genre paintings in Europe, 1865-68, and 1873-83; later in New York, making portraiture his prin. work. Died 1907.

BUTLER, George Frank, physician, author; b. Moravia, N.Y., Mar. 15, 1857; s. Isaac and Asenath (Chase) B.; grad. Baldwin's Acad., Groton, N.Y., 1874; pharmacist, Pittsfield, Mass., 1874-78; in sheep and drug business, southwestern Kan., 1878-86; M.D., Rush Med. Coll., Chicago, 1889; (hon. A.M., Valparaiso U., 1908); m. Nannie Blanche Porter, Mar. 21, 1882. Lecturer med. pharmacy and materia medica,

Rush Med. Coll., 1889-92; prof. materia medica, therapeutics and clin. medicine, Northwestern U. Women's Med. Sch., 1890-96, Coll. Phys. and Surg., Chicago, 1892-1906; prof. medicine, Dearborn Med. Coll., 1905-06; prof. internal medicine, Chicago Post-Grad. Med. Sch., 1905-07; med. supt. Alma Springs Sanitarium, Alma., Mich., 1900-05; prof. and head dept. therapeutics, and prof. clin. and preventive medicine, Chicago Coll. Medicine and Surgery, 1906-15, emeritus, 1915—; pres. faculty and prof. diseases of kidneys and nervous system, Practitioners' Coll., Chicago, 1910-12; co. phys. of Cook Co., Ill., Nov. 1911-13; med. dir. North Shore Health Resort, Winnetka. Author: Textbook of Materia Medica, Therapeutics and Pharmacology, 1896. Home: Wilmette, Ill. Died June 22, 1921.

BUTLER, Glentworth Reeve, M.D.; b. Phila., Dec. 31, 1855; s. J(ames) Glentworth and Evelyn E. (Reeve) B.; A.B., Hamilton Coll., 1877, A.M., 1880; M.D., L.I. Coll. Hosp., Brooklyn, 1880; Sc.D., Hamilton, 1904; LL.D., Wesleyan, 1908; m. Antoinette Willson, Jan. 1884; 1 dau., Antoinette Reeve (Mrs. Brower Hewitt). In practice of medicine in Brooklyn; asst. phys., St. Mary's Gen. Hosp., 1882-91, M.E. Hosp., 1885-91; chief 2d med. div., M.E. Hosp., 1891-1906, phys.-in-chief, 1906—; attending phys., Brooklyn Hosp., 1902—, sr. phys., 1913. U.S. pension examining surgeon, 1889-93; contract surgeon, U.S.A., Aug.-Nov. 1917; maj., later lt. col., M.C., U.S.A., Sept. 1918-May 1919; mem. advisory med. bd. Dept. of Health, New York, Fellow Am. Climatol. Assn., Am. Coll. Physicians. V.p. Packer Inst., 1905—. Presbyn. Republican. Author: Emergency Notes, 1889; Diagnostics of Internal Medicine, 1901. Home: Brooklyn, N.Y. Died Dec. 6, 1926.

BUTLER, Howard Crosby, univ. prof.; b. Croton Falls, N.Y., Mar. 7, 1872; s. Edward Marchant and Helen Belden (Crosby) B.; A.B., Princeton, 1892, A.M., 1893; post-grad. Columbia Sch. of Architecture, Am. Schs. of Classical Studies, Rome, Athens; univ. fellow in archeology, Princeton, 1893, 1897; fellow Am. Sch. Classical Studies, Rome, 1897-98; unmarried. Organized and conducted archæol. expdns. in Syria, 1899-1900, 1904-05, 1909; prof. history of architecture, Princeton, 1905—. Resident master of Graduate Coll., Princeton; dir. Am. excavations at Sardis in Asia Minor. Mem. Archæol. Inst. America (hon.), A.I.A., Am. Acad. of Arts and Letters. Author: Scotland's Ruined Abbeys, 1900; The Story of Athens, 1902; etc. Drexel Gold Medalist, 1910. Address: Princeton, N.J. Died Aug. 15, 1922.

BUTLER, Howard Russell, artist; b. New York, Mar. 3, 1856; s. William Allen and Mary R. (Marshall) B.; B.S., Princeton U., 1876, M.F.A., 1923; LL.B., Columbia, 1882; m. Virginia Hays, Nov. 25, 1890. Practiced law, New York, 1881-84. Painter in oil; hon. mention, Paris Salon, 1886, Pa. Acad., 1888; medals, Paris Expn., 1889, 1900, Chicago Expn., 1893, Atlanta, 1895, Phila. and St. Louis, Buffalo, San Francisco expns.; Carnegie prize, N.A.D., 1916; 2d prize, Duxbury Expn., 1917. Founder, 1889, pres., 1889-1906, Am. Fine Arts Soc.; pres. Carnegie Music Hall, 1896-1905. Accompanied the U.S. Naval Obs. Expdn. to Baker, Ore., and painted the solar eclipse of June 8, 1918 (painting owned by Am. Mus. Natural History); painted solar eclipses of Sept. 10, 1923, Lompoc, Calif., and of Jan. 24, 1925, Middletown, Conn.; apptd. supervisor of Am. Mus. Natural History on astron. exhibits, 1925. Paintings on exhbn. in Mus. of Natural History, Met. Mus., Lotos Club, etc., also has painted portraits of many prominent citizens, including 13 portraits of the late Andrew Carnegie for libraries, A.N.A., 1898; N.A., 1902. Home: Princeton, N.J. Died May 22, 1934.

BUTLER, Hugh, lawyer; b. Lanarkshire, Scotland, May 31, 1840; ed. pub. and pvt. schs. and acads. in Scotland, 1846-53, St. Lawrence Acad., Ky., 1854-56, Fulton Sem., Lewistown, Ill., 1857-59; admitted to Ill. bar, 1862; m. Annie Duke Thatcher, Feb. 1872. Removed to Central City, Colo., 1863, to Denver, 1874; pros. atty. Gilpin Co., Colo., 1864-67; mem. Territorial Council of Territorial Legislative Assembly, Colo. Ty., 1867-71, 1874-75; mayor Central City, 1872-73; chmn. Dem. State Central Com., 1876-77. Lecturer on common law pleading, U. of Colo. Home: Denver, Colo. Died 1913.

BUTLER, James Davie, educator; b. Rutland, Vt., Mar. 15, 1815; grad. Middlebury Coll., 1836 (A.M.; LL.D.); Andover Theol. Sem., 1840; m. Anna, d. Joshua Bates, pres. Middlebury Coll., 1845. Prof. ancient languages, Norwich, Vt., Univ., 1845-47; held Cong. pastorates, 1847-54; prof. ancient languages, Wabash Coll., Ind., 1854-58; same Univ. of Wis., 1858-67; then engaged in lecturing and occasional preaching. Author: Butleriana, M13; also main text of Armsmear Colt's Memorial 1866; writer in The Nation continuously, 1879—. Home: Madison, Wis. Died 1905.

BUTLER, James Gay, capitalist; b. Saugatuck, Mich., Jan. 23, 1840; s. William G. and Eliza (McKennan) B.; student U. of Mich., 1858-61, leaving coll. to enlist in Union Army; B.S., same univ., 1904; m. Maggie Leggat, Oct. 15, 1868. Mem. 3d Mich. Cav. 4½ yrs., advancing to maj., and comdg. regt. during last 8 mos. of service; entered manufacture of tobacco in St. Louis, 1866, and became dir. Am. Tobacco Co. (retired). Rep. candidate for mayor of St. Louis, 1880; mem. bd. dirs. La. Purchase Expn., 1903-04. Presbyn. Home: St. Louis, Mo. Died Aug. 22, 1916.

BUTLER, John Ammi, lawyer; b. Milwaukee, Oct. 14, 1851; s. Ammi R. R. and Orvilla L. (Tanner) B.; B.A., Yale, 1874; studied at Göttingen and Leipzig; m. Fanny L. Dana, Oct. 25, 1877. Admitted to bar, 1877, and practiced at Milwaukee; retired, 1884, traveled abroad, 1885-91; then occupied with civic reform work. Founder Milwaukee Municipal League, 1894 (pres. 8 terms), Milwaukee City Club, 1909 (1st pres.), Wis. Civ. Service League, 1905 (pres.); mem. exec. com. Nat. Municipal League, Council Nat. Civ. Service Reform League. Corr. for Chicago Times and other papers in '80s. Home: Milwaukee, Wis. Died June 17, 1923.

BUTLER, John Gazzam, brig. gen. U.S.A.; b. Pittsburgh, Pa., Jan. 23, 1842; s. John Bartlet and Catherine Selina (Gazzam) B.; ed. Western U. of Pa., and grad. U.S. Mil. Acad., 1863; m. Eliza Miller Warnick, Jan. 26, 1866. Second lt. 4th Arty., June 11, 1863; advanced through grades to col., Aug. 16, 1903; brig. gen. Jan. 21, 1904. Served with Battery M, 4th U.S. Arty. in Army of the Cumberland, Tenn., campaign; bvtd. 1st lt., Sept. 20, 1863, "for gallant and meritorious services in battle of Chickamauga;" transferred to ordnance corps, Jan. 1864; served on various spl. duties during 40 yrs.; retired Jan. 22, 1904. Episcopalian. Died Aug. 17, 1914.

BUTLER, John George, clergyman; b. Cumberland, Md., Jan. 28, 1826; ed. Allegheny Acad., Cumberland, Md.; attending Pa. Coll. and Theol. Sem., Gettysburg, Pa. (D.D., Pa. Coll., 1868); pastor St. Paul's English Luth. Ch., 1849-73; Luther Pl. Memorial Ch., 1873—, both at Washington, D.C.; one of 1st hosp. chaplains apptd. by Pres. Lincoln; served through Civil war in and around Washington; chaplain U.S. Ho. of Reps., 1869-75; U.S. Senate from 1866 for several yrs.; for about 30 yrs. prof. homiletics and ch. history, Howard Univ.; many yrs. Washington corr. Lutheran's Observer and Lutheran Evangelist; editor of latter. Died 1909.

BUTLER, John Wesley, clergyman; b. Shelburne Falls, Mass., Oct. 13, 1851; s. William and Julia (Crompton) B.; prep. edn. Boston Latin Sch. and Passaic (N.J.) Collegiate Inst.; student Boston U. Sch. of Theology, 1871-74; (D.D., Baker U., Kan., 1889); m. Sara Aston, Aug. 13, 1878. Missionary M.E. Ch. in Mexico, 1873—, then treas. and atty. Missionary Soc. of M.E. Ch. in Mexico; pastor in Mexico City 10 yrs.; presiding elder or dist. supt., 1890—. Pres. Mexican Meth. Inst., Puebla, 2 yrs. Author: Sketches of Mexico, 1894; Silver Anniversary of Methodism in Mexico (Spanish), 1898; Mexico Coming Into Light, 1907. Died Mar. 17, 1918.

BUTLER, Joseph Green, Jr., mfr.; b. Temperance Furnace, Mercer Co., Pa., Dec. 21, 1840; s. Joseph Green and Temperance (Orwig) B.; ed. pub. schs.; m. Harriet Voorhes Ingersoll, Jan. 10, 1866; children—Mrs. Blanche Butler Ford (dec.), Mrs. Grace Ingersoll McGraw, Henry A. Began as bookkeeper with James Ward & Co., Niles, O., 1857, financial mgr., 1858-63; with Hale & Ayer, Chicago, 1863-66; mgr. Girard Iron Co., 1866-78; mgr. Brier Hill Iron & Coal Co., 1878-1912; pres. Portage Silica Co.; v.p. Brier Hill Steel Co., 1912-17, Ohio Steel Co., 1896-1906; chmn. bd. Bessemer Limestone & Cement Co. Mem. Industrial Commn. to France, 1916; originator and pres. McKinley Birthplace Memorial Assn., Niles, O.; erected and presented to Youngstown, The Butler Art Inst. Republican. Author: Life of McKinley, 1900; Presidents I Have Seen and Known, 1910; A Journey Through France in Wartime, 1917; Fifty Years of Iron and Steel, 1917; Recollections of Men and Events—an Autobiography. Home: Youngstown, O. Died Dec. 19, 1927.

BUTLER, Louis Fatio, insurance pres.; b. Hartford, Conn., July 23, 1871; s. John Hartwell and Ida deM. (Fatio) B.; grad. Hartford High Sch., 1889; m. Alice Goodrich, Oct. 28, 1902. With Travelers Ins. Co., Hartford, Conn., 1890—, becoming asst. sec., 1904, sec., 1907-12, v.p., 1912-15, pres., 1915—; also pres. Travelers' Indemnity Co. Trustee Hartford Retreat for Insane. Mem. com. to report on plan of insurance for officers and men of U.S. Army and Navy. Home: Hartford, Conn. Died Oct. 23, 1929.

BUTLER, Marion, senator; b. Sampson Co., N.C., May 20, 1863; s. Wiley and Romelia B.; A.B., U. of N.C., 1885; m. Florence Faison, Aug. 31, 1893; children—Pocahontas, Marion, Edward F., Florence F., Wiley. Taught in an academy, 3 yrs.; purchased the Clinton (N.C.) Caucasian, 1888, removing it to Raleigh, 1894; admitted to bar, 1899; in practice, Raleigh and Washington. Largely interested in agr. Mem. N.C. Senate, 1890; led and won fight to establish state univ. for girls at Greensboro, N.C.; led and won fight to secure appropriation to save the old state university at Chapel Hill, N.C.; author of the state ry. commn. law, also of the six per cent interest law; led fight to improve the public schools; left Dem. party, 1892, and assisted in organizing Peoples party; chmn. Nat. Exec. Com., same, 1896-1904; then affiliated with Rep. party. U.S. senator, N.C., 1896-1901; author of the law establishing the present rural free delivery system; secured first favorable report on bill to establish postal savings banks; urged the establishment of the parcels post; led fight for appropriation to build the first modern submarine boat. Pres. State Farmers' Alliance, 1891. Nat. Farmers' Alliance and Industrial Union, 1894; trustee and mem. exec. com. of U. of N.C., 1891-99. Del. Rep. Nat. Convs., 1912, 16, 20, 24, 28, 32. Home: Elliott, N.C. Died June 3, 1938.

BUTLER, Matthew Calbraith, lawyer, U.S. senator; b. nr. Greenville, S.C., Mar. 8, 1836; s. Dr. Williams and Jane T. (Perry) B.; ed. S.C. coll., 1853-56, leaving in jr. yr.; m. Feb. 21, 1858, Maria Simkins Pickens. Admitted to S.C. bar, 1856; practiced at Edgefield Court House; elected to legislature, 1859; served in C.S.A., capt. to maj. gen., losing right leg at battle of Brandy Sta., June 9, 1863; elected to S.C. legislature, 1866; U.S. senator from S.C., 1877-89; Democrat; apptd. maj. gen. U.S. vols. for service in Spanish-Am. war, May 28, 1898; after war sent on com. with Admiral Sampson and General Wade, U.S.A., to assist Spanish gov. in evacuating Island of Cuba to be turned over to Cuban govt.; resigned commn. Pres. Mexican Mining and Exploration Co. Died 1909.

BUTLER, Nathaniel, educator; b. Eastport, Me., May 22, 1853; s. Nathaniel and Jennette (Loring) B.; A.B., Colby U., 1873, A.M., 1876 (D.D., 1895, LL.D., 1903); m. Florence Reeves Sheppard, 1881 (died June 21, 1902); 2d, Lillian M. Googins, of Chicago, Dec. 12, 1903. Asso. prin. Ferry Hall Female Coll., Lake Forest, Ill., 1873-76, Highland Hall Coll. for Women, Highland Park, Ill., 1876-79, prin. same, 1880-84; master Yale Sch. for Boys, Chicago, 1879-80; ordained Bapt. ministry, 1884; prof. rhetoric and English lit., old U. of Chicago, 1884-86; prof. Latin, 1886-89, prof. English lang. and lit., 1889-92, U. of Ill.; acting dir. Univ. Extension Div., 1893-94, Univ. Extension asso. prof. English lit. and dir. Univ. Extension Div., 1894-95, U. of Chicago; pres. Colby Coll., 1895-1901; prof. edn. and dir. co-operative work, 1901—, dean Coll. of Edn., 1905-09, and dean of Univ. Coll., 1916-23, asst. to pres., 1924—, U. of Chicago. Del. U. of Chicago to World's Congress on Univ. Extension, London, 1894. Author: Bellum Helveticum (Latin text-book, 5th edit.), 1900. Home: Chicago, Ill. Died Mar. 3, 1927.

BUTLER, Pierce, jurist; b. Dakota Co., Minn., Mar. 17, 1866; B.S., Carleton Coll., Northfield, Minn., 1887. Admitted to Minn. bar, 1888, practicing law in St. Paul until Jan. 1923; nominated by President Harding to be asso. justice Supreme Court of the United States, Nov. 23, 1922, confirmed by Senate, Dec. 21, 1922, and took seat Jan. 2, 1923. Died Nov. 16, 1939.

BUTLER, Richard, mfr.; b. Birmingham, O., Aug. 9, 1831; went to New York, 1845; employed in commercial house, 1846-52; partner William H. Cary & Co., 1851-79; then mfr. hard rubber goods; from 1883 pres. Butler Hard Rubber Co. of Butler, N.J.; one of founders and long trustee Metropolitan Museum of Art; mem. New York Chamber of Commerce, etc.; Chevalier Legion of Honor of France; 8 yrs. staff officer, N.Y. Nat. Guard, reaching rank of maj. Died 1902.

BUTLER, Robert Gordon, lawyer; b. New York, Nov. 22, 1860; grad. Harvard, 1883, Columbia Law Sch., 1885; m. 1888, Mary Leland Thorp. Mem. New York bar. Editor Questions and Answers, New York Sun, 1886-1903; editor of correspondents' columns of newspapers in various parts of the country, 1892-98. Edited "Sun in Fun" by Philip Henry Welsh, 1888 S3. Home: South Orange, N.J. Died 1906.

BUTLER, Robert Reyburn, congressman; b. Butler, Tenn., Sept. 24, 1881; s. William Roderick and Rebecca Caroline (Grayson) B.; prep. edn., Holly Springs Coll., Butler; L.L.B., Cumberland U., Lebanon, Tenn., 1903; married, 1911; 1 dau., Elizabeth Anabelle. Admitted to Tenn. bar, 1903, and began practice at Mountain City; moved to Condon, Ore., 1906, The Dalles, Ore., 1911. Formerly circuit judge, 11th Jud. Dist., Ore.; mem. Ore. State Senate, 1913, 15, 25, 27; Rep. presdl. elector, 1908, 16; mem. 70th (unexpired term) and 71st and 72d Congresses (1928-33) 2d Ore. Dist. Home: The Dalles, Ore. Died Jan. 7, 1933.

BUTLER, Scot, pres. Butler Coll. (dept. liberal arts, Univ. of Indianapolis); grad. Northwestern Christian Univ. (now Butler Coll.), 1868 (A.M., LL.D.); studied Halle and Berlin; prof. Latin language and literature, 1871—, Butler Coll. Home: Irvington, Ind. Died Jan. 15, 1931.

BUTLER, Smedley Darlington, officer U.S.M.C.; b. West Chester, Pa., July 30, 1881; s. Thomas Stalker and Maud (Darlington) B.; Haverford Sch., 1898; m. Ethel C. Peters, June 30, 1905; children—Ethel Peters (wife of Capt. John Wehle, U.S. Marine Corps), Smedley Darlington, Thomas Richard. Appointed to U.S.M.C., Apr. 8, 1898; promoted through grades to col., Mar. 9, 1919; brig. gen. (temp.), 1918-21; brig. gen., March 5, 1921; maj. gen., July

5, 1929; retired, Oct. 1, 1931. Leave of absence to act as dir. Dept. of Safety, Phila., 1924-25. Served as comdr. Camp Pontanezen, Brest, France, Oct. 15, 1918-July 31, 1919. Awarded 2 congressional medals of honor, for capture of Vera Cruz, Mexico, 1914, and for capture of Ft. Riviere, Haiti, 1917; D.S.M. (U.S.), 1919. Quaker. Candidate for Republican nomination, U.S. Senate, Pa., 1932. Lecturer. Home: Newton Square, Pa. Died June 21, 1940.

BUTLER, Tait, editor, veterinarian; b. Hastings Co., Ont., Can., July 24, 1862; s. James W. and Arvilla (Sine) B.; Collegiate Inst., St. Mary's, Ont.; V.S., Ont. Vet. Coll., Toronto, Can., 1885; m. Dell Bell, Aug. 8, 1893; children— Eugene, Seta. Prof. vet. sci., veterinarian Expt. Sta., Agrl. Coll. of Miss., 1891-96; editor, pub. Southern Farm Gazette, Starkville, Miss., 1895-98; prof. vet. sci. and bacteriology, Kan. State Agrl. Coll., and state veterinarian of Kan., 1900-01; prof. vet. sci., N.C. Coll. of Agr., 1901-06; state veterinarian of N.C., 1901-08; dir. Farmers' Insts. of N.C., 1904-08; editor Progressive Farmer, Memphis, Tenn., 1909—; v.p. Progressive Farmer Co. of Birmingham, Ala., Raleigh, N.C., Memphis, Tenn., and Dallas, Tex. Awarded medal by Am. Farm Bur. Fed., 1934, for distinguished service to organized agr. Author: Practical Arithmetic (with F. L. Stevens and Adeline T. Chapman Stevens), 1908. Home: Memphis, Tenn. Died Jan. 13, 1939.

BUTLER, Thomas S., congressman; b. Uwchland Tp., Chester Co., Pa., Nov. 4, 1855; ed. at various schs. and Normal Sch., West Chester; admitted to bar of Chester Co. Was judge 15th Jud. Dist., Pa., several yrs.; mem. 55th to 57th Congresses (1897-1903), 6th Pa. Dist., and 58th to 70th Congresses (1903-29), 7th Pa. Dist. Republican. Home: West Chester, Pa. Died May 26, 1928.

BUTLER, William, U.S. dist. judge eastern dist. Pa., Feb. 19, 1879-99; b. Chester Co., Pa., Dec. 22, 1822; attended school until 15 yrs. old; worked on W. Chester Village Record 4 yrs.; bought interest in and became asso. editor Norristown, Pa., Herald and Free Press; studied law; admitted to bar, Dec., 1845; returned to West Chester; dist. atty., 1856; pres. judge, 15th jud. dist., Pa., 1861-79. Home: West Chester, Pa. Died 1909.

BUTLER, William Allen, lawyer; b. Albany, N.Y., Feb. 20, 1825; s. Benjamin F. Butler (atty. gen. U.S. in cabinets of Jackson and Van Buren); grad. Univ. City of New York, 1843; studied law with his father; established practice in New York. Author: Nothing to Wear (a satirical poem); Martin Van Buren (biography); Mrs. Limber's Raffle; Oberammergau; etc. Home: Yonkers, N.Y. Died 1902.

BUTLER, William Allen, lawyer; b. N.Y. City, July 14, 1853; s. William Allen and Mary R. (Marshall) B.; bro. of Charles Henry and Howard Russell B.; A.B., Princeton, 1876; LL.B., Columbia, 1878; m. Louise T. Collins, Oct. 1, 1884. Admitted to bar, 1878, and then in practice at New York; then mem. Butler, Wyckoff & Reid; formerly mem. of Wallace, Butler & Brown, successors to Butler, Notman & Mynderse. Dir. Employers' Liability Assurance Corp., Hanover Fire Ins. Co., Franklin Trust Co., Brunswick Site Co.; trustee Seamen's Savings Bank. Treas. Church Extension Com. Presbytery of New York; mgr. Presbyn. Hosp., New York. Home: New York, N.Y. Died July 1, 1923.

BUTLER, William Frederick, publisher; b. Cincinnati, O.; s. DeWitt Clinton and Adeline Matilda (Saxton) B.; ed. high schs., Cincinnati and Milwaukee, Wis.; unmarried. In wholesale grocery and life ins. bus. until 1903; then head of William F. Butler, pubs. Ch. organist and choir dir. since age of 12. Compiler and pub.: The Art of Living Long (translated from the Italian of Luigi Cornaro), 1903; He Shall Speak Peace, 1915; Blessed Art Thou Among Women, 1916; Good Tidings of Great Joy, 1916. Home: Milwaukee, Wis. Died Mar. 28, 1926.

BUTLER, William Morgan, senator; b. New Bedford, Jan. 29, 1861; s. Rev. James D. and Eliza B. (Place) B.; LL.B., Boston U., 1884; m. Minnie F. Norton, July 15, 1886 (died 1905); m. 2d, Mary Lothrop Webster, Jan. 1, 1907. Practiced in New Bedford until 1895, then at Boston; pres. Hoosac Mills Corp., Butler, Prentice & Co., Inc., West End Thread Corp., Quissett Mill. Mem. Mass. Ho. of Rep., 1890, 91, Mass. State Senate, 1892-95 (pres. last 2 yrs.); mem. commn. to revise statues of Mass., 1896-1900. Mason. Mem. Rep. Nat. Com. (chmn., 1924; mgr. Coolidge campaign, 1924); chosen chmn. of Rep. Nat. Committee, 1924; apptd. U.S. senator from Mass., Nov. 13, 1924, for term ending Nov. 1926. Home: Boston, Mass. Died Mar. 29, 1937.

BUTLER, William Morris, neurologist; b. Maine, Broome Co., N.Y., Mar. 26, 1850; s. of William (M.D.) and Nancy (Smith) B.; A.B., Hamilton Coll., Clinton, N.Y., 1870, A.M., 1874; M.D., Coll. Phys. and Surg. (Columbia), 1873; post-grad. work in nervous diseases, Bellevue Med. Coll., L.I. Med. Coll., École de Médecine, Paris, and under Dr. Charcot, La Salpêtrière, Paris; Dr. Déjerine, La Salpêtrière, session 1914; m. Mary Bradford, Oct. 9, 1874; 1 son, Bradford; m. 2d, Anna Clarke; m. 3d, Ann L. Pell. Began practice, Montclair, N.J., 1873; specialist in nervous and mental diseases, Brooklyn, 1883—; 1st asst. physician, Middletown State Homœ. Hosp., 1874-83, later consulting alienist same; prof. mental diseases, N.Y. Homœ. Coll. and Flower Hosp., 1904-17; retired. Mem. N.Y. State Bd. Med. Examiners, 1892-1903. Hon. mem. Western N.Y. Homœ. Soc. Mason. Author: Mental Diseases and Their Homœopathic Treatment, 1910. Home: Brooklyn, N.Y. Died June 23, 1940.

BUTLER, Willis Howard, clergyman; b. Bangor, Me., Oct. 3, 1873; s. Henry Hersey and Inez (Lunt) B.; A.B., Princeton, 1895; B.D., Union Theol. Sem., 1898; D.D., Williams, 1926; m. Mary Helen Wales, Dec. 21, 1898; children—Barbara (Mrs. Chester Tappan), Virginia. Ordained Congl. ministry, 1898; pastor First Ch., Williamstown, Mass., 1898-1903, Edwards Ch., Northampton, 1903-12; asso. pastor Old South Ch., Boston, 1912-19; pastor Asylum Hill Ch., Hartford, Conn., 1919—. Home: Hartford, Conn. Died Oct. 22, 1930.

BUTNER, Henry W., army officer; b. Pinnacle, N.C., Apr. 6, 1875; s. Frank A. and Sarah E. B.; grad. U.S. Mil. Acad., 1898, Staff College, 1906, Army War Coll., 1920; unmarried. Commissioned 2d lt. arty., Apr. 26, 1898; promoted through grades to col., May 15, 1917; brig. gen., temporary, Oct. 1, 1918; brig. gen., permanent, Mar. 7, 1930; maj. gen., Feb. 1, 1936. Died Mar. 13, 1937.

BUTT, Archibald Willingham, army officer; b. Augusta, Ga., Sept. 26, 1866; s. Joshua Willingham and Pamela Robertson (Boggs) B.; grad. U. of the South; unmarried. Apptd. capt. a.q.m. vols., Jan. 2, 1900; hon. disch. from vol. service, June 30, 1901; apptd. capt. q.m. U.S.A., Feb. 2, 1901; maj., Dec. 1911. Served as q.m. in P.I., Mar. 1900-June 1903; depot q.m., Washington, July 1903-Sept. 1906, Havana, Sept. 1906-Apr. 1908; personal aide to President Roosevelt, Apr. 1908-Mar. 4, 1909; personal aide to President Taft, Mar. 4, 1909—. Home: Washington. Died Apr. 15, 1912.

BUTTE, George Charles; b. San Francisco, Calif., May 9, 1877; s. Charles Felix and Lena Clara (Stoes) B.; B.A., Austin (Tex.) Coll., 1895, LL.D., 1921; B.A., U. of Tex., 1903, M.A., 1904; studied U. of Berlin, 1911-12; J.U.D., Heidelberg U., 1913; studied École de Droit, Paris, 1913-14; m. Bertha Lattimore, Aug. 31, 1898. Admitted to bar Tex., 1903, Okla., 1904, Supreme Court of U.S., 1907; practiced at Muskogee, Okla., 1904-11; retired to travel and study in Europe; prof. law, U. of Tex., 1914—, dean, 1923-24. Rep. candidate for gov. of Tex., 1924; atty. gen. of Porto Rico, 1925-28; special asst. to atty. gen. of U.S., 1928-30; vice gov. Philippine Islands, Dec. 31, 1930-July 1, 1932; acting gov. gen. part of 1931 and 1932; acting gov. of Porto Rico, 3 times, 1926 and 27; associate justice Supreme Court of P.I., 1932-36. At request R.R. Commn. of Tex., 1920, granted year's leave to organize Oil and Gas Conservation Dept. and draft regulations; apptd., 1920, by Gov. Hobby, as mem. com. to draft Pub. Utilities law. Served as chief of fgn. intelligence sect. of Gen. Staff, U.S. Army, title of maj., Oct. 5, 1918-Mar. 10, 1919. Republican. Mason. Author: Great Britain and the Panama Canal, 1913; Amerikanische Prisengerichtsbarkeit, 1913. Home: Manila, P.I. Died Jan. 18, 1940.

BUTTENWIESER, Moses, college prof.; b. Beerfelden, Germany, Apr. 5, 1862; s. Simon and Bella Pauline (Saalheimer) B.; student U. of Würzburg, 1881-84; U. of Leipzig, 1889-95; Ph.D., U. of Heidelberg, 1896; m. Ellen Clune, Jan. 11, 1897; children—Paul, Hilda, Ellen, Laurence. Prof. Bibl. exegesis, Hebrew Union Coll., Cincinnati, 1897—. Author: Die Hebrüische Elias-Apokalypse, 1897; Outline of Neo-Hebraic Apocalyptic Literature; The Prophets of Israel, 1914; The Book of Job, 1920; The Psalms, 1937. Home: Cincinnati, O. Died Mar. 11, 1939.

BUTTERFIELD, Consul Willshire, author; b. Mexico, N.Y., July 28, 1824; ed. in various schools and academies and, 1845-46, in State Normal Sch., Albany, N.Y.; m. Mira Scroggs, May 8, 1854 (dec.); 2d, Letta M. Reicheneker, Mar. 30, 1858. Taught school and was, 1847-48, county supt. schools, Seneca Co., O.; went to Calif. overland, 1849; defeated for State supt. public instruction on independent ticket by small vote; sec. Ohio & Ind. R.R., 1853-54; practiced law, Bucyrus, O., 1855-75; removed to Madison, Wis., 1875, and to South Omaha, Neb., 1888. Author: History of the Discovery of the Northwest by John Nicolet in 1634; History of Brule's Discoveries and Explorations, 1610-1626; History of George Rogers Clark's Conquest of the Illinois and the Wabash Towns, 1778 and 1779. Home: South Omaha, Neb. Died 1899.

BUTTERFIELD, Daniel, soldier, banker; b. Oneida Co., N.Y., Oct. 31, 1831; grad. Union Coll., 1849, A.B., A.M., LL.D.; m. Julia Lorillard Safford, 1887. Studied law, but entered commercial life; was lt. col. 7th regt. and col. 12th N.Y. militia; took regt. to front, 1861; rose to maj. gen. vols., Nov. 1862; col. 5th inf., regular army, July 1, 1863; comd. 5th corps, Fredericksburg; wounded at Gaines' Mill and at Gettysburg; chief of staff, Army Potomac; chief of staff 11th and 12th corps, Chattanooga campaign; comd. div. 20th corps, Atlanta campaign; designed and established system of badges for army corps; bvtd. brig. gen. and maj. gen. U.S.A.; medal of honor from Congress for gallantry at Gaines' Mill; resigned from army, 1869; U.S. sub-treasurer, New York, 1869-70. Pres. Steam Boat and Ferry Co.; pres. Nat. Bank, Cold Spring-on-Hudson, where he resided. Died 1901.

BUTTERFIELD, Kenyon Leech, educator; b. Lapeer, Mich., June 11, 1868; s. Ira H. and Olive F. (Davison) B.; B.S., Mich. State Coll., 1891; M.A., U. of Mich., 1902; LL.D., Amherst Coll., 1910; R.I. State Coll. of Agr. and Mechanic Arts, 1921; m. Harriet E. Millard, Nov. 28, 1895; children—Howard Millard, Victor Lloyd. Pres. R.I. Coll. Agr. and Mechanic Arts, 1903-06; pres. and head div. rural social science, Mass. Agrl. Coll., 1906-24; pres. Mich. State Coll., 1924-28; counsellor on rural work, Internat. Missionary Council, 1928—. Home: Asbury Park, N.J. Died Nov. 25, 1935.

BUTTERFIELD, Ora Elmer, lawyer; b. Brattleboro, Vt., Nov. 9, 1870; s. Oscar Holland and Rosalia Edna (Elmer) B.; grad. Child's Business Coll., Springfield, Mass.; LL.B., U. of Mich., 1891; m. Amy Iola Dunklee, Sept. 14, 1893. Admitted to Mich. bar, 1891, and practiced in Ann Arbor until 1902; served as Circuit Ct. commr., city atty. and alderman; local atty. M.C. R.R., 1896-1902; gen. atty. same, Detroit, 1902-09; became asst. gen. solicitor N.Y.C. R.R., 1909; later devoting entire attention to state and federal regulation of rys. Republican. Died Dec. 22, 1916.

BUTTERWORTH, George Forrest, lawyer; b. New York, Dec. 10, 1853; s. Henry H. and Helen S. B.; A.B., Columbia, 1874, LL.B., 1876, A.M., 1877; m. Alice Crawford. Mem. Strong & Cadwalader, New York, many yrs.; firm now Cadwalader, Wickersham & Taft; dir. and mem. exec. com. Lawyers Title & Trust Co.; trustee Fulton Trust Co. Gov. New York Skin and Cancer Hosp.; dir. Norwalk Hosp.; mem. vestry Ch. of the Incarnation, N.Y. City. Home: New York, N.Y. Died Mar. 13, 1928.

BUTTERWORTH, Hezekiah, asst. editor Youth's Companion, 1870-94; b. Warren, R.I., Dec. 22, 1839; common school edn.; traveled extensively in U.S., Europe, Canada, So. America, Cuba, etc. Author: Zig-Zag Journeys (numerous vols.); Great Composers; The Knight of Liberty; In the Boyhood of Lincoln; The Patriot Schoolmaster; many other juvenile books; also Songs of History; Poems for Christmas, Easter and New Year; In Old New England; Popular History of So. America; A New England Miracle, 1903. Died 1905.

BUTTERWORTH, William, mfr.; b. Maineville, O., Dec. 18, 1864; s. Benjamin and Mary Ellen (Seiler) B.; ed. pub. schs., Cincinnati and Washington, D.C.; M.E., Lehigh U., 1889; hon. Dr. Business Adminstrn., Syracuse U.; LL.D., Augustana College, Rock Island, Ill.; m. Katherine Mary Deere, June 22, 1892. In employ U.S. Govt. at Paris Expn., 1889; pvt. sec. U.S. commr. of patents, 1891-92; admitted to Ill. bar, 1892; settled in Moline, Ill., 1892; began as asst. to buyer, 1892, then buyer, treas., in charge of operations, about 1897, pres. Deere & Co., after death of Charles H. Deere, 1907-30, chmn. bd., 1930—, also officer or dir. subsidiary cos.; chmn. bd. Moline Nat. Bank. Home: Moline, Ill. Died May 31, 1936.

BUTTON, Frank Christopher, educator; b. Oquawka, Ill., Nov. 19, 1863; s. Marion Francis and Phebe E. (Phelps) B.; ed. pub. schs., Ill.; grad. theol. dept. Transylvania U., 1887; hon. A.M., Bethany (W.Va.) Coll., 1908; m. Hattie Bishop, Dec. 24, 1889; children—Mrs. Hattie Harber, Mrs. Phebe Shankland, Ida Harrison, Frank W. Founder, and prin., 1887-1911, Morehead (Ky.) Normal Sch.; also founder Corbin (Ky.) Acad. (now part of city school system); state supervisor rural schs. of Ky., 1911-23; pres. State Normal Sch. for Eastern Ky., 1923-30, emeritus. Served as mayor, also pastor Christian (Disciples) Ch., Morehead. Republican. Mason. Author: (with others) Elementary State Course of Study of Kentucky, 1915; History of Education in Kentucky, 1914. Home: Morehead, Ky. Died Apr. 24, 1932.

BUTTRICK, Wallace, chmn. Gen. Edn. Bd.; b. Potsdam, N.Y., Oct. 23, 1853; s. Charles H. and Polly Dodge (Warren) B.; ed. Ogdensburg Acad., 1868-69, Potsdam Normal Sch., 1871-72; pvt. tuition, 1876-80; grad. Rochester Theol. Sem., 1883; D.D., U. of Rochester, 1898; L.H.D., Union, 1914; LL.D., Bowdoin, 1925; m. Isabella Allen, Dec. 1875. Ordained Bapt. ministry, 1883; pastor First Ch., New Haven, Conn., 1883-89, First Ch., St. Paul, Minn., 1889-92, Emmanuel Ch., Albany, N.Y., 1892-1902; sec. Gen. Edn. Bd., 1902-17, pres., 1917-23, chmn., 1923—; chmn. Internat. Edn. Bd., 1924—; mem. Rockefeller Foundation, Internat. Health Bd., China Med. Bd. Home: Scarsdale, N.Y. Died May 27, 1926.

BUTTS, Annice Esther Bradford (Miss), educator; b. Rome, N.Y., Sept. 22, 1844; d. David Knight and Emily (Wilcox) B.; ed. pvt. home schs., Rome Acad., Vernon Acad. and Stanwix Sem. (grad. 1867); A.M., Washington Univ., 1898. Prin. Joliet W. Div. High Sch., 1867-71, teacher Dearborn Sem., Chicago, 1871-77; prin. 54th St. Sch., 1881-86; established 1886 and then conducted Kenwood Inst., a pvt. sch., from 1893 an affiliated acad. of Univ. of Chicago. Home: Chicago, Ill. Died 1904.

BUTTZ, Henry Anson, theologian; b. Middle Smithfield, Pa., Apr. 18, 1835; A.B., Princeton, 1858, A.M., 1861; student Theol. Sem. Reformed Ch., N.J.; A.M., Wesleyan, 1866; (D.D., Princeton, 1875, Wesleyan, 1903; LL.D., Dickinson, 1885); m. Emily Hoagland, Apr. 11, 1860. Entered M.E. ministry, 1858; pastor Millstone, N.J., 1858, Irvington, N.J., 1859, Woodbridge, N.J., 1860-61, Mariners' Harbor, S.I., N.Y., 1862-63, Paterson, N.J., 1864-66, Morristown, N.J., 1867-69; instr., 1867, adj. prof. Greek and Hebrew, 1868-70, prof. N.T. Greek and exegesis, 1871—, pres., 1880-1912, pres. emeritus, Drew Theol. Sem. Mem. Gen. Conf., 1884-1912, Ecumenical Conf., Toronto, 1912, M.E. Centennial Conf., 1884. Author: Epistle to the Romans in Greek, with textual and grammatical references. Home: Madison, N.J. Died Oct. 6, 1920.

BUXTON, (William) Albert, theologian, judge; b. Londonderry, Vt., June 16, 1861; s. Stephen A. and Laura (Haynes) B.; brother of L(auren) Haynes B.; A.B., Brown U., 1882, A.M., 1885; student Harvard Div. Sch., 1883-86, A.M., 1886, Univs. of Bonn and Heidelberg (Germany), 1887-88; also grad. 3 yrs.' course each in law and medicine; Ph.D., Bethany Coll., 1897; LL.D., Milligan Coll., 1905; Sc.D., Southern Christian Coll., 1921; m. Inez M. Parsons, May 27, 1883; 1 dau., Laural Albertine (Mrs. Stephen Bertram Hobbs); m. 2d, Maude Damuth, Oct. 12, 1897 (died 1905); children—Mrs. Lucile Marsh, Cary Morgan, Teresa Louise. Pastor Christian churches, Hutchinson, Kan., Fairbury, Neb., Norfolk, Va., Salt Lake City, Utah, Pueblo, Colo.; pres. N.W. Christian Coll., 1895-97; pres. and chancellor Tex. Christian U., 1898-1901; pres. Dexter (Mo.) Christian Coll., 1902-04; dean Christian U., Canton, Mo., 1904-08. Municipal judge, Centralia, Wash., 1918-21. Dem. candidate for state supt. edn., S.D., 1890. Mason. Author: Spanish Grammar; Elements of Psychology; and vol. of poetry. Lived at Hagerstown, Ind. Died Aug. 25, 1930.

BUXTON, L(auren) Haynes, surgeon; b. Londonderry, Vt., July 15, 1859; s. Stephen A. and Laura (Haynes) B.; brother of (William) Albert B.; ed. at Leland and Gray Sem., Townshend, Vt.; M.D., U. of Vt., 1884; U. of Vienna, Austria, 1907; (LL.D., Central U. of Ia., 1907); m. Ella G. Hooey, Dec. 25, 1882. Mem. city council and bd. of edn., Guthrie, Okla.; later, head dept. of oto-laryngology, Med. Dept. U. of Okla. State supt. of public health, 1898-1902; sec. med. exam. board and pres. Insane Commn. of Okla., 1897-1901. Home: Oklahoma City, Okla. Died Oct. 11, 1924.

BYARS, William Vincent, writer, editor; b. Covington, Tenn., June 21, 1857; s. James and Mary J. H. (Vincent) B.; ed. by his father (prin. Tipton Male High Sch., Covington), gaining classical and scientific edn.; m. Loula Clement, d. Rev. Charles Francis Collins, June 15, 1880. Asso. editor Weekly Record, Covington, Tenn., 1877-78; on city staff St. Louis Daily Times, 1879, St. Louis Globe-Democrat, 1880; city and editorial staff, Missouri Republican and its successor, St. Louis Republic, 1881-93 (except 1 yr. on editorial staff St. Louis Chronicle); editorial staff Morning World and contbr. to Evening World, New York, 1893-97; editorial and local contbr. to Harper's Weekly, 1897-98. Editor: The Handbook of Oratory; The Science of Expression; managing editor The World's Best Essays, The World's Best Orations, The Woman's Athenæum, 10 vols. each. Collector and editor of The Gratz Papers (1750-1850), 1914-15. Washington corr. War Congress, 1917-18. Home: Kirkwood, Mo. Died June 21, 1938.

BYE, Frank Paxson, educator; b. Buckingham, Pa., Feb. 23, 1868; s. John Hart and Helen M. (Paxson) B.; B.E., Pa. State Normal Sch., West Chester, 1893, M.E., 1895; spl. student New York U.; B.S., U. of Pa., 1907; student Law Sch. and economics, Grad. Sch., same; student econs., U. of Berlin, 1911-13; m. Christine Antonia Faas, 1893. Teacher in pub. schs., Del., 1888-91; prin. high schs., Kennett Sq., Pa., 1893-96; supt. pub. schs., Chester Co., Pa., 1896-99; dir. Darlington Sem., 1899—, dir. and psychologist, Vocational Coll.; lecturer in industry, U. of Pa., 1914—. Republican. Home: Lansdowne, Pa. Died Jan. 12, 1931.

BYERLY, William Elwood, mathematician; b. Phila., Dec. 13, 1849; s. Elwood B.; A.B., Harvard, 1871, Ph.D., 1873, m. Alice Worcester Parsons, May 28, 1885; children—Robert Wayne, Francis Parkman; m. 2d, Anne Carter Wickham Renshaw, July 23, 1921. Asst. prof. mathematics, Cornell, 1873-76; asso. prof. mathematics, 1876-81, prof., 1881-1913, prof. emeritus, Harvard. Fellow Am. Acad. Arts and Sciences, etc. Author: Elements of Differential Calculus, 1879; Elements of Integral Calculus, 1881; An Elementary Treatise on Fourier's Series and Spherical, Cylindrical and Ellipsoidal Harmonics, 1893; Problems in Differential Calculus, 1895; Generalized Coördinates, 1916; Introduction to the Calculus of Variations, 1917. Died 1935.

BYERS, Maxwell Cunningham, ry. pres.; b. Pittsburgh, Pa., Feb. 2, 1878. Asst. engr. on various divs., Pa. Lines west of Pittsburgh, 1897-1902; asst. engr. maintenance of way, B.&O. Ry., 1902-03; div. engr. same rd., 1903-04; asst. engr. maintenance of way, asst. to gen. mgr. and engr. maintenance of way, St.L.&S.F. R.R., 1904-09; chief engr. and chief engr. operation, same rd., 1909-13; asst. to pres. G.N. Ry., 1913-14; asst. to pres. Western Md. Ry., 1914-18; federal gen. mgr. Western Md. Ry., Cumberland Valley and Cumberland & Pa. rys., 1918-20; pres. Western Md. R.R., Baltimore, Mar. 1920—. Died Sept. 23, 1930.

BYERS, Samuel Hawkins Marshall, soldier, author; b. Pulaski, Pa., July 23, 1838; s. James M. and Parmela (Marshall) B.; moved with parents to Oskaloosa, Ia., 1852; studied law; hon. degrees State U. of Ia., Penn Coll. and Grinnell Coll.; m. Margaret Bilmour, 1869; children—Lawrence and Helen (both dec.). Enlisted as pvt. 5th Ia. Inf., 1861; served 4 years; wounded at Champion Hills; promoted adj.; taken prisoner at Chattanooga and spent 14 mos. in Libby and other prisons; escaped at Columbia, S.C., and served on Sherman's staff; selected to carry first news of Carolina victories to Gen. U.S. Grant and President Lincoln; brevetted maj.; consul at Zürich and consul gen. to Italy and later to Switzerland; recalled by President Cleveland after 20 yrs. service, returning to Ia., 1903; later settled at Los Angeles, Calif. Author: Complete Poems, 1914; The Bells of Capistrano, 1917; The Pony Express, and other Poems, 1925; In Arcady (verse), 1929, etc. While in mil. prison wrote famous song, "Sherman's March to the Sea." Died May 24, 1933.

BYERS, William Newton, st. ry. dir. and v.p., Feb. 1885—; b. Madison Co., O., Feb. 22, 1831; s. Moses W. and Mary A. B.; ed. country schools, Madison Co., O., winters, and Acad. West Jefferson, O., 1848-49; m. Elizabeth M. Sumner, g. d. of Gov. Lucas, late of Ohio, later Gov. of Ia., Nov. 16, 1854. Govt. surveyor, 1851, as deputy, first in Ia., later in Ore., Wash., Neb. and finally in Colo.; brought 1st newspaper office to Colo. and founded Rocky Mountain News, April 23, 1859; edited it for over 19 yrs.; in first legislature of Neb., and first constl. conv. of Colo. Republican. Home: Denver, Colo. Died 1903.

BYFIELD, Joseph (surname changed from Beifield to Byfield, July 1917), hotel man; b. Hungary, Aug. 22, 1853; came to U.S., 1867; ed. common schs.; m. Fannie Grossman, May 25, 1876; children—Albert Henry, Eugene Victor, Ernest Lessing. In employ of Field, Leiter & Co., mchts., 1869-78; in cloak business, 1878-1902; pres. Hotel Sherman Co., 1902—; pres. Fulton Market Cold Storage Co. Originator of plan, organizer and nat. chmn. of assn. of hotel men who furnished the U.S. Army with 240 cooks for each of the 16 cantonments, 1917, making 3,840 cooks in all. These cooks trained about 40,000 men to cook for the army; letters of commendation received from Sec. of War Newton Baker and Maj. Gen. Henry G. Sharpe. Mem. Art Inst. Chicago (life), Field Mus. Republican. Jewish religion. Home: Chicago, Ill. Died Sept. 17, 1926.

BYFORD, Henry Turman, gynecologist; b. Evansville, Ind., Nov. 12, 1853; s. Dr. William H. and Anne (Holland) B.; grad. Williston Sem., 1870; M.D., Chicago Med. Coll. (Northwestern U.), 1873; m. Lucy Larned, Nov. 8, 1882. Engaged in practice in Chicago; prof. gynecology, Coll. of Medicine of U. of Illinois, Chicago, 1892-1913, emeritus; cons. gynecologist, St. Luke's and Chicago Lying-In hosps. Fellow American Coll. Surgeons. Author: Manual of Gynecology; To Panama and Back, 1908; Diseases of Women (with late Dr. William Heath Byford). Joint author: American Text Book of Gynecology; Keating and Coe's Clinical Gynecology; Kelly and Noble's Operative Gynecology. Home: Chicago, Ill. Died June 5, 1938.

BYINGTON, Ezra Hoyt, clergyman-author; b. Hinesburgh, Vt., Sept. 3, 1828; grad. Univ. of Vt., 1852 (A.M., 1855; D.D., 1890); grad. Andover Theol. Sem., 1857. Congl. pastor at Windsor, Vt., 1859-69; Brunswick, Me., 1870-78; Monson, Mass., 1880-87. Librarian N.E. Historic Genealogical Soc., 1892-93; m. Ann Eliza Hoyt, 1858; m. 2d, Louisa J. Workman, 1887. Author: History of Congregational Church in Hinesburgh, Vt., Windsor, Vt., and New Haven, Vt. (3 vols.); The Puritan in England and New England. Home: Newton, Mass. Died 1901.

BYLES, Axtell J., oil inst. exec.; b. Titusville, Pa., Oct. 21, 1880; s. Julius and Mary (Axtell) B.; student Lawrenceville (N.J.) Sch., 1898-99; B.S., Princeton, 1903; student Pittsburgh Law Sch. 2 yrs.; m. Florence Payne, Sept. 6, 1905; children—Julius, Axtell. Admitted to bar, 1905; formerly pres. Tidewater Asso. Oil Co., etc.; became pres. Am. Petroleum Inst., New York. Republican. Presbyn. Home: Ardsley-on-Hudson, N.Y. Died Sept. 28, 1941.

BYLLESBY, Henry Marison, elec. engr.; b. Pittsburgh, Pa., Feb. 16, 1859; s. Rev. DeWitt Clinton and Sarah (Mathews) B.; ed. Lehigh U., Pa.; m. Margaret Stearns Baldwin, June 15, 1882. Was associated with Thomas A. Edison in the early days of electric lighting in N.J., and has been identified with many movements and advances in elec. enterprises. Pres. H. M. Byllesby & Co., engrs., Chicago; also officer and dir. pub. service cos. in Ala., Ark., Okla., Ia., Colo., etc. Commd. lt. col. U.S.A., and assigned to hdqrs. of Chief Signal Officer, Washington. Purchasing agt. in Great Britain and Scandinavian countries for A.E.F., hdqrs. London, June-Dec. 1918, when hon. disch. Awarded D.S.O. (British). Died May 1, 1924.

BYNE, Arthur, architect, author, painter; b. Phila., Pa., Sept. 25, 1883; s. William A. and Ann (Klauder) B.; grad. Sch. of Architecture, U. of Pa., 1905; student Am. Acad. in Rome, 1906-07; m. Mildred Stapley, 1910. Designer with Howells & Stokes, N.Y. City, 1908-14; curator of Mus. of Hispanic Soc. America, 1914-18; lived in Spain, 1916—. Exhibited water colors, New York and Madrid. Silver medal, San Francisco Expn., 1915; Gran Cruz del Merito Militar (Spain). Mem. Architectural League (New York); hon. mem. A.I.A. Author: (with wife) Spanish Ironwork, 1914; Rejeria of the Spanish Renaissance, 1915; Spanish Architecture of the Sixteenth Century, 1916; Decorated Wooden Ceilings in Spain, 1917; Spanish Interiors and Furniture, 1920, 28; Provincial Houses in Spain, 1924; Spanish Gardens and Patios, 1924; Majorcan Houses and Gardens, 1928. Home: Madrid, Spain. Died July 1935.

BYNUM, William Dallas, congressman; b. Newberry, Ind., June 26, 1846; s. Daniel A. B.; B.S., Ind. U., 1869. Admitted to bar, 1869; practiced at Washington, Ind., 1869-81, Indianapolis, 1881—. City atty., Washington, 1871-75, mayor, 1875-79; presdl. elector, 1876; mem. Ind. Ho. of Rep., 1882-83 (speaker 1883); mem. 49th to 53d Congresses (1885-95); mem. commn. to revise laws of U.S., 1900-06. Active in organization of Nat. (Gold-Standard) Dem. party, 1896 (chmn. nat. com., 1896-98). Home: Indianapolis, Ind. Died Oct. 21, 1927.

BYNUM, William Preston, lawyer; b. McDowell Co., N.C., Aug. 1, 1861; s. Benjamin F. and Charity Henrietta (Morris) B.; A.M., Trinity Coll., N.C., 1883; LL.D., U. of N.C., 1922; m. Mary F. Walker, Mar. 9, 1892. Admitted to N.C. bar, 1884; solicitor for Jud. Dist. No. 5, 1895-98; judge Superior Court, 1898-99; spl. U.S. atty., 1899-1903; mem. com. to assist in revision of rules of practice for Courts of Equity of U.S., 1911-12; mem. commn. to revise system of court procedure and formulate uniform system of interior courts in N.C., 1915-16; mem. Nat. Conf. Commrs. on Uniform State Laws. Home: Greensboro, N.C. Died Jan. 7, 1926.

BYRAM, George Logan, army officer; b. Noxubee Co., Miss., Jan. 19, 1862; s. George and Sallie I. (Moseley) B.; student U. of Ala., 1878-81; grad. U.S. Mil. Acad., 1885; m. Jane Lockhart Skiles, Jan. 23, 1889; 1 dau., Cornelia (wife of John E. Lewis, U.S.A.). Commd. 2d lt. 1st Cav., June 14, 1885; promoted through grades to col., and retired July 1916. Participated in Sioux campaign, 1890-91; in operations against Apache Kid, 1893; duty with Colo. N.G., 1893-97; wounded in battle at Las Guasimas, Cuba, June 24, 1898; recommended for Medal of Honor by Maj. James M. Bell, 1st Cav.; acting judge advocate Dept. of the Colo., 1898-99; in Philippines, 1899-1903; acting insp. gen., Jan.-July 1901; q.m. 6th Cav., 1901-05; participated in expedition against renegade Utes, from Utah, in S.D. and Mont., 1906; again in Philippines, 1907-10; comd. expdn. which annihilated Jikiri's band of Moro pirates, July 4, 1909. On Mexican border different periods, 1914-15; recalled to active duty Sept. 1, 1917, as comdt. War Prison Barracks No. 3, Ft. Douglas, Utah. Awarded D.S.C. "for extraordinary heroism in action," at Las Guasimas, Cuba. Mem. Mil. Order of Caraboa. Democrat. Presbyn. Home: Hollywood, Calif. Died June 16, 1929.

BYRD, Adam Monroe, congressman; b. Sumter Co., Ala., July 6, 1859; removed to Miss. when 8 yrs. old; ed. common schs. and Cooper Inst., Daleville, Miss.; LL.B., Columbian U., Lebanon, Tenn., 1884. Supt. edn., Neshoba Co., Miss., 1887-89; mem. Miss. Senate, 1889, 1890, 1892, Ho. of Rep., 1895; apptd. pros. atty., 10th Jud. Dist., Miss., 1896; judge 6th Chancery Dist., Miss., 1897; reapptd., 1901; mem. 58th to 61st Congresses (1903-11), 5th Miss. Dist. Democrat. Home: Philadelphia, Miss. Died June 21, 1912.

BYRD, Richard Evelyn, lawyer; b. Austin, Tex., Aug. 13, 1860; s. William and Jennie Meriweather (Rivers) B.; U. of Va., 1879-81; U. of Md., 1882-83; m. Elinor Bolling Flood, Sept. 15, 1886. Admitted to Va. bar, 1884; commonwealth atty., Frederick Co., Va., 1884-1904; mem. Va. Ho. of Del., 1906-14 (speaker 1908-14). Del.-at-large, Dem. Nat. Conv., 1912; mem. Ednl. Commn., Virginia, 1908-12; mem. State Tax Commn., 1910-12. U.S. dist. atty.,

Western Dist. of Va., Apr. 14, 1914-June 1, 1920 (resigned); special asst. to atty. gen. U.S., June 1920-Mar. 1921 (resigned). Mem. State Commn. Efficiency and Economy, 1916-18; chmn. State Industrial Council of Safety, 1917. Died Oct. 23, 1925.

BYRNE, Austin Thomas, civil engr.; b. Belfast, Me., Sept. 8, 1859; s. Michael J. and Ellen (Cashin) B.; m. Rebina Jardin, Apr. 16, 1890; children—Austin St. Clair, Louise Evelyn (dec.), Oliver Thomas, Terence Julius. Engaged as civ. engr., 1876—. Author: Highway Construction, 1892; Inspection of Materials and Workmanship Employed in Construction, 1898. Home: Ardonia, N.Y. Died May 24, 1934.

BYRNE, Bernard Albert, soldier; b. Newport Barracks, Ky., Oct. 19, 1853; s. Maj. Bernard Myles and Louisa (Albert) B.; ed. Columbian (now George Washington) U.; m. Bertha, d. Albert Barnitz, Feb. 11, 1892. Apptd. from D.C., 2d lt. 6th Inf., Oct. 15, 1875; promoted through grades to lt. col. 28th Inf., June 15, 1906; retired at own request, over 30 yrs.' service, July 13, 1906. Awarded Congressional Medal of Honor, July 1, 1902, "for gallantry at Bobong Negros, P.I., July 19, 1899." Home: Los Altos, Calif. Died 1910.

BYRNE, Charles Alfred, dramatist, author; b. London, Eng., 1848; ed. Brussels and Paris (Coll. Louis le Grand). Founded Dramatic News, 1875; Truth, 1879; Journalist, 1884; Dramatic Times, 1881; Evening Standard, 1883. Wrote, in conjunction with Arthur Wallack, a play called Coward Conscience; also the following comic operas produced at various periods: Pearl of Pekin, Castles in the Air, Venus, Princess Nicotine, Isle of Champagne, The Normandy Wedding, Isle of Gold, Bangdoolah of Swat. Died 1909.

BYRNE, Charles Christopher, brig. gen.; b. Pikesville, Baltimore Co., Md., May 7, 1837; s. Charles (M.D.) and Emeline (Cole) B.; ed. Mt. St. Mary's Coll. Emmitsburg, Md.; M.D., U. of Md., 1895; m. Henrietta P. Colt, Oct. 4, 1876. Entered U.S.A. as asst. surgeon, June 23, 1860; attained rank of asst. surgeon-gen.; retired by operation of law, May 7, 1901, with rank of col.; advanced to rank of brig. gen.; retired by act of Apr. 23, 1904. Died Nov. 8, 1921.

"BYRNE, Donn" (Brian Oswald Donn-Byrne), author; b. N.Y. City, Nov. 20, 1889; s. Tomas Fearghail and Jane D'Arcy (McParlane) Donn-Byrne; ed. University Coll., Dublin, Ireland (hon. B.A., 1909); studied English lit., Paris and Leipzig; m. Dorothy Mary Elizabeth Cadogan, of Waterford and Dublin, Ireland, Dec. 2, 1911. Author: Stories Without Women, 1915; The Strangers' Banquet, 1919; The Foolish Matrons, 1920; Messer Marco Polo, 1921; The Wind Bloweth, 1922; Changeling, 1923; Blind Raftery, 1924; O'Malley of Shanganagh, 1925; Hangman's House, 1926; Brother Saul, 1927. Home: Kilbrittain, County Cork, Ireland. Died June 19, 1928.

BYRNE, Frank M., governor; b. Volney, Allamakee Co., Ia., Oct. 23, 1858; pub. sch. edn.; m. Emma Beaver; children—Carroll, Beaver, Francis John, Malcolm, Joseph Donald, Emmons. Moved to Sioux Falls, Dak. Ty., 1879, took up homestead in McCook Co., 1880; located in Faulk Co., S.D., 1888; extensive farmer and real estate dealer. Mem. first State Senate, 1890, also sessions of 1907, 09; lt. gov. of S.D., 1909-13, gov., 1913-17; commr. State Dept. Agr., 1922—. Republican. Conglist. Mason. Home: Faulkton, S.D. Died Dec. 25, 1927.

BYRNE, John, ry. official; b. Md., 184—; s. John and Elenor B.; ed. by pvt. tutors, in country sch. and local acad. Began ry. service as rodman in engr. corps, and later became identified with ry. operations of late Collis P. Huntington; was gen. agt. Southwest System; pres. Scioto Valley & N.E. Ry. Co., Central N.Y. & Western R.R. Co., etc.; was mem. Flood Commn. for relief of flood sufferers in Ohio, 1884. Now chmn. Pittsburgh, Shawmut & Northern R.R. Co., Shawmut Mining Co. Catholic. Organized 1896, Democratic Honest Money League of America, as pres. of which took active part in promoting election of McKinley in 1896 and 1900, and of Roosevelt in 1904. Home: New York. Died 1905.

BYRNE, Thomas Sebastian, bishop; b. Hamilton, O., July 29, 1841; s. Eugene and Mary Anne (Reynolds) B.; grad. St. Mary's of the West, 1865; at Am. Coll., Rome, 3 yrs.; (D.D., Pope Leo XIII, 1887). Ordained R.C. priest, 1869; devoted himself to literature and teaching in Mt. St. Mary's Sem.; later had charge of the Cathedral at Cincinnati; pres. Mt. St. Mary's of the West, 1887-94; apptd. bishop of Nashville, May 10, 1894, consecrated July 25 following. Wrote, Man from a Catholic Point of View (read at Parliament of Religions, 1903), and other pamphlets, chiefly religious. Died Sept. 4, 1924.

BYRNE, William, Roman Catholic clergyman; b. in Ireland, 1836; was vicar-gen. of Archbishop Williams, of Boston; now pastor St. Cecilia Ch., Boston. Author: Catholic Doctrine; Devout Manual. Died Jan. 9, 1912.

BYRNES, Charles Metcalfe, M.D., neurologist; b. Claiborne Co., Miss., Nov. 4, 1881; s. Charles Ralston and Helen (Metcalfe) B.; student La. State U.; B.S., U. of N.C., 1902; M.D., Johns Hopkins, 1906; m. Louise Alexander McCosh, Sept. 1, 1920; 1 dau., Louise Metcalfe. Demonstrator in anatomy, Johns Hopkins, 1902-03; adj. prof. anatomy, U. of Va., 1906-09; instr. in clin. neurology, Johns Hopkins, 1909, asso., 1918—; lecturer in neuropathology, Univ. of N.C., 1935; neurologist Church Home and Infirmary, Baltimore. Contbr. to Forchheimer's Therapeusis of Internal Disease, 1913, and Tice's Practice of Medicine, 1920. Home: Baltimore, Md. Died Nov. 29, 1936.

BYRNS, Joseph W., congressman; b. Cedar Hill, Tenn., July 20, 1869; s. James H. and Mary E. (Jackson) B.; student Vanderbilt U. (acad. dept.), 2 yrs.; LL.B., Vanderbilt U., 1890; m. Julia Woodard, Aug. 23, 1898; 1 son, Joseph W. Practiced at Nashville, 1891—; mem. Tenn. House of Rep., 3 terms, 1895-1900 (speaker, 1899), Senate, 1901; Dem. presdl. elector, 1904; mem. 61st to 72d Congresses (1909-33), 6th Tenn. Dist., and 73d and 74th Congresses (1933-37), 5th Tenn. Dist.; majority leader 73d Congress, and speaker of House, 74th Congress. Methodist. Mason. Home: Nashville, Tenn. Died June 4, 1936.

BYRON, William Devereux, congressman; b. Danville, Va., May 15, 1895; s. Col. Joseph C. and Jane (Wilson) B.; student Phillips Exeter Acad. and Pratt Inst.; m. Katherine Edgar; 5 children. Mem. 76th Congress (1939-41), 6th Md. Dist. Home: Williamsport, Md. Died Feb. 27, 1941.

C

CABANA, Oliver, Jr., banker, mfr.; b. Island Pond, Vt., Feb. 9, 1865; s. Oliver and Edmire (Rainville) C.; ed. pub. schs. and business coll.; m. Isabelle Josephine Pilliard, June 2, 1886; children—Isabel Josephine, Ethel Adelaide, Oliver Frederick. Organizer, 1885, mgr. and later pres. Buffalo Specialty Co., name changed to Liquid Veneer Corp., of which was pres.; pres. Buffalo Specialty Co., of Elma, N.Y., G. A. Hosmer Oil Co., Samuel C. Rogers & Co., Liberty Safe Deposit Co., Wright-Hargreaves Mines, Ltd., Pure Penn Petroleum Co.; pres. and treas. Oliver Cabana, Jr., Inc.; chmn. bd. Liberty Bank of Buffalo; mng. dir. Liquid Veneer Co., Ltd., London, Eng.; controlling dir. Le Suer Oil Corp., Peerless Belting Co.; propr. Pine Grove Farms. Pres. Sun and Diet Health Foundation; mem. N.Y. State Bd. of Housing, N.Y. State Waterways Assn., Nat. Rivers and Harbors Congress, Am. Forestry Assn.; dir. U. of Buffalo; v.p. Central Park Clinic. Mem. Am. Red Cross, Y.M.C.A. Democrat. Home: Buffalo, N.Y. Died Jan. 21, 1938.

CABANISS, Edward Harman, lawyer; b. at Forsyth, Monroe Co., Ga., Oct. 1, 1857; s. George Augustus and Juliet (McKay) C.; A.B., Mercer U., Macon, Ga., 1875, M.A.; student U. of Va. Law Sch., 1875; m. Martha F. Jelks, Dec. 13, 1882; children—Robert W., Edward H., Jelks H., Gerry, William J. Began practice, Union Springs, 1882; removed to Birmingham, 1887; sr. mem. Cabaniss & Johnston. Mem. Ala. Senate, from 32d Dist., 1886. Democrat. Baptist. Home: Birmingham, Ala. Died Mar. 1936.

CABANISS, Henry Harrison, newspaper publisher; b. Forsyth, Ga., June 21, 1848; s. Judge Elbridge Gerry and Sarah (Chipman) C.; A.B., U. of Ga., 1869; m. Sarah E. Royston. Publisher of the Atlanta Journal, 1887-1903, Augusta Chronicle, 1903-05. Asst. sec. Ga. Senate 18 yrs. Formerly v.p. the Associated Press of America; formerly dir. Am. Newspaper Assn. and pres. Southern Newspaper Pub. Assn. Home: Atlanta, Ga. Died Sept. 12, 1934.

CABEEN, Charles William, univ. prof.; b. Kalamazoo, Mich., Jan. 30, 1859; s. David and Celeste A. (Childs) C.; B.S., U. of Wis., 1882, M.L., 1883; A.M., Harvard, 1892; sr. fellow in German, U. of Chicago, 1892-93; studied U. of Grenoble, France, 1903-04, Docteur de l'Université, 1904; m. Sarah Amelia Clark, July 15, 1885. Prin. high schs., at Baraboo, DePere, and Neenah, Wis., 1882-91; prof. German, Oberlin Coll., 1893-95; prof. French and later of Romance langs., Syracuse U., 1895—. Republican. Congregationalist. Editor: Les Oberlé, by René Bazin, 1905; Voltaire's Zaire, 1910. Died June 16, 1925.

CABELL, Benjamin Francis, pres. Potter Coll., 1889—; b. Campbellsville, Ky., June 6, 1850; s. Thomas Jefferson C.; ed. Bedford, Ind., 1866-1870; grad. Wesleyan Univ., Delaware, O.; m. Ellen Douglas Patterson, June 15, 1876. Prof. in Warren Coll. (now Ogden Coll.), Bowling Green, Ky., 1875; elected pres. Cedar Bluff Coll., Warren Co., Ky., 1877. Methodist. Died 1909.

CABELL, De Rosey Carroll, army officer; b. in Ark., July 7, 1861; grad. U.S. Mil. Acad., 1884, Army War Coll., 1913. Commd. 2d lt. 8th Cav., June 15, 1884; advanced through grades to brig. gen. N.A., Dec. 17, 1917; maj. gen., Oct. 1, 1918; remanded to regular rank of col. after the war. Participated in Geronimo Indian campaign, 1885-86; Sioux Indian campaign, 1890-91; China Relief Expdn., 1900; Philippines campaigns, 1900-02; chief of staff Punitive Expdn. into Mexico, 1915-16; D.S.M., 1919. Then retired. Home: San Diego, Calif. Died Mar. 15, 1924.

CABELL, George Craghead, lawyer; b. Danville, Va., Jan. 25, 1837; ed. Danville Acad.; grad. law dept., Univ. of Va., 1857; commonwealth atty., 1858-61; in C.S.A., 1861-65, private to col., 18th Va. inf. —3 times wounded. Mem. Congress, 1875-87; then city atty. Democrat. Home: Danville, Va. Died 1906.

CABELL, James Alston, lawyer; b. Richmond, Va.; s. Gen. Henry Coalter (C.S.A.) and Jane (Alston) C.; g.s. William H. C., gov. Va., 1805-08, judge of the General Ct., 1808-11, judge Supreme Ct. of Appeals, 1811-51, and pres. Supreme Ct. of Appeals, 1842-51; grad. Richmond Coll. and U. of Va.; m. Ethel Hoyt Scott, June 12, 1895; children—Ethel Alston (Mrs. F. Lewis Barroll), Kathrine Hamilton (Mrs. Chas. W. Morris), James Alston Cabell (dec.), Dorothy Temple (Mrs. Herman Allyn), Margery Wade (dec.). Prof. chemistry, Central U. of Ky., 1876-78; admitted to bar, 1879; elected to Richmond City Council, 1884; mem. of Va. legislature, 1893-97 (Dem. floor leader, 1896-97); chmn. Va. Commn. of Uniformity of Legislation in U.S., 1893-1902; took a prominent part in framing Negotiable Instruments Act; chmn. com. on uniform insurance legislation; mem. State Bd. Charities and Corrections, 1908-12. Revived Va. Soc. of the Cincinnati and was 1st pres. of temporary organization, 1889-96; pres. Va. Soc. S.R., 1895-1901. Mason. Legal Bd. Selective Service Draft; speaker for war time activities, etc. Episcopalian; sr. warden Rivanna Parish. Has written numerous scientific, hist. and biog. papers. Home: "Point of Fork," Columbia, Va. Died July 22, 1930.

CABELL, William Lewis, lawyer; b. Danville, Va., Jan. 1, 1827; grad. U.S. Mil. Acad., 1850; lt. 7th U.S. Inf., 1850-58; capt. q.m.'s dept., 1858; served on Gen. Harney's staff on Utah expdn., 1858; ordered to rebuild old Ft. Kearney on the Platte River, Neb., Jan. 1859; stationed at Ft. Arbuckle, in Indian Ty., 1860; 1860-61 engaged in building Fort Cobb, in Indian country occupied by the Comanches, Kiowas, and other wild tribes; resigned Mar. 1861; in C.S.A., Apr. 1861-Oct. 1864, becoming brig. gen.; captured on a raid into Kansas; prisoner of war until Apr. 28, 1865. After war practiced law at Ft. Smith, Ark., 1865-72; in Dallas, Tex., 1872—; 4 times mayor of city; U.S. marshal Northern Dist. Tex., 1885-89. Home: Dallas, Tex. Died 1911.

CABLE, Benjamin Stickney, asst. sec. of commerce and labor; b. Rock Island, Ill., Sept. 24, 1872; s. late Ransom R. and Josephine (Stickney) C.; A.B., Yale, 1895; LL.B., Columbia, 1898. In office of Lowden, Estabrook & Davis, 1898-99; entered law department of the C.,R.I.&P. Ry., 1899; atty. for Ill. same, 1904-09; asst. sec. of commerce and labor, 1909—. Independent in politics. Home: Washington, D.C. Died Sept. 27, 1915.

CABLE, Benjamin Taylor, congressman; b. Georgetown, Ky., Aug. 11, 1853; s. Philander L. and Mary (Taylor) C.; m. Maria C. Benton, June 5, 1882. Mem. 52d Congress (1891-93); declined renomination; mem. Dem. Nat. Com., 1892-96; chmn. western branch, same, 1892; was one of organizers of Nat. (Gold) Dem. party, 1896; del.-at-large Nat. (Gold) Dem. Conv., Indianapolis, 1896; returned to regular ranks, 1898, becoming mem. Ill. Dem. State Com.; chmn. exec. com. of Dem. Congressional Com., 1902. Home: Rock Island, Ill. Died Dec. 13, 1923.

CABLE, George Washington, author; b. New Orleans, Oct. 12, 1844; s. George W. and Rebecca (Boardman) C.; ed. pub. schs.; (hon. A.M., Yale, 1883; Litt.D., Washington and Lee, 1882, Yale, 1901, Bowdoin, 1904); m. Louise S. Bartlett, Dec. 7, 1869 (died 1904); m. 2d, Eva C. Stevenson, Nov. 24, 1906; father-in-law of A. L. P. Dennis. Served 4th Miss. Cav., C.S.A., 1863-65; for a time reporter on New Orleans Picayune, 1865-79; wrote stories for Scribner's Monthly; devoted to literature, 1879—. Founded, 1887, the Home Culture Clubs, now Northampton (Mass.) People's Inst., designed for the ednl. and esthetic culture of wage-earning people. Mem. Am. Acad. of Arts and Letters. Author: Old Creole Days, 1879, 1880, 1895; The Grandissimes, 1880, 1895, 1907; Dr. Sevier, 1885, 1894; Silent South, 1885; Bonaventure, 1888; John March, Southerner, 1894; Strong Hearts, 1899; The Cavalier, 1901; Posson Jone and Père Raphael, 1909; Gideon's Band, 1914; The Amateur Garden, 1914; Lovers of Louisiana, 1918. Died Jan. 31, 1925.

CABLE, Ransom R., chmn. bd., The Chicago, Rock Island & Pacific Ry., 1898—; b. Athens Co., O., 1834, and in early life moved to Rock Island, Ill., where for many years he was engaged in coal mining; became interested in ry. business, becoming pres. of Rockford, Rock Island & St. Louis R.R., 1870; elected dir. C.,R.I.&P. Ry. Co., 1877; asst. to pres., 1879; v.p. and gen. mgr., 1880; pres., 1883. Was also for several yrs. pres. of M.&St.L.; then also chmn. of bd. of Burlington, Cedar Rapids & North Ry. Co., and pres. R.I. & Peoria Ry. Co. Home: Rock Island, Ill. Died 1909.

CABOT, Arthur Tracy, surgeon; b. Boston, Jan. 5, 1852; s. Samuel and Hannah Lowell (Jackson) C.; A.B., Harvard, 1872, A.M., 1878, M.D., 1876; post-grad. studies Vienna and Berlin, 1876-77; m. Susan Shattuck, Aug. 16, 1882. Consulting surgeon Mass. Gen. Hosp., Children's Hosp., N.E. Hosp. for Women and Children; chmn. Mass. Commn. on Hospitals for Consumptives. Fellow Harvard U.; trustee Boston Mus. Fine Arts. Fellow Am. Surg. Assn., Am. Acad. Arts and Sciences. Died Nov. 4, 1912.

CABOT, Carolyn Sturgis, author; b. Concord, Mass., Apr. 13, 1846; d. William Ellery and Ellen K. (Fuller) Channing; sister of Walter and Edward Channing; ed. pvt. sch.; m. Follen Cabot, Sept. 20, 1865 (died 1905). Mem. Boston Browning Soc., Boston Authors' Club, etc. Author: Six Stories in the Child's Hour, 1898; Sketches of Nantucket, Mass., 1899; Football Grandma, 1905. Home: Boston. Died Jan. 26, 1917.

CABOT, Ella Lyman, teacher; b. Boston; d. Arthur Theodore and Ella (Lowell) Lyman; spl. student Radcliffe Coll., 1889-91, 1897-1900; grad. courses in logic and metaphysics, at Harvard Coll., 1900-04; m. Richard Clarke Cabot, Oct. 26, 1894. Teacher ethics and psychology in Boston pvt. schs., 1897—; formerly teacher Garland Sch. of Homemaking, Wellesley; teacher Pine Manor Junior Coll., Wellesley; mem. State Bd. Edn., 1905—. Author: Everyday Ethics, 1906; Report State Board of Education, 1907; Ethics for Children, 1910; A Course in Citizenship, 1914; Volunteer Help to the Schools, 1914; Our Part in the World, 1918; Seven Ages of Childhood, 1921; Temptations to Right Doing, 1929. Address: Cambridge, Mass. Died Sept. 20, 1934.

CABOT, Frederick Pickering, lawyer; b. Brookline, Mass., June 15, 1868; s. Francis and Louisa (Higginson) C.; A.B., Harvard, 1890, A.M., 1893, LL.B., 1893. Admitted to bar, 1893, and began practice at Boston; asst. U.S. atty., Dist. of Mass., 1896-97; mem. Hurlburt, Jones & Cabot, 1897-1916; justice Boston Juvenile Court; pres. Judge Baker Foundation; pres. and dir. Fisher Mfg. Co., and Winthrop Mills Co. Pres. trustees Boston Symphony Orchestra; trustee Wentworth Inst.; mem. council Radcliffe Coll. Home: Boston, Mass. Died Jan. 1932.

CABOT, Henry Bromfield, lawyer; b. Boston, Mass., Feb. 28, 1861; s. Walter Channing and Elizabeth Rogers (Mason) C.; A.B., Harvard, 1883; LL.B., Law Sch., Harvard U., 1887; studied U. of Heidelberg, 1884; m. Anne McMaster Codman, Nov. 15, 1892. Trustee Boston Personal Property Trust; trustee Business Property Associates, Duluth Real Estate Associates, Minneapolis Real Estate Associates, St. Paul Central Associates, Seattle Real Estate Associates, etc. Home: Brookline, Mass. Died Nov. 30, 1932.

CABOT, Philip, prof. business adminstrn.; b. Beverly Farms, Mass., Aug. 11, 1872; s. James Elliot and Elizabeth (Dwight) C.; A.B., Harvard University, 1894; LL.D., Juanita College, 1936; m. 2d, Gertrude Glidden, Sept. 11, 1937; children (by 1st marriage)—Sylvia (Mrs. A. M. Walker), Faith (Mrs. P. J. W. Pigors). Began in office of William Minot, trustee, Boston, 1894-1904; mgr. of real estate trusts, 1904-10; mgr. of electric pub. utilities, 1910-18; partner White, Weld & Co., 1912-18. Lecturer in public utility management, Harvard, 1924-27, prof. same, 1927-35, prof. of business adminstrn., 1935—. Home: Boston, Mass. Died Dec. 25, 1941.

CABOT, Richard Clarke, M.D.; b. Brookline, Mass., May 21, 1868; s. James Elliot and Elizabeth (Dwight) C.; A.B., Harvard U., 1889, M.D., 1892; LL.D., University of Rochester, N.Y., 1930; L.H.D., Syracuse U., 1934; m. Ella Lyman, Oct. 26, 1894. Physician to outpatients, Mass. Gen. Hosp., 1898-1908, asst. visiting phys., 1908-12, chief med. staff, 1912-21; asst., 1899-1903, instr. in medicine, 1903-08, asst. prof., 1908-19, prof. clin. medicine, 1919-33, Harvard Med. Sch.; lecturer philosophy, Prof. Josiah Royce's Harvard Sem. course in logic, 1903-04; prof. social ethics, Harvard U., 1920-34. Maj. U.S.A. Med. Reserve Corps, 1917-18, lt. col., 1918; service in France, 1917-19. Unitarian. Pres. Nat. Conf. of Social Work, 1931; pres. Mass. Anti-Saloon League, 1931-33. Awarded gold medal by Nat. Inst. Social Sciences, 1931. Fellow Am. Acad. Arts and Sciences. Author: Physical Diagnosis, 10 edits., 1901-30; Social Service and the Art of Healing, 2 edits., 1909-28; Differential Diagnosis, Vol. I, 4 edits., 1911-19, Vol. II, 3 edits., 1915-24; What Men Live By, 1914; Laymen's Handbook of Medicine, 1916, revised edit., 1937; Social Work, 1919; Facts on the Heart, 1926; Adventures on the Borderlands of Ethics, 1926; The Meaning of Right and Wrong, 1933; The Art of Ministering to the Sick (with Russell L. Dicks), 1936; Christianity and Sex, 1937. Home: Cambridge, Mass. Died May 8, 1939.

CADISCH, Gordon Francis, economist, educator; b. N.Y. City, Mar. 30, 1894; s. John and Frances (Pleva) C.; B.S., U. of Ill., 1917; M.B.A., New York U., 1924; Ph.D., Georgetown U., Washington, D.C., 1927, chartered life underwriter, 1931; studied Coll. City of N.Y., George Washington U., and U. of Md.; unmarried. Asst. in Physics Lab., Nat. Electric Lamp Assn., Nela Park, Cleveland, 1911-13; with investment firms, New York, 1917-22; asst. and asso. economist Bur. Agrl. Economics, U.S. Dept. Agr., 1922-24; instr. in economics, U. of Md., 1925-27, asso. prof. and asst. to dean, 1927-29; extension economist, U. of Ill., summer 1929; prof. economics and dir. Sch. of Business Administration, State Coll. of Wash., 1930-35; dean Hudson Coll. of Commerce and Finance of St. Peter's Coll., Jersey City, N.J., 1935—. Conglist. Mason. Author: (with Nils A. Olsen, C. O. Brannen, and R. W. Newton) Farm Credit, Farm Insurance, and Farm Taxation, 1924. Home: New York, N.Y. Died Oct. 5, 1937.

CADMAN, S(amuel) Parkes, clergyman; b. Wellington, Salop, Eng., Dec. 18, 1864; s. Samuel and Betsy (Parkes) C.; ed. Wesleyan Coll., Richmond, Surrey; D.D., Wesleyan (Conn.) and Syracuse univs., 1898, Yale and New York U., 1925; S.T.D., Columbia, 1913, Yale, 1925; L.H.D., U. of Vt., 1913; Litt.D., Wesleyan U., Bloomington, Ill., Dickinson Coll., 1926; LL.D., Syracuse U., 1922, Muskingum Coll., New Concord, O., 1927, Miami U., 1928, Bates Coll. and Rollins Coll., 1931; m. Lillian Esther Wooding, Buxton, Eng., 1889; children—Frederick Leslie, Marie Isabel, Lillian Esther. Pastor Metropolitan Temple, N.Y. City, 1895-1901, Central Congl. Ch., Brooklyn, 1901—; acting pres. Adelphi Coll., Brooklyn, 1911-13. Pres. Federal Council Chs. of Christ in America, 1924-28; radio minister of same, 1928—. Has served as spl. lecturer Yale Div. Sch.; Shepherd lecturer Bangor Theol. Sem.; Carew lecturer Hartford Theol. Sem.; Earl lecturer U. of Calif.; Cole lecturer Vanderbilt U. Del. to Gt. Britain for Tercentennial of Mayflower's Sailing, 1920; rep. of clergy of New York at 300th anniversary of founding of the first Christian Church of that city, 1928; chmn. Am. sect. of Stockholm Conf. on Life and Work, 1925; pres. Church and Drama League, 1926, 30. Comdr. Royal Order of Vasa (Sweden), 1932; gold medalist Nat. Inst. Social Sciences. Author: William Owen, A Biography, 1912; The Three Religious Leaders of Oxford, 1916; Ambassadors of God, 1920, 2d edit., 1921; Christianity and the State, 1924; Lure of London, 1925; Imagination and Religion, 1926; The Christ of God, 1929; Every Day Questions and Answers, 1930; The Parables of Jesus, 1931; The Prophets of Israel, 1933; The Pursuit of Happiness, 1935. Home: Brooklyn, N.Y. Died July 12, 1936.

CADWALADER, Charles Evert, physician; b. Phila., Nov. 5, 1839; s. John and Henrietta Maria (Bancker) C.; grad. Univ. of Pa., 1858; A.M., M.D., 1861; m. Mary B. Ryan, July 15, 1897. During Civil war served pvt. 1st City troop; capt. 6th Pa. cav., and on gen. staff Army of the Potomac as aid to Gens. Hooker and Meade with bvt. rank of lt. col. In med. practice, 1861—; and lived in same house in which he was born. Active from 1872 in polit., med. and social reform. Home: Philadelphia. Died 1907.

CADWALADER, John, lawyer; b. Phila., June 27, 1843; s. Judge John and Henrietta Maria (Bancker) C.; A.B., U. of Pa., 1862, A.M., 1865 (LL.D., same, 1912); m. Mary Helen Fisher, Apr. 17, 1866. Admitted to bar, 1864 and began practice at Phila.; mgr. and pres. Pa. Instn. for the Blind, 1870—. Pres. Baltimore & Phila. Steamboat Co. Dir. pub. schs., 1875-85; collector, port of Phila., 1885-89; jury commr. U.S. Circuit Ct. Democrat. Trustee U. of Pa. Pres. gen. Soc. War of 1812. Chmn. Appeal Bd. for draft in Phila. Home: Philadelphia, Pa. Died Mar. 11, 1925.

CADWALADER, John Lambert, lawyer; b. Trenton, N.J., Nov. 17, 1837; s. Thomas and Maria (Gouverneur) C.; bro. of Richard McCall C.; A.B., Princeton, 1856, A.M., 1859; LL.B., Harvard, 1860; (LL.D., Princeton, 1897, U. of Pa., 1908, Harvard, 1913). In practice in New York for many years under name Strong & Cadwalader; asst. sec. of state U.S., under Hamilton Fish, 1874-77. Pres. N.Y. Pub. Library; pres. N.Y. Bar Assn., 1906-07; trustee Met. Mus. of Art, Carnegie Instn. of Washington, Carnegie Endowment for Peace, Princeton U. Home: New York. Died Mar. 11, 1914.

CADWALADER, Richard McCall, lawyer; b. Trenton, N.J., Sept. 17, 1839; s. Thomas and Maria (Gouverneur) C.; bro. of John Lambert C.; A.B., Princeton, 1860, A.M., 1863; LL.B., Harvard, 1863; m. Christine Biddle, Nov. 23, 1873. Admitted to bar, 1864, and then in practice at Phila. Mem. S.R. (v.p. Gen. Soc., pres. Pa. Soc.); gov. Pa. Soc. of Colonial Wars; gov. gen. of Gen. Soc. Colonial Wars. Netherland Soc. Author: Law of Ground Rents; Fort Washington and the Encampment at White Marsh (address to and published by Pa. Soc. S.R.), 1901. Homes: Fort Washington, Pa., and Phila. Died Dec. 9, 1918.

CADWALLADER, Isaac Henry, physician; b. Waynesville, O., Aug. 29, 1850; s. John Thomas and Rachel (Farquhar) C.; ed. Lincoln (Ill.) U., finishing jr. course 1869; M.D., Rush Med. Coll., Chicago, 1875; m. Ella C. Brown, 1896. Began practice St. Louis, 1875; lectured on materia medica and therapeutics Woman's Med. Coll., 3 yrs.; on staff, 1891—. phys in charge, 1900—, Mo. Bapt. Sanitarium. Mason Home: St. Louis, Mo. Died July 22, 1919.

CADWALLADER, Starr, settlement worker; b. Howard, N.Y., June 11, 1869; s. Joseph Shepard and Anne E. (Starr) C.; A.B., Hamilton Coll., 1893, A.M., 1896; grad. Union Theol. Sem., 1896; m. Harriet E. Gomph, July 30, 1896; children—Elizabeth (dec.), Starr. Was engaged in Y.M.C.A. work, 1887, 1888 and 1890; teacher in pvt. schs., 1892-95; head worker Goodrich Settlement, Cleveland, 1896-1903 (trustee, 1903—, sec., 1906—); sch. dir. of Cleveland, 1902-05; sec. bd. trustees, Cleveland Sch. of Art, 1905-08; supt. of sanitation, 1908-10; trustee Kent State Normal Sch., 1912-14; mem. Ohio Bd. of Adminstrn., 1913-15; chmn. Cuyahoga Co. Selective Service Bd., 1917-18; dir. Civilian Relief and mgr. Lake Div. Am. Red Cross, 1918-23; exec. sec. Cleveland Hosp. Council, 1924—; mem. advisory com. Cleveland Asso. Charities. Home: Cleveland, O. Died June 26, 1926.

CADY, Daniel Leavens, poet, lawyer; b. West Windsor, Windsor County, Vt., Mar. 10, 1861; s. John Wesley and Mary Ann (Leavens) C.; prep. edn., Kimball Union Acad. and Montpelier Sem.; Ph.B., U. of Vt., 1886, L.H.D., 1909; Litt.D., Norwich U., 1924; m. Mary Elizabeth Wells, Oct. 6, 1913. Practiced law in N.Y. City as mem. Powell & Cady, 1894-1912; retired to Vt., 1913. Was one of three poets on behalf of State of N.Y. for Champlain Celebration, 1909; official poet State of Vt. for Bennington Battle Sesquicentennial, 1927. Democrat. Episcopalian. Author: Rhymes of Vermont Rural Life, Series I, 1919, Series II, 1922, Series III, 1926; also (pamphlets) Champlain and Lake Champlain, 1926; The Hill of Bennington, 1927. Home: Burlington, Vt. Died Apr. 1, 1934.

CADY, Edward Hammond, banker; b. Cleveland, O., Nov. 23, 1866; s. Seth Minard and Amelia (Read) C.; ed. pub. schs., Cleveland; m. Emma Page Watson, Sept. 29, 1899; children—Watson Chichester, Suzanne Morgan. Began as clk. in ry. office; clk. Ohio Nat. Bank, Cleveland, 1888-95; teller Union Nat. Bank, 1895-1901, asst. cashier, 1901-06; cashier Ohio Savings Bank & Trust Co., Toledo, O., 1906-12, v.p. 1912-13; pres. Guardian Trust & Savings Bank, 1913; pres. Commerce Guardian Trust & Savings Bank, 1922-31, retired. Republican. Unitarian. Home: Pasadena, Calif. Died Aug. 13, 1934.

CADY, George Luther, clergyman; b. Lamont, Mich., June 3, 1868; s. James F. and Silence P. (Hard) C.; A.B., Olivet Coll., Mich., 1890 (first honors), M.A., 1903, D.D., 1930; D.D., Ia. Coll., Grinnell, 1903; m. Florence V. O'Loughlin, Mar. 20, 1894. Teacher and lecturer on sociology, State Univ. of Ia., 1902-03; ordained Congl. ministry, 1894; pastor Benton Harbor, Mich., 1894-96, Geneseo, Ill., 1896-1900, Iowa City, Ia., 1900-05, Dubuque, Ia., 1905-08, Boston, 1908-16, Plymouth Congl. Ch., Lansing, Mich., 1916-17; nat. sec. Am. Missionary Assn., New York, 1917—. Mason. An authority on penology and charities, Negro, Indian, Oriental and Spanish American, in America and Hawaiian Islands. Home: Chesham, N.H. Died Nov. 23, 1939.

CADY, J. Cleveland, architect; b. Providence, R.I.; s. Josiah and Lydia C.; acad. edn., Colchester and Plainfield acads., Trinity Coll., Conn., A.M., 1880 (LL.D., 1905); m. Emma M. Bulkley, 1881. Engaged in practice of architecture, 1870—; sr. mem. Cady & Gregory; first important building was that of the Brooklyn Art Assn., followed by buildings for Yale U., some 15 in number, including Dwight Hall, Chittenden Library, Law Sch. bldg., the labs., and two halls for the scientific sch., the Yale Infirmary and other structures; also Met. Opera House, Am. Mus. Natural History, the later buildings of the Presbyn. Hosp. and the New York Hosp., Skin and Cancer Hosp., Bellevue Med. Schs., and the Hudson St. Hosp., New York; buildings for Williams, Trinity and Wesleyan univs., chs., commercial buildings and dwellings in various parts of the U.S. Contbr. to Outlook, Independent, Homiletic Review, etc. Pres. N.Y. Skin and Cancer Hosp.; gov. Presbyn. Hosp.; v.p. N.Y. City Mission; trustee Berea (Ky.) Coll. Mem. A.I.A. Presbyn. Home: New York, N.Y. Died Apr. 17, 1919.

CADY, Philander Kinney, clergyman; b. Cincinnati, O., Oct. 23, 1826; s. David K. and Ann Eliza C.; A.B., Woodward Coll., 1843, A.M., 1847; grad. Gen. Theol. Sem., 1847; (hon. M.A., Trinity, 1856; S.T.D., Columbia, 1868, Gen. Theol. Sem., 1895); m. Helen S. Hamilton, June 11, 1863. Deacon, 1850, priest, 1851, P.E. Ch.; rector Trinity Ch., W. Troy, N.Y., 1851-57, Grace Ch., Newark, N.J., 1857-66, Christ Ch., Poughkeepsie, N.Y., 1866-76, St. James' Ch., Hyde Park, N.Y., 1876-89; prof. evidences of natural and revealed religion, Gen. Theol. Sem., 1889-1902, emeritus. Died Aug. 30, 1917.

CAETANI, Gelasio, diplomat; b. Rome, Italy, Mar. 7, 1877; s. Onarato, Duke of Sermoneta, and Ada (Wilbraham); grad. Eng. sch. at Rome, 1901; E.M., Columbia U., 1903. Capt. Royal Engrs., 1915-19;

del. Paris Peace Conf., 1919; alderman, City of Rome, 1920; mem. Parliament, 1921-22; now A.E. and P. from Italy to U.S. Catholic. Died Oct. 23, 1934.

CAFFERY, Donelson, lawyer; b. parish of St. Mary, La., Sept. 10, 1835; ed. at St. Mary's Coll., Md.; studied law in La. and admitted to bar; served in C. S. A., 1861-65; after war lawyer and sugar planter; mem. State Constitutional Conv., 1879; State senator, 1892; Democrat. Affiliated with Nat. (Gold) Democrats, 1896; U.S. senator, 1893-1901. Home: Franklin, La. Died 1906.

CAFFIN, Charles Henry, art critic; b. Sittingbourne, Kent, Eng., June 4, 1854; s. Rev. Charles Smart and Harriet C.; grad. Oxford U., 1876; engaged in scholastic work and 6 yrs. in theatrical work; m. Caroline Scurfield, 1888. Came to U.S., 1892; engaged in decoration dept., Chicago Expn., 1893; at New York, 1897—; was art critic Harper's Weekly and one of art critics New York Evening Post; art critic New York Sun, 1901-04; late Am. editor The Studio; lecturer Univ. Extension Assn., Pa. Acad. Fine Arts, and Yale Sch. Fine Arts. Author: American Masters of Painting, 1902; American Masters of Sculpture; How to Study Pictures; The Story of American Painting; Old Spanish Masters, engraved by Timothy Cole; Guide to Pictures, Appreciation of the Drama, Story of Dutch Painting; Story of Spanish Painting, 1910; How to Study Architecture, 1915. Art critic of the New York American. Home: New York, N.Y. Died Jan. 15, 1918.

CAHILL, Edward, lawyer; b. Kalamazoo, Mich., Aug. 3, 1843; s. Abraham and Frances Maria (Marsh) C.; ed. Kalamazoo Coll.; m. Lucy Crawford, June 11, 1867. Enlisted as pvt. Co. A, 89th Ill. Inf., Aug. 1862; disch. for disability, Dec. 1862; apptd. by President Lincoln, 1st lt. 102d U.S.C.T., Dec. 1863; promoted capt., Jan. 1864; mustered out, Sept. 30, 1865. Admitted to bar, 1866; practiced in Clinton and Ionia cos., Mich., 1866-71, at Chicago, 1871-73, Lansing, Mich., 1873—; counsel for State of Mich. in important cases. Pros. atty., Ingham County, Mich., 1877-81; apptd. justice Supreme Ct., Mich., for unexpired term (1890-91) of James V. Campbell, deceased. Pres., trustee Edward W. Sparrow Hosp. Assn. Mem. Nat. Conf. Commrs. on Uniform State Laws. Address: Lansing, Mich. Died July 26, 1922.

CAHILL, Marie (Mrs. D. V. Arthur), actress; b. Brooklyn; m. Daniel V. Arthur. First appearance, in "Kathleen Mavourneen," Brooklyn; later appeared in "A Tin Soldier," and other musical comedies; starred in "Nancy Brown," 1902-03, and in "Molly Moonshine," 1904; created title rôle of Mary Montgomery, in "Marrying Mary," 1906-07; played Betty Barbeau in "The Boys and Betty," at Wallack's Theatre, New York, 1908, Judy Evans in "Judy Forgot," Casino Theatre, New York, 1911. Died Aug. 23, 1933.

CAHILL, Michael Harrison, ry. official; b. Lexington, O., Nov. 19, 1874; s. Michael J. and Jane E. (Murphy) C.; ed. high sch., Lexington; m. Ethel B. White, Sept. 1902; 1 dau., Margaret Cromwell (Mrs. Gilbert Winslow Colby). With B.&O. R.R. Co., 1891-1920, successively messenger boy, telegraph operator, train dispatcher, trainmaster, asst. supt. and supt., serving as supt. on 5 divisions and as gen. supt. Pa. and Md. dists.—except a short period as supt. Buffalo div. D.,L.&W. Ry.; with S.A.L. Ry., 1920-28, 1st as gen. mgr., and as v.p. in charge of operations, 1922-28; chmn. bd. M.K.&T. Lines, 1928—, also pres., 1930—. Home: Dallas, Tex. Died Mar. 26, 1940.

CAHILL, Michael Henry, lawyer; b. Thurston, N.Y., Sept. 17, 1886; s. James and Margaret (McMahon) C.; grad. Corning (N.Y.) Free Acad., 1908; LL.B., Georgetown U., 1911; m. Gertrude E. Lovejoy, Oct. 29, 1919. Began as reporter, Corning (N.Y.) Evening Leader, 1904; in office of comptroller of currency, Washington, D.C., 1910-11; nat. bank examiner, 1913-15; mem. Cheney, Cahill & Costello (Corning), 1915-18; asst. cashier, trust officer and asst. v.p. Irving Nat. Bank, New York, 1919-25; pres. Utica (N.Y.) Nat. Bank & Trust Co., 1925-28, Plaza Trust Co., New York, 1928-30, Park Row Trust Co., 1929-30; mem. Cahill & Tanner, Corning, N.Y., 1930—. Apptd. dist. atty. Steuben County, Jan. 1936. Dem. chmn., Steuben County, 1916-18, and 1934-36; asst. counsel to banking and currency com., U.S. Ho. of Rep., 1912; chmn. legislative com. of N.Y. State Bankers Assn., 1926; v.p. Am. Bankers Assn., 1926-27. Served as 1st lt., Chem. Warfare Service, U.S. Army, World War. Apptd. flood control commr. of N.Y., 1936. Democrat. Catholic. Home: Corning, N.Y. Died Apr. 29, 1939.

CAHILL, Thaddeus, inventor; b. Ia., 1867; s. Timothy and Ellen (Harrington) C.; grad. Oberlin (O.) High Sch., 1884; studied Oberlin Acad., 1884-85, and in laboratories; LL.B., Columbian (now George Washington) U., 1892, LL.M., 1893, D.C.L., 1900; unmarried. Admitted to bar, 1894, practiced several yrs. Invented the elec. typewriter; invented process of producing music electrically, known as telharmony; pioneer in U.S. of art of distributing music electrically from a central sta. to receiving telephones on premises of subscribers; also inventions in composing machines, heat engines, wireless telephony and wired-wireless; removed laboratory from Washington to Holyoke, Mass., 1902, and to New York, 1911. Jeffersonian Democrat. Episcopalian. Home: New York, N.Y. Died Apr. 12, 1934.

CAHOON, Edward Augustus, banking; b. Lyndon, Caledonia Co., Vt., Aug. 20, 1862; s. Charles Shaw and Charlotte (Chase) C.; A.B., Amherst, 1883; m. Mabel Howel, Apr. 26, 1894 (died 1902); children—Mrs. Katharine Wilson, Mrs. Louise Keller, Mabel; m. 2d, Laura Hedgcoxe, of Roswell, N.M., Aug. 15, 1908; 1 son, Dan H. Located in New Mexico, 1884; in cattle business until July 1887; entered Albuquerque Nat. Bank, 1887; organized Bank of Roswell, 1890; sole mgr. of bank from its origin. Pres. First Nat. Bank of Roswell; v.p. P. V. Lumber Co.; dir. Roswell Hardware Co. Mayor of Roswell, 1897. Del. Rep. Nat. Conv., 5 times between 1900-1928; chmn. Rep. Co. Com., Chaves Co., 22 yrs.; mem. Rep. Central Com. State of N.M., 20 yrs. Mem. Bd. of Regents, N.M. Mil. Inst.; v.p. Carnegie Pub. Library, Roswell. Presbyn. Mason. Home: Roswell, N.M. Died Dec. 23, 1934.

CAILLE, Augustus, M.D.; b. at Madison, Ind., Apr. 1, 1854; s. William and Ernestine (Hof) C.; Huguenot descent; grad. New York Coll. Pharmacy, 1873; M.D., U. of Würzburg, 1877, Coll. of Phys. and Surg. (Columbia), 1881; m. Emily Guth, 1879; m. 2d, Rita E. Seibold. In practice of medicine, New York, 1878—; prof. children's diseases, New York Post-Grad. Med. Sch., 1890—; consulting physician N.Y. Post-Grad., Lenox Hill hospitals. Del. Internat. Med. Congress, Berlin. Fellow Am. Congress on Internal Medicine, Am. Coll. of Physicians, N.Y. Acad. Medicine. Author: Diagnosis and Treatment of Disease, 1906; Prevention and Treatment of Disease, 1918. Deceased.

CAIN, James William, college pres.; b. New Haven, Conn., Sept. 1, 1860; s. P. J. and Mary (Kelley) C.; A.B., Yale U., 1884, A.M., 1893; LL.D., St. John's College, 1903, U. of Pittsburgh, 1912, also Washington Coll., 1928; m. Rose Cecilia Mallahan, Dec. 25, 1890; children—James Mallahan, Virginia Mary, Rosalie Cecelia, Edward Cain (lt. U.S.M.C., killed Feb. 15, 1919), Genevieve. Began teaching in evening schs. of New Haven, 1880; prin. of an evening sch., 1881-84; prin. Lewiston (Pa.) Acad., 1884-86; prof., 1886-1903, v.p., 1892-1903, St. John's Coll., Annapolis, Md.; pres. Washington Coll., Chestertown, Md., 1903-18; v.p. U.S. Fidelity & Guaranty Co., Baltimore, 1918—. Pres. bd. sch. trustees, Annapolis, Md., 1897-1901; mem. Md. State Bd. Edn. (ex-officio); Md. Edn. Commn. Author: Financial History of the United States, 1933. Home: Baltimore, Md. Died Oct. 13, 1938.

CAIN, Walter, editor; b. Pontotoc, Miss., Aug. 21, 1862; s. John Savely and Martha (Worsham) C.; B.A., U. of Miss., 1880; B.L., Vanderbilt, 1883; m. Adelaide Douglas, Dec. 19, 1901 (died Nov. 25, 1919); 1 son, Byrd Douglas. Began as reporter Nashville American, 1883, editor in chief, 1892-94; editor in chief Memphis News-Scimitar, 1906-12; asso. editor Nashville Banner, 1917-21, editor in chief, 1921—. Democrat. Episcopalian. Home: Nashville, Tenn. Deceased.

CAIN, William, univ. prof.; b. Hillsboro, N.C., May 14, 1847; s. William and Sarah Jane (Bailey) C.; A.M., N.C. Mil. and Poly. Inst., 1865; (LL.D.); unmarried. Engring. practice, 1868-74, 1880-82; prof. mathematics and civ. engring., Carolina Mil. Inst., 1874-79, S.C. Mil. Acad., Charleston, 1882-89; prof. mathematics, U. of N.C., 1889—. Author: Theory of Voussoir Arches, Solid and Braced Elastic Arches, Steel-Concrete Arches and Vaulted Structures, Bridges, Retaining Walls, Symbolic Algebra (all in Van Nostrand's Science Series), 1874-1909; A Brief Course in the Calculus, 1905; Earth Pressure, Retaining Walls and Bins, 1916. Died 1930.

CAIRNS, Anna Sneed, coll. pres.; b. New Albany, Ind., Mar. 19, 1841; d. Rev. Samuel K. and Rachel O. (Crosby) Sneed; grad. Monticello Sem., 1858; studied Latin, Greek and Hebrew with her father and Bishop Dunlop; m. John G. Cairns, 1881 (died 1895). Founder, 1861, and since pres. Forest Park U. (for young women), St. Louis. Legislative and legal supt. Mo. W.C.T.U.; supt. of labor, Nat. W.C.T.U. Addressed Nat. Ho. of Rep. in its sessions, an honor never accorded to any woman before, except to Dorothea Dix; delivered 30 prohibition addresses in Tex. Home: St. Louis, Mo. Died Sept. 1, 1930.

CAIRNS, Charles Andrew, ry. official; b. Cleveland, O. Began as messenger in gen. offices Cleveland, Columbus, Cincinnati & Indianapolis Ry., at Cleveland, 1878; stock clk., later chief clk., pass. dept. combined C.,C.,C.&I., Indianapolis & St. Louis and Dayton & Union rys., 1889; chief clk. pass. dept., 1889-90; asst. gen. pass. and tkt. agt., 1890-92, Chicago, St. Paul & Kansas City Ry.; in gen. pass. dept. C.&N.W. Ry., 1892-95; successively asst. gen. pass. and ticket agt., 1895-1903; gen. pass. and ticket agt., Mich., 1903—, same rd. Died July 1, 1933.

CAIRNS, William B., univ. prof.; b. Ellsworth, Wis., June 4, 1867; s. George W. and Abbie S. (Leavitt) C.; A.B., U. of Wis., 1890, A.M., 1892, Ph.D., 1897; m. Dora E. Bateman, June 21, 1893 (died 1917); children—William Bateman (killed in action, France, July 30, 1918), George Walter. Instr. rhetoric, 1893-97, English, 1897-1900, asst. prof., 1900-01, asst. prof. Am. literature, 1901-17, asso. prof., 1917—, University of Wis. Mem. summer faculty, Columbia, 1911, 1912; del. Conf. English and Am. profs. of English, and lecturing at English univs., 1920. Has edited sch. and coll. text books. Author: On the Development of American Literature, 1815-33, 1897; Forms of Discourse, 1896, 1909; History of American Literature, 1912; American Literature for Secondary Schools, 1914; British Criticisms of American Writers, 1783-1815, 1918; British Criticisms of American Writers, 1815-1833, 1922. Home: Madison, Wis. Died Aug. 2, 1932.

CAJORI, Florian, college prof.; b. St. Aignan, near Thusis, Switzerland, Feb. 28, 1859; s. George and Catherina (Camenisch) C.; came to U.S., 1875; B.S., U. of Wis., 1883, M.S., 1886; student Johns Hopkins; Ph.D., Tulane, 1894; LL.D., U. of Colo., 1912, Colo. Coll., 1913; Sc.D., U. of Wis., 1913; m. Elizabeth G. Edwards, Sept. 3, 1890; 1 son, Florian Anton. Asst. prof. mathematics, 1885-87; prof. applied mathematics, 1887-88, Tulane U.; prof. physics, 1889-98, mathematics, 1898-1918, dean dept. of engring., 1903-18, Colo. Coll.; prof. history of mathematics, U. of Calif., 1918—. Fellow Am. Acad. Arts and Sciences: Author: A History of Mathematics, 2 ed., 1919; A History of Elementary Mathematics, 2 ed., 1917; A History of Physics, 1899; Early Mathematical Sciences in North and South America, 1928; Mathematics in Liberal Education, 1928; Career of F. R. Hassler, 1929; History of Mathematical Notations (2 vols.), 1928-29. Deceased.

CALDER, Alexander Milne, sculptor; b. Aberdeen, Scotland, Aug. 23, 1846; s. Alexander and Margaret (Milne) C.; studied Royal Institute of Arts, Edinburgh; s. Kensington, London; Pa. Acad. Fine Arts; m. Margaret Stirling, Nov. 26, 1868; father of Alexander Stirling C. Designed and modeled equestrian statue of Gen. George G. Meade, Fairmount Park Art Assn., Phila., 1887; sculpture (independent and attached), City Hall, Phila., 1873-94; of busts in bronze, for Union League, Sharswood Memorial, in Supreme Ct., McArthur, Memorial, for city, colossal statue of William Penn in Bronze, 1894; four colossal groups ("races") in bronze and other groups and figures for pub. and pvt. monuments. Republican. Presbyn. Home: Philadelphia, Pa. Died June 14, 1923.

CALDWELL, Alexander, senator; b. Drake's Ferry, Pa., Mar. 1, 1830; common sch. edn.; m. Pace A. Heise. Private in his father's (Capt. James Caldwell's) co. in Mexican war, father being killed in battle, City of Mexico, Sept. 13, 1847. Officer Columbia (Pa.) Bank, 1853-61; engaged, 1861-70, transporting mil. supplies to frontier posts and bldg. railroads in Kansas; elected U.S. senator, 1871; resigned, 1873. Republican. Pres. Kansas Mfg. Co., mfrs. wagons and farm implements, 1877-97; pres. 1st Nat. Bank of Leavenworth, Kan., 1897—. Died May 1917.

CALDWELL, Burns Durbin, ry. official; b. at Placerville, Calif., Apr. 27, 1858; s. J. M. and Jennie C.; ed. high schs., Chambersburg, Pa. Entered ry. service, 1875, as clerk in auditor's office, Vandalia Line, at Terre Haute, Ind., chief clerk gen. passenger and ticket office, Vandalia Line, St. Louis, 1881-86; same, Mo.P. and St. Louis, Iron Mountain and Southern roads, 1886-88; asst. gen. passenger and ticket agt., same, 1888-92; chmn. Western Passenger Assn., Chicago, 1892-99; traffic mgr. D.,L.&W. R.R. Co., 1899-1902; v.p. traffic dept., same, 1902-11; pres. Wells Fargo & Co., Oct. 1911—; chmn. bd. Am. Ry. Express Co., July 1, 1918—. Home: Orange, N.J. Died Sept. 25, 1922.

CALDWELL, Charles Pope, lawyer; b. Bastrop County, Tex., June 18, 1875; s. Charles G. C.; LL.B., U. of Tex., 1898, Yale, 1899; m. Frances Morrison, July 20, 1907; 1 son, Charles Morrison. Admitted to N.Y. bar, 1900. Del. Dem. Nat. Conv., 1912; mem. 64th to 66th Congresses (1915-21), 2d N.Y. Dist.; apptd. asso. justice Ct. of Special Sessions, N.Y. City, 1926. Maj., Ordnance Corps, World War, 1918; founder Veterans' Mountain Camp, Tupper Lake, N.Y. Mason. Home: Kew Kardens, L.I. Died July 31, 1940.

CALDWELL, Clifford Douglass, pres. Interlake Iron Corp.; b. Bristol, Tenn., Oct. 16, 1872; s. Rev. George Aiken and Margaret (Brooks) C.; desc. of Anthony Caldwell of Virginia, a Continental soldier at Yorktown, 1781; ed. King Coll., Bristol, 1885-88, LL.D., 1935; m. Jane Wood, Oct. 9, 1895 (died 1928); m. 2d, Charlotte Goodlett, Apr. 19, 1930. Employed in bank, 1888-96; in coal business developing own interests in Va. and W.Va., 1896-1914; in Chicago, 1914—; v.p. By-Products Coke Corp., Chicago, 1916-21, pres., 1921-29, and of successor, Interlake Iron Corp., 1929—. Served on Com. of Coal

Production, U.S. Govt., Washington, 1917-18. Dir. Am. Iron and Steel Inst. Republican. Presbyn. Home: Chicago, Ill. Died Apr. 16, 1940.

CALDWELL, Eugene Craighead, theologian; b. Rock Hill, S.C., Aug. 17, 1876; s. Alfred Shorter and Lizzie (Hutchison) C.; A.B., Hampden-Sydney (Va.) Coll., 1898, A.M., 1899, LL.D., 1923; B.D., Union Theol. Sem. in Virginia, 1904; D.D., Austin Coll., Sherman, Tex., 1910; m. Margaret Beverley McCormick, Feb. 9, 1904 (died, 1929); children—Virginia Beverley, Caroline Elizabeth, Eugene Craighead. Prof. English, Hampden-Sydney Coll., 1898-99, Hoge Mil. Acad., Blackstone, Va., 1899-1901; Hoge fellow, Union Theol. Sem. in Va., 1904-05; ordained Presbyn. ministry, 1905; pastor Leaksville and Wentworth, N.C., 1905-06; Ball prof. O.T. lang. and exegesis, Austin (Tex.) Theol. Sem., 1906-14; prof. O.T. lang. and exegesis, 1914-15, prof. N.T. exegesis, 1915—, Union Theol. Sem. in Va. Stone lecturer, Princeton Theol. Sem., 1918. Died Dec. 12, 1931.

CALDWELL, Eugene Wilson, physician; b. Savannah, Mo., Dec. 3, 1870; s. W. W. and Camilla (Kellogg) C.; B.S., U. of Kan., 1892; M.D., Univ. and Bellevue Hosp. Med. Coll. (New York U.), 1905; special student of the College of Physicians and Surgeons (Columbia), 1898-99; m. Elizabeth Perkins, 1913. Engaged in experiments in wireless telephony (with L. I. Blake) for United State Lighthouse Establishment, 1893-95; asst. engring. dept. New York Telephone Co., 1895-97; from 1897 has devoted nearly all time to experimental work with Röntgen rays and to their practical application in diagnosis. Inventor Caldwell Liquid Interrupter, spl. forms of Röntgen ray tubes for therapeutic uses and many other appliances used with Röntgen rays. Prof. Röntgenology, Coll. Phys. and Surg. (Columbia), Mar. 1917—. Commd. capt. Med. O.R.C., 1917, maj., 1918, in active service. Author: The Röntgen Rays in Therapeutics and Diagnosis (with William A. Pusey), 1903. Home: New York, N.Y. Died June 23, 1918.

CALDWELL, Frank Merrill, army officer; b. Rochester, N.Y., Nov. 8, 1866; s. Walter Lester and Jane (Carter) C.; grad. U.S. Mil. Acad., 1890; distinguished grad. Army Sch. of the Line, 1909; grad. Army Staff Coll., 1910; m Mary Hay, June 6, 1894; children—Dorothy (Mrs. C. F. Beach), Jane Carter (Mrs. Harrison Lobdell), Mary Hay (Mrs. David Bath). Commissioned 2d lieut. 3d Cav., June 12, 1890; promoted through grades to brig. gen., Jan. 18, 1925. Served as lt. col. 4th Wis. Inf., Spanish-Am. War; detailed in Insp. Gen.'s Dept., 1916-18; brig. gen. N.A., Apr. 12, 1918-Oct. 31, 1919, World War; comdr. 75th Inf. Brig., 38th Div., May 15-Oct. 14, 1918; comdr. 83rd Inf. Brig., 42d Div., 1918-19; insp. gen., 1920-21; chief of staff, Gen. Staff Corps, 6th Corps Area, 1921-24; comdg. harbor defenses of P.I., 1925-27, harbor defenses of Pacific Coast, 1928-31; retired Nov. 30, 1931. Died Mar. 8, 1937.

CALDWELL, George Brinton; b. Dunkirk, N.Y., Aug. 24, 1863; s. Charles Melville and Mary Ann (Kelner) C.; ed. high sch. and business coll.; m. Lucy Smith Patrick, Oct. 14, 1886 (died May 1922); 1 dau., Mrs. A. R. Gibbons; m. 2d, Marion Haley Andrews, July 14, 1923. City clk., Greenville, Mich., 1886; bank bookkeeper, 1884-90; state accountant of Mich. and sec. State Bd. of Equalization, 1891, 1892; nat. bank examiner, Mich. and Ind., 1893-99; asst. cashier Merchants Nat. Bank, Indianapolis, Ind., 1899-1902; became identified, 1902, with investment bond business with Am. Trust and Savings Bank, Chicago; v.p. Continental and Commercial Trust & Savings Bank, Chicago, 1910-15; organized, 1911, Investment Bankers Assn. America and was its first president, serving two yrs., 1912, 13; pres. Sperry & Hutchinson Co., New York, 1915-23; pres. Caldwell, Mosser & Willamen, investment bankers, 1923-25, 1926-30; now pres. Geo. B. Caldwell & Co.; v.p. U.S. Bond & Mortgage Corp., New York. Conglist. Mason. Home: Bronxville, N.Y. Died May 27, 1933.

CALDWELL, George Chapman, prof. chemistry, Cornell, 1868-1903; b. Framingham, Mass., Aug. 14, 1834; grad., B.S., Lawrence Scientific School, Harvard, 1855; (Ph.D., Göttingen, Germany, 1857); m. Rebecca Stanley Wilmarth, 1861. Prof. chemistry and physics, Antioch Coll., Ohio, 1859-62; prof. chemistry, 1864-67, v.p., 1867-68, Agrl. Coll. of Pa.; prof. emeritus, Cornell, 1903. Home: Ithaca, N.Y. Died 1907.

CALDWELL, Henry Clay, judge; b. Marshall County, W.Va., Sept. 4, 1832; moved with family to Iowa, 1837; ed. in common schs.; admitted to bar, 1852. Pros. atty., Van Buren County, Ia., 1856-58; mem. Iowa legislature, 1859-61; maj., lt. col. and col. 3d Ia. Cav., 1861-64; U.S. dist. judge, Eastern Dist. of Ark., 1864-90; U.S. circuit judge, 8th Jud. Circuit, 1890-1903; resigned. Died Feb. 15, 1915.

CALDWELL, Howard Walter, univ. prof.; b. Bryan, O., Aug. 26, 1853; s. Walter Earl and Emily (McGowan) C.; Ph.B., U. of Neb., 1880, A.M., 1894; prin. Lincoln High Sch., 1881-82; student Johns Hopkins, 1882-83; traveled in Europe, 1892; m. Lisbeth Barnes, June 25, 1890. Adj. and asso. prof. history, 1883-92, prof. Am. history and jurisprudence, 1892-1905, head prof. Am. history, 1906—, U. of Neb. In Europe, 1911-12, and worked for some months in Record Office, London, on Vice-Admiralty Courts in the Colonies. Author: History of the United States, 1815-61, 1896; Source History of United States, 1909; Outlines With References for American History, 1783-1877, 1910. Home: Lincoln, Neb. Died Mar. 2, 1927.

CALDWELL, James Henry, mech. engr.; b. Mobile, Ala., Mar. 21, 1865; s. Edward Holland and Carolina Amelia (Shields) C.; B.S., Rensselaer Poly. Inst., 1886; m. Margery Josephine Christie, May 3, 1887. Engr. and v.p. Mobile (Ala.) Gas & Electric Co., 1886-1904; engr. Ludlow Valve Co., Troy, N.Y., 1888-94, v.p. and gen. mgr., 1894-1908, pres., 1908-30, chmn. bd., 1930—; elected pres. Troy Trust Co. upon its orgn., 1902; resigned, 1913; treas. Rensselaer Improvement Co.; trustee and 1st v.p. Troy Savings Bank; v.p. Troy & Greenbush, Rensselaer & Saratoga, Albany & Vermont, Troy & Bennington, Troy & Schenectady, Troy & Lansingburg, Cohoes & Lansingburg railways, etc. Vice-pres. and trustee Rensselaer Poly. Inst.; pres. Samaritan Hosp., Troy Pub. Library; sr. past pres. Troy Chamber Commerce. Democrat. Episcopalian. Home: Troy, N.Y. Died Nov. 1931.

CALDWELL, Jesse Cobb, clergyman, educator; b. Clay County, Mo., Jan. 15, 1873; s. Robert and Mildred (Cobb) C.; A.B., Transylvania Coll., Lexington, Ky., 1896; grad. Coll. of the Bible, Lexington, Ky., 1897; B.D., Div. Sch. of Yale U., 1903; LL.D., Transylvania, 1916; m. Mary, d. Congressman E. E. Settle, of Owenton, Ky., Oct. 18, 1898; children—Elisabeth, Mildred; m. 2d, Ruth O. Wilkinson, Aug. 10, 1927. Ordained ministry Disciples of Christ, 1897; pastor Christian Ch., Owenton, Ky., 1897-1902; prin. Caldwell Acad., Owenton, 1900-02; pastor First Christian Church, Selma, Ala., 1903-07, 1st Ch., Wilson, N.C., 1907, also dean Atlantic Christian Coll., Wilson; pres. same coll., 1908-16; dean Coll. of the Bible, Drake U., Des Moines, Ia., 1916-37, prof. History of Religion, 1937—. Democrat. Home: Des Moines, Ia. Died Feb. 22, 1941.

CALDWELL, John Curtis, soldier; b. Lowell, Vt., Apr. 17, 1833; s. George M. and Betsey (Curtis) C.; A.B., Amherst, 1855; m. Martha Helen Foster, May 15, 1857. Prin. Washington Acad., E. Machias, 1855-61; col. 11th Me. Inf., Nov. 12, 1861; brig. gen. vols., Apr. 28, 1862; bvtd. maj. gen. vols., Aug. 19, 1865, for faithful and meritorious services; hon. mustered out, Jan. 15, 1866; pres. Mil. Commn., Washington, 1864-65. Admitted to Me. bar, 1866; mem. Me. Senate and adj. gen., 1867-69. Removed to Kan., 1883, chmn. State Bd. Pardons, 1885-92; Am. consul at Valparaiso, Chile, 1869-70; chargé d'affaires ad interim to Chile, Aug.-Dec. 1870; minister resident, 1874-76, chargé d'affaires, 1876-81, Uruguay and Paraguay; consul at San José, Costa Rica, 1897-1909. Died Aug. 30, 1912.

CALDWELL, John Lawrence, lawyer; b. in Bourbon County, Kan., July 16, 1875; s. Thomas Anderson and Mary Alice (Hamman) C.; grad. Kansas Normal College; m. Evelyne de Lambert, June 11, 1902. Teacher dist. and high schs. 5 yrs.; mem. Kan. Senate, from 8th Dist., 1901-04; practiced law at Fort Scott, Kan.; pros. atty., Bourbon County, Kan., 2 terms, 1907-11; Dem. candidate for Congress from 2d Kan. Dist., 1910 (defeated); del. Dem. Nat. Conv., Baltimore, Md., 1912; apptd. E. E. and M. P. to Persia, June 6, 1914. Mason. Died Dec. 6, 1922.

CALDWELL, John Williamson, univ. prof.; b. Charleston, S.C., Jan. 31, 1842; s. John W. and Martha Catherine (Coates) C.; A.B., Coll. of Charleston, 1861, A.M., 1868; M.D., Va. State Med. Coll., 1864; pvt. and asst. surgeon C.S.A., 1861-65; m. Mary Palmer, Sept. 20, 1865. Practiced medicine, New Orleans, 1865-74; Stewart prof. of natural sciences, Stewart Coll. (afterward Southwestern Presbyn. U.), Clarksville, Tenn., 1874-84; curator Tulane U. Mus., 1885; prof. chemistry and geology, 1886-1907, emeritus, Tulane U. Died 1923.

CALDWELL, Joseph Pearson, editor; b. Statesville, N.C., June 16, 1853; s. Joseph Pearson (M.C.) and Amanda (McCullough) C.; pub. sch. edn.; m. Maggie Spratt, June 14, 1877 (died 1893); m. 2d, Addie W. Williams, Sept. 9, 1900. Editor Statesville Landmark (weekly), 1880-92, Charlotte (N.C.) Daily Observer, 1892-1909. Mayor of Statesville, 1886-90; dir. State Hosp. for Insane, 1880-1909 (chmn. bd., 1884-1909). Died 1911.

CALDWELL, Joshua William, lawyer; b. Athens, Tenn., Feb. 3, 1856; s. Alfred C.; grad. Univ. of Tenn., 1875 (A.M., 1895); m. Kate Moore Barnard, Nov. 20, 1883. Admitted to Tenn. bar, 1877; trustee State Univ. and State Deaf and Dumb School; lecturer on Tenn. laws and constl. history of Tenn., U. of Tenn. Author: Constitutional History of Tennessee, 1895, 2d edit., 1907; Bench and Bar of Tennessee, 1898. Home: Knoxville, Tenn. Died 1909.

CALDWELL, Morley Albert, univ. prof.; b. nr. Lebanon, Ind., Oct. 4, 1877; s. John Hubert and Margaret Ann (Williams) C.; A.B., Indiana U., 1904, A.M., 1905; Ph.D., Harvard, 1908; m. Mary Etta Armstrong, Aug. 8, 1909 (died 1928); m. 2d, Edith A. Sanford, Aug. 11, 1931. Prof. of philosophy and psychology and head of dept., Ursinus Coll., 1908-11; prof. of philosophy and psychology and head of dept., U. of Louisville, 1911—. Unitarian. Died Mar. 15, 1938.

CALDWELL, Samuel Cushman, editor; b. Carlisle, Pa., Apr. 10, 1836; s. Prof. Merritt and Rosamond (Cushman) C.; A.B., Dickinson Coll., 1858, A.M., 1861 (D.C.L., 1899); admitted to bar, Portland, 1861, New York, 1863; m. Charrie Forshee, Mar. 20, 1883. Asst. editor The Methodist, New York, 1866-69; on staff New York World, 1869-72, New York Tribune, Sept. 1, 1872—; editor New York Tribune Farmer, 1902-11. First pres. Village of Pelham, N.Y., 1896-98. Republican. Home: Pelham Heights, N.Y. Died Jan. 23, 1923.

CALDWELL, Victor Bush, banker; b. Omaha, Neb., Feb. 14, 1864; s. Smith S. and Henrietta M. (Bush) C.; A.B., Yale, 1887; m. Nellie R. Hugus, Oct. 10, 1888. Engaged in banking business at Omaha, Neb., 1887; now pres. U.S. Nat. Bank; trust officer U.S. Trust Co.; dir. Union Stock Yards Co.; pres. J. W. Hugus & Co., Denver, Colo. Republican. Episcopalian. Home: Omaha, Neb. Died Dec. 26, 1915.

CALEY, Katharine, educator; b. Princeton, Minn.; d. of Dr. Daniel A. and Sophronia M. (Groff) C.; student St. Mary's Hall, Faribault, Minn., U. of Minn.; A.B., U. of Wash., 1917. Successively teacher St. Mary's Hall (Faribault), Annie Wright Sem., asso. prin. Orton Sch. for Girls, and prin. St. Nicholas Sch. (Seattle); now prin. St. Mary's Hall, Faribault. Episcopalian. Died Aug. 23, 1938.

CALEY, Llewelyn N., clergyman; b. Eng., July 4, 1859; s. M. Lawrence and Ellen (Twinch) C.; grad. London Coll. of Divinity, 1884; B.D., Phila. Div. Sch., 1904; D.D., U. of the South, 1919; m. Ella K. Walker, July 1889; children—Rev. N. Herbert, William L., Kathleen F. (wife of Dr. Paul K. Musselman), Edith A. (Mrs. Bland S. Killpatrick), Arthur L. Came to U.S., 1890, naturalized citizen, 1895. Deacon, 1884, priest, 1885, P.E. Ch.; rector Church of the Nativity, Phila., Pa., 1893-1908, St. Jude and the Nativity, Philadelphia, 1908-20, St. Martin's Ch., Oak Lane, Phila., 1921—. Republican. Author: The Church Handbook, 1914. Home: Philadelphia, Pa. Died Apr. 15, 1932.

CALFEE, John Edward, educator; b. Arcola, Dade Co., Mo., Feb. 7, 1875; s. James Buford and Elizabeth (Wilkins) C.; Park Coll., Parkville, Mo., 1905, LL.D., 1919; A.M., Columbia, 1914; grad. student at U. of Chicago and at U. of Mo.; m. Margaret Irene Ballantyne, Aug. 28, 1906; children—Cleland Ballantyne (dec.), John Douglas, Margaret Elizabeth. Prin. Hyden Acad., 1905-07; prof. natural science, Tusculum Coll., 1907-08; prof. mathematics, Normal Dept. Berea Coll., 1908-16; pres. Asheville Normal and Teachers Coll., 1916-37; personality and vocational counselor Cecil's Business Coll. Field study 1 yr. of ednl. social and econ. problems of isolated regions of Southern mountains; organizer Asheville Summer Sch.; organizer student thrift banks, to teach banking business and thrift. Presbyn. Author: Calfee's Rural Arithmetic; Doing the Impossible; Chapel Talks; What Next?. Home: Arden, N.C. Died Nov. 28, 1940.

CALHOUN, Abner Wellborn, physician; b. Newnan, Ga., Apr. 16, 1845; s. Dr. A.B.C.; ed. common schs., Newnan; in C.S.A., 1861-65; studied medicine; spent 3 yrs. in Vienna and Berlin studying diseases of the eye, ear and throat; (LL.D., U. of Ga.); m. Louise Phinizy, Sept. 25, 1877. Prof. ophthalmology and oto-laryngology, Atlanta Med. Coll.; pres. Atlanta Coll. Phys. and Surg. (consolidation of Atlanta and Southern med. colls.), 1900—; oculist and aurist Grady, Wesleyan Memorial and St. Joseph's hosps. Home: Atlanta, Ga. Died 1910.

CALHOUN, Alexander McConnell, ry. executive; b. Nebraska City, Neb., May 1, 1871; s. Simeon Howard and Matilda (McMechan) C.; grad. high sch., Nebraska City, 1888; unmarried. Clk., supt's. office, Mo.P. Ry., Atchison, Kan., 1890-96; clk. to claim agt. St. Louis Southwestern R.R., Pine Bluff, Ark., 1896-97, claim agt., Tyler, Tex., 1897-99; chief clk. to supt. K.C.S. Ry., Pittsburg, Kan., Apr.-June 1899, claim agt., Texarkana, Tex., 1899-1903; chief clk. to gen. storekeeper and gen. mgr. D.&R.G. R.R. Co., Denver, Colo., 1903-05; chief clk. to gen. mgr. C.,H.&D. Ry., Cincinnati, Mar.-June 1905; chief clk. to pres. K.C.S. Ry., Kansas City, Mo., 1905-10, asst. to pres., 1910-18; asst. to federal mgr. K.C.S. Ry., Kansas City, Mexico & Orient R.R. Midland Valley R.R. Co., Houston, E.&W. Tex. Ry., Mo.&N.Ark. Ry. Co., 1918-20; asst. to pres., and v.p., K.C.S. Ry., 1924—, then also sec.; v.p. and asst. to pres. Texarkana & Ft. Smith Ry. Co.; pres. or v.p. numerous cos. Republican. Home: Kansas City, Mo. Died May 16, 1935.

CALHOUN, David Randolph, dry goods mcht.; b. Hartford, Conn., Feb. 28, 1858; s. George W. and Sarah R. (Giles) C.; ed. Smith Acad., Dunellen, N.J.; m. Marie Gardner Whitmore, Nov. 25, 1901.

Entered employ of Ely, Janis & Co., wholesale dry goods, St. Louis, 1878, firm inc., 1883, as Ely & Walker Dry Goods Co., of which was elected pres. 1903. Home: Clayton, Mo. Deceased.

CALHOUN, Hall Laurie, clergyman, educator; b. Conyersville, Tenn., Dec. 11, 1863; s. John Shelton and Martha Louisa (Hall) C.; grad. Coll. of the Bible, Lexington, Ky., 1892 (1st honors); A.B., Ky. U., 1892 (1st honors); B.D., Yale Div. Sch., 1902; A.M., Harvard, 1903, Ph.D., 1904; m. Mary Ettah Stacey, Dec. 31, 1890; children—Mary Ettah, John Laurie, James Edwin, Margaret Lee, Dorothea Eloise. Teacher in Acad. of Ky. U., 1892-93; evangelist, Ch. of Christ, 1893-96; minister Franklin, Tenn., 1896-1900; prof. Georgia Robertson Christian Coll., Henderson, Tenn., 1900-01; Hopkins scholar, Harvard, 1902-03, Williams fellow, 1903-04; prof. Coll. of the Bible, 1904-17, dean, 1909-17; prof. of O.T. lit., Bethany (W.Va.) Coll., 1917-25; asso. pres. Freed-Hardeman Coll., Henderson, Tenn., 1925-26; pastor, 1926—, Belmont Av. Ch. of Christ, Nashville. Mem. Internat. S.S. Lesson Com., 1908-16. Democrat. Home: Nashville, Tenn. Died Sept. 4, 1935.

CALHOUN, John, clergyman; b. McKeesport, Pa., Sept. 22, 1863; s. James and Sarah Elizabeth (McClure) C.; A.B., Princeton, 1886; grad. Princeton Theol. Sem., 1892; D.D., Ursinus Coll., 1909; m. Louise B. Johnstone, July 31, 1900; children—Sarah Elizabeth, John Adley. Ordained ministry Presbyn. Ch. in U.S.A., 1892; asst. pastor Germantown, Pa., 1892-96; pastor Mt. Airy Presbyn. Ch., Phila., Pa., 1896—. Trustee Wilson Coll., Chambersburg, Pa., Lincoln U. Commr. to Gen. Assembly Presbyn. Ch. in U.S.A., 3 times; mem. 1st bd., Ministerial Sustentation Fund, Presbyn. Ch. in U.S.A.; vice-moderator Synod of Pa., Presbyn. Ch., 1933. Home: Philadelphia, Pa. Died Oct. 16, 1937.

CALHOUN, John Calwell, financier; b. nr. Demopolis, Ala., July 9, 1843; s. Andrew Pickens and Margaret Maria (Green) C.; g.s. John Caldwell Calhoun, v.p. of U.S., 1825-29; brother of Patrick C.; ed. Thalian Acad., nr. Pendleton, S.C.; entered S.C. Coll., class of 1863, but left to enter C.S.A. at battle of Ft. Sumter; served in cav. through war, becoming capt.; m. Linnie Adams (1870), grandniece Richard M. Johnson (v.p. U.S., 1837-41). Planter after war in Ala., Miss. and Ark.; del.-at-large from Ark. to Cotton Expn., Louisville, 1883, New Orleans, 1884; v.p. conv. in Washington, 1884, which memorialized Congress with reference to improvement of Miss. River; spl. ambassador to France of S.A.R., 1897. Pres. Baltimore Coal Mining & Railroad Co., Albertite Oilite & Cannel Coal Co., Ltd. Home: New York, N.Y. Died Dec. 18, 1918.

CALHOUN, William James, diplomat; b. Pittsburgh, Oct. 5, 1848; s. Robert and Sarah (Knox) C.; acad. edn., Union Sem., Poland, O.; m. Alice D. Harmon, Dec. 26, 1875 (died 1898); m. 2d, Lucy Monroe, 1904. Admitted to bar, 1875; practiced at Danville, Ill., 1875-98, Chicago from 1900; sr. mem. Calhoun, Lyford & Sheean, 1904; western counsel Baltimore & Ohio R.R. Co. Special commr. for President McKinley to Cuba in 1897; mem. U.S. Interstate Commerce Commn., 1898-1900; spl. commr. for President Roosevelt to Venezuela, 1905; E.E. and M.P. to China, Dec. 1909-Aug. 1, 1913. Republican. Died Sept. 19, 1916.

CALIFF, Joseph Mark, brig. gen.; b. E. Smithfield, Pa., Aug. 31, 1843; s. Hosea and Mary (Pierce) C.; ed. pub. schs. and acads.; m. Katharine Wendell Hardy, June 4, 1902. Commd. 2d lt., U.S.C.T., Oct. 8, 1863; 1st lt., Mar. 5, 1865; bvt. capt., Mar. 13, 1865; hon. mustered out, Oct. 13, 1866; apptd. 2d lt., 3d U.S. Arty., Aug. 17, 1867; honor grad. Arty. Sch., 1871; 1st lt., capt., maj., arty. corps, 1875-1901; lt. col., May 20, 1904; brig. gen., Mar. 24, 1906; retired, Mar. 28, 1906. Served during Civil War in Va., and Dept. of the South; comd. battery of field arty. in Cuba and P.R. during Spanish-Am. War. Author: History of the 7th Regiment, United States Colored Troops, 1878; Notes on Military Science, 1889, 1906. Home: Towanda, Pa. Died Dec. 9, 1914.

CALKINS, Franklin Welles, author; b. Iowa Co., Wis., June 5, 1857; s. John Franklin and Abigail (Welles) C.; desc. Sir Jean Carmont Calquens, granted estate in Wales, 1066; unmarried. Was lawyer, contractor in ry. building, real estate broker and ranchman; early explorer Black Hills country; familiar with a number of Indian tongues and with animal and bird life of plains and mountains. Author: Tales of the West (3 vols.), 1893; The Cougar-Tamer, 1899; My Host, the Enemy, 1901; Two Wilderness Voyages, 1903; The Wooing of Tokala, 1907; Betty Canteen, A Romance, 1924. Home: Elsinore, Calif. Died Dec. 20, 1928.

CALKINS, Harvey Reeves, clergyman; author; b. Valparaiso, Ind., Apr. 11, 1866; s. William Thomas and Arabella Thurza (Reeves) C.; A.B., Northwestern U., 1888, A.M., 1891; B.D., Garrett Bibl. Inst., 1890; traveled and studied in Europe, 1890-91, and 1896; m. Helen M. Pearsons, July 8, 1890 (died 1893); m. 2d, Ida Von Holz, Oct. 3, 1894; 1 dau., Helen Deborah. Ordained M.E. ministry, 1892; pastor Castle Rock, Colo., 1891, Haymarket Ch., Denver, 1892-93, Sheffield Av. Ch., Chicago, 1894-98; missionary field evangelist, 1898-1900; missionary in India, 1900-10; del. World's Missionary Conf., Edinburgh, 1910; del. Gen. Conf., M.E. Ch., 1912, reserve, 1916 and 1920; stewardship sec. Commn. on Finance, M.E. Ch., 1912-18; stewardship editorial dir. Methodist Centenary, 1919-20; lecturer in schools of China, 1920-21; missionary, India, 1922-29; cons. sec. Laymen's Econ. Fellowship, 1929-31; dir. stewardship schs. of religion for Bd. of Edn. of M.E. Church, 1932-36; literary research, 1937—. Author: Victory of Mary Christopher, 1903; Mind of Methodism, 1905; A Man and His Money, 1914; Stewardship Starting Points, 1916; Ganga Dass, 1916; The Centenary at Old First, 1919; Ten Weeks, 1920; The Christian Renaissance, 1933. Home: Evanston, Ill. Died Feb. 16, 1941.

CALKINS, Lyman Darrow, clergyman; b. Brooklyn, N.Y., Jan. 13, 1845; s. Daniel O. and Lydia (Clark) C.; A.B., Williams, 1867, A.M., 1870; Union Theol. Sem., 1867-68; Princeton Theol. Sem., 1868-70; (D.D., Emporia Coll., Kan., 1900); m. Mary Hepburn Rankin, May 13, 1874. Ord. Presbyn. ministry, 1871; pastor Muncy, Pa., 1871-73, Park St. Congl. Ch., W. Springfield, Mass., 1873-83, Presbyn. Ch., S. Salem, N.Y., 1883-86, Trinity Presbyn. Ch., Brooklyn, 1886-89, Far Rockaway, 1890-1901; stated supply, Grace Ref. Episcopal Ch., Brooklyn, 1902-03, Ref. Ch. of Reconciliation, 1903-06, Presbyn. Ch., Newtown, 1906, Bay Ridge Ch., Brooklyn, 1906—. Republican. Home: Westfield, N.J. Died Feb. 18, 1917.

CALKINS, Mary Whiton, coll. prof.; b. Hartford, Conn., March 30, 1863; d. Wolcott and Charlotte Grosvenor (Whiton) C.; A.B., Smith Coll., 1885, A.M., 1887; student Clark U., 1890-91, Harvard, 1893-95; Litt.D., Columbia, 1909; LL.D., Smith 1910; unmarried. At Wellesley Coll., 1891—, becoming research prof. philosophy and psychology. Author: Introduction to Psychology, 1901, 1905; Der doppelte Standpunkt in der Psychologie, 1905; The Persistent Problems of Philosophy, 1907, 08, 17, 25; A First Book in Psychology, 1910, 14; The Good Man and the Good, 1918. Home: Newton, Mass. Died Feb. 27, 1930.

CALKINS, Ransom M., ry. official; b. Ogdensburg, N.Y., Aug. 12, 1863; s. James F. and Sarah C.; ed. pub. schs.; m. Corina Bell., Sept. 9, 1884. Began as clk. and telegraph operator, C.,M.&St.P. Ry., at Monticello, Ia., 1879; successively local agt., various points in Ia., 1881-92, agt. at Kansas City, Mo., 1892-96, div. freight and pass. agt. at Mason City, Ia., 1896-98, same rd.; gen. freight and pass. agt., Des Moines, Northern & Western Ry., at Des Moines, 1898-99; asst. gen. freight agt., C.,M.&St.P. Ry., at Chicago, 1899-1909; gen. freight and pass. agt., Chicago, Milwaukee & Puget Sound Ry. and Mont. R.R., at Butte, Mont., 1909-10; traffic mgr. Chicago, Milwaukee & Puget Sound Ry., 1910-13; traffic mgr. Puget Sound Lines, C.,M.&St.P. Ry., 1913-17; v.p. in charge of traffic, at Chicago, 1917-18, pres. Oct. 15, 1918, v.p., 1920-26, asst. to receiver, 1926—, C.,M.&St.P. Ry. Co. Mason. Died Dec. 4, 1932.

CALKINS, Wolcott, clergyman; b. Corning, N.Y., June 10, 1831; s. James and Sarah (Trowbridge) C.; A.B., Yale, 1856 (class valedictorian on presentation day, De Forest Gold Medal); Union Theol. Sem., 1859-60; U. of Halle, and travel in Europe, 1860-62; (D.D., Hamilton Coll., 1887); m. Charlotte Grosvenor Whiton, June 6, 1860; 1 dau., Mary Whiton C. Ordained Congl. ministry, 1862; pastor First Ch. of Christ, Hartford, Conn., 1862-64, Calvary Ch., Phila., 1864-66; preached to soldiers in Army of Potomac, 1865; pastor N. Presbyn. Ch., Buffalo, N.Y., 1866-80, Eliot Ch., Newton, Mass., 1880-95, Montvale Ch., Woburn, Mass., 1896—. Author: Life of Matthew W. Baldwin, Locomotive Builder, 1866; Keystones of Faith, 1888; Parables for Our Times, 1901. Home: Newton, Mass. Died Dec. 31, 1924.

CALL, Edward Payson, newspaper pub.; b. W. Cambridge, Mass., Nov. 2, 1855; s. Henry Edwin and Emily Payson (Call) C.; bro. of Annie Payson C.; ed. Brimmer Sch., Boston; m. Mary Marshall, Nov. 2, 1887. Pvt. sec. to late R. M. Pulsifer, pub. Boston Herald, 1875-82; advertising mgr. Boston Herald, 1884-88, Royal Baking Powder Co., 1888-93, Philadelphia Press, 1893-97; pub. the New York Evening Post, 1897-1902, New York Mail and Express, Oct. 1902-04, New York Commercial, 1904-07; mgr. The Daily Club, 1908-09; asst. business mgr. New York Times, 1909-13; business mgr. Jour. Commerce, 1913—. Home: Larchmont Manor, N.Y. Died May 19, 1919.

CALL, Manfred, M.D., educator; b. Richmond, Va., Dec. 17, 1876; s. Manfred and Sallie (Watt) C.; M.D., Med. Coll. of Va., 1899; grad. study Johns Hopkins, Mass. Hosp. and Good Samaritan Dispensary, N.Y.; m. Martha Amanda Clopton, Oct. 24, 1904; children—Manfred III, Elizabeth Somerville, John Daniel. Began practice at Richmond, Va., 1900; prof. clin. medicine, Med. Coll. of Va. Democrat. Presbyn. Home: Richmond, Va. Died Sept. 13, 1936.

CALL, Rhydon Mays, judge; b. Fernandina, Fla., Jan. 13, 1858; s. George William and Sarah (Stark) C.; B.L., Washington and Lee U., 1878; m. Ida Holmes, Apr. 11, 1887. Admitted to Va. bar, 1878, Fla. bar, 1881; judge 4th Jud. Circuit, Fla., 1893-1913; judge U.S. Dist. Court, Southern Dist. of Fla., Apr. 1, 1913—. Democrat. Baptist. Home: Jacksonville, Fla. Died 1928.

CALL, Wilkinson, senator; b. Russelville, Ky., Jan. 9, 1834. Went to Fla. in boyhood; served as adj. gen. in C.S.A. during Civil War; then in law practice at Jacksonville, Fla.; elected U.S. senator by Fla. Legislature, 1865, but was not seated; presdl. elector-at-large, 1872, 1876; mem. Dem. Nat. Exec. Com., 1876; U.S. senator, 1879-85, 1885-91, 1891-97. Died 1910.

CALLAHAN, Ethelbert, lawyer; b. Licking Co., O., Dec. 17, 1829; s. John and Margaret (Brown) C.; ed. pub. schs.; (LL.D., McKendree Coll., 1894); m. Mary Barlow Jones, June 27, 1854. Removed to Ill., 1849; editor Wabash (Ill.) Sentinel, 1853-54, Marshall (Ill.) Telegraph, 1854-55; admitted to bar, 1859, and then in practice at Robinson, Ill.; mem. Callahan, Jones & Lowe; also scientific farmer. Mem. 29th, 37th, 38th and 39th Ill. Gen. Assemblies; presdl. elector, 1880, 1886. Republican. Mason. Methodist. Home: Robinson, Ill. Died June 20, 1918.

CALLAHAN, Patrick Henry, varnish mfr.; b. Cleveland, O., Oct. 15, 1866; s. John Cormic and Mary Anna (Connolly) C.; ed. St. John's High Sch. and Spencerian Business Coll., Cleveland; m. Julia Laure Cahill, Jan. 20, 1891; children—John Mitchell, Robert Emmet, Edith Dee. With Glidden Varnish Co., Cleveland, 1886-92; sales mgr. Louisville Varnish Co., 1892, later pres. Served as col. on staffs of 2 govs. of Ky.; chmn. K.C. Com. of War Activities, World War; U.S. del. to Geneva Conf. on Alcoholism; v.p. Ky. Interracial Commn., Ky. Crime Commn.; mem. Nat. Exec. Coms. World's Alliance for Friendship, Catholic Com. for Internat. Peace, Catholic Industrial Conf., Nat. Catholic Charities Conf. (v.p.). Pres. Nat. Paint, Oil and Varnish Assn., 1913-14; treas. Louisville Grand Opera Assn., 1930-33, Reconstruction Finance Corp., Kentucky, 1933-34, Nat. Labor Relations Board, Kentucky, 1934-35. Decorated Order of Knight of St. Gregory by Pope Pius XI, 1922. Recipient of Newman Foundation Award, 1931. Vice chmn. World Fellowship of Faiths; trustee Ky. State Industrial Coll. Democrat. Catholic. Home: Louisville, Ky. Died Feb. 4, 1940.

CALLAN, John Gurney, univ. prof.; b. Northfield, Conn., Apr. 7, 1875; s. Michael John and Olive Rebecca (Gurney) C.; B.S. in E.E., Mass. Inst. Tech., 1896; m. Martha Towns Litchfield, July 25, 1900 (now dec.); children—Malcolm Frederic (dec.), Rosalie Dorothea (Mrs. Sven A. Baeckström), Priscilla Elsa Gurney (Mrs. Georges Lucien Houle), Hildegarde Muriel (Mrs. Donald T. Whittemore), John Gurney, Paul Litchfield. Began active career with the Edison Electric Illuminating Co., Boston, 1897, General Electric Company, experimental and engring. depts. and commercial engring., 1897-1909; mech. and elec. engr. of Arthur D. Little Co., Boston, 1909-15; prof. steam and gas engring., U. of Wis., 1915-20; prof. industrial management, Grad. Sch. of Business Administration, Harvard, 1920—, also consulting work. War work on investigation of marine Diesel engines in Great Britain, 1917-18. Chmn. Cotton Textile State Industrial Relations Bd. for Mass. Republican. Mem. Ch. of New Jerusalem (Swedenborgian). Has taken out about 70 patents, principally in connection with steam turbines. Home: Cambridge, Mass. Died Dec. 30, 1940.

CALLAN, Peter A., M.D., ophthalmologist; b. 1845; M.D., Univ. Med. Coll. (New York U.), 1867. House surgeon, Charity Hosp., 1867-68; asst. surgeon U.S. Navy, 1869-72; attending eye surgeon, Central Dispensary, 1874, Demilt Dispensary, 1877; formerly surgeon to N.Y. Eye and Ear Infirmary, now consulting surgeon; ophthalmologist to Columbus and St. Vincent's hosps.; pres. med. bd. St. Joseph's Hosp., Yonkers. Fellow Am. Coll. Surgeons. Home: Yonkers, N.Y. Died Oct. 1932.

CALLAN, Robert Emmet, army officer; b. Baltimore, Md., Mar. 24, 1874; s. Frank J. and Sarah (Riley) C.; grad. U.S. Mil. Acad., 1896; m. Margaret Valentine Kelly, Oct. 10, 1912. Commd. add. 2d lt. 5th Arty., June 12, 1896; promoted through grades to lt. col., July 19, 1916; col. (temp.), Aug. 5, 1917; brig. gen. N.A., Aug. 8, 1918; brig. gen. regular army, June 9, 1921, maj. gen., Apr. 1, 1931. In campaign, Western Puerto Rico, 1898; instr. mathematics, U.S. Mil. Acad., 1899-1903; mem. Torpedo Bd., Ft. Totten, 1904-07; asst. to chief of Coast Arty., 1907-12; comdr. Fort Andrews, Mass., 1912-14; pres. Coast Arty. Bd., Ft. Monroe, Va., 1914-15; duty Gen. Staff Corps, Philippine Dept., 1915-17; organized 65th Regt. Heavy Arty., and arrived in France in command of regt., Apr. 8, 1918; chief of staff of Army Arty., 1st Army, June-Aug. 1918; comdr. 33d Heavy Arty. Brig., Aug.-Dec. 1918; mem. Arty. Mission in France, Italy, Eng. and U.S. Jan.-May 1919; assigned duty with technical staff, Ordnance Dept., June 1, 1919. Grad. Army War Coll., June 1, 1921; comdg. 2d Coast Arty. Dist. Hdqrs., Ft. Totten, N.Y., July-Nov. 1921; comdg. Panama Coast Arty. Dist. Hdqrs., Ft. Amador, C.Z., 1921-24; comdg. Third Coast Arty. Dist., and Coast Arty. Sch., Ft. Monroe, Va., 1924-29; comdg. Hawaiian Separate Coast Arty. Brigade, hdqrs., Ft. De Russy, July 1929-Jan. 1931; asst. chief of staff, War Dept., Washington, Jan. 1931-Jan. 1935; comdg. 3d Corps Area, Hdqrs. Baltimore, Md., Feb. 18, 1935-Jan. 31, 1936; retired. Awarded D.S.M.; Commander Order of the Crown (Italy); Officer Legion of Honor (France). Catholic. Died Nov. 20, 1936.

CALLANDER, Cyrus N., surgeon; b. 1865; M.D., Trinity Med. Coll., Ontario, Can., 1897. Practiced at Fargo, N.D., 1899—; staff surgeon St. John's and St. Luke's hosps.; orthopedic surgeon Fargo Clinic. Fellow Am. Coll. Surgeons. Home: Fargo, N.D. Died July 1930.

CALLAWAY, Enoch Howard, lawyer; b. Wilkes County, Ga., July 19, 1862; s. Brantly Mercer and Lucy B. (Howard) C.; A.B., U. of Ga., 1881; m. Mary Eugenia Jones, Feb. 23, 1888 (died 1901); children—Mrs. Catherine Lee, Brantly, Mrs. Gena Merry. Admitted to Ga. bar, 1885; practiced, Waynesboro, 1885-97. then Augusta; in partnership with E. F. Lawson, 1886-93, with Hon. J. R. Lamar, 1905-11, when he became justice U.S. Supreme Court, with Congressman William M. Howard, 1914-31. Dem. presdl. elector on Cleveland ticket, 1888; mayor of Waynesboro, 1889; mem. Ga. State Senate, 1890-91; judge Superior Court, Augusta Circuit, 1895-99; mem. State Tax Commn., 1918-19. Trustee U. of Ga.; pres. bd. Med. Dept., U. of Ga.; trustee Mercer U., Macon, Ga. Baptist. Home: Augusta, Ga. Deceased.

CALLAWAY, Fuller Earle, cotton mfr.; b. La Grange, Ga., July 15, 1870; s. Abner Reeves and Sarah J. (Howard) C.; ed. pub. schs.; m. Ida J. Cason, Apr. 28, 1891. Began as porter in local dry goods store; established, on borrowed capital, 1888, a 5 and 10 cent store which developed into dept. store and wholesale dry goods business; entered cotton mfg., 1900; chmn. bd. Callaway's Dept. Stores, La Grange Nat. Bank, La Grange Savings Bank, La Grange Ins. Agency, Callaway Development Co., Manchester Development Co., Milstead Mfg. Co., Manchester Cotton Mills. and other cos.; chmn. bd. J. T. Perkins Co., Inc., Brooklyn, N.Y., and of Callaway Mills, Inc., New York. Asst. commissary gen. Ga. N.G., 1903-07, rank of lt. col.; railroad commr. of Ga., 1907, 08. Upon request of Franklin K. Lane, sec. of interior, undertook, 1917, with substantial results, to secure coöperation of mine owners and producers in Ga. and Ala. to increase production of pyrites; apptd. mem. governing bd. of field div. Council of Nat. Defense, Sept. 20, 1918, also spl. com. on higher edn.; chmn. Commn. on European Representation, World Cotton Conf., 1919, and now v.p. World Cotton Conf. for U.S.; represented the public as mem. Conf. on Industrial Relations, Washington, D.C., Oct. 1919; named by vote of Southern mill officials, Sept. 1921, as one of 7 leaders of Southern textile industry. Democrat. Baptist. Home: La Grange, Ga. Deceased.

CALLAWAY, Morgan, Jr., univ. prof.; b. Cuthbert, Ga., Nov. 3, 1862; s. Rev. Dr. Morgan and Eliza Mary (Hinton) C.; A.B., Emory Coll., Ga., 1881, A.M., 1884; Ph.D., Johns Hopkins, 1889; LL.D., Southern Methodist U., 1924; m. Loru Hamah Smith, Aug. 3, 1920. Adj. prof. English, Emory Coll., 1881-83; prof. English, Southwestern U., Tex., 1884-86 and 1889-90; univ. scholar, 1887-88, fellow, 1888-89, Johns Hopkins; asst. prof. English, 1890-91, adj. prof., 1891-93, asso. prof., 1893-98, prof., 1898—, faculty research lecturer, 1925, U. of Texas. Democrat. Methodist. Author: The Infinitive in Anglo-Saxon, 1913; Studies in the Syntax of the Lindisfarne Gospels, 1918; The Historic Study of the Mother-Tongue, 1925; The Temporal Subjunctive in Old English, 1931; The Consecutive Subjunctive in Old English, 1933. Editor: The Select Poems of Sidney Lanier, 1895. Home: Austin, Tex. Died Apr. 3, 1936.

CALLAWAY, Samuel Rodger, pres. of Am. Locomotive Co., June 1901—; b. Toronto, Ont., Dec. 24, 1850; entered service of Grand Trunk R.R., 1864; later in employ of Canadian Express Co. and Great Western Ry.; supt. Detroit & Milwaukee Ry., 1875; mgr. Chicago & Grand Trunk, 1880; v.p. Union Pacific, 1884; pres. Toledo, St. Louis & Kansas City Ry., 1887-95; pres., 1885, New York, Chicago & St. Louis; pres. Lake Shore & Mich. Southern, 1897-98; pres. N.Y. Central & Hudson River R.R., 1898-1901; dir. in numerous ry. and other corporations. Died 1904.

CALLBREATH, James Finch, sec. emeritus Am. Mining Congress; b. White Lake, Sullivan County, N.Y., Dec. 2, 1858; LL.B., U. of Denver, 1895; teacher pub. schs., 1877-80; editor Sullivan County (N.Y.) Republican, 1886-88; chmn. Sullivan County Rep. Com., 1887-90; gen. ins. business, 1888-92; editor and pub. Mining Reporter, Denver, 1894-1901; law practice, Denver, 1895-1906; mem. Denver Charter Conv., 1903; mem. Denver City Council, 1904-06; sec. Am. Mining Congress, 1904-34. Pres. Denver Chamber of Commerce, 1903-04. Mason. Home: Washington, D.C. Died Aug. 4, 1940.

CALLENDER, Edward Belcher, lawyer, author; b. Boston, Mass., Feb. 23, 1851; s. Henry and Adeline Jones (Stoddard) C.; A.B., Harvard, 1872; Harvard Law Sch., 1873-74; unmarried. Admitted to bar, 1875, practiced at Boston. Mem. Mass. Ho. of Rep., 1879, 1897, 1898, 1901, 1902, 1903, Senate, 1904, 1905. Republican. Author: Thaddeus Stevens—Commoner, 1882; The Leg Pullers, or Politics as She Is Applied, 1894; The Gigantic Meddler, 1901; Fugitive Poems, 1906. Home: Dorchester, Mass. Died Feb. 5, 1917.

CALLENDER, Guy Stevens, univ. prof.; b. Harts Grove, O., Nov. 9, 1865; s. Robert Foster and Lois (Winslow) C.; A.B., Oberlin Coll., 1891; A.B., Harvard, 1893, A.M., 1894, Ph.D., 1897; (hon. A.M., Yale, 1907); m. Harriet Rice, June 14, 1904. Instr. polit. economy, Wellesley Coll., 1895-96, Harvard, 1897-1900; Daniel B. Fayerweather prof. polit. economy and sociology, Bowdoin, 1900-03; prof. polit. economy, Yale, 1903—. Author: Selections From the Economic History of the United States, 1765-1850, 1909. Died Aug. 8, 1915.

CALLENDER, (William) Romaine, musician; b. South Shields, Eng., Aug. 16, 1857; s. Edwin and Jane (Carr) C.; ed. Wright pvt. sch. and Dr. Addison's coll. prep. sch.; studied science at Mechanics Inst., and Marine Sch., South Shields, and at Lit. and Philos. Inst., Newcastle-on-Tyne; studied piano, organ, harmony and composition under pvt. tutors; m. Ella Cordelia Andrews, Aug. 2, 1878. Came to Can., 1876, to U.S., 1889; editorial and publicity work for several yrs. with J. B. Lippincott Co., Phila.; also publicity work with Canadian rys. and Canadian Govt.; prin. Metropolitan Coll. of Music, Phila., 1900—. Formerly dir. Haydn Orchestral Soc. and conductor Brantford (Can.) Philharmonic Soc.; organist Grace Episcopal and Zion Presbyn. chs., Brantford. Episcopalian. Author: Teachers' Manual and Elementary Method (piano), 1911; Prison-Flower, Kermadec Romance (novels), 1912, etc.; composer pieces for organ, compiler and editor. Inventor of pneumatic and electric organ actions, automatic telephone exchange system, autographic piano recording and reproducing apparatus, etc. Home: Philadelphia, Pa. Died July 1, 1930.

CALLENDER, Walter Reid, merchant; b. Providence, R.I., Feb. 28, 1872; s. Walter and Ann Oswald (Crow) C.; grad. high sch., Providence, 1890; A.B., Yale, 1894, A.M., 1897; m. Mrs. Ivy Lee Edinger, Feb. 10, 1927. Began in merchandising business with Brown, Thomson & Co., Hartford, Conn., 1894; mem. Callender, McAuslan & Troup Co., dept. store, 1897—, pres. and treas., 1921—; sec. and treas. Boston Store Land Co. Police commr., Providence, 1910-13. Trustee R.I. Hosp., Providence Pub. Library. Conglist. Home: Providence, R.I. Died Apr. 29, 1932.

CALLERY, James Dawson, street ry. pres., mfr.; b. Pittsburgh, Nov. 11, 1857; s. James and Rose (Downing) C.; m. Marcella Hawley (died 1899); m. 2d, Julia W. Callery, June 4, 1902; children—William, Francis A., George Lewis, Mrs. Marcella Heron, Mrs. Frederic R. Coudert, Jr. Began business life in his father's leather mfg. business; became identified with street ry. interests in Pittsburgh and Allegheny; then chmn. bd. Pittsburgh Rys. Co.; pres. Diamond Nat. Bank; mem. exec. com. Phila. Co., Duquesne Light Company. Home: Pittsburgh, Pa. Died May 1932.

CALLEY, Walter, clergyman; b. Dover, Del., Aug. 19, 1858; s. Manlove H. and Elizabeth Brown (England) C.; ed. Belford Lit. Inst. and by pvt. tutors; grad. Crozer Theol. Sem., 1880; (D.D., Denison U., 1903); m. Florence Morgey, June 1880 (died 1888); children—Walter E. (dec.), Donald M.; m. 2d, Alice R. Huston, June 1890 (died 1896); children—Alice C. (wife of Dr. Thomas E. Jones), Charles H. (dec.); m. 3d, Irene Hopkins, Feb. 3, 1898 (died 1917); 1 son Francis D.; m. 4th, Eva Brantly Helm, Dec. 2, 1925. Ordained Baptist ministry, 1880; pastor Bethlehem, Pa., 1880-82, Lehigh Av. Church, Phila., 1882-91, Emmanuel Church, Cambridge, Mass., 1891-93, Tabernacle Church, Boston (noted institutional ch.), 1893-1902, Upland Ch. (at seat of Crozer Theol. Sem.), 1905-09, First Ch., Jamaica Plain, Boston, 1909-Oct. 1, 1917. Spl. student of penology and sociology; 5 yrs. mem. Bd. State Visitors for Prisons of Pa. One of founders Prospect Union Instn. for edn. of workingmen, in connection with Harvard U. Gen. sec. Bapt. Young People's Union America, and mng. editor of Service (official organ), 1902-05. Author: Great Christian Truths; What Jesus Taught. Home: Cambridge, Mass. Died Dec. 21, 1928.

CALLISTER, Edward Henry, publisher; b. Salt Lake City, Utah, Dec. 29, 1862; s. Edward and Ann (Cowley) C.; common sch. edn.; m. Louisa J. Eddington, Sept. 6. 1888. Began in printing business Salt Lake City, 1878; gen. mgr. Herald-Republican Pub. Co. (pub. of The Herald-Republican), Sept. 1913—. Mem. City Council, Salt Lake City, 1896-1900; chmn. Rep. State Central Com., 1900; U.S. internal revenue collector for Dist. of Mont. (Utah, Ida. and Mont.), July 13, 1901—. Mormon. Home: Lake City, Utah. Died Nov. 23, 1917.

CALLOW, John Michael, mining engr., metallurgist; b. Northrepps, Norwich, Norfolk, Eng., July 7, 1867; s. Michael John and Emily (Neave) C.; ed. in England; came to U.S., 1890; m. Roberta More, 1893; children—Bessie Roberta, Margaret Roper More, Francis Marie, Michael John. Engr. and draftsman with Stearns, Roger Mfg. Co., 1892-93; engr. Metallic Extraction Co., 1894; operating mines and mills in San Juan Co., Colo., 1895-96; on engring. staff Samuel Newhouse, 1898-1901; pvt. practice, 1901-06, inventing Callow settling tank and Callow traveling belt screen; pres. and mgr. Gen. Engineering Co., New York, 1906—; designed and built 500-ton plant for Nat. Copper Co., Mullan, Ida., installing pneumatic flotation cells, 1912; designing and constrn. engr., Mt. Isa Mines, Australia, 1928-31. Originator of pneumatic flotation in treatment of ores; awarded 18 patents. Awarded Douglas medal by Am. Inst. Mining and Metall. Engrs., 1925, for achievements in non-ferrous metallurgy. Mason. Episcopalian. Died July 27, 1940.

CALLOWAY, Alfred W., coal operator; b. Manchester, Eng., June 21, 1872; s. Charles William and Alice (Woodward) C.; brought to U.S., 1882; ed. pub. schs., Brooklyn, N.Y.; m. Mary B. Henshey, Nov. 15, 1893. Began as rodman Cresson div., Pa. R.R., 1888; asst. supt., later gen. mgr., Rochester & Pittsburgh Coal & Iron Co., and affiliated cos., Punxsutawney, Pa., 1893-1913; pres. Davis Coal & Coke Co., Baltimore, Md., 1913—, Buffalo & Susquehanna Coal & Coke Co., 1925—; also pres. Pittsburgh Terminal Coal Co., 1917-23; chmn. bd. Buxton & Landstreet Co. Dir. bituminous coal distribution under Fuel Administration, Feb. 1918-July 1919. Republican. Baptist. Home: Merion, Pa. Died Sept. 13, 1926.

CALTHROP, Samuel Robert, clergyman; b. Swineshead Abbey, Lincolnshire, Eng., Oct. 9, 1829; ed. St. Paul's Sch., London, and Cambridge U.; (L.H.D.). Came to U.S., 1853; ordained Unitarian ministry, 1860. Author: Experimental Theology and Experimental Religion; God in His World, 1905; The Supreme Reality. Home: Syracuse, N.Y. Died 1917.

CALVE, Emma, operatic singer; b. France, 1866; convent edn.; m. Alnor Gaspari, Mar. 1910. Début 1882, at Théâtre de la Monnaie, Brussels (Massenet's "Herodiade"), 1882; first appeared in Paris in "Aben Hamet," 1884; as Carmen and as Santuzza, in "Cavalleria Rusticana," at the Opera Comique; sang in same Covent Garden, London, 1892; came to Met. Opera House, New York, 1893, as Carmen; retired from stage, 1910. Home: Aveyron, France. Died Jan. 6, 1942.

CALVERLEY, Charles, sculptor; b. Albany, N.Y., Nov. 1, 1833; ed. there; moved to New York, 1868. Has executed many groups and figures; specially noted for portrait busts, in bronze, of Horace Greeley, John Brown, Peter Cooper, Elias Howe, etc. A.N.A., 1872, N.A., 1875. Home: Caldwell, N.J. Died Feb. 26, 1914.

CALVERT, John Betts, editor; b. Preble, Cortland County, N.Y., Aug. 29, 1852; s. James Alexander and Olive Adaline (Betts) C.; A.B., U. of Rochester, 1876, A.M., 1879; grad. Union Theol. Sem., 1879; D.D., Shurtleff, 1894, Colgate, 1915; m. Mary Dows Mairs, Dec. 10, 1885. Prin. high sch., McLean, N.Y., 1871-72; licensed to preach, 1875; ordained Baptist ministry, 1880; asst. pastor Calvary Bapt. Ch., New York, 1881-87; bought Baptist Weekly, 1888, changed name to Christian Inquirer, of which was pres. and one of editors, until it consolidated with the Examiner, 1895; became stockholder of the Examiner Co. and one of editors of the Examiner until 1912. Corr. sec., 1879-86, pres. 1886-1907, Bapt. Missionary Conv. of N.Y. Trustee U. of Rochester from 1899, of Cook Acad., 1900-10 (pres. bd. 1905-10); pres. Inst. of Applied Music, 1910—. Author: The Impartial Christ, 1915; Men Who Have Meant Much to Me, 1918; Ministering in a Wide Field, 1922. Home: Irvington-on-Hudson, N.Y. Died Jan. 13, 1928.

CALVERT, Thomas Elwood, engr.; b. near Phila., Pa., Sept. 10, 1849; s. Isaac and Phoebe (Rhodes) C.; Ph.B., Yale, 1870; widower. Began ry. service in engring. dept. of C.,B.&Q. R.R., 1871, and was supt. lines west of the Mo. River, 1875-1905, and chief engr. of the entire system, 1905—. Republican. Home: Chicago, Ill. Died Dec. 19, 1916.

CALVERTON, Victor Francis (George Goetz), writer, lecturer; b. Baltimore, Md., June 25, 1900; s. Charles and Ida Janette (Geiger) C.; student Baltimore City Coll.; A.B., Johns Hopkins, 1921; unmarried. Founder, 1923, and editor The Modern Quarterly (now The Modern Monthly); editor dept. of book review of Book League Monthly; lit. editor Ray Long and Richard R. Smith, Inc. Author: The

Newer Spirit, 1925; Sex Expression in Literature, 1926; The Bankruptcy of Marriage, 1928; Three Strange Lovers (a trilogy), 1929; The New Ground of Criticism, 1930; American Literature at the Crossroads, 1931; The Liberation of American Literature, 1931; For Revolution, 1932; The Passing of the Gods, 1934; The Man Inside (novel), 1936; The Awakening of America, 1939; Where Angels Dared to Tread, 1939; Between Two Wars, 1940. Editor of An Anthology of American Negro Literature, 1929; The Making of Man, 1931. Co-editor: Sex in Civilization, 1929; The New Generation, 1930; Woman's Coming of Age, 1931; The Making of Society, 1937. Author of monthly dept. "The Cultural Barometer" in Current History (mag.); author bi-monthly dept. in Hollywood Tribune (mag.). Home: Baltimore, Md. Died Nov. 20, 1940.

CALVIN, Edgar Eugene, ry. official; b. Indianapolis, Ind., Oct. 16, 1858; s. Newton and Aseneth C.; ed. pub. schs.; m. Alida Frances Man, Sept. 15, 1881. Telegraph operator Indianapolis, Cincinnati & Lafayette R.R., 1875-76; telegraph operator and sta. agt., 1877-82; train dispatcher, conductor and trainmaster, 1882-87, U.P. Ry.; div. supt. Mo. P. Ry., 1887-91; supt. Ida. div. U.P. Ry., 1891-95; gen. supt. I.&G.N. RR., 1895-97; gen. supt., 1897-1903, asst. gen. mgr., 1903-04, Ore. Short Line R.R.; v.p. and gen. mgr. Ore. R.R. & Navigation Co., 1904-05; v.p. and gen. mgr. S.P. Co., 1905-13, also v.p. constrn. and operation same company, and v.p. and gen. mgr. O.S.L. R.R., 1913-16; elected pres. U.P. R.R., July 1, 1916; apptd. federal mgr. L.A.&S.L. R.R., O.,P.& E. Ry., St. Joseph & Grand Island Ry., St. Joseph Terminal R.R.; Salina Northern R.R., U.P. R.R., O.S.L. R.R.; v.p. U.P. System Lines, Mar. 1920—. Died Mar. 17, 1938.

CALVIN, Samuel, geologist; b. Wigtonshire, Scotland, Feb. 2, 1840; s. Thomas and Elizabeth C.; came to U.S. at 11; attended Lenox Coll., Hopkinton, Ia., but did not graduate on account of enlistment in Union Army, 1864; (hon. A.M., 1875, LL.D., 1904, Cornell Coll., Ia.; Ph.D., Lenox, 1888); m. M. Louise Jackson, Sept. 5, 1865. Prof. geology, State U. of Ia., 1874—, State geologist of Ia., 1892-1904, and 1906—; one of editors Am. Geologist, 1888-1905; mem. Nat. Advisory Bd. on Fuels and Structural Materials. Home: Iowa City, Ia. Died 1911.

CALVO, Joaquin Bernardo, diplomat; b. San José, Costa Rica, July 10, 1857; ed. San José; m. María de León, June 24, 1881. Founded 1st daily paper in Costa Rica, 1885; mem. War Claims Commn., 1885; gov. province of Cartago, 1886; sec. Costa Rica delegation to Internat. Am. Conf., Washington, 1889; del. to the Monetary Conf. and chargé d'affaires of Costa Rica at Washington, 1892; sec. Costa Rica Commn. to World's Fair, Chicago, 1893; minister of Costa Rica to U.S., 1896—, and to Mexico, 1908—. Del. of Costa Rica to 2d Internat. Am. Conf., Mex., 1901-02; del. Central Am. Peace Conf., 1907. Catholic. Died Nov. 22, 1915.

CALWELL, Charles Sheridan, banker; b. Philadelphia, Pa., Oct. 16, 1871; s. James Madison and Mary (Kilpatrick) C.; ed. pub. sch. and Central High Sch.; m. Eleanor Parker. Pres. Corn Exchange Nat. Bank, Phila., 1910—. Republican. Unitarian. Died May 6, 1932.

CAMAC, Charles Nicoll Bancker, M.D.; b. Phila., Pa., Aug. 6, 1868; s. William and Ellen (McIlvaine) C.; A.B., U. of Pa., 1892, M.D., 1895; student, Guy's Hosp. Med. Sch., London, 1893; Johns Hopkins U. Med. Sch., grad. studies, 1895-97; m. Julia Augusta Metcalfe, Nov. 17, 1897; m. 2d, Christie M. Fraser, May 25, 1935. Instr. physiology, U. of Pa., 1895; asst. resident phys., Johns Hopkins Hosp., 1896-97; organizer and dir. lab. of clin. pathology, 1899-1905, instr. physical diagnosis, chief of med. clinic, lecturer in medicine, 1905-09, prof. clin. medicine, 1909-10, Cornell U. Med. Coll., New York; asst. prof. clin. medicine, College Physicians and Surgeons (Columbia), 1910-38; visiting phys., 1899-1916, cons. physician, 1916-35, N.Y. City Hospital; cons. physician, N.Y. Polyclinic Hosp. and Med. Sch., 1934-36 (emeritus prof. medicine). During World War served as physician in American War Hospital, England, and Ocean Ambulance Hospital, Belgium; chmn. Physicians, Surgeons and Dentists Fund for purchase of hosp. instruments and equipment for French mil. hosps., 1916; med. dir. Gouverneur Hosp. of the Bellevue and Allied hosps., N.Y. City, 1916-23; cons. phys., 1923—. Commissioned 1st lt. Med. R.C., Apr. 1917; student officer, Camp Greenleaf, Ft. Oglethorpe, Ga., and Sch. of Gas Defense, Ft. Sill, Okla.; apptd. instr. in gas defense, Inf. Sch. of Arms, U.S. Army, Ft. Sill, Okla., Sept. 1917; promoted maj., Med. R.C., Oct. 1917; apptd. med. chief U.S. Army Gen. Hosp. No. 6, Ft. McPherson, Ga., Oct. 1917; apptd. dir. Officers' Training Sch., Ft. McPherson, Apr. 1918; promoted lt. col. M.C., Nov. 1918; apptd. med. chief Gen. Hosp. No. 38, Eastview, N.Y., Jan. 1919; hon. disch., July 1919. Author: Imhotep to Harvey—The Backgrounds of the History of Medicine, 1931. Home: Altadena, Calif. Died Sept. 27, 1940.

CAMDEN, Johnson Newlon, capitalist; b. Lewis County, Va., Mar. 6, 1828; 2 yrs. at West Point; practiced law and was pros. atty., 1851-56, and with Exchange Bank of Va., Weston, 1854-57, holding both positions at same time; identified with 1st petroleum operations of W.Va.; organized Camden Consolidated Oil Co., afterward merged in Standard Oil Co.; was dir. Standard Oil Co.; pres. Monongahela River R.R. and W.Va. and Pittsburgh R.R.; pres. 1st Nat. Bank of Parkersburgh, 1862—. Was defeated for gov., W.Va., 1872; U.S. senator from W.Va., 1881-87, 1893-95. Democrat. Home: Parkersburgh, W.Va. Died 1908.

CAMERON, Edward Herbert, psychologist; b. Yarmouth, N.S., Can., Jan. 24, 1875; s. William Jack and Mary Eliza (Allen) C.; grad. N.S. Normal Sch., Truro, N.S., Can., 1894; B.A., Acadia U., Wolfville, N.S., 1900; B.A., Yale, 1903, Ph.D., 1906; m. Annie Louise O'Donnell, 1906; children—Winifred Wesley, Mary Louise. Teacher pub. schs., N.S., 5 yrs.; came to U.S., 1902, naturalized citizen, 1916; instr. psychology 1906-10, asst. prof., 1910-14, asst. prof. edn., 1914-20, Yale; prof. ednl. psychology, U. of Ill., 1920—, and dir. summer session same, 1931—. Baptist. Author: Psychology and the School, 1921; Educational Psychology, 1927. Home: Urbana, Ill. Died Dec. 20, 1938.

CAMERON, Henry Clay, educator; b. Shepherdstown, Va., Sept. 1, 1827; s. John and Anna (McFall) C.; grad. Princeton, 1847 (A.M., 1850; Ph.D., 1866) Princeton Theol. Sem., 1855; D.D., Rutgers Coll. and Wooster Univ., 1875; m. Mina Chollet (niece Prof. A. Guyot), Sept. 14, 1858. Connected with Greek dept., Princeton, 1852—; prof. Greek, 1855-1902; emeritus prof., 1902—; instr. in Latin for a time and in French, 1859-70; attended lectures at U. of Paris and Coll. of France, 1857-58. In addition to Greek chair was librarian, 1865-72; editor of gen. catalogue, 1866-86; clerk of the faculty, 1882-1902. Ordained to Presbyn. ministry, 1863; 3 times mem. Gen. Assembly Presbyn. Ch. Mem. Bd. of Visitors U.S. Mil. Acad.; chaplain at West Point 2 summers. Author: The History of the American Whig Society; Old Princeton, Its Battle, Its Cannon, Etc. Died 1906.

CAMERON, James Donald, sec. of war; b. Middletown, Pa., May 14, 1833; s. Simon C. (U.S. senator and sec. of war in President Lincoln's cabinet); A.B., Princeton, 1852, A.M., 1855; m. Mary McCormick, (died 1874); m. 2d, 1878, Elizabeth, d. Judge Sherman, of Ohio and niece of Gen. W. T. Sherman. Clerk, cashier, and then pres. Nat. Bank of Middletown; pres. Northern Central R.R. Co., of Pa., 1863-74; had large coal, iron and mfg. interests. Sec. of War in cabinet of President Grant, May 22, 1876-Mar. 3, 1877; elected U.S. senator, 1877, for unexpired term of his father, resigned, and reëlected, serving until 1897; del. Rep. Nat. Convs., 1868, 1880; chmn. Rep. Nat. Com., 1880. Home: Harrisburg, Pa. Died Aug. 30, 1918.

CAMERON, John M., lawyer; b. Ottawa, Can., Sept. 18, 1867; s. Neil and Mary (McRae) C.; LL.D., Carthage (Ill.) Coll.; m. Anna M. Iverson, Jan. 1, 1895 (died 1917); children—Alan Campbell, Juliette Alice (dec.), Anita Cecelia (Mrs. Christian Sorensen). Lived in Chicago, 1869-95, Riverside, Ill., 1895—; admitted Ill. bar, 1889, practicing at Chicago; mem. Cameron & Heath; dir. Chicago Crime Commn., Citizens Assn. of Chicago. Trustee Village of Riverside, 1901-05, pres. board, 1905-09; pres. Board Edn. Riverside-Brookfield High Sch., 1920-32. Republican. Episcopalian. Home: Riverside, Ill. Died Jan. 2, 1939.

CAMERON, Roderick William, shipping merchant; b. Glengarry Co., Canada, July 25, 1825; ed. in dist. school at Kingston; chartered a ship, 1852, at New York, in which a party of young Canadians made a voyage to Australia; established as shipping merchant; then head of R. W. Cameron & Co., New York, with branches in London and Sydney, N.S.W.; was Union volunteer in 79th N.Y. vols., 1861; has remained a British subject; hon. commr. from Australia to Centennial Expn., 1876; from Canada to Sydney Expn., 1879; and Melbourne Expn., 1880; knighted, 1883; widower. Home: New York, N.Y. Died 1900.

CAMERON, William Evelyn, governor; b. at Petersburg, Va., Nov. 29, 1842; s. Walker Anderson and Elizabeth Byrd (Walker) C.; ed. Petersburg Classical Acad., N.C. Mil. Acad., Washington U., St. Louis; graduation prevented by Civil War; m. Louisa Clara Egerton, Oct. 1, 1868. In C.S.A. from May, 1861; served pvt. to asst. adj. gen. in all battles of Lee's army from Seven Pines to fall of the Confederacy; wounded at 2d Manassas; surrendered at Appomattox. Edited leading newspapers in Va., 1866-76; admitted to bar, 1876. Mayor of Petersburg, 1876-82; governor of Va., 1882-86; mem. Constl. Conv., 1891-92. Democrat. Author: Life and Character of Robert E. Lee, 1902; History of the Chicago Exposition, 1903; The World's Fair, 1904. Now editor-in-chief The Virginian-Pilot, Norfolk, Va. Home: Norfolk, Va. Died Jan. 26, 1927.

CAMINETTI, Anthony, commr. gen. immigration; b. Jackson, Calif., July 30, 1854; s. Rocco and Ballestina (Giusto) C.; ed. at Jackson, Oakland and San Francisco; m. Ella E. Martin, May 28, 1881. Admitted to Calif. bar, 1877; dist. atty., Amador Co., Calif., 1877-82; mem. Calif. Assembly, 25th, 32d and 33d sessions; State Senate, 27th and 28th sessions; mem. Congress, 1891-95; presdl. elector on Cleveland ticket, 1888; del. Dem. Nat. Conv., 1896; received vote of his party for U.S. Senator (15th ballot) at 33d session Calif. legislature, 1899; apptd. commr. gen. of immigration. Author of the law known as the "Caminetti Law," passed by Congress, 1893, under which hydraulic mining was resumed in Calif., and chmn. of Calif. commn. for the revision and reform of the law. Died Nov. 17, 1923.

CAMMACK, Ira Insco, educator; b. Hamilton Co., Ind., Feb. 16, 1858; s. James and Edith (Pearson) C.; B.S., Earlham Coll., 1884; post-grad. work, summers, U. of Chicago, Columbia, U. of Calif., Stanford; m. Lulu King Dove, Apr. 3, 1886; children—Edith (wife of Dr. F. C. Touton, v.p., U. So. Calif.), Harriett (dec.). Prin. Union High Sch., Westfield, Ind., 1885-86, Lathrop Elementary Sch., 1886-97; asst. prin. Central High Sch., 1897-1901; prin. Central High Sch., 1901-11; asst. supt. schs., 1911-13, supt. schs., 1913-28, supt. emeritus, 1928—, all in pub. schs. of Kansas City, Mo. Introduced sch. gardens; special schs. for atypical and underprivileged children; industrial schs. for both boys and girls; sch. nurses; dental service, etc. Established Jr. High schs.; Jr. Coll.; Teachers' Coll. to prepare resident students for Kansas City schs., and to provide extension professional courses for teachers in service. Mem. Friends' Ch. (Quaker). Mason. Home: Los Angeles, Calif. Died Sept. 1939.

CAMMACK, James William, lawyer; b. nr. English, Ind., July 15, 1869; s. William Butler and Elizabeth (Franks) C.; B.S., Nat. Normal U., Lebanon, O., 1891; law study, same, 1892, and summer sch. 2 terms, U. of Mich.; m. Nellie Allen, Apr. 27, 1898; children—Allen Berriman, Eleanor Ray, James William, Emma Louise (Mrs. J. Davis), Lawrence Dowe, Marjorie (dec.), Owen Floyd, Edward Jackson. Began practice at Owenton, Ky., 1892. Mem. Ky. State Senate, 1904-07; circuit judge, 15th Jud. Dist., Ky., 1907-16, atty. gen. of Kentucky for term 1928-32. Mem. bd. regents Eastern Ky. State Normal Sch. and Teachers Coll. Democrat. Baptist. Mason. Home: Owenton, Ky. Died Feb. 5, 1939.

CAMP, Charles Wadsworth, author; b. Phila., Pa., Oct. 18, 1879; s. Charles Henry and Emma (Martin) C.; A.B., Princeton, 1902; m. Madeleine Barnett, Dec. 27, 1906; 1 dau., Madeleine Lengle. Reporter and corr., New York Evening Sun, 1902-05; editorial dept., McClure's Mag., 1905-06; mng. editor, Met. Mag., 1906-09; corr. in Europe for Collier's Weekly, 1916. Formerly mem. Co. H, 7th Regt. N.G.N.Y.; grad. 1st O.T.C., Plattsburg, N.Y., 1917; 2d lt., 305th F.A.; participated in Vosges and Oise-Aisne campaigns; hon. disch., May 10, 1919. Episcopalian. Author: Guarded Heights, 1921; Hidden Road, 1922; The Communicating Door, 1923; The Barbarian, 1925; Forbidden Years, 1930; (play) Evil Tongues, prod. by W. A. Brady, New York, 1915; dramatization of The M. K. Curse, prod. at Grand Guignol, Paris, 1923. Died Oct. 31, 1936.

CAMP, David Nelson, educator, retired; b. Durham, Conn., Oct. 3, 1820; s. Elah and Orit (Lee) C.; ed. Hartford Acad. and under pvt. tutors; A.M., Yale, 1853; m. Sarah Adaline Howd, June 25, 1844 (died 1883). Teacher and supt. in pub. schs., Conn., for many yrs. and lect. teachers' insts.; was prin. Conn. Normal Sch., state supt. schs., Conn., 1856 to 1866; prof. geography, history and mental philosophy, St. John's Coll., Annapolis, Md., 1867-69; mem. Conn. Ho. of Rep., 1889-90; pres. New Britain Inst., Congl. Missionary Soc. of Conn.; trustee City Library, New Britain; v.p. New Britain Nat. Bank. Republican. Author: Globe Manual, 1864; American Year Book, 1869; History of New Britain, 1889. Home: New Britain, Conn. Died Oct. 19, 1916.

CAMP, Irving Luzerne; b. Waterbury, Conn., Sept. 2, 1879; s. Luzerne M. and Julia Crosby (Hitchcock) C.; grad. Wilbraham (Mass.) Acad., 1900; m. Gertrude Pease, Oct. 9, 1902; 1 son, Irving Luzerne. Began as clk. with father in retail coal business, 1900; with Frank Miller Coal Co., Waterbury, until 1903; salesman, Dickson & Eddy, N.Y. City, 1903-16; treas. Martin-Camp Co., 1916-17, pres., 1917; treas. McCann-Camp Co. (reorgn. of same co.), 1918; organizer, 1920, and pres. Producers Coal & Coke Co. until 1932; was organizer, 1923, and pres. Camp-Osgood-Sleppy, Inc., and of Winder Coal Mining Co. and served as pres. Lehigh Coal Co.; retired from coal business, 1932; Civil Service Commr., New Rochelle, N.Y., 4 yrs. Dir. Conemaugh Valley Memorial Hosp., Johnstown Asso. Charities, Johnstown Council Boy Scouts of America. Republican. Methodist. Mason. Home: Johnstown, Pa. Died Sept. 25, 1934.

CAMP, Walter, author; b. New Haven, Conn., Apr. 7, 1859; A.B., Yale, 1880, A.M.; m. Miss

Sumner, sister of Wm. G. Sumner. Chmn. bd. New Haven Clock Co.; dir. Peck Bros. Co. Trustee, Hopkins Grammar Sch. Author: The Substitute, Jack Hall of Yale; Old Ryerson; Danny Fists; Captain Danny; Danny the Freshman; Bridge Don'ts; Auction Bridge Don'ts; Auction Bridge Up to Date; Pocket Bridge Book; Book of College Sports; American Football; Football Facts and Figures; Football; Yale, Her Campus, Class-Room and Athletics; Drives and Puts (with Lillian Brooks), 1899; Keeping Fit All the Way; Athletes All; Training for Sports; Handbook of Health. Home: New Haven, Conn. Died Mar. 4, 1925.

CAMPANARI, Giuseppe, operatic baritone; b. Venice, Italy, Nov. 17, 1858; s. of Antonio and Louiga (de Bazan) C.; played 'cello at La Scala, Milan; engaged by Boston Symphony Orchestra, 1884, and took up vocal studies in America; m. Edvige Ziffer, of Trieste, 1880. Sang title rôle in "Faust," with Emma Yuch Opera Co.; later engaged by Walter Damrosch for series of concerts in New York; with Hinrich's Opera Co., Phila., creating the part of Tonio, in "Il Pagliacci"; with Maurice Grau Opera Co., New York, and for many yrs., a leading singer of Metropolitan Opera Co.; has appeared in the prin. opera houses of Europe and frequently on tours in U.S. Home: New York, N.Y. Died May 31, 1927.

CAMPANINI, Cleofonte, musical dir.; b. Parma, Italy, Sept. 1, 1860; studied at Royal Conservatory, Parma; m. Eva Tetrazzini, of Florence, Italy, May 15, 1887. First conducted at Parma, 1881; reputation spread rapidly through Italy, later Europe and S. America; prin. condr. Royal Opera, Covent Garden, London, during its most fruitful and artistic period, 1897-1906; first came to America, 1883; dir. Manhattan Opera Co., New York, 1906-09; gen. mus. dir. Chicago and Phil. opera cos., 1910-13, gen. mgr., 1913—; notable in productions of "Salome," "Natoma," "The Secret of Susanne," "Cendrillon," "Le Jongleur de Notre Dame," "Thaïs," "Louise," "Pelleas et Melisande," "Samson and Delilah," "Dejanire," "Cleopatre," "Monna Vanna," etc. Hon. citizen of Parma, and recipient of many orders from crowns of Italy, Austria, Spain and Portugal, also from govts. of Brazil and Argentina. Mason. Home: Parma, Italy. Died Dec. 19, 1919.

CAMPAU, Daniel J., lawyer; b. Detroit, Mich., Aug. 20, 1852; s. Daniel J. and Mary (Palms) C.; ed. Fordham, N.Y.; married. Admitted to bar, 1879; practiced 20 yrs.; devoted time to real estate holdings. Collector customs, Detroit, 1886-90; chmn. Dem. State Central Com., Mich., 1890; mem. Dem. Nat. Com., Mich., for many yrs. and chmn. campaign com. same, 1906. Home: Grosse Pointe Farms, Mich. Died Oct. 5, 1927.

CAMPBELL, Albert James, lawyer; b. Dec. 12, 1857; ed. at Agrl. Coll., Lansing, Mich.; m. Ella J. Mann, Apr. 23, 1879. Admitted to bar, 1881; pros. atty. of Lake County, Mich., 3 yrs.; city atty. of Livingstone, Mont., 1 yr.; elected to Mont. legislature, 1896; mem. Congress from Mont., 1899-1901. Democrat. Home: Butte, Mont. Died 1907.

CAMPBELL, Alfred Hills, educator; b. Litchfield, N.H., Sept. 28, 1850; s. Smith and Sophia (Hills) C.; grad. Bridgewater (Mass.) Normal Sch., 1870, McCollum Inst., Mt. Vernon, N.H., 1872; A.B., Dartmouth, 1877, A.M., 1880; Ph.D., U. of Vt., 1888; Univs. of Leipzig and Jena, 1895-96; m. Hattie E. Winchester, 1877; m. 2d, Marian E. Blake, July 20, 1893. Taught in elementary schs., 1870-72; prin. Kingston (N.H.) Acad., 1877-79; asso. prin. Cushing Acad., Ashburnham, Mass., 1879-84; prin. Johnson (Vt.) Normal Sch., 1884-95, Plymouth (N.H.) Normal Sch., 1896-1900; supt. schs., S. Hadley, Mass., 1900-04, Glastonbury, Conn., 1904-07; prin. Campbell Sch. for Girls, 1903—; 1st v.p. and dean Home Corr. Sch., Springfield, Mass., and prin., Normal Dept., 1907—. Mgr. Am. Teachers' Agency, 1908-17; pres. White Mountain Summer Sch. for Teachers, 1889. Republican. Conglist. Home: Windsor, Conn. Deceased.

CAMPBELL, Charles Atwood, prof. Biblical lit.; b. De Soto, Ia., June 18, 1872; s. Rev. William and Emma Charlotte (Atwood) C.; B.S., Kan. State Agrl. Coll., 1891; grad. study Emporia (Kan.) Coll., 1892-93; grad. Auburn (N.Y.) Theol. Sem., 1896; D.D., U. of Denver, 1908; m. Caroline V. Lovell, June 18, 1896. With Kan. State Expt. Sta. and U.S. Biol. Survey, 1891-92; instr. in logic and rhetoric, Auburn Theol. Sem., 1894-95; ordained ministry Presbyn. Ch., 1896; pastor successively, Providence, R.I., Philadelphia, Denver, Colo., Dayton, O., 1896-1917; pastor 1st Presbyn. Ch., Elizabeth, N.J., 1917-26; lecturer and instr., Summer Student Confs., 1903-19; prof. Bibl. lit. and instr. in entomology, also dean of Knowles Memorial Chapel, Rollins Coll., Winter Park, Fla., 1926—. Author: Handbook in Entomology, 1927; Traditions of Hartwood, 1929. Home: Winter Park, Fla., and Hartwood, N.Y. Died Jan. 7, 1939.

CAMPBELL, Charles Diven, prof. music; b. Anderson, Ind., Aug. 3, 1877; s. David Wallace and Mary Anna (Diven) C.; Heidelberg Coll., Germany, 1894-96, U. of Heidelberg, 1896-97; A.B., Ind. U., 1898; U. of Strassburg, Germany, 1900-05, Ph.D., 1905; Harvard, 1905-06; m. Marion Elizabeth Grimes, Aug. 15, 1917. Instr. German, 1906-08, prof., 1908-10, asso. prof. music, 1910—, also head dept. of music, Ind. U. Composer and dir. music for Ind. centennial pageants, at Indianapolis, Bloomington and Corydon, 1916. Home: Bloomington, Ind. Died Mar. 29, 1919.

CAMPBELL, Chester I., dir. industrial expns.; b. Providence, R.I., May 16, 1869; s. Henry J. and Sarah C.; ed. pub. schs.; m. Mary Alice Little, Sept. 12, 1893. Dir. indsl. expns. from 1898; dir. U.S. Govt. war expns., World War; mayor of Quincy, Mass., 1915. Conglist. Mason. Home: Boston, Mass. Deceased.

CAMPBELL, Edmond Ernest, college pres.; b. Waynesboro, Pa., Jan. 21, 1859; s. John Francis (D.D.) and Martha Catherine (Gatewood) C.; A.B., Roanoke Coll., Salem, Va., 1879, A.M., 1884; Ph.D., Susquehanna U., Selinsgrove, Pa., 1893; m. Sarah Agnes Zufall, Sept. 22, 1887 (died 1896); children—Annie Catherine, Mary Agnes (dec.), Emma and Nellie (twins), Clara Evelyn, William Ernest; m. 2d, Grace Koser, Dec. 21, 1897; children—Daniel, Grace Josephine, John Francis, Jane Eliza. Prof. mental and moral science, Kee Mar. Coll., Hagerstown, Md., 1882-88, Staunton (Va.) Female Sem., 1888-90; pres. Irving College and Music Conservatory for Young Women, Mechanicsburg, Pa., July 1, 1891. Pres. Bd. of Health, Mechanicsburg. Democrat. Lutheran. Home: Mechanicsburg, Pa. Died Aug. 4, 1926.

CAMPBELL, Edward De Mille, chemist; b. Detroit, Mich., Sept. 9, 1863; s. James Valentine and Cornelia (Hotchkiss) C.; B.S. in Chemistry, U. of Mich., 1886; m. Jennie M. Ives, 1888. Chemist Ohio Iron Co., Zanesville, 1886-87, Sharon (Pa.) Iron Co., 1887-88, Dayton (Tenn.) Coal & Iron Co., 1888-90; asst. prof. metallurgy, 1890, jr. prof. metallurgy and metall. chemistry, 1893, jr. prof. analytical chemistry, 1896, prof. chem. engring. and analytical chemistry, 1902, dir. chem. lab. and prof. chem. engring. and analytical chemistry, 1905, prof. chemistry and dir. chem. lab., 1914, prof. chemistry and metallurgy and dir. chem. lab., 1920—, all U. of Mich. Cons. chemist, Ordnance Dept. at large, Oct. 1917 to close of War. Home: Ann Arbor, Mich. Died Sept. 18, 1925.

CAMPBELL, Edward K., judge; b. Washington County, Va., Apr. 17, 1858; s. James C. and Ellen (Kernan) C.; ed. Emory and Henry Coll., Va., 1875-76; law dept. U. of Va., 1882-83; m. Loula E. Brown, Apr. 24, 1888; children—Mary, Jean. Admitted to bar in Va., 1883; removed to Birmingham, Ala., 1884; was mem. Campbell & Johnston. Chief justice U.S. Ct. of Claims, 1913-28, resigned. Mem. Dem. State Exec. Com.; chmn. Dem. Congressional Com., Birmingham. Mem. M.E. Ch., South. Home: Washington, D.C. Deceased.

CAMPBELL, Felix, mcht.; b. Brooklyn, 1829; left pub. sch. at 12 to learn printing trade with Brooklyn Daily Eagle; 1848-51, mechanic; 1851-61, foreman; later in business for himself in steam heating and engring.; pres. bd. of supervisors, Kings County, 1858; fire commr. of Brooklyn in old vol. days; mem. Centennial Com. apptd. by Gov. Tilden, 1876; mem. Brooklyn bd. of edn. 12 years; mem. Congress, 1883-91; Democrat. Pres. People's Trust Co. and the Brevoort Savings Bank. Home: Brooklyn, N.Y. Died 1902.

CAMPBELL, George Hollister, ry. official; b. Mendon, Ill., Sept. 15, 1856; s. Rev. Alexander Bennett and Ann Maria (Hollister) C.; bro. Rev. Wm. R. Campbell; ed. pub. schs. and Denmark (Ia.) Acad.; m. Lilian T. Lyman, Aug. 25, 1887; children—Anna May (dec.), William Lyman, Isabel McCown, George Murray. Began as telegrapher C.,B.&Q. Ry., and later held various positions on Wabash and Mo.P. rys. until 1888; joint agt. Big Four, C.&O., and L.&N. rys., at Cincinnati, 1888-96; with B.&O. R.R. Co., 1896—, at Baltimore, later at New York as gen. supt. and v.p. N.Y. lines, asst. to pres., at Baltimore, 1910—; dir. and mem. exec. com. Ky. & Ind. Terminal R.R.; pres. B.&O. Stores, Inc. (New York), Camden Warehouses (Baltimore), Fairport (O.) Warehouse & Elevator Co., Balto. & Ohio Warehouse Co. (Cincinnati). Republican. Presbyn. Died Dec. 25, 1930.

CAMPBELL, Gilbert Whitney, clergyman, educator; b. Billings, Mo., Nov. 2, 1883; s. Alexander and Emma (Combs) C.; A.B. and A.M., Ky. U., 1908; B.D., Yale, 1909, A.M., 1910; Ph.D., U. of Halle, Germany, 1914; m. Mary A. Gillette, Sept. 4, 1917; children—Everett Whitney, Edward Dwight. Fellow and asst., psychol. lab., Yale, 1910-12; prin. Easton Acad., Easton, Conn., 1912-13; ordained ministry Christian (Disciples) Ch., 1906; pastor Pawnee City, Neb., 1915-16; evangelist, Australia, 1916-17; dean of Kansas City (Mo.) Sch. of Religious Pedagogy, 1917-19; pastor Orrick and Holt, Mo., 1920-24; pastor University Ch., Alfred, N.Y., 1927-29; head of dept. philosophy and edn. and dir. bur. of appmts., Alfred U., 1924-35, head dept. philosophy, 1935—. Chmn. Allegany County Com. on Mental Hygiene. Mason. Author: Fiktives in der Lehre von den Empfindungen, 1915. Home: Alfred, N.Y. Deceased.

CAMPBELL, Harry Huse, steel expert; b. W. Roxbury, Mass., Mar. 10, 1859; s. John H. C. and Caroline E. (Huse) C.; B.S., in mining engring., Mass. Inst. Tech., 1879; unmarried. Began in a minor capacity, 1879, with Pa. Steel Co., and advanced through various positions, including gen. supt. and gen. mgr.; metall. engr. same, Sept., 1905—, and also of Md. Steel Co., Spanish-Am. Iron Co. Investigated the scientific principles of open hearth process of making steel. Republican. Unitarian. Author: The Manufacture and Properties of Iron and Steel, 1895, 4th edit., 1906. Home: Steelton, Pa. Deceased.

CAMPBELL, Henry Colin, newspaper editor; b. Wild Rose, Waushara County, Wis., Apr. 3, 1862; s. Henry and Margaret (Strehorn) C.; ed. pub. schs., Milwaukee; m. Emma Marcotte Doolittle, Sept. 5, 1888. Reporter, Apr. 1883-92, city editor, 1892, Evening Wisconsin, Milwaukee; city editor, 1894-98, mng. editor, 1898-1913, asst. editor, Oct. 1913—, Milwaukee Journal. Mem. Milwaukee School Board, 1901-05; pres. Milwaukee Charter Conv., 1908. Chevalier, Legion of Honor, Oct. 1919. Trustee Lawrence Coll., Appleton, Wis. Episcopalian. Author: Wisconsin in Three Centuries (4 vols.). Home: Milwaukee, Wis. Died Jan. 2, 1923.

CAMPBELL, Henry Donald, univ. dean; b. Lexington, Va., July 29, 1862; s. John Lyle and Harriet Peters (Bailey) C.; A.M., Washington and Lee U., 1882, Ph.D., 1885; univs. of Berlin and Heidelberg, 1886-88; Sc.D., U. of Pittsburgh, 1912; LL.D., Tulane U., 1930; m. Martha Miller, July 18, 1888; children—Henry Donald (dec.), Edmund Douglas, Ben Miller (dec.), Robert Bailey. Prof. geology and biology, 1887-1920, prof. geology, 1920—, dean, 1906-32, acting pres., Jan.-July, 1912, Washington and Lee U.; historian of the University. Pres. Southern Assn. Colls. and Secondary Schs., 1930. Fellow Geol. Soc. of Am., A.A.A.S. Home: Lexington, Va. Deceased.

CAMPBELL, Henry Munroe, lawyer; b. Detroit, Mich., Apr. 18, 1854; s. James V. and Cornelia (Hotchkiss) C.; Ph.B., U. of Mich., 1876, LL.B., 1878, LL.D., 1916; m. Caroline B. Burtenshaw, Nov. 22, 1881; children—Henry Munroe, Douglas. Admitted to bar, 1877; sr. mem. Campbell, Bulkley & Ledyard, Detroit; chmn. bd. Union Trust Co.; pres. Russel Woods Co., River Rouge Improvement Co.; v.p., counsel Parke, Davis & Co.; dir. counsel Charcoal Iron Co. of America, Cass Farm Co., Delray Land Co. An organizer Detroit Naval Reserve, and comd. 3d div. as sr. lt. Pres. Detroit Naval Reserve during Spanish-Am. War. Del. State Constl. Conv., 1907. Chmn. Legal Advisory Bd., Wayne County, 1917-18. Republican. Episcopalian. Home: Detroit, Mich. Died Mar. 16, 1926.

CAMPBELL, H(enry) Wood, dental surgeon; b. Amherst, Va., July 9, 1866; s. Rev. Thomas Horace and Henry Virginia (Wood) C.; D.D.S., U. of Md., 1889; m. Emmie Eley, June 4, 1895; children—Seth Eley, Thomas Wood, Margarette Elizabeth, Emily Louise. Practiced at Suffolk, 1889—. Pres. Suffolk Bldg. and Loan Assn. Mem. City Council, Suffolk, 1903-19 (pres. 1905-09). Mem. med. advisory bd. under Selective Service Act, 1918. Pres. Va. State Bd. Dental Examiners, 1896-1921; mem. com. from Nat. Assn. Dental Examiners in conjunction with Carnegie Ednl. Foundation to create a nat. bd. of dental examiners. Fellow Am. Coll. of Dentists. Mason. Democrat. Mem. M.E. Ch., S. Home: Suffolk, Va. Died Mar. 31, 1931.

CAMPBELL, Herbert Grant, coll. prof.; b. Hale, Ia., Dec. 15, 1868; s. John H. and Sarah A. (Pike) C.; grad. Epworth (Ia.) Sem., 1891; Ph.B., Cornell Coll., Mt. Vernon, Ia., 1896; M.A., Columbia, 1902; studied Union Theol. Sem., 1902-03, Berlin and Heidelberg, 1910-11; m. Pearl E. Reeder, Sept. 1, 1897. Deacon, 1896, elder, 1900, M.E. Ch.; minister, Akron, Ia., 1897-99, Sheldon, 1899-1901; v.p. and prof. philosophy, Morningside Coll., 1904-07, prof. philosophy and psychology, 1907—. Founder and conductor (with wife) "Morningside Tours" in Europe, 1914—, except during World War. Y.M.C.A. war service in France, 1917-19; with U.S. Army Ednl. Corps, Mar.-July 1919. Officer de l'Instruction Publique (France). Home: Sioux City, Ia. Died Apr. 1934.

CAMPBELL, James A., mfr.; b. 1854. Pres. The Youngstown Sheet & Tube Co., 1906-30, chmn. bd., 1930-31, retired with title of chairman emeritus. Home: Youngstown, O. Died Sept. 20, 1933.

CAMPBELL, James Archibald, clergyman, educator; b. Harnett Co., N.C., Jan. 13, 1862; s. Rev. Archibald Neill and Humy (Betts) C.; A.B., Wake Forest (N.C.) Coll., 1911, D.D., 1926; m. Cornelia Pearson, Nov. 18, 1890; children—Leslie Hartwell, Arthur Carlyle, Elizabeth Pearson (Mrs. Archibald Edgar Lynch). Ordained ministry Bapt. Ch., 1886; pastor Spring Branch, 1889—, Buie's Creek, 1892—, Coats, 1908—. Founded Buie's Creek Acad., 1887, and continued as its head until the acad. became a jr. coll., 1926, under title of Campbell Coll., of which was pres. (767 students in 1926); pres. Bank of Buie's Creek. Trustee Wake Forest Coll. Home: Buie's Creek, N.C. Died Mar. 18, 1934.

CAMPBELL, James Daniels, lawyer; b. Bridgewater, Pa., Jan. 14, 1839; s. Matthew Fairman and Margaret Ann (Daniels) C.; acad. edn., Shirleysburg, Pa.; m. Ada Katherine Campbell, Sept. 17, 1863. Admitted to bar, 1859; practiced at Huntingdon; 2d lt. 5th Pa. Vols., 90 days, and capt. Co. D, 49th Pa. Vols., 1861-63; resumed practice of law, 1864; dist. atty., Huntingdon Co., and co. solicitor until Mar. 1866; practiced at Davenport, Ia., 1866-80; was asst. city solicitor and city solicitor, Davenport, and gen. atty. or counsel for various rys.; removed to N.Y., 1880, as counsel for Austin Corbin and associates in superintending legal work of reorganizing and consolidating rys. on L.I.; later chief counsel of financiers in acquiring control and reorganizing finances of Central R.R. Co. of N.J. Spl. counsel to pres. and management, 1887-90, gen. solicitor and head legal dept., Oct. 1890-Jan. 1, 1910, Phila. & Reading Ry. Co.; retired Jan. 1, 1910. Home: Wyncote, Pa. Died Dec. 1925.

CAMPBELL, James E., governor; b. Middletown, O., July 7, 1843; s. Dr. Andrew and Laura P. (Reynolds) C.; acad. edn.; served in U.S.N., 1863-65; m. Elizabeth Owens, Jan. 4, 1870. Admitted to bar, 1865, and then practiced at Hamilton and Columbus, O.; pros. atty., Butler Co., O., 1876-80; mem. 48th to 50th Congresses (1883-89); seat in 48th Congress unsuccessfully contested and was not seated until June 20, 1884; gov. of Ohio, 1890-92; unsuccessful candidate for reëlection, 1891 and 1895. Democrat. Home: Columbus, O. Died Dec. 17, 1924.

CAMPBELL, James Romulus, congressman; b. Crook Tp., Hamilton Co., Ill., May 4, 1853; s. John and Mary (Coker) C.; ed. U. of Notre Dame, Ind.; admitted to bar, 1877; m. Kittie B. Benson, Dec. 18, 1879. Pub. McLeansboro Times, 1879-99; pres. First Nat. Bank (McLeansboro), Campbell Milling Co. (Carmi, Ill.). Mem. Ill. Ho. of Rep., 1884-88, Senate, 1888-96; mem. 55th Congress (1897-99), as Democrat; resigned seat in Congress, 1898. Col. 9th Ill. Vols., June 28, 1898; hon. mustered out, May 20, 1899; lt. col. 30th U.S.V. Inf., July 5, 1899; brig. gen. vols., Jan. 3, 1901; hon. disch., Mar. 25, 1901; served in Cuba and P.I. Home: McLeansboro, Ill. Died Aug. 12, 1924.

CAMPBELL, James U., judge; b. Prince Edward Island, Can., Aug. 29, 1866; s. John and Mary (McDougall) C.; ed. Prince of Wales Coll., 1883-84; studied law privately; m. Anna C. Pauling, Aug. 7, 1901; 1 dau., Mary A. (Mrs. Walter F. Patrie). Came to U.S., 1887, naturalized, 1893. Began as teacher pub. schs., 1884; admitted to Ore. bar, 1893; practiced at Oregon City, Ore., until 1909; mem. State Legislature, 1907, 1909; apptd. judge of Circuit Court, 5th Jud. Dist. of Ore., 1909, elected 4 times; elected justice Supreme Court of Ore., 1930, chief justice, 1935—. Enlisted in 2d Ore. Regt., U.S. Vols., Spanish-Am. War, served in Philippines; hon. disch. as 1st lt. Republican. Mason. Home: Salem, Ore. Died July 16, 1937.

CAMPBELL, John, soldier; b. New York, Sept. 16, 1821; s. Archibald and Mary C.; apptd. asst. surgeon, U.S.A., Dec. 1847; served in war with Mexico and afterward at several posts; promoted surgeon, May 1861, serving throughout Civil war; bvtd. col.; promoted lt. col., 1877, and col., and retired Sept. 16, 1885; commd. brig. gen., U.S.A., retired Apr. 23, 1904. Home: Cold Spring, N.Y. Died 1905.

CAMPBELL, John, judge; b. Monroe Co., Ind., Sept. 13, 1853; s. James M. and Nancy C.; A.B., State U. of Iowa, 1877, LL.B., 1879, A.M., 1882; LL.D., Colorado Coll., 1909, State U. of Iowa, 1913, State U. of Colo., 1934; m. Harriet J. Parker, June 28, 1881. Admitted to bar, 1880; practiced at Colo. Springs, 1880-89; city atty., 1880-83; co. atty., El Paso Co., 1884-85; mem. Ho. of Rep., 1885, Senate, 1887; judge Dist. Court, 1889-95; asso. justice Supreme Court, 1895-1913; apptd. asso. justice Colo. Supreme Court, to fill vacancy caused by death of Morton S. Bailey, May 20, 1922, elected for unexpired term, Nov. 1922, and for 2 full terms, 1926-46. Republican. Dean emeritus Law Sch., U. of Colo. Trustee Colo. Coll. 40 yrs.; mem. Pub. Library Commn. of Denver. Home: Denver, Colo. Died Jan. 1, 1938.

CAMPBELL, John A(lexander), banker, mfr.; b. Shushan, N.Y., Jan. 31, 1856; s. Peter and Mary Jane (McIntosh) C.; grad. Collegiate Inst., New York, 1873; A.B., Princeton, 1877, hon. A.M., 1907; m. Fannie Cleveland, Oct. 30, 1879; 1 dau., Fannie Cleveland (Mrs. Elzey Stuart Aitkin). Treas. Internat. Pottery Co., Trenton, N.J., 1879-1906; gen. mgr. Trenton Potteries Co., 1906-10, pres., 1910-32, chmn. bd., 1932—; dir. Trenton Banking Co., 1898-1900, v.p., 1900-04, pres., 1904-27 and 1930-35, chmn. bd., 1927-30 and 1935—; pres. United N.J. R.R. and Canal Co., 1928—; chmn. bd. Trenton Savings Fund Soc.; pres. Del. & Bound Brook Railroad Co. Mem. N.J. State Exemption Bd., World War, also treas. War Emergency Com. of Trenton and chmn. Am. Red Cross drives. Pres. N.J. State Bd. Tenement House Supervision 15 yrs.; pres. Pa.-N.J. Free Bridge Commission 8 yrs.; pres. of Trenton and Mercer County Soldiers and Sailors War Memorial Commn., 1929—. Pres. Trenton Free Pub. Library; pres. bd. Prospect St. Presbyn. Ch. Mem. N.J. and Trenton hist. socs. Awarded Trenton Times Civic Cup, 1927. Republican. Home: Trenton, N.J. Died June 2, 1938.

CAMPBELL, John Bulow, chmn. bd. Campbell Coal Co.; b. Atlanta, Ga., Dec. 15, 1870; s. John Bulow and Margaret Virginia (Orme) C.; ed. Ga. Mil. Coll., Milledgeville, Ga., 1886-89; m. Laura Graflin Berry, Apr. 20, 1904; 1 dau., Virginia Orme. With B. O. Campbell (now Campbell Coal Co.), 1885—, chmn. bd., 1929—; dir. and mem. exec. com. Coca Cola Co., Trust Co. of Ga. Trustee Agnes Scott Coll.; chmn. bd. trustees and chmn. investment com. Berry Schs.; chmn. exec. com. and dir. Columbia Theol. Sem.; chmn. bd. dirs. Rabun Gap-Nacoochee Sch.; curator Atlanta Hist. Soc.; trustee Y.M.C.A.; dir. Atlanta Art Assn.; mem. adv. com. Emory Univ. Presbyn. Mason. Home: Atlanta, Ga. Died June 28, 1940.

CAMPBELL, John Charles; b. La Porte, Ind., Sept. 14, 1867; s. Gavin and Anna Barbara (Kipp) C.; A.B., Williams, 1892; B.D., Andover Theol. Sem., 1895; m. Grace H. Buckingham, 1895 (died 1905); m. 2d, Olive A. Dame, Mar. 21, 1907. Prin. of a mountain acad. in Ala., 1895-98; teacher pub. schs., Stevens Point, Wis., 1898-99; prin. Mountain Acad., Tenn., 1909; supt. secondary edn., Piedmont Coll., Demorest, Ga., also dean and pres., 1901-07; traveled in Sicily and Italy, 1907-08; with Russell Sage Foundation, 1908—, now sec. Southern Highland Div. (rural welfare work). Conglist. Home: Asheville, N.C. Died May 2, 1919.

CAMPBELL, John Henry, lawyer; b. Tuscola, Ill., Sept. 19, 1868; s. William J. and Milla (Smith) C.; LL.B., George Washington University, 1891, LL.M., from same, 1892; m. Estelle Freet, Apr. 15, 1890 (died 1910); children—William, Helen (Mrs. Webster H. Land), Ruth (Mrs. Horace W. Day); m. 2d, Elise W. Nave, Mar. 30, 1916. Employed in U.S. Treasury Dept., 1888-94; atty. in charge of pardons, Dept. of Justice, 1894-1901; moved to Ariz., 1901; asst. U.S. atty., Ariz., 1902-05; asso. justice Supreme Court of Ariz., 1905-12; chancellor U. of Ariz., Oct. 1921—. Rep. presdl. elector for Ariz., 1924. Home: Tucson, Ariz. Died June 1928.

CAMPBELL, John Lyle, prof. physics and astronomy, Wabash Coll., 1850—; b. Salem, Ind., Oct. 13, 1827; s. David G. C.; grad. Wabash Coll., 1849 (A.M., 1852; LL.D., Ind. State Univ., 1876); m. Mary E. Johnston, July 27, 1854. Civ. engr., 1849-50; in 1866 made 1st suggestion to Mayor McMichael of Phila. concerning Centennial Expn., 1876; Centennial Commr. for Ind., 1874-78; sec. U.S. Centennial Commn., 1875-78; pres. Ind. Bd. of Commrs. for Columbian Expn., Chicago, 1893; asst. U.S. Coast and Geodetic Survey, 1881-89. Home: Crawfordsville, Ind. Died 1904.

CAMPBELL, John TenBrook, surveyor; b. nr. Montezuma, Ind., May 21, 1833; s. Joseph and Rachel (TenBrook) C.; ed. dist. schs.; one term Western Manual Labor Acad.; m. Annie Butterfield, Dec. 15, 1864. Capt. Co. H, 21st Ind. Vols., 1861; right leg permanently crippled in battle, Baton Rouge, La., Aug. 5, 1862; resigned, Oct. 29, 1862; asst. provost-marshal, 7th Congl. Dist. of Ind., June 24-Nov. 4, 1863; treas. Parke Co., Ind., 2 terms; asst. assessor internal revenue, 1870; Republican; later Greenbacker; returned to Rep. party, 1890; defeated for state senate as Greenbacker, 1870; journal clerk, Ind. Senate, 1878; 1st asst., Ind. Bur. of Statistics, 1878-83; co. surveyor 10 yrs. Devised 5 new problems in trigonometry as applied to surveying; also 2 new problems in curve work, with formula for application in practice. Home: Rockville, Ind. Deceased.

CAMPBELL, Josiah A. Patterson, judge; b. Waxaw Settlement, S.C., Mar. 2, 1830; s. Rev. R. B. and Mary (Patterson) C.; ed. Camden Acad. and Davidson Coll., N.C.; (LL.D., U. of Miss.); admitted to bar, 1847; m. Eugenia E. Nash, May 23, 1850. In practice Kosciusko, Miss., 1848-65, except war period; at Jackson, Miss., 1876—. Mem. Ho. of Rep., 1851-59 (speaker, 1859); one of 7 Miss. dels. to conv. which organized Confed. States; capt. lt. col. of inf. and col. of cav., C.S.A., 1862-65; judge Circuit Ct., 1865-70; judge of Supreme Ct., 1876-94 (chief justice 6 yrs.). Mem. Miss. Code Commn., 1870; prepared Miss. code, 1880, still almost wholly in force. Democrat. One of the 49 who signed the constitution of the Confed. States of America. Home: Jackson, Miss. Died Jan. 10, 1917.

CAMPBELL, Killis, univ. prof.; b. Enfield, King William Co., Va., June 11, 1872; s. Robert Camm and Alice (Hawes) C.; Coll. of William and Mary, 1888-90, 1893-94, B.A., 1894; B.Litt., Peabody College for Teachers, 1892; fellow, Johns Hopkins, 1897-98, Ph.D., 1898; student British Mus. and Bodleian Library, summers, 1897, 1902, 04; m. Mary Hogg Aitken, June 26, 1902; children—Mrs. Alice Hawes Patton, Mrs. Catherine Wiley McConchie, Mary Aitken, Killis, Hawes. English master, Culver (Ind.) Mil. Acad., 1898-99; instr. English, U. of Tex., 1899-1906, adj. prof., 1906-11, asso. prof., 1911-18, prof., 1918—, also research prof., 1930-31. Democrat. Mem. Disciples of Christ. Author: The Seven Sages of Rome with Special Reference to the Middle English Versions, 1898; The Mind of Poe and Other Studies, 1933. Home: Austin, Tex. Died Aug. 8, 1937.

CAMPBELL, Macy, college prof.; b. Pleasanton, Ia., Aug. 12, 1879; s. Duncan and Alida (Hulse) C.; M.Di., Ia. State Teachers Coll., 1905; B.A., State U. of Ia., 1911; spl. work, Ia. State Coll. Agr., 1912; m. Amabel Hart, Aug. 24, 1904; children—Lee Loren, Alida Catherine, Dorothy Mabel, Malcolm Seerley, Mary Frances. Teacher rural schs. 3 yrs.; supt. schs., Alden, Ia., 1905-09, West Liberty, 1912-13; head dept. rural edn. Ia. State Teachers Coll., 1913—. County chmn. Liberty Loan, Am. Red Cross, and United War Work campaigns, 1918-19; state dir. sch. Thrift Campaign for Ia., 1918-20; mem. Central Ednl. Com. of 7th Federal Reserve Dist. of U.S. Republican. Author of Little Lessons in Thrift, and various bulls. on improvement of rural edn. Home: Cedar Falls, Ia. Died Apr. 16, 1927.

CAMPBELL, Marius Robison, geologist; b. Garden Grove, Ia., Sept. 30, 1858; s. Alvah W. and Eliza (Davis) C.; ed. in common schs.; taught country schs.; attended Ohio-State U., 1885-86; m. Margaret Stevenson, Nov. 5, 1890. Civ. engr. on ry. construction, 1886-88; geologist in U.S. Geol. Survey, 1889—. Fellow Geol. Soc. America. Home: Washington, D.C. Died Dec. 7, 1940.

CAMPBELL, Mrs. Patrick (Beatrice Stella Campbell), English actress; b. London, Eng., Feb. 9, 1865; d. John and Louisa (Romanini) Tanner; ed. in England and Paris; m. Patrick Campbell, 1884 (killed in S. Africa, 1900). First professional appearance as Sophia Moody, in "Bachelors," at Alexandra Theatre, Liverpool, Oct. 22, 1888; later with Ben Greet's Co.; has made several Am. tours; appeared in U.S. in "The Ambassador's Wife," 1910. Died Apr. 9, 1940.

CAMPBELL, Patrick Thomas, supt. schools; b. Jersey City, N.J., Apr. 14, 1871; s. Thomas and Mary (Houghton) C.; student Boston Latin Sch., 1885-89; A.B., Harvard, 1893; Dr. of Education, honoris causa Colby, 1934; m. Edith T. Hayes, Aug. 28, 1899; children—Thomas, Edith. Teacher Medford High Sch., 1893-97; jr. master and later master, Boston Latin Sch., 1897-1908, head of dept. of history, 1908-20, head master, 1920-29; asst. supt. Boston Pub. Schs., 1929-31, supt., 1931—. Mem. bd. visitors Harvard Summer Sch. and Univ. Extension. Democrat. Catholic. Died Feb. 12, 1937.

CAMPBELL, Philip Pitt, lawyer, congressman; b. Cape Breton, N.S., Apr. 25, 1862; s. Daniel A. and Mary (McRae) C.; A.B., Baker U., 1888, A.M., 1891, LL.D., 1917; m. Helen E. Goff, Nov. 23, 1892. Admitted to bar, 1889; in practice at Pittsburg, Kan., 1889-1903. Mem. 58th to 67th Congresses (1903-23), 3d Kan. Dist.; elected Speaker of the House, Jan. 1923, and served until March 4, 1923; parliamentarian of Rep. Nat. Conv., Cleveland, 1924. Home: Arlington, Va. Died May 26, 1941.

CAMPBELL, Prince Lucian, univ. pres.; b. Newmarket, Mo., Oct. 6, 1861; s. Thomas Franklin and Jane Eliza C.; grad. Christian Coll., Ore., 1879; A.B., Harvard, 1886; (LL.D., Pacific U., 1911, U. of Colo., 1913); m. Eugenia J. Zieber, Sept. 12, 1887 (died 1891); m. 2d, Susan A. Church, Aug. 20, 1908. Prin. State Normal Sch., Monmouth, Ore., 1890-1902; pres. U. of Ore., 1902—. Mem. State Text-Book Commn., 1901, Ore. State Bur. of Mines and Geology, Ore. State Library Commn. Mem. exec. com. Y.M.C.A. of Ore. and Ida. Chmn. Ore. State Council Defense com. on scientific research, 1918. Home: Eugene, Ore. Died Aug. 14, 1925.

CAMPBELL, Ralph Emerson, judge; b. in Butler Co., Pa., May 9, 1867; s. Washington and Ann Eliza C.; B.S., Ind. Normal U., 1891, A.B., 1892; LL.B., U. of Kan., 1894; married. Asst. gen. solicitor at S. McAlester, I.T., and Little Rock, Ark., 1895-1901, gen. atty. in Okla. Ty., 1901-03, for Choctaw, Okla. & Gulf R.R.; in gen. practice at S. McAlester, 1905-07; U.S. dist. judge, for Eastern Dist. of Okla., Nov. 16, 1907-Sept. 1, 1918, resigned; gen. atty. Cosden Cos., Tulsa, Okla., Sept. 1918—. Republican. Methodist. Home: Tulsa, Okla. Died Jan. 9, 1921.

CAMPBELL, Richard, lawyer; b. in Ireland, Oct. 28, 1872; s. Felix and Mary (Connolly) C.; brought to U.S. in early youth; LL.B., Georgetown U., 1899; unmarried. Clk., bookkeeper and newspaper reporter; apptd. asst. in office of atty. gen. of P.I., 1902; apptd. dist. atty. Moro Province, 1906, and mem. Legislative Council; judge Court of First Instance, 1908-17 (resigned); then mem. Gilbert, Campbell & McCool, New York, N.Y. Died Oct. 16, 1935.

CAMPBELL, Richard Kenna, commr. naturalization; b. Lynchburg, Va., Aug. 7, 1853; s. Nathaniel Henry and Mary Cabell (Cralle) C.; Norwood High Sch., Nelson County, Va.; Baltimore City Coll.; B.L., U. of Md. Law Sch., 1874; m. Frances Grace Cabell, June 7, 1876; children—Nathaniel Henry (dec.), Anna Barraud (dec.), Philip B. Practiced in Baltimore, 1874-76; farmer and editor till 1894; entered U.S. Immigration Service, 1894, and became atty. for Immigration Bur.; apptd. mem. Presdl. Commn. on Naturalization, 1905; chief Naturalization Div., Dept. of Commerce and Labor, Washington, 1906-13; commr. of naturalization in charge of Bur. of Naturalization in Dept. of Labor, 1913-24, retired; mem. Bd. of Review, Jan. 1, 1923. Democrat. Swedenborgian. Died May 24, 1931.

CAMPBELL, R(obert) Granville, prof. polit. science; b. Glenwood, Va., Feb. 11, 1879; s. Alexander Doak and Estaline (Bell) C.; A.B., Washington and Lee U., 1898, M.A., 1899; fellow in political science, Johns Hopkins, Ph.D., 1908; m. Ellin North Moale, June 20, 1908. Asst. prof. economics, commerce and polit. science, 1908-12, adj. prof., 1912-16, asso. prof., 1916-20, prof. polit. science, 1920—, Washington and Lee U. Spl. lecturer on citizenship with army ednl. corps, A.E.F., in France, and economic investigation U.S. Shipping Bd., at London, Eng., 1919. Delta Kappa. Democrat. Presbyn. Mason. Author: Neutral Rights and Obligations in the Anglo-Boer War, 1908. Prof. govt., U. of Va., summers 1923, 24. Home: Lexington, Va. Died Oct. 17, 1932.

CAMPBELL, Theodorick Pryor, educator; b. Nottoway C.H., Va., Oct. 10, 1861; s. Thomas Harris and Fanny (Pryor) C.; A.B., Hampden-Sidney Coll., 1881, A.M., 1883, LL.D., 1922; studied univs. of Berlin and Chicago; m. Anna Montgomery Johnson, Nov. 9, 1887. Prin. Farmville Male Acad., 1881-82; asso. prin. Wytheville Male Acad., and prof. mathematics, Plumer Memorial Coll., 1882-84; prin. Montgomery Male Acad., 1884-89; prof. German and Latin, Montgomery Female Coll., 1885-87; prof. and head of Dept. of Modern Langs., Va. Poly. Inst., 1889—; dean of faculty, 1905-07 (resigned), dean of gen. faculty, 1910-24 (resigned). Democrat. Presbyn. Home: Blacksburg, Va. Died July 1928.

CAMPBELL, Thomas Joseph, editor; b. New York, Apr. 29, 1848; ed. St. Francis Xavier Coll.; entered Soc. of Jesus; became prof. of belles lettres and rhetoric at St. John's, Fordham, and St. Francis Xavier colls.; ordained R.C. priest in Belgium, 1880. Provincial New York, Md. Province, S.J., May 1889; pres. St. John's Coll., Fordham, N.Y., 1885-89, and 1896-99; asso. editor Messenger of the Sacred Heart, 1900-10; editor of America, 1910—. Home: New York, N.Y. Died Dec. 14, 1925.

CAMPBELL, Thomas Mitchell, governor; b. Rusk, Tex., Apr. 22, 1856; s. Thomas D. and Racheal (Moore) C.; ed. pub. schs.; attended Trinity U., Tehuacana, Tex., 1873-74; admitted to bar, 1878. Master in chancery, 1889-91, receiver, 1891-92, gen. mgr., 1892-97, I.&N.G. R.R. Gov. Tex. for terms 1907-09, 1909-11. Democrat. Home: Palestine, Tex. Died Apr. 1, 1923.

CAMPBELL, Thomas W., clergyman; b. Three Rivers, P.Q., Can., Sept. 24, 1851; s. Rev. Thomas C. and Harriet C. (Burrell) C.; grad. Victoria U., 1879; m. Sarah A., Nov. 26, 1879, d. Rev. H. Cheesbrough, supt. Wesleyan mission, Bahamas, later of Toronto, Can. Ordained Meth. ministry, 1879; asso. editor Christian Guardian, Toronto, Ont., 1878-80; served in Methodist and afterward R.E. ministry in Can.; elected bishop Ref. Episcopal Ch. in Can., 1891; presiding bishop, 1894-97; united with Presbyterian Ch., 1898; pastor Noble St. Presbyn. Ch., Brooklyn, 1899-1905. Home: Richmond Hill, L.I. Died Mar. 26, 1918.

CAMPBELL, William, metallurgist; b. Gateshead-on-Tyne, England, June 24, 1876; s. Thomas and Franceska (Albrecht) C.; grad. Civil Service Dept., King's Coll., London, 1892; St. Kenelms Coll., Oxford, 1892-94; Durham U. Coll. Science, 1894-97, A.Sc., 1896, B.Sc., 1897, M.Sc., 1903, Sc.D., 1905; Royal Sch. of Mines, London, 1899-1901; Ph.D., Columbia, 1903, A.M., 1905, Sc.D., 1928; m. Estelle M. Campbell. Demonstrator in metallurgy and lecturer in geology, Durham Coll. of Science, 1898-99; "Royal Exhbn. of 1851" research scholar, Royal Sch. of Mines, London, 1899-1901; univ. fellow, Columbia, 1902, Barnard fellow, 1903; lecturer on European geology, 1903-06, instr. in metallurgy, 1904-07, adj. prof., 1907-12, asso. prof., 1912-14, prof., 1914-24, Howe prof., 1924—, Sch. of Mines, Columbia. Metallographer Technologic Branch U.S. Geol. Survey, 1907-11; metallographer Bur. of Mines, same, 1911-21; lecturer on metallurgy, U.S. Naval Acad. Post-Grad. Sch., 1913. Editor Sch. of Mines Quarterly, 1910; asst. editor Internat. Jour. of Metallography, Jour. Indsl. and Engineering Chemistry. Fellow Geol. Soc. London, New York Acad. Sciences (v.p. 1911). Awarded Saville Shaw Medal, Soc. Chem. Industry (British), 1903; Carnegie Scholarship, Iron and Steel Inst., 1903; Research Grant, Carnegie Instn., 1905. Mem. com. on alloy steel, Nat. Research Council; metallurgist, Navy Yard, New York, 1917; mem. advisory com. U.S. Bur. of Standards; lt. comdr. U.S. N.R.F., 1918, comdr., 1919-29; advisory metallurgist, Navy Yard, New York, 1921-26; advisory metallurgist, Bd. of Transportation, N.Y. City. Episcopalian. Mason. Home: New York, N.Y. Died Dec. 16, 1936.

CAMPBELL, William Alexander, editor; b. nr. Lincoln, Neb., May 8, 1881; s. John A. and Josephine (Faulkner) C.; special courses, U. of Neb.; m. Maud L. Carter, Apr. 30, 1903; 1 son, William Carter. Reporter Denver Republican during Cripple Creek strike, financial editor and editorial writer, Sioux City Tribune, 1904-07; financial editor, Omaha Bee, 1907-09; asst. to L. W. Hill, pres. G.N. Ry., 1910-13; editor and pub. Helena Daily Independent, 1913—; pres. Four Range Ranch Co. Mem. and spl. agt. State Council of Defense, World War. Republican. Presbyterian. Mason. Home: Helena, Mont. Died Dec. 15, 1938.

CAMPBELL, William Francis, surgeon; b. Brooklyn, N.Y., Nov. 7, 1867; s. Alexander and Catharine (Bennett) C.; A.B., New York U., 1887; M.D., Long Island Coll. Hosp., 1892; married. Practiced in Brooklyn, 1892—; prof. surgery, Long Island Coll. Hosp., 1910—; surgeon in chief, Trinity Hosp.; attending surgeon Meth. Episcopal Hosp. Maj. surgeon 2d Brigade, N.G.N.Y., 1908-13; maj. with Am. Red Cross in France, June-Nov. 1918. Fellow Am. Coll. Surgeons; mem. A.M.A., Med. Soc. State N.Y. (pres., 1913). Republican. Conglist. Mason. Home: Bayville, L.I. Died Sept. 7, 1926.

CAMPBELL, William Rogers, clergyman; b. Rushville, Ill., Feb. 2, 1855; s. Rev. Alexander Bennett and Anna Maria (Hollister) C.; B.A., Williams Coll., 1876; Boston U. Law Sch., 1876-77; grad. Andover Theol. Sem., 1881; (D.D., Williams, 1906); m. Angeline Crosby, Mar. 7, 1895. Ordained Congl. ministry, 1881; pastor Highland Congl. Ch., Boston, Sept. 1881—. Mem. bd. visitors Andover Theol. Sem.; pres. Congl. Ednl. Soc.; dir. Congl. S.S. and Pub. Soc., Congl. Home Missionary Soc. Republican. Home: Boston, Mass. Died Jan. 29, 1935.

CAMPBELL, William Taggart, clergyman; b. Antrim, O., July 21, 1836; s. William and Ann (Lawrence) C.; A.B., Monmouth Coll., Ill., 1870, A.M., 1873; (D.D., Hanover Coll., Ind., 1883); m. Cleveland, Jennie C. Logue (19 yrs. prof. English lit., Monmouth Coll.), July 31, 1889. Ordained U.P. ministry, 1871; pastor Little York, Ill., 1871-75, Second Ch., Monmouth, Ill., 1875-1901 (retired); engaged in ch. ednl. work, 1901—. Corr. secretary Bd. Edn., U.P. Ch., 1878—; moderator Gen. Assembly U.P. Ch., 1907-08. Died Apr. 10, 1912.

CAMPBELL, William Wallace, pres. emeritus U. of Calif., astronomer; b. on farm, Hancock Co., O., Apr. 11, 1862; s. Robert Wilson and Harriet (Welch) C.; B.S., U. of Mich., 1886; hon. M.S., 1899; Sc.D., Western U. of Pa., 1900, U. of Mich., 1905, U. of Western Australia, 1922, Cambridge U., 1925, Columbia U., 1928, U. of Chicago, 1931; LL.D., U. of Wis., 1902, U. of Calif., 1932; m. Elizabeth Ballard Thompson, Dec. 28, 1892; children—Wallace, Douglas, Kenneth. Prof. mathematics, U. of Colo., 1886-88; instr. astronomy, U. of Mich., 1888-91; astronomer, 1891-1930 (emeritus), acting dir., 1900, dir., 1901-30, emeritus, Lick Observatory; pres. U. of Calif., 1923-30, emeritus. In charge Lick Obs. eclipse expdn. to India, Jan. 1898, Ga., May 1900, Spain, Aug. 1905, Flint Island, Jan. 1908, Kiev, Russia, Aug. 1914, Goldendale, Wash., June 1918, Wallal, Western Australia, Sept. 1922; mem. expdn. to Lower Calif., Mexico, Sept. 1923. Silliman lecturer, Yale, 1909-10; William Ellery Hale lecturer, Nat. Acad. Sciences, 1914; Halley lecturer, Oxford, 1925. Lalande prize (gold medal), Paris Acad. Sciences, 1903; gold medal, Royal Astron. Soc., 1906; Draper gold medal, Nat. Acad. Sciences, 1906; Janssen prize (gold medal), Paris Acad. Sciences, 1910; Bruce gold medal, 1915. Comdr. Order of Leopold II, 1919; Officer Legion of Honor (France), 1927; comdr. Order Crown of Italy, 1928. Trustee Carnegie Instn. (Washington), Internat. House (Berkeley, Calif.). Mem. Am. Acad. Arts and Sciences. Author: The Elements of Practical Astronomy, 1899; Stellar Motions, 1913; Stellar Radial Velocities (with collaboration of J. H. Moore), 1928. Home: San Francisco, Calif. Died June 14, 1938.

CAMPBELL, Willis Cohoon, orthopedic surgeon; b. Jackson, Miss., Dec. 18, 1880; s. Charles C. and Lula (Cohoon) C.; M.D., U. of Va., 1904; m. Elizabeth Yerger, June 30, 1908; children—Louise, Willis, Elizabeth, George. Practiced at Memphis, Tenn., 1906—; prof. of orthopedic surgery, U. of Tenn. Coll. of Medicine, 1910—; consultant in orthopedic surgery, Bapt. Memorial and St. Joseph's hosps., U.S. Marine Hosp. No. 12; chief of staff Dr. Willis C. Campbell Clinic, Crippled Children's Hosp., Hosp. for Crippled Adults; attending orthopedic surgeon Methodist Hosp. Fellow Am. Coll. Surgeons. Democrat. Episcopalian. Author: Orthopedic Surgery, 1930; Orthopedics of Childhood (monograph), 1927; Operative Orthopædics, 1939. Home: Memphis, Tenn. Died May 4, 1941.

CAMPHOR, Alexander Priestly, bishop; b. Soniat, Jefferson Parish, La., Aug. 9, 1865; s. Perry and Elizabeth C.; Leland U., 1879-80; New Orleans U., 1880-89; Gammon Theol. Sem., S. Atlanta, Ga., 1893-95; Union Theol. Sem., and Columbia U., 1896; U. of Chicago, summers, 1912-14; m. Mamie A. R. Weathers, Nov. 19, 1895. Prof. mathematics, New Orleans U., 1889-93; pastor M.E. Ch., Germantown, Pa., 1895, St. John's Ch., Orange, N.J., 1896; pres. Coll. of West Africa, Monrovia, Liberia, 1897-1907; pres. Central Ala. Inst., Birmingham, 1908-16; bishop M.E. Ch. for Africa, 1916—. Trustee Coll. for West Africa, Central Ala. Inst. Del. Gen. Conf. M.E. Ch., 1904, 12, World's Missionary Conf., Edinburgh, 1910. Mem. African Soc., Freedman's Aid Instn. M.E. Ch., Southern Sociol. Congress. Author: Missionary Story Sketches, 1909. Home: Monrovia, Liberia, West Africa. Died Dec. 11, 1919.

CANADA, William Wesley, consul; b. in Stony Creek Twp., Ind., June 8, 1850; s. David and Mary Ann (Moore) C.; ed. high and State Normal schs., Ind.; admitted to bar, 1874; m. Carrie E. Moore, Dec. 9, 1875. Chmn. Randolph Co. (Ind.) Rep. Central Com., 1890-1907; consul at Vera Cruz, Mex., June 1897—. Home: Winchester, Ind. Died May 17, 1921.

CANBY, William Marriott, banker; b. Phila., Mar. 17, 1831; s. Marriott and Eliza Tatnall (Sipple) C.; academic edn. at Wilmington, Del., and Westtown, Pa.; m. Edith Dillon Mathews, June 15, 1870. Pres. Wilmington Savings Fund Soc., 1881—; pres. Wilmington Inst.; receiver Wilmington & Western R.R.; pres. Del. Western R.R. Republican. Home: Wilmington, Del. Died 1904.

CANDLER, Allen Daniel, governor; b. Lumpkin Co., Ga., Nov. 4, 1834; s. Daniel G. and Nancy C. (Matthews) C.; A.B., Mercer U., Ga., 1859, A.M., 1866 (LL.D., 1908); m. Eugenia Williams, Jan. 12, 1864. Served pvt. to col., C.S.A., 1861-65; founded Clayton High Sch., and was prin. same, 1859-61 and 1867-69; v.p. Monroe Female Coll., 1865-66; pres. Bailey Inst., 1870-71; mem. Ga. Ho. of Rep., 1872-78, Senate, 1879-80; was pres. of a ry., 1879-92; mem. 48th to 51st Congresses (1883-91); sec. of state of Ga., 1894-98; gov. Ga., 1898-1902; state historian, 1903—. Democrat. Home: Atlanta, Ga. Died 1910.

CANDLER, Asa G., capitalist; b. nr. Villa Rica, Carroll Co., Ga., 1851; s. Samuel Charles and Martha (Beall) C.; common sch. ed.; m. Lucy Elizabeth Howard, Jan. 15, 1878. Apprentice in drug business, Cartersville, Ga., 1870-73; clerk in drug store of Dr. Howard, Atlanta, 1873-78; mem. Hallman & Candler, druggists, 1878-82, and successors until sold out, 1899; was organizer and pres. Central Bank & Trust Corp., Atlanta Warehouse Co. Pres. bd. trustees and chmn. finance com. Emory Univ.; gave $50,000 to Emory Coll., $1,000,000 to Emory Univ., $75,000 to Wesley Memorial Fund. Methodist. Democrat. Home: Druid Hills, Atlanta, Ga. Died Mar. 12, 1929.

CANDLER, Charles Murphey, lawyer, chmn. railroad commn.; b. Decatur, Ga., Mar. 17, 1858; s. Milton A. and Eliza C. (Murphey) C.; A.B., U. of Ga., 1877, LL.D., 1924; m. Mary H. Scott, Oct. 26, 1882; children—Laura Eliza, George Scott, Rebekah, Milton Anthony, Charles Murphey. Admitted to Ga. bar, 1880; mem. Ga. Ho. of Rep., four terms (resigned 1909), State Senate, 1904-06; apptd. mem. R.R. Commn. of Ga., Apr. 1909, for unexpired term of 2 yrs.; elected for terms, 1911-17, 1917-23 (chmn. bd.); mem. C. M. and Scott Candler, 1923—. Democrat. Trustee Agnes Scott Coll. Presbyn. Mason. Home: Decatur, Ga. Died Aug. 1935.

CANDLER, Warren A., bishop; b. Carroll Co., Ga., Aug. 23, 1857; s. Samuel Charles and Martha (Beall) C.; A.B., Emory Coll., 1875 (D.D., 1888, LL.D., 1897); m. Nettie Curtright, Nov. 21, 1877; children—Mrs. Annie Florence Sledd, John Curtright, Samuel Charles, Warren Akin (dec.), Emory Candler (dec.). Entered North Ga. Conf., M.E. Ch., S., 1875; continued in pastorate until July 1886; pres. Emory Coll., 1888-98; bishop M.E. Ch., S., 1898—. Asst. editor Christian Advocate, Nashville (organ M.E. Ch., S.), 1886-88. Del. Gen. confs., 1886, 90, 94, 98, Ecumenical Conf., 1891, 1911. Chancellor of Emory U., 1914-21. Author: Christus Auctor, 1899; High Living and High Lives, 1901; Great Revivals and the Great Republic, 1905; Practical Studies in the Fourth Gospel, 1913; Life of Thomas Coke, 1923; Current Comments on Timely Topics, 1926; Life of Bishop Charles B. Galloway, 1927; The Christ and The Creed, 1927; Easter Meditations, 1930; Young J. Allen, the Man Who Seeded China, 1931. Home: Atlanta, Ga. Died Sept. 25, 1941.

CANDLER, William, hotelman; b. Atlanta, Ga., Jan. 24, 1890; s. Asa Griggs and Lucy Elizabeth (Howard) C.; ed. pub. schs.; m. Bennie Irene Teabeaut, Feb. 3, 1913; children—Rena Elizabeth, William. Sec. and treas. Coca Cola Co., 1909-26; pres. Callan Court Co., 1920—; pres. and treas. of Atlanta Biltmore Hotel Co., 1923—; vice-pres. Coca Cola Bottling Co. of New York, 1925—; pres. Atlanta Baggage & Cab Co.; vice-pres. 1st Mut. Bldg. & Loan Assn., Asa G. Candler, Inc., Dunlap & Co. Formerly chmn. of governing board Nation's Business. Former chmn. Forward Atlanta Advertising Campaign. Former dir. U.S. Chamber Commerce, Atlanta Community Chest. Methodist. Mason. Home: Atlanta, Ga. Died Oct. 2, 1936.

CANEVIN, J(ohn) F(rancis) Regis, bishop; b. Westmoreland Co., Pa., June 5, 1852; ed. St. Vincent's Sem., Westmoreland Co. Ordained priest R.C. Ch., 1879; rector St. Mary's Ch., Pittsburgh, Pa., until 1884; asst. at Cathedral, Pittsburgh, 1881-86; chaplain St. Paul's Orphan Asylum, Pa. Reform Sch. and the Western Penitentiary, 1886-88; diocesan chancellor, Pittsburgh, 1888-93; pastor St. Philip's Ch., Crafton, Pa., 1893-95; rector Cathedral, Pittsburgh, 1895-1903; consecrated titular bishop of Sabrata, and coadjutor Diocese of Pittsburgh, Feb. 24, 1903; succeeded Bishop Phelan upon death of latter, Dec. 20, 1904. Address: Pittsburgh, Pa. Died Mar. 22, 1927.

CANFIELD, George Folger, lawyer; b. New York, Aug. 21, 1854; s. Albert Warren and Elizabeth Irene H. C.; A.B., Harvard, 1875, LL.B., 1880; studied law and history at German univs., 1875-77; m. Sarah Kittredge, Feb. 24, 1884 (died 1897); 1 son, George Dana; m. 2d, Frances M. Marshall, Sept. 20, 1904; children—Maynard M. (dec.), Robert W., Franklin O., Mary M., Elizabeth B. Admitted to bar, 1881, then in practice at New York; mem. Satterlee & Canfield. Lecturer, 1892-94, prof. law, 1894-1930, emeritus, Columbia Univ. Pres. Atlanta & Charlotte Air Line Ry. Co.; v.p. Morris Plan Co., Bronx Refrigerating Co. Home: New York, N.Y. Died Nov. 15, 1933.

CANFIELD, James Hulme, librarian; b. Delaware, O., Mar. 18, 1847; s. Rev. Dr. E. H. and Martha C. (Hulme) C.; grad. Williams Coll., 1868 (A.M., LL.D., 1893; Litt.D., [Oxon] 1902); m. Flavia A. Camp, 1873. In railroad building in Iowa and Minn., 1868-71; admitted to Mich. bar, 1872; practiced law at St. Joseph, Mich., 1872-77; prof. history, State Univ. of Kan., 1877-91; chancellor Univ. of Neb., 1891-95; pres. Ohio State Univ., 1895-99; librarian, Columbia Univ. from 1899. Author: The College Student and His Problems, 1902. Died 1909.

CANFIELD, Roy Bishop, M.D.; b. Lake Forest, Ill., July 22, 1874; s. Eli Lake and Sarah Maria (Bishop) C.; A.B., U. of Mich., 1897, M.D., 1899; studied U. of Friedrich Wilhelm, Berlin, Germany; m. Leila Marchant Harlow, Aug. 6, 1907. Interne, Mass. Charitable Eye and Ear Infirmary, 1900-01; chief of clinic, Jansensche Klinik und Poliklinik, Berlin, 1903; asst. surgeon, Manhattan Eye, Ear and Throat Hosp., New York, 1904; attending laryngologist, N.Y. City Clinic for Laryngeal Tuberculosis, 1904; clin. prof. diseases of ear, nose and throat, Med. Sch., U. of Mich., 1904-05; prof. oto-laryngology, same, 1905—; oto-laryngologist in chief to Univ. Hosp., 1904. Commd. maj. Med. C. U.S.A., Sept. 1917; chief of ear, nose and throat sect., Base Hosp., Camp Custer, till ordered to Neuro-Surg. Sch. and Rockefeller Inst., New York; chief of surg. service Base Hosp. 76, A.E.F.; later surg. consultant Base Sec. III; hon. disch., Jan. 11, 1918. Fellow Am. Coll. Surgeons. Protestant. Home: Ann Arbor, Mich. Died May 12, 1932.

CANFIELD, William Walker, author; b. Ellicottville, N.Y., July 6, 1857; s. Hervey W. and Electa A. (McLouth) C.; common sch. edn.; m. Mary L. Gastmann, Jan. 15, 1879 (died 1906); children—Fred W., Mrs. Mabel H. Hemmens; m. 2d, Fanny G. Howard, Nov. 9, 1909 (died 1928). Author: White Seneca, 1911; At Seneca Castle, 1912; The Sign Above the Door, 1913. Editor Utica Observer-Dispatch. Home: Utica, N.Y. Died Aug. 28, 1937.

CANNON, Annie Jump, astronomer; b. Dover, Del., Dec. 11, 1863; d. Wilson Lee and Mary Elizabeth (Jump) C.; B.S., Wellesley, 1884, M.A., 1907; spl. work in astronomy, Radcliffe Coll.; D.Sc., U. of Del., 1918; Dr. Astronomy, U. of Groningen, Holland, 1921; LL.D., Wellesley Coll., 1925; D.Sc., Oxford U., 1925, Oglethorpe, 1935; Mt. Holyoke, 1937. Asst. Harvard Coll. Obs., 1897-1911, curator astron. photographs, 1911-38, William Cranch Bond astronomer and curator, 1938—. In course of photographic work has discovered 300 variable stars, 5 new stars, 1 spectroscopic binary and numerous stars having bright lines or variable spectra; has completed a catalogue of 272-150 stellar spectra which fills ten quarto volumes of the annals, all of which are published; made an extension to the catalogue, giving the spectra of fainter stars. Author of various Harvard Coll. Obs. Annals. Awarded Henry Draper medal, for investigations in astro. physics, 1931; Ellen Richards Research prize, 1932. Home: Cambridge, Mass. Died Apr. 1941.

CANNON, Austin Victor, lawyer; b. Streetsboro, O., June 9, 1869; s. Artemus M. and Leonora (Wells) C.; B.S., Buchtel Coll. (now U. of Arkon), 1892; m. Marian E. Cook, June 9, 1896 (died 1923); children—Rudolf A., Victor M., Josephine (Mrs. Richard H. Watt). Admitted to Ohio bar, 1892, Supreme Court of U.S., 1914; then mem. Cannon, Spieth, Taggart, Spring & Annat; v.p. and gen. counsel Electric Vacuum Cleaner Co.; dir. and gen. counsel City Ice & Fuel Co. Chmn. Cuyahoga County Relief Com.; mem. Cleveland Welfare Fedn., Cleveland Community Fund Council. Democrat. Unitarian. Home: Cleveland Heights, O. Died Sept. 27, 1934.

CANNON, Frank Jenne, senator; b. Salt Lake City, Utah, Jan. 25, 1859; s. George Quayle and Sarah (Jenne) C.; A.B., U. of Utah, 1878; m. Martha Anderson Brown, Apr. 8, 1878 (died 1908); 2d, May Anderson Brown, sister of 1st wife, June 29, 1909. In printing business, 1878—; also interested in mines. Del. Rep. nat. convs., 1892, 1896; candidate for del. to 53d Congress, 1892; del. to 54th Congress (1895-97); U.S. senator, 1896-99; Democrat, 1900—; state chmn. Dem. party 1902. Author: Under the Prophet in Utah (with Harvey J. O'Higgins), 1911; Brigham Young and His Mormon Empire (with George L. Knapp), 1913. Home: Denver, Colo. Died July 25, 1933.

CANNON, Henry White, banker; b. Delhi, N.Y., Sep. 27, 1850; s. George Bliss and Ann Eliza (White) C.; grad. Del. Lit. Inst., Delhi; hon. A.M., Dartmouth, 1899. Married; children—George Curtis, Henry White. Engaged in banking as clerk and teller, 1st Nat. Bank, Delhi, N.Y.; moved to St. Paul, 1870, and became teller 2d Nat. Bank; organized, 1871, Lumberman's Nat. Bank, Stillwater, Minn., and was cashier and acting pres. until 1884; comptroller of the currency, U.S., 1884-Feb. 1, 1886; v.p. Nat. Bank of the Republic, New York, Feb.-Oct. 1886; pres. Chase Nat. Bank, 1886-1904, chmn. bd., 1904-11, then dir. Was chmn. clearing house com., N.Y. Clearing House Assn.; was aqueduct commr., New York; del. Internat. Monetary Conf., Brussels, 1892. Died April 27, 1934.

CANNON, James Graham, banker; b. Delhi, N.Y., 1858; s. George Bliss and Ann Eliza W(hite) C.; bro. Henry White C. (q.v.); m. Charlotte B. Bradley. Pres. Fourth Nat. Bank of New York; chmn. bd. H.W. Johns-Manville Co.; v.p. and dir. Packard Commercial Sch. Co.; dir. Fifth Avenue Bank, Mechanics & Metals Nat. Bank, Guarantee Co. of N. America, Fidelity Trust Co., Met. Trust Co., U.S. Guarantee Co., Asso. Land Co., Agrl. Credit Co.; trustee Asso. Simmons Hardware Co.; Franklin Sav. Bank, U.S. Casualty Co. Trustee New York Univ. Mem. Internat. Com. Y.M.C.A.; pres. bd. trustees Hahnemann Hosp.; pres. and mem. Bronx Parkway Commn.; v.p. Chamber of Commerce. Author: Clearing Houses—Their History, Methods and Administration. Home: Scarsdale, N.Y. Died July 5, 1916.

CANNON, John, railroad exec.; b. Cairo, Ill., May 16, 1872; s. John and Mary (Stapleton) C.; ed. pub. schs., Cairo; m. Adelaide Miserae, Nov. 11, 1905; children—Lucille (Mrs. J. L. Matthews), Adelaide (Mrs. C. J. Lawrence), John. With Ill. Central Railroad, 1886-1905, advancing from messenger-clerk to trainmaster; supt. Mo. Pacific Railroad, 1905-15, gen. supt., 1915-17, gen. supt. transportation, 1917-20, asst. gen. mgr., 1920-25, gen. mgr, 1925—, also v.p., 1926—. Democrat. Mason. Home: St. Louis, Mo. Died Sept. 14, 1941.

CANNON, John Franklin, clergyman; b. in Cabarrus Co. N.C., Jan. 3, 1851; s. John Maxwell and Eliza Deborah (Robinson) C.; A.B., Davidson Coll., N.C., 1869; post-grad. U. of Va., 1869-70; grad. Union Theol. Sem., Va., 1873; (D.D., Southwestern Presbyn. U., 1888); m. Mary Lupton, Feb. 24, 1880. Ordained ministry Presbyn. Ch. of U.S. (Presbyn. Ch., S.), 1873; pastor, Leesburg, Va., 1873-81, Shelbyville, Tenn., 1881-88, Grand Av. (now Westminster) Ch., St. Louis, 1888—. Moderator Gen. Assembly, Presbyn. Ch. of U.S., 1899. Democrat. Home: St. Louis, Mo. Died Mar. 12, 1920.

CANNON, Joseph Gurney, congressman; b. Guilford, N.C., May 7, 1836; s. Dr. Horace F. and Gulielma (Hollingsworth) C.; admitted to Ill. bar, 1858; (LL.D., U. of Ill., 1903); m. Mary P. Reed, Jan. 1862. State's atty., 27th Jud. Dist. of Ill., 1861-68; mem. 43d to 51st Congresses (1873-91), 53d to 57th Congresses (1893-1903), 12th Ill. Dist. and 58th to 62d Congresses (1903-13), 64th to 66th Congresses, 1915-21), 18th Ill. Dist.; chmn. Com. on Appropriations, 51st, 55th, 56th and 57th Congresses; speaker U.S. Ho. of Rep., 58th, 59th, 60th and 61st Congresses (1903-11); received 58 votes for presdl. nomination, Rep. Nat. Conv., Chicago, 1908. Republican. Home: Danville, Ill. Died Nov. 12, 1927.

CANNON, Le Grand Bouton, retired banker. Served in Civil war, 1861-65; v.p. Am. Protective Tariff League; dir. in many corporations. Mem. Met. Mus. Art, Loyal Legion. Home: New York, N.Y. Died 1906.

CANRIGHT, Dudley Marvin, clergyman, author; b. Kinderhook, Mich., Sept. 22, 1840; s. Hiram and Loretta (Richardson) C.; ed. high sch., Coldwater, Mich., and acad., Albion, N.Y.; m. Lucretia Cranson, Apr. 11, 1867; m. 2d, Lucy Hadden, Apr. 24, 1881. Licensed to preach, 7th Day Adventist Ch., 1864, ordained, 1865; continued with the ch. until 1887, and became a leader in the denomination; was for 2 yrs. mem. com. of 3 having oversight of work throughout the world; prof. theology Battle Creek, Mich., Coll., 1886; united with regular Bapt. Ch., Feb., 1887; pastor Otsego, Mich., 1887-90, Berean Ch., Grand Rapids, 1891-96, then emeritus. Author: Matter and Spirit, 1881; Seventh Day Adventists Renounced, 1887, 14th edit., 1915; Lord's Day, from neither Catholics nor Pagans, 1915; Life of Mrs. E. G. White, Seventh Day Adventist Prophetess, Her Claims to Divine Inspirations Refuted, 1917. Home: Grand Rapids, Mich. Died May 12, 1919.

CANT, William Alexander, judge; b. Westfield, Marquette Co., Wis., Dec. 23, 1863; s. John and Jessie (Cameron) C.; grad. State Teachers Coll., St. Cloud, Minn.; LL.B., U. of Mich., 1885; m. Carrie E. Graham, Sept. 7, 1886 (died 1923). Began practice at Duluth, Minn., 1886; mem. Minn. Ho. of Rep., 1895; city atty. of Duluth, 1895-96; judge of Dist. Court, Minn., 1897-1923; U.S. dist. judge, Dist. of Minn., by apptmts. of Presidents Harding and Coolidge, July 1, 1923—. Republican. Conglist. Home: Duluth, Minn. Died Jan. 12, 1933.

CANTILLON, William David, ry. official; b. Janesville, Wis., Aug. 5, 1861. Began with C.&N.W. Ry., as brakeman and conductor, 1875-91, trainmaster, at Milwaukee, 1891-93, asst. supt., at Milwaukee, 1893-97, supt. Minn. and Dak. div., at Winona, Minn., 1897-1901, asst. gen. supt., at Chicago, 1901-02, gen. supt., 1902-06, asst. gen. mgr., 1906-10, and gen. mgr., Nov. 1910—. Home: Chicago, Ill. Died Dec. 13, 1914.

CANTOR, Jacob Aaron, lawyer; b. New York, Dec. 6, 1854; s. Henry and Hannah C.; LL.B., Univ. Law Sch., 1875; m. Lydia Greenebaum, Sept. 23, 1897 (dec.). Admitted to bar, 1876; then practiced law, New York; mem. N.Y. Assembly, 1885—, Senate, 1889-98 (Dem. leader); was pres. of Senate and acting lt. gov., 1893-94, and chmn. com. on finance; pres. Borough of Manhattan (on reform ticket), 1902-04; received votes for gov. in Dem. State Conv., Saratoga, 1902; chmn. com. of highways and parks of New York Improvement Commn.; chmn. New York Commn. on Congestion of Population, apptd. by the mayor, May 17, 1910. Elected to 63d Congress (1913-15), 20th N.Y. Dist., to succeed Francis B. Harrison. Apptd. pres. Dept. of Taxes and Assessments, Greater City of New York, Jan. 1, 1918. Home: New York, N.Y. Died July 2, 1921.

CANTRELL, Deaderick Harrell, lawyer; b. Little Rock, Ark., June 14, 1868; s. William Armour and Ellen Maria (Harrell) C.; prep. edn. St. John's Coll., Little Rock; Washington and Lee U., 1886-87; studied law in offices of John M. Moore and Judge Henry Clay Caldwell, Little Rock; m. Catherine Emrich, July 31, 1918. Practiced at Little Rock, 1899—; mem. Rose, Hemingway, Cantrell & Loughborough, 1905—; dir. Ark. Power & Light Co. Served as 2d lt. Ark. N.G., 1893; state chmn. for Ark., Am. Red Cross, 1917. Dir. Ada Thompson Memorial Home. Democrat. Chancellor P.E. Ch., Diocese of Ark. Mason. Home: Little Rock, Ark. Died Apr. 4, 1934.

CANTRILL, James Campbell, congressman; b. Georgetown, Ky., July 9, 1870; s. Judge James E. and Jennie (Moore) C.; ed. Georgetown (Ky.) Coll.; m. Carrie Payne, 1893 (died 1913). Farmer; active in work of organizing tobacco growers of Ky., 1906—. Chmn. Scott Co. (Ky.) Dem. Com., 1895-97; mem. Ky. Ho. of Rep., 1897-1901, Senate, 1901-05; chmn. joint caucus Ky. Legislature, 1904; nominated for Congress, 1904 (declined); mem. 61st to 66th Congresses (1909-21), 7th Ky. Dist. Pres. Am. Soc. of Equity for Ky., 1908. K.T. Home: Georgetown, Ky. Died Sept. 2, 1923.

CANTRILL, James E., justice Ky. Court of Appeals. Democrat. Home: Frankfort, Ky. Died 1908.

CANTWELL, James William, educator; b. nr. Douglass, Tex., Mar. 6, 1868; s. of John T. and Martha T. C.; A.B., Baylor U., Waco, Tex., 1893, A.M., 1903; A.B. Yale, 1894; LL.D., Baylor, 1917; m. Ada Westmoreland, May 24, 1895; children—James W., Ada Carolyn, Robert W., Christine W., Conan W. Began as teacher in country schs.; prin. Southwestern Acad., Magnolia, Ark., 1894-1901; supt. schs., Texarkana, Ark., 1901-02, Corsicana, Tex., 1902-08, Ft. Worth, Tex., 1908-15; pres. Okla. A. and M. Coll., 1915-21; supt. State Juvenile Training Sch., Gatesville, Tex., 1922-23; supt. schs. and pres. of Junior Coll., Wichita Falls, Tex., 1923—. Democrat. Methodist. Mason. Mem. State Council of Defense, 1917. Home: Wichita Falls, Tex. Died Apr. 2, 1931.

CAPEN, Charles Laban, lawyer; b. Union Springs, N.Y., Jan. 31, 1845; s. Luman W. and Eliza (Munger) C.; A.B., Harvard, 1869, A.M., 1872; m. Ella E. Briggs, Oct. 27, 1875. Began practice at Bloomington, 1871; mem. William, Burr & Capen, 1871-1902, Williams & Capen, 1902-04; prof. law of corps., bailments and carriers, personal property, damages, and legal ethics, Bloomington Law Sch. (Ill. Wesleyan U.), 1903-25, dean, 1913-25 (retired). Mem. State Bd. of Edn. many yrs.; mem. Bd. State Normal Schs. of Ill. Presbyn. Mason. Home: Bloomington, Ill. Died May 31, 1927.

CAPEN, Elmer Hewitt, pres. Tufts Coll., 1875—; b. Stoughton, Mass., April 5, 1838; grad. Tufts, 1860; (D.D., St. Lawrence Univ., 1879; LL.D., Buchtel Coll., 1899); m. Letitia H. Mussey; 2d, Mary L. Edwards. Elected to Mass. legislature, 1859, while still in coll.; attended Harvard Law School; admitted to bar, 1864; practiced at Stoughton for short time; then studied theology; ordained pastor of Independent Christian Ch., Gloucester, Mass., 1865; pastor 1st Universalist Ch., Providence, R.I., 1870-75; mem. Mass. State Bd. of Edn. Died 1905.

CAPEN, Samuel Billings, mcht.; b. Boston, Dec. 12, 1842; s. Samuel Childs and Anne Capen (Billings)

C.; grad. English High Sch., Boston, 1858; (hon. A.M., Dartmouth, 1893; LL.D., Oberlin, and Middlebury, 1900); m. Helen Maria Warren, Dec. 8, 1869. Entered carpet store of Wentworth & Bright, Boston, 1859; became partner of William E. Bright, 1863, the firm finally becoming Torrey, Bright & Capen Co., of which has been sec., treas. and dir. Pres. Congl. S.S. and Pub. Soc., 1882-99 (v.p., 1899—), A.B.C.F.M., 1899—, Watch and Ward Soc., 1904-09; v.p. Am. Congl. Assn., 1903—; dir. Boston City Missionary Soc.; trustee United Soc. Christian Endeavor; pres. Boston Municipal League, 1894-99; mem. Boston Sch. Com., 1889-92 (pres. 1892); pres. bd. trustees Wellesley Coll., 1905—; chmn. exec. com. Laymen's Missionary Movement of U.S. and Can. Active in Boston Indian Citizenship Com.; chmn. Com. of Arrangements for 2d Internat. Congl. Council, Boston, 1899. Home: Jamaica Plain, Mass. Died Jan. 29, 1914.

CAPERS, Ellison, P.E. bishop of S.C., 1893—; b. Charleston, S.C., Oct. 14, 1837; s. William and Susan C.; grad. S.C. Mil. Acad., Nov. 18, 1857; asst. prof. same, 1858-60; m. Charlotte Rebecca Palmer, Feb. 24, 1859. Served maj., lt. col., col. and brig. gen. in C.S.A., 1861-65; severely wounded at Jackson, Miss., May 14, 1863; at Chickamauga, Sept. 20, 1863, and at Franklin, Tenn., Nov. 30, 1864; sec. state S.C., 1867-68. Entered P.E. ministry, 1867; rector Christ Ch., Greenville, S.C., for 20 yrs.; St. Paul's Selma, Ala., 1 yr.; Trinity, Columbia, S.C., 6 yrs. Home: Columbia, S.C. Died 1908.

CAPERS, John G., lawyer; b. Anderson, S.C., Apr. 17, 1866; s. late Rt. Rev. Ellison and Charlotte Rebecca (Palmer) C.; bro. William Theodotus C.; ed. S.C. Mil. Acad., Charleston, 1881-85; LL.B., S.C. Coll., 1887; m. Lilla Trenholm, June 18, 1895. Admitted to bar, 1887; Democrat until 1896, when, upon nomination of Bryan, he became a supporter of McKinley, and joined Rep. party; campaigned for McKinley and Roosevelt, 1900; asst. U.S. atty., Dept. of Justice and U.S. Ct. of Claims, 1894-1901; U.S. dist. atty. for S.C., 1901-06; U.S. internal revenue commr., June-Dec. 1, 1907, and Sept., 1909. Mem. Rep. Nat. Com., 1904-12. Died Sept. 5, 1919.

CAPERTON, William Banks, admiral U.S.N.; b. Spring Hill, Tenn., June 30, 1855; s. Samuel B. and Mary Jane (Childress) C.; desc. John Caperton, from Scotland to Va. abt. 1753; Spring Hill Academy; B.Sc., U.S. Naval Acad., 1875; grad. Naval War Coll., 1896; m. Georgie Washington Blacklock; 1 daughter, Marguerite. Ensign, U.S. Navy, Aug. 3, 1877; promoted through grades to read adm., Feb. 13, 1913; advanced to rank of adm., retired, June 30, 1919. Served on various ships and stas., 1875-96; Naval Intelligence, Washington, D.C., 1896; U.S.S. Brooklyn, 1897; exec. officer U.S.S. Marietta, 1899; insp. ordnance Naval Gun Factory, 1901; exec. officer U.S.S. Prairie, 1904; Naval War Coll., 1904; lighthouse inspector 15th Dist., 1907; comdr. U.S.S. Denver, 1908, U.S.S. Maine, 1909; naval sec. Lighthouse Bd., 1910; Naval War Coll., 1910; mem. Naval Examining and Retiring Bd., 1912; comdt. Naval Sta., Newport, R.I., and 2d Naval Dist., 1913; apptd. comdr. in chief Atlantic Reserve Fleet, Nov. 25, 1914; comdr. Cruiser Squadron of Atlantic Fleet, 1916; in command naval forces that intervened in Haiti, 1915-16; comdr. Naval Forces, Vera Cruz, 1915; comdr. naval forces intervening and suppressing Santo Domingo Revolution, 1916; designated comdr. in chief U.S. Pacific Fleet, July 28, 1916, with rank of admiral. In charge patrol of east coast of S. America during World War; rep. with rank of A.E. and P. at inauguration of President Alves, of Brazil, also spl. naval del. at inauguration of Dr. Brum, as president of Uruguay, 1919; relieved of command of fleet, Apr. 30, 1919; retired June 30, 1919. Decorations: Spanish Campaign; Cuban Pacification; Mexican Service medal; Haitian Campaign; Dominican Campaign; Victory Medal—patrol clasp; D.S.M. with citation; Bust of Bolivar (Venezuela); Grand Officer Southern Cross (Republic Brazil). Founder and hon. mem. Mil. Order Foreign Wars of U.S. (European comdry., Paris, 1927); hon. life mem. Mil. Order Foreign Wars of U.S. (comdg. gen. 1914-17), Mil. Order World War, etc. Died Dec. 21, 1941.

CAPLES, Martin Joseph, ry. official; b. Ireland, Apr. 28, 1864; s. Phillip and Mary Ann (English) C.; m. Helen Stanley Hutchinson, Mar. 12, 1901. Came to America, 1869; rodman and div. engr., Boston & Lowell R.R., 1883-87; r.r. surveys and hydraulic mining, S. America, 1887-89; resident engr. on constrn. and engr. in charge maintenance of way, Norfolk & Western Ry., 1889-99; engr. maintenance of way and trainmaster, Columbus, Sandusky & Hocking R.R., 1901-02; treas. and supt. later gen. mgr., Pocahontas Coal & Coke Co., 1902-04; supt. Norfolk & Western Ry., 1904-05; gen. mgr. and chief engineer, South & Western Ry. and its successor, the Carolina, Clinchfield & Ohio Ry., and v.p. and gen. mgr. same rd., 1905-11; 4th v.p. Chesapeake & Ohio and Hocking Valley rys., 1911-14; v.p. Hocking Valley Ry. and C.&O. Ry., 1914-18; v.p. Seaboard Air Line Ry. Co., 1918-28; then in cons. practice on constrn. and operation of railroads. Home: Norfolk Va. Died July 29. 1931.

CAPPS, Charles R., ry. official; b. Norfolk, Va., Mar. 4, 1871; s. Leonard O. and Mary F. (James) C.; ed. Roanoke (Va.) Coll., 1886-88. Began as messenger, Seaboard & Roanoke R.R., 1888, later clk. in gen. frt. office same rd., to 1895; gen. frt. agt., Seaboard Air Line, 1895-1900; gen. frt. agt. combined system, Seaboard Air Line Ry., 1900-09, frt. traffic mgr. for receivers, July-Dec. 1909, v.p., Dec. 1, 1909-15, 1st v.p., Nov. 23, 1915, same rd.; apptd. traffic asst. U.S.R.R. Adminstrn., Southern Region, Jan. 1918, Allegheny Region, June 1918; re-elected 1st v.p. S.A.L. Ry., Nov. 1, 1919; v.p. Marion Southern R.R.; v.p. Raleigh & Charleston, Chesterfield & Lancaster, Tampa Northern, Tampa & Gulf Coast, East & West Coast and Florida Central & Gulf, also Macon, Dublin & Savannah, Charleston, Monroe & Columbia, Tavares & Gulf, Jacksonville, Gainesville & Gulf rys.; v.p., dir. Baltimore Steam Packet Co. Home: Norfolk, Va. Died July 31, 1936.

CAPPS, Washington Lee, naval officer; b. Portsmouth, Va., Jan. 31, 1864; s. Washington Tazewell and Frances (Bernard) C.; grad. U.S. Naval Acad., 1884; B.S., U. of Glasgow, 1888, D.Sc., 1912; m. Edna Ward, d. of Rear Admiral and Mrs. Aaron Ward, of Roslyn, L.I., 1911. Promoted ensign, July 1, 1886; apptd. asst. naval constructor, June 6, 1888; promoted naval constructor, Jan. 28, 1895. Served on the U.S.S. Tennessee, and on the staffs of Rear Admirals Luce and Jouett, 1884-86; spl. duty Glasgow, Scotland, and abroad, 1886-89; Navy Dept. and Cramp's Shipyard, 1889; Navy Yard, New York, 1889-92; Bur. of Constrn. and Repair, Navy Dept., 1892-95; superintending constrn. for the Navy at Union Iron Works, San Francisco, 1896-98; spl. duty on staff of Admiral Dewey, comdr.-in-chief Asiatic sta., 1898-99; superintended raising of several sunken Spanish ships; mem. Bd. Inspection and Survey, Washington, 1899-1901; then head of the construction dept. of Navy Yard, New York, 1901-03; chief constr. of the Navy and chief of Bur. Constrn. and Repair, with rank of rear admiral, 1903-07, re-apptd., 1907; resigned as chief of bur., Oct. 1910, and given permanent commn., as chief constr., with rank of rear admiral, from Oct. 1, 1910. Spl. duty abroad, 1909 and 1910-11; spl. duty as mem. Navy Yd. Commn., 1916-35, as pres. Navy Compensation Bd., 1917-35; pres. Naval War Claims Bd., 1925-35; pres. bds. on hull changes for U.S. naval vessels bldg. on Atlantic Coast, 1912-28. Gen. mgr. Emergency Fleet Corp., July-Dec. 1917. U.S. commr. Internat. Maritime Conf., London, 1913. and chmn. Conf. Com. on Safety of Constrn.; transferred to retired list, 1928, but continued on active duty by request of sec. of navy. Awarded Navy D.S.M. "for exceptionally meritorious services in a position of great responsibility" during the World War; specially commended, 1924, for services on Naval Compensation Board during preceding seven years. Remained on duty as mem. Navy Yard Commn., pres. Navy Compensation Bd., and pres. Naval War Claims Bd. until day of death, at his home, May 31, 1935.

CAPRON, Adin Ballou, congressman; b. Mendon, Mass., Jan. 9, 1841; s. Carlisle W. and Abby (Bates) C.; ed. Woonsocket High Sch. and Westbrook Sem., nr. Portland, Me.; sergt. and sergt. maj. 2d R.I. Inf., June 5-Oct. 11, 1861; 2d lt., Oct. 11, 1861; 1st lt., July 24, 1862; 1st lt. Signal Corps U.S.A., Mar. 3, 1863; bvtd. capt. and maj. vols., Mar. 13, 1865, "for faithful and meritorious services during the war"; hon. mustered out, Sept. 1, 1865. Miller and grain dealer. Mem. R.I. Ho. of Rep., 1887-92 (speaker, 1891-92); Rep. candidate for 53d Congress, 1892; mem. 55th to 61st Congresses (1897-1911), 2d R.I. Dist. Address: Smithfield, R.I. Died 1911.

CAPSTICK, John Henry, congressman; b. Lawrence, Mass., Sept. 2, 1856; s. John and Mary A. (Hulme) C.; ed. pub. schs. and Mowry and Goff's Mil. Acad., Providence, R.I.; m. Ella F. Blake, May 1, 1882. Engaged in dyeing, printing and bleaching textile fabrics, Montville, N.J., until 1913 (retired); pres. Consolidated Realty Co.; v.p. Morristown Trust Co.; mem. 64th Congress (1915-17), 5th N.J. Dist. Mem. 1st Inf. Cadets, Providence, R.I., 1870-71. Republican. Presbyn. Mason. Died Mar. 16, 1918.

CARAWAY, Thaddeus H., senator; b. Stoddard Co., Mo., Oct. 17, 1871; A.B., Dixon Coll., Tenn., 1896. Admitted to Ark. bar, 1900, and began practice at Lake City; elected pros. atty. 2d Jud. Circuit of Ark., 2 terms, 1908, 12; mem. 63d to 66th Congresses (1913-21), 1st Ark. Dist.; mem. U.S. Senate from Ark., 2 terms, 1921-33. Democrat. Home: Jonesboro, Ark. Died Nov. 6, 1931.

CARBONE, Agostino, vocal teacher; b. Genoa, Italy, May 19, 1856; ed. Conservatory of Music, Genoa. Engaged at grand opera houses, Paris, London, St. Petersburg, Lisbon, etc. Came to U.S., first time, season, 1881-82, engaged with Strakosh's Italian opera co.; was also mem. of Gerster's and Campanini's operatic concert cos.; later with Abbey and Grau grand opera cos. during seasons of 1887-88, 1890-91, 1891-92, 1894-95, 1895-96, 1898-99. In Italy he was selected by the foremost operatic composers to create leading rôles in many operas. Died Mar. 27, 1915.

CARD, Benjamin Cozzens, soldier; b. in R.I., Feb. 15, 1825. Apptd. from Kan., 1st lt. 12th U.S. Inf. and capt. asst. q.m., Sept. 27, 1861; col. q.m. vols., Aug. 2, 1864-Jan. 1, 1867; maj. q.m., June 6, 1872; lt. col. deputy q.m. gen., Aug. 31, 1883; retired by operation of law, Feb. 15, 1889; advanced to rank of col. retired, by act of Apr. 23, 1904. Bvtd.: maj., lt. col. and col., Mar. 13, 1865, "for faithful and meritorious services during the war," brig. gen., Mar. 13, 1865, for same in q.m. dept. during the war. Died Feb. 14, 1916.

CARDEN, Cap R., congressman; b. Hart Co., Ky., Dec. 17, 1866; s. William P. and Frances (King) C.; ed. pub. schs.; m. Mamie Hubbard, Mar. 7, 1900; children—Mary E., Frances McElroy. Began practice in Hart Co., 1895; served as sheriff and as county atty.; organized Glenbrook Power Co. and Munfordville Bridge Co.; mem. 72d Congress, 4th Ky. Dist. (1931-33), and 73d Congress (1933-35), Ky. at large. Democrat. Baptist. Home: Munfordville, Ky. Died June 13, 1935.

CARDEN, William Thomas, lawyer; b. Honolulu, T.H., Mar. 3, 1888; s. John Joseph and Anna Diane (Woodard) C.; B.L., U. of Calif., 1911; LL.B., Harvard, 1914; m. Florence Gavin Cassidy, Mar. 23, 1916. Dep. city and county atty., Honolulu, 1915-17; mem. Pub. Utilities Commn., T.H., 1916-21 (chmn. 1916-21); U.S. atty. Dist. of Hawaii, July 6, 1922—, term of 6 yrs. Republican. Home: Honolulu, T.H. Died Oct. 19, 1924.

CARDOZO, Benjamin Nathan, jurist; b. New York, N.Y., May 24, 1870; s. Albert and Rebecca Washington (Nathan) C.; A.B., Columbia, 1889, A.M., 1890, LL.D., 1915; LL.D., Yale, 1921, New York U., 1922, U. of Mich., 1923, Harvard Univ., 1927, St. John's College, Brooklyn, 1928, St. Lawrence, Williams, Princeton and Pennsylvania, 1932, Brown and U. of Chicago, 1933, Univ. of London, 1936; L.H.D., Yeshiva, 1935; unmarried. Admitted to New York bar, 1891; justice of Supreme Court of N.Y., for term 1914-28; designated to serve as judge Court of Appeals, Feb. 2, 1914; apptd. to permanent court Jan. 15, 1917; elected for full term as asso. judge Ct. of Appeals, 1917; elected for full term as chief judge Ct. of Appeals, 1927; apptd. asso. justice Supreme Court of U.S., Feb. 15, 1932. Hebrew. Author: Jurisdiction of New York Court of Appeals, 1909; The Nature of the Judicial Process, 1921; The Growth of the Law, 1924; The Paradoxes of Legal Science, 1928; Law and Literature and Other Essays, 1931. Died July 9, 1938.

CAREW, James, actor; b. Goshen, Ind., Feb. 5, 1878; ed. pub. schs. and business coll., Chicago, Chicago Conservatory of Music and Columbia U., New York; cashier for A. C. McClurg & Co., Chicago, several yrs.; m. Ellen Terry, Mar. 22, 1907. Began professional career, Chicago, 1898; leading man with Amelia Bingham, 1901-02, Maxine Elliott, 1904-05, and others; leading man with Ellen Terry, 1906—, playing in Captain Brassbounds' Conversion and The Good Hope. Home: Chicago, Ill. Died Apr. 4, 1938.

CAREY, Archibald James, bishop; b. Atlanta, Ga., Aug. 25, 1867; s. Jefferson Alexander and Anna Bell C.; ed. Atlanta U., U. of Chicago, Chicago Theol. Sem.; hon. A.M. and Ph.D., Brown U.; D.D., Wilberforce; m. Elizabeth Hill Davis, Dec. 18, 1890. Ordained A.M.E. ministry, 1891; pastor Bethel Ch. (Athens), Mt. Zion Ch. (Jacksonville, Fla.), various chs. in Chicago; bishop of Ky. and Tenn., A.M.E. Ch., May 13, 1921—. Speaker at 100th Anniversary of Perry's Victory, Put-In-Bay, Mich., 1912, and at Ecumenical Conf., London, Eng., 1921. Chmn. Selective Service Bd. No. 5, Chicago, World War; mem. Ill. Constl. Conv., 1920-22. Trustee Wilberforce U.; chancellor Turner Normal Coll., Shelbyville, Tenn. Republican. Mason. Home: Chicago, Ill. Mar. 23, 1931.

CAREY, Arthur Astor, social worker; b. Rome, Italy, Feb. 23, 1857; s. John and Mary Alida (Astor) C.; A.B., Harvard, 1879; studied in Europe, 1881-82, 1885-87; m. Agnes Whiteside, of London, Eng, Oct. 15, 1889. Founder Naval Div. of Boy Scouts, in Mass. Author: New Nerves for Old, 1914; The Scout Law in Practice, 1915; Boy Scouts at Sea, 1917. Home: Waltham, Mass. Died June 16, 1923.

CAREY, Asa Bacon, brig. gen.; b. Windham Co., Conn., July 12, 1835; s. James B. C.; apptd. from Conn., and grad. U.S. Mil. Acad., 1858; m. Laura M., d. Hon. S. B. Colby, of Vt., July 29, 1867. Commd. 2d lt. 7th Inf., Oct. 1858; advanced through grades to col. asst. p.m. gen., June 10, 1898; brig. gen. p.m. gen., U.S.A., Jan. 30, 1899; retired operation of law, July 12, 1899. Bvtd.: maj., Mar. 28, 1862, "for gallant and meritorious services in battle of Apache Cañon, N.M."; lt. col., Mar. 13, 1865, for same in war against Navajo Indians. Author: Legislative History of Pay Department U.S. Army. Home: Vineyard Haven, Mass. Died Apr. 4, 1912.

CAREY, Charles Henry, lawyer; b. Cincinnati, O., Oct. 27, 1857; s. Samuel Doak and Martha Louisa (Fenton) C.; Ph. B., Denison U., 1881, LL.D., 1931; LL.B., Cincinnati College, 1883; degree M.A. in Pub. Service, U. of Ore., 1927; m. Mary N. Bidwell, Sept. 24, 1884 (died 1928). Engaged in practice of law at Portland, 1883-1932, except 1888-89, Detroit, Mich.; senior mem. Carey, Hart, Spencer & McCulloch for many yrs., retiring Dec. 31, 1932; apptd. by gov., corp. commr. of Ore., resigned Apr. 15, 1937. Ore. counsel for various railways, public service corps., industrial and commercial cos. Municipal judge, Portland, 1892-95; one of founders and pres. Multnomah Law Library. Mem. Rep. Nat. Com., 1904-08; chmn. Rep. Congressional Com., 1894-98. Trustee Portland Art Assn. (pres. 1928-34; councillor bd. trustees, 1935—); mem. State Commn. on Reform in Jud. Procedure, chmn., 1921-22. Mem. Am. Council Inst. of Pacific Relations and of Am. Group at 3d Biennial Conference, Kyoto, Japan, 1929. Mason. Author: Index-Digest of the Oregon and Washington Reports, 1888; History of Oregon, 1922; A General History of Oregon (2 vols.), 1935. Editor: The Oregon Constitution, 1926; The Journals of Theodore Talbot, 1931; Lansford W. Hasting's Emigrants' Guide to Oregon and California, 1933. Awarded medallion by Société des Artistes Français for services during World War. Home: Portland, Ore. Died Aug. 26, 1941.

CAREY, Henry Westonrae, lumberman; b. New York, Sept. 21, 1850; s. T. Westonrae and Mary (Ramsay) C.; A.B., Coll. City of New York, 1870; m. May M. Ransom, May 4, 1879. On change and in pub. business in New York for several yrs.; removed to Manistee, Mich., 1881; pvt. sec. to R. G. Peters, lumberman, 1881-1906; sec. and treas., R. G. Peters Salt & Lumber Co., 1887-1907; an organizer, 1903, and pres. Mich. Maple Co., and Hemlock Bark Co., 1903-06; pres. Lakewood Lumber Co. (Grand Rapids), Wolverine Oil Co. (Manistee); v.p. Peters Lumber & Shingle Co. (Benton Harbor); treas. Gillette Roller Bearing Co. (Grand Rapids); sec. Manistee & Luther R.R. Co., Batchelor Cypress Lumber Co. (Fla.); also in business for self as buyer and seller of lumber lands. Regent U. of Mich., 1901-10; mem. Rep. State Exec. Com., 1886-1902; mem. Eastlake (Mich.) Sch. Bd., 1882—. Was capt. 22d Regt., N.Y.S.N.G.; p.m. gen. Mich. N.G., 1892-96. Home: Eastlake, Mich. Died 1911.

CAREY, Joseph, clergyman; grad. Gen. Theol. Sem., New York, 1864 (hon. M.A., St. Stephen's Coll., Annandale, N.Y., 1878; D.D., LL.D.). Deacon, 1864, priest, 1865, P.E. Ch.; rector Grace Church, Waterford, N.Y., 1864-68, Ballston Spa, 1868-73; archdeacon of Troy, 1877—. Deputy to Gen. Conv. P.E. Ch., 1884—. Trustee Gen. Theol. Sem., 1882—. Home: Saratoga Springs, N.Y. Died June 1913.

CAREY, Joseph Maull, governor; b. Milton, Del., Jan. 19, 1845; s. Robert Hood and Susan (Davis) C.; partial course at Union Coll.; LL.B., U. of Pa., 1864; (LL.D., Union, 1894). Admitted to bar, 1867; practiced 2 yrs. in Phila.; m. Louisa David, Sept. 1877. Went to Wyo., 1869, and then interested in cattle raising and real estate; pres. several large cos. U.S. dist. atty., Wyo. Ty., 1869-71; justice Supreme Ct., 1872-76; mem. U.S. Centennial Commn., 1872-76; mem. Rep. Nat. Com., 1876-96; mayor Cheyenne, 1881-85; del. 49th to 51st Congresses (1885-91); introduced bill which admitted Wyo. to statehood, 1890; author of the "Carey Act"; elected U.S. senator, Nov. 15, 1890, and resigned from House; term expired 1895; gov. of Wyo., term 1911-15. Republican. V.p. Fed. Land Bank, Omaha. Trustee Wyoming U. Home: Cheyenne, Wyo. Died Feb. 5, 1924.

CAREY, Miriam Eliza, librarian; b. Peoria, Ill., Feb. 21, 1858; d. Rev. Isaac Eddy and Eliza Ann (Wright) C.; ed. Rockford (Ill.) Sem., Oberlin Coll., U. of Chicago; student U. of Ill. Library Sch., 1898-99. Librarian Pub. Library, Burlington, Ia., 1899-1906; supervising librarian inst. under Ia. State Bd. Control, 1906-08 (first apptmt. of the kind in U.S.); supervising librarian inst. under Minn. Bd. Control, 1909-27; instr. U. of Minn. Library Sch., 1930-36. Field rep. A.L.A. Hosp. War Service, 1918-19, and chmn. A.L.A. Com. on Instn. Libraries, 1913-23. Republican. Conglist. Home: St. Paul, Minn. Died Jan. 9, 1937.

CAREY, Robert Davis, senator, irrigation enterprises; b. Cheyenne, Wyo., Aug. 12, 1878; s. Joseph Maull and Louisa (David) C.; Hill Sch., Pottstown, Pa.; A.B., Yale, 1900; m. Julia B., d. Brig. Gen. H. B. Freeman, Sept. 5, 1903; children—Sarah Darlington, Joseph Maull. Pres. J. M. Carey & Brother, Inc.; pres. Wheatland Industrial Co., Wyoming Development Co., Wheatland Roller Mill Co., Converse County Bank (Douglas, Wyoming). Pres. Wyo. State Fair Commn., 1909-10. Chmn. Rep. Central Com., Converse Co., Wyo., 1908-09; mem. Prog. Nat. Com. for Wyo., 1912-16; treas. Prog. State Com. Chmn. Wyo. State Highway Commn., 1917-18; mem. State Council Defense, 1917-18. Gov. Wyo., 1919-23; apptd. chmn. Agrl. Conf. to investigate and report on agrl. situation in U.S., 1924; elected U.S. senator, Nov. 9, 1930, to fill unexpired term of late Senator Francis E. Warren and for full term expiring 1937. Episcopalian. Home: Careyhurst, Wyo. Died Jan. 17, 1937.

CARHART, Daniel, civil engr.; b. Clinton, N.J., Jan. 28, 1839; s. Charles and Christianna (Bird) C.; C.E., Poly. Coll. of Pa., 1859, M.C.E., 1869; Sc.D., Western U. of Pa., 1897; m. Josephine R. Stoy, Apr. 17, 1867. Practicing civ. engring., 1859-68; asst. prof. and prof. civ. engring. Poly. Coll. of Pa., 1868-78; prof. mathematics and civ. engring., 1882-92, dean collegiate and engring. depts., 1892-1908, emeritus prof. civ. engring., 1908—, Western U. of Pa. (now U. of Pittsburgh). Author: Plane Surveying (text-book), 1888, 1902; Field Book for Civil Engineers, 1893, 1902. Apptd., Aug. 1913, by the pres. of Civ. Service Commn., leading advisor on the bd. to pass upon the eligibility of applicants to fill positions as sr. civ. engr. in the Interstate Commerce Commission under the act providing for the valuation of properties of common carriers. Home: Pittsburgh, Pa. Died Dec. 7, 1926.

CARHART, Henry Smith, physicist; b. Coeymans, N.Y., Mar. 27, 1844; s. Daniel S. and Margaret (Martin) C.; A.B., Wesleyan, Conn., 1869, A.M., 1872; student Yale, 1871-72, Harvard, 1876, U. of Berlin, 1881-82; (LL.D., Wesleyan, 1893, U. of Mich., 1912; Sc.D., Northwestern, 1912); m. Ellen M. Soule, Aug. 30, 1876. Prof. physics and chemistry, Northwestern U., 1872-86; prof. physics, 1886-1909, emeritus prof., 1909—, U. of Mich. Mem. Internat. Jury of Awards, Paris Expn., of Electricity, 1881; pres. Bd. Judges, Dept. Electricity, Chicago Expn., 1893; mem. Jury of Awards, Buffalo Expn., 1901; U.S. del. Internat. Elec. Congress, Chicago, 1893, St. Louis, 1904; guest of Brit. Assn. Adv. Science to S. Africa, 1905; mem. preliminary conf. on elec. units and standards, Berlin, 1905; U.S. del. to conf., same, London, 1908; del. U. of Mich. to Darwin Centennial Celebration, Cambridge, Eng., 1909. Author: University Physics, 1894-96; Electrical Measurements (with G. W. Patterson), 1895; High School Physics (with H. N. Chute), 1901; College Physics, 1910; First Principles of Physics (with H. N. Chute), 1912; Physics with Applications (with H. N. Chute), 1917. Home: Pasadena, Calif. Died Feb. 13, 1920.

CARHARTT, Hamilton, cotton mfr.; b. Macedon Locks, Wayne Co., N.Y.; s. George and Lefa (Wylie) C.; ed. public schs. and Racine (Wis.) Coll.; m. Annette Welling, Dec. 22, 1882. Began in wholesale business, firm of Welling & Carhartt, Grand Rapids, 1882; removed to Detroit, 1884, and established Hamilton Carhartt & Co., wholesale furnishing goods, changed, 1899, to mfr. men's working apparel, as Hamilton Carhartt Mfr. (Inc.), and, 1915, to Hamilton Carhartt Cotton Mills (Toronto, Ont., and Liverpool, Eng.; mfg. concentrated at Carhartt Park at the foot of the Sweet Lick mountains, Ky.), pres. of mills. Episcopalian. Home: Carhartt Park, Irvine P.O., Ky. Deceased.

CARKIN, Seth Ballou, business educator; b. South Hope, Maine, Sept. 27, 1885; s. William and Mary (Fogler) Carkin; B.S. in Edn., U. of Rochester, 1924; studied U. of Pa., Boston U. and Simmons Coll., Boston; m. Alice M. Williams, Sept. 21, 1912; children—Mary Sumner, Janice Williams. Began as teacher St. Johnsbury (Vt.) Acad., 1913, later teacher high schs., Rochester; dir. business edn., Rochester, 1919-25; pres. Packard Commercial School, N.Y. City, 1925—, also instr. Sch. of Edn., New York U.; served as instr. summer sessions Simmons Coll., N.Y. State Coll. for Teachers (Albany), U. of Rochester and New York Univ. Mem. Regents Syllabus Revision Com. in charge of revision of commercial syllabus for Univ. of State of N.Y., 1923-24; pres. Rochester Teachers Assn., 1924-25; mem. exec. com., Eastern Commercial Teachers Assn., 3 yrs., sec. 4 yrs., pres., 1929; pres. N.Y. City Gregg Shorthand Teachers Assn., 1934-35. Home: New York, N.Y. Died Apr. 27, 1938.

CARL, Francis Augustus, commr. Chinese customs; b. Osyka, Miss., July 16, 1861; s. Francis Augustus and Mary (Bredon) C.; ed. J. D. Stewart Inst., Memphis, Tenn.; m. Mary Ruth Collins, June 16, 1898. Joined the Chinese Maritime Customs, 1881; promoted to be commr., 1889, and officiated as such in the treaty ports of China till Aug. 1921 (retired). Imperial vice-commr. for China, St. Louis Expn., 1904; asso. del. for China, Internat. Opium Commn., Shanghai, Feb. 1909; del. for China, Internat. Opium Conf., The Hague, Dec. 1911. Granted civil rank of 3d class, China, Apr. 1893, and of 2d class, Jan. 1903; decorations, Officer Double Dragon, 1893, Grand Officer Double Dragon, 1912, Officer Chia Ho, 1914, Grand Officer Chia Ho, 1917. Died Jan. 5, 1930.

CARL, Katharine Augusta, artist; b. in La.; d. Francis Augustus and Mary (Bredon) C.; grad. State Female Coll., Memphis, Tenn., 1882; studied art under Bouguereau and Gustave Courtois, Paris; unmarried. Portraits: Tze Hsi, Empress Dowager of China, now in U.S. Nat. Mus.; Prince El Hadj, Algeria; H. E. Tseng, former Lord Chamberlain to Emperor Hsuan Tong of China, known under family name of Pu-Yi (now emperor Kang Teh of Manchukuo); H. E. Li Yuan Hung, 2d Pres. Republic of China; Sir Richard Dane; Paul S. Reinsch, U.S. minister to China; Col. Robertson, mil. attaché British Legation; Miss Belle Skinner, New York. Orders Double Dragon (China) and Flaming Pearl (Manchu). Author: (and illustrator) With the Empress Dowager of China, 1905. Home: New York, N.Y. Died Dec. 7, 1938.

CARL, William Crane, organist; b. Bloomfield, N.J., March 2, 1865; ed. in Paris, France, under Alexander Guilmant; hon. Mus.D., New York U., 1911; unmarried. Was organist and musical dir. First Presbyn. Ch., dir. Guilmant Organ Sch., New York. Made extensive organ tours in Europe and America (including 7 to Pacific Coast, and 1 to the Klondike; gave nearly 200 organ concerts in 1st Presbyn. Ch., New York; appeared as soloist with Theodore Thomas, Emil Paur, Walter Damrosch, the People's Symphony orchestras, the Worcester Festival, etc.; displayed the great organ at St. Louis Exposition for the jury of awards, besides a series of concerts. Officier de l'Instruction Publique (France), 1909. Chevalier Legion of Honor (France), 1924. Author: Several Songs and Organ Arrangements, 1892. Editor: Masterpieces for the Organ, 1898; Thirty Postludes for the Organ, 1900; Novelties for the Organ, Book I and II; Master Studies for the Organ; Guilmant Organ-pieces, 3 vols.; Ecclesiastiæ Organum (Voluntaries for the Church Service); Festival Organ Music (5 vols.), for Christmas, Easter, Funerals, Weddings, or Festivals of the Church, 1915; historical Organ Collection. Died Dec. 8, 1936.

CARLAND, John Emmett, judge; b. in Oswego Co., N.Y., Dec. 11, 1853; s. Capt. John (U.S.A.) and Emily C.; m. Albertine Knaack, Sept. 29, 1884. Admitted to bar, 1875; U.S. dist. atty., Dak. Ty., 1885-88; asso. justice Supreme Ct., 1888-89; U.S. dist. judge Dist. of S.D., Aug. 31, 1896-Dec. 12, 1910; apptd. additional U.S. circuit judge, Dec. 12, 1910, and designated to serve on U.S. Commerce Ct. for 2 yrs.; assigned to U.S. Ct. of Appeals, 8th Circuit, Dec. 26, 1913. Mem. N.D. Constl. Conv., 1889. Home: Washington, D.C. Died Nov. 11, 1922.

CARLE, Frank Austin, newspaperman; b. Spencerport, N.Y., July 21, 1851; s. John and Catherine Melissa (Spencer) C.; ed. U. of Wis., 1869-71; B.S., U. of Mich., 1874; m. Mary Elizabeth Bardeen, May 15, 1878 (died 1895). In newspaper work, 1876—; mng. editor St. Paul Pioneer Press, 1880-88; in Washington, 1888-89; mng. editor Portland (Ore.) Oregonian, 1889-97; in charge editorial page New York Commercial-Advertiser, 1897-1900; in Europe, 1900-01; in charge editorial page Minneapolis Tribune, 1901-12; editorial writer Minneapolis Journal, 1913-16, retired. In Ordnance Dept., Washington, "dollar-a-year" work, 1917-18. Republican. Home: Minneapolis, Minn. Died 1930.

CARLE, Richard (Charles N. Carleton), actor, playwright; b. Somerville, Mass., July 7, 1871; s. Edgar W. Carleton; high sch. edn., Somerville, Mass.; married. Began stage career, Bijou Theatre, New York, Sept. 20, 1891; playing in "The Spring Chicken," 1906-07, "Mary's Lamb," 1909-10, etc. Author: (plays) "Mam'selle 'Awkins"; "The Storks"; "The Tenderfoot"; "The Mayor of Tokio"; "The Hurdy Gurdy Girl"; "The Maid and the Mummy"; "Jumping Jupiter"; and adapter of "The Spring Chicken" and "Mary's Lamb," "The Chief Nut" (from story by Irvin S. Cobb). Died June 28, 1941.

CARLETON, Bukk, G., surgeon; b. Whitefield, N.H., Nov. 11, 1856; s. Ebenezer and Lucia M. (Dexter) C.; ed. Littleton (N.H.) High Sch., 1870-73; M.D., N.Y. Homœ. Med. Coll., 1876; med. dept. U. City of New York, 1876-77; (hon. A.M., Rutgers, 1907); m. Sarah E. Robinson, Nov. 19, 1879 (died 1901); 2d, Clarice E. Griffith, Mar. 23, 1903. Mem. house staff, 1876-77, pathologist, 1877-81, visiting phys., 1881-95, genito-urinary surgeon, 1895—, Homœ. and Metropolitan hosps., Dept. Pub. Charities, New York; demonstrator anatomy, 1879-80, adj. prof. of anatomy, 1880-82, N.Y. Homœ. Medical Coll.; cons. genito-urinary surgeon Hahnemann Hosp., 1897—; prof. genito-urinary surgery, 1902-10, med. ethics and clin. urology, 1910—, New York Homœ. Med. Coll. and Hosp. Author: Urological and Venereal Diseases, 1905. Died Oct. 20, 1914.

CARLETON, Henry Guy, playwright; b. Ft. Union, N.M., June 21, 1856; s. Gen. James Henry (U.S.A.) and Sophia Garland (Wolfe) C.; ed. Santa Clara Coll., Cal., 1865-70. Apptd. 2d lt. 8th U.S. Cav., Oct. 21, 1873, served in Miles' campaign against Kiowas and Arapahoes, Tex., 1874-75; resigned, Aug. 1, 1876; asso. editor New Orleans Times, 1876-79; spl. writer Chicago Tribune, 1880-81, New York Times, 1882-83; lit. editor Life, 1883-85; spl. writer New York World, 1886-89; dramatic author, 1881—. In elec. work, 1889-1903; took out 34 patents on elec. devices. Was adj. La. Field Arty., 1877; adj. 1st La. Inf., 1877-80. Mem. Com. of 200, N.Y. Centennial of Washington Inaugural, 1889. Plays: (produced) Memmon (tragedy, blank verse), 1881; Victor Durand, 1885; The Pembertons, 1889; The Lion's Mouth, 1890; Ye Earlie Trouble, 1891; Princess of Erie, 1892; A Guilded Fool, 1892; The Butterflies, 1894; That Imprudent Young Couple, 1896; Ambition, 1896; Colinette, 1898; Jack's Honeymoon, 1903. Also adaptations: Never Again; Ladies First; Girl from Maxim's etc. Home: Atlantic City, N.J. Died 1910.

CARLETON, Mark Alfred, plant pathologist; b. Jerusalem, O., Mar. 7, 1866; s. Lewis D. and Lydia Jane (Mann) C.; B.Sc., Kan. Agrl. Coll., 1887,

M.Sc., 1893; m. Amanda Elizabeth Faught, Dec. 29, 1897. Cerealist, U.S. Dept. Agr., 1894—. Agrl. explorer for U.S. Govt. in Russia and Siberia, 1898-99; cereal expert, then plant pathologist Cuyamel (Honduras) Fruit Co. Has introduced several new grain crops from foreign countries, including especially the durum wheat industry; in charge U.S. grain exhibit and mem. jury of awards, Paris Expn., 1900; chmn. group 84, jury of awards, St. Louis Expn., 1904. Given leave of absence 15 mos., 1912-13, to conduct work of the Pa. Chestnut Tree Blight Commn. Decorated with order Mérite Agricole by French Govt. Died 1925.

CARLETON, Murray, merchant; b. Cumberland, Md., Sept. 1, 1852; s. Henry D. and Mary Ellen (Boogher) C.; ed. high sch., 1 yr.; m. Annie Laurie Hays, June 26, 1884. Worked at printing business 5 yrs.; removed to St. Louis, 1873; became connected with Henry Bell & Son, wholesale dry goods, and continued with same house and its successors; then pres. Carleton Dry Goods Co. Trustee Robert Barnes Estate. Mem. M.E. Ch., S. Trustee Y.M.C.A. Home: St. Louis, Mo. Died Mar. 2, 1926.

CARLETON, Will, poet; b. Hudson, Mich., Oct. 21, 1845; B.S., Hillsdale (Mich.) Coll., 1869, later A.M. (Litt.D.). In newspaper work, Hillsdale, Detroit, Chicago, Boston, and New York several yrs.; became editor of Everywhere (monthly), Brooklyn. Lecturer and reader from own works throughout U.S. and Europe. Author: Farm Ballads; Farm Legends; Farm Festivals; Young Folks' Rhymes; City Ballards; City Legends; City Festivals; Rhymes of Our Planet; The Old Infant, and Similar Stories; Songs of Two Centuries, 1902; Poems for Young Americans, 1906; In Old School Days, 1907; Drifted In, 1907; A Thousand Thoughts, 1908; Correct Affinities; Ghosts, or Dreams? Home: Brooklyn, N.Y. Died Dec. 18, 1912.

CARLEY, Patrick J., congressman; b. County Roscommon, Ireland, 1866; brought to U.S. in childhood; ed. pub. schs. In building business, Brooklyn, N.Y., many yrs.; pres. P. J. Carley Building Co., P. J. Carley & Sons, N.Y. City. Mem. 70th to 73d Congresses (1927-35), 8th N.Y. Dist. Democrat. Died Feb. 25, 1936.

CARLIN, Charles Creighton, congressman; b. Alexandria, Va., Apr. 8, 1866; s. William H. and Frances E. C.; LL.B., Nat. Law U., Washington, 1891; m. Lillian Broders, Oct. 1891. In law practice at Alexandria, Va.; postmaster of Alexandria during Cleveland's 2d term; presdl. elector, 1904; elected to 60th Congress, Nov. 5, 1907, for unexpired term (1907-09) of John F. Rixey, deceased; reëlected 61st to 66th Congresses (1909-21), 8th Va. Dist. Democrat. Home: Alexandria, Va. Died Oct. 14, 1938.

CARLIN, James Joseph, college pres.; b. Peabody, Mass., Apr. 14, 1872; s. James and Mary (O'Rourke) C.; A.B., A.M., Boston Coll., 1892; studied classics, Jesuit Novitiate, Frederick, Md., 1892-96, philosophy and sciences, Woodstock (Md.) Sem., 1896-99, theology, sacred scripture and cannon law, same sem., 1904-08. Joined Soc. of Jesus, 1892; prof. of Latin, Greek and English, Georgetown U., 1899-1904; ordained priest R.C. Ch., 1907; lecturer on scholastic philosophy, Holy Cross Coll., Worcester, Mass., 1910-12; asst. to provincial of Md., 1912-18; pres. Holy Cross Coll., 1918—. Died Oct. 1, 1930.

CARLIN, William Passmore, brig. gen., retired. Nov. 24, 1893; b. Greene Co., Ill., Nov. 24, 1829; grad. U.S. Mil. Acad., 1850. Bvtd. 2d lt., 6th regt., U.S. inf., and served with regt. until 1861, participating in Sioux war, 1855-56; Cheyenne, 1857; Mormon rebellion, 1858. Apptd. col. 38th Ill. vol. inf., 1861; comd. 4,500 men, battle of Fredericktown, Mo., Oct. 21, 1861; promoted brig. gen. vols., Nov. 29, 1862, and bvt. maj. gen., U.S.A. After being mustered out of vol. army, was returned to rank maj., regular army; promoted brig. gen., U.S.A., May 17, 1893, and assumed command dept. of the Columbia; retired by age limit. Home: Carrollton, Ill. Died 1903.

CARLISLE, Charles Arthur, mfr.; b. Chillicothe, O., May 3, 1864; s. Meade Woodson Clay and Emma V. (Barr) C.; ed. Chillicothe, O., pub. schs., and by his mother; in ry. service, 1886-91; m. Anne, d. late Clement Studebaker, of South Bend, Ind., Sept. 17, 1891. Pres. Perkins Corp., Milmore Corp., and Products Conservation Co. Col. on staffs Govs. Mount and Durbin, of Ind., 1897-1905. Trustee Y.M.C.A. Republican. Methodist. Mason. Home: South Bend, Ind. Died Sept. 2, 1938.

CARLISLE, James Henry, pres. Wofford Coll., 1875-1902; b. Winnsboro, S.C., May 4, 1825; grad. S.C. Coll., 1844; (A.M., LL.D., Southwestern Univ., Texas); m. Margaret Jane Gryce, 1848. Prof. Mathematics, Wofford Coll., 1854—; emeritus. Editor of Lives of Ascham and Arnold and The Young Astronomer. Home: Spartanburg, S.C. Died 1909.

CARLISLE, John Griffin, sec. of the treasury; b. Campbell (now Kenton) Co., Ky., Sept. 5, 1835; s. L. H. and Mary A. (Reynolds) C.; pub. sch. edn.; admitted to bar, 1858; m. Mary Jane Goodson, Jan. 15, 1857. Mem. Ky. Ho. of Rep., 1859-61, Senate, 1866-71; del.-at-large Dem. Nat. Conv., 1868; lt. gov., Ky., 1871-75; alternate presdl. elector-at-large 1876; mem. 45th to 51st Congresses (1877-91); speaker of the House, 48th, 49th, 50th Congresses (1883-89); resigned from Ho. of Rep. May 26, 1890, to become U.S. senator, for unexpired term of James B. Beck, deceased; resigned from Senate, Feb. 4, 1893; sec. of the treasury, in cabinet of President Cleveland, 1893-97. Democrat. Affiliated with Nat. (gold standard) Dem. Party, 1896; practiced at New York from 1897. V.p. Anti-Imperialist League (Boston). Died 1910.

CARLISLE, John Nelson, lawyer; b. Preble, Cortland Co., N.Y., Aug. 24, 1866; s. William S. and Catharine Rose (Burdick) C.; grad. Watertown (N.Y.) High Sch., 1884; m. Carrie C. Brown. Admitted to N.Y. bar, 1889, to U.S. courts, 1902; practices in Watertown; city attorney of Watertown, 1891-92; mem. Bd. of Edn., 1901-04; pub. service commr., 2d Dist., N.Y., 1910-12; chmn. Com. of Inquiry, State of N.Y., 1913; state commr. of highways, 1913-15; advisor to state commr. of highways, Mar. 1-Aug. 1, 1915; mem. Black River Regulating Dist. Bd. (water storage); pres. Northern N.Y. Utilities, Inc., of Watertown, N.Y.; pres. The Power Corp. of New York. Mem. N.G.N.Y., 1895-1910 (maj. 1st Regt., 1905-10). Trustee Cornell U., 1909-15. Democrat. Universalist. K.T. Home: Watertown, N.Y. Died July 21, 1931.

CARLISLE, Marcus Lee, clergyman; b. Pendleton, S.C., Oct. 13, 1863; s. Rev. F. John Mason and Elisabeth Catherine (Sharp) C.; A.B., Wofford Coll., Spartanburg, S.C., 1883, D.D., 1901; m. Annie Margaret Rast, Feb. 17, 1887; children—Charles Heber (dec.), Aiken Rast. Ordained ministry M.E. Ch., S., 1887; pastor Clifton, S.C., 1887, Walhalla, 1888-90, Camden, 1891-94, Chester, 1895-96, Central Ch., Spartanburg, 1897-1900, Washington St. Ch., Columbia, 1901-04, Bethel Ch., Charleston, 1905-06, Marion, 1907; presiding elder Spartanburg Dist., 1908-11; pastor Buncombe St. Ch., Greenville, 1912-15; presiding elder Greenville Dist., 1916; pastor St. John's Ch., Anderson, 1917-20, Washington St. Ch., Columbia, 1921-24, Central Ch., Spartanburg, 1925—. Del. Gen. Conf. M.E. Ch., S., 1906, 1910, 1922; del. Ecumenical Meth. Conf., London, 1921; mem. Commn. on Constn. M.E. Ch., S. Pres. bd. trustees Columbia Coll. Democrat. Died Nov. 8, 1927.

CARLL, John Franklin, geologist; b. Long Island, N.Y., May 7, 1828; ed. Union Hall Acad., Jamaica, L.I.; m. Hannah A. Burtis, Nov. 15, 1853 (died 1859); 2d, Martha Tappan, Oct. 28, 1868. Published Daily Eagle, Newark, N.J., 1849-53; civil engr. and surveyor at Flushing, L.I., 1853-61; settled in Pleasantville, Pa., 1864, becoming identified with oil development; invented static pressure sand-pump, removable pump chamber and other devices now used in oil operations; in 1874 received an apppmt. on the geol. survey of Pa. and as asst. in charge of the oil regions; compiled 7 vols. of the State reports; then in practice as cons. geologist. Died 1904.

CARLSEN, Carl Laurence, author; b. Alameda, Cal., Feb. 19, 1880; s. Carl Frederick and Laura Bendicte (Larsen-Kaäe) C.; B.L., U. of Calif., 1901; m. Iva Rhoda Cutler, Aug., 1904. Began as teacher at Solana, P.I., 1902; teacher high sch., Tulare, Calif., 1904-06, Sonora, 1906; prin. high sch., Lodi, Calif., 1906-09; high sch. teacher, San Francisco, 1909-20; dir. part-time edn., San Francisco Pub. Schs., July 1920—. Methodist. Author: The Taming of Calinga, 1916; The Son of Pio, 1919. Home: San Francisco, Calif. Deceased.

CARLSEN, Emil, painter; b. Copenhagen, Denmark, Oct. 19, 1853; s. I. A. S. and Dorothea (Raa) C.; ed. Copenhagen, Denmark. Awarded Inness prize, Salmagundi Club; Shaw purchase prize, Soc. of Am. Artists; gold medal, St. Louis Epxn., 1904. Webb prize, Soc. of Am. Artists, 1905; Inness gold medal, Nat. Acad. Design, 1907; medal of third class, Carnegie Inst., Pittsburgh, 1908; medal, Internat. Expn., Buenos Aires, 1910; Temple gold medal, Pa. Acad. of Fine Arts, 1912; Walter Lippincott prize, Pa. Acad., 1913; gold medal of honor, Panama-Pacific Internat. Expn., San Francisco, 1915; Jennie Sesnan gold medal, Pa. Acad. Fine Arts, 1916; Saltus gold medal, Nat. Acad. Design, 1916; Carnegie prize, 1919; gold medal, Sesquicentennial Internat. Expn., 1926. Represented in Met. Mus. of Art, New York; Brooklyn Inst. Arts and Sciences; Nat. Gallery of Art and Corcoran Gallery Fine Arts, Washington; Albright Art Gallery, Buffalo; R.I. School of Design; Art Inst. Chicago; Pa. Acad. Fine Arts; John Herron Art Inst., Indianapolis, N.A., 1906; mem. Nat. Inst. Arts and Letters. Address: New York, N.Y. Died Jan. 4, 1931.

CARLSON, George Alfred, governor; b. Alta, Buena Vista Co., Ia., Oct. 23, 1876; s. Charles August and Louisa Piternilla (Gustafson) C.; Ped.B., Colo. State Normal Sch., 1898; Ph.B., U. of Colo., 1902; LL.B., 1904; m. Rosa Lillian Alps, Aug. 29, 1906 (died 1922); children—Elaine Bessie, George Alfred, John Swink, Juanita Rose; m. 2d, Louise Avery Crose, Mar. 11, 1924. Admitted to Ida. bar, 1904, and practiced at Lewiston; removed to Colo., 1905, and practiced at Ft. Collins; dist. atty. 8th Judicial Dist., Colo., 1908-15; gov. of Colo., 1915-17; resumed practice of law at Denver. Republican. Presbyn. Mason. Home: Denver, Colo. Died Dec. 6, 1926.

CARLTON, Albert E., banker; b. Warren, Ill., Feb. 20, 1866; s. Horace Milton and Amelia Caroline C.; grad. Beloit (Wis.) Coll.; m. Ethel Frizzel, Dec. 4, 1902. Moved to Colo., 1889; engaged in coal business at Cripple Creek, 1891; later interested in banking and mining; pres. Cresson Consol. Gold Mining & Milling Co., Golden Cycle Mining and Reduction Co., United Gold Mines Co., Cripple Creek Central Ry. Co., Holly Sugar Corp. Home: Colorado Springs, Colo. Died Sept. 7, 1931.

CARLTON, Caleb Henry, brig. gen.; b. Cleveland, Sept. 1, 1836; s. C. C. and Jane (Stow) C.; grad. U.S. Mil. Acad., 1859; m. Sara Pollock, Mar. 3, 1863. Bvt. 2d lt. 7th Inf., July 1, 1859; commd. 2d lt. 4th Inf., Oct. 12, 1859; 1st lt., May 14, 1861; capt. June 30, 1862; col. 89th Ohio Inf., July 7, 1863; hon. mustered out of vol. service, June 23, 1865; assigned to 10th Cav., Dec. 15, 1870; maj. 3d Cav., May 17, 1876; lt. col. 7th Cav., Apr. 11, 1889; col. 8th Cav., Jan. 30, 1892; brig. gen., June 28, 1897; retired at own request after 40 yrs.' service, June 30, 1897. Bvt. maj., July 4, 1862, for Peninsular campaign; lt. col., Sept. 20, 1863, for battle of Chickamauga, Ga. Died Mar. 21, 1923.

CARLTON, Leslie Gilbert, mining exec.; s. Horace Milton and Amelia Caroline C.; head of Carleton interests in Cripple Creek (Colo.) mining dist.; pres. Golden Cycle Corp., which owns Golden Cycle, Cyanide Mill (one of the largest of the kind in the U.S.), Pike's Peak Fuel Co., United Gold Mines Co., Midland Terminal R.R.; pres. First Nat. Bank (Cripple Creek); head of Cresson Consol. Gold Mining & Milling Co. and other cos. Home: Colorado Springs, Colo. Died Sept. 4, 1938.

CARMACK, Edward Ward, U.S. senator Tenn., 1901-07; b. nr. Castilian Springs, Sumner Co., Tenn., Nov. 5, 1858; academic edn.; studied law; practiced at Columbia, Tenn.; mem. legislature, 1884; on editorial staff, Nashville American, 1886-88; founded Nashville Democrat, 1888; and when it was merged into the American became editor-in-chief of latter; in 1892 became editor Memphis Commercial; m. Elizabeth Cobey Dunnington, Apr. 1890. Del. Nat. Dem. Conv., 1896; mem. Congress, 1897-1901, 10th Tenn. dist. Democrat. Home: Memphis, Tenn. Died 1908.

CARMALT, James Walton, lawyer; b. Montrose, Pa., Oct. 24, 1872; s. James E. and Charlotte (Churchill) C.; A.B., Hamilton Coll., 1895; studied law Columbia and New York law schs.; m. Katherine I. Crupper (nee McCuen), 1918; children (adopted)—Leonard Berkeley, John Scott, Wilbur Brooke, Eveline Theresa. Admitted to N.Y. bar, 1898; practiced at New York, 1898-1909, largely engaged in street ry. transportation work during the same period; with Interstate Commerce Commn., 1909-18; asso. with the Hon. Louis D. Brandeis in preparation and presentation of Rate Advance Case, 1913-14; chief examiner Interstate Commerce Commn., 1914-18; mem. staff War Industries Bd., 1918; asst. to gen. counsel U.S. Railroad Administration, 1918-19; practiced at Washington, 1919—. Apptd. mem. Nat. Mediation Bd., 1934. Home: Washington, D.C. Died Dec. 2, 1937.

CARMALT, William Henry, surgeon; b. Friendsville, Pa., Aug. 3, 1836; s. Caleb and Sarah (Price) C.; ed. boarding schs. in Pa., N.J. and Va.; M.D., Coll. Phys. and Surg. (Columbus), 1861; hon. A.M., Yale, 1881; m. Laura Woolsey Johnson, Dec. 8, 1863; children—Ethel, Laurance Johnson, Geraldine Woolsey. In practice, New York, 1861-69; studied in Germany, 1869-74; lecturer ophthalmology and otology, 1876-79, prof. same, 1879-81, prof. principles and practice of surgery, 1881-1907, emeritus, Yale; consulting surgeon, New Haven Hosp. and pres. Gen. Hosp. Soc. of Conn. Fellow Am. Surg. Assn. (pres. 1907). Home: New Haven, Conn. Died July 17, 1929.

CARMAN, Augustine Spencer, clergyman, educator; b. Ashland, O., July 1, 1859; s. Rev. Isaac Newton and Julia Ann (Spencer) C.; student U. of Ill. 2 yrs.; A.B., U. of Rochester, 1882 (valedictorian); grad. Rochester Theol. Sem., 1885; D.D., Denison, 1910, U. of Rochester, 1913; m. Myra Elizabeth Hanscomb, May 5, 1886; children—Raymond Spencer, Charles Augustine, Newton Hanscomb, Eleanor Joy. Ordained Bapt. ministry, 1885; pastor Lincoln Park Ch., Cincinnati, O., 1885-88, 1st Ch., Ann Arbor, Mich., 1888-93, 1st Ch., Springfield, O., 1893-98; ednl. sec. Denison U., 1898-1909; pastor 1st Ch., Marietta, O., 1909-17; sec. Ill. Bapt. Bd. of Beneficence, 1918-20; prof. ch. history, Northern Baptist Sem., Chicago, 1920-29 (emeritus). Pres. Chicago Baptist Ministers' Conf., 1920-21; hist. sec. Chicago Bapt. Assn.; trustee Denison U., 12 yrs., Ohio Bapt. Edn. Soc., 23 yrs., Ohio Bapt. Conv., 23 yrs. Republican. Home: San Diego, Calif. Died Feb. 6, 1941.

CARMAN, (William) Bliss, poet; b. Fredericton, N.B., Apr. 15, 1861; s. William and Sophia Mary (Bliss) C.; A.B., U. of N.B., 1881, A.M., 1884;

U. of Edinburgh, 1882-83; Harvard, 1886-88; read law 2 yrs.; (LL.D., U. of N.B., 1906); unmarried. Office editor The Independent, New York, 1890-92; editor Chap Book, Boston, 1894. Author: Songs from Vagabondia (with Richard Hovey), 1894; More Songs from Vagabondia (with same), 1896; Last Songs of Vagabondia (with same), 1900; Pipes of Pan, No. 1, 1902; Pipes of Pan, No. 2, 1903; Pipes of Pan, Nos. 3, 4 and 5, 1904-05; Poems, Collected Edition (2 vols.), 1905; Friendship of Art, 1904; The Making of Personality, 1907; Gate of Peace, 1907; Rough Rider, 1909; A Painter's Holiday, 1911; Echoes from Vagabondia, 1912; Daughters of Dawn (with Mary Perry King), 1913; Earth Deities (with same), 1914; April Airs, 1916; Far Horizons, 1925. Home: New Canaan, Conn. Died June 8, 1929.

CARMAN, Ezra Ayers; b. Metuchen, N.J., Feb. 27, 1834; s. M. F.and Ann Maria (Ayers) C.; early edn. in Middlesex Co., N.J.; grad. Western Mil. Inst., Ky., 1855; asst. prof. mathematics Univ. of Nashville, Tenn., 1855-56 (A.M., U. of Nashville, 1858); m. Ada Salmon, Nov. 22, 1859. Civil pursuits, 1859-60; lt. col. 7th N.J. inf., Sept. 5, 1861; col. 13th N.J. inf., July 8, 1862, and bvt. brig. gen., U.S.V., Mar. 13, 1865; served in Army of the Potomac, Sept. 1861-Sept. 1863; in Army of the Cumberland, Sept. 1863, to end of war, June 8, 1865. Comptroller Jersey City, 1871-75; chief clerk U.S. Dept. of Agr., July 1877-Apr. 1885; mem. Antietam Battlefield Bd., Oct. 1894-July 1898; chmn. Chickamauga and Chattanooga Park Commn., June 1905—. Republican. Died 1909.

CARMICHAEL, Henry, chemist; b. Brooklyn, Mar. 5, 1846; s. Daniel and Eliza C.; A.B., Amherst, 1867, A.M., 1870; Ph.D., Göttingen, 1871; m. Annie Darling Cole (writer, composer). Prof. chemistry, Iowa Coll., 1871, Bowdoin Coll., 1872-86; lecturer Me. Med. Sch., 1872-86; state assayer of Me., 1872-86; lecturer M.I.T., 1899-1901. Moved to Boston, 1886; inventor of processes for manufacture of fibreware, of soda and bleach by electrolysis, and many others; expert in patent causes; assayer, metallurgist and inventor metall. processes. Home: Malden, Mass. Died 1924.

CARMODY, Thomas, lawyer; b. Milo, Yates Co., N.Y., Oct. 9, 1859; s. Thomas and Mary (Connors) C.; ed. Penn Yan Acad., N.Y.; Cornell U., 1878-81; m. Margaret Caviston, Aug. 19, 1891 (died 1911). Admitted to bar, 1886; apptd. dist. atty., Yates Co., by Gov. D. B. Hill, 1889; chief examiner to State Civil Service Commn., 1893-96; elected atty.-gen., N.Y., Nov. 1910, reëlected, Nov. 1912. Trustee Keuka Coll., N.Y., Union Coll., Schenectady, N.Y. Was mem. Carmody & Kellogg. Democrat. Catholic. Home: Mt. Vernon, N.Y. Died Jan. 22, 1922.

CARNAHAN, George Holmes, corp. official; b. Cadiz, O., Mar. 16, 1879; s. Andrew Henderson and Elizabeth (Wood) C.; ed. pub. schs. and under instr. in engring.; m. Lucetta Butt, Apr. 29, 1913; children—Charlott E., George H., William T. Mining business, Leadville, Colo., Mexico and Ecuador, 1896-1902; in Mexico as gen. supt. of mines for Cia Metalurgica Mexicana and subsidiaries, 1903-09; mgr. mines, mills and smelters, Tezuitlan Copper Co., 1910-14; pres. and chmn. bd., 1915—, Intercontinental Rubber Co., Cia Ganadera y Textil de Cedros, Continental-Mexican Rubber Co., Continental Rubber Co. of N.Y., Cia Explotadora de Hule, Sociedad Anónima; chmn. bd. Penyon Syndicate. Inventor of improved process of extracting rubber from guayule shrub, and of nitrate of soda from Chilean ores. Fellow Am. Geog. Soc. Died Mar. 20, 1941.

CARNAHAN, Herschel L., lawyer; b. Aledo, Ill., Aug. 31, 1879; s. Porter M. and Jennie (McCrory) C.; ed. Monmouth Coll., 1894-96; studied law under William Collier; m. Hattie Helmer, Nov. 29, 1907. Admitted to Calif. bar, 1904; law partner of William Collier, Riverside, Calif., 1904-12; in practice at Los Angeles, 1920—. State commr. of corps., Calif., 1915-18; mem. State Tax Commn., Calif., 1927-28; apptd. co-receiver Julian Petroleum Corp., 1927; lt. gov., Calif., 1928-31; state bldg. and loan commr., Calif., 1931. Pres. Nat. Assn. Securities Commrs. and Attys Gen., 1917-18. Republican. Home: Los Angeles, Calif. Died Mar. 31, 1941.

CARNAHAN, James Richards, lawyer; b. Tippecanoe, Ind., Nov. 18, 1840; s. Rev. James Aikman and Martha A. C.; ed. Wabash Coll.; m. Susan Elizabeth Patterson, Nov. 7, 1867. Left coll. 1861 and enlisted as private 11th inf.; mustered out, 1865, with rank of capt.; returned to Wabash Coll. at close of war and was grad. June 1866; grad. Ind. Law School, 1867; comdr. dept. of Ind., G.A.R., 2 terms, 1882-83; adj.-gen. Ind., brig. gen. comdg. Ind. Nat. Guard, 1881-85; elected maj. gen. Uniform Rank, Knights of Pythias, May 1, 1884, and continuously thereafter. Was U.S. Commr. for Ind. for Cotton Centennial Expn., New Orleans, 1884-85. Commr. for Ind., Chickamauga Nat. Mil. Park, 1894—; pres. bd. trustees Ind. State Soldiers' Home, 1895—. Address: Indianapolis, Ind. Died 1905.

CARNEGIE, Andrew, philanthropist; b. Dunfermline, Fifeshire, Scotland, Nov. 25, 1835; came with family to U.S., 1848, settling in Pittsburgh; (lord rector, St. Andrew's U., 1903-07, LL.D., 1905; lord rector, Aberdeen U., 1912-14, and LL.D.; also LL.D., univs. of Glasgow, Edinburgh, Birmingham, Manchester, McGill U. [Montreal], Queen's Coll. [Toronto], Erskine Coll., Allegheny Coll., U. of Pa., Brown U., Cornell U., Hamilton Coll.; Dr. Polit. Science, U. of Groningen); m. Louise Whitfield, 1887. First work was as weaver's asst. in cotton factory, Allegheny, Pa.; telegraph messenger boy in Pittsburgh office of Ohio Telegraph Co., 1851; learned telegraphy, entered employ Pa. R.R. and became telegraph operator, advancing by promotions until he became supt. Pittsburgh div. Pa. system; joined Mr. Woodruff, inventor of the sleeping car, in organizing Woodruff Sleeping Car Co., gaining through it nucleus of his fortune; careful investments in oil lands increased his means; during Civil War served as supt. mil. rys. and govt. telegraph lines in the East. After war developed iron works of various kinds and established, at Pittsburgh, Keystone Bridge Works and Union Iron Works. Introduced into this country Bessemer process of making steel, 1868; was principal owner a few years later of Homestead and Edgar Thomson Steel Works, and other large plants as head of firms of Carnegie, Phipps & Co. and Carnegie Bros. & Co.; interests were consolidated, 1899, in the Carnegie Steel Co., which in 1901 was merged in the United States Steel Corp., when he retired from business. Has given libraries to many towns and cities in the U.S. and Great Britain, and large sums in other benefactions, including $24,000,000 to Carnegie Inst., Pittsburgh; $5,200,000 to New York for the establishment of branch libraries; $22,000,000 to Carnegie Instn. of Washington; $10,000,000 to Scotch universities; $5,000,000 to fund for benefit of employes of Carnegie Steel Co.; $1,000,000 to St. Louis Pub. Library; $5,000,000 to the Carnegie Hero Fund Commn., Pittsburgh; $1,150,000 to the Carnegie Hero Fund Trust, Dunfermline, Scotland (for Great Britain); $1,000,000 to the Hero Fund for France; $1,-500,000 to the Hero Fund for Germany; $230,000 to the Hero Fund for Belgium; $125,000 to the Hero Fund for Denmark; $200,000 for the Hero Fund for Holland; $230,000 to the Hero Fund for Sweden; $130,000 to the Hero Fund for Switzerland; $750,000 to the Hero Fund for Italy; $125,000 to the Hero Fund for Norway; $3,500,000 to the Carnegie Dunfermline Trust; $1,500,000 for the Peace Temple at The Hague; $1,500,000 to United Engring. Soc. Total benefactions exceed $300,000,000, including over $60,000,000 for over 3,000 municipal library bldgs.; also building and grounds for Pan-Am. Union, Washington, 1906; $16,250,000 for Foundation for Advancement of Teaching in U.S., Can. and Newfoundland. Life trustee Carnegie Corp. of New York ($125,000,000 foundation to carry on various works in which he has been engaged). Hon. mem. Am. Inst. Architects, Am. Soc. M.E., Am. Inst. Mining Engrs.; trustee Cornell U., 1890—. Comdr. Legion of Honor, France, 1907; Grand Cross, Order of Orange Nassau; Grand Cross, Order of Danebrog. Has received freedom of 54 cities of Great Britain and Ireland. Author: An American Four-in-Hand in Britain, 1883; Round the World, 1884; Triumphant Democracy, 1886; The Gospel of Wealth, 1900; The Empire of Business, 1902 (translated into 8 langs.); The Life of James Watt, 1906; Problems of Today, 1909. Died Aug. 11, 1919.

CARNELL, Laura Horner, educator; b. Phila., Sept. 7, 1867; d. Lafayette and Rebecca Wood (Ayars) C.; grad. Phila. Normal Sch., 1886; studied U. of Chicago, Cornell U. and Cambridge, Eng.; B.A., Temple U., Phila., 1898, Litt.D., 1902; unmarried. Teacher in pub. schs., Phila., 1885-93; prin. Woman's Dept., Temple U., 1893-97; acting dean, 1897-1905, dean Univ. Corp. and lecturer on history of art, 1905—, asso. pres., 1925—, Temple U. Asso. editor Woman's Atheneum, and author of numerous articles and biog. sketches. Mem. Phila. Bd. Edn. Home: Philadelphia, Pa. Died Mar. 30, 1929.

CARNEY, Francis Joseph, lawyer; b. Cambridge, Mass., Oct. 13, 1876; s. Francis Henry and Katharine C.; A.B., Boston Coll., Newton, Mass., 1898; LL.B., Harvard, 1901; m. Elizabeth Pauline Palmer, Oct. 17, 1906; children—Bernadette (Mrs. John W. Shyne), Marianne (Mrs. Richard J. Donovan), Katharine. Admitted to Mass. bar, 1901, and then practiced in Boston; sr. partner Carney, Lynch & Killion; dir. various business and ins. companies; prof. of constl. law and legal ethics, Boston Coll., 1929-36. Mem. Sinking Fund Commn., Cambridge, 1914-24; treas. Minot Village Assn. A leader in a nat. campaign, beginning 1935, as chmn. of the Com. on Ethics and Grievances of Am. Bar Assn., to raise the standard of professional conduct. Democrat. Catholic. Home: Minot, Mass. Died July 28, 1939.

CARNEY, Frank, geologist; b. Watkins, N.Y., Mar. 15, 1868; s. Hugh and Esther R. (Beahan) C.; Starkey Sem., Eddytown, N.Y.; A.B., Cornell U., 1895, Ph.D., 1909; m. Mary E. Keegan, June 26, 1890; children—Esther L. (Mrs. H. H. Martin), Ewart Gladstone, Harry Beahan, Mary F. (Mrs. J. W. Cunnick), Frances E. (Mrs. P. A. Knoedler). Instr., 1887-90, prin., 1894-95, Starkey Sem.; instr. Keuka Inst., 1895-1900; asst. in geology, Cornell U., 1901, and instr., Cornell Summer Sch. of Geography, 1901-04; v.prin. Ithaca High Sch., 1901-04; prof. geology, 1904-14, prof. geology and geography, 1915-17, Denison Univ.; chief geologist, Nat. Refining Co., 1917—, in charge of Land Department, 1923-29; prof. geology and geography, Baylor Univ., 1929—. Lecturer on geography, Summer Sch., U. of Va., 1909-11; prof. geology, Summer Quarter U. of Chicago, 1912; acting prof. geology, U. of Mich., 1912-13; prof. geography, Cornell Summer Sch., 1914-16. Asst. geologist Ohio Geol. Survey, 1907-17. Baptist. Mason. Died Dec. 13, 1934.

CAROTHERS, Wallace H(ume), chemist; b. Burlington, Ia., Apr. 27, 1896; s. Ira Hume and Mary Elizabeth (McMullen) C.; B.S., Tarkio (Mo.) Coll., 1920; M.S., U. of Ill., 1921, Ph.D., 1924; grad. study U. of Chicago; m. Helen E. Sweetman, Feb. 21, 1936. Instr. chemistry, Tarkio Coll., 1918-20, U. of S.D., 1921-22, U. of Ill., 1924-26, Harvard, 1926-28; research chemist du Pont Co., Wilmington, Del., 1928—; co-inventor of important new synthetic rubbers. Editor: Organic Syntheses, 1933; asso. editor Jour. Am. Chem. Soc., 1930—. Home: Wilmington, Del. Died Apr. 29, 1937.

CARPENTER, Alva Edwin, clergyman; b. Pawtucket, R.I., Mar. 21, 1855; s. Alva and Mary E. (Allen) C.; A.B., Brown U., 1879; B.D., Gen. Theol. Sem., New York, 1882; m. Anna M. Greene, Sept. 13, 1883 (died 1906); children—George Washington Greene, Mrs. Anna Clarke Meader; m. 2d, Janet D. Grieve, Aug. 3, 1915. Deacon, 1882, priest, 1883, P.E. Ch.; pastor Apponang, R.I., 1882-83, Middlebury, Vt., 1883-89, Warren, R.I., 1889-1902, Manton, R.I., 1902-27, rector emeritus; instr. in church history of American church, Army Training Center, Providence, R.I., 1928—. Mem. public sch. committees, Middlebury, Vt., 1886-89, Warren, R.I., 1890-1902 (supt. public schools, Warren, R.I., 1893-1902), Johnston, R.I., 1903-06; asso. editor Convocation Messenger, Providence, R.I., 1893-1901; examining chaplain Diocese of R.I., 1893—; dean of Convocation of Providence, 1922—. Hon. mem. R.I. Soc. of Cincinnati. Local fuel com. under U.S. Fuel Administration, 1917. Died Dec. 14, 1931.

CARPENTER, B. Platt, governor; b. Stanford, N.Y., May 14, 1837; s. Morgan and Maria (Bockee) C.; A.B., Union Coll., 1857, A.M., 1860; m. Esther, d. Stephen Thorne, of Poughkeepsie, N.Y., 1860. Admitted to bar, 1858; dist. atty. Dutchess Co., N.Y., 1858; appointed by President Lincoln, assessor of internal revenue, 12th N.Y. Dist., 1864; mem. N.Y. Constl. Conv., 1867-68; temporary chmn. Rep. State Conv., 1872; mem. N.Y. Senate, 1875; judge Dutchess Co., N.Y., 1876-83; chmn. Rep. State Com., N.Y., 1881; nominee for lt. gov., N.Y., 1882; gov. of Mont. Ty., 1884-85; mem. Mont. Constl. Conv., 1889; mem. Mont. Code Commn. Home: Chula Vista, Calif. Died Dec. 24, 1921.

CARPENTER, Benjamin, merchant; b. Chicago, Sept. 16, 1865; s. George B. and Elizabeth Curtis (Greene) Carpenter; S.B., Harvard Univ., 1888; m. Helen Graham Fairbank, Sept. 18, 1893; children—Benjamin, Jr., Cordelia Fairbank (wife of Dr. N. S. Davis, III), Elizabeth Webster (Mrs. Thos. L. Marshall), Fairbank. In business, 1888—; pres. Geo. B. Carpenter & Co.; v.p. Anniston (Ala.) Cordage Co. Lt. col., Q.M.R.C., on active duty July 1917-Feb. 1919. Mem. Art Inst., Chicago (life), Chicago Hist. Soc. (life), Field Mus. (life). Home: Chicago, Ill. Died Feb. 23, 1927.

CARPENTER, Charles Carroll, clergyman; b. Bernardston, Mass., July 9, 1836; s. Dr. Elijah W. and Vallonia (Slate) C.; ed. Goodale Acad., Williston Sem., Kimball Union Acad., Meriden, N.H.; Andover Theol. Sem.; (A.M., Hamilton Coll., 1869, Dartmouth, 1887); m. Feronia N. Rice, May 1, 1862. Ordained Congl. ministry, 1860; missionary in Labrador, 1858-65; cashier U.S. Christian Commn., armies operating against Richmond, 1864-65; supt. Lookout Mountain (Tenn.) Ednl. Instns., 1866-72; pastor, S. Peabody, Mass., 1875-80, Mt. Vernon, N.H., 1880-85. Editor Andover (Mass.) Townsman, 1887-89; contbg. editor The Congregationalist, 1886-1906. Died Aug. 19, 1918.

CARPENTER, Charles E(verly), mfr.; b. Phila., Pa., Feb. 21, 1863; s. Rev. Aaron Everly and Mary Ann (Banes) C.; ed. Friends Central Sch. and under pvt. teachers in chemistry and engring.; m. Florence R. Browne, Oct. 29, 1881. With E. F. Houghton & Co., mfrs. of oils and leather for industries, since beginning of active career, except a few yrs. as professional billiardist, roller skater and prize fighter; then pres., chmn. exec. com. and gen. mgr. E. F. Houghton & Co. Organizer, and chmn. campaign com. City Party, Phila., which defeated the Rep. orgn. in 1905, 06. Republican. Mason. Home: Philadelphia, Pa. Died Apr. 6, 1929.

CARPENTER, Charles Lincoln, civil engr.; b. Amherst, Mass., June 17, 1867; s. Charles Carroll and Feronia N. (Rice) C.; B.S., Dartmouth, 1887; C.E., Thayer Sch. Civ. Engring. (Dartmouth), 1889; m. Charlotte Florence Sullivan, Dec. 15, 1892; children—James Sullivan, Thomas Rice, Charles Carrol. On surveys and constrn. Nicaragua Canal, Nicaragua Canal Co., 1889-91; asst. engr. with Boston Bd. of Survey, 1891-98; mining in Alaska, 1898-1900; locating Boston & Worcester R.R., 1900-01; asst. engr., location and constrn., Cuba R.R., Cuba, 1901-02; with U.S. engr. corps, dredging in Boston Harbor, 1902-04; with Isthmian Canal Commn. in Panama as asst. engr. on surveys, 1904-06, resident engr. in direct charge of Gatun Locks, 1906-08, in charge Gatun Dam and Porto Bello Quarry, 1906-07; supt. constrn. for J. G. White & Co., on reconstruction of Cuba Eastern R.R., 1908-09; gen. mgr. and chief engr. Guantanamo & Western R.R., which is the Cuba Eastern R.R. reorganized, 1909-11; supt. Ponce & Guayama R.R., Dec. 1911-12; v.p. and gen. mgr. Central Aguirre Sugar Co., Puerto Rico, 1912—; v.p. and gen. mgr. Central Machete Co., 1920—; v.p. Santa Gabel Sugar Co. Died Sept. 28, 1929.

CARPENTER, Edmund Janes, author; b. N. Attleboro, Mass., Oct. 16, 1845; s. Rev. George M. and Sarah L. (Walcott) C.; Ph.B., Brown U., 1866 (Litt.D., 1905); m. Lydia Etta Snow, Nov. 12, 1873. Engaged in mercantile pursuits until 1878; entered journalism, 1878; on staffs newspapers in Providence, R.I., New Haven, Conn., and Boston; editorial writer and literary editor Boston Daily Advertiser, 1884-96. Author: Hellenic Tales, 1906; The Mayflower Pilgrims, 1917. Did essential work in collaboration with author on "Letters and Memoirs of Chancellor Kent." by William Kent, 1898. Home: Milton, Mass. Died Feb. 21, 1924.

CARPENTER, Eugene R., brain surgeon; b. Knobnoster, Mo., Oct. 5, 1873; s. William D. and Emma (Shanks) C.; student U. of Mich., 1894-97; M.D., Jefferson Med. Coll., Phila., Pa., 1898 (winner de Schweinitz medal on ophthalmology, Dercums neurol. prize, and the otol. prize); interne Kings Co. Hosp., 1898-99; post-grad. work, Manhattan Eye and Ear Hosp., New York Eye and Infirmary, also Vienna and London, 1907-08; m. Lucile Snyder, July 20, 1916. Practiced at Dallas, Tex., 1921—. Maj. Med. R.C.; retired capt. U.S.A. Fellow Am. Coll. Surgeons. Democrat. Baptist. Mason. Designer of numerous surg. instruments. Home: Dallas, Tex. Died Oct. 11, 1934.

CARPENTER, Francis Bicknell, portrait painter; b. Homer, N.Y., 1830; self-taught in art except for 6 months' instruction in Syracuse, 1844; went to New York, 1851, became asso. of Acad., 1852; painted many portraits of presidents, statesmen and other celebrites, also the historical painting, President Lincoln Signing Emanicaption Proclamation, now at the capitol, Washington. Author: Six Months in the White House with Abraham Lincoln. Died 1900.

CARPENTER, Frank George, traveler, corr.; b. Mansfield, O., May 8, 1855; s. George F. and Jennette L. C.; A.B., U. of Wooster, 1877, A.M., 1880 (Litt.D., 1911); m. Joanna D. Condict, Jan. 10, 1883. Began newspaper work as legislative corr. Cleveland Leader, at Columbus, 1879; in European and Egyptian travel, 1881; Washington corr. Cleveland Leader, 1882; corr. Am. Press Assn., 1884, New York World, 1887; trip round the world for newspaper syndicate and Cosmopolitan Mag., 1888-89; newspaper tour to Mexico, 1891, to Russia, Germany and England, 1892, to China, Japan and Korea, 1894; in S. America, 25,000 miles of travel, 1898; in Philippines, China, Java, Australia and New Zealand, 1900; to investigate Am. "commercial invasion" in England, France, Germany, Russia, Holland, Belgium, Norway, Sweden, Denmark, 1902; to Panama, Cuba and Can., 1905; in Africa part of 1906-07, going from Morocco to Egypt and from Cairo to the Cape; in Asia investigating awakening of China, Korea and Japan, 1908; in India, Turkey, Palestine and Egypt, 1909; letter-writing tour of Central America and Panama, 1912; in Mexico during the revolution, 1913; letter-writing tour of South America, 1914, Alaska, 1915, 16, of U.S., investigating industries of the war, 1917, 18; letterwriting tour through Europe, 1922, 23. Author: Carpenter's Readers of Commerce and Industry; How the World Is Fed, 1907; How the World Is Clothed, 1909; How the World Is Housed, 1911; Around the World with the Children, 1917; Carpenter's New Geographical Readers—South America, 9121, Europe, 1922, North America, 1922, Asia, 1923, Africa, 1923. Home: Washington, D.C. Died June 18, 1924.

CARPENTER, Frank Pierce, paper mfr.; b. Chichester, N.H., Oct. 28, 1845; s. David Morrill and Mary (Perkins) C.; grad. high sch., Concord, N.H., 1863; hon. M.A., Dartmouth, 1915, LL.D., 1929; m. Elenora Blood, 1872 (died 1910); children—Aretas, Mary (Mrs. Charles B. Manning). One of founders and pres. Burgess Sulphite Fibre Co. (now Brown Co.); pres. Amoskeag Paper Mills, 1885—; treas. Mechanics Savings Bank; mem. bd. of dirs. N.H. Fire Ins. Co. (mem. finance com.), Amoskeag Nat. Bank, Amoskeag Trust Co., Boston & Me. R.R., Hanover Fire Ins. Co.; trustee Amoskeag Mfg. Co. Chmn. Manchester Park and Playground Commn.; trustee Currier Gallery of Art, Balch Hosp., Carpenter Memorial Library (chmn. bd.). Pres. Franklin Street Congl. Soc. Donor Carpenter Memorial Library as memorial to wife, Carpenter Art Gallery to Dartmouth Coll., building to Manchester Historic Assn.; co-donor Parish House Franklin St. Congl. Ch. Home: Manchester, N.H. Died Apr. 1938.

CARPENTER, Frederic Ives, educator; b. Monroe, Wis., Nov. 29, 1861; s. William O. and Lucetta (Spencer) C.; A.B., Harvard, 1885; student France and Germany, 1885-86, Union Coll. of Law, Chicago, 1886-87; Ph.D., U. of Chicago, 1895; m. Emma, d. C. W. Cook, of Chicago, Dec. 12, 1888. Docent, 1895-97, instr., 1897-1902, asst. prof., 1902-04, asso. prof. English, 1904-10, prof., 1910-11, U. of Chicago. Author: Metaphor and Simile in the Minor Elizabethan Drama, 1895; Reference Guide to Edmund Spencer, 1923. Editor: English Lyric Poetry, 1500-1700, 1897; Leonard Cox, The Arte or Crafte of Rhethoryke, 1530 (reprint of the first English Rhetoric), 1899. Selections from the Poetry of Lord Byron, 1900; Ben Jonson's The Case Is Altered, 1902; Lewis Wager's Life and Repentance of Marie Magdalene 1567, 1902. Pres. Menominee Land & Iron Co., Northern Land & Iron Co. Trustee Newberry Library, Chicago. Chmn. Santa Barbara (Calif.) Chapter Am. Red Cross, 1918-19. Home: Barrington, Ill. Died Jan. 28, 1925.

CARPENTER, Frederic Walton, zoölogist; b. Millbrook, N.Y., May 12, 1876; s. Franklin T. and Jane (Willets) C.; B.S., New York U., 1899; A.M., Harvard, 1902, Ph.D., 1904; studied Neurol. Inst., Frankfort-on-Main, Germany, 1908, univs. Berlin and Munich, 1910-11; m. Dorothy E. Dresler, June 26, 1906. Asst. in zoölogy, Harvard, 1901-03; lecturer in biology, summer sch. New York U., 1904, 05; instr. in zoölogy, 1904-08, asso., 1908-10, asst. prof., 1911-13, Univ. Ill.; dir. Bermuda Biol. Sta., summer, 1909; J. P. Morgan prof. biology, Trinity Coll., Conn., July 1, 1913—. Mem. editorial bd. of Folia Neuro-Biologica. Q.m., Am. Red Cross Sanitary Training Detachment No. 2, 1917; asso. field dir., later field dir., hosp. service of Am. Red Cross, at U.S.A. Base Hosp., Camp Devens, Mass., June 21, 1918-July 1, 1919. Died Mar. 1, 1925.

CARPENTER, George Oliver, retired mfr.; b. Wakefield, Mass., Feb. 17, 1852; s. George Oliver and Maria J. (Emerson) C.; prep. edn., Park Latin Sch. and English High Sch., Boston; spl. course, Mass. Inst. Tech., 1869-70; m. Caroline G. Greeley, Apr. 7, 1880; children—George Oliver, Kenneth Greeley (dec.). Began in employ St. Louis Lead & Oil Co., 1870, advancing to pres.; v.p. Madison Coal Co., and St. Louis & Eastern R.R. Co., 1889-95; v.p. St. Louis, Peoria & Northern R.R., 1895-99; v.p. Nat. Lead Co., 1907-33, dir., 1891-1933, mgr., St. Louis, 1891-1929; dir. St. Louis Smelting & Refining Co., 1892-1934, 1st v.p., 1893-1934. Col. 1st Regt. Mo. N.G., 1879-80. Dir. St. Louis Pub. Library, 1901-35, pres. 1911-35; mem. bd. Washington U.; mem. Tower Grove Park Bd., 1892-1924 (ex-pres.). Republican. Unitarian. Home: St. Louis, Mo. Died Dec. 2, 1939.

CARPENTER, George Rice, prof. rhetoric Columbia, 1893—; b. on coast of Labrador, Oct. 25, 1863; grad. Harvard, 1886; studied in Berlin, Paris, 1886-88; instr. Harvard, 1888-90; prof. English, Mass. Inst. of Tech., 1890-93; (D.C.L., Univ. of the South, 1907); m. Mary Seymour, 1890. Author: Elements of Rhetoric, 1899; Life of Longfellow, 1901; Life of Whittier, 1903; Teaching of English, 1903. Editor: Latham's Letters of Dante, 1891; American Prose, 1898; also of Longmans' English Classics. Home: New York, N.Y. Died 1909.

CARPENTER, Gilbert Saltonstall, brig. gen. U.S. Army, retired, Jan. 1900; b. Medina, O., Apr. 17, 1836; s. Judge James G. C.; grad. Western Reserve Coll., 1859; admitted to Ohio bar, 1861; m. Elizabeth Thacher Balch, Mar. 1863. Entered army as lt., 19th Ohio vol. inf., 1861; 18th U.S. inf., 1861-66; bvtd. capt. for gallantry, battle Stone River; served in Indian campaigns; maj. 4th U.S. inf.; lt. col. 7th inf.; promoted brig. gen. vols. for gallantry at El Caney, from Sept. 21, 1898, to May 12, 1899; as col. 18th inf. comd. at the battles of Jaro and Pavia, Island of Panay, P.I. Was made brig. gen. U.S.A. and retired Jan. 1900. Home: Montclair, N.J. Died 1904.

CARPENTER, Horace Francis; b. Pawtucket, Oct. 19, 1842; s. Horace and Charlotte C.; grad. high sch., Pawtucket; spl. course in analyt. chemistry, Brown U., 1860-61; m. Jennie Hastings, Feb. 23, 1895. Began in gold and silver refining business, 1860; retired from firm of H. F. Carpenter & Son, 1912; discoverer of process of extracting gold and silver from photographic waste; also discovered process of obtaining chemically pure gold for commercial purposes. Treas. N.E. Mfg. Jewelers and Silversmiths' Assn. 18 yrs. Trustee and mem. library com. of William H. Hall Free Library Corp. Republican. Episcopalian. Mineralogist and conchologist; regarded as the leading authority in R.I. on mollusks; presented City of Providence his library on natural history (237 vols.) and his collection of 1,200 species and varieties of minerals and 4,000 species of shells, consisting of 75,000 specimens; discovered 3 new shell-bearing mollusks. Home: Edgewood, R.I. Died Feb. 28, 1937.

CARPENTER, John Slaughter, rear admiral; b. Louisville, Ky., May 18, 1860; s. John Slaughter and Ellen Blake (Cosby) C.; ed. pub. and pvt. schs. and under pvt. tutor; studied law Columbian (now George Washington) U.; m. Charlotte Freeman Clark, Oct. 8, 1889; 1 dau., Evelyn Fessenden (Mrs. Everard Stowell Pratt). Apptd. fleet pay clk., European Sta., 1877, and by President Arthur as asst. p.m. with rank of ensign, Oct. 29, 1881; promoted through grades to rear adm., 1921 (the first officer of Supply Corps to reach permanent flag rank in U.S. Navy, upon recommendation of Selection Bd.); retired May 18, 1924. Attached to Battleship Texas, Spanish-Am. War, and participated in Battle of Santiago and minor engagements; served twice as asst. p.m. gen.; fleet p.m. Pacific Sta., 1903-05; then in charge Supply Corps Sch. of Application, Washington, D.C., and of gen. edn. activities in Supply Corps. Awarded Sampson medal with 6 bars, Spanish-Am. War medal, Victory medal, also letter of commendation Navy Dept. for services in World War. Home: Washington, D.C. Died June 24, 1929.

CARPENTER, Julia Wiltberger, physician; b. Cincinnati; d. Isaac B. (M.D.) and Susan (Ellmaker) C.; M.D., Woman's Med. Coll., Phila., and was interne in Woman's Hosp., Phila.; spent 2 yrs. at McMicken U. of Cincinnati, studying practical chemistry, and 2 yrs. in hosps. of Vienna and Paris; unmarried. Began practice, Cincinnati, Nov. 1878; prof. physiology, Laura Memorial Woman's Med. Coll.; on staff Presbyn. Hosp. Home: Cincinnati, O. Died May 24, 1915.

CARPENTER, Louis George, consulting engr.; b. Orion, Mich., Mar. 28, 1861; s. Charles K. and Jennette (Coryell) C.; B.S., Mich. Agrl. Coll., 1879, M.S., 1883; D.Eng. from same college, 1927; U. of Mich., winters, 1881-82, 1883-84; Johns Hopkins, 1885-86, 1887-88; m. Mary J. C. Merrell, Feb. 17, 1887 (died 1921); children—Charles L. (capt. U.S. Army), Jeannette (Mrs. Roe Emery); m. 2d, Katherine M. Warren, Sept. 30, 1922. Asst. and asst. prof. mathematics, Mich. Agrl. Coll., 1881-88; prof. engring. and physics, Colo. Agrl. Coll., 1888-1911. Irrigation engr., Colo. Expt. Station, later dir. of station, 1899-1910; irrigation expert U.S. Dept. of Agr.; organized 1st systematic instrn. in irrigation engring. and investigation in that line, 1888; spl. agt. and field geologist U.S. artesian wells investigation, 1890; expert in irrigation litigation, U.S. vs. Rio Grande dam, Elephant Butte Internat. Case; state engr., Colo., 1903-05; consulting engr. and irrigation expert for state in suit of state of Kan. against Colo., of Wyo. against Colo., etc.; cons. engr. many important dams, irrigation and hydraulic enterprises, etc.; mem. bd. arbitration selected by both parties as referee and chmn. to settle electric lighting controversy at Colo. Springs, 1907; mem. Irrigation Commn. of British Columbia, 1907-08, to determine foundations for new water code (adopted by B.C. Parliament, 1908); arbitrator chosen by both sides in dispute over waters of North Platte, U.S. vs. Wyo., 1920; expert for Pueblo, Canon City and Salida in stopping pollution of Arkansas River by mining debris; cons. engr. preparing case for Colo. in Wyo. vs. Colo., etc. Served in World War as dir. Dept. of Information, vice-chmn. Explosives Bd., Edn. of Drafted Soldiers, etc. Chevalier du Mérite Agricole, France, 1895; gold medals, Paris and Portland expns. Mem. Colo. State Council Defense, 1917-19. Home: Denver, Colo. Died Sept. 12, 1935.

CARPENTER, Louis Henry, brig. gen.; b. Glassboro, N.J., Feb. 11, 1839; s. Edward and Anna Maria (Howey) C.; A.B., Central High Sch., Phila., 1856; student Univ. of Pa., class 1859; unmarried. Pvt., corporal and sergt. cos. C. and L, 6th U.S. Cav., Nov. 1, 1861-Sept. 20, 1862; 2d lt. 6th Cav., July 17, 1862; advanced through grades to brig. gen. U.S.V., May 4, 1898; hon. disch., June 12, 1899; brig. gen. U.S.A., Oct. 18, 1899; retired at own request, over 30 yrs.' service, Oct. 19, 1899. Bvtd.: 1st lt., July 3, 1863, for Gettysburg; capt., Sept. 19, 1864, for Winchester, Va.; maj. and lt. col., Mar. 13, 1865, for gallant and meritorious services during the war; col., Oct. 18, 1868, for Beaver Creek, Kan.; col. volunteers, Sept. 28, 1865, for meritorious services during the war; awarded Congressional Medal of Honor, Mar. 26, 1898, for distinguished conduct during Indian campaign in Kan. and Colo., Sept. and Oct., 1868, and in forced march, Sept. 23-25, 1868, to the relief of Forsyth's scouts. Served in Army of Potomac in Civil War, participating in many battles, and as a.d.c. to Gen. Sheridan; served on Indian frontier, 1866-79; comd. Ft. Robinson, Neb., 1883-85, Ft. Myer, Washington, 1887-91; dir. Cav. Sch. of Application, Ft. Riley, Kan., 1892; pres. bd. to revise cav. tactics, 1896; comd. Ft. Sam Houston, Tex., 1897-98; comd. 1st Div., 3d Corps, and 3d Div., 4th Corps, in Spanish-Am. War; mil. gov. Province of Puerto Principe, 1898-99. Home: Philadelphia. Died Jan. 21, 1916.

CARPENTER, Newton Henry, bus. mgr. Art Inst. of Chicago; b. Olmsted Falls, O., May 17, 1853; s. William Sears and Lucina (Horr) C.; Oberlin (O.) High Sch., 1 yr., U.S. Mil. Acad., 2½ yrs., class of 1876; m. Hattie Lewis, Dec. 25, 1879. Began active career with Chicago Acad. of Design, Dec. 1876, reorganized 1878, incorporated as Acad. of Fine Arts, 1879, and name changed to Art Inst. of Chicago, 1881, of which was sec. until 1916, then bus. mgr. Dir. and treas. Am. Fedn. of Arts; dir. Municipal Art League. Mem. I.N.G., 1877-82. Republican. Conglist. Died May 27, 1918.

CARPENTER, Reid, farmer; b. Mansfield, O., June 6, 1853; s. George F. and Jennette (Reid) Carpenter; B.A., Coll. of Wooster, Ohio, 1875; law study U. of Mich., 1877. Reorganized Mansfield Street Ry. and Elec. Co., Card Elec. Co., and Humphreys Pump Co., Mansfield, O.; pres. Citizens Nat. Bank, Mansfield, 1901-17; mem. Carpenter & Ross, importers and breeders of pure bred Shorthorn and Aberdeen Angus cattle. Home: Mansfield, O. Deceased.

CARPENTER, Rolla Clinton, engr.; b. Orion, Mich., June 26, 1852; s. Charles K. and Jennette (Coryell) C.; brother of Louis George and William Leland C.; B.S., Mich. Agrl. Coll., 1873, M.S.; C.E., U. of Mich., 1875; M.M.E., Cornell, 1888; (LL.D., Mich. Agrl. Coll., 1906); m. Marion Dewey, 1876. Instr. and prof. of mathematics and civ. engring., Mich. Agrl. Coll., 1875-90; asso. prof. engring., 1890-95, prof. exptl. engring., 1895-1917, Cornell U. (emeritus). Consulting engr. for Helderburg, Cayuga Lake, Quaker Portland, Great Northern, Belleville Portland, Cal. and Atlas Portland cement companies. Constructed numerous power stas. for elec. rys.; patent expert in several important cases; engr. for City of New York for high pressure pumping engines, 1911-12; engr. for Kopper's Co.; Brooklyn pumping engines, 1914; lighting and heating of city buildings, 1913-16; high pressure fire system, City of Baltimore, 1911. Judge of machinery and transportation, Chicago Expn., 1893, Buffalo Expn., 1901, Jamestown Expn., 1907. Author: Experimental Engineering (8 edits.), 1890, 1902; Heating and Ventilating (6 edits.), 1898, 1910; The Gas Engine (with Prof. Diedrichs); Heating and Ventilation (New Internat. Ency. and Kidder's Architectural Pocket Book). Home: Ithaca, N.Y. Died Jan. 19, 1919.

CARPENTER, William E., banker; b. Cloverland, Clay County, Ind., Nov. 17, 1857; s. Jacob A. and Evelyn V. (Grass) C.; ed. Westfield (Ill.) Coll. and Terre Haute (Ind.) Business Coll.; m. Mary B. Price, Jan. 31, 1884; children—Jay V., Guy O., Don P., Van W. Organized, July 1899, and was secretary, mgr. and dir., The Brazil Trust Co. Trustee Northwest Ind. Conf., DePauw U., Methodist Hospital, Indianapolis; mem. bd. mgrs. Preachers' Aid Soc.; dir. Battle Ground Camp Meeting Assn. Mem. Gen. Confs., M.E. Ch., 6 times to 1932; mem. Gen. Miss. Com. and Bd. Sunday Schs., M.E. Ch., also of Gen. Edn. Com. and The Men's Brotherhood; supt. First M.E. Ch. S.S. of Brazil for 35 yrs. Chmn. Ind. Dry Fedn., which secured prohibitory legislation for the state, 1916. Mem. commission apptd. by Am. Com. for Relief in Near East to visit Armenia in Turkey. Del. Ecumenical M.E. Conf. of the World, London, 1921; mem. Com. Conservation and Advance and Adminstrn. Com., M.E. Ch.; trustee First M.E. Ch., Brazil, Ind. Independent Republican. Mason. Home: Brazil, Ind. Died Aug. 21, 1937.

CARPENTER, William Henry, educator; b. Utica, N.Y., July 15, 1853; s. William Penn and Sarah C.; ed. Utica Acad. and Cornell, Leipzig and Freiburg in Baden (Ph.D., 1881); A.B., Hamilton Coll., 1881; fellow Johns Hopkins, 1881-83; m. Anna Morgan Douglass, July 2, 1884; children—William Morgan, Rhys, John Tilney. Instr. rhetoric and lecturer on N. European lit., Cornell, 1883; instr. German and Scandinavian langs., 1883-89, asst. prof. same, 1889-90, adj. prof. Germanic langs. and lits., 1890-95, prof. Germanic philology, 1895-1902, Villard prof. Germanic philology, 1902-26, provost of univ., 1912-26, Columbia U. (emeritus). Author: Grundriss der Neuisländischen Grammatik, 1881. Home: Downingtown, Pa. Died Nov. 25, 1936.

CARPENTER, William Leland, lawyer; b. Orion, Mich., Nov. 9, 1854; s. Charles K. and Jennette (Coryell) C.; brother of Rolla Clinton and Louis George C.; B.S., Mich. State Coll., 1875; LL.B., U. of Mich., 1878, LL.D., 1913; m. Elizabeth C. Ferguson, Oct. 15, 1885 (died 1927); children—Lela (Mrs. Frederick G. Buesser), Rolla L. (dec.). In practice, Detroit, 1878-94; judge Circuit Court, Wayne County, Mich., 1894-1902; justice Supreme Court, 1903-08; resigned Sept. 15, 1908, and resumed practice at Detroit; counsel for Butzel, Eaman, Long, Gust & Bills. Del. Rep. Nat. Conv., 1912; temporary and permanent chmn. Rep. State Conv., Mich., 1915. Republican. Home: Detroit, Mich. Died Jan. 7, 1936.

CARR, Camillo Casatti Cadmus, brig. gen.; b. Harrisonburg, Va., Mar. 3, 1842; s. Dr. Wattson and Maria (Graham) C.; prep. edn. Wheeling, Va., and Chicago; entered University of Chicago, 1859, left in senior yr. before graduation to enter army (hon. A.M., 1873); m. Mrs. Marie C. Camp, Nov. 1878 (dec.). Served pvt. to regimental sergt. maj. 1st U.S. cav., Aug. 15, 1862; advanced through grades to brig. gen., Aug. 17, 1903. Bvtd. 1st lt. (Todd's Tavern), May 6, 1864; capt. (Winchester, Va.), Sept. 19, 1864; maj. (Nez Percé campaign, Idaho), Aug. 20, 1877. Wounded Todd's Tavern, Va., and in battle of Cedar Creek, Va., Oct. 19, 1864. Engaged in Apache campaigns, Ariz., 1866-69, 1871-73, and 1881-82; Nez Percé campaign, 1877; Bannock campaign, 1878, etc.; over 20 yrs. campaigning in Indian country; asst. instr. and instr. cav. in U.S. Inf. and Cav. Sch., Ft. Leavenworth, Kan., 1885-94; insp. gen. Dept. Columbia, 1894-95; command in western part of P.R., 1898-99; comd. regt. in P.I., 1900-01; comdg. post and comdt. Sch. of Application for Cav. and Field Arty. at Ft. Riley, Kan., 1901; comd. Dept. of Mo., Jan. 15-Feb. 24, 1904, Dept. of Dak., 1904-06; retired by operation of law, Mar. 3, 1906. Died July 24, 1914.

CARR, Ceylon Spencer, physician, editor; b. Herrickville, Pa., Jan. 6, 1850; s. Ezekiel and Susannah (Marsh) C.; grad. Towanda (Pa.) High Sch., 1872; student Univ. Med. Coll. (New York U.), 1874-76; M.D., Chicago Homœ. Med. Coll., 1877; m. Ida A. Smalley, Oct. 4, 1876. Began practice in Elmira, N.Y., 1877; removed to Columbus, O., 1889; editor Columbus Medical Journal. Mem. Bd. of County Visitors (pres.), Work House Bd. (dir.), Blind Relief Commn., Columbus Humane Soc., etc. Home: Columbus, O. Deceased.

CARR, Clarence Alfred, rear admiral; b. Crawford County, Pa., July 26, 1856; s. Alfred B. and Chloe R. (Stebbins) C.; grad. U.S. Naval Acad., 1879; M.E., Stevens Inst. Tech., 1884; m. Blanche Lanman, Oct. 19, 1898. Asst. engr. U.S. Navy, June 10, 1881; chief engr., Apr. 24, 1898; transferred to line as lt., Mar. 3, 1899; lt. comdr., Sept. 28, 1901; comdr., July 22, 1906; capt., July 1, 1910; rear adm., Sept. 26, 1919. Insp. machinery, Seattle, 1902-04; fleet engr. Coast Squadron, and in charge steam engring. on Texas, 1904-06; head dept. steam engring., Navy Yard, Mare Island, Calif., 1906-10; insp. machinery, Bayonne, N.J., 1911-17; engr. officer, Navy Yard, Phila., July 1917-Sept. 1919; insp. machinery, 3d Naval Dist., N.Y. City, Sept. 1919. Catholic. Retired July 22, 1921. Home: New London, Conn. Died Mar. 9, 1930.

CARR, Clark E(zra), author, lawyer; b. Boston Corners, Erie County, N.Y., May 20, 1836; s. Clark Murwin and Delia Ann (Torrey) C.; bro. late Gen. Eugene Asa Carr; student Knox Coll., Ill., 1851-56; LL.B., Albany Law Sch., 1858; (LL.D., Knox Coll., 1908); m. Grace Mills, Dec. 31, 1873. In practice at Galesburg, Ill., 1858-94, retired. On staff Gov. Yates (Ill.) with rank of col. during Civil War; postmaster Galesburg, 1861-85; U.S. minister plenipotentiary to Denmark, 1889-93. Del. Rep. Nat. Conv., 1864, del.-at-large, 1884; commr. of Ill. for Soldiers' Nat. Cemetery at Gettysburg, 1863; mem. Conf. U.S. Consuls-Gen., Paris, 1889; inaugurated Am. Indian Corn Kitchen, Paris, Expn., 1900; pres. Ill. Commission, Omaha Expn., 1898; trustee and mem. exec. bd. Knox Coll., 1881—; dir. Galesburg Public Library, 1898—. Author: The Illini, 1904; Lincoln at Gettysburg, 1906; My Day and Generation, 1908; The Railway Mail Service, 1909; Life of Stephen A. Douglas, 1909. Home: Galesburg, Ill. Died Feb. 28, 1919.

CARR, Clyde Mitchell, merchant; b. (of Va. parentage) in Will County, Ill., July 7, 1869; s. Richard Baxter and Margaret (Mitchell) C.; prepared for Princeton at Lake Forest Acad.; student Northwestern U., 2 yrs.; m. Lillian Van Alstyne, 1894. Pres. Joseph T. Ryerson & Son, Chicago; dir. C.G.W. R.R., Corn Exchange Nat. Bank. Trustee Art Inst. Chicago, Chicago Plan Commn.; pres. Orchestral Assn. Democrat. Presbyn. Home: Lake Forest, Ill., and Chicago. Died June 5, 1923.

CARR, Elias, farmer, governor; b. Bracebridge, Edgecombe Co., N.C., Feb. 25, 1839; ed. in private schools and Univ. of Va.; since then has conducted the ancestral farm at his native place. County commr. 15 years; pres. County and State Farmers' Alliance; one of the committee that drafted the Ocala resolutions of that organization; commr. from N.C. to World's Columbian Expn.; trustee State Agrl. and Mech. Coll. of N.C. several years; gov. N.C., 1893-97. Democrat. Home: Old Sparta, N.C. Died 1900.

CARR, Eugene Asa, brig. gen.; b. Concord, N.Y., Mar. 20, 1830; s. Clark Murwin and Delia Ann (Torrey) C.; brother of Clark Ezra C.; apptd. from N.Y., and grad. U.S. Mil. Acad., 1850; m. Mary P. Magwire, 1865. Bvt. 2d lt. mounted riflemen, July 1, 1850; 2d lt., June 30, 1851; advanced through grades to col. 3d Ill. Cav., Aug. 16, 1861; commd. brig. gen. vols., Mar. 7. 1862, "for distinguished services in battle of Pea Ridge, Ark.;" hon. mustered out of vol. service, Jan. 15, 1866; maj. 5th Cav., July 17, 1862; lt. col. 4th Cav., Jan. 7, 1873; transferred to 5th Cav., Apr. 10, 1873; col. 6th Cav., Apr. 29, 1879; brig. gen., July 19, 1892. Bvtd. lt. col., Aug. 10, 1861, "for gallant and meritorius services in battle of Wilson's Creek, Mo.;" col., May 7, 1863, for same in action of Black River Bridge, Miss.; brig. gen., Mar. 13, 1865, for same in capture of Little Rock, Ark.; maj. gen., Mar. 13, 1865, for same in the field during the war; also maj. gen. vols., Mar. 11, 1865; awarded Congressional Medal of Honor, Jan. 16, 1894, "for distinguished gallantry in battle of Pea Ridge, Ark." Served on frontier from Missouri River to Pacific and from Mont. to Tex.; was wounded in Texas, 1854, and was in 13 Indian fights; served through Civil War, and was at the battles of Wilson Creek, Mo., Pea Ridge, Ark. (wounded there 3 times), battles of Clarendon, Poison Spring and Jenkins Ferry, Ark., Port Gibson, Champion Hills, Black River Bridge, siege and capture of Vicksburg, siege and capture of Mobile. Received resolutions of thanks from legislatures of Neb., Colo. and N.M.; retired, Feb. 15, 1893. Died 1910.

CARR, George H., lawyer; b. Whitehall, N.Y., Nov. 23, 1852; s. William H. and Elizabeth (Armstrong) C.; student Beloit (Wis.) Coll., 1870, Jennings Sem., Aurora, Ill., 1871-73, State U. of Ia., 1874-76; m. Emma E. Parker, June 15, 1876. Admitted to bar, 1877; in practice at Des Moines, Ia., 1894—; sr. mem. Carr, Carr & Evans, 1908—. Judge 4th Jud. Dist., Ia., 1887-94; mem. Ia. Ho. of Rep., 2 terms, 1896-98. Republican. Del.-at-large Universal Congress Lawyers and Jurists, St. Louis, 1904. Home: Des Moines, Ia. Died Dec. 6, 1918.

CARR, Harry, newspaperman; b. Tipton, Ia., Mar. 27, 1877; s. Henry Clay and Louise (Low) C.; ed. high sch.; m. Alice Eaton, 1902; children—Donald Eaton, Patricia Josephine (Mrs. Walter Everett Morris). With Los Angeles (Calif.) Times from 1897, war corr. and Washington corr. and editor, now mem. bd. dirs. and contbr. daily column, "The Lancer"; formerly exec. and writer and supervisor of movie stories for D. W. Griffith, Cecil B. DeMille, Mack Sennett, Jesse Lasky, Erich Von Stroheim, etc. Vice-pres. League for Preservation of San Juan Bautista. Republican. Episcopalian. Author: Old Mother Mexico; The West Is Still Wild. Home: Tujunga, Calif. Died Jan. 10, 1936.

CARR, Henry James, librarian; b. Pembroke, N.H., Aug. 16, 1849; s. Col. James Webster and Jane D. (Goodhue) C.; ed. grammar and high schs., Manchester, N.H., and Grand Rapids, Mich.; accountant and cashier in commercial and ry. offices, 1867-86; partial law course at U. of Mich.; admitted to Michigan bar, 1879, but did not practice; m. D. Edith Wallbridge, May 13, 1886. Librarian Pub. Library, Grand Rapids, 1886-90; organized Free Pub. Library, St. Joseph, Mo., 1890-91; librarian Scranton Pub. Library, 1891—. Mem. A.L.A. (treas. 1886-93, recorder, 1894-95, v.p. 1896, sec. 1898-1900, pres. 1900-01). Home: Scranton, Pa. Died May 21, 1929.

CARR, Herbert Wildon, prof. philosophy; b. London, Eng., Jan. 16, 1857; s. Benjamin Wildon and Catharine (Anscomb) C.; Brown scholar and medallist, Stationers' Sch., London; King's Coll., London U.; hon. D.Litt., Durham U., 1912; LL.D., U. of Southern Calif., 1926; m. Margaret Geraldine Spooner, Dec. 20, 1890; children—Joan (Mrs. Fred I. Tomlinson), Ursula (Mrs. Charles A. Birnstingl), Teresa (Mrs. Armytage Noel Bryan-Brown). Became mem. of London Stock Exchange, 1879, retired 1908; head of dept. of psychology, King's Coll., 1914; prof. of philosophy, U. of London, 1918—; visiting prof. philosophy, U. of So. Calif., 1925—. Author: Henri Bergson, 1910; The Problem of Truth, 1911; The Philosophy of Change, 1914; The Philosophy of Benedetto Croce, 1917; The Principle of Relativity, 1920; A Theory of Monads, 1921; The Scientific Approach to Philosophy, 1924; Changing Backgrounds in Religion and Ethics, 1927; The Unique States of Man, 1928; The Freewill Problem, 1928; Leibniz, 1929. Home: Los Angeles, Calif. Died July 8, 1931.

CARR, John Foster, educator, author, lecturer; b. New York, Aug. 23, 1869; s. John Foster and Annie Sarah (Clark) C.; ed. Friends' Sch., Providence, R.I., Yale, and B.A., M.A., Brasenose Coll., Oxford; student Inner Temple, London; m. Emma Lilian Dana, June 21, 1916 (died 1921). Began writing, 1903; chief work has been in connection with immigration, and Americanization and edn. of the immigrant; founder and dir. Immigrant Publn. Soc.; Chevalier Order of the Crown of Italy, 1912; Officer Order of the Crown of Italy, 1920. Author: Guide to United States for the Italian Immigrant (in Italian and English), 1910; Guide to the United States for the Polish Immigrant, 1912; Guide to the United States for the Jewish Immigrant (in Yiddish and English), 1913; Immigrant and Library—Italian Helps, 1914; War's End—The Italian Immigrant Speaks of the Future, 1918; The Declaration of Independence, Its Story and Its Message, 1924. Home: New York, N.Y. Died Dec. 30, 1939.

CARR, Julian Shakespeare, mfr.; b. Chapel Hill, N.C., Oct. 12, 1845; s. John Wesley and Eliza P. C.; grad. Univ. of N.C.; served in Barringer's brigade, Hampton's Corps, C.S.A., Army of Northern Va. Engaged in business; pres. Bull Durham Tobacco Co., First Nat. Bank of Durham, Ormond Mining Co.; v.p. N.C. Joint Stock Bank; dir. Durham Hosiery Mills. Pres. bd. Durham Pub. Library; trustee N.C. Children's Home Soc. U. of N.C.,

Meth. Orphanage, Woman's Coll. (Greensboro, N.C.) Training Sch. for Colored People (Durham), Coll. (colored people) (Augusta, Ga.), Am. U. (Washington, D.C.), Old Ladies' Home (Durham), Confed. Home for Women (Fayetteville, N.C.), Methodist Chautauqua (Junaluska, N.C.), etc.; pres. Confed. Soldiers' Home (Raleigh, N.C.); mem. Durham Bd. of Edn. Formerly maj. gen. comdg. N.C. Div. U.C.V.; lt. gen. comdg. Army Northern Va., also former comdr. in chief U.C.V., then hon. comdr. in chief for life. Del. Ecumenical Meth. Conf., London, and Robert Raikes S.S. Centennial. Vol. aide to Herbert C. Hoover, federal food administrator, Washington, 1917-19. Home: Durham, N.C. Died Apr. 29, 1924.

CARR, Lewis E., lawyer; b. Salisbury, Herkimer Co., N.Y., Mar. 10, 1842; s. Eleazer and Hannah (Carr) C.; acad. edn., Fulton and Fairfield, N.Y.; LL.B., Albany Law Sch., 1864; m. Ruth Duke, of Kingston, Ont., Apr. 21, 1864 (died 1907). Admitted to bar, 1864, and began practice at Port Jervis, N.Y.; counsel for N.Y.,L.E.&W. R.R. Co. in Orange, Rockland, Sullivan and Del. cos., N.Y., 1872-94; resident counsel D.&H. Co. at Albany, 1894—. Dist. atty., Orange Co., 1872-75; mem. commn. to propose amendments to N.Y. constn., 1890; mem. bd. edn., Port Jervis, 16 yrs. Republican. Mason. Home: Albany, N.Y. Died Apr. 1, 1929.

CARR, Lucien, curator; b. Lincoln Co., Mo., Dec. 1829; A.B., St. Louis U., 1846, later A.M. Asst. curator Peabody Mus. of Am. Archæology and Ethnology, Harvard, 1877-94. Mem. Am. Acad. Arts and Sciences. Author: The Mounds of the Mississippi Valley Historically Considered; Missouri (a brief history), 1888; Prehistoric Remains of Kentucky (with N. S. Shaler). Home: Cambridge, Mass. Died Jan. 27, 1915.

CARR, Samuel, financier; b. Boston, Nov. 18, 1848; s. Samuel and Louisa Hall (Trowbridge) C.; high sch. edn., Newton, Mass.; m. Susan Waters Tarbox, Sept. 10, 1872. Dir. Old Colony Trust Co., 1st Nat. Bank (Easton, Mass.), Am. Agrl. Chem. Co., Ames Shovel & Tool Co., Boston Elevated Ry. Co., Boston Consol. Gas Co., etc.; trustee Mass. Gas Cos., N.E. Transportation Co., Am. Sugar Refining Co., Pray Bldgs. Trust, Boston Five Cents Savings Bank, Business Real Estate Trust, Embankment Land Co., Union Copper Land & Mining Co., estates of Oliver and Frederick L. Ames. Organist and director of music Old South Church, Boston, for many yrs.; pres. N.E. Conservatory of Music. Homes: Manchester, Mass., and Boston. May 29, 1922.

CARR, William John, judge; b. Brooklyn, Oct. 10, 1862; s. Cornelius and Mary (Gallagher) C.; A.B., Coll. of St. Francis Xavier, New York, 1882; (LL.D., Villanova Coll., 1904, St. Francis Xavier, 1907, Fordham, 1912); m. Julia Mary Fryer, Oct. 12, 1887. Admitted to bar, 1884, and practiced at Brooklyn; mem. bar of State and Federal cts., including U.S. Supreme Ct. Clk. Supreme Ct., Kings Co., 1891-93; commr. U.S. Circuit Ct., Brooklyn, 1895-96; asst. corp. counsel, City of New York, 1898-1902, in charge law dept. of city in Borough of Brooklyn; justice Supreme Ct., N.Y., Jan. 1, 1907—; term expiring Dec. 31, 1920; designated by governor as justice Appellate Div. Democrat. Catholic. Home: Brooklyn, N.Y. Died Aug. 5, 1917.

CARR, William Kearny, researcher; b. in Warren Co., N.C., Aug. 17, 1860; s. the late Gov. Elias and Eleanor (Kearny) C.; Hillsboro (N.C.) Mil. Acad., 1873-76; U. of Va., 1877-78; m. Martina Van Riswick, June 5, 1885. Engaged in sale and mfr. of cotton at Norfolk, Va., and N.C., 1878-90; dir. Rocky Mt. (N.C.) Cotton Mills; study and research in phys. sciences at Washington, 1890—. Home: Washington, D.C. Died Oct. 7, 1915.

CARRÉ, Henry Beach, theologian; b. New Orleans, La., June 9, 1871; s. Walter Willie and Elvira Adams (Beach) C.; A.B., Tulane U. of La., 1895; B.D., Bibl. Dept., Vanderbilt U., 1898; studied univs. of Berlin and Marburg, Germany, 1898-1900; Ph.D., U. of Chicago, 1913; m. Mary O. Vaughan, Mar. 22, 1906. In merc. business to 1889; ordained ministry M.E. Ch., S., 1893; pastor, Jackson, La., and prof. Centenary Coll. of La., 1900-02; pres. Centenary Coll. of La., 1902-03; prof. Bibl. theology and English exegesis, 1903-19, prof. O.T. lang. and lit., 1920—, Vanderbilt U. Mem. Gen. Council World League Against Alcoholism, 1919—. Supt. of platform and schools Monteagle S.S. Assembly, 1917-20. Overseas service with Y.M.C.A., in Les Foyers du Soldat, Apr. 1, 1918-Apr. 1, 1919; overseas representative of Sigma Chi Fraternity, 1918-19. Democrat. Author: Paul's Doctrine of Redemption. Died Jan. 30, 1928.

CARRÈRE, John Merven, architect; b. of Am. parents in Rio de Janeiro, Brazil, Nov. 9, 1858; ed. in Switzerland; grad. École des Beaux Arts, Paris, 1882. Partner with Thomas Hastings in firm, Carrère & Hastings, 1884—. The firm were architects of the Ponce de Leon and Alcazar hotels, St. Augustine, Fla., the New York Pub. Library, also for Nat. Acad. of Design and many other notable buildings. Fellow Am. Inst. Architects. Home: New York, N.Y. Died 1911.

CARRICK, Manton Marble, sanitarian; b. near Keatchie, La., Aug. 17, 1879; s. White L. and Cammie Rozina (Thompson) C.; grad. Dallas Acad., 1897; M.D., Tex. Christian U., 1901; also post-grad. work in clinics of Chicago, New York, Boston and Philadelphia; m. Mai Connor Gordon, July 15, 1926. Asst. house surgeon, T.&P. Ry. Hosp., Marshall, Tex., 1899; resident phys., Parkland Hosp., 1900; quarantine officer State of Tex., 1906; asst. supt. State Epileptic Colony, Abilene, Tex., 1910-11; supt. Tex. State Lepers' Colony, 1912; pres. Tex. State Bd. of Health, and State health officer; chmn. pub. health com. United Charities, Dallas; prof. preventive medicine, Baylor U. Coll. of Medicine, 1914; dir. pub. health, City of Dallas, Aug. 20, 1927; has made sanitary surveys of many cities and towns of U.S. Surgeon (R.) U.S. Public Health Service. Retired as maj., Med. Corps, U.S. Army. Awarded scholarship in gen. medicine, New York Post-Grad. Med. Sch. and Hosp., 1925, also scholarship in diseases of children by same, 1926. Democrat. Episcopalian. Mason. Home: Dallas, Tex. Died Sept. 17, 1932.

CARRIER, Augustus Stiles, clergyman; b. Ripley, N.Y., Dec. 30, 1857; s. Augustus Hart and Susan A. (Bandelle) C.; A.B., Yale, 1879; Andover Theol. Sem., 1881-82; grad. Hartford Theol. Sem., 1884; univs. of Leipzig and Berlin, 1885-87, Semitic langs. a splty.; (D.D., 1893, LL.D., 1913, Parsons Coll.); m. Anne C. Dennis, July 15, 1885. Ordained Presbyterian ministry, 1884. Prof. Hebrew and O.T. exegesis, McCormick Theol. Sem., 1892—. Republican. Home: Chicago, Ill. Died Sept. 4, 1923.

CARRIER, Wilbur Oscar, clergyman; b. Marshall, Mich., Feb. 28, 1860; s. Edwin Burt and Cornelia Clarcy (Root) C.; A.B., Albion Coll., 1883, A.M., 1895; grad. Auburn Theol. Sem., 1886; D.D., Ripon, 1898; LL.D., Alma, 1916; m. Myrtle Jene Pitts, May 5, 1885; children—Ralph Wilbur, Cornelia C. (Mrs. Andrew Weaver). Ordained Presbyn. ministry, 1886; pastor Shortsville, N.Y., 1886-88, Wausau, Wis., 1889-1900, Belden Av. Ch., Chicago, 1900-04; pres. Carroll Coll., Waukesha, Wis., 1904-17 (emeritus); supt. Ch. Extension Bd. Presbytery of Chicago, 1917-18; in Asia in interest of foreign missions, 1920-21; pastor Third Ch., Chicago, 1921-24. Moderator Presbyn. Synod of Wis., 1894; mem. bd. dirs. McCormick Theol. Sem. Republican. Home: Evanston, Ill. Died Aug. 12, 1939.

CARRIGAN, Clarence, consular service; b. San Rafael, Calif., Mar. 22, 1880; A.B., St. Ignatius Coll., San Francisco, 1899. Clk. subsistence dept. U.S. Army, 1900-01; 2d lt. Arty. Corps, U.S. Army, 1901-07 (resigned); in oriental-art business, San Francisco, 1907-09; v. and dep. consul, St. John, N.B., 1910-13; same at Lyon, France, 1912-13; consul at Grenoble, France, 1913-15; v. consul, London, Eng., 1915-16; became consul at Lyon, France, 1918, at Milan, Italy, 1921; then consul gen. at Montevideo, Uruguay. Died Dec. 22, 1929.

CARRIGAN, William L., artist; b. San Francisco, Calif., Sept. 21, 1868; s. Andrew and Jane (Hackett) C.; student Jesuit Coll., San Francisco; pupil of Emil Carlsen; unmarried. Began painting, 1906; asst. to U.S. Naval attachè, Lisbon, Portugal, 1917-18. Awarded silver medal, Washington Soc. Am. Artists, 1914; silver medal, Panama-Pacific Expn., San Francisco, 1915; Walter L. Clarke portrait prize, Grand Central Art Gallrey, New York, 1931; Conn. prize for best work, New Haven Paint and Clay Club, 1934; Berstow prize for landscape, Stockbridge Exhibition, 1934. Decorated St. Tiago da Espada of Portugal. Democrat. Catholic. Home: Falls Village, Conn. Died Oct. 27, 1939.

CARRINGTON, Edward Codrington, lawyer; b. Washington, D.C., Apr. 10, 1872; s. Edward Codrington and Florida Troupe (Harrison) C.; ed. under pvt. tutors; m. Ethel Stuart Coyle, Oct. 5, 1899. Admitted to Md. bar, 1894, and began practice in Baltimore; mem. Carrington & Carrington, Baltimore and New York; specializes in corp. law. Mem. staff of Gov. Goldsborough, with rank of col. Campaign manager for Md. for Theodore Roosevelt, primary election, 1912; del. at large, Rep. Nat. Conv., Chicago, same yr.; signed call for Progressive Nat. Conv., 1912, and later del. at large to same; mem. Progressive Nat. Com., 1912, and chmn. Progressive State Com., Md.; after presdl. election, 1912, led movement in Md. to unite Reps. and Progressives; regular Rep. nominee for U.S. Senate, 1914 (defeated); Rep. nominee for pres. Borough of Manhattan, 1931. Chmn. bd. and pres. Hudson River Navigation Corp.; chmn. bd. Hudson River Steamboat Co.; pres. Americana Corp.; v.p. Eastwood Corp. Episcopalian. Home: Loreley, Md. Died Dec. 30, 1938.

CARRINGTON, Frances Courtney, author; b. Franklin, Tenn., Jan. 14, 1845; d. Robert and Eliza Jane Courtney; m. Lt. G. W. Grummond, 18th U.S. Inf., 1865 (killed in Fetterman Massacre, Dec. 21, 1866); 2d, Henry Beebe Carrington, 1871. Spl. guest at Chicago Sanitary Fair for services as nurse to wounded Union soldiers during Civil War. Author: The Flag in Dixie; Army Life on the Plains; History of Indian War of 1866-67; The Sheridan Celebration of 1908. Home: Hyde Park, Mass. Died 1911.

CARRINGTON, Henry Beebee, brig. gen.; b. Wallingford, Conn., Mar. 2, 1824; A.B., Yale, 1845, A.M., 1848; Yale Law Sch., 1847; (LL.D., Wabash Coll., 1878); m. Margaret Irvin McDowell (author "Absaraka, Home of the Crows"); m. 2d, Frances Courtney, 1871 (widow of Lt. G. W. Grummond); father of James Beebee C. Practiced law, Columbus, O., 1848-61 (Dennison & Carrington); chmn. com. to organize new party, July 13, 1854; adj. gen., 1857-61; escort of legislatures of Ky. and Tenn. to Columbus; of Prince of Wales from Cincinnati to Columbus; of Pres.-elect Lincoln from Springfield to Columbus; at beginning of war moved 9 militia regts. into Western Va.; apptd. col. 18th U.S. Inf., May 14, 1861, and brig. gen. vols., Nov. 29, 1862; served in important commands; also comd. Dist. of Ind.; organized and sent to front 120,000 Ind. vols.; exposed disloyal "Sons of Liberty;" rejoined Army of Cumberland, 1865; opened wagon route to Mont., through Wyo., 1866; comd. Rocky Mountain Dist.; planned and built Ft. Phil Kearney; in active war with the opposing Sioux; wounded in skirmish with the Sioux Indians; comd. Ft. McPherson, Neb., and Ft. Sedgwick, Colo.; detailed as mil. prof. Wabash Coll.; on increased disability retired from active service, 1870; in 1875 was granted access by Great Britain and France to all revolutionary archives; surveyed and mapped the battlefields; made treaty with Flathead Indians of Mont., 1889; in 1891 moved the Indians through Missoula, across Mission Ridge Range to the Rocky Mountains, to Jocko Reservation, Western Mont.; took detailed census of Six Nations, N.Y., and Cherokees, N.C., 1890. Author: Washington, the Soldier, 1899. Home: Hyde Park, Mass. Died Oct. 26, 1912.

CARRINGTON, James Beebee, editor; b. Columbus, O.; s. Henry Beebee and Margaret Irvin McDowell (Sullivant) C.; A.M., Wabash Coll., 1898. Formerly associate editor of Scribners. Lecturer on art and nature topics, and contbr. to mags. Home: New York, N.Y. Died July 14, 1929.

CARRINGTON, William Thomas, educator; b. Callaway County, Mo., Jan. 23, 1854; s. Judge William and Susan (Fisher) C.; ed. Kirksville Normal Sch., Westminster Coll., U. of Mo.; m. Mary Holloway, Aug. 19, 1879 (died 1930); children—Will, Paul. Prin. town schs., 1876-83; asst. state supt. pub. schs., 1883-87; prin. Springfield (Mo.) High Sch., 1887-99; state supt. public schs., 1899-1907; pres. State Normal Sch., 4th dist., Springfield, 1907-18; became dir. vocational education, Missouri State Dept. of Public Schools, June 1919; retired. Editor and pub. Mo. School Journal, 1883-87. Author: Missouri School Reports, 1899-1907; Course of Study for Rural and Village Schools; Elements of Agriculture for Public Schools; Biography of Mrs. Carrington; Education in Missouri. Home: Jefferson City, Mo. Died Jan. 21, 1937.

CARROLL, B. Harvey, consular service; b. Waco, Tex., Mar. 3, 1874; s. Benajah Harvey and Ellen Virginia (Bell) C.; B.A., Baylor U., 1892; LL.B., U. of Tex., 1894; Th.M., Southern Bapt. Theol. Sem., Louisville, Ky., 1899, Th.D., 1900; studied U. of Chicago, summer, 1899; M.A., Ph.D., magna cum laude, U. of Berlin, 1902; m. Daisy Crawford, Aug. 6, 1895. Bapt. ministry, 1895-1905; head, dept. of history and polit. economy, Baylor U., 1902-04; editorial staff Houston Chronicle, 1906-14; editor Stylus, 1912; apptd. Am. consul at Venice, Italy, Apr. 24, 1914; consul at Naples, Oct. 4, 1918 to March 20, 1920, then consul at Cadiz, Spain. Chaplain and capt. 1st Vol. Tex. Cav., Spanish-Am. War, 1898; lt. col. and a.d.c. Tex. N.G., staff of Gov. Lanham. In war zone, Italy, May 24, 1915-Oct. 4, 1918; del. Am. Red Cross, Venice, Oct. 1917-June 1918; established 1st relief stations, 1st free kitchens and 1st hosp. of Am. Red Cross in Italy. Cavaliere Ufficiale della Corona d'Italia, 1917; Italian War Cross, for valor, 1918; Campaign medal, 1919. Democrat. Author: Die Annextion von Texas, Ein Beitrag zür Geschichte der Monroe Doctrin (thesis), 1902; Political History of Europe, 1815-1848, 1904; The High Priest of the Lost Temple (Art and Archæology, July 1921). Home: Houston, Tex. Died Mar. 30, 1922.

CARROLL, Benajah Harvey, clergyman; b. nr. Carrollton, Miss., Dec. 27, 1843; s. Benajah and Mary Elisa (Mallard) C.; ed. Baylor U., Independence (now Waco), Tex. (hon. A.M.; D.D., U. of Tenn.; LL.D., Keochi Coll., La.); m. Ellen Bell, 1866; 2d, Hallie Harrison, of Waco, 1899. Served in C.S.A. 4 yrs.; ordained Bapt. ministry, 1866; pastor chs. in Burleson Co., Tex.; 1st Ch., Waco, 1871-99; apptd. corr. sec. Tex. Bapt. Edn. Commn., 1899; dean Bible Dept., Baylor U., 1902-10; pres. Southwestern Bapt. Theol. Sem., 1910—. Democrat. Mason. Author: Baptist Doctrines, 1912; Lectures on Revelation, 1913; Lectures on Genesis, 1913; also 2 vols. of sermons, etc. Died Nov. 11, 1914.

CARROLL, Beryl F., governor; b. Davis Co., Ia., Mar. 15, 1860; s. Willis and Christena C.; grad. N. Mo. State Normal Sch., Kirksville, Mo., 1884; LL.D., Simpson Coll., 1909; m. Jennie Dodson, June 15, 1886; children—Paul Willis, Jean Franklin.

Teacher country schs. of Ia., and in graded schs. of Mo., 1884-89; engaged with brother as live stock dealer, Bloomfield, Ia., 1889-91; became editor Davis County Republican, 1891; presdl. elector 6th Iowa District, 1892; Rep. candidate for Ia. Ho. of Rep., 1893; mem. Ia. Senate, 1895-98 (resigned); postmaster of Bloomfield, Ia., 1898-1902; state auditor of Ia. 3 terms, 1903-09; gov. of Ia., 1909-11, 1911-13; chmn. bd. Commercial Finance Corp.; pres. Carroll Investment Co. Republican. Methodist. Home: Des Moines, Ia. Died Dec. 16, 1939.

CARROLL, Charles, educator, author, lawyer; b. Providence, R.I., June 8, 1876; s. William and Mary E. (Sheehan) C.; A.B., Brown U., 1898, A.M., 1913, Ph.D., 1915; LL.B., Harvard, 1901; LL.D., Providence (R.I.) Coll., 1931; m. Gertrude V. Gariepy, Oct. 2, 1902; children—Charles, William. Admitted to R.I. bar, 1901, and since practiced at Providence; prof. Rhode Island edn., and law and govt., R.I. Coll. of Edn., 1916—; also prof. sch. law and administration, R.I. State Coll., 1898-1930; dir. vocational education of Rhode Island. Trustee of Providence College, 1929—. Catholic. Author: Outlines of Government of Rhode Island, 1923; Outlines of History of Rhode Island, 1924; also wrote the Rhode Island State song, "Rhode Island," 1919; Rhode Island and the Constitution of the United States, 1933. Editor of Quarterly Jour. of R.I. Inst. of Instr. Home: Providence, R.I. Died Feb. 4, 1936.

CARROLL, Charles Chauncey, clergyman, educator; b. Waco, Tex., Apr. 23, 1876; s. Benajah Harvey and Ellen Virginia (Bell) C.; grad. mil. dept. Baylor U., 1896, B.O., 1897, B.Litt., 1898, D.D., 1920; studied U. of Chicago, 1899; m. Maria Annette Williams, Oct. 2, 1900; children—Mary Edna, Dorothy Virginia, Annette Williams. Vice-pres. Mt. Lebanon (La.) Coll., 1900; ordained ministry Bapt. Ch., 1900; pastor Natchitoches and Robelene, La., later Calvert, Tex., until 1904; in charge home mission work, Havana, Cuba, under Home Mission Bd., Southern Bapt. Conv., 1904; pastor successively Ocala, Fla., Owensboro, Ky., Winchester, Ky., and supply at Shreveport, La., and Beaumont, Tex., until 1919; chair of Bible doctrines, etc., Bapt. Bible Inst., New Orleans, La., 1919-28, also pastor New Sight Baptist Ch., nr. Brookhaven, Miss. Enlisted Troop G, 1st Regt., Tex. Vol. U.S. Cav., 1898, Spanish-Am. War; apptd. sergt. asst. chaplain gen. U.S.C.V., 1909, 10. Democrat. Mason. Author: Synthesis and Analysis of the Poetry of Sidney Lanier, 1910; Outline of Bible Doctrines, 1922. Home: Natchitoches, La. Died Feb. 4, 1936.

CARROLL, Henry, soldier; b. in N.Y., May 20, 1838. Served pvt., sergt. and 1st sergt., Co. E, 3d Arty., Jan. 13, 1859-Jan. 13, 1864; pvt. and sergt., Co. G, 3d Arty., Feb. 3-June 4, 1864; promoted through grades to lt. col., 6th Cav., May 23, 1896; apptd. brig. gen., vols., June 8, 1898; hon. disch., Nov. 30, 1898; col. 7th Cav., Mar. 29, 1899; retired at own request after 40 yrs.' service, May 6, 1899; advanced to rank of brig. gen. retired, by act of Apr. 23, 1904. Bvtd. maj., Feb. 27, 1890, for action against Indians on main fork of Brazos River, Tex., Sept. 16, 1869, and against Indians in San Andreas Mts., N.M., Apr. 7, 1880 (severely wounded). Died 1908.

CARROLL, Henry King, author; b. Dennisville, N.J., Nov. 15, 1848; s. Henry King and Charlotte (Johnson) C.; ed. pub. schs.; LL.D., Syracuse U., 1885; m. Annie Barnes, Oct. 9, 1872. Religious and polit. editor The Independent, 1876-98; in charge census of chs., 11th census, 1890; U.S. commr. to Porto Rico, 1898-99; 1st asst. corr. sec. Meth. Missionary Soc., 1900-08; sec. Am. Exec. Com. of World Missionary Com., Edinburgh, 1910; exec. sec. Western Sect. Ecumenical Meth. Conf., 1911, 21; sec. Ecumenical Meth. Conf., Toronto, 1911; asso. sec. Federal Council of Churches of Christ in America, 1913-16; corr. sec. Asbury Memorial Assn. and Ecumenical Meth. Commn.; del. 5 times to Gen. Conf. M.E. Ch. Author: Religious Forces of the United States, 1893; Missionary Growth of the Methodist Episcopal Church; First Methodist Society in America, Francis Asbury Centenary Volume; Francis Asbury in the Making of American Methodism. Home: Plainfield, N.J. Died Jan. 21, 1931.

CARROLL, Howard, journalist; b. Albany, N.Y., 1854; ed. old Henry St. Grammar Sch., New York, Hanover, Germany, and Geneva, Switzerland. Entered newspaper work as reporter New York Times, of which he later became traveling corr.; spl. Washington corr., 1877; reported yellow fever epidemic in South; distinguished by his advocacy of Gov. Packard of La. and Gov. Chamberlain of S.C.; declined offer of private sec. to Pres. Arthur and post of minister to Belgium. Was candidate for congressman-at-large. Chief of arty., N.Y., 1895-98; 4th Cav., Jan. 7, 1873; transferred to 5th Cav., insp. gen. N.Y. troops, Spanish-Am. War. Pres. Sicilian Asphalt Paving Co., Asphalt Co. of Canada. Author: A Mississippi Incident; Twelve Americans, Their Lives and Times; (play) The American Countess. For interest in German affairs, decorated by German Emperor with Order of the Red Eagle. Homes: Tarrytown, N.Y., and N.Y. City. Died Dec. 30, 1916.

CARROLL, James, physician, army surgeon; b. in Eng., June 5, 1854; s. James and Harriet (Chiverton) C.; ed. Albion House Acad., Woolwich, Eng., to 1869; grad. med. dept., Univ. of Md., 1891; post-grad. course pathology, Johns Hopkins Hosp., 1891; in bacteriology, 1892; m. Jennie M. George Lucas, May 1888. Associated with late Maj. Walter Reed, surgeon U.S.A., in study of Sanarelli's supposed yellow fever bacillus, 1897-1902, U.S. and Cuba. To justify experimentation on other persons, voluntarily submitted to bite of a contaminated mosquito that had previously been caused to bite 3 well-marked cases of yellow fever. Within 4 days was taken ill and suffered a severe attack of the disease. First lt. and assistant surgeon U.S.A. Prof. bacteriology and clinical microscopy, Army Med. Sch.; prof. bacteriology, Washington Post-Grad. Sch.; prof. bacteriology and pathology, med. dept. George Washington Univ.; curator Army Med. Museum. Home: Washington, D.C. Died 1907.

CARROLL, James Bernard, judge; b. Lowell, Mass., Jan. 10, 1856; s. Patrick and Bridget (O'Rourke) C.; A.B., Holy Cross Coll., Worcester, Mass., 1878, LL.D., 1912; LL.B., Boston U. Law Sch., 1880; m. Mary E. Corbett, 1884. Began practice Springfield, Mass., 1881; city solicitor, 1886-88; chmn. Industrial Accident Bd., 1911; judge Superior Court, Mass., 1914; justice Supreme Judicial Court, Jan. 1915—. Knight of St. Gregory, 1925. Mem. Knights of Columbus. Home: Springfield, Mass. Died Jan. 8, 1932.

CARROLL, James Jordan, bishop of Nueva Legovia. Died Apr. 11, 1913.

CARROLL, James Milton, clergyman, educator; b. Monticello, Ark., Jan. 8, 1852; s. Benajah and Mary Eliza (Mallard) C.; moved to Tex., 1858; A.B., Baylor U., 1878, A.M., 1879 (D.D.); m. Sudie Eliza Womble, Dec. 22, 1870. Ordained missionary Bapt. ministry, 1874; pastor, Anderson, Tex., 1878-79, Corpus Christi, 1880-82, Lampasas, 1882-87, Taylor, 1887-88; agt. Bapt. foreign mission work for Tex., 1888-92; corr. sec. Bapt. Gen. Conv. of Tex., 1892-95; agt. Baylor Female Coll., 1895-97 (reduced debt more than $40,000); corr. sec. Tex. Bapt. Edn. Commn., 1898-1901; pastor 1st Ch., Waco, 1902-03; again corr. sec. Edn. Com. and endowment sec., Baylor U., 1903-05; pres. and builder San Marcos (Tex.) Acad., 1905-11; pres. Howard Payne Coll., Brownwood, Tex., 1913-15 (resigned); pastor Riverside Park Ch., San Antonio, Tex., 1916-18; has written a history of Texas Baptists; long active in S.S. and temperance work. Democrat. Built Carroll Coll., at McAllen, Tex. Home: McAllen, Tex. Died Jan. 10, 1931.

CARROLL, John D., judge; b. Oldham County, Ky., Oct. 1854; s. A. J. and Eliza (Collins) C.; ed. pub. schs., Oldham County, short time; m. Harriett Hunter Sanford, 1894; children—John S., Lewis. Admitted to bar and practiced at New Castle. Mem. Ky. Ho. of Rep., 2 terms, 1881-84; mem. Ky. Constl. Conv., 1890-91; commr. to revise laws of Ky., 1892-94; chmn. Dem. State Central and Exec. coms., 1892-95; commr. Ct. of Appeals of Ky., 1906-07; judge Ct. of Appeals, 1907-20; retired from bench and resumed practice of law at Frankfort. Edited and compiled Ky. Statutes, 5 edits., 1894, 99, 1903, 09, 15; editor Ky. Codes of Practice, 5 edits., 1885, 95, 1900, 06, 13. Home: Frankfort, Ky. Died Jan. 4, 1927.

CARROLL, John F., banker. Was Tammany leader in the old 20th assembly dist.; clerk of grand jury, 1879; clerk 7th dist. civil ct.; clerk ct. of spl. sessions; clerk courts of oyer, terminer and gen. sessions, 1891-98; resigned; sachem and mem. exec. com. Tammany Hall. Dir. Adirondack Trust Co., Saratoga Springs, N.Y.; v.p. 14th St. Bank; dir. New Amsterdam Nat. Bank, New Amsterdam Safe Deposit Co., Wall St. Exchange Bldg. Assn. Home: New York, N.Y. Died 1911.

CARROLL, John Francis, newspaperman; b. St. Clair, Pa., June 15, 1858; s. Thaddeus and Catherine (Jordan) C.; ed. State Normal Sch., Millersville, Pa.; took a yr.'s course in medicine Western Reserve U.; m. Florence Hurlbut, May 1, 1889. Entered newspaper work, 1876; on staff Missouri Republican, St. Louis, 1879; city editor Omaha Bee, 1880-81; cowboy in Wyo. and Mont., 1882-84; employed on Cleveland Leader, 1884; subsequently entered med. dept. Western Reserve U., but did not graduate. Editor Cheyenne (Wyo.) Leader for 8 yrs. preceding 1895; went through celebrated Wyo. Rustler war, taking side of the small ranchmen. Managing editor Denver Post for 6 yrs. and gen. mgr. Denver Times; statistician for Colo. Fuel & Iron Co.; became pub. and part owner The Evening Telegram, Portland, Ore. "Father" of the annual Rose Festival at Portland; Carroll Pub. Market (municipal) named for him, 1914. Home: Portland, Ore. Died Dec. 4, 1917.

CARROLL, John Haydock, lawyer; b. in Erie County, N.Y., June 27, 1857; s. Michael and Margaret (Doolin) C.; ed. in Quaker schs. in Ind.; m. Priscilla Woodrow, Dec. 17, 1880. Admitted to Ohio bar, 1880, Mo. bar, 1881; pros. atty., Putnam County, Mo., 1883-89; practiced in St. Louis, 1889—; gen. atty. C.,B.&Q. R.R. Co., N.P. Ry. Co.; and G.N. Ry.; pres. Vinsonhaler Shoe Co. Was col. on staff Gov. D. R. Francis; del. Dem. nat. convs., 1888, 1900, alternate-at-large, 1892. Died Nov. 29, 1931.

CARROLL, John Joseph, priest; b. Enniscrone, County Sligo, Ireland, June 24, 1856; s. Francis C. and Mary (Howley) C.; came to U.S. in infancy; 6 yrs.' course in St. Michael's Coll., Toronto, Ont.; grad. St. Joseph's Provincial Theol. Sem., Troy, N.Y., 1879. Asst. Cathedral of Holy Name, Chicago, 1880; soon after rector St. Thomas Ch., Chicago; distinguished as a Gaelic writer and scholar. Elected at conv. 1898 chmn. Gaelic History, at conv. 1901, Nat. Librarian Gaelic League of America. Author: Notes and Observations on the Aryan Race and Tongue, 1894; Prechristian Occupation of Ireland by the Gaelic Aryans, 1908; Ancient History of Ireland (Gaelic and English, 2 vols.); Tale of the Wanderings of the Red Lance (in Gaelic and English). Translated into Gaelic verse, The Rubaiyat of Omar Khayyam, 1909. Home: Chicago, Ill. Deceased.

CARROLL, John Lee, governor; b. Homewood, near Baltimore, Md., Sept. 30, 1830; great g.s. Charles C. of Carrollton, a "signer"; ed. Roman Catholic Coll., Georgetown, D.C., Emmittsburg, Md., St. Mary's and Harvard Law Sch.; admitted to bar, 1851; m. Anita Phelps (died 1873); 2d, Mary Carter, d. late Judge L. P. Thompson, of Staunton, Va. Mem. Md. Senate, 1867, 1871; gov. of Md., 1876-80. Democrat. Pres.-gen. Nat. Soc. S.R. Home: Ellicott City, Md. Died 1911.

CARROLL, John P., bishop; b. Dubuque, Ia., Feb. 22, 1864; s. Martin and Catherine (O'Farrell) C.; ed. St. Raphael's Parochial Sch., Dubuque, until 1877, St. Joseph's Coll., Dubuque, until 1883, Grand Sem., Montreal, Can., until 1889, when grad. D.D. Ordained R.C. priest, July 7, 1889; apptd. prof. mental philosophy, Sept. 12, 1889, and pres., Sept. 12, 1894, St. Joseph's Coll., Dubuque; apptd. bishop of Helena, Mont., Sept. 12, 1904. Died Nov. 4, 1925.

CARROLL, (Alexander) Mitchell, educator, editor; b. Wake Forest, N.C., June 2, 1870; s. Rev. Dr. John L. and Sarah G. (Mitchell) C.; A.B., A.M., Richmond (Va.) Coll., 1888; Ph.D., Johns Hopkins, 1893; univs. of Leipzig and Berlin, 1893-94; m. Carolyn Moncure Benedict, Sept. 6, 1897. Prof. Greek, Richmond Coll., 1895-97; mem. Am. School Classical Studies, Athens, 1897-98; reader in classical archæology, Johns Hopkins, 1898-99; prof. classics, 1899-1910, prof. archæology and history of art, 1910—, George Washington U. Author: Aristotle's Poetics, c.XXXV, in the Light of the Homeric Scholia, 1895; Greek Women, 1907; Early Christian Women (joint author), 1907. Editor The Attica of Pausanias, with Introduction, Notes and Excursuses (College Series of Greek Authors), 1907. Dir. and editor Art and Archæology; dir. Art and Archæology Press, Inc. Decorated with Order of the Redeemer (Greek), 1918. Home: Washington, D.C. Died Mar. 3, 1925.

CARROLL, Thomas F., lawyer; b. near Rochester, Nov. 23, 1854; s. James and Mary (Kennedy) C.; ed. pub. schs.; m. Ella M. Remington; m. 2d, Julia Agnes Mead, Aug. 19, 1889; children—Charles, Katharine, Lee. Admitted to bar, 1879; sr. mem. Carroll, Kirwin & Hollway; v.p. and gen. counsel Grand Rapids, Grand Haven & Muskegon Ry. Co.. Postmaster, Grand Rapids, 1894-98; 1st Dem. elector-at-large, Mich., 1904; mem. Bd. of Estimates, Grand Rapids, 1906. Home: Grand Rapids, Mich. Deceased.

CARROLL, William Henry, lawyer; b. Panola County, Miss., Feb. 18, 1843; s. Gen. William H. and Elisabeth (Breathitt) C.; student U. of Tenn. through sr. yr.; m. Mattie McKay, June 15, 1888. Enlisted in C.S. Army at outbreak of Civil War, drilling a regt. raised by father; became mem. staff of Gen. Thomas H. Bradley, as vol. and aide; was made adj. 37th Tenn. Regt.; in comd. of Gen. James R. Chalmer's escort; resigned shortly before close of war on account of ill health. Engaged in cotton business in Memphis; admitted to bar, 1875; asso. in practice with Julius A. Taylor, later with Gen. Chalmers; then mem. Carroll & Scott. For many yrs. a leading figure in Tenn. politics; chmn. Dem. State Central Com.; del. Dem. Nat. Conv., 1876, 1880; Dem. presdl. elector from Tenn., 1900. Home: Memphis, Tenn. Died 1916.

CARRUTH, Charles Theodore, art lecturer; b. Dorchester, Mass., May 22, 1851; s. Charles and Mary Anna (Bachi) C.; student Mass. Inst. Tech.; m. Anna Kent, June 5, 1884; 1 son, Charles. Traveled extensively in Europe and made spl. studies of the Florentine renaissance; has delivered illustrated lectures at many of the univs. and most of the art museums of U.S.; lectures on Giotto, Donatello, della Robbia, Fra Angelico, Domenico Ghirlandaio, Botticelli, Michaelangelo, Raphael. Episcopalian. Home: Cambridge, Mass. Died 1926.

CARRUTH, (Fred) Hayden, writer; b. near Lake City, Minn., Oct. 31, 1862; s. Oliver P. and Mary (Veeder) C.; student U. of Minn., 1881-82; m. Ettie

L. Gorton, June 28, 1884 (died 1929); children—Oliver Edward, Gorton Veeder, Paul Hayden, Max Irwin. In newspaper work in Minneapolis, 1882-83; conducted the Estelline Bell, in Dak., 1883-86; served as editorial writer on New York Tribune, 1888-92; editor Editor's Drawer dept. of Harper's Magazine, 1900-02; on staff Woman's Home Companion, May 1905—, writer of The Postscript page of same magazine, 1915—. Author: The Adventures of Jones, 1895; The Voyage of the Rattletrap, 1897; Mr. Milo Bush and Other Worthies, Their Recollections, 1899; Track's End, 1911. Home: Briarcliff Manor, N.Y. Died Jan. 3, 1932.

CARRUTH, Louis, oil refiner; b. Groton, N.Y., June 18, 1850; s. James Blake and Betsey (Thompson) C.; ed. Fredonia (N.Y.) Acad. and N.Y. State Normal and Training Sch., Fredonia; m. Frances J. Massey, June 4, 1878; children—William Massey, Harold Massey, Alice Massey. Cashier Meriam and Morgan Paraffine Co., Cleveland, 1875-87; successively sec., v.p. and pres. Canfield Oil Co., 1887—; pres. Canfield Tank Line Co., The Stockbridge Co. Presbyterian. Home: Cleveland Heights, O. Died Dec. 8, 1936.

CARRUTH, William Herbert, univ. prof.; b. Osawatomie, Kan., Apr. 5, 1859; s. James H. and Jane (Grant) C.; A.B., U. of Kan., 1880, A.M., 1883; A.M., Harvard, 1889, Ph.D., 1893; m. Frances Schlegel, June 10, 1882 (died 1908); 2d, Katharine Morton, 1910. Asst., 1880-82, prof. modern langs., 1882-87, prof. German lang. and lit., and v.p., 1887-13, U. of Kan.; prof. comparative lit. Stanford, 1913—. Pres. Nat. League of Unitarian Laymen, 1909. Author: Letters to American Boys, 1907; Each in His Own Tongue. 1906. Home: Grand Rapids, Mich. Died Dec. 15, 1924.

CARRY, Edward Francis, mfr.; b. Ft. Wayne, Ind., May 16, 1867; s. Joseph J. and Margaret C. (Stoops) C.; ed. pub. schs.; m. Mabel D. Underwood, Nov. 28, 1893; children—Mrs. Ermina Nicholson, Mrs. Margaret Cudahy. Sec. Wells & French Co. until 1899; with Am. Foundry Co., 1899-1915, advancing to 1st v.p. and mgr.; pres. Haskell & Barker Car Co., Inc., Jan. 1916-22; pres. The Pullman Co., 1922—. V. chmn. Shipbuilding Labor Adjustment Bd., Sept. 1917; dir. operations U.S. Shipping Bd., Sept. 1917-Oct. 1918; trustee Emergency Fleet Corp., Aug. 1918-Jan. 1919; chmn. Port and Harbor Facilities Commn., U.S. Shipping Bd., Mar. 1918-Jan. 1919. Republican. Catholic. Home: Chicago, Ill. Died Apr. 24, 1929.

CARRYL, Guy Wetmore, author; b. New York, March 4, 1873; grad. Columbia, 1895; editor Munsey's Mag., 1895-96; Paris rep. Harper & Bros., 1897-99; foreign corr. Munsey's Outing, Collier's, etc., 1900-02. Author: Fables for the Frivolous, 1898; Mother Goose for Grown-Ups, 1900; Grimm Tales Made Gay, 1902; The Lieutenant-Governor, 1903; The Will of Andrew Vane, 1903; Zut, and Other Parisians, 1903. Home: Swampscott, Mass. Died 1904.

CARSE, Matilda Bradley, W.C.T.U. worker; b. Saintfield, nr. Belfast, Ireland; d. John and Catherine (Cleland) Bradley; has lived almost continually in Chicago, 1858—; m. Thomas Carse (died 1870). Pres. Chicago Central W.C.T.U., 1878—; founder of Bethesda Day Nursery and Talcott Day Nursery of Chicago W.C.T.U.; founded, and pres. 18 yrs., Woman's Temperance Publishing Assn.; mem. Bd. of Lady Mgrs., Chicago Expn.; first woman mem. Bd. of Edn., Cook Co., Ill. Founder Woman's Temple in Chicago, and for yrs. has devoted her energies toward freeing it from debt and making it a memorial to Frances E. Willard. Died June 3, 1917.

CARSON, Adam Clarke, judge; b. Enniskillen, Ireland, Jan. 14, 1869; s. Samuel and Annie (Lougheed) C.; came to U.S., 1885; LL.B., U. of Va., 1893; m. Eleanor Barnard Conrad, May 12, 1908. Admitted to bar, 1893; judge Court of First Instance, P.I., 1901-04; asso. justice Supreme Court of P.I., 1904—. Capt. 4th U.S. Vol. Inf., Army of Occupation, Cuba, 1898-99; capt. 28th U.S. Vol. Inf., P.I., 1899-1901; col. and judge adv. gen. Philippine N.G., 1917-18; lt. col. 1st Regt. Inf., 1st Philippine Div., 1918. Mem. bd. dirs. Am. Y.M.C.A., Manila. Democrat. Home: Manila, P.I. Died May 23, 1941.

CARSON, Hampton Lawrence, lawyer; b. Phila., Feb. 21, 1852; s. Joseph (M.D.) and Mary (Hollingsworth) C.; A.B., U. of Pa., 1871, A.M., LL.B., 1874; LL.D., Lafayette, 1898, Western U. of Pa., 1904, U. of Pa., 1906; admitted to bar, Apr. 1874; m. Anna Lea Baker, Apr. 14, 1880. Prof. law, U. of Pa., 1895-1901; atty. gen. of Pa., 1903-07. Republican. Sec. Constl. Centennial Commn., 1887. Author: Law of Criminal Conspiracies as Found in American Cases; History of the One Hundredth Anniversary of the Promulgation of the Constitution of the United States (2 vols.); History of the Supreme Court of the United States. Mem. Commn. to Revise Constitution of Pa., 1920. Address: Philadelphia, Pa. Died July 18, 1929.

CARSON, Howard Adams, civil engr.; b. Westfield, Mass., Nov. 28, 1842; s. Daniel B. and Mary (Pope) C.; B.S., Mass. Inst. Tech., 1869; (hon. A.M., Harvard, 1906); m. Nancy Wilmarth, 1870. Asst. engr. Providence Water Works, 1871; in charge sewer constrn., Providence, 1873; prin. supt. constrn., Boston main drainage, 1878; designed, 1887, and later was chief engr., N.Met. and Charles River Valley sewerage systems for Mass.; chief engr. Boston Transit Commn., 1894-1909, bldg. the Boston subway, the E. Boston tunnel and the Washington St. tunnel; has been cons. engr. in various parts of the country, including double-track ry. tunnel under Detroit River. Author of annual reports as chief engr. Met. Sewerage, 1890-94, and as chief engr. Boston Transit Commn., 1894-1909, and other engring. reports. Trustee Mass. Inst. Tech. Home: Malden, Mass. Died Oct. 26, 1931.

CARSON, John Fleming, clergyman; b. Phila., Jan. 28, 1860; s. William and Margaret (Fleming) C.; A.B., U. of Pa., 1881; grad. Allegheny Theol. Sem., 1885; (D.D., Ursinus Coll., 1893, LL.D., 1911); m. Bessie McKnight, Feb. 9, 1886. Ordained to ministry, May 20, 1885; minister First Ref. Presbyn. Ch., Brooklyn (now Central Presbyn. Ch.). Moderator Gen. Assembly Presbyn. Ch. U.S.A., 1911-12. Chmn. Nat. Service Commn. Presbyn. Ch. U.S.A. Pres. Stony Brook Sch. for Boys, Stony Brook Assembly. Author: Married Life in Sacred Story, 1897; The Bible and Infidelity, 1899; The Word of Authority, 1914. Died Sept. 2, 1927.

CARSON, John Miller, newspaperman; b. Phila., June 18, 1838; s. Thomas and Jane C.; ed. Phila.; m. Annie L. Miller, Nov. 28, 1861. Lt. and capt. 27th Pa. Inf., 1861-64; newspaper work at Phila. until 1873; night editor National Republican, Washington, 1873-74; asst. corr. New York Times, 1874-77; chief Times Washington bur., 1877-82; chief Washington bur. of Philadelphia Public Ledger, 1882-1902; chief consolidated bureaus of Philadelphia Ledger and New York Times, 1902-05; chief Bur. of Manufacturers, Dept. Commerce and Labor, June 1, 1905-Sept. 1910; U.S. commercial agt., Sept. 1910—. As clerk Ways and Means Com. Ho. Rep. assisted in forming tariff act of 1883 and "McKinley Bill" of 1890. Home: Washington, D.C. Died Sept. 29, 1912.

CARSON, John Renshaw, research engr.; b. Pittsburgh, Pa., June 28, 1887; s. John D. and Ada R. (Johnston) C.; B.S., Princeton, 1907, E.E., 1909, M.S., 1912; grad. study Mass. Inst. Tech., 1907-08; D.Sc., Brooklyn Poly. Inst., 1936; m. Frances Atwell, July 22, 1913; 1 son, John R. Instr. in physics, Princeton, 1912-14; engr. transmission theory development, Am. Telephone & Telegraph Co., 1914-34; research mathematician, Bell Telephone Labs., N.Y. City, 1934—. Awarded Liebmann Memorial prize, Inst. Radio Engrs., for invention in radio and contbns. to math. theory of electric circuits, 1924; Elliott Cresson medal, Franklin Inst., for contributions to the art of electrical communication, 1939. Author: Electric Circuit Theory and the Operational Calculus, 1927; Elektrische Ausgleichvorgänge und Operatorenrechnung, 1929. Home: New Hope, Pa. Died Oct. 31, 1940.

CARSON, Norman Bruce, surgeon; b. Somerset, Pa., Nov. 9, 1844; s. James O'Hara and Barbara (Bruce) C.; ed. pvt. schs. and Washington U.; M.D., St. Louis Med. Coll., 1868; studied U. of Vienna, 1869-70; D.Sc., Washington U., 1925; m. Susan Ross Glasgow, Apr. 23, 1888; 1 son, Wm. G. Bruce. Began practice at St. Louis, 1868; served as surgeon, pres. staff, St. Louis Mullanphy Hosp.; mem. med. dept. Washington U., 1898-1914; retired 1923. Home: St. Louis, Mo. Died Aug. 9, 1931.

CARSON, William Waller, civil engr.; b. Adams Co., Miss., June 2, 1845; s. Dr. James Green and Catherine (Waller) C.; pvt. and sergt. maj. 4th La. Cav., C.S.A., 1863-65; C.E., Washington Coll. (now Washington and Lee U.), 1868; M.E., 1869; m. Rachel Finnie, Dec. 23, 1880; children—Katherine Waller, James Finnie (dec.), Emma Finnie, William Waller. Instr. engring., Washington Coll., 1868-69; prof. mathematics, Davidson Coll., 1877-83; prof. civ. engring., U. of Tenn., 1885-1916 (emeritus). Engr. on various rys. and on city, river and other public works. Comdr. Fred Ault Camp No. 5, U.C.V., 1912—. Home: Knoxville, Tenn. Died Feb. 7, 1930.

CARSS, William Leighton, congressman; b. Pella, Marion Co., Ia., Feb. 15, 1865; s. James and Annie (Parks) C.; collegiate edn., Des Moines, Ia.; m. Lilian Burnside, Dec. 21, 1898; 1 dau., Elizabeth Anne. Locomotive engr.; mem. 66th Congress (1919-21), and 69th and 70th Congresses (1925-29), 8th Minn. Dist. Democrat. Episcopalian. Mason. Home: Proctor, Minn. Died May 31, 1931.

CARSTENS, Christian Carl, social worker; b. Bredstedt, Germany, Apr. 2, 1865; s. Broder and Christina Maria (Ibsen) C.; A.B., Grinnell Coll., 1891; A.M., U. of Pa., 1900, Ph.D., 1903; m. Blanche E. McMeans, June 21, 1893; children—Constance Carol, Ariel Candace (Mrs. Dane Farnsworth Smith), Cedric Stephens. Prin. Creston (Ia.) High Sch., 1895-96, Marshalltown (Ia.) High Sch., 1896-99; asst. sec. Phila. Soc. for Organizing Charity, 1900-03; asst. sec. N.Y. Charity Organization Soc., 1903-07; gen. sec. Mass. Soc. for Prevention of Cruelty to Children, 1907-20; exec. dir. Child Welfare League of America, 1921—. Chmn. of one of four sections of White House Conf. on Child Health and Protection, 1930; rep. of U.S. at Pan.-Am. Child Welfare Congress, Havana, 1927. Republican. Home: Forest Hills, New York, N.Y. Died July 4, 1939.

CARSTENS, J. Henry, surgeon; b. Kiel, Germany, June 9, 1848; s. John H. and Marie (Mordhorst) C.; came to U.S. with parents early in life; ed. German-Am. Sem., Detroit; M.D., Detroit Med. Coll., 1870; m. Hattie Rohnert, Oct. 18, 1870. Practiced Detroit, 1870—; chief of staff Harper Hosp.; pres. of faculty and prof. abdominal and pelvic surgery, Detroit Coll. Medicine and Surgery; cons. obstetrician, Woman's Hosp. and House of Providence. Republican. Home: Detroit, Mich. Died Aug. 7, 1920.

CARSTENSEN, Gustav Arnold, clergyman; b. St. Croix, Danish West Indies, June 15, 1851; s. George John Bernard and Mary Ann (Sempill) C.; B.A., Hobart Coll., Geneva, N.Y., 1873, M.A., 1878, D.D., 1910; S.T.B., Gen. Theol. Sem., 1876; M.A., New York U, 1902; m. Mary Rutherford Thomas, Jan. 17, 1877; 1 dau., Grace. Deacon and priest, P.E. Ch., 1876; missionary, St. John's Ch., Elkhart, Ind., 1876-77; rector Grace Ch., Toledo, O., Christ Ch., Meadville, Pa., St. Paul's Ch., Erie, Pa., St. Paul's Ch., Indianapolis, Ind., Christ Ch., Riverdale, N.Y., until 1917, Holy Rood Ch., N.Y. City, 1918 (emeritus). Gen. sec. P.E. Ch. Congress in U.S., 1905-20. Chaplain 158th Regt., Ind. Vols., Spanish-Am. War. Democrat. Mason. Author: The Parochial Mission, 1888; Qoheleth and Contemporary Greek Philosophy, 1903. Home: Flushing, Long Island, N.Y. Died June 26, 1941.

CARSTENSEN, John, ry. official; b. New York, N.Y., Aug. 14, 1854; s. George John Bernard and Mary Ann (Sempill) C.; ed. Cayuga Lake Acad., Aurora, N.Y., 1865-68, Alexander Mil. Inst., White Plains, N.Y., 1868-70, Rural High Sch., Clinton, N.Y., 1870-71; m. Adele Thacher Robin, Aug. 1, 1877. In service N.Y.C. & H.R. R.R. Co., 1871—; v.p. in charge accounting dept., 1903—; v.p. N.Y. Central R.R. Co., 1915—, and officer or dir. many other subsidiary lines. Home: Scarsdale, N.Y. Died Apr. 14, 1921.

CARTER, Bernard, lawyer; b. in Prince George's County, Md., July 20, 1834; s. Charles H. and Rosalie Eugenia (Calvert) C.; A.B., St. James' Coll., Md., 1852, A.M., 1855; LL.B., Harvard, 1855; (LL.D., Trinity Coll., 1894); m. Mary B., d. David Ridgely, of White Marsh, Md., Apr., 1858; father of John Ridgely C. Began practice in Baltimore, 1855; mem. first branch, City Council, 1869-70; mem. Md. Constl. Conv., 1867; became prof., Md. Univ. Law Sch., 1878; city solicitor, Baltimore, 1883-89; provost U. of Md., 1895—. One of counsel of Pa. R.R. Co. and all affiliated roads. Democrat. Home: Baltimore, Md. Died June 13, 1912.

CARTER, Charles David, congressman; b. near Boggy Depot, an old fort in Choctaw Nation, Ind. Ty., Aug. 16, 1868; s. Benjamin Winsor and Serena Josephine (Guy) C.; ed. in dist. sch. and Chickasaw Manual Labor Acad., Tishomingo, Ind. Ty.; m. Gertrude Wilson, Dec. 29, 1891 (died 1901); children—Stelle LeFlore, Italy Cecile (Mrs. Frank Ernst), Julia Josephine (Mrs. Gus A. Welch), Benjamin Wisner; m. 2d, Mrs. Cecile Jones, Jan. 8, 1911. Worked on ranch and clerk in store until 1892; auditor pub. accounts, Chickasaw Nation, 1892-94; supt. schs., Indian Ty., 1894-96; mem. Chickasaw council, 1897; mining trustee Ind. Ty., 1900-04; mem. Carter & Cannon, fire ins., 1905—. Sec. 1st Dem. Exec. Com., proposed State of Okla., June-Dec. 1906; mem. 60th to 69th Congresses (1907-27), 3d Okla. Dist. Methodist. Mason. Address: Ardmore, Okla. Died Apr. 9, 1929.

CARTER, Charles Francis, clergyman; b. Chicopee Falls, Mass., June 14, 1856; s. Timothy Walker and Eliza Harriet (Bayley) C.; grad. Williston Sem., 1874; A.B., Yale, 1878; grad. Andover Theol. Sem., 1882, post-grad. work 1 yr.; D.D., Marietta (O.) Coll., 1917; m. Harriet Fidelia Herrick, May 28, 1884 (died 1923); children—Thomas Walker (deceased), Dwight Herrick, Lyon, Frederic Dewhurst. Ordained ministry Congl. Ch., 1883; pastor successively Union Ch., Manchester, N.H., College Street Ch., Burlington, Vt., Hancock Ch., Lexington, Mass., Park Ch., Hartford, Conn., Immanuel Ch. (union of Park and Farmington Av. chs.) until 1927 (emeritus). Chmn. exec. com. Nat. Council Congl. Chs., 1913-25; pres. bd. trustees Andover Theol. Sem.; trustee Williston Acad. Author: Decision Day Talks, 1925. Home: Hartford, Conn. Died Feb. 26, 1928.

CARTER, Charles Frederick, author; b. Jones County, Ia., Apr. 8, 1863; s. John Woodford and Caroline Matilda (Keller) C.; ed. dist. sch., Dixon County, Neb.; m. Edna Althea Fall, June 8, 1903. Mem. editorial staff Chicago Inter Ocean, 1889-92, Chicago Tribune, 1892-94, New York News, 1896, Denver News, 1897, New York Times and Journal, 1898; Sunday editor Brooklyn Eagle, 1899-1905. Author: Katooticut (children's story), 1899; When Railroads Were New,

1909 (centenary edit., 1926); On Secret Service in Mexico, 1919; Big Railroading, 1919. Compiler: Wedding Day in Literature and Art, 1900. Editor The South American and El Norte Americano, Mar.-Nov. 1915. Dir. publicity, League to Enforce Peace, 1916-17, Nat. Assn. Protection Am. Rights in Mexico, 1919; spl. rep. (publicity) New York Central Lines, 1923-32. Home: New York, N.Y. Died Dec. 10, 1939.

CARTER, Edward Carlos, civil engr.; b. Waverly, Ill., Jan. 11, 1854; s. George and Louisa J. (Smith) C.; C.E., Rensselaer Poly. Inst., 1876; m. Fannie G. Fairbank, Dec. 16, 1880; children—Edward Fairbank, Paul Epler, Gertrude. Rodman, draftsman and mech. engr., 1870-77, asst. engr. on Kansas City extension, C.&A. R.R., 1877-78; prin. asst. engr. on Mississippi River observations, 1878; asst. engr. constrn., Indianapolis, Decatur & Springfield Ry., 1879-80; resident engr. Wabash, St. Louis & Pacific Ry., 1880-84, asst. to chief engr., 1884-85; asst. and contracting engr., Detroit Bridge & Iron Works, 1885-87; prin. asst. engr. C.&N.W. Ry., 1887-99, chief engr., 1899-1914; later cons. engr. Home: Evanston, Ill. Died Dec. 23, 1930.

CARTER, Emma Smuller, author; b. New York, N.Y.; d. Rev. Henry W. and Amelia H. (Miller) Smuller; ed. largely pvt. instrn., home and foreign travel; m. James Carter, Sept. 30, 1885. Founder Y.W.C.A. of Williamsport, Pa.; mem. various clubs and beneficent socs. Presbyn. Traveled in Europe, 1881, 1902, in Europe and the Orient, 1904, 1907, in the Romance countries, 1911. Mem. D.A.R. Author: A Golden Sunset, 1889; Lays of the Lake, 1911. Asso. editor and large contbr. to "Songs of Work and Worship," 1899. Died Oct. 16, 1928.

CARTER, Francis Beauregard, judge; b. Neel's Landing, Jackson County, Fla., Aug. 12, 1861; s. Francis M. G. and Sarah Yancy (Boone) C.; common sch. edn.; m. Margaret H. Dickson, Apr. 27, 1885 (died 1932); children—Francis Beauregard, Philips John, Eugenia Wood, Helen Mae, Mrs. Pattie Williams Gatzke, John Hardin, Dickson Herndon, Margaret Henrietta. Admitted to bar, 1882; practiced in Jackson County, 1882-97; asso. justice Supreme Court, Fla., 1897-1905 (resigned); judge 1st Jud. Circuit, 1905-07 (resigned); mem. Blount & Blount & Carter, 1907-21, mem. Carter & Yonge, 1921—. Democrat. Home: Pensacola, Fla. Died Jan. 9, 1937.

CARTER, Franklin, coll. pres.; b. Waterbury, Conn., Sept. 30, 1837; s. Preserve Wood and Ruth Wells (Holmes) C.; student Yale, 1855-57; A.B., Williams, 1862, A.M., 1864, Ph.D., 1877; student U. of Berlin, 1863-64, 1872-73; (LL.D., Union, 1881, Yale, 1901, Williams, 1904, S.C. Coll., 1905); m. Sarah Leavenworth Kingsbury, Feb. 24, 1863; 2d, Mrs. Elizabeth Sabin Leake, d. Dr. H. L. Sabin, of Williamstown, Mass., Feb. 10, 1908. Prof. Latin, Williams, 1865-72; prof. German, Yale, 1872-81; pres. Williams Coll., 1881-1901; resigned; later lecturer on Theism; pres. of Clarke Sch. for the Deaf, 1896—. Mem. Mass. State Bd. Edn., 1896-1900; presdl. elector, 1896; trustee Williams Coll., 1881-1901, Phillips Acad., Andover, Mass., 1881-1902; trustee American College, Madura, India. Corporate mem. A.B.C.F.M.; pres. Mass. Home Missionary Soc., 1896-1901. Fellow Am. Acad. Arts and Sciences; A.A.A.S. Author: Life of Mark Hopkins, 1892; an edition of Goethe's Iphigenie auf Tauris. Home: Williamstown, Mass. Died Nov. 22, 1919.

CARTER, George Robert, governor; b. Honolulu, H.I., Dec. 28, 1866; s. H. A. P. and S. A. (Judd) C.; Ph.B., Sheffield Scientific Sch. (Yale), 1888; m. Helen Strong, Apr. 19, 1892. Mem. Hawaiian Senate, 1901-03; sec. H. Ty., Feb. 22-Nov. 23, 1903; gov. H. Ty., 1903-07. Progressive. Dir. Hawaiian Trust Co., Bank of Hawaii, C. Brewer & Co., Ltd., Alexander & Baldwin, Ltd. Home: Honolulu, H. Ty. Died Feb. 11, 1933.

CARTER, George William, clergyman; b. Rosario, Argentine Republic, Jan. 4, 1867; s. Thomas and Emeline Mary (England) C.; B.A., Wesleyan U., Conn., 1892, M.A., 1899; B.D., Drew Theol. Sem., 1893; fellow Oxford U., Eng., 1894-95; M.A., Yale, 1899; Ph.D., New York U., 1900; D.D., Wesleyan U., Conn., 1929; m. Urania M. Smith, Dec. 12, 1896 (died 1915); m. 2d, Miriam Anna Pope, June 28, 1922. Ordained M.E. ministry, 1893; asst. pastor Trinity Ch., New York, 1893-94; pastor St. Paul's Ch., Hartford, Conn., 1895-98, West Haven Ch., New Haven, Conn., 1898-99, Sea Cliff, N.Y., 1899-1907; gen. sec. New York Bible Soc., 1907—. Instituted Universal Bible Sunday. Joined Reformed Ch. in America, 1911. Author: A Comparison Between Zoroastrianism and Judaism, 1900; The Faith of the Presidents. Home: New York, N.Y. Died Mar. 19, 1930.

CARTER, Henry Rose, sanitarian; b. Clifton Plantation, Caroline Co., Va., Aug. 25, 1852; s. Henry Rose and Emma Caroline (Coleman) C.; C.E., U. of Va., 1873; post-grad. work in mathematics and applied chemistry, same, 1874, 1875; M.D., U. of Md. Sch. of Medicine, 1879; m. Laura Hook, Sept. 29, 1880. Entered Marine Hosp. Service (now U.S. Pub. Health Service), as asst. surgeon, May 5, 1879; passed asst. surgeon, July 1, 1882; surgeon Feb. 1, 1892; sr. surgeon, Oct. 15, 1912; asst. surgeon gen. by spl. act of Congress, Mar. 4, 1915—. Has devoted attention mainly to sanitation in connection with yellow fever and malaria, beginning at the Ship Island Quarantine Sta. on Gulf of Mexico, 1888; had charge in control of several yellow fever epidemics in Southern states; discoverer, 1900-01, of extrinsic incubation of yellow fever, this announcement leading to later discovery of Dr. Walter Reed, that mosquitoes are carriers of yellow fever; inaugurated quarantine system in Cuba, 1899, 1900. Democrat. Episcopalian. Mem. Rockefeller Yellow Fever Commn., sent to Central and S. America, 1916; in charge malarial work for U.S.P.H.S., 1917 and 1918, with special reference to anti-malarial measures for cantonments; yellow fever work, Peru, S.A., and sanitary advisor Peruvian Govt., 1920-21. Mem. Yellow Fever Council, Internat. Health Bd., Rockefeller Foundation; hon. chmn. Nat. Malaria Com., also vice permanent sec. Name was presented for Nobel prize, 1904, by Maj. Sir Ronald Ross. Home: Washington, D.C. Died Sept. 14, 1925.

CARTER, Herbert DeWayne, ry. official; b. Watertown, N.Y., Oct. 16, 1860; s. of Hubbard Earl and Fanny P. (Rugg) C.; ed. pub. schs.; m. Emma Louise Brown, Dec. 15, 1880. Messenger Dominion Telegraph Co., 1873; telegraph operator Montreal Telegraph Co., Watertown, 1874-75; telegraph operator, clk., chief clk. gen. frt. office, Rome, Watertown & Ogdensburg R.R., 1875-88; clk. div. frt. office Phila. & Erie R.R., and Northern Central Ry., Williamsport, Pa., 1888-90; clk. gen. frt. office, Phila. & Reading Ry., 1890-91; asst. gen. frt. and pass. agt., Adirondack & St. Lawrence Ry., 1891-93; div. frt. agt. and gen. agt. pass. dept., N.Y.C.& H.R. R.R., Herkimer and Malone, N.Y., 1893-1902; asst. gen. frt. agt., same, and West Shore Rd., New York, 1902-04; gen. frt. agt. West Shore Rd., 1904-06; gen. frt. agt., N.Y.C.&H.R. R.R., 1906-07; asst. frt. traffic mgr., New York Central Lines east of Buffalo, May 15, 1907—. Home: Yonkers, N.Y. Died Jan. 18, 1914.

CARTER, Herbert Swift, physician; b. Orange, N.J., Sept. 19, 1869; s. Aaron and Sarah (Swift) C.; B.A., Princeton, 1892, M.A., 1895; M.D., Coll. Phys. and Surg. (Columbia), 1895; post-grad. work, U. of Berlin, Germany, 1898-99; m. Mabel S. Pettit, Jan. 12, 1898; children—Mrs. Alida C. Agar, Herbert S., Alan. Asst. in pathology, Cornell Med. Sch., 1889-1900; asso. in clin. medicine, Columbia, 1908—; cons. phys. Presbyn., Lincoln, N.Y. Skin and Cancer, Booth Memorial, Northern Westchester hosps. Fellow N.Y. Acad. Medicine. Episcopalian. Author: Diet Lists of the Presbyterian Hospital, 1913; Nutrition and Clinical Dietetics. Home: New York, N.Y. Died Oct. 1927.

CARTER, James Coolidge, lawyer; b. Lancaster, Mass., Oct. 14, 1827; grad. Harvard, 1850, Harvard Law School, 1853; established practice in New York; apptd. by Gov. Tilden, 1875, mem. of commn. to devise a form of municipal govt. for the cities of the State. Author: The Codification of Our Common Law; also many papers on professional and local subjects. Died 1905.

CARTER, James Madison Gore, physician; b. Johnson Co., Ill., Apr. 15, 1843; s. Rev. William B. and Mary A. (Deans) C.; A.B., St. John's Coll., 1874; M.D., Northwestern U., 1880; A.M., McKendree Coll., 1881, Ph.D., 1887; Sc.D., Lake Forest U., 1887; m. Eunice R. Northrop, 1873 (died 1887); m. 2d, Mrs. Emogene P. Earle, June 18, 1890. Served in Co. K, 60th Ill. Vols., 1861-65; was at Island No. 10, Corinth, Nashville, Murfreesboro, Chattanooga to Atlanta, with Sherman to the sea, through Carolinas to Rockingham, N.C., where was captured and taken to Libby Prison. Prof. pathology and hygiene, 1891-95, clin. and preventive medicine, 1895-99, prof. emeritus, Coll. of Phys. and Surg., Chicago. Author: Outlines of Medical Botany of the United States, 1888; Catarrhal Diseases of the Respiratory Organs, 1895; Diseases of the Stomach, 1902. Home: Los Angeles, Calif. Died Mar. 3, 1919.

CARTER, James Richard, paper mfr.; b. Boston, Mass., Jan. 4, 1849; s. Richard B. and Lucy Lazell (Hobart) C.; ed. Boston pub. schs.; m. Carrie, d. Rev. Chauncey and Eunice (Lakey) Giles, of New York, Oct. 15, 1873. Founded Carter, Rice & Co., paper mfrs., 1871; half owner, treas. and mgr. Carter, Rice & Co. Corp. since its incorp., 1884; treas. Carter's Ink Co., 1896—; pres. Carter, Rice & Carpenter Paper Co. (Denver), Nashua (N.H.) Gummed & Coated Paper Co.; trustee and executor of estates. Treas. Gen. Conv. New Jerusalem Ch., 1900; dir. New Ch. Theol. Sch. Home: West Newton, Mass. Died Sept. 13, 1923.

CARTER, Jesse Benedict, educator; b. New York, June 16, 1872; s. Peter and Mary Louise (Benedict) C.; student New York U., 1889-90; A.B., Princeton, 1893; U. of Leipzig, 1893-94; univs. of Berlin and Göttingen, 1894-95; Ph.D., U. of Halle, 1898; (L.H.D., Princeton, 1913); m. Kate Benedict Freeman, Jan. 22, 1902. Instr. Latin, 1895-97, asst. prof., 1898-1902 prof., 1902-07, Princeton; prof. Latin, 1904-07, dir., 1907-12, Am. Sch. Classical Studies in Rome, dir. Am. Acad. in Rome, 1913—. Lecturer on Roman Religion, U. of Wis., summer, 1900. Democrat. Episcopalian. Author: De Deorum Cognominibus, 1898; The Roman Elegiac Poets, 1900; Epitheta Deorum, 1902; Virgil's Æneid, 1903; The Religion of Numa, 1906; The Religious Life of Ancient Rome, 1911. Died July 21, 1917.

CARTER, Jesse McIlvaine, army officer; b. in Mo., Apr. 12, 1863; grad. U.S. Mil. Acad., 1886; married; children—Clara McIlvaine (dec.), Betty Landon, Mary Allen. Commd. 2d lt. 3d Cav., July 1, 1886; promoted through grades to brig. gen., Nov. 16, 1917; maj. gen. N.A., Aug. 8, 1918; brig. gen. U.S.A., retired, Oct. 1, 1921. Duty Gen. Staff, 1909-13; assigned to Militia Bur., War Dept., 1916, chief of bur., 1917; organized and comd. 11th (Regular) Div., Aug. 1918-Feb. 1919. Awarded D.S.M., Feb. 13, 1919, "for exceptionally meritorious and conspicuous service to U.S. Govt." Mgr. Tex. properties Missouri-Lincoln Trust Co. Home: Magnet, Tex. Died June 23, 1930.

CARTER, Joseph Newton, judge; b. Hardin Co., Ky., Mar. 12, 1843; s. William P. and Martha (Mays) C.; B.S., Ill. Coll., 1866; LL.B., U. of Mich., 1868; (LL.D., Ill. Coll., 1898); m. Ellen D. Barrell, Dec. 3, 1879. Practiced law, Quincy, Ill., 1869-94; mem. legislature, 1879 and 1881; judge Supreme Ct. of Ill., 1894-1903 (chief justice, 1898); resumed practice, 1903. Home: Quincy, Ill. Died Feb. 6, 1913.

CARTER, Mrs. Leslie, actress; b. Lexington, Ky., June 10, 1862; m. Leslie Carter, May 26, 1880; m. 2d, W. L. Payne, July 13, 1906. Début at Broadway Theatre, New York, as Kate Graydon, in "The Ugly Duckling," Nov. 10, 1890; appeared later in musical comedy; played in "The Heart of Maryland," at Washington, D.C., 1895; frequently toured U.S., appearing in "Zaza," "Adrea," "La Tosca," "The Second Mrs. Tanqueray," etc. Died Nov. 13, 1937.

CARTER, Orrin Nelson, judge; b. Jefferson Co., N.Y., Jan. 22, 1854; s. Benajah and Isabel (Cole) C.; A.B., Wheaton (Ill.) Coll., 1877, LL.D., 1899; LL.D., Northwestern, 1925; m. Nettie J. Steven, Aug. 1, 1881; children—Allan J., Ruth G. Admitted to bar, 1880; co. supt. schs., Grundy Co., Ill., 1882-84; state's atty., Grundy Co., 1884-88; removed to Chicago, 1889; atty. for Sanitary Dist. of Chicago, 1892-94; co. judge, Cook Co., 1894-1906; justice Supreme Court of Ill., 1906-24. Republican. Conglist. Chmn. Charter Conv., Chicago, 1905-06. Home: Evanston, Ill. Died Aug. 15, 1928.

CARTER, Samuel Fain, banker; b. Huntsville, Ala., Sept. 14, 1857; s. John Quincy Adams and Mildred Ann (Richards) C.; ed. pub. schs.; m. Carrie E. Banks, Jan. 23, 1882. Began as printer's apprentice in newspaper office, Sherman, Tex., 1870; with Galveston News, 1876-81; bookkeeper, Long & Co., shingle mills, Beaumont, and Village Mills, Tex., 1884, later sec. and business mgr.; moved to Houston, 1892, entered lumber business, and owner Emporia Lumber Co.; disposed of lumber interests, 1907, and organized Lumbermen's Nat. Bank, now the Second Nat. Bank, of which was chmn. of board; pres. Houston Building Co. Democrat. Chmn. bd. trustees First M.E. Ch.; mem. Y.M.C.A. Home: Houston, Tex. Died Mar. 1, 1928.

CARTER, Thomas Coke, bishop; b. Carroll County, Tenn., Jan. 1, 1851; s. Reuben Ellis and Sarrah (Herron) C.; A.B., De Pauw U., 1875, A.M., 1878; (D.D., De Pauw U., and Ohio U., Athens; LL.D., Southern Normal Univ., Huntington, Tenn., 1905); m. Maggie Brown, Dec. 26, 1875. Ordained to U. B. ministry, 1869; was prin. W. Tennessee Sem.; pres. Tullahoma Coll., 4 yrs.; pastor, 1875-80; editor the Advocate, 1883-92; missionary in China, 1880-81; supt. of work of the ch. in the south, 1894-1905; bishop, 1905—. Mem. Gen. confs., 1884, 1888. Centennial Conf., 1884. Home: Chattanooga, Tenn. Died Feb. 27, 1916.

CARTER, Thomas Henry, senator; b. in Scioto County, O., Oct. 30, 1854; common sch. edn.; engaged in farming, railroading and sch. teaching for several yrs.; removed from Burlington, Ia., to Helena, Mont., 1882; m. Ellen L. Galen. Del. to 51st Congress, Mont. Ty., 1889-91, and upon admission of Ty. to statehood was elected first representative to same Congress; commr. U.S. Gen. Land Office, Mar. 1891-July 1892; chmn. Rep. Nat. Com., 1892-96; U.S. senator, 1895-1901, 1905-11. Pres. U.S. Commn. to St. Louis Expn., 1901-04. Home: Helena, Mont. Died 1911.

CARTER, Walter Steuben, lawyer; b. Barkhamsted, Conn., Feb. 24, 1833; s. Evits and Emma (Taylor) C.; ed. dist. sch.; admitted to bar, Middletown, Conn., 1855; m. Antoinette Smith, Oct. 8, 1855; m. 2d, Mary Boyd Jones, Dec. 18, 1867; m. 3d, Harriet Cook, Dec. 1, 1870. Mem. bd. edn., 1856-58; lived in Milwaukee, 1858-69; compiler Wis. Code, 1859; U.S. commr. and master in chancery U.S. Circuit Court, 1859, 1862; trustee Lawrence Univ., 1864-65; practiced in Chicago, 1869-72, and N.Y., 1872— (became head Carter, Hughes & Dwight). Pres. dept music, Brooklyn Inst., 8 yrs.; trustee Syracuse Univ., 1896—; hon. asso. Guild Am. Organists from organization; donor organ New York Av. M.E. Ch., Brooklyn; builder chapel and founder library and cemetery, Barkhamsted, Conn.; noted helper of young lawyers. Mem. Am. Mus. Natural History, Met. Mus. Art, New York Bot. Gardens. Home: Brooklyn, N.Y. Died 1904.

CARTER, William Harding, major gen. U.S. Army; b. Nashville, Tenn., Nov. 19, 1851; s. Samuel Jefferson and Anne (Vaulx) C.; ed. pvt. and pub. schs., Nashville and Ky. Mil. Inst., Frankfort; mounted messenger in Civil War, 1864-65; grad. U.S. Mil. Acad., 1873; m. Ida Dawley, Oct. 27, 1880. Apptd. 2d lt. 8th Inf., June 13, 1873; promoted through grades to maj. gen., Nov. 13, 1909. Awarded Congressional Medal of Honor "for distinguished bravery in action against Apache Indians at Cibicu Creek, Ariz., Aug. 30, 1881;" D.S.M., World War. Student of army orgn. and adminstrn.; chiefly responsible for tech. details of army orgn., 1901-03. Comdg. 2d Div. U.S. Army, 1913, Hawaiian Dept., Jan. 1914-15; retired by operation of law, Nov. 19, 1915; recalled for active service, Aug. 26, 1917; comd. Central Dept., Chicago, Aug. 1917-Feb. 1918. Author: Horses, Saddles and Bridles, 4th edit., 1918; From Yorktown to Santiago with the Sixth Cavalry, 1900; Old Army Sketches, 1906; Giles Carter of Virginia, 1909; The American Army, 1915; Life and Services of Lieutenant General Chaffee, 1917. Died May 24, 1925.

CARTER, William Henric, clergyman; b. Utica, N.Y., Oct. 27, 1829; s. Joseph and Sarah (Whaley) C.; A.B., New York Univ., 1850; (LL.D., U. of Vincennes, 1868; D.D., Univ. of Ind., 1869; Ph.D., New York Univ., 1872); m. Harriet A. Hyde, Aug. 16, 1853. Ordained to P.E. ministry, 1853; pastor, Hamburg, N.J., 1853-59, Vincennes, Ind., 1859-69, Bloomfield, N.J., 1869-74, Passaic, N.J., 1874-77, Tallahassee, Fla., 1879—. Prin. Orange County Inst., N.Y., 1855-6; was prof. mathematics, Vincennes U., and Univ. of Fla.; chaplain 60th Ind. Vols., Civil War, Fla. Ho. of Reps., 1 session, Fla. State Hosp. for Insane, 1881—; deputy to Gen. Conv. P.E. Ch., 8 sessions. Home: Tallahassee, Fla. Died 1907.

CARTER, William Samuel; b. Austin, Tex., Aug. 11, 1859; s. Samuel Miles and Margaret Frances (Oliphant) C.; student Agrl. and Mech. Coll. of Tex., 2 yrs.; m. Mary Evelyn Gorsuch, Dec. 26, 1880 (died 1892); m. 2d, Julia I. Cross, Nov. 27, 1902. Locomotive fireman and engr. on rys. in Tex., Colo. and Mexico, 1879-94; editor and mgr. Locomotive Firemen and Enginemens Magazine, 1894-1903; gen. sec. and treas. Brotherhood of Locomotive Firemen and Enginemen, 1904-08, pres., 1909-18; dir. Div. of Labor of U.S. R.R. Administration, Feb. 11, 1918-Mar. 1, 1920. Pres. Brotherhood of Locomotive Firemen and Engineers, Cleveland, Mar. 1, 1920—. Democrat. Mason. Died Mar. 15, 1923.

CARTON, John Jay, lawyer; b. Genesee County, Mich., Nov. 8, 1856; s. John and Ann (Maguire) C.; ed. dist. schs. and high sch., Flushing, Mich., teaching at intervals, 1873-77; admitted to bar, 1884; m. Addie C. Pierson, Nov. 22, 1898. In mercantile houses Flushing, 1877-80; mem. law firm Durand (George H.) & Carton until death of sr. partner, 1903, later Carton & Gault; pres. First Nat. Bank of Flint and its successor, Nat. Bk. of Flint, 1899-1916. County clk. Genesee County, 1880-84; city atty., Flint, 1890, 91; mem. Mich. Ho. of Rep., 1899-1905 (speaker, 1901, 03); pres. State Constl. Conv., 1907. Republican. Mason. Home: Flint, Mich. Died Aug. 26, 1934.

CARTWRIGHT, James Henry, judge; b. Maquoketa, Ia. Ty., Dec. 1, 1842; s. Barton Hall and Chloe Jane (Benedict) C.; ed. Rock River Sem., Mt. Morris, Ill.; capt. 140th Ill. Inf., Civil War; LL.B., U. of Mich., 1867; m. Hattie L. Holmes, Nov. 26, 1873. Practiced at Oregon, Ill., 1867-88; judge 13th Jud. Circuit, Ill., 1888-95; judge Appellate Ct., 1891-95; justice of Supreme Court, 1895— (chief justice, 1899-1900, 1905-06, 1908-09, 1914-15, 1920-21). Republican. Home: Oregon, Ill. Died May 18, 1924.

CARTY, John J., elec. engr.; b. Cambridge, Mass., Apr. 14, 1861; ed. Cambridge Latin Sch.; D.Engring., Stevens Inst. Tech., 1915, New York U., 1922; D.Sc., U. of Chicago, Bowdoin, 1916, Tufts, 1919, Yale, 1922, Princeton, 1923; LL.D., McGill, 1917, U. of Pa., 1924; m. Marion Mount Russell, Aug. 8, 1891; 1 son, John Russell. Began with Bell System in Boston, 1879, served in various positions, including chief engr. New York Telephone Co., 1889-1907, chief engr. Am. Telephone & Telegraph Co., 1907-19, v.p. same, 1919-30. A pioneer in development of telephone, for which invented many improvements. Trustee of Carnegie Instn., Washington, Carnegie Corp. (New York). Fellow Am. Academy of Arts and Sciences, American Institute E.E. (pres. 1915-16); hon. mem. Franklin Inst., etc. Longstreth medal, 1903, and Franklin medal, 1916, Franklin Inst.; Edison medal, 1918, Am. Inst. E.E.; John Fritz medal, 1928, engring. societies. Commd. maj. Signal Officers' R.C., Jan. 1917; col. (temp.) U.S. Army, 1917; served on staff chief signal officer U.S. Army, and in France on staff chief signal officer A.E.F.; signal officer during armistice, in charge of communications, Am. Commn. to Negotiate Peace; brig. gen. U.S. Army Res. Decorated D.S.M. (U.S.); Officer Legion of Honor (French), Order Rising Sun and Order Sacred Treasure (Japanese). Home: Winter Park, Fla. Died Dec. 27, 1932.

CARUS, Emma, actress; b. Berlin, Germany, Mar. 18, 1879; d. Carl and Henrietta (Rohland) Carus; came to America, 1883; ed. pvt. schs., Brooklyn; m. Harry James Everall, June 25, 1905. On the stage from age of 15; 1st important appearance as Lady Muriel, in "The Giddy Throng," New York Theatre, 1900; remained with that theatre till 1903, creating parts in musical comedies; played leading parts in "The Defender," "The Wild Rose," "The Darling of the Gods," "The Medal and the Maid," "Woodland," etc., and as Mary in "Forty-five Minutes From Broadway," appeared as star in "The Motor Girl," co-star with Eddie Foy in "Up and Down Broadway," star in "The Wife Hunters," in "Broadway Honeymoon"; in vaudeville, 1915—. Died Nov. 18, 1927.

CARUS, Paul, editor, author; b. at Ilsenburg, Germany, July 18, 1852; s. Dr. Gustav and Laura (Krueger) C.; ed. in Gymnasium at Stettin, U. of Strassburg; Ph.D., U. of Tübingen, 1876; m. Mary Hegeler, Mar. 29, 1888. Editor, The Open Court, and The Monist, Chicago. Author: The Ethical Problem; Primer of Philosophy; Religion of Science; Karma; Nirvana; Eros and Psyche; Crown of Thorns; The Chief's Daughter; Godward; Nature of the State; Surd of Metaphysics; Sacred Tunes; Amitabha; Rise of Man; Story of Samson; Bride of Christ; God, an Enquiry Into Man's Highest Ideals; The Pleroma, an Essay on the Origin of Christianity; Truth on Trial; Personality and the Interpersonal; Nietzsche and other Exponents of Individualism; Mechanistic Principle and the Non-Mechanical; Principle of Relativity from the Standpoint of the Philosophy of Science; Truth and Other Poems; K'ung Fu Tze (dramatic poem); Goethe; The Venus of Milo. Home: La Salle, Ill. Died Feb. 11, 1919.

CARUSI, Charles Francis, lawyer, educator; b. Washington, D.C., May 19, 1873; s. Eugene and Frances (Stanford) C.; A.B., Georgetown U., 1894; LL.B., Nat. U. of Law, Washington, D.C., 1896, LL.D., 1920; m. Marie Abernethy Cassin, Sept. 18, 1900; children—Francis Cassin (dec.), Helen Cassin (wife of Maj. Emmanuel E. Lombard), Eugene Cassin. Admitted to N.Y. bar, 1896, and began practice in N.Y. City; moved to Washington, 1900; chancellor Nat. U. of Law, 1924—. Mem. N.Y.N.G., 1896-1900; served with U.S. Vols., Porto Rico, Spanish-Am. War. Pres. Bd. of Edn., D.C., 1926—. Mason. Author: Government Contracts and Claims, 1910. Contbr. to Am. Law Rev., Nat. Univ. Law Rev. Home: Washington, D.C. Died Feb. 5, 1931.

CARUSO, Enrico, operatic tenor; b. Naples, Italy, Feb. 25, 1873; s. Marcellius and Anna (Baldini) C.; began to sing in chs. of native city at 11; studied under Guglielmo Vergine 3 yrs.; m. Dorothy Benjamin, Aug. 20, 1918. Made début in "L'Amico Francesco," at Nuovo Theatre, Naples, 1894; later toured Italy and Sicily and was engaged for 4 seasons at La Scala, Milan; sang in St. Petersburg, Moscow, Warsaw, Rome, Paris, London, and leading cities of Germany, being hailed as one of most promising young tenors Italy had produced; came to America, and was received with great acclaim at Metropolitan Theatre, New York, Nov. 23, 1903; won his great successes in the entire Italian and French repertoire; sang frequently in U.S. Home: Florence, Italy. Died Aug. 2, 1921.

CARVALHO, David Nunes, expert in handwriting and inks; b. Phila., Sept. 29, 1848; s. Solomon N. (artist) and Sarah (Solis) C.; brother of Solomon Solis C.; student of New York Free Acad. (now N.Y. Coll.); spl. studies in organic chemistry, photography, light and color; m. Annie Abrams, Mar. 22, 1876. Handwriting expert, 1872—. Died June 29, 1925.

CARY, Annie Louise (Mrs. Charles M. Raymond), prima donna; b. Wayne, Me., Oct. 22, 1841; d. Dr. Nelson Howard and Maria (Stockbridge) C.; grad. Gorham (Me.) Female Sem., 1862; studied under Lyman W. Wheeler, Boston, and Giovanni Corsi, Milan; début in Italian opera, Copenhagen; afterward, under Strakosch and Mapleson, sang principal contralto and mezzo-soprano rôles of grand opera, Europe and America; m. Charles Monson Raymond, banker, of New York, 1882, and retired from professional life. Home: Norwalk, Conn. Died Apr. 3, 1921.

CARY, Austin, forester; b. East Machias, Me., July 31, 1865; s. Charles and Mary C.; A.B., Bowdoin, 1887, A.M., 1890; studied biology, Johns Hopkins and Princeton univs., 1888-91; D.Sc., Bowdoin Coll., 1922; instr. Dept. Geology and Biology, Bowdoin, 1887-88; m. Lelia J. Chisholm, Oct. 8, 1916 (died 1917). In employ of forest commr., Me., and Forestry Div., U.S. Dept. Agr., 1893-96; forester for Berlin Mills Co., Portland, Me., 1898-1904; taught, spring terms, Yale Forest Sch., 1904-05; asst. prof. forestry, Harvard, 1905-09; supt. state forests, N.Y., 1909-10; U.S. forest service, 1910-35. Democrat. Conglist. Author: Woodsman's Manuel, 1909. Home: Brunswick, Me. Died Apr. 28, 1936.

CARY, Charles, M.D.; b. Buffalo, N.Y., 1852; s. Walter (M.D.) and Julia (Love) C.; ed. pub. and pvt. schs.; M.D., U. of Buffalo, 1875; student in France 1 yr., and Belgium 18 months, and spent a yr. in travel in Europe; m. Evelyn Rumsey, 1879 (dec.). In practice of medicine at Buffalo, 1879—; prof. anatomy 11 yrs., prof. materia medica and therapeutics 10 yrs., prof. clin. medicine 12 yrs., U. of Buffalo; attending phys. and mem. bd. dirs. Buffalo Gen. Hosp.; mem. council U. of Buffalo. Pres. Buffalo Cremation Co., Ltd. Chmn. bd. trustees N.Y. State Inst. for Research in Malignant Disease. Home: Buffalo, N.Y. Died Dec. 8, 1931.

CARY, Edward, editorial writer; b. Albany, N.Y., June 5, 1840; s. Joseph and Lydia (Chase) C.; A.B., Union Coll., 1863; (hon. Litt.D. from same, 1915); m. Elisabeth Luther, Apr. 27, 1864; was father of Elisabeth Luther Cary. Editor Brooklyn Union, 1863-70; editorial writer New York Times, 1871—. Author: Life of George William Curtis (Am. Men of Letters Series). Home: Brooklyn, N.Y. Died May 23, 1917.

CARY, Elisabeth Luther, author; b. Brooklyn, N.Y., 1867; d. Edward and Elisabeth (Luther) Cary; ed. by pvt. instrn.; studied art for 10 yrs. under Eleanor C. Bannister and Charles Melville Dewey; unmarried. Editor and owner The Scrip until 1908; writer on art, New York Times, 1908—. Translator: Recollections of Middle Life, from French of Francisque Sarcey, 1893; Russian Portraits, from the French of Vte. E. Melchior Vogüé, 1895; The Land of the Tawny Beasts, 1895. Author: Alfred Tennyson, His Homes, His Friends and His Work, 1898; The Rossettis, Dante, Gabriel and Christina, 1900; William Morris, 1902; Ralph Waldo Emerson, Poet and Thinker, 1904. Editor: Poems of Dante Gabriel Rossetti, 1903. Home: Brooklyn, N.Y. Died July 13, 1936.

CARY, George Lovell, theologian; b. Medway, Mass., May 10, 1830; s. William H. and Lydia D. (Lovell) C.; A.B., Harvard, 1852, A.M., 1857, hon. Alumnus Div. Sch.; (L.H.D., Allegheny Coll., 1893); m. Mary Isabella Harding, Mar. 12, 1854. Prof. Greek and Latin, Antioch Coll., Ohio, 1856-62; prof. N.T. lit., 1862-1902, pres., 1890-1902, became prof. emeritus, Meadville Theol. Sch. Some time pres. Meadville Library, Art and Hist. Assn. Author: Introduction to the Greek of the New Testament, 1878; The Synoptic Gospels, with a Chapter on the Text Criticism of the New Testament (Vol. I, International Handbooks to the New Testament), 1900; The Metric of Hymnody. Home: Meadville, Pa. Died 1910.

CARY, Glover H., congressman; b. Calhoun, Ky., May 1, 1885; s. Remus G. and Henrieta (Allen) C.; ed. Prof. Wayland Alexander's pvt. sch., Owensboro, Ky., and Centre Coll., Danville; m. Bessie W. Miller, Apr. 4, 1906; children—William Ree, Sarah Ghee, Elizabeth, Helen, Glover H. Admitted to Ky. bar, 1909, and began practice at Owensboro; mem. Cary, Miller & Kirk; pres. Hartford (Ky.) Deposit Bank. Mem. Ky. Ho. of Rep., 1914, 16, and spl. session, 1917; county atty., McLean County, 1918-22; commonwealths atty. 6th Jud. Dist. of Ky., 1922-31; mem. 72d and 74th Congresses (1931-33 and 1935-37), 2d Ky. Dist., and 73d Congress (1933-35), Ky. at large. Democrat. Methodist. Mason. Home: Owensboro, Ky. Died Dec. 5, 1936.

CARY, Henry Nathaniel, newspaperman; b. Racine, Wis., Feb. 11, 1858; s. Lucius C. and Emile (Kenea) C.; pub. sch. edn., La Cygne, Kan.; m. Susie L. Wustenfeldt, Sept. 9, 1885. Learned printer's trade on La Cygne Journal, 1872-76; removed to Milwaukee, Wis., 1876; reporter, 1880-82, mng. editor, 1882-83, Milwaukee Sentinel; mng. editor Chicago Times, 1889-92; gen. western mgr. N.Y. Asso. Press, 1892; mng. editor of New York Times, 1893, St. Louis Post-Dispatch, 1897; in Cuba in charge of field staff New York World, Spanish-Am. War, 1898; publisher The Verdict, New York, 1899-1900; mng. editor New York Morning Telegraph, 1903, later pub. same; gen. mgr. Detroit Free Press, 1907-08; gen. mgr. St. Louis Republic, 1908-10; gen. mgr. Chicago Newspaper Publishers' Assn., 1911—. Democrat. Home: Chicago, Ill. Died Nov. 23, 1922.

CARY, Robert John, lawyer; b. Milwaukee, Wis., Feb. 6, 1868; s. Alfred L. and Harriet Maria (Van Slyke) C.; A.B., Harvard, 1890, A.M., 1892; m. Fanney Caruthers, Jan. 18, 1913; 1 dau., Catherine Cary. Began practice at Chicago, 1892; mem. Glennon, Cary, Walker & Murray; moved to New York, 1920; v.p. and gen. counsel N.Y.C. Lines. Presbyn. Home: New York, N.Y. Died Nov. 6, 1929.

CARY, William Joseph, congressman; b. Milwaukee, Mar. 22, 1865; orphaned at 11, with 5 younger children; ed. pub. schs. and St. John's Acad., Milwaukee; m. Alma Clark, 1889. Became messenger boy at 13, telegraph operator at 19. Elected alderman, Milwaukee, 1900, 1902, sheriff of Milwaukee County, 1904; mem. 60th to 65th Congresses (1907-

19), 4th Wis. Dist. Republican. Home: Milwaukee, Wis. Died Jan. 2, 1934.

CASANOWICZ, Immanuel Moses, archæologist; b. Zholudok, Russia, July 25, 1853; studied at the Evangelische Predigerschule, and U. of Basle, Switzerland, 1876-83; Ph.D., Johns Hopkins, 1892. Instr. Latin and Greek, Evangelische Predigerschule, Basle, Switzerland, 1880-81; instr. Hebrew and ch. history, German Theol. Sch. of Newark, Bloomfield, N.J., 1883-86; in Oriental dept., 1892—, became asst. curator div. old world archæology, U.S. Nat. Museum. Author: Paronomasia in the Old Testament, 1894. Home: Washington, D.C. Died Sept. 26, 1927.

CASE, Carl Delos, clergyman, author; b. Plainview, Minn., Mar. 11, 1868; s. Douglas Royal and Mary (Owen) C.; U. of Minn., 1887-88; B.A., Colgate Univ., 1891; U. of Chicago, 1892-96, B.D., 1898, Ph.D., 1899; (D.D., Colgate, 1912); m. Ellen Mae Jenkins, Apr. 9, 1896. Ordained Bapt. ministry, 1896; pastor 1st Ch., South Bend, Ind., 1896-1900, 1st Ch., Terre Haute, 1900-02, 1st Ch., Montclair, N.J., 1902-04, Hanson Place Ch., Brooklyn, 1904-08, Delaware Av. Ch., Buffalo, 1908-18, Oak Park, Ill., 1918—. Mason. Author: The Masculine in Religion, 1906; The Incarnation and Modern Thought, 1908; My Christ, 1917. Home: Oak Park, Ill. Died Jan. 25, 1931.

CASE, Clifford Philip, clergyman; b. Jersey City, N.J., Oct. 22, 1873; s. Philip and Amanda V. (Edwards) C.; A.B., Rutgers Coll., 1897, A.M., 1900; grad New Brunswick Theol. Sem., 1900; (D.D., Hope College, Mich., 1916); m. Jeannette McAlpin Benedict, Dec. 9, 1902. Ordained ministry Ref. (Dutch) Ch. in America, 1900; asst. pastor West End Collegiate Ch., New York, 1900-02; pastor Six-Mile Run, Franklin Park, N.J., 1902-07; pastor First Ch., Poughkeepsie, N.Y., 1907-14, when the First and Second Ref. chs. of Poughkeepsie merged into the Ref. Dutch Ch. of Poughkeepsie, of which was pastor, Jan. 1914—. Permanent clk. Gen. Synod of Ref. Ch. in America, June 1915—. Mem. Bd. of Supts. New Brunswick Theol. Sem.; mem. Bd. of Domestic Missions of Ref. Ch. in America; trustee Vassar Inst., Poughkeepsie, N.Y.; mem. Dutchess County Bd. of Child Welfare; mem. Corp. of Pringle Memorial Home, Poughkeepsie. Camp pastor, Camp Merritt, N.J., 1918; sec. Ministerial Pension Commn., Ref. Ch., 1919—. Home: Poughkeepsie, N.Y. Died Mar. 8, 1920.

CASE, Nelson, lawyer; b. Falls, Pa., Apr. 22, 1845; s. Chauncy and Mary Elma (Roberts) C.; grad. Ill. Normal U., Normal, Ill., 1866; LL.B., U. of Mich. Dept. of Law, 1869; (LL.D., Baker U., 1908); m. Mary E. Claypool, Feb. 22, 1872 (died 1892); m. 2d, Georgiana Reed, May 31, 1900. Practiced in Oswego, Kan., 1869—; has appeared as counsel in the state courts, U.S. Dist. and Circuit Courts, and U.S. Supreme Court; apptd. probate judge for Labette County by Gov. St. John, 1880, and elected and served 2 terms; regent State Normal Sch., Emporia, Kan., 6 yrs., etc. Has served as chmn. Rep. County Central Com., and del. state convs. Helped organize Deming Investment Co., of which was pres. and gen. counsel 18 yrs.; gen. counsel C. M. Condon & Co. State Bank 25 yrs. Trustee Baker U., 1883—, and pres. bd., 1897—; trustee Oswego Coll., 1887—; prominent in Sunday Sch., ednl. and temperance work. Methodist. Author: History of Labette County, 1893; European Constitutional History, 1902; Constitutional History of the United States, 1904; The Story of Little Town (hist. romance), 1915. Home: Oswego, Kan. Died July 8, 1921.

CASE, Theodore Spencer, M.D.; b. Jackson, Ga., Jan. 26, 1832; grad. Marietta, 1851; A.M. (Ph.D., U. of Kansas City); grad. Starling Med. Coll., Columbus, O., 1856; settled in Kansas City; edited Medical Review, 1860-61; 2d lt., 25th Mo. inf., June, 1861; served until end of the war, becoming col. and quartermaster-gen. of Mo.; curator Univ. of Mo., 1866-68; postmaster Kansas City, 1873-75; prof. chemistry, Kansas City Med. Coll.; was editor Kansas City Review of Science and Industry, 1873-85. Author: History of Kansas City. Home: Kansas City, Mo. Died 1900.

CASE, Walter Summerhayes; b. Savannah, Ga., Jan. 26, 1885; s. James McNaughton and Florence Adele (Weigel) C.; B.A., Williams Coll., 1906; spl. grad. work, New York U. Sch. of Commerce, Accounts and Finance, 1907-09; m. Mary Soule Hadley, Sept. 25, 1908; children—Hadley, Donald Sloane, Dorothy, Rosemary. Financial work and bond salesman, 1907-10; European agt. Ladenburg, Thalmann & Co., later mgr. bond dept. with power of atty., 1910-16; founder, 1916, pres. and dir. Case, Pomeroy & Co., Inc., a private investment co., patterned after the British plan with a specialized research organization; in later years activities were particularly devoted to mineral and petroleum exploration and development in N. and S. America, Africa and Australia. Conglist. Home: Essex Fells, N.J. Died Oct. 6, 1937.

CASE, William Scoville, judge; b. Tariffville, Conn., June 27, 1863; s. William C. and Margaret (Turnbull) C.; A.B., Yale, 1885; (LL.D., Trinity, 1919); m. Elizabeth Nichols, Apr. 8, 1891. Admitted to bar, 1887; clerk of bills, Conn. Legislature, 1887-89; law clerk U.S. Patent Office, 1891-93; judge Ct. of Common Pleas, Conn., 1897-1901; judge Superior Ct. of Conn., Oct. 1, 1901-19; asso. justice Supreme Court of Errors of Conn., Aug. 23, 1919—. Republican. Author: Forward House, 1895. Wrote History of Granby, in Memorial History of Hartford County, 1884. Home: Hartford, Conn. Died Feb. 28, 1921.

CASEY, Edward Pearce, architect; b. Portland, Me., June 18, 1864; s. Gen. Thomas Lincoln and Emma (Weir) C.; g.s. of Major Gen. Silas Casey; C.E., Columbia U., 1886, Ph.B., 1888; École des Beaux Arts, Paris, 3 years; m. Lilian Berry, June 20, 1929. Architect for completion of Congressional Library Bldg., Washington, 1892-97; one of the 6 equal prize winners on New York City Hall competition (in which were 134 competitors), 1893; joined with Prof. William H. Burr, of Columbia, in competing for design for new memorial bridge across Potomac River at Washington, winning 1st prize, 1900; won the first prize in competition for the Grant monument, in Washington, 1902; architect of the Memorial Continental Hall and Conn. Av. Viaduct, Commodore Barry monument, Washington, D.C., also of N.Y. State monuments on battlefields of Antietam and Gettysburg; architect of bldg. for Am. Coll., Beirut, Syria, also U.S. Govt. bldg., Sault Ste. Marie, Mich. Former mem. 7th Regt. N.G., N.Y. Fellow Am. Inst. Architects. Republican. Episcopalian. Home: New York, N.Y. Died Jan. 2, 1940.

CASEY, Francis de Sales, art editor; b. Corning, N.Y., Jan. 12, 1882; s. Jeremiah L. and Ellen (Casey) C.; ed. pub. schs., N.Y. City; m. Susette Muriel Maguire, June 27, 1909; children—Helen Marie, Francis de Sales. Joined the staff of Collier's Weekly, 1897, became asst. art editor 1903, art editor 1913-20; also art editor, Housekeeper, 1912, and the Flying Magazine, 1912; on staff of Life as art editor, 1920-28; v.p. Fine-Arts Engraving Co., 1929—. Vice chmn. div. pictorial publicity, Com. on Pub. Information, 1917-18. Home: New York, N.Y. Deceased.

CASEY, John J., congressman; b. Wilkes-Barre Tp., Pa., May 26, 1875; s. Andrew P. and Mary C. (McGrath) C.; ed. pub. and parochial schs.; m. Sarah C. Lally, Aug. 1, 1900; children—Andrew A., John J., James A., Walter C., Edward D., Marie E., Catherine R., Sara C., Lawrence, Robert, Matthew (dec.). Learned plumbing trade and held office of president of local union and internat. rep. in Journeymen Plumbers, Gas Fitters and Steamfitters Union of U.S. and Can., 1895-1913 (resigned); mem. Pa. Ho. of Reps., 1907-08; nominated for sec. internal affairs, Pa., by Keystone Party of Pa., 1910; mem. 63d, 64th, 66th and 67th Congresses (1913-17, and 1919-23), 11th Pa. Dist., and elected to 70th Congress (1927-29), 12th Pa. Dist. Democrat. Commr. of conciliation U.S. Dept. of Labor, 1917; mem. advisory counsel to Sec. of U.S. Dept. of Labor, 1918; labor advisor, industrial relations div. and dir. labor adjustment bd., Emergency Fleet Corp. U.S. Shipping Board, 1918-19. Catholic. Home: Wilkes-Barre, Pa. Died May 5, 1929.

CASEY, Lyman R., senator; b. York, N.Y., May 6, 1837; s. Lyman and Annie M. C.; m. Harriet M Platt, Aug. 8, 1861. Mcht. and mfr., Detroit, 1867-73; traveled in U.S. and abroad, 1872-79; mgr. Carrington & Casey Land Co., Jamestown, N.D., cultivators of thousands of acres, 1882-1907; retired. Was commr. on organization of Foster County, N.D.; U.S. senator from N.D., 1889-93. Was many yrs. trustee, N.D. Agrl. Coll. Died Jan. 26, 1914.

CASEY, Silas, rear adm.; b. E. Greenwich, R.I., Sept. 11, 1841; s. Gen. Silas and Abbie (Pearce) C.; apptd. to U.S. Naval Acad. from N.Y., 1856, grad. 1860; m. Sophie Gray Heberton, Oct. 1865. Midshipman, June 15, 1860; promoted through grades to rear admiral, Mar. 3, 1899. Served on the Niagara, 1860-62; engagements with batteries at Pensacola, Fla., Oct. 1861; served on Wissahicken, S. Atlantic Blockading Squadron, 1862-63; engagements with Ft. McAllister, 1862; Quaker City, N. Atlantic Blockading Squadron, 1863-65; first attack on Charleston under Admiral Dupont; attack on Ft. Fisher, Dec. 1864; Winooski, Atlantic Squadron, 1865-67; Naval Acad., 1867-69; various duties to 1897; comdt. Navy Yard, League Island, 1897-1901; comdr.-in-chief, Pacific Fleet, 1901-03; retired, Sept. 11, 1903. Died Aug. 14, 1913.

CASEY, Thomas Lincoln, army officer; b. at West Point, N.Y., Feb. 19, 1857; s. Gen. Thomas Lincoln and Emma (Weir) C.; brother of Edward Pearce C.; ed. pvt. schs., Washington and Sheffield Scientific Sch., Yale, class of 1877; grad. U.S. Mil. Acad., 1879; m. Laura Welsh, June 1, 1898. Second lt. corps of engrs., June 13, 1879; 1st lt., June 17, 1881; capt., July 23, 1888; maj., July 5, 1898; lt. col., Sept. 26, 1906; col., Sept. 21, 1909. In charge of defense of Hampton Roads, Va., during Spanish-Am. War, and at many stations in charge of works of river and harbor improvement; asst. astronomer, under Prof. Newcomb, Transit of Venus expedition, Cape of Good Hope, 1882; Greer County Commn., Tex., 1886; Miss. River Commn., 1902-06, and numerous other spl. bds.; in charge of U.S. engrng. exhibit, St. Louis Expn., 1904; mem. and engr. sec. Light House Board, 1906-10; retired from active service, Mar. 1, 1912. Home: Washington, D.C. Died Feb. 3, 1925.

CASHMAN, Joseph Thomas, lawyer; b. Providence, R.I., Dec. 20, 1876; s. John and Mary Ann (Kane) C.; student Brown, 1896-99; LL.B., Georgetown U., 1902; m. Mabel Clare Christy, Dec. 31, 1906; 1 son, Joseph Thomas. Admitted to N.Y. bar, 1904, and began practice in N.Y. City; field sec. Nat. Security League, 1918. An authority on radicalism in U.S.; initiated "slacker vote" campaign through Nat. Security League; lecturer on preparedness in Eastern States, 1915-17, and throughout U.S. in support of U.S. Constitution and against subversive movement and ratification of 20th Amendment; frequent lecturer on Constitutional questions and questions appertaining to matters of government. Govt. appeal agt. Draft Bd. No. 15, New York, 1917-19; comdr. Junior Naval Reserve; past nat. pres. Civil Legion. Roman Catholic. Author: America Asleep, 1923; Government by Default, 1923; Give the Constitution a Chance, 1924; Should the Child Labor Amendment Be Ratified?, 1925; Socialism and the Twentieth Amendment, 1925; Wars of Defense Are Always Justifiable, 1925; What Socialism Is Doing in the United States, 1926; The Meaning of Citizenship, 1929. Home: New York, N.Y. Died Feb. 5, 1936.

CASKODEN, Edwin ("Charles Major"), author; b. Indianapolis, Ind., July 25, 1856; s. Stephen and Phœbe A. M.; educated common schools, Shelbyville and Indianapolis; m. Alice Shaw, Sept. 27, 1885. Admitted to bar, and engaged in practice at Shelbyville. Author: When Knighthood Was in Flower, 1898; Bears of Blue River, 1900; Dorothy Vernon of Haddon Hall, 1902; A Forest Hearth, 1903; Yolanda, Maid of Burgundy, 1905; Uncle Tom Andy Bill, 1908; A Gentle Knight of Old Brandenburg, 1909; The Little King, 1910. Home: Shelbyville, Ind. Died Feb. 13, 1913.

CASPARI, Charles, Jr., pharmacist; b. Baltimore, May 31, 1850; s. Charles C.; prep. edn. Sch. of Arts and Sciences, U. of Md.; Ph.G., Md. Coll. of Pharmacy, 1869; (Phar.D., U. of Md., 1905). Prof. pharmacy, 1879—, dean, 1902—, Md. Coll. of Pharmacy (U. of Md.). Author: Treatise on Pharmacy, 1895 (5th edit., 1916). Home: Baltimore, Md. Died Oct. 13, 1917.

CASS, Alonzo Beecher, telephone official; b. Albion, N.Y., July 4, 1856; s. Pliny C. and Amanda M. C.; ed. Albion Acad.; m. Emily F. Tufts, June 21, 1885; m. 2d, Martha Tufts, Aug. 1906. Settled at Los Angeles, 1888; mem. Cass Bros. Stove Co., later Crandall & Cass and then v.p. Cass, Smurr, Damerel Co.; v.p., 1902-06, pres., 1906-16, Home Telephone & Telegraph Co., Los Angeles, and pres. of its successor, Southern Calif. Telephone Co., 1916—; pres. Cass, Howard & Sanford, Inc., bonds; also v.p. Cass, Stewart & Co.; dir. Security Trust & Savings Bank. Furnished 7 sons to the war; active in bond sales and Red Cross Work; was mem. Nat. War Work Council Y.M.C.A. and pres. Los Angeles Y.M.C.A. Republican. Presbyn. Mason. Home: South Pasadena, Calif. Died Mar. 11, 1924.

CASS, Joseph Kerr; b. Coshocton, O., Oct. 10, 1848; s. Abner Lord and Margaret (Kerr) C.; A.B., Kenyon Coll., 1868; m. Sarah Margaret Anderson, Feb. 19, 1879; children—Charles Anderson, Margaret Kerr, Anne Stevenson. Began as surveyor Grand Rapids & Ind. Ry., 1869; with Pa. R.R., Pittsburgh, 1872-76; partner Morrison, Bare & Cass Paper Co., 1876-81, Morrison & Cass Paper Co., 1881-99; dir. and v.p. W.Va. Pulp & Paper Co., 1899-1905, chmn. bd., 1909—. Republican. Presbyn. Died Nov. 1, 1938.

CASSATT, Alexander Johnston, pres. Pa. R.R. Co., June 1899—; b. Pittsburgh, Dec. 8, 1839; ed. Univ. of Heidelberg and Rensselaer Poly. Inst.; m. Lois Buchanan, niece James Buchanan, 15th President U.S. Engaged locating ry. in Ga., 1859-61; entered service of Pa. R.R. as rodman, 1861; asst. engr. Phila. & Trenton R.R., 1863; resident engr. Phila. & Erie R.R., 1864; supt. motive power and machinery Pa. R.R., 1867; gen. supt. Pa. system, 1870; gen. mgr. lines east of Pittsburgh, 1871-74, 3d v.p., 1874-80, 1st v.p., 1880-82, resigned v.p., Sept. 30, 1882; elected dir. Sept. 12, 1883. Home: Philadelphia, Pa. Died 1906.

CASSATT, Mary, artist; b. Pittsburgh, Pa.; sister of late A. J. Cassatt, pres. Pa. R.R.; went to Europe to study art, 1875; lived in Spain some time, studying Velasquez' work, then went to Paris and was influenced by Manet and Degas; unmarried. Exhibited in the Impressionist expns., Paris, never at the Salon. Returned to America 1898 for a few months and exhibited portraits and paintings at Durand-Ruel's. Died June 14, 1926.

CASSEDY, John Irvin, seminary pres.; b. Blanchester, O., Aug. 8, 1856; s. Laurence and Martha

(Irvin) C.; B.S., Ohio Wesleyan U., 1885 (hon. A.M., 1907); m. Luellia Vesta Harvey, Aug. 12, 1886 (died 1910); m. 2d, Stephana Prager, June 12, 1912. Prin. Norfolk (Va.) Coll., 1889-94; founded, 1894, and then pres. and gen. mgr., National Park Seminary, Forest Glen, Md. Died 1916.

CASSELBERRY, William Evans, physician; b. Phila., Sept. 6, 1858; s. Jacob Rush and Ellen Lane (Evans) C.; M.D., U. of Pa., 1879; interne Germantown Hosp., Phila., 1879-81; post-grad. courses at U. of Vienna, 1881-82, London Throat Hosp., 1882; m. Lillian Hibbard, June 23, 1891. In practice in Chicago, 1883—; prof. therapeutics, 1883-94, laryngology, 1894—, Northwestern Univ. Med. Sch.; laryngologist to St. Luke's Hosp. Republican. Episcopalian. Home: Chicago, Ill. Died July 11, 1916.

CASSIDY, George Washington, clergyman; b. Boston, Apr. 20, 1863; s. James and Maria (Barnes) Cosgrave; lost parents in childhood and was adopted by Hillary S. and Elizabeth Cassidy; ed. Kan. Normal Coll., Fort Scott, Kan.; A.B., William Jewell Coll., 1890; A.M., 1911; grad. Rochester Theol. Sem., 1898; D.D., Ottawa (Kan.) U., 1911, D.D., William Jewell Coll., 1914; m. Hester Purl, Aug. 4, 1886; children—Lorena Elanor, Henry Kenneth. Taught sch. intermittently, 1884-92; ordained Bapt. ministry, May 1891; pastor, Cherryvale, Kan., 1892-93; 1st Ch., Fort Scott, 1893-95; Canaseraga, N.Y., 1895-96; Hilton, N.Y., 1896-98; Walnut Hills Ch., Cincinnati, 1898-1901; Terrace Park, Ohio, 1902; 1st Ch., Wichita, Kan., Feb. 1903-Dec. 1914; joint dist. sec. Southwestern Dist. Am. Bapt. Home Mission Soc. and Am. Bapt. Foreign Mission Soc., Wichita, Kan., 1914-19; pastor 1st Bapt. Ch., Sioux City, Ia., 1920-21; exec. sec. and dir. of promotion, Ia. Bapt. Conv., 1921-22; pastor First Av. Ch., Hutchinson, Kan., 1922-24; spl. denom. work, 1924-25; acting pastor Immanuel Ch., Salt Lake City, Utah, 1925-26; acting pastor First Ch., Long Beach, Calif., 1927-28; mem. bd. mgrs. Am. Bapt. Foreign Mission Soc., 1925-28, field sec., 1928-30; pastor Immanuel Ch., Long Beach, Calif., 1931-36, retired, 1936; then acting pastor in several chs. Mem. exec. com. Northern Bapt. Conv., 1910-16. Trustee Ottawa, U., 1904—. Mason. Home: Wichita, Kan. Died Mar. 15, 1941.

CASSIDY, (Ira D.) Gerald, artist; b. Cincinnati, O., Nov. 10, 1879; s. Edwin B. and Olive E. (Crouch) C.; ed. Art Inst., Cincinnati, under Duvenick (first prize for drawing); Nat. Acad. Design and Art Students' League, New York; m. Sarah Craus Snowden; m. 2d, Mrs. Perlina Sizer Davis, Jan. 10, 1912. Regular exhibitor New York, Boston and in Calif.; awarded grand prize and gold medal for murals in Indian Art Gallery, Panama-Calif. Expn., 1915; represented in San Diego Mus.; Freer Collection, Washington, D.C.; Canton (China) Christian Coll.; N.M. Mus. of Fine Arts, Santa Fe; Mus. of Fine Arts, Houston, Tex.; McPherson (Kan.) High Sch.; Golden (Colo.) High Sch.; N.Y. Pub. Library; Luxembourg Gallery, Paris; Albertina Mus., Vienna; also in pvt. galleries of U.S., France and Germany. Mem. Chicago Galleries Assn. (awarded prizes in semiannual exhbns., 1928, 29, 30, 31). Home: Santa Fe, N.M. Died Feb. 12, 1934.

CASSIDY, Massilon Alexander, city supt. schs.; b. Morristown, Tenn., Aug. 22, 1856; s. Jeremiah Alexander and Martha Matilda (Jackson) C.; ed. Reagan College, 4 yrs.; M.A., U. of Ky.; m. Martha C. Rogan, 1882; children—Henry Duncan, Martha, Perry Rogan, Margaret. Studied law and licensed to practice, 1879; elected supt. schs., Fayette Co., Ky., 1886, and supt. Lexington (city) schs., 1888; in ednl. work continuously, 1886—. Leader of movement and author of first bill to reform sch. system of Ky. Democrat. Presbyn. Short story writer; dialect reader. Author of "Golden Deeds System" of character education. Home: Lexington, Ky. Died Dec. 21, 1928.

CASSINO, Samuel Edson, publisher; b. Salem, Mass., Jan. 4, 1856; s. John Trask and Harriet Lucretia (Phelps) C.; grad. St. Johnsbury (Vt.) Acad., 1872, Peabody Acad. Science, Salem, 1875, Agassiz Sch. Zoölogy, Pennikeese Island, 1875; m. Melvina King Osborn, Jan. 31, 1877; children—Margherita Osborn, Leslie Phelps (dec.), Herman Edson, Harold Lorence. Began to publish books, 1877; pub. Little Folks Magazine for 30 years, Naturalists' Directory (31 edits.). Entomologist. Editor The Lepidopterist. Conglist. Republican. Home: Salem, Mass. Died Nov. 6, 1937.

CASSODAY, John B., justice, 1880—, chief justice, 1895—, Supreme Court of Wis.; b. Herkimer Co., N.Y., July 7, 1830; moved to Tioga Co., Pa., when 3 years old; worked for board while securing occasional few months' attendance in dist. school; worked in summer and taught in winter to secure means to attend Wellsboro Acad. one term, Knoxville Acad. 2 terms, and Alfred Acad. (grad.); special studies in Univ. of Mich. and Albany Law School; (LL.D., Beloit Coll., 1881, Univ. of Wis., 1905). Practiced law, Janesville, Wis., 1857-80; mem. Wis. legislature, 1865, and speaker, 1877; del. Nat. Rep. Conv., 1864, 1880; prof. constl. law, Univ. of Wis. Author: Cassoday on Wills. Home: Madison, Wis. Died 1907.

CASTELLO, Eugene, artist; b. Phila., Pa., Jan. 12, 1851; s. Alexander Harrison and Ann Maria (Laws) C.; ed. pub. schs. and Pa. Acad. Fine Arts, under Schussele and Eakins; traveled and studied abroad at intervals, 1885-1903; m. Virginia Jones, Nov. 23, 1904. Teacher of drawing, LaSalle Coll., Phila., 1886, North East Manual Training Sch., Phila., 1892; draftsman and designer art metal work and furniture, etc. Designed sword of honor presented Rear Admiral W. P. Sampson by State of N.J., 1899; (in collaboration) "Avenue of Fame," for G.A.R., 1890; John Welsh Memorial, Phila., 1886. Exhibited: (paintings) Chicago Expn., 1893, St. Louis Expn., 1904; Salon de l'Union Internationale des Arts et des Lettres, Paris, 1909; Expn. Art and History, Rome, 1911; Nat. Acad. Design, N.Y. Water Color Club, Corcoran Galley, Pa. Acad. Fine Arts, Art Inst. of Chicago, etc.; (sculpture) Universelle Expn., Ghent, 1913; Pa. Acad. Fine Arts, 1903; Expn. Medallic Art, New York, 1910. Awarded bronze medal, for paintings, Am. Art Soc., 1904; prize for best design, Arts and Craft Club, Phila., 1905; medal for painting, Am. Art Soc., 1904; prize for Charter mem. Phila. Chapter A.I.A., 1870, Art Workers' Guild, 1892; mem. Fellowship of Pa. Acad. Fine Arts, Am. Art Soc., L'Union Internationale des Arts et des Lettres; medalist Am. Numismatic Society. Home: Philadelphia, Pa. Died Mar. 3, 1926.

CASTLE, Frederick Albert, M.D.; b. Fabius, N.Y., Apr. 29, 1842; was matriculated at Albany Med. Coll., and when war broke out became med. cadet on hosp. service until 1863, when became acting asst. surgeon U.S. Navy; grad. Bellevue Hosp. Med. Coll., 1866, and settled in New York. Has held hosp. appmts. and been mem. of faculty of the coll. in various capacities; on editorial staff Medical Record, 1872-76, and editor New Remedies, 1873, when it became the American Druggist of which he also became editor. Died 1902.

CASTLE, Henry Anson, lawyer; b. near Quincy, Ill., Aug. 22, 1841; s. Timothy Hunt and Julia A. (Boyd) C.; A.M., McKendree Coll., Ill., 1862; pvt. and sergt. maj. 73d Ill. Vols., 1862-63; capt. 137th Ill. Vols., 1864; admitted to bar, 1864; m. Margaret Jaquess, Apr. 18, 1865. In practice, Quincy, Ill., 1864-66, St. Paul, Minn., 1866—; editor and pub. of St. Paul Daily Dispatch, 1876-85; adj. gen. Minn., 1875-76; mem. Minn. Ho. of Rep., 1873; postmaster St. Paul, 1892-6; auditor U.S. Post Office Dept., 1897-1904; counsel U.S. Postal Commn., 1907. Republican. Pres. St. Paul Chamber of Commerce, 1893; pres. bd. trustees Minn. Soldiers' Home, 1887-99. Author: The Army Mule and Other War Sketches, 1897; History of Saint Paul, 1911; History of Minnesota, 1915. Home: St. Paul, Minn. Died Aug. 16, 1916.

CASTLE, Nicholas, bishop; b. Bristol, Ind., Oct. 4, 1837; s. W. H. and Harriet (Van Brunt) C.; ed. in frontier sch. house and by pvt. effort; m. Miss C. A. Hummer, 1861 (died 1879); 2d, Ellen Livingood, 1881. Entered ministry U.B. Ch., 1857; was traveling pastor and presiding elder in Ind. and Mich.; elected bishop 1877, emeritus, 1905—. Author: The Witness of the Holy Spirit; Fifty Years in the Ministry; The Exalted Life. Mem. Bd. of Bishops; dir. Bonebrake Theol. Sem., Foreign Missionary Soc. of U.B. Ch., Home Missionary Soc., Ch. Erection Soc., Bd. of Edn., Bd. of Control of S.S. Brotherhood and Young People's Work. Home: Philomath, Ore. Died Apr. 18, 1922.

CASTLE, William, vocal dir. Chicago Musical Coll., 1891—; b. Eng., Dec. 22, 1836; ed. in Phila.; m. Hetty M. Warren, 1863. Studied music in New York, London and Milan, Italy; leading tenor of English opera for 30 years; made début as singer in concert in New York, 1861; in opera, New York, 1864; sang in Europe, 1872-74; retired from stage, 1891; original in America of "Paul," in Victor Massè's opera of Paul and Virginia; "Romeo" in Gounod's Romeo and Juliet; and many other well known works. Died 1909.

CASTLE, William Richards, lawyer; b. Honolulu, P.I., Mar. 19, 1849; s. Samuel Northrup and Mary Ann (Tenney) C.; Oahu Coll., Honolulu; Oberlin Coll., O., hon. A.M., 1887; Harvard Law Sch.; Columbia Law School, LL.B., 1873; m. Ida Beatrice Lowrey, Oct. 12, 1875. Practiced in New York, 1874-76, then in Honolulu; atty. gen. Kingdom of Hawaii, Feb.-Nov. 1876; mem. Legislature of Hawaii, 1878, 1886, 87, 88 (pres., 1887, 1888); annexation commr. Hawaii to U.S., 1893; Hawaiian minister resident in Washington, D.C., 1895; pres. Bd. of Edn., Republic of Hawaii, 1896; pres. and atty. Honolulu Gas Co., Ltd., S. N. Castle Estate. Republican. Congregationalist. Home: Honolulu, Hawaii. Died June 5, 1935.

CASTLEBERRY, John Jackson, clergyman; b. Savannah, Tenn., Apr. 13, 1877; s. George Washington and Sarah Graham (Mahan) C.; grad. Coll. of the Bible, Transylvania U., Ky., 1900; B.D., Yale, 1917; studied Harvard and Chicago U.; D.D., Lincoln Memorial Univ., 1924; LL.D. from Transylvania U. in 1935; m. Annie Porter, Feb. 8, 1903; 1 son, John Porter. Ordained ministry Disciples of Christ, 1900; pastor Springfield, Tenn., 1900-04, Union City, 1904-09, 1st Ch., Mayfield, Ky., 1909-20, Walnut Hills Ch., Cincinnati, O., 1920—. Pres. Congress of Disciples of Christ, 1921-22; pres. Tenn. Christian Missionary Conv., Ky. Christian S.S. Conv.; formerly mem. bd. mgrs. United Christian Missionary Soc. of Disciples of Christ; mem. bd. mgrs. Bethesda Hosp., Cincinnati; mem. bd. Cincinnati Asso. Charities; trustee Coll. of the Bible, Lexington, Ky., Am. Christian Missionary Soc.; mem. Am. Seminar in Europe, 1926; formerly pres. Cincinnati Fedn. of Chs. Mason. Author: The Soul of Religion, 1926. Deceased.

CASTLEMAN, John Breckinridge, retired; b. Fayette County, Ky., June 30, 1841; s. David and Virginia (Harrison) C.; ed. Transylvania U., from which, at 19, entered C.S.A. at outbreak of war; trooper Morgan's cav., 1861-Oct. 1864, and maj. of Morgan's old regt.; comd. expdn. to release Confederate prisoners confined in Ill. and Ind., when he was captured and placed in solitary confinement 9 months, being released on parole, July, 1865, to leave the U.S. never to return; parole revoked by President Johnson; studied in Europe; LL.B., U. of Louisville, 1868; m. Alice Barbee, Nov. 24, 1868. Mgr. Royal Ins. Co. of Liverpool, 1869-1902. Adj. gen. Ky. under Gov. Knott; chmn. Dem. State Central Com., 1890-92; comdg. officer Louisville Legion, 1878—; pres. Louisville bd. park commrs., 1891—; enlisted the 1st regt. Ky. Vol. Inf., 1898, for service Spanish-Am. War, which participated in P.R. campaign; apptd. brig. gen. U.S.V.; declined commn. of brig. gen. U.S. Army tendered by President McKinley; comd. Ky. troops during troubles following assassination of Gov. Goebel. His fellow citizens in Ky. have erected in his honor an equestrian statue in recognition of distinguished pub. service. Author: Active Service. Home: Louisville, Ky. Died May 23, 1918.

CASTLEMON, Harry, author. See Charles Austin Fosdick.

CASWELL, Mary S. (Mrs. George A.), educator; b. Paris, Me.; d. of Mark and Alice Deering; ed. acads. and pvt. schs. in N.E.; m. George A. Caswell, 1879 (dec.). Founded, 1883, and prin., 1883-89, The Caswell Sch., Portland, Me.; founded, 1889, became prin. The Marlborough Sch. for Girls, Los Angeles, Calif. Episcopalian. Died Feb. 11, 1924.

CASWELL, Thomas Hubbard, lawyer; sovereign grand comdr., Supreme Council, A and A, Scottish Rite Masons, 33 degree, for southern jurisdiction, U.S.A., Oct. 1895-99; b. Exeter, N.Y., Aug. 10, 1825; ed. there and St. Mary's Coll., Ky.; licensed as lawyer, Nov. 8, 1848; went to Calif., 1849; m. Mary Jones, Jan. 9, 1853. Judge 2 terms (8 yrs.), Nevada County, Calif.; moved to San Francisco, 1878; grand sec. Grand Chapter, Royal Arch Masons, and grand recorder, Grand Commandery, Knights Templar, Calif., 1878, to Feb. 1899; resigned. Author: Hand Book of the Chapter; also other book. Home: San Francisco, Calif. Died 1900.

CASWELL, Thomas Thompson, rear adm.; b. Providence, R.I., Jan. 4, 1840; s. Alexis and Esther Lois (Thompson) C.; A.M., Brown U., 1861; widower. Apptd. from R.I. asst. p.m. U.S. Navy, Sept. 9, 1861; p.m., 1863; pay insp., 1881; pay dir., 1892; retired with rank of rear admiral, June 1899. Home: Annapolis, Md. Died July 18, 1913.

CATE, Horace Nelson, lawyer; b. Sevier County, Tenn., Jan. 19, 1863; s. Nelson Newman and Margaret (Scruggs) C.; ed. Carson & Newman Coll., Jefferson City, Tenn., 1879-81; m. Lily Early, June 15, 1893. Admitted to Tenn. bar, 1888; mem. firm of Pickle, Turner & Cate, of Newport, Tenn., 1890-95, Cate & Hooper, 1894-1901; mem. State Senate, 4th Senatorial Dist., 1903-05; judge Ct. of Civil Appeals, Tenn., by appmt. of Gov. Hooper, to fill vacancy, Feb. 1911-Sept. 1912; returned to gen. practice; mem. Turner, Cate & Cate, 1923—. Republican. Baptist. Mason. Home: Knoxville, Tenn. Died Apr. 11, 1925.

CATES, Charles Theodore, Jr., lawyer; b. Maryville, Tenn., Mar. 6, 1863; s. Charles T. and Martha Victoria (Kidd) C.; B.A., Maryville Coll., 1881, LL.D., 1909; m. Emma J. Parham, Nov. 3, 1886. Read law in office of father; admitted to bar before 21 yrs. of age, 1883; practiced with father, 1883-89; removed to Knoxville, 1889; mem. Howe & Cates, 1889-91, Hood & Cates (Gen. R. N. Hood) until death of partner, 1892, Templeton & Cates, 1893-98, later Shields, Cates & Mountcastle, then member Cates, Smith & Long. Atty. gen. of Tenn., 2 terms, 1902-18, resigned, 1913, to resume law practice; mem. Dem. State Exec. Com., 1898-1900. Methodist. Home: Knoxville, Tenn. Died Oct. 15, 1938.

CATHCART, William, Bapt. clergyman; b. Londonderry, Ireland, Nov. 8, 1825; ed. Univ. of Glasgow, and Horton, now Rawdon Coll., Yorkshire, England (D.D., U. of Lewisburg, 1873); came to U.S., 1853, becoming minister in Phila. Pres. Am. Bapt. Hist. Soc. Author: The Baptists and the American Revolution; The Papal System; Baptist Encyclopædia, etc. Home: Hoyt, Pa. Died 1908.

CATHCART, William Ledyard, engr.; b. Mystic, Conn., Aug. 12, 1855; s. William and Eliza (Caldwell) C.; ed. U. of Pa., 1871-73; grad. U.S. Naval Acad., 1875. Served in Engr. Corps U.S. Navy on N. and S. Atlantic, S. Pacific and Asiatic squadrons; resigned from Navy, 1891, to enter pvt. business; treas. mfg. co., 1891-97; prof. marine engring., Webb Acad. of Naval Architecture, New York, 1897-99; adj. prof. mech. engring., Columbia, 1899-1903; prof. engring., Webb Inst. Naval Architecture, N.Y. City, 1918—. Apptd. chief engr. U.S. Navy, and ordered to spl. duty as asst. to engr.-in-chief, Navy Dept., during Spanish-Am. War; apptd. lt. comdr. U.S.N. R.F., and on spl. duty office of engr.-in-chief, U.S. Navy, World War; later promoted to comdr. U.S.N. R.F. Author: Machine Design, 1903; Elements of Graphic Statics, with Prof. J. Irvin Chaffee, 1910; A Short Course in Graphic Statics (with same), 1911. Mem. Griffin & Cathcart, consulting engrs. Home: Germantown, Philadelphia, Pa. Died Mar. 1925.

CATHERWOOD, Mary Hartwell, author; b. (Hartwell) Luray, Licking Co., O., Dec. 16, 1847; grad. Female Coll., Granville, O., 1868; m. James S. Catherwood, Dec. 27, 1887. Author: Romance of Dollard; Story of Tonty; Lady of Fort St. John; Queen of the Swamp; Rocky Fork. Home: Chicago, Ill. Died 1902.

CATLIN, Albertus Wright, officer U.S.M.C.; b. Gowanda, N.Y., Dec. 1, 1868; s. Buckley Dary and Adeline (Cook) C.; grad. U.S. Naval Acad., 1890; grad. Army War Coll., May 1917; m. Carrie Abbott, Aug. 29, 1902 (died 1915); m. 2d, Martha Ellen Gallant, Aug. 22, 1917; 1 dau., Martha Ellen. Commd. 2d lt. U.S.M.C., July 1, 1892; promoted through grades to brig. gen., and retired Dec. 10, 1919. Comd. marine guard, U.S.S. Maine when destroyed in Havana Harbor, 1898; comd. marines on S.S. St. Louis during Spanish-Am. War; in Philippines, 1902-04; comd. first marines landed in Cuba, 1906, and served there until 1909; comd. marines from fleet, landed at Vera Cruz, Mexico, Apr. 21-22, 1914; comd. 6th Regt. Marines, 4th Brigade, 2d Div., 1st A.C., A.E.F., 1917-18; wounded in action at Belleau Wood, June 6, 1918; assigned as comdr. 1st Brigade Marines, Hayti, Nov. 1918. Awarded Congressional Medal of Honor "for distinguished conduct," at Vera Cruz, Apr. 22, 1914; Croix de Guerre with Palm, and Legion of Honor (French) for service at Château Thierry, June 1918. Republican. Methodist. Home: Washington, D.C. Died May 31, 1933.

CATLIN, Charles Albert, chemist; b. Burlington, Vt., May 10, 1849; s. Henry Wadhams and Mary Cobb (Mayo) C.; bro. of Henry Guy and Robert Mayo C.; B.S., U. of Vt., 1872, Ph.B., 1873 (Sc.D., 1913); special course Mass. Inst. Tech., 1894, 95; m. Frances L. Herrick, June 20, 1877. Chemist, Rumford Chem. Works, Providence, 1873-75 and 1878—. Inventor and patentee of chem. processes and applications, many of which relate to mfr. of phosphates for dietetic purposes. Trustee U. of Vt. and R.I. Hosp. Author: Baking Powders, 1899. Home: Providence, R.I. Died Apr. 2, 1916.

CATLIN, Isaac Swartwood, brig. gen.; b. Owego, N.Y., July 8, 1835; s. Nathaniel and Jane (Brodhead) C.; ed. Owego; m. Virginia H. S. Bacon, Oct. 1862. Raised 1st co. of vols. for the Civil War on the day of Mr. Lincoln's call for 75,000 troops; capt. 3d N.Y. Inf., May 14, 1861; resigned Mar. 14, 1862; 1st lt., adj. 109th N.Y. Inf., Aug. 2, 1862; lt. col., Aug. 28, 1862; col., July 29, 1864; hon. mustered out, June 4, 1865; capt. 45th U.S. Inf., May 6, 1867; retired with rank of col., May 6, 1870; brig. gen. U.S.A. retired by act of Apr. 23, 1904. Bvtd.: brig. gen. vols., Mar. 13, 1865, "for gallant and meritorious services during the war"; maj. gen., Mar. 13, 1865, for same in battles before Petersburg, Va. (lost right leg); maj., May 6, 1867, for same in Battle of Wilderness; lt. col., May 6, 1867, for same at Petersburg; awarded Congressional Medal of Honor "for most distinguished gallantry in action at the explosion of the mine at Petersburg." Asst. U.S. dist. atty., 1871; elected dist. atty., Kings Co., 1877; reelected, 1880; nominated for mayor of Brooklyn, 1885; nominated for Congress, but declined nomination, 1893; offered, but declined, nomination for lt. gov., 1896; originally Republican, then Cleveland Democrat; supported war policy of Presidents McKinley and Roosevelt. Then retired from business. Writing "Memoirs of Civil and Military Career." Home: Brooklyn, N.Y. Died Jan. 19, 1916.

CATLIN, Robert Mayo, mining engr.; b. Burlington, Vt., June 8, 1853; s. Henry Wadhams and Mary Cobb (Mayo) C.; B.S., U. of Vt., 1872, C.E., 1873, hon. E.M., 1902; Sc.D., Rutgers, 1918; m. Ann E. Robertson, June 15, 1882; children—Bessie Margery, Mary Helen, Robert Mayo. Engaged as mining engineer, 1875; co. surveyor, Elko Co., Nev., 1876; supt. Navajo Mining Co., Tuscarora, Nov. 1880; supt. Victorine Gold Mining Co., 1882; supt. Navajo, Belle Isle, N. Belle Isle, N. Commonwealth and Del Monte mines (Tuscarora), and, 1893, of Commonwealth and Nevada Queen mines (Tuscarora); gen. mgr. (under John Hays Hammond), of 8 deep level mines, Johannesburg, Transvaal, 1895-1906; gen. supt. N.J. Zinc Co., 1906-30; v.p. Sussex County Trust Co., Franklin, N.J. Acting cons. engr. of the Consolidated Gold Fields of South Africa, Ltd. Home: Oakland, Calif. Died Nov. 22, 1934.

CATLIN, Roy George, clergyman; b. Washington Twp., Pa., May 26, 1883; s. William Edward and Liona (Hostettler) C.; student Thiel Coll., Greenville, Pa., 1901-04; A.B., Wittenberg Coll., Springfield, O., 1905; grad. Chicago Luth. Theol. Sem., 1908; D.D., Carthage (Ill.) Coll., 1920; m. Eva Coates, Aug. 26, 1907 (dec.); children—Robert Leroy, Eleanor Onah; m. 2d, Mertie Sanders, Sept. 22, 1934. Ordained Lutheran ministry, 1908; pastor Decatur, Ill., 1908-31; pres. Ill. Synod United Luth. Ch. America, July 1, 1931—; an incorporator, 1920, Ill. Synod, of which is pres.; dir. Rock River (Ill.) Assembly; pres. Synodical Bd. of Home Mission and Ch. Extension. Editor Ill. Synod Bull. Home: Maywood, Ill. Died Sept. 17, 1937.

CATON, Arthur J., lawyer; b. Ottawa, Ill., 1851; s. John Dean and Laura A. (Sherrill) C.; grad. Phillips Exeter Acad., 1869; Hamilton Coll., 1873; admitted to bar, 1873; began practice in Chicago; has been receiver Chicago & Southern Ry. Co.; married. Home: Chicago, Ill. Died 1904.

CATOR, George, retired mcht.; b. Baltimore, May 10, 1856; s. Benjamin F. and Sallie (McNamara) C.; A.B., Johns Hopkins, 1901, Ph.D., 1902; attended lectures Johns Hopkins, 1896-1902; unmarried. Entered business 1872; became mem. Armstrong, Cator & Co., jobbers of millinery and notions, 1878; retired, 1892; dir. in several corps.; pres. Am. Bonding Co., 1904-14; pres. Mt. Vernon-Woodberry Mills, Inc., 1915-16. Baltimore, Md. Died Feb. 25, 1932.

CATRON, Thomas Benton, senator; b. Lafayette Co., Mo.; s. John and Mary (Fletcher) C.; A.B., A.M., U. of Mo.; m. Julia A. Walz, Apr., 1877. Began practice of law in N.M., 1867; mem. N.M. legislature several terms; atty. gen. N.M., 1869-72; U.S. atty. Dist. of N.M., 1872-79; del. from N.M. to Congress, 1895-97; elected to U.S. Senate Mar. 27, 1912, and drew term which expired Mar. 4, 1917. Republican. Mason. Home: Santa Fe, N.M. Died May 15, 1921.

CATT, George William, civ. engr.; b. Davenport, Ia., March 9, 1860; s. Alfred B. and Mary C.; grad. Iowa State Coll., 1879-82; studied civ. engring. and law.; m. Carrie Lane Chapman, 1890. Chief Engr., San Francisco Bridge Co., 1887-92; pres. and engr. N.Y. Dredging Co., 1893-99; pres. and engr. Atlantic Gulf and Pacific Co. (engrs. and contractors), 1899; builders of dry docks for U.S. Govt., at League Island and Mare Island Navy Yards, together with harbor improvements. Died 1905.

CATTELL, Edward James ("Francis H. Hardy") statistician; b. Phila., Dec. 8, 1856; s. Elijah G. and Catharine (Hardy) C.; ed. private schs., U.S., England and Germany; D.Sc., Temple U., 1917; unmarried. Traveled extensively in Europe and East; during 10 yrs. residence abroad, contbr. on econ., geog. and polit. topics to English mags. and jours. (under pen-name). Editor Foreign Commercial Guide of Philadelphia Commercial Museum. Then corr. sec. Atlantic Deeper Waterways Assn.; asst. gen. sec. Founders Week Celebration, 1909; statistician, City of Phila., and editor of "Philadelphia," the city's newspaper, June 1, 1909—; field dir. Phila. Chamber of Commerce. Author: (novels) The Mills of God, 1897; To the Healing of the Sea. Home: Philadelphia, Pa. Died Jan. 6, 1938.

CATTELL, Henry Ware, medical editor; b. Harrisburg, Pa., Oct. 7, 1862; s. Rev. William C. (pres. Lafayette Coll.) and Elizabeth (McKeen) C.; A.B., Lafayette, 1883, A.M., 1886; U. of Leipzig, 1883-84; M.D., U. of Pa., 1887; unmarried. Demonstrator of morbid anatomy, U. of Pa., 1892-97; dir. Ayer Clin. Lab., Pa. Hosp., 1899-1901; pathologist at different times to Blockley, Presbyn., and other Phila. hosps.; expert in many murder trials. Served in France as a major, 1918-19, and had charge of the post mortem records of the A.E.F., and was pathologist to Base Hosp. No. 17 and to the Central Med. Dept. Laboratory; grad. Oct. 13, 1925, Med. Field Service Sch., U.S.A., Carlislie, Pa.; lt. col. Med. Res., U.S.A. (Ret.). Editor Internat. Med. Magazine, 1894-97, Internat. Clinics, 1900-03, 1910-16, 1922-32 (edited 78 vols. before retiring). Del. of U.S. to 5th Internat. Congress of Military Medicine and Pharmacy, London, 1929. Republican. Presbyn. Author: Post-Mortem Pathology, 1903, 05, 06. Editor: Lippincott's Medical Dictionary, 1910, 3d edition, 1913. Translator: Ziegler's Special Pathological Anatomy, 1896-97. Home: Brown Mills, N.J. Died Mar. 8, 1936.

CATTELL, William Ashburner, civil engr.; b. Princeton, N.J., June 16, 1863; s. Rev. Thomas W. (Ph.D.) and Anna C. (Ashburner) C.; C.E., Lafayette Coll., 1884; m. Jennie W. Woodhull, Sept. 17, 1889. Asst. engr., State Bd. of R.R. Assessors, N.J., and later on preliminary location surveys for A.,T.&S.F. R.R. in Kan. and Ind. Ty., 1884-89; asst. chief engr., constrn. L.I. R.R., 1889-97; consulting practice, New York, 1897-1905; cons. engr. for E. H. Rollins & Sons, San Francisco, on various projects, 1905-08, including Western Pacific R.R.; report for Hirsch Syndicate, Ltd., London, on Valdez-Yukon R.R. project in Alaska; chief engr. Clear Lake Power and Irrigation project, also the Trona Ry.; cons. engr. San Francisco-Oakland Terminal Rys., Peoples Water Co., Los Angeles Ry. Corp. Gen. consulting practice, San Francisco, 1908-17; mem. Cattell, Howard & Ashton, 1917. Commd. maj., Engr. R.C., Mar. 1, 1917; ordered to active duty, Dec. 28, 1917; at Camp Lee, Va., Jan. 5-Feb. 22, 1918; staff duty Office Chief of Engrs., Washington, in charge of hist. unit, Feb. 23, 1918-Sept. 30, 1919. Mason. Home: Washington, D.C. Died Oct. 10, 1920.

CATTELLE, Wallis Richard, author; b. in Eng., Dec. 30, 1848; s. James Wallis and Martha (Skeels) C.; ed. common schs. and under tutors; m. Berenice J. Seaman, Oct. 20, 1875. Came to America, 1868; dealer in precious stones. Republican. Author: Precious Stones, 1903; The Pearl, 1907; The Diamond, 1911. Home: Tenafly, N.J. Died Nov. 12, 1912.

CATTERALL, Ralph Charles Henry, univ. prof.; b. Bolton, Eng., Mar. 29, 1866; s. Ralph Charles Henry and Caroline (Reed) C.; came to America with parents, Sept. 1869; A.B., Bucknell U., 1891; A.B., Harvard, 1892; Ph.D., U. of Chicago, 1902; m. Helen Honor Tunnicliff, June 24, 1896. Instr. in history, U. of Chicago, 1894-1902; asst. prof. history, 1902-05, prof. modern European history, 1905—, Cornell U. Democrat. Episcopalian. Author: The Second Bank of the United States, 1902. Home: Ithaca, N.Y. Died Aug. 2, 1914.

CATTS, Sidney Johnston, governor; b. nr. Pleasant Hill, Ala., July 31, 1863; s. Capt. S. W. and Adeline R. (Smyly) C.; ed. Agrl. and Mech. Coll. of Ala., Howard Coll., Ala., and Ala. Poly. Inst.; LL.B., Cumberland U. Law Sch., Tenn., 1882. Licensed Bapt. ministry, 1885, ordained, 1886; pastor in Ala. at Mt. Gilead, Benton, Farmersville, Shiloh, Ackeville, Steep Creek, Letohatchee, Ft. Deposit and Tuskegee, and again at Ft. Deposit until 1904 (resigned from ministry). Candidate for Congress, 5th Ala. Dist., 1904; removed to Florida; gov. of Florida, term 1918-21. Democrat. Candidate for U.S. Senate, 1919. Died Mar. 9, 1936.

CAULDWELL, Leslie Giffen, artist; b. New York, Oct. 18, 1861; s. William and Eliza Ellen C.; studied art, Julian Acad., Paris, 1884; pupil of Boulanger, Lefebvre, Carolus-Durant. Had pictures admitted to Paris Salon, 1886 and 1888; also Paris Expn., 1889, Salon, Champs de Mars, 1890, 1, 2, 3, 4, 6; also to Soc. British Artists and Royal Acad., London, and at Liverpool and Berlin, and Nat. Acad. Design and Soc. Am. Artists, New York; then exhibited his paintings in various Am. cities and at World's Fair. In 1896 took up decorating and furnishing of interiors as a profession; commenced in Paris, 1897-98, in "The Hotel Ritz," followed in 1899 with the "Carlton Hotel," London; received gold medal, Paris Expn., 1900, for artistic interior work at the British Pavilion and Waring & Gillow's exhibit in British sect. Mgr. N.Y. branch of E. Alavoine & Co. of Paris, interior decorators, 1907—. Home: New York, N.Y. Died Apr. 9, 1941.

CAULK, John Roberts, surgeon; b. McDaniel, Md., Oct. 30, 1881; s. Frank Ernest and Sarah D. (Wrightson) C.; B.A., St. Johns Coll., Annapolis, Md., 1901, M.A., 1902; student Georgetown U., 1901-02; M.D., Johns Hopkins, 1906; m. Bessie Jenifer Harrison, June 1, 1910; children—John Robert, Marion Elizabeth. Interne and asst. resident phys. Union Protestant Infirmary, Baltimore, Md., 1906-07; asst. resident surgeon, dept. urology, Johns Hopkins Hosp., 1907-10; came to St. Louis, Mo., 1910; prof. clin. genito-urinary surgery, Washington U.; asst. surgeon Barnes Hosp.; asso. surgeon St. Louis Maternity Hosp.; urologist St. Luke's, St. Louis Children's and Jewish hosps., Evang. Deaconess Home and Hosp., St. Louis County Hosp. Comdt. of cadets and maj. of bn., St. Johns Coll., 1900-01; instr. Army Sch. of Urology, Barnes Hosp., World War. Fellow Am. Coll. Surgeons. Democrat. Episcopalian. Home: Clayton, Mo. Died Oct. 13, 1938.

CAUSEY, William Bowdoin, civil engr.; b. Suffolk, Va., June 24, 1865; s. Charles Henry and Martha Josephine (Prentis) C.; ed. pvt. schs.; unmarried. Began as chairman Atlantic & Danville R.R., Va., 1883; with engring. depts. various rys., including U.P. Ry., N.Y.,N.H.&H. R.R., C.&N.W., C.&A. R.R., C.G.W. R.R., also was chief engr. E.J.&E. Ry., supt. Ill. lines C.&A. R.R., supt. C.G.W. Ry.; v.p. and gen. mgr. Norwood-White Coal Co., Des Moines, Ia., 1914-17; city mgr. Norfolk, Va., 1923-25; then v.p. White Construction Co. and M. E. White Co., gen. contractors, Chicago. Commd. capt. engrs., June 13, 1917, and assigned to 17th Engrs., U.S.A.; landed in France Aug. 1917; maj., Mar. 1918; lt. col., Sept. 1918; mem. Am. sect. Inter-Allied Mission sent to Vienna from Paris by Supreme War Council to investigate financial, economic and fuel transportation conditions in former Austro-Hungarian Empire, Dec. 1918-July 1919; was coal and transp. expert of the Mission, pres. Allied Ry. Mission, Austro-Hungary, Jan.-Oct. 1919; tech. adviser to Austrian Govt., Sept. 1919-July 1923; then lt. col. O.R.C., U.S.A. Asst. U.S. commr. to

Century of Progress Expn., Chicago, July 1932-Apr. 15, 1935. Decorated Officer Legion of Honor (France); Order of Saint Sava 2d class (Kingdom of the Serbs, Croats and Slovenes—Jugo-Slavia); The Great Silver Cross of Honor (Republic of Austria); citation from Gen. Pershing "for distinguished services" in France. Republican. Episcopalian. Mason. Home: Chicago, Ill. Died Aug. 10, 1936.

CAVANAUGH, John William, college prof.; b. Leetonia, O., May 21, 1870; s. Patrick and Elizabeth (O'Connor) C.; Litt.B., U. of Notre Dame, 1890; studied theology same; (D.D., Ottawa U.; LL.D., Notre Dame, 1921); ordained priest, Apr. 21, 1894. Asso. editor Ave Maria Magazine, 1894-1905; rector of Holy Cross Sem., 1898-1905; prof. English lit., 1902-06; pres. U. of Notre Dame, 1905-19; prof. spl. English, Holy Cross Coll., Brookland, D.C., 1919-20; prof. English, U. of Notre Dame, 1920-31. Chmn. of Compliance Bd. of NRA; apptd. by gov., chmn. State Commn. of Liquor Control. Mem. Nat. Council and Nat. Ednl. Com., Boy Scouts. Author: Priests of Holy Cross, 1904; The Modesty of Culture, 1931. Editor: Biography of Knute K. Rockne, 1931. Home: Notre Dame, Ind. Died Mar. 22, 1935.

CAVERNO, Charles, clergyman; b. Strafford, N.H., Aug. 19, 1832; s. Jeremiah and Dorothy Kingman (Balch) C.; A.B., Dartmouth, 1854, A.M., 1857; (LL.D., U. of Colo., 1891); m. Abbie H. Smith, Nov. 14, 1859; 2d, Anna C. Matson, Sept. 11, 1888. Admitted to bar, 1856; in practice at Milwaukee, 1857-63; mem. Wis. Ho. of Rep., 1861. Student Chicago Theol. Sem., 1865-66; ordained Congl. ministry, 1866; pastor, Waukesha, Wis., 1864-65, Lake Mills, Wis., 1866-71, Amboy, Ill., 1871-74, Lombard, Ill., 1874-88, Boulder, Colo., 1888-98. Del. Congl. Nat. councils, 1895, 1898. Author: Divorce, 1889; Narrow Ax in Biblical Criticism, 1897; Chalk Lines Over Morals, 1898; The Ten Words, 1899; Theism et als., 1902; Reminiscences of the Eulogy of Rufus Choate on Daniel Webster, 1914. Home: Lombard, Ill. Died Sept. 29, 1916.

CAWEIN, Madison Julius, author; b. Louisville, Ky., Mar. 23, 1865; s. William and Christiana C.; high sch. edn.; m. Gertrude McKelvey, June 4, 1903. Mem. Nat. Inst. Arts and Letters. Author: Blooms of the Berry, 1887; The Triumph of Music, 1888; Accolon of Gaul, 1889; Lyrics and Idyls, 1890; Poems of Nature and Love, 1893; Idyllic Monologues, 1898; The Vale of Tempe (poems), 1905; Nature-Notes and Impressions (prose and verse), 1906; Complete Poetical Works (5 vols.), 1907; An Ode, in Commemoration of the Founding of the Massachusetts Bay Colony, 1908; The Giant and the Star, 1909; Poems, selected by the author, with Foreword by William Dean Howells; The Republic, 1913; Minions of the Moon, 1913. Home: Louisville, Ky. Died Dec. 7, 1914.

CAYVAN, Georgia (Miss), retired actress; b. Bath, Me., 1858; father died when she was quite young; attended sch. until she was 18, but began giving readings and recitations when she was 14; appeared as Hebe in early production of Pinafore by Boston Ideals; studied elocution under Lewis B. Monroe, Dublin, N.H. Made professional debut as Dolly Dutton in Hazel Kirke, at Madison Sq. Garden; later played Daisy Brown in The Professor, and the principal female rôle in Œdipus Tyrannus under George Riddle, which brought her into prominence. Afterward created parts of Lisa in the White Slave, Sara in Siberia, Hattie in Old Shipmates, Lura in Romany Rye; later leading lady at California Theatre, San Francisco, then successively at Madison Sq. Theatre, in Dion Boucicault's Co. (1887), leading lady in Daniel Frohman's Lyceum Theatre Co., 1887-94; resting in Europe, 1894-95; starring with her own co. in several plays, 1896-97; from 1897 in retirement because of incurable mental breakdown. Was given testimonial benefit by her professional friends Jan. 13, 1903. Died 1906.

CAZEDESSUS, Eugene Romain, realtor; b. at Baton Rouge, La., Apr. 21, 1872; s. Romain and Annie Mary (Ritsch) C.; ed. Magruders Collegiate Inst., Baton Rouge; m. Elvira Erwin Craft, Sept. 9, 1908; children—Camille Erwin, Eugene Romain. Began as asst. bookkeeper Bank of Baton Rouge, 1892, cashier, 1910-18, v.p., 1918-28, pres., 1928-33; commr. pub. parks and sts., Baton Rouge; pres. La. Investment Co., Realty Developers, Inc., Caz-perk Realty, Inc., The Richland Co., Cleon Land Development Co., La. Central Land Co., Cazedessus Sales Co., Bridge City Realty Co., Zadok Realty Co.; sec. Triad Co., Provident Bldg. & Loan Assn. Pres. bd. supervisors of elections, Baton Rouge, 1916—; mem. La. constl. conv., 1921; mem. bldg. com., Sch. Bd., Baton Rouge; v.p. board of supervisors La. State Univ. Chmn. advisory bd. Our Lady of the Lake Sanitarium; mem. exec. com. Baton Rouge chapter Am. Red Cross; dir. Baton Rouge Chamber of Commerce. Democrat. Home: Baton Rouge, La. Died Feb. 1938.

CAZIARC, Louis Vasmer, brig. gen.; b. Boston, July 4, 1844; s. Etienne and Maria Louisa Susetta (de Rochemont) C.; ed. pub. schs., Boston; (M.A., Bowdoin Coll., 1879); m. Esther Alexander Ritchie, 1873. Served as sergt. and 1st sergt., Co. I, 38th Mass. Vol. Inf., Aug. 16, 1862-Apr. 19, 1864; 1st lt. 89th U.S.C.T., Apr. 24, 1864; promoted through grades to col. Arty. Corps, Jan. 23, 1904; brig. gen. and retired at own request, after over 40 yrs.' service, 1906. Bvtd. capt. vols., Mar. 26, 1865, for campaign against city of Mobile, Ala. Was a.d.c. to Gen. George L. Andrews, 1864-65, to Gen. Canby, U.S.A., and adj. gen. 1st, 2d and 5th mil. districts and Dept. of Columbia, 1866-73; was mil. prof. and acting prof. internat. and constl. law, Bowdoin Coll.; exec. officer signal and weather bureau, 1881-84; adj. Arty. Sch., Ft. Monroe, 1887-91; served in Cuba on staffs of Gens. Bates, Wilson, Ludlow and Wood, 1898-1901. Home: Charleston, S.C. Died June 19, 1935.

CECIL, John Giles, physician; b. Monticello, Ky., Nov. 20, 1855; s. Russell Howe and Lucy Anne (Phillips) C.; bro. of Russell C.; B.S., Princeton, 1876; M.D., Hosp. Coll. of Medicine, Louisville, Ky., 1879; m. Elizabeth, d. Rev. Stuart Robinson, of Louisville, Nov. 28, 1882. Adj. prof. obstetrics, 1886-92, prof. materia medica, therapeutics and pub. hygiene, 1899-1905, prof. principles and practice of medicine and clin. med., 1905—, and mem. exec. com., U. of Louisville; prof. obstetrics, Ky. Sch. Medicine, 1892-93; prof. principles and practice of medicine, Louisville Coll. Medicine, 1893-99. Trustee pub. schs., Louisville, short time. Presbyterian. Home: Louisville, Ky. Died Dec. 12, 1913.

CECIL, Russell, clergyman; b. Monticello, Ky., Oct. 1, 1853; s. Russell Howe and Lucy Anne (Phillips) C.; bro. of John Giles C.; A.B., Princeton, 1874, A.M., 1877; grad. Princeton Theol. Sem., 1878; student, U. of Edinburgh, 1878-79; traveled in Europe and Orient, 1879; (D.D., Southwestern Presbyn. U., Clarksville, Tenn., 1893, Princeton, 1895); m. Alma Miller, Jan. 19, 1881. Ordained Presbyn. ministry, Nov. 13, 1879; pastor, Nicholasville, Ky., 1879-85, Maysville, Ky., 1885-89, Selma, Ala., 1889-1900, 2d Ch., Richmond, Va., 1900—. Moderator, Synod of Va., 1910-11; moderator, Gen. Assembly Presbyn. Ch. U.S., 1911-12; chmn. exec. com. of publ.; mem. Council Reformed Chs., holding Presbyn. System; chmn. com. of Southern Presbyn. Ch. in World's Conf. Faith and Order. Trustee Southwestern Presbyn. U., 1893-95, Agnes Scott Inst., Decatur, Ga., 1895-99; pres. trustees Columbia (S.C.) Theol. Sem., 1898-1900; dir. Union Theol. Sem. Democrat. Author: Three Discourses on Baptism, 1892; Education for the Ministry, 1894; In Trust with the Gospel, 1897; Handbook of Theology, 1923. Home: Richmond, Va. Died June 15, 1925.

CELL, George C., educator; b. St. Thomas, Franklin Co., Pa., Feb. 20, 1875; s. John W. and Mary Ellen C.; A.B., Baker U., Baldwin, Kan., 1901; S.T.B., Boston U., 1904; grad. student U. of Berlin, 1904-07, Ph.D., 1907; Ph.D., Boston U., 1908; m. Cornelia Ella Clark, June 26, 1901; children—George Preston (dec.), Clark Wesley, Cornelia Ellen. Prof. historical theology, Boston U. Sch. of Theology, 1908—, also mem. exec. com. Grad. Sch., same univ., 1912-32; chmn. Sch. Com. North Reading, Mass., 1921-27. Mem. Am. Acad. of Arts and Sciences, 1932—. Mem. Progressive Party State Com. of Mass., 1912. Mem. N.E. Conf. M.E. Ch. Mason. Author: A Workable Income Tax, 1901; The Decay of Religion, 1923; The Temperance Revolution, 1930; The Organization of the Temperance Revolution into American Laws, 1932; The Rediscovery of John Wesley, 1935. Home: Reading, Mass. Died Apr. 18, 1937.

CERMAK, Anton Joseph, mayor; b. Prague, Bohemia, May 9, 1873; s. Anton and Catherine (Frank) C.; came to U.S. with parents, 1874; ed. pub. schs., Braidwood, Ill., high sch. and business coll., Chicago; m. Mary Horejs, Dec. 15, 1894 (died 1928); children—Lillian (Mrs. Richey V. Graham), Ella (wife of Frank J. Jirka, M.D.), Helen (Mrs. Floyd M. Kenlay). Engaged in coal mining in Ill. until 1892; in coal and wood business, Chicago, until 1908; organized, 1908, and partner Cermak & Serhant, real estate; pres. Lawndale Bldg. & Loan Assn., 1907—; dir. Lawndale Nat. Bank. Sec. United Societies and Liberty League, 1908; dir. 26th St. Business Men's Assn. Mem. 43d, 44th, 45th and 46th Gen. Assemblies of Ill.; mem. City Council, Chicago, 1912-18; pres. Bd. of Commrs. Cook County, 1922-31; mayor of Chicago for term 1931-35. Chmn. Cook Co. Dem. Com. (mem. nominating com.). Mason. Home: Chicago. Died Mar. 6, 1933.

CESNOLA, Louis Palma di, trustee and dir. Metropolitan Museum of Art, 1878—; b. Rivarolo, Piedmont, Italy, June 29, 1832; ed. in Turin (LL.D., Columbia; also Princeton). At 17 took part in war against Austria for independence of Italy and was promoted lt. on battlefield at Novara, 1849, for merit; came to New York, 1860; apptd., 1861, maj., then lt. col., 11th N.Y. cav.; promoted col., 4th N.Y. cav., 1862; at the battle of Aldie, Va., was severely wounded, taken prisoner and 9 months in Libby Prison; promoted brig. gen.; U.S. consul at Cyprus, 1865-77; made extensive archæol. explorations, unearthed statues, inscriptions, sarcophagi, architectural remains, vases, terracottas, bronzes, gold and silver jewels at Curium, etc.; all are now exhibited in the Metropolitan Museum of Art; awarded, Dec. 1897, Congressional medal of honor; gold medal and several knightly orders from King of Italy. Author: Cyprus: Its Cities, Tombs and Temples. Died 1904.

CESSNA, Orange Howard, clergyman, educator; b. Kenton, O., July 31, 1852; s. Jonathan Wilson and Elizabeth Jane (Mathews) C.; B.S., Ia. State Coll. Agr. and Mechanic Arts, 1872; B.D., Garrett Bibl. Inst., Evanston, Ill., 1885, D.D., 1900; hon. M.A., Cornell Coll., 1901; m. Lillian May Wheeler, Aug. 31, 1881 (dec.); children—Ethyl, Frank Wheeler (dec.). Ordained M.E. ministry, 1885; pastor Nunda, Ill., 1885-87, Belvidere, 1887-91, 1st Ch., Elgin, 1891-93, Dixon, 1893-98, Wesley Ch., Chicago, 1898-1900; head of dept. of history and psychology, 1900-21, prof. psychology, 1921—, also chaplain, Ia. State Coll. Agr. and Mechanic Arts, 1900—. Republican. Home: Ames, Ia. Died Oct. 22, 1932.

CHACE, Arnold Buffum, cotton mfr.; b. Valley Falls, R.I., Nov. 10, 1845; s. Samuel B. and Elizabeth (Buffum) C.; A.B., Brown U., 1866, A.M., 1869 (Sc.D., 1892); studied Lawrence Scientific Sch. (Harvard), 1867, École de Médecine, Paris, 1868; m. Eliza C. Greene, Oct. 24, 1871. Began in cotton mfg. business at Valley Falls, R.I., 1869; treas. Valley Falls Co. Trustee, 1876—, treas., 1882-1900, then chancellor Brown U. Home: Albion, R.I. Died Feb. 28, 1932.

CHACE, Jonathan, senator; b. Fall River, Mass., July 22, 1829; s. Harvey and Hannah (Wood) C.; ed. Friends Sch., Providence; (hon. A.M., Brown U., 1882); m. Jane C. Moon, Oct. 12, 1854. Mem. firm of J. H. & J. Chace, cotton mfrs.; pres. Phœnix Nat. Bank. Mem. R.I. Senate, 1876-78; mem. 47th and 48th Congresses (1881-85); elected U.S. senator, 1885, to fill unexpired term (1885-87) of Henry B. Anthony, deceased, and resigned from Congress; reelected for term, 1887-93, but resigned from senate, Apr. 9, 1889. Republican. Trustee Brown U., 1892—. Home: Valley Falls, R.I. Died June 30, 1917.

CHADBOURNE, George Storrs, clergyman; b. Somersworth, N.H., Dec. 30, 1833; s. Samuel and Sophronia W. (Odiorne) C.; A.B., Wesleyan U., Conn., 1858, A.M., 1861 (D.D., 1883; S.T.D., Claflin, 1884); m. Martha M. Ransom, June 14, 1898. Teacher, 1858-63, asso. prin., 1860-63, Troy Conf. Acad., Vt.; ordained M.E. ministry, 1858; in ministry of the ch. 50 yrs., Troy and N.E. confs.; presiding elder Boston and Cambridge dists., 1886-94; del. Gen. Confs., M.E. Ch., 1888-92; prof. ednl. instns., 5 yrs.; trustee and sec. Ch. Aid Soc. of N.E. Conf., etc. Home: Melrose, Mass. Died Aug. 22, 1923.

CHADBOURNE, Thomas Lincoln, lawyer; b. Houghton, Mich., 1871; s. Thomas Lincoln and Georgina (Kay) C.; student U. of Mich., 1890-91; m. Emily R., d. late R. T. Crane, of Chicago, Nov. 7, 1896 (dec.); m. 2d, Mrs. Grace (Runnion) Wassall, 1906 (died 1919); 1 son, Leroy; m. 3d, Marjorie, d. late Dr. H. Holbrook Curtis, of New York, 1920; children—Marjorie, Leila. Admitted to bar, 1892; began practice in Milwaukee, Wis.; removed to Chicago, 1895, later to New York; mem. Chadbourne, Stanchfield & Levy; officer or dir. many corps. Home: Brookville, L.I., N.Y. Died June 15, 1938.

CHADDOCK, Charles Gilbert, M.D.; b. Jonesville, Mich., Nov. 14, 1861; s. Gilbert and Anna (Sinclair) C.; student lit. dept., U. of Mich., 1879-80, M.D., 1885; post-grad. studies, U. of Munich, and hosps. of Paris; m. Adelaide Gowans Macpherson, Dec. 18, 1890. Asst. med. supt. Northern Mich. Asylum, 1889-92; resided in Germany, 1888-89, in France, 1896-1900; prof. nervous diseases, 1892—; then prof. emeritus diseases of the nervous system, med. dept. of St. Louis U. Fellow Am. Psychiatric Assn. Translator: Psychopathia Sexualis (Krafft-Ebing), 1892; Hypnotism (same), 1889; Suggestive Therapeutics (von Schrenck-Notzing), 1895; Insanity (Krafft-Ebing), 1904. Author: Outline of Psychiatry; Sexual Crimes; Hamilton's System of Legal Medicine; Peterson and Haines' Text-Book of Legal Medicine and Toxicology. Home: St. Louis, Mo. Died July 20, 1936.

CHADDOCK, Robert Emmet, statistician; b. Minerva, O., Apr. 16, 1879; s. David C. and Alwilda A. (Brothers) C.; B.A., Wooster (O.) College, 1900; M.A., Columbia U., 1907, Ph.D. from same, 1908; LL.D., Wooster Coll., 1929; m. Rose A. Fallbush, July 16, 1910; 1 dau., Helen Roberta. Teacher Wooster Coll., 1900-05; instr. economics, Columbia, 1907-09; asst. prof. economics and statistics, Wharton Sch. of Finance (U. of Pa.), 1909-11; asst. prof. statistics and economics, 1911-12, asso. prof., 1912-22, prof. sociology and statistics, 1922—, Columbia. Chmn. advisory com. to dir. of census, apptd. by Am. Statis. Assn.; mem. advisory council Milbank Memorial Fund; mem. Am. Com. of Internat. Union for the Scientific Investigation of Population Problems; chmn. advisory com. on research, Welfare Council N.Y. City, vice-chmn. com. on research in med. economics. Republican. Presbyn. Author: (thesis) Ohio Before 1850, 1908; (with others) Statistical Sources for Demographic Studies of Greater New York, 1920, 23; Principles and Methods of Statistics,

1925; Exercises in Statistical Methods, 1928; (with others) Population of the City of New York, 1890-1930, 1932. Home: New York, N.Y. Died Oct. 21, 1940.

CHADSEY, Charles Ernest, educator; b. Nebraska City, Nebraska, Oct. 15, 1870; s. Franklin and Sallie Maria (Barnum) C.; A.B., Leland Stanford Jr. U., 1892, A.M., 1893; A.M., Columbia, 1894, Ph.D., 1897; Litt.D., Denver U., 1909; m. Callie Worth Price, June 29, 1897; 1 son, Charles Price. Prin. Durango High Sch., 1894-97; supt. city schs., Durango, 1897-1900; supt. North Side schs., Denver, 1900-03; asst. city supt. schs., 1904-07, supt. city schs., Sept. 1, 1907-Aug. 1912, Denver; supt. public schs., Detroit, Aug. 1912-Mar. 1919; supt. schs., Chicago, Mar.-June 1919; prof. ednl. administration, U. of Chicago, summer quarter, 1919; dean Coll. of Edn., U. of Ill., Sept. 1919—. Lecturer on School Problems, U. of Colo., 1900-03; on administration and modern ednl. movements, U. of Wis., 1911. Pres. dept. of superintendence, N.E.A., 1911-12; mem. Ednl. Council, N.E.A. Congregationalist. Author: The Struggle Between President Johnson and Congress Over Reconstruction, 1897. Joint author of Efficiency Arithmetic, Chadsey-Spain Readers, America in the Making. Home: Urbana, Ill. Died Apr. 12, 1930.

CHADWICK, Charles Wesley, engraver; b. Red-Hook-on-the-Hudson, N.Y., Feb. 8, 1861; s. Rev. T. W. and Mary F. C.; A.B., Wesleyan U., Conn., 1884, A.M.; studied wood engraving under Frederick Juengling, William Miller and Frank French; m. Agnes F. Hardy, Oct. 30, 1902; children—John Vincent, Sumner Stone (dec.), Donald Hardy, Charles W. Work has appeared mostly in Century Magazine and Scribner's Magazine; later engaged in finishing and engraving halftone plates. Exhibited at Paris Expn., 1900; bronze medal, Buffalo Expn., 1901, St. Louis Expn., 1904; silver medal, Panama Expn., San Francisco, 1915. Home: Milford, Conn. Died Aug. 25, 1940.

CHADWICK, Clarence Wells; b. Rensselaerville, N.Y.; s. Aaron and Emma S. (Wells) C.; grad. Poly. Inst. Brooklyn, 1884; B.S. in M.E., Worcester Poly. Inst., 1888; C.S.B., Mass. Metaphysical Coll., 1907; m. Ida Louise Fleming, June 30, 1898. Began as practitioner Christian Science, 1891, as teacher, 1908, as lecturer, 1913; has lectured throughout U.S., Can., British Isles, New Zealand, Australia, Africa, China, Japan, etc.; retired from lecture field, 1923. Mem. Christian Science Bd. of Lectureship, 1913-23. Republican. Home: Omaha, Neb. Died Nov. 10, 1933.

CHADWICK, French Ensor, rear adm.; b. Morgantown, W.Va., Feb. 29, 1844; s. Daniel Clark and Margaret Eliza (Evans) C.; apptd. to U.S. Naval Acad. from W.Va., 1861, grad. 1864; m. Cornelia J. Miller, Nov. 20, 1878. Ensign, Nov. 1, 1866; promoted through grades to rear adm., Oct. 11, 1903. Summer of 1864, was attached to the Marblehead in pursuit of the Confederate steamers Florida and Tallahassee; various assignments to 1882; naval attaché, Am. Embassy, London, 1882-89; comd. Yorktown, 1889-91; chief, intelligence office, 1892-93; chief Bur. of Equipment, 1893-97; comd. New York, and chief of staff of Admiral Sampson, during war with Spain, participated in the most important engagements in the Atlantic during the war, and was advanced 5 numbers in rank for eminent and conspicuous conduct in battle; pres. Naval War Coll., Newport, 1900-03; duty in connection with Naval War Coll., 1903-04; comdr.-in-chief S. Atlantic Squadron, 1904; retired, Feb. 28, 1906. Mem. Nat. Inst. Arts and Letters. Interested in municipal government, on which he often wrote and spoke. Mem. Newport Representative Council 2 terms, and mem. Newport Park Commn. Author: Causes of the Civil War (Am. Nation Series, Vol. XIX), 1906; Relations of the United States and Spain, 1776-1898. Home: Newport, R.I. Died Jan. 27, 1919.

CHADWICK, George Whitefield, conductor, composer; b. Lowell, Mass., Nov. 13, 1854; hon. A.M., Yale, 1897; LL.D., Tufts, 1905. Dir. N.E. Conservatory of Music. Composed 5 overtures (Rip Van Winkle, Thalia, Melpomene, Adonais, Euterpe); 3 symphonies, opera Judith, various choral works, and smaller orchestral works—songs, string quartettes, etc.; ode for dedication of Chicago Expn., 1893. Mem. Am. Acad. Arts and Letters. Address: Boston. Died Apr. 4, 1931.

CHADWICK, James Read, M.D.; b. Boston, Nov. 2, 1844; grad. Harvard Med. School, 1871; m. Katherine Maria Lyman, 1871. Went to Europe; began practice in Boston, 1873; specialist in gynecology, founder, sec. (1876-82), and pres. (1897) Am. Gynecol. Soc.; librarian Boston Med. Library, 1875—; 1st pres. Harvard Med. Alumni Assn., 1891-94. Home: Boston. Died 1905.

CHADWICK, John White, pastor 2d Unitarian Soc. of Brooklyn, 1864—; b. Marblehead, Mass., Oct. 19, 1840; grad. Cambridge Div. School, 1864; m. Annie Horton Hathaway, June 28, 1865. Author: A Book of Poems; Cap'n Chadwick, Marblehead Skipper and Shoemaker, 1906. Died 1904.

CHADWICK, Stephen James, judge; b. Roseburg, Ore., Apr. 28, 1863; s. Stephen Fowler and Jane Ann (Smith) C.; ed. Willamette U. and U. of Ore.; LL.D., Whitman College, 1927; m. Emma Plummer, Mar. 2, 1887; children—Claire Leslie (Mrs. Herndon Jansen Maury), Harriet Jane (Mrs. Arthur Thompson Karr), Stephen Fowler, Elizabeth. Admitted to bar, 1885; practiced at Colfax, Wash.; mayor, Colfax, 1891-93; mem. Bd. State Land Commrs., 1894-97; judge Superior Ct., Whitman Co., 1900-08; asso. justice Supreme Ct. of Wash. for terms 1908-15, 1915-21 (chief justice for term, 1919-21); resigned June 1, 1919, to resume private practice; mem. Chadwick & Chadwick, Seattle, Wash. Democrat. Home: Seattle, Wash. Died Nov. 19, 1931.

CHAFFEE, Adna Romanza, lt. gen. U.S.A.; b. Orwell, O., Apr. 14, 1842; s. Truman B. and Grace (Hyde) C.; ed. pub. schs. of Ohio; (LL.D., Tufts Coll., 1905); m. Annie Frances Rockwell, Mar. 31, 1875. Pvt., sergt. and 1st sergt., Troop K, 6th Cav., July 22, 1861-May 12, 1863; 2d lt. 6th Cav., Mar. 13, 1863; advanced through grades to maj. gen. U.S.V., July 8, 1898; hon. disch., Apr. 13, 1899; brig. gen. U.S.V., Apr. 13, 1899; maj. gen., July 19, 1900; col. 8th U.S. Cav., May 8, 1899; maj. gen., Feb. 4, 1901; lt. gen., Jan. 9, 1904. Bvtd.: 1st lt., July 3, 1863, for Gettysburg; capt., Mar. 31, 1865, for Dinwiddie C.H., Va.; maj., Mar. 7, 1868, for engagement with Indians, Paint Creek, Tex., Mar. 7, 1868; lt. col., Feb. 27, 1890, for Red River, Tex., Aug. 30, 1874, and against Indians at Big Dry Wash, Ariz., July 17, 1882. Served in Army of Potomac during Civil War; mostly on the plains, 1865-98; in Spanish-Am. War comd. 3d Brigade, 2d Div., 5th Army Corps, June-Aug. 1898; comd. 2d Div., 5th Corps, Aug.-Sept., 1st Div., 4th Corps, Nov.-Dec. 1898; chief of staff, Div. of Cuba, Dec. 25, 1898-May 1900; comd. China relief expdn., June 24, 1900-May 21, 1901; comd. Div. of the Philippines, July 4, 1901-Oct. 1, 1902; comd. Dept. of the East, 1902-03; asst. to chief of staff, 1903-04; chief of staff, U.S.A., Jan. 9, 1904-Feb. 1, 1906; retired at own request, over 40 yrs.' service, Feb. 1, 1906. Died Nov. 1, 1914.

CHAFEE, Adna Romanza, army officer; b. Junction City, Kan., Sept. 23, 1884; s. Adna Romanza and Anna Frances (Rockwell) C.; B.S., U.S. Mil. Acad., 1906; grad. Mounted Service Sch., Ft. Riley, Kan., 1908, advanced course, same, 1912, Gen. Staff Coll., Langres, France, 1917, Sch. of the Line, Ft. Leavenworth, Kan., 1921, Army War Coll., Washington, D.C., 1925; m. Ethel Warren Huff, Dec. 15, 1908; 1 son, Adna Romanza. Commd. 1st lt., 1912, advanced through grades to brig. gen., Nov. 1, 1938; maj. Inf., Nat. Army, and assigned as adj., 81st Div., Camp Jackson, S.C., 1917; served in St. Mihiel and Meuse-Argonne offensives and with Army of Occupation, World War; comdg. gen. 7th Cavalry Brigade (mechanized), 1938—. Awarded D.S.M. Episcopalian. Died Aug. 22, 1941.

CHAFFEY, Andrew M., banker; b. Kingston, Ont., Can., Apr. 9, 1874; s. George and Annette Augusta (McCord) C.; brought to U.S., 1881, naturalized citizen, 1898; ed. Prince Alfred College, Adelaide, South Australia; LL.D., University of Southern Calif., 1935; m. Maud Taylor Macalister, of Dublin, Ireland, July 21, 1900; children—Maud Elswood (Mrs. J. Derry Kerr), Kathleen Macalister (Mrs. J. B. Murray), Andrew Stewart. Agt. Union Bank of Australia and Royal Bank of Australia, Mildura, Australia, 1896-97; pres. Imperial (Calif.) Water Co. No. 1, 1900; organizer First Nat. Bank of Imperial, 1901, First Nat. Bank of Ontario (Calif), 1902; organizer and was pres. Am. Savings Bank, Los Angeles (name now California Bank), then chmn. bd. Mem. Calif. State Council of Defense and chmn. Allies' Aid Assn., World War; dir. Community Development Assn. Trustee and treas. U. of Southern Calif.; trustee Chaffey Coll. Trust. Republican. Episcopalian. Mason. Home: Los Angeles, Calif. Died July 16, 1941.

CHAFFIN, Lucien Gates, organist; b. Worcester, Mass., Mar. 23, 1846; A.B., Brown U., 1867; m. Gertrude Sidway, Oct. 16, 1876 (dec.); 1 dau., Mrs. Ethel Balthasar. Headmaster St. Mark's Sch., Southboro, Mass., and Heathcote Sch., Buffalo, N.Y., and prof. Latin, Hobart Coll., several yrs. Many yrs. concert organist; exhibitor of great organ at Centennial Expn., Phila., 1876; organist at cathedrals in Boston, Buffalo and other large cities; sec. People's Symphony Concerts, New York; mus. editor Buffalo Express, 1879-83, N.Y. Commercial Advertiser, 1884-90. Episcopalian. Author: Song-Writing and Song-Making. Home: Montclair, N.J. Died May 26, 1927.

CHAFIN, Eugene Wilder, temperance advocate; b. E. Troy, Wis., Nov. 1, 1852; s. Samuel E. and Betsey (Pollard) C.; ed. pub. schs.; LL.B., U. of Wis., 1875; m. Carrie A. Hunkins, Nov. 24, 1881. Admitted to bar, 1875; in practice at Waukesha, 1876-1900; supt. Washingtonian Home, Chicago, 1901-04. Active as speaker and organizer in temperance and prohibition movements. Prohibition candidate for Congress, Wis., 1882, Chicago, 1902; for atty. gen. Wis., 1886, 1900, for gov. Wis., 1898, and for atty. gen. Ill., 1904; for President of U.S., 1908, 1912. Admitted to bar Supreme Ct. of U.S., 1909; removed to Ariz., 1909. Home: Long Beach, Calif. Died Nov. 30, 1920.

CHAILLÉ, Stanford Emerson, physician; b. Natchez, Miss., July 9, 1830; s. William H. and Mary (Stanford) C.; A.B., Harvard, 1851, A.M., 1854; M.D., U. of La. (then Tulane), 1853 (LL.D., 1901); student in Europe, 3 yrs.; m. Laura Mountfort, Feb. 23, 1857. Surg. and med. insp. C.S.A., Army of Tenn., 1862-65; demonstrator of anatomy, etc., 1858-68, prof. physiology, pathology, anatomy, hygiene, 1868-1908, dean, 1885-1908, emeritus, Tulane U. Author: Origin and Progress of Medical Jurisprudence. Home: New Orleans, La. Died 1911.

CHAILLÉ-LONG, Charles, soldier, diplomat; b. Princess Anne, Somerset Co., Md., July 2, 1842; s. Littleton Long of Chaillé and Anne Mitchell (Costen) Long; ed. Washington Acad., Md., 1860; LL.B., Columbia, 1880; m. Marie Amélie Hammond, July 16, 1890. Served all ranks to capt., 11th Md. Vols., 1862-65; apptd. lt. col. Egyptian army, 1869; chief 1st, 2d and 3d sects. gen. staff, Egyptian army, 1869-73; chief staff to Gen. Gordon, gov. gen. Egyptian Soudan, 1874-77; executed treaty with King M'Tesa, annexing Uganda to Egypt, 1874; discovered Lake Ibrahim, solving problem of Nile source, Aug., 1874; wounded at M'Rossi, Aug. 17, 1874; cited in general orders No. 18, decorated Cross Medjidieh, for expdns. Niam-Niam and East Coast Africa; promoted col. and bey, Nov. 16, 1874; retired Aug. 31, 1877. Acting consul of U.S. at Alexandria, when titular agents had abandoned consulate, June-Aug., 1882, making consulate refuge for all nationalities after bombardment; decorated Cross Osmanieh; sec. legation and consul gen. U.S. to Corea, 1887-89; sec. Universal Postal Congress, Washington, 1897; sec., Aug. 1897, and chargé d' affaires, Oct. 1897-Sept. 1898, U.S. Spl. Commn. to Paris Expn., 1900. Chevalier Légion d' Honneur of France; hon. mem. Institut Égyptien. Gen. assembly of Md. conferred by unanimous vote resolutions of thanks and gold medal for services to science and valiant conduct in Central Africa and Egypt, Mar. 3, 1904; awarded gold medal by Am. Geog. Soc. for final solution of Nile source problem, Feb. 15, 1910. Died Mar. 24, 1917.

CHALFANT, Harry Malcolm; b. Washington County, Pa., June 26, 1869; s. Henry Sweitzer (M.D.) and Lucinda (Crow) Chalfant; grad. California (Pa.) State Normal Sch., 1886; A.B., Washington and Jefferson Coll., 1892, A.M., 1895, D.D., 1922; m. Elizabeth Fitz Randolph, Apr. 22, 1896; children—Jean Elizabeth (Mrs. Allan F. Gwynne), Mary Fitz Randolph (Mrs. Carl Heath Kopf), Dorothy Lynde, Beulah Carol, Anna Louise. Ordained M.E. ministry, 1893; pastorates in Pa. until 1909; editorial staff Pittsburgh Christian Advocate, 1902-08; editor Keystone Citizen, 1909-10; editor American Issue (Pa. edit.), 1910-32; dist. supt. Anti-Saloon League, 1932—. Del. Gen. Conf., M.E. Ch., 1928; mem. nat. exec. com. Anti-Saloon League of America. Republican. Author: Father Penn and John Barleycorn, 1920; Paying the Fiddler (play), 1929; These Agitators and Their Idea, 1931. Home: Narberth, Pa. Died Nov. 10, 1932.

CHALIAPIN, Feodor (Ivanovitch), basso; b. Kazan, Russia, Feb. 14, 1873. Sang with operetta co., 1890-91; studied with Usatov, at Tiflis, 1892; appeared in grand opera in Petrograd, 1895; sang in Paris, 1906; with Met. Opera Co., New York, 1906-08; made several tours of U.S. Author: Man and Mask, 1932. Home: Paris, France. Died Apr. 12, 1938.

CHALKLEY, Lyman, lawyer, educator; b. Richmond, Va., Oct. 20, 1861; s. Otway Hebron and Susan Marian (Jordan) C.; Richmond Coll.; grad. U. of Va., 1882; studied law, Columbia U. and univs. of Berlin and Bonn; LL.B., Washington and Lee U., 1889; m. Eleanor Desha Breckinridge, June 27, 1899; children—Preston Breckinridge (dec.), Marian (dec.), Lyman, Issa Desha (Mrs. Ernest B. Harper). Began practice of law at Covington, Va., 1889; elected by Va. legislature judge Dist. of Allegheny and Craig cos., 1891, term of 6 yrs.; apptd. after 2 yrs., by Gov. O'Ferrall, to hold court for Augusta Co., and moved to Staunton; elected by legislature, 1893, for unexpired term, and resigned judgeship of Allegheny and Craig; judge Dist. of Augusta and Highland, 1898-1904; moved to Lexington, Ky.; apptd. dean Ky. U. (Transylvania), 1895, and revived the law dept.; dean Law Sch., U. of the South, Sewanee, Tenn., 1907-10; prof. law, U. of Ky., 1910-31, prof. emeritus, 1931—, dean Coll. of Law, 1923. Trustee Margaret Hall, Versailles, Ky. Democrat. Episcopalian: historiographer Diocese of Lexington. Mason. Home: Lexington, Ky. Died Apr. 21, 1934.

CHALMERS, Hugh, mfr.; b. Dayton, O., Oct. 3, 1873; s. Thomas and Jeanette (Bell) C.; ed. pub. schs. and bus. coll.; m. Frances L. Houser, Aug. 22, 1901; children—Helen Janet, Hugh, Frances H. (dec.), Bruce, Peggy. Began in office with Nat. Cash Register Co., Dayton, at 14, v.p. and gen. mgr., 1900-07; has served as pres. E. R. Thomas Detroit Motor Co. and its successors, Chalmers-Detroit Motor Co.

and Chalmers Motor Co.; dir. Chrysler Corp. Home: Bloomfield Hills, Mich. Died June 2, 1932.

CHALMERS, James, educator; b. Strathroy, Ont., Can., Nov. 22, 1859; s. Andrew and Catherine (Doyle) C.; bro. of William Wallace and Thomas C.; student U. of Mich., 1887; A.B., Eureka (Ill.) Coll., 1888, Ph.D., 1889; fellow U. of St. Andrews, Scotland, 1897-99; D.D., Wheaton (Ill.) Coll., 1902; LL.D., Western Mich. Coll., 1904; m. Elizabeth Anderson, Aug. 30, 1888; children—James Anderson, William Wallace, Elizabeth, Robert Burns, Margaret, Agnes, Herbert Wallace. Prof. English, Eureka Coll., 1888-89, Ohio State U., 1889-94; pres. Wis. State Normal Sch., 1894-97; pastor Congl. Ch., Elgin, Ill., 1899-1902; pres. S.D. State Coll., 1902-06; pastor Congl. Ch., Fitchburg, Mass., 1906-14; supt. schs., Fitchburg, 1914-17; pres. State Teachers College, Framingham, Mass., 1917-31. Lecturer on literature, Columbia summer sessions, 1921—; Saturday lecturer Boston U., 1922—. Mem. Mass. State Bd. of Edn., 1915-17. Mason. Author: Bible Emblems and Oriental Imagery, 1900; Seven Churches, 1913. Home: Framingham, Mass. Died Jan. 7, 1937.

CHALMERS, Louis Henry, lawyer; b. Jamestown, O., Jan. 13, 1861; s. James Clark and Hariet (Jenkins) C.; ed. grammar and high schs., Jamestown; LL.B., Cincinnati (Ohio) Coll. Law Sch., 1884; m. Laura E. Coats, Jan. 13, 1891. Practiced in Phoenix, Ariz., 1884—; mem. Chalmers, Fennemore & Nairn; chmn. of board, 1928—, also pres., 1929—, Phoenix Nat. Bank, Phoenix Sav. Bank & Trust Company, atty. Nev. Cons. Copper Co.; solicitor for Ariz. for A.,T.&S.F. Ry.; etc. City atty., Phoenix, 1889, 1890; mem. Legislative Assembly of Ariz., 1891-93 (chmn. judiciary com.). Democrat. Mason. Home: Phoenix, Ariz. Died Feb. 19, 1934.

CHALMERS, Robert Scott, clergyman; b. Dundee, Scotland, Jan. 22, 1882; s. William and Helen Walker (Miller) C.; ed. Edinburgh U.; hon. M.A., Kenyon Coll., 1922, D.D., 1931; m. Adela W. Burnet, 1905; children—Margaret Burnet, William Scott, James Burnet. Deacon, 1914, priest, 1915, P.E. Ch.; deacon St. Paul's Ch., Akron, O., 1914-15; rector Trinity Ch., Tiffin, 1915-18, St. Mark's Ch., Toledo, 1918-24; dean St. Matthew's Cathedral, Dallas, Tex., 1924-30; rector Grace and St. Peter's Ch., Baltimore, 1930—. Mem. Nat. Council P.E. Ch., term 1924-30; mem. Standing Com. Diocese of Dallas, Evergreen (Colo.) Summer Conf.; mem. Standing Com. Diocese of Md., 1930—. Trustee Donaldson Sch. (Ilchester, Md.), St. James' Sch. for Boys. Mason. Home: Baltimore, Md. Died Apr. 12, 1935.

CHALMERS, Stephen, author; b. Dunoon, Scotland, Feb. 29, 1880; s. Stephen and Katharine Maria (McFarland) C.; ed. Dunoon Grammar Sch.; m. 2d, Helen A. Brereton, 1924. Went to Jamaica, W.I., 1898; sub-editor The Daily Gleaner, Kingston, 1901; with newspapers, N.Y. City, 1902-07. Author: The Vanishing Smuggler, 1909; When Love Calls Men to Arms, 1910; The Trail of a Tenderfoot, 1911; A Prince of Romance, 1911; Footloose and Free, 1912; The Beloved Physician—Edward Livingston Trudeau, 1915; The Penny Piper of Saranac, 1916; The Hermit Thrush (verse), 1927; House of the Two Green Eyes, 1928; The Crime in Car 13, 1930; The Affair of the Gallows Tree, 1931; The Whispering Ghost, 1932; Blood on the Heather, 1933; Campobello Days With F. D. R. (essay), 1933. Home: Laguna Beach, Calif. Died Dec. 14, 1935.

CHALMERS, Thomas, clergyman, educator; b. Algoma, Mich., Jan. 8, 1869; s. Andrew and Catherine (Doyle) C.; brother of James and William Wallace Chalmers; A.B., Harvard, 1891; studied univs. of Marburg, Germany, and St. Andrew's, Scotland; D.D., Dartmouth, 1908; m. Maude Virginia Smith, June 20, 1894; children—Thomas Lewis (dec.), Marjorie, Philip Owen, Donald Creighton, Virginia, Mary Eleanor, Barbara, Duncan Macfarlane, Douglas. Ordained, Congl. ministry, 1894; pastor, Port Huron, Mich., 1894-1900; dean Mich. Mil. Acad., 1895-96; pastor 1st Ch., Manchester, N.H., 1900-16; was prin. and propr. Allen-Chalmers School, Newton, Mass.; prof. history Boston Univ., 1920—; winter lecturer at Rollins Coll., Fla. Author of The Juvenile Revival, Alexander Campbell in Scotland, The Town Church of Manchester, Franco-American Goodwill (reprint of Articles in La Nouvelle Revue, Paris). Pres. Pembroke (N.H.) Sanatorium, 1908-16. Pres. Rep. State Conv., N.H., 1912; elected mem. N.H. Senate, 1912 (Rep. caucus nominee for pres. Senate, 1913). Mason. Home: Winter Park, Fla. and Hyannisport, Mass. Died July 4, 1940.

CHALMERS, Thomas Stuart, mfr.; b. Chicago, Sept. 21, 1881; s. William James and Joan (Pinkerton) C.; grad. St. Paul's School, Concord, N.H., 1899; student mech. engring. course, Cornell U., 1899-1904; unmarried. Pres. Chalmers & Williams, Inc., mining and crushing machinery; v.p. Fraser & Chalmers, Inc. Republican. Episcopalian. Home: Chicago Heights, Ill.. Died Mar. 26, 1923.

CHALMERS, William Everett, denominational sec.; b. Paterson, N.J., Nov. 13, 1868; s. Alexander Keith and Sarah (Morrison) C.; A.B., Brown U., 1893; B.D., U. of Chicago, 1897; (D.D. from Central U. of Iowa, 1915); m. Mary Duncklee Maynard, May 11, 1897; children—Ruth S. (Mrs. A. L. Rogers), Paul Maynard, William Ellison, Gordon Keith. Ordained Baptist ministry, 1897; pastor Parmly Memorial Ch., Jersey City, N.J., 1897-98, West End Ch., Brooklyn, 1899-1903, Waukesha, Wis., 1903-06, Morgan Park Ch., Chicago, 1906-11; gen. sec. Bapt. Young People's Union of America, 1911-15; sec. for religious edn. of Am. Baptist Publication Soc. Progressive. Author: The Coming School of the Church; Church School Objectives; A Church School Program; Church School Improvement; The Church and the Church School. Home: Merwood, Pa. Died Apr. 5, 1928.

CHALMERS, William James, mfr.; b. Chicago, July 10, 1852; s. Thomas and Janet (Telfer) C.; ed. pub. grammar and high schs., Chicago; m. Joan, d. late Allan Pinkerton, Oct., 1878. After leaving school was apprenticed to the Eagle Works Mfg. Co., of which his father was then gen. supt.; in 1872 became associated with his father in the firm of Fraser & Chalmers, of which was made v.p. and treas. upon incorporation, 1889, pres., 1891; built works at Erith, Kent., Eng., 1889, known as Fraser & Chalmers, Ltd.; united with Allis Engine Works at Milwaukee, the Bullock Works, Cincinnati, Gates Iron Works, Chicago, and Dickson Works, Scranton, Pa., as the Allis-Chalmers Co., 1901, of which was chmn. exec. com., v.p. and treas. until 1906 (retired); with Chalmers & Williams, mfrs. mining machinery, Chicago, 1911—; pres. Bates Expanded Steel Truss Co. Formerly mem. Chicago Bd. of Edn., and a dir. World's Columbian Expn.; then life trustee Field Museum of Natural History and Science. Died Dec. 10, 1938.

CHAMBERLAIN, Abiram, governor; b. Colebrook, Conn., Dec. 7, 1837; s. Abiram and Sophronia Ruth (Burt) C.; ed. Williston Sem., Easthampton, Mass.; (LL.D., Wesleyan U., 1903); m. Charlotte E. Roberts, Nov. 21, 1872. Banker, 1863—; pres. Home Nat. Bank of Meriden, Conn., Winthrop Hotel Co.; v.p. Meriden Savings Bank; dir. Meriden & Waterbury R.R. Co., Meriden Cutlery Co., etc. Served in Meriden City Council; mem. Conn. Ho. of Rep., 1877; state comptroller, 1901-02; gov. of Conn., 1903-05. Republican. Home: Meriden, Conn. Died 1911.

CHAMBERLAIN, Alexander Francis, anthropologist; b. Kenninghall, Eng., Jan. 12, 1865; s. George and Maria (Anderton) C.; grad. Toronto (Can.) U., 1886, A.M., 1889; Ph.D., Clark U., 1892; m. Isabel Cushman, 1898. Then prof. anthropology, Clark U. Made spl. investigations of the Kootenay (British Columbia) Indians under auspices British Assn., 1891. Editor Jour. Am. Folk-Lore, 1900-08; dept. editor Am. Anthropologist; co-editor Jour. of Religious Psychology. Alderman-at-large, Worcester, 1905; chmn. Lincoln Centenary Com., Worcester, 1909. Author; Child and Childhood in Folk Thought, 1896; The Child—A Study in the Evolution of Man, 1900; Poems, 1904. Home: Worcester, Mass. Died Apr. 8, 1914.

CHAMBERLAIN, Daniel Henry, governor, S. Carolina; b. W. Brookfield, Mass., June 23, 1835; s. Eli C.; prep. edn. Phillips Acad., Andover, Mass., and high school, Worcester; grad. Yale Univ., 1862, A.M., 1867 (LL.D., Univ. of S.C.); grad. Harvard Law School, 1863; m. Alice C. Ingersoll, Dec., 1869. Served in Union army; capt. 5th Mass. colored inf., 1864-65; cotton planter, S.C., 1866 del. S.C. Constl. Conv., 1868; atty. gen. S.C., 1868-72; gov. S.C., 1874-77. Home: Columbia, S.C. Died 1907.

CHAMBERLAIN, Eugene Tyler, b. Albany, N.Y., Sept. 28, 1856; s. Frank and Celia Deborah (Tyler) C.; A.B., Harvard, 1878; m. Mary Lee Barnette, Apr. 17, 1900 (died 1904). Asso. editor Albany Journal, polit. corr. at Albany for Boston, New York, Phila. and Washington papers, and editor Albany Argus, 1882-93; U.S. commr. of navigation, Dec. 1893-Sept. 1, 1921, when attached to Bur. Foreign and Domestic Commerce. Am. del. Internat. Conf. on Safety at Sea, London, 1913. Home: Albany, N.Y. Died June 28, 1929.

CHAMBERLAIN, Francis Asbury, banker; b. Bangor, Me., Apr. 20, 1855; s. James T. and Caroline (Emery) C.; removed with parents to Minn., 1857; student Univ. of Minn.; m. Frances Taft Foss., May 23, 1883. Began as collector Merchants Nat. Bank, Minneapolis; later was pres. Security Nat. Bank, and chmn. bd. dirs. First & Security Nat. Bank, now First Nat. Bank & Trust Co., of which became chmn. exec. com. Republican. Methodist. Mason. Home: Minneapolis, Minn. Died Dec. 17, 1940.

CHAMBERLAIN, Frank, retired; b. Romulus (now Varick), N.Y., Dec. 1826; s. Jacob P. and Catherine (Kuney) C.; was 2 yrs. at Geneva (now Hobart) Coll., then entered Yale, but was unable to complete course of graduation because of failing eyesight; studied law under Gov. William H. Seward, but did not enter profession; m. Celia Deborah Tyler, 1850 (died 1894); father of Eugene Tyler C. Engaged in grain and milling business, Seneca Falls, until 1852; then at Albany, 1st in commn. grain and flour business, later in elevator and milling business. Lt. col. 10th N.Y.N.G., which entered U.S. service in 1862; apptd. and confirmed by Gov. Fenton and senate as commissary gen. with rank of brig. gen. Was one of 5 charter mems. 1st Nat. Bank; was pres. Capital City Ins. Co., Bd. of Trade of Albany, Young Men's Assn. of Albany, East Albany Gas Light Co. Mason. Author: Truth, Hudson Tercentenary, 1909. Home: Albany, N.Y. Died 1910.

CHAMBERLAIN, Frederick Stanley, banker; b. New Britain, Conn., Aug. 19, 1872; s. Valentine Burt and Anna I. (Smith) C.; pub. sch. edn.; m. Irene B. Robinson, Nov. 19, 1896; 1 son, James Robinson. Connected with Mechanics Nat. Bank, New Britain, 1889-1907; cashier New Britain Nat. Bank, 1907-26, pres., 1926—. Mem. City Council, New Britain, 1904-08; city treas., 1908-16; pres. Bd. of Finance and Taxation, 1907-15; mem. Conn. Ho. of Rep., 1909; treas. State of Conn., 1915-19. Republican. Conglist. Home: New Britain, Conn. Died July 27, 1936.

CHAMBERLAIN, George Earle, senator; b. nr. Natchez, Miss., Jan. 1, 1854; s. Charles Thomson and Pamelia A. (Archer) C.; A.B. and B.L., Washington and Lee U., 1876; m. Sarah Newman Welch, May 21, 1879; children—Charles Thomson, Mrs. Lucie Blair, Mrs. Marguerite Gaither, Mrs. Carrie Lee Wood, George Earle, Mrs. Fannie Tevis. Went to Ore., 1876; mem. Ore. Ho. of Rep., 1880; dist. atty., 3d Jud. Dist., 1884-86; atty. gen., 1891-95; dist. atty., 4th Jud. Dist., 1900-04; elected gov. for terms, 1903-07, 1907-11; resigned, 1909, on election as U.S. senator, for term 1909-15; reëlected for term 1915-21; mem. U.S. Shipping Board, 1921-23, resigned. Democrat. Author of the Chamberlain mil. preparedness bill, 1918. Home: Washington, D.C. Died July 9, 1928.

CHAMBERLAIN, Henry, mcht., farmer; b. Pembroke, N.H., March 17, 1824; s. Moses and Mary (Foster) C.; ed. Pembroke and Concord, N.H.; came to Mich. with father's family in 1843; m. Sarah J. Nash, Jan. 16, 1851; 2d, Mrs. Rebecca Vandevanter Ames, Nov. 19, 1856. Founder of village of Three Oaks, Mich., 1850; held many local offices; mem. State legislature, 1849; mem. bd. of control Mich. Agrl. Coll., 1883-89, 1891-97; received the votes of his party 3 times for Congress, 3 times for U.S. senator and once for gov. Democrat. Mason. Engaged on a history of the early settlements of the southwest towns of Berrien Co., Mich. Home: Three Oaks, Mich. Died 1907.

CHAMBERLAIN, Henry Richardson, newspaper corr.; b. in Ill., Aug. 25, 1859; s. Thomas C.; pub. sch. edn.; m. Abbie L. Sanger, 1883. In newspaper work, 1877—; mng. editor New York Press, 1888, Boston Journal, 1891-92; London corr. New York Sun, 1892—; mgr. Laffan News Bur. Author: Six Thousand Tons of Gold. Died 1911.

CHAMBERLAIN, Hiram Sanborn, capitalist; b. Franklin, Portage Co., O., Aug. 6, 1835; s. Leander and Susanna (Willey) C.; ed. Eclectic Inst. (now Hiram Coll.), Hiram, O., M.A., 1889; (LL.D., U. of Chattanooga, 1910); m. Amelia I. Morrow, Sept. 4, 1867. Enlisted as pvt. 2d Ohio Vol. Cav., Aug. 24, 1861; commd. 2d lt., July 7, 1862; 1st lt., acting regtl., brigade and div. q.m., capt. and a.q.m., being chief q.m. Eastern Div. of Tenn., hdqrs. at Knoxville, during last 18 mos. of service; took part in many campaigns and battles; on staff Gen. Stoneman in raid through N.C. and Va.; mustered out Oct. 26, 1865. Organized Knoxville Iron Co., 1867; an organizer of Roane Iron Co., 1868, Citico Furnace Co., 1882; then pres. Roane Iron Co., Belt Ry. of Chattanooga, Citico Furnace Co.; v.p. Columbian Iron Wks., Knoxville Iron Co., 1st Nat. Bank. Pres. bd. trustees, U. of Chattanooga. Republican. Mason. Home: Chattanooga, Tenn. Died Mar. 15, 1916.

CHAMBERLAIN, Isaac Dearborn, labor leader; b. Fredericktown, O., Oct. 20, 1840; s. Uriah T. C., anti-slavery leader and one of founders Oberlin Coll.; academic edn.; m. Lida Bennet, Oct. 31, 1872. Served in 18th Pa. Cav., Kilpatrick's div., Army Potomac; 1 yr. in Custer's command; army corr. Erie Gazette, Cleveland Leader and other papers; teacher graded and high schs.; many yrs. editor and publisher at Pueblo, Colo. Past Gen. Master Workman; elected Nov. 1902, gen. sec.-treas. Knights of Labor and mgr. Knights of Labor Journal. Died June 1918.

CHAMBERLAIN, Jacob, missionary Ref. (Dutch) Church; b. Sharon, Connecticut, April 13, 1835; s. Jacob and Anna (Nutting) C.; grad. Western Reserve Coll., O., 1856; Theol. Sem. in New Brunswick, N.J., 1859; Coll. Phys. & Surg., New York, and Western Reserve Med. Coll., Cleveland (D.D., LL.D.); m. Charlotte Birge, Sept. 7, 1859. In Dec. 1859, went as med. and evangelistic missionary to the Arcot Mission, Southern India; then resided in Madras Presidency, except during 4 vacations in America. Stationed 1st at Palamaner, then at Mandanapalle, 1863-1901; from 1901 engaged in lit. work in Telugu and Tamil languages. Chmn. com. for bringing out new version of Bible in Telugu language, 1873-94; translator Liturgy of Ref. Ch. into Telugu; also author in Telugu of hymn book and Oriental Illustrated Bible Dictionary. Author: In the Tiger Jungle, 1896; The Cobra's Den, 1900. Died 1908.

CHAMBERLAIN, Joshua Lawrence, soldier, governor; b. Brewer, Me., Sept. 8, 1828; s. Joshua and Sarah Dupee (Brastow) C.; A.B., Bowdoin, 1852, A.M., 1855; grad. Bangor Theol. Sem., 1855; (LL.D., Pa. Coll., 1866, Bowdoin, 1869); m. Frances Caroline Adams, Dec. 7, 1855. Lt. col. 20th Me. Inf., Aug. 8, 1862; col., May 20, 1863. Congressional Medal of Honor for "daring heroism, holding position Little Round Top and carrying Great Round Top, in battle of Gettysburg, July 2, 1863"; comdg. brigade 5th Corps, Aug. 15; promoted brig. gen. U.S.V. on field of battle, June 18, 1864, by General Grant for "meritorious and efficient services in battle and specially gallant conduct in leading his brigade against the enemy in the assault on Petersburg"; bvtd. maj. gen. U.S.V., Mar. 29, 1865, for "conspicuous gallantry in action"; apptd. to command parade at formal surrender of Lee's army, Appomattox, Apr. 1865; comdg. 1st Div. 5th Corps thence to dissolution of Army of the Potomac; assigned to spl. command from that date; declined colonelcy regular army, and hon. disch. Jan. 15, 1866; thrice wounded. Gov. of Me., 1866-71; maj. gen., Me., charged with protection of peace and institutions of the state in absence of civil govt. and contest thereover, 1879-80. Prof. rhetoric and oratory, 1856-62, modern langs., 1861-65, rhetoric and oratory, 1865-66, trustee, 1867—, pres., 1871-83, prof. mental and moral philosophy, 1874-79, lecturer polit. science and pub. law, 1883-85, Bowdoin Coll. U.S. commr. Paris Expn., 1878; medal from French Govt. for his services there. Pres. Soc. Army of Potomac, 1884; comdr. Loyal Legion U.S., 1866, G.A.R. of Me., 1903; pres. Me. branch Am. Nat. Red Cross; sr. v.p. Am. Bible Soc.; life mem. A.B.C.F.M. U.S. surveyor of customs, port of Portland, 1900—; leave of absence to visit Egypt to observe methods of English rule, 1901. Home: Brunswick, Me. Died Feb. 24, 1914.

CHAMBERLAIN, Leander Trowbridge, clergyman; b. W. Brookfield, Mass., Sept. 26, 1837; s. Eli and Achsah (Forbes) C.; A.B., Yale, 1863; acting asst. paymaster and later naval storekeeper and judge adv., in S. Pacific Squadron, U.S.N., 1863-67; grad. Andover Theol. Sem., 1869; (D.D., U. of Vt., 1879); m. Frances, d. Isaac Lea, LL.D., of Phila., 1890 (died 1894). Ordained Congl. ministry, 1869; pastor New England Ch., Chicago, 1869-76, Broadway Ch., Norwich, Conn., 1876-83, Classon Av. Presbyn. Ch., Brooklyn, 1883-90; resigned. Supt. relief, North Div., Chicago, after great fire of 1871; first rep. sec. in U.S. of McAll Mission of France; aided in organizing Am. McAll Assn.; a founder Brooklyn Inst. Arts and Sciences; pres. U.S. Evang. Alliance; sec.-treas. Am. and For. Christian Union; v.chmn. Nat. Com. Arbitration bet. U.S. and Great Britain; custodian and patron nat. collection of gems in Nat. Mus., Washington; curator eocene mollusca, and patron Acad. Natural Sciences, Phila.; hon. asso. Smithsonian Instn. Del. S.S. Centennial, London, 1880, Pan-Presbyn. Council, London, 1888, World's Conf. Evang. Alliances, Florence, Italy, 1891. Author: Suffrage and Majority Rule; True Doctrine of Prayer, 1906. Died May 10, 1913.

CHAMBERLAIN, Mary Crowninshield Endicott; b. Salem, Mass.; d. Hon. William C. Endicott (Sec. of War U.S., 1885-89) and Ellen (Peabody) Endicott; m. Rt. Hon. Joseph Chamberlain, M.P., for W. Birmingham, Sec. of State for the Colonies in Lord Salisbury's and Mr. Balfour's cabinets, Nov. 15, 1888. Home: Birmingham, England. Died July 2, 1914.

CHAMBERLAIN, Mellen, jurist-librarian; b. Pembroke, N.H., June 4, 1821; grad. Dartmouth, 1844 (LL.D., 1885); legal edn. at Dane Law School, Cambridge, Mass.; m. Martha Ann Putnam, June 6, 1849 (died 1887); began practice in Boston, 1849; held several municipal offices and was member of both houses of Massachusetts legislature; appointed, 1866, judge, and later chief justice, municipal court, until 1878; librarian-in-chief, Boston Public Library, 1878-90; resigned because of ill-health. Home: Chelsea, Mass. Died 1900.

CHAMBERLAIN, Montague, ornithologist; b. St. John, N.B., Apr. 5, 1844; s. Samuel M. and Catherine W. (Stevens) C.; ed. pvt. schs., St. John, until 1858; m. Anna Sartoris Prout, June 15, 1907. Bookkeeper 18 yrs., and partner, 1885-87, firm of J. & W. F. Harrison, wholesale grocers, St. John; recorder Harvard U., 1889-93, sec., 1893-1900, Lawrence Scientific Sch. For 10 yrs. was active mem. of Canadian army; retired with rank of capt. Editor: Popular Handbook of the Birds of the United States and Canada, by Thomas Nuttall, 1903. Home: Groton, Mass. Died 1924.

CHAMBERLAIN, Oscar Pearl, civil engr.; b. Pittstown, N.Y., Nov. 26, 1870; s. Alonzo Bradner and Laura Arceville (Munson) C.; A.B., Central High Sch., Phila., 1885; A.B., U. of Pa., 1889; unmarried. Rodman and asst. engr., Pa. R.R., 1889-1902; asst. engr., C.G.W. Ry., 1902-04; div. engr., N.P. Ry., 1904-05; chief engr. C.&I.W. R.R., 1905—; chief operating engr. Dolese & Shepard Co., 1910—; gen. mgr. Union Paving Co.; v.p. and gen. mgr. Dolese & Shepard Co., 1913. Republican. Home: LaGrange, Ill. Died Dec. 10, 1932.

CHAMBERLAIN, Paul Mellen, cons. mech. engr.; b. Three Oaks, Mich., Feb. 28, 1865; s. Henry and Rebecca (Van Devanter) C.; B.S., Mich. Agrl. Coll., 1888; M.E., Cornell, 1890; m. Olivia Langdon Woodward, Apr. 23, 1891 (died 1920); children—Rebecca Van Devanter (Mrs. Elmer J. Baker, Jr.), Wheelock Paul, Olivia Langdon (Mrs. Clinton G. Johnson), Julia Ada (Mrs. Frank Alexander Farnham III); m. 2d, Margaret Phelps Graham, Feb. 21, 1935. Assistant engr. Frick Co., 1890-92; mech. engr. Hercules Iron Works, Aurora, Ill., 1892-93; asst. prof. mech. engring., Mich. Agrl. Coll., 1893-96; asst. prof. drawing and design, 1896-99, prof. mech. engring., 1899-1906, Lewis Inst., Chicago; cons. practice, Los Angeles, 1906-07; chief engr. The Underfeed Stoker Co. of America, Chicago, 1907-10; cons. practice, 1910-17; inventor of various machines. Commd. maj., Ordnance R.C., Oct. 3, 1917; called into active service, Nov. 1, 1917; insp. ordnance, Toledo, O., Dec. 1917-Feb. 1919, Cleveland Dist. Claims Bd., Feb.-July 1919; apptd. chmn. Chicago Dist. Salvage Bd., Oct. 1919; comdg. officer Chicago and St. Louis Ordnance dists., Apr.-Dec. 1920; disch. Dec. 28, 1920. Home: Keene, N.Y. Died May 27, 1940.

CHAMBERLAIN, Samuel Selwyn, newspaper editor; b. Walworth, N.Y., Sept. 25, 1851; s. Ivory C. and Mary (Ingalls) C.; ed. New York U., class of 1871; m. Mary T. Munson, Sept. 15, 1873. On editorial staff Newark Advertiser, 1873-74, New York Herald, 1875-79, New York World, 1879-80, New York Evening Telegram, 1881-83; founded, 1884, and edited, Le Matin, Paris, 1884-86; editor San Francisco Examiner, 1889-95; editor-in-chief New York American, 1905-07, and supervising editor of all of W. R. Hearst's newspapers until 1907; editor Cosmopolitan Magazine, 1907-08, San Francisco Examiner, 1909. Died Jan. 25, 1916.

CHAMBERLAIN, William Isaac; b. Madras, India, Oct. 10, 1862; s. Jacob and Charlotte (Birge) C.; A.B., Rutgers, 1882, A.M., 1886, LL.D., 1935; B.D., New Brunswick Theol. Sem., 1886; Ph.D., Columbia, 1900; D.D., Rutgers Coll., 1912; m. Mary Eleanor Anable, June 18, 1891; children—Eleanor (dec.), Alma Birge. Ordained Ref. Ch. ministry, 1886; evangelistic and ednl. missionary in Arcot Mission (Madanapalle, Chittoor, Vellore), India, 1887-1905; established, 1898, and pres. until 1905, Voorhees Coll., Vellore, India; prof. logic and mental philosophy, Rutgers Coll., 1906-09; corr. sec. Bd. Foreign Missions, Ref. Ch. in America, 1909-35, retired. Pres. Gen. Synod Ref. Ch. in America, 1908-09, Alliance of Reformed Churches, 1923-24. Pres. bd. trustees Fukien Christian U., Fuchow, China, 1920-35; trustee Am. U. (Cairo, Egypt), Rutgers U. On tour visitation missions in Japan, China, India, Korea, Arabia, 1916 and 1920. Author: Education in India from B.C. to 1900 (Columbia Univ. Contbns. to Philosophy and Education), 1899. Home: New York, N.Y. Died Sept. 28, 1937.

CHAMBERLAINE, William, army officer; b. in Va., Mar. 1, 1871; grad. U.S. Mil. Acad., 1892; honor grad. Arty. Sch., 1896. Commd. add. 2d lt. 2d Arty., June 11, 1892; advanced through grades to brig. gen., Dec. 18, 1918. Duty U.S. Mil. Acad., 1899-1901; asst. to chief of arty., War Dept., May 1901-Oct. 1903; mem. Coast Arty. Bd., 1903-06; mem. Gen. Staff, 1906-10; asst. chief of staff, Philippines Div.; dir. Coast Arty. Sch., 1911-13; adj. gen. Fort Totton, 1917; organized and took to France 6th Prov. Regt. Coast Arty., Aug. 1917; chief of arty. 2nd Div., May and June 1918, during capture by marines of Belleau Woods; comd. gen. ry. arty. A.E.F.; comd. ry. arty. St. Mihiel and Meuse-Argonne operations; comd. gen. coast arty. training center; detailed Gen. Staff Corps, 1919, chief staff Hawaiian Dept. Officier de l'Legion l'Honneur; Croix de Guerre with Palm. Died June 9, 1925.

CHAMBERLAYNE, Catharine Jane, educator; b. Toledo, Can.; d. Ashley Taylor and Cynthia Sheffield (Thompson) C.; A.B., Elmira Coll. for Women, 1865; studied lit. and French in Paris; unmarried. Lady prin. Lasell Sem., 9 yrs., Cincinnati Wesleyan Coll., 6 yrs., Wilbraham Acad., 7 yrs.; founded 1892, and became prin., Miss Chamberlayne's School for Girls. Home: Boston, Mass. Died Apr. 16, 1920.

CHAMBERLAYNE, Churchill Gibson, clergyman, educator; b. Richmond, Va., Dec. 23, 1876; s. John Hampden and Mary Walker (Gibson) C.; student McCabe's Univ. Sch., Petersburg, Va., 7 yrs.; B.A., U. of Va., 1901; student Theol. Sem. of Va., 1901-04, B.D., 1927; U. of Halle-Wittenberg, 1904-06, M.A. and Ph.D., 1906; LL.D., Hampden Sydney Coll., 1926; m. Elizabeth Breckinridge Bolling, June 22, 1911; children—Edward Pye, John Hampden. Deacon, 1904, priest, 1914, P.E. Ch.; missionary Albemarle County, Va., 1906-07; teacher and chaplain Gilman Country Sch., Baltimore, Md., 1907-11; founder, 1911, and then headmaster, St. Christopher's Sch. (formerly the Chamberlayne Sch.), Richmond, Va. Democrat. Died Apr. 3, 1939.

CHAMBERLAYNE, Lewis Parke, college prof.; b. Richmond, Va., June 3, 1879; s. John Hampden and Mary Walker (Gibson) C.; U. of Va., 1896-99, 1901-02, B.A. and M.A., 1902; U. Berlin, 1905-06; U. Halle, 1906-08; A.M. and Ph.D., Halle, 1908; m. Elizabeth Weldon Claiborne Mann, June 27, 1911. Classical master, Locust Dale Acad., Va., 1900; Latin master, Kenyon Mil. Acad., Ohio, 1901; prof. Latin, Southern Female Coll., Petersburg, Va., 1903; Latin and German master, Chestnut Hill Acad., Pa., 1903-05; instr. in Latin, Amherst, 1908-10; prof. ancient langs., U. of S.C., June 1910—; prof. Latin, Chautauqua Instn. summer schs., 1910-14; prof. Latin, George Peabody Coll. summer session, 1915. Democrat. Episcopalian. Home: Columbia, S.C. Died Dec. 14, 1917.

CHAMBERLIN, Chester Harvey, ry. official; b. Natchez, Miss., Sept. 14, 1859; A.B., Stewart Coll., Clarksville, Tenn., 1879. Rodman, levelman and transitman, T.&P. Ry., 1881-82; transitman on surveys and resident engr. on constrn., Yazoo & Miss. Valley Ry., 1883-85; locating engr., Ferrocarril del Norte, Guatemala, 1885-86; engr. land surveys, U.S. Govt., 1886-89; asst. engr., Nicaragua Canal surveys, locating engr. and engr. of constrn. Nicaragua Canal Ry., 1889-91; apptd. asst. engr. maintenance, T.&P. Ry., 1891; later locating and constructing engr. of branches and div. engr. La. div.; later chief engr. same road. Home: Dallas, Tex. Died July 14, 1922.

CHAMBERLIN, Henry Barrett, lawyer, dir. Chicago Crime Commn.; b. Washington, Mar. 10, 1867; s. Arthur Schofield and Maria Louise (Barrett) C.; ed. public schools; LL.B., Union Coll. of Law, 1888; LL.D., Northwestern U., 1934; m. Irene Celene Byrne, Aug. 17, 1903; children—Byrne (dec.), Henry Barrett, John Byrne, William Charles. Editor and publisher The Guardsman, military newspaper, 1886-92; reportorial work on Herald, Tribune, Inter Ocean, Times, Record, all of Chicago; night mgr. City Press Assn., 1891; with Laffan Bureau and New York Sun, 1894; in charge of various depts. Omaha World-Herald, 1895-96. In charge dispatch-boat Hercules of the Chicago Record during Spanish-Am. War, 1898; was between the fire of fleets off Santiago, July 3, only newspaper boat there during battle; cruised 35,000 miles covering news and stories throughout Cuba, P.R. and W.I.; city editor Chicago Record, 1898-1901; editor The Voter (magazine); mng. editor Chicago Record-Herald, Dec. 7, 1910-13; editor-in-chief Chicago Record-Herald, 1913-14; editor Chamberlin's Magazine, and pres. Chamberlin Service Assn. Col. insp. gen. I.N.G. Asst. sec. Municipal Voters' League, 1901-04; sec. state legislation com. City Council of Chicago, 1906-08; asst. sec. Chicago Charter Conv., 1906-09; sec. Chicago Plan Commn., 1909-10; asst. sec. Cleveland Memorial Assn.; mem. Chicago Com. on the Liquor Problem. Mgr. news bur. for 7th Fed. Reserve Dist., 2d liberty loan; chmn. War Dept. "Smileage" campaign for Chicago and Cook Co.; operating dir. Chicago Crime Commn.; dir. Scientific Crime Detection Laboratory; pres. Am. Inst. Criminal Law and Criminology; dir. of inquiry Ill. Prison Inquiry Commn.; mem. Central States Probation and Parole Conf.; del. Am. Prison Assn., Nat. Parole Conference; mem. exec. com. Legislative Voters League; mem. Citizens' Com. on Criminal Court and County Jail Bldgs., Mayor's Committee. Spl. asst. state's atty. Writer of "Stories of the Streets and of the Town" in Chicago Record-Herald; author "Parole in Illinois." Episcopalian. Democrat. Mason. Home: Chicago, Ill. Died July 7, 1941.

CHAMBERLIN, Joseph Edgar, editor; b. Newbury, Vt., Aug. 6, 1851; s. Abner and Mary (Haseltine) C.; ed. in Wis.; m. Ida E. Atwood, June 26, 1873; children—Helen, Charles (dec.), Elisabeth, Corda (dec.), Raymond (dec.), Eleanor; m. 2d, Leonilda Farnese Lowry, June 8, 1915; m. 3d, Jenny Le Royer, Oct. 30, 1926. Was connected with staff Chicago Times, 1871-81; editor Newport (R.I.) Daily News, 1881-82, Fall River (Mass.) Daily Herald, 1882-84, Boston Record, 1884-86; mem. of staff of the Boston Transcript, 1886-1901; asst. editor Youth's Companion, 1890-1901; literary editor, editorial writer and art critic, New York Evening Mail, 1901-15; editorial writer, Boston Transcript, 1915-33; writer of "Listener" and "Nomad" columns, Boston Transcript. War corr. New York Evening Post, in Cuba, 1898. Author: The Listener in the Town, 1896; The Listener in the Country, 1896; Life of John Brown (in Beacon Biographies), 1899; The Ifs of History, 1907; The Boston Transcript—A History of Its First Hundred Years, 1931. Home: Boston, Mass. Died July 6, 1935.

CHAMBERLIN, Thomas Chrowder, geologist; b. Mattoon, Ill., Sept. 25, 1843; A.B., Beloit Coll., 1866, A.M., 1869; grad. science, U. of Mich., 1868-69 (Ph.D., univs. of Mich. and Wis., 1882; LL.D., U. of Mich., Beloit Coll., Columbian U., 1887, U. of Wis., 1904, Toronto U., 1913; Sc.D., U. of Ill., 1905, U. of Wis., 1920); m. Alma Isabel Wilson, 1867. Prof. natural science, State Normal Sch., Whitewater, Wis., 1869-72; prof. geology, Beloit, 1873-82, Columbian, 1885-87; pres. U. of Wis., 1887-92; prof. and head dept. of geology and dir. Walker Mus., U. of Chicago, 1892-1919 (prof. emeritus). Asst. state geologist, Wis., 1873-76, chief geologist, 1876-82; studied glaciers of Switzerland, 1878; U.S. geologist in charge of glacial div., 1882-1907; geologist Peary Relief Expdn., 1894; cons. geologist, Wis. Geol. Survey; commr. Ill. Geol. Survey; cons. geologist U.S. Geol. Survey; investigator fundamental problems of geology, Carnegie Instn., 1902-09; research asso., same instn., 1909—; mem. commn. for Oriental Ednl. Investigation, 1909. Fellow Am. Acad. Arts and Sciences. Author: Geology of Wisconsin; General Treatise on Geology (with R. D. Salisbury), 1906; The Origin of the Earth, 1916. Home: Chicago, Ill. Died Nov. 15, 1928.

CHAMBERS, Edward, ry. official; b. Waukegan, Ill., Feb. 16, 1859; ed. pub. schs. Began with A., T.&S.F. Ry., 1878; frt. handler, clk., foreman and cashier at Pueblo, Colo., agt., San Diego and Los Angeles, Calif., asst. gen. frt. agt., Los Angeles, and gen. frt. agt. lines west of Albuquerque, to 1905; became asst. frt. traffic mgr. Coast Lines, San Francisco, 1905, later v.p., in charge of traffic, at Chicago until resigned; apptd. dir. transportation of U.S. Food Administration and U.S. Grain Corp., July 1917; dir. div. of traffic of U.S. R.R. Administration, Jan. 1918-May 1920, also mem. War Industries Bd.; re-apptd. v.p. in charge of traffic, A.,T. &S.F. Ry., Mar. 1920. Died Feb. 11, 1927.

CHAMBERS, Francis T., patent lawyer; b. Cincinnati, Mar. 3, 1855; s. Francis T. and Elizabeth Lea (Febiger) C.; Ph.B., Sheffield Scientific Sch. (Yale), 1875; studied law in office of William Henry Rawle; LL.B., U. of Pa., 1877; m. Nanette Schuyler Bolton, June 10, 1890 (died 1912); children—Katharine Schuyler, Mrs. Christine Chambers Gray, Francis T. Began practice, Phila., 1877; asso. with late George Harding, 1878-88; alone, 1888—, in federal cts. throughout U.S. Mem. bd. dirs. Franklin Inst. Republican. Episcopalian. Homes: Philadelphia, and Penllyn, Pa. Died Nov. 9, 1939.

CHAMBERS, Frank Taylor, rear admiral; b. Louisville, Ky., July 1, 1870; s. Henry and Annie Cowan (Weisiger) C.; A.B., Male High Sch., Louisville, 1888; C.E., Rensselaer Poly. Inst., 1892; m. Mrs. Florence Newell Pease, Feb. 14, 1920. Apptd. jr. lt. C.E. Corps U.S.N., July 19, 1897; promoted through grades to rear adm., Apr. 6, 1927. Mem. Chesapeake & Delaware Canal Commn., 1905, 06, Nat. Advisory Bd. on Fuels and Structural Materials, 1906-07, Army and Navy Bd., 1908, studying and reporting upon Deep Draft Ship Canal between Chesapeake and Delaware bays, also upon deep draft ship channel from Golden Gate, San Francisco, to Mare Island Navy Yard; apptd. mem. Navy Yard Commn., 1917; chief engr. and mem. port facilities com. U.S. Shipping Bd.; visited Eng. and France, 1918, and reported on port and harbor facilities, information to be applied to improvement of home ports; cons. engr. on port facilities to Bd. of Engrs. for Rivers and Harbors, War Dept.; rep. of Navy Dept. on Assn. of Port Authorities; then dir. Naval Petroleum Reserves and Naval Oil Shale Reserves. Mem. Permanent Internat. Commn., Permanent Internat. Assn. of Navigation Congresses. Died Nov. 10, 1932.

CHAMBERS, Henry Edward, author, educator; b. New Orleans, Mar. 28, 1860; s. Joseph A. and Maria (Charles) C.; ed. pub. and pvt. schs.; post-grad. Tulane U., 1890-92; fellow Johns Hopkins, 1893-94; m. Ellen White Taylor, Dec. 27, 1883; children—John Taylor, Henry Edward. Taught in rural schs., La., 1877-81; prin. Mineral Springs (Ark.) High Sch., 1881-82; pres. Monticello Male and Female Coll., 1882-83; prin. Monticello High Sch., 1883-84; supt. schs., Beaumont, Tex., 1884-85; prin. McDonough Sch., New Orleans, 1885-87; prof. science, New Orleans Boys' High Sch., 1887-90; asst. prof. science, Tulane U., 1890-93; prin. Monroe (La.) High Sch., 1894-96; prof. English, 1896-1901. English and elocution, 1902-05, New Orleans Boys' High Sch.; in lit. work, 1905—. Editor Progressive Teacher, 1885-89; founder and editor, 1893-94, and business mgr., 1907-08, Louisiana School Review. Organized, 1893, first supt., dir. 10 yrs., v.p., 1897, pres., 1902, La. State Chautauqua; pres. dept. secondary edn. N.E.A., 1890; La. State Teachers' Inst. conductor and training teacher La. State Normal Sch., 1901-02. Founder and pres. The Chambers Agency, Inc., 1905-12; v.p. La Valliere Co., 1914—. Author: Constitutional History of Hawaii, 1896; West Florida (Hist. Cartography), 1898; Mississippi Valley Beginnings, 1922; Subjectivity of Certain Economic Concepts, 1924; History of Louisiana, State and People (3 vols.), 1925. Home: New Orleans, La. Died Mar. 8, 1929.

CHAMBERS, James, clergyman; b. Holbrook, Ont., Can., Mar. 1, 1851; s. Maj. Robert and Catherine Lucas (Nesbitt) C.; B.A., Princeton, 1872, M.A., 1875; Princeton Theol. Sem., 1875 (D.D., 1890); m. Jessie Irene Buell, Aug. 29, 1877. Ordained Presbyn. ministry, 1875; pastor Sherburne, N.Y., 1875-82, Calvary Ch., New York, 1882-1900; corr. Nat. Bank of Norwich, N.Y., Jan. 1901—. Delivered sermon in 1894 that started campaign against Tammany; 3 times moderator Presbytery of New York; mem. 5 Gen. Assemblies; editor Church Work, 12 yrs. Life mem. A.B.C.F.M. Home: Norwich, N.Y. Died 1911.

CHAMBERS, Julius, author and editor; b. Bellefontaine, O., Nov. 21, 1850; s. Joseph and Sarabeila C.; prep. course Ohio Wesleyan U.; grad. Cornell U., 1870; studied at Columbia Coll. Law Sch., 1877-79; later read law with U.S. Atty. Gen. Benjamin H. Brewster, Phila.; m. Ida L. Burgess; m. 2d, Margaret Belvin. Joined New York Tribune, 1870, under Horace Greeley; personally equipped expdn. to headwaters of Miss. River and discovered Elk Lake, Minn., beyond Itaska, June 9, 1872, since officially recognized source of Miss. River; on staff New York Herald in various capacities and in many parts of the world, 1873-89, editor Herald, 1886-89; 1st editor Paris Herald; mng. editor New York World, 1889-91; devoted to travel and lit. work, 1891—. Spent winter, 1900-01, in Egypt; spl. corr. at various times in Madrid, Havana, Paris, London, Rome and Washington. Nonresident lecturer on journalism, Cornell U., 1903, 04, New York U., 1910. Writer of "Walks and Talks," a daily newspaper feature in Brooklyn Eagle, 1904—. Fellow Royal Geog. Soc., London. Author: The Mississippi River and Its Wonderful Valley. Home: New York, N.Y. Died Feb. 12, 1920.

CHAMBERS, Mary Davoren, editor, writer; b. Ireland, 1865; d. John Griffin and Frances (Davoren) Molony; diploma, Pratt Inst., Brooklyn, N.Y., 1898; B.S. in Edn., Columbia, 1905, A.M., 1908; m. James Chambers, 1885 (died 1885). Teacher Girls' Hebrew Tech. Sch., New York, 1897-98; teacher normal domestic sci. dept., Pratt Inst., 1898-1902; supervising teacher household arts, Brooklyn Vacation Schs., 1899-1902; prof. domestic economy and head dept., Millikin U., Decatur, Ill., 1903-06; prof. chemistry and home economics, Rockford (Ill.) Coll., 1906-14, also head dept.; asso. editor Am. Cookery (mag.), Boston, Mass., 1918—. Catholic. Author: Principles of Food Preparation, 1914; The Art of Story-Writing (with J. Berg Esenwein), 1914; Guide to Laundry Work, 1915; Breakfasts, Luncheons and Dinners, 1920; Nature Secrets, 1923; A Book of Unusual Soups, 1923; Teens and Twenties, 1923; One-Piece Dinners, 1924; Care and Training of Boys and Girls, 1925; More Teens and Twenties, 1927; Table Etiquette, 1929. Home: Boston, Mass. Deceased.

CHAMBERS, Robert, missionary; b. North Norwich, Ont., May 1, 1849; s. Robert and Catharine Lucas (Nesbitt) C.; B.A., Queen's U., Kingston, Ont., 1866; B.D., Princeton Theol. Sem., 1870; (D.D., Queen's U., 1897); m. Elizabeth Lawson, Dec. 31, 1872. Ordained ministry Presbyn. Ch. of Can., 1870; pastor at East Williams and Whitby, Ont., 1870-79; missionary A.B.C.F.M., 1879—; at Erzerum, Armenia, 1879-88; traveling in U.S. and addressing Congl. chs., 1888-91; missionary in charge, Province of Ismidt, Turkey, 1891—. Organized local conf. Evang. chs.; established self-supporting boarding sch. for boys; founded orphanage after massacres of 1895-96; instrumental in saving town of Bardizag and neighboring villages from massacre. Died Apr. 2, 1917.

CHAMBERS, Robert Craig, mine mgr., capitalist; b. Lexington, O., Jan. 16, 1832; academic edn.; m. Eudora A. Tolles, 1884 (dec.). Went to Calif., 1850; became placer miner and later merchant; sheriff Plumas Co., Calif., 1858-62; later quartz miner; went to Utah, 1870; in 1872, with late George Hearst, bought Ontario mine, which he managed and which paid $13,500,000 in dividends; State senator, Utah, 1895-99. Home: Salt Lake City, Utah. Died 1901.

CHAMBERS, Robert William, author, artist; b. Brooklyn, N.Y., May 26, 1865; s. William and Caroline (Boughton) C.; student Académie Julian, Paris, 1886-93; m. Elsa Vaughn Moller, July 12, 1898. First exhibited in Salon, 1889; illustrator for Life, Truth, Vogue, etc. Author: Ashes of Empire, 1897; The Cambric Mask, 1899; Outsiders, 1899; Cardigan, 1901; The Maid-At-Arms, 1902; Outdoor-Land, 1902; Forest Land, 1905; Iole, 1905; The Fighting Chance, 1906; Hide and Seek in Forestland, 1909; Ailsa Paige, 1910; Bluebird Weather, 1912; The Common Law, 1913; Athalie, 1915; The Dark Star, 1915; The Better Man, 1915; The Girl Philippa, 1916; The Restless Sex, 1917; The Moonlit Way, 1918; In Secret, 1918; The Crimson Tide, 1919; Slayer of Souls, 1920; Little Red Foot, 1921; Eris, 1923; The Hi-jackers, 1923; The Girl in Golden Rags, 1924; The Man They Hanged, 1925; The Drums of Aulone, 1926; The Sun Hawk, 1927; The Rogue's Moon, 1927; also "The Witch of Ellangowan," drama produced at Daly's Theatre and written for Miss Ada Rehan; "Iole," musical comedy, prod. New York, 1913. Mem. Nat. Inst. Arts and Letters. Home: Broadalbin, N.Y. Died Dec. 16, 1933.

CHAMBRÉ, A(lbert) St. John, clergyman; b. London, Eng.; a direct descendant of John de la Chambré, a noble knight in the train of William of Normandy; came to America, 1850; chaplain 1st and 8th N.J. Vols., 1861-65; deacon, 1880, priest, 1881, P.E. Ch.; rector Ch. of the Ascension, Fall River, 1881-84, St. Anne's Ch., Lowell, Mass., 1884—. First arch-deacon of Lowell, and mem. Standing Com., Diocese of Mass.; dean of the Eastern Convocation; trustee and mem. examining bd., Gen. Theol. Sem., New York; trustee and v.p. St. Mark's Sch., Southboro, Mass.; pres. Lowell Instn. for Savings, Lowell, Mass.; a founder and trustee Lowell Day Nursery, and Lowell Gen. Hosp.; pres. Battles Home for Old Men; trustee, v.p. Rogers Hall Sch. Author: The Apostles' Creed (a collection of sermons), 1898; Seven Words from the Cross (addresses), 1905. Home: Lowell, Mass. Died 1912.

CHAMPION, Charles Sumner, patent lawyer; b. Washington, D.C., Jan. 22, 1871; s. Charles and Catherine Elizabeth (Hyde) C.; ed. grammar and high schs., Washington, D.C.; studied law N.Y. Univ. Law Sch.; m. Charlotte Amelia Flentjé, June 26, 1895. Practiced in Washington, D.C., Phila., Hartford and N.Y. City, 1888-1901, for or against leading inventors of U.S. and Europe, including Thomas A. Edison, Francis H. Richards and Dr. Werner von Siemens; practiced in N.Y. City, 1901—; a pioneer in movement in N.Y. State, 1905, for direct primary nominations. Home: Montclair, N.J. Died July 31, 1916.

CHAMPION, Fritz Roy, newspaper pub.; b. Schenectady, N.Y., Feb. 28, 1878; s. Austin L. and Deborah (Van Antwerp) C.; grad. Union Classical Inst., Schenectady, 1895; Ph.B., Union Coll., Schenectady, 1899; m. Anna M. Jones, June 28, 1905; 1 son, Van Antwerp (dec.). Began as reporter Schenectady Union Star, 1897, pub., 1917—; v.p. and mgr. Schenectady Union Pub. Co.; sec. and treas. Union-Star Bldg. Corp.; dir. Citizens Trust Co. Served as sergt. N.Y. Vol. Inf., U.S.A., Spanish-Am. War; commr. of jurors, Schenectady County, 1905-21. Trustee Ingersoll Memorial for Aged Men, Children's Home. Republican. Mem. First Ref. Ch. Home: Schenectady, N.Y. Died Jan. 21, 1933.

CHAMPLIN, Edwin Ross ("Clarence Fairfield"), editor; b. E. Westerly, R.I., May 4, 1854; s. Samuel Anthony and Mary Bliven (Ross) C.; ed. Westerly pub. schs.; m. Georgie A. Butler, Apr. 25, 1877; children—Charles Laurence, John Butler. At 16 was a "Young Contributor" to Our Young Folks, Boston; edited and published young people's monthlies at Westerly, R.I., 1870-74; night editor Norwich, Conn., Morning Bulletin, 1872; asst. editor Danbury (Conn.) News, 1874; mem. staff New York Daily Tribune, 1877; asst. editor Attleboro (Mass.) Chronicle, 1878; reporter Providence Daily Journal, at Westerly, 1879-84; conducted "Table Talk" dept. of Literary World, Boston, 1885-86; privately engaged in lit. work, 1884-88; editor and reporter, Fall River (Mass.) Daily Evening News, 1888-1910; lit. editor Gloucester (Mass.) Daily Times, 1901-09. Then engaged in lit. work, and on staff Fall River Evening Herald. Author: (verse) Heart's Own, 1886; Lover's Lyrics and Other Songs, 1888; On the White Birch Road, 1891. Home: Worcester, Mass. Died Sept. 8, 1928.

CHAMPLIN, John Denison, author; b. Stonington, Conn., Jan. 29, 1834; s. John D. and Sylvia (Bostwick) C.; A.B., Yale, 1856, A.M., 1866; m. Franka E. Colvocoresses, Oct. 8, 1873. Admitted to bar, 1859; practiced short time; later newspaper writer and editor; devoted to literature from 1869. Author: Young Folks' Cyclopædia of Common Things, 1879; Young Folks' Cyclopædia of Persons and Places, 1880, 99, 1911; Young Folks' Astronomy, 1881; Young Folks' History of War for the Union, 1881; Young Folks' Cyclopædia of Games and Sports (with Arthur E. Bostwick), 1890; Young Folks' Cyclopædia of Literature and Art, 1901; Young Folks Cyclopædia of Natural History, 1905. Died Jan. 8, 1915.

CHAMPLIN, John Wayne, lawyer; b. Kingston, N.Y., Feb. 17, 1831; s. Jeffrey C. C.; ed. Rhinebeck Acad., 1846; Harpersfield Acad.; Stamford Sem.; Delaware Lit. Inst.; spl. studies engring. and law (hon. LL.D., Univ. of Mich.); m. Ellen More, Oct. 1, 1856. In 1854 removed from Harpersfield, N.Y., to Grand Rapids, Mich. Was admitted to bar, June 1855; city atty., 1857; judge Recorder's court, 1861; mayor Grand Rapids, 1867; judge Supreme Court, 1884-91. Prof. law, Univ. of Mich., 1892-96. Democrat. Home: Grand Rapids, Mich. Died 1901.

CHAMPNEY, Benjamin, artist; b. New Ipswich, N.H., Nov. 20, 1817; s. Benjamin and Rebecca (Brooks) C.; academical edn.; m. Mary C. Brooks, July 1853; m. 2d, Mrs. Margaret Stevenson, June 26, 1879. Went to Boston, 1834; began study of art, 1837; studied painting in Paris, 1841-48; exhibited several pictures in Paris Salon. Was landscape and flower painter, occupied with White Mountain scenery and the wild flowers of New England. Owned summer cottage and spent summers at North Conway, N.H. Author: Sixty Years' Memories of Art and Artists, 1900. Address: Woburn, Mass. Died 1907.

CHAMPNEY, Elizabeth Williams, author; b. (Williams) Springfield, O., Feb. 6, 1850; d. Judge Samuel B. and Caroline (Johnson) Williams; A.B., Vassar, 1869; m. J. Wells Champney, 1873 (died 1903). Traveled in Europe; wrote many papers for Harper's and Century. Pres. bd. mgrs. Messiah Home for Children. Author: Romance of the Feudal Chateaux, 1900; Romance of the Renaissance Chateaux, 1901; Romance of the Bourbon Chateaux, 1903; Romance of the French Abbeys, 1905; Romance of Italian Villas, 1906; Romance of Roman Villas, 1908; Romance of Imperial Rome, 1910. Part author: Romance of Old Belgium, 1915; Romance of Old Japan, 1917; Romance of Russia from Rarik to Bolshevik, 1921. Home: Seattle, Wash. Died Oct. 13, 1922.

CHAMPNEY, James Wells, artist; b. Boston, July 16, 1843; began art edn. with wood engraver in Boston; studied in Europe under Edouard Frère, Paris, and at Antwerp Acad., 1868-69; m. Elizabeth Williams, May 15, 1875. In 1882 made asso. mem. Nat. Acad.; has painted genre pictures, and after 1883 pastel portraits of many notables; exhibitor oil paintings at Phila. Centennial, 1876, and pastels at World's Columbian Expn., 1893. Died 1903.

CHANCE, Henry Martyn, cons. engr.; b. Phila., Pa., Jan. 18, 1856; s. Jeremiah Chambers and Augusta (Mitchell) C.; C.E., U. of Pa., 1874; M.D., Jefferson Med. Coll., 1881; m. Lilie E. Mickley, Apr. 20, 1882; children—Edwin Mickley, Thomas Mitchell (died 1933). In gen. consulting practice, 1884—; developed, 1921—, sand flotation process for cleaning coal, an invention of Thomas M. Chance, largely used in cleaning Pa. anthracite coal, and also bituminous coal. Home: Philadelphia, Pa. Died Feb. 19, 1937.

CHANCE, Jesse Clifton, brig. gen.; b. Alliance, O., Jan. 26, 1843; s. Henry and Charlotte Temple (Trego) C.; ed. pub. schs., Alliance, O., m. Elizabeth Hafford Roberts, April 8, 1867; m. 2d, Jean Sleeth McWatty, September 1, 1887. Enlisted private Company E, 25th Ohio Infantry, August 9, 1862; mustered out of vol. service as 2d lt., Apr. 16, 1866; apptd. 2d lt. 13th U.S. Inf., Jan. 22, 1867, and after serving through every grade was retired from active service, Aug. 15, 1903, with rank of brig. gen. U.S.A., after more than 40 yrs.' service. Methodist. Republican. Home: Petersburg, Fla. Died May 16, 1914.

CHANCE, Julie Grinnell, see Gordon, Julien.

CHANCELLOR, Charles Williams, physician; b. Spottsylvania Co., Va., Feb. 19, 1831; s. Maj. Sanford and Fannie L. (Pound) C.; ed. Georgetown Coll., 1848, U. of Va., 1851; M.D., Jefferson Med. Coll., Phila., 1853; m. Mary Archer Taliaferro, Mar. 1864 (died 1865); m. 2d, Martha A. Butler, Feb. 28, 1868. Med. dir., Gen. Pickett's div., C.S.A., 1863-65; prof. surgery and dean, Washington U., 1868-75; sec. State Bd. Health, Md., 1875; pres. Md. State Insane Asylum, 1880; U.S. consul, Havre, France, 1893-97. Author: Treatise on Mineral Waters; Sewage Disposal; The Climate of the Eastern Shore of Maryland. Deceased.

CHANCELLOR, Eustathius A., M.D.; b. Chancellorsville, Va., Aug. 29, 1854; s. Dr. James Edgar and Josephine D. (Anderson) C.; ed. U. of Va., 1871-74, M.D., 1876; clin. studies U. of Pa., 1876; M.D., U. of Md., 1877; A.M., St. Louis U., 1885; unmarried. Practiced at Charlottesville with his father, 1879-80; then in St. Louis; one of founders, 1885, and prof. cutaneous and venereal diseases, 1885-90, Beaumont Hosp. Med. Coll.; supreme med. dir. Legion of Honor, 1886; supervising med. examiner for Missouri Royal Arcanum, 1890; medical dir. with rank of lt. col. Mo. N.G., 1891-96. Med. examiner and adjuster for life, accident, health and liability ins. cos. Deceased.

CHANDLER, Albert Brown, pres. Postal Telegraph and Cable Co.; b. W. Randolph, Vt., Aug. 20, 1840; s. William Brown and Electa (Owen) C.; acad. edn.; learned telegraphy; m. Marilla Eunice Stedman, Oct. 11, 1864. Mgr. Western Union Telegraph, Bellaire, O., 1858-59; in service Cleveland & Pittsburgh Ry., 1859-63; in U.S. mil. telegraph service, 1863-66; chief clerk in office of gen. supt. Eastern div., Western Union Telegraph, and later also supt. 6th dist., 1866-75; asst. gen. mgr., sec.-treas., v.p. and pres., Atlantic & Pacific Telegraph Co., 1875-82; pres. Fuller Electric Co., 1881-84; counsel, 1884, receiver, 1885-86 and elected pres. 1886, Postal Telegraph and Cable Co.; retired, Dec. 1911. Home: Brooklyn, N.Y. Died Feb. 2, 1923.

CHANDLER, Alfred Dupont, lawyer; b. Boston, May 18, 1847; s. Theophilus Parsons and Elizabeth Julia (Schlatter) C.; A.B., Harvard, 1868; studied law with father and R. H. Dana, Jr.; student Harvard Law Sch. part of 1869; m. Mary Merrill Poor, Dec. 27, 1882. Admitted to Mass. bar, 1869, U.S. Supreme Ct., 1877; with firm Porter, Lowry & Soren, New York, 1871; in practice at Boston, 1872—. Drafted Senator Windom's bill for creation of nat. savings banks, 1880, making argument before Senate finance committee; appeared frequently before Mass. legislative coms. on municipal and state matters. Chmn. Selectmen and various municipal bds., Brookline, 1884-85-86; trustee Brookline Pub. Library, 1874-76; leader in many movements, local and state, for reform and advancement. Home: Brookline, Mass. Died Aug. 26, 1923.

CHANDLER, Algernon Bertrand, Jr., educator; b. Bowling Green, Va., May 12, 1870; s. Algernon Bertrand and Julia Yates (Callaghan) C.; B.A., U. of Va., 1893, M.A., 1893; studied Washington and Lee U. and Cornell U.; m. Blanche Montgomery, July 23, 1902. Practiced law, Atlanta, Ga., 1895-97; teacher, Miss Ellett's Sch. for Girls (Richmond, Va.), Nolley's Sch. for Boys (Richmond), and prin. high sch., Clifton Forge, Va., until 1903; prin. elementary schs., Richmond, 1903-10; prof. English, Va. Mechanics' Inst., Richmond, 1907-10; dean State Normal Sch. for Women, Fredericksburg, Va., 1915-19, pres., 1919—. V.p. State Teachers' Assn., 1905-08, 1915-19; mem. State Bd. Sch. Examiners, 1910-12. Mem. Christian (Disciples) Ch. Author: Va. Supplement Frye's Higher Geography. Home: Fredericksburg, Va. Died Sept. 20, 1928.

CHANDLER, Charles, college prof.; b. Pontiac, Mich., Jan. 15, 1850; s. Jonathan and Vashti (Lamdin) C.; A.B., U. of Mich., 1871, A.M., 1874; U. of Berlin, 1891-92; m. Adelaide Isadore Murray, Aug. 16, 1876. Teacher langs., high sch., Pontiac, 1871-74; instr. Latin, 1874-76, prof., 1876-91, Denison U., Granville, O.; prof. Latin, U. of Chicago, 1892—. Republican. Baptist. Mason. Home: Chicago, Ill. Died Nov. 14, 1938.

CHANDLER, Charles deForest, aeronautics; b. Cleveland, O., Dec. 24, 1878; s. Francis Marion and Effie May (Barney) C.; student Case Sch. of Applied Science, 1899-1901; grad. Army Signal Sch., Fort Leavenworth, Kan., 1911; unmarried. Served as 1st lt. U.S. Vol. Signal Corps, June 1898-May 1899; apptd. 1st lt. U.S.A., Feb. 2, 1901, and advanced through grades to col., Aug. 5, 1917; trans. to Air Service, July 1, 1920; retired, Oct. 18, 1920; aeronautic editor Ronald Press Co., 1925—. Served in Spanish-Am. War, Philippine Insurrection, Punitive Expdn. in Mexico; chief of balloon sect., Air Service, U.S.A., in France, World War. Comdr. U.S. Cableship Burnside, laying of 1st submarine cables to Alaska, 1903-04; 1st winner of Lahm trophy for balloon racing, 1907; comdr. 1st Army aviation sch., College Park, Md., 1911-13. Awarded D.S.M. (U.S.); Officer Legion of Honor (France). Republican. Author: Free and Captive Balloons (with R. H. Upson), 1926; Balloon and Airship Gases (with W. S. Diehl), 1926. Home: Washington, D.C. Died May 18, 1939.

CHANDLER, Charles Frederick, chemist; b. Lancaster, Mass., Dec. 6, 1836; student Lawrence Scientific Sch. (Harvard), univs. of Berlin and Göttingen; A.M., Ph.D., Göttingen, 1856; (hon. M.D., New York U., 1873; LL.D., Union, 1873; Sc.D., Oxford, 1900; Ph.D., Göttingen, 1906; LL.D., Columbia Univ., 1911). Prof. chemistry, Union College, 1857-64; one of organizers, and prof. analytical and applied chemistry, Columbia Sch. of Mines, 1864-77; adj. prof. chemistry and med. jurisprudence Coll. Phys. and Surg., 1872-76; prof. chemistry, 1877—, dean Faculty of Mines, 1864-97, dean Faculty of Science, 1897, Columbia; then prof. organic chemistry, and pres. New York Coll. of Pharmacy. Chemist and later pres. Met. Bd. of Health, 1867-84. Asso. editor (with his brother, Prof. W. H. C.) American Chemist, 1870-77; chem. editor Johnson's Encyclopedia. Address: New York, N.Y. Died Aug. 25, 1925.

CHANDLER, Charles Henry, coll. prof.; b. New Ipswich, N.H., Oct. 25, 1840; s. James and Nancy (White) C.; A.B., Dartmouth, 1868, A.M., 1871; m. Eliza Francena Dwinnell, Aug. 17, 1868 (died 1894); father of Elwyn Francis C. Taught in various acads.; prof. Antioch Coll., O., 1871-81; prof. chemistry and physics, 1881-83, mathematics, 1883-1906, emeritus, 1906—, Ripon College. Local historian, 1908—. Home: New Ipswich, N.H. Deceased.

CHANDLER, Francis Ward, architect; b. Boston, Sept. 30, 1844; s. Samuel Ward C.; grad. Lancaster Acad., Mass., 1861; pvt. 53d Mass. Vols., 1862-63; studied architecture; m. Alice Daland, Oct. 12, 1882. With Messrs. Ware & Van Brunt, architects, Boston, 1864-67; student in Paris, 1867-69; asst. in architectural dept., Mass. Inst. Tech., 1869-70; asst. architect Treasury Dept., Washington, 1871-74; in partnership with E. C. Cabot, Boston, 1874-88; prof. architecture, 1888-1911, Mass. Inst. Tech.; prof. emeritus, 1911; hon. mem. A.I.A.; mem. bd. Art Commrs. City of Boston, 1898-1908; advisory architect to mayor of Boston, 1896-1900. Author: Construction Details, prepared for the use of the students of Mass. Institute of Tech., 1892; Notes on Limes, Cements, Mortars and Concretes, 1892. Home: Boston. Died Sept. 8, 1926.

CHANDLER, Izora (Mrs.), artist, author; grad. Coll. of Fine Arts of Syracuse Univ. as Bachelor of Painting; studied in Europe; on her return received degree of Master of Painting from Syracuse University; specialty is portraiture and miniatures upon ivory; illustrator for various publishers; art and music critic for The Christian Advocate, New York. Chmn. com. on art, Woman's Press Club, New York. Author: Three of Us; A Dog of Constantinople (illustrated by herself); Elvira Hopkins of Tompkins Corners; (with M. W. Montgomery) Told in the Gardens of Araby, 1905. Died 1906.

CHANDLER, John Gorham, brig. gen.; b. Lexington, Mass., Dec. 31, 1830; s. Daniel and Susannah C.; grad. U.S. Mil. Acad., 1853; m. Mrs. Louise Carnegie Maurice, Oct. 9, 1890. Bvt. 2d lt., 3d Arty., July 1, 1853; commd. 2d lt., Dec. 24, 1853; 1st lt., May 31, 1856; regtl. adj., Dec. 27, 1857-May 17, 1861; capt. asst. q.m., May 17, 1861; lt. col. q.m. vols., Jan. 1, 1863-Aug. 1, 1865; maj. q.m., Jan. 18, 1867; lt. col. deputy q.m.-gen., Mar. 4, 1879; col. asst. q.m. gen., Dec. 11, 1892; retired by operation of law, Dec. 31, 1894; advanced to rank of brig. gen. retired, by act of Apr. 23, 1904. Bvtd. maj., lt. col. and col., Mar. 13, 1865, "for faithful and meritorious services during the war." Home: Los Angeles. Died June 21, 1915.

CHANDLER, Julian Alvin Carroll, college pres.; b. at Guineys', Caroline County, Va., Oct. 29, 1872; s. Joseph A. (M.D.) and Emuella Josephine (White) C.; A.B., William and Mary Coll., 1891, A.M., 1892; Ph.D., Johns Hopkins, 1896; LL.D., Richmond Coll., 1904; m. Lenore Burten Duke, July 10, 1897. Instr. history and English, William and Mary Coll., 1891-92; prin. pub. schs., Houston, Va., 1892-93; instr. Morgan Coll., Baltimore, 1894-96; dean faculty, 1896-99, acting pres., 1899-1900, Woman's Coll., Richmond; acting prof. history and lit., Richmond Coll., 1897-1900; prof. English, same, 1900-04, dean Richmond Acad., 1902-04; editor for Silver, Burdett & Co., publishers, 1904-07; editor Va. Journal of Education, Richmond, 1907-09; prof. history, Richmond Coll., 1908-09; supt. of schs., Richmond, July 1909-July 1919; chief of rehabilitation div. for disabled soldiers Federal Bd. for Vocational Edn., Oct. 1918-Apr. 1919; pres. Coll. of William and Mary, Williamsburg, Va., July 1, 1919—. Lecturer in Virginia Summer School of Methods; dir. history and edn., Jamestown Expn., 1907. Author: Representation in Virginia, 1896; History of Suffrage in Virginia, 1899; Geography of Virginia (joint author), 1902; Makers of Virginia History, 1904; Makers of American History (joint author), 1904; Colonial History (joint author), 1907; Our Republic (joint author), 1910. Home: Williamsburg, Va. Died May 31, 1934.

CHANDLER, Seth Carlo, astronomer; b. Boston, Sept. 17, 1846; s. Seth and Mary (Cheever) C.; ed. Boston English High Sch.; (LL.D., DePauw Univ., Ind., 1891); m. Carrie M. Herman, Oct. 20, 1870. Aid, U.S. Coast and Geod. Survey, 1864-70; life ins. actuary, 1870-85; editor Astronomical Journal, 1896—. Received the Watson gold medal and the gold medal of the Royal Astron. Soc. of Eng. Fellow Am. Acad. Arts and Sciences. Home: Wellesley Hills, Mass. Died Dec. 31, 1913.

CHANDLER, Walter Marion, lawyer, author; b. Yazoo Co., Miss., Dec. 8, 1867; s. King David and Mary Frances (Harrison) C.; ed. U. of Miss., Tulane U., univs. of Berlin and Heidelberg, Univ. of Va., Univ. of Mich.; LL.B., Univ. of Mich., 1897; unmarried. Cowboy and school teacher for several yrs. in Tex.; practiced at Dallas, Tex., 1897-1900; served as 1st asst. state's atty., Dallas Co.; lecturer, Tex.-Colo. Chautauqua, summer of 1900; moved to New York and resumed practice, 1900. Lecturer and Rep. campaign speaker; mem. 63d to 65th and 67th Congresses (1913-19 and 1921-23), 19th N.Y. Dist. Author: The Trial of Jesus from a Lawyer's Standpoint (2 Vols.), 1908; The Jew—a Tribute by a Gentile. Home: New York, N.Y. Died Mar. 16, 1935.

CHANDLER, William Eaton, secretary of the Navy; b. Concord, N.H., Dec. 28, 1835; s. Nathan S. and Mary Ann (Tucker) C.; LL.B., Harvard, 1854; admitted to bar, 1855; (A.M., 1866, LL.D., 1901, Dartmouth). In law practice Concord, N.H., from 1855; reporter decisions Supreme Ct. of N.H., 1859; mem. N.H. Ho. of Rep., 1862, 1863, 1864, 1881 (speaker 1863-64); solicitor and judge adv. gen., Navy Dept., Mar. 9-June 17, 1865; 1st asst. sec. of the treasury, June 17, 1865-Nov. 30, 1867; apptd. solicitor gen. of U.S., Mar. 31, 1881, but rejected by Senate; sec. of the Navy, in cabinet of President Arthur, 1882-85; organized Greeley relief expdn., 1884; U.S. senator, for unexpired term (1887-89) of Austin F. Pike, deceased; reëlected for terms 1889-95, 1895-1901; pres. Spanish Treaty Claims Commn., 1901-07. Del.-at-large Rep. nat. convs., 1868, 1880; sec. Rep. Nat. Com. during Grant's administration; mem. N.H. Constl. convs., 1876, 1902. Home: Concord, N.H. Died Nov. 30, 1917.

CHANDLER, William Henry, professor chemistry, 1871—, dir. of library, 1878—, Lehigh Univ.; b. New Bedford, Mass., Dec. 13, 1841; ed. at Union Coll.; chemist for various cos., 1861-67; instr. Columbia School Mines, 1868-71. Fellow Chem. Soc. of London; mem. chem. socs. of Paris and New York. Brother of Charles Frederick Chandler. Home: S. Bethlehem, Pa. Died 1906.

CHANDLER, William Henry, traffic mgr.; b. Greenville, Ala., Jan. 13, 1871; s. Charles Henry and Catherine (Flowers) C.; ed. pvt. schs.; m. Margaret Blight, Jan. 12, 1898; 1 son, Desmond Blight. Clk., wholesale grocery, 1887-90; chief rate clk., L.&N. R.R., Montgomery, Ala., 1890-92, C. of Ga. Ry., Savannah, Ga., 1892-95, Ocean S.S. Co., N.Y. City, 1895-97, at Savannah, 1897; industrial traffic mgr. for Francis H. Leggett & Co. and Seacoast Canning Co., N.Y. City, 1898-1908; New England freight agt. for A.B.&A. R.R. and Brunswick and Tex. City S.S. companies, Boston, 1908; industrial traffic mgr., Boston Chamber Commerce, 1909-12, Merchants Assn. of New York, 1912-14; mgr. traffic bur., Merchants Assn. of New York, 1924—; Eastern traffic asst.

federal coördinator of transportation, 1933-35. Chmn. legislative com. Shippers Conf. of Greater New York; mem. exec. com. Nat. Industrial Traffic League, N.E. Traffic League. Mem. N.E. rate com., U.S. R.R. Adminstrn., during federal control. Mason. Author: Express Service and Rates, 1912. Compiler: Merchants Parcel Post and Express Guide, 1914. Home: Upper Montclair, N.J. Died Dec. 2. 1939.

CHANEY, Lucian West, statistician; b. Heuvelton, N.Y., June 26, 1857; s. Lucian West and Happy T. (Kinney) C.; A.B., Carleton Coll., 1878, B.S., 1879, M.S., 1882, D.Sc., 1916; Woods Hole, Mass., 1890-95; m. Mary E. Hill, June 20, 1882. High sch. prin. and supt. schs., Faribault and Glencoe, Minn., 1879-82; instr. biology, 1882-83, prof., 1883-1908, Carleton Coll.; spl. agt. U.S. Bur. of Labor on dangerous occupations of women and children, 1907-09; expert in accident prevention, U.S. Bur. Labor Statistics, 1909—. Explored in Rocky Mountains, Mont., 1895, 1903, 1905; visited several glaciers for first time; one bears name of Chaney Glacier. Author numerous bulls. of the U.S. Bur. of Labor. Died May 6, 1935.

CHANEY, Novetus Holland, educator; b. near New Vienna, O., Mar. 4, 1856; s. John Alexander and Mary Catherine (Holmes) C.; Wilmington Coll., Ohio; Ohio Wesleyan U., Delaware, O., 1892-94; summer terms, U. of Chicago and U. of Pa.; m. Anna R. Roush, Aug. 12, 1880. Teacher country and village schs. 6 yrs.; supt. schs. Washington C.H., Ohio, 1886-98, Chillicothe, 1898-1902, Youngstown, Sept. 1902—. Mem. State Bd. Sch. Examiners, Ohio, 1908-13. Trustee Y.M.C.A., Youngstown. Republican. Methodist. Mason. Home: Youngstown, O. Died Apr. 23, 1925.

CHANLER, William Astor, congressman; b. Newport, R.I., June 11, 1867; s. Hon. John Winthrop and Margaret Astor (Ward) C.; bro. of Lewis Stuyvesant C.; ed. St. John's Sch., Ossining, N.Y., Phillips Acad., Exeter, N.H., and Harvard, class of 1887 (hon. A.M., 1895); m. Minnie Ashley, 1903. Has traveled and explored in Africa. Mem. N.Y. Assembly, 1897; member 56th Congress (1899-1901), 14th N.Y. Dist. Democrat. Capt. asst. adj. gen. vols., May 10, 1898; participated in Battle of Santiago; received spl. commendation from Gen. Shafter; hon. disch. Sept. 30, 1898. Fellow Royal Geog. Soc. (London); hon. mem. Königliche Geographische Gesellschaft (Vienna). Author: Through Jungle and Desert; Travels in Eastern Africa. Home: Barrytown, N.Y. Died Mar. 4, 1934.

CHANNING, Edward, historian; b. Dorchester, Mass., June 15, 1856; s. William Ellery and Ellen K. (Fuller) C.; A.B. from Harvard, 1878, A.M., Ph.D., 1880; LL.D. from U. of Mich., 1921; Litt.D. from Columbia U., 1926; m. Alice Thacher, July 22, 1886; children—Alice, Elizabeth Torrey. Instructor, 1883-87, assistant prof., 1887-97, prof. history, 1897-1913, McLean prof. ancient and modern history, 1913—, Harvard U. Mem. Am. Acad. of Arts and Letters. Author: Town and County Government in the English Colonies of North America, 1884; The Narragansett Planters, 1886; The Navigation Laws, 1890; English History for American Readers (with Thomas Wentworth Higginson), 1893; The United States of America, 1765-1865 (in Cambridge History Series), 1896; Students' History of the United States, 1898; First Lessons in United States History, 1903; History of the United States, Vol. I, The Planting of a Nation in the New World (1000-1660), 1905; Vol. II, A Century of Colonial History (1660-1760), 1908; Vol. III, The American Revolution (1761-1789), 1912; Vol. IV, Federalists and Republicans (1789-1815), 1917; Vol. V, The Period of Transition (1815-1848), 1921; Vol. VI, The War for Southern Independence, 1925. Awarded Pulitzer Prize ($2,000) for the best book of 1925 upon history of U.S. (6th vol. of History of the U.S.). Died Jan. 7, 1931.

CHANNING, Grace Ellery (Grace Ellery Channing-Stetson), writer; b. Providence, R.I., Dec. 27, 1862; d. William Francis (M.D.) and Mary Jane (Tarr) Channing; g.d. Rev. William Ellery Channing; ed. pvt. schs.; m. Charles Walter Stetson, 1894 (died July 20, 1911). Republican. Author: The Sister of a Saint, 1895; The Fortune of a Day, 1900; Sea Drift (verse), 1899. Editor: Dr. Channing's Note Book; War Letters of Edmond Genet, 1918. Home: New York, N.Y. Died Apr. 4, 1937.

CHANNING, Walter, alienist; b. Concord, Mass., Apr. 14, 1849; s. William Ellery and Ellen K. (Fuller) C.; brother of Carolyn Sturgis Cabot and Edward C.; ed. Chauncy Hall Sch. and, 1867-68, Mass. Inst. Tech.; M.D., Harvard U., 1872; (LL.D., Tufts, 1900); m. Anna K. Morse, June 25, 1878. Hon. fellow Clark U., 1890-92; asst. phys., N.Y. State Asylum for Insane Criminals, 1875-77; 1st asst. phys., State Insane Hosp., Danvers, Mass., 1878-79; supt. pvt. hosp. for mental diseases, 1879—; prof. mental diseases, Tufts Med. Sch., 1895-1903; chmn. bd. trustees Boston State Hosp., 1908-14. Address: Brookline, Mass. Died Nov. 1921.

CHANNING, William Ellery, poet and essayist; b. Boston, Nov. 29, 1818; ed. Boston Latin School and Harvard; lived some time in Ill. and Ohio; m. Ellen, d. Timothy Fuller (dec.). Spent several yrs. in newspaper and mag. work. Author: Thoreau, the Poet-Naturalist. Home: Concord, Mass. Died 1901.

CHANNON, Frank Ernest, author; b. Cheltenham, Gloucestershire, Eng., July 18, 1870; s. Daniel Walkley and Eliza Ann (Rawlinson) C.; ed. pvt. sch.; diplomas, Coll. of Preceptors and Soc. Science, Letters and Art, London; m. Lenora Flood, Sept. 8, 1894. Came to U.S., 1891; engaged in jewelry business until 1898; served in U.S.N. during and after Spanish-Am. War, 1898-99. Author: An American Boy at Henley, 1910; Henley's American Captain, 1912. Compiler: Handgrips, 1913. Editor Vineland Republican. Dir. Vineland Chamber of Commerce; sec. Unitarian Bd. of Trustees; trustee Vineland Hist. and Antiquarian Soc.; sec. local council Boy Scouts America. Home: Vineland, N.J. Died Nov. 22, 1920.

CHANUTE, Octave, engineer; b. Paris, France, Feb. 18, 1832; s. Joseph and Eliza (De Bonnaire) C.; came to U.S., 1838; ed. pvt. schs., New York; (Dr. Engring., U. of Ill., 1905); m. Annie James, Mar. 12, 1857. Civ. engr. on various rys., 1849-63; chief engr. C.&A. R.R., 1863-67, Sundry Kan. R.R., 1867-73, Erie R.R., 1873-83; pres. Chicago Tie Preserving Co., 1893—. Author: The Kansas City Bridge (with George Morison), 1870; Progress in Flying Machines, 1894. Home: Chicago, Ill. Died 1910.

CHAPELLE, Placide Louis, R. C. archbishop; b. diocese of Mende, France, Aug. 28, 1842; came to U.S., 1859; took complete theol. and philos. courses at St. Mary's Coll.; taught in St. Charles Coll., 1863-65; ordained priest, 1865; (D.D., St. Mary's, 1868); in missionary work, 1865-70; asst. pastor (1870) and later pastor, St. John's Ch., and of St. Joseph's, Baltimore; pastor St. Matthew's, Washington, 1882; prominent as theologian and pres. theol. confs. in Baltimore and Washington; apptd., 1891, coadjutor bishop to Archbishop Salpòinte, with right of succession, and consecrated titular bishop of Arabissus; promoted archbishop (titular to Sebaste, May 1893); on resignation of Archbishop Salpòinte became archbishop of Santa Fé, Jan. 1894; apptd., Nov. 1897, archbishop of New Orleans; apptd. apostolic delegate, by the Pope, of Cuba and Puerto Rico, Sept. 16, 1898; apptd. by the Pope apostolic delegate of the Philippine Islands, Sept. 1899. Died 1905.

CHAPIN, Alfred Clark, congressman; b. S. Hadley, Mass., Mar. 8, 1848; s. Ephraim and Josephine (Clark) C.; A.B., Williams, 1869; LL.B., Harvard, 1871; (LL.D., Williams, 1909); m. Grace Stebbins, Feb. 24, 1884. Admitted to bar, 1872, and then in practice at New York. Mem. N.Y. Assembly, 1882-83 (speaker 1883); comptroller, N.Y., 1884-87; mayor, Brooklyn, 1888-91; mem. 52d Congress, 1891-92, 2d N.Y. Dist., resigned, Nov. 16, 1892; railroad commr., N.Y., 1892-97. Democrat. Home: New York, N.Y. Died Oct. 21, 1936.

CHAPIN, Anna Alice, author; b. New York, Dec. 16, 1880; d. F. W. (M.D.) and Anna J. (Hoppin) C.; ed. under pvt. instrn.; studied music under Harry Rowe Shelley, New York; m. Robert Peyton Carter, 1906. Author: The Story of the Rhinegold, 1897; Wonder Tales from Wagner, 1898; Wotan, Siegfried and Brünnhilde, 1898; Masters of Music, 1901; Babes in Toyland (with Glen McDonough), 1904; Humpty Dumpty, 1905; The Heart of Music, 1906; Königskinder, 1911; The Eagle's Mate, 1914; Greenwich Village, 1917. Died Feb. 26, 1920.

CHAPIN, Augusta J., Universalist minister; b. Lakeville, nr. Rochester, N.Y.; d. Almon Morris and Jane (Pease) C., descendant in 8th generation of Deacon Samuel Chapin of Springfield, Mass.; studied in Olivet Coll. and Univ. of Mich. (A.M., U. of Mich., 1884; D.D., Lombard Univ., 1893), in active ministry, 1859—; ordained Universalist minister, Dec. 3, 1863. Has held pastorates Mich., Iowa, Pa., Ill., Neb., N.Y.; writer and lecturer on art and literature; extension lecturer in English, U. of Chicago; lecturer in literature and art, Lombard Univ.; chmn. Woman's Gen. Com., World's Parliament of Religions, Chicago, 1893. Home: New York, N.Y. Died 1905.

CHAPIN, Benjamin Chester, dramatist; b. Bristolville, O., Aug. 9, 1874; s. Warren Ely and Catherine (Taylor) C.; grad. Bristolville High Sch., 1890, New Lyme (O.) Inst., 1892; studied various univs.; unmarried. Platform lecturer and entertainer, 1892-98; engaged in presenting "Lincoln," a dramatic monologue, 1902-05; produced an original 4-act drama, same title, in New York, 1906; has made many tours of U.S. as lecturer, actor and dramatist. Author, dir. and producer of a series of 10 moving picture features founded on the early life struggles of Abraham Lincoln; gen. dir. Benjamin Chapin studios, Ridgefield Park, N.J.; pres. Charter Features Corp. of New York. Home: Ridgefield Park, N.J. Died June 3, 1918.

CHAPIN, Charles Frederic, newspaperman; b. S. Hadley, Mass., Aug. 3, 1852; s. Enoch Cooley and Harriet J. (Abbe) C.; A.B., Yale, 1877; m. Katharine Mattison, Oct. 12, 1877; children—Carl Mattison, Mrs. Barbara Russell and Mrs. Harold A. Marvin (twins), latter dec. Editor Waterbury American, 1878—. Home: Waterbury, Conn. Died Oct. 27, 1926.

CHAPIN, Charles Sumner, school adminstr.; b. Westfield, Mass., Oct. 19, 1859; s. Rev. Daniel Ely and Betsey (Hancock) C.; A.B., Wesleyan U., Conn., 1880, A.M., 1883; spl. student Clark U., 1897; (D.Sc., Brown U., 1908); m. Minnie Gertrude Fisher, Aug. 3, 1886. Prin. Brookfield (Mass.) High Sch., 1881-82; asso. teacher Worcester Classical High Sch., 1882-84; mem. Mass. bar and practiced law with Hon. John R. Thayer, Worcester, 1884-86; supt. schs. Middletown, Conn., 1886-87; asso. teacher Hartford Pub. High Sch., 1887-90; prin. Fitchburg (Mass.) High Sch., 1890-96, Westfield (Mass.) State Normal Sch., 1896-1901, R.I. State Normal Sch., 1901-08, Montclair (N.J.) State Normal Sch., July 1, 1908—. Home: Montclair, N.J. Died Mar. 21, 1924.

CHAPIN, Charles Value, health officer; b. Providence, R.I., Jan. 17, 1856; s. Joshua B. and Louise (Value) C.; A.B., Brown U., 1876; M.D., Bellevue Hosp. Med. Coll. (New York U.), 1879; Sc.D., Brown, 1909, R.I. State Coll., 1932; LL.D., Yale, 1927; m. Anna Augusta Balch, May 6, 1886; 1 son, Howard M. House physician Bellevue Hosp., 1879-80; supt. of health, Providence, 1884-1932, then emeritus; prof. physiology, Brown U., 1886-96; city registrar of Providence, 1889-1932. Lecturer, Harvard Med. Sch., 1909, Harvard-Mass. Inst. of Tech. School for Health Officers, 1913-22, Harvard School of Hygiene, 1923-35; spl. agent of A.M.A. for study of state sanitation, 1913. Providence City Hosp. named Charles V. Chapin Hosp., 1931. Author: Sources and Modes of Infection, 1910; State Public Health Work, 1916; How to Avoid Infection, 1917; Changes in Type of Contagious Disease, 1926. Mem. med. advisory bd. Am. Red Cross, World War. Fellow Am. Acad. Arts and Sciences, Royal Soc. Medicine (Eng.). Awarded Marcellus Hartley gold medal by Nat. Acad. of Sciences, 1928; Sedgwick memorial medal for distinguished service in pub. health, 1929; Susan Colver Rosenberger special honor medal, Brown U., 1935. Home: Providence, R.I. Died Jan. 31, 1941.

CHAPIN, Henry Barton, clergyman; b. Rochester, N.Y., Sept. 14, 1827; s. Hon. Moses and Lucy Terry (Barton) C.; A.B., Yale U., 1847, A.M., 1850; Union Theol. Sem., 1851-52; Princeton Theol. Sem., 1852-54; (hon. Ph.D., Princeton, 1868, D.D., 1891); m. Harriet Ann Smith, Feb. 22, 1854; father of Henry Dwight C. Ordained Presbyterian ministry, 1854; city missionary, New York, 1854-56; pastor Second Ch., Steubenville, O., 1856-58, Third Ch., Trenton, N.J., 1858-66; asso. prin. Edgehill Sch., Princeton, N.J., 1866-67; prin. Chapin Collegiate Sch., New York, 1867-1903, prin. emeritus, 1903-07. Recording sec. U.S. Evang. Alliance, 1871—; chaplain Soc. Cincinnati in R.I., 1884—; chaplain-gen. Soc. of the Cincinnati, 1905; chaplain Presbyn. Home for Aged Women, New York, 1900—. Died July 7, 1914.

CHAPIN, Henry Edgerton, biologist; b. Wilbraham, Mass., May 9, 1859; s. Samuel W. and Maria (Damon) C.; B.Sc., Mass. Agrl. Coll., Amherst, Mass., and Boston U., 1881; post-grad. student chemistry and biology, Johns Hopkins, 1886-87; M.Sc., Mich. Agrl. Coll., 1893; (Sc.D., McKendree Coll., 1908); m. Eudora M. Hoffman, June 29, 1893. Taught in secondary schs. and engaged in agrl. journalism, 1881-86; teacher Pa. State Normal Sch., 1888-90; prof. biology, Ohio U., 1891-1900; instr. in biology and physiography, high sch., New York, 1900—. Lecturer and mem. Council Brooklyn Inst. Arts and Sciences and pres. dept. of botany, 1904-14; editor "Tomahawk," mag. of Alpha Sigma Phi, 1916-21. Capt. Ohio N.G., 1892-93; capt. New York reserve list for commd. officers, 1917—. Joint author: Chapin's and Rettger's Elementary Zoölogy and Guide, 1896. Died Mar. 1922.

CHAPIN, Howard Millar, librarian; b. Providence, R.I., May 11, 1887; s. Charles V. and Anna Augusta (Balch) C.; A.B., Brown U., 1908; m. Hope Caroline, d. Gov. D. Russell Brown, of R.I., Apr. 10, 1912. In various lines of business until 1912; librarian R.I. Hist. Soc., 1912—, also Shepley Library, 1917-25; business mgr. Brown Alumni Magazine Co., 1912-15. Chmn. R.I. State Geographical Board. Author: Murthy's Cattage, 1911; Titanic Disaster, 1913; The Printing Press of the French Fleet, 1914; Cartography of Rhode Island, 1915; Cameo Portraiture in America, 1918; Dogs in Early New England, 1920; New England Vessels in the Louisbourg Expedition, 1923; Bermuda Privateers, Vol. I, 1923, Vol. II, 1925; Rhode Island Privateers in King George's War, 1926; Privateering in King George's War (1739-48), 1928; Roger Williams and the King's Colors, 1928; The New England Flag, 1929; Emblems of Rhode Island, 1930; Sachems of the Narragansetts, 1931; American Municipal Arms, 1932; Civic Heraldry in America, 1935. Compiler: Bibliography of Rhode Island, 1914; Documentary History of Rhode Island, Vol. I, 1916, Vol. II, 1920; Canadian Municipal Arms, 1937; etc. Editor of Rhode Island Court Records, Vol. I, 1920, Vol. II, 1922; Rhode Island Land Evidences, 1921; Records of the Town of Warwick.

R.I., 1926. Presented, with wife, the Peter Chapin collection of books on dogs to Coll. of William and Mary, Williamsburg, Va. Home: Providence, R.I. Died Sept. 18, 1940.

CHAPIN, John Bassett, physician; b. New York, Dec. 4, 1829; s. William and Elizabeth H. (Bassett) C.; A.B., Williams Coll., 1850; M.D., Jefferson Med. Coll., Phila., 1853; (LL.D., Jefferson, and Williams); m. Harriet E. Preston, Mar. 18, 1858. Resident phys. N.Y. Hosp. State Lunatic Asylum, 1854, Brigham Hall, Canandaigua, 1860-69; med. supt. State Hosp., Willard, N.Y., 1869-84; phys.-in-chief, Pa. Hosp. for Insane, Phila., 1884-1911. In a public communication, 1862, recommended changes in asylum construction which would provide for segregation of insane in detached blocks, according to classes and conditions; views were adopted in Willard Hosp. Author: Compendium of Insanity for Physicians and Students, 1899. Retired, June 1911. Died Jan. 18, 1918.

CHAPIN, Robert Coit, economist; b. Beloit, Wis., Jan. 4, 1863; s. Aaron Lucius and Fanny (Coit) C.; B.A., Beloit Coll., 1885; B.D., Yale, 1890; U. of Berlin, 1894-95; Ph.D., Columbia, 1909; m. Winogene Grabill, Dec. 25, 1907. Prof. history, Drury Coll., Mo., 1890-92; prof. economics, Beloit Coll., 1892—. Sec. N.Y. Charities Conf. Com. on Standard of Living (on leave of absence from coll.), 1907. Author: Standard of Living Among Workingmen's Families in New York City, 1909. Home: Beloit, Wis. Died Sept. 12, 1913.

CHAPIN, Roy Dikeman, mfr.; b. Lansing, Mich., Feb. 23, 1880; s. Edward C. and Ella (King) C.; student U. of Mich., 1899-1901, hon. M.A., 1922; m. Inez Tiedeman, Nov. 4, 1914; children—Roy D., Joan K., John C., Sara A., Daniel, Marian. Identified with automobile business in Detroit from 1901; gen. sales mgr. Olds Motor Works, 1904-06; organizer E. R. Thomas-Detroit Co., 1906, and treas. and gen. mgr. same, 1906-08; also treas. and gen. mgr. of its successor, the Chalmers-Detroit Motor Co., 1908-10; pres. Hudson Motor Car Co., 1910-23, chmn. bd., 1923-33, pres., 1933—; sec. of commerce in Cabinet of President Hoover, 1932-33. Chmn. Highway Transport Com., Council Nat. Defense, 1917-18. V.p. and dir. Detroit Symphony Soc.; dir. Detroit Community Fund; chmn. Highway Transport Com. of Internat. Chamber Commerce; pres. Sixth Internat. Road Congress, Washington, 1930. Home: Grosse Point Farms, Mich. Died Feb. 16, 1936.

CHAPLIN, Winfield Scott, engr.; b. Glenburn, Me., Aug. 22, 1847; s. Col. Daniel and Susan D. (Gibbs) C.; grad. U.S. Mil. Acad., 1870; (hon. A.M., Union Coll., 1885; LL.D., Harvard, 1893; Doc. of Tech., Imperial Univ. of Japan, 1915); m. Harriet B. Caldwell, 1873. Second lt. 5th U.S. Arty., 1870-72; civil engr., on ry., 1872-73; prof. mech. engring., Me. State Coll., 1873-76; prof. engring., Imperial U. of Japan, 1877-82; prof. mathematics and adj. prof. physics, Union Coll., 1883-86; prof. engring. and dean, Lawrence Scientific Sch. (Harvard), 1886-91; chancellor Washington U., 1891-1907. Decorated Order of the Rising Sun (Japan). Fellow Am. Acad. Arts and Sciences. Home: San Antonio, Tex. Died Mar. 12, 1918.

CHAPLINE, Jesse Grant, educator; b. Waverly, Mo., Jan. 13, 1870; s. William Purnell and Sallie Ann C.; ed. St. Louis Coll.; m. Anne J. Johnson, May 12, 1909; children—Marjorie Anne, Dorothy Jane, Jesse Grant. Founder and president of the La Salle Extension University; pres. Marye Safety Nut Corp.; dir. Commercial Research Corp. Vice-pres. Nat. Home Study Council. Writer on sales and business topics. Home: Chicago, Ill. Died July 3, 1937.

CHAPMAN, Arthur, writer; b. Rockford, Ill., June 25, 1873; s. George and Sarah (Tole) C.; pub. sch. edn.; m. Lillian Mathewson Eddy, June 27, 1895 (died Feb. 26, 1923); children—John Arthur, Arthur Seaverns, Neil Thomas, Lillian Esther (dec.); m. 2d, Kathleen Caesar, July 12, 1924. Reporter Chicago Daily News and contbr. verse to that paper, 1895-98; with Denver Republican, 1898-1913; mng. editor Denver Times, 1916-19; removed to New York; Sunday staff writer, New York Herald Tribune until 1925, then contributed to magazines. Author: Out Where the West Begins, 1917; Cactus Center, 1921; Mystery Ranch, 1921; The Story of Colorado, 1924; John Crews, 1926; The Pony Express, 1932. Home: New York, N.Y. Died Dec. 4, 1935.

CHAPMAN, Carlton Theodore, artist; b. New London, O., Sept. 18, 1860; ed. Oberlin, O.; art edn. Nat. Acad. Design, and Art Students' League, New York, Julian Acad., Paris; m. Aurélie M. Reynaud, Nov. 8, 1911. Specialty, marines and landscapes; silver medal, Boston, 1892; medal, Chicago Expn., 1893, Atlanta Expn., 1895, Buffalo Expn., 1901, Charleston Expn., 1902; mem. Internat. Jury of Awards, St. Louis Expn., 1904. War corr. and artist, Harper's Weekly, Spanish-Am. War, 1898, N.A. Home: New York, N.Y. Died Feb. 12, 1925.

CHAPMAN, Elverton R., banker; b. New York, Aug. 5, 1848; s. Rev. Carlos R. and Susan M. (Beardsley) C.; ed. Fredonia (N.Y.) Acad., Mt. Union Coll., Alliance, O., Eastman's Business Coll., Poughkeepsie, N.Y., grad. 1864; LL.B., Columbian (then George Washington) U., 1871; thrice married; m. 3d, Mrs. Lucille N. Nelson, May 1908; children—Carlos B. (dec.), Melville D. (dec.), Cornelia C. (Mrs. P. N. Furber), Amabel M. (Lady Eardley-Wilmot), Virginia M. (Countess de Bellissen-Durban), Elverton Reginald (dec.). Mem. Co. G, 86th Ohio Inf., 1862; mem. 77th Regt., N.G.S.N.Y., 1864; chief stamp div., Internal Revenue Dept., Washington, 1875-79; in contracting business, 1879-84; banker and broker, 1884—; mem. Moore & Schley, 1888-1901; E. R. Chapman & Co., 1901-06; firm retired from business, selling seat on N.Y. Stock Exchange. Treas.; pres. Flatbush Gas Co., Newtown Gas Co., Jamaica Gas Light Co., Woodhaven Gas Co., Richmond Hill Gas Co., Elliott-Chapman Coal & Coke Co., Chapman Investment Co., Elverton Land Co., Ala. Iron & Steel Co. Episcopalian. Republican. Home: Great Neck, L.I. Died Dec. 22, 1928.

CHAPMAN, Ervin S., clergyman; b. Defiance Co., O., June 23, 1838; s. George W. and Narcissa (Hopkins) C.; ed. pub. schs. and pvt. tuition; (hon. A.M., Westfield Coll., Ill., 1872; D.D., Lebanon Valley Coll., Pa., 1882; LL.D., Otterbein U., O., 1904); m. Adelia Haymaker, Oct. 2, 1860. Com. clerk U.S. Ho. of Rep., 1864-69; entered U.B. ministry, 1870, ordained 1872; transferred to Presbyn. Ch., 1883; pastor in Ohio, Wyo., Calif., 1870-98; supt. California Anti-Saloon League, and editor The Searchlight, its official organ, 1898-1914. Author: Particeps Criminis. The Story of a California Rabbit Drive. Originator of the "Stainless Flag" movement. Home: Berkeley, Calif. Died Aug. 30, 1921.

CHAPMAN, Francis, lawyer; b. Burlington, N.J., Aug. 19, 1869; s. Samuel (M.D.) and Mary Elizabeth (Hopkins) C.; Washington Acad., Princess Anne, Md.; LL.B., U. of Pa., 1891; unmarried. Practiced, Phila., 1891—; mem. faculty of law, Temple U., 1902—, and dean Sch. of Law, July 1906—. Republican. Presbyn. Author: Pennsylvania Mechanics Lien Law, 1909; Principles of the Law of Evidence, 1930. Home: Philadelphia, Pa. Died May 2, 1939.

CHAPMAN, Frank Elmo, hospital dir.; b. St. Louis, Mo., Dec. 27, 1884; s. Alonzo Loring and Elizabeth Mason (Foster) C.; grad. high schs., St. Louis; m. Vida May Black, Dec. 27, 1911; 1 dau., Elizabeth Scott. In charge of med. dept. St.L.&S.F. R.R., 1906-11; in charge St. Louis City Hosp., 1911-15; in charge Mount Sinai Hosp., Cleveland, O., 1915—; mem. editorial bd. Modern Hospital. Mason. Author: Hospital Organization and Operation, 1924. Home: Cleveland, Ohio. Died 1931.

CHAPMAN, Henry Cadwalader, physician; b. Phila., Aug. 17, 1845; s. George William and Emily (Markoe) C.; grad. Univ. of Pa., 1864 (A.M.), med. dept. same, M.D., 1867; M.D., Jefferson Med. Coll., 1878; studied 3 yrs. in Europe; m. Hannah Neylee Megargee, Dec. 2, 1876. Resident physician Pa. Hosp. and lecturer on anatomy and physiology, Univ. of Pa., 1870; prof. institutes of medicine and med. jurisprudence, Jefferson Med. Coll., 1880; coroner's physician, Phila., 1876-81. Mem. Phila. Acad. Natural Sciences, 1868—, curator same, 1875—; fellow Coll. Physicians, Phila., 1880; prosector Zoöl. Soc., Phila. Author: Evolution of Life; History of the Discovery of the Circulation of the Blood; Treatise upon Human Physiology; Medical Jurisprudence and Toxicology, 1903. Home: Philadelphia. Died 1909.

CHAPMAN, Henry Leland, college prof.; b. Bethel, Me., July 26, 1845; s. Elbridge and Delinda Twitchell (Kimball) C.; A.B., Bowdoin College, 1866, A.M., 1869; grad. Bangor Theol. Sem., 1869; (D.D., Bowdoin, 1890, LL.D., 1908); m. Emma Caroline Smith, Aug. 21, 1870 (dec.). Prof. English lit., Bowdoin Coll., 1875—. Pres. board of trustees Bangor Theol. Sem. Republican. Conglist. Home: Brunswick, Me. Died Feb. 24, 1912.

CHAPMAN, J. Wilbur, clergyman; b. Richmond, Ind., June 17, 1859; s. Alexander Hamilton and Lorinda (McWhinney) C.; bro. of Edwin Garner C.; A.B., Lake Forest (Ill.) U., 1879; grad. Lane Theol. Sem., 1882; (D.D., U. of Wooster, 1898; LL.D., Heidelberg U., Ohio, 1910); m. Irene E. Steddon, May 10, 1882 (died 1886); 2d, Agnes Pruyn Strain, Nov. 4, 1888 (died 1907); 3d, Mabel Cornelia Moulton, Aug. 30, 1910. Ordained Presbyn. ministry, 1882; pastor First Ref. Ch., Albany, 1884-90; Bethany Presbyn. Ch., Phila., 1890-93; evangelist, laboring in all parts of the country, 1893-96; again pastor Bethany Ch., Phila., 1896-1900; pastor Fourth Ch., New York, 1900-05; exec. sec. Gen. Assembly's Com. on Evangelistic Work for the Presbyn. Ch., from Jan. 1, 1903; now rep.-at-large for Evangelistic Com. of Presbyn. Ch. Author: And Peter; The Lost Crown; The Secret of a Happy Day; The Surrendered Life; Spiritual Life of the Sunday School; Chapman's Pocket Sermons, 1911; Revival Sermons, 1911; When Home Is Heaven, 1917. Moderator Gen. Assembly Presbyn. Ch. U.S.A., Dallas, Tex., May 1917. Home: Jamaica, L.I., N.Y. Died Dec. 25, 1918.

CHAPMAN, James Crosby, prof. edn.; b. Nottingham, Eng., July 23, 1889; s. James (D.D.) and Annie (Thompson) C.; B.Sc., U. of London, 1909, D.Sc., 1913; B.A., U. of Cambridge, 1912; Ph.D., Columbia, 1914; m. Daisy Rogers, Oct. 20, 1917. Came to U.S., 1913, naturalized citizen, 1923. Asso. prof. experimental edn., Western Reserve U., 1914-20; asso. prof. ednl. psychology, Yale, 1920—. Conglist. Author: Homogeneous Rontgen Radiation, 1913; Individual Differences in Improvement, 1914; Scientific Measurement of Classroom Products, 1917; Trade Tests, 1921; Principles of Education, 1924. Home: New Haven, Conn. Died July 15, 1925.

CHAPMAN, John Jay, author; b. New York, N.Y., 1862; s. Henry G. C.; A.B., Harvard, 1884, A.M., 1885; L.H.D., Hobart, 1900; read law, admitted to bar, 1888; m. Minna Timmins, July 2, 1889; m. 2d, Elizabeth W. Chanler, Apr. 23, 1899. Not in practice since 1898. Author: William Lloyd Garrison, 1913; Songs and Poems, 1919; A Glance Toward Shakespeare, 1922; Letters and Religion, 1923; Dante (essay and transls.), 1927. Home: Barrytown, N.Y. Died Nov. 3, 1933.

CHAPMAN, Pleasant Thomas, congressman; b. on farm in Johnson County, Ill., Oct. 8, 1854; A.B., McKendree Coll., Ill., 1876. Admitted to bar, 1878, then in practice at Vienna, Ill. County supt. schs., Johnson County, Ill., 1877-82; county judge, 1882-90; mem. Ill. Senate, 1890-1902; mem. 59th to 61st Congresses (1905-11), 24th Ill. Dist. Republican. Home: Vienna, Ill. Died Jan. 31, 1931.

CHAPMAN, Robert Hollister, topographic engr.; b. New Haven, Conn., July 29, 1868; s. Charles Wesley and Etta (Sperry) C.; ed. Corcoran Scientific School, Washington, D.C.; m. Frances Beardsley Andrews, June 1, 1907. With U.S. Geol. Survey, 1880—; has made topographic surveys and explorations in prin. Western and Southern states, maps of portion of Death Valley and adjacent deserts and high Sierras, Cal.; sent to Ottawa, May 1909, to introduce U.S. topographic methods in Geol. Survey of Can.; in charge of field work, on Vancouver Island, 1909, 1910, 1911; acting supt. Glacier Nat. Park, Mont., 1912; returned to U.S. Geol. Survey, 1913. Maj., Engrs. R.C. and on active duty, June 1917. Author many bulletins published by governments of United States and Canada. Personal explorations in Northern Selkirks, B.C., 1915, and Northern Canadian Rockies, 1919. Home: Washington, D.C. Died Jan. 11, 1920.

CHAPMAN, Mrs. Woodallen, writer, lecturer; b. Lakeside, O., June 25, 1875; d. Chilion B. and Mary A. (Wood) Allen; grad. Ann Arbor (Mich.) High Sch., 1895; student U. of Mich., 1895-98; m. William Brewster Chapman, Feb. 19, 1902. Began writing and lecturing, 1895; asso. editor American Motherhood, 1904-07; nat. supt. purity dept. W.C.T.U., 1908-11; on staff Ladies' Home Journal, 1910-13; field sec. N.Y. Social Hygiene Society, 1915-18; sec. women's work, Am. Social Hygiene Assn.; lecturer under women's sect. social hygiene div. of Commn. on Training Camp Activities of War Dept.; chmn. social hygiene com. pub. health dept. of Gen. Fedn. of Women's Clubs. Author: Life Sketch of Dr. Mary Wood-Allen, 1908; The Moral Problem of the Children, 1909; How Shall I Tell My Child?, 1911; In Her Teens, 1914. Died Oct. 27, 1923.

CHAPPELL, Walter Franklin, surgeon; b. in Ont., Can., Sept. 26, 1856; s. Robert and Mary (Moore) C.; M.D., Toronto U., 1879; m. Louise Graves, Jan. 31, 1893. Surgeon, Manhattan Eye, Ear and Throat Hosp., 1887—; prof. clin. laryngology, Coll. Phys. and Surg. (Columbia), 1910—. Fellow Am. Surg. Assn., Royal Coll. Surgeons, Eng. Republican. Episcopalian. Died Oct. 19, 1918.

CHAPPELLE, William D., bishop; b. Winnsboro, S.C., Nov. 16, 1857; ed. Fairfield Normal Institute, Allen Univ., Columbia, S.C.; (A.M., D.D., LL.D., Ph.D.); m. Miss R. C. Palmer, Apr. 25, 1900. Ordained A.M.E. ministry, 1881; editor A.M.E. S.S. lit., 1900-08; pres. Allen U., 1908-12; bishop A.M.E. Ch., May 23, 1912—. Pres. Gen. Ednl. Bd., A.M.E. Ch.; pres. bd. trustees Allen U.; connectional trustee Wilberforce U., Xenia, O. Mason. Author: Sermons and Addresses (2 vols.). Became chancellor Allen Univ. Has contributed much money to the development of Allen Univ. Home: Columbia, S.C. Died June 15, 1925.

CHARLES, Benjamin Hynes; b. Chester, Ill., Apr. 26, 1866; s. Benjamin Hynes and Achsah Susan (Holmes) C.; A.B., Westminster Coll., Fulton, Mo., 1885, A.M., 1888, LL.D., 1930; LL.B., Yale, 1891; m. Nancy McCandless Horne, June 30, 1903; children—Benjamin Hynes III, Robert Horne, William Hamill. Admitted to Mo. bar, 1892, and began practice in St. Louis; mem. Charles & Lackey, 1898-1900; asso. city counselor, St. Louis, 1903-10; practiced alone, 1910-17; mem. Charles & Rutherford, 1917-27, then alone. Trustee Westminster Coll. (pres. bd.). Democrat. Presbyn. Home: St. Louis Co., Mo. Died May 22, 1937.

CHARLTON, Earle Perry, merchant, mfr.; b. Chester, Conn., June 19, 1863; s. James Duncan and

Lydia A. (Ladd) C.; ed. pub. schs. of Norwich and Hartford, Conn.; m. Ida May Stein, June 19, 1889; children—Earle Perry, Ruth (Mrs. Frederick M. Mitchell), Virginia (Mrs. Kenneth C. Lincoln). Began at 17 with Thomas E. Newell Co., 5 and 10 cent business, Boston; associated with S. H. Knox of Buffalo, N.Y., 1889, in same line of business, locating first store at Fall River, Mass.; separated from partner, 1895, dividing stores, and organized the E. P. Charlton Co.; pioneer in opening 5 and 10 cent stores west of the Rocky Mountains and in Canada; one of the founders of F. W. Woolworth Co., 1912, at which time was operating 54 stores; built Charlton Mills, Fall River, 1909; pres. Charlton Mills; v.p. F. W. Woolworth Co.; trustee Eastern Mass. Street Ry. Mem. War Industries Bd. and Purchasing Dept. of War Dept., 1918. Trustee Tufts Coll., Truesdale Hosp., Union Hosp. Decorated by Govt. of France. Republican. Conglist. Mason. Home: Fall River, Mass. Died Nov. 20, 1930.

CHARLTON, George James, ry. official; b. Hamilton, Ont., Sept. 9, 1860; s. James and Mary C.; ed. pub. and pvt. schs.; m. Elizabeth Hilton, 1883. Since 1875 continuously in the service of the C.&A. R.R. and its successor, the C.&A. Ry., beginning as messenger boy in the gen. pass. dept.; gen. pass. agt., 1901-09; pass. traffic mgr., Dec. 1, 1909—. Home: Oak Park, Ill. Died Jan. 28, 1929.

CHARLTON, James, ry. official; b. Botnal Co., Northumberland, Eng., May 15, 1832. Entered ry. service, Apr., 1847, and served from jr. clerk to chief clerk and cashier, Newcastle & Carlisle Ry.; then with Great Western Ry. of Can.; asst. to chief clerk, 1857, auditor and gen. pass. agt., until Mar., 1870; gen. pass. and ticket agt., N. Mo. R.R., 1870-71; gen. pass. and ticket agt., C.&A. R.R., 1871-1900; chmn. Transcontinental Passenger Assn., at Denver, 1900-01, at Chicago, Oct., 1901—. Home: Chicago, Ill. Died Nov. 19, 1913.

CHARLTON, Loudon, concert mgr.; b. Monmouth, Ill., Dec. 15, 1869; s. James Beauvard and Lucy Abigail (Gow) C.; ed. high sch., Omaha, Neb.; m. Helen Stanley, opera singer, Oct. 3, 1917. Concert mgr. in New York, 1899; Nordica, Sembrich, Stanley, Melba, Kubelik, Gabrilowitsch, Novães, Flonzaley, Toscanini, La Scala Orchestra, etc., have been under his management; retired. Home: Stamford, Conn. Died Apr. 27, 1931.

CHARLTON, Paul, judge; b. Harrisburg, Pa., Nov. 2, 1856; s. Samuel Templeton and Clare (Porter) C.; A.B., Yale, 1878; m. Helen Wanstall, Jan. 8, 1908. Admitted to bar, 1882; practiced at Harrisburg, Pa., 1882-88, Omaha, Neb., 1888-1905; law officer, Bur. Insular Affairs, War Dept., May, 1905-Aug., 1911; U.S. district judge for Puerto Rico, Aug. 1, 1911-Dec. 15, 1912; resumed practice at San Juan. Lecturer on Colonial Administration, Coll. Polit. Sciences, Geo. Washington U.; asso. editor Buletin de Colonization Comparée, Brussels. Home: San Juan, P.R. Died June 4, 1917.

CHARLTON, Walter Glasco, judge; b. Savannah, Ga., June 5, 1851; s. Robert Milledge and Margaret (Shick) C.; student U. of Va., 1869-72; m. Mary Walton Johnston, Feb. 11, 1874. Asst. solicitor-gen. Eastern Jud. Circuit of Ga., 1873-77; solicitor-gen. same, 1881-85; alderman of Savannah 3 terms; chmn. Dem. Co. Com., Chatham Co., Ga., 3 terms; temporary chmn., Dem. State Conv., 1883; pres. Congressional Conv. 1st dist., 1886; then judge Superior Ct., Eastern Jud. Circuit of Ga. Pres. Ga. Soc. S.R., Ga. Soc. of the Cincinnati, Oglethorpe Monument Assn. of Ga. Episcopalian. Democrat. Home: Savannah, Ga. Died Feb. 13, 1917.

CHARTRAND, Joseph, bishop; b. St. Louis, Mo., May 11, 1870; s. Joseph and Margaret C. Ordained priest by Bishop Chatard, Sept. 24, 1892; consecrated bishop coadjutor by Cardinal Falconio, Sept. 15, 1910, bishop of Indianapolis, Ind., Sept. 7, 1918. Died Dec. 8, 1933.

CHASE, Arthur Horace, librarian (retired); b. Concord, N.H., Feb. 16, 1864; s. William M. and Ellen S. (Abbott) C.; A.B., Dartmouth, 1886, A.M., 1893; law student Boston U., 1888; m. Alice M. Fisk, Sept. 17, 1888 (died 1924); children—Mrs. Marjorie Fisk Merrill, Robert Martin; m. 2d, Alice M. Pray, June 17, 1925. Admitted to N.H. bar, 1890; state librarian, N.H., 1895-1923, also clk. N.H. Supreme Court; sec. Com. to Revise Pub. Laws, 1923. Congregationalist. Republican. Died Feb. 24, 1930.

CHASE, Benjamin E., mfr., banker; b. Floyd, N.Y., Aug. 2, 1843; s. Stephan C. and Laura A. C.; ed. Vernon (N.Y.) Acad.; m. Marilla A. Murty, Sept. 19, 1870. Pres. Central Bank of Rochester, East Side Savings Bank; treas. Chamber Commerce; dir. Am. Fruit Product Co., Gen. Ry. Signal Co., Lyceum Theatre Co., N.Y.&Ky. Co., Pfaudler Co.; trustee Rochester Trust & Safe Deposit Co. (all of Rochester, N.Y.); pres. Ludlow & Southern Ry. Co. of Calif.; v.p. Peck & Chase Co. (Los Angeles); treas. Nat. Casket Co. of Oneida, N.Y. Home: Rochester, N.Y. Died Mar. 27, 1915.

CHASE, Benjamin Franklin, consul; b. Woodward Tp., Pa., Feb. 1, 1869; s. John M. and Tabitha S. (Williams) C.; LL.B., U. of Mich. Dept. of Law, 1891; m. Clemma B. Hayes, Aug. 4, 1896. Practiced law in Clearfield, Pa.; consul at Catania, Italy, 1905-07; apptd. consul to Zanzibar, 1907, but did not go to post; consul, at Leeds, Eng., 1909-13; Leghorn, Italy, 1913-14, Fiume, Hungary, Nov. 1914-July 1916, San José, Costa Rica, 1916 (in charge Am. interests, San José, Costa Rica, during revolutionary period, 1918-20); consul at Trondhjem, Norway, until closed consulate, Nov. 1921, then consul at Messina, Italy; home on sick leave, 1923-24. Republican. Baptist. Mason. Home: Clearfield, Pa. Died Nov. 23, 1925.

CHASE, Charles E., fire ins.; b. Dubuque, Ia., Mar. 29, 1857; s. George L. and Calista M. (Taft) C.; grad. Hartford High Sch., 1876; m. Helen Smith Bourne, June 9, 1886. Connected with Hartford Fire Ins. Co., at Hartford local agency, 1877-80, at home office, 1880—, 2d asst. sec., 1880-1903, v.p., 1903-08, pres., 1908-13, now chmn. bd.; chmn. bd. Hartford Accident & Indemnity Co., Hartford Live Stock Co.; chairman bd. Sanborn Map Co. of N.Y.; trustee Soc. of Savings; Hartford National Bank & Trust Co., The Bankers Trust Co. (Hartford). Pres. Hartford Board of Underwriters, 1894-1906; mem. Hartford Chamber of Commerce. Home: Hartford, Conn. Died Aug. 3, 1933.

CHASE, Charles Parker, banker; b. W. Newbury, Mass., May 6, 1845; s. Samuel Sewall and Eunice Noyes (Colby) C.; A.B., Dartmouth Coll., 1869, A.M., 1872; m. Fanny Huntington, July 30, 1874. Prof. Latin, Olivet (Mich.) Coll., 1872-78; tutor Greek, 1870-72, instr. polit. economy, 1884-92, treas., 1890-1916 (treas. emeritus), Dartmouth College. President Dartmouth Nat. Bank (cashier, 1878-92); v.p. Dartmouth Savings Bank; pres. Mascoma Electric Light & Power Co., 1912—. Republican. Conglist. Home: Hanover, N.H. Died Aug. 10, 1923.

CHASE, Emory Albert, judge; b. Hensonville, N.Y., Aug. 31, 1854; s. Albert and Laura O. (Woodworth) C.; ed. Ft. Edward Collegiate Inst., 1873-74; m. Mary E. Churchill, June 30, 1885. Practiced law at Catskill, N.Y.; 1st v.p. Catskill Savings Bank; supervisor Town of Catskill, 1890; mem. bd. edn., 1882-96 (pres. 1891-96); justice Supreme Ct. of N.Y., 3d Dist., terms, 1896-1910, 1910-24; judge Appellate Div. of Supreme Ct., 1901-06; judge Ct. of Appeals of N.Y., Jan. 9, 1906—. Republican. Address: Catskill, N.Y. Died June 25, 1921.

CHASE, Ethan Allen, nurseryman; b. Turner, Me., Jan. 18, 1832; s. Col. Nathaniel and Eunice (Westcott) C.; 6th generation from Aquila C., Newbury, Mass.; ed. Hebron Acad., Me.; m. Augusta Field, Nov. 3, 1860; father of Lewis Nathaniel C. Taught sch. in Ga., 1852-53; began nursery business, 1856; moved to Rochester, N.Y., 1868, and organized firm of Chase Bros., N.E. Nurseries; later established branch houses in Augusta, Me., Montreal, Toronto, St. Louis, New York, Chicago and Richmond, Va.; with brothers, established Ala. Nursery Co., Huntsville, 1889, of which became pres.; moved to Riverside, Calif., 1891, and with sons organized Chase Nursery Co.; organized, 1901, and pres. Nat. Orange Co. Mem. Bd. of Supervisors, Monroe Co., N.Y., 1877; mem. Com. of Fifteen to draw up charter for City of Riverside, 1907; declined nomination as first mayor of Riverside; del.-at-large Rep. Nat. Conv., Chicago, 1908. Home: Riverside, Calif. Died Oct. 9, 1921.

CHASE, Frank David, industrial engr.; b. Riverside, Ill.; s. David Fletcher and Emily Frances (Tabor) C.; B.S. in C.E., Mass. Inst. Tech., 1901. Pres. 1913—, Frank D. Chase, Inc., engineers and architects, specialists in design of industrial and mercantile bldg., operating throughout U.S. Home: Evanston, Ill. Died July 23, 1937.

CHASE, Frank Herbert, librarian; b. Portland, Me., Apr. 22, 1870; s. Hazen M. and Fannie L. (Hale) C.; A.B., Yale, 1894, Ph.D., 1896; m. Mary Hollands McLean (A.B., Wellesley, 1896), June 30, 1903. Teacher Cheshire (Conn.) Acad., 1896-97; traveled and studied (Berlin) in Europe, 1897-98; tutor in English, Yale, 1898-1900; traveled in Near East, 1900-01; instr. in English, Bates Coll., 1901-02; prof. English, Centre Coll., Ky., 1902-04; prof. English lit., Beloit Coll., 1904-11; with Boston Public Library, 1911—, custodian Spl. Libraries until 1916, custodian Bates Hall, 1916-23, reference librarian, 1923—. Was prof. English Summer Sch., Oberlin Coll. Organized Wisconsin Assn. of English Teachers (first pres.); librarian University Club (Boston); sec. Episcopalian Club of Mass. Jr. warden Ch. of St. John the Evangelist, Hingham, Mass. Author: Bibliographical Guide to Old English Syntax, 1896; Bibliography of American Art and Artists before 1835, 1918. Died Dec. 12, 1930.

CHASE, Frederick Augustus, prof. natural sciences, Fisk Univ., Nashville, Tenn., 1872—; b. King's Ferry, N.Y., Jan. 29, 1833; studied at Union Coll. and Univ. of Mich.; m. Julia Augusta Spence, 1863 (died 1880). Took spl. courses in science and engring.; theology at Auburn Theol. Sem. Ordained Presbyn. clergyman; held several pastoral and teaching charges until 1872. Died 1904.

CHASE, Frederick Lincoln, astronomer; b. Boulder, Colo., June 28, 1865; s. George Franklin and Augusta Ann (Staples) C.; A.B., U. of Colorado, 1886; Ph.D., Yale, 1891; unmarried. Asst. in Yale Obs., 1890; asst. astronomer, 1891-1911, acting dir. same, 1910-13. Wrote: Heliometer Triangulation of the Victoria Comparison Stars (Annals of the Cape Observatory, 1897); Triangulation of the Principal Stars of the Cluster in Coma Berenices (trans. Yale Univ. Obs., Vol. I, Part V, 1896); Parallax Investigations on 163 Stars, mainly of Large Proper Motion (trans. Yale Univ. Obs., Vol. II, Part I, 1906); Parallax Investigations on 35 Selected Stars, Vol. II, Part II, 1910; Parallax of 41 Southern Stars, Vol. II, Part III, 1912; Catalogue of Yale Parallax Results, Vol. II, Part IV, 1912. Home: Boulder, Colo. Died Nov. 8, 1933.

CHASE, George, univ. dean; b. Portland, Me., Dec. 29, 1849; s. David T. and Martha E. C.; A.B., Yale, 1870; LL.B., Columbia U. Law School, 1873; admitted to N.Y. bar, 1873; m. Eva R. Hawley, Nov. 25, 1884. Instr. and asst. prof. municipal law, 1873-78, prof. criminal law, torts, and procedure, 1878-91, Columbia; dean New York Law School, 1891—. Author: Chase's edition Blackstone's Commentaries for American Students; Stephens' Digest of the Law of Evidence; Chase's Cases on Torts. Home: New York, N.Y. Died Jan. 8, 1924.

CHASE, George Colby, college pres.; b. Unity, Me., Mar. 15, 1844; s. Joseph and Jane C. (Dyer) C.; A.B., Bates Coll., 1868, A.M., 1871; student Cobb Div. Sch., 1870-71; grad. student, Harvard, 1871-72; Univ. College, London, 1891-92; (D.D., Colby, 1895; LL.D., U. of Colo., 1895, U. of New Brunswick, 1898, Bowdoin, 1902); m. Emma Francette Millett, June 12, 1872 (died 1913). Teacher Greek and Latin, New Hampton Lit. Instn., 1868-70; prof. rhetoric and English lit., 1872-94, pres. and prof. psychology and logic, 1894—, Bates Coll. Mem. Commn. on the Ch. and Social Service of Fed. Council of Churches of Christ in America. Home: Lewiston, Me. Died May 27, 1919.

CHASE, George Francis, army officer; b. Macomb, Ill., July 29, 1848; s. Rev. James M. and Salina (Venable) C.; grad. U.S. Mil. Acad., 1871; m. Nannie, d. of Col. Ely McClellan, U.S.A., Oct. 30, 1888. Commd. 2d lt. 9th Inf., June 12, 1871; promoted through grades to col. 12th Cav., Oct. 2, 1906; brig. gen., May 16, 1912; retired on account of age, July 29, 1912. Served in Dept. of Platte, 1871-80, participating in many campaigns against Indians and in Tongue River, Rosebud, Slim Buttes, Fort Robinson and Hat Creek battles; at U.S. Arty. Sch., 1880-82; duty against Apaches, 1882-85; comd. squadron of cav. on Texas frontier, 1892; at Chickamauga Park, 1898; provost marshal gen. 2d Army Corps, 1898-99; in P.I., 1899-1900 and 1903-05; comd. 15th Cav. in Cuba, 1906-07; duty, Washington, D.C., 1912. Mem. Mil. Order Carabao, Order of Indian Wars of U.S., Vet. Army of Philippines. Died Dec. 13, 1925.

CHASE, George Lewis, underwriter; b. Millbury, Mass., Jan. 13, 1828; s. Paul Cushing and Sarah Pierce C.; grad. Millbury Acad., 1847; m. Calista M. Taft, Jan. 8, 1858. In ins. business from 1847; then pres. Hartford Fire Ins. Co.; v.p. Society for Saving; trustee Conn. Trust Co.; dir. Am. Nat. Bank. Home: Hartford, Conn. Died 1908.

CHASE, Harold Taylor, newspaperman; b. Wilkes-Barre, Pa., Apr. 13, 1864; s. Edward Henry and Elizabeth (Taylor) C.; A.B., Harvard, 1886; m. Annie Thompson, Jan. 15, 1890; children—Ethel Eugenia (Mrs. David G. Nethercot), Hamilton. Began newspaper work on Wilkes-Barre Record, 1886; editor Topeka Daily Capital, 1895—. Mem. Spl. State Tax Code Commn. for revision of state tax system, 1929. Home: Topeka, Kan. Died June 22, 1935.

CHASE, Henry Sabin, financier, mfr.; b. Waterbury, Conn., Oct. 1, 1855; s. Augustus S. and Martha (Starkweather) C.; B.A., Yale, 1877; m. Alice Morton, Apr. 4, 1889. Began in business, 1877; pres. Chase Rolling Mill Co., Waterbury Mfg. Co., Am. Printing Co., The A. S. Chase Co., Chase Metal Works; dir. numerous cos.; trustee, etc., in fiduciary capacity. Treas. sinking fund, City of Waterbury; Independent Republican. Home: Waterbury, Conn. Died Mar. 4, 1918.

CHASE, Isaac McKim, mech. engr.; b. Baltimore, May 27, 1837; s. Alexander and Mary Ann (Cruser) C.; grad. Md. Inst.; m. Emeline Hall, Apr. 1, 1878. Entered Washington Navy Yard, 1868, becoming master mechanic; expert in marine propellers and propulsion. Author: Screw Propellers and Marine Propulsion, 1895; Art of Pattern Making, 1903. Died 1903.

CHASE, J(ason) Franklin; b. Boston, Mar. 7, 1872; s. Jason Lincoln and Emma (Coutant) C.; B.A., Wesleyan U., Conn., 1896; S.T.B., Boston U., 1901; m. Bertha Newell, June 19, 1901; children—J(ason) Newell, Lois Eaton. Ordained M.E. ministry, 1900; pastor Essex, Mass., 1900-01, West Roxbury, 1901-06, Allston, 1906-07; sec. N.E. Watch and Ward Soc., Boston, 1907—. Del. Internat. Purity Fedn., 1913, 14, 15, 17. N.E. exec. of Commn.

on Training Camp Activities, 1917-18. Began fight against "dope traffic," Boston, 1908; active in "white slave" movement. Pres. Chace-Chase Family Assn. Republican. Author: The Dope Evil, 1912; The First Corps of Moral Engineers U.S.A., 1917; The Challenge of Diamond Hill, 1919. Home: West Roxbury, Mass. Died Nov. 3, 1926.

CHASE, Jehu Valentine, naval officer; b. Pattersonville, La., Jan. 10, 1869; grad. U.S. Naval Acad., 1890. Ensign, July 14, 1892; lt., Mar. 3, 1899; promoted through grades to rear admiral, Jan. 1, 1922. Served on Newport, Spanish-Am. War, 1898; comd. Whipple, 1902-05. Hull, 1905; comdr. Naval Torpedo Sta., Newport, R.I., 1905-07; navigator Kearsarge, 1907-08; flag sec. to comdr. 3d squadron Pacific Fleet, 1908-10; aide on staff comdr. in chief Pacific Fleet, 1910; comd. Tallahassee, 1910-11; insp. ordnance, Whitehead Torpedo Works, Weymouth, Eng., 1911-12; comd. Monterey, 1912-13, Cincinnati, 1913-14; mem. spl. bd. on ordnance, Navy Dept., 1914-17; apptd. comdr. Minnesota, 1917; comdr. fleet base force, 1923; later mem. Gen. Board of U.S. Navy; retired, Feb. 1, 1933. Died May 24, 1937.

CHASE, John Carroll, civil engr.; b. Chester, N.H., July 26, 1849; s. Charles and Caroline (Chase) C.; grad. Pinkerton Acad. (Derry, N.H.), 1869; student Mass. Inst. of Tech., 1870-71; m. Mary Lizzie Durgin, Oct. 21, 1871 (died 1927); children—Caroline Louise (wife of Raffaele Lorini, M.D.), Benjamin (dec.), Alice Durgin (wife of Samuel C. Prescott, S.B., Sc.D.); m. 2d, Florence Anne Buchanan, July 14, 1928. Began as civil engr., 1871; asst. engr. on water works constrn., N.H. and Mass., 1871-77; asst. engr. on Elevated R.R. constrn., New York, 1877-79; asst. cashier, N.Y. Custom House, 1880-81; supt. Clarendon Water Works, Wilmington, N.C., 1881-97; city surveyor and engr., Wilmington, 1886-94; gen. practice as civil engr., 1871-1907; pres. and treas. The Benjamin Chase Co., Derry, N.H., 1907—. Mem. N.C. State Bd. of Health, 1893-97. Trustee and sec. Pinkerton Acad.; trustee and treas. Taylor Library, Derry, N.H. Republican. Mason. Author: History of Chester, N.H., 1926; Descendants of Aquila and Thomas Chase, 1928; Descendants of William Chase. Home: Derry, N.H. Died Apr. 1936.

CHASE, J(oseph) Smeaton, author; b. London, Eng., Apr. 8, 1864; s. Samuel C. (pub.) and Jane (Evans) C.; ed. London Elementary Sch. and Haverstock Hill, N. London; came to U.S., 1890; m. Isabel, d. William M. and Anna M. (Pierrepont) White, of Utica, N.Y., 1917. Interested in sociol. work in Calif.; settlement resident, Bethlehem Institutional Ch., Los Angeles, many yrs. Author: Yosemite Trails, 1911; California Coast Trails, 1913; The California Padres and Their Missions (with Charles F. Saunders), 1915; California Desert Trails, 1919; Our Araby, 1920. Home: Palm Springs, Calif. Died Mar. 29, 1923.

CHASE, Lewis (Nathaniel), author; b. Sidney, Me., June 27, 1873; s. Ethan Allen and Augusta (Field) C.; A.B., Columbia, 1895, A.M., 1898, Ph.D., 1903; studied, Harvard, Grenoble; m. Pearl Rowell Mikesell; m. 2d, Emma Service Lester. Was an actor with Creston Clarke Co. in Shakespearean and other legitimate rôles, 1895-96; asst. and tutor comparative lit., Columbia, 1899-1902; lecturer on lit. subjects, 1902-03; instr. and asst. prof. English, Ind. U., 1903-07; prof. English and dir. summer session, U. of Louisville, 1907-08; lecturer, U. of Bordeaux, 1909-10; instr. and lecturer on contemporary poetry, U. of Wis., 1916-17; actg. asst. prof. U. of Rochester, 1917-19; prof. English studies, Aligarh (India) Muslim U., 1919-22; with Yenching, Peking Nat. and Penking Normal univs., 1921-25; extension lecturer U. of Calif., Southern Br., 1925-27; visiting prof. Calif. Inst. Tech., 1926; with Union Coll. Schenectady, N.Y., 1927-29, Duke U., 1929-31, Brown U., 1931-33, Asheville Normal Coll., summers, 1933—. Author: The English Heroic Play, 1903; Bernard Shaw in France, 1910; Poe and His Poetry, 1913. Editor: (in part with P. A. Rashid) Western Classics for Eastern Students. Co-editor of Brown Univ. project for publication of life and works of Thomas Holley Chivers. Home: Washington, D.C. Died Sept. 23, 1937.

CHASE, Robert Howland, alienist; b. Salem, Mass., Jan. 30, 1845; s. William Henry and Elizabeth (Howland) C.; student Haverford Coll., 3 yrs. (hon. A.M., 1885); M.D., U. of Pa., 1869; m. Amanda Howe Adams, Oct. 10, 1871 (died 1885); m. 2d, Jane Sovereign Rumsey, Apr. 21, 1897. Asst. phys. Govt. Hosp. for Insane, Washington, 1872-80; med. supt., male dept. State Hosp. of Insane, Norristown, Pa., 1880-93; med. supt. Friends' Hosp., Phila., many yrs. from 1893. V.p. sect. of psychol. medicine, Internat. Med. Congress, Washington. Author: General Paresis, 1902; Mental Medicine and Nursing, 1914; The Ungeared Mind, 1917. Home: Wyncote, Pa. Died Mar. 13, 1921.

CHASE, Solon, farmer; b. Chase's Mills, Me., Jan. 14, 1822; s. Isaac and Eunice C.; ed. local schs. and Gorham Sem.; engaged in farming. Was one of the leading and most active campaigners for the Greenback Labor Party in its campaigns from 1876 to 1884. Widower. Home: Chase's Mills. Me. Died 1909.

CHASE, William Martin, lawyer; b. Canaan, N.H., Dec. 28, 1837; s. Horace and Abigail S. (Martin) C.; B.S., Dartmouth, 1858 (hon. A.M., 1879, LL.D., 1898); m. Ellen S. Abbott, Mar. 18, 1863. Admitted to bar, 1862; in practice, Concord, N.H., 1862-91, and 1908—; dir. First Nat. Bank (pres. 1883-85). Clerk N.H. Senate, 1871; various local offices; chmn. commn. to codify and revise the public laws of the state, upon whose report the pub. statutes were adopted at Jan. session, 1891; asso. justice Supreme Ct., N.H., 1891-1907; mem. N.H. Senate, 1909-11. Democrat. Trustee Dartmouth Coll., 1890—. Home: Concord, N.H. Died Feb. 3, 1918.

CHASE, William Merritt, artist; b. Franklin, Ind., Nov. 1, 1849; early study under B. F. Hayes in Indianapolis, J. O. Eaton, New York, A. Wagner and Piloty, Munich. Established studio in New York; received medal, Phila., 1876; hon. mention, Paris, 1881; honors, Munich, 1883; silver medal, Paris Salon, 1889; 1st prize Cleveland Art Assn., 1894; Shaw prize, Soc. Am. Artists, 1895; gold medal of honor, Pa. Acad. Fine Arts, 1895; gold medal, Paris Expn., 1900. Specialties, portraits and figure pieces. N.A., 1890; mem. Am. Acad. Arts and Letters. Home: New York, N.Y. Died Oct. 25, 1916.

CHASE, William Sheafe, clergyman; b. Amboy, Lee County, Ill., Jan. 11, 1858; s. Newton Simpson and Harriet Fish (Peckham) C.; A.B., Brown U., 1881, A.M., 1885, D.D., 1912; B.D., Episcopal Theol. Sch., 1885; m. Susan Gladding Collins, Jan. 11, 1887 (died 1897); 1 son, Newton Gladding; m. 2d, Fannie Louise Jackson, Apr. 27, 1914; 1 dau., Dorothy Briggs. Deacon, 1885, priest, 1886, P.E. Ch.; asst. minister Emmanuel Ch., Boston, Sept.-Oct. 1885; rector St. James Ch., Woonsocket, R.I., 1885-1902; hon. canon Cathedral of the Incarnation, Garden City, L.I., and chaplain St. Paul's Sch., 1902-05; rector Christ Ch., Bedford Av., Brooklyn, 1905-32 (rector honorarius). Pres. Religious Union for World Peace, 1937—. Member International Reform Fedn. (supt. 1926-36, pres. 1936-37), Lord's Day Alliance of U.S. (dir.), Soc. for Prevention of Crime (dir.). Four-minute man, World War. Author: Catechism on Motion Pictures in Inter-State Commerce (New York Civic League), 1922; Amicus Curiæ, to U.S. Supreme Court Against Repeal of the 18th Amendment, 1933; The Spirit for the New Era, 1934. Home: Kings Park, N.Y. Died July 16, 1940.

CHATARD, Francis Silas Marean, bishop; b. Baltimore, 1834; grad. Mt. St. Mary's, Emmitsburg, Md.; M.D., U. of Md. Decided to enter ch.; became student at St. Urban Coll., Rome, and earned D.D. degree, 1863. Became vice-rector and then rector Am. Coll., Rome; apptd. and consecrated, 1878, bishop of diocese of Vincennes; established episcopal residence at Indianapolis, Ind. Author: Christian Truths, etc. Died Sept. 7, 1918.

CHATBURN, George Richard, civil engr.; b. near Magnolia, Ia., Dec. 24, 1863; s. Jonas Wellington and Mary (Burton) C.; B.C.E., Ia. State Coll., 1884, C.E., 1910; A.M., U. of Neb., 1897; Dr.Engring. from Iowa State Coll., 1928; m. Anna Murphy, July 21, 1889; children—Mary Frances, Alice (dec.), George Richard. Teacher dist. schs., Shelby County, Ia., 1884-85; prin. sch., Plattsmouth, Neb., 1885-89; supt. pub. schs., Humboldt, Neb., 1889-91, Wymore, 1891-94; instr. and adj. prof. civ. engring., 1894-1905. asso. prof. and prof. applied mechanics and machine design, 1905—, U. of Neb., also head dept. applied mechanics and machine design; ry. and highway consulting engr. During World War had charge of publicity and instructional work of S.A.T.C., U. of Neb. Republican. Mason. Author: Highway Engineering, 1921; Highways and Highway Transportation, 1923. Home: Lincoln, Neb. Died Jan. 30, 1940.

CHATFIELD, Thomas Ives, judge; b. Owego, N.Y., Oct. 4, 1871; s. Thomas Ives and Lucy B. (Goodrich) C.; A.B., Yale U., 1893; LL.B., Columbia, 1896; m. Laura D. Ayer, June 7, 1899. Admitted to N.Y. bar, 1896, and engaged in practice at New York until 1906; asst. U.S. atty., in Brooklyn, 1902-06; U.S. dist. judge, Eastern Dist. of N.Y., 1907—. Republican. Home: Brooklyn, N.Y. Died Dec. 24, 1922.

CHATFIELD, Walter Henry, army officer; b. New Haven, Conn., Mar. 11, 1852; s. John L. and Mary A. (Riggs) C.; ed. high sch., Waterbury, Conn.; Episcopal Acad., Cheshire, Conn.; m. Frances May Rains, Dec. 21, 1880. Pvt. and corpl. Co. G, and q.-m. sergt. 7th Cav., 1878-80; commd. 2d lt. 5th Inf., Oct. 4, 1880; promoted through grades to col. Inf., May 30, 1914; assigned to 2d Inf., Sept. 1, 1915; retired, Mar. 11, 1916. Served in the Indian country 10 yrs., Cuba 2 yrs., Philippines 2½ yrs., Hawaii 6 mos. On active duty, Feb. 1917-Aug. 1919, recruiting and at Port of Embarkation, Hoboken, N.J. Episcopalian. Home: New York, N.Y. Died June 30, 1922.

CHAUVENET, Regis, mining engr.; b. Phila., Pa., Oct. 7, 1842; s. William and Catharine (Hemple) C.; bro. of William Marc C.; A.B., Washington U., 1862, A.M., 1864 (LL.D., 1900); B.S., Harvard, 1867; m. Virginia Mellon, Dec. 20, 1887. Analytical chemist, St. Louis, 1871-83; chemist to Mo. Geol. Survey and city gas insp., St. Louis, 1872-75; pres. and prof. chemistry and metallurgy, Colo. Sch. of Mines, 1883-1902; resigned to devote attention to practice as mining engr. Author: Chemical and Metallurgical Calculations, 1911. Home: Denver, Colo. Died Dec. 6, 1920.

CHEEVER, David Williams, surgeon; b. Portsmouth, N.H., Nov. 30, 1831; s. Charles Augustus and Adeline (Haven) C.; A.B., Harvard, 1852; M.D., 1858 (LL.D., 1893); m. Annie C. Nichols, Oct. 9, 1860. Sr. surgeon, Boston City Hosp., 1864—; prof. surgery, 1882-92, emeritus prof., 1893—, Harvard; emeritus surgeon City Hosp., 1913—. Sr. fellow Am. Surg. Assn. Author: Medical and Surgical Reports of City Hospital (5 vols.). Home: Boston, Mass. Died Dec. 27, 1915.

CHEEVER, Harriet A., author; b. Boston, Mass.; married. Author: Little Miss Boston, 1890; Jacky Lee, 1894; St. Rockwell's Little Brother, 1894; Little Jolliby's Christmas, 1895; The Fairies of Fern Dingle, 1896; A Rescued Madonna, 1896; Links of Gold, 1897; Little Mr. Van Vere of China, 1898; The Strange Adventures of Billy Trill, 1898; Ted's Little Dear, 1900; A Little American Girl in India, 1900; Madam Angora, 1901; Dr. Robin, 1902; Maid Sally, 1902; Elm Cove, 1902; Gypsy Jane, 1903; Lord Dolphin, 1903; Mother Bunny, 1903; Lou, 1904; Lady Spider, 1904; The Rock Frog, 1904; Tommy Joyce and Tommy Joy, 1905; Josie Bean; Flat Street, 1905. Home: Newton, Mass. Deceased.

CHENEY, Albert Nelson, editor, angling writer, fish culturist; b. Glens Falls, N.Y., May 3, 1849; s. Albert Nelson and Annah (Hunt) C.; ed. Glens Falls Acad., Sedgwick School, Mass., Abbott School, Mass., and Alexander Mil. Inst., New York; m. Mary Louise Rosekrans, Oct. 10, 1872. State fish culturist N.Y., 1895—. Fishery editor Shooting and Fishing; formerly 9 yrs. contributor to Forest and Stream, conducting "Angling Notes;" to American Angler; to London Fishing Gazette, etc.; donater to fisheries. Pres. Nat. Fisheries Congress; v.p. Internat. Fisheries Soc.; capt. Nat. Guards State of N.Y. Home: Glens Falls, N.Y. Died 1901.

CHENEY, Charles Edward, bishop; b. Canandaigua, N.Y., Feb. 12, 1836; s. Dr. E. Warren and Altie W. C.; A.B., Hobart, 1857; studied theology, Alexandria (Va.) Theol. Sem.; (D.D., Grinnell Coll., Ia., 1871; S.T.D., Hobart, 1908); m. Clara Emma Griswold, Apr. 25, 1860. Ordained P.E. ministry, 1858; was rector Christ Ch., Chicago; leader in organizing Reformed Episcopal Ch.; consecrated missionary bishop of the Northwest, Dec. 14, 1873, still being rector of Christ Ch.; made bishop of Synod of Chicago, 1878. Pres. Synod of Reformed Episcopal chs. of Central States, 1905, 1907. Author: Twenty-eight Sermons, 1880; What Do Reformed Episcopalians Believe?, 1888; The Enlistment of the Christian Soldier, 1893; A King of France Unnamed in History, 1902; The Second Norman Conquest of England, 1907; A Belated Plantagenet, 1914. Died Nov. 15, 1916.

CHENEY, Ednah Dow, author; b. Boston, June 27, 1824; d. Sargent S. and Ednah P. Littlehale; m. Seth Wells Cheney, artist, 1853. Was active in the Freedman's Aid movement; sec., 1862-87, and then pres. New England Hosp. for Women and Children; prominent in other socs. Author: Handbook for American Citizens, 1864; Child of the Tide, 1874; Life, Letters and Journals of Louisa M. Alcott, 1889; Stories of the Olden Time, 1890; Reminiscences, 1902, etc. Home: Jamaica Plain, Mass. Died 1904.

CHENEY, Elmer Erwood, business man; b. Champaign Co., O., July 2, 1861; s. James Henry and Beatrice (Tullis) C.; A.B., Ohio Wesleyan U., 1883; LL.B., Cincinnati Law Sch., 1885; m. Cora May Burnham, Feb. 28, 1889; children—Helen (Mrs. Paul C. Slater), Ruth (Mrs. Harry E. Campbell). Admitted to O. bar, 1885, and began practice at Urbana; pres. Champaign Nat. Bank of Urbana, 1917—; pres. and treas. Western Mutual Fire Ins. Co., 1918—; pres. Champaign Telephone Co., 1926—; pres. The Brand-Neer Co. Judge Probate Ct., Champaign Co., 1897-1903. Republican. Methodist. Mason. Home: Urbana, O. Died May 10, 1934.

CHENEY, James William, librarian; b. Newburyport, Mass., Jan. 22, 1849; A.B., Dartmouth, 1870, A.M., 1875; m. Margaret Kline Staver, July 19, 1887. Taught sch., 1870-87, most of the time as prin. of high schs. and acads.; librarian War Dept. Library, 1897-1914, when it was consolidated with the Army War Coll. Library; librarian Gen. Staff, U.S.A. Ch. organist, from 1864; organist and choirmaster, Old St. Paul's P.E. Ch. Mason. Hon. mem. Nat. Inst. Social Sciences. Home: Washington, D.C. Died Oct. 20, 1917.

CHENEY, Jerome Lucius, judge; b. Baldwinsville, N.Y., June 18, 1863; s. Lucius Harrison and Frances (Averill) C.; ed. Southeast Mo. State Teachers Coll.; m. Mary Frances Shorey, June 4, 1889 (died 1924); children—James Lucius (dec.), Karl Shorey, Jerome Kent. Admitted to N.Y. bar, 1884, and began prac- Cheney & Shinaman; White, Cheney, Shinaman & O'Neill, 1893-1918; Cheney & Melvin, 1919-20 Pub.

service commr., 2d N.Y. dist., 1918; 1st dep. atty. gen. of N.Y., 1919-20; justice, Supreme Court, N.Y., 1921—. Republican. Unitarian. Mason. Home: Syracuse, N.Y. Died Nov. 29, 1932.

CHENEY, John Moses, judge; b. Milwaukee, Wis., Jan. 6, 1859; s. Joseph Young and Juliette (McNab) C.; grad. N.H. Lit. Instn., New Hampton, 1881; LL.B., Boston U. Law Sch., 1885; m. Elizabeth Alexander, Nov. 23, 1886. Admitted to practice, Mass. Supreme Ct., Boston, 1885; began practice at Orlando, Fla., 1886; organizer and prin. owner Orlando Light & Water Co.; supervisor U.S. Census, 2d Dist. of Fla., 1900; Rep. candidate for Congress, 2d Dist. of Fla., 1900, 04; U.S. atty. Southern Dist. of Fla., 1906-12; Rep. candidate for gov. of Fla., 1908; U.S. dist. judge, Southern Dist. of Fla., Aug. 1912-Mar. 4, 1913; resumed practice; Rep. candidate for U.S. Senate, 1920. Unitarian. Home: Orlando, Fla. Died June 2, 1922.

CHENEY, John Vance, author; b. Groveland, N.Y., Dec. 29, 1848; s. Simeon Pease and Christiana (Vance) C.; grad. Geneseo Acad., Geneseo, N.Y., at 17; asst. prin. there 2 yrs. later; m. Abbey Perkins, 1876; m. 2d, Mrs. Sara Barker Chamberlin, July 11, 1903. Practiced law, New York, 1875-76; librarian Free Public Library, San Francisco, 1887-94, Newberry Library, Chicago, 1894-1909. Mem. Nat. Inst. Arts and Letters. Author: Lyrics, 1901 (poems), 1905; The Time of Roses (poems), 1908; At the Silver Gate (poems), 1911. Home: San Diego, Calif. Died May 1, 1922.

CHENEY, Orion Howard, lawyer, banker; b. Bloomington, Ill., Jan. 23, 1869; s. Lewis Howard and Mary Elizabeth (West) C.; student Drake U. and U. of Mich.; LL.B., New York U., 1897; m. Margaret Danforth, June 26, 1909; children—Lewis West, Ward Danforth. Practiced at N.Y. City as head of Cheney, Schenck & Stockell, 1903-08; supt. of banks, State of N.Y., 1909-11; pres. Pacific Bank, 1911-25; v.p. Am. Exchange-Pacific Nat. Bank, 1925-26; formerly v.p. Irving Trust Co.; pres. Parkway Spencer Corp., Scarsdale Improvement Corp.; v.p. Scarsdale Nat. Bank & Trust Co. Republican. Presbyn. Home: Patterson, N.Y. Died Jan. 17, 1939.

CHENEY, Person Colby, mfr.; b. Holderness (now Ashland), N.H., Feb. 25, 1828; academic edn.; (A.M., Dartmouth, 1876); m. S. Anna Moore, May 22, 1850 (died 1858); m. 2d, Mrs. Sarah (White) Keith, June 29, 1859. Mfd. paper at Peterboro, N.H., 1854-66, removing to Manchester, N.H.; then a mfr. of paper, chem. fibre, leather board and wood pulp. Mem. N.H. legislature, 1853-54; was q.m. with rank of lt., 13th N.H. vols., Aug. 1862-Aug. 1863; compelled to resign on account of sickness, and at his own expense put in a 3-yrs.' substitute; R.R. commr. N.H., 1864-67; mayor Manchester, 1871; gov. N.H., 1875-76; U.S. senator for short term of 49th Congress to fill unexpired term of late Senator Austin F. Pike; U.S. minister to Switzerland, 1892-93; mem. Rep. Nat. Com., 1892-1900; since its orgn., 1874—; pres. People's Savings Bank. Home: Manchester, N.H. Died 1901.

CHENEY, Warren, author; b. Canandaigua, N.Y., Sept. 3, 1858; s. Dr. William Fitch and Frances Elizabeth (Sheldon) C.; bro. of William Fitch C.; Ph.B., U. of Calif., 1878; LL.B., Hastings Law Sch., 1881; m. May L. Shepard, May 1883. Editor Mining Press, San Francisco, 1879; asst. editor and part owner The Californian, 1881-82; editor and owner The Overland Monthly, 1882-83; corr. San Francisco Chronicle in Balkan Peninsula, 1883-84; in charge Calif. ednl. exhibit, Chicago Expn., 1893; real estate dealer, 1894—. Progressive. Author: Yosemite in Color, 1887; The Flight of Helen and Other Poems, 1891; The Way of the North (novel), 1905; The Challenge (novel), 1906; His Wife (novel), 1907. Home: Berkeley, Calif. Died Mar. 27, 1921.

CHENEY, William Atwell, lawyer; b. Boston, Mass., Feb. 18, 1848; s. Benjamin F. and Martha Stearns (Whitney) C.; ed. pub. schs. and acad. and by pvt. study; m. Annie E. Skinner, 1871 (died 1916). Admitted to Calif. bar, 1878; county judge, 1878-80; mem. Calif. Senate, 1880-83; judge Superior Court at Los Angeles, Calif, 1885-91; lecturer on constl. law, U. of Southern Calif. Sch. of Law, 1904-12; gen. counsel Los Angeles Gas & Electric Corp., 1891—. Republican. Unitarian. Home: Los Angeles, Calif. Died Aug. 10, 1925.

CHENEY, William Fitch, M.D.; b. Canandaigua, N.Y., Sept. 6, 1866; s. Dr. William Fitch and Frances Elizabeth (Sheldon) C.; B.Litt., U. of Calif., 1885; M.D., Cooper Med. Coll., San Francisco, 1889; Johns Hopkins Med. Sch., 1898; m. Mary St. Clair Garnett, July 7, 1892. Prof. principles and practice of medicine, Cooper Med. Coll., 1898—; clin. prof. of medicine, med. dept. Leland Stanford Jr. U., 1909-32, emeritus. Fellow Am. Coll. Phys. Home: San Francisco, Calif. Died Apr. 10, 1941.

CHENOWETH, Alexander Crawford, cons. engr.; b. Baltimore, June 5, 1849; s. Rev. George Davenport and Frances Ann (Crawford) C.; A.B., Dickinson Coll., 1868, A.M., 1869 (LL.D., 1908); course in engring. Rensselaer Poly. Inst.; m. Catherine Richardson Wood, Apr. 19, 1876. Engaged on engring. force of Prospect Park, Brooklyn, 1870; asst. engr. Middletown-New Haven R.R., 1871, Brunswick & Western R.R., Ga., 1872; asst. under Gen. George Green, pub. works, Washington; contractor for dock and ry. work, West Shore R.R., 1882; cons. engr. to Gen. M. Prado, President of Peru; prepared foundation for Bartholdi Statue of Liberty, Bedloe's Island, N.Y., 1884; apptd. asst. engr. Croton Aqueduct Commn., New York, Feb. 16, 1885, resident engr. in charge Croton Aqueduct, July 26, 1889; resigned, 1895, to enter into constrn. work for U.S. Govt. at Sandy Hook; contractor for drainage work, D.C., 1896, built Nagle Av., New York, 1898; specialist in foundation work; pres. Chenoweth Concrete Revetment Co. Served in 7th Regt. N.G.N.Y.; was 1st lt. Vet. A.C. and Washington Continental Guard. Episcopalian. Democrat. Home: New York, N.Y. Died Apr. 13, 1922.

CHENOWETH, Catherine Richardson, philanthropical worker; b. New York, N.Y.; d. late Hon. Fernando Wood (mayor, congressman, etc.); ed. pvt. French sch.; m. Alexander Crawford Chenoweth, Apr. 19, 1876 (died 1922); children—Maud C. (dec.), Catharine R. (dec.), Alexander Fernando Wood. Traveled in Holland, studying its history and people; foundress Soc. of Daughters of Holland Dames. Collected funds for hosp. ship "Maine," for wounded in South African War; mem. Red Cross Soc., apptd. by the London com. Del. to Internat. Peace Conf., New York, 1907; mem. Eugenic Congress in London, 1912; del. to Internat. Peace Congress, Geneva, Switzerland, 1912; del. Internat. Peace Congress, The Hague, Holland, 1913; mem. New York com. for celebrating the 100 years of peace between English speaking peoples, 1914-15. Mem. Commn. on Training Camp Activities of War and Navy Depts., 1917. Eugenic Congress, 1921. Home: New York, N.Y. Died Apr. 11, 1928.

CHERRY, Henry Hardin, educator; b. Bowling Green, Ky., Nov. 16, 1864; s. George W. and Frances Martha (Stahl) C.; grad. Southern Normal Sch. and Bowling Green Business U., 1889; m. Bessie Fayne, Apr. 1896; children—Mrs. Josephine Lowman, Mrs. Elizabeth Sims, Henry Hardin. Assumed charge, in 1892, of Southern Normal School and Bowling Green Business U., then a private institution enrolling only 78 students in 1 year; has given entire time to the school from then; now known as Western Ky. State Teachers Coll., of which became pres. Pres. College Heights Foundation. Mem. State Ednl. Commn. and the Exec. Council. Methodist. Democrat. Chmn. publicity com. and speakers bur. of State Council Defense. Author: Our Civic Image and our Government, 1906; Education the Basis of Democracy, 1926. Home: Bowling Green, Ky. Died Aug. 1937.

CHERRY, Kathryn Evelyn (wife of William W. Cherry, M.D.), artist; b. Quincy, Ill.; d. of Jacob and Catherine (Richard) Bard; art. edn., Washington U. Sch. Fine Arts, New York Sch. Arts; pupil of Paul Cornoyer, Richard Miller, Arthur Dow and Hugh Breckenridge; study in Europe 1 yr.; m. William W. Cherry, M.D., Apr. 4, 1892. Head of art dept., Principia Acad., St. Louis, 1914—. Awarded gold medal, La. Purchase Expn., St. Louis, 1904; gold medal, Atlan Club, Chicago, 1907; 2d prize, annual Thumb Box, St. Louis, 1918; 1st landscape prize, Sedalia, Mo., 1918; $500 prize, St. Louis, 1919; 1st landscape prize, St. Louis, 1920; 2d landscape prize, Sedalia, 1920; 1st landscape prize, St. Louis, 1921; grand prize, best work of art, St. Louis, 1922; Art Inst. gold medal, Kansas City, Mo., 1922; 1st prize, Sedalia, 1922; Chamber of Commerce prize, St. Louis, 1923; 1st landscape prize, St. Louis, 1924; 2d landscape prize, Sedalia, 1924; bronze medal, Kansas City Art Inst., 1926; $500 purchase prize, St. Louis, 1926; $200 purchase prize, Chicago, 1927; 3d prize, Sedalia, 1929. Home: St. Louis, Mo. Died Nov. 19, 1931.

CHESEBROUGH, Robert Augustus, mfr.; b. London, Eng., Jan. 9, 1837; s. American parents; reared and ed. in New York. Began mfr. of petroleum products, 1858; discovered and patented, 1870, the substance now known as vaseline; became trustee Chesebrough Mfg. Co. Republican candidate for Congress, 1894. Home: Spring Lake, N.J. Died Sept. 8, 1933.

CHESHIRE, Fleming Duncan, consul; b. Brooklyn, N.Y., Mar. 4, 1849; ed. in pub. and pvt. schs.; unmarried. In mercantile life, China, 1869-77; acting interpreter to consulate at Foochow, 1877-78; apptd. vice-consul at Foochow, Aug. 7, 1878; in charge consulate, Foochow, 1878-79, Canton, 1879-80; interpreter to consul-gen., Shanghai, 1880-82, in charge consulate, 1882-84; interpreter to legation at Peking, 1884-1900, Chinese sec. to legation, 1900-01; Chinese sec. to spl. plenipotentiary of the U.S., Apr.-Sept. 1901; consul-gen. at Mukden, 1904-06; consul-gen.-at-large, July 1, 1906-Aug. 22, 1912, consul-gen. at Canton. Methodist. Died June 13, 1922.

CHESHIRE, Joseph Blount, bishop; b. Tarboro, N.C., Mar. 27, 1850; s. Rev. Joseph Blount and Elizabeth Toole (Parker) C.; A.B., Trinity Coll., 1869, A.M., 1872; D.D., U. of N.C., 1890, U. of the South, 1894, Trinity Coll., Hartford, Conn., 1916; m. Annie Huske Webb, Dec. 17, 1874; children—Mary Parker (dec.), Elizabeth Toole, Sarah Frances, Joseph Blount, Annie Webb, Haywood Parker (dec.), Katharine Moore (dec.), James Webb, Godfrey; m. 2d, Elizabeth Lansdale, July 19, 1899. Admitted to bar, 1872; in practice 1872-78; deacon, 1878, priest, 1880, P.E. Ch.; rector Chapel Hill, 1878-81, St. Peter's, Charlotte, N.C., 1881-93; consecrated coadjutor bishop Oct. 15, 1893, becoming bishop of N.C. on death of Bishop Lyman, Dec. 13, 1893. Trustee U. of the South, 1885—. Author: History of the Protestant Episcopal Church in Confederate States, 1911. Home: Raleigh, N.C. Died Dec. 27, 1932.

CHESNUT, Victor King, chemist, botanist; b. Nevada City, Calif., June 28, 1867; s. John A. and Henrietta S. (King) C.; B.S., U. of Calif., 1890; grad. student U. of Chicago and Columbian (now George Washington) U.; m. Olive Branch Spohr, July 18, 1899; children—George S., Alma E., Frank T., Gertrude V. Asst. in chemistry, U. of Calif., 1890-93; asst. botanist in charge of poisonous plant investigations, Bur. of Plant Industry, U.S. Dept. Agr., 1894-1904; prof. chemistry and geology, Mont. Agrl. Coll.; chemist Mont. Expt. Sta., 1904-07; collaborator, poisonous plant investigations, U.S. Dept. of Agr., 1904-06; asst. chemist, div. of drugs, 1907-16, asst. chemist, Phytochemical Lab., 1916-24, asso. chemist, 1924-33, Bur. Chemistry, U.S. Dept. Agr., Food and Drug Administration; retired on pension, July 1, 1933. Elder in Presbyterian Ch. Author: Principal Poisonous Plants of the United States, 1898; Determination of Pepsin in Liquids, 1913 and 1916; Determination of the Proteoclastic Activity of Papaya latex and the Detection of Enzyme Adulterants, 1916; (with F. B. Power) An Improved Method for the Quantitative Determination of Caffeine in Vegetable Material, 1919; Ilex Vomitoria as a Native Source of Caffeine; The Odorous Constituents of Apples, 1920, 22; Odorous Constituents of Peaches, 1921; Methyl Anthranilate in Grape Juice, 1921; The Odorous Constituents of the Cotton Plant, 1925; The Nonvolatile Constituents of the Cotton Plant, 1926. Home: Hyattsville, Md. Died Aug. 1938.

CHESNUTT, Charles Waddell, author; b. Cleveland, O., June 20, 1858; married Susan U. Perry, 1878. Nine yrs. teacher in public schs. of North Carolina; at 23 became prin. State Normal Sch., Fayetteville, N.C.; in 1884 spent some months as newspaper writer in New York; admitted to Ohio bar, 1887, and began practice in Cleveland. Mem. Cleveland Chamber of Commerce. Author: Conjure Woman, 1899, 1929; Life of Frederick Douglass, in Beacon Biographies, 1899. Home: Cleveland, O. Died Nov. 15, 1932.

CHESTER, Albert Huntington, prof. chemistry and mineralogy, Rutgers Coll., 1892—; b. Saratoga Springs, N.Y., Nov. 22, 1843; s. Albert Tracy and Elizabeth (Stanley) C.; grad. (M.E.) Columbia Sch. of Mines, 1868; Ph.D. in course, 1878 (Sc.D., Hamilton, 1892); m. Alethea Sandford Rudd, 1869 (died 1891); m. 2d, Georgiana Waldron Jenks, 1898. Had large practice as mining engr.; was, 1870-92, prof. chemistry, Hamilton Coll., N.Y. Author: Dictionary of the Names of Minerals, 1886-97; Catalogue of Minerals with Their Chemical Compositions and Synonyms, 1896. Home: New Brunswick, N.J. Died 1903.

CHESTER, Alden, judge; b. Westford, N.Y., Sept. 4, 1848; s. Alden and Susan G. (Draper) C.; desc. on father's side from Samuel Chester of Groton, Conn., on mother's from James Draper of Roxbury, Mass., also from Elder William Brewster of Mayflower. ed. Westford Lit. Inst.; LL.B., Columbia, 1871; L.H.D., Union Coll., N.Y., 1928; m. Lina, d. Ezra R. Thurber, of E. Worcester, N.Y., Oct. 5, 1871 (died 1921); 1 dau., Mrs. Amy C. Merrick. Practiced with Andrew S. Draper, Albany, N.Y., 1871-87, alone, 1887-95; deputy clerk N.Y. Assembly, 1874, 76; asst. U.S. atty., Northern Dist. N.Y., 1882-85; asst. corp. counsel, City of Albany, 1894-95; mem. commn. to prepare uniform charter for cities of the second class, 1895; justice, Supreme Court of N.Y., 3d Dist., 1895-1918; justice, Appellate Div., 3d Dept., 1902-09; official referee of Supreme Court, 1918—; trustee Albany Exchange Savings Bank, 1899—, v.p., 1904—. Mem. Bd. Pub. Instruction, Albany, 1881-84 (pres. 1884); trustee Albany Acad. for Girls, 1897—, pres., 1904—; trustee Albany Med. Coll., 1900—, v.p., 1904—; pres. bd. govs. Union U.; mem. faculty Albany Law Sch., 1897—, and lecturer on federal judicial system; trustee Albany Coll. Pharmacy. Republican. Author: Legal and Judicial History of New York (3 vols.), 1911; Courts and Lawyers of New York, 1609-1925 (3 vols.), 1925. Died Feb. 12, 1934.

CHESTER, Colby Mitchell, rear adm.; b. New London, Conn., Feb. 29, 1844; s. Melville and Frances E. (Harris) C.; apptd. to U.S. Naval Acad. from Conn., 1859, grad. 1863; m. Melancia Antoinette Tremaine, Nov. 25, 1873. Ensign, Oct. 1, 1863; promoted through grades to rear adm., Aug. 10, 1903; retired. Served on Richmond, W. Gulf Blockading Squadron, 1863-65; participated battle of Mobile

Bay, and capture of Ft. Morgan, Aug. 1864; capture of Mobile, Apr. 1865; various assignments to 1888; mem. commn. to select site for navy yard on Pacific Coast, 1888-90, Bur. of Navigation, 1890-91; comdt. cadets U.S. Naval Acad., 1891-94; Navy Yard, New York, 1894-95; comd. Richmond, 1896, Newark, 1896-97, Minneapolis, May-July 1897; comdr.-in-chief S. Atlantic Squadron, 1897-98; Cincinnati, 1898-99; gen. insp. Kentucky, 1899-1900; comd. Kentucky, 1900-01; Naval War Coll., 1901-02; supt. Naval Obs., 1902-06; comd. spl. service squadron to witness total eclipse of sun, 1905, retired, Feb. 28, 1906; spl. duty in Bur. of Equipment and in Europe until July 1908. Prof. naval science, Yale U., 1917; supt. naval units of Yale and Brown univs., and comdt. U.S. Naval Unit, Yale U., until Apr. 1919. Engaged for 15 yrs. under apptmt. from President Roosevelt in establishing open door for Am. trade in Western Asia. Pres. Inter-ocean Engring. Co.; negotiating concessions for construction of railroads and development of mines and oil wells in Ottoman empire. Wrote Diplomacy of the Quarter-Deck; The Monroe Doctrine. A pioneer of the "A.B.C. policy." Died May 4, 1932.

CHESTER, Eliza, author. See Harriet Eliza Paine.

CHESTER, Frank Dyer, linguist; b. Newton Lower Falls, Mass., Dec. 2, 1869; s. Charles Edward and Miranda (Burgess) C.; grad., with Franklin medal, English High Sch., Boston, 1886; A.B., Harvard, 1891, A.M., 1892, Ph.D., 1894 (spl. studies in Arabic lang. and lit.); instr. Semitic langs., 1892-95; studied as Rogers fellow of Harvard U. in Damascus, Syria, 1895-96, and in Budapest, Hungary, 1896-97; unmarried. Consul, 1897-1904, consul gen., 1904-08, at Budapest, Hungary; instr., Chestnut Hill Acad., Phila., 1909, Cascadilla Sch., Ithaca, N.Y., 1910-11, Milton (Mass.) Acad., 1912-13; genealogist and historian of Chester and Dyer families, 1912—. Republican. Unitarian. Home: Boston, Mass. Died June 14, 1938.

CHESTER, George Randolph, author; b. in Ohio, 1869. Left home at an early age and engaged in various occupations; began newspaper work as a reporter on Detroit News; later on Cincinnati Enquirer, becoming Sunday editor of latter; began writing for newspaper syndicate and later for mags. Author: Get-Rich-Quick Wallingford, 1908; Cash Intrigue, 1909; Making of Bobby Burnit, 1909; Art of Short Story Writing, 1910; Young Wallingford; Early Bird, 1910; Five Thousand an Hour, 1911; The Jingo; A Tale of Red Roses, 1912; Wallingford and Blackie Daw, 1913; Wallingford in His Prime, 1913. Also in collaboration with his wife, Lillian Chester, The Ball of Fire, 1914; Cordelia Blossom, 1914; Runaway June, 1915; The Enemy, 1915. Plays: (with Lillian Chester) Cordelia Blossom, 1914; Pay, 1915. Died Feb. 26, 1924.

CHESTER, Samuel Hall, clergyman; b. Mt. Holly, Ark., Jan. 17, 1851; s. Charles and Caroline (Yemans) C.; A.B., Washington and Lee U., 1872; grad. Union Theol. Sem. in Va., 1875; D.D., Davidson Coll., N.C., 1890; m. Susan W. Willard, Apr. 15, 1884. Ordained Presbyn. ministry, 1875; pastor Castanea Grove, N.C., 1875-82, Hawfields and Cross Roads chs., 1883-88, Franklin, Tenn., 1888-91, 2d Ch., Nashville, 1891-92. Sec. Foreign Missions of Presbyn. Ch. in U.S., 1894-1911, sec. foreign correspondence same, 1911-27 (emeritus); editor foreign dept. Missionary Survey. Mem. bd. corporators Presbyn. Ministers' Fund, Phila. Democrat. Mason. Author: Lights and Shadows of Mission Work in the Far East, 1915; Pioneer Days in Arkansas, 1927. Home: Montreat, N.C. Died Apr. 27, 1940.

CHESTERMAN, William Dallas, mng. editor Richmond Dispatch; b. Hanover Co., Va., July 10, 1845; ed. in Richmond; m. Mildred V. Davis, Feb. 27, 1867. At 17 enlisted in C.S.A.; was shot in thigh at Petersburg, June 17, 1864; became clerk of bureau exchange of prisoners. On Richmond Examiner, 1865; Richmond corr. Petersburg Index; business mgr. Enquirer; later city editor; reporter, Dispatch, 1873; then city editor; then v.p., then pres. and mng. editor. Home: Richmond. Va. Died 1904.

CHETLAIN, Augustus Louis, soldier; b. St. Louis, Dec. 26, 1824; s. Louis and Julia (Droz) C.; ed. com. schs.; m. Emily Tenney, Oct. 1847; m. 2d, Mrs. Melancthon Smith, Apr. 6, 1865; father of Arthur Henry C. Assisted in raising a co. of Galena (Ill.) vols., and elected capt., Apr. 18, 1861; lt. col., 12th Ill. Inf., May 2, 1861; col., Apr. 2, 1861; brig. gen. vols., Dec. 18, 1863; bvtd. maj. gen. vols., June 18, 1865, for gallant and meritorious services during the war; mustered out, Jan. 15, 1866. Asst. U.S. collector internal revenue, Utah, 1867-69; U.S. consul gen., Brussels, 1869-72; mem. bd. of edn., Chicago, 1876-77; organized Home Nat. Bank, Chicago, 1872, and was its pres.; organized Industrial Bank of Chicago, 1891, and elected its pres.; retired. Author: Recollections of Seventy Years, 1898. Home: Chicago, Ill. Died Mar. 15, 1914.

CHEW, Beverly, banker; b. Geneva, N.Y., Mar. 5, 1850; s. Alexander Lafayette and Sarah Augusta (Prouty) C.; Hobart Coll., Geneva; m. Clarissa Taintor Pierson, Dec. 11, 1872 (died 1889). Asst. sec., 1887-90, sec., 1890-1900, 2d v.p., 1900-14, v.p., 1914-20, Met. Trust Co.; dir. New Netherland Bond & Mortgage Co., Geneva Trust Co., The Nat. Bank of Geneva. Sec. N.Y. Soc. Library. Home: Geneva, N.Y. Died May 21, 1924.

CHEW, Ng Poon, editor; b. Sun Ning, Canton Province, China, Mar. 14, 1866; s. Ng Yip and Wong (Shee) Hok; ed. pub. schs., Occidental Sch., San Francisco, 1884-89, San Francisco Theol. Sem., 1889-92; Litt.D., U. of Pittsburgh, 1913; m. Chun Fah, of San Francisco, May 4, 1892; children—Mansie C., Effie B., Rose B., Edward C., Caroline B. Was placed by parents to prepare for Taoist priesthood, but converted to Christianity; entered ministry at San Francisco; Nov. 1899, resigned from ministry and pub. 1st Chinese illustrated weekly; established the Chung Sai Yat Po, the 1st Chinese daily paper in America, 1899, of which is mng. editor; advisor to Chinese consulate gen., 1906-13; vice consul of China at San Francisco, 1913—; pres. Chung Sai Yat Po Pub. Co. Mem. Mt. Hermon Assn., Yick Lung Co., Dan Sang Tong Co. Presbyn. Mason. Author: Non-Exclusion, 1905; Treatment of Exempt Classes of Chinese in America, 1907. Home: Oakland, Calif. Died Mar. 13, 1931.

CHEW, Samuel Claggett, physician; b. Baltimore, July 26, 1837; s. Dr. Samuel and Henrietta (Scott) C.; grad. Princeton U., 1856; M.D., U. of Md., 1858; (LL.D., 1907); m. Agnes R. Marshall, June 1884. In practice of medicine in Baltimore from 1858; prof. medicine, U. of Md., 1864—. Pres. trustees Peabody Inst., Baltimore. Episcopalian. Address: Roland Park, Md. Died Mar. 22, 1915.

CHICHESTER, Richard Henry Lee, judge; b. Fairfax Co., Va., Apr. 18, 1876; s. Daniel McCarty and Agnes Robinson (Moncure) C.; prep. edn., St. John's Acad., Alexandria, Va.; student U. of Va.; m. Virginia Belle Wallace, June 11, 1895; children—Daniel McCarty, Mary Wallace (Mrs. John L. Wilson), Richard Henry Lee. Admitted to Va. bar, 1892, and began practice at Fairfax; comonmwealth's atty. Stafford Co., 1895-98; county judge, Stafford and King George counties, 1898-1904; judge Circuit Court, Va., 1910-25; asso. judge spl. Court of Appeals, Va., 1923-25; asso. judge, Supreme Court of Appeals, Va., 1925—, for term ending Jan. 31, 1929. Pres. Free Lance Star Pub. Co. Democrat. Episcopalian. Home: Falmouth, Va. Died Feb. 3, 1930.

CHICKERING, Charles A., congressman; b. Harrisburgh, N.Y., Nov. 26, 1843; academic edn.; m. Emma B. Stanton, Dec. 15, 1870. Taught in Lowville Acad.; school commr. Lewis Co., 1865-75; mem. N.Y. Assembly, 1879-81; clerk of assembly, 1884-90; has been chmn. Lewis Co. Rep. Committee and sec. State committee. Mem. Congress, 1893—. Republican. Chmn. Com. on Railways and Canals, 54th and 55th Congresses. Home: Copenhagen, N.Y. Died 1900.

CHICKERING, John White, coll. prof.; b. Bolton, Mass., Sept. 11, 1831; s. Rev. John White and Frances E. (Knowlton) C.; A.B., Bowdoin, 1852, A.M., 1855; grad. Bangor Theol. Sem., 1860; m. Luciana Jameson, 1856. Ordained Congl. ministry, 1859; pastor Springfield, Vt., 1860-63, Exeter, N.H., 1865-70; prof. natural science, Gallaudet Coll., Washington, D.C., 1870—. Died Nov. 9, 1913.

CHIDWICK, John Patrick Sylvester, clergyman; b. New York, Oct. 23, 1863; s. John Bagley and Margaret (O'Reilly) C.; A.B., Manhattan Coll., 1883, A.M., 1885; St. Joseph's Sem., 1883-87; (D.D., from Pope Pius X, 1910; LL.D., Manhattan, 1912, Fordham, 1916). Ordained priest R.C. Ch., 1887; pastor St. Ambrose Ch., New York, Mar. 1904-Aug. 1909; chaplain U.S. Navy, 1895-1903; aboard U.S.S. Maine, Cincinnati, during Spanish-Am. War, U.S.S. New York, 1900-03, also at Washington Navy Yard and New York Navy Yard; pres. St. Joseph's Sem., Dunwoodie (Yonkers), N.Y., Aug. 1909—. Made Domestic Prelate by Pope Pius X, 1916. Was 1st chaplain New York Police Dept., 1906, and Spanish War Vets, 1906; chaplain N.Y. State Soc. United Spanish War Vets., 1916—. Dir. Catholic Ch. Extension Soc.; trustee Catholic Summer Sch. of America, Catholic Inst. for Blind. Died Jan. 13, 1935.

CHIERA, Edward, orientalist; b. Rome, Italy, Aug. 5, 1885; s. Albert and Amalia (Malaguti) C.; B.D., Crozer Theol. Sem., Chester, Pa., 1911, Th.M., 1912; A.M., U. of Pa., 1911, Ph.D., 1913; m. Sylia Moretti, Aug. 3, 1913; children—William, Helen. Instr. in Assyriology, U. of Pa., 1913-19, instr. in Semitics, 1919-22, asst. prof. Assyriology, 1922-26; research fellow, Imperial Ottoman Mus., summer 1923; ann. prof., Am. Sch. Oriental Research, Baghdad, and dir. excavations at Nuzi, Iraq, 1924-25; prof. Assyriology, U. of Pa., 1926-27; field dir. Am. Sch. Oriental Research and dir. excavations at Nuzi, 1927-28; prof. Assyriology, U. of Chicago, 1927—; dir. Oriental Inst. excavations at Khorsabad, Iraq, 1928. Editor Assyrian Dictionary, U. of Chicago, 1927—; coop. editor Am. Jour. Semitic Langs, 1927—. Decorated Chevalier Crown of Italy, 1918. Republican. Baptist. Author: Legal and Administrative Documents from Nippur, 1914; Lists of Personal Names from the Temple School of Nippur, 3 parts, 1916-19; Catalogue of the Babylonian Cuneiform Tablets in the Princeton University Library, 1921; Selected Temple Accounts from Telloh, Yokha and Drehem, 1922; Old Babylonian Contracts, 1922; Sumerian Religious Texts, 1924; Adoption Documents, 1927; Declarations in Court, 1930; Sumerian Lexical Texts, 1930; Exchange and Security Documents, 1931. Home: Chicago, Ill. Died June 20, 1933.

CHILCOTT, Ellery Channing, agriculturist; b. E. Hamburgh, N.Y., Apr. 8, 1859; s. Benjamin Franklin and Philenda (Freeman) C.; ed. common schs. and Friends' Inst. there; (M.S., S.D. Agrl. Coll., 1898); m. Alice Bushley, Jan. 2, 1884; children—Ellery Franklin, Ralph Waldo, Amos Huerd, Minnie (Mrs. Edwin A. Reeves). U.S. deputy surveyor, 1882-92; owned and managed stock ranch, Campbell County, S.D., 1883-92; mem. S.D. Senate, 1892; prof. agr., 1892-97, prof. geology and agronomy and vice dir., 1897-1905, S.D. Agrl. Coll.; agriculturist U.S. Expt. Sta., S.D., 1893-1905; in charge of dry land agrl. investigations, Bur. of Plant Industry, Dept. Agr., 1905—; organizer of Central Great Plains Field Station, near Cheyenne, Wyo., for U.S. Dept. Agr., 1928-29. Mem. S.D. State Bd. Agr., 1901-02; collaborator U.S. Dept. Agr. Cereal Investigations, 1902. During summer and fall of 1918 was head of an agrl. mission sent to France and Algeria by the U.S. Dept. of Agr. at the request of the French High Commn. Author of numerous bulls. and reports, U.S. Dept. Agr. Home: Vienna, Va. Died Nov. 14, 1930.

CHILD, Clement Dexter, physicist; b. Madison, O., May 15, 1868; s. Increase and Artemisia (Lincoln) C.; grad. Normal Sch., Fredonia, N.Y., 1886; A.B., U. of Rochester, 1890; Ph.D., Cornell U., 1897; studied Berlin and Cambridge, Eng., 1897-98; m. H. Aerion Stiles, June 26, 1902; children—Aileen Mary (adopted), James Alfred. Instr. in physics, Cornell U., 1893-97; prof. physics, Colgate U., 1898—. Republican. Baptist. Author: Electric Arcs, 1913. Home: Hamilton, N.Y. Died July 15, 1933.

CHILD, Edwin Burrage, artist; b. Gouverneur, N.Y., May 29, 1868; s. Rev. Jonathan Bush and Sarah Jane (Burnham) C.; A.B., Amherst, 1890, hon. M.A., 1925; studied art at Art Students' League, New York, 1891, and pupil of John LaFarge; m. Anna G. Sykes, Sept. 18, 1894; children—Katherine Edwina, Bradford, Sargent Burrage, Edwin Burrage (dec.). Asst. of John LaFarge in glass work and mural painting several yrs.; exhibited regularly in Soc. Am. Artists and Nat. Acad. Design, and other annual exhbns. Illustrator of many articles in Scribner's and other periodicals. Engaged chiefly in portrait painting from 1910. Painted portraits of Judge Bassett Moore, John Dewey, Dwight W. Morrow, Lyman Abbott, L. B. Rainey, etc. Awarded medal for landscape, St. Louis Expn., 1905. Rep. in Brooklyn Mus., Columbia U., Coll. of City of N.Y., Amherst Coll., Mass. Agrl. College, Mich. State Coll., Yale, Case Sch. of Applied Science, Nat. Mus. of Art, Washington, D.C., etc. Lecturer on art in residence, Amherst Coll., 1924-25. Died Mar. 10, 1937.

CHILD, Frank Samuel, clergyman; b. Exeter, N.Y., Mar. 20, 1854; s. Henry Horatio and Betsey (Brand) C.; A.B., Hamilton Coll., 1875, A.M., 1878; grad. Union Theol. Sem., 1878; (D.D., Hamilton, 1896; L.H.D., Alfred, 1903); m. Lizzie J., d. Gen. John Lilly, of Lafayette, Ind., Oct. 21, 1880. Ordained Congl. ministry, 1879; pastor Greenwich, Conn., 1878-81, New Preston, Conn., 1884-88, First Ch., Fairfield, Conn., 1888—. Corporate mem. A.B.C.F.M.; trustee Francis A. Palmer Fund (corr. sec.), Rollins Coll., Palmer Inst., and Aged Christian Ministers' Home; dir. Fairfield Memorial Library. Author: An Old New England Town, 1895; The Colonial Parson of New England, 1896; Fairfield—Ancient and Modern; A Church of the Established Religion in Connecticut; A Country Parish, 1911. Died May 4, 1922.

CHILD, George Newport, supt. schs.; b. Clover, Utah, Feb. 11, 1869; s. John Joseph and Elizabeth Ann (De St. Jeor) C.; grad. normal dept. Brigham Young U., 1896; B.S., U. of Utah, 1912; m. Florence Willes; children—George, Lionel, Florence, Mildred, Margaret, Edith; m. 2d, Julia Alleman, June 3, 1908; children—Julia, John, Richard. Teacher, pub. schs., Midway, Utah, 1890-91; prin. schs., Lehi, Utah, 1896-1906; asst. cashier State Bank of Lehi, 1907-11; county supt. schs., Utah County, 1909-11; supervisor grammar grade schs., Salt Lake City, 1911-15; asst. supt. schs., Salt Lake City, 1915-19; state supt. pub. instrn., Utah, 1919-20; city supt. schs., Salt Lake City, 1920—. Rotarian. Died July 9, 1932.

CHILD, Richard Washburn, author, diplomat; b. Worcester, Mass., Aug. 5, 1881; s. Horace Walter and Susan Sawyer (Messinger) C.; A.B., Harvard, 1903, LL.B., 1906, LL.D., 1924; m. Maude Parker, Aug. 1916; children—Anne, Constance; m. 2d, Eva Sanderson, Sept. 1927; m. 3d, Dorothy G. Everson, Sept. 1931. Was admitted to bar, 1906. Asst. to Frank A. Vanderlip in war finance work, U.S. Treasury, 1917-18; editor Collier's Weekly, 1919; A.E. and P. to Italy, May 1921-Feb. 1924. Founder Council on Foreign Relations. Chief rep. of U.S. at Conf. of

Genoa, 1922, at Conf. of Lausanne, 1922. Chmn. National Crime Commn., Republicans for Roosevelt National League. Decorated Order of St. Maurice and St. Lazarus (Italy), Order of Crown of Italy. Author: Jim Hands, 1910; The Man in the Shadow, 1911; The Blue Wall, 1912; Potential Russia, 1916; Bodbank, 1916; Vanishing Men, 1919; Velvet Black, 1920; Fresh Waters, 1924; A Diplomat Looks at Europe, 1925; Battling the Criminal; Writing on the Wall, 1928; Pitcher of Romance, 1930; also collaborator with Mussolini on his autobiography, 1927. Home: Newport, R.I. Died Jan. 31, 1935.

CHILDS, Arthur Edward, elec. engr., ins. pres.; b. Montreal, Can., Sept. 16, 1869; s. George and Christian C.; B.Sc., McGill U., 1888, M.S., 1892; asso., 1891, and fellow Central Tech. Coll., London, Eng., 1893; m. Alice Grant Moen, Feb. 1, 1894; children—Philip Moen, Alice Muriel. Began as wireman, with Canadian Gen. Electric Co. and became asst. to Dr. Coleman Sellers in development of Niagara Falls power plant; dist. engr. Westinghouse Elec. & Mfg. Co., Phila., 1893-95, and later N.E. mgr. Electric Storage Battery Co., Boston; organized, 1896, the Light, Heat & Power Corp. to acquire lighting, heating and power plants in the Eastern states, and became actively connected with a large number of gas, electric light and power cos.; one of organizers, 1902, and pres. Columbian Nat. Life Ins. Co.; pres. Am. Investment Securities Co., Hotel Somerset Co., Mass. Lighting Cos., Mass. Utilities Investment Co. (chmn. bd.). Republican. Conglist. Home: Boston, Mass. Died Nov. 9, 1933.

CHILDS, Eleanor Stuart, author; b. Orange, N.J., June 24, 1876; d. Edward and Isabel Liddon (Coxe) Patterson; ed. at home, in pvt. sch. and by travel, spending 3 yrs. in East Africa; m. Harris Robbins Childs, Dec. 15, 1903. Author: Stonepastures, 1896; Averages, 1898; The Postscript, 1908; Romance of Ali, 1913. Contbr. to Scribner's and McClure's magazines of several serials which have been translated into French and German; short story, "The Deeper Diagnosis," in Harper's, 1915. Home: New York, N.Y. Died 1920.

CHILDS, Henry A., jurist; b. Carlton, N.Y., July 17, 1836; s. Levi L. and Ann M. C.; academic edn. Albion and Macedon acads.; grad. Williams Coll. (LL.D.); m. Julia B. Freeman, Nov. 16, 1859. Judge Supreme Court, N.Y., 1882—; term expiring 1906. Republican. Home: Medina, N.Y. Died 1906.

CHILDS, Thomas Spencer, clergyman; b. Springfield, Mass., Jan. 19, 1825; s. Joshua and Susan (King) C.; A.B., New York U., 1847, A.M., 1850; grad. Princeton Theol. Sem., 1850; (D.D., New York U., 1862); m. Mary E. Porter, Mar. 7, 1855; m. 2d, Jane Lawrence Perkins, Aug. 24, 1864. Ordained Presbyn. ministry, 1852; pastor First Ch., Hartford, Conn., 1851-66, First Ch., Norwalk, Conn., 1866-70; prof. bibl. and ecclesiastical history, Hartford Theol. Sem., 1871-79; prof. mental and moral science, U. of Wooster, 1880-82; pastor Washington, 1882-90; joined P.E. ministry, 1890; first archdeacon of Washington, 1894-1901; rector Ch. of Chevy Chase, Washington, 1901-11; asso. rector St. John's 1911—. Commr. to negotiate with Ute Indians, 1888. Author: Claims of the Ministry on Young Men (prize essay), 1885. Home: Chevy Chase, Md. Died Mar. 21, 1914.

CHILDS, William Hamlin, mfr.; b. Hartford, Conn., Mar. 7, 1857; s. Gordon H. and Julia (Richards) C.; ed. Hartford High Sch.; m. Nellie Spencer, July 20, 1881. Chmn. bd. Bon Ami Co.; dir. Congoleum Co., Inc. (exec. com.), Crucible Steel Co. of America, Continental Baking Corp. Apptd. June 1917, chairman sub-com. on coal tar by-products, under com. on raw materials of Council Nat. Defense. V.p. Merchants' Assn. Republican. Presbyn. Home: Brooklyn, N.Y. Died Nov. 2, 1928.

CHILTON, Arthur Bounds, lawyer; b. Montgomery, Ala., July 14, 1890; s. Claudius Lysias and Mabel (Pierce) C.; prep. edn., Starke's Univ. Sch., Montgomery, Ala.; LL.B., U. of Ala., 1916; m. Fanny Wheeler, Aug. 18, 1917; children—Arthur Bounds, John Morgan, Horace Duval, Francis Wheeler. Practiced at Montgomery (except during war period), 1916—; prof. law, U. of Ala., 1920-22; U.S. atty., Middle Dist. of Ala., June 10, 1931—. Entered 1st O.T.C., Ft. McPherson, May 1917; commd. capt. Coast Arty. Res. Corps, Aug. 1918; overseas, Mar. 1918-Jan. 1919; in information sect., Army Arty., 1st Army, staff of Maj. Gen. Douglas MacArthur; participated in St. Mihiel and Meuse Argonne offensives; lt. col. on staff of Gov. Graves of Ala., 1927-31. Methodist. Mason. Home: Montgomery, Ala. Deceased.

CHILTON, Horace, senator; b. Smith Co., Tex., Dec. 29, 1853; s. George W. and Ella (Goodman) C.; ed. at Tyler, Tex.; read law and admitted to bar; m. Mary W. Grinnan, Feb. 20, 1877; children—George, Mrs. Mary Scurlock, Benjamin, Mrs. Christine O'Brien, Thomas (dec.), Mrs. Ella Boren, William (dec.), Arch (dec.). Asst. atty. gen. Tex., 1881-83; apptd. U.S. senator by Gov. Hogg, Apr. 1891, for unexpired term of John H. Reagan, resigned; failed of election when legislature convened, 1892, but was elected as successor to Richard Coke, term 1895-1901. Democrat. In practice, Dallas, Tex., 1906—. Home: Dallas, Tex. Died June 12, 1932.

CHILTON, William Edwin, senator; b. St. Albans, W.Va., Mar. 17, 1858; s. William Edwin and Mary Elizabeth (Wilson) C.; ed. pub. and pvt. schs., pvt. tutors, and Shelton Coll.; m. Mary Louise Tarr, Dec. 19, 1892. Began law practice at Charleston, W.Va., 1880; admitted to Supreme Court of U.S., 1891; apptd. pros. atty., Kanawha Co., 1883, for unexpired term; Dem. nominee for same, 1884; nominee for W.Va. Senate, 1886; chmn. Dem. State Exec. Com., 1892; sec. of state, W.Va., 1893-97; U.S. senator, W.Va., term 1911-17; then in practice of law. Candidate for U.S. Senate, Aug. 1934. Apptd. col. N.G. of W.Va., 1897. Mason. Home: Charleston, W.Va. Died Nov. 7, 1939.

CHIPERFIELD, Burnett Mitchell, congressman; b. Dover, Ill., June 14, 1870; s. Rev. Thomas and Hannah M. (Reynolds) C.; ed. Hamline Univ., 1888-89 (non-grad.); m. Clara Louise Ross, Nov. 12, 1895; children—Margaret Ross (dec.), Robert Bruce, Claude Burnett. Began law practice, Canton, Ill., 1891; identified with much important litigation in Ill.; mem. Chiperfield & Chiperfield. City atty., Canton, 1894-96; state's atty., Fulton Co., Ill., 1896-1900; sec., trustee W. Ill. State Normal Sch., 1901-05; mem. Ill. Ho. of Rep., 8 yrs., 1903-13 (chmn. judiciary com., 1909-11); chmn. com. of House and Senate which made extensive investigations and submitted exhaustive report concerning submerged and shore lands owned by the State; mem. 64th Congress (1915-17), Ill. at large, also 71st and 72d Congresses (1929-33), 15th Ill. Dist.; del. to Rep. Nat. Conv., 1920, 36. Adjutant and lt. col. 1st Cav. Ill. N.G., also judge advocate gen.; organized regt. Spanish-Am. War; mem. mil. staff several Ill. govs.; assisted, 1917, in writing draft law and regulations for World War; asst. to provost marshal gen. of U.S.A., in charge 1st draft in Ill. until Aug. 1917; commd. major, judge advocate general's dept. O.R.C., 1917; judge advocate 33d Div., U.S.A., Camp Logan, Houston, Tex., and in France; div. liaison officer; judge advocate gen. 3d Army Corps, Army of Occupation, in Germany, in charge civil affairs area across Rhine; judge advocate gen. State of Ill., for 10 years, rank of col.; retired, 1934, with rank of brig. gen., after 30 years' service with Ill. N.G. Cited for "exceptionally meritorious and conspicuous service," by Gen. Pershing, and for "gallantry in action against the enemy," by comdr. 33d Div., A.E.F.; recommended on 4 distinct occasions for D.S.M. Pres. First Nat. Bank, Canton. Mem. Bd. Cons. Biologists and Conservationists, Emergency Conservation Com.; mem. Nat. Council Jews and Christians. Methodist. Home: Canton, Ill. Died June 24, 1940.

CHIPMAN, John Sniffen, hosiery mfr.; b. Easton, Pa., June 20, 1899; s. William Evan and Harriet Louise (Sniffen) C.; student Lawrenceville (N.J.) Sch., 1912-17, Lafayette Coll. (Easton, Pa.), 1917-19; m. Emilie Bacon Michler, July 29, 1922; children—William Evan, Frank Louis. With Chipman Knitting Mills, Easton, Pa., 1919—, pres., Feb. 10, 1932—; v.p. Chas. Chipman's Sons Co., Inc., 1931—; also pres. Chipman Spinning Mills, Easton, Pa. Served in U.S.N., World War. Republican. Episcopalian. Mason. Home: Easton, Pa. Died Oct. 28, 1940.

CHIPMAN, Norton Parker, judge; b. Milford, O., Mar. 7, 1838; s. Norman and Sarah Wilson (Parker) C.; prep. edn., Washington Coll. and Mt. Pleasant Acad., Ia.; LL.B., Cincinnati Law Sch., 1859; m. Mary Isabel Holmes, Jan. 30, 1865. Began practice at Washington, Ia., 1859; lt. Co. H, and adj. 2d Ia. Inf., 1861; commd. maj., Sept. 23, 1861; col. and a.a.d.c., Apr. 17, 1862, staff of Maj. Gen. Samuel R. Curtis; brig. gen. vols., Mar. 13, 1865, "for meritorious service in Bureau of Military Justice"; hon. mustered out, Nov. 30, 1865, and resumed practice of law. Apptd. sec. District of Columbia, 1871 (resigned and elected); del. to Congress from D.C., 1871-75; removed to California, 1875, and engaged in law practice; commr. Supreme Ct. of Calif., 1897-1905; apptd. presdg. justice Dist. Ct. of Appeals, 3d Dist., San Francisco, 1905, and elected to same office, Nov. 1906. Pres. Calif. State Bd. of Trade; dir. Calif. Development Bd. Republican. Episcopalian. Died Feb. 1, 1924.

CHIPMAN, William Pendleton, author; b. Old Mystic, Conn., May 11, 1854; s. Charles Packer and Kate (Pendleton) C.; A.B., Brown U., 1875, A.M., 1878; Rochester Theol. Sem., 1876-77; D.D., Presbyn. Coll. of S.C., 1890; m. Lillie B. Phillips, Jan. 23, 1877; children—Charles Phillips, William Browning, Jennie (dec.). Ordained Bapt. ministry, 1877; pastor Quidnessett Ch., Davisville, R.I., 1877-83, First Ch., Peabody, Mass., 1883-85; preacher, Barnwell C.H., S.C., 1885; pastor First Ch., Walton, N.Y., 1886-88, Central Ch., Pawling, N.Y., 1888-92, First Ch., Essex, Conn., 1892-1900, First Ch., Damariscotta, Me., 1900-06; retired from active pastorate, 1906, and engaged in lit. work until 1911; pastor Olivet Ch., Hartford, Conn., Mar. 1, 1911-Oct. 1, 1916. Author: The Black Forge Mills, 1889; (serials) Cruise of the Red Dragon, 1921-22, and Rockcleft, 1930. Home: Hartford, Conn. Died Feb. 28, 1937.

CHISHOLM, Hugh J., capitalist; b. Niagara-on-the-Lake, Can., May 2, 1847; was train newsboy on Grand Trunk Ry. at 13, studied in evening classes at a business coll. in Toronto, gradually secured control of news routes on trains of Grand Trunk Ry. east to Portland, Me., taking his brothers into partnership and steadily added to this business. Sold out Canadian business and purchased his brothers' interests in N.E.; located in Portland and added publishing to his interests; m. Henrietta Mason, 1872. Became interested in wood-pulp business late in 70's; began mfr. of indurated fibre ware, organized Somerset Fibre Co.; mfg. wood-pulp at Fairfield; established, 1881, Umbagog pulp mill at Livermore Falls on Androscoggin River, and later organized the Otis Falls Pulp Co.; developed water power at Rumford Falls, organizing Rumford Falls Power Co.; organized and is pres. Portland & Rumford Falls Ry., Rumford Falls & Rangeley Lakes R.R.; with William A. Russell and others organized Internat. Paper Co., and on death of Mr. Russell became its pres. and Nov. 1907, chmn. bd. dirs. until 1909; then pres. Oxford Paper Co. Home: New York, N.Y. Died July 8, 1912.

CHISHOLM, William, retired; b. Montreal, Can., May 22, 1843; ed. public schools of Cleveland, O., and 3 yrs., 1861-64, at Polytechnic Coll., Phila.; left before graduation to accept gen. management Union Rolling Mill, Chicago, 1864-80; later pres. Cleveland Rolling Mill Co.; m. Mary H. Stone, Sept. 22, 1864. Home: New York, N.Y. Died 1905.

CHISHOLM, William, Sr., inventor, mfr.; b. Scotland, Aug. 12, 1825; was a sailor, then, 1847-52, builder at Montreal; removed, 1852, to Cleveland, O.; became mgr. Cleveland Rolling Mills, then mfr. of spikes, bolts, etc.; discovered practical method for manufacture of screws from Bessemer steel; organized Union Steel Co.; invented new method for mfg. steel shovels and spades; also invented new method of steam hoisting and pumping engines, conveyors for coal and ore, etc. Home: Cleveland, O. Died 1908.

CHISLETT, Howard Roy, surgeon; b. Salt Lake City, Utah, Apr. 6, 1862; s. John and Mary Ann (Stockdale) C.; M.D., Hahnemann Med. Coll. and Hosp., Chicago, 1888; post-grad. work London, Berlin, Vienna; m. Maude A. Codington, 1896. Interne in Hahnemann Hosp., 1888-89; lecturer on minor surgery, Hahnemann Med. Coll., 1889-91; prof. surgery and clin. surgery, 1897-1920, dean, 1903-09, pres., 1910-16, Hahnemann Med. Coll.; attending surgeon to Cook Co. Hosp., 1893-1900, to Hahnemann Hosp., 1893-1920, to Streeter's Hosp., 1900-20, to Chicago Memorial Hosp., 1920—. Republican. Home: Chicago, Ill. Died June 13, 1931.

CHITTENDEN, Frank Hurlbut, entomologist; b. Cleveland, O., Nov. 3, 1858; s. S. King and Harriet M. C.; ed. Cleveland, O., and Cornell U., licentiate, 1881 (hon. Sc.D., Western U. of Pa., 1904); unmarried. Asst. entomologist, U.S. Dept. Agr., Apr. 25, 1891—; entomologist, truck crop insect investigations, 1917—. Author: Insects Injurious to Vegetables; also bulls. and other papers on econ. and tech. entomology published by the U.S. Dept. Agr. Home: Washington, D.C. Died Sept. 15, 1929.

CHITTENDEN, Hiram Martin, brig. gen.; b. Western N.Y., Oct. 25, 1858; s. William F. and Mary Jane (Wheeler) C.; apptd. from N.Y., and grad. U.S. Mil. Acad., 1884; grad. Engr. Sch. of Application, 1887; m. Nettie M. Parker, Dec. 30, 1884. Second lt. engrs., June 15, 1884; 1st lt., Dec. 31, 1886; capt., Oct. 2, 1895; lt. col. chief engr. vols., May 9, 1898-Feb. 25, 1899; maj. engrs., Jan. 23, 1904; lt. col., July 28, 1908; brig. gen., Jan. 25, 1910. Had charge govt. works in Yellowstone Nat. Park and on Missouri, Ohio and other Western rivers; also of reservoir surveys in arid regions; chief engr. 4th Army Corps in Spanish-Am. War, 1898; retired for disability incident to the service, Feb. 10, 1910. Mem. Fed. commn. on Yosemite Nat. Park, 1904, commn. of engrs. on Sacramento flood control; port commr., Port of Seattle, Sept. 5, 1911-Oct. 15, 1915; cons. engr. Spring Valley Water Co., San Francisco, 1912, and on Dayton, O., flood problem, 1914-15. Author: Yellowstone National Park (12 edits.). Died Oct. 9, 1917.

CHITTENDEN, J(onathan) Brace, college prof.; b. Milford, Conn., May 13, 1864; s. Richard H. and Lucy (Brace) C.; B.S., Worcester Poly. Inst., 1888; A.B., Harvard, 1889, A.M., 1890, Kirkland fellow, 1891, Parker fellow, 1892; A.M., Ph.D., Konigsberg, Prussia, 1892; m. Evelyn Louise Betts, July 11, 1900. Instr. mathematics, Princeton, 1892-94, Columbia, 1894-99; prof. mathematics, Brooklyn Poly. Inst., 1899—. Formerly instr. mathematics, Cooper Inst., New York. Admitted to N.Y. bar, 1901. Served as pvt. Vet. Corps Arty., and as 1st lt. 23d Inf., N.Y. Guard, 1917-18. Author: Functions of Lamè, 1893. Home: Brooklyn, N.Y. Died 1928.

CHITTENDEN, William Lawrence, author; b. Montclair, N.J., Mar. 23, 1862; s. Henry A. and Henrietta (Gano) C.; ed. Montclair, N.J. Began work as a reporter for New York newspaper; went to Tex. in 1883, as traveling salesman and corr., with borrowed capital of $50.00. Started the Chittenden cattle ranch at Anson, Jones County, Tex., with his uncle, late Hon. S. B. Chittenden, congressman, of Brooklyn, in 1887; and bought the business soon after; developed farm and ranch of about 10,000 acres, with colony of 45 families, town site, railroad and other interests in Tex., Palm Beach, Fla., and N.J. Contbr. verse and other matter to periodicals under pen-name of "Larry Chittenden." Known as "poet ranchman." Author: Ranch Verses, 1893 (now in the 16th edit.); Bermuda Verses, 1909; Lafferty's Letters; etc. Founded unique autograph free public library at Christmas Cove, Me. Died Sept. 24, 1934.

CHITWOOD, Joseph Howard, lawyer; b. Rocky Mount, Va., Mar. 14, 1877; s. Henry Clay and Gillie Anne (Divers) C.; A.B., William and Mary Coll., 1903; LL.B., U. of Va., 1905; m. Ruth Elizabeth Peddicord, Sept. 12, 1913; 1 son, Randolph. Began practice at Roanoke City, 1906; became mem. Woods, Chitwood, Coxe & Rogers. Mem. Va. Ho. of Dels., 1907-08; asst. U.S. atty., Western Dist. of Va., 1914-20; U.S. atty., same dist., June 8, 1920-May 11, 1921 and from Jan. 16, 1934. Mem. bd. of visitors William and Mary Coll., 1906-14; mem. Commn. to suggest revision Va. Constn. Democrat. Baptist. Home: Roanoke, Va. Died Feb. 21, 1940.

CHIVERS, Elijah Eynon, Baptist clergyman; b. Maesteg, Glamorganshire, South Wales, Oct. 8, 1850; s. John M. and Ann C.; ed. Swansea, S. Wales; grad. Haverfordwest, S. Wales; D.D., Hamilton Theol. Sem., Colgate Univ.; m. Jane E. Shires, Oct. 4, 1871. Pastor 1st Bapt. Ch., Waterford, N.Y., 1870-72; Prospect Av. Bapt. Ch., Buffalo, 1872-94; dist. sec. Am. Bapt. Missionary Union, 1894-97; gen. sec. Bapt. Young People's Union of America, and editor of Bapt. Union, 1897-1901; pastor 6th Av. Bapt. Ch., Brooklyn, 1901-03; field sec. Am. Bapt. Home Mission Soc., 1903—. Died 1907.

CHOATE, Charles Francis, ry. pres.; b. Salem, Mass., May 16, 1828; s. Dr. George and Margaret Manning (Hodges) C.; bro. of William Gardner and Joseph Hodges C. (both q.v.); A.B., Harvard, 1849, A.M., 1852, LL.B., 1853; (hon. A.M., Dartmouth, 1872); m. Elizabeth W. Carlile, Nov. 7, 1855; father of Sarah Choate Sears and Charles Frances Choate, Jr. Admitted to bar, 1855; in practice Boston, 1855-78; counsel, 1865-78, dir., 1872—, pres., 1878-1907, old Colony R.R. Co.; pres. Mass. Hosp. Life Ins. Co., 1901—, Essex Co., 1902—; v.p. N.E. Trust Co., 1887—. Mem. Corp. Mass. Inst. Tech.; pres. Boston Commercial Club, 1898-1900. Home: Boston, Mass. Died 1911.

CHOATE, Charles Francis, Jr., lawyer; b. Cambridge, Mass., Oct. 23, 1866; s. Charles Francis and Elizabeth W. (Carlile) C.; brother of Sarah Choate Sears; A.B., Harvard, 1888; m. Louise Burnett, June 15, 1892. Pres. Appleton Co.; dir. N.Y.,N.H.&H. R.R. Co., Mchts. Nat. Bank of Boston, Appleton Co., Am. Telephone & Telegraph Co.; v.p. Mass. Hosp. Life Ins. Co. Regent Smithsonian Instn., 1908—. Home: Southboro, Mass. Died Nov. 30, 1927.

CHOATE, Isaac Bassett, author; b. S. Otisfield, Me., July 12, 1833; s. Ebenezer, Jr. and Eliza (Barker) C.; A.B., Bowdoin Coll., 1862, A.M., 1865 (Litt.D., 1907); m. Sophia P. Thompson, Sept. 25, 1866. Author: With Birds and Flowers, 1895; Wells of English, 1892; Obeyd, the Camel Driver, 1899; Apollo's Guest, 1907; The Singing Heart, 1912; Through Realms of Song, 1914; The Praise of Song, 1914. Home: Boston, Mass. Died Oct. 7, 1917.

CHOATE, Joseph Hodges, diplomatist; b. Salem, Mass., Jan. 24, 1832; s. George and Margaret Manning (Hodges) C.; brother of Charles Francis and William Gardner C.; A.B., Harvard, 1852, LL.B., 1854, A.M., 1860; (LL.D., Amherst, 1887, Harvard, 1888, Cambridge, 1900, Edinburgh, 1900, Yale, 1901, St. Andrew's, 1902, Glasgow, 1904, Williams, 1905, U. of Pa., 1908, Union, 1909, McGill, 1913, Toronto U., 1915; D.C.L., Oxford, 1902); m. Caroline Dutcher Sterling, Oct. 16, 1861. Admitted to bar, Massachusetts, 1855, N.Y., 1856; identified with many famous cases; one of the com. of 70 which broke up the Tweed ring, 1871; chmn. of its subcommittee on elections; secured reinstatement Gen. Fitz John Porter to his army rank, etc.; pres. of N.Y. Constl. Conv., 1894; candidate for U.S. senator, 1897; U.S. ambassador to Great Britain, 1899-1905; elected Bencher of the Middle Temple, England, Apr. 10, 1905; ambassador and 1st del. U.S. to Internat. Peace Conf. at The Hague, 1907; v.p. Am. Soc. for Judicial Settlement Internat. Disputes. Trustee Met. Mus. of Art, Am. Mus. Natural History from foundation of each; gov. N.Y. Hosp., 1877—; trustee Equitable Life Assurance Soc., Dec. 1913—. Home: New York, N.Y. Died May 14, 1917.

CHOATE, Joseph Kittredge, managing engr.; b. Salem, Mass., Aug. 22, 1853; s. George C. S. (M.D.) and Susan (Kittredge) C.; B.S. in C.E., U. of Colo., 1899. With engr. corps, Central Park, N.Y. City, 1873-74; asst. engr. Dept. Pub. Works, N.Y. City, 1874-77, and chief engr. constrn., 1877-79; supervisor and asst. engr. Pa. Railway, 1879; prin. asst. engr. construction, Erie R.R., 1879-84; supt. U.P. Ry., 1884-96; consulting practice, 1896-1913; v.p. J. G. White Management Corp., 1913—; pres., Morris County Traction Co.; v.p. Manila Electric Corp., Augusta-Aiken Ry. & Electric Co., Staten Island Edison Corp., Helena Light & Ry. Co., Richmond Light & R.R. Co. Home: New York, N.Y. Died June 19, 1928.

CHOATE, William Gardner, judge; b. Salem, Mass., Aug. 30, 1830; s. George and Margaret Manning (Hodges) C.; A.B., Harvard, 1852, LL.B., 1854, A.M., 1860; m. Mary Lyman Atwater, June 29, 1870. In practice at New York, 1856—; mem. Choate, Larocque & Mitchell. U.S. dist. judge, Southern Dist., N.Y., 1878-81. Pres. Harvard Club, 1872-74. Died Nov. 14, 1920.

CHOLMELEY-JONES, R(ichard) G(ilder); b. New York, N.Y., Oct. 8, 1884; s. E. and Elmira (Gilder) C.; ed. pub. schs., under pvt. tutors and at Wharton Sch. of Finance (U. of Pa.). In ins. business, 1899-1903; with Review of Reviews, 1903-17, the last 7 yrs. as advt. mgr.; reorganized work of the recruiting com. of N.Y. City under Mayor's Com. of Nat. Defense, Sept. 1917; at request of sec. of war, organized sale of 2d Liberty Loan Bonds through U.S. Army, bonds to amount of $86,000,000 being disposed of; commd. capt. adj., U.S. Army, Nov. 1917; and sent to France to assist in organizing the War Risk Sect. of A.E.F. of which became chief; promoted to lt. col.; hon. disch., Feb. 5, 1919; dir. Bur. of War Risk Ins., May 19, 1919—. Episcopalian. Home: New York, N.Y. Died Feb. 21, 1922.

CHOPIN, Kate, author; b. (O'Flaherty) St. Louis, Feb. 8, 1851; grad. Sacred Heart Convent, St. Louis, 1868; m. Oscar Chopin, 1870 (dec.). Lived in La. 14 years; now in St. Louis. Author: At Fault, 1891; Bayou Folk, 1894; A Night in Acadie, 1897; The Awakening, 1899, etc. Died 1904.

CHOUTEAU, Pierre, engr.; b. St. Louis, July 30, 1849; s. Charles P. and Julia Augusta (Gratiot) C.; ed. tech. schs., St. Louis and Royal School of Arts, Mines and Manufacturers, Liege, Belgium; m. Lucille M. Chauvin, Nov. 27, 1882. Has devoted leisure to invention of various devices and appliances now in gen. use; has also done much in collection and preservation of ancient documents, papers and books illustrating early conditions and history of St. Louis; originated project for commemoration of centennial anniversary of purchase of La. Ty., being chmn. of several preliminary coms., which originated the La. Purchase Expn., of which he served as 8th v.p. Home: St. Louis, Mo. Died 1910.

CHRISMAN, Edward Robert, army officer; b. Connersville, Ind., Aug. 13, 1866; s. Jesse Swisher and Catharine Verlinda (Price) C.; grad. U.S. Mil. Acad., 1888, Sch. of Submarine Mining, Willetts Point, N.Y., 1892; m. Florence Isabella Ryan, Mar. 28, 1892; children—Catharine Verlinda, Ord Gariché. Commd. 2d lt. inf., U.S.A., 1888, and advanced through grades to col., May 15, 1917; retired Jan. 31, 1921; brig. gen. on retired list, June 21, 1930; prof. mil. science and tactics, S.D. State College, 1909-11; on active duty as prof. mil. science and tactics, U. of Idaho, 1919-36, comdt. of cadets, 1932-35, prof. military science and tactics, emeritus for life, by act of Congress, approved Apr. 15, 1936, comdt. of cadets, emeritus, by board of regents, University of Idaho, 1935. Participated in Sioux Indian Campaign, 1890-91; Spanish-American War, Cuba, 1898 (cited for gallantry in action); Philippine Insurrection, 1899-1902; Leyte Campaign, Pulujan (P.I.) Outbreak, 1906-07; served in Panama Canal Zone, and brig. gen. comdg. U.S. forces in Puerto Rico, World War. Mason. Home: Moscow, Ida. Died Jan. 15, 1939.

CHRISMAN, Oscar, paidologist; b. Gosport, Ind., Nov. 16, 1855; s. Benjamin and Eliza (Bastian) C.; grad. Ind. State Normal Sch., 1887; A.B., Ind. U., 1888, A.M., 1893; fellow in Clark U., 1892-94; student in Jena and Berlin, 1894-96; Ph.D., U. of Jena, 1896; m. Drusilla Lukenbill, Oct. 6, 1883; children—Chrisman, Oscie Drusilla (Mrs. R. D. Gladding, dec.). Teacher pub. schs., 1876-83, prin., 1883-85; prin. Longfellow Sch., Houston, Tex., 1888-89; supt. schs., Gonzales, Tex., 1889-92; prof. Kan. State Normal Sch., 1896-1901; prof. of paidology, 1902-26, also prof. psychology, 1904-22, Ohio Univ. Republican. Methodist. Formulated idea of the science of the child, 1893, originated the term paidology, and has since made this his life's work. Author: The Historical Child, 1920. Home: Athens, Ohio. Died Feb. 2, 1929.

CHRISTENSEN, Niels, merchant; b. Beaufort, S.C., Apr. 21, 1876; s. Niels and Abbie M. (Holmes) C.; ed. Allen Sch., West Newton, Mass., and Brookline (Mass.) High Sch.; m. Katherine Wales Stratton, Dec. 12, 1912; children—Niels, Anne Wales, Stratton, Andrea. Pres. Beaufort Gazette Pub. Co. and editor Beaufort Gazette, 1903-22; partner N. Christensen & Sons, Beaufort, 1906-25; pres. Christensen Realty Co. Mem. S.C. State Senate, 1904-24; mem. com. to investigate State Dispensary, 1905-06, State Fisheries, 1905, State Hospital for Insane, 1908, State Printing, 1913, State penitentiary, 1924; chmn. Senate Finance Com., 1914-24; mem. Dem. State Exec. Com., 1906-17, 1922-26; pres. Farmers and Taxpayers League of S.C., 1931-33; sr. tech. advisor U.S. Social Security Bd., 1936. Ensign and lt. U.S.N., World War. Pres. State Chamber Commerce, S.C., 1920-22. Unitarian. Home: Beaufort, S.C. Deceased.

CHRISTIAN, Edmund Adolph, psychiatrist; b. Detroit, Sept. 7, 1857; s. Edmund Potts and Mary (Hawley) C.; A.B., University of Michigan, 1879, M.D., 1882, honorary A.M., 1906; m. Augusta Baldwin, Jan. 24, 1894; children—Mrs. Isabel White, Mrs. Margaret Perry, Mrs. Dorothea Clark. Asst. phys. 1882, asst. med. supt., 1889, med. supt., 1894—, Eastern Michigan Asylum (Pontiac State Hosp.). Mem. leading med. societies. Republican. Episcopalian. Home: Pontiac, Mich. Died Feb. 5, 1935.

CHRISTIAN, Eugene, author, dietitian; b. nr. McMinnville, Tenn., May 30, 1860; s. William Thornton and Harriet (Freeman) C.; Irving Coll., Warren Co., 1 yr.; m. Mollie Griswold, Apr. 30, 1889; children—Eugenia, Lorita. Traveled for mercantile house until 1894; in mercantile bus., Atlanta, Ga., 1894-97; mfg. Binghamton, N.Y., 1897-1900; settled in N.Y. City, 1900; began teaching and practicing as dietitian; was prosecuted by Med. Soc. of N.Y. City, and by decision of Supreme Court of New York established right of food scientist to diagnose and prescribe diet as a remedy for disease; founded Am. Vitamin Food Co., Westfield, Mass. Pres. Christian Realty Co., New York, Christian-Boice Corp. and Hotel Co., St. Petersburg (Fla.) Christian Foundation; chmn. bd. Canada Health Foods, Ltd., Toronto, Can. Author: Ency. of Diet (5 vols.), 1913; How to Live 100 Years, 1914; 24 Lessons in Scientific Eating, 1915; Eat and Be Well, 1916; Encyclopedia of Cookery (4 vols.), 1919. Home: Forest Hills, L.I., N.Y. Died Mar. 10, 1930.

CHRISTIAN, John Tyler, clergyman; b. Lexington, Ky., Dec. 14, 1854; s. Marion Washington and Amanda (Martinie) C.; B.A., Bethel Coll., Russellville, Ky., 1876, M.A., 1882, D.D., 1888; made 7 trips to Europe, for post-grad. work; LL.D., Keachie Coll., La., 1898; m. Evelyn G. Quin, Dec. 19, 1878 (died 1919); children—Eloise Graham, John Tyler, William Langdon. Ordained Baptist ministry, 1876; pastor, Tupelo, Miss., 1877-78, Sardis, 1879-83, Chattanooga, Tenn., 1883-86; missionary sec., Miss., 1887-92; pastor, East Ch., Louisville, Ky., 1892-1900, La Salle Av. Ch., Chicago, 1900-04, 2d Ch., Little Rock, 1904-10; missionary sec. Ark., 1910-13; pastor First Bapt. Ch., Hattiesburg, Miss., 1913-19; prof. Christian history and librarian, Baptist Bible Inst., New Orleans, La., 1919—. Chmn. Religious Welfare Com. of Camp Shelby. Mason. Author: Immersion the Act of Christian Baptism, 1891; A History of the Baptists, 1923; History of the Baptists of Louisiana, 1923. Home: New Orleans, La. Died Dec. 18, 1925.

CHRISTIE, Alexander, archbishop; b. Highgate, Vt., 1850; removed with parents to Minn.; ed. St. John's U. (Minn.) and Sem. of Notre Dame, Montreal, Can. Ordained priest R.C. Ch., 1877; pastor Waseca, Minn., 13 yrs., Ascension Parish, Minneapolis, 4 yrs., St. Stephen's Ch., Minneapolis, 4 yrs.; consecrated bishop of Vancouver Island, B.C., June 29, 1898; archbishop See of Ore., Apr. 11, 1899—. Home: Portland, Ore. Died Apr. 6, 1925.

CHRISTIE, James, mech. engr.; b. nr. Ottawa, Can., Aug. 28, 1840; s. Thomas A. and Elizabeth (Holmes) C.; ed. pub. schs., Ottawa; m. Miss M. J. Maxwell, 1866. Served U.S.A., 1863. Machinist's apprentice, Detroit and Phila.; bridge builder, 1872-76; mem. town council and mayor, Phillipsburg, N.J., 1874; chief mech. engr. Pencoyd Iron Works, 1876—, and Am. Bridge Co., 1899-1905. Awarded Norman medal, Am. Soc. C.E., 1884. Home: Philadelphia, Pa. Died 1912.

CHRISTIE, Luther Rice, clergyman; b. Halifax Co., N.C., Feb. 3, 1873; s. Thomas Hervey and Martha Henry (Barfield) C.; ed. Trinity Coll., Durham, N.C., and Richmond (Va.) Coll.; D.D., Mercer U., Macon, Ga., 1910; m. Blanche Wilson, June 21, 1899; children—Mrs. T. M. Forbes, J. Thomas. Ordained Bapt. ministry, 1898; pastor successively Spurgeon Memorial Ch., Norfolk, Va., Windsor, Va., Valdosta, Ga., 1st Ch., Columbus, Ga., 1909-17; gen. sec. Shorter Coll., Rome, Ga., 1917-18; pastor 1st Ch., Savannah, Ga., 1918-22, 1st Ch., Meridian, Miss., 1922-26, Ponce de Leon Ch., Atlanta, Ga., 1926-33, Fourth Av. Ch., Louisville, Ky., 1933-35, First Ch., Tallahassee, Fla., 1935—. Vice-pres. Ga. Bapt. Conv., 1907; pres. Home Mission Bd. of Southern Bapt. Conv., 1928-29. Mason. Home: Tallahassee, Fla. Died Nov. 30, 1939.

CHRISTIE, Thomas Davidson, missionary; b. Sion Mills, Co. Tyrone, Ireland, Jan. 21, 1843; s. James and Eliza (Reid) C.; pvt. to 1st sergt. 1st Battery Minn. Light Arty., 1861-65; A.B., Beloit Coll., 1871, A.M., 1874; B.D., Andover Theol. Sem., 1877;

(D.D., New York U., 1893; LL.D., U. of Aberdeen, 1904); m. Carmelite Brewer, Mar. 14, 1872. Taught in U. of Wis., 1871-72, Beloit Coll., 1872-74; ordained Congl. ministry, Aug. 21, 1877; prof. ch. history and N. T. Greek, Marash (Turkey) Theol. Sem., 1877-93; pres. St. Paul's Coll., Tarsus, 1893—. Compelled to leave Turkey, July 1915, and was pastor in Southern Calif., and Y.M.C.A. sec. at Camp Kearney until 1919, when returned to Tarsus via Pacific; wife "held the fort" alone in Tarsus 4 yrs. Died May 25, 1921.

CHRISTIE, William Wallace, mech. engr.; b. Paterson, N.J., July 12, 1866; s. James C. and Louisa (Jones) C.; grad. high sch., Paterson, N.J., 1882, spl. student, Cornell, 1889-91; spl. musical edn. (organ); m. Carrie E. Ker, Mar. 14, 1895. In practice as mech. engr. from 1882. Republican. Author: Chimney Formulæ and Tables, 1897; Chimney Design and Theory, 1899; Furnace Draft, 1901; Boiler Waters; Scale, Corrosion, Foaming, 1906; Furnace Draft, Its Production and Mechanical Methods, 1905. Editor Mech. Section Foster's Electrical Pocket Book, 1909; Water: Its Purification and Use in the Industries, 1912. Home: Ridgewood, N.J. Died Apr. 13, 1925.

CHRISTISON, J(ohn) Sanderson, physician; b. Brechin, Forfarshire, Scotland, Mar. 13, 1856; s. Rev. Robert and Martha (Sanderson) C.; ed. schs. at Glasgow, Wigan, Upholland, Edinburgh and London; came to U.S. with parents, 1875; M.D., U. of City of New York, 1877; unmarried. Was asst. physician N.Y. City Lunatic Asylum, acting surgeon to Workhouse (prison) Blackwell's Island; asst. physician New York City Insane Asylum; acting physician Bellevue Hosp., outdoor dept.; later asst. physician Wis. State Hosp. for Insane; then in private practice. Sec. Criminological Soc. of Chicago. Author: Crime and Criminals (2 edits.), 1898, 1901; Brain in Relation to Mind, 1899; Farmer Kilroy, 1902; The Tragedy of Chicago—A Study in Hypnotism, 1906. Died 1908.

CHRISTMAN, W(illiam) W(eaver), poet, farmer; b. Delanson, N.Y., May 30, 1865; s. Spencer and Nancy Augusta (Weaver) C.; ed. pub. schs.; m. Phebe Catherine Bradt, Oct. 6, 1887; children—William Shenstone, Emily Davenport (Mrs. Bert J. Chrysler), Spencer, Nancy Augusta (Mrs. Ellsworth W. Avery), Philip Sidney, Duane Coffin, Henry Esmond, Walden, James Lansing. Spent entire life farming. Democrat. Mason. Awarded Burroughs medal by John Burroughs Memorial Assn. for best nature book pub. in 1934. Author: Songs of the Helderhills, 1926; Songs of the Western Gateway, 1930; Wild Pasture Pine, 1934. Home: Delanson, N.Y. Died Feb. 26, 1937.

CHRISTY, Samuel Benedict, metallurgist; b. San Francisco, Calif., Aug. 8, 1853; s. James C.; Ph.B., U. of Calif., 1874; studied mining and metallurgy U. of Calif., 1874-79; (Sc.D., Columbia, 1902); m. Sarah Adele Field, Feb. 22, 1881. Grad. student and instr. analytical chemistry, 1874-79, instr. mining and metallurgy, 1879-85, prof., 1885—, U. of Calif. Life mem. Calif. Acad. Sciences (corr. sec., 1881-86). Patented, 1900, improved process for recovering gold and silver from dilute cyanide solutions. Home: Berkeley, Calif. Died Nov. 30, 1914.

CHRYSLER, Walter Percy, mfr. motor cars; b. Wamego, Kan., Apr. 2, 1875; s. Henry and Anna Maria (Breyman) C.; desc. of Tuenis Van Dolsen, who was first male child born in New Amsterdam (now Manhattan), New York; grad. of high sch., Ellis, Kansas; m. Della V. Forker, June 5, 1901 (died 1938); children—Thelma (Mrs. Byron C. Foy), Bernice (Mrs. E. W. Garbisch), Walter, Jack. From machinist's apprentice with r.r. to supt. motive power and machinery of C.G.W. Ry. at age of 33; apptd. asst. mgr. Pittsburgh works of Am. Locomotive Co., 1910, mgr., 1911; works mgr. Buick Motor Co., 1912-16, pres. and gen. mgr., 1916-19; v.p. in charge operations Gen. Motors Corp., 1919-20; exec. v.p. Willys-Overland Co., 1920-22; served as chmn. reorganization com. Maxwell Motor Corp.; became chmn. bd. Chrysler Corp. Republican. Episcopalian. Mason. Home: New York, N.Y., and Great Neck, L.I., N.Y. Died Aug. 18, 1940.

CHURCH, Alonzo, lawyer; b. Chicago, Ill., Oct. 31, 1870; s. Alonzo and Mary (Robbins) C.; A.B., Princeton, 1892, A.M., 1895. Reporter on Newark (N.J.) Daily Advertiser, 1892-94; sec. and counsel Essex County Park Commn., 1894-1908; admitted to N.J. bar, 1898, as counselor, 1901; mem. Munn & Church, 1902-22; mem. State Bd. Bar Examiners, 1908-22, chmn., 1922; apptd. standing advisory master, 1915; vice chancellor of N.J., 1922-32; again in law practice, 1932—. Democrat. Presbyterian. Mason. Home: Newark, N.J. Died Feb. 20, 1937.

CHURCH, Arthur Latham, mech. engr.; b. Phila., Pa., Oct. 11, 1858; s. William A. and Elizabeth I. (Barker) C.; B.S., U. of Pa., 1878; m. Louise Brant, Dec. 5, 1888; 1 son, Herbert. In machine shop and draughting room of The William Cramp & Sons Ship & Engine Bldg. Co., Phila., 1878-82; with engine depts. of steamships Queen of the Pacific, City of Peking and Granada, and draughtsman Union Iron Works, San Francisco, 1882-84; chief engr. Franklin Inst. Elec. and Novelties Exhbns., Phila., 1884-85; supt. Spring Garden Inst., 1885-86; with Baldwin Locomotive Works, Phila., 1886—, now sec. and asst. treas. Trustee U. of Pa.; mgr. Preston Retreat, Spring Garden Inst., Univ. Hosp. Republican. Home: Philadelphia, Pa. Died June 25, 1931.

CHURCH, Augustus Byington, coll. pres.; b. N. Norwich, N.Y., Jan. 11, 1858; s. Austin William and Catherine (Conklin) C.; A.B., St. Lawrence U., 1886; theol. course St. Lawrence Theol. Sch., 1887-88; (hon. A.M., Buchtel Coll., 1899; D.D., St. Lawrence, 1901; LL.D., Tufts, 1905); m. Anne Atwood, Sept. 5, 1889. Ordained to Universalist ministry, 1889; pastor First Universalist Ch., S. Berwick, Me., 1888-90, N. Adams, Mass., 1890-97, Akron, O., 1897-1901; acting pres., 1901, pres., 1902—, Buchtel Coll. Town supt. schs., S. Berwick, Me., 1890; mem. sch. bd., N. Adams, Mass., 1896-97. Republican. Home: Akron, O. Died Nov. 6, 1912.

CHURCH, Earl D., commr. of pensions; b. Rockville, Conn.; s. Philo H. and Jennie T. (Ide) C.; grad. high sch., Rockville, 1890; student Yale, 1891-92; m. Elysabeth Remington, Sept. 26, 1905. With Travelers Ins. Co., 1896-1929, pvt. sec. to pres., 1896-1901, supt. life policy loan div., 1905-18, in casualty agency dept., 1920-29, asst. supt. of agencies, 1929; U.S. commr. of pensions, May 24, 1929—. Served as maj., later lt. col., Ordnance Dept., U.S. Army, 1917-20; took part in Battle of Cambrai, on the Somme, at Verdun, in battles of St. Mihiel and the Argonne. Awarded D.S.M. (U.S.); Croix de Guerre with bronze star (France); Gen. H.Q. citation certificate for "exceptionally meritorious and conspicuous service"; French citation at St. Mihiel; cited in 80th Div. gen. orders in battle of Argonne. Pres. Bd. of Councilmen, Hartford, 1905-06, Bd. of Aldermen, 1907-08. Republican. Home: Washington, D.C. Died May 9, 1930.

CHURCH, Edward Bentley, P.E. clergyman; prin. Irving Inst., San Francisco, 1881—; b. Greenville, Miss., Sept. 7, 1844; s. Edward B. C. (M.D.); grad. Kenyon Coll., 1867; A.M., 1870; studied in Theol. Sem. of Ohio and Phila. Divinity School; made deacon, 1868; ordained priest, 1874; m. Frances Augusta Kellogg, 1869. Went to Calif., 1869, and was head master of private schools until he established Irving Inst., for higher edn. of young ladies; is also asst. minister Trinity Ch., San Francisco, Grand Chaplain F. and A.M. of Calif., 1896-1902. Home: San Francisco. Died 1904.

CHURCH, Francis Pharcellus, editor; b. Rochester, N.Y., Feb. 22, 1839; s. Pharcellus and Chara Emily C.; prep. edn. Charles Anthon's Latin Sch., New York; grad. Columbia Coll., 1859, A.M., 1861; studied law in office of Judge Hooper C. Van Vorst, New York; m. Elizabeth Wickham. In editorial work, 1860—; editor Galaxy Mag. and, in association with brother, Col. William Conant Church, of the Army and Navy Journal and the Internal Revenue Record; also editorial writer New York Sun, 1874—. Mem. Sons Revolution, Nat. Sculpture Soc. Home: New York, N.Y. Died 1906.

CHURCH, Frank Henry, clergyman, publisher; b. Toledo, O., Mar. 24, 1858; s. Roger Wadsworth and Eliza Prudence (Hall) C.; Trinity Coll., Conn., 1882, M.A., 1895; grad. Berkeley Div. Sch., 1885; m. Virginia Easton Hobart, June 3, 1886 (died 1920); m. 2d, Alice Elizabeth Wilson, May 1, 1924. Deacon, 1885; priest, 1886; P.E. Ch.; curate St. Andrew's Ch., Meriden, Conn., 1885-86, St. Phillip's Ch., Putnam, 1886-89, Trinity Ch., San Francisco, 1889-91, St. Luke's Ch., San Francisco, 1891-93; sec. Diocese of Calif., 1893-96; rector St. Luke's Ch., Tacoma, Wash., 1896-99; vicar St. Paul's Ch., College Point, N.Y., 1900-04; curate Trinity Chapel, N.Y. City, 1904-06; vicar Chapel of the Messiah, N.Y. City, 1906-11; Cathedral staff missions, San Francisco, 1911-15; editor Pacific Churchman, 1914-21; sec. Diocese of Calif., 1921—. Founder and mgr. Bur. of Information and Supply, San Francisco, 1893-96, 1911—. Republican. Home: Alameda, Calif. Died Apr. 6, 1927.

CHURCH, Frederick Edwin, landscape painter; b. Hartford, N.Y., May 4, 1826; pupil of Thomas Cole; established studio in New York; academician Nat. Acad. Design, 1849. His Great Fall at Niagara, now in the Corcoran Gallery, Washington, received medal at Paris Expn., 1867. Home: Hudson, N.Y. Died 1900.

CHURCH, Frederick Stuart, artist; b. Grand Rapids, Mich., Dec. 1, 1842; s. Thomas B. and Mary Elizabeth (Stuart) C.; pub. sch. edn.; in employ Am. Express Co., Chicago, 1855-61; served as pvt. Union Army more than 3 yrs.; studied Chicago Acad. Design and later Nat. Acad. Design and Art Students' League, New York; unmarried. Painter of figures and animals; has exhibited at various exhbns. U.S. and Europe. N.A., 1885. Died Feb. 18, 1923.

CHURCH, George Hervey, officer corps.; b. Columbus, Ga., July 23, 1855; s. Moses Hall and Caroline (Hall) C.; ed. pvt. schs.; C.P.A., Univ. State of N.Y., 1901; m. Myra Dickinson, dau. Franklin Harrison Carter, of N.Y. City, June 29, 1899. Began at 17 in employ of Bound & Co., bankers and brokers, New York; later with Clark, Walcott & Co., and J. C. Walcott & Co. until 1882; entered business on own account as pub. accountant and auditor, 1885; mem. Church & McCulloh, 1909-12; has served as trustee of over 60 trusts; now pres. and treas. The Fidelity Co., Wyoming Land Co.; v.p. New Amsterdam Gas Co.; treas. Va. Terminal Ry. Co., Virginian & Western Ry. Co., Virginian Ry. Co.; trustee Terminal Warehouse Co. Treas. and trustee Miriam Osborn Memorial Home Assn. Republican. Presbyn. Home: New York, N.Y. Died July 27, 1935.

CHURCH, Henry Ward, coll. prof.; b. St. Joseph, Mich., June 25, 1887; s. William Barnes and Grace Blakesley (Ward) C.; artist's diploma in pipe organ, Univ. Sch. of Music, Ann Arbor, Mich., 1906; A.B., U. of Mich., 1908, A.M., 1909, Ph.D., 1915; m. Helen Farr, June 28, 1911; children—William Farr Church, Alice Grace Church. Teaching asst. in German, U. of Mich., 1908-09; teacher French and German, Interlaken Sch., LaPorte, Ind., 1909-10, Asheville (N.C.) Sch., 1910-12; prof. modern langs., Monmouth (Ill.) Coll., 1912-18; prof. Romance langs. and lit., Allegheny Coll., 1919—. Ednl. sec. Army Y.M.C.A., camps Dodge and Taylor, also Am. dir. Foyer du Soldat, Camp Sathonay (Ain), France, 1918-19. Methodist. Home: Meadville, Pa. Died July 11, 1938.

CHURCH, Irving Porter, univ. prof.; b. Ansonia, Conn., July 22, 1851; s. Dr. Samuel P. and Elizabeth (Sterling) C.; C.E., Cornell, 1873, M.C.E., 1878; m. Elizabeth P. Holley, June 15, 1881. Asst. and asso. prof. civil engring., 1876-92, prof. applied mechanics and hydraulics, 1892-1916 (emeritus), Cornell Univ. Author: Statics and Dynamics for Engineering Students, 1886; Mechanics of Materials, 1887; Hydraulics and Pneumatics, 1889 (these three afterward published as Mechanics of Engineering, 1890); Notes and Examples in Mechanics, 1892; Diagrams of Mean Velocity of Water in Open Channels, 1902; Hydraulic Motors, 1905; Mechanics of Internal Work, 1910. Home: Ithaca, N.Y. Died May 8, 1931.

CHURCH, John Adams, mining engr.; b. Rochester, N.Y., Apr. 5, 1843; s. Rev. Pharcellus and Chara E. (Conant) C.; bro. of William Conant C.; E.M., Columbia, 1867, Ph.D., 1879; studied in Europe, 1868-70; m. Jessie A. Peel, July 30, 1884. Acting prof. mineralogy and metallurgy, Columbia School of Mines, 1872-73; editor Engineering and Mining Journal, 1872-74; on U.S. Geog. and Geol. Survey, and examined Comstock Lode; prof. mining and metallurgy, State U. of Ohio, 1878-81; became supt. Tombstone (Ariz.) Mill & Mining Co.; in service of Viceroy Li Hung Chang, opening silver mines in Mongolia and introducing Am. methods and machinery, 4 yrs., 1886-90; now practicing as mining engr. Author: Notes on a Metallurgical Journey in Europe, 1875; The Comstock Lode, 1880; Report on Artesian Wells in Arizona, 1882; etc. Home: New York, N.Y. Died Feb. 12, 1917.

CHURCH, Melville, lawyer; b. Utica, N.Y., Dec. 16, 1856; s. Truman Kilborn and Julia Maria (Benedict) C.; grad. St. John's Acad., Alexandria, Va., 1871; LL.B., 1879, LL.M., 1880, L.P.M., 1895, LL.D., 1921, Columbian (now George Washington) U.; admitted to bar, 1879; m. Sarah H. Durant; children—Durant, Melville Durant, Kortright, Helen Durant, Mallory Durant, Heyliger, Kilborn (dec.), Maxwell Durant. Delegate of U.S. to Internat. Union for Protection of Industrial Property, 1911. Episcopalian. Home: Washington, D.C. Died Oct. 10, 1935.

CHURCH, William Conant, editor; b. Rochester, N.Y., Aug. 11, 1836; s. Rev. Pharcellus and Chara E. (Conant) C.; bro. of John Adams C.; ed. Boston Latin Sch.; m. Mary Elizabeth Metcalf, Apr. 2, 1863. With father, engaged in editing and publishing New York Chronicle, 1855-60; became publisher New York Sun, 1860; Washington corr. New York Times, 1861-62, until apptd. capt., U.S.V., Oct. 4, 1862; received bvts. of maj. and lt. col.; with his brother established, 1863, the Army and Navy Journal, and in 1866, the Galaxy mag.; govt. commr. to inspect N.P. R.R., 1882. With George W. Wingate established Nat. Rifle Assn. and was its first president, and became hon. director for life; one of founders and a fellow in perpetuity, Met. Mus. of Art; life mem. and dir. N.Y. Zoöl. Soc.; original mem. Mil. Order Loyal Legion U.S. (sr. vice comdr.). Author: Life of John Ericsson; Life of Ulysses S. Grant, etc. Home: New York, N.Y. Died May 23, 1917.

CHURCH, William E., lawyer; b. Brooklyn, N.Y., Dec. 7, 1841; s. John R. and Anstiss (Howard) C.; A.B., Williams Coll., 1861; studied law at Morristown, N.J., 1861-62, and New York, 1865-66; enlisted in 11th N.Y. Cav., Aug. 1862; served in Md., Va., and La.; apptd. asst. adj. gen. vols. with rank of capt., Mar. 29, 1865, and assigned to 1st Brigade, 1st Div., 13th Army Corps; went with his command, in May, 1865, to occupy Shreveport, La., and to receive the surrender of Kirby Smith's army; was post adj. of Shreveport until Aug. and afterward on staff of Gen. Sheridan until mustered out, Oct. 23, 1865; m. Mary Jones, Nov. 2, 1870. Admitted to N.Y. bar.

1866; practiced there until 1872; at Morristown, N.J., 1872-83; asso. justice Supreme Ct. of Dak. Ty., 1883-87; located in Chicago, 1890; sr. mem. Church & McMurdy. Republican. Apptd. judge-advocate, Dept. Ill., G.A.R., July 1913. Home: Evanston, Ill. Died Apr. 20, 1917.

CHURCH, William Howell, educator; b. Bath, N.Y., Nov. 1, 1869; s. Edwin Lawrence and Augusta (Bull) C.; A.B., Hamilton Coll., Clinton, N.Y., 1892, A.M., 1895; post-grad. work Johns Hopkins, 1896-97; m. Edith Gray, July 9, 1904 (died 1924); 1 son, William Bull. Master in Berkeley Sch., N.Y. City, 1892-96, 1897-1902; headmaster, Nathan Hale Sch., New York, 1902-08; asso. prof. mathematics, Carnegie Inst. Tech., Pittsburgh, Pa., 1908-10; headmaster, George H. Thurston Sch., Pittsburgh, 1910-15; St. Albans Sch., Washington, D.C., 1915—. Episcopalian. Deceased.

CHURCHILL, Charles Samuel, civil engr., ry. official; b. New Britain, Conn., Sept. 22, 1856; s. Samuel W. and Ellen (Hubbard) C.; C.E., Sheffield Sci. Sch. (Yale), 1878; m. Anna D. Green, Nov. 11, 1885. Ry. surveys and constrn., Conn. and Pa., 1879-81; div. engr. constrn., Pittsburgh & Lake Erie R.R., 1881-84; prin. asst. engr. constrn., Schuylkill Valley div. Pa. R.R., 1884-87; engr. maintenance of way, Shenandoah Valley R.R., 1887-88; engr. in charge Ohio extension of N.&W. Ry., May-Oct. 1888, engr. maintenance of way, 1888-1903, chief engr., 1903-14, chmn. valuation com., 1913-14, asst. to pres. and chief of valuation, 1914-18, Norfolk & Western Ry. System; v.p. N.&W. Ry. Co., 1918-26, in charge purchases, real estate and valuation, 1920-26, also chmn. coms. representing Southern group of rys. on federal valuation, 1913-26, and engaged in ventilation of ry. tunnels; retired from ry. service, Oct. 1, 1926; cons. engring. practice. Elected hon. mem., 1931, Am. Ry Engring. Assn., "in recognition of outstanding contributions to the science of railway engineering." Home: Roanoke, Va. Died Jan. 25, 1934.

CHURCHILL, George Bosworth, coll. prof.; b. Worcester, Mass., Oct. 24, 1866; s. Ezra and Myra Jane (Bosworth) C.; A.B., Amherst Coll., 1889, A.M., 1892; post-grad. U. of Pa., 1892-94; univs. of Strassburg, 1894-95, Berlin, 1895-97, Ph.D., 1897; m. Belle E. Whittier, Aug. 24, 1893. Teacher Worcester High Sch., 1889-92, William Penn Charter Sch., Phila., 1892-94; asso. editor Cosmopolitan Magazine, 1897-98; asso. prof. English and pub. speaking, 1898-1903, asso. prof. English lit., 1903-05, prof. same, 1905—, Amherst College. Has lectured much before learned and lit. assns., especially on the drama. Am. editorial representative Jahrbuch der Deutschen Shakespeare Gesellschaft. Republican. Author: Richard III Up to Shakespeare, 1900; Descriptive Catalogue of the Latin University Plays of England in the time of Elizabeth (with Prof. Wolfgang Keller), 1898. Editor: The Country Wife and The Plain Dealer (by William Wycherley), 1923; Shakespeare's Richard III, 1912. Mem. Mass. Senate, 1917, 18, 19. Home: Amherst, Mass. Died July 1, 1925.

CHURCHILL, John Charles, lawyer; b. Mooers, N.Y., Jan. 17, 1821; s. Samuel and Martha (Bosworth) C.; grad. Middlebury Coll. (Vt.), 1843 (A.M., LL.D.); legal edn. Harvard Law Sch. (LL.D., Hamilton Coll.); m. Catharine Thomas, Sept. 11, 1849, d. Lawrence Sprague, surgeon U.S. Army (dec.). Admitted to bar July, 1847; mem. Congress, 1867-71; justice Supreme Court, N.Y., 1881-1902; Republican. Pres. Oswego Bar Assn.; Oswego State Normal and Training Sch. Bd. Home: Oswego, N.Y. Died 1905.

CHURCHILL, John Wesley, prof. homiletics and pulpit oratory Andover Theol. Sem.; b. Fairlee, Vt., May 26, 1839; grad. Harvard, 1865, A.M., 1868 (D.D., Dartmouth); grad. Andover Theol. Sem., 1868; m. Mary Donald, July 27, 1869. Has given instruction in elocution in Brown Univ., Wellesley Coll., Mt. Holyoke Sem., Abbott Acad., Phillips Acad., Smith Coll., Harvard Divinity School and Dartmouth Coll. One of editors Andover Review, 1884-94. Trustee Abbott Acad., Andover, and of the School of Expression, Boston; mem. Bd. of Preachers, Dartmouth. Home: Andover, Mass. Died 1900.

CHURCHILL, Joseph Richmond, lawyer; b. Dorchester, Mass., July 29, 1845; s. Asaph and Mary (Brewer) C.; A.B., Harvard, 1867, LL.B., 1869; m. Mary Cushing, Feb. 21, 1871. Admitted to bar, 1869; justice Municipal Ct., Dorchester Dist. of Boston, 1870—. Student and writer on bot. subjects; contbr. to Rhodora; prepared "List of Plants Growing Naturally in Milton, Mass.," for History of Town of Milton, published by town. Home: Dorchester, Mass. Died Feb. 14, 1933.

CHURCHILL, Lady Randolph Spencer (Mrs. George Cornwallis-West); b. Brooklyn; d. Leonard and Clara (Hall) Jerome; ed. principally in Paris; m. Rt. Hon. Lord Randolph Henry Spencer Churchill, son of the seventh Duke of Marlborough, 1874 (died 1895); m. 2d, George Cornwallis-West, Scots Guards, only son Col. Cornwallis-West, of N. Wales, July 28, 1900 (divorced, 1913). Former propr. and editor Anglo-Saxon Review; chmn. Am. ladies hosp. ship Maine, S. Africa. Imperial Order Crown of India, 1885; Lady of Grace of St. John of Jerusalem, 1901; Royal Red Cross, 1902; v.p. Ladies' Grand Council, Primrose League. Author: The Reminiscences of Lady Randolph Churchill, 1908; His Borrowed Plumes (play), 1909; The Bill (play), 1913. Home: London, England. Died June 29, 1921.

CHURCHILL, Thomas J., planter; b. Louisville, Ky., Mar. 10, 1824; s. Col. Samuel C.; grad. St. Mary's Coll., Ky.; studied law Transylvania Univ., Lexington, Ky.; m. Annie Maria, d. Senator A. H. Sevier, July 31, 1849; First col., Humphrey Marshall's regt. cav., in war with Mexico; postmaster Little Rock, Ark., during Buchanan's administration; col. 1st regt. mounted riflemen in Civil war; promoted to brig. gen. for gallant conduct and afterwards to maj. gen.; State treas. Ark. for 3 terms; gov. Ark., 1881-83. Home: Little Rock, Ark. Died 1905.

CHURCHILL, Thomas William, lawyer; b. N.Y. City, Nov. 28, 1862; s. William and Mary (Casey) C.; A.B., Coll. of City of New York, 1882; student of Columbia Law Sch.; LL.B., New York U., Law Sch., 1888; (LL.D., Manhattan, 1915). Served as supt. bonded warehouses, Port of New York, and deputy fire commr., N.Y. City; mem. Churchill, Marlow & Hines. Pres. Bd. of Edn. City of New York, 1913-16. Home: New York, N.Y. Died May 7, 1934.

CHURCHILL, William, philologist; b. Brooklyn, Oct. 5, 1859; s. William and Sarah (Starkweather) C.; A.B., Yale, 1882; U.S. consul general, Samoa, 1896-99, also judge of Consular Ct. and receiver and custodian revenues of Samoa; U.S. consul gen. Tonga, 1897-99; dept. editor New York Sun, 1902-15. Editor Malayo-Polynesian dept. Standard Dictionary, 1912. Fellow Royal Anthropol. Inst. of Great Britain and Ireland, 1912. Asso. in primitive philology, Carnegie Inst., Washington, 1915; dir. division of foreign lang. publs. of Com. on Pub. Information, Washington, 1917-18. Author: Polynesian Wanderings, 1910; Beach-la-Mar (trade speech of the Western Pacific), 1911; Easter Island, Rapanui Speech and the Peopling of Southeast Polynesia, 1912; Sissano, Movements of Migration within and through Melanesia; Club Types of Nuclear Polynesia, 1917. Home: Washington, D.C. Died June 9, 1920.

CHURCHMAN, John Woolman, bacteriologist; b. Burlington, N.J., Jan. 8, 1877; s. Horace and Edith Anna (Woolman) C.; A.B., Princeton, 1898, A.M., 1901; M.D., Johns Hopkins, 1902; A.M., Yale University, 1915; m. Martha Bertrand Jaramillo, Oct. 27, 1923. Resident house officer and clin. asst. in surgery, Johns Hopkins Hosp., 1902-05; vol. asst. Surg. Clinic, Breslau, Germany, 1905-06; asst. resident surgeon and resident surgeon, Johns Hopkins Hosp., 1906-11; instr. in surgery, Johns Hopkins, 1909-11; asst. prof. surgery, 1912-14, prof. 1914—, Yale, also acting head of dept.; médecin chef Hôp. Militaire, 32 bis, Château de Passy, France, 1916; attending surgeon and acting surgeon in chief, New Haven Hosp. and Dispensary; prof. of exptl. therapeutics and dir. Lab. of Exptl. Therapeutics, Cornell U. Med. Sch. Maj., Med. R.C.; pres. Bd. Examiners of Med. R.C., State of Conn. Fellow Am. College of Surgeons and of the N.Y. Acad. of Science. Officier de l'Instruction publique, and Officier d'Académie, France. Awarded Alvarenga prize, College Physicians of Philadelphia, 1921. Republican. Home: New York, N.Y. Died July 12, 1937.

CHUTE, Arthur Hunt, author; b. Stillman Valley, Ill., Apr. 19, 1890; s. Arthur Crawley and Ella Maude (Hunt) C.; B.A., Acadia U., Can., 1910; studied Harvard and Edinburgh U.; m. Lorna Pitt, of Hamilton, Bermuda, Sept. 15, 1919; 1 dau., Audrey. Newspaper reporter, Edinburgh, Scotland, 1912, later on London newspapers; war corr. 1st and 2d Balkan wars, 1912-13; with Turkish Army in Thrace, later with the Greeks at Janina; with Gen. Funston in Mexico, 1914; officer in France with 1st Canadian contingent, 1914-17. Engaged in war propaganda work in U.S., 1918. Baptist. Author: The Real Front, 1918; The Land of Youth, 1922; The Roaring Forties, 1923; Mutiny of the Flying Spray, 1925; Far Gold, 1927; The Crested Seas, 1928. Died Sept. 22, 1929.

CHUTE, Arthur Lambert, surgeon; b. Georgetown, Mass., Aug. 12, 1869; s. Richard and Susan (Nelson) C.; M.D., Harvard Med. Sch., 1895; m. Eliza R. Swift, Sept. 26, 1899; children—Richard, Mary, Oliver Swift. House officer, Mass. Gen. Hosp., 1894-95, Boston Lying-in Hosp., 1895; genito-urinary surgeon, St. Elizabeth's Hosp.; cons. surgeon, Newton Hosp.; etc.; instr. genito-urinary surgery, 1906, then asst. prof., Tufts Med. Coll. Home: Boston, Mass. Died Jan. 12, 1934.

CHUTE, Horatio Nelson, physicist; b. Grovesend, Ont., Can., Dec. 26, 1847; s. Walter and Catherine C.; ed. Woodstock Coll., Ont., 1860-63; B.S., U. of Mich., 1872, M.S., 1875; m. M. Lucretia Clappison, Aug. 21, 1872. Prin. Aylmer pub. schs., Ont., 1866-69; asst. prof. Latin, Woodstock Coll., Ont., 1869-70; engaged in astron. work under Dr. J. C. Watson, 1872-73; instr. physics, Ann Arbor High Sch., 1873-1922. Author: Practical Physics, 1889; Physical Laboratory Manual, 1894; Elements of Physics (with Henry S. Carhart), 1892-97; Laboratory Note-Book, 1898; A Laboratory Guide, 1913. Home: Ann Arbor, Mich. Died 1928.

CILLEY, Gordon Harper, editor; b. Lenoir, N.C., Oct. 11, 1874; s. Clinton Albert and Emma Sofia (Harper) C.; ed. high sch., Hickory, N.C.; m. Maud E. Shuford (died 1912); m. 2d, Marcella Ruth, Apr. 12, 1913; children—Alda Virginia, Adelaide Campbell, Mary Josephine. Began newspaper work with Charlotte (N.C.) Observer, 1895; asst. news editor Phila. Record, 1899-1909; advt. mgr. John Wanamaker, Phila., 1909-25; pres. Cilley & Sims, advertising, 1925-26; managing editor Phila. Record, 1926-28; editor Main Line Daily Times, 1930-32; dir. publicity John Wanamaker, Phila., 1932-34. Served as corporal, N.C. Volunteers in Cuba, Spanish-Am. War, 1898; maj. O.R.C. Democrat. Episcopalian. Author: Maxims of John Wanamaker (with Russell H. Conwell), 1924; also newspaper series, Advertising for Profit, 1929. Home: Paoli, Pa. Jan. 17, 1938.

CILLEY, Jonathan Longfellow, physician; b. Cincinnati, Jan. 25, 1838; s. Jonathan and Sarah (Lee) C.; grad. Harvard, 1858, Miami Med. Coll., 1866, Med. Coll. of Ohio, 1879; m. Apr. 26, 1869, Mary P. Hubbard. Served hosp. steward 137th Ohio vol. inf. and as acting master's mate in Mississippi squadron, U.S.N., during Civil War. Began practice in Cincinnati, 1866; taught anatomy Miami Med. Coll., 1871-88, Med. Coll. of Ohio, 1878-99; was prof. physiology, Ohio Coll. Dental Surgery, 5 yrs.; lecturer on artistic anatomy several yrs. at Cincinnati Mus. Art Acad.; then teaching art anatomy in New York. Republican. Home: Brooklyn, N.Y. Died 1903.

CILLEY, Jonathan Prince, soldier; b. Thomaston, Me., Dec. 29, 1835; s. Jonathan and Deborah (Prince) C.; A.B., Bowdoin, 1858; admitted to bar, 1860; m. Caroline A. Lazell, Oct. 10, 1866; m. 2d, Abby (Butler) Burpee, Dec. 25, 1897. Capt. 1st Me. Cav., Oct. 19, 1861; maj., May 15, 1862; lt. col., July 1, 1864; hon. mustered out, Aug. 1, 1865. Bvtd.: col. vols., Mar. 13, 1865, "for gallant and meritorious services during the war"; brig. gen. vols., June 12, 1865, for same. In practice, Rockland, Me., 1865—; mem. Ho. of Rep., 1867; U.S. ct. commr., 1867-80; adj. gen. of Me., 1876-78; editor Maine Bugle, 1894. Author: Cilley Genealogy, 1879; The Mount Desert Widow, 1896. Died Apr. 7, 1920.

CIST, Henry Martyn, soldier, lawyer; b. Cincinnati, Feb. 20, 1839; s. Charles and Janet W(hite) C.; grad. Farmer's (now Belmont) Coll., 1858, A.M.; studied law; m. Mary E. Morris, g.d. U.S. Senator Thomas A. Morris of Ohio, Sept. 22, 1868; m. 2d, Jennie E., d. Martin Bare, Cincinnati, April 12, 1882. Enlisted April 21, 1861, pvt. 6th Ohio vols.; became 2d lt. 52d Ohio vol. inf.; adj. 74th Ohio vols.; post adj. Camp Chase during confinement of prisoners of war captured at Ft. Donelson; served in middle Tenn., 1862; adj. Miller's brigade, Sept. 1862; later asst. adj. gen. Dept. of the Cumberland, on staff Gens. Rosecrans and Thomas; resigned Jan. 4, 1866; attained rank of maj. and asst. adj. gen., with bvts. of lt. col., col. and brig. gen. After war practiced law, Cincinnati; mayor of College Hill, O., 2 terms; corr. sec. Army of the Cumberland, 1869-92 (edited 20 ann. reports of soc.). Author: The Army of the Cumberland, 1882; Life of Maj. Gen. George H. Thomas (with late Col. Donn Piatt). Died 1902.

CLAASSEN, Peter Walter, biologist; b. Hillsboro, Kan., Mar. 17, 1886; s. Deitrich and Elizabeth (Wall) C.; grad. normal course, McPherson (Kan.) Coll., 1909; A.B., U. of Kan., 1913, A.M., 1915; Ph.D., Cornell U., 1918; m. Evelyn Strong, Dec. 22, 1917; children—Sarah Evelyn, Richard Strong. Prin. pub. sch., Hillsboro, Kan., 1909-11; asst. state entomologist of Kan., 1913-15; instr. biology, Cornell U., 1915-16; asst. prof. entomology, U. of Kan., 1916-17; asst. prof. biology, Cornell U., 1918-26, prof., 1926—; prof. biology (leave of absence), Tsing Hua Coll., Peking, China, 1924-25. Republican. Presbyn. Specialized in study of plecoptera. Author: Laboratory Text in General Biology; Plecoptera Nymphs of North America. Home: Ithaca, N.Y. Died Aug. 16, 1937.

CLABAUGH, Harry M., judge; b. Cumberland, Md., July 16, 1856; s. G. W. C.; LL.B., U. of Md., 1878; m. dau. of John A. Swope. Practiced law, Baltimore, until 1880, in Carroll County, Md., 1880-1904. Candidate for Md. Senate, 1885; chmn. Rep. State Central Com., 1891-99; atty. gen. of Md., 1895-1904; chief justice Supreme Ct. of D.C., Nov. 16, 1903—. Home: Washington, D.C. Died Mar. 6, 1914.

CLAFLIN, Arthur Whitman, wholesale and mfg. druggist; b. Providence, R.I., Oct. 10, 1852; s. George Lyman and Louisa Sisson (Whitman) C.; grad. Mowry and Goff's English and Classical Sch., 1869; m. Alice M. Howard, Mar. 15, 1881; children—Louisa Howard, Albert Whitman. Began as clk. in father's drug firm, Snow, Claflin & Co., Providence, 1869; partner Geo. L. Claflin & Co., 1885, and pres. from inc., 1903, as the Geo. L. Claflin Co.; pres. Workingmen's Loan Assn.; trustee Peoples Savings Bank. V.p. R.I. Coll.

Pharmacy and Allied Sciences. Pres. Providence Charitable Fuel Soc.; mem. bd. mgrs. and auditor Home for Aged Men and Aged Couples; mem. bd. mgrs. R.I. Elective Protective Co. Home: Providence, R.I. Died Jan. 12, 1926.

CLAFLIN, John, merchant; b. Brooklyn, N.Y., July 24, 1850; s. Horace B. and Agnes (Sanger) C.; A.B., Coll. City of New York, 1869; m. Elizabeth Stewart Dunn, June 27, 1890. Traveled in Europe and the East, July 1869-July 1870; crossed the South Am. continent from Pacific Coast at 10° S. latitude to Atlantic Coast at equator, 1877; entered wholesale dry goods business with father's firm, H. B. Claflin & Co., Oct. 1870; mem. of firm, Jan. 1873. Organized The H. B. Claflin Co. to take on the business of H. B. Claflin & Co., June 1890; organized Asso. Merchants Co., May 1900, and United Dry Goods Cos., May 1909, and pres. to 1914, when retired; trustee of many financial and charitable corps. Pres. Chamber of Commerce of state of N.Y., 1913-14. Independent Republican. Home: Morristown, N.J. Died June 11, 1938.

CLAFLIN, William, mcht., gov.; b. Milford, Mass., Mar. 6, 1818; s. Lee and Sarah (Adams) C.; ed. Brown Univ. (LL.D., Wesleyan, 1868); also Harvard Univ.; was in leather business, St. Louis, and afterward in Boston; mem. Mass. legislature, 1849-52; State senator, 1860-61; gov., 1869-71; mem. Congress, 1877-81; was chmn. Rep. Nat. Exec. Com., 1868-72. Twice married. Home: Newtonville, Mass. Died 1905.

CLAGETT, John Rozier, maj. U.S. Army; b. Washington, D.C., Apr. 1852; of family settled in Md. under Lord Baltimore; ed. under private tutors. Second lt. 23d inf., 1875; promoted 1st lt., 1884; capt., 1892; maj. 2d inf., Mar. 2, 1901; m. Cornelia M., d. Col. H. M. Black, U.S. Army, Jan. 1884. Served on Crook's campaign against Northern Cheyenne Indians, 1876-77; on duty at St. Louis during riots, 1877; on campaign against Northern Cheyenne Indians when they broke from reservation in Indian Ty., 1878; campaigns against Ute Indians, Colo., 1880; Apache Indians, Ariz., 1882. Served on 2d Philippine expdn., May 1898; engaged in assault and capture Manila, Aug. 1898; defense of Manila during Tagalog insurrection, Feb. 1899; on expdn. to Sulu Islands, May 1899, and took possession of same; returned to U.S. in command Home Battalion 25th inf. after 2 yrs.' service in Philippines. Died 1902.

CLAGHORN, Kate Holladay, author; b. Aurora, Ill.; d. Charles and Martha (Holladay) Claghorn; removed to New York in infancy; A.B., Bryn Mawr Coll., 1892; Ph.D., Yale, 1896; unmarried. Research work for U.S. Industrial Commn., 1900-01, U.S. Census Office, 1902; asst. registrar of records, 1902-06, registrar of records, 1906-12, Tenement House Dept., City of New York; mem. permanent staff N.Y. Sch. of Philanthropy (now N.Y. Sch. of Social Work), 1912-32. Author: College Training for Women, 1897; Juvenile Delinquency in Rural New York, 1918; The Immigrant's Day in Court, 1923. Home: Greenwich, Conn. Died 1938.

CLAIBORNE, John Herbert, M.D.; b. Brunswick County, Va., Mar. 10, 1828; s. Rev. J. G. and Mary Elizabeth (Weldon) C.; grad. U. of Va., 1848, A.M., 1851; Jefferson Med. Coll., 1850; m. Miss S. J. Alston; m. 2d, Annie L. Watson. Established practice in Petersburg, Va., 1851; mem. Va. Ho. Reps., 1855-56; State senate, 1857, 1861-62; surgeon in C.S.A., 1861-65; mem. many med. socs.; became specialist in diseases of women and children. Author: The Old Virginia Doctor; Clinical Reports from Private Practice; 75 Years in Old Virginia; etc. Home: Petersburg, Va. Died 1905.

CLAIBORNE, William Stirling, clergyman; b. Amherst County, Va.; s. William R. and Alice (Clay) C.; Roanoke Coll., 1891-97, D.D., 1925; U. of South, 1897-1901; m. Minnie M. Marlow, July 17, 1902; 1 dau., Alice V. Deacon, 1899, priest, 1901, P.E. Ch.; rector, Sewanee, Tenn., 1900-13; became archdeacon of Sewanee and prof. pastoral theology, DuBose Memorial Ch. Training Sch. Trustee of U. of South, 1908—, also trustee DuBose Tr. Sch. and Emerald Hodgson Hosp. Founder St. Andrew's Sch. for Mountain Boys, Sewanee; reëstablished St. Mary's on the Mountain (industrial sch. for girls); established and became v.p. Emerald-Hodgson Hospital; founder and acting v.p. DuBose Memorial Ch. Training Sch., Monteagle, Tenn. Chaplain U.S. Army, 1917; chaplain 42d (Rainbow) Div. with rank of 1st lt.; promoted to capt., May 8, 1919. Author: Ray in the Mountains, 1916; Twenty-one Years in the Mountains of Tennessee. Founder and editor Theology, a jour. of religious thought. Home: Monteagle, Tenn. Died Jan. 7, 1933.

CLANCY, Frank Willey, lawyer; b. Dover, N.H., Jan. 15, 1852; s. Michael Albert and Lydia Ardilla (Willey) C.; ed. Prep. Dept., Columbian (now George Washington) U., and Dover and Rochester high schs., N.H.; Spencerian Business Coll., Washington; LL.B., Law Sch., Columbian U., 1873; m. Charlotte Jane Cawthorne Swallow, Oct. 30, 1879. Clk. in law offices of Hon. William E. Chandler, Washington, D.C., about 3 yrs., U.S. Coast Survey Office, 3 yrs.; clk. Dist. Ct., 2d Dist. of N.M., 1875-76; sec. to Richard C. McCormick, asst. sec. of treasury, 1877, and to same as commr.-gen. to Paris Expn., 1878; clk. Dist. Ct., 1st Dist. of N.M., at Santa Fe, 1879-83, and clk. of Sup. Ct., 1880-83; mem. Constl. Conv. of N.M. Ty., 1889; mayor of Albuquerque, 1897-98; dist. atty. at Albuquerque, 1901-09; atty. gen. N.M. Ty., 1909-12; atty. gen. State of N.M., Jan. 1912-Jan. 1917; counsel for State in case against State of Tex. Mem. bd. regents U. of N.M., 1889-1912. Engaged in practice most of time in N.M., 1874—. Home: Santa Fe, N.M. Died Sept. 1, 1928.

CLANCY, John Richard, congressman; b. Syracuse, N.Y., Mar. 8, 1859; s. Richard V. and Eliza A. C.; ed. pub. schs.; m. Elenora V. Kopp, Apr. 29, 1886. Mfr. hardware specialties, 1885—; mem. 63d Congress (1913-15), 35th N.Y. Dist. Democrat. Long identified with civic and philanthropic affairs; pres. Syracuse Chamber Commerce; v.p. N.Y. State Coll. of Forestry, at Syracuse U. Chmn. exec. com. Onondaga County Savings Bank. Mem. Central N.Y. Park Commn. Home: Syracuse, N.Y. Died 1932.

CLAPP, Charles Horace, geologist; b. Boston, Mass., June 5, 1883; s. Peleg Ford and Mary Lincoln (Manson) C.; B.S., Mass. Inst. Tech., 1905, Ph.D., 1910; studied Harvard, 1911; m. Mary R. Brennan, Apr. 19, 1911; children—Daniel Brennan, Michael Manson, Mary Lincoln, Francis Coyle, Lucy Ford, Prudence, Paul, Margaret. Instructor geology and mining, Univ. of N.D., 1905-07, also asst. state geologist; instr. geology, Mass. Inst. Tech., 1907-10; with Geol. Survey of Can., 1908-13; prof. geology, U. of Ariz., 1913-16; prof. geology, Mont. State Sch. of Mines, 1916-21, pres., 1918-21; pres. State U. of Mont., 1921—. Dir. and geologist Mont. Bur. Mines and Metallurgy, 1919-22; asst. geologist U.S. Geol. Survey, 1914-25. Democrat. Unitarian. Home: Missoula, Mont. Died May 9, 1935.

CLAPP, Cornelia Maria, zoölogist; b. Montague, Mass., Mar. 17, 1849; d. Richard and Eunice Amelia (Slate) C.; grad. Mt. Holyoke Coll., 1871; Ph.B., Syracuse U., 1888, Ph.B. and Ph.D., 1889; Ph.D., U. of Chicago, 1896; studied at Penikese, 1874, and at Marine Biol. Lab., Woods Hole, 1888-1902, during summer sessions carried on investigations; unmarried. Prof. zoölogy, Mt. Holyoke Coll., 1896-1916. Home: Montague, Mass. Died Jan. 1, 1935.

CLAPP, Edward Bull, univ. prof.; b. at Cheshire, Conn., Apr. 14, 1856; s. Rev. Charles Wells and Jane Pray (Bassett) C.; A.B., Ill. Coll., 1875; Ph.D., Yale, 1886; Berlin, 1884-85; (LL.D., Illinois Coll., 1914); m. May Mattoon Wolcott, Dec. 22, 1886. Prof. Greek, Ill. Coll., 1882-90; asst. prof. Greek, Yale, 1890-93; prof. Greek, U. of Calif., Jan. 1, 1894-1917 (retired). Prof. Greek, American School Classical Studies at Athens, 1907-08. Conglist. Editor: Homer's Iliad (books 19-24), 1899. Chmn. editorial bd. of U. of Calif. publs. in classical philology. Home: Berkeley, Calif. Died Feb. 6, 1919.

CLAPP, Edwin Jones, publicist; b. Hudson, Wis., Sept. 9, 1881; s. Newell Harvey and Sarah Elizabeth (Jones) C.; A.B., Yale, 1904; studied in Germany, 1907-10; Ph.D., U. of Berlin, 1910; m. Susanna Clifford Nelson, July 17, 1907; children—Amy Nelson, Edwin Jones. Instr. polit. economy, Yale, 1910-11; asst. prof. trade and transportation, Sch. of Commerce, New York U., 1911-12; spl. traffic commr., Directors of the Port of Boston, 1912-14; prof. economics, New York U., 1914-20. Chief of economics sect., Information and Edn. Service, U.S. Dept. of Labor, 1918-19; gen. mgr. Fifty-Fifty Corp., 1919; sec. treas. Exporters' Encyclopedia Co., 1919-20; cons. economist, 1920-21; financial editor New York American, 1922-23, editor, 1924; staff corr. Hearst newspapers, 1925; editorial staff, Los Angeles Examiner, 1926; financial and editorial writer Hearst newspapers, 1927-28; asst. to W. C. Durant, 1929. Christian Scientist. Author: The Navigable Rhine, 1911; The Port of Hamburg, 1911; Economic Aspects of the War, 1915; The Port of Boston, 1916; Railway Traffic, 1917; The Port of Charleston, 1921. Died Aug. 7, 1930.

CLAPP, Elmer Frederick, surgeon; b. St. Lawrence Co., N.Y., Apr. 10, 1843; s. William and Harriett (Anderson) C.; ed. in Ill. pub. schs. and Normal (Ill.) U.; M.D., Bellevue Hosp. Med. Coll. (New York U.), 1870; m. Carolina M. Ringer Barrett, Dec. 19, 1877 (died 1892). In Union Army, 1861-65; prof. anatomy, med. dept., Ia. State U., 1871-88; pres. Mercy Hosp., 1872-88; surgeon C.,R.I. &P., and Burlington, Cedar Rapids & Northern rys. Home: Iowa City, Ia. Died Apr. 12, 1917.

CLAPP, Frank Leslie, prof. edn.; b. Forest Hill, Ind., Aug. 21, 1877; s. Elias and Mary Ann (Amick) C.; B.S., Lincoln (Ill.) Coll., 1911; A.M., U. of Ill., 1912; Ph.D., U. of Wis., 1914; m. Anna Bertha Marmein, 1903. Teacher rural schs., prin. and supt. pub. schs. until 1909; prof. edn., U. of Colo., 1914-19; prof. edn., U. of Wis., 1919—. Presbyn. Author: Clapp's Drill Books in Arithmetic, 1925. Joint Author: Better Teaching, 1926; Introduction to Education, 1928; Number Games and Stories; Technique of Study to Accompany Introduction to Education, 1931. Joint inventor of Clapp-Young Self-Marking Test Device. Home: Madison, Wis. Died Mar. 23, 1937.

CLAPP, Henry Austin, clerk Supreme jud. court of Mass.; b. Dorchester, Mass., July 17, 1841; grad. Harvard, 1860 (A.M.); grad. Harvard Law School; practiced in Boston until apptd. to present position; principally known as dramatic critic and lecturer on Shakespeare. Author: Reminiscences of a Dramatic Critic, 1902. Died 1904.

CLAPP, Herbert Codman, M.D.; b. Boston, Jan. 31, 1846; s. John C. and Lucy B. (Blake) C.; A.B., Harvard, 1867, A.M. and M.D., 1870; m. Mary O. Richardson, Jan. 31, 1878; children—Theodora White, Lucy Blake, Marion Lazell. Specialist in diseases of the chest; instr. in auscultation and percussion, 1877-85, prof. diseases of the chest, 1885-1915, emeritus, Boston U. Sch. of Medicine; cons. phys. in diseases of the chest to Mass. Homœ. Hosp., Boston; visiting phys. to Mass. State Sanatorium for Incipient Consumptives, Rutland, Mass., 1898-1907; cons. phys. Cullis Consumptives' Home, Dorchester 1895-1919. Author: Auscultation and Percussion (13 edits.), 1878-1902; Is Consumption Contagious? 1880. Home: Brookline, Mass. Died Apr. 30, 1929.

CLAPP, Moses Edwin, senator; b. Delphi, Ind., May 21, 1851; s. Harvey Spaulding and Abbie Jane (Vandercook) C.; LL.B., U. of Wis., 1873; m. Hattie Allen, Dec. 30, 1874. Admitted to bar, 1873; in practice at Hudson, Wis., 1873-81, Fergus Falls, Minn., 1881-91, St. Paul, 1891-1901. Co. atty. St. Croix Co., Wis., 1878-80; atty. gen. Minn., 1887-93; candidate for Rep. nomination for gov., 1896; elected U.S. senator, Jan. 19, 1901, to succeed late C. K. Davis; reëlected for terms 1905-11, 1911-17; resumed the practice of law, Washington, 1918. Home, Washington, D.C. Died Mar. 6, 1929.

CLAPPER, Samuel Mott Duryea; chmn. bd. Gen. Refractories Co.; v.p. Cannon Mills, Inc.; treas. Ewing Thomas Corp.; chmn. bd. Schlicter Jute Cordage Co., Mortgage Service Co.; dir. Central Pa. Nat. Bank, Delaware County Nat. Bank of Chester (Pa.), Fire Assn. of Phila., Reliance Ins. Co., Guaranty Co. of North America. Died Jan. 19, 1940.

CLARE, Arthur James, consul; b. Barbados, May 8, 1864. Apptd. v. consul, Barbados, May 9, 1901; vice and deputy consul, 1902-05; consul, 1905-08; consul at Georgetown, Guiana, 1908-11, at Bluefields, Jan. 21, 1911—. Died Oct. 22, 1915.

CLARE, Israel Smith, historian; b. Lancaster Co., Pa., Nov. 24, 1847; ed. State Normal Sch., Millersville, Pa., 1868-70; m. Mrs. Annis S. Bartel; 2d, Mrs. Louisa Williams. Editor Cram's Magazine, 1899-1901, The Rostrum Magazine (Lancaster, Pa.), 1901-02. Candidate National party for Congress, 1878. Author: Illustrated Universal History, 1876; Complete Historical Compendium, 1884; Unrivaled History of the World, 5 vols., 1890; British-Boer War Souvenir, 1900; Illustrated History of All Nations, 15 vols., 1906; True History of the Human Race, 1921. Contbr. hist. maps, Peale's edit. Ency. Britannica (maps, colonial period U.S.), 1890; Cram's Universal Atlas, 1890; Cram's Ancient and Modern Atlas of the World, 1901. Socialist. Home: Lancaster, Pa. Died Mar. 1, 1924.

CLARITY, Frank Edmund, ry. official; b. Sauk Centre, Minn., Sept. 10, 1877; s. Michael and Hannah (Connolly) C.; ed. pub. schs.; m. Kittie Mary McKanna, 1905. Began as car checker, G.N. Ry., 1894, and advanced through various positions to chief clk. to gen. supt. Western Dist., at Seattle, Wash., 1911; insp. transportation, 1912-13, supt. transportation, 1913-17, asst. gen. mgr., 1917-18, D.&R.G. Ry.; transportation asst. and asst. regional dir. Central Western Region at Chicago, U.S. R.R. Administration, 1918-20; v.p. and gen. mgr. Ft. Worth & Denver City Ry. and Wichita Valley Ry., 1920—; pres. and gen. mgr. Rapid City, Black Hills & Western R.R., 1931—. Republican. Catholic. Home: Rapid City, S.D. Died Dec. 27, 1933.

CLARK, Albert Warren, missionary; b. Georgia, Vt., June 27, 1842; s. Rufus King (M.D.) and Elvira A. (Hinckley) C.; A.B., U. of Vt., 1865, A.M., 1868; studied Union Theol. Sem., 1865-67, grad. Hartford Theol. Sem., Conn., 1868; (D.D., Univ. of Vt., 1893); m. Ruth E. Pirie, Mar. 20, 1884. Ordained Congl. ministry, 1868; pastor in Conn., 1868-72; missionary A.B.C.F.M., Prague, Bohemia, 1872—; preaches in German and Bohemian. Dir. Nat. Bible Soc. of Scotland, in Austria and Poland. Served as sergt. 12th Vt. Vols., 1862-63; participated in Battle of Gettysburg. Author: (in Bohemian) The Worth of the Soul; The Way of Truth. Died June 7, 1921.

CLARK, A(lonzo) Howard, editor; b. Boston, Apr. 13, 1850; s. Thatcher and Abby (Carnes) C.; ed. Wesleyan U. (hon. M.A., 1906); m. Alice Morrow, June 25, 1881. In mercantile business, New York, 1867-75; in charge of U.S. Fish Commn. Sta., at Gloucester, Mass., and spl. agt. 10th Census, 1879-80; curator div. of history, U.S. Nat. Mus., and editor Smithsonian Instn., Washington, 1881—. Asst. U.S. commn. to London Internat. Expn., 1883; expert commr. and mem. Internat. Jury Awards, Paris

Expn., 1889. Del. Internat. Geog. Congress, Paris, 1889. Sec. Am. Hist. Assn., 1889-1908, and curator, 1889—; sec. gen. and registrar gen. Sons of the Am. Revolution. Decorated with cross Officier du Mérite Agricole of France. Author: Fishery Industries of United States; Whale and Seal Fisheries; Food Industries of the World, in Paris Reports. Died Dec. 31, 1918.

CLARK, B(enjamin) Preston, trustee, merchant; b. Boston, Mass., Oct. 8, 1860; s. Benjamin C. and Adeline K. (Weld) C.; Amherst, 1877-81; m. Josephine F. Allen, Jan. 21, 1890. Mem. B. C. Clark & Co.; pres. Plymouth Cordage Co.; dir. U.S. Smelting, Refining & Mining Co., Asso. Industries of Mass. Consul for Hayti at Boston, 1897—. Trustee Cambridge Theol. Sem.; trustee Mass. Homœ. Hosp.; treas. Mass. Bible Soc., Lincoln House Assn., Newsboys' Reading Room Assn. Episcopalian. Home: Cohasset, Mass., and Boston. Died Jan. 1939.

CLARK, Champ, congressman; b. Anderson Co., Ky., Mar. 7, 1850; s. John Hampton and Aletha Jane (Beauchamp) C.; ed. common schs., Ky. U., Bethany Coll. and Cincinnati Law School; (LL.D., Bethany College, W.Va., 1914); m. Genevieve Bennett, Dec. 14, 1881. Pres. Marshall Coll., W.Va., 1873-74; admitted to bar, 1875; in practice, Bowling Green, Mo., 1880—. City atty. Louisiana, Mo., and Bowling Green, Mo., 1878-81; presdl. elector, 1880; pros. atty. Pike Co., Mo., 1885-89; mem. Mo. Ho. of Rep., 1889-91; mem. 53d (1893-95) and 55th to 66th (1897-1921) Congresses, 9th Mo. Dist.; mem. Com on Ways and Means. Permanent chmn. Dem. Nat. Conv., St. Louis, 1904, and chmn. com. to notify Judge A. B. Parker of his nomination for Presidency; minority leader of the House, 2d Session 60th Congress and in 61st Congress; speaker 62d, 63d, 64th, 65th Congresses (1911-19). Led on 27 ballots for Dem. presdl. nomination, having a clear majority on eight at Baltimore Conv., 1912; Dem. minority leader in 66th Congress. V.p. Trans-Miss. Congress, Denver. Home: Bowling Green, Mo. Died Mar. 3, 1921.

CLARK, Charles Dickson, U.S. judge for eastern and middle dists. of Tenn., Jan. 21, 1895—; b. Laurel Cove, Tenn., Oct. 7, 1847; grad. (B.A.) Burritt Coll., same county, 1871; grad. (B.L.) law dept., Cumberland Univ., Lebanon, Tenn., 1873; admitted to Tenn. bar, 1874; practiced at Manchester, Tenn., 1876-83, and at Chattanooga, 1883-95; at 16 entered C.S.A., Sept., 1864, serving on staff Gen. George G. Dibrell and under Gen. Joseph Wheeler; after war practiced law. Home: Chattanooga, Tenn. Died 1908.

CLARK, Charles Edgar, rear adm.; b. Bradford, Vt., Aug. 10, 1843; s. James Dayton and Mary (Sexton) C.; apptd. from Vt., and grad. U.S. Naval Acad., 1863; (LL.D., U. of Pa., 1905); m. Marie L. Davis. Promoted ensign, Oct. 1, 1863; advanced through grades to rear adm., June 16, 1902. Served on board Ossipee, W. Gulf Blockading Squadron, 1863-65; battle of Mobile Bay, and capture of Ft. Morgan, Aug., 1864; Vanderbilt, Pacific Squadron, 1865-67; comd. Ranger, 1883-86, Mohican, 1893-94, Monterey, 1896-98; comd. battleship Oregon during the cruise from San Francisco to Key West, and in the battle of Santiago, July 3, 1898; for eminent and conspicuous conduct in this battle was advanced 6 numbers in rank; was again advanced 7 additional numbers in rank, and promoted rear-adm., June 16, 1902; gov. Naval Home, Phila., 1901-04; pres. Naval Examining and Retiring Bd., 1904-05; retired, Aug. 10, 1905. Home: Washington, D.C. Died Oct. 1, 1922.

CLARK, Charles Finney, pres. The Bradstreet Co., 1876—; b. Preble, N.Y., Aug. 30, 1836; s. Rev. Gardner K. and Lucy Bement C.; ed. acad., Homer, N.Y.; m. Sarah M. Wilder, June, 1862 (dec.); 2d, Ellen M. Fogg, 1870. Entered law office Crane & Wesson, Detroit, 1857; corr. Bradstreet's, 1858, and from 1859 has made its interests his life work. V.p. and dir. Washington Trust Co. Mem. Chamber of Commerce, State of N.Y. Home: Morristown, N.J., and N.Y. City. Died 1904.

CLARK, Charles Heber, author; b. Berlin, Md., July 11, 1841; s. Rev. William J. C.; ed. Georgetown, D.C. In journalism from 1865; later became owner of an industrial jour. in Phila.; writer upon econ. subjects. Was for 10 yrs. sec. of Manufacturers' Club, Phila., and edited the Manufacturer, club's jour. Author (under pen name of Max Adeler): Out of the Hurly Burly; Captain Bluitt; In Happy Hollow; The Quakeress, 1905; etc. Home: Conshohocken, Pa. Died Aug. 10, 1915.

CLARK, Charles Hopkins, newspaper editor; b. Hartford, Conn., Apr. 1, 1848; s. Hon. Ezra and Mary (Hopkins) C.; A.B., A.M., Yale, 1871; L.H.D., Trinity Coll., 1910; m. Ellen Root, 1873 (died 1895); children—Horace Bushnell, Mrs. Mary Hopkins Welch; m. 2d, Matilda C. Root, Nov. 1899. Connected with the Hartford Courant, 1871—, editor-in-chief, 1890—. Pres. and dir. Hartford Courant Co. Mem. Conn. Constl. Conv., 1902; dir. State Reformatory, 1909—, Hartford Pub. Library. Fellow Corp. of Yale U., 1910-25; trustee Wadsworth Athenæum, Watkinson Library (Hartford). Republican. Conglist. Home: Hartford, Conn. Died Sept. 5, 1926.

CLARK, Charles Martin, pres. The Bradstreet Co.; b. Boston, Mass., Nov. 5, 1873; s. Charles Finney and Ellen Marcia (Fogg) C.; prep. edn., Cutlers Sch., N.Y. City; E.E., Columbia Sch. of Mines, 1897; m. Eliza Rolston Milligan, June 14, 1897; children—Katharine (Mrs. John Starr Taber), Charles Martin. Treas. The Bradstreet Co., 1904-26, pres., 1926—; pres. Bradstreet Co. of Me., Bradstreet Realty Corp., Bradstreet's Adjustment Service. Served with Emergency Fleet, World War. Episcopalian. Home: New York, N.Y. Died July 25, 1935.

CLARK, Charles Walker, capitalist; b. Deer Lodge, Mont., Nov. 3, 1871; s. William Andrews (U.S. Senator) and Katherine Louise (Stauffer) C.; A.B., Yale, 1893; m. Katharine Quinn Roberts, June 30, 1896 (died 1904); m. 2d, Cecilia Tobin, Aug. 4, 1904; m. 3d, Elizabeth W. Judge, Aug. 22, 1925. Engaged extensively in mining in Mont. and Ida.; gen. mgr. United Verde Copper Co., Jerome, Ariz., to 1922, pres., 1931—. Home: San Mateo, Calif. Died Apr. 8, 1933.

CLARK, Charles William, baritone singer; b. Van Wert, O., Oct. 15, 1865; s. William Asbury and Virginia Adelia (Mahan) C.; ed. High Sch., Van Wert; Methodist Coll., Ft. Wayne, Ind.; studied music with F. W. Root, Chicago, and George Henschel and A. Randagger, London; m. Jessie Baker, Nov. 7, 1888. Appeared first with Theodore Thomas Orchestra, Chicago, 1897; made 6 tours in America, reëngaged, 1913, 1914; toured Germany twice, also England, Ireland, Scotland, Italy and Portugal. Sang at Birmingham Festival, Liverpool Philharmonic concerts, Halle Orchestra, many times; also Broadwood concerts, Boosey Ballad concerts, etc. Dir. vocal dept. Bush Conservatory, Chicago. Home: Chicago, Ill. Died Aug. 3, 1925.

CLARK, Clarence Don, senator; b. Sandy Creek, Oswego Co., N.Y., Apr. 16, 1851; s. Oratia D. and Laura A. (King) C.; ed. common schs. and Ia. State U.; admitted to bar, 1874; taught sch.; m. Alice Downs, Aug. 6, 1874; children—George Laurance (dec.), Laura Alice, Margaret Helen, Frances Dorothy (dec.). In practice, Delaware Co., Ia., 1874-81, Evanston, Wyo., 1881—; pros. atty., Uinta Co., Wyo., 1882-86; apptd. asso. justice Supreme Court of Wyo., Ty., 1889, but declined; mem. 51st and 52d Congresses (1889-93); U.S. senator, 1895-99, to fill vacancy caused by failure of legislature to elect; reëlected for terms, 1899-1905, 1905-11, 1911-17; chmn. com. on Judiciary and mem. Com. on Finance, Pub. Lands, Railroads, etc. Apptd. mem. Internat. Joint Commn., July 1919, retired, May 1929. Home: Evanston, Wyo. Died Nov. 18, 1930.

CLARK, Clarence Munroe, banker; b. Germantown, Pa., Aug. 27, 1859; s. Edward White and Mary Todhunter (Sill) C.; A.B., U. of Pa., 1878; m. Mary Newbold Taylor, Nov. 13, 1884 (died 1918). Mem. E. W. Clark & Co., bankers, 1900—; dir. Commonwealth & Southern Corp., Consumers Power Co., Denver Tramway Corp., Germantown Trust Co., etc. Home: Philadelphia, Pa. Died June 29, 1937.

CLARK, David L., osteopathic phys.; b. Hillsboro, Ia., Mar. 21, 1868; s. Leonard B. and Louisa (Mendenhall) C.; D.O., Iowa-Am. Sch., Osteopathy, Kirksville, Mo., 1898; grad. study Los Angeles (Calif.) Coll. Osteopathy, 1910; wife dec.; children—Everett D., Alma Ruth (Mrs. Clarence Synder), Lulu Pearl (Mrs. James P. Grant, Jr.); m. 2d, J. Virginia Frey (D.O.), Nov. 1, 1914; 1 son, Robert Arthur. Began practice at Sherman, Tex., 1898; moved to Denver, 1905; trustee Income Securities Co., South Bend, Ind. Mem. Colo. State Bd. Med. Examiners, 1916—. Mgr. boy choir, Co-operative Club, Denver, 1922. Republican. Methodist. Home: Denver, Colo. Died Feb. 20, 1936.

CLARK, Davis Wasgatt, clergyman; b. New York, N.Y., July 28, 1849; s. Davis Wasgatt and Mary Johnson (Redman) C.; A.B., Ohio Wesleyan U., 1871, A.M., 1873; S.T.B., Sch. of Theology, Boston U., 1875; D.D., Ohio U., 1894; m. Fannie Deleno Jones, June 3, 1880 (dec.); children—Davis Wasgatt, William Armstrong, Jesse Redman, Robert Rutledge (dec.). Entered M.E. ministry, 1875; principal pastorates Columbus, Dayton, Cincinnati, and Covington, Ky.; dist. supt. Cincinnati Dist., 1900-05; supt. Methodist Union, Cincinnati, 1911-12. Republican. Author: From a Cloud of Witnesses, 1892; The American Child and the Moloch of Today, 1907; Child Labor and the Social Conscience, 1924; The President of the United States of America, 1932. Home: Boston, and Annisquam, Mass. Died July 25, 1935.

CLARK, Edgar Erastus, interstate commerce commissioner; b. Lima, N.Y., Feb. 18, 1856; s. Henry Dean and Nancy Elizabeth (Jones) C.; ed. Genesee Wesleyan Sem., Lima, N.Y.; m. Lovenia Jenkins, Sept. 1, 1880 (died 1903); children—Frank C., Elizabeth M., Florence, Marshall E., Helen H.; m. 2d, Agnes English Barnes, June 28, 1911; children—Mary B., Edgar E., Jr. Entered ry. service in 1873 and remained therein until 1889, when he entered the service of the Order of Ry. Conductors of America as Grand Senior Conductor; Grand Chief Conductor, same, 1890-1906. Mem. Interstate Commerce Commn., Aug. 28, 1906-Aug. 31, 1921; then mem. firm Clark & La Roe. Republican. Mem. bd. apptd. to report on Adamson 8-hour law, 1916; ex-officio mem. R.R. War Bd., 1917. Mason. Home: Monrovia, Calif. Died Dec. 1, 1930.

CLARK, Edson Lyman, clergyman; b. Easthampton, Mass., Apr. 1, 1827; s. Ithamar and Ursula (Lyman) C.; A.B., Yale, 1853; grad. Union Theol. Sem., 1858; m. Jane Elizabeth Stone, Dec. 8, 1858. Ordained Congl. ministry, 1859; pastor Dalton, Mass., 1858-67, N. Bradford, Conn., 1867-77, Southampton, Mass., 1877-86, Norwich Hill, Mass., 1886-87, Charlemont, Mass., 1889-92, Peru, Mass., 1893-98. Author: The Arabs and the Turks, 1876; The Races of European Turkey, 1878; Fundamental Questions, Chiefly Relating to the Early Hebrew Scriptures, 1882. Home: Dalton, Mass. Died Feb. 1913.

CLARK, Edward, architect U.S. Capitol, 1865—; b. Phila., 1822; common school and academic edn.; m. Evaline F. Freeman, Dec. 13, 1860. Studied architecture under Thomas U. Walter; became asst. to latter on his apptmt. as architect of the U.S. Capitol extension and succeeded him when he resigned, 1865; apptd. by Congress on commn. for completion of Washington monument; has served on various other commns. for Govt. work, including that for construction of Congressional Library. Is trustee Corcoran Gallery of Art; mem. various scientific socs. Mem. A.I.A. Home: Washington, D.C. Died 1902.

CLARK, Edward Lord, clergyman; b. Nashua, N.H., Feb. 3, 1838; s. Peter and Susan (Lord) C.; grad. Brown Univ., 1858, Andover Theol. Sem., 1863 (D.D., Williams, 1880); m. Susan Grafton, Aug. 11, 1863. Ordained to Congl. ministry, Boston, Aug. 8, 1861; chaplain 12th Mass. vols., 1861-62; pastor 1st Ch. N. Bridgewater, Mass., 1863-66, New Haven, Conn., 1867-73, Presbyn. Ch. of the Puritans, New York, 1873-93, Central Congl. Ch., Boston, 1893-1902. Author: Daleth-Egypt Illustrated, 1863; Israel in Egypt, 1873 M4. Home: Kennebunkport, Me. Died 1910.

CLARK, Edward P., journalist; b. Huntington, Mass., Oct. 21, 1847; s. Rev. Perkins K. C.; grad. Yale, 1870 (editor Yale Literary Mag.); m. Kate P. Upson, Jan. 1, 1874. Entered journalism, Springfield (Mass.) Republican, 1870; mng. editor, 1872-79; Washington corr., 1879-81; then editor Milwaukee Sentinel; editorial writer New York Evening Post, 1885—. Home: Brooklyn, N.Y. Died 1903.

CLARK, Emmons, soldier; b. Huron, N.Y., Oct. 14, 1827; s. William and Sophronia (Tillotson) C.; grad. Hamilton Coll., 1847; m. Adelia Augusta Hallett, Nov. 15, 1859. In commercial pursuits in New York, 1850-66; apptd. fire commr., Metropolitan dist., 1868, and consul to Havre by Pres. Harrison, 1889, but declined both positions. Enlisted private Co. B, 7th regt., N.G.S.N.Y., 1857; promoted 1st sergt., 1859; 2d lt., 1859; 1st lt., 1859; capt., 1860; mustered into U.S. service as capt., 1861; served as such in campaigns, 1861-62-63; promoted to col. 7th regt., 1864, and after serving in that capacity 25 yrs. was, by spl. act of legislature of N.Y., promoted to bvt. brig. gen. Sec. Bd. of Health, New York, 1866-1901. Mem. 7th Regt. Vet. Assn., 7th Regt. Active and Vet. League. Author: History of the Seventh Regiment of New York. Died 1905.

CLARK, Eugene Francis, sec. Dartmouth Coll.; b. Portland, Me., Aug. 10, 1879; s. Francis Edward and Harriet Elizabeth (Abbott) C.; A.B., Dartmouth, 1901, A.M., 1905; A.M., Harvard, 1908, Ph.D., 1915; studied univs. of Marburg and Freiburg; m. Martha Gay Haskell, Sept. 19, 1906 (died 1922); children—Barbara (dec.), Alden Haskell. Instr., DeMerritt Sch., Boston, 1902-06; asst. prof. German, Dartmouth Coll., 1908-19, prof., 1919—, also sec., 1918—. Mng. editor Dartmouth Alumni Mag.; sec. Dartmouth Alumni Assn., Dartmouth Alumni Council and Dartmouth Secretaries Assn. Student S.A.T.C., Plattsburg, N.Y., July-Sept. 1918; 2d lt. inf., U.S.A., Sept. 16, 1918; personnel officer and adj. S.A.T.C., Univ. of Rochester, N.Y.; hon. disch., Dec. 21, 1918. Editor Gen. Catalogue of Dartmouth Coll., 1769-1925. Republican. Conglist. Home: Hanover, N.H. Died Feb. 21, 1930.

CLARK, Francis Edward, founder United Soc. Christian Endeavor; b. Aylmer, P.Q., of N.E. parentage, Sept. 12, 1851; s. Charles C. Symmes; orphaned at 8, and adopted by his uncle, Rev. E. W. Clark, and assumed his name; A.B., Dartmouth, 1873; Andover Theol. Sem., 3 yrs.; D.D., Dartmouth, 1889; LL.D., Ia. Coll., 1902; m. Harriet E. Abbott, Oct. 3, 1876; children—Mrs. Maude Williston Chase, Eugene Francis, Harold Symmes, Sydney A., Faith Phillips. Became pastor Williston Ch., Portland, Me., which from a small mission he built up to a large Congl. ch.; founded, Feb. 1881, the Soc. of Christian Endeavor, which has extended throughout the world; pastor Phillips Ch., South Boston, 1883-87; devoted 44 yrs. to Christian Endeavor work as pres. United Soc. Christian Endeavor (pres. emeritus); served as pres. World's Christian Endeavor Union, and editor of The Christian Endeavor World (hon. editor); traveled around the world 5 times in interest of the work.

Author: Young People's Prayer Meetings, 1887; Fellow Travelers, 1898; The Great Secret, 1895; Training the Church of the Future, 1902; Christian Endeavor Manual, 1903. Editor: The Continent of Opportunity; Old Homes of New Americans, 1912; The Holy Land of Asia Minor, 1914; Christ and the Young People, 1916; In the Footsteps of St. Paul, 1917; Our Italian Fellow Citizens, 1919; The Gospel of Out-of-Doors, 1920. Univ. preacher at Cornell and other colls. Homes: Sagamore Beach, and Boston, Mass. Died May 25, 1927.

CLARK, F(rancis) Lewis; b. Bangor, Me., June 21, 1861; s. Jonathan Greenleaf and Harriet (Brown) C.; A.B., Harvard, 1883; m. Winifred Wiard, 1892. Mem. Clark & Curtis, Spokane, Wash., and built flour mills and elevators, 1885-89; receiver First Nat. Bank, Spokane, 1893; sr. mem. Clark & Sweeny, mining, Wardner, 1894-98, and v.p. Exchange Nat. Bank several yrs.; an organizer, and v.p. Spokane Inland Empire Ry.; then pres. Consol. Improvement Co., Hillyard Townsite Co., Ry. Land & Improvement Co. Retired. Overseer Whitman Coll., Wash. Republican. Conglist. Home: Hayden Lake, Ida. Died Jan. 16, 1914.

CLARK, Fred Pope, M.D.; b. Stockton, Calif., Aug. 25, 1865; s. Asa and Mary Elizabeth (Mountjoy) C.; M.D., Cooper Med. Coll., San Francisco, 1887; m. Edith Helena Cross, May 7, 1889. Practiced at Stockton, 1887—; propr. Clark's Sanatorium for Nervous and Mental Diseases; dir. City Bank, Stockton. Served as capt. and asst. surgeon Calif. N.G. Mem. Native Sons of Calif. Republican. Presbyn. Mason. Address: Stockton, Calif. Died Nov. 17, 1929.

CLARK, Frederic Simmons, woolen mfr.; b. Boston, Oct. 9, 1850; s. Nathan and Miranda Dearborn (Bean) C.; grad. English High Sch., Boston, 1867; m. Isabella W., d. of Gov. Talbot, of Mass., June 6, 1883; children—Mrs. Isabella H. Eaton, Thomas Talbot, Frederic S., Lincoln. In employ of Rice, Kendall & Co., wholesale paper, Boston, 1867-83; became connected with the Talbot (woolen) Mills, 1883, treas. and gen. mgr., 1884-1907, pres. and treas., 1907-13, pres., 1913—; trustee Franklin Savings Bank, Boston. Pres. Am. Assn. Woolen and Worsted Mfrs., 1910-11, dir., 1911-17; v.p. Nat. Assn. Wool Mfrs., Boston, 1904-17, pres. 1918-20, dir. 1921. Chmn. war service com. of the Wool Mfg. Industry, 1918-19; mem. Nat. Industrial Conf. Bd., 1916—. Trustee Lowell Textile Sch., 1898-1918, Howe Sch., Billerica, Mass. Republican. Unitarian. Mason. Home: North Billerica, Mass. Died Feb. 18, 1929.

CLARK, Frederick John, editor; b. McHenry Co., Ill., July 22, 1857; s. George Milo and Lucretia (Ball) C.; ed. common schs.; m. Jeannette Glessner, May 8, 1884. Actively identified with The Northwestern Miller (weekly publ.), 1874—, and then northwestern editor of same; v.p. Miller Pub. Co. Home: Minneapolis, Minn. Died May 12, 1917.

CLARK, Frederick Timothy, surgeon; b. Granville, Mass., Mar. 27, 1874; s. William Calvin and Mary Newberry (Ripley) C.; M.D., Albany Med. Coll. (Union U.), 1896; m. Emily Fletcher Rogers, June 18, 1902. Interne Albany City Hosp., 1896-97; asst. phys. Hudson River State Hosp., Poughkeepsie, N.Y., 1897-1900; settled in Westfield, Mass., 1901; surgeon in charge Eye, Ear, Nose and Throat Dept., Noble Hosp.; surgeon Sarah Gillet Home and Shurtleff Mission. Fellow Am. Coll. Surgeons, 1913. Conglist. Mason. Capt. M.C., U.S.A., Oct. 2, 1918; maj., Dec. 1918; chief eye, ear, nose and throat dept. Gen. Hosp. 1, New York; hon. disch., Oct. 25, 1919. Home: Westfield, Mass. Died Aug. 16, 1927.

CLARK, Gaylord Parsons, prof. physiology in Coll. of Medicine, Syracuse Univ., 1891—; b. Syracuse, N.Y., Nov. 12, 1856; s. Charles Parsons and Aurelia Lyons Nolton C.; grad. Williams Coll., 1877 (A.M.); Coll. of Medicine, Syracuse Univ. (M.D.), 1880; m. Jessie H. Suydam, June 15, 1881. Home: Syracuse, N.Y. Died 1907.

CLARK, George Archibald; b. Eden Prairie, Minn., Nov. 7, 1864; s. James and Prudence (Sterritt) C.; B.L., U. of Minn., 1891, M.A., 1911; m. Jennie Chestnut Corriston, Dec. 24, 1891. With Stanford U. from 1891, sec., 1896-09, academic sec., 1909—. Sec. Bering Sea Fur Seal Commn., 1896-97; sec. Internat. Fur Seal Conf., Washington, D.C., 1897, also joint sec. conf. fur seal experts; spl. fur seal investigator, Pribilof Islands, seasons of 1909, 12, 13. Author: (with David Starr Jordan) Vols. I and II, Report of Fur Seal Commn., 1896-97. Deceased.

CLARK, George Crawford, banker; b. St. Louis, Aug. 3, 1845; A.B., Coll. City of New York, 1863. Mem. Clark, Dodge & Co. of New York; dir. City Investing Co.; trustee Atlantic Mutual Insurance Co., Seamen's Bank for Savings. Treas. and dir. Brearley Sch. (Ltd.), and Gen. Memorial Hosp. Home: New York, N.Y. Died Feb. 24, 1919.

CLARK, George Thomas, librarian; b. San Francisco, Dec. 7, 1862; s. Robert and Augusta (Caryl) C.; B.S., U. of Calif., 1886; m. Annie Douglas, June 8, 1892 (deceased); 1 son, Douglas. Asst. librarian, U. of Calif., 1886-87; deputy state librarian, 1887-90, classifier, 1890-94, Calif. State Library; librarian San Francisco Pub. Library, 1894-1907, Stanford U., Aug. 1, 1907, retired, Dec. 31, 1927; dir. Univ. Libraries (Stanford) emeritus. Joint compiler of Index to Laws of California, 1850-93. Author: Leland Stanford, War Governor of California, Railroad Builder and Founder of Stanford University, 1931. Home: Palo Alto, Calif. Died Oct. 19, 1940.

CLARK, George Whitefield, clergyman; b. S. Orange, N.J., Feb. 15, 1831; s. John B. and Rebecca (Ball) C.; and related to Abraham Clark, the "signer"; A.B., Amherst, 1853, A.M., 1856; grad. Rochester Theol. Sem., 1855; (D.D., Rochester, 1872); m. Susan C. Fish, Sept. 6, 1855. Ordained Bapt. ministry, 1855; pastor New Market, N.J., 1855-59, Elizabeth, N.J., 1859-68, Ballston Spa, N.Y., 1868-73, Somerville, N.J., 1873-77; financial agt. and missionary Am. Bapt. Pub. Soc., 1880-1908; missionary, 1908—. V.p. trustees Peddie Inst. Author: Harmony of the Gospels, 1870; Harmony of the Acts, 1884; (9 vols. of). Home: Hightstown, N.J. Deceased.

CLARK, Grover, writer, educator; b. of Am. parentage, Osaka, Japan, Dec. 14, 1891; s. Cyrus Alonzo and Harriet (Gulick) C.; B.A., Oberlin, 1914; M.A., U. of Chicago, 1918; m. Kathryn Bird, Feb. 19, 1916; children—Mary Elise, John Carter. Engaged in teaching and magazine work in Japan, 1918-20; mem. faculty, National U., Peking, China, 1920-27; editor, Peking Leader, 1921-29, and pres. The Peking Leader, Inc., 1924-29; Peking corr. Christian Science Monitor, 1921-26; editor The Week in China, 1924-29; mem. exec. com. China Internat. Famine Relief Commn., 1928-30, asso. exec. dir., 1929-30; consultant on Far Eastern affairs, N.Y. City, 1930-36. Lecturer, Columbia Univ., 1930-33. Trustee China Inst. in America, 1930—; mem. Am. council Inst. Pacific Relations, 1931—; chmn. Round Table on Far East, University of Va. Inst. Public Affairs, 1933—; visiting lecturer in modern history, Wellesley College, 1934-35; asso. editor American Observer, 1936-37; prof. economics, U. of Denver, 1937—. Author: Today's Government, 1919; Some Problems of Republican Government (in Chinese), 1923; Tibet, China and Great Britain, 1924; Manchuria, an Economic Survey, 1931; Economic Rivalries in China, 1932; Rayon and Textiles in American Industry and Trade, 1934; The Great Wall Crumbles, 1935; A Place in the Sun, 1936; The Balance Sheets of Imperialism, 1936. Home: Denver, Colo. Deceased.

CLARK, Harry Granville, ry. official; b. Leavenworth, Kan., July 8, 1875; s. Barton C. and Drucilla (Baker) C.; C.E., U. of Kan., 1898; m. Mabel Fishburne, Nov. 7, 1908; children—Harry G., Hall Barton, Suzanne. Began as chainman, A., T. & S.F. Ry., 1898; with C., B. & Q. Ry. Co., as rodman and transitman, in Ia., until Oct. 1900; resident engr. and div. engr. Western div., Choctaw, Okla. & Gulf R.R. (now part of R.I. System), and div. engr. Pan Handle and Ark. divs., C.,R.I.&P. Ry., 1900-05; dist. engr. Choctaw dist., same rd., 1905-09, and continued with same co. successively as trainmaster Ark. and Okla. divs., asst. to v.p., chief engr., asst. to pres., v.p. and exec. asst. to trustees, May 1927—. Republican. Presbyn. Home: Glencoe, Ill. Died Jan. 1935.

CLARK, Harvey Cyrus, lawyer; b. in Morgan Co., Mo., Sept. 17, 1869; s. James C. and Melissa (Myers) C.; Wentworth Mil. Acad., Lexington, Mo., 1887-88; A.B., Scarrett Coll., Neosho, Mo., 1891; m. Sudye C. Berry, Dec. 7, 1909. Admitted to Mo. bar, 1893; mem. Graves & Clark until partner was elected chief justice of Mo., 1908; pros. atty. Bates Co., 1896-1901; apptd. dist. atty. Mo.P. Ry., 1910; atty. for K.C. Southern Ry. Co., Western Coal Mining Co., etc. Commd. capt. 2d Mo. Inf., Oct. 8, 1888; maj., July 1, 1897; lt. col. 6th Mo. Inf., July 20, 1898, and served during Spanish-Am. War; brig. gen. Mo. N.G., Feb. 2, 1899; comd. Mo. troops on Mexican border, June 19-Dec. 31, 1916; brig. gen. N.A., Aug. 5, 1917; apptd. comdr. 60th Depot Brigade, Camp Doniphan, Okla., Aug. 5, 1917; hon. disch. account physical disability, Dec. 26, 1917; apptd. adj. gen. of Mo., Jan. 1, 1918. Democrat. Presbyn. Mason. Home: Nevada, Mo. Died Apr. 1921.

CLARK, Horace Spencer, lawyer; b. Huntsburg, O., Aug. 12, 1840; s. Joseph M. P. and Charlotte (Brainerd) C.; ed. in Ohio public schools, Iowa State Univ.; m. Harriet E. Betts, May 3, 1864. 1st lt. Co. E, 73d Ohio vol. inf., discharged on account of wounds at Gettysburg, July 3, 1863; judge of Mattoon City Court; State senator Ill., 1880-84; delegate at large Rep. Nat. Conv., 1888; comdr. G.A.R., dept. of Ill., 1891; Rep. elector at large, 1896, and chmn. Electoral Coll., Ill.; brig. gen. comdg. 2d brigade Ill. Nat. Guard. Republican. Home: Mattoon, Ill. Died 1907.

CLARK, Howard J., lawyer; b. Cass Co., Ia., Jan. 9, 1868; s. Riley P. and Juliet Porter (Davis) C.; prep. edn., Oakfield Acad.; LL.B., Drake U., 1892; m. Florence Graham, Sept. 25, 1894; children—Howard J., Helen Louise. Admitted to bar, 1892, and engaged in gen. practice in all courts; sr. partner Clark, Byers & Garber; dir. and gen. counsel Iowa-Des Moines Nat. Bank & Trust Co.; gen. counsel Valley Savings Bank. Chmn. Rep. State Conv.; candidate for U.S. Senate, 1926. Mem. bd. trustees and chmn. Com. of Coll. of Law, Drake Univ. Conglist. Mason. Home: Des Moines, Iowa. Died Feb. 16, 1940.

CLARK, Imogen, author; b. New York; d. George H. and Phillie (Beatty) C.; ed. Mme. da Silva's French and English Sch., and pvt. tutors; unmarried. Author: Will Shakespeare's Little Lad, 1897; Rhymed Receipts, 1912; Suppose We Play, 1925; Suppose We Do Something Else, 1927; Old Days and Old Ways, 1928. Editor: The Robert Collyer Anthology, 1911. Home: New York, N.Y. Died Jan. 2, 1936.

CLARK, Isaac, theologian; b. Canterbury, Conn., June 30, 1833; s. Isaac (M.D.) and Susan (Tracy) C.; A.B., Yale, 1856, A.M., 1859; Union Theol. Sem., 1858-59; grad. Andover Theol. Sem., 1861; (D.D., Howard, 1896); m. Sophie T. Hastings, Jan. 1, 1862. Ordained Presbyn. ministry, 1861; pastor Elmira, N.Y., 1861-68, First Congl. Ch., Aurora, Ill., 1868-72, Elm Pl. Ch., Brooklyn, 1872-74, Rondout, 1874-82, Edwards Ch. (Congl.), Northampton, Mass., 1882-91; prof. theology, homiletics and English exegesis, 1891—, dean Sch. of Theology, 1901—, Howard U., Washington, D.C. Died Sept. 2, 1918.

CLARK, Isaiah Raymond, lawyer; b. Windsor, Vt., Jan. 1, 1853; s. Ripley and Mary A. (Raymond) C.; A.B., Dartmouth, 1873; m. Katherine Cummings, Nov. 13, 1878. Admitted to Mass. bar, 1876, and began practice at Boston; pres. Thorndike Co., Otis Co.; v.p. Androscoggin Mills. Republican. Baptist. Home: Cambridge, Mass. Died Sept. 19, 1933.

CLARK, J. Scott, univ. prof.; b. Copenhagen, N.Y., Sept. 23, 1854; s. Hon. Nathan and Eliza A. C.; A.B., Syracuse U., 1877, A.M., 1880 (Litt.D., 1898); m. Carrie L. Johnson, Jan. 5, 1885. Prin. Evanston High Sch., 1879-82; instr., 1882-86, prof. rhetoric, English criticism and elocution, 1886-92, Syracuse U.; prof. English lang., Northwestern U., 1892—. Author: A Practical Rhetoric, 1886; A Briefer Practical Rhetoric, 1888; English Literature by an Inductive Method, 1891; A Chart of English and American Literature, 1891; The Art of Reading Aloud, 1892; A Study of English Prose Writers, 1898; A Study of English and American Poets, 1900; Macaulay's Life of Jonson (Van Dyke series), 1905; The Shorter Poems of Robert Browning, 1909. Home: Evanston, Ill. Died 1911.

CLARK, J(ames) Ross, banker; b. Connellsville, Pa., Apr. 10, 1850; s. John and Mary (Andrews) C.; pub. schs. and acad.; m. Miriam Evans, Apr. 16, 1878. Engaged in mining, banking and sugar beet industry, in the West, for many yrs.; moved to Los Angeles, 1892; v.p. Los Angeles & Salt Lake R.R., 1901-21; dir. Citizens Nat. Bank, Los Angeles, 1894—, chmn. bd., 1924—; dir. U. P. Ry. Republican. Conglist. Mason. Home: Los Angeles, Calif. Died Sept. 19, 1927.

CLARK, James Truman, ry. pres.; b. Auburn, N.Y., Nov. 20, 1852; s. William and Sarah Jane C.; ed. pub. schs.; m. Fannie May Arnold, Jan. 28, 1880. Began as messenger boy I.C. R.R., 1870; clk. gen. offices C.&N.W. Ry., Chicago, 1873-80; gen. agt. same rd., at Omaha and Council Bluffs, 1880-83; asst. traffic mgr., Jan.-Nov. 1883, asst. gen. freight agt., 1883-84, gen. frt. agt., 1884-96, gen. traffic mgr., 1896-99, 2d v.p. in charge of traffic, from June 5, 1899, jurisdiction extending over operating and construction depts., from Mar. 9, 1909, pres., May 23, 1916—, C.,St.P.M.&O. Ry. Trustee St. Paul Art Inst. Presbyn. Home: St. Paul, Minn. Died Sept. 8, 1922.

CLARK, James Waddey, justice; b. Allisona, Tenn., Dec. 8, 1877; s. Joseph P. and Cora Belle (Waddey) C.; LL.B., Cumberland U., Lebanon, Tenn., 1909; m. Anna Paullin, May 1, 1917; children—Ann Paullin, Jim, Mary Louise, John Marshall. Began practice in Atoka County, Okla., 1909; mem. Okla. Ho. of Rep., 1911; county atty. Atoka County, 1913-16; mem. Dem. State Central Com., 1922-25; justice Supreme Court of Okla., Jan. 1925-33; vice chief justice, 1931-33. Mem. M.E. Ch., S. Mason. Home: Atoka, Okla. Died Feb. 24, 1939.

CLARK, Jesse Redman, life ins. pres.; b. Cincinnati, Oct. 31, 1854; s. Davis Wasgatt and Mary Johnson (Redman) C.; ed. Chickering Inst. and Woodward High Sch., Cincinnati, and Ohio Wesleyan U.; m. Carrie Marqua, Sept. 19, 1883. Cashier, 1878-80, dir., 1880—, treas., 1886-1906, pres., 1906—, Union Central Life Ins. Co. Republican. Methodist. Home: Avondale, Cincinnati. Died Sept. 25, 1921.

CLARK, John Bates, political economist; b. Providence, Jan. 26, 1847; s. John Hezekiah and Charlotte (Huntington) C.; student Brown U., 2 yrs.; A.B., Amherst, 1872, A.M., 1878, Ph.D., 1890; univs. of Heidelberg and Zürich, 2½ yrs.; LL.D., Princeton, 1896, Amherst, 1897, U. of Christiania, Norway, 1911, Columbia U., 1929; Doctor of Polit. Science, U. of Tubingen, Germany, 1928; m. Myra A. Smith, Sept. 28, 1875; children—Frederick Huntington, Alden Hyde, John Maurice, Helen Converse. Prof. polit. economy and history, Carleton Coll., 1877-81; prof.

history and polit. science, Smith Coll., 1882-93; prof. polit. economy, Amherst, 1892-95; prof. polit. economy, Columbia, July 1, 1895-1923. Lecturer polit. economy, Johns Hopkins, 1892-95; editor Political Science Quarterly, 1895-1911; dir. div. of economics and history, Carnegie Endowment for Internat. Peace, 1911-23. Trustee Smith Coll., 1898-1920. Author: The Philosophy of Wealth, 1885; The Distribution of Wealth, 1899; The Control of Trusts, 1901; The Problem of Monopoly, 1904; Essentials of Economic Theory, 1907; The Modern Distributive Process (with F. H. Giddings); Control of Trusts (enlarged edit., with J. M. Clark). Home: New York, N.Y. Died Mar. 21, 1938.

CLARK, John Bullock, lawyer; b. Fayette, Mo., Jan. 14, 1831; grad. Harvard Law School, 1854; served in C.S.A., lt. to brig. gen.; resumed law practice at Fayette, Mo.; mem. Congress, 1873-83; then clerk of House of Reps. several yrs. Died 1903.

CLARK, John Edward, M.D.; b. England, Jan. 13, 1850; s. Fred J. and Ellen (Petley) C.; came to America, 1856; ed. Victoria Coll., Toronto; M.D., U. of Mich., 1877; m. Frances Hutchins, June, 1887; children—Harold E., Frances. In practice at Detroit, 1877—; prof. gen. chemistry and physics, Mich. Coll. of Medicine, 1879-85, Detroit Coll. of Medicine, 1885—; dean dept. pharmacy and prof. chemistry and toxicology, Detroit Coll. of Medicine, 1892—. Surgeon-gen. Mich. N.G., 1892; pres. U.S. Pension Examining Bd., 1899—; then chemist and analyst Wayne Co., Mich. Mem. Detroit Bd. of Edn., 1893-97 (pres., 1895); pres. Detroit Pub. Library Commn., 1902. Author Clark's Physical Diagnosis and Urine Analysis, 1890; Laboratory Technique for Medical Students, 1900. Home: Detroit, Mich. Died Sept. 19, 1934.

CLARK, John Emory, mathematician; b. Northampton, N. Y., Aug. 8, 1832; s. Rev. John and Sarah Miller (Foote) C.; A.B., U. of Mich., 1856, A.M., 1859; (hon. A.M., Yale, 1873); m. Caroline C. Doty, Aug. 20, 1856 (dec.). Professor of mathematics, Mich. State Normal Sch., 1856-57; asst. prof. mathematics, U. of Mich., 1857-59; studied at univs. of Heidelberg, Munich and Berlin, 1859-60; U.S. deputy surveyor in Dak., 1861-62, in Colo., 1869; capt. and maj. 5th Mich. Cav., 1862-65; bvtd. lt. col. U.S. Vols., Mar., 1865; prof. mathematics and astronomy, Antioch Coll., 1866-72; asst. astronomer, Northern Boundary Commn., 1872; prof. mathematics, 1873-1901, emeritus, Sheffield Scientific Sch. (Yale). Home Springfield, Mass. Died Jan. 3, 1921.

CLARK, John Goodrich, gynecologist; b. Wayne Co., Ind., June 4, 1867; s. Thomas E. and Nancy (Goodrich) C.; ed. Earlham Coll. and Ohio Wesleyan U.; M.D., U. of Pa., 1891; post-grad. work Johns Hopkins and univs. of Leipzig and Prague; married. Asso. in gynecology, Johns Hopkins, 1899; prof. gynecology, U. of Pa., 1899—; gynecologist in chief, University Hospital. Mem. Gen. Med. Com. of Council Nat. Defense, 1917—. Pres. Clin. Congress of Surgeons of N. America, 1917. Home: Philadelphia, Pa. Died May 4, 1927.

CLARK, John Howe, rear adm.; b. Greenland, N.H., Apr. 16, 1837; s. Samuel Wallace and Rebecca E. (Howe) C.; A.B., Dartmouth Coll., 1857; M.D., Harvard, 1862; unmarried. Entered U.S.N. as asst. surgeon, Oct. 19, 1861; promoted surgeon, May 14, 1867; med. insp., Jan. 8, 1885; med. dir., Mar. 4, 1893; retired with rank of rear adm., Apr. 16, 1899. Home: Amherst, N.H. Died Nov. 30, 1913.

CLARK, John Marshall; b. White Pigeon, Mich., Aug. 1, 1836; s. Robert, Jr. and Mary E. (Fitch) C.; C.E., Rensselaer Poly. Inst., 1856; m. Mary Louise Qua, Jan. 7, 1873. Removed to Chicago, 1847; civil engr. on I.C. R.R., 1856-59; practiced at Denver, 1859-62, where he was part propr. of the original townsite; in 1862 went to Santa Fé in employ of govt. to survey pub. land in N.M. and while so engaged secured records and documents of the dept., saving them from the raid made into N.M., by the Confederates by taking them, under escort, to Ft. Union; was aid on staff of Gen. Donaldson of Union Army and also served, with same rank, under Brig. Gen. Stough, at battle of Apache Cañon. Returned to Chicago, 1864; dir. and pres. Chicago Telephone Co. Mem. Chicago Common Council, 1869-71; Rep. candidate for mayor against Carter H. Harrison, Sr., 1881; later mem. Chicago Bd. of Edn.; collector port of Chicago, 1890-94; pres. first Bd. of Civil Service Commrs., 1895-97. Home: Chicago, Ill. Died Aug. 6, 1918.

CLARK, Joseph Bourne, clergyman; b. Sturbridge, Mass., Oct. 7, 1836; s. Rev. Dr. Joseph S. and Harriet Bates (Bourne) C.; A.B., Amherst, 1858, A.M., 1861; grad. Andover Theol. Sem., 1861; (D.D., Amherst, 1884); m. Clara N. Herendeen, Oct. 23, 1878. Ordained Congl. ministry, 1861; pastor First Ch., Yarmouth, 1861-68, Central Ch., Newtonville, 1868-72, Central Ch., Jamaica Plain, Boston, 1872-79; sec. Mass. Home Missionary Soc., 1879-82; sec. Congl. Home Missionary Soc., 1882—. Author: Leavening the Nation, 1903; "Blue-Sky," The Life of Harriet Caswell Broad, 1911. Home: Brooklyn, N.Y. Died July 10, 1923.

CLARK, Kate Upson, author; b. Camden, Ala., Feb. 22, 1851; d. Edwin and Priscilla (Maxwell) Upson; grad. Wheaton Coll., Norton, Mass., 1869. hon. Litt.D., 1919; grad. Westfield (Mass.) Normal Sch., 1872; m. Edward Perkins Clark, journalist, Jan. 1, 1874 (died 1903); children—Charles Upson, John Kirkland, George Maxwell. Taught in Cleveland (O.) Central High Sch., 1872-73; has edited many periodicals and depts. Lecturer on lit., ednl. and domestic topics. Mem. exec. com. philol. dept. Brooklyn Inst., 1910. Trustee Wheaton Coll., 1907—. Author: The Dole Twins, 1906; The Adventures of Spotty, 1907; Donald's Good Hen, 1907; Art and Citizenship, 1917; Teaching the Child Patriotism, 1918; etc. Died Feb. 17, 1935.

CLARK, L. Pierce, M.D.; b. Ingleside, N.Y., June 15, 1870; s. Frank L. and Almira (Pierce) C.; Naples (N.Y.) Acad.; M.D., Univ. Med. Coll. (New York U.), 1892. Consulting neurologist, Manhattan State Hosp., 1893—, Craig Colony for Epileptics, 1893—; visiting neurologist, Randalls Island Hosp. and Sch. for Mental Defectives, 1894—. Trustee Letchworth Village for Mental Defectives, Theills, N.Y. Author: Clinical Studies in Epilepsy, 1900; Diagnosis of Organic Nervous Diseases (with Christian A. Herter), 1907; Neurological and Mental Diagnosis (with A. Ross Diefendorf), 1908. Editor: Archives of Psychoanalysis, 1926-27. Died Dec. 3, 1933.

CLARK, Lester Williams, judge; b. Brookline, Mass., Jan. 22, 1854; s. Lester Manzer and Maria Isabella (Williams) C.; B.A., Harvard, 1875; LL.B., Columbia, 1878; admitted to bar, 1878; m. Irene M. de Ma Carty, Oct. 20, 1883. Justice Supreme Court of N.Y., for term 1907-20. Republican. Home: New Brighton, N.Y. Died Sept. 22, 1922.

CLARK, Lewis Whitehouse, justice supreme court of N.H., 1877—; b. Barnstead, N.H., Aug. 19, 1828; grad. Dartmouth, 1850 (LL.D., 1888); practiced law from 1851 until elected to bench. Home: Manchester, N.H. Died 1900.

CLARK, Mallie Adkin, M.D.; b. Russell Co., Ala., Sept. 1, 1866; s. Adoniram Judson and Abi (Morris) C.; A.B., Mercer U., 1885, A.M., 1888, LL.D., 1911; M.D., Bellevue Hosp. Med. Coll. (New York U.), 1890; m. Irma Murphey, June 7, 1894; children—Mallie Adkin (dec.), Olaf Judson (dec.), Irma (wife of Dr. Ralph G. Newton), Martha (Mrs. Emmette H. Baker), Milledge Adoniram (dec.), Carroll Murphey (dec.), Verna. Began practice at Bluffton, 1890; moved to Barnesville, 1892, to Macon, 1897; prof. materia medica, Dept. of Pharmacy, Mercer U., 1905-09; lecturer in med. jurisprudence, same univ., 1898—. Mem. Com. Nat. Defense, Ga., World War, also chmn. Dist. Advisory Bd. (medical). Mem. Bd. Trustees Mercer U., and chmn. exec. com. Fellow Am. Coll. Physicians. Democrat. Missionary Baptist. Home: Mason, Ga. Deceased.

CLARK, Marguerite, actress; b. Cincinnati, O.; d. A. J. and Helen (Golden) C.; ed. pvt. sch. and Ursuline Convent, Brown Co., O., to 13, later under pvt. teachers; m. H. P. Williams, Aug. 15, 1918. Début in Baltimore, under management of Milton Aborn, 1900; featured with DeWolf Hopper Co.; starred in musical comedy with Jefferson DeAngelis: starred in "Wishing Ring," "King of Cadoma" and "Baby Mine"; appeared in all-star casts, revivals of "Lights o' London" and "Jim the Penman"; played 2 rôles in Little Theatre, New York, 1912 and 1913, appearing evenings with John Barrymore, in "Anatol," and starring afternoons and Saturday mornings in "Snow White"; played title rôle in "Prunella," 1913-14. Began appearing in films with Famous Players, 1914; pictures released—"Wild Flower"; "The Crucible"; "Goose Girl"; loaned by Famous Players to Lasky Co., and appeared in "Pretty Sister of Jose"; "Gretna Greene"; "Seven Sisters"; "Helene of the North"; "Still Waters"; "Princess and Pauper"; "Mice and Men," etc. Home: Los Angeles, Calif. Died Sept. 25, 1940.

CLARK, Melville, piano mfr.; b. Oneida Co., N.Y.; s. Thomas W. and Susan M. (Medole) C.; ed. pub. schs. and commercial coll.; m. Elizabeth Baughman, Oct. 1, 1873. Began mfg. organs, Oakland, Calif., 1875; removed to Quincy, Ill., 1876, Chicago, 1880; became mem. Story & Clark, mfrs. of organs, 1884; firm began mfr. of piano, 1894; dissolved partnership, 1899; organizer, 1900, and pres. Melville Clark Piano Co. Extensive experimenter in field of pneumatics. Invented and put on market first 88-note piano player, revolutionizing the player piano industry of the world; built first player, 1901. Invented, 1911, the recording machine which reproduces the temperament and tech. peculiarities of the pianist playing a grand piano to which recorder is attached; used for cutting music rolls. Progressive. Home: Chicago, Ill. Died Nov. 5, 1918.

CLARK, Melvin Green, supt. schs.; b. Belleville, N.Y., Mar. 6, 1868; s. Milo R. and Lamira A. (Truesdell) C.; Union Acad., Belleville, N.Y.; Oswego (N.Y.) State Normal Sch.; A.B., A.M., Greer Coll., Hoopeston, Ill., 1898; studied U. of Chicago; hon. LL.D., Buena Vista Coll., Storm Lake, Ia., 1924; m. Mary E. Miller, 1891 (died 1909); children—Harry M., Wilson T., M. Robert; m. 2d, Colleen Hogan, 1913; 1 dau., Dorothy J. Supt. schs., Greenville, Ill., 1898-1901, Princeton, Ill., 1901-06, Streator, Ill., 1906-11, Sioux City, Ia., 1911—. Chairman State Committee Vocational Education, Iowa, 1912-14; member State Advisory Board of Vocational Edn., 1917-25. Republican. Presbyn. Mason. Author: Motived Language, 1919; Habituated Arithmetic, 1919; Applied English, 1924; Progress and Patriotism, 1924; Language in Use, Book I, 1925, Book II and Book III, 1926. Home: Sioux City, Ia. Died Feb. 5, 1931.

CLARK, Nathaniel Walling, clergyman; b. Plattsburg, N.Y., Feb. 12, 1859; s. George Lafayette and Jane (Walling) C.; A.B., Wesleyan U., Conn., 1879, A.M., 1882; B.D., Drew Theol. Sem., Madison, N.J., 1883; studied U. of Bonn, 1890, U. of Heidelberg, 1891-93; (D.D., New York U., 1899, Wesleyan, 1901); m. Felicia Hemans Buttz, Aug. 22, 1883. Ordained M.E. ministry, 1883; pastor, Phila., 1883-85, Englewood, N.J., 1886-89; prof., Martin Inst., Frankfurt-on-the-Main, Germany, 1889-93; pres. Reeder Theol. Sch., Rome, 1893-1901; traveling sec. for Europe and Levant of World's Student Christian Fedn., 1901-03; pres., Methodist Coll., Rome, 1903-05; supt., M.E. Ch., Rome Dist., 1904—. Home: Madison, N.J. Died Mar. 12, 1918.

CLARK, Olynthus B., prof. history; b. near Bloomington, Ill., Jan. 30, 1864; s. Abia and Anna (Joder) C.; S.B., Eureka (Ill.) College, 1896, A.M., 1900, LL.D. from same college, 1926; student of U. of Chicago, 1900, 1903; Ph.D., Columbia U., 1911; m. Lilly E. Rowell, Dec. 29, 1892; children—Lawrence, Ralph (dec.), Anna Laura (Mrs. Reginald Thompson), Margaret, Alfred Rowell. Teacher public schools, McLean Co., Ill. Field Secretary, 1896-97, prin. Prep. Sch., 1897-99; professor edn. and history, 1899-1904, Eureka Coll.; prof. history, Drake U., 1904-32 (emeritus). Curator State Hist. Soc. of Ia., 1906-11. Pres. Nat. Inter-Collegiate Prohibition Assn., 1898-99. Mem. Ch. of Christ (Disciples). Chmn. Commn. on Internat. Relations, Des Moines, 1925-32; founder Ia. Br. League of Nations Assn., 1923 (pres. 1927-29). Author: Outlines of Civil Government in the United States, 1907; The Politics of Iowa During the Civil War and Reconstruction, 1911. Home: Des Moines, Ia. Died Sept. 9, 1936.

CLARK, Robert Carlton, prof. of history; b. Thorp Spring, Tex., Mar. 4, 1877; s. Addison and Sara (McQuigg) C.; A.B., Tex. Christian U., 1894, A.M., 1895; A.M., U. of Tex., 1901; Ph.D., U. of Wis., 1905; m. Anna W. Wallace, Sept. 9, 1909 (died 1922); children—Catherine Louise, Edith Elizabeth, Wallace Carlton; m. 2d, Marguerite Straughan, June 13, 1925; 1 dau., Ruth Anna. Prof. of history, Epworth U., Oklahoma City, 1904-05, Pa. Normal Sch., Bloomsburg, 1905-07; prof. of history, U. of Ore., 1907—, head dept. of history, 1920—. Fellow Tex. Hist. Soc. Democrat. Author: Beginnings of Texas, 1907; A History of Oregon (with G. V. Blue and R. H. Down), 1925; A History of the Willamette Valley, Oregon, 1927. Editor of Ore. Hist. Quarterly, 1937—. Home: Eugene, Ore. Died Dec. 4, 1939.

CLARK, Rufus Wheelwright, P.E. clergyman; b. Portsmouth, N.H., May 29, 1844; s. Rev. Rufus Wheelwright C. (D.D.) and Eliza Walton C.; grad. Williams, 1865 (A.M., 1868; D.D., 1890); Gen. Theol. Sem., New York, 1868; m. Lucy G., d. Gov. William Dennison of Ohio, April 9, 1874. Deacon, 1867; priest, 1868; rector St. John's, Portsmouth, N.H., 1868-71; Trinity Ch., Columbus, O., 1871-77; St. Paul's, Detroit, Mich., 1877-1906. Mem. New England Soc. of Mich. (pres.), Soc. of Colonial Wars. Chaplain gen. S.A.R. Author: The Church in Thy House; Addresses, Religious and patriotic. Died 1909.

CLARK, Samuel M., congressman-editor; b. on farm in Van Buren Co., Ia., Oct. 11, 1842; admitted to bar, 1864; editor Keokuk Gate City, 1866—; mem. Congress, 1895-99. Republican. Home: Keokuk, Ia. Died 1900.

CLARK, Solomon Henry, univ. prof.; b. New York, July 24, 1861; s. M. S. and Elizabeth (Goldsmith) C.; ed. Coll. City of New York, and Queen's Coll., Kingston, Can.; Ph.B., U. of Chicago, 1897; m. Anna Maud Fralick, Aug. 19, 1889. Lecturer, Queen's U., Can., 1886-87, Trinity Coll., 1888-92, McMasters Coll., 1890; reader in elocution, 1892-94, instr., 1894-97, asst. prof. pub. speaking, 1897-1901, asso. prof. and head of dept. of pub. speaking, 1901—, U. of Chicago. Prin. Chautauqua (N.Y.) Sch. of Expression, from 1896. Author: Mental Technique; How to Read Aloud; Principles of Vocal Expression and Literary Interpretation (with W. B. Chamberlain), 1895; How to Teach Reading in the Public Schools, 1898; Practical Public Speaking (with F. M. Blanchard), 1899; Handbook of Best Readings, 1902; Interpretation of the Printed Page, 1915. Home: Highland Park, Ill. Died Dec. 29, 1927.

CLARK, Theodore Minot, architect; b. Boston, Aug. 20, 1845; grad. Harvard, 1866; m. Jeannette French, Nov. 11, 1879. Prof. bldg. and architecture, in charge dept. of architecture, Mass. Inst. Tech., 1881-88. Fellow Am. Inst. Architects, Soc. of Arts,

London; mem. Internat. Inst. of Public Art, Brussels. Author: Rural School Architecture, 1880; Building Superintendence (15 edits.), 1884-1903; Architect, Owner and Builder Before the Law, 1894; En Voyage; The Care of a House, 1903. Died 1909.

CLARK, Thomas Arkle, univ. dean; b. Minonk, Ill., May 11, 1862; s. William G. and Dorothy (Metcalf) C.; B.L., U. of Ill., 1890; grad. student, U. of Chicago, 1894, Harvard, 1898-99; Litt.D., Knox Coll., 1923, Coll. of Wooster, 1924; m. Alice V. Broaddus, Aug. 24, 1896. Instr. English and Latin, U. of Ill. Acad., 1891-93; instr. English, U. of Ill., 1893-95; asst. prof. rhetoric, 1895-99, prof., 1899, acting dean, Coll. Lit. and Arts, 1900-01, dean undergraduates, 1901, dir. summer session, 1903, dean of men, 1909-31; retired. Author: English Composition in State Course of Study; English Composition in the Grades; Great American Authors; Great English Authors; The Sunday Eight O'Clock, 1916; The Fraternity and the College, 1916; The Fraternity and the Undergraduate; The High School Boy and His Problems; Discipline and the Derelict; When You Write a Letter. Home: Urbana, Ill. Died July 18, 1932.

CLARK, Thomas Collier, judge; b. Flint, Mich., Oct. 27, 1860; s. George T. and Mary E. (Duxbury) C.; ed. U. of Mich., 1877-79; m. Edith M. Smith, Jan. 29, 1896. Was connected with C.&W.M. Ry. and D.,L.&N. R.R. Co. in various capacities, 1879-91; practiced law at Muskegon, Mich., 1891-93; removed to Chicago, 1893; mem. Smiley & Clark, 1895-10; elected judge Superior Ct., Cook Co., Nov. 1910, term expiring Dec. 1916; assigned by the Supreme Ct. of Ill., to Appellate Ct. of 1st Dist. of Ill., Feb. 1911, and continued serving on reassignment made June 1912. Democrat. Episcopalian. Home: Evanston, Ill. Died Feb. 19, 1915.

CLARK, Thomas Harvey, lawyer; b. Pine Level, Ala., Nov. 16, 1857; s. of Henry William and Mary (Wright) C.; A.B., Howard Coll., Ala., 1877; post-grad., Harvard, 1878-79, law, U. of Va., 1882; m. Caroline Marks, Apr. 13, 1887 (died 1909). Practiced law at Montgomery from 1880; editor, Selma (Ala.) Times, 1886; on staff Montgomery Advertiser, 1887. Asst. sec. Ala. Senate, 1882-86; rec. sec. to the gov., 1887-90. Mem. City Council, Montgomery, 1890-92; mem. Ala. Ho. of Rep., 1892-96 (speaker, 1894-96); Nat. Dem. sound money nominee for Congress, 1896; law librarian of Congress, 1897-1903; reporter U.S. Ct. of Customs Appeals, Washington, since its orgn., Apr. 1910. Home: Montgomery, Ala. Died June 17, 1915.

CLARK, Thomas March, P.E. bishop of R.I., 1854—; b. Newburyport, Mass., July 4, 1812; ed. at Phillips Acad., Andover; grad. Yale, 1831; studied Princeton Theol. Sem., 1831-35 (D.D., Union Coll., N.Y., 1851, Brown, 1860; LL.D., Cambridge, Eng., 1867). In 1835 licensed to preach in Presbyn. Ch., Newburyport, Mass., but next yr. took deacon's and priest's orders in P.E. Ch. Rector Grace Ch., Boston, 1836-43; St. Andrew, Phila., 1844-47; Trinity Ch., Boston, 1847-51; Christ Ch., Hartford, 1851-54. Presiding bishop of P.E. Ch. in U.S., 1899—. Author: Formation of Character; Primary Truths of Religion; Readings and Prayers as Aid in Private Devotion; Reminiscences (1895); The Dew of Youth; Early Discipline and Culture; The Efficient Sunday School Teacher. Home: Providence, R.I. Died 1903.

CLARK, Walter, judge; b. Halifax Co., N.C., Aug. 19, 1846; s. David and Anna M. (Thorne) C.; A.B., U. of N.C., 1864, A.M., 1867 (LL.D., 1888); m. Susan W., d. Gov. and U.S. Senator and Sec. of Navy W. A. Graham of N.C., Jan. 28, 1874. Lt. col. C.S.A., 1864, at 17 yrs. of age; admitted to bar, 1868; judge Superior Ct. of N.C., 1885-89; judge Supreme Ct., 1889-1902, chief justice, Jan. 1, 1903—. Author: Annotated Code of Civil Procedure, 3d edition. Translated from original French, Constant's Memoirs of Napoleon, 3 vols., 1895. Home: Raleigh, N.C. Died May 19, 1924.

CLARK, Walter, artist; b. Brooklyn, Mar. 9, 1848; s. Daniel Candee and Helen Maria (Ballard) C.; began study of art, 1876; pupil Nat. Acad. of Design, Prof. Wilmarth and Art Students' League; entered studio of J. S. Hartley and followed sculpture 5 yrs.; began landscape work, 1881, and received much instruction from late George Inness; m. Jennie Woodruff Clark, June 15, 1876; father of Eliot Candee C. Splty., landscapes; exhibited at Chicago Expn., 1893, Paris Expn., 1900; silver medal for picture "In Early Leaf," Buffalo Expn., 1901; Inness gold medal for picture "Gloucester Harbor," Nat. Acad. Design; silver medal, St. Louis Expn., 1904. N.A., 1909. Home: Bronxville, N.Y. Died Mar. 12, 1917.

CLARK, Walter Appleton, artist, illustrator; b. Worcester, Mass., 1876; pupil of H. Siddons Mowbray and William M. Chase; m. Anne Hoyt, 1902. Best known by his cover designs and illustrations on Scribner's Mag. Instr. Art Students League, New York; silver medal, Paris Expn., 1900; silver medal, Pan-Am. Expn., 1901. Died 1906.

CLARK, Walter Loane, lawyer; b. McKean Co., Pa., Oct. 27, 1878; s. Robert Yealdhall and Ella L. (Loane) C.; student Baltimore City Coll., LL.B., U. of Md. Sch. of Law, 1902; unmarried. Admitted to Md. bar, 1903; gen. counsel Md. Casualty Co., Baltimore, 1911-21; in gen. practice, 1921—; formerly instr. in ins., Johns Hopkins U., now instr. in evidence, U. of Md. Sch. of Law. Pres. City Service Commn., Baltimore. Democrat. Episcopalian. Home: Baltimore, Md. Died July 3, 1941.

CLARK, Walton, engr.; b. Utica, N.Y., 1856; s. Erastus and Frances A. (Beardsley) C.; ed. High Sch., Utica; M.E., Sc.D.; m. Alice M. Shaw (died); 1 son, Frank Shaw; m. 2d, Louise Beauvais, 1885; children—Walton, Theobald Forstall, Beauvais, Darthela. Began in New Orleans, 1873, and has been identified with pub. service corps.; cons. engr. United Gas Improvement Co., Phila. Republican. Home: Chestnut Hill, Pa. Died 1934.

CLARK, William Andrews, senator; b. nr. Connellsville, Pa., Jan. 8, 1839; s. John and Mary (Andrews) C.; ed. Laurel Hill Acad., and other acads.; studied law Mt. Pleasant (Ia.) U.; m. Kate L. Stauffer, Mar. 1869 (died 1893); 2d, Anna E. La Chapelle, May 25, 1901. Did not enter legal profession; taught sch., Mo., 1859-60; went to Colo., 1862, to Mont., 1863; then banker, mine-owner, having large interests; pres. or dir. United Verde Copper Co., Mayflower, Moulton, Ophir Hill Consolidated mining cos., L.A.&S.L. R.R., Butte Elec. Ry. Co., Clark-Mont. Realty Co., Colusa-Parrot Mining & Smelting Co., Los Alamitos Sugar Co., Mont. Land Co., Natural Mineral Water Co., W. A. Clark & Bro., bankers, Butte, Mont., Waclark Realty Co., Waclark Wire Co. State orator, representing Mont. at Centennial Expn., 1876. Major Butte battalion, leading it in Nez Percé campaign, 1878; pres. Constl. convs., 1884, 1889; commr. from Mont. to New Orleans Expn., 1884; Dem. candidate for del. to Congress, 1888; nominated by Democrats for U.S. senator, 1890, and claimed election, but was denied seat; candidate for U.S. senate, 1898, and elected; a contest ensued at Washington, but before investigation concluded he resigned; elected U.S. senator by legislature for term, 1901-07. Mason. Home: Butte, Mont. Died Mar. 2, 1925.

CLARK, William Andrews, Jr., miner, capitalist; b. Deer Lodge, Mont., Mar. 29, 1877; s. U.S. Senator William Andrews and Katherine Louise (Stauffer) C.; ed. pub. schs. of Garden City, L.I., and Los Angeles, and Drisler Sch., N.Y. City; B.L., U. of Va., 1899; m. Mabel Duffield Foster, June 19, 1901 (dec.); 1 son, William Andrews; m. 2d, Alice G. McManus, May 7, 1907 (deceased). Admitted to bar by Supreme Court of Mont., 1900, and practiced 7 yrs.; started, 1905, and developed the Elm Orlu Mine, at Butte, Mont.; built the Timber Butte Mill, 1911; v.p. and dir. United Verde Copper Co. Founded Los Angeles Philharmonic Orchestra, 1919. Episcopalian. Home: Butte, Mont. (also Los Angeles, Calif.). Died June 14, 1934.

CLARK, William Arthur, psychologist; b. Manchester, O., May 23, 1853; s. Samuel Elison and Sarah Ann (Kirker) C.; Nat. Normal U., Lebanon, O., 1871-72, 1883-85, A.B., 1885; Harvard, 1893-94, 1898-99, A.M., 1899; U. of Chicago, 1899-1900, Ph.D., 1900; (hon. Ped.D., Nat. Normal U., 1894; LL.D., Hastings Coll., Neb., 1912); m. Irene Holbrook, July 28, 1886. Teacher and supt. pub. schs., Ohio, 1872 81; supt. Ohio Soldiers' and Sailors' Orphans' Home schs., Xenia, O., 1881-83; prof. mathematics, Nat. Normal U., 1883-93; prof. philosophy and dean of faculty, Western Normal Coll., Lincoln, Neb., 1894-95; teacher pedagogy, 1895-98, pres., 1900-04, Neb. State Normal Sch., at Peru, Neb.; teacher psychology and pedagogy and dean of faculty, Neb. State Normal School, Kearney, Neb., 1905-12; head prof. of edn. and psychology, Mo. State Normal School, Sept. 1912—. Republican. Presbyterian. Author: Suggestion in Education (doctor's thesis), 1900; Syllabus of Pedagogy, 1910; Syllabus of Psychology, 1913. Home: Kirksville, Mo. Died Nov. 17, 1918.

CLARK, William Braddock, underwriter; b. Hartford, Conn., June 29, 1841; s. A.N. (formerly propr. Hartford Courant) and Emily I. (Braddock) C.; ed. grammar and high schs.; m. Caroline H. Robbins; m. 2d, Rachel Whittier Root, Aug. 30, 1905. In fire ins. from boyhood; became chmn. bd.Ætna Ins. Co.; dir. Travelers Ins. Co., First Nat. Bank, Soc. for Savings. Alderman and water commr. Home: Hartford, Conn. Died Aug. 6, 1927.

CLARK, William Bullock, geologist; b. Brattleboro, Vt., Dec. 15, 1860; s. Barna A. and Helen C. (Bullock) C.; A.B., Amherst, 1884; Ph.D., U. of Munich, 1887; continued studies in Berlin and London; (LL.D., Amherst, 1908); m. Ellen C. Strong, Oct. 12, 1892. Instr. and asso., 1887-92, asso. prof., 1892-94, prof. geology, and dir. Geol. Lab., from 1894, Johns Hopkins. Asst. geologist, 1888-94, geologist, 1894-1907, coöperating geologist, 1907—, U.S. Geol. Survey; dir. Md. Weather Service, 1891—; state geologist, 1896—; commr. for state of Md. on re-survey of Mason and Dixon line, 1900-06; mem. and exec. officer Md. State Forestry Commn., 1906—; mem. White House Conf. on conservation, 1908; mem. Md. State Conservation Commn., 1908-12. Asso. editor Jour. of Geology., 1896—; pres. Children's Aid Soc., Baltimore, 1901—. Author: The Eocene Deposits of the United States, 1891; The Physical Features of Maryland, 1906; The Mesozoic and Cenozoic Echinadermata of the United States, 1915. Home: Baltimore, Md. Died July 27, 1917.

CLARK, William Heermans, editor; b. Lyons, N.Y., Aug. 12, 1848; s. William and Amelia R. (Heermans) C.; desc. on both paternal and maternal sides of commissioned officers of Am. Army in Revolutionary War; student Hamilton Coll., 1865-66; A.B., Union Coll., 1868, A.M., 1871; m. Helen Street, Dec. 31, 1879. Admitted to bar, 1869; practiced at Lyons, N.Y., 1869-76; purchased Cortland Standard, 1876; pres. Cortland Standard Printing Co. from 1893; pres. Norwich Pub. Co., 1903—. Mem. N.Y. Assembly, 1875; mem. Rep. State Com., 1880-81; chmn. local bd. mgrs. State Normal and Training Sch., Cortland, 1891-1926; postmaster of Cortland, 1911-15. Presbyn. Chmn. Cortland County orgn., for 3d-5th Liberty loans. Home: Cortland, N.Y. Died Mar. 1928.

CLARKE, Albert, economist; b. Granville, Vt., Oct. 13, 1840; s. Jedediah and Mary (Woodbury) C.; grad. Barre, Vt., Acad., 1859; (hon. A.M., Dartmouth, 1888); m. Josephine Briggs, Jan. 21, 1864. Enlisted 13th Vt. Inf., Aug., 1862; thrice promoted; comd. co. Gettysburg and captured cannon and prisoners. Practiced law at Montpelier, Vt., 1859-65; editor and most of time propr. St. Albans (Vt.) Messenger, 1868-80; on staff Boston Daily Advertiser, 1883-85; pres. Vt. & Can. R.R., 1885-86; editor and mgr. Rutland (Vt.) Herald, 1886-89; sec. Home Market Club, Boston, July, 1889—. Col. on staff of Gov. Dillingham of Vt., 1865; mem. Vt. senate, 1874; mem. Mass. Ho. of Rep., 1896-98; editor Home Market Bull. (then Profectionist Mag.), 1899—; mem. U.S. Industrial Commn., 1899-1902 (chmn. 1901-02). Judge adv. gen. G.A.R., 1897. Home: Brookline, Mass. Died 1911.

CLARKE, Alfred, mech. engr.; b. Leicester, Eng., June 4, 1849; s. Thomas Alfred William and Susanna (Cott) C.; ed. pub. schs., Leicester, and dept. of science and art, S. Kensington, London; m. Lucia Evelyn Whiting, Nov. 3, 1880. Came to America, 1874; chief engr., Bradley Fertilizer Co., N. Weymouth, Mass., 1876-77; supt. Kitson Machine Co., Lowell, Mass., 1877-85, and while there invented and patented improvements in cotton machinery then in general use; gen. mgr. Prospect Machine & Engine Co., Cleveland, O., 1885-87; asso. with Arthur E. Childs in founding The Light, Heat & Power Corp., Boston, which led to formation of the Mass. Lighting Cos., owning a number of gas, electric light and power cos. in Mass. Republican. Mem. Ch. of England. Mason. Home: Walpole, N.H. Died Apr. 27, 1922.

CLARKE, Andrew Stuart Currie, clergyman; b. Omagh, Co. Tyrone, Ireland, Oct. 28, 1859; s. Joseph and Mary Ann (Johnston) C.; came to U.S. with parents, 1873; grad. Westminster Coll., Fulton, Mo., 1886, McCormick Theol. Sem., 1889; D.D., Bellevue (Neb.) Coll., 1906; LL.D., James Millikin U., 1930; m. Mattie McCluer, Apr. 1889; m. 2d, Belle M. Oliver, Sept. 22, 1897; children—David Marquis, Ruth (Mrs. E. M. Callis), Elizabeth (Mrs. Angus M. Stuart), Robert Edward. Ordained Presbyn. minister, 1889; pastor Piper City, Ill., 1889-91, Elmira, Ill., 1891-1900, Immanuel Ch., Chicago, 1900-02, Lowe Av. Ch., Omaha, Neb., 1902-07, Second Ch., Evanston, Ill., 1907-23; moderator Presbytery of Chicago, 1914-15; moderator Synod of Ill. Presbyn. Ch., 1924-25. Trustee Synod of Ill. (chmn. com. on Christian edn.); exec. sec. Ill. Presbyn. Edn. Fund; sec. Presbyn. Home; dir. and teacher, McCormick Theol. Sem. Y.M.C.A. sec., overseas, 1918-19. Republican. Mason. Episcopalian. Home: Butte, Mont. (also Los Angeles, Calif.). Died June 2, 1934.

CLARKE, Augustus Peck, physician; b. Pawtucket, R.I., Sept. 24, 1833; s. Seth Darling and Fanny (Peck) C.; A.B., Brown U., 1861, A.M., 1887; M.D., Harvard, 1862; m. Mary Hannah Gray, Oct. 23, 1861. Surgeon, U.S.A., 1861-65; bvtd. lt. col., vols., 1865; med. student univs. of Paris and Leipzig, 1865-66; prof. gynecology and abdominal surgery, 1893-1901, dean, 1894-1901, Coll. Phys. and Surg., Boston. Mem. 9th Internat. Med. Congress, Washington, 1887, 10th, Berlin, 1890, 11th, Rome, 1894, 12th, Moscow, 1897 (hon. pres. sect. obstetrics and gynecology in latter), 13th, Paris, 1900, 14th, Madrid, 1903, 15th, Lisbon, 1906; v.p. Pan-Am. Med. Congress, Washington, 1893, Mexico, 1896, Havana, 1901, Panama, 1904. Fellow Mass. Med. Soc. Home: Cambridge, Mass. Died Apr. 22, 1912.

CLARKE, Bascom B., editor; b. Lexington, Va., June 24, 1851; s. James Francis and Lucy (Frances) C.; self-ed.; m. Mahettie Belle Watkins, Oct. 9, 1873; children—Frank M., Joseph Byron (dec.), Alice Belle (dec.), Harry Donald (dec.), James Leonard. Began in publishing business at Madison, Wis., 1898; pres. Clarke Pub. Co.; editor Am. Thresherman and founder Brotherhood of Threshermen. Republican. Methodist. Mason. Author: Uncle Silas' Gospel of Freemasonry, 1920; The Gospel of De Molay, 1924. Home: Madison, Wis. Died Mar. 17, 1929.

CLARKE, Benjamin Franklin, prof. mech. engring., Brown U.; b. Newport, Me., July 14, 1831; grad. Brown Univ., 1863 (A.M., 1866; Sc.D., 1897); m. Mary Elizabeth Reynolds, Aug. 2, 1864. Long connected with faculty of Brown Univ.; acting pres., 1896-97, 1898-99 (emeritus prof., 1905—). Home: Providence, R.I. Died 1908.

CLARKE, Caspar Purdon, Kt., dir. Met. Mus. of Art; b. London, Eng., Dec. 21, 1846; s. Edward Marmaduke C.; ed. in England and France (LL.D., McGill U., Montreal); m. Frances Susannah Collins, 1866. Was keeper art collections and asst. dir. and afterward dir. of Art Mus., S. Kensington, London, until July, 1905; dir. Met. Mus. of Art, New York, Sept. 1, 1905—. Chevalier Legion d'Honneur, France, 1878; Companion of the Order of the Indian Empire, 1883; created knight, 1902; Comdr. Victorian Order, 1905; Commander's Cross Order of the Crown (German). Died 1911.

CLARKE, Charles Cameron, prof. French; b. New York, May 4, 1861; s. Charles Cameron and Sarah Ruth (McCutchin) C.; A.B., Yale, 1883, M.A., 1908; Columbia Law Sch., 1886; post-grad. work Université Libre, Brussels, 1895, Sorbonne, Paris, 1896-97; m. Valentine Lemaieur, June 2, 1896; 1 son, Charles Lemaieur. Instr. in French, 1898-1903, asst. prof., 1903-08, prof., June 30, 1908—, Yale. Republican. Episcopalian. Author: The French Subjunctive, 1900; Common Difficulties of French, 1909; Concerning French Verse, 1922; Molière and the Doctors, 1923. Home: New Haven, Conn. Died Jan. 28, 1935.

CLARKE, Charles Lorenzo, elec. engr.; b. Portland, Me., Apr. 16, 1853; s. Daniel and Mary Lewis (Bragg) C.; B.S., with honors, Bowdoin, 1875, M.S., 1879, C.E., 1880; m. Helen Elizabeth Sparrow, 1881; 1 son, John Curtis; m. 2d, Henriette Mary Augusta Willatowski, 1894; children—Mary Willatowski (dec.), Daniel William; m. 3d, Edna Florence Thurston, Aug. 30, 1916; 1 son, Charles Lorenzo. Became asst. Edison lab., Menlo Park, N.J., 1880; chief engr. parent Edison Electric Light Co., 65 Fifth Av., New York, 1881-84; engr. Telemeter Co., New York, 1884-87, Gibson Electric Co. (storage batteries), 1887-89; cons. practice, 1889-1901; cons. engr. Bd. of Patent Control, Gen. Electric Co. and Westinghouse Electric & Mfg. Co., 1901-11; cons. engr. General Electric Co., 1911-31, retired Nov. 1, 1931. Intalled first (now historically noted) Edison electric lighting central station system, 1882, with central station at 257 Pearl St., New York. Republican. Protestant. Author: Diagonal Functions, 1937. Patentee of several inventions. Home: Newton, Mass. Died Oct. 9, 1941.

CLARKE, Clement George, clergyman; b. Candor, N.Y., Feb. 21, 1869; s. Leroy and Martha (Scovel) C.; B.S., Kans. State Agrl. Coll., 1888; B.A., Yale, 1895, B.D., 1900 (De Forest gold medal and C. Wyllys Betts prizes); m. Mattie Cobb, June 11, 1891; children—Helen Isabel, Dana Cobb, Clement Cobb. Ordained ministry Congl. Ch., 1900; pastor successively Plainville, Conn., Minneapolis, Peoria, Ill., to 1916; denom. work., Ill., 1916-17; war work with Internat. Y.M.C.A., lecturer on sex hygiene, 1917-19; with World Ch. Movement, 1920; pastor Springfield, Vt., 1920-23, First Ch., Portland, Ore., 1923-29, Austin Congl. Church, Chicago, 1929-30. Republican. Author: (brochures) The Greatness of God, 1908; The Appeal to Experience, 1912. Home: Wagoner, Okla. Died Mar. 1, 1940.

CLARKE, Creston, actor; b. Phila., Aug. 20, 1865; s. John Sleeper C., and nephew late Edwin Booth, actor; attended Coll. of St. Croix, Paris, France; grad. Hampstead Collegiate School, London, 1886; m. Adelaide Prince, actress, Apr. 17, 1895. Began professional career in London, 1882; 1st appearance on Am. stage at Wallack's, New York; has attained success in tragic rôles. Author: The Last of His Race (drama). Part author of The Ragged Cavalier (comedy drama). Died 1910.

CLARKE, Dumont, banker, capitalist; b. Newport, R.I., Oct. 1, 1840; ed. pvt. acad., Newport. Pres. Am. Exch. Nat. Bank; mem. bd. mgrs. Adams Express Co.; trustee Caledonian Ins. Co., Mut. Life Ins. Co., The Mackay Cos., Press Pub. Co.; dir. Del. & Hudson Co., Norfolk & Southern Ry. Co., L.I. R.R. Co., L.I. Consol. Electric Cos., Algoma Central & Hudson Bay Ry. Co., Home Ins. Co., Fidelity & Casualty Co., N.Y., etc. Home: Dumont, N.J. Died 1909.

CLARKE, Edith Emily, librarian; b. Syracuse, N.Y., Nov. 5, 1859; d. Rev. Joseph Morison and Emily (Balis) C.; Ph.B., Syracuse U., 1881; taught in various schs., 1881-87; grad. N.Y. State Library Sch., 1889; unmarried. Chief cataloguer, Columbia U. library, 1889-90; head cataloguer, Newberry Library, Chicago, 1890-94; arranged library of Woman's Bldg., Chicago Expn., 1893; chief of cataloguing, Library of Pub. Documents, Washington, D.C., 1895-98; librarian, U. of Vt., 1898-1909; instr., Library Sch. of Syracuse U., 1910-14, and in library schs. of Riverside and Los Angeles, Calif., 1916. Author: Guide to the Use of United States Government Publications, 1918. Home: Syracuse, N.Y. Died Nov. 22, 1932.

CLARKE, Edmund Arthur Stanley, capitalist; b. Ottawa, Can., Jan. 21, 1862; s. Thomas Curtis and Susan Harriet (Smith) C.; A.B., Harvard, 1884; m. Louisa Hall Ward, Feb. 10, 1890; children—Mrs. Marion Montagu Brown-Serman, Mrs. Louise Bodman. Pres. of Bonzano Rail Joint Co.; v.p. Can. Joint Co. Sec. Am. Iron and Steel Inst., Jan. 1, 1923—. Home: Seabright, N.J. Died May 15, 1931.

CLARKE, Eliot Channing, engr.; b. Boston, May 6, 1845; s. Rev. Dr. James Freeman and Anna (Huidekoper) C.; A.B., Harvard, 1867; studied civ. engring. 1 yr. Mass. Inst. Tech.; m. Alice de Vermandois Sohier, Apr. 4, 1878 (died 1901). Practiced as civ. engr. in different parts of U.S., in connection with building rys., bridges, tunnels, water works and sewerage systems, 1868-86; treas. of cotton mill, 1886-1904. Fellow Am. Acad. Arts and Sciences (treas. 13 yrs.). Author: Report of a Commission Appointed to Consider a General System of Drainage for the Valleys of Mystic, Blackstone and Charles Rivers, 1886 (state publ.); Astronomy from a Dipper, 1909. Home: Boston, Mass. Died May 4, 1921.

CLARKE, Ernest Perley, editor; b. Alna, Me., Dec. 13, 1859; s. John P. and Angie (Perkins) C.; prep. edn., Kents Hill (Me.) Sem.; A.B., Wesleyan U., Conn., 1885, A.M., 1888, LL.D., 1925; m. Louise M. Harvey (M.D.), July 3, 1898. On U.S. Geol. Survey part of 1885; editor Ontario (Calif.) Record, 1885-94; mng. editor Riverside (Calif.) Daily Press, 1894—. Mem. bd. mgrs. Southern Calif. State Hosp., 1898-1913; mem. Calif. State Bd. of Edn., 1913-26, and from 1928; trustee U. of Southern Calif., 1916—; del. to Gen. Conf. Meth. Ch., 1912. Represented Calif. at Conf. of Governors in 1925, conf. of 11 Western states, Salt Lake City, Utah, 1929. Republican. Methodist. Home: Riverside, Calif. Died Sept. 20, 1933.

CLARKE, Francis West, editor; b. Atlanta, Ga., Apr. 7, 1885; s. Col. Edward Young and Nora (Harrison) C.; ed. pvt. tutors and Southern Business U.; also studied voice, piano and pipe organ; m. Laura Belle Burdine, Oct. 14, 1925. Began at 18 as sec. to Hon. Clark Howell, editor and gen. mgr. The Atlanta Constitution; became state news editor same, later city editor, then mng. editor and asst. to gen. mgr. from 1929. Mem. Am. Press Com., under Carnegie Foundation for Internat. Peace, touring Japan, China, Manchuria and Korea, 1929. Presbyn. Home: Atlanta, Ga. Died Feb. 20, 1938.

CLARKE, Frank G., congressman-lawyer; b. Wilton, N.H., Sept. 10, 1850; grad. Dartmouth, 1873; admitted to bar, 1876; began practice at Peterboro; mem. house of representatives of N.H., 1885, 1891 (speaker, 1891); State senator, 1889; col. on mil. staff Gov. Hale, 1885-87; member Congress from 2d N.H. dist., 1897—; present term expiring 1901; Republican; m., Fannie A. Brooks, 1876. Home: Peterboro, N.H. Died 1901.

CLARKE, Frank Wigglesworth, chemist; b. Boston, Mar. 19, 1847; s. Henry Ware and Abby Mason (Fisher) C.; S.B., Lawrence Scientific Sch. (Harvard), 1867; D.Sc., Columbian, 1891, Victoria, Manchester, 1903; LL.D., Aberdeen U., 1906, U. of Cincinnati, 1914; m. Mary P. Olmsted, Sept. 9, 1874. Instr. Cornell, 1869; prof. chemistry, Howard U., Washington, D.C., 1873-74; prof. chemistry and physics, U. of Cincinnati, 1874-83; chief chemist U.S. Geol. Survey and hon. curator minerals, U.S. Nat. Museum, 1883—. Hon. pres. Internat. Com. on Chem. Elements. Chevalier de la Légion d'Honneur; Wilde medallist, Manchester (Eng.) Literary and Philos. Soc., 1903. Mem. Internat. Jury Awards, Paris Expn., 1900. Author: Weights, Measures and Money of All Nations; Elements of Chemistry; Constants of Nature; Report on the Teaching of Chemistry and Physics in the United States, 1881; Elementary Chemistry (with Louis M. Dennis), 1902; Laboratory Manual of Elementary Chemistry (with same), 1902. Home: Washington, D.C. Died May 23, 1931.

CLARKE, George Herbert, univ. prof.; b. Gravesend, Eng., Aug. 27, 1873; s. George Kerry Mitchell and Anne (Mann) C.; came to Can., 1881, U.S., 1896; B.A., McMaster U., Toronto, Can., 1895; M.A., 1896, Litt.D., 1923; unmarried. Editorial journalism at Chicago, 1897-1901; prof. English lit., Mercer U., Ga., 1901-05; lecturer, various summer sessions, Peabody Coll. for Teachers, and prof. Eng. lit., same coll., 1908-11; lecturer summer sch. of the South, Knoxville, Tenn., 6 sessions; summers, Cornell, 1921, 24, U. of Va., 4 summers; asso. prof. English, 1911-12, prof. English, 1912-19, U. of Tenn.; prof. and head Dept. of English, U. of the South, 1919-25; editor of Sewanee Rev., 1919-25; prof. and head Dept. of English, Queen's U., Kingston, Ont., Can., 1925—. Lecturer before various colls. and socs. Mem. staff, War Trade Intelligence Dept., etc., London, Eng., 1916-17. Engaged in travel and lit. work in Europe, 1922-23. Mason. Episcopalian. Author: At the Shrine and Other Poems, 1914; The Hasting Day, 1930. Editor: Bacon's Essays, 1905; Selected Poems of Shelley, 1907; Some Early Letters and Reminiscences of Sidney Lanier, 1907; A Treasury of War Poetry, 1917, 2d series, 1919; Selected Poems of Browning, 1928. Died 1932.

CLARKE, George W., governor; b. Shelby Co., Ind., Oct. 24, 1852; s. John and Eliza J. (Akers) Clarke; moved to Ia. with parents, 1856; A.B., Oskaloosa (Ia.) Coll., 1877; LL.B., law dept., Ia. State U., 1878; LL.D., Drake U., 1916; m. Miss Arletta Greene, June 25, 1878; children—Fred G., Chas. F., Mrs. Portia Van Meter, Mrs. Frances A. Kinnick. Admitted to Ia. bar, 1878; practiced at Adel, Ia.; mem. Ia. Ho. of Rep. 4 terms, Jan. 1900-Jan. 1907 (speaker of House, 1904-07); lt. gov. of Ia., 2 terms, 1909-13, gov. 2 terms, 1913-17; dean Coll. of Law, Drake U., 1917-18; practiced law, Des Moines, 1918-21. Republican. Home: Adel, Ia. Died Nov. 28, 1936.

CLARKE, Helen Archibald, author; b. Phila.; d. Hugh Archibald and Jane M. (Searle) C.; ed. under governesses at pvt. sch., grad. musical dept., U. of Pa.; unmarried. Hon. mem. Boston Browning Soc., New York Browning Soc., Am. Poetry Assn. (v.p.), Poetry Soc. of London (v.p.). Editor: (with Charlotte Porter) Poems of Robert Browning, 2 vols., 1896; The Ring and the Book, 1897; Robert Browning's Complete Poetical Works, 12 vols., 1898; Mrs. Browning's Complete Works, 6 vols., 1900; Shakespeare Studies—Macbeth, 1902; The Pembroke Edition of Shakespeare, 12 vols., 1903. Author: Browning's England; Browning's Italy; "Longfellow's Country"; Guide to Mythology; Ancient Myths in Modern Poets; Hawthorne's Country, 1910; Poets' New England; Browning and His Century. Founder and dir. The Symposium. Home: Boston, Mass. Died Feb. 8, 1926.

CLARKE, Hopewell, mining; b. Williamsport, Pa., Mar. 10, 1854; s. Hopewell and Mary A. (Strebeigh) C.; ed. pub. schs. Dickinson Sem., Wiliamsport, and spl. study in civ. and mining engring.; m. Rosetta Cline, Nov. 18, 1884. Entered engring. dept. Pa. R.R., 1871; engr. for various rys. in Minn., 1880-83; surveyor, land examiner and chief clerk N.P. R.R., 1883-88; land commr. St. Paul & Duluth R.R., 1888-99; then engaged in the development of mines, especially on the Mesabi Iron Range, with which and the settlement of Northern Minn. he was early identified. During controversy over the source of Miss. River made survey of its headwaters; report pub. in Science, 1886. Mason. Home: St. Paul, Minn. Died Feb. 3, 1931.

CLARKE, James Franklin, missionary; b. Buckland, Mass., Jan. 31, 1832; s. Benjamin Franklin and Sarah (Chapin) C.; B.A., Amherst, 1854; B.D., Andover Theol. Sem., 1858; (D.D., Amherst, 1894); m. Isabella Graham Davis, Apr. 14, 1859 (died 1894); 2d, Marion C. Beach, Jan. 16, 1896 (died 1897). Ordained Congl. ministry, 1858; pastor Bridgewater, Vt., 1858-59; missionary A.B.C.F.M., Philippopolis, Turkey, and Bulgaria, Sept., 1859—. Founder, 1860, and trustee Samokove Collegiate and Theol. Inst. Organized over 30 temperance socs. Died July 1916.

CLARKE, James P., senator; b. Yazoo City, Miss., Aug. 18, 1854; s. Walter and Ellen (White) C.; ed. pub. schs., later in acads. Miss.; LL.B., U.of Va., 1878; admitted to bar, 1878; removed to Helena, Ark., 1879; m. Sallie, d. Francis M. Moore, of Helena, Ark., Nov. 10, 1883. In practice, Helena, 1879-97, Little Rock, 1897—; mem. Ark. Ho. of Rep., 1886, 1887, Senate, 1888-92 (pres. 1891, and ex-officio lt. gov.); atty. gen. of Ark., 1893-94; gov., 1895-97; U.S. senator, 1903-09, 1909-15, and 1915-21. Mem. Dem. Nat. Com. Home: Little Rock, Ark. Died Oct. 1, 1916.

CLARKE, John Davenport, congressman; b. Hobart, N.Y., Jan. 15, 1873; s. Capt. W. J. and Emaline (Davenport) C.; Ph.B., Lafayette Coll., 1898; post-grad. work Colorado Coll.; LL.B., Brooklyn Law Sch., 1911; m. Marian Williams, 1905; 1 son, John Duncan. Formerly with Oliver Mining Co. (subsidiary of Carnegie Steel Co.); and asst. to sec. of mines of U.S. Steel Corp.; identified with various mining cos., also practicing lawyer, and farmer. Mem. 67th, 68th, 70th to 72d Congresses (1921-25, 1927-33), 34th N.Y. Dist. Sponsor for Clarke-McNary Bill establishing nat. reforestation policy. Republican. Home: Fraser, N.Y. Died Nov. 5, 1933.

CLARKE, John Mason, geologist; b. Canandaigua, N.Y., Apr. 15, 1857; s. Dr. Noah T. and Laura Mason (Merrill) C.; brother of Lorenzo Mason C.; A.B., Amherst, 1877, A.M., 1882; U. of Göttingen, 1882-84; (Ph.D., Marburg, 1898; LL.D., Amherst, 1902, Johns Hopkins, 1915; Sc.D., Colgate, 1909, U. of Chicago, 1916, and Princeton U., 1919), m. Fannie V. Bosler, 1895. Professor of geology and mineralogy, Smith Coll., 1881-84; lecturer geology, Mass. State Agrl. Coll., 1885-86; asst. N.Y. State paleontologist, 1886; prof. geology and mineralogy, Rensselaer Poly. Inst., 1894—; asst. state geologist, 1894, state paleontologist, 1898-1904, state geologist and paleontologist and dir. State Mus. and Science Dept., U. State of N.Y., 1904—. Hayden gold medal, 1908; gold medal Permanent Wild Life Protection Fund, 1920; wampum keeper of Iroquois Nation; Spindiaroff prize, Internat. Congress of Geologists, Stockholm, 1910. Chmn. geol. com. Nat. Research Council, 1917. Pres. Albany Inst., and Hist. and Art Soc.; trustee Dudley Obs., Schuyler Mansion. Fellow Am. Acad. Arts and Sciences, Geol. Soc. America (pres. 1916-17), Paleontol. Soc. (1st pres.). Mem. Nat. Research Council (chmn. geology); v.p. Nat. Parks Assn.; mem. Nat. Council Boy Scouts America. Author: Sketches of Gaspé; The Magdalen Islands; Heart of Gaspé; The Life of James Hall; Organic Dependence and Disease; L'Ile Percée. Home: Albany, N.Y. Died May 29, 1925.

CLARKE, John Proctor, judge; b. Florence, Italy (of Am. parents), Apr. 23, 1856; s. Isaac Edwards and Mary (Proctor) C.; grad. Yale, 1878; LL.D., 1917; studied law at Northampton, Mass., admitted to Mass. bar, Oct. 1880; m. Sarah M. Parker, June 25, 1884 (dec.); 1 son, Robert Parker; m. 2d, Mrs. Ida Hatch Cambell, July 8, 1924. Asst. U.S. atty., Southern Dist. N.Y., 1881-86; mem. Hascall, Clarke & Vander Poel to Mar. 1, 1895; asst. corp. counsel New York in Mayor Strong's adminstrn. until Jan. 1, 1898; apptd. justice Supreme Ct. of N.Y., 1900; elected, 1901; reëlected by all parties, 1915; assigned to Appellate Div. 1st Department, Oct. 1905; reassigned, Oct. 1910, and Oct. 1915; presiding justice Jan. 1, 1916-Dec. 31, 1926; mem. Clarke and Kresel, 1926-30; apptd. official referee for life, N.Y. Supreme Court, Jan. 1, 1930. Home: Larchmont, N.Y. Died Jan. 12, 1932.

CLARKE, John Sleeper, comedian; b. Baltimore, 1833; made début in Boston, 1851; became a star comedian; later lessee, with Edwin Booth, his brother-in-law, of theatres—at the same time—in Philadelphia, New York and Boston; he went to London, 1867, where for years he was the lessee and manager of the Haymarket Theatre; then sole owner Strand Theatre, London, and Wall Street Theatre, Philadelphia; retired. Died 1899.

CLARKE, John Vaughan, banker; b. Chicago, Oct. 15, 1862; s. John V. and Elizabeth (Bertrand) C.; ed. pub. schs., St. Ignatius and Barnes acads., until 18; m. Bertha English, 1889. Entered Hibernian Bank, 1882, of which his father (who died 1892) was pres.; succeeded his father as pres., 1892. Home: Chicago, Ill. Died 1911.

CLARKE, Joseph Ignatius Constantine, playwright; b. Kingstown, Ireland, July 31, 1846; s. William and Ellen (Quinn) C.; came to U.S., 1868; m. Mary Agnes Cahill, June 18, 1873. On editorial staff New York Herald, 1870-83; mng. editor New York Journal, 1883-95; editor Criterion, 1898-1900; Sunday editor New York Herald, 1903-06; chief of publicity dept. Standard Oil Co., Apr. 1906-July 1913. Dir. Tuinucu Sugar Co. Pres. gen. Am. Irish Hist. Soc., 1913-23; then mem. of exec. council; pres. Nat. Art Theater Society; dir. Am. Dramatists. Plays: Heartsease; (in collaboration) For Bonnie Prince Charlie; The First Violin; Her Majesty; Lady Godiva; Great Plumed Arrow; The Prince of India. Author: Robert Emmet, a Tragedy, 1888; Malmorda, a Metrical Romance, 1893; The Fighting Race and other Poems and Ballads, 1911; Japan at First Hand, 1918; My Life and Memories, 1925. Traveled in Japan and China, 1914, writing descriptive articles for New York Sun. Home: New York, N.Y. Died Feb. 27, 1925.

CLARKE, Rebecca Sophia ("Sophie May"), author; b. Norridgewock, Me., Feb. 22, 1833; d. Asa and Sophie (Bates) C.; ed. Norridgewock, Me.; writer, 1863—. Author: Little Prudy Stories (6 vols.), 1863-65; Dotty Dimple Stories (6 vols.), 1867-69; Little Prudy's Flyaway Series (6 vols.), 1870-73; Quinnebasset Series (6 vols.), 1871-91; Flaxie Frizzle Stories (6 vols.), 1876-84; Little Prudy's Children Series (6 vols.), 1894-1901. Home: Norridgewock, Me. Died 1906.

CLARKE, R(ichard) Floyd, lawyer; b. Columbia, S.C., Oct. 14, 1859; s. Lemuel C. and Caroline B. (Clarkson) C.; A.B., Coll. City of New York, 1880, A.M., 1899; LL.B., cum laude, Columbia, 1882. Mng. clerk, Olcott & Mestre, 1882-83, mem. firm, 1883-84; sr. mem. Clarke & Culver, 1885-1903. Counsel for various large corps. and in matters involving internat. litigation. Author: The Science of Law and Law Making, 1898. Homes: Stony Creek, Conn., and New York, N.Y. Died Sept. 16, 1921.

CLARKE, Richard Henry, lawyer; b. Washington, July 3, 1827; s. Walter and Rachel (Boone) C.; lineal desc. of Robert Clarke, one of the founders of Md., 1634; A.B., Georgetown U., 1846, A.M., 1849 (LL.D., 1872, and St. John's Coll.); m. Ada Semmes, near relative of Admiral Raphael Semmes of C.S.N., 1858. Admitted to bar, 1848; practiced at Washington, 1848-64, New York, 1864—; was asso. with Charles O'Conor in some important cases. Pres. N.Y. Catholic Protectory. Author: Illustrated History of the Catholic Church in the United States; Lives of the American Catholic Bishops; Old and New Lights on Columbus; Life of Pope Leo XIII. Home: New York, N.Y. Deceased.

CLARKE, Robert, publisher; b. Annan, Dumfrieshire, Scotland, May 1, 1829; removed with parents to Cincinnati, O., 1840; ed. in Woodward Coll. there. Founded publishing and bookselling house of Robert Clarke & Co., later The Robert Clarke Co., of which he is pres. Has written on archaeol. and hist. subjects, and edited Col. George Rogers Clarke's Campaign in the Illinois; Pioneer Biographies; etc. Fellow Am. Soc. Adv. Science. Home: Glendale, O. Died 1899.

CLARKE, Samuel Fessenden, college prof.; b. Geneva, Ill., June 4, 1851; s. Samuel Nye and Polly Hooper (Patten) C.; Ph.B., Sheffield Scientific Sch. (Yale), 1878; Ph.D., Johns Hopkins, 1879; A.M., Williams, 1891; asst. to the U.S. Fish Commn., 1874-75; fellow and asst. in biology, Johns Hopkins, 1876-81; m. Elizabeth Crocker Lawrence, Apr. 5, 1892. Lecturer, Smith Coll., 1881; prof. natural history, Williams Coll., 1881-1916, emeritus. Fellow A.A.A.S., Am. Acad. Arts and Sciences. Trustee Marine Biol. Lab., Woods Hole, Mass. Home: Williamstown, Mass. Died Aug. 1, 1928.

CLARKE, Thomas Benedict, art collector; b. New York, Dec. 11, 1848; s. George W. and Mary J. C.; ed. Washington Collegiate Inst., New York; m. Fanny E. Morris, Nov. 14, 1871. Founder of the composition prize at the Nat. Acad. Design. Well known as an art collector and connoisseur. Mem. Chamber of Commerce. Home: New York, N.Y. Died Jan. 18, 1931.

CLARKE, Thomas Shields, sculptor; painter; b. Apr. 25, 1860; s. Charles J. and Louisa (Semple) C.; A.B., Princeton, 1882; studied painting and sculpture at École des Beaux Arts, Paris, and in Rome and Florence, for 11 yrs.; m. Adelaide Knox, 1887. Exhibited works and won many medals at London, Madrid, Berlin, Paris, Chicago Expn., and at expns. of San Francisco and Atlanta, Ga. Has executed many large works in bronze and marble for New York, San Francisco, Chicago and other cities. Pictures in museums of Boston and Phila. A.N.A. Home: Lenox, Mass. Died Nov. 15, 1920.

CLARKE, Walter Irving, editor; b. Pittsfield, Mass., Dec. 30, 1868; s. Thomas Richard and Clarissa Ellen (Clark) C.; grad. high sch., New Brunswick, N.J., 1885; m. Adaline Louise Gardner, June 26, 1890 (died 1925); children—Bruce Addison, Rosemary, Roger Winthrop, Fremont Fairfield, Iris; m. 2d, Mildred Williams Witham, Nov. 24, 1926. Member editorial staff New York World, 1887-89; editor Omaha Bee, 1901, Chicago Chronicle, 1903, Phila. Pub. Ledger, 1904-10, Boston Herald, 1910-12, Boston American, 1913-18; publicity dir. Presbyn. Ch. U.S.A., 1918—. Chmn. Nat. Religious Publicity Council (interdenominational). Republican. Presbyn. Editor Religion and Publicity Manuals, General Assembly Daily News, and Presbyterian Press. Home: Swarthmore, Pa. Died July 5, 1934.

CLARKE, William Fayal, editor; b. near Richmond, Va., May 12, 1855; s. Dr. Dougan and Sarah J. (Bates) C.; parents moved to Ind., 1856; student, Earlham Coll., to senior yr., Litt.D., 1925; m. Katharine Strickland, of Lakewood, Ont., May 28, 1903. On editorial staff St. Nicholas, 1873—; succeeded Frank R. Stockton as asst. editor, 1878, asso. editor, 1893-1905, and became editor-in-chief on the death of Mary Mapes Dodge, 1905; retired from editorship and active work 1927. Home: Scarsdale, N.Y. Died Aug. 23, 1937.

CLARKE, William Hawes Crichton, lawyer; b. Washington, D.C., July 15, 1882; s. William James Patmore and Sarah (Richardson) C.; studied medicine and law George Washington U., LL.D., Oglethorpe U., 1928; m. Elizabeth Macpherson Crichton, June 15, 1905 (divorced 1932); children—Douglas Richardson, James Malcolm; m. 2d, Ruth McNamara Work, Dec. 28, 1937. Admitted to Patent Office Bar, 1902; Supreme Court and Court of Appeals of District of Columbia, 1906; Supreme Court of U.S., 1911; Supreme Court of N.Y., 1913; counsel Kellogg Co. (Battle Creek, Mich.), Iodent Chem. Co., Am. Booksellers Assn., Am. Fair Trade League, Alliance Against Food Frauds, Panama-Pacific Expn. Co., etc.; partner of late Edward Bruce Moore, commr. of patents under Presidents Roosevelt, Taft and Wilson, in firm of Moore & Clarke; ran for Congress, 5th Dist. N.J., 1918; resided in India, 1903-04. Radio commentator; chmn. Assn. for a World Constl. Conv.; chmn. Air Services Memorial Com. Author: Fields of Faith, Ideals and Reals, Creed-Prayer of Spiritual Evolution and of notebooks deposited at Emerson Hall, Harvard U. Home: Mountain Lakes, N.J., and N.Y. City. Died Jan. 2, 1942.

CLARKE, William Horatio, organist; b. Newton, Mass., Mar. 8, 1840; s. Horatio and Elvira (Richards) C.; ed. Dedham, Mass., pub. and high schs.; m. Eliza T. Richardson, Dec. 18, 1861. Was organist from 1856, Boston, Indianapolis, Toronto and Rochester; retired from professional life, 1892. Author: Outline of the Structure of the Pipe Organ. Home: Reading, Mass. Died Dec. 11, 1913.

CLARKE, William Newton, theologian; b. Cazenovia, N.Y., Dec. 2, 1841; s. Rev. William and Urania (Miner) C.; A.B., Madison (now Colgate) U., 1861, A.M., 1863; grad. Hamilton Theol. Sem., 1863; (D.D., Colgate, 1878, Yale, 1900, U. of Chicago, 1901); m. Emily A. Smith, Sept. 1, 1869. Ordained Bapt. ministry, 1863; pastor Keene, N.H., 1863-69, Newton Centre, Mass., 1869-80, Montreal, 1880-83; prof. New Testament interpretation, Toronto Bapt. Coll., 1883-87; pastor Hamilton, N.Y., 1887-90; prof. Christian theology, 1890-1908, ethics and apologetics, 1908—, Colgate U. Author: Outline of Christian Theology, 1898; What Shall We Think of Christianity?, 1899; A Study of Christian Missions, 1900; The Use of the Scriptures in Theology, 1905; The Christian Doctrine of God, 1909. Home: Hamilton, N.Y. Died 1912.

CLARKSON, Coker Fifield, manager and editor; b. Des Moines, Ia., May 11, 1870; s. James S. and Anna (Howell) C.; A.B., Harvard, 1894; Harvard Law Sch., 1894-96; m. Lucy Miller Corkhill, 1898. Admitted to Phila. bar, 1896; practiced with Alexander & Magill, Phila., 1896-98; removed to New York, 1898, and practiced with Tracy, Boardman & Platt, later in own office as tech., corp. and patent atty.; became head of engring. dept. Assn. of Licensed Automobile Mfrs., operating under Selden patent; edit. 2 volumes mech. branch bulls. and reports of tests; inaugurated and edited A.L.A.M. Digest of Current Technical Literature; mgr. and head of publicity deppartment A.L.A.M., 1909; sec. and gen. mgr. Soc. Automotive Engrs., which took over engring. work of A.L.A.M., 1910—. Mem. automotive products sect. of War Industries Bd., Council of Nat. Defense; Internat. Aircraft Standards Bd.; sec. war truck com. Q.M. Dept., U.S. Army, 1917; sec. Soc. Automotive Engrs., ordnance com. Home: Scarborough, N.Y. Died June 4, 1930.

CLARKSON, Grosvenor B.; b. Des Moines, Ia., Sept. 13, 1882; s. James S. and Anna (Howell) C.; ed. De Lancey Sch., Phila., and Berkeley Sch., New York. Reporter for New York Mail and Express, 1901-02, later staff corr. and spl. work; in charge investigation criminal cases, U.S. Interior Dept., 1904-06, Southern Dist. of N.M. (collected all evidence in Tallmadge land fraud cases); on resigning declined one of chief inspectorships of the dept., covering 52 U.S. land offices, and secretaryship of U.S. Embassy in Russia; in gen. and advertising business, New York, 1909-16; asst. to Chmn. Howard E. Coffin, of Com. on Industrial Preparedness, U.S. Naval Consulting Board, which inventoried 27,000 Am. industrial plants for mil. purposes, 1916; in this work also directed first Am. ednl. campaign for industrial preparedness for war; apptd. asst. to dir. U.S. Council of Nat. Defense, Feb. 1917; apptd. sec. Council of Nat. Defense and the Advisory Commn., Mar. 3, 1917; acting dir., July 1918, dir. council, Dec. 1918-Mar. 1, 1920; Sept. 1918; mem. War Risk Bur. Advisory Commn., July 1919—; chmn. Interdepartmental Defense Bd., Nov. 7, 1919-Mar. 1, 1920; sr. fellow and councillor Engring. Economics Foundation. Author: Industrial America in the World War—The Strategy Behind the Lines (introd. by Georges Clémenceau), 1923, 2d edit., 1924. Home: Scarborough-on-Hudson, N.Y. Died Jan. 23, 1937.

CLARKSON, James C., politician; b. Brookville, Ind., May 17, 1842; s. Coker Fifield and Elizabeth (Goudie) C.; ed. pub. schs., Ind. and Ia.; m. Anna Howell, Dec. 26, 1867; father of Coker Fifield C. Established and operated, 1856-62, sta. and 28-mile section on "Underground Railway," and helped over 500 runaway slaves from Mo., Ark. and Tex. into Canada, meeting John Brown in work; editor-in-chief and co-propr., Iowa State Register, Des Moines, 1868-89. Chmn. Ia. Rep. State Com., 1869-71; declined mission to Switzerland, 1869; postmaster, Des Moines, 1871-77; 1st asst. postmaster gen., 1889-90; mem. Rep. Nat. Com., 1880-96 (12 yrs. mem. Exec. Com., 12 yrs. vice chmn., 2 yrs. chmn.); pres. Rep. League U.S., 1891-92; surveyor of customs, New York, 1902-10. Organized and was pres. of the cos. which built the C.,B.&Q. (1874) and Wabash rys. into Des Moines, and also of the Des Moines Northern and Des Moines N.W. rys., 1882-84; pres. N.Y.&N.J. Bridge Co., New York. Home: Tarrytown, N.Y. Died May 31, 1918.

CLARKSON, Richard Perkinhon, journalist; b. Brookville, Ind., 1840; learned printing trade on Brookville American, owned by his father; moved with family to Grundy County, Ia., 1855; printer in office of Des Moines Register several months in 1861; enlisted, Oct. 1861, in Co. A, 12th Ia. inf.; captured at Shiloh, Apr. 6, 1862, and spent 7 months in Confederate prison; returned to regt. and served to end of war; worked on the family farm, 1865-70, when he, with his father, Coker F., and brother, James S. C., bought Iowa State Register; the sons bought the father's interest, 1872; and in 1889 James S. sold his interest to R. P. C., who, with his sons, conducted the paper until its sale, July 1, 1902, to George E. Roberts; m. Aggie Green, Sept. 4, 1867. U.S. pension agt. for Iowa-Neb. dist., Feb. 1, 1903—. Home: Des Moines, Ia. Died 1905.

CLARKSON, W(illiam) Palmer, lawyer, mfr.; b. Essex County, Va., Feb. 13, 1867; s. James L. and Loulie C. (Turner) C.; LL.B., St. Louis Law Sch., 1889; LL.D., Culver-Stockton Coll., 1937; m. Marie Soulard, d. Gen. John W. Turner, of St. Louis, Oct. 18, 1897; children—John Turner, Marie Louise, Palmer. Began practice at St. Louis, 1889; atty. for Mo. Southern R.R. Co., Fidelity and Casualty Ins. Co., Clarkson Sawmill Co., 1889-1902; atty. and sec. Pioneer Cooperage Co., St. Louis, 1902-22, pres., 1922—; pres. Soulard Investment Co., Brown Estate Co. Mem. Bd. of Edn., St. Louis, 1902-10; trustee Christian Coll., National City Christian Ch. (Washington, D.C.); pres. board of trustees Union Av. Christian Ch. (treas. building fund); pres. Christian Board of Publ.; former v.p. St. Louis Ch. Fedn.; mem. met. board dirs. Y.M.C.A. Mem. Christian (Disciples) Ch. Democrat. Home: St. Louis, Mo. Died Dec. 27, 1940.

CLARY, Albert G., commodore U.S. Navy, retired 1874; b. Mass., 1812; apptd. to navy, May 8, 1832; served in Pacific squadron, 1834-36; naval sch., New York, 1837; passed midshipman, July 8, 1839; lt., Apr. 11, 1845; served in Mexican war; comd. U.S.S. Anacostia, Potomac flotilla, 1861; engagement Aquia Creek, May 31, and battle Port Royal, Nov. 7, 1861; comdr., July 16, 1862, in blockade service to end of Civil War; capt., Nov. 21, 1866; commodore, 1873. Died 1902.

CLASSEN, Anton H., pres. Okla. Street Ry.; b. Pekin, Ill., Oct. 18, 1861; s. Anton C.; B.L., U. of Mich., 1887; m. Ella D. Lamb, 1903. Settled in Okla., 1889; active in development of the state and the City of Okla.; pres. Okla. Street & Interurban Ry. Co. (Oklahoma City), The Classen Co., Okla. City Bldg. & Loan Assn. Receiver and register U.S. Land Office, Okla. City, 6 yrs. Republican. Methodist. Mason. Died Dec. 30, 1922.

CLASSON, David Guy, congressman; b. Oconto, Wis., Sept. 27, 1870; s. William J. and Adaline (Legr) C.; LL.B., U. of Wis., 1891; m. Myrtie L. Orr, Apr. 15, 1899; children—Mrs. Abigail Lange, Brooks (dec.), Mrs. Edna Leigh, Mary Orr, Richard Orr, Peggy Lawson. Admitted to Wis. bar, 1891, and began practice in Oconto; mem. Classon & O'Kelliher. County judge of Oconto County, 1894-98; mayor of Oconto, 1898-1900; city atty. 6 yrs.; pres. Bd. Edn. and Bd. Fire Commrs.; mem. 65th to 67th Congresses (1917-23), 9th Wis. Dist.; judge 20th Judicial Circuit, Wis., 1928-30. Republican. Mason. Home: Lena, Wis. Died Sept. 6, 1930.

CLATWORTHY, Linda May, librarian; b. Dayton, O.; d. Rev. Frederick (D.D.) and Emma Crawford (Payne) C.; Denison U. (Ohio), Vassar Coll., Northwestern U.; B.L.S., U. of Ill. Library Sch., 1900; Ph.B., U. of Denver, 1915. Began library work with U. of Pa. Library, and Pub. Library, Evanston, Ill.; with Pub. Library and Mus., Dayton, O., 1900-13, librarian, 1905-13; library organizing in the West, 1914-19; librarian U. of Denver from Sept. 1921. Lecturer library schools, U. of Illinois, Ind. Library Commn. and Lake Chautauqua. Pres. Ohio Library Assn., 1911; chmn. spl. com. on cataloging, 1904-09; mem. Colo. Library Assn. (pres. 1931), A.L.A. (advisory com. on revised edit. list of subject headings for use in dictionary catalogs, 1912; council, 1924-30). Baptist. Joint editor: Bibliography of Food Economy and Bibliography of the Economics of Textiles and Clothing, 1918. Home: Denver, Colo. Died Jan. 15, 1933.

CLAUSE, William Lewis, mfr.; b. Homer, O., Nov. 6, 1858; s. David and Lovina (Andreas) C.; ed. pub. schs., Akron, O.; m. Elizabeth Ann Fish, Apr. 13, 1881; children—Alice Elizabeth (Mrs. Wilson A Campbell), Luella Ruth (Mrs. George Graham Bell), Robert Lewis. With various mfg. cos., Akron, until 1889; sec. Diamond Plate Glass Co., Kokomo, Ind., 1889-95; sales agt., 1895-1905, pres., 1905-16, chmn. bd., 1916—, Pittsburgh Plate Glass Co.; also pres. Columbia Chem. Co., 1899—. Dir. Chamber Commerce U.S., Pittsburgh Chamber Commerce; v.p. Pa. State Chamber Commerce. Trustee U. of Pittsburgh, Grove City Coll., Sewickley Valley Hosp. Assn. Republican. Home: Sewickley, Pa. Died Oct. 7, 1931.

CLAUSSEN, Julia, operatic singer; b. Stockholm, Sweden; studied music, Stockholm and Berlin; m. Capt. Theodore Claussen; children—Sonja Dagmar, Gunborg Julia. Joined Royal Opera, Stockholm, 1903, and mastered nearly all mezzo-soprano and contralto parts in standard operas; prima donna mezzo soprano of Chicago Grand Opera Co., 1912-17, and of Royal Opera, Covent Garden, London, and Théâtre des Champs Elysées, Paris, 1914; became mem. Metropolitan Opera Co., New York, 1917, Ravinia (Ill.) Opera Company, 1927. Became an American citizen, 1920. Court singer to King Gustavus V of Sweden, and decorated with Literis et Artibus. Fellow Royal Acad. Music, Stockholm (Jenny Lind and Christine Nilsson medals). Among principal rôles are Fides in "Le Prophète"; Dalila in "Samson et Dalila"; Anita in "La Navarraise"; Brünnhilde in "Die Walküre"; Kundry in "Parsifal"; Amneris in "Aïda"; Orfeo in Gluck's "Orfeo." Died May 1, 1941.

CLAXTON, Kate, actress; b. Somerville, N.J.; d. Spencer Wallace and Josephine (Martinez) Cone; g.d. Rev. Spencer Houghton Cone; m. Charles A. Stevenson, Mar. 3, 1878. First professional engagement with Miss Lotta, Chicago, 1870; fall of same year joined Augustin Daly's 5th Av. Theatre, New York; became mem. A. M. Palmer's Union Square Theatre, spring of 1872; left Union Sq. Theatre Co. to star in "Conscience," 1876; traveled with own co. until 1904; best remembered for performance in "Frou Frou," "Called Back," "The Double Marriage," "Pauvrette," Ogarita in "The Sea of Ice," and the blind girl in "The Two Orphans." Home: Larchmont Manor, N.Y. Died May 5, 1924.

CLAY, Albert Tobias, orientalist; b. Hanover, Pa., Dec. 4, 1866; s. John Martin and Mary Barbara C.; A.B., Franklin and Marshall Coll., 1889; grad. Mt. Airy Theol. Sem., 1892; Ph.D., of U. of Pa., 1894; (hon. A.M., Yale, 1910; LL.D., Pa. Coll.. 1913, and Litt.D., Muhlenberg Coll., Pa., 1918); m. Elizabeth Sommerville McCafferty, June 11, 1895. Assyrian fellow, 1892-93, instr. Hebrew, 1892-95, U. of Pa.; instr. O.T. theology, Chicago Luth. Sem., 1895-99; instr. in Hebrew, Mt. Airy Theol. Sem., 1905-10; lecturer in Hebrew, Assyrian, and Semitic archæology, 1899-1903, asst. curator Babylonian and Semitic antiquities, 1899-1910, asst. prof. Semitic philology and archæology, 1903-09, prof., 1909-10, U. of Pa.; Laffan prof. Assyriology and Babylonian lit., Yale, 1910—. Curator Yale Babylonian Collection, 1912—; Reinicker lecturer, Episcopal Theological Seminary, Alexandria, Va., 1908; annual prof., Am. Sch. of Oriental Research in Jerusalem, 1919-20. Mem. Archaeol. Inst. America (v.p., 1917—; apptd. to visit Bagdad and arrange for establishment of Sch. of Oriental Research, 1920, 23), Am. Oriental Soc. (librarian 1912—, treas.). Author: Business Documents of Murashu Sons, dated in the reign of Darius II (2 vols.); Documents from Temple Archives of Nippur, dated in the region of Cassite Rulers (3 vols.); Legal and Commercial Transactions, dated in the Assyrian and Neo-Babylonian and Persian Periods; Aramaic Endorsements, O.T. and Semitic Studies, in memory of W. R. Harper; Amurru, the Home of the Northern Semites; Personal Names of the Cassite Period; Business Transactions of the First Millennium B.C.; Legal Documents from Erech, Seleucid Era, Epics, Hymns, Omens and Other Texts, vols. I, II and IV, and II of Babylonian Records in the Library of J. Pierpont Morgan; Miscellaneous Inscriptions in the Yale Babylonian Collection; The Empire of the Amorites; Neo-Babylonian Letters from Erech; A Hebrew Deluge Story in Cuneiform; The Origin of Biblical Traditions; also (with H. V. Hilprecht) Business Documents of Murashu Sons of Nippur, dated in the reign of Artaxerxes I; (with Morris Jastrow, Jr.) An Old Babylonian Version of the Gilgamesh Epic. Home: New Haven, Conn. Died Sept. 14, 1925.

CLAY, Alexander Stephens, senator; b. Cobb County, Ga., Sept. 25, 1853; A.B., Hiawassee Coll., 1875. Admitted to bar, 1877, and began practice at Marietta. Mem. City Council, 1880-82; mem. Gen. Assembly, 1884-87 and 1889-90 (speaker, 1886-87, 1889-90); pres. Ga. Senate, 1892-94; chmn. Dem. State Exec. Com., 1894-97; U.S. senator, 1897-1903, 1903-09, 1909-15. Home: Marietta, Ga. Died 1910.

CLAY, Brutus Junius, diplomat; b. Madison County, Ky., Feb. 20, 1847; s. Cassius Marcellus and Mary Jane (Warfield) C.; C.E., U. of Mich., 1868, M.A., 1918; m. Pattie Amelia Field, Feb. 20, 1872 (dec.); children—Belle Lyman, C. Field, Orville M., Mary N., Charlotte E.; m. 2d, Lalla-R. Fish Marsteller, Jan. 15, 1895. Began in wholesale and retail grocery business at Richmond, Ky., 1868, later conducted cotton plantations in Mississippi and farms in Ky. and Illinois, also mfg. lumber, quarrying, mining, etc.; tendered position of U.S. minister to Argentina, 1897, but declined; U.S. commr. to Paris Expn., 1900; E.E. and M.P. to Switzerland, 1905-10. Life mem. Inst. of Geneva, Switzerland, 1909. Republican. Presbyn. Home: Richmond, Ky. Died June 2, 1932.

CLAY, Cassius Marcellus, lawyer; b. Madison County, Ky., Oct. 19, 1810; grad. Yale, 1832; became abolitionist as result of a speech of William Lloyd Garrison, though his parents were slave-holders; mem. Ky. legislature 3 terms; practiced law in Lexington; in 1845 issued there The True American, an anti-slavery paper. The office was mobbed, but afterward he printed the paper in Cincinnati, but circulated it in Ky.; served with gallantry as officer of vols. in Mexican war; was minister to Russia, 1861-69. Home: White Hall, Ky. Died 1903.

CLAY, Cecil, veteran soldier, U.S. civ. service official; b. Phila., Pa., Feb. 13, 1842; s. Joseph Ashmead and Cornelia (Fletcher) C.; grad. Univ. of Pa., 1859, A.M.; m. Anna Wood Kester, June 8, 1865. Capt. 58th Pa. vols. Feb., 1862; maj. Sept. 30, 1864; lt. col. Nov. 19, 1864; col. Nov. 20, 1864; bvtd. col. and brig. gen. U.S.V.; mustered out Jan. 24, 1866; congressional medal of honor for distinguished bravery at storming of Ft. Harrison, Va., Sept. 29, 1864 (lost right arm and was badly wounded in left hand). Pres. St. Lawrence Boom & Mfg. Co., 1870-79; 1883 to 1903, chief clerk, now gen. agt. U.S. Dept. of Justice. Col. 2d D.C. Nat. Guard, 1887-97. Pres. Bd. Reform Sch., D.C. Home: Washington, D.C. Died 1907.

CLAY, Christopher Field, lawyer; b. Richmond, Ky., Dec. 19, 1874; s. Brutus Junius and Pattie Amelia (Field) C.; student Williams, 1893-94; LL.B., U. of Colo., 1898; m. Elinor Wise, June 1899; 1 dau., Katherine Belle (Mrs. William Covinton Benton). In practice of law at Denver, 1898—; mem. Clay & Benton; pres. Clay Petroleum Co.; counsel and dir. Creede Mines Co.; atty. and dir. Trinity Royalties Co.; counsel Canadian Exploration Co., Frontier Developments Co. Mem. legal advisory bd., Denver, World War. Republican. Mason. Home: Denver, Colo. Died Dec. 6, 1939.

CLAY, John, farming, banking, livestock commn.; b. Winfield, Berwickshire, Scotland, Apr. 24, 1851; s. John and Patricia (Thomson) C.; ed. St. Andrews and Edinburgh U.; m. Euphemia Forrest, 1881 (dec.); m. 2d, Stella Rintoul, 1925; 1 son, John. Came to U.S., 1874, naturalized citizen, 1888. Began farming in Scotland, 1867; mgr. of farm nr. Brantford, Ont., Can., 1879-82; engaged in ranching in the West, livestock commn. and banking; pres. John Clay & Co., livestock commn.; chmn. bd. Stock Growers Nat. Bank, Cheyenne, Wyo. Author: My Life on the Range, 1924; John Clay, a Scottish Farmer, 1908. Home: Chicago, Ill. Died Mar. 17, 1934.

CLAY, Laura; b. Madison County, Ky., Feb. 9, 1849; d. Gen. Cassius Marcellus and Mary Jane (Warfield) C.; ed. pvt. schs., U. of Mich. and Ky. State Coll. Active for many yrs. in club, church, temperance and civ. service reform work, also in promotion of laws for rights of women and children; pres. Ky. Equal Rights Assn., 1888-1910; auditor U.S. Woman Suffrage Assn. 16 yrs. Mem. W.C.T.U. Democrat. Episcopalian. Home: Lexington, Ky. Died June 29, 1941.

CLAY, William Rogers, judge; b. Fayette County, Ky., Nov. 9, 1864; s. Samuel, Jr., and Mary Katherine (Rogers) C.; A.B., Transylvania Univ., 1885, LL.D. from same, 1935; LL.B., Georgetown U., 1888, LL.M., 1889; m. Anne Field Clay, June 14, 1900; children—William Rogers, Sidney Warfield. Admitted to Mo. bar, 1887, and began practice with judge A. H. Waller, as Waller & Clay, Moberly, Mo.; pvt. sec. to U.S. Senator James B. Beck, 1887-90; settled in Lexington, 1890, and formed partnership with Judge M. C. Alford (later lt. gov. of Ky.); supt. schs., Lexington, 1892-1903; city solicitor, 1904-07; commr. Court of Appeals of Ky., 1907-21; judge same court, 1921—, chief justice, 1927-28, 1935-36. Mem. Bd. Arbitration to settle wage dispute between ry. clerks and I.C. RR., 1927, between shopmen and C.&O. Ry., 1923; apptd. mem. com. to report on dispute between train and engine service employees and T.&P. Ry., 1929. Trustee Transylvania U. Democrat. Mem. Ch. of Disciples. Home: Frankfort, Ky. Died Aug. 15, 1938.

CLAYBERG, John Bertrand, lawyer; b. Cuba, Ill., Oct. 8, 1853; s. George and Elizabeth (Baughman) C.; ed. Cuba, Ill.; LL.B., U. of Mich., 1875; m. Katheryn C. Edwards, Sept. 10, 1878. Admitted to bar, 1875; employed by Judge Thomas M. Cooley in works on Taxation and Torts, 1874-76; moved to Mont., 1884, atty. gen. Mont., 1889; non-resident lecturer on mining law and irrigation, U. of Mich., mining law, Columbia, also School of Mines, Mont.; chief commr. of the Supreme Ct. of Mont., 1903-05. Hon. dean Law Dept., U. of Mont., and prof. mining law. Home: San Francisco, Calif. Died May 18, 1921.

CLAYPOLE, Edward Waller, geologist; b. England, June 1, 1835; grad. U. of London, B.A., 1862; B.Sc., 1864; D.Sc., 1888. Has been engaged in teaching for 40 yrs.; now prof. geology and biology, Poly. Inst., Pasadena, Calif.; was for a time on geol. survey of Pa. Author of many papers and essays on geol. and biol. subjects. Mem. geol. socs. of London, Edinburgh and America. Home: Pasadena, Calif. Died 1901.

CLAYTON, Bertram Tracy, army officer; b. Clayton, Ala., Oct. 19, 1862; s. Gen. Henry De Lamar and Victoria Virginia (Hunter) C.; bro. of Henry De Lamar C.; student of U. of Ala., 1880-82; grad. U.S. Mil. Acad., 1886; m. Louise M. Brasher, June 12, 1887; m. 2d, Mary D. Watson, Sept. 2, 1907. Second lt. 11th Inf., July 1, 1886; resigned, May 31, 1888, to enter civil engring. practice at Brooklyn. Adj. 13th Regt. N.G.S.N.Y., 1890; maj. and engr. 2d Brigade, 1894; organized troop C and elected capt., 1896, comdg. same during Spanish-Am. War; in action at Coama, P.R., Aibonito Pass; col. 14th Regt., N.G.S.N.Y., 1899-1901. Mem. 56th Congress (1899-1901), 4th N.Y. Dist. Democrat. Apptd. capt. and q.-m. U.S. Army, Feb. 2, 1901; maj. and q.-m., Mar. 3, 1911. As constructing q.-m. had charge of completing the new riding hall and the erection of the new academic bldg. of the U.S. Mil. Acad., 1911-13; was q.-m. of U.S. troops in Canal Zone to 1917; chief q.-m. 1st Div., 1st Army Corps, A.E.F. in France, 1917—. Died May 30, 1918.

CLAYTON, Henry De Lamar, judge; b. Barbour County, Ala., Feb. 10, 1857; s. Maj. Gen. (C.S.A.) Henry De Lamar and Victoria Virginia (Hunter) C.; A.B., U. of Ala., 1877, LL.B., 1878; m. Virginia Ball

Allen, 1882 (died 1883); m. 2d, Bettie, d. late Samuel M. Davis, Georgetown, Ky., 1910. In practice, Clayton, Ala., 1878-80, Eufaula, Ala., 1880-1914; register in chancery, Barbour County, 1880-84; mem. Ala. Gen. Assembly, 1890-91; presdl. elector, 1888, 1892; mem. Dem. Nat. Com., 1888-1914; U.S. dist. atty. Middle Dist., Ala., 1893-96; mem. 55th to 63d Congresses (1897-1915), 3d Ala. Dist.; resigned from Congress, May 1914; U.S. dist. judge, Middle and Northern Dist. of Ala., May 1914—. Was chmn. Com. on Judiciary, 62d and 63d Congresses; author of The Clayton Act; chmn. Dem. caucus, 60th Congress; permanent chmn. Dem. Nat. Conv., Denver, 1908. Episcopalian. Home: Montgomery, Ala. Died Dec. 21, 1929.

CLAYTON, Powell; b. Bethel, Pa., Aug. 7, 1833; s. John and Ann (Clark) C.; ed. pub. schs. and Partridge Mil. Acad., Bristol, Pa.; studied civ. engring., Wilmington, Del.; went to Kan., 1855. In civ. engring. practice to 1861; city engr. Leavenworth, Kan., 1859-61; capt. 1st Kan. Inf., May 29, 1861; lt. col. 5th Kan. Cav., Dec. 28, 1861; col., Mar. 7, 1862; brig. gen. vols., Aug. 24, 1864; hon. discharged, Aug. 24, 1865; m. Adaline McGraw, Dec. 14, 1865. Purchased and settled upon a plantation near Pine Bluff, Ark., after close of war; removed to Eureka Springs, Ark., 1882, where same yr. built the Eureka Springs Ry.; later built the st. ry. and as chmn. water and sewer boards constructed sewer system and water works there; pres. Crescent Hotel Co., Eureka Springs, and dir. Mo.&N.Ark. Ry. Co. Active in politics from orgn. of Rep. party; mem. State Central Com., Ark., 1867—; mem. Rep. Nat. Com., 1872-1913 (except about 3 yrs.). Gov. of Ark., 1868-71; U.S. senator, 1871-77; attended every Rep. Nat. Conv., 1872-1912; mem. com. of arrangements Rep. Nat. Conv., St. Louis, 1896, and mem. exec. com. Rep. Nat. Com. and chmn. of speaker's bur., at New York, during following campaign; Am. ambassador to Mexico, 1897-1905. Address: Washington, D.C. Died Aug. 25, 1914.

CLAYTON, Victoria Virginia, author; b. near Charleston, S.C., June 10, 1832; d. John L. and Sarah Elizabeth (Bowler) Hunter; ed. Christ's Coll. nr. Macon, Ga.; m. Mr. Clayton, Jan. 9, 1850. Author: White and Black under the Old Regime, 1899. Home: Eufaula, Ala. Died 1908.

CLAYTON, Willis Sherman, banker; b. San Jose, Calif., Oct. 10, 1864; s. James Atkins and Anna (Thomson) C.; Ph.B., U. of the Pacific, 1884; m. Anna A. Bradley, May 15, 1889; children—James Bradley, Willis Sherman. Pres. First Nat. Bank, from 1907, then chmn.; pres. Clayton Investment Co.; sec. Jas. A. Clayton & Co. Republican. Mason. Home: San Jose, Calif. Died Aug. 23, 1940.

CLAYTOR, Thomas Ash, M.D., b. West River, Md., July 14, 1869; s. Richard and Helen (Ash) C.; M.D., Med. Dept., U. of Pa., 1891; interne Germantown Hosp., Phila., 1891-92, Pa. Hosp., 1892-94; m. Helen Niernsée, June 30, 1904; children—Richard, Louise N. Formerly prof. clin. medicine, George Washington Univ.; consulting physician to Garfield Hospital; apptd., 1925, attending specialist internal medicine, U.S. Vets. Hospital No. 32. Actg. asst. surgeon U.S. Army, Spanish-Am. War, 1898, and in World War. Democrat. Episcopalian. Home: Washington, D.C. Died June 4, 1941.

CLEARWATER, Alphonso Trumpbour, judge; b. West Point, N.Y., Sept. 11, 1848; s. Isaac and Emily Baoudoin (Trumpbour) C.; ed. Anthon Grammar Sch., New York, Kingston Acad.; LL.D., Rutgers, 1903, for distinction in pub. service; m. Anna Houghtaling, d. Col. William D. Farrand, of San Francisco, 1875. Admitted to bar, 1871; dist. atty., Ulster County, N.Y., 1877, reëlected, 1880 and 1883; declined nomination for Congress, 1884 and 1886; county judge Ulster County, 1889-98; apptd. justice Supreme Ct. to succeed Alton B. Parker, then elected chief judge Ct. of Appeals. At request of David Dudley Field prepared many of the provisions of the Penal Code and Code of Criminal Procedure of New York; apptd., 1895, commr. to supervise transl. from Dutch into English of the Dutch Records of Ulster County (1661-1684), and completed work, 1898. Many times del. to nat., state and senatorial convs. of Rep. Party; del. Universal Congress Lawyers and Jurists, St. Louis, 1904. Trustee Rutgers Coll., Kingston City Hosp.; probation commr. of N.Y., 1909-10, and from 1913 (v.p., 1919—); pres. State Reservation Commn. of Niagara Falls from 1918; del. at large New York Constl. Conv., 1915. Collector early Am. silver. A founder Holland Soc. (trustee and pres.); hon. life fellow Met. Museum Art; hon. mem. St. Andrew's Soc., Charleston, S.C. Apptd., 1916, mem. State Reservation Commn. of Niagara Falls. Pres. Kingston br. Nat. Security League, 1916; pres. Zoning Bd. of Appeals, Kingston; chmn. "four-minute men," etc. Appointed, 1920, mem. conv. to consider and adopt rules of civil practice in the courts of N.Y.; apptd., 1921, mem. conv. to revise the judiciary article of the Constitution of the State of N.Y. Home: Kingston, N.Y. Died Sept. 23, 1933.

CLEARY, Alfred John, engr.; b. San Francisco, Calif., June 24, 1884; s. Patrick and Julia Agnes (Tarpey) C.; B.A., U. of San Francisco, 1902; B.S., U. of Calif., 1906; m. Marie Alouise Ryan, Mar. 2, 1918; children—Alfred John, Louis Xavier. Cons. engr. for State of Calif. on development of its water resources, 1921-30; chief engr. Construction Co. of N. America, in charge of Hetch Hetchy tunnel, Muscle Shoals analysis and bid, Kennet project, and San Francisco-Oakland Bridge via Rincon Hill; pioneer engring. on Mokelumne River water supply project and American River Reservoir development, in Sacramento-San Joaquin Delta; formerly chief asst. city engr. of San Francisco, and acting city engr.; apptd. city adminstr. of San Francisco, Jan. 8, 1932. Catholic. Author: The Engineering Works of San Francisco, 1915. Home: San Francisco, Calif. Died Feb. 16, 1941.

CLEARY, Peter Joseph Augustine, brig. gen.; b. Malta, N.Y., Nov. 7, 1839; s. Patrick and Laura (Celli) C.; gen. edn. at Queen's U., Ireland; M.D., Royal Coll. Surgeons, London, 1860; m. Sarah M., d. Judge Charles Fleming Keith, of Athens, Tenn., Sept. 28, 1865. Apptd. from N.Y., asst. surgeon U.S.V., Oct. 4, 1862; surgeon U.S.V., Apr. 13, 1863; hon. mustered out, Aug. 10, 1865; asst. surgeon U.S. Army, Oct. 9, 1867; capt. asst. surgeon, Dec. 26, 1867; maj. surgeon, Jan. 30, 1883; lt. col. deputy surgeon gen., Nov. 15, 1897; col. asst. surgeon gen., Feb. 4, 1901; brig. gen., Aug. 6, 1903. Bvtd. lt. col. vols., Aug. 9, 1865, "for faithful and meritorious services." Served during Civil War chiefly with Army of the Cumberland, participating in Chickamauga campaign and siege of Chattanooga; in regular service on Western frontier, Western Tex., Ind. Ty., Colo., Ariz., N.M., etc.; chief surgeon Dept. of Tex., 1896-98, 1900-03, Dept. of the Gulf, 1898-1900; retired at own request, Aug. 7, 1903. Died Nov. 5, 1914.

CLEARY, William E., congressman; b. Ellenville, N.Y.; ed. pub. grammar and high schs.; m. Mary Riley, 1874. Lighterage business, New York, 1879—. V.p. Bay Ridge Hosp., N.Y. Bd. Trade and Transportation. Elected to 65th Congress, Mar. 5, 1918, for unexpired term (1918-19), 8th N.Y. Dist., of Daniel J. Griffin; reëlected to 66th, 68th and 69th Congresses (1919-21, 1923-27), same dist. Mem. N.Y. Chamber of Commerce, Brooklyn Chamber of Commerce. Home: Brooklyn, N.Y. Died Dec. 19, 1932.

CLEAVELAND, Elizabeth Hannah Jocelyn, writer; b. New Haven, Conn.; d. Nathaniel (portrait painter) and Sarah Atwater (Plant) Jocelyn; ed. in boarding sch., New Haven, later pupil of E. A. Andrews of Latin Grammar fame; grad. Chautauqua, class of 1886; m. Rev. James Bradford Cleaveland, Sept. 8, 1852 (died 1889). For many yrs. contbr. of poems to The Congregationalist, New York Observer, etc. Author: No Sects in Heaven and Other Poems, 1868, rev. edit., 1909, limited number edition, 1902. Home: New Haven, Conn. Died 1911.

CLEAVELAND, Livingston Warner, lawyer; b. S. Egremont, Mass., Jan. 31, 1860; s. Rev. James Bradford and Elizabeth Hannah (Jocelyn) C.; lineal desc. of Governor Bradford and John Howland; g.s. Nathaniel Jocelyn, portrait painter, engraver; LL.B., Yale, 1881 (class sec.), M.L., 1888; m. Mrs. Frances (Ferrins) Dowkontt, Apr. 8, 1912. Admitted to bar, 1881; mem. New Haven Bd. of Councilmen, 1891-92, Bd. of Finance, 1891; judge of probate, Dist. of New Haven, 6 terms, 1895-1907; received 158 votes for nomination as gov. of Conn., Rep. State Conv., 1902. Chmn. N.H. County Bar Exam. Com. on Moral Character until 1924; chmn. Selective Service Bd., Div. 1, City of New Haven, 1917. Dir. Union & New Haven Trust Co. Moderator Conn. Congl. Conf., 1905; chmn. State Y.M.C.A., 1910-18 (pres. state conv. 1903, 09, 1913-18); supt. City Mission S.S., 1889-1925; a nat. mgr. Am. S.S. Union. Deacon United (Congl.) Ch., New Haven; mem. Pilgrim Memorial Fund Commn. of 100 apptd. by Nat. Council Congl. Chs. Joint author: Probate Law and Practice of Conn., 1915. Home: New Haven, Conn. Died Mar. 6, 1929.

CLEAVES, Arthur Wordsworth, clergyman; b. Boston, Mass., Mar. 20, 1876; s. Emery and Elizabeth (Groocock) C.; grad. Coburn Classical Inst., Waterville, Me., 1894; A.B., Colby Coll., 1898, D.D., 1920; B.D., Newton Theol. Sem., 1901; m. Mary Elden Nudd, July 17, 1901; children—Emery Nudd, Alfred Sargent, Arthur Bailey, Richard Dalton. Ordained Bapt. ministry, 1901; pastor First Ch., North Scituate, Mass., 1901-06, Newburyport, Mass., 1906-20; on editorial staff Newburyport News and Gloucester Times, 1910-20; editor The Baptist, Chicago, 1920-22; pastor First Ch., Providence, R.I., Sept. 1922—. Trustee Newton Theol. Instn. and mem. various denom. bds.; pres. Am. Bapt. Foreign Mission Soc., 1935-36. Republican. Mason. Home: Providence, R.I. Died Oct. 18, 1940.

CLEAVES, Henry Bradstreet, governor; b. Bridgton, Me., Feb. 6, 1840; s. Thomas and Sophia (Bradstreet) C.; acad. edn.; (hon. A.M., Bowdoin, 1897); pvt. to 1st lt. U.S.V., 1862-65. Admitted to bar, 1868; practiced at Bath, Me., 1868-69, Portland from 1869. Mem. Me. Ho. of Rep., 1876-77; city solicitor, Portland, 1877-79; atty. gen. of Me., 1880-85; gov., 1893-97. Republican. Home: Portland, Me. Died June 22, 1912.

CLEBORNE, Christopher James, naval officer; b. Edinburgh, Scotland, Dec. 16, 1838; grad. Univ. of Pa., 1860. Apptd. from Pa., asst. surgeon U.S. Navy, May 9, 1861; promoted past asst. surgeon, Oct. 26, 1863; surgeon, Nov. 24, 1863; med. insp., Jan. 7, 1878; med. dir., Sept. 18, 1887; retired with rank of rear admiral, Nov. 10, 1899. During Civil War attached to various ships and participated in destruction of the Alvarado, Aug. 5, 1861, expdn. to Stono River; operations off Mobile, both attacks on Ft. Fisher, etc. Judge advocate Naval Retiring Bd., 1865, 1867; served in European Squadron, 1872-74; Naval Sta., Portsmouth, N.H., 1875-78, 1881-84; fleet surgeon N. Atlantic Squadron, 1879-81; mem. Med. Examining Bd., 1884-87; dir. naval hosps., Norfolk, Va., 1888-91, Chelsea, Mass., 1891-94, Norfolk, Va., 1894-99, Phila., Jan.-Nov. 1899. Home: Washington, D.C. Died 1909.

CLEEMANN, Richard Alsop, physician; b. Phila., Pa., Feb. 22, 1840; s. G. B. C. and Claramond (Colquhoun) C.; A.B., U. of Pa., 1859, A.M., M.D., 1862; unmarried. Resident phys. Hosp. of P.E. Ch., 1862; acting asst. surgeon U.S. Army, 1862-64; phys. St. Mary's Hosp., 1872-79; mem. bd. health, Phila., 1879-87; dir. Charities and Corrections, Phila., 1887-92; mem. (became pres.) State Quarantine Bd. of Pa., 1893—; mem. bd. mgrs. Pa. Instn. for Instruction of Blind. Fellow Coll. of Phys. Phila. Home: Philadelphia, Pa. Died 1912.

CLEGG, Moses Tran, bacteriologist; b. Red Bluff, Ark., Sept. 1, 1876; s. Joseph Thomas and Ida Neal (Daugherty) C.; Siloam Springs (Ark.) High Sch.; U. of Ark., 1892, 93, 96; m. Edna Wisner, July 26, 1911. Mem. U.S. Army Hospital Corps, Mar. 31, 1899-Apr. 1, 1902, serving through Philippine insurrection; asst. bacteriologist in Bureau of Science, Philippine Civ. Service, Apr. 2, 1902-Sept. 1910; in U.S. Pub. Health and Marine Hosp. Service as asst. dir. U.S. Leprosy Investigation Sta., Hawaii, 1910-15; bacteriologist, U.S. Public Health Service, San Francisco, 1916-17; supt. Queen's Hosp., Honolulu, H.T., 1918—. Mason. Died Aug. 9, 1918.

CLELAND, Herdman Fitzgerald, prof. geology; b. Milan, Ill., July 13, 1869; s. David James and Margaret (Betty) C.; Gates Coll., Neligh, Neb.; B.A., Oberlin, 1894; Ph.D., Yale, 1900; post-grad. work, U. of Neb., 1895, U. of Chicago, 1896, Cornell U., 1901; m. Helen Williams Davison, 1910; children—Margaret Jane, Elizabeth Davison; m. 2d, Emily Leonard Wadsworth, 1925. Asst. in geology, Cornell U., 1900-01; instr. in geology and botany, 1901-04; asst. prof. geology and mineralogy, Williams, 1905-07, prof. geology from 1907; instr., Cornell Summer Sch., 1900-02, U. of Tenn. Summer Sch., 1904. Mem. Internat. Geol. Congress, Mexico, Belgium and Spain; Internat. Geog. Congress, Geneva, Switzerland. Author: Fossils and Stratigraphy of the Middle Devonic of Wisconsin, 1911; Physical and Historical Geology (2 vols.), 1917; Practical Applications of Geology and Physiography, 1920; Our Prehistoric Ancestors, 1928; Why Be an Evolutionist, 1930. Home: Williamstown, Mass. Died Jan. 24, 1935.

CLELAND, McKenzie, lawyer, lecturer; b. Delhi, N.Y., Oct. 8, 1860; s. William J. and Judith (Wilson) C.; A.M., Monmouth (Ill.) Coll., 1882 (LL.D., 1911); LL.B., Washington U., St. Louis, 1884; m. Mary L. Norton, June 16, 1887. Admitted to bar, June 15, 1884; mem. Phelps & Cleland, 1897-1906; judge Municipal Court of Chicago, 1906-10; mem. Cleland, Lee & Phelps, 1911—. Dir. and v.p. Moody Bible Inst. United Presbyn. Republican. Pres. Nat. Probation League, Mother's Pension League, Anti-Revolver League America; Am. pres. Berean Band; dir. Family Altar League; pres. Englewood (Ill.) Y.M.C.A. 6 yrs. Author of 1st mothers' pension law; founder Chicago "Parting of the Ways." Home: Chicago, Ill. Died Feb. 12, 1924.

CLELAND, Thomas Hann, clergyman; b. Woodford County, Ky., Mar. 31, 1843; s. John W. and Emily M. (Taylor) C.; A.B., Centre Coll., Ky., 1863; grad. Princeton Theol. Sem., 1866; (D.D., U. of Wooster, 1880); m. Louise Mitchell, Oct. 24, 1866 (died 1911). Ordained Presbyn. ministry, 1867; pastor, Council Bluffs, Ia., 1866-82, Keokuk, Ia., 1882-88, Springfield, Mo., 1888-94, First Ch., Duluth, Minn., 1894-1906; dist. sec. for northwest of Am. Tract Soc., 1906-08; pastor Third Ch., New Albany, Ind., 1908-13, Knox Church, Minneapolis, Feb. 1913—. One of founders Parsons Coll., Fairfield, Ia., and Corning (Ia.) Acad.; dir. McCormick Theol. Sem., Chicago, 25 yrs.; trustee Macalester Coll., St. Paul; charter mem. Bd. of Aid for Colls. and Acads. Presbyn. Ch., Chicago. Moderator Presbyn. Synod Minn., 1903-04; pres. annual session of Presbyn. Ministers' Fund, Phila., Jan. 23, 1905. Home: Minneapolis, Minn. Died Aug. 26, 1916.

CLEM, John Lincoln, army officer; b. Newark, O., Aug. 13, 1851; s. of Roman and Mary (Weber) C.; grad. Arty. School, Ft. Monroe, Va., 1875; m. Anita Rossetta, d. General W. H. French, U.S. Army, May 24, 1875 (died 1899); m. 2d, Bessie, d. Daniel Sullivan, of San Antonio, Tex., Sept. 23, 1903; children—John L., Anne E. Attempted to enlist as drummer in 3d Ohio and 22d Mich. vols., May 1861, but was rejected on account of youth; enlisted as drummer, 22d Michigan Inf., May 1, 1862; promoted sergt. at battle of Chickamauga, Sept. 20, 1863; apptd. 2d lt. 24th U.S. Inf., Dec. 18, 1871; promoted through grades to brig. gen., Aug. 13, 1915, retired as maj. gen., Aug. 29, 1916. Chmn. Fredericksburg-Spottsylvania Battle Grounds Commn. With Army of Cumberland, Civil War, and participated in battles of Shiloh, Chickamauga, Perryville, Stone River, Resaca, Kenesaw, Atlanta, Nashville, etc. Chief q.-m. Philippine Div., 1903-06, Dept. of Tex., 1906-11, Dept. of the Lakes, Chicago, 1911-15. Republican. Catholic. Home: San Antonio, Tex. Died May 13, 1937.

CLEMENS, Charles Edwin, prof. music; b. Plymouth, Eng., Mar. 12, 1858; s. Philip Blake and Hannah Theresa (Brown) C.; ed. Royal Coll. of Music, London, Eng.; Mus.D., Western Reserve U., 1915; m. Mrs. Alice Lepehne, of London, Oct. 29, 1896. Played the organ publicly at 8 and at 11 won, in competition, position of organist in Christ Ch., Devonport; official organist of the Royal Chapel, Berlin, and prof. of organ and theory of music, Klindworth-Scharwenka Conservatorium, 1889-96; organist St. Paul's Episcopal Ch., Cleveland, 1896-1911, Euclid Av. Presbyn. Ch. (now Ch. of the Covenant), 1911-27; prof. music and organist Western Reserve U., 1899—. Concert organist; gave recitals at Buffalo and St. Louis expns. Author: Modern Progressive Pedal Technique (2 vols.), 1894; Modern School for the Organ, 1907. Home: Cleveland, O. Died Dec. 27, 1933.

CLEMENS, Samuel Langhorne ("Mark Twain"), author, humorist; b. Florida, Mo., Nov. 30, 1835; s. John Marshall and Jane (Lampton) C.; ed. common schs., Hannibal, Mo.; (hon. M.A., Yale, 1888, Litt.D., 1901; LL.D., U. of Mo., 1902; Litt.D., Oxford, Eng., 1907); apprenticed to printer at 12; short time was Mississippi River pilot; became, 1861, pvt. sec. to his brother (apptd. territorial sec., Nev.); m. Olivia L. Langdon (died at Florence, Italy, June 5, 1904.) City editor Virginia City (Nev.) Enterprise, 1862; alternated between mining and newspaper work until, becoming noted as a humorist, he began lecturing and writing books; founded, 1884, pub. house of C. L. Webster & Co., failure of which involved him in heavy losses; its debts have been paid by proceeds of lectures and books; has traveled extensively. Mem. Am. Acad. Arts and Letters. Author: The Jumping Frog, 1867; The Innocents Abroad, 1869; Autobiography and First Romance, 1871; The Gilded Age, 1873 (with late C. D. Warner); Roughing It, 1872; Sketches New and Old, 1873; Adventures of Tom Sawyer, 1876; Punch Brothers, Punch, 1878; A Tramp Abroad, 1880; The Prince and the Pauper, 1880; The Stolen White Elephant, 1882; Life on the Mississippi, 1883; The Adventures of Huckleberry Finn, 1885; A Yankee at the Court of King Arthur, 1889; The American Claimant, 1892; Merry Tales, 1892; The £1,000,000 Bank Note, 1893; Puddinhead Wilson, 1894; Tom Sawyer Abroad, 1894; Joan of Arc, 1896; Following the Equator, 1898; The Man That Corrupted Hadleyburg, 1900; A Double-Barreled Detective Story, 1902; Articles on Christian Science, 1903; A Dog's Tale, 1903; Eve's Diary, 1905; A Horse's Tale, 1906; The $30,000 Bequest, 1906; Christian Science, 1907; Autobiography of Mark Twain (appearing serially); Captain Stormfield's Visit to Heaven. 1908. Home: "Stormfield," Redding, Conn. Died 1910.

CLEMENS, William Marshall, editor, pub.; b. Louisville, Ky., Apr. 30, 1876; s. John Marshall (M.D.), and Ella Virginia (Robinson) C.; grad. Louisville Male High Sch., 1891; student Center Coll., Danville, Ky.; m. Cora Genevieve Wolfe, Nov. 27, 1901. Began as reporter Louisville Courier Journal and Times, 1895; city editor Cincinnati Post, 1904; news editor Indianapolis Sentinel, 1905; mng. editor Memphis News-Scimitar, 1906, Birmingham News, 1912; editor Mobile Item, 1915; mgr. Mobile Chamber Commerce, 1916; mng. editor Atlanta Georgian, 1920, Knoxville Journal, 1922; asst. to publisher of Gannett Newspapers, 1925-28; editor and mgr. Flushing (L.I.) Journal, 1929-31. Served as pvt. and sergt. 1st Ky. U.S. Vol. Inf., Spanish-Am. War, 1898; later adj. 1st Ky. N.G.; branch officer Emergency Fleet Corp., 1917-19. Presbyn. Mason. Home: Lexington, Ky. Died Nov. 23, 1932.

CLEMENS, William Montgomery, author, genealogist; b. Paris, O., Jan. 16, 1860; s. John (Cameron) and Sarah Elizabeth (Flickinger) C.; ed. Akron (O.) High Sch. and Buchtel Coll.; m. Rosa A. Garfield, Aug. 11, 1881 (died 1886); children—Rhea, Nina (dec.); m. 2d, Kate Fowler Lott, June 28, 1887 (died 1900); children—Marian, Florence. On staff Pittsburgh Leader, 1879, Pittsburgh Dispatch, 1880, Cleveland Plain Dealer, 1882, Los Angeles Tribune, 1889, San Francisco Chronicle, 1890-94; criminologist New York World, 1907-08. Revision editor Ridpath's Library Universal Literature, 1905; editorial staff Ency. Americana, 1903-04; founder Literary Life, Chicago, 1884, and Genealogy Magazine, New York, 1912. Author: Life of Mark Twain, 1891; Life of Theodore Roosevelt, 1898; Life of Admiral Dewey, 1898; The

Clemens Chronology, 1913; Ancestry of Mary Baker Eddy, 1924; American Marriage Records Before 1699, 1926; North and South Carolina Marriage Records from Colonial Days to the Civil War, 1927. Historian and genealogist Clemens, Cameron and Montgomery families. Editor and founder of the Biblio Magazine, 1921. Home: Somerset, Bermuda. Died Nov. 25, 1931.

CLEMENT, Charles Maxwell, army officer; b. Sunbury, Pa., Oct. 28, 1855; s. John Kay and Mary S. (Zeigler) C.; ed. Sunbury and Klinesgrove acads. and at mil. acad., Burlington, N.J.; m. Alice Virginia Withington, Nov. 19, 1879. Began practice in Sunbury, 1878; deputy sec. Commonwealth of Pennsylvania, 1890-91; sec., later chmn. Rep. County Com. Northumberland County, 1879-88. Enlisted as pvt. Co. E, 8th Inf. N.G. Pa., Sept. 3, 1877; 1st lt., May 6, 1878; advanced through grades to maj. gen., Pa. Div., Dec. 22, 1915; retired, Apr. 1, 1919; maj. gen. N.A., Aug. 5, 1917. Served as lt. col. 12th Inf., Spanish-Am. War, 1898; maj. gen. 7th Pa. Div., Mexican border, 1916-17; comdg. 28th Div., Camp Hancock, Ga., Aug. 1917; hon. disch. Dec. 11, 1917. Republican. Episcopalian. Mason. Home: Sunbury, Pa. Died Sept. 9, 1934.

CLEMENT, Clay, actor, playwright; b. Green Tp., Ill., Dec. 21, 1863; s. Christian and Sarah (Young) Geiger; ed. El Paso, Ill.; grad. prep. dept. U. of Chicago, 1892, undergrad. U. of Chicago, class of 1897; read law in Chicago with Judge W. L. Snell 1 yr.; actor, 1884—; m. Matti E. Marshall, July 4, 1888 (died 1896); m. 2d, Kathleen Kerrigan, Sept. 5, 1906. Author: (plays) The New Dominion, 1894; A Southern Gentleman, 1897; Ping Pong, 1902. Dramatized, In Hampton Roads, 1904; Sam Houston (with John McGovern and Jesse Edson), 1906. Died 1910.

CLEMENT, Edmond, tenor singer; b. Paris, France, 1871; s. Georges and Souveraine (Baume) C.; ed. Polytechnic, Chartes and Conservatoire, Paris, under Prof. Warot; m. Lea Borel, of Paris, 1894. Made début in Gounod's "Mireille"; identified with the Opera Comique, Paris, many yrs.; has sung in leading cities of Europe and America; became mem. Metropolitan Opera Co., New York, 1909; most popular rôle, Don José in "Carmen." Chevalier Legion d'Honneur. Home: Paris, France. Died Feb. 22, 1928.

CLEMENT, Edward Henry, journalist; b. Chelsea, Mass., Apr. 19, 1843; s. Cyrus and Rebecca Fiske (Shortridge) C.; A.B., Tufts, 1864, A.M., 1875 (Litt.D., 1904); m. Gertrude Pound, 1869 (died 1895); m. 2d, Josephine Hill Russell, Mar. 20, 1898. Editor Savannah Daily News, 1865-67; brief engagements on Boston papers; night editor and city editor N.Y. Tribune during John Russell Young's editorship, 1867-69; mng. editor Newark Daily Advertiser, 1869-72; propr. Elizabeth Daily Journal, 1873-75; asst. editor, 1875-81, editor-in-chief, 1881-1906, Boston Transcript. Home: Concord, Mass. Died Feb. 7, 1920.

CLEMENT, Ernest Wilson, teacher, author; b. Dubuque, Ia., Feb. 21, 1860; s. Jesse and Lucetta H. (Blood) C.; A.B., U. of Chicago, 1880, A.M., 1883; m. Nellie Hall, Aug. 26, 1887; children—Mrs. Ione Clarke, Mrs. Ruth Hoyer, Edward Jesse. Teacher Atlanta (Ga.) Bapt. Sem., 1881-82, Burlington (Ia.) Collegiate Inst., 1882-84, Wayland Acad., Beaver Dam, Wis., 1884-87, High Sch., Mito, Japan, 1887-91, Hyde Park High Sch. and Kenwood Inst., Chicago, 1891-94; prin. Duncan Acad., Tokyo, Japan, 1894-1911; teacher First Higher Sch., Tokyo, 1911-27. Acting interpreter, U.S. legation, Tokyo, 1896-97, 1906-07; librarian, Asiatic Soc. of Japan, 1896-1900 and 1911-15, recording sec., 1907-09, v.p., 1916-21; editor of the Japan Evangelist, 1899-1909; editor Christian Movement in Japan, 1907-09; spl. corr. Chicago Daily News, 1895-1920. Baptist. Author: A Handbook of Modern Japan, 1903; Japanese Floral Calendar, 1904; Christianity in Modern Japan, 1905; Hildreth's Japan as It Was and Is (rev. edit.), 1906; Short History of Japan, 1915. Decorated Fifth Class of Rising Sun (Japan), 1927. Home: Floral Park, N.Y. Died Mar. 11, 1941.

CLEMENT, George Clinton, bishop; b. Mocksville, N.C., Dec. 23, 1871; s. Albert Turner and Eveleanor (Carter) C.; B.A., Livingstone Coll., Salisbury, N.C., 1898, M.A., 1904, D.D., 1906; LL.D., Wilberforce U., 1929; m. Emma Clarissa Williams, May 25, 1898; children—Abby Evelyn, Rufus Early, Frederick Albert, John Clinton (dec.), Ruth Elizabeth, George Williams, James Addison, Emma Mills. Ordained A.M.E. Zion ministry, 1893; pastor in N.C. at Cleveland, 1894, Zebu, 1895-97, China Grove, 1897-98, Charlotte, 1898-99, Salisbury, 1899-1900, and Louisville, Ky., 1900-04; editor Star of Zion, 1904-16; mgr. A.M.E. Zion Publn. House, 1914-16; elected bishop, May 1916, in charge 3d Dist. Trustee A.M.E. Zion Publn. House, Livingstone Coll., Atkinson Coll. Mem. exec. com. and chmn. commn. Church and Race Relations, Fed. Council of Churches; mem. exec. com. Meth. Ecumenical Council. Del. to Ecumenical Conf. on Methodism, Toronto, 1911, London, 1921, Atlanta, 1931. Mem. Commn. on Interracial Relations. Assn. Study of Negro Life and History. Democrat. Mason. Author: Boards for Life's Building, 1925. Home: Louisville, Ky. Died Oct. 23, 1934.

CLEMENT, Percival Wood, governor; b. Rutland, Vt., July 7, 1846; s. Charles and Elizabeth (Wood) C.; student Trinity Coll., Hartford, Conn., 1864-68; m. Maria H. Goodwin, 1868. Clk. and partner Clement & Sons, marble quarries, 1871-76; engaged in banking, 1876; pres. Rutland R.R. Co., 1882-1902; pres. Bristol R.R. Co. Owner Rutland Herald. Mayor of Rutland, 1897-99, 1911-12; mem. Vt. Ho. of Rep., 1892, Vt. Senate, 1900-02, 1911-12; gov. of Vt., 1919-20, inclusive. Republican. Home: Rutland, Vt. Died Jan. 9, 1927.

CLEMENT, Stephen Merrell, banker; b. Fredonia, N.Y., Nov. 4, 1859; s. Stephen Malory and Sara Elizabeth (Leonard) C.; A.B., Yale, 1882; m. Caroline Jennette Tripp, Mar. 27, 1884. Pres. Marine Nat. Bank, Buffalo, Buffalo Steamship Co.; v.p. Rogers Brown Iron Co.; dir. Ont. Power Co., Great Southern Lumber Co., New Orleans Gt. Northern R.R. Pres. Buffalo Clearing House. Mem. S.A.R. Home: Buffalo, N.Y. Died Mar. 26, 1913.

CLEMENTS, Courtland Cushing, lawyer; b. Blooming Grove, Ind., Mar. 26, 1843; s. James Morris and Catherine (Ferris) C.; ed. pub. sch., New Castle, Ind., and U.S. Naval Acad.; m. Ella, d. Gen. William Grose, of New Castle, Aug. 26, 1868. Midshipman, U.S. Navy, 1860-63; acting receiver, U.S. Land Office, Colo., 1864-68; register, U.S. Land Office, Utah, 1868-69; U.S. surveyor gen., Utah., 1869-74. Admitted to bar, 1865; in practice at Washington from 1880. Republican. Methodist. Home: Washington, D.C. Died Oct. 19, 1933.

CLEMENTS, Edward Bates, Republican Nat. Committeeman; b. Washington, D.C., May 10, 1861; s. John Thomas and Mary Sophia (Brush) C.; prep. edn., St. James Acad., Macon, and Bryant & Stratton Bus. Coll., St. Joseph, Mo.; M.D., Howard U., 1881; m. Elizabeth Barclay (died 1921). Practiced at Macon, Mo., 1881-1921. Was mem. city council and mayor, Macon; later mem. Mo. Ho. of Rep.; mem. Rep. State Com., Mo., from 1903, formerly chmn.; mem. Rep. Nat. Com., 1924—. Mason. Home: Macon, Mo. Died June 19, 1935.

CLEMENTS, Judson C., interstate commerce commissioner; b. Walker County, Ga., Feb. 12, 1846; ed. pvt. sch. and acad. Pvt. and 1st lt. in C.S.A., 1864-65; law student Cumberland U., 1868; admitted to bar, 1869; m. Lizzie E. Dulaney, Dec. 2, 1886. In practice, LaFayette, Ga., 1869-92; county sch. commr., Walker County, 1871; mem. Ga. Ho. of Rep., 1872-76, Senate, 1877; mem. 47th to 51st Congresses (1881-91), 7th Ga. Dist.; mem. U.S. Interstate Commerce Commn., Mar. 1892—. Democrat. Home: Rome, Ga. Died June 18, 1917.

CLEMENTS, Newton N., mcht.; b. Tuscaloosa County, Ala., Dec. 23, 1837. Mem. Ala. legislature, 1870-78, twice speaker; mem. Congress, 1878-80; candidate for gov., Ala., 1900. Home: Tuscaloosa, Ala. Died 1900.

CLEMENTS, Robert, theologian; b. Schenectady, N.Y., July 19, 1869; s. John and Anna Neish (Harvey) C.; grad. Union Classical Inst., Schenectady, 1886; A.B., Union Coll., Schenectady, 1891; grad. Auburn Theol. Sem., 1894; D.D., Parsons Coll., 1921; D.D., Union Coll., 1931; m. Edith Louise Winnett, Dec. 4, 1900 (died 1931); children—Ellen North (Mrs. Chester W. Hamblin), John. Ordained ministry Presbyn. Ch., 1894; pastor Cuba, N.Y., 1894-1900, First Ch., Cortland, N.Y., 1900-07, First Ch., Erie, Pa., 1907-20, Austin Ch., Chicago, 1920-28; prof. pastoral theology and polity, Presbyn. Theol. Sem. (formerly McCormick Theol. Sem.), 1928—; Pres. Bd. of Ch. Extension of Presbytery of Chicago; pres. Chicago Ch. Fedn. With Y.M.C.A. World War. Republican. Mason. Home: Chicago, Ill. Died Apr. 1, 1936.

CLEMENTS, William Lawrence, mfr.; b. Ann Arbor, Mich., Apr. 1, 1861; s. James and Agnes (Macready) C.; B.S., U. of Mich., 1882; m. Jessie N. Young, Feb. 7, 1887; m. 2d, F. Katharine Fisher, Apr. 22, 1931. Mfg. business, Bay City, Mich., 1887-1924 (retired); pres. Industrial Works, 1898-1924. Regent University of Mich., 1909-33. Republican. Founder William L. Clements Library, U. of Mich., and donor of library and building. Home: Bay City, Mich. Died Nov. 6, 1934.

CLEMONS, Charles Frederic, judge; b. Manchester, Vt., Oct. 9, 1871; s. Seneca Sherman C. (M.D.) and Anna (Danforth) C.; B.A., Yale, 1895; LL.B., Nat. U. Law Sch., Washington, 1898, LL.M., 1899; m. Virginia Armstrong Patten, Sept. 10, 1902. Editorial bd. Yale News, 1894-95; chmn. Yale Law Journal, 1897-98; admitted to Conn. bar, 1898; practiced at Butte, Mont., 1900-1901, Honolulu, H.T., from 1902. Sec. Commn. to Revise Laws of Hawaii, 1904-05; U.S. dist. judge, Dist. H.T., 1911-17 (resigned). Republican. Mem. commn. to revise laws of Hawaii, revision of 1915, 1913-15. Chancellor P.E. Diocese H.T., 1907-11; dir. Honolulu Y.M.C.A., 1913-23; dir. P.E. Ch. in Hawaiian Islands. Died Sept. 17, 1925.

CLENDENIN, Frank Montrose, clergyman; b. Washington, D.C., Sept. 17, 1853; s. George and Charlotte

(Humphreys) C.; Princeton Univ., 1879 (S.T.D., Nashotah, 1893); m. Gabrielle, d. late Horace Greeley, of New York, Apr. 23, 1891. Former Presbyterian minister; deacon P.E. Ch., 1880; rector St. George's Ch., Belleville, Ill., 1880-83, Grace Ch., Cleveland, O., 1883-87, St. Peter's Ch., Westchester, N.Y. City, 1887-1917. A leader in municipal battle of 5 yrs., resulting in annexing Westchester to N.Y. City. Author: Idols by the Sea, and Other Sermons; The Name of the Church; The Comfort of the Catholic Faith. Home: Chappaqua, N.Y. Died Aug. 19, 1930.

CLENDENIN, Henry Wilson, editor; b. Schellsburg, Pa., Aug. 1, 1837; s. Samuel Miller and Elizabeth (Henry) C.; ed. pvt. schs. and tutors; m. Mary E. Morey, Oct. 23, 1877; children—Harry Francis, George Morey, Clarence Rees, Mrs. Marie Etta Ghering. Pvt. Co. I, 20th Pa. Vol. Inf. during Civil War. Began newspaper work on Burlington (Ia.) Hawkeye, 1852; afterward with various papers; editor and part owner Keokuk (Ia.) Constitution, 1876-81; editor and part owner from 1881, pres. corp. from 1887, Ill. State Register. Mem. Dem. State Com., Ill., 1884-88. Postmaster Springfield, 1886-90. Mem. bd. dirs. Lincoln Pub. Library, Springfield. Conglist. Home: Springfield, Ill. Died July 18, 1927.

CLEPHANE, James Ogilvie, lawyer, financier; b. Washington, D.C., Feb. 21, 1842; s. James and Ann (Ogilvie) C.; m. Pauline M. Harrison, Oct. 9, 1867. In early life became interested in the typewriter and other inventions, and expended much capital in their development; under his direction the first Sholes or Remington typewriter was built; brought C. T. Moore from W.Va. in 1871 and had him construct the Moore Typewriter and Linomatrix machine, of which companies he became officer and dir.; these cos. were subsequently merged with the Am. Planograph Co., of which he became v.p. and dir.; suggested to Mr. Ottmar Mergenthaler the idea of a typesetting machine and furnished the means whereby was evolved the present successful linotype machine. Later was assisted by Whitelaw Reid, William C. Whitney and Ogden Mills; organized Am. Graphophone Co. to develop invention of the graphophone of Profs. Graham Bell and Summer Tainter; also organizer and pres. Horton Basket Machine Co., the Locke Steel Belt Co., and the Aurora Mining Co.; pres. Oddur Mfg. Co. Home: Englewood, N.J. Died 1910.

CLEVELAND, Abner Coburn, cattleman, miner, politician; b. Me., Nov. 17, 1839; ed. public schs. in Me. till 1857; m. Kate M. Peters, Jan. 19, 1868. Mem. Nev. legislature, 1869; State senate, 1870-74; commr. to Washington to settle territorial indebtedness, 1871; presdl. elector, 1888 and 1892; candidate for gov., 1894; delegate Rep. Nat. Conv., 1892, 1896; left conv. with silver Reps., 1896; independent candidate U.S. senate, 1898; stumped the state for Republican ticket, 1900. Rep. nominee for gov. Nev., 1902; defeated by John Sparks, fusion candidate. Home: Cleveland, Nev. Died 1903.

CLEVELAND, Clement, surgeon; b. Baltimore, Md., Sept. 29, 1843; s. Anthony B. and Mary Woods (Manning) C.; A.B., Harvard, 1867, A.M., 1870; M.D., Coll. Phys. and Surg. (Columbia), 1871; diploma City Hosp., 1872, Woman's Hosp., 1873; m. Annie Ward Davenport, June 17, 1874 (dec.); children—Henry Davenport, Clement, Elsie (Mrs. Robert G. Mead). Attending surgeon, City Hosp., 1873-80; attending surgeon, 1882-1915, surg. dir., 1915-20 (emeritus), Woman's Hosp., 1912-16 (emeritus); cons. surgeon, Memorial Hosp., 1882—. Home: New York, N.Y. Died 1934.

CLEVELAND, Grover (Stephen Grover Cleveland), President of the United States; b. Caldwell, N.J., Mar. 18, 1837; s. Rev. Richard Falley and Ann (Neal) C.; family removed to Onondaga County, N.Y., 1841; attended village sch. and clerked in store; teacher in Inst. for Blind, New York, 1 yr.; (LL.D., Princeton, 1897); m. Frances Folsom, June 2, 1886. Went to Buffalo, 1855, became clerk in law offices of Rogers, Bowen & Rogers, 1855, and was admitted to bar, 1859; asst. dist. atty. Erie County, 1863-66; sheriff Erie County, 1870-73; established law practice; in 1881 was elected mayor of Buffalo. His veto of extravagant appropriations directed outside attention to him and led to his nomination and election as gov. the following year; in 1884 elected Pres. of U.S. as Democrat, over James G. Blaine, Republican, by majority of 37 electoral votes; in 1888 again Democratic nominee, but defeated by Benjamin Harrison; returned to law practice, locating in New York; in 1892 again elected President as Democrat, defeating Pres. Harrison; in 1896 the Democratic party having declared for the free coinage of silver in the platform of its Nat. Conv., Mr. Cleveland withheld his support from the ticket and platform. He took up his residence, after his second retirement from the White House, at Princeton, N.J. Elected trustee, holding a majority of the stock of the Equitable Life Assurance Soc. of U.S., June 10, 1905. Chmn. Assn. of Life Ins. Presidents, Jan. 1907—. Mem. exec. com. Nat. Civic Federation. Trustee Princeton Univ. Home: Princeton, N.J. Died 1908.

CLEVELAND, Helen M., author; b. Sheffield, Mass.; d. Frederick and Clara (Mansfield) C.; fitted for coll. by mother; completed a course in State Normal Sch., took spl. course in Boston Univ., and in 1888 in Univ. of Mich., followed by original study in English literature and history in Europe; unmarried. Taught State Normal Sch., Platteville, Wis., later prin. Windsor (Conn.) High Sch., and afterward teacher of English and history in two female sems. Edited Young People's Mag., Boston, 1890-94; engaged in lit. work. Author: Stories of Brave Old Times, 1904. Mem. staff of Modern Women and Teacher's Mag. Home: Boston, Mass. Died 1909.

CLEVELAND, Rose Elizabeth (Miss), author; b. Fayetteville, N.Y., 1846; d. Rev. Richard Falley and Ann (Neal) Cleveland (sister of President Grover Cleveland); removed 1853, to Holland Patent, N.Y., where her father was Presbyn. pastor (died 1854); teacher several yrs.; was mistress of the White House from Mar. 1885, until her brother's marriage, June 1886; lived in New York several yrs.; later in Europe. Author: George Eliot's Poetry and Other Studies; The Long Run (novel). Home: Dark Harbor, Me. Died 1918.

CLEVER, Conrad, clergyman; b. Shippensburg, Pa., Feb. 11, 1848; s. George and Isabella (Kelso) C.; student Pa. Coll.; A.B., Franklin and Marshall Coll., 1870; D.D., Ursinus Coll., 1889; m. M. Elisabeth Everhart, June 6, 1879; 1 dau., Elisabeth I. Ordained ministry Ref. Ch. in U.S., 1873; pastor Columbia, Pa., 1873-79, Baltimore, Md., 1879-1904, Christ Ch., Hagerstown, Md., 1904—. Pres. Bd. of Publication Ref. Ch. in U.S.; trustee Mercersburg Acad. Home: Hagerstown, Md. Died Feb. 19, 1935.

CLEWELL, John Henry, college pres.; b. Winston-Salem, N.C., Sept. 19, 1855; s. John David and Dorothea (Shultz) C.; grad. Moravian Coll., A.B., 1875, later A.M. (Ph.D., 1900); B.D., Moravian Theol. Sem., 1877; diploma, Union Theol. Sem.; m. Alice C. Wolle, June 1882. Moravian clergyman. Pres. Salem Acad. and Coll. (founded, 1802), 1884-1909; pres. Moravian Sem. and Coll. for Women, Bethlehem, Pa. (founded, 1742), 1909—. Author: History of Wachovia in North Carolina, 1902. Deceased.

CLEWS, Henry, banker; b. Staffordshire, Eng., Aug. 14, 1840; s. James C.; studied for ministry, but left sch. to enter mercantile life at New York, whither father had taken him on a visit; (Ph.D.; LL.D.); m. Lucy Madison Worthington, of Ky. (grand-niece President Madison; g.g.d. Gen. Andrew Lewis, next in command to Washington in Rev. War). After panic of 1857, organized banking firm of Stout, Clews & Mason, which later became Livermore, Clews & Co.; at outbreak of Civil War apptd. by Sec. of Treas. S. P. Chase, govt. financial agt. for sale of bond issues to continue the war; organized, 1877, and became head of Henry Clews & Co. Apptd. fiscal agt. of U.S. Govt. for all foreign nations (as recognition of services in placing bond issues during Civil War); adviser and agt. in organizing new financial system of Japan (on recommendation of President Grant). Decorated Comdr. Order of the Rising Sun, Japan, 1908. Twice declined portfolio of sec. of the treas., and Rep. nomination for mayor of New York; also declined office of collector of port of New York; originated, organized and nominated 65 members of the Com. of Seventy. Republican. Trustee Ohio Northern U. Mem. N.Y. Chamber of Commerce, Stock Exchange. Author: Twenty-eight Years in Wall Street, 1885; The Wall Street Point of View, 1900; Fifty Years in Wall Street, 1908; Speeches and Essays, 1910. Home: New York, N.Y. Died Jan. 31, 1923.

CLEWS, James Blanchard, banker; b. Dunkirk, N.Y., Aug. 4, 1869; s. John and Sabina (Dayman) C.; g.s. James Clews, mfr. of celebrated Clews pottery, Staffordshire, Eng.; grad. Chamberlain Coll., Randolph, N.Y., 1888; m. Mrs. Leta Nichols Livingston, 1909 (died 1919); 1 dau., Leta; m. 2d, Mary Ann Payne, Oct. 2, 1926. In banking business, 1890—; head Henry Clews & Co., bankers; pres. Toledo, Ann Arbor and North Mich. R.R. during reorganization period; dir. of many corps. Republican. Episcopalian. Home: New York, N.Y. Died Dec. 17, 1934.

CLIFFE, Adam C., judge; b. Sycamore, Ill., June 25, 1869; s. Thomas and Mary Ann (Collins) C.; high sch., Sycamore; LL.B., Northwestern U.; m. Edna Sitts, Sept. 12, 1900. Began practice at Sycamore; was mem. Ill. Ho. of Rep. and Senate (twice pres. protem.); circuit judge 16th Judicial Dist. of Ill., 1920-23 (resigned); U.S. district judge, Northern Dist. of Ill., Jan. 4, 1923—. Republican. Mason. Home: Sycamore, Ill. Died June 12, 1928.

CLIFFORD, Chandler R., publisher; b. Boston, Mass., Feb. 23, 1858; s. Samuel W. and Mary Anette (Ford) C.; ed. English High and Boston Latin schs.; m. Eva M. Davidson, Sept. 15, 1885; children—Cora T., George J., Irene B. Pres. Clifford & Lawton, pubs., The Am. Silk Journal, The Upholsterer and Interior Decorator, text books and annuals, 1888—. First pres. Am. Trade Press Assn.; founder Am. Assn. Interior Decorators; chmn. Design Registration League; mem. internat. jury, Louisiana Purchase Expn., 1905, Panama-Pacific Expn., 1915, Hoover delegation to Paris Expn. of New Art, 1925. Awarded Silver Service Testimonial by Decorative Trades, 1913. Republican. Episcopalian. Mason. Author: The Philosophy of Color, 1904; The Decorative Periods, 1906; Color Value, 1907; Rugs of the Orient, 1911; Period Furnishings, 1911; The Lace Dictionary, 1913; "Junk Snupper" and stories of antique collecting, 1927, 28, 29. Home: New York, N.Y. Died Mar. 1935.

CLIFFORD, Charles Warren, lawyer; b. New Bedford, Mass., Aug. 19, 1844; s. John H. and Sarah Parker (Allen) C.; A.B., Harvard, 1865, A.M., 1868; studied law with Judge Edmund H. Bennett, Taunton, 1865-67; Harvard Law Sch. and John C. Dodge, Boston, 1867-68; m. Frances L. Wood, May 5, 1869 (died 1872); m. 2d, Wilhelmina H. Crapo, Mar. 15, 1876 (died 1909). Admitted to bar, 1868; commr. on revision of judiciary system of Mass., 1876; civil service commr. of Mass., 1884-88; commr. revision of statutes of Mass., 1898-1901; U.S. commr.; commr. on revision of Building Laws, 1904; pres. St. Luke's Hosp., New Bedford. Republican. Took part in Internat. Arbitration at The Hague, June 1902, between U.S. and Russia, as counsel for owners of "Cape Horn Pigeon." V.p. New Bedford Instn. for Savings; trustee Masonic Bldg. Assn.; dir. Am. Unitarian Assn., 1901-06. Fellow Am. Acad. Arts and Sciences. Address: New Bedford, Mass. Died Sept. 14, 1923.

CLIFT, Albert Earl, ry. official; b. Urbana, Ill., Oct. 15, 1869; s. Perry Poole and Emma E. (Apperson) C.; ed. pub. schs.; m. Letitia M. Yeats, Feb. 10, 1892. Brakeman and conductor I.C. R.R., 1888-92; conductor C.,C.,C.&St.L. Ry., 10 mos., 1892-93; again with I.C. R.R., consecutively conductor, engine foreman, yardmaster, acting trainmaster and trainmaster, 1893-1905, supt. Freeport (Ill.) div., 1905-07, St. Louis div., 1907-10, gen. supt. Southern lines, at New Orleans, 1910-12, gen. supt. Northern and Western lines at Chicago, 1912-17, asst. gen. mgr. and gen. mgr., 1917-23, v.p. in charge operation, 1923-24, sr. v.p., 1924-29; pres. Central of Georgia Ry. Co. and Ocean Steamship Co. of Savannah, from Mar. 1, 1929; pres. Macon Terminal Co., Albany Passenger Terminal Co. Home: Savannah, Ga. Died May 30, 1931.

CLIFTON, Charles, automobile mfr.; b. Buffalo, N.Y., Sept. 20, 1853; s. Henry and Elizabeth (Dorsheimer) C.; ed. Highland Mil. Acad., Worcester, Mass., 1869-70; m. Grace Gorham, Jan. 22, 1891. Associated with Pierce-Arrow Motor Car Co. from 1897, then chmn. bd.; dir. Marine Trust Co. Pres. Buffalo Gen. Hosp., Buffalo Fine Arts Acad. Officer N.G.N.Y., 1881-93. Mem. Nat. Automobile Chamber of Commerce (pres. 1912-27); Chevalier Legion of Honor (France). Republican. Unitarian. Home: Buffalo, N.Y. Died June 21, 1928.

CLINCH, Edward Sears, lawyer; b. New York, N.Y., Nov. 8, 1846; s. Frederick and S. Sophia (Demilt) C.; B.S., Coll. City of New York, 1865; LL.B., Columbia, 1867; m. Cornelia B. Todd, Sept. 15, 1869. In practice at New York, 1868—; presdl. elector, 1904; justice Supreme Ct. of N.Y., 1906. Republican. Baptist. Pres. Northern Bapt. Conv. Home: New York, N.Y. Died Nov. 24, 1924.

CLINCH, R(ichard) Floyd, coal; b. Ga., 1865; s. Duncan L. and Susan A. (Hopkins) C.; ed. pvt. schs. in Ga. and Cheltenham Acad., Pa.; m. Katharine S. Lay, 1890; children—Duncan L., Margaret L. Connected with the Joliet Steel Co., 1883-89; mem. Crerar, Clinch & Co., coal and iron, 1889 until incorporated as Crerar Clinch Coal Co., becoming pres. of latter co.; also pres. Chicago Auditorium Assn., Traverse City (Mich.) State Bank, Hannah & Lay Co., Hannah & Lay Mercantile Co., North Shore Material Co.; v.p. Chicago, North Shore & Milwaukee R.R. Co., Chicago, Aurora & Elgin R.R. Co., Chicago Rapid Transit Co. Democrat. Episcopalian. Home: Winnetka, Ill. Died Nov. 7, 1930.

CLINE, Sheldon Scott, newspaperman; b. Nelsonville, O., Aug. 27, 1874; s. Lemuel J. and Martha (Bowman) C.; ed. pub. schs.; m. Mary Brigham, June 18, 1902; children—John Henry, Martha Edna, Mary Josephine, Catherine Elizabeth, Lucy Sheldon, Jane Brigham, Sheldon S., Marjorie Ann. Began newspaper work at Akron, O., 1895; settled in Washington, D.C., 1900; asst. mng. editor Washington Star, 1922-28, mng. editor, 1928—. Home: Falls Church, Va. Died May 18, 1928.

CLINE, Walter Branks, public utilities; b. Sacramento, Calif., Nov. 15, 1862; s. William and Maria C.; ed. pub. schs., San Francisco; m. Clara Emily Smith, 1885. Broker's clk., San Francisco, 1878-80; accountant Pacific Gas Improvement Co. and its predecessors, 1882-89, also sec., mgr. Pacific Lighting Co.; pres. Los Angeles Gas & Electric Corp., 1889-1924, chmn. bd. 1924—. Died July 22, 1932.

CLINEDINST, B(enjamin) West, artist; b. Woodstock, Va., 1860; s. Barnet M. and Mary C. (South) C.; ed. Va. Mil. Inst.; art edn. at École des Beaux Arts, Paris; pupil of Cabanel and Bonnât; m. Emily

Gertrude Waters, June 5, 1888; children—Josephine Herwig, Wendel Waters. Specialty genre pictures and portraits; illustrator of books of Hawthorne, Stevenson, Parkman, Cable, Page, Bret Harte, Mark Twain, etc.; later portraits of Theodore Roosevelt, Admiral Peary, Gen. Curtis Lee, Edward Echols, Gen. E. W. Nichols. Awarded Evans prize, Am. Water Color Soc., 1900; medal, Buffalo Expn., 1901, Charleston Expn., 1902. N.A., 1898. Home: Pawling, N.Y. Died Sept. 12, 1931.

CLINKSCALES, John George, teacher, lecturer; b. Abbeville Co., S.C., May 28, 1855; s. George Brownlee and Eliza Ann (Black) C.; A.B., Wofford Coll., Spartanburg, S.C., 1876; A.M., 1889; studied Johns Hopkins and Cornell U.; LL.D., Erskine Coll., Due West, S.C., 1912; m. Sallie C. Hutto, Mar. 14, 1878. Prof. mathematics, Williamston (S.C.) Female Coll., 1881-82, Columbia Female Coll., 1887-92, Clemson Agrl. and Mech. Coll., 1893-99, Wofford Coll., 1899—; County supt. edn. Anderson Co., S.C., 1882-86. Lt. col. on staff of Gov. Haygood, 1880-84; candidate for gov. of S.C. on compulsory edn. platform, 1914. Democrat. Methodist. Author: How Zach Come to College, 1907. Home: Spartanburg, S.C. Died Jan. 1, 1942.

CLINTON, George, lawyer; b. Buffalo, N.Y., Sept. 7, 1846; s. George W. and Laura C. (Spencer) C.; LL.B., Columbia, 1868; m. Alice Thornton, Jan. 17, 1872. Practiced at Buffalo from 1875; now sr. mem. Clinton, Clinton & Striker. Has been mem. various commns.; chmn. commn. to investigate expenditures upon canal improvements, etc.; mem. Internat. Waterways Commn., 1902—. President Merchants Exchange (now Buffalo Chamber of Commerce). Mem. N.Y. State Constl. Conv., 1915. Home: Buffalo, N.Y. Died June 1934.

CLINTON, George Perkins, botanist; b. Polo, Ill., May 7, 1867; s. John Waterbury and Carrie Adelia (Perkins) C.; B.S., U. of Ill., 1890, M.S., 1894; M.S., Harvard, 1901, Sc.D., 1902; m. Anna J. Lightbody, Aug. 9, 1892; 1 son, Harry Lightbody (dec.). Asst. botanist Ill. Agrl. Expt. Sta., and asst. in botany, U. of Ill., 1890-1902; botanist Conn. Expt. Sta., 1902—; lecturer forest pathology, Yale Univ., 1915-26, research asso., 1926-1929. Fellow Am. Acad. Arts and Sciences. Author bot. monograph and expt. sta. bulls. dealing with parasitic fungi. Home: New Haven, Conn. Died 1937.

CLINTON, George Wylie, bishop; b. Cedar Creek Tp., S.C., Mar. 28, 1859; s. Jonathan and Rachel C. (both slaves); grad. Brainerd Inst., Chester, S.C.; grad. junior classical course S.C. U., 1878; studied theology, Livingstone Coll., Salisbury, N.C.; (A.M., Livingstone Coll., 1893; D.D., Wilberforce, 1894, LL.D., 1906); m. Marie Louise Clay, Feb. 6, 1901. In Ministry A.M.E. Zion Ch. from 1879; taught 12 yrs. Lancaster (S.C.) High Sch., and Union (S.C.) graded schs.; pres. Atkinson Lit. and Indsl. Coll., Madisonville, Ky., 8 yrs. Founded A.M.E. Zion Quarterly Rev., 1889, and edited it 2 yrs.; editor Star of Zion, 1902-06; elected bishop, 1896. Now pres. Negro Young People's Endl. and Religious Congress; was 1st mgr. A.M.E. Zion Pub. House; pres. Bd. Publn.; del. Ecumenical Conf.; mem. exec. com. Fed. Council of Chs. of Christ in America; v.p. and life mem. Internat. S.S. Assn. Trustee Livingstone and Atkinson colls. Author: The Negro in the Ecumenical Conference of 1901; The Three Alarm Cries, 1906; Tuskegee Lectures, 1907; Christianity Under the Searchlight, 1909. Address: Charlotte, N.C. Died May 12, 1921.

CLINTON, Louis Adelbert, agriculturist; b. Grand Rapids, Mich., Feb. 13, 1868; s. Frederick Henry and Rhoby Ann (Allen) C.; B.S., Mich. Agrl. Coll., 1889, M.S., 1901; post-grad. Cornell Univ., 1901-02; m. Florence Ada Seage, Sept. 16, 1892. Asst. to dir. Mich. Expt. Sta., 1890-93; asst. prof. agr., Clemson Coll., S.C., 1893-95; asst. agriculturist, Cornell U. Expt. Sta., 1895-1902; dir. Storrs Agrl. Expt. Sta., and prof. agronomy, Conn. Agrl. Coll., 1902-12; agriculturist in charge of farm management N. Atlantic States for U.S. Dept. Agr., 1912-15; agrist. and asst. chief, Office of Extension North and West, for U.S. Dept. Agr., 1915-18; dir. agrl. extension, Rutgers Coll. and State U. of N.J., 1918—. Lecturer before farmers' insts. in Mich., N.Y., Pa., Del., Conn., Mass., N.H. and R.I. Home: New Brunswick, N.J. Died Jan. 21, 1923.

CLIPPINGER, Erle Elsworth, educator; b. Eau Claire, Mich., Sept. 27, 1875; s. Henry Gilbert and Mary Edna (Johnson) C.; grad. Mich. State Normal Coll., 1899; A.B., U. of Mich., 1903, A.M., 1904; student Harvard Grad. Sch., 1907-08; m. Laura Isabel Minturn, Sept. 9, 1911. Asst. prof. of English, Ind. State Normal Sch., Terre Haute, 1904-18; prof. of English, Eastern Division Ind. State Normal School (now Ball State Teachers College), Muncie, 1918-37 (emeritus). Author: Illustrated Lessons in Composition and Rhetoric, 1912; Teachers' Manual of Composition and Rhetoric, 1914; Written and Spoken English, 1917, enlarged edit., 1933; Children's Literature (with C. M. Curry), 1921. Home: Muncie, Ind. Died Jan. 6, 1939.

CLORAN, Timothy, univ. prof.; b. nr. Cuyahoga Falls, O., Jan. 9, 1869; A.B., Adelbert Coll. (Western Reserve U.), 1891; U. of Berlin, 1897-98; U. of Strassburg, 1898-99, Ph.D., 1901; U. of Paris, 1904-05; U. of Madrid, 1905-06; m. Lauretta Edith Murphy, Sept. 7, 1899. Instr. in Latin and Greek, Geneva (O.) High Sch., 1891-93; prof. French, German and Greek, Shurtleff Coll., Ill., 1893-97; prof. modern langs., U. of Ida., 1899-1900; adj. prof. Romance langs., Vanderbilt U., Tenn., 1900-04; asst. prof. Romance langs., 1906-07, prof., Jan. 1, 1908—, U. of Ore.; studied in Europe on leave of absence, 1931-32. Democrat. Conglist. Author of a philol. study of "Angier's Anglo-Norman French Translation of the Dialogues of Gregory the Great" (manuscript 24766 of the Nat. Library, Paris), 1901. Editor: Chateaubriand's Atala, 1911. Home: Eugene, Ore. Died Dec. 8, 1935.

CLOSE, Charles William, author; b. Bangor, Me., Sept. 4, 1859; s. Charles William and Emily Augusta (Steward) C.; ed. Bangor pub. schs.; Ph.D. and S.S.D., Spiritual Science U., Chicago, 1888. Editor and pub. The Free Man (monthly New Thought mag.), 1897-1901, The Phrenopathic Journal, 1903; pres. Bangor Co-operative Printing Co., 1903-07. Republican. Editor and pub. of Old and New, monthly, 1910. Home: Bangor, Me. Deceased.

CLOSE, Stuart, M.D.; b. Oakfield, Fond du Lac Co., Wis., Nov. 24, 1860; s. David and Sophronia (Wells) C.; matriculated U. of Pacific Med. Dept., San Francisco, 1882; M.D., New York Homœ. Med. Coll., 1885; m. Evangeline L. Lewis, Apr. 21, 1885; children—May Lewis (Mrs. Ralph Kirkman), Elizabeth Stuart, Bernard Wells. Internist, specializing in homœ. therapeutics; prof. homœ. philosophy, New York Homœ. Med. Coll. and Flower Hosp., 1909-13; founder Brooklyn Hahnemannian Union, 1896. Vol. Med. Service Corps, 1918. Democrat. Conglist. Author: The Genius of Homœopathy; Lectures and Essays on Homœopathic Philosophy, 1923. Home: Brooklyn, N.Y. Died June 26, 1929.

CLOSSON, Henry Whitney, brig. gen.; b. Whitingham, Vt., June 6, 1832; s. Henry and Emily (Whitney) C. Grad. U.S. Mil. Acad., 1854; m. Olivia A. Burke, Oct. 26, 1857; m. 2d, Julia W. Terry, June 2, 1868. Commd. 2d lt. 1st Arty., July 1, 1854; advanced through grades to col. 4th Arty., Apr. 25, 1888; retired by operation of law, June 6, 1896; advanced to rank of brig. gen. retired, by act of Apr 23, 1904. Bvtd. maj., July 8, 1863, for services at capture of Port Hudson, La.; lt. col., Aug. 23, 1864, for services at capture of Ft. Morgan, Ala. Served on frontier against Indians in Tex. and Fla., until 1861; in defense of Ft. Pickens, 1861-62; chief arty dist. of Pensacola, May-Dec. 1862; comdg. Baton Rouge, La., to Mar. 1863; on Teche campaign comdg. arty. of Gen. Grover's div., 19th Army Corps, Mar.-Aug. 1863; chief arty., 19th Army Corps, Oct. 1863-July 1864; chief arty. Mobile expdn., engaged in sieges of Forts Gaines and Morgan; chief arty. and ordnance cav. corps, Middle Mil. Div., Nov.-Dec. 1864. Home: Washington, D.C. Died July 16, 1917.

CLOSSON, William B(axter Palmer), artist; b Thetford, Vt., Oct. 1848; s. David Wood and Abigail (Palmer) C.; schs. and acad., Thetford; studied art, Lowell Inst. and Evening Art Sch., Boston; m. Grace W. Gallaudet Kendall, Apr. 20, 1907. Followed engraving on wood, 1866-94, then painting in pastel and oil. Awarded diploma, silver medal and spl. gold medal, Mass. Charitable Mechanics' Assn.; medals World's Fair (Chicago), Buffalo Expn., St. Louis Expn., Paris Salon, for proofs of engravings on wood. Represented by paintings in Nat. Gallery of Art, Columbia Instn. for the Deaf (Washington), Nat. Arts Club (N.Y.). Republican. Methodist. Home: Magnolia, Mass., and Newton, Mass. Died May 30, 1926.

CLOTHIER, Isaac Hallowell, mcht.; b. Phila., Nov. 5, 1837; s. Caleb and Hannah Fletcher (Hallowell) C.; ed. Friends' Sch., Phila.; (hon. A.M., Swarthmore Coll., 1903); m. Mary Clapp Jackson, Sept. 1, 1864; father of Morris Lewis C. Received business training in firm of George D. Parrish, Phila.; mem. Morris, Clothier & Lewis, Phila., 1861-68, Strawbridge & Clothier, 1868-95; retired, Jan. 1, 1895. Dir. Girard Trust Co., Fourth St. Nat. Bk. Trustee Swarthmore Coll.; trustee Williamson Free Sch. of Mech. Trades, Merchants' Fund, Free Library of Phila. Republican. Mem. Soc. of Friends. Home: Wynnewood, Pa. Died Jan. 15, 1921.

CLOUD, James Henry, clergyman, educator; b. Chambersburg, Ind., Apr. 26, 1862; s. Hiram and Miriam (Osborne) C.; grad. Ill. Sch. for the Deaf, Jacksonville, Ill., 1880; B.A., Gallaudet Coll., Washington, D.C., 1886, M.A., 1889, D.D., 1914; Summer Sch. of Physical Edn., Chautauqua, N.Y., and Harvard U.; m. Lulu O. Herdman, Oct. 4, 1892; children—Mary Kendall (Mrs. George M. Flint), John Keble, George Herbert, Daniel Tuttle. Deacon, 1889, priest, 1893, P.E. Ch.; asst. minister All Souls Ch. for the Deaf, Phila., Pa., 1890; minister St. Thomas Mission for the Deaf, and missionary, St. Louis, Mo., Sept. 1890—; also prin. Gallaudet Sch. for the Deaf (a pub. sch.), 1890-1922; missionary to the deaf in Dioceses of Mo., W. Mo., Neb. and Ky. Home: St. Louis, Mo. Died Oct. 20, 1926.

CLOUD, Marshall Morgan, surgeon; b. Carroll Co., Va., Oct. 9, 1868; s. Columbus Henry and Mary Emily (Parker) C.; M.D., honor medalist, U. of Kan., 1892; grad. U.S.A. Med. Sch., 1897; B.S., U. of Southern Calif., 1904, A.M., 1906; grad. study Stanford, 1905, U. of Chicago, 1906; m. Mary Frances Moore, June 19, 1894; children—Dorothy (Mrs. Frederick B. Pinkus), Marguerite (Mrs. Allison J. Wallace, Jr.), Mary, Frances. Asst. supt. Kan. State Hosp., Topeka, 1893-95; commd. 1st lt., Med. Corps, U.S.A., 1896, and advanced through grades to maj., 1919; retired for disability in line of duty, 1921; clin. prof. ophthalmology, U. of Southern Calif., 1910-13, prof. mil. medicine, 1920-23; ophthalmologist, Nat. Soldiers Home, Sawtelle, Calif., 1910-13; same, Santa Fe Ry., 1910-21; examining surgeon, U.S. Pension Bur.; on staff Hollywood Hosp. and Gen. Hosp., Los Angeles; partner Angeles Mesa Land Co.; owner Cloud Heights Subdivision, La Crescenta, Calif. Comdr. div. hosp., Mobile, Ala., Miami, Fla., and Anniston, Ala., Spanish-Am. War; served on operations div., commd. personnel br., Gen. Staff, World War. Fellow Am. Coll. Surgeons. Democrat. Episcopalian. Author: Sanitary Analysis of Water, 1905; Curing Our Nerves, 1934; Facts About Alcoholic Drinks, 1934. Inventor, with M. F. Volkman, of horizontal-base range finder for artillery fire, 1904. Home: Los Angeles, Calif. Died 1937.

CLOUGH, David Marston, governor; b. Lyme, N.H., Dec. 27, 1846; family removed in 1855 to Waupaca, Wis., and in July 1857, to Spencer Brook, Minn.; ed. in country schs.; m. Addie Barton, 1868. From boyhood worked in lumber business, and at 35 was at head of one of largest lumber firms of Minn. Mem., 1885, and later pres. City Council, St. Paul; mem. Minn. Senate, 1887-91; elected lt. gov., 1892 and 1894; became gov. on election of Gov. Knute Nelson to U.S. Senate, Jan. 31, 1895; elected gov., 1896, term expiring Jan. 1899. Home: Everett, Wash. Died Aug. 28, 1924.

CLOUGH, George Albert, architect; b. Bluehill, Me., May 27, 1843; s. Asa and Louisa (Ray) C.; ed. Bluehill Acad.; studied architecture with Snell & Gregeson, Boston, 1863-69; m. Amelia M., d. Lyman Hinckley, of Thetford, Vt., 1876. Opened office on his own account, 1869; first city architect of Boston, 1873-83; architect numerous sch., ch., municipal, hosp., ecclesiastical and other bldgs., Boston and elsewhere. Home: Brookline, Mass. Died 1910.

CLOUGH, W. P., ry. official. Was asst. to pres., St. Paul, Minneapolis & Manitoba Ry., to 1887, v.p. same rd., and its successor, the G.N. Ry., 1887-1901; 4th v.p. and gen. counsel. Northern Securities Co., 1901; dir. C.,B.&Q. R.R. Co., Colo. & Southern Ry. Co., Colo. Midland Ry. Co., Crow's Nest Pass Coal Co.; then chmn. Northern Pacific Ry. Co.; v.p. Northern Express Co. Died Aug. 18, 1916.

CLOUS, John Walter, army officer; b. Württemberg, Germany, June 9, 1837; s. John and Fredericka (Dieterle) C.; ed. in the higher schs. of Germany; began the study of civil law; came to the U.S., 1855; m. Caroline M. Strickle, Nov. 24, 1874. Served as pvt. 9th Inf., Feb. 2, 1857-Nov. 5, 1860; pvt. and corp. and q.m. sergt. 6th Inf., Feb. 9, 1860-Nov. 29, 1862; 2d lt. to capt. 38th Inf., Jan. 22, 1867; transferred to 24th Inf., Nov. 11, 1869; maj. and judge advocate, Apr. 1, 1886; lt. col. and deputy judge adv. gen., Feb. 12, 1892; brig. gen. U.S.V., Sept. 21, 1898; hon. disch. from vols., Mar. 24, 1899; col. and judge adv., Feb. 2, 1901; brig. gen. and judge adv. gen. U.S.A., May 22, 1901; retired at own request after over 40 yrs'. service, May 24, 1901. Twice bvtd. for gallant conduct at Gettysburg, Pa.; adj. gen. 2d Mil. Dist. during reconstruction, 1866-67; acting a.d.c. to Maj. Gen. Sheridan during Indian campaign, 1868-69; finished law studies and admitted to bar U.S. Supreme Court; served on frontier and Indian campaigns, 1868-86; commended in War Dept. orders for gallant conduct in Indian engagement, 1872; asst. to judge adv. gen., 1886-90; prof. law, U.S. Mil. Acad., 1890-95; on staff Maj. Gen. Merritt to 1898; on staff Maj. Gen. Miles while in the field during Spanish-Am. War; sec. and counsel of commn. for evacuation of Cuba, Aug. 20, 1898-Jan. 10, 1899; on staff Maj. Gen. Brooke as judge advocate to May 21, 1901. Home: New York, N.Y. Died 1908.

CLOVER, George Frederick, clergyman; b. Lanesboro, Mass., June 12, 1866; s. Rev. Lewis P. (D.D.) and Sarah Ann (Ackerman) C.; student Hobart Coll., 1889, D.D., 1930; M.A., Columbia, 1916; m. Laura Brand, Apr. 22, 1896. Deacon, 1890, priest, 1891, P.E. Ch.; rector Calvary Ch., Homer, N.Y., 1891-92; asst. pastor and asst. supt. St. Luke's Hosp., 1892-1900; pastor and supt. same, 1900—; canon and registrar Cathedral of St. John the Divine, 1905-14; hon. canon, Cathedral St. John the Divine. Pres. Hosp. Conf. of Greater New York, 1906-15; pres. Hosp. Bur. Standards and Supplies; pres. Asso. Outpatients Clinics, 1915-22; trustee United Hosp. Fund. Home: New York, N.Y. Died July 18, 1937.

CLOVER, Richardson, rear adm.; b. St. James' Coll., Hagerstown, Md., July 11, 1846; s. Rev. Lewis

P. and Sarah Ann (Ackerman) C.; grad. U.S. Naval Acad., 1867; m. Mary Eudora, d. late Senator John F. Miller, May 19, 1886. Ensign, Dec. 18, 1868; master, Mar. 21, 1870; lt., Mar. 21, 1871; lt. comdr., May 19, 1891; comdr., Sept. 14, 1897; capt., Apr. 11, 1902; rear adm., Oct. 9, 1907. Served in various stas. and depts., with 22 yrs. of sea service; in charge survey of S.E. Alaska, 1885-86; hydrographer Bur. of Navigation, 1889-93; chief Office Naval Intelligence, 1897-98; mem. bd. on constrn. of vessels, Navy Dept., 1897-99; mem. war and strategy bd., Mar. 15 to Apr. 25, 1898; comd. U.S.S. Bancroft, May 1, 1898, to end of Spanish War; returned to Naval Intelligence Office; naval attaché, London, 1900-03; comdg. U.S.S. Wisconsin, Asiatic Sta., 1904-05; pres. Bd. of Inspection and Survey, 1906-08; retired, 1908. Home: Washington, D.C. Died Oct. 14, 1919.

CLOVER, Samuel Travers, newspaperman; b. London, Aug. 13, 1859; academic edn.; m. Mabel Hitt, Apr. 3, 1884. Began newspaper career, 1880, by making trip around the world; worked on newspapers in Dak. 5 yrs.; as staff corr. Chicago Herald reported Cheyenne Indian uprising, 1890, and Messiah outbreak among the Sioux, 1891; present at final "ghost dance" led by Sitting Bull, and is believed to be the last white man who saw that chief alive; only newspaper man with vigilantes through Johnson Co. war, Wyoming, 1892; etc. Became mng. editor Chicago Evening Post, 1894; later editor and pub. Los Angeles Graphic; editor and pub. Richmond (Va.) Evening Journal, 1916-22; pres. and editor Los Angeles Saturday Night, 1922—. Author: Paul Travers' Adventures; Glimpses Across the Sea; Rose Reef to Buluwayo; On Special Assignment; A Native Son; Browsings in an Old Book-Shop; King Hal's Fifth Wife. Home: Los Angeles, Calif. Died May 28, 1934.

CLOW, Harry Beach, pres. Rand, McNally & Co.; b. Allegheny, Pa., Feb. 11, 1870; s. James B. and Matilda (Ross) C.; ed. pub. schs.; grad. North Div. High Sch., Chicago, 1885; m. Elizabeth F. McNally, Jan. 6, 1892; children—Helen, Marion, Harry B. Began with James B. Clow & Sons, 1885, later sec. until 1907, now dir.; pres. Rand, McNally & Co. from 1907. Republican. Presbyn. Home: Chicago, Ill. Died Aug. 4, 1933.

CLOWRY, Robert Charles, capitalist; b. Will Co., Ill., Sept. 8, 1838; pub. sch. edn.; m. Caroline A. Estabrook, Aug. 29, 1865 (died 1896). Capt. asst. q.m. vols., Oct. 27, 1863; bvtd. maj. and lt. col. vols., Mar. 13, 1865, "for meritorious services and devoted application to duty"; hon. mustered out, May 31, 1866. In charge mil. telegraph lines, 1863-66; after the war served in various capacities with Western Union Telegraph Co., of which was pres. and gen. mgr., Apr., 1902-Nov. 23, 1910; was also pres. and gen. mgr. of its subsidiary cos. Home: Tarrytown, N.Y. Died Feb. 26, 1925.

CLUETT, Robert, mfr.; b. Birmingham, Eng., June 14, 1844; ed. pub. schs. of Troy, and Troy Acad.; m. Elizabeth Marchisi, May 19, 1868; m. 2d, Mrs. Emily R. Webster, Aug. 1, 1917. Became mem. George B. Cluett, Bro. & Co., mfrs. shirts and collars, Troy, 1866; after several changes in personnel, firm was incorporated, 1901, as Cluett, Peabody & Co., of which was v.p., 1901-02, pres., 1902-Apr. 30, 1907 (retired); v.p. Nat. City Bank, Troy. Pres. Troy Y.M.C.A. (presented commodious bldg. to the organization, fully equipped and furnished); v.p. Samaritan Hosp. (Troy); an organizer Troy Civic League (pres. to 1907). Elder 2d Presbyn. Ch., Troy. Home: Troy, N.Y. Died Nov. 25, 1927.

CLUTE, Walter Marshall, artist; b. Schenectady, N.Y., Jan. 9, 1870; s. Walter Swits and Elizabeth (Marshall) C.; ed. Union Classical Inst., Schenectady, 1896; Art Students' League, New York, 1897-99; Julian Acad., Paris, 1900-01; m. Beulah Mitchell, Dec. 26, 1900. Corr. and staff artist Chicago Daily News, during Cuban Campaign, Spanish-Am. War, Apr.-July 1898; instr. and lecturer Art Inst., Chicago, 11 yrs. Awarded Mrs. Julius Rosenwald prize, Art Inst., Chicago, 1910; Arché Club Purchase, 1911. Mem. Faculty, Art Inst. Chicago, Summer Sch. of Painting, Saugatuck, Mich. Unitarian. Home: Park Ridge, Ill. Died Feb. 3, 1915.

CLUTZ, Jacob Abraham, theologian; b. Adams Co., Pa., Jan. 5, 1848; s. Henry and Hannah (Buffington) C.; A.B., Pa. Coll., 1869; grad. Luth. Theol. Sem., Gettysburg, Pa., 1872; (D.D., Pa. Coll., 1889; LL.D., Midland Coll., Fremont, Neb., 1920); m. Liberty A. Hollinger, Sept. 4, 1872. Pastor Luth. chs. at Newville, Pa., and Baltimore, 1872-83; gen. sec. Luth. (Gen. Synod) Bd. of Home Missions, 1883-89; pres. Midland Coll., Atchison, Kan., 1889-1904; also prof. homiletics and Christian ethics, Western Theol. Sem., Atchison, 1894-1904; pastor St. James' Ch., Gettysburg, 1904-09; prof. practical theology, Luth. Theol. Sem., Gettysburg, 1909—. Sec. Luth. Bd. Foreign Missions, 1877-83; pres. Luth. Gen. Synod, Lebanon, Pa., 1891; treas. Luth. Bd. of Home Missions (Gen. Synod), 1905-13; pres. same, 1913-15; sec. ways and means com. to effect merger of Luth. Gen. Synod, Gen. Council, and United Synod in the South, 1917-18; mem. exec. bd. United Luth. Ch. in Am., 1918-24. Trustee Pa. Coll., 1908—. Co-editor Lutheran Quarterly from 1909. Home: Gettysburg, Pa. Died Sept. 7, 1925.

CLYDE, John Cunningham, clergyman; b. White Deer Valley, Pa., Oct. 22, 1841; served in 72d Ill. Vols., 1861-63; deputy provost marshal, Columbus, Ky.; A.B., Lafayette Coll., 1866, A.M., 1869; grad. Princeton Theol. Sem., 1869; (D.D., Maryville Coll., Tenn., 1885); m. Martha Hallock Coffin, Oct. 26, 1869. Licensed, 1868; ordained, 1869, Presbyn. ministry; stated supply, Centreville, Iowa, 1869-70, Shenandoah, Pa., 1870-72; pastor Frazer, Pa., 1872-79, Bloomsbury, N.J., 1879-1901. Chaplain Lafayette Post 217, G.A.R. Author: History of the Irish Settlement of Pennsylvania; Reminiscences of the Irish Settlement. Home: Easton, Pa. Died Jan. 28, 1915.

CLYDE, William Gray, pres. Carnegie Steel Co.; b. Chester, Pa., July 29, 1868; s. John Edward and Emma Bertha (Ott) C.; grad. Pa. Mil. Coll., Chester, 1888, hon. Dr. Applied Science, 1924; m. Margaret Burns Johnson, Nov. 5, 1890; children—Emma Clyde (Mrs. Edwin Hodge, Jr.), William J. Began as civ. engr., Ryan & McDonald, Baltimore, Md., 1890; supt. plate mills, Wellman Steel & Iron Co., Thurlow, Pa.; supt. South Works, Ill. Steel Co., Chicago, 1895; sales mgr. Am. Steel Hoop Co., 1898; with Carnegie Steel Co. from 1902, salesman, Cleveland, O., 1903, asst. gen. mgr. sales, Pittsburgh, Pa., 1904-18, v.p. and gen. mgr. sales, 1918-25, pres., 1925—; pres. Clairton Steel Co., Clairton By-Products Coke Co., Clairton Land Co., Carnegie Land Co., Girard Land Co., Conneaut Land Co., Sharon Land Co., Sharon Coke Co., Bessemer Electric Power Co. Trustee Pa. Mil. Coll., Carnegie Inst., Carnegie Inst. Tech., Carnegie Library; dir. 5th Avenue Assn. of Pittsburgh. Episcopalian. Mason. Home: Pittsburgh, Pa. Died Mar. 23, 1931.

CLYDE, William Pancoast, ship owner; b. Claymont, Del., Nov. 11, 1839; s. Thomas and Rebecca (Pancoast) C.; M.A., Trinity Coll., Conn., 1862; m. Emeline F. Hill, Jan. 18, 1865. Was head William P. Clyde & Co., Clyde Steamship Co. Episcopalian. Home: New York, N.Y. Died Nov. 18, 1923.

CLYMER, Meredith, M.D.; b. Phila., June 6, 1817; g.s. George C., signer Declaration of Independence; grad. Univ. of Pa., 1835; (M.D., 1837); studied also in Paris, London and Dublin; practiced medicine about 10 yrs. in Phila. holding several professorships there; physician and consulting physician to Phila. Hosp.; physician-in-chief Cholera Hosp., Phila., 1849; prof. practice of medicine, Hampden-Sidney Coll., Richmond, Va. Settled in New York and in 1851 became prof. practice of medicine Univ. of N.Y., and, 1871, prof. mental and nervous diseases Albany Med. Coll.; surgeon U.S. vols., and med. dir. dept. of the South during Civil war. Home: New York, N.Y. Died 1902.

COADY, Charles Pearce, congressman; b. Baltimore, Md., Feb. 22, 1868; A.B., Baltimore City Coll., 1886; m. Milly Stuart Kenly, Jan. 21, 1901; children—Charles Pearce, Alice Ford, John Morris, James O'Connor. Admitted to Md. bar, 1894, and then in practice at Baltimore. Elected to Md. Senate for terms 1908-12, 1912-16; resigned, 1913; elected to 63d Congress, Nov. 4, 1913, for unexpired term (1913-15), of George Konig, deceased; reëlected 64th to 66th Congresses (1915-21), 3d Md. Dist. Democrat. Home: Baltimore, Md. Died Feb. 16, 1934.

COAKLEY, Cornelius Godfrey, physician; b. Brooklyn, Aug. 14, 1862; s. George Washington (LL.D.) and Isabelle (Hoe) C.; A.B., Coll. City of New York, 1884, A.M., 1887; M.D., Univ. Med. Coll. (1st honor), 1887; m. Sept. 10, 1890. Interne Bellevue Hosp., 1887-88; dir. histology dept., Loomis Lab.; lecturer anatomy, 1889-90, instr. histology, 1889-96, New York U.; clin. prof. laryngology, 1898-1905, prof., 1905-14, Univ. and Bellevue Hosp. Med. Coll.; prof. laryngology and otology, Coll. Phys. and Surg. (Columbia) from 1914; cons. surgeon, ear, nose and throat service, Bellevue Hosp.; attending otolaryngologist, Presbyterian Hosp.; cons. surgeon, Neurol. Inst., Babies Hosp., Sloan Maternity Hosp., Skin and Cancer Hosp., Southampton Hosp. Author: Diseases of the Nose and Throat, 1899. Home: Sagaponack, L.I. Died Nov. 22, 1934.

COALE, Robert Dorsey, college dean; b. Baltimore, Md., Sept. 13, 1857; s. George Buchanan and Caroline (Dorsey) C.; C.E., Pa. Mil. Acad., 1875; Ph.D., Johns Hopkins, 1881; hon. M.D., U. of Md., 1912; m. Mina C. Howison, Nov. 15, 1892. Asst. in chemistry, Johns Hopkins, 1881 to 1883; prof. chemistry and toxicology, U. of Md., 1884—; dean combined med. colls., U. of Md., May 29, 1900—. Col. 5th Md. Vol. Inf., U.S.A., May-Sept. 1898. Home: Baltimore, Md. Deceased.

COAN, Charles Florus, prof. history; b. Dayton, O., Apr. 30, 1886; s. John Leet and Marjorie Sarah (Hanger) C.; Whitman Coll., Walla Walla, Wash., 1904-07; A.B., U. of Wash., 1908; M.L., U. of Calif., 1915, Ph.D., 1920; m. Mary Leanor Wright, Mar. 9, 1924; 1 son, John Victor. Asst. supt. Tung Wen Inst., Amoy, China, 1910-12; head history dept., Alameda (Calif.) High Sch., 1915-18; asso. prof. history, State U. of N.M., 1920-21, prof., 1922—. Cons. editor of Social Science. Author: History of New Mexico, 1925. Home: Albuquerque, N.M. Died Sept. 19, 1928.

COAN, Titus Munson, author; b. Hilo, H.I., Sept. 27, 1836; s. Titus and Fidelia (Church) C. (missionaries); A.B., Williams, 1859, A.M., 1884; M.D., Coll. Phys. and Surg. (Columbia), 1861. Interne Bellevue and army hosps., 1861-63; asst. surgeon in Admiral Farragut's squadron, U.S. Navy, 1863-65; founded, 1880, and then dir. New York Bur. of Revision; editor Topics of the Time. Author: Ounces of Prevention, 1888; Hawaiian Ethnography, 1899; Polynesian Charm, 1901; Climate of Hawaii, 1901. Died May 8, 1921.

COAPMAN, Eugene H., ry. official; b. Aug. 15, 1865. Messenger boy and telegraph operator, C.M.,& St.P. Ry., 1880-83; train dispatcher, later supt. of telegraph, Ia. Central Ry., 1883-86; train dispatcher, C.,M.&St.P. Ry., 1886-90; train dispatcher, later trainmaster, I.C. R.R., Clinton, Ill., 1890-1901; trainmaster, A.,T.&S.F. Ry. in Ariz., 1901-02; supt. Danville div. Southern Ry., 1902-05; asst. gen. supt. and gen. mgr., Eastern dist., same rd., Greensboro, N.C., 1905-08; mgr. entire Southern Ry. System, 1908-10; gen. mgr. from Jan. 1910, also v.p. from Oct. 1910; apptd. federal mgr. same. Died Jan. 5, 1921.

COAR, John Firman, univ. prof.; b. of Am. parents, Berlin, Germany, July 26, 1863; s. Firman Wood and Lucinda Elizabeth (Blake) C.; came to America, 1870; grad. Kaiser Wilhelm Gymnasium, Cologne, Germany, 1884; U. of Bonn, 1884; Boston U. Law Sch., 1885-86; Harvard, 1896-1900, A.M., 1897, Ph.D., 1900; m. Emily Laura Miller, Nov. 10, 1886; 1 son, Herbert Greenleaf. Head dept. modern langs., Park Inst., Allegheny, Pa., 1891-92; prin. Adams (N.Y.) Collegiate Inst., 1893-94, Canandaigua (N.Y.) Acad., 1894-95; instr. German lang., Harvard, 1896-1903; prof. Germanic langs. and lits., Adelphi Coll., Brooklyn, 1903-14, U. of Rochester, 1914-15, then at U. of Alberta, Can., retired, 1934. Lecturer of the Deutsche Akademie at German univs., 1934-35. Dir. Germanistic Soc. of America and rep. of the soc. in Germany and Austria, 1911-12; pres. German sect. Brooklyn Inst. Arts and Sciences, 1904-14. Fellow Am. Geog. Soc. Founder, 1923, and organizer the Liberal League, its first exec. sec. and then chmn.; corr. mem. Schiller Akademie. Awarded silver medal by Deutsche Akademie. Author: Studies in German Literature in the Nineteenth Century, 1903; Modern German Literature (monograph), 1909; History of German Literature, Eighteenth Century, 1916; Democracy and the War, 1917; The Old and the New Germany, 1923; The Peace of Nations, 1928; Reparations and Debts—An Analysis and Synthesis (pamphlet), 1929, also pub. in a German adaptation under title "Reparationen und Schulden," 1929; Sprache und Volk, 1935; Democracy and World Trade, 1935. Editor: Goethe's Torquato Tasso, 1908. Home: Kingston, Mass. Died June 26, 1939.

COATES, Charles Edward, chemist; b. Baltimore, Aug. 13, 1866; s. Charles Edward and Anna Hunter (Roberts) C.; A.B., Johns Hopkins, 1887; Königliche Bergacademie, Freiberg in Sachsen, 1888; U. of Heidelberg, 1889; Ph.D., Johns Hopkins, 1891; LL.D. from Louisiana State University, 1934; m. Ollie Maurin, June 26, 1901; children—Charles Hunter, Victor Maurin, Jesse, Caroline Pennock. Prof. chemistry, St. John's Coll., 1891-93, La. State U., 1893—; dean Audubon Sugar Sch., 1907-37, then emeritus, also dean Coll. of Pure and Applied Sci., 1931. Dir. Institute for Industrial Research, 1931. Episcopalian. Herty medalist, 1938. Home: Baton Rouge, La. Died Dec. 27, 1939.

COATES, Edward Hornor, pres. Pa. Acad. Fine Arts; b. Phila., Nov. 12, 1846; s. Joseph Potts Hornor and Elisa Henri (Troth) C.; A.B., Haverford Coll., 1864; m. Florence Earle, Jan. 7, 1879. Chmn. Com. on Instruction, 1883-90, pres., 1890-1906, Pa. Acad. Fine Arts. Chmn. Muybridge Commn. for Investigation of Animal Locomotion, U. of Pa., 1883. A founder Contemporary Club, Phila., 1886; pres. Gilbert Stuart Memorial Assn., 1890, Transatlantic Soc. of America, 1900; pres. Corp. for Relief of Widows and Children of Clergymen in Commonwealth of Pa. Dir. Pa. Co. for Insurances on Lives & Granting Annuities, Phila. Saving Fund Soc., Ins. Co. of N. America. Gold medal of honor, Pa. Acad. Fine Arts, 1915. Home: Philadelphia, Pa. Died Dec. 23, 1921.

COATES, Edwin Morton, brig. gen.; b. New York, Jan. 29, 1836; s. Charles and Catherine (Staley) C.; ed. Albany (N.Y.) Acad.; m. Isaelta Stewart, Oct. 1882. Mem. Chicago Zouaves, Col. E.E. Ellsworth commdg., 1859-60; entered Union Army, Apr. 1861, as 1st lt. N.Y. Fire Zouaves; 2d lt. 2d N.Y. Dragoons, June 1861; 2d lt. 2d U.S. Cav., Aug. 5, 1861; transferred to 12th Inf., Sept. 20, 1861; 1st lt., Oct. 24, 1861; advanced through grades to col. 7th Inf., July 23, 1898; retired, Jan. 29, 1900; advanced to rank of brig. gen. retired, by act of Apr. 23, 1904. Bvtd. capt., Aug. 1, 1864, "for gallant services in battle of the Wilderness and during the campaign before Richmond." Died Sept. 13, 1913.

COATES, Florence Earle, author; b. Phila.; d. George H. and Ellen Frances (Von Leer) Earle; ed. pvt. sch. in N.E. and Convent Sacred Heart, France; studied also at Brussels; m. Edward Hornor Coates, Jan. 7, 1879. Pres. Browning Soc., Phila., 1895-1903 and 1907-08; a founder Contemporary Club, Phila., 1886, also Transatlantic Soc. of America. Unanimously elected poet laureate of Pa. by State Fedn. of Women's Clubs. Author: (poems) Poems, 1898; Mine and Thine, 1904; Lyrics of Life, 1909; Ode on the Coronation of King George V, 1911; The Unconquered Air and Other Poems, 1912; Poems, 2 vols., 1916; Pro Patria, 1917. Home: Philadelphia, Pa. Died Apr. 6, 1927.

COATES, Foster, journalist. Entered newspaper work as boy on New York Commercial, finally becoming its mng. editor; later mng. editor Mail and Express, news editor the Press, and editor Evening World; then mng. editor New York American. Syndicate writer and contbr. to mags. Home: New York, N.Y. Died Nov. 17, 1914.

COATES, Henry Troth, publisher; b. Phila., Sept. 29, 1843; s. George Morrison and Anna (Troth) C.; grad. Haverford Coll., 1862 (A.M.); m. Estelle Barton Lloyd, June 25, 1874. Publisher, 1868—. Editor: Comprehensive Speaker, 1871; Fireside Ency. of Poetry, 1878; Children's Book of Poetry, 1879. Author: Short History of the American Trotting and Pacing Horse, 1901. Home: Berwyn, Pa. Died 1910.

COATES, Joseph Hornor (Hornor Cotes), author; b. Phila.; s. George Morrison and Anna (Troth) C.; A.B., U. of Pa.; m. Elizabeth Gardner Potts (dec.); children—George Morrison, Mrs. Ella Mary Bishop, Henry Troth, Beulah, Anna Morrison, Joseph Collins (dec.), Josiah Langdale (dec.), Sydney Hornor, Sherman Gardner. Has engaged in various lines of mercantile and mfg. bus., and in cattle ranching in the West and as mag. editor. Mem. bd. dirs. Athenæum of Phila. Life mem. Hist. Soc. of Pa.; hon. life mem. Acad. Fine Arts (Phila.); mem. Acad. Nat. Sciences (Phila.). Episcopalian. Author: The Counterpart, 1909; The Spirit of the Island, 1911; Would an Act of Congress Granting Independence to the Philippines be Valid Under the Constitution, 1916. Home: Berwyn, Pa. Died Dec. 13, 1930.

COATES, Thomas Jackson, educator; b. Pikeville, Ky., Mar. 17, 1867; s. Aaron Thompson and Jalana (Wells) C.; State Coll., Lexington, Ky.; Emmons Blaine Sch., Chicago; A.B., Southern Normal Sch., Bowling Green, Ky., 1904, A.M., 1906; m. Dellah D. Myers, Oct. 11, 1893. Teacher, country schs., 1883-89; prin. Greenville pub. schs., Ky., and editor Muhlenburg Echo, 1889-95; supt. schs., Princeton, Ky., 1895-1907, Richmond, Ky., 1907-11; state supervisor of rural schs. of Ky., 1911-16; pres. Eastern Ky. State Normal Sch., Aug. 1916—. Democrat. Presbyn. Mason. Home: Richmond, Ky. Died Mar. 17, 1928.

COBB, Albert Clifford, lawyer; b. Rockland, Me., Aug. 27, 1860; s. John Clifford and Hannah Maria (Hawkes) C.; grad. Westbrook Sem., Portland, Me., 1877; A.B., Bowdoin Coll., 1881; m. Annie Storer Littlefield, Sept. 15, 1886; children—Frederick Littlefield, Helen C. (Mrs. Mac Martin), Grace Manson (dec.), Marion Clifford. Admitted to Minn. bar, 1884, and began practice at Minneapolis; mem. Cobb, Hoke, Benson, Krause & Faegre; dir. and mem. exec. com. Northwestern Nat. Bank of Minneapolis, Minn. Loan & Trust Co. Trustee 1st Universalist Soc. Minneapolis. Republican. Home: Minneapolis, Minn. Died Dec. 5, 1933.

COBB, Amasa, lawyer; b. Crawford Co., Ill., Sept. 27, 1823; s. John and Nancy (Briggs) C.; ed. Crawford Co., Ill., public schools; m. Dec. 26, 1849, Mrs. Sudduth (died 1896). Served in Mexican war, 6th regt., Ill. vols., 1 yr. as private soldier; served in both houses Wis. legislature, 2 yrs. each; was speaker lower house; col. 5th Wis. vol. inf., June 4, 1861-Dec. 27, 1862; comd. regt. in battle of Williamsburg, May 5, 1862; comd. Hancock's brigade at battle of Antietam, Sept. 17, 1862; raised and comd. 43rd regt. Wis. vols., Sept. 10, 1864, to July 7, 1865; received bvt. rank of brig. gen. for gallant and meritorious service at Williamsburg, Golden's farm, Malvern Hill and Antietam. Was elected to Congress 4 times, twice while in actual mil. service; mem. Congress, 1863-71; mayor of Lincoln, Neb., 1873; judge Supreme Court, Neb., 1878-92 (4 yrs. chief justice). Republican. Home: Los Angeles, Calif. Died 1905.

COBB, Andrew Jackson, judge; b. Athens, Ga., Apr. 12, 1857; s. Howell and Mary Ann (Lamar) C.; A.B., U. of Georgia, 1876, LL.B., 1877 (LL.D., same university, 1921); m. Starkie Campbell, Mar. 3, 1880 (died 1901). In practice at Athens, Ga., from 1877; prof. law, U of Ga., 1884-93; dean Atlanta Law Sch., 1893-98, city atty., Athens, 1887-91; mem. bd. edn., 1886-89 (pres. 1889); asso. justice Supreme Ct., Ga., 1896-1907 (presiding justice, 1905-07); resigned; resumed practice of law at Athens, 1908-17; judge Superior Court, for Western Circuit of Ga., 1917-21; professor of law, U. of Ga., 1921—; practiced at Athens, 1921—. Mem. State Bd. of Pub. Welfare, 1921-23. Lecturer Y.M.C.A. Law School, Atlanta, 1905-06; lecturer constl. law and procedure, U. of Ga., 1908-21, on constl. law, Sch. of Commerce same, 1913-17. Presdl. elector state at large and pres. Electoral Coll. of Ga., 1912. Chmn. permanent commn. of Ga. Bar Assn. on Revision of Jud. System and Procedure in Courts, 1911—; mem. legislative commn. on Revision of Procedure in Courts, 1913. Trustee U. of Ga., 1891-93 and 1915-21, N. Ga. Agrl. Coll., 1916-18, Lucy Cobb Inst., Athens, 1907—(pres. bd. 1910—); chmn. bd. deacons Athens Bapt. Ch., 1911—; chmn. exec. com. Ga. Bapt. Conv.; trustee Ga. Med. Coll., 1918-21, State Normal Sch., 1919-21; chmn. State Memorial Commn. of Ga., 1919—; "Four-Minute Speaker" during war; asst. judge advocate U.C.V. of Ga., with rank of maj., 2 terms; brig. comdr. Sons of Confederate Vets., 1918-19. Author of the Athens, Ga., Dispensary law, first legally established dispensary for sale of liquors in U.S. Mason. Home: Athens, Ga. Died Mar. 27, 1925.

COBB, Calvin, publisher; b. Cleveland, July 15, 1853; s. Lucius Marcus and Mary (McMillan) C.; m. Fanny H. Lyon, Feb. 7, 1878 (died 1917); children—Lyon Cobb (dec.), Margaret. Editor and pub. Idaho Statesman, 1889—. Republican. Presbyn. Home: Boise, Ida. Died Nov. 6, 1928.

COBB, Collier, geologist; b. Mt. Auburn Plantation, Wayne Co., N.C., Mar. 21, 1862; s. Needham B. (D.D.) and Martha Louisa (Cobb) C.; student Wake Forest Coll., hon. Sc. D., 1917; student University of North Carolina; A.B., Harvard University, 1889, A.M., 1894; m. Mary L. Battle, Jan. 27, 1891 (died 1900); children—Wm. Battle, Collier, Mary Louisa; m. 2d, Lucy P. Battle, Apr. 6, 1904 (died 1905); m. 3d, Mary Knox Gatlin, Oct. 27, 1910. Taught in pub. schs. of N.C.; lecturer in State normal schs.; asst. Harvard, 1888-90; instr. Mass. Inst. Tech., 1890-92; prof. geology, U. of N.C., 1892; Kenan research prof., 1920-21, studying shore lines N. Pacific, Gulf of Mexico, and Caribbean Sea. Taught geology, summer, Harvard, 1891, Knoxville, 1902, 09, Biltmore Forest Sch., 1905-12, Cornell, 1928, and U. of N.C.; student of moving sands, coast lines and soils. Mem. Baltimore Conf. on China-America Relations, 1925. Fellow Geol. Soc. America, A.A.A.S., Assn. Am. Geographers. Edited and published small illustrated paper, 1871-75; pub. map of North Carolina, 1879, 6 editions. Author: Where the Wind Does the Work; Human Habitations; Landes and Dunes of Gascony; Pocket Dictionary of Common Rock and Rock Minerals, 2d edit., 1915; Geography of North Carolina, 1880, 5th edit., 1915. Discoverer of Enfield horse, in early Pleistocene deposits of N.C. Home: Chapel Hill, N.C. Died Nov. 28, 1934.

COBB, Cyrus, sculptor, painter; b. Malden, Mass., Aug. 6, 1834 (twin brother of Darius C.); s. Rev. Sylvanus C. (D.D.) and Eunice (Hale) C.; pursued art from boyhood; grad. Boston Univ. Law School, 1873, and practiced law until 1879, to advance, in conjunction with his brother, his life purpose to nationalize Am. Art. He then resumed his art; has executed many statues and busts; soldiers' monument at Cambridge, and other groups; in painting has executed many historic scenes and portraits; served in the 44th Mass. vols. in Civil war; m. Emma Lillie, Jan. 1, 1866. Author: Sonnets to the Great Masters (with portraits reproduced from drawings by himself); Veteran of the Grand Army (novel); etc. Home: Allston, Mass. Died 1903.

COBB, Darius, artist; b. Malden, Mass., Aug. 6, 1834; s. Rev. Sylvanus C. and Eunice (Hale) C.; twin brother late Cyrus C.; pub. sch. edn.; served in 44th Mass. Vols. through Civil War; m. Laura M. Lillie, Jan. 1, 1866. Painter of portraits and landscapes, and especially well known for his large exhbn. paintings of scriptural and hist. scenes and groups. Has been art critic of the Boston Traveler; also lectured on art; contbr. of blank verse to Boston Transcript, etc. After many yrs.' work, completed (1914) his head of Christ, which is regarded as his masterpiece; has exhibited this painting (entitled "The Master") in chs. of leading cities of the U.S.; also pvt. exhbns. before the President, and other govt. officials at Washington, D.C. Died Apr. 23, 1919.

COBB, Ebenezer Baker, clergyman; b. Auburn, N.Y., Oct. 23, 1855; s. Ebenezer Baker and Eleanor Matilda (Brownell) C.; A.B., Hamilton Coll., 1875, D.D., 1895; m. Helen Mills Starr, Aug. 11, 1886. Ordained Presbyn. ministry, 1880; pastor, Ramapo, N.Y., 1880-86, Second Ch., Elizabeth, N.J., 1886-1925, pastor emeritus, 1925—. Treas., 1890—, also pres. trustees, 1895—, Synod of N.J.; mem. Bd. of Foreign Missions, Presbyn. Ch., 1903—; pres. bd. trustees Bloomfield (N.J.) Theol. Sem., Presbyn. Home for Aged (Belvidere, N.J.); mem. bd. of founders Nanking (China) Univ. Home: Elizabeth, N.J. Died Oct. 15, 1940.

COBB, Frank Irving, editor New York World; b. in Shawnee Co., Kan., Aug. 6, 1869; s. Minor H. and Mathilde A. C.; m. Delia S. Bailey, 1897; m. 2d, Margaret Hubbard Ayer, Oct. 2, 1913. Editorial writer, Detroit Evening News, 1896-1900, Detroit Free Press, 1900-04, New York World, May 1904—. Address: The World, New York. Died Dec. 21, 1923.

COBB, Henry Ives, architect; b. Brookline, Mass., Aug. 19, 1859; s. Albert A. and Mary R. (Candler) C.; ed. pvt. and pub. schs. and at Mass. Inst. Tech.; S.B., Harvard, 1880; m. Emma M. Smith, 1882; children—Henry Ives, Cleveland, Leonore Amory, Candler, Elliot, Boughton, Russell. He entered an architect's office in Boston and moved to Chicago, 1881; architect for Chicago Opera House, Newberry Library, U. of Chicago, Ch. of the Atonement, Albany (N.Y.) Savings Bank, Liberty Tower, Harriman Bank (N.Y. City), etc.; one of Nat. Bd. of Architects of Chicago Expn., 1893; spl. architect for U.S. Govt., 1893-1903; gen. practice, including the U.S. Govt. bldgs. at Chicago, League Island, Annapolis, etc., and the American U. at Washington, D.C. Home: New York, N.Y. Died Mar. 27, 1931.

COBB, Henry Nitchie, clergyman; b. New York, Nov. 15, 1834; s. Sanford and Sophia Lewis (Nitchie) C.; brother of Sanford Hoadley C.; A.B., Yale, 1855, A.M., 1858; Union Theol. Sem., 1856-57; (D.D., Rutgers, 1878); m. Matilda E. Van Zandt, May 17, 1860. Ordained Presbyn. ministry, 1860; missionary to Persia under A.B.C.F.M., 1860-62; pastor Ref. Ch. in America, 1866-81; corr. sec. Bd. of Foreign Missions, Ref. Ch. in America, 1882—. Tours of the world visiting mission fields, 1891-92, 1904-05. Author: Far Hence—A Budget of Letters from Our Mission Fields in Asia, 1893. Home: E. Orange, N.J. Died 1910.

COBB, Herbert Edgar, prof. mathematics; b. Searsmont, Me., July 4, 1860; s. David Barnabas and Mary Crocker (Post) C.; grad. Me. Wesleyan Sem. and Female Coll., Kent's Hill, 1883; A.B., Wesleyan U., Conn., 1887, A.M., 1890; U. of Chicago, 1892-95; U. of Berlin, 1905-06; m. Sara Maxson, Mar. 11, 1890. Teacher mathematics, Me. Wesleyan Sem. and Female Coll., 1887-90; instr. mathematics, U. of Colo., 1890-92; lecturer univ. extension div., U. of Chicago, 1892-96; instr. mathematics, 1896-99, asst. prof., 1899-1906, prof., 1906—, Lewis Inst., Chicago. Author: Elements of Applied Mathematics, 1911. Home: Chicago. Died Mar. 1, 1938.

COBB, John Blackwell, capitalist; b. Caswell County, N.C., Oct. 5, 1857; s. Henry Wellington and Mary (Howard) C.; ed. pvt. schs., Caswell County, N.C.; m. Pricie Perkins Millner, Jan. 4, 1881. Borrowed $500 at 19, and engaged in leaf tobacco business; became connected with Am. Tobacco Co., as buyer of leaf tobacco, 1890, and v.p. same, 1896-1908, also dir. and officer affiliated cos. (retired, 1908); dir. and mem. exec. com. United Drug Co. Methodist. Mason. Home: Stamford, Conn. Died Apr. 9, 1923.

COBB, John Candler, trustee; b. Brookline, Mass., May 10, 1858; s. Albert A. and Mary Russell (Candler) C.; grad. Brookline High Sch., 1874; spent 1 yr. abroad in study and travel; m. Leonore Smith, Dec. 9, 1879; children—John Candler, Mrs. Emma May Foot, Augustus S., Stanley, Mrs. Florence Brooks, Mrs. Beatrice Smart, Mrs. Hildegarde B. Forbes. In mercantile business, Boston, New York and Chicago, 1 yr. each, 1876-79; mem. E. Indian shipping firm of Albert A. Cobb & Co., 1879 until firm was dissolved, 1892; mem. successor firm, Cobb & Co., 1892—; organizer and mgr. South Bay Wharf & Terminal Co., purchased by N.H. R.R. Co., 1907; dir. Mut. Boiler Ins. Co.; trustee and dir. City Land Co., Boston; dir. and chmn. of bondholders com. of New York Railways Co. until reorganization, 1925. Republican. Presdl. elector, 1896. Unitarian. Mem. Boston Chamber of Commerce (v.p., 1909-11), Nat. Tariff Commn. Assn. (pres., 1909-14). Home: Milton, Mass. Died Dec. 30, 1933.

COBB, John Nathan, author, naturalist; b. Oxford, N.J., Feb. 20, 1868; s. Samuel S. and Louise (Richards) C.; ed. pub. schs.; m. Harriet C. Bidwell, Oct. 18, 1898; 1 dau., Genevieve Catherine. Newspaper reporter and editor, 1886-90; field agt. U.S. Bur. Fisheries, 1895-1904; asst. Alaska salmon agt., with same bur., 1904-12; editor Pacific Fisherman, Seattle, Wash., 1913-17; dir. Coll. of Fisheries, U. of Wash., Seattle, 1919—. Mem. Advisory Scientific Bd., Internat. Fisheries Commn., 1925—. Mem. Am. Fisheries Soc., Pacific Fisheries Soc. (pres., 1921, 23). Conglist. Author: The Canning of Fishery Products, 1919; Fish Cookery (with Mrs. Evelene Spencer), 1921. Deceased.

COBB, Joseph Pettee, physician; b. Abington, Mass., June 12, 1857; s. Edward White and Elmina (Howard) C.; A.B., Harvard, 1879; M.D., Hahnemann Med. Coll., Chicago, 1883; m. Edith H. Persens, Sept. 18, 1882. Adj. prof., 1889-93, prof. physiology, embryology and histology, 1893-98, sr. prof. pediatrics, 1898—, and now pres. Hahnemann Med. Coll.; prof. diseases of children, Hahnemann Hosp., 1893—. Pres. Chicago Soc. of the New Jerusalem Ch. Home: Chicago, Ill. Died Dec. 23, 1924.

COBB, Levi Henry, clergyman; b. Cornish, N.H., June 30, 1827; s. Levi and Calista S.C.; ed. Dartmouth Coll. and Andover Theol. Sem., D.D., 1881; m. Harriet J. Herrick, Jan. 12, 1858. Sec. Congl. Ch. Bldg. Soc., 1882-1903; sec. emeritus, 1903—, mng. editor Congregational Work, 1898-99; editor Church Building Quarterly, 1882—. Home: Maynard, Mass. Died 1906.

COBB, Nathan Augustus, scientist, educator; b. Spencer, Mass., June 30, 1859; s. William H. and

Jane A. (Bigelow) C.; both of English Puritan stock; B.Sc., Worcester Poly. Inst., 1881; Ph.D., U. of Jena, 1888, honors under Haeckel, Hertwig, Lang and Stahl; m. Alice Vara Proctor, Aug. 8, 1881; children—Russell Harding (dec.), Margaret Vara, Victor, Roger (dec.), Mrs. Frieda Blanchard, Mrs. Ruth Ross, Mrs. Dorothy Adams. Teacher pub. schs., Spencer, 1877-78; prof. chemistry and natural science, Williston Sem., Mass., 1881-87; appointee British Assn. Adv. Science, Naples Zoöl. Sta., 1888-89; locum tenens prof. biology, Sydney U., N.S.W., 1890-91; pathologist Dept. of Agr., N.S.W., 1891-98; mgr. Wagga Expt. Farm, 1897-98; agrl. commr. N.S.W. to U.S. and Europe, 1898-1901; pathologist Dept. Agr., N.S.W., 1901-04; dir. div. Physiology and Pathology, Hawaiian Sugar Planters' Expt. Sta., Honolulu, 1904-07; agrl. technologist, Dept. of Agr., 1907—; acting asst. chief, Bur. Plant Industry, Dept. Agr., Jan. 1, 1911—. Awarded medal by Nat. Cotton Mfrs. Assn. "for work in establishing methods of determining the properties and value of cotton." Home: Falls Church, Va. Died 1932.

COBB, Samuel Ernest, banker; b. Salina, Kan., Dec. 17, 1870; s. H. S. and Nancy (Tucker) C.; ed. pub. schs. of Kan. and Commercial Coll., St. Louis, Mo.; m. Josephine Joseph, Oct. 27, 1897; children—Theo, Ray (dec.), Mateel (dec.). Began in banking business at El Dorado, Kan., 1898; moved to Topeka, 1909; chmn. bd. of Bank of Topeka, Prudential Trust Co.; dir. Burns State Bank, Victory Life Ins. Co., Kan. Life Ins. Co., Menninger Sanatorium Corp. A leader and treas. war drives in Kan.; mem. Southwest Div. Am. Red Cross; treas. Near East Relief. Trustee Washburn Coll., Topeka. Republican. Mason. Home: Topeka, Kan. Died Nov. 3, 1927.

COBB, Sanford Hoadley, clergyman; b. New York, Feb. 4, 1838; s. Sanford and Sophia Lewis (Nitchie) C.; brother of Henry Nitchie C.; A.B., Yale, 1858; grad. Princeton Theol. Sem., 1862; m. Mary Elizabeth Capen, Nov. 9, 1865. Ordained Presbyn. ministry, 1864; pastor Reformed ch., Schoharie, N.Y., 1864-71, Presbyn. ch., Saugerties, N.Y., 1871-83, Westminster Presbyn. Ch., Grand Rapids, Mich., 1885-94, Presbyn. ch., Greenwich, Conn., 1900-01. Tour of the world visiting mission fields, 1883-84. Author: The Story of the Palatines, 1897; The Rise of Religious Liberty in America, 1902. Died 1910.

COBB, Seth Wallace, mcht.; b. Southampton Co., Va., Dec. 5, 1838; s. Benjamin and Margaret (Wallace) C.; ed. pub. schs., Va.; m. Zoe Desloge, Oct. 3, 1876. Enlisted C.S.A., 1861, as orderly sergt. of arty.; served throughout Civil War in Army of Northern Va., reaching rank of bvt. maj.; for a time with Gov. Cameron of Va., edited the Petersburg Index; went to St. Louis, 1867; pres. Merchants' Exchange, 1886, and with others obtained charter for Merchants' Bridge and was pres. of the company that built it; mem. Congress, 1891-97; refused renomination and engaged in grain business until retired, 1902; 5th v.p. and dir. La. Purchase Expn. Co.; Cleveland Democrat. Catholic. Home: St. Louis, Mo. Died 1909.

COBB, William Henry, librarian; b. Rochester, Mass., Apr. 2, 1846; s. Rev. Leander and Julia Ann (Scribner) C.; A.B., Amherst, 1867 (D.D., 1892); m. Emily Wollaston Wiggins, Oct. 30, 1872. Ordained Congl. ministry, 1872; pastor Chiltonville, Plymouth, Mass., 1872-76; acting pastor Medfield, Mass., 1876-78; pastor Uxbridge, Mass., 1878-87; librarian Congl. Library and asst. treas. Am. Congl. Assn., Boston, Dec. 1, 1887—. Supt. schs., Uxbridge, 1886-87. One of 3 editors and pubs. Jour. Biblical Literature, 1889-1915. Author: A Criticism of Systems of Hebrew Metre, 1905; The Meaning of Christian Unity, 1915; Seven Centuries Illustrated in the Congregational Library, 1921. Home: Newton Center, Mass. Died May 1, 1923.

COBB, William Titcomb, gov., mfr.; b. Rockland, Me., July 23, 1857; s. Francis and Martha C.; A.B., Bowdoin, 1877, A.M., 1880 (LL.D., Bowdoin and U of Me., 1905); m. Lucy C. Banks, June 14, 1882. Was long engaged in lime mfg. business, title of Cobb-Wight Co.; pres. Bath Iron Works, later receiver; gov. of Me., 1905-09. Republican. Trustee Bowdoin Coll., 1908—. Home: Rockland, Me. Died July 24, 1937.

COBBEY, Charles Elliott, clergyman, educator; b. Beatrice, Neb., July 9, 1885; s. Joseph Elliott and Lottie Wilhelmina (Schell) C.; student Butler Coll., Indianapolis, 1904-05; A.B., Cotner Coll., Bethany, Neb., 1909, D.D., 1922; m. Mabel Mussette Snyder, June 30, 1909. Began ministry, Disciples of Christ, at 17; pastor, Columbus, Ind., 1903-06, Chester, Neb., 1907-10; evangelistic work and pastor, Eureka, Mont., 1911-12; pastor 1st Ch., Omaha, 1913-22; pres. Cotner Coll., Oct. 3, 1922—. Religious work dir. Y.M.C.A., Camp Cody, summer 1917; in charge Y.M.C.A. religious work in Italy, July 1918-Sept. 1919. Mem. Nat. Ednl. Bd. and Nat. Bd. Mgrs., Disciples of Christ. Mason. Home: Bethany, Neb. Died Sept. 11, 1925.

COBBEY, Joseph Elliott, lawyer; b. Clarksville, Mo., Nov. 5, 1853; s. Joseph Elliott and Harriet J. C.; A.B., State Agrl. Coll. of Ia., 1876; LL.B., Simpson Coll. (now Drake U.), 1877; m. Lottie W. Schell, July 30, 1879. Admitted to bar, 1877, and then in practice at Beatrice. Prepared a new statute for Territory of N.M. preparatory to statehood, 1908. Republican. Author: Law of Replevin, 1890; Law of Chattel Mortgages, 1893; Consolidated Statutes of Nebraska, 1891-93; Code of Nebraska, Annotated, 1901; Annotated Statutes of Nebraska (2 vols.), 1903. Home: Beatrice, Neb. Deceased.

COBE, Ira Maurice, investments; b. Boston, Oct. 29, 1866; s. Mark H. and Eva (Morris) C.; ed. Boston U.; m. Annie E. Watts, Mar. 19, 1892. Admitted to Suffolk bar, Boston, 1888, and practiced in Boston 4 yrs.; joined, 1892, in organizing present firm of Cobe & McKinnon, investments, Chicago; pres. Assets Realization Co.; chmn. bd. Chicago City Ry. Co.; dir. Chicago Title & Trust Co., etc.; chmn. governing com. Chicago City and Connecting Rys. Republican. Home: Chicago, Ill. Died July 9, 1931.

COBERN, Camden McCormack, theologian; b. Uniontown, Pa., Apr. 19, 1855; s. Simon Peter and Mary Ellen (McCormack) C.; A.B., Allegheny Coll., 1876, A.M., 1878; S.T.B., Boston U., 1883, Ph.D., 1885; student in Eng. and Germany, 1889-90; (D.D., Allegheny Coll., 1891; Litt. D., Lawrence Coll., Wisconsin, 1908); m. Ernestine Craft, Sept. 4, 1883. Ordained M.E. ministry, 1878; pastor in Erie Conf., 1876-81, Detroit Conf., 1883-96, Colo. Conf., 1896-1901, in Chicago, 1901-06; prof. English Bible and philosophy of religion, Allegheny Coll., Sept. 1906—. Del. Gen. Conf., 1896; mem. joint commn. for the preparation of a common hymnal for the M.E. Ch. and M.E. Ch., S., 1900-04, etc. Hon. sec. Egyptian Exploration Fund. Author: Critical Commentary on the Books of Ezekiel and Daniel (Whedon Series), 1901; The New Archeological Discoveries and Their Bearing upon the New Testament and upon the Life and Times of the Primitive Church, 1917, 4th edit., 1921. Served in British sect. in France, rank of 1st lt., Red Cross, 1919. Home: Meadville, Pa. Died May, 1920.

COBLEIGH, Nelson Simmons, newspaperman; b. Wilbraham, Mass., June 29, 1845; s. Nelson Ebenezer C. (D.D., LL.D.) and Charlotte Maria (Simmons) C.; A.B., McKendree Coll., Ill., 1862, A.M., 1865; Harvard, 1863-64; grad. Lewis Normal Inst. Phys. Edn., Boston, 1864; hon. A.M., Yale, 1865, Wesleyan, 1866; m. Martha Abbie Rice, June 29, 1869; children—Nellie Stephens, Grace Rice (dec.), Harriet Esty and Charles Nelson (twins, both dec.), Henry Rice. Reporter, Boston Daily Advertiser, 1865-67; city editor, Cleveland Daily Leader, 1868-69; city editor, later asso. editor, Cleveland Plain Dealer, 1869-90; on staff, 1890—, foreign editor, 1893-1923, New York World. Mem. Cleveland City Council, 1875-77 (v.p. 1 yr.). Democrat. Home: White Plains, N.Y. Died Mar. 3, 1927.

COBLENTZ, Emory Lorenzo, lawyer, corp. exec.; b. nr. Middletown, Md., Nov. 5, 1869; s. Edward Livingston and Lucinda F. (Bechtol) C.; grad. high sch., Middletown, Md.; studied law in the office of Charles W. Ross, of Frederick, Md.; LL.D., Franklin and Marshall College, 1926; m. Amy A. Douh, Sept. 26, 1893 (died Feb. 4, 1904); children—Mrs. Ruth Swank, Mrs. Naomi Winston, Esther Douh (Mrs. Frank C. Englesing), Miriam A. (Mrs. John C. Saur); m. 2d, Mary V. Kefauver, May 15, 1906; children—Mary Virginia (dec.), Helen O. (Mrs. Arthur E. Fox). Practiced at Frederick, 1897—; organized and was pres. Potomac Edison Co., Frederick, Md., until 1923, then mem. board and exec. com.; v.p. and dir. Economy Silo and Mfg. Co.; dir. Potomac Light & Power Co. (Martinsburg, W.Va.), South Penn Power Co. (Waynesboro, Pa.), Northern Va. Power Co. (Winchester). Mem. Md. State Senate (chmn com. on edn. and com. on revaluation and assessments), term 1930-34; mem. State Bd. of Edn., Md., 1924-36. Mem. Bd. State Aid and Charities, Md., 1912-16; v.p., dir. and chmn. finance com. Hood College (Frederick, Md.). Mem. Md. legislature, 1920, and majority floor leader of House; chmn. and dir. Md. Dept. of Welfare, 1922-24. Mem. Board Home Missions, Evang. and Reformed Ch., 1917—. Democrat. Mason. Home: Middletown, Md. Died Aug. 6, 1941.

COBLENTZ, Virgil, chemist; b. Springfield, O., Mar. 12, 1862; s. John Philip and Susan (Zitzer) C.; grad. Wittenberg Coll.; Ph.G. and Pharm.M., Phila. Coll. Pharmacy, 1882; Ph.D., U. of Berlin, 1891; M.D., U. of Wuerzburg, 1895; m. Anna Bauer, of Strassburg, Mar. 7, 1889. Prof. materia medica and toxicology, Cincinnati Coll. Pharmacy, 1884-87; prof. chemistry, New York Coll. Pharmacy (Columbia), 1891-1911; chief chemist, E. R. Squibb & Sons, N.Y. City, 1911-17; pathologist to Hazard Hosp., Long Branch, N.J. Chmn. N.Y. sect. Soc. Chem. Industry of Gt. Britain, 1902-04, N.Y. sect. Verein Deutscher Chemiker, 1909-14; mem. com. of revision of U.S. Pharmacopœia, 1900-20. Mason. Author: Handbook of Pharmacy, 1895; The Newer Remedies, 1897; Sadtler and Coblentz Medical and Pharmaceutical Chemistry, 1899; Volumetric Analysis. Home: West End, N.J. Died 1932.

COBURN, Foster Dwight, sec. Kan. Dept. Agr.; b. Jefferson Co., Wis., May 7, 1846; s. Ephraim W. and Mary Jane (Mulks) C.; ed. common schs.; hon. M.A., Baker Univ.; LL.D., Kan. State Agrl. Coll.; m. Lou Jenkins, Sept. 8, 1869. Served in the Civil War in the 135th and later in the 62d Ill. Inf.; from 1867 a resident of Kan.; was a farmer and stockman in Franklin Co.; sec. Kan. Dept. Agr., 1882, and Jan. 1894-Jan. 1914. Was editor of the Kansas City Live-Stock Indicator nearly 6 yrs.; has been a regent of the State Agrl. Coll. under 4 appmts. and pres. and v.p. of bd.; pres. Kan. State Temperance Union 4 terms. Chief of dept. of live stock, St. Louis Expn., 1904; mem. bd. mgrs. Kansas State Fair. Apptd. U.S. senator from Kan., June 4, 1906, but declined. Author: Alfalfa; The Book of Alfalfa; Swine in America. Was chmn. Draft Appeal Bd., 1st dist. Kan., 1917. V.p. Prudential Trust Co., and Capitol Bldg. & Loan Assn. Home: Topeka, Kan. Deceased.

COBURN, John, lawyer; b. Indianapolis, Ind., Oct. 27, 1825; s. Henry P. C.; grad. Wabash Coll., 1846, A.M., 1852; LL.D., 1898; studied law at Indianapolis; m. Caroline A. Test, Mar. 9, 1852. Mem. Ind. legislature, 1850-51; judge Court of Common Pleas, 1859-61; col. 33d regt., Ind. vols., Sept. 16, 1861-Sept. 20, 1864; bvt. brig. gen. for gallant and meritorious services; served in Army of the Cumberland; judge of circuit court, 1865-66; mem. Congress, 1867-75; mem. U.S. Hot Springs (Ark.) Commn., 1877-79; judge Supreme Court of Mont., 1884-86; Whig and Republican. Home: Indianapolis, Ind. Died 1908.

COCHEMS, Henry Frederick, lawyer; b. Sturgeon Bay, Wis., Jan. 11, 1875; s. Mathias and Eliza (Wagener) C.; grad. Sturgeon Bay High Sch., 1890; LL.B., Law Dept., U. of Wis., 1897; LL.B., Harvard Law Sch., 1900; unmarried. Practiced in Milwaukee, 1900; spl. asst. dist. atty., Milwaukee Co., 1905; mem. Cochems & Wolfe; sec. Republican State Central Com., Wisconsin, 1904; chmn. speakers' bur. Progressive Nat. Com., 1912. Home: Milwaukee, Wis. Died Sept. 23, 1921.

COCHRAN, Alexander G., lawyer; b. Allegheny City, Pa., Mar. 20, 1846; s. John Turner and Anna (Richardson) C.; ed. pub. and pvt. schs. and Phillips Acad., Andover, Mass.; studied law Columbia Law Sch., and admitted to bar, 1866; m. Mary Virginia Andrews, June 1, 1869. Practiced at Pittsburgh, 1866-74; mem. 44th Congress (1875-77), 2d Pa. Dist.; defeated for 45th Congress; Democrat. Mem. spl. com. to S.C. to investigate Tilden-Hayes election and spl. com. to investigate whisky frauds in St. Louis. Apptd. gen. solicitor M.P. Ry., 1888; v.p. M.P. and Iron Mountain lines, Oct. 1, 1904-Dec. 1, 1909, when retired. Was gen. solicitor Cotton Belt and Internat. Great Northern Ry. Judge adv. Mo. N.G. on staff of Brig. Gen. Clarke. Episcopalian. Home: St. Louis, Mo. Died May 1, 1928.

COCHRAN, Andrew McConnell January, judge; b. Maysville, Ky., Feb. 4, 1854; s. Robert Armstrong and Harriet Frances (January) C.; A.B., Centre Coll., Ky., 1873, A.M., 1878; LL.B., Harvard, 1877; LL.D., Ky. U., 1916, Centre Coll., Ky., 1919; m Lucy B. McElroy, May 24, 1882; children—John McElroy, Mrs. Harriet Duke, Robert Armstrong. Admitted to bar, 1877, and practiced at Maysville, 1877-1901; U.S. dist. judge, Eastern Dist. of Ky., July 1, 1901—. Republican. Presbyn. Home: Maysville, Ky. Died June 12, 1934.

COCHRAN, Carlos Bingham, chemist; b. Albion, Mich., July 1, 1854; s. Isaac Cook and Julia A. (Bingham) C.; B.A., U. of Mich., 1877, M.A., 1888, Sc.D., 1907; m. Sarah B. Marshall, July 16, 1885. Microscopist and hygienist to Pa. State Bd. Agr., 1884—; chemist to Pa. dairy commr., 1885-95, to Phila. Milk Exchange, 1890-1905; chemist dairy and food division, Dept. Agr., 1895-1918; mem. West Chester Bd. Health, 1897—; prof. natural sciences, 1879, prof. physical sciences, 1895-1903, prof. chemistry, 1903-09, West Chester State Normal Sch.; chemist, Charles E. Hines Co., Phila., 1918—. Home: West Chester, Pa. Died 1929.

COCHRAN, Charles Fremont, congressman, editor; b. Kirksville, Mo., Sept. 27, 1848; s. W. A. and Laetitia (Smith) C.; lived at Atchison, Kan., 1860-85; ed. common schs.; m. Louise M. Webber, Apr. 27, 1868. Became printer; editor, 1868—; also lawyer; pros. atty. Atchison Co., Kan., 4 yrs.; has lived at St. Joseph, Mo., 1885—; mem. Mo. senate, 6 yrs.; mem. Congress from 4th Mo. dist., 1897-1905; Democrat. Home: St. Joseph, Mo. Died 1906.

COCHRAN, David Henry, educator; b. Springville, N.Y., July 5, 1828; s. Samuel and Catherine (Gallup) C.; grad. Hamilton Coll., 1850 (A.M., Ph.D., LL.D.); commenced teaching at age of 15; worked his way through coll. by teaching and lecturing; m. Harriet Stryker Rawson, 1851. Prof. natural science, Clinton Liberal Inst., 1850-52; prin. Fredonia Acad., 1852-55; prof. chemistry and physics, N.Y. State Normal Coll., 1855 (pres., 1856-64); pres., 1864-1900, Brooklyn Collegiate and Poly. Inst. (granted power to confer B.S. and B.A. degrees, 1870; chartered as coll., 1890); resigned (retired). Pres. Am. Soc. for Regulation of Vivisection; hon. mem. Brooklyn Inst. Arts and Sciences; v.p. Am. Humane Assn.; trustee Hamilton Coll. for 30 yrs. Died 1909.

COCHRAN, Ernest Ford, judge; b. Anderson, S.C., Sept. 12, 1865; s. John Robert and Grace Greenwood (Arnold) C.; grad. U. of Va., LL.B., 1888; m. Mary Virginia Lewis, Sept. 6, 1900; 1 son, Ernest F. (dec.). Admitted to S.C. bar, 1889, and began practice at Anderson; U.S. commr., 1889-91; asst. U.S. atty., Dist. of S.C., 1891-92, 1898-1905; city atty., Anderson, 1898-1900; U.S. atty., Dist. of S.C., 1906-14, and for Western Dist. of S.C., 1921-23 (resigned); U.S. dist. judge, Eastern Dist. of S.C., Nov. 24, 1923—. Republican. Baptist. Home: Charleston, S.C. Died Mar. 5, 1934.

COCHRAN, George G., ry. official; b. Sandusky, O., Dec. 31, 1842; entered railroad service as clerk in freight and ticket offices Cincinnati, Dayton & Eastern R.R., Oct. 1858; held clerkships and other positions up to 1871; asst. gen. frt. agt., 1871-74, gen. frt. agt. Atlantic & Great Western Ry. (now N.Y.,Pa.&O. R.R.), 1874-87; western frt. traffic mgr., 1887-93, traffic mgr. New York, Lake Erie & Western, and Chicago & Erie R.R.'s, 1893-95; 4th v.p. Erie R.R., Dec. 1, 1895-July 1, 1900; western frt. traffic mgr. Erie R.R. and frt. traffic mgr. Chicago & Erie R.R., July 1, 1900—. Home: Cleveland, O. Died 1905.

COCHRAN, Harry King, merchant; b. Staunton, Va., Nov. 20, 1853; s. James Addison and Jane Annis (Davis) C.; grad. Culpeper High Sch., Va., 1869; m. N. Irene Haney, Jan. 9, 1884. Mgr. for Standard Oil Co. at Dallas, Tex., Chattanooga, Savannah, St. Louis and Little Rock until 1884; then in grain and grain products business. Mem. Progressive Nat. Com., 1912—. Episcopalian. Home: Little Rock, Ark. Died Mar. 2, 1913.

COCHRAN, Samuel Poyntz, fire ins.; b. Lexington, Ky., Sept. 11, 1855; s. John Carr and Samuella Tannehill (Dewees) C.; grad. high sch., Covington, Ky., 1873; m. Sue Webb Higgins, July 3, 1883. Began as ins. insp., Cincinnati, 1873; in gen. agency office J. W. Cochran & Son, Lexington, Ky., 1874-76; in local ins. business, Covington, 1876-81; spl. agt. Lancashire Ins. Co., Cincinnati, 1881, then with Phœnix Ins. Co. of Hartford, Conn., under H. M. Magill, Cincinnati; in Tex. for Phœnix, 1881-83; with Springfield Fire & Marine Ins. Co., Mar.-July 1883; entered employ of Dargan & Trezevant, Dallas, Tex., July 1, 1883, became partner, Jan. 1, 1884, name changed to Trezevant & Cochran, July 1, 1888. Pres. Mut. Bldg. Assn., Dallas Scottish Rite Cathedral Assn. Mem. bd. regents U. of Tex. and of Park Bd., Dallas; mem. bd. dirs. State Fair of Tex. and Dallas Chamber Commerce. Democrat. Christian Scientist. Mason. Chmn. trustees Shriners' Hosps. for Crippled Children, life mem. Imperial Council of the Shrine. Home: Cedar Springs, Tex. Died Feb. 11, 1936.

COCHRAN, Thomas, banker; b. St. Paul, Minn., Mar. 20, 1871; s Thomas and Emilie B. (Walsh) C.; B.A., Yale, 1894; m. Martha A. Griffin, Sept. 30, 1910 (died 1914). Pres. Liberty Nat. Bank, New York, 1914-17; partner J. P. Morgan & Co., Jan. 1, 1917—; chmn. exec. com. Bankers Trust Co.; dir. Bankers Trust Co., Braden Copper Co., Copper River & N.W. Ry. Co., Kennecott Copper Corp. Trustee New York Assn. for Improving Condition of Poor, Phillips Acad., Andover, Mass.; dir. Milbank Memorial Fund. Mem. New York Chamber of Commerce. Home: New York, N.Y. Died Oct. 29, 1936.

COCHRAN, William J(oseph) Hamilton, newspaperman; b. St. Louis Co., Mo., Nov. 16, 1878; s. James and Elizabeth (Hamilton) C.; ed. pub. schs. and under pvt. tutors; m. Isabella Meagher, June 21, 1915. Asst. sporting editor and reporter, St. Louis Post-Dispatch, 1896-1900; with Ft. Smith (Ark.) Times, 1900-03; reporter and polit. writer, St. Louis Star, 1904-05; mng. editor Joplin (Mo.) American, 1906; polit. writer, St. Louis Republic, 1907-12, Chicago Tribune, 1912-14; Washington corr. St. Louis Republic, 1914-19. Mem. staff Gov. Joseph W. Folk of Mo.; sec. Mo. Dem. League, 1912; dir. publicity western hdqrs., Dem. Nat. Com., 1916; dir. publicity Dem. Nat. Com., 1920; gen. newspaper writing and publicity work, 1920—. Catholic. Home: Washington, D.C. Died Aug. 1, 1925.

COCHRANE, Charles Henry, author; b. Lacon, Ill., Sept. 3, 1856; s. John and Annie Deborah (Hamilton) C.; ed. in acad. and under pvt. tutelage; m. Cora V. Miller, Nov. 23, 1877 (died 1881); m. 2d, Priscilla E. Applegate, 1884. Co-founder Salem (Mass.) Evening News, 1880; founder Marlborough (N.Y.) Record, 1885; one of editors Standard Dictionary, 1890-93; established pub. business now known as The Shakespeare Press, 1908. Sec. N.Y. Typothetæ, 1898-1903; founder and sec. N.Y. Master Printers' Assn., 1902. Author: Punctuation and Capitalization, 1910. Home: West Hoboken, N.J. Died Sept. 14, 1940.

COCHRANE, Henry Clay, brig. gen.; b. Chester, Pa., Nov. 7, 1842; s. James L. and Sarah Jane (Gillespie) C.; ed. Upland Normal Sch. and Friends' Central High Sch., Phila.; m. Elizabeth F., d. Capt. E. P. Lull, U.S.N., June 30, 1887. Apptd. in naval service, Sept. 7, 1861; served in Civil War, in railroad strikes of 1877, Spanish-Am. War, Boxer campaign, China, 1900, and in P.I.; retired with rank of brig. gen., Mar. 10, 1905. Was present at bombardment of Alexandria, Egypt, by the British, 1882, and at coronation of Czar, Alexander III, Moscow, 1883; maj. of marine battalion that held the heights at Guantanamo, Cuba, June, 1898; detailed as gov. of Manzanillo; comd. 1st brigade of marines in P.I. and acted as gov. Peninsula of Cavite, 1900-01; comd. regt. marines in Boxer war in China. Decorated with Cross of Legion of Honor by Pres. Carnot of France for services at Universal Expn., 1889; has Civil War, Spanish War, China and Philippine medals. Republican. Episcopalian. Home: Chester, Pa. Died Apr. 27, 1913.

COCHRANE, John McDowell, jurist; b. Mercersburg, Pa., Mar. 8, 1859; s. James and Caroline A. C.; ed. Minneapolis High Sch., business coll., Univ. of Minn. and Univ. of Mich.; grad. Mich. Law Sch., 1881; m. Francis Merrill, Mar. 8, 1884. Admitted to bar, 1881; probate judge 4 yrs., dist. atty. 4 yrs., Supreme Court reporter 11 yrs., judge Supreme Court N.Dak., 1902—. Republican. Prof. constl. and criminal law, Univ. of N.Dak. Home: Grand Forks, N.D. Died 1904.

COCHRANE, John Taylor, ry. official; b. Tuscaloosa, Ala., June 24, 1873; s. William Gilbert and Lily (Taylor) C.; student U. of Ala.; m. Alice Searcy, (died 1922); children—John T., George S.; m. 2d, Katharine S. Crampton, Nov. 1925. Began in employ Tuscaloosa Belt Railway, 1893, rebuilt and extended same; builder of Ala., Tenn. & Northern Ry., later Tombigbee Valley R.R. and Mobile Terminal & Ry. Co.; the three companies consol. as the Ala., Tenn. & Northern R.R. Corp., of which was pres.; financed and built the Mississippian Ry. and the Ala. & North Western R.R.; also financed the Mobile-Baldwin Bridge; officer or dir. various corps. Pres. Mobile Sch. Bd., Mobile Chamber Commerce; trustee Ala. Coll. for Girls; nat. counsellor U.S. Chamber of Commerce. Awarded Kiwanis loving cup, 1925, as "Mobile's most useful citizen." Home: Mobile, Ala. Died Jan. 12, 1938.

COCKE, Lucian Howard, lawyer; b. Hollins College, Va., March 27, 1858; s. Charles L. and Susanna V. (Pleasants) C.; student Richmond (Va.) Coll., 1873-76; A.B., Washington and Lee U., 1878; LL.B., U. of Va., 1881; m. Lelia M., d. Dr. Francis H. Smith, of U. of Va., Sept. 17, 1885 (died 1899); children—Charles Francis, Mrs. William H. Goodwin, Mrs. S. K. Funkhouser, Lucian H.; m. 2d, Mrs. Sarah Cobb Hagan (Johnson), Oct. 30, 1903. In law practice at Roanoke, Va., 1881; mem. Penn & Cocke, 1884-95, Cocke & Glasgow, 1896-1904; gen. atty. Norfolk & Western R.R., 1904; v.p .Nat. Exchange Bank, Hollins Coll., Roanoke; rector Washington and Lee U. Mayor of Roanoke, 1882-84; city solicitor, 1884-88. Democrat. Baptist. Home: Roanoke, Va. Died Nov. 14, 1927.

COCKE, William Horner, educator; b. City Point, Va., Sept. 12, 1874; s. Henry Teller and Elizabeth Welsh (Horner) C.; C.E., Va. Mil. Inst., 1894; B.L., Washington U., 1898; Army Gen. Staff College, Langres, France, 1918; LL.D., Washington and Lee U., 1929; m. Anne Jeannette Owen, Dec. 20, 1905. Comdt. cadets and prof. mathematics, Kemper Mil. Acad., Booneville, Mo., 1894-97; practiced law, St. Louis, Mo., 1899-1907; founder, 1907, pres. until 1936, Southern Acid & Sulphur Co. (formerly Commercial Acid Co.), St. Louis, Mo.; supt. Va. Mil. Inst., Oct. 1, 1924-July 1, 1929; apptd. mem. board visitors of same instn., 1930. Served as 1st lt. 4th Mo. Inf. (U.S. Vols.), Spanish-Am. War; maj. Inf., U.S.A., 1917-19, World War; brig. gen. Va. Volunteers, 1924; aide on staff gov. of Va., 1930. Chmn. Va. Assn. Against the Prohibition Amendment. Democrat. Episcopalian. Home: Claremont, Va. Died June 9, 1938.

COCKRAN, W(illiam) Bourke, congressman; b. in Co. Sligo, Ireland, Feb. 28, 1854; s. Martin and Harriet (Knight) C.; ed. in Ireland and France; (LL.D., St. Francis Xavier Coll., 1887; Georgetown Coll., D.C., 1900, Manhattan Coll., 1902); came to U.S., 1871; taught in pvt. acad.; later prin. of a pub. sch. in Westchester Co., N.Y.; admitted to bar, 1876, soon becoming prominent in N.Y. City politics; m. Anne, d. Henry Clay Ide, Nov. 5, 1906. Del. Dem. State Conv., 1881; made noteworthy speeches at Dem. Nat. convs., 1884 and 1892, opposing nomination of Cleveland; mem. 50th Congress (1887-89) and 52d and 53d Congresses (1891-95), as Democrat; in 1896 became advocate of the gold standard and campaigned for McKinley; on issue of anti-imperialism returned to Dem. party, 1900, and campaigned for Bryan; elected to 58th Congress, Feb. 23, 1904, for unexpired term (1904-05) of George B. McClellan, resigned; reelected to 59th and 60th Congresses (1905-09), 12th N.Y. Dist.; was not candidate for reëlection, 1909; resumed law practice at New York; mem. 67th Congress (1921-23), 16th N.Y. Dist. Died Mar. 1, 1923.

COCKRELL, Egbert Railey, college pres.; b. Platt Co., Mo., Apr. 2, 1873; s. H. Cliff and Sadie (Railey) C.; LL.B., Ia. Coll. of Law, Des Moines, Ia., 1898, LL.M., 1904; A.B., Tex. Christian U., Ft. Worth, Tex., 1900; A.M., Drake U., Des Moines, 1902, LL.D., 1923; studied Columbia, Oxford U., U. of Liverpool, U. of Chicago; m. Dura Brokaw, May 26, 1898; children—Dura Louise, Vardaman. Practiced law at Bozeman, Mont., 1897-99; prof. government, Tex. Christian U., 1899-1921, dean Coll. of Law, 1917-19; practiced in Tex.; mayor of Ft. Worth, two terms, 1921-24; pres. William Woods Coll., Fulton, Mo., Sept. 1924—. Teacher S.A.T.C., at Tex. Christian U., World War; col. on staff gov. of Mo., 1932—. Vice chmn. Reconstruction and Relief Commn. of Mo., 1933—. Pres. League of Tex. Municipalities, 1922-23; pres. Southwestern Polit. Science Assn., 1923—. Admitted to Mo. bar, 1926. Democrat. Mem. Disciples of Christ; pres. Mo. Conv. Disciples of Christ, 1931. Mason. Established dept. of govt. at Tex. Christian U. Home: Fulton, Mo. Died Sept. 1934.

COCKRELL, Francis Marion, senator; b. Johnson Co., Mo., Oct. 1, 1834; s. Joseph and Nancy (Ellis) C.; grad. Chapel Hill Coll., Lafayette Co., Mo., 1853; m. Miss Stapp, 1853 (died 1860); 2d, Anne E. Mann, 1867 (died); 3d, Anna Ewing, 1874. Admitted to bar, 1855; practiced at Warrensburg, Mo.; served in C.S.A., capt. to brig. gen. Resumed practice after war; U.S. senator, 5 terms, 1875-1905; Democrat; was chmn. Com. on Appropriations in 53d Congress, etc. Mem. Interstate Commerce Commission, Mar. 5, 1905-Dec. 31, 1910; U.S. commr. to reëstablish boundary between Tex. and N.M., Mar. 9, 1911—. Dir. Columbia Instn. for Deaf and Dumb. Civilian mem. Bd. of Ordnance and Fortifications, 1913. Home: Warrensburg, Mo. Died Dec. 13, 1915.

COCKRELL, Joseph Elmore, lawyer; b. Johnson County, Mo., Dec. 27, 1859; s. J. V. C. and Jane (Douglas) C.; A.B., Washington and Lee U., 1880, A.M., 1881, LL.B., 1882 (awarded Cincinnati oration, 1881); LL.D., Emory U.; m. Emma Lee Meadors, Jan. 25, 1885; children—Mrs. Mary Cockrell Cockrell, Mrs. Jane Adams, Mrs. Josephine C. Watkin, Mrs. Anne Stewart. Moved with parents to Tex., 1864; admitted to Tex. bar, 1882, and began practice at Sherman, Tex.; spl. dist. judge in West Tex., by apptmt. of Gov. Ross, 1892-93; gen. counsel and dir. Southwestern Life Ins. Co., from 1915; pres. Dallas Nat. Bank from 1920; mem. Cockrell, McBride, O'Donnell & Hamilton. Chmn. bd. trustees Southern Methodist U., also acting dean law dept.; mem. Com. on Constn. of M.E. Ch., S., 1922-26; state chmn. Tex. State Non-Partisan League; dir. Civic Fedn., Dallas. Democrat. Methodist. Mason. Died, Dallas, Tex., Apr. 7, 1927.

COCKRILL, Ashley, lawyer; b. Little Rock, Ark., Nov. 8, 1872; s. Sterling R. and Mary A. (Freeman) C.; mother g.d. Chester Ashley; Little Rock U., 1885-88; U. of Va., 1889-92; law dept. U. of Ark., 1893-94; m. Jennie Mitchell, Dec. 30, 1896; children—James Mitchell, Sterling R., Chester Ashley, Harry Howard, Jane, Anne. Admitted to Ark. bar, 1894, later to U.S. Dist. Court, U.S. Circuit Court of Appeals and Supreme Court of U.S.; practiced with father (chief justice Supreme Court of Ark), from 1896 until latter's death, 1901; then mem. Cockrill & Armistead. City atty., Little Rock, 1902-06; mem. sch. bd., 1909-12. Democrat. Episcopalian. Chancellor Diocese of Ark., 5 yrs. Home: Little Rock, Ark. Died Apr. 4, 1932.

COCKRUM, John Barrett, lawyer; b. Oakland City, Ind., Sept. 12, 1857; s. William M. and Lucretia C.; ed. pub. schs., Oakland City; LL.B., Cincinnati Law Coll., 1879; m. Josephine C. Bittrolff, Jan. 25, 1880. Admitted to Ind. bar, 1879; asst. U.S. dist. atty. for Ind., at Indianapolis, 1889-93; asst. gen. atty. L.E.&W. and Ft. Wayne, Cincinnati & Louisville rys., 1893-95, later gen. atty.; then gen. solicitor N.Y.,C.&St.L. R.R. (L.E.&W. dist.). Republican. Died Apr. 15, 1937.

COCKS, William Willets, congressman; b. Old Westbury, L.I., N.Y., July 24, 1861; s. Isaac H. and Mary Titus (Willets) C.; ed. Swarthmore (Pa.) Coll.; m. Caroline R. Hicks, July 24, 1901 (died 1901); 2d, Jessie Wright, Apr. 29, 1911. Engaged in farming on Long Island from 1875; trustee Roslyn (L.I.) Savings Bank. Mem. N.Y. Senate, 1900-02, Assembly, 1903-04; mem. 59th to 61st Congresses (1905-11), 1st N.Y. Dist.; Republican. Mem. Bd. Mgrs. Swarthmore Coll.; trustee Friends' Acad., Locust Valley, L.I. Home: Old Westbury, L.I. Died May 4, 1932.

COCO, Adolphe Valery, lawyer; b. La., Mar. 21, 1857; s. Adolphe Dominique and Heloise (Sheldon) C.; La. State U., 1872-73; A.M., St. Vincent's Coll., Cape Girardeau, Mo., 1877; LL.B., Tulane U., 1881; m. Catharine Malone, July 10, 1877. Began practice at Marksville, La., 1881; dist. judge, parishes of Avoyelles, Rapides and Natchitoches, 1888-96; mem. La. State Constl. Conv., 1898; atty. gen. of La., 1916-24. Democrat. Catholic. Home: Marksville, La. Died Dec. 23, 1927.

CODD, George Pierre, judge; b. Detroit, Mich., Dec. 7, 1869; s. George C. C.; A.B., U. of Mich., 1891; m. Kathleen Warner, Oct. 2, 1894; children—

dell. In practice at Detroit, from 1892. Asst. city atty., 1893-96; alderman, 1902, 1903, 1904; mayor Detroit, 1905-06; was circuit judge of Wayne Co. Regent U. of Mich., 1909-10; mem. 67th Congress (1921-23), 1st Mich. Dist.; again circuit judge, 1924—. Republican. Presbyn. Mason. Home: Detroit, Mich. Died Feb. 16, 1927.

CODDINGTON, Wellesley Perry, univ. prof.; b. Sing Sing (now Ossining), N.Y., Oct. 23, 1840; s. David Cook and Hannah (Perry) C.; A.B., Wesleyan U., Conn., 1860, A.M., 1866; (S.T.D., Hamilton, 1880); m. Louisa Guibord, July 23, 1863 (dec.). Teacher mathematics, Troy Conf. Acad., Poultney, Vt., 1860-62; teacher ancient langs., Amenia (N.Y.) Sem., 1862-63; entered M.E. ministry, 1863; prin. Amenia Sem., 1863-64; teacher Greek, 1864-65, prin., 1865, Cazenovia (N.Y.) Sem.; prof. modern langs., 1865-66, Greek and Latin, 1867-70, Genesee (N.Y.) Coll.; prof. Greek and ethics, 1870-91, philosophy, 1891—, Syracuse U. Home: Syracuse, N.Y. Died Aug. 13, 1913.

CODMAN, Charles Russell, lawyer; b. Paris, France (while parents were abroad), Oct. 28, 1829; s. Charles Russell and Anne (Macmaster) C., of Boston; A.B., Harvard, 1849, A.M., 1852, LL.B., 1852; m. Lucy Lyman Paine, d. Russell Sturgis, Feb. 28, 1856. Practiced in Boston, Mass.; subsequently in business inherited from his father. Mem. Sch. Com. of Boston, 1861-62; col. 45th Mass. Vols. (Cadet Regt.), 1862-64; mem. Mass. Senate, 1864-65, Ho. of Rep., 1872-75 (chmn. com. on judiciary, 1874-75); Rep. candidate for mayor of Boston, 1878. Overseer of Harvard, 1878-97 (pres. of bd., 1880, 1881, 1887); pres. Mass. Homœ. Hosp.; trustee Westborough Insane Hosp.; mem. State Bd. of Insanity. Home: Brookline, Mass. Died Oct. 5, 1918.

CODMAN, Ernest Amory, surgeon; b. Boston, Mass., Dec. 30, 1869; s. William C. and Elizabeth (Hurd) C.; A.B., Harvard, 1891, M.D., 1895; m. Katharine Putnam Bowditch, Nov. 16, 1899. Practiced in Boston, 1895—; asst. visiting surgeon, Mass. Gen. Hosp., 1899-1914, then cons. surgeon; lecturer on surgery, Harvard Med. Sch., 1913-14. Fellow Am. Coll. Surgeons. Author: The Shoulder, 1934. Home: Boston, Mass. Died Nov. 23, 1940.

CODMAN, Julian, lawyer; b. Cotuit, Mass., Sept. 21, 1870; s. Charles Russell and Lucy L. P. (Sturgis) C.; A.B., Harvard, 1892, LL.B., 1895; m. Norah Chadwick, Apr. 27, 1897; children—Lucy Sturgis, Hester Schuyler. Admitted to Mass. bar, 1895, and then practiced at Boston; with C. P. Greenough, 1897-1902; mem. Warren, Perry & Codman, 1902-10, Wheelwright & Codman, 1910-26; then asso. with David F. Sibley; pres. Fabreeka Belting Co. Commd. Q.M. Dept., U.S.A., 1916; capt. Q.M. Dept., World War, 1917-19; with A.E.F. 9 mos.; lt. col. J. A. Gen's. Dept., O.R.C., 1924-26. Gen. counsel for A.F. of L. and all assns. opposed to prohibition in hearings before House and Senate coms. on bills for the modification of the Volstead Act. Home: Boston, Mass. Died Dec. 29, 1932.

CODMAN, Robert, bishop; A.B., Harvard, 1882; LL.B., 1885; (S.T.D., Trinity Coll., Conn., 1900; D.D., U. of Bishop's Coll., Lennoxville, P.Q., 1904). Practiced law at Boston, 1885-91; theol. student, 1891-94; deacon, 1893, priest, 1894, P.E. Ch.; asst. All Saints' Ch., Ashmont, Mass., 1894-95; rector St. John's, Roxbury, Boston, 1895-1900; consecrated bishop Diocese of Me., 1900. Home: Portland, Me. Died Oct. 7, 1915.

CODMAN, Russell Sturgis, trustee; b. Boston, Mass., Oct. 20, 1861; s. Charles Russell and Lucy Lyman Paine (Sturgis) C.; A.B., Harvard, 1883; m. Anna Kneeland Crafts, Aug. 1, 1891. Trustee Central Bldg. Trust, Congress Street Associates, Cross Roads Associates, Dwelling House Associates; dir. Boston Storage Co. Life mem. Am. Mus. Natural History. Home: Manchester, Mass. Died May 16, 1941.

CODY, William Frederick, scout, showman; b. Scott Co., Ia., Feb. 26, 1846; father killed in the "Border war" in Kan.; pony express rider, 1860-61; Govt. scout and guide and mem. 7th Kan. Cav., 1861-65; m. Louisa Frederici, Mar. 6, 1866. Contracted to furnish Kan. Pacific Ry. with all the buffalo meat required to feed the laborers engaged in construction, and in 18 months (1867-68) killed 4,280 buffaloes, earning name of "Buffalo Bill," by which he is best known; govt. scout and guide, 1868-72, serving in operations against Sioux and Cheyenne; mem. Neb. Legislature, 1872; joined 5th Cav. as scout, 1876. In battle of Indian Creek killed Yellow Hand, Cheyenne chief, in hand-to-hand fight; 1890-91, gen. Neb. N.G., Sioux outbreak; headquarters Pine Ridge Agency; Battle of Wounded Knee. At head of "Wild West Show," 1883—. Judge-advocate-gen. Wyo. N.G.; pres. Shoshone Irrigation Co. Co-author: The Great Salt Lake Trail. Home: Cody, Wyo. Died Jan. 10, 1917.

COE, Edward Benton, clergyman; b. Milford, Conn., June 11, 1842; s. David Benton and Rebecca (Phœnix) C.; A.B., Yale, 1862; Union Theol. Sem., 1862-63; dianapolis Morris Plan Bank. Actively identified with

John Warner, George Calvin, Mrs. Kathleen C. Bry- LL.D., 1893; S.D.T., Yale, 1885); m. Mary Jenks, d. late Rev. Richard Salter Storrs, June 11, 1874. Street prof. modern langs., (Yale, 1864-79); ordained Ref. Ch. in America ministry, 1879; pastor, 1879-99. sr. minister, 1896—, Collegiate Ch., New York. Pres. Gen. Synod, 1898. Trustee Rutgers Coll., 1887—, of Robert Coll., Constantinople, 1894—, of Leake and Watts Orphan House, 1896—, Columbia U., 1896—; mgr. Presbyn. Hosp., 1896—. Author: Life Indeed, 1899. Home: New York, N.Y. Died Mar. 19, 1914.

COE, Frantz Hunt, surgeon; b. St. Charles, Ill., Nov. 25, 1856; grad. Univ. of Mich., 1879; med. dept. same, 1888; surgeon Northern Pacific Ry., and Seattle Traction Co.; sec. State Med. Soc. of Wash. Home: Seattle, Wash. Died 1904.

COE, Henry Clarke, gynecologist; b. Cincinnati, Feb. 21, 1856; s. Erastus Pease and Mary (Ross) C.; A.B., Yale, 1878, A.M., 1881; M.D., Harvard, 1881, Columbia, 1882; M.R.C.S., Eng., 1884; m. Sara Livingston Werden; children—Fordyce B., Henry C., Arthur P. Practiced at N.Y. City from 1884; prof. gynecology, Univ. and Bellevue Hosp. Med. Coll. (New York U.), 1896-1915 (emeritus); consulting surgeon to Bellevue, Woman's, Memorial, Polyclinic, and Beth Israel hosps. Col. M.C.U.S.A., 2 yrs. foreign service in war; then col. U.S.A., Ret. Fellow Am. Coll. Surgeons. Republican. Episcopalian. Home: New York, N.Y. Died Apr. 21, 1940.

COE, Henry Waldo, M.D.; b. Waupun, Wis., Nov. 4, 1857; s. Samuel B. (M.D.) and Mary J. (Chronkhite) C.; desc. of Robert Coe, Plymouth, Mass., 1634; student U. of Minn., 1874-76; student med. dept. U. of Mich., 1877-78; M.D., Long Island Coll. Hosp., 1880; m. Viola May Boley, 1883 (dec.); children— George Clifford, Wayne Walter, Earl Alphonso; m. 2d, Elsie Ara Waggoner, Mar. 25, 1915. Began practice at Mandan, 1880; mem. N. Dak. Ho. of Rep., 1885-87; settled in Portland, Ore., 1891; has served as consulting neurologist, State Hosp. for Insane (Salem), Multnomah County Hosp., State Instn. for Defective Youths (Vancouver, Wash.), etc.; founder, 1893, and med. dir. Morningside Hosp. (300 beds) for treatment of mental and nervous diseases; editor, 1893—, the Medical Sentinel; formerly prof. nervous and mental diseases, Willamette U.; mem. State Senate, 1905-07. Republican. Conglist. Mason. Art student, especially as to bronzes; presented heroic bronze equestrian statues of Roosevelt and Joan of Arc, and bronze heroic figures of George Washington and of Abraham Lincoln to City of Portland. Home: Portland, Ore. Died Feb. 15, 1927.

COEFIELD, John, labor official; b. Petroleum Center, Pa., June 18, 1869; s. John and Isabella (Wright) C.; ed. Franklin (Pa.) High Sch.; m. Ethel B. McKinnon; children—Isabelle, Florence. Began as plumber's apprentice; then 4th vice pres. Am. Fed. of Labor and gen. pres. United Assn. of Journeymen Plumbers and Steamfitters of the U.S. and Canada. Mem. Plumbers Local 442, San Francisco, Calif. Home: Washington, D.C. Died Feb. 8, 1940.

COERNE, Louis Adolphe, composer, educator; b. Newark, N.J., Feb. 27, 1870; s. Adolphe M. and Elizabeth (Homan) C.; German and French schs.; grad. Boston Latin Sch., 1888; Harvard, 1888-90, Ph.D., 1905; studied harmony and composition under Prof. J. K. Paine; violin under Franz Kneisel; organ and composition under Rheinberger, Royal Acad. Music, Munich, 1890-93; grad. with honors, 1893; (Mus.D., Olivet Coll. [Mich.], 1910); m. Adele Turton, Dec. 14, 1897. Mus. dir. Buffalo (N.Y.) Liedertafel, Buffalo Vocal Soc., Ch. of the Messiah, 1894 -97; music. dir. Trinity Ch., Arion Club, Maennerchor, Columbus, O., 1897-99; composing and pubg. in Europe, 1899-1902; in charge music dept. Harvard Summer session, 1903; asso. prof. music, Smith Coll., 1903-04; research work at Harvard and in New York, 1904-05; composing and pubg. in Germany and Denmark, 1905-07; mus. dir. Troy, N.Y., 1907-09; dir. Conservatory of Music, Olivet Coll., 1909-10; dir. Sch. of Music and prof. history and science of music, U. of Wis., 1910-15; organist and choirmaster First Congl. Ch., Madison, and musical dir. Madison Maennerchor (hon.), 1910-15, 2d Congl. Ch., New London, Conn., 1918-19; prof. music, Conn. College, 1915—; editor sch. and coll. music dept., Oliver Ditson Co., Boston, 1920—. Mason. Republican. Episcopalian. Author: Evolution of Modern Orchestration, 1908 (accepted as thesis by Harvard for Ph.D. degree). Composer of 182 works, numerous sets of vocal and instrumental music, etc. Home: New London, Conn. Died 1922.

COES, Mary, college dean; b. Worcester, Mass., Mar. 24, 1861; d. Aury Gates and Lucy Gibson (Wyman) C.; A.B., Radcliffe Coll., 1887, A.M., 1897; unmarried. Sec., 1894-1910, dean from 1910, Radcliffe Coll. Mem. Bd. Associates of Radcliffe Coll., Bd. of Govt. Women's Ednl. and Industrial Union (Boston). Conglist. Home: Cambridge, Mass. Died Aug. 16, 1913.

COFFEY, Alexander Brainard, educator; b. Sedalia, Mo.; s. Rufus Lafayette and Martha (Fowler) C.; M.S.D., 1st State Normal Sch., Kirksville, Mo., 1900;

France and Germany, 1864-67; (D.D., Rutgers, 1881, studied Hastings Coll. of Law, San Francisco; A.B., Stanford U., 1903; A.M., Columbia, 1904); unmarried. Teacher and supt. schs., Calif., to 1895; asso. editor Pacific Ednl. Journal, 1895-96; ednl. editor Overland Monthly, 1896-98; dean Dept. of Edn., U. of Wash., 1898-1901; resident lecturer, U. of Wis., 1904-05; prof. philosophy and edn., Coll. of William and Mary, Va., 1905-07; dean Teachers Coll., La. State U., 1907—. Lecturer Summer Extension Sch., Norfolk, Va., 1905, 06, 07; dir. summer sessions, State U. of La., 1909—; editor La. School Review, 1908-11. Democrat. Mason. Home: Baton Rouge, La. Deceased.

COFFEY, James Vincent, judge; b. New York, Dec. 14, 1846; s. James C.; ed. in New York, 1852-54, Bridgeport, Conn., 1854-57, Nevada City, Calif., 1863; studied in law offices in New York, Virginia City, Nev., and San Francisco; admitted to bar, 1869; (Ph.D., Santa Clara Coll., Calif.; LL.D., St. Ignatius' Coll., San Francisco); unmarried. Editor San Francisco Examiner for 6 yrs., while also practicing law; elected to State Assembly, 1875-78; chmn. San Francisco delegation each session; chmn. Dem. Co. Conv. 1878, and its unanimous nominee for Constl. Conv.; nominated for atty. gen. Calif., 1879, but declined; judge Superior Ct. of San Francisco, 1882—, term expired 1918 (presiding judge, 1887, 1907). Dem. nominee for justice Supreme Ct., 1890, and led ticket several thousand votes; voted for in Calif. Legislature, 1899, as Dem. choice for U.S. senator; declined nomination for Congress 4th Calif. Dist., 1900. Home: San Francisco, Calif. Died Jan. 15, 1919.

COFFEY, James V., lawyer; b. Troy, N.Y., Apr. 18, 1879; s. James W. and Nora (Hartigan) C.; grad. LaSalle Inst., Troy, 1896; LL.B., Albany Law School, 1901; LL.D., Manhattan College, N.Y. City, 1932; m. Helen Scallen, June 30, 1909; children— Eugene V., Helen, Mary Louise, Florence, Jane, James, Martha. Admitted to N.Y. bar, 1901, and practiced at Troy; apptd. justice Supreme Court, 3d Dist. of N.Y., Mar. 4, 1925, confirmed by Senate, Mar. 5, 1925, for term ending Dec. 31, 1925; apptd. mem. Judicial Council for State of N.Y., June 28, 1934. V.p. and dir. Troy Trust Co.; trustee Troy Savings Bank. V.p. and trustee Albany Law Sch.; pres. T.C.M.O. Asylum; dir. Troy Boys' Club. Democrat. Catholic. Home: Troy, N.Y. Died Apr. 24, 1937.

COFFEY, Robert Calvin, surgeon; b. Caldwell Co., N.C., Oct. 20, 1869; s. Patterson Vance and Nancy Martitia (Estes) C.; prep. edn., Globe (N.C.) Acad.; M.D., Ky. Sch. of Medicine, Louisville, Ky., 1892; m. Clarissa Ellen Coffey, Aug. 9, 1893; children— Jay Russell, Wilson Bryan, Robert Mayo. Began practice at Moscow, Ida., 1892; moved to Portland, Ore., 1900; owner and chief surgeon Dr. Robert C. Coffey Clinic and Hosp. Fellow Am. Coll. Surgeons. Democrat. Presbyterian. Devised method of treatment of gastro-enteroptosis, entitled the "hammock operation." Wrote monograph on Gastroptosis; chapter on Diseases of the Pancreas, in Binnie's Regional Surgery. Home: Portland, Ore. Died Nov. 9, 1933.

COFFIN, Charles Albert, financier, mfr.; b. Somerset Co., Me., Dec. 1844; s. Albert and Anstrus (Varney) C.; LL.D., Union, 1914, Bowdoin, 1922, Princeton, 1924; M.A., Yale, 1919; m. Caroline, d. Rev. E. Russell, of Holbrook, Mass., Sept. 1872; children—E. R. (dec.), Mrs. Starling W. Childs, Alice S. Pres. Gen. Electric Co. from its organization until June 1913, and chmn. bd. until May 1922. Organized War Relief Clearing House for France and her allies, early in 1915, later consol. with Am. Red Cross; active in work of Am. Red Cross throughout the war. Decorated officer Legion of Honor (French); comdr. Order of Leopold II (Belgian); Order of St. Sava (Serbian). Home: Locust Valley, L.I. Died July 14, 1926.

COFFIN, Charles E., banker, author; b. Salem, Ind.; s. Zachariah T. and Caroline (Armfield) C.; ed. high sch. and bus. coll.; m. Mary H. Birch, 1897; children—Clarence Eugene, Jean Fletcher (Mrs. J. H. Ingram), Carolyn (Mrs. Charles H. Bradley, Jr.). In real estate bus., Indianapolis, 1870-99; organized 1899, and ex-pres. Central Trust Co.; financed constrn. of Indianapolis & Eastern Traction Co., 1902-03, and was v.p. same; pres. Indiana Savings and Investment Co.; treas. Star Pub. Co. (pubs. Indianapolis Star); dir. Polk Sanitary Milk Co. Republican. Methodist. Mason. Author: The Gist of Whist, 1895; The Gist of Auction Bridge, 1907. Home: Indianapolis, Ind. Died Oct. 15, 1934.

COFFIN, Charles Franklin, lawyer, life ins. official; b. Indianapolis, Ind., June 2, 1856; s. Benjamin Franklin and Emily Jane (Harlan) C.; A.B., DePauw U., 1881 (winner interstate oratorical prize); A.M., 1884; m. Sarah I. Dowling, Oct. 26, 1887; children—Charles Franklin, Jean Dionis, Natalie Cornelia. Supt. of Schools, New Albany, Ind., 1882-84; practiced law, Wichita, Kan., 1887-93; returned to Indianapolis and became dean, DePauw Law Sch., 1893; an organizer State Life Ins. Co., 1894, and then gen. counsel, also dir. Peoples State Bank, In-

Indianapolis Chamber of Commerce many yrs., v.p., 1917-18, pres., 1919-21, then hon. life mem. bd. (membership increased from 1,000 to over 4,000 in that time), also mem. U.S. Chamber Commerce, Internat. Chamber Commerce (del. to orgn., 1920). Mem. bd. mgrs. M.E. Ch. Bd. of Edn. for Colored People, 12 yrs.; del. to Meth. Ecumenical Council, London, 1921. Republican. Mason. Home: Indianapolis, Ind. Died Dec. 16, 1935.

COFFIN, Frank G., clergyman, educator; b. Marshall Co., Ia., June 14, 1874; s. George Hartman and Joanna (Maronda) C.; A.B., Legrand (Ia.) Christian Inst., 1897; A.M., Iowa Christian Coll., Legrand, 1899; D.D., Palmer Coll., Albany, Mo., 1907; m. Lula May Klump, Nov. 15, 1894; children—Ruth Mabel (wife of Dr. John H. Randall), Marie Florence (Mrs. Ephraim E. Wylie). Ordained ministry Christian Ch., 1891; pastor successively Chelsea, Ia., Montezuma, Ia., Madrid, Ia., Dayton, O., Albany, N.Y., until 1919; pres. Palmer Coll., 1919-28; asso. editor The Congregationalist and Herald of Gospel Liberty, also pastor Congl.-Christian Federated Ch., Columbus, O., 1928—. Co-moderator Gen. Council of Congl.-Christian Chs.; moderator Central Ohio Congl.-Christian Assn.; pres. Ohio Pastors' Conf. Pres. Gen. Conv. Christian Ch. in U.S. and Can.; v.p. Federal Council of Chs. of Christ in America. Trustee World's Christian Endeavor Union. Mason. Author: The Church Facing the Future, 1922. Home: Columbus, O. Died June 9, 1941.

COFFIN, Howard Earle, cons. engr.; b. West Milton, O., Sept. 6, 1873; s. Julius V. and Sarah E. (Jones) C.; U. of Mich., 1893-96, 1900-02, B.S. in M.E., 1911, as of 1903, hon. Dr. Engring., 1917; LL.D., Mercer U., Macon, Ga., 1929; ScD., Ga. Sch. of Tech., 1931; m. Matilda V. Allen, Oct. 30, 1907 (died 1932). With the U.S. Civil Service, 1896-1900; chief of exptl. dept., Olds Motor Works, Detroit and Lansing, 1902-05, and chief engr., 1905-06; v.p. and chief engr., E. R. Thomas Detroit Co., 1906-08; v.p. and cons. engr., Chalmers Detroit Motor Co., 1908-10; v.p. and cons. engr. Hudson Motor Car Co., 1910-30; pres. Nat. Air Transport, Inc., 1925-28, chmn. bd., 1928-30; chmn. bd. Sea Island Co., Southeastern Cottons, Inc. Mem. Naval Consulting Board, 1915—; mem. Advisory Commn. of Council of Nat. Defense, 1916-18, and chmn. Aircraft Board of U.S., 1917-18; mem. Am. Aviation Mission, 1919; mem. Morrow Bd., 1925. Home: Sea Island Beach, Ga. Died Nov. 21, 1937.

COFFIN, Lorenzo S., philanthropist; b. on farm, Alton, N.H., Apr. 9, 1823; s. Stephen and Deborah C.; studied prep. dept. Oberlin Coll., 18 months; m. Cynthia Curtis, 1848 (dec.); 2d, Mary C. Chase, 1857. Taught 1 yr. in Geauga Sem. (James A. Garfield and Lucretia Randolph, later Mrs. Garfield, were among his pupils); located claim of land nr. Ft. Dodge, Ia.; pvt., orderly sergt., q.m. sergt. and chaplain 32d Iowa Inf. in Civil War; after war preached 16 yrs. Mem. State Bd. R.R. Commrs. Ia., 1883-88; author of state and nat. legislation compelling adoption of safety appliances in coupling cars and running trains, with result of saving many lives; started White Button temperance movement among railroad men, 1893; pres. R.R. Temperance Assn.; help found, nr. Chicago, Home for Aged and Disabled R.R. Men, and is at its head; pres. State Anti-Saloon League of Ia.; established on his own farm "Hope Hall," a home for disch. convicts. Prohibition party nominee for gov., 1907; United Christian Party nominee for V.P. of U.S., 1908. Home: Ft. Dodge, Ia. Died Jan. 17, 1915.

COFFIN, O(wen) Vincent, governor; b. Union Vale, N.Y., June 20, 1836; s. Alexander H. and Jane (Vincent) C.; acad. edn.; (LL.D., Wesleyan U., 1896); m. Ellen Elizabeth Coe, June 24, 1858 (died July 23, 1912). Salesman and mfrs.' agt., N. Y., 1853-61; spl. mem. business firm, 1863-68; mem. N.Y. com. of U.S. Christian Commn., 1861-65; pres. Brooklyn Y.M.C.A., 1863-64. Resident of Middletown, Conn., 1864—; sec.-treas. and dir. Farmers and Mechanics' Savings Bank, 1864-78; pres. Middlesex Fire Assurance Co., 1884—, and identified with numerous other corps. Mayor of Middletown, 1872-73; mem. Conn. Senate, 1887-91; gov. of Conn., 1895-97. Republican. Home: Middletown, Conn. Died Jan. 3, 1921.

COFFIN, Selden Jennings, astronomer; b. Ogdensburg, N.Y., Aug. 3, 1838; s. late Prof. James Henry and Aurelia M. (Jennings) C.; A.B., Lafayette Coll., 1858, A.M., 1861; grad. Princeton Theol. Sem., 1864; (Ph.D., Hanover Coll., 1876); m. Mary A. Angle, N.J., Dec. 22, 1875 (died 1889); 2d, Emma F. Angle, Dec. 23, 1891. Tutor and adj. prof. mathematics, 1864-76, prof., 1876-86, registrar, 1886-1904, prof. astronomy, 1873—, Lafayette Coll. Ordained Presbyn. ministry, 1874. Author: Conic Sections, 1878; Record of the Men of La Fayette, 1891. Compiled his father's The Winds of the Globe, 1876; revised Olmsted's Astronomy, 1882. Home: Easton, Pa. Died Mar. 15, 1915.

COFFIN, Thomas Chalkley, congressman; b. Caldwell, Ida., Oct. 25, 1887; s. Sherman M. and Jessie (Phelps) C.; student Phillips Exeter Acad., 1903-06, Sheffield Scientific Sch. (Yale), 1907-08, Law Sch. (Yale), 1908-10; m. Aileen Franklin, Nov. 11, 1920; 1 dau., Jeanne. Admitted to Ida. bar, 1911, and began practice at Pocatello; asst. atty. gen. of Ida., 1913-15; mayor of Pocatello, 1931-33; mem. 73d Congress (1933-35), 2d Ida. Dist. Served as 2d class petty officer, U.S. Navy, World War. Democrat. Episcopalian. Mason. Home: Pocatello, Ida. Died June 8, 1934.

COFFIN, William, consul gen.; b. Brooklyn, N.Y., Oct. 8, 1877; s. Charles A. and Alice E. (Gale) C.; ed. St. Paul's Sch., Concord, N.H.; m. Mabel Sands Rees, Oct. 1905; children—Patricia, Miriam. In mercantile business, Tenn. and Ky., 1894-1900, New York, 1900-06; apptd. after examination Am. consul at Maskat, Arabia, June 28, 1906; consul at Tripoli, 1908-10; Jerusalem, 1910-13; on spl. duty in U.S. in connection with 12th Internat. Congress of Navigation, Phila., May-June 1912; apptd. consul gen. at Budapest, Hungary, Sept. 1913, at Christiania, Norway, July 21, 1917, at Stockholm, Sweden, Nov. 5, 1917; assigned to Dept. of State, Apr. 1, 1918; consul gen. at Berlin, Germany, Dec. 1, 1919—. Died Feb. 14, 1927.

COFFIN, William Anderson, painter; b. Allegheny, Pa., Jan. 31, 1855; s. James Gardiner and Isabella Catharine (Anderson) C.; A.B., Yale, 1874 (B.F.A., 1901); studied art in U.S., 1874-77; in Paris under Léon Bonnât, 1877-82; unmarried. Opened studio in New York, 1882, painter of landscapes and figure pieces; has frequently exhibited at Paris Salon, Nat. Acad. and Soc. American Artists, New York. Awards: Hallgarten prize, Nat. Acad., 1886; medal, Paris Expn., 1889; Webb prize, Soc. Am. Artists, 1891; gold medal, Art Club, Phila., 1898; silver medal, Charleston Expn., 1902, St. Louis Expn., 1904. Art critic New York Evening Post and The Nation, 1886-91, The Sun, 1896-1900. Dir. Fine Arts, Buffalo Expn., 1901; mem. New York advisory bd. to art dept. Panama-Pacific Internat. Expn. Represented in permanent collections Met. Mus., New York, Nat. Collection, Washington, Municipal Gallery, Venice, Italy, Fine Arts Acad., Buffalo, Brooklyn Inst. Arts and Sciences, Brooks Memorial Art Gallery, Memphis, Tenn., etc.; N.A.; mem. Archtl. League, New York. Apptd. by French Govt., 1915, hon. attaché to French Commn. to Panama Expn., San Francisco; pres. com. for exhibition, by invitation of French Govt., of painting and sculpture by Am. artists at Luxembourg Museum, Oct.-Nov. 1919; pres. Am. Fine Arts Soc.; hon. pres. Fraternité des Artistes, Paris. Chevalier Legion of Honor of France, 1917. Home: New York, N.Y. Died Oct. 26, 1925.

COFFIN, William Sloane, corp. official; b. N.Y. City, Apr. 18, 1879; s. Edmund and Euphemia (Sloane) C.; B.A., Yale, 1900, M.A., 1904; hon. M.A., New York U., 1923; m. Catherine Butterfield, Sept. 14, 1920; children—Edmund, William S., Margaret. Pres. Company of Master Craftsmen, Oneida-craft, Inc., Henry Williams Co., Creekfront Realty Co.; v.p. City Housing Corp.; dir. W. & J. Sloane. Pres. Child Edn. Foundation, N.Y. City Mission Soc., Met. Mus. of Art; trustee Provident Loan Soc. Chevalier Legion of Honor (France). Republican. Presbyn. Home: New York, N.Y. Died Dec. 16, 1933.

COFFMAN, De Witt, naval officer; b. Shenandoah Co., Va., Nov. 28, 1854; grad. U.S. Naval Acad., 1876; married; 1 son, Richard Boush. Ensign, July 10, 1879; promoted through grades to vice adm., June 19, 1916. Served on Terror during Spanish-Am. War; comd. Boston, 1905-07; insp. charge naval magazine, Fort Mifflin, Pa., 1907-08; in charge naval magazine, St. Julien's Creek, 1908-09; comd. New Jersey, 1909-11; comdt., Navy Yard, Boston, Mar. 18-Nov. 6, 1914, Naval War College, Newport, Nov. 7-Dec. 3, 1914; comdr. 3d Div. Atlantic Fleet to Apr. 15, 1916, 6th Div. Atlantic Fleet to June 19, 1916; promoted vice admiral, June 19, 1916, and battleship squadron comdr. Atlantic Fleet (comdr. Atlantic Fleet, Aug.-Oct. 22, 1917); comd. Battleship Force Two until Aug. 30, 1918; comd. 5th Naval Dist. and Naval Operating Base, Hampton Roads, Va.; retired by operation of law, Nov. 28, 1918; commd. vice adm., retired, June 21, 1930. Mem. Bd. of Awards, Medals and Honors, Navy Dept., until Oct. 30, 1919. Died June 27, 1932.

COFFMAN, Leroy Mallon, clergyman; b. Warsaw, Ill., July 14, 1867; s. George C. and Lettie G. (Bailey) C.; student Burlington (Ia.) Coll., 1885; B.A., Drake U. Des Moines, Ia., 1887; B.D., McCormick Theol. Sem., 1891; D.D., Ohio U., 1905; m. Lula Pamela Washburn, Sept. 5, 1894; children—Alden W., Donald Drake, Ruth Priscilla. Ordained Presbyn. ministry, 1891; mng. editor "The World" dept. of The Interior, Chicago, 1892-93; pastor successively LaGrange, Ind., Warsaw, Sidney, O., until 1908, First Ch., Davenport, Ia., 1908—. Trustee Parsons Coll., Fairfield, Ia. Address: Davenport, Ia. Died Sept. 27, 1934.

COFFMAN, Lotus Delta, pres. U. of Minn.; b. Salem, Ind., Jan. 7, 1875; s. Mansford E. and Laura E. (Davis) C.; grad. Ind. State Normal Sch., Terre Haute, Ind., 1896; A.B., Ind. State U., 1906, A.M., 1910; Ph.D., Columbia Univ., 1911; LL.D., Indiana U. and Carleton Coll., 1922, Columbia, 1929, U. of Mich., 1931, Northwestern, 1935, U. of S.D., 1936, Williams Coll., 1936; D.S. in Edn., George Washington U., 1930; L.H.D., U. of Denver, 1930; m. Mary Emma Farrell, Dec. 28, 1899; children—Mrs. Catharine Farrell Knudtson, William Mansford. Principal and supt. schs., Ind., 1896-1907; supervisor Training Sch., Charleston, Ill., 1907-09; scholar, 1909-10, lecturer, 1910-11, Columbia; supervisor Training Sch., Charleston, Ill., 1911-12. Prof. edn., U. of Ill., 1912-15, dean Coll. of Education, U. of Minn., 1915-20; pres. U. of Minn., July 1, 1920—. Visiting prof. for Carnegie Endowment for Internat. Peace to New Zealand and Australia, 1931; rep. Carnegie Corp. of N.Y. to univs. and scientific socs. of New Zealand and Australia, 1931; visiting lecturer, U. of Philippines, 1932. Expert consultant to U.S. Dept. Interior, Land Grant Coll. Survey, 1928-30 and Nat. Survey of Sch. Finance, 1931; consultant Joint Commn. on the Emergency in Edn., N.E.A., 1933-35. Mem. bd. curators Stephens Coll.; mem. bd. overseers Chevy Chase Sch.; mem. Am. Advisory Council Yenching U., Peiping, China; mem. Commn. on Edn. of Unemployed Youth for Minn., 1933-34; mem. edn. com. of Boy Scouts of America; mem. group of Am. educators to study ednl. methods in Soviet Russia, as guests of govt., summer 1928; chmn. Commn. of Inquiry on Public Service Personnel, 1933-35, Am. Youth Commn., 1935—. Am. Council on Education, 1935—, Ednl. Policies Commn. of N.E.A. and Dept. of Superintendence, 1935—. Adviser to surgeon gen. on edn. of disabled soldiers, during the war. Pres. Nat. Soc. for Study of Edn., 1917-18, Nat. Soc. Coll. Teachers of Edn., 1917-18; pres. North Central Assn. of Colls. and Secondary Schs., 1921-22, hon. mem.; pres. Assn. Urban Univs., 1921-22; pres. and chmn. exec. com. Am. Council on Schs., 1921-23; pres. Nat. Assn. of State Univs., 1930; mem. Nat. Council of Edn., Nat. Advisory Com. on Edn.; mem. Com. on Scientific Aids to Learning of Nat. Research Council, 1937—; sec. board trustees Carnegie Foundation for Advancement of Teaching; mem. board trustees Carnegie Corp., New York; mem. U.S. Commn. on Cooperation in Pan-Am. Child Welfare Work. Republican. Baptist. Author: Teacher Training Departments in Minnesota High Schools, 1920; The State University: Its Work and Problems, 1934. Co-author: Reading in Public Schools (with T. H. Briggs), 1908; How to Teach Arithmetic (with J. C. Brown), 1913; The Supervision of Arithmetic (with W. A. Jessup), 1915; Better Service Personnel (Com. of Inquiry Pub. Service Personnel), 1935; Land Utilization in Minnesota—A State Program for the Cut-Over Lands (Minn. Land Utilization Com.), 1934. Made ednl. surveys, N.D., 1916, Kan., 1922, Tex., 1925, Rutgers Univ., 1927, Missouri, 1930, Calif., 1932, Ga., 1932, N.C., 1932, New York Univ., 1932, Atlanta (Ga.), 1933, U. of Chicago-Northwestern U. Merger, 1933. Home: Minneapolis, Minn. Died Sept. 22, 1938.

COGGESHALL, Edwin Walter, lawyer; b. New York, N.Y., July 26, 1842; s. Giles H. and Marianna C.; LL.B., Columbia, 1867; m. Anna Walter, June 8, 1870. Admitted to N.Y. bar, 1867, and began practice at N.Y. City; organized Lawyers Title Ins. Co., 1887, and pres. until 1912; chmn. bd. Lawyers Title & Guaranty Co., Lawyers Trust Co.; pres. Lawyers Realty Co.; dir. Lawyers Westchester Mortgage & Title Co. Society of Friends. Home: New York, N.Y. Died Mar. 31, 1929.

COGGESHALL, Henry James, lawyer; b. Waterville, N.Y., Apr., 28, 1845; s. Dr. James Stirling and Deidama (Rurey) C.; ed. Waterville Sem.; admitted to bar, 1866; m. Lillian Alene Terry, Jan. 1, 1867. Asst. dist. atty., 1868-71; mem. N.Y. assembly, 1873; clerk Oneida County, 1880-83; State senator, 1884-1901, reëlected, 1904; mem. Waterville bd. of edn., 16 yrs. Republican. Home: Waterville, N.Y. Died 1907.

COGGINS, Paschal Heston ("Sidney Marlow"), author; b. Phila., Pa., Jan. 10, 1852; s. Paschal and Mary (Williamson) C.; resided in Calif., 1855-68; L.B., U. of Pa., 1872; m. Caroline Leonard, Oct. 9, 1876. In law practice, 1873-1915. Author: (under pen-name) Harry Ambler, 1891; Moncasket Mystery, 1893; (under own name) Law (a handbook), 1895; Parliamentary Law, 1909; Going Down to Jericho; Dolly Brown of Vassar; "Why Not" Fuller. Home: Oakland, Calif. Died Nov. 14, 1917.

COGHILL, George Ellett, anatomist; b. Beaucoup, Ill., Mar. 17, 1872; s. John Waller and Elisabeth (Tucker) C.; student Shurtleff Coll., Alton, Ill., 1891-94; A.B., Brown, 1896, Ph.D., 1902, D.Sc., 1934; M.S., U. of N.M., 1899; Sc.D., Pittsburgh, 1931, Denison, 1933; m. Muriel Anderson, Sept. 13, 1900; children—Robert De Wolf, James Tucker, Louis Waller, Muriel, Benjamin Anderson. Asst. prof. biology, U. of N.M., 1899-1900; prof. biology, Pacific U., Forest Grove, Ore., 1902-06; prof. biology and embryology, Willamette U., Salem, Ore., 1906-07; prof. zoölogy, Denison U., Granville, O., 1907-13; asso. prof. anatomy, U. of Kan., 1913-15, prof., 1915-25, head of dept., 1918-25, sec. Sch. of Medicine, 1918-24; prof. comparative anatomy, Wistar Inst. Anatomy and Biology, 1925-27, mem. bd. advisers,

Wistar Inst., 1926—, mem. inst., 1927-36; mng. editor Jour. Comparative Neurology, 1927-33; visiting lecturer on advanced anatomy, Univ. Coll., London, 1928. Awarded Daniel Giraud Elliot gold medal in 1934 by National Academy of Sciences. Baptist. Author: Anatomy and the Problem of Behavior, 1929. Home: Gainesville, Fla. Died July 23, 1941.

COGHLAN, Charles F., actor-dramatist; b. London, Eng., 1848, son of a clergyman; trained for the bar, which he gave up for the stage; was leading man at Prince of Wales Theatre, London; came to U.S. in 1880 and appeared as Captain Absolute in "The Rivals." Has taken leading parts in numerous productions; starred in "The Royal Box." Author: "Jocelyn;" "Lady Barter;" (written for his sister, Rose Coghlan). Died 1899.

COGHLAN, Joseph Bullock, naval officer; b. Frankfort, Ky., Dec. 9, 1844; s. Cornelius and Lavinia (Fouke) C.; apptd. to U.S. Naval Acad. from Ill., 1860, graduated 1863. Promoted ensign, May 28, 1863; advanced through grades to rear adm., Apr. 11, 1902. Served Sacramento spl. service, 1863-65; Brooklyn, Brazilian Squadron, 1865-67; training-ship Portsmouth, 1868; Hydrographic Office, 1871-73; sick leave, 1873-74; comd. Saugus, 1875-76, Colorado, 1877, Monongahela, 1877-79, receiving-ship Independence, 1879-82, Adams, 1883-84; Navy Yard, Mare Island, 1886-88; comd. Mohican, 1888-90; insp. ordnance, Navy Yard, League Island, 1891-94; light-house insp. 8th dist., 1894-97; comd. Richmond, Feb., Mar., 1897; comd. Raleigh, Asiatic Fleet, during war with Spain, 1898; participated in battle of Manila Bay, May 1, 1898; advanced 6 numbers in rank for eminent and conspicuous conduct in battle of Manila Bay; comdt., Naval Sta., Puget Sound, 1899-1900; Naval War Coll., 1901; capt. of yard, Navy Yard, New York, 1901-02; 2d in command of N. Atlantic Fleet, 1902-04; comdt., Navy Yard, New York, 1904-07; retired, Dec. 9, 1906. Died 1908.

COGHLAN, Rose, actress; b. Peterboro, Eng., 1853; played soubrette parts Theatre Royal, Cheltenham, Eng., later becoming leading lady; went to London and traveled through the provinces in burlesque and comedy. Came to U.S., 1872, with Lydia Thompson, soon after joining E. A. Sothern, returned to Eng. and supported Barry Sullivan; leading lady with Wallack, 1880-89. Has starred in various cos. in U.S. and England; naturalized Am. citizen, July 1902, and engaged in stock raising in Montana. Home: New York, N.Y. Died Apr. 2, 1932.

COGSWELL, Frederick Hull, author, court reporter; b. New Preston, Conn., Mar. 11, 1859; s. Egbert and Mary Eliza (Hull) C.; grad. Conn. Lit. Instn., Suffield, Conn., 1881; studied law at Yale Law Sch. and Univ. of Mich.; m. Clara Knowles Wood, Sept. 12, 1882. Official reporter Superior Court, New Haven, 1884—. Republican. Author: A Compendium of Phonography, 1884; The Regicides, 1896; Art Work of New Haven, 1896; (joint author) Historic Towns of New England, 1898. Home: New Haven, Conn. Died 1907.

COGSWELL, Hamlin Elisha, musical dir.; b. Silvara, Pa., Sept. 26, 1852; s. Niram Jackson (M.D.) and Caroline P. C.; Wyoming Sem.; (hon. Master of Music, Syracuse U., 1903); m. Dorothy Tewksbury, 1875. Bandmaster, 13th Regt. Band, and choir master, Scranton, Pa., 1876-85; dir. Elmira City Band, Trinity Choir and Choral Club, 1886-89; dir. Conservatory of Music, Mansfield, Pa., 1887-97; supervisor music, Symphony Orchestra, Binghamton, N.Y., 1897-99, Syracuse, 1899-1903; dir. Conservatory of Music, Mansfield, 1903-06, Indiana (Pa.) Normal Conservatory of Music, 1906-15; dir. public school music, Washington, 1915—. Dir. Chautauqua (N.Y.) Summer Sch. of Music, 4 yrs.; teacher Summer Sch., Cornell U., 1915-17. Republican. Conglist. Author: School Room Echoes; The Institute. Home: Washington, D.C. Died Apr. 7, 1922.

COGSWELL, James Kelsey, naval officer; b. Milwaukee, Sept. 27, 1847; s. George and Celestia Anne Jeannette (Stone) C.; ed. Milwaukee Univ., St. Aloysius Acad. and pub. schs., 1855-60, Racine Coll. Grammar Sch., 1860-62, U.S. Naval Acad. at Newport, R.I., and Annapolis, Md., grad. 1868; m. Annie Miller Hatch, July 16, 1884. Midshipman, S. Pacific Sta., U.S.S. Powhatan, 1869; ensign U.S.S. Saginaw, 1870-71, wrecked on Ocean Island, Pacific Ocean; master on Saranac and flagship Pensacola, Pacific Sta.; promoted in turn to lt., lt. comdr.; served on Ticonderoga, Essex, Kearsarge, Tallapoosa, Marion on N. and S. Atlantic Stas.; shore duty at Torpedo Sta., Newport, R.I., and at Hydrographic Office, Washington; Portsmouth (N.H.) Navy Yard, ins. ordnance S. Boston Iron Works, Navy Yard, Washington; U.S. Battleship Oregon, 1897-98; promoted comdr., 1899; lighthouse insp., 1st dist.; comdr. Marietta and Isla de Luzon, Asiatic Sta., Philippine Islands; promoted capt., 1904; comd. U.S.S. Cleveland, N. Atlantic Sta., 1903-04; retired with rank of rear-admiral, 1904. Advanced 5 numbers for service as exec. officer on U.S.S. Oregon in Spanish War and battle of Santiago. Episcopalian. Democrat. Home: Portsmouth, N.H. Died 1908.

COGSWELL, William Brown, mfr.; b. Oswego, N.Y., Sept. 22, 1834; s. David and Mary (Barnes) C.; ed. Syracuse and Seneca Falls, N.Y.; attended Rensselaer Poly. Inst., 1850-52 (hon. C.E., 1884); twice married; m. 2d, Cora Louise Brown, Apr. 29, 1902. Apprentice Lawrence (Mass.) Machine Shop, 1852-55; asst. supt. Marietta & Cincinnati R.R., 1856-59; in U.S.N., 1861-65; erecting and operating blast furnaces at Franklin Iron Works, Oneida Co., N.Y., 1869-73; in charge mines La Motte Estate, Mo., 1874-79; established Solvay Process Co. (chem. works; soda products), 1881, of which was v.p. and mng. dir. Home: Syracuse, N.Y. Died June 7, 1921.

COGSWELL, William Sterling, lawyer; b. Jamaica, N.Y., Dec. 29, 1840; s. William Johnson and Alma Canfield (Sterling) C.; A.B., Trinity Coll., Conn., 1861, A.M., 1867; m. Henrietta Spader, Apr. 18, 1872. First lt. Co. I, 5th Conn. Inf., July 22, 1861; detailed to signal service, Aug. 1861; capt. Nov. 1861; major, Aug. 1863; lt. colonel, Nov. 1864; not mustered as lt. col. because regt. then had less than requisite number of men; bvtd. lt. col. U.S.V.; mustered out, Aug. 1865; served under Banks until Antietam, then in Army of Potomac until after Gettysburg; transferred to Army of Cumberland, 1863; with Thomas until after capture of Atlanta; went with Sherman to the Sea and through the Carolinas to Raleigh. Engaged in law practice, 1866—; in Brooklyn, N.Y., until 1899; then in New York (Manhattan). Pres. Maple Grove Cemetery Assn.; commr. of taxes of City of New York, 1902-04. Episcopalian. Republican. Trustee Trinity Coll., Brooklyn Law Library; mem. chapter of the Cathedral, Diocese of L.I. Home: Jamaica, L.I., N.Y. Died July 18, 1935.

COHAN, George M(ichael), comedian; b. Providence, R.I., July 4, 1878; s. Jerry John and Helen Frances (Costigan) C.; m. Ethel Levy, actress; 1 dau., Georgette; m. 2d. Agnes Nolan, July 4, 1908; children—Mary Helen, Helen Frances, George M. First appearance, Haverstraw, N.Y., at 9 yrs. of age, in "Daniel Boone"; appeared in "Peck's Bad Boy," 1890; later in vaudeville, in "The Four Cohans"; starred in "Little Johnny Jones," 1904-06; in "George Washington, Jr.," 1906-07. Author: (plays) "The Wise Guy"; "The Governor's Son" (3 act comedy); "Running for Office"; "Little Johnny Jones" (prod. 1904); "Forty-five Minutes from Broadway" (prod. 1905); "George Washington, Jr.," (prod. 1906); "Popularity" (prod. 1906); "The Talk of New York"; "Fifty Miles from Boston" (prod. 1907); "The Man Who Owns Broadway" (prod. 1908); "The Yankee Prince" (prod. 1909); "Get-Rich-Quick Wallingford" (prod. 1910); "The Little Millionaire" (prod. 1911); "Seven Keys to Baldpate" (prod. 1913); "Hit-the-Trail Holiday," 1915; "The Tavern," 1920; "The Song and Dance Man," 1923; "American Born," 1925; "The Baby Cyclone" (farce), 1927; "The Merry Malones" (musical play), 1927; "Billie" (musical play), 1928; "Gambling drama," 1929; also many popular songs. Starred in play "I'd Rather Be Right," 1937-38. Died Nov. 5, 1942.

COHEN, Charles Joseph, mfr.; b. Phila., Pa., Sept. 21, 1847; s. Henry and Matilda (Samuel) C.; ed. Dr. Faires' Classical Inst., Phila., and Dr. Ihne's Instn., Liverpool, Eng.; m. Clotilda Florance Cohen, Oct. 13, 1880; children—Henry Barnet (dec.), Albert Morris, Eleanor Florance. Pres. Charles J. Cohen Co., mfrs. envelopes and paper. Mem. bd. dirs. Phila. Chamber of Commerce, 1900— (pres. 1913-15); trustee Fairmount Park Art Assn., 1877— (pres., 1916—); mem. bd. mgrs. Phila. Fountain Soc., 1907-23 (pres. 1916-23); pres. Portuguese Jewish Congregation Mikve Israel (board managers); charter member board trustees Gratz College (treasurer, 1895-1900; v.p., 1923-24); charter member, pres. Y.M.H. Assn.; mem. Jewish Theol. Sem. Am. (Phila. br.), Federation of Jewish Charities. Mem. Home Defense Reserve, 1918-19; mem. Asso. Soc. Am. Red Cross (life). Republican. Author: Rittenhouse Square, Past and Present, 1922; History of The Penn Club, 1924. Home: Philadelphia, Pa. Died Sept. 24, 1927.

COHEN, Jacob (da Silva) Solis, M.D.; b. New York, Feb. 28, 1838; s. Myer David and Judith Simirah (da Silva Solis) C.; brother of David Solis and Solomon Solis C.; ed. Central High Sch., Phila.; M.D., Univ. of Pa., 1860; LL.D., Jefferson Med. Coll. and Temple U., 1912; m. Miriam Bingswanger, Feb. 10, 1874. Asst. surgeon 26th Pa. Regt., 1861; later asst. surgeon U.S.N., with Dupont's expdn. to Port Royal and S. Atlantic Blockading Squadron until Jan. 1864; then acting asst. surgeon in army hosps., Phila., to end of war; in practice at Phila., 1866—, with spl. attention to diseases of throat and chest; hon. prof. laryngology, Jefferson Med. Coll., Phila.; emeritus prof. diseases of the throat, Phila. Polyclinic and Coll. for Graduates in Medicine; cons. phys. Hosp. for Insane, S.E. Dist. Pa. Author: A Treatise on Inhalation; Diseases of the Throat; Croup in Its Relations to Tracheotomy; The Throat and the Voice. Home: Philadelphia, Pa. Died Dec. 22, 1927.

COHEN, John Sanford, editor; b. Augusta, Ga., Feb. 26, 1870; s. Philip Lawrence and Ellen Gobert (Wright) C.; prep. edn., Richmond Acad. (Augusta, Ga.), Shenandoah Valley Acad.; U.S. Naval Acad., 1885-86; LL.D., Washington and Lee U., 1924; m. Julia Lowry Clarke, Nov. 11, 1897; children—John Sanford, Mary Clarke. Began newspaper work on Augusta Chronicle, later on staff New York World; war corr. Spanish-Am. War, sailing with fleet under Admiral Bob Evans; identified with Atlanta Journal most of time, 1890, editor, 1917—, also pres. Atlanta Journal Co.; served as Washington corr. and spl. writer on politics. Commd. 1st lt. Co. A, 3d Ga. U.S. Vol. Inf., 1898, Spanish-Am. War; promoted capt. and maj.; was with Army of Occupation in Cuba. Originator Nat. Highway, built under joint supervision of Atlanta Journal and New York Herald, from N.Y. City to Jacksonville, Fla.; aided building of "Greater Emory University," Atlanta, and refounding Oglethorpe U., Atlanta; patron of art and music; dir. Atlanta Music Festival Assn.; trustee Georgia School of Technology. Mem. Dem. Nat. Com. from Ga., Apr. 1924—. Apptd. U.S. senator to fill vacancy caused by death of William J. Harris, Apr. 25, 1932, term ending Jan. 10, 1933; vice chmn. Dem. Nat. Com., 1932—. Episcopalian. Mason. Home: Atlanta, Ga. Died May 13, 1935.

COHEN, Katherine M., sculptor and painter; b. Phila., Mar. 18, 1859; d. Henry and Matilda (Samuel) C., of England; ed. pvt. sch., and Ogontz, Pa., until 16; then pvt. lessons in literature, art, languages, etc.; Pa. Acad. Fine Arts, Art Students' League, New York, under St. Gaudens and 6 yrs. in Paris, and 6 yrs. in Italy; unmarried. Hon. mem. Am. Art Assn., Paris, New Century Club, Phila. Engaged in sculpture, 1880—; prin. works portraits and bas reliefs; decorative works—Romola, Lorna Doone, Rabbi-ben-Ezra, Priscilla, Maid Marion, The Israelite (life size statue), portrait of Gen. Beaver for Smith Memorial, Fairmount Park, Phila., paintings of figure and landscape, miniatures on ivory, etc. Home: Philadelphia, Pa. Died Dec. 14, 1914.

COHEN, Lewis, artist; b. London, Eng., 1857; s. Solomon L. and Caroline C.; came with parents to America, 1859; B.A., Dartmouth, 1878; studied art in London and Paris under Alphonse Legros, J. Watson Nicoll and A. S. Cope; unmarried. Spent 20 yrs. in London; exhibited in Royal Acad., Paris Salon and in prin. Am. cities. A.N.A. Home: New York, N.Y. Died Aug. 4, 1915.

COHEN, Lily Young, editor, author; b. Charleston, S.C.; d. J. Barrett and Marie (Young) C.; pvtly. ed. Mem. editorial staff Neale Pub. Co., 1912—; asso. editor Neale's Monthly, 1912-14; translates from English into French, German, Spanish and Esperanto, and from those languages into English; editor of more than 100 published vols. Episcopalian. Writer for motion picture producers; writes critically on lit., painting, the plastic arts, Oriental rugs and tapestries. Author: Lost Spirituals, 1928. Died June 1, 1930.

COHEN, Mendes, civil engr.; b. Baltimore, May 4, 1831; s. David I. C.; ed. pvt. schs.; studied engring., 1847-51, in locomotive works Ross Winans, Baltimore; m. 1865. In engr. corps and other service of B.&O. R.R., 1851-55; asst. supt. Hudson River R.R., 1855-61; pres. and supt. Ohio & Miss. R.R. (of Ill.), 1861-63; then in spl. service of Phila. & Reading; comptroller and asst. to pres. Lehigh Coal & Navigation Co., 1868-71; pres. Pittsburgh & Connellsville, 1872-75; afterward retired from active professional work; mem. bd. apptd. by Pres. Cleveland, 1894, to examine and report route for Chesapeake and Delaware Ship Canal; chmn. sewerage commn., Baltimore, 1893-1904. Died Aug. 13, 1915.

COHEN, William Nathan, lawyer; b. New York, N.Y., May 7, 1857; s. Nathan and Ernestine (Erdmann) C.; A.B., Dartmouth, 1879, A.M., 1884, LL.D., 1899; LL.B., Columbia, 1881; unmarried. Engaged in practice in New York; justice Supreme Court of N.Y., 1897-98. Republican. During the war was chmn. Draft Bd. and later chmn. Ocean Advisory Com. of U.S. Shipping Bd., which sat as a court to determine the compensation to be made to owners of vessels requisitioned by U.S. Govt. Died Feb. 26, 1938.

COHEN, William W., congressman; b. Brooklyn, N.Y., Sept. 6, 1874; s. Benjamin and Fredericka (Kronacher) C.; ed. pub. schs.; m. Sophie Dazian, Feb. 4, 1902. Began in brokerage business, N.Y. City, 1902. Mem. 70th Congress (1927-29), 17th New York District. Trustee and mem. exec. com. Daughters of Jacob; dir. Hosp. for Joint Diseases, Fedn. of New York Guild for Jewish Blind; hon. dep. chief of Fire Department. Democrat. Hebrew. Mason. B'nai B'rith. Home: New York, N.Y. Died Oct. 12, 1940.

COHN, Adolphe, univ. prof.; b. Paris, France, May 29, 1851; s. Albert and Mathilde (Lowengard) C.; B.èsL., U. of Paris, 1868, LL.B., 1873, A.M. (archiviste Paléographe École Nationale des Chartes), Paris, 1874; vol. in French Army during Franco-German War, July 1870-Feb. 1871; came to U.S., 1875; m. Marian Loys Wright, Apr. 6, 1887 (died 1888); 2d, Madeleine Merlin, June 4, 1904. Tutor and instr. French, Columbia, 1882-84; instr. and asst. prof French, Harvard, 1884-91; prof. Romance langs. and lits., Columbia Univ., 1891-1916; retired, June 30, 1916. Officier Légion d'Honneur; Knight Crown of Italy. Author: Voltaire's Prose (with Prof. B. D. Woodward), 1897; Le Sage's Gil Blas (with R. Sanderson), 1889; Montaigne (in French Classics for English Readers), 1907. Died Feb. 13, 1930.

COHN, Morris M., lawyer; b. New Albany, Ind., Mar. 14, 1852; s. Mathias A. and Therese (Koebner) C.; ed. grammar schs., Cincinnati, and pvt. instrn. in German and Hebrew and in law; m. Addie M. Ottenheimer, Aug. 19, 1883. Admitted to bar, 1873; city atty., Little Rock, 2 years; school dir. 3 yrs.; prof. law sch., U. of Ark., several yrs. Mem. Com. for Admission to Bar to Supreme Ct., and Federal Ct. at Little Rock. Dir. Little Rock Board of Trade; v.p. for Arkansas, Sound Money League; trustee Little Rock Pub. Library. Democrat. Author: The Growth of Law, 1882; Introduction to the Study of the Constitution (extra vol. XI of Hist. Series of Johns Hopkins Univ.), 1892. Home: Little Rock, Ark. Died Apr. 3, 1922.

COILE, Samuel Andrew, clergyman; b. Dandridge, Tenn., Jan. 18, 1857; s. John Leonard and Mary Elizabeth (Bettis) C.; A.B., Tusculum Coll., Greeneville, Tenn., 1879, A.M., 1884; Lane Theol. Sem., Cincinnati, O., 1880-83; studied U. of Chicago; (D.D., Gale [Wis.] Coll., 1895); m. Mary Carleton Speck, June 30, 1887. Ordained Presbyn. ministry, 1883; pastor Greeneville, Tenn., 1883-95, Ft. Sanders Ch., Knoxville, 1895-1901; pres. Tusculum Coll., 1901-07; pastor Lebanon, Tenn., 1907-14; pres. Cumberland U., 1914-16; pastor Maryville, Mo., 1916-20, McCausland Av. Ch., St. Louis, Jan. 18, 1920—. Trustee Tusculum Coll., 1883-1907. Republican. Mason. Home: St. Louis, Mo. Died May 9, 1923.

COIT, Arthur Clinton, lyceum mgr.; b. Shalersville, O., Apr. 8, 1869; s. Burton O. and Lucy Ann (Connor) C.; student Hiram Coll. to jr. yr.; B.S., Buchtel Coll., Akron, O., 1890; m. Myrta Critchlow, Nov. 2, 1893. Began in lyceum and chautauqua bus., at Cleveland, O., 1895, and was pres. Coit Lyceum Bur., Coit-Alber Chautauquas (Cleveland), Coit-Alber Independent Chautauqua Co. (Chicago), Dominion Chautauqua (Toronto, Can.), Coit-Alber Lyceum Bur. (Boston), Coit-Alber Bur. (New York), Coit-Neilson Lyceum Bur. (Pittsburgh). Retired, 1924. Overseas Y.M.C.A. sec., 1918. Democrat. Methodist. Mason. Home: Los Angeles, Calif. Died Aug. 3, 1929.

COIT, J(ames) Milnor, teacher; b. Harrisburg, Pa., Jan. 31, 1845; s. Rev. Joseph H. C.; prep. edn. St. Paul's Sch., Concord, N.H.; A.B., Hobart Coll., 1865, A.M., 1868; (Ph.D., Dartmouth, 1881; Sc.D., Hobart, 1905); m. E. Josephine Wheeler, Oct. 1867. Mgr. Cleveland Tube Works, 1873-75; master in natural sciences, 1876—, vice-rector, 1904-06, acting rector till July 1, 1906, St. Paul's Sch., Concord, N.H.; engaged in research work, U. of Munich, 1909; was head master, Coit Sch. (for Am. boys), Munich, Germany. Pres. Am. Red Cross Com. and chmn. Children's Relief Com., Munich. Died 1925.

COIT, John McLean, patent lawyer; b. Cheraw, S.C., Dec. 9, 1869; s. James C. and Sarah E. (McLean) C.; B.S. in C.E., U. of S.C., 1891; LL.B., Columbian (now George Washington) U., Washington, D.C., 1895; unmarried. Asst. examiner, 1891-1900, law examiner, 1900-06, examiner in chief, 1906-07, U.S. Patent Office; mem. Watson, Coit, Morse & Grindle. Democrat. Presbyn. Home: Washington, D.C. Died May 11, 1926.

COIT, Joseph Howland, clergyman, educator; b. Wilmington, Del., Sept. 11, 1831; grad. St. James Coll., Md., 1851 (D.D., Hobart, 1888; LL.D., Dartmouth, 1889). Ordered deacon, 1854; ordained priest, 1855. Asst. prof. mathematics and physics, St. James' Coll., 1856-60, prof. same, 1860-64; chaplain Hobart Coll., 1864; vice rector, 1865-95, rector from June, 1895, St. Paul's Sch., Concord, N.H. Author: Memorials of St. Paul's School; also chapters in The Life of Bishop Kerfoot. Died 1906.

COIT, Joshua, clergyman; b. New London, Conn., Feb. 4, 1832; s. Robert and Charlotte (Coit) C.; A.B., Yale, 1853; grad. Andover Theol. Sem., 1856; student Univ. of Halle, 1857, Univ. of Berlin, 1858; m. Mary L. Chandler, Oct. 10, 1860. Ordained Congl. ministry, 1860; pastor Brookfield, Mass., 1860-70; sec. Mass. Prison Commn., 1870-73; pastor Lawrence St. Ch., Lawrence, Mass., 1873-83; sec., 1883-1905, treas., 1905—, Mass. Home Missionary Soc. Home: Winchester, Mass. Died 1907.

COIT, Judson Boardman, univ. prof.; b. Central Square, N.Y., June 5, 1849; s. James J. and Miriam (Owen) C.; A.B., Syracuse U., 1875, A.M., 1878, Ph.D., 1881; m. Ellen M. Alden, Aug. 19, 1875. Prof. mathematics, Dickinson Seminary, Williamsport, Pa., 1875-79; student asst. in observatory, Ann Arbor, 1879-80; taught mathematics, Central High Sch., Cleveland, 1880-82; asst. prof. mathematics and astronomy, 1882-84, prof., 1884-1915, prof. astronomy, 1915—, acting dean of Grad. Sch., 1911-12, Boston U. Died July 26, 1921.

COKE, Henry Cornick, lawyer; b. Norfolk, Va., May 30, 1856; s. William W. and Lucy (Cornick) C.; student William and Mary Coll., 1875-76; LL.B., U. of Va., 1878; m. Roberta Rosser, 1884 (died 1888); children—Roberta, Rosser; m. 2d, Margaret Johnson, Apr. 16, 1890; children—Richard Wellesley, Lucy W., Anne B., Henry C. Admitted to Va. bar, 1878; moved to Dallas, 1881; sr. mem. Coke & Coke; atty. for state of Tex. in first Railroad Commn. suit in Tex.; represented Standard Oil Cos. when sued by State; chmn. bd. of First Nat. Bank in Dallas. Democrat. Episcopalian. Home: Dallas, Tex. Died July 10, 1933.

COKER, David Robert, plant breeder, agrl. and cotton expert; b. Hartsville, S.C., Nov. 20, 1870; s. James Lide and Susan (Stout) C.; A.B., Univ. of S.C., 1891; hon. D.Sc. from Duke Univ., 1930; LL.D., U. of N.C., 1931; LL.D., Coll. of Charleston, 1935; D.Sc., Clemson Coll., 1937; m. Jessie Ruth Richardson, Sept. 10, 1894 (died 1913); children—Katherine, Hannah, Eleanor, Robert, Samuel; m. 2d, Margaret May Roper, 1915; children—Martha, Mary, Carolyn. Originator of varieties of staple cotton widely planted in the U.S. and elsewhere; pres. J. L. Coker & Co., merchants; mem. Coker Cotton Co.; pres. Coker's Pedigreed Seed Co. Mayor of Hartsville, S.C., 1902-04; chmn. S.C. Council of Defense, World War, also of Federal Food Administration for S.C.; mem. Nat. Agrl. Advisory Com.; mem. Nat. Agrl. Commn. to Europe, 1918, S.C. Land Settlement Commission; mem. Business Advisory Council of Dept. of Commerce. Trustee U. of S.C., Coker Coll. for Women. Awarded McMaster medal, U. of S.C. Democrat. Home: Hartsville, S.C. Died Nov. 28, 1938.

COKER, James Lide, paper mfr.; b. Society Hill, S.C., Jan. 3, 1837; s. Caleb and Hannah (Lide) C.; ed. St. David's Acad., Society Hill, S.C. Mil. Acad., Charleston, S.C., and Lawrence Scientific Sch. (Harvard U.); (LL.D., U. of S.C.); m. Susan Stout, Mar .28, 1860 (died 1904). Capt. and maj. 6th S.C. Inf. C.S.A., 1861-65; wounded nr. Chattanooga, Oct., 1863. Mem. S.C. Ho. of Rep., 1864, 65, 66. Mcht. and mfr. at Hartsville, S.C., 1866—; mem. Norwood & Coker, cotton and naval stores, Charleston, 1874-81; organized, 1881, and pres. Darlington (S.C.) Nat. Bank; 1st pres. Darlington Mfg. Co., 1884; built short line ry., Floyd to Hartsville, S.C., 1889; pres. Carolina Fiber Co., Southern Novelty Co.; partner J. L. Coker & Co.; dir. Hartsville Cotton Mill, Hartsville Oil Mill, Bank of Hartsville (pres. until 1910). Democrat. Baptist. Trustee Coker Coll. for Women, Hartsville. Home: Hartsville, S.C. Died June 25, 1918.

COLAHAN, John Barron, Jr., lawyer; b. Phila., Pa., May 18, 1848; s. John B. and Mary Dorothea (Zell) C.; A.B., Central High Sch., Phila., 1866; St. Joseph's Coll., law dept. U. of Pa.; m. Mary Ophelia Cowton, Apr. 14, 1873. Admitted to bar, 1869; dir. The Land Title & Trust Co. Pres. Pa. State Bar Assn. (twice v.p., many yrs. chmn. exec. com.); v.p. Am. Bar Assn.; chmn. bd. censors Law Assn., Phila. Vice-pres. Welcome Soc. Mem. commission to examine into industrial conditions and draft laws for the prevention and settlement of industrial accidents. Chmn. Legal Advisory Bd., 1917-18. Catholic. Republican. Home: Philadelphia, Pa. Died Mar. 5, 1920.

COLBY, Albert Ladd, metallurgist; b. New York, N.Y., June 26, 1860; s. John Ladd (M.D.) and Mary Ann C.; student Coll. City of New York; Ph.B., Columbia Sch. of Mines, 1881; m. Agnes Wilson Lee, June 20, 1894. Engaged in steel metallurgy, 1886—; sec. of Assn. Am. Steel Mfrs., 1897-1905; U.S. Juror, Paris Expn., 1900; iron and steel commr., St. Louis Expn., 1904. Author: American Standard Specifications for Steel, 1902; Reinforced Concrete in Europe, 1909. Home: Bethlehem, Pa. Died May 2, 1924.

COLBY, Branch Harris, civil engr.; b. Cherry Valley, O., July 20, 1854; s. Lewis and Celestia (Rice) C.; C.E., U. of Mich., 1877, post-grad. course in mining engring., 1877-78; m. Minnie Bary, June 28, 1883; children—Vine (Mrs. Charles O. McCasland), Dorothy (Mrs. Victor H. Lawn). Asst. on survey of Great Lakes, 1875-78; U.S. asst. engr., Miss. River, 1878-84; in pvt. practice, 1885-89; U.S. asst. engr. in charge of survey of Portage Lake Ship Canal, 1888-89, for Straight Channel, Sandusky (O.) Harbor, 1889; U.S. asst. engr. Miss. River Commn., 1889-90; prin. asst. engr. sewer dept., St. Louis, 1890-95; sewer commn. and mem. Bd. of Pub. Improvements, 1895-99; civ. and consulting engr. Am. Car & Foundry Co., 1900; pvt. practice, 1901, until retired. Engineer on building steel ships at Hog Island Pa., 1917; supervised constrn. Govt. Island Shipyard, San Francisco, July-Dec. 1918; mem. bd. to investigate and report upon condition and operation of ship yards upon Atlantic Coast; resident engr. in charge of constrn. of a dry dock, marine ry. and repair plant at Jacksonville, Fla. Mem. Mich. Nat. Guard, 1873-76. Unitarian. Mason. Home: Normal, Ill. Died Jan. 3, 1933.

COLBY, Clara Bewick, lecturer; b. England; d. Thomas and Clara (Willingham) Bewick; brought to America in early girlhood; Ph.B., U. of Wis. Editor and pub. The Woman's Tribune, 25 yrs. V.p. Woman's Nat. Press Assn.; mem. Internat. Woman's Franchise Club, London. Apptd. del. Internat. Moral Edn. Congress, London, 1908, and del. Internat. Races Congress, London, 1911; apptd. del. Internat. Woman Suffrage Alliance, Budapest, and Internat. Peace Congress, The Hague, 1913. Corr. sec. and chmn. Congl. Com. Fed. Suffrage Assn.; hon. v.p. Internat. New Thought Alliance. Home: Portland, Ore. Deceased.

COLBY, Frank C(arleton); b. McHenry Co., Ill.; s. Frank and Georgiana W. (Jewett) C.; D.D.S., Chicago Coll. Dental Surgery (Lake Forest U.), 1892; m. Mary A. Bayrd. In drug business as clerk, 1882-88; in gen. mercantile business, 1888-90; in practice of dentistry, 1892-1909; Christian Science practitioner, 1909—; first reader First Ch., Detroit, 1909-12; served on Bible Lesson Com., Christian Science Ch., 1919-22; pres. 1st Ch. of Christ, Scientist, Boston, Mass., 1928. Republican. Mason. Home: Brookline, Mass. Died 1939.

COLBY, Frank Moore, editor; b. Washington, Feb. 10, 1865; s. Stoddard Benham and Ellen Cornelia (Hunt) C.; A.B., Columbia, 1888, A.M., 1889; spl. studies political sciences, Columbia; m. Harriet Wood Fowler, Dec. 30, 1896. Acting prof. history, Amherst Coll., 1890-91; lecturer history, Columbia, 1891-95; instr. history and economics Barnard Coll., 1891-95; prof. economics, N.Y. U., 1895-1900; editor New Internat. Ency., 1900— (revised, 1913-16, sup., 1923-24), and New Internat. Year Book, 1907—. On editorial staff Johnson's Cyclopedia, dept. of history and polit. science, 1893-95; editor Internat. Cyclopedia, 1898 edit., Internat. Year Book, 1898-1902; editorial writer New York Commercial Advertiser, 1900-02; Am. editor Nelson's Ency., 1905-06; lit. reviewer for Harper's Weekly, Mar.-June 1913; staff writer and contbr. to New Republic, Vanity Fair, North Am. Review, etc. Author: Outlines of General History, 1900; Imaginary Obligations, 1904; Constrained Attitudes, 1910; The Margin of Hesitation, 1921. Died Mar. 3, 1925.

COLBY, Franklin Green, merchant; b. Brooklyn, Aug. 10, 1858; s. Solomon B. and Margerette Coffin (Hill) C.; ed. common sch. and acad., Phillipsburg, N.J.; m. 2d, Josephine Wood, Feb. 1, 1892. Engaged largely in foreign business as exporter and importer and mfr. in Manila, P.I.; retired. Volunteer work for allied govts. during war. Has lived abroad many years. Life mem. N.Y. Hist. Soc. and Arts Club; mem. Met. Mus. of Art. Interested in the fine arts. Home: Andover, N.J. Died June 4, 1941.

COLBY, Gardner, civil service officer; b. E. Orange, N.J., Sept. 12, 1864; s. Gardner and Martha L. (Hutchings) C.; A.B., Brown U., 1887, A.M., 1890; m. Fanny Hazard Curtis, Mar. 21, 1888. Pres. and treas. Everett Pulp & Paper Co., and treas. Everett Land Co., 1893-1901; treas. Kinsman Block Signal Co., 1906-08, sec. and chief examiner N.J. Civ. Service Commn., May 23, 1908—. Trustee Brown U., 1896—, Colgate U.; sec. Lincoln Fund Com.; trustee Dodge Memorial Fund. Republican. Baptist. Home: East Orange, N.J. Died Nov. 4, 1917.

COLBY, Harrison Gray Otis, rear adm.; b. New Bedford, Mass., Jan. 28, 1846; s. Harrison Gray Otis and Jane Standish (Parker) C.; grad. U.S. Naval Acad., 1867; m. Mary Catherine Thompson, Apr. 20, 1881 (dec.); 1 son, Francis Thompson. Promoted through grades to capt., June 18, 1902; rear adm. and retired, Jan. 28, 1908. Served on U.S.S. Dakotah during Civil War; comdr. U.S.S. Hannibal and 2d Dist. coast defense, also selecting proper vessels for the govt. to purchase during Spanish-Am. War; capt. of Olympia; comdr. European Squadron, 1904-05; in command cruiser div. N. Atlantic Fleet, winter, 1904-05; comdr. spl. squadron to Havana, Mar. 1905. Was exec. officer yacht "America" in race for the Queen's Cup with the "Cambria" and other yachts; afterwards in command of "America"; comdr. U.S. Coast and Geod. Survey schooner "Eagre" (late "Mohawk") and steamer "Blake"; then hydrographic insp. of U.S. Coast and Geod. Survey; insp. 2d Light House Dist. With Mrs. Colby worked in Paris for Am. Fund for French Wounded and Am. Red Cross, 1916-18; ordered to active duty U.S.N., Sept. 1918. Home: Boston, Mass. Died Nov. 3, 1926.

COLBY, Henry Francis, clergyman; b. Boston, Nov. 25, 1842; s. Gardner and Mary L. (Roberts) C.; A.B., Brown U., 1862, A.M., 1865 (D.D., 1882); grad. Newton Theol. Instn., 1867; ordained Bapt. ministry, 1868; m. Mary Lizzie Chamberlin, May 5, 1870. Pres. Am. Bapt. Missionary Union, 1865-68; pastor First Ch., Dayton, O., 1868-1903. Pres. Ohio Bapt. Conv., 1883-86; trustee, 1872—, pres. bd., 1890—, Denison U.; pres. Miami Valley Hospital. Home: Dayton, O. Died May 8, 1915.

COLBY, James Fairbanks, prof. law; b. St. Johnsbury, Vt., Nov. 18, 1850; s. James K. and Sarah A. (Pierce) C.; A.B., Dartmouth, 1872; LL.B., Columbian (now George Washington) U., 1875; A.M., Yale, 1877; (LL.D., Dartmouth, 1901); unmarried. Admitted to bar, D.C., 1875, Conn., 1878, N.H. 1889; practiced at New Haven, Conn., 1878-85. Instr. economics and history, Sheffield Scientific Sch. (Yale), 1879-81; lecturer on internat. law, Yale Law Sch., 1883-85; Parker prof. law and polit. science,

1885-1916, then prof. emeritus, Dartmouth. Lecturer jurisprudence and international law, Boston University Law School, 1905—. Clerk Com. Revision of Laws, Ho. of Rep., 43d Congress; sec. New Haven Civ. Service Reform Assn., 1881-85; mem. N.H. Forestry Commn., 1893-98; del. N.H. Constl. Conv., 1902. Editor Manual of N.H. Constitution, 1902, 2d edit., 1912, and of A Sketch of English Legal History by F. W. Maitland and F. C. Montague, 1915. Home: Hanover, N.H. Died Oct. 21, 1939.

COLBY, J(une) Rose, teacher; b. Cherry Valley, O., June 1856; d. Lewis and Celestia (Rice) C.; A.B., U. of Mich, 1878, A.M., 1885, Ph.D., 1886. Taught algebra, Ann Arbor High Sch., 1878-79, Latin and Greek, Flint (Mich.) High Sch., 1879-83; studied Radcliffe Coll., 1883-84, U. of Mich., 1884-86; taught lit., Peoria (Ill.) High Sch., 1886-92; preceptress, prof. lit., 1892-1909, prof. lit., 1909-31, prof. emeritus of lit., 1931—, Illinois State Normal U. Instructor in Columbia U., summer session, 1909. Editor, with introduction and notes, Silas Marner, by George Eliot, 1900; Quentin Durward, by Scott, 1912. Author: Some Ethical Aspects of Later Elizabethan Tragedy, 1886; Literature and Life in School, 1906. Home: Normal, Ill. Died May 11, 1940.

COLBY, Leonard Wright, soldier, lawyer; b. Ashtabula Co., O., Aug. 5, 1846; s. Rowell and Abigail (Livingston) C.; A.B. and C.E., U. of Wis., 1871, LL.B., 1872, A.M., 1874; m. 2d, Marie C. Miller; 1 son, Paul Livingston. Judge of 18th Jud. Dist. of Neb.; asst. atty. gen. of U.S., 1890-93; mem. Neb. Senate, 2 terms. Republican. Pvt. Co. B, 8th Ill. Inf., June 12, 1864-Oct. 16, 1865; served in Sioux Indian campaign, 1890-91, comdg. brigade of Neb. troops; lt. to brig. gen. Neb. N.G.; brig. gen. U.S. Vols., June 3, 1898-Feb. 24, 1899, in Spanish-Am. War; adj. gen., Neb., 1901-03. Organized Cuban-Am. Vol. Legion, 1897. Chairman Gage County Defense Council, U.S. Govt. Draft Agt. Mason. Mem. Christian Ch. Home: Beatrice, Neb. Died Nov. 15, 1925.

COLBY, William Irving, educator; b. Warner, N.H., Oct. 29, 1852; s. B. S. and Maria (Harriman) C.; ed. pub. schs., Warner, N.H.; grad. Chicago Coll. of Elocution; teacher of German, 1881—. Widower. Extensive traveler. Author: Der Lehrer (German Reader and Conversation Book), 1888; Practical Synopsis of German Grammar, 1893; Der Leitstern, 1895; Key to German Grammar, 1897; Literal Translation of Der Lehrer, 1903. Deceased.

COLCOCK, F(rancis) Horton, lawyer; b. Huntsville, Ala., June 19, 1855; s. Col. Charles Jones and Lucy Frances (Horton) C.; desc. of Revolutionary ancestry; C.E., Union Coll., Schnectady, N.Y., 1877; (LL.D., U. of Ala.); m. Mary Robert Jones, Aug. 4, 1880. Studied law in office of Gen. James Conner, Charleston, S.C., and admitted to bar, 1879; mem. Howell, Murphy & Colcock, of Hampton and Walterboro, S.C., 1880-82; teacher Porter Mil. Acad., 1886-94; asst. prof. mathematics, 1894-99, prof., 1899-1907, prof. mathematics and astronomy, 1907-15, dean dept. Physics and Engring., 1907-08, dean Dept. Engring. and Mathematics, 1907-12, U. of S.C.; resumed practice, June 1915, then at Beaufort, S.C.; also planter. Was commr. of co. schs. of Charleston Co., S.C., and commr. pub. schs. of Charleston, rearganizing same; v.p. Nat. Rivers and Harbors Congress; mem. Good Roads Congress, Washington, D.C., 1911 (com. on orgn.). Democrat. Episcopalian. Home: Bluffton, S.C. Died Nov. 13, 1925.

COLCORD, Charles Francis, capitalist; b. Bourbon Co., Ky., Aug. 18, 1859; s. Col. William R. and Maria Elizabeth (Clay) C.; self-educated; m. Harriet Scoresby, Sept. 1884. Left Ky. and went to Nueces Co., Tex., when a small boy; range rider in West Tex. at 12; made run into Okla., 1889, staking lots in Oklahoma City; organizer, 1898, and first pres. Commercial Nat. Bank, Oklahoma City; entered oil business, 1903, drilling first wells at Red Fork, Okla.; discovered (in partnership with Robert Galbreath) Glen Pool, the great oil field of Okla., 1906; organizer, 1908, and then pres. Local Building & Loan Assn., Oklahoma City; pioneer in Healdton, Loco and Duncan oil fields; built 12 story Colcord Bldg., Oklahoma City, 1910; discovered and developed the South Bend, Tex., oil field during 1917-21; pres. Okla. Biltmore Hotel. First chief of police of Oklahoma City, 1889; first sheriff, Okla. County, 1889-90; dep. U.S. marshal, 1893-98. Member Oklahoma Chamber Commerce (pres. 1914). Democrat. Mason. Home: Oklahoma City, Okla. Died Dec. 1934.

COLCORD, Roswell Keyes, supt. U.S. Mint; b. Scarsport, Me., April 25, 1839; s. James and Eliza C.; ed. in pub. schs. Has lived in Nev. 44 yrs.; gov. of Nev., 1890-94; supt. U.S. Mint, Carson City, Nev., Nov. 1, 1898—. Died Oct. 30, 1939.

COLDEN, Charles J., congressman; b. on farm, Peoria Co., Ill., Aug. 24, 1870; s. John Wesley and Susan Harriett (Gingrich) C.; B.S., Country Coll., Stanberry, Mo., 1893; m. Jessie F. McGrew, Aug. 16, 1891; children—Archie John, Vi June (Mrs. Lester L. Hawthorne), Abbie Bel; m. 2d, Clara Norman, Feb. 12, 1914; 1 son, Charles J. Teacher in common schs., 1889-96; editor and pub. Parnell (Mo.) Sentinel, 1896-1900; established Nodaway Forum, Maryville, Mo., 1901, sold out interest, 1907; in building business, Kansas City, Mo., 1908-11; realty investment business San Pedro, Calif., 1912-23; retired. Elected to Mo. Assembly, 1901-03; mem. Los Angeles City Council, 1925-29; apptd. mem. and pres. Los Angeles Harbor Commn., 1923; mem. 73d and 74th Congresses (1933-37), 17th Calif. Dist. Mem. City Planning Assn. of Los Angeles (pres. 4 terms), Playground Commn. of Los Angeles; pres. San Pedro Chamber of Commerce, 1922-24; pres. bd. of regents State Teachers College, Maryville, Mo., 1905-08. Democrat. Home: San Pedro, Calif. Died Apr. 15, 1938.

COLE, Aaron Hodgman, biologist; b. Greenwich, N.Y., Oct. 21, 1856; s. Morgan C. (M.D.) and Lydia Ann (Hodgman) C.; A.B., Colgate U., 1884, A.M., 1887; grad. student Johns Hopkins, 1889, U. of Chicago, 1893, 1896, 1898; m. Emma Sarah Mason, Dec. 29, 1885. Instr. natural sciences, Peddie Inst., 1884-88; lecturer in zoölogy and geology, Colgate, 1888-92; instr. zoölogy, Cold Spring Harbor Biol. Laboratory, 1893; lecturer in biology, U. of Chicago, extension div., 1895-1906; instr. of biology, Chicago Teachers College, 1906—. Instr. technique of biol. projection and anesthesia of animals, U. of Chicago, 1901. Popular lecturer on bacteriology, 1895—; then delivering popular lectures on vital phenomena of lower animals and plants. Inventor of scientific apparatus, eye-shields, and of methods of highly magnifying on screen images of microscopic animals and plants; demonstrated method of "teaching biology from living plants and animals with a projection microscope," 1905; discovered a successful method of culture for amœba, and a method of showing the movement of sap in the leaves of plants. Asso. editor United Editors Ency. and Dictionary and author of articles on "The Projection Microscope and Its Use" and "Anesthesia of Animals and Plants." Author and publisher: Manual of Biological Projection and Anesthesia of Animals, 1907. Home: Chicago, Ill. Died Dec. 31, 1913.

COLE, Alfred Dodge, physicist; b. Rutland, Vt., Dec. 18, 1861; s. Israel D. and Alice (Ware) C.; A.B., Brown, 1884, A.M., 1887; studied Johns Hopkins, 1884-85, Summer Sch., Harvard, 1888, Berlin, 1894-95, Summer Sch., Cornell, 1897, U. of Chicago, summers, 1898, 1899, 1900, 1904; m. Emily Downer, June 18, 1889. Instr. chemistry and physics, 1885-87, acting prof., 1887-88, prof., 1888-1901, Denison U.; prof. physics, Ohio State U., 1901-07, Vassar Coll., 1907-08; prof. of physics and head of dept., Ohio State U., 1908-26; prof. physics, 1926—. Trustee Denison U., Ohio., 1901-07, 1911—. Research guest, Nat. Bur. of Standards, Washington, and U. of Berlin, 1912-13. War work on electron radio receivers U.S. Navy lab., Washington, summer 1917, and U.S. Bur. Standards, summer 1918. Deceased.

COLE, Carlos Merton, supt. schs.; b. Durand, Ill., Feb. 22, 1872; s. Edward Van Sickle and Flora Marie (Crowley) C.; A.B., Grinnell (Ia.) Coll., 1895; (A.M., Colorado Coll., Colorado Springs, Colo., 1915; LL.D., Denver U., 1916); m. Catharine Newland, June 25, 1896. Prin. Atlantic (Ia.) High Sch., 1896-99; supt. public schs., Atlantic, 1899-1907; sec. Messenger Loan & Trust Co., Atlantic, 1907-08; prin. Sioux City High Sch., 1908-10; supt. Colorado Springs pub. schs., 1910-15; supt. Denver pub. schs., July 1, 1915—. Republican. Methodist. Mason. Home: Denver, Colo. Deceased.

COLE, Charles Cleaves, lawyer, jurist; b. Hiram, Me., May 22, 1841; ed. Hiram, Fryeburgh and Kent's Hill, Me.; grad. Harvard Law School, 1867. Served private to capt. in Cos. I and E, 17th Me. inf., in Civil War, from Aug. 1862 to close; admitted to bar, Portland, Me., Oct. 1866; practiced law, 1867-71, at West Union, Doddridge Co., W.Va., and was pros. atty. of co.; practiced at Parkersburg, W.Va., 1871-79; city solicitor there 4 yrs.; practiced in Washington, 1879-93; U.S. atty. for D.C., 1891-93; asso. justice Supreme Court, D.C., 1893-1901; resigned and resumed practice. Died 1905.

COLE, Charles F., lawyer; b. Wyandot Co., O., June 13, 1871; s. David D. and Mary C. (Bell) C.; A.B., Little Rock U., 1894; m. Ella M. F. Hamblen, May 2, 1901; children—Charles F., Karia, S. Hamblen, Dorothea P., Rena Agnes. Referee in bankruptcy 24 yrs., then mem. Cole & Poindexter; many times del. to Rep. Nat. Conv. and twice chmn. Rep. State Conv. of Ark.; Rep. nominee for U.S. Senate, 1920, 24; U.S. dist. atty., Eastern Dist. of Ark., 1922-30. Methodist. Home: Batesville, Ark. Died Jan. 22, 1933.

COLE, Charles Knox, physician; b. Plainfield, Ill., Apr. 5, 1852; s. Charles Nelson and Lovisa Brainerd (Wood) C.; grad. Lincoln U., Ill., 1872; M.D., Miami Med. Coll., 1878; studied Berlin, Paris, Vienna, New York; (A.M., Taylor U., 1892); m. Harriet Gillet, June 1881. Went to Mont., 1880; mem. city council, Helena, 1883-84; pres. Mont. Senate, 1889; pres. State Bd. Med. Examiners, Mont., 1892; treas. U.S. Bd. Pension Examiners, Helena, 1892; co. physician Lewis and Clarke Co., Mont., 1893; chief surgeon Mont. Cent. Ry., 1887; removed to New York. Pres. Am. Acad. Ry. Surgeons, 1894; fellow Am. Surg. Assn. Pres. A. Schrader's Son, Inc., mfrs., New York. Home: Chelsea-on-Hudson, N.Y. Died Feb. 27, 1920.

COLE, Chester Cicero, chief justice Supreme Court of Iowa; b. Oxford, N.Y., June 4, 1824; s. Samuel and Alice (Pullman) C.; grad. Oxford Acad., 1846; studied Harvard Law School, 1846-48; m. Amanda M. Bennett, June 25, 1848. Engaged in law practice Aug. 11, 1848; judge and chief justice Supreme Court Iowa, 1864-76; then resigned and returned to practice; prof. law, 42 yrs., dean, 1892-1907, Ia. Coll. of Law. Editor Western Jurist (legal monthly), 1866-81; edited annotated edn. Iowa Reports (12 vols.). Home: Des Moines, Ia. Deceased.

COLE, Cornelius, senator; b. Lodi, N.Y., Sept. 17, 1822; s. David and Rachel (Townsend) C.; M.A., Wesleyan U., Conn., 1847; m. Olive Colegrove, Jan. 6, 1853. Admitted to bar, 1848; went to Calif., 1849, and worked in gold fields 1 yr.; resumed practice, 1850; mem. Rep. Nat. Com., 1856-60; dist. atty. Sacramento City and County, 1859-62; mem. 38th Congress, 1863-65; mem. U.S. Senate, 1866-73 (chmn. com. on appropriations). Mem. Pioneer Soc. of Calif. Home: Los Angeles, Calif. Died Nov. 3, 1924.

COLE, Cyrenus, editor, congressman; b. Pella, Ia., Jan. 13, 1863; s. Aart and Henrica (de Booy) C.; A.B., Central Coll., 1887, Litt.D., 1937; unmarried. With Des Moines Register, 1888-98; acquired interest in Cedar Rapids Republican, 1898, later founded Evening Times; elected to Congress, July 19, 1921, to fill vacancy; reëlected 68th to 72d Congresses (1923-33), 5th Ia. District. Author: From Four Corners to Washington, 1920; From Washington to Four Corners, 1922; I Remember, I Remember, A Book of Recollections, 1936. Home: Cedar Rapids, Ia. Died Nov. 14, 1939.

COLE, David, clergyman; b. Spring Valley, N.Y., Sept. 22, 1822; s. Rev. Isaac D. and Anna Maria (Shatzel) C.; grad. Rutgers Coll., 1842 (D.D., Franklin and Marshall Coll., 1865); m. Abigail Dean Wyckoff, Apr. 18, 1844. Private teacher, 1842-51; prin. of acad., Trenton, N.J., 1851-57; prof. languages, N.J. State Normal Sch., 1857-58; had studied privately for the ministry while engaged in edn1. work; was ordained by Ref. Ch. in America, Nov. 23, 1858; pastor Ref. Ch., E. Millstone, N.J., 1858-63; prof. Greek, Rutgers Coll., 1863-66; pastor First Ref. Ch., Yonkers, N.Y., 1865-97; retired 1897. Pres. Gen. Synod Ref. Ch., 1884. Mem. London Missionary Conf., 1888; same yr. also mem. London Session Alliance of Ref. Chs. (mem. exec. com. Am. sect.). Home: Yonkers, N.Y. Deceased.

COLE, Eli Kelley, officer U.S.M.C.; b. Carmel, N.Y., Sept. 1, 1867; s. Oncken Willard and Cornelia (Walker) C.; grad. U.S. Naval Acad., 1888; Army War Coll., 1908; m. Emilie de R. Maxwell, May 10, 1893; 1 son, Maxwell. Apptd. 2d lt. U.S.M.C., July 1, 1890; promoted through grades to maj. gen. June 3, 1924. Comd. Marine Barracks, Puget Sound, 1899-1901; duty Philippines, 1902-03; comd. marine battalion, Panama, 1903-04; duty Marine Barracks, Washington, 1904-05; with 2d Regt. and post, Olongapo, P.I., 1905-06; comd. battalion fortifying Grande Island, P.I., 1907; comd. marine regt., spl. duty, Panama, 1908, 10; duty Marine Barracks and Sch. of Application, Port Royal, S.C., 1909-11; duty Office of Maj. Gen. Comdt., Marine Corps, Navy Dept., 1911-14; comd. Marine Barracks, Annapolis, Md., 1915; comd. 2d Regt., 1st Provisional Brigade of Marines, Haiti, 1915-16; apptd. comdr. 1st Provisional Brigade of Marines, Haiti, Nov. 10, 1916; comd. Marine Barracks and Recruit Depot, Parris Island, S.C., Jan.-Aug. 1918; comd. 5th Brigade, U.S. Marines, A.E.F., Sept. 1918-Apr. 1919; comd. 1st Depot Div. (41st), A.E.F., Oct. 1918-Jan. 1919; comd. Am Embarkation Center A.E.F., Jan.-Feb. 1919; spl. duty hdqrs. U.S. Marine Corps, May 1919; comdg. Marine Barracks, Navy Yard, Phila., June-July 1919, Marine Barracks, Parris Island, S.C., 1919-24, Marine Barracks, Quantico, Va., 1925-27; comdg. gen. Dept. of Pacific, hdqrs. San Francisco, July 2, 1927—. Home: Carmel, N.Y. Died July 4, 1929.

COLE, Frank Nelson, univ. prof.; b. at Ashland, Mass., Sept. 20, 1861; s. Otis and Frances Maria (Pond) C.; A.B., Harvard, 1882, A.M., Ph.D., 1886; m. Martha Marie Streiff, July 26, 1888. Lecturer mathematics, Harvard, 1885-87; instr. and asst. prof. mathematics, U. of Mich., 1888-95; prof. mathematics, Columbia, 1895—. Died May 27, 1926.

COLE, George E., mfr., governor; b. Trenton, N.Y., Dec. 23, 1826; s. Nathan and Laura (Hill) C.; ed. Hobart Hall Inst., Holland Patent, N.Y.; went to Ore.; m. Mary E. Cardwell, Oct. 9, 1853. Mem. Territorial legislature, Ore., 1851-53; clerk U.S. Dist. Court, Ore., 1859-60; del. to Congress from Wash. Ty., 1863-65; gov. Wash., 1867; postmaster Portland, Ore., 1873-81; treas. Spokane County, Wash., 1889-93. Was identified with mining and mfg. interests. Author: Early Oregon, 1905. Home: Spokane, Wash. Died 1906.

COLE, George E., printer; b. Jackson, Mich., Mar. 2, 1845; s. Ichabod and Sarah H. C.; ed. pub. schs., Jackson; m. Lois T. Milnes, June 20, 1878. Pvt. 10th Mich. Inf. 2 yrs. in Civil War. In business as stationer and printer, Chicago, Mar. 1878—. Independent in politics. Organized, 1896, pres., 1896-99, Municipal Voters' League; pres. Citizens' Assn. 2 yrs.; pres. Legislative Voters' League; chmn. exec. com. Initiative and Referendum League of Ill. Home: Wilmette, Ill. Died Aug. 19, 1930.

COLE, George Lamont, archeologist; b. Lockport, N.Y., June 8, 1849; s. David Cole and Cynthia (Griggs) C.; A.B., Albion (Mich.) Coll., 1869, A.M., 1872; D.D., 1893; m. Ida J. Upright, Sept. 20, 1871. Ordained M.E. ministry, 1869; pastor Olivet, Mich., 1869, Frankfort, 1871, Charlevoix, 1872, Jonesville, 1875, Rockford, 1876, Cannonsburg, 1877, Plainwell, 1879, Paw Paw, 1881, St. Joseph, 1884, Long Beach, Calif., 1887; gen. sec. 14th Gen. Conf. Epworth League, 1890, also supt. Long Beach Chautauqua Assembly; pastor Epworth Ch., Los Angeles, 1892, Santa Paula, 1895, Burbank, 1896, 1897. Has given a portion of each year, from 1892, to research work in the Am. southwest, making a spl. study of the ruins of the ancient cliff dwellers and of the life, manners and customs of the Pueblos; has lectured extensively on these subjects before schs., colleges, institutes, etc. Has furnished archeol. and ethnol. collections for the museums of Bethany Coll., Lindsborg, Kan., the Northwestern U., U. of Wis., Museum für Volkerkunde, Berlin, Germany, Museum of the Southwest, Los Angeles, Calif., Heye Museum of Archeology, N.Y. City, etc. Curator of Museum, Venice, Calif. Home: Los Angeles, Calif. Died May 11, 1918.

COLE, George W., judge; b. Humphrey, N.Y., Dec. 31, 1858; s. Stephen S. and Lemira P. (Berry) C.; ed. high sch.; m. Lucia Ellen Weber. Admitted to N.Y. bar, 1884, and practiced in Salamanca; dist. atty., Cattaraugas County, 1902-14; apptd. justice Supreme Court of N.Y., 8th Dist., by gov., May 23, 1916, and elected for term Jan. 1, 1917-Dec. 31, 1930. Republican. Mason. Home: Salamanca, N.Y. Died Mar. 30, 1923.

COLE, George Watson, bibliographer, librarian; b. Warren, Conn., Sept. 6, 1850; s. Munson and Antoinette Fidelia (Taylor) C.; ed. Phillips Acad., Andover, Mass.; admitted to bar, 1876; practiced until 1885; grad. Library Sch., Columbia, 1888; hon. L.H.D., Trinity Coll., Conn., 1920; married. Cataloguer, Pub. Library, Fitchburg, Mass., 1885-86; librarian Pratt Inst., Brooklyn, 1886-87; asst. in Newberry Library, Chicago, 1888-90; librarian Free Pub. Library, Jersey City, N.J., 1891-95; resigned to devote himself to bibliog. work; librarian Henry E. Huntington Library and Art Gallery, San Marino, Calif., Oct. 1, 1915-Oct. 1, 1924 (emeritus). Inventor of a size-card for measuring books in accordance with the standard adopted by A.L.A., which is in general use in Am. libraries. Life mem. A.L.A. (treas. 1893-96), Bibliog. Soc. America (life, pres. 1916-21). Fellow Am. Geog. Soc. Compiler: Check-List of English Literature to 1640 in Library of Henry E. Huntington, 1919; Additions and Corrections to same, 1920; Bibliography—a Forecast, 1920; Cataloguing of Rare Books in Henry E. Huntington Library, 1923, Henry E. Huntington Library and Art Gallery, 1923; Elizabethan Americana, 1925; Bibliographical Pitfalls—Linked Books, 1926. Collaborator in Bibliog. Soc. (London), Short-Title Catalogue of English Books (1475-1640), 1926; Early Library Development in New York State (1800-1900), 1927. Address: Pasadena, Calif. Died Oct. 10, 1939.

COLE, Henry Tiffany, chmn. bd. U.S. Radiator Corp.; b. Cleveland, O., June 29, 1870; s. Delos O. and Isabella (Tiffany) C.; ed. pub. schs.; m. Alice Jerome Day, 1900; children—Eunice Tiffany (Mrs. R. Halstead Mills), Ruth Spencer (Mrs. C. Lamar Brace). With H. Scherer & Co., wholesale hardware, Detroit, 1887-93; vice-pres. and treas. U.S. Heater Co., 1902-10; v.p. and treas. U.S. Radiator Corp., 1910-21, became pres., 1921, then chmn. bd.; pres. Pacific Steel Boiler Corp. Mem. Detroit Bd. of Commerce. Republican. Episcopalian. Home: Grosse Pointe, Mich. Died June 7, 1938.

COLE, Jean Dean, educator; b. Albany, N.Y., Nov. 9, 1873; d. Walter Dougherty and Margaret (Mitchell) Cole; grad. Albany Teachers Training Sch., 1892; B.A., Mt. Holyoke Coll., 1900; studied Columbia and Oxford U., Eng. Teacher Albany High Sch., 1900-05; with Mt. Vernon Sem., Washington, D.C., from 1905, successively teacher until 1917, asso. head mistress, 1917-22, head mistress, 1923—, also chmn. bd. Mem. Grad. Council Mt. Holyoke Coll. Presbyterian. Died Apr. 21, 1939.

COLE, John Nelson, editor, pub.; b. Andover, Mass., Nov. 4, 1863; s. George S. and Nancy E. (Bodwell) C.; ed. pub. schs.; m. Minnie White Poor, Sept. 21, 1886. Manager and treasurer of Andover Townsman, 1887—; trustee Andover Savings Bank; mem. Mass. House of Rep., 1903-08 (speaker of House, 1906, 7, 8); chmn. Mass. Commn. of Efficiency and Economy, 1913-14; chmn. Boston Industrial Development Bd., 1914-16; chmn. Mass. Commn. on Waterways and Pub. Lands, 1916-19; state commr. of Public Works, 1920—; dir. Port of Boston. Republican. Conglist. Mem. Boston Chamber Commerce; pres. Am. Assn. of Port Authorities; v.p. Atlantic Deeper Waterways Assn. Mason. Home: Andover, Mass. Died Oct. 18, 1922.

COLE, Louis Maurice; b. Chicago, Ill., Mar. 24, 1870; s. Samuel (M.D.) and Ricka (Dinkelspiel) C.; ed. high sch. and business coll.; m. Frida Hellman, Jan. 6, 1904. Began as bookkeeper for Kutner-Goldstein Co., Hanford, Calif., 1887, later mgr. for same co. at Hanford, Fowler and Lemoore, Calif.; gen. mdse. business on own account, Huron, Calif., 1895-97, elec. specialties, Chicago, 1898; traveling salesman, 1899-1900; mgr. Dinkelspiel Bros. dept. store, Bakersfield, Calif., 1901-03; treas. Simon Levi Co., wholesale produce, Los Angeles, 1903-16; pres. Royal Packing Co., 1916—; pres. Cudahy Land Co., Boulevard Land Co., Small Farms Co., Walnut Park Mutual Water Co.; v.p. Washington Sq. Land Co. U.S. food adminstr. for Los Angeles, 1918-19; mem. Los Angeles Chamber of Commerce (pres. 1914). Mem. B'nai B'rith (pres.). Mason. Republican. Home: Los Angeles, Calif. Died Sept. 28, 1930.

COLE, Nathan, Jr., promoter; b. St. Louis, Mo., Mar. 16, 1860; s. Nathan (mayor of St. Louis) and Rebecca Lane (Fagin) C.; Shurtleff Coll., Upper Alton, Ill., 1878-80; m. Mary Ellen Corbett, Aug. 28, 1881. In newspaper work, St. Louis, 1877-80; co-founder, 1881, and 1st editor, Los Angeles Daily Times; newspaper work in Calif., Ore. and Ariz., 1882-85; real estate, Los Angeles, 1886-87; built ry. from Los Angeles to Pasadena, 1888; developed Littlerock Colony, Calif., 1889-1904; built and operated beet sugar factories at Visalia and Corcoran, Calif., 1905-09; dir., and asso. in management San Joaquin Valley Sugar Co. Alternate del. Rep. Nat. Conv., 1896; mem. nat. com. Silver Rep. party, 1897; received complimentary vote of Dem. minority of Calif. Legislature for U.S. senator, 1898; del.-at-large Silver Rep. Nat. Conv., Kansas City, 1900 (mem. conf. com. of 15); chmn. Dem. Co. Conv., Los Angeles, 1904; police commr., Los Angeles, 1907-09; Calif. mem. Dem. Nat. Com., 1908—, and mem. exec. com. same. Baptist. Mason. Home: Berkeley, Calif. Died 1921.

COLE, Nelson, brig. gen. U.S. vols.; veteran officer of vols. in Civil war; after war engaged in business in St. Louis; has been prominent in G.A.R.; apptd., May 28, 1898, from civil life, brig. gen. U.S.V., and placed in command 3d brigade, 2d div., 2d corps. Home: St. Louis, Mo. Died 1899.

COLE, Ralph Dayton, congressman; b. Vanlue, O., Nov. 30, 1873; s. John W. and Sarah (McCrea) C.; Ph.B., Findlay Coll., 1896; diploma, Ohio Normal U., Ada, 1898. Taught sch.; deputy clerk Hancock County, O., 2 yrs.; admitted to bar, 1899; in practice at Findlay, O.; mem. Ohio Ho. of Rep., 1898-1902; mem. 59th to 61st Congresses (1905-11), 8th Ohio Dist. Republican. Home: Findlay, O. Died Oct. 15, 1932.

COLE, Richard Beverly, M.D.; pres. faculty med. dept., Univ. of Calif., 1876—; b. Manchester, Va., Aug. 12, 1829; ed. Del. Collegiate Inst.; grad. Jefferson Med. Coll., Phila., 1849; mem. Royal Coll. Surgeons, England, 1864; m. Eugenie Irene Bonaffon, Oct. 4, 1848. Practiced Phila., 1849-52; then at San Francisco; consulting surgeon State Women's Hosp., Calif., 1870-80; gynecologist county hosp., 1878—; prof. obstetrics and gynecology, U. of Pacific, 1858-64; same chair, med. dept., U. of Calif., 1870—. Fellow Brit. Gynec. Soc., Obstet. Soc., London. Surgeon gen., Calif., 1868-72. Several yrs. chmn. State Dem. Com., Calif., etc. Deceased.

COLE, Samuel Valentine, coll. pres.; b. Machiasport, Me., Dec. 29, 1851; s. Isaac T. and Catherine Sophia (Valentine) C.; A.B., Bowdoin, 1874, A.M., 1877; grad. Andover Theol. Sem., 1887; (D.D., 1898, LL.D., 1912, Bowdoin); m. Annie Maria Talbot, Apr. 11, 1880 (died 1906); m. 2d, Helen Emma Wieand, Aug. 22, 1917. Tutor rhetoric and instr. Latin, Bowdoin, several yrs.; ordained and installed pastor Trinitarian Congl. Ch., Taunton, Mass., 1889-97; pres. Wheaton Sem., Norton, Mass., 1897-1912, and its successor, Wheaton Coll., 1912—. Trustee Bowdoin Coll., 1901— (v.p. bd., 1912—); pres. Bowdoin Alumni Assn. of Boston and Vicinity, 1916-18; mem. board visitors Andover Theol. Sem., 1907-21 (pres. bd., 1912-21). Author: In Scipio's Gardens and Other Poems, 1901; The Life That Counts, 1905; Fidelissima, 1908; The Great Grey King and Other Poems, 1914. Home: Norton, Mass. Died May 6, 1925.

COLE, Samuel Winkley, musician; b. Meriden, N.H., Dec. 24, 1848; s. Deacon Converse and Mary A. (Winkley) C.; took semi-classical course at Kimball Union Acad., 1867; studied music under various teachers and at N.E. Conservatory of Music. Began professional career at Portsmouth, N.H., 1877; organist Clarendon St. Bapt. Ch., Boston, 1882-94; teacher, later supt., dept. of sight-singing, N.E. Conservatory of Music, 1883-1925; was also supervisor music, Brookline, Mass., and Dedham, Mass.; teacher pub. school music methods, Boston U., 1906-13. Dir. People's Singing Class movement in Boston, and conductor People's Choral Union, 1897-1911 (emeritus). Author: Child's First Studies in Music; New England Course in General Sight-Reading. Compiled New England Conservatory Course in Sight Singing (3 vols.). Home: Brookline, Mass. Deceased.

COLE, Theodore Lee, law bookseller; b. Albany, N.Y., Dec. 26, 1852; s. John Jay and Mary Pohlman (Lee) C.; ed. Galesville U., 1866-67; Ph.B., U. of Wis., 1871; m. Kate Dunn Dewey, Aug. 20, 1885 (died 1922); 1 son, Felix. Law bookseller, 1874—; with Soule, Thomas & Wentworth, and their successors F. H. Thomas & Co. and the F. H. Thomas Law Book Co., St. Louis, until 1890; head of T. L. Cole and Statute Law Book Co., Washington, D.C., 1890-1931. Mem. Williamstown Institute of Politics. Home: Montclair, N.J. Died Jan. 27, 1932.

COLE, Timothy, wood engraver; b. London, Eng., 1852; s. Skinner C.; emigrated to U.S., 1857; burned out by Chicago fire of 1871; returned to New York penniless; entered employment of Century Magazine (then Scribner's), 1875; m. Annie Carter, 1875. Went to Europe to engrave the Old Masters, 1883; finished 1st Italian series, 1892, Dutch and Flemish series, 1896, English series, 1900, Spanish series, 1907, French series, 1910; was engaged on Old Masters in Am. pub. and pvt. galleries. Awarded diploma, Chicago Expn., 1893; first class gold medal, Paris Expn., 1900; grand prix, St. Louis Expn., 1904 (only grand prize given for wood engraving). Hon. mem. Soc. of Sculptors, Painters and Engravers, London; N.A., 1908; mem. Am. Acad. Arts and Letters, 1913; hon. M.A., Princeton U., 1914. Author: Notes to Old Italian Masters, first published monthly in Century Magazine, 1889-92. Home: Poughkeepsie, N.Y. Died May 17, 1931.

COLE, Whitefoord R., ry. official; b. Nashville, Tenn., Jan. 14, 1874; s. Edmund W. and Anna Virginia (Russell) C.; B.A., Vanderbilt U., 1894; m. Mary Conner Bass, Apr. 21, 1901; 1 son, Whitfoord Russell. Pres. L.&N. R.R. Co.; dir. Louisville, Henderson & St. Louis Ry. Co., N.C.&St.L. Ry., Nashville & Decatur R.R Co., Atlanta & West Point R.R. Co., Western Ry. of Ala., Chicago, Indianapolis and Louisville Ry. Co., Am. Cyanamid Co., Southern Bell Telephone & Telegraph Co., Am. Nat. Bank, Am. Trust Co., Fruit Growers Express Co. Fidelity & Columbia Trust, Co.; dir. Louisville Br. Federal Res. Bank of St. Louis, Louisville Bd. of Trade. Pres. bd. trustees Vanderbilt U.; trustee Meharry Med. Coll., Carnegie Inst. of Washington, Brookings Instn. Home: Louisville, Ky. Died Nov. 17, 1934.

COLE, William Carey, naval officer; b. Chicago, Ill., Aug. 23, 1868; s. Jirah Delano and Julia Elizabeth (Tucker) C.; grad. U.S. Naval Acad., 1889; grad. Naval War College, 1916; m. Minnie Wetmore, Aug. 13, 1895; 1 dau., Mrs. Louise Chapin. Ensign, July 1, 1891; lt. jr. grade, Jan. 13, 1899; promoted through grades to rear admiral, Dec. 31, 1921. Served on Dolphin, Spanish-Am. War, 1898; various assignments to 1917; apptd. comdr. Frederick, Apr. 10, 1917, comdr. Nevada to Oct. 10, 1918; U.S. Dutch ship mission, May 17, 1919; operations, Navy Dept., Nov. 1919; comdg. Spl. Service Squadron, Apr. 22, 1922; chief of staff U.S. Fleet, Aug. 6, 1923; comdt. Navy Yard, Norfolk, Va., Nov. 16, 1925; comdg. Battleship Div. Four, Battle Fleet, 1928-29, Scouting Fleet, June 21, 1929-July 1930; comdr. 12th Naval Dist., San Francisco, 1930-32; retired, Sept. 1, 1932. Baptist. Died May 28, 1935.

COLE, William Isaac, sociologist; b. Machias, Me., Mar. 21, 1859; s. Isaac T. and Catherine Sophia (Valentine) C.; A.B., Bowdoin, 1881 (Phi Beta Kappa), A.M., 1884; S.T.B., Andover Theol. Sem., 1888. Ordained Congl. ministry, 1889; pastor Houlton (Me.), 1889-94; resident, South End House, Boston, as settlement worker, 1894-1913; sec. South End House Assn., 1896-1913; resident lecturer in applied sociology, 1913-16, prof. applied sociology, 1916-26, Wheaton Coll., Norton, Mass. Contbr. chapters in The City Wilderness, 1898, and Americans in Process, 1902. Republican. Home: Nantucket, Mass. Died Sept. 27, 1935.

COLEMAN, Algernon, prof. French.; b. News Ferry, Va., Aug. 9, 1876; s. Henry Embry and Sallie Chalmers (Crump) C.; A.B., A.M., U. of Virginia, 1901; Ph.D., Johns Hopkins U., 1913; m. Mary Boggs Gude, Dec. 23, 1913 (died 1929); 1 dau., Mary Gude. Instr. modern langs., Culver (Ind.) Mil. Acad., 1901-05; 2d and 1st asst., Norfolk (Va.) Acad., 1906-10; instr. French, 1913-15, asst. prof., 1915-18, asso. prof., 1918-19, prof., 1919—, U. of Chicago. Mng. editor Modern Lang. Jour., 1919-22. Author: Literary Development of Flaubert, 1914; Sources and Structure of Salammbo (with P. B. Fay), 1914. Collaborator in revision of Fraser and Squair's French Grammar, 1921; Intermediate French, 1925; Teaching of Modern Foreign Languages in the U.S., 1929; Analytical Bibliography of Modern Language Teaching, 1933; experiments and studies in Modern Language Teaching, 1934; Graded French Readings, 1934. Home: Chicago, Ill. Died Aug. 8, 1939.

COLEMAN, Alice Blanchard; b. Boston, May 7, 1858; d. James W. and Ellen Maria (Blanchard) Merriam; grad. Bradford (Mass.) Acad., 1878; m. George W. Coleman, June 30, 1891. Honorary president Council of Women for Home Missions; hon. pres. Woman's Am. Baptist Home Mission Soc.; mem. bd. mgrs. (Bapt.) Bd. of Edn.; mem. Foreign Policy Assn.; trustee Spelman Coll., Atlanta, Ga., Atlanta University. Home: Boston, Mass. Died Oct. 22, 1936.

COLEMAN, Benjamin Wilson, judge; b. Ballsville, Va., July 1, 1869; s. John and Arabella (Smith) C.; B.L., Richmond Coll. (now U. of Richmond), 1892; m. Martha L. Attleton, June 6, 1906; children—Elizabeth (Mrs. Judson D. Levensaler), Virginia (dec.), Margaret, John Attleton. Admitted to Colo. bar, 1893; practiced in Denver, 1893-97, Cripple Creek, 1897-1906; removed to Nev., 1906, and practiced in Ely; judge Dist. Court, 9th Nev. Dist., 1911-15; asso. justice Nev. Supreme Court, 1915—, and chief justice, 1919-20, 1925-26, 1931-33, 1937-38. Lecturer on law of contracts, Northwestern U., summer 1925. Mem. advisory staff Narcotic Research Assn.; ex-chmn. bd. visitors, U. of Nev. Mason. Home: Carson City, Nev. Died Feb. 25, 1939.

COLEMAN, Chapman, consul. Apptd 2d sec. Am. Legation at Berlin, May 8, 1874; apptd. sec. of legation at Peking, July 5, 1884, but declined; apptd. sec. of legation at Berlin, Sept. 15, 1884; apptd. sec. of the Reciprocity Commn., Oct. 1897, and upon the retirement of the spl. commr. plenipotentiary in spring of 1907, assumed charge until discontinuance of the commn., June 30, 1906; consul at Roubaix, France, 1906-08, at Rome, Italy, June 10, 1908-July 1915. Deceased.

COLEMAN, Charles Caryl, painter; b. Buffalo, N.Y., 1840; s. John Hull and Charlotte Augusta C.; went to Europe, 1859, to study art, but returned and served 3 yrs. in Union Army in Civil War. From 1866 resided in Europe, painting in London, Paris and Rome. Bronze medal, Chicago Expn., 1893; silver medal, Buffalo Expn., 1901, A.N.A., 1881; hon. mem. Buffalo Fine Arts Acad. (Albright Gallery). Home: Island of Capri, Italy. Died Dec. 5, 1928.

COLEMAN, Charles Philip, mfr.; b. Baltimore, Md., Mar. 28, 1865; s. William Wheeler and Ellen Gibbons (Hiss) C.; M.E., Lehigh U., 1888; m. Helen Douglas, d. Nelson S. Rulison, 2d P.E. bishop of Pa., Jan. 27, 1891; children—Douglas Rulison, Leighton Hammond. With Lehigh Valley R.R., in various capacities, 1888-97; purchasing agt. and asst. to pres., Bethlehem Steel Co., 1897-98; gen. purchasing agt., Lehigh Valley R.R., 1898-1903; sec.-treas. Singer Sewing Machine Co., 1903-10; pres. Saurer Motor Co., 1910, Internat. Motor Co., 1911-13; v.p. Internat. Steam Pump Co., 1913, co-receiver and receiver, 1914-16; v.p. Worthington Pump & Machinery Corp. (reorganization of Internat. Steam Pump Co.), 1916-18, pres. 1918—; also pres. Worthington Co., Inc., Henry R. Worthington. Democrat. Episcopalian. Home: Palisades, N.Y. Died Apr. 13, 1929.

COLEMAN, Cynthia Beverley Tucker, charter mem. and chmn. for Va. of George Washington Memorial Assn.; b. Saline Co., Mo., Jan. 18, 1832; d. Judge Beverley Tucker (1784-1851) of Williamsburg, Va.; m. Henry Augustine Washington, 1852; m. 2d, Charles Washington Coleman, M.D. (1826-94), 1861. One of founders and incorporators and 1st v.p. Assn. for Preservation of Va. Antiquities. Home: Williamsburg, Va. Died 1908.

COLEMAN, Frank Joseph, judge; b. N.Y. City, Mar. 24, 1886; s. Frank Joseph and Catherine (Scanlan) C.; A.B., Coll. City of New York, 1906; LL.B., New York Law Sch., 1909; m. Marjorie Sands Pyne, Oct. 19, 1921; children—Margery, Joan, Patricia. Began as sec. to Justices McLaughlin and Finch of Supreme Court of N.Y., 1911; asst. dist. atty. New York Co., 1914-16; justice Municipal Court City of New York, 1918-23; Republican leader of 15th Assembly Dist., New York County, 1924-27; judge U.S. Dist. Court, Southern Dist. of N.Y., 1927—. Served as pvt. arty., U.S.A., in U.S., World War. Catholic. Home: Larchmont, N.Y. Died Mar. 14, 1934.

COLEMAN, George Whitfield, clergyman; b. Perry, N.Y., Oct. 10, 1830; s. John and Julia C.; acad. edn. Wyoming Acad., 1850-57; m. 2d, Mrs. Laura J. Warren, Nov. 25, 1898. Ordained to Free Methodist ministry, 1863; 3d gen. supt. (bishop) F. M. Ch., 1886-1903; retired. Home: Gainesville, N.Y. Died 1907.

COLEMAN, Leighton, P. E. bishop of Del., Oct. 18, 1888—; b. Phila., May 3, 1837; s. Rev. John C. (D.D.) and Louisa Margaretta (Thomas) C.; grad. Gen. Theol. Sem., New York, 1861; (A.M., Trinity, 1865; LL.D., Hobart, 1888; S.T.D., Racine, 1875); m. 1861, Frances Elizabeth, d. Alexis Irenée du Pont. Deacon, 1860, priest, 1862; rector St. Luke's Ch., Bustleton, Pa., 1861-63, St. John's Ch., Wilmington, Del., 1863-66, St. Mark's, Mauch Chunk, Pa., 1866-74, Trinity Ch., Toledo, O., 1874-79; in England, 1879-87; rector Ch. of the Redeemer, Sayre, Pa., 1887-88. Author: History of the Lehigh Valley, 1872; The Church in America, 1895; History of the American Church, 1901; etc. Died 1907.

COLEMAN, Lewis Minor, lawyer; b. University, Va., May 20, 1861; s. Lewis Minor (lt. col. 1st Va. Arty.) and Mary Ambler (Marshall) C.; mother g.d. Chief Justice John Marshall; M.A., U. of Va., 1882, B.L., 1886; m. Julia Wingate Boyd, d. Maj. Charles H. Boyd, of Portland, Me., Sept. 7, 1892. Prin. Univ. Sch., Charleston, S.C., 1882-85; admitted to Tenn. bar, 1886, and practiced in Chattanooga; then mem. Coleman & Frierson. Promoted reforms in criminal cost system of Tenn., 1897; mem. com. to notify Woodrow Wilson of his nomination as Pres. of U.S.; U.S. atty. Eastern Dist. of Tenn., by appmt. of Pres. Wilson, 1913-17; mem. Local Bd. No. 2, Hamilton Co., Tenn., under Selective Service Act, 1917—. Home: Chattanooga, Tenn. Died Oct. 18, 1918.

COLEMAN, Thomas Davies, M.D.; b. Augusta, Ga., Jan. 13, 1865; s. Dr. John S. and Carolina Wyatt (Starke) C.; A.B., Ky. U., 1885, A.M., 1902; U. of Ga. (M.D., ad eundem); post-grad. Johns Hopkins, 1886-87; M.D., Univ. Med. Coll. (New York U.), 1890; m. Annie Lee Adams, June 18, 1890. Asst. physiology, Johns Hopkins, 1887-88; asst. physiology, medical dept. U. City of New York, 1889-90; prof. physiology, 1893-95, physiology and pathology, 1895-1901, medicine, 1901—, principles and practice of medicine, 1903—, med. dept. U. of Ga.; pres. Bd. of Health, Augusta, Ga., Jan. 1903-May 1904; cons. physician Univ. Hospitals; U.S. Pub. Health Hosp. for psychiatric cases. Maj. Med. R.C., 1917, hon. disch., Feb. 1, 1919; lt. col. O.R.C. Fellow Am College Physicians. Home: Augusta, Ga. Died Aug. 2, 1927.

COLEMAN, Thomas Wilkes, banker, planter; b. Eutaw, Ala., Mar. 31, 1833; s. James C. and Martha (Anderson) C.; A.B., Princeton, 1853, later, A.M.; (LL.D., U. of Ala.); admitted to bar, Supreme Ct. of Ala.; m. Frances Jane Wilson, Oct. 1, 1860. Was solicitor of state of Ala. about 15 yrs., later chancellor, then judge of Supreme Ct. for many yrs. Opposed secession though never doubting constitutional right of state to secede; served in C.S.A.; surrendered at Vicksburg, Miss.; subsequently wounded at battle of Missionary Ridge; del. Ala. Constl. convs., 1865, 1901, chmn. in 1901 conv. of com. to frame article on suffrage and elections, prin. author of suffrage article providing for qualified suffrage. Democrat. Pres. Merchants and Farmers Bank, Eutaw. Chmn. exec. com. bd. trustees U. of Ala. (and pres. bd. pro tem.) many yrs. Presbyn. Home: Eutaw, Ala. Died Nov. 9, 1920.

COLEMAN, Walter Moore, author; b. Chappell Hill, Tex., Dec. 21, 1863; s. William Ludlow (M.D.) and Maria Jane (Stewart) C.; grad. Sam Houston Normal Inst., Huntsville, Tex., 1879; A.B., Washington and Lee U., Va., 1889; studied U. of Berlin, 1889-90, Royal Sch. of Science, 1890; m. Satis Narrona Barton, Mar. 13, 1896. Prin. Belton High Sch., 1884-87; prof. biology Sam Houston Normal Inst., 1890-08; research in Physiol. Inst., U. of Berlin, 1908-09, and in London Hosp., 1909-10. Democrat. Author: Hygienic Physiology, 1905; First Course in Biology (co-author), 1908. Home: Corpus Christi, Tex. Deceased.

COLEMAN, William Emmette, orientalist; b. Shadwell, Va., June 19, 1843; ed. in Lancasterian Sch., Richmond, Va.; asst. librarian Richmond, Va., Library, 1854-57; actor of "old men" parts and stage mgr., 1862-67 and 1870-74; dramatized several novels for stage—notably "East Lynne," 1864. Became Republican, 1859, 1st one in Richmond, Va.; mem. Rep. State Central Com. of Va., 1869-70; v.p. Va. State Woman's Right Assn., 1870; clerk q.-m.'s dept. U.S. Army, 1874—; chief clerk, same in San Francisco, 1883-91. Pres. Golden Gate Religious and Philos. Soc., San Francisco, for yrs.; mem. advisory councils Psychic Science Congress and World's Congress of Evolutionists, Chicago, 1893; mem. prin. Oriental socs. in America and Europe. Home: Alameda, Calif. Deceased.

COLEMAN, William Magruder, lawyer; b. Brookeville, Md., Mar. 3, 1874; s. Samuel Henry and Lavinia (Magruder) C.; ed. pub. schs.; m. Lillian Worthy, July 15, 1899. Admitted to N.Y. bar, 1896, and also practiced in N.Y. City; v.p., gen. counsel, and dir. Republic Ry. & Light Co., Central States Electric Corp.; v.p., dir. Republic Corp., Utilities Securities Corp.; sec., dir. and gen. counsel, Mahoning & Shenango Ry. & Light Co. Home: New York, N.Y. Died Jan. 21, 1921.

COLER, Bird Sim; b. Champaign, Ill., Oct. 9, 1867; s. William N. C.; ed. Poly. Inst. and Andover Acad.; married. Entered his father's banking house as clerk and later became partner W. N. Coler & Co.; v.p. Greensboro Pub. Service Corp. Candidate for alderman-at-large, Brooklyn, 1892; Dem. candidate for gov. N.Y., 1902; elected comptroller City of New York, 1897; pres. Borough of Brooklyn, Jan. 1, 1906-Dec. 31, 1909. Del. Dem. Nat. Conv., 1896. Author: Municipal Government, as illustrated by the Charter, Finances and Public Charities of New York, 1900; The Financial Effects of Consolidation, Municipal Government and Tunnels and Bridges. Home: New York, N.Y. Deceased.

COLES, J(onathan) Ackerman, surgeon; b. Newark, N.J., May 6, 1843; s. Dr. Abraham (M.D., Ph.D., LL.D.) and Caroline E. (Ackerman) C.; A.B., Columbia, 1864, A.M., 1867; M.D., Coll. Phys. and Surg. (Columbia), 1868 (Harsen prize, 1867, for best written clin. rep. on med. and surg. cases in New York Hosp.); studied in Eng. and European univs. and hosps., 1877-78; (LL.D., Hope Coll., 1903); unmarried. Pres. Union County (N.J.) Med. Soc., 1891; patron and trustee N.J. Hist. Soc.; fellow Met. Mus. of Art. Has traveled extensively over both continents. Gave for Lincoln Park, Newark, Ives' life-size bronze historic Indian group; for Washington Park, Newark, bronze bust of his father, by J. Q. A. Ward, mounted on pedestal having for a base a 7-ton boulder from vicinity of Plymouth Rock; gave to people of N.J. the painting (now in State House, Trenton) of "Good Samaritan," by Daniel Huntington and Paul De La Roche; to Admiral Dewey, as a souvenir of his victory in Manila Bay, he sent a Barye allegorical bronze of an eagle and dead heron; to the univs. of Oxford and Cambridge, Eng., and to the American Embassy, London, has given replica life-size bronze busts by Jean Antoine Houdon of George Washington and Benjamin Franklin; also to the Met. Museum of Art, Columbia, Yale, Harvard and other univs. and instns. throughout the U.S. many valuable works of art. Mem. and one of founders Valley Forge Library; hon. v.p. Am. Tract Soc.; mem. bd. advisors Canton (China) Christian Coll.; hon. regent Lincoln Memorial U., Md. His library is noted for its collection of original MSS., among which are those bearing signatures of Ferdinand and Isabella, Pope Gregory III, Napoleon Bonaparte, Queen Victoria, original autograph letters and documents of all the presidents of the U.S., the original MS. of the national anthem, "America," an original autograph poem in its entirety by Edwin Arnold, with other original autograph works in whole or in part by poets and scholars. Presented city of Newark for Museum of Art and Pub. Library paintings, rare books, bronzes, marbles and other works, valued at over $2,000,000. Home: Scotch Plains, N.J. Died Dec. 16, 1925.

COLEY, Francis Chase, passenger traffic mgr.; b. Monroe, Conn., Jan. 21, 1866; s. Rev. James Edward and Mary Gray (Huntington) C.; ed. pvt. schs.; m. Cornelia Kelsey Hurlbutt, June 1, 1893; children—Ambrose Hurlbutt (dec.), James Edward II, Cornelia Kelsey (Mrs. Walter William Lathrop). Began as stenographer, passenger dept. N.Y.,N.H.&H. R.R. Co., 1888, chief clk., 1889-1905, asst. gen. passenger agt., 1905-22; gen. passenger agt., same r.r. and N.E. Steamship Co., 1922-24, passenger traffic mgr., 1924—. Episcopalian. Home: Westport, Conn. Died May 1, 1934.

COLEY, William Bradley, surgeon; b. Westport, Conn., Jan. 12, 1862; s. Horace Bradley and Clarine Bradley (Wakeman) C.; B.A., Yale, 1884; M.D., Harvard, 1888; New York Hosp., 1890; hon. A.M., Yale, 1910, Harvard, 1911; m. Alice Lancaster, June 4, 1891; children—Bradley Lancaster, Malcolm (deceased), Helen Lancaster (Mrs. William Boone Nauts). In practice as physician, 1888—; cons. surgeon Memorial Hospital; surgeon in chief emeritus Hospital for Ruptured and Crippled; surgeon in chief Mary McClellan Hosp. (Cambridge, N.Y.); cons. surgeon Fifth Avenue Hosp. and Sharon (Conn.) Hosp. Fellow Am. Surgical Assn.; Am. Coll. Surgeons; hon. mem. Assn. of Surgeons of Great Britain and Ireland. Author: Twentieth Century Practice of Medicine—part on Cancer (Vol. XVII), 1897; Hernia (in Dennis' System of Surgery), 1896; Hernia (in Warren and Gould's International Text Book of Surgery), 1898; Chapter on Hernia, in Progressive Medicine, 1898—; Hernia (in Keen's Surgery), 1907. Home: New York, N.Y. Died Apr. 16, 1936.

COLGATE, Gilbert, mfr.; b. Orange, N.J., Dec. 15, 1858; s. Samuel and Elizabeth Ann Breeze (Morse) C.; A.B., Yale, 1883; m. Florance Buckingham Hall, June 7, 1888; children—Mrs. Elizabeth Rumbough, Mrs. Florance Greble, Mrs. Grace Rumbough, Gilbert, Robert Bangs. Began with Colgate & Co., becoming chmn. of bd.; became dir. Colgate-Palmolive-Peet Co. Republican. Presbyn. Home: New York, N.Y. Died Jan. 5, 1933.

COLGATE, James Boorman, banker; b. New York, March 4, 1818; head of James B. Colgate & Co., bankers; became, 1864, pres. bd. of trustees, Colgate Univ., Hamilton, N.Y. In connection with it he built and endowed Colgate Acad., and in 1890 the name of the univ. was changed to Colgate Univ. Home: Yonkers, N.Y. Died 1904.

COLGATE, Russell; A.B., Yale U., 1896; m. Josephine B. Kirtland. Pres. Internat. Council of Religious Edn. Dir. Colgate-Palmolive Peet Co. Trustee Colgate U., Colgate-Rochester Div. Sch. Home: West Orange, N.J. Died July 31, 1941.

COLGATE, Sidney Morse, mfr.; b. Orange, N.J., Sept. 11, 1862; s. Samuel and Elizabeth Ann (Morse) C.; A.B., Yale, 1885; m. Caroline Bayard Dod, Oct.

16, 1894; children—S. Bayard, Mrs. Edward P. F. Eagan, Mrs. Howard C. Taylor, Jr. Chmn. board Colgate-Palmolive-Peet Co. Served as chmn. War Service Com. of Soap Industry. Baptist. Home: Orange, N.J. Died Nov. 10, 1930.

COLGROVE, Philip Taylor, lawyer; b. Winchester, Ind., Apr. 17, 1858; s. Charles H. and Catherine (Van Zile) C.; ed. schs. of Mich. and Olivet Coll.; m. Carrie M. Goodyear, Apr. 29, 1897. Admitted to Mich. bar, 1879, to Supreme Court of U.S., 1910; pros. atty., Barry Co., Mich., 1883-89; mem. Mich. Senate 1 term; city atty., Hastings, several terms; presdl. elector, 1892; campaigned for Rep. Nat. Com., 1900, and for State Com. many years. Pres. State League of Rep. Clubs. Comdr. Supreme Lodge K.P. of the World, 1896. Home: Hastings, Mich. Died Feb. 1930.

COLIE, Edward Martin, lawyer; b. Milburn, N.J., Oct. 27, 1852; s. Daniel F. and Elizabeth S. (Dayton) C.; A.B., Coll. City of N.Y., 1873; m. Caroline Matilda Runyon, Sept. 4, 1878; children—Edward M., Dayton, Runyon, Margaret, Frederic R. Admitted to bar, 1876; mem. E. M. & Runyon Colie; judge in Equity, under apptmt. as advisory master N.J. Court of Chancery. V.p. Orange (N.J.) Bur. Asso. Charities. Pres. Alumni of Coll. City of New York 2 terms. Presbyn. Author: John Ruskin as an Ethical Teacher, 1894. Home: E. Orange, N.J. Died May 6, 1931.

COLLAR, William Coe, head master; b. Ashford, Conn., Sept. 11, 1833; s. Charles and Mary Ann C.; A.B., Amherst, 1859, A.M., 1864; (hon. A.M., Harvard, 1870; L.H.D., Amherst, 1901); m. Hannah Caroline Averill, Feb. 24, 1858; m. 2d, Mary Evelyn Cornwall, of Rome, N.Y., Jan. 5, 1893. Master, 1857-67, head master, 1867-1907, Roxbury (Mass.) Latin Sch. Mem. Boston Sch. Com., 1878-81; mem. Harvard Sch. Exam. Bd., 1892-96. Fellow Am. Acad. Arts and Sciences. Author of a series of books on Latin and Greek langs. Home: Waban, Mass. Died Feb. 27, 1916.

COLLBRAN, Henry, ry. and mining operator; b. London, Eng., Dec. 24, 1852; s. Edward and Mary (Barnard) C.; pub. sch. education; m. Amabel Maurice Merrill, Mar. 22, 1902. Came to America, 1881; in charge of various traffic depts. Chicago, New Orleans & Tex. Pacific Ry., 1881-88; gen. mgr. Colo. Midland Ry., 1888-93; built Cripple Creek Ry. and pres. Midland Terminal Ry. of Colo., 1893-96; went to Korea, 1896; built 1st steam ry. in Korea and afterwards 1st electric ry. and lighting system, and 1st water works system (Seoul Water Works); then operating 2 large mining concessions in Korea. Pres. Seoul Mining Co. (Suan concession), Collbran-Bostwick Development Co. (Kapsan concession, copper property, 90x50 miles in extent). Naturalized as Am. citizen at Colorado Springs, Colo., June 20, 1891. Died Feb. 15, 1925.

COLLEDGE, William A., educator; b. Edinburgh, Scotland, Nov. 28, 1859; s. Joseph and Margaret J. (Whiteman) C.; Established Church Normal Coll., Glasgow, Scotland, 1879-82; studied in London, Eng., 1883-86; D.D., Adrian (Mich.) Coll., 1892; m. Frances Marshall, May 1902; 1 son, Edward Wilson. Ordained Congl. ministry, 1887; in pastorate, 1887-1903; extension lecturer, English lit., U. of Chicago, 1902; editor Technical World, 1903; prof. English lit., Armour Inst., Chicago, 1904. Was editor in chief New Standard Ency. and History of the World, 1906; then v.p. La Salle Extension U. Lecturer and head dept. of edn., Redpath Lyceum Bur., 1911—. Fellow Royal Geog. Soc., 1894. Wrote: History of Theatrical Art; The Beginnings of Modern Drama; etc. Died Jan. 9, 1927.

COLLETT, John, geologist and farmer; b. Eugene, Ind., Jan. 6, 1828; grad. Wabash Coll., 1847 (A.M., 1850; Ph.D., 1879); M.D., Central Med. Coll. State senator (Ind.), 1870-73; asst. State geologist, 1870-78; member New State House Commn., 1878-79; chief bureau of statistics and geology, 1879-80; State geologist, 1881-85. Has published numerous geol. reports, 6 vols., 110 papers, 22 maps and gen. sections, nearly 2,000 figures, most of which were since copied by Mo. and Pa. Unmarried. Home: Indianapolis, Ind. Died 1899.

COLLIER, Barron, capitalist; b. Memphis, Tenn., Mar. 23, 1873; s. Cowles Miles and Hannah (Shackelford) C.; ed. pub. schs., Memphis; Doctor of Commercial Science, Oglethorpe Univ.; m. Juliet Gordon Carnes, Nov. 26, 1907; children—Barron, Samuel Carnes, C. Miles. Began in advertising brokerage bus. at Memphis, 1890; moved to New York, 1900; pres. Barron G. Collier, Inc., Street Railways Advt. Co., Collier Advt. Service, Inc., Broadway Surface Advt. Corp., Florida Gulf Coast Hotels, Inc., Inter-County Telephone & Telegraph Co., Collier Bros., Inc., Collier Service Corp., Empire State Development Co., Collier Fla. Coast Hotels, Pacific Rys. Advt. Co., Phila. Advt. Co., United Brokerage Co., Western Advt. Co., United Stores Land & Improvement Co.; member board of dirs. Baltimore Commercial Bank, Eastern Advt. Co., Gainsborough Studios, Charles Marchand Co. Mem. exec. bd. and chmn. Com. on Publicity of Am. Transit Assn. Mem. Sheriff's Jury, N.Y. City, 1913—; spl. dep. police commr. in charge Bur. of Pub. Safety, N.Y. City, 1922-25; dep. sheriff West Chester County, N.Y.; consul gen. at large Republic of Georgia. Decorated Chevalier Order of Crown of Italy; Chevalier Order of Crown of Belgium; Great Silver Cross of Merit (Austria); Certificate of the Solidaridad (Republic of Panama); Order of Pro Georgiæ Libertate (Republic of Georgia); Comdr. Order of Crown of Rumania; Compagnon Grand Croix Order of St. Lazare; Star and Badge (Spanish Am. Acad. of Science and Arts); Yellow Cross of Dedication (Portugal); Order of the Red Cross of Esthonia. Mem. Pontifical Acad. of Tiberina. Largest land owner in Fla. Acting pres. Boy Scout Foundation of Greater New York; a founder and trustee Museum City of New York; mem. exec. bd. and dir. Boy Scouts of America; chmn. advisory com. Internat. World Police; commr. in charge foreign relations and chmn. com. in charge foreign relations, Internat. Assn. of Chiefs of Police. Life mem. Nat. Inst. Social Sciences; mem. Chamber of Commerce of State of New York, Internat. Chamber of Commerce, Italy-America Society, Rockefeller Center Club, France-America Soc., Inc., New York Southern Soc., The Pilgrims, Sons of Confederate Vets., Va. Hist. Soc., Tennessee Soc., United Hunts Racing Assn., Internationaler Club of Baden-Baden (Germany), Soc. of Arts and Sciences, Fla. Hist. Soc., N.Y. Board of Trade. Home: New York, N.Y. Died Mar. 13, 1939.

COLLIER, David Charles; b. Central City, Colo., Aug. 14, 1871; s. David C. and Martha Maria (Johnson) C.; ed. pub. high sch.; m. Ella May Copley, Jan. 1, 1896 (divorced); children—David Copley (dec.), Ira Clifton; m. 2d, Ruth E. Everson, Nov. 14, 1915 (died 1916); m. 3d, Clytie B. Lyon, Dec. 13, 1919; step-dau., Clytie B. Admitted to the Calif. bar, 1891; admitted to bar of U.S. Supreme Court, 1907; and practiced at San Diego until 1905; admitted to bar of state of Illinois, 1929. Organized, 1904, Ralston Realty Co., later succeeded by D. C. Collier & Co.; was for 5 yrs. head of Panama-Calif. Expn., San Diego, 1915, first as dir. gen., later as pres.; dir. and commr. gen. Panama-Calif. Internat. Expn., San Diego, 1916; dir. San Diego Mus.; bd. mgrs. Am. Sch. of Research, Santa Fe, N.M.; apptd. commr. gen. by President Harding to represent U.S. at Brazilian Centennial Expn., 1922; apptd. 1925, dir. gen. Sesqui-Centennial Internat. Expn., Philadelphia; expn. consultant, Republic of Panama, 1925-26; assisted in initiating Chicago World's Fair for 1933, 1927; dir. gen. Order of Liberty Bell, 1930; was in practice of law; pres. Bay Trust Co. Lieut. col. on the staff of Governor J. N. Gillette, Calif., 1907-11; del. to Rep. state, county and city convs., and mem. central coms. Mason. Home: San Diego, Calif. Died Nov. 13, 1934.

COLLIER, George Haskell, univ. prof.; b. Mina, N.Y., Mar. 5, 1827; s. George and Susan Warner (Haskell) C.; grad. N.Y. State Normal Sch. (now Coll.), Albany, 1847; A.B., Oberlin, 1853, A.M., 1856; (LL.D., U. of Neb., 1881; Ph.D., Pacific U., Forest Grove, Ore., 1883); m. Sybel Sumner Smith, Dec. 19, 1853. Began teaching pub. schs., Chautauqua County, N.Y., 1845; prof. mathematics, Wheaton (Ill.) Coll., 1856-66; prof. natural science, Pacific U., Ore., 1866-76; prof. mathematics, Willamette U., 1876-79; prof. physics, 1879-95; prof. emeritus, 1895—. U. of Ore. Mem. Ore. Legislature, 1872-74. Republican. Trustee Pacific U. many yrs. from 1872. Thrice moderator, Ore. Congl. Assn. Home: Eugene, Ore. Died Mar. 14, 1916.

COLLIER, James William, congressman; b. near Vicksburg, Miss., Sept. 28, 1872; LL.B., U. of Tenn., 1894; m. Emma H. Klein, 1900. Mem. Miss. Ho. of Rep., 1895-96; circuit clerk of Warren County, Miss., 1899-1908 (resigned); mem. 61st to 72d Congresses (1909-33), 8th Miss. Dist. Democrat. Home: Vicksburg, Miss. Died Sept. 28, 1933.

COLLIER, Peter Fenelon, publisher; b. Carlow, Ireland; ed. Mt. St. Mary's Coll., Cincinnati, O.; m. Katherine Louise Dunne. Founder and pub. Collier's Weekly and head of P. F. Collier & Son, publishers. Home: New York, N.Y. Died 1909.

COLLIER, Price, author; b. May 25, 1860; s. Robert Laird and Mary (Price) C.; early edn. Geneva, Switzerland, Leipzig, Germany; B.D., Harvard, 1882; m. Katharine Delano, 1893. European editor of the Forum, 2 yrs. Officer U.S. Navy during Spanish-Am. War, 1898. Author: A Parish of Two, 1903; England and the English, from an American Point of View, 1909; Germany and the Germans from an American Point of View, 1913, etc. Home: Tuxedo Park, N.Y. Died Nov. 3, 1913.

COLLIER, Robert Joseph, editor, pub.; b. New York, N.Y., June 17, 1876; s. late Peter Fenelon and Katherine Louise (Dunne) C.; A.B., Georgetown U., Washington, 1894; student Oxford U., Eng., 1 yr.; Harvard, 1 yr.; m. Sara Stewart Van Alen, July, 1902. Since father's death, Apr. 24, 1909, head of P. F. Collier & Son, pubs. of Collier's Weekly, of which he is editor. Initiated Lincoln Farm Assn. which raised, by popular subscription, funds for purchase of the old Lincoln farm in Ky. and erected granite memorial at log-cabin where Lincoln was born; memorial formally accepted by U.S. Govt., Sept. 4, 1916. Home: New York, N.Y. Died Nov. 9, 1918.

COLLIN, (Henry) Alonzo, physicist; b. Hillsdale, N.Y., Aug. 14, 1837; s. Henry Augustus and Sarah Ann (White) C.; A.B., Wesleyan U., Conn., 1858, A.M., 1862; (Sc.D., Upper Ia. U., 1888); m. Chloe Matson, June 30, 1868. Prof. mathematics and natural science, 1860-68, natural sciences, 1868-81, Cornell Coll.; prof. chemistry and exptl. physics, U. of Neb., 1881-82; prof. physics and chemistry, 1882-99, physics, 1899-1906, emeritus, 1906, Cornell Coll. Home: Mt. Vernon, Ia. Died Apr. 17, 1918.

COLLIN, Frederick, judge; b. Benton, N.Y., Aug. 2, 1850; s. Henry Clark and Maria (Park) C.; bro. of Charles Avery C.; A.B., Yale, 1871, A.M., 1874; m. Alice L. Bacon, June 30, 1900. Admitted to bar, Oct. 26, 1876, and practiced at Elmira; member Reynolds & Collin, 1876-86, Reynolds, Stanchfield (John B.) & Collin, 1886-Oct. 1910. Corp. counsel, Elmira, 1891-92, mayor, 1894-98; pres. bd. of edn., 1889-94, 1899-1910; apptd. by Gov. Hughes, Oct. 1910, judge Ct. of Appeals, N.Y.; elected, Nov. 1910, for term expiring Dec. 31, 1920. Democrat. Presbyterian. Pres. Arnot Art Gallery, Elmira. Home: Elmira, N.Y. Died Nov. 26, 1939.

COLLINGS, Crittenden Taylor, chmn. bd. Standard Oil Co. of Ky.; b. Big Spring, Ky., Oct. 20, 1848; s. James and Letitia (Beard) C.; ed. pub. schs.; m. Annie Bell, Nov. 7, 1876. Chmn. bd. Standard Oil Co. of Ky., 1919—. Home: Louisville, Ky. Died Dec. 24, 1924.

COLLINGS, Harry Thomas, prof. commerce; b. Troy, N.Y., Mar. 25, 1880; s. Henry and Catherine (Sullivan) C.; A.B., Colgate, 1903, A.M., 1906, Sc.D., 1925; Ph.D., Yale, 1910; studied in Germany, France, Belgium, Mexico; m. Gracia Blair Darrow, July 27, 1910. Instr., Colgate, 1904-08; fellow, Yale, 1909; instr. Yale, 1909-13; prof. Pa. State Coll., 1913-18; prof. economics, U. of Pa., 1920-27; prof. commerce, same, 1927—, dir. grad. course in bus. administration, 1932—. Trade adviser for Argentina and Uruguay, War Trade Bd., 1918; U.S. trade commissioner in Belgium, 1919; spl. agt. Dept. of Commerce, 1920; visiting prof. from U. of Pa., in Mexico, summer 1923; made investigations on internat. trade in Chile, Argentina and Brazil, summer 1924; lecturer at Furman Inst. of Politics, 1925, at Univ. of Kiel, Germany, 1927, U. of Chicago, 1928, Inst. Internat. Relations, 1928, Inst. of Politics, 1928, 29, U. of Leipzig, Germany, 1929, U. of Southern Calif., 1930, univs. of Berlin, Leipzig, and Hamburg, 1932. Republican. Methodist. Author: (with L. B. Smith) The Economic Position of Argentina during the War, 1920; Business Economics, 1925; Die Kapitelexpansion der Vereinigten Staaten in Latein Amerika, 1927; Die Handelsbeziehungen Zwischen den Vereinigten Staaten und Latein Amerika, 1930. Editor: Business Ency. Revised (10 vols.), 1931. Mem. bd. of associates (editors) Current History Mag., Scholarship Com. of John Simon Guggenheim Foundation. Home: Germantown, Philadelphia, Pa. Died Aug. 28, 1934.

COLLINGS, Kenneth Brown, writer; b. Lincoln, Neb., Sept. 22, 1898; s. Franklin Wallace and Mary Deborah (Brown) C.; student of law George Washington U., 1916-19; student Army and Navy Acad., Washington, D.C., 1917; m. Luceille Hendley Smoot, Oct. 20, 1917 (divorced); 1 son, Kenneth Hendley; m. 2d, Mary Katherine Dovel, Nov. 12, 1927; 1 son, Kirby Brown Dovel. Served as private, later corpl., 3d D.C. Inf. (Nat. Guard), on Mexican Border, 1916; 2d lt., later 1st lt. and capt. (naval aviator), U.S. Marine Corps, 1917-22, with A.E.F., 1918, and service in Haiti, 1920-21; officer in Marine Corps Reserve, 1922—; naval aviator, 1917—. Broker, 1922-23, ins. underwriter in aviation hazards, 1923—; licensed civil pilot, 1927—; chief pilot and chief instr. Newark Air Service, 1928-29; pilot Pan Am. Airways, 1929; free lance writer and foreign corr., 1935—, covering Italo-Ethiopian War for Liberty Mag., 1935, German occupation of Sudetenland, 1938, and 2d World War on German-Russian front, 1939; lecturer, 1937—. Nat. trustee Marine Corps League (also one of incorporators). Author: With Allenby in the Holy Land (with L. J. Thomas), 1938; Just for the Hell of It, 1938; These Things I Saw, 1939. Home: Rockville Centre, L.I., N.Y. Died May 6, 1941.

COLLINGS, Samuel Posey, physician, surgeon; b. Rockville, Ind., Feb. 4, 1845; s. Spotsard and Rebecca S. (Mattox) C.; bro. of Howard Paxton C.; M.D., Jefferson Med. Coll., Phila., 1870; m. Sarah E. Louden, June 2, 1875 (died 1910). Practiced, Phila., 1870-72, Indianapolis, 1872-78, Hot Springs, Ark., 1878—; was demonstrator of anatomy, Ind. Med. Coll., and Coll. Phys. and Surg.; visiting surgeon Indianapolis City Hosp.; then cons. surgeon and mem. bd. govs. St. Joseph's Hosp., Hot Springs. Democrat. Presbyn. Del. 17th Internat. Med. Congress, London, Eng., 1913; fellow Am. Coll. Surgeons Mason. Home: Hot Springs, Ark. Died Mar. 16, 1917

COLLINGWOOD, Francis, civil engr.; b. Elmira, N.Y., Jan. 10, 1834; acad. edn., Elmira, N.Y.; C.E., Rensselaer Poly. Inst., 1855; m. Eliza W. Bonnett. City engr. Elmira, 1865-69; asst. engr. East River

Bridge constrn., New York, 1869-83; expert examiner New York Civ. Service, 1895—; lecturer on foundations, New York U., 1895-1904. Awarded Thelford medal and Thelford premium by Brit. Inst. C.E., 1884. Home: Elizabeth, N.J. Died 1911.

COLLINGWOOD, Herbert Winslow, editor; b. Plymouth, Mass., Apr. 21, 1857; s. Joseph W. and Rebecca W. (Richardson) C.; B.S., Mich. Agrl. Coll., 1883, LL.D., 1906; highest honors in agriculture, U. of Wis., 1912; m. Lulie D. Sullivan, Apr. 5, 1888. Editor Southern Live Stock Journal, Starkville, Miss., 1883-85; editor Rural New Yorker, 1885—, editor-in-chief, 1900. Candidate for Congress, 1906. Author: Hope Farm Notes, 1921; Adventures in Silence, 1923; Cape Cod Ramblings, 1925, etc. Home: Woodcliff Lake, Bergen Co., N.J. Died Oct. 21, 1927.

COLLINS, Alfred Quinton, artist, illustrator; pupil of Bonnât. Asso. Nat. Academician, 1901; mem. Soc. Am. Artists, Century Assn. Home: New York, N.Y. Died 1903.

COLLINS, Atwood, banker; b. Hartford, Conn., Sept. 19, 1851; s. Erastus and Mary (Atwood) C.; desc. of John Collins, of Boston and Braintree, Mass., about 1640; A.B., Yale, 1873; student Columbia Law Sch., New York, 1879-80; admitted to bar, 1880; m. Mary Buel Brace, June 9, 1880; children—Frederick Starr, Elinor B., Marion A. (Mrs. Matthew G. Ely), Emily B. In brokerage business, 1880-95; v.p., 1895-96, pres., 1896-1922, chmn. bd., 1922-25, then dir. U.S. Security Trust Co.; v.p. Soc. for Savings. Mem. Council, 1888-89, alderman, 1889-91, health commr., 1886-88, charity commr., 1904-07—all of Hartford. Pres. Charity Orgn. Soc.; v.p. Am. Sch. for the Deaf; trustee Hartford Sem. Foundation; mem. exec. com. Conn. Humane Soc. Republican. Conglist. Del. Nat. Congress of Irrigation, Phoenix, Ariz., 1896. Home: Hartford, Conn. Died May 8, 1926.

COLLINS, Clinton DeWitt, M.D.; b. Lomira, Wis., Sept. 5, 1866; s. DeWitt C. and Catherin (Lerch) C.; M.D., Hahnemann Med. Coll., Chicago, 1889; M.D., Rush Med. Coll., 1890; post-grad. work, Vienna, Austria, 1895, 1900; m. Lucy Heinemann, Aug. 3, 1910; 1 dau., Lucy Ann. Practiced in Chicago, 1889—; prof. dermatology, Chicago Medical School. Republican. Home: Chicago, Ill. Died Oct. 15, 1932.

COLLINS, Cornelius Van Santvoord, criminologist; b. Greenwich, N.Y., June 20, 1856; s. Thomas and Elizabeth (Vallance) C.; ed. pub. schs.; m. Ida S. Salmson, 1879. Dry goods mcht., Troy, 1877-98; police commr., Troy, 1888-90; Sheriff Rensselaer Co., N.Y., 1905-08; supt. state prisons of N.Y., 1898-1911; mem. Rep. State Central Com., 24 yrs.; postmaster of Troy, 1923—. Mason. Home: Troy, N.Y. Died June 1926.

COLLINS, Edgar Thomas, army officer; b. Williamsport, Pa., Mar. 7, 1873; s. Jeremiah and Katharine (Hyde) C.; grad. U.S. Mil. Acad., 1897; honor grad. Army Sch. of the Line, 1910, grad. Army Staff Coll., 1911, Army War Coll., 1917, 20; m. Margaret, d. late Col. J. J. Van Horn, Oct. 5, 1898; children—Margaret Katharine (Mrs. Frederick Viehe Armistead), Mary Elizabeth (Mrs. Allison J. Barnett). Commd. add. 2d lt. inf., June 11, 1897; promoted through grades to brig. gen., Nov. 3, 1924; lt. col. and col. N.A., Aug. 5, 1917-Aug. 31, 1919. Participated in battles around Santiago, Cuba, Spanish-Am. War, 1898; numerous engagements in Philippine Insurrection; with A.E.F., in France, World War; twice assigned to Gen. Staff. Awarded D.S.M. (U.S.); Officer Legion of Honor (French). Episcopalian. Died Feb. 10, 1933.

COLLINS, Edward Day, educator; b. Hardwick, Vt., Dec. 17, 1869; adopted son I. D. R. and Mary E. (Tenney) C.; B.A., Yale, 1896, Ph.D., 1899; m. Ruth Mary Colby, July 8, 1903; children—Ruth Mary, Paul Tenney, Alice Rutherford. Instr. history, Yale, 1899-1901; treas. and mng. dir. Canadian Carbonate Co., 1902-04; publicity mgr. Tabard Inn Corp., Phila., 1904; prin. State Normal Sch., Vt., 1905-09; prof. pedagogy, 1909-21, actg. pres., 1918-19 and 1921, provost, 1919-21, comptroller, 1923-25, Middlebury Coll. Pres. Vt. Congl. Conf., 1929-30. Republican. Home: Middlebury, Vt. Died Jan. 1, 1940.

COLLINS, Edwin R., editor; b. Rhonerville, Calif., Apr. 21, 1876; s. Edwin R. and Eleanor (Palmer) C.; ed. high sch., and Whitman Coll., Walla Walla, Wash.; m. Margaret E. Flint, June 15, 1909. War corr., 1898-99; city editor Walla Walla Union, 1900-02; telegraph editor Portland Journal, 1903; city editor Portland Telegram, 1904-05; night editor Los Angeles Examiner, 1906-07; editor Daily Optic, Las Vegas, N.M., 1908; Sunday editor Boston American, 1909-11; news editor Los Angeles Evening Herald, 1911-12; news editor Chicago American, 1913; mng. editor Los Angeles Evening Herald, 1913—, also connected with the Ledger, Tacoma, Wash., and San Francisco Examiner; editorial supervisor Hearst afternoon newspapers on the Pacific Coast. Mem. Co. I, 1st Wash. Vol. Inf., Spanish-Am. War and Philippine Insurrection; participated in battles of Santa Ana, Pasig, Morong, Tai-Tai, Calamba, Pateros and Taguig. Mem. Army, Navy and Marine Corps Res. Officers Assn. Home: Los Angeles, Calif. Died Aug. 25, 1933.

COLLINS, Everell Stanton, lumberman, banker; b. Cortland, N.Y., Mar. 30, 1866; s. Truman Doud and Mary (Stanton) C.; ed. Allegheny Coll., Meadville, Pa. (non-grad.); m. Mary Emma Laffey, Feb. 7, 1899; children—Alton Laffey, Grace Esther, Truman Wesley. Began lumbering in Pa., 1885; moved to Ostrander, Wash., 1889; then pres. Ostrander Ry. & Timber Co., Curtis, Collins & Holbrook Co., Ostrander Logging Co.; owner of Cook Oil Lease (Mayburg, Pa.). Mem. Washington legislature, 1903. Trustee Willamette U., Coll. of Puget Sound. Republican. Methodist. Mason. Home: Portland, Ore. Died Dec. 18, 1940.

COLLINS, Foster K(yle), surgeon; b. Xenia, O., May 15, 1871; s. James W. and Ruth A. (Kyle) C.; B.S., Monmouth (Ill.) Coll., 1894; M.D., Medico-Chirurg. Coll., Phila., 1899; m. Pearl G. Clark, Sept. 5, 1900; children—Donald C., Jean R. Began practice at Phila., 1899, at Los Angeles, Calif., 1915—, prof. operative surgery, Coll. Med. Evangelists, Los Angeles, 1919-26; then asso. prof. surgery; dir. Hollywood Clara Barton Memorial Hosp., 1924-31; then sr. surgeon Los Angeles Gen. Hosp. Served as chief of surgery, Base Hosp., 107, France, 1918; maj. Med. R.C. Examiner in surgery, Nat. Bd. Med. Examiners. Fellow Am. Coll. Surgeons; fellow founders group Am. Board of Surgery. Republican. Presbyn. Home: Hollywood, Calif. Died Sept. 18, 1939.

COLLINS, George Lewis, physician; b. Providence, R.I., Feb. 10, 1852; s. George L. and Laura S. (Capron) C.; Ph.B., Brown U., 1873; M.D., Harvard, 1879; studied U. of Leipzig; attended lectures, Paris, Vienna and Berlin; unmarried. Has been visiting phys. and surgeon to various R.I. hosps. and charitable orgns.; cons. phys. to Providence Lying-In Hosp., R.I. R.C. Orphan Asylum, R.I. State Sanatorium; cons. surgeon to R.I. and St. Joseph's hosps. Trustee Brown U., Providence Lying-In Hosp. Home: Providence, R.I. Died June 17, 1940.

COLLINS, George Stuart, college prof.; b. New Rochelle, N.Y., Sept. 25, 1862; s. of Rev. William Force and Susan (Stuart) C.; Ph.D., U. of Leipzig, 1892; m. Frances C. Wilson McFarland, Dec. 24, 1892; children—Helen Stuart, Kenneth Maynard, Donald Wilson. Prof. German lang. and lit., 1892-1905, prof. Spanish, 1893-1905, prof. modern langs. and lits., 1905-08, prof. German and Spanish, 1908-17, prof. modern langs., 1917-33, emeritus, Brooklyn Poly. Inst.; prof. German, Long Island Coll. Hosp., 1914-16. Author: Dryden's Dramatic Theory and Praxis (Ph.D., thesis), 1892. Editor: Selections from the Works of Jean Paul Friedrich Richter, 1898. Home: Manhasset, L.I. Deceased.

COLLINS, Gilbert, judge; b. Stonington, Conn., Aug. 26, 1846; s. Daniel P. C.; privately ed.; studied law in office; (LL.D., Rutgers, 1899); m. Harriet Kingsbury Bush, June 2, 1870 (died 1917). Admitted to bar and practiced law in Jersey City, Dixon & Collins till Apr., 1875, Collins & Corbin, 1875-97; mayor Jersey City, 1884-86; justice Supreme Ct. of N.J., Mar. 8, 1897-Jan. 17, 1903, when he resigned to resume law practice and firm of Collins & Corbin was reëstablished. Republican. Home: Jersey City, N.J. Died Jan. 29, 1920.

COLLINS, Guy N., botanist; b. Mertensia, N.Y., Aug. 9, 1872; s. George and Maria Anne (Hathaway) C.; prep. edn., high sch., Syracuse, N.Y.; student Syracuse U., 1890-91; m. Christine Hudson, Aug. 3, 1903; children—George Briggs, Perez Hathaway. Asst. botanist Bur. Plant Industry, U.S. Dept. Agr., 1901-10, botanist, 1910-20, botanist in charge bio-physical investigations, 1920—. Conducted explorations in Liberia for N.Y. Colonization Soc., 1891-97; visited Mexico, Guatemala, Costa Rica, Puerto Rico and Haiti for U.S. Dept. Agr. Author: Economic Plants of Puerto Rico (with O. F. Cook), 1903; also numerous articles on tropical agr. and genetics of maize. Home: Lanham, Md. Died Aug. 14, 1938.

COLLINS, Herman LeRoy, newspaperman; b. Hepburn, Pa.; s. John and Catherine (Hyde) C.; A.B., Lafayette (Pa.) College, 1887, A.M., 1891, Litt.D., 1914; m. Marion H., dau. of S. C. and E. Long of Philadelphia, May 22, 1913; 1 son, Herman LeRoy. Formerly news editor, mng. editor and financial editor, Philadelphia Press; mem. editorial staff Philadelphia Public Ledger beginning 1913, writing over pen name of "Girard"; later editor and pres. Phila. Evening Telegraph; now asso. editor Phila. Inquirer; also writing under name of "Girard." Newspaper and mag. corr., London, Eng., 1901. Republican. Episcopalian. Home: Cynwyd, Pa. Died Oct. 7, 1940.

COLLINS, Hubert Edwin, cons. engr.; writer; b. Boonesboro, Ia., Mar. 27, 1872; s. Mahlon Day and Keturah Ann (Williams) C.; ed. high sch., Clarinda, Ia.; m. Ethelyn Ella Cropsey, June 30, 1897. Machinist and erecting engr., Lake Erie Engring. Works, Buffalo, N.Y., 1891-96; operating engr., New York & Queens Co. Electric Light & Power, Long Island City, N.Y., 1896-98; supt. shops and gen. mgr. in charge engring., Ambrose Machinery Co., Brooklyn, N.Y., 1898-1902; cons. and advisory engr., 1902—. Teacher of power plant design, Sch. of Fine Arts, Columbia, 1911-12. Conducted coal survey of Oneida and Herkimer counties, World War; N.Y. State Res. officer, Wright-Martin Aircraft Corp.; mem. mil. police, Utica. Sec. Inst. Operating Engrs. (N.Y. City); mem. Coal Survey Commn. of Federated Engrs. (Washington, D.C.). Mason. Methodist. Author: Valve Setting, Shaft Governors, Erecting Work, Boilers, Steam Turbines, Pumps, Knocks and Kinks, Pipes and Belting, Shafting, Pulleys and Belting (9 vols.), 1907-08; Warpath and Cattle Trail, 1928. Home: Utica, N.Y. Died Oct. 31, 1932.

COLLINS, J(ames) Franklin, botanist; b. North Anson, Me., Dec. 29, 1863; s. James H. and Josephine (Witherell) C.; ed. pub. schs. N. Anson and Providence, R.I.; (hon. Ph.B., Brown U., 1896); unmarried. Moved to Providence, R.I., 1873; art metal worker, 1879-99; became interested in botany in 1883 (pvt. study); curator, Brown U. Herbarium, 1894-1911 and 1924-1938; instr. in botany, 1899-1905, asst. prof., 1905-11, head dept., 1906-11, demonstrator, 1913-25, lecturer, 1925-38, Brown U.; pathologist, U.S. Dept. Agr., 1911-33, retired. Author: Illustrated Key to the Trees of Northeastern North America (with H. W. Preston), 1912. Home: Edgewood, R.I. Deceased.

COLLINS, John Bartholomew, commodore, U.S. Navy; b. New Orleans, Jan. 20, 1850; s. Bartholomew and Ann (Douglas) C.; grad. U.S. Naval Acad., 1870; widower. Midshipman, July 26, 1866; promoted through grades to capt., Feb. 28, 1906; commodore and retired, June 30, 1909. Served in Behring Sea, Atlantic, Pacific and Indian oceans, on the prin. rivers—Mississippi, Rio Grande, Orinoco, Amazon, Rio de la Plata, Guayaquil, Columbia, etc.; on the Wilmington during war with Spain; comd. Princeton, Rainbow, Brooklyn, Indiana, and at navy yards, Pensacola, Fla., Mare Island, Calif., and Phila. Mason. Home: Annapolis, Md. Died Apr. 12, 1917.

COLLINS, John Joseph, bishop; b. Maysville, Ky., Nov. 15, 1857; s. John and Hannah (Glenn) C.; ed. St. Mary's Sem. (Cincinnati), Mt. St. Mary's Coll. (Emmitsburg, Md.), Woodstock (Md.) Coll.; D.D., LL.D. Mem. Soc. of Jesus (Jesuits); ordained priest R.C. Ch., Aug. 29, 1891; in Jamaica, 1894-1902; returned to U.S. and Mission Bd. 2 yrs.; rector Fordham U., 1904-06, introducing depts. of law and medicine into univ. during rectorship; apptd. administrator apostolic, Jamaica, 1906, also superior S.J. in Jamaica; apptd. bishop of Antiphellos, Aug. 9, 1907, consecrated, Oct. 28, 1907. Erected Holy Trinity Cathedral (Kingston); resigned as vicar apostolic of Jamaica, 1920. Died Nov. 1934.

COLLINS, Joseph William, chmn. Mass. Fish and Game Commn., Oct. 31, 1899—; b. Isleboro, Me., Aug. 8, 1839; s. David and Eliza B. (Sawyer) C.; primary edn. in small country schs.; self-taught in higher branches on shipboard; worked on fishing schooner from a boy of 10 yrs. old, and later comd. schooners sailing from Gloucester, Mass.; m. Pauline Coombs, Mar. 1, 1861 (died 1894); m. 2d, Sallie Atkinson, Apr. 14, 1897. Made statist. inquiry into fisheries of New England for 10th Census 1879-80, and for U.S. Fish Commn., with which he remained connected until Dec. 1892. Was on staff of U.S. commr. Internat. Fisheries Expns. Berlin, 1880, London, 1883; U.S. commr. to Bergen Expn., Norway, 1898. Apptd. in charge Div. of Fisheries, U.S. Fish Commn., 1888; chief department Fish and Fisheries, World's Columbian Expn.; organized, 1884, and was hon. curator until 1893, sect. of Naval Architecture, U.S. Nat. Museum. One of contributors to Century Dictionary; edited Fishing Gazette, 1893-94; pres. Commercial Fisheries Assn., 1894. Made Chevalier of St. Olaf by Norwegian govt., 1898. Hon. mem. various European fishery and scientific socs. Awarded diploma for invention, Berlin, 1880; 2 silver medals for invention and diploma for spl. services, London, 1883; spl. gold medal of honor by German Govt., 1894, and honor medal, 1893, as "one of the makers of the World's Columbian Expn." Home: Brighton, Mass. Died 1904.

COLLINS, Loren Warren, judge; b. Lowell, Mass., 1838; s. Charles P. and Abigail C. (Libby) C.; removed to Minn., 1854; served in Civil War in 7th Minn. Regt., 1861-65; bvtd. capt.; admitted to bar; m. Ella M. Stewart, Sept. 4, 1878 (dec.). County atty. Stearns County, 10 yrs.; mem. Minn. Legislature, 1881-83; judge 7th Jud. Dist., Minn., 1883-87, asso. justice Supreme Ct. of Minn., 1887-Apr. 1, 1904; resigned. Unitarian. Home: Minneapolis, Minn. Died Sept. 27, 1912.

COLLINS, Lorin Cone, lawyer, jurist; b. Wapping, Conn., Aug. 1, 1848; s. Lorin Cone and Mary (Bemis) C.; student Ohio Wesleyan U., Delaware, O.; B.A., Northwestern U., 1872, M.A., 1874; m. Nellie Robb, Sept. 17, 1873; children—Carrie May (dec.), Lorin Cone, III, Helen Robb (dec.), Grace, George Robb. Admitted to Ill. bar, 1874, and began practice at Chicago; apptd. judge Circuit Court of Cook County, Ill., Dec. 1884; elected to same office, 1885, reelected, 1891; resigned, 1893, and resumed practice as mem. Collins, Goodrich, Darrow & Vincent; mem. Collins & Fletcher, 1895-1905; asso. justice Supreme Court of Canal Zone, 1905-11; admitted to practice in New Mexico, 1912, and resided and practiced there until 1922; returned to Chicago and employed in spl. cases only. Mem. Ill. Ho. of Rep., 1879, 81, 83 (speaker of House, 1883). Trustee Northwestern U. 20 yrs. Republican. Methodist. Mason. Home: Sawyer, Mich. Died Oct. 18, 1940.

COLLINS, Matthew Garrett, oil producer; b. Robbins, Westmoreland County, Pa., Feb. 25, 1874; s. Oliver Cromwell and Mary Elizabeth (Rodibaugh) C.; ed. pub. schs.; m. Effie Craig, Dec. 19, 1898. Went to work at 12; began mfr. of silk on small scale, 1896, and developed business to $2,000,000 yearly in 10 yrs.; entered exporting business, principally oils and chemicals, 1912; asso., 1916, with Gov. Charles N. Haskell, of Okla., in developing the Middle States Oil Co.; became pres. Interstate Gasoline Co. Trustee Drew Sem. for Young Women, Carmel, N.Y. Republican. Methodist. Mason. Home: Lake Mahopac, N.Y. Died June 26, 1925.

COLLINS, Michael Francis, newspaper pub.; b. Troy, N.Y., Sept. 27, 1854; s. Patrick and Alice C.; ed. pub. schs. and Christian Brothers' Acad.; m. Caroline E. O'Sullivan, Dec. 20, 1880. Owner and editor Troy Observer, 1879—. Mem. N.Y. Assembly, 1886-87, Senate, 1888-90, 1894-95. Democrat. Home: Troy, N.Y. Died Dec. 22, 1928.

COLLINS, Patrick A., lawyer; b. Fermoy, Ireland, Mar. 12, 1844; came to U.S. (Chelsea, Mass.), 1848; worked at different occupations from the age of 12 to 22, devoting his evenings to study; grad. Harvard Law School, 1871; admitted to bar, 1871; mem. Mass. legislature, 1868-69; State senator, 1870-71; mem. Congress, 1883-89; consul-gen. of U.S. at London, 1893-97; judge-advocate-gen. of Mass., 1875; mayor of Boston, 1902-03. Died 1905.

COLLINS, Paul Valorous, writer; b. Camden, Preble Co., O., July 22, 1860; s. Samuel and Abigail Jane (Patton) C.; student Univ. of Minn., Univ. of Toulouse (France); studied art, Art Students' League, New York, 1884-85; m. Mary Graves Rhoads, June 20, 1889. Reporter, Dayton Herald, 1880, Cincinnati Commercial Gazette, 1883; went to Paris, France, to study art, but became cable corr. New York Tribune and other Am. papers; interviewed DeLesseps when he returned from Panama inspection, and Pasteur when he first announced successful treatment of hydrophobia; editor and propr. St. Peter (Minn.) Tribune, 1887-90; prin. owner Northwestern Agriculturist, Minneapolis, 1893-1915. Prog. Republican nominee for gov. of Minn., 1912; then mgr. Paul V. Collins Internat. Newspaper Syndicate, Washington and London; mag. and newspaper writer; interviewed Benito Mussolini for Outlook Mag., 1927. Enlisted in Q.M.C. (vol.), U.S.A., Apr. 1917; in service with A.E.F. 2 yrs.; participated in Lys defensive and Meuse-Argonne advance; capt. Q.M.C. Presbyn. Mason. Author: A Baton of a Heart, 1888; The True in Fine Art, 1888; A Country Romance, 1898; What Farmers Use, 1903; Readjusted Compensation (novel), 1930. Home: Washington, D.C. Died Mar. 8, 1931.

COLLINS, Varnum Lansing, college prof.; b. Hong Kong, China, Dec. 1, 1870; s. Varnum Daniel and Mary L. H. (Ball) C.; A.B., Princeton, 1892, A.M., 1895; m. Princetta Lee Hanger, Nov. 20, 1901; children—Princetta Lansing (dec.), Varnum Lansing. Prof. Greek and Latin, Moores Hill Coll., Ind., 1892-93; reference librarian, Princeton U., 1896-1906; asst. prof. modern langs., 1906-12, prof. French lang. and lit., 1912—, Princeton U.; also clerk of the faculty, 1912—, acting sec., 1917-20, sec., 1920—. Episcopalian. Author: The Continental Congress at Princeton, 1908; Early Princeton Printing, 1911; Princeton (Am. Univ. and College Series), 1914; Guide to Princeton, 1919; Howard Crosby Butler, 1923; President Witherspoon, a Biography, 1925; Princeton Past and Present, 1931. Compiler: (with F. P. Hill) Books, Pamphlets and Newspapers Printed at Newark, N.J., 1876-1900, 1902; General Biog. Catalogue, Princeton U., 1908. Editor: Brief Narrative of the Ravages of the British and Hessians at Princeton, 1776-1777, 1906; Witherspoon's Lectures on Moral Philosophy, 1912; Princeton in the World War, 1932. Home: Princeton, N.J. Died Oct. 9, 1936.

COLLIS, Charles H. T., lawyer; b. Cork, Ireland, Feb. 4, 1838; s. William and Mary Anne (Lloyd) C.; academic edn. in Eng.; m. Septima M. Levy, Dec. 13, 1861. Enlisted Union army, April, 1861; served until surrender of Gen. Lee as pvt., sergt., maj., capt., col., brig. gen., maj. gen. Participated in all battles of Army of Potomac, excepting Gettysburg; after war twice elected city solicitor, Phila.; 15 yr. dir. of city trusts; commr. public works, New York, during the Strong adminstrn. Republican. Home: New York, N.Y. Died 1902.

COLLISON, Wilson, author, playwright; b. Gloucester, O., Nov. 5, 1893; s. John Byron and Mary Elizabeth (Gardner) C.; grad. common schs., Columbus, O., 1908; m. Anzonetta Lloyd, Feb. 10, 1920. Mem. Authors' League of America. Republican. Author: (plays) Up in Mabel's Room (with Otto Harbach), 1919; The Girl in the Limousine (with Avery Hopwood), 1919; Getting Gertie's Garter (with Avery Hopwood), 1921; Desert Sands, 1924; The Vagabond, 1927; Red Dust, 1927; (novels) The Murder in the Brownstone House, 1929; Murder in the Rain, 1930; Diary of Death, 1930; Blonde Baby, 1931; A Woman in Purple Pajamas (under pseud. Willis Kent), 1931; Expensive Women, 1931; Farewell to Women, 1932; Red Haired Alibi, 1932; Shy Cinderella, 1932; Millstones, 1933; One Night with Nancy, 1933; Sexational Eve, 1933; Congo Landing, 1934; Second Mrs. Lynton, 1935; Save a Lady, 1935; Dame Dark, 1935; Begins with Murder, 1936; Long Glittering Isle, 1936. Home: Beverly Hills, Calif. Died May 24, 1941.

COLLITZ, Hermann, philologist; b. Bleckede, Hanover, Feb. 4, 1855; grad. Gymnasium Johanneum at Lüneburg, 1875; student philology, Göttingen, 1875-79, Berlin, 1879-82; A.M., Ph.D., Göttingen, 1878; L.H.D., U. of Chicago, 1916; m. Klara Hechtenberg, Aug. 13, 1904. Asst. librarian, 1883-86, instr. Sanskrit and comparative philology, U. of Halle, 1885-86; asso. prof. German, 1886-97, prof. comparative philology and German, 1897-1907, Bryn Mawr Coll.; prof. Germanic philology, Johns Hopkins U., 1907-27 (emeritus), lecturer in Linguistic Institute, 1928 and 1931. Author: Die Verwantschaftsverhältnisse der Griechischen Dialekte, 1885; Die neueste Sprachforschung, 1886; Das Schwache Praeteritum und seine Vorgeschichte, 1912. Editor: Sammlung der Griechischen Dialektinschriften, 4 vols., 1884-1915; Bauer's Waldeck Dialect Dictionary, Leipzig, 1902; Hesperia (Schriften zur Germanischen Philologie), 1912—. Home: Baltimore, Md. Died May 13, 1935.

COLLYER, Robert, clergyman; b. Keighly, Yorkshire, Eng., Dec. 8, 1823; s. Samuel and Harriet (Norman) C.; learned blacksmith trade, which he followed after coming to U.S., 1850; m. Anne Armitage, Apr. 1850. Was Methodist local preacher, but became a Unitarian in 1859; became Unitarian missionary in Chicago; founded and was pastor Unity Ch. there, 1860-79; then pastor Ch. of the Messiah, New York (pastor emeritus). Author: Augustus Conant, Illinois Pioneer and Preacher, 1905; Father Taylor, 1906; Clear Grit, 1913; Some Memories; Thoughts for Daily Living. Home: New York, N.Y. Died Nov. 30, 1912.

COLMAN, Norman Jay, sec. of agr.; b. nr. Richfield Springs, Otsego Co., N.Y., May 16, 1827; s. Hamilton and Nancy (Sprague) C.; ed. dist. sch. and sem.; removed to Ky., 1847; taught sch.; LL.B., Louisville Law Sch., 1851; (LL.D., U. of Mo., 1905; D.Agr., U. of Ill., 1905); m. Clara Porter, 1851 (died 1863); m. 2d, Catherine Wright, 1866 (died 1897). Practiced law, New Albany, Ind., 1850-52; elected dist. atty., 1852; removed to St. Louis, 1852; established Colman's Rural World, and became its editor; dean of agrl. editors in U.S. Alderman St. Louis, 1855-56; lt. col. 85th Enrolled Mo. Militia, in Civil War; mem. Mo. Ho. of Rep., 1865-66; defeated for lt. gov., 1868, elected for term 1875-77; U.S. commr. of agr., 1885-89, and when dept. was elevated to an exec. branch of the govt., became first sec. of agr., U.S., Feb. 11-Mar. 4, 1889. Democrat. Issued call, and presided over conv. of dels. from agrl. colls. in U.S., 1885, and urged adoption of laws upon Congress creating the present system expt. stas. in connection with agrl. colls. in U.S.; selected by a commn. to head the govt. horse-breeding farm at Ft. Collins, Colo., for the establishment of a breed of Am. trotting-bred carriage horses. Officier du Merite Agricole, France, 1889. Home: St. Louis, Mo. Died 1911.

COLMAN, Samuel, painter; b. Portland, Me., Mar. 4, 1832; s. Samuel and Pamela (Chandler) C.; studied art, New York, under Asher B. Durand, and 1860-62, in Spain, France, Italy and London; returned to Europe again, 1871-76; opened studio New York, 1854; m. Anne Lawrence Dunham, 1862; 2d, Lillie Margaret Gaffney, 1903. Principal pictures: the Ships of the Western Plains (Union League Club); Moonrise in Venice, and The Spanish Peaks, Colorado (Met. Mus. of Art); Mosque of Side Bou Hac, Algeria (New York Public Library). A.N.A., 1860, N.A., 1864; a founder and 1st pres., 1866-67, Am. Soc. Painters in Water Colors. Author: Nature's Harmonic Unity, 1913. Died Mar. 27, 1920.

COLQUITT, Oscar Branch, governor; b. Camilla, Ga., Dec. 16, 1861; s. Thomas J. and Ann E. (Burkhalter) C.; ed. common schs.; m. Alice Murrell, Dec. 9, 1885; children—Rawlins Murrell, Sidney Burkhalter, Oscar Branch, Mrs. Mary Alice Laubaugh, Walter Fuller (dec.). Mem. Tex. Senate, 1895-99; state revenue agt., 8 mos., 1898; mem. state tax commn., 1899-1900; railroad commr., 1903-11; gov. of Tex. 2 terms, 1911-15; engaged in oil business; mem. U.S. Bd. of Mediation, May 1929—. Democrat. Methodist. Home: Dallas, Tex. Died Mar. 8, 1940.

COLQUITT, Walter T., lawyer; m. Julia Dunning. In practice law, Atlanta; mem. Colquitt, MacDougald, Troutman & Arkwright. Home: Atlanta, Ga. Died May 16, 1937.

COLSON, David Grant, lawyer; b. Middlesboro, Ky., April 1, 1861; academic edn.; taught school; took junior course in law, Ky. Univ., 1879-80; examiner and spl. examiner, U.S. Pension Bureau, 1882-86; mem. Ky. legislature, 1887-88; Rep. nominee for State treas., Ky., 1889; mayor of Middlesboro, 1893; elected mem. Congress, 11th Ky. dist., for term 1897-99, but left Congress, 1898, to command 4th Ky. regt. inf., U.S.V., in Spanish-Am. war. Republican. Home: Middlesboro, Ky. Died 1904.

COLSTON, Edward, lawyer; b. Berkeley County, Va., Apr. 22, 1844; s. Edward and Sarah Jane (Brockenborough) C.; prep. edn. Episcopal High Sch., Alexandria, Va.; LL.B., Washington and Lee U., 1867, LL.D.; m. Sally Coles Stevenson, Oct. 19, 1875 (dec.); m. 2d, Mary W. Stevenson, June 2, 1896 (dec.). Practiced at Cincinnati, O., 1870—; mem. Hoadly, Johnson & Colston, 1874-87, Harmon, Colston, Goldsmith & Hoadly, 1887—; gen. counsel Cincinnati, New Orleans & Tex. Pacific Ry., 1887—. Served in Army of Northern Va., C.S.A., 2 yrs. and 7 mos., 1862-65. Episcopalian. Home: Cincinnati, O. Died Sept. 20, 1928.

COLSTON, William Ainslie, lawyer; b. Louisville, Ky., Nov. 3, 1873; s. John William and Belle (Ainslie) C.; LL.B., Jefferson Sch. of Law, Louisville, 1907; m. Cora Virginia Brown, 1923; children—Margaret Virginia, Ann Ainslie. Began as messenger in mail dept., L.&N. R.R., and continued with the rd. in various positions in accounting dept. and in law dept. up to gen. solicitor; dir. finance, Interstate Commerce Commn., Washington, D.C., 1920-22; v.p. and gen. counsel N.Y.,C.&St.L. R.R., at Cleveland, O., 1922-32, v.p. in charge corporate relations, Jan. 1932—; dir. Railroad Credit Corp. Served as capt. 1st Ky. Inf., Spanish-Am. War; col. 138th F.A. and comdg. 63d F.A. Brigade, A.E.F., World War. Democrat. Episcopalian. Home: Shaker Heights, Cleveland, O. Died Nov. 6, 1934.

COLT, Le Baron Bradford, senator; b. Dedham, Mass., June 25, 1846; s. Christopher and Theodora G. (DeWolf) C.; A.B., Yale, 1868; LL.B., Columbia, 1870; A.M., Brown, 1882; LL.D., Columbia, 1904, Yale, 1905, Brown, 1914; m. Mary Louise Ledyard, Dec. 17, 1873. Practiced law, Chicago, 1872-74; moved to Bristol, R.I., 1875; practiced at Providence, R.I., 1875-81; mem. R.I. House of Rep., 1879-81; U.S. dist. judge, Dist. of R.I., 1881-84; U.S. circuit judge, 1st Jud. Circuit, July 6, 1884-1913; U.S. senator, 1913-19, 1919-25. Republican. Home: Bristol, R.I. Died Aug. 18, 1924.

COLT, Samuel Pomeroy, lawyer; b. Paterson, N.J., Jan. 10, 1852; s. Christopher and Theodora G. (DeWolf) C.; bro. of Le Baron Bradford C.); Mass. Inst. Tech., 1870-73; LL.B., Columbia, 1876; m. Elizabeth M. Bullock, Jan. 12, 1881. Admitted to N.Y. bar, 1876, R.I., 1877; in practice at Providence, 1877-87; founded, 1887, pres., 1887-1908, chmn. of bd., 1908—, Industrial Trust Co., Providence; reorganized, 1888, and became pres., Nat. India Rubber Co., Bristol; pres. U.S. Rubber Co., 1901-18, then chmn. bd.; dir. or officer of about 40 other corps. On staff Gov. Henry Lippitt, with rank of col., 1875-77; mem. Gen. Assembly, 1876-79; asst. atty. gen., 1879-81; atty. gen., 1882-85. Home: Bristol, R.I. Died Aug. 13, 1921.

COLTON, Charles Henry, bishop; b. New York, N.Y., Oct. 15, 1848; s. Patrick Smith and Teresa Augusta (Mullin) C.; grad. St. Francis Xavier Coll., 1872, St. Joseph's Sem., Troy, N.Y., 1876; ordained priest, R.C. Ch., June 10, 1876. Asst., 1876-86, pastor, 1886-1903, St. Stephen's Ch., New York; chancellor archdiocese, N.Y., 1896-1903; consecrated bishop diocese of Buffalo, Aug. 25, 1903. Author: Seedlings, 1906; My Trip to Rome and the Holy Land, 1906; Buds and Blossoms, 1910. Died May 9, 1915.

COLTON, Elizabeth Avery, prof. English; b. Choctaw Nation, Ind. Ty., Dec. 30, 1872; d. Rev. James Hooper and Eloise (Avery) Colton; student Mt. Holyoke Coll., 1891-93; B.S., Columbia, 1903, A.M., 1905. Instr. English, Wellesley, 1905-08; prof. English, Meredith Coll., Raleigh, N.C., 1908-21. Presbyterian. Author: (pamphlets) Southern Colleges for Women, 1911; Standards of Southern Colleges for Women, 1912; Improvements in Standards of Southern Colleges, 1900, 1913—; The Various Types of Southern Colleges for Women, 1916, and others. Home: Morganton, N.C. Died Aug. 25, 1924.

COLTON, George Henry, college prof.; b. Nelson, O., Oct. 10, 1848; s. John Belden and Mary Lucretia (Tilden) C.; prep. edn., Nelson Acad. of Hiram (O.) Coll.; B.S., Hiram Coll., 1871, M.S., 1874, Ph.B., 1880; studied engring., U. of Mich., 1 yr.; U. of Chicago, summer 1902; m. Clara A. Taylor, Nov. 14, 1873. Division engr. on railway, 1872-73; professor physical science, Hiram Coll., 1873—; mem. Ohio Constl. Convention, 1912. Republican. Invented and patented the underfeed house-heating furnace. Home: Hiram, O. Died June 4, 1927.

COLTON, George Radcliffe, governor; b. Galesburg, Ill., Apr. 10, 1866; s. Francis C.; ed. Knox Coll., Ill. Ranchman in N.M., 1881-86; mem. Neb. Ho. of Rep., 1889-90; nat. bank examiner Dist. of Neb.,

1897; went to P.I. as lt. col. 1st Neb. Vol. Inf.; organized customs service at Manila upon Am. occupation, and served with it until 1905, then went to Santo Domingo and organized Dominican customs receivership under the modus vivendi between U.S. and Santo Domingo; insular collector of customs for P.I., 1907-09; drafted and presented to Congress the tariff for Philippines, enacted by spl. session of Congress, 1909; also took part in drafting provisions of the Payne Bill relating to free trade between the U.S. and Philippines; gov. P.R. Nov. 7, 1909-Nov. 15, 1913. Mason. Home: New Canaan, Conn. Died Apr. 7, 1916.

COLVER, William Byron; b. Wellington, O., Sept. 26, 1870; s. Byron Henry and Josephine Lillian (Noble) C.; prep. edn. high sch., Cleveland; student law dept. Ohio State U., 1891-92; m. Pauline Simmons, Apr. 14, 1897; 1 dau., Polly Anne. Admitted to Ohio bar, 1892, and practiced in Cleveland and Sandusky, 1892-94; telegraph editor Cleveland Plain Dealer, 1894-95, Cleveland Press, 1896-98; New York and Washington corr., Scripps-McRae League, 1898-1900; editor Newspaper Enterprise Assn., and corr. in Orient, 1901-04; tax inquisitor, Cuyahoga County (Cleveland), 1905-06; sec. Municipal Traction Co., Cleveland, 1906-07; pres. and gen. mgr. Newspaper Enterprise Assn., Chicago, 1907-12; editor in chief "Clover Leaf" Publs., St. Paul, Minn., 1912-17; mem. Federal Trade Commn., Mar. 15, 1917-Sept. 25, 1920 (chmn. June 8, 1918-July 1, 1919); mem. price fixing com. of War Industries Bd., 1918-19; organized pulp and paper sect. of War Industries Bd., 1918; gen. editorial mgr. Scripps-Howard Newspapers; pres. and gen. mgr. Newspaper Enterprise Assn.; gen. mgr. Newspaper Information Service, Inc.; treas. Atlantic Shores Corp., Miami, Fla. Home: Washington, D.C. Died May 28, 1926.

COLVIN, George; b. Willisburg, Ky., Sept. 7, 1875; s. William Arthur and Lucy Madison (Harris) C.; A.B., Centre Coll., Danville, Ky., 1895; studied law, 1896-97; m. Mary Claybrooke McElroy, Jan. 20, 1903; children—Mary, William. Mem. legal dept. Louisville Title Co. 3 yrs.; supt. schs., Springfield, 1900-20; state supt. edn., Ky., 1920-24; pres. U. of Louisville, 1926—. Republican. Mem. Christian (Disciples) Ch. Mason. Died July 22, 1928.

COLVIN, Stephen Sheldon, college prof.; b. Phenix, R.I., Mar. 29, 1869; s. Stephen and Clara Anna (Turner) C.; grad. Worcester (Mass.) Acad., 1887; Ph.B., Brown U., 1891, A.M., 1894; U. of Berlin, 1895-96, U. of Strassburg, 1896-97 (Ph.D., 1897), Clark U., 1897-1901; m. Edna F. Boothman, Oct. 1891 (deceased); 2d, Eva M. Collins, June 1895. On staff of Providence Journal, 1891-93; instr. rhetoric, Brown U., 1892-95; instr. English, high schs., Worcester, 1897-1901; asst. prof. psychology, 1901-04, asso. prof., 1904-07, prof., 1907-12, U. of Ill.; prof. ednl. psychology, Brown U., 1912—. Asst. prof. philosophy, Brown U., 1903-04. Lecturer at Boston U., 1919—. Author: The Thing in Itself of Schopenhauer, 1897; Some Facts in Partial Justification of the Dogma of Formal Discipline, Urbana, 1909; The Learning Process, 1911; Human Behavior (with W. C. Bagley), 1913; Introduction to High School Teaching, 1917. Home: Providence, R.I. Died July 15, 1923.

COLVIN, Verplanck, ry. pres.; b. at Albany, N.Y., Jan. 4, 1847; s. Andrew James and Margaret Crane (Alling) C.; ed. Albany Acad. and by pvt. tutors; unmarried. Studied law under his father and practiced for short time; studied geology, geodesy and topography, and began, 1865, exploration of Adirondacks wilderness at his own expense; made, by law, supt. N.Y. State Land Survey, 1905. Determined latitudes and longitudes and heights of chief mountains of Northern N.Y.; discovered, 1869, and in 1872 determined position and elevation of Lake Tear-of-the-Clouds, highest lake source of Hudson River. Pres. N.Y. Canadian Pacific Ry., July 1, 1902—. Lectured on higher surveying and geodesy, Hamilton Coll., 1881; del. 1st Am. Forestry Congress, 1882; Rep. nominee for state engr. and surveyor, 1891; rep. N.Y., 1893, in reception of Duke of Veragua and family (desc. of Columbus). Trustee Albany Inst. (pres.); life mem. Geog. Soc. and Am. Inst. Mining Engrs.; life fellow A.A.A.S. At request of Gov. Hughes of N.Y., wrote an important paper opposing change in U.S. Constitution. Home: Albany, N.Y. Died 1920.

COLVOCORESSES, George Partridge, rear adm.; b. Norwich, Vt., Apr. 3, 1847; s. George M. and Eliza Freelon (Halsey) C.; grad. U.S. Naval Acad., 1869; hon. A.M., Norwich U., Vt., 1898; m. Mary D. Baldwin, Oct. 7, 1875; children—Edith Baldwin (dec.), George Musalas, Harold. Captain's clk. on board ships Supply and Saratoga, 2 yrs., in Civil War; commd. ensign, 1870; master, 1872; lt., 1875; lt. comdr., 1897; comdr., 1900; capt., 1905; retired as rear admiral June 1907. Advanced 5 numbers in grade "for eminent and conspicuous conduct at Battle of Manila Bay." Served in nearly all parts of the world; instr. Naval Acad., 1886-90 and 1893-96; comdt. of midshipmen, 1905-07; served at Torpedo Sta., War Coll., and in comd. Naval Sta., Key West; comd. U.S. Ships Lancaster, Yankee and Newark. Episcopalian. Home: Litchfield, Conn. Died Sept. 11, 1932.

COLWELL, Nathan Porter, M.D.; b. Osceola, Ia., May 25, 1870; s. Fernando N. and Mary Ellen (Shields) C.; M.D., Rush Med. Coll., Chicago, 1900; m. Agnes Louise Peterson, May 5, 1903; children—Nathan Porter, Ethel Florence. Began practice, Chicago, 1900; asso. instr. Rush Med. Coll., 1900-06; sec. Council on Med. Edn. of Am. Med. Assn., 1906—; collaborator U.S. Bur. Edn., 1913-30; managing editor of the Federation Bulletin of Fedn. of State Med. Bds. of U.S., 1915—. Contract surgeon, assigned to Office of Surgeon Gen. U.S. Army, 1918. Republican. Presbyn. Mason. Home: Wilmette, Ill. Died Jan. 6, 1936.

COMAN, Charlotte Buell, artist; b. Waterville, N.Y.; d. Chauncey Buell; studied in Paris with Harry Thompson and Emille Vernier; remained in France and Holland 6 yrs.; widow. Paints landscapes; received medal at Midwinter Expn., Cal.; Shaw memorial prize, Soc. Am. Artists; several prizes Woman's Art Club; 2d prize Washington Soc. Artists, 1906, etc. A.N.A., 1910. Home: New York, N.Y. Died 1924.

COMAN, Henry Benjamin, judge; b. Morrisville, N.Y., Dec. 8, 1858; s. Benjamin F. and Harriet E. (White) C.; ed. Cazenovia Sem.; m. Lucy Sandford Dana, Sept. 20, 1888. Admitted to bar, 1880, and practiced at Morrisville, 1880-1907. Clerk Madison Co. Surrogate Ct., 1881-90; deputy atty.-gen., N.Y., 1899-1902; justice Supreme Ct. of N.Y. for term Jan. 1, 1907-Dec. 31, 1920. Republican. Presbyn. Home: Oneida, N.Y. Died Jan. 10, 1912.

COMAN, Katharine, coll. prof.; b. Newark, O., Nov. 23, 1857; d. Levi P. and Martha (Seymour) C.; Ph.B., U. of Mich., 1880. Professor history, 1883-1900; prof. economics, 1900-1913 (emeritus) Wellesley Coll. Author: The Growth of the English Nation, 1895; History of England, 1899; History of England for Beginners, 1901; English History As Told by English Poets (with Katharine Lee Bates, 1902; Industrial History of the United States, 1905; Economic Beginnings of the Far West, 1911. Home: Wellesley, Mass. Died Jan. 11, 1915.

COMAN, Wilber Edmund, ry. exec.; b. Portage, Wis.; s. Edmund and Marion Winona (Seaton) C.; ed. high sch.; m. Madeline C. Zan, June 8, 1898; 1 son, Edmund Zan. Began as messenger boy, C.B. & Q. R.R., 1888; with Kansas City, Springfield & Memphis Ry. to 1890, U.P. R.R., at Portland, Ore., 1890-97; gen. agt. Ore.-Wash. R.R. & Navigation Co., Butte, Mont., 1897; same, Ore. Short Line R.R., Portland, 1897-1901, at Salt Lake City, Utah, 1901-02; became asst. gen. freight agt. Ore.-Wash. R.R. & Navigation Co., Portland, 1902; gen. freight and passenger agt., S.P. Co., Portland, to 1910; gen. freight and passenger agt., later traffic mgr. Spokane, Portland & Seattle Ry., 1910-13; v.p. and gen. mgr. Northwestern Electric Co., Portland, 1913-19; same, Wash. Water Power Co., Spokane, 1919-21; western traffic mgr. N.P. Ry., 1921-28, asst. to pres., Jan.-July 1928, v.p., July 1928—. Home: Seattle, Wash. Died June 10, 1939.

COMBA, Richard, soldier; b. in Ireland, July 11, 1837; m. Frances Mary Logan, Nov. 23, 1874. Enlisted in U.S.A. as pvt., Jan. 30, 1855; served as such and as non-commissioned officer, 7th inf., to March 26, 1863; apptd. 2d lt. 7th inf. Feb. 19, 1863; advanced through grades to col. 5th Inf. June 30, 1898. Brevets: 1st lt., July 2, 1863 (in the field); capt. and maj., U.S.A., March 13, 1865, for gallantry in battle of Gettysburg, Pa.; lt. col., Feb. 27, 1890; for gallant services in action against Indians at Big Hole, Mont., Aug. 9, 1877. Comd. 12th inf. in Santiago campaign and battle of El Caney, Cuba; bri. gen. vols. Sept. 7, 1898, for distinguished service in Cuba; comd. 2d brigade, 1st div., 4th corps; hon. disch. vol. service, Apr. 15, 1899; comd. 5th inf. in Philippines; comd. province of Abra, Northern Luzon, P.I., 1900-01; brig. gen. U.S.A., retired. Died 1907.

COMBS, Gilbert Raynolds, musician; b. Phila., Jan. 5, 1863; s. Robert Lorton and Mary Porter (Moorhead) C.; ed. Eastburn Acad., Phila.; in piano, organ, string instruments and musical composition under best Am. and foreign masters; hon. Mus. D., Capital Coll. Oratory and Music, Columbus, O., 1931; m. Rose Wrigley, May 12, 1886. Pianist, organist, player of string orchestral instruments; orchestral and chorus conductor; dir. and piano teacher Combs Broad St. Conservatory of Music, which he founded 1885. One of founders and pres. Sinfonia Nat. musical fraternity; a founder and v.p. National Association of Schools of Music. Mason. Author: Introductory Steps and Science of Piano Playing; (brochure) The Combs Science of the Art of Piano Playing. Composer for orchestra, piano, voice and violin. Home: Mt. Airy, Phila. Died June 14, 1934.

COMBS, Leslie, diplomat; b. Little Compton, R.I., July 31, 1852; s. Gen. Leslie and Mary Elizabeth (Brownell) C.; student Transylvania U., through sophomore yr.; m. Mary C., d. Daniel Swigert, of Spring Station, Ky., Oct. 18, 1876. Engaged since manhood in fine stock raising and tobacco planting; also rancher in Tex. and Indian Ty., several yrs.; pension agt. for Ky., 1898-1900; resigned, becoming chmn. Rep. Exec. Com., Ky., 1900; reapptd. pension agt. for Ky., 1900-02; E.E. and M.P. to Guatemala and Honduras, 1902-06, to Peru, Dec. 19, 1906-Mar. 1911, resigned. Presented with a gold vase by Govt. of Guatemala as souvenir of the Peace Conf. of the Marblehead, 1906. Organized Prog. party in Ky., 1912. Home: Lexington, Ky. Died Nov. 18, 1940.

COMER, Braxton Bragg, governor; b. Barbour Co., Ala., Nov. 7, 1848; s. John Fletcher and Catherine Lucinda (Drewry) C.; U. of Ala., class of 1865; A.M., Emory and Henry Coll., 1869; m. Eva J. Harris, Oct. 1, 1872; children—Mrs. Sally B. Lathrop, J. Fletcher, J. McD., Mrs. Catherine Buck, Mrs. Mignon Smith, Mrs. Bevelle Nabers, Braxton B., Mrs. Eva Ryding, Hugh M. Extensive farmer in Ala.; also interested in milling and cotton mfg. Mem. Commr's Court, Barbour Co., Ala., 1874-80; pres. Ala. R.R. Commn., 1905-07; gov. of Ala., 1907-11; mem. U.S. Senate by apptmt., to fill vacancy occasioned by death of Senator Bankhead, Mar.-Nov. 1920. Democrat. Home: Birmingham, Ala. Died Aug. 15, 1927.

COMER, Edward Trippe, mfr., planter; b. Barbour Co., Ala., Aug. 1, 1856; s. John Fletcher and Catherine Lucinda (Drewry) C.; ed. Southern U. and U. of Ala. Chmn. bd. Bibb Mfg. Co., Macon, Ga.; pres. E. T. Comer Co., Millhaven, Ga.; pres. Chattanooga & Gulf Ry. Co. Home: Savannah, Ga. Died Mar. 31, 1927.

COMERFORD, Frank, judge; b. Chicago, Sept. 25, 1879; s. Isaac and Jane (Linane) C.; ed. Northwestern Univ. Law Sch.; LL.B., Ill. Coll. of Law, 1904; m. Lyela Brandeis, Nov. 10, 1926. Nominated and elected, as Dem., for representative from 2d Dist., 1904; expelled by Ill. legislature, Feb. 8, 1905, for attacking alleged corrupt methods at Springfield; reëlected as independent, Apr. 4, 1905; police atty. of Chicago under Mayor Dunne, then judge of the Superior Court of Cook County. In 1919, as public prosecutor, won the first battle against American Bolsheviki, convicting William Bross Lloyd and others for conspiracy against the govt. Author: "The New World." Home: Chicago, Ill. Died Aug. 29, 1929.

COMEY, Arthur Messinger, chemist; b. Boston, Nov. 10, 1861; s. Elbridge C. and Josephine L. (Messinger) C.; A.B., Harvard, 1882; Ph.D., U. of Heidelberg, 1885; m. Kate Coleman, Sept. 9, 1885; 1 son—Arthur Coleman Comey. Instr. in chemistry, Harvard, 1885-89; prof. chemistry, Tufts Coll., 1889-93; analyt. and cons. chemist, Boston, 1893-1906; dir. Eastern (research) Lab. of E. I. du Pont de Nemours & Co., Chester, Pa., 1906-20, chem. dept. Wilmington, Del., 1920-21. Fellow Am. Acad. Arts and Sciences. Author: Dictionary of Chemical Solubilities, 1896, 2d edit., 1921. Chmn. sub-com. on explosives Nat. Research Council, 1917. Home: Cambridge, Mass. Died Apr. 6, 1933.

COMFORT, Anna Manning, physician; b. Trenton, N.J., Jan. 19, 1845; d. Alfred C. and Elizabeth (Price) Manning; ed. in. Boston; M.D., New York Med. Coll. for Women, 1865; m. George Fisk Comfort, Jan. 19, 1871 (died 1910). First woman med. graduate to practice in Conn.; later specialist in gynecology, in practice in New York and Syracuse. Pioneer suffragist and club woman; mem. Sorosis Club, 1870—. Home: New York, N.Y. Died Jan. 11, 1931.

COMFORT, George Fisk, educator, author; b. Berkshire, N.Y., Sept. 20, 1833; s. Silas C. (D.D.) and Electra (Smith) C.; A.B., Wesleyan U., Conn., 1857, A.M., 1860; studied art, philosophy and history, Europe, 1860-65; studied and traveled in Europe, Orient, 1879, 1887, 1891; (L.H.D., U. of the State of N.Y., 1888; L.L.D., Syracuse U., 1892); m. Anna Manning, Jan. 19, 1871. Prof. æsthetics and modern langs., Allegheny Coll.; Pa., 1865-68; lecturer Christian art and archæology, Drew Theol. Sem., 1868-72; prof. modern langs. and æsthetics, 1872-93, also æsthetics and history of fine arts and organized, and dean Coll. Fine Arts, 1873-93, Syracuse U.; originated in this coll. degrees in fine arts (architecture, painting, sculpture and music); organized Syracuse Mus. of Fine Arts, 1896, of which he is dir. Organized, 1869, sec., 1869-76, Am. Philol. Assn.; organized Central N.Y. Soc. of Artists, 1901; a founder Met. Mus. of Art, New York, 1869-72. Author: Art Museums in America; Modern Languages in Education; a series of German text books. Home: Syracuse, N.Y. Died 1910.

COMFORT, Will Levington, novelist; b. Kalamazoo, Mich., Jan. 17, 1878; s. Silas H. and Jane (Levington) C.; ed. grammar and high schs., Detroit; m. Mrs. Adith Duffie-Mulholland, Sept. 30, 1900; children—Jane Levington, John Duffie, Tom Tyrone. Served in 5th U.S. Cav. during Spanish-Am. War, 1898; war corr. in P.I. and China for Detroit Journal Newspaper Syndicate, 1899; in Russia and Japan during war for Pittsburgh Dispatch Newspaper Syndicate, 1904. Author: Fate Knocks at the Door, 1912; Midstream, 1914; Lot & Company, 1915; Child and Country, 1916; The Hive, 1918; This Man's World,

1921; The Public Square, 1923; Somewhere South in Sonora, 1925; Samadhi, 1927; Apache, 1931. Home: Los Angeles, Calif. Died Nov. 2, 1932.

COMLY, Samuel Pancoast, rear adm.; b. Woodbury, N.J., July 13, 1849; s. Nathan Folwell and Mary (Wood) C.; grad. U.S. Naval Acad., 1869; m. Laura L. Carpenter, Dec. 17, 1884; m. 2d, Mrs. Hannah L. Hamill, Aug. 14, 1895. Promoted ensign, 1870; advanced through grades to rear adm., 1909. Practice cruise to Europe in Sabine, 1869-70; on Juniata in Polaris search expdn. to Greenland, 1874; on Adams, in S. Atlantic and S. Pacific, 1876-79; on various ships until apptd. insp. ordnance and steel, Midvale Steel Works, and mem. Spl. Torpedo Bd., 1886-89; on Alliance, China, Japan, and various Pacific ports, 1890-93; navigator Indiana, 1895-98 and during Spanish-Am. War; in action San Juan, P.R., bombardments of Santiago and destruction of Cervera's fleet; comd. training ship Alliance, 1901-02; insp. 4th lighthouse dist.; Phila., 1904-05; comd. Battleship Alabama, 1905-07; mem. Light House Bd., 1907-09; in comd. 4th div. U.S. Atlantic Fleet, June 10, 1909-Jan. 1910, 3d div. until Oct. 1910; court martial duty, Oct. 1910, until retired, July 13, 1911. Home: Woodbury, N.J. Died April 10, 1918.

COMPARETTE, T(homas) Louis, museum dir.; b. Dekalb Co., Ind., Apr. 9, 1868; s. Alexander Charles and Mary Jane (Forder) C.; student U. of Wooster, O., 1889-92; A.B., U. of Mich., 1893; Ph.D., U. of Chicago, 1901; Am. Sch. of Antiquities, Rome, 1901-02, univs. of Halle and Berlin, 1903-04; unmarried. Prof. Greek and Latin, Tex. Christian U., Waco, Tex., 1893-97; asst. in Latin, U. of Mo., 1905; curator Numismatic Collection, U.S. Mint, Phila., 1905—. Compiled catalogue of the Coins and Medals in the Numismatic Collection of U.S. Mint at Phila., 1912-13-14; Guide (book) to the Collection, 1913; Debasement of the Silver Coinage under the Emperor Nero, 1914; Aes Signatum, 1919; Descriptive Catalog Selected Greek Coins, 1921. Home: Philadelphia, Pa. Died July 3, 1922.

COMPTON, Alfred George, educator; b. London, Eng., Feb. 1, 1835; s. William and Elizabeth G. C.; A.B., Coll. City of New York, 1853, A.M.; m. Frances E. Feeks, June 10, 1874. Teacher mathematics, 1853-1911; prof. physics, 1902, acting pres., 1902-Sept. 15, 1903, Coll. City of New York. Author: A Manual of Logarithmetic Computations, 1881; First Lessons in Wood-Working; First Lessons in Metal-Working, 1890; The Speed-Lathe (Compton and De Groodt), 1898; Some Common Errors of Speech, 1898. Died Dec. 12, 1913.

COMPTON, Charles Elmer, army officer; b. Mauricetown, N.J., Jan. 28, 1836. Served as 1st sergt. Co. A, and sergt. maj. 1st Ia. Inf., May 7-Aug. 21, 1861; commd. capt. 11th Ia. Inf., Oct. 19, 1861; hon. mustered out of vol. service, May 4, 1863; maj. 47th U.S.C.T., May 5, 1863; lt. col. 53d U.S.C.T., Dec. 9, 1864; hon. mustered out, Mar. 8, 1866; maj. 40th Inf., July 28, 1866; assigned to 6th Cav., Dec. 15, 1870; lt. col. 5th Cav., Apr. 29, 1879; col. 4th Cav., Oct. 19, 1887; brig. gen. vols., May 4, 1898; hon. discharged from vol. service, Dec. 6, 1898; retired for age, June 9, 1899; advanced to rank of brig. gen. retired, by act of Apr. 23, 1904. Bvtd. lt. col., Mar. 2, 1867, for campaign against Mobile, Ala.; col., Feb. 27, 1890, for action against Indians on Red River, Tex., Aug. 30, 1874. Home: Washington, D.C. Died 1909.

COMPTON, Elias, college prof.; b. Glendale, O., Aug. 3, 1856; s. Wilson Martindale and Elizabeth (Hunt) C.; student Nat. Normal Sch., Lebanon, O., 1873-75; A.B., Coll. of Wooster, 1881, A.M., 1884, Ph.D., 1889; Western Theol. Sem., 1881-83; Clark U., summer 1892; 6 mos.' study in philosophy in library of British Mus., 1908-09 (D.D., Wabash, 1903); m. Otelia C. Augspurger, Aug. 3, 1886; children—Karl Taylor, Mary Elesa (Mrs. C. H. Rice), Wilson Martindale, Arthur Holly. Instr. English, Latin and mathematics, 1883-84, asst. prof. English, 1884-1900, prof. philosophy, 1887-1928, dean, 1899-1921, actg. pres., Apr.-Oct. 1919, Coll. of Wooster, emeritus 1928. Pres. Confer. of Ohio Coll. Presidents and Deans, 1921-22. Editor of the Wooster Quarterly, 1887-1910. Author: A Short History of Philosophy. Made tour of Asia for study of missions and edn., 1926-27. Clergyman in Presbyterian Ch. Home: Wooster, O. Died May 2, 1938.

COMPTON, George Brokaw, lawyer; b. Ovid, N.Y., Dec. 21, 1883; s. Charles Covert and Catherine (Little) C.; A.B., Columbia, 1909; LL.B., 1913, valedictorian; unmarried. Farm manager, 1899-1900; began as railway postal clerk in 1901; U.S. customs insp., 1905-13; editor Columbia Alumni News, 1911-14; organizer Columbia Alumni Fed. and exec. sec., 1913-14; admitted to N.Y. bar, 1914; state transfer tax appraiser (N.Y. County), 1915-20; mem. Peaslee and Compton, 1920-23, Compton and Delaney, 1923-31, Compton, Dillon and Clark, 1931—; dir. Nat. Bondholders Corp., United Air Lines Transport Corp. (chmn. stockholders protective com. 1934), Alma Egan Hyatt Foundation; mem. N.Y. City Charter Revision Commn., 1934; spl. master Federal Court to determine fairness and feasibility of plan of reorganization of Hotel Waldorf-Astoria Corp., 1934-36; trustee in bankruptcy Greyling Realty Corp. and 10 affiliated mortgage and subsidiary corps. in reorganization of Nat. Surety Co., 1934-36. Capt. F.A., 2d Army, U.S.A., in Marbache sector and Metz offensive, comdr. of a battalion and recommended for promotion, World War; now maj. O.R.C.; one of organizers of Am. Legion, organizer and first comdr. in N.Y. County; resigned as county comdr., Mar. 1920, in personal protest of nat. exec. com. for bonuses for ablebodied, was first Legion official to make public stand in opposition; presided at reception to King Albert of Belgians, Madison Sq. Garden, 1919; presented Legion standard of colors to Prince of Wales, 1920. Chairman Fusion Speakers Bureau, Mayoralty Campaign, New York, 1933; chmn. Mayor's Committee to Welcome Columbia Univ. Football team, Rose Bowl champions, 1933-34. Vol. organizer for Rep. Nat. Com. and campaign mgr. Hughes Nat. Coll. Men's League, 1916; mgr. campaign for new city charter, New York, 1936. Awarded conspicuous Columbia Alumni service medal, 1933. Presbyn.; trustee Fourth Presbyn. Ch., New York. Home: New York, N.Y. Died Mar. 24, 1938.

COMPTON, Loulie, educator; b. Nashville, Tenn.; ed. Nashville Acad., Nashville Coll. for Young Ladies; unmarried. Teacher various schs. for women, Tex., 8 yrs., then in charge dept. of English, Ward's Sem., Nashville; a founder and asso. prin. and business mgr. Birmingham (Ala.) Seminary. Died 1912.

COMSTOCK, Albert H., mcht.; b. Pontiac, Mich., Feb. 22, 1847; s. Elkanah and Eliza (Holden) C.; ed. high sch.; m. Elizabeth Hadley, Jan. 25, 1875; 1 dau., Margueret (Mrs. Charles W. Andrews). Bank cashier, Saginaw, Mich., for 30 yrs., until 1895; settled in Duluth, Minn., 1895, and then engaged in hardware business; pres. Marshall-Wells Building Corp.; v.p. Marshall-Wells Co., Marshall-Wells Co., Ltd. (Winnipeg, Can.), Marshall-Wells Alberta Co., Ltd. (Edmonton), Marshall-Wells B. C., Ltd. (Vancouver). Chmn. Minn. Com. for Deep Waterway to the Sea; mem. Duluth Chamber Commerce. Republican. Episcopalian. Awarded bronze plaque by Legion of Honor on being chosen as first in Hall of Fame of Duluth for services to the Commonwealth, Apr. 4, 1925. Home: Duluth, Minn. Died Nov. 22, 1926.

COMSTOCK, Anna Botsford, natural history artist and wood engraver; b. Otto, N.Y., Sept. 1, 1854; d. Marvin and Phebe (Irish) Botsford; grad. Chamberlain Inst., Randolph, N.Y., 1873, Cornell, 1878; studied art at Cooper Union and under John P. Davis; m. John Henry Comstock, Oct. 7, 1878. Exhibited Chicago Expn., 1893, Paris Expn., 1900; bronze medal for wood engraving, Buffalo Expn., 1901. Asst. prof. Cornell extension work in Nature Study, 1899; lecturer Stanford extension work, 1899-1900; asst. prof., 1913-20; prof. nature study, 1920-22, Cornell U. (emeritus). Associate dir. of Am. Nature Assn. Author: Ways of the Six-Footed; How to Keep Bees; Handbook of Nature-Study, 1911; The Pet Book, 1914; Bird, Animal, Tree and Plant Notebooks, 1914. Editor Nature Study Review, 1917-23. Chosen by the Nat. League of Women Voters in 1923 as one of the 12 greatest living Am. women. Home: Ithaca, N.Y. Died Aug. 24, 1930.

COMSTOCK, Anthony, sec. N.Y. Soc. for Suppression of Vice; b. New Canaan, Conn., Mar. 7, 1844; s. Thomas A. and Polly A. (Lockwood) C.; ed. Wyckoff's Acad., New Canaan, and high sch., New Britain, Conn.; his brother Samuel having been killed in Battle of Gettysburg, volunteered to fill his place in col., 1863; mustered out, July 1865; served under Gen. Gilmore in 3d separate brigade, Dept. of South; m. Margaret Hamilton, Jan. 25, 1871. Sec. and spl. agt. New York Soc. for Suppression of Vice, May 1873—; postoffice insp. New York, 1873—; was prominent in Y.M.C.A. As sec. and spl. agt. New York Soc. for Suppression of Vice and P.O. insp. has brought about 3,670 criminals to justice and destroyed 160 tons of obscene literature and pictures, etc. Republican. Presbyn. Author: Frauds Exposed, 1880; Gambling Outrages, 1887; Morals vs. Art, 1888; Traps for the Young, 1890. Home: Summit, N.J. Died Sept. 21, 1915.

COMSTOCK, Cyrus Ballou, brig. gen.; b. West Wrentham, Mass., Feb. 3, 1831; s. Nathan and Betsey (Cook) C.; grad. West Point, 1855, in engrs.; m. Elizabeth Blair, Feb. 3, 1869. Bvt. 2d lt. engrs., July 1, 1855; advanced through grades to col., Apr. 7, 1888; bvtd. maj., July 4, 1863, for gallant and meritorious services in siege of Vicksburg; lt. col., May 6, 1864, for same in battle of the Wilderness; col., Jan. 15, 1865, for same in capture of Ft. Fisher; brig. gen., Mar. 13, 1865, for same in campaign ending with capture of Mobile; col. and brig. gen. vols., Jan. 15, 1865, for same in capture of Ft. Fisher; maj. gen. vols., Mar. 26, 1865, for same during campaign against Mobile. Chief engr. Army of the Potomac, 1862-63; sr. engr. at siege of Vicksburg; chief engr. in assault and capture of Fort Fisher, N.C.; sr. a.-d.-c. to Lt. Gen. U. S. Grant, 1864-66; col. a.-d.-c. to Generals Grant and Sherman, 1866-70. Mem. and pres. Miss. River Commn.; mem. permanent Bd. Engrs. for Fortifications; retired, Feb. 3, 1895; advanced to rank of brig. gen. retired, by act of Apr. 23, 1904. Author: Primary Triangulation of the U.S. Lake Survey. Edited Some Descendants of Samuel Comstock of Providence, R.I., 1905. Died 1910.

COMSTOCK, Frank Mason, college prof.; b. Le Roy, N.Y., May 20, 1855; s. Samuel Francis and Mary Mason (Turner) C.; A.B., C.E., Union College, Schenectady, 1876, A.M., 1879, Ph.D., 1891, L.H.D. from same, 1926; m. Louise Brown, June 29, 1882; 1 son, William Steele Brown. On New York Adirondack survey, 1876; prin. Le Roy Academic Inst., 1879-91; prof. natural history and descriptive geometry, Case Sch. of Applied Science, 1891—; acting pres. same, 1912-13. Home: Cleveland, O. Died Mar. 7, 1929.

COMSTOCK, George Cary, astronomer; b. Madison, Wis., Feb. 12, 1855; s. Charles Henry and Mercy (Bronson) C.; Ph.B., U. of Mich., 1877; LL.B., U. of Wis., 1883 (LL.D., U. of Ill., 1907; Sc.D., U. of Mich., 1907); admitted to bar, but never practiced; m. Esther Cecile Everett, June 12, 1894; 1 dau., Mary (Mrs. George Carey). Recorder and asst. engr. U.S. Lake Survey, 1874-78; asst. engr. on improvement Miss. River; asst. astronomer Washburn Obs.; computer Nautical Almanac Office; prof. mathematics and astronomy, Ohio State U., 1885-87; prof. astronomy, 1887-1922, dir. Washburn Obs., 1889-1922, dir. and dean Grad. Sch., 1906-20, U. of Wis., retired, 1922. Fellow Am. Acad. Arts and Sciences. Author: Method of Least Squares, 1890; Text-Book of Astronomy, 1900; Field Astronomy for Engineers, 1902; The Sumner Line as an Aid to Navigation, 1919. Home: Beloit, Wis. Died May 21, 1934.

COMSTOCK, John Henry, entomologist; b. Janesville, Wis., Feb. 24, 1849; s. Ebenezer and Susan (Allen) C.; B.S., Cornell, 1874; grad. student Yale, 1874-75, U. of Leipzig, 1888-89; m. Anna Botsford, Oct. 7, 1878. Instr. entomology, 1875-77, asst. prof., 1877-78, Cornell; U.S. entomologist, Washington, 1879-81; prof. entomology, invertebrate zoölogy, Cornell U., 1882-1914 (emeritus). Lecturer on zoölogy, Vassar College, 1877; non-resident prof. entomology, Leland Stanford Jr. U., 1891-1900. Author: Insect Life; Notes on Entomology; Introduction to Entomology; How to Know the Butterflies (with his wife); The Spider Book; The Wings of Insects. Home: Ithaca, N.Y. Died Mar. 20, 1931.

COMSTOCK, Solomon Gilman, congressman; b. Argyle, Me., May 9, 1842; s. James Madison and Louisa M. (Gilman) C.; acad. edn.; law student U. of Mich., 1868-69; m. Sarah Ball, May 27, 1874; children—Ada L., Jessie M., George M. Admitted to bar, 1869; in practice at Moorhead, Minn., 1870—. County atty. Clay Co., Minn., 1872-78; mem. Minn. Ho. of Rep., 1875-82, Senate, 1882-88; mem. 51st Congress (1889-91), 5th Minn. Dist.; Republican. Mem. State Normal Sch. Bd. and regent U. of Minn. Home: Moorhead, Minn. Died June 3, 1933.

COMSTOCK, Theodore Bryant, mining engr., geologist; b. Cuyahoga Falls, O., July 27, 1849; s. Calvin J. and Amelia (Hanford) C.; B. Agr., Pa. State Coll., 1868; B.S., Cornell, 1870 (Sc.D., 1886); m. Blanche Huggins, Dec. 9, 1880. First asst. and photographer, Morgan expdn. to Brazil, 1870; prof. natural sciences, Pellham Priory, N.Y., 1871-72, pvt. sch., Cincinnati, 1873; geologist, Capt. W. A. Jones' N.W. Wyo. and Yellowstone Park expdn., 1873; founder, and dir. Kirtland Summer Sch. of Natural History, Cleveland, 1875; acting prof. geology and paleontology (founded dept. of econ. geology), Cornell, 1875-79; prof. mining engring. and physics, U. of Ill., 1885-89; asst. state geologist of Tex., 1889-91; founder and dir. Ariz. Sch. of Mines, 1891-95; pres. U. of Ariz., 1893-95. Asst., Harvard Summer Sch. of Geology, 1876; led expdn. to N.W. Ty., Can., 1877; asst. state geologist of Ark., 1887-88; dir. Ariz. Agrl. Expt. Sta., 1894. Pres. Calif. Farm & Home Builders; cons. engr. some of the largest mining cos. in the world; sec. and chief engr. Bd. of Pub. Utilities, Los Angeles, 1910-12. V.p. (presiding) Nat. Irrigation Congress, Los Angeles, 1893; mem. exec. com. Trans-Mississippi Congress, 1892-94. Author: Outline of Geology, 1878. Editor, Bulletin Southern California Academy Sciences, 1901. Home: Los Angeles, Calif. Died July 26, 1915.

CONANT, Alban Jasper, artist; b. Chelsea, Vt., Sept. 24, 1821; grad. Gouverneur Wesleyan Sem., 1844; (hon. A.M., Madison U., Hamilton, N.Y., and U. of Mo., 1871); m. Sarah M. Howes, 1845 (died 1867); 2d, Brianna C. Bryan, 1869. Was curator U. of Mo. 8 yrs.; chmn. commn. under U.S. land grant; founded sch. of mines and metallurgy, supervisor 3 yrs.; apptd., 1880. Délégué Correspondant Institution Ethnographique, Paris. Painted portraits of Lincoln, Sherman, Anderson at Sumter, judges of Ct. of Appeals, and Supreme Ct. of U.S. and cabinet secretaries, 4 portraits of Henry Ward Beecher, Dr. James McCosh, Bishop H. C. Potter, Burial of De Soto, etc. Author: The Archæology of the Missouri Valley (republished in many European transls.); Footprints of Vanished Races in the Mississippi Valley; My Acquaintance with Abraham Lincoln, etc. Died Feb. 3, 1915.

CONANT, C(arlos) Everett, philologist; b. Cabot, Vt., Nov. 27, 1870; s. Henry Clay and Medora (Reed) C.; A.B., Lawrence Coll., Wis., 1892, A.M., 1899; grad. student and instr. Greek, U. of Minn., 1892-93; Ph.D., U. of Chicago, 1911; m. Julie Laubmeyer, Feb. 1, 1908. Prof. langs., Chaddock Coll., Ill., 1893-94; asso. prof. Latin and German, Benzonia (Mich.) Coll., 1894-95; prof. Greek and Latin, Lincoln U., Ill., 1895-98; asst. in Latin and German, Kalamazoo (Mich.) Coll., 1898-99; instr. German and Spanish, Washburn Coll., Kan., 1900-01; supervising teacher, Bur. Edn., P.I., 1901-04; transl. N.T. (1st 5 books) into Bisaya (a Phil. lang.) for Am. Bible Soc., 1902-04, and of Luke's Gospel into Ibanag for the same soc., 1905; govt. translator and interpreter of Spanish and native langs., Manila, 1904-07; traveled Asia, Africa, and Europe, 1907-08; studied Univ. of Leipzig, winter semester, 1907-08; prof. modern langs., U. of Chattanooga, 1908-10 and 1912-21; asst. prof. Romance langs., Carleton Coll., Northfield, Minn., 1921-22; European travel and study, 1922-23. Fellow in Sanskrit and comparative philology, U. of Chicago, 1910-11, and lecturer in Indonesian philology, U. of Chicago, summer quarters, 1908, 10, 11 and 13; acting asso. prof. comparative philology (head dept.), Ind. U., 1911-12; prof. French, Tulane U., summer, 1917; prof. Spanish, Peabody Coll., Nashville, summers, 1919-21. Author: The Pepet Law in Philippine Languages, 1912. Home: Boston, Mass. Died Jan. 27, 1925.

CONANT, Charles Arthur, economist; b. Winchester, Mass., July 2, 1861; s. Charles E. and Marion (Wallace) C.; ed. grammar and high schs., supplemented by pvt. study; unmarried. Washington corr. Springfield Republican and other jours., 1889-1901; treas. Morton Trust Co., New York, 1902-06; dir. Manila R.R., Nat. Bank of Nicaragua, Credit Clearing House. Dem. candidate for Congress, Harvard U. Dist., 1894. Del. Gold Dem. Conv., 1896; spl. commr. War Dept. in Philippines, 1901; invited to Mexico, 1903, to aid in plans for monetary reform; mem. commn. on Internat. Exchange of U.S., 1903; mem. spl. com. of N.Y. Chamber of Commerce on currency reform, 1906, which reported in favor of a central bank. Tech. del. of U.S. to Internat. Conf. on Bills of Exchange, The Hague, 1910 and 1912; visited Nicaragua to prepare plan of monetary reform, winter of 1911-12. Author: A History of Modern Banks of Issue, 4th edit., 1909; The United States in the Orient, 1900; Alexander Hamilton, 1901; Wall Street and the Country, 1904; The Principles of Money and Banking (translated into French), 2 vols., 1905. Home: New York, N.Y. Died July 5, 1915.

CONANT, Charlotte Howard, educator; b. Greenfield, Mass., Feb. 3, 1862; d. Chester Cook and Sarah (Howard) C.; A.B., Wellesley, 1884; unmarried. Associated, 1893, with Florence Bigelow in establishing Walnut Hill Sch. (prep. sch. for girls), of which is prin. Episcopalian. Alumna trustee Wellesley Coll., 1918—. Mem. D.A.R. Home: Natick, Mass. Died Jan. 19, 1925.

CONANT, Frederick Odell, merchant, banker; b. Portland, Me., Oct. 1, 1857; s. Richard Odell and Emma (Loring) C.; desc. of Roger Conant; A.B., Bowdoin, 1880, A.M., 1883; m. Eva Merrill, 1883; children—Elizabeth M., Persis L. (Mrs. Hugh W. Babb), Richard O., Reginald O. Pres. Conant, Patrick & Co., York Utilities Co., Marine Hardware Equipment Co., Conant Corp., Fidelity Trust Co. (exec. com.). Was formerly mem. Common Council and Bd. of Aldermen, Portland. Overseer Bowdoin Coll.; trustee North Yarmouth Acad., Portland Pub. Library. Mason. Author: History and Genealogy of the Conant Family, 1887. Home: Portland, Me. Died Aug. 6, 1928.

CONANT, Helen Peters Stevens, author; b. Methuen, Mass., Oct. 9, 1839; ed. by private tutors; spent two years in Europe studying languages and literature; m. Samuel Stillman Conant (dec.), late mng. editor Harper's Weekly. Author: The Butterfly Hunters; Primers of German and Spanish Literature (in Harper's School Classics). Home: Brooklyn, N.Y. Died 1899.

CONANT, Levi Leonard, mathematician; b. Littleton, Mass., Mar. 3, 1857; s. Levi and Annie W. (Mead) C.; A.B., Dartmouth, 1879, A.M., 1887; A.M., Ph.D., Syracuse, 1893; m. Laura M. Chamberlain, July 24, 1884 (died 1911); m. 2d, Emma B Fisher, June 19, 1912. In public school work, 1879-87; prof. mathematics, Dak. Sch. of Mines, 1887-90; post-grad. student mathematics, Clark U., 1890-91; prof. mathematics, Worcester Poly. Inst., 1891—, and acting pres., 1911-13. Mem. Worcester Bd. Edn. (chmn., 1909), Mass. State Bd. Edn., 1909-14. Republican. Author: The Number Concept—Its Origin and Development, 1894; Original Exercises in Plane and Solid Geometry, 1905; Plane and Spherical Trigonometry, 1909; Logarithmic and Trigonometric Tables, 1909. Editor Jour. of Worcester Poly. Inst., 1897-1905. Home: Worcester, Mass. Died Oct. 11, 1916.

CONANT, Thomas Oakes, editor; b. Hamilton, N.Y., Oct. 15, 1838; s. Thomas Jefferson and Hannah O'Brien (Chaplin) C.; ed. Collegiate Inst., Rochester, N.Y.; Brooklyn Poly. Inst.; (LL.D., Mercer U., Macon, Ga.); m. Martha Wilson, Jan. 29, 1862 (died 1907). Clk. U.S. Assay Office, New York, 1861-93; contbg. editor, 1872-93, asst. editor, 1893-94, editor-in-chief, 1895-12, cons. editor, Oct. 1, 1912—, The Examiner (Bapt. weekly), New York; pres. The Examiner Co., 1895-12. Mem. Press Com. Lake Mohonk Conf. Republican. Baptist. Home: New Brunswick, N.J. Died Feb. 1913.

CONATY, Thomas James, bishop; b. Ireland, Aug. 1, 1847; s. Patrick and Alice (Lynch) C.; Montreal Coll., 1863-67; grad. Coll. of the Holy Cross, 1869, Montreal Theol. Sch., 1872; (D.D., Georgetown U., 1889; J.C.D. and D.D., Laval U., Quebec, 1896); ordained R.C. ministry, 1872; pastor Church of the Sacred Heart, Worcester, Mass., 1880-97; selected by Am. Catholic bishops, trustees of univ., to succeed Bishop Keane as rector Catholic U., Washington, Oct. 22, 1896, and apptd. to position by Pope Leo XIII, Nov. 20, 1896, who also conferred upon him, June 19, 1897, the title of Domestic Prelate and nominated him Titular Bishop of Samos, Oct. 5, 1901; consecrated by Cardinal Gibbons, Baltimore, Nov. 24, 1901; apptd. to see of Monterey and Los Angeles, Cal., Mar. 27, 1903. Author: Bible Studies, for use in colleges and schools, 1898. Died Sept. 18, 1915.

CONBOY, Sara Agnes, labor advocate; b. Boston, Mass., Apr. 3, 1870; d. Michael and Sara (Mellyn) McLaughlin; ed. pub. schs.; m. Joseph P. Conboy (dec.). Elected sec.-treas. United Textile Workers of America, Oct. 1915; was one of 5 women selected by President Wilson, and only woman representing labor at President Wilson's conf., 1918; rep. A.F. of L. at British Trades Union Congress, Portsmouth, Eng., 1920; mem. exec. bd. Nat. Com. on Prisons and Prison Labor; chmn. advisory bd. vocational training in pub. schs., New York; one of the 4 women selected by President Harding for the unemployment conf., Washington, Sept. 1921; mem. N.Y. State Housing Commn., 1923. Democrat. Catholic. Home: Brooklyn, N.Y. Died Jan. 8, 1928.

CONDEE, Robert Asa, agriculturist; b. San Diego, Calif., Dec. 25, 1875; s. Asa and Eliza (Isaminger) C.; student of agr., U. of Calif.; m. Mae S. Newcomb; children—Newcomb, Gwendolyn M. Engaged in farming, southern Calif., 1892-96; clk. bd. of supervisors, Riverside Co., Calif., 1897-1900; hort. insp., Riverside County, 1901-02; agrl. adviser, 1903-13; supt. agr. and dir. edn., Calif. Jr. Republic, a farm sch. for problem boys, 14 to 18, Chino, Calif., 1914—; prin. Chino Vocational High Sch. Regent U. of Calif. Pres. Calif. state bd. agr., Calif. Agrl. Soc., Calif. State Fair; dir. Calif. State Chamber of Commerce; mem. agrl. com. Los Angeles Chamber of Commerce. Republican. Mason. Died Oct. 4, 1930.

CONDIT, Blackford, retired Presbyterian minister; b. Sullivan Co., Ind., Aug. 6, 1829; was taken by his parents to Terre Haute, Ind., when about 3 yrs. old; grad. Wabash Coll., 1854; Lane Theol. Sem., Cincinnati, 1857 (D.D., Marietta Coll., 1889). Licensed by presbytery of Cincinnati, 1856; ordained by presbytery of Erie, 1859; pastor Fulton St. Presbyn. Ch., Cincinnati, 1 yr.; studied in Union Theol. Sem., New York, and Andover (Mass.) Theol. Sem.; traveled 9 months in Europe; m. Sarah L. Mills, 1862. Pastor 2d Presbyn. Ch., Terre Haute, Ind., 1868-75; resigned because of failing health; trustee Wabash Coll., 1871-96; resigned; stated clerk Vincennes Presbytery, 1875-95; resigned. Author: History of the English Bible, 1882, 1896; Short Studies of Familiar Bible Texts, 1898; History of Early Terre Haute, 1900. Died 1903.

CONDICT, George Herbert, electrical engr.; b. Newark, N.J., Mar. 7, 1862; s. J. Elliot and Sarah (Johnson) C.; ed. schs. New York and Phila., and U. of Pa.; m. Anna Neill, Jan. 10, 1888; children—Elizabeth Richards, Margaret, Harold Vail. Entered employ Central Gas Light Co., San Francisco, 1882; built gas works in Calif. and Ore.; connected with Pacific Coast Electric Constrn. Co., 1884; Pacific Coast agt. Van Depoele Electric Co., 1885; visited Chicago and was asst. to Mr. Van Depoele in electric ry. and lighting experiments; installed Van Depoele's exhbn. trolley line, New Orleans Expn., 1885; afterward in electric constrn. in Calif.; invented improved controller, which has ben important factor in electric ry. development; was gen. mgr. Electric Car Co. of America; deevloped improved storage batteries and in 1894 built, at Merrill, Wis., 1st storage battery plant to be used as auxiliary to provide for fluctuations of ry. load; became chief engr. Electric Vehicle Co., 1897, and cons. engr. other automobile companies; v.p. and gen. mgr. Electro-Dynamic Co., 1903-06; now cons. electric and mech. engr. Mem. Common Council, Plainfield, N.J., 1917-20. Mem. com. of examiners Naval Cons. Bd., 1917-19; mem. tech. advisory com. War Claim Bd., War Dept., Washington, 1919-20. Home: Plainfield, N.J. Died Apr. 9, 1934.

CONDON, John Thomas, dean law sch; b. Port Gamble, Wash., Sept. 20, 1865; s. John Stephenson and Catherine C.; U. of Wash., 1875-79; LL.B., U. of Mich., 1891; LL.M., Northwestern U., 1892; m. Marion Uranah Clark, June 24, 1903. Asst. in charge of evidence, Northwestern U., 1891-92; returned to Seattle, Wash., 1892; prof. law and dean Sch. of Law, U. of Wash., 1899—, then dean of faculties. Democrat. Home: Seattle, Wash. Died Jan. 5, 1926.

CONDON, Randall Judson, supt. schs.; b. Friendship, Me., July 10, 1862; s. James and Hannah Y. (Oram) C.; A.B., Colby, 1886, A.M., 1901; Harvard Summer Sch., 1909, LL.D., Colby, 1913, U. of Cincinnati, 1925; m. Eliza Alice Sturtevant, Apr. 30, 1889; 1 dau., Katharine Eleanor. Prin. Richmond High Sch., 1886-89; mem. Me. Ho. of Rep., 1886-88; nominated for Senate, 1888; dist. supt. schs., Templeton, Mass., 1889-91; supt. schs., Everett, Mass., 1891-1902, Helena, Mont., 1902-10, Providence, R.I., 1910-12, Cincinnati, 1913-29. Sec. Mont. State Text-Book Commn., 1906-10. V.p. Nat. Congress of Parents and Teachers, 1926—; U.S. del. Internat. Ednl. Conf., The Hague, 1914; del. to Geneva conv., Internat. Ednl. Assn., 1929. Trustee Lincoln Memorial U., 1917-23; mem. Ohio State Bd. of Edn., 1918-21; trustee Colby Coll., 1925—; chmn. Americanization Com. (Cincinnati), 1916—. Mem. Cincinnati Chamber Commerce. Independent Democrat. Baptist. Author: Kindergarten Creed; Montana Supplement to Frye's Geography; also various ednl. monographs. Editor of Atlantic Readers, also of Atlantic Monthly Press, 1924-25. Home: Friendship, Me. Died Dec. 25, 1931.

CONE, Hutchinson, Ingham, naval officer; b. Brooklyn, Apr. 26, 1871; s. Daniel Newman and Annette (Ingham) C.; removed with parents in infancy to Fla.; grad. Fla. Agrl. Coll., 1889; grad. U.S. Naval Acad., 1894; m. Patty Selden, Oct. 16, 1900; children—Elizabeth, Hutchinson I.; m. 2d, Julia Mattes, Dec. 17, 1930. Commissioned asst. engr., May 23, 1896; jr. lt., July 1, 1899; lt., Feb. 9, 1902; lt. comdr., Jan. 1, 1908. Served on U.S.S. Baltimore during war with Spain; was in Manila Bay, May 1, 1898, and during war; comdr. torpedo boat Dale on trip from Hampton Roads to Manila, 1903; comdr. flotilla of torpedo boats on voyage from Hampton Roads to San Francisco, 1908; fleet engr. Atlantic Fleet, on trip around the world, June 1908-Mar. 1909; head Bur. Steam Engring. with rank of rear-admiral and engr.-in-chief, May 21, 1909; then exec. officer Utah; comdg. U.S.S. Dixie; marine supt. Panama Canal; in command U.S. Naval Aviation Forces, foreign service, Aug. 1917-Oct. 1918; wounded on bd. S.S. Leinster when she was sunk in the Irish Sea by a German submarine, Oct. 10, 1918; retired, July 11, 1922; served as v.p. and gen. mgr. U.S. Shipping Bd. Emergency Fleet Corpn. (resigned 1925); apptd. commr. U.S. Shipping Bd., 1928; now chmn. board Moore and McCormack Co., Inc. Distinguished Service Medal (U.S. Navy), Comdr. Order British Empire (mil. br.), Distinguished Service Order (British), Officer Legion of Honor (French), Order of St. Maurice and St. Lazarus (Italian). Episcopalian. Home: Washington, D.C. Died Feb. 12, 1941.

CONE, Orello, educator, author; b. Nov. 16, 1835; s. Daniel N. and Emily (Sadd) C.; ed. Woodstock and Cazenovia Acads., N.Y., and St. Paul's Coll., Mo. (D.D. Lombard U.); m. Miss M. N. Pepper, 1864. Taught in public schools; prof. Biblical langs. and lit., St. Lawrence U. (1865-80); pres. Buchtel Coll., O., 1880-96; prof. Bib. Theology St. Lawrence Univ., 1900—. Author: The Gospel and Its Earliest Interpretations, 1893. Editor: Internat. Handbooks of the New Testament, 4 vols., (author vol. 3), 1899-1901 P2. Home: Canton, N.Y. Died 1905.

CONGDON, Charles Harris, song leader, author; b. Nelson, Pa., Dec. 18, 1856; s. Benjamin D. and Sarah (Campbell) C.; grad. State Normal Coll., Mansfield, Pa., 1876; m. Anna R. McWilliams, Apr. 29, 1887. Teacher country schs., 1876-78; introduced music in pub. schs., Brainerd, Minn., 1884; dir. music, pub. schs., St. Paul, 1885-98; grouped 2,200 sch. children to represent the Stars and Stripes, at Nat. Encampment, G.A.R., St. Paul, 1896; moved to Chicago, 1898; originated with Robert Foresman and Eleanor Smith, system of teaching music to children in pub. schs., discarding the "scale-method" and substituting pure song material; official song-leader Progressive Party, and led singing at Progressive Conv. at Chicago, also at Roosevelt rallies, Madison Sq. Garden, New York; organized pageant at Jersey City, N.J., 1919, for Gen. War Fund. Unitarian. Author: Congdon Music Readers (series), 1908-23; (with Charles B. Gilbert) Congdon Pamphlet Readers, 1910. Home: Marshall's Creek, Pa. Died Mar. 23, 1928.

CONGDON, Charles Howard, newspaper pub.; b. Trumansburg, N.Y., Aug. 31, 1870; s. Rev. Noyes Banzett and Esther Elizabeth (King) C.; prep. edn., Genesee, Wesleyan Sem., Lima, N.Y., 1889-92; student Syracuse U., 1893-97; m. Martha E. Caldwell, Sept. 1, 1898. Pub. Geneva (N.Y.) Courier, 1900-04; v.p. Geneva Daily Times, 1904-07; pub. gen. mgr., sec. and treas. Watertown (N.Y.) Daily Times, 1908—. Pres. Jefferson County Tuberculosis Com., Chaumont Library. Republican. Presbyn. Mason. Died July 30, 1933.

CONGDON, Chester Adgate, lawyer; b. Rochester, N.Y., June 12, 1853; s. Sylvester L. and Laura J. (Adgate) C.; A.B., Syracuse U., 1875; m. Clara H. Bannister, Sept. 29, 1881. Admitted to N.Y. bar, 1877; removed to Minn., 1879; mem. Billson & Congdon, 1892—; v.p. Am. Exchange Nat. Bank. Asst. U.S. atty., Dist. of Minnesota, 1881-6; mem. Minn. Ho. of Rep., 1909-11. Republican. Home: Duluth, Minn. Died Nov. 21, 1916.

CONGDON, Edward Chester, mining; b. St. Paul, Minn., Mar. 1, 1885; s. Chester Adgate and Clara Hesperia (Bannister) C.; grad. Hill Sch., Pottstown, Pa., 1904; A.B., Yale, 1908; m. Dorothy House, May 5, 1920; children—Mary Mecracken, Stephen House, Thomas Edward. Began in father's office, Duluth, 1908, continuing in business there after the death of father, 1916; principally exploration and mine development; dir. First and Am. Nat. Bank of Duluth. Served as 2d lt., O.R.C., 1916-17; capt., inf., U.S.A., Camp Dodge, 1917. Dir. St. Luke's Hosp. Assn. of Duluth, Duluth Community Fund. Republican. Conglist. Home: Duluth, Minn. Died Nov. 27, 1940.

CONGDON, Joseph William, judge; b. New York, Nov. 26, 1844; s. George and Sarah A. (Wentz) C.; acad. edn. Binghamton, N.Y.; m. Kate De Forest Burlock, Jan. 3, 1867. From Feb. 1, 1886, engaged as mfr. silk products; formerly pres. Phœnix Silk Mfg. Co. (Paterson, N.J.), Adelaide Silk Mills (Allentown, Pa.), Tilt Silk Mills (Pottsville, Pa.). Was alderman, Paterson, N.J., 1879-83; pres. Railroad Commn. of N.J., 1907-08; asso. judge Ct. of Errors and Appeals of N.J., Mar. 1909—. Republican. Served in N.G. S.N.Y., lt. and capt. 22d Regt., and col. 22d Regt. Veteran Corps, New York; formerly maj. comdg. Paterson (N.J.) Light Guard, lt. col. comdg. 1st Battalion N.G.N.J.; commd. brig. gen. and insp. gen. N.G.N.J. Mason. Home: Paterson, N.J. Died May 1, 1914.

CONGER, Edwin Hurd, diplomatist; b. Knox County, Ill., March 7, 1843; grad. Lombard U., Galesburg, Ill., 1862; served in Civil War, 1862-65; became bvt. maj.; grad. Albany Law School, 1866; m. Sarah Pike, June 21, 1886; practiced law, Galesburg, Ill., 1866-68; from 1868 farmer, stockman and banker in Iowa; State treas. Iowa, 1882-85; mem. Congress, 1885-91; minister to Brazil, 1891-93; again apptd. minister to Brazil, 1897; transferred to China, 1898; was in Peking during Boxer Siege; conducted negotiations on part of U.S. after capture of Peking by allies. Was head of commn. which negotiated new commercial treaty with China, of Oct. 8, 1902. Apptd. ambassador to Mex., 1905; resigned, Aug., 1905. Mason. Home: Des Moines, Ia. Died 1907.

CONGER, Everett Lorentus, clergyman; b. Cherry Grove, Ill., Dec. 23, 1839; s. Lorentus Everett and Mary Willard (Hurd) C.; A.B., Lombard U., Galesburg, Ill., 1861, A.M., 1863; B.D., St. Lawrence U., Canton, N.Y., 1863; (D.D., Buchtel Coll., Akron, O., 1890); m. Harriet A. Drowne, Sept. 21, 1874. Ordained Universalist ministry, 1863; pastor Monroe, Wis., 1863-67, Taunton, Mass., 1867-72, Concord, N.H., 1872-80; financial agt. and prof. pastoral theology, Lombard U., 1880-87; pastor Pasadena, Calif., 1887-94, emeritus. Trustee Throop Poly. Inst. (now Throop Coll. of Tech.) from its foundation, 1890, now v.p. Sec. N.H. Univ. Conv., 1874-80; pres. Calif. Univ. Conv. for many yrs. Donor $1,000 oratorical prize, Throop Coll. Tech. on subject of Peace. Home: Pasadena, Calif. Died Nov. 17, 1914.

CONGER, John William, coll. pres.; b. Jackson, Tenn., Feb. 20, 1857; s. P. D. W. and E. J. C.; A.B., Southwestern Bapt. U., 1878, A.M., 1883 (LL.D., 1902); m. Tennie C. Hamilton, Oct. 9, 1884. Pres. Odd Fellows' Coll., 1880-83, Searcy Coll., 1883-85; organized, 1886; pres., 1886-1907, Ouachita Bapt. Coll.; pres. Union U., Jackson, Tenn., 1907-09, Central Coll., Conway, Ark., 1911-20 (emeritus). Pres. Ark. Bapt. State Conv. Home: Ft. Smith, Ark. Died Apr. 1924.

CONGER, Seymour Beach, newspaperman; b. Port Huron, Mich., Oct. 11, 1876; s. Clinton Barker and Cornelia Elvira (Smith) C.; A.B., U. of Mich., 1900, A.M., 1903; m. Lucile Bailey, Sept. 14, 1910; children—Seymour Beach, Kyril Bailey, Clinton B. Mem. staff Evening Press, Grand Rapids, Mich., 1899-1902; corr. Associated Press, 1903-19; at St. Petersburg, Russia, during revolution and Russo-Japanese War, 1904-10; dir. Berlin bur., Asso. Press, 1910-17. War corr. attached to German and Austro-Hungarian forces on all fields of the European war until rupture of relations with Germany; at Paris peace conf., 1919, covering for Asso. Press submission of German and Austrian treaties and signature of peace at Versailles. Foreign adviser to the War Trade Bd., Washington, during 1918; chief corr. Public Ledger, Phila., in Central and Eastern Europe, 1920-25; Feature writer Booth Newspapers, 1926-30; partner Keen, Conger & Knauth, 1931—. Pvt. 32d Mich. Inf., Spanish-Am. War; later 2d lt., 2d Regt., Mich. N.G. Episcopalian. Home: Ann Arbor, Mich. Died July 12, 1934.

CONGLETON, Jerome Taylor, banker; b. Newark, N.J., Aug. 25, 1876; s. Joseph Norton and Mary Isabel (Wade) C.; student New York Law Sch.; m. Jessie Oakley Tobin, Oct. 16, 1901; children—Richard J., Jerome Taylor. Admitted to N.J. bar, 1899; mem. Congleton, Stallman & Hoover, 1917—; pres. United States Trust Co. of Newark, 1933—. Alderman City of Newark, 1906-11, corp. counsel, 1917-28, mayor, 1928-33. Mem. Essex Co. Tax Bd., 1910-17. Republican. Methodist. Home: Newark, N.J. Died Dec. 10, 1936.

CONKLIN, Charles, clergyman; b. Nyack, N.Y., Feb. 10, 1855; s. John Nathaniel and Elizabeth (Storms) C.; ed. St. Lawrence U., Canton, N.Y., 1874-76, D.D., 1904; M.A., Lombard Coll., Galesburg, Ill., 1888; m. Lillian Hazen, Jan. 18, 1882 (died 1890); m. 2d, Florence Green Newcomb, May 3, 1892. Ordained Universalist ministry, 1876; pastor Mt. Vernon, N.Y., 1876-79, Troy, 1879-82, Chelsea, Mass., 1882-85, Ch. of the Redeemer, Chicago, 1885-91 (built new ch. edifice), Boston, Mass., 1891-93, Springfield, 1893-1902; supt. Universalist chs. in Mass. and sec. Mass. Universalist Conv., 1902-14; pastor Beacon Universalist Ch., Brookline, Mass., 1914-22, Universalist Ch., Canton, Mass, 1922—. Chmn. bd. of trustees Foxboro Home for Aged Universalists. Republican. Mason. Home: Canton, Mass. Deceased.

CONKLIN, Jennie Maria Drinkwater, author; b. (Drinkwater) Portland, Me., Apr. 14, 1841; ed. public schools there and at Greenleaf's Inst., Brooklyn; m. Rev. Nathaniel Conklin, Mar. 17, 1880. Author: Electa; Fifteen; Uncle Justice Seth's Will; The Fairfax Girls; Second Best; Set Free; Fourfold; Other Folk; Miss Prudence Cromwell; The Story of Hannah; Looking Seaward; Dorothy's Islands; Goldenrod Farm; Shar Burbank; Dolly French's Household, and others. Home: New Vernon, N.J. Died 1900.

CONKLIN, Roland Ray; b. Urbana, Ill., Feb. 1, 1858; s. Joseph Okell and Julia (Hunt) C.; grad. U. of Ill., 1880, M.Litt., 1891; m. Mary Macfadden, May 4, 1898 (died 1919). A founder of the Jarvis-Conklin Mortgage Trust Co., Kansas City, Mo.; v.p. North Am. Trust Co., New York, 1895-1900; resigned to devote attention to personal investments, and financial undertakings in Cuba; a founder, 1900, and dir. Nat. Bank of Cuba; pres. Jucaro & Moron Ry. Co., Havana Telephone Co.; v.p. Central Cuba Sugar Co.; pres. N.Y. Motorbus Co., Chicago Motorbus Co. Mem. Am. Mus. Natural History, Met. Mus. Art., Mo. Soc. of New York (pres. 1912-13). Home: Huntington, L.I., N.Y. Died Jan. 2, 1938.

CONKLIN, William Augustus, zoölogist; b. New York, Mar. 17, 1837; s. Benjamin and Netta (Adams) C.; ed. pub. schs.; D.V.S., Columbia Vet. College, 1884; Ph.D., Manhattan Coll., 1886. Connected with Central Park, New York, 1858-98, dir. zoöl. dept., 1865-98; engaged in importing wild animals, 1898—. Editor Journal of Comparative Medicine and Veterinary Archives, 1878-93. Home: New York, N.Y. Died June 17, 1913.

CONKLIN, William Judkins, physician; b. Sidney, O., Dec. 1, 1844; s. Dr. H. S. and Ann (Blake) C.; A.B., Ohio Wesleyan U., 1866, A.M., 1869; M.D., Ohio Med. Coll., Cincinnati, 1868; m. Miss Beckel, 1875. Phys. to Dayton Hosp. for Insane, 1869-71; prof. physiology, 1875-78, diseases of children, 1878-86, Starling Med. Coll., Columbus, O. Pres. Ohio State Med. Soc., 1890; pres. Dayton Pub. Library Mus., 1899—. Address: Dayton, O. Died Oct. 1916.

CONLEY, John Wesley, clergyman; b. nr. Cedar Rapids, Ia., Nov. 20, 1852; s. Lewis and Betsey (Hutchins) C.; A.B., State U. of Ia., 1877, A.M., 1880; B.D., U. of Chicago, 1881; (D.D., Des Moines U., 1896); m. Sarah Elizabeth Clyde, July 19, 1878. Ordained Baptist ministry, 1879; pastor First Ch., Joliet, Ill., 1881-89, First Ch., Oak Park, Ill., 1889-92; instr. Div. Sch., U. of Chicago, 1892-93; pastor First Ch., St. Paul, Minn., 1893-98, Oak Park, Ill., 1898-1902, Omaha, Neb., 1902-10, Fresno, Calif., 1910-15. Republican. Author: The Church at Libertyville, 1906; The Young Christian and the Early Church, 1908; History of Baptist Young People's Union of America, 1913. Home: Cannon Falls, Minn. Deceased.

CONLEY, William Gustavus, governor; b. Kingwood, W.Va., Jan. 8, 1866; s. Maj. William and Mary (Freeburn) C.; LL.B., W.Va. U., 1893, LL.D., 1929; m. Bertie Ison Martin, July 14, 1892; children—William G. (dec.), Marion (dec.), Lillian (Mrs. Vincent Legg), Donald Martin, James Stalnaker. Teacher, pub. schs., 1886-91; supt. schs., Preston Co., 1891-93; admitted to W.Va. bar, 1893, and began practice at Parsons; pros. atty., Tucker Co., 1896-1904; mem. city council, Parsons, 1897-99; mayor of Parsons, 1901-03; editor and part owner Parsons Advocate, 1896-1903; mem. city council, Kingwood, 1903-05, mayor of Kingwood, 1906-08; apptd. atty. gen., W.Va., 1908, to fill vacancy; elected to same office, 1908, for term 1909-13; mem. and v.-chmn. State Bd. of Edn., 1924-29; gov. of W.Va., for term 1929-33. Hon. mem. Nat. Council of U.S. Ednl. Assn. Asst. sec. Rep. Nat. Conv., 1896. Mem. advisory council U.S. Law Review. Republican. Methodist. Mason. Home: Charleston, W.Va. Died Oct. 21, 1940.

CONN, Granville Priest, surgeon; b. Hillsboro, N.H., Jan. 25, 1832; s. William and Sarah (Priest) C.; ed. Norwich U., 2 yrs. (hon. A.M., 1881); M.D., Dartmouth, 1856; m. Helen M. Sprague, May 25, 1858. Practiced in Vt., 1856-62; asst. surgeon 12th Vt. Vols., 1862-63; in practice at Concord, N.H., 1863—; city phys., Concord, 1872-76; mem. U.S. Bd. Pension Examiners, 1872-85; mem. N.H. Bd. R.R. Commrs., 1877-81; pres. N.H. State Bd. Health, 1881—; lecturer on hygiene, 1886-96, prof., 1896—, Dartmouth Coll.; surgeon B.&M. Ry., 1880—. Compiler and editor History of the New Hampshire Surgeons in the War of the Rebellion. Home: Concord, N.H. Died Mar. 24, 1916.

CONN, Harry L., lawyer; b. Van Wert, O., 1869; s. Perry C. and Sophronia (Saltzgaber) C.; ed. common, high schs., preparatory acad. and law course; m. Minnie Irene Balyeat, 1898. Admitted to Ohio bar, 1894; pros. atty. Van Wert County, 1903-08; commr. of insurance of Ohio, 1923; elected judge Ohio Supreme Court, 1924; then mem. Conn & Stroup, lawyers, Van Wert; chmn. bd. First Nat. Bank, Van Wert. Permanent chmn. bd. trustees The Marsh Foundation (charitable trust). Home: Van Wert, O. Died June 14, 1939.

CONN, Herbert William, biologist; b. Fitchburg, Mass., Jan. 10, 1859; s. Reuben Rice and Harriet E. (Harding) C.; A.B., Boston U., 1881, A.M.; Ph.D., Johns Hopkins, 1884; m. Julia M. Joel, Aug. 5, 1885. Instr. biology, 1884-86, asst. prof., 1886-88, prof., 1889—, Wesleyan U. Dir Cold Spring Harbor Biol. Lab., 1889-97; bacteriologist, Storrs Expt. Sta., 1890-1906; dir. lab. of Conn. State Bd. Health, 1905—; lecturer, Trinity Coll., 1887-89. Specialist on the bacteriology of dairy products. Author: The Story of the Living Machine, 1899; The Method of Evolution, 1900; An Elementary Physiology and Hygiene for Use in Schools, 1903; practical Dairy Bacteriology, 1907; Introductory Physiology and Hygiene (rev. edit.), 1908; Biology (an introd. study for use in colls.), 1912; Elementary Physiology and Hygiene (for upper grammar grades), 1913; Social Heredity and Social Evolution, 1914; Bacteria, Yeasts, and Molds in the Home, 1917; Physiology and Health (rev. edit.), 1924. Home: Middletown, Conn. Died Apr. 18, 1917.

CONN, Ulysses Sylvester, educator; b. Middletown, Ind., Mar. 16, 1865; s. Charles L. and Mary (Jones) C.; student Nat. Normal U., Lebanon, O.; A.B., Valparaiso (Ind.) Univ., 1891, A.M., 1901; spl. student U. of Chicago; LL.D. from Neb. Wesleyan U., 1922; m. Cammie Baum, Aug. 23, 1893; 1 dau., Ardath. Began teaching at 19; prin. and supt. schs., Ind. and Ill.; supt. schs., Wayne, 1895-1901; in business Fargo, N.D., 1901-05; head Dept. of Mathematics, Fremont (Neb.) Coll., 1905-07; supt. schs., Columbus, 1907-10; pres. Wayne State Teachers Coll., Aug. 1910—. Republican. Mem. Christian (Disciples) Ch. Mason. Home: Wayne, Neb. Died Jan. 28, 1936.

CONNAH, Douglas John, artist, art educator, lecturer; b. N.Y. City, Apr. 20, 1871; s. John and Anna Maria (Dalhousie Duff) C.; ed. Royal Acad. (Weimar), Royal Acad. (Dusseldorf), Academie Julien (Paris); studied under Count Von Kaulkreuth, Baron von Gebhardt, Jules Lefebre, Benjamin Constant, Jean Paul Laurens and William Merritt Chase; m. Nora Leslie, of London, Eng., Oct. 1893; children—John Ferris, Douglas Duff, William Ludlow; m. 2d, Kay Hardy, Oct. 6, 1926. Dir. New York Sch. of Art, 1896-1911, Shinnecock Summer School of Art, 1897-1900, New Sch. of Design, 1911-24; co-dir. from 1925, N.Y. Sch. of Design (also called Am. Sch. of Design), chartered by Regents of the Univ. of State of New York; formerly dir. of summer schs. in Windsor Mountain, Vt., Essex, Mass., Wellfleet and Orleans, Cape Cod, and Deep River, Conn. Exhibited in Paris Salon, Royal Acad., Nat. Acad. Design, World's Fair (Chicago). Home: Essex, Conn., and New York, N.Y. Died Aug. 23, 1941.

CONNELL, Charles R., congressman; b. Scranton, Pa., Sept. 22, 1864; s. Hon. William and Annie (Lawrence) C.; ed. Williston Acad., Easthampton, Mass.; m. Elizabeth R. Shafer, Sept. 26, 1889. Pres. Lackawanna Mills, Scranton Button Co.; v.p. Third Nat. Bank, Scranton; dir. South Side State Bank, Scranton; mem. 67th Congress (1921-23), 10th Pa. Dist. Republican. Home: Scranton, Pa. Died Sept. 26, 1922.

CONNELL, Horatio, bass-baritone; b. Phila., Pa., Mar. 15, 1876; s. Horatio Pennock and Anne (Laylock) C.; ed. pvt. and pub. schs., Phila.; studied voice with Julius Stockhausen, of Frankfort-on-the-Main, Germany, 1900-04; m. Blanche Dobbins, Sept. 18, 1901. Began professionally as lieder singer in Germany; various tours in England, 1904-09; returned to U.S., 1909; concert and oratorio singer; has appeared at Worcester (Mass.) Festival, Chicago North Shore Festival, Ann Arbor (Mich.) Festival, Bach Festival (Bethlehem, Pa.), and as soloist with New York, Phila. and Minneapolis symphony orchestras, Chicago Apollo Club, etc.; head of vocal dept. Chautauqua Instn., summer session, 1916—; mem. voca faculty, Juilliard Grad. Sch., New York, dept. of relief for deserving musicians, Theodore Presser Foundation. Republican. Unitarian. Author: Master Vocal Exercises. Home: Philadelphia, Pa. Died Nov. 16, 1936.

CONNELL, Karl, surgeon; b. Omaha, Neb.; s. William J. and Mattie (Chadwick) C.; M.D., Coll. Physicians and Surgeons, Columbia, 1900; m. Frank Hovey-Roof, Sept. 28, 1922; children—Barbara, Karl, Francis Chadwick. Aso. in surgery, Columbia, 1910-14; asst. attending surgeon Roosevelt Hosp., New York, 1908-19; prof. of surgery, Creighton U., 1919-24; pres. Connell Apparatus, 1930—. Served as maj. Med. Corps, N.G., 1907-17; mil. surgery, France, 1914; observer in Germany and Austria, 1915; mem. Med. Council of Nat. Defense, 1916-17; Mexican Border Service, 1917; maj. Chem. Warfare Service, U.S. Army, with A.E.F., 1917-19; cited for meritorius service; decorated D.S.M. (U.S.). Pres. Presbyn. Hosp., Omaha, 1920-24. Fellow Am. Coll. Surgeons. Author: Surgical Therapeusis. Holds 10 patents on anesthetic apparatus, etc. Died Oct. 18, 1941.

CONNELL, Richard E., congressman; b. Poughkeepsie, N.Y., Nov. 16, 1857; s. Richard and Ann (Phelan) C.; ed. parochial and pub. schs.; m. Mary E. Miller, Nov. 12, 1890. Reporter, 1887, editor 1891—, Poughkeepsie News Press. Active in Dem. politics as speaker, 1884—; police commr., Poughkeepsie, 1892-94; Dem. nominee for Congress, 1896, for N.Y. Assembly, 1898-1900; inheritance tax appraiser, Dutchess Co., N.Y., 1907-09; mem. 62d Congress (1911-13), 21st N.Y. Dist. Del. Dem. Nat. Conv., Kansas City, 1900, St. Louis, 1904. Address: Poughkeepsie, N.Y. Died Oct. 30, 1912.

CONNELL, William, congressman, coal operator; b. Cape Breton, Nova Scotia, Sept. 10, 1827; self-ed.; taken in infancy by parents to what is now Hazleton, Pa.; worked in mines as driver boy; rose steadily; became mgr. of mines of Susquehanna & Wyoming Valley R.R. and Coal Co.; purchased the plant, 1870, and organized William Connell & Co.; pres. 3d Nat. Bank of Scranton. Mem. Pa. Rep. Com.; mem. Congress, 1897-1903, 1th Pa. dist. Republican. Home: Scranton, Pa. Died 1909.

CONNELL, William Lawrence, mine operator; b. suburb of Scranton, Pa., Oct. 14, 1862; s. James and Jessie English C.; ed. pub. and private schs.; m. Lillian Harrington, Jan. 13, 1886. Was mem. Hill & Connell, furniture dealers, Scranton; was organizer, 1891, and mgr. Enterprise Coal Co., later pres. and gen. mgr. Green Ridge Coal Co.; etc. Mayor of Scranton, 1893-96 and 1902-06; mem. Conciliation Bd., Pa., 1903— (apptd. under prov. of Anth. Coal Strike Commn.); mem. Mine Cave Commn. by apptmt. of Gov. Tener. Republican. Methodist. Mason. Home: Scranton, Pa. Died Dec. 9, 1923.

CONNELL, William Phillips, mcht., banker; b. Nashville, Tenn., Aug. 24, 1874; s. Allen Prince and Ella Knox (Phillips) C.; B.S., Vanderbilt U., 1896, M.S., 1897; spl. course in engring., same univ., 1898; m. Eleanor Garig, Jan. 21, 1903 (died 1905); m. 2d, Ernestine Lake, Jan. 4, 1919. In mercantile business, Baton Rouge, 1900—; pres. Baton Rouge Brick Yard, Baton Rouge Lumber Co., Baton Rouge Water Works Co.; was chmn. bd. and from Jan. 1918, active pres. La. Nat. Bank. Pres. Bd. of Pub. Works, Baton Rouge, 1904, sec., 1906. Democrat. Mason. Home: Baton Rouge, La. Died Feb. 14, 1932.

CONNELL, Wilson Edward, banker; b. Bell Co., Tex., Apr. 12, 1858; s. Wm. A. and Louise (Wills) C.; largely self-ed.; m. Hattie Millican, Jan. 30, 1881. Began as cashier with 1st Nat. Bank, Midland, Tex., 1890; with First Nat. Bank, Ft. Worth, Tex., 1898, later v.p., then pres., then chmn. bd.; v.p. Cicero Smith Lumber Co.; largely interested in cattle business. Republican. Baptist. Mason. Died May 5, 1936.

CONNELLEY, Clifford Brown; b. Monongahela City, Pa., Mar. 26, 1863; s. George and Elizabeth (Brown) C.; Teachers College (Columbia); Western U. of Pa.; hon. M.A., Sc.D., Duquesne U.; m. Katherine J. Seiferth Culp, Jan. 12, 1889; children—Ella, Katherine. Practical experience with Robinson & Rea, Westinghouse Elec. & Mfg. Co.; asst. to John Haliburton, engr., Phila.; instr. Mech. Dept. and supt. shops, Western U. of Pa.; prin. Fifth Ward Manual Training Sch., Allegheny, Pa.; organized industrial work for City of Allegheny and was cons. supervisor Pittsburgh Indsl. Schs.; dean Sch. of Applied Industries, Carnegie Inst. Tech.; sec.-treas. Marine Mfg. & Supply Co.; dir. Allegheny Carnegie Free Library. Mem. Bd. of Edn. and City Council, Pittsburgh; truste Duquesne U.; mem. Frick Ednl. Fund Commn.; pres. Fineview Bd. of Trade, Pittsburgh. Mem. Allegheny Co. Council Boy Scouts of America; chmn. of Selective Draft Bd., Allegheny Co. Republican. Methodist. Home: Schenley Park, Pittsburgh, Pa. Deceased.

CONNELLEY, William Elsey, author; b. Johnson Co., Ky., Mar. 15, 1855; s. Constantine and Rebecca J. (McCarty) C.; principally self-ed.; hon. A.M., Baker U., Kan., 1911; m. Julia F. Witten, Feb. 18, 1874; m. 2d, Sarah A. Fife, Jan. 13, 1885. Taught sch., Johnson Co., 1872-80, Wyandotte Co., Kan., 1881-82; co. clerk Wyandotte Co., 1883-87; in wholesale lumber business, Springfield, Mo., 1888-92; connected with banking interests, Kansas City, Kan., 1892. Wrote call for the first meeting of oil men in Kan., Jan. 1905, which resulted in organization of Kansas Oil Producers' Assn. and began the crusade against Standard Oil Co. which resulted in the dissolution of that corp. by the Supreme Court U.S. Republican. Mason. Author: The Provisional Government of Nebraska Territory, 1899; Quantrill and the Border Wars, 1909; Eastern Kentucky Papers, 1910; Life of Preston B. Plumb, 1913; History of Kansas (5 vols.), 1917; History of Kentucky (5 vols.), 1922; Indian Myths, 1928. Prepared only vocabulary ever written of Wyandot language and made extensive investigations in language and history of Delawares, Shawnees and other tribes. Has large collection of MS. relating to N.Am. Indians and hist. subjects relating to Ky. and the West. Died July 15, 1930.

CONNELLY, Celia Logan, author, playwright; b. (Logan) Phila., 1837; d. Cornelius Ambrosius and Eliza (Ackley) Logan (sister Olive Logan); childhood in Cincinnati; grad. at private academy. Early in life on the stage, but left it when she married M. K. Kellogg, Am. painter (dec.). Began literary career in London under tutelage of Charles Reade. After Civil War returned to U.S.; m. 1872, James H. Connelly (died 1903). Author: Her Strange Fate, 1891; Sarz, a Story of the Stage, 1891; An American Marriage (drama); Gaston Cadol, and other plays. Died 1904.

CONNELLY, James H., author; b. Pittsburgh, 1840; began newspaper work on Cincinnati Columbian, 1857; from then connnected with Pittsburgh Chronicle, San Francisco Chronicle, New York Sun, Chicago Tribune, etc. Was 1st lt. 145th N.Y. vols. in Civil War; m. Celia Logan, 1872. Author: My Casual Death. Died 1903.

CONNER, Benjamin Coulbourn, clergyman, educator; b. Marion, Md., Jan. 5, 1850; s. Nathan C. and Sallie (Coulbourn) C.; ed. Williamsport-Dickinson Sem., Pa., 1867-71; A.B., Wesleyan U., Conn., 1876, A.M., 1879 (D.D., 1911); Psi Upsilon, Phi Beta Kappa; m. Bettie S. Tyler, Aug. 16, 1877. Prof. natural sciences, Dickinson Sem., 1876-79; joined Central Pa. Conf., M.E. Ch., 1878; pastor, Sinnemahoning, 1880, Grace Ch., Williamsport, 1881-83, Ridge Av. Ch., Harrisburg, 1884-86, 1st Ch., York, 1887-91, Mulberry St. Ch., Williamsport, 1892-94, 1st Ch., Bloomsburg, 1895-99, Ridge Av. Ch., Harrisburg, 1900-02, 1st Ch., Altoona, 1903-05; supt. Altoona Dist., 1906-11; apptd. supt. Danville Dist., Mar. 1912; pres. Dickinson Sem., July, 1912—. Mem. Gen. Conf. M.E. Ch., Chicago, 1900, Baltimore, 1908, Minneapolis, 1912. Mem. bd. mgrs. Foreign Missions, 1900-12. Home: Williamsport, Pa. Died Aug. 18, 1921.

CONNER, Eli Taylor, mining engr.; b. Mauch Chunk, Pa., Mar. 1, 1864; s. William Isaac and Anna Elizabeth (Hawk) C.; ed. pub. schs. E. Mauch Chunk, 1870-79; m. Florence Isabel Towar, June 30, 1887 (died 1889); m. 2d, Caroline Yarnall Minshall, Sept. 21, 1893; children—Margaret Yarnall (Mrs. Henry H. Strater), Walter Leisenring, Caroline Minshall, Eli Taylor. Operator and asst. chief clk. C.R.R. of N.J., Mauch Chunk, 1879-82; rodman, chainman, transitman, engr. and asst. supt. Sandy Run, Pond Creek Harleigh Collieries of M. S. Kemmerer & Co., 1882-88; supt. Mt. Jessup (Pa.) Coal Co., Ltd., Florence Coal Co., Dupont, Pa., and Spring Brook Coal Co., Moosic, Pa., 1888-96; supt. Shamokin Div. Lehigh Valley Coal Co., 1896, Wyoming Div., 1897-1902; apptd. gen. supt. Webster Coal & Coke Co., 1902, merged with Pa. Coal & Coke Co. of which was gen. mgr. until 1907; gen. mgr. New River Collieries Co. of W.Va., 1907-09; cons. coal mining engr. in Phila., N.Y. City and Scranton, Pa., 1909—. Republican. Episcopalian. Home: Scranton, Pa. Died Jan. 3, 1938.

CONNER, James Keyes, civil engr.; b. Wabash, Ind., Apr. 12, 1871; s. Ovid Washington and Annie (Keyes) C.; ed. pub. schs. and Rose Poly. Inst.; m. Winifred Lamport, June 24, 1896. Asst. engr. and supvr. of track, C.C.C. & St. L. Ry. Co., 1895-99; asst. engr., B. & O. R.R., 1899-1900; asst. engr., designer and engr. N.Y.C. Lines, 1900-06; 1st asst., engr., 1906-14, chief engr., Feb. 10, 1914—. L.E. & W. R.R. Co. Republican. Presbyn. Home: Indianapolis, Indiana. Died May 18, 1925.

CONNER, Phineas Sanborn, M.D.; b. West Chester, Pa., Aug. 23, 1839; grad. Dartmouth, 1859 (LL.D., 1884); Jefferson Med. Coll., March 8, 1861; asst. surgeon U.S.A., 1862-66, retiring as bvt. maj.; from then in practice in Cincinnati; m. Julia E. Johnston, Dec. 17, 1873. Prof. surgery Med. Coll. of Ohio, and in Dartmouth Coll.; mem. President's commn. to investigate War Dept., 1898. Home: Cincinnati, O. Died 1909.

CONNERS, William James, newspaper pub.; b. Buffalo, N.Y., Jan. 3, 1857; common sch. edn. until 13, when started to work on steamboat. Freight contractor, 1885—; in asphalt and stone paving business, 1888; propr. Buffalo Enquirer, Dec. 1895—, Buffalo Courier, May 1897—. Built yacht Enquirer, which held record for greatest speed on fresh water, tendered it to U.S. Govt., which accepted it, spring of 1898. Chmn. Dem. State Com., 1906-10; chmn. Perry Centennial State Com., 1912-13. Commodore Buffalo Motor Boat Club, 1912-13. Organized the Great Lakes Transit Corp., 1916, and bought all the ry. operated steamships on the Great Lakes, comprising 3 passenger vessels and 21 freighters, total gross tonnage 95,190, chmn. of board. Tendered high speed steam yacht, Mary Alice, 1916, to U.S. govt., which accepted it; volunteered for U.S. service at Am. terminals in France, 1917. Bought, 1918, and reclaimed 7,000 acres of the Everglades in Fla.; tract now cultivated in sugar cane and fruit; leased, Nov. 1921, New York Central car repair shops, located at East Buffalo, now called the Wm. J. Conners Car Shops; built, 1924, the Conners Highway, a length of 51 miles, through the Fla. Everglades, affording a cross-state route from the Atlantic to the Gulf; established the Conners Foundation, July 1925, with fund of $1,000,000, for relief of the poor in City of Buffalo. Home: Buffalo, N.Y. Died Oct. 5, 1929.

CONNERY, Lawrence J(oseph), congressman; b. Lynn, Mass., Oct. 17, 1895; s. William Patrick and Mary Theresa (Haven) C.; ed. Lynn High Sch., St. Mary's (Kan.) Coll., Georgetown U. Sch. of Law; m. Geneva Mildred Butler, June 24, 1936. Sec. to the late Congressman William P. Connery, Jr. (brother), 1923-37; elected to fill unexpired term of his brother William P. Connery to 75th Congress on Sept. 28, 1937; elected to 76th Congress (1939-41), 7th Mass. Dist. Served as private to sergt., 9th Mass. Inf., on Mexican border, 1916; served with 101st Inf., 26th Div., U.S. Army, 1917-19; with A.E.F., 19 months, in all major engagements. Democrat. Home: Lynn, Mass. Died Oct. 19, 1941.

CONNERY, William Patrick, Jr., congressman; b. Lynn, Mass., Aug. 24, 1888; s. William P. and Mary T. (Haven) C.; student Montreal (Can.) Coll., 1902-04, Holy Cross Coll., Worcester, Mass., 1904-08, hon. M.A., 1925; m. Marie Antoinette Manseau, May 7, 1912; I dau., Marie Therese. Actor with Bush Temple Stock Co., Chicago, 1909; with George M. Cohan, musical and dramatic productions, Margaret Anglin, Irene Franklin; later candy mfr., Lynn. Mem. 68th to 74th Congresses (1923-37), 7th Mass. Dist.; reëlected to 71st Congress on both Republican and Democratic tickets. Enlisted in 101st Inf., U.S.A., Aug. 23, 1917; served 19 mos. with A.E.F. in France; promoted regtl. color sergt., Sept. 25, 1918; hon. disch. Apr. 28, 1919. Admitted to bar of D.C., Oct. 1934. Democrat. Home: Lynn, Mass. Died June 15, 1937.

CONNESS, John, U.S. senator; b. Ireland, Sept. 22, 1821; s. Walter and Mary (Williams) C.; came to U.S. at age of 13; ed. in New York; m. Mary Russell Davis, 1869. Learned trade of piano-maker; worked in New York; went to Calif., 1849; was miner and mcht.; mem. Calif. legislature, 1853-4 and 1860-61; candidate for lt. gov., 1859; Union Dem. candidate for gov., 1861; U.S. senator from Calif. as Union Republican, 1863-69. Later removed to Mass., and engaged in farming pursuits. Home: Mattapan, Mass. Died 1909.

CONNOLLY, Christopher Powell, writer; b. Wappingers Falls, N.Y., Dec. 23, 1863; s. James and Jane (Mackay) C.; self-ed. except 2 yrs. in primary sch.; m. Mary Ellen Fallon, June 6, 1888; children—Mary Alice, Lillian Kathryn, Helen, Walter James. Wrote "Story of Montana," which ran 8 mos. in McClure's Mag., 1906-07; "Big Business and the Bench," 6 mos. in Everybody's Mag., 1912, etc. Admitted to bar, N.Y., N.J. and Mont., and pros. atty. Butte, 1897-99 and 1899-1901; practiced at Newark, N.J., 1901—. Republican. Home: East Orange, N.J. Died Nov. 8, 1933.

CONNOLLY, James Austin, congressman; b. Newark, N.J., Mar. 8, 1843; s. William and Margaret (Maguire) C.; acad. edn.; m. Mary Dunn, Feb. 9, 1862. Admitted to bar, 1861; pvt. to maj. and bvtd. lt. col., 123d Ill. Vols., 1862-65; mem. Ill. Ho. of Rep., 1873-75; U.S. atty., Southern Dist., Ill., 1876-85, 1889-93; apptd. solicitor of the treasury by President Arthur, and confirmed by Senate, but declined; mem. 54th and 55th Congresses (1895-99), 17th Ill. Dist. Republican. Comdr. Ill. Dept. G.A.R., 1910-11. Home: Springfield, Ill. Died Dec. 15, 1914.

CONNOLLY, Maurice, congressman; b. Dubuque, Ia., 1877; s. Thomas and Ellen (Brown) C.; A.B., Cornell U., 1897; LL.B., cum laude, New York U., 1898; post-grad. work Balliol Coll., Oxford, Eng., and U. of Heidelberg, Germany; unmarried. Pres. Connolly Mfg. Co., Dubuque, 1904—; v.p. Dubuque Fire & Marine Ins. Co., etc.; mem. 63d Congress (1913-15), 3d Ia., Dist.; Dem. primary nominee for U.S. senator, June, 1914; chmn. Ia. State Dem. Convention, 1914. Regent and mem. exec. com. Smithsonian Instn. Commd. capt. Aviation Sect. Signal Corps, July 5, 1917. Adj. Aviation Sch., Rantoul, Ill.; promoted to maj., Aviation Sect. Signal Corps U.S.A., Oct. 23, 1917; exec. officer temporarily in command Wilbur Wright Aviation Sch., Fairfield, O.; reserve mil. aviator, 1918; flew for Liberty Loans; chief corr. br., Dept. Mil. Aeronautics,

Washington; recruiting officer, Hazelhurst Aviation Field, L.I., 1919. Internat. Pilot's License. Home: Dubuque, Ia. Died May 29, 1921.

CONNOLLY, Michael William, editor; b. L'Isle des Allumette, Can., Mar. 2, 1853; acad. edn. at Montreal; worked in Tex., 1874-87; in Memphis, 1888—. Was editor Memphis Commercial-Appeal and News-Scimitar; now editorial writer on News Scimitar and editor of Elkdom, Memphis. Home: Memphis, Tenn. Deceased.

CONNOR, George L.; b. Brooklyn, Aug. 23, 1846. Entered transportation service Aug., 1868, as clerk in treasurer's office Narragansett Steamship Co.; auditor pass. and frt. receipts, Apr. 1873-Mar. 1874; gen. pass. agt. same co., Mar.-June, 1874; gen. pass. agt. Old Colony Steamboat Co. (Fall River Line), 1874-94; also gen. pass. and ticket agt. Old Colony R.R., 1887-93; pass. traffic mgr. N.Y., N.H. & H. R.R., 1893-1908; retired. Home: New York, N.Y. Died Sept. 3, 1921.

CONNOR, George Whitfield, judge; b. Wilson, N.C., Oct. 24, 1872; s. Judge Henry Groves and Kate (Whitfield) C.; A.B., U. of North Carolina, 1892, LL.D., 1928; m. Bessie, d. J. C. Hadley, of Wilson, N.C., May 30, 1894; children—John Hadley (dec.), Henry Groves (dec.), Mary Hadley (Mrs. Thomas H. Leath), Elizabeth Goodman (Mrs. J. W. Harrelson). Prin. Goldsboro (N.C.) High Sch., 1892-94; supt. pub. schs., Wilson, 1894-97; in mercantile business as J. C. Hadley & Co. and Hadley, Harriss & Co., Wilson, N.C., 1897-1912; began law practice, 1899. Chmn. Bd. of Edn., Wilson Co., N.C., 1899-1908; mem. N.C. Ho. of Rep., 1909, 11, 13 (speaker of House, 1913); mem. Commn. on Constl. Amendments, N.C., 1913; judge Superior Courts, 2d Dist, term 1913-24; asso. justice Supreme Court of N.C., 1924—. Chmn. Commn. for Improvement of Laws of N.C., 1931. Lecturer in Law School, University of N.C. Trustee Univ. of N.C., 1905-09. Democrat. Episcopalian. Home: Raleigh, N.C. Died Apr. 23, 1938.

CONNOR, Henry Groves, judge; b. Wilmington, N.C., July 3, 1852; s. David and Mary C. (Groves) C.; ed. in town schs., Wilson, N.C.; (LL.D., U. of North Carolina, 1908); m. Kate Whitfield. Practiced at Wilson, N.C., 1873-85 and 1893-1903; mem. N.C. Senate, 1885; judge Superior Ct., 1885-93; mem. Ho. of Rep., 1899 (speaker) and 1901; asso. justice Supreme Court of N.C., 1903-09; apptd. U.S. dist. judge, Eastern Dist. of N.C., June 1, 1909. Democrat. Episcopalian. Home: Wilson, N.C. Died Nov. 23, 1924.

CONNOR, Leartus, ophthalmologist; b. Coldenham, N.Y., Jan. 29, 1843; s. Hezekiah and Caroline (Corwin) C.; A.B., Williams Coll., 1865, A.M., 1868; M.D., Coll. Phys. and Surg. (Columbia), 1870; m. Anna A. Dame, Aug. 10, 1870. In practice, Detroit, 1871—; lecturer on chemistry, 1871-72, prof. physiology and clin. medicine, 1872-79, prof. didactic and clin. ophthalmology and otology, 1878-81, sec., 1875-81, Detroit Med. Coll.; attending phys., St. Mary's Hosp., 1872-78; ophthalmic and aural surgeon, Harper Hosp., 1881-1906, Children's Hosp., 1887-1909. Home: Detroit, Mich. Died 1911.

CONNOR, Ray, M.D.; b. Detroit, Mich., Nov. 1, 1876; s. Leartus (M.D.) and Anna Amelia (Dame) C.; A.B., Williams, 1897; M.D., Johns Hopkins, 1901; unmarried. Asst. and house surgeon, Manhattan Eye and Ear Hosp., New York, 1901-03; practiced in Detroit, 1903—, as aurist and oculist; formerly asst. clin. prof. ophthalmology, Detroit Coll. Medicine and Surgery; staff Providence Hosp., Children's Free Hosp. Commd. capt. Med. O.R.C., Aug. 1, 1917. Fellow Am. Coll. Surgeons, Am. Acad. Medicine. Republican. Presbyn. Home: Detroit, Mich. Died Apr. 20, 1933.

CONNOR, Selden, soldier, pension agent; b. Fairfield, Me., Jan. 25, 1839; s. William and Mary C.; A.B., Tufts Coll., 1859 (LL.D., 1876); m. Henrietta W. Bailey, Oct. 20, 1869. Pvt. 1st Vt. Inf., May 2-Aug. 15, 1861; lt. col. 7th Me. Inf., Aug. 22, 1861; col. 19th Me. Inf., Jan. 11, 1864; brig. gen. vols. June 11, 1864; wounded in battle of the Wilderness, 1864; hon. mustered out Apr. 7, 1866. Assessor of Internal Revenue, 1869; gov. of Me., 3 terms, 1876-78; U.S. pension agt., 1882-86, and again, 1897-1914. Republican. Home: Augusta, Me. Died July 9, 1917.

CONNOR, Washington Everett, financier; b. New York, Dec. 15, 1849; ed. pub. sch., 1 yr. in Free Acad. (now Coll. City of N.Y.). Clerk in banking house of H. C. Stimson & Co.; mem. N.Y. Stock Exchange, Oct. 6, 1871; established as broker; formed partnership with late Jay Gould, 1881, firm being W. E. Connor & Co., and George J. Gould became a mem. on attaining his majority. Mr. Gould retired from Wall street, 1886, Mr. Connor following in 1887. Died Feb. 23, 1935.

CONNOR, William Ott, banker; b. Hamburg, Tenn., Oct. 8, 1852; s. William David and Julia C. (Hines) C.; ed. grammar sch.; m. Hattie Crowdus; 1 son, Eugene C.; m. 2d, Lula Mays, d. of Enoch Grigsby Mays, of S.C., June 8, 1882; children—Mrs. Dorothy Austin, Brevard Mays. Gen. mgr. Sanger Bros., dept. store, Dallas, 1877-1920; founder Republic Nat. Bank and pres., 1920, then chmn. bd.; also officer or director other cos. First mayor of Highland Park; one of first members Park Bd., City of Dallas. Treas. Near East Relief Funds. Republican. Episcopalian. Mason. Home: Highland Park, Tex. Died Feb. 5, 1934.

CONOVER, Adams Jewett, banker; b. Dayton, O., Jan. 12, 1850; s. Peter Post and Mary E. (Dolley) C.; ed. pub. schs., Dayton; m. Anna E. Hendrickson, Sept. 19, 1872. Clerk in Post Office, Dayton, 2 yrs.; then in coal business, title of Conover Bros., later Conover & Hayden; identified with Gem City Stove Co., 1885—, was sec. and treas.; founder, and first pres. Dayton Savings & Trust Co., later chmn. bd. Methodist. Wrote: (brochures) A Glimpse of the Millennium, 1903; The Man Higher Up, 1910; Temperance, 1914; Economic Aspects, 1915; The Story of the Trust Companies, 1916. Home: Dayton, O. Died Oct. 1928.

CONOVER, Charles H., mcht.; b. Easton, Pa., July 12, 1847; removed with parents to Buffalo, N.Y., at age of 12; ed. pub. and high schs. Began in employ of Pratt & Co., hardware, Buffalo, 1863; removed to Chicago, 1871, and entered employ of Hibbard & Spencer (wholesale hardware) as buyer; upon incorp. of Hibbard, Spencer, Bartlett & Co., 1881, became dir. and sec., later gen. mgr., and, 1904, v.p.; dir. Nat. Bank of the Republic; v.p. Chicago Hist. Soc. Episcopalian. Home: Chicago, Ill. Died Nov. 4, 1915.

CONQUEST, Ida, actress; b. New York, June 1882; d. Alfred John and Elza Curpless Moriner; m. Cavalier Riccardo Bertelli, of Genoa, Italy, Oct. 23, 1911. Début as Constance in "The Transgressor," with Olga Nethersole, in Palmer's Theatre, New York, 1894; ingénue in Empire Stock Co., Empire Theatre, 1896; leading lady with John Drew in "Tyranny of Tears," "Second in Command" and "Richard Carvel," 1902; leading lady with William Gillette in "Sherlock Holmes"; with Nat Goodwin as Helena in "Midsummer Night's Dream," 1903; starred under Charles Frohman, in "Girl with the Green Eyes," 1904; also leading lady with Richard Mansfield in "Old Heidelberg," "Ivan the Terrible," etc.; leading lady with William Collier, in "On the Quiet," London and New York, 1905; appeared as Ann Whitfield, in "Man and Superman," 1906, and later played in "The Wolf" and "Little Brother of the Rich"; appeared with Nazimova, as Asta, in "Little Eyolf," 1910; starred in "The Talker," 1911; retired from stage. Home: Elmsford, N.Y. Died July 12, 1937.

CONRAD, Arcturus Z., clergyman; b. Shiloh, Ind., Nov. 26, 1855; s. Jacob E. and Margaret E. (Slagle) C.; A.B., Carleton Coll., 1882, A.M., 1885, D.D., 1891; grad. Union Theol. Sem., 1885; Ph.D., New York U., 1891; m. Harriett N. Adams, Aug. 26, 1885; m. 2d, Jean Livingston, Nov. 9, 1932 (died 1937). Ordained Presbyn. ministry, 1885; pastor Ainslie St. Presbyn. Ch., Brooklyn, 1885-90, First Congl. Ch., Worcester, Mass., 1890-1902, Park St. Congl. Ch., Boston, Nov. 1905—. Summer preacher Carrs Lane, Birmingham, City Temple, London, Renfield St. Free Ch., Glasgow. Pres. N.E. Home for Deaf Mutes; pres. Lord's Day League. Author: Jesus Christ at the Crossroads, 1924; Comrades of the Carpenter, 1926; Seven Finalities of Faith, 1926. Home: Cambridge, Mass. Died Jan. 22, 1937.

CONRAD, Carl Nicholas, clergyman; b. Rochester, N.Y., Apr. 30, 1858; s. Nicholas and Mary (Rohr) C.; A.B., Muhlenberg Coll., Allentown, Pa., 1879, A.M., 1882; grad. Luth. Theol. Sem., Phila., 1882; Ph.D., Thiel Coll., Greenville, Pa., 1897; S.T.D., Harriman U., Tenn., 1900, D.D., 1901; m. Catharine A. Heech, Oct. 31, 1895 (died 1930); 1 son, Irving Carl (dec.). Ordained Evang. Luth. ministry, 1882; pastor Concordia Church, Rochester, N.Y., 1882—. Organized chs. in N.Y. at Brockport, Byron Centre, Bethlehem Ch., Rochester, Concordia Mission, Charlotte, West Henrietta, Kendall, and Ch. of Concord, Greece, N.Y. Editor The Hausfreund 25 yrs. Mem. Am. Acad. Polit. and Social Science, Nat. Probation Assn., Gideon Soc., Rochester Chamber Commerce, Chi Phi. Author: Erroneous Views of Our Life, Epicurean Philosophy; Gospel Truths; Conversation with God, 1901; Christian Narratives, 1901; Martin Luther, the Great Reformer; History of Lutheran Concordia Ch., 1877-1927. Died June 8, 1932.

CONRAD, Frank, elec. engr; b. Pittsburgh, Pa., May 4, 1874; s. Herbert M. and Sadie (Cassidy) C.; ed. pub. schs., Pittsburgh; hon. D.Sc., U. of Pittsburgh, 1928; m. Flora Selheimer, June 18, 1902; children—Francis H., Crawford J., Jane L. Began as bench-hand, Westinghouse Elec. & Mfg. Co., Pittsburgh, 1890; became gen. engr., 1914, asst. chief engr., 1921—. Early experimenter in radio, using phonograph records and local talent for broadcasting, 1919; exptl. programs developed into Station KDKA, first on the air, Nov. 2, 1920. Has patented over 200 inventions including round watt-hour electric meter, pantagraph trolley for electric trains, electric clock and devices for automobile starting, lighting and ignition. Served in U.S. Army during World War; then lt. comdr. U.S. Naval Reserve. Awarded Edison medal of Am. Inst. Elec. Engrs., 1931; John Scott medal of City of Phila., 1933; Morris Liebman prize by Inst. Radio Engrs., 1936; Lamme medal by Am. Inst. Elec. Engrs., 1936. Home: Wilkinsburg, Pa. Died Dec. 11, 1941.

CONRAD, Frowenus, abbot; b. Auw, Aargau, Switzerland, Nov. 2, 1833; s. Johann and Gertrude (King) C.; entered Order of St. Benedict at Engelberg, Switzerland, 1853; ordained priest, 1856; sent to America, 1873; founded New Engelberg, a monastery of his order, at Conception, Mo., which was erected into an abbey, called Conception Abbey, 1881. Father Conrad becoming its first abbot. Head of Swiss-Am. Congregation of Benedictines, 1898—; pres. Conception (Mo.) Classical Coll. Died Mar. 24, 1923.

CONRAD, Henry Clay, judge; b. Bridesburg, Pa., Apr. 25, 1852; s. Aaron and Sarah Walker (Pennypacker) C.; ed. Reynolds Classical Acad., Wilmington, Del.; LL.B., Harvard, 1873; m. Sarah J. Longaker, Feb. 20, 1884 (died 1899); children—Edith L. (wife of Dr. H. Croskey Allen), Rachel L. (Mrs. Walter T. Baker). Admitted to bar, 1874 and practiced at Wilmington; pres. bd. of edn., Wilmington, 1880-82; pres. city council, 1882-85; Rep. nominee for mayor, 1885; city solicitor, 1897-1901; postmaster, 1906-09; asso. judge Supreme Court of Del., term 1909-21. Republican. Methodist. Author: Thones Kunders and His Children (genealogy of the Conrad family), 1901. History of the State of Delaware, 3 vols., 1907. Home: Georgetown, Del. Died Oct. 24, 1930.

CONRAD, Stephen, author. See Stephen Conrad Stuntz.

CONRIED, Heinrich, theatrical mgr.; b. Bielitz, Silesia, Austria, Sept. 13, 1855; s. Joseph and Bertha C.; grad. Oberealschule, Vienna; A.M., U. of Pa.; m. Augusta Sperling, 1888. For yrs. engaged in management of theatrical and operatic cos.; then mgr. of Irving Place Theatre, and of Met. Opera House as successor to Maurice Grau. Received decoration, Order of Crown, from German Emperor; cross of knighthood of Franz Joseph Order, Austria; Order for Art and Science of Italy and Belgium; Order of Crown from King of Italy; Order of Knighthood from the Grand Duke of Meiningen. Hon. mem. bd. on Germanic langs. and lits. at Harvard and Vassar. Home: New York, N.Y. Died 1909.

CONROY, Joseph H. Ordained priest, R.C. Ch., June 11, 1881; consecrated bishop, May 1, 1912; succeeded to the See, Nov. 21, 1921; created asst. at Pontifical Throne, May 30, 1931; now bishop of Ogdensburg. Died Mar. 20, 1939.

CONRY, Michael Francis, congressman (Democrat); b. Shenandoah, Pa., Apr. 2, 1870; taught sch. 7 yrs.; LL.B., U. of Mich., 1896. Asst. corp. counsel, New York, 2 yrs.; mem. 61st to 64th Congresses (1909-17), 15th N.Y. Dist. Died Mar. 2, 1917.

CONSTANT, Samuel Victor, lawyer; b. New York, Sept. 9, 1857; A.B., Columbia, 1880, LL.B., 1888; m. Florence E., d. Capt. James Price, R.N.R., of Monmouth House, Waterloo, Eng., June 22, 1883. Admitted to bar, 1882; has traveled extensively; student of Oriental langs. and archeologist; mem. numerous socs.; prominent as chmn. of com. in movement for relief of Armenian Christians. Home: New York, N.Y. Died 1910.

CONVERSE, C(harles) Crozat, lawyer, composer; b. Warren, Mass., Oct. 7, 1832; s. Maxey Manning and Anne (Guthrie) C.; ed. U.S. and Germany; LL.B., Albany Law Sch., 1861; (LL.D., Rutherford Coll., N.C., 1895); m. Miss Eliza Jane Lewis, Jan. 14, 1858. Composer: Im Frühling, Am. and other overtures and symphonic works for full orchestra, used by Theodore Thomas, Anton Seidl and other orchestral directors; also much church and other music, including words and music of hymn "God For Us." Home: Highwood, N.J. Died Oct. 18, 1918.

CONVERSE, Costello C., mfr.; b. Jamaica Plain, Mass., Sept. 22, 1848; s. James W. and Emeline C. C.; ed. Chauncy Hall Sch., Boston; m. M. Ida Converse, Jan. 4, 1882. Pres. Grand Rapids Plaster Co., Boston; dir. many cos. Republican. Baptist. Home: Boston, Mass. Died Nov. 30, 1931.

CONVERSE, Edmund Cogswell, capitalist; b. Boston, Mass., Nov. 7, 1849; s. James C. and Sarah Ann (Peabody) C.; ed. Boston Latin Sch.; m. Jessie Macdonough Green, Jan. 2, 1879 (dec.); m. 2d, Mary Edith Dunshee, Jan. 30, 1914. Dir. Bankers' Trust Co., Fidelity Phenix Ins. Co., Internat. Nickel Co., Am. Bank Note Co., etc.; v.p. Texas and Pacific Coal Co. Home: Greenwich, Conn. Died Apr. 4, 1921.

CONVERSE, Francis Bartlett, clergyman, journalist; b. Richmond, Va., June 23, 1836; s. Rev. Dr. Amasa and Flavia (Booth) C.; ed. Phila. Central High Sch., Univ. of Pa. and Princeton Theol. Sem.; m. Ellen Pollard, 1866. Entered Presbyn. ministry, 1862; began editorial work on the Christian Observer, of which his father was editor, in 1857; has from then been its editor and publisher and head of Converse

& Co., its publishers. Home: Louisville, Ky. Died 1907.

CONVERSE, Frederick Shepherd, composer; b. Newton, Mass., Jan. 5, 1871; s. Edmund Winchester and Charlotte Augusta (Shepherd) C.; A.B., Harvard Univ., 1893; studied music at Kgl. Akademie der Tonkunst, Munich; hon. Mus.D., Boston U., 1933; m. Emma Cecil Tudor, June 6, 1894; children—Louise (Mrs. J. S. Morgan, Jr.), Augusta C. (Mrs. D. M. McElwain), Marie T. (Mrs. G. A. McCook), Virginia (Mrs. P. C. Cabot), Frederick (dec.), Elizabeth, Edmund W. (dec.). Instr. harmony, N.E. Conservatory of Music, 1899-1901; instr. music, 1901-04, asst. prof., 1904-07, Harvard; prof. theory and composition, N.E. Conservatory of Music, also dean faculty, 1931-38; v.p. Boston Opera Co., 1911-14. Capt. 13th Regt. Mass. N.G., 1918-19; mem. Nat. Com. in Charge Music in Training Camps, 1918-19. Mem. American Acad. of Arts and Letters. Composer: Op. 1, Sonata in A; Op. 2, Suite for Piano; Op. 9, Festival of Pan; Op. 11, Night and Day; Op. 12, La Belle Dame Sans Merci; Op. 14, Three Love Songs; Op. 17, Two Songs for Soprano Voice; Op. 18, Quartet in A minor; Op. 20, Two Songs for Low Voice; Op. 20, No. 2, Silent Noon; Op. 22, Laudate Dominum; The Mystic Trumpeter (a fantasy for orchestra); opera, The Pipe of Desire; oratorio, Job; opera, "The Sacrifice"; symphonic poem, "Ormazd"; opera, "The Immigrants"; cantata, "The Peace Pipe"; tone poem, "Ave atque Vale"; symphony, C minor; symphony, E major; photo music drama, "The Scarecrow"; "Fantasie" (for piano and orchestra); tone poem, "Song of the Sea"; "From the Hills" (piano); Elegy (orchestra); "Fantasy" (for orchestra); "Flivver Ten Million"; tone poem "California"; Trio for violin, violoncello and pianoforte; "The Pirate" (for male chorus); Concertino for Piano and Orchestra; Symphonic Suite for Orchestra—American Sketches; Two Songs for Soprano Voice, Harp and Flute; Tone Poem for Soprano Voice and Orchestra—Prophecy; String Quartet in E minor; Symphony in F major; Symphony No. VI in F minor; Rhapsody for Clarinet and Orchestra; Theme and Variations for Chamber Orchestra. Home: Westwood, Mass. Died June 8, 1940.

CONVERSE, George Albert, naval officer; b. Norwich, Vt., May 13, 1844; s. Shubael and Luvia (Morrill) C.; ed. Norwich pub. schs., 1852-58, Norwich U., 1858-61; grad. U.S. Naval Acad., 1865 (B.S., Norwich U.); m. Laura Shelby Blood, Dec. 1871. Served on steam sloop Canandaigua, European squadron, 1865-67; promoted ensign, Dec. 1, 1866; promoted through grades to rear adm., Nov. 8, 1904. In torpedo service, 1869-72; on Asiatic Sta., 1872-74; instr. Torpedo Sta., 1874-77; served in U.S.S. Marion, 1877-79, Lancaster, 1883-84; instr. Torpedo Sta., 1885-89; comdg. Enterprise, 1890-91; in Bureau of Ordnance, 1891-92; in charge Torpedo Sta., 1893-97; comd. U.S.S. Montgomery, cruiser, N. Atlantic squadron, 1897-99; in Bur. of Navigation, 1899-1901; comdg. battleship Illinois, 1901-03; chief Bur. of Equipment, 1903-04; chief Bur. of Ordnance, Mar. 15 to Aug. 1, 1904; chief Bur. of Navigation, Aug. 1, 1904—. Home: Norwich, Vt. Died 1909.

CONVERSE, Harriet Maxwell, author; b. Elmira, N.Y.; d. Thomas and Maria (Purdy) Maxwell; left motherless in infancy and went to live with aunt at Milan, O., where she was educated; m. Franklin Converse, 1861. Traveled in U.S. and Europe until 1866, contributing to press under pen-name of "Musidora" and "Salome." Formally adopted by Seneca Indians, 1884 (as her father and grandfather before her had been). Defender of rights of N.Y. Indians and worked hard to secure defeat of bill in N.Y. Legislature, 1891, aimed to deprive Indians of their lands; after its defeat was elected a mem. of Seneca Nat. Council and also installed as a chief of the Six Nations. Author: Sheaves (poems); Myths and Legends of the Iroquois Indians, 1903. Home: New York, N.Y. Died 1903.

CONVERSE, Harry E., rubber mfr.; b. Malden, Mass., 1863; s. Elisha Slade and Mary D. (Edmands) C.; pub. sch. edn.; m. Mary Caroline Parker, Dec. 2, 1891. Pres. Boston Rubber Shoe Co., Bay State Rubber Co.; dir. Am. and U.S. rubber cos., Rubber Mfrs. Mut. Insurance Co., etc. Home: Marion, Mass. Died Dec. 1920.

CONVERSE, James Booth, clergyman; b. Phila., Pa., Apr. 8, 1844; s. Rev. Dr. A. and Flavia (Booth) C.; A.B., Princeton, 1865, A.M., 1868; grad. Union Theol. Sem., Va., 1870; m. Queen Campbell, June 30, 1874; 2d, Eva Almeda Dulaney, Feb. 14, 1881. Ordained Presbyn. ministry, 1871; pastor Drummondtown, Va., 1869-71; editor Christian Observer, 1872-79; evangelist, 1879-81; pastor Blountville, Tenn., 1881-87; evangelist, 1888; editor Christian Patriot, 1890-95. Home: Morristown, Tenn. Died 1914.

CONVERSE, John Heman, locomotive builder; b. Burlington, Vt., Dec. 2, 1840; s. Rev. John Kendrick and Sarah (Allen) C.; A.B., U. of Vt., 1861 (LL.D., 1897); m. Elizabeth Perkins Thompson, July 9, 1873. Pres. Baldwin Locomotive Works, Phila.; dir. Phila. Nat. Bank, Franklin Nat. Bank, etc. Vice moderator Gen. Assembly, Presbyn. Ch., U.S., 1900. Trustee Princeton Theol. Sem. and U. of Vt. Home: Philadelphia, Pa. Died 1910.

CONVERSE, Marquis Mills, pres. Converse Rubber Shoe Co.; b. Lyme, N.H., Oct. 23, 1861; ed. pub. schs.; m. Alice H. Sargent, Oct. 23, 1884; children—Frieda, Harold, John, Ralph, Dorothy. Engaged in mfr. of shoes, 1887-1928; pres. Converse Rubber Shoe Co., 1908-28; retired. Dir. Eastern States Agrl. and Indsl. League, Mass. State Chamber Commerce. Republican. Conglist. Home: Andover, Mass. Died Feb. 9, 1931.

CONWAY, Edwin Stapleton, mfr.; b. Province of Ont., Can., 30 miles from Detroit, Mich., 1850; moved to Wis. at age of 7, and from there to Lake City, Minn., where he remained until 1868; ed. common schs. and at the Wesleyan Sem., West Eau Claire, Wis. Became connected with W. W. Kimball & Co., pianos, 1871, in charge of wholesale business of firm in Chicago, 1876-82, becoming sec., 1882-1905, v.p., 1905—. Republican. Baptist. Home: Oak Park, Ill. Died Nov. 4, 1919.

CONWAY, John Severinus, artist, sculptor; b. Dayton, O., Feb. 21, 1852; s. James Davies and Ellen Maria Louise (Brannon-Ghent) C.; ed. pub. schs., Chicago; pupil of Conrad Diehl, Chicago; student École des Arts Decoratifs and Académie des Beaux Arts, Paris, France; studied with Jules Lefebvre and Gustave Boulanger, painters, and Aimee Millet, sculptor, Paris; m. Agatha Milone, of Rome, Italy, Nov. 10, 1884. Exhibited at Soc. In Arte Libertas, Rome, Italy, and Soc. Am. Artists, New York. Prin. works: large mural painting in Chamber of Commerce, and Wis. Soldiers' Monument, Milwaukee; statue of Okla., at St. Louis Expn., 1893, etc. Democrat. Died Dec. 24, 1925.

CONWAY, Katherine Eleanor, editor; b. Rochester; d. James and Sarah Agatha C.; ed. acads. of the Sacred Heart, Rochester and New York, and St. Mary's Acad., Buffalo; unmarried. Editorial asst., 1883, asso. editor, 1890-1905, mng. editor, 1905-08, The Pilot; mng. editor The Republic, Boston, June 1908—; also adj. prof., St. Mary's Coll., Notre Dame, Ind., 1911-15. Awarded the Lætare Medal by U. of Notre Dame, 1907. Awarded the Papal decoration, "Pro Ecclesia et Pontifice," by Pope Pius X in 1912. Author: The Golden Year of the Good Shepherd in Boston, 1918; Fifty Years with Christ the Good Shepherd, 1925; The Color of Life (poem), 1926. Home: Boston, Mass. Died Jan. 2, 1927.

CONWAY, Moncure Daniel, author; b. Stafford Co., Va., March 17, 1832; grad. Dickinson Coll., Pa., 1849; Harvard Div. School, B.D., 1854 (M.A., Dickinson, 1853; L.H.D., same, 1892); m. Ellen Davis Dana (dec.). In 1849-50 studied law; in Meth. ministry 1850-52; became a Unitarian and, 1854-56, minister Unitarian Ch., Washington; 1856-61, Unitarian Ch., Cincinnati. Edited The Dial, Cincinnati, and later the Boston Commonwealth; wrote The Rejected Stone and many pamphlets and articles favoring emancipation of slaves; lectured in England and became, 1863-84, minister at South Pl. Chapel, London; on staff London Daily News, and Pall Mall Gazette. Author: Lives of Edmund Randolph, Thomas Paine (transl. into French), Hawthorne and Thomas Carlyle; Barons of the Potomack and Rappahannock; Emerson at Home and Abroad; Autobiography. Died 1907.

CONWAY, Patrick, band leader; b. nr. Troy, N.Y., July 4, 1867; s. Martin and Bridget (Dane) C.; ed. Homer (N.Y.) Acad., and Ithaca Conservatory of Music; m. Alice Randall, Dec. 28, 1893; children—Paul Randall (dec.), Mrs. Katherine White. Instr. Cornell U. Cadet Band, 1895-1908; organized Conway's Band, 1908, and from then its leader; founded Conway Mil. Band Sch., Ithaca, N.Y., 1922; has played many important seasonal engagements. Camp band instr., Camp MacArthur, Tex., Aug.-Dec. 1918; commd. capt. Aviation Sect., U.S. Army; mem. O.R.C. Democrat. Catholic. Home: Ithaca, N.Y. Died June 10, 1929.

CONWELL, Russell Herman, clergyman; b. Worthington, Mass., Feb. 15, 1843; s. Martin and Miranda C.; ed. Wilbraham Acad.; entered Yale, law dept., 1860; LL.B., Albany Law Sch., 1866; (D.D., Temple U., Phila., 1898, LL.D., 1900); m. Sarah F. Sanborn, 1874. Capt. to lt. col. U.S.V., 1862-65; admitted to bar, 1865; practiced at Minneapolis, 1865-67; immigration agt. State of Minn. to Germany, 1867-68; foreign corr. New York Tribune and Boston Traveler, 1869-71; practiced law at Boston, 1871-79; ordained Bapt. ministry at Lexington, Mass., 1879; pastor Grace Ch., Phila., 1881-91. The Bapt. Temple, 1891—; founded, 1888, and became pres. Temple U., Phila. Founded Garretson Hosp., and Samaritan Hosp. Lyceum lecturer from 1860. Author: Acres of Diamonds, 1888; Observation, 1916; What You Can Do With Your Will Power, 1917; Effective Prayer, 1920; The Angel's Lily, 1920; Sermons for Occasions, 1921; Unused Powers, 1922; Why Lincoln Laughed, 1922; Borrowed Axes, 1923. Home: Philadelphia, Pa. Died Dec. 6, 1925.

COOK, Albert John, naturalist; b. Owosso, Mich., Aug. 30, 1842; s. Ezekiel and Barbara Ann (Hodge) C.; B.S., Mich. Agrl. Coll., 1862, M.S., 1865 (D.Sc., 1905); studied at Harvard, 1867-88; m. Mary H. Baldwin, June 30, 1870; m. 2d, Mrs. Sarah J. Eldredge, July 3, 1897. Instr. mathematics, 1867-69, prof. zoölogy and entomology, 1868-93, curator Gen. Mus., 1875-93, entomologist Expt. Sta., 1888-91, Mich. Agrl. Coll.; prof. biology, Pomona Coll., Cal., 1893-1911; state commr. of horticulture Cal., Oct. 1911—. Conductor Univ. Extension work in agr., U. of Cal., 1894-1905. Author: Manual of the Apiary; Injurious Insects of Michigan; Silo and Silage; Maple Sugar and the Sugar Bush; Birds of Michigan; California Citrus Culture, 1913. Died Sept. 29, 1916.

COOK, Albert Stanburrough, univ. prof.; b. Montville, N.J., Mar. 6, 1853; s. Frederick Weissenfels and Sarah (Barmore) C.; B.S., Rutgers, 1872, M.S., 1875; student Göttingen, Leipzig, 1877-78, London, Jena, 1881-82; Ph.D., Jena, 1882; hon. M.A., Rutgers, 1882, Yale, 1889; L.H.D., 1889, LL.D., 1906, Rutgers; Litt.D., Princeton, 1918; m. Emily Chamberlain, June 1, 1886; children—Mildred Emily, Sidney Albert; m. 2d, Elizabeth Merrill, June 7, 1911. Tutor mathematics, Rutgers, 1872-73; teacher Freehold (N.J.) Inst., 1873-77; asso. in English (organized the dept.), Johns Hopkins, 1879-81; prof. English, U. of Calif., 1882-89; prof. English lang. and lit., Yale, 1889-1921 (emeritus). Sec. Nat. Conf. on entrance exams. in English, 1897-99; co-editor for English of Jour. of English and Germanic Philology, 1897-1905; founder of annual prizes in poetry at Yale (1897) and U. of Calif. (1909). Author: The Art of Poetry, 1892; First Book in Old English, 1894; The Authorized Version of the Bible and Its Influence, 1910; The Date of the Ruthwell and Bewcastle Crosses, 1912; Literary Middle English Reader, 1915; The Old English Elene, Phœnix, and Physiologus, 1919; The Possible Begetter of the Old English Beowulf and Widsith, 1922; The Old English Andreas and Bishop Acca of Hexham, 1924; Cynewulf's Part in our Beowulf, 1925. Then editor from 1898 of Yale Studies in English (70 vols.), and numerous selections from English lit. Died. Sept. 1, 1927.

COOK, Alfred Newton, chemist; b. Cornell, Ill., Feb. 22, 1866; s. Ira and Harriett Ann (DeVelbiss) C.; grad. Geneseo (Ill.) Normal Sch., 1886; B.S., Knox Coll., Galesburg, Ill., 1890; Ph.D., U. of Wis., 1900; m. Annie G. McClelland, July 10, 1894; children—Herbert Edward, Harold Lewis. Prof. natural sciences, Amity Coll., College Springs, Ia., 1892-94; prof. chemistry and physics, Upper Ia. U., 1894-98; asst. in chemistry, U. of Wis., 1898-1900; prof. chemistry, Morningside Coll., 1900-04; prof. chemistry, U. of S. Dak., 1904-20; prof. of chemistry, Occidental Coll., Los Angeles, 1924—. State food and drug commr., S. Dak, 1909-13. Republican. Conglist. Mason. Deceased.

COOK, Ansel Granville, surgeon; b. Glasgow, Scotland, Apr. 18, 1862; s. Capt. William and Harriet (Blish) C.; ed. Friends Acad., New Bedford, Mass., Pierce Acad., Middleboro; M.D., Coll. Phys. and Surg. (Columbia), 1887; Sc.D., Trinity Coll., Conn., 1926; m. Annah H. Richardson, June 30, 1891; children—Katherine Cary (Mrs. Alfred Ely Pulford, dec.), Ellenor Richardson, Harriet Huntington (Mrs. Bayard Carter). Practiced at Hartford, Conn., 1887—; was orthopedic surgeon, gen. surgeon, now cons. surgeon Hartford Hosp.; consulting surgeon Litchfield Co. Hosp. (Windsted, Conn.), Middlesex (Conn.) Hosp., Municipal Hosp. (Hartford). Capt. Med. R.C., 1917, and in charge of orthopedic surgery and instrn. in a group of Southern camps; at Ft. Sam Houston, Tex., Jan. 1918-Mar. 1919; commd. maj., M.C., U.S.A., June 1918; lt. col. M.R.C., U.S.A., Apr. 13, 1920. Fellow Am. Coll. Surg. Home: Hartford, Conn. Died Jan. 25, 1933.

COOK, Carroll Blaine ("Dixie Carroll"), author; b. Great Bend, Pa., Nov. 27, 1883; s. Calvin Benson and Clara May (Close) C.; ed. high sch. and under pvt. tutors; m. Rose Margaret Steble, Feb. 8, 1908. Reporter New York Sun, 1903-07; with Western Newspaper Union, 1909-21; fishing and out-doors editor Chicago Daily Herald, 1913-17, Chicago Daily News, 1918—; editor Nat. Sportsman Magazine, Boston, 1917—. Mem. New York Naval Reserves, 1903; mem. Gov. Lowden's Nat. Guard Commn. of Ill., 1917-20. Mem. Am. Anglers' League (pres. 1916-20). Mason. Author: Lake and Stream Game Fishing, 1917; Fishing, Tackle and Kits, 1919; Goin' Fishin', 1920. Has fished and hunted throughout U.S. and Canada. Home: Chicago, Ill. Died June 11, 1922.

COOK, Charles Alston, judge; b. Warrenton, N.C., Oct. 7, 1848; s. Rev. Charles Marshall and Havana Lenoir (Alston) C.; ed. U. of N.C., 1866-68; A.B., Princeton, 1870, A.M., 1873; (A.M., U. of N.C., 1881); m. Marina Williams Jones, Oct. 11, 1871. Solicitor Warren Co. Ct., 1878-80; Rep. nominee for atty. gen. N.C., 1884; state senator, 1886-88, 1894-96; U.S. atty., Eastern Dist. N.C., 1889-93; mem. N.C. Ho. of Rep., 1896-98; trustee U. of N.C., 1889-1901; asso. justice Supreme Ct., N.C., 1901-03; resumed practice at Muskogee, Okla. Mem. Okla. Ho. of Rep., 1908-10; nominee for justice Supreme Ct. of Okla., 1912; mem. State Bar Commn., 1911—. Republican. Has served capt. and col. State Guard of N.C.; brig. gen. on retired list. Home: Muskogee, Okla. Died Oct. 21, 1916.

COOK, Charles Augustus, clergyman; b. Lowville, Ont., Can., Aug. 3, 1856; s. of Robert B. and Sarah E. (Kelsey) Cook; Pastor's Coll., London, Eng.; spl. work Queen's U., Kingston, Ont.; (D.D., William Jewell Coll., Mo., 1907); m. Emma Matthews, July 6, 1880; children—Charles Montrose (dec.), Emma May (dec.), Cecil Albert, Luetta Sarah, Gordon LeRoy. Ordained Baptist ministry, 1879; pastor Kingston, Ont., 1879-83, Parliament St. Ch., Toronto, 1883-88, Bloomfield, N.J., 1888-1903; recording sec., N.J. Bapt. Conv., 6 yrs.; supt. Christian stewardship campaign in Northern states, 1903-09; joint dist. sec. Yellowstone dist., for Am. Bapt. Home and Foreign Missions soc., 1909-15; pastor Spokane, Wash., 1915-16, First Ch., Butte, Mont., 1916-21, Seattle, Wash., 1921-29, retired. Author: Stewardship, 1900; Stewardship and Missions, 1908; God's Will and Our Life, 1922; The Larger Stewardship, 1923; Money Power, 1933. Home: Seattle, Wash. Died Mar. 31. 1940.

COOK, Charles Sumner, lawyer, banker; b. Portland, Me., Nov. 18, 1858; s. Obadiah Gould and Christiana S. (Perry) C.; grad. Nichols Latin Sch., 1877; A.B., Bates Coll., 1881; married Miss Annie Jefferds Reed, Oct. 23, 1889; children—Lydia McDonald, Robinson. Prin. high sch., Waldoboro, Me., 1882-83; admitted to Me. bar, 1886, and began practice at Portland, with Symonds & Libby; now cons. counsel Cook, Hutchinson, Pierce & Connell; also chmn. bd. Nat. Bank of Commerce (Portland). Mem. bd. dirs. Nat. Traders Bank until 1906; organizer, 1906, Fidelity Trust Co., of which was successively dir., v.p., pres. and chmn. bd., company having absorbed Nat. Traders Bank, 1906, Portland Trust Co., 1910, U.S. Trust Co., 1926; elected, 1910, pres. Brunswick Electric Light & Power Co. and dir. Sagadahock Light & Power Co., merged as Bath & Brunswick Light & Power Co., of which was pres. until company was absorbed by Central Me. Power Co., 1915. Mem. Governor's Council, 1899-1905, chmn., 1901-02. Republican. Conglist. Home: Portland, Me. Died Feb. 9, 1939.

COOK, Charles T., merchant; b. New York, May 17, 1835; ed. pub. and pvt. schs. Entered service of Tiffany & Co., New York, 1847; asst. treas., 1868, v.p., 1875-1902; since death of Charles L. Tiffany, 1902, has been pres. Tiffany & Co. Officer Légion d' Honneur, France, 1900; decorated cross of royal order Crown of Italy, 1904. Home: New York, N.Y. Died 1907.

COOK, David C., editor, pub.; b. East Wooster, N.Y., Aug. 28, 1850; s. Ezra S. and Permilla (Milk) C.; m. Marguerite Murat, 1875; children—George E., David C. Editor and pub. S.S. publs., 1875—, growing to 43 separate titles, combined circulation exceeding 4,500,000; pres. David C. Cook Pub. Co. Home: Elgin, Ill. Died July 29, 1927.

COOK, Ermond Edson, editor; b. Dalton, O., Jan. 21, 1874; s. William Campbell and Ella (Fletcher) C.; ed. high sch., Dalton; m. Mary Elsie Eckard, July 21, 1897; children—Clare Eckard, Mary Eleanor, Helen Louise. Began as reporter on Columbus Press-Post, 1895; city editor, mng. editor and editor of Columbus Citizen; became editor in chief of Central Group (Ohio) of Scripps-Howard newspapers with headquarters in Cleveland, 1922; returned to Columbus, 1927, as editor in chief of same group newspapers which position he still holds and in addition is editor of The Citizen. Methodist. Republican. Mason. Home: Columbus, O. Died May 3, 1931.

COOK, Fayette Lamartine, educator; b. Ottawa Co., Mich., Aug. 22, 1850; s. Martin William and Mary Elizabeth (Barnes) C.; grad. State Normal Sch., Winona, Minn., 1866; took pvt. instrn. under Irwin Shepard and others; (LL.D., U. of S.Dak., 1915); m. Wenona Culbertson, Aug. 25, 1892. Taught country and village schs., 3 yrs., and in Minneapolis Commercial Coll. 1 yr.; supt. city schs., Sauk Centre, Minn., 1872-74; teacher State Normal Sch., Winona, 1877-79; co. supt. schs., Olmsted Co., 1882-84; pres. S.D. State Normal Sch., 1885-1919 (emeritus). Was state instr. in 38 teachers' insts. in Minn. Home: Spearfish, S.D. Died Sept. 17, 1922.

COOK, Francis Augustus, rear adm.; b. Northampton, Mass., May 10, 1843; s. Gen. Benjamin E. and Elizabeth Christine (Griffin) C.; apptd. from Mass. and grad. U.S. Naval Acad., 1863; m. Carrie Earle, Sept. 3, 1868. Promoted ensign, Oct. 1, 1863; advanced through grades to rear adm., Mar. 21, 1903. Served Seminole, W. Gulf Blockading Squadron, 1863-65; Vanderbilt, N. Pacific Squadron, 1865-67; N. Atlantic Squadron, 1867-68; Naval Acad., 1868-70; receiving ship Independence, 1870-71; Saranac, 1871-72; Richmond, 1872-74; receiving ship Sabine, 1874-76; Plymouth, 1876-79; Naval Acad., 1879-83; light house insp. 11th dist., 1883-86; comd. Ranger, 1886-89; insp. of ordnance, Boston, 1890-92; equipment officer, Navy Yard, Boston, 1892-93; asst. Bur. of Navigation, 1893-96; comd. Brooklyn, 1896-99; advanced 5 numbers in rank "for eminent and conspicuous conduct in battle," while in command of Brooklyn, at battle of Santiago de Cuba with Admiral Cevera's Squadron, July 3, 1898; mem. Naval Examining and Retiring Bd., 1899-1903; retired, Sept. 5, 1903. Home: Northampton, Mass. Died Oct. 8, 1916.

COOK, Frederick Albert, physician, explorer; b. Callicoon Depot, N.Y., June 10, 1865; s. Dr. Theodore Albert and Magdalene C. (the family name has been changed from Koch to Cook); ed. Brooklyn, 1878-85; Callicoon, N.Y., 1871-78; M.D., Univ. of New York, 1890; m. Mary Fidell Hunt, June 10, 1902. Decorations: Order of Leopold, Belgium; gold medal of Royal Soc., Belgium; silver medal, Royal Geog. Soc., Belgium; mem. Am., Nat. and Phila. Geog. socs., Kings Co. Med. Soc. Was surgeon of the Peary Arctic expdn., 1891-92; surgeon of the Belgium Antarctic expdn., 1897-99, led expdns. to explore and climb Mt. McKinley, 1903-06. Author: Through the First Antarctic Night, 1900; To the Top of the Continent, 1907. Home: Brooklyn, N.Y. Died Aug. 5, 1940.

COOK, George Brinton, state supt. instrn.; b. White Oak, Ky., May 31, 1868; s. Wylie and Delilah (Nickell) C.; ed. Central Coll., Fayette, Mo.; U. of Chicago; (LL.D., University of Arkansas, 1916); m. Greta Chambers, Apr. 7, 1899. Supt. schs. Hot Springs, Ark., 1890-1908; state supt. instrn. of Ark. several yrs. from 1908; then supt. Mena (Ark) city schs. Pres. trustees State Normal Sch.; trustee U. of Ark.; mem. Jury Awards, St. Louis Expn., 1904. Democrat. Mason. Home: Mena, Ark. Deceased.

COOK, George Cram, author; b. Davenport, Ia., Oct. 7, 1873; s. Edward Everett and Ellen Katherine (Dodge) C.; U. of Ia., 1889-92; A.B., Harvard, 1893; Heidelberg, 1894; U. of Geneva, 1895; m. Sara Herndon Swain, May 19, 1902; 2d, Mollie A. Price, Jan. 21, 1908; 3d, Susan Glaspell, Apr. 14, 1913. Taught in U. of Ia., 1895-99, Leland Stanford Jr. U., 1902-3. Asso. lit. editor, Chicago Evening Post, 1911. Author: In Hampton Roads (novel), 1899; Roderick Taliaferro, a Story of Maximilian's Empire, 1903; Evolution and the Superman, 1906; The Chasm (novel), 1911; Battle Hymn of the Workers, 1912; The C.T.U., 1914; Suppressed Desires (play), 1915, book, 1920; The Athenian Women (play), 1917; Tickless Time (play) prod., 1919, book, 1920; The Spring (play) prod., 1921, book, 1921. Dir. Provincetown Players, 1915—. Home: Provincetown, Mass. Died Jan. 14, 1924.

COOK, George Frederick, physician; b. Hamilton, O., Sept. 4, 1846; s. Robert W. and Susan (Devon) C.; ed. pub. schs., Eaton, O., and under pvt. tutelage; studied medicine under Drs. J. P. Brookins and A. H. Stephens, of Eaton, and Dr. Carter, of Holden, Mo.; M.D., Med. Coll. of Ohio, 1872; m. Sallie J. Pryor, Sept. 29, 1868 (died Apr. 23, 1874); 2d, Octavia Emma, d. Dr. R. E. Pryor, of Seven Mile, O., 1877; father of R(obert) Harvey C. Practiced in Somerville, O., 1872-86, at Oxford, 1886—; med. supt. Oxford Retreat (pvt. hosp.); pres. Oxford Nat. Bank. Republican. Presbyn. Mason. Home: Oxford, O. Died 1910.

COOK, Henry Clay, brig. gen.; b. Fall River, Mass., Sept. 29, 1837; s. Joseph S. and Minerva (Warren) C.; ed. pub. schs. and Pierce Acad., Middleboro, Mass.; m. Teresa Valdes Thom, July 12, 1877. Second lt. 2d R.I. Inf., June 5, 1861; mustered out, Aug. 7, 1861; apptd. 1st lt. 16th U.S. Inf., Aug. 5, 1861; advanced through grades to col. 5th Inf., Apr. 17, 1897; retired for disability in line of duty, 1898; advanced to rank of brig. gen. retired, by act of Apr. 23, 1904. Bvtd. capt., Sept. 1, 1864, for Atlanta campaign and battle of Jonesboro, Ga. Served in Army of Potomac and participated in various battles and campaigns in middle Tenn., and later in Ga.; after war served at various points in south and on reconstruction duty until 1877; served in campaign against Nez Perce and Bannock Indians in Ida. and Mont., 1877-79; later on different frontier posts. Home: Fall River, Mass. Died Feb. 22, 1916.

COOK, Joel, congressman; b. Phila., Mar. 20, 1842; s. Joel and Mary Paul (Yerkes) C.; bro. of Richard Yerkes C.; A.B., Central High Sch., Phila., 1859; m. Mary J. Edmunds, Sept. 19, 1865. Admitted to bar, 1863; adopted journalism as profession; war corr. with Army of Potomac, 1862-63; on editorial staff Public Ledger, 1865-1906, and its financial editor, 1883-1906; on staff of foreign corrs. London Times, 1865-1907. Mem. 60th and 61st Congresses (1907-11), 2d Pa. Dist. V.p. and treas. United Security Life Ins. & Trust Co. Pres. Phila Bd. Trade. Author: England, Picturesque and Descriptive. Home: Philadelphia, Pa. Died 1910.

COOK, John, soldier; b. Belleville, Ill., June 12, 1825; s. Daniel P. (for whom Cook Co., Ill., was named) and Julia (Edwards) C.; mother d. of Gov. Ninian Edwards of Ill.; ed. Ill. Coll.; m. Susan A. Lamb, October 20, 1847; 2d, Mary E. Baker, Sept. 16, 1889. Was in dry goods and later in real estate business, Springfield, Ill.; mayor, 1855; sheriff Sangamon Co., 1856; q.m. gen. of Ill., prior to Civil War; comd. first regt. raised in Ill.; served through war, comd. 3d brigade, Gen. Charles F. Smith's Div., at Ft. Donelson; received the messenger bearing surrender of Ft. Donelson and transmitted it, through Gen. Smith, to Gen. Grant; promoted brig. gen., Mar. 21, 1862; later bvtd. maj. gen. Gov. Yates (war gov.) on behalf of people of the state presented him with beautiful sword in token of appreciation of services and conduct at Ft. Donelson. Mem. Ill. legislature, 1868; agt. for Brule Sioux Indians, 1879. Home: Ransom, Mich. Died 1910.

COOK, John Williston, normal sch. pres.; b. Oneida Co., N.Y., Apr. 20, 1844; s. Harry Dewitt and Joanna (Hall) C.; grad. Ill. State Normal U., 1865; (A.M., Knox, 1891; LL.D., Blackburn, 1896, U. of Ill., 1904); m. Lydia Farnham Spofford, Aug. 26, 1867. Prin. pub. schs., 1865-66; teacher Ill. State Normal U., 1866-90; pres. same, 1890-99; pres. Northern Ill. State Normal Sch., DeKalb, Ill., July 1, 1899-Aug. 1, 1919, since lecturer for same. Lecturer on ednl. subjects, 1870—; editor and pub. Ill. Schoolmaster, 1874-76 (with E. C. Hewett); same of Ill. Sch. Jour., 1883-84 and 1884-86 (with R. R. Reeder). Pres. Ill. State Teachers' Assn., 1880, Normal Dept. N.E.A., 1896, N.E.A., 1904. Author: Educational History of Illinois, 1912. Home: Chicago, Ill. Died July 16, 1922.

COOK, Joseph, lecturer, author; b. Ticonderoga, N.Y., Jan. 26, 1838; s. William Henry and Merrett (Lamb) C.; grad. Phillips Acad., Andover, 1857; 2 yrs. at Yale; 2 yrs. at Harvard, grad. 1865 (LL.D., Howard Univ.); studied 4 yrs. at Andover Theol. Sem.; licensed to preach, after 4 yrs. in pulpit went abroad and spent 2 yrs. chiefly in Germany and England in travel and study; m. Georgiana Hemingway, June 30, 1877. From 1875 has lectured in all English-speaking countries; made with his wife a tour of the world as lecturer, 1880-82; for 25 yrs. Monday lecturer to great audiences in Boston. After lecturing tour in Australia in 1895, returned by way of Japan to America, on account of illness, but resumed Boston Monday lectures, 1900, giving his 251st lecture Jan. 7, 1901. Author: Boston Monday Lectures (11 vols.), 1876-88; Current Religious Perils. Died 1901.

COOK, Otis Seabury, lawyer; b. New Bedford, Mass., July 30, 1873; s. William and Cornelia A. (Seabury) C.; LL.B., Harvard, 1896, Boston U., 1897; m. Katharine Lee Mathews, Dec. 13, 1899; children—Seabury, Helen, Barbara. Admitted to Mass. bar, 1897, and began practice at New Bedford; mem. Knowlton Perry & Cook, succeeded by Cook, Brownell & Taber, 1910—; pres. Morris Plan Co.; dir. Safe Deposit Nat. Bank, Wamsutta Mills, Union Street Ry. Co., The Pairpoint Corp. Mem. Com. of 100 and Selective Draft Bd., World War. Formerly mem. Sch. Com. of New Bedford; trustee New Bedford Free Pub. Library. Home: New Bedford, Mass. Died Feb. 3, 1939.

COOK, Paul, mfr., banker; b. Albany, N.Y., Sept. 13, 1847; s. George Hammell (C.E., Ph.D., LL.D.) and Mary Halsey (Thomas) C.; A.B., Rutgers, 1866, A.M., 1869; m. Esther M. Curley, Apr. 25, 1875 (died 1892); children—William Gurley (dec.), Sarah Williamson, Margaret Cooper, George Hammell, Esther Dorothea; m. 2d, Anna Loomis Beveridge, Oct. 24, 1894; children—Janet Beveridge, Alison Loomis, Ellis Beveridge. Pres. W. & L. E. Gurley, mfrs. civ. engring. instruments, Troy; v.p. Union Street Ry. Co., The Pairpoint Corp. Mem. treas. Troy & Bennington R.R. Pres. bd. trustees Russell Sage Coll., Emma Willard Sch.; Troy Cemetery Assn.; pres. Leonard Hosp., Lansingburg; treas. Rensselaer Poly. Inst.; mem. Bd. of Edn., Lansingburg; mem. bd. govs. Marshall Infirmary. Presbyn. Home: Lansingburg, N.Y. Died July 30, 1926.

COOK, Philip, bishop; b. Kansas City, Mo., July 4, 1875; s. John D. S. and Rosalie (Barlow) C.; A.B., Trinity Coll., Conn., 1898; Gen. Theol. Sem., 1902, S.T.D., 1922; D.D. from St. John's College, Md., and Trinity, 1921; LL.D., Temple U., Phila., 1933; m. Anita Levin, June 1904 (died 1906); m. 2d, Adeline Bassett, 1911; children—Josephine, Harriett, Adeline, Phyllis, George T., Philip, John S. Deacon and priest, P.E. Ch., 1902; missionary, N. Dak., 1902-04; asst. minister, later vicar Chapel of Incarnation, New York, 1904-11; rector St. Mark's Ch., San Antonio, Tex., 1911-16, Ch. of St. Michael and All Angels, Baltimore, 1916-20; consecrated bishop of Del., Oct. 14, 1920. Deputy to Gen. Conv. from W. Tex., later from Md.; pres. of National Council, P.E. Church, 1934. Y.M.C.A. sec., A.E.F., in France, 1918, with 77th Div. Mason. Chaplain gen. S.A.R., 1927-28. Home: Wilmington, Del. Died Mar. 25, 1938.

COOK, Richard Briscoe, clergyman; b. Baltimore, Nov. 11, 1838; s. Columbus E. and Catherine (Graffin) C.; A.B., Columbian (now George Washington) U., 1863, Greek tutor, 1863-64, A.M., 1866 (D.D., 1882); m. Louisa Love, d. Daniel S. and Maria (Carr) Kerfoot, of Va., 1866. Ordained Bapt. ministry, 1864; pastor Holmesburg Ch., Phila., 1864-74, 2d Ch., Wilmington, Del., 1875-93, New Castle, Del., 1893-99, Calvary Ch., Wilmington, 1899-1901. Manager and v.p. Am. Bapt. Hist. Soc., 1876—, also treas.; pres. Phila. Conf. of Ministers, 1874-75;

moderator Phila. Assn. of Bapt. Chs., 1883-84 trustee, 1878-92, chmn. hist. com., 1881-94); sec. Nat. Bapt. Bible Conv., Saratoga, 1883; mem. bd. Nat. Bapt. Edn. Soc., 1888-91, when the present U. of Chicago was started; organized (with Dr. Henry G. Weston) Del. Bapt. Union Assn., 1878. Vice-pres. bd. of Nugent Home and Fund, Phila. Home: Wilmington, Del. Died May 1916.

COOK, Richard Yerkes, banker; b. Phila., Feb. 25, 1845; s. Joel and Mary Paul (Yerkes) C.; A.B., Central High Sch., Phila., 1862, A.M., 1865; m. Lavinia Borden, 1868. Importer of English, French and German goods, 1868-85; elected pres. Guarantee Trust and Safe Deposit Co., 1890; v.p. Pa. Warehousing Co.; dir. Lehigh Coal & Navigation Co., Finance Co. of Pa., Real Estate Trust Co., A. Coburn & Co. (Inc.). With Geo. H. Earle, Jr., took charge of Philadelphia Record after failure and death of William Singerly and rehabilitated it as a valuable newspaper property, and by its sale at large price enabled Chestnut St. Nat. Bank to pay depositors in full. Episcopalian. Home: Lansdowne, Pa. Died Dec. 8, 1917.

COOK, Robert George, M.D.; b. Canandaigua, N.Y., Aug. 4, 1864; s. George and Caroline (Bull) C.; A.B., Harvard, 1886; M.D., Coll. Phys. and Surg. (Columbia), 1889; m. Mary Belle Strong, June 2, 1892. Interne Roosevelt Hosp., New York, 1889-91; asst. phys. St. Lawrence State Hosp., 1891-95; in pvt. practice, Rochester, N.Y., 1895-1908; neurologist St. Mary's Hosp., Rochester, 1896-1908; attending neurologist out-patient dept. Rochester City Hosp., 1895-1908; cons. neurologist Rochester State Hosp., 1905-08; resident phys. and treas. Brigham Hall (pvt. hosp. mental and nervous disorders), 1908-29, now cons. physician. Republican. Conglist. Home: Canandaigua, N.Y. Died Oct. 25, 1940.

COOK, Samuel A., congressman; b. Ontario, Can., Jan. 28, 1849; removed to Wis. with parents, 1855; common sch. edn.; served Co. A, 2d Wis. Cav., in Civil War; m. Jennie Christie, 1876 (died 1895). Farmer until 1872; gen. mdse. bus., Marathon Co., Wis., 1872-81; pres. S. A. Cook Mfg. Co., Neenah, Wis., Alexandria Paper Co. Mayor Neenah, Wis., 1889; mem. Wis. Ho. of Rep., 1890-91; mem. 54th Congress (1895-97), 6th Wis. Dist.; declined renomination; candidate for U.S. senator from Wis., 1898. Home: Neenah, Wis. Died Apr. 4, 1918.

COOK, Samuel C., judge; b. Oxford, Miss., July 13, 1857; s. Milas Jasper and Martha Ann (Bumpass) C.; student short time U. of Miss.; LL.B., Law Dept., U. of Miss., 1878; m. Lizzie M. Murphy, Oct. 25, 1882. Began practice at Durant, Miss., 1878; mem. Miss. Ho. of Rep., 3 terms, 1886, 1890, 1892-94; atty. for Yazoo-Miss. Delta Levee Bd., 1900-02; circuit judge 11th Circuit, Miss., by apptmt. of Govs. Longino, Vardeman and Noel, 1902-12; resigned May, 1912, and apptd. by Gov. Brewer asso. justice Sup. Ct., Miss., term, 1912-21. Trustee (ex-officio) State Library. Democrat. Methodist. Home: Clarkesdale, Miss. Died Feb. 15, 1924.

Cook, Virgil Y., soldier, mcht., planter; b. Boydville, Ky., Nov. 14, 1848; s. William D. and Pernecia (Dodds) C.; business edn.; entered C.S.A. at age of 14; 8 months in 12th Ky. Cav., transferred to 7th Ky. Mounted Inf., Forrest's cav. corps, participating in battles and campaigns of that command and paroled at Columbus, Miss., May 16, 1865; m. Mildred, d. Capt. Enos Lamb, 1871. From 1866 has lived in Ark.; conducted mercantile business at Grand Glaize, Olyphant and Elmo; also a plantation of 4,000 acres in the Oil Trough Valley, Upper White River; retired. Officer Ark. N.G. many yrs., retiring with rank of maj. gen.; col. 2d Ark. Inf. during Spanish-Am. War; served in 2d Brigade, 2d Div., 3d and 4th Corps and 1st Separate Brigade, 2d Corps, comdg. at frequent intervals as sr. col. each these brigades and was for ten days in command of all the U.S. troops stationed at Camp Shipp, Anniston, Ala.; mustered out with regt., Feb. 25, 1899. Comdr. Tom Hindman Camp 318, U.C.V., Newport, Ark., many yrs.; also adj. gen. and chief of staff Ark. Div. U.C.V.; maj. gen. 2 yrs.; was maj. gen. comdg. 3d Div. Forrest's Cav. Corps, U.C.V.; now lt. gen. comdg. Trans-Miss. Dept. U.C.V. Trustee U. of Ark 6 yrs.; was mem. State Bd. Confed. Pensions; mem. bd. mgrs. endowment fund Hendrix Coll., Conway, Ark.; pres. Ark. Hist. Soc.; pres. trustees Confed. Vet. Pub. Co., Nashville, Tenn., official organ U.C.V. Home: Batesville, Ark. Died Dec. 3, 1922.

COOK, Walter, architect; b. New York, N.Y., July 23, 1846; s. Edward and Catharine (Ireland) C.; A.B., Harvard, 1869, A.M., 1872; studied at Royal Poly. Sch., Munich; École des Beaux Arts, Paris, returning to U.S., 1877; m. Louise Sprague, Feb. 25, 1900. In practice, New York, 1877—; mem. N.Y. Art Commn., 1905-07; was mem. jury for New York Pub. Library and for competition for U. of Cal.; cons. architect Bd. of Estimate and Apportionment, and of Court House Bd., New York, A.N.A.; dir. Am. Inst. Architects (pres., 1912-13). Home: New York, N.Y. Died Mar. 25, 1916.

COOK, William Henry, M.D., editor and pub. Chicago Medical Observer; b. New York, N.Y., 1832; grad. Syracuse Med. Coll., 1851 (A.M., Lawrence Univ., Appleton, Wis.); m. Catherine Ann Maseker, 1851; m. 2d, Rebecca E. Smith, 1893. Dean and prof. Physio-Med. Inst., Cincinnati, for 25 years; pub. Medical Recorder, Cincinnati, 30 years; pres. and prof. Coll. Med. and Surg., Chicago, 1897—. Author: Medical and Operative Surgery; Science and Practice of Medicine; Physiological Dispensatory; Family Medicine and Hygiene; Woman's Book of Health; etc. Died 1899.

COOK, William Henry, judge; b. Philadelphia, Miss., Sept. 15, 1874; s. William Buford and Mary Ellen (Greer) C.; grad. Lexington (Miss.) Normal Coll.; A.B., U. of Miss., 1896, LL.B., 1898; m. Bertha Bagby Beardslee, June 14, 1904; children—Martha Louise, Bessie Bagby, William Henry. Admitted to Miss. bar, 1898, and began practice at Hattiesburg; police judge, Hattiesburg, 1903-04; judge Circuit Court of Miss., 1906-10; dist. atty., 1919; judge Supreme Court of Miss., 1920—, last term ended 1940. Dem. presdl. elector, 1912. Baptist. Home: Jackson, Miss. Died Oct. 5, 1937.

COOK, William Wallace, author; b. Marshall, Mich., Apr. 11, 1867; s. Charles Ruggles and Jane Elizabeth (Bull) C.; ed. in schs. at Ottawa, Kan., Lafayette, Ind., and Cleveland, O.; m. Anna Gertrude Slater, 1891 (died 1913); m. 2d, Mary A. Ackley, 1926. Court reporter, journalist, contbr. to Detroit Free Press, Puck and Truth Mags. until 1898. Author: His Friend the Enemy, 1903; New Fiction Series, 1909-11; Around the World in Eighty Hours, 1925; also author of Plotto: A New Method of Plot Suggestion for Writers of Creative Fiction, 1927, and others. Home: Marshall, Mich. Died July 20, 1933.

COOK, William Wilson, lawyer; b. Hillsdale, Mich., Apr. 16, 1858; s. John Potter and Martha (Wolford) C., of Cayuga County, N.Y.; desc. in 9th generation from Gov. William Bradford; A.B., U. of Mich., 1880, LL.B., 1882. Admitted to N.Y. bar, 1883, practiced as corp. lawyer, N.Y. City, until 1921. Author: Cook on Corporations (8 edits.); Power and Responsibility of the American Bar, 1922; Principles of Corporation Law, 1924; American Institutions and Their Preservation, 1927, 1929. Donor of the Lawyers' Club Bldg., and the Martha Cook Bldg., at Univ. of Mich., also the Legal Research Bldg. and the John P. Cook Bldg. Home: New York, N.Y. Died June 10, 1930.

COOK, Willis Clifford; b. Gratiot, Wis., Oct. 5, 1874; s. Alfred and Sarah (Cole) C.; LL.B., U. of Wis., 1895; m. Mary Butler Miller, 1899; 1 son, Alfred L. Began practice at Plankinton, S.D., 1899; county judge of Aurora Co., S.D., 1900-02; mem. S.D. Senate 2 terms, 1905-09; chmn. Rep. State Central Com., 1906-12; mem. Rep. Nat. Com. for S.D., term 1916-24; E.E. and M.P. to Venezuela, 1921-29. Past pres. S.D. Soc. S.A.R. Home: Sioux Falls, S.D. Died Jan. 5, 1942.

COOKE, A(rthur) Wayland, lawyer; b. Murfreesboro, N.C., Apr. 24, 1876; s. Henry Harrison and Elizabeth Florence (Maddrey) C.; prep. edn., Murfreesboro and Franklin (Va.) Male acads., 1890-95; A.B., A.M. and LL.B., Wake Forest (N.C.) Coll., 1900; m. Annie M. Owen, Oct. 13, 1904; children—Arthur Owen, William Owen. Admitted to N.C. bar, 1900, and began practice at Greensboro; partner Stedman & Cooke, 1900-10; city atty. of Greensboro, 1910-16; partner Cooke & Fentress, 1916-20, Cooke & Smith, 1920-22; postmaster of Greensboro, 1916-22; emergency judge Superior Court, 1926, became clk., 1930; judge of Juvenile Court, Guilford County, 1930—; atty. Greensboro Sch. Dist., 1928-30; dir. Security Life & Trust Co., Winston-Salem, N.C. Mem. Legislative Commn. on Revision of Laws of N.C. Relating to Estates, 1935-36 and 1937-39. Dir. N.C. Baptist State Hosp., Oak Ridge (N.C.) Inst. Democrat. Baptist. Home: Greensboro, N.C. Died Aug. 27, 1940.

COOKE, Edmund Vance, author and lecturer; b. Port Dover, Canada, June 5, 1866; s. Edmund and Matilda (Vance) C.; educated common schools; m. Lilith Castleberry, Oct. 21, 1897; children—Merrill Vance (dec.), Dolores Felice (dec.), Martha Castleberry, Paula (dec.), Edmund Vance. Lecturer with lecture-entertainments, 1893—. Author: Rimes to Be Read, 1897, 1905; Impertinent Poems, 1903, 1907; Chronicles of the Little Tot, 1905; Told to the Little Tot, 1906; Little Songs for Two, 1909; I Rule the House, 1910; The Story Club, 1912; The Uncommon Commoner, 1913; Just Then Something Happened, 1914; Cheerful Children (for schools), 1923; Companionable Poems, 1924; From the Book of Extenuations, 1926. Home: Cleveland, O. Died Dec. 18, 1932.

COOKE, George Anderson, judge; b. New Athens, O., July 3, 1869; s. Thomas and Vanceline (Downing) C.; A.B., Knox Coll., 1892, LL.D., 1922; m. Sarah Blee, Oct. 20, 1896; children—Margerie (Mrs. Robert P. McBride), Martha (Mrs. Claude E. Canning), George Blee, Thomas Blee. Practiced at Aledo; partner of Judge Guy C. Scott, 1896-1900. Mem. Ill. Ho. of Rep., 33d Dist., 1902-06; elected judge Supreme Ct. of Ill., 4th Dist., Sept. 25, 1909, to fill unexpired term of Judge Guy C. Scott; re-elected, 1912; chief justice, June 1913-June 1914; resigned 1918; mem. Cooke, Sullivan & Ricks, Chicago, Jan. 1, 1919—. Democrat. Presbyn. Mason. Home: Chicago, Ill. Died Dec. 6, 1938.

COOKE, George Henry, rear adm.; b. Phila., Pa., Dec. 12, 1836; s. Christopher and Dorothea C.; ed. Phila. pub. schs.; M.D., Phila. Med. Coll.; m. Mrs. Sarah Lyon Atkinson, Oct. 16, 1873. Apptd. from N.J., asst. surgeon U.S.N., Sept. 22, 1862; passed asst. surgeon, Jan. 20, 1866; surgeon, Feb. 20, 1870; med. insp., Sept. 15, 1888; med. dir., Sept. 29, 1895; retired Dec. 12, 1898; advanced to rank of rear admiral, June 29, 1906, for services during Civil War. Home: Waverly, Ala. Died Feb. 15, 1924.

COOKE, George Willis, author; b. Comstock, Mich., Apr. 23, 1848; s. Hiram and Susan Jane (Earl) C.; ed. Olivet Coll., Mich., Jefferson Inst., Wis.; studied theology, Meadville Theol. School, Pa.; m. Lucy Nash, Sept. 4, 1872. Entered Unitarian ministry, 1872; pastor Grand Haven, Mich., Indianapolis, Ind., Dedham and Lexington, Mass., and Dublin, N.H.; retired from active ministry, 1899, and thereafter devoted to lit. and lecturing. Lecturer at Rand Sch. of Social Science, New York, and Boston Sch. of Social Science. Author: Ralph Waldo Emerson—His Life, Writings and Philosophy, 1881; George Eliot, a Critical Study, 1883; Guide Book to the Poetic and Dramatic Writings of Robert Browning, 1891; Unitarianism in America. Editor: (with intro. and notes) Poetic and Dramatic Works of Robert Browning (Riverside Edit.), 1899; A Bibliography of James Russell Lowell, 1907; A Bibliography of Ralph Waldo Emerson, 1907; 3 vols. of a complete edit. of the Works of Theodore Parker, 1907; The Social Evolution of Religion, 1911, 1920. Socialist. Home: Boston, Mass. Died Apr. 30, 1923.

COOKE, Jay, banker; b. Sandusky, O., Aug. 10, 1821; s. Hon. Eleutheros C.; went to work at 15; became clerk, 1838, and later partner, E. W. Clark & Co., bankers, Phila.; founded, 1860, house of Jay Cooke & Co., which handled larger part of the $2,000,000,000 bonds issued by U.S. during war; afterward handled large enterprises, including building of Northern Pacific R.R., but in depression of 1873 the firm failed and a panic resulted; finally made a new fortune; later large owner of Western land. Home: Ogontz, Pa. Died 1905.

COOKE, Lorenzo Wesley, brig. gen.; b. Round Top, N.Y., June 8, 1847; s. Amos B. and Lucy A. (Smith) C.; ed. pub. schs.; m. S. Emma Beatty, Nov. 4, 1869. Served pvt. to brig. gen. U.S.A., 1862-1906; retired, Mar. 24, 1906, at own request, over 40 years' service. Home: Santa Barbara, Cal. Died Feb. 15, 1915.

COOKE, Lorrin Alanson, gov. Conn.; b. New Marlboro, Mass., April 6, 1831; s. Levi and Amelia (Todd) C.; ed. acad. at Norfolk, Conn.; m. Matilda E. Webster, 1858 (died 1868); m. 2d, Josephine E. Ward, 1870. Taught school several yrs.; then farmed, Colebrook, Conn. Elected to legislature, 1856, as representative of town; removed to Riverton, Conn., 1869; for yrs. mgr. Eagle Scythe Co. State senator, 1882, 1883; pres. pro tem senate, 1884; lt. gov., 1885-87 and 1895-97; gov., 1897-99. Home: Hartford, Conn. Died 1902.

COOKE, Marjorie Benton, author; b. Richmond, Ind.; d. Joseph Henry and Jessie (Benton) C.; Ph.B., U. of Chicago, 1899. Began writing for mags., 1899; monologist, touring U.S., 1902—. Author: Modern Monologues, 1903; Dramatic Episodes, 1905; Plays for Children, 1905; More Modern Monologues, 1907; The Girl Who Lived in the Woods, 1910; Dr. David, 1911; To a Mother, 1911; The Twelfth Christmas (dramatic poem), 1911; Bambi, 1914; The Incubus, 1915; The Dual Alliance, 1915; Cinderella Jane, 1916; The Threshold, 1917; The Cricket, 1918. Died Apr. 26, 1920.

COOKE, Richard Joseph, bishop; b. N.Y. City, Jan. 31, 1853; s. Richard and Joana (Geary) C.; grad. E. Tenn. Wesleyan U., 1880; D.D., U. of Tenn.; LL.D., Williamette U.; L.H.D., Chattanooga U.; m. Eliza Gettys Fisher, Apr. 20, 1881 (died 1904); children—Richard Warren, James Fisher, William Rule, Francis Joyce; m. 2d, Ella B. Fisher, of Athens, 1908. Entered M.E. ministry, 1873, ordained 1876; pastor, student at Berlin U., traveled through Germany, France, Italy; prof. N.T. exegesis and hist. theology, Chattanooga U., 1889-1912, v.-chancellor, 1893, actg. pres., 1897; editor Methodist Advocate Journal, 1891-1912; book editor M.E. Ch., 1904-12; biship M.E. Ch., May 1912—. Mem. Gen. Conf. M.E. Ch. 5 times, Ecumenical Conf., Eng., 1901; commr. on Federation of Episcopal Methodism, on Common Hymnal, on Constn., on Revision of the Ritual of the M.E. Ch.; fraternal del. from M.E. Ch. to the British and Irish Wesleyan Conf., Eng. and Ireland, 1906; sec. commn. on jud. procedure M.E. Ch., 1908; mem. Commn., on Unification of M.E. Ch. and M.E. Ch., S. Author: The Historic Episcopate, 1896; History of Ritual M.E. Church, 1900; The Wingless Hour; Incarnation and Recent Criticism; The Church and World Peace; Religion in Russia Under the Soviets. Home: Athens, Tenn. Died Dec. 25, 1931.

COOKE, Walter Platt, lawyer; b. Buffalo, N.Y., Apr. 28, 1869; s. Josiah P. and Alice (Baker) C.; LL.B., Cornell U., 1891; LL.D., U. of Rochester, 1928; m. May Louise Perry, 1894; children—Mrs. Katharine Cooke Porter, Carlton P. Practiced in Buffalo, 1891—; then member Kenefick, Cooke, Mitchell & Bass; chmn. bd. Marine Trust Co.; chmn. bd. and gen. counsel Gt. Southern Lumber Co., New Orleans, Gt. Northern R.R. Co.; executor, trustee various estates. Chmn. council U. of Buffalo (acting chancellor, 1920-22), trustee Cornell U., Buffalo Fine Arts Acad., Buffalo State Teachers College, Buffalo Seminary. Manager Buffalo State Hospital, for the Insane, 1901-04; dir. Buffalo Pub. Library, 1902-17; chmn. Endowment Fund Com. U. of Buffalo, 1919. Served as chmn. Liberty Loan orgns., Buffalo, during 4 Liberty Loan campaigns, and mem. exec. com. Red Cross campaign, United War Work campaign and advisory com. Capital Issues Com. Pres. Arbitral Tribunal of Interpretation, to decide controversies between Germany and the Reparations Commn., 1925-26; U.S. citizen mem. Reparation Commn. (Paris), 1926-27. Decorated grand Officer Legion of Honor (France); grand Officer Order of Leopold (Belgium); grand Officer Order Sts. Maurice and Lazare (Italy). Republican. Presbyn. Home: Buffalo, N.Y. Died Aug. 4, 1931.

COOKE, William Parker, dentist; b. Milford, Mass., Mar. 15, 1859; s. George Lamb and Emma Augusta (Clarke) C.; grad. high sch., Milford; studied dentistry under father; D.M.D., Harvard Dental Sch., 1881; m. Caroline Lucia Wicks, Nov. 10, 1892. Practiced in Boston, 1881—; instr. in operative dentistry, 1887-90, clin. lecturer, 1890-92, instr. in crown and bridge work, 1892-95, also in metallurgy, 1895-1900, asst. prof. mech. dentistry, 1900-07, asst. prof. prosthetic dentistry, 1907-08, prof., 1908, prof. preventive dentistry and oral hygiene, 1918—, Harvard Dental Sch., also mem. Administrative Bd. Republican. Methodist. Home: Newton Center, Mass. Died Aug. 1931.

COOKSON, Walter John, mayor; b. Pascoag, R.I., Apr. 17, 1876; s. William Henry and Susan (Chappell) C.; ed. Post Business Coll., Worcester, Mass., 1900-01; student Army Sch., Ft. Riley, Kan., 1910-12, Army Sch. for Officers, San Antonio, Tex., 1912; m. Susan Alice Dennison, Apr. 2, 1902; children—Russell Maynard, Dorothy Louise (Mrs. Beaumont J. Kiniry). Began as salesman, 1896; sales mgr. Fuller-Warren Co., Troy, N.Y., 1915-30, Andes Range Co., Geneva, N.Y., 1930-32, Universal Appliance Co., Boston, 1933-35; mayor of Worcester, Mass., 1935—. Mem. Worcester Sch. Com., 1907-33 (chmn. 1920-33); chmn. bd. trustees Worcester Pub. Sch. Athletic Field. Republican. Mason. Home: Worcester, Mass. Deceased.

COOLBRITH, Ina Donna, author; b. in Illinois, of N.E. parentage; went in early childhood across the great overland trail to Calif.; ed. pub. schs. of Los Angeles; unmarried. Librarian Oakland (Calif.) Pub. Library, 1874-93, Mercantile Library, San Francisco, 1897-99, Bohemian Club, San Francisco, 1899-1906. Pres. Panama-Pacific Expn. Congress of Authors and Journalists, 1915 (invested with poet-laureateship of Calif.). Author: A Perfect Day and Other Poems, 1884; The Singer of the Sea; Songs from the Golden Gate, 1895; associated with Bret Harte in the Overland Monthly during his editorship. Died Feb. 29, 1928.

COOLE, Thomas Henry; b. Douglas, Isle of Man, Feb. 13, 1868; s. Thomas and Catherine Jane (Christian) C.; came to U.S., 1888; A.B., Baker U., Baldwin, Kan., 1897, D.D., 1924; M.D., Northwestern U., 1906; post-grad. studies New York, London and Peking; m. Cora Louisa (Shepard) Boynton, June 4, 1897; children—Douglas Paul, Mona Ruth (Mrs. Leland West Mann), Arthur Braddan. Entered ministry M.E. Ch., 1896; pastor in Kan. 6 yrs., in Chicago, 4 yrs.; med. missionary in China, 1906—, supt. Foochow (China) Union Christian Hosp., 1928—. Fellow China Med. Bd. Died June 3, 1930.

COOLEY, Alford Warriner, judge; b. Westchester, N.Y., Apr. 9, 1873; s. James Calvin and Agnes (Medlicott) C.; A.B., Harvard, 1895; Columbia Law Sch. 1895-97; m. Eusan Dexter Dalton, Dec. 1, 1904. Admitted to N.Y. bar, 1898; insp. common schs., New York, 1896-98; mem. N.Y. Assembly, 1900-01; clk. Surrogate's Ct., Westchester Co., N.Y., 1901-03; U.S. civil service commr., 1903-06; asst. atty. gen. U.S., 1906-09; asso. justice Supreme Ct. of N.M., 1909-July 1, 1910, resigned. Episcopalian. Republican. Home: Silver City, N.M. Died July 19, 1913.

COOLEY, Charles Horton, univ. prof.; b. Ann Arbor, Mich., Aug. 17, 1864; s. Thomas M. and Mary E. (Horton) C.; A.B., U. of Mich., 1887, Ph.D., 1894; m. Elsie Jones (A.B., U. of Mich., 1888), July 24, 1890; children—Rutger Horton, Margaret Horton (Mrs. James A. Kennedy, dec.), Mary Elizabeth. Statistical work in Interstate Commerce and Census Bur., Washington, 1889-91; asst. polit. economy, 1892-95, instr. sociology, 1895-99, asst. prof., 1899-1904, prof., 1904—, U. of Mich. Pres. Am. Sociol. Soc.,

1918. Author: Human Nature and the Social Order, 1902; Social Organization, 1909; Social Process, 1918; Life and the Student, 1927. Home: Ann Arbor, Mich. Died May 8, 1929.

COOLEY, Edwin Gilbert, educator; b. Strawberry Point, Ia., Mar. 12, 1857; s. Gilbert and Martha C.; student State Univ. of Ia.; Ph.B., U. of Chicago, 1895; life diploma as teacher in Ia., 1889; (LL.D., U. of Ill., 1905); m. Lydia A. Stanley, Jan. 1, 1878. Began teaching in Ia., 1879; supt. schs., Cresco, Ia., 1885-91; prin. high sch., Aurora, Ill., 1891-93, La Grange, Ill., 1893-1900; supt. schs., Chicago, 1900-09; pres. D. C. Heath & Co., Boston, Mar. 1, 1909-10; ednl. commr. of Commercial Club of Chicago studying industrial schs. in Europe and America, 1910-15; dir. junior activities, Central Div. Am. Red Cross, Jan.-July. 1918; prin. continuation schools, Chicago, Dec. 1, 1918—. Business mgr. of S.A.T.C., Ill., Wis. and Mich., to Dec. 1, 1918. Decorated Order Franz Josef (Austria), 1905. Pres. Ill. State Teachers' Assn., 1904; pres. N.E.A., 1907-08. Home: La Grange, Ill. Died Sept. 28, 1923.

COOLEY, Hollis Eli, theatrical mgr.; b. New York, May 7, 1859; s. Eli and Wealthy Hyde (Shepard) C.; ed. Williston Sem., Easthampton, Mass., Springfield (Mass.) High Sch. and Deerfield Acad.; m. Lillian Eliza Lombard Wallace, July 3, 1883. Mgr. Turner Opera House, Wichita, Kan., 1884-86; bus. mgr. Ninth St. Theatre, Kansas City, Mo., 1887-91; mgr. Hopkin's Trans-Oceanics, 1892, Kimball Opera Co., 1893, Wild East, Chicago Expn., 1893, John Kernell, 1894; gen. mgr. Davis & Keogh, 1894-95, Bijou Circuit & Star Theatre, 1895-98, Charles E. Blaney, 1898-99, Gus Hill, 1900-05, Henry W. Savage, 1905-07, all of New York; sec. Nat. Assn. Theatrical Producing Mgrs., Jan. 1908-June 1909; gen. mgr. for Felix Isman; gen. manager War Dept. Commn. on Training Camp Activities, Mil. Entertainment Service, 1917—. Trustee Actors' Fund America. Mason. Republican. Conglist. Home: Great Kills, S.I., N.Y. Died Aug. 2, 1918.

COOLEY, LeRoy Clark, physicist; b. Point Peninsula, N.Y., Oct. 7, 1833; s. James and Sally (Clark) C.; grad. N.Y. State Normal Coll., 1855; A.B., Union Coll., 1858, M.A., 1861. Ph.D., 1870; m. M. Rossabella Flack, May 30, 1859. Prof. mathematics, Fairfield Acad., 1858-59; prof. physical science, N.Y. State Normal Coll., 1860-74; prof. physics and chemistry, 1874-94, physics, 1894-1907 (emeritus), Vassar Coll., Poughkeepsie, N.Y. Author: New Text-Book of Physics, 1880; New Text-Book of Chemistry, 1881; Beginner's Guide to Chemistry, 1886; Laboratory Studies in Chemistry, 1894; Student's Manual of Physics, 1897. Died Sept. 20, 1916.

COOLEY, Lyman Edgar, civil engr.; b. Canandaigua, N.Y., Dec. 5, 1850; s. Albert Blake and Achsah (Griswold) C.; bro. of Mortimer Elwyn C.; C.E., Rensselaer Poly. Inst., 1874; (hon. E.D., U. of Mich., 1915); m. Lucena McMillan, Dec. 31, 1874. Taught in Canandaigua Acad., 1871-72; prof. Northwestern U., 1874-77; asso. editor Engineering News, 1876-78; asst. engr. ry. bridge over Mo. River, Glasgow, Mo., 1878; asst. U.S. engr. on Miss. and Mo. River improvements, 1878-84; editor Am. Engineer, 1884; promoter and consecutively asst. and chief engr. and trustee, cons. engr. Chicago Sanitary Dist.; mem. Internat. Deep Waterways Commn., 1895-96; consulting engr. on contractors' and engrs.' trip to Nicaragua, 1897-98; advisory engr. investigation of $9,000,000 expenditure Erie Canal, State of N.Y., 1898; made econ. investigation on deep waterway, lakes to Atlantic, 1899; cons. engr. Union Water Co., Denver, 1899-1904; mem. U.S. Postal Commn. on pneumatic tubes for mail in cities, 1901; advising engr. on water works appraisement, Omaha, 1904; engr. water power project by damming Miss. River at Keokuk, and other projects; cons. engr. Rochester, N.Y., on location of barge canal, 1905; and Grand Rapids, Mich., on flood problem, 1905-10, Saginaw, 1912; sec. and cons. engr. Internat. Improvement Commn. of Ill., 1906-09; cons. engineer Lakes-to-the-Gulf Deep Waterways Assn., 1909—, and Sanitary Dist. of Chicago, 1912-15; chmn. Commn. on Sewage Disposal and Water Power Development, Sanitary Dist. of Chicago, 1912-15. Lecturer Ill., Wis., and Mich. univs. Author: The Lakes and Gulf Waterway; The Diversion of the Waters of the Great Lakes; The Illinois Valley Problem. Home: Evanston, Ill. Died Feb. 3, 1917.

COOLEY, Roger William, lawyer; b. Decorah, Ia., Dec. 25, 1859; s. Judge Ezekiel E. and Jennie M. (Rhodes) C.; Litt.B., U. of Mich., 1882; LL.M., U. of N.D., 1913; m. Eliza W. Booth, Mar. 17, 1887; 1 son, John Booth. Admitted to Minn. bar, 1884; sec. commn. to revise laws of Dak., 1887; asso. editor Century Digest, 1896-1902; instr. in ins., St. Paul Coll. of Law, and spl. lecturer law schs., univs. of Minn., Mich., Chicago, 1906-11; prof. law, U. of N.D., 1911-20; prof. law, Sch. of Jurisprudence Am. U., 1920-22; prof. law, U. of N.D., 1923—, acting dean, 1927-28, dean, 1929—. Spl. legal adviser, Bur. War Risk Ins. (U.S. Vets. Bur.), 1918-23. Author: Briefs on the Law of Insurance (5 vols.), 1905; Supplement to Briefs on the Law of Insurance (2 vols.), 1919, 2d edit. (8 vols.), 1927. Home: Grand Forks, N.D. Died Nov. 7, 1931.

COOLEY, Stoughton, writer; b. Savanna, Ill., Apr. 23, 1861; s. Stoughton and Clarissa (Mays) C.; ed. pub. schs. Savanna; m. Nellie Wilson, July 9, 1885 (died 1902); children—Ruth (dec.), Norma. With acctg. dept. C.&N.W. Ry., 1884-1907; free lance writer for many yrs. on politics and polit. economy; with D. C. Heath & Co., pubs., Boston, 1909-10; on Miss. steamboat, in cotton trade, out of New Orleans, 1910-12; editorial writer and writer spl. articles Chicago Record Herald, later Chicago Herald, 1912-18; co-editor The Public, 1913-18, later editor same and of "Taxation," New York; then editor Tax Facts and sec. Tax Relief Assn. of Calif. Clubs: City, "X." Author: The Captain of the Amaryllis. Active in social and economic reform; advocate of the "California Plan" of progressive tax exemption to industry. Home: Los Angeles, Calif. Died May 31, 1934.

COOLIDGE, Algernon, M.D.; b. Boston, Jan. 24, 1860; s. Algernon and Mary (Lowell) C.; A.B., Harvard, 1881, M.D., 1886; m. Amy P. Lothrop, Dec. 15, 1896; children—Anne, Algernon Lothrop, Thornton. Was in practice at Boston, 1888—; phys. for diseases of throat, Mass. Gen. Hosp., 1893-1920, trustee, 1921; clin. instr. laryngology, 1893-1906, asst. prof., 1906-11, prof., 1911-25, prof., emeritus, 1925—, Harvard Med. Sch. Author: Diseases of the Nose and Throat, 1915. Home: Boston, Mass. Died Aug. 16, 1939.

COOLIDGE, Archibald Cary, univ. prof.; b. Boston, Mar. 6, 1866; s. Joseph Randolph and Julia (Gardner) C.; brother of John Gardner. Joseph Randolph, Jr., and Julian Lowell C.; A.B., Harvard, 1887, LL.D., 1916; studied U. of Berlin 1 term; École des Sciences Politiques, Paris and Freiburg, in Baden, Ph.D., 1892; unmarried. Acting sec. Am. Legation, St. Petersburg, winter of 1890-91; private sec. to uncle, T. J. Coolidge, minister to France, spring of 1892; sec. Am. Legation at Vienna, 1893; instr. history, 1893-99, asst. prof., 1899-1908, prof., 1908—, dir. of University Library, 1911—, Harvard U. With Taft party to P.I., 1905-06; Harvard lecturer at the Sorbonne and other French univs., 1906-07; U.S. and Harvard del. to Pan-Am. Scientific Congress, Santiago, Chile, 1908-09; Harvard exchange prof. at U. of Berlin, 1913-14. Visited Sweden and Northern Russia as spl. agt. of State Dept., 1918; chief of mission in Vienna, 5 months, and in Paris 3 months, attached to Peace Conf., 1919; joined Am. Relief Administration, Russia, 1921—. Fellow Am. Acad. Arts and Sciences. Author: The United States as a World Power, 1908; The Origins of the Triple Alliance, 1917. Editor of "Foreign Affairs." Home: Brookline, Mass. Died Jan. 14, 1928.

COOLIDGE, Calvin, thirtieth President of the U.S.; b. Plymouth, Vt., July 4, 1872; s. John C. and Victoria J. (Moor) C.; A.B., Amherst, 1895; LL.D., Amherst, 1919, also from Tufts, Williams, Bates, Wesleyan, U. of Vt.; studied law with Hammond & Field, Northampton, Mass.; m. Grace Anna Goodhue, Oct. 4, 1905; children—John, Calvin (dec.). Began practice, Northampton, 1897; councilman, Northampton, 1899; city solicitor, 1900-01; clk. of courts, 1904; mem. Gen. Court of Mass., 1907-08; mayor of Northampton, 1910-11; mem. State Senate, 1912-15 (pres. Senate, 1914-15); lt. gov. of Mass., 1916, 17, 18; gov. of Mass., 2 terms, 1919, 20; elected v.p. of U.S. for term 1921-25; became President after death of Warren G. Harding, the oath of office being administered by his father, a notary public, at the paternal home in the village of Plymouth, Vt., at 2:47 morning of Aug. 3, 1923; elected President, term Mar. 4, 1925-Mar. 3, 1929. Dir. N.Y. Life Ins. Co. Visited Havana, Cuba, Jan. 15-17, 1928, and delivered address before Pan-Am. Conf. Conglist.; hon. moderator, Nat. Council Congl. Chs., 1923—. Home: Northampton, Mass. Died Jan. 5, 1933.

COOLIDGE, Charles Allerton, architect; b. Boston, Nov. 30, 1858; s. David Hill and Isabella (Shurtleff) C.; A.B., Harvard, 1881, hon. Dr. of Arts, 1906; spl. student in architecture, Mass. Inst. Tech.; m. Julia Shepley, Oct. 30, 1889. Entered office H. H. Richardson, architect, Boston, 1882; partner Shepley, Rutan & Coolidge, 1886-1914, Coolidge & Shattuck, 1914-July 1, 1924, then of Coolidge, Shepley, Bulfinch & Abbott; partner Coolidge & Hodgdon, Chicago, until 1930. Built Stanford Univ., Calif.; Ames Bldg., Southern Terminal Sta., and new Harvard Med. Sch. bldgs., Boston; Chicago Pub. Library, Chicago Art Inst., Law Sch. and Commons of U. of Chicago; freshman halls, Harvard U.; Merchants Nat. Bank, Boston; new bldgs. for Rockefeller Inst., New York; Med. Sch. and Hosp. Group, Vanderbilt U., Nashville; Med. Sch. Western Reserve U., Cleveland; Med. Sch. and Hospital for U. of Chicago; dormitories and Memorial Chapel, Harvard; N.Y. City Hosp. Group, etc. Apptd. mem. U.S. Commn. on Fine Arts. Chevalier Légion d'Honneur, France, 1900; mem. Order of the Cincinnati. Republican. Home: Boston, Mass. Died Apr. 1, 1936.

COOLIDGE, Charles Austin, brig. gen.; b. Boston, July 19, 1844; s. Charles Austin and Anna Maria (Rice) C.; B.S., Norwich (Vt.) U., 1863; M.D., Wooster Med. Coll., Cleveland, O., 1873; m. Sophie Wager Lowry, Nov. 19, 1867. Pvt. Co. H, 16th U.S.

Inf., Oct. 22, 1862; commd. 2d lt., May 14, 1864; promoted through grades to col. 7th Inf., Mar. 2, 1901; brig. gen. and retired, Aug. 9, 1903. Bvtd. maj., Feb. 27, 1890, for gallant services in action against Indians at the Big Hole, Mont., Aug. 9, 1877 (thrice wounded); served in Cuba, P.I., and China during Boxer troubles, 1900. Episcopalian. Home: Detroit, Mich. Died June 1, 1926.

COOLIDGE, Cora Helen, college pres.; b. Westminster, Mass.; d. Hon. Frederick Spaulding and Ellen D. (Allen) C.; grad. Cushing Acad., Ashburnham, Mass., 1887; B.L., Smith Coll., Mass., 1892; summer courses, univs. of Chicago and in Göttingen, Germany; M.A., Washington and Jefferson Coll., 1915; Litt.D., Pa. Coll. for Women, 1917. Dean Cushing Acad., 1904-06; dean, 1906-17, pres. from 1922, Pa. Coll. for Women. Home: Pittsburgh, Pa. Died Mar. 12, 1933.

COOLIDGE, Dane, novelist, naturalist; b. Natick, Mass., Mar. 24, 1873; s. Francis and Sophia (Whittemore) C.; A.B., Stanford U., 1898; Harvard, 1898-99; m. Mary E. B. Roberts, July 30, 1906. Field collector (mammals) for Stanford U., in Nev., summer 1895, for British Mus., in Lower Calif., summer, 1896, for U.S. Biol. Survey, in Southern Calif., summer, 1897; field collector (live animals, birds, reptiles) for U.S. Nat. Zoöl. Park, in Calif., 1898, for N.Y. Zoöl. Park, in Ariz. and Calif., 1899; field collector (mammals), for U.S. Nat. Museum in Italy and France, 1900. Republican. Unitarian. Author: The Desert Trail, 1915; Rimrock Jones, 1916; Shadow Mountain, 1917; The Fighting Fool, 1918; Silver and Gold, 1918; Wunpost, 1919; The Man Killers (Maverick Basin), 1920; Lost Wagons, 1920; The Scalplock, 1922; Not Afraid, 1923; Lorenzo the Magnificent (The Riders from Texas), 1924; War Paint, 1928; Horse Ketchum, 1929; The Navajo Indians (with Mary R. Coolidge), 1930; Maverick Makers, 1931; Sheriff Killer, 1932; Fighting Men of the West, 1932; Jess Roundtree—Texas Ranger, 1933; Silver Hat, 1934; Long Rope, 1935; Wolf's Candle, 1935; Snake-bit Jones, 1936; Rawhide Johnny, 1936; Death Valley Prospectors, 1936; The Trail of Gold, 1937; Ranger Two-Rifles, 1937; Texas Cowboys, 1937; Arizona Cowboys, 1938; Comanche Chaser, 1938; Hell's Hip Pocket, 1938; The Last of the Seris (with Mary Roberts Coolidge), 1939; Gringo Gold, 1939; Old California Cowboys, 1939; Wally Laughs-Easy, 1939. Home: Berkeley, Calif. Died Aug. 8, 1940.

COOLIDGE, Harold Jefferson, lawyer; b. of Am. parents, Nice, France, Jan. 22, 1870; s. J. Randolph and Julia (Gardner) C.; A.B., magna cum laude, Harvard, 1892, LL.B., 1896; m. Edith Lawrence, Feb. 19, 1903; children—Harold Jefferson, Lawrence, Emily Fairfax. Admitted to Mass. bar, 1896, and then practiced at Boston; mem. Loring, Coolidge, Noble & Boyd; specialized in care of trust property; dir. Nat. Shawmut Bank, Mass. Hosp. Life Ins. Co.; pres. bd. Isabella Stewart Gardner Mus.; trustee Univ. Associates. Has been interested in travel, literary work, the collection of books and pictures, and in the acquiring and management of land needed for development of Harvard Univ., in the building and management of the Army and Navy Y.M.C.A. of Charlestown, Mass., in the Parish of the Advent, Boston—as mem. exec. and finance com. Trustees or Donations of P.E. Ch., and in development of farming and forest lands in Va. and N.H. Republican. Episcopalian. Author: Life and Letters of Archibald Cary Coolidge, 1932. Home: Boston, Mass. Died July 31, 1934.

COOLIDGE, John Gardner, diplomat; b. Boston, July 4, 1863; s. Joseph Randolph and Julia (Gardner) C.; great-great-grandson of Thomas Jefferson; bro. of Archibald Cary C.; A.B., Harvard, 1884; m. Helen Granger Stevens, Apr. 29, 1909. Left U.S. in 1887 and spent 3 yrs. traveling in the Far East, then 4 yrs. in S.A. and 4 yrs. mainly in Europe; was in Cuba, July 1898, and in the Philippines in early part of 1899, later visiting Samoa, the South Sea Islands, and Australia. Acted as U.S. vice-consul at Pretoria, S. Africa, 1900 (1st yr. of Boer War); sec. legation and chargé d'affaires, Peking, 1902-06; sec. embassy and chargé d'affaires, City of Mexico, 1907-08; apptd. E.E. and M.P. to Nicaragua, July 1, 1908, resigned Nov. 26, 1908; spl. agt. of Dept. of State to assist the Am. ambassador at Paris, Nov. 27, 1914-Aug. 1917; spl. asst. in Dept. of State, July 1918-Aug. 1919. Republican. Unitarian. Author: Random Letters from Many Countries, 1924; A War Diary in Paris, 1914-17, 1931. Fellow Royal Geog. Soc. (London). Home: Boston, Mass. Died Feb. 28, 1936.

COOLIDGE, J(oseph) Randolph, architect, retired; b. Boston, May 17, 1862; s. Joseph Randolph and Julia (Gardner) C.; A.B., Harvard, 1883, A.M., 1884; Dresden Poly., 1884; U. of Berlin, 1885; Mass. Inst. Tech., 1888-90; École des Beaux Arts, Paris, 1891-94; m. Mary Hamilton Hill, Oct. 28, 1886; children—Joseph Randolph, Mrs. Julia Richards, Mary Eliza, Hamilton (dec.), John Gardner, Oliver Hill, Mrs. Eleonora Works, Roger Sherman. Consultant in architecture for Coolidge & Carlson, Boston. Trustee State Library (Concord, N.H.), Wentworth Library (Sandwich, N.H.). Fellow A.I.A. Mem. N.H. Ho. of Reps., 1925-28. Unitarian. Home: Center Harbor, N.H. Died Aug. 8, 1928.

COOLIDGE, Louis Arthur, asst. sec. of the treasury; b. Natick, Mass., Oct. 8, 1861; s. William L. and Sarah Isabella (Washburn) C.; bro. of William Henry C.; A.B., Harvard, magna cum laude, 1883; m. Helen I. Pickerill, Jan. 2, 1890. On staff Springfield Republican, 1883-88; pvt. sec. to Henry Cabot Lodge, 1888-91; Washington corr., 1891-1904; dir. Lit. Bur., Rep. Nat. Com., 1904; asst. sec. of treas., Feb. 1908-Apr. 1909; treas. and dir. United Shoe Machinery Co., 1909—; v.p. and dir. Am. Zinc, Lead and Smelting Co. Chmn. welfare dept. Nat. Civic Fedn.; chmn. nat. com. on welfare work of Council Nat. Defense; mem. Federal Shipbuilding Wage Adjustment Bd.; mem. Inter-Am. High Commn. (U.S. sect.); dir. League for Preservation Am. Independence (pres. Mass. br.), 1919-20; dir. Constl. Liberty League of Mass.; dir. Community Service of Boston. Pres. Coolidge Family Assn., 1920-23. Del. at large Mass. Constl. Conv., 1917. Chmn. Mass. com. to welcome returning soldiers, sailors and marines, 1918-19; pres. Sentinels of the Republic; v.p., dir. The Boys' Club of Boston, Inc. Author: An Old Fashioned Senator—Life of Orville H. Platt, 1910; Life of U.S. Grant, 1916. Home: Milton, Mass. Died May 31, 1925.

COOLIDGE, Sherman, clergyman; b. Goose Creek, Wyo., 1863; s. Banasda and Ba-ah-noce (Arapahoe Indians); ed. Shattuck Mil. Sch., Faribault, Minn., 1877-80; B.D., Seabury Div. Sch., 1884; Hobart Coll., 1887-90; m. Grace D. Wetherbee, Oct. 8, 1902; children—Sarah Lucy, Sophie Austin Hope. Deacon, 1884, priest, 1885, P.E. Ch.; missionary most of time from 1884 in Wyo., among white people and Shoshone and Arapahoe tribes of Indians; had charge of Indian field in western Okla. under Bishop F. K. Brooke, 1910-12; hon. canon St. John's Cathedral, Denver. Delegate Gen. Missionary Council, Washington, 1903. Has traveled widely throughout U.S., lecturing on the Indian problem from the Indian standpoint. Mem. Com. of One Hundred on Indian Affairs of the Dept. of Interior. Mem. Colo. State Museum, Denver, Chamber of Commerce of Colorado Springs. Republican. Home: Colorado Springs, Colo. Died Jan. 1932.

COOLIDGE, Sidney, corp. official; b. Boston, Mass., Mar. 8, 1864; s. Algernon and Mary (Lowell) C.; A.B., Harvard, 1911, as of 1886; m. Mary L. Colt, Aug. 1891; children—Mary Lowell, Sidney, Edmund Jefferson, Thomas B., John Lowell (dec.), Helen, Francis Lowell, Philip. With Hannibal & St. Joseph R.R., 1886-92, C.,B.&Q. R.R., 1892-98; asst. treas. Stark Mills, Manchester, Mass., 1898-99, treas., 1899-1901; treas. Fore River Ship & Engine Co., Quincy, Mass., 1901-03; treas. Lowell Bleachery, 1903-26; pres. Lowell Bleachery-South, 1922-26; pres. Nat. Fabric & Finishing Co., Boston, 1924-27. Pres. Emerson Hosp., Concord, Mass., 1925-27. Home: Concord, Mass. Died June 24, 1939.

COOLIDGE, T(homas) Jefferson, diplomat; b. Boston, Aug. 26, 1831; s. Joseph and Ellen Wayles (Randolph) C.; A.B., Harvard, 1850, A.M., 1853 (LL.D., 1902); m. Hetty Sullivan Appleton, 1852; father of T(homas) Jefferson C., Jr. Began business in firm Gardiner & Coolidge, East India mchts.; pres. A.,T.&S.F. R.R., and Ore. R.R. & Navigation Co.; dir. Old Colony Trust Co., Mass. Hosp. Life Ins. Co., Amoskeag Mfg. Co. Mem. Pan-Am. Congress, 1889; tax commr., 1892; U.S. minister to France, 1892-93; mem. Joint High Commn. to adjust disputes between England and U.S., 1898-99. Republican. Overseer Harvard, 1886-97; gave Jefferson Physical Research Lab. to Harvard; gave library bldg. to Manchester, Mass. Home: Boston, Mass. Died Nov. 17, 1920.

COOLIDGE, T(homas) Jefferson, Jr., banker; b. Boston, Mar. 16, 1863; s. T(homas) Jefferson and Hetty Sullivan (Appleton) C.; A.B., Harvard, 1884; m. Clara Amory, Sept. 30, 1891. Started Old Colony Trust Co., 1890, pres., 1890-1903, chmn. exec. com., 1910—; dir. Bay State Trust Co., Am. Telegraph & Telephone Co., Edison Electric Illuminating Co., etc. Pres., dir. Lawrence Mfg. Co.; trustee Suffolk Savings Bank for Seamen and Others. Democrat. Home: Manchester, Mass. Died Apr. 14, 1912.

COOLIDGE, William Henry, lawyer; b. Natick, Mass., Feb. 23, 1859; s. William L. and Sarah Isabella (Washburn) C.; A.B., Harvard, 1881; studied Harvard Law Sch.; m. May Humphreys, Oct. 3, 1887; children—Isabelle (Mrs. Samuel S. Stevens), William Humphreys, Katherine (Mrs. Geoffroy S. Smith). Admitted to bar, 1885; practicing at Boston. Was asst. counsel Boston & Lowell R.R. Corp., and after its lease to Boston & Me. R.R., 1887, remained as atty. that corp.; partner Strout & Coolidge, 1889-98, Coolidge & Hight, 1898-1930; dir. numerous companies. Republican. Home: Manchester, Mass. Died May 28, 1936.

COOMBS, C(harles) Whitney, organist; b. Bucksport, Me., 1859; s. Luther Augustine and Caroline (Whitney) C.; ed. abroad; Mus. Doc., Syracuse U., 1922; unmarried. Organist Am. Ch., Dresden, Saxony, 1887-91, Ch. of Holy Communion, New York, 1891-1908, St. Luke's Ch., New York, 1908—. Composer: (cantatas) Vision of St. John; The First Christmas; The Ancient of Days; The Sorrows of Death; Light Eternal. Died Jan. 24, 1940.

COOMBS, Frank L., congressman; b. Napa, Calif., Dec. 27, 1853; s. Nathan and Isabel (Gordon) C.; LL.B., Columbian (now George Washington) U., 1875; m. Belle M. Roper, Dec. 27, 1879. Admitted to bar, 1876; dist. atty. Napa Co., Calif., 1879-84; mem. Calif. Assembly, 1887, 1889, 1891 and 1897 (speaker 1891-1897); Am. minister to Japan, June, 1892-Aug., 1893; state librarian of Calif., 1898-99; U.S. atty. Northern Dist. of Calif., 1898-1901; mem. 57th Congress (1901-03), 1st Cal. Dist. Republican. Practiced law in Napa, Calif. Home: Napa, Calif. Died Oct. 5, 1934.

COOMBS, William Jerome, banker; b. Jordan, N.Y., Dec. 24, 1832; s. Charles (soldier in War of 1812) and Mary (Wooleaver) C.; ed. Jordan Acad.; m. Josephine Adams, Oct. 21, 1856 (died 1915). Merchant, foreign business, 1855-95; a pioneer in organizing and developing the export business of the U.S.; at time of retirement, 1895, had active business relations with every country in the world. Pres. Mfrs. Trust Co., Brooklyn, 1896-1903; chmn. advisory bd. Title Guaranty & Trust Co., 1903—; pres. S. Brooklyn Savings Instn., 1904—. Apptd. govt. dir. Union Pacific R.R. with spl. commn. to collect the debt of over $124,000,000, which was collected under his direction. Candidate for 51st Congress, 1888; mem. 52d and 53d Congresses, 1891-95. Democrat. Was selected to succeed John G. Carlisle as sec. of treas., when latter's appmt. to Supreme Court was contemplated; offered postmaster generalship, which declined in favor of William L. Wilson; apptd. mem. Interstate Commerce Commn., which also declined. Trustee of Brooklyn Inst. Arts and Sciences, 1888—, Brooklyn Soc. for Prevention of Cruelty to Children, and Brooklyn Art Assn.; pres. Municipal Art Soc.; mem. advisory council Pratt Inst. Chmn. spl. com. empowered by Congress to investigate Reading Combine, 1891. Home: Brooklyn, N.Y. Died Jan. 14, 1922.

COON, Charles Lee, educator; b. Lincoln Co., N.C., Dec. 25, 1868; s. David A. and Frances E. (Hovis) C.; A.B., Lenoir Coll., Hickory, N.C., 1887; LL.D. from U. of N. Car., 1926; m. Carrie Louise Sparger, Oct. 21, 1903; children—Frances Elizabeth (Mrs. John T. Baxter), Mary Moore, Charles Lee. Teacher dist. schs., N.C., 1886-97; teacher high sch., Charlotte, 1897-99; supt. schs., Salisbury, 1899-1903; sec. Bur. of Information, Southern Edn. Bd., Knoxville, Tenn., 1903-04; supt. N.C. Negro Normal Schs., 1904-07; supt. pub. schs., Wilson, N.C., 1907-13, Wilson City and County pub. schs., 1913—. Sec. N.C. Child Labor Com., 1904-16. Democrat. Lutheran. Author: The Beginnings of Public Education in North Carolina (1790-1840), 1908; North Carolina Schools and Academies (1790-1840), 1915. Home: Wilson, N.C. Died Dec. 23, 1927.

COON, Stephen Mortimer, lawyer; b. Hastings, N.Y., Apr. 18, 1845; s. Stephen D. and Sarah (Haight) C.; A.B., U. of Rochester, 1870, A.M., 1873; LL.B., Hamilton Coll., 1873; m. Mary F. Coit, Nov. 23, 1870. Prin. acad., Mexico, N.Y., 1872-74; admitted to bar, 1873, and entered practice at Oswego, N.Y.; treas. Oswego Canal Co., Oswego Dock & Land Co.; trustee Oswego Co. Savings Bank. Lecturer internat. law, Syracuse U., 1898—. Asst. dist. atty. Oswego Co., 1877-78; corp. counsel and atty. for city of Oswego, 1879-82; spl. U.S. dist. atty. Northern Dist. N.Y., 1880; mem. N.Y. Assembly, 1888-89. Republican. Mem. local bd. Oswego State Normal Training Sch., 1887—; mem. bd. mgrs. St. Lawrence State Hosp. for Insane, Ogdensburg, N.Y., 1902—(pres.); trustee Cazenovia Sem. Home: Oswego, N.Y. Died Apr. 9, 1913.

COONE, Henry Herbert, educator; b. York Inst., Alexander Co., N.C., Nov. 1, 1869; s. Rev. Thomas Albert and Mary Caroline (Smith) C.; ed. Clay Hill Sem., Mocksville, N.C., and Statesville (N.C.) Acad.; read law under Maj. H. Bingham, Statesville; m. Brownie Howlett, Nov. 9, 1905. Formerly printer, later editor and proofreader; connected with Draughon Text-Book Co. and Draughon's Practical Business Coll., Nashville, 1906—, then pres. and owner of both. Democrat. Methodist. Mason. Author: The Sentence Analyzed, Capitalized, Punctuated, 1904 (revised edition); Draughon's Practical Speller-Dictionary, 1910. Co-author: Draughon's Progressive Bookkeeping, 1917. Home: Nashville, Tenn. Died May 28, 1937.

COONEY, Frank H., governor; b. Norwood, Ont., Canada, Dec. 31, 1872; s. John W. and Mary (O'Callaghan) C.; ed. common schs.; m. Emma May Poindexter, Dec. 27, 1899; children—Francis, John, Walter, Merlie, Tyler, Virginia, Rody. Began as grocery clerk, 1888; salesman for Paulson Grocery Co., Butte, 1891-94; grocery mdse. broker, 1894-1933. Elected lt. gov. of Mont., 1932, gov. filling unexpired term of J. E. Erickson, Mar. 14, 1933. Democrat. Catholic. Home: Missoula, Mont. Died Dec. 15, 1935.

COONEY, Michael, brig. gen.; b. Muroe, Co. Limerick, Ireland, May 1, 1837; s. Maurice and Anne (Ryan) C.; ed. pvt. and Nat. schs. in Ireland; m. Catherine Connolly, July 23, 1868. Pvt. Troop A, 1st Cav., Dec. 4, 1856; corp., May 1, 1859; sergt., Mar. 10, 1860; disch. at end of enlistment, Dec. 4, 1861; reënlisted Dec. 18, 1861; served 1st sergt. and q.-m. sergt. to Dec. 30, 1864; capt. 5th U.S.C. Cav., Jan. 1, 1865; mustered out of service Mar. 16, 1866; 1st lt. U.S. Cav., July 28, 1866; capt., Jan. 1, 1868; maj., Dec. 10, 1888; lt. col., June 2, 1897; col., June 9, 1899; retired Sept. 12, 1899; advanced rank of brig. gen. retired by act of Apr. 23, 1904. Catholic. Home: Washington, D.C. Died Sept. 10, 1928.

COONEY, Percival John, author; b. Peterboro, Can., May 19, 1871; s. John Ward and Mary A. (O'Callaghan) C.; student Ottawa (Can.) Univ. 1 yr., Pratt Inst., Brooklyn, 1902-03; m. Emma Wilhemena Keppner, Sept. 16, 1904; children—Byron Arthur, John P. Teacher pub. schs. and newspaper work, Butte, Mont., 1897-1902; editor and mgr. Telegram, Deadwood, S.D., 1904-08; dir. manual arts pub. schs., Ontario, Calif., 1908-10, South Pasadena, 1910-12, Los Angeles, 1912-16; scenario dept. Am. Film Co., Santa Barbara, 1917; dir. manual arts and visual education, high sch., Imperial City, Calif., 1917-19, Perris, Calif., 1919-20; dramatic critic and mem. advisory bur., Palmer Photoplay Corp., Los Angeles, 1921; dir. Americanization work with foreigners, high sch., El Monte, Calif., 1921—. Democrat. Author: (novels) Dons of the Old Pueblo, 1914; Kinsman, 1917. Home: El Monte, Calif. Died Mar. 17, 1932.

COONLEY, Lydia Avery (Ward, Lydia Avery Coonley), author; b. Lynchburg, Va.; d. Benjamin F. and Susan (Look) Avery; ed. Louisville, Utica, and Phila.; lived in Louisville; m. John C. Coonley, 1867 (died 1882); 2d, Henry Augustus Ward, 1897 (died 1906). Lived in St. Louis, 1867-68, Louisville, 1868-73, Chicago, 1873—. Author: Under the Pines, and Other Verses, 1895; Our Flag, cantata (music by Dr. George F. Root), 1896; Singing Verses for Children, 1897; Magic Hour (cantata); Love Songs, 1898; Christmas in Other Lands; Washington and Lincoln; The Melody of Life, 1921; The Melody of Love, 1921; The Melody of Childhood, 1921. Home: Wyoming, N.Y. Died Feb. 1924.

COONTZ, Robert Edward, naval officer; b. Hannibal, Mo., June 11, 1864; s. Benton and Mary Bacon (Brewington) C.; prep. edn. Ingleside Coll., Palmyra, Mo., 1878-79, Hannibal (Mo.) Coll., 1879-80; grad. U.S. Naval Acad., 1885; LL.D. from University of Missouri in 1926; Dr. Naval Science, Pennsylvania Mil. Acad., 1930; m. Augusta Cohen, Oct. 31, 1890; children—Lt. Kenneth Lee, U.S.N. (dec.), Bertha. Commissioned ensign U.S.N., July 1, 1887; promoted through grades to rear adm., Dec. 24, 1917; adm., Oct. 24, 1919. Was in Alaskan service six years, becoming proficient as pilot in those waters; exec. officer Nebraska, on voyage of fleet around the world, 1908; comdt. of midshipmen, U.S. Naval Acad., 1910-11; gov. of Guam, 1912-13; comdg. officer Georgia, 1913-15, winning fleet gunnery trophy; apptd. comdt. Navy Yard, Puget Sound, July 20, 1915; ordered to command 7th Div., U.S. Atlantic Fleet, Aug. 31, 1918; asst. for Naval Operations, 1918; made trip to Pacific with U.S. Fleet, U.S.S. Wyoming, flagship; confirmed by the Senate as Chief of Naval Operations, Oct. 24, 1919; comdr. in chief U.S. Fleet, Aug. 4, 1923-Oct. 3, 1925; comdg. fleet on Hawaiian-Australian-New Zealand Cruise; comdt. 5th Naval Dist. Nov. 30, 1925; retired, 1928; recalled, 1930, to assist in investigation of Alaska railroads. Medals Spanish-Am. War, Philippine Insurrection, Vera Cruz, World War; D.S.M.; awarded Am. Legion D.S.M., Oct. 15, 1923; War Mothers' Medal, 1930. Comdr. Gen. Mil. Order Foreign Wars, 1920-23. Democrat. Mem. M.E. Ch., S. Mason. Home: Bremerton, Wash. Died Jan. 26, 1935.

COOPER, Charles Champlin, settlement worker; b. New Orleans, Mar. 20, 1874; s. Benjamin Henry and Clara (Puryear) C.; B.Litt., Central U., Ky., 1899; D.Sc., U. of Pittsburgh, 1924; m. Sarah Bedinger, Sept. 14, 1912; children—Benjamin Bedinger, Wade Folger, Harriet Elizabeth, Jonathan Cilley. Began in social work, Union Bethel, Cincinnati, 1905; exec. dir. Kingsley Assn., Pittsburgh, Oct. 1910—. Advisory bd., Workshop for Blind, Pittsburgh; pres. and mem. exec. com. Nat. Fedn. Settlements. Mem. nat. council, Foreign Policy Assn.; corr. mem. Commn. on Race Relations of The Inquiry; mem. advisory bd. Children's Aid Soc. of Allegheny Co., Pa.; mem. Council of Chs. (Pittsburgh); pres. University Extension Soc. (Pittsburgh); pres. and mem. bd. Community Sch. of Pittsburgh. Presbyn. Home: Pittsburgh, Pa. Died Dec. 25, 1930.

COOPER, Charles Lawrence, brig. gen.; b. New York, Mar. 6, 1845; s. James G. and Mary E. (Bradford) C.; ed. pub and pvt. schs. of New York; m. Flora Green, Dec. 20, 1865. Enlisted May 27, 1862, in 71st N.Y. State Militia, and, with exception of brief period after Civ. War, has been continuously in service, taking part in many campaigns against Indians on the plains, and participating in Porto Rico campaign in war with Spain. Served, enlisted man and officer, in U.S.V., during Civ. War, apptd. 2d lt. in regular service, July 28, 1866; promoted successively, reaching rank of col. 5th U.S. Cav.; apptd. brig. gen. U.S.A., Aug. 16, 1903; retired, Aug. 17, 1903. On duty with Nat. Guard of Colo., June 30, 1904—. Episcopalian. Republican. Deceased.

COOPER, Clayton Sedgwick, author, lecturer; b. Henderson, N.Y., May 24, 1869; s. Ira Sedgwick and Julia Augusta (Dix) C.; A.B., Brown U., 1894; Union Theol. Sem., 1895-96; grad. Rochester Theol. Sem., 1898; A.M., Columbia, 1907; spl. study, Harvard and U. of Chicago, 1898 and 1901; m. Elizabeth Goodnow, Feb. 3, 1912. Student sec. Internat. Com. Y.M.C. Assns., 1894-95; gen. sec. 23d St. Branch Y.M.C.A., New York, 1895-98; ordained Bapt. ministry, 1898; pastor Washington St. Ch., Lynn, Mass., 1898-1902; college secretary for U.S. and Can., Internat. Com. Y.M.C. Assns., 1902-12; world tour under auspices World Student Christian Fedn., among students of India, Ceylon, China, Korea and Japan, 1909; spent 1½ yrs. visiting England, Europe, Africa and Asia, investigating ednl. and industrial conditions, 1912, 13; investigation in S.A., 1916, 17; seven months industrial investigation, Spain, N. Africa and Near East, 1927. Editor Ednl. Foundations, 1915-17, Nat. Marine, 1917-18; editorial dir. W. R. Grace & Co., New York, 1918-22; editor Miami (Fla.) Tribune, 1924-25; dir. City Nat. Bank, Miami. Regent, U. of Miami. President Com. of 100, Miami Beach. Republican. Baptist. Author: The Bible and Modern Life, 1911; The Brazilians and Their Country, 1917; Foreign Trade Markets and Methods, 1921; Understanding Italy, 1923; Latin-America, Men and Markets, 1927; Understanding Spain, 1928. Home: Miami Beach, Fla. Died Oct. 12, 1936.

COOPER, Colin Campbell, artist; b. Phila.; s. Colin Campbell (M.D.) and Emily (Williams) C.; brother of Samuel Williams C.; studied Pa. Acad. Fine Arts, Phila., Julian Académie and other art schs., Paris; spent much time in Europe painting figure and archtl. subjects; m. Emma Lampert, June 9, 1897 (died 1920); m. 2d, Marie H. Frehsee, March 9, 1927. Has made a specialty of views in American and European cities, and "sky-scrapers"; represented in Art Museum, Cincinnati; Boston Art Club; St. Louis Museum; Pa. Acad. Fine Arts; Phila. Art Club; Memorial Art Gallery, Rochester; Reading Museum, Pa.; Fine Arts Gallery, San Diego; collection of the French Govt., Paris. Awarded bronze medal, Atlanta Expn., 1895; Evans prize, New York, 1903; Sesnan gold medal, 1904; commemorative gold medal, as mem. Internat. Jury of Awards, St. Louis Expn., 1904; gold medal, Art Club, Phila., 1905; bronze medal, State Fair, Dallas, Tex., 1910; silver medal, Internat. Fine Arts Expn., Buenos Aires, 1910; gold and silver medals, Panama P.I. Expn., 1915; Beal prize, N.Y. Water Color Club, 1911; Hudnut prize, N.Y. Water Color Club, 1918; Lippincott prize, Pa. Acad., 1919; hon. mention, Fine Arts Gallery, San Diego, 1931. Home: Santa Barbara, Calif. Died Nov. 6, 1937.

COOPER, Courtney Ryley, writer; b. Kansas City, Mo., Oct. 31, 1886; s. Baltimore Thomas and Catherine (Grenolds) C.; ed. pub. schs., Kansas City; ran away from sch. and became clown in circus; m. Genevieve R. Furey, Dec. 20, 1916. Spl. writer, Kansas City Star, 1910-12, New York World, 1912, Chicago Tribune, 1913, Denver Post, 1913; press agt. Sells-Floto Circus and Col. W. F. Cody (Buffalo Bill), 1914-15. Pvt. U.S. Marines, Aug. 1, 1918; later commd. 2d lt. and sent to France to collate hist. matter concerning marines. Author: The Eagle's Eye (with W. J. Flynn); Dear Folks at Home (with K. F. Cowing), 1919; Memories of Buffalo Bill (with Mrs. W. F. Cody), 1919; The Cross Cut, 1921; The White Desert, 1922; Under the Big Top, 1923; The Last Frontier, 1923; Lions 'n' Tigers 'n' Everything, 1924; High Country, 1926; Oklahoma, 1926; Annie Oakley, Woman at Arms, 1927; The Golden Bubble, 1928; Sawdust and Solitude (with Lucia Zora), 1928; Challenge of the Bush, 1929; Go North Young Man, 1929; Avalanche, 1929; Caged, 1930; Ghost Country, 1930; Mystery of Four Abreast, 1930; Trigger Finger, 1930; End of Steel, 1931; Circus Day, 1931; Old Mom, 1934; Poor Man's Gold, 1935; The Pioneers, 1937. Also numerous photoplays, including "Weary River" and "Wild Cargo," "The Plainsman," Did much assignment work for Saturday Evening Post, particularly on northern frontier of Can.; active in interpreting work of Fed. Bur. of Investigation in mags. as well as in book "Ten Thousand Public Enemies," 1935, "Here's to Crime," 1937, and "Designs in Scarlet," 1939. Collaborator with J. Edgar Hoover, dir. Federal Bur. of Investigation, on mag. articles, books and motion pictures on crime subjects. Mem. faculty Nat. Police Inst., U.S. Dept. of Justice. Died Sept. 29, 1940.

COOPER, Edward, mcht.; b. New York, Oct. 26, 1824; s. Peter C., philanthropist; ed. in public schools and Columbia Univ.; asso. with his brother-in-law, Abram S. Hewitt, in Cooper, Hewitt & Co., owners Trenton Iron Works, N.J. Steel Works, etc.; was active in New York City politics as Democrat; one of leaders in overthrow of Tweed ring; mayor New York, 1879-81. Died 1905.

COOPER, Emma Lampert, artist; b. Nunda, N.Y.; d. Henry and Jenette (Smith) Lampert; grad. Wells Coll., Aurora, N.Y.; began study of art N.Y., Cooper Union, and Art Students' League, and with Miss Agnes D. Abbatt in water colors; later went abroad several times for study in Paris and to sketch in Holland, Italy, etc.; m. Colin Campbell Cooper, June 9, 1897. Had charge of art dept. Foster Sch., Clifton Springs, 2 yrs., of painting classes at Mechanics' Inst., Roshester, 1893-97. Medal, Chicago Expn., 1893; bronze medal, Atlanta Expn., 1895; exhibited Paris Expn., 1900; two bronze medals, St. Louis Expn., 1904; medal, Woman's Art Club Expn., 1907. Home: New York, N.Y. Died July 30, 1920.

COOPER, Frank Irving, architect; b. Taunton, Mass., May 8, 1867; s. Joseph J. and Mary A. (Nichols) C.; grad. Chauncy Hall School, Boston, 1885; studied architecture under Henry Van Brunt and engineering under Harry Keith, of Boston; m. Anna Wellington Sawyer, Oct. 16, 1890; children—Edward Irving, Frank Lakelin, Gregory. Draftsman and supt., Shepley, Rutan & Coolidge, Boston; practiced in Pittsburgh, Pa., 1890-92, Boston, 1892—; pres. Frank Irving Cooper Corp.; architect Bristol Co. Court House, Taunton, Mass.; Clark Hall, Amherst; Memorial Hall, Bridgewater; Library Bldg., Medford; high schs. in Mass., R.I. and Conn.; dormitories for Ashburnham Acad., and Deerfield Acad.; administration Building, N.E.A., Washington; 11 sch. bldgs. for Argentine Govt.; etc. Executed models of sch. houses for U.S. Bur. of Edn., for Internat. Congress of Hygiene and Demography, Washington, D.C., 1912; models for Canadian Govt., 1914; del. 4th Internat. Congress Hygiene, Buffalo, N.Y., 1913. Gold medal for designs for sch. bldgs., Jamestown Expn., 1907. Member expert com. on air conditioning Capitol, Washington, D.C., 1928-29. Home: Wayland, Mass. Died Oct. 23, 1933.

COOPER, Frederic Taber, author; b. New York, May 27, 1864; s. Varnum Eugene and Mary Hurlbut (Taber) C.; A.B., Harvard, 1886; LL.B., Columbia, 1887, A.M., 1891, Ph.D., 1895; m. Edith Redfield, Nov. 29, 1887. Assistant in Latin, Columbia, 1891-94; asso. prof. Latin and Sanskrit, New York U., 1895-1902; lit. editor New York Commercial Advertiser, 1898-1904, New York Globe, until June, 1904; editor The Forum, 1907-09. Presbyn. Author: History of the Nineteenth Century in Caricature (with Arthur Bartlett Maurice), 1904; The Craftsmanship of Writing, 1911; Some American Story Tellers, 1911; Some English Story Tellers, 1912; Translation of Montessori's Pedagogical Anthropology, 1913; Thomas Alva Edison, 1914. Home: New York. Died May 19, 1937.

COOPER, Henry Allen, congressman; b. Walworth Co., Wis., Sept. 8, 1850; A.B., Northwestern U., 1873; LL.B., Union Coll. of Law, Chicago, 1875. In law practice at Racine, Wis.; dist. atty. Racine Co., 1880-86; del. Rep. Nat. Conv., 1884, 1908, 1924; mem. bd. edn., Racine, 1886-87; mem. Wis. Senate, 1887-89; mem. 53d to 65th Congresses (1893-1919) and 67th to 71st Congresses (1921-31), 1st Wis. Dist. Home: Racine, Wis. Died Mar. 1, 1931.

COOPER, Henry Ernest, lawyer; b. New Albany, Ind., Aug. 28, 1857; s. William Giles C.; ed. common schs. of Boston; LL.B., Boston U., 1878; m. Mary E. Porter, Oct. 2, 1883. Admitted to bar, Suffolk Co., Mass., 1878; located in Honolulu, 1890; chmn. com. of safety, Hawaiian Revolution, Jan. 14-17, 1893; on Jan. 17, 1893, read proclamation abrogating monarchial govt. in H.I. and establishing provisional govt.; mem. Advisory Council, Provisional Govt., Jan.-Mar. 1893; judge Circuit Ct., 1st Circuit, H.I., 1893-95; minister foreign affairs, 1895-99; acting pres. Republic of Hawaii, Jan. 9-Mar. 1898; minister of pub. instrn., June 1896-Mar. 1899; atty. gen. Hawaii, Mar. 1899-June 1900; minister of the interior ad interim, 4 terms; minister of finance ad interim, 3 terms; pres. bd. of health, Mar. 1899-Jan. 5, 1900; apptd. 1st sec. H.T., June 14, 1900; retired; engaged in practice of law. Republican. Home: Honolulu, H.T. Died May 15, 1929.

COOPER, Hugh Lincoln, hydraulic engr.; b. Sheldon, Minn., Apr. 28, 1865; s. George Washington and Nancy (Marion) C.; grad. High Sch., Rushford, Minn., 1883; hon. LL.D., Univ. of Mo.; Eng.D., Syracuse U. and Rensselaer Poly. Inst.; m. Frances Bliss Graves, Oct. 12, 1892; children—Agnes (Mrs. Ralph M. Sheldon), Elizabeth (Mrs. John R. Hardin, Jr.). Began bridge engring., 1883; chief engr. and supt. Chicago Bridge & Iron Co., 1890, 1891; engaged in hydraulic engring. as applied to power development for electric uses, 1891—; designed and largely built works totaling over 2,000,000 h.p. and costing over $200,000,000, in U.S., Canada, Brazil, Chile, Mexico, Russia and Egypt, the prin. being the hydro-electric plant of the Miss. River Power Co. at Keokuk, Ia., Toronto Power Co.'s plants at Niagara Falls, Penn. Water & Power Co., at Holtwood, Pa., 620,000 h.p. water power project at Muscle Shoals,

Ala., and 750,000 h.p. water power and navigation project in Ukraine, Russia. Hon. prof. civil engineering Republic of Brazil Govt. Sch. of Engineering. Republican. Conglist. Home: Stamford, Conn. Died June 24, 1937.

COOPER, Irving Steiger, bishop; b. Santa Barbara, Calif., Mar. 16, 1882; s. Augustus Steiger and Mary F. (Naftel) C.; U. of Calif., 1902-06; studied at Adyar, Madras, India; m. Susan L. Warfield, Apr. 8, 1927. Nat. lecturer for Theos. Soc., 1908-19; nat. organizing sec. Order of the Star in the East, 1912-19; ordained priest Old Catholic Ch., 1918; consecrated regionary Bishop of Liberal Catholic Ch. for U.S., 1919. Author: Methods of Psychic Development, 1911; Ways to Perfect Health, 1912; The Secret of Happiness, 1912; Theosophy Simplified, 1915; Reincarnation—The Hope of the World, 1917. Home: Ojai, Calif. Died Jan. 17, 1935.

COOPER, Jacob, educator, clergyman; b. Butler Co., O., Dec. 7, 1830; s. Jacob and Elizabeth (Walls) C.; grad. Yale, 1852; Berlin, Ph.D., 1854; studied theology at Theol. Sem., Edinburgh, Scotland (S.T.D., Columbia Univ., 1874; D.C.L., Jena, 1873; LL.D., Tulane Univ., 1895); m. Caroline Macdill, May 31, 1855 (died 1857); m. 2d, Mary Linn, July 20, 1865. Prof. Greek, Centre Coll., Ky., 1855-66; chaplain 3d Ky. regt. (Union) inf., 1862-63; editor Danville (Ky.) Quar. Rev., 1861-65; corr. editor Bibliotheca Sacra, 1895; prof. Greek, Rutgers Coll., 1866-83; prof. elect, ethics and metaphysics, U. of Mich., 1883-84; prof. philosophy and logic, Rutgers, 1893—. Republican. Presbyn. clergyman. Home: New Brunswick, N.J. Died 1904.

COOPER, James Wesley, clergyman; b. New Haven, Conn., Oct. 6, 1842; s. James Ford and Cornelia (Walkley) C.; A.B., Yale, 1865, A.M., 1879; grad. Andover Theol. Sem., 1868; (D.D., Olivet, 1886); m. Nellie E. Hilliard, Aug. 13, 1868. Asst. adj. gen. on staff Gov. William A. Buckingham, of Conn., 1865-66; ordained Congl. ministry, 1868; pastor Rockport, Mass., 1868-71, Lockport, N.Y., 1871-78, New Britain, Conn., 1878-1903; corr. sec., 1903-10, v.p., 1910-14, Am. Missionary Assn., New York. Chaplain 1st Regt. Conn. N.G., 1878-88; mem. Corp., Yale Univ., 1885—; trustee Hampton (Va.) Inst., Talladega (Ala.) Coll. Corporate mem. A.B.C.F.M., 1884-1914; mem. Internat. Congl. Council, London, 1891, Boston, 1899. Home: Hartford, Conn. Died 1916.

COOPER, Job A., banker-stock-raiser; b. Bond Co., Ill., Nov. 6, 1843; grad. Knox Coll., Galesburg, Ill., 1865 (A.M., 1868); served in 137th Ill. vol. inf. during Civil War; for 25 years was engaged in banking and stockraising in Colo.; gov. of Colo., 1899-91. Republican. Died 1899.

COOPER, Oscar Henry, educator; b. Carthage, Tex., Nov. 22, 1852; s. Dr. William Henry and Catherine Hunter (Rosser) C.; A.B., Yale, 1872; grad. student Yale and U. of Berlin, Germany; LL.D., Peabody Normal Coll., 1892, and Baylor U., Tex., 1914; Litt.D., Simmons U., 1925; m. Mary Bryan Stewart, Nov. 24, 1886; children—Oscar Henry, Jackson Stewart, Hubert Newton, Mary Theodosia. Tutor, Yale, 1881-84; state supt. edn., Tex., 1886-90; supt. schs., Galveston, 1890-96; pres. Baylor U., 1899-1902, Simmons Coll., 1902-09; prof. philosophy and edn., Simmons U., 1915, also chmn. faculty. Visiting prof. history and philosophy of edn., U. of Tex., 1928-29. President Assn. of Texas Colleges, 1923. Mem. exec. bd. Conf. for Edn. in Tex., advisory council, Simplified Spelling Bd. Author: History of Our Country, also 4 vols. ednl. reports and about 100 published ednl. addresses. Home: Abilene, Texas. Died Aug. 22, 1932.

COOPER, Philip Henry, rear adm.; b. Camden, N.Y., Aug. 5, 1844; s. Hiram H. and Delia A. (Murdock) C.; grad. U.S. Naval Acad., 1863; m. Katharine Jordena Foote, June 24, 1884. Ensign, May 28, 1863; promoted through grades to rear adm., Feb. 9, 1902. Served on Constellation, 1863, Richmond, 1863-65; participated in battle of Mobile Bay, siege of Ft. Morgan; exec. officer of Richmond at surrender of ram Webb in Miss. River; served Powhatan, 1865-67; Naval Acad., 1868-69; Sabine, 1869-79; Tehuantepec surveying expdn., 1870-71; Plymouth, 1871-73; Naval Acad., 1873-74; exptl. battery, 1876; comdg. Alliance, 1881, Swatara, 1882-84; Navy Yard, Norfolk, Va., 1886-88; Bd. Inspection, 1889; comdg. Swatara, 1890-91, San Francisco, 1894; supt. Naval Acad., 1894-98; comd. U.S.S. Chicago, Dec. 1898-Oct. 1899; comd. Iowa, June 1900-Apr. 1901; supt. 2d naval dist., July 1902-Jan. 1903; sr. squadron comdr., Asiatic Sta., Mar. 1903; comdr.-in-chief Asiatic Fleet, 1904; retired Aug. 5, 1904. Home: Morristown, N.J. Died Dec. 29, 1912.

COOPER, Sam Bronson, congressman; b. Caldwell Co., Ky., May 30, 1850; family removed to Tyler Co., Tex., 1850; common sch. edn.; m., 1873. Admitted to bar, 1872; practiced at Beaumont, Tex.; co. atty. Tyler Co., 1876-80; mem. Tex. Senate, 1881-85 (pres. pro tem. 1 term); collector internal revenue, 1885-87; mem. 53d to 58th Congresses (1893-1905) and 60th Congress (1907-09), 2d Tex. Dist. Chmn. Tex. delegation Dem. Nat. Conv., 1900; chmn. Dem. State Conv., Tex., 1904; apptd. by President Taft mem. U.S. Bd. Gen. Appraisers, New York. Home: Beaumont, Tex. Died Aug. 21, 1918.

COOPER, Samuel Williams, lawyer; b. Phila., Mar. 5, 1860; s. Collin Campbell (M.D.) and Emily (Williams) C.; br. of Colin Campbell C.; studied at home with tutor; LL.B., U. of Pa., 1881; m. Homie Weldon, Dec. 28, 1893. Admitted to Phila. bar, 1881; independent in politics. Author: Confessions of a Society Man, 1887; Three Days, 1889; Think and Thank, 1890. Home: Philadelphia, Pa. Died Jan. 13, 1939.

COOPER, Theodore, cons. engr.; b. Cooper's Plains, N.Y., Jan. 12, 1839; s. John and Elizabeth (Evans) C.; C.E., Rensselaer Poly. Inst., 1858; unmarried. Engr. officer U.S.N., 1861-72; asst. prof. Naval Acad., 1865-68; with Capt. James B. Eads, 1872, in charge mfg. and constrn. St. Louis bridge; later resident engr. in charge of its erection; engr. and supt. after its completion; later, supt. Delaware Bridge Co.'s shops and asst. gen. mgr. and supt. Keystone Bridge Co.; asst. engr. in charge constrn. of the 1st elevated railroads in New York; from 1879 cons. engr. in charge of many important bridges, aqueducts, buildings, railroad shops, etc.; was one of the 5 expert engrs. selected by the President to determine the Hudson River bridge span; cons. engr. for N.Y. Pub. Library and for the Quebec bridge; mem. bd. of experts on Manhattan Bridge plan, 1903; retired. Authority on iron and steel constrn. Home: New York, N.Y. Died Aug. 24, 1919.

COOPER, William Alpha, univ. prof.; b. Batesville, O., Oct. 29, 1868; s. Azariah C. and Lucy Wilson (Gebhart) C.; A.B., Marietta (O.) Coll., 1892, A.M., 1897; student U. of Bonn, Germany, 1892-93, U. of Leipzig, 1893-94, U. of Paris, 1894, Stanford U., 1901-04, U. of Berlin, 1908-09; Litt.D., Marietta Coll., 1917; Ehrendoktor der Philosophie, Univ. of Köln, 1934; m. Mary H. Grosvenor, June 17, 1897 (died 1919); 1 son, Grosvenor William; m. 2d, Anna M. Tietjen, Sept. 2, 1920. Instr. German and French, Marietta Coll., 1895-99, prof., 1899-1901; asst. prof. German, Stanford U., 1901-09, asso. prof., 1909-17, prof., 1917-34, also head dept. Germanic languages, 1917-34 (emeritus). Republican. Conglist. Translator: Albert Bielschowsky's Life of Goethe, 3 vols., 1906-08; Fontaine's Effi Briest, 1914. Edited Moser's Der Bibliothekar, 1902. Died Sept. 19, 1939.

COOPER, William Irenaeus, banker; b. Waverly, N.J., Jan. 12, 1857; s. Sylvanus and Henrietta (Price) C.; student Stevens Inst. Tech., 1873-75; m. Lillie Slater, Jan. 12, 1882 (died 1887). Connected with Nat. State Bank, Newark, N.J., 1876—, pres., 1911—. Mem. Delta Tau Delta. Republican. Presbyn. Home: Newark, N.J. Died June 17, 1931.

COOPER, William John, prof. edn.; b. Sacramento, Calif., Nov. 24, 1882; s. Wm. James and Belle Stanley (Leary) C.; A.B., U. of Calif., 1906, A.M., 1917; Ed.D., U. of Southern Calif., 1928; LL.D., Whittier (Calif.) Coll., 1927, Coll. City of Detroit, 1929, Birmingham Southern Coll., 1930, Lafayette College, Easton, Pa., 1931, Dickinson College, Carlisle, Pa., 1932; Litt.D., Rhode Island State College, 1931; Sc.D. in Edn., George Washington U., 1931; Pd.D., N.Y. State Teachers College, 1931; m. Edna Curtis, Aug. 19, 1908; children—William Curtis, Elizabeth Fales, John Stanley. Asst. dept. history, U. of Calif., 1905-06; teacher of Latin and history, high sch., Stockton, Calif., 1907-10; head of history dept., sr. high sch. and 4 jr. high schs., Berkeley, 1910-15; supervisor social studies, pub. schs. Oakland, 1915-18; dist. supt. schs., Piedmont, 1918-21; city supt. schs., Fresno, 1921-26; supt. schs., San Diego, 1926; state supt. pub. instrn. and state dir. of edn., Calif., 1927-29; U.S. commr. of edn., 1929-33; prof. of edn., George Washington U., 1933—; mem. Federal Bd. for Vocational Edn., Com. on Licensure D.C., 1930-33; also instr. in edn., summer sessions, U. of Calif., 1919, 20, 24, 26, 27, U. of Ore., 1923; part-time instr. in edn., Fresno State Coll., 1923-26, Johns Hopkins U., spring 1932. Business mgr. War Dept. com. on edn. and spl. training, Western States, 8 mos., 1917-18. Regent U. of Calif. Episcopalian. Mason. Home: Chevy Chase, D.C. Died Sept. 19, 1935.

COOPER, William Knowles, Y.M.C.A. sec.; b. Phila., Pa., Nov. 1, 1867; s. James Brown and Annie (Knowles) C.; ed. pub. schs., Phila.; Master of Humanics, Internat. Y.M.C.A. Coll., Springfield, Mass., 1912; LL.D. from Dist. of Columbia Coll., 1929; m. Jessie Shaver, Nov. 24, 1896; children—Anna K. (dec.), William K., Jr., Martha M. Gen. sec. Y.M.C.A., Norristown, Pa., 1890-92, Brooklyn, N.Y., 1892-98, Springfield, Mass., 1898-1908, Washington, D.C., 1908—; teacher in Y.M.C.A. training schs.; dir. Federal-Am. Nat. Bank; mem. Crane Parris & Co., investment bankers. Arbitrator in labor disputes, baking industry, 1921, Washington Street Ry., 1924. Chmn. Real Estate Valuation Commn., 1928. Trustee Internat. Y.M.C.A. Coll., Am. Univ. Mem. Federal Council Chs. in America (exec. com.), Nat. Council Boy Scouts America, Nat. Y.M.C.A. Conglist. Mason. Home: Washington, D.C. Died Jan. 17, 1932.

COOPERRIDER, George T., clergyman, editor; b. Licking Co., O., Mar. 20, 1852; s. George and Margaret (Trout) C.; A.B., Capital U., Columbus, O., 1875, A.M., 1878; grad. Columbus Theol. Sem., 1877; m. Caroline N. Rosenfeld, Mar. 26, 1878. Ordained Luthern ministry, 1877; in active pastorates, 1877-1901; asso. editor Lutheran Standard, 1898-1902; editor-in-chief same, 1903-09. Author: Be True, 1890; The Lamb of God, 1902; The Last Things, 1911; In His Service, 1913. Home: Columbus, Ohio. Died Aug. 1916.

COOVER, John Edgar, prof. psychology; b. Remington, Ind., March 16, 1872; s. John Calvin and Elizabeth Hadessa (Keller) C.; Ped.B., Colo. State Normal School, 1898; A.B., Stanford, 1904, A.M., 1905, Ph.D., 1912; m. Margaret Evelyn Brooks, June 3, 1905; 1 son, Calvin Clay. Various lines of business, and principal schools of Colo. and Calif., until 1910; assistant in department psychology, Stanford, 1910, asso. prof., 1921-30, prof., 1930—; asso. prof. psychology, Johns Hopkins, 1927-28. Capt. S.C., U.S.A., 1918-19, at Med. Research Lab., Hazelhurst Field, Mineola, L.I., N.Y., Psychol. Sect. Mason. Author: Formal Discipline from the Standpoint of Experimental Psychology, 1916; Experiments in Psychical Research at Leland Stanford, Jr. University, 1917; Metapsychics and the Incredulity of Psychologists (Chapt. XI, "The Case For and Against Psychial Belief"), 1927; The Quantitative Measurement of Higher Mental Processes in the Pioneer Studies of H. Ebbinghaus (Analysis 51, in "Methods in Social Science"), 1931. Joint Author: The Weise-Coover Kinæsthetic Method of Typing, 1924. Home: Stanford University, Calif. Died Feb. 19, 1938.

COPE, Henry Frederick, educator; b. London, Eng., June 17, 1870; s. Albert and Elizabeth (Davies) C.; ed. elementary schs., London, Govt. Boys' Sch., Enfield, S. Kensington, Dept. Sciences and Arts, London, and pvt. tutors; came to U.S., 1891; studied theology, Southern Bapt. Theol. Sem., A.B., Ripon Coll., 1908; (hon. A.M., Oberlin Coll., 1911; D.D., Washburn Coll., 1911); m. Elizabeth Erwin, Aug. 9, 1893. Ordained Bapt. ministry, 1893; pastor Rochester, N.Y., 1894-95, Plano, Ill., 1895-98, Dillon, Mont., 1898-1903; engaged in teaching and spl. lit. work, Chicago, 1903-04; asst. sec., 1905-07, gen. sec., Feb. 7, 1907—. Religious Edn. Assn.; editor Religious Education (mag.), 1906—. Author: The Modern Sunday School in Principle and Practice, 1907; Levels of Living, 1908; The Friendly Life, 1909; The Efficient Layman, 1910; Efficiency in the Sunday School, 1912; Religious Education in the Family, 1915; The Modern Sunday School and Its Present-Day Task, 1916; Religious Education in the Church, 1917; The School in the Modern Church, 1919; Parent and Child, 1921; The Week-Day Church School, 1921; Principles of Christian Service, 1921. Home: Chicago, Ill. Died Aug. 3, 1923.

COPELAND, Foster, banker; b. Evansville, Ind., Mar. 9, 1858; s. Guild and Eliza Jane (Foster) C.; ed. pub. schs. and business coll.; m. Martha Hoge Thomas, Jan. 26, 1893; children—Alfred Thomas, Eleanor Foster, Mrs. Martha Wilcox, Foster. Began as errand boy in father's office, New York, 1876; removed to Columbus, O., as a bookkeeper, 1882; treas. H. C. Godman Co., shoe mfrs., 1889-99; pres., 1899-1905, City Deposit Bank, and of its successor, The City Nat. Bank, 1905-27; chmn. bd. City-Nat. Bank of Commerce (now City Nat. Bank & Trust Co.), 1927—; v.p. Forrest Realty Co. Pres. Jury Commn., Franklin County, O., 1908-13. Pres. Columbus Home for the Aged; hon. treas. Anti-Saloon League of America; trustee Columbus Y.M.C.A. (pres. 10 yrs.); dir. Columbus Acad. Presbyn. Republican. Mason. Home: Columbus, O. Died 1935.

COPELAND, Frederick Kent, engineer; b. Lexington, Mass., Aug. 22, 1855; s. Robert Morris and Josephine G. (Kent) C.; B.S. in C.E., Mass. Inst. Tech., 1876; m. Anna L. Boyd, Dec. 7, 1884; children—Margaret Boyd (Mrs. N. H. Blatchford, Jr.), Frederick W. With operating dept. C.,B.&Q. R.R., 1876-78; coal mining engr. in Ia., 1878-80; mining engr. in Colo., 1882-84; organized, 1884, Diamond Prospecting Co., merged, 1892, with Sullivan Machinery Co., mine and quarrying machinery (pres.). Democrat. Home: Winnetka, Ill. Died Nov. 10, 1928.

COPELAND, Guild Anderson, editor; b. Evansville, Ind., Dec. 2, 1862; s. Guild and Eliza J. (Foster) C.; A.B., Williams, 1883; post-grad. work Columbian (now George Washington) U., 1883-86, B.S.; m. Jennie S. Copeland, June 19, 1903; children—Sara Foster, Guild. Engaged in newspaper work, 1889; editor Boston Daily Advertiser, 1903-17; resigned to enter on a study of agrl. conditions; founder and mng. editor Kenosha (Wis.) Herald, 1919; editor Richmond (Ind.) Item, 1920—. Home: Richmond, Ind. Died Apr. 30, 1925.

COPELAND, Royal Samuel, U.S. senator; b. Dexter, Mich., Nov. 7, 1868; s. Roscoe P. and Frances J. (Holmes) C.; Mich. State Normal Coll.; M.D.,

U. of Mich., 1889; post-grad. in medicine in Eng., France, Germany, Switzerland, Belgium; hon. A.M., Lawrence U., 1897, Hahnemann Coll., Phila., Pa., 1921; LL.D., Syracuse U., 1923; Oglethorpe U., 1927; D.Sc., Temple U., 1934; m. Frances Spalding, July 15, 1908. Practiced, Bay City, Mich., 1890-95; house surgeon, University Hosp., 1889-90; asst. to prof. ophthalmology and otology, 1889-90, prof. ophthalmology, 1895-1908, U. of Mich.; dean N.Y. Flower Hosp. Med. Coll. and prof. ophthalmology, 1908-18; commr. of health and pres. Bd. of Health, N.Y. City, 1918-23; U.S. senator, term 1923-29, re-elected for terms, 1929-35 and 1935-41. Mayor of Ann Arbor, Mich., 1901-03, pres. Board of Edn., 1907-08. Delegate Meth. Ecumenical Conf., London, 1900; treas. Nat. Bd. of Control Epworth League, 1900-08. Fellow Am. College of Surgeons. Mem. N.Y. State Com., Med. Sect. of Council Nat. Defense, 1917. Author: (with A. E. Ibershoff) Refraction (text book), 1899-1905; The Health Book, 1924; Dr. Copeland's Home Medical Book, 1935. Home: Suffern, N.Y. Died June 17, 1938.

COPELAND, Theodore, clergyman; b. Blountsville, Ala., Nov. 18, 1867; s. Silas Virgil and Mary Jane (Yeilding) C.; ed. Southern Univ., 1885-88; Vanderbilt U., 1888-89; D.D., McKendree Coll., Lebanon, Ill., 1908; m. Kate Phillips, July 6, 1892; children—Theodore, David P., Mary Katherine, Ophelia, Virgil. Ordained M.E. Ch., S., ministry, 1891; pastor St. Paul's Ch., Birmingham, Ala., 1902-03, 1st Ch., Grenada, Miss., 1903, St. Luke's Ch., Columbus, Ga., 1904-06, Rayene Memorial Ch., New Orleans, 1906, St. Paul's Ch., St. Louis, 1907-11, Cabanne Ch., St. Louis, 1911-15, Central Av. Ch., Hot Springs, Ark., 1915-17 (built $90,000 ch.); engaged in evangelistic work. Ark. rep. in conf. of U.S. Food Administration, Washington, 1917. Home: Dallas, Tex. Deceased.

COPELAND, Walter Scott, editor, pub.; b. Jackson, N.C., Mar. 14, 1856; s. Winfield Scott, M.D., and Catherine (Randolph) C.; ed. pvt. acads., N.C., and U. of Va.; m. Mary A. Christian, Oct. 13, 1885 (dec.), 1 dau., Mrs. Katherine C. Lacy; m. 2d, Grace B. Cunningham, Apr. 26, 1906; children—Elizabeth Randolph, Randolph Scott. Began newspaper work with Petersburg Index-Appeal, 1881; editor Danville (Va.) Register, 1886-94, Richmond (Va.) Times and Times Dispatch, 1894-1909; pub. and editor Newport News (Va.) Press and Times Herald, 1909—; pres. The Daily Press, Inc. Democrat. Episcopalian. Home: Newport News, Va. Died July 24, 1928.

COPLIN, William Michael Late, M.D.; b. Clarksburg, W.Va., Nov. 1, 1864; s. Jacob and Martha (Davisson) C.; ed. State Normal, Lindsley Inst., Mount Union Coll.; M.D., Jefferson Med. Coll., Phila., 1886; m. Isabella H. Moffat, Apr. 7, 1887. Prof. pathology, Jefferson Med. Coll., 1896, emeritus; pathologist to Phila. Hosp., 1892—; dir. dept. of pub. health and charities, Phila., 1905-07; med. dir. Jefferson Hosp., 1907-12. Major Med. O.R.C., 1917, and dir. Base Hosp. No. 38; col. M.R.C., 1919. Author: Manual of Pathology (5th edit.), 1911; Textbook of Practical Hygiene (2d edit.). Home: Atlantic City, N.J. Died May 29, 1928.

COPP, Arthur Woodward, newspaperman; b. Madison, Wis., July 26, 1868; s. Ezra Putnam and Josephine Rachel (Woodward) C.; public sch. edn.; unmarried. Telegraph operator for various railroads in Middle West and on Pacific Coast, also for Western Union and Postal Telegraph cos.; began as writer sporting news for United Press, San Francisco, 1893; reporter Associated Press, Chicago, 1895-1901; corr. same, Salt Lake City, Utah, 1901-05, Denver, 1908-11, also at Chicago and Atlanta, Ga.; service in Cuban Campaign before Santiago, July 1898, and at Juarez, Mexican revolution, May 1911; supt. Western Div. Asso. Press, Sept. 10, 1911—. Presbyn. Home: San Francisco, Calif. Deceased.

COPP, Owen, M.D.; b. Salem, N.H., Jan. 12, 1858; s. Millet Goodwin and Rowena (Wentworth) C.; A.B., Dartmouth, 1881; M.D., Harvard, 1884; m. Hattie Grace Sargent, June 15, 1886. Asst. phys. Taunton (Mass.) Insane Hosp., 1885-95; supt. Mass. Hosp. for Epileptics, Monson, Mass., 1895-99; exec. sec. Mass. Bd. of Insanity, Boston, 1899-1911; phys.-in-chief and administrator Pa. Hosp. Dept. for Mental and Nervous Diseases, Phila., Sept. 1911-22; consultant for development Pa. Hosp., 1922-29. Home: Philadelphia, Pa. Died Apr. 18, 1933.

COPPÉE, Henry St. Leger, asst. U.S. engr. in charge of U.S. levees in Miss.; b. West Point, N.Y., 1853; C.E., Lehigh Univ., 1872; engr. on rys., 1872-76; with Bethlehem (Pa.) Iron Co., 1876-78; from 1878 in U.S. Engr. Corps in improvement of rivers and harbors in Southwest; mem. Am. Soc. Civ. Engrs., and received its Roland prize, 1896, for paper on Bank Revetment on the Mississippi; mem. and State sec. for Miss. Mil. Order of Foreign Wars of the U.S. Home: Greenville, Miss. Died 1901.

COPPENS, Charles, educator, author; b. Turnhout, Belgium, May 24, 1835; s. Peter Hubert and Caroline (Vaes) C.; ed. St. Joseph's Coll., Turnhout; St. Louis U.; Fordham U., New York; joined Soc. of Jesus, 1853. Prof. Latin and Greek, St. Louis U., 1855-59, St. Xavier Coll., Cincinnati, 1859-62, Normal Sch., Florissant, Mo., 1865-75; prof. Latin, Greek and English, St. Louis U., 1875-80; pres. St. Mary's Coll., Kan., 1881-84; prof. philosophy, Detroit Coll., 1886-91, Creighton U., Omaha, 1896-05; lectured meanwhile on med. jurisprudence, later in Chicago; now prof. philosophy and history of philosophy, Loyola U., Chicago. Author: Practical Introduction to English Rhetoric, 1885; Art of Oratorical Composition, 1886; Moral Principles and Medical Practice, 1898; Systematic Study of the Catholic Religion, 1903; Mystic Treasures of the Holy Mass, 1904; Brief History of Philosophy, 1909; Who Are the Jesuits?, 1911; Spiritual Instructions for the Religious, 1914. Home: Chicago, Ill. Died Dec. 14, 1920.

COPPINGER, John Joseph, army officer; b. Co. of Cork, Ireland, Oct. 11, 1834; s. William J. and M. (O'Brien) C.; ed. pvt. schs.; m. Alice, d. late James G. Blaine, 1870. Was lt. and capt. in Roman Army; chevalier for gallantry at La Roca, 1860; came to U.S., 1861; commd. capt. 14th Inf., Sept. 30, 1861; col. 15th N.Y. Cav., Jan. 27, 1865; hon. mustered out vol. service, June 17, 1865; transferred to 23d Inf., Sept. 21, 1866; maj. 10th Inf., Mar. 20, 1879; lt. col. 18th Inf., Oct. 31, 1883; col. 23d Inf., Jan. 15, 1891; brig. gen., Apr. 25, 1895; maj. gen. vols., May 4, 1898; retired from U.S.A., by operation of law, Oct. 11, 1898; hon. disch. from vol. service, Oct. 31, 1898. Bvtd. maj., June 12, 1864, for battle of Trevillian Sta., Va.; lt. col., Oct. 19, 1864, for battle of Cedar Creek, Va.; col., Dec. 1, 1868, for operations against Indians, 1866-68. Home: Washington, D.C. Died 1909.

COQUILLETT, Daniel William, entomologist; b. McHenry Co., Ill., Jan. 23, 1856; s. Francis Marquis Lafayette and Sarah Ann (Cokelet) C.; ed. dist. sch.; studied entomology and kindred sciences at home at odd moments, principally at night; married. Taught dist. sch., 1876; prepared, 1880, for Tenth Annual Rept., state entomologist of Ill., a descriptive paper on the caterpillars of U.S., with analytical keys to groups and species. Contributor on applied entomology Germantown Telegraph, 2 yrs.; asst. state entomologist of Ill., 1881, and wrote major portion Eleventh Annual Rept.; removed to Southern Calif., 1882; assisted Matthew Cooke on two works on entomology, 1883; investigated, 1885, for U.S. Dept. Agr., outbreak of destructive grasshoppers in Central Calif. and perfected method for destroying them by use of poisoned mash; also investigated for same, 1886, cottony cushion scale insect, infesting citrus trees in Southern Calif.; investigation suspended Aug. 1, 1886, for want of funds; experimented on own account with poisonous gases for destroying these and other noxious insects on trees and plants, inaugurating the hydrocyanic gas treatment; from 1887 in employ U.S. Dept. Agr.; asst. entomologist, Sept. 1893—; removed to Washington, 1893; apptd., 1896, hon. custodian diptera, U.S. Nat. Museum. Died 1911.

CORBETT, Henry Winslow, banker; b. Westboro, Mass., Feb. 18, 1827; acad. edn.; in mercantile life, Cambridge, N.Y., and New York, 1840-50; went to Oregon, 1851, mcht., 1851-67, then banker; U.S. senator, Ore., 1867-73; Republican senatorial candidate, 1898; pres. Security Savings and Trust Co. and 1st Nat. Bank, Portland; m. Emma L. Ruggles. Home: Portland, Ore. Died 1903.

CORBETT, Hunter, clergyman; b. Leatherwood, Pa., Dec. 8, 1835; s. Ross M. and Fannie C. (Orr) C.; grad. Jefferson Coll., Pa., 1860; student Western Theol. Sem., 1860-62; grad. Princeton Theol. Sem., 1863; (D.D., Washington and Jefferson, 1886, LL.D., 1902); m. Lizzie Culbertson, June 4, 1863; m. 2d, Mary C. Nixon, Sept. 16, 1875. Ordained Presbyn. ministry, 1863; foreign missionary in China, 1863—. Moderator Presbyn. Gen. Assembly, 1906. Author: (in Chinese) Church History (2 vols.); Ten Commandments; Benevolence. Died Jan. 11, 1920.

CORBETT, Lee Cleveland, horticulturist; b. Watkins, N.Y., Oct. 21, 1867; s. J. Wallace and Lucia M. C.; B.S., Cornell, 1890, M.S., 1896; D.Agr., U. of Md., 1921; m. Evelyn L. Northrup, Mar. 23, 1893 (died 1931); children—Ruth Eleanor, Frances Lee (Mrs. Colston E. Warne), Roger Bailey, Laurence Ward, Thurston Lee; m. 2d, C. Louise Phillips, Feb. 22, 1936. Asst. horticulturist, Cornell, 1891-93; prof. horticulture and forestry, S.D. Agrl. Coll., 1893-95, W.Va. U., 1895-1901; horticulturist, U.S. Dept. Agr., 1901-13; asst. chief, Bur. Plant Industry, U.S. Dept. Agr., 1913-15; in charge hort. and pomol. investigations, U.S. Dept. Agr., 1915-29, prin. horticulturist; retired. Del. Internat. Inst. Agr., Rome, 1920. Author: Garden Farming, Intensive Farming. Also Agrl. Expt. Sta. bulls. of Cornell U., S.D., W.Va., and U.S. Dept. Agr., and articles in yearbook of latter. Home: Washington, D.C. Died July 13, 1940.

CORBETT, Timothy, bishop; b. Mendota, Minn., July 10, 1858; s. Timothy and Anna (Kenrick) C.; ed. Coll. of Meximiux, France, and Sulpician seminaries at Montreal, Can., and Brighton, Mass. Ordained priest R.C. Ch., 1886; asst. in Diocese of St. Paul, Minn., 1886-89; pastor Cathedral, Duluth, 1886-1910; consecrated bishop of Crookston, Minn., May 19, 1910. Died July 20, 1939.

CORBIN, Daniel C., ry. pres.; b. in N.H., 1837. Constructed the first ry. the Coeur d'Alene dist., connecting with N.P. R.R., 1886-87, which sold to latter, 1888; built Spokane Falls & Northern Ry., 1889, connecting Canadian Pacific R.R. with Spokane, Wash.; also built other connecting rys. in Northwest; pres. Spokane Internat. R.R., operating in connection with Canadian Pacific Ry. Home: Spokane, Wash. Died June 29, 1918.

CORBIN, Henry Clark, army officer; b. Clermont Co., O., Sept. 15, 1842; s. Shadrach and Mary Anne C.; reared on farm; ed. common schools and 2 yrs. in private acad.; studied law, 1860-61; m. Edith Agnes Patten, Nov. 6, 1901. Entered U.S.V., 2d lt. 83d Ohio Inf., July 28, 1862; advanced through ranks to col. U.S.C.T., Sept. 23, 1865; bvtd. brig. gen. U.S.V., Mar. 13, 1865, for meritorious services; hon. mustered out, Mar. 26, 1866; bvtd. maj., Mar. 2, 1867, for gallant and meritorious services in action at Decatur, Ala., and lt. col., Mar. 2, 1867 for same at Nashville. Entered regular army as 2d lt. 17th U.S. Inf., May 11, 1866; promoted through grades to lt. gen. U.S.A., Apr. 15, 1906; retired, Sept. 15, 1906. Served 10 yrs. on plains in Kan., N.Mex., Ariz. and Tex.; in Mar. 1877, detailed for duty at Executive Mansion; sec. Sitting Bull Commn. With Pres. Garfield at the time he was shot and at his bedside at Elberon, where he died. In recognition of his services, and the part he took in war with Spain, Congress conferred upon him rank of maj. gen. Comd. Atlantic Div., 1904; conducted army maneuvers, Manassas, Va., Sept., 1904; comd. Philippine Div., 1904, Northern Div., 1906. Home: Washington, D.C. Died 1909.

CORBIN, Henry Pinkney, civil engr.; b. Franklin, N.C., Oct. 5, 1867; s. Harvey Leander and Lucinda Hasseltine (Brendle) C.; ed. pub. schs.; m. Lulu Hannah White, June 1, 1899. Served as surveyor and engr. various irrigation projects in Colo.; owner 2 live stock ranches in Colo.; mem. Dem. State Central Com., Colo., 1898-04; presdl. elector, 1912; cons. engr. Internat. Boundary Commn., U.S. and Mexico, Oct. 7, 1914—. Baptist. Mason. Home: Foxton, Colo. Died Feb. 1922.

CORBIN, Philip, mfr.; b. Willington, Conn., Oct. 26, 1824; s. Philip C.; acad. edn.; m. Francina F. Whiting, June 21, 1848. Began as mfr. with his brother and Edward Doen, under title of Doen, Corbin & Co., 1849; firm name changed to Corbin, Whiting & Co., and in 1852 to P. & F. Corbin; firm consolidated with the North & Stanley Co., 1854, of which was sec., later sec. and treas. and pres.; organized, 1882, Corbin Cabinet Lock Co. (pres.); mem. P. & F. Corbin, and Russell & Erwin Mfg. Co., merged with the Am. Hardware Corp., 1902, of which became pres.; pres. Corbin Screw Corp., Corbin Motor Vehicle Co., 1903—; pres. New Britain Machine Co., Savings Bank of New Britain, D. C. Judd Co., Calumet Bldg. Co., Porter & Dyson. Mem. Conn. Ho. of Rep., 1884, Senate, 1888. Republican. Home: New Britain, Conn. Died 1910.

CORBITT, Charles Linwood; b. Boykins, Va., Oct. 21, 1862; s. James Madison and Martha (Whitney) C.; student Suffolk Mil. Acad., 1878-80, Richmond Coll., 1880-83; studied law, U. of Va. Summer Sch., 1885, 86, and practiced at Boykins, 1886-94; Th.M., Southern Bapt. Theol. Sem., 1897; m. Josephine Weston, Nov. 21, 1899; children—Martha Ann, Linwood Percy (dec.), Josephine Weston, Charles Whitney. Ordained Bapt. ministry, 1897; pastor Millwood, Rockland and Bethel chs., in Valley of Va., 1897-98, Red Bank, Northampton Co., 1898-1906; became supt. Bapt. Orphanage of Va., 1906; pastor, Townsend, Va., 1929—. Democrat. Mason. Home: Townsend, Va. Died Aug. 23, 1934.

CORCORAN, Francis Vincent, educator; b. Pittsburgh, Pa., May 6, 1879; s. Martin and Rose (McDermott) C.; prep. edn., St. Mary's Sem., Perryville, Mo.; student St. Mary's Scholasticate; grad. St. Thomas Acad. of Philosophy, Rome, Italy; study at Minerva (now Angelica) Coll., Rome, 1901-03, Ph.D., S.T.D. Mem. Congregation of the Mission (founded by St. Vincent de Paul); ordained at Paris, France, July 27, 1902; prof. philosophy, Kenrick Sem., St. Louis, Mo., 1903-07, prof. theology, 1907-30, vice-pres. of sem., 1926-30; also head of dept. of philosophy, Webster Coll., Webster Groves, Mo., 1917-30; asso. editor Western Watchman, St. Louis, 1916-25; chmn. administrative bd. of corporate colls., St. Louis Univ., 1926-30; pres. De Paul Univ., Chicago, 1930-35; superior Los Angeles (Calif.) Coll., 1936—. Mem. Knights of Columbus. Died Jan. 28, 1939.

CORCORAN, John William, lawyer; b. Batavia, N.Y., June 14, 1853; ed. Clinton (Mass.) public schools; Holy Cross Coll., Worcester, Mass.; St. John Univ., Fordham, N.Y. (LL.D., 1893); grad. Boston Univ. Law Sch., 1875; began practice Clinton, Mass., 1875; m. Margaret J. McDonald, Apr. 28, 1881. Town solicitor, 1883-92; Dem. nominee for atty. gen.

Mass., 1886 and 1887, defeated; Dem. candidate for lt. gov. Mass., 1888, 1889, 1890, 1891; judge adv. gen. on Gov. Russell's staff, 1891-92; chmn. Mass. bd. mgrs. World's Columbia Expn.; a justice Mass. superior court, May 1, 1892, to Nov. 1893, resigned; then law partner Patrick A. Collins. Receiver, 1886, Lancaster Nat. Bank, and paid all creditors in full; for 21 yrs. chmn. school bd.; from 1881 mem. bd. of water commrs., Clinton, Mass. Chairman Dem. State Com. 5 yrs. Home: Clinton, Mass. Died 1904.

CORDLEY, Arthur Burton, college dean; b. Pinckney, Mich., Feb. 11, 1864; s. Charles and Esther (Hicks) C.; B.S., Mich. Agrl. Coll., 1888, M.S., 1901, hon. D.Sc., 1917; grad. student Cornell U., 1900, 1907; hon. LL.D., Ore. State College, 1932; m. Mary Celia McLouth, July 5, 1893; 1 dau., Dorothea McLouth. Asst. in entomology, Mich. Agrl. Coll., 1888-90; asst. entomologist, Vt. Expt. Sta., 1890-91; asst. entomologist, U.S. Dept. Agr., 1891-93; farmer, 1893-95; prof. zoölogy and entomologist, Expt. Sta., Ore. Agrl. Coll., 1895-1913, dir. sta., 1914-20, dean of agr., 1907-31 (emeritus), Ore. Agrl. Coll. Pres. Corvallis Orchard Co. Republican. Conglist. Mason. Home: Corvallis, Ore. Died Nov. 1, 1936.

CORDOVA-DAVILA, Félix; b. Vega Baja, P.R., Nov. 20, 1878; LL.B., Nat. U., Washington, D.C., LL.M.; m. Mercedes Diaz, 1906; children—George L., Felix L., Henry, Aida. Practiced in Porto Rico; judge Court of Caguas, 1904; judge Municipal Court of Manati, 1904-08; later judge Dist. Court of Guayama, Dist. Court of Arecibo, Dist. Court of San Juan; resident commr. at Washington, D.C., from Puerto Rico, 1917-32; asso. justice Supreme Court of P.R., 1932-38; resigned, Feb. 28, 1938. Died Dec. 3, 1938.

COREA, Luis Felipe, diplomatist, lawyer; b. Granada, Nicaragua, Aug. 25, 1864; s. Simon and Ramona (Briceño) C.; ed. Nat. Coll., Granada, and grad. (LL.D.) Central Univ. of Guatemala. Prof. history, philosophy and mathematics, Central Univ., after graduation; prof. philosophy and history in various colls. in Guatemala; judge at Totonicapam and asso. judge, Quezaltenango, and at same time prof. internat. law, Western U. of Guatemala. Given title of doctor of laws and apptd. sec. legation, Republic of Central America, in Washington, 1896; apptd. chargé d'affaires same republic few months later; chargé d'affaires of Nicaragua, 1898; E.E. and M.P. of Nicaragua to U.S., 1899-1909; minister to Mexico City, 1901; del. 1st Pan-Am. Customs Congress. Galston & Corea, New York, 1909. Del. to Phila. Commercial Congress; chmn. Nicaraguan Commn., Buffalo Expn., 1901; del. 2d Internat. Am. Congress, Mex., 1900-09, to Cuba, 1906-09; mem. Johnson, gress, New York, 1902; non. v.p. Internat. Geographic Congress, 1904; del. to 3d Internat. Am. Congress, Rio de Janeiro, 1906, to Central Am. Peace Conf., Washington, 1907, to 2d Pan-Am. Scientific Congress, 1915-16. Proclaimed candidate for president of Nicaragua by the Republican Liberal Party, 1924. Order of Bust of Liberator Bolivar, and Medal of Public Instruction of Venezuela. Home: New York, N.Y. Died Apr. 27, 1932.

COREY, Charles Henry, Baptist clergyman; b. New Canaan, N.B., Dec. 12, 1834; grad. Acadia Coll., Nova Scotia, 1858 (A.M., D.D.); grad. Newton Theol. Sem., 1861 (D.D., Richmond Coll., Va.; Baylor Univ., Texas; McMaster Univ., Canada). Shortly after ordained minister, but soon resigned charge and served with U.S. Christian Commn. to end of the war; in 1867 became prin. Augusta, Ga., Inst.; from 1868 pres. Richmond, Va., Theol. Sem. for training colored ministers. Author: Reminiscences of 30 Years' Labor Among the Colored People of the South. Home: Richmond, Va. Died 1899.

COREY, Fred Daniel, pub. utilities; b. nr. Watertown, N.Y., May 27, 1863; s. Daniel M. and Angeline (Kennedy) C.; LL.B., U. of Buffalo, 1892; m. Winifred Eaton, Apr. 18, 1925; children—Winifred Wilma, Ann. Teacher pub. schs., 6 yrs.; admitted to N.Y. bar, 1892, and practiced at Buffalo until 1915; pres. Niagara, Lockport & Ontario Power Co., 1915—; chmn. exec. com. Buffalo, Niagara & Eastern Power Corp.; pres. Bradford Electric Co., Lockport & Newfane Power & Water Supply Co., Lower Niagara River Power & Water Supply Co.; v.p. Niagara Share Corp., Old Fort Niagara Assn.; treas. and dir. Hotel Touraine Co., Delaware & Johnson Corp. Republican. Presbyn. Home: Lake View, N.Y. Died Feb. 1936.

COREY, William Ellis, capitalist; b. Braddock, Pa., May 4, 1866; s. Alfred A. and Adaline (Fritz) C.; ed. pub. schs. and Duff's Coll., Pittsburgh; twice married; m. 2d, Mabelle Gilman, May 14, 1907. At 16 entered chem. laboratory of Edgar Thomson Steel Works; went to Homestead Steel Works, 1887, becoming supt. plate mill, 1889, supt. armor plate dept., 1893, succeeded Charles M. Schwab as gen. supt., 1897; pres. Carnegie Steel Co., 1901-03, U.S. Steel Corp., 1903-11; dir. numerous corps. Home: New York, N.Y. Died May 11, 1934.

CORKEY, Alexander, clergyman; b. Glendermott, Londonderry, Ireland, Oct. 27, 1871; s. Joseph (LL.D.) and Isabella (Sloane) C.; Foyle Coll. and Magee Coll., Londonderry; grad. McCormick Theol. Sem., Chicago, 1899; post-grad. work, New Coll., Edinburgh, Scotland, 1900; (hon. A.B., Tabor Coll., Ia., 1902, D.D., 1910); m. Olive Ranney, Sept. 20, 1893. Ordained Presbyn. ministry, 1899; pastorates, Malvern, Ia., 1901-02, Fairfield, Ia., 1902-05, Cedar Bluffs, Neb., 1906-10, Wayne, Neb., 1910—; spl. lecturer on sociology, Bellevue Coll., Neb. Democrat. Author: The Truth About Ireland, 1910; The Victory of Allan Rutledge, 1910; The Testing Fire, 1911; For Conscience Sake, 1912; The Vision of Joy, 1913. Home: Wayne, Neb. Died Oct. 28, 1914.

CORLISS, Augustus Whittemore, soldier; b. N. Yarmouth, Me., Mar. 25, 1837; s. Robert Elwell and Asenath (Field) C.; grad. N. Yarmouth (Me.) Acad., 1851; widower. Served in Civil War from 1862 as lt. col. 2d R.I. Cav.; after war was 2d lt. and later 1st lt., 15th U.S. Inf.; capt. 8th U.S. Inf.; maj. 7th U.S. Inf., 1897; lt. col. 2d U.S. Inf., 1899; col. 2d U.S. Inf., 1901; brig. gen. U.S.A. retired, Apr. 23, 1904. Republican. Home: Denver, Colo. Died 1908.

CORLISS, Charles Albert, corp. official; b. Troy, N.Y., Oct. 16, 1868; s. Wilbur Fisk and Julia (Parmlee) C.; B.A., Williams, 1890; m. Anne Parrish, Dec. 29, 1915. Pres. Lamont, Corliss & Co., selling agents, 1903—; pres. Pond's Extract Co. Republican. Presbyn. Home: Englewood, N.J. Died Feb. 9, 1936.

CORLISS, John Blaisdell, congressman; b. Richford, Vt., June 7, 1851; s. Hezekiah and Lydia (Round) C.; grad. Vt. Meth. U., 1871; LL.B., Columbian (now George Washington) U., 1875; m. Elizabeth N. Danforth, Dec. 5, 1877. Admitted to bar, 1875, and began practice at Detroit; sr. mem. Corliss, Leete & Joslyn; pres. Mich. Lubricator Co., Shipman Coal Co., of Pa. City atty., Detroit, 1882-86; prepared 1st complete charter for Detroit which was passed by legislature, 1884, and remains in force; mem. 54th to 57th Congresses (1895-1903), 1st Mich. Dist. Republican. Home: Detroit, Mich. Died Dec. 24, 1929.

CORN, Samuel Thompson, judge; b. Nicholasville, Ky., Oct. 8, 1840; s. Ellis and Emily (Thompson) C.; A.B., Princeton, 1860; m. Emma Blackburn, Aug. 10, 1876. Admitted to bar, 1863; practiced at Carlinville, 1866-86, Evanston, Wyo., 1890-97, Cheyenne, Wyo., 1905, Ogden, Utah, 1906—. Justice Supreme Ct. of Wyo., 1886-90 and 1897-1904 (chief justice, 1903-04). Democrat. Home: Ogden, Utah. Died Jan. 28, 1925.

CORNELIUS, Charles Over, author, architect; b. Sewickley, Pa., Sept. 9, 1890; s. Charles Edwin and Katharine Courtney (Shurtleff) C.; A.B., Princeton, 1913; B.S., Mass. Inst. Tech., 1916; m. Louise, d. Walter Russell, of N.Y. City, Sept. 10, 1932. Began in office Frank A. Colby, architect, N.Y. City; with Met. Mus. Art, 1917—; asst. curator dept. decorative art, same, 1918-24, asso. curator Am. art, 1925—; in practice as architect, Jan. 1931—. Presbyn. Author: Furniture Masterpieces of Duncan Phyfe, 1922; The American Wing (with R. T. H. Halsey), 1924; Early American Furniture, 1926. Died July 14, 1937.

CORNELIUS, Mary Ann, author; b. Pontiac, Mich., Sept. 25, 1827; d. Lewis Whiting and Elvira (Bagley) Mann; ed. at Pontiac, Mich.; m. Samuel Cornelius, D.D., 1850 (dec.). Extensively engaged in philanthropic work; was given a free reading room and free circulating library. Author: Little Wolf, 1880; Uncle Nathan's Farm, 1897; The White Flame, 1900; Why? or, A Kansas Girl's Query, 1905. Home: Chicago, Ill. Died Apr. 18, 1918.

CORNELIUS, Samuel Anderson, clergyman; b. Mt. Jackson, Pa., Nov. 20, 1857; s. Maxwell and Mary (Anderson) C.; A.B., U. of Wooster, O., 1882; A.M., 1885; grad. Union Theol. Sem., 1885; D.D., Wooster, 1897; m. Harriet Canfield, May 25, 1886. Ordained Presbyn. ministry, 1885; pastor Phillipsburg, Pa., 1885-89, Santa Cruz, Calif., 1889-91, Oil City, Pa., 1891-1915. Moderator of Synod of Pa., 1912-13, and mem. exec. commn. of Synod; rep. Gen. Assembly of Presbyn. Ch. at Princeton Centennial, 1912. Republican. Home: Wooster, O. Died Feb. 15, 1932.

CORNELL, Alonzo B.; b. Ithaca, N.Y., Jan. 22, 1832; s. Ezra C., founder Cornell Univ.; ed. Ithaca Acad.; became telegraph operator and later telegraph mgr.; owned line of steamboats on Cayuga Lake; v.p. and cashier 1st Nat. Bank of Ithaca, 1864-69; dir., 1868-99, Western Union Telegraph Co.; defeated as Republican candidate for lt. gov., 1868; surveyor of customs, New York, 1869-73; mem. and speaker N.Y. assembly; chmn. Rep. State Central Com., 1870-78; naval officer, port of New York, 1876-78; gov. N.Y., 1880-83; had large financial interests. Home: Ithaca, N.Y. Died 1904.

CORNELSON, George Henry, clergyman; b. Orangeburg, S.C., Nov. 2, 1869; s. George Henry and Angie M. (Holman) C.; B.S., S.C. Mil. Acad., 1888; A.M., Davidson (N.C.) Coll., D.D., 1906; student McCormick Theol. Sem.; B.D., Columbia (S.C.) Theol. Sem., 1895; spl. courses, U. of Chicago and Free Ch. Coll., Edinburgh, Scotland, 1895-96; m. Emma F. Bailey, Nov. 10, 1897; children—George Henry, Rose Bailey. Ordained ministry Presbyn. Ch. in U.S., 1896; pastor successively Malvern, Ark., Aiken, S.C., Concord, N.C., Moore Memorial Ch., Nashville, Tenn., until 1909, First Ch., New Orleans, 1909-27; v.p. City Investment Co., Gentilly Terrace Co., Rose Hill, Inc. Cadet capt. Prize Co. B, S.C. Mil. Acad., 1888. Trustee Mountain Retreat Assn., Montreat, N.C. Democrat. Mason. Home: New Orleans, La. Died Mar. 5, 1928.

CORNER, George Washington, Jr.; b. Baltimore, Md., May 1, 1862; s. George W. and Mary J. (Dungan) C.; ed. Pembroke Sch. and Friends' Acad., Baltimore; m. Florence Elmer Evans, Nov. 27, 1888; children—George Washington III, Henry Evans, Hester King. Mem. Rouse, Hempstone & Co., merchants, Baltimore, 1895; treas. Rouse, Hempstone & Co., Inc., 1917-26; sec. same firm in liquidation; asst. treas. Baltimore Equitable Soc., fire ins., 1928-30, treas., 1930—; chmn. bd. Baltimore Goodwill Industries; v.p. Central Savings Bank. Mem. Public Bath Commn. of Baltimore, 1900-05; treas. bd. of trustees Home for the Aged, M.E. Ch., Baltimore, 1911-15; dir. Boys' Home Soc. of Baltimore, 1910-15; pres. bd. trustees Baltimore Y.M.C.A. Pres. Samuel Ready Sch. for Girls; trustee Goucher Coll., 1933-36. Republican. Home: Baltimore, Md. Died Sept. 20, 1938.

CORNER, Thomas Cromwell, portrait painter; b. Baltimore, Md., Feb. 2, 1865; s. William Henley and Camilla (Cromwell) C.; ed. pub. schs., Baltimore; studied art, Md. Inst. Design (Baltimore), Art Students' League (New York), Académie Julian (Paris); unmarried. Exhibited at Nat. Acal. Design, New York; Pa. Acad. Fine Arts, Phila.; Corcoran Gallery of Art, Washington, D.C.; Baltimore Mus. of Art. Portraits on permanent exhbn. in State Capitol and City Hall, Albany, N.Y.; Annapolis, Md.; Richmond, Va.; U.S. Court House, Harrisburg, Pa.; Johns Hopkins U., Baltimore. Trustee Baltimore Mus. of Art. Democrat. Unitarian. Home: Baltimore, Md. Died Sept. 4, 1938.

CORNETET, Noah E., clergyman, educator; b. Mowrystown, O., June 2, 1867; s. Lewis C. and Leah (Winkle) C.; B.A., Otterbein Coll., Westerville, O., 1896, M.A., 1902, Litt.D., 1921; m. Nannie E. Holladay, May 9, 1889; children—Dwight Lowell, Hazel Lois Miller, Wendell Hillis, Russell Lewis, Mary Grace. Ordained ministry U.B. in Christ, 1890; pastor Halisville and Cynthiana (O.), 1889-92, Newark (O.), Trenton (Mo.) and Logan (O.), 1895-1901; prof. Greek, Otterbein Coll., 1901—, dean, 1921—. Teacher of a men's Bible class. Sec. Ohio State Assn. Sch. Bd. Members 4 yrs.; mem. Bd. of Edn., Westerville, 11 yrs. (pres.). Author: Prayer a Means of Spiritual Growth, 1904. Home: Westerville, O. Died Nov. 13, 1931.

CORNING, Charles Robert, judge; b. Concord, N.H., Dec. 20, 1855; s. Robert Nesmith and Mary Lougee (Woodman) C.; ed. Phillips Academy, Andover, Mass., and Harvard Law Sch.; (hon. A.M., Dartmouth, 1887); unmarried. Mem. N.H. Ho. of Rep., 1878-83, Senate, 1889; asst. atty. Dept. of Justice, Washington, 1889-93; probate judge, Concord, N.H., 1899—. Mayor of Concord, 1903-09, pres. Bd. of Edn., 1900-08; trustee State Normal Sch. Republican. Author: Aalesund to Tetuan, 1888. Home: Concord, N.H. Died Oct. 18, 1924.

CORNING, Frederick Gleason, mining engr.; b. Brooklyn, Mar. 27, 1857; s. Rev. James Leonard and Sarah Ellen (Deming) C.; ed. Realschule, Stuttgart, Germany, Stuttgart Poly. Royal Sch. of Mines, Freiberg, 4½ years, M.E., 1879; LL.D., U. of Pittsburgh, 1911; m. Marion Adeline Vernon, June 18, 1891. Practiced as mining engr. and metallurgist in U.S., Central and S. America and Can.; from 1897 has been at head of cos. operating gold and silver mines in Mexico, S.A. and Can. Pres. The Exploration Co. of New York. Hon. senator in Freiberg Mining Acad. Home: New York, N.Y. Died July 12, 1937.

CORNING, J(ames) Leonard, neurologist; b. Stamford, Conn., Aug. 26, 1855; s. Rev. James Leonard and Sarah Ellen (Deming) C.; bro. of Frederick Gleason C.; ed. Riverview Mil. Acad., Poughkeepsie, N.Y.; U. of Heidelberg; M.D., U. of Würzburg, 1878; (hon. A.M., Williams Coll., 1888; LL.D.); m. Julia Crane, May 12, 1883. Discoverer spinal anæsthesia, 1885; demonstrated that the action of certain medicinal substances, notably stimulants and sedatives, may be increased and prolonged while subject remains in compressed air; also first to inject liquid paraffin into the tissues and solidify it in loco; consultant in nervous and mental diseases to various hosps., New York. Author: Carotid Compression, 1882; Brain Rest, 1883, Brain Exhaustion; Local Anæsthesia, 1886; Hysteria and Epilepsy, 1888; A Treatise on Headache and Neuralgia, 1888; Pain in Its Neuro-Pathological and Neuro-Therapeutic Relations, 1894. Died Aug. 24, 1923.

CORNISH, Ed(ward), banker; b. Ark., Oct. 25, 1871; s. Eli and Sarah Jane (Benton) C.; grad. high sch., Monticello, Ark.; Eastman Business Coll., Poughkeepsie, N.Y., 1888; m. Hilda Kahlert, July 20, 1902; children—Edith (Mrs. Raymond F. Low), Hilda (Mrs. James M. Cootes), Ed(ward), Sylvia, Merion, Don. Mem. Cornish & England, 1900-02; v.p. State Nat. Bank, 1902-04; pres. Am. Bank, 1904-11; v.p. German Nat. Bank, 1911-17; v.p. Am. Nat. Bank, 1917-19; v.p. Am. Bank of Commerce & Trust Co., 1919-21, pres. 1921-24; later pres. Am. Southern Trust Co. (all of Little Rock, Ark.); then pres. First Am. Bank & Trust Co., West Palm Beach, Fla. Pres. Bd. of Commerce, Little Rock, 1918. Democrat. Home: West Palm Beach, Fla. Died Nov. 5, 1928.

CORNISH, Edward Joel, chmn. bd. Nat. Lead Co.; b. Sidney, Ia., Dec. 15, 1861; s. Col. Joel N. and Virginia (Raymond) C.; student Tabor (Ia.) Coll., 1875-78; A.B., State U. of Ia., 1881, LL.B., 1882; m. Mrs. Levi Carter, 1909. Began practice at Omaha, 1882; asst. city atty., 1892-96; park commr., 1896-1912; as atty. for Levi Carter Estate, became pres. Carter White Lead Co., 1903; sold out to Nat. Lead Co., 1906, but continued as pres.; apptd. mgr. Chicago br. Nat. Lead Co., 1908; v.p. Nat. Lead Co., 1910-16, pres., 1916-33, chmn. bd., 1933—; pres. Lakeside Ice Co., Omaha; chmn. bd. Patino Mines & Enterprises Consol., Inc. Republican. Mason. Home: Cold Spring, N.Y. Died May 3, 1938.

CORNISH, Leslie Colby, judge; b. Winslow, Me., Oct. 8, 1854; s. Colby Coombs and Pauline Bailey (Simpson) C.; A.B., Colby U., 1875; Harvard Law Sch., 1879-80; (LL.D., Colby, 1904; Bowdoin Coll., 1918, U. of Maine, 1920); m. Fannie Woodman Holmes, Oct. 10, 1883. Admitted to the bar, 1880; mem. Me. legislature, 1878; mem. State Bd. Bar Examiners, Me., 5 yrs.; asso. justice Supreme Judicial Court of Me., Mar. 31, 1907-17, and apptd. chief justice, June 25, 1917. Pres. Augusta Savings Bank, 1905—(trustee from 1892). Trustee Lithgow Library, 1883— (pres. bd., 1094—); chmn. bd. trustees Colby Coll.; trustee Coburn Classical Inst., 1901—; dir. Am. Unitarian Assn., Boston, 1904-13 and 1919—; pres. Me. Unitarian Assn., 1917-18. Mem. Am. Acad. Arts and Sciences, 1923. Republican. Home: Augusta, Me. Died June 24, 1925.

CORNISH, Lorenzo Dana, civil engr.; b. Lee Centre, N.Y., Mar. 30, 1877; s. James Bennett and Frances Emeline (Ward) C.; C.E., Syracuse U., 1902; m. Mary Elizabeth Brodhead, Jan. 15, 1901 (died 1911); 1 son, Eugene Brodhead; m. 2d, Jeanette Welsh, May 18, 1916. Jr. U.S. civ. engr. and supt. constn., at Pittsburgh, 1902-06; asst. engr. Internat. Consulting Bd. Panama Canal, 1906; designing engr. Isthmian Canal Commn., 1907-13; prin. asst. engr. Am. Red Cross Bd. Engrs., China, 1914; prin. U.S. engr., U.S. Engr. Dept., Cincinati, O., 1915-17; asst. chief engr., 1919, became chief engr., 1928, Div. of Waterways, State of Ill., building Waterways, Lockport to La Salle. Served as pvt. Co. C, 3d N.Y. Vols., June-Oct. 1898; capt. 15th Engrs., U.S.A., June 11, 1917-Feb. 13, 1919; maj., Feb. 13-Oct. 30, 1919; hon. disch. Oct. 30, 1919. Republican. Baptist. Home: Chicago, Ill. Died May 12, 1934.

CORNISH, William D., ry. official; pres. Southern Pacific R.R., U. P. Land Co.; v.p. U. P. R.R. Co., Ore. Short Line R.R. Co., Ore. R.R. & Navigation Co., Leavenworth, Kan. & Western Ry., Portland & Asiatic Steamship Co., S. P. Co.; dir. San Pedro, Los Angeles & Salt Lake R.R., Wells, Fargo & Co., Spokane Union Depot Co., N. P. Terminal Co. of Ore. Died 1908.

CORNMAN, Oliver Perry, author; b. Phila., Aug. 26, 1866; s. Samuel and Jane (Fife) C.; grad. Central High Sch., Phila.; Ph.D., U. of Pa., 1899; unmarried. Supervisor North West Sch., Phila.; dist. supt. Phila. pub. schs., 1906-09, asso. supt., July, 1909—. Lecturer child psychology, U. of Pa., 1897—. Author: Brief Tropical Survey of U.S. History (with Oscar Gerson), 1902; Physiology Primer (with same), 1902; Spelling in the Elementary School, 1902. Home: Philadelphia, Pa. Died 1930.

CORNOYER, Paul, artist; b. St. Louis; pupil of Lefebvre, Benjamin Constant, and Louis Blanc, Paris, and St. Louis Sch. Fine Arts. Awarded 1st prize, Am. Art Assn. Exhbn., 1890; gold medal, Assn. Painters and Sculptors, St. Louis, 1895; Shaw, Inness, Evans prizes, Salmagundi Club, Phila. Art Club, Nat. Arts Club; hon. mention, Art Club, Phila. Represented in St. Louis Mus., Dallas (Tex.) Mus., pvt. collection of William M. Chase, etc. A.N.A., 1909. Died June 17, 1923.

CORNWALL, Edward Everett, M.D.; b. Buenos Aires, Argentine Republic, July 2, 1866; s. Nathaniel O. and Mary A. (West) C.; Ph.B., Wesleyan U., Conn., 1887; M.D., Coll. Phys. & Surg. (Columbia), 1890; unmarried. Resident phys. Presbyn. Hosp., New York, 1890-92; ship surgeon, Netherlands-Am. S.S. Co., 1892; practicing in Brooklyn, 1893—; attending phys. to Williamsburg Hosp., 1904-27, Norwegian Hosp., 1906—; cons. phys. Bethany Deaconesses Hosp., 1910—, Broad St. Hosp., 1922-26, Southside Hosp., 1928—, Brooklyn Eye and Ear Hosp., 1929—, St. John's Hosp., 1932—; prof. internal medicine, Brooklyn Post-Grad. Med. Sch., 1907-11. Fellow Am. Coll. Physicians (council 1915-20). Author: Clinical Treatise on Diseases of the Heart, 1917; William Cornwall and His Descendants, 1901. Died Oct. 6, 1940.

CORNWALL, Henry Bedinger, chemist; b. Southport, Conn., July 29, 1844; s. Rev. Nathaniel Ellsworth and Susan Peyton Ellsworth (Bedinger) C.; A.B., Columbia, 1864, A.M., 1867, E.M., 1867, Ph.D., 1888; student Royal Acad. Mining, Freiberg, 1866-68; (hon. A.M., Princeton U., 1896); m. Mary Hall Porter, June 3, 1875. Asst. gen. chemistry and metallurgy, 1864-66, asst. gen. chemistry, 1868-70, Columbia; supt. mining co. in Mexico, 1870-71; prof. applied chemistry and mineralogy, 1873-1910 (emeritus), Princeton U. Author: A Manual of Blow-Pipe Analysis, 1882; etc. Died Apr. 1, 1917.

CORNWALLIS, Kinahan, lawyer, editor; b. London, Eng., Dec. 24, 1839; s. William Baxter Kinahan C. (barrister-at-law) and Elizabeth (Cornwallis); collegiate edn.; m. Annie Louise Tisdale; m. 2d, Elizabeth Chapman (both dec.). Entered British colonial civil service; 2 yrs. in Melbourne, Australia; located in New York, 1860, as one of editors of The Herald; as Herald corr., accompanied Prince of Wales on Am. tour; admitted to N.Y. bar, 1863; financial editor and gen. editorial writer New York Herald, 1860-69; editor and propr. The Knickerbocker Magazine, afterward of The Albion; from 1886 editor and propr. Wall Street Daily Investigator, now Wall Street Daily Investor. Author: The Song of America and Columbus, 1892; The Conquest of Mexico and Peru, 1893; The War for the Union, or the Duel Between North and South, 1899. Home: New York, N.Y. Died Aug. 15, 1917.

CORNYN, John Hubert, newspaperman; b. Wingham, Ontario, Canada, July 6, 1875; s. William and Eleanor (Glazier) C.; B.A., Toronto U., 1895; post-grad. studies 2 yrs. in Germany and France. Newspaper work, Toronto, N.Y. City, Cuba and Mexico; dir. and prin. Mexico City Grammar and High Sch., 1901-05; prin. Pan-Am. Coll., 1908-09; prof. English and Greek, Nat. U. of Mexico, 1910-13, post-grad. English lit., 1925-26; prof. Romance langs., Birmingham (Ala.) Southern Coll., 1918-19, Southwestern U., 1919-20; was mng. editor Mexican papers; head Chicago Tribune Foreign News Bur., Mexico City, 1920-32. War corr. at front in Mexican revolutions, 1910-14 and 1920-29. Professor Aztec lang. and lit., Mexican Nat. U. Summer Sch., 1923-31. Owner and mgr. Quetzalcoatl Palace, tourist hotel, Mexico City, Mexico. Latin Am. editor of Ency. Americana, 1915-1920. Author: Mexican Fairy Tales, 1908; King of Reeds and Rushes, 1908; In the Name of Our Lady, 1909; Old Maya, 1909; Don Juan of Córdoba, 1910; Diaz and Mexico (in Spanish), 1910; Around the Wigwam Fire (Indian hero tales), 1920; When the Camp Fire Burns (Glooskap stories), 1923; Cuentos Mexicanos, 1925; The Song of Quetzalcoatl (an ancient saga translated from Aztec), 1930; The Song of the Ages (Aztec), 1936; Song of Tetzauteotl (Aztec saga), 1938. Also made many translations of tales, songs and comedies from Aztec into Spanish and English. Demonstrated the metric form of Ancient Aztec documents and showed that these contain the greater part of the lost literature of the ancient Mexicans. Engaged in research in Indian langs. of Mexico. Died Dec. 23, 1941.

CORRADO, Gaetano, corp. official; b. Marietta, O., Oct. 29, 1887; s. Cataldo and Marie Josephine C.; ed. pub. schs.; m. Angeline Bell, Sept. 25, 1913; children—Albert, Josephine, Gloria. Began in employ of Pittsburgh, McKeesport & Connellsville St. Ry. Co., later in gen. mdse. and banking business; in charge foreign dept. Colonial Nat. Bank of Connellsville, 1908-16; pres. and gen. mgr. Bell Coal & Coke Co., Corrado & Galiardi Constrn. Co.; pres. Penn-Yough Contracting Co., Bradford Coal Co., Faywest Coal Co., and 10 other coal cos.; chmn. bd. Vanderbilt Coal & Coke Co.; v.p. Yough-Cville Coal & Coke Co.; treas. Crawford Coal & Coke Co.; dir. Yough Brewing Co. Trustee Connellsville State Hosp. Republican. Catholic. Home: Connellsville, Pa. Died June 4, 1938.

CORRIGAN, Michael Augustine, R.C. archbishop N.Y., 1885—; b. Newark, N.J., Aug. 13, 1839; s. Thomas and Mary (English) C.; ed. St. Mary's Coll., Wilmington, Del.; grad. Mt. St. Mary's, Emmitsburg, Md., 1859; Am. Coll., Rome, D.D., 1864; prof. dogmatic theology and sacred scripture, 1864-68; pres., 1868-73, Seton Hall Coll., Orange, N.J.; adminstr. diocese Newark, 1870-73; bishop Newark, N.J., 1873; coadjutor, with right of succession, under title Archbishop of Petra, Sept. 26, 1880, to Cardinal-Archbishop McCloskey of New York. Died 1902.

CORRIGAN, Owen Bernard, bishop; b. Baltimore, Md., Mar. 5, 1849; s. John and Rosanna (McDonald) C.; ed. St. Charles Coll., Baltimore, 1864-68, St. Mary's Sem., 1868, Am. Coll. at Rome, 1869-73. Ordained priest R.C. Ch., in Rome, 1873; asst., St. Peter's Ch., Baltimore, 1873-84; built, and 1st pastor St. Gregory's Ch., 1884-1919; vicar gen., July 6, 1908; apptd. titular bishop of Macra and auxiliary to Cardinal Gibbons, Sept. 29, 1908; consecrated, Jan. 10, 1909. Home: Baltimore, Md. Died Apr. 8, 1929.

CORRUCCINI, Roberto, singer, teacher; b. Macerata, Italy, June 7, 1859; s. Pietro and Carolina (Gentili) C.; ed. gymnasium of Macerata; studied music with Faustini, at Istituto Musicale, Macerata, and grad. from same sch. in violin, under Romagnoli; student voice and singing with Domenico Concordia; m. Katherine Linton, Jan. 17, 1917; 1 son, Robert Joe. Played in orchestra at Bologna, Italy, 1879-84; operatic début as Dulcamara, in L'Elisir d'Amore, at Teatro Vaccai, Tolentino, 1885; sang comic bass parts in theatres of Italy, also at Budapest, Vienna and Lisbon, and 4 yrs. in Russia; came to U.S., 1906; prompter under Campanini, at Manhattan Opera House, New York, 1907; toured extensively with Abraamson and Bonci grand opera cos., with Melba in Australia, with Constantino Grand Opera Co., Bessie Abbott, etc.; mus. dir. and condr. Portland Opera Assn.; mus. condr. Holy Rosary Ch. Republican. Catholic. Home: Portland, Ore. Died Apr. 30, 1926.

CORSER, Harry Prosper, author, clergyman; b. Portageville, N.Y., Apr. 13, 1864; s. John Farmer and Hattie E. (Smith) C.; Ph.B., Lafayette Coll., 1885, M.S., 1888; grad. Union Theol. Sem., 1896; unmarried. Teacher pvt. schs., 1885-93; ordained Presbyn. ministry, 1896; pastor Flagstaff, Ariz., 1896-98, Wrangell, Alaska, 1899-1903; in charge P.E. Ch., Wrangell, 1904—, deacon and priest, 1907—; rep. Alaska at Pacific Coast Provincial Synod, 1925-31. Official lecturer Pacific Coast S.S. Co. Republican. Author: The Totem Lore of Alaska, 1910, 4th edit., 1921; Jack and Tom (stories for boys), 1915-16; Through the Ten Thousand Islands of Alaska; History of Alaska, 1929; Totem Lore and Land of the Totem, 10th edit., 1932. Home: Wrangell, Alaska. Died Feb. 2, 1936.

CORSON, Caroline Rollins, author; b. France; ed. France and Germany; m. Prof. Hiram Corson. Has written valuable articles on Faust, Machiavelli, Victor Hugo, etc., besides translations and other literary contributions. Transl. Paul Janet's Elements of Morals, 1884. Home: Ithaca, N.Y. Died 1901.

CORSON, David Birdsall, educator; b. nr. Millville, N.J., Feb. 17, 1864; s. David P. and Mary (Birdsall) C.; grad. Trenton State Normal Sch., 1884; Pd.M., New York U., 1893, Pd.D., 1913, Ph.D., 1924; LL.D., Alfred, 1921; m. Kate Thomson, 1893; children—David Noble, Frances (Mrs. Herbert P. Greenwood), Mary (Mrs. John R. McCune, Jr.). Prin. elementary schs. and supt. schs., Rahway; asst. supt. schs., Newark, N.J., 1905, supt., 1918-27. Organized courses for teachers in service, now Newark Inst. Arts and Sciences; v.p. Nat. Dept. of Superintendence; pres. N.J. Council of Edn. Republican. Presbyn. Died Apr. 30, 1935.

CORSON, Dighton, judge; b. Somerset Co., Me., Oct. 21, 1829; s. Isaac and Nancy C.; acad. edn., Waterville, Me. Admitted to bar, 1853; in practice at Milwaukee, Wis., 1853-61, in Nev., 1861-76, at Deadwood, S.D., 1877-89. Mem. Wis. Ho. of Rep., 1857-58; dist. atty., Milwaukee Co., Wis., 1859-60; dist. atty., Storey Co., Nev., 1861-65; mem. S.D. Constl. convs., 1885, 1889; judge Supreme Ct. of S.D., 1889-1913. Republican. Home: Deadwood, S.D. Died May 7, 1915.

CORSON, Hiram, univ. prof.; b. Phila., Nov. 6, 1828; s. Joseph D. and Ann Eliza (Hagey) C.; acad. edn.; (A.M., Princeton, 1864; LL.D., St. John's Coll., Md., 1878; Litt.D., Princeton, 1903); m. Caroline Rollin, of Paris, France, Sept. 13, 1854 (died 1901); father of Eugene Rollin C. Connected with Smithsonian Instn. library, 1849-56; lecturer on English lit., Phila., 1859-65; prof. moral science, history and rhetoric, Girard Coll., 1865-66; prof. Anglo-Saxon and English langs. and lit., St. John's Coll., 1866-70; prof. English lit., 1870-1903 (emeritus), Cornell. Author: Chaucer's Legende of Goode Women, with introduction and notes, 1863; An Introduction to the Study of Robert Browning's Poetry, 1886; An Introduction to the Study of Shakespeare, 1889; The Voice and Spiritual Education, 1896; Selections from Chaucer's Canterbury Tales, with introduction, notes and glossary, 1896; An Introduction to the Prose and Poetical Works of John Milton, 1899. Home: Ithaca, N.Y. Died 1911.

CORSON, Oscar Taylor, author, lecturer; b. on farm nr. Camden, O., May 3, 1857; s. William and Eliza (McBurney) C.; ed. pub. schs. and Ohio Wesleyan U., hon. A.M., 1888; LL.D., Wooster, 1907; m. Ella May Jacoby, Aug. 2, 1881. Teacher country schs., 1875-78; prin. Fair Haven (O.) Sch., 1878, 79; supt. schs., Camden, 1880-83, Granville schs., 1884-87, Cambridge schs., 1887-91; state commr. common schs. Ohio, 1892-98; editor Ohio Ednl. Monthly (founded, 1852), 1895-1918; lecturer on edn., Western Coll., Oxford, O. Republican. Presbyn. Trustee Ohio State U., 1899-1913. Author of Ohio State School Reports, 6 vols., 1892-98; Our Public Schools; Abraham Lincoln—His Words and Deeds, 1927. Home: Oxford, O. Died Apr. 14, 1928.

CORTELYOU, George Bruce, Secretary of the Treasury; b. New York, July 26, 1862; s. Peter C.,

Jr., and Rose (Seary) C.; grad. Hempstead (L.I.) Inst., 1879, State Normal Sch., Westfield, Mass., 1882; LL.B., Georgetown U., 1895; LL.M., Columbian (now George Washington) U., 1896; LL.D., Georgetown, 1903, Ky. Wesleyan U., 1905, U. of Ill., 1905, George Washington University, 1932; m. Lily Morris, d. Dr. Hinds, pres. Hempstead Inst., Sept. 15, 1888. General law and verbatim reporter, New York, 1883-85; prin. of prep. schs., New York, 1885-89. Entered pub. service, 1889, and was pvt. sec. to various officials, including postoffice insp., New York, surveyor of port of New York, 4th asst. postmaster gen.; stenog. to President Cleveland, Nov. 1895; exec. clerk, Feb. 1896; asst. sec. to President McKinley, July 1, 1898, sec., Apr. 13, 1900, reapptd., Mar. 15, 1901; reapptd. by President Roosevelt, Sept. 16, 1901; 1st sec. of Dept. of Commerce and Labor, Feb. 16, 1903-July 1, 1904; postmaster gen., Mar. 7, 1905-Mar. 4, 1907; sec. of the treasury, Mar. 4, 1907-Mar. 8, 1909, in cabinet of President Roosevelt. Chmn. Rep. Nat. Com., 1904-07. Pres. Consolidated Gas Co. of New York, 1909-35; dir. New York Life Ins. Co., D. Appleton-Century Co. Hon. pres. McKinley Nat. Memorial Assn.; pres. Miriam Osborn Memorial Home Assn. Home: Huntington, L.I., N.Y. Died Oct. 23, 1940.

CORTHELL, Arthur Bateman, civil engr.; b. Whitman, Mass., July 3, 1860; s. James Hosea and Charlotte (Almy) C.; ed. Providence High Sch., 1875-77; Brown U., 1877-81 (hon. A.M., 1898); m. Lena Cynthia Foster, Sept. 26, 1882. Draftsman with Hereshoff Mfg. Co., Bristol, R.I., 1878-81; rodman, city engineer's office, Providence, Mar.-June 1881; again with Hereshoff Mfg. Co., June-Sept. 1881; asst. engr., supervisor and div. engr., N.Y., West Shore & Buffalo R.R., 1881-84; civ. engr. Knickerbocker Ice Co., New York, 1884-86; prin. asst. engr., Fitzgerald & Mallory Construction Co., building railroads for M.P. Ry., in Kan. and Colo., 1886-87; 1st asst. engr. constrn. Sioux City Bridge over Missouri River, 1887-88; asst. engr. on Thames River bridge, 1888-89, N.Y., Providence & Boston R.R., 1889-92; 1st asst. engr. Providence passenger sta. and approaches, 1892-97; prin. asst. engr. on constrn. South Sta. for Boston Terminal Co., Boston, 1897-99; with Westinghouse, Church, Kerr & Co., Boston, 1899-1900; resident engr. Boston Terminal Co., 1900-02; terminal engr. N.Y.C.&H.R. R.R., at New York, 1902-06; asst. exec. Grand Central Sta. architects, 1906-08; sec. and cons. engr. auxiliary facilities com., Grand Central Terminal, 1908-11; chief engr. B.&M. R.R., July 1911—. Mason. Home: Winchester, Mass. Died May 1924.

CORTHELL, Elmer Lawrence, civil engr.; b. S. Abington (now Whitman), Mass., Sept. 30, 1840; s. James Lawrence C.; A.B., Brown U., 1867, A.M., 1868 (Sc.D., 1894); m. Emily T. Davis, 1867 (died 1884); m. 2d, Marie Küchler (b. Switzerland), 1900. Served pvt. to capt. of battery 1st R.I. Light Arty., 1861-65; began civil engring. Providence, 1867; served on ry. surveys and constrn., Ill. and Mo.; chief engr. bridges over Mississippi River, Hannibal and Louisiana, Mo.; also levees on Miss.; resident engr. in constrn. Mississippi jetties with James B. Eads; chief engr. Atlantic & Pacific Ship Ry., to build ship ry. over Isthmus of Tehuantepec, Mex., with Capt. Eads; chief engr. constrn. N.Y., West Shore & Buffalo Ry.; cons. engr. bldg. rys. into Chicago; asso. chief engr. several large bridges over Mo., Ohio and other rivers; chief engr. Merchants Bridge, St. Louis, Brazos River jetties, Tex., Tampico Harbor Works, Mex.; consulting engr. Nat. Pub. Works Argentine Govt., 1900-02; mem. advisory bd. of engrs., 1903-05, to build 1,000-ton barge canals, N.Y. State, to cost over $100,000,000; chief engr. Port of Para, Brazil, and Rio Grande do Sul. Contbr. articles Jetties, Levees, Ship Canals, Ship Railways, etc., in Johnson's Cyclopedia; Railway Passenger Stations of the World, in Ency. Americana, 1904, etc. Home: North Egremont, Mass. Died May 16, 1916.

CORTHELL, Nellis Eugene, lawyer; b. Franklinville, N.Y., Nov. 14, 1861; s. Lathrop Vinton and Phoebe (Morris) C.; grad. Ten Broeck Free Acad., Franklinville, 1879; moved to Wyo., 1880; studied law in office Stephen W. Downey, Laramie; m. Eleanor M. Quackenbush, June 30, 1885; children—Evelyn, Morris Eliot, Miriam, Gladys, Robert Clinton, Huron Decatur, Irving Eugene. Admitted to Wyo. bar, 1883. Democrat. Home: Laramie, Wyo. Died Aug. 21, 1932.

CORTISSOZ, Ellen Mackay Hutchinson, author; b. New York; m. Royal Cortissoz. Art editor New York Tribune. Author: Songs and Lyrics. Editor (with E. C. Stedman): The Library of American Literature (11 vols.). Home: New York, N.Y. Died Aug. 13, 1933.

CORWIN, Arthur Mills, M.D.; b. Honolulu, H.I., Mar. 24, 1864; s. Eli (D.D.) and Henrietta S. (Howell) C.; A.B., Princton, 1887, A.M., 1899; M.D., Rush Med. Coll., 1890; grad. study, Berlin, 3 mos.; m. Fannie L. Hastings, 1893 (died 1922); 1 dau., Sylvia (Mrs. L. M. Francisco); stepdaughter, Mary W. Hastings (Mrs. Herbert E. Bradley); m. 2d, Mrs. Marion Dwyer, July 1924; step-son, Harold R. Dwyer. Demonstrator physical diagnosis, Rush Medical Coll., and attending phys. Central Free Dispensary, dept. chest, nose and throat, 1892-1902; prof. diseases throat and nose, Chicago Clin. Sch. and Ill. Post-Grad. Med. Sch., 1902-13; prof. physical diagnosis, Coll. Phys. and Surgeons, 1903-13; formerly attending phys. tuberculosis dept., Cook County Hosp., and attending laryngologist, West Side and Sheridan Park hosps.; formerly asso. prof. laryngology, Chicago Coll. Medicine and Surgery. Dir. publicity and edn., Chicago Dept. of Health, 1915-16; mem. editorial staff Chicago Medical Recorder; dir. Valmora Sanitarium for tuberculosis. Dir. Anti-Saloon League of Ill. Fellow Am. Coll. Surgeons. Author: Outline Physical Diagnosis of the Chest, 1892. Home: Chicago, Ill. Died Sept. 9, 1933.

CORWIN, Edward Tanjore, clergyman; b. New York, July 12, 1834; s. Edward Caldwell and Mary Ann (Shuart) C.; A.B., Coll. City of N.Y., 1853, A.M., 1856; New Brunswick Theol. Sem., 1856; (D.D., Rutgers, 1872, Litt.D., 1911); m. Mary Esther Kipp, July 25, 1861; father of Charles Edward C. Ordained Ref. Church in America ministry, 1857; pastor Paramus, N.J., 1857-63, Millstone, N.J., 1863-88; rector of Hertzog Hall, New Brunswick, N.J., 1888-95; pastor Greendale, N.Y., 1895-97; agt. of Gen. Synod to make researches in Holland concerning history of colonial chs. of N.Y. and N.J., 1897-98; edited documents obtained in Holland, for State of New York, 1898-1905. Pres. Gen. Synod, 1891. Author: Manual of Reformed Church in America, 4 editions, 1859-1902; The History of the Reformed Church in America (Vol. VIII, American Church History Series), 1895; Ecclesiastical Records of New York, 6 vols., 1901-05. Died June 23, 1914.

CORWIN, Richard Warren, M.D., surgeon; b. Binghamton, N.Y., May 24, 1852; s. Walter Scott and Rhoda (Little) C.; student scientific course, Cornell, 1871-74; M.D., U. of Mich., 1878; interne St. Luke's Hosp., Chicago, 1879-81; studied in European hosps., 1893, 1900; LL.D., U. of Colo., 1905; hon. A.M., U. of Denver, 1906; unmarried. Instr. comparative anatomy and microscopy, U. of Mich., 1874-78; chief surgeon from 1881, supt. sociol. dept. from 1900, Colo. Fuel & Iron Co.; chief surgeon Colo. & Wyo. Ry., Crystal River Ry.; div. surgeon Mo.P. Ry.; local surgeon D.&R.G. Ry., C.&S. Ry.; prof. surgery U. of Colo. Lecturer on med., sociol. and other themes; asst. editor "Physicians and Surgeons," 1878-84. Pres. Colo. State Conf. Charities and Corrections, 1906; mem. bd., Colo. State Prison Assn., 1906; Colo. State Normal Sch., 8 yrs., Colo. State Bd. of Health, 5 yrs., Colo. State Agrl. Coll., 1905—, Pueblo Sch. Bd., 1892—. First lt. C.N.G., 1883-84; capt. and 1st asst. surgeon, 1884-87; maj. and surgeon, 1887-98; col. and surgeon-gen., 1898; col. and a.-d.-c., 1903, 1904, 1907, 1908. Fellow Am. Coll. Surgeons. Republican. Protestant. Mason. Home: Pueblo, Colo. Died June 1928.

CORWIN, Robert Gilbert, lawyer; b. Lebanon, O., Dec. 7, 1877; s. Robert Boake and Sarah Bankson (Baker) C.; B.S., Nat. Normal U., Lebanon, 1898; m. Louise Snyder, Oct. 14, 1909; children—Mary Louise, Robert Knox, Charles Frederick Snyder, Gilbert. Admitted to O. bar, 1901, and then practiced in Dayton; mem. McMahon, Corwin, Landis & Markham; chmn. Montgomery Co. Com. Civil Works Adminstrn., Dayton Juvenile Counseling Bureau; mem. Governor's School Survey Commn., Employment Exchange Adv. Bd.; past pres. Dayton Council of Social Agencies, Dayton Art Inst., Dayton Bur. of Community Service; dir. Nat. Assn. of Community Chests and Councils; mem. Sherrill State Survey Com.; referee Nat. Railroad Adjustment Bd. and Ry. Express Agency Labor Disputes; pres. Dayton Boys Club; v.p. Dayton Lawyers Club, pres. bd. trustees Dayton Pub. Library; trustee Ohio Inst., Ohio League for Constl. Rights, Ohio State Library Assn. Received Civitan Civil Award, 1930. Home: Dayton, O. Died Oct. 26, 1940.

CORY, Charles Barney, ornithologist; b. Boston, Jan. 31, 1857; s. Barney and Eliza A. B. C.; ed. Boston schs. and Lawrence Scientific Sch. (Harvard), 1879; m. Harriet W. Peterson, May 29, 1883. Hon. curator of ornithology, Boston Soc. Natural History until 1905; hon. curator of ornithology, 1895-1906, prof. and hon. curator dept. zoölogy, 1906—, Field Mus. Natural History, Chicago. Pres. Am. Ornithologists' Union, 1904-05; fellow Zoöl. and Linnean socs. London. Author: Catalogue of West Indian Birds; Hunting and Fishing in Florida; The Birds of Eastern North America; How to Know the Shore Birds of North America; How to Know the Ducks, Geese and Swans of North America; The Birds of the West Indies; Key to the Water Birds of Florida; Hunting and Fishing in Florida; Key to the Birds of Eastern North America; The Birds of Illinois and Wisconsin. Home: Chicago, Ill. Died July 29, 1921.

CORY, Clarence Linus, electrical engr.; b. Lafayette, Ind., Sept. 4, 1872; s. Thomas and Carrie (Stoney) C.; B.M.E., Purdue U., 1889, E.D., 1914; M.E., Cornell, 1891; m. Mayme Pritchard, Dec. 25, 1905; 1 dau., Marion Elizabeth. Prof. elec. engring. Highland Park College, Des Moines, Ia., 1891-92; prof. elec. engring., 1892—, and dean Coll. Mechanics, 1901—, U. of Calif. In practice as cons. elec. and mech. engr., San Francisco, Jan. 1, 1899—. Asst. dir. U.S. explosive plants, in charge of elec. power supply, 1917-18. Home: Berkeley, Calif. Died Aug. 2, 1937.

COSBY, Frank Carvill, naval officer; b. Louisville, Ky., Apr. 10, 1840; s. Fortunatus and Ellen (Blake) C.; ed. in Ky. and Washington, to 1854; receiving teller. U.S. Treasury, 1854-57; m. Charlotte M. Spencer, Dec. 6, 1864. Capt.'s clerk, U.S.N., 1857-61; paymaster Potomac flotilla, 1861-63; depot paymaster S. Atlantic squadron, 1863-64, participating in engagements on Potomac and Rappahannock rivers, off Charleston, etc.; paymaster Baltimore and Annapolis stas., 1865-68; Honolulu, H.I., 1868-69, and various other stas. until became fleet paymaster, European sta., 1877-81; various duties to 1897; mem. Bd. Inspection and Survey of Naval Vessels, 1897-98; pres. Naval Examining Bd., 1897-1901; gen. insp. pay corps U.S.N. with rank of capt., 1898-1902; pay dir. with rank of rear admiral, retired. Home: Washington, D.C. Died 1905.

COSBY, George Blake, receiver public moneys of Calif.; b. Louisville, Ky., Jan. 19, 1830; s. Fortunatus and Ellen (Blake) C.; ed. private schools; clerk in commn. house; entered West Point, Sept. 1, 1848; bvt. lt. mounted rifles, July 1, 1852; 2d lt., Sept. 16, 1853; 2d lt. cav., Mar. 3, 1855; 1st lt., May 1, 1856; capt., May 9, 1861. Entered C.S.A. as capt. cav.; was chief of staff to Gens. Magruder and Buckner; promoted brig. gen., Jan. 20, 1863; comd. cav. brigade under Gen. Earl Van Dorn. After war went to Calif., where was adj. gen. 5 yrs., and held various other govt. and state offices. Home: Sacramento, Calif. Died 1909.

COSDEN, Joshua S., oil producer; b. Kent Co., Md., July 8, 1882; s. John and Anna Cosden; ed. pub. schs., Baltimore, Md.; m. Eleanor Neves. Engaged in oil business, Bigheart, Okla., 1908; organizer, 1913, later pres. Cosden & Co., oil refiners; was also pres. Cosden Pipe Line Co., Cosden Oil & Gas Co.; became pres. Cosden Oil Co., Fort Worth, Tex. Died Nov. 17, 1940.

COSGRIFF, James E., banker; b. Burlington, Vt.; m. Mildred Dobson; children—Walter, Marian. Moved to Utah; engaged in woolgrowing many yrs.; pres. Continental Nat. Bank & Trust Co., Salt Lake City. At personal expense engaged Australian wool expert, 1913, at $10,000 a yr. for about 4 yrs. to teach woolgrowers of West, free of charge, the Australian methods of preparing wool for the market; also engaged in same work himself, 1909-17, without expense to woolgrowers. Died Sept. 17, 1938.

COSGROVE, Henry, R.C. bishop; b. Williamsport, Pa., 1834; s. John and Bridget C.; removed to Dubuque, Ia., 1845; ordained priest, 1857; asst. pastor, 1857, of St. Marguerite's Ch., Davenport, and its pastor, 1862. Apptd. vicar gen. diocese of Davenport, Ia., 1882, and 1884, on death of Bishop McMullen, was apptd. his successor. Died 1906.

COSHOW, Oliver Perry, judge; b. Brownsville, Ore., Aug. 14, 1863; s. Oliver Perry and Sarah Elizabeth (Cochran) C.; ed. pub. schs. and Univ. of Ore. (nongrad.); LL.D., Linfield College, McMinnville, Ore.; m. Elizabeth Kay (died 1925); children—Elizabeth Ann (Mrs. E. B. Stewart, dec.), Minnie Hazel (Mrs. K. H. Pickens), Lenore Dale (Mrs. Charles F. Thompson), Bertha Leone (Mrs. John L. McClintock). Admitted to Ore. bar, 1890, and began practice at McMinnville; moved to Roseburg, 1897; mem. State Senate, Ore., 1905-09; mem. Bd. of Higher Curricula, 1909-20; asso. justice Supreme Court of Ore., term 1924-30, chief justice, 1929-30. Trustee Linfield Coll., McMinnville, Ore., 1893—. Baptist; pres. Bapt. State Conv. 2 yrs. Mason. Deceased.

COSTELLO, Frederick Hankerson, author; b. Bangor, Me., Sept. 24, 1851; s. David E. and Rosina A. (Hankerson) C.; ed. common schs. and pvt. tutors; married. Local agt. for R. G. Dun & Co.'s mercantile agency, Jan. 1889—. Author: On Fighting Decks in 1812, 1899; A Tar of the Old School, 1900; Nelson's Yankee Boy, 1904; Suredart, 1909; Morgan's Youngest Rifleman, 1913; The Girl with Two Selves, 1913. Home: Bangor, Me. Died Aug. 2, 1921.

COSTER, Frank Donald. The sketch of the then president of McKesson & Robbins, Inc., published in Volume 20 under this name is the only instance—during nearly five decades of continuous publication involving over 77,000 biographees—of a fictitious biographee foisting himself on the editors of Who's Who. Those holding certain outstanding civilian and official positions, including the presidencies of concerns whose securities are quoted on the New York Stock Exchange, are arbitrarily listed in Who's Who. This imposter became so qualified on being elected president of the important drug house of McKesson & Robbins, Inc. He had for years successfully hoodwinked banks. boards of directors, famous clubs' admission committees, trade organizations, stock exchanges and scores of leading business men and officials. It later developed he had had falsified birth certificates filed which apparently substantiated his biographical data, to which he added fraudulent educational information. Although buried as Coster, he was actually Phillip Musica, an ex-convict.

COSTIGAN, Edward Prentiss, senator; b. King William Co., Va., July 1, 1874; s. George Purcell and Emilie (Sigur) C.; A.B., Harvard U., 1899; m. Mabel G. Cory, June 12, 1903. Admitted to Utah bar, 1897, and began practice at Denver, 1900; an organizer, and atty. of Honest Election League, Denver, 1903-06, Law Enforcement League, 1906-08; atty. for Anti-Saloon League in local option litigation before Colo. Supreme Court; chmn. Dry Denver Campaign Com., 1910; an organizer Direct Primary League and Direct Legislation Leagues of Colo.; pres. Civil Service Reform Assn. of Denver; an organizer of Citizens Party which carried municipal election, 1912; a founder of Prog. Party, 1912, and its candidate for governor of Colo., 1912, 14. Represented Colorado merchants, Denver Chamber of Commerce and Ariz. commercial interest, etc., in freight rate litigation before Interstate Commerce Commn.; atty. for United Mine Workers of America at time of Congressional investigations of Colo. Coal Strike 1914; atty. for defendants in murder trials growing out of strike, securing, in last case tried, acquittals, Mar. 1916, for all defendants. Mem. U.S. Tariff Commn., 1917-28, resigned. Mem. U.S. Senate, term 1931-37. Democrat. Home: Denver, Colo. Died Jan. 17, 1939.

COSTIGAN, George Purcell, Jr., prof. law; b. Chicago, July 19, 1870; s. George Purcell and Emilie (Sigur) C.; A.B., Marvard, 1892, A.M., 1894; LL.B., 1894; LL.D., U. of Neb., 1913; m. Maud Whittemore, Mar. 31, 1896; 1 son, Henry Dunster. Practiced in Salt Lake City, Utah, 1894-99, at New York, 1899-1900, at Denver, Colo., 1900-05; instr. law, 1900-04, prof., 1904-05, Denver Law Sch.; prof., 1905-07, dean, 1907-09, Coll. of Law, U. of Neb.; prof. law, Northwestern U., Chicago, 1909-22; prof. law U. of Calif., 1922—. Editor-in-chief Ill. Law Review, 1909-16. Congregationalist. Author: American Mining Law, 1908; The Performance of Contracts, 1911, 2d edition, 1927. Editor: Cases on Wills, Descent and Administration, 1910, 2d edit., 1929; Cases on Mining Law, 1912; revised edit., 1929; Cases and Other Authorities on Legal Ethics, 1917; 2d edit., 1933; Cases on Contracts, 1921, 2d edit., 1932; Cases on Trusts, 1925. Home: Berkeley, Calif. Died Nov. 18, 1934.

COTHRAN, Thomas Perrin, judge; b. Abbeville, S.C., Oct. 24, 1857; s. James Sproull and Emma Chiles (Perrin) C.; ed. U. of Va., 1876-78; m. Ione Smith, of Abbeville, Jan. 6, 1886. Admitted to S.C. bar, 1878, and began practice at Abbeville. Mem. S.C. Ho. of Rep., 1904-10, 1914-21 (speaker of House, 1918-21); chmn. Dem. State Conv., 1920; asso. justice Supreme Court of S.C., Jan. 28, 1921—, 2d term ended Jan. 28, 1939. Presbyn. Mason. Home: Greenville, S.C. Died Apr. 11, 1934.

COTTEN, Sallie Southall, clubwoman; b. Lawrenceville, Va., June 13, 1846; d. Thomas James and Susan Swepson (Sims) Southall; grad. Greensboro (N.C.) Female Coll., 1864; m. Robert Randolph Cotten, Mar. 14, 1866; children—Agnes (Mrs. Julian B. Timberlake), Bruce, L.A., Mrs. R. B. Wiggin, Preston, Mrs. D. B. Wesson. Lady mgr. for N.C. at World's Fair, Chicago, 1893 (both nat. and state bds.), also at Atlanta and Charleston expns.; mem. N.C. Fedn. of Women's Clubs (pres., 1911-13; hon. pres.); dir. for N.C. Gen. Fedn. Women's Clubs, 1916-20; hon. chmn. woman's com. N.C. Div. Council Nat. Defense; mem. Nat. Congress of Mothers (hon. v.p.). Mem. N.C. Dem. Exec. Com. Episcopalian. Home: Farmville, N.C. Deceased.

COTTER, James Edward, lawyer; b. Ireland, Mar. 29, 1847; s. James and Margaret (Callaghan) C.; came to America, 1855; ed. pub. schs. and Bridgewater (Mass.) State Normal Sch.; m. Mary A. Walsh, Oct. 1874; children—Esther M., Alice E., Mary Alma, Anna, Sara F. Admitted to Middlesex bar, 1874, and practiced in state and federal courts; admitted to bar Supreme Court of U.S., 1892. Mem. sch. com., 1886-88 (chmn., 1888), and town counsel, 1878-1902, Hyde Park, Mass.; counsel for Dedham, Walpole, and City of Marlborough in sewer litigation; apptd. counsel Federal Trust Co., of Boston, upon its incorporation, 1899; mem. Cotter & Fagan, Boston. Commd. by Gov. Douglas, 1905, to visit Eng. and report to Mass. Gen. Court on sliding scale of rates as applied to gas cos., according to resolutions of Gen. Court; apptd. by Gov. Walsh, 1915, chmn. of commn. to settle labor controversy in Holyoke, Mass. Mem. advisory com. Mass. Gen. Hosp. Del. Dem. Nat. Conv., and presdl. elector, 1904; presdl. elector at large, 1908. Died Aug. 22, 1933.

COTTER, Joseph B., R.C. bishop; b. Liverpool, England, 1844; came to U.S., 1850; ed. in St. Paul, Minn., and St. Vincent, Pa.; theol. studies at St. John's Univ., Collegeville, Minn.; ordained priest, 1871; pastor St. Thomas Ch., Winona, Minn., 1871-89; consecrated 1st bishop, see of Winona, 1889; was 3 terms pres. Catholic Total Abstinence Union of America. Home: Winona, Minn. Died 1909.

COTTERAL, John Hazleton, judge; b. Middletown, Ind., Sept. 26, 1864; s. William W. and Vorintha E. (Burr) C.; student U. of Mich., 1883-84; LL.D., Okla. City U., 1925; m. Lulu Evans, Sept. 17, 1890 (died 1920); m. 2d, Ruth Morrow, Sept. 1, 1928. Began practice of law at Garden City, Kan., 1885; removed to Guthrie, Okla., 1889; chmn. Okla. delegation to Rep. Nat. Conv., 1904; nom. as candidate Supreme Court of Okla., 1907; U.S. dist. judge, Western Dist. of Okla., Nov. 1907-28; apptd. U.S. circuit judge, May 1928. Mem. Christian Ch. Home: Guthrie, Okla. Died Apr. 22, 1933.

COTTINGHAM, Irven A., civil engr.; b. St. Marys, Tex., Oct. 14, 1866; C.E., Agrl. and Mech. Coll. of Tex. Began as asst. engr. S. P. Co., 1889; div. engr. Galveston, Harrisburg & San Antonio Ry., until 1904; successively engr. maintenance of way and asst. gen. mgr. Houston & Tex. Central R.R. at Houston, 1904-16; spl. engr. in charge of valuation work Sunset Central Lines, 1916-18; chief engr. Texas lines of S. P. Co., 1918-22; engaged in pvt. practice and cons. engr. on valuation, Southern Pacific lines, Tex. and La.; retired, 1932. Home: Houston, Tex. Died Nov. 8, 1934.

COTTMAN, James Hough, business man; b. Baltimore, Feb. 4, 1847; s. James Stewart and Elizabeth McEldery (Boggs) C.; ed. pvt. schs., Baltimore; m. Caroline Cary Chubb, Nov. 30, 1871. Merchandise broker, Baltimore, 1867—; sr. mem. J. H. Cottman & Co.; pres. Palmetto Phosphate Co., 1894—; dir. Eutaw Savings Bank, Continental Trust Co. Democrat. Episcopalian. Mason. Was 1st lt. Co. A, 5th Regt. Md. N.G. Died Nov. 1919.

COTTMAN, Vincendon Lazarus, rear adm.; b. Donaldsville, La., Feb. 13, 1852; s. Thomas Edmond Huff and Marie Louise (de Tournillon) C.; grad. U.S. Naval Acad., 1872. Ensign, July 15, 1873; master, May 9, 1878; lt., Jan. 8, 1885; lt. comdr., July 1, 1898; comdr., May 15, 1902; capt., Jan. 15, 1907; rear adm., Nov. 7, 1910. Sec. Internat. Marine Conf., Washington, 1889-90; served at Guam and Manila, 1899; comdt. Navy Yard, Puget Sound, Wash., and 13th naval defense dist., 1910-14; retired, Feb. 13, 1914. Home: Seattle, Wash. Died Mar. 15, 1917.

COTTON, Alfred Cleveland, physician; b. Griggsville, Ill., May 18, 1847; s. Porter and Elvira (Cleveland) C.; drummer and pvt. Co. F., 137th Ill. Inf., in Civil War; grad. Ill. State Normal U., 1869; M.D., Rush Med. Coll., Chicago, 1878; (A.M., Ill. Coll., 1887); m. Nettie U. McDonald, May 2, 1893. Home: Chicago, Ill. July 12, 1916.

COTTON, Charles Stanhope, naval officer; b. Milwaukee, Feb. 15, 1843; s. Lester Holt and Mary Ann C.; apptd. to U.S. Naval Acad. from Wis., 1858; ordered into active service, May, 1861; m. Aug. 30, 1865, Miss R. C. Robertson. Promoted ensign, Nov. 11, 1862; advanced through grades to rear adm., Feb. 27, 1900. Served on St. Lawrence, 1861; on Minnesota, N. Atlantic Blockading Squadron, 1861-63; participated in action between Merrimac and Monitor and the fleet in Hampton Roads, Mar. 1862; on Iroquois, 1863; Oneida, W. Gulf Blockading Squadron, 1864-65; in battle of Mobile Bay, and at surrender of Ft. Morgan, 1864; Shenandoah, Asiatic Sta., 1865-69; duty at Naval Acad., 1869-70; various duties to 1898; comd. Harvard during Spanish War, 1898; Navy Yard, Mare Island, 1898-99; comd. receiving-ship Independence, 1899-1900; mem. Naval Retiring Bd., 1900; commandant Navy Yard, Norfolk, 1900-03; comdr.-in-chief European Squadron, 1903-04; retired, Feb. 16, 1904. Died 1909.

COTTON, Frederic Jay, surgeon; b. Prescott, Wis., Sept. 24, 1869; s. Joseph Potter and Isabella (Cole) C.; A.B., Harvard, 1890, A.M., 1894; M.D., Harvard Med. Sch., 1894; surg. house officer, Mass. Gen. Hosp.; post-grad. work, Coll. Phys. and Surg., New York, U. of Vienna; m. Jane Baldwin, Feb. 8, 1902. Practiced, Boston, 1897—; asst. surgeon, Children's Hosp., 1897-1902; surgeon Boston City Hospital, 1902-1931; surgeon Beth Israel Hospital, 1923-27; asst. in surgery, Harvard Med. Sch., 2 yrs., 1903-04; asst. prof. surgery, Tufts Coll. Med. Sch., 1906-10; lecturer in surgery, Harvard Med. Grad. School. Acting asst. surgeon at Montauk Pt., U.S.A., for 2 mos. during Spanish-Am. War; maj. M.C.U.S.A., 1918-19; consultant in surgery, U.S. Pub. Health Service, 1919—. Fellow Am. Surg. Assn., Am. Coll. Surgeons (a founder). Presbyn. Author: Dislocations and Joint Fractures, 1910. Home: Boston, Mass. Died Apr. 14, 1938.

COTTON, Henry Andrews, medical dir.; b. Norfolk, Va., May 19, 1869; s. George Adolphus and Mary Della (Biggs) C.; grad. Baltimore Poly. Inst., 1894; spl. student Johns Hopkins, 1895; M.D., U. of Md., 1899; studied Royal U., Munich, under Prof. Kraepelin, 1905-06; spl. research student, in Pathol. Lab., same, under Prof. Alzheimer, 1906-07; hon. A.M., Saint John's Coll., 1914; m. A. Delha Keys, Oct. 15, 1903; children—Henry Andrews, Adolph G. Asst. phys., City Asylum, Bay View, Baltimore, 1899-1900, Worcester (Mass.) State Hosp., 1900-03, Danvers (Mass.) State Hosp., 1903-07; med. dir. N.J. State Hosp., Nov. 51, 1907—. Served U.S.A., 6 mos., Hosp. Corps, Chickamauga, Spanish-Am. War, 1898; maj. Medical Corps, U.S. Army, World War. Democrat. Presbyn. Author: Defective, Delinquent and Insane (Vanuxem lectures, Princeton, 1921). Engaged in investigation of relation of physical factors to causation of mental disorders. Died May 8, 1933.

COTTON, Jesse Lee, theologian; b. Pulaski, Pa., Apr. 28, 1862; s. William and Eliza Ann (Kerchoff) C.; A.B., Westminster Coll., New Wilmington, Pa., 1885; grad. Western Theol. Sem., Allegheny, Pa., 1888; post-grad. study, same, 1888-89; D.D., Grove City (Pa.) Coll., 1904; LL.D., Centre Coll., Danville, Ky., 1918; m. Lizzie Hickman Miller, June 6, 1889; children—Eliza Ethelwyn (dec.), John Vincent, William Miller, Jesse Lee (dec.), Gladys Hickman. Ordained Presbyn. ministry, 1889; pastor Slippery Rock and N. Liberty, Pa., 1889-93, Parnassus, Pa., 1893-95, Coraopolis, Pa., 1895-1908; instr. Semitics, Princeton (N.J.) Theol. Sem., 1907-10; prof. Hebrew and O.T. exegesis, Louisville (Ky.) Presbyn. Theol. Sem., 1910—. Republican. Home: Anchorage, Ky. Died Dec. 14, 1937.

COTTON, Joseph Bell, lawyer; b. Albion, Ind., Jan. 6, 1865; s. John and Elizabeth (Riddle) C.; B.S., Mich. State Coll., 1886, LL.D., 1927; m. Louise Hubbell, Jan. 4, 1900; children—Josephine (Mrs. Hale Holden, Jr., dec.), Mary Louise (Mrs. Phelps Kelley), John Mather. Admitted to bar, 1888, practicing at Duluth until 1916, then at New York, specializing in corp. and mining law; gen. solicitor Lake Superior Consolidated Iron Mines, and Duluth, Missabe & Northern Ry. Co., 1893-1909, also Duluth & Iron Range R.R. Co., Oliver Iron Mining Co., Minn. Iron Co. (subsidiary cos. of U.S. Steel Corp.), 1901-09; spl. counsel at Duluth for same and allied interests, 1909-16; gen. counsel Greene Cananea Copper Co. The Am. Metal Co., Ltd., Consolidated Coppermines Corp., etc. Republican. Mem. Minn. House of Representatives, 1893. Home: New York, N.Y. Died Aug. 5, 1940.

COTTON, Joseph Potter, lawyer; b. Newport, R.I., July 22, 1875; s. Joseph P. and Isabella (Cole) C.; A.B., Harvard, 1896, A.M., 1897, LL.B., 1900; m. Jessie I. Child, Feb. 24, 1906. Began practice in N.Y. City, 1900; mem. Cravath, Henderson & de Gersdorff, 1907-08, Spooner & Cotton, 1910-19, McAdoo, Cotton & Franklin, 1919-21, Cotton & Franklin, 1921-29; undersecretary of state, 1929—. Served as counsel Alaskan Engring. Commn., New York State Commn. on Workmen's Compensation; cons. counsel Fed. Reserve Bd., with U.S. Food Administration, Dec. 1917; European rep. U.S. Food Administration, 1918; mem. Interallied Finance Council. Home: New York, N.Y. Died Mar. 10, 1931.

COTTON, William Joseph Henry, univ. prof.; b. Philadelphia, Feb. 17, 1878; s. George Ward and Helena (Kramer) C.; A.B., Temple U., Phila., 1906; A.M., U. of Pa., 1911, Ph.D., 1914; grad. study U. of Berlin, 1928-29; m. Minnie Lord, Sept. 20, 1906; 1 son, Albert Henry. Instr. in mathematics, Temple U., 1903-08; also clk., Corn Exchange Nat. Bank, 1906-08; ednl. dir., Kensington (Phila.) Y.M.C.A., 1908-11; spl. teacher, high sch., Camden, N.J., 1911-13; head of commercial dept., high sch., Wilmington, Del., 1913-16; commercial teacher, high sch., Germantown, Phila., 1916-20; prof. economics and business adminstrn., Duke U., 1920—. Baptist. Home: Durham, N.C. Died Sept. 11, 1932.

COTTON, William Wick, lawyer; b. Lyons, Ia., Dec. 13, 1859; s. Aylett R. and Laura Finch (Wick) C.; B.S., Pa. State Normal School, Millersville, Pa., 1878; LL.B., Columbia U., 1882; m. Fannie C. Collingwood, Aug. 29, 1888. Apptd. asst. to gen. solicitor, U.P. R.R. Co., Omaha, 1888; gen. atty. Pacific div., U.P. at Portland, Ore., 1889, and when road passed into hands of Ore. R.R. & Navigation Co., became gen. atty. latter co. Apptd. by Ore. legislature, 1901, with U.S. Dist. Judge Charles B. Bellinger, to prepare MSS. for new edit. of laws and codes of Ore. Joint Author: Bellinger and Cotton's Annotated Laws of Oregon, 1902. Home: Gresham, Ore. Died 1918.

COTTRELL, Elias, bishop; b. near Holly Springs, Miss., Jan. 31, 1853; s. Daniel and Ann (Mull) C.; ed. by father; taught in pub. schs.; theol. course, Walden U., Nashville, Tenn., 1878-79; (D.D., Rust U., 1895); m. Catherine Davis, Jan. 1, 1880. Licensed to preach, Colored M.E. Ch., Nov., 1875; ordained deacon, 1877, elder, 1878; mem. Gen. Conf., 1882-94; elected bishop, 1894. Book agt., 1882-86; ednl. commr., 1890-94; fraternal messenger, Gen. Conf., M.E. Ch., Omaha, 1892. Trustee, gen. mgr. and treas., Miss. Industrial Coll., Holly Springs, Miss. Republican. Mason. Died Dec. 5, 1937.

COUCH, Albert Irving, pres. Essex Savings Bank; b. Webster, N.H., July 12, 1867; s. Walter S. and Sarah (Webster) C.; grad. high sch., Lawrence, Mass., 1885; m. Alice Mabel Eaton. Bookkeeper, Edison Electric Illuminating Co., Lawrence, 1885-89; teller Essex Savings Bank, Lawrence, 1889-1901; treas. Lawrence Savings Bank, 1901-02; treas. Essex Savings Bank, 1902-24, pres., 1924—. Republican. Conglist. Home: Lawrence, Mass. Died 1936.

COUCH, Harvey Crowley, utility exec.; b. Calhoun, Ark., Aug. 21, 1877; s. Thomas Gratham and

Mamie (Heard) C.; ed. Southwestern Acad., Magnolia, Ark.; hon. degrees from Hendrix Coll., Baylor U and Subiaco Coll.; m. Jessie Johnson, Oct. 4, 1904; children—Johnson Olin, Harvey Crowley, Kirke, Catherine, William Thomas. Began as clk. in drug store, 1897; in ry. mail service, 1897-1904; organizer, 1904, operator until 1912, North La. Telephone Co.; organizer, 1913 and pres. Ark. Power & Light Co., also organizer and pres. Miss. Power & Light Co., 1925-36, and La. Power & Light Co., 1925-36; pres. La. & Ark. Ry., 1928-32; pres. White River Power Corp.; pres. Southwestern Div. NELA, 1930-31; chmn. bd. Kansas City Southern Ry. Co., also pres., 1939—. Mem. bd. mgrs. Lehigh Coal & Navigation Co., 1939. Mem. bd. Reconstruction Finance Corp., 1932-34. Fed. Fuel Administrator, Ark., World War. Dir. Ark. State Flood Commn. and Am. Red Cross, 1927; Ark. Drought Relief, 1930, Ark. Centennial Commn., 1936. Trustee Hendrix Coll., George Peabody Coll. for Teachers, Conway State Teachers Coll., Southern Meth Univ. Councillor Chamber Commerce of U.S. Democrat. Meth. Mason. Rotarian. Selected by 8 local orgns. to receive Commercial Loving Cup, 1925. Selected by citizens as Arkansas' most outstanding citizen and presented with plaque in recognition of services to nation and state in fields of economics, industry and edn., 1933. Home: Pine Bluff, Ark. Died July 30, 1941.

COUDEN, Albert Reynolds, rear adm.; b. Michigan City, Ind., Oct. 30, 1846; s. Reynolds and Margaret S. (Marshall) C.; apptd. to U.S. Naval Acad. from Utah, 1863, grad. 1867. Promoted ensign, Dec. 18, 1868; advanced through grades to rear-adm., July 12, 1907. Summer of 1864 was in active service on board Marion in pursuit of Confederate steamer Florida; various duties to 1896; charge naval proving ground, Indian Head, 1896-1900; comd. Wheeling, 1900-01, Mohican, 1901-02; commandant Naval Sta., Cavite, 1902-04; gen. insp. of ordnance for navy, 1904-06; comd. Louisiana, 1906-07; mem. bd. on Crozier and Brown systems wire wound guns, 1907; later pres. Bd. Naval Ordnance; retired, Oct. 30, 1908. Recalled to active duty, Sept. 1917, with Bur. Navy Ordnance, War Industries and U.S. Shipping bds.; released from active duty, Nov. 1919. Died Apr. 7, 1923.

COUDEN, Henry Noble, chaplain U.S. Ho. of Rep.; b. Marshall Co., Ind., Nov. 21, 1842; s. Joseph G. and Eliza (Chase) C.; grad. State School for the Blind, Columbus, O.; Divinity Sch., St. Lawrence U., Canton, N.Y. (D.D.); ordained Universalist clergyman, 1878; m. Harriet Dunbar, Jan. 26, 1886. Served in Union Army, Apr. 1861-July 1863; hon. disch. by reason of wound in battle which destroyed sight. Chaplain Ho. of Rep., 1895—. Died Aug. 22, 1922.

COUDERT, Frederic René, lawyer; b. New York, 1832, of French parentage; grad. Columbia Coll., 1850; (J.U.D., Columbia, 1887; LL.D., Seton Hall and St. John's Coll., Fordham); admitted to N.Y. bar, 1853; head of firm of Coudert Bros.; public speaker and lecturer; del. of N.Y. Chamber of Commerce to Internat. Congress, Antwerp, for framing internat. rules of gen. average, 1877; mem. of Pres. Cleveland's Venezuela Boundary Commn., 1896-98; govt. dir. Union Pacific R.R., 1885-88; govt. receiver Union Pacific R.R., 1892-98; counsel of U.S., before Internat. Behring Sea Commn., Paris, 1893-95. Cross Legion of Honor of France and other decorations. Home: New York, N.Y. Died 1903.

COUES, Elliott, naturalist; b. Portsmouth, N.H., Sept. 9, 1842; grad. Columbian Univ., 1861; (M.D., 1863; hon. A.M., 1862; Ph.D., 1869). Medical cadet to asst. surgeon U.S. army (filling all intermediate grades), 1862-81, resigned; was prof. anatomy and zoölogy in several colleges; was surgeon and naturalist U.S. Northern Boundary Commn., 1873-76; sec. and naturalist U.S. Geol. and Geog. Survey of the Territories, 1876-80; long connected with Smithsonian Instn. Member Nat. Acad. Sciences; one of the founders and v.p.'s Am. Ornithologists' Union; mem. and corr. mem. on nearly 50 Am. and fgn. scientific and psychical societies. Author: Key to North American Birds; Field Ornithology; Birds of the Northwest; Fur-Bearing Animals; Monographs of North American Rodentia; Birds of the Colorado Valley; New England Bird Life; Biogen, a Speculation on the Origin and Nature of Life; The Daemon of Darwin; Kuthumi; Can Matter Think; Buddhist Catechism; A Woman in the Case; Signs of the Times; Citizen Bird; etc. Was chmn. gen. and joint coms. of Psychical Science Congress, World's Congress Auxiliary, 1893. Died 1899.

COUES, Samuel Franklin, rear adm.; b. in N.H., Sept. 17, 1825. Apptd. asst. surgeon U.S.N., Feb. 25, 1851; surgeon, Apr. 26, 1861; med. dir., Aug. 15, 1876; retired, June 29, 1906, with rank of rear admiral for services during Civil War. Pres. Naval Examining Bd., Phila., 1884-87; in charge Naval Hospital, Chelsea, Mass., Mar.-Sept. 1887. Home: Cambridge, Mass. Died May 1, 1916.

COUGHLIN, John William, physician; b. June 9, 1860; s. William and Abigail C.; M.D., Coll. Phys. and Surg., Baltimore, 1885 (head of class of 220). Practiced, Fall River, Mass., 1885—; mayor of Fall River 4 terms, 1891-95; chmn. Dem. State Com., Mass., 1896; Dem. candidate for lt. gov. of Mass., 1901; mem. Dem. Nat. Com., 1908—. Catholic. Home: Fall River, Mass. Died Dec. 3, 1920.

COUGHLIN, William Thomas, surgeon; b. Ont., Can., Apr. 25, 1873; s. Thomas and Ellen (O'Reilley) C.; prep. edn., Collegiate Inst., Barrie, Ont.; M.D., Washington U., St. Louis, 1901; post-grad. work, London Hosp. and univs. of Paris and Heidelberg; unmarried. Interne St. Louis City Hosp., 1901-02; instr. in anatomy, Washington U., later in surgery; asst. prof. surgery, St. Louis U. Sch. of Medicine, 1911-16, prof., 1916—, head of dept., 1920—; surgeon-in-chief St. Mary's Hosps. (St. Louis Univ.). Fellow Am. Coll. Surgeons. Served in France as maj. and lt. col. Med. Corps, U.S.A., 1918-19. Catholic. Home: St. Louis, Mo. Died May 22, 1940.

COULSTON, John Bishop, hotelman; b. Ellisburg, Pa., May 22, 1869; s. John and Stella (Bishop) C.; ed. pub. schs.; m. Nora Seibert, Nov. 10, 1891; children—John T., George S., Lillian M. Banking business from 1890; pres. Maryland Hotel Co., Wildwood Ranch Co., Edgemont Ranch Co., Calif. Foothill Fruit Co. Maj. Am. Red Cross, at head of South Intermediate and Southern zones, Lyons, France, World War. Pres. Pasadena Chamber of Commerce; dir. and nat. councilor to U.S. Chamber of Commerce. Democrat. Episcopalian. Mason. Home: Pasadena, Calif. Died Aug. 2, 1928.

COULTAS, Andrew Jackson, clergyman; b. New York, Aug. 26, 1853; s. Andrew Jackson and Emily Davies (Woodman) C.; A.B., Wesleyan U., 1880, A.M., 1883 (D.D., 1906); m. Rachel A. C. West, 1880. Ordained M.E. ministry, 1880; pastor North Ch., Fall River, Mass., 1880, 1881. Mystic Bridge, Conn., 1882-84, Sachem St. Ch., Norwich, 1885-87, Federal St. Ch., New London, 1888-91, St. Paul's Ch., Fall River, Mass., 1892-96, Chestnut St. Ch., Providence, R.I., 1897, Trinity Union Ch., Providence, 1898-1901; presiding elder Providence Dist., 1902-07; dist. supt. New Bedford Dist., 1908—. Mem. Bd. of Foreign Missions of M.E. Ch.; trustee Wesleyan U., E. Greenwich (R.I.) Acad. Del. Quadrennial Gen. Conf., Chicago, 1900, Los Angeles, 1904; del. 4th Ecumenical Meth. Conf., Toronto, 1911. Home: Fall River, Mass. Died Mar. 9, 1920.

COULTER, John Merle, botanist; b. Ningpo, China, Nov. 20, 1851; s. Moses Stanley and Caroline E. (Crowe) C.; A.B., Hanover Coll., 1870, A.M., 1873, Ph.D., 1882; Ph.D., Ind. U., 1884; m. Georgie M. Gaylord, Jan. 1, 1874. Botanist, U.S. Geol. Survey in Rocky Mountains, 1872-73; prof. natural sciences, Hanover Coll., 1874-79; prof. biology, Wabash Coll., 1879-91; pres. and prof. botany, Ind. U., 1891-93; pres. Lake Forest U., 1893-96; prof. and head dept. botany, U. of Chicago, 1896-1925; adviser of Boyce Thompson Inst. Plant Research, Yonkers, N.Y., 1925—. Prin. Bay View Summer Univ., 1893-96, Winona Summer Sch., 1895-98; founder and editor Botanical Gazette, 1875—. Fellow Am. Acad. Arts and Sciences, A.A.A.S. (gen. sec. 1901, pres. 1918); pres. Chicago Acad. of Sciences; mem. Nat. Research Council, 1923—. Author: Manual of Rocky Mountain Botany, 1885; Manual of Texan Botany, 1891; Plant Relations, 1899; Plant Structures, 1899; Plant Studies, 1902; Morphology of Gymnosperms (with Charles J. Chamberlain), 1901; Morphology of Angiosperms (with same), 1903; A Text-book of Botany, 1906; Elementary Studies in Botany, 1913; Fundamentals of Plant Breeding, 1914; Evolution of Sex in Plants, 1914; Plant Genetics, 1918. Died Dec. 23, 1928.

COULTON, George A.; vice-chmn. bd. Union Trust Co. of Cleveland; dir. Cleveland Savings & Loan Co., Electric Controller & Mfg. Co., Ferry Cap & Set Screw Co., Midland Steel Products Co., Wheeling & Lake Erie R.R. Co. Home: Cleveland, O. Died May 18, 1933.

COUNCILL, William Hooper, coll. pres.; b. a slave, Fayetteville, N.C., July 12, 1848; s. William and Mary Jane C.; ed. 3 yrs. in school, Stevenson, Ala., 1865-67; engaged in teaching 1867 (Ph.D., Morris Brown Coll.); m. Maria H. Weeden, Sept. 5, 1885. Studied law and admitted to the Supreme Court of Ala., 1883, but has continued teaching; chief enrolling clerk, Ala. Ho. Reps., 1872-74; receiver gen. land office, Northern Dist., Ala., 1875; organized 1875, and became pres., Agrl. and Mech. Coll. at Normal. Founder, and editor 1877-84, Huntsville Herald; associated with Bishop Turner in his work for redemption of Africa. Contbr. to Arena, Forum, etc. Mem. A.M.E. Ch. Home: Normal, Ala. Died 1909.

COUNCILMAN, William Thomas, pathologist; b. Pikesville, Md., Jan. 1, 1854; s. Dr. John T. and Christiana Drummond (Mitchell) C.; ed. St. John's Coll., Annapolis, Md.; M.D., U. of Md., 1878; student univs. of Vienna and Leipzig; hon. A.M., Harvard, 1899, Johns Hopkins, 1902; LL.D., Md. U., 1907, McGill, 1911; m. Isabella Coolidge, Dec. 17, 1894; children—Isabella Coolidge (Mrs. Frank Wigglesworth), Christiana Drummond (Mrs. William Otho Potwin Morgan), Elizabeth Lydia. Asso., and asso. prof. pathology, Johns Hopkins, 1886-91; Shattuck prof., Harvard, 1892, now emeritus. Fellow Am. Acad. of Arts and Sciences, Phila. Acad. Medicine. Home: York Village, Me. Died May 26, 1933.

COUNSELMAN, Charles, mcht.; b. Baltimore, Md., 1849; s. Jacob and Mary C.; ed. pub. schs., Baltimore. Went to Chicago, 1869; clerk in commn. trade, 1869-71; then senior mem. Counselman & Day and Charles Counselman, commission mchts. Home: Chicago, Ill. Died 1904.

COUNTRYMAN, Edwin, lawyer; b. Fort Plain, N.Y., May 2, 1833; s. Solomon and Catherine (Diefendorf) C.; ed. common sch.; studied law in office at Cherry Valley, N.Y.; m. Mary Ann Thompson, Jan. 1, 1858 (dec.). Admitted to bar, 1854; dist. atty. Otsego Co., 1860-62; register in bankruptcy, 19th Congressional Dist., N.Y., 1867-73; justice Supreme Ct. of N.Y., 1874; mem. N.Y. Constl. Conv., 1894. Independent in politics and religion. Home: Albany, N.Y. Died June 13, 1914.

COUPAL, James Francis, surgeon U.S.A.; b. Quincy, Mass., Jan. 26, 1884; s. Moses Edward and Mary Ann (Hayes) C.; B.S., Tufts Coll., 1906, M.D., 1909, M.S., 1928; m. Martha L. Wilfert, June 23, 1916. Began practice at Boston, 1910; commd. lt. M.R.C., June 18, 1915; capt. med. dept. Mass. N.G., June 19, 1916; maj. M.C., U.S.A., Feb. 17, 1919; maj. M.C. (regular army), July 1, 1920; apptd. White House physician, July 1, 1924; apptd. col. U.S.A., by act of Congress, Mar. 1928; resigned July 12, 1929. Republican. Author of Gas Gangrene Chapter, U.S. Medical History of World War. Home: Washington, D.C. Died Jan. 3, 1935.

COURSAULT, Jesse Harliaman, educator; b. Bellaire, O., Mar. 23, 1871; s. Theodore Graigver and Anna Elizabeth (Brookie) C.; A.B., Ohio State U., 1893, A.M., 1898; A.M., Harvard, 1900; Ph.D., Columbia, 1907; m. Edith Logan Snyder, Nov. 28, 1907; children—Ruth Logan, Theodore Gregver. Teacher, Central and South high schs., Columbus, O., 1894-1903; mem. faculty, U. of Mo., 1905—, then prof. the history and philosophy of edn.; chmn. faculty Sch. of Edn., same, 1917-18, and dean, 1918-23. Mem. faculty Cornell U., on leave from U. of Mo., 1915-16; teacher summer sessions, Ohio State U., 1914, 17; spl. lecturer and teacher in summer session of Territorial Normal Sch., Honolulu, Hawaii, 1925. Mem. Disciples of Christ. Author: The Learning Process, 1907; Principles of Education, 1920. Became editor in 1913 of edn. series of bulls. pub. by U. of Mo. Co-editor U. of Mo. Studies (a quarterly of research), 1928—. Chmn. U. of Mo. Com. on Accredited Schs. and Colls, 1923—. Home: Columbia, Mo. Died June 24, 1937.

COURTENAY, William Ashmead, mfr.; b. Charleston, S.C., Feb. 4, 1831; s. Edward Smith and Elizabeth (Wade) C.; had few ednl. facilities in boyhood; with brother conducted bookselling and publishing business in Charleston, 1850-60; m. Miss Julia Anna Francis, 1854. Officer C.S.A., 1861-65; in shipping and commission business, Charleston, 20 yrs.; comdr. Washington Light Inf. and instrumental in erecting monuments to Col. William Washington of the Revolution, 1858, to Gen. Daniel Morgan, 1881, and the Heroes of Cowpens, to the 114 dead of the Washington Light Inf. in the war between the States, and to Gen. R. S. Ripley, C.S.A.; mayor of Charleston, 1879-87; declined 3d reëlection. Elected trustee Peabody Ednl. Fund, 1887; founded large cotton mfg. interest and mill, Newry, S.C., 1893. Home: Columbia, S.C. Died 1908.

COURTENAY, William Howard, ry. official; b. Louisville, Ky., July 30, 1858; s. Robert Graham and Annie Christian (Howard) C.; C.E., Rensselaer Poly. Inst., 1879; m. Isabel Stevenson Clark, Apr. 27, 1893; children—Erskine Howard, James Clark. With engring. dept. L.&N. R.R. Co., 1879—; prin. asst. engr., 1891-1905, became chief engr., 1905, cons. engr., 1933. Home: Louisville, Ky. Died Mar. 15, 1934.

COURTIS, Frank, naval officer; b. Cincinnati, O., June 18, 1844; s. James F. and Jane (Cook) C.; ed. schs. of Cincinnati, 1850-59, acad., Oakland, Calif., 1859-62; grad. U.S. Naval Acad., 1866, as midshipman; m. Maude Carleton, Apr. 17, 1883. Promoted ensign Mar. 12, 1868, master Mar. 12, 1869, lt. Mar. 21, 1870, lt. commdr. Mar. 2, 1885, commdr. July 10, 1894, capt. July 23, 1900; rear admiral, and retired for physical disability, Sept. 27, 1901. Served on various duties and stas.; commd. U.S.S. Essex, 1898-1900; at War Coll., 1900, until placed on sick leave. Died 1908.

COURTIS, William Munroe, mining engr.; b. Boston, Mass., Jan. 7, 1842; s. William and Mehitable (Appleton) C.; A.B., Harvard, 1864, A.M., 1867; studied civ. engring., Lawrence Scientific Sch. (Harvard), 1 yr.; 3 yrs. at Royal School of Mines, Freiberg; m. Lizzie Easton Folger, Apr. 2, 1873. Was supt. and gen. mgr. of many mines and smelting works in Mich., Colo., Cal., N.M., etc., and cons. engr. to extensive operators; was chief engr. on survey of Santo Domingo, etc.; patented improved mill apparatus for saving waste in tailings. Interested in the search for potash in the U.S. to which devoted 5 yrs. and traveled 100,000 miles. Home: Highland Park, Detroit. Died 1922.

COURTLEIGH, William Louis, actor; b. Guelph, Ont., June 28, 1869; s. Stephen and Elizabeth (Phelan) C.; grad. pub. sch., St. Louis, 1887; m. Helen Cross, Mar. 17, 1890 (died 1908); m. 2d, Edna Conroy, Apr. 29, 1912. Began career as actor, Sept. 1, 1888. Mem. Actors' Order of Friendship, Actors' Soc. of America. Home: Rye, N.Y. Died Dec. 27, 1930.

COURTNEY, Frederick, bishop; b. Plymouth, England, Jan. 5, 1837; s. Rev. Septimus and Elizabeth (Wilshin) C.; ed. Christ's Hosp., London, 1845-51, King's Coll., London, 1862-64, T.A. (theol. asso.), 1864; (D.D., Racine Coll., 1881, U. of King's Coll., Windsor, N.S., 1888; D.C.L., Trinity Coll., Toronto, 1889, Lennoxville College, Can., 1895); m. Caroline Louisa Nairn, Northumberland, Eng., July 11, 1865. Deacon, 1864, priest, 1865, Ch. of England; curate Hadlow, Kent, Eng., 1864-65; incumbent Charles' Chapel, Plymouth, Eng., 1865-70, St. Jude's Ch., Glasgow, 1870-76; asst. minister St. Thomas' Ch., New York, 1876-80; rector St. James', Chicago, 1880-82, St. Paul's, Boston, 1882-88; bishop of Nova Scotia, 1888-1904; rector St. James', New York, 1904-15 (emeritus). Pres. Ch. Temperance Soc., 1906—. Home: New York, N.Y. Died Dec. 29, 1918.

COURTNEY, Joseph William, neurologist; b. Cambridge, Mass., Aug. 9, 1868; A.B., Harvard, 1890, M.D., 1893; married; children—Paul Graham, Gerald, Suzette. In practice at Boston, 1893—; asst. phys., diseases of the nervous system, Boston City Hosp., 1893-1909; phys. in chief, dept. diseases of mind and nervous system, Carney Hosp., Boston, 1909-19. Former lecturer on neurology, Harvard Grad. Sch. Medicine. Author: The Conquest of Nerves, 1911. Home: Boston, Mass. Died June 6, 1929.

COURTNEY, Walter, surgeon; b. Moore, Ont., Can., Sept. 18, 1856; s. Angus and Janet (McCash) C.; ed. pub. schs. and Strathroy Collegiate Inst., Can.; M.D., U. of Mich., 1883 (hon. M.A., 1908); m. Hildegarde von Jasmund, Feb. 10, 1885 (died 1922). Chief surg. eastern div. N.P. Ry., 1888-1913. Fellow Am. Coll. Surgeons. Home: Brainerd, Minn. Died June 23, 1924.

COUSE, E(anger) Irving, artist; b. Saginaw, Mich., Sept. 3, 1866; s. M. S. and Mary J. (Price) C.; pupil Nat. Acad. Design, New York, and Bouguereau, Fleury and École des Beau Arts, Paris; m. Virginia Walker, Sept. 5, 1889; 1 child, Kibbey Whitman. Awards: Shaw prize for black and white at Salmagundi Club, 1899, Proctor prize, 1900; 2d Hallgarten prize, Nat. Acad. Design, 1900, 1st Hallgarten prize, 1902; hon. mention, Paris Expn., 1900, Buffalo Expn., 1901; bronze medal, St. Louis Expn., 1904; Isidor gold medal, 1911, Carnegie prize, 1912, and Altman prize, 1916, N.A.D.; silver medal, Panama P.I. Expn., 1915, Isidor prize, Salmagundi Club, 1917; W. Lippincott prize of $300 P.A.F.A., 1921. His best known pictures are: "The Forest Camp," "An Indian Camp," "The War Pony" (Indian subjects) and "Adoration of the Shepherds" (in Grace M.E. Ch., Harrisburg, Pa.); rep. in permanent collections of Brooklyn Inst. Arts and Sciences, Smith Coll. Mus., at St. Paul, Minn., Dallas, Tex., and Detroit Mus. of Art, Nat. Gallery, Washington, Montclair Art Mus., Omaha Gallery, Met. Mus., New York, Santa Barbara Mus., Fort Worth Mus., Toledo Mus., Milwaukee Art Inst., Nashville Art Assn., Ranger Fund Purchase, N.A.D., 1921, etc. A.N.A., 1902, N.A., 1911. Studio: Taos, N.M. Died Apr. 23, 1936.

COUSENS, John Albert, college pres.; b. Brookline, Mass., Nov. 17, 1874; s. John Emmons and Sarah Catherine (Wiggin) C.; A.B., Tufts Coll., 1898; LL.D., St. Lawrence U. and Lombard Coll., 1922, Tufts Coll., 1930; m. Elizabeth Frances Edwards, July 2, 1906. Pres. Tufts Coll., Sept. 1, 1919—, also trustee. Pres. Brookline Savings Bank (chmn. investment com.); dir. Brookline Trust Co. Republican. Universalist. Home: Chestnut Hill, Mass. Died July 2, 1937.

COUSINS, Robert Bartow, educator; b. Fayetteville, Ga., July 21, 1861; s. Isaac William and Mary Elizabeth (Bennett) C.; A.B., U. of Ga., 1882; studied U. of Chicago, 1900; LL.D., Southwestern U., 1926; m. Dora M. Kelly, Sept. 5, 1885; children—Mary Mabel (dec.), Robert B., Ralph Pittman, Wayne Kelly, Edith Blair, William Gregg (dec.). Teacher in rural schs. of Ga., and high sch., Longview, Tex., until 1883; supt. pub. schs., Mineola, 1885-87, Mexia, 1887-1903; state supt. pub. instrn., Tex., 1905-10; pres. West Tex. State Normal Coll., 1910-18; supt. schs., Houston, Tex., 1921-24; pres. Tex. Coll. of Arts and Industries, Kingsville, Tex., 1924—. Democrat. Methodist. Mason. Author: (with Joseph Abner Hill) American History for Schools, 1913. Home: Kingsville, Tex. Died Mar. 3, 1932.

COUSINS, Robert Gordon, congressman; b. Cedar County, Ia., 1859; s. James and Mary (Dallas) C.; B.C.E., Cornell Coll., Ia., 1881, also C.E., LL.D., 1904; unmarried. Admitted to bar, 1882, and entered practice at Tipton, Ia.; mem. Ia. Ho. of Reps., 1886-87; presdl. elector, 1888; pros. atty., Cedar Co., 1888-90; mem. 53d to 60th Congresses (1893-1909), 5th Ia. Dist., retiring while chmn. of Foreign Affairs Com. Lectures: Lincoln and the Great Commander; Thomas B. Reed; Alexander Hamilton; The Making and Unmaking of the Constitution; and many others. Home: Tipton, Ia. Died June 21, 1933.

COUZENS, James, senator; b. Chatham, Ont., Can., Aug. 26, 1872; s. James J. and Emma (Clift) C.; ed. pub. schs.; m. Margaret A. Manning, Aug. 31, 1898. Began mfr. of automobiles in 1903. Formerly pres. Bank of Detroit and Highland Park State Bank; was v.p. gen. mgr. and treas. Ford Motor Co. of Detroit, v.p. Ford Motor Co. of Can., Ltd., dir. Ford Motor Co. of England, Ltd., and dir. Detroit Trust Co.; served as pres. Detroit Bd. of Commerce, and dir. U.S. Chamber Commerce; chmn. for Wayne County of U.S. Fuel Administration, World War; served as commr. Police Dept. and commr. Street Rys.; mayor of Detroit, 1919-22; mem. U.S. Senate, 1922—, apptd. to fill vacancy, Nov. 29, 1922, and elected, 1924, to fill unexpired term of Truman H. Newberry and for full term, 1925-31, reëlected for term 1931-37. Presbyn. Republican. Home: Pontiac, Mich. Died Oct. 22, 1936.

COVERT, John Cutler, journalist; b. Norwich, N.Y., Feb. 11, 1839; s. Jacob and Phebean (Cutler) C.; ed. in printing office; became good tech. printer; speaks French, German, Italian, Spanish; m. Amelia A. Dutcher, 1871. Began newspaper work on Cleveland Leader, of which he became editor; mem. Ohio Legislature 2 terms; U.S. consul at Lyons, France, 1897-1909; in newspaper work at Lyons, for French and Am. newspapers, 1909—. Republican. Wrote treatise on the silver question, 1896, which was distributed by Rep. Nat. Com. Decorated by French Minister of Pub. Instrn. Officer of French Academy, 1904. Died Jan. 14, 1919.

COVERT, William Chalmers, clergyman; b. Franklin, Ind., Oct. 4, 1864; s. Albert Newton and Susan Elizabeth (Magill) C.; B.A., Hanover (Ind.) Coll., 1885, A.M., 1888; grad. Presbyn. Theol. Seminary, Chicago, 1888; D.D., Hanover, 1905, D.Litt., 1933; LL.D., Blackburn Coll., Carlinville, Ill., 1917; S.T.D., Waynesburg Coll., Waynesburg, Pa., 1924; m. Alice Brown Hudson, May 14, 1890; children—Hudson, Katharine (Mrs. L. H. Nichols), Seward. Ordained Presbyn. ministry, St. Paul, Minn., Sept. 1888; pastor, St. Paul Park, 1888-92, Merriam Park Ch., St. Paul, 1892-1900, First Ch., Saginaw, Mich., 1900-05, 41st St. Ch., Chicago, 1905-12, First Presbyn. Ch., Chicago, 1913-24; gen. sec. Bd. of Christian Edn. of Presbyn. Ch., 1924-34; visiting prof. homiletics, Western Theol. Sem., Pittsburgh, 1939-40; mem. Federal Council Chs. of Christ in America; mem. exec. com. Council of Ch. Bds. of Edn. and of exec. com. World Alliance of Internat. Friendship Through the Chs. Awarded Silver Buffalo, Boy Scouts of America, 1939. Dir. Presbyn. Theol. Sem.; trustee Hood Coll. for Women; vice chmn. Save the Children Fedn., chmn. Nat. Protestant Com. on Scouting; moderator Gen. Assembly Presbyn. Ch., 1935. Author: Glory of the Pines; Wildwoods and Waterways, 1914; New Furrows in Old Fields; Religion in the Heart, 1926; Christ and Culture, 1930; Facing Our Day, 1934; Handbook to the Hymnal, 1935; With Cross and Crown in Every Land (pageant), 1937. Home: Germantown, Philadelphia, Pa. Died Feb. 4, 1942.

COVILLE, Frederick V(ernon), botanist; b. Preston, N.Y., Mar. 23, 1867; s. Joseph Addison and Lydia (More) C.; A.B., Cornell U., 1887; D.Sc., George Washington U., 1921; m. Elizabeth Harwood Boynton, Oct. 4, 1890; children—Arthur Boynton (dec.), Stanley, Katharine, Cabot, Frederick. Instr. botany, Cornell, 1887-88; asst. botanist, 1888-93, botanist, 1893—, U.S. Dept. Agr.; curator U.S. Nat. Herbarium, 1893—; acting dir. Nat. Arboretum, 1929—. Procured foundation of the Desert Botanical Lab. by Carnegie Instn. Fellow (v.p. botany, 1902) A.A.A.S. Author: Botany of the Death Valley Expdn.; Standardized Plant Names (joint author); and many bot. papers. Awarded George Robert White medal of honor, Mass. Hort. Society, 1931. Home: Washington, D.C. Died Jan. 9, 1937.

COVINGTON, Harry Franklin, prof. pub. speaking; b. Snow Hill, Md., Apr. 6, 1870; s. George W. and Sallie (Dennis) Bishop C.; A.B., Princeton, 1892, A.M., 1895; m. Priscilla Upshur, Oct. 25, 1905. Asst. in oratory, 1893-98, asst. prof. oratory, 1898-1904, asst. prof. English, 1904-11, prof. pub. speaking and debate, 1911—, Princeton. Episcopalian. Author: The Fundamentals of Debate, 1918. Asso. editor Quarterly Jour. of Speech Edn. Home: Princeton, N.J. Died July 16, 1928.

COVINGTON, J(ames) Harry, judge, lawyer; b. Talbot County, Md., May 3, 1870; s. James H. and Emma V. C.; ed. pub. schs. and Md. Mil. Acad.; LL.B., U. of Pa., 1894; m. Ethel K. Rose, Apr. 4, 1899. Admitted to bar, 1894, and practiced at Easton, Md. Dem. nominee for Md. Senate, 1901; state's atty., Talbot Co., 1903-09; mem. 61st to 63d Congresses (1909-15), 1st Md. Dist.; apptd. chief justice Supreme Court of D.C. by President Wilson, and resigned from 63d Congress, Sept. 30, 1914; resigned, June 1, 1918, to resume practice of law. Mem. U.S. Railroad Wage Commn., 1918. Professor of law, Georgetown U., 1914-19. Episcopalian. Home: Washington, D.C. Died Feb. 4, 1942.

COWAN, Andrew, merchant, mfr.; b. Ayrshire, Scotland, Sept. 29, 1841; s. William Strong and Margaret Isabella (Campbell) C.; ed. pub. schs., Auburn, N.Y., and Madison (now Colgate) U.; m. Mary E. Adsit, Feb. 23, 1864; 2d, Anna L. Gilbert, Utica, Jan. 13, 1876. Enlisted as pvt. Co. B, 19th N.Y. Inf., Apr. 16, 1861; assisted in raising 1st N.Y. Independent Battery which was mustered into service Nov. 23d, 1861, and served as capt. same, from Jan., 1862; bvtd. maj. and lt. col., and comd. Arty. Brigade, 6th Corps Army of Potomac in campaign ending at Appomattox; hon. mustered out June 23, 1865. Head of Andrew Cowan & Co., established 1866, wholesale hardware, leather and mill supplies, Louisville; pres. Nat. Oak Leather Co.; v.p. Louisville Leather Co. Mem. 1st and 2d bds. of Park Commrs. which established Louisville Park System, 1891-95, and pres. bd., 1907-08; trustee Am. Printing House for the Blind, from 1897, pres., 1906-18; pres. Ky. Inst. for Edn. of the Blind, 1896-1900, 1908-12; charter mem. and councilor Asso. Charities. Republican. Baptist. Home: Louisville, Ky. Died Aug. 23, 1919.

COWAN, Frank, author; b. Greensburg, Pa., Dec. 11, 1844; s. Edgar C. (U.S. senator); ed. Mt. Pleasant and Jefferson colls.; M.D., Georgetown Med. Coll., 1869. Sec. U.S. Senate Com. on Patents, 1862; studied law; admitted to bar, 1865; one of Pres. Andrew Johnson's secretaries, 1865-9; practiced medicine, Greensburg, Pa., after 1869, but soon returned to the law; editor and propr. Frank Cowan's paper (industrial), Greensburg, 1872-75; gen. supt. Westmoreland Hosp., 1895-96. Has traveled extensively in Europe, Asia, Africa, S. America and Australia, and entered Corea before that country had made any treaties with foreign nations; now devoting attention to fruit culture and writing. Author: Curious Facts in the History of Insects; Zomara, a Romance of Spain; Fact and Fancy in New Zealand; Dictionary of Proverbial Phrases Relating to the Sea; Australianisms. Home: Greensburg, Pa. Died 1905.

COWARD, Edward Fales, playwright; b. New York, Sept. 6, 1862; s. Edward and Ellen S. (Fales) C.; ed. Lyons Collegiate Inst., New York; LL.B., Columbia, 1883; m. Mabel Ridgway, Dec. 4, 1890; children—Edward Fales (dec.), Thomas Ridgway, Eleanor Josephine Fales (Mrs. John Howard Mallon). Best known as amateur actor; for 57 yrs. played continuously a total of 212 rôles; dramatic editor and critic New York Evening Sun, 2 yrs., New York World, 6½ yrs.; spl. writer for The Theatre. Author: "Hearts Are Trumps," 3-act comedy, prod. by Strollers; adapter of "The Belle's Stratagem" (version formerly acted by Julia Marlowe); King Stephen; part author musical comedy, "The Lady from Chicago," prod. by Strollers; also (with J. Cheever Goodwin and Jas. T. Waldron) "Around New York in 80 Minutes," a musical comedy, prod. Koster & Bial's, New York, 1900; Klytemnestra. Home: New York, N.Y. Died Aug. 29, 1933.

COWDERY, Edward Gilmore; b. North Andover, Mass., Oct. 4, 1856; s. William S. and Eliza J. (Wilson) C.; ed. Mass. Inst. Tech.; m. Jennie Van Fleet Burr, May 19, 1887; children—Louise Mansfield (Mrs. Charles Baird Willard), Corene, Chester Van Fleet. Began as civil engr., Toledo, O., until 1875; then with the Toledo Gas Light & Coke Co., until 1877, engr. with Milwaukee (Wis.) Gas Co., 1877-82; with Peoples Gas Light & Coke Co., Chicago, 1882-84; supt. Milwaukee Gas Light Co., 1884-93, and v.p. and gen. mgr. same, 1893-1903; v.p. and gen. mgr. Laclede Gas Light Co., St. Louis, 1903-07; v.p. Peoples Gas Light & Coke Co., Chicago, 1907-15, pres., 1915-19; chmn. bd. Counselman & Co., investment bankers, Chicago, 1919—. Republican. Conglist. Home: Kenilworth, Ill. Died Jan. 13, 1932.

COWELL, Hervey Sumner, educator; b. W. Lebanon, Me., Oct. 10, 1855; s. Rev. David Barker and Christiana (Coffin) C.; A.B., Bates Coll., Lewiston, Me., 1875, A.M., 1878, hon. Pd.D., 1916; m. Abbie Flora Cobb, June 12, 1879. Prin. Clinton Grove Sem., Weare, N.H., 1875-76, Francestown (N.H.) Acad., 1876-83, Arms Acad., Shelburne Falls, Mass., 1883-87, Cushing Acad., Ashburnham, Mass., 1887-1926; made prin. emeritus and continuing teaching in same academy. Home: Ashburnham, Mass. Died July 6, 1929.

COWEN, Benjamin Rush, clerk U.S. Courts, Southern dist. Ohio, 1884—; b. Moorfield, O., Aug. 15, 1831; s. Benjamin Sprague and Anne Wood C.; ed. St. Clairsville, O.; studied medicine; m. Ellen Thoburn, Sept. 19, 1854. Engaged in journalism, 1848; chief clerk Ho. of Reps., Ohio, 1860-61; private, 1st lt., maj., bvt. lt. col., col. and brig. gen. vols., U.S.A.; sec. of State, Ohio, 1862; adjt. gen., Ohio, 1864-68; asst. sec. of Interior, U.S., 1871-77; Republican; mem. M.E. Ch. Del. Nat. Rep. Conv., 1868, 1876, Ecumenical Meth. Conf., London, 1881. Mason. Mem. Ohio Centennial Commn., 1903; Hamilton Co. Memorial Bd., Nat. Geographic Soc. Author: Our Beacon Light, 1884; Our Civilization the

COWEN 267 COX

Product of Christianity, 1889; Do Missions Pay?, 1891. Home: Cincinnati. Died 1908.

COWEN, John King, lawyer, ry. official; b. Millersburg, O., Oct. 28, 1844; s. Washington C.; prep. edn. Vermillion Inst., Hayesville, O.; taught sch., Millersburg, 1862-63; grad. Princeton (head of class), 1866; taught in high sch., Millersburg, and later prin. of acad. at Shreve, O.; studied law Univ. of Mich.; admitted to bar, Canton, O., 1868 (Maj. William McKinley being one of examiners). Practiced Mansfield, O., 1868-72; counsel Baltimore & Ohio R.R. Co., 1872-76, gen. counsel, 1876-96, and from June 1901, pres. Baltimore & Ohio R.R., 1896-1901; also receiver same, 1896-99. Mem. Congress, 1885-87, as free trader, opposed by Gorman wing of party; reëlected to Congress 1894 from 4th Md. dist. In gen. practice as head firm Cowen, Cross & Bond. Home: Baltimore, Md. Died 1904.

COWHERD, William Strother, congressman; b. Jackson Co., Mo., Sept. 1, 1860; s. Charles J. and Emily S. C.; A.B., U. of Mo., 1881, LL.B., 1882; m. Jessie Kitchen, Sept. 25, 1889. Admitted to bar, 1882, and began practice at Kansas City; asst. pros. atty., Jackson Co., 1885-89; 1st asst. city counselor, 1890-92; mayor Kansas City, 1892-94; mem. 55th to 58th Congresses (1897-1905), 5th Mo. Dist.; Dem. nominee for gov. of Mo., 1908. Died June 20, 1915.

COWIE, David Murray, M.D.; b. Moncton, N.B., Nov. 19, 1872; s. James S. and Isabel Henderson (Harris) C.; student Battle Creek (Mich.) Coll., 1889-92; M.D., U. of Mich., 1896; internal medicine, U. of Heidelberg, 1908; m. 2d, Anna Marion Cook, M.D., June 13, 1908; 2 children—David Bruce (by 1st marriage), Margaret Lucy (by 2d marriage). Gen. practice at Ann Arbor, Mich., 1896-1900; specialized in internal medicine and pediatrics from 1900; 1st asst. in internal medicine, Univ. of Mich., 1896-1906, instr. pediatrics, 1906-07, clin. prof., 1907-09, clin. prof. pediatrics and internal medicine, 1909-18, and prof. of same, 1918-20, prof. pediatrics and infectious diseases, 1920—; phys. in chief Dept. of Pediatrics and Infectious Diseases, U. of Mich. Hosp.; med. dir. Cowie Private Hosp., established 1912. Served with M.R.C., World War. Fellow Am. Coll. Physicians, Am. Acad. Pediatrics, A.A.A.S. Republican. Episcopalian. Asso. editor Am. Jour. Diseases of Children, 1912-24. Home: Ann Arbor, Mich. Died Jan. 27, 1940.

COWIE, Thomas Jefferson, naval officer; b. Montezuma, Ia., Feb. 15, 1857; s. George and Margaret (Duffus) C.; ed. pub. and pvt. schs., Washington, D.C.; m. Susie A. Gedney, Feb. 15, 1881; 1 dau., Mrs. Clyde R. Robinson. Apptd. asst. p.m. U.S.N., June 16, 1880; promoted through various grades to p.m. gen. with rank of rear admiral, July 1, 1910; was also chief Bur. of Supplies and Accounts. Originator and promoter of navy pay bill whereby the pay of all officers and enlisted men of the army, navy and marine corps was increased; intelligence officer on bd. U.S.S. Monocacy during Japanese-Chinese War, Navy liberty loan officer during World War; presented by sec. of Treas. with first Liberty Loan medal made of German cannon, and highly praised by the Sec. of the Navy for service rendered. Sr. vice comdr. in chief Mil. Order World War, 1922-29, comdr. in chief, 1929-30. Sec. and treas. Navy Mutual Aid Assn., 1921—. Mason. Died July 16, 1936.

COWIN, John Clay, lawyer; b. Warrensville, O., Jan. 11, 1846; s. Thomas and Margaret C.; A.B., Ohio State U.; student Union Law Coll., 1867; m. Ella L. Benton, 1870. Dist. atty., Omaha, 1868-72; was spl. U.S. atty. during receivership of U.P. R.R., apptd. by President Cleveland, 1893 (recovered prin. and interest amounting to $64,000,000 due U.S. Govt.). Home: Omaha, Neb. Died Dec. 20, 1918.

COWLES, Alfred, lawyer; b. Chicago, Ill., Jan. 5, 1865; s. Alfred and Sarah Frances (Hutchinson) C.; A.B., Yale, 1886, post-grad., 1886-87, Yale Law Sch., 1887-88; Northwestern Coll., Coll. of Law, Chicago, 1888-89; m. Elizabeth Cheney, Nov. 28, 1890; children—Alfred, 3d, Knight Cheney, John Cheney, Thomas Hooker (dec.). Admitted to Ill. bar, 1889, and thereafter practiced in Chicago, except from 1898 to 1901, during which time was engaged in the management of The Chicago Tribune. Republican. Unitarian. Home: Chicago, Ill. Died Jan. 15, 1939.

COWLES, Alfred Hutchinson, engineer; b. Cleveland, Dec. 8, 1858; s. Edwin C. (founder and editor Cleveland Leader) and Elizabeth (Hutchinson) C.; Ohio State U., 1875-77; Cornell, 1877-82; m. Helen J. Wills, Nov. 1906. With bro. Eugene H., organized, 1885, The Electric Smelting & Aluminum Co., pres., 1895—; pres. Cowles Detergent Co., 1923—, Pecos Copper Co., 1902-21. V.p. Cleveland Leader Printing Co., 1898-1904. Awarded Elliott Cresson and John Scott Legacy medals, Franklin Inst., 1886; medal, Paris Expn., 1889. With bro., Eugene H. Cowles, was a pioneer in electric smelting, beginning in 1884. Fellow Am. Inst. Elec. Engrs., A.A.A.S. Home: Sewaren, N.J. Died Aug. 13, 1929.

COWLES, Augustus Woodruff, college pres.; b. Reading, N.Y., July 12, 1819; s. Alvah C. and Harriet (Woodruff) C.; A.B., Union Coll., 1841, A.M., 1844; Union Theol. Sem., 1843-46; (D.D., Union, 1895; LL.D., Hamilton, 1887); m. Frances C. Goold, June 15, 1847. Ordained Presbyn. ministry, 1847; pastor Brockport, 1847-56; pres., 1856-89, pres. emeritus and prof. Christian evidences and art criticism, until 1906, Elmira Coll.; retired. Home: Elmira, N.Y. Died Mar. 15, 1913.

COWLES, Edward, physician; b. Ryegate, Vt., July 20, 1837; s. George and Mary (Bradley) C.; A.B., Dartmouth, 1859, A.M., 1861, M.D., 1863; M.D., Coll. Phys. and Surg. (Columbia), 1863; fellow by courtesy, Johns Hopkins, 1887-88; (LL.D., Dartmouth, 1890); m. Harriet M. Wainwright, Dec. 25, 1865. Asst. phys. Retreat for the Insane, Hartford, Conn., 1863; capt. asst. surgeon U.S.A., 1863-72; resident phys. and supt., Boston City Hosp., 1872-79; med. supt., McLean Hosp. (for treatment of insane), 1879-1903; prof. mental diseases, Dartmouth Med. Sch., 1885-1914, emeritus; instr. mental diseases, Harvard Med. Sch., 1889-1914; trustee, 1890-1908, non-resident lecturer mental diseases, 1904—, Clark U. Republican. Conglist. Home: Plymouth, Mass. Died July 25, 1919.

COWLES, Henry Chandler, botanist; b. Kensington, Conn., Feb. 27, 1869; s. Henry Martyn and Eliza (Whittlesey) C.; A.B., Oberlin Coll., 1893; fellow in geology and botany, 1895-97, lab. asst., 1897-98, Ph.D., 1898, U. of Chicago; Sc.D., Oberlin, 1923; m. Elizabeth Waller, June 25, 1900; 1 dau., Harriet Elizabeth. Prof. natural sciences, Gates Coll., Neb., 1894-95; spl. field asst. U.S. Geol. Survey, summer, 1895; instr. botany, 1902-07, asst. prof., 1907-11, asso. prof., 1911-15, prof., 1915—, chmn. dept. of botany, 1925-34 (emeritus), U. of Chicago. Pres. ecology sect., Internat. Bot. Congress, 1930. Conglist. Author: Vegetation of Sand Dunes of Lake Michigan, 1899; Plant Societies of Chicago, 1901; Text-book of Plant Ecology, 1911; Plant Societies of Chicago and Vicinity, 1913. Editor Botanical Gazette, 1925-34. Home: Chicago, Ill. Died Sept. 12, 1939.

COWLES, James Lewis, writer; b. Farmington, Conn., Sept. 14, 1843; s. James and Jane L. C.; A.B., Yale, 1866, LL.B., 1888; m. Martha L. Gwaltney, June 2, 1870 (died June 10, 1893); father of Genevieve Almeda C. Admitted to Conn. bar, 1888; never practiced; has devoted last 25 years to the solution of the railroad problem and to the study of the postal service. Mem. Cobden Club of England; asso. with various reform clubs; sec. Conn. Reform Club, 1888; founded Postal Progress League of Mass., 1902; organized the World Postal League in Jan. 1914. Author: A General Freight and Passenger Post, 3 edits., 1896-98. Styled "Father of the Parcel Post." Home: New York, N.Y. Died Oct. 22, 1922.

COWLES, John Guiteau Welch, real estate; b. Oberlin, O., Mar. 14, 1836; s. Rev. Henry and Alice (Welch) C.; A.B., Oberlin, 1856, A.M., 1859 (LL.D., 1898); grad. Oberlin Theol. Sem., 1859; m. Lois M. Church, Aug. 26, 1859; m. 2d, Beatrice Walker, Aug. 24, 1904. Ordained Congl. ministry, 1859; pastor, Bellevue, Ohio, 1859-61; chaplain 55th Ohio Vol. Inf., 1861-62; pastor, Mansfield, O., 1862-65, E. Saginaw, Mich., 1865-71; editor Cleveland Leader, 1871-73; engaged in real estate operations, Cleveland, 1873-1913; retired, 1913, and removed to San Diego, Calif. Pres. Cleveland Chamber Commerce, 1896-97, Cleveland Bd. Park Commrs., 1902-13; trustee Oberlin College, 1874—, Cleveland Mus. Art, Cleveland Sch. Art, Y.M.C.A. Republican. Home: San Diego, Calif. Died June 17, 1914.

COWLES, Julia Darrow, author; b. Norwalk, O., Jan. 6, 1862; d. Francis Vincent and Elmina (Jones) Darrow; grad. Central High Sch., Buffalo, N.Y., 1880; studied English lit. under Prof. Maria L. Sanford, U. of Minn. Summer Sch., and in spl. classes; course in story telling, Northwestern Conservatory, Minneapolis; m. Francis Dana Cowles, Oct. 16, 1884. Dept. editor, The Housekeeper, 1903-06; has specialized in lit. for children and in story telling to children. Author: Robinson Crusoe Reader, 1906; Our Little Athenian Cousin of Long Ago, 1913; Our Little Roman Cousin of Long Ago, 1913; Our Little Spartan Cousin of Long Ago, 1914; The Art of Story Telling, 1914; Our Little Macedonian Cousin of Long Ago, 1915; Favorite Fairy Tales Retold, 1915; Favorite Folk Tales Retold, 1916; Going to School in Animal Land, 1917; The Queer Little Tailor, 1917; Indian Nature Myths, 1918; Plays and Poems (dramatic readers), grades I-V, 1917-18. Home: Minneapolis, Minn. Died Sept. 6, 1919.

COWLES, Maude Alice, artist; b. Farmington, Conn., Feb. 23, 1871; d. James L. and Martha L. C.; ed. by private teachers; studied art at Miss Porter's school, Farmington; 2 yrs. at Yale Art School; 1 yr. at Cowles Art School, Boston; unmarried. In Europe, 1880-83; 2 yrs. in Ala.; with twin sister, Genevieve Cowles, worked as illustrator for mags. and publishers, 1894—; now especially interested in making designs for stained glass windows; received award of bronze medal at Paris Expdn., 1900, Pan-Am. Expn., 1901, and St. Louis Expn., 1904, for drawing. Home: Farmington, Conn. Deceased.

COWLES, Torris Zalmon, editor; b. Geneva, N.Y., Feb. 8, 1845; s. Zalmon J. and Sarah (Hoover) C.; common sch. edn. to 15; m. Ellen M. Crooks, 1866 (died 1885); m. 2d, Emma F. Bliss, Apr. 18, 1888. Enlisted as musician 2d Minn. Vol. Inf., Aug. 1861; hon. mustered out, May 26, 1862; learned printer's trade, Rochester, Minn., 1862-65; reporter Chicago Evening Post, 1866-67, Chicago Times, 1867-68; sporting editor, 1868-75, night editor, 1875-83, Chicago Tribune; editor American Sports, 1883-86; night editor Chicago Times, 1886-88; mng. editor Pioneer Press, St. Paul, 1888-92, Dispatch, 1892-93; with Asso. Press, 1894-95; editor New York Commercial and Shipping List, 1897; editor Am. Economist, Oct. 18, 1897—. Republican. Home: New York, N.Y. Died Dec. 3, 1919.

COWLES, Walter Cleveland, rear adm.; b. Conn., July 11, 1853; grad. U.S. Naval Acad., 1873. Advanced through various grades and promoted rear admiral U.S.N., Jan. 14, 1911; comd. Naval Sta., Havana, Cuba, Dec., 1910-Mar., 1913; comd. Pacific Fleet, Apr. 1913-Mar. 1914, Asiatic Fleet, May, 1914-July 1915; retired July 11, 1915. Died Nov. 25, 1917.

COWLES, William Lyman, educator; b. Belchertown, Mass., Apr. 11, 1856; s. Samuel Dunton and Emily S. (Towne) C.; A.B., Amherst, 1878, L.H.D., 1925; post-grad. study, U. of Berlin, 1883-84; m. Martha Snell Hall, Aug. 16, 1905. Prof. Latin, Amherst, 1880-1925, now prof. emeritus. Lecturer on Latin lit., Smith Coll., 1886-94. Mem. mng. com. Am. Sch. at Rome; trustee Monson Acad. Republican. Conglist. Address: Amherst, Mass. Died May 12, 1926.

COWLES, William Sheffield, rear adm.; b. Farmington, Conn., Aug. 1, 1846; s. Thomas and Elizabeth (Sheffield) C.; grad. U.S. Naval Acad., 1867. Promoted ensign, U.S.N., 1869; master, 1870; lt., 1871; lt. comdr., 1892; comdr., June 5, 1899; capt., Nov. 2, 1902; rear admiral, Apr. 23, 1908. Served on Mediterranean, Pacific, North Atlantic and Asiatic stas.; served on Isthmus of Panama, guarding property of Am. citizens, 1884; naval aide to Sec. of the Navy, in charge naval militia, 1891-92; naval attaché, U.S. Embassy, London, 1893-97; comd. the Fern, 1897-98, Topeka, 1898-99; asst. to Bur. of Navigation, Sept. 30, 1899, and naval aide to the President; comdg. Missouri, 1903-05; chief Bur. of Equipment, and mem. Bd. Constrn., Feb. 1906; retired, Aug. 1, 1908. Naval rep. to Tercentenary Celebration, Quebec, July, 1908; chief Bur. Equipment until 1910. Mem. Borough Council, Farmington, 3 yrs.; naval aide to Gov. Holcomb, of Conn., 1914; mem. Conn. Ho. of Rep., 1916; enlisted in Farmington Home Guard, 1917; detailed Conn. River Patrol, later to staff Maj. Gen. Lucien Burpee, comdg. Conn. Home Guard; chmn. naval and mil. com. Conn. Council Defense. Home: Farmington, Conn. Died May 1, 1923.

COWLEY, Charles, lawyer; b. Gloucestershire, Eng., Jan. 9, 1832; s. Aaron and Hannah (Price) C.; ed. by pvt. tutors at Lowell, Mass.; (hon. LL.D., Norwich Univ., 1885); unmarried; admitted to bar, 1856. Capt. Wamesit Rifles, 1861; paymaster U.S. steamer Lehigh, 1864; judge advocate South Atlantic blockading squadron, 1864-65; with fleet brigade in battles of Honey Hill and Gregory's Landing, S.C.; entered Charleston with Admiral Dahlgren, Feb. 18, 1865; with Dahlgren when his flagship was sunk by Confederate torpedo at Winyah Bay, S.C., Mar. 1, 1865; resumed law practice in Lowell and Boston, 1865; as counsel for the Knights of St. Crispin obtained an act incorporating their Grand Lodge, being the first trade union ever incorporated, 1870. Agitated for, 1869-74, and obtained enactment of the 10-hours law in Mass. Edited, 1877, Dahlgren's Maritime International Law, the first text-book on that subject used in the Naval War Coll., Newport, R.I. Author: History of Lowell, 1868; Famous Divorces of All Aages, 1878; Historical Sketch of Middlesex County, 1878; Leaves from a Lawyer's Life Afloat and Ashore, 1879; Our Divorce Courts, 1879; Reminiscences of James C. Ayer and the Town of Ayer, 1879; Memoir of Josiah Gardner Abbott; Siege of Charleston and Savannah, 1903. Home: Lowell, Mass. Died 1908.

COWPER, Harry Mattingly ("Holmes Cowper"), tenor soloist; b. Dundas, Ont., Can., Mar. 4, 1870; s. Roland Frederick and Sara Ann (Bishop) C.; Quaker Coll., Pickering, Ont., to 1888; pupil Frederick Walker, London, Eng., 1895-97; George Ferguson, Berlin; Vergenet, Paris; Gottschalk, Chicago; m. Kate Holmes, Aug. 12, 1895; children—Marian Jennie Holmes, Gerald Holmes (dec.), Muriel Grace (Mrs. Willard Parrish). Tenor soloist with leading choral and oratorio socs., including 9 appearances with Apollo Club (Chicago), Theodore Thomas Orchestra, Pittsburgh Orchestra, Cincinnati Orchestra, Boston Festival, etc.; ch. positions, London and Chicago; teacher singing and interpretation Am. Conservatory of Music, Chicago, 1897-1900, Sherwood Sch. of Music, 1900-02; pvt. teacher, 1902-09; dean Coll. of Fine Arts and prof. singing, Drake U., 1909—. Song leader, Camp Dodge, Ia., Oct. 1917-Apr. 1919. Episcopalian. Home: Des Moines, Ia. Died July 2, 1934.

COX, Abraham Beekman, civil engr.; b. New York, N.Y., April 16, 1844; s. Abraham Beekman and

COX 268 COX

Levantia White (Livingston) C.; grad. Yale, 1864; C.E. Rensselaer Poly. Inst., 1867; m. April 30, 1873, Augusta McBlair, d. late U.S. Senator John C. Ten Eyck of N.J. (died 1876). Practiced civ. engring 1st in R.R. work, afterward building iron bridges until 1876; retired. Home: Cherry Valley, N.Y. Died 1906.

COX, Archibald, lawyer; b. Smyrna, Del., Nov. 26, 1874; s. Rowland and Fanny Cummins (Hill) C.; A.B., Harvard, 1896, LL.B., 1899; m. Frances Bruen Perkins, June 7, 1911; children—Archibald, Elizabeth Evarts, Mary Davenport, Robert Hill, Maxwell Evarts, Louis Anthony, Rowland Johns. Practiced in New York 1899—; practice largely devoted to matters of unfair competition, trade-marks, copyrights and patents. Democrat. Episcopalian. Home: Plainfield, N.J. Died Feb. 28, 1931.

COX, Attilla, lawyer; b. Owenton, Ky., Feb. 21, 1875; s. Attilla and Kate (Martin) C.; student law dept. U. of Louisville, New York Law Sch., 1898; m. Carrie Rogers Gaulbert, Nov. 22, 1898; 1 dau., Harriet Rogers (Mrs. John V. Collis). Admitted to Ky. bar, 1898, and began practice at Louisville, Ky.; mem. Trabue, Doolan & Cox, 1903-11, Cox & Wells, 1920-30. Dir. of Louisville & Nashville R.R. Co., Fidelity & Columbia Trust Co., etc. Served as maj. judge advocate U.S.A., with A.E.F. in France, 1918-19; served as mem. Franco-American Transportation Commn. Decorated Officier d'Académie, with Palms (France); Pilsudski Medal (Poland). Democrat. Episcopalian. Home: Louisville, Ky. Deceased.

COX, Charles Elbridge, judge; b. Hamilton Co., Ind., Feb. 21, 1860; s. Aaron and Mary Ann (Skaggs) C.; common sch. edn.; studied law under Justice William E. Niblack, of Supreme Court of Ind.; m. Emma M. Cooley, June 10, 1884; children—Mrs. Elinor Karsten, Samuel Leslie, Charles E. Admitted to Ind. bar, 1889; associated with preceptor in practice at Indianapolis, 1889, until latter's death, 1893; librarian Ind. Supreme Court, 1883-89; chief deputy pros. atty., Marion Co., Ind., 1891-94; city judge, Indianapolis, 2 terms, 1895-99, declined 3d term; unanimously nominated judge of Criminal Court, 1902, but entire ticket defeated; justice Supreme Court of Ind., term 1911-17. Democrat. Conglist. Home: Indianapolis, Ind. Died Feb. 4, 1936.

COX, Charles Finney, ry. officer; b. Richmond Co., N.Y., Jan. 16, 1846; A.B., Oberlin, 1869 (hon. A.M., 1889); m. Mrs. Helen M. Fake, Apr. 30, 1878. Treas. L.S.&M.S. Ry. Co., M.C. Ry. Co., C.,C.C.& S.L. Ry. Co., N.Y.,C.&S.L. Ry. Co., L.E.&W. Ry. Co., and other subsidiary cos. in the N.Y. Central system. Mem. Council N.Y. Acad. Sciences; one of the scientific directors N.Y. Bot. Garden. Home: Yonkers, N.Y. Died Jan. 24, 1912.

COX, Douglas Farley, marine insurance; b. N.Y. City, Jan. 28, 1867; s. James Farley and Maria (McIntosh) C.; student Columbia, 1886-87; m. Dora Andrews Harris, Nov. 21, 1905; 1 son, Douglas Farley. Pres. Appleton & Cox, Inc., 1920—; dir. Westchester Fire Insurance Company, Seaboard Fire & Marine Insurance Company, North River Insurance Company; trustee Seamen's Bank for Savings (New York). Mem. Nat. Bd. of Marine Underwriters (pres. 1912-15), Bd. of Underwriters (marine) of New York (pres. 1924, 25), Am. Inst. Marine Underwriters (pres. 1926-27), Nat. Automobile Underwriters Conf. (pres. 1916-18). Republican. Episcopalian. Home: West Orange, N.J. Died Apr. 9, 1940.

COX, Eleanor Rogers, author; b. Enniskillen, Ireland; d. Patrick and Anne (McCaffery) C.; came with family to U.S. in childhood; ed. St. Gabriel's High Sch., New York, and under pvt. tutors; unmarried. Contbr. poems, notably those dealing with Celtic myth and legend, to Century Magazine, Smart Set, Harper's Weekly, New York Sunday Times Magazine, etc.; also contbr. short stories, poems and essays to various mags.; editor Inisfail (ednl. lit. mag.), 1922-25. One of poets chosen by com. of Poetry Soc. America to represent Am. poetry from 1900-19. Catholic. Author: A Hosting of Heroes, 1911; Latter Day Poetry of Ireland, 1913; Singing Fires of Erin, 1916; Finovar of the Fair Eyelids, 1918; Austin Dobson, Poet and Friend, 1921; Andrew Lang, 1922; Lord Byron, 1923. Home: New York, N.Y. Died Jan. 17, 1931.

COX, G(eorge) Howland, banker; b. Fairhaven, Mass., Oct. 9, 1854; s. James Valentine and Mercy Nye (Howland) C.; ed. U.S. Mil. Acad. (non-grad.); m. Ella, d. Zenas and Mary (Tobey) Whittemore, of New Bedford, Mass., Sept. 25, 1877; 1 son, George Howland. Clk. in Mt. Washington Glass Works, New Bedford, 1872-74; in employ of Calumet & Hecla Mining Co., 1875-1902; dir. and treas. Cambridge Trust Co., 1902-09, then pres. and chmn. bd.; pres. Bd. of Park Commrs., Cambridge, 1893; sec. and treas. Met. Improvement League; mem. State Armory Commn., 1901—. Trustee Cambridge Home for Aged People, Cambridge Hosp.; pres. Cambridge Bd. of Trade. Mason. Home: Cambridge, Mass. Died Mar. 1931.

COX, Guy Henry, geologist; b. Lehigh, Ia., May 4, 1882; s. Edward Henry and Ada (Wilson) C.; B.S., Northwestern U., 1905; studied Sch. of Mines, U. of Calif., 1906; M.A., U. of Wis., 1908, Ph.D., 1911; E.M., Mo. Sch. of Mines and Metallurgy (U. of Mo.), Rolla, 1914; m. Kittie May Gates, Dec. 27, 1909. Geol. work in Wis., Wyo., Ill., summers 1904-11; instr. geology, U. of Calif., 1909; asst. prof. mineralogy and petrology, 1910-11, prof. geology and mineralogy, 1911-20, Mo. Sch. of Mines and Metallurgy. Civilian supervision govt. training camp, sections A and B, Rolla, Mo., 1917-18. Mem. Cox & Radcliffe, cons. engrs., 1917-19; chief geologist, Jersey Oil Co., 1920—. Methodist. Author: Field Methods in Petroleum geology, 1920. Home: Pine Bluff, Ark. Died 1922.

COX, Henry Joseph, meteorologist; b. Newton, Mass., Apr. 5, 1863; s. Thomas and Hannah M. (Perkins) C.; A.B., Harvard, 1884; hon. A.M., Norwich U., 1887, and ScD., 1914; m. Mary Cavanagh, Sept. 8, 1887; children—Henry Perkins, Arthur Cavanagh, Paul Greenwood (killed in action nr. Soissons, France, 1918). Prof. Norwich U., 1886-88; in weather service from Aug. 1, 1884; sr. meteorologist, July 1, 1924—; became sr. in charge North Central Forecast Dist., Chicago; also in charge of corn and wheat region service of Weather Bur., and formerly in charge spl. researches in agrl. meteorology. Fellow Am. Meteorol. Soc. (councilor). Author: Weather Bureau Records in Court; Lantern Slides in Teaching of Meteorology (Bull. 3, Geog. Soc. Chicago); Recent Advances in Meteorology; Notes of a Meteorologist in Europe; The Weather Bureau and the Cranberry Industry; Weather and Climate of Chicago; Weather Forecasting in United States (joint author); Influence of Great Lakes upon Movement of Storms; Thermal Belts and Fruit Growing in North Carolina Mountain Region. Home: Chicago, Ill. Died Jan. 7, 1930.

COX, J. Elwood, banker, mfr.; b. Rich Square, N.C., Nov. 1, 1856; s. Jonathan E. and Elizabeth A. (Hare) C.; ed. Guilford Coll., N.C., Earlham Coll., Richmond, Ind., and business coll., Baltimore; m. Bertha E. Snow, Oct. 23, 1878. Pres. Commercial Nat. Bank; dir. First Nat. Bank, Thomasville, N.C., Greensboro (N.C.) Loan & Trust Co., Virginia Trust Co., Richmond, Jefferson Standard Life Ins. Co., Greensboro, N.C.; also pres. High Point (N.C.) Savings and Trust Co.; dir. Southern Expn. Bldg. (cost $1,000,000), High Point, High Point Hotel Co. Rep. nominee for gov. N.C., 1908. Mem. Friends Ch. Mem. N.C. State Highway Commn., 1921—; chmn. bd. trustees Guilford Coll. and High Point pub. schs. Mem. exec. council and pres. nat. bank sect. of Am. Bankers' Assn., 1917, treas., 1923; apptd., 1921, on State Highway Commn. of N.C., to expend $50,000,000 on highways; mem. com. from N.C. on War Finance Corp.; trustee George Peabody Coll. for Teachers, Duke Endowment. Home: High Point, N.C. Died Mar. 29, 1932.

COX, Jacob Dolson, lawyer, governor; b. Montreal, Canada (parents natives of U.S.), Oct. 27, 1828; spent boyhood in New York; removed to Ohio, 1846; grad. Oberlin, 1851; m. Helen C., 1849, dau. Rev. Chas. G. Finney, pres. Oberlin Coll. Studied law and settled in practice at Warren, O.; mem. State senate, 1859-61. Was brig. gen. Ohio militia, at breaking out of Civil war; served from Va. to Sherman's march, first as brig. gen. U.S. vols., then as maj. gen., promoted for services at Antietam. Since war in law practice in Cincinnati. Gov. Ohio, 1866-67; U.S. sec. of the interior, 1869-70; congressman, 1877-79; pres. Cincinnati Univ., 1885; dean Cincinnati Law School, 1881-97. Author: Atlanta; The March to the Sea; etc. Home: Oberlin, O. Died 1900.

COX, Joseph Winston, judge; b. Bridle Creek, Va., Oct. 19, 1875; s. Melville B. and Martha E. (Fulton) C.; prep. edn., Bridle Creek Acad.; grad. George Peabody Coll. for Teachers, 1896; LL.B., George Washington, 1901; m. Emma P. Leckie, Oct. 18, 1905; children—Joseph W., Melville B., Leckie, Carol McNeir. In gen. practice of law at Washington, D.C., 1901-30; instr. Georgetown U. Law Sch., 1913-15; spl. asst. to atty. gen. U.S. in enforcement of anti-trust laws and matters arising in spl. war activities of U.S., 1914-19; mem. District Selective Service Bd., D.C., 1917-18; regional counsel U.S. R.R. Administration, 1919-20; professorial lecturer, George Washington U., 1928-30, adjunct prof., 1930—; asso. justice Supreme Court D.C. (now Dist. Court of U.S. for D.C.), 1930—. Home: Washington, D.C. Died Sept. 9, 1939.

COX, Katherine Hamilton Cabell; b. Richmond, Va.; d. Gen. Henry Coalter (C.S.A.) and Jane C. (Alston) Cabell; ed. pvt. schs., Richmond and New York; m. Maj. Herbert Augustine Claiborne (C.S.A.), Feb. 1, 1882 (died 1902); children—Jeanie Alston (dec.), Herbert Augustine, Hamilton Cabell; m. 2d, Gen. William Ruffin Cox (C.S.A.), June 21, 1905. Pres. Colonial Dames of America in the State of Va., 1897—; pres. Nat. Soc. Colonial Dames of America, 12 yrs., now hon. pres. (Kate Cabell Cox scholarship in Am. history, founded at U. of Va. in her honor by Nat. Soc. Colonial Dames of America); v. chmn. woman's com. Va. div. Council of Nat. Defense; mem. bd. govs. Am. br. Sulgrave Instn. Episcopalian. Home: Richmond, Va. Died Dec. 25, 1925.

COX, Kenyon, painter; b. Warren, O., Oct. 27, 1856; s. Gen. Jacob Dolson and Helen (Finney) C.; nephew Frederick Norton Finney; studied in Cincinnati and Phila., in Paris under Carolus Duran and Gérôme, 1877-82; returned to New York; (hon. A.M., Yale U., 1910; D.Litt., Oberlin [Ohio] Coll., 1912, and Dartmouth Coll., 1915)); m. Louise Howland King, June 30, 1892. Pictures principally portraits and figure pieces; painted 2 decorations in Library of Congress, 1 in Walker Art Gallery, Bowdoin Coll., 1 in Minn. State Capitol, 1 in Citizens Bldg., Cleveland, 8 in Ia. State Capitol, 1 in Essex Co. Ct. House, Newark, 1 in Luzerne Co. Ct. House, Wilkes-Barre, Pa., 1 in Public Library, Winona, Minn., and frieze in court room, Appellate Ct., New York, and other decorative pictures; modeled one of the statues on the Brooklyn Inst. Bldg.; awarded medal of honor for mural painting, Architectural League, 1910; mosaics in dome and paintings in Senate Chamber, Wis. State Capitol; etc. Fellow A.N.A., 1900, N.A., 1903; pres. of the Mural Painters; mem. Am. Acad. Arts and Letters, etc. Part author: Modern French Masters (edited by John C. Van Dyke), 1896; The Nineteenth Century, 1901. Author: Mixed Beasts, 1904; Old Masters and New, 1905; Painters and Sculptors, 1907; The Classic Point of View, 1911; Artist and Public, 1914; Winslow Homer, 1914; Concerning Painting, 1917. Died Mar. 17, 1919.

COX, Palmer, author, artist; b. Granby, P.Q., Can., Apr. 28, 1840; s. Michael and Sarah (Miller) C.; grad. Granby Acad., unmarried. Lived in San Francisco, 1863-75, contributing to Golden Era and Alta Californian; from 1875 has lived in New York. His specialty is original humorous pictures illustrating his own books. Author: Squibs of California, or Every-Day Life Illustrated, 1875 (same re-written as Comic Yarns, 1889); Hans Von Pelter's Trip to Gotham, 1876; How Columbus Found America, 1877; That Stanley, 1878; The Brownies, Their Book, 1887; Queer People, 1888; Queer People with Wings and Stings, 1888; Queer People with Paws and Claws, 1888; Another Brownie Book, 1890; The Brownies at Home, 1893; The Brownies Around the World, 1894; The Brownies Through the Union, 1895; The Brownies Abroad, 1899; The Brownies in Fairyland (cantata, 1895; Palmer Cox's Brownies, spectacular play in 3 acts, 1895; The Brownies in the Philippines, 1904; The Palmer Cox Brownie Primer, 1906; Brownie Clown in Brownie Town, 1907; The Brownies' Latest Adventures, 1910; The Brownies Many More Nights, 1913; The Brownies and Prince Florimel, 1918. Home: Granby, P.Q., Can. Died July 24, 1924.

COX, Walter Smith; b. Georgetown, D.C., Oct. 25, 1826; studied in private school; grad. Georgetown Coll., 1843 (A.M., 1844); grad. Harvard Law School, 1847; (LL.D., Columbian). Practiced law in Washington until 1879; asso. justice Supreme Court of D.C., March, 1879; retired July 1, 1899; prof. law school, Columbian Univ., since 1874; author of a work on practice, for students; presided as judge on trial of Guiteau, assassin of Garfield, Nov., 1881, to Feb., 1882. Died 1902.

COX, William Ruffin, cotton planter; b. in Halifax Co., N.C., Mar. 11, 1832; s. Hon. Thomas and Olivia (Norfleet) C.; A.B., Franklin Coll., Tenn., 1851, A.M., 1853; LL.B., Lebanon (Tenn.) Law Sch., 1853; admitted to bar, 1853; practiced, Nashville, 1853-57; m. a d. James S. Battle, 1857 (died 1880); 2d, Fannie A., d. Rt. Rev. T. B. Lyman, of Raleigh, N.C.; 3d, Mrs. Kate C. Claiborne, June, 1905. Commd. maj. 2d N.C. Inf., C.S.A., 1861; lt. col., col. and brig. gen.; wounded 11 times. Pres. Chatham Coal Field R.R., 1866; solicitor, 4th Jud. Dist., 1868-74; chmn. Dem. State Exec. Com., 5 yrs.; del.-at-large Dem. Nat. Conv., 1876; judge 6th Jud. Dist., N.C., 1877-80; mem. 47th to 49th Congresses (1881-87); sec. U.S. Senate, 1893-99. Grand Master Grand Lodge of Masonry in N.C., 4 yrs.; has been pres. N.C. Agrl. Soc. Chmn. Dem. State Exec. Com.; trustee U. of the South, 1883. Home: Penelo, N.C. Died Dec. 26, 1919.

COX, William Van Zandt, banker; b. near Zanesville, O., June 12, 1852; s. Col. Thomas J. and Lucy Ann (Van Zandt) C.; A.B., Ohio Wesleyan U., 1874, A.M., 1884 (Phi Beta Kappa, LL.D., 1919); m. Juliet H. Emery, Oct. 27, 1886. Admitted to Ohio bar, 1877; message clk., Ohio State Senate, 1877-78; entered service U.S. Nat. Mus., 1879; sec. and disbursing officer, Internat. Fisheries Exhbn., London, 1883; represented Smithsonian Instn. at Minneapolis Expn., 1887, Northwest Ty. Centennial, Marietta, O., 1888; financial officer Smithsonian Instn. and U.S. Nat. Mus., Chicago Expn., 1893, Cotton States Expn., Atlanta, 1896; sec. and exec. officer gvt. bd. management, Tenn. Centennial Expn., Nashville, 1897, Trans-Miss. Expn., Omaha, 1898, Pan-Am. Expn., Buffalo, 1901, La. Purchase Expn., 1904, Jamestown Tercentennial, 1907; sec. joint com. celebration 100th anniversary establishment of seat of govt. in D.C., 1900; mem. exec. com., Com. of 100 to Celebrate 100 Years of Peace Between Great Britain and U.S. Pres. 2d Nat. Bank, Washington,

1901; v.p. Washington Market Co.; mem. exec. com. Nat. Savings & Trust Co., Washington Title Ins. Co. Democrat. Presbyn. Trustee Howard U.; pres. Bd. of Edn., D.C., 1910. Chmn. Selective Service Bd., D.C., 1917-18. Mem. currency commn., executive council and federal legislative com., Am. Bankers' Assn.; treas. Dem. Nat. Com., D.C., 1912; treas. Wilson and Marshall Inaugural Com., 1913, etc. Author: (with H. M. Northrup) Life of Samuel S. Cox (his uncle), Syracuse, 1899; (monograph), Settlement of the Northwest Territory, 1896; The Last Mayor of Washington, 1917. Home: Brightwood, D.C. Died July 24, 1923.

COX, Wilson Naylor, banker; b. Terre Haute, Ind., Nov. 11, 1876; s. Benjamin Guille and Elizabeth Ellen (Naylor) C.; student Phillips Exeter Acad., Exeter, N.H.; LL.B., Columbia, 1900; m. Lassie M. Gardenhire, Oct. 10, 1907; children—Wilson N., Francis G., Benjamin G. and John R., twins. Admitted to N.Y. bar, 1900, Ind. bar, 1900, and practiced at Terre Haute until 1921; pres. Terre Haute Nat. Bank, 1921-27, Terre Haute Nat. Bank & Trust Co., 1927-32, Terre Haute First Nat. Bank, 1932—; dir. Terre Haute Mutual Savings Assn. Treas. Ind. State Teachers Coll. Republican. Episcopalian. Home: Terre Haute, Ind. Died July 9, 1938.

COXE, Alfred Conkling, judge; b. Auburn, N.Y.; s. Rev. Samuel Hanson and Eliza (Conkling) C.; g.s. of Judge Alfred Conkling, nephew Senator Roscoe Conkling and Bishop Arthur Cleveland Coxe; A.B., Hamilton Call., 1868; (LL.D., Columbia, 1904); m. Maryette, d. Judge Charles H. Doolittle, of Utica, N.Y., 1878. Admitted to bar, 1868; practiced Utica, N.Y., 1868-82; U.S. dist. judge, Northern Dist. of N.Y., 1882-1902; U.S. circuit judge, 2d Jud. Circuit, 1902-17, retired. Home: Hartford, Conn. Deceased.

COXE, Frank Morrell, brig. gen.; b. Phila., Mar. 4, 1844; s. Charles W. and Sarah H. C.; ed. pub. schs., Phila. Served pvt. to capt. and bvt. col., U.S.V., during Civil War; transferred to regular army as capt. 40th Inf., July 28, 1866; transferred to 25th Inf., Apr. 20, 1869; maj. p.m., Mar. 3, 1875; lt. col. deputy p.m. gen., Feb. 24, 1896; col. asst. p.m. gen., Feb. 1, 1899; brig. gen. Jan. 23, 1904; retired at own request over 39 yrs.' service Jan. 24, 1904. Principally on line and staff duty on plains and frontier for past 30 yrs. Died Sept. 15, 1916.

COXE, James Clarke Watson, clergyman; b. Ft. Ann, N.Y., July 9, 1837; s. John Todd and Polly Baker (Nelson) C.; M.A., Wesleyan U., Conn., 1865; Ph.D., Cornell Coll., Ia., 1876 (D.D., Wesleyan, 1881; L.H.D., Ia. Wesleyan U., 1906); m. Mary F. Shaw, 1862 (died, 1889); 2d, Mrs. Zerilda A. Caldwell, Aug. 29, 1892 (died 1904); 3d, Mrs. Amelia Holden, Feb. 9, 1907. Ordained M.E. ministry, 1864; pastor Bellows Falls, Vt., 1864, Groton, 1865-67, Lyndon, 1868, Springfield, Vt., 1869-70, Montpelier, 1871-72; prin. Vt. Methodist Sem., Montpelier, 1873-74; pastor Burlington, Ia., 1874-77, Washington, Ia., 1877-79, Oskaloosa, 1879-82, Brooklyn, Ia., 1882-85; field sec. S.S. Union (M.E. Ch.), 1885-92; presiding elder, 1895-1901; pastor Knoxville, Ia., 1901-03, Oskaloosa, 1904-09, superannuated, 1911. Trustee Wesleyan U., 1874-78, Ia. Wesleyan U., 1880-92. Del. Gen. Conf., M.E. Ch., 1872, 1884, 1888, 1900, reserve del., 1896; fraternal del. from Gen. Conf. to Nat. Council Congl. Chs., 1872; mem. Book Com. M.E. Ch., 1884-88; mem. bd. of control Epworth League, 1900-04. Republican. Mason. Home: Los Angeles, Cal. Died July 28, 1914.

COXE, Macgrane, lawyer; b. Huntsville, Ala., May 29, 1859; s. Robert E. and Eliza (Davies) C.; A.B., Yale, 1879; LL.B., Columbia, 1881; (hon. A.M., Yale, 1908); m. Lena Townsend Crawford, Aug. 28, 1888. In practice at New York, 1881—; asst. U.S. dist. atty., Southern Dist., N.Y., 1885-89; apptd. U.S. commr. U.S. Circuit Ct. for same dist., Dec. 1, 1889; U.S. minister to Guatemala and Honduras, 1896-97; U.S. referee in bankruptcy since Dec. 5, 1899. Lecturer on law and practice in bankruptcy, Yale, 1906—. Mem. Bd. Visitors U.S. Naval Acad., 1908. Author: The Sterling Furnace and the West Point Chain, 1906; Chancellor Kent at Yale, 1908; Analogous Provisions of the Bankruptcy Acts of 1898 and 1867, 1907, rev. edit., 1911. Home: Southfields, N.Y., and N.Y. City. Died Apr. 20, 1923.

COXE, William Briscom, marine engr.; b. Reading, Pa., Feb. 25, 1869; s. Charles Chauncey and Annie Ellen (Griscom) C.; grad. Royal Tech. Coll., Charlottenburg, Berlin, 1891; served apprenticeship as marine engr., with J. & G. Thompson, Clyde Bank, Scotland, also with North German Lloyd repair plant, Bremerhaven, Germany; m. Helen Baer, Apr. 30, 1904. Fgn. rep. and asst. gen. supt. William Cramp & Sons Shipbuilding Co., Phila., 1898-1904; delivered to Russia, from Cramps, the battleship Retvizan and the cruiser Variag; to Japan, the cruiser Kasagi; pres. Harlan & Hollingsworth Corp., Wilmington, Del., 13½ yrs.; pres. Reading Paper Mills Co.; gen. mgr. for Pusey & Jones Co. of the Wilmington and Gloucester, N.J., plants. Served as sr. lt. U.S.N., Spanish-Am. War, 1898; dist. mgr. Emergency Fleet Corp., Delaware River Dist., World War, 1917-19. Pres. Atlantic Coast Shipbuilders' Assn., 1917-20. Democrat. Episcopalian. Mason. Home: Bellevue, Del. Died July 4, 1927.

COXE, William Ellery C., iron and coal sales agt.; b. Phila., June 12, 1837; A.B., 1855, A.M., 1860; Phila. High School; m. Frances Yeomans, June 12, 1866. At Fairmount Rolling Mill, 1855-62; private in Commonwealth art., 1861; afterward supt. and mgr. for several railroads, iron mills, etc., including Lochiel Iron Co., Phila. & Reading Coal and Iron Co., Montour Iron and Steel Co.; v.p. Columbus & Hocking Coal and Iron Co., 1890-92; now sales agt. for Cambria Steel Co., and Pa. R.R. coal; pres. Reading, Pa., Hosp., 1880-90; v.p. Toledo Chamber of Commerce, 1898. Home: Toledo, O. Died 1904.

COY, Edward Gustin, head master Hotchkiss Sch., 1892—; b. Ithaca, N.Y., Aug. 23, 1844; grad. Yale, 1869 (A.M.); studied in Univ. of Berlin; m. Helen E. Marsh, Nov. 25, 1873. Instr. Williston Sem., Easthampton, Mass., 2 yrs.; tutor Yale, 1 yr.; instr. Greek, Phillips Acad., Andover, 19 yrs., until 1892. Author: Greek for Beginners; First Greek Reader; etc. Home: Lakeville, Conn. Died 1904.

COY, Eliah Washburn, high sch. prin.; b. Thorndyke, Me., Dec. 6, 1832; s. Eliah and Sallie (Dyer) C.; A.M., Brown U., 1858; Ph.D., Princeton, 1886; m. Gena L. Harrington, Aug. 12, 1863. Prin. high sch., Peoria, Ill., 1858-71; practiced law, Peoria, 1862-65; in charge of high sch. dept. State Normal Sch., Normal, Ill., 1871-73; prin. Hughes High Sch., Cincinnati, 1873—. Editor Ill. Teacher, 1870-71. Pres. Nat. Council Edn., 1893-94; pres. Ohio State Teachers' Assn., 1901; pres. N. Central Assn. Colls. and Secondary Schs., 1908-09. Republican. Author: Latin Lessons for Beginners, 1896. Home: Avondale, Cincinnati. Died Mar. 29, 1915.

COYE, William Henry, furniture consultant; b. Grand Rapids, Mich., Mar. 30, 1863; s. Albert and Mary (Pugh) C.; ed. pub. schs.; m. Mary Gilbertson, Oct. 5, 1882; children—Mary Ethel (dec.), Nina Belle, Clarence William. Employed in furniture factories, Grand Rapids, until 1886; supt. factory, Milwaukee, 1886, Oshkosh, 1887; factory mgr. successively at Burlington (Ia.), Kankakee (Ill.), Marshfield (Wis.), 1888-1900; mgr. and treas. Coye Furniture Co., Stevens Pt., Wis., 1900-17; counsel for Nat. Furniture Mfrs.' Assn. from 1917, also counsel from 1919 for Southern Furniture Mfrs.' Assn. Republican. Presbyn. Home: Grand Rapids, Mich. Died Jan. 15, 1929.

COYLE, James Edwin, clergyman; b. Westpark Drum, nr. Athlone, Ireland, Mar. 23, 1873; s. Owen and Margaret Laetitia (Durney) C.; Mungret Coll., Limerick, Ireland; A.B., Royal U. of Ireland; grad. Collegio Americano del Nord (North Am. Coll.), Rome, Italy; U. of Propaganda, Rome. Ordained priest R.C. Ch., at Rome, 1896; missionary, at Cathedral, Mobile, Ala., 1896-99; rector McGill Inst., 1899-1904; apptd. pastor St. Paul's Ch., Birmingham, 1904, irremovable rector same, June 1913; dean of North Ala., 1915. Hon. mem. Syrian Young Men's Soc., Birmingham, and various Italian socs.; chaplain K. of C., A.O.H.; mem. Drama League. Editor. The Catholic Monthly. Home: Birmingham, Ala. Died Aug. 11, 1921.

COYLE, Robert Francis, clergyman; b. Roseneath, Ont., Can., July 28, 1850; s. James and Ann C.; ed. in Can., 1856-64; grad. Wabash Coll., 1877 (D.D., 1890; LL.D., Westminster Coll., 1892); studied theology, Auburn (N.Y.) Theol. Sem., 1878-79; m. J. Adella Haviland, June 4, 1885. Ordained Presbyn. ministry, 1879; pastor, Fort Dodge, 1879-85, Fullerton Av. Ch., Chicago, 1885-91, First Ch., Oakland, Calif., 1891-1900, Central Ch., Denver, 1900—. Moderator Presbyn. Gen. Assembly at Los Angeles, 1903. Author: Foundation Stones, 1887; Workingmen and the Church, 1896; The Christianity of Christ, 1892; The Church and the Times (sermons), 1905. Deceased.

COYLE, Robert McCurdy, ins. broker; b. Cincinnati, O., July 17, 1860; s. James Huston and Susan (McCurdy) C.; student U. of Pa.; m. Margaret Ivins, Jan. 25, 1901. Began in ins. brokerage business, Phila., 1888; sr. partner Robert M. Coyle & Co., 1892—; dir. Real Estate Land Title & Trust Co. Mem. commn. to study and revise ins. laws of state of Pa. Vice-pres. Wanamaker Inst. of Industries; chmn. Williamson Free Sch. of Mech. Trades; supt. Bethany Presbyn. S.S. Dir. Phila. Fire Patrol. Republican. Author: Fenceless France, 1907. Home: Philadelphia, Pa. Died Feb. 24, 1936.

COYNE, John Nicholas, soldier; b. New York, Nov. 14, 1839; s. John Nicholas and Hannah Anne (Park) C.; ed. schs. and acads. New York and Can.; m. Pauline M. Hemingway, June 6, 1894. Served in 7th regt. N.G.S.N.Y., Apr.-June 1861, in response to Lincoln's first call for troops; then pvt. to capt. 70th N.Y. vols. until July 1, 1864, then as capt., Hancock's Vet. Corps to end of war. Bvtd. maj. and lt. col. for gallantry at Williamsburg, Fair Oaks and Bristoe Sta., Va., and Gettysburg, Pa.; Congressional Medal of Honor for bravery and capture of Confederate flag at Williamsburg, Va.; wounded at Fair Oaks and Gettysburg. Now chief clerk disbursing dept. New York Custom House. Author: History of the Third Army Corps; History of the Excelsior Brigade. Home: East Orange, N.J. Died Mar. 4, 1907.

CRABBE, John Grant, college president; b. Mt. Sterling, O., Nov. 29, 1865; s. Thomas W. and Julia Catherine (Baughman) C.; A.B., Ohio Wesleyan U., 1889, A.M., 1892, Pd.D., 1913, Ped.M., Ohio U., 1897; LL.D., Berea, 1909, State U. of Ky., 1911; Ped.D., Miami U., 1909; m. Jennie Florence Graff, Jan. 29, 1889. Supt. pub. schs., Ashland, Ky., 1890-1907; state supt. pub. instrn. of Ky., Jan. 6, 1908-Apr. 9, 1910; pres. Eastern Ky. State Normal School, Richmond, Ky., Apr. 9, 1910-Sept. 1, 1916; pres. Colo. State Teachers Coll., Greeley, Colo., 1916—. Republican. Methodist. Rotarian. Mason (32°). Home: Greeley, Colo. Died Jan. 20, 1924.

CRABTREE, Charlotte ("Lotta"), actress; b. New York, 1847. First stage appearance when 6, at Petaluma, Calif.; 10 yrs. later made her New York début at Niblo's Garden, followed by a Western starring tour with her parents. Played in Eng. and U.S. for 30 yrs.; as the Marchioness in "Little Nell," and in "Firefly," "Topsy," "Musette," "Bob," "Nitouche," "The Little Detective," etc., met with great success. Died Sept. 25, 1924.

CRABTREE, Frederick, engineer; b. Bramley, York, Eng., Feb. 1, 1867; s. Joseph and Isabella (Clegg) C.; grad. high sch., Lawrence, Mass.; B.S. in Chemistry, Mass. Inst. Tech., 1889; m. Mary Odessa Moore, Aug. 30, 1894. Chemist, Ill. Steel Co., 1889, Nat. Tube Co., 1890-1900; supt. Western Steel Co., 1900-01; supt. blast furnace, Colo. Fuel & Iron Co., 1901-04; prof. mining and metallurgy, Colo. Coll., 1904-06; prof. mining and metall. engring., Carnegie Inst. Tech., 1906—. Republican. Episcopalian. Home: Pittsburgh, Pa. Died Feb. 14, 1925.

CRADDOCK, Charles Egbert, author. See Mary Noailles Murfree.

CRAFT, Clarence Christian, M.D., magnetician; b. Gaston, S.C., Sept. 28, 1880; s. of David Elmore and Mary Louisa (Richter) C.; B.S., S.C. Mil. Acad., 1902; M.D., George Washington U., 1909; m. Charlotte Maye Thomas, Dec. 6, 1911; children—Hume Richter, Warren Frederick. Aid, U.S. Coast and Geod. Survey, 1903-05, on U.S.S. Patterson, assisting in making soundings for Army and Navy cable, from Cape Flattery to Sitka, Alaska, summer of 1903; surveying harbor of Kiska, Aleutian Is., summer of 1904, and survey of H.I., Oct. 1904-Mar. 1905; magnetic observer in various states, 1905-07; computer Dept. Terrestrial Magnetism, Carnegie Instn. of Washington, to 1909; magnetic observer, Comdr. Peary's auxiliary ship Erik, July-Oct. 1908, going as far north as Etah, Greenland; surgeon and magnetic observer aboard yacht Carnegie from Aug. 3, 1909-June 1, 1911; in pub. health work, Florence, S.C., 1914-16, and from Sept. 1, 1921. Home: Hickory, N.C. Died May 25, 1935.

CRAFT, Edward Beech, electrical engr.; b. Cortland, Trumbull Co., O., Sept. 12, 1881; s. Charles C. and Nora A. (Trowbridge) C.; prep. edn., high sch., Warren, O.; D. Engring., Worcester Poly. Inst., 1926; m. Mary Ann Richards, Oct. 21, 1902; 1 dau., Clara Virginia. With Warren (O.) Electric and Specialty Co., 1898-1902 (last 2 yrs. as supt. lamp dept.); with dept. design of communication equipment, Western Electric Co., Chicago, 1902-07; development engr., in charge telephone apparatus design, Western Electric Co., New York, 1907-17; asst. chief engr. same, in charge development and design, 1917-22; chief engr. same and Internat. Western Electric Co., 1922-25; exec. v.p. Bell Telephone Labs., Inc., New York, 1925—. Capt. Signal Corps, U.S.A., Mar. 1917; maj., Dec. 1917; tech. adviser U.S. Navy, London, June-Oct. 1918. Vice chmn. div. of engring. and industrial research Nat. Research Council; chmn. bd. Engring. Socs. Library; mem. of council Am. Inst. Weights and Measures. Republican. Home: Hackensack, N.J. Died Aug. 20, 1929.

CRAFT, Frost, clergyman; b. Lawrenceburg, Ind., July 12, 1846; s. William Edward and Amelia Grace (Pell) C.; A.B., Ind. Asbury (now De Pauw) U., 1870, A.M., 1873 (D.D., 1888); m. Julia S. Shuler, Oct. 16, 1877 (died 1891). Ordained M.E. ministry, 1870; pastor 3d St. Ch., Indianapolis, 1874, Patterson Ch., Indianapolis, 1874-75, Berry St. Chapel, Ft. Wayne, Ind., 1875-78, Noblesville, 1878-82, Grace Ch., Richmond, Ind., 1882-85, Trinity Ch., Evansville, 1885-87, Trinity Ch., Lafayette, 1887-92, First Ch., Bloomington, Ill., 1892-97, Decatur, Ill., 1897-1901, Trinity Ch., Denver, 1901-4, Capitol Hill Ch., Denver, 1904-10, University Park Ch., Denver, 1910—. Republican. Died Mar. 3, 1919.

CRAFTS, James Mason, chemist; b. at Boston, Mar. 8, 1839; s. R. A. and Marian (Mason) C.; S.B., Lawrence Scientific Sch. (Harvard), 1858; (LL.D., 1898); studied chemistry at Bergacademie, Freiberg, and univs. of Heidelberg and Paris, 1850-55; m. Clemence Haggerty, June 13, 1868. Examined mines in Mex., 1866-67; prof. chemistry and dean chem. faculty, Cornell, 1868-71; prof. chemistry, 1871-80, organic chemistry, 1892-97, pres., 1898-1900, Mass. Inst. Tech.; engaged in chem. research, Boston, 1900—. Jecker Prize, Paris Acad. Sciences, 1885; chevalier Legion of Honor, France, 1885. Fellow Am. Acad. Arts and Sciences; mem. Nat. Acad. Sciences; hon. mem. Royal Inst. Great Britain. Author: Qualitative Chemical Analysis, 1870. Also published Researches Upon Silicic Compounds, 1865; Arsenic Ethers, a Method of Synthesis by Means of Chloride of Aluminum, 1879; Studies in Thermometry, 1880; Catalysis in Concentrated Solutions, 1908; Thermometry, 1913-15. Home: Boston, Mass. Died June 20, 1917.

CRAFTS, Leo Melville, M.D.; b. Minneapolis, Minn., Oct. 3, 1863; s. Maj. Amasa and Mary Jane (Henry) C.; B.L., U. of Minn., 1886; M.D., Harvard, 1890; m. Amelia I. Burgess, Sept. 4, 1901. House phys., Boston City Hosp., 1889-91; practiced in Minneapolis, 1892—; prof. nervous and mental diseases, 1893-1908, dean, 1897-1903, Hamline Med. Sch., also trustee Corp. Hamline Med. Sch.; visiting neurologist various hosps. Pres. Progressive Club, Hennepin Co., 1912; v.-chmn. Prog. State Central Com., 1912. Mem. Com. Am. Physicians on Med. Preparedness, Med. Advisory Bd. of U.S. Selective Service, etc.; del. Internat. Congress of Medicine, London, 1913; del. to Internat. Neurol. Congress, Berne, Switzerland, 1931. Pres. Minn. State S.S. Assn., 1893-95. Congregationalist. Chief neurologist on special neuro-psychiatric bd., examining the command at Camp Funston, summer 1918; attending specialist in neuro-psychiatry for U.S. Vet. Bur. Author of text book on Epidemic Encephalitis and numerous monographs on med. topics. One of originators of movement for Minn. Nat. Park and Forest Reserve. Home: Minneapolis, Minn. Died Sept. 22, 1938.

CRAFTS, Wilbur Fisk, clergyman; b. at Fryeburg, Me., Jan. 12, 1850; s. Rev. Frederick A. C.; A.B., Wesleyan U., Conn., 1869, A.M., 1871; B.D., Boston U., 1871; Ph.D., Marietta Coll., 1896; m. Sara Jane Timanus, May 1, 1874. Methodist minister, 1867-79, Congl., 1880-83, Presbyn., 1883—; pastor various chs. Active in Sunday sch. work, 1871—: founded Am. Sabbath Union, 1889; lectured throughout U.S. as its field sec., 1889-90; founded, 1895, and supt. Internat. Reform Bureau. Chief editor Christian Statesman, 1901-03; 20th Century Quarterly, 1896—. Author: Through the Eye to the Heart, 1873; Wagons for Eye Gate, 1874; Trophies of Song, 1874; Childhood, the Text-Book of the Age, 1875; The Ideal Sunday School, 1876; Fireside Talks on Genesis, 1877; Song Victories, 1877; The Bible and the Sunday School, 1878; The Two Chains, 1878; The Coming Man Is the Present Child, 1879; Illustrations of the International Sunday School Lessons, 1879; Symbols and System in Bible Reading, 1879; Normal Outlines, 1879; Rescue of Child-soul, 1880; Normal Half-hours, 1881; Plain Uses of the Blackboard (with his wife), 1881; Talks to Boys and Girls about Jesus, 1883; Teacher's Edition of the Revised Testament, 1883; Successful Men of To-day, 1883; Must the Old Testament Go?, 1884; Talks and Stories of Heroes and Holidays, 1884; The Sabbath for Man, 1884; Rhetoric Made Racy, 1884; The Temperance Century, 1885; Reading the Bible with Relish, 1887; The Civil Sabbath, 1890; Practical Christian Sociology, 1895; Social Progress, 1896; Before the Lost Arts, 1900; Protection of Native Races against Intoxicants and Opium, 1900; The March of Christ Down the Centuries, 1902; Patriotic Studies, 1906; Internationalism (translated into Japanese and Arabic), 1908; World Book of Temperance (with his wife), 1908; Prohibition Handbook, 1911; Bible in School Plans in All Lands; Bible Stories and Poems, 1914; Made in Mayflower Land, 1920; History of National Prohibition, 1920; That Boy and Girl of Yours and Other Addresses, 1921. Chairman official U.S. delegates Internat. Congress on Alcoholism, London, 1911; U.S. del. Purity Congresses, 1915, 16; mem. Union Nat. Commn. to frame amendment for constl. prohibition, 1915, 16; mem. Presbyn. Social Service Commn.; mem. United Com. War Time Activities, 1917—. Home: Washington, D.C. Died Dec. 27, 1922.

CRAGIN, Edwin Bradford, physician; b. Colchester, Conn., Oct. 23, 1859; s. Edwin T. and Ardelia E. (Sparrow) C.; A.B., Yale, 1882 (hon. A.M., 1907); M.D., Coll. Phys. and Surg. (Columbia), 1886; m. Mary R. Willard, May 23, 1889. Lecturer obstetrics, 1898-99, prof., 1899—, prof. gynecology, 1904—, Coll. Phys. and Surg., New York; attending obstetrician and gynecologist, Sloane Hospital for Women; consulting obstetric surgeon, City Maternity Hosp., and New York Nursery and Child's Hosp. Republican. Author: Essentials of Gynecology; A Text Book of Obstetrics. One of authors of American Text-Book of Gynecology. Address: 10 W. 50th St., New York. Died Oct. 21, 1918.

CRAGO, Thomas Spencer, congressman; b. Carmichaels, Pa., Aug. 8, 1866; s. John N. and Permelia (Spencer) C.; A.B., Waynesburg Coll., 1892, Princeton U., 1893; m. Margaret Leah Hoge, Oct. 27, 1897; children—Leah A., John Hughes, Ruth Constance. Admitted to Pa. bar, 1894, and practiced in Waynesburg; mem. 62d Congress (1911-13), 23d Pa. Dist. and 64th to 67th Congresses (1915-23), Pa. at large; spl. asst. to atty. gen. of U.S., 1923-24. V.p. Union Deposit & Trust Co.; dir. South Pa. T. & T. Co., River Coal & Coke Co. Trustee Waynesburg Coll., Southwestern State Normal Sch., California, Pa. Served in Spanish-Am. War, capt. Co. K, 10th Regt. Pa. Vols., later in Philippines, lt. col. 10th Regt., N.G. Pa. Republican. Presbyn. Mason (33°). Home: Waynesburg, Pa. Died Sept. 12, 1925.

CRAIG, Alexander Righter, secretary A.M.A.; b. Columbia, Pa., July 31, 1868; s. Alexander (M.D.) and Eleanor Margaretta (Righter) C.; A.B., Franklin and Marshall College, Pa., 1890, A.M., 1893; M.D., Med. Dept., U. of Pa., 1893 (class pres.); D.Sc., Franklin and Marshall Coll., 1920; m. Florence C. Bromwell, Oct. 17, 1899. Resident physician Phila. Poly. Hosp., 1893-4; practiced at Phila. till 1895, Columbia, Pa., 1895-1906, Phila., 1906-11; sec. A.M.A., 1911—. Pres. Am. Acad. Medicine, 1912. Home: Chicago, Ill. Died Sept. 2, 1922.

CRAIG, Alfred Edwin, clergyman; b. Wellington Co., Ont., Can., July 28, 1861; s. George Francis and Eliza (Orr) C.; A.B., Northwestern U., 1890; B.D., Garrett Bible Inst., 1890; Ph.D., Syracuse U., 1896; D.D., Albion Coll., 1901, Garrett Bibl. Inst., 1909, Northwestern U., 1911; m. Clara Tucker, May 5, 1892. Ordained M.E. ministry, 1885; pastor, Hillsdale, Mich., 1890-93, Benton Harbor, 1893-95, Albion, 1895-1901, Ottumwa, Ia., 1901-05, Broad St. Ch., Columbus, O., 1905-10, Grace Ch., Wilmington, Del., 1910-11; pres. Morningside Coll., Sioux City, Ia., 1911-18; pastor Trinity Ch., Evansville, Ind., 1918—. Republican. Home: Evansville, Ind. Deceased.

CRAIG, Alfred M., judge; b. Edgar Co., Ill., Jan. 15, 1833; s. David and Minty C.; A.B., Knox Coll., 1853 (LL.D.); m. Elizabeth P. Harvey, Aug. 4, 1856; 2d, Mary Davis, July 22, 1908. Admitted to bar, 1854, and began practice, Knoxville, Ill.; state's atty., 1856; co. judge Knox Co., 1861-65; del. Ill. Constl. Conv., 1870; justice Supreme Ct. of Ill., 1873-1900; after leaving bench has devoted entire time to large farming and banking interests. Trustee and mem. exec. com. Knox Coll.; apptd. mem. Ill. Tax Commn., Mar., 1910. Home: Galesburg, Ill. Died 1911.

CRAIG, Asa Hollister, farmer; b. Caldwell, Wis., Dec. 19, 1847; s. Perry and Maria (Hollister) C.; ed. common sch. and Albion (Wis.) Acad. (non-grad.); m. Rebecca Birthrong, July 5, 1873 (died Jan. 16, 1923); 1 dau., Alice Craig (Mrs. Charles H. Edgerton). Teacher pub. schs. until 1872; county supt. schs., 1873, 1890-95; engaged in farming, 1875—; postmaster, Mukwonago, Wis., 1914-23; apptd. capt. of all postmasters in Wis. for sale of Treasury Saving Certificates and personally sold over $40,000 worth. Originated and developed "Craig's Honey Melon," "Craig's Silver Bantam" and "Craig's Giant Bantam" sweet corn. Democrat. Conglist. Mason (32°). Author: Craig's Common School Question Book, 1872; Parliamentary Practice, 1875; Pros and Cons, 1897; Christian Persecutions, 1899. Home: Mukwonago, Wis. Died July 4, 1934.

CRAIG, Charles Patton, exec. dir. Great Lakes-St. Lawrence Tidewater Assn.; b. Limestone Twp., Clarion Co., Pa., July 4, 1858; s. William Thompson and Katherine (Patton) C.; A.B., Lafayette Coll., Easton Pa., 1883, A.M., 1886; LL.B., U. of Pa., 1886; m. Florence Cameron, Dec. 10, 1890; children—Kathryne Patton (dec.), Margaret Patton. Began practice at Duluth, 1886; pres., treas. and mgr. Charles P. Craig & Co., investments; pres. Great Lakes Securities Co.; pres. Highland Co.; sec., treas. and mgr. Greysolon Farms Co.; v.p. at large and exec. dir. Great Lakes-St. Lawrence Tidewater Assn.; exec. sec. St. Lawrence Commn. of U.S. by apptmt. of President Coolidge. Organizer and pres. for 15 yrs. Jean Duluth Farm Co.; was chmn. Minn. Commn. on Efficiency and Economy which produced an administrative code for State of Minn.; active in starting the movement against the "Pittsburgh-plus" freight charges on steel. Apptd. col. on staff gov. of State of Ky., 1933. Ex-pres. Minn. State Agrl. Soc.; ex-pres. and mgr. Minn. State Fair. Republican. Presbyterian. Home: Washington, D.C. Died Oct. 1, 1935.

CRAIG, Donald Alexander, newspaper corr., magazine writer; b. Brookville, Pa., Nov. 24, 1883; s. William Franklin and Mary (Fields) C.; grad. high sch., 1903; student George Washington U. Dept. of Law, 1903-04; m. Elisabeth May Adams, Oct. 12, 1909; children—Donald Alexander, Elisabeth Adams (Mrs. Albert Alexander Clagett). Began newspaper work as reporter on Washington (D.C.) Evening Star, 1903; became mem. congressional and polit. staff, same, 1907; joined Washington staff New York Herald, 1909; corr. of Herald and of Louisville (Ky.) Courier-Journal, Toronto (Ont.) Evening Telegram, etc., till 1913; mgr. New York Herald's Washington Bur. and corr. Paris Herald, 1913-23; corr. N.Y. Evening Sun, 1923-25; corr. various newspapers, 1921—; also engaged in newspaper, mag. and hist. writing and research and radio broadcasting. Presbyn. Dir. of special activities and foreign participation, U.S. George Washington Bicentennial Commn., 1931-33. Spl. agent for sec. of Interior in enforcement of oil code; also investigations for Civil Works Adminstrn., 1933-34; in exec. office of U.S. Govt. Nat. Emergency Council, 1935. Home: Washington, D.C. Died Sept. 28, 1936.

CRAIG, Frank, banker; b. Ghent, Ky., Apr. 29, 1870; s. Albert G. and Laura H. C.; A.B., U. of Kan., 1891; m. Florence Washburne, 1895; 1 son, Albert Pike. Admitted to bar, Wichita, 1891, practiced there and at McAlester until 1901; cashier State Nat. Bank, McAlester, 1901-02; organizer, 1901, and pres. City Nat. Bank. Mem. Okla. Bankers' Assn. (pres. 1904-05). Regent U. of Okla., term 1921-28. Democrat. Presbyn. Mason (33°), Sovereign Grand Insp. Gen. for Okla. of Scottish Rite Freemasonry. Home: McAlester, Okla. Died July 14, 1926.

CRAIG, John, horticulturist; b. at Lakefield, P.Q., Can., Apr. 27, 1864; s. William and Mary (Hamilton) C.; Ia. State Coll., 1885-88; asst. Ia. Expt. Sta., 1888-89; horticulturist Dominion Expt. Sta., Ottawa, Can., 1890-97; B.S., Ia. State Coll., 1898; M.S. in agr., Cornell U., 1899; m. Florence Augusta Slater, Nov. 1895. Prof. horticulture and forestry, Ia. State Coll., 1899-1900; prof. extension teaching, 1900-03, horticulture, 1903—, Cornell U. Editor National Nurseryman, 1904—; pres. N. Fla. Pecan Co., S. Ga. Pecan Co., Empire-Ga. Pecan Co. Mem. Jury of Awards, Chicago Expn., 1893, St. Louis Expn., 1904, Nat. Apple Show, Spokane, Wash., 1908. Mason (32°). Author: Practical Agriculture, revised edit., 1901. Contbr. to Cyclopedia of American Horticulture. Home: Ithaca, N.Y. Died Aug. 12, 1912.

CRAIG, Joseph Davis, physician; b. Albany, N.Y., Oct. 5, 1856; s. William H. and Ruth E. (Davis) C.; A.B., Union Coll., 1880, A.M., 1883; M.D., Albany Med. Coll., 1884. Demonstrator, asst. and lecturer anatomy, 1886-92, adj. prof., 1892-1902, prof., 1902-16, curator mus., 1888-16, Albany Med. Coll.; attending phys., Albany Hospital, 1894-16; consulting phys. Albany Hosp., 1915—; health officer, 1900-14. Republican. Presbyn. Mason (33°). Home: Albany, N.Y. Died 1923.

CRAIG, Joseph Edgar, naval officer; b. Medina, N.Y., Feb. 24, 1845; s. Joseph and Elizabeth Warren (Herring) C.; m. Alethe Lowber, July 29, 1868, grad. U.S. Naval Acad., 1865; ensign, Dec. 1, 1866; advanced through grades to rear admiral, Dec. 28, 1904. Comdr.-in-chief European Squadron, Feb. 10-May 18, 1902; capt. of the yard, U.S. Navy Yard, Norfolk, Va., Feb. 2, 1903-Dec. 30, 1904; spl. duty Bur. of Navigation, Jan.-Mar. 1905; commandant Navy Yard, League Island, Pa., 1905-07; retired, Feb. 24, 1907. Author: Azimuth, 1887; Negative-Reciprocal Equations, 1893. Home: Washington, D.C. Died June 21, 1925.

CRAIG, Katherine L., educator; b. Colo., Apr. 1876; d. Hugh Harvey and Hester (Foote) C.; ed. U. of Colo. and Mo. Valley Coll.; Ph.B., State Teachers' Coll., Colo., 1906. Elected supt. pub. instrn. of Colo., 1904, reëlected, 1906, 20, 26 and 28; field sec. Colo. Woman's Coll., 1909-10; teacher of lit. in the public schools of Denver, Colo., 1910-20; later supt. of schools, State of Colo. Author: Primary Geography (illustrated by herself), 1907; Craig's Brief History of Colorado. Writer of fiction. Contbr. to New Teachers' and Pupils' Cyclo., New Students' Reference Work, The Woman's Athenæum. Home: Denver, Colo. Died 1934.

CRAIG, Locke, governor; b. Bertie Co., N.C., Aug. 16, 1860; s. Andrew Murdock and Clarissa Rebecca (Gilliam) C.; A.B., U. of N.C., 1880, LL.D., 1915; m. Annie Burgin, Nov. 18, 1891. Admitted to N.C. bar, 1883, and practiced at Asheville; dist. elector, 1892; elector for state at large, 1896; mem. N.C. Ho. of Rep., 1899, 1901; gov. of N.C., 1913-17. Democrat. Home: Asheville, N.C. Died June 9, 1925.

CRAIG, Thomas Bigalow, artist; b. Phila., Feb. 14, 1849; s. Gerritt and Eleanor Frances C.; ed. pub. and pvt. schs., Phila.; spl. art studies; m. Daisy W. Beach, June 3, 1896. Exhibited Pa. Acad. Fine Arts, 1869, Nat. Acad. Design, 1881. Has pictures owned by Boston Art Club, Pa. Acad. Fine Arts, etc. A.N.A. Home: Rutherford, N.J. Died Sept. 1, 1924.

CRAIG, William Bayard, clergyman; b. St. John, N.B., Dec. 7, 1846; s. Dr. William and Mary (Harding) C.; B.A., State U. of Iowa, 1872, M.A., 1876; Yale Div. Sch., 1874; (D.D., U. of Colo., 1893; LL.D., Drake U., 1896); m. Priscilla E. Milliken, June 26, 1874; m. 2d, Emma Pickrell, Oct. 29, 1885; m. 3d, Mary Carpenter, 1908. Ordained Christian (Disciples) ministry, 1874; pastor Iowa City, Ia., 1876-82, Denver, Colo., 1882-94 (built two large city chs.), San Antonio, Tex., 1892-97; chancellor Drake U., Des Moines, Ia., 1896-1902; pastor Central Christian Ch., Denver, 1902-09, Lenox Av. Union Ch. (Disciples), New York, 1909-11, Christian Church, Redlands, Calif., 1911—Home: Redlands, Calif. Died Sept. 5, 1916.

CRAIG, William Benjamin, congressman; b. Selma, Ala., Nov. 2, 1877; s. George and Alvena (White) C.; LL.B., Cumberland U., 1898; m. Irene Kunst, Dec. 2, 1903. Mem. law firm Craig & Craig, Selma. Referee in bankruptcy and U.S. commr., middle dist., Ala., 1900-03; mem. Ala. Senate, 1903-07; mem. 60th and 61st Congresses (1907-11), 4th Ala. Dist. Democrat. Presbyn. Capt. Co. C, 2d Inf. Ala. N.G. Home: Selma, Ala. Died Nov. 27, 1925.

CRAIG, William Edward, clergyman; b. Chester, O., Oct. 14, 1874; s. Edward William and Eliza (Coleman) C.; A.B., Ohio Wesleyan U., 1902; S.T.B., Boston U., 1907; D.D., Davis and Elkins Coll., 1916; m. Flora Virginia Shimer, Feb. 27, 1907; children—William E., Jean Shimer, Ina Virginia, John Robert. Ordained M.E. ministry, 1907; pastor successively in W.Va., at Huntington, Williamstown, Middlebourne, Elkins, Wheeling and Clarksburg. Chaplain Camp Lee, World War. Served as pres. Ministerial Bd., Wheeling, 4 yrs. Republican. Mason. Home: Clarksburg, W.Va. Deceased.

CRAIG, Willis Green, theologian; b. Danville, Ky., Sept. 27, 1834; s. William and Martha E. (Green) C.; A.B., Centre Coll., Ky., 1852, Danville Theol. Sem., 1860; (D.D., Centre Coll., 1875; LL.D., Princeton, 1893); m. Amelia Owsley, Oct. 24, 1861. Ordained Presbyn. ministry, 1862; pastor First Ch., Keokuk, Ia., 1862-82; prof. of ecclesiastical history, 1882-91, Cyrus H. McCormick prof. didactic and polemic theology, 1892—, McCormick Theol. Sem. Moderator Gen. Assembly Presbyn. Ch. U.S.A., Washington, 1893. Home: Chicago, Ill. Died 1911.

CRAIGHEAD, Erwin, newspaper man; b. Nashville, Tenn., Apr. 4, 1852; s. James B. and Ellen Kirkman (Erwin) C.; student Racine (Wis.) Coll.; B.Litt., U. of Nashville, 1872; post-grad. student Middle Temple, London, England, and U. of Leipzig; LL.D., U. of Ala., 1906; admitted to Tenn. bar, 1876, but never practiced; m. Lura Harris, Dec. 12, 1878; 1 son, Frank. In journalism, 1877—; music critic and editorial writer, New Orleans Times, 1878-80; mng. editor New Orleans Daily States, 1880-82; city editor, 1882-84, mng. editor from 1884, also editor and v.p. from 1923, editor emeritus, 1926, Mobile Register. Pres. Mobile Commercial Club, 1897-98, Mobile Symphony Orchestra, 1910-11, Iberville Hist. Soc. of Mobile, 1913-17; 1st dist. trustee Ala. State Dept. of Archives and History, 1915-23. Democrat. Author: From Mobile's Past, 1925. Home: Mobile, Ala. Died Feb. 3, 1932.

CRAIGHILL, William Price, chief of engrs. U.S.A.; b. Charlestown, Va., July 1, 1833; grad. West Point, 1853; (LL.D., Washington and Lee, 1897); m. Mary A. Morsell, Oct. 14, 1856; m. 2d, Rebecca Churchill Jones, Sept. 22, 1874. Assigned to engr. corps and superintended work on Ft. Sumter, 1854-55, and Ft. Delaware, 1858; several yrs. instr. West Point; built defenses of Pittsburgh, 1863; bvtd. lt. col., Mar. 1865, for services at Cumberland Gap; afterward engaged on defenses of New York and Baltimore, and many public works. Mem. Light House Bd. several yrs., also of Bd. Consulting Engrs. to Dept. of Docks of City of New York; after centennial of Surrender of Cornwallis, 1881, built the monument at Yorktown, Va., which, though ordered to be built by Continental Congress, did not have funds provided until over a century later; colonel engineers, Jan. 10, 1887; brig. gen., chief of engrs. U.S.A., May 10, 1895, until retired, Feb. 1, 1897. Dir., 1892-93, pres., 1894-95, hon. mem., Mar. 23, 1896—, Am. Soc. Civ. Engrs.; 7 times deputy from W.Va. to Gen. Conv. P.E. Ch. Author: Army Officers' Pocket Companion, 1862. Address: Charles Town, W.Va. Died 1909.

CRAIGIE, David Johnston, army officer; b. Broomieside, Scotland, Dec. 6, 1840; s. George and Helen (Young) C.; ed. at various schs. and pvt. teachers; m. Florence Mortimer, Apr. 1869. Served as 1st lt., 8th Ia. Inf., Sept. 12, 1861-July 25, 1864; capt. asst. adj. gen. vols., July 2, 1864; hon. mustered out, Sept. 19, 1865; 2d lt., May 11, 1866; advanced through grades to brig. gen., Aug. 12, 1903; retired, Aug. 13, 1903. Bvtd. 1st lt., Mar. 2, 1867, for battle of Shiloh, Tenn.; capt., Mar. 2, 1867, for battle of Iuka, Miss. Served in P.I., 1901-03. Home: Oskaloosa, Ia. Died Dec. 14, 1913.

CRAIGIE, Pearl Mary-Teresa ("John Oliver Hobbes"); author; b. Boston, Nov. 3, 1867; d. John Morgan and Laura Hortense (Arnold) Richards; ed. under private tutors, also at Paris and Univ. Coll., London; m. Reginald Walpole Craigie, in England, Feb., 1887. Received into Roman Catholic Ch., 1892. Author: Some Emotions and a Moral, 1891; The Sinner's Comedy, 1892; A Study in Temptations, 1893; A Bundle of Life, 1894; Journey's End in Lovers' Meeting (proverb in one act, written for Miss Ellen Terry); The Gods, Some Mortals and Lord Wickenham, 1895; The Herb Moon, 1896; School for Saints, 1897; Osborn and Ursyne, tragedy in blank verse, 1899; Robert Orange, 1900; The Serious Wooing, 1901; Tales About Temperaments, 1902; Love and the Soul Hunters, 1902; The Vineyard, 1903; The Flute of Pan, 1905. Plays: The Ambassador (prod. London, 1898); A Repentance (prod. same, 1899); The Wisdom of the Wise, comedy (prod. same, Nov. 1900); part author The Bishop's Move, 1902; The Flute of Pan (prod. Shaftesbury Theatre, London, 1904). Home: London, Eng. Died 1906.

CRAIL, Joe, congressman; b. Fairfield, Ia., Dec. 24, 1877; s. Benjamin Franklin and Nancy Ralston (McCrackin) C.; A.B., Drake U., Des Moines, Ia., 1898; student Ia. Coll. of Law, Des Moines, Ia.; m. Gladys Adelaide Schmidt, Feb. 10, 1920; children—Gladys Adelaide, Jo. Admitted to bar, 1902, and practiced at Los Angeles; associated with twin bro., Charles S., until latter was elected to bench of Superior Court of Los Angeles Co., 1918. Served as vol. Spanish-Am. War, 1898, and continued until evacuation of Cuba by U.S. Army, 1902; chmn. Rep. State Central Com. for Southern Calif., 1918-20; mem. 70th to 72d Congresses (1927-33), 10th Calif. Dist. Member Christian (Disciples) Ch. Home: Los Angeles, Calif. Died Mar. 2, 1938.

CRAM, George F., publisher; b. Lowell, Mass., May 20, 1842; s. Joseph T. and Anna D. (Blanchard) C.; early edn. in Lowell schs.; ed. Wheaton (Ill.) Coll., 1862; m. Martha A. Hiatt, Oct. 3, 1865 (died 1907). Served in Union Army, 1862-65. Began publishing maps and atlases, 1867. Author: Hand Book of Geography, 1882; Minette, a Tale of the Crusades, 1901. Home: Chicago, Ill. Died May 24, 1928.

CRAMBLET, Thomas E., college pres.; b. Tappan, O., Sept. 17, 1862; s. Jacob and Sarah C.; student Scio Coll., 1879-80, Ohio State U., 1880-82; A.B., Mt. Union Coll., 1885, A.M., 1888; classical graduate in Coll. of the Bible, Ky. U., 1887; (LL.D., Western U. of Pa., 1902); m. Della S. Weaver, May 31, 1887. In ministry of Christian (Disciples) Ch., 1887—; pastor Mentor, O., 1887-88, Salem, O., 1888-91, First Christian Ch., Omaha, 1891-96, East End Christian Ch., Pittsburgh, 1896-1901; pres. Bethany (W.Va.) Coll., 1901—. Home: Bethany, W.Va. Died June 22, 1919.

CRAMER, Harriet Laura, newspaper pub.; b. in Dodge Co., Wis., Feb. 14, 1848; d. Charles Grandison and Alice (Doyle) Barker; ed. Madam Hoffman's select sch., N.Y. City; m. William E. Cramer, editor The Evening Wisconsin, Milwaukee, Wis., June 24, 1869 (died 1905). Began newspaper work in office of Evening Wisconsin, 1864; pres. Evening Wisconsin Co., taking active part in management from death of husband to June 1918, when sold the paper; then treas. Wisconsin Printing Company. Home: Milwaukee, Wis. Died Feb. 5, 1922.

CRAMER, Stuart Warren, mfr.; b. Thomasville, N.C., Mar. 31, 1868; s. John Thomas and Mary Jane (Thomas) C.; grad. U.S. Naval Acad., 1888; studied Sch. of Mines (Columbia), 1888-89; Sc.D., N.C. State Coll., 1929; m. Bertha Hobart Berry, June 24, 1889 (died 1895); children—Katharine (wife of James R. Angell, pres. Yale U.), Stuart Warren; m. 2d, Kate Stanwood Berry, Sept. 7, 1896 (died 1897); m. 3d, Rebecca Warren Tinkham, Jan. 28, 1902; 1 son, George Bennett. Resigned from U.S.N., 1888; assayer in charge U.S. Assay office, Charlotte, N.C., 1889-93; engr. and mgr. D. A. Tompkins Co., Charlotte, 1893-95; mill engr. and contractor, Charlotte, designing or equipping nearly one-third of cotton mills in South, 1895-1918; pres. and treas. Mays Mills, Mayflower Mills, Cramerton Mills, Inc. Owner of Mayfarm and Orchards; officer or director of various financial, manufacturing and railway corps. Granted about 60 U.S. and foreign patents as result of research in industry, trade chemistry and physics. Organizer and first comdr. N.C. Naval Reserve, 1890-93; mem. Bd. Visitors, U.S. Naval Acad., 1912-26; life mem. U.S. Naval Inst., 1889; state chmn. for N.C. of Navy League of U.S.; mem. production engineering com. Council Nat. Defense, World War; was also mem. war service com. and advisory tax board of Treasury Dept. Mem. Am. Cotton Mfrs. Assn. (pres. 1916-17), Nat. Council Am. Cotton Mfrs. (pres. 1917-18, 1920-27), Nat. Assn. Cotton Mfrs. (medalist 1913); Cotton Textile Inst. (1st v.p.). Mem. Nat. Industrial Conf. Board; mem. Am. com. of Internat. Chamber of Commerce, 1923, Nat. Com. on Inheritance Taxation, 1925; mem. executive com. Nat. Business Survey Conf., 1929. Mem. Tax Com. U.S. Chamber of Commerce. Del. to Rep. Nat. Conv., 1928, 32; (mem. com. to notify Herbert Hoover of presdl. nomination); chmn. finance com. N.C. Rep. State Exec. Com. and campaign mgr., 1928; mem. nat. advisory com., President's Orgn. on Unemployment Relief, 1931; mem. President's Conf. on Home Building and Home Ownership (chmn. sub-com. on industrial decentralization and housing), 1931. Dir. and treas. The Textile Foundation. Mem. Cotton Textile Code Authority under NRA. Episcopalian. Author: Useful Information for Cotton Manufacturers (4 vols.), 1904-09. Home: Cramerton, N.C. Died July 2, 1940.

CRAMER, W(illiam) Stuart, clergyman; b. Frederick Co., Md., Apr. 12, 1873; s. Milton Clay and Julia (Crouse) C.; A.B., Franklin and Marshall Coll., 1898, D.D., 1921; grad. Theol. Sem. Ref. Ch. in U.S., 1898-1901; spl. student Oxford U., 1907; m. Margaret White Snader, Apr. 17, 1907; children—W. Stuart, Julia Margaret. Ordained ministry Ref. Ch. in U.S., 1901; asso. pastor First Ch., Lancaster, Pa., 1901-03, pastor, 1903—. Asst. sec. Gen. Wartime Com. of Chs., 1918; mem. exec. com. Federal Council Chs. of Christ in America; mem. Gen. Com. Army and Navy Chaplains, Commn. on France and Belgium, Commn. on Relations of Religious Bodies in Europe. Mem. Continuation Com. Memorial Ch., Château Thierry, France, and dedicated the ch., 1924. Pres. Eastern Synod, Reformed Ch., 1927-28. Republican. Mason. Author: History of the First Reformed Ch., 1904. Home: Lancaster, Pa. Deceased.

CRAMP, Charles Henry, ship builder; b. at Phila., May 9, 1828; s. William and Sophia (Miller) C.; grad. Central High Sch., Phila.; (Sc.D., U. of Pa.); m. Hannah Ann Cox, 1850; m. 2d, Amy Jane Cox, 1870. Learned ship-building trade, 1845; became a partner in William Cramp & Sons, largest ship-building enterprise in the U.S., which has built many of the finest naval and mcht. vessels now afloat. Home: Philadelphia, Pa. Died June 6, 1913.

CRAMP, Walter Concemore, surgeon; b. Hamilton, N.Y., April 12, 1878; s. Concemore Richard and Eliza Mary (Smith) C.; A.B., Colgate, 1900, D.Sc., 1923; M.D., Columbia, 1904; m. Louise Mason, June 5, 1904 (divorced); 1 son, Walter Mason; m. 2d, Elizabeth Pendleton, Apr. 2, 1928 (died 1935). Practiced surgery in N.Y. City, 1904—; asst. prof. surgery Bellevue Med. Sch., 6 yrs.; visiting surgeon Willard Parker Hosp., St. Francis Hosp., Bellevue Hosp., Hosp. for Deformation of Joint Diseases, etc. Republican. Episcopalian. Home: New York, N.Y. Died Feb. 18, 1941.

CRAMPTON, Charles Albert, chemist; b. Davenport, Ia., Feb. 18, 1858; s. Albert Aulich and Harriet Jones (Weaver) C.; B.L., Ph.C., U. of Mich., 1882; A.C., Purdue, 1882; M.D., Columbian (now George Washington) U., 1884; m. Lillie Dunn, June 25, 1890. Asst. chemist, U.S. Dept. Agr., 1883-90; chemist, 1890-93, chief chemist, 1893-1910, Internal Revenue Bur., Treas. Dept.; chief div. food and drug products, Institute Industrial Research, Washington, 1910—. Home: Bethesda, Md. Address: Institute of Industrial Research, Washington. Died July 26, 1915.

CRANDALL, Charles Henry, author; b. at Greenwich, N.Y., June 19, 1858; s. Henry Sargent and Mary Carmichael (Mills) C.; ed. Greenwich; m. Kate Virginia Ferguson, June 19, 1884 (deceased); m. 2d, Mary Vere Davenport, Nov. 26, 1891. Lived 17 yrs. on farm where born; 5 yrs. in mercantile life; 5 yrs. reporter, corr. and editor, New York Tribune. Mem. Am. Inst. Art, Science and Letters. Author: The Season, 1883; Representative Sonnets, 1891; Wayside Music (poems), 1893; The Chords of Life (poems), 1898; Songs from Sky Meadows (poems); Saratoga, dedicatory poem, read at the Battle Monument, Schuylerville, N.Y., Oct. 18, 1912; Liberty Illumined (poems), 1918; Songs for the Boys in Khaki, 1918. Home: Stamford, Conn. Died 1923.

CRANDALL, Charles Lee, civil engr.; b. Bridgewater, N.Y., July 20, 1850; s. Peter B. and Eunice C. (Priest) C.; family removed to Ithaca, 1868; C.E., Cornell, 1872; served in architect's office and asst. ry. engr., 1872-74; m. Myra G. Robbins, Aug. 20, 1878. City engr., Ithaca, N.Y., 1870-91; instr. civ. engring, 1874-75, asst. prof., 1875-91, asso. prof., 1891-95, prof. ry. engring. and geodesy, 1895-1908, prof. ry. engring., 1908—, in charge of Coll. of Civil Engring., 1903-06, Cornell. Author: Tables for Computation of Railway and Other Earthwork, 1886, 1893, 1902, 1907; Notes on Descriptive Geometry, 1888, 1893; Notes on Shades, Shadows and Perspective; The Transition Curve, 1893, 1899; Text-Book on Geodesy and Least Squares, 1907; (joint author) Field Book for Railroad Surveying, 1909. Home: Ithaca, N.Y. Died Aug. 25, 1917.

CRANDALL, Charles Spencer, pomologist; b. Waverly, N.Y., Oct. 12, 1852; s. Richard Orson and Marie Louise (Cushman) C.; B.S., Mich. Agrl. Coll., 1873, M.S., 1889; m. Maud Bell, June 9, 1897. Asst., dept. of horticulture, Mich. Agrl. Coll., 1885-89; prof. botany and horticulture, Colo. Agrl. Coll., 1890-1900; instr. horticulture, 1902-03, asst. prof., 1903-06, asso. prof., 1907-10, prof. pomology, Sept. 1, 1911—, U. of Ill. Home: Urbana, Ill. Died July 12, 1929.

CRANDALL, Floyd Milford, physician; b. at Belfast, N.Y., May 2, 1858; s. Charles Milford (M.D.) and Deborah J. (Wood) C.; grad. Geneseo Normal Sch., 1880; M.D., Univ. Med. Coll. (New York U.), 1884; unmarried. Interne Bellevue Hosp., 1884-85; attending physician, Northwestern Dispensary, 1889-90; lecturer on diseases of children, 1889-93, adj. prof., 1893—, New York Polyclinic; surgeon New York Skin and Cancer Hosp., 1890-98; consulting phys., Infants' and Children's hosps.; state med. examiner of N.Y., 1907—. Editor The Archives of Pediatrics; editorial writer New York Medical Journal, 1889-95; mng. editor Gaillard's Medical Journal, 1893-95. Sec. sect. diseases of children, Pan-

American Medical Congress, 1893; pres. West End Medical Soc.; pres. sect. on pediatrics, N.Y. Acad. Medicine; pres. N.Y. Co. Med. Soc.; pres. Soc. Alumni Bellevue Hosp.; sec. N.Y. State Med. Soc. Author: How to Keep Well, 1903. Home: New York, N.Y. Died Nov. 19, 1921.

CRANDALL, Francis Asbury, editor, librarian; b. Carbondale, Pa., Nov. 28, 1837; s. Rev. Andrew Jackson and Amelia (Fink) C.; ed. at Cazenovia (N.Y.) Sem.; m. Annie A. Jones, Sept. 17, 1861 (died 1907). Learned printer's trade; foreman in charge state printing of Ia., 1856-57; editor and publisher Linn County Register, Marion, Ia., 1857; news and asso. editor Utica Morning Herald, 1860-62; editor and publisher, Cazenovia Republican, 1862-63, Utica Evening Telegraph, 1863-66, Scranton Republican (founding daily morning issue 1867), 1866-69, Mississippi Valley Review, St. Louis, 1869-70, Oswego (N.Y.) Evening Press, 1870-73, Erie (Pa.) Gazette (founded Sunday edition 1875), 1873-80; mng. editor Buffalo Morning Express, 1877-86; editor Providence Evening Telegram, 1886-88; mng. editor Buffalo Morning Courier, 1888-93, Buffalo Evening Times, 1894-95; 1st U.S. supt. of documents, 1895-97, organizing that work; librarian of pub. documents, Govt. Printing Office, 1897-1906; acting chief editor, Govt. Printing Office, 1907; chief, reference section, 1907-13, dir. lit. div., Jan. 1, 1914—, Public Documents Office. Home: Washington, D.C. Died July 9, 1915.

CRANDALL, Lathan Augustus, clergyman; b. Plymouth, N.Y., Sept. 20, 1850; s. Rev. J. M. and Lucy A. (Sisson) C.; A.B., Hillsdale Coll., 1873, A.M., 1874; ordained Free Bapt. ministry, 1873; pastor Free Baptist chs., Racine, Wis., 1874-76, Fairport, N.Y., 1876-79; B.D., Rochester Theol. Sem., 1881; (D.D., Hillsdale, 1889); m. Nellie L. Hart, Dec. 8, 1892. Ordained Bapt. ministry, 1881; pastor Owego, N.Y., 1881-84, 23d St. Ch., New York, 1884-89, Euclid Av. Ch., Cleveland, 1889-92, Memorial Ch., Chicago, 1892-1904, Trinity Ch., Minneapolis, 1904-20; editor The Baptist, 1920-21; asso. pastor Hyde Park Bapt. Ch., Chicago, 1921—; chmn. Am. Com. of Baptist World Alliance, 1905; president Interdenominational Commission of Minn., 1908; chmn. child welfare com., Civic and Commerce Assn., 1911; v.p. Children's Protective Soc.; trustee Carleton Coll., Frances Shimer Sem. Author: A Calm View of Christian Science, 1900; Days in the Open, 1914; Henry Lyman Morehouse, A Biography, 1919. Home: Chicago, Ill. Died July 20, 1923.

CRANDON, Le Roi Goddard, surgeon, author; b. Chelsea, Mass., Jan. 15, 1873; s. Daniel Goddard and Florence Jane (Pillsbury) C.; A.B., Harvard, 1894, A.M., 1909; M.D., 1898; m. Mina Stinson; 1 son, John Howland. Began practice at Boston, 1898; instr. surgery, Harvard Med. Sch., 1903-18; visiting surgeon Boston City Hosp., 1903-18. Capt. Med. Corps, U.S.N.R.F., 1917-18; consulting surgeon Chelsea (Mass.) Memorial Hosp., Home Memorial Hosp. (New London, Conn.); surgeon in chief Whidden Memorial Hosp., Everett, Mass. Author: Surgical After-Treatment, 1911. Home: Boston, Mass. Died Dec. 28, 1939.

CRANE, Aaron Martin, author; b. Glover, Orleans Co., Vt., Feb. 13, 1839; s. John and Nancy (Martin) C.; ed. pub. schs., acad. and 1 term Newbury (Vt.) Sem.; m. Lida D. Flint, Jan. 16, 1867. Pvt. Co. I, 1st Vt. Cav., Aug. 11, 1862; promoted 1st lt. Co. E, 18th Regt., U.S.C.T., Aug. 2, 1864, and afterwards to capt., serving until May 1865; pub. Rep. paper, Winchester, Va., 1865-69; assessor internal revenue, 1869, until office abolished by law, 1873, then continued as spl. agt. in charge at various cities until 1884. Republican. Author: Right and Wrong Thinking and Their Results, 1906, 12th edit., 1911; A Search After Ultimate Truth, 1910. Homes: Boston, Mass., and Norfolk, Va. Died 1914.

CRANE, A(ugustus) W(arren), M.D.; b. Adrian, Mich., Nov. 13, 1868; s. Nathan Seeley and Julia Etta (Chaffee) C.; student lit. dept. U. of Mich., 1889-90, M.D., 1894, M.A., 1932; m. Caroline Bartlett, Dec. 31, 1896; children—Juliana Bartlett, Warren Bartlett. Practiced at Kalamazoo, 1894-1907; specialized as diagnostician, 1915—; investigator of X-rays, 1897—. Chmn. Kalamazoo Co. sect. Mich. State Com. of Med. Preparedness, and mem. Mich. Med. Advisory Bd. No. 12, 1917-18; apptd. mem. Nat. Research Council, 1919. Pres. Am. Roentgen Ray Soc., 1916 (Caldwell lecturer for 1932); pres. Kalamazoo Acad. Medicine, 1908. Acting editor Am. Jour. Roentgenology, 1917-18, later mem. editorial bd. Awarded gold medal, 1921, by Radiol. Soc. of N. America "in recognition of achievement in science of radiology." Mem. People's Ch. Home: Kalamazoo, Mich. Died Feb. 20, 1937.

CRANE, (Robert) Bruce, painter; b. New York, Oct. 17, 1857; s. Solomon Bruce and Leah (Gillespie) C.; ed. pub. schs., New York; studied painting under A. H. Wyant; m. Ann Brainerd, Nov. 15, 1904; children—A. Bruce, Ann. Splty. Am. landscapes; exhibited Nat. Acad. Design, 1879; awarded Webb prize, Soc. Am. Artists, 1897; bronze medal, Paris Expn., 1900; George Inness gold medal, Nat. Acad. Design, 1901; silver medal, Buffalo Expn., 1901; gold medal, St. Louis Expn., 1904; silver medal, Charleston Expn., 1907; bronze medal, Carnegie Inst., 1909; gold medal, Nat. Acad. Design, 1912; silver medal, Panama P.I. Expn., 1915; Ranger purchase prize, Nat. Acad. Design, 1919. A.N.A., 1889, N.A., 1901. Home: Bronxville, N.Y. Died Oct. 29, 1937.

CRANE, Caroline Bartlett; b. Hudson, Wis.; d. Lorenzo D. and Julia A. (Brown) Bartlett; grad. Carthage (Ill.) Coll., 1879, M.A., 1882; studied U. of Chicago; LL.D., Kalamazoo Coll., 1917; LL.D., Carthage (Ill.) Coll., 1923; m. Dr. Augustus Warren Crane, Dec. 31, 1896; children—Juliana Bartlett, Warren Bartlett. Teacher, 1879-83; newspaper writer and city editor, 1883-86; pastor All Souls' Ch., Sioux Falls, S.D., 1886-89, called to First Unitarian Ch., Kalamazoo, Mich., and there ordained as minister of liberal religion, 1889; out of the Unitarian Ch. organized and built, 1893, a new creedless institutional "People's Church"; resigned pastorate, 1899; then engaged in lit. work and in social and sanitary surveys of cities, under local or state auspices; has made sanitary surveys of 62 cities in 14 states under auspices of local organizations and state bds. of health. Chief lit. works: "U. S. Inspected and Passed," 1913 (a criticism of Federal Meat Inspection); "Everyman's House," 1924. Chmn. Woman's Com. (Mich. Div.) Council of Nat. Defense; and chmn. Mich. State Woman's Com. on Preparedness during the war. Mem. Council Nat. Municipal League; dir. Am. Civic Assn., Mich. Housing Assn., Mich. League of Women Voters; pres. Mich. Assn. for Old Age Security; on staff consultants Nat. Tuberculosis Assn. Home: Kalamazoo, Mich. Died Mar. 24, 1935.

CRANE, Cephas Bennett, clergyman; b. Marion, N.Y., Mar. 28, 1833; s. Wheeler Ingalls and Almena (Riddell) C.; Hamilton Coll., Clinton, N.Y.; A.B., U. of Rochester, 1858, A.M., 1864, D.D., 1868; grad. Rochester Theol. Sem., 1860; m. Mary Adelia Day, 1865. Ordained Bapt. ministry, 1860; pastor, Hartford, Conn., 1860-78, Boston, 1878-84, Concord, N.H., 1885-96; minister-at-large, 1896—. Trustee Rochester Theol. Sem., Newton (Mass.) Theol. Instn. Home: Cambridge, Mass. Died Jan. 4, 1917.

CRANE, Charles Alva, clergyman; b. Quincy, Ill., Nov. 16, 1853; s. Rev. James L. and Elizabeth (Mayo) C.; ed. Springfield, Ill., pub. schs.; Garrett Biblical Inst., Evanston, Ill. (D.D.); m. Sallie Hitt, Nov. 24, 1866. Entered M.E. ministry in Ill. Conf., 1878, holding several pastorates in that conf. (last 1st M.E. Ch., Danville); then pastor 1st M.E. Ch., Colo. Springs, Colo.; then pastor People's Temple, Boston. Home: Boston, Mass. Died 1907.

CRANE, Charles Kittredge, narcotics research; b. Dalton, Mass., Aug. 28, 1881; s. Zenas and Ellen Judith (Kittredge) C.; Ph.B., Sheffield Scientific Sch. (Yale), 1903; m. Margaret Diana Wilson, 1914 (divorced 1926); 1 son, Peter. With Z. and W. M. Crane, paper mfrs., Dalton, Mass., 1903-11; asst. hon. sec. Lord Knutsford's Shell Shock Hosps., London, 1914-17; research on internat. narcotics problem, 1925—. Republican. Conglist. Home: Pasadena, Calif. Died Jan. 24, 1932.

CRANE, Charles Richard; b. Chicago, Aug. 7, 1858; s. Richard Teller and Mary (Prentice) Crane; ed. public schs, Chicago; LL.D., Harvard, 1922, U. of Wis., 1922, Coll. of William and Mary, 1924; m. Cornelia W. Smith, 1881; children—Richard, Frances, Josephine (Mrs. H. C. Bradley), John. Entered the Crane Co., Chicago, mfrs. of valves, fittings, etc., and after serving in various capacities became 1st v.p., 1894, pres., Jan. 1912-14. V.chmn. finance com., Wilson campaign, 1812, mem. President's Spl. Diplomatic Commn. to Russia, 1917; Am. commr. on mandates in Turkey, 1919; Am. minister to China, May 1920-June 1921. Hon. adviser Nat. Government of China. Pres. Municipal Voters' League, Chicago. Home: New York, N.Y. Died Feb. 15, 1939.

CRANE, Frank, journalist; b. Urbana, Ill., May 12, 1861; s. James L. and Elizabeth (Mayo) C.; Ph.B., Ill. Wesleyan U., 1892; D.D., Neb. Wesleyan U., 1894; m. Ellie C. Stickel, Sept. 26, 1883. Ordained M.E. ministry, 1882; pastor Trinity and Hyde Park M.E. chs., Chicago, 1896-1903; pastor Union Congl. Ch., Worcester, Mass., 1904-09. Entered journalism, 1909; editorial writer syndicate of 100 newspapers. Editor of Current Opinion. Author: The Religion of Tomorrow, 1899; Vision, 1907; The Song of the Infinite, 1909; Human Confessions, 1911; God and Democracy, 1911; Lame and Lovely, 1912; Foot Notes to Life, 1913; War and World Government, 1915; Just Human, 1915; Adventures in Common Sense, 1916; The Looking Glass, 1917; Christmas and the Year Round, 1917; 400 Four minute Essays (10 vols.), 1919; The Crane Classics (10 vols.), 1920; Why I Am A Christian, 1924, Everyday Wisdom (10 vols.), 1927. Home: Los Angeles, Calif. Died Nov. 6, 1928.

CRANE, George Francis, banker; b. Boston, Apr. 21, 1852; s. Dr. P. M. and Susan (Hooker) C.; pub. sch. edn.; m. Katharine P. Oliver, Nov. 9, 1888. For many years a partner in Baring, Magoun & Co., bankers, but retired from active business, 1904; v.p. Seamen's Bank for Savings; chmn. bd. Columbia Ins. Co. of N.J.; dir. various corps. Comptroller Trinity Corporation; trustee St. Luke's Hosp., P.E. Soc. for Promoting Religion and Learning. Home: New York, N.Y. Died Sept. 24, 1933.

CRANE, (Harold) Hart, writer; b. Garrettsville, O., July 21, 1899; s. Clarence A. and Grace Edna (Hart) C.; ed. pub. schs., Warren and Cleveland, O.; short extension course in advertising, Western Reserve; unmarried. Mechanic bench hand, shipyard "bolter-up," newspaper reporter, book clerk, advertising writer, 1916-25. Awarded Helen Waire Levinson prize, Poetry—A Mag. of Verse, 1930; awarded John Simon Guggenheim fellowship for creative writing abroad, 1931-32. Author (verse): White Buildings, 1926; The Bridge, 1930; Collected Poems, 1933. Home: Chagrin Falls, O. Died Apr. 1932.

CRANE, Louis Burton, clergyman; b. Mt. Sterling, Ill., Apr. 23, 1869; s. Frederic D. and Adelaide (Wells) C.; A.B., Princeton, 1891, A.M., 1894; Princeton Theol. Sem., 1894; student univs. of Berlin, Erlangen, Giessen; D.D., Knox Coll., 1916; m. Josephine Hopkinson Smith, Oct. 25, 1899 (died May 8, 1908); children—Louis Burton, Frederic Marshall, Alex Crawford, Mary Josephine; m. 2d, Mabel Schuyler, July 9, 1910; children—Mabel Schuyler, Schuyler. In Presbyn. ministry, 1896-1902 (First Ch., Princeton, N.J., and Calvary Ch., Buffalo); Congl. clergyman, 1902-05; prof. N.T. lit. and interpretation, Chicago Theol. Sem., 1902-05; supply 2d Presbyn. Ch., Scranton, Pa., 1905-06; pastor Brainerd Union Presbyn. Ch., Easton, Pa., Dec. 1906-Apr. 1910; pastor Westminster Presbyn. Ch., Elizabeth, N.J., 1910—. Mem. Exec. Com. Presbyn. Ch. in U.S.A., 1921-23; lecturer Stone Foundation, Princeton Theol. Sem., 1921. Dir. Princeton Theol. Sem., 1909-29. Author: The Teaching of Jesus Concerning the Holy Spirit, 1905; Intermediate and Senior Graded Sunday School Lessons, for Presbyterian Board of Publication and S.S. Work, 1913-21. Home: Elizabeth, N.J. Died Oct. 1934.

CRANE, Michael Joseph, bishop; b. Ashland, Pa., Sept. 8, 1863; s. Patrick and Ann (Monaghan) C.; entered St. Charles Sem., Overbrook, Pa., 1880; post-grad. course, Catholic U. of America, 1889-90; D.D. Ordained priest R.C. Ch., 1889; apptd. pastor St. Francis de Sales' Ch., Phila., 1903; vicar gen. and consultor to the Archdiocese of Phila., 1919; consecrated bishop of Curium and auxiliary bishop of Phila., Sept. 19, 1921. Home: Philadelphia, Pa. Died Dec. 26, 1928.

CRANE, R. B., banker; b. Berea, O., Jan. 1, 1857; s. Rezin H. and Mary Jane (Chaney) C.; self educated; m. Myrtle C. Cowdrick, Oct. 19, 1893. Engaged in candy business, Toledo, O., 1870-83; mem. Meagley & Crane, wholesale grocers, later Crane & Robinson, wholesale fruit and produce, 1883-93; began in banking with Holcomb Nat. Bank, 1893, advancing to mgr.; was organizer, Commerce Trust Co. (later Commerce Guardian Trust & Savings Bank), pres., 1921-24, chmn. bd., 1924—; pres. Magnolia Land & Lumber Co.; v.p. Franklin Printing & Engraving Co.; dir. M. E. Wilcox Co. Mason (32°, Shriner). Home: Toledo, O. Died Feb. 20, 1929.

CRANE, Ralph Thompson, banker; b. Montclair, N.J., May 22, 1878; s. James B. and Elizabeth (Thompson) C.; ed. pub. schs., Montclair; m. Lois A. Johnson, Sept. 10, 1902; children—James B. and Ralph T. Began as clerk, Montclair Savings Bank, 1896, becoming treas. then v.p.; partner Ludwig & Crane, 1914-18; with Federal Reserve Bank, New York, 1918-21; partner Brown Brothers & Co., 1921-31, Brown Brothers Harriman & Co., 1931-34; v.p. Brown Harriman & Co., Inc., 1934—; dir. various corps. Served in Spanish-Am. War. Pres. Investment Bankers Assn. of America, 1935. Died May 5, 1938.

CRANE, Richard, diplomat; b. Denver, Colo., Aug. 12, 1882; s. Charles R. and Cornelia (Smith) C.; B.S., Harvard, 1904; m. Ellen Douglas Bruce, Sept. 22, 1909; 1 dau., Ellen Bruce (Mrs. Frederick S. Fisher, Jr.). Became connected with The Crane Co., Chicago, 1904, later with Eaton, Cole & Burnham Co., Bridgeport, Conn., and pres. of its successor, The Crane Valve Co., 1910-14; also v.p. the Crane Co., Chicago. Elected commr. Rivers and Harbors Commn., 1909; mem. Pub. Safety Commn., Chicago and Cook Co., Ill., 1913-15; pvt. sec. to Robert Lansing, sec. of State, 1915-19; U.S. minister to Republic of Czecho-Slovakia, 1919-21; treas. Birdneck Realty Corp. Fellow Am. Geog. Soc. Awarded Great Cross Order of White Lion (Czecho-Slovakia); Polonia Restituta (Poland). Home: Westover, Va. Died Oct. 3, 1938.

CRANE, Richard Teller, manufacturer; b. Paterson, N.J., 1832; spent early life chiefly in labor. having little time for study; twice married; father of Charles Richard C. Learned and worked at machinist's trade in Paterson, Brooklyn and New York until 1855, when he removed to Chicago, where his uncle, Martin Ryerson, helped him to start in business by giving him a small piece of land on which to build a brass foundry; later joined by brother, Charles S. Crane, in firm of R. T. Crane & Bro.; began making steam heaters, 1858; added iron foundry, 1862; built 4-story factory, 1864; later incorporated business as Northwestern Mfg. Co., later reorganized as Crane Bros. Mfg. Co. and later as Crane Co., mfrs. pipe and fittings. In 1867 started mfr. of elevators (freight and passenger), which as The Crane Elevator Co. grew to very large proportions. Home: Chicago, Ill. Died 1912.

CRANE, Richard Teller, Jr., mfr.; b. Chicago, Ill., Nov. 7, 1873; s. Richard Teller and Mary (Prentice) C.; Ph.B., Sheffield Scientific Sch. (Yale), 1895; m. Florence Higinbotham, June 4, 1904; children—Cornelius, Florence. In 1896, entered works of The Crane Co. (established 1855, inc. 1865) in the foundries, entering the office in the city sales dept. in 1897, 2d v.p., 1898, pres., 1914—. Home: Chicago, Ill. Died Nov. 7, 1931.

CRANE, R(obert) Newton, lawyer; b. Long Branch, N.J., Apr. 1, 1848; s. Rev. John and Hannah (Wilde) C.; B.A., Wesleyan U., Conn., 1867, M.A., 1870; m. Mary Frances Allen, Nov. 1873. On editorial staff Newark (N.J.) Daily Advertiser, 1867-69; founder, with Richard Watson Gilder, Newark Morning Register, 1869; mng. editor St. Louis Globe Democrat, 1873; U.S. consul at Manchester, Eng., 1874-80; admitted to bar, St. Louis, 1880, U.S. Supreme Ct., 1881; called to English bar, 1894; representative U.S. Govt. in S. African Deportation Claims Commn., 1901; agt. U.S. Govt. in Samoan arbitration award, 1903; U.S. Govt. dispatch agt., 1904. Chancellor P.E. Diocese of Mo., 1894. Grand deacon Grand Lodge of Eng., 1908; grand herald Great Priory of K.T. of Eng., 1907. Home: London, Eng. Died May 6, 1927.

CRANE, Stephen, author; b. Newark, N.J., Nov. 1, 1871; ed. there; also took partial course at Lafayette Coll. Entered journalism at 16; for years reporter and writer of newspaper sketches; from 1896 devoted time chiefly to story-writing; corr. New York Journal in Graeco-Turkish war, 1897; while on his way to Cuba, 1897, was shipwrecked and spent some time in an open boat until rescued. Author: Maggie, a Girl of the Streets; The Black Riders, and Other Lines; The Red Badge of Courage; George's Mother; The Little Regiment; The Open Boat; The Third Violet; The Eternal Patience; etc. Home: Hartwood, N.Y. Died 1900.

CRANE, Thomas Frederick, educator; b. New York, July 12, 1844; A.B., Princeton, 1864, A.M., 1867, Ph.D., 1883, Litt.D., 1903; m. Sarah Fay Tourtellot, July 10, 1872 (died 1912); 1 dau., Frederika Crane (Mrs. G. B. Muchmore). Prof. langs., 1868-73, Spanish and Italian, 1873-84, Romance langs., 1884-1909, dean Coll. of Arts, 1896-1902, dean Univ. Faculty, 1902-09, acting pres., 1899, emeritus, 1909, acting pres., 1912-13, Cornell U. Author or Editor: Italian Popular Tales; The Exempla, or Illustrative Stories from the Sermons of Jacques de Vitry, Tableaux de la Révolution Française, Le Romantisme Français; la Société Française au Dix-Septième Siècle; Chansons Populaires de la France; Boileau's Les Héros de Roman; Rotrou's Saint Genest and Venceslas; Italian Social Customs of the Sixteenth Century; Pez's Liber de Miraculis Mariæ. Home: Ithaca, N.Y. Died Dec. 9, 1927.

CRANE, William H., actor; b. Leicester, Mass., Apr. 30, 1845; s. Amaziah Brito and Mary Sophia C.; début Utica, N.Y., July 13, 1863; married 1870. Was with Mrs. Harriet Holman's Opera Co. for 7 years, Oates Opera Co., 4 yrs. Became leading comedian Hooley's Stock Co., Chicago; appeared with Stuart Robson, Park Theatre, New York, in "Our Boarding House," 1877, followed by numerous successes, including the two Dromios in Shakespeare's "Comedy of Errors," ending with "The Henrietta." Appeared in star rôles in "The Senator," "On Probation," "For Money," "The American Minister," "Brother John," "Fool of Fortune," "The Pacific Mail," 1892, "A Virginia Courtship," 1898, "Worth a Million," 1898-99, "The Head of the Family," 1899; appeared for 3 yrs. as David Harum in play of that name, 1900; followed by "The Spenders," "Business is Business," "Les Affaires sont Les Affaires," "Father and the Boys," 1907-10; "The Senator Keeps House," 1911, and a revival of Bronson Howard's "The Henrietta." Died Mar. 7, 1928.

CRANE, William Iler, educator, writer; b. Delaware Co., O., Aug. 27, 1866; s. Elbert and Eleanor Barrett (Iler) C.; Ohio Wesleyan U., 1886-88; A.B., Ohio U., 1900, A.M., 1902; m. Ione A. Oliver, Dec. 24, 1891. Taught country schs., 1884-86; supt. in Ohio schs., 1888-94; head English dept., Steele High Sch., Dayton, O., 1894-1900; supt. schs., Marshalltown, Ia., 1902-05; editor and mgr. ednl. dept., D. Appleton & Co., New York, 1913-16. Author: Changing the Viewpoint, 1905; Wheeler's Graded Literary Readers (with W. H. Wheeler), 1919. Died Apr. 3, 1924.

CRANE, W(inthrop) Murray, senator; b. Dalton, Mass., Apr. 23, 1853; s. Zenas Marshall and Louise (Laflin) C.; ed. public schools and Williston Sem.; (A.M., Williams, 1897; LL.D., Harvard, 1903); m. Mary Benner, 1880 (died 1884); m. 2d, Josephine Porter, 1906. Mem. Crane & Co., paper mfrs., also mfg. paper used for currency. Lt. gov. of Mass., 1897-99, gov., 1900-02; apptd., Oct. 12, 1904, and elected Jan. 1905, U.S. senator, to fill vacancy for unexpired term (1904-07) of George F. Hoar, deceased; reëlected for term 1907-13. Mem. Rep. Nat. Com., 1892-1900 and from 1904. Home: Dalton, Mass. Died Oct. 2, 1920.

CRANE, Zenas Marshall, paper mfr.; b. Dalton, Mass., Mar. 5, 1878; s. Zenas and Ellen J. (Kittredge) C.; student Hotchkiss Sch., Lakeville, Conn., 1893-96; A.B., Yale, 1900; unmarried. Entered paper mfg. business, 1900; v.p. Crane & Co., Inc.; v.p. and chmn. exec. com. Pittsfield Third Nat. Bank & Trust Co.; trustee City Savings Bank of Pittsfield; dir. and mem. finance com. Berkshire Life Ins. Co.; dir. B.&A. R.R. Co. Mem. Finance Com., Town of Dalton. Served with Near East Relief in Russian Caucasus, 1919-20. Republican. Conglist. Home: Dalton, Mass. Died Apr. 29, 1936.

CRANMER, Gibson L., lawyer; b. Cincinnati, Feb. 20, 1826; grad. Woodward Coll. there, 1847; sec. of Wheeling conv., June 1861, called to reorganize govt. of Va.; mem. gen. assembly, Va., 1855-56; 1st clerk reorganized house of delegates of Va.; was pres. Antietam Nat. Cemetery Assn. when it was handed over to Nat. Govt.; was judge, municipal court of Wheeling, 8 yrs.; mem. Wheeling bd. of edn. Home: Wheeling, W.Va. Died 1903.

CRANNELL, Philip Wendell, theologian; b. Albany, N.Y., Dec. 26, 1861; s. Matthew and Laura Adell (Prink) C.; A.B., Dartmouth, 1882 (commencement speaker); grad. Rochester Theol. Sem., 1888 (commencement speaker); D.D., Ottawa, U., Kan., 1901, Dartmouth, 1913; m. Fannie Eleanor Grout, Apr. 2, 1884; children—Effie Euretta (dec.), Mrs. Florence Crannell Means. Prin. pub. schs., Le Raysville, Pa., 1882-83; supt. schs. and prin. high sch., Luverne, Minn., 1883-84; actg. pastor South Alabama, N.Y., 1886-87; ordained Bapt. ministry, 1888; pastor Baldwinsville, N.Y., 1888-94, Corning, N.Y., 1894-1900, 1st Ch., Topeka, Kan., 1900-04; prof. homiletics and pastoral theology, 1902—, 1st pres. Kansas City Bapt. Theol. Sem., 1903-26; head dept. of religion, Colo. Woman's Coll., Denver, 1927-31. Republican and Prohibitionist. Author: The Lesson Analyzed, 1910; The Survival of the Unfit, 1915; Crannell's Pocket Lessons, 1917-32; Character Crises in the Old Testament, 1920; The Book of Books—How to Appreciate the Bible, 1921; Seams of Glory, 1926. Home: Denver, Colo. Died Dec. 2, 1936.

CRANSTON, Earl, bishop; b. Athens, O., June 27, 1840; s. Earl and Jane (Montgomery) C.; A.B., Ohio U., 1861, A.M., 1866, LL.D., 1897; D.D., Allegheny, 1882; m. Martha A. Behan, Oct. 7, 1861; 1 son, Earl Montgomery; m. 2d, Laura Martin; children—Ethel, Laura Alden, Ruth; m. 3d, Lucie M. Parker, of Cincinnati, Ohio, Nov. 5, 1905. 1st sergt. to captain in Ohio infantry and W.Va. cav., 1861-64. Ordained M.E. ministry, 1867; pastor Marietta, O., 1867, Portsmouth, O., 1868-69, Columbus, Ohio, 1870, Winona, Minn., 1871, Jacksonville, Ill., 1872-74, Evansville, Ind., 1874-75, Cincinnati, 1875-78. Denver, Colo., 1878-80; presiding elder, 1880-84; pub. agt. M.E. Ch., 1884-96; elected bishop, 1896. Episcopal visitor, China, Japan, Korea, 1898-1900, also Mexico, P.R., H.Ty. and European missions; commr. for M.E. Church on the union of Methodism in Japan, 1907; resident bishop at Washington, D.C., 1904-16; retired, 1916. Chmn. Commn. for Unification of Methodism. Author: Breaking Down of the Walls, 1916. Home: New Richmond, O. Died Aug. 19, 1932.

CRANWELL, Thomas George, mfr.; b. Baltimore, Dec. 2, 1862; s. George William and Clara Belle (Holton) C.; ed. pub. schs.; m. Elizabeth Lloyd Fenn, Oct. 24, 1906. Founded firm of Thomas G. Cranwell & Co., Baltimore, 1889; dir. Norton Tin Plate & Can Co., 1898-1901; v.p. Am. Can Co., 1901-04; an organizer, 1904, pres. Continental Can Co., Inc., until 1927, chmn. bd., Jan. 1927—; dir. Vulcan Detinning Co., Syracuse Trust Co. Asst. chief of tin sect. War Industries Bd., Washington, World War. Trustee Syracuse Free Dispensary, Syracuse Boys Club. Republican. Methodist. Home: New York, N.Y. Died Jan. 9, 1935.

CRAPO, Philip M., insurance; b. Freetown, Mass., June 30, 1844; s. Philip C.; ed. public and high schools, New Bedford, Mass.; served in Union army in Civil war; studied law; m. Ruth A. Ray, Sept. 6, 1870. Gen. agt. Conn. Mut. Life Ins. Co., 1868-82, financial corr., 1882—. Chiefly instrumental in securing Iowa Soldiers' Home, and prominent in securing erection of Iowa Soldiers' Monument; secured public park for Burlington which bears his name; mainly instrumental in establishment of free public library, contributing nearly one-half the cost of fine library bldg.; pres. bd. trustees Free Public Library; pres. bd. park commrs. Republican. Home: Burlington, Ia. Died 1903.

CRAPO, Stanford Tappan; b. New Bedford, Mass., June 13, 1865; s. William W. and Sarah (Tappan) C.; A.B., Yale, 1886; m. Emma C. Morley, Oct. 10, 1894; children—William W., Catherine, Mary M. Began at Saginaw, Mich., in local freight dept. of Flint & Pere Marquette R.R., 1887; successively supt's. clk., div. supt., asst. to gen. mgr., 1891-94, gen. mgr., 1894-1900, and gen. mgr. at Detroit, Pere Marquette R.R., 1900-03; engaged in production of coal and cement, 1903; dir. Federal Reserve bank. Home: Detroit, Mich. Died Jan. 26, 1939.

CRAPO, William Wallace, lawyer; b. Dartmouth, Mass., May 16, 1830; s. Henry H. and Mary A. (Slocum) C.; A.B., Yale, 1852, LL.D., 1882; student Harvard Law Sch.; (LL.D., Williams Coll., 1910); m. Sarah A. D. Tappan, Jan. 22, 1857 (dec.). City solicitor, New Bedford, 1855-67; mem. Mass. Legislature, 1857; mem. 44th to 47th Congresses (1875-83); head of law firm Crapo, Clifford & Prescott; pres. Acushnet Mill Corp., Potomska Mill, and Institution for Savings, New Bedford, and connected with many other banking and industrial enterprises. Home: New Bedford, Mass. Died Feb. 28, 1926.

CRAPSEY, Algernon Sidney, author; b. Fairmount, O., June 28, 1847; s. Jacob Tomkins and Rachel (Morris) C.; ed. pub. sch. to 12 and in business 12 to 15; mem. Co. B, 79th Ohio Inf., 1862; in business, 1863-69; ed. St. Stephen's Coll. and Sem., 1869-72; S.T.D., Hobart Coll., Geneva, N.Y., 1900; m. Adelaide Trowbridge, 1875; children—Philip T. (dec.), Emily M. (dec.), Adelaide (dec.), Paul B., Rachel M., Algernon S., Ruth E. (dec.), Marie Louise, Arthur H. Deacon, 1872, priest, 1873, P.E. Ch.; on staff of Trinity Ch., New York, 1872-79; rector St. Andrew's, Rochester, N.Y., 1879-1906; deposed for heresy, Dec. 4, 1906. Parole officer State of N.Y., 1914. Author: Five Joyful Mysteries, 1883; Voice in the Wilderness; The Disunion of Christendom, 1900; Sarah Thorne, 1900; The Greater Love, 1901; Religion and Politics, 1906; The Re-Birth of Religion, 1907; The Rise of the Working Class, 1914; The Ways of the Gods, 1920; The Last of the Heretics, 1924. Founder of The Brotherhood, Rochester, 1907. Home: Rochester, N.Y. Died Dec. 31, 1927.

CRARY, George Waldo, dermatologist; b. Brooklyn, N.Y., Jan. 3, 1864; s. George and Sarah Matilda (Durkee) C.; Poly. Inst. of Brooklyn, 1870-81; M.D., Coll. Phys. and Surg. (Columbia U.), 1885; Berlin, 1899-1900, Vienna, 1900-01; m. Julia Treadwell Ogden, Apr. 30, 1891. House surgeon, Bellevue Hosp., New York, 1887; inst. physiol. chemistry, Post-Grad. Med. Sch., 1888-89; attending surgeon, out-door dept., 1886-99, asst. attending surgeon, 1895-99, Roosevelt Hosp.; asst. demonstrator anatomy, Coll. Phys. and Surg., 1897-99; attending dermatologist, Cornell Med. Sch., New York, 1902-06; asst. consulting dermatologist, New York Lying-in Hosp., 1903-05; cons. dermatologist, Gen. Memorial Hosp., N.Y. Infant Asylum, Manhattan Eye, Ear and Throat Hosp., Nursery and Child's Hosp. Republican. Presbyn. Home: New York, N.Y. Died Nov. 1925.

CRATTY, Mabel, Y.W.C.A. official; b. Bellaire, O.; d. Charles Campbell and Mary (Thoburn) C.; B.L., Ohio Wesleyan U., 1890, LL.D., 1922. Teacher Wheeling (W.Va.) Female Sem., and high schs., Kent and Delaware, O., until 1900; prin. high sch., Delaware, 1900-04; asso. gen. sec. Am. Com. Y.W.C.A., Chicago, 1904-06; exec. sec. Home Dept. of Nat. Bd. Y.W.C.A. of U.S.A., hdqrs. N.Y. City, 1906-09; gen. sec. Nat. Bd., 1906—. Methodist. Home: New York, N.Y. Died Feb. 27, 1928.

CRAVATH, Erastus Milo, pres. Fisk Univ. 1875—; b. Homer, N.Y., July 1, 1833; grad. Oberlin Coll., 1857; theol. dept., 1860 (A.M.; D.D., Iowa Coll.); m. Ruthanna Jackson, Sept. 18, 1860. Chaplain 101st regt., Ohio vol. inf., 1864-65; connected with Fisk Univ. from time founded. Home: Nashville, Tenn. Died 1900.

CRAVATH, Paul Drennan, lawyer; b. Berlin Heights, O., July 14, 1861; s. Erastus M. and Ruth (Jackson) C.; ed. Brooklyn Poly. Inst.; studied 2 yrs. in Europe; A.B., Oberlin, 1882, A.M., 1887; LL.B., Columbia, 1886, LL.D., 1923; admitted to bar, 1886; m. Agnes Huntington, Nov. 15, 1892. Prize tutor in law, Columbia, 1886-89; mem. Cravath, deGersdorff, Swaine & Wood. Mem., representing U.S. Treasury, of "House Mission" to the Inter-Allied War Conf., Paris, Dec. 1917; advisory counsel of Am. Mission to the Inter-Allied Council on War Purchases and Finance, London and Paris, 1918. Awarded D.S.M. by Gen. Pershing, 1919; Chevalier Legion of Honor (French), 1919; Grand Officer Order of the Crown (Italian), 1921; hon. Bencher of Gray's Inn, London, 1918; Knight Comdr. Order S.S. Maurizio e Lazzaro, 1923; Officer of the Crown of Roumania, 1923. Pres. Metropolitan Opera Assn. Home: 36 E. 72d St., New York, and Locust Valley, L.I. Office: 15 Broad St., New York, N.Y. Died July 1, 1940.

CRAVEN, Alfred, civil engr.; b. Bound Brook, N.J., Sept. 16, 1846; s. Thomas Tingey and Emily (Henderson) C.; grad. U.S. Naval Acad., 1867; m. Nina Florence Browne; children—Lucy Egerton, Emily Henderson, Truxtrin Tingey (dec.), Nana Florence. Resigned as master, U.S.N., 1871; engaged in geol. survey and irrigation work, Calif., and in mining engring., Calif. and Nev., 1871-84; div. engr. new Croton Aqueduct, N.Y. City, 1884-95; in charge constrn. Jerome Park Reservoir, 1895-1900; apptd. div. engr. Rapid Transit Commn., N.Y. City, 1900, and was in charge constrn. of sect. of subway at 42d St. and Broadway to 104th St.; dep. chief under same commn., 1905-07; dep. engr., subway constrn. of Pub. Service Commn., 1st Dist. N.Y., 1907-10; acting chief engr., later chief engr. in charge constrn. dual system of subways for N.Y. City, 1910-16; was consulting engr. Pub. Service Commn. and its successor, the Transit Constrn. Commn. Apptd. by Sec. of Navy, as one of two representatives of Am. Soc. C.E. on Naval Consulting Bd., 1915. Awarded Civil War Medal by Act of Congress, 1908. Republican. Episcopalian. Home: Pleasantville, N.Y. Died Sept. 30, 1926.

CRAVEN, Elijah Richardson, clergyman; b. Washington, March 28, 1824; grad. Princeton, 1842 (A.M., 1845; D.D., 1859); Princeton Theol. Sem., 1848 (LL.D., Lafayette, 1890); m. Hannah T. Sanderson, 1852; m. 2d, Elizabeth G. Moore, 1867. Studied law, 1842-44; tutor mathematics, Princeton, 1846-49; ordained, 1850; pastor, Somerville, N.J., 1850-54; Newark, N.J., 1854-87; trustee Princeton; dir. Princeton Theol. Sem.; chmn. com. revision Book of Discipline, Presbyn. Ch. (North), 1878-84; moderator Gen. Assembly Presbyn. Ch. (North), 1885; pres. bd. dirs., German Theol. Sem., Newark, 1889-1902; sec. Presbyn. Bd. Publ. and S.S. Work, 1887-1904, emeritus. Home: Philadelphia, Pa. Died 1908.

CRAVEN, George Warren, electrical engr.; b. Helena, Mont., Apr. 1, 1871; s. Robert Martin and Mary Eleanor (Frasier) C.; B.S. in E.E., Mass. Inst. Tech., 1898; m. Marthell Arnold of Butte, Mont., June 30, 1903. Engr. with Highland Boy's Smelter, Murray, Utah, 1899; engr. with Butte Water Co.'s steam pumping plant, 1901; engr. Boston & Mont. Consol. Copper & Silver Mining Co., 1901-03; with Mont. Power Co., 1903—, also cons. practice; pres. Mont. State Sch. of Mines, 1921-27. Democrat. Methodist. Mason. Home: Butte, Mont. Deceased.

CRAVENS, Ben, congressman; b. Ft. Smith, Ark., Jan. 17, 1874; s. William Murphy and Mary Eloise (Rutherford) C.; student Louisville (Ky.) Mil. Acad., and Staunton (Va.) Mil. Acad.; B.L., U. of Mo., 1893; s. Carolyn Dyal, Dec. 19, 1895; children—Fadjo, Nancy (Mrs. William M. Eads). City atty. Ft. Smith, 1896-1900; dist. atty. 12th Jud. Dist. of Ark., 1900-06; mem. 60th to 63d and 73d to 75th Congresses (1907-15 and 1933-39), 4th Ark. Dist. Democrat. Home: Fort Smith, Ark. Died Jan. 13, 1939.

CRAVENS, John William, educator; b. Center Valley, Ind., Oct. 1, 1864; s. William Reece and Sarah Ruth (Bray) C.; grad. Central Normal Coll., Danville, Ind., 1884; A.B., Indiana U., 1897, A.M., 1920; m. Emma Lucille Krueger, Oct. 1, 1891 (died 1898); 1 dau., Ruth Ralston; m. 2d, Mellie Parker Greene, June 28, 1916. Editor Danville Gazette, 1884-85; supt. schs., Monroe Co., Ind., 1887-90; clk. Monroe Co. Circuit Court, 1890-94; editor Bloomington World, 1893-1906; registrar Ind. U., 1895-1915, sec., 1915—, also sec. bd. of trustees. Chmn. Monroe Co. Dem. Central Com., 1890-96; mem. Ind. Ho. of Rep., 1898-1902; mem. Dem. Central Com. of Ind., 1916-18. Presbyn. Mason. Home: Bloomington, Ind. Died Aug. 10, 1937.

CRAVER, Samuel Porch, clergyman; b. at Franklinville, N.J., Apr. 26, 1847; s. James Abbott and Hannah (Porch) C.; A.B., Iowa (now Grinnell) Coll., 1871; B.D., Boston U. Sch. of Theology, 1875; (D.D., Ia. Wesleyan, 1887); m. Laura E. Gassner, Sept. 22, 1875. Ordained M. E. ministry, 1875; missionary in Mexico, 1876-95, in S. America, 1895—; various positions, as pastor, dist. supt., etc.; pres. Theol. Sem. E. South Am. Conf. M.E. Ch., Montevideo, also treas. Bd. Foreign Missions same conf. Died Oct. 31, 1919.

CRAWFORD, Andrew Murray, lawyer; b. Cannonsville, Delaware Co., N.Y., Jan 29, 1853; s. James Nelson and Joanna Adelia (Owens) C.; ed. Walton (N.Y.) Acad.; m. Florence Watson, Oct. 22, 1885. Admitted to N.Y. bar, 1878; removed to Marshfield, Ore., 1880; receiver, U.S. local land office, 1890-94; mem. Ore. Ho. of Rep., 1897; atty. gen. of Ore., 1902-14. Republican. Episcopalian. Mason. Home: Portland, Ore. Died Jan. 29, 1925.

CRAWFORD, Andrew Wright, lawyer; b. Lower Merion Township, Montgomery Co., Pa., Dec. 24, 1873; s. John Y. and Violetta Virginia (Wright) C.; A.B., U. of Pa., 1893, LL.B., 1897; student civ. engring., Mass. Institute Tech., 1893-94, Columbia Law Sch., New York, 1894-96; m. Clotilde Florance Cohen, Apr. 19, 1906. Asst. city solicitor, Phila., 1906-11; prof. law of real property, of landlord and tenant, of negotiable instruments and sales, Law Dept., Temple U., 1908-23. Sec. City Parks Assn. of Phila., 1900; trustee Fairmont Park Assn., 1903-22; sec., 1922—; editor city planning section of Public Ledger, 1913; mem. exec. com. Nat. Conf. on City Planning, 1910-25; sec. Art Jury of Phila., 1911—; dir. Nat. Housing Assn., 1913—, Am. Federation of Arts, 1915—; field sec. Am. Civic Assn., 1918-20. Republican. Protestant. Home: Philadelphia, Pa. Died June 27, 1929.

CRAWFORD, Arthur, writer; b. Montreal, Can., July 2, 1867; s. James David and Annie Rosina (Smith) C.; grad. Lincoln Coll., Sorel, P.Q., 1884, Royal Mil. Coll., Kingston, Ont., 1888; m. Anne Goy, of Sheffield, Eng., Apr. 18, 1895. Began as actor in drama "Dartmoor," 1892; with "A Night Off" co., and Lyceum Co., 1895; left stage, 1896, and then engaged in writing verses, paragraphs, jokes, etc., for Puck, Judge, Life, and other humorous publs.; furnishes artists with ideas for humorous pictures ("A.C." after artist's name indicating source of the idea). Home: New Rochelle, N.Y. Died Nov. 1922.

CRAWFORD, Edward Grant, banker, b. Kelso, Cowlitz Co., Wash., Apr. 23, 1868; s. Peter W. and Zillah C.; ed. pub. schs.; m. Ida M. Goss, 1888. Sec. treas. Crawford-Marshall Co., Portland, Ore.; mgr. Vancouver Nat. Bank, 1901-19; pres. Lumberman's Nat. Bank, Portland, 1911-17; 1st v.p. U.S. Nat. Bank (consolidation of Lumberman's and U.S. nat. banks), 1917—. Republican. Mason (32°). Home: Portland, Ore. Died May 12, 1923.

CRAWFORD, Edwin Robert, banker, mfr.; b. Mifflin Twp., Allegheny Co., Pa., Feb. 13, 1870; s. James Chambers and Mathilda Jane (Wigham) C.; ed. Southwestern State Normal Sch., California, Pa.; m. Mary Edmonds, Sept. 3, 1923. Began as office boy U.S. Iron & Tin Plate Mfg. Co., McKeesport, Pa., 1885, and advanced to sec.; traveling auditor Am. Tin Plate Co., 1899-1902; pres. McKeesport Tin Plate Co., 1902—; dir. Washington Tin Plate Co., First Nat. Bank of Duquesne, National Bank of McKeesport, National Can Co., Inc., Mellon Nat. Bank. Mem. Pa. State Commn. to study municipal consolidation; mem. Sch. Bd., Duquesne, 1896-1902. Trustee McKeesport Hosp. Republican. Presbyn. Mason (32°, K.T., Shriner). Home: Duquesne, Pa. Died Sept. 13, 1936.

CRAWFORD, Eugene Lowther, clergyman; b. Glenville, Ala., Jan. 12, 1871; s. Robert Blakeley (D.D.) and Martha Frances (Stephenson) C.; prep. edn., Barton Acad., Mobile, Ala.; A.B., Southern U., Greensboro, Ala., 1891; D.D., Birmingham-Southern Coll., Birmingham, Ala., 1925; m. Martha Ginder Thorington, Oct. 30, 1902 (died Mar. 19, 1911); children—Frances (Mrs. Eugene Robbins), Lucile (Mrs. Alexander Waller), Martha; m. 2d, Mrs. Sudie Hughes Harrison, Sept. 5, 1914. Licensed ministry M.E. Ch., S., 1893, ordained, 1897; pastor chs. in Ala. and Tex. until 1919; presiding elder, 1919-22; sec. Bd. of Edn. and Christian Edn. Movement, Ala. Conf., M.E. Ch., S., 1923-24; presiding elder, 1925-27; gen. sec. Bd. Temperance and Social Service, M.E. Ch., S., 1927—. Formerly chaplain Sons Confed. Vets., Ala. Mem. Gen. Conf. M.E. Ch., S., 1922, asst. sec., 1926. Democrat. Mason (K.T.), K.P., Odd Fellow. Home: Washington, D.C. Died Sept. 1, 1934.

CRAWFORD, Francis Marion, novelist, historian; b. Bagni di Lucca, Italy, Aug. 2, 1854; s. Thomas C. (sculptor) and Louisa Ward C.; ed. St. Paul's Sch., Concord, N.H., and Trinity Coll., Cambridge, Eng.; studied Oriental languages while corr. for newspapers; m. 1884, Elizabeth, d. Gen. Hiram Berdan. Edited Indian Herald, Allahabad, India, 1879-80. Author: Mr. Isaacs, 1882; Dr. Claudius, 1883; A Roman Singer, 1884; To Leeward, 1884; An American Politician, 1884; Zoroaster, 1885; A Tale of a Lonely Parish, 1886; Marzio's Crucifix, 1887; Paul Patoff, 1887; Sarinesca, 1887; With the Immortals, 1888; Greifenstein, 1889; Sant' Ilario, 1889; A Cigarette Maker's Romance, 1890; Khaled, 1891; The Witch of Prague, 1891; The Three Fates, 1892; The Children of the King, 1892; Don Orsino, 1892; Marion Darche, 1893; Pietro Ghislero, 1893; The Novel—What It Is, 1893; Katherine Lauderdale, 1894; Love in Idleness, 1894; The Ralstons, 1894; Constantinople, 1895; Casa Braccio, 1895; Adam Johnstone's Son, 1895; Taquisara, 1896; A Rose of Yesterday, 1897; Corleone, 1897; Ave Roma Immortalis (hist.), 1898; Via Crucis, 1899; In the Palace of the King, 1900; The Rulers of the South (hist.), 1900 (reprinted 1904, under the title, Sicily, Calabria and Malta); Marietta, a Maid of Venice, 1901; Cecilia, a Story of Modern Rome, 1902; The Heart of Rome, 1903; Whosoever Shall Offend, 1904; Soprano, a Portrait, 1905; Venetian Gleanings (hist.), 1905; A Lady of Rome, 1906; Arethusa, 1907; The Little City of Hope, 1907;—all Ml. Play: Francesca da Rimini (prod. by Sarah Bernhardt in Paris, 1902). Died 1909.

CRAWFORD, F(rederick) Stuart, editorial writer; b. Lyons, Ia., May 28, 1876; s. Sidney and Harriet Phinney (Peak) C.; A.B., Amherst Coll., 1897; m. Mabel Rosemond McLean, Sept. 11, 1902; children—F(rederick) Stuart, S(idney) Peak. With New York Tribune, 1897-1915, polit. writer, 1906-15; sec. law dept., City of N.Y., 1915-18; polit. writer New York Sun, Sun-Herald and Herald, 1918-24; asst. to vice chmn. Charles D. Hillis of Rep. Nat. Com. and later exec. sec. com. legislation of New York County Rep. Com., 1924-25; a sec. of President Calvin Coolidge, 1925-29; editorial writer New York Herald Tribune, 1929—. Republican. Conglist. Home: Brooklyn, N.Y. Died Mar. 9, 1936.

CRAWFORD, George Gordon, engineer, metallurgist; b. Madison, Ga., Aug. 24, 1869; s. George Gilmore and Margaret Reed (Howard) C.; B.S., in mech. engring., Ga. Sch. of Tech., Atlanta, 1890, Sc.D., 1931; Karl-Eberhard U., Tübingen, Germany, 1891-92; m. Margaret Richardson, Feb. 1, 1911. Chemist, 1892-94, draughtsman, 1894-95, Edgar-Thomson Works; asst. supt. Edgar-Thompson Blast Furnaces, Carnegie Steel Co., 1895-97; supt. blast furnaces and steel works, Nat. Tube Co., McKeesport, Pa., 1897-99; supt. Edgar-Thomson Blast Furnaces, Carnegie Steel Co., 1899-1901; mgr. nat. dept. Nat. Tube Co., McKeesport, Pa., 1901-07; pres. Tenn. Coal, Iron & R.R. Co., Birmingham, Ala., 1907-30; pres. Jones & Laughlin Steel Corp., Pittsburgh, 1930—. Mem. metall. advisory bd. Carnegie Inst. Tech. Dir. Am. Iron and Steel Inst. Home: Pittsburgh, Pa. Died Mar. 20, 1936.

CRAWFORD, James Pyle Wickersham, coll. prof.; b. Lancaster, Pa., Feb. 19, 1882; s. James and Corinne (Wickersham) C.; A.B., U. of Pa., 1902, grad. work, 1902-04, Ph.D., 1906; univs. of Grenoble, Madrid and Freiburg, 1904-06; Litt.D., Franklin and Marshall, 1925; m. Florence May Wickersham, June 3, 1909; 1 dau., Harriet de B. Instr. Romance langs., U. of Pa., 1906, prof., 1914—. Commd. capt. U.S.A., June 1918 and assigned duty at Washington, D.C.; mil. attaché to Colombia, S.A., Jan.-July, 1919; hon. discharged Aug. 1919; commd. maj. O.R.C., Nov. 1919. Author: Life and Works of Suarez de Figueroa, 1907; Spanish Composition, 1910; Temas Españoles, 1922; Spanish Drama before Lope de Vega, 1923 (revised edit. 1937); Un viaje por España, 1931; Spanish Pastoral Drama, 1915; First Book in Spanish, 1919. Editor: Tragedia de Narciso, 1909. Editor of Modern Language Journal, 1920-24, Hispanic Review, 1933—. Home: Philadelphia, Pa. Died Sept. 22, 1939.

CRAWFORD, Jerry Tinder, church official; b. Clayton, Hendricks Co., Ind., May 28, 1865; s. William English and Huldah Jane (Tinder) C.; B.Litt., Ottawa (Kan.) U., 1892; D.D., 1917; B.D., Div. Sch. U. of Chicago, 1897; m. Belle Nordyke, Oct. 4, 1900. Taught sch., 1885-87; prin. Oswego High Sch., 1886-87; ordained ministry Bapt. Ch., 1892; pastor successively Phillipsburg, Kan., Parkside (Chicago), Warrensville, Ill., and Parsons, Kan., until 1907; exec. sec. and gen. missionary Kan. Bapt. Conv., 1907-36; editor The Kansas Baptist, 1907-36; acting pres. Kansas City Bapt. Theol. Sem., 1936-37; pres. Sunset Home Soc. for Aged. Del. Bapt. World Alliance, Stockholm, 1923. Republican. Home: Topeka, Kan. Died Feb. 15, 1938.

CRAWFORD, John Martin, banker; b. Herrick, Pa., Oct. 18, 1845; s. John S. and Clarissa C.; A.B., Lafayette Coll., 1871; M.D., Pulte Med. Coll., Cincinnati, 1878, Miami Med. Coll., 1881 (LL.D.); m. Cora Hayward, Apr. 18, 1888. Prof. physiology and physical diagnosis, Pulte Med. Coll., 1881-89; U.S. consul gen. to Russia, 1889-94; U.S. Commr. of Chicago Expn. to Russia. Lecturer on the ancient Finns, and on European and Asiatic Russia. Translator of the Kalevala (the epic of Finland); editor and translator of The Industries of Russia (5 vols.); Agriculture, Trade, Manufacturers, Mines and Mining, Siberia and the Great Siberian Railway. Pres. Western Acad. Medicine, 1888. Home: Cincinnati, O. Died Aug. 4, 1916.

CRAWFORD, John Raymond, prof. Latin; b. Chicago, Ill., July 4, 1886; s. William Henry and Jennie May (Foote) C.; A.B., Allegheny Coll., 1906; A.M., Harvard, 1908, Ph.D., 1916; studied U. of Munich, 1908-09, Am. Sch. Classical Studies in Rome, 1909-10, 1913-14, U. of Grenoble, summer, 1910; m. Pauline Avery, July 22, 1913; children—William Avery, John Avery. Acting prof. Greek and Latin, Upper La. U., 1906-07; asst. in classics, Harvard, 1911-12; instr. classical philology, Columbia, 1912-17; asst. prof. Roman archæology, same, 1917-19; prof. Latin and head dept. Greek and Latin, Lafayette Coll., 1919—. Served as candidate officer and 2d lt. inf., U.S. Army, May-Dec. 1918. Methodist. Home: Easton, Pa. Died Apr. 15, 1929.

CRAWFORD, John Wallace (Capt. Jack), author; b. Co. Donegal, Ireland, Mar. 4, 1847; s. John Austin and Susie (Wallace) C.; came to U.S. in boyhood; ran away from home to enlist, but was several times refused because of youth; finally joined 48th Pa. Vols.; severely wounded; while in hosp. at W. Phila., was taught to read and write by Sister of Charity; m. Anna M. Stokes, 1869. After war went West; became govt. scout; served under Gen. Crook in Sitting Bull campaign, 1876 (apptd. chief of scouts); and in campaigns against Apaches in N.M.; retired from army life, 1886; miner and ranchman in N.M. many yrs.; went to Klondike, 1898; returned after 2 winters. Author: The Poet Scout—A Book of Song and Story, 1885; Campfire Sparks, 1888; Tat, a drama in 3 acts (prod. Alta Theatre, San Francisco, Oct., 1900); Fonda, drama in 3 acts; Colonel Bob, drama (with Marie Madison), 1909; Private Brown, serial story; Whar' the Hand o' God Is Seen, and other poems, 1911; also many short stories. Home: San Marcial, N.M. Died Feb. 27, 1917.

CRAWFORD, Leonard Jacob, lawyer; b. Newport, Ky., Apr. 29, 1860; grad. Hughes High Sch., Cincinnati, 1880; LL.B., Cincinnati Law Coll., 1882; m. Ella J. Horner, Jan. 16, 1883. Admitted to Ky. bar, 1882; Rep. candidate for atty. gen. of Ky., 1891. Pres. Rep. State League of Ky., 1893-95; pres. Nat. Rep. League, 1897. Mem. com. to prepare for Gen. Assembly, bills for re-districting state, amendments to election laws, etc., 1909. Home: Newport, Ky. Deceased.

CRAWFORD, Mary Caroline, author; b. Boston, Mass., May 5, 1874; d. James George and Mary (Coburn) C.; student Girls' Latin Sch., Boston, Radcliffe Coll., class of 1898; grad. Sch. for Social Workers, Boston, 1907. Lit. critic Boston Budget, 1902; sec. Women's Trade Union League, 1907-08, Ford Hall Meetings, 1908-21; mgr. Old South Meeting House Forum, 1914—; counselor in social service advertising. Episcopalian. Author: The Romance of Old New England Rooftrees, 1902; The Romance of Old New England Churches, 1903; The College Girl of America, 1904; Among Old New England Inns, 1907; St. Botolph's Town, 1908; Old Boston Days and Ways, 1909; Romantic Days in Old Boston, 1910; Goethe and His Woman Friends, 1911; Romantic Days in the Early Republic, 1912; The Romance of the American Theatre, 1913, 25; Social Life in Old New England, 1914; In the Days of the Pilgrim Fathers, 1920; Famous Families of Massachusetts, 1930. Home: Boston, Mass. Died Nov. 15, 1932.

CRAWFORD, Medorem, army officer; m. Yamhill Co., Ore., Jan. 27, 1844; s. Medorem (capt. U.S.V.) and Adaline (Brown) C.; grad. U.S. Mil. Acad., 1867, Arty. Sch., 1875; (hon. A.M., Bowdoin Coll., 1881); m. Rita Shreve Carter, Jan. 15, 1874; 2d, Lola Goodall, Jan. 14, 1885. Commd. 2d lt. 2d Arty., June 17, 1867; promoted through grades to brig. gen., Jan. 3, 1908; retired Jan. 27, 1908. On duty, Ft. Vancouver, Wash., 1867-68; with 1st expdn. to Alaska, where was shipwrecked, 1868-70; Tex., Mexican border and in Old Mexico, 1878-79; prof. mil. science, Bowdoin Coll., 1879-81; served in Cuba, and chief ordnance officer, div. and dept. of Cuba, 1898-01; comd. Ft. Kenay, Alaska, 1869-70; Pirotecnia militar, Habana, Cuba, 1899-01; comd. Ft. Schuyler, 1901-03, Ft. McHenry, 1903-05, Ft. Wadsworth, 1905-08. Republican. Home: Washington, D.C. Died Aug. 11, 1921.

CRAWFORD, Morris Barker, physicist; b. Sing Sing (now Ossining), N.Y., Sept. 26, 1852; s. Morris D'Camp and Charlotte (Holmes) C.; A.B., Wesleyan U., Conn., 1874, A.M., 1877; univs. of Leipzig and Berlin, 1877-80; m. Caroline L. Rice, Dec. 25, 1883; children—Holmes (dec.), Frederick North (dec.), Margaret. Instr. physics, Wesleyan U., 1880-81, asso. prof., 1881-84, prof., 1884-1921, emeritus. Home: Middletown, Conn. Died Oct. 9, 1940.

CRAWFORD, Robert A., banker; b. London, Eng., Aug. 22, 1855; s. Alexander and Mary Ann C.; ed. Plainfield (N.J.) Acad.; m. Melissa Beaty, Mar. 25, 1876. Brought to U.S., 1858, naturalized, 1875. Began as pvt. banker, at Altoona (Ia.) Exchange Bank, 1875; then chmn. bd. Valley Savings Bank; exec. v.p. University State Bank; pres. Reiley Investment Co. Treas. and dir. Drake U., Ia. Methodist Hosp. Republican. Mason. Home: Des Moines, Ia. Died Aug. 7, 1937.

CRAWFORD, Samuel Johnson, governor; b. Lawrence Co., Ind., Apr. 15, 1835; s. William and Jane (Morrow) C.; prep. edn. graded schs., Bedford, Ind.; read law, Bedford, and admitted to bar, 1856; LL.B., Cincinnati Law Sch., 1858; removed to Garnett, Kan., 1859; m. Isabel M. Chase, Nov. 27, 1866. Capt. 2d Kan. Cav., May 14, 1861; col. 83d U.S.C.T., Nov. 1, 1863; resigned, Nov. 7, 1864; bvtd. brig. gen. vols., Mar. 13, 1865 "for meritorious services"; col. 19th Kan. Cav., 1868. Farming in Kan., 1869—. Mem. Kan. Ho. of Rep., 1861; gov. of Kan., 1865-69. Author: Kansas in the Sixties. Home: Topeka, Kan. Died Oct. 21, 1913.

CRAWFORD, Thomas Dwight, lawyer; b. Warren, Ark., Dec. 21, 1860; s. Alexander Lafayette and Melinda Parthenia (Harrington) C.; A.B., Davidson Coll., N.C., 1882; LL.B., U. of Va., 1884; m. Elizabeth Daviess Williams, Oct. 8, 1890; children—John Williams, Phyllis Crawford. Admitted to Ark. bar, 1884; asst. atty. gen. of Ark., 1889-90; reporter Supreme Court of Ark., 1890-1913, and 1920—; asst. atty. St.L.I.,M.&S. Ry. Co., 1913-15. Democrat. Presbyn. Author Digest of Arkansas Decisions (7 vols.), 1917-30; Digest of Oklahoma Decisions (8 vols.), 1913-25; Digest of Tennessee Decisions (vols. 1 to 157), 1929. Editor Arkansas Reports (vols. 53-105), 1891-1913, also vols. 141-190. Apptd. to digest Statutes of Ark., 1919. Died May 2, 1936.

CRAWFORD, Walter Joshua, lawyer; b. Mt. Vernon, Tex., Feb. 25, 1873; s. Joshua S. and Lou (Eddins) C.; A.B., U. of Tex., 1895, B.L., 1897; m. Cora Shults, Dec. 12, 1901. Admitted to Tex. bar, 1897, and practiced in Beaumont; mem. Smith & Crawford; v.p. Beaumont Hotel Co.; dir. Internat. Lumber & Export Co., Gulf Export & Trans. Co., First Nat. Bank. Referee in bankruptcy, 1897-1904; chmn. Jefferson Co. Dem. Com., 1903-05; mem. Tex. State Dem. Exec. Com., 1906-08. Home: Beaumont, Tex. Died Feb. 19, 1924.

CRAWFORD, William Alfred, newspaper man; b. Belfast, Ireland, Jan. 20, 1874; s. William and Margaret Archer (Kennedy) C.; ed. pub. and pvt. schs.; unmarried. With the Chicago Chronicle, 1900, city and news editor Chicago Inter Ocean, 1900-05; Washington corr., and night mgr. Associated Press, 1905-14; chief of Washington staff, Central News of America, and Central News of London, Ltd., 1914-24; accompanied President Wilson to Peace Conf. in Paris, and to Great Britain, Italy, France and Belgium; covered the Conf. on Limitation of Armaments (Washington, D.C.), 1921. Home: Washington, D.C. Died July 2, 1926.

CRAWFORD, William Campbell, educator; b. Warren, Me., Jan. 19, 1862; s. Alexander and Sarah Rebecca (Henderson) C.; A.B., Colby Coll., 1882, A.M., 1885, L.H.D., 1914; m. Cora A. King, Dec. 1891 (died Mar. 11, 1893); m. 2d, Mabel A. Spooner, July 11, 1898. Supt. schs., Waterville, Me., 1888-91; instr. pedagogy, Colby Coll., 1890-91; sec. Am. Inst. of Instrn., 1902-07; dir. Boston Trade School, 1911-35. Trustee Colby Coll., Brighton Five Cent Savings Bank. Republican. Unitarian. Home: Boston, Mass. Died Apr. 28, 1938.

CRAWFORD, William L., lawyer; b. Estell, Clay Co., Ky., Jan. 23, 1839; s. J. D. and Catharine C.; ed. McKinzie Inst., Clarksville, Tex.; studied law in office of D. B. Culberson, Jefferson, Tex.; admitted to bar, 1866, and began practice at Jefferson, Tex., same year; m. Kate Lester Lamar, Oct. 1, 1896. Lt. col. 19th Tex. Inf., C.S.A., 1861-65; mem. Constl. Conv., Tex., 1875; mem. law firm Crawford & Lamar (L. Q. C. Lamar), Dallas, 1903—. Home: Dallas, Tex. Died Feb. 17, 1920.

CRAWFORD, William Thomas, congressman; b. Haywood Co., N.C., June 1, 1856; acad. edn.; LL.B., U. of N.C., 1890; m. Inez Coman, 1892. Admitted to bar, 1891, and practiced at Waynesville, N.C. Mem. N.C. Ho. of Rep., 1884-88; presdl. elector, 1888, 1904; mem. 52d and 53d Congresses (1891-95), 9th N.C. Dist.; elected to 56th Congress, but was unseated by majority of 1 vote in Ho. of Rep., for Richmond Pearson; mem. 60th Congress (1907-09), 10th N.C. Dist.; Democrat. Home: Waynesville, N.C. Died 1913.

CRAWFORD, William Webb, banker; b. Eutaw, Ala., Aug. 27, 1867; s. Robert and Frances Elizabeth (Webb) C.; ed. pub. schs. of St. Louis, Mo.; m. Juliet I. Cherry, June 21, 1891. In banking business in Birmingham, Ala., 1887—; pres. Am. Trust & Savings Bank, 1905-30; vice-chmn. bd. First Nat. Bank of Birmingham; dir. Sloss Sheffield Steel & Iron Co., Alabama Great Southern Railroad Co. Democrat. Presbyn. Mason. Home: Birmingham, Ala. Died Jan. 15, 1934.

CRAWFORD-FROST, William Albert, clergyman; b. Owen Sound, Ont., Can., Oct. 29, 1863; s. William and Louisa (Crawford) F.; B.A., U. of Toronto, 1884, M.A., 1886; grad. divinity, Wycliffe Coll., Toronto, 1887; spl. course Baltimore Med. Coll., 1897; m. Damaris Constance Ings, Aug. 28, 1889; children—John, Ernest (dec.), William Arthur. Explored Rainy River country for Toronto Globe, 1886. Deacon, 1888, priest, 1889, P.E. Ch.; curate, St. Paul's, Charlottetown, P.E.I., 1888; rector, St. George's, New Glasgow, N.S., 1889-92, Ch. of the Redeemer, Merrick, L.I., 1892-96, Memorial Ch. of the Holy Comforter, Baltimore, 1896-1903; instr. chemistry, Baltimore Med. Coll., 1904-06; rector, St. Mary's, Emmorton, Md., 1910—. Invented a thought recorder, 1902; passenger car, 1904; trolley device, 1906; tri-plane, 1907; house cooling system, 1908; safety aeroplane, combined parachute and aeroplane, etc., 1911; automobile fender, 1912; spring auto wheel, 1913; poison gsa respirator, 1915; wave energy motor, 1920; torpedo obstructing projectile, 1921; elevated bumper, 1926; deeded claim against British Govt. in re poison gas respirator to Viscount Knutsford and Trustees of London Hospital, 1927. Original model of poison gas respirator, made June 1, 1915, installed in Tech. Mus., Edgewood Arsenal, Md., Jan. 23, 1933, at request of chief chemist. Author: Old Dogma in a New Light, 1896; The Philosophy of Integration, 1906; A New Theory of Evolution, 1926; The Way Out, 1931; Fourteen Points of a Wheat-based Currency, 1933; The Poison Theory of The Resurrection, 1935. Home: Baltimore, Md. Died Mar. 3, 1936.

CRAWLEY, Edwin Schofield, univ. prof.; b. Phila., July 31, 1862; s. Joseph S. and Elmira (Hammell) C.; B.S., U. of Pa., 1882, Ph.D., 1892; m. M. Annie Reckefus, Apr. 3, 1888 (died 1908); children—Mildred, Marion; m. 2d, Marjorie Bond, Mar. 1, 1924. Instr. civ. engring., 1882-85, instr. mathematics, 1885-89, asst. prof., 1889-99, Thomas A. Scott prof. mathematics, 1899—, U. of Pa. Author: Elements of Plane and Spherical Trigonometry, 1889, 96, 1907, 14; Tables of Logarithms, 1899; Short Course in Plane and Spherical Trigonometry, 1902; One Thousand Exercises in Trigonometry, 1914; Analytic Geometry (with Prof. H. B. Evans), 1918; Trigonometry (with Prof. H. B. Evans), 1922. Home: Philadelphia, Pa. Died Oct. 18, 1933.

CRAWSHAW, William Henry, univ. dean; b. Newburgh, N.Y., Nov. 6, 1861; s. Charles and Mary (Lodge) C.; A.B., Colgate U., 1887, A.M., 1889, L.H.D., 1930; student, Oxford U., Eng., 1900-01; traveled and studied in Europe, 1894, 1900-01, 1904, 1910-11; Litt.D., U. of Rochester, 1909; LL.D., Syracuse, 1910; m. Jennie Louise Broughton, Dec. 26, 1888. Instr. English and elocution, 1887-89, asso. prof. English, 1889-93, prof. English lit., 1893-1917, and prof. general literature, 1917-30, dean, 1897-1930, dean and prof. gen. lit. emeritus, 1930—, acting pres., 1897-99, 1907, 1908, pres. pro tem., 1908-09, Colgate U.; academic dean, Univ. Cruise Around World, 1929-30, exec. dean, 1930-31. Asso. mem. Nat. Inst. Arts and Letters. Baptist. Author: The Interpretation of Literature, 1896; Dryden's Palamon and Arcite, 1898; Literary Interpretation of Life, 1900; The Making of English Literature, 1907, rev. edit., 1924; The Genius of Christ, 1917; The Indispensable Soul, 1931; My Colgate Years, 1937. Home: Hamilton, N.Y. Died July 2, 1940.

CREED, Wigginton Ellis, lawyer, public utility executive; b. Fresno, Calif., Feb. 8, 1877; s. William Henry and Georgia Hindman (Ellis) C.; A.B., U. of Calif., 1898; m. Isabel Hooper, Oct. 15, 1904; children—Stanwood Cooper (dec.), Isabel Payson, Patricia Perry, Elizabeth Ellis, Margery Meserve. Began law practice at San Francisco, 1900; mem. Titus, Wright & Creed, 1902-07, Titus & Creed, 1907-15, Creed, Jones & Dall, 1915-22; retired from practice of law, 1922. Assisted in reorganizing Peoples Water Co., 1915-17, and was made pres. reorganized co., East Bay Water Co., 1917; also pres. Pacific Gas & Electric Co., C. A. Hooper & Co. (lumber), Columbia Steel Co.; dir. Wells Fargo Nev. Nat. Bank, Associated Oil Co., East Bay Water Co., and various other corps. Regent U. of Calif., 1918-20; trustee Calif. Instn. for Deaf and Blind, 1905-13; trustee Hooper Foundation, and Mills Coll. Republican. Episcopalian. Home: Piedmont, Calif. Died Aug. 6, 1927.

CREEGAN, Charles Cole, college pres.; b. Brighton, Ia., May 29, 1850; s. Daniel and Mary Ann (McKee) C.; B.S., Lebanon Normal Coll., 1869, A.M., 1872; B.D., Oberlin Theol. Sem., 1879; (D.D., Syracuse U., 1886); m. Melissa W. Williams, May 10, 1872 (died July 31, 1897); 2d, Harriet Miriam Stephenson, Oct. 7, 1899. Ordained Congl. ministry, 1875; pastor, Wakeman, O., 1875-80; supt. home missions, Colo., 1880-82; sec. home missions, New York, 1882-88; field sec., 1888-93; dist. sec. and gen. agt., 1893-1909, A.B.C.F.M.; pres. Fargo (N.D.) Coll., 1909—. Trustee Internat. Med. Missionary Soc.; founder and dir. Mindena Med. Assn.; trustee Hospital Talas, Turkey; dir. Am. Coll., Madura, India, Am. and Foreign Christian Union, New York; corporate mem. A.B.C.F.M. Author: Great Missionaries of the Church, 1896; Pioneer Missionaries, 1903. Home: Fargo, N.D. Died Jan. 3, 1939.

CREELMAN, James, editor; b. at Montreal, Can., Nov. 12, 1859; ed. Canadian pub. schs. and Talmage's Lay Theol. Coll.; m. Alice L. Buell, 1891. In service of New York Herald as reporter, corr. and editorial writer, 1887-89; editor London edition, 1890. Paris edition, 1891-92, New York Evening Telegram; British editor Cosmopolitan Magazine, 1893; war corr. New York World, Japanese War, 1894; New York Journal, Græco-Turkish War, 1897. Cuban War, 1898, Philippine War, 1899; captured Spanish flag and was shot and almost mortally wounded after he received surrender of Spanish commandant at El Caney, Cuba, 1898; had charge editorial page and later was Washington corr. New York Journal; spl. and editorial writer New York World, 1900-06; asso. editor Pearson's Magazine, 1906-10; pres. Municipal Civil Service Commn., New York, 1911-12; asso. editor New York Evening Mail, 1912—. Mem. New York Bd. Edn., 1911—. Has interviewed Leo XIII, King George of Greece, the Emperor of Korea, President Faure, Prince Bismarck, H. M. Stanley, Louis Kossuth, Count Tolstoi; made extensive investigation of massacre of Armenians in Asia Minor, 1909. Author: On the Great Highway, 1901; Eagle Blood, 1902; Why We Love Lincoln, 1908; Diaz, Master of Mexico, 1911. Home: New York, N.Y. Died Feb. 12, 1915.

CREEVEY, Caroline Alathea Stickney (Mrs. John K. Creevey), author; b. Union City, Mich.; d. John Newton and Mary (Hale) Stickney; spent childhood and youth in Rockville, Conn.; A.B., Wheaton Sem. (now Wheaton Coll.), Norton, Mass., 1863; m. John Kennedy Creevey, of New York, Aug. 20, 1866. Author: Recreations in Botany, 1893; Flowers of Field, Hill and Swamp, 1895; Harper's Guide to Wild Flowers, 1912; Daughter of the Puritans, 1916; At Random, 1920. Home: New York, N.Y. Died 1920.

CREHORE, William Williams, civil engr.; b. Cleveland, Feb. 3, 1864; s. John Davenport and Lucy (Williams) C.; A.B., Yale, 1886, Ph.B. (Sheffield Scientific Sch.), 1888; m. Anna Ballard, July 11, 1888. Prin. Hemenway High Sch., Norfolk, Va., 1888-90; practicing as civ. engr., 1890—; pres. Typewriting Telegraph Co., 1906—. Author: Tables and Diagrams for Use of Engineers and Architects, 1894; Protection's Brood, 1912. Contributor to engring. jours.; also chapter on Modern High Buildings in DuBois' Stresses in Framed Structures, 1896; chapter on Theoretical Considerations of Design in Foster's Wooden Trestle Bridges, 1894. Home: Westfield, N.J. Died Sept. 13, 1918.

CREIGHTON, Elmer Ellsworth Farmer, electrical engr.; b. Vallejo, Calif., 1873; A.B., Leland Stanford Jr. U., 1895, E.E., 1897; Sorbonne, Paris, 1898; École Supérieure de l'Électricité, Paris, 1898-1900; unmarried. Engr. exptl. dept. Stanley Elec. Mfg. Co., Pittsfield, Mass., 1902-04; protective apparatus developments and research, Gen. Elec. Co., 1904; asst. prof. of elec. engring., Union U., 1904-06; consulting engr. with Gen. Electric Co., also inventor and developer of elec. protective apparatus, 1912—. Author of many tech. papers pub. in Trans. Am. Inst. Elec. Engr. from 1906. Home: Schenectady, N.Y. Died Jan. 12, 1929.

CREIGHTON, James Edwin, univ. prof.; b. Pictou, N.S., Apr. 8, 1861; s. John and Mary C. (O'Brien) C.; A.B., Dalhousie Coll., Halifax, 1887; student univs. of Leipzig and Berlin; Ph.D., Cornell, 1892; LL.D., Queen's U., 1903, and Dalhousie U., 1914; m. Katherine F. McLean, Dec. 20, 1892. Instr. philosophy, 1889-92, asso. prof., 1892-95, prof. logic and metaphysics, 1895—, and dean of the Graduate School, 1914-23, Cornell U. Am. editor Kant-Studien, 1896—; co-editor, 1894-1902, editor, 1892—, Philosophical Review. Pres. Am. Philos. Soc. 1902-03. Author: An Introductory Logic, 1898, 1909. Translator: Wundt's Human and Animal Psychology (with Edward B. Titchener), 1894; Paulsen't Kant—His Life and Philosophy (with Albert Lefevre), 1902. Home: Ithaca, N.Y. Died Died Oct. 8, 1924.

CREIGHTON, John Thraie, lawyer; b. Springfield, Ill., July 17, 1884; s. James Asbury and Mary Catherine (Newman) C.; A.B., U. of Mich., 1908, J.D., 1910; m. Helen Davidson Jones, Oct. 22, 1921. Began practice with Brown & Hay, Springfield, 1910; mem. firm Brown, Hay & Creighton, 1912-21. With War Trade Bd., Jan. 1, 1918-June 1919; specialized in investigations of enemy controlled chem. companies in U.S. and later chief of investigations War Trade Intelligence; rep. of War Trade Bd. on advisory sales com. of alien property custodian; apptd. spl. asst. to atty. gen. of U.S., June 1919, in charge Alien Enemy Div. and of Bur. of Investigation; directed parolment and repatriation of interned alien enemies; reorganized Bur. of Investigation, 1920-21; resigned from Dept. of Justice, 1921; with trust dept. Nat. City Bank of New York, 1921—, and v.p. City Bank Farmers Trust Co., 1930—. Trustee Legal Research Foundation of U. of Mich. Mem. govt. relations com. Nat. Research Council, 1919-21. Founder, dir. Grand Central Sch. of Art. Mem. exec. com. N.Y. Corporate Fiduciaries Assn., 1930-34, v.p., 1936-38, pres., 1938-40. Home: Ossining, N.Y. Died May 13, 1941.

CREIGHTON, William Henry, engineer; b. Cincinnati, June 29, 1859; s. Peter and Mary A. (Woods) C.; grad. U.S. Naval Acad., 1882; m. Mathilda Mathis, Dec. 26, 1904; 1 son, William Henry. Asst. engr. U.S. Steamships Lackawanna and Mohican, to 1887; prof. engring., Purdue U., 1887-91; chief engr. U.S.C.S. Blake, 1891; retired from naval service, 1892; prof. mech. and sugar engring, 1894-1930, dean Coll. of Tech., 1911-19, Tulane U.; ordered to active duty U.S.N., Apr. 6, 1917. Democrat. Catholic. Author: The Steam Engine and Other Heat Motors, 1907, 3d edit., 1911. Has taken out number of patents on sugar making machinery. Home: New Orleans, La. Died Jan. 24, 1933.

CREITZ, Charles Erwin, church official; b. Lynnport, Pa., Oct. 24, 1865; s. Alvin F. and Caroline (Oswald) C.; A.B., Franklin and Marshall Coll., Lancaster, Pa., 1889, D.D., 1910; grad. Eastern Theol. Sem., Lancaster, 1892; m. Wilhelmina Schafer, Aug. 30, 1900; children—George Alvin, Mary Louise. Ordained ministry Ref. Ch. in U.S., 1892; pastor Weissport, Pa., 1892-95, Huntingdon, Pa., 1895-99; field agent Board of Home Missions, 1899-1900; pastor St. Paul's Memorial Reformed Ch., Reading, Pa., 1900-37, retired. Pres. Bd. of Foreign Missions Ref. Ch. in U.S., 1924—; visited Japan and China, 1926. Trustee and pres. Bethany Orphans' Home; pres. Hope Rescue Mission. Democrat. Home: Easton, Pa. Died Sept. 20, 1940.

CREMER, Jacob Theodoor, diplomat; b. Zwolle, Holland, June 30, 1847; s. Jacob Theodoor and Louise (Toewater) C.; ed. in Holland; m. Annie Hermine Hogan, of Penang, Straits Settlements, Jan. 16, 1873. Went to Netherlands, East Indies, in employ of Netherlands Trading Soc., 1868; head mgr. Deli Co. (tobacco plantations), 1871-83; returned to Amsterdam as head mgr. Deli Ry. Co., 1883; mem. 2d Chamber States General (Ho. of Rep.), 1884-97; minister for the colonies, 1897-1901; again mem. 2d Chamber States General, 1901-05; pres. Netherlands Trading Soc., at Amsterdam, 1906-12; mem. 1st Chamber States General (Senate), 1912—; spl. envoy of Queen of Netherlands to Hudson-Fulton Celebration, New York, 1909; M.P. and E.E. from Netherlands to U.S., 1918—. Mem. bd. administrators Suez Canal Co., Paris, France; mem., later pres., Internat. Opium Confs., The Hague, 1911, 12, 13, 14. Died Aug. 14, 1923.

CRENSHAW, Bolling Hall, prof. mathematics; b. Greenville, Ala., May 18, 1867; s. Walter Henry and Sarah (Anderson) C.; B.S., Ala. Polytechnic Institute, 1889, M.E., 1890, LL.D., 1932; m. Willie Glenn, Apr. 29, 1896; children—Mary Glenn (Mrs. Carl E. Wideberg), Sarah Hall. Railroad construction work, 1890-91; instr. mech. engring. and mathematics, 1891-96, asso. prof., 1896-1905, prof. mathematics and head of dept., 1905—, Ala. Poly. Inst. Democrat. Presbyn. Co-Author: Crenshaw & Derr's Plane Trigonometry, 1923; Crenshaw & Killebrew's Analytic Geometry and Calculus, 1925; Crenshaw & Harkin's College Algebra, 1929; Crenshaw, Pirenian & Simpson's Mathematics of Finance, 1930. Home: Auburn, Ala. Died Nov. 25, 1935.

CRENSHAW, H(ervey) F(iles), lawyer; b. Mongomery, Ala., Aug. 6, 1875; s. James Hervey and Mary Childers (Files) C.; B.S., Vanderbilt U., 1896; Legal edn. at Georgetown U. and private study; m. Pauline Smith, Dec. 26, 1900; children—Hervey Files, James Chauncey, Hathaway (wife of Lt. Robert Goldthwaite, U.S.N.). Began as school teacher, 1896; admitted to Ala. bar, 1907, practiced since then in Montgomery; mem. Rushton, Crenshaw & Rushton; v.p. Brown Printing Co., Montgomery. Commr. on Uniform State Laws. Trustee Vanderbilt U. Pres. Ala. State Bar Assn., 1935-36, Montgomery Bar Assn., 1925-26. Democrat. Presbyn. Home: Montgomery, Ala. Died Mar. 22, 1938.

CRESSEY, George Croswell, clergyman; b. Buxton, Me., Apr. 1, 1856; s. George W. and Sarah (Croswell) C.; A.B., Bowdoin, 1875, A.M., 1878, D.D., 1899; Ph.D., U. of Leipzig, 1880; grad. Andover Theol. Sem., 1884; m. Lilian Maling, Apr. 19, 1888. Prof. modern langs., Washburn Coll., Topeka, Kan., 1880-82; entered Unitarian ministry, 1884; pastor, Bangor, Me., 1884-90, Salem, Mass., 1890-96, Northampton, Mass., 1896-1901, Portland, Ore., 1901-06, Effra Rd. Ch., London, 1907-13, Ch. of the Redeemer, New Brighton, N.Y., 1914-24. Lecturer Unitarian Coll., Manchester, Eng., 1912, Meadville Theol. Sch., 1914 and 1928-35. Del. of Am. Unitarian Assn. to Nat. Unitarian Assembly, in Eng., 1906, 27, American British and Fgn. Unit. Assns. to Nat. Liberal Conv., Holland, 1907. Author: The Essential Man, 1895; Mental Evolution, 1894; Philosophy of Religion, 1892; The Doctrine of Immortality in Liberal Thought, 1897; Soul-Power, 1899; Outline of Unitarian Belief, 1905; A Talk with Young People on Liberal Religious Thoughts, 1912; The Distinctive Thought of Liberal Christianity, 1921. Home: Stoughton, Mass. Died Oct. 26, 1938.

CRESSLER, Alfred Miller, banker; b. Fort Wayne, Ind., Sept. 19, 1877; s. Alfred David and Elizabeth Esther (Murray) C.; prep. edn., Hill Sch.; B.A., Yale, 1902, M.A., 1908; m. Jeannette Morton Stacey, Apr. 21, 1917. With Kerr Murray Mfg. Co., gas plant equipment, Fort Wayne, 1903-13, treas., 1906-13; with W. H. Fillmore & Co., investment bankers, Cincinnati, O., 1916-25, mem. firm, 1921-25; mem. Haydock, Cressler, Lamson & Co., investment counsel, Cincinnati, 1926-29; v.p. and investment officer, Central Trust Co., 1930—; dir. The Stearns & Foster Co.; dir. and v.p., The Stacey Engineering Co. Served with Ordnance Dept., U.S.A., Cincinnati dist., 1917-18; mem. Claims Bd., 1919. Trustee Cincinnati Art Mus. (treas. 1930—), Mercantile Library, Better Housing League (treas. 1926—), Cincinnati Soc. Natural History, Diocese of Episcopal Ch. of Southern Ohio (treas. 1934—). Republican. Episcopalian. Home: Cincinnati, O. Died Nov. 19, 1939.

CRESSON, W(illiam) Penn, author, diplomat; b. Claymount, Del., Sept. 17, 1873; s. Hilbourne Thompson (M.D.) and Elizabeth (Vaux) C.; m. Margaret French, Jan. 10, 1921; student U. of Pa., 1895, École des Beaux Arts, Paris, 1897-1902 (student of the 1st class); followed Prof. Sorel's course at the École de Sciences Politiques, 1902; Ph.D., Columbia, N.Y., 1922. Practiced architecture, Washington, D.C., 1905-07; ranching in Nev., 1907-09; sec. of Am. Legation at Lima, Peru, 1909-12; 2ed sec. Am. Embassy, London, 1912-13; sec. Am. Legation, Quito, Ecuador, 1913-14, Panama, 1914-15; sec. Am. Embassy, Petrograd, May 21, 1915-17; sec. Am. Legation, Lisbon, Portugal, Aug. 1917; retired; asst. prof. internat. law Princeton, 1920-21; lecturer on diplomatic history, Georgetown U., 1924-27; Fletcher prof. of internat. law and diplomacy, Tufts Coll., 1927-28, 1928-29. Apptd. a diplomatic sec. Conf. on Limitation of Armament, Washington, 1921-22, and of VI Pan-Am. Conf., Havana, 1928. Commd. lt. A.S., S.O.R.C., Sept. 1917; capt. A.S., Jan. 1918; chief Am. Mil. Mission Belgian General Hdqrs.; maj. M.I.O.R.C. Decorated Chevalier Order of Leopold, with Croix de Guerre. Republican. Episcopalian. Author: Persia—The Awakening East, 1908; The Cossacks—Their History and Country, 1919; The Holy Alliance—The European Background of the Monroe Doctrine, 1922; Diplomatic Portraits, 1923; Francis Dana—A Puritan Diplomat of the Court of Catherine the Great, 1931. Home: Stockbridge, Mass. Died May 12, 1932.

CRESSY, Wilfred Wesley, prof. English, Oberlin Coll., March 8, 1899—; b. Bucksport, Me., July 8, 1867; grad. Harvard, 1892 (A.M., Cornell); m. Lilian R. Fitz, June 3, 1890 (died Feb. 16, 1897). Supt. public schools, Heron Lake, Minn., 1887-88; same, Jackson, Minn., 1888-90; tutor in English, 1892-93, instructor of same, Oberlin Acad., 1893-94; asso. prof. English, Oberlin Coll., 1894-99. Dean of college dept., 1899. Home: Oberlin, O. Died 1909.

CRESSY, Will Martin, actor, playwright; b. Bradford, N.H., Oct. 29, 1863; s. Frank and Annette Miriam (Ring) C.; ed. pub. schs., Concord, N.H.; m. Blanche May Dayne, Jan. 19, 1890. Made first appearance on stage at Norwalk, Conn., Sept. 19, 1889, in Frost & Fanshawe Repertoire Company; later with numerous companies, including 6 yrs. in "The Old Homestead"; in vaudeville (with wife) Dec. 19, 1899—, visiting all prin. countries of world. Has written 170 one-act plays. Served as an entertainer with A.E.F., in France, 8 months. Home: St. Petersburg, Fla. Died May 8, 1930.

CREW, William Binford, judge; b. Chester Hill, Morgan Co., O., Apr. 1, 1852; s. Fleming and Sarah (Patterson) C.; ed. Westtown Coll., Ohio State and Union Law Sch., 1874; m. Elizabeth Worrall, May 9, 1876. Pros. atty. Morgan Co., O., 1876; mem. Ohio Legislature, 1889; judge Ct. of Common Pleas, 8th Jud. Dist., 1891-1902; apptd. judge Supreme Ct., Ohio, July 19, 1902, to fill vacancy caused by death of Hon. M. J. Williams; elected judge, Nov. 4, 1902. Republican. Home: Cleveland, O. Died 1912.

CREWS, Ralph, lawyer; b. Mt. Vernon, Ill., Mar. 29, 1876; s. Seth Floyd and Helena Ridgway (Slocum) C.; Hyde Park High Sch., Chicago; LL.B., Chicago Coll. of Law, 1897; m. Elizabeth Stuart Sherman, June 17, 1901; children—Mary Arthur, Elizabeth Ridgway, Ralph. Admitted to Ill. bar, 1897, and practiced at Chicago until 1917; mem. law firm Shearman & Sterling, New York, 1919—. Dir. National City Co., Old Ben Coal Corp., Austin Machinery Corp., Brokaw & Co. Maj., lt. col. and col. Ordnance Dept., U.S.A., 1917-18; in charge contract sect., later spl. asst. to chief of ordnance, Washington, D.C. Republican. Episcopalian. Home: New York, N.Y. Died Sept. 6, 1926.

CRICHTON, Alexander Fraser, banker; b. N.Y. City, Nov. 2, 1878; s. Alexander Fraser and Harriet (Steele) C.; ed. Poly. Inst. of Brooklyn; m. Florence Elizabeth Ametrano, Nov. 2, 1898; children—Florence Elizabeth (Mrs. Victor McLean Day), Lillian Fraser (Mrs. Brooks Darlington). Supt. Planet Mills, Brooklyn, 1898-1900, treas. and gen. mgr., 1900-11; owner Wilmington (Del.) Jute Mills, 1911—; pres. Union Nat. Bank, Wilmington, 1921-35: Republican. Presbyn. Home: Wilmington, Del. Died Apr. 26, 1939.

CRILE, Dennis Rider Wood, surgeon; b. Baltic, O., May 27, 1891; s. Austin D. and Winifred Augusta (Wood) C.; B.S., U. of Wis., 1914; M.D., Harvard, 1917; m. Mary Dorothea Webb, Jan. 1, 1919; children—Dennis Michael, Dorothea Mary. Asst. prof. surgery, U. of Ill. Coll. Medicine. Served in France and Belgium, with Harvard Unit under British May 1916-Aug. 1918; in Eng., Aug. 1918-July 1919; commd. hon. capt. Royal Army M.C. Contbr. to medical jours., and chapters dealing with compound fractures in Ochsner's Surgical Diagnosis and Treatment. Originator of method of resuscitation of dying persons by injection of adrenalin into the heart. Died Mar. 21, 1937.

CRIM, John William Henry, lawyer; b. Loudoun Co., Va., Mar. 31, 1879; s. John Joseph and Sarah Gulielma (Brown) C.; normal grad.; William and Mary College, LL.D., 1926; LL.B., N.Y. Law Sch., 1906; m. Mary Amelia Goodyear, Jan. 12, 1910; 1 dau., Barbara. Admitted N.Y. bar, 1907, spl. agt. Dept. of Justice, 1906; spl. asst., asst. U.S. atty., or spl. asst. U.S. atty. gen., in N.Y., 1907-13, conducting cases against a number of railroads and large shippers and against various corps. and pools under act to regulate commerce and anti-trust act; practiced in N.Y. City, 1913-21; defended Charles S. Mellen and other dirs. in case of U.S. vs. N.Y.,N.H. &H. R.R. Co.; spl. asst. U.S. atty., 1921; investigated income tax frauds, collecting $1,000,000 for the Govt.; asst. atty. gen. of U.S., 1921-23; personally conducted investigations resulting in conviction of Congressman John Langley, Gaston B. Means and others; directed investigation resulting in indictment of Thomas P. Miller, former alien property custodian; coöperated in investigation resulting in impeachment of U.S. Judge English; as spl. asst. atty. gen., 1924-25, prosecuted Charles R. Forbes and John W. Thompson for fraud in U.S. Vets.' Bur. Home: Martinsville, N.J. Died July 2, 1933.

CRIMMINS, John Daniel, contractor; b. at New York, N.Y., May 18, 1844; s. Thomas and Johanna (O'Keefe) C.; ed. St. Francis Xavier Coll. Partner in his father's contracting business, 1864; in 1873, head of the firm; built many important public works in New York and elsewhere, often employing as many as 12,000 men; has been New York City park commr. and Dem. presdl. elector; mem. Constl. Conv.; several times chosen as arbitrator to settle strikes. Pres. Met. Traction Co., Essex & Hudson Land Improvement Co.; v.p., dir. New York Mortgage & Security Co.; dir. 5th Av. Bk., Chelsea Realty Co., U.S. Realty & Improvement Co., Pa. Tunnel & Terminal R.R. Co., U.S. Realty & Improvement Co., Encyclopædia Press; trustee Provident Loan Soc. of N.Y. Trustee or mgr. in a number of Catholic charitable instns. Created Knight Commander Order of St. Gregory the Great by Pope Leo XIII, 1901. Home: New York, N.Y. Died Nov. 9, 1917.

CRIPPEN, Henry Durrell, pres. The Bon Ami Co.; b. Lawrence, Kan., July 6, 1876; s. Joseph J. and Helen Francis (Durell) C.; ed. St. Johns Mil. Acad., Salina, Kan., Jarvis Hall, Denver, Colo., and Phillips Exeter (N.H.) Acad.; m. Marie Virginia Huston, June 15, 1898; 1 son, Huston Durell. Began as clk., 1896; became treas., sec. and gen. mgr. Bon Ami Co., N.Y. City, then pres. and gen. mgr.; v.p. and gen. mgr. The Orford Soap Co., Bon Ami, Ltd. of Can.; pres. The Whitehall Co.; vice chmn. bd. The Bon Ami Co. of Australia, Ltd. Pres. and dir. Associated Grocery Manufacturers of America, 1928, dir. and treas., 1931—. Home: New York, N.Y. Died Oct. 26, 1935.

CRISP, Charles R., congressman; b. Ellaville, Ga., Oct. 19, 1870; s. Charles Frederick and Clara (Burton) C.; pub. sch. edn.; m. Jennie Hollis, Dec. 5, 1907; 1 son, Charles Frederick. Admitted to Ga. bar; elected to 54th Congress to serve out unexpired term of father, late speaker of the House; judge of the City Court, Americus, 1900-11; resigned to accept position of parliamentarian 62d Congress, under Speaker Clark; parliamentarian Dem. Nat. Conv., Baltimore, 1912; elected mem. 63d to 72d Congresses (1913-33), 3d Ga. Dist.; resigned, Oct. 7, 1932; mem. U.S. Tariff Commn., Oct. 1932-Jan. 1933; resigned to practice law in Washington. Methodist. Home: Americus, Ga. Died Feb. 7, 1937.

CRISWELL, George Stuart, judge; b. Venango Co., Pa., Apr. 7, 1850; s. Robert Chesney and Hannah (Nickle) C.; ed. pub. schs., and acad.; m. Flora Smith, Nov. 26, 1879; children—Chesney H., Elisha W., George S., Clarence C. Read law with late Henry A. Miller; admitted to Pa. bar, Sept. 30, 1875; practiced alone at Franklin, Pa., 1875-87. Mem. Pa. Ho. of Rep., 1885-88 (chmn. Judiciary General Com., session of 1887); apptd., 1895, by Gov. Hastings, pres. judge of Venango Co. (28th Jud. Dist.), and elected to same office for term of 10 yrs., Nov. 1895; reelected, 1905, 1915. Republican. Mem. Pa. N.G., 1876-82. Trustee Edinboro State Normal Sch. Presbyn. Mason. Home: Franklin, Pa. Died 1928.

CRITTENDEN, Thomas Theodore, lawyer; b. Shelby Co., Ky., Jan. 2, 1832; s. Henry and Anna Maria C.; ed. Cloverport, Ky., and Centre Coll., Danville, Ky., grad. 1855; m. Carrie W. Jackson, Nov. 13, 1856. Lt. col. 7th Mo. cav., from May, 1862, to close Civil war; after war practiced law; filled an unexpired term as atty. gen. of Mo.; mem. Congress, 1877-81, 7th dist., Mo.; gov. Mo., 1881-85; U.S. consul gen. at city of Mexico, 1893-97; resumed practice of law. Home: Kansas City, Mo. Died 1909.

CROASDALE, Stuart, mining engr.; b. Delaware Water Gap, Pa., Nov. 21, 1866; s. Evan Thomas and Ellen (Andre) C.; of early Quaker ancestry in America; B.S. in chemistry, Lafayette Coll., Easton, Pa., 1888, M.S., Ph.D., 1891; m. Elma G. Shaw, 1891; children—Dorothy, Ernest Shaw, Evan Thomas. Was chief chemist, Holden Lixiviation Works, Aspen, Colo., 1891-93, Gillette (Colo.) Reduction Works, 1894-95, Globe Smelting & Refining Co., Denver, 1896-1900; cons. practice, 1900—; cons. engr. Anaconda Copper Co., Mont., 1903, Burro Mt. Copper Co., 1903-07, Calumet & Ariz. Copper Co., 1912-13, and many other cos., including Utah Copper Co., Nipissing Mines Co., etc.; pres. Alma Gold Corporation, Denver, Colo. Pioneer in smelter smoke investigation, and commercial leaching of copper ores; inventor, volatilization process for treatment of ores, improved process for concentration of ores, hydometallurgical process for teatment of mercury ores, etc. Republican. Home: Denver, Colo. Died Sept. 30, 1934.

CROCKER, Charles Henry, bookseller; b. Sacramento, Calif., Aug. 29, 1865; s. Henry S. and Clara Ellen (Swinerton) C.; U. of Calif., 1883-86; m. Carlotta L. Steiner, June 21, 1905. Treas., 1886-1904, pres., 1904-19, H. S. Crocker Co., wholesale stationers and printers, San Francisco. Lt. comdr. U.S.N. R.F., World War. Republican. Home: San Francisco, Calif. Died May 6, 1935.

CROCKER, Francis Bacon, electrical engr.; b. New York, N.Y., July 4, 1861; s. Henry H. and Mary (Eldridge) C.; E.M., Columbia, 1882, Ph.D., 1894 (hon. M.S., 1914); unmarried. Instr. elec. engring., 1889-92, adj. prof., 1892-93, prof., 1893-1914, Columbia. Founder and v.p. C. & C. (Curtis & Crocker) Electric Co., 1887, and Crocker-Wheeler Electric Co., 1889. Pres. Am. Inst. Elec. Engrs., 1897-98, N.Y. Elec. Soc., 1889-92. Author: Management of Electrical Machinery, 8th edit., 1908; Electric Lighting, 8th edit., 1908; Electric Motors, 2d edition, 1911. Home: Ampere, N.J. Died July 9, 1921.

CROCKER, George, capitalist; s. Charles C. Pres. and dir. Capay Valley Land Co., Carbon Hill Coal Co., Crocker Estate Co. (San Francisco), Rocky Mountain Coal & Iron Co., Zwoyer Fuel Co.; v.p. and dir. Guatemala Central R.R. Co., Kansas City, Mexico & Orient Ry. Co., Oakland Water Front Co., Pacific Improvement Co.; dir. Internat. Banking Corp., Crocker-Woolworth Nat. Bank (San Francisco), Cuba R.R. Co., Detroit City Gas Co., Federal Sugar Co., etc. Home: New York, N.Y. Died 1909.

CROCKER, George Glover, lawyer; b. at Boston, Mass., Dec. 15, 1843; s. Uriel and Sarah Kidder (Haskell) C.; A.B., Harvard, 1864, A.M., 1867, LL.B., 1866; m. Annie Bliss Keep, June 19, 1875. Admitted to bar, 1867, and practiced at Boston; dir. Plymouth Cordage Co., Sampson Cordage Works. Mem. Mass. Ho. of Rep., 1873-75, Senate, 1880-84 (pres. 1883-84); chmn. Mass. Bd. R.R. Commrs., 1887-92; chmn. Boston Transit Commn., 1894—; chmn. joint bd. on Met. Improvements, 1909-10. Author: Principles of Procedure in Deliberative Bodies, 1894; From the Stage-coach to the Railroad Train and the Street Car, 1900. Home: Boston, Mass. Died May 26, 1913.

CROCKER, Henry E.; b. Barnstable, Mass., June 13, 1848; s. Wilson and Elizabeth C. (Wright) C.; Wesleyan Acad., Wilbraham, Mass., 1869-70; M.A., Bates Coll., Me.; m. Helen Howard Scudder, July 28, 1870. Capt. of barge on Hudson River at 16; teacher on Indian reservation; later in Mass., becoming supt. schs., Dedham; with Ginn & Co., pubs., 3 yrs.; v.p. Fisk Teachers' Agency, and mgr. New York office, 1891—. Mayor of Haworth, N.J., 2 terms, 1908-12. Republican. Conglist. Home: Haworth, N.J. Died Feb. 11, 1918.

CROCKER, Uriel Haskell, lawyer; b. Boston, Mass., Dec. 24, 1832; s. Uriel C.; grad. Harvard, 1853; practiced law in Boston; m. Clara G. Ballard, 1861; m. 2d, Annie J. Fitz, 1893. Author: Notes on Common Forms; Notes on the Public Statutes of Massachusetts (two books of Massachusetts law). Home: Boston, Mass. Died 1902.

CROCKER, William Henry, banker; b. Sacramento, Calif., Jan. 13, 1861; s. Charles and Mary Ann (Deming) C.; Ph.B., Sheffield Scientific Sch. (Yale), 1882; m. Ethel W. Sperry, Oct. 6, 1886. Engaged in the banking business, 1883—; pres. Crocker First Nat. Bank, The Crocker Investment Co., Provident Securities Co., Crocker Estate Co., Pacific Improvement Co.; dir. of Pacific Telegraph & Telephone Co., Met. Life Ins. Co., Pacific Mutual Life Insurance Co., Pacific Gas & Electric Co. Regent U. of Calif. Mason (33°). Home: Burlingame, Calif. Died Sept. 25, 1937.

CROCKETT, Charles Winthrop, educator; b. Macon, Ga., Oct. 6, 1862; s. Earlsworth and Elizabeth (Holden) C.; A.B., Mercer U., Macon, Ga., 1879, A.M., 1886 (LL.D., 1913); C.E., Rensselaer Poly. Inst., 1884; m. Marie Merritt Haydock, Dec. 1, 1887; children—Gladys M. (Mrs. F. N. Billingsley), Charles H., Doris L., Winthrop M. Asst. prof. of mathematics and astronomy, Rensselaer Polytechnic Inst., 1884-93; prof. same, 1893-1934, emeritus. Democrat. Christian Scientist. Author: Explanation of the Principles and Operation of the Mannheim Slide Rule, 1891; Calculus Notes, 1903; Plane and Spherical Trigonometry, 1896; Logarithmic and Trigonometric Tables, 1896; Methods for Earthwork Computations, 1908; Mathematical Review, Arithmetic, Algebra, Geometry, 1912; Questions on Astronomy, 1913; Algebra Review, 1924; Elements of Spherical and Practical Astronomy, 1928. Home: Troy, N.Y. Died Dec. 30, 1936.

CROCKETT, Eugene Anthony, otologist; b. Calais, Me., Oct. 22, 1867; s. Frederick and Susan (George) C.; M.D., Harvard, 1891; m. Elizabeth Le Bourgeois, July 28, 1900. Has served as prof. otology, Harvard Med. Sch., and chief of staff Eye and Ear Infirmary of same. Commr. Red Cross Service, Italy, 1917-18; maj. Med. Corps, O.R.C. Home: Ipswich, Mass. Died June 13, 1932.

CROCKETT, Walter Hill, author; b. Colchester, Vt., June 26, 1870; s. Charles Whipple and Martha Hannah (Hill) C.; ed. Mt. Hermon (Mass.) School; hon. A.M., Middlebury (Vt.) College, 1928; m. Kate Manville Chamberlain, June 14, 1902; children—Eleanor Alice (Mrs. Elvidge F. Cleveland), Charles Newton, Elizabeth. Mem. editorial staff Burlington Free Press, 1895-1901; news editor St. Albans (Vt.) Messenger, 1901-09; mng. editor Montpelier Journal, 1909-13; dir. Vt. State Publicity Bur., 1913—; lecturer on journalism and Vermont history, U. of Vt. Rep. presdl. elector, 1912; pres. Bd. of Aldermen, Burlington, 1925-27; elected state senator, 1927 and 1929; chmn. State Constl. Revision Com., 1929—. Conglist. Author: History of Vermont; History of Lake Champlain; Life of George F. Edmunds. Home: Burlington, Vt. Died Dec. 8, 1931.

CROCKETT, William Day, author, educator; b. Sterling, N.Y., June 16, 1869; s. John Boyd and Emily Baxter (Robinson) C.; A.B., Hamilton Coll., 1890, A.M., 1895; grad. Auburn Theol. Sem., 1893; A.M., U. of Pa., 1915; student U. of Pa., 1914-16, Columbia, 1917, Am. Acad. in Rome, 1922-23; hon. Pd.D., Temple U., 1920; m. Sarah Frances Gates, Sept. 12, 1911. Ordained Presbyn. ministry, 1893; pastor Canton, Pa., later Carpinteria, Calif., until 1902; prof. English lit., State Normal Sch., Mansfield, Pa., 1902-06; with Pa. State Coll., 1906—, as instr. English and history, 1906-07, English and Latin, 1907-09, asst. prof., 1909-18, asso. prof. Latin, 1918-20, prof. Latin lang. and lit., 1920—, also head classical lang. dept. Republican. Author: A Harmony of Samuel, Kings and Chronicles, 1895. Author and editor (with Wm. J. Rolfe) of A Satchel Guide to Europe, annual edits., 1924—. Home: State College, Pa. Died Oct. 19, 1930.

CROCKETT, William Goggin, pharm. chemist; b. Tazewell, Va., Jan. 9, 1888; s. John Ward and Mary Grace (Hopkins) C.; student Hampden-Sydney Coll., 1906-08, D.Sc., 1939; Pharm.D., Columbia U., 1913; M.S., New York U., 1917; m. Ethel May Dulin, Dec. 27, 1919; 1 dau., Mary Leila. Chemist Dept. of Health, New York, 1914-16; asst. in chemistry, New York U., 1916-17; chemist E. R. Squibb & Sons, Brooklyn, N.Y., 1917; chemist E. I. du Pont de Nemours & Co., Wilmington, Del., 1919; prof. of pharmacy, Baylor U., Dallas, Tex., 1920; prof. of pharmacy, Med. Coll. of Va., 1920—. Served as sergt. 1st class Research Div., Chem. Warfare Service, Am. Univ. Expt. Sta., Washington, D.C., 1917-18. Mem. revision com. U.S. Pharmacopoeia, term 1930-40. Presbyn. Mason. Home: Richmond, Va. Died Oct. 29, 1940.

CROES, John James Robertson, civ. engr.; b. Richmond, Va., Nov. 25, 1834; s. Rev. Robert Brown and Helen (Robertson) C.; grad. Coll. of St. James, Md., 1853; unmarried. In practice as civ. engr., 1856—; resident engr. first high masonry dam in U.S. at Boyd's Corners, N.Y., 1865-70; topog. engr., New York Park Dept., 1872-78; chief engr., Suburban Rapid Transit R.R., New York, 1885-91; made expert reports on Quaker Bridge Dam (New York Aqueduct Commn.), 1888, New Croton dam and reservoir, 1901, and on New York water supply to Comptroller, 1899, and Merchants' Assn., 1900; consulting engr., N.Y. State Health Dept., 1903-05. Has made numerous reports on water supply, sewage, etc., to various cities. Pres. Am. Soc. Civil Engrs., 1901. Home: Yonkers, N.Y. Died 1906.

CROFFUT, William Augustus, author; b. Redding, Conn., 1835; s. Benedict and Harriet N. (Hull) C.; ed. common schs.; (Ph.D., Union Coll.); m. Margaret Marshall; m. 2d, Bessie B. Nicholls. In newspaper work, 1852—; pvt. U.S.A., in Civil War; phonographic reporter and corr. on many leading jours. Was some time editor Minneapolis Tribune, New York American, Rochester (N.Y.) Democrat, New Haven (Conn.) Palladium, American Architect, Hearth and Home, and Daily Post, Washington. Exec. officer U.S. Geol. Survey, 1888-94. In 1899, organized and became sec. Anti-Imperialist League; pres. Liberty League. Author: Helping Hand for American Homes; War History of Connecticut; The Vanderbilts; Folks Next Door; A Midsummer Lark; The Open Door of Dreamland; The Lord's Day or Man's; Labor's Riddle Guessed At; Fifty Years in Camp and Field, being a Diary of Maj. Gen. Ethan Allen Hitchcock; The Crimson Wolf (novel). Home: Washington, D.C. Died Aug. 31, 1915.

CROFT, Albert Jefferson, clergyman; b. Middlebury Center, Pa., Feb. 25, 1877; s. Lavern Lent and Vilona Helena (West) C.; Ph.B., Syracuse U., 1906; S.T.B., Boston U., 1909; studied Union Theol. Sem., summers 1927, 28; m. Anna Elizabeth Williams, June 26, 1907; children—Thomas Lavern, Albert Jefferson. Ordained M.E. ministry, 1909; pastor successively Spring Valley, Minn., North Ch. and Prospect Ch., both Minneapolis, Kingsley Ch., Milwaukee, to 1918; chaplain U.S. Army, 1918-20; pastor Endion Ch., Duluth, Minn., First Ch., Lincoln, Neb., Asbury Ch., Salisbury, Md., First Ch., Wichita, Kan., until 1931, Grace Ch., Springfield, Mo., 1931—. Trustee Burge Hosp. and Ozark Wesleyan Coll. Republican. Home: 603 S. Jefferson St., Springfield, Mo. Died July 15, 1933.

CROFT, Delmer Eugene, writer, lecturer; b. Enosburg, Vt., July 27, 1864; s. Joseph Benjamin and Pamelia Ann (Buck) C.; B.S., U. of Vt., 1889; completed Pond's course in theology; m. Helen B. Somers. Ordained Bapt. ministry, 1892; held pastorates in Vt., Mass. and N.Y.; lyceum lecturer, 1897—. An organizer Progressive Party in Conn., 1912. Author: (mental science pamphlets) Supreme Personality, 1914; Supreme Miracles, 1915; Supreme Self-Command, 1916; Supreme Love Thrills, 1917. Home: New Haven, Conn. Died Aug. 15, 1925.

CROFT, Edward, army officer; b. Greenville, S.C., July 11, 1875; s. Edward and Mary Eliza (Pearson) C.; student S.C. Mil. Acad., 1892 to 1896; grad. Inf.-Cavalry School, 1904, School of Line, 1920, General Staff School, 1921, Army War College, 1924; m. Maribel Williams, February 8, 1905; 1 son, Edward. Second lieutenant, Infantry, U.S.A., July 9, 1898; advanced through grades to major, May 15, 1917; lt. col., Inf., N.A., Aug. 5, 1917, col., June 17, 1918; lt. col., U.S.A., July 1, 1920; advanced through grades to maj. gen., May 6, 1933; chief of Inf., U.S.A., May 6, 1933—. Decorated Silver Star, Purple Heart (M.S.A.). Episcopalian. Mason. Died Jan. 28, 1938.

CROFT, George William, congressman, lawyer; b. Newberry, S.C., Dec. 20, 1846; s. Theodore Gaillard and Eliza Webb (D'Oyley) C.; prep. edn. at the Citadel, Charleston, S.C., 1863-64; attended Univ. of Va., 1866-67; studied law under Gov. B. F. Perry, Greenville, S.C.; m. Florence E. McMahon, April 17, 1873. Admitted to bar, 1869; president S.C. Bar Association, 1892, 1901. Elected to S.C. senate,

1880; mem. House of Representatives, S.C., 1882 and 1900; mem. Congress, 2d S.C. dist., 1903-05. Democrat. Home: Aiken, S.C. Died 1904.

CROFTAN, Alfred Careno, physician; b. New York, N.Y., Apr. 11, 1871; ed. Gymnasium, Germany, and univs. of Berlin and Paris; M.D., Coll. Phys. and Surg., Chicago, 1897; post-grad. work, Vienna; m. Elizabeth Hubbard, Feb. 9, 1900. Practiced internal medicine, Chicago, 1902—; prof. medicine, Chicago Post-Grad. Sch.; phys.-in-chief St. Mary's Hosp., etc. Author: Clinical Urinology; Clinical Therapeutics. Home: Chicago, Ill.; and Keene Valley, N.Y. Died Aug. 22, 1938.

CROGMAN, William Henry, Sr., univ. pres.; b. St. Martins, W.I., May 5, 1841; s. William and Charlotte (Chippendale) C.; orphaned when he was 12 yrs. old; A.B., Atlanta U., 1876, A.M., 1879, Litt.D., 1901; LL.D., Clark U., Atlanta, Ga., 1901; m. Lavinia C. Mott, July 10, 1878; children—Charlotte, Edmund Loring (dec.), William Henry, Ada, Leonidas Chase, Albert Keith (dec.), Marcellus Parks (dec.), Edith Genevieve. Prof. classics from 1876, and pres., 1903-10, Clark U., S. Atlanta, Ga.; retired 1921. Mem. Univ. Senate of M.E. Ch., 1892-1900. Home: South Atlanta, Ga. Died Oct. 15, 1931.

CROKER, Richard, politician; b. Clonakilty, County Cork, Ireland, Nov. 23, 1841; brought to U.S. at age of 7; ed. pub. schs., N.Y. City; m. Elizabeth Frazier, Nov. 1873; m. 2d, Bula Benton Edmondson (a Cherokee Indian, from Oklahoma), Nov. 26, 1914. Learned machinist's trade; entered politics, 1865; elected alderman, N.Y. City, 1868, 1870 and 1883; coroner 2 terms, 1873-79; fire commr., 1883; city chamberlain, 1889-90. Was an opponent of the Tweed ring; prominent in Tammany Hall and recognized as its leader for 17 yrs.; especially active in campaign of 1897 when Robert A. Van Wyck was elected first mayor of Greater New York. Lived in Ireland, 1907-19. Home: New York, N.Y. Died Apr. 29, 1922.

CROLL, William M., congressman; b. Upper Macungie, Lehigh Co., Pa., Apr. 9, 1866; student Keystone State Normal Sch., Kutztown, Pa., 2 yrs., 1880-82; grad. Eastman Business Coll., Poughkeepsie, N.Y., 1882; m. Annie M. Kuhns, June 20, 1889; children—Amy Blanche (Mrs. P. Fred Eisenbrown), Mabel Alma (Mrs. Lee Filbert). Gen. mdse. bus., as Smith & Croll, Maxatawny, 1889-97; became mem. firm Heffner, Gilbert & Croll, clothiers, Reading, Pa., 1897, later Croll & Keck; dir. Berks Co. Trust Co., Nat. Bank of Topton. Co. treas. Berks Co., Pa., 1909-12; naval officer at Phila., 1913-18; mem. 68th Congress (1923-25), 14th Pa. Dist. Lutheran. Mason (32°). Home: Reading, Pa. Died Oct. 22, 1929.

CROLY, Herbert, author; b. New York, N.Y., Jan. 23, 1869; s. David Goodman and Jennie (Cunningham) C.; Coll. City of New York, 1884-85; Harvard, 1886-87, 1895-99; m. Louise Emory, May 30, 1892. Editor Architectural Record, 1900-06, and on staff same until 1913; editor The New Republic, Nov. 1914—; also pres. The New Republic Co. Mem. Nat. Inst. Arts and Letters. Author: Promise of American Life, 1909; Marcus Alonzo Hanna—His Life and Work, 1912; Progressive Democracy, 1914; Willard Straight, 1924. Home: New York, N.Y. Died May 17, 1930.

CROLY, Jane Cunningham ("Jenny June"), author; b. (Cunningham) Market Harborough, Eng., Dec. 19, 1829; came to U.S. with family when 10 yrs. old, settling at Poughkeepsie, N.Y.; m. David G. Croly, journalist, 1856 (died 1889). Editor Demorest's Mag., 1860-87; held editorial positions on papers and mags. over 40 yrs.; started the duplicate system of correspondence which suggested the modern syndicate. First regular woman corr. of New Orleans Delta, Richmond Enquirer, Louisville Jour., 1856-58; late of New Orleans Picayune, Baltimore American (15 yrs.); etc. Founded Woman's Cycle (afterward New Cycle), 1889, to represent associated interests of women, and sustained it 8 yrs. Called 1st Woman's Congress in New York, 1856, and the 2d, 1869; founded Sorosis, 1868, was its pres., 1868-70, 1876-86. Severe accident crippled her in 1898. Author: Talks on Women's Topics, 1869; For Better or Worse, 1875; Cookery Book for Young Beginners; History of the Woman's Club Movement in America. Died 1901.

CROMER, George Benedict, lawyer; b. Newberry Co., S.C., Oct. 3, 1857; s. Thomas H. and P. M. C.; A.B., Newberry Coll., 1877, A.M., 1879; LL.D., Wittenberg, 1901, Muhlenberg, 1901; m. Caro J. Motte, Oct. 11, 1883 (died 1888); children—Mrs. Marguerite Moise (dec.), Carolyn; m. 2d, Harriet S. Bittle, Nov 27, 1890; children—George B. (dec.), Beale Holland. Prof. in Newberry Coll., 1877-81; admitted to bar, Dec. 1881, practiced law until Jan. 1896; pres. Newberry Coll., 1896-1904; resumed law practice, 1904. Mayor of Newberry, 1886-90, and 1905. Pres. trustees Newberry Coll.; chmn. State Bd. Charities and Corrections, S.C., 1915-19. Home: Newberry, S.C. Died Sept. 25, 1935.

CROMWELL, Bartlett Jefferson, rear admiral U.S. Navy; b. nr. Springplace, Ga., Feb. 9, 1840; s. Andrew Forgison and Sarah (Ragon) C.; apptd. to U.S. Naval Acad. from Neb., 1857, grad. 1861; m. Lizzie S. Huber, Dec. 31, 1866. Midshipman, June 3, 1861; promoted through grades to rank of rear admiral, Mar. 3, 1899. Participated in attacks on Morris Island and Battery Gregg; comdg. captured Confed. Ram Atlanta, on passage from Port Royal to Phila., Sept. 14, 1863; insp. ordnance, Navy Yard, Phila., 1874-78; Navy insp. ordance, Navy Yard, Phila., 1874-78; Navy Yard, Portsmouth, 1882-84; comd. naval rendezvous, Phila., 1884-85; Navy Yard, League Island, 1886-89; ordnance duty, 1889-90; comd. Omaha, 1890-91; capt. of yard, Navy Yard, Norfolk, 1891-94; comd. Atlanta, 1894-95; mem. Naval Examining Bd., 1895-98; commandant, Naval Sta., Havana, Cuba, 1899; pres. Naval Retiring Bd., 1899-1900; commandant, Navy Yard, Portsmouth, 1900-01; comdr.-in-chief, S. Atlantic Station, May-July, 1901, European Station, 1901-02; retired, Feb. 9, 1902. Home: Washington, D.C. Died June 24, 1917.

CROMWELL, Frederic, capitalist; A.B., Harvard, 1863. Has been treas. and trustee Mutual Life Ins. Co. of N.Y. more than 21 yrs. Dir. Morris & Essex R.R. Home: New York, N.Y. Died June 22, 1914.

CROMWELL, George, lawyer; b. Brooklyn, N.Y., July 3, 1860; s. Henry Bowman and Sarah (Seaman) C.; grad. Brooklyn Poly. Inst., 1878 (salutatorian); A.B., with honors, Yale, 1883; traveled in Europe, Egypt and Palestine, 1883-84; student Columbia U. Sch. of Law, 1884-86; m. Hermine de Rouville, June 1, 1915. Admitted to N.Y. bar, 1886; in Elihu Root's office, 1885-89; with Butler, Stillman & Hubbard, in charge of admiralty dept., 1889-97; practicing alone at N.Y. City, 1897—; also pres. Dongan Hills Realty Co. Mem. N.Y. Assembly, 1888, Senate, 1915-18; pres. Richmond County Park Commn., 1897; pres. Borough of Richmond, 1898-1913, inclusive; mem. Charter Revision Com., New York, 1900, also New York Charter Commn., 1908-09, N.Y. City Com. on Taxation, 1914; mem. New York Charter Commn., 1923. Dir. and trustee Staten Island Inst. Arts and Sciences. Republican. Conglist. Mason (32°). Home: Dongan Hills, S.I., N.Y. Deceased.

CRONAU, Rudolf, author; b. Solingen, Germany, Jan. 21, 1855; s. Rudolf Cronau and Helene (Waldeck) C.; ed. high schs. and Acad. of Art, Dusseldorf, Germany; m. Margarethe Taenzler, Feb. 8, 1888. Came to America, 1880; Am. rep. Cologne Gazette, 1883-99; writer, traveler and lecturer, 1877—. Author: History of the Sward Industry of Solingen (pub. Stuttgart), 1885; From Wonderland to Wonderland (2 vols., Leipzig), 1886; Travels in the Lands of the Sioux (Leipzig), 1886; In the Wild West—Trips of an Artist (Braunschweig), 1890; America—the History of Its Discovery from Ancient to the Present Time (2 vols., pub. in Germany and Spain), 1892 (award Chicago Exposition, 1893); Our Wasteful Nation (New York), 1908; Three Centuries of German Life in America (Berlin), 1909, 2d edit., 1925 (awarded $2,000, Univ. of Chicago); The British Black Book, 1915; German Achievements in America, 1916, 3d edit., 1917; Woman Triumphant, 1919; In the Realm of Clouds and Gods, 1919; The Discovery of America and the Landfall of Columbus—The Last Resting Place of Columbus, 1921; The Army of the American Revolution and Its Organizer, 1923; Prohibition and the Destruction of the American Brewing Industry, 1926. Home: Philipse Manor, N.Y. Died Oct. 27, 1939.

CRONIN, Con P., librarian; b. Charlestown, Mass., Apr. 27, 1871; s. Patrick and Nora Cranston (Coleman) C.; ed. pub. schs., Boston; m. Lillian Elizabeth Rood, Dec. 20, 1898; children—Lillian Elizabeth, Margaret Eleanor, Stanley Rood, Katherine Nichols. County recorder, Yuma Co., Ariz., 1896-1905, lacking one term; insp. U.S. Dept. of Commerce and Labor, 1907-12; sec. Ariz. Senate, 1912-15; Ariz. State law and legislative reference librarian, 1915—. Chmn. State Board of Library Examiners. Sergt. B Troop, 1st U.S. Vol. Cav. ("Rough Riders"), 1898; became ill and did not see foreign service. Democrat. Author: Cronin's Annotations to the Arizona Codes and Session Laws. Home: Phoenix, Ariz. Died Mar. 14, 1932.

CRONIN, Marcus Daniel, army officer; b. Worcester, Mass., Jan. 9, 1865; grad. U.S. Mil. Acad., 1887, Army War Coll., 1911; m. Helen Hannay, Aug. 2, 1893. Commd. 2d lt., June 12, 1887; promoted through grades to col., May 15, 1917; brig. gen. N.A., Aug. 5, 1917. Instr. U.S. Mil. Acad., 1893-97; regimental adj. 25th Inf., 1898-99, 1903-07; in Santiago Campaign, Cuba, 1898; col. and asst. chief Philippine Constabulary, 1915-17 (acting chief part of time); officer Gen. Staff, 1908-10; apptd. comdr. 163d Inf. Brigade, Camp Gordon, Ga., 1917. Died Aug. 12, 1936.

CRONKHITE, Adelbert, army officer; b. N.Y., Jan. 5, 1861; grad. U.S. Mil. Acad., 1882, Arty. Sch., 1886. Commd. 2d lt. 4th Arty., June 13, 1882; promoted through grades to brig. gen., 1917; maj. gen. N.A., Aug. 5, 1917; maj. gen. U.S.A., Mar. 7, 1921. Operations against Sioux Indians, 1891; prof. mil. science and tactics, Mich. Mil. Acad., Orchard Lake, 1891-92; q.m. and commissary, F.A. Brig., Cuba and P.R., 1898; q.m., 1904-07; insp. gen.'s dept. and arty. officer, 1907-11; comdg. coast defenses, Eastern N.Y., 1911-14, coast defenses Panama and Panama Canal Dept., 1914-17; at Camp Lee and in A.E.F. comdg. 80th Div., 9th and 6th A.C., Sept. 1917-May 28, 1918; service on British front, St. Mihiel and Meuse-Argonne; retired Feb. 1, 1923. Died June 15, 1937.

CROOK, Alja Robinson, chief State Museum Div.; b. Circleville, O., June 17, 1864; s. Rev. Isaac and Emma (Wilson) C.; A.B., Ohio Wesleyan U., 1887; studied in British Mus., Jardin des Plantes (Paris), univs. of Berlin, Zürich and Munich, 1889-92; Ph.D., U. of Munich, 1892; m. Florence Wayne Purdum, Dec. 28, 1904; children—Elinor Josselyn, William Henry, Robert Purdum, Frederick Sherwood, Richard Bradford. Supt. Mt. Carmel, O., pub. schs., 1887-89; prof. natural history, Wheaton (Ill.) Coll., 1892-93; prof. mineralogy and economic geology, Northwestern U., 1893-1906; curator Ill. State Mus. Natural History, 1906-17; chief State Museum Div. of Ill., dept. of registration and edn., 1917—. Pres. Ill. Acad. Science, 1914-15 (sec. 1908-10, 1915-16). Pres. Springfield Christian Laymen's Federation; v.p. Ill. State S.S. Assn.; pres. Ill. Conf. M.E. Laymen's Assn. Author: Guide to Mineral Collection. Home: Springfield, Ill. Died May 30, 1930.

CROOK, Isaac, clergyman and educator; b. Crossenville, Perry Co., O., Dec. 10, 1833; s. John and Anna (Sherwood) C.; A.B., Ohio Wesleyan U., 1859, A.M., 1862; (D.D., Cornell Coll., Ia., 1875; LL.D., Neb. Wesleyan, 1896); m. Emma Wilson, of Delaware, O., July 25, 1860. Ordained M.E. ministry, 1864; pastorates in Ohio, Ill., Mich., Minn. and Ky.; pres. U. of the Pacific, 1891-92; chancellor Neb. Wesleyan U., 1892-96; pres. Ohio U., 1896-98; pastor Ironton, O., 1898-1902; presiding elder Chillicothe Dist., 1902-08; lecturer, Del. Ecumenical Conf., Edinburgh, 1910. Author: Character Sketch of Hon. C. C. White, of Crete, Nebraska, 1896; Life of Jonathan Edwards, 1903; John Knox, the Scotch and Scotch-Irish, 1905; Earnest Expectation, a Volume in Second Series Methodist Pulpit, 1905; The Great Five, First Faculty Ohio Wesleyan University, 1907. Home: Spokane, Wash. Died Feb. 20, 1916.

CROOK, James King, physician; b. Allenton, Ala., Feb. 25, 1859; s. Hon. James Alexander and Sarah (Stover) C.; ed. pvt. schs., acads. and instrs.; M.D., Univ. Med. Coll. (New York U.), 1880; (hon. A.M., U. of Ala., 1893). Resident phys. city instns. on Blackwell's and Ward's Islands, 1880-81; attending phys. diseases heart and lungs, Bellevue Hosp., outdoor dept., 1884-94; clin. asst., 1883, instr., 1884-98, adj. prof., 1898-1904, dept. clin. medicine, Post-Grad. Med. Sch. Mem. and del. 2d Pan-Am. Med. Congress, City of Mexico, 1896; del. Brit. Med. Assn., 1897, 1903. Contbr. on clin. medicine, diseases of the heart and lungs and climatology to current literature. Home: New York, N.Y. Deceased.

CROOK, James Walter, college prof.; b. Bewdley, Ont., Can., Dec. 21, 1858; s. Richard and Jane (Sackville) C.; A.B., Oberlin Coll., 1891; studied U. of Wis., 1892-93, U. of Berlin, 1893-94, Columbia, 1894-95, Ph.D., 1898; m. Eva M. Lewis, Sept. 13, 1883. Prof. economics, Amherst Coll., 1895—. Mem. Mass. State Bd. of Labor and Industries, 1913—. Author: German Wage Theories, 1898. Home: Amherst, Mass. Died Oct. 22, 1933.

CROOKER, Florence Kollock, minister; b. Waukesha, Wis., Jan. 19, 1848; d. William Edward and Ann Margaret (Hunter) Kollock; grad. St. Lawrence U., theol. dept., 1875; (hon. A.M., U. of Wis., 1882); m. Rev. Joseph Henry Crooker, June 18, 1896. Organized, and pastor Stewart Av. Universalist Ch., Chicago, 1878-92; pastor Universalist Ch., Pasadena, Calif., 1892-95, St. Paul's Universalist Ch., Jamaica Plain, Mass., 1904-Sept. 1910. Pres. Woman's Centenary Assn., Universalist Ch. of America, 1901-03. Home: Lexington, Mass. Died Apr. 21, 1925.

CROOKER, Joseph Henry, clergyman; b. Foxcroft, Me., Dec. 8, 1850; s. Orin Barrows and Eliza Ann (Cobb) C.; grad. Ypsilanti Union Sem., 1870; S.T.D., St. Lawrence U., 1900; D.D., U. of Nashville, 1901; m. Frank E. Burt, 1872; m. 2d, Florence Kollock, June 18, 1896 (died 1925). In Bapt. ministry 5 yrs.; entered Unitarian ministry, 1877; pastor Madison, Wis., 1881-91, and built large ch. there; established Unitarian congregation at Helena, Mont., 1891-97; pastor Ann Arbor, Mich., 1898-1905, Roslindale Ch., Boston, 1905-12. Pres. Unitarian Temperance Soc. 10 yrs. Author: The Church of Today; The Church of Tomorrow; Shall I Drink?, 1914. Home: Kansas City, Mo. Died May 29, 1931.

CROOKS, Ezra Breckenridge, univ. prof.; b. Clinton, Ky., Oct. 6, 1874; s. James David and Mary Elizabeth (Bugg) C.; B.A., Central Coll., Fayette, Mo., 1899; M.A., Vanderbilt, 1901; S.T.B., Harvard, 1908, M.A., 1909, Ph.D., 1910; m. Mary Elizabeth Groves, Sept. 10, 1902 (died 1906); m. 2d, Mary Lasher, Sept. 8, 1909; children—Anna Elizabeth, James Lasher. Editor St. Louis Christian Advocate, 1901; ednl. missionary M.E. Ch., S., Brazil, 1902-06; asst. in depts. philosophy and history, Harvard, 1910-11; asst. prof. philosophy, Northwestern U., 1911-13; head dept. philosophy and edn., Randolph-Macon Woman's Coll., Lynchburg, Va., 1913-22; head dept. philosophy and social sciences, U. of Del., 1922—.

Dir. publicity U.S. Food Administration in Va., 1917-18; went to France under Y.M.C.A. and was with Portuguese Troops, British 5th Army. Democrat. Methodist. Home: Newark, Del. Died Mar. 8, 1941.

CROPSEY, James Church, judge; LL.B., Columbia, 1893. Admitted to N.Y. bar, 1893, and practiced in Brooklyn; counsel to police commr., Brooklyn, 1897; commr. of police, N.Y. City, 1910-11; dist. atty. Kings Co., 1912-16; justice Supreme Court of New York, 2d Dist., term 1916-30. Home: Brooklyn, N.Y. Died June 16, 1937.

CROPSEY, Jasper Francis, artist; b. Rossville, N.Y., Feb. 18, 1823; m. Maria Cooley, 1847. Studied architecture for 5 years, then turned attention to landscape painting, studying under Edward Maury, and afterward in Europe; established studio in New York, 1863; mem. Nat. Acad., 1851—; one of founders Am. Water Color Soc. Home: Hastings-on-Hudson, N.Y. Died 1900.

CROPSEY, Nebraska, Miss, supervisor elementary schs., Indianapolis. Died Mar. 1916.

CROSBY, Dick J., agricultural educator; b. Elbridge, Mich., Oct. 2, 1866; s. Daniel Way and Agnes (Colestock) C.; B.S., Mich. Agrl. College, 1893, M.S., 1901; m. Mary Lilian Wheeler, July 2, 1902; children—Alan Wheeler, Ruth, Richard Collier; m. 2d, Adelaide J. Irwin, Oct. 5, 1914. Taught rural schs., 1885-89, and winters during coll. course; instr. in English and coll. editor, Mich. Agrl. Coll., 1893-99; asst. in office of expt. stas., 1901-08, head of agrl. edn. service, 1908-13, U.S. Dept. of Agr.; specialist in agrl. edn. on part time; prof. extension teaching, N.Y. State Coll. of Agr., 1915—. Republican. Conglist. Home: Ithaca, N.Y. Died Nov. 15, 1926.

CROSBY, Edward Harold, writer; b. Boston, Mass., 1859; s. Edward and Eliza A. (Nichols) C.; grad. Boston High Sch., 1874; m. Medora B. Robbins, June 7, 1883. Became connected with Boston Post, 1886, dramatic critic, 1890—. Amateur electrician; has taken out 10 Am. and European patents; invented one of first dry batteries put on the market. Author: Radiana, 1909; The Evolution of Fredda, 1911; (plays) The Hour of Reckoning; The Catspaw; A Modern Parasite; The Cup of Memory; The Hand of an Enemy; A Lesson in Realism; The Man Who Grew Young; The Menace; Pants and Petticoats, 1919; Naughty Florence, 1920; On the QT, 1920; My Greenwich Village Girl, 1921; Behind the Screen, 1922; The Taming of Helen, 1925; Married or Not?, 1927; His Stenographer, 1928. Home: Boston, Mass. Died Dec. 1, 1934.

CROSBY, Ernest Howard, author, social reformer; b. New York, Nov. 4, 1856; s. Rev. Howard C. (1826-91); grad. Univ. of New York, 1876, Columbia Coll. Law School, 1878; in law practice, New York, 1878-89; mem. N.Y. Assembly, 1887-89; nominated by Pres. Harrison and apptd. by Khedive, judge internat. court, Alexandria, Egypt, 1889; resigned, 1894, and returned to New York. Visited Count Tolstoy in Russia on his way home; under influence of latter's writings has since devoted attention to social reform. One of founders and 1st pres. Social Reform Club, 1894; pres. N.Y. Anti-Imperialist League, 1900-05; chmn. com. N.Y. Friends of Russian Freedom, 1905; m. Fanny Schieffelin, 1881. Author: Plain Talk in Psalm and Parable, 1899; Captain Jinks, Hero, 1902; Swords and Plowshares, 1902; Tolstoy and His Message, 1904; Broad-Cast (poems), 1905; Tolstoy as a Schoolmaster, 1905; William Lloyd Garrison, Non-Resident and Abolitionist, 1905. Home: Rhinebeck, N.Y. Died 1906.

CROSBY, Fanny (Mrs. Frances Jane Van Alstyne), writer of hymns; b. Southeast, N.Y., Mar. 24, 1820; when 6 weeks old became blind from application of hot poultices to her eyes during an illness, the poultices destroying the optic nerve. At 15 entered the Inst. for Blind, New York; teacher there, 1847-58 in English grammar and rhetoric, and Roman and American history. Wrote words to many songs for George F. Root, the composer. Her first hymn was written for William B. Bradbury; has written more than 6,000 hymns in all, among them being: "Safe in the Arms of Jesus;" "Jesus, Keep Me Near the Cross" and "Jesus the Water of Life Will Give." Among her songs are "There's Music in the Air" and "Hazel Dell." Author: The Blind Girl, and Other Poems, 1844; Monterey, and Other Poems, 1849; A Wreath of Columbia's Flowers, 1858; Bells at Evening, and Other Poems, 1898; Memories of Eighty Years, 1906. Home: Bridgeport, Conn. Died Feb. 12, 1915.

CROSBY, Frederic Van Schoonhoven, railway official; b. Troy, N.Y., Mar. 15, 1860; s. Edward Nicoll and Elizabeth Maria (Van Schoonhoven) C.; spl. student Sch. of Mines (Columbia), 1876-77; traveled for several yrs.; m. Julia Floyd Delafield, Nov. 11, 1896. Second sec. Am. Legation, Berlin, Germany, 1884-90; gold mining brokerage business, Colorado Springs, Colo., until 1898; treas. U.P. System, 1898—; dir. Wells Fargo & Co. Express, 1909-10, Southern Pacific R.R. Co. of Mexico, 1909-13. Pres. and chmn. exec. com. Herman Knapp Memorial Eye Hosp. Served as pvt. Co. K, 7th Regt., N.Y.N.G. Home: Tuxedo Park, N.Y. Died Dec. 2, 1920.

CROSBY, George Harrington, ry. official; b. at Hillsboro, Ill.; s. of H. W. and Susan (Willis) C.; ed. pvt. schs., and Notre Dame (Ind.) U.; m. Jennie M. Wolcott, May 19, 1880. Held various positions on Hannibal & St. Joseph R.R. and C.,B.&Q. Ry., 1872-81; gen. frt. agt. Kansas City, St. Joseph & Council Bluffs R.R., St. Joseph, Mo., 1881-83; 1st asst. gen. frt. agt. and gen. agt., Denver, 1883-90, gen. frt. agt., Omaha, 1890-1902, Burlington & Mo. River R.R.; asst. frt. traffic mgr., 1902-05, frt. traffic mgr., Feb. 1, 1905—, C.,B.&Q. Ry. Home: Chicago, Ill. Died Mar. 29, 1927.

CROSBY, Herbert Ball, army officer; b. Fairmount, Kan., Dec. 24, 1871; s. George Heman and Jane (Ball) C.; grad. U.S. Military Acad., 1893; m. Catharine Adelaide Dakin, Feb. 11, 1902; children—George Dakin, Richard Lansing (dec.), Jane, Gordon Willard. Commd. 2d lt., 1893; promoted through grades to lt. col., 1917; commd. col. 351st Inf., N.A., Aug. 5, 1917; col. Cav., regular army, July 1, 1920. Served in Cuba, 1898-1901; in Mindanao, P.I., campaigns against Moros, 1903-05; in France, 1918-19; was instr. service schs. and asst. comdr. War Coll.; apptd. chief of cav., rank of maj. gen., Mar. 21, 1926, term of 4 yrs.; retired from active service, 1930; commr. of D.C. for term 1930-33; moved to San Antonio, Tex., to enter banking, Nov. 1933. Home: San Antonio, Tex. Died Jan. 11, 1936.

CROSBY, James Ott, lawyer; b. at Caldwell, Warren Co., N.Y., Mar. 22, 1828; s. Nathan and Melinda (Bishop) C.; ed. Seneca Falls Acad., 1835-36, Fredonia (N.Y.) Acad., 1844, Fowler's Law Sch., Cherry Valley, N.Y., 1848; LL.D., Upper Ia. Univ., 1918; m. Caroline C. Gibbs, Apr. 29, 1851. Entered law office, Ellicottville, N.Y., 1844; taught sch. 3 winter terms; employed in co. clerk's and land offices; admitted to N.Y. bar, 1849; removed to Ia., 1854; practiced law until 1900, retired. Pres. Ia. State and Clayton Co. bar assns. Progressive Republican. Home: Garnavillo, Ia. Died May 23, 1921.

CROSBY, John Schuyler, soldier; b. Albany Co., N.Y., Sept. 19, 1839; s. Clarkson Floyd and Angelica (Schuyler) C.; grad. U. City of New York, 1855; m. Harriet Van Rensselaer, June 26, 1863. One of the first Americans to cross S. America from Valparaiso, Chili, to Montévidio, Uruguay, 1856; 2d lt. U.S.A., Apr. 5, 1861; 1st lt., Aug. 28, 1861; capt. a.-d.-c. vols., 19th Army Corps, June 3, 1863; hon. mustered out of vol. service, Aug. 1, 1866; lt. col. and a.-d.-c. to Lt. Gen. Sheridan, Mar. 13, 1869-July 31, 1870; resigned, Dec. 31, 1870. Bvtd.: capt., Apr. 12, 1863, "for gallant and meritorious services in action at Ft. Bisland, La."; maj., Apr. 9, 1864, for same at battle of Pleasant Hill, La.; lt. col., Mar. 13, 1865, for same during the war; also maj. and lt. col. vols., Feb. 15, 1865. Apptd. by Gov. Seymour, col. 7th N.Y. Heavy Arty., 1863, but continued to serve on staff duty; served in Army of the Potomac during Civil War; afterward in Indian campaigns as adj. gen. with Gens. Sheridan and Custer. Personally thanked by President Lincoln for carrying dispatches. Gov. Mont., 1882-84; 1st asst. postmaster-gen., 1883-86; school commr., New York, 1889; Republican. Died Aug. 8, 1914.

CROSBY, Peirce, naval officer, retired; b. nr. Chester, Pa., Jan. 16, 1824; ed. private school; apptd. midshipman from Pa., 1838; served through all grades to rear adm., retiring, 1883, after 45 years' service; served wtih distinction in the Mexican and Civil wars, participating in numerous engagements; commanded South Atlantic station, 1882; Asiatic station, 1883. Died 1899.

CROSBY, Sheldon Leavitt, diplomatic service; b. N.Y. City, Nov. 9, 1879; s. Henry Ashton and May (Leavitt) C.; ed. pvt. tutors at home and Eng. and German schs., Dresden, Germany. In business, New York, 10 yrs.; apptd. 3d sec. of Embassy, London, Mar. 1, 1910; sec. Legation and consul gen. Bangkok, 1912-14; 2d sec. of Embassy, Madrid, 1914-15; temporarily assigned to Embassy at Vienna at outbreak Austro-Italian War, May 1915; 2d sec. of Embassy, Vienna, 1915-17, 1st sec. Embassy, London, 1917-19; at Rome, 1919-20; counsellor of Legation, Stockholm, 1920-21, of Embassy, Rio de Janeiro, Oct. 1921-24, of Embassy, Constantinople, 1924-30 (chargé d'affaires and acting high commr., 1926); counsellor of Embassy, Madrid, 1930-32, Warsay, 1932-35; retired, 1935. Died July 10, 1936.

CROSBY, Stephen Moody, banker; b. Salisbury, Mass., Aug. 14, 1827; grad. Dartmouth, 1849, Harvard Law School, 1852; m. Anna Hayden, Oct. 18, 1855. Served through war, reaching bvt. rank of lt. col.; mem. Mass. legislature, 1869; State senator, 1870-71; State dir. Boston & Albany R.R., 1871-72; commr. of Hoosac tunnel, 1874-75; treas., 1870-83; pres. Massachusetts Trust Co., 1883—; pres. Boston Art Club, 1890—. Home: Boston, Mass. Died 1909.

CROSBY, William Otis, geologist; b. Decatur, O., Jan. 14, 1850; s. Francis William and Hannah Everett (Ballard) C.; B.S., Mass. Inst. Tech., 1876; m. Alice Ballard, Sept. 4, 1876. Was engaged in mining in N.C. and Colo.; mem. faculty of Mass. Inst. Tech., 1883-1907, retired. Consulting geologist, chiefly engaged in original research; spl. geologist, U.S. and N.Y. surveys, U.S. Reclamation Service, U.S. Army Engineers, Met. Water Bd. of Mass., Bd. of Water Supply, New York; geologic investigations in connection with engring. projects in U.S., Can., Mexico, Alaska and Spain. Author: Contributions to the Geology of Eastern Massachusetts, 1880; Common Minerals and Rocks, 1881; Guide to Mineralogy, 1886; Tables for the Determination of Common Minerals, 1887; Guide to Dynamical Geology and Petrography, 1892; Geology of the Boston Basin, 1893-94; Geology of Long Island. Home: Jamaica Plain, Mass. Died Dec. 31, 1925.

CROSLEY, Walter Selwyn, rear adm.; b. East Jaffrey, N.H., Oct. 30, 1871; s. Rev. William Jacob and Charlotta (Davis) C.; grad. U.S. Naval Acad., 1893; m. Pauline de Launay Stewart, July 3, 1895; children—Floyd Stewart (lt. U.S.N., retired), Paul Cunningham (lt. U.S.N.). Commd. ensign July 1, 1895; promoted through grades to rank of rear admiral, Feb. 17, 1927. Participated in Brazilian Revolution, 1893, railroad riots, Calif., 1894, Spanish-Am. War, 1898, Philippine Insurrection, 1900, West Indian Campaign, Haitian Occupation, 1915, Santo Dominican Occupation, 1916, World War, 1917-18; naval attaché at Constantinople, 1910-12, Petrograd, Russia, 1917-18, at Madrid, Spain, 1918; commandant of 7th Naval Dist., Key West, Fla., 9th Naval District at Chicago, Ill., Fifteenth Naval District at Balboa, C.Z.; commanded Squadron One, Fleet Base Force and Battleship Division 3. Elected dir. of Internat. Hydrographic Bur., Monte Carlo, Monaco, Apr. 1937. Decorated Navy Cross, Sampson medal, Spanish campaign medal, Philippine campaign medal, Haitian campaign medal, Dominican campaign medal, Victory medal with star, Chinese Order of Wen Hu, Haitian Medal of Honor. Died Jan. 6, 1939.

CROSMAN, Charles Sumner; b. Lynn, Mass., June 3, 1858; s. John Henry and Deborah Wing (Holway) C.; A.B., LL.B., Haverford Coll., 1878; A.B., Harvard, 1879; LL.B., Columbian (now George Washington) U., 1883; m. Sarah E. Fuller, Sept. 1, 1885. Teacher in families of members of Supreme Court, Senate, Ho. of Rep., and foreign legations, Washington, D.C., 1879-84; head master Haverford Sch., 1884-1912; tour. around the world, 1912-13; lecturer and in charge tours de luxe, Raymond & Whitcomb Co., 1913-15; lecturer Curtis Pub. Co., 1915-17; speaker U.S. Food Administration and U.S. Shipping Bd., 1918; mgr. New York Office Fisk Teachers' Agency. Mem. Friends Ch. (Quaker). Home: Brooklyn, N.Y. Died Dec. 16, 1926.

CROSS, Arthur Lyon, univ. prof.; b. Portland, Me., Nov. 14, 1873; s. Emerlous D. and Charlotte (Noyes) C.; A.B., Harvard, 1895; A.M., 1896, Ph.D., 1899; student Berlin and Freiburg, 1897-98; unmarried. Asst. in history, Harvard, 1895-97, 1898-99; instr. history, U. of Mich., 1899-1904, asst. prof., 1904-07, jr. prof., 1907-11, prof., 1911-16, Hudson prof. English history, 1916—. Editor: Selected Documents from the Shelburne Papers, 1928; chapter on Great Britain and Ireland in A Guide to Historical Literature, 1931. Author: The Anglican Episcopate and the American Colonies, 1902, 2d edit., 1924; A History of St. Andrew's Church, 1906; A History of England and Greater Britain, 1914; A Shorter History of England and Greater Britain, 1920, 3d edit., 1939. Home: Ann Arbor, Mich. Died June 21, 1940.

CROSS, Charles Robert, physicist; b. Troy, N.Y., Mar. 29, 1848; s. George and Lucy Ann (Brown) C.; B.S., Mass. Inst. Tech., 1870; m. Mariana Pike, July 15, 1873 (died 1900). Instructor, 1870-71, as st. prof., 1871-75, prof., 1875-76, Thayer prof. physics, 1877-1917, emeritus prof., 1917, dir. Rogers Laboratory, 1885-1917, Mass. Inst. Tech. (the first course in elec. engring. in U.S. leading to a degree was established at the inst., at his instance, 1882). Home: Brookline, Mass. Died Nov. 16, 1921.

CROSS, Edward Weeks, clergyman; b. Cannon Falls, Minn., Feb. 12, 1885; s. Rowland Stevenson and Mary Elizabeth (Weeks) C.; A.B., Carleton Coll., 1907; Union Theol. Sem., 1909-10; B.D., Oberlin Coll., 1911; D.D., Grinnell (Ia.) Coll., 1923; m. Bessie Louise Dougherty, Oct. 19, 1915; children—Elizabeth, Robert Dougherty, Rowland Edward. Ordained Congl. ministry, 1911; pastor Livingston, Mont., 1911-15, First Ch., Grinnell, 1915-25; Y.M.C.A. sec. and chaplain U.S.A., 1st Div., in France, Sept. 1917-Feb. 1919 (cited for bravery); pastor Union Congl. Ch., Richmond Hill, N.Y., 1925-37, First Ch. of Christ (Congl.), Springfield, Mass., 1927—. Chmn. Commn. on Evangelism and Devotional Life of Congl. Chs., 1929-34; pres. Home Bd. of Missions of Congl. and Christian Chs. Home: Springfield, Mass. Died Nov. 2, 1939.

CROSS, George, clergyman; b. Bewdley, Ont., Can., Sept. 21, 1862; s. Henry and Elizabeth (Crook) C.; Woodstock Coll., 1883-85; A.B., U. of Toronto, 1888; B.Th., McMaster U., 1894, A.M., 1895, D.D., 1907; Ph.D., U. of Chicago, 1900; m. Lucy Viola Bullis, Dec. 21, 1887; children—Olive Agnes, Bessie Anne. Ordained Bapt. ministry, 1888; pastor Ormond, Ont.,

1887-89, Calgary, Alta., 1889-92, Carleton Place, Ont., 1894-97, Aylmer, Ont., 1898-1901; prof. history, McMaster U., 1901-09; prof. systematic theology, Newton Theol. Instn., 1909-12; prof. systematic theology, Rochester Theol. Sem., 1912—. Author: The Theology of Schleiermacher, 1911; What Is Christianity?, 1918; Creative Christianity, 1922; Christian Salvation, 1925. Home: Rochester, N.Y. Died Jan. 19, 1929.

CROSS, Joseph, judge; b. nr. Morristown, N.J., Dec. 29, 1843; s. William and Sarah M. C.; A.B., Princeton, 1865, A.M., 1868; studied law at Columbia Law Sch. and with Hon. W. J. Magie; admitted to bar, 1868; married, Oct. 19, 1870. Mem. law firm Magie & Cross, 1869-80, Cross & Noe, 1880-1905; U.S. dist. judge, Dist. of N.J., 1905—. Judge Dist. Ct. City of Elizabeth, 1888-91; mem. N.J. Assembly, 1894-95 (speaker, 1895), Senate, 1899-1905 (pres. 1905). Republican. Presbyn. Home: Elizabeth, N.J. Died Oct. 29, 1913.

CROSS, Judson Newell, lawyer; b. Philadelphia, Jefferson Co., N.Y., Jan. 16, 1838; s. Rev. Gorham and Sophia (Murdock) C.; studied and taught in Oberlin Coll., 1855-61; when he enlisted with the 100 Oberlin students who formed Co. C, 7th Ohio inf., becoming 1st lt.; served through Western Va. campaign under Gens. McClellan, Rosecrans and Cox and was editor of The Ohio Seventh, 1st Union paper pub. by Union soldiers, from a press captured from the enemy. Severely wounded and captured at battle of Cross Lanes, but recaptured by Maj. Rutherford B. Hayes; promoted capt., Nov. 1861, but because of wounds given spl. duty to close of war. Later commandant post at Madison, Ind.; adj. gen. mil. dist. Ind.; asst. provost marshal and on staff mil. gov. of dept. at Washington, D.C. Grad. Albany Law Sch., 1866. Practiced law, Lyons, Ia., 1866-75; mayor Lyons, 1871; practiced at Minneapolis, 1875—; city atty., 1883-87; mem. Minneapolis bd. park commrs., 1883; mem. U.S. bd. immigration commrs. sent to Europe by U.S. Govt., 1891. Republican. Home: Minneapolis, Minn. Died 1901.

CROSS, Richard James, banker; b. Liverpool, Eng., Nov. 3, 1845; s. William and Anna Chalmers (Wood) C.; ed. Marlborough Coll., Eng.; m. Matilda Redmond, June 3, 1872; m. 2d, Annie Redmond, of New York, May 16, 1885. Mem. banking firm of Morton, Bliss & Co., 1875-99, retired. Home: Newfoundland, N.J. Died Mar. 30, 1917.

CROSSLEY, Frederic Beers, lawyer, educator; b. Glen Eyre, Pa., Dec. 2, 1872; s. Thomas and Mary (McRoy) C.; Harvard, 1895-97; LL.B., Northwestern U., 1899, hon. M.A., 1922; m. Susan E. Jenkins, Aug. 2, 1904; children—Frederic McRoy (dec.), Martha Jenkins, Jean Campbell. Admitted to Ill. bar, 1899, and practiced at Chicago; sec. Sch. of Law, Northwestern U., 1901-29, then prof. law; librarian Elbert H. Gary Library of Law, 1903-32. Mng. dir. Jour. Am. Inst. Criminal Law and Criminology; sec. Northwestern U. Press. Mem. bd. govs. Chicago Y.M.C.A. Schs.; mem. Chicago Crime Commn. (dir.), Scientific Crime Detection Lab., Air Law Inst. Republican. Congregationalist. Home: Chicago, Ill. Deceased.

CROSWELL, James Greenleaf, head master; b. Brunswick, Me., Aug. 29, 1852; s. Andrew and Caroline (Greenleaf) C.; A.B., Harvard, 1873; post-grad. work at U. of Bonn; (hon. M.A., Hobart, 1913); m. Letitia Brace, May 10, 1888. Was tutor St. Mark's Sch., Southboro, Mass., and at Harvard Coll., 1873-78; asst. prof. Greek and Latin, Harvard, 1883-87; head master, Brearley Sch., New York, 1887—. Home: New York, N.Y. Deceased.

CROTHERS, Austin L., governor; b. nr. Conowingo, Cecil Co., Md., May 20, 1860; s. Alpheus and Margaret Aurelia (Porter) C.; ed. pub. schs. and W. Nottingham Acad.; LL.B., U. of Md., 1880; unmarried. Admitted to bar, 1880, and practiced at Elkton, Md.; dir. First Nat. Bank. State's atty., Cecil Co., 1891-95; mem. Md. Senate, 1897-1901; defeated for senate, 1902, 06; judge 2d Jud. Circuit, 1906; gov. of Md., 1908-12. Democrat. Home: Elkton, Md. Died May 25, 1912.

CROTHERS, Samuel McChord, clergyman; b. Oswego, Ill., June 7, 1857; s. Hon. John M. and Nancy (Foster) C.; A.B., Wittenberg College, 1873; A.B., Princeton, 1874; Union Theol. Sem., 1874-77; Harvard Div. Sch., 1881-82; D.D., Harvard, 1899; Litt.D., St. Lawrence U., 1904, Princeton, 1909, Western Reserve, 1923; m. Louise M. Bronson, Sept. 9, 1882. Ordained Presbyn. ministry, 1877; pastor Eureka, Nev., 1877-78, Gold Hill, Nev., 1878, Santa Barbara, Calif., 1879-81; entered Unitarian ministry, 1882; pastor Brattleboro, Vt., 1882-86, St. Paul, 1886-94, First Ch., Cambridge, Mass., 1894—. Preacher to Harvard U. Author: Members of One Body, 1894; Miss Muffet's Christmas Party, 1901; The Gentle Reader, 1903; The Understanding Heart, 1903; The Pardoner's Wallet, 1905; The Endless Life, 1905; By the Christmas Fire, 1908; Oliver Wendell Holmes and His Fellow Boarders, 1909; Among Friends, 1910; Humanity Speaking, 1912; Three Lords of Destiny, 1913; Meditations on Votes for Women, 1914; Pleasures of an Absentee Landlord, 1916; The Dame School of Experience, 1919; How to Know Emerson, 1920; The Cheerful Giver, 1923. Home: Cambridge, Mass. Died Nov. 9, 1927.

CROTHERS, Thomas Davison, physician; b. W. Charlton, N.Y., Sept. 21, 1842; ed. Ft. Edward Sem., N.Y.; M.D., Albany Med. Coll., 1865; m. Mrs. S. B. Risedorph, 1872. Practiced at West Galway, N.Y., 1866-70; began practice, Albany, 1870; asst. professor practice of medicine, Albany Med. Coll., 1871; asst. phys. N.Y. Inebriate Asylum, Binghamton, 1875-78; supt. Walnut Hill Asylum, Hartford, Conn., 1878-80; pres. and supt. Walnut Lodge Hosp., Hartford, 1880—. Editor Journal of Inebriety, 1876—; prof. nervous and mental diseases, and dean, Coll. Phys. and Surg., Boston. Author: Disease of Inebriety, 1893; Drug Habits and Their Treatment, 1901; Morphinism and Other Drug Diseases, 1902; Clinical Study of Inebriety, 1911. Home: Hartford, Conn. Died Jan. 1918.

CROUCH, Calvin Henry, mech. engr.; b. Oswego, N.Y., Apr. 25, 1870; s. Henry Theodore and Ruth Lydia (Kenyon) C.; M.E., Cornell U., 1892; m. Della U. Newman, Oct. 6, 1898. Coll. vacations spent in machine shops; spl. apprentice, Ames Iron Works, Oswego, N.Y., 1892-93; machinist with Rome, Watertown & Ogdensburg R.R., Oswego, 1893-94; erecting engr. Deane Steam Pump Co., Holyoke, Mass., 1894-97; instr. in machine shop practice, Williamson (Pa.) Free Sch. of Mech. Trades, 1897-1900; traveling engr., erecting locomotives in Europe for Baldwin Locomotive Works, 1900-01; dean U. of N.Dak. Coll. Mech. and Elec. Engring., 1901-16; prof. mech. engring. and dir. of shops Coll. of Engring., U. of N.D., 1916-19; actg. dean and prof. engring., New Hampshire Coll., 1919-20; dean Coll. of Technology and prof. mech. engring., U. of N.H., 1920-25; mech. engr. with E. L. Phillips & Co., New York, 1925-32. Republican. Baptist. Mason. Home: Grantwood, N.J. Died July 13, 1937.

CROUNSE, Lorenzo, farmer; b. Sharon, Schoharie Co., N.Y., 1834; worked in his father's tannery when young; common school edn. and 2 terms in N.Y. Conf. Sem., Schoharie Co.; taught school; studied law; admitted to practice, 1857; entered army, 1861, as capt., Battery K, 1st regt., N.Y. light art.; wounded while holding Beverly Ford on Rappahannock in 2d Bull Run under Pope; disabled for long time and resigned; m. Mary E. Griffiths, 1860 (died 1882). Removed to Neb., 1864; mem. Territorial legislature, 1866; justice Supreme Court, Neb., 1867-72; mem. Congress, 1873-77; internal revenue collector, dist. of Neb., 1879-83; Asst. Sec. U.S. Treasury, 1891-92; gov., Neb., 1893-95; elected Nov. 1900, State senator, 10th dist. Neb. Republican. Home: Omaha, Neb. Died 1909.

CROUTER, A(lbert) L(ewis) Edgerton, educator; b. Belleville, Ont., Can., Sept. 15, 1846; s. Abraham Lewis and Elizabeth Eliza (German) C.; ed. pub. and pvt. schs.; studied Franklin Inst. and U. of Pa.; (M.A., Gallaudet Coll., Washington, 1886; LL.D., Ill. Coll., Jacksonville, 1894); m. June Yale, 1895. Teacher, 1867-84, supt., 1884—, Pa. Instn. for the Deaf and Dumb. Dir. and pres. Am. Assn. to Promote Teaching Speech to Deaf. U.S. del. Internat. Conf. Teachers of Deaf, Edinburgh, 1907. Republican. Episcopalian. Home: Philadelphia, Pa. Died June 26, 1925.

CROW, Herman Denton, judge; b. Delaware, O., Apr. 15, 1851; s. Thomas Denton and Henrietta (Downs) C.; A.B., Ohio Wesleyan U., 1871, A.M., 1887, LL.D., 1911 (LL.D., Washington State College, 1908); m. Martha Florence Mendenhall, Oct. 24, 1877. Admitted to Ohio bar, 1873; practiced at Urbana, 1875-86, Winfield, Kan., 1886-90, Spokane, Wash., 1890-1905. City solicitor, Urbana, 1876-81; mem. state exec. com. League Rep. Clubs of Kan., 1888; mem. Wash. Senate, 1 short and 1 full term, 1898-1903 (chmn. jud. com. 8th Assembly); Rep. presdl. elector, 1904; apptd. justice Supreme Ct. by Gov. Mead, Jan. 1905; elected on Rep. ticket for short term, 1906-09, and for full term, on non-partisan ticket, 1909-15; reëlected for term 1915-21; was chief justice, 1913-15. Regent Wash. State Coll., 1901-05. Congregationalist. Home: Spokane, Wash. Deceased.

CROW, Martha Foote, author; b. Sacketts Harbor, N.Y.; d. Rev. John Bartlit and Mary Pendexter (Stilphin) Foote; Ph.B., Syracuse U., 1876, Ph.D., 1885; m. John M. Crow, archæologist, 1884 (died 1891). Preceptress, Ives Sem., Antwerp, N.Y., 1876-77; lady prin., Waynesburg (Pa.) Coll., 1877-78; teacher, Newton (Mass.) High Sch., 1878-82; lecturer and president's asst., Wellesley Coll., 1882-84; lady prin., Ia. (now Grinnell) Coll., Ia., 1884-91; asst. prof. English lit., U. of Chicago, 1892-1900; asst. prof. English lit. and dean of women, Northwestern U., 1900-05. Author: Elizabethan Sonnet-Cycles (4 vols.), 1896; The World Above, 1905; Elizabeth Barrett Browning (in Modern Poets and Christian Teaching Series), 1908; Harriet Beecher Stowe, a Biography, 1913; The American Country Girl, 1915; LaFayette (biography), 1916; Christ in the Poetry of Today (anthology American poets), 1917. Home: Chicago, Ill. Died Jan. 1, 1924.

CROW, William E., senator; b. German Twp., Fayette Co., Pa., Mar. 10, 1870; A.B., Waynesburg Coll. Admitted to Pa. bar, 1895; apptd. asst. dist. atty., Pa., 1896, and elected to same office, 1898, term of 3 yrs.; chmn. Rep. County Com., Fayette Co., 1899-1901; mem. State Senate, 3 terms, 1906-18, twice elected pres. pro tem; chmn. Rep. State Com., 1913-18; apptd. mem. U.S. Senate by Gov. Sproul, Oct. 1921, to fill unexpired term of Philander C. Knox, deceased, for term expiring Mar. 3, 1923. Home: Uniontown, Pa. Died Aug. 2, 1922.

CROWDER, Enoch Herbert, army officer; b. in Mo., Apr. 11, 1859; s. John Herbert and Mary C. (Weller) C.; grad. U.S. Mil. Acad., 1881; LL.B., U. of Mo., 1886; LL.D., Harvard, Columbia, Brown, Princeton, U. of Mich., U. of Mo., Havana; unmarried. Commd. 2d lt. 8th Cav., June 11, 1881; 1st lt., July 5, 1886; maj. judge advocate, Jan. 11, 1895; lt. col. judge advocate vols., June 22, 1898, apptd. lt. col. 39th Vol. Inf., Aug. 17, 1899; hon. discharged from vol. service, May 6, 1901; lt. col. judge advocate U.S.A., May 21, 1901; brig. gen. vols., June 20, 1901; hon. discharged from vol. service, June 30, 1901; col. judge advocate U.S.A., Apr. 16, 1903; brig. gen. and judge advocate gen. U.S.A., Feb. 14, 1911; maj. gen. and judge advocate gen. U.S.A., Oct. 6, 1917; retired Feb. 14, 1923. Comdr. of troop in Geronimo and Sitting Bull campaigns; mem. commn. to stave off hostilities between Americans and Filipinos, 1899; served on Supreme Ct. Bench Philippine Islands. Served in Philippine Islands, 1898-1901; in Manchuria, with Japanese Army, Apr. 1904-May 1905; in Cuba, Sec. of State and Justice, 1906-08; provost marshal gen. U.S.A., May 1917-July 1919; reapptd. judge advocate gen. U.S.A., Feb. 15, 1919. Del. 4th Pan-Am. Conf., Argentina, July-Aug. 1910; E.E. and M.P. on spl. mission to Chile, Sept. 1910. A.E. and P. to Cuba, 1923-27 (retired). Awarded D.S.M. "for especially meritorious and conspicuous service" as provost marshal gen. during the war, Dec. 1918; Comdr. Legion of Honor (French); Knight Comdr. Order of St. Michael and St. George (British); comdr. Mil. Order of the Crown (Italian); 3d Order of Rising Sun (Japanese); Order of Cespedes (Cuban). Died May 7, 1932.

CROWDER, Frank Warfield, clergyman; b. Baltimore, Md., June 6, 1869; s. Alexander N. and Deborah J. (Warfield) C.; Randolph-Macon Coll., Va., 1885-88; A.B., Dickinson Coll., 1890; B.D., Drew Theol. Sem., 1893; Ph.D., U. of Tübingen, Germany, 1894; D.D., Brown U., 1920; m. Louetta Plitt, Apr. 11, 1893. Minister M.E. Ch., 1894-1900; lay asst. Procathedral, New York, 1900-01; deacon and priest, P.E. Ch., 1901; rector Christ Ch., New Brighton, N.Y., 1901-10, Grace Ch., Providence, R.I., 1910-16, St. James Ch., New York, 1916—. Trustee Cathedral of St. John the Divine, etc. Home: New York, N.Y. Died 1932.

CROWE, Thomas Bennett, engring. consultant; b. Emporia, Kan., Sept. 6, 1876; s. Alexander Fulton and Sophia (Bennett) C.; E.M., Colo. Sch. of Mines, 1900; m. Blanche Stonehouse, Oct. 19, 1901. Mine foreman Ophelia Tunnel, Cripple Creek, Colo., 1900-03; assayer, chemist, metallurgist and supt. mills, Portland Gold Mining Co., Cripple Creek and Colorado Springs, Colo., 1903-22; cons. engr. The Merrill Co., San Francisco, Calif., 1922—; best known as consultant, designer, builder and operator ore reduction plants; inventor and co-inventor metall. processes and apparatus. Republican. Mason. Home: Palo Alto, Calif. Died Nov. 13, 1940.

CROWELL, Chester Theodore, writer; b. Cleveland, O., Oct. 14, 1888; s. William Theodore and Adelaide (Chichester) C.; ed. pub. schs.; m. 2d, Mrs. Evelyn Miller Pierce, Oct. 24, 1935. Editor Mexican Herald, City of Mexico, 1908-09; editorial writer San Antonio (Tex.) Express, 1909-11; mng. editor Austin (Tex.) Statesman, 1911-16; staff corr. Dallas News, later on staff New York Evening Post; spl. asst. to sec. of the treasury (U.S.), 1935. Author: Recovery Unlimited—The Monetary Policy of the Roosevelt Administration, 1936. Died Dec. 26, 1941.

CROWELL, Edward Payson, educator; b. Essex, Mass., Sept. 7, 1830; s. Robert C. (D.D.) and Hannah (Choate) C.; A.B., Amherst, 1853, A.M., 1856; Andover Theol. Sem., 1856-58; (D.D., Williams, 1880); m. Mary H. Warner, Aug. 13, 1861. Licensed Congl. preacher, 1859; teacher Latin and Greek, Williston Sem., Easthampton, Mass., 1853-55; tutor, 1855-56, prof. Latin and instr. in German, 1858-64, prof. Latin lang. and lit., 1864-1908, prof. emeritus Latin lang. and lit., 1908—, dean of faculty, 1880-94, Amherst Coll. Mem. Mass. Ho. of Rep., 1879. Home: Amherst, Mass. Died 1911.

CROWELL, James Foster, civil engr.; b. Oct. 13, 1848; s. John and Catherine (Roney) C.; grad. Poly. Coll. of Pa., June 27, 1867; m. Anna McK. Whiting, Jan. 27, 1881. Home: Flushing, N.Y. Died Mar. 29, 1915.

CROWELL, James McMullin, clergyman; b. Phila., June 9, 1827; s. Elisha and Susan (McMullin) C.; grad. (4th in class) Coll. of N.J. (Princeton), 1848, A.M., 1851, Princeton Theol. Sem., 1851, also D.D.;

m. June 12, 1851. Ordained to Presbyn. ministry, 1851; held pastorates at Chester Co., Pa., the Presbyn. Ch., Phila. (now the Tabernacle), St. Peter's Presbyn. Ch., Rochester, N.Y., and Woodland Presbyn. Ch., Phila. Pres. Bd. of Edn. Presbyn. Ch.; mem. Presbyn. Bd. of Home Missions, Presbyn. Bd. of Publ. Home: Philadelphia, Pa. Died 1908.

CROWELL, John, clergyman; b. Phila., June 22, 1814; s. James and Mary (Gardner) C.; coll. course began Univ. of Pa., 1830; grad. Princeton, 1834, A.M., 1837, D.D., 1869; divinity course Princeton Theol. Sem., supplemented by private study in Phila.; m. Katharine Roney, Oct. 21, 1840. Ordained to Presbyn. ministry, June 5, 1840; pastor West Chester, Pa., 1840-50; Orange, N.J., 1850-63; Odessa, Del., 1867-78; acting pastor Stirling, N.J., 1884-88; sec. bd. edn., E. Orange, N.J., 1889—. Republican. Author: Republics—Popular Government An Appointment of God, 1871 P6; Christ in All the Scriptures, P6. Home: East Orange, N.J. Died 1909.

CROWELL, John Franklin, economist; b. York, Pa., Nov. 1, 1857; s. Daniel and Sarah Ann C.; A.B., Yale, 1883, Larned scholar in philosophy, 1885-86; Ph.D., Columbia, 1897; student U. of Berlin, 1898; Litt.D., U. of N.C., 1889; LL.D., Trinity Coll. (now Duke U.), Durham, N.C., 1917; m. Laura K. Getz, 1887 (died 1888); m. 2d, Carrie H. Pascoe, 1891. Prin. Schuylkill Sem., Fredericksburg, Pa., 1883-84 and 1886-87; pres. Trinity Coll., N.C., 1887-94; head dept. economics and sociology, Smith Coll., Mass., 1895-97; expert agt., U.S. Industrial Commn., and expert on Internal Commerce, Bur. of Statistics, Treasury Dept., 1900-04; ednl. dir. Intercontinental Correspondence U., Washington, 1904-06; editorial staff Wall St. Journal, New York, 1906-15; exec. officer Chamber of Commerce of State N.Y., 1915-17; economist and financial statistician, Internal Revenue Office, Washington, 1918; dir. World Market Inst. of New York, 1919—; retired 1921. Author: The True Function of the American College; A Program of Progress; Taxation in American Colonies; The Logical Process of Social Development; The Distribution of Farm Products in the United States; The Iron and Steel Trade of the United States; The Lumber Trade of the United States; Ship Building and the Shipping Policy of the United States, Internal Commerce of the United States, 1902; Report to War Dept. on Deepening Mississippi River, 1903; Trusts and Competition, 1915; Revised Work of Wall Street, 1920. Home: Washington, D.C. Died Aug. 6, 1931.

CROWELL, John Stephen, publisher; b. Louisville, Ky., Jan. 7, 1850; s. Stephen Bruen and Jane (Graham) C.; ed. public schools, Louisville; m. Ella C. Mangold, Nov. 20, 1877. In 1877, founded and established the publishing house of Mast, Crowell & Kirkpatrick, which afterward became The Crowell Pub. Co., proprs. the Woman's Home Companion and the Farm and Fireside; dir. First Nat. Bank (Springfield, O.), Columbia Life Ins. Co. (Cincinnati). Pres. trustees New City Hosp. (Springfield), Western Coll. for Women (Oxford, O.); pres. Springfield Bd. of Trade, Springfield Coll. and Sem. Presbyn. Home: Springfield, Ohio. Died Aug. 17, 1921.

CROWELL, Katharine Roney, author; d. Rev. John (D.D.) and Catherine (Roney) C.; unmarried. Author: China for Juniors, Japan for Juniors, Africa for Juniors, Alaska for Juniors, 1902-05; Coming Americans, Great Voyages, 1906; Pioneers, Star 49? 1908, 1911; The Call of the Waters, 1908; Fair America, 1910; Best Things in America, 1911; Bearers of the Torch, 1917. Home: Litchfield, Conn. Died Apr. 1926.

CROWELL, Luther Childs, inventor; b. West Dennis, Cape Cod, Mass., Sept. 7, 1840; s. Francis B. Crowell (sea capt.); ed. West Dennis, Pine Grove Sem., Harwich, Mass., 1844-56, Pierce's Acad., Middlebury, Mass., 1856-57; m. Mrs. Margaret D. Howard, Aug. 18, 1863. In merchant marine service, 1857-61. Invented an aerial machine, 1860; invented and patented metallic tie paper bag, 1867; square bottomed grocers' paper bag, also machine for making same, 1872; also (placed in Boston Herald, 1873) first mechanism for associating webs of paper in printing, by which the multiple newspaper is produced; also the supplement newspaper press, and the double and quadruple presses, pamphlet printing and combined wire binding machines; has received 280 patents from U.S. for printing machinery alone; since 1879 engaged with R. Hoe & Co. Died 1903.

CROWLEY, Henry J., engineer; b. Unionville, Conn., 1865; s. Robert and Ann (O'Reilly) C.; ed. high sch.; m. Serena Virginia Ford, Nov. 25, 1892. Served as apprentice in mech. and elec. engring., later in constrn. electric light plants and as chief of students' course in elec. engring., Thomson-Houston Elec. Co.; dist. mgr. Gen. Elec. Co., at Atlanta, Ga., 1890-93; ry. mgr. Gen. Elec. Co., Philadelphia, 1893-99; gen. mgr., Am. Ry. Co., constrn. and operation of pub. utilities, 1899—; v.p. in charge construction of plants and operation of about 30 subsidiary corps. in 12 states. Republican. Catholic. Home: Philadelphia, Pa. Died Oct. 27, 1924.

CROWLEY, Mary Catherine, author, editor; b. Boston; d. John Colman and Mary J. (Cameron) C.; grad. Coll. Sacred Heart, New York; unmarried. Engaged in lit. work, 1887—, beginning as contbr. of poems and short stories to Wide Awake, St. Nicholas, Ladies' Home Journal, Pilot, etc., later of special articles to Boston Globe and syndicates (sometimes under pen-name "Janet Grant"); editor Catholic Missions Magazine, and "The Annals," New York, 1907-12. Authority on early history of Detroit; one of collaborators on Memorial History of Detroit. Author: Merry Hearts and True, 1889; Happy-Go-Lucky, 1890; Apples Ripe and Rosy, 1893; The City of Wonders, 1894; The Sentinel of Metz, 1897; An Every Day Girl, 1900; Tilderee, 1900; A Daughter of New France, 1901; The Heroine of the Straits, 1902; Love Thrives in War, 1903; In Treaty with Honor, 1906. Home: Ridgewood, N.J. Died May 14, 1920.

CROWNHART, Charles Henry, lawyer; b. Fond du Lac Co., Wis., Apr. 16, 1863; s. Napoleon and Mahitable (Burgess) C.; student River Falls (Wis.) Normal Sch., 1884-86; LL.B., U. of Wis., 1889; LL.D., Marquette U., 1929; m. Jessie E. Evans, July 1895; children—Jesse George, Charles H. Began practice at Ellsworth, Wis., 1889; moved to Superior, 1891, to Madison, 1911; chmn. Wis. Industrial Commn., 1911-15; reviser of statutes for State of Wis., 1921-22; justice Supreme Court, Wis., apptd. by gov., 1922, elected, 1923, for 10-year term. Dist. atty. Douglas Co., Wis., 1901-05; mem. Bd. Normal Sch. Regents, 1905-12. Republican. Elk. Home: Madison, Wis. Died May 2, 1930.

CROWNINSHIELD, Arent Schuyler, naval officer; b. Seneca Falls, N.Y., Mar. 14, 1843; s. Jacob and Mary Miller (Schuyler) C.; grad. U.S. Naval Acad., 1863; m. Mary Bradford, July 27, 1870. Ensign, May 28, 1863; promoted through grades to rear adm., Mar. 16, 1902. Served in both attacks on Ft. Fisher, Civil War; lighthouse insp. 1st dist., 1882-85; comd. nautical sch.-ship St. Mary's, 1887-91; Navy Yard, New York, 1891-92; comd. Kearsarge, 1892-93; senior mem. bd. of inspectors, Navy Yard, New York, 1893-94; comd. receiving-ship Richmond, 1894-95, Maine, 1895-97; chief of Bureau of Navigation with the rank of rear adm., 1897-1902; comdr.-in-chief European Sta., 1902-03; was mem. Bd. of Naval Strategy during war with Spain; retired, Mar. 20, 1903. Home: Mt. Desert, Me. Died 1908.

CROWNINSHIELD, Caspar Schuyler, consul; b. Nice, France, June 1, 1871; s. Arent Schuyler and Mary (Bradford) C.; ed. pvt. tutelage; studied painting New York Art League and pupil of Jean Paul Laurens and Benjamin Constant, Paris; studied for consular service at Washington; m. Grace Nadine Snelling, Feb. 7, 1907. Mem. Paris Expn. Commn., 1898-1900; consul at Castellammare di Stalia, Italy, 1901-07; at Naples, Italy, 1907—. Died 1910.

CROWNINSHIELD, Frederic, artist; b. Boston, Nov. 27, 1845; s. Edward A. and Caroline M. (Welch) C.; A.B., Harvard, 1866; studied art, France and Italy; m. Helen S. Fairbanks, 1867. Specialty: mural painting and stained glass windows; also landscape in oils and water-colors. Instr. of drawing and painting, Mus. Fine Arts, Boston, 1879-85; also lecturer on artistic anatomy; dir. Am. Acad. in Rome, 1909-11. Pres. Fine Arts Federation, New York, 1900-09; A.N.A. Author: Mural Painting, 1887; Pictoris Carmina (poems), 1900; A Painter's Moods (poems), 1902; Tales in Metre, and Other Poems, 1903; Under the Laurel (poems), 1907; Villa Mirâfiore (poems), 1912. Died Sept. 13, 1918.

CROWNINSHIELD, Mary Bradford, author; d. Judge John Melancthon and Sarah Elizabeth (Hopkins) Bradford; m. Arent Schuyler Crowninshield, July 27, 1870 (died 1908). Author: Latitude 19°—A Romance of the West Indies; Where the Trade Wind Blows; All Among the Light-Houses; The Light-House Children Abroad; Plucky Smalls; San Isidro; The Archbishop and the Lady, 1900; Valencia's Garden. Home: Mt. Desert, Me. Died Oct. 14, 1913.

CROWSON, Benjamin Franklin, educator; b. Parksley, Va., Apr. 11, 1889; s. Levin Thomas and Sarah Ayres (Rew) C.; B.S., Va. Mil. Inst., 1910, M.A., 1926; student U. of Pa., summers 1914, 21, U. of Va., summer 1924; m. Gladys Anita Wright, June 26, 1915; children—Benjamin Franklin, Levin Thomas III (dec.), Gladys Wright. Comdt. cadets, Millersburgh (Ky.) Mil. Inst., 1910-11; asst. prof. Va. Mil. Inst., 1911-15, co-dir. summer sessions, 1913, 15, 16, asso. prof. English, 1920-27; supervising prin. Roanoke (Va.) Jr. High Sch., 1915-16; prin. Charlotte Hall Sch., 1916-20, and 1927—. Dir. County Trust Co. of Md. Capt. field arty., Va. Vols., 1911-1915, lt. col. engrs., same, 1920-28. Democrat. Episcopalian. Mason. Home: Charlotte Hall, Md. Died July 12, 1938.

CROZER, Samuel Aldrich, manufacturer, capitalist; b. Aston Twp., Delaware Co., Pa., Dec. 25, 1825; s. John P. C.; m. Abigail Cheney, 1854. Entered his father's mills at 17; has extensive interests in iron and coal mines, etc. Pres. Crozer Theol. Sem. from founding, 1868; pres. Nat. Bapt. Council for Missionary Purposes 50 yrs., Bapt. Publication Soc., Pa. Training Sch. for Feeble Minded Children at Elwyn; mgr. Deaf and Dumb Asylum, Phila.; pres. Upland (Pa.) Borough Council over 30 yrs. Has personally erected many Bapt. chs. in Delaware Co., Pa.; gave large tract of land to city of Chester, Pa., for pub. park. Home: Upland, Pa. Died 1910.

CROZIER, Herbert William, cons. engineer; b. San Francisco, Calif., June 28, 1875; s. William J. and Elizabeth (Mackeon) C.; student Cogswell Poly. Engring. Sch., San Francisco, 1891-92, Mechanics Inst. Schs., San Francisco, 1892-95; B.S., U. of Calif., 1899; m. Elizabeth Hyde, June 9, 1904; children—Elizabeth (Mrs. Milton G. Mauer), Hallett; m. 2d, Mary E. Sevison, Feb. 22, 1925. Engaged in constrn. work, Pacific Electric Ry., between Vallejo and Napa, Stockton and Sacramento; with Ore. Electric Ry., 1902-1905; hydro-electric installation on Stanislaus River, Calif., 1905-09; hydro-electric exploration on Klamath River, Calif., 1912-15, same and development work, Hoh, Queets, Cowlitz, North and Columbia rivers, Wash., 1922; cons. engr., State of Nev. (mem. Ariz.-Nev. Engrs. Conf., Ariz., Nev. and Calif. Engrs. Conf., Boulder Canyon project), 1923-26; appraisal commr. Islais Creek Reclamation Dist., San Francisco, and cons. engr. Nev.-Colo. River Commn., 1927-28; v.p. Calif. Desert Products Co. Rep. Monterey Breakwater before Bd. Engrs. for Rivers and Harbors, Washington, D.C., 1929; West Coast Naval Airship Base, Sunnyvale, Calif., before House Naval Affairs Committee, 1930; Redwood Harbor project before U.S. dist. engrs., 1931. Cons. engr., Central Valley project, 1935; project mgr. Boulder-Pioche project, 1936-37. Home: San Francisco, Calif. Died Apr. 14, 1939.

CROZIER, Norman Robert, supt. schs.; b. Sardis, Miss., Sept. 14, 1877; s. Robert Haskins and Mary Elizabeth (Reinhardt) C.; B.A., U. of Tex., 1899; Litt.D., Austin Coll., 1925; LL.D., Southern Methodist U., 1931; m. Anne Starke Gardner, Dec. 23, 1902; children—Norman Robert, Isabelle Gardner (dec.), Mary Catherine. Teacher and prin. various high schs.; supt. schs., Dallas, Tex., 1924—. Dir. Summer Normal Sch., Southern Methodist U., 1917; lecturer in edn. U. of Tex., summer of 1920; dir. of Summer Normal Sch., U. of Tex., 1921, 22, 23; mem. bd. of consultants, Nat. Survey of School Finance, 1931-32. Pres. N.E.A., 1930-31. Democrat. Presbyn. Home: Dallas, Tex. Died Sept. 4, 1940.

CRUCE, Lee, governor; b. Crittenden Co., Ky., July 8, 1863; s. James Winlock and Jane (Hill) C.; ed. Marion (Ky.) Acad., 1 yr., and Vanderbilt U., Nashville, 1 yr.; m. Chickie LaFlore, June 21, 1893 (died 1903); 1 dau., Lorena Jane. In law practice, Ardmore, Indian Ty., 1891-1901; cashier, 1901-03, pres., 1903-10, Ardmore Nat. Bank. Gov. of Okla., term 1911-15. Democrat. Presbyn. Trustee Hargrove Coll., Ardmore. Mason (32°). Home: Ardmore, Okla. Died Jan. 16, 1933.

CRUGER, Mary, novelist; b. Oscawana, N.Y., May 9, 1834; d. Hon. Nicholas and Eliza (Kortright) C.; after the death of her parents built her present home, devoting herself to literature. Author: Hyperæsthesia, 1886; A Den of Thieves, or the Lay Reader of St. Mark's, 1886; The Vanderheyde Manor-House, 1887; How She Did It, 1888; Brotherhood, 1891. Home: Montrose, N.Y. Died 1908.

CRUIKSHANK, Alfred B., lawyer, author; b. Fredericton, N.B., Can., Sept. 8, 1847; s. John and Matilda J. C.; came to U.S., 1863; LL.B., New York U., 1874; m. Jessie Goodliff, (died 1909); m. 2d, Elisa Ruiz, Jan. 4, 1911. Served as pvt. 2d Mass. Cav., Sept. 1864-June 1865; practiced at N.Y. City, 1874-1919 (retired). Episcopalian. Mason. Author: The True Character of Hamlet, 1918; Popular Misgovernment in the United States, 1920. Died Oct. 9, 1933.

CRUM, William Demos, diplomatic service; b. Charleston, S.C., Feb. 9, 1859; s. Darius and Charlotte C.; grad. Avery Normal Inst., Am. Missionary Sch., Charleston, 1875; student, U. of S.C.; M.D., Howard U., Washington, 1881; m. Ellen Craft, of London, Eng., Oct. 19, 1883. Practiced medicine at Charleston, 1881-1910. Collector, port of Charleston, 1904-10; Am. minister resident and consul gen. to Liberia, June 13, 1910—. Died Dec. 7, 1912.

CRUMBACKER, William Pollock, alienist; b. Wheeling, Va. (now W.Va.), Dec. 20, 1857; s. John Hubbs (M.D.) and Hannah Jane (Pollock) C.; M.D., Med. Coll. of Ohio (now med. dept. U. of Cincinnati), 1882; post-grad. work in neurology and psychiatry, New York Polyclinic, 1892, in hosps. Great Britain and Ireland, 1897-98; m. Emma L. Bower, Nov. 13, 1888. Practiced with father at Antrim, Guernsey Co., O., 1882-84; asst. phys. Athens Asylum (now Athens State Hosp.), 1884-89; gen. practice, Cambridge, O., 1889-90; supt. Athens Asylum, 1890-92; supt. W.Va. Hosp. for Insane, Weston, W.Va., 1893-97; supt. Independence (Ia.) State Hosp., 1902—. Died May 14, 1920.

CRUMMER, Le Roy, M.D.; b. Elizabeth, Ill., Apr. 15, 1872; s. Benjamin F. and Mary Louise (DonKersley) C.; B.S., U. of Mich., 1893; M.D., Northwestern U. Med. Sch., 1896; Litt.D., U. of Mich., 1929; m. Myrtle A. Kelley, July 20, 1922. Began practice at Omaha, Neb., 1897; prof. medicine, U. of Neb.,

1919-25, emeritus; then prof. history of medicine, U. of Calif. at San Francisco and U. of Southern Calif. at Los Angeles. Served as capt., Med. Corps, U.S.A., World War. Republican. Author: Clinical Features of Heart Disease, 1925. Editor: An Introduction to the Study of Physic (by Wm. Heberden), 1929. Collector of early med. books and manuscripts. Home: Los Angeles, Calif. Died Jan. 1, 1934.

CRUMP, Rousseau O., congressman; b. Pittsford, N.Y., May 20, 1843; ed. in schools there and in Rochester, N.Y.; established in lumber business at Plainwell, Mich.; located and built mill in W. Bay City, 1881; formed Crump Mfg. Co., 1884, and has large lumber interests; was 4 years alderman, and, 1892-96, mayor of W. Bay City, Mich.; member Congress from 10th Mich. dist., 1895-1901. Republican. Home: West Bay City, Mich. Died 1901.

CRUMPACKER, Edgar Dean, congressman; b. Laporte Co., Ind., May 27, 1851; s. Theophilus and Harriet (Emmons) C.; ed. common schs. and Valparaiso Acad.; admitted to bar, 1876; m. Charlotte A. Lucas, Apr. 20, 1879. Pros. atty. 31st Jud. Dist., Ind., 1884-88; judge Appellate Ct. of Ind., 1891-93; mem. 55th to 62d Congresses (1897-1913), 10th Ind. Dist. Republican. Home: Valparaiso, Ind. Died May 19, 1920.

CRUMPACKER, Maurice Edgar, congressman; b. Valparaiso, Ind., Dec. 19, 1886; s. Edgar Dean and Charlotte (Lucas) C.; grad. Culver (Ind.) Mil. Acad., 1905; A.B., U. of Mich., 1909; studied law, Harvard 1909-12; m. Cully Cook, Oct. 8, 1913; 3 sons. Admitted to Ore. bar, 1912, and began practice at Portland; spl. dep. dist. atty., Multnomah Co., Ore., 1921; mem. 69th Congress (1925-27), 3d Ore. Dist. Served as capt. U.S. Army, World War. Republican. Protestant. Home: Portland, Ore. Died July 24, 1927.

CRUMPTON, Washington Bryan; b. Camden, Wilcox Co., Ala., Feb. 24, 1842; s. Henry Tally and Matilda Smith (Bryan) C.; student Georgetown Coll., Ky., 2 yrs.; m. Ellen Cochran, 1872 (died 1899); m. 2d, Florence Harris, 1910. Served with Co. H, 37th Miss. Inf., 3 yrs., as pvt. sergt. and lt.; wounded 3 times (Vicksburg, Atlanta and Nashville). Ordained Bapt. ministry, 1870; pastorates in several country and village chs. in Ala. and 1st Ch., Meridian, Miss. In gen. denom. work, 1855—; corr. sec. Bapt. Mission Bd. of Ala., for 28 yrs., emeritus, 1915. Editor Alabama Baptist, 1895. Pres. Anti-Saloon League of Ala., from its beginning. Trustee Southern Bapt. Theol. Sem., Louisville; pres. Ala. Bapt. State Conv., 1917—. Democrat. Author: The Adventures of Two Alabama Boys, 1912; A Book of Memories, 1921. Home: Montgomery, Ala. Deceased.

CRUNDEN, Frederick Morgan, librarian; b. Gravesend, Eng., Sept. 1, 1847; s. Benjamin Robert and Mary (Morgan) C.; came to U.S. in infancy; A.B., Washington U., 1868, A.M., 1872 (LL.D., 1905); m. Kate Edmondson, 1889. Prin. grammar schools, St. Louis, 1869-72; prof. Washington U., 1872-76; librarian St. Louis Pub. Library, 1877-1909. Mem. A.L.A. (pres. 1890); v.p. Internat. Library Conf., London, 1897; chmn. library sect. Internat. Congress Arts and Sciences, St. Louis, 1904. Home: St. Louis, Mo. Died 1911.

CRUZ, Anibal, diplomat; b. Falca, Chile, Aug. 2, 1865; s. Rafael and Zoila (Diaz) C.; LL.B., U. of Chile, 1884; m. Isidora Huneeus, June 8, 1896. Sec. of legation, agt. and counsel for Chile, 1891; prof. administrative law, U. of Chile, 1896; U.S. and Chilean Claims Commn., 1899; mem. Chilean Congress, 1903-07; sec. of War, Chile, 1904; Chilean minister to Mexico, 1907, to U.S., 1907—. Roman Catholic. Died 1911.

CRYER, Matthew Henry, oral surgeon; b. Manchester, Eng., July 21, 1840; s. Henry and Elizabeth (Cookson) C.; grad. Phila. Dental Coll., 1876; M.D., U. of Pa., 1877; m. Martha Gates Phillips, June 17, 1889. Came to America, 1851; enlisted in 6th Ohio Cav., 1861, and advanced to maj., Apr. 8, 1865; participated in Shenandoah Valley campaign, 1862, battles of the Wilderness, Trevilian Station, Mallory's Cross Roads, St. Mary's Ch. (two horses shot under him); wounded at Deep Harbor, Va., July 28, 1864; in command of regt. at Battle of Boydton Plank Road, Oct. 27, 1864, and at Battle of Appomattox; opened the last fight between Grant and Lee, Apr. 9, 1865. Practiced in Phila., 1877—; prof. oral surgery, U. of Pa., 1898—; visiting surgeon, Phila. Gen. Hosp.; consulting dental surgeon, Univ. Hosp. Republican. Author: Regional Anatomy, 1886; Studied of Internal Anatomy of the Face, 1901; Imperial Stereoscopic Anatomy of Head (with D. J. Cunningham and David Waterston), 1909. Wrote chapter on Extraction of Teeth, in American Text-Book of Operative Dentistry, and one on General Hygiene of Mouth, in Musser and Keller's Handbook of Practical Treatment. Home: Lansdowne, Pa. Died Aug. 12, 1921.

CUBBERLEY, Ellwood Patterson, univ. prof.; b. Andrews, Ind., June 6, 1868; s. Edwin Blanchard and Kate (Coryell) C.; A.B., Ind. U., 1891; A.M., Columbia, 1902, Ph.D., 1905; LL.D., U. of Ia., 1923, Indiana U., 1934; m. Helen Van Uxem, June 15, 1892. Prof. and pres. Vincennes U., 1891-96; city supt. schs., San Diego, Calif., 1896-98; asso. prof. edn., Stanford Univ., 1898-1906, prof., 1906-33, dean sch. edn., 1917-33, dean emeritus, 1933. Mem. Baltimore Ednl. Commn., 1911, Butte Sch. Survey Bd., 1914, and Nat. Sch. Finance Inquiry, 1921-24; dir. Portland (Ore.) Sch. Survey, 1913, Salt Lake City Sch. Survey, 1915, Oakland (Calif.) Sch. Survey, 1915; mem. Ednl. Research Com., Commonwealth Fund, 1920-25. Adviser Calif., N.M., Wash. sch. legislative commns., 1920-21. Awarded Butler Silver Medal, Columbia Univ., 1915; University Medal, 1933. Republican. Author: Syllabus of Lectures on the History of Education, 1902, 2d edition, 1904; School Funds and Their Apportionment, 1905; Certification of Teachers, 1906; Changing Conceptions of Education, 1909; The Improvement of Rural Schools, 1911; Rural Life and Education, 1913, revised edit. 1922; State and County Educational Reorganization, 1914; Portland School Survey, 1915; Public School Administration, 1915, 22, 29; School Organization and Administration, 1916; Public Education in the United States, 1919, revised edit., 1934; A History of Education, 1921; Readings in the History of Education, 1921; A Brief History of Education, 1922; The Principal and His School, 1923; An Introduction to the Study of Education, 1925; 2d edit. with W. C. Eells, 1933; State School Administration, 1927; (with E. C. Elliot) State and County School Administration, Source Book, 1915; (with J. B. Sears) Cost of Education in California, 1924; Readings in Public Education in the United States, 1934. Dept. editor, Monroe's Cyclopedia of Education, 1911-13. Home: Stanford University, Calif. Died Sept. 15, 1941.

CUBBERLY, Fred, lawyer; b. Chillicothe, Mo., Oct. 28, 1869; s. George and Sarah (Frazier) C.; common sch. edn.; m. Etta Hancock, Oct. 21, 1903; children—Hazel Hancock (Mrs. James F. Merrin), Helen Frazier (Mrs. E. B. Mann). Admitted to Fla. bar, 1898; U.S. commr. Northern Dist. of Fla., 1898-1908; apptd. U.S. collector of customs, Cedar Keys, Fla., by Pres. Roosevelt, 1902, reapptd., 1906; resigned Feb. 1909; U.S. atty. Northern Dist. of Fla., 1908—; city atty. Cedar Keys, 1909-11; judge Municipal Court Gainesville, Fla., 1914-16; again U.S. dist. atty., by appmt. of President Coolidge, 1923; city atty. Gainesville, Fla., 1916-17. Sec. Rep. State Com., 1927; del. Rep. Nat. Conv., 1920. Republican. Home: Gainesville, Fla. Died Aug. 11, 1932.

CUCKSON, John, Unitarian minister; b. Caistor, Lincolnshire, Eng., Jan. 25, 1846; s. John and Rebecca (Fardell) C.; ed. Unitarian Coll., Manchester, Eng., 1865-68, Queen's Coll., Liverpool, Eng., 1868-72; m. Sarah M. Evans, Mar. 4, 1868. Minister Hamilton Rd. Ch., Liverpool, Eng., 1868-72, Newhall Hill Ch., Birmingham, Eng., 1872-81, Bradford, Eng., 1881-84, Springfield, Mass., 1884-92, Arlington St. Ch., Boston, 1892-1900, Plymouth, Mass., 1901—. Republican. Died 1907.

CUDAHY, Edward Aloysius, Sr., packer; b. Milwaukee, Wis., Feb. 1, 1860; s. Patrick and Elizabeth (Shaw) Cudahy; ed. pub. schs., Milwaukee; m. Elizabeth Murphy, Nov. 27, 1884 (died 1937); children—Edward A., Eugenia (Mrs. Frank E. Wilhelm), Helen (Mrs. Austin H. Niblack), Florence (Mrs. Vaughan C. Spalding), Alice (Mrs. John N. Stearns, Jr.). Began with Armour Packing Co., Chicago, 1875; asso. with brother Michael and established the Armour-Cudahy Packing Co., South Omaha, Neb.; title later changed to The Cudahy Packing Co., became pres., 1910, chmn. bd., 1926. Catholic. Home: Chicago, Ill. Died Oct. 18, 1941.

CUDAHY, John, packer; b. Callan, County Kilkenny, Ireland, Nov. 2, 1843; s. Patrick and Elizabeth (Shaw) C.; came to U.S., 1849, parents settling in Milwaukee; attended pub. schs. until 14 yrs. old; m. Mary Nolan, 1873; m. 2d, Margaret F. O'Neil, 1882. At 14 to 17 worked in packing house of Ed. Roddis, Milwaukee, later 4 yrs. with John Plankinton and Plankinton & Armour; then in fruit and ornamental tree business until 1870; afterward in employ of Milwaukee packing firms; became partner Chapin & Co., Chicago, 1875, firm becoming Chapin & Cudahy, 1877, and later Cudahy Packing Co.; also partner with his brother, Michael, in Cudahy Brothers Co., packers, of Milwaukee. Home: Chicago, Ill. Died Apr. 23, 1915.

CUDAHY, Michael, merchant; b. Callan, Co. Kilkenny, Ireland, Dec. 7, 1841; s. Patrick and Elizabeth (Shaw) C.; came to U.S., 1849, family settling in Milwaukee; married; became employe in packing house, 1855; became packing house mgr. and meat insp.; partner in Armour & Co., 1873-90; then pres. Cudahy Packing Co., packers, Omaha, Sioux City and Los Angeles. Home: Chicago, Ill. Died 1910.

CUDAHY, Patrick, packer; b. Callan, Co. Kilkenny, Ireland, Mar. 17, 1849; s. Patrick and Elizabeth (Shaw) C.; came to United States, 1849, parents settling in Milwaukee; ed. in pub. schs., Milwaukee; m. Annie A. Madden, 1877. Began business life at 12 as a delivery boy for a Milwaukee grocer; at 14 entered employ Roddis Packing Co.; later worked for Layton & Co., Lyman & Wooley, and Plankinton & Armour, becoming supt., 1874, and a partner, 1876, in latter; with brother John bought Mr. Plankinton's interest, 1888, firm becoming Cudahy Bros.; moved plant to Cudahy, nr. Milwaukee, 1893; organizing Cudahy Bros. Co., of which was pres. until 1915. Home: Milwaukee, Wis. Died July 25, 1919.

CUDDEBACK, Allan W(inter), pub. utility exec.; b. Cuddebackville, N.Y., April 11. 1868 s. Thomas and Sally J. (Cogdil) C.; student Cornell U., 1890-91, Stanford U., 1891-94; m. Hester Beatty, Oct. 30, 1901; children—Thomas M., Louise B.; m. 2d, Edith A. Finley, July 24, 1929. With U.S. Coast and Geodetic Survey, 1904-05; asst. engr. Metropolitan Street Ry., N.Y. City, 1905-06; same, Newark (N.J.) Water Supply, 1898-1926; engr., supt. 1926-30, v.p. and gen. mgr. Passaic (N.J.) Water Supply; v.p. and gen. mgr. Federal Water Service Corp., N.Y. City, 1926-33; pres. New York Water Service Corp., 1931—. Pres. Am. Water Works Assn, 1926. Republican. Protestant. Home: New York, N.Y. Died Dec. 4, 1938.

CUDDEBACK, William Herman, judge; b. Orange Co., N.Y., Mar. 25, 1852; s. Lewis Cuddeback and Caroline (Thompson) C.; Cornell U., 1870-74; unmarried. Admitted to N.Y. bar, 1877; practiced at Goshen, 1877-85, Buffalo, 1885-1913; chmn. Dem. County Com. of Erie Co., 1895-98; corp. counsel, City of Buffalo, 1898-1902; asso. judge Court of Appeals of N.Y., term 1913-26. Presbyn. Home: Buffalo, N.Y. Died Aug. 16, 1919.

CUENY, Elizabeth, concert mgr.; b. Flint, Mich.; d. Meinrad and Elizabeth (Wimmer) C.; grad. Perry Sch. Oratory and Dramatic Art, St. Louis, 1904. Began business career at 16; newspaper writer, corr., booking of artists; concert management, 1915—; established Civic Music League, St. Louis Chamber Music Soc., and has represented many of the leading artists and orgns. in St. Louis. Sec. woman's com., Council of Nat. Defense, Mo., 1916. Mem. Nat. Concert Mgrs. Assn. (sec.-treas., 1918-22; pres. 1922-23). Died Mar. 29, 1931.

CULBERSON, Charles A., senator; b. Dadeville, Ala., June 10, 1855; s. David B. (congressman from Tex., for 22 yrs.) and Eugenia (Kimbal) C.; grad. Va. Mil. Inst., 1874; law student U. of Va., 1876-77; settled in Tex., 1856; in practice at Dallas., 1887—. Was co. atty. Marion Co.; atty. gen., 1890-94; gov. of Tex., 2 terms, 1894-98; U.S. senator, terms 1899-1905, 1905-11, 1911-17, 1917-23. Died Mar. 19, 1925.

CULBERTSON, Emma Valeria (Pintard) Bicknell, physician; b. New Albany, Ind., Dec. 2, 1854; d. John C. and Mary P. C.; ed. by governess and tutors at home and in Europe; A.B., Vassar, 1877, A.M., 1881; M.D., Woman's Med. Coll. of Pa., 1881; unmarried. Attending surgeon N.E. Hosp. for Women and Children, 1891—. Home: Boston, Mass. Deceased.

CULBERTSON, Henry Coe, clergyman; b. Cincinnati, July 11, 1874; s. James Coe (M.D.) and Sarah (Pogue) C.; A.B., U. of Cincinnati, 1895; student Columbia Law Sch., 1896-98; B.D., U. of Chicago, 1900; D.D., Lenox, 1910; LL.D., Mo. Valley, 1914; Litt.D., Carroll, 1919; m. Irene A. Blood, July 16, 1923; children—Horace Coe, Henry Alvin. Asst. pastor Presbyn. Ch., Lake Forest, Ill., 1901-02; ordained Presbyn. ministry, 1902; pastor Iola, Kan., 1902-07; pres. Coll. of Emporia, 1907-17; pres. Ripon (Wis.) Coll., 1918-21; lecturer and circuit mgr. Radcliffe Chautauqua System, 1921-23; pastor Plymouth Congl. Ch., Los Angeles, 1923-25, Mesa Congl. Ch., 1925-27; on merger of Plymouth and Mesa Chs., 1927, under name Plymouth Congl. Ch. became pastor of new organization; pastor (with Dr. C. F. Aked) of All Souls' Ch. (Congl.), Los Angeles, 1929-30; pastor First Congl. Ch., Lorain, O., 1930—. Pres. Congl. Ministerial Union, 1925-26; v.p. Ministerial Assn. of Los Angeles (all denominations), 1927, pres., 1929. Mason. Author: Evolution Helps Christianity, 1927; Songs of the Twelve Apostles, 1927. Died Mar. 2, 1933.

CULBERTSON, James Coe, physician, editor; b. Miami Co., O., Dec. 19, 1840; s. William and Mary Ann C.; M.D., Bellevue Hosp. Med. Coll., 1865; m. Virginia B. Clark, May 10, 1865 (died 1866); 2d, Sarah Pogue, Apr. 22, 1873 (died 1884); 3d, Sophie W. Braun, June 18, 1888. Entered army, pvt. Co. D, 5th Ohio Inf., Apr. 19, 1861; became hosp. steward U.S.A., Sept. 18, 1862; asst. surgeon, 137th Ohio Inf., May 10, 1864; after war in med. practice at Cincinnati; editor and pub. Cincinnati Lancet-Clinic, 1873—; editor Journal A.M.A., 1891-93; prof. principles and practice of medicine, Cincinnati Coll. Medicine and Surgery, 1893—. Mem. Cincinnati Bd. of Aldermen, 1884-88, Bd. of Edn., 1896—. Author: Luke, the Beloved Physician, 1899. Republican. Died 1908.

CULBERTSON, John J., v.p. Southland Cotton Oil Co.; b. Mar. 16, 1853; s. John J. and Amelia (Fonshill) C.; dist. sch. edn.; m. Emily Lee; children—John J., Emily Lee, Florance Fonshill. **Employed**

with dry goods commn. merchants in New York until 1883, then came South to Ala. and in 1884 built his first cotton oil mill in Paris, Tex; sold out to Am. Cotton Oil Trust; mgr. Southern Cotton Oil Company's plant, Little Rock, Ark., 1887, later mgr. Houston, Tex., plant; organized, 1891, Paris Oil and Cotton Co., and later built and operated mills at Corsicana, Ladonia, Temple and Waxahachie, Tex., and Oklahoma City, Wynnewood and Chandler, Okla., Shreveport, La., and Jackson, Miss., organized Southland Cotton Oil Co., of which was v.p. Dir. Federal Reserve Bank, of Dallas Tex., from orgn., 1914. Presented citizens cup of Paris, 1926. Sr. warden Episcopal Ch. Died Sept. 27, 1932.

CULIN (Robert) Stewart, museum dir., curator; b. Phila., July 13, 1858; s. John and Mira (Barrett) C.; ed. Nazareth Hall, Pa.; m. Alice (Mumford) Roberts, Apr. 11, 1917. Director U. of Pa. Mus., 1892-99; curator ethnology, Brooklyn Inst. Mus., 1903—. Made numerous scientific expdns. to Japan, Korea, China and India, and among Am. Indian tribes. Knight of Royal Order of Isabella the Catholic; Officer Order of the White Lion (Czechoslovakian). Author: Korean Games, 1896; Chess and Playing Cards, 1896; American Indian Games, 1905. Home: Brooklyn, N.Y. Died Apr. 8, 1929.

CULKINS, William Clement, business exec.; b. May 12, 1868; s. John and Elizabeth Jane (Steed) C.; attended high sch., Ironton, O., 1886; m. Ida Nicholson, Feb. 14, 1906; children— William Burton (dec.), John Paul (dec.), Florence Louise (Mrs. Edward Joseph Koper). Began as sch. teach, 1887; successively editor Daily Irontonian, N.Y. corr. Commercial Gazette of Cincinnati, city editor Cincinnati Post, Washington (D.C.) corr. Scripps-McRae Press Assn., polit. writer Cincinnati Times-Star, dir. and sec. Hotel Gibson Co., pres. Hyde Park Bldg. & Loan Co., v.p. and gen. mgr. Columbia Life Ins. Co., dept. mgr. Equitable Life Assurance Soc. of N.Y.; city auditor Cincinnati, 1906-08; dir. Cincinnati Street Rys., 1917-21; then exec. sec. Ohio Valley Improvement Assn.; a pioneer in river improvement, and regarded as an authority on organization work. Republican. Episcopalian. Mason. Home: Cincinnati, O. Died July 21, 1936.

CULLEN, Edgar Montgomery, judge; b. Brooklyn, Dec. 4, 1843; s. Dr. Henry J. and Eliza (McCue) C.; A.B., Columbia, 1860, A.M., 1863, LL.D., 1892; LL.D., Union College, 1905, and Harvard U., 1915; unmarried. Second lt. 1st U.S. Inf., Mar. 24, 1862; 1st lt., Sept. 29, 1863; col. 96th N.Y. Inf., Dec. 26, 1862; hon. mustered out of vol. service, Mar. 21, 1865; resigned from U.S.A., Apr. 9, 1865. Admitted to bar, 1867; asst. dist. atty., 1872-75; engr.-in-chief, with rank of brig. gen. on staff of Gov. Tilden, 1875; justice Supreme Ct. of N.Y., 1880-Dec. 31, 1913, when retired by law; was asso. judge Ct. of Appeals, 1900-04, chief judge on nomination of both parties, Nov. 1904-Dec. 1913. Democrat. Home: Brooklyn, N.Y. Died May 23, 1922.

CULLEN, Glenn E(rnest), university prof.; b. Isle Saint George, O., Apr. 1, 1890; s. Charles and Emma (Gould) C.; A.B., U. of Mich., 1912, B.Chem. Engring., 1913; Ph.D., Columbia, 1917; m. Marie Wherry, June 22, 1917; children—Mary Alice, Donna Jean, Glenn Wherry. Research chemist at Rockefeller Inst. for Med. Research, New York, 1913-22; asso. prof. research, medicine, U. of Pa., 1922-24, prof. biochemistry, Vanderbilt U., 1924-31; traveling fellow, Rockefeller Foundation, 1924-25; prof. biochemistry, Grad. Sch., and prof. research pediatrics, Coll. of Medicine, U. of Cincinnati, 1931—; dir. laboratories of Children's Hosp. Research Foundation, 1931—. Served as capt. Sanitary Corps, World War. Pres. Am. Soc. Biol. Chemists, 1937-39. Writer on enzymes, antiseptics, chemistry of blood in health and disease, diseases of children. Home: Cincinnati, O. Died Apr. 11, 1940.

CULLER, Joseph Albertus, univ. prof.; b. on farm in Wayne Co., O., Mar. 5, 1858; s. Michael and Barbara C.; A.B., U. of Wooster, 1884, later A.M., Ph.D., 1900; m. Isabella Carnes, 1887. Prin. high schs., Cambridge, O., 1884-85, Kenton, O., 1885-1900; supt. schs., Kenton, O., 1900-01, Bowling Green, O., 1901-03; prof. physics, Miami U., 1903-26, emeritus. Presbyn. Republican. Author: 1st, 2d and 3d Book of Physiology, 1904; First Book in Physics, 1905; High School Book of Physics, 1906; General Physics for Colleges, Mechanics and Heat, 1909; Electricity, Electromagnetic Waves and Sound, 1913; Physics for College Freshmen, 1922. Home: Oxford, O. Died May 18, 1937.

CULLINAN, Joseph Stephen, corp. official; b. Sharon, Pa., Dec. 31, 1860; s. John Francis and Mary (Considine) C.; ed. pub. schs.; m. Lucie Halm, of Lima, O., Apr. 14, 1891 (she died Oct. 26, 1929); children—John Halm (dec.), Craig Francis, Nina Jane, Mrs. Margaret Anna Wray, Mrs. Mary Catherine Cravens. Pres. Texas Co., 1903-13; organizer, 1916, and pres. of American Republics Corp. of Delaware. Mem. bd. dirs. C.R.B., Ednl. Foundation; chmn. advisory council and dir. Intracoastal Canal Assn. of La. and Tex.; mem. exec. com. Goethals Memorial Commn.; pres. Mount Rushmore Nat. Memorial Soc. of Black Hills; chmn. Mt. Rushmore Nat. Memorial Commn., dir. Nat. Rivers and Harbors Congress, mem. Nat. Industrial Conf. Bd. Mem. Chamber of Commerce of the U.S.; mem. nat. advisory council Am. Liberty League. Home: Houston, Tex. Died Mar. 11, 1937.

CULLISON, James Buchanan, judge; b. New London, Ia., Sept. 21, 1857; s. Elisha and Matilda (McCabe) Cullison; Valparaiso (Ind.) Normal Sch., 1881-82, and Kirksville (Mo.) State Normal Sch., 1882; m. May Mary Sharp, July 30, 1882; children—James B., June Beatrice (Mrs. William John Otjen), Tyra Gladstone, Irene Margaret (Mrs. Wm. Jordan Vaught), May Elizabeth (Mrs. John W. R. Myers), Douglas Lincoln, Cecelia Jennette (Mrs. Glenn Willis Johnston). Teacher pub. schs., 1875-82; admitted to Kan. bar, 1888; register U.S. Land Office, Enid, Okla., 1897-1902; probate judge and county judge, Garfield Co., Okla., 1904-11; dist. judge, 21st Okla. Dist., 1911-29; asso. justice Supreme Court of Okla., Jan. 14, 1929, for term ending Jan. 1935. Republican. Mason. Home: Enid, Okla. Died Sept. 11, 1936.

CULLOM, Shelby Moore, senator; b. Monticello, Wayne Co., Ky., Nov. 22, 1829; s. Richard Northcraft and Elizabeth (Coffey) C.; family removed to Tazewell Co., Ill., 1830; acad. edn. Rock River Sem., Mt. Morris, Ill., 2 yrs.; (LL.D., U. of Ill., 1903); went to Springfield, 1853, to study law; has since resided there; admitted to Ill. bar, 1855; m. Hanna M. Fisher, Dec. 12, 1855 (died 1861); m. 2d, Julia Fisher, May 5, 1863 (died 1909). Was city atty. and continued to practice law until 1865; presdl. elector on Fillmore ticket, 1852; mem. Ill. Ho. of Rep., 1856, 1860-61, 1872, 1873-74 (speaker, 1861, 1873); mem. 39th to 41st Congresses (1865-71); apptd., by President Lincoln, 1862, with George S. Boutwell and Charles A. Dana to pass upon accounts of U.S. q.m. and commissary officers; chmn. Ill. delegation Rep. Nat. Conv., Phila., 1872, and placed Gen. Grant in nomination for the Presidency; gov. of Ill., 1876-83, resigned; U.S. senator, 1883—. Republican. Home: Springfield, Ill. Died Jan. 28, 1914.

CULLOP, William Allen, congressman; b. Knox Co., Ind., Mar. 28, 1853; s. William W. and Maria J. (Patterson) C.; A.B., Hanover Coll., Ind., 1878, A.M., 1883; m. Mrs. Artie Goodwin, June 1898. Admitted to bar, 1881, and practiced at Vincennes, Ind. Pros. atty., 12th Jud. Dist. of Ind., 1882-86; mem. Ind. Ho. of Rep., 1890-94 (chmn. com. on ways and means and leader of majority in House); mem. 61st to 64th Congresses (1909-17), 2d Ind. Dist. Presbyterian. Home: Vincennes, Ind. Died Oct. 9, 1927.

CULMER, Henry L. A., painter; b. Davington, Kent Co., Eng., Mar. 25, 1854; s. Frederick and Mary (Kennett) C.; ed. free schs., London, to 10; came to America, 1867; m. Annette Susan Wells, Dec. 31, 1878. Job printer and pub., Salt Lake City, 1876-82; mem. firm of G. F. Culmer & Bros., wholesale mchts., 1882—; sec. and treas. Culmer Paint & Glass Co., Kyune Graystone Co.; dir. Nat. Bank of the Republic, 1890-1900; editor and pub. Salt Lake Journal of Commerce, 1881-90. Painter of landscapes; State of Utah presented a painting by him, "The Great Augusta Bridge," to President Taft, as a souvenir of his visit, Aug. 1909. Home: Salt Lake City, Utah. Died Feb. 10, 1914.

CULP, John M., railway official; b. Harrisville, W.Va., Apr. 28, 1849; s. Amos and Cevina Ann (Heaton) C.; ed. high sch., 1864-65; m. Juliet B. Edmonds, Oct. 15, 1889. Became clerk to chief clerk, gen. frt. agent's office, L.&N. R.R., 1870; gen. frt. agt., L.&N. R.R. System, 1880-91; asst. traffic mgr. Richmond & Danville Ry., 1891-94; traffic mgr., 1894-1902, 4th v.p., 1902-04, 3d v.p., at Washington, D.C., 1904-06, v.p., in charge of traffic, Dec. 14, 1906—, Southern Ry.; v.p. Northern Ala. Ry., Va. & Southwestern Ry. Deceased.

CULVER, Charles Mortimer, M.D.; b. West Troy (now Watervliet), N.Y., Sept. 28, 1856; s. Cyrus Lee and Mary Ann (Bullock) C.; A.B., Union Coll., 1878, A.M., 1881; M.D., Albany Med. Coll., 1881; Wilhelm Friedrich U., Berlin, 1881-82; U. of Paris, 1882-83; m. Jessie Munsell, May 10, 1887; children—Cyrus Lee, Mary. In practice at Albany, 1883-1927; specialized in treatment of eye; ophthalmic surgeon Albany Orphan Asylum. Pres. Class of 1878, Union Coll., 1875-76, then sec.; alumni trustee Union Coll., 1888-92; pres. Albany Presbyn. Union, 1906-07; pres. Albany Citizens' Union, 1907; pres. Albany Civic League, 1908-11; pres. Progressive Democrats, Albany, 1910. Mem. Am. Acad. Medicine (1st v.p., 1901-02). Home: Delmar, N.Y. Died May 8, 1938.

CULVER, Helen, philanthropist; b. Little Valley, N.Y., Mar. 23, 1832; d. Lyman and Emeliza (Hull) C.; grad. Randolph (N.Y.) Acad., 1853; unmarried. Established pvt. sch., Sycamore, Ill., 1853; prin. primary sch. and teacher in grammar and high schs., Chicago, 1854-61; matron mil. hosps. at Murfreesboro, Tenn., under U.S. Sanitary Commn., 1863; entered real estate business, 1868, with her relative, Charles J. Hull, in Chicago, operating extensively in properties in the city and all over the West. After death of Charles J. Hull she built and endowed (1895) the four Hull Biol. Laboratories for U. of Chicago. Trustee Hull House Assn. from its organization, 1895. Died Aug. 19, 1925.

CULVER, Raymond B., coll. pres.; b. Branch Co., Mich., July 11, 1887; s. Frank Dwight and Sarah Maria (Walter) C.; Mus.B., Linfield Coll., 1910, A.B., 1914; A.B., Yale, 1916, B.D., A.M., 1921, Ph.D., 1924; m. Annabel Wood, Sept. 25, 1917; children—Josephine, John Howard. Grad. sec. Yale Y.M.C.A., 1916, sec. Y.M.C.A. Nat. War Work Council, 1917; ordained ministry Bapt. Ch., 1921; asso. minister 1st Congl. Ch., Waterbury, Conn., 1922-24; sec. Nat. Council Y.M.C.A.'s (student div.), 1924-36; prof. of bible and religious edn., Linfield Coll. (McMinnville, Ore.), 1933-36; pres. Frances Shimer Jr. Coll., Mt. Carroll, Ill., 1936—. Served as ensign U.S.N., 1918. Baptist. Author: Horace Mann and Religion in the Massachusetts Public Schools, 1929. Deceased.

CUMMING, Charles Atherton, artist; b. Knox Co., Ill., Mar. 31, 1858; s. George Paxton and Eliza Ellen (Atherton) C.; studied art at Chicago Acad., and Académie Julian, Paris, under Boulanger, Lefebvre and Benj. Constant. Founder, 1895, and dir. Cumming Sch. of Art (no applied arts and crafts), Des Moines, Ia.; established the Dept. of Graphic and Plastic Arts at State U. of Ia., 1910, and its head, 1910-27; organizer, 1915, and supt., 1915-27, Dept. of Graphic and Plastic Arts of Ia. State Fair and Expn.; decorator State Hist. Bldg., Pub. Library Bldg., etc. Painted mural decoration, "The Departure of the Indians from Ft. Des Moines," in Polk County Court House, Des Moines; 19 portraits in memorial collection Ia. Hist. Gallery, Des Moines; 8 portraits in memorial collection of Ia. State U.; landscapes in Women's Club Gallery, Des Moines; etc. Founder Ia. Art Guild, 1914; mem. Ia. Art Soc. (pres. 1897). Died Feb. 16, 1932.

CUMMINGS, Amos, congressman, journalist; b. Conkling, N.Y., May 15, 1841; entered father's printing office at 12; served in army in Civil War; was sergt. maj. in 26th N.J. inf. Afterward filled editorial positions on Tribune and Sun; mem. Congress from N.Y. dists., 1887-1903. Democrat. Died 1902.

CUMMINGS, Charles Amos, architect; b. Boston, June 26, 1833; s. Amos and Rebecca (Hopkins) C.; grad. Rensselaer Poly. Inst., 1850; m. Margaret Kimball, Oct. 12, 1869. Pres. Boston Soc. Architects, 1896-1902; mem. Boston Art Commn., 1890-92. Trustee Boston Athenæum, Boston Museum of Fine Arts. Author: History of Architecture in Italy from the Time of Constantine to the Dawn of the Renaissance, 1901 H5. Various articles in North American Review, Christian Examiner and other periodicals; collaborator in the Cyclo, of Architecture. Died 1905.

CUMMINGS, Clara Eaton, educator; b. Plymouth, N.H., July 13, 1855; d. Noah Cummings; grad. N.H. Normal School, Plymouth, N.H.; studied at Wellesley Coll., 1876-79; at Zurich U., 1886-87. Died 1906.

CUMMINGS, D(avid) Mark, capitalist; b. Pekin, Ill., Feb. 18, 1866; s. Columbus R. and Sarah M. C.; A.B., Yale, 1887; m. Ruth Dexter, 1893. Began as a banker and broker, Chicago, with Watriss, Breese & Cummings; on the death of father, 1897, succeeded him in the management of many of his large financial enterprises. Home: Chicago, Ill. Died Feb. 29, 1932.

CUMMINGS, Edward, clergyman; b. Colebrook, N.H., Apr. 20, 1861; s. Edward Norris and Lucretia Frances (Merrill) C.; grad. Woburn (Mass.) High Sch., 1879; A.B., Harvard, 1883, A.M., 1885; studied Harvard Law, Divinity, and Grad. schs., 1883-85; instr. English, Harvard and Radcliffe, 1885-87; Robert Treat Paine fellow in social sci., Harvard, 1888-91 (first incumbent of this fellowship); studied at École Libre des Sciences Politiques, Sorbonne and Coll. de France, Paris, and U. of Berlin; m. Rebecca Haswell Clarke, June 25, 1891; children—Edward Estlin, Elizabeth Frances. Instr. sociology, 1891-93, asst. prof., 1893-1900, Harvard; minister S. Congl. Ch., Boston, 1900-25 (succeeding late Edward Everett Hale, minister emeritus); minister emeritus First Church in Boston after merger of S. Congl. with First Ch., 1925. Gen. sec. World Peace Foundation, 1916—. Home: Boston, Mass. Died Nov. 2, 1926.

CUMMINGS, George W., journalist; b. Ill.; grad. Ind. State U., 1872; m. Dec. 10, 1879, Josephine de Fontaine. Journalist, 1882—; v.p. Am. Press Assn. Home: New York, N.Y. Died 1904.

CUMMINGS, James Howell, mfr.; b. Goshen, Pa., Aug. 7, 1867; s. John and Sarah E. (Thompson) C.; pub. sch. edn.; m. Anna C. Richards, Feb. 22, 1890. Began as office boy, John B. Stetson & Co. (hat mfrs.), Phila., 1882; became sec. J. B. Stetson Co., 1891, 2d v.p., 1901, and pres., 1906—; dir. many corps. Pres. Stetson Hosp., Phila. Republican. Methodist. Home: Philadelphia, Pa. Died Apr. 28, 1928.

CUMMINGS, John, statistician, economist; b. Colebrook, N.H., May 18, 1868; s. Edward Norris and Lucretia Frances (Merrill) C.; A.B., Harvard,

1891, A.M., 1892; Ph.D. in Polit. Economy, U. of Chicago, 1894; m. Carry Rebecca Howe, Dec. 3, 1902; 1 dau., Frances Ellen. Teacher economics and statistics Harvard, 1894-1900; editorial staff New York Evening Post, 1900; asst. prof. polit. economy, U. of Chicago, 1902-10; expert spl. agt. Census Bur., 1910-16; research expert Joint Congressional Commn. on Nat. Grants for Vocational Edn., 1914; statistician Vocational Surveys, Richmond, Va., 1914, Evansville and Indianapolis, Ind., 1915-16; editor and statistician Federal Bd. for Vocational Edn., 1917-23; statistician and economist Div. of Research and Statistics, Federal Reserve Bd., 1924-30; chief of research and statistical service, Federal Bd. for Vocational Education, 1930-33; chief of research and statistical service, vocation edn., U.S. Office of Edn., 1933—. Author: Poor Laws of Massachusetts and New York, 1895; Negro Population (Census Bur.), 1790-1815, 1918; Statistical Work of the Federal Government (in History of Statistics), 1918; Statistics (with Prof. W. B. Bailey), 1920; Statistics and Graphics, 1923. Home: 3029 Q St., Washington, D.C. Died June 26, 1936.

CUMMINGS, Wilbur Love, lawyer; b. Springfield, O., May 19, 1881; s. Finley Ogden and Rachel (Litler) C.; A.B., Kenyon Coll., 1902, hon. LL.D., 1928; LL.B., Columbia U., 1905; m. Marian Engle, Apr. 15, 1912; children—Wilbur L., Molly. Admitted to New York and Wash. bars, 1905; practiced law Seattle, 1905-18; mem. firm Sullivan & Cromwell, New York, 1918—; dir. many corps. Trustee Kenyon Coll. Republican. Died July 26, 1941.

CUMMINS, Albert Baird, senator; b. Carmichaels, Pa., Feb. 15, 1850; s. Thomas Layton and Sarah (Baird) C.; coll. edn. at Waynesburg, Pa.; LL.D., Waynesburg Coll., 1903, Cornell Coll., Ia., 1904; studied surveying and became asst. chief engr. Cincinnati, Richmond & Ft. Wayne R.R.; studied law in offices of McClellan & Hodges, Chicago; m. Ida L. Gallery, June 24, 1874. Admitted to Ill. bar, 1875; practiced Chicago, 1875-78; removed to Des Moines, Ia., 1878; mem. Ia. Ho. of Rep., 1888; candidate for U.S. senator, 1894 and 1900; chmn. Rep. State Conv., 1892 and 1896; mem. Rep. Nat. Com., 1896-1900; gov. of Ia., 1902-04, 1904-06, 1906-08; U.S. senator, 1908-27; succeeded Calvin Coolidge as pres. of Senate, Aug. 1923. Home: Des Moines, Ia. Died July 30, 1926.

CUMMINS, Albert Wilson, editor; b. Smyrna, Del., Oct. 25, 1867; s. David J. and Juliet (Polk) C.; B.S., Lafayette Coll., 1888, M.S., 1896; unmarried. Mng. editor Wilmington Morning News, 1892-1907; editor and v.p. Evening Journal, Wilmington, 1907-12; editor Morning News, 1912—. Episcopalian. Mason (32°). Home: Wilmington, Del. Died Feb. 14, 1935.

CUMMINS, John, lawyer; b. Angola, Ind., May 13, 1838; s. William and Almira C.; ed. pub. schs.; m. 2d, Sarah L. Henshaw, June 10, 1895. Admitted to bar Supreme Court, Ore., 1862; mem. Ore. legislature, 1862; removed to Ida., 1863; probate judge Owyhee Co., Ida., 1863; mem. and pres. Territorial Council (upper house of legislature), 1864-65; U.S. collector internal revenue, 1865-66; asso. justice Supreme Ct., Ida., 1866-68; went east, 1868; practiced in New York, 1872-1906; mayor Roselle Park, N.J., 1901-03; removed to Portland, Ore., 1906. Died Oct. 30, 1916.

CUMMINS, William J., mfr.; b. Paris, Tenn., Dec. 9, 1861; s. Hiram F. and Susan (Courts) C.; grad. Montgomery Bell Acad., Nashville, 1882; m. Emma Mai Benson, Oct. 8, 1885; children—Lena Hillman (Mrs. Lee W. Adams), Mary Sue (Mrs. Frederic Leake), Shirley (Mrs. Martin J. Condon, Jr.). Vice-pres. and gen. mgr. Bon Air Coal & Iron Corp., Nashville, 1916-26; chmn. exec. com. Tenn. Products Corp. (consol. of Bon Air Coal & Iron Corp., Bon Air Chem. Co., Chattanooga Coke & Gas Co. and furnaces and operation of J. J. Gray, Jr., Rockdale, Tenn.); pres. Wholesale Merchants Warehouse Co. (owners of Cummins Station); vice chmn. Doctors Essential Foods Co. Democrat. Mem. Christian (Disciples) Ch. Died Feb. 24, 1936.

CUMNOCK, Robert McLean, college prof.; b. Scotland, May 31, 1840; s. Robert McLean and Margaret (Goodlet) C.; A.B., Wesleyan U., 1868, A.M., 1871; L.H.D., Dickinson Coll., 1903; Litt.D., Northwestern U., 1905; LL.D., U. of Southern Calif., 1927; m. Annie Webster, June 27, 1877. Prof. rhetoric and elocution, Northwestern U., from 1868, now emeritus. Author: Cumnock's Choice Readings, 1881; Cumnock's School Speaker, 1887. Methodist. Died Nov. 27, 1929.

CUNLIFFE-OWEN, (Philip) Frederick, editor; b. at London, Eng., Jan. 30, 1855; s. late Sir Philip (K.C.B.) and Lady (née Baroness von Reitzenstein) C.; m. Countess Marguerite, d. late Comte Jules du Planty de Sourdis. One of editors of New York Tribune, 1889. V.p. Pilgrims Soc. America; dir. St. George's Soc. New York. Grand officer (with star) Order of Charles III of Spain; Osmanieh, Turkey; commander Order of the Crown, Italy; Legion d'Honneur, France; l'Instruction Publique, France; Orange-Nassau, Netherlands, etc. Died June 30, 1926.

CUNNIFF, Michael Glen; b. Boston, Feb. 7, 1875; s. Bernard and Mary Ellen (Mooney) C.; A.B., Harvard, 1898, A.M., 1899; m. Everesta Spink, Apr. 10, 1903. Instr. in English, Harvard, 1898-1900, U. of Wis., 1900-01; lit. editor World's Work, mag., 1901-03, mng. editor, 1903-07; partnership with brother, Bernard, buying, selling and operating mines, 1907—; pres. Commonwealth Exploration Co. Mem. Ariz. Constl. Conv., 1910 (chmn. style, revision and compilation com.); mem. Ariz. State Senate, 1912-15 (pres.); commr. from Ariz. to Conf. on Uniform State Laws, 1912—. Home: Crown King, Ariz. Died Dec. 23, 1914.

CUNNINGHAM, Andrew Chase, officer U.S. Navy, civ. engr.; b. Mohawk, Herkimer Co., N.Y., Feb. 15, 1858; s. Thomas and Celeste (Chase) C.; grad. U.S. Naval Acad., 1879, C.E., Rensselaer Poly. Inst., 1885; m. Jessie E. Thomas, 1879. Line officer U.S.N. until 1883, when resignation was accepted; took up study of civ. engring.; followed profession until Spanish-Am. War, in which served as vol. ensign; at end of war apptd. to corps of civ. engrs. U.S.N. Inventions cover floating dry docks, coaling ships at sea, and burning of liquid fuel. Republican. Died Jan. 13, 1917.

CUNNINGHAM, Andrew Oswald, civil engr.; b. Rangoon, Burma, July 8, 1866; s. Gen. Percy S. (British Army) and Annie Sarah (Stroud) C.; ed. South Eastern Coll., Eng., 1879-83; came to U.S., 1883; B.C.E., U. of Minn., 1894; m. Georgia Townsend Quinn, July 11, 1903. Rodman and leveler on N.P. R.R., 1886-88; land surveyor in N.D., 1890-91; draftsman, 1894-95, and asst. engr., 1895-96, Gillette-Herzog Mfg. Co., Minneapolis; gen. contracting and engring., and southern agt. for Schultz Bridge & Iron Co., Pittsburgh, 1896-98; with Pittsburgh Reduction Co., designing improvements in old bldgs. at Niagara Falls and making designs for new bldgs. and improvements at New Kensington Works, 1898-99; in gen. cons. and civ. engring. bus., 1899-1900; contracting mgr. in charge estimates, designs and bids, for Am. Bridge Co., Cleveland, 1900-02; bridge engr., 1902-05; chief engr. Wabash R.R., 1905-23; in pvt. practice as cons. engr. Mayor University City, 1924—. Deceased.

CUNNINGHAM, David West, engineer; b. Boston, Dec. 24, 1829; s. Andrew and Abby L. (West) C.; ed. Chauncy Hall Sch. and Lawrence Scientific Sch. (Harvard); m. Mary B. S. Fuller, 1859 (died 1869); 2d, Caroline S. Thomas, 1873. Commenced as civ. engr. asst. in Boston water works, 1848; later civ. engr. on railroads in U.S. and Can., and 6 yrs. in Chile, S.A., on r.r. and govt. work; was engaged in construction Charleston water works and Lowell water works; sewerage systems, Lowell, Mass., and Stillwater, Minn.; chief asst. engr. for Boston water works additional supply, 6 yrs.; built Tarkio Valley R.R.; was consulting engr., Minneapolis water works; worked 4-section wheat farm in N.D. until 1894, when he removed to Calif. Died May 11, 1916.

CUNNINGHAM, Edward Henry, mem. Federal Reserve Bd.; b. Burlington, Wis., Dec. 14, 1869; s. P. H. and Hannah (Nagle) C.; ed. common and high schs.; m. Ida F. Scovel, Aug. 28, 1893. Farming in Ia., 1889—; mem. Ia. Ho. of Rep. 3 terms, 1909-13 (speaker of Ho., 1913); sec. Ia. Farm Bur. Federation, 1920-23; mem. Federal Reserve Bd., 1923—. Republican. Conglist. Mason. Home: Cresco, Ia. Died Nov. 28, 1930.

CUNNINGHAM, Frank Simpson, merchant; b. Bourbon, Ind., Apr. 16, 1866; s. Oliver W. and Bethia Ann (Simpson) C.; ed. high sch., Goshen, Ind.; m. Lucy E. Baty, Sept. 14, 1893; 1 son, Capt. Oliver Baty (killed in battle, World War). With Butler Bros., wholesale gen. mdse., Chicago, 1886—, pres., 1918-39, chmn. bd., 1939—. Pres. Cradle Soc.; trustee Northwestern U., Evanston Hosp. Republican. Episcopalian. Home: Evanston, Ill. Died Dec. 1, 1941.

CUNNINGHAM, Henry Vincent, lawyer, banker; b. Roxbury, Mass., Aug. 13, 1865; s. Patrick Joseph and Bridget Louise (Curley) C.; LL.B., Boston U., 1887; A.M., Boston Coll., 1892; LL.D., St. Francis Xavier, N.Y., 1908; m. Anna Elizabeth Madigan, June 27, 1894; children—John Madigran, Winifred Adams, Albert Whittier (dec.), Henry Vincent, Albert Whittier (dec.). Admitted to Mass. bar, 1887, and began practice at Boston; pres. Union Savings Bank, Boston, 1917—; dir. and counsel U.S. Fidelity & Guaranty Co. of Baltimore. Decorated Knight of St. Gregory (Pope Pius X). Democrat. Catholic. Died Mar. 14, 1930.

CUNNINGHAM, I. A., educator; b. Crawfordsville, Ind., June 23, 1895; s. George and Anna (McLain) C.; ed. Purdue Summer Sch., Winona Lake, Ind.; student Wabash College, Indiana; m. Frances Jane Spence Housel, Apr. 4, 1923. children—Charles Claire, Paul E. (by adoption); Efficiency engr. Goodyear Tire & Rubber Co., Akron, O., 1917-20; v.p. Schafer Housing Assn., Chicago, 1923-25; organizer, and mgr. Camp Hoosier for Boys, Winona Lake, 1920-23; pres. Columbia (Tenn.) Mil. Acad., 1925—. Served in Personnel Div., U.S.A., 8 mos., World War. Episcopalian. Mason. Deceased.

CUNNINGHAM, Joseph Oscar, lawyer; b. Lancaster, N.Y., Dec. 12, 1830; s. Hiram Way and Eunice (Brown) C.; student Baldwin Inst., Berea, O., and Oberlin Coll.; LL.B., Union Law Sch., Cleveland, 1859; m. Mary M. McConoughey, Oct. 13, 1853. Mem. firm Cunningham & Flynn, pubs. Urbana Union, 1853-58; admitted to Ill. bar, 1856, and to Supreme Ct. of U.S., 1880; retired from law practice, 1905. Donor of Cunningham Children's Home, Urbana, 1895. Judge County Ct. of Champaign Co., Ill., 1861-65. Trustee, U. of Ill., 1867-73, McKendree Coll., Lebanon, Ill., 1897-98. Mem. of Gen. Conf. M.E. Ch., 1896, 1900. Home: Urbana, Ill. Died Apr. 1917.

CUNNINGHAM, Louis Wyborn, judge; b. Ripley Co., Ind., Aug. 14, 1863; s. Samuel C. V. and Phebe (Jessup) C.; ed. high sch. State Normal Sch., Terre Haute, Ind., and Union Christian Coll., Ind.; m. Emma Ingraham, July 25, 1887 (died 1930); 1 son, Wyborn Ingraham. Admitted to bar, Nov. 17, 1893; practiced law at Colorado Springs, Colo., 1893—; county judge, El Paso Co., Colo., 1899-1900; (dist. judge, 4th Dist. of Colo., 1901-07); justice Colo. Court of Appeals, 1911-15 (presiding judge, 1913-15). Democrat. Home: Colorado Springs, Colo. Died Apr. 21, 1939.

CUNNINGHAM, Milton Joseph, lawyer; b. Caddo (now DeSoto) Parish, La., Mar. 10, 1842; s. John Hamilton and Anne (Buie) C.; ed. Homer Coll.; m. Emma Mai Blouin, Aug. 7, 1895. Began teaching school soon after 16th birthday, reading law at intervals; applied himself exclusively to the study of law from Dec. 1860; enlisted, Apr. 1861, on outbreak of Civil War, as pvt. in 2d La. Inf.; served in Army of Northern Va.; wounded at Malvern Hill, Gettysburg and Spottsylvania Court House; at close of war resumed study of law and practiced, 1866—; dist. atty., 1872-75; mem. La. Ho. of Rep., 1879; mem. La. Constl. Conv., 1879; mem. La. Senate, 1880-84; atty. gen. of La., 3 terms, 1884-88, 1892-1900. Democrat. Home: New Orleans, La. Died Oct. 19, 1916.

CUNNINGHAM, Paul Davis; b. Monroe Co., Ga., Nov. 27, 1869; s. Sumner Archibald and Laura N. (Davis) C.; ed. public schools Monroe Co., Ga., 1878-85; undergraduate Emory Coll., Oxford, Ga.; unmarried. Engaged in ry. location and construction, from rodman to asst. resident engr., July 1887, to Feb. 1890; resident engr. ry. construction, June 1890, to March 1891; hydrographic work engr. dept., U.S.A., Oct. 1891; topographical work Internat. Boundary Commn., U.S. and Mexico, 1892-94; U.S. asst. engr. Internat. Boundary Commn., U.S. and Mexico, 1894-96; engr. clerk, N.W. and S.W. divs., engr. dept., U.S.A., 1896-98; asst. to chief engr. on duty at headquarters of army, July 1898-Jan. 1899; prin. asst. engr., Engr. Dept., Dept. of Havana, Cuba, Jan.-Dec. 1899; acting chief engr. Dept. of Havana, Dec. 1899-April 1900; chief engr. City of Havana, April-Aug. 1900; cons. engr. U.S. Internat. Boundary Commn. (U.S. and Mexico), 1900—. Home: El Paso, Tex. Died 1901.

CUNNINGHAM, Richard Hoope, neurologist; b. Richmond, Va., July 1, 1865; student U. of Va., 1883-85; M.D., Med. Coll. of Va., 1886; M.D., Columbia, 1888; student Heidelberg, 1890-91. Lecturer on nervous and mental diseases, Med. Coll. of Va., 1893-94; demonstrator in physiology, Columbia, 1895-98; clin. asst. in neurology, Vanderbilt Clinic, 1895-1902; instr. electrophysiology, Columbia, 1902-06; neurologist and chief of clinic, Dept. of Neurology, Vanderbilt Clinic, 1906—. Home: New York, N.Y. Died Feb. 24, 1937.

CUNNINGHAM, Russell McWhorter, physician; b. Mt. Hope, Ala., Aug. 25, 1855; s. Moses Winslow and Nancy Caroline (Russell) C.; M.D., Bellevue Hosp. Med. Coll., 1879; m. Miss S. L. Moore, Aug. 1876; 2d, Annice Taylor. Mem. Ala. Ho. of Rep., 1880-81; phys. to State Penitentiary, 1881-85; local surgeon Tenn. Coal, Iron & R.R. Co., 1885-1914; mem. Ala. Senate, 1896-1900 (pres. 1898-99); mem. Ala. Constl. Conv., 1901; lt. giv. of Ala., 1903-07 (acting gov., Apr. 1904-Mar. 1905). Democrat. City health officer of Birmingham, 1913—. Past Grand Master Grand Lodge of Masons; past Grand Comdr. Grand Commandery K.T. Died 1922.

CUNNINGHAM, Sumner Archibald, journalist; b. in Bedford Co., Tenn., July 21, 1843; s. John Washington Campbell and Mary A. (Buchanan) C.; reared on farm; ed. country schs.; m. Laura N. Davis, Nov. 27, 1866. Pvt. and orderly sergt. Co. B, 41st Tenn. Inf., and sergt. maj. of regt. Engaged in dry goods business, then established book store at Shelbyville, Tenn.; bought and edited Shelbyville Commercial, 1870-73; bought Chattanooga (Tenn.) Daily Times, 1876, sold it to Adolph S. Ochs, present owner, 1880; established, 1893, Confederate Veteran. Democrat. Cumberland Presbyterian. Home: Nashville, Tenn. Died Dec. 20, 1913.

CUNNINGHAM, Thomas F., shipping; b. New Haven, Conn., Dec. 15, 1864; s. Thomas and Elizabeth (Birne) C.; ed. pub. schs., New Haven; unmarried. With Miss. Shipping Co., New Orleans, La., 1918—, pres., 1919—; pres. West Grain Trimming Co., Public Belt R.R. (New Orleans); dir. Pub. Service Co., Am. Steamship Agencies Co., Hibernia Nat. Bank, Lykes Bros.-Ripley Steamship Co., New Orleans Bd. of Trade (pres. 1920-24). Vice pres. and chmn. Miss. Valley Assn. Died Nov. 24, 1937.

CUPPLES, Samuel, mfr.; b. Harrisburg, Pa., Sept. 13, 1831; s. James and Elizabeth (Bigham) C.; pub. sch. edn.; m. Amelia Kells, 1854. Began in a grocery store at Pittsburgh, 1843; entered employ of A. O. Tylor, pioneer mfr. of woodenware in the West, 1846; began mfr. of woodenware on own account as Samuel Cupples & Co., largest enterprise in the country in its line, 1851; became pres. Samuel Cupples Wooden Ware Co., Samuel Cupples Real Estate Co., Samuel Cupples Envelope Co. Methodist. Home: St. Louis, Mo. Died 1912.

CUPPY, Hazlitt Alva, editor; b. Shelburn, Ind., Oct. 3, 1863; s. Rev. W. T. and Martha Ann C.; B.S., Franklin Coll., Ind., 1888; studied Oxford U. (Eng.), 1889-90; Berlin, 1890-91; M.A., Ph.D., Heidelberg, 1891-92; U. of Paris, 1892; m. Elizabeth Overstreet, 1895. Founder and editor Altruistic Review, 1893-95; editor Baptist Union, 1895-97; dir. U. of Chicago Press, 1896-98; pub. and editor of Public Opinion, 1898-1906. Author: Rise of the Anglo-Indian Empire. Home: Lititz, Pa. Deceased.

CURLEY, Daniel J., bishop; b. N.Y. City, June 16, 1869; s. Michael J. and Margaret (Swan) C.; A.B., A.M., St. Francis Xavier's Coll., N.Y. City; studied philosopy, St. Joseph's Sem., Troy; S.T.L., North Am. Coll., Rome, Italy. Ordained priest R.C. Ch., 1894; pastor Ch. of Our Lady of Solace, 1902-23; apptd. sec. to Archbishop Corrigan, 1901; consecrated bishop of Syracuse, 1923. Died Aug. 3, 1932.

CURLEY, Edward W., congressman; b. Easton, Pa.; ed. pub. schs. and Coll. City of N.Y.; married. Engaged in bldg. industry 25 yrs.; was pres. Stanley Hoist & Machine Co., N.Y. City, dealers in builders' and contractors' machinery and equipment; mem. Bd. of Aldermen, N.Y. City, 1916-35; elected to 74th Congress from 22d N.Y. Dist. at spl. election, Nov. 1935, to fill vacancy caused by death of A. J. Griffin; mem. 75th Congress (1937-39), same dist. Democrat. Died Jan. 7, 1940.

CURLEY, Frank E., lawyer; b. Walton, Ky., Sept. 22, 1877; s. Thomas F. and Dora (Northcutt) C.; LL.B., Cincinnati Coll., 1897; m. Amy Trippel, Oct. 9, 1912; children—Marie A., Gene F., Frank E. Admitted to Ky. bar, 1897, and began practice at Walton; moved to Tucson, 1906. Mem. State Bd. Bar Examiners; commr. from Ariz. of Nat. Commn. on Uniform State Laws; mem. bd. dirs. Ariz. Industrial Congress. Pres. Ariz. State Bar Assn., 1926-27. Democrat. Mason (32°). Home: Tucson, Ariz. Died Dec. 24, 1929.

CURREY, John, lawyer; b. in Westchester Co., N.Y., Oct. 4, 1814; s. Thomas and Rebecca (Ward) C.; ed. acads. and Wesleyan U.; studied law in office of Hon. William Nelson, Peekskill, N.Y., 1839-42; admitted to N.Y. bar, 1842; (LL.D., Williams Coll., 1870); m. Cornelia Scott, Sept. 1845 (died 1877); m. 2d, Cornelia Ferris, 1881. Practiced law Peekskill, 1842-47, Kingston, N.Y., 1847-49; went to Calif., 1849; practiced law in San Francisco; was Whig while that party existed, then joined anti-slavery wing of Dem. party and was its candidate for gov. of Calif., 1859; elected judge Supreme Ct., Calif., 1863; served 1 term; retired from practice for a few years because of partial loss of eyesight, but resumed after sight was sufficiently restored. Died Dec. 18, 1912.

CURREY, J(osiah) Seymour, author; b. Peekskill, N.Y., Oct. 2, 1844; s. James and Eliza (Ferris) C.; ed. Northwestern U., 1 yr.; m. Mary Corell, Nov. 24, 1875. Moved with parents to Will Co., Ill., 1857; enlisted 67th Ill. Vols., 1862, and again, 134th Ill. Vols., 1864, serving about 8 mos.; became an accountant; largely engaged in hist. writing in later yrs. Trustee Evanston Pub. Library, 1886-1908 (pres. bd.); an organizer, 1898, and pres. Evanston Hist. Soc.; Ill. State Hist. Soc. (hon. v.p.). Progressive. Conglist. Author: Chicago: Its History and Its Builders, 1912; The Story of Old Fort Dearborn, 1912; Makers of Illinois, 1913. Home: Evanston, Ill. Died Dec. 25, 1928.

CURRIE, Donald Herbert, sanitarian; b. in Jefferson Co., Mo., Mar. 25, 1876; s. Daniel McNeil and Martha (Dent) C.; M.D., Washington U., 1899; m. Helen Hope Hanson, May 10, 1900. Apptd. asst. surgeon U.S.P.H. Service, July 25, 1899; passed asst. surgeon, 1904; surgeon, 1912. At Hygienic Lab., Washington, 1900-01; served in plague epidemic, San Francisco, 1901-05, yellow fever epidemic, New Orleans, 1905; boarding officer San Francisco Quarantine Sta., 1905-07; on duty in Honolulu, 1907-11, in Calif., 1911-13; state health officer, Calif. (leave of absence), 1914-15; dir. U.S. Leprosy Sta., Honolulu, 1909-11, 1915-17; was sanitary adviser to gov. of Hawaii; apptd. quarantine officer, Boston, Mass., Aug. 1917. Represented U.S. in Internat. Leprosy Conf., Bergen, Norway, 1909. Episcopalian. Elk. Died Dec. 23, 1918.

CURRIE, George Graham, author; b. Province of Quebec, Can., June 6, 1867; s. Francis P. and Ellen H. (Hanna) C.; ed. pub. schs.; m. Miss Rickards, of Bocaratone, Fla.; m. 2d, Miss Angevine, 1906; children—Francis Angevine, Margaret Marion Imogen. Began traveling at 19 and visited many parts of N. America, also spent 2 yrs. in Europe; made 500-mile trip in canoe, from Juneau, Alaska, to the Skeena River, B.C.; admitted to Fla. bar, 1897; organizer and first pres. Farmers Bank and Trust Co.; pres. Currie Investment & Title Guaranty Co.; mayor of West Palm Beach, and treas. Dade Co., Fla. Author: Sonnets and Love Songs, 1912; In the Other Man's Place, 1913; Epitaphs, Epigrams and Other Ephemera, 1914; Songs of Florida, and Other Verse, 1921; Women in Her Infinite Variety (London), 1925. Known as the "poet laureate" of Florida. Died Sept. 5, 1926.

CURRIER, Albert Dean, lawyer; b. Osceola, Stark Co., Ill., July 29, 1861; s. Jonathan T. and Martha J. (Hoblit) C.; B.S., Northwestern U., 1884; spl. work in Mass. Inst. Tech., 2 yrs., and at same time attending Boston U. Law Sch.; also studied law in offices of John H. Hamline and Elbridge Hanecy; m. Anna D. Thomas, Nov. 22, 1910; children—Mariana T., Martha Josephine. Wrote for Chicago Times and Chicago Evening Journal, 1884-85 and 1886-87. Admitted to bar, 1889; was receiver of John Alexander Dowie under appmt. of U.S. Dist. Court, Dec. 1903. Mem. com. Ill. Tariff Reform League, 1889-90; dir. Am. Acad. in Rome. Home: Evanston, Ill. Died Feb. 18, 1931.

CURRIER, Amos Noyes, educator; b. Canaan, N.H., Oct. 13, 1832; grad. Dartmouth, 1856 (A.M.; LL.D., Des Moines Coll.); m. Celia A. Moore, Sept. 9, 1868. Prof. ancient languages, Central Coll., Pella, Ia., 1857-67; private 8th Ia. inf., and commissary 11th Mo. cav., 1861-65; prof. ancient languages, U. of Ia., and then Latin, 1867—; dean Coll. Liberal Arts, same, 1887—; acting pres., 1898-99. Pres. Ia. State Teachers' Assn., 1898. Died 1909.

CURRIER, Charles Francis Adams, college prof.; b. E. Kingston, N.H., Mar. 17, 1862; s. Ezra F. and Isabella T. (Webster) C.; A.B., Harvard, 1887, A.M., 1888; studied 1 yr. at U. of Berlin and 1 yr. at Paris; m. Florence M. Morton, Dec. 26, 1892. Prof. history and polit. science, Mass. Inst. Tech., 1891—. Died Sept. 6, 1919.

CURRIER, Charles Warren, bishop; b. St. Thomas, West Indies, Mar. 22, 1857; s. Warren Green and Deborah (Heyliger) C. (father native of N.Y.); ed. St. Thomas, W.I., until 1871, Province of Limburg, Holland, 1871-80; grad. Roermond, Holland; studied philosophy and theology, Wittem, Holland, 1874-80. Ordained R.C. ministry, 1880; missionary in Surinam, Dutch Guiana, 1881-82; came to U.S., 1882; pastor St. Mary's, Washington, 1900. Del. Internat. Congress Americanists, Spain, 1892, Stuttgart, 1904, Buenos Aires, 1910. Traveled through S. America, 1910; apptd. bishop of Matanzas, Cuba, and consecrated in Rome, Italy, July 1913; resigned Feb. 1915 and returned to U.S. Author: Carmel in America, 1890; Dimitrios and Irene, Historical Romance, 1893; History of Religious Orders, 1894; Church and Saints, 1897; The Rose of Alhambra, Historical Romance, 1898; Cuba, What Shall We Do With It?, 1898; Mission Memories, 1898; The Divinity of Christ, 1898; A Child of Mary, 1897; The Mass, 1899; Lands of the Southern Cross; A Visit to South America, 1911. Died Sept. 23, 1918.

CURRIER, Frank Dunklee, congressman; b. Canaan, N.H., Oct. 30, 1853; s. Horace S. and Emma C. (Plastridge) C.; ed. Kimball Union Acad., Meriden, N.H., and Dr. Hixon's Sch., Lowell, Mass.; (hon. A.M., Dartmouth, 1901); m. Adelaide H. Sargent, May 31, 1890. Admitted to bar, 1874; in practice, Canaan, N.H., 1875—; mem. N.H. Ho. of Rep., 1879; sec. Rep. State Com., 1882-90; clerk N.H. Senate, 1883-87; del. Rep. Nat. Conv., 1884; pres. N.H. Senate, 1887-89; naval officer of customs, Port of Boston, 1890-94; speaker N.H. Ho. of Rep., 1899-1901; mem. 57th to 62d Congresses (1901-13), 2d N.H. Dist. Died Nov. 25, 1921.

CURRIER, J. Frank, artist; b. Boston, Nov. 21, 1843; s. Joseph S. and Catherine (Barrows) C.; ed. pub. schs., Boston and Roxbury, Mass., until 15; attended Lowell Inst. evening class; studied with Samuel Gerry and William Hunt; went to Europe, 1868, studied at acad. at Antwerp 1½ yrs., then to acad. at Munich; received medal in drawing class, then for short time in painting class; m. Catherine Appleton, Nov. 1873. Distinguished as landscape painter. Home: Roxbury, Mass. Died 1909.

CURRY, Albert Bruce, clergyman; b. Climax, Decatur Co., Ga., July 16, 1852; s. Calvin Alexander and Jane Elizabeth (Gregory) C.; grad. Columbia (S.C.) Theol. Sem., 1875; studied U. of Va., 1877-79; D.D., Southwestern Presbyn. U., Clarksville, Tenn., 1897; m. Mary Elizabeth Quarterman, Sept. 26, 1883. Ordained Presbyn. ministry, 1875; pastor Darien, Ga., 1875-78, 1879-83, Gainesville, Fla., 1883-94, Birmingham, Ala., 1894-1903, 2d Ch., Memphis, Tenn., 1903-31, emeritus. Moderator Gen. Assembly Presbyn. Ch. of U.S., St. Louis, Mo., 1921. Mem. bd. dirs., Synod of Tenn., Presbytery of Memphis, Ky. Theol. Sem., Louisville, Ky., Southwestern Coll. of Miss. Valley, Memphis, Tenn. Died Dec. 3, 1939.

CURRY, Charles Forrest, congressman; b. Naperville, Ill., Mar. 14, 1858; s. Charles Henry Madren and Emma Jane (Kimball) C.; ed. Episcopalian Acad., Mineral Point, Wis.; m. Lillie Alice Siperly, Oct. 5, 1891 (died 1898); children—Florence Alice, Charles F. Mem. Calif. Assembly, 1887; supt. Sta. B, postoffice, San Francisco, 1890-94 (resigned); county clk., 1894-98; sec. of state, Calif., 1899-1911; mem. 63d to 71st Congresses (1913-31), 3d Calif. Dist. Republican. Mason. Author: Alien Land Laws and Alien Rights; Anthropology of the Japanese People. Home: Sacramento, Calif. Died Oct. 10, 1930.

CURRY, Edward Rufus, church official; b. Windsor, N.S., Can., Nov. 15, 1858; s. Elisha and Mary Ann (Dill) C.; B.A., Acadia U., 1881; B.D., Morgan Park (Ill.) Theol. Sem., 1887; D.D., Grand Island (Neb.) Coll., 1911; m. Laura C. Clinch, Dec. 13, 1883; children—Alice Clinch (Mrs. A. A. Engstrom), Estelle Ruth (Mrs. Robert Laird), Charles K., Margaret (Mrs. I. B. Dumm), Robert Kingdon. Ordained Bapt. ministry, 1887; pastor successively First Ch., Fremont, Neb., First Ch., Jackson, Mich., Clinton Av. Ch., Newark, N.J., First Ch., Flint, Mich., Calvary Ch., Omaha, First Ch., Boulder, Colo., First Ch., Bozeman, Mont., until 1925; exec. sec. Mont. Bapt. Conv., 1925—. Trustee Linfield Coll. (McMinnville, Ore.), Billings Polytechnic Bapt. Hosp. (St. Paul, Minn.). Mem. Bd. of Edn. Northern Bapt. Conv., 1910—. Home: Bozeman, Mont. Deceased.

CURRY, Jabez Lamar Monroe, educator; b. Lincoln Co., Ga., June 5, 1825; grad. Univ. of Ga., 1843; Dane Law School, Harvard, 1845 (LL.D., Mercer U., Ga., and U. of Ga.). Mem. Ala. legislature, 1847-48, 1853-54, 1855-56; mem. Congress, 1857-61; mem. Confederate Congress, 1861-65; aide on staff Gens. Jos. E. Johnson and Jos. Wheeler, and lt. col. of cav., C.S.A., 1864-65; pres. Howard Coll., Ala., 1866-68; prof. English philosophy and constitutl. and internat. law, Richmond Coll., Va., 1868-81; U.S. minister to Spain, 1885-88; pres. Bd. of Foreign Missions of Southern Bapt. Conv. and of Bd. Trustees Richmond Coll.; pres. Southern History Assn., etc. Is gen. agt. Peabody Edn. Fund and of John F. Slater Edn. Fund. Author: Protestantism, How Far a Failure, 1870; Struggles and Triumphs of Virginia Baptist, 1873; Establishment and Disestablishment, or Progress of Soul Liberty in the United States; Francis Strother Lyon as Commissioner and Trustee of Alabama, 1889; Constitutional Government in Spain, 1889; William Ewart Gladstone, 1891; The Southern States of the American Union in Their Relation to the Constitution and the Resulting Union, 1895; History of the Peabody Edn. Fund, 1898; Civil History of the Confederate Government, 1901. Died 1903.

CURRY, James Bernard, clergyman; b. New York, Dec. 29, 1856; s. Peter and Ellen (Horgan) C.; A.B., Coll. of St. Francis Xavier, New York, 1878; Sem. of North Am. Coll., Rome, 1878-83. Ordained R.C. priest, 1883; pastor Ch. of St. James, New York, 1901—. Active in neighborhood and prison work; originator of anti-cocaine legislation in N.Y. Wrote: The Little Catholic's Choral; What the Settlement Clubs Stand For; Hymns and Miscellanies. Died June 26, 1932.

CURRY, Samuel Silas, educator; b. Chatata, Tenn., 1847; s. James Campbell C.; A.B., Grant U., 1872; A.M., Boston U., 1878, Ph.D., 1879; (Litt.D., Colby, 1905). Snow prof. oratory, Boston U., 1879-88; acting Davis prof. elocution, Newton Theol. Instn., 1884-1919; instr. elocution, Harvard, 1891-94, Yale Div. Sch., 1892-1902, Harvard Div. Sch., 1896-1902, and Union Theol. Sem., New York, 1919—. Founder and pres. School of Expression, Boston. Author: Province of Expression, 1891; Lessons in Vocal Expression, 1895; Imagination and Dramatic Instinct, 1896; Vocal and Literary Interpretation of the Bible, 1903; Foundations of Expression; Browning and the Dramatic Monologue, 1908; Mind and Voice, 1910; Little Classics for Vocal Expression, 1912; Spoken English, 1913; The Smile, 1915; How to Add Ten Years to Your Life, 1915. Home: Boston, Mass. Died Dec. 24, 1921.

CURRY, William Melville, clergyman; b. Bloomington, Ind., Oct. 1, 1867; s. David S. and Margaret (Fullerton) C.; A.B., U. of Kan., 1893; D.D., Geneva Coll., Beaver Falls, Pa., 1916; m. Juliet Titsworth, Aug. 15, 1893 (died 1924); children—Paul R., W. Lawrence; m. 2d, Laura Hensel, 1927. Ordained ministry Presbyn. Ch., 1896; pastor successively Limesville, Pa., Lima, O., Parnassus, Pa., 4th Ch., Trenton, N.J., until 1920, 9th Presbyn. Ch., Philadelphia, Pa., 1920—. Mem. Sch. Commn., Trenton, 1916-20. Chmn. com. on evangelism, N.J. Synod, Presbyn. Ch., 1918; moderator, Synod of Pa., 1929-30. Republican. Mason. Author: Pastor's Corner, 1927; Illustrative Stories, 1929. Deceased.

CURTIN, Jeremiah, author; b. Milwaukee, Wis., 1840; s. David and Ellen (Furlong) C.; grad. Harvard, 1863; sec. of Legation of U.S., 1864-70; acting consul gen. of U.S., 1865-66, in Russia. Actively connected with Bureau of Ethnology, Smithsonian, Instn., 1883-91. Returned, 1901, from journey around the world, via Russia, Siberia, Amoor River, China and Japan. Spent 3 months, 1900, among Buriats, the only tribe of Mongols who have retained the great horse sacrifice and preserved the spendid creation myths of their race. Distinguished linquist and philologist, knowing, it is said, 70 languages. Visited Indian tribes, U.S. and Canada, 1902. Married. Author: Myths and Folf-Tales of Ireland; Myths and Folk-Tales of the Russians, Western Slavs and Magyars; Hero-Tales of Ireland; Fairy Tales of Ireland; Creation Myths of Primitive America and Their Relation to the Religious and Mental History of Mankind; The Mongols; Religion and Ideas of the Mongol Race. Best known by his translations from the Polish of Quo Vadis and 8 other works of Henryk Sienkiewicz, and from the Russian of Michael Zagoskin's Tales of Three Centuries; Count Alexis Tolstoi's Prince Serebryani; On the Field of Glory; also, from Polish, The Argonauts (Orzeszko) and The Pharaoh and the Priest (Glovatski). Home: Bristol, Vt. Died 1906.

CURTIN, Roland Gideon, physician; b. Bellefonte, Pa., Oct. 29, 1839; s. Constans and Mary Anne (Kinne) C.; grad. Williston Sem., 1859; M.D., U. of Pa., 1866; Ph.D., 1871; (hon. A.M., Lafayette Coll., 1883); m. his cousin, Mrs. Julia (Taylor) Robinson, Mar. 21, 1882. Consulting phys. Rush Hosp. for Consumptives, St. Timothy, Jewish and Douglas hosps, Presbyterian Hosp., Phila.; surgeon U.S. Geol. Survey, 1868; U.S. Naval Storekeeper, 1862-66; lecturer on physical diagnosis, U. of Pa., 1875-95. Pres. Am. Climatol. Assn., 1892-93, Phila. Med. Club, 1905, Phila. Co. Med. Soc., 1904, Am. Soc. of Tropical Medicine, 1905. Author: Influenza (with Dr. E. W. Watson), 1893; Vol. IV, Phila. Hospital Reports (with Dr. D. E. Hughes), 1911; Medical Pilgrimage to Panama, 1905. Home: Philadelphia, Pa. Died Mar. 14, 1913.

CURTIS, Alfred Allen, R. C. bishop; b. Somerset Co., Md., July 4, 1831; early edn. in schs. of Somerset Co.; ordained deacon P.E. Ch., 1856; in charge of St. John's Ch., Worcester, Mass.; priest P.E. Ch., 1859; resigned from P.E. ministry, 1870; received into R.C. Ch., Apr. 18, 1872, by Bishop John Henry Newman, London. Returned to U.S.; entered Sem. St. Sulpice, Baltimore; ordained priest, Dec. 18, 1874. Apptd. asst. Baltimore cathedral and pvt. sec. archbishop until consecrated, Nov. 16, 1886, Bishop of Wilmington. Resigned bishopric Jan. 23, 1896, receiving titular see of Echinus, June 25, 1896; remained bishop administrator of Wilmington until May 2, 1897; apptd. by Cardinal Gibbons vicar gen. of Baltimore, 1898. Died 1908.

CURTIS, Augustus Darwin, illuminating engr.; b. Hawley, Pa., Oct. 14, 1865; s. George B., M.D., and Augusta (Cook) C.; ed. Honesdale (Pa.) High Sch. and Athanæum, Chicago, Ill.; student Art Inst. Chicago; m. Marette Hotchkin, 1891; children—Kenneth, Darwin. Sec. M. & M. Box Co., Marinette, Wis., 1890-1900; was half owner and bus. mgr. Popular Mechanics; pres. Curtis Lighting, Inc., Chicago, New York and Antwerp, 1900—. Former mem. Ill. N.G. Republican. Presbyn. Mason. A pioneer in development of indirect lighting. Died Apr. 29, 1931.

CURTIS, Charles, vice pres. of U.S.; b. N. Topeka, Shawnee Co., Kan., Jan. 25, 1860; ed. common schs.; m. Annie E. Baird, Nov. 27, 1884; children—Mrs. Permelia George, Harry K., Mrs. Leona Knight. Admitted to bar, 1881, and began practice at Topeka; county atty., Shawnee Co., 1884-88; mem. 53d to 60th Congresses (1893-1909); elected U.S. senator, Jan. 23, 1907, for unexpired term of J. R. Burton, resigned, succeeding Hon. A. W. Benson, apptd. ad interim, and resigned seat in 60th Congress; re-elected to Senate for 4 terms, 1907-33; elected vice president of U.S. for term 1929-33. Died Feb. 8, 1936.

CURTIS, Charles Albert, army officer; b. Hallowell, Me., Oct. 4, 1835; s. Charles Stubbs and A. F. (Ham) C.; B.A., Bowdoin Coll., 1861; m. Harriet L. Hughes, May 17, 1866. Second lt. U.S.A., Apr. 14, 1862; 1st lt., Mar. 30, 1864; retired, Dec. 15, 1870, on account of wounds received in line of duty; advanced to rank of capt. of inf. retired, by act of Apr. 23, 1904. Bvtd. capt., Sept. 27, 1865, for meritorious services during the war. Prof. mil. science and tactics in various instns., 1870—; col. Wis. N.G. Episcopalian. Author: Captured by the Navajos, 1904. Home: Madison, Wis. Died 1907.

CURTIS, Charles Boyd, lawyer; b. Penn Yan, N.Y., Sept. 24, 1827; s. Samuel F. and Amelia (Boyd) C.; grad. Hamilton Coll., N.Y. (A.M.); admitted to N.Y. bar, 1849; served in Civil war, capt. 57th regt. N.Y. vols., 1861; m. Isabel Douglass, Aug. 23, 1876. Author: Catalogue of the Works of Velasquez and Murillo, London, 1883; Rembrandt's Etchings, 1888. Died 1905.

CURTIS, C(harles) Densmore, prof. archæology; b. Augusta, Me., Oct. 16, 1875; s. Charles Alphonso and Blanche (Densmore) C.; B.A., Pomona Coll., 1900; M.A., U. of Colo., 1901; unmarried. Mem. Am. Expdn. for the excavating of Cyrene, Tripoli, 1910-11; fellow Am. Acad. in Rome, 1912-15; then asso. prof. archæology, Am. Acad. in Rome. Died June 8, 1925.

CURTIS, Cyrus Hermann Kotzschmar, publisher; b. Portland, Me., June 18, 1850; s. Cyrus L. and Salome A. (Cummins) C.; ed. N.E. pub. schs.; m. Louisa Knapp, Mar. 10, 1875 (died Feb. 25, 1910); 1 dau., Mary L. (Mrs. Edward Bok); m. 2d, Mrs. Kate S. Pillsbury (a second cousin), Aug. 2, 1910. Went to Phila. in 1876; became pub. Tribune and Farmer; later established Ladies Home Journal; head of Curtis Publishing Co., pubs. Ladies' Home Journal, The Country Gentleman and Saturday Evening Post, latter established by Benjamin Franklin, 1728. Purchased The Public Ledger, 1913, New York Evening Post, 1923. Died June 7, 1933.

CURTIS, David A., writer; b. at Norwich, Conn., Oct. 19, 1846; s. David R. and Sophia C. T. (Lazell) C.; ed. Poly. Inst., Brooklyn, 1 yr., Columbia Law Sch., 1 yr., pvt. sch., Huntsville, Ala., ½ yr.; m. Lizzie Dungate. Was reporter, editor, writer, corr., contbr. for nearly all the New York newspapers and mags., 1873—; also syndicate writer; splty. fiction; noted for his poker stories in New York Sunday Sun. Was librarian of New York City, 1892, 1893. Agnostic. Author: Beyond Hypnotism, 1902; Queer Luck, 1899; Science of Draw Poker, 1901; Stand Pat, 1906; Old Man Greenhut and His Friends, 1911; Finality, 1920. Died May 23, 1923.

CURTIS, Edward, physician; b. Providence, R.I., June 4, 1838; s. George and Julia (Bridgham) C.; A.B., Harvard, 1859, A.M., 1862; M.D., U. of Pa., 1864; m. Augusta Lawler Stacey, Nov. 16, 1864; father of Constance and Natalie C. Entered army as med. cadet, Sept. 6, 1861; acting asst. surgeon, May 5, 1863; asst. surgeon, Mar. 30, 1864; bvtd. capt. and maj. U.S.A., Mar. 13, 1865, "for faithful and meritorious services during the war"; resigned, June 7, 1870. Lecturer, 1871-73, prof. materia medica and therapeutics, 1873-86, emeritus, 1886, Coll. Phys. and Surg. (Columbia); med. dir. Equitable Life Assurance Soc., 1876-1904; retired, 1904. Author: Manual of General Medicinal Technology, 1883; Months and Moods; A Fifteen-year Calendar, 1903; Nature and Health, 1906. Died Nov. 28, 1912.

CURTIS, Edward Lewis, theologian; b. at Ann Arbor, Mich., Oct. 13, 1853; s. Rev. William S. (pres. Knox Coll., Ill.) and Martha A. (Leach) C.; A.B., Yale, 1874; grad. Union Theol. Sem., 1879; studied in Germany, 1879-81; (hon. Ph.D., Hanover Coll., Ind., 1886; D.D., Yale, 1891); m. Laura E. Ely, Apr. 27, 1882. Ordained Presbyn. ministry, Nov. 19, 1883; instr., 1881-86, prof. O. T. literature and exegesis, 1886-91, McCormick Theol. Sem., Chicago; Holmes prof. Hebrew, Yale Div. Sch., 1891—. Author: Commentary on Chronicles (International Critical Commentary), 1910. Died 1911.

CURTIS, Edwin Upton, lawyer; b. Roxbury, Mass., Mar. 26, 1861; s. George and Martha Ann (Upton) C.; A.B., Bowdoin, 1882, A.M., 1885 (LL.D., 1914); m. Margaret M. Waterman, Oct. 27, 1897. Admitted to bar, 1885; clerk, City of Boston, 1889-90; sec. Rep. City Com., 1888; mayor of Boston, 1895; asst. U.S. treas. at Boston, 1906; mem. Met. Park Commn., 1896-1916; collector of customs, port of Boston, 1909-13. Trustee Institution for Savings in Roxbury and its Vicinity; dir. Nat. Rockland Bank of Roxbury; dir. U.S. Trust Co. Police Commr. for City of Boston, Dec. 30, 1918—. Died Mar. 28, 1922.

CURTIS, F(rederick) Kingsbury, lawyer; b. N.Y. City, Feb. 3, 1863; s. Judge William E. and Mary Ann (Scovill) C.; prep. edn., St. Paul's Sch., Concord, N.H.; A.B., Yale, 1884; LL.B., Columbia, 1886; LL.D., Lincoln Memorial U., 1930; m. Cornelia Day McLanahan, June 14, 1905; children—Helen Kingsbury (Mrs. H. Pelham Curtis), Cornelia McLanahan (Mrs. Laurence M. Lombard). Admitted to N.Y. bar, 1886, and practiced since at N.Y. City; owner Insular Line and Ocean Freight Line until 1916; pres. Conn. Steel Co., 1920-22; chmn. bd. Am. Tube & Stamping Co., 1923-26; pres. Ramapo, Inc.; dir. Regal Shoe Co. Mem. bd. mgrs. Seamens Ch. Inst.; trustee Vassar Coll., Soc. for Relief of Half-Orphan and Destitute Children (pres.), Camp Fire Girls (v.p.), Mus. of Am. Indian, Heye Foundation. Chmn. Serbian Aid Fund, World War. Decorated Order St. Sava (Servia). Democrat. Episcopalian. Died Mar. 4, 1936.

CURTIS, Frederick Smillie, educator; b. Stratford, Conn., Feb. 8, 1850; s. Calvin and Elizabeth Augusta (Wicks) C.; Ph.B., Sheffield Scientific Sch. (Yale), 1869, post-grad., 1870; m. Ida Jewell Whiting, Oct. 29, 1873; children—Mrs. Chloe Baker, Gerald Beckwith, Lawrence. Prof. mathematics and natural science, State Normal Sch., West Chester, Pa., 1871-72; asst. prof. chemistry, Swarthmore Coll., 1872-75; founder, 1875, and prin. Curtis Sch. for Young Boys. Mem. Bd. Edn. of Brookfield, 1894-1915; moderator State Conf. Congl. Chs., 1902; del. 3d Internat. Congl. Council, Edinburgh, 1908. Mem. Alumni Advisory Bd., Yale. Home: Brookfield Center, Conn. Died Feb. 9, 1930.

CURTIS, George Carroll, geographic sculptor; b. Abington, Mass., July 15, 1872; s. George E. and Mary Adeline (Browne) C.; S.B., Harvard, 1896; grad. work in physiography and geographic modeling, 1895-98; m. Helen Louise Waters. Asst. in geol. dept., Harvard Univ.; asst. field geologist, U.S. Geol. Survey; model Met. Boston (for State of Mass.), gold medal, Paris, 1900 (aerial perspective first applied to topog. models); studied with Heim in Zurich; made, for U.S. Senate (Congressional Library), models (1) Washington City, 1902 (2) Washington City as proposed future development—1st Am. city to be modeled on a photographic survey; gold medal, Geog. Models, St. Louis, 1904; rep. Nat. Geog. Soc., Dixie Expdn. to W. Indian eruptions; first to reach crater of La Soufrière; discovered new summit of Mt. Pelee; Curtis Geography Models of land form types; year among Coral Islands, S. Pacific, for Agassiz Mus. Coral Id. Bora Bora, 1st naturalistic landscape model to be made in America; sailed single handed, in study of coast, from Me. to Newfoundland, 1910-11, made photographic survey of Kilauea crater, for Harvard U.; went around the World examining volcanoes, 1913; landscape paintings in relief of Josemite, Niagara, and Grand Canyon, 1923-25. Author: (and illustrator) Topography of the Region about Boston, 1900. Deceased.

CURTIS, George Martin, mfr.; b. Oxford, N.Y., Apr. 1, 1844; s. John S. and Elizabeth M. (Carpenter) C.; ed. pub. schs. and Mt. Morris (Ill.) Sem.; m. Ettie Lewis, Sept. 4, 1872. Began mfr. sash, doors, etc., Clinton, Ia., 1867; v.p. City Nat. Bank, Clinton; dir. McCloud River Lumber Co., Calif.; officer or dir. Curtis Bros. & Co., Curtis Door & Sash Co., Curtis & Yale Co., Curtis, Towle & Paine Co., etc. Mem. Ia. Ho. of Rep., 1887-88; mem. 54th and 55th Congresses (1895-99) 2d Ia. Dist.; del. 3 Rep. Nat. convs. Presbyn. Mason (33°). Address: Clinton, Ia. Died Feb. 9, 1921.

CURTIS, George Milton, lawyer; b. Worcester, Mass., June 18, 1843; ed. pvt. tutors and Bapt. Acad., Worcester. Served in 3d Battalion, Mass. Rifles, Civ. War; admitted to bar after war and practiced, New York; mem. N.Y. Assembly 2 terms; asst. corpn. counsel, New York, 1 term; judge marine ct., 1868-74. Appeared in many important criminal and civ. causes; defended and saved from gallows Col. Buford of Ky., indicted for murder of Chief Justice Elliott; appeared in Stetson will case, Boston, Bowman will case, New York, 1876; was counsel in the Dr. Helmbold insanity cases, Phila. and elsewhere; the Coffin lunacy case, New York, 1888; Hayes forgery case, 1893; of counsel in La. Lottery case; appeared for Mrs. Craven-Fair in Fair deed case, Calif., 1897; of counsel in Jeanette inquiry before Congress; successfully defended William Reinlander against charge of murder and insanity, etc. Died May 14, 1915.

CURTIS, George Munson, business man; b. Meriden, Conn., May 27, 1857; s. George Redfield and Augusta (Munson) C.; ed. Cheshire (Conn.) Acad. and Trinity Coll., Hartford, Conn. (hon. A.M., 1911); m. Sophie Phillips Mansfield, Nov. 30, 1886. Sec., treas., dir. Meriden Gas Light Co., Meriden Electric Light Co.; treas., dir. Internat. Silver Co., Meriden Britannia Co. of Hamilton, Ont., Home Nat. Bank, Meriden Savings Bank, Meriden Trust & Safe Deposit Co., Standard Silver Co. of Toronto, Can. Republican. Episcopalian. Trustee Curtis Home Corp. (charitable instn. for orphans and old ladies), Curtis Memorial Library. Died Aug. 28, 1915.

CURTIS, Georgina Pell, writer; b. at New York, Feb. 19, 1859; d. Alfred Leonard and Maria Elizabeth (Hill) C.; ed. pvt. tutors and St. Mary's (P.E.) Sch., New York; convert to R.C. Ch. Author: The Romance of a Chap Book, 1914; The Bridge of Victory, 1914; Faith in the Wilderness, 1921. Home: Elizabeth, N.J. Died April 25, 1922.

CURTIS, Heber Doust, astronomer; b. Muskegon, Mich., June 27, 1872; s. Orson B. and Sarah E. (Doust) C.; A.B., U. of Mich., 1892, A.M., 1893; Ph.D., U. of Va., 1902; m. Mary D. Rapier, July 12, 1895; children—Margret Evelyn (Mrs. Alexander Walters), Rowen Doust, Alan Blair, Baldwin Rapier. Prof. Latin, Napa Coll., 1894-97; prof. mathematics and astronomy, U. of the Pacific, 1897-1900; fellow in astronomy, Leander McCormick Obs., U. of Va., 1900-02; asst. 1902-04, asst. astronomer, 1904-06, Lick Obs.; acting astronomer in charge of the D. O. Mills Expdn. to the Southern Hemisphere, 1906-09; astronomer, Lick Obs., 1909-20; dir. Allegheny Obs., 1920-30; dir. obs. of U. of Mich., 1930—. Observed 11 total solar eclipses—Georgia, 1900, Sumatra, 1901, Labrador, 1905, Russia, 1914, Washington, 1918, Mexico, 1923, New Haven, 1925, Sumatra, 1926, 29, Nevada, 1930, Maine, 1932; in charge Lick Observatory Eclipse Sta., Labrador, 1905. Mem. Nat. Acad. Sciences. Died Jan. 8, 1942.

CURTIS, Henry G., lawyer; b. Licking Co., O., Nov. 3, 1839; grad. Central U. of Iowa, 1861; A.M., 1866; m. Mary A. Fisher, Apr. 4, 1864. Taught in common schools to procure means for coll. course; enlisted private, Co. E, 8th Ia. inf.; promoted sergt

Miss. River Marine Brigade, U.S.V.; asst. sec. Iowa senate, 1864-65; admitted to bar, 1865; mem. bd. trustees, Central U. of Ia., gave $25,000 to its endowment; on council of administration, G.A.R., and was aide to Gen. Alger when comdr.-in-chief; distinguished as Republican orator and writer; was a mem. the U.S. Insular Commn. Address: Atlantic, Ia. Died 1901.

CURTIS, H(enry) Holbrook, laryngologist; b. New York, Dec. 15, 1856; s. Judge William Edmond and Mary A. (Scovill) C.; Ph.B., Yale, 1877, M.D., 1880; m. Josephine Allen, June 19, 1884. Specialist in laryngology and otology, New York City; consulting laryngologist to Minturn Diphtheria and Scarlet Fever Hosp. Fellow Royal Med. Soc. (England); pres. Am. Laryngol., Rhinol. and Otol. Soc. Author: Voice Building and Tone Placing, 1894. Died May 14, 1920.

CURTIS, Howard Junior, judge; b. Stratford, Conn., June 29, 1857; s. Freeman L. and Georgiana (Howard) C.; A.B., Yale, 1881, LL.B., 1883; m. Ellen V. Talbot, of Stratford, June 5, 1888; children—Howard W. (dec.), John Talbot, Violetta. Practiced with Judge G. W. Wheeler, at Bridgeport, Conn., 1883-93; judge Civil Court of Common Pleas, Fairfield Co., Conn., 1893-1907; judge Superior Court of Conn., 1907-29; judge Supreme Court of Errors of Conn., term 1920-28, retired 1927. Democrat. Episcopalian. Home: Stratford, Conn. Died Sept. 24, 1931.

CURTIS, Isabel Gordon, editor; b. Huntly, Aberdeenshire, Scotland, Apr. 24, 1863; d. Peter and Elizabeth (Ragg) Gordon; ed. Gordon Sch., Huntly, and Milne's Acad., Fochabers, Scotland; came to America, 1886; m. Francis Curtis, Aug. 6, 1896. Did gen. lit. work, 1886-90; lit. editor New England Homestead, and Farm and Home, 1892-96; dramatic editor Springfield Homestead, 1896; associated with husband as editor Binghamton Chronicle, 1896-1900; asso. editor Good Housekeeping, 1900-03; editor woman's dept. Success Magazine until 1911. Author: The Making of a Housewife, 1906; The Woman from Wolverton, 1912; The Lapse of Enoch Wentworth, 1913; The Congresswoman, 1914. Died Dec. 23, 1915.

CURTIS, John Green, physiologist; b. New York, Oct. 29, 1844; s. George and Julia (Bridgham) C.; A.B., Harvard, 1866, A.M., 1869; M.D., Coll. Phys. and Surg. (Columbia), 1870; (LL.D., Columbia, 1904); m. Mrs. Martha (McCook) Davis, Oct. 20, 1871. Apptd. jr. asst. Bellevue Hosp., Apr. 1, 1869, sr. asst., Oct. 1, 1869, house surgeon, Apr. 1, 1870, attending surgeon, 1876-80; asst. and demonstrator of anatomy, 1870-75, adj. lecturer, 1875-76, adj. prof. physiology, 1876-83, prof. physiology, 1883, emeritus prof. physiology, 1909, Coll. Phys. and Surg. Joint Author: American Text-book of Physiology, 1896. Died Sept. 20, 1913.

CURTIS, John Jay, publisher; b. nr. Indianapolis, Ind., Jan. 21, 1857; s. Hiram King and Harriet Elizabeth (Little) C.; grad. North Western Christian (now Butler) U., 1873; m. Bertha Justine Loeper, Apr. 27, 1903. Began with Bowen, Stewart & Co. (now Bobbs-Merrill & Co.), book pubs., Indianapolis, 1873, successively mgr. retail dept., sec. and vice-pres., established New York office, 1898, Hollywood office, 1920, pres., 1926—. Republican. Episcopalian. Mason. Known as "dean of modern book advertising"; originator of colored pictorial book jackets. Died July 22, 1931.

CURTIS, Newton Martin, soldier; b. De Peyster, N.Y., May 21, 1835; s. Jonathan and Phebe (Rising) C.; attended Gouverneur Wesleyan Sem., 1854-55; (LL.D., St. Lawrence U., 1906). Postmaster, De Peyster, 1857, 1861; capt. 16th N.Y. Inf., May 15, 1861; lt. col. 142d N.Y. Inf., Oct. 22, 1862; col., Jan. 21, 1863; bvtd. brig. gen. vols., Oct. 28, 1864, for distinguished services nr. New Market, Va.; maj. gen. vols., Mar. 13, 1865, for gallant and meritorious services at capture of Ft. Fisher; awarded medal of honor, May 28, 1891, for being the 1st man at Ft. Fisher, Jan. 15, 1865, to pass through stockade; hon. mustered out, Jan. 15, 1866. Mem. N.Y. legislature, 1884-90; pres. N.Y. State Agrl. Soc., 1880; sec. N.Y. Agrl. Expt. Sta., 1879-85, pres., 1885-90; mem. Congress St. Lawrence-Jefferson dist., 1891-93, St. Lawrence-Saratoga dist., 1893-97. Asst. insp. gen. Nat. Home for Disabled Vol. Soldiers, 1898—. Pres. Soc. Army of the Potomac, 1907-08. Author: From Bull Run to Chancellorsville, 1906 P2. Home: Ogdensburg, N.Y. Died 1910.

CURTIS, Oakley Chester, governor; b. Portland, Me., Mar. 29, 1865; s. William and Amanda (Randall) C.; ed. pub. schs.; m. Edith L. Hamilton, Nov. 24, 1886. Mgr. Randall & McAllister, wholesale coal, 1894—; dir. Casco Mercantile Trust Co., Portland Safe Deposit & Trust Co., U.S. Trust Co.; alderman, Portland, 1901; member Maine House of Representatives, 1903-04; Senate, 1905-08; mayor of Portland, 4 yrs., 1911-14; chmn. High School Commn. (for new bldg.); gov. of Me., 1915, 16. Democrat. Conglist. Mason (32°). Home: Falmouth, Me. Died Feb. 22, 1924.

CURTIS, Olin Alfred, theologian; b. Frankfort, Me., Dec. 10, 1850; s. Reuben and Mary (Gilbert) C.; ed. pub. schs., Lawrence Coll. (A.M., S.T.D., LL.D.); Boston U. (B.D.); post-grad. in philosophy and theology, Leipzig, Erlangen, Marburg and Edinburgh. M.E. pastor, Janesville, Wis., 1880-83, Milwaukee, 1883-86, Chicago, 1888-89; prof. systematic theology, Boston U., 1889-95, Drew Theol. Sem., Sept. 1896-1914; emeritus. Author: Elective Course of Lectures in Systematic Theology; The Christian Faith; Personal Submission to Jesus Christ. Home: Leonia, N.J. Died Jan. 9, 1918.

CURTIS, Sumner (Macomber), newspaper man; b. Madison, Wis., Nov. 14, 1868; s. Joseph Walker and Julia Ella (Macomber) C.; B.L., U. of Wis., 1889; m. Henriette Gregory, July 3, 1906. Polit. and legislative corr. at Wis. State Capital for Milwaukee Sentinel and Chicago Tribune, 1889-91; Washington corr. Milwaukee Sentinel, 1891-94; reporter Chicago Times-Herald, 1895-97; war corr. New York Herald, 1898; with Chicago Record-Herald, 1904-14, polit. editor, 1905, in charge Washington bur. and editorial writer, 1906-1910, Washington corr., 1910-14; spl. agt. of Dept. of State, attached to Am. Embassy at Berlin, 1914; polit. corr. Washington (D.C.) Post, 1915-16; with lit. dept. Am. Red Cross War Council, 1917-19; editor Nat. Red Cross Bulletin, 1918—. Apptd. asst. to chmn. Rep. Nat. Com., 1923. During Spanish-Am. War was in charge, at different times, of dispatch boats Sommers N. Smith, Miñdora and Golden Rod, in West Indian waters. Died at Denver, Colo., June 24, 1923.

CURTIS, Wardon Allan, author; b. in N.M., Feb. 1, 1867; s. Capt. Charles Albert (U.S.A.) and Harriet Louise (Hughes) C.; A.B., U. of Wis., 1889; unmarried. Since graduation engaged in journalism, with Chicago Daily News, 1910-13, Boston Herald, 1913-16; sec. Publicity Commn. of N.H., 1921-25; editorial writer Manchester Union, 1924-28. Author: Strange Adventures of Mr. Middleton, 1903. Home: Ashland, N.H. Died Jan. 20, 1940.

CURTIS, William Buckingham, editor; b. Salisbury, Vt., Jan. 17, 1837; academic edn. (2½ yrs. at Wabash Coll.); in mercantile business until 1878; then editor; better known as amateur athlete and oarsman. Unmarried. Home: Brooklyn, N.Y. Died 1900.

CURTIS, William Edmond, lawyer; b. New York, June 2, 1855; s. Judge William Edmond and Mary A. (Scovill) C.; A.B., Trinity Coll., 1875, A.M., 1878 (LL.D., 1902); LL.B., Columbia, 1877; unmarried. In practice at New York, 1877—. Mem. State Com. apptd. by Syracuse "Anti-Snapper" Conv., 1892; asst. sec. U.S. Treasury, 1893-97; mem. New York Aqueduct Commn., 1902-05; del. Dem. Nat. Conv., 1904. Conducted negotiations which resulted in purchase of gold by U.S. Govt., Feb. 1895, to sustain pub. credit and was sent to Europe to deliver $31,000,000 of the bonds issued therefor. Trustee Trinity Coll. Died Aug. 20, 1923.

CURTIS, William Eleroy, journalist; b. Akron, O., Nov. 5, 1850; s. Eleroy and Harriet (Coe) C.; A.B., Western Reserve Coll., 1871 (Litt.D., 1901; L.H.D., Amherst, 1907); m. Cora Belle Kepler, Dec. 23, 1874. On staff of Chicago Inter Ocean, 1873-87; Washington corr. Chicago Record, 1887-1901, Chicago Record-Herald, 1901—. Special commr. from U.S. to Central and S.Am., Republics; exec. officer Internat. Am. Conf., 1889-90; dir. Bur. Am. Republics, 1890-93; chief Latin-Am. dept. and hist. sect., Chicago Expn., 1891-93; commr. of Chicago Expn. to Madrid, and spl. envoy to the Queen Regent of Spain and Pope Leo XIII, 1892. Author: Tibbalses Folks, 1875; A Summer Scamper, 1881; The Life of Zachariah Chandler, 1879; Children of the Sun, 1882; Capitals of Spanish America, 1886; The Land of the Nihilist, 1887; Trade and Transportation, 1889; Handbook to the American Republics, 1890; Guatemala, 1891; Costa Rica, 1891; Ecuador, 1891; Venezuela—A Land Where It Is Always Summer, 1891; The United States and Foreign Powers, 1892, 1899; The Existing Autographs of Columbus, 1893; Relics of Columbus, 1893, same; Recent Discoveries Concerning the Early Settlement of America in the Archives of the Vatican, 1894; The Yankees of the East, 1896; To-day in France and Germany, 1897; Between the Andes and the Ocean, 1901; The True Thomas Jefferson, 1901; The Turk and His Lost Provinces, 1902; Denmark, Sweden and Norway, 1903; The True Abraham Lincoln, 1903; To-day in Syria and Palestine, 1904; Modern India, 1905; Egypt, Burma and the British East Indies, 1905; One Irish Summer, 1909. Died 1911.

CURTIS, William Franklin, college pres.; b. nr. Souderton, Bucks Co., Pa., Feb. 12, 1873; s. William Henry and Elizabeth Seiple (Miller) C.; A.B., Franklin and Marshall Coll., Pa., 1898, LL.D., 1926; grad. Theol. Sem. of the Reformed Ch., Lancaster, Pa., 1901; Litt.D., Muhlenberg Coll., 1913; m. Anna Frances Denlinger, June 11, 1901; children—Elizabeth Mae, William D. Ordained Ref. Ch. in U.S. ministry, 1901; pastor St. Paul's Ref. Ch., Kansas City, Mo., 1901-08; pres. Cedar Crest Coll. for Women, Allentown, Pa., 1908—. Republican. Mason (32°). Home: Allentown, Pa. Died May 5, 1941.

CURTIS, William John, lawyer; b. Brunswick, Me., Aug. 28, 1854; s. John and Letitia (Bammer) C.; A.B., Bowdoin Coll., 1875, LL.D., 1913; admitted to Me. bar, 1878; Columbia Law Sch., 1878; admitted to N.Y. bar, 1879; m. Angeline Sturtevant Riley, June 13, 1881; children—Katharine (Mrs. Henry H. Pierce), Helen (Mrs. E. L. Taylor), Lena (Mrs. Arthur Poillon), William J., Mildred (Mrs. Walter Hughson). In practice at New York, 1879—. Organized the Cleveland Anti-Snap Movement in N.J., 1892; organized Independent Dem. Sound Money Movement in N.J., 1896; del.-at-large and chmn. N.J. delegation to Indianapolis Independent Dem. Conv., 1896. Trustee and chmn. finance com. Bowdoin Coll. Episcopalian. Died Oct. 8, 1927.

CURTIS, William Samuel, dean law sch.; b. Newport, Wayne Co., Ind., June 19, 1850; s. William C. and Elizabeth R. (Harker) C.; ed. McKendree Coll., 1869-70; A.B., Washington U., 1873; LL.B., St. Louis Law Sch., 1876; (LL.D., Washington, 1905); m. Hope Goodson, 1881. Practiced law, Omaha, Neb., 1876-94; dean St. Louis Law Sch. (law dept. Washington U.), 1894-1915, emeritus, 1915. Del. Universal Congress Lawyers and Jurists, St. Louis, 1904. Unitarian. Died May 1916.

CURTISS, Charles Chauncey, business man; b. Chicago, July 31, 1847; s. James (twice mayor of Chicago) and Mary (Kimball) C.; ed. pub. schs. and under pvt. tutelage; m. Addie Louise Miller, May 24, 1877; children—Charles DeLaskie (dec.), Marjorie Kimball, James, Marion. Messenger in telegraph office at Champaign, Ill., 1862; clerk in dry goods store, Champaign, 1863-64; pvt. Co. B, 135th Ill. Vol. Inf., May-Oct. 1864; clerk ordnance depot, Nashville, Tenn., 1864-66; salesman Field, Palmer & Leiter, Chicago, 1866-67; clerk at Pittsburgh, Pa., 1867-68; in co. recorder's office, Chicago, 1868; bookkeeper, Lyon & Healy, Chicago, 1869-72; partner in music pub. house of F. S. Chandler & Co. and Chandler & Curtiss, 1872-75; mgr. and treas. Root & Sons Music Co., 1875-81, Curtiss & Mayer, 1881-89; pres. Manufacturers' Piano Co., 1890-95; projector of Fine Arts Bldg., completed May 1, 1898, and v.p., treas. and dir. An organizer of Ill. Civil Service Reform League; mem. Citizens' Assn., Municipal Voters' League, Legislative Voters' League, etc. Charter mem. and sec. Apollo Mus. Club. Died Mar. 26, 1928.

CURTISS, Glenn Hammond, inventor, aviator; b. Hammondsport, N.Y., May 21, 1878; s. Frank R. and Lua (Andrews) C.; ed. pub. schs.; m. Lena P. Neff, 1898; 1 son, Glenn Hammond. Former pres. G. H. Curtiss Mfg. Co., Curtiss Aeroplane Co., Curtiss Motor Co., Curtiss Engring. Co., Curtiss Aeroplane & Motor Corp.; dir. Curtiss Aeroplane & Motor Corp., Curtiss Flying Service. Early began expts. with motor vehicles, establishing motorcycle factory at Hammondsport, 1902. Set speed records for motorcycle, riding his own machines, 1905; at Ormond Beach, Florida, 1907, made record for mile of 46⅖ seconds with 110 pound motorcycle. Designed aeronautical motors for dirigibles with Capt. T. S. Baldwin, 1907-09, building for U.S.A., Dirigible No. 1; director of experiments for Aerial Expt. Assn., 1907-09, and supervised construction of and piloted "June Bug," July 4, 1908, for first public flight of mile in U.S., winning Scientific American trophy; experimented with the "Loon," an aeroplane fitted with pontoons, 1908; won Gordon Bennett cup and prix de la Vitesse at Rheims, France, Internat. Aviation Meet as rep. Aero Club America, Aug. 1909, with aeroplane and motor of Curtiss design; won N.Y. World prize of $10,000 in flight from Albany to New York in 2 hours, 51 minutes, May 29, 1910; made public demonstration of hydroaeroplane, Jan. 1911, with which had been experimenting for number of years, following demonstration of this invention with that of flying boat (awarded prize by Aero Club America, 1912). Established flying schs. at Hammondsport, San Diego, Buffalo, Newport News, Miami, Atlantic City, 1909-19; introduced flying boat to Brazil, Russia, Austria, Italy and Germany, 1913-14; designed and built for Rodman Wanamaker, the "America," the first multi-motored flying boat, and first heavier-than-air flying craft designed for transatlantic flight, 1914. With J. N. Willys expanded Curtiss factories to meet war demands of Great Britain, Russia, and U.S., 1917. Developed "Wasp" (holder of world's records for speed, climb, and altitude) and other types of aeroplanes, flying boat types, and with U.S. Navy, the Navy-Curtiss flying boats 1, 2, 3 and 4, the latter of which made the first Atlantic crossing, May 16-27, 1919. Hon. mem. Nat. Aeronautic Assn., 1924. Author: (with Augustus Post) Curtiss Aviation Book. Home: Hammondsport, N.Y. Died July 23, 1930.

CURTISS, Ralph Hamilton, astronomer; b. Derby, Conn., Feb. 8, 1880; s. Hamilton Burton and Emily Wheeler (Curtiss) C.; B.S., U. of Calif., 1901, Ph.D., 1905; m. Mary Louise Welton, June 17, 1920. Asst. Astron. Obs., U. of Calif., 1900; mem. Lick Obs. Eclipse Expdn. to Sumatra, 1901; fellow at Lick Obs., 1901-04; Carnegie asst., same, 1904-05; astronomer,

Allegheny Obs., 1905-07; asst. prof. astronomy, 1907-11, asso. prof., 1911-18, prof., 1918—, U. of Mich., and asst. dir. Detroit Obs., dir., 1927—. Principal line of investigation, the properties of stars having bright line spectra in Classes B to A of the Draper Classification. Died Dec. 25, 1929.

CURTISS, Samuel Ives, Congl. theologian; b. Union, Conn., Feb. 5, 1844; s. Samuel Ives and Eliza (Ives) C.; grad. Amherst, 1867 (D.D., 1883); grad. Union Theol. Sem., 1870 (Ph.D., Leipzig, 1876; Lic. Th., U. of Berlin, 1878; D.D., Iowa Coll., 1878; Amherst, 1881); m. Mrs. Laura W. Sessions, May 10, 1870. Engaged in missionary work, New York; ordained in New York Presbytery, 1874; pastor Am. Chapel, Leipzig, 1874-78; became, 1878, prof. Biblical lit., Chicago Theol. Sem.; later changing to chair of Old Testament literature and interpretation; pres. Chicago City Missionary Soc., 1888-98, 1899-1903. Author: (transl.) Bickell's Outlines of Hebrew Grammar, 1877; The Name Machabee, 1876; The Levitical Priests, 1877; De Aaronitici Sacerdotii atque Thoræ Elohisticæ Origine, 1878; A Plea for a More Thorough Study of the Semitic Languages in America, 1879; Delitzsch, Messianic Prophecies (transl.), 1880, 1891; Delitzsch Old Testament History of Redemption (transl.), 1881; Moses and Ingersoll, 1881; The Old Testament in "Current Discussions in Theology," 1888-90; Franz Delitzsch, 1890; Ezekiel and His Times in "The Bible as Literature," 1896; MSS. in "The People's Bible History," 1896; Primitive Semitic Religion Today, 1902. Died 1904.

CURTS, Lewis, clergyman; b. Hocking Co., O., Mar. 24, 1847; s. John and Elmira (Leist) C.; B.S., Cornell Coll., Ia., 1869, M.S., 1872 (D.D., 1889); m. Electa Bardwell, Dec. 25, 1871; m. 2d, Ella Randolph, Oct. 29, 1901. Pvt. Co. F, 24th Ia. Vols., in Civil War. Entered M.E. ministry in Rock River Conf., 1870; in pastorates, 1870-85, 1889-91, and from 1900; presiding elder, 1885-89, 1891-92; western publishing agent M.E. Ch., 1892-1900; pastor Gary Memorial Ch., Wheaton, Ill., 1901-03; asst. pastor First Ch., Chicago, 1903-05; retired 1905. Mem. bd. trustees M.E. Ch.; trustee Cornell Coll., Ia. Died Feb. 19, 1928.

CURWEN, John, physician; b. Montgomery Co., Pa., Sept. 20, 1821; grad. Yale, 1841; med. dept., U. of Pa., 1844; asst. physician, 1844-51; physician-in-chief and supt., 1851-81, Pa. State Lunatic Hosp., Harrisburg; commr. for erection State Hosp. for Insane, at Danville, 1868-72, and for State Hosp. at Warren, 1873-82; physician-in-chief and supt. Pa. State Hosp., Warren, 1881-1900. Married twice. Died 1901.

CURWEN, Samuel M.; pres. J. G. Brill Co., The Brill Corp., G. C. Kuhlman Car Co., Am. Car Co., Wason Mfg. Co., Electric Ry. Equipment Securities Corp. Home: Haverford, Pa. Died Mar. 29, 1932.

CURWOOD, James Oliver, author; b. Owosso, Mich., June 12, 1878; s. James Moran and Abigail (Griffin) C.; ed. lit. dept., U. of Mich.; married. In newspaper work 7 yrs.; asst. editor and editor, News-Tribune, Detroit; resigned to take up lit. work exclusively, 1907. Republican. One of the foremost authorities on matters pertaining to the Canadian Northland; spent several mos. each year in the wilds, traveling as far north as Arctic coast; the only American ever employed by the Canadian Government as an exploratory and descriptive writer. Active worker for national wild life and forest conservation. Author: The Courage of Captain Plum, 1908; The Wolf Hunters, 1908; The Great Lakes, 1909; The Gold Hunters, 1909; The Danger Trail, 1910; The Honor of the Big Snows, 1911; Philip Steele, of the Royal Mounted, 1911; Flower of the North, 1912; Isobel, 1913; Kazan, 1914; God's Country and the Woman, 1915; The Hunted Woman, 1916; The Grizzly King, 1917; Baree, Son of Kazan, 1917; The Courage of Marge O'Doone, 1918; Nomads of the North, 1919; The River's End, 1919; The Valley of Silent Men, 1920; The Flaming Forest, 1921; The Country Beyond, 1922; The Alaskan, 1923; A Gentleman of Courage, 1924; The Ancient Highway, 1925; The Black Hunter, 1926. Home: Owosso, Mich. Died Aug. 13, 1927.

CURZON, Mary Victoria (Lady Curzon); b. Chicago, Ill.; d. L. Z. Leiter; m. Jan., 1895, Hon. George Nathaniel Curzon, who became under sec. Foreign Affairs and Privy Councillor, Aug. 1895, and Viceroy of India, Jan., 1899. He was created an Irish baron with the title of Lord Curzon (of Kedleston), June 23, 1898. Died 1906.

CUSACK, Thomas Francis, bishop; b. New York, Feb. 22, 1862; s. James and Honora (Boland) C.; grad. St. Francis Xavier Coll., 1880. Ordained priest, R.C. Ch., 1885; superior N.Y. Diocesan Mission Soc., 1897-1904; consecrated auxiliary bishop of New York, Apr. 25, 1904; apptd. bishop of Albany, Sept. 2, 1915. Died July 12, 1918.

CUSHING, Charles C(yprian) S(trong) (Tom Cushing), playwright; b. New Haven, Conn., Oct. 27, 1879; s. William Lee and Mary Lewis (Strong) C.; prep. edn., Westminster Sch., Simsbury, Conn.; A.B., Yale, 1902; unmarried. With entertainment dept., Y.M.C.A., in France, World War. Author: Sari (musical comedy), 1912; Thank You, 1921; Blood and Sand, 1921; Laugh, Clown, Laugh, 1924; The Devil in the Cheese, 1926; La Gringa, 1927; Barely Proper, 1931. Home: New Haven, Conn. Died Mar. 6, 1941.

CUSHING, Ernest Watson, surgeon; b. Boston, Jan. 17, 1847; s. Thomas and Elizabeth A. (Baldwin) C.; A.B., Harvard, 1867; M.D., Coll. of Phys. and Surg. (Columbia), 1871; (LL.D., Tufts Coll., 1898); m. Maria von Ralenowsky, of Vienna, Austria, Dec. 27, 1873. In practice at Boston, 1874—; prof. abdominal surgery and gynecology, Tufts Med. Sch., 1895-13. Editor Annals of Gynecology and Pediatry, 1887-1903. Episcopalian. Mem. bd. dirs. Robert Bent Brigham Hosp. Died Aug. 27, 1916.

CUSHING, Grafton Dulany, lawyer; b. Boston, Mass., Aug. 4, 1864; s. Robert Maynard and Olivia Donaldson (Dulany) C.; A.B., Harvard, 1885, A.M., 1888, LL.B., 1888; unmarried. Practiced at Boston, 1888—; trustee Mut. Life Ins. Co. of New York. Mem. Boston Sch. Com. 6 yrs. (pres. 2 yrs.); mem. Mass. Ho. of Rep., 1906-14 (speaker, 1912-14); elected lt. gov. 1915. Pres. Rep. Club of Mass. 2 yrs.; del. Rep. Nat. Conv., 1912; pres. Rep. City Com. of Boston. Dir. and pres. Mass. Soc. Prevention of Cruelty to Children; v.p. Pub. Sch. Assn.; chmn. Mass. State Child Labor Com.; trustee of Donations of the P.E. Ch.; trustee Isabella Stewart Gardner Museum. Died May 31, 1939.

CUSHING, Harvey, surgeon; b. Cleveland, O., Apr. 8, 1869; s. Henry Kirke and Betsey M. (Williams) C.; A.B., Yale, 1891, hon. A.M., 1912, Sc.D., 1919; A.M. and M.D., Harvard, 1895, Sc.D., 1931; hon. fellow Royal Coll. Surgeons, Eng., 1913, Ireland, 1918, Edinburgh, 1927; M.D., hon. causa, Belfast, 1918, Strasbourg and Brussels, 1930, Budapest and Bern, 1931, Paris, 1933; Sc.D., Washington U., 1915; LL.D., Western Reserve U., 1919, Cambridge, 1920, Edinburgh and Glasgow univs., 1927; Litt.D., Dartmouth Coll., 1929; m. Katharine Stone Crowell, June 10, 1902; children—Mary Benedict, Betsey, Henry Kirke, Barbara. Engaged in practice surgery, 1895-1933; asso. prof. surgery, etc., Johns Hopkins, 1902-12; prof. surgery, Harvard, and surgeon-in-chief, Peter Bent Brigham Hosp., 1912-32; Sterling prof. neurology, Yale, 1933—. Dir. U.S.A. Base Hosp., No. 5, attached to B.E.F., in France, May 1917-Mar. 1919; sr. consultant in neurol. surgery, A.E.F., 1918; col. M.C. D.S.M. (U.S.); Companion of the Bath; Officier Légion d'Honneur. Mem. Nat. Acad. Sciences; pres. Am. Neurol. Assn., 1923, Am. Coll. Surgeons, 1923. Charles Mickle fellowship, U. of Toronto, 1922; Cameron prize, U. of Edinburgh, 1924; Lister medal (London), 1930. Author: The Pituitary Body and Its Disorders, 1912; Tumors of the Nervus Acusticus, 1917; The Life of Sir William Osler, 1925 (Pulitzer prize); A Classification of the Gliomata (with P. Bailey), 1925; Consecratio Medici and other Essays, 1928; Intracranial Tumours, 1932; Pituitary Body and Hypothalamus, 1932. Died Oct. 8, 1939.

CUSHING, Henry Platt, geologist; b. Cleveland, Oct. 10, 1860; s. Henry Kirke and Betsey M. (Williams) C.; Ph.B., Cornell U., 1882; post-grad. work, same, 1882-83, 84, 85, M.S., 1884, Ph.D., 1909; Columbia, 1883-84; U. of Munich, 1891-92; m. Florence E. Williams, June 3, 1886. Prof. of geology, Western Reserve U., 1892—; geologist on the N.Y. state Geol. Survey, 1893—. Died Apr. 14, 1921.

CUSHING, Howard Gardiner, artist; b. Boston, 1869; s. Robert and Olivia (Dulany) C.; grad. Groton Sch., 1887; A.B., Harvard, 1891; studied at Académie Julien, Paris, 1891-96; m. Boston, Nov. 7, 1904. A.N.A., 1906. Deceased.

CUSHING, John Pearsons, educator; b. Lansingburg, N.Y., Sept. 5, 1861; s. Alvin Matthew (M.D.) and Elizabeth H. (Pearsons) C.; student Boston U., 1878-80; A.B., Amherst, 1882, A.M., 1885; Ph.D., U. of Leipzig, 1894; m. Alice Blyth Bullions, June 25, 1890. Prof. economics and history, Knox Coll., 1894-1900; headmaster high sch., New Haven, Conn., 1900-11, Hamden Hall Sch., New Haven, 1911—. Conglist. Mason. Died Apr. 6, 1941.

CUSHING, John Thayer, newspaper pub.; b. Lowell, Mass., Oct. 24, 1887; s. George Russell and Katherine (Moran) C.; student Dartmouth Coll., 1904-07, U.S. Mil. Acad., 1907-08; m. Ruth Marian Ellis, Oct. 18, 1913; children—William Thayer, Whitney, Sarah Sharp. Reporter St. Albans (Vt.) Messenger, 1908-12, editor, 1912-27; business mgr. Washington Herald, 1927-28, pub. same, 1928-30; pub. Washington Times, 1928-30, Boston Record, 1930—; pres. Northeastern Pub. Co., 1930-36; v.p. and dir. New England Newspaper Pub. Co., 1937—. Conglist. Mason. Died Sept. 24, 1938.

CUSHING, Samuel Tobey, army officer; b. Providence, R.I., Sept. 14, 1839; s. George W. and Sarah (Cooke) C.; early edn. common schools, Providence; grad. West Point Mil. Acad., July 1, 1860; m. Kate Dewey, May 27, 1869. Bvtd. 2d lt., Jan. 1861; 1st lt., Feb. 1862; capt., Feb. 1863; capt. subsistence dept., May 1863; maj. by bvt., Aug. 1888; maj. subsistence dept., Jan. 1897; brig. gen. and commissary gen. U.S. Army. In New Mex. during Navajo war, 1860-61; signal officer, and during Civil War, 1862-63, chief signal officer Army of the Potomac; chief commissary of subsistence in field during Bannock War, 1878. Died 1901.

CUSHING, William Erastus, lawyer; b. Cleveland, Sept. 23, 1853; s. Henry Kirke (M.D.) and Betsey M. Williams) C.; A.B., Western Reserve (now Adelbert) Coll., 1875; LL.B., Harvard Law Sch., 1878; m. Carolyn J. Kellogg, June 4, 1884. Mem. law firm Cushing, Hopkins & Lamb, Cleveland. Mem. Ohio State Bd. of Commrs. on Uniform Laws, 1902-5. Trustee Western Reserve U., Adelbert Coll., and University Sch., Cleveland. Died Dec. 19, 1917.

CUSHING, William Lee, educator; b. Phippsburg, Me., July 24, 1849; s. Samuel Woodward and Mary Ann (Mereen) C.; B.A., Yale, 1872, M.A., 1876; m. Mary Lewis Strong, Apr. 6, 1876. Rector Hopkins Grammar Sch., 1873-85; founded, 1888, and then headmaster, Westminister Sch. Home. Simsbury, Conn. Died Dec. 11, 1921.

CUSHMAN, Allerton Seward, chemist; b. (U.S. Consulate) Rome, June 2, 1867; s. Edwin and Emma (Crow) C.; B.S., Worcester Poly. Inst., 1888; Freiberg, and Heidelberg, 1889-90; A.M., Harvard, 1896, John Harvard fellow, Ph.D., 1897; pvt. to capt., 6th Mass. Vol. Inf., 1898; m. Sarah Dunn Hoppin, June 20, 1901 (died 1921); children—Charles Van Brunt, Agnes Hoppin (dec.). Asso. prof. chemistry, Bryn Mawr Coll., 1900-01; asst. dir. Office of Pub. Roads, U.S. Dept. Agr., and chemist in charge of investigations, 1902-10; founder and dir. Inst. of Industrial Research, Washington, 1910-24. Commd. maj. Ordnance R.C., June 4, 1917; stationed at Frankford Arsenal, Pa.; promoted lt. col. Ordnance, U.S.A., Jan. 1918; discharged Dec. 1918. Prin. researches: extraction of potash from feldspathic rocks; use of ground rock as fertilizer; properties of road materials; cause and prevention of the rusting of iron and steel. Franklin medal, 1906. Author: The Corrosion and Preservation of Iron and Steel, 1910; Chemistry and Civilization, 1920, 2d edit., 1925. Died May 1, 1930.

CUSHMAN, Austin Sprague, lawyer; b. Duxbury, Mass., Sept. 9, 1827; s. late Robert Woodward C., D.D. (Bapt. clergyman) and Lucy (Sprague) C.; grad. Brown, 1848; admitted to Mass. bar, 1853; of N.Y., 1879; m. Carrie L. Hathaway, Nov. 17, 1861. Clerk in U.S. War Dept., 1849; collaborated with Dr. Stone in reporting (by Isaac Pitman's phonography) trial of Dr. Webster for murder of Dr. Parkman (published 1850); private sec. to Pres. Fillmore, 1852; 3d lt. U.S. Revenue Marine Service, 1853; U.S. Commr., Mass. dist., May 24, 1855; lt. in 3d Mass. inf., 1858-61; promoted adj. 3d regt. Apr. 19, 1861; on duty at burning of Gosport Navy Yard—among first troops in Va.; raised co.; capt. and maj., 47th Mass. inf., 1862-63; U.S. register bankruptcy, 1867; practiced admiralty and patent law; sec. Am. Patent Protective Assn.; editor Republic Mag., 1890. Prominent in G.A.R.; was 1st post comdr. in New England and 1st dept. comdr. of Mass. 32° Mason. Died 1907.

CUSHMAN, Francis W., congressman; b. Brighton, Ia., May 8, 1867; grad. Pleasant Plain Acad., Ia., 1884; studied law and admitted to bar; mem. Congress, 1899-1909, at large, Wash. Republican. Home: Tacoma, Wash. Died 1909.

CUSTER, Elizabeth Bacon, author; b. (Bacon) Mich., about 1844; m. Feb. 1864, Gen. George Armstrong Custer, and was with him at various posts until his death, 1876. Author: Boots and Saddles, or Life in Dakota with General Custer; Tenting on the Plains; Following the Guidon. Died Apr. 4, 1933.

CUTCHEON, Byron M., lawyer, soldier, congressman; b. Pembroke, N.H., May 11, 1836; s. James M. and Hannah (Tripp) C.; grad. U. of Mich., 1861; A.M., LL.B., 1866; m. Marie Annie Warner, June 22, 1863. Served in Civil war, capt. and maj. 20th Mich., 1862; lt. col. and col., 1863; bvt. brig. gen., 1865. Admitted to bar, 1866; regent Univ. of Mich., 1875-83; mem. Congress, 1883-91; mem. U.S. Bd. of Ordnance and Fortification, 1891-95. Editorial writer, 1895-98; practicing law, 1898—. Republican. Home: Grand Rapids, Mich. Died 1908.

CUTCHEON, Franklin W(arner) M.; b. Dexter, Mich., Mar. 6, 1864; s. Byron M. and Marie A. (Warner) C.; Ph.B., U. of Mich., 1885; studied law, same univ., 1885; m. Sarah Gibson Flandrau, Feb. 5, 1891. Began practice of law at St. Paul, Minn., 1885; moved to New York, 1899; retired, 1924. Sec.-gen. Am. Red Cross (war council), 1917. Commd. capt. Q.M.R.C., Dec. 17, 1917; lt. col. U.S.A., May 8, 1918; chmn. Bd. of Contracts and Adjustments A.E.F., Jan. 30, 1918, to Nov. 13, 1918; thereafter adviser to spl. rep. of sec. of war in Europe; dir. U.S. War Finance Corp., 1920; U.S. citizen mem. Reparation Commn., 1927-29. Decorated D.S.M.; Grand Officer Legion of Honor (French); Grand Officer Order of Leopold (Belgian); Companion St. Michael and St. George (British); Officer Order of Crown of Italy. Chmn. bd. trustees Santa Barbara (Boys) Sch. Died Nov. 12, 1936.

CUTHBERT, Lucius Montrose; b. Phila., Aug. 17, 1856; s. Rev. James Hazzard and Julia Elizabeth (Turpin) C.; A.B., A.M., Columbian (now George Washington) U., 1876, LL.B., 1878; m. Gertrude Hill, Oct. 24, 1900. In law practice at Denver, 1881-1903; lecturer on Roman law, Law Sch. of U. of Colo. Pres. United Oil Co. and Inland Oil & Refining Co. Del. Universal Congress Lawyers and Jurists, St. Louis, 1904. Episcopalian. Republican. Home: Denver, Colo. Died Dec. 11, 1915.

CUTLER, Arthur Hamilton, head master; b. Holliston, Middlesex Co., Mass., Jan. 26, 1849; s. Hon. Elihu, Jr. and Rebekah (Temple) C.; A.B., Harvard, 1870; (hon. Ph.D., Princeton, 1885); m. Elizabeth Jones (Wilson), Aug. 2, 1890. Organizer and head master The Cutler School, New York, 1876. Sec. National Conf. on Mathematics, Harvard, 1893, Columbia, 1896; pres. School-masters' Assn. of New York, 1897. Died June 21, 1918.

CUTLER, Charles Frederic, capitalist. Pres. and dir. N.Y. Telephone Co., N.Y. & Pa. Telephone & Telegraph Co., N.Y. & N.J. Telephone Co., Hudson River Telephone Co., Empire State Telephone Co., Central N.Y. Telephone & Telegraph Co., Empire City Subway Co.; also trustee or dir. many cos. Died 1907.

CUTLER, Condict Walker, M.D.; b. Morristown, N.J., Feb. 27, 1859; s. Augustus W. and Julia R. (Walker) C.; B.S., Rutgers Coll., 1879, M.S., 1882, Sc.D., 1929; M.D., Coll. Phys. and Surg. (Columbia), 1882; m. Cora Carpenter, Jan. 30, 1884; 1 son, Condict W. Prof. dermatology, U. of Vt., 1892-95; visiting physician, city hosps., 1897-98; phys.-in-chief New York Dispensary, 1888-1902. Author: Manual of Differential Medical Diagnosis, 1886; Differential Diagnosis of the Diseases of the Skin, 1896; Essentials of Physics and Chemistry, 1885; Practical Lectures in Dermatology, 1894. Died July 9, 1930.

CUTLER, Elbridge Gerry, physician; b. Farmington, Me., Sept. 7, 1846; s. John Lewis and Abigail Doty (Belcher) C.; A.B., Harvard, 1868, M.D., 1872; post-grad. med. courses, univs. of Berlin, Vienna, Prague, and Strassburg; m. Fanny Gore Bradford, Oct. 7, 1885. Began med. practice, 1874; asst. in pathology, 1878-84, in clin. medicine, 1884-88, instr. theory and practice of medicine, 1888-1908, Harvard Med. Sch. Consulting phys. Mass. Gen. Hosp. Author: Percussion Outlines (with Dr. George M. Garland), 1887. Republican. Unitarian. Home: Boston, Mass. Died 1929.

CUTLER, Everett Alonzo, clergyman; b. Green Prairie, Minn., June 3, 1873; s. William A. and Mary (Denny) C.; Earlham Coll., Richmond, Ind., 1888-90; A.B., Hanover Coll., Ind., 1893, A.M., 1896, D.D., 1911; grad. McCormick Theol. Sem., Chicago, 1896; m. Mary Hutchison, of Clarence, Ill., June 30, 1903. Ordained Presbyn. ministry, 1896; pastor Clarence, Ill., 1896-99, Westminster Ch., Milwaukee, 1899—. Moderator Synod of Wis., 1902-03; pres. Wis. Federation of Chs. Trustee Carroll Coll., Waukesha, Wis., 1909—; dir. Wis. Humane Soc., 1905—. Grand Chaplain of Grand Lodge of Masons of Wis., 1914—. Originator of a system of comparative biography, worked out in two compilations, "The Olympiads" and "Noted Men and Women of America." Died Jan. 7, 1917.

CUTLER, Harry Morton, insurance; b. Montpelier, Vt., Dec. 15, 1867; s. Marcus Morton and Carney (Gray) C.; ed. pub. schs.; m. Helen Hyde, May 14, 1890; children—Richard Hyde, Elizabeth F. (Mrs. Rollo K. Blanchard), Edward De Lorne. Began with First Nat. Bank, Montpelier, 1884, teller, 1886-88, asst. cashier, 1888-89; with Nat. Life Ins. Co., Montpelier, 1889—, v.p., 1917—, chmn. new bldg. com., 1921—, and of finance com., 1922—. Republican. Unitarian. Died May 13, 1930.

CUTLER, Ira Eugene, college prof.; b. Putnam, Conn., Oct. 8, 1863; s. Frederick and Georgia Ann Frances (Stead) C.; B.S., Albion (Mich.) Coll., 1893, LL.D., 1919; A.M., U. of Denver, 1906; studied at U. of Chicago; m. Amelia Perkins, Aug. 1, 1894; children—Alice Zilpha, Marian Frances, Owen Perkins, Marjorie Mitchell, Laura Ann. Teacher of science, Menominee, Mich., 1895-97; supt. schs. Crystal Falls, Mich., 1897-98; with U. of Denver, 1898—, becoming prof. zoölogy. U.S. Govt. expert work upon Indian corn, 1916-20, developing many promising hybrids; had the largest pharm. and botanic garden in the Middle West; extensive geol. researches in the Florissant Dist., Colo. Commd. staff capt. R.O.T.C., U. of Denver, 1918; chmn. Colo. State Com. on Sch. Gardening. Conglist. Died May 25, 1936.

CUTLER, James Goold, banker; b. Albany, N.Y., Apr. 24, 1848; s. John N. and Mary E. (Goold) C.; ed. Albany Acad.; m. Anna K. Abbey, Sept. 27, 1871. Architect by profession, retired from practice, 1894; pres. Cutler Mail Chute Co.; chmn. bd. Lincoln-Alliance Bank; also trustee of Rochester Savings Bank. Commr. to draft charter of cities of second class, 1895; presdl. elector, 1896; comms. public safety, Rochester, 1900; mayor of Rochester, 1904-07. Pres. Rochester Chamber of Commerce, 1896; trustee U. of Rochester; pres. Municipal Art Commn., City Planning Advisory Bd., until 1922; trustee Rochester Bur. Municipal Research. Hon. mem. A.I.A.; was pres. Western N.Y. State Assn. Architects 3 terms. Episcopalian. Republican. Died Apr. 21, 1927.

CUTLER, John Christopher, governor; b. Sheffield, Eng., Feb. 5, 1846; s. John and Elizabeth (Robinson) C.; ed. in pvt. schs. in Eng.; m. Sarah Elizabeth Taylor, Apr. 3, 1872; children—Mrs. Elizabeth T. Jenkins, John C., Alfred T., Mabel B., Harold G., Mrs. Hazel A. Beck. Began business in Utah, July 1877, as agt. Provo Woolen Mills, and in 1895 incorporated under name of Cutler Bros. Co., of which was pres.; pres. Deseret Nat. Bank, Salt Lake City, 1911—; dir. many corps.; v.p. Beneficial Life Ins. Co. Was county clk. Salt Lake Co., 1884-90; gov. of Utah, 1905-09. Republican. Mormon. Deceased.

CUTLER, Otis Henderson, mfr.; b. N.Y. City.; s. Otis Nelson and Mary Frye (Tebbetts) C.; ed. Rockland Mil. Acad. (Nyack, N.Y.), Washington (D.C.) Law U.; m. Mary A. Straut. Clk. U.S. Senate, 1884-95; mem. N.Y. Assembly, 1895, 1896, 1897; sec. North River Bridge Co., 1895-1900; gen. mgr. Ramapo Foundry Co., 1900-02; v.p. and gen. mgr., 1902-03, pres., 1903-16, chmn. bd., 1916—, Am. Brake Shoe & Foundry Co.; chmn. bd. Hale & Kilburn Co., 1912-15; chmn. bd. Bucyrus Co., 1912-15; dir. Baldwin Locomotive Works, 1912-16; chmn. bd. Bronze Metal Co.; dir. many corps. Republican. Episcopalian. Mason (K.T.). Mgr. insular and foreign div. of Am. Red Cross, 1917-19. Home: Suffren, N.Y. Died Mar. 4, 1922.

CUTLER, Ralph William, banker; b. Newton, Mass., Feb. 21, 1853; s. Eben and Caroline Elizabeth (Holman) C.; grad. English High Sch., Boston (Franklin medal), 1869; m. Grace Dennis, Jan. 6, 1880. In employ of wholesale grocery firm, Boston, 1869-80; removed to Hartford; treas., 1880-87, pres., 1887—, Hartford Trust Co. Mem. Court of Common Council, Hartford, 1883-84; fire commr., 1896-1902; commr. Bd. of Finance, 1905—. Republican. Conglist. Home: Hartford, Conn. Died Oct. 31, 1917.

CUTTEN, Arthur W.; b. Guelph, Ont., Can. Came to U.S. at age of 18; interested in numerous business enterprises, including operations on boards of trade and stock exchanges. Home: Chicago, Ill. Died June 24, 1936.

CUTTER, Benjamin, musician; b. Woburn, Mass., Sept. 6, 1857; s. Ephraim (q.v.) and Rebecca Smith (Sullivan) C.; ed. Warren Acad., Woburn, Mass.; pupil in violin of Eichberg (Boston), Singer (Stuttgart), 1877-81; theoretical studies, Emery (Boston), Götschius and Seifriz (Stuttgart); m. Isabel Mason, Apr. 18, 1899. Teacher of violin, 1882, of harmony, 1888—, and of harmonic analysis, 1898—, N.E. Conservatory of Music. Mem. Boston Symphony Orchestra under Henschel and Gericke. Published compositions: Mass in D, chamber music, and choral music, religious and secular. Author: Exercises in Harmony, 1901; Harmonic Analysis, 1902; How to Study Kreutzer, 1903. Died 1910.

CUTTER, Charles Ammi, librarian, Forbes Library, Northampton, Mass., 1894—; b. Boston, Mass., March 14, 1837; grad. Harvard, 1855, Div. School, same, 1856; m. Sarah Fayerweather Appleton, 1863. Asst. Harvard Coll. Library, 1861-68; librarian Boston Athenæum, 1869-93, and editor of its catalogue, 5 vols., 1874-82; editor Library Jour., 1881-93. Author: Rules for a Dictionary Catalog; The Expansive Classification. Home: Northampton, Mass. Died 1903.

CUTTER, Ephraim, physician, food expert; b. Woburn, Mass., Sept. 1, 1832; s. Benjamin and Mary (Whittemore) C.; B.A., Yale, 1852, M.A., 1855; M.D., Harvard, 1856; M.D., U. of Pa., 1857; (LL.D., Ia. Coll., 1887); spl. lab. work in Sheffield Scientific Sch. and at Harvard under Oliver Wendell Holmes and J. P. Cooke; m. Rebecca Smith Sullivan, 1856 (died 1899); m. 2d, Mrs. Anna L. Davidson, 1901. Practiced at Woburn, Boston and New York, 1875—. Inventor of many surg. and gynecol. instruments, and procedures in relation to same; successfully with George B. Harrimon, D.D.S., of Boston, in 1876, used in microphotography of blood and sputum the higher and highest power lenses extant then and now. Mem. 9th and 10th Internat. Med. Congresses. Mem. Com. of One Hundred, Mass. Soldiers' Fund, 1861; was spl. military agt. during Civil War. Author: Versions and Flexions and Food in Motherhood; Fatty Ills and Their Masquerades (with John A. Cutter); Food—Its Relation to Health and Disease (with same), 1907. A pioneer of Am. laryngology; has studied the morphology of raw beef, 1854—; proved that the galvanic currents penetrate the human body, 1871; discovered tuberculosis cattle test, 1894; etc. Died Apr. 24, 1917.

CUTTER, K(irtland) K(elsey), architect; b. Cleveland, Ohio, Aug. 20, 1860; s. William Lemen and Caroline Atwater (Pease) C.; ed. Brooks Military Academy, Cleveland; studied art at Art Students' League, New York, and in Europe for several yrs.; m. Mary Corbin, Oct. 5, 1892 (divorced 1896); m. 2d, Katharine Phillips Williams, Feb. 19, 1906 (died 1933). Settled at Spokane, 1885. Designed Ida. State Bldg. at Chicago Expn., 1893; Rainier Club Bldg., Seattle, Wash.; Kirtland Hall (Sheffield Scientific Sch., Yale); Western Union Life Ins. Bldg., Spokane Club Bldg., Davenport Hotel, and others in Spokane; Carnegie Camp, Raquette Lake, Adirondacks; Lloyd Lodge, New Forest, near Ringwood, Eng.; Glacier Nat. Park Hotel, Lake McDonald, Mont.; Chronicle Bldg., Spokane; Thornewood, American Lake, Wash.; Lewis-Clark Hotel, Lewiston, Ida.; and many pvt. residences. Died Sept. 26, 1939.

CUTTER, William Dick, educator; b. Brooklyn, N.Y., Sept. 14, 1878; s. John Dicks and Adelaide Cornelia (Paulk) C.; A.B., Yale, 1899; M.D., Johns Hopkins, 1905; grad. study U. of Berne, 1900; m. Margaret F. M. Moir, 1908; children—Adelaide Cornelia, Katherine Ellen, Margaret Elizabeth, Ruth Dick. Asst. in physiol. chemistry, Coll. Phys. and Surgeons, Columbia, 1899-1901; resident phys. and surgeon, French Hosp., N.Y. City, 1905-06; mem. hosp. staff Copper Queen Consol. Mining Co., Bisbee, Ariz., 1906-10; prof. physiology and pharmacology, U. of Ga., 1911-19; sec. State Bd. Med. Examiners, Albany, N.Y., 1919-23; dean N.Y. Post Grad. Med. Sch., 1923-28; dean Sch. of Medicine, U. of Southern Calif., 1928-31; sec. Council on Med. Edn., and Hosps., A.M.A., 1931—. Republican. Presbyn. Died Jan. 22, 1942.

CUTTING, Bronson, senator; b. Oakdale, L.I., N.Y., June 23, 1888; s. William Bayard and Olivia Peyton (Murray) C.; Harvard, 1910; unmarried. Moved to Santa Fe, N.M., 1910; pres. N.M. Printing Co., 1912-18, Santa Fe New Mexican Pub. Corp., 1920—; pub. Santa Fe New Mexican, El Nuevo Mexicano; dir. Sunmount Sanatorium Co.; apptd. senator, Dec. 1927, to fill unexpired term of Andrieus A. Jones, dec., and elected Nov. 1928, for full term ending Mar. 3, 1935. Commd. capt. U.S.A., Aug. 5, 1917; asst. mil. attaché, Am. Embassy, London, 1917-18. Regent N.M. Mil. Inst., 1920; chmn. bd. commrs. N.M. State Penitentiary, 1925. Treas. Prog. State Central Com., 1912-14, chmn., 1914-16; mem. exec. com. N.M. Taxpayers' Assn., 1915-17. Decorated British Mil. Cross. Episcopalian. Home: Santa Fe, N.M. Died May 6, 1935.

CUTTING, Charles Sidney, judge; b. Highgate Springs, Vt., Mar. 1, 1854; s. Charles A. and Laura E. (Averill) C.; ed. high sch., Hastings, Minn.; A.B., Willamette U., Salem, Ore., 1875; LL.D., U. of Mich., 1907; m. Annie E. Lytle, June 27, 1876; 1 son, Robert M. After leaving coll. was asst. editor Cedar Rapids (Ia.) Times; prin. high sch., Palatine, Ill., 1874-80; admitted to Ill. bar, Jan. 17, 1879; practiced at Chicago; master in chancery Circuit Court of Cook Co., Ill., 1890-93; judge of Probate Court of Cook Co., terms 1899-1914 (resigned in 1913, before expiration of term, to resume practice of law). Republican. Mem. Cook Co. Bd. Edn. 9 yrs. (ex-pres.); ex-pres. Palatine (Ill.) Bd. of Edn. Mason (32°). Mem. Ill. Constitutional Conv., 1920. Died Apr. 17, 1936.

CUTTING, Churchill Hunter, pres. Am. Bible Soc.; b. Southbridge, Mass., Sept. 12, 1842; s. Sewall Sylvester and Elisabeth Eddy (Brown) C.; ed. pub. schs.; m. Mary Augusta Dutton, May 5, 1864 (died 1909). Mgr. Am. Bible Soc., 1882-1916, v.p. 1916-19, pres., Apr. 1919—. Dir. Am. Bapt. Foreign Missionary Union, 1893-1911; mem. exec. com. Japan Soc. Republican. Died Apr. 23, 1924.

CUTTING, Mary Stewart, author; b. New York, N.Y., June 27, 1851; d. Gen. Ulysses (U.S.V.) and Mary (Stewart) Doubleday; ed. 2 yrs. at Hobart Hall, New York, and 1 yr. at Moravian Sem., Bethlehem, Pa.; m. Charles Weed-Cutting, Dec. 29, 1875 (died 1893). As a girl wrote verses which were published in Lippincott's and little stories for the Young Christian Soldier (church mission paper). Episcopalian. Author: Little Stories of Married Life, 1902; Heart of Lynn, 1904; Little Stories of Courtship, 1905; More Stories of Married Life, 1906; The Suburban Whirl, 1907; The Wayfarers, 1908; Just for Two, 1909; The Unforeseen, 1910; Lovers of Sanna, 1912; Refractory Husbands, 1913; The Blossoming Rod, 1914; Some of Us Are Married, 1920. Home: Orange, N.J. Died Aug. 10, 1924.

CUTTING, R(obert) Fulton, financier; b. N.Y. City, June 1852; s. Fulton and Justine (Bayard) C.; A.B., Columbia, 1871, A.M., 1875, LL.D., 1904; m. Nathalie C. P. Schenck (died 1875); 1 son, R. Bayard; m. 2d, Helen Suydam, Jan. 1883; children—Helen Suydam, Elisabeth McEvers, Fulton, Charles Suydam, Ruth Hunter. Officer or dir. in numerous corps. Home: Tuxedo Park, N.Y. Died Sept. 21, 1934.

CUTTING, Starr Willard, univ. prof.; b. W. Brattleboro, Vt., Oct. 14, 1858; s. Henry Maynard and Cornelia Liscom (Starr) C.; A.B., Williams Coll., 1881, A.M., 1892; studied univs. of Leipzig and Geneva, 1886-88; grad. student, 1890-91, Ph.D., 1892, Johns Hopkins; m. Mary Edith Derby, Sept. 11, 1889; children—Winifred, Edith, Clifton. Prin. Deerfield (Mass.) Acad., 1881-86; prof. modern langs., U. of S.D., 1888-90; prof. German and French, Earlham Coll., Ind., 1891-92; asst. prof. German, 1892-94, asso. prof., 1894-1900, prof. German lit., 1900-06, prof. and head of dept. Germanic languages and literatures, 1906-23, U. of Chicago. Author: Der Konjunktiv bei Hartmann von Aue, 1894; critical edition of Lessing's Minna von Barnhelm, 1899; The Modern German Relatives Das and Was, 1904; Robert Wesselhoeft, Jena Burschenschafter, German Revolutionary, and American Citizen, 1911; Gutzkow and Young Germany, 1913; An American Estimate of the Salient Features of Modern German Life, 1914; Uber die Schriften des Jenaer Burschenschafters und Amerikanischen Arztes Robert Wesselhoeft, 1917; Heinrich von Treitschke's Treatment of Turner and Burschenschafter in his Deutsche Geschichte im Neunzehntnen Jahrhundert, 1922. Died Oct. 18, 1935.

CUTTING, W(illiam) Bayard, lawyer; b. New York, Jan. 12, 1850; s. Fulton and Justine (Bayard) C.; brother of R(obert) Fulton C. (q.v.); A.B., Columbia, 1869, LL.B., 1871, A.M., 1872; m. Olivia Murray, Apr. 26, 1877. Admitted to bar, 1871, and then in practice at New York; trustee U.S. Trust Co.; dir. Am. Exchange Nat. Bank, Southern Pacific Co., Norfolk & Southern Ry. Co., Commercial Union Assurance Co., Ltd. (London), Commercial Union Fire Ins. Co., City & Suburban Homes Co., Tropical Land Co., Ltd. Civil service commr., 1896-97. Trustee Columbia U., 1880—. Died Mar. 1, 1912.

CUYLER, Cornelius Cuyler, banker; mem. firm Cuyler, Morgan & Co., bankers. Dir. Mercantile Trust Co., Mobile & Ohio R.R. U.S. Guarantee Co., Casualty Co. of America, U.S. Mortgage & Trust Co., Guarantee Co. N. America, J. G. White Co., Ltd., Princeton Inn Co. Trustee Princeton Univ. Pres. Inst. Musical Art City of New York; treas. Am. Sch. of Classical Studies in Rome. Married. Home: New York, N.Y. Died 1909.

CUYLER, Theodore Ledyard, clergyman; b. Aurora, N.Y., Jan. 10, 1822; s. B. Ledyard and Louisa Frances (Morrell) C.; grad. Princeton, 1941 (D.D., LL.D.); Princeton Theol. Sem., 1846; m. Annie E. Mathiot, 1853. Ordained to ministry, 1848; after 3 other pastorates was, 1860-90, pastor Lafayette Av. Presbyn. Ch., Brooklyn; resigned to enter upon a ministry at large; active in temperance and philanthropic work. Author: Stray Arrows; Cedar Christian; The Empty Crib; Wayside Springs; Right to the Point; Thought Hives; God's Light on Dark Clouds; Pointed Papers; Heart Life; From the Nile to Norway; Newly Enlisted, or Talks to Young Converts; The Young Preacher; How to Be a Pastor; Stirring the Eagle's Nest; Christianity in the Home; Beulah-Land; Mountain-tops with Jesus; Help and Good Cheer, 1902 B1; Recollections of a Long Life—An Autobiography, 1902 B1; Our Christmastides, 1904. Died 1909.

CUYLER, T(homas) De Witt, lawyer; b. Phila., Sept. 28, 1854; s. Theodore and Mary (De Witt) C.; B.A., Yale, 1874; LL.D., Lafayette, 1916, Yale, 1920; m. Frances Lewis, May 3, 1881. Admitted to bar, 1876; judge advocate gen. N.G. Pa.; dir. Pa. R.R. Co., Equitable Life Assurance Soc., and other corps.; chmn. Assn. Ry. Executives. Home: Haverford, Pa. Died Nov. 2, 1922.

CZARNOMSKA, Marie Elizabeth Josephine, educator; b. N.Y. City; d. Isydor and Letitia (Coakley) C.; grad. Packer Collegiate Inst., Brooklyn; later studied under tutors; A.M., Smith Coll., 1904. Prin. girls' dept., Classical Inst., Schenectady, N.Y., 1875-77; teacher, St. Mary's Sch., Raleigh, N.C., 1877-80, Packer Collegiate Inst., 1880-81; prin. St. Mary's Sch., Raleigh, 1881-88; prof. English lit., Smith Coll., 1888-1904; dean of women and lecturer on Eng. and Bibl. lit., U. of Cincinnati, 1904-09; studied in Egypt, 1910; student of Semitics, 1916-19, and instr. O.T. lit., 1918-21, Columbia U. Ext.; prof. Biblical and comparative lit., Sweet Briar (Va.) Coll., 1919-30. Author: The Authentic Literature of Israel (2 vols.), 1924-1928. Died May 22, 1938.

D

DABNEY, Edwin, lawyer; b. Comanche Co., Tex., Feb. 3, 1876; s. Edwin Thomas and Ninnie (Dickenson) D.; grad. high sch., Blanket, Tex., 1896; LL.B., U. of Tex., 1903; m. Emma Adams, June 20, 1904 (dec.); 1 dau., Amber Jane; m. 2d, Jewel Cooper, Feb. 14, 1929. Admitted to Tex. bar., 1903, and began practice at De Leon; county judge, Comanche Co., 1906-08; moved to Altus, Okla., 1910, and practiced there until 1919; mem. Okla. Ho. of Rep., 1919-23; asst. to atty. gen. of Okla., 1923-27, atty. gen., 1927-30; oil and gas atty. to Corp. Com., 1932-35; representing oil companies, 1935—. Managed State Dem. Campaign, 1922. Democrat. Mason. Home: Oklahoma City, Okla. Died May 16, 1938.

DABNEY, Lewis Stackpole, lawyer; b. Fayal, Azores, Dec. 21, 1840; s. Frederick and Roxana (Stackpole) D.; A.B. Harvard, 1861; 2d lt., 1st lt. and capt., 2d Regt. Mass. Vol. Cav., 1862-65; on staff Gen. C. C. Augur, 1864-65; admitted to bar, 1863, and began practice at Boston; m. Apr. 22, 1867, Clara Bigelow (died 1899). Home: Boston, Mass. Died 1908.

DABO, Theodore Scott, painter; b. New Orleans, La., Oct., 1877; s. Ignace Scott and Madeleine (Oberle) D.; bro. of Leon D.; ed. at New Orleans and Detroit; painting in École des Arts Decoratifs and École des Beaux Arts, Paris; traveled extensively and studied painting independently. Ceased painting, 1890, owing to irreconcilable views of teachers and his own ideas; studied natural law and optics and made discoveries in atmosphere, luminosity and vibration that have since made his paintings quoted; returned to New York, 1900, and entered various exhbns.; subsequently exhbns. at London, Paris and elsewhere. Studio: Billancourt (Seine), France. Died Nov. 17, 1928.

DA COSTA, (John) Chalmers, surgeon; b. Phila., Nov. 15, 1863; s. George T. and Margaretta (Beasley) D.; prep. edn. Friends' Central Sch., Phila.; grad. U. of Pa., sci. dept., 1882; M.D., Jefferson Med. Coll., 1885; m. May R. Brick. Resident phys. Phila. Hosp., 1885-86; asst. phys. insane dept. Phila. Hosp., 1886-87; asst. demonstrator anatomy, Jefferson Med. Coll., 1887; asst. surgeon Jefferson Hosp., 1887; demonstrator of surgery, Jefferson Med. Coll., 1891, clin. prof. surgery, same, 1898, prof. surgery, 1900; Samuel D. Gross prof. of surgery, 1901—. Surgeon to Phila. Hosp., 1895—, to St. Joseph's Hosp., 1896—. Comdr. U.S.N.R.F. Fellow Am. Surg. Assn., Coll. Physicians of Phila. Author: A Manual of Modern Surgery, 1895-1925 (10 edits.). Editor of English edition of Zuckerkandl's Operative Surgery, 1899, and new Am. edit. of Gray's Anatomy, 1905. Home: Philadelphia, Pa. Died May 16, 1933.

DA COSTA, Jacob M., M.D.; b. St. Thomas, W.I., Feb. 7, 1833; grad. Jefferson Med. Coll., Phila., 1852; studied subsequently in Vienna and Paris; established practice, Phila., 1854 (LL.D., Univ. of Pa. and Harvard); became lecturer in clinical medicine, Jefferson Med. Coll., 1864, and in 1872 prof. theory and practice of medicine; emeritus prof., 1891; pres. Coll. of Phys. of Phila., 1895. Author: Harvey and His Discovery; Strain and Over-Action of the Heart; Medical Diagnosis. Home: Philadelphia. Died 1900.

DA COSTA, John C., Jr., physician; b. Pottstown, Pa., June 13, 1871; s. John C. and Mary Gould (Meigs) D.; M.D., Jefferson Med. Coll., 1893; m. Elizabeth S. Hays, Oct. 24, 1905. First lt. and asst. surgeon U.S.V., 1898-99; asso. prof. of medicine, Jefferson Med. Coll.; attending phys. Jefferson Hosp.; consulting phys., Northwestern Gen. Hosp.; hematologist German Hosp. Fellow Coll. Physicians Phila., A.M.A. Soc. Author: Clinical Hematology, 2d edit., 1905; Surgical Hematology (in Keen's System of Surgery), 1906; Principles and Practice of Physical Diagnosis, 3d edit., 1915; Diseases of the Blood (in Hare's System of Therapeutics); Secondary Anemia (in Sajous' Cyclopedia of Practice of Medicine). Home: Philadephia, Pa. Died Apr. 26, 1919.

DADANT, Camille Pierre, apiarist; b. Langres, France, Apr. 6, 1851; s. Charles and Gabrielle (Parisot) D.; came to America, 1863; ed. in France and pub. schs., Hamilton, Ill.; m. Mary Marinelli, Nov 1, 1875; children—Louisa G. (Mrs. L. G. Saugier), Valentine, Louis C., Henry C., Maurice G., Clemence S., Harriette G. (Mrs. F. A. Bush). Associated with his father, as Dadant & Son, in bee culture, and publisher of book, The Hive and Honey Bee, 1874-1902; with 3 sons and 2 daughters as Dadant & Sons, 1902—; began mfr. of bee comb foundations, 1879; editor Am. Bee Journal, 1912—. Mem. Nat Bee Keepers' Assn. (ex-sec., v.p., pres., later treas.). Editor and reviser of various edits. of The Hive and Honey Bee (by L. L. Langstroth), 1888—. Decorated Order of the Crown for services rendered Belgian bee-keepers during World War. Author: First Lessons in Bee-Keeping, 1915; Bee Primer; The Dadant System of Bee-Keeping. Home: Hamilton, Ill. Died Feb. 25, 1938.

DADE, Alexander Lucien, army officer; b. in Ky., July 18, 1863; grad. U.S. Mil. Acad., 1887, Inf. and Cav. Sch., 1893; Army War Coll., 1910. Comd. 2d lt. 13th Inf., June 12, 1887; trans. to 10th Cav., Feb. 27, 1888; 1st lt. 2d Cav., June 13, 1895; trans. to 3d Cav., Nov. 7, 1895; maj. 47th Vol. Inf., Sept 9, 1899; hon. disch. vols., June 30, 1901; capt. 13th U.S. Cav., Feb. 2, 1901; promoted maj., 1911, col., 1917, Cav.; brig. gen. N.A., Oct. 29, 1917. Assigned as dir. aviation training, Central Dept., hdqrs., Chicago, Mar. 1918; hon. disch. as brig. gen., Signal Corps Aviation Sect., May 3, 1918; col. (cav.), Insp Gen.'s Dept., May 24, 1918; duty in office Insp. Gen., Feb. 12, 1919; dept. insp., Central Dept., Chicago, Feb. 13, 1919-Sept. 30, 1920 (retired). Died Jan. 8, 1927.

DAEGER, Albert Thomas, archbishop; b. N. Vernon, Ind., Mar. 5, 1872; s. George A. and Frances (Kriech) D.; A.B., St. Francis Coll., Cincinnati, O., 1889; entered Novitiate of Friars-Minor, Oldenburg, Ind., 1889, and studied at St. Francis and St. Clement, Cincinnati, O., St. Boniface, Louisville, Ky., and Sem., Oldenburg, Ind. Ordained priest R.C. Ch., July 25, 1896; asst. priest Our Lady of Sorrows Ch., Kansas City, Mo., 1896-97; asst. St. Francis de Sales Ch., Lincoln, Nebr., 1897-1900. pastor, 1900-02; pastor Pena Blanca, N.M., 1902-10, Farmington, 1910-17, Jemes, 1917-19; apptd. archbishop of Santa Fe, N.M., Mar. 9, 1919, consecrated May 7, 1919. Died Dec. 2, 1932.

DAGER, Forrest Eugene, clergyman; b. Germantown, Phila., Nov. 10, 1855; s. Molton C. R. and Wilhelmina (Bockins) D.; Germantown Acad.; U. of Pa., 1875; D.D., Temple U., 1894; m. Mary Ellen Hall, June 28, 1887. Ordained R.E. ministry, 1878; pastor Ch. of the Redemption, Brooklyn, N.Y., 1878-81, Emmanuel Ch., Phila., 1881-1900, St. Paul's Ch., Phila., 1901—. V.p., 1895, and senior prof., oratory and homiletics, Temple U. Home: Philadelphia, Pa. Deceased.

DAGGETT, Aaron Simon, army officer; b. Greene Corner, Me., June 14, 1837; s. Aaron and Dorcas C. (Dearborn) D.; ed. Greene, Me., Monmouth Acad., Me., and Wesleyan Sem., Bates Coll.; m. Rose Bradford, June 14, 1865. Enlisted in Co. E, 5th Me. Inf., Apr. 27, 1861; 2d lt., 1st lt., capt., maj., same, 1861-63; lt. col. 5th U.S. Vet. Vol. Inf., Jan. 23, 1865; hon. mustered out, May 10, 1866; capt. 16th U.S. Inf., July 28, 1866; maj. 13th Inf., Jan. 2, 1892; lt. col. 25th Inf., Oct. 1, 1895; brig. gen. vols., Sept. 21-Nov. 30, 1898; col. 14th Inf., Mar. 31, 1899; brig. gen., Feb. 21, 1901. Bvts.: col. and brig. gen. vols., Mar. 13, 1865, "for gallant and meritorious services during the war"; maj., Mar. 2, 1867, for same in battle of Rappahannock Sta., Va., Nov. 7, 1863; lt. col., Mar. 2, 1867, for same in battle of the Wilderness. Participated in battles of First Bull Run, West Point, Gaines Mill, Savage Sta., White Oak Swamp, Malvern Hill, Va., Crampton's Gap, Antietam, Fredericksburg, Marie's Heights, Salem Church, Va., Gettysburg, Rappahannock Station, Mine Run, Wilderness, Spottsylvania C.H., North Anna, Coal Harbor, Petersburg, Va.; in Spanish-Am. War, served in Santiago campaign, taking part in battle of El Caney; in Philippines engaged at Imus river and Bacoor; in China at Yangtsun, Peking and Imperial City; retired, Mar. 2, 1901. Author: America in the China Relief Expedition, 1903. Home: Washington, D.C. Died May 14, 1938.

DAGGETT, Ellsworth, mining engr.; b. Canandaigua, N.Y., May 24, 1845; s. Rev. Oliver Ellsworth and Elizabeth (Watson) D.; Ph.B., Sheffield Scientific Sch. (Yale), 1864; post-grad. courses in chemistry there, 1864-65; 1 yr. upon mineralogy and blow-piping elsewhere, 1865-66; 1 yr. at Bergakademie, Berlin, 1874-75; m. June Spencer, June 24, 1874. In practice as mining engr., 1866—; connected with Geol. Survey of 40th parallel, 1870; U.S. surveyor-gen., Utah, 1888-92; U.S. del. to Am. Mining Congress, Portland, Ore., Aug. 20, 1904. Home: Salt Lake City, Utah. Died 1923.

DAGGETT, Mabel Potter, writer; b. Syracuse, N.Y.; d. of Albert P. and Sara Louise (Hobbie) Potter; B.A., Syracuse U., 1895; m. John Duval Daggett, Nov. 2, 1901. Editor woman's page, The Post-Standard, Syracuse, 1895-1900, Sunday North American, Phila., 1900-01; spl. writer New York Sunday World, 1902-03; asso. editor Hampton's Mag., 1907-08, The Delineator, 1908-11, 1919-20, Equal Rights, 1923. Author: In Lockerbie Street—A Little Appreciation of James Whitcomb Riley, 1909; Women Wanted, 1918; also articles leading to Delineator child rescue campaign, 1909. Spl. commr. to France for Butterick Pub. Co., French war relief, 1919. Home: (country) Rock Tavern, N.Y. Died Oct. 14, 1927.

DAGGETT, Mary Stewart, author; b. Morristown, Ohio, May 30, 1856; d. John B. (D.D.) and Nancy (McGregor) Stewart; grad. Steubenville (O.) Sem., 1873; m. Charles D. Daggett, 1875. Author: Mariposilla, 1895; The Broad Aisle, 1899; The Higher Court, 1911; The Yellow Angel, 1914. Also, The Second Son, Chinese play in 3 acts (prod. Valley Hunt Club, Pasadena, Calif., 1917). Active in war camp community recreation and Liberty Loan drives. Home: Pasadena, Calif. Died Mar. 9, 1922.

DAHL, Theodore H., clergyman; b. Norway, Apr. 2, 1845; s. Thore and Anna (Thorgerson) Halvorson; ed. Christiania, Norway; came to U.S., 1865; studied theology at Paxton, Ill., now Augustana Coll. and Theol. Sem., Rock Island, Ill. (D.D., 1905); m. Rebekke Lina Gjertson, Dec. 27, 1867. Ordained Luth. ministry; pres. United Norwegian Luth. Ch. of America, 1902—; chmn. Bd. of Regents, Sem. United Norwegian Luth. Ch., St. Anthony Park, Minn.; also chmn. Bd. of Regents, St. Olof Coll., Northfield, Minn., etc. Decorated by King Haakon VII of Norway, with insignia Knights of St. Olof Order, 1908. Home: Minneapolis, Minn. Died Jan. 18, 1923.

DAHLMAN, James Charles, mayor; b. Tex., Dec. 15, 1856; s. Charles and Mary D.; ed. pub. schs.; m. Hattie Abbott, Dec. 20, 1884. Mem. city council, Chadron, Neb., 1884-87, mayor, 1894-95; sheriff of Dawes Co., Neb., 3 terms, 1888-94; del. Dem. Nat. Conv., 1892; apptd. sec. State Bd. Transportation, Neb., 1897; chmn. Dem. State Conn., 1896-1900; mem. Dem. Nat. Com., 1900-08, and apptd. on exec. com; 6 times elected mayor of Omaha, present term, 1925-28; U.S. marshal for Neb., 1920-21. Home: Omaha, Neb. Died Jan. 21, 1930.

DAILEY, Morris Elmer, educator; b. Warrick Co., Ind., Apr. 14, 1867; s. William and Ann E. (Pluck) D.; Simpson Coll., Indianola, Ia.; A.M., Ind. U.,

1897; Harvard U., summer, 1898; Cal. U. summers, 1900-05; (LL.D., Drake U., 1901); m. Frances Jones, Aug. 15, 1912. Supt. schs., Fresno, Calif., 1897-99; teacher history, 1899-1900, pres., 1900—, State Normal Sch., Calif., San Jose. Lecturer in edn., Stanford U., 1908—. Republican. Methodist. Mason. Home: San Jose, Calif. Died July 5, 1919.

DAINGERFIELD, Elliott, artist; b. Harper's Ferry, Va., Mar. 26, 1859; s. John E. P. and Matilda (Brua) D.; ed. in schs., acad., and by pvt. tutor at Fayetteville, N.C.; studied drawing and painting in New York with pvt. teacher and at Art Students' League; m. Roberta Strange French; m. 2d, Anna E. Grainger, Dec. 30, 1895; children—Marjorie Jay, Gwendoline. First exhibited at Nat. Acad. Design, 1880; studied in Europe, 1897; commd. to paint the Lady Chapel of the Ch. of St. Mary the Virgin, New York, 1902; pub. lecturer on art; head of Permanent Art Sch., Blowing Rock, N.C. Notable paintings: Madonna and Child (property of Haley Fiske); Child of Mary (silver medal); The Story of the Madonna (prize, 1902); Slumbering Fog (Met. Museum of Art), etc. Silver medal, Buffalo Expn., 1901; Clarke prize, Nat. Acad. Design, 1902. N.A., 1906; mem. Fine Arts Fedn., N.Y. Water Color Club. Author: (monographs) George Inness, 1911; R. A. Blakelock, 1914. Died Oct. 22, 1932.

DAINGERFIELD, Foxhall Alexander, author; b. Harrisonburg, Va., Sept. 15, 1887; s. Algernon Grey and Elizabeth (Thomas) D.; ed. Transylvania U., Lexington, Ky., and Washington and Lee U.; unmarried. Actor with Mrs. Fiske, later with Robert Hilliard. Author: Ghost House, 1924; The White and Gold Lady, 1925; The Silver Urn, 1926; Wilderness House, 1927; That Gay Nineties Murder, 1928; The Linden Walk Tragedy, 1929; The House Across the Way; The Unknown Quantity. Democrat. Episcopalian. Home: Washington, D.C. Died Oct. 17, 1933.

DAISH, John Broughton, lawyer; b. Quincy, Mich., Jan. 26, 1867; s. Silas S. and Mattie A. (Broughton) D.; A.B., Johns Hopkins, 1888; LL.B., Georgetown U., 1899, LL.M., 1900; m. Grace W. Markel, Sept. 21, 1890. Has practiced at Washington, 1900—. Methodist. Author: Equity Pleading and Practice (joint author), 1901; Cases Common Law Pleading (joint author), 1903; Procedure Interstate Commerce Cases, 1909. Home: Washington, D.C. Died 1918.

DAKE, Charles Laurence, prof. geology; b. Chaseburg, Wis., Apr. 2, 1883; s. George E. and Mary A. D.; A.B., U. of Wis., 1911, A.M., 1912; Ph.D., Columbia, 1922; m. Ella Hildagarde Falkenstern, 1912; children—Laurence Falkenstern, Helen Elizabeth, Emilie Louise. Asst. in geology, Williams Coll., 1912-13; asst. prof. of geology, Sch. of Mines and Metallurgy (U. of Mo.), 1913-18, asso. prof., 1918-21, prof., 1921—. Asst. Wis. Geol. and Natural History Survey, summer 1910; geologist Mo. Bureau Geology and Mines 16 summers, Wyo. Geol. Survey, summer 1916. Cons. commercial work, several summers. Author: (with others) Field Methods in Petroleum Geology, 1921; Interpretation of Topographic and Geologic Maps, 1925. Home: Rolla, Mo. Died 1934.

DALAND, Judson, M.D.; b. N.Y. City, July 11, 1860; s. Benjamin A. and Jane Ann (Hunseker) D.; M.D., U. of Pa., 1882; practiced in Phila., 1882—; prof. clin. medicine, Medico-Chirurg. Coll., Phila., 1903-16; became prof. medicine, Grad. Sch., U. of Pa., 1916 (emeritus). Commd. 1st lt. Med. R.C., U.S.A., May 12, 1911; resigned to become 1st lt. jr. grade, Med. R.C., U.S.N., June 4, 1913; surgeon, rank of lt. comdr., Naval Coast Defense Reserve, July 7, 1917; comdr. U.S.N.R.F.; med. insp. with rank of comdr., July 22, 1919. Served at U.S. Naval Hosp., Phila.; made tour of inspection U.S. Naval hosps., 1917; served through epidemic of influenza, fall of 1918. Editor Internat. Med. Mag., 1891-95; editor Internat. Clinics, 14 vols., 1891-99. Republican. Mason. Home: Philadelphia, Pa. Died Aug. 14, 1937.

DALAND, William Clifton, college pres.; b. New York, Oct. 25, 1860; s. William Batchelder and Alexina Janet (Kenworthy) D.; A.B., Poly. Inst., Brooklyn, 1879; grad. Union Theol. Sem., New York, 1886; A.M., Alfred U., 1887; (D.D., Milton Coll., 1895, Alfred U., 1903); m. Agnes B. Norton, Sept. 10, 1884. Ordained Seventh Day Bapt. ministry, 1886; pastor Leonardsville, N.Y., 1886-91, Westerly, R.I., 1891-96, London, Eng., 1896-1900, Leonardsville, N.Y., 1900-02; pres. Milton Coll., Sept. 1902—. Home: Milton, Wis. Died June 21, 1921.

DALE, Alan (Alfred J. Cohen), dramatic critic; b. Birmingham, Eng., May 14, 1861; ed. King Edward's Sch. there; passed senior and junior "local" exams., Oxford U.; m. Carrie Livingston Frost, 1886. Engaged in journalism in New York; dramatic critic New York Evening World, 1887-95, then with New York Journal, later with the New York American, then with Cosmopolitan News Service. Author: Jonathan's Home; A Marriage Below Zero; An Eerie He and She; My Footlight Husband; Miss Innocence; Familiar Chats with Queens of the Stage; An Old Maid Kindled; A Moral Busybody; Conscience on Ice; His Own Image; A Girl Who Wrote, 1902; Wanted—A Cook; The Great Wet Way, 1909; The Madonna of the Future, 1918; When a Man Commutes, 1918. Died May 21, 1928.

DALE, Frank, lawyer; b. DeKalb Co., Ill., Nov. 26, 1849; ed. pub. schs., Leland, Ill.; settled at Wichita, Kan., 1872. Admitted to bar, Wichita, 1876; pros. atty. Wichita and Sedgwick cos., Kan., 1880-85; register U.S. Land Office, Wichita, 1885-89; located at Guthrie, Okla., 1889; asso. justice, May to Sept., 1893; chief justice, 1893-98, Supreme Court of Okla. Ty.; resumed practice; mem. Dale & Bierer. Address: Guthrie, Okla. Died Feb. 12, 1930.

DALE, Harry Howard, congressman; b. New York, Dec. 3, 1868; ed. pub. schs., Brooklyn; studied law New York Law Sch. Admitted to N.Y. bar, 1891; mem. N.H. Ho. of Rep., 5 terms; atty. for comptroller State of N.Y. in transfer tax proceedings affecting County of Kings, 1911-12; mem. 63d to 65th Congresses (1913-19, 4th N.Y. Dist. Home: Brooklyn, N.Y. Died Nov. 17, 1935.

DALE, Porter Hinman, senator; b. Island Pond, Vt., Mar. 1, 1867; s. George N. and Helen (Hinman) D.; ed. Phila. and Boston and 2 yrs. under James E. Murdoch, actor; studied law with father; m. Amy K. Bartlett, 1891 (died 1907); m. 2d, Augusta M. Wood, 1910. Admitted to Vermont bar, 1896, to practice in U.S. courts, 1900; formerly engaged in lumber, electric and banking enterprises. Chmn. Rep. State Conv. Vt., 1898, 1919; chief dep. collector of customs, Island Pond, 1897-10 (resigned); mem. Vt. Senate, 1910, 12; mem. 64th to 67th Congresses (1915-23), 2d Vt. Dist., elected 68th Congress (resigned); mem. U.S. Senate, 1923-27 (spl. election), and term 1927-33. Conglist. Home: Island Pond, Vt. Died Oct. 6, 1933.

DALE, Thomas Henry, congressman; b. Daleville, Pa., June 12, 1846; s. William and Susan (Hodgson) D.; ed. Daleville pub. schs.; Eastman's Business Coll., Poughkeepsie, N.Y.; grad. Wyoming Sem., Pa., 1869; m. Grace Rounds, Aug. 20, 1870. Enlisted in response to Gov. Curtin's call for emergency men, in Pa. Vols. in Civ. War. In wholesale produce and coal business, 1870-1901; now pres. Anthracite Trust Co., Scranton, Pa.; dir. Traders' Nat. Bank, also several local corps. Elected prothonotary, Lackawanna Co., Pa., 1882, 1885, 1888; mem. 59th Congress (1905-7), 10th Pa. Dist. Trustee Albright Memorial Library, Scranton, and of Wyoming Sem., Kingston, Pa. Republican. Mem. M.E. Ch. Home: Scranton, Pa. Died Aug. 21, 1912.

DALE, Thomas Nelson, cons. geologist; b. New York, N.Y., Nov. 25, 1845; s. Thomas Nelson and Sarah Patten (Monson) D.; gen. edn. Europe and Williston Sem., Mass.; geol. training under Zittel and Pumpelly; m. Margaret Brown, Dec. 22, 1874; children—Sarah, Norman Brown, Nelson Clark, Oswald, Margaret, Arthur. Connected with U.S. Geol. Survey, 1885-1920, geologist, 1892-1920. Instr. geology and botany, Williams Coll., 1893-1901. Author: The Marbles of Western Vermont, 1912; Slate in the United States, 1914; The Commercial Granites of New England, 1923; etc. Home: Pittsfield, Mass. Died Nov. 16, 1937.

DALL, William Healey, naturalist; b. Boston, Aug. 21, 1845; s. Rev. Charles Henry Appleton and Caroline (Healey) D.; ed. pub. schs.; pupil in natural sciences under Louis Agassiz; spl. courses anatomy and medicine; hon. A.M., Wesleyan, 1888; D.Sc., U. of Pa., 1904; LL.D., George Washington U., 1915; m. Annette Whitney, Mar. 3, 1880; children—Charles Whitney, Marcus Hele, Marion, William Austin (dec.). Lt. in Internat. Telegraph Expdn. to Alaska, 1865-68; in U.S. Coast Survey, Alaska, 1871-84; paleontologist, U.S. Geol. Survey, 1884-1925; also from 1880, hon. curator U.S. Nat. Mus.; also prof. invertebrate paleontology, Wagner Inst. of Science, Phila., Feb. 1893—. Mem. Nat. Acad. of Sciences; fellow Am. Acad. of Arts and Sciences. Author: Tribes of the Extreme Northwest; Scientific Results of the Exploration of Alaska; Reports on the Mollusca of the Blake Expedition; Alaska and Its Resources; Coast Pilot of Alaska; Biography of Spencer Fullerton Baird. Died Mar. 27, 1927.

DALMORÈS, Charles, operatic tenor; b. Nancy, France, Dec. 31, 1871; studied at Conservatory, Nancy, and became proficient in French horn and cello; refused admission to classes for singing in Paris, on ground that he was too good a musician to waste time in becoming an inferior singer; apptd. prof. of French horn, at Conservatory, Lyons, at 23; studied under Prof. Dauphin, of Conservatory, Lyons, later mastering one opera a month, mainly alone; studied Italian opera under Franz Emerich, Berlin. Début at Rouen, 1899; sang in "Lohengrin," at Beyreuth, 1908; has appeared as Nicias in "Thaïs," as Julien in "Louise," Pelleas in "Pelleas and Melisande," Herod in "Salome," Samson in "Samson and Delilah," Vinicius in "Quo Vadis," etc.; with the Chicago Grand Opera Co. several seasons from 1912. Home: Coppet, Switzerland. Died Dec. 6, 1939.

DALRYMPLE, Louis, cartoonist; b. Cambridge, Ill., Jan. 19, 1866; ed. Pa. Acad. Fine Arts, Art Students' League, New York; m. Mary A. Goode. Illustrator for leading comic and other journals. Died 1905.

DALRYMPLE, William Haddock, veterinarian; b. Scotland, Apr. 23, 1856; s. Thomas and Mary Eleanor (Haddock) D.; Stranraer Acad.; M.R.C.V.S., Glasgow Vet. Coll., 1886; m. Mary Isabel Umpleby, of Snaith, Yorkshire, Eng., Aug. 27, 1891. Mem. vet. staff, Irish Privy Council, Dublin, 1888; came to America, 1889; prof. comparative medicine, La. State U., and veterinarian La. Expt. stas., 1889-93 and 1897-1919; former dean Coll. Agriculture, same univ.; v. dir. La. Agrl. Expt. Stas. Former editor live stock dept., New Orleans Picayune; former sec. La. State Agrl. Soc. and La. Stockbreeders' Assn.; former mem. staff of collaborators, Am. Vet. Review; pres. U.S. Expt. Sta. Vet. Med. Assn., 1901-02, Am. Vet. Med. Assn., 1907-08, U.S. Live Stock Sanitary Assn., 1908-09; mem. exec. com. Nat. Live Stock Assn., 1902, 3, 4; v. p. La. State Sanitary Assn. Fellow Glasgow Vet. Med. Soc., A.M.A., A.A.A.S.; mem. Internat. Congress on Tuberculosis (Washington, D.C.), 1908, 15th Internat. Congress on Hygiene and Demography (Washington), 1912; reporter on anthrax for the U.S., 10th Internat. Vet. Congress, London, 1914. Presbyn. Author: Veterinary Obstetrics and Livestock Sanitation. Hon. v.p. Baton Rouge Chamber Commerce. Mem. Agrl. Advisory Com. of U.S. Food Administration for La., 1917. Former editor, Jour. Am. Vet. Med. Assn. Home: Baton Rouge, La. Died Sept. 17, 1925.

DALTON, Henry George, corp. official; b. Cleveland, O., Oct. 3, 1862; s. Frederick and Ellen (Gordon) D.; ed. pub. schs.; LL.D., Kenyon Coll., 1927; m. Julia Kaufholz, Jan. 19, 1886. Began in employ of Pickands, Mather & Co., Cleveland, June 15, 1883, mem. of co., 1893—; chmn. bd. Youngstown Sheet & Tube Co., 1932—; pres. Interlake Steamship Co. Mem. steel com., War Industries Bd., World War; apptd. by President Coolidge to investigate U.S. Merchant Marine; apptd. mem. Advisory Shipping Com. Trustee Western Reserve U., Cleveland Mus. of Art, Trinity Cathedral, Kenyon Coll., Lakeside Hosp. Episcopalian. Home: Cleveland, O. Died Dec. 27, 1939.

DALTON, Mary Louise, librarian, hist. writer; b. Wentzville, Mo.; d. William R. and Harriet Ursula (Walker) D.; ed. pub. sch., St. Charles Co., Lindenwood Coll., Mo., and pvt. sch. in New York; unmarried. Editorial writer and asst. Sunday editor, St. Louis Republic, 1895-1901; librarian Mo. Hist. Soc., 1903—. Awarded silver medal for work as collaborator in history, La. Purchase Expn., 1904. Mem. and was 3 yrs. State historian, D.A.R.; now historian of Confederate Memorial Soc. of Mo. Wrote several chapters in and was one of the editors of History of La. Purchase Expn., 1905. Home: St. Louis, Mo. Died 1907.

DALTON, W(illiam) R(obert) Inge, physician; b. Livingston, Ala., Dec. 6, 1841; s. Dr. Robert Hunter and Jane (Martin) D.; ed. Aberdeen, Miss.; and U.S. Naval Acad., 1859-61; M.D., St. Louis Coll. Phys. and Surg., 1884; m. Hattie Ursula Walker, Apr. 2, 1867; 2d, Helen Louise Hillebrand, Jan. 19, 1907. Served 4 yrs. in Confederate navy and army, 1 month in Peruvian navy and 4 months in Brazilian navy. Prof. dermatology and syphilography, N.Y. Sch. Clin. Medicine; dermatologist Met. Hosp. and Dispensary, and West Side German Dispensary. Home: Seattle, Wash. Died May 26, 1931.

DALY, Arnold (Peter Christopher), actor; b. Brooklyn, N.Y., Oct. 4, 1875; s. Joseph J. and Mary (Arnold) D.; St. Patrick's Acad., Brooklyn; m. Mary Blythe, July 1, 1901. Employed as office boy in the office of Charles Frohman; made first appearance on stage in "The Jolly Squire," with Fanny Rice, 1892; New York début, Herald Sq. Theatre, as Chambers in "Pudd'nhead Wilson," 1895; played at Garrick Theatre, London, as Henry Mackintosh, in "Too Much Johnson," 1898; appeared at the Criterion, New York, with Julia Marlowe, as Jack Negley, in "Barbara Frietchie," 1899; later in "Are You a Mason?" "The Way of the World," "The Girl from Dixie," "Mrs. Warren's Profession," "The Boys of Company B," "The Return from Jerusalem," etc.; played prin. parts in "Arms and the Man," in London, Eng., 1911. Gained prominence as producer of plays written by George Bernard Shaw. Died Jan. 13, 1927.

DALY, Augustin, dramatist and theatrical mgr.; b. Plymouth, N.C., July 20, 1838; ed. at Norfolk, Va.; dramatic critic on New York dailies, 1859-69; became prominent as adapter of German and French plays; from 1869 has managed theaters in New York; is also lessee and mgr. of Daly's Theater, London; besides adaptations, has written Under the Gaslight; Divorce; Pique; and other original plays. Died 1899.

DALY, Charles Frederick, ry. official; b. Canton, Ill., July 6, 1865. Operator and ticket agent, pass. and ticket agt., clerk in gen. pass. office at Omaha, 1878-88, C.,B.&Q. Ry.; chief clerk to gen. pass. and ticket agt., 1888-89, asst. gen. pass. agt., 1889-90, gen. pass. agt., 1890-1902, L.E.&W. R.R.; chief asst. gen. pass. agt., L.S.&M.S. Ry., 1902-05; pass. traffic mgr. same rd., and M.C. Ry. and L.E.&W. Ry., at Chicago, Feb.-Dec. 1905; pass. traffic mgr., N.Y.C. Lines east of Buffalo, hdqrs. in New York, 1905-06; v.p. same lines east and west of Buffalo, in charge of matters pertaining to passenger traffic, 1906-08; v.p. in charge of all traffic N.Y.C. Lines, Nov. 24, 1908—. Died Jan. 6, 1928.

DALY, Charles Patrick, jurist; b. New York, Oct. 31, 1816; ed. in New York public schools; worked as clerk in Savannah, afterwards sailor before the mast, and later mechanic; studied law; admitted to bar, 1837 (LL.D., Columbia Univ.); mem. N.Y. assembly, 1843; apptd., 1844, judge court of common pleas for city of New York; held the office for 42 years until retired, 1886, under constl. age limitation; was 27 years chief justice of the court; was member State Constl. Conv., 1867; mem. of many scientific societies; pres. Am. Geog. Soc., 1864—. Author: First Settlement of the Jews in N. America; 16 vols. of law reports, etc. Died 1899.

DALY, J(ohn) Burrwood, congressman; b. Philadelphia; A.B., La Salle Coll., Philadelphia, also A.M. and LL.D.; LL.B., U. of Pa. Admitted to Pa. bar and practiced in Phila.; asst. city solicitor 12 yrs.; mem. faculty La Salle Coll.; mem. 74th and 75th Congresses (1935-39), 4th Pa. Dist. Democrat. Home: Philadelphia, Pa. Died Mar. 13, 1939.

DALY, Joseph Francis, lawyer; b. Plymouth, N.C., Dec. 3, 1840; s. Denis and Elizabeth T. D.; ed. New York; (LL.D., St. John's Coll., 1883, Villanova, 1902); m. Emma Robinson Barker, Nov. 19, 1873 (died 1886); 2d, Mary Louise Smith, June 18, 1890. Resident of New York, 1849—; admitted to bar, 1862; judge Ct. Common Pleas, N.Y., 1870-96 (chief justice, 1890-96); justice Supreme Ct. of N.Y., 1896-98; U.S. law commr., P.R., 1900. Mem. bd. of mgrs. R.C. Orphan Asylum; mem. advisory bd. St. Vincent's Hosp.; mem. bd. Trinity Coll., Washington. Home: New York, N.Y. Died Aug. 6, 1916.

DALY, Marcus, mgr. Anaconda mine and smelter; b. in Ireland, 1842; in Mont., 1876—; was gen. mgr. Alice silver mine; transferred to Anaconda; practical miner and assayer; member Constl. Convention, 1884; candidate before legislature for U.S. Senate, 1899. Democrat. Home: Anaconda, Mont. Died 1900.

DALY, William D., congressman, 7th N.J. dist. for term 1899-1901; b. Jersey City, N.J., 1851; ed. in public schools; began study of law, 1870; admitted to bar as atty. and later made counselor; built up an extensive practice, especially in criminal cases; asst. U.S. dist. atty., 1886-89; del. Nat. Dem. conventions, 1888 and 1892; mem. N.J. assembly, 1891; judge Hoboken dist. court, 1891-92; State senator, 1892-98. Democrat. Home: Hoboken, N.J. Died 1900.

DALZELL, John, congressman; b. New York, Apr. 19, 1845; s. Samuel and Mary (McDonnell) D.; removed to Pittsburgh, 1847; A.B., Yale, 1865; widower. Admitted to bar, 1867; for yrs. one of the attys. for Pa. R.R. Co. for all its Western lines; also atty. for many corps. in Allegheny Co., Pa. Mem. 50th to 62d Congresses (1887-1913), 30th Pa. Dist.; mem. coms. on Rules, and Ways and Means, 54th to 62d Congresses; del. Rep. nat. convs., 1904, 08. Regent Smithsonian Instn. Died Oct. 3, 1927.

DALZELL, William Sage, lawyer; b. Pittsburgh, Pa., Aug. 17, 1868; s. John and Mary Louise (Duff) D.; A.B., Yale, 1891; student law schs. of Harvard and U. of Pa. (non-grad.); m. Mary Ruth Hough, Oct. 4, 1893 (died 1916); m. 2d, Elizabeth (Guilford) Prestley, of Lansdowne, Pa., Oct. 1918. Began practice with Dalzell, Scott & Gordon and mem. of firm, 1897-1906; mem. of Dalzell, Fisher & Dalzell until 1929, now Dalzell, Dalzell, McFall & Pringle; firm represents Pa. R.R. System and other corps. Republican. Episcopalian. Home: Pittsburgh, Pa. Died Sept. 27, 1934.

DAM, Henry Jackson Wells, dramatist; b. San Francisco; s. Alphonso and Lucy E. D.; grad. U. of Calif.; Ph.B.; m. Dorothy Dorr (actress), 1892. Engaged in dramatic composition from 1891. Has produced in England and America the following plays: Diamond Deane; The Silver Shell; The Shop Girl; The White Silk Dress; La Coquette; A King of Fools; La Madeleine; Skipper & Co.; The Red Mouse. Contbr. Strand mag., McClure's, etc.; won first $1,500 prize in first Black Cat story competition. Mem. Royal Instn., London; Société des Auteurs et Compositeurs Dramatiques of France. Died 1906.

DAME, Frank Libby, electrical engr.; b. Boston, Mar. 21, 1867; s. Seth T. and Josephine R. (Libby) D.; E.E., Mass. Inst. Tech., 1889; m. Mary Elizabeth Elvidge, 1906; children—Frank E., Edward L., Robert O. Engr. Portland (Ore.) office of Westinghouse Co., 1889-90; supt. Vancouver (B.C.) Ry. & Light Co., 1891-92; engr. local office Gen. Electric Co., 1892-93; in charge ry. property, Tacoma, Wash., 1893-1901; engr. local cos., Gen. Electric Co., 1901-09; v.p. Electric Bond & Share Co., 1909-12; official various Public Utilities cos., 1912-24; now pres., chmn. exec. com. North American Co.; chmn. bd exec. com. Cleveland Electric Illuminating Co., North Am. Edison Co., Wired Radio, Inc.; pres. Edison Securities Co., North Am. Utilities Securities Corp., Sixty Broadway Building Corp., Western Power Corp.; v.p., mem. exec. com. and dir. Union Electric Light & Power Co.; dir. numerous cos. Episcopalian. Home: Garden City, N.Y. Died Dec. 30, 1933.

DAME, Harriet Patience, pres. Army Nurses' Assn., Washington; b. Barnstead, N.H., Jan. 5, 1815; ed. public schools; unmarried. Moved to Concord, N.H., 1846; when war broke out went to front with 2d N.H. regt., in hospital dept.; served as army nurse 4 years and 8 months. Remained in Washington; clerk in Treasury Dept., June 1867-Feb. 1896. Injured by being run down by a woman bicyclist and now walks on crutches. Home: Concord, N.H. Died 1900.

DAMM, Henry Christian Augustus, consular service; b. West Bloomfield, Wis., Jan. 19, 1874; s. Conrad and Maria (Markworth) D.; B.A., U. of the South, 1907, M.A., 1909; m. Alice Mary Ann Purdue, June 11, 1902; children—Alice Clara (Mrs. Swan Erickson), Florence Elisabeth, Henry Thomas, Frieda Mildred. Teacher pub. schs., Fla., 1898-1904, Sewanee (Tenn.) Mil. Acad., 1904, 09; consul at Cornwall, Ont., Can., 1909-12, Stettin, Germany, 1912-15, Aix la Chapelle, 1915-17, Stavanger, 1917-18, Vardo and Kirkenes, 1918, Christiania, Norway, 1918, Copenhagen, Denmark, 1919, Malaga, 1920-21, Valencia, Spain, 1921-22, Nogales, Mexico, 1922—. Mem. Foreign Service Assn. Episcopalian. Died Aug. 24, 1929.

DAMON, Alonzo Willard, insurance pres.; b. Norwell, Mass., Feb. 11, 1847; s. Davis and Lucy (Damon) D.; ed. pub. schs., Boston; unmarried. Began with Washington Fire & Marine Ins. Co. of Boston, 1862, sec., 1880-87; spl. agt. for N.E. of Franklin Fire Ins. Co., 1888-89; spl. agt. for N.E., 1890-91, asst. sec., 1891-95, pres., 1895—, Springfield Fire & Marine Ins. Co.; trustee N.E. Investment & Security Co., Springfield Instn. for Savings; dir. Springfield St. Ry. Co., 3d Nat. Bk., Springfield, etc. Pres. Nat. Bd. Fire Underwriters, 1910. Commr. of Sinking Fund, City of Springfield. Republican. Unitarian. Home: Springfield, Mass. Died Jan. 7, 1924.

DAMON, George Alfred, consulting engr.; b. Chesaning, Mich., Apr. 7, 1871; s. Brazil Monroe and Martha Angeline (Gould) D.; B.S. in elec. engring., U. of Mich., 1895; m. Harriett Diller, June 8, 1904; children—George Alfred, Harriet Antha. On staff Electrical Industries, World's Fair, Chicago, 1893; in shops of Fisher Electric Works, Detroit, 1894; draftsman and engr. with Bion J. Arnold, Chicago, 1895-1900; mng. engr. The Arnold Co., in charge design and constrn. railroad shops, elec. rys., hydroelectric plants and industrial work, 1900-08; asso. with Mr. Arnold in reports on subway operation and constrn., New York, transportation problems of Pittsburgh and Los Angeles, Calif., and surrounding dists., etc., 1911; dean engring., Throop Coll. of Tech. (Calif. Inst. Tech.), 1911-17. Cons. engr. Bd. Pub. Utilities, Los Angeles, 1912-13; tech. dir. City Planning Com. of Pasadena, 1915-17; cons. engr. City Plan, San José, 1917; consultant City Plan, Long Beach, Calif., 1918-19; mem. Zoning Commn., Pasadena, 1923. Republican. Presbyn. Fellow Am. Inst. E.E.; chmn. Joint Tech. Socs., Los Angeles, 1918-19, Am. City Planning Inst.; charter mem. City Planning Assn., Los Angeles (pres. 1918-19, sec. 1922, 25); mem. Los Angeles Co. Regional Planning Commn., 1922-26 (v. chmn. 1923-25); co-ordinator for "Damon-Jubb Plan" for Los Angeles Union Depot, started Dec. 1933; program chmn. Pasadena 60th Anniversary Celebration, 1934. Author: Inter and Intra Urban Transit and Traffic as a Regional Planning Problem (proc. Nat. Conf. City Planning), 1923; The Influence of the Automobile on Regional Transportation Problems (trans. Am. Soc. C.E.), 1925. Home: Pasadena, Calif. Died June 23, 1934.

DAMON, Lindsay Todd, educator; b. Brookline, Mass., Nov. 8, 1871; s. David and H. Emmeline (Todd) Damon; A.B., Harvard, 1894; m. Julia O'Neill, June 30, 1896 (died 1926); m. 2d, Bertha Clark Pope, Mar. 11, 1928. Asst. in English, Harvard, 1894-96; instr. English, U. of Chicago, 1896-1901; asso. prof. rhetoric, Brown U., 1901-05, prof. rhetoric, 1905-11, prof. of English, 1911-36, prof. emeritus, 1936—. Editor: Lake English Classics, etc., 1897—. Author (with Robert Herrick): Herrick and Damon's Composition and Rhetoric, 1899. Home: Alton, N.H. Died May 6, 1940.

DAMON, William Emerson, author; b. Windsor, Vt., Nov. 15, 1838; ed. Kimball Union Acad., Meriden, N.H.; m. Alma C., d. Timothy B. Otis, of Windsor, Vt., Feb. 14, 1865. Supt. credit dept. Tiffany & Co., New York. Well known as amateur naturalist; mem. N.E. Soc., Scientific Alliance, New York, N.Y. Micros. Soc., N.Y. Mycol. Club. Zoöl. Soc., etc. Author: Ocean Wonders. Died 1911.

DAMROSCH, Frank Heino, musical dir.; b. Breslau, Germany, June 22, 1859; s. Leopold and Helene (von Heimburg) D.; ed. Coll. City of N.Y.; studied music with Pruckner, Jean Vogt and von Inten; hon. Mus. D., Yale, 1904; m. Hetty Mosenthal, Jan. 10, 1888. Conductor Denver Chorus Club, 1882-84; supervisor music, pub. schs., Denver, 1884; chorus master, Met. Opera House, New York, 1885-91; comdr. Harmonic Soc., Newark, N.J., 1886-87, Choral Club, New York, 1891-95, People's Choral Union and Singing Classes, 1892-1912, Musical Art Soc., New York, 1893-1920, Musurgia (male chorus), 1891-97, Orpheus Club, Phila., 1897-1905, Eurydice Chorus (female), Phila., 1897-1905; dir. music, New York pub. schs., 1897-1905; comdr. Oratorio Soc., New York, and of Symphony Concerts for Young People, 1898-1912; Mendelssohn Glee Club, 1904-09; organizer and dir. Inst. of Musical Art, 1905—. Was lt. Colo. Nat. Guard, 1884. Home: New York, N.Y. Died Oct. 22, 1937.

DANA, Charles Edmund, art critic; b. Wilkes-Barré, Pa., Jan. 18, 1843; s. Brig. Gen. Edmund L. and Sarah Helen (Peters) D.; C.E., Union Coll., 1865; studied art in Paris under Luminais, architecture at Royal Acads., Dresden and Munich; m. Emilie H. Woodbury, Nov. 29, 1870. Asst. engr. Pa. R.R., 8 yrs.; prof. art. U. of Pa., 1893-1904; lecturer same, 1904—. Dir. Library Co. of Phila.; trustee Pa. Mus. and Sch. of Industrial Art; v. p. Pa. Instn. for Deaf and Dumb, Fairmount Park Art Assn.; mem. Chicago and St. Louis juries of awards, gold medal, Phila. Art Club, 1891. Wrote Glimpses of English History, 4 volts.; Great Seal of England and Some Others. Home: Philadelphia. Died Feb. 1, 1914.

DANA, Charles Loomis, M.D.; b. Woodstock, Vt., Mar. 25, 1852; s. Charles and Charitie Scott (Loomis) D.; A.B., Dartmouth, 1872, A.M., 1875, LL.D., 1905; M.D., Nat. Med. Coll., 1876; M.D., Columbia, 1877; LL.D., Edinburgh U., 1927; m. Lillian Farlee; children—Marjorie F. (Mrs. William T. Barlow), Elizabeth (dec.), Charles Loomis (dec.). Prof. nervous diseases, Cornell U. Med. Coll., New York, 1902—. Pres. N.Y. Acad. Medicine, 1914-16. Author: Textbook of Nervous Diseases and Psychiatry, 1892. Home: Woodstock, Vt. Died Dec. 12, 1935.

DANA, Edward Salisbury, mineralogist; b. New Haven, Conn., Nov. 16, 1849; s. James Dwight and Henrietta F. (Silliman) D.; A.B., Yale, 1870, A.M., 1874, Ph.D., 1876; studied Heidelberg and Vienna; m. Caroline, d. William Brooks Bristol, of New Haven, Oct. 2, 1883; children—Mary Bristol (Mrs. Alexander C. Brown), James Dwight, William Bristol. Tutor 1874-79, curator mineral collection, 1874-1922, asst. prof. natural philosophy, 1879-90, prof. physics, 1890-1917, and prof. emeritus, 1917—, Yale U. Trustee of Peabody Mus., 1885-1929; editor Am. Jour. of Science, 1875—. Fellow Am. Acad. of Arts and Sciences; mem. Nat. Acad. Sciences. Author: Text-book of Mineralogy, 1877, new edit., 1898; Text-book of Elementary Mechanics, 1881; Dana's System of Mineralogy, 6th edit., 1892; Minerals and How to Study Them, 1895. Home: New Haven, Conn. Died June 16, 1935.

DANA, Francis E., lawyer; b. Brooklyn, Jan. 21, 1836; s. Alexander H. and Augusta C. (Radcliff) D.; grad. Columbia Grammar Sch., New York, 1852; m. Julia, d. Rev. William Ives Budington, of Brooklyn, Oct. 7, 1869 (she died Mar. 29, 1897). Admitted to bar, 1858, and then in practice at Brooklyn; admitted to bar, U.S. Supreme Court, Mar. 7, 1873; in partnership with Freeman Clarkson from Apr., 1871, in firm of Dana & Clarkson; has won many important cases in N.Y. Court of Appeals. Was 7 yrs. mem. Bd. of Edn. of Brooklyn (6 yrs. chmn. law com.), and has served on Bd. of Health of Summit, N.J. Conglist. Republican. Home: Summit, N.J. Died June 1910.

DANA, Israel Thorndike, physician; b. Marblehead, Mass., June 6, 1827; s. Rev. Samuel and Henrietta Bridges D.; M.D., Harvard, 1850; pursued med. studies abroad for 2 yrs.; settled in Portland, Me., 1852; specialist in diseases of heart and lungs; attending physician Maine Gen. Hosp., and prof. materia medica and theory and practice of medicine in Med. School of Maine, attached to Bowdoin Coll. Home: Portland, Me. Died 1904.

DANA, John Cotton, librarian; b. Woodstock, Vt., Aug. 19, 1856; s. Charles and Charitie Scott (Loomis) D.; A.B., Dartmouth, 1878; studied law, Woodstock, Vt., 1878-80; m. Adine Rowena Wagener, Nov. 15, 1888. Land surveyor, Colo., 1880-81; admitted to N.Y. bar, 1883; civ. engr. Colo., 1886-87. Librarian, Denver Pub. Library, 1889-97, City Library, Springfield, Mass., 1898-1902, Free Pub. Library, Newark, N.J., 1902—. Dir. Newark Mus. Assn., since foundation, 1909. Author: Libraries, Addresses and Essays, 1916; The New Museum; American Art, 1914, Gloom of the Museum, 1917; The Installation of a Speaker; Suggestions, 1921; also wrote The Industrialist is an Artist, Art is All in Your Eye, Art's Best Friends are the Advertisers, Should Museums be Useful, Changes in Library Methods in a Changing World, all 1927. Home: Newark, N.J. Died July 21, 1929.

DANA, Lynn Boardman, musician; b. Middleport, N.Y., Oct. 15, 1875; s. William Henry and Emma Jane (Tuttle) D.; ed. Dana's Musical Inst., Warren,

O., Mus.B., Master in the Art of Music, Doctor of Music; pupil in piano of Anton de Kontski, Jacob Schmitt, William H. Sherwood, Robert Goldbeck; in theory of William H. Dana, J. D. Cook; m. Retta C. Nimocks, June 21, 1901; 1 son, Lynn B. Concert pianist and accompanist, 1896—; dir. Dana's Symphony Orchestra, 1906—; pres. Dana's Mus. Inst.; actively connected with music dept. Chautauqua Instn. for 15 yrs.; dean music dept. McKinley Memorial Assn., Niles, Ohio; dir. Nat. Music Convention and Chautauqua, Lockport, N.Y.; dir. of music and organist First M.E. Ch.; dir. Grotto Glee Club, Warren, O., and Warren Masonic Chorus; founder Tau Delta Beta, nat. musical fraternity; trustee Warren Y.M.C.A.; pres. Warren Bd. of Edn., 3 yrs. Mem. Nat. Council Boy Scouts of America; mem. exec. bd. Salvation Army; dir. Trumbull County Health Bd. Mem. Company C, 2d Ohio Inf., Spanish-Am. War, 1898. Mason (32°). Composer: (anthem) As Moses Lifted Up the Serpent, 1903; (oratorio) Triumph of Faith, 1917; Concerto in D Minor for piano and orchestra, 1931; musical setting to pageant, The Challenge, 1933; (Male Choruses) Prayer Perfect, and Still, Still With Thee. Home: Warren O. Died Sept. 22, 1941.

DANA, Napoleon Jackson Tecumseh, soldier; b. Ft. Sullivan, Eastport, Me., Apr. 15, 1822; s. Capt. Nathaniel G. D., 1st U.S. arty.; ed. Portsmouth Acad., N.H., 1833-38; grad. U.S. Mil. Acad., West Point, 1842; m. Sue Lewis Martin Sandford, 1844. Engaged in Mexican war, 1st with Gen. Taylor from beginning through siege of Fort Brown and campaign of Monterey, and next with Gen. Scott in siege of Vera Cruz and battle of Cerro Gordo; was banker in St. Paul, 1855-61; was col. 1st Minn. vols. at Ball's Bluff in Civil war, then brig. gen. in all battles of Army of the Potomac up to and including Battle of Antietam; then maj. gen. and comdg. div. and corps and dept. to end of war. Was wounded at Cerro Gordo and again at Antietam. After war engaged in mining in west; gen. agt. Am. Russian Commercial Co. in Alaska and Washington, 1866-71; afterward connected with several railroads; retired. Died 1905.

DANA, Paul, editor; b. New York, Aug. 20, 1852; s. late Charles Anderson and Eunice (Macdaniel) D.; A.B., Harvard, 1874; LL.B., Columbia, 1878; m. Mary, d. William Butler Duncan, 1884 (dec.); children—Janet, Anderson, Duncan. Maj. ordnance, 1st Brigade, N.G.S.N.Y., on staff Gen. Louis Fitzgerald, 1883; commr. pub. parks, New York, 1891; became connected with New York Sun, 1880 (of which his father was editor) and on death of his father, 1897, succeeded him as editor; retired 1903. Was mem. Com. for Relief in Belgium, in Namur, May and June 1915. Died April 7, 1930.

DANA, Richard Henry, lawyer; b. Cambridge, Mass., Jan. 3, 1851; s. Richard Henry D., Jr., and Sarah (Watson) D.; A.B., Harvard 1874, LL.B., 1877; m. Edith Longfellow, Jan. 10, 1878 (died 1915); children—Richard Henry, Henry W. Longfellow, Frances A. (Mrs. H. C. de Rham, II), Allston, Edmund T., Delia F.; m. 2d, Mrs. James G. Mumford, née Helen Ford, Feb. 25, 1922. Admitted to bar, 1877. Organized Asso. Charities of Boston, 1878-79; drafted Civil Service Reform Act (Mass., 1884), and the first Australian Ballot Act passed in U.S. (Mass., 1888); editor Civil Service Record, 1889-92; as a commr. Charles River Dam, made report to legislature, 1903. Pres. N.E. Conservatory of Music, 1891-98, Boston Y.M.C.A., 1890-91, Cambridge Civil Service Reform Assn., 1897-01; chmn. council Nat. Civ. Serv. Ref. League, 1905-12, pres. 1913-23. Fellow Am. Acad. Arts and Sciences. Author: Double Taxation in Massachusetts, 1895; intro. and notes to speeches in Stirring Times and Letters to a Son, 1910; intro. and concluding chapter to Two Years Before the Mast, 1911; Hospitable England in the Seventies, 1921. Home: Cambridge, Mass. Died Dec. 16, 1931.

DANA, Richard Turner, civil engr.; b. Lenox, Mass., June 13, 1876; s. Richard Starr and Florine (Turner) D.; Ph.B. in C.E., Sheffield Scientific Sch. (Yale), 1896; m. Mary R. Meredith, 2d, Apr. 22, 1902. With maintenance of way dept., Erie R.R., 1896-1902; cons. practice in N.Y. City, 1902—, chief engr. Construction Service Co.; pres. Codex Book Co.; v.p. and treas. Construction Service Co.; sec. and treas. R. T. & D. T. Dana Co. Served in 1st Div. Naval Battalion, Conn. N.G., 2 yrs., 130th Separate Co., 1 yr. Republican. Episcopalian. Mason. Author: Cost Keeping and Management Engineering (with H. P. Gillette), 1909; Rock Drilling (with W. L. Saunders), 1911; Handbook of Construction Equipment, 1921, 26. Joint author: Mechanical and Electrical Cost, 1918; Construction Costkeeping and Management, 1922; Concrete Computation Charts, 1922; The Bridge at Windsor (Vt.) and Its Economic Implications, 1926; The Human Machine in Industry, 1927. Home: New York, N.Y. Died Aug. 26, 1928.

DANA, Stephen Winchester, clergyman; b. Canaan, N.Y., Nov. 17, 1840; s. Rev. John Jay and Mary A. (Freeman) D.; A.B., Williams Coll., 1861; prin. acad., Hinsdale, Mass., 1861-63; student Union Theol. Sem., New York, 1863-66; (D.D., Williams, 1880); m. Rebecca R. Paul, Oct. 1, 1868; m. 2d, Eleanor H. Crocker, July 12, 1883. Ordained Presbyn. ministry, 1867; pastor Second Ch., Belvidere, N.J., 1866-68, Walnut St. Ch., Phila., July 1, 1868—. Pres. N.E. Soc. of Pa., 4 yrs.; dir. Union Theol. Sem.; trustee Lincoln U. Republican. Author: Woman, Her Possibilities and Limitations, 1899. Died 1910.

DANA, William Franklin, judge; b. Somerville, Mass., June 26, 1863; s. Thomas and Mary C. (Baldwin) D.; A.B., Harvard, 1884, LL.B., 1887. Mem. Dana & Bates, and Choate & Dana, and practiced alone, Boston, 1887-1906; councilman, alderman at large, v.p. Bd. of Aldermen, Newton, 1897-1900; mem. Mass. Ho. of Rep., 1901, 1902, 1903, Senate, 1904, 1905, 1906 (pres., 1905-06); justice Superior Court of Mass., July 9, 1906—. Wrote: Optimism of Ralph Waldo Emerson (Bowdoin prize essay, 1886). Home: Newton, Mass. Died Aug. 5, 1920.

DANA, William Henry, musician; b. Warren, O., June 10, 1846; s. Junius and Martha (Potter) D.; ed. Williston Sem., Easthampton, Mass.; musical edn., Kuliak's Conservatory of Music, Berlin, and Royal Acad. of Music, London; m. Emma Jane Tuttle, 1870. Served in both Eastern and Western armies during Civil War. Fellow Am. Coll. Musicians of U. of New York; bronze medal and diploma of Expn. at Bologna, Italy, 1888, for excellence of his musical text-books. In 1880 began series of tours, traveling over Europe and in Scandinavia, Russia and Arctic regions. Pres. Dana's Musical Inst. Author: Dana's Practical Thorough Bass, 1874; Dana's Practical Harmony, 1880; Dana's Practical Counterpoint, 1885; Guide in Orchestration, 1879; Guide in Military Band Arranging, 1880; The National School for Cornet, 1890. Home: Warren, O. Died Feb. 1916.

DANA, William Parsons Winchester, artist; b. Boston, Mass., Feb. 18, 1833; s. Samuel D.; ed. Boston Latin Sch.; studied art École des Beaux Arts and under Le Poittevin; m. Anna Bronson, 1855. Maintained a studio in N.Y. City, 1862-70; lived abroad from 1870. Marine landscape and figure painter; Gold Medal at Paris Expn., 1878; 1st prize figure painting, Pa. Acad. Fine Arts, 1881. Died Apr. 8, 1927.

DANCY, Alexander Brown, ophthalmologist, otologist; b. Holly Springs, Miss., Dec. 23, 1877; s. Col. Clifton (C.S.A.) and Sarah Torian (Brown) D.; student Southwestern Bapt. Univ., Jackson, Tenn., 1894-95, 1896-97; M.D., U. of Louisville, 1900, Vanderbilt U., 1902; interne N.Y. Polyclinic, 1902-03; certificate New York Ophthalmic and Aural Inst., 1903; Royal London (Eng.) Ophthalmic Hosp., 1903-04; spl. certificate Am. Bd. for Ophthalmic Examinations, 1916, also Am. Bd. Otolaryngology; course in advanced Ophthalmology, Harvard, 1917; m. Mary Eloise Happel, June 6, 1911; children—Mary Happel, Alexander Brown. Practiced at Jackson from 1904; ophthalmologist and otolaryngologist Crook Sanatorium, also Memorial Hosp.; dir. Second Nat. Bank, Jackson. Mem. Med. Advisory Bd. No. 35, Jackson, 1917-18, World War; consultant Unit No. 2, U.S.P.H.S.; cons. E.E.N.T. U.S. Veterans' Bur., Dist. No. 5, Jackson. Mem. Tenn. Governing Com. Gorgas Memorial; trustee West Tenn. Coll.; v.p. Jackson Y.M.C.A. Fellow Am. Acad. Ophthalmology and Otolaryngology, Am. Coll. Surgeons. Democrat. Methodist. Home: Jackson, Tenn. Died June 10, 1933.

DANDRIDGE, N(athaniel) Pendleton, surgeon; b. Cincinnati, O., Apr. 16, 1846; s. Alexander Spotswood and Martha Eliza Hunt (Pendleton) D.; A.B., Kenyon Coll., 1866, A.M., 1873; attended Med. Coll. of Ohio, 1 yr. and afterward pursued med. studies in Paris and Vienna; M.D., Coll. of Phys. and Surg. (Columbia), 1870. Prof. surgery, Miami Med. Coll., 1880-1907; surgeon to Cincinnati Hosp. and Episcopal Hosp. for Children. Fellow Am. Surg. Assn. Home: Cincinnati, O. Died 1910.

DANDY, George Brown, colonel U.S.A.; b. Macon, Ga., Feb. 11, 1830; s. Rev. James Hervey and Charlotte (Temple) D.; who moved to N.J. same year; ed. private schools, N.J.; m. Anne Eliza Slaughter, Feb. 11, 1873. Enlisted April, 1847, in 10th Inf., raised for service in Mexican War, and served until its close; began study of medicine, Salem, N.J.; cadet U.S. Mil. Acad., 1849-52; pvt., sergt., and 1st sergt. Co. A, 1st Arty., 1854-57; promoted through grades to col. 100th N.Y. Inf., Aug. 29, 1862; hon. mustered out of vol. service, Aug. 28, 1865; maj. q.m., Mar. 3, 1875; lt. col. deputy q.m. gen., Nov. 11, 1887; retired, Feb. 11, 1894; advanced to rank of col. retired, by act of Apr. 23, 1904. Bvts.: maj., Sept. 6, 1863, "for distinguished and gallant conduct in siege of Ft. Wagner, S.C."; lt. col., Aug. 14, 1864, "for gallant services in action at Deep Bottom, Va."; col., Mar. 13, 1865, "for gallant and meritorious services at Fort Gregg, Va."; brig. gen., Mar. 13, 1865, for same in the field during the war. Served in Spokane Indian expdn. and Snake expdn.; assigned to duty Gen. McClellan's headquarters; captured Folly Island, S.C.; took part in assault and capture Morris' Island and Ft. Wagner, S.C.; battles at Port Walthall Junction, Drury's Bluff, Deep Bottom, Deep Run, Fussell's Mills and siege of Petersburg, Va.; placed in command 3d Brigade, 1st Div., 24th Army Corps; 1865 took prominent part in assault and capture of Ft. Gregg, south of Petersburg, Va., and comd. his brigade at Appomattox C.H., last battle of war. Since war in q.m. dept.; built Fort Phil Kearney at base of Big Horn Mountains, 1866, and Ft. Abraham Lincoln, N.D., 1873-75; in charge gen. depot q.m. and subsistence depts., Yuma, Ariz., 1868; later at various cities. Hon. mem. Buffalo Hist. Soc. Home: Omaha, Neb. Died 1911.

DANFORD, Lorenzo, congressman, lawyer; b. Belmont Co., O., Oct. 18, 1829; reared on farm; ed. common schools and 2 years at coll. at Waynesburg, Pa. Admitted to bar, 1854; pros. atty., Belmont Co., 1857-61; in Union army from April, 1861, as private, lt. and capt. until Aug., 1964; presdl. elector, 1864 and 1892; member Congress, 16th Ohio dist., 1873-79, and 1895—. Republican. Chmn. Com. Immigration and Naturalization, 55th Congress. Home: St. Clairsville, O. Died 1899.

DANFORTH, Elliott, lawyer; b. Middleburg, N.Y., March 6, 1850; s. Judge P. S. D.; ed. public schools and Schoharie Acad.; admitted to bar 1872; pres. village of Bainbridge 3 terms; deputy State treas., 1884-89; State treas., 1889-93; chmn. Dem. State Com., 1896-98; Dem. nominee for lt. gov., N.Y., 1898; pres. 1st Nat. Bank of Bainbridge. Home: New York, N.Y. died 1906.

DANFORTH, Henry Gold, congressman; b. Town of Gates (now part of Rochester), N.Y., June 14, 1854; s. George Franklin and Frances Jeanette (Wright) D.; A.B., Harvard, 1877, LL.B., 1880; m. Edwine L. Blake, Nov. 8, 1888. Admitted to bar, 1880, and since in practice at Rochester. Mem. 62d Congress (1911-13), 32d N.Y. Dist., and 63d and 64th Congresses (1913-17), 39th Dist. Republican. Unitarian. Mem. bd. mgrs., N.Y. State Reformatory, Elmira, 1900-02; trustee Rochester Gen. Hosp., Reynolds Library. Editor: New York Court of Appeals Digest, 1884; U.S. Supreme Court Digest, 1886; Digest of New York Supreme Court Reports, 1902. Died Apr. 8, 1918.

DANFORTH, Isaac Newton, physician; b. Barnard, Vt., Nov. 5, 1835; s. A. H. and Elvira (Bosworth) D.; M.D., Dartmouth, 1862 (hon. A.M., 1881); m. Elizabeth Skelton, June 9, 1869; m. 2d, Mary McPherson Barnes, Jan. 12, 1898. In practice at Chicago, 1866; lecturer pathology, 1870-81, prof. pathology and histology, 1881-83, Rush Med. Coll.; prof. pathology and renal diseases, Chicago Med. Coll., 1883-92; prof. of pathology and renal diseases, 1875-98, dean, 1895-99, Woman's Med. Sch., Northwestern U.; hon. phys. St. Luke's Hosp. Home: Chicago, Ill. Died 1911.

DANIEL, Ferdinand Eugene, editor; b. Greenville (now Emporia) Co., Va., July 18, 1839; s. R. W. T. and Hester Jordan (Adams) D.; ed. pub. schs., Vicksburg, Miss., 1850-56, Jackson, Miss., 1856-60; M.D., New Orleans Sch. of Medicine, 1862; m. Minerva Patrick, July 4, 1863; m. 2d, Fanny Ragsdale Smith, Oct. 10, 1872; m. 3d, Josephine Draper, June 3, 1903. Pvt. 18th Miss. Inf., C.S.A., May-Sept., 1861; surgeon (maj.), C.S.A., upon exam. before Army Bd. Med. Examiners, Army of Tennessee, Tupelo, Miss.; commd. July 8, 1862; registrar Army Bd. Med. Examiners, July-Nov., 1862; judge advocate, gen. court martial, Army of Tenn., Nov., 1862-Feb., 1863, at Chattanooga; in charge Confederate hosps. at Chattanooga, Tenn., Marietta, Kingston, and Covington, Ga., and Lauderdale, Miss., until close of war. Practiced medicine and surgery, Galveston, Tex., 1866-75, Jackson, Miss., 1875-80, in Texas, 1880-85; retired and founded Texas Med. Jour., July, 1885, editing and publishing it. Sec. Texas Quarantine Dept., 1890-98; had charge at Lake Miss. of epidemic of yellow fever, 1878; U.S. quarantine officer, Vicksburg, Miss., 1879. Prof. anatomy and later of surgery, Tex. Med. Coll., Galveston, 1867-68. Pres. Am. Internat. Congress on Tuberculosis, 1905-06. Democrat. Author: Recollections of a Rebel Surgeon, 1899; The Strange Case of Dr. Bruno, 1906. Home: Austin, Tex. Died May 14, 1914.

DANIEL, John Warwick, senator; b. Lynchburg, Va., Sept. 5, 1842; s. Judge William, Jr. and Sarah A. (Warwick) D.; ed. at Lynchburg Coll. and Dr. Gessner Harrison's Univ. Sch.; (LL.D., Washington and Lee, 1883, U. of Mich., 1887); in C.S.A. of Northern Va. throughout war; wounded 4 times; became adj. gen. on Gen. Early's staff; studied law, U. of Va., 1865-66; admitted to bar, 1866; m. Julia E. Munnell, 1869. Mem. Va. House of Delegates, 1869-72, Senate, 1875-81; presdl. elector, 1876; defeated for gov. of Va., 1881; mem. 49th Congress (1885-87); U.S. senator, 1887-93, 1893-99, 1899-1905, 1905-11, and reëlected, Jan. 1910, for term 1911-17. Author: Attachments Under the Code of Virginia; Negotiable Instruments; etc. Home: Lynchburg, Va. Died 1910.

DANIELL, Moses Grant, educator, author; b. Boston, Sept. 9, 1836; s. George Keith and Hannah Adams (Grant) D.; grad. Harvard, 1863 (A.M.); master Everett School, Dorchester, Mass., 3 yrs.; master Roxbury Latin School, 17 yrs.; prin. Chauncy Hall School, Boston, 12 yrs.; now in editorial dept.

Ginn & Co., Boston. Mem. Boston Handel and Haydn Soc. (treas. 20 yrs.). Author: Exercises in Latin Composition, 1889; New Latin Composition, 1897; (with William C. Collar) The Beginners' Latin Book, 1886; First Latin Book, 1894; Exercises in Greek Composition, 1893; First Year Latin, 1901. Editor: (with Prof. J. B. Greenough and Prof. B. L. D'Ooge) The New Cæsar, 1898, and Second Year Latin, 1899; (with Prof. Greenough) Sallust's Catiline, 1901. Home: Roxbury, Mass. Died 1909.

DANIELLS, William Willard, chemist; b. Oakland Co., Mich., 1840; s. Nathaniel I. and Lucinda (Reed) D.; B.S., Mich. Agrl. Coll., 1864, M.S., 1867; Lawrence Scientific Sch. (Harvard), 1867; Halle and Berlin, 1881; (D.Sc., Mich. Agrl. Coll., 1897); m. Hontas Augusta Peabody, June 21, 1871. Asst. in chemistry, Mich. Agrl. Coll., 1864-68; prof. chemistry, 1868-68, prof. agrl. and analytical chemistry, 1869-70, prof. chemistry, 1879-1907 (emeritus), U. of Wis. Chemist Wis. State Geol. Survey, 1872-76; asst. U.S. Geol. Survey, 1882-83; mem. Wis. State Bd. Health, 1885-89. Home: Madison, Wis. Died Oct. 12, 1912.

DANIELS, Arthur Hill, educator; b. East Medway (now Millis), Mass., Oct. 19, 1865; s. Elijah Breck and Roxa (Boyden) D.; A.B., Olivet (Mich.) Coll., 1887; B.D., Yale Univ., 1890; Ph.D., Clark U., 1893; traveled and studied in Europe, 1909-10; m. Eunice Dean, July 21, 1898. Instr. philosophy, 1893-95, asst. prof., 1895-99, prof., Sept. 1, 1899—, acting dean Coll. of Lit. and Arts, Feb. 1911-July 1913, asst. dean Grad. Sch., Nov. 1, 1918, actg. dean, 1919-21, dean, 1921-33, U. of Ill., acting pres., 1933-34, also acting dean Coll. Liberal Arts and Sciences, Oct. 1925-Apr. 1926, 1927-28 and 1931-33, acting pres. and prof. of philosophy emeritus, 1934—. Died Apr. 2, 1940.

DANIELS, Charles Herbert, clergyman; b. Lyme, N.H., July 6, 1847; s. William Pomeroy and H. Ann (Stark) D.; bro. of Fred Harris D.; B.A., Amherst, 1870; graduate of Union Theol. Sem., 1873; (D.D., Amherst, 1892); m. Mary L. Underwood, May 28, 1884. Ordained Congl. ministry, 1873; pastor Montague, Mass., 1873-76, Vine St. Ch., Cincinnati, 1876-83, Second Ch., Portland, Me., 1883-88; dist. sec. at New York, 1888-93, corr. sec. at Boston, 1893-1903, A.B.C.F.M.; pastor Grace Ch., South Framingham, Mass., 1903-11. Home: Wellesley, Mass. Died Aug. 3, 1914.

DANIELS, Charles Nelson, consul; b. Barre, N.Y., July 2, 1849; s. Nelson Fitch and Alenda (Clark) D.; Prep. Sch., Shurtleff Coll., Upper Alton, Ill., 2 yrs.; m. Susie E. Little, Dec. 28, 1877. Postmaster, Willimantic, Conn., 1890-94; judge of probate, Dist. of Windham Co., Conn., 1897-01; auditor of Conn., 1903; Am. consul, Sheffield, Eng., 1903-12, Sherbrooke, Can., Aug., 1912-13. Republican. Unitarian. Home: Willimantic, Conn. Died Dec. 17, 1916.

DANIELS, Frank, actor; b. Dayton, O., 1860; ed. pub. schs., Boston; m. Elyzebeth Wiley Sanson ("Bessie Sanson"), 1895. First appeared on stage as the Sheriff in "Chimes of Normandy," at Chelsea, Mass., 1879; was with Gayety Theatre, Boston; toured in "An Electric Doll"; first appeared in Eng., 1883; played in "Little Puck," for 7 years, later in "The Idol's Eye," "Miss Simplicity," "The Office Boy," "The Tattooed Man," "The Pink Lady," "Wizard of the Nile," "Sergeant Brue," "Girl in the Train," etc. Home: Rye, N.Y. Died Jan. 12, 1935.

DANIELS, Fred Harris, mech. engr.; b. Hanover Centre, N.H., June 16, 1853; s. William Pomeroy and H. Ann (Stark) D.; brother of Charles Herbert D.; M.E., Worcester Poly. Inst., 1873; spl. study in chemistry, under Dr. Thomas M. Drown, of Lafayette Coll.; m. Sarah Lydia White, May 17, 1883. Entered employ Washburn & Moen Mfg. Co., Worcester, 1873, and became gen. supt. and chief engr.; visited Europe, and made spl. studies of advanced methods in mfr. of iron, steel, etc.; apptd. chief engr., Am. Steel & Wire Co. when latter acquired business of Washburn & Moen Co., 1899, and became dir. in co., 1902; apptd. chmn. bd. of engrs. U.S. Steel Corp. when latter acquired interests of Am. Steel & Wire Co., 1901; pres. Washburn & Moen Co., and Worcester Wire Co., 1900—; also mem. bd. engrs. Ind. Steel Co., Gary, and Minn. Steel Co., Duluth. Awarded grand prize and gold medal, Paris Expn., 1900, for achievements in development of wire industry. Republican. Conglist. Home: Worcester, Mass. Died Aug. 30, 1913.

DANIELS, George Henry, gen. passenger agt. N.Y. Central & Hudson River R.R., Apr. 1, 1889-1907; b. Hampshire, Ill., Dec. 1, 1842; rodman engr. corps, N. Mo. R.R.; gen. freight and pass. agt. Chicago & Pacific R.R., 1872-80; gen. ticket agt. Wabash, St. Louis & Pacific, 1880-82; commr. Iowa Trunk Line Assn., Jan.-Oct. 1882; commr. Colo. R.R. Assn., 1882-85; also commr. Utah Traffic Assn., 1884-85; commr. Central Pasenger Com., Jan.-July 1886; asst. commr., 1886-87; vice-chmn., 1887-89, Central Traffic Assn.; also chmn. Eastbound Passenger Com., 1886-89. Home: Buffalo, N.Y. Died 1908.

DANIELS, Joseph Leonard, educator; b. Medway (now Millis), Mass., Aug. 1, 1833; s. Paul and Eliza (Breck) D.; A.B., Yale, 1860, A.M., 1863; grad. Yale Div. Sch., 1863; travel and study in Europe, 1873 and 1888; (D.D., Yale, 1894; LL.D., Olivet, 1905); m. Julia Burrage Allen, Nov. 26, 1863 (died 1903); 2d, Mrs. Minerva Tenney Ellis, Mar. 24, 1907. Asst. librarian, Yale Coll. Library, 1862, 1863; prin. Guilford (Conn.) Inst., 1863-65; prof. Greek, 1865-1906, trustee, 1875-89, acting pres., 1892-93 and 1904, Olivet Coll.; librarian Olivet Coll. Library, 1865-73, 1883-1908. Ordained Congl. ministry, 1876; preached at Olivet Coll., 1880-89; pastor Tryon, N.C., 1909-13, emeritus. Republican. Chaplain Mich. Soc. S.R. Home: Tryon, N.C. Died Oct. 22, 1924.

DANIELS, William S., Washington corr. St. Louis Republic, 1897—; b. Springfield, Mass., Feb. 3, 1861; s. M. T. and Isabella G. Daniels; academic edn. Springfield, Mass.; m. Elizabeth Duvall, 1886. Was stenographer in P.O. Dept.; afterwards P.O. insp.; sec. to v.p. of U.S., 1893-97. Democrat. Home: Brookland, D.C. Died 1904.

DANN, Hollis Ellsworth; b. Canton, Pa., May 1, 1861; s. Judson and Harriet (Harding) D.; grad. Canton High Sch., 1879, Elmira (N.Y.) Business Coll., 1887; music sch., Rochester, N.Y., 1879-80; pvt. instrn., Boston, 1881-83; Mus. D., Alfred U., 1906; m. Lois Hanford, July 10, 1890; children—Hollis Hanford, Margaret Louise, Roger Lewis and Robert Harding (twins). Teacher, voice and piano, 1884-86; prin. Havana (N.Y.) Acad., 1886-87; dir. music, Ithaca schs., 1887-1905; conductor Ithaca Choral Club, 1890-1900; condr. Sage Chapel Choir, Cornell U., 1903-21; condr. Annual Music Festivals, Cornell U., 1904-21; instr. in music, 1903-04, asst. prof., 1904-06, prof. and head dept. of music, 1906-21, Cornell U.; state dir. of music, Pa., 1921-25; head dept. of music edn., New York U., 1925—. Dir. Pa. Summer Session for Supervisors of Music, West Chester, 1922-24; dir. Cornell U. Glee Club, 1889-1921; chmn. music council New York Bd. of Regents, 1910-21; War Dept. song leader, Camp Taylor, Louisville, Ky., 1918-19. Mem. faculty New Sch. of Methods, Boston, 1896-1906; pres. Music Supervisors Nat. Conf., 1920; condr. 1st Nat. High Sch. Chorus, Chicago, 1928-30, Detroit, 1931; condr. Nat. Supervisors Chorus, Chicago, 1934. Republican. Presbyterian. Author: Hollis Dann Music Course, 1915-19; New Manual for Teachers, 1929. Compiler: Christmas Carols and Hymns, 1910; School Hymnal, 1910; Assembly Songs, Vol. I, 1911, Vol. II, 1914; Complete Manual for Teachers, 1912; Standard Anthems, Vol. I, 1917, Vol. II, 1921, Vols. III and IV, 1925; Hollis Dann Song Series, Books 1, 2 and 3, 1935; Conductors Book (guide to song interpretation), 1935. Died Jan. 3, 1939.

DANNAT, William T., painter; b. New York, 1853; pupil of Munich Acad. and Munkacsy. Medal, Paris Salon, 1883; exhibited Paris Expn., 1900. Chevalier, 1889, officer, 1897, comdr., 1900, Legion of Honor, France. Pres. Paris Soc. of Am. Painters; mem. Nat. Inst. Arts and Letters. Gold medal Buffalo Expn., 1901. Died Mar. 12, 1929.

DANNELLY, John Milton, clergyman; b. Camden, Ala., Sept. 19, 1855; s. James Patrick and Louisa Olivia (Gordon) D.; ed. high sch.; (D.D., Southern U., Greensboro, Ala., 1908); m. Lena Augusta Stephens, Dec. 23, 1886. Entered M.E. Ch., S., ministry; pastor in Ala. at Louisville, Wetumpka, Fort Deposit, Bolling and Dothan, Pensacola, Fla., Troy, Ala., and Opelika, Ala.; presiding elder Montgomery Dist., Ala. Conf. Trustee, and financial agt., 1907—, Woman's Coll. of Ala.; pres. Mutual Aid Soc. and mem. bd. edn., Ala. Conf.; dir. Preachers' Interstate Inst., Biloxi, Miss. Chaplain Ala. N.G., on staff Gov. B. B. Comer, with rank of col., 1907-11. K.P. Died Dec. 1931.

DANNER, Harris Leslie, judge; b. near Astoria, Ill., Feb. 13, 1888; s. Aaron B. and Mallissa (Moore) D.; student Rushville (Ill.) Normal Sch., 1904-05; LL.B., Valparaiso (Ind.) Univ., 1909; m. Helen M. Trueblood, Apr. 6, 1921. Teacher rural schs., Schuyler County, Ill., 1906-08; admitted to Okla. bar, 1909, and practiced in Oklahoma City, 1909-38; justice of Supreme Court of Okla., Dec. 1, 1938—. Mem. Bar Commn., State of Okla., 1924-29, chmn., 1929; mem. Com. of Bar Examiners, Okla., 1929-36, pres., 1935; trustee Children's Museum; trustee Rose Hill Cemetery (pres. bd). Served as private, U.S. Army, World War; commd. capt. Judge Adv. Gen. Reserve. Democrat. Mason. Mem. Disciples of Christ Ch. Home: Oklahoma City, Okla. Died Jan. 7, 1941.

DANNER, Peter C., vicar general and chancellor; b. Pittsburgh, Pa., Dec. 24, 1875; s. William and Teresa (Hartman) D.; A.B., 1899, A.M., 1900, S.T.B., 1902, St. Mary's Univ. Sem., Baltimore, Md.; LL.D., Duquesne U., Pittsburgh. Ordained priest R.C. Church, 1903; asst. pastor St. John Baptist Ch., Scottdale, Pa., 1903; dir. Catholic Missionary Aid Soc., 1909; asst. chancellor, 1910, chancellor, 1919, vicar general, 1921—, Diocese of Pittsburgh. Died Feb. 13, 1939.

DANZIGER, Henry, editor; b. Tarnowitz, Prussia, Feb. 7, 1852; s. Ignatius and Charlotte D.; acad. edn. in Germany; came to U.S. 1864; LL.B., Cincinnati Law Sch., 1883; admitted to bar, 1883; m. Mrs. Rosa Lutz, 1906. Editor-in-chief of Cincinnati Volksblatt, 1887—. Mem. board examiners Cincinnati pub. schs., 1885—. Died March 16, 1935.

DARBY, Edwin Tyler, dentist; b. Binghamton, N.Y., Aug. 21, 1845; s. Rev. Chauncey and Mary Ann (Short) D.; Cortland Acad., Homer, N.Y.; D.D.S., Pa. Coll. Dental Surg., 1865; M.D., U. of Pa., 1878, LL.D., 1915; m. Carolyn B. Thomas, 1866. Prof. operative dentistry, Pa. Coll. Dental Surgery, 1876-78; prof. operative dentistry and dental histology, U. of Pa., 1878-1919; retired Sept. 1923, after 60 yrs.' continuous practice. Home: Lansdowne, Pa. Died Dec. 11, 1929.

DARBY, John Eaton, physician; b. S. Williamstown, Mass., Aug. 20, 1835; s. William and Electa (Edwards) D.; A.B., Williams Coll., 1858; M.D., Western Reserve Med. Coll., 1861; m. Julia Frances Wright, Apr. 11, 1861 (died 1867); 2d, Emma Maybell Cox, May 1, 1872 (died 1888). Prof. Latin and Greek, Cleveland Inst., 1858-60; demonstrator anatomy, Western Reserve Med. Coll., 1861-2; surgeon in Civil War, 1862-66; surgeon Cleveland & Pittsburgh R.R., 1867-87; visiting phys. Lakeside Hosp., 1867-87; mem. med. bd. City Hosp., 1895-1908; prof. materia medica and therapeutics, 1867-1906, emeritus prof. therapeutics, 1906, Western Reserve Med. Coll. Died Jan. 4, 1918.

DARBY, William Johnson, clergyman; b. in Lyon Co., Ky., Nov. 17, 1848; s. George F. and Mary (Wyatt) D.; A.B., U. of Mich., 1869, A.M., 1872; B.D., Cumberland U., 1871; (D.D., Lincoln U., Ill., 1882); m. Mary Belle Lambert, May, 1874. Pastor Cumberland Presbyn. Ch., Evansville, Ind., 1871-89; gen. mgr. publishing work, C. P. Ch., 1889-91; sec. Bd. Ministerial Relief, 1892-1901; ednl. sec. C. P. Ch., 1895—. Chiefly instrumental in establishing Woman's Bd. Missions, Bd. of Ministerial Relief (now v.p.) and Christian Endeavor Soc., C. P. Ch. Asst. sec. Presbyn. Bd. of Edn., 1906-11; field sec. for Bd. Relief Presbyn. Ch. U.S.A.; pres. trustees James Milliken U., Decatur, Ill. Republican. Home: Evansville, Ind. Died Feb. 11, 1921.

DARGAN, Edwin Charles, clergyman; b.. Darlington Co., S.C., Nov. 17, 1852; s. John O. B. (D.D.) and Jane Frances (Lide) D.; A.M., Furman U., 1873, Litt. D., 1920; grad. Southern Bapt. Theol. Sem. (then at Greenville, S.C.), 1877; D.D., Washington and Lee, 1888; LL.D., Baylor U., Tex., 1904; m. Lucy A. Graves, June 12, 1878; children—Edwin Preston, John Herbert (dec.), Ethel Forrester (dec.), Mary Lydia (dec.), Henry McCune. In mission work summer of 1874; supplied First Bapt. Ch., Wilmington, N.C., summers of 1875-76; ordained Bapt. ministry, 1876; pastor Botetourt Springs (now Hollins), Big Lick (now Roanoke) and Bonsack, Va., 1877-81, First Ch., Petersburg, Va., 1881-87, Dixon, Calif., 1887-88, Citadel Sq. Ch., Charleston, S.C., 1888-92; prof. in Southern Bapt. Theol. Sem., Louisville, 1892-1907; pastor Glen's Creek Ch., Woodford Co., Ky., 1892-94, 1906-07, First Ch., Macon, Ga., June 1907-Aug. 1917; editor of S.S. Lesson Helps of S.S. Bd. of Southern Bapt. Conv., Nashville, Tenn., Aug. 1917-27. Pres. Southern Baptist Conv., 1911-13; chmn. Internat. S.S. Lessons Com., 1920-21. Author: Notes on Colossians (in Am. Commentary), 1890; Ecclesiology, 1897, 1905; A History of Preaching, Vol. I, 1905, Vol. II, 1912; The Doctrines of Our Faith, 1905; Harmony Hall, Recollections of an Old Southern Home, 1912; An Exposition of the Epistle to the Romans, 1914; The Changeless Christ, and Other Sermons, 1918; The Hope of Glory and Other Sermons, 1919; The Art of Preaching in the Light of Its History, 1922; The Bible Our Heritage, 1924. Died Oct. 26, 1930.

DARGAN, Edwin Preston, prof. French lit.; b. Barboursville, Va., Sept. 7, 1879; s. Edwin Charles and Lucy Augusta (Graves) D.; B.A., Bethel Coll., Russellville, Ky., 1899; U. of Va., 1899-1902; Ph.D., Johns Hopkins, 1906; m. Esterelle Vere Riddett, Cannes, France, June 28, 1910; children—Avise Ethel, Rosamund Vere, Marjorie. Instr. Romance langs., U. of Va., 1906-07, adj. prof., 1907-10; asst. prof. of French, U. of Calif., 1910-11; asst. prof. French lit., 1911-15, asso. prof., 1915-18, prof. since 1918, U. of Chicago. Democrat. Author: The Aesthetic Doctrine of Montesquieu, 1907; Hylas and Other Poems, 1910; Honoré de Balzac—A Force of Nature, 1932; Anatole France, 1937. Joint Author: History of French Literature (with W. A. Nitze), 1922, 3d edit., 1938. Died Dec. 13, 1940.

DARLING, Charles Kimball, lawyer; b. Corinth, Vt., June 28, 1864; s. Joseph and Mary Alice (Knight) D.; grad. Barre (Vt.) Acad., 1881; A.B., 1885, A.M., 1893, Dartmouth; cadet for 2 yrs. at U.S. Mil. Acad., West Point; LL.B., 1896, Boston U. Law Sch.; m. Elizabeth R. Holmes, 1903. Admitted to bar, 1896, and began practice in Boston; instr. criminal law, Boston Univ. Law Sch., 1896-99; U.S. marshal for Dist. of Mass., 1899-1908; clk. U.S. Circuit Court of Appeals, 1st Circuit, U.S. Circuit Court and U.S. Dist. Court, Dist. of Mass

1908-14; also U.S. commr.; referee in bankruptcy, Suffolk Co. Dist., 1914—. Has been prominent in mil. affairs, 1887—, when he was apptd. sergt. maj. 6th Regt. Mass. Vol. Militia, adjt., 1889, maj., 1893; served in Spanish-Am. War as sr. field officer of regt.; elected and commd. col. of regt. after it again became part of M.V.M.; retired brig. gen., M.N.G., 1904. Comdr. in chief Sons of Veterans, 1897-98. Died Dec. 29, 1926.

DARLING, Charles William, soldier, historical writer; b. New Haven, Conn., Oct. 11, 1830; s. Rev. Charles Chauncey D.; ed. N.Y. Univ.; became mem. mil. cabinet of Gov. E. D. Morgan, N.Y.; aide on staff Gen. B. F. Butler, Army of the James; mil. engr.-in-chief, N.Y., on staff of Gov. R. E. Fenton, with rank of brig. gen.; m. Angeline E. Robertson. Was several yrs. pres. Y.M.C.A., Utica, N.Y.; corr. sec. Oneida Hist. Soc.; writer on hist. subjects; received decoration for gratuitous service rendered in connection with hist. literature from Soc. of Science, Letters and Art of London. Home: Utica, N.Y. Died 1905.

DARLING, Flora Adams, author; b. Lancaster, N.H., 1840; d. Harvey and Nancy Dustin (Rowell) Adams; m. Gen. Edward Darling and moved to La. Her husband became a Confederate officer and was killed in the Civil War. Founder, dir. gen. Daughters of the Revolution and United States Daughters, 1812; v.p. Lamperti School of Music; also Edward Irving Darling Mus. Soc., founded in memory of her son, an Am. composer. Author: History D.A.R. and D.R. Societies of Patriotic Organizations, 1901-15; The Senator's Daughter; Senator Athens, C.S.A.; Memories of Virginia, 1907, etc. Died 1909.

DARLING, John Augustus ("August Mignon"), soldier; b. Bucksport, Me., June 7, 1835; s. Amos Buck and Caroline (Hooper) D.; grad. Pa. Mil. Acad., 1849; m. Encarnacion Yniguez, Jan. 28, 1866; 2d, Clara L. Hastings, Oct. 22, 1895. Commd. 2d lt. U.S. Arty., Aug. 5, 1861; 1st lt., May 31, 1862; hon. mustered out, Jan. 1, 1871; apptd. capt. arty., Apr. 24, 1878, with former rank and date of commn. from Dec. 9, 1867; assigned to 1st Arty., Mar. 20, 1879; maj. 5th Arty., July 1, 1892; transferred to 3d Arty., Oct. 7, 1896; retired at his own request, being 62 yrs. of age, June 7, 1897; advanced to rank of lt. col. retired, by act of Apr. 23, 1904. Bvtd. capt. and maj., Mar. 13, 1865, "for gallant and meritorious services during the war." Has published many well-known vocal and instrumental compositions in U.S. and Europe, under pen-name August Mignon. Home: Bucksport, Me. Deceased.

DARLING, Samuel Taylor, pathologist; b. Harrison, N.J., 1872; s. Edmund Adams and Sarah Ann (Patterson) D.; M.D., Coll. Physicians and Surgeons, Baltimore, 1903; m. Nannyrle Llewellyn, Feb. 18, 1905. Chief of Lab., Panama Canal, 1906-15; with Gen. Gorgas on sanitary mission to Rand mines and Rhodesia, South Africa, 1913-14; chmn. bd., under Rockefeller Foundation, to investigate causes of anemia among people of Malaya, Java and Fiji, 1915-17; prof. hygiene and dir. labs. of hygiene, Faculdade de Medicina e Cirurgia de Sao Paulo, Brazil, 1917-20. Fellow (by courtesy) Sch. Hygiene and Pub. Health, Johns Hopkins U., 1921. Home: Baltimore, Md. Died May 21, 1925.

DARLING, William Lafayette, civil engr.; b. Oxford, Mass., Mar. 24, 1856; s. William E. and Cynthia M. (Steere) D.; B.S., Worcester Poly. Inst., 1877, hon. Dr. Engring., 1927; m. Alice E. Bevans, Apr. 15, 1901. Engaged in constrn. and maintenance of steam rys. in various capacities, mostly with the Northern Pacific, 1878-1901; chief engr. St. Andrew's Bay & Chipley R.R., in Fla., 1884; engr. terminals for Burlington R.R., St. Paul and Minneapolis, 1885; chief engr. location and constrn. of Duluth, Watertown & Pacific Ry. and chief engr. Yankton, Sioux Falls R.R., for City of Yankton, later built by G.N. Ry., 1887-88; construction branch lines for N.P. Ry., 1888-91; chief engr. N.P. System, 1901-03; chief engr. Rock Island System, 1903-05, also v.p. Gulf Constrn. Co., building line for the Rock Island between St. Louis and Kansas City; late in 1905 made report on extension of Milwaukee Road from Butte, Mont., to Pacific Coast; chief engr. N.P. Ry., Jan. 1906-Oct. 1916, also v.p. and engr. in charge of engring. and constrn. of Portland & Seattle Ry. from Spokane to Portland; also pres. Union Depot Co., 1906-09. Apptd. asso. mem. U.S. Naval Consulting Bd., 1916; mem. U.S. commn. of ry. experts to Russia, May 1917-Jan. 1918; in nat. and state war work, 1918; cons. engr., St. Paul, 1919-21; mem. Bd. of Economics and Engring. of Nat. Assn. Owners of Ry. Securities, 1922-May 1923; then cons. practice, St. Paul, Minn. Died Oct. 27, 1938.

DARLINGTON, Charles Francis, lawyer; b. Brooklyn, N.Y., Nov. 1, 1860; s. Thomas and Hannah Anne (Goodliffe) D.; A.B., Princeton, 1882, A.M., 1884; LL.B., Columbia, 1884; m. Letitia Craig O'Neill, 1903; children—Charles Francis, Caroline Craig. Practiced in N.Y. City, succeeding father as head of Darlington & Jenkins; retired 1912. With Naval br. Y.M.C.A., etc. Republican. Home: Mount Kisco, N.Y., and N.Y. City. Died Dec. 28, 1938.

DARLINGTON, James Henry, bishop; b. Brooklyn, N.Y., June 9, 1856; s. Thomas and Hannah Anne (Goodliffe) D.; A.B., New York U., 1877, A.M., 1880, D.D., 1895; grad. Princeton Theol. Sem., 1880; Ph.D., Princeton, 1884; LL.D., St. John's, Md., 1905, LL.D., Dickinson, 1907, Lafayette College, Pa., 1927; D.C.T., Halki Greek Sem., Constantinople, 1923; m. Ella Louise Bearns, July 26, 1888; children—Rev. Henry Vane Bearns, Alfred William Bearns (dec.), Rev. Gilbert Sterling Bancroft, Eleanor Townsend (Mrs. J. Ellis Fisher), Rev. Elliott Christopher Bearns, Kate Brampton. Deacon and priest, P.E. Ch., 1882; asst. 1882-83; rector, 1883-1905, Christ Ch., Brooklyn; consecrated first bishop of Harrisburg, Apr. 26, 1905. Archdeacon, Brooklyn, 1896-98; lecturer New York U., 1902-03; chaplain, 47th regt., N.G.S.N.Y. Served as lt. col. on staff gov. of Pa.; mem. Com. Pub. Safety of Pa., World War; declined appmt. on U.S. commn. to Russia. Pres. Serbian Relief Fund in U.S.; hon. v.p. Am. Peace Soc.; mem. advisory com. Nat. Probation Assn. Officer Legion of Honor (France); Grand Comdr. Order Redeemer (Greece); Officer Order St. Sava (Serbia); Comdr. Order Queen Isabella la Catolica (Spain); Comdr. Order of Crown (Italy); Comdr. Order of Leopold II (Belgium). Mason. Knight of Holy Sepulchre (Patriarch of Jerusalem), 1922. Chmn. Commn. to Confer with Eastern Orthodox Chs. and the Old Catholics from Episcopal Ch. of U.S., 1910-25, visiting Constantinople, Athens, etc., 1920, arranging and having signed Concordat between Eastern and Western Chs.; spoke at Pilgrim Fathers' Celebration, Plymouth, Eng., Tercentennial, 1920; rep. Episcopal Ch. Commn. and Am. Bible Soc. in Egypt and Holy Land, 1923, also of Epis. Ch., Life and Work Conf., Stockholm, 1925; dedicated statue of Lincoln, Westminster, London; rep. of Am. Ch. at 1600th Anniversary Nicene Creed, Westminster Abbey, 1925; presented gift of Am. Huguenots to Queen of Holland, at The Hague. Author: In Memoriam; Little Rhymes for Little People; Pastor and People, 1902; Verses by the Way, 1923, 4th series, 1929. Editor of The Hymnal of the Church; composer of hymn tunes, songs, instrumental music, also symphony, "The Sea and the Sea Gulls," 1929. Home: Newport, R.I. Died Aug. 14, 1930.

DARLINGTON, Joseph James, lawyer; b. Due West, S.C., Feb. 10, 1849; s. Henry Dixson and Charlotte Georgiana (Blease) D.; A.B., Erskine Coll., Due West, 1868, A.M., 1872; LL.B., Columbian (now George Washington) U., 1875; (LL.D., Georgetown U., 1888); m. Elizabeth Rachel Meador, July 21, 1885 (died 1890). In practice at Washington, D.C., 1875—; dir. Federal Nat. Bank. Pres. Washington City Orphan Asylum; pres. Baptist Home of D.C.; trustee Erskine Coll. Democrat. Baptist. Died June 24, 1920.

DARLINGTON, Thomas, lawyer; b. Blooming Grove, N.Y., Aug. 29, 1826; s. Peter and Maria (Wilde) D.; ed. common schools Orange Co., N.Y.; admitted as atty. at law and solicitor and counsellor in chancery, June 3, 1847, in New York; in active practice for over 56 yrs.; m. Hannah A. Goodliffe, 1850. Whig, then Republican. Offered territorial chief justiceship, 1872, but declined; appeared against Guiteau, the assassin of President Garfield, 1882; sr. mem. Darlington, Crane & Jenkins, New York, N.Y. Died 1903.

DARNALL, Carl Rogers, army officer; b. Weston, Tex., Dec. 25, 1867; s. Joseph Rogers and Mary Ellen (Thomas) D.; student Carlton Coll., Bonham, Tex., and Transylvania U., Lexington, Ky.; M.D., Jefferson Med. Coll., Phila., 1890; grad. Army Med. Sch., Washington, D.C., 1897; m. Annie Estella Major, Apr. 27, 1892; children—Joseph Rogers, William Major, Carl Robert. Commd. 1st lt. and asst. surgeon, U.S.A., Oct. 26, 1896, and advanced through grades to col., May 15, 1917; brig. gen., Dec. 5, 1929; comdr. Army Med. Center, Washington, D.C., 1929-31, retired Dec. 31, 1931. Served in Spanish-Am. War, Philippine Insurrection, Boxer Rebellion, World War. Fellow Am. Coll. Surgeons. Award: D.S.M. (U.S.). Died Jan. 18, 1941.

DARNALL, William Edgar, surgeon and gynecologist; b. Pearisburgh, Va., 1869; s. Henry T. and Margaret Poague (Johnstone) D.; A.B., Washington and Lee U., 1892; M.D., U. of Va., 1895; m. Elizabeth Nesbitt, Feb. 27, 1907; children—William Edgar, Jean Mauzy. Began practice, Covington, Va., 1895; removed to Atlantic City, N.J., 1896; gynecologist and pres. of staff, Atlantic City Hosp.; surgeon Bamburger Home, Longport, N.J. Cons. surgeon to the Home for Incurables (Longport), North Am. Sanitarium for treatment of surg. tuberculosis; cons. gynecologist Atlantic City Municipal Hosp. Pres. Atlantic Co. Mosquito Extermination Commission; pres. N.J. Bd. Med. Examiners, 1933; diplomate mem. Nat. Bd. Obstetrics and Gynecology. Pres. trustees Atlantic City Fre Pub. Library. Fellow Am. Coll. Surgeons, A.A.A.S., A.M.A. (v.p. 1914). Democrat. Presbyn. Home: Atlantic City, N.J. Died Dec. 27, 1937.

DARNELL, Henry Faulkner, clergyman; b. London, Eng., June 24, 1831; s. Rev. James D.; ed. Trinity Coll., Dublin, and Queen's Coll., Cambridge; (D.D., Kenyon Coll., 1875); m. Augusta Balfour, of Cheltenham, Eng., 1857. Classical master, Royal Sch., Raphoe, Ireland, 1853-56; deacon, 1858; priest, 1859, P.E. Ch., asst. at Strensall and Bossal, Eng., 1858-60; rector Stanstead, Que., 1860-61, St. John's, Que., 1861-74; prin. and chaplain, Hellmuth Colls., Can., 1874-83; canon Christ Ch. Cathedral, London, Ont., and pvt. and examining chaplain, Huron, Ont., 1877-83; rector Avon, N.Y., 1883-1904, St. Mary's, Detroit, 1905-07. Home: Phillipsburg, N.J. Died Jan. 1917.

DARROW, Clarence (S.), lawyer; b. Kinsman, O., Apr. 18, 1857; ed. Ohio pub. schs.; admitted to bar, 1878; twice married; 1 son (1st marriage), Paul. Formerly corp. counsel City of Chicago, and atty. for North Western Ry. Has been identified with many prominent cases of recent yrs., notably in cases against monopolies, including litigation against gas trust in Chicago, litigation for City of Chicago against Street Ry. Co.; chief counsel for anthracite miners in the anthracite coal strike arbitration at Scranton and Phila., 1902-03, commn. apptd. by President Roosevelt; counsel in Debs strike case and large number of labor injunction and labor conspiracy cases on side of labor; platform speaker. Elected Ill. Legislature, 1902. Active in polit. campaigns as Independent Democrat. Counsel for McNamara brothers in Los Angeles Times dynamite case, 1911; atty. for defendants in Moyer, Haywood and Pettibone case, for murder of Governor Steunenburg, of Ida.; atty. for Loeb and Leopold, Chicago, 1924, and for Scopes evolution case, Dayton, Tenn., 1925; atty., Kidd conspiracy case in Oshkosh, Wis.; O. Sweet case in Detroit; Fortescue-Massie case in Honolulu. Author: Prohibition Mania; Persian Pearl (essays); Resist Not Evil; Farmington (novel); An Eye for an Eye; Crime, Its Cause and Treatment; The Story of My Life, 1932; Infidels and Heretics (with Wallace Rice), 1933. Home: Chicago, Ill. Died Mar. 13, 1938.

DARSIE, Marvin Lloyd, prof. edn.; b. Cleveland, O., Feb. 18, 1887; s. Lloyd and Cora Belle (Marvin) D.; Lewis Inst., Chicago, 1903-06; B.S., Hiram (O.) Coll., 1908; A.M., Stanford, 1912, Ph.D., 1924; m. Grace Wharton, June 23, 1910; children—Marvin Lloyd, Jean Elisabeth, Barbara Ann. High sch. instr., Kendallville, Ill., Glendale, Calif., and Los Angeles, 1908-14; instr. in edn., Los Angeles State Normal Sch., 1914-19; asst. prof. edn., U. of Calif. at Los Angeles, 1919-27, prof. edn., 1927—, dean of Teachers Coll., 1922—. Mem. Disciples of Christ Ch. Author: (monograph) Mental Capacity of American Born Japanese Children, 1926. Died Jan. 24, 1940.

DART, Carlton Rollin, civil engr.; b. Lansing, Mich., Feb. 1, 1862; s. Rollin Charles and Sarah Elizabeth (Darling) D.; B.S., Mich. Agrl. Coll., 1881; post grad. in engring., U. of Mich., 1882-83; m. Ella Weinland, Feb. 8, 1908 (died 1923). Asst. to city engr., Lansing, Mich., 1881-82; draftsman Marquette & Western R.R., Marquette, Mich., 1883-84, G.R.&I. Ry., Grand Rapids, 1885-86; asst. engr., U.P. System, on constn. of terminals, 1886-91; in gen. engring. work, 1891-97; in bridge, structural and waterway engring., 1897—; bridge engr. Sanitary Dist. of Chicago, Feb., 1901-11, asst. chief engr., 1912, chief bridge engr., 1913-21, cons. engr. and bridge engr., Chicago, 1921—. Died June 23, 1929.

DART, Henry Plauché, lawyer; b. Fort St. Philip, La., Feb. 5, 1858; s. Henry and Mary (Plauché) D.; ed. pub. schs., New Orleans, and by pvt. study in law office; m. Mary Lytle, d. Judge W. F. Kernan, of Clinton, La., Sept. 23, 1882 (died 1912); children Henry P., William K. (dec.), May W., John, Benjamin W., Sally, Edith (Mrs. H. Grady Price). Admitted to La. bar, 1879, to practice before Supreme Court of U.S., 1893; sr. mem. Dart & Dart, New Orleans; pres. Harvey Canal & Improvement Co., Joseph Rathborne Lumber Co.; lecturer on History of the Law in Louisiana, Loyola U., 1920-22. Chmn. com. on admission and disbarment, Supreme Court of La., 1898-1908, also of Centenary Celebration Com. of Supreme Court of La., 1913; projector, and mem. New Orleans Court House Commn., 1906-21 (pres. 1916-21); chmn. U.S. Legal Advisory Bd. for New Orleans, 1917. Editor La. Hist. Quarterly, 1922—; pres. La. State Mus, 1926—; archivist La. Hist. Soc. Democrat. Methodist. Supervised recovery of Records of the French Superior Council of La. (1717-69) and Spanish Judicial Records of La. (1769-1803); wrote history of Superior Court of Ty. of Orleans (1804-12) and of Supreme Court of La. (1813-1912). Died Sept. 27, 1934.

D'ARVILLE, Camille, actress; b. Holland, 1863; 1st appeared in opera, Strand Theatre, London; came to U.S., 1888, to take rôle of Anita in "The Queen's Mate," Broadway Theatre, New York. Became mem. of Casino Co. and later of The Bostonians; then with E. E. Rice's Co. and after that as a star at the head of her own company. Died Sept. 9, 1932.

DARWIN, Charles Carlyle, librarian; b. Paris, Tenn., Jan. 27, 1848; s. Charles and Mary (Platt) D.; A.B., Oberlin, 1868, A.M., 1873; Union Theol. Sem., 1868-70; m. Gertrude Bascom, Nov. 25, 1880 (died 1911). Lit. work in New York, co-worker with Dr. Lyman Abbott, 1870-72; prof. Hebrew, Howard U., 1872; librarian in Library of Congress, Washington, in charge of Smithsonian Library, 1872-82; librarian, 1882-1902, bibliographer, 1902-11, U.S. Geol. Survey; also librarian Bureau of Ethnology, Smithsonian Instn., 1882-94; bibliographer, Bur. of Soils, Dept. Agr., 1911-22. Deceased.

DARWIN, Gertrude Bascom; b. Middlebury, Vt., May 19, 1855; d. William Franklin and Anne Field (Strong) Bascom; A.B., Vassar, 1878; finished art studies Geneva and Dresden, 1878-79; m. Charles Carlyle Darwin, Nov. 25, 1880. Pres. Aurora (W.Va.) Library Assn., 1893; librarian-gen., 1897-99, treas.-gen., 1899-1903; historian-gen., 1909-11, Nat. Soc. D.A.R.; nat. v.p. in charge of orgn. of local socs. Children of the Am. Revolution, 1903-07. Author of several D.A.R. reps.; asst. probation officer, Juvenile Court, Washington, D.C., 1906—. Died 1911.

DASHIELL, William Robert, army officer; b. Mecklenburg Co., Va., Apr. 3, 1863; s. Thomas M.D.; grad. U.S. Mil. Acad., 1888; Army Sch. of the Line, 1909; Army War Coll., 1915; m. Ida L. Pearson, Nov. 6, 1889. Commd. add. 2d lt. 8th Inf., June 11, 1888; promoted through grades to col., May 15, 1917; brig. gen. N.A., Apr. 12, 1918. Served in Sioux Indian campaign, 1890-91; prof. mil. science and tactics, N. Ga. Agrl. Coll., 1892-95; at posts in Ariz. and Utah, 1896-99; in Philippines in comd. Co. C, 24th Inf., 1899; with Lawton's Column on march through San Isidor and San José; again in Philippines, 1906-08; comd. Madison Barracks, N.Y., Feb.-May 1908; comdt. Va. Poly. Inst., 1909-11; at Ft. Sheridan, Ill., 1911-13, Texas City, Tex., 1913-14; Army War Coll., Washington, D.C., 1914-15, Ft. Shafter, H.T., 1915-17. Organized 43d Inf. at Ft. Douglas, Utah, Aug.-Nov. 1917; at Camp Pike, Ark., 1917-18, New Orleans, Feb.-May 1918, Camp Forrest, Ga., May-June 1918, Camp Upton, N.Y., June-July 1918; arrived in France, July 26, 1918; apptd. comdr. 11th Brigade Inf., 6th Div., 5th Army Corps, A.E.F., July 1918; in training area to Sept. 3; in Vosges sector, Sept. 3-Oct. 12; comd. div. in support of 1st Army during Meuse-Argonne drive, Oct. 26-Nov. 6; occupied Artoise, Nov. 4-6; marched to Verdun, Nov. 6-12, 1918; left France for U.S., June 5, 1919; assigned sta. Schofield Barracks, H.T., July 12, 1919. Home: Norfolk, Va. Died Mar. 16, 1939.

DASKAM, Walter Duryee, banker; b. New Haven, Conn., Sept. 18, 1865; s. Theodore James and Sara (Stanley) D.; grad. King Sch., Stamford, Conn., 1882; m. Harriet Agnes Tilley, June 3, 1897; 1 dau., Elizabeth Stanley (Mrs. Wilton A. Pierce). Began as messenger, Stamford (Conn.) Nat. Bank, 1882, clk., 1882-91; treas. Stamford Trust Co., 1891-1918, v.p., 1918-23, pres., 1923—. Corpl., Conn. N.G., 1884-90, capt., 1917-19. Treas., Town of Stamford, 1894-1903, mem. bd. finance, 1914-23. Republican. Episcopalian. Died Jan. 22, 1932.

DATER, Alfred Warner, utility exec.; b. Brooklyn, N.Y., Aug. 23, 1872; s. Jacob Henry and Adda Helen (McMurray) D.; student Brooklyn Poly. Inst., 1886-92; Ph.B., Yale, 1895; m. Grace Carroll Ferguson, Nov. 23, 1898; children—Walton Ferguson, Alfred Warner, Philip. Began as machinist apprentice, 1895; machinist Pa. R.R., Fort Wayne, Ind., 1895-97; asst. gen. supt. Kings Co. Electric Light & Power Co., Brooklyn, 1897-98; treas. Edison Electric Illuminating Co., Brooklyn, 1898-1903; treas. Stamford (Conn.) Gas & Electric Co., 1904-11, v.p. and gen. mgr., 1911-17, pres., 1917—; pres. Stamford Savings Bank, Morewood Realty Co.; v.p. Stamford Water Co. Vice-pres. Stamford Hosp.; mem. nat. exec. bd. Boy Scouts of America. Episcopalian. Home: Stamford, Conn. Died Feb. 21, 1938.

DAUGHERTY, Charles M., statistician; b. Waynesville, O., Feb. 19, 1854; s. James Henry and Permelia A. (Goe) D.; A.B., U. of Mich., 1878; m. Susan Peyton Telfair, Aug. 26, 1886. Corr. Chicago Inter Ocean, at Atlanta, Ga., 1878-79; in 2d comptroller's office, U.S. Treasury Dept., Washington, 1880-85; care of agrl. and timber interests in northern Ind., 1886-93; with U.S. Dept. of Agr., 1894—; European agt. of Dept., at London, 1905-07; chief of div. of research and ref., Bur. of Statistics, Washington, D.C., 1908-13, statis. scientist, 1918—. Died July 10, 1919.

DAUGHERTY, Harry Micajah, atty. gen. of U.S.; b. Washington C.H., Ohio, Jan. 26, 1860; s. John H. and Jane A. (Draper) D.; LL.B., U. of Mich., 1881; m. Lucie Walker, Sept. 3, 1884 (dec.). Began practice at Washington C.H., 1881; moved to Columbus, O., 1893; mem. Daugherty, Todd & Rarey, 1902-21. Mem. Ohio Ho. of Rep. from Fayette Co., 2 terms, 1890-94; atty. gen. of U.S. in cabinet of Presidents Harding and Coolidge, Mar. 4, 1921-Mar. 28, 1924 (resigned); acquitted of charges of conspiracy to defraud the U.S. Govt., 1927. Methodist. Author: The Inside Story of the Harding Tragedy (with Thomas Dixon), 1932. Home: Columbus, O. Died Oct. 12, 1941.

DAUGHERTY, Lewis Sylvester, zoölogist; b. Belmont Co., Ohio, Aug. 10, 1857; s. Samuel and Rachel Ann (Mechem) D.; student, Ill. State Normal U., Normal, Ill., 1881-82; B.S., U. of Ill., 1889, M.S., 1893; grad. student, U. of Chicago, 1894-96; Ph.D., Ill. Wesleyan U., 1901; spl. study, various summer schs. and in univs. of Germany, 1907; m. Millie Crum, July 8, 1885. Prof. science, 1889-92, biology, 1892-94, Township High Sch., Ottawa, Ill.; prof. natural science, 1897-1900, zoölogy, 1900-13, State Normal Sch., Kirksville, Mo.; prof. zoölogy and chemistry, Mo. Wesleyan Coll., 1913—. Republican. Methodist. Mason. Author: (with wife) Principles of Economic Zoölogy, 1912; Field and Laboratory Guide, 1912. Home: Cameron, Mo. Died Feb. 28, 1919.

DAULTON, George, author; b. Knox Co., Mo., Oct. 18, 1861; s. Francis Marion and Annie Victoria (Bitler) D.; ed. at home; m. Agnes Warner McClelland, Dec. 9, 1900. Life mem. Shakespeare Soc. of New York. Author: The Helter-Skelters, 1909. Home: New Brighton, N.Y. Died Jan. 29, 1913.

D'AUNOY, Rigney, med. dean; b. New Orleans, La., Aug. 8, 1890; s. Joseph and Zelina (Chretien) D'A.; B.S., Tulane U., New Orleans, 1910, M.D., 1914; unmarried. Asst. pathologist, New Orleans Dispensary, 1916-17; asst. pathologist Charity Hosp. of La., 1919-24, pathologist and dir. of albs., 1928—; instr. in pathology and bacteriology, Tulane U., 1919-24; prof. of pathology and bacteriology, La. State U. Sch. of Medicine, 1931—, dean, 1937—. Served as dir. of labs., Base Hosp. No. 86 A.E.F., 1917-19. Decorated Commendatore, Royal Crown of Italy, 1939. Democrat. Catholic. Home: New Orleans, La. Died Sept. 17, 1941.

DAVENPORT, Bennett Franklin, medico-legal expert; b. Cambridge, Mass., May 28, 1845; s. Charles and Joan Fullerton (Hagar) D.; A.B., Harvard, 1867, A.M., 1870, M.D., 1871; M.D., Coll. Phys. and Surg. (Columbia), 1871; studied U. of Tübingen 1 yr.; m. Annie Emeline Coolidge, July 23, 1873; children—Grace Coolidge (Mrs. Henry J. Winslow), John C., Anna C. (Mrs. Clifford M. Holland), Benita C. Began gen. practice of medicine at Boston; from 1875, when was apptd. coroner for Suffolk Co., Mass., devoted mostly to medico-legal specialties, among them being the expert examination of questioned documents to determine the authorship of the handwriting; expert upon many of the more notable court trials; expert for State Record Commn. upon the official record ink, 1895—. Prof. chemistry, Mass. Coll. Pharmacy, 1879-86; dairy insp., City of Boston, 1882-85; chemist, Mass. State Bd. Health, 1882-92, State Dairy Bur., 1892-1921; chmn. Watertown health, park and water bds. Delegate for the revision of U.S. Pharmacopœia, 1880, 90, 1900. Home: Watertown, Mass. Died June 2, 1927.

DAVENPORT, Eugene, agriculturist; b. Woodland, Mich., June 20, 1856; s. George Martin and Esther (Sutton) D.; B.S., Mich. Agrl. Coll., 1878, M.S., 1884, M.Agr., 1895, LL.D., 1907; D.Sc. from Iowa State College, 1920; also LL.D., Univ. of Ky., 1913, Univ. of Ill., 1931; m. Emma Jane Coats, Nov. 2, 1881 (now dec.); children—Dorothy (dec.), Margaret (Mrs. H. B. Tukey, dec.). Asst. botanist Expt. Sta., 1888-89, prof. practical agr. and supt. of farm, 1889-91, Mich. Agrl. Coll.; pres. Collegio Agronomica, Sao Paulo, Brazil, 1891-92; dean Coll. of Agr., Univ. of Ill., 1895-1922; dir. Agrl. Expt. Station, and prof. thremmatology, U. of Ill., Sept., 1896-1922 (emeritus). Author: Principles of Breeding, 1907; Education for Efficiency, 1909; Domesticated Animals and Plants, 1910; Vacation on the Trail, 1923; The Farm, 1927. Republican. Conglist. Home: Woodland, Mich. Died Mar. 31, 1941.

DAVENPORT, Frances Gardiner, historian; b. Stamford, Conn., Apr. 30, 1870; d. Amzi Benedict and Jane Joralemon (Dimon) D.; Barnard Coll., New York, 1890-91; A.B., Radcliffe Coll., Cambridge, Mass., 1894, A.M., 1896; London (Eng.) Sch. of Economics, 1897; Assn. of Collegiate Alumnæ, European fellowship, 1902-03, studied at Cambridge, Eng.; fellow U. of Chicago, 1903-04, Ph.D., 1904; unmarried. Instr. history, Erasmus Hall High Sch., Brooklyn, 1898-1901, Vassar Coll., 1904-05; asst. in dept. hist. research, Carnegie Instn., Washington, D.C., 1905—. Author: The Economic Development of a Norfolk Manor, 1906. Compiler of List of Printed Original Materials for English Manorial and Agrarian History, 1894; (joint) Guide to the Manuscript Materials for the History of the United States to 1783, in the British Mus., etc., 1908. Editor of European treaties bearing on the history of the U.S. to 1648, 1917. Deceased.

DAVENPORT, Frederick Parker, clergyman; b. Troy, N.Y., June 3, 1853; s. Charles P. and Jannette R. D.; grad. St. Stephen's Coll., 1873 (D.D., 1888); Gen. Theol. Sem., 1876; m. June 7, 1883, Fanny N. Willis, Metropolis, Ill. P.E. clergyman; tutor Seabury Divinity Sch., 1875-76; instr. cannon law, Western Theol. Sem., Chicago, 1886; from 1886 mem. and from 1892 chmn. com. on canons Gen. Conv. of the Episcopal Ch.; pres. standing com. Diocese of Tenn. Rector Ch. of Redeemer, Cairo, Ill., 1881-91, Calvary Ch., Memphis, 1891-1905; prof. canon law and ch. history, Western Theol. Sem., Chicago, July, 1905—. Died 1909.

DAVENPORT, George Edward, botanist; b. Boston, Mass., August 3, 1833; educated Boston schs.; has resided in Medford from 1875; devoted much attention to botany research; best known for his work on the ferns. One of founders Middlesex Field Club, which became Middlesex Inst.; became mem., 1872, of Mass. Hort. Soc. to which he gave, 1875, his collection of ferns now known as the Davenport Herbarium; was made life mem. of soc. and given Appleton gold medal. Has written various monographs and papers on ferns. Home: Medford, Mass. Died 1907.

DAVENPORT, Herbert Joseph, univ. prof.; b. Wilmington, Vt., Aug. 10, 1861; s. Charles N. and Louise (Haynes) D.; Ph.B., U. of S.D., 1894; Harvard Law Sch., 1884-86; U. of Leipzig, 1890; École des Sciences Politiques, Paris, 1890-91; Ph.D., U. of Chicago, 1898; m. Harriet Crandall, Jan. 6, 1911; children—Martin Warren, John Byrne. Prin. high sch., Lincoln, Neb., 1899-1902; instr. polit. economy, 1902-04, asst. prof., 1902-07, asso. prof., 1907-08, U. of Chicago; head dept. polit. economy, 1908-14, and dean School of Commerce, 1914-16, Univ. of Missouri; prof. economics, Cornell Univ., 1916—. Democrat. Author: Outlines of Economic Theory, 1896; Elementary Economic Theory, 1898; Principles of Grammar (Davenport and Emerson), 1898; Value and Distribution, 1908; Economies of Enterprise, 1913. Home: Ithaca, N.Y. Died June 16, 1931.

DAVENPORT, Homer Calvin, cartoonist; b. Silverton, Ore., March 8, 1867; reared on farm in Ore.; never attended art schools; no school edn. Has been jockey; railroad fireman; clown in circus. Given employment, 1892, on San Francisco Examiner; taken to New York by W. R. Hearst, 1895; from 1895 on New York Journal; originated the Mark Hanna $-mark suit of clothes and the giant figure of the trusts in 1899; his work caused attempt to pass anti-cartoon bill in New York, 1897. In 1906 was granted permission by the Sultan of Turkey to export 27 Arabian horses from the desert of Arabia to America (said to be the only real Arabian horses in America); en route to the desert he drew the only picture ever made of the Sultan; while there was made the desert Brother of Akmut Haffez, the great Bedouin. Author: Davenport's Cartoons; The Bell of Silverton, and Other Short Stories of Oregon; The Dollar or the Man? 1900. Home: Morris Plains, N.J. Died May 2, 1912.

DAVENPORT, Ira, capitalist; b. Hornellsville, N.Y., June 28, 1841; State senator, 1877-81; State comptroller, 1881-83; defeated for re-election, 1883; defeated for gov. by D. B. Hill, 1885; mem. Congress, 1885-89. Republican. Home: Bath, N.Y. Died 1904.

DAVENPORT, James Henry, surgeon; b. Fall River, Mass., Mar. 17, 1862; s. William and Julia Slocum (Gifford) D.; Ph.B., Brown U., 1883; M.D., U. of Vt., 1885; M.D., Harvard, 1887; unmarried. Interne R.I. Hosp., Providence, 1885-86, Boston Lying-In Hosp., 1887; asst. surgeon dept. of gynecology, R.I. Hosp., 1888-95, surgeon, 1895-1917, cons. surgeon, 1917—. Maj. surgeon, R.I.N.G., 1903-08. Mem. City Council, Providence, 1912-14. Dir. Providence Athenaeum, 1918-21. Democrat. Unitarian. Mason. Author: Literary Doctors of Medicine, 1926. Died Oct. 15, 1928.

DAVENPORT, James LeRoy, U.S. commr. of pensions; b. Hinsdale, N.H., Jan. 27, 1845; s. Lockhart and Mary C. (Merrill) D., and desc. of Thomas D., Dorchester, Mass., about 1640; ed. common schs. and Harris Acad., nr. Brattleboro, Vt.; m. Ella A. Carpenter, Dec. 6, 1868. Pvt. Co. B, 40th Wis. Inf., 1864-65; clk. in store, Keene, N.H., 1866-70; traveling salesman, Boston house, 1870-71; clk. U.S. Pension Bur., 1881-97, 1st deputy commr. of pensions, 1897-1909, commr. of pensions, Nov. 27, 1909-13. Republican. Home: Keene, N.H. Died Apr. 2, 1914.

DAVENPORT, James Sanford, judge; b. nr. Gaylesville, Ala., Sept. 21, 1864; s. W. A. J. and Amanda C. D.; family moved to Conway, Ark., 1880; ed. acad., Greenbrier, Ark.; read law under Col. G. W. Bruce, Conway; m. Gulielma Ross, 1892 (died 1898); m. 2d, Byrd Ironside, June 15, 1907 (both citizens by blood of Cherokee Nation); children—Millard D. (dec.), Grace, Mrs. Dorothy Radle. Admitted to bar, 1890; moved to Muskogee, Ind. Ty., 1890, to Vinita, Okla., 1893; mem. lower house of Cherokee legislature 2 terms, 1897-1901 (speaker of House, 1900-01); an atty. for Cherokee Nation, 1899-1907; mayor of Vinita 2 terms, 1903-05; mem. 60th Congress (1907-09) and 62d to 64th Congresses (1911-17), 3d and 1st Okla. dists.; became judge Criminal Court of Appeals of Okla., Jan. 1927. Democrat. Presbyn. Died Jan. 3, 1940.

DAVENPORT, John Gaylord, clergyman; b. Wilton, Conn., Nov. 24, 1840; s. Charles Augustus and Sarah Maria (Gaylord) D.; A.B., Williams, 1863, A.M., 1866 (D.D., 1893); studied Union Theol. Sem., 1864-65; tutor, Williams Coll., 1865-67, and studied with Dr. Mark Hopkins during same time; m. Alice Westcott, Nov. 29, 1866. Ordained Congl. ministry, July 1, 1868; pastor Park St. Ch., Bridgeport, Conn., 1868-81, 2d Ch., Waterbury, 1881-1911 (emeritus).

Moderator Conn. Gen. Congl. Ministers, 1897. Author: The Fulfillment, 1900; Something Beyond, and Other Poems, 1914; Life of Moses Stuart; Experiences and Observations by the Way—an Autobiography, 1917. Home: Waterbury, Connecticut. Died June 9, 1922.

DAVENPORT, R(euben) Briggs, journalist, author; b. New York, N.Y.; s. David Marshall and Hannah (Briggs) D.; ed. Coll. City of N.Y., 1869-71. Mem. staff of New York Herald, 1872-82; spl. corr. U.S. Govt. gold expdn. Black Hills and Sioux Indian reservation, 1875; with Gen. Crook's column in Sioux Cheyenne uprising; was a volunteer scout in the famous "Starvation March" from the Yellowstone to the Black Hills; established the Morning News, New Haven, Conn., 1882; asso. editor Morning News, Paris, 1884-85; editor Star and Herald, Panama, 1886; editorial writer Chronicle, San Francisco, 1886-87; resumed editorship Morning News, New Haven, 1890; lit. editor New York Commercial Advertiser, 1895-96. Spl. corr. Asso. Press in Haiti, Jamaica and Cuba during Spanish-Am. War; later corr. New York Times, and Public Ledger, in London and Paris; lit. critic Continental Daily Mail, Paris, 1914-17; editor Am. soldiers' edition of La Petite Gironde, Bordeaux, 1918-19; chief editorial writer Paris edition The New York Herald, July 1920—. Quaker. Author: The Yorktown Campaign, 1881; Loyal Arms, 1886; The Death Blow to Spiritualism, 1888; The Genesis (1st vol. of a history of the German-European War), 1916; L'Énergie Britannique et la Guerre (in French), 1916; What the British Empire is Doing in the War (London), 1916; The Nobler Love (a romance of American life), 1928. Died Mar. 11, 1932.

DAVENPORT, Richard Graham, rear adm., U.S.N.; b. Washington, D.C., Jan. 11, 1849; s. Capt. Henry Kollock (U.S.N.) and Jennie Brent (Graham) D.; apptd. from Ga., Sept. 29, 1864, and grad. U.S. Naval Acad., 1869; instrn. in torpedoes and electricity at torpedo station, Newport, R.I., 1875 and 1881; ordnance instrn. duty, Washington, D.C., Navy Yard, in winter 1880-81; attended course of lectures in internat. law and naval science, Naval War Coll., Newport, terms of 1887 and 1902; m. Serena Hale Gilman, Nov. 20, 1884. Commd. ensign U.S.N., July 12, 1870; promoted through grades, retiring after more than 42 yrs.' active service, June 30, 1907, as commodore, while in command of 1st class battleship Georgia. On shore duty served as aid to rear adm. representing Navy Dept. at Centennial Expn., Phila., 1875-76; on temporary duty at Chicago Expn., 1893; served as mem. Bd. Civ. Service Examiners for Nautical Experts. Pres. permanent Gen. Court Martial, also navigation and equipment officer and sr. mem. bd. of inspection, Labor Bd. and Wages Bd., Navy Yard, Washington, D.C., May 1902-Aug. 1906, also mem. Naval Examining and Retiring bds., 1906; asst. to chief of Bur. of Navigation and in charge of the detail of officers, Bur. of Navigation, 1897-98, and in charge from time to time of various divisions of the Hydrographic Office, Bur. Navigation; afloat served as a midshipman and as watch and division officer, navigating and exec. officer in N. Atlantic, S. Atlantic, Pacific, Asiatic, Training and European squadrons, also as aid on staff of comdr.-in-chief of Asiatic Sta., served as flag lt. to Commodore J. C. Watson, during war with Spain, 1898-99, 2d in command of fleet blockading on coast of Cuba, and later comdr.-in-chief Eastern Squadron; was attached to and aboard U.S.S. Oregon, off Santiago, Cuba, when Spanish gen. comdg. capitulated; as a lt. comdr. in command U. S.S. Fishhawk, investigated radius of dispersion of star fish in waters of Narragansett Bay, and in 1898-99, with party of scientists aboard, made biol. survey of waters around island of Puerto Rico and vicinity, and as comdr. in 1900-02 comd. U.S. training ship Essex and as capt. comd. battleship Georgia at opening of Jamestown Expn., 1907. Awarded West India Campaign Medal, War with Spain, 1898-99, and (Admiral) Sampson Medal, with bars for naval engagements. During World War on active duty, Jan. 26, 1918-June 1, 1919, at Navy Yard, Brooklyn, as sr. mem. Permanent Bd. of Investigation. Home: Washington, D.C. Died May 30, 1926.

DAVEY, James Charles, clergyman, educator; b. New York, N.Y., Sept. 19, 1869; s. Patrick C. and Louisa B. (Gilhooley) D.; B.A., St. Francis Xavier's Coll., New York, 1897, M.A., 1906; theol. studies, Woodstock (Md.) Coll. Ordained priest R.C. Ch., 1908; prof. Latin, Greek and English, St. Joseph's Coll., Phila., 1901-05; v.p. and dean Brooklyn (N.Y.) Coll., 1908-10; research work, St. Andrew-on-Hudson, 1910-11; v.p. and dean St. Joseph's Coll., Phila., 1911-14; pres. same, and rector Gesu Ch., Phila., 1914-18; v.p. and dean Gonzaga Coll., Washington, D.C., 1918-28; v.p. and dean St. Peter's Coll., Jersey City, N.J., 1928-29, treas., 1929-32; asst. rector, St. Joseph's Ch., Phila., and Moderator, St. Joseph's Cath. Action Club, 1932—. Mem. Knights of Columbus. Died Nov. 1935.

DAVEY, John, tree surgeon; b. Somersetshire, Eng., June 6, 1846; s. Samuel and Ann (Shopland) D.; largely self-ed.; m. Bertha A. Reeves, Sept. 21, 1879. Learned floriculture and landscape architecture, Torquay, Eng., 1866-72; came to U.S. and settled at Warren, O., 1873; moved to Kent, O., 1881; introduced tree surgery, 1890; pres. Davey Tree Expert Co. and Davey Inst. Tree Surgery (school), 1908—. Mem. Christian (Disciples) Ch. Author: The Tree Doctor, 1901; A New Era in Tree Growing, 1905; Davey's Primer on Trees and Birds, 1905; Instruction Books on Tree Surgery and Fruit Growing, Nos. 1-23, 1914. Home: Kent, O. Died Nov. 8, 1923.

DAVEY, Robert C., congressman, mcht.; b. New Orleans, Oct. 22, 1853; grad. St. Vincent's Coll., Cape Girardeau, Mo., 1871; elected to State senate, 1879, 1884 and 1892; pres. pro tempore of senate, sessions of 1884 and 1886; judge 1st recorder's court, New Orleans, 1880-88; defeated for mayor of New Orleans, April 1888; mem. Congress, 1891-93, and 1897-1909, 2d La. dist. Democrat. Home: New Orleans, La. Died 1908.

DAVIDSON, Alfred James, ry. official; b. Decatur, Ill., Apr. 14, 1863; grad. high sch., Lexington, Ill., 1880. Began with C.&A. R.R., 1880, as station baggage master, later night telegraph operator, day operator and station agt.; foreman transfer platform of what is now St.L.S.W. Ry., at Birds Point, Mo., 1884-85; bill clk. and baggage master at Waco, same rd., 1885-88; later train dispatcher, clk. in div. supt.'s office and clk. gen. freight office; chief train dispatcher and train master San Antonio and Aransas Pass Ry., 1888-93; supt. Northern div. G.,C.&S.F. Ry., at Ft. Worth, Tex., 1893-98; supt. transportation St.L.&S.F. R.R. at St. Louis, 1898-1901; gen. supt. same rd., 1901-04; pres., same rd., C.&E.I. R.R. and Evansville & Terre Haute R.R. to 1909; supt. Portland div., Spokane, Portland & Seattle Ry., 1914-17, later gen. supt. now gen. manager. Deceased.

DAVIDSON, Anstruther, M.D.; b. Watten, Scotland, Feb. 19, 1860; s. George and Ann (Macadam) D.; M.B., C.M., U. of Glasgow, 1881, M.D., 1887; came to U.S., 1889; in med. practice, Los Angeles, 1889—; m. Alice Merritt, June 24, 1897; children—Ronald A., Merritt T. Student and investigator in botany and entomology; has described several new species of plants. Fellow Southern Calif. Acad. Sciences (pres. 1893-94), editor of its Bull., 1902—. Asso. prof. dermatology, U. of Southern Calif., 1909—. Author: Plants of Los Angeles County, 1892; Flora of Southern California, 1923. Died April 3, 1932.

DAVIDSON, Augustus Cleveland, clergyman; b. Franklin Co., Mo., Dec. 3, 1846; s. Samuel M. and America A. D.; A.B., Georgetown (Ky.) Coll., 1871, A.M., 1874; D.D., 1886, LL.D., 1904, Howard Coll., Ala.; LL.D., Georgetown Coll., Ky., 1920; m. Elizabeth Stevenson Keene, Nov. 17, 1874; children—Mattie C. (Mrs. T. F. Seale), Allan Keene (dec.), Marion Tabb, Harry Frazer. Ordained Bapt. ministry, 1871; pastor, Eminence, Ky., 1871-76, Bloomington, Ind., 1876-79, Aurora, Ind., 1879-84, Marion, Ala., 1884-87, 1st Ch., Covington, Ky., 1887-93; pres. of Georgetown Coll., 1893-98; pastor South Side Ch., Birmingham, Ala., 1898-1906, Murfreesboro, Tenn., 1906-08, 1st Ch., Covington, Ky., 1908-12, became pastor, Livingston, Ala., 1912, then pastor emeritus and 5th Sunday pastor. Dean of Ala. Bapt. Preachers' Sch. Died Mar. 31, 1938.

DAVIDSON, Benjamin, merchant; b. Slutzk, Russia, Aug. 15, 1859; s. H. L. and Cima (Lazinski) D.; ed. pvt. sch.; m. Ida Frank, 1888 (died 1906); children—Tess (Mrs. Oswaldo de Zuliani), Edith (Mrs. Paul Segnitz), Leon, Frank; m. 2d, Blanche Hart, 1911. Came to U.S., 1881, naturalized citizen, 1886. Settled in Sioux City, Ia., 1882; dealer in housewares; asso. in mercantile business with brother, 1884; then pres. Davidson Bros. Co. Republican. Jewish religion. Mason. Home: Sioux City, Ia. Died Oct. 31, 1927.

DAVIDSON, Charles, univ. prof.; b. Streetboro, O., July 29, 1852; s. David Botsford and Jeannette Patty (Parker) D.; A.B., Ia. Coll., 1875, A.M., 1878; grad. student, Yale, 1876-77; spl. student of English with Dr. Albert S. Cook, U. of Calif., 1887-90; grad. student English, Yale, 1891-92, Ph.D., 1892; m. Hannah Amelia Noyes, Aug. 21, 1878. Teacher in Mitchell Sem., Ia., 1877-79; founder, and prin. Minneapolis Acad., 1879-84; prin. pub. schs., The Dalles, Ore., 1884-86; master in English, Belmont (Calif.) Sch., 1887-93; asst. prof. English, Ind. U., 1893-94; asso. prof. English, Adelbert Coll., Cleveland, 1894-96; English insp. for U. of State of N.Y., 1896-1904; prof. edn., U. of Me., 1906-11; prof. with graduate classes in English, U. of Chicago, summer term, 1895. Author: English Mystery Plays; Necessary Equipment for Teachers of English; English a Factor in the Training of a Business Man; A Guide to English Syntax; English in the Secondary School; Motor Work and Formal Studies in Primary Grades; Active Citizenship, 1915. Home: Claremont, Calif. Died 1919.

DAVIDSON, Edwin Lee, mfr.; b. Parkersburg, W.Va., Nov. 3, 1863; s. Fred E. and Virginia (Mitchell) D.; ed. pvt. sch.; m. Nettie R. Johnson, June 9, 1887; 1 dau., Dorothy Burdette (dec.). President and general manager The Parkersburg Mill Co.; vice-president Community Savings & Loan; dir. Parkersburg Corrugated Box Co. Chmn. Liberty Loan and Am. Red Cross drives, World War. Pres. Y.M.C.A., Parkersburg, Parkersburg Bd. of Commerce. Democrat. Methodist. Home: Parkersburg, W.Va. Died Feb. 24, 1941.

DAVIDSON, George, geodesist, astronomer; b. Nottingham, Eng., May 9, 1825; s. Thomas and Janet (Drummond) D.; came to U.S., 1832; A.B., Central High Sch., Phila., 1845, A.M., 1850; (Ph.D., Santa Clara Coll., 1876; Sc.D., U. of Pa., 1889; LL.D., U. of Calif., 1910); m. Ellinor Fauntleroy, Oct. 5, 1858. Secretary to Prof. A. D. Bache, supt. Coast Survey, 1845-46; member U.S. Coast and Geod. Survey, 1845-95; in geod. field and astron. work in Eastern states, 1845-50; in coast survey work of Calif., Ore., Wash. and Alaska, 1850-95, in charge of Pacific Coast work, 1868-95; hon. prof. geodesy and astronomy, 1870—, regent, 1877-84, prof. geography, 1898—, U. of Calif. Expert U.S. mints, Phila. and San Francisco, 1872, 85, 86; mem. U.S. Irrigation Commn. Cal., 1873-74, India, Egypt, etc., 1875; mem. U.S. Advisory Bd. of Harbor Improvement, San Francisco, 1873-76; in charge Transit of Venus Expdn. to Japan, 1874, to N.M., 1882; mem. Miss. River Commn., 1888-90; spl. agt. U.S. 9th Internat. Geod. Congress, Paris, 1889. Medal, Paris Expn., 1878; Daly gold medal, Am. Geog. Soc., 1908; decorated with Order of St. Olof, Norway, 1907. Fellow Am. Acad. Arts and Sciences, A.A.A.S. Died Dec. 1, 1911.

DAVIDSON, Hannah Amelia, editor, author; b. Campello, Mass., Oct. 29, 1852; d. Spencer Williams and Mary (Packard) Noyes; A.B., Ia. (now Grinnell) Coll., 1878, A.M., 1881; m. Charles Davidson, Aug. 21, 1878; 1 dau., Enid Amelia (dec.). Studied Sanskrit and taught, 1878-79; prin. and teacher Greek, Latin and English history, Minneapolis Acad., 1879-84; taught history and English composition, The Dalles (Ore.) High Sch., 1884-85; student politics, finance and economics, grad. dept., U. of Minn., 1885-86, Am. colonial instns. and politics, grad. dept. U. of Calif., 1886-87; taught history and English, Belmont Sch., Calif., 1887-93; student grad. dept., U. of Chicago, economics, history and politics, summer terms, 1894-95; lecturer on literary art in fiction and the drama, Wellesley and Mt. Holyoke colls.; dir. summer classes for study of English, 1902—. Author: Reference History of the United States, 1892; Literary Study for Busy People; The Gift of Genius. Author, editor and publisher of The Study-Guide Series (10 books); also Study-Guide Courses; also edited, with aids to study and critical essays, Riverside Literature Series edits., Silas Marner, Vicar of Wakefield, House of Seven Gables, etc. Home: Claremont, Calif. Died Nov. 29, 1932.

DAVIDSON, Harlan Page, academy pres.; b. Hookset, N.H., Sept. 15, 1838; s. Samuel and Lydia (Jackman) D.; attended Norwich U., 1863-64; (A.M., Lafayette Coll.); m. Adelaide S. Ford, May 16, 1866. Has taught sch. 51 yrs.; founded, 1888, pres. from 1902, Northwestern Mil. Acad., Highland Park, Ill. Prohibitionist. Alderman Highland Park, 3 terms; candidate for Congress, 7th Ill. Dist., 1900, for presdl. elector, 1904. Col. Ill. N.G. Pres. Northwestern Summer Naval Sch., 1902, Sheridan Rd. Pub. Co., 1904. Died Jan. 20, 1913.

DAVIDSON, Irville Fay, college prof.; b. Weymouth, Mass., Jan. 26, 1875; s. Jonas Keith and Henrietta Cordelia (Nash) D.; A.B., Harvard, 1897; A.M., U. of Chicago, 1908; A.M., St. Stephen's, 1907, L.H.D., 1914; m. Helen Van Wagner, Sept. 4, 1901; children—Dorothy, John Irville. Teacher St. Thomas Hall, Holly Springs, Miss., 1897-98; teacher Mt. Pleasant Mil. Acad., Ossining, N.Y., later Lakewood (N.J.) Sch., 1900-04; instr. Latin and Greek, 1898-1900 and 1904-13, prof., 1913—, also library dir., 1904-26, dean, 1918-25, and actg. pres., Feb.-July 1919, St. Stephen's Coll. (now Bard Coll.). Home: Annandale-on-Hudson, N.Y. Died Dec. 27, 1940.

DAVIDSON, Israel (adopted surname Davidson), educator, author; b. Yanova, Russia, May 27, 1870; s. David Wolf and Rebecca (Cohen) Movshovitz; came to U.S., 1888; B.A., Coll. City of New York, 1895; fellow in Semitics, Columbia, 1900, Ph.D., 1902; Dr. Hebrew Law, Hebrew Union College, 1937; Dr. Hebrew Letters, Dropsie College, 1937; m. Carrie Dreyfuss, Sept. 3, 1906; children—Gladys, Jessica. Prof. mediæval Hebrew lit., Jewish Theol. Sem. of America, 1915—. Visiting prof. at Hebrew U. in Jerusalem, 1926. Awarded 1st Bialik prize of $1,000, 1936, for the most outstanding work in Hebrew literature published between 1933 and 1935. Author: Parody in Jewish Literature, 1907. Editor or transl.: Sepher Shaashuim (a book of mediæval lore), 1914; Saadia's Polemic against Hiwi Al-Balkhi, 1915; Mahzor Yannai, 1919; Selected Religion Poems of Solomon Ibn Gabirol, 1923; Thesaurus of Mediæval Hebrew Poetry (4 vols.), 1924-33. The Book of the Wars of the Lord, 1934. Home: New York, N.Y. Died June 27, 1939.

DAVIDSON, James Henry, congressman; b. Colchester, N.Y., June 18, 1858; s. James and Ann (Johnson) D.; ed. Walton (N.Y.) Acad.; LL.B., Albany Law Sch., 1884; m. Niva T. Wilde, Oct. 8, 1889.

Admitted to bar, 1884; practiced at Princeton, Wis., 1887-92, Oshkosh, Wis., 1892—. Dist. atty., Green Lake Co., 1888; chmn. Rep. Congressional Com., 1890-96; city atty., Oshkosh, 1895-97; mem. 55th to 62d Congresses, 1897-1913 (55th to 57th, 6th Dist., 58th to 62d, 8th Dist.); reëlected to 65th Congress (1917-19), 6th Dist. Home: Oshkosh, Wis. Died Aug. 6, 1918.

DAVIDSON, James O., governor; b. Norway, Feb. 10, 1854; s. Ole and Ingabor (Jenson) D.; ed. pub. and parochial schs., Norway; came to U.S., 1872; m. Helen Bliss, Feb. 19, 1883. Engaged in milling and mercantile business at Soldier's Grove, Wis., from 1877. Mem. Wis. legislature, 1893-99; state treas., 1899-1903; lt.-gov., 1903-06, becoming gov., Jan. 1, 1906, on resignation of Gov. La Follette, who was elected to U.S. Senate; elected gov. of Wis., for terms, 1907-09, 1909-11. Pres. State Bd. of Control, Feb. 1915—. Republican. Died Dec. 16, 1922.

DAVIDSON, James Wheeler, financial agt.; b. Austin, Minn., June 14, 1872; s. Charles H. and Mary (Wheeler) D.; grad. Northwestern Mil. Acad., Highland Park, Ill.; m. Lillian Dow, Oct. 9, 1906; 1 dau., Marjory Dow. Mem. Peary Arctic Expdn. to N. Greenland, 1893-94; war corr. with Chinese Army, 1895, with Japanese Army, 1895-96; mem. Botel Tobago Exploring Party, 1896; spl. corr. in Formosa, 1897; apptd. U.S. consular agt. for Tamsui, Formosa, 1897; consul for Formosa and Loochoo Islands, June 1898; U.S. commercial attaché, stationed Shanghai, Apr.-July 1904; consul at Nanking, Aug.-Sept. 1904; consul for Antung, Manchuria, Jan. 1904-Feb. 1905; special agent Dept. of State in charge Consulate General, Shanghai, 1904-05; v.p. and mng. dir. Staples & Co., Ltd., 1905-07; pres. and mng. dir. Crown Lumber Co., Ltd., 1908-14; v.p. and gen. mgr. Beiseker & Davidson, Ltd., 1917. Vice-pres. Rotary Internat., 1926-27, gen. commr., 1928-31, organizing Rotary Clubs in Greece, Palestine, Egypt, India, Burma, Ceylon, Straits Settlements, Federated Malay States, Java, Sumatra, Siam and China. Decorated Order of the Rising Sun (Japan). Author: Formosa Camphor and Its Future, 1895; A Review of the History of Formosa, 1896; Formosa Under Japanese Rule, 1903; The Island of Formosa, Past and Present, 1903. Home: Calgary, Alberta, Can. Died July 18, 1933.

DAVIDSON, James Wood, clerk U.S. Treasury Dept., author; b. Newberry Co., S.C., Mar. 9, 1829; s. Alexander and Sarah J. D. D.; grad. S.C. Coll. (now U. of S.C.), 1852 (A.M., 1855). Prof. Greek, Mt. Zion Collegiate Inst., Winnsboro, S.C., 1854-59; then taught the classics in Columbia, S.C.; was adjt., 13th regt., S.C. vols., in Stonewall Jackson's army corps, under Lee in Va., during Civil war; after war engaged in journalism; moved to Washington; 1873-84, lived in New York; m. Mrs. Josephine Allen, 1884, and moved to Lake Worth, Dade Co., Fla.; mem. Fla. State Constl. Conv., 1886; legislature, 1887; is still a citizen there, though from 1887 clerk in Treasury Dept., residing in Washington. Author: The Living Writers of the South, 1869; A School History of South Carolina. Home: West Palm Beach, Fla. Died 1905.

DAVIDSON, Louis Rogers, mining, mfg.; b. Connellsville, Pa., May 8, 1866; s. Daniel Rogers and Margaret Clark (Johnston) D.; ed. Pa. Mil. Coll., and Mass. Inst. Tech.; m. Mary Agnew Quay, Jan. 29, 1896; 1 dau., Agnes Quay (Mrs. Willard H. Johnstone). Brick mfg. business, West Bridgewater, Pa., 1890-96; with Atlantic Refinery Co., Pittsburgh br., 1896-99; successively sec., treas., gen. mgr. N.Y. State Steel Co. (now The Donner Steel Co.), 1907-10; organizer, 1910, became pres. Davidson Ore Mining Co.; v.p. Davidson, Connellsville Coal & Coke Co. Republican. Presbyterian. Mason. Home: Buffalo, N.Y. Died Aug. 28, 1941.

DAVIDSON, Robert James, chemist; b. Armagh, Ireland, Apr. 3, 1862; s. John and Hannah (Donaldson) D.; B.S., S.C. Coll., 1885, A.M., 1887; m. Anna Maria, d. of John McLaren McBryde (q.v.), May 2, 1892. Tutor in chemistry, S.C. Coll., 1885-88, asst. prof. and sec. of faculty, Univ. of S.C., 1888-91; asst. chemist, S.C. Expt. Sta., 1888-90; chemist, Va. Expt. Sta., 1891-1907; prof. chemistry, 1891—, dean scientific dept., 1903—, Va. Poly. Inst., Blacksburg, Va. Democrat. Episcopalian. Del. Internat. Congress Applied Chemistry, London, 1909. Died Dec. 19, 1915.

DAVIDSON, Samuel Presley, lawyer; b. Mt. Zion, Ill., Oct. 8, 1847; s. John and Mary (Campbell) D.; A.B., Lincoln (Ill.) U. at head of class, 1869, A.M., 1879 (LL.D., 1901); m. Sidna J. Houser, July 24, 1889. Admitted to Ill. bar, 1870, Neb. bar, 1873, U.S. Supreme Court bar, 1888; began practice at Lincoln, Ill., 1870; removed to Tecumseh, Neb., 1872; has been judge Dist. Ct., Neb.; atty. and dir. Tecumseh Nat. Bank Presbyn. Republican. Deceased.

DAVIDSON, Theodore Fulton, lawyer; b. Waynesville, N.C., Mar. 30, 1845; s. Allen Turner and Elizabeth Adaline (Howell) D.; ed. Col. Stephen Lee's Classical Sch., Asheville, N.C.; apptd. to U.S. Naval Acad. but did not enter on account of Civil War; studied law under Judge Baily of Asheville, 1867-68; m. Sallie K. Alexander, Nov. 6, 1866 (died 1886); 2d, Sally L. Carter, Oct. 12, 1893. Entered C.S.A., Apr. 1861; sergt. maj. 39th Regt. N.C. Vols., 1861-62; a.-d.-c. on staff Brig. Gen. Robert B. Vance, until close of war, serving in Ky., Tenn., Ga. and Western N.C. Began law practice, 1868, as mem. A. T. & T. F. Davidson; later Davidson & Martin, Davidson & Jones, and Davidson, Bourne & Parker; counsel Wachovia Bank & Trust Co.; v.p., counsel N.C. Elec. & Power Co., W. T. Weaver Power Co. Solicitor Clay Co., N.C., 1868; mem. N.C. Ho. of Rep. 4 terms, 1878-1903; atty. gen. of N.C. 2 terms, 1885-93; mayor of Asheville; presiding justice of Criminal Ct. of Buncombe Co., 1894. Chancellor diocese Missionary Diocese of Western N.C., etc. Democrat. Episcopalian. Home: Asheville, N.C. Died June 11, 1931.

DAVIDSON, Thomas, author; b. Deer, Aberdeenshire, Scotland, Oct. 25, 1840; grad. U. of Aberdeen (first graduate and Greek prizeman), 1860; was master of several schools in Scotland and England, 1860-66; then in America, 1866-75; settled in Cambridge, Mass. Author: The Parthenon Frieze and Other Essays; Giordano Bruno, and the Relation of His Philosophy to Free Thought; The Place of Art in Education; Aristotle, and Ancient and Modern Educational Ideals; Prolegomena to Tennyson's "In Memoriam"; The Education of the Greek People, and Its Influence on Civilization; etc. Died 1900.

DAVIDSON, Wilbur Leroy, clergyman; b. Woodsfield, O., Apr. 3, 1853; s. William A. and Margaret (McGregor) D.; A.B., Scio Coll., 1870; B.D., Drew Theol. Sem., 1876; (D.D., Claflin U., 1889); m. Belle Clark, 1890. Ordained M.E. ministry, 1876; in pastorates, 1876-86; field agt. S. S. Union, 1886-89; field agent Chautauqua Literary and Scientific Circle, 1895-1902; supt. instrn. at 15 Chautauquas, 1887-1911; sec. The Am. Univ., 1899-1908; mgr. Nat. Chautauqua Bur., July, 1908—. Lyceum lecturer. Del. Ecumenical Meth. Conf., London, 1901. Home: Cleveland, O. Died Sept. 1913.

DAVIDSON, William Mehard, supt. schools; b. Jamestown, Pa., May 8, 1863; s. Thomas Houston and Anna (Mehard) D.; grad. Kan. State Normal Sch., Emporia, 1886; A.B., Kan. State U., 1892; LL.D., U. of Neb., and Miami U., 1909, Bethany College, 1916, U. of Pittsburgh, 1917, Duquesne U., 1929; m. Nettie Adams, July 11, 1888; 1 dau., Helen Mehard. Taught in rural schs. of Lyon Co., Kan., 1882-84; city editor on Emporia, Kan., newspaper, 1885-86; prin. Atwood, Kan., schs., 1886-87; prin. Quincy Sch., 1887-88, and of Lincoln Sch., 1888-92, Topeka, Kan.; supt. pub. schs., Topeka, Kan., 1892-1904; supt. pub. schs., Omaha, Neb., 1904-11; supt. pub. schs., Washington, D.C., 1911-14, Pittsburgh, Pa., Jan. 1, 1914—. Republican. Presbyn. Author: History of the United States, 1902. Editor of series of Classics and School Readings, 1900-03. Home: Pittsburgh, Pa. Died July 27, 1930.

DAVIES, Acton, dramatic critic; b. St. Johns, Quebec, Can., 1870; s. Lt. E. Whitacre D.; high sch. edn., St. Johns; went to New York, 1887; reporter, 1890-93, became dramatic critic, 1893, New York Evening Sun. Was corr. New York Sun in Cuba and P. R., and was with the marine corps during the fight at Guantanamo. Home: New York, N.Y. Died June 12, 1916.

DAVIES, Arthur B., painter; b. Utica, N.Y., 1862; studied under Dwight Williams and in Art Inst. of Chicago and at New York; married. Began as illustrator for St. Nicholas Mag.; rep. of the Romantic school in painting; 1st exhibited Internat. Soc. of Sculptors, Painters and Gravers, London; since in various exhbns. throughout U.S.; represented in permanent collections of Art Inst. of Chicago, Met. Mus. of Art, New York, etc. Silver medal, Buffalo Expn., 1901; hon. mention, Carnegie Inst., Pittsburgh, 1913. Home: Rockland Lake, N.Y. Died Oct. 24, 1928.

DAVIES, David Charles; b. Wales, June 23, 1866; s. Robert Joseph and Frances (Humphreys) D.; Univ. Coll. Sch., London, 1879-82; Univ. Coll. of Wales; m. Abbie Stuart Poole, Dec. 18, 1912. Came to U.S., 1888. Began as clk. with Marshall Field & Co., 1889; became connected with Field Mus. of Nat. History, 1894, dir. and trustee, 1921—. Fellow A.A.A.S. Mason. Home: Chicago, Ill. Died July 14, 1928.

DAVIES, Hywel, mining engr.; b. Breconshire Co., Wales, Sept. 26, 1859; s. Howell and Tydfil (Watkins) D.; ed. pub. schs.; m. Sarah Williams, of Wales, 1883 (died 1886); m. 2d, Ella C. Brooks, 1888; children—Hywel Brooks, Alwilda Tydfil, Winnefred Jeannette (dec.), Arthur Wayne, Paul Drummond, Alleine Blodwen, Helen Gwendolen, John Franklyn. Teacher and bookkeeper, 1875-85; came to U.S., 1885, naturalized citizen, 1892. In charge mine office of East Tenn. Coal Co., later supt. until 1890; gen. mgr. du Pont mining operations in 3 counties in Ky., 1890-1912; consulting and mining engr. coal cos. Southern States and Mexico. Govt. mediator Colo. coal strike, 1914, Eastern Ohio coal strike, 1915. Alaska Govt. railroad strike, 1916; commr. of conciliation U.S. Dept. Labor, 1914—; Govt. labor adminstr. copper industry, World War; sole referee Calif. oil industry, 1919-21; mem. Govt. commn. on labor conditions in Hawaiian Islands, 1922. Trustee Ky. State U., 1908-14. Republican. Baptist. Mason. Home: Los Angeles, Calif. Died Feb. 17, 1927.

DAVIES, James; b. Stockport, Eng., Apr. 17, 1870; s. Shem and Catherine (O'Rourke) D.; Ph.B., Boston U., 1900, M.A., 1905; Ph.D., Leipzig, 1906; m. Grace Golden, Dec. 25, 1909; children—James Golden, Helen Caroline, John Edward, Barbara Jane, Mary Verna, Diane. Came to U.S., 1888, naturalized, 1900. Lecturer on English lit., U. of Leipzig, 1905-09; mem. faculty, U. of Minn.; music editor, editorial writer, Minneapolis Tribune; lecturer on musical lit. and civic subjects. Mason. Home: Minneapolis, Minn. Died Jan. 7, 1940.

DAVIES, John Rumsey, clergyman; b. Abergavenny, Eng., Aug. 9, 1855; s. Thomas Y. and Hester A. R. D.; grad. Lafayette Coll., 1881; Princeton Theol. Sem., 1883; (D.D., Lafayette, 1892); m. Isabella Moffatt, Dec. 12, 1883. Ordained by Presbytery of Lackawanna, 1883; pastor Avoca, Pa., 1883-87, Tyrone, Pa., 1887-93, Fourth Av. Ch., New York, 1893-88, Bethlehem Ch., Phila., 1898—. Dir. Princeton Theol. Sem.; pres. Presbyn. Bd. of Ministerial Relief. Died Mar. 15, 1919.

DAVIES, John Vipond, civil engr.; b. Swansea, South Wales, Oct. 13, 1862; s. Andrew and Emily (Vipond) D.; Wesleyan Coll., Taunton, Eng.; U. of London; m. Ruth Ramsey, Apr. 16, 1895 (died 1931). Engaged in coal mining, steel mfr. and other engring. work to 1889, when came to New York and employed as engr. with late Austin Corbin; chief asst. engr. tunnel under East River for East River Gas Co.; pres. Jacobs & Davies, Inc., cons. engrs., New York; v.p., chief engr. Hudson & Manhattan R.R.; chief engr. in charge design and constrn., W.Va. Short Line R.R. and Kanwaha & Pocahontas R.R. in W.Va.; chief engr. Atlantic Av. improvement, L.I. R.R., Brooklyn; consulting engr. Brooklyn Rapid Transit Co.; cons. engr. City of Detroit for water supply tunnel under Detroit River; engr. in charge for contractors of terminal improvement of N.Y.C. R.R., New York City; designed and built 4 tunnels under Hudson River and under New York, Jersey City and Hoboken, for Hudson & Manhattan R.R.; constrn. engr. for 26 aqueduct tunnels, aggregating 18 miles, in Mexico; one of bd. of 3 engrs. on constrn. of Moffat Tunnel in Rocky Mountains nr. Denver; firm prepared original studies for Pa. R.R. tunnels under North and East Rivers, New York; engr. in charge Astoria Tunnel, Consol. Gas. Co. of N.Y.; engr. in charge constrn. Hales Bar Dam across Tenn. River at Chattanooga; engr. in charge constrn. intake and discharge tunnels of N.Y. Edison Co.; on constrn. bridge or tunnel crossing of Miss. River at New Orleans; mem. bd. cons. engrs. N.Y. State Bridge and Tunnel Commn. and N.J. interstate Bridge and Tunnel Com. (vehicular tunnel under Hudson River, 1912-22); one of two engrs. on tunnel and bridge crossing of San Francisco Bay. Awarded Telford gold medal by the Institute of Civil Engineers, 1914; Norman gold medal, 1913, and Thomas Fitch Rowland prize, 1917, by Am. Soc. C.E.; Fowler professorial award, 1930. Episcopalian. Home: Flushing, N.Y. Died Oct. 4, 1939.

DAVIES, Julian Tappan, lawyer; b. New York, N.Y., Sept. 25, 1845; s. Judge Henry Ebenezer and Rebecca Waldo (Tappan) D.; bro. of William Gilbert D.; served in 22d N.Y. Vols, participating in Gettysburg campaign; A.B., Columbia, 1866; LL.B., 1868, A.M., 1869; also read law in office of Alexander W. Bradford; m. Alice, d. Henry H. Martin, of Albany, Apr. 22, 1869. Admitted to bar, 1867; on death of Mr. Bradford succeeded, under his will, to part of practice of his office; later asso. with his father; sr. mem. Davies, Auerbach & Cornell, New York. Counsel for New York elevated rys. and Manhattan Ry. Co., 1884-1914; trustee Mut. Life Ins. Co., 1882—, Title Guarantee & Trust Co. Compiled the statutes and decisions of N.Y. relating to taxation, 1886. Died May 6, 1920.

DAVIES, Thomas Frederick, P.E. bishop of Michigan, 1889—; b. Fairfield, Conn., Aug. 31, 1831; grad. Yale, 1853 (D.D., Yale and Univ. of Pa.; LL.D., Hobart); Berkeley Divinity School, 1856; was prof. Hebrew there; m. Mary L. Hackstaff. Deacon, 1856; priest, 1857; rector 1st of St. John's Ch., Portsmouth, N.H.; then St. Peter's Ch., Phila., until 1889. Died 1905.

DAVIES, Thomas Frederick, bishop; b. Phila., July 20, 1872; s. late Bishop Thomas Frederick and Mary Lang (Hackstaff) Davies; ed. P.E. Acad., Phila., 1883-89; B.A., Yale, 1894, M.A., 1907; B.D., Gen. Theol. Sem., New York, 1897, D.D., 1911; D.D., Amherst College, 1912; m. Anne Thayer Patten, Feb. 24, 1930. Became deacon, 1897, priest, 1898, P.E. Ch.; asst. minister Ch. of the Incarnation, New York, 1897-1900; rector Christ Ch., Norwich, Conn., 1901-03, All Saints, Worcester, Mass., 1903-11; elected bishop of Western Mass., May 10, 1911; elected pres. Province of New England, 1927. Served for Y.M.C.A. with A.E.F. in France, Sept.-Nov. 1918. Home: Springfield, Mass. Died Aug. 25, 1936.

DAVIES, William Gilbert, lawyer; b. New York, Mar. 21, 1842; s. Judge Henry Ebenezer and Rebecca Waldo (Tappan) D.; bro. of Julien Tappan D.; B.A.

Trinity Coll., Conn., 1860 (LL.D., 1906); U. of Leipzig, 1860-61; admitted to bar, 1863; m. Lucie Carter, d. Alexander H. Rice, of Boston, Dec. 15, 1870. Mem. 22d N.Y. Inf., Gettysburg Campaign, 1863; adj. 4th Regt., N.G.S.N.Y., 1866-69; entered service of Mut. Life Ins. Co., 1866, asst. in law dept., 1870-85, gen. solicitor, 1885-94; commr. for widening Elm St., New York, 1896-1904. Democrat. Home: New York, N.Y. Died July 26, 1910.

DAVIES, William Walter, univ. prof.; b. Llangybi, Cardiganshire, S. Wales, May 10, 1848; s. David and Mary D.; A.B., Ohio Wesleyan U., 1872, A.M., 1875; B.D., Drew Theol. Sem., 1874; A.M., Ph.D., U. of Halle, 1877; studied Faculte Libre, Lausanne, Switzerland, and The Sorbonne, Paris; m. Mary E. Chase, Dec. 25, 1879 (died 1909); m. 2d, Mrs. Madeline B. Sharp, June 27, 1911 (died 1921). Ordained to Methodist Episcopal ministry, 1878; pastor Dover, Ohio, 1878-79; instr. Hebrew and modern langs., 1879-83, adj. prof., 1883-84, prof. Hebrew and German, 1884—, Ohio Wesleyan U. Editor dept. archæology and bibl. research, Meth. Review, 1894—, critical notes in S.S. Teachers' Jour., 1895-97. Author: The Universal Bible Ency. (2 vols.), 1903; The Codes of Hammurabi and Moses, 1905. Home: Delaware, O. Died May 5, 1922.

DAVIESS, Maria Thompson, author; b. Harrodsburg, Ky.; d. John Burton Thompson and Leonora (Hamilton) D.; grad. Science Hill, Shelbyville, Ky., 1891; spl. lit. course, Wellesley, 1891-92; studied painting in Julien, Delecluse and Vite schs., Paris, 1902-04. Miniature painter, 1905—; art jewelry worker; gold medal, Nashville Art Club; exhibited in Paris Salon, 1904-05. Author: Treasure Babies, 1911; The Tinder Box, 1913; Phyllis; Bluegrass and Broadway, 1919; Matrix, 1920; Seven Times Seven. Home: New York, N.Y. Died Sept. 3, 1924.

DAVIS, Abel; b. Chicago, Dec. 26, 1874; s. Peter and Keile (Hochsberger) D.; LL.B., Northwestern U., 1901, LL.D., 1930; m. Marjorie Mayer, Dec. 28, 1922; children—Florence, Abel, Jean A. Admitted to Ill. bar, 1901; mem. Gardner, Stern, Anderson & Davis until 1904, Stern, Anderson & Davis, 1910-12. Mem. Ill. Ho. of Rep., 1902-04; Cook County recorder, 1904-12; mem. Ill. State Constl. Conv., 1920; v.p. Chicago Title & Trust Co., 1912-31, chmn. bd., 1931—. Served as pvt. in Cuba, Spanish-Am. War; maj. on Mexican border; col. 132d Inf. in France, World War; brig. gen. 66th Inf. Brig., Ill. N.G.; retired from Ill. Nat. Guard, Jan. 1935. Mem. Chicago Plan Commn.; trustee Century of Progress Expn., Chicago, 1933, Chicago Community Trust, John Crerar Library. Awarded D.S.M., D.S.C. (U.S.); Officer Legion of Honor (France). Republican. Reformed Jewish religion. Mason. Home: Glencoe, Ill. Died Jan. 7, 1937.

DAVIS, Albert Gould, lawyer; b. Brooklyn, N.Y., Oct. 19, 1871; s. Owen Warren, Jr., and Abby (Gould) D.; B.S., Mass. Inst. Tech., 1892; LL.B., Nat. Univ., Washington, D.C., 1896, LL.M., 1897; m. Agnes H. Shaw, June 26, 1898; 1 dau., Lilian Gould (Mrs. Van Ness Philip); m. 2d, Pauline C. Lunt, June 4, 1929. Engr. Davis-Colby Ore Roaster Co., 1893-94; asst. examiner U.S. Patent Office, 1894-96; began patent practice, Washington, 1896; mgr. patent dept. Gen. Electric Co., 1897-1919, v.p., 1919-33; mem. Pennie, Davis, Marvin & Edmonds, May 1, 1933-Sept. 15, 1937; practicing law independently, 1937—. Fellow Am. Inst. Elec. Engrs. Republican. Home: New York, N.Y. Died Apr. 25, 1939.

DAVIS, Andrew McFarland, antiquarian; b. Worcester, Mass., Dec. 30, 1833; S.B., Lawrence Scientific Sch. (Harvard), 1854 (hon. A.M., Harvard, 1893); m. Henrietta Parker Whitney, Oct. 23, 1862. Admitted to N.Y. and Mass. bars; later went to Cal., became partner with his brother, Horace, in mfg. business; later returned to Cambridge, Mass., becoming an antiquarian. Fellow Am. Acad. Arts and Sciences. Author: Currency and Banking in the Province of Massachusetts Bay, 1900; Tracts Relating to the Currency of Massachusetts Bay, 1902; The Confiscation of John Chandler's Estate, 1903; Colonial Currency Reprints; The Origin of the National Banking System, 1910; Certain Old Chinese Notes or Chinese Paper Money, 1915. Home: Cambridge, Mass. Died Mar. 27, 1920.

DAVIS, Arnold Lyman, lawyer; b. Winthrop, Ia., May 27, 1873; s. Napoleon J. and Mary A. (Arnold) D.; A.B., U. of S.D., 1895, LL.D., 1936; LL.B., U. of Michigan, 1898; m. Charlotte Kennedy, Sept. 19, 1900; children—Marion J., Marjorie C. Admitted to Michigan bar, 1898, New York bar, 1899, and began practice at N.Y. City; then mem. Davis, Wagner, Heater and Hallett. Mem. advisory bd. Bankers Investment Trust of America; dir. many companies. V.p. and dir. Am. Foreign Trade Zone, Inc.; v.chmn. Am. Defense Soc.; v.p. Com. of Americans. Republican. Baptist. Home: New York, N.Y. Died Sept. 11, 1940.

DAVIS, Arthur Powell, civil engr.; b. Decatur, Ill., Feb. 9, 1861; s. John and Martha P. D.; grad. State Normal Sch., Emporia, Kan.; B.S., Columbian (now George Washington) U., 1888, Sc.D., 1917; D.Eng., Ia. State Coll., 1920; m. Elizabeth Brown, June 20, 1888 (died Apr. 13, 1917); children—Mrs. Rena Peck, Mrs. Florence Eslin, Mrs. Dorothy Smith, Mrs. Elizabeth Smith; m. 2d, Marie MacNaughton, June 19, 1920. Topographer U.S. Geol. Survey, 1884-94, conducting surveys and explorations in Ariz., N.M., and Calif.; hydrographer in charge of all govt. stream measurements, 1895-97; hydrographer in charge hydrographic exam. of Nicaragua and Panama canal routes, 1898-1901; chief engr., U.S. Reclamation Service, 1906-14, dir. same, 1914-23. Consulting engr., Panama Canal, 1909. Examined and reported on irrigation in Puerto Rico, 1909; in Turkestan, 1911; mem. bd. of engrs. reporting on flood control in China, 1914; cons. engr. on many high dams; mem. joint conf. on standard specifications for Portland cement, 5 yrs.; tech. adviser to U.S. on Pecuniary Claims Arbitration, London, 1923. Chief engr. and gen. mgr. East Bay Municipal Utility Dist., Oakland, Calif., 1923-29; built large reservoir on Mokelumne River, aqueduct and tunnels, 95 miles long, now delivering mountain water to Oakland, San Francisco and eight other cities around San Francisco Bay; chief cons. engr. for irrigation projects in Turkestan and Transcaucasia 2 yrs. Fellow Am. Acad. Arts and Sciences, Washington Soc. Engrs. (pres. 1907; hon. mem. 1923). Author: Irrigation Works Constructed by the U.S. Government, 1917. Home: Oakland, Calif. Died Aug. 7, 1933.

DAVIS, Asa Barnes, surgeon; b. Preston, Conn., Sept. 28, 1861; s. Charles Crandall and Harriet Frances (Barnes) D.; grad. Vermont Acad., Saxtons River, Vt., 1886; M.D., Columbia, 1889; m. Alma L. Fisher, Oct. 28, 1896 (died 1902); children—Annette (Mrs. Allan S. Locke), Asa Barnes. Junior and house surgeon, Memorial Hosp., N.Y. City, 1889-90; resident physician, Midwifery Dispensary (now Lying-In Hospital), 1890-1902, asst. attending surgeon, 1892-1903, med. dir. and attending surgeon, 1903-18; also attending surgeon Demilt Dispensary, 1906; chief surgeon Lying-In Hosp., 1918—; cons. gynecologist, Vassar Bros. Hosp., Poughkeepsie. Fellow A.M.A., Am. Coll. Surg. Republican. Baptist. Home: New York, N.Y. Died 1930.

DAVIS, Beale, author; b. Petersburg, Va., Sept. 1886; s. Richard Beale and Nannie Warwick (Hall) D.; A.B., Randolph-Macon Coll., Ashland, Va. B.L., U. of Va.; unmarried. With U.S. Diplomatic Corps, 1914-21; served as sec. Legation at Port au Prince, Hayti, 2d sec. Legation at Copenhagen and 2d sec. Embassy, at London and Madrid; negotiated and signed treaty between U.S. and Hayti, 1915. Democrat. Author: One Way Street, 1924; The Goat Without Horns, 1925. Home: Hopewell, Va. Died Nov. 1, 1929.

DAVIS, Boothe Colwell, educator; b. nr. Jane Lew, Lewis Co., W.Va., July 12, 1863; s. Samuel D. and Elizabeth (FitzRandolph) D.; A.B., Alfred U., 1890, D.D., 1901; B.D., Yale, 1893; Ph.D., Nat. Normal U., 1897; LL.D., Temple U., 1926; m. Estelle W. Hoffman, June 18, 1893. Ordained Seventh-Day Bapt. ministry, 1893; pastor Alfred, N.Y., 1893-95; pres. Alfred U., 1895-1933; pres. N.Y. State Coll. of Ceramics, 1900-33; pres. N.Y. State Sch. of Agr. at Alfred U., 1908-33 (pres. emeritus). Pres. Council of Ch. Boards of Edn., 1929. Author: Country Life Leadership. Home: Holly Hill, Fla. Died Jan. 16, 1942.

DAVIS, Byron Bennett, surgeon; b. Fayette, Wis., June 14, 1859; s. William Bennett and Martha Electa (Haywood) D.; A.B., U. of Neb., 1882; M.D., Minn. Coll. Hosp., 1884; post-grad. work, U. of Berlin; m. Sophia Myers, June 7, 1887; (died 1922); 1 son, Herbert H.; m. 2d, Florence E. Davis, Sept. 3, 1925. Practiced in Omaha, Neb., 1894—; chief surgeon, Immanuel Deaconess Inst.; attending surgeon Bishop Clarkson Memorial and Nebraska M.E. hosps.; former prof. principles of surgery and clin. surgery, U. of Neb., now prof. surgery and chmn. of dept.; regent Univ. of Neb., 1887-93. Died Apr. 1933.

DAVIS, Carroll Melvin, clergyman; b. Campo Seco, Calif., Sept. 9, 1857; s. Thomas F. and Sarah M. (Chase) D.; B.A., U. of California, 1879, M.A., 1882; LL.D., from University of Mo., 1924; m. Maud Reber, Oct. 12, 1897 (died 1903). Deacon, 1881, priest, 1883, P.E. Ch.; rector, St. Paul's Ch., Sacramento, Calif., 1881-87; diocesan missionary, Mo., 1887-89; dean, Christ Ch. Cathedral, St. Louis, 1889-1921; domestic sec. Domestic and Foreign Missionary Soc. of P.E. Ch., 1921-30. Hon. canon Christ Ch. Cathedral. Republican. Mason. Was army chaplain in France, 1917. Home: St. Louis, Mo. Died Mar. 2, 1932.

DAVIS, Charles Albert, geologist; b. Portsmouth, N.H., Sept. 29, 1861; s. Lewis Gilman and Cyrena Frances (Peirce) D.; A.B., Bowdoin, 1886, A.M., 1889; Cornell Sch. of Forestry, 1 semester, 1900-01; Ph.D., U. of Mich., 1905; m. Frances Margaret Humphreys, Aug. 26, 1886. Teacher natural science, Hyde Park (Ill.) High Sch., 1886-87; prof. natural science, 1887-96, prof. biology and geology, 1896-1900, Alma (Mich.) Coll.; instr. forestry, 1900-05, curator Herbarium, 1905-08, U. of Mich.; peat expert U.S. Geol. Survey, 1907-10, Bur. of Mines, Washington, July 1, 1910-12; fuel technologist, 1912-14, geologist, 1914—. Field agent, Mich. Geol. Survey 1896-1907; instr. geology, U. of Mich. Summer School, 1900, 1901; field asst., U.S., Geol. Survey, 1904. Editor Jour. of Am. Peat Soc., 1907—. Republican. Conglist. Fellow Geol. Soc. America, A.A.A.S. Died Apr. 9, 1916.

DAVIS, Charles Belmont, author; b. Phila., Pa., Jan. 24, 1868; s. late L. Clarke and Rebecca Blaine (Harding) D.; A.B., Lehigh U., 1887; m. Pauline Turgeon, of Ottawa, Can., Jan. 17, 1914. U.S. consul at Florence, Italy, 1893-97; dramatic editor New York Herald Tribune, N.Y. City. Author: The Borderland of Society, 1898; The Stage Door, 1908; The Lodger Overhead, 1909; Tales of the Town, 1911; In Another Moment, 1913; Nothing a Year, 1915; Her Own Sort, 1917. Died Dec. 9, 1926.

DAVIS, Charles Edward Law Baldwin, brig. gen.; b. New Haven, Conn., Feb. 16, 1844; s. Charles S. A. and Mary Jeannette (Downs) D.; 1 yr. in acad. dept., Yale, 1861-62; grad. U.S. Mil. Acad., 1866; unmarried. Second lt. engrs., U.S.A., June 18, 1866; 1st lt., Mar. 7, 1867; capt. Sept. 12, 1877; maj., Apr. 7, 1888; lt. col., May 3, 1901; col., Oct. 15, 1905; brig. gen., Jan. 29, 1908; retired, Feb. 16, 1908. Served in the depts. of the Atlantic, Gulf, and Lakes, Pacific Coast, and P.I. Home: Atlantic City, N.J. Died June 1, 1925.

DAVIS, Charles Gilbert, M.D.; b. Clay Co., Mo., Oct. 14, 1849; s. Dr. George W. and Mary W. (Brooks) D.; grad. Western Christian U., Ottumwa, Kan., at 17; grad. Cincinnati Eclectic Med. Inst.; M.D., U. of Va., 1873; asst. physician Quarantine Hosp., St. Louis, Mo., 1 yr.; M.D., ad eundem, Mo. Med. Coll.; practiced 1 yr. at Mulberry, Mo.; studied in France, 1892-93; m. Isabella Braden, Jan. 19, 1876; m. 2d, Caroline May Doggett, Aug. 25, 1904. In practice at Chicago, 1876—, formerly attending phys., Cook County Hosp.; clinic, Lakeside Hospital; pres. Wannita Hot Springs Radium Sanitarium. Author: The Philosophy of Life; Why Not Now? Died Oct. 31, 1928.

DAVIS, Charles Harold, artist; b. Amesbury, Mass., Jan. 7, 1856; s. James H. and Elizabeth L. (Coffin) D.; studied, Art Mus. Sch., Boston, 3 yrs. and under Lefebvre and Boulanger, Julian Acad., Paris; remained in France 10 yrs. and exhibited in Salon for 10 yrs.; m. Angele Legarde, of Paris, 1884 (died 1897); m. 2d, Frances Thomas, d. Dr. Edwin Tyler Darby, of Philadelphia, April 9, 1900. Resided at Mystic, Conn., 1890—; landscape painter; represented in Met. Mus.; Corcoran Gallery and Nat. Collection, Washington, D.C.; Pa. Acad. Fine Arts; Art Inst., Chicago; Carnegie Inst., Pittsburgh; Mus. Fine Arts, Boston; City Mus., St. Louis; Art Mus., Syracuse; Art Mus., Worcester, Mass.; R.I. Sch. of Design, Providence; Art Mus., Minneapolis, etc. Awarded $2,000 prize, Prize Fund Exhbn., Am. Art Assn., New York, 1887; gold medal, Mass. Charitable Mechanics Assn., Boston; grand gold medal, Atlanta Expn., 1895; Lippincott prize ($500), Pa. Acad. Fine Arts; silver medal, Buffalo Expn., 1901, St. Louis Expn., 1904, Buenos Aires Expn., 1910; Norman Wait Harris prize ($300), Chicago, 1914; gold medal, San Francisco Expn., 1915; Altman prize ($1,000), N.A.D., 1917; Jennie Sesson gold medal, Pa. Acad. Fine Arts, 1919; 2d Clark prize, Corcoran Gallery, 1920; Saltus medal, N.A.D., 1921; Logan prize, $1,000, Prize Exhbn., Grand Central Art Galleries, New York, 1928. N.A., 1906. Died Aug. 5, 1933.

DAVIS, Charles Henry, rear adm.; b. Cambridge, Mass., Aug. 28, 1845; s. late Rear Admiral C. H. D.; apptd. from Mass., and grad. U.S. Naval Acad., 1864. Ensign, Nov. 1, 1866; master, Dec. 1, 1866; lt., 1868; lt. comdr., 1869; comdr., 1885; capt. 1898; rear admiral, U.S.N., Aug. 24, 1904. Served on various stas. and duties; connected with the various expdns. for determination of the difference of longitude by means of submarine telegraph cables; supt. Naval Obs., 1897-98; comd. auxiliary cruiser, Dixie, N. Atlantic Squadron, Apr.-Sept., 1898; returned to Naval Obs.; comd. Alabama, 1902; div. comdr. battleship squadron, 1904; U.S. commr. Internat. Commn. of Inquiry on N. Sea incident, Paris, 1904-05; comdr. 2d Squadron Atlantic Fleet, 1905; retired by operation of law, Aug. 28, 1907. Author: Chronometer Rates as Affected by Temperature and Other Causes; Telegraphic Determination of Longitude; Life of Rear Admiral Davis, 1899; etc. Apptd. mem. Perry's Victory Centennial Commn., 1912. Died Dec. 27, 1921.

DAVIS, Charles Henry Stanley, physician; b. Goshen, Conn., Mar. 2, 1840; s. Dr. Timothy Fisher and Moriva (Hatch) D.; M.D., Univ. Med. Coll. (New York U.), 1866; studied in hosps., New York, Boston, Paris, London; m. Caroline Elizabeth Harris, 1868. In practice at Meriden, Conn., 1868—; phys. Curtis Home for Orphans and Old Ladies, 1886-1908; phys. State Sch. for Boys, 1895-1900 (trustee, sec., treas., 1894-99). Mem. Conn. Ho. of Rep., 1873, 1885, 1886; mayor, Meriden, 1887-88; city treas., 1898-99; pres. bd. Edn., 1898-1908. Well known as archeologist and philologist; editor Biblia, jour. of Oriental archeology, 1887—; asso. editor Am. Antiquarian and Oriental Journal, 1906—. Author: The Voice as a Musical Instrument, 1873; Greek and Roman Stoicism and Some of Its Disciples, 1903. Home: Meriden, Conn. Died Nov. 1917.

DAVIS, Charles Lukens, brig. gen.; b. New Brighton, Pa., Feb. 27, 1839; s. Benjamin and Elizabeth (Hamill) D.; ed. Lawrenceville (N.J.) High Sch.; m. Margaretta M. S. Bowers, 1880. Civ. engr. on rys. in Pa. and Del. before Civ. War; pvt. Commonwealth Arty. of Pa. and 2d lt. 31st Pa. Inf., Aug. 20, 1861; promoted through grades to col. 5th U.S. Inf., July 11, 1901; brig. gen., Jan. 26, 1903. Bvtd. maj. vols., Apr. 9, 1865, "for gallant and meritorious services during operations resulting in the fall of Richmond"; capt. U.S.A., Mar. 2, 1867, for same in campaign from the Rapidan to the James; maj. U.S.A., Mar. 2, 1867, for same in siege of Petersburg. Chief signal officer, Dept. of Va. and N.C., 1862; mem. exam. bd. of officers at New Orleans for appmt. in signal corps, 1863; served with Army of Potomac, 1863-65; chief signal officer Army of Potomac, Jan. 1, 1865; served on Mexican and Indian frontiers, 1866-93; coll. duty, N.C., 1893-97; with gov. of N.C., organizing and discharging vols., 1898-99; mil. collector customs, P.R., 1899-1900; comd. Governor's Island, N.Y., 1900-01; Philippines, Apr. 1901-Dec. 1902; retired, Feb. 10, 1903. Home: Schenectady, N.Y. Died Nov. 10, 1919.

DAVIS, Charles Palmer, editor, publisher; b. Woburn, Mass., Nov. 7, 1859; s. Thomas George and Margaret Anne (Davison) D.; ed. pub. schs., and by pvt. study; m. Minerva Porter, Nov. 24, 1887. Began newspaper work on Woburn Advertiser, 1876; with New York Herald, 1884-86, Dallas (Tex.) News and El Paso Tribune, 1886, Boston Globe, 1887-91; founder, 1902, Current Events (weekly), of which is editor and chief owner; dir. and treas. Am. Edn. Press, Inc., and of Ednl. Press Co. Dem. candidate for Congress, 1st Mass. Dist., 1898. Home: New York City. Died June 21, 1921.

DAVIS, Charles Russell, congressman; b. Pittsfield, Ill., Sept. 17, 1849; moved to Le Sueur Co., Minn., 1853; grad. St. Peter High Sch., 1865; pvt. instrn. and bus. coll., 1865-68; read law with Hon. Alfred Wallin (chief justice, N. Dak.); m. Emma Haven, 1874; children—Isabel Haven (Mrs. Walter C. Poehler), Russell Haven. Admitted to bar, 1872, and began practice at St. Peter, Minn. Co. atty., Nicollet Co., 14 yrs.; city clerk and city atty., St. Peter, 18 yrs.; mem. Minn. Ho. of Rep., 1888-90, Senate 1890-94; mem. 58th to 68th Congresses (1903-25), 3d Minn. Dist. Republican. Capt. Minn. N.G., 4 yrs. Home: St. Peter, Minn. Died July 29, 1930.

DAVIS, Cushman Kellogg, U.S. senator; b. Henderson, N.Y., June 16, 1838; moved in childhood to Waukesha, Wis.; grad. Univ. of Mich., 1857; studied law and began practice in Waukesha; served in Union army, 1861-64, as lt. and asst. adj. gen.; began practice of law at St. Paul, 1865. Member Minn. legislature, 1867; U.S. dist. atty. for Minn., 1868-73; gov., 1874-75; elected U.S. senator in 1887 and again in 1893, present term expiring, 1899. Republican. Mem. Peace Commn. to Paris, 1898; chmn. Foreign Relations Committee, 55th Congress. Author: The Law in Shakespeare. Home: St. Paul, Minn. Died 1900.

DAVIS, David Jackson, U.S. dist. judge; b. Weedowee, Ala., Oct. 15, 1878; s. Dora Franklin and Callie Rebecca (Satterwhite) D.; student Phillips Acad., Andover, Mass., 1899-1901; LL.B., Yale, 1906; m. Mary Helm, May 1, 1912; 1 dau., Marjorie Helm. Admitted to Ala. bar, 1906; practiced in Birmingham, 1906-35, holding partnerships at various times with Hugo L. Black, Jim Davis, Hugh A. Locke; recorder city of Birmingham, 1915; U.S. dist. judge, 1935—. Democrat. Mem. Christian Ch. Mason. Home: Birmingham, Ala. Died Dec. 7, 1938.

DAVIS, Earl J., lawyer; b. Saginaw, Mich., Oct. 23, 1885; s. John E. and Ida D.; grad. high sch., Saginaw, 1905; LL.B., U. of Mich., 1909; m. Lenore F. Cowles, May 8, 1914; 1 dau., Jean Lenore. Began practice as mem. Otto & Davis, Saginaw, 1909; mem. Dist. War Bd., Lansing, Mich., 1917-18; U.S. dist. atty., Eastern Dist. of Mich., 1922-24 (resigned); asst. atty. gen. of U.S., 1924-25; apptd. atty. for U.S. Senate Com. investigating Bur. of Internal Revenue, Aug. 1, 1925; spl. asst. to U.S. atty. gen., to handle matter of improvement of River Rouge, 1926; spl. counsel to Sec. of Treasury in tax case, 1927; spl. asst. atty. gen. of U.S., to try East Chicago conspiracy cases, 1929; successful counsel for defense Calif. homestead cases, 1933. Mem. Mich. Naval Brigade until 1914. Republican. Home: Detroit, Mich. Died Nov. 9, 1936.

DAVIS, Edith Smith, temperance worker; b. Milton, Wis., Jan. 20, 1859; d. Richard and Elizabeth (Clayton) Smith; A.B., Lawrence U., Appleton, Wis., 1879, A.M., 1882, Litt.D., 1907; post-grad. work, Wellesley; m. Rev. John Scott Davis, D.D., Oct. 4, 1884. Teacher English lit., Clark U., Atlanta, Ga., 1881-84; active in temperance work, 1884—; asst. to Frances E. Willard in White Cross and social purity work; pres. Milwaukee W.C.T.U.; supt. bur. of scientific temperance investigation and dept. of scientific temperance instrn. in pub. schs. and colls., World's and Nat. W.C.T.U., 1905—. Methodist. Home: Milwaukee, Wis. Died Mar. 19, 1917.

DAVIS, Edward, brig. gen.; b. Louisville, Ky., July 7, 1845; s. Benjamin Outran and Susan Fry (Speed) D.; grad. U.S. Mil. Acad., 1867; m. Margaret J. Davis, Sept. 18, 1867. Commd. 2d lt. 5th Ky. Vol. Cav., Sept. 20, 1862; resigned, Nov. 2, 1863; commd. 2d lt. 3d U.S. Arty., June 17, 1867; 1st lt., Apr. 14, 1873; grad. Arty. Sch., 1876; capt., Sept. 1, 1896; maj. asst. adj. gen. vols., May 12, 1898; hon. disch. from vols., Apr. 15, 1899; maj. arty. corps, U.S.A., July 1, 1901; asst. adj. gen., Dec. 3, 1902; lt. col. Arty. Corps, Jan. 23, 1904; asst. adj. gen., June 22, 1904; brig. gen., Apr. 11, 1905; retired at own request after 40 yrs.' service, Apr. 12, 1905. Bvtd. 1st lt., June 17, 1867, "for gallant and meritorous services in battle of Chickamauga, Ga., Sept. 19 and 20, 1863." Died Aug. 2, 1918.

DAVIS, E(dward) Gorton, landscape architect; b. Cincinnati, O., May 7, 1880; s. George Francis and Lucy (Gorton) D.; B.S., Denison U., Granville, O., 1905; m. Marion Briggs, 1908; children—Dorothea, Edward Gorton. Associated with Bryant Fleming, Buffalo, in practice of landscape architecture, 1905-11; prof. and head dept. of landscape architecture, Cornell U., 1911—. Republican. Episcopalian. Home: Ithaca, N.Y. Died May 23, 1930.

DAVIS, Effa Vetina, M.D.; b. Freedom, Ill.; d. Frederick Jenkins and Nancy Janet (Foot) D.; grad. Morris (Ill.) Normal Sch., 1887; M.D., Woman's Med. School (Northwestern U.), 1891. Practiced in Chicago, 1891—; formerly clin. asst. prof. of obstetrics, Rush Med. Coll. and Northwestern U. Women's Med. Sch.; then phys. in chief and mem. bd. Chicago Maternity Hosp. and Training School. Dir. Chicago Council Medical Women (pres.). Republican. Unitarian. Died Oct. 28, 1936.

DAVIS, Ellery Williams, univ. dean; b. Oconomowoc, Wis., Mar. 29, 1857; s. Lothrop Wilson and Sarah Angeline D.; B.S., U. Wis., 1879; Ph.D., Johns Hopkins, 1884; m. Annie T. Wright, June 20, 1886. Prof. mathematics, Fla. Agrl. Coll., 1884-88, S.C. Coll., 1888-93, U. of Neb., 1893—; also dean Coll. Arts and Science, U. of Neb., 1901—. Author: An Introduction to the Logic of Algebra, 1889; The Calculus, 1912. Home: Lincoln, Neb. Died Feb. 2, 1918.

DAVIS, Frank, Jr., lawyer; b. New Richmond, O., Sept. 26, 1875; s. Frank and Elizabeth (Short) D.; B.A., Amherst, 1898; studied Cincinnati Law Sch.; m. Nancy P. House, Sept. 12, 1900. Practiced at Batavia, 1900-10; spl. counsel to atty. gen. of Ohio, 1911-14; mem. Bd. Examiners for Admission to Bar of Ohio, 1913-20; mem. McGee, Davis & Boulger, Columbus, 1914-16; asso. with Hoyt, Dustin, McKeehan & Andrews, Cleveland, O., 1918-19; asst. atty. gen. of U.S., 1919-21; became mem. Palmer, Davis & Scott, Washington, D.C. Democrat. Presbyn. Died Dec. 29, 1929.

DAVIS, Fred Henry, judge; b. Greenville, S.C., May 18, 1894; s. Fred Henry and Annie E. (Pearson) D.; grad. high sch., 1914; m. Frances M. Chambers, Feb. 3, 1921; children—Marilyn, Hazel Anice. Admitted to Fla. bar, 1914, bar of Supreme Court of U.S., 1921, and began practice at Tallahassee, Fla.; gen. county atty., Wakulla Co., 1916-25; spl. asst. U.S. atty., northern dist., Fla., 1917; county pros. atty., Leon Co., 1919-20; spl. counsel Fla. R.R. Commn., 1925-27. Served as pvt., later 2d lt. inf., U.S.A., 1918. Mem. Fla. Ho. of Rep. (speaker 1927), 1920-28; apptd. atty. gen. of Fla., 1927, elected to same office, 1928; apptd. justice Supreme Court, Fla., 1931, chief justice, 1933-35, justice, 1935—. Mem. Commn. for Reform of Pleading and Practice, Fla., 1926. Democrat. Methodist. Mason. Home: Tallahassee, Fla. Died June 20, 1937.

DAVIS, Frederick Henry, banker; b. Fairfield, Ia., June 10, 1853; s. Thomas and Elizabeth (Bennion) D.; ed. high sch., Indianapolis, Ind., and Episcopal Acad., Cheshire, Conn.; m. Nellie S. Clarkson, May 11, 1876; children—Thomas L., Mrs. Helen Roberts, Elizabeth, Mrs. M. D. Bohling. Began in banking business with First Nat. Bank, Omaha, Neb., 1872, then chmn. of bd. Republican. Episcopalian. Died Apr. 5, 1935.

DAVIS, George Breckenridge, army officer; b. Ware, Mass., Feb. 13, 1847; s. Solomon B. and Sarah (Dunbar) D.; grad. U.S. Mil. Acad., 1871; LL.B., Columbian (now George Washington) Univ., 1891; m. Ella I. Prince, July 6, 1871. Sergeant and q.m. sergeant, Co. I, and q.m. sergt. 1st Mass. Cav., Sept. 10, 1863-June 16, 1865; 2d lt. 1st Mass. Cav., June 17, 1865; hon. mustered out, June 26, 1865; cadet U.S. Mil. Acad., 1867-71; 2d lt. 5th Cav., June 12, 1871; 1st lt., May 9, 1877; capt., Aug. 21, 1888; maj. judge-adv., Dec. 10, 1888; lt. col. deputy judge-adv. gen., Aug. 3, 1895; prof. law and history, U.S. Mil. Acad., 1895-1901; col. judge-adv., May 22, 1901; brig. gen. judge-advocate gen. U.S.A., May 24, 1901; retired with rank of major gen., Feb. 13, 1911. Del. plenipotentiary to Geneva Conf., 1906, and to Second Peace Conf. at The Hague, 1907; mem. bd. com. Nat. Soldiers' Home, D.C. Author: Military Law, 1898; Military Laws of the United States, 1907; Elements of International Law, 1908. Home: Washington, D.C. Died Dec. 15, 1914.

DAVIS, George Royal, dir. gen. World's Columbian Expn., 1890-94; b. Palmer, Mass., 1840; prepared for college at Williston Sem., but enlisted as private, 8th Mass., 1861; served through war; rose to col., 3d R.I. cav.; received staff appointment regular army, but resigned, 1871; located in Chicago; mem. Congress, 1879-85; treas. Cook Co., Ill., 1886-90; long a member and officer Nat. Republican Committee; m. Gertrude Schulin, 1867. Home: Chicago, Ill. Died 1899.

DAVIS, George Samler, college pres.; b. New York, Oct. 22, 1858; s. Robert Vernon and Mary (Samler) D.; B.S., Coll. City of N.Y., 1880; LL.D., New York U., 1908; m. Emilia Wickham Suydam, July 3, 1888. Teacher pub. schs., 1880-87; asst. supt. schs., 1887-96, asso. city supt., 1896-1908, New York; became pres. Hunter Coll., City of N.Y., 1908 (emeritus). Episcopalian. Home: Kew Gardens, L.I., N.Y. Died Jan. 7, 1931.

DAVIS, George Whitefield, maj. gen.; b. Thompson, Conn., July 26, 1839; s. George and Elizabeth (Grow) D.; ed. Nichols Acad., Dudley, Mass., and State Normal Sch., New Britain, Conn.; m. Carmen Atocha, Apr. 30, 1870. Q.m. sergt. 11th Conn. Inf., Nov. 27, 1861; disch., Apr. 5, 1862; 1st lt. 11th Conn. Inf., Apr. 5, 1862; promoted through grades to brig. gen. U.S.V., May 4, 1898; hon. disch., Apr. 14, 1899, brig. gen. U.S.V., Apr. 14, 1899; col. 23d U.S. Inf., Oct. 19, 1899; brig. gen., Feb. 2, 1901; maj. gen., July 21, 1902. Bvtd.: Maj. vols., Mar. 13, 1865, "for faithful and meritorious services during the war." Asst. engr. in completion of Washington Nat. Monument, 1878-85; instr. in Inf. and Cav. Sch., Ft. Leavenworth, Kan., 1888-89; mgr. of a mfg. enterprise, Chicago, 1889-1900; mil. gov., Puerto Rico, 1899-1900; provost marshal gen. Div. of Philippines, 1901; comdg. Dept. of Mindanao and Luzon, P.I., 1901-02, Div. of Philippines, 1902-03; gen. mgr. and v.p. Nicaragua Canal Constrn. Co., 1900-03; retired by operation of law, July 26, 1903. Spl. duty in office of Sec. of War, 1903-06; pres. Bd. Publ. Official Records of Union and Confederate Armies, 1904-06; mem. Isthmian Canal Commn., 1904-05; gov. Panama Canal Zone, 1904-05; chmn. bd. of cons. engrs. on type of Panama Canal, 1905-06; E.E. and M.P. to Guatemala on spl. mission, 1907; spl. agt. Dept. of State to Govt. of Guatemala, 1913. Mem. Am. Nat. Red Cross (chmn. Central Com., 1907-15). Died July 12, 1918.

DAVIS, Gwilym George, surgeon; b. Altoona, Pa., July 20, 1857; s. Thomas Rees and Catherine (Fosselman) D.; A.B., Central High Sch., Phila., 1876, A.M., 1881; M.D., U. of Pa., 1879; M.D., U. of Göttingen, 1881; M.R.C.S., Eng., 1880; (LL.D., Lafayette Coll., 1911); unmarried. Resident phys., Pa. Hosp., 1881-82; surgeon to St. Joseph's, Episcopal, German, and Orthopedic hosps. many years.; asso. prof. applied anatomy, 1900-11, prof. orthopedic surgery, 1911—, U. of Pa.; orthopedic surgeon, Phila. Gen. Hosp., 1902-14; surgeon, Orthopedic Hosp. Republican. Lutheran. Fellow Am. Surg. Assn., Phila. Acad. Surgery, Coll. Phys. Phila. Mason. Author: The Principles and Practice of Bandaging, 1891; Applied Anatomy, 1910. Chief surgeon Widener Sch. for Crippled Children. Apptd. mem. advisory bd. on orthopedics of Gen. Md. Bd. of Council of Nat. Defense, Aug. 1917. Home: Philadelphia. Died June 16, 1918.

DAVIS, Harry Phillips; b. Somersworth, N.H., July 31, 1868; s. Harrison B. and Helen M. (Horne) D.; M.E., Worcester Poly. Inst., 1890, E.E., 1891; m. Agnes L. Taylor, June 29, 1892; children—Mrs. Louise D. Rockwell, Harry Ransom. With Westinghouse Elec. & Mfg. Co., 1891—; organized detail engring. dept.; apptd. asst. chief engr., 1904, mgr. of engring., 1909, asst. to 1st v.p. 1910, v.p. in charge mfg. and engring. activities, 1911—; v.p. Westinghouse Inter Works Ry., Turtle Creek & Allegheny R.R. Co.; chmn. bd. and dir. Nat. Broadcasting Co., Audio Vision Appliance Co. Republican. Episcopalian. Awarded many patents in elec. appliances. Home: Pittsburgh, Pa. Died Sept. 10, 1931.

DAVIS, Henry Edgar, lawyer; b. Washington, D.C., March 15, 1855; A.B., Princeton, 1876, A.M., 1879; LL.M., Columbian (now George Washington) U., 1879; (LL.D., Nat. U., 1898). Admitted to bar, 1879; asst. atty. of District of Columbia, 1885-89; U.S. atty. for D.C., 1897-99; prof. common law practice and lecturer on the history of law, Columbian U., 1888-97; prof. evidence, pleading and mercantile law, and lecturer on history of law, Nat. Univ., D.C., Oct. 1897—. Deceased.

DAVIS, Henry Gassaway, senator; b. Baltimore, Md., Nov. 16, 1823; s. Caleb and Louisa (Brown) D.; ed. at county schools, but being left fatherless went to work young; m. Kate A., d. Judge Gideon Bantz, of Frederick, Md., 1853; father-in-law of late Stephen B. Elkins. Became supt. of a plantation, then brakeman, conductor, and later agt. at Piedmont, W.Va., of the B.&O. R.R.; later mcht. and a leading collier; projected and carried on to success the West Va. Central & Pittsburgh Ry., which was sold to the Wabash, 1902; then built the Coal & Coke Ry. of W.Va., of 200 miles, of which is pres.; also pres. Davis Trust

Co. of Elkins, etc. Mem. Ho. of Del., W.Va., 1865, Senate, 1868-71; U.S. senator, 1871-83, declining reelection. Del. to 6 Dem. Nat. convs.; del. to 1st, chmn. of dels., 2d Pan-Am. Congress; mem. U.S. Permanent Pan-Am. Ry. Com. Democratic nominee for Vice-President of U.S., 1904. Home: Elkins, W.Va. Died Mar. 11, 1916.

DAVIS, Herbert Burnham, prin. training sch.; b. Charlestown, Mass., Aug. 17, 1867; s. Jacob Burnham and Mary Ann (Perkins) D.; A.B., Bates Coll., Me., 1890; scholar Clark U., Mass., 1906, fellow in psychology, 1907, Ph.D., 1908; m. Lena J. Pratt, Dec. 20, 1893; children—Irene, Christine. Teacher in pub. schs., 1886-88; instr., Nichols Latin Sch., Lewiston, Me., 1889, Arms Acad., Shelburne Falls, Mass., 1890-91, Cushing Acad., Ashburnham, Mass., 1891-97; instr. and v.prin., Wesleyan Acad., Wilbraham, Mass., 1897-1906; supt. Training Dept., 1908, prin., 1909-12, Southwestern State Normal Sch., California, Pa.; prin. Pittsburgh Training Sch. for Teachers, 1912—; cons. psychologist, Morals Court, Pittsburgh. Methodist. Home: Pittsburgh, Pa. Died Sept. 14, 1928.

DAVIS, Herman S(tearns), astronomer; b. Milford, Del., Aug. 6, 1868; s. Thomas Josiah and Mary Jane (Potter) D.; prep. edn., Wilmington Conf. Acad., Dover, Del., and Phillips Acad., Andover, Mass.; A.B., cum laude, Princeton, 1892, grad. study, 1892-93, A.M., 1912; Univ. fellow in astronomy, Columbia, 1893-95, A.M., 1894, Ph.D., 1895; m. Coreita Register Hoffecker, May 24, 1894; 1 son, Herman Stearns. Asst. astronomer, U.S. eclipse expdn. to W. Africa, 1889-90; teacher of astronomy and geodesy, Columbia, 1895-99; lecturer, Bd. of Edn., N.Y. City, 1896-99, 1905-07; asst. U.S. Coast and Geodetic Survey, 1900; dir. Internat. Latitude Observatory, Gaithersburg, Md., 1900-05; cons. engr. and auditor, N.Y. City and Pittsburgh, Pa., 1905-10; sec. to pres. Gulf Refining Co., Pittsburgh, 1910-20; sec.-treas. Indian River Fruit & Vegetable Co., Indian River Grove & Farming Co., Dupont Land Co., Indian River Corp., Matson Oil Co. Astronomer, Carnegie Instn., Nat. Acad. Sciences. Am. editor Astronomischer Jahresbericht, 1900-14; dir. New Reduction of Piazzi's Star Catalog, 1895—. Republican. Methodist. Mason. Author: Glossary to Homer's Iliad, 1888; Parallax of Eta Cassiopeiæ, 1895; Catalogue of 62 Stars about Eta Cassiopeiæ, 1895; Computation Forms for the Use of Classes in Practical Astronomy, 1897; An Abbreviated Form for Least Square Solutions, 1898; Private Cipher-Book, 1911; Dictionary of Telegraphic Code-Words, 1912. Home: Pittsburgh, Pa. Died May 23, 1933.

DAVIS, Horace, mfr.; b. Worcester, Mass., Mar. 16, 1831; s. John D. (gov. Mass.) and Eliza (Bancroft) D.; A.B., Harvard, 1849; (LL.D., U. of the Pacific, 1889, Harvard, 1911, U. of Calif., 1912); studied law, but went to San Francisco, 1852, and became mfr.; retired; m. Edith S., d. Rev. Thomas Starr King, 1875 (died 1909). Mem. 45th and 46th Congresses (1877-81); mem. Rep. Nat. Com., 1880-88; presdl. elector, 1884; pres. U. of Calif., 1887-90. Trustee Leland Stanford Jr. U. (pres. bd.); pres. Calif. Sch. Mech. Arts. Pres. Nat. Conf. of Unitarian Chs.; v.p. Am. Unitarian Assn. Home: San Francisco. Died July 13, 1916.

DAVIS, Irving Gilman, prof. agrl. economics; b. Poland, Me., Apr. 25, 1885; s. John Gilman and Juniata S. (Dunn) D.; A.B., Bates Coll., 1906; student Mass. Agrl. Coll., 1909-10; Ph.D., Harvard U., 1937; m. Alice I. Sawin, Aug. 18, 1914; children—Elizabeth V., Irving Gilman, Robert Sawin. Teacher rural sch., 1902-03; prin. and teacher high sch., 1907-12; instr. agrl. secondary sch., 1913-14; in agrl. extension work, 1915-18; acting dir. Conn. Agrl. Extension Service, 1918-19; prof. agrl. economics, Conn. State Coll., 1920—. Chmn. Advisory Com. on Agr. of Social Science Research Council. Progressive Republican. Conglist. Mason. Home: Storrs, Conn. Died Mar. 15, 1939.

DAVIS, J. Frank (James Francis), author; b. New Bedford, Mass., Dec. 20, 1870; s. James and Ann (Francis) D.; ed. pub. schs., New Bedford and Brockton, Mass.; m. Clara Franklin Draper, Oct. 7, 1896. Newspaperman, salesman and publicity work, 1886-1904; spl. writer Boston American, 1904-07; mng. editor Boston Tribune, 1907; spl. polit. writer Boston Herald, 1908; city editor Boston Traveler, 1908-09, asso. editor, 1910; state supervisor Tex. Writers' Project, Work Projects Administration, 1935—. Republican. Mason. Author: Almanzar, 1918; The Chinese Label, 1920; Almanzar Evarts, Hero, 1925; The Road to San Jacinto, 1936; (plays) The Ladder, 1926; Gold in the Hills, 1930; Ladies' Night, 1934; (one-act plays) Freckles; Appearances; Midnight. Home: San Antonio, Tex. Died Apr. 6, 1942.

DAVIS, James, bishop; b. Tinvawn, Co. Kilkenny, Ireland, 1852; s. James and Margaret D.; ed. under Carmelite fathers, at Knocktopher, parish of Donemagin, Ireland, and at Carlow. Ordained priest, R.C. Ch., Kildare, Ireland, 1878; came to America, 1878; had charge of St. Peter's congregation, Windham, also St. Michael's Ch., Holbrook, Ia., 1878-84; consecrated coadjutor bishop of Davenport and titular bishop of Milopotamus, Nov. 30, 1904; consecrated bishop of Davenport, Dec. 22, 1906, succeeding Bishop Cosgrove (dec.). Died Dec. 2, 1926.

DAVIS, James Cox, lawyer; b. Keokuk, Ia., Sept. 2, 1857; s. Caleb F. and Caroline T. (Cox) D.; ed. Keokuk pub. schs. and Hellmuth Boys' Coll., London, Ont.; m. Clara B. Mooar, Dec. 10, 1884 (died 1895); children—Daniel M., Ora (Mrs. Robert Fullerton, Jr.), Caroline Thistle (Mrs. John T. Corley); m. 2d, Louise M. Pomeroy, Aug. 15, 1901; children—James C., Jr., Joseph P., Frank W. Admitted to bar, 1877; practiced at Keokuk, 1877-1903; city solicitor, 1881-83, mayor, 1885-87; apptd. gen. atty. for Iowa of C.&N.W. Ry. Co., Jan. 1, 1903, and moved to Des Moines. Apptd. gen. solicitor C.&N.W. R.R., under federal administration, Apr. 23, 1918, and moved to Chicago; apptd. gen. counsel U.S. R.R. Administration, June 15, 1920, and moved to Washington; apptd. (1921) dir. gen. railroads and agt. of the President in liquidating and settling controversies rising out of federal control (resigned, 1926); mem. Davis, McLaughlin & Hise, 1926—. Episcopalian. Home: Des Moines, Ia. Died Aug. 31, 1937.

DAVIS, Jeff, senator; b. Little River Co., Ark., May 6, 1862; s. Lewis W. and Mary D.; ed. Russellville, Ark.; LL.B., Vanderbilt U., 1884; admitted to bar, 1884; m. Ina McKenzie, 1882 (dec.); m. 2d, Leila, d. Dr. Wallace A. Carter, of Ozark, Ark., Oct. 12, 1911. Pros. atty. 5th Jud. Dist., Ark., 1892; atty. gen. of Ark., 1898; gov. Ark., 1900-07; U.S. senator, 1907-13. Del.-at-large Dem. Nat. Conv., 1904. Home: Little Rock, Ark. Died Jan. 3, 1913.

DAVIS, John, asso. judge U.S. Court of Claims, Jan. 20, 1885—; b. Newton, Mass., Sept. 16, 1851; studied in Univs. of Heidelberg, Berlin and Paris; (A.M., Harvard). Held several minor diplomatic posts, and became, 1874, clerk of court of Ala. Claims; practiced law, Washington and New York; asst. counsel for U.S. before Franco-Am. Claims Commn., 1881; asst. sec. of State, 1882-85. Died 1902.

DAVIS, John Chandler Bancroft, reporter U.S. Supreme Court, Nov., 1883—; b. Worcester, Mass., Dec. 29, 1822; s. Gov. John D., of Mass.; grad. Harvard, 1840; (LL.D., Columbia); studied law and began practice; sec. U.S. legation, London, 1849-53; practiced law, New York, and at same time Am. corr. London Times, 1854-61; mem. N.Y. legislature, 1869; asst. sec. of state, U.S., 1869-71, and 1873-74; agt. U.S. Govt. before Geneva Court of Arbitration, Alabama Claims, 1871; U.S. minister to Germany, 1874-77; judge U.S. Court of Claims, 1878-82. Author: The Massachusetts Justice; The Case of the United States Before the Tribunal of Arbitration at Geneva; Treaties of the United States, With Notes; Mr. Fish and the "Alabama" Claims; numerous vols. U.S. Supreme Court Reports. Died 1907.

DAVIS, John Charles, banker; b. Ireland, March 14, 1852; ed. Westbury and Salisbury, Eng.; m. Jan., 1883, Ella M. Castiday. Organized 1st Nat. Bank, Rawlins, Wyo., 1891; cashier 8 yrs. Organized Bank of Rifle, Colo.; Bank of Steamboat, Colo.; Bank of Meeker, Colo.; Bank of Craig, Colo.; pres. Bank of Hayden, Colo., Bank of Palisade, Colo.; pres. and gen. mgr. J. W. Hughes & Co.; organized Davis-Bridaham Drug Co., Denver, 1901. Mem. State Constl. Conv., 1890; chmn. bd. co. commrs., 1890-1901; mayor Rawlins, 1892; chmn. delegation to Rep. Nat. Conv., 1897; chmn. Rep. State Central Com., 1898. Candidate U.S. Senate, 1893 and 1899. Home: Denver, Colo. Died 1909.

DAVIS, John D., theologian; b. Pittsburgh, Pa., Mar. 5, 1854; s. Robert and Anne Williams (Shaw) D.; A.B., Princeton, 1879, A.M., 1882; Ph.D., 1886; grad. Princeton Theol. Sem., 1883; U. of Bonn, 1879-80, Leipzig, 1884-86; D.D., Princeton, 1898; LL.D., Washington and Jefferson, 1902; m. Marguerite Scobie, June 13, 1889; children—Jean Scobie, Nathaniel Penistone, Anne Wallis, Marguerite, Philip Haldane, Lois Elizabeth. Instr. Hebrew, 1883-84, 1886-88, prof. Hebrew and cognate langs., 1888-92, Semitic philology and O.T. history, 1892-1900, Oriental and O.T. lit., 1900—, Princeton Theol. Sem. Author: Genesis and Semitic Tradition, 1894; A Dictionary of the Bible, 1898, 4th edit., 1924. Writer of critical notes in Westminster Teacher, July 1899-Dec. 1907. Died June 21, 1926.

DAVIS, John Francis, lawyer; b. Angel Island, San Francisco Bay, Calif., June 5, 1859; A.B., magna cum laude, Harvard, 1881; LL.B., Hastings Coll. of Law (U. of Calif.), 1884; traveled and studied in Europe 2 yrs.; m. Lillian Parks, Nov. 26, 1896; children—Mary Lillian (wife of Leland Stanford Lathrop, Jr.), Ruth Margaret (Mrs. Walter P. Busher), John Parks, Janet Frances. Judge of the Superior Court of Amador County, California, 1892-94 (resigned); mem. Calif. Senate, sessions of 1899, 1900, 1901; settled at San Francisco, 1903; code commr. of Calif., 1903-07; mem. Bd. Fire Commrs., San Francisco, 1914-24 (pres. most of time); pres. Calif. Hist. Survey Commn., 1915-23; civil service commr., San Francisco, Jan. 7, 1924—. Apptd. mem. Commn. on Calif. Representation at the Statuary Hall, Washington, D.C., 1927 (elected chmn.). Republican. Catholic. Home: San Francisco, Calif. Died May 3, 1930.

DAVIS, J(ohn) McCan, author; b. Fulton Co., Ill., Nov. 19, 1866; s. Martin L. and Nancy F. (McCan) D.; ed. pub. and normal schs.; m. Florence Flower Packard. Began writing for newspapers at 15; official ct. reporter Fulton Co., Ill., 1887; removed to Springfield, 1888; became newspaper corr., editor and publisher; admitted to Ill. bar, 1895, and practiced law. Active in Rep. politics of Ill.; sec. Ill. State Bd. of Arbitration, 1897-1904; clk. Ill. Supreme Ct., 1908-14; Rep. nominee for Congress, Ill.-at-large, 1914. Author: The Early Life of Abraham Lincoln (with Ida M. Tarbell), 1896; Abraham Lincoln—His Book, 1901; The Breaking of the Deadlock, 1904; How Abraham Lincoln Became President, 1909. Home: Springfield, Ill. Died May 11, 1916.

DAVIS, John Merrill, educator; b. Harrisonville, O., Nov. 16, 1846; s. William and Samantha (Chase) D.; pvt. 188th Ohio Vols., 7 mos., 1865; A.B., Ohio U., Athens, 1873, A.M. 1876; Ph.D., U. of Wooster 1886; (D.D., Ohio U., 1896); m. Jane Elliott Boyd, June 22, 1876. Taught in Ohio U., 1872-74, in Ridgeville Col., Ind., 1874-78, in Rio Grande Coll., 1879-1919, pres., 1887-1911, prof. psychology and ethics, 1911-19. Mem. Conf. Bd. Free Bapt. Ch., 1892-95; del. Inter-Ch. Conf., New York, 1906, Federal Council Chs. of Christ in America, Phila., 1908, St. Louis, 1916, Nat. Rivers and Harbors Congress, Washington, 1908; pres. Ohio Free Baptist State Assn., 1906-07; mem. advisory council Ohio Rural Life Assn., 1916—. Retired from active work, 1919. Home: Rio Grande, O. Died Nov. 11, 1920.

DAVIS, John Moore Kelso, brig. gen.; b. Washington, Jan. 31, 1844; s. Dr. A. McD. and Martha (Kelso) D.; 1st lt. 3d Md. Cav., July 1863; apptd., Sept. 1863, from Ark. and grad. U.S. Mil. Acad., 1867; honor grad. Arty. Sch., 1869; m. Fanny Sanger, June 7, 1870. Commd. 2d lt. 1st Arty., June 17, 1867; promoted through grades to brig. gen. U.S.A., May 25, 1907. Comd. Dept. of the Gulf, July 1907-Jan. 31, 1908; retired by operation of law, Jan. 31, 1908. Home: Hartford, Conn. Died May 20, 1920.

DAVIS, John Patterson, lawyer, author, economist; b. Niles, Mich., May 27, 1862; grad. Univ. of Mich., 1885 (A.M., Ph.D., 1894). Admitted to bar, Berrien Co., Mich., 1888; practiced Omaha, Neb., 1888-92; asst. in history and economics, Univ. of Mich., 1894-95; in law practice in Idaho, 1895—. Author: The Union Pacific Railway, a Study of Political and Economic History, 1894 G6; also articles in reviews. Home: Nampa, Ida. Died 1903.

DAVIS, John William, gov. R.I.; b. Rehoboth, Mass., Mar. 7, 1826; lived on farm until 1844; ed. in public schools in Mass., and private school, Pawtucket, R.I.; in summers, 1844-50, in mason and civ. engring. work, teaching school winters; in grain trade, Providence, 1850-90; attending to trust estates, 1890—. Mem. and pres. town council, 1882; reelected, 1885; State senator, 1885-1886, 1893; U.S. appraiser foreign merchandise for Providence, R.I., customs dist., 1886; gov. R.I., 1887 and 1890; mem. Nat. Dem. Conv., 1884-1892, 1900; mayor of Pawtucket, 1897; mem. State House Commn., 1890. While gov. instituted searching investigation and reform in prison discipline; secured constl. amendment extending elective franchise to all citizens upon uniform qualifications; reform ballot law, and establishment of Coll. of A. & M. Art. Home: Pawtucket, R.I. Died 1907.

DAVIS, John Williams, engr.; b. Petersburg, Va., Nov. 21, 1887; s. Richard Beale and Annie Warwick (Hall) D.; prep. edn., Petersburg Acad., 1897-1904; Randolph Macon Coll., Ashland, Va., 1904-06; M.E., Cornell U., 1910; M.S., U. of Ill., 1917; m. Elizabeth Grimes Walker, Oct. 22, 1921; children—John Williams, Elizabeth Walker, Timothy Pickering. Instructor in elec. engring., Harvard U., 1910-11, Vanderbilt, 1912-13, Stanford, 1913-14, Univ. of Ill., 1914-17; also with various engring. firms for short periods, 1910-17; research in helium gas, U.S. Bur. Mines (inventor process for separation of helium from natural gas), 1919-25; head of development div., later head of tech. dept. Atmospheric Nitrogen Corp., Syracuse, N.Y., and Hopewell, Va., 1925-29; has been cons. engr., Atmospheric Nitrogen Corp. and The Solvay Process Co., 1929— (inventor of improvements in processes for nitrogen fixation). Mem. commn. to Toronto, Can., on establishment of schs. of mil. aeronautics in U.S., 1917; asst. in establishment of sch. of mil. aeronautics at U. of Ill., 1917; adj. Flying Dept., U.S.A., Kelly Field, San Antonio, Tex., later asst. to exec. officer U.S. Air Service, Washington, D.C., and later in charge helium work for Air Service, World War; reserve mil. aviator, capt. Air Service Reserve. Democrat. Home: Petersburg, Va. Died Oct. 4, 1938.

DAVIS, John Woodbridge, civil engr.; b. New York, Aug. 19, 1854; s. Dr. Edwin Hamilton and Lucy (Woodbridge) D.; C.E., Columbia School of Mines, 1878 (Ph.D., 1880); began practice as civ. engr., New York. Devised plan for sending life lines ashore from ships by means of kites; in April, 1893, with cooperation of U.S. Govt., sent out a stout life line, dragged by a large steerable kite, from Brenton Reef lightship to Brenton's Point, a tongue of land 1¾ miles distant. Author: Dynamics of the Sun, 1891. Died 1902.

DAVIS, Joseph Baker, engr.; b. Westport, Mass., July 31, 1845; s. Ebenezer Hathaway and Mehitabel C. (Gifford) D.; C.E., U. of Mich., 1868; m. Mary H. Baldwin, July 10, 1872. Asst. prof. civ. engring., 1872-91, prof. geodesy and surveying, 1891-1910, asso. dean dept. engring., 1904-07, U. of Mich.; chief engr. St. Clair Flats Survey, Mich., 1899-1902. Retired, 1910. Home: Dexter, Mich. Died Mar. 9, 1920.

DAVIS, Joseph Phineas, engr.; b. Northboro, Mass., Apr. 15, 1837; s. William E. and Almira L. (Sherman) D.; C.E., Rensselaer Poly. Inst., 1856; unmarried. Asst. engr. on constrn. of Brooklyn water wks., 1856-61 and 1865; topog. engr., Govt. Peru, S.A., 1861-65; chief engr. Brooklyn park commrs., 1866; prin. asst. engr. on constrn. St. Louis water works, 1867-69; chief engr. on constrn. Lowell (Mass.) water works, 1870-71; chief engr. Boston Water Bd., 1872; city engr., Boston, 1873-80; chief engr. Am. Bell Telephone Co. and its successor, Am. Telephone & Telegraph Co., 1880-1905; cons. engr. Croton Aqueduct Commrs., 1884-86, Mass. State Bd. Health, 1886-1904, Met. Water Bd., Mass., 1895-1907, Met. Sewerage Commrs., Mass., 1898. V.p. and gen. mgr. Met. Telephone Co., New York, 1880-86; pres. Hudson River Telephone Co., 1889-95, Westchester Telephone Co., 1890-93. Home: Yonkers, N.Y. Died Mar. 31, 1917.

DAVIS, Kary Cadmus, agrl. educator; b. Decatur, Ill., Oct. 7, 1867; s. John and Martha (Powell) D.; B.S., Kan. State Agrl. Coll., 1891, M.S., 1894; grad. Kan. State Normal Sch., Emporia, 1892; Ph.D., Cornell, 1900; m. Fanny Elisabeth Waugh, Aug. 19, 1896; children—Douglas Powell, Louise Davis. Prin. State High Sch., Austin, Minn., 1892-98; science teacher, State Normal Sch., St. Cloud, Minn., 1900-01; prof. horticulture, W.Va. U. and Expt. Sta., Morgantown, 1901-02; prin., Dunn Co. Sch. Agr., Menomonie, Wis., 1902-07; dean, State Sch. Agr., Canton, N.Y., 1907-08; prof. agronomy and prin. agrl. short courses, State Agrl. Coll. (Rutgers), New Brunswick, N.J., 1908-13; prof. agrl. edn., Knapp Sch. of Country Life (George Peabody Coll. for Teachers), Nashville, Tenn., 1913—. Conductor 11 summer training schs. for teachers in Minn., Wis. and N.J.; prof. agr., U. of Va. Summer Sch., 1908-12. Author: Productive Farming, 1911; School and Home Gardening, 1917; Productive Plant Husbandry, 1917; Horticulture for Schools, 1919; New Agriculture for High Schools, 1923; Farm Projects and Problems, 1927; Horticulture Enterprises, 1929; Modern Productive Farming, 1932. Joint author: Soils Laboratory Manual, 1915; How to Teach Agriculture, 1921; Field Crop Enterprises, 1930; Livestock Enterprises, 1930. Editor, Laboratory Manual Series, 5 vols.; Lippincott's Farm Manuals, 18 vols.; Farm Life Text Series, 6 vols.; Farm Enterprise Series, 10 vols., etc. Died Mar. 4, 1936.

DAVIS, Katharine Bement, sociologist; b. Buffalo, N.Y., Jan. 15, 1860; d. Oscar B. and Frances (Bement) D.; A.B., Vassar, 1892; fellow in polit. economy, U. of Chicago, 1897-98, 1899-1900, Ph.D., 1900; foreign fellow N.E. Women's Ednl. Assn., 1898-99, Berlin and Vienna; LL.D., Mt. Holyoke, 1912, Western Reserve, 1914; A.M., Yale, 1915; unmarried. Supt. N.Y. State Reformatory for Women, 1901-14; commr. of correction, N.Y. City, by appmt. of Mayor Mitchel, Jan. 1, 1914-Dec. 28, 1915; chmn. Parole Commn., 1915-17; dir. sect. on Women's work, div. social hygiene of Commn. on Training Camp Activities, 1918; gen. sec. Bur. Social Hygiene, 1918-28; retired. Home: Asilomar, Calif. Died Dec. 10, 1935.

DAVIS, Lemuel Clarke, editor; b. nr. Sandusky, O., Sept. 25, 1835; common school edn.; entered newspaper life, and in 1869 became editor Phila. Inquirer; later editor Public Ledger; m. Rebecca Harding, 1863; father of Richard Harding and C. Belmont Davis. Author: The Stranded Ship, etc. Home: Philadelphia, Pa. Died 1904.

DAVIS, Leonard Moore, artist; b. Winchendon, Mass., May 8, 1864; s. Charles Robert Wilson and Maria (Gilson) D.; student Coll. City of N.Y., Art Students League, 1884-89, Academie Julian (under Laurens, Lefebvre and Constant and of Ecole des Beaux Arts, Paris, 1889-90, 1894-95; m. Viola Henriette Russell, June 14, 1913. Began as woodfinisher, printer, lithographic artist, 1884; portrait painter, art teacher, gold miner in Alaska, landscape painter; lecturer on art in relation to human development and "Alaska, the Beautiful" for Bd. of Edn., New York, for 9 years. Awarded silver medal Panama-Pacific Expn., 1915. Represented in exhbns. at Brandus Galleries, New York, 1910, Am. Mus. of Natural History, 1913, 18, 28, British Empire Expn., 1923, St. James's Palace, London, 1924, Union League Club, New York, 1926, Parliament Bldg., Victoria, B.C., 1929; permanently represented in Am. Mus. of Natural History Planetariums by 27 views of the aurora borealis, children's ward of Los Angeles Co. Gen. Hosp. by mural "Involution and Evolution," also in State Mus. of N.M., Seattle Pub. Library, etc. Republican. Mason. Home: Tarzana, Calif. Died May 5, 1938.

DAVIS, Lyman Edwyn, clergyman, editor, author; b. Perrysburg nr. Toledo, O., Dec. 28, 1854; s. John Wesley and Martha (Powers) D.; U. of Neb., 1872-73; A.B., Adrian (Mich.) Coll., 1877, A.M., 1881, LL.D., 1912; D.D., Kansas City U., 1902; m. Ella H. Hood, Oct. 23, 1877; children—Laura (Mrs. Frederick Crisp), Marion (Mrs. Arthur Hugh Davis). Ordained ministry M.P. Ch., 1877; pastor, Tarrytown-on-Hudson, N.Y., 1878, Rockville Center, N.Y., 1882, Brooklyn, 1887, Middletown, N.Y., 1890, Albany, 1893, Saratoga, N.Y., 1895, Grace Ch., Pittsburgh, 1896-1913. Pres. Gen. Conf. M.P. Ch., 1912-20. Editor Meth. Recorder, 1913-29; editor Meth. Protestant-Recorder, 1929—. Studied social conditions in London, Eng., writing for Am. Syndicates on "Life Studies of London." Mem. exec. com. Federal Council Chs. of Christ in America and of Nat. Reform Assn. Mem. Gen. War Time Commn. of the Churches and of nat. com. on army and navy chaplains. Author: Jonathan Twigg; The Scepter of Washington; Social Doctrines of Christianity; Democratic Methodism in America; The Creed of Bethlehem. Home: Baltimore, Md. Died Aug. 13, 1930.

DAVIS, Mary Evelyn Moore ("Mollie E. Moore"), author; b. Talladega, Ala., 1852; d. Dr. John and Marian Lucy (Crutchfield) Moore, reared on Texas plantation; m. Maj. Thomas Edward Davis, 1874. Author: Minding the Gap, and Other Poems; In War Times at La Rose Blanche; Under the Man-Fig; An Elephant's Track, and Other Stories; Under Six Flags; Wire Cutters, 1899; The Queen's Garden, 1900; Jaconetta; The Price of Silence, 1907. Died 1909.

DAVIS, Milton Fennimore, army officer, educator; b. Mantorville, Minn., Nov. 15, 1864; s. Evan Richard and Julia Ann (Ryder) D.; grad. U.S. Mil. Acad., 1890; hon. M.A., U. of Ore.; m. Bessie Aitken Hall; children—Margaret Hall (wife of Frank A. Pattillo, U.S.A.), Dorothy (dec.), Helen Dorman, Milton F. Commd. 2d lt. cav., June 12, 1890; promoted through grades to maj., June 14, 1909 (retired); lt. col., ret., July 9, 1918; col. ret., May 29, 1921. Mapped Yosemite and Sequoia parks and Sierra Forest Reserve, 1891-96; explored Grand Canyon of the Colorado, 1895; adj. gen. 3d Brigade, Philippine Insurrection, 1900-03; exec. sec. of staff, Inf. and Cav. Sch., U.S.A., 1903-07; with Gen. Staff and aide to chief of staff, 1907-09; made comdt., sec. and treas. New York Mil. Acad., 1909, now supt. Served as chief of training and executive, U.S. Air Service, World War; brig. gen. A.C. Res., 1920. Silver star citation "for gallantry" at Battle of Santiago, 1898; D.S.M., World War. Sec. treas. New York Mil. Acad. Realty Co.; v.p. Cornwall Nat. Bank. Fellow Am. Geog. Soc. Mem. Chamber of Commerce of U.S. (nat. councillor), Hudson Valley Federated Chamber of Commerce (pres.); nat. councillor Boy Scouts America. Republican. Presbyn. Mason. Died May 31, 1938.

DAVIS, Nathan Smith, M.D.; b. Greene, N.Y., Jan. 9, 1817; s. Dow and Eleanor Smith D.; ed. common school and Cazenovia Sem.; grad. Coll. Phys. & Surg., Fairfield, N.Y., 1837; (A.M., Northwestern; LL.D., Ill. Wesleyan); m. Anna Maria Parker, Mar. 1838. Practiced medicine at Vienna and Binghamton, N.Y., and 1847-49, at New York; from 1849 at Chicago. Lecturer, Coll. Phys. & Surg., New York, 1848; prof. Rush Med. Coll., Chicago, 1849-59; one of founders, 1859, of Chicago Med. Coll. (now med. dept. Northwestern U.); prof. there for 30 yrs. and dean of faculty until 1898, resigned. Was editor of The Annalist, New York; afterward of Chicago Med. Journal, and later of Chicago Med. Examiner; 6 yrs. editor of Journal of the A.M.A. One of founders of Mercy Hosp., and one of its physicians over 40 yrs.; a founder and trustee Northwestern Univ., Union Coll. of Law (prof. med. jurisprudence), and Washingtonian Home for Reformation of Inebriates. Author: Prniciples and Practice of Medicine; Medical Education and Reform. Home: Chicago, Ill. Died 1904.

DAVIS, Nathan Smith, physician; b. Chicago, Sept. 5, 1858; s. Dr. Nathan Smith and Anna Maria (Parker) D.; A.B., Northwestern U., 1880, A.M., 1883; M.D., Chicago Med. Coll., 1883, and began practice in Chicago; post-grad. course in Heidelberg, and Vienna, 1885; m. Jessie B. Hopkins, Apr. 16, 1884. Asso. prof. pathology, 1884-86, prof. principles and practice of medicine and of clin. medicine, 1886—, and formerly dean, Northwestern U. Med. Sch.; phys. to Mercy Hosp., 1883—, Wesley Hosp., 1899—, St. Luke's Hosp., 1909—. Mem. 9th Internat. Med. Congress, Pan-Am. Med. Congress, etc.; v.p. U.S. Pharmacopœia Conv., 1910; formerly chmn. sect. of therapeutics and pharmacology and sec. of sect. of medicine, A.M.A.; chmn. sect. of medicine, Ill. State Med. Soc. Trustee Northwestern U., Chicago Y.M.C.A., Wesley Hosp.; chmn. bd. scientific govrs., Chicago Acad. Science. Author: Consumption, How to Prevent It and How to Live With It; Diseases of the Lungs, Heart and Kidneys; Diet in Health and Disease. Home: Chicago, Ill. Died Dec. 21, 1920.

DAVIS, Nathaniel French, univ. prof.; b. Lake Village (now Laconia), N.H., June 11, 1847; s. John and Rhoda French (Maxfield) D.; A.B., Brown U., 1870, A.M., 1873; U. of Göttingen, 1892-93; (LL.D., Colby, 1894); m. Lydia Martin Bellows, Dec. 23, 1878. In engineering dept., Providence Water works, 1870-71; instr. Riverview Mil. Acad., Poughkeepsie, N.Y., 1871-73; v.prin. and prof. mathematics and physics, Keystone State Normal Sch., Kutztown, Pa., 1873-74; instr. mathematics, 1874-79, asst. prof., 1879-89, asso. prof., 1889-90, prof. pure mathematics, 1890-1915 (emeritus), Brown U. Sec. N.E. Coll. Entrance Certificate Board, 1902-1913, pres., 1913-15; mem. commn. to investigate pub. sch. system of city of Providence, 1898-99. Home: Cambridge, Mass. Died May 17, 1921.

DAVIS, Nelson Fithian, biologist; b. Seeley, N.J., Aug. 10, 1872; s. George D. and Frances (Moore) D.; Sc.B., Bucknell U., Lewisburg, Pa., 1895, Sc.M., 1896, Sc.D., 1903; student Marine Biol. Lab., Cold Spring Harbor, L.I., N.Y., summers, 1895, 96; m. Nellie Taylor, 1899 (died 1904); children—Nelson Fithian, Frances Moore; m. 2d, Ella Marion Briggs, 1905. With biol. dept. Bucknell U., 1898—, prof. biology and head of dept., 1910—; instr. biology, Marine Biol. Lab., Cold Spring Harbor, summers, 1898-1903; in charge zoölogy, U. of Vt. Summer Sch., 1914. Republican. Presbyn. Mason. Home: Lewisburg, Pa. Died Nov. 11, 1939.

DAVIS, Noah, lawyer; b. Haverhill, N.H., Sept. 10, 1818; removed to Albion, N.Y., 1825; academic edn.; admitted to bar, 1841; practiced in Gaines, then in Buffalo; justice N.Y. Supreme Court, 1857-68, resigned; mem. Congress, 1869-70; Rep.; U.S. atty., Southern dist., N.Y., 1870-72; again justice Supreme Court, N.Y., 1872-87; resumed practice in New York. The cases of Stokes for murder of Fisk, and of William M. Tweed for official malfeasance, were tried before him. Died 1902.

DAVIS, Noah Knowles, educator; b. Phila., May 15, 1830; s. Rev. Noah D. (founder Am. Bapt. Publ. Soc.); A.B., Mercer U., Ga., 1849, A.M., 1853 (Ph.D., 1885; LL.D., Baylor U., 1872, Furman U. 1909); m. Ella Hunt, Nov. 25, 1856. Prof. natural science, Howard Coll., Ala., 1852-59; prin. Judson Female Inst., Ala., 1859-65; pres. Bethel Coll., Russellville, Ky., 1868-73; prof. philosophy, 1873-1906 (emeritus), U. of Va. Baptist. Democrat. Author: Elements of Deductive Logic, 1890; Elements of Psychology, 1892; Elements of Inductive Logic, 1895; Elements of Ethics, 1900; Synopsis of Events in Life of Jesus of Nazareth, 1900. Home: University, Va. Died 1910.

DAVIS, Oscar King, newspaperman; b. Baldwinsville, N.Y., Jan. 13, 1866; A.B., Colgate, 1888, A.M., 1892, Litt.D., 1914; m. Jessie Bates Johnson, Apr. 6, 1899; children—Margaret, Oscar King. Spl. corr. New York Sun and Harper's Weekly at Manila, during Spanish-Am. War, Philippine Insurrection, and in China during the troubles of 1900; spl. corr. N.Y. Herald with First Japanese Army, 1904; Washington corr. New York Times and Phila. Public Ledger, 1907-12; was sec. Progressive Nat. Com., 1912, and in charge publicity dept.; spl. corr. Chicago Tribune in China, 1915, of New York Times in Berlin, 1916-17. Del. from U.S. to First Pan-Am. Postal Congress, Buenos Aires, 1921, v.p. of Congress; sec. Nat. Foreign Trade Council, 1917—. Author: Our Conquests in the Pacific; At the Emperor's Wish; Dewey's Capture of Manila; Sherreaf's Exclusive, and other stories; The Storm Birds (with Reginald Schroeder); Released for Publication. Home: Bronxville, N.Y. Died June 3, 1932.

DAVIS, Ozora Stearns, theologian; b. Wheelock, Vt., July 30, 1866; s. Alexander Warner and Caroline (Burroughs) D.; A.B., Dartmouth, 1889; grad. Hartford (Conn.) Theol. Sem., 1894; A.M., Ph.D., U. of Leipzig, 1896; (D.D., Ia. Coll., 1906, Dartmouth, 1909; LL.D., Colo. Coll., 1921, Washburn Coll., 1922); m. Grace Emeline Tinker, Nov. 17, 1896. Ordained Congl. ministry, 1896; prin. White River Junction High Sch., 1889-91; pastor First Ch., Springfield, Vt., 1896-99, Central Ch., Newtonville, Mass., 1899-1904, South Ch., New Britain, Conn., 1904-08; pres. Chicago Theol. Sem., 1909-29, now pres. emeritus and prof. of practical theology. Author: The Pilgrim Faith, 1913; Using the Bible in Public Address, 1916; At Mother's Knee, 1916; Meeting the Master, 1917; The Gospel in the Light of the Great War, 1919; Evangelistic Preaching, 1921; Comrades in the Great Cause, 1921; Preaching the Social Gospel, 1922; Preaching by Layman, 1923; Principles of Preaching, 1924; Preaching on Church and Community Occasions, 1929. Moderator of the Congl. Ch., 1927-29. Died Mar. 15, 1931.

DAVIS, Raymond Cazallis, librarian; b. Cushing, Me., June 1836; s. George and Katharine (Young) D.; student U. of Mich., 1855-57 (hon. A.M., 1881); m. Ellen Regal, July 6, 1880. Made voyage around the world, 1849-51. Librarian, 1877-1905, librarian emeritus and lecturer on books and reading, from Oct. 1, 1905, U. of Mich.; retired, 1914. Home: Ann Arbor, Mich. Died June 10, 1919.

DAVIS, Rebecca (Blaine) Harding, author; b. Washington, Pa., June 24, 1831; d. Richard and Rachel Leet (Wilson) Harding; m. L. Clarke Davis, Mar. 4, 1863 (died 1904); mother of Richard Harding and Charles Belmont D. Author: Margaret Howth, Waiting for the Verdict, Dallas Galbraith, A Law Unto Herself, Kitty's Choice, John Andross, Kent Hampden, Natasqua, Silhouettes of American Life, Frances Waldeaux, Doctor Warrick's Daughters, Bits of Gossip, etc. Home: Philadelphia. Died 1910.

DAVIS, Reuben Nelson, museum dir.; b. Lemon, Pa., Apr. 13, 1858; s. Charles R. and Julia A. (Sheldon) D.; grad. Wyoming Sem., Kingston, Pa., 1880; Ph.B., Ill. Wesleyan U., 1902; m. Sarah M. Evans, 1883; children—Harold E., Jennie E., Catherine. Formerly teacher high schs. and Y.M.C.A.; curator Everhart Mus., Scranton, Pa., 1912-24, dir., 1924—. Conducted nat. history expdn. to Panama, 1921. Republican. Presbyn. Mason. Author: Butterflies of Lackawanna County, Pa., 1914; The Nature of Gravitation, 1931. Home: Dunmore, Pa. Died Jan. 1934.

DAVIS, Richard Beale, lawyer; b. Hickory Ground, Va., Feb. 5, 1845; s. Williams Thomas and Elizabeth Taylor Corbin (Beale) D.; A.B., Randolph-Macon Coll., Va., 1861; pvt. Co. E, 12th Va. Inf., C.S.A., 1862-65; LL.B., U. of Va., 1870; m. Annie Warwick Hall, Apr. 20, 1875. In practice at Petersburg, Va., 1871—; mem. Va. Ho. of Dels., 1875-77, 1902-04; city atty., Petersburg, 1879-81; asst. atty. gen., Va., Jan. 1911—. Mem. legislative com. to revise the statutes, 1902; trustee Randolph-Macon Coll., 1876—; pres. board Va. Normal School, 1914—. Democrat. Methodist. Home: Petersburg, Va. Died July 11, 1917.

DAVIS, Richard Harding, novelist, playwright; b. Phila., Pa., 1864; s. the late L. Clarke and Rebecca Blaine (Harding) D.; brother of Charles Belmont D.; ed. Lehigh and Johns Hopkins univs.; m. Cecil, d. J. M. Clark, of Chicago, Apr. 4, 1899 (divorced 1912); m. 2d, Bessie McCoy. War corr. of London Times and New York Herald in Turkish-Greek, Spanish-American, South African and Russian-Japanese wars. Fellow Royal Geog. Society, London. Author: Soldiers of Fortune, 1899; Gallagher and Other Stories; The Princess Aline; Our English Cousins; Van Bibber and Others; About Paris; The Rulers of the Mediterranean; Three Gringos in Venezuela; Cuba in War Time, 1898; A Year from a Correspondent's Note-Book, 1898; Stories for Boys, Cuban and Porto Rican Campaigns, 1898; Cinderella and Other Stories; Dr. Jameson's Raiders; Exiles; The King's Jackal, 1898; The Lion and the Unicorn, 1899; The West from a Car Window; Episodes in Van Bibber's Life, 1899; With Both Armies in South Africa, 1900; In the Fog, 1901; Ranson's Folly, 1902; Captain Macklin, 1902; The Bar Sinister, 1904; Real Soldiers of Fortune, 1907; The Scarlet Car; The Congo and Coasts of Africa; Vera, the Medium; The White Mice; Once Upon a Time, 1910; The Man Who Could Not Lose, 1911; The Red Cross Girl, 1912; The Lost Road, 1913; Boy Scout, 1914; With the Allies, 1914; Somewhere in France, 1915. Plays: Taming of Helen; Ranson's Folly; The Dictator; The Yankee Tourist; Who's Who? Zone Police, 1914. Home: Mount Kisco, N.Y. Died Apr. 12, 1916.

DAVIS, Richmond Pearson, army officer; b. Statesville, N.C., June 23, 1866; s. Hayne and Mary Williams (Pearson) D.; grad. U.S. Mil. Acad., 1887; grad. torpedo course, Willets Pt., N.Y., 1889 (1st in class); m. Bertha Marie Bouvier. Commd. 2d lt. 2d Arty., June 12, 1887; promoted through grades to col., Jan. 24, 1914; brig. gen. N.A., Aug. 5, 1917; brig. gen. regular army, Dec. 1, 1922; major general, Oct. 4, 1927. Instructor, asst. prof. and acting prof. chemistry and electricity, U.S. Mil. Acad., 1891-96, 1898-1904, 1906; dir. Sch. Submarine Defense, Fort Totten, N.Y., 1904-06, Coast Arty. Sch., Ft. Monroe, Va., 1907-11; asst. chief C.A., 1911-12, 1915-16; assisted materially in development of coast arty. service, development of system of submarine mines; apptd. comdr. 162d F.A. Brigade, Camp Pike, Ark., Aug. 1917; comdr. 151st F.A. Brigade at St. Mihiel and Camp de Songe, France, 1918-19, also chief of arty., 9th Corps; comdr. coast defenses, Manila Bay, 1919-21; comdr. Coast Arty. Sch., Ft. Monroe, Va., 1921-22, 22d Brigade, Hawaii, 1922-29, retired, Dec. 22, 1929. Episcopalian. Died Sept. 16, 1937.

DAVIS, Robert Stewart, publisher The Call, Phila.; b. Phila., Pa., April 23, 1839; ed. Phillips Acad., Andover, Mass.; grad. Yale, 1860 (A.M.). Studied law, but later entered journalism; m. Mary L. Molten, 1868. Home: Philadelphia, Pa. Died 1911.

DAVIS, Royal Jenkins, newspaperman; b. Ridgefarm, Ill., Nov. 29, 1878; s. Jonah M. and Ella (Jenkins) D.; A.B., Earlham (Ind.) Coll., 1898, Haverford (Pa.) Coll., 1899, Harvard, 1900; m. Louise Stanton, June 27, 1906; children—Royal Stanton, J. Stanton (dec.), William Wiles, Emily Louise, Jane Virtue. Mng. editor The American Friend, Phila., 1901-02; staff Chicago Tribune, 1903; prof. English and history, Guilford (N.C.) Coll., 1904-06; prof. English St. John's Coll., Annapolis, Md., 1906-10; editorial writer, 1910—, lit. editor 1914-20, New York Evening Post. Lecturer New York U., 1910-20. Mem. Corp. Haverford Coll. Trustee Sec. for Ethical Culture, New York. Author: America's View of the Sequel, 1916; The Boys' Life of Grover Cleveland, 1925. Died Oct. 20, 1934.

DAVIS, Samuel T., M.D.; b. Huntington Co., Pa., March 6, 1838; s. Henry D.; served 4 yrs. in his father's blacksmith shop; fought with distinction, 1861-64 in Civil war, attaining rank asst. adj. gen.; grad. Long Island Coll. hosp., 1865; practiced at Millersville, Pa., 10 yrs.; removed to Lancaster, Pa., 1874; specialist in surgery and gynecology. Mem. Lancaster City Council, 1878-81 (pres. 1881) and now mem. same; mem. State legislature, 1885-87. Republican. Took active part in securing passage of State pharmacy law and law creating a State bd. of health, of which he became mem., 1889, and pres., 1892-94, and 1900—. Pres. of Select Council, 1905—. Died 1908.

DAVIS, Stephen Brooks, lawyer; b. Middletown, Conn., Nov. 18, 1874; s. Stephen Brooks and Harriet Southmaid (Woodward) D.; A.B., Wesleyan U., 1895; LL.B., Yale, 1897; m. Mary LaRue, June 4, 1903; children—Stephen, Marion, Jane. Admitted to Conn. bar, 1897, N.M. bar, 1898; dist. atty. 4th Dist. of Ty. of N.M., 1903-08; asst. U.S. atty., N.M., 1908-12, U.S. atty., 1912-13; asso. justice Supreme Court of N.M., 1921-22; rep. of N.M. on Colorado River Commn., 1921-22; solicitor Dept. of Commerce, Washington, D.C., 1923-27; counsel for U.S. on St. Lawrence Waterways Commn.; federal rep. on North Platte River Commn.; mem. First Constl. Conv. of State of N.M., 1911; mem. U.S. delegation to Preliminary Conf. on Oil Pollution of Navigable Waters, 1926; vice chmn. Internat. Radiotelegraph Conf., Washington. Republican. Conglist. Compiler: New Mexico Statutes Annotated, 1915. Wrote: The Law of Radio Communication (Awarded Linthicum Foundation prize by Northwestern U. Law Sch., 1927). Home: New York, N.Y. Died Feb. 24, 1933.

DAVIS, Thomas Davis, physician; b. Morgantown, Va. (now W.Va.), Apr. 20, 1846; s. Rev. James and Margarett Wilson (Long) D.; A.B., Washington and Jefferson Coll., 1866, A.M., 1869, Ph.D., 1902; M.D., Jefferson Med. Coll., Phila., 1870; m. Elizabeth D. McCay, Sept. 25, 1873. Resident Phys., Phila. Hospital (Blockley), 1870-71; practiced Dayton, O., 1872-77, Pittsburgh, 1877—. U.S. pension examiner, Dayton, 1874-77; surgeon Soldiers' Home, Dayton, 2 yrs., Mercy Hosp., Pittsburgh, 12 yrs., St. Francis Hosp., 14 yrs., Passavant Hosp., 18 yrs.; prof. and lecturer Pa. Coll. for Women, 8 yrs. Trustee and dir. Western Theol. Sem., 1898—. Mem. Am. Acad. Arts and Sciences. Republican. Presbyn. Home: Pittsburgh, Pa. Died Apr. 3, 1916.

DAVIS, Thomas Edward, editor; b. Bedford, Va., Sept. 25, 1835; s. Judge Micajah and Ellen Phillips D.; grad. U. of Va., 1858; subsequently studied medicine and law but did not practice; m. Mary Evelyn, d. Dr. John Moore, at Houston, Tex., 1874. Joined C.S.A., May, 1861; became adj. 21st Va. Cav., maj. and asst. adj. gen.; fought in numerous engagements, and at close of the war removed to Mont. and engaged in mining. Located in Galveston, Tex., 1871, where was engaged in business several yrs.; entered journalism, 1876, at Houston, founding Houston Telegram; joined staff of New Orleans Picayune, 1879, and editor 1884 till its sale and consolidation with Times-Democrat, New Orleans, 1914. Died Feb. 20, 1917.

DAVIS, Thomas Francis, army officer; b. N.Y. City, May 8, 1853; s. James and Mary A. (Lennon) D.; grad. U.S. Mil. Acad., 1875; m. Paulina S. Hart, May 12, 1886 (died 1910). Commd. 2d lt., 15th U.S. Inf., June 16, 1875; promoted through grades to brig. gen., May 16, 1913. Collector of customs, Santiago, Cuba, 1899; mil. sec. and adj. gen. by detail, 1905; gov. Lanao Dist., Mindanao Province, P.I., 1909; comd. 5th Brigade, 2d Div., U.S.A., Galveston, Tex., 1913-14, 6th Brigade, Texas City, Tex., and Naco and Douglas, Ariz., Feb. 1, 1914; comdg. Ariz. Dist. and 3d Provisional Inf. Div., Douglas, Ariz., to May 8, 1917, when retired by operation of law. Catholic. Home: El Paso, Tex. Died Dec. 10, 1935.

DAVIS, Varina Jefferson (Varina Jefferson-Davis); b. Natchez, Miss., May 7, 1826, g.d. Gov. Richard Howell of N.J., and d. William Burr and Margaret (Kempe) Howell; ed. Madame Grelaud's Sch., Phila., and by pvt. teachers at home; m. Jefferson Davis of Warren Co., Miss., Feb. 25, 1845. He was elected to Congress, Nov. 1845; resigned June 1846, to go to Mexican war, from which he returned severely wounded, and they went to live at his Brierfield plantation, Davis Bend, Warren Co., Miss. Was with husband in Washington where he was U.S. senator, 1847-52; sec. of war, 1853-57; U.S. senator, 1857-61; and in Richmond during the time he was pres. of the Confederate States, 1861-65. During first yr. of Mr. Davis' imprisonment was not permitted to be with him, but was permitted to remain with him during second year at Fortress Monroe. They went to England, 1867-70; lived in Memphis, Tenn., 1870-78, then removed to Beauvoir Station, on the Mississippi Coast. Acted as his amanuensis when he wrote his Decline and Fall of the Confederate Government. Since husband's death, 1889, has written numerous criticisms and articles for newspapers and mags. Property is in Miss., but lives in New York for health reasons. Has 4 sons and one daughter dead; one daughter living, Margaret Howell Davis, now Mrs. I. A. Hayes, Colorado Springs, Colo. Author: Jefferson Davis: A Memoir by His Wife, 1890. Home: Brierfield, Warren Co., Miss., and Elkridge, La. Died 1906.

DAVIS, Vernon Mansfield, judge; b. New York, N.Y., Jan. 29, 1855; s. Robert Vernon and Mary (Samler) D.; A.B., Coll. City of N.Y., 1876, A.M., 1880; LL.B., Columbia, 1879; m. Harriet, d. Rev. Francis Lobdell, of Buffalo, June 17, 1885. Admitted to bar, 1879; asst. 1885-96, and dist. atty., 1896-97; commr. of edn. of City of N.Y., 1899-1902; became justice Supreme Ct. of N.Y., 1st Dist., 1903. Democrat. Pres. Soc. for Prevention of Cruelty to Children, 1901-04; mem. Soc. Med. Jurisprudence. Home: New York, N.Y. Died Apr. 17, 1931.

DAVIS, Warren Blair, editor, pub.; b. Charlestown, Mass., Sept. 12, 1877; s. John McIntyre and Catherine (Connolly) D.; ed. pub. schs.; m. Ethilda Claribel Rutherford, Fenelon Falls, Can., Dec. 14, 1904; children—John Rutherford, Dorothy, Marion. Began as reporter Charlestown Enterprise, 1896; reporter Boston (Mass.) Journal, 1896-1904; asst. city editor Boston American, 1904-08; city and mng. editor Anaconda (Mont.) Standard, 1908-26; editor and pub. Missoula (Mont.) Sentinel and Daily Missoulian, 1926—; pres. Missoulian Pub. Co. Pres. Western Mont. Council Boy Scouts of America. Universalist. Died Sept. 1, 1939.

DAVIS, Webster, lawyer; b. Ebensburgh, Pa., June 1, 1862; s. Daniel J. and Elizabeth D.; student Lake Forest U., 1883-84, U. of Kan., 1885-86; admitted to bar, 1886, LL.B., U. of Mich., 1887. Practiced law, Kansas City, Mo., 1887-96, Seattle, Wash., 1904-07, Los Angeles, 1907—; lecturer. Spl. deputy surveyor of customs, western dist. Mo. and Kan., 1888-92; defeated for Congress, 1892; mayor of Kansas City, 1894-96; asst. sec. of the Interior, 1897-1900. Republican. Home: Los Angeles, Calif. Died Feb. 22, 1923.

DAVIS, William Horace, statistician; b. Holyoke, Mass., July 21, 1871; s. George Washington and Julia Rawson (Hastings) D.; student Amherst, 1889-90; A.B., Harvard, 1893, M.D., 1897; studied in Vienna, Austria, 1899; m. Mabel A. C. Johnson, Dec. 3, 1898; children—Crown Hastings, George William, Dorothy, Roger Maxfield (dec.), Richard Mackworth (dec.), Barbara, Kenneth, Gordon. Surg. house officer Mass. Gen. Hosp., 1898; practiced in Boston, Mass., 1900-16; in charge vital statistics, Boston Health Dept., 1908-16; chief statistician for vital statistics, U.S. Census Bur., Washington, D.C., 1916—. Home: Chevy Chase, D.C. Died Jan. 8, 1929.

DAVIS, Will(iam) J(ames), theatrical mgr.; b. on farm, Washtenaw Co., Mich., Feb. 8, 1844; s. Thomas Gleason and Ann Isabella (McWhorter) D.; ed. public schools, Elkhart, Ind.; m. Jessie Bartlett, 1880 (died 1905); m. 2d, Mary Ellen O'Hagan, June 12, 1907. Served U.S. Navy, 1861-65; in business offices, Chicago, 1866-69; in internal revenue service in Miss., 1869-73; later in ry. service, Chicago; became advance agt. and mgr. of theatrical cos.; leased Haymarket Theatre, Chicago, 1887; mgr. Columbia Theatre, Chicago, 1890-1900; mem. Hayman & Davis Co., owners of Illinois Theatre, Chicago; retired from active theatricals, 1914; was one of the owners and mgrs. of the ill-fated Iroquois Theatre; was prosecuted for this disaster, but after tedious trial was acquitted. Home: Crown Point, Ind. Died May 16, 1919.

DAVIS, William Morris, geographer, geologist; b. Phila., Pa., Feb. 12, 1850; s. Edward M. and Maria (Mott) D.; S.B., Lawrence Scientific Sch. (Harvard), 1869, M.E., 1870; Sc.D., U. of Cape of Good Hope, 1905; Ph.D., U. of Greifswald, 1906; Ph.D., U. of Christiania, 1911; S.D., U. of Melbourne, 1914; m. Ellen B. Warner, Nov. 25, 1879 (died 1913); m. 2d, Mary M. Wyman, Dec. 12, 1914 (died 1923); m. 3d, Lucy L. Tennant, Aug. 13, 1928. Asst., Nat. Obs., Cordoba, Argentina, 1870-73; joined faculty Harvard U., 1876, prof. geology, 1899-1912 (emeritus). Fellow Am. Acad. Arts and Sciences, A.A.A.S. Was decorated Chevalier Legion of Honor (France). Author: Elementary Meteorology, 1894; Physical Geography, 1898; Practical Exercises in Physical Geography, 1908. Gold medalist of Harvard Travellers Club, Am. Geog. Soc., Geog. Socs. of Phila. and Chicago, Acad. Natural Sciences, Phila., Royal Geog. Soc. London, Geog. Soc. Stockholm. Republican. Unitarian. Died Feb. 5, 1934.

DAVIS, William R., lawyer; b. Washington Co., Ia., Feb. 26, 1850; s. George Washington and Ellen Rebecca (Walker) D.; A.B., U. of Calif., 1874, A.M., 1877; m. M. Otteline Towne, Apr. 3, 1879. Admitted to Calif. bar, 1877; spl. counsel city of Oakland, in litigation to recover municipal control of its water front on Bay of San Francisco, begun 1893, ended successfully, 1910; now spl. counsel for Oakland in litigation against pvt. water supply co. Mayor of Oakland, 1887-88. Has canvassed state many times in nat. campaigns for Rep. party. Mason. Home: Oakland, Calif. Died Mar. 17, 1915.

DAVIS, William Stearns, educator, author; b. Amherst, Mass., Apr. 30, 1877; s. William Vail Wilson and Rebecca Frances (Stearns) D.; A.B., Harvard, 1900, A.M., 1901, Ph.D., 1905; m. Alice Williams Redfield, Sept. 5, 1911. Lecturer at Radcliffe Coll., 1904-05; instr. Beloit (Wis.) Coll., 1906-07; asso. prof. mediæval and modern European history, Oberlin, 1907-09; prof. history, U. of Minn., 1909-27. Author: A Friend of Cæsar, 1900; God Wills It, 1901, Belshazzar, 1902; A Victor of Salamis, 1907; Outline History of the Roman Empire, 1909; The Friar of Wittenberg, 1912; Readings in Ancient History, 1913; A Day in Old Athens, 1914; A History of France, 1919; A Short History of the Near East, 1922; Life on a Mediæval Barony, 1923; The Beauty of the Purple, 1924; The White Queen, 1925; Europe Since Waterloo, 1926; Gilman of Redford, 1927. Home: Exeter, N.H. Died Feb. 15, 1930.

DAVIS, William Thomas, lawyer, author; b. Plymouth, Mass., Mar. 3, 1822; grad. Harvard, 1842; m. Abby Burr Hedge, Nov. 19, 1849. Admitted to bar, Boston, 1849; State senator, 1858-59; Rep. presdl. elector, 1872. Head of Plymouth town govt. many yrs.; pres. Pilgrim Soc.; hon. mem. Conn. Hist. Soc., Old Colony Hist. Soc. Author: History of Plymouth; Ancient Landmarks of Plymouth; History of Bench and Bar of Massachusetts; History of the Judiciary of Massachusetts; Plymouth Memories of An Octogenarian, 1907. Editor: Plymouth Town Records, 3 vols.; New England States, 4 vols.; vol. 6 of Original Narratives of Early American History. Home: Plymouth, Mass. Died 1907.

DAVIS, William Warren; b. Cambridge, Mass., Aug. 8, 1862; s. William and Adelia Merriam (Carter) D.; ed. pub. schs.; m. Daisy R. Jones, Nov. 5, 1885; children—Dorothy (Mrs. George A. Tyler), Marjorie (dec.), Marguerite (Mrs. John A. High). Mgr. Norfolk House, Boston, 1886-1905, Riverbank Court Hotel Co., Cambridge, 1905-32. Mem. City Council, Boston, 1894; mem. Mass. Ho. of Rep., 1895-96, Mass. State Senate, 1897-98, governor's council, 1899-1900; Rep. presdl. elector, Mass., 1924. Pres. First Ch. of Christ, Scientist, Boston, 1929-30; now exec. supervisor of Christian Science Benevolent Assns., Chestnut Hill, Mass., and San Francisco, Calif., Christian Science Pleasant View House, Concord, N.H. Food Administrator, Cambridge, and chmn. exemption bd., World War. Republican. Home: Boston, Mass. Died Sept. 21, 1941.

DAVIS, William Watts Hart, journalist; b. Southampton Twp., Pa., July 27, 1820; s. John and Amy (Hart) D.; grad. Norwich Univ., 1842; instr. Mil. Acad. Portsmouth, Va., 1842-44; admitted to bar, 1846; entered Harvard Law Sch., 1846, but left to enlist in Mass. regt. for Mexican War; mustered out at close, July 19, 1848, as capt.; practiced law 5 yrs. in N.M., 1853-57, as U.S. dist. atty., atty. gen., sec. of Ty., acting gov., supt. Indian affairs, and supt. pub. bldgs.; published Santa Fé Gazette (Spanish and English) 2½ yrs.; engaged in journalism, 1858—; comd. co., regt., brig., and div. in Civil War, reaching bvt. rank brig. gen.; shot 3 times; twice Dem. nominee for Congress, defeated with party; U.S. commr. Paris Expn., 1878; U.S. pension agt., Phila., 1885-89. Home: Doylestown, Pa. Died 1910.

DAVIS, William Z., judge; b. Loydsville, O., June 10, 1839; s. Dr. Bushrod W. and Harriet (Hatcher) D.; academic edn.; LL.D., Ohio Wesleyan, 1909; m. Harriet M. Search, Dec. 3, 1868 (died 1901); m. 2d, Jessie Myer, Sept. 9, 1903. Served 3 months' enlistment, 4th Ohio regt., 1861; reënlisted in 96th O. Vols., remaining in service until physically disabled and hon. discharged; admitted to bar, 1862; practiced at Marion, O., 1864-1900; elected judge of Supreme Court of Ohio, 1899, to succeed Hon. Joseph P. Bradbury, from Feb. 9, 1900, but, Judge Bradbury having resigned, was apptd., Jan. 10, 1900; reëlected for term 1906-12; retired, Dec. 31, 1912. Home: Columbus, O. Died Dec. 18, 1926.

DAVIS, Wirt, brig. gen.; b. Richmond, Va., May 28, 1839; s. John F. and Delight T. D.; ed. Hampden-Sidney Coll. and U. of Va.; m. Anna J. Berry, 1884. Served as pvt. and corp. Co. K, 1st Cav., promoted through grades to col. 3d Cav., Jan. 10, 1900; retired at own request, after 40 yrs.' service, Apr. 29, 1901; advanced to rank of brig. gen. retired, by act of Apr. 23, 1904. Bvtd.: "for gallant and meritorious services in Civ. War"; 1st lt., Sept. 19, 1863 (for Chickamauga); capt., Feb. 20, 1864 (cav. expdn. in Miss.); maj., Apr. 2, 1865 (capture of Selma, Ala.); also bvtd. lt. col., Feb. 27, 1900, "for gallant services on N. fork of Red River, Texas, Sept. 29, 1872," and in action against Indians in the Big Horn Mountains, Mont., Nov. 25, 1870. Died Feb. 10, 1914.

DAVISON, Charles, surgeon; b. on farm, Lake Co., Ill., Jan. 13, 1858; s. Peter and Martha Maria (Whedon) D.; M.D., Northwestern U. Med. Sch., 1883; (A.M., Northwestern U., 1917); interne Cook County Hospital, 1883-84; m. Mary Lavinia Kidd, Oct. 20, 1887; 1 son, Charles Marshall. In practice at Chicago, 1884—; asst. surgeon, Ill. Charitable Eye and Ear Infirmary, 1887-92; attending surgeon, Cook Co. Hosp., 1894-1926 (pres. med. staff, 1917-19, chief dept. surgery, 1919-20), emeritus, attending surgeon, West Side Hosp., 1896-1907; surgeon-in-chief University Hosp., 1918—; surgeon Research and Edn. Hosp., 1925-26; prof. surgery, Chicago Clin. Sch., 1896-1907; prof. surg. anatomy, 1899-1900, adj. prof. surgery, 1900-05, prof. same 1905-26, head of dept. of surgery, 1917-26 (emeritus), Coll. of Medicine, U. of Ill., Chicago. One of founders West Side Hosp. and of University Hosp.; trustee U. of Ill., 1906-11. Fellow Founder's Group Am. Bd. of Surgery. Founder and fellow Am. Coll. Surgeons. Methodist. Republican. Mason. Author: Autoplastic Bone Surgery, 1916. Home: River Forest, Ill. Died Jan. 18, 1942.

DAVISON, Henry Pomeroy, banker; b. Troy, Pa., June 13, 1867; s. George B. and Henrietta (Pomeroy) D.; acad. edn., S. Williamstown, Mass.; LL.D., U. of Pa., 1913, Yale, Harvard, Columbia, Princeton, Williams, Bowdoin, New York U.; m. Kate Trubee, 1893. Teller, Astor Pl. Nat. Bank, New York, 1891-94; asst. cashier, 1894-95, cashier, 1895-98, v.p., 1898-99, pres., 1899-1902, Liberty Nat. Bank; elected v.p. First Nat. Bank, 1902; now mem. firm J. P. Morgan & Co., N.Y. City, chmn. exec. com. and dir. Bankers Trust Co.; dir. First Security Co., Am. Foreign Securities Co., N.J.&N.Y. R.R. Co., Guaranty Safe Deposit Co. Chmn. War Council Am. Red Cross, 1917-19; elected chmn. gov. bd. World League of Red Cross Societies, Paris, May 1919. Trustee, treas. Am. Mus. Natural History. Knight Order Crown of Italy; Comdr. Legion of Honor (French), 1918. Died May 6, 1922.

DAVISON, John, educator; b. West Newton, O., July 22, 1858; s. Amaziah and Eliza J. (Nye) D.; B.Sc., Ohio Northern U., Ada, O., 1889, M.Sc., 1892, M.Litt., 1902, D.Pd., 1912; m. Clara E. Hay, Mar. 24, 1886. Prof. literature, Lima, Coll., 1895-1900; prof. lit., Ohio Northern U., 1900-05; supt. pub. schs., Lima, 1905-15; v.p. Ohio Northern U., also dean Coll. of Edn., 1915—. Republican. Methodist. Author: American Literature, 1904; English Literature, 1905. Home: Lima, O. Died July 20, 1924.

DAVISON, Peter Weimer, army officer; b. Waupun, Wis., May 15, 1869; s. James and Sarah (Weimer) D.; grad. U.S. Mil. Acad., 1892; m. Esther Fleming, Apr. 11, 1913. Commd. 2d lt. 22d Inf., June 11, 1892; 1st lt., Apr. 26, 1898; capt. a. q.-m. vols., May 12, 1900; hon. disch. vols., Mar. 21, 1901; capt. 26th Inf., U.S.A., Feb. 2, 1901; advanced through grades to col. N.A., Aug. 5, 1917; brig. gen. (temp.), Aug. 8, 1918-Oct. 31, 1919. Served on Gen. Staff, 1910; a.d.c. to Maj. Gen. J. Franklin Bell, 1911-12; with allied armies, Tientsin, China, fall of 1913; served in Mont., 1892-96, Neb., 1896-98; a.d.c. to Gen. Ludlow during Spanish-Am. War, serving in campaign in Cuba, and in action at El Caney and Santiago; with regt. in Philippines, 1899-1902, 1903-05, 1911-Sept. 1914; on Tex. border, 1914-15; in Alaska, 1908-10 and 1916-Sept. 1917; comd. 166 Depot Brigade, Oct. 1917-June 1918; comd. 8th Inf. to Sept. 1918, and as brig. gen. comd. 16th Div., Oct. 1918-Feb. 1919; comd. Ft. D. A. Russell, Cheyenne, Wyo., to May 1919; duty at Port of Embarkation, New York, May 1919—. Recommended twice, 1899, for brevet, "for gallantry in action," in Philippine Campaign; awarded Naval Cross, "for distinguished services," 1919. Mason. Episcopalian. Died Feb. 12, 1920.

DAVISSON, Albert Eugene, educator; b. Crawfordsville, Ind.; s. Gideon Leigh and Mary Ann (Bowyer) D.; ed. Sugar Grove Inst., Tippecanoe Co., Ind., 1876-79, Ind. State Normal Sch., Terre Haute, 1879-82; spl. student Purdue U. 1892; A.B., U. of Neb., 1898; m. Emma Reed, Aug. 25, 1886. Prin. high sch., Rochester, Ind., 1882-86; supt. town schs., Camden, Ind., 1886-92; 1st asst., 1892-93, prin., 1893-96, prof. Latin and prin., 1894-96, prep. dept. N.M. Agrl. Coll.; head master, 1897-99, dir., 1899-1901, prof. economics and prin., 1901-08, head prof. agrl. edn. and prin., 1908—, Sch. of Agr., U. of Neb. at Lincoln. Univ. extension lecturer. Mason. Died 1911.

DAVY, John M., jurist; b. Ottawa, Ont., June 29, 1835; removed to Rochester when 6 months old; brought up on farm; ed. com. schs. and Monroe Acad., E. Henrietta, N.Y.; studied law; was law student when Civil war broke out; assisted in raising and became 1st lt. 108th N.Y. Vols.; served until 1863, when he was hon. disch. because of illness; resumed law study; admitted to bar, 1863; dist. atty. Monroe Co., 1868-71; collector of customs, Rochester, 1872-75; mem. Congress, 1875-77. Judge Supreme Court, 7th jud. dist., N.Y., 1889-1905; retired. Republican. Home: Rochester, N.Y. Died 1909.

DAWES, Anna Laurens, author; b. North Adams, Mass., May 14, 1851; d. late U.S. Senator Henry Laurens and Electa (Sanderson) D.; sister of Chester Mitchell D.; ed. Maplewood Inst., Pittsfield, Abbot Acad., Andover; unmarried. Washington corr. Springfield Republican, Boston Congregationalist and Christian Union, 1871-83. Trustee Smith Coll., 1889-96; mem. Mass. State bd. mgrs. Chicago Expn., 1892-93; mem. bd. lady mgrs. St. Louis Expn., 1902-04. V.p. Mass. Anti-Suffrage Soc. until 1919; pres. Wednesday Morning Club, Pittsfield, 1879—; chmn. Child Labor Com., Boston, 1916; dir. Mass. Prison Assn., Boston, 1916; v.p. Indian Industries League, Boston. Officer or mem. missionary, philanthropic and civic orgns. Author: How We Are Governed, 1885; The Modern Jew, His Present and Future, 1886; Charles Sumner, 1892. Home: Pittsfield, Mass. Died Sept. 25, 1938.

DAWES, Chester Mitchell, lawyer; b. N. Adams, Mass., July 14, 1855; s. late U.S. Senator Henry Laurens and Electa (Sanderson) D.; bro. of Anna Laurens D.; A.B., Yale, 1876; LL.B., Boston U., 1878; m. Ada B. Laflin, May 12, 1881. Admitted to bar, 1878; gen. solicitor, 1900-09, gen. counsel, 1909—, C.,B.&Q. Ry. Co. Presdl. elector, 1896; mem. Chicago Bd. of Edn., 1899-1902, and 1907-10; Republican. Home: Chicago, Ill. Died Apr. 12, 1917.

DAWES, Henry Laurens, lawyer; b. Cummington, Mass., Oct. 30, 1816; s. Mitchel D.; grad. Yale, 1839; (LL.D., Williams, 1869; Yale, 1889); edited Greenfield Gazette, and later the Adams Transcript; admitted to bar, 1842; mem. Mass. legislature, 1848-50; Mass. senate, 1850-52; Constl. Conv., 1853; Mass. atty. for Western dist. Mass., 1854-57; mem. Congress, 1857-73; U.S. senator, 1875-93; chmn. Commn. to the Five Civilized Tribes, Indian Ty., 1893. Home: Pittsfield, Mass. Died 1903.

DAWES, Rufus Cutler, business man; b. Marietta, O., July 30, 1867; s. Gen. Rufus R. and Mary Beman (Gates) D.; A.B., Marietta Coll., 1886, A.M., 1889, LL.D., 1933; LL.D., Northwestern U., 1931, U. of Wis., 1933; LL.D., Wabash Coll., 1936; m. Helen B. Palmer, June 3, 1893. Business life has been spent in organizing and managing gas and electric light cos.; pres. Union Gas & Electric Co., Met. Gas & Electric Co., Dawes Bros., Inc. Mem. Ill. State Pension Laws Commn., 1918-19; del. State Constl. Conv., 1920. Adviser to Am. members of experts com. which prepared the "Dawes Plan" of reparations settlement; asst. to Owen D. Young, first agt. of gen. reparations. Was pres. Century of Progress Expn., Chicago; pres. Mus. of Science and Industry, Chicago. Republican. Author: Dawes Plan in the Making. Presented with bronze tablet as "Chicago's most distinguished citizen," Rotary Club, 1934. Home: Evanston, Ill. Died Jan. 8, 1940.

DAWLEY, Frank E., farm expert; b. Elbridge, N.Y., Sept. 10, 1863; s. William Walker and Charlotte A. (Lamson) D.; ed. Munro Collegiate Inst.; spl. work in chemistry and agr.; m. Carrie L. Barnes, June 16, 1891; children—Marian B., Laura A., Helen F., Katherine L., Lamson E., Dorothy J. Has devoted attention largely to scientific breeding of horses, cattle, sheep and poultry and the domestication of fur-bearing wild animals, in which is regarded as an authority; founder and owner of Dotshome Farms and Karakul Fur Sheep Farms. Awarded gold medal for alfalfa hay exhibit, San Francisco Expn., 1915. One of first to introduce pure Karakul sheep, producing Persian lamb fur, in America; organized Am. Karakul Fur Sheep Record Assn. Dir. N.Y. State Farmers' Insts., 1896-1908. Trustee Cornell U. Sec. Am. Cheviot Sheep Soc. 20 yrs. (awarded gold medal by world soc. for services to Cheviot breed); master of Onondaga Pomona Grange. N.Y. state appraiser of animals, Dept. Agriculture and Markets, 1917-33. Republican. Home: Fayetteville, N.Y. Died June 13, 1936.

DAWLEY, Thomas Robinson, Jr., writer; b. New York, Apr. 18, 1862; s. Thomas Robinson and Antoinette (Hoxsie) D.; ed. high sch. Brooklyn, 1 year; m. Rosalie Janez, Jan. 1891; children—Grace, Antoinette, Thomas Robinson, Bradley Lee, Hattie May (dec.). Left home at 17; went to Liverpool on cattle ship; tramped from Liverpool to London; later in printing business, New York; traveled in Central America, W.I., Spain and France; after 10 yrs. absence returned to New York; taught dist. sch. on Block Island; studied law, Providence, R.I.; went to Cuba for Harper's Weekly, 1896; visited insurgent camps and went out with Spanish troops arrested several times, finally confined in Morro Castle 2 weeks; expelled from island by Gen. Weyler; returned to Cuba following yr.; with army of Gen. Gomez; vol. aid on staff Gen. Miles in Spanish-Am. War; transferred to Gen. Shafter's staff, 1898; after taking of Santiago, published 1st Am. daily newspaper in Cuba, The Times of Cuba; incarcerated under old Spanish jud. system at Havana, and newspaper plant seized by judicial authorities; returned to New York, then went to Spain for Century Co.; spl. commr. Outlook, Pan-Am. Congress, Mexico, 1901; U.S. del. Internat. Coffee Congress, New York, 1902. Traveled through island of Santo Domingo, 1904, and at request of President Roosevelt, made a report on the polit. and sociol. conditions there; spl. agt. of Bur. of Labor, 1907-09, and as such assigned to investigate, under an act of Congress, the effect of factory employment upon the women and children drawn from the farms to the cotton mills of the South; made an exhaustive investigation of rural conditions in the southern Appalachians, 1912. Author: Cuba, Annual Cyclopedia, 1897, and various contributed articles, idem, 1902. On editorial staff Providence Journal, 1916-17; went to Guatemala and attempted to introduce welfare work; adjudicator of compensation claims, War Risk Bur., Washington, D.C., 1919; returned to Guatemala, 1920; participated in revolution and overthrow of Estrada Cabrera, and apptd. official publicist by the succeeding government; founder of the "Casa del Niño" for the care and instruction of poor children; after overthrow of Herrera government, returned to New York, 1922. Home: New York, N.Y. Died June 2, 1930.

DAWSON, Allan, newspaperman; b. Hudson, Wis., Oct. 7, 1866; s. Allan and Anna (Cleland) D.; brother of Thomas Cleland D.; A.B., Hanover (Ind.) Coll., 1888; studied law, St. Paul, 1888-90; m. Nell M. Perkins, Oct. 9, 1895. Entered printing office, Hudson, Wis., 1880, at age of 14; reporter, 1891, city editor, 1892, Des Moines (Ia.) Register; editorial writer Sioux City Journal, 1892-93; editor Sioux City Tribune, 1894-95; editor and half propr. Des Moines (Ia.) Leader, 1895-1903; chief editorial writer New York Globe and Commercial Advertiser, New York, 1903—. Died June 24, 1923.

DAWSON, Arthur, artist; b. Crewe, Eng., Mar. 9, 1858; s. Rev. John Godfrey and Anna (Kent) D.; A.B., St. Saviour's Coll.; studied art at S. Kensington Sch. (medalist); pupil of David Law and William Morris; m. Adelaide Kent, Aug. 18, 1883. Came to America, 1887; naturalized U.S. citizen; studio in Chicago, 10 yrs. removed to New York, 1898. A founder of Chicago Soc. of Artists; was chmn. advisory com. Municipal Art Soc., Chicago; had charge restoration of pictures belonging to Pub. Library, New York, and U.S. Mil. Acad. (official portrait painter of latter). Art critic. Works, 1921, portraits of John Barton Payne, Generals Tillman, Barry, Biddle, and McArthur; E. H. Harriman, Dr. Henry L. Smith of Washington and Lee Univ., Dr. George H. Denny of Univ. of Ala. Mem. Artists' Fund Society, New York. Democrat. Episcopalian. Home: Richmond, Va. Died Aug. 22, 1922.

DAWSON, Benjamin Elisha, orificial surgeon; b. Madison, Mo., July 10, 1852; s. John W. and Mary Ann (Welch) D.; dist. and select schs.; M.D., Ohio Med. Coll., Cincinnati, 1875; M.D., Eclectic Med. U., Kansas City, Mo., 1903; (hon. A.M., Potomac U., Washington, 1913); m. Mary G. Crawford, Nov. 21, 1875 (dec.); m. 2d, Dr. Minnie E. Willson, June 29, 1919. Practiced, Howard Co., Mo., 1875-79, Windsor, Mo., 1879-88; gave up practice on account of poor health; pastor, Christian Ch., Odessa, Mo., 1890-94, Rockport, 1895-96, Farragut, Ia., 1896, Butler, Mo., 1896-99, Belton, 1909-02; resumed practice of medicine at Belton, 1903; removed to Kansas City, 1908, and established pvt. hosp. for orificial surgery. Pres. and prof. orificial and gen. surgery, Eclectic Med. U., 1910; supt. Am. Hosp., 1914-16; mem. staff Grace Hosp. Compiler and Author: Orificial Surgery, 1912. Author: Give The Child a Chance, 1915. Prohibitionist. Mason. Home: Kansas City, Mo. Died Feb. 13, 1922.

DAWSON, Clyde C., lawyer; b. Dallas Co., Ia., Feb. 8, 1864; s. Jesse W. (M.D.) and Caroline (Price) D.; spl. course, Denver U., 2 yrs.; LL.B., U. of Mich., 1888; m. Kathryn Russell, Sept. 23, 1899; children—Katharine, Clyde C. Practiced in Canon City, 1889-1910, at Denver, 1910—; became mem. Dawson & Wright; has given much attention to irrigation and corp. law. Rep. candidate for U.S. Senate, 1912. Mem. bd. dirs. Chamber of Commerce of U.S., 1920-23. During fall and winter of 1923-24 served as mem. Fed. Finding Commn., apptd. by sec. of the Interior to make a complete review of the operations of the Federal Reclamation Service since its inauguration; the report of this commn. was transmitted to Congress by President Coolidge with spl. message commending it to the consideration of that body. Home: Denver, Colo. Died June 21, 1927.

DAWSON, George Ellsworth, educator; b. Berkeley Springs, W.Va., Dec. 23, 1861; s. Jefferson Berlin and Martha Jane (Durham) Berlin; father died in Civil War, mother moved to Ill., remarried, and son was adopted by stepfather and has borne stepfather's name; prep. edn. Mt. Morris (Ill.) Acad. and Carthage (Ill.) Coll.; A.B., U. of Mich., 1887; U. of Leipzig, Germany, 1888-89; Ph.D., Clark U., Worcester, Mass., 1897; m. Susie Charlotte Reber, Aug. 4, 1887; children—Harold (dec.), Paul Reber, Ruth Agnes. Prin. Oil City (Pa.) High Sch., 1889-91; prof. English, Agrl. Coll., S.D., 1891-93; instr. English, U. of Mich., 1893-95; fellow in psychology, Clark University, 1895-97; professor psychology, Bible Normal College, Springfield, Mass., 1897-1901; head of hist. dept., Pratt Institute, Brooklyn, 1901-02; prof. psychology, Hartford Sch. of Religious Pedagogy, 1902-19, Internat. Y.M.C.A. Coll., Springfield, 1919-25. Prof. edn., Mt. Holyoke (Mass.) Coll., 1903-08; dir. child study dept., Henry Barnard Sch., Hartford, Conn., 1908-16; dir. psychol. lab., Springfield pub. schs., 1913—. Republican. Conglist. Author: The Child and His Religion, 1909; The Right of the Child to Be Well Born, 1912. Home: W. Springfield, Mass. Died 1936.

DAWSON, George Walter, artist, teacher; b. Andover, Mass., March 16, 1870; s. Jackson Thornton and Mary (McKenna) D.; grad. West Roxbury High Sch., Boston, 1887; grad. Mass. Normal Art Sch., Boston, 1893; studied Pa. Acad. Fine Arts; hon. degree A.E.D., U. of Pa., 1921; unmarried. Instr. drawing, 1893, asst. prof., 1907, prof. from 1911, U. of Pa. Water color artist; paints gardens, landscapes and flowers, in Europe and America; has occasionally designed gardens. Mem. jury for selection of water colors, St. Louis Expn., 1904, San Francisco Expn., 1915, also mem. jury of awards of honors at latter and of Sesquicentennial Internat. Expn., Phila., 1926; dir. Phila. Sch. of Design for Women. Fellow Pa. Acad. Fine Arts. Republican. Episcopalian. Died Feb. 5, 1938.

DAWSON, Lemuel Orah, clergyman, educator; b. Chambers Co., Ala., Apr. 24, 1865; s. Andrew Jackson and Marie Antoinette (Bailey) D.; A.B., Howard Coll., Birmingham, Ala., 1886, D.D., 1897; grad. Southern Bapt. Theol. Sem., Louisville, Ky., 1889; post-grad. work, same sch., 1890; studied in Germany and at Columbian (now George Washington) U., and U. of Ala.; m. Margaret Samuel Lewis, Oct. 30, 1890; children—Andrew Lewis, Eugene Reese. Entered Bapt. ministry, 1884, ordained, 1888; pastor Mt. Vernon Ch. in Woodford Co., Ky., 1888-92, Tuscaloosa, Ala., 1892-1924; prof. Bible and church history, Howard Coll., 1924—, also pastor Edgewood Ch., Birmingham. Pres. Ala. Bapt. State Conv. 3 terms; chmn. ednl. commn., same; pres. Southern Bapt. Young People's Union 10 terms; pres. Rotary Internat. 1 yr. Mem. Ala. Bapt. State Exec. Com.; mem. Bd. of Relief and Annuities of Southern Baptist Convention, also mem. ednl. bd.; trustee Central Female College, Southern Baptist Theol. Sem., Druid City Hosp., Tuscaloosa; mem. exec. com. Southern Bapt. Ednl. Assn. Democrat. Author: Light Spots, 1933; After Fifty Years—A State, A Father and A Son, 1935. Home: Birmingham, Ala. Died Jan. 14, 1938.

DAWSON, Mary, writer; b. Phila, Pa.; d. William and Margaret (Sweeney) D.; ed. Acad. Sacred Heart, Phila.; Acad. of Visitation, Georgetown, S.C.; studied under pvt. tutors in America and Paris, France. Was on staff Phila. Press, editor woman's supplement Phila. North American, and mem. staff Butterick Publs. Author: Book of Parties and Pastimes, 1912; Book of Frolics, 1912; Money-Making Entertainments, 1915; The Mary Dawson Game Book, 1916. Home: Whitestone, L.I., N.Y. Died 1922.

DAWSON, Thomas Cleland, diplomat; b. Hudson, Wis., July 30, 1865; s. Allan and Anna (Cleland) D.; bro. of Allan D.; A.B., Hanover Coll., Ind., 1883, A.M., 1898; Harvard, 1884-85; LL.B., Cincinnati Law Sch., 1886; m. Luiza Guerra Duval, of Porto Alegre, Brazil, Apr. 5, 1900. Published country newspaper, Enterprise, Fla., 1882-84; admitted to bar, 1886; practiced law, Des Moines, Ia., 1886-89; legislative corr. and later city editor Iowa Daily Register, Des Moines, 1890-91; practiced law Council Bluffs, Ia., 1891-97; asst. atty. gen. of Ia., 1891-94; sec. U.S. Legation to Brazil, 1897-1904; 5 times chargé d'affaires of legation; minister resident and consul gen. of U.S. to Santo Domingo, 1904-07; E.E. and M.P. to Colombia, 1907-09, to Chile, 1909-10; chief Div. of Latin Am. Affairs, Dept. of State, 1910; E.E. and M.P. to Panama, 1910; spl. agt. to Nicaragua, 1910; spl. commr. to Honduras, 1911; spl. ambassador to Venezuelan Centennial, 1911; resident diplomatic officer of Dept. of State, 1911—. Presbyn. Author: South American Republic, 2 vols., 1903-04. Home: Council Bluffs, Ia. Died May 1, 1912.

DAWSON, William James, clergyman, author; b. Towcester, Northampton, Eng., Nov. 21, 1854; s. Rev. William James and Susan (Waller) D.; ed. Didsbury Coll., Manchester; D.D., Oberlin Coll., 1905; m. Jane Powell, 1879. Ordained Wesleyan minister, 1875; held various appmts. until 1892, when resigned and became pastor Highbury Quadrant Congl. Ch., London; del. Meth. Ecumenical Council, Washington, 1891; moved to U.S., 1905; has lectured widely on lit. and hist. subjects; now pastor emeritus, 1st Ch., Newark, N.J. Author: The Threshold of Manhood, 1889; Makers of English Poetry, 1890; Makers of English Prose, 1899; The Man Christ Jesus, 1901; The Evangelistic Note, 1905; Makers of English Fiction, 1905; The Empire of Love, 1907; The Reader's Library (with C. W. Dawson), consisting of The Great English Letter-Writers, The Great Essayists, The Great Short Story Writers, 1909; The Book of Courage, 1911; American Hymnal, 1913; The Autobiography of a Mind, 1925. Home: Newark, N.J. Deceased.

DAWSON, William Leon, ornithologist; b. Leon, Ia., Feb. 20, 1873; s. William Edwy and Ada Eliza Sarah (Adams) D.; Washington U., 1887-90; A.B., Oberlin, 1897, A.M., 1903; B.D., Oberlin Theol. Sem., 1899; m. Frances Etta Ackerman, May 1, 1895; children—William Oberlin, Giles Edwin, Barbara Dorothy. Ordained Congl. ministry, 1899; pastor North Ch., Columbus, O., 1900-02; organizer Wheaton Pub. Co., Columbus, 1902, Occidental Pub. Co., Seattle, Wash., 1905, Birds of Calif. Pub. Co., 1911, Birds of Ohio Pub. Co., 1926, Birds of Fla. Pub. Co., 1927. Dir. Internat. Mus. Comparative Oölogy, Santa Barbara, Calif. Progressive. Author: The Birds of Ohio, 1903; The Birds of Washington (2 vols.), 1909; The Birds of California (4 vols.), 1923. Home: "Los Colibris," Mission Canyon, Santa Barbara, Calif. Died Apr. 30, 1928.

DAWSON, William Mercer Owens, governor; b. Bloomington, Md., May 21, 1853; s. Francis and Leah (Knight) D.; ed. pub. and pvt. schs.; m. Luda Neff, 1879; m. 2d, Maude Brown, 1899. Editor, 1873-1891, owner, 1875-1891, Preston Co. (W.Va.) Journal; admitted to bar, 1892, and since in practice at Kingwood and Charleston. Chmn. Rep. Co. Com., Preston Co., 1875-88; mem. W.Va. Senate, 1881-88; chmn. Rep. State Com., 1891-1904; clerk Ho. of Dels., 1895; mayor, Kingwood, 1890-91; sec. of state of W.Va., 1897-1905; gov., 1905-09. Republican. Home: Charleston, W.Va. Died Mar. 12, 1916.

DAWSON-WATSON, Dawson, artist, craftsman; b. London, Eng., July 21, 1864; s. John and Jane Dawson (Edmondson) Dawson-Watson; ed. grammar sch. Southsea, Hants, Eng.; pupil of Mark Fisher, R.A., Carolus Duran, Aime Morot, Luc Olivier Merson, Chartran, Leon Glaize, Raphäel Collin; m. Mary Hoyt Sellar, May 30, 1888; children—Edward Dawson, Hilda Rosalind (Mrs. Rolf Georg Overland). Came to U.S., 1893. Art dir. Hartford (Conn.) Art Soc., 1893-96; art teacher, Byrdcliffe Colony, Woodstock, N.Y., 1903, St. Louis (Mo.) Sch. Fine Arts, 1904-15, Springfield Art Assn., 1915-17; also art dir. St. Louis Industrial Exhbn., 1914, St. Louis Centennial, 1918. Served as sergt. 2d Vol. Bn. Royal Welsh Fusiliers, 1882. Painter in oils and water colors, wood carver, mezzotint engraver, textile designer, scenic artist, costume designer. Represented in collection of Springfield (Ill.) Art Assn., City Art Mus., St. Louis, New Haven (Conn.) Clay and Palette Club, Lotos Club, N.Y. City, Vanderpool Memorial Gallery, Chicago, Witte Memorial Mus., San Antonio, Tex., etc. Awarded $5,000 prize, nat. sect. Tex. Wildflower Competition, 1927; hors de concours, same, 1928; hon. mention, portrait, Austin, 1928; spl. landscape prize, Nashville, Tenn., 1928; $1,000 prize, Tex. sect., and $1,000 prize, cotton field sect., Tex. Wildflower Competition, 1929; popular vote prize, Southern States Art League, 1929; landscape prize, Miss. Art Soc., 1929; Alice Huger Smith water color prize, Southern States Art League, 1931; popular vote purchase prize, Simmons Univ., Abilene, Tex. Episcopalian. Mem. advisory board of The Living Age. Home: San Antonio, Tex. Died Sept. 3, 1939.

DAY, Addison Blanchard, utilities; b. Chicago, Mar. 19, 1874; s. Alphonso C. and Elnora (Blanchard) D.; ed. pub. and high schs.; m. Mabel C. Godfrey, Mar. 14, 1900; children—Herbert Godfrey, Robert Addison. Began as salesman Los Angeles Lighting Co., Feb. 1, 1895, and continued through various offices with its successor, Los Angeles Gas & Electric Corp., of which was pres. and gen. mgr., 1928-37; chmn. bd. Southern Calif. Gas Co.; dir. Southern Fuel Co., Industrial Fuel Supply Company, Pacific Indemnity Co. Trustee U. of Southern Calif., Calif. Junior Republic; mem. advisory council U. of Southern Calif. Coll. Engring. Republican. Conglist. Home: Los Angeles, Calif. Died Nov. 28, 1939.

DAY, Benjamin Franklin, rear adm.; b. Plymouth, O., Jan. 16, 1841; s. Benjamin Franklin and Prussia Bunnell (King) D.; apptd. to U.S. Naval Acad. from Ohio, 1858; resigned, Nov. 24, 1860; reinstated, June 29, 1861; m. Flora Inez Baldwin, Sept. 22, 1869; children—Philip Baldwin, Benjamin Clark. Lt., Aug. 1, 1862; promoted through grades to rear admiral, Mar. 29, 1899. Served New London, on Colorado, W. Gulf Blockading Squadron, 1861-64; wounded in a night engagement, July 9, 1863; on Saugus, N. Atlantic Blockading Squadron, 1864-65; engagements with Howlett House batteries in James River, and attacks on Ft. Fisher; Tuscarora, 1865-68; Contocook, 1868-70; Hydrographic Office, 1870-71; Ticonderoga, 1871; Congress, 1871-74; receiving-ship New Hampshire, 1874-75; comd. Manhattan, 1875-76, Rio Bravo, 1877-78; Navy Yard, Norfolk, 1879-80; light-house insp. 8th dist., 1881-84; comd. Mohican, 1885-88; Navy Yard, Boston, 1889-92; comd. Boston, 1892-93, Baltimore, 1894-96; pres. Steel Bd., 1896-97; mem. Naval Exam. and Retiring bds., 1897-1900; retired 1900. Home: Buena Vista, Va. Died July 3, 1933.

DAY, Charles, mech. engr.; b. at Phila., May 15, 1879; s. Richard H. Day; M.E., U. of Pa., 1899. Began engring. work in Phila., 1899; mem. Dodge & Day, specializing in engring. management and constrn. work, 1901-11; pres. Day & Zimmermann, 1911-26; chmn. bd. Day & Zimmermann, Inc., 1926—. Superintendent of installation of power plant machinery, Phila. Export Expn., 1899; asst. supt. and engr. works for Link Belt Engring. Co., 1900-01; dir. Pennsylvania R.R., Fidelity-Phila. Trust Co., United Gas Improvement Co. Has lectured before Grad. Sch. of Business Administration, Harvard, and at Columbia; mem. civilian bd. apptd. by Sec. of Navy to investigate the efficiency of the navy yards; mem. Storage Com. of Gen. Munitions Bd. during World War; mem. Depot Bd. apptd. by Sec. of War; engring. advisor

Col. House's Commn.; spl. mission to France for Sec. of War; trustee Emergency Fleet Corp. Mem. bd. mgrs. Franklin Inst.; trustee U. of Pa. Republican. Author: Industrial Plants, 1911. Home: Chestnut Hill, Pa. Died May 10, 1931.

DAY, Charles Orrin, theologian; b. Catskill, N.Y., Nov. 8, 1851; s. Charles Henry and Sarah Collins (Porter) D.; A.B., Yale, 1872; grad. Andover Theol. Sem., 1877; Yale Div. Sch., 1884-85; (D.D., Dartmouth, 1901, Ia. Coll., 1901; LL.D., Norwich U.); m. Mary Hiland Hull, June 25, 1879. Ordained Congl. ministry, 1877; city missionary, Montreal, 1877-78; pastor Williamsburg, Mass., 1879-84, Brattleboro, Vt., 1885-98; sec. Congl. Ednl. Soc., 1898-1901; pres. and Bartlet prof. homiletics and practical theology, Andover Theol. Sem., 1901-08. Chaplain 1st Vt. Vols. at Chickamauga, 1898. Home: Andover, Mass. Died 1910.

DAY, Clarence, author; b. New York, N.Y., 1874; s. Clarence S. and Lavinia (Stockwell) D.; grad. St. Paul's Sch., Concord, N.H.; B.A., Yale, 1896, hon. M.A., 1926; m. Katharine Briggs Dodge, 1928; 1 dau. Author: This Simian World, 1920; The Crow's Nest, 1921; Thoughts Without Words, 1928; God and My Father, 1932; In the Green Mountain Country, 1934; Life with Father, 1935; Life with Mother (edited by wife), 1937. Home: New York, N.Y. Died Dec. 28, 1935.

DAY, David Talbot, geologist; b. E. Rockport (Lakewood), O., Sept. 10, 1859; s. Willard Gibson and Caroline (Cathcart) D.; A.B., Johns Hopkins, 1881, Ph.D., 1884; m. Elizabeth Eliot Keeler, Mar. 17, 1886. Demonstrator chemistry, U. of Md., 1884-85; chief, mining and mineral resources div., 1886-1907, expert in charge petroleum investigations, U.S. Geol. Survey, 1907-14; cons. chemist U.S. Bureau Mines, Washington, 1914-20. Exhibitor Centennial Exhbn., 1876; spl. agt. U.S. Geol. Survey, 1883-85; in charge petroleum exhibits, Chicago Expn., 1893; dir. of mining, Cotton States and Internat. Expn., Atlanta, 1896; sec. Jury of Awards, Tenn. Centennial, 1897; dir. of mining, Trans-Miss. Expn., 1898; in charge petroleum, etc., Phila. Centennial, 1899, Paris Expn., 1900; in charge mining, Buffalo Expn., 1901; hon. chief dept. of mines and metallurgy, St. Lewis Expn., 1904; hon. commr. of mining, Lewis and Clark Expn., Portland, Ore., 1905, Jamestown Expn., 1907; U.S. commr. Internat. Commn. for Petroleum Tests, 1907-09; pres. fuel sect., Internat. Congress Applied Chemistry, 1912. Compiler of Mineral Resources of the United States, 1885-1904. Author: Day's Handbook of the Petroleum Industry. Home: Washington, D.C. Died Apr. 15, 1925.

DAY, Edmund, playwright; b. New York, Oct. 28, 1866; s. William A. and Jennie Elmer (De Vere) D.; pub. sch. and pvt. edn.; m. Patty Montgomery Chandler, Dec. 1, 1900. Dramatic editor Detroit Tribune, 1898-99. Author: The Futurity Winner; The Cardinal's Edict; The Head Waiters; Behind the Mask; The Round Up. Died June 24, 1923.

DAY, Edward Cason, lawyer; b. Cynthiana, Ky., Mar. 20, 1862; s. Alfred and Mary Frances (Cason) D.; B.A., Washington and Lee U., 1880, B.L., 1883; unmarried. Practiced at Cincinnati, O., 1883-87; mem. editorial bd. West Pub. Co., St. Paul, Minn., 1887-90; practiced at Livingston, Mont., 1890-96; in practice at Helena, Mont., 1896—. Mem. School Board, Helena, 1898-1920; mem. Mont. Ho. of Rep., 1899, 1913, 15; city atty. Helena, 1904-05, 1918-21; U.S. atty. dist. of Mont., 1918-20. Was state chmn. Am. Red Cross drives, and U.S. and Y.M.C.A. war work. Trustee St. Peter's Hosp. (Helena), P.E. Diocese of Mont. Pres. Helena Y.M.C.A.; v.p. State Y.M.C.A., Mont. Democrat. Mason. Died June 7, 1936.

DAY, Edward Charles, newspaper editor; b. Denver, Colo., Jan. 3, 1886 ;s. Thomas William and Margaret Vincentia (Ducey) D.; student Sacred Heart Grade and High Sch., Denver, 1891-1903; m. Mary Ellen Sampson, July 4, 1907; children—Edward Charles, Jr., Maxine Elizabeth (Mrs. Edward F. Burke), William Thomas (dec.). Copy boy, later state, sports, city, news editor Denver Times, 1904-26; mng. editor Denver Evening News, 1926-28, Rocky Mountain News, 1928-31; mng. editor Denver Post, 1931—. K.C. Deceased.

DAY, Erastus Sheldon, consul; b. Colchester, Conn., July 7, 1836; s. Elihu M. and Jane E. (Buell) D.; ed. dist. sch. in Westchester, in town of Colchester, and Wilbraham (Mass.) Acad.; m. Catherine G. Olmsted, Aug. 29, 1864. Practiced law at Colchester, 1861-97. Mem. Conn. Ho. of Rep., 1862, 64, 74; clerk Conn. Senate, 1863; judge of probate, dist. of Colchester, 2 terms; chmn. Rep. State Com., 1886-90; U.S. consul at Bradford, Eng., 1897-1909. Home: Colchester, Conn. Died Aug. 30, 1921.

DAY, Fisk Holbrook, physician; b. Richmond, N.Y., Mar. 11, 1826; s. Rev. Warren and Lydia Lovell (Holbrook) D.; ed. Geneva, N.Y., Lyceum, 1837-38; Ithaca Acad., 1845-46; attended first course med. lectures at med. dept. New York U., 1847-48; grad. Jefferson Med. Coll., Phila., 1849; m. Caroline D. Perry, of Middlesex, N.Y., Sept. 1851; m. 2d, Frances A. Williams, Nov. 3, 1859; now widower. Began med. practice, 1849; located at Wauwautosa (suburb of Milwaukee), Jan. 1, 1854; apptd. one of Milwaukee Co. physicians, 1860, and had charge of county poor, and Co. Hosp. for Sick and Insane for more than 20 yrs. Retired from practice, 1893. Home: Lansing, Mich. Died 1903.

DAY, Frank Miles, architect; b. Phila., Apr. 5, 1861; s. Charles and Anna (Miles) D.; B.S., Univ. of Pa., 1883; (hon. M.A., Yale, 1916); studied architecture at Univ. of Pa. and 3 years in Europe; m. Anna Blakiston, Nov. 5, 1896. Practicing architecture, 1887—. Trustee Am. Acad. in Rome. Fellow A.I.A. (past pres.); hon. corr. member Royal Inst. British Architects; mem. Nat. Inst. Arts and Letters; A.N.A., 1910. Home: Mt. Airy, Pa. Died June 16, 1918.

DAY, George Armstrong, judge; b. Union Co., Ia., Nov. 10, 1859; s. James Gamble and Minerva C. (Manly) D.; B.S., Tabor (Ia.) Coll., 1882; LL.B., State U. of Ia., 1883; m. Sarah Brown, Feb. 13, 1889. Began law practice at Omaha, Neb., 1883; dep. atty. gen. of Neb., 1895, 96; mem. Supreme Court Commn., 1901-02; judge Dist. Court, 4th Jud. Dist. (Omaha), 1902-19; justice Supreme Court of Neb., term Feb. 1919-Jan. 1923; reëlected 1922 for term expiring 1929. Republican. Conglist. Mason. Home: Omaha, Neb. Died Dec. 20, 1927.

DAY, George Calvin, naval officer; b. Bradford, Vt., Nov. 8, 1871; grad. U.S. Naval Acad., 1892. Ensign, July 1, 1894; promoted through grades to rear adm., July 18, 1925. Served on Topeka during Spanish-Am. War, 1898; exec. officer, Hancock, 1906-07; navigator Connecticut, 1907-09; comd. Preston, 1909-10; comd. Div. 7, Torpedo Flotilla, Atlantic Fleet, 1910-11; in charge navy publicity bur., N.Y. City, 1911-13; exec. officer, New York, 1914-15; comd. Brooklyn, 1915-16; duty Naval Obs., Washington, 1917; comd. America, on transport service, Aug. 1917-Sept. 1918; comd. Montana, Sept. 1918-June 1919; at Naval War Coll., June 1919-July 1920; spl. duty Canal Zone, July-Sept. 1920; comd. Pennsylvania, Sept. 1920-May 1921; duty Navy Dept. (submarines), June 1921-July 1923; comd. submarines, Pacific, Aug. 1923-Aug. 1925; apptd. comdt. 15th Naval Dist. also Naval Operation Base, Canal Zone, Sept. 1, 1925-June 8, 1927; comdg. Light Cruisers, Div. 2, June 27, 1927-29; pres. Bd. of Inspection and Survey, 1929-35; retired Dec. 1, 1935. Home: New York, N.Y. Died Nov. 3, 1940.

DAY, George Edward, prof. Hebrew lang. and lit., Yale, 1866—, emeritus; b. Pittsfield, Mass., March 19, 1815; grad. Yale, 1833; Yale Theol. Sem., 1838; asst. instr. in Hebrew there, 1838-40; Congl. pastor Marlboro, and Edwards Ch., Northampton, Mass., 1840-51; prof. Bibl. lit., Lane Theol. Sem., 1851-66; dean Yale Divinity Sch., 1888-95. Established and edited Theol. Eclectic, 1863-71, when it united with the Bibliotheca Sacra, Andover, Mass. Home: New Haven, Conn. Died 1905.

DAY, George Edward, author; b. N. Dana, Mass., Sept. 21, 1864; s. Horace J. and Mary Jane (Chamberlain) D.; grad. Internat. Y.M.C.A. College, Springfield, Mass., 1893 (B.H., 1908; M.A., Norwich U., 1909); studied at Harvard U., 1908-1909; m. Nettie M. Fisher, June 30, 1897. In Y.M.C.A. work, 1890—; gen. sec. Y.M.C.A., Somerville, Mass., 1905-17, Army Y.M.C.A., Aug. 1917—. Author: Wild Rose and Thistle, 1885; A Wilderness Cry, 1906. Home: Somerville, Mass. Died Oct. 31, 1919.

DAY, Holman Francis, author; b. Vassalboro, Me., Nov. 6, 1865; s. Capt. John R. and Mary (Carter) D.; A.B., Colby Coll., 1887 (Litt.D., 1907). Mng. editor publs. of Union Pub. Co., Bangor, 1889-90; editor and propr. Dexter (Me.) Gazette; spl. writer for Lewiston (Me.) Journal; Me. rep. Boston Herald; mng. editor Lewiston Daily Sun. Maj. and mil. sec. on staff Gov. John F. Hill of Maine, 1901-04. Author: Up in Maine (verse), 1900; Pine Tree Ballads, 1902; Kin O' Ktaadn (prose and verse), 1904; Squire Phin (novel), 1905 (dramatized as The Circus Man, prod. Chicago, Aug. 1909); Along Came Ruth (play, prod. New York, 1914); Blow The Man Down, 1916; The Rider of the King Log, 1919; When Egypt Went Broke, 1920; All Wool Morrison, 1921; The Loving Are the Daring, 1923; Leadbetter's Luck, 1923; Clothes Make The Pirate, 1925; John Lang, 1926; When the Fight Begins, 1926; Starwagons, 1928; Ships of Joy, 1932. Address: Monterey, Calif. Died Feb. 19, 1935.

DAY, James Roscoe, univ. chancellor; b. Whitneyville, Me.; s. Thomas and Mary (Plummer) D.; A.B., Bowdoin College, 1874; (D.D., Wesleyan, 1883, Dickinson, 1883; S.T.D., Bowdoin, 1894; LL.D., Northwestern, 1896; D.C.L., Cornell Coll., Ia., 1904; L.H.D., Syracuse Univ., 1915, LL.D., 1921); m. Anna E. Richards, 1873. Ordained M.E. ministry, 1872; pastor Bath, Me., 1872-74, Portland, Me., 1876-78, Boston, 1881-82, New York, 1883-85 and 1889-93; chancellor Syracuse U., 1893-1922, chancellor emeritus, 1922—. Elected bishop M.E. Ch., 1904, but declined. Author: The Raid on Prosperity; My Neighbor The Working Man. Died Mar. 13, 1923.

DAY, Jerome J., mining; b. Truckee, Calif., Dec. 26, 1876; s. Henry Loren and Helen (Powers) D.; student Gonzaga Coll., Spokane, Wash., 1891-92, U. of Ida., 1894-97 and 1902; m. Lucy Mary Mix, Jan. 21, 1903; children—Bernice Eugenia (Mrs. John F. Malony), Jerome J. (dec.). Pres. Tamarack & Custer Consolidated Mining Co., 1912—; also pres. Sherman Lead Co., Coeur d'Alene Hardware & Foundry Co., Wallace Realty Co. Mem. Ida. State Senate, 3 terms; mem. Ida. State Bd. of Edn., 1933-39; regent U. of Idaho, 1933-39. Democrat. Catholic. Home: Moscow, Ida. Died Mar. 9, 1941.

DAY, Jesse Erwin, chemistry; b. Yorkshire, O., Feb. 16, 1888; s. John and Mary Elizabeth (Smith) D.; grad. Miami U. Acad., 1907; A.B., Miami U., 1911; A.M., Ohio State U., 1913, Ph.D., 1917; m. Frances Elizabeth Leech, Aug. 26, 1913; children—Cora Elizabeth, Donald Erwin. Fellow in chemistry, Ohio State U., 1911-12, asst. in chemistry, 1912-15; instr. in chemistry, La. State U., 1915-17; instr. in same, O. State U., 1917-18, asst. prof., 1918-20; chemist Nat. Electric Light Assn., summer 1920; asst. prof. chemistry, U. of Wis., 1920-23; same, Ohio State U., Columbus, 1923, asso. prof., 1928, prof., 1932—. Active in Liberty Loan drives, World War, also for Community Chest and K.C. Methodist. Died Apr. 19, 1935.

DAY, John Boynton Wilson, clergyman; b. Charlestown, Mass., Aug. 4, 1874; s. Marcellus and Mary J. (Wilson) D.; A.B., Tufts Coll., 1897; S.T.B., Harvard Div. Sch., 1900; m. Gertrude L. Watson, June 28, 1904. Ordained Unitarian ministry, 1900; pastor Unity Ch., Amherst, Mass., 1900-03, Channing Ch., Dorchester, 1903-06, Fall River, 1906-15. All Souls' Ch., Greenfield, 1915-19; rep. Am. Unitarian Assn. at Tokyo, Japan, 1919-22; minister Ch. of Our Father, Lancaster, Pa., 1924-29. Home: Wilton, N.H. Died 1936.

DAY, John Dabney, banker; b. Ladonia, Tex., Nov. 19, 1872; s. Samuel and Nancy (Bourland) D.; grad. Hill's Business Coll., Waco, Tex.; completed course in law; m. Nancy Adams Hayden, Feb. 9, 1902. An organizer, 1907, and cashier Traders State Bank, Dallas; bank consolidated, 1910, with First State Bank, of which was cashier and mng. dir.; 1st v.p. City Nat. Bank, Dallas, 1915-20; v.p. First Nat. Bank, Los Angeles, Calif., 1920-22; pres., 1922—, Citizens Nat. Bank, comprising group made up of Citizens Trust & Savings Bank, Citizens Nat. Co. and Citizens Nat. Bank; dir. Equitable Eastern Banking Corp. (New York); mem. Southern Calif. Bd. of Nat. Surety Co. Chmn. for Tex. of com. to procure Red Cross nurses, World War, and active in Liberty Loan drives. Democrat. Baptist. Home: Los Angeles, Calif. Died June 22, 1929.

DAY, John Francis, banker; b. Utica, N.Y., Oct. 14, 1853; s. Horace Burch (M.D.) and Harriett Amelia (Rust) D.; ed. pub. and pvt. schs.; m. Fanny Jane Williams, Oct. 30, 1878; children—Laura D. (Mrs. Frederick H. Cookinham), Irvin Williams, Louise D. (Mrs. Allen E. Trunbore). Banking official at Utica, N.Y., 1899—; formerly chmn. board dirs. Utica Trust & Deposit Co.; trustee Utica Cemetery Assn. Trustee Diocese of Central N.Y., Diocesan Fiscal Corp., House of the Good Shepherd, St. Luke's Home and Hosp. Episcopalian. Mason. Died Jan. 11, 1941.

DAY, John William, clergyman; b. Woburn, Mass., June 13, 1861; s. John Weeks and Julia (Clark) D.; student Meadville Theol. Sch., 1881 to 1882, D.D., 1921; S.T.B., Harvard Divinity Sch., 1885; m. Anne Bigelow, June 6, 1887; children—John Freeman, Anthony Bigelow, Joseph Tuckerman. Ordained ministry Unitarian Ch., 1886; pastor Newport, 1885-87, Ithaca, N.Y., 1887-90, Hingham, Mass., 1890-99, St. Louis, Mo., 1899-1924, Kennebunk, Me., 1925-32. Unitarian and Universalist. Editorial contbr. to Boston Transcript, 1893-99; a leading editorial writer Christian Register, Boston, 1896-1918. Worker for Am. Red Cross, 1918; asst. sec. War Y.M.C.A., Camp Taylor, Louisville, Ky., 1918; speaker, Liberty Bond campaigns, 1918-19. Vice-pres. Me. Unitarian Conf., 1925; mem. council Nat. Unitarian Conf. Republican. Home: Kennebunk, Me. Deceased.

DAY, L. B., judge; b. Westboro, Mo., Feb. 3, 1889; s. Frank and Sarah (Rowan) D.; grad. high sch., Albion, Neb., 1907; A.B., Creighton U., Omaha, 1911, A.M. from same univ., 1913, LL.B., 1914; LL.D., U. of Omaha, 1934; m. Neva Emma Grimwood, Apr. 10, 1916; children—Frank Edmund, Robert Grimwood, L.B. Admitted to Nebraska bar, 1914, began practice at Omaha; judge Dist. Court, Omaha, 1920-29; asso. justice Supreme Court of Neb., Jan. 3, 1929, for term 1929-35. Democrat. Presbyn. Mason. Home: Omaha, Neb. Died Nov. 22, 1938.

DAY, Richard Edwin, author; b. Granby, N.Y., Apr. 27, 1852; s. Richard and Susan L. (Huggins) D.; A.B., Syracuse U., 1877, A.M., 1878 (Litt.D., 1899); m. Frances E. Northrop, Apr. 22, 1880. Asst. editor, Northern Christian Advocate, 1879-80; asso. editor, Syracuse Daily Standard, 1880-99; on staff regents' office, Albany, N.Y., 1899-1904; editor in state historian's office, 1904-29. Author: Lines in the Sand, 1878; Thor—A Drama, 1880; Lyrics and Satires, 1883; Poems, 1888; New Poems, 1909; Dante—a

Sonnet Sequence, and Other Poems, 1924; (with Arthur Pound) Sir William Johnson (biography), 1930. Home: Albany, N.Y. Died Dec. 14, 1936.

DAY, Robert Henry, judge; b. Ravenna, O., July 3, 1867; s. Luther and Ellen I. (Barnes) D.; student U. of Mich., 1885-88, and in law dept., 1888-89; LL.B., Cincinnati Law Sch., 1891; m. Mary L. Hunt, June 27, 1898; children—Elizabeth Hunt, Margaret Hubbel. Admitted to Ohio bar, 1891, and began practice at Massillon; pros. atty. Stark Co., O., 1900-06; judge Court of Common Pleas, Stark Co., 1911-23; asso. justice Supreme Court of Ohio, 1923—. Mem. Draft Bd., World War. Republican. Episcopalian. Home: Columbus, O. Died Sept. 29, 1933.

DAY, Sarah J., poetic writer; b. Cincinnati, O., Nov. 5, 1860; d. Timothy Crane and Mary J. (Johnson) D.; grad. Packer Collegiate Inst., 1879. Author: Mayflowers to Mistletoe (verse), 1900; Fresh Fields and Legends Old and New, 1909; Wayfares and Wings, 1924; The Man on a Hilltop (biography), 1931. Won prize, Brooklyn Inst. Arts and Sciences, for poem, Battle of Long Island, 1913. Home: Englewood, N.J. Died May 11, 1940.

DAY, Thomas Fleming, editor; b. Weston-Super-Mare, Eng., Mar. 27, 1861; s. Edward Hartsinck and Georgina Sarah (Mant) D.; ed. New York; m. Anne Pirine Dunham, 1889. Editor The Rudder and pres. Rudder Pub. Co., 1890—. Writer of prose and verse; specially known as writer on yachting. Hon. mem. Springfield, Columbia, Brooklyn, Hampton Roads, Huguenot and 49 yacht clubs. Author: Songs of Sea and Sail, 1895; On Yachts and Yacht Handling, 1899; Hints to Young Yacht Skippers, 1902; On Yacht Sailing, 1904. Home: New York, N.Y. Died Aug. 19, 1927.

DAY, William A., lawyer; b. Wilmington, Del.; s. Isaac and Mary (Lowe) D.; auditor U.S. Treasury Dept., 1885-89; spl. asst. to atty. gen. of U.S. in cases under the interstate commerce and anti-trust laws, 1901-03; asst. atty. gen. U.S. in charge of prosecution of trust cases, Mar., 1903-05; v.p. Equitable Life Assurance Soc. of U.S., 1906-11, pres. Apr. 20, 1911—. Home: New York, N.Y. Died Apr. 9, 1928.

DAY, William Baker, univ. prof.; b. Peru, Ill., Feb. 15, 1871; s. Minthorne M. and Caroline Mary (Stockdale) D.; Ph.G., Chicago Coll. Pharmacy, 1892; M.Pharm., Phila. Coll. Pharmacy, 1917; m. Bertha P. Quinn, 1896 (died 1916); children—Helen May, Charlotte (Mrs. Ivan D. Carson); m. 2d, Marietta Carothers, 1920. Practiced as pharmacist Chicago; prof. botany, U. of Ill. Sch. of Pharmacy, 1898-1913, prof. materia medica and botany, 1913—, also acting dean, 1913-19, dean, 1919—. Republican. Conglist. Author: Introduction to Plant Histology, 1908. Home: Oak Park, Ill. Died Dec. 10, 1938.

DAY, William Cathcart, prof. chemistry Swarthmore (Pa.) Coll.; b. Urbana, O., May 30, 1857; s. Willard G. and Caroline Cathcart Day; grad. Johns Hopkins Univ. (Ph.D.); spl. studies in chemistry and physics; m. Jane Leamy, Baltimore, Dec. 27, 1884. Articles in Am. Chemical Jour., Analysis of Chrome Iron Ore, Oxidation of Brom. Cymene; Action of Carbon Dioxide on Sodium Aluminate; Production of Asphalt from Organic Materials; also wrote a series of tech. reports for U.S. Geol. Survey. Deceased.

DAY, William Louis, judge; b. Canton, O., Aug. 13, 1876; s. William Rufus and Mary Elizabeth (Schaefer) D.; grad. Williston Sem., 1896; LL.B., U. of Mich., 1900; m. Elizabeth E. McKay, Sept. 10, 1902. Admitted to bar, 1900, and practiced at Canton; city solicitor, 1906-08; U.S. atty., Northern Dist. Ohio, 1908-11; U.S. dist. judge, May 13, 1911-May 1, 1914, resigned; resumed practice as mem. Squire, Sanders & Dempsey, Cleveland. Republican. Lutheran. Home: Cleveland, O. Died July 15, 1936.

DAY, William Plummer, rear adm.; b. New York, Sept. 30, 1848; s. William Harrison and Mercy Carter (Church) D.; grad. U.S. Naval Acad., 1869; m. Jenetta Maria Eliza Grace Master, of Bath, Eng., Mar. 3, 1873. Promoted ensign, July 12, 1870; master, Oct. 31, 1871; lt., Jan. 23, 1875; lt. comdr., Jan. 1, 1897; comdr., Dec. 12, 1899; capt., Jan. 12, 1905; retired as rear adm., U.S.N., June 11, 1906. Served successively on Juniata, Franklin, Powhatan, Wyoming, Dictator, receiving ships Vermont and Colorado, Despatch, Wyandotte, Passaic, and Hartford, 1869-79; Quinnebaug, 1881-84; Powhattan, 1884; Yantic, 1885; Alliance, 1886-89; Franklin, 1891-93; exec. officer Bancroft and Machias, 1893; Franklin, 1894; Machias, 1894-96; exec. officer Richmond, 1897-98; New Orleans, 1898-99; comd. Vixen, 1899-1900; light house insp. 13th dist., 1900-02; comd. Mohican, 1902-04; lighthouse insp. 12th dist., 1904-05; Navy Yard, Mare Island, Calif., 1905-06. Died Dec. 28, 1919.

DAY, William Rufus, jurist; b. Ravenna, O., Apr. 17, 1849; s. Luther Day (chief justice of Ohio) and Emily (Spalding) D.; B.S., U. of Mich., 1870; read law in offices of Judge Robinson, Ravenna, O., and attended law lectures, U. of Mich., 1871-72; (LL.D., U. of Mich., 1898, Coll. City of N.Y., 1899); m. Mary Elizabeth Schaefer, 1875 (died 1912). Admitted to bar, 1872, and practiced at Canton. Judge Ct. Com. Pleas, 1886-90; apptd., 1889, U.S. dist. judge, Northern Dist. of Ohio, but because of failing health resigned before taking office; appdt. asst. Sec. of State, Mar. 1897; succeeded John Sherman as Sec. of State, Apr. 26, 1898, but in Sept., 1898, was succeeded by John Hay, and became chmn. U.S. Peace Commrs. at Paris, at close of war with Spain; U.S. circuit judge, 6th Circuit, 1899-1903; asso. justice Supreme Court of U.S., Feb. 1903—. Home: Washington, D.C. Died July 9, 1923.

DAYTON, Alston Gordon, judge; b. Philippi, Va. (now W.Va.), Oct. 18, 1857; s. Spencer and Sarah (Bush) D.; A.B., W.Va. U., 1878, A.M., 1880; m. Columbia M. Sinsel, Nov. 26, 1884. Admitted to bar, 1878; pros. atty., Upshur Co., W.Va., to fill unexpired term, 1879; pros. atty. Barbour Co., W.Va., 1884-88; mem. 54th to 58th Congresses (1895-1905), 2d W.Va. Dist.; reëlected to 59th Congress, but apptd. U.S. dist. judge, Northern Dist. of W.Va., 1905. Republican. Home: Philippi, W.Va. Died July 30, 1920.

DAYTON, Charles Willoughby, judge; b. Brooklyn, N.Y., Oct. 3, 1846; s. Abram Child and Maria A. (Tomlinson) D.; entered Coll. City of New York, 1861; LL.B., Columbia, 1868; m. Laura A., d. Dr. John B. and Rebecca (Stanford) Newman, of New York, Jan. 29, 1874. Practiced law at New York, 1868-1906. Mem. N.Y. Assembly, 1881; presdl. elector and sec. electoral coll., N.Y., 1884; postmaster New York, 1893-97; justice Supreme Ct. of N.Y., 1st dist., 1906-20. Democrat. Home: New York, N.Y. Died 1910.

DAYTON, George Draper, merchant, banker; b. Clifton Springs, N.Y., Mar. 6, 1857; s. David Day (M.D.) and Caroline (Draper) D.; LL.D., Macalester Coll., St. Paul, 1932; D.Litt. Jamestown Coll., 1933; m. Emma Willard Chadwick, Dec. 17, 1878; children—David Draper (dec.), Caroline (Mrs. W. F. Hayden), George Nelson, Josephine (wife of Rev. F. H. Blair). Settled in Minn., 1883; founder, 1902, since pres. The Dayton Co., Minneapolis, dept. store, employing 2800 persons; pres. Dayton Investment Co., Dayton Foundation, and J. B. Hudson, Inc. Active in promoting diversified farming in the Northwest, also in land reclamation. Mem. Capital Issues Com. World War. Dir. or trustee Macalester Coll. (St. Paul), Biddle Univ. (N.C.), Presbyn. Bd. of Nat. Missions, Presbyn. Ch. in U.S.A., Presbyn. Theol. Sem. (Chicago), Union City Mission, Goodwill Industries, Bd. of Church Extension, Y.W.C.A. Republican. Died Feb. 18, 1938.

DAYTON, James Henry, rear adm.; b. South Bend, Ind., Oct. 25, 1846; s. Daniel and Anna M.D.; apptd. from Ind. and grad. U.S. Naval Acad., 1866; unmarried. Ensign, Apr. 1868; master, Mar. 6, 1869; lt., Mar. 27, 1870; lt. comdr., Nov. 1884; comdr., Jan. 1894; capt., Mar. 29, 1900; rear adm., Feb. 28, 1906. Served on various duties and stas.; comd. Detroit, 1897-99; comdt. naval sta., San Juan, Oct. 11, 1899; comd. Chicago, 1901-03; pres. Naval Bd. Inspection and Survey, 1904-05; comdg. Philippine Squadron, Asiatic Fleet, 1906-07; comdr.-in-chief Pacific Fleet, 1907-08; retired Oct. 25, 1908. Court-martial duty, Jan. 1918-May 1919. Home: South Bend, Ind. Died Nov. 15, 1938.

DAYTON, William Lewis, lawyer; b. New Germantown, N.J., Sept. 5, 1864; s. Charles Henry and Mary Ellen (Thornton) D.; State Normal Sch., Trenton, N.J., 1882-84; Rutgers Coll., 1885-87; LL.B., Columbia, 1889; m. Elizabeth Harrington, Oct. 5, 1904. Practiced at Denver, Colo., 1889—; mem. Dayton & Denious. Mem. Colo. State Pardon Bd., 1896, 1903. Mem. Selective Service Bd. and Mil. Training Camps Com., Denver, during war period. Republican. Presbyn. Mason. Died Dec. 27, 1921.

DAZEY, Charles Turner, dramatist; b. Lima, Ill., Aug. 13, 1855; s. Mitchell and Albina (Conover) D.; student Coll. of Arts, Lexington, Ky.; A.B. (class poet), Harvard, 1881; (hon. A.M., Ill. Coll., 1892); m. Lucy Harding, July 12, 1887. Served on Harvard Advocate while at coll.; began dramatic composition, 1880. Plays: An American King; That Girl from Texas; War of Wealth; In Old Kentucky; The Suburban Home Folks; The Stranger; When Fran Came Home. Collaborator: In Mexico; An American Lord; The Captain and the Three Lights; The Sign of the Rose; A Night Out. Screen Plays: Wolf Lowry; Redemption of Dave Parcey; Behind the Mask; Shifting Sands, etc. Co-author: Manhattan Madness, The Sea Master, New York Luck, The Flower of Faith, Peggy Leads the Way. Home: Quincy, Ill. Died Feb. 9, 1938.

DEALEY, James Quayle, univ. prof., editor.; b. Manchester, Eng., Aug. 13, 1861; s. George and Mary Ann (Nellins) D.; A.B., Brown U., 1890, A.M., 1893, Ph.D., 1895; D.Litt., Baylor U., 1930; m. Clara Learned, Aug. 7, 1890; children—William Learned, Hermione Louise, Clara Elizabeth, James Quayle. Prof. langs. and history, Normal Coll., Denton, Tex., 1890; instr. langs., Vt. Acad., Saxtons River, 1891-93; instr. Latin, 1893-95, prof. social and polit. science, 1895-1928, Brown, now emeritus; editor Dallas News, 1929—; exchange prof. and lecturer, China, 1921; lecturer at Naval War Coll., 1916-28. Author: Text-book of Sociology (with Dr. Lester F. Ward), 1905; The Family in its Sociological Aspects, 1912; Growth of State Constitutions, 1915; Sociology—Its Development and Application, 1921; State and Government, 1921; Foreign Policies of the United States, 1927; Political Situations in Rhode Island, 1928. Home: Dallas, Tex. Died Jan. 22, 1937.

DEAN, Alexander, play director; b. Newburyport, Mass., May 6, 1893; s. of Joseph Flanders and Maria Fisher (Alexander) D.; A.B., Dartmouth, 1916; study, "47 Workshop," Harvard, 1917; m. Virginia Dixon, Aug. 23, 1928. Actor, appearing with John Drew, Rose Coghlan, Margaret Illington, and others; instr. English and dir. dramatics, U. of Mont., 1920-22; dir. Little Theatre, Dallas, Tex., 1922-23; asso. prof. dramatic art and lit., Sch. of Speech, Northwestern U., 1923-27; asst. prof. play production, Yale, 1927-33, asso. prof., 1933—. Dir. North Shore Theatre Guild of Chicago, 1923-27. Dir. Stuart Walker Co., Dayton, O., 1926; guest dir. Berkshire Playhouse, Stockbridge, Mass., 1929, 31; dir. Yale Univ. Dramatic Assn., 1929-33; chmn. drama com. Bur. of Recreation, New Haven; dir. Cape Playhouse, summer 1933; mng. dir. South Shore Players, Cohasset, Mass., summers 1934—; staged N.Y. City production of "Russet Mantle," 1936; "Laughing Woman," 1937, "In Clover," 1938. Served as 2d lt. Air Service, World War. Wrote: Just Neighborly; Little Theatre Organization and Management, 1926; Rosamunde (libretto), 1928; A Syllabus of Play Directing, 1931. Home: New Haven, Conn. Died July 29, 1939.

DEAN, Bashford, zoölogist, armor expert; b. New York, Oct. 28, 1867; A.B., Coll. City of New York, 1886; A.M., Columbia, 1889, Ph.D., 1890; m. Mary Alice, d. Isaac Michael Dyckman, of Kingsbridge, N.Y., 1893. Tutor natural history, Coll. City of New York, 1886-90; instr. biology, 1891-96, adj. prof. zoölogy, 1896-1904, prof. vertebrate zoölogy, 1904-27, hon. prof., 1927—, Columbia. Asst. N.Y. State Fish Commn., 1886-88; asst., 1889-92, biologist, 1900-01, spl. investigator U.S. Fish Commn.; dir. Biol. Lab., Cold Spring Harbor, N.Y., 1890; mem. Advisory Bd., New York Aquarium, 1902—; curator of herpetology and ichthyology, 1903-26, hon. curator of ichthyology, 1926—, Am. Mus. Natural History; curator arms and armor, Met. Mus. Art, 1903—; prof. Fine Arts, New York U., 1925; pres. Dyckman Inst., curator Dyckman House Mus. Trustee N.Y. Museum. Chevalier Legion of Honor. Adviser on armor U.S. War Dept.; maj. of Ordnance U.S.A.; mem. Mission to France, Belgium, England, 1917. Author of numerous works on palæichthyology and embryology of fishes (myxinoid, chimæroid and ganoid), and of bibliography of fishes (50,000 titles). Many pubs. on armor and arms. Home: Riverdale, New York, N.Y. Died Dec. 6, 1928.

DEAN, Francis Winthrop, mill engr., architect; b. Taunton, Mass., May 24, 1852; s. Samuel Augustus and Charity Williams (Washburn) D.; S.B., Lawrence Scientific Sch. (Harvard), 1875; m. Lydia Clarkson Hale Cushing, Mar. 8, 1893 (died Sept. 15, 1926); children—Samuel Winthrop, Francis Hale. Instructor in civil engineering, Harvard Engineering Sch., 1874-82; entered office of E. D. Leavitt, Cambridge, Mass., as spl. asst., and afterwards draftsman and insp. of machinery; chief draftsman, 1886-89; opened an office in Boston, 1889; head of Dean & Main, engrs. and architects, 1893-1907. With Emergency Fleet Corp., Jan. 1, 1918-Oct. 1, 1920; now practicing as engr. and architect. Mem. Bd. of Sewer and Water Commrs., Lexington, Mass., 7 yrs. Fellow, Am. Soc. M.E. (v.p. 1895-97). Home: Lexington, Mass. Died May 25, 1940.

DEAN, James Renwick, judge; b. St. Louis, Mo., Sept. 15, 1862; s. Henry and Ellen Margaret (Armour) D.; prep. edn., pub. schs., and Decorah (Ia.) Inst.; LL.B., U. of Mich., 1885, supplemented by lectures in lit. dept.; m. Jennie E. Sutton, Jan. 14, 1892. Practiced in Chicago, 1885-89; removed to Broken Bow, Neb., 1890; co. atty., Custer Co., Neb., 1895-99; city atty. Broken Bow 3 terms; mem. Bd. of Edn., Broken Bow, 10 yrs.; apptd. judge Supreme

DEAN, James Theodore, army officer; b. Ironton, O., May 12, 1865; s. Ezra Van Ness and Charlotte Anne (Weaver) D.; grad. U.S. Mil. Acad., 1887; grad. Army War Coll., Washington, 1911; unmarried. Commd. 2d lt. 3d inf., June 12, 1887; 1st lt. 14th Inf., Aug. 14, 1894; maj. chief ordnance officer vols., July 18, 1898; hon. mustered out vols., May 12, 1899; capt. 10th Inf. U.S.A., Mar. 2, 1899; promoted through grades to brig. gen. N.A., Aug. 5, 1917; retired, rank brig. gen. U.S.A., June 21, 1930. Maj. and chief ordnance officer in Puerto Rico and Cuba, Spanish-Am. War; in Alaska, 1906-08, P.I., 1912-15; apptd. comdr. 156th Inf. Brigade, Camp Dix, Wrightstown, N.J., Aug. 25, 1917, and in France, 78th Div., May 1918-May 1919; was in St. Mihiel and Meuse-

Court of Neb. by Gov. Sheldon for term, 1909-10; and elected for term 1917-23, on ticket without party designation; reëlected on non-political ballot, 2 terms, 1923-35. Democrat. Wilson presdl. elector-at-large, 1912. Commr. to Presbyn. Gen. Assembly, 1906. Mason. Home: Lincoln, Neb. Died Jan. 5, 1936.

Argonne campaigns; col. 29th U.S. Inf., Aug. 15, 1919-Aug. 23, 1920; apptd. adj. gen. Aug. 23, 1920; adj. Philippine Dept., Manila, P.I., Dec. 2, 1920-Nov. 18, 1922; col. 11th U.S. Inf., Dec. 12, 1922-Feb. 25, 1924; in charge New York Dist. Gen. Recruiting Service assigned Apr. 23, 1924; asst. chief of staff 77th Div. Organized Reserves, N.Y. City, Jan. 28, 1927-Sept. 3, 1928 (retired). Died June 15, 1939.

DEAN, John, jurist; b. Williamsburg, Pa., Feb. 15, 1835; ed. Williamsburg Acad. and Washington Coll.; admitted to bar, 1855, Supreme Court bar, 1871. Supt. Blair Co. Sch., 1857-59; practiced law with Hon. S. S. Blair, 1859-64; dist. atty., Pa., 1867-71; presiding judge, 24th jud. dist., Pa., 1871-92; justice Supreme Court, Pa., 1892—; term expires 1913. Republican. Deceased.

DEAN, John Candee, mfr. and astronomer; b. Deansboro, N.Y., Sept. 15, 1845; s. John and Harriet R. (Peck) D.; scientific course, Whitestown Sem., Utica, N.Y.; Sc.D., Lombard Coll., Galesburg, Ill., 1917. Entered iron foundry and machine business, 1867; now pres. and treas. Dean Bros. Co., mfrs. pumping and condensing machinery. Republican. Unitarian. Author: "Life of Count Rumford," "Astronomical Superstitions," "Mysteries of Matter." Home: Indianapolis, Ind. Died Dec. 31, 1928.

DEAN, John Marvin, clergyman; b. Cobleskill, N.Y., Oct. 14, 1875; s. John Marvin and Eva (Müller) D.; ed. pub. schs.; m. Alice Beatrice Fisken, Jan. 19, 1903. Entered Bapt. ministry, 1894; evangelistic work, 1894-96; pastor, Reynoldsville, Pa., 1897-98; spl. work under Internat. Com. Y.M.C.A. among U.S. troops in P.I., 1899-1901; pastor Tabernacle Ch., Seattle, 1902-09, First Ch., San Jose, Calif., 1910-11; with Men and Religion Forward Movement of N. America, 1911-12; pastor 2d Bapt. Ch., Chicago, 1912-17, and pres. Northern Bapt. Theol. Sem., 1913-18. Founder Aiken Inst. Soc. Settlement, Chicago, 1913. Mil. training camps, 1916, 17; commd. capt. inf., Ill. Reserve Militia, 1917; chaplain Am. Red Cross, 1918; chaplain U.S.A., 1918-19, attached 8th Div. Sanitary Train; chaplain O.R.C., U.S.A., 1919; supervising chaplain U.S. Res. with Civilian Conservation Corps, 1934. Evangelist, 1919-21; pastor First Ch., Pasadena, Calif., 1921-27; minister Hinson Memorial Ch., Portland, 1927-29; also pres. Western Baptist Theol. Sem., Portland, 1927-29. Author: The Miracle on Hermon, 1921; The Undying Torch, 1926; Portland Sermons, 1929; Unrhymed Sonnets of the Sunset Trail, 1929. Address: Greensburg, Pa. Died Nov. 10, 1935.

DEAN, John Ward, author; b. Wiscasset, Me., Mar. 13, 1815; youth in Portland, Me., later lived at Providence, R.I.; more recently at Boston (hon. A.M., Dartmouth, 1869); librarian and prominent mem. New England Historic-Geneal. Soc.; editor New England Hist. and Geneal. Register, and 9 vols. New England Bibliopolist, 1880-98. Home: Medford, Mass. Died 1902.

DEAN, Richard Crain, rear admiral; b. Harrisburg, Pa., May 27, 1833; s. Alexander Tracy and Mary Adeline (Crain) D.; student Yale; M.D., Jefferson Med. Coll., 1854; (hon. A.M., Yale, 1854); m. Anna Mulford, 1856; m. 2d, Sarah Elizabeth Bingham, 1888. Apptd. asst. surgeon U.S.N., Apr. 7, 1856; promoted past asst. surgeon, Mar. 25, 1861; surgeon, Aug. 1, 1861; med. insp., June 8, 1873; med. dir., June 10, 1880; retired May 27, 1895; advanced to rank of rear admiral, June 29, 1906, for services during Civil War. Served on various vessels and at various stas. during Civil War; fleet surgeon N. Atlantic Fleet, 1876-77; sr. mem. Examining Bd., 1877-79; mem. Bd. of Inspection, 1879-80; mem. Naval Examining and Retiring Bds., 1886-87; mem. Examining Bd., Washington, 1891-93, pres., 1902-03. Died 1910.

DEAN, Robert Augustus, lawyer; b. Fall River, Mass., Oct. 19, 1881; s. Gardiner Turner and Rachel (Allen) D.; A.B., Harvard, 1903, LL.B., 1905; m. Marion Eddy, Oct. 17, 1907. Practiced at Fall River, 1905-18; mem. Mass. Constl. Conv., 1917; became connected with legal dept. U.S. Shipping Bd., 1918, gen. counsel, 1919-20. Mem. Am. Bar Assn. Republican. Conglist. Home: Washington, D.C. Died Dec. 30, 1924.

DEAN, Walter Lofthouse, painter; b. Lowell, Mass., June 4, 1854; s. Benjamin and Mary Anne D.; ed. Boston grammar and high schs.; studied art in Mass. State Normal Art Sch., Mass. Inst. Tech., Boston, and Julian Acad., Paris, under Boulanger and Jules Lefebvre; m. Katharine Bates Whiting, July 1, 1874. Received 3 medals Mass. Mechanics' Assn. Has important paintings, Fitchburg (Mass.) Art and Library Bldg., Ayer (Mass.) Library, Boston Art Club collection; medal St. Louis Expn., 1904; has exhibited in most important exhbns. in this country and abroad. Home: Boston, Mass. Died Mar. 14, 1912.

DEAN, William Blake, merchant; b. Pittsburgh, Sept. 26, 1838; s. William and Aurelia (Butler) D.; ed. pub. schs., Pittsburgh and Bolmar Acad., W. Chester, Pa.; went to St. Paul, 1856; m. Mary C. Nicols, Oct. 18, 1860. Established wholesale iron and heavy hardware business in St. Paul, in 1860, in firm of Nicols & Dean, now Nicols, Dean & Gregg; dir. G.N. Ry. Co., First Nat. Bank, State Savings Bank, Northwestern Trust Co., etc. Trustee Mut. Life Ins. Co. of N.Y., 1907—. Trustee McCormick Theol. Sem., Chicago. Republican. Presbyn. Mem. Minn. Senate, 1891-95; presdl. elector on Blaine and Logan ticket, 1884. Home: St. Paul, Minn. Died Dec. 5, 1922.

DEAN, William John, merchant; b. St. Paul, Minn., Sept. 11, 1869; s. William Blake and Mary Catharine (Nicols) D.; ed. The Hill Sch., Pottstown, Pa.; m. Laura Cannon Winter, June 19, 1894; children—William W. (dec.), Mrs. Walter Kennedy, Winter, Mrs. Harold Waterworth, George W., Mrs. Robert B. F. Wylie, Mrs. A. E. Floan, Mrs. Robert C. Palmer. With Nicols, Dean & Gregg, heavy hardware, St. Paul, 1887—, mem. firm, 1894, treas., 1906, later v.p. and treas., and pres. and treas., 1921—; dir. First Nat. Bank, First Trust Co., etc. Mem. Mil. Training Camps Com., World War, also mem. Capital Issues Com., 9th Federal Dist. Trustee St. Paul Acad., Wilder Charity. Mem. U.S. Chamber Commerce (dir. exec. com.). Republican. Presbyn. Home: St. Paul, Minn. Died Feb. 4, 1941.

DEANE, John Hall, lawyer; b. in Canada; served in U.S. Vols., 1862-64, U.S.N., 1864-65; A.B., U. of Rochester, 1866, A.M., 1870. Gave $100,000 to U. of Rochester; has made other noteworthy gifts to Bapt. instns. Trustee U. of Rochester, Vassar Coll. Life mem. Am. Geog. Society. Died June 20, 1923.

DEANE, Ruthven, ornithologist; b. Cambridge, Mass., Aug. 20, 1851; s. Charles and Helen Elizabeth (Waterston) D.; ed. at Cambridge; m. Martha R., d. Henry A. Towner, of Chicago, Dec. 16, 1885; children—Charles, Henry Towner. Fellow Am. Ornithologists' Union, 1883—; pres. Ill. Audubon Soc., 1898-1914; mem. Chicago Acad. Sciences. Home: Chicago, Ill. Died Mar. 20, 1934.

DEANE, Walter, botanist; b. Boston, Apr. 23, 1848; s. Charles and Helen Elizabeth (Waterston) D.; A.B., Harvard, 1870; m. Margaret Chapman Coolidge, Dec. 31, 1878. Pvt. tutor, 1870-71; instr. St. Mark's Sch., Southborough, 1871-78; instr. John P. Hopkinson's pvt. sch., 1878-95; pvt. tutor, 1895-97; associated with William Brewster in his ornithol. mus., as asst. in charge, 1897-1907. Compiled and edited, Flora of the Blue Hills, Middlesex Fells, Stony Brook and Beaver Brook Reservations of the Met. Park Commn. Home: Cambridge, Mass. Died July 30, 1930.

DE ANGELIS, Jefferson, comedian; b. San Francisco, Nov. 30, 1859; s. John and Susan D.; ed. common schs., San Francisco, Philadelphia, and New York; m. Florence Conliffe, 1882; m. 2d, Charlotte Elliott, Jan. 1, 1931. Entered the theatrical profession as a child, appearing in single act in vaudeville, 1874; toured Australia, China, Japan, Burma, India, S. Africa, etc., with own co., 1880-84; with McCaull Opera Co., 1887-90; leading comedian, Casino, N.Y. City, 1890-93; under own management, 1902-05; starred in Fantana, 1904, The Great White Way, 1907, The Beauty Spot, 1908; has played rôle of Ko-Ko in 12 productions of the Mikado, and sung in more than 100 operas; dramatic performances include, "Revelry," "School for Scandal," "The Royal Family," "Apron Strings." Mason. Co-author: A Vagabond Trouper, 1932. Home: Long Island City, N.Y. Died Mar. 20, 1933.

DE ANGELIS, Pascal Charles Joseph, judge; b. Holland Patent, N.Y., Jan. 27, 1850; s. William Webb and Elizabeth (Burlingame) D.; A.B., Cornell, 1871; LL.B., and LL.D., Hamilton College; m. Annie Jackson, 1880. Admitted to Pa. bar in 1873, to N.Y. bar, 1875; practiced in Utica, 1875-1907; justice Supreme Court, 5th Dist., State of N.Y., 1907-20; justice Appellate Div., 4th Dept., 1916-20. Mem. bd. mgrs., Utica State Hosp., 1886-93; mem. Bd. of Edn., Utica. Republican. Home: Utica, N.Y. Died May 2, 1932.

DEARBORN, George Van Ness, psychiatrist; b. Nashua, N.H., Aug. 15, 1869; s. Cornelius Van Ness and Louisa Frances (Eaton) D.; 7th generation from Godfreye D., Exeter, New Hampshire, 1637, and John Eaton of Haverhill, 1638; Litt.B., Dartmouth, 1890; M.D., Coll. Phys. and Surg. (Columbia), 1893; A.M., Harvard, 1896; Ph.D., Columbia, 1899; m. Blanche V. S. Brown, June 18, 1893; 1 dau., Lucia Eaton (Mrs. Seabury B. Hough). Assistant in philosophy, Harvard, 1896; asst. in physiology, Harvard Med. Sch., 1899; prof. and dir. lab. of physiology, 1900-16, Tufts College; professor psychology and education, Sargent Normal School, Cambridge, 1906-21; instr. psychology, School of Eugenics, Boston, 1912-15; cons. physiologist and psychologist, Forsyth Dental Infirmary for Children, Boston, 1913—; Med. Corps, U.S.A., Apr. 29, 1918; 158th Depot Brig., Camp Sherman, Ohio, neuropsychiatric board; chief of neuropsychiatric service, Camp Devens, Mass., Base Hosp., May 1919, until discharge, July 2, 1919. Asst. phys. for nervous diseases, Boston City Hosp., 1919-21; phys. August (Me.) State Hosp., June-Nov. 1921; surgeon (R) U.S.P.H.S., neuropsychiatric sect., Sept. 28, 1921—; med. officer expert, U.S. Vets.' Bureau, 1924. Med. O.R.C., U.S.A., 1922. Fellow Boston Soc. Natural History, Am. Psychiat. Assn. Republican. Mason. Author: The Emotion of Joy, 1899; A Textbook of Human Physiology, 1908; Moto-Sensory Development, 1910; Relations of Mind and Body, 1914; The Physiology of Exercise, 1918; The Influence of Joy, 1916; How to Learn Easily, 1916; The Psychology of Clothing, 1918; Physiology and Hygiene. Editor: Our Senses Series, 1916. Home: Maplewood, N.J. Died Dec. 12, 1938.

DEARBORN, Henry M., prof. dermatology New York Homœ. Med. Coll. and Hosp., 1893—; b. Epsom, N.H., Nov. 1846; studied Harvard Med. Coll.; grad. Bowdoin Med. Coll., 1869; located in New York, 1880; visiting physician Metropolitan Hosp., 1883—; prof. principles and practice medicine, New York Med. Coll. and Hosp. for Women, 1883-1903; asso. editor N. A. Journal of Homœopathy, 1883-91; cons. dermatologist Flower Hosp., and cons. physician several hosps., New York and Brooklyn; m. Sadie Smith, London, Eng., Jan. 1873. Author: Diseases of the Skin, 1903. Died 1904.

DEARBORN, John, pres. Warren Bros. Co.; b. Dorchester, Mass., Mar. 27, 1868; s. John Langdon and Sarah (Abbott) D.; grad. Boston Inst. Tech., 1890; m. Adelina L. Toel., Mar. 29, 1922. In investment business, Boston, 1890-1906; with Warren Bros. Co., roofing and paving, Boston, 1906—, vice-pres. and treas., 1907-20, pres., 1920—; pres. Warren Bros. Co. of Argentina, Bio-Chemic Fertilizer Co., Warren Bros. Co. of Chile. Home: Boston, Mass. Died June 6, 1930.

DEARHOLT, Hoyt E., M.D.; b. Reedsburg, Wis., Mar. 2, 1879; s. Sylvester J. and Adelaide (Mackey) D.; M.D., Rush Med. Coll. (U. of Chicago), 1900; m. Edith Tweeden, Aug. 31, 1907; children—John Winslow, Dorothy Mary (Mrs. T. W. Goodrich). Began practice at Milwaukee, 1902; one of founders, 1903, and mng. editor Wis. Med. Journal until 1910; one of founders River Pines Sanatorium, Stevens Point, Wis., 1905; orthopedic surgeon, Milwaukee County Hosp., 1905-07, Milwaukee Children's Hosp., 1906-10; exec. sec. Wis. Anti-Tuberculosis Assn., 1910—; asso. prof. and chief of Health Instruction Bur., Univ. Extension Div., U. of Wis., 1913-20. Vice chmn. and sec. Wis. Com. Internat. Congress on Tuberculosis, 1907-08; sec. and treas. Miss. Valley Conf. on Tuberculosis, 1919-20, pres., 1925. Mem. Wis. Conf. Social Work (dir.). Died July 12, 1939.

DEARING, John Lincoln, missionary; b. Webster, Me., Dec. 10, 1858; s. Joseph Henry and Susan Vinton (Adams) D.; A.B., Colby Coll., 1884, A.M., 1894 (D.D., 1900); grad. Newton Theol. Instn., 1889; m. Mary Lyon Hinckley, July 27, 1891. Ordained Bapt. ministry, 1889; went to Japan as missionary Am. Bapt. Missionary Union, 1889; pres. and prof. theology and ethics, Yokohama Bapt. Theol. Sem., 1894-1908; gen. missionary supt. Am. Bapt. Missionary Union for Japan, China and the Philippines, 1908-11. Lectured in America, part of 1899-1900; again in America, engaged in Laymen's Missionary Movement, Feb. 1909-Aug. 1910; traveled extensively in China, 1910-11. Dir. Nat. Y.M.C.A. of Japan; corr. mem. Asiatic Soc. of Japan, Japan Soc. of London, Yokohama Lit. Soc. (pres. 1912, 13). Republican. Author: Outline of Theology (Japanese), 1895. Deceased.

De ARMOND, David A., congressman, lawyer; b. Blair Co., Pa., March 18, 1844; reared on farm; ed. in common schools and at Williamsport Dickinson Sem.; practiced law at Butler, Mo.; presdl. elector, 1884; State senator, circuit judge and Mo. Supreme Court commr. Mem. Congress, 6th Mo. dist., 1891-1909. Democrat. Home: Butler, Mo. Died 1909.

DEARTH, Henry Golden, artist; b. Bristol, R.I., 1864; s. John W. and Ruth Marshall D.; pupil École des Beaux Arts, and Anmé Morot; m. Cornelia Van Rensselaer Vail, Feb. 26, 1896. Webb prize, Soc. Am. Artists, 1893; bronze medal, Paris Expn., 1900, silver medal, Buffalo Expn., 1901, Charleston, 1902. A.N.A., 1902, N.A., 1906. Died Mar. 28, 1918.

DEASY, Luere B., judge; b. Gouldsboro, Me., Feb. 8, 1859; s. Daniel and Emma L. (Moore) D.; student Eastern State Normal Sch., Castine, Me.; m. Emma M. Clark, Dec. 15, 1885. Admitted to Me. bar, 1884, and practiced at Bar Harbor; formerly mem. Deasy & Lynam, and pres. Me. Senate; justice Supreme Court of Me. until 1930, chief justice, Sept. 1929-Feb. 7, 1930; in practice of law, 1930—. Republican. Unitarian. Mason. Home: Bar Harbor, Me. Died Mar. 13, 1940.

DEAVER, John B., surgeon; M.D., U. of Pa., 1878; (Sc.D., Franklin and Marshall; LL.D., Villa Nova). Emeritus prof. of surgery, U. of Pa.; surgeon in chief to Lankenau Hosp. Fellow Am. Coll. Surgeons, Am. Surg. Assn. Author: Surgical Anatomy (3 vols.); Appendicitis, Its History, Pathology, Treatment, 4th edit., 1905; Enlargement of the Prostate (with A. P. C. Ashhurst), 1895; Surgery of the Upper Abdomen (with same), Vol. 1, 1909; Diseases of the Breast. Home: Philadelphia, Pa. Died Sept. 25, 1931.

DEAVOURS, Stone, lawyer; b. Iuka, Miss., Dec. 10, 1867; s. John and Adeline Katherine (Moore) D.; LL.B., with spl. distinction, U. of Miss., 1892;

m. Mary Elizabeth Clayton, Aug. 28, 1889; children—Adeline Katherine (dec.), Ernestine Clayton, Burns Moore (dec.), Anne, Dinah, Jack, Mary Elizabeth. Admitted to Miss. bar, 1892, and began practice at Paulding; removed to Laurel, Miss., 1901; dean School of Law, U. of Miss., 1930—. Mem. bd. trustees Miss. Dept. Archives and History, Eastman Memorial Foundation (Laurel). Mem. Dem. Nat. Com. from Miss. Democrat. Mason. Died Sept. 20, 1933.

DE BELLEVILLE, Frederic, actor; b. in Belgium, 1857; began stage career in England, played with success there and in Australia before coming to U.S.; 1st gained distinction in this country as Count de Carojac in "The Banker's Daughter." Has been leading man with Union Square Co., Frohman's Stock Co., sub-star to Clara Morris, Rose Coghlan, Mrs. Fiske and with Liebler & Co., Klaw & Erlanger, Charles Dillingham, and Charles Frohman. Home: Malba-on-the-Sound, L.I., N.Y. Died Feb. 26, 1923.

DE BLOIS, George Lewis, trustee; b. Newton, Mass., Aug. 17, 1867; s. George Lewis and Amanda M. (Fuller) De B.; A.B., Harvard, 1889; m. Mary B. Brooks, Nov. 23, 1899; 1 dau., Elizabeth. In real estate business, Boston, many yrs.; then trustee Barristers Hall Trust, Boston Real Estate Trust, David Sears Real Estate Trust, Essex Street Trust, Factory Buildings Trust, Kimball Building Trust, Hotel Trust, Longwood Trust, Paddock Building Trust, Park Building Trust, South Street Trust, South Terminal Trust, Tremont Building Trust, Provident Instn. for Savings; dir. New England Trust Co.; treas., dir. State Street Exchange; treas. Fifty Associates. Republican. Episcopalian. Home: Boston, Mass. Died May 4, 1939.

DEBOE, William J., senator; b. Crittenden Co., Ky., 1849; acad. edn.; M.D., U. of Louisville; practiced medicine few yrs.; admitted to bar. In law practice, Marion, Ky.; supt. schs., Crittenden Co.; mem. Rep. State Central Com., 12 yrs.; candidate for Congress, 1892; mem. Ky. Senate, 1893-96; U.S. senator, 1897-1903. Del. Rep. Nat. Conv., 1888, del.-at-large and chmn. Ky. delegation, 1896. Home: Marion, Ky. Died June 15, 1927.

DE BOER, Joseph Arend, life underwriter; b. Warffum, Province of Groningen, Holland, June 17, 1861; s. Jan Arend and Anje Peiter (Kuiper) D.; came to U.S. in boyhood; A.B., Dartmouth, 1884, A.M., 1887 (Sc.D., 1909); m. Augusta Charles Featherly, Dec. 23, 1885. Master Holderness Sch. for Boys, Plymouth, N.H., 1884-85; prin. Montpelier Union and Washington Co. grammar schs., Montpelier, Vt., 1885-89. Elected actuary, 1889, dir. and sec. 1897, 2d v.p. 1900, 1st v.p. 1901, pres. from Mar., 1902, Nat. Life Ins. Co. Mem. Vt. Senate, 1900, Ho. of Rep., 1908-09. Trustee Washington Co. Grammar Sch., St. Johnsbury Acad., Montpelier Sem., Wood Art Gallery, sec. permanent sch. fund commn. of Vt. Charter mem. Actuarial Soc. of America; v.p. Vt. Hist. Soc. Home: Montpelier, Vt. Died Dec. 25, 1915.

DE BOOY, Theodoor, archeologist, explorer; b. Hellevoetsluis, The Netherlands, Dec. 5, 1882; s. C. J. G. and Mary (Hobson) de B.; ed. Royal Inst.; m. Elizabeth Hamilton Smith, Mar. 29, 1909. Came to U.S., 1906; naturalized citizen, 1916; in charge West Indian archeol. work of Mus. of Am. Indian, New York, 1911—. Explored previously unknown regions of Santo Domingo and Venezuela; conducted archeol. investigations in Bahamas, Cuba, Jamaica, Hayti, Santo Domingo, Turks and Caicos Islands, Margarita, Trinidad, Martinique, Venezuela and Virgin Islands of U.S. Commander Order of Liberator of Venezuela. Democrat. Author: The Newly Acquired Virgin Islands of the U.S. and the British Virgin Islands, 1918. Home: Yonkers, N.Y. Died Feb. 18, 1919.

DeBOW, Charles Louis, clergyman; b. La Grange, Ind., Sept. 12, 1881; s. John H. and Laura J. (Hildebrand) D.; ed. Valparaiso U.; studied voice under pvt. teacher; D.D., Okla. U., 1923; m. Myrtle B. Gardner, Jan. 4, 1905; children—Lenore Josephine, Barbara Jane. Teacher, pub. schs., Ind., 1904-05; ordained ministry M.E. Ch., 1906; pastor successively Corunna, Wakarusa, Ligonier and La Grange, Ind., until 1918, First Ch., Dallas, Tex., 1918-22, First Ch., Oklahoma City, 1923-25, First Ch., Cleveland, 1926-33, Trinity Ch., Kansas City, 1933—. Sec. Okla. Ann. Conf., M.E. Ch., 3 yrs.; del. Gen. Conf. M.E. Ch., 1924 and 1932. Mem. Ind. Council of Defense, World War, also active in war savings campaign. Republican. Mason. Home: Kansas City, Mo. Died Jan. 3, 1937.

de BOWER, Herbert Francis; b. Dane, Wis.; s. Gerd and Mary (Buffmire) de B.; LL.B., U. of Wis., 1896. Practiced at Madison, Wis., several yrs.; developed organization for extensive training in business and law; founded Alexander Hamilton Inst., New York, 1909; v.p. and chmn. exec. com.; dir. various other cos. Capt. Signal R.C. attached to Hdqrs. U.S.A., A.E.F., 1917-19. Commr. of Conciliation, Dept. of Labor, 1922. Author: Advertising Principles, 1917. Co-author of Effective Speech, 1927. Home: Long Beach, N.Y. Died Mar. 16, 1940.

DEBS, Eugene Victor, lecturer, organizer; b. Terre Haute, Ind., Nov. 5, 1855; s. Daniel and Marguerite (Betterich) D.; common sch. edn.; m. Katherine Metzel, June 9, 1885. Locomotive fireman on Terre Haute & Indianapolis R.R., 1871-74; wholesale grocery house of Hulman & Co., 1875-79; city clerk of Terre Haute, 1879-83; mem. Ind. Legislature, 1885; grand. sec. and treas. Brotherhood of Locomotive firemen, 1880-93; pres. Am. Railway Union, 1893-97; chmn. Nat. Council Social Democracy, 1897-98; candidate Social Dem. Party for President, 1900. As pres. Am. Railway Union won a large strike on the Great Northern Ry.; while managing the still larger strike of Western roads in 1894 was charged with conspiracy, but acquitted; then he was charged with violation of an injunction and sent to jail for six months for contempt of court. Candidate of Socialist Party for President U.S., 1904, 08, 12; convicted of violation of espionage act, Sept. 1918, and sentenced by U.S. Judge David C. Westenhaver to 10 yrs.' imprisonment in penitentiary; decision sustained by Supreme Court of U.S., Mar. 10, 1919; entered prison Apr. 13, 1919. Died Oct. 20, 1926.

DeBUSK, Burchard Woodson, prof. ednl. psychology; b. nr. Shelbyville, Ind., Oct. 23, 1877; s. William and Emma Catherine (Woodard) DeB.; Central Normal Coll., Danville, Ind.; A.B., Ind. U., 1904; Ph.D., Clark U., 1915; m. Matella Druley, June 8, 1905. Prof. psychology and edn., Southwestern Coll., Winfield, Kan., 1904-08; acting dir. Psychol. Lab., U. of Ind., 1908-09; fellow Clark U., 1909-10, 1914-15; asso. prof. psychology, Colo. Teachers Coll., 1910-14; prof. ednl. psychology, U. of Ore., 1915—; mem. faculty U. of Calif. 4 summers. Republican. Conglist. Home: Eugene, Ore. Died July 29, 1936.

DE CAMP, Joseph Rodefer, artist; b. Cincinnati, 1858; s. Lambert and Lydia (Garwood) D.; pupil of T. S. Noble at Cincinnati Sch.; Royal Acad., Munich, and Duveneck, Florence, Italy; m. Edith Franklin Baker, Sept. 1891. First prize City Hall Decorative competition, Phila.; Temple gold medal, Pa. Acad. Fine Arts, 1899; hon. mention, Paris Expn., 1900; gold medal, St. Louis Expn., 1904; Beck portrait medal, Phila., 1911. Mem. Nat. Inst. Arts and Letters, "Ten Am. Painters." Home: Medford, Mass. Died Feb. 11, 1923.

DE CAMP, William Scott, engr. in mining and forestry; b. Powerville, N.J., Nov. 10, 1846; common school edn.; studied engring; mining operations confined to magnetic ores of New Jersey, forestry to Herkimer and Lewis counties, N.Y. First wife died, Aug. 26, 1895; again married March 19, 1900. Died 1905.

DE CASTRO, Hector, consular officer; b. Constantinople, Turkey, June 30, 1849; ed. Vienna, Austria, 1857-60, Paris, France, 1863-70 (grad.); moved to U.S. 1885, naturalized 1885; m. Grace A. Aldrich, Feb. 12, 1889. V.p. Commercial Cable Co., 1883-90; sec. Intercontinental R.R. Commn., Washington, 1890-1902. U.S. consul gen. at Rome, June 1897—. Republican. Died 1909.

DECHERT, Henry Martyn, lawyer, financier: b. Reading, Pa., March 11, 1832; s. Elijah and Mary W. (Porter) D.; A.B., Yale, 1850; m. Esther S. Taylor, Sept. 15, 1857. First lt. 25th and 40th Pa. Vols., 1862-63. Admitted to bar and has long practiced in Phila.; also identified with large financial interests; 20 yrs. pres., then 1st chmn. bd., Commonwealth Title Ins. & Trust Co. First pres. trust sect. Am. Bankers' Assn., 1896-97. Pres. Pa. State Asylum for Chronic Insane, 19 yrs. Mason. Home: Philadelphia. Died May 27, 1918.

DECHERT, Henry Taylor, lawyer; b. Philadelphia, Feb. 2, 1859; s. Henry Martyn and Esther S. (Taylor) D.; A.B., U. of Pa., 1879, LL.B., 1881; desc. of Gen. Andrew Porter; m. V. Louise Howard, Jan. 30, 1896. In practice at Phila., 1881—. Lt. col. 2d Regt., N.G. of Pa. in U.S. service Spanish Am. War; after close of war elected col. of regt., serving 5 yrs. and then declined reëlection. Home: Philadelphia. Died Oct. 14, 1915.

DE CISNEROS, Eleonora, opera singer; b. New York; d. John C. and Eleonor (Small) Broadfoot; ed. St. Agnes Sem., Brooklyn; studied grand opera singing with Mme. Murio Celli; m. Count Francois G. de Cisneros, Nov. 16, 1900. Début Met. Opera House, New York, season 1899-1900; has sung at Rome, Milan, Madrid, Lisbon, Vienna, St. Petersburg, Berlin, Covent Garden, London, Rio Janeiro, Mexico City, New York (Metropolitan Opera House), also in Australia with Melba, and in extensive concert tours. Member Chicago Opera Assn., 1910-16. Was decorated by Am. Red Cross for war work. Guest appearances, 1921, New York, spl. operatic rôles. Mem. Wagnerian Opera Co. (in America), 1923-24, singing Brünhilde in "Walküre," Ortrud in "Lohengrin," etc. Died Feb. 3, 1934.

DECKER, Benton Clark, naval officer; b. Lima, N.Y., Dec. 28, 1867; grad. U.S. Naval Acad., 1887. Ensign, July 1, 1889; promoted through grades to capt., July 1, 1913; rear admiral, temporary, July 1, 1918. Served on Indiana, Spanish-Am. War, 1898; insp. powder, Wilmington, Del., 1899-1901; on Helena, and Philippine service, 1901-04; Naval Acad., 1904-06; navigator and exec. Virginia, 1906-09; War Coll. and Dept., 1909-10; on Chester, 1910-12; War Coll., 1912-14; on Tennessee, 1914-15; Washington, 1915-16; War Coll., 1916-17; naval attaché, Madrid, 1917-18; Naval Sta., New London, 1918-19; 7th Naval Dist. and Naval Sta., Key West, 1919; Naval Operating Base, Hampton Roads, Aug.-Dec. 1920; 1st Naval Dist., Boston, Mass., Dec. 1920—. Died Mar. 22, 1933.

DECKER, Martin Snyder, pub. service commr.; b. Rosendale, N.Y., Jan. 4, 1858; s. John Taylor and Martha (Keator) D.; ed. pub. schs. and pvt. tuition; m. Petronella Wurts Beaver, Jan. 8, 1887. Deputy co. clerk Ulster Co., 1882-87; docket clk. Interstate Commerce Commn., 1887-93; asst. sec. Interstate Commerce Commn., 1893-1907, also chief examiner; spl. examiner to hear and report upon cases before the Federal Commn. under the Hepburn railroad law, 1906-07; pub. service commr. 2d Dist., N.Y., 1907-15, chmn. Pub. Service Commn., 2d Dist., 1913-14. Has been largely consulted in railroad and other public utility regulation cases. Democrat. Presbyn. Died 1928.

DECKER, Sarah Platt (Mrs.), president of Gen. Fedn. of Women's Clubs; has been v.p. of Nat. Federation and has been pres. of the Woman's Club of Denver. Died July 7, 1912.

DeCORMIS, Louis, clergyman; b. Norfolk, Va., Jan. 14, 1846; s. Edward and Martha (Whitelock) D.; and direct descendant on maternal side of Edmund Freeman, Colonial deputy gov. with Gov. Bradford, Plymouth Colony, Mass.; A.B., Kenyon Coll., 1870; B.D., Episcopal Theol. Sch., Cambridge, Mass., 1873; (D.D., Northern Ill. Coll., 1893; LL.D., Ewing Coll., 1900); m. Isabel Gibbs, Nov. 15, 1882. Deacon and priest, P.E. Ch., 1873; rector St. John's, Taunton, Mass., 1873-76, St. Stephen's, Lynn, 1876-85; 1st asst. minister, St. Ann's, Brooklyn, 1885-87; rector All Saint's Ch., Great Neck, L.I., 1887-95 (built ch. and rectory), St. Paul's Ch., Columbia, Pa., 1895-1901; removed to Cambridge, Mass., 1901; in charge St. Paul's, Boston, 1909. Republican. Died Mar. 3, 1916.

De COU, Branson, travel lecturer; b. Philadelphia, Pa., Oct. 20, 1892; s. Walter E. and Margaret (Mull) De C.; grad. Blair Acad., Blairstown, N.J., 1909; student Stevens Inst. Tech., 1910-12; m. Florence Chapman, Nov. 27, 1915 (divorced); m. 2d, Elsie Vera Stanley, Mar. 28, 1932. Lecturer on travel, illustrated, and under gen. title of "Dream Pictures," 1915—. Subjects: Forty lectures covering practically every country in the world. Home: Hollywood, Calif. Died Dec. 12, 1941.

De COURCY, Charles A., judge; b. Lawrence, Mass., Sept. 23, 1857; s. John and Mary (Lalor) D.; ed. pub. schs. and Georgetown U.; LL.B., Boston U., 1878; (LL.D., Georgetown, 1904); admitted to bar, 1881; m. Elisabeth May Roberts, Sept. 8, 1886. Practiced at Lawrence, Mass., 1881-1902; asst. dist. atty., 1883-89; asso. judge Superior Ct. of Mass., 1902-11; justice Supreme Jud. Ct. of Mass., Sept. 27, 1911—. Member bd. visitors Harvard U. and of Boston U. Law Sch.; mem. bd. regents Georgetown U.; fellow and v.p. Am. Inst. of Criminal Law and Criminology; v.p. Mass. Conf. Charities. Died Aug. 22, 1924.

DEDERICK, Peter Kells, capitalist; b. Columbia Co., N.Y., Feb. 1, 1838; s. Philip W. and Anna Maria (Kells) D. (both of Revolutionary ancestry); ed. Hudson River Inst.; m. Marietta Michael, 1864 (also of Revolutionary ancestry). Began in mfg. business at Albany, N.Y., 1860; founding what is known as Dederick Agrl. and Machine Works now conducted by P. K. Dederick's Sons; established branch works at Montreal, Can., Chicago, and St. Louis, and interested large operators in European countries, under foreign patents, 1876. Has been granted several hundred Am. and foreign patents in various classes. Home: Albany, N.Y. Died 1911.

DEEKS, William Edgar, M.D., specialist in tropical medicine; b. Williamsburg, Ont., Can., Apr. 23, 1866; s. William and Rosanna (Merkley) D.; prep. edn., Collegiate Inst., Kingston, Ont.; A.M., McGill U., 1889, M.D., 1893; m. Clara Cramer Strunk, Sept. 18, 1915; 1 dau., Kathleen Cramer. Came to U.S., 1914, naturalized citizen, 1924. Began practice at Montreal, Can., 1894; gen. mgr. med. dept., United Fruit Co., N.Y. City, editor of annual report of dept., 1915—. Fellow Am. Coll. Surgeons. Home: New York, N.Y. Died July 24, 1931.

DEEMER, Horace Emerson, judge; b. Bourbon, Ind., Sept. 24, 1858; s. John A. and Elizabeth (Erwin) D.; ed. State U. of Ia., 1873-75, LL.B., 1879; (LL.D., State U. of Ia., and Cornell Coll., 1904); m. Jeannette Gibson, July 12, 1882. In practice at Red Oak, 1879-86; judge 15th Jud. Dist., 1887-94; justice Supreme Ct. of Ia., 1894— (chief justice, 1898, 1904, 10, 15). Republican. Lecturer, 1895-1904, hon. prof. jurisprudence, 1904—, State U. of Ia. Pres. Art Inst. of Des Moines. Mem.

Com. on Uniform State Laws. Author: Grand Juries, Cyclopedia of Law and Procedure, 1906; Pleading and Practice of Iowa, 1915. Home: Red Oak, Ia. Died 1917.

DEEMS, Edward Mark, clergyman; b. Greensboro, N.C., Apr. 22, 1852; s. Charles Force (D.D., LL.D.) and Anna (Disosway) D.; A.B., Princeton, 1874, A.M., 1877; grad. Princeton Theol. Sem., 1877; Ph.D., New York U., 1893; D.D., Alfred U., 1904; m. Virginia Watkins Price, Apr. 17, 1884; children—Charles P., Elsie, Virginia, William H., Edward M., Robert D. (dec.). Licensed to preach by Presbytery of New York, 1877; ordained by Presbytery of Denver, Oct. 1877; pastor Central Ch., Longmont, Colo., 1877-79, Westminster Ch., New York, 1880-89, First Ch., Hornellsville, N.Y., 1890-1909; chaplain Am. Seamen's Friend Soc., New York, 1909-13, Sailors' Snug Harbor, New Brighton, N.Y., Nov. 15, 1913—. Moderator Presbytery of New York, 1885; commr. to Gen. Assembly from N.Y. Presbytery, 1887, from Steuben Presbytery, 1897; stated clerk and treas. Steuben Presbytery, 1898-1908. Home: New Brighton, N.Y. Died Aug. 7, 1929.

DEEMS, J(ames) Harry, musician; b. Baltimore, Feb. 4, 1848; s. Gen. James Monroe and Mary Isabelle (Flack) D.; ed. Baltimore City Coll., and St. Timothy's Hall, Md.; studied music under his father, also in Stuttgart, Wurttemberg; m. Mollie White, July 9, 1872; m. 2d, May Adams, Oct. 26, 1892. Organist First Bapt. Ch., Baltimore, 1861-74, and from 1902, Brown Memorial Presbyn. Ch., 1874-79, Franklin Sq. Bapt. Ch., 1879-95, Mt. Vernon M.E. Ch., 1895-1902. Prof. music, Baltimore City Coll., 1868-69, Western Female High Sch., 1868-78, Eastern Female High Sch., 1884-1901; supt. music, Baltimore pub. schs., 1868-1901. Active mem. Y.M.C.A. Author: New American Musical Reader, 1 and 2, 1892, No. 3, 1896; The Divinity of the Secular and The Secularity of the Divine. Home: Baltimore, Md. Died Apr. 24, 1931.

DEERE, Charles Henry, mfr.; b. in Vt., Mar. 28, 1837; s. John and Demaris (Lamb) D.; moved in infancy to Grand Detour, Ill., and 1847 to Moline, Ill.; m. Mary Little Dickinson, Sept. 26, 1862. He succeeded his father, John Deere, who established the plow works which are now incorporated as Deere & Co.; also pres. Deere & Mansur Co., mfrs. of cotton and corn planters, and pres. of other cos., outgrowth of these mfrs.; John Deere Plow Co., St. Louis, Dallas, New Orleans, Kansas City, Denver, Omaha, Portland and Indianapolis; Deere Implement Co., San Francisco, and Deere & Webber Co., Minneapolis. Home: Moline, Ill. Died 1907.

DEERING, Charles, mfr.; b. Paris, Maine, 1852; s. of William and Abby (Barbour) D.; grad. U.S. Naval Acad., 1873; m. Anna Case, 1875 (died 1876); m. 2d, Marion, daughter of Gen. William D. Whipple, U.S.A., 1883. Served as officer in the navy until 1881, when resigned and became sec. of the Deering Harvester Co., until that business was merged, with the other leading harvester interests, in the Internat. Harvester Co., of which was chmn. bd. many yrs. Home: Miami, Fla. Died Feb. 5, 1927.

DEERING, Frank Prentiss, lawyer; b. Jacksonville, Calif., June 10, 1855; s. James Henry and Mary Ann Reed (Brackett) D.; A.B., U. of Calif., 1875, LL.B. and A.M., 1881; m. Mabel Clare Craft, Nov. 22, 1902; 1 dau., Francesca. Admitted to Calif. bar, 1879, and began practice at San Francisco; mem. firm Myrick & Deering and Scott. Trustee Leland Stanford Jr. Univ., 1916—; trustee San Francisco Pub. Library, San Francisco Law Library (pres.), St. Luke's Hosp., Society for Prevention of Cruelty to Animals. Republican. Episcopalian. Annotated political, penal, civil and civil procedure codes of Calif. (the first work of the kind in U.S.). Home: San Francisco, Calif. Died May 18, 1939.

DEERING, James, mfr.; b. 1859; s. William and Clara (Hamilton) D.; ed. Northwestern U. and Mass. Inst. of Tech. (non-grad.). Officer of Deering Harvester Co., until 1902; v.p. Internat. Harvester Co., 1902, then dir.; was pres. Internat. Harvester Co. of N.J. Home: Miami, Fla. Died Sept. 21, 1925.

DEERING, William, mfr.; b. Paris, Me., Apr. 25, 1826; s. James and Eliza (Moore) D.; ed. in Readfield Sem.; m. Abby Barbour, Oct. 31, 1849; m. 2d, Clara Hamilton, Dec. 15, 1857. Engaged in a woolen mill, and later in the dry-goods business; became mem. of wholesale and commn. dry goods house of Deering, Milliken & Co., of Portland and New York; established in the harvester business at Plano, Ill., 1873; was pres. Deering Harvester Co., and William Deering & Co.; retired. Home: Evanston, Ill. Died Dec. 9, 1913.

DEETER, Paxson, lawyer; b. Reading, Pa., Dec. 23, 1880; s. Ammon S. and Lydia K. (Paxson) D.; B.S., U. of Pa., 1903, LL.B., 1906; m. Helen M. Bowen, 1911. Admitted to Pa. bar, 1906, and began practice at Phila.; lecturer in law, Wharton Sch. (U. of Pa.), 1906-11; dir. Atwater Kent Mfg. Co. Served as capt. Ordnance Dept., U.S.A., 1918-19. Sec. and trustee Atwater Kent Foundation, Inc. Republican. Presbyn. Home: Bryn Mawr, Pa. Died June 24, 1933.

DEFEBAUGH, James Elliott, editor; b. Williamsburg, Pa., Mar. 28, 1854; s. James Elliott and Elizabeth Ann (Kinney) D.; ed. pub. schs.; m. Annie E. Carhart, 1883. Learned printer's trade, and followed it until 1881; sec. Burlington (Ia.) Y.M.C.A., 1881-82; represented the Shoe and Leather Reporter of New York, and other eastern papers, at Chicago, 3 yrs.; acting sec. of the Lumberman's Exchange and Lumber Mfrs. Assn. of the Northwest, 1885, and was corr. of several eastern trade jours.; established The Timberman, 1886; assumed editorial and business management of The Young Men's Era, internat. official organ of the Y.M.C.A., 1893-96, in connection with his other interests; consolidated the Timberman and Northwestern Lumberman, Jan. 1, 1899, and became its editor and publisher. Presbyn. Home: Chicago, Ill. Died 1909.

DE FOE, Louis Vincent, dramatic critic; b. Adrian, Mich., July 18, 1869; s. James Vincent and Rebecca Phoebe (Young) D.; B.Litt., U. of Mich., 1891; m. Isabelle Ethellyn Brewer, Nov. 1, 1905. With Chicago Tribune as Sunday editor, New York corr., dramatic critic, etc., 1891-99; dramatic critic New York World, 1899—, taking frequent trips to Europe to observe foreign stage; contbr. monthly critical article to Red Book Magazine, Chicago, 1905-13. Republican. Home: New York, N.Y. Died Mar. 13, 1922.

DE FOREST, Henry S., congressman; b. Schenectady, N.Y., Feb. 16, 1847; s. Obadiah L. and Sarah (Vedder) D.; ed. Union Classical Inst., Poughkeepsie, N.Y.; m. Lucie E. Van Epps, Sept. 6, 1876. Engaged in real estate and banking at Schenectady, 1883—. City recorder, 1881-85; mayor, 1885-87, 1889-91; mem. 62d Congress (1911-13), 23d N.Y. Dist. Republican. Died Feb. 13, 1917.

DE FOREST, Henry Wheeler, lawyer, capitalist; b. New York, Oct. 29, 1855; s. of Henry Grant and Julia Brasher (Weeks) D.; A.B., Yale, 1876; LL.B., Columbia, 1878; m. Julia Gilman Noyes, Aug. 15, 1898; children—Julia Mary, Alice Delano. In law practice at New York, 1878—; dir. and mem. exec. com. S.P. Co.; dir. and mem. exec. com. Tex. & New Orleans R.R. Co., Western Union Telegraph Co., Guaranty Trust Co., Hudson Trust Co. of N.J., etc.; trustee The Bank for Savings. Member bd. mgrs. N.Y. Bot. Garden; gov. New York Hosp.; trustee Presbyn. Hosp. Homes: N.Y. City, and Cold Spring Harbor, L.I. Died May 28, 1938.

DE FOREST, Lockwood, artist; b. New York, June 23, 1850; s. Henry G. and Julia Mary (Weeks) D.; ed. New York and abroad; studied art with Herman Corrode, Rome, 1869, Frederic E. Church and James M. Hart, 1870; in Egypt, Syria and Greece, 1875-76, Greece and Egypt, 1877-78, India, 1881-82; m. Meta Kemble, Nov. 11, 1880. Founded workshops at Ahemedabad, India, for the revival of wood carving, 1881; exhibited by spl. request at the 1st Indian Exhbn., Lahore, 1882, the prin. things being purchased for the India Mus. at S. Kensington, London. Medals for best carving, Colonial Exhbn., London, 1886, Chicago, 1893, A.N.A., 1891, N.A., 1898. Home: Santa Barbara, Calif. Died Apr. 3, 1932.

de FOREST, Marian, writer; b. Buffalo, N.Y.; d. Cyrus H. and Sarah Germain (Sutherland) D.; grad. Buffalo Sem. Mgr. Buffalo Musical Foundation, Inc. Episcopalian. Author: (play) Erstwhile Susan, prod. New York, 1915; (with Jessie Bonstelle) Little Women Letters from the House of Alcott, 1914. Dramatized Louisa M. Alcott's Little Women (prod. New York, 1912, London, 1919). Collaborated with Zona Gale in series of radio dramalogues, "Neighbors" for Nat. Broadcasting Co., 1933. Home: Buffalo, N.Y. Died Feb. 17, 1935.

DE FOREST, Robert Weeks, lawyer; b. New York, Apr. 25, 1848; s. Henry G. and Julia Brasher (Weeks) D.; A.B., Yale, 1870, A.M., 1873, LL.D., 1904; LL.B., Columbia, 1872; LL.D., Hamilton Coll., 1919, New York U., 1923; also studied at U. of Bonn; m. Emily Johnston, Nov. 12, 1872. Admitted to bar, 1871; joined father's and uncle's law firm, Weeks, Forster & De Forest; then with brother, Henry W., and sons, Johnston and Henry L., in firm of De Forest Bros. Gen. counsel Central R.R. of N.J., 1874-1924; pres. Hackensack (N.J.) Water Co., 1885-1926, chmn. bd., 1926—; pres. Dolphin Jute Mills, Seawaren Improvement Co.; vice-pres. N.Y. & Long Branch R.R. Co. Chmn. N.Y. State Tenement House Commn., 1900; pres. Nat. Conf. Charities and Correction, Atlanta, 1903; pres. Municipal Art Commn., New York, 1905-29; v.p. Am. Red Cross; pres. Russell Sage Foundation; pres. Nat. Housing Assn. Home: New York, N.Y. Died May 6, 1931.

DEFREES, Joseph Holton, lawyer; b. Goshen, Ind., Apr. 10, 1858; s. James McKinney and Victoria (Holton) D.; ed. Earlham Coll., Richmond, Ind., and Northwestern U., Ill.; m. Harriet McNaughton, Oct. 4, 1882. Admitted to Ind. bar, 1880; moved to Chicago 1888; mem. Defrees, Brace & Ritter, later Defrees, Buckingham & Eaton; dir. pres. Windermere Co. V.p. Civic Federation, 1912-14; dir. Chicago Legal Aid Soc., 1912-13; pres. Chicago Assn. Commerce, 1914; v.p. Chamber Commerce U.S.A., 1915-19 (chmn. exec. com., 1916-19; pres., 1920-21); mem. Ill. Chamber Commerce. Mem. President's Conf. on Unemployment, Washington, D.C., 1921; mem. U.S. Sect. Inter-Am. High Commn., 1st Pan Am. Financial Congress, 1921-22; Chevalier Legion of Honor (France). Home: Chicago, Ill. Died Feb. 5, 1929.

DE GRAFF, Lawrence, judge; b. Apple River, Ill., June 24, 1871; s. Hiram and Sarah (Eplett) D., A.B., Dixon (Ill.) Coll., 1892; LL.B. and LL.M., Ill. Coll. of Law, 1896; Ph.B., U. of Chicago, 1898; m. Grace L. Clark, Aug. 14, 1901; children—Lawrence, Barbara Grace. Began practice at Chicago, Ill., 1896; moved to Des Moines, 1898; 1st asst. atty. gen. of Ia., 1904-07; pros. atty. Polk Co., Ia., 1907-10; judge Dist. Court, 9th Jud. Dist. of Ia., 1910-21; justice Supreme Court of Iowa, 1921-33. Professor of law at Drake Law Sch., 1918-23; lecturer on real property, Northwestern U. Sch. of Law, summer, 1923. Republican. Methodist. Mason. Author: Outlines in American Government, 1898; Outlines in Economics, 1900; Pharmacy Law, 1918. Home: Des Moines, Ia. Died July 7, 1934.

de GRAFFENRIED, Edward, lawyer; b. Sawyerville, Ala., Jan. 31, 1861; s. Emanuel T. and Sue Howard (Seay) deG.; M.A., Southern U., Greensboro, Ala., 1880; m. Mary Meriwether, June 2, 1886. Began practice with uncle, Gov. Thomas Seay, at Eutaw, 1882; mem. Ala. Constl. Conv., 1901; confidential legal adviser to gov. of Ala., 1910; asso. judge Court of Appeals of Ala., 1910, 11; asso. justice Supreme Court of Ala., 1912-15; resigned and resumed practice at Tuscaloosa, Ala. Democrat. Mem. M.E. Ch. S. Home: Tuscaloosa, Ala. Died Apr. 5, 1922.

DE GRAFFENRIED, Reese Calhoun, congressman, lawyer; b. Franklin, Tenn., 1859; grad. Univ. of Tenn., 1878; Lebanon, Tenn., Law School, 1879; practiced in Tenn. 1 yr.; went to Texas; connected with construction Texas & Pacific R.R. until 1883, then in law practice at Longview, Tex.; elected co. atty., but resigned 2 months later; presidential elector, 1888; defeated for Congress, 1890; mem. Congress, 3d Texas dist., 1897-1903; m. Annie Elizabeth Berry. Democrat. Home: Longview, Tex. Died 1902.

DE GRAW, Peter Voorhees, 4th asst. postmaster gen.; b. Princeton, N.J., Feb. 1, 1853; s. Abraham Paul and Susan Norris (Lowrey) D.; ed. pub. schs.; m. Emma Louisa Doerr, Oct. 16, 1876. Began as ry. telegrapher at S. Amboy, N.J.; one of the "Big 8" to man for N.Y. Associated Press first leased wire for handling press matter exclusively, 1874; mem. Associated Press staff at Washington, 1875-82; with Western Asso. Press, 1882-83; Washington mgr. of same, 1884-85, of United Press, 1885-86; Southern mgr. United Press and asst. gen. mgr. Southern Associated Press, 1886-97; in commercial business, Phila., 1897-1901. Fourth asst. postmaster gen., Mar. 17, 1905-13; v.p. Postal Life Ins. Co. of New York, 1913—. Home: Washington, D.C. Died Aug. 22, 1914.

DE GROOT, William A., lawyer; b. Brooklyn, N.Y., Nov. 27, 1869; s. Alexander and Jane (McCullough) D.; prep. edn., Wesleyan Acad., Wilbraham, Mass.; A.B., Dickinson Coll. (Pierson prize for oratory); student N.Y. Univ. Law Sch.; m. Grace Lester Atkins, June 13, 1900; children—Alfred Hugo, Ethel Jane, Helen Marie, Lester Atkins. Admitted to N.Y. bar, and began practice in Brooklyn; mem. N.Y. Assembly 5 terms until 1909; asst. U.S. atty. Eastern Dist. of N.Y., 1923-25, U.S. atty., Nov. 13, 1925—. Founder Richmond Hill Record; supt. S.S. 10 yrs.; organizer Temple Forum (for young men). Republican. Methodist. Mason. Home: Richmond Hill, N.Y. Died Mar. 1, 1932.

DE HART, William Henry, clergyman; b. New Brunswick, N.J., Mar. 21, 1837; s. Nicholas B. and Abigail (Voorhees) D.; A.B., Rutgers, 1865, A.M., 1868; grad. New Brunswick Theol. Sem., 1868 (D.D., Rutgers, 1900); m. Janette, d. James S. Rich, M.D., of Bucks Co., Pa., May 12, 1870. Ordained Reformed Ch. in America ministry, 1868; pastor, Churchville, Bucks Co., Pa., 1868-71, New York, 1871-77, Jamaica, L.I., N.Y., 1877-87, Bethlehem, N.Y., 1887-88, Third Ch., Raritan, N.J., 1888-1911; retired. Stated clerk, Gen. Synod, 1894—. Home: Plainfield, N.J. Died Feb. 14, 1916.

DE HASS, Wills, physician, anthropologist; b. Washington Co., Pa., July 4, 1817; s. Gen. Charles (desc. Gen. John Philip De Hass of the Revolution) and Myra (Fields) D.; ed. Western Univ. and Washington and Jefferson Coll., Pa.; studied medicine with Dr. Joseph P. Gazzam, Pittsburgh, and attended lectures at Jefferson Coll., Phila.; m. Amanda M. Hoblitzell, May 4, 1837. Practiced medicine in Va., Louisville and Washington; early turned attention to hist. and scientific studies; extensively investigated Am. pre-historic archeology; asso. Bur. of Ethnology, Smithsonian Instn.; consul to Yucatan. Recruited 77th Ohio regt. from border cos. of Va. and Ohio and comd. advance in Sherman's div. at Shiloh; was active in Va. supporting the Union, the restoration of the state govt., and final separation to form the new commonwealth of W.Va. Home: Philadelphia. Died 1910.

DE HAVEN, Franklin, painter; b. Bluffton, Ind., Dec. 26, 1856; s. Nathaniel and Fannie D.; pupil of George H. Smilie; m. Elizabeth Woodcock, Dec. 17, 1902. Splty. landscapes; Inness prize, Salmagundi Club, 1900, Shaw prize, same, 1901; hon. mention, Buffalo Expn., 1901; silver medal, Charleston Expn., 1903, St. Louis Expn., 1904, Nat. Arts Club, 1921; Vezin prize, 1916, Plimpton prize, 1925, Salmagundi Club; oil painting prize, National Arts Club, 1931. Represented in Evans' Collection, Nat. Gallery, Washington; Brooklyn Mus. of Arts and Sciences; Salmagundi Club; Nat. Arts Club; Butler Art Mus., Youngstown, Ohio. N.A., 1920. Home: New York, N.Y. Died Jan. 10, 1934.

DE HAVEN, John Jefferson, judge; b. St. Joseph, Mo., Mar. 12, 1845; s. Jacob D.; went to Calif., 1849; pub. sch. edn.; m. Zernah Jane Ball, June 24, 1872. Admitted to bar, 1866; dist. atty., Humboldt Co., 1867-69; mem. Ho. of Rep., 1869, Senate, 1871-74; city atty., Eureka, Calif., 1878-80; Rep. candidate for Congress, 1882; judge Superior Ct., 1884-89; mem. 51st Congress (1889-91), resigned Oct. 1, 1890; asso. justice Supreme Ct. of Calif., 1891-95; U.S. dist. judge, Northern Dist. of Calif., June 8, 1897—. Died Jan. 26, 1913.

DEILER, John Hanno, prof. German, Univ. of La., and Tulane Univ., 1879—; b. Altoetting, Upper Bavaria, Germany, Aug. 8, 1849; s. Konrad and Magd. (Ebenbeck) D.; grad. Royal Normal Coll., Freising; studied at Royal Polytechnic Inst., Munich; m. Wilhelmina Saganowski, Dec. 9, 1872. Knight of the Order of the Prussian Crown, Dec. 15, 1898; teacher public schools, Munich, until 1871; prin. German school, New Orleans, 1872-79; founder of German Archives and of German singing socs. in New Orleans, La.; pres., 1896—, Nat. Union "North-american Sængerbund;" reëlected, 1903-07; pres. German Soc. for Protection of German Immigrants; pres. New Orleans Quartette Club and pres. New Orleans German Gazette Publishing Co., Ltd. Author: Geschichte der Deutschen Presse in New Orleans, 1900; Deutschen am unteren Mississippi und die Creolen Eine vergessene deutsche Colonie, 1902; Die ersten deutscher Abstammung, 1904. Contributor to the New Orleans German Gazette and Am. mem. Redaktions-Ausschuss "Deutsche Erde," and other papers of Germany and U.S. Home: New Orleans, La. Died 1909.

DEININGER, William; chmn. bd. General Baking Co., New York, N.Y. Died Sept. 7, 1941.

DEITRICH, Theodore C., newspaperman, motion pictures; b. New Brighton, Pa., Feb. 8, 1876; s. Jacques and Anna Barbara (Burri) D.; ed. pub. schs.; m. Helen Fallon, Nov. 23, 1900. Reporter Pittsburgh Times, 1896, later becoming mng. editor Pittsburgh Dispatch and Gazette-Times; spl. writer of the Chicago Chronicle, 1902-05; entered W. R. Hearst organization, 1905; editorial staff New York American, Chicago Examiner, San Francisco Examiner, then New York American, 1911-15; dir. publicity and advertising Hearst Metrotone News and Cosmopolitan Productions. Author: The Panama Canal, 1912; India, 1913. Home: New York, N.Y. Died Jan. 6, 1935.

DE KALB, Courtenay, mining engr.; b. Loudoun Co., Va., Sept. 18, 1861; s. E. E. and Emma A. De K.; acad. education; m. Frances Douglas. Practiced as mining engr. in Western and Southern states; went on expdns. through Brazil up the Amazon River and through Peru, Ecuador, Central America and Mexico; prof. mining and metallurgy, U. of Mo., 1895-98, Queen's U., Can., 1898-1901; mgr. San Fernando mine, Durango, Mex., 1901-02, Exposed Treasure mine, Calif., 1902-05; asso. editor Mining and Scientific Press, San Francisco, 1908-10; pres. and gen. mgr. Pacific Smelting & Mining Co., Guaymas, Mexico, 1910-12; asso. editor Mining and Scientific Press, 1917-19; trade commr. U.S. Dept. of Commerce, for investigation of mineral resources of Spain, Portugal and Morocco, 1919-20; cons. engr., New Orleans; and Roadside Mine, Ariz., 1921-25; prof. mining engring., U. of Ala., 1925-26; investigations in Spain and other countries for St. Joseph Lead Company, 1926-27. Lectured De Pauw Univ., 1925. Author: Handbook of Explosives; Nicaragua Canal—Ours or England's; A Visit to King Solomon's Mines; Fixed Nitrogen for National Defense. Home: New York, N.Y. Died Sept. 2, 1931.

DE KAY, Charles, author, critic; b. Washington, July 25, 1848; s. Commodore George C. and Janet (Drake) D.; A.B., Yale, 1868; m. Edwalyn, d. Edward Lees Coffey of Dublin, Ireland, maj. British forces in India, June 4, 1888; children—Phyllis Dunboyne (Mrs. Edward Basil Bury), Helena van Brugh, Katharine Finola (Mrs. Robert Woodhouse Barbour), Adrian Barton Drake, Rodman Drake, Marion Eckford (Mrs. Peyton Rous), Charles Ormonde, Sylvia Octavia. Lit. and art editor New York Times, 1876-94; art editor New York Evening Post, 1907. Am. consul gen. at Berlin, 1894-97. Asso. editor Art World, New York, 1915-17. Mem. Nat. Inst. Arts and Letters. Author: The Bohemian, 1878; Hesperus and Other Poems, 1880; Vision of Nimrod, 1881; Vision of Esther (dramatic poems), 1882; Love Poems of Louis Barnaval, 1883; Life and Works of Barye, Sculptor, 1889; Bird Gods (study of myths and religions in Ancient Europe), 1898; Life and Works of Louis C. Tiffany. Home: East Hampton, L.I., N.Y. Died May 23, 1935.

DE KNIGHT, Clarence Woods, lawyer; b. Rocky Mount, Va., Sept. 23, 1867; s. William Francis and Roselia (Pettibone) D.; ed. Columbian Prep. Sch., and Coll. (now George Washington) U., LL.B., 1891, LL.M., 1892, Master of Patent Law, 1896; admitted to bar, 1892; unmarried. Was pvt. sec. to late Senator Arthur Pue Gorman and others; sec. com. on naval affairs, U.S. Senate, U.S. Armor Factory Bd., P. R. Evacuation Com.; an asst. sec. Nat. Rep. Conv., 1900; counsel for Queen Liliuokalani of H.I.; counsel for contractors, ry., shipping and other corps., before Congress and exec. depts. Ct. of Claims, and Supreme Ct. of U.S., Washington; dir. and counsel Samana Bay Co. of Santo Domingo. Del. to 3d Congress of Internat. Chamber of Commerce, Brussels, 1925, 4th Congress, Stockholm, 1927, 5th Congress, Amsterdam, 1929, 6th Congress, Washington, 1931; mem. Nat. Council of Nat. Economic League to represent D.C.; mem. nat. advisory council of Am. Peace Soc. Mason. Home: Washington, D.C. Died Nov. 22, 1936.

DE KOVEN, (Henry Louis) Reginald, composer; b. Middletown, Conn., April 3, 1861; s. Rev. Henry and Charlotte (Le Roy) D.; grad. Oxford, 1880; (Mus. Doc., Racine Coll.); studied music, Stuttgart, Florence, Paris and Vienna; m. Anna Farwell, May 1, 1884. Has served as musical critic on various New York publs., Harper's Weekly, New York World, etc. Founder and conductor The Washington Symphony Orchestra. Pres. Manuscript Soc., 1897-98; mem. Nat. Inst. of Arts and Letters. Composer (operas): The Begum; Don Quixote; Robin Hood; The Fencing Master; The Algerian; Rob Roy; The Knickerbockers; The Tzigane; The Mandarin; The Highwayman; The Three Dragoons; Papa's Wife; Foxey Quiller; Little Duchess; Maid Marian; Red Feather; Happyland; Student King; The Snowman; The Golden Butterfly; The Beauty Spot; The Wedding Trip; Her Little Highness; grand opera, The Canterbury Pilgrims, prod. Met. Opera House, N.Y., Mar. 1917; A Masque of American Drama. Also over 300 songs, including "Oh, Promise Me," and "A Recessional." Died Jan. 16, 1920.

DE KROYFT, S(usan) Helen A(ldrich), author; b. Rochester, N.Y., Oct. 29, 1818; d. Obed and Melintha (Potter) Aldrich; grad. Lima Coll., N.Y., 1843; m. Dr. William De Kroyft, of Rochester, who died on the wedding day from injuries received in falling from a carriage; a month later she lost her sight. Author: A Place in Thy Memory, 1849, revised edit., 1905; The Story of Little Jakey, 1871; Darwin and Moses, 1875; Mortara, 1888; The Foreshadowed Way, 1901; The Soul of Eve, 1904. Home: Dansville, N.Y. Died Oct. 25, 1915.

DELABARRE, Frank Alexander, orthodontist; b. Conway, Mass., Apr. 8, 1868; s. Edward and Maria L. (Hassell) D.; A.B., Amherst, 1890, fellow, 1890-91; Boston Dental Coll., 1891-92; D.D.S., U. of Pa., Dental Dept., 1894; M.D., U. of Pa. Med. Dept., 1895; m. Anna E. Sweeney, 1893; children—Lawrence, Katharine, Dorothy. In practice in Boston, 1895—; asst. prof. orthodontia, 1907-10, prof., 1910-18, Tufts Coll. Dental Sch.; chief of staff orthodontia department and dean Postgrad. Sch. of Orthodontia. Forsyth Dental Infirmary for Children, 1914-19; consultant Mass. Dept. of Health; lecturer, Tufts Coll. Dental Sch., Harvard Univ. Dental Sch. Member dental advisory com., Mass. Dept. Pub. Health. Fellow Am. Coll. Dentists. Home: Greenbush, Mass. Died Apr. 15, 1938.

DELAFIELD, Francis, physician; b. New York, Aug. 3, 1841; s. Dr. Edward and Julia (Floyd) D.; A.B., Yale, 1860; M.D., Coll. Phys. and Surg. (Columbia), 1863; studied London, Berlin and Paris; (LL.D., Yale, 1890, Columbia, 1904); m. Katherine Van Rennsselaer, Jan. 17, 1870. Surgeon New York Eye and Ear Infirmary, 1871; pathologist, Roosevelt Hosp., 1871; physician Bellevue Hosp., 1874, consulting phys., 1885—; adj. prof., 1875-82, prof. pathology and practice of medicine, prof. emeritus, 1901—, Coll. Phys. and Surg. Author: Studies in Pathological Anatomy (2 vols.), 1882; Hand Book of Pathological Anatomy and Histology (with Dr. T. Mitchell Prudden, 1885, 5th edit., 1897. Home: New York, N.Y. Died July 17, 1915.

DELAFIELD, Richard, banker; b. New Brighton, S.I., N.Y., Sept. 6, 1853; s. Rufus King and Eliza (Bard) D.; ed. Anthon Grammar Sch.; m. Clara Foster Carey (died 1909); m. 2d, Edith P. Fesser (died 1925). At early age engaged in mercantile pursuits; sr. partner Delafield & Co. of New York, Chicago and San Francisco, which house he founded; pres. Nat. Park Bank of New York for 22 yrs., chmn. bd. 7 yrs.; trustee, Trinity Church Corp., Am. Surety Co., etc. Vestryman and sr. warden Trinity Ch. Died Aug. 3, 1930.

DE LAMAR, Joseph Raphael, capitalist; b. Amsterdam, Holland, Sept. 2, 1843; s. Maximilian and Johanna (Teune) D.; early life spent on shipboard; pvt. edn.; unmarried. Identified with various financial interests and mine owner and operator; dir. Am. Bank Note Co., Coronet Phosphate Co., Canadian Mining & Exploration Co., Dome Mines Co., Manati Sugar Co.; v.p. Internat. Nickel Co. Home: New York, N.Y. Died Dec. 1, 1918.

DELAMATER, Nicholas B., physician; b. Albany, Co., N.Y., Feb. 21, 1847; s. Ira M. and Elizabeth (Beebe) D.; A.B., Harvard, 1868; studied law 1 yr.; M.D., Chicago Homœ. Medical Coll., 1873; m. Ella J. Link, Nov. 3, 1870. Specialist in mental and nervous diseases; professor mental and nervous diseases, Hahnemann Med. Coll., Chicago. Home: Chicago, Ill. Died Mar. 11, 1915.

DELANCEY, Darragh, sculptor; b. East Orange, N.J., July 31, 1870; s. James and Anna (Spencer) D.; B.S., Mass. Inst. Tech., 1890; B.F.A., Yale Sch. of Fine Arts, 1925; m. Harriet Tooker Gallup, Oct. 30, 1897; children—Harriet Anna (dec.), Anna Halsted, Darragh, Margaret Spencer. With Eastman Kodak Co., Rochester, N.Y., 1890-1900 (built original plant and operated it 9 yrs.); in charge of mfg., Library Bur., Boston, 1900-02; with Stanley Instrument Co., Gt. Barrington, Mass., and Waterbury Buckle Co. until 1914. Chmn. 2d Dist. Bd., Conn., World War; also chief of industrial furlough sect., Adj. Gen.'s Office, Washington, D.C., dir. industrial relations, U.S. Shipping Bd., and expert, Central Bur. of Planning and Statistics; then devoting attention to sculpture. Trustee Dime Savings Bank, Waterbury, Conn. Republican. Conglist. Wrote: Manual of Selective Service and Industrial Furlough (pub. U.S. Govt.), 1918. Awarded 2d mention, sculpture, Beaux Arts Inst. Design, New York, 1923, 1st mention, 1924. Exhibitor Nat. Acad., Archtl. League New York. Prin. works: Exedra, Great Barrington, Mass.; war memorial, Newton, Conn. Home: Waterbury, Conn. Died Nov. 15, 1937.

DE LANCEY, Edward Floyd, lawyer; b. Mamaroneck, N.Y., Oct. 23, 1821; eldest son of the late Rt. Rev. W. H. De Lancey; grad. Hobart, 1843; attended Harvard Law School, 1844-45; admitted to bar, 1846; m. Josephine M. De Zeng, 1848. Practiced in New York; prominent in hist. organizations; corr. sec. N.Y. Hist. Soc. Author: History of Mamaroneck; Origin and History of Manors in the Province of New York; The Capture of Ft. Washington the Result of Treason. Home: Ossining, N.Y. Died 1905.

DE LAND, Charles Victor, journalist; b. N. Brookfield, Mass., July 25, 1828; removed with family to Mich., 1830; learned printing trade; founded, 1849, editor and propr., 1849-61, Jackson Citizen; sec. of the provisional com. of 16 to organize an anti-Nebraska party, and as such drafted, printed and circulated the call for the 1st Rep. State Conv. in the U.S., held at Jackson, Mich., July 6, 1854; m. Mary Elizabeth Perry, 1859. Clerk Ho. Reps., 1857-59; mem. State senate, 1861-62; served, private to bvt. brig. gen. in Civil War; 3 times severely wounded, twice prisoner of war; consul to Cadiz, Spain, 1865; established Saginaw Daily Enterprise, 1866; collector internal revenue, 1874-80; state senator, 1873-74; established Saginaw Daily Herald, 1876; retired to farm, 1883. Rep. presdl. elector, 1892; apptd. to revise and compile tax laws of Mich., 1893; apptd. State tax statistician, 1895. Author: History of Jackson County, 1830-1900. Home: Summit, Mich. Died 1903.

DELAND, Ellen Douglas, author; b. Lake Mahopac, N.Y., Sept. 3, 1860; d. Thorndike and Elizabeth (Rawle) Deland; grad. pvt. sch., New York, 1878; unmarried. Author: Oakleigh; Katrina; A Successful Venture; Malvern; Alan Ransford; Three Girls of Hazelmere; Josephine; A Little Son of Sunshine, 1906; The Friendship of Anne; Miss Betty of New York, 1908; The Girls of Dudley School, 1911; The Fortunes of Phoebe, 1912; Country Cousins, 1913; Cyntra, 1915; The Waring Girls, 1917; Clyde Corners, 1918; The Secret Stairs, 1921. Home: Dedham, Mass. Died Feb. 22, 1923.

DeLANEY, Matthew A., medical officer U.S. Army; b. Waymart, Pa., Mar. 6, 1874; s. Sylvester and Elizabeth (Burns) DeL.; grad. Pa. Normal Inst., 1896; M.D., U. of Pa., 1898; grad. Army Med. Sch., Washington, 1902; studied U. of Vienna, 1913-14; C.P.H., Harvard U. Sch. of Health, 1928; hon. D.Sc. from Dickinson College, 1935; m. Elizabeth Voltz, Apr. 17, 1918. With Med. Dept., U.S.A., Feb. 6, 1901—; promoted through grades to brig. gen., Jan. 1, 1932. Served in Philippine Insurrection; White House physician under President Taft, 1909-13; served in Mexican border trouble, 1916; went to France in command Pa. Base Hosp. No. 10, May 1917; liaison officer Brit. War Office, London, comdg. all Am. med. officers with Brit. Army, 1918; exec. officer Surgeon General's Office, 1919-21; surgeon Field Arty. Sch., Ft. Sill, Okla., 1924, Camp Devens, Mass., 1927-28; med. adviser in pub. health and sanitation to Gov. Gens. Henry L. Stimson and Dwight Davis, of Philippines, 1928-31; corps area surgeon Fifth Corps Area, 1931;

asst. surgeon gen., 1931-36; comdt. Med. Field Service Sch., Carlisle, Pa., 1933-36, retired. Fellow Am. Coll. of Surgeons, Am. Pub. Health Assn., Am. Coll. Physicians, A.M.A. Awarded D.S.M. (U.S.); Order St. Michael and St. George (British); mentioned in dispatches for "gallantry in the field" by Field Marshal Sir Douglas Haig; member Order of St. Lazare of Jerusalem. Died Nov. 1, 1936.

DELANEY, Peter A., lawyer; b. Albany, N.Y., Dec. 20, 1864; s. Peter H. and Eliza S. (Finn) D.; grad. Albany High Sch., 1884; LL.B., Cornell Law Sch., 1889; m. Mary C. O'Brien, Sept. 21, 1893. Admitted to N.Y. bar, 1889; asst. dist. atty., Albany, N.Y., 1899-1902; mem. Rosendale, Hessberg, Delaney & Haines. Democrat. Catholic. Home: Albany, N.Y. Died Feb. 21, 1914.

DELANO, Eugene, banker; A.B., Williams Coll., Mass., 1866, later A.M. Mem. Brown Brothers & Co., bankers, N.Y. City; trustee Seamen's Bank for Savings, N.Y. Life Ins. Co. Trustee Williams Coll., 1900—. Home: New York, N.Y. Died Apr. 2, 1920.

DELANO, Francis Henry, rear adm.; b. Mt. Carmel, O., Apr. 14, 1848; s. Henry Franklin and Maria (Carter) D.; apptd. from Mass., and grad. U.S. Naval Acad., 1867; m. Evelina Frances Paine, Jan. 29, 1874. Ensign, Dec. 1868; promoted through grades to capt., Oct. 1903; rear adm., June 29, 1905, and retired at own request. Served on Susquehanna, Contoocook and Yantic, N. Atlantic Fleet, 1867-69; Mohican, Pacific Fleet, and Ashuelot, Asiatic Fleet, 1870-73; Portsmouth, Pacific Fleet, 1874-75; on various stas. and duties to 1896; flagship Olympia, Asiatic Fleet and Minneapolis, N. Atlantic Fleet, and comd. Fish Hawk, N. Atlantic Fleet,1896-98; ordnance officer navy yard, Boston, 1898-99; comdg. training ships Alliance and Topeka, and Marietta, N. Atlantic Fleet, 1899-1902; capt. of yard, navy yard, League Island, Pa., Mar.-Dec., 1902; ordnance officer navy yard, Portsmouth, 1902-03; Naval War Coll. and comdg. Dixie, Jan.-Nov., 1903; assigned to court martial duty and served as comdg. officer of receiving ship Lancaster, 1903-05. Died Jan. 31, 1929.

DELANY, John Bernard, R.C. bishop; b. Lowell, Mass., Aug. 9, 1864; s. Thomas and Catherine (Fox) D.; ed. Lowell (Mass.) pub. schs. and Boston Coll., grad. 1887; entered theol. sem. of St. Sulpice, Paris, France, 1887, and ordained priest at Paris, 1891, by Cardinal Richard (D.D.). After serving as asst. priest 7 yrs. was named chancellor of diocese and sec. to bishop of Manchester; founded the Guidon Mag. and was its editor 5 yrs.; elected 2d bishop of Manchester, N.H., on death of Bishop Bradley. Consecrated Sept. 8, 1904. Died 1906.

DELANY, John Joseph, judge; b. 1861; A.B., St. Francis Xavier Coll., 1885 (LL.D.); LL.B., Columbia, 1888. Associated in most of the important municipal litigation in New York, 1890—; corporation counsel of City of New York, 1904-06; justice Supreme Ct. of N.Y., term 1910-24. Democrat. Died July 14, 1915.

DELANY, Patrick Bernard, electrician; b. Kings Co., Ireland, Jan. 28, 1845; s. James and Margaret D.; ed. pvt. and parochial schs., Ireland and U.S.; m. Annie M. Ovenshine, Mar. 31, 1869. Learned telegraphy in Hartford, Conn., worked at same, office boy to supt. of lines; expert operator, newspaper corr., editor and writer. Inventor 150 patents, covering anti-induction cables, synchronous multiplex telegraphy. Awarded gold medal and diploma Internat. Inventions Exhibition, London, 1885; automatic systems for ocean cables; rapid machine telegraphy for land lines; vox Humana talking machines; etc. Claims to have perfected system of automatic telegraphy, transmitting and plainly recording 3,000 words per minute over single wire; also patented method for locating submerged metallic bodies. Awarded Elliott Cresson gold medal twice, and John Scott legacy medal, Franklin Inst.; gold medal, Buffalo Expn., 1901, St. Louis Expn., 1904. Home: South Orange, N.J. Died Oct. 19, 1924.

DELANY, Selden Peabody, clergyman; b. Fond du Lac, Wis., June 24, 1874; s. Edmund and Evelyn (Selden) D.; B.A., Harvard, 1896; Western Theol. Sem., Chicago, 1899; unmarried. Deacon and priest, P.E. Ch., 1899; Curate St. Paul's Cathedral, Fond du Lac, 1899, St. John's Ch., Roxbury, Boston, 1899-1900; vicar St. Stephen's, Menasha, Wis., 1900-02; rector Grace Ch., Appleton, Wis., 1902-07; dean All Saints' Cathedral, Milwaukee, 1907-15; associate rector Ch. of St. Mary the Virgin, New York, Nov. 1, 1915-29, rector, 1929-30; joined Catholic Ch., June 1930; ordained priest in Rome, 1934. Author: Difficulties of Faith, 1906; The Ideal of Christian Worship, 1909; The Value of Confession, 1913; The Religion of the Prayer Book, 1919; Christian Practice, 1920; The Parish Priest, 1926; Why Rome, 1930. Died July 5, 1935.

DE LARME, Alonzo Alvin, clergyman; b. Jefferson Co., Pa.; s. Francis and Clarissa (Smith) D.; grad. Classical and Scientic Inst., Mt. Pleasant, Pa., 1885; A.B., Ind. U., 1887, 1890; grad. Crozer Theol. Sem., 1890; D.D., Furman U., Greenville, S.C., 1910; m. Ethel Charlotte Kirkham, June 14, 1905. Ordained Bapt. ministry, 1890; pastor successively Hope Ch., New Haven, Conn., First Church, Norristown, Pa., First Ch., Paterson, N.J., First Ch., McKeesport, Pa., until 1916, First Ch., Omaha, Neb., 1916—; built $100,000 ch. at Paterson and $150,000 ch. at Omaha. Mem. bd. mgrs. Neb. Bapt. State Conv. Republican. Prohibitionist. Baptist. Knight of Malta. Author: History of the First Baptist Church of Morristown, Pa., 1897; History of the First Baptist Church of Paterson, N.J., 1905; History of the First Baptist Church of Omaha, Neb., 1925. Home: Omaha, Neb. Died Mar. 28, 1930.

DELATOUR, Henry Beeckman, surgeon; b. New York, N.Y., Mar. 27, 1866; s. Albert J. and Josephine (Labatut) D.; student Coll. City of New York; M.D., Coll. Phys. and Surg. (Columbia), 1887; m. Jeannie May Peck, Oct. 16, 1895. Asst. surgeon, 1888-96, surgeon, 1905-10, Methodist Hosp.; surgeon Norwegian Hosp., 1890—, St. John's Hosp., 1896—; surgeon Long Island Coll. Hosp., also clin. prof. surgery, 1896-1906; surgeon-in-chief Jewish Hosp., 1906-12; cons. surgeon Babylon, Jamaica, Huntington and Methodist hospital; chief ambulance service, N.Y. City, 1904-12. Fellow Am. Coll. Surgeons. Major Med. R.C. U.S.A., in charge of surg. service, Camp Upton, 1918. Republican. Episcopalian. Home: Brooklyn, N.Y., also Bay Port, L.I., N.Y. Died 1930.

DELAUP, Sidney Philip, surgeon; b. New Orleans, La., June 5, 1863; s. Alfred and Josephine (Gastinel) B.Sc., Tulane, 1883, M.D., 1890; m. Gabrielle Roux, Jan. 8, 1900. Practiced at New Orleans, 1890—; prof. genito-urinary and rectal surgery, New Orleans Polyclinic (Tulane U.), 19—. Pioneer and advocate of spinal analgesia in the U.S. Democrat. Catholic. Home: New Orleans, La. Died Oct. 29, 1923.

DE LEON, Daniel, editor; b. Curacao, an island off the coast of Venezuela, Dec. 14, 1852; A.M., and Ph.B., U. of Leyden; came to U.S. from Europe, 1872; LL.B., Columbia, 1878. Prize lecturer on Latin-American diplomacy, Columbia, 1886-91; joined Knights of Labor, 1888, and in 1895, as the result of a split, he led in forming the Socialist Trade and Labor Alliance, of which he was an officer until its merging into the Industrial Workers of the World, 1905; was active in the Nationalist movement; joined Socialist Labor party, Oct. 1890, becoming editor of its English organ; editor Weekly People, 1892—, Daily People, 1900—. Home: Pleasantville, N.Y. Died May 11, 1914.

DE LEON, Edwin Warren, insurance pres.; b. Charleston, S.C., Aug. 6, 1868; s. Harmon Hendricks and Caroline Agnes (Moïse) DeLeon; A.B., Randolph-Macon Coll., Va., 1886; LL.B., Columbia, 1889; m. Frances Moïse, Jan. 23, 1901. New York mgr. Travelers Ins. Co. (liability dept.), 1893-98; mgr. for N.Y., N.J. and Conn., of Md. Casualty Co., 1898-1903; v.p. and gen. mgr., 1903-09, pres., 1909-16, Casualty Co. of America; pres. E. W. DeLeon, Inc., 1916—. Author: Law of Liability, 1900; Manual of Liability Insurance, 1911. Home: New York, N.Y. Died 1918.

DE LEON, Thomas Cooper, author; b. Columbia, S.C., May 21, 1839; s. Dr. M. H. and R. L. DeL.; ed. schs. Washington, D.C., Rugby Acad., and Portland, Me., and Georgetown (D.C.) Coll.; auditor Topog. Engr. Bur., Washington, 1858-61; went South; in C.S.A., 1861-65; conducted Cosmopolite Mag., Baltimore, 1865-66; in New York newspaper and mag. work, 1866-67; mng. editor and later sole editor Mobile Register, 1868-76; owner and editor The Gossip and The Gulf Citizen, Mobile, 1873-96; mgr. Gossip Pub. Co., 1888-97; lessee Mobile Theatre, 1873-85. Managed Interstate Blue and Gray drill and encampment, 1885, Nat. Drill, Washington, 1887; organized (1873) Mobile Mardi Gras Carnival, and managed it 25 yrs.; invented and designed carnivals of Pensacola, 1874, 1875, Vicksburg, 1876, 1st Baltimore, "Oriole," 1881, Albany, N.Y., Bi-Centennial, 1886, and other celebrations. Totally blind from 1903; called "The Blind Laureate of the Lost Cause." Author: South Songs (edited), 1866; Out of the Sulphur (prize novel—Tales from Town Topics), 1895; Confederate Memories, 1899; History of Creole Carnivals, 1899; Tales from the Coves, 1903; The Passing of Arle Haine, 1905; Belles, Beaux and Brains of the 60's, 1907. Home: Mobile, Ala. Died Mar. 19, 1914.

DE LESTRY, Edmond Louis, editor; b. Lake Charles, La., Jan. 1, 1860; s. Charles F. and Marguerite (de la Mont) D.; prep. edn., Gymnasium, Frankfort, Germany; U. of Louvain, 1877-81, M.A.; m. Rosamond M. Hedlund, 1890; children—Marguerite N. (Mrs. E. C. Staples), Robert Fredrick. Newspaper writer, St. Louis, 1881; mem. editorial staff Helena Herald, 1882-89; with St. Paul Daily Globe, 1900-07; founded, 1897, and ed. Western Mag. (now Northwest Magazine); served as editor St. Paul Graphic, and as mng. dir. Midwest News Bur.; retired. Prominent in promotion of good roads movement; v.p. Associated Highways of Minn. Woodman, Elk. Episcopalian. Author: Leaves from a Note Book, 1897; Splinters, 1925. Asso. author: St. Paul and Ramsey County, Minnesota, in the World War, 1929. Home: St. Paul, Minn. Died Dec. 18, 1933.

de LIMA e SILVA, R., diplomat; b. Porto Alegre, Rio Grande do Sul, Brazil; s. Field Marshal de Lima e Silva; ed. Pedro II Coll., 7 yrs., S. Paulo Law Sch., 5 yrs.; m. Juliet de Covarrubias. Was sec. Legation or Embassy at Vienna, Buenos Aires, Washington, London, Brussels, Japan and Norway; minister of Brazil to Ecuador, Bolivia, Switzerland, Poland and Spain; A.E. and P. to Japan, Mexico, now to U.S. Decorated Grand Cross Order of Rising Sun (Japan); Polonia Restituta (Poland); Order of Isabella the Catholic (Spain). Died Aug. 2, 1935.

De LISSER, Horace, chmn. Ajax Rubber Co.; b. Jamaica, B.W.I., Sept. 18, 1866; s. Edmund and Hannah (Lopez) D.; ed. pub. schs., N.Y. City; m. Ione Magaard, Aug. 8, 1911. Organized Ajax Rubber Co., Inc., 1903, chmn. bd., 1910—; also chmn. Racine Rubber Co.; v.p. Earl Motors, Inc. V.p. Rubber Assn. of America, Broadway Assn. Trustee Met. Mus. Art. Republican. Christian Scientist. Mason. Home: Great Neck, L.I., and N.Y. City. Died June 27, 1923.

DELK, Edwin Heyl, clergyman; b. Norfolk, Va., Aug. 15, 1859; s. Edwin Holoman and Margaret (Esher) D.; desc. Roger Delk, of Va., 1647; M.A., Central High Sch., Phila., Pa., 1880; D.D., Luth. Theol. Sem., Gettysburg, Pa., 1901; m. Ella Buehler, 1884; m. 2d, Adeline Grim Miller, Jan. 19, 1905. Ordained Luth. ministry, 1882; pastor Schoharie, N.Y., 1882-85, Hagerstown, Md., 1885-1902, St. Matthew's Ch., Phila., 1902-29; lecturer on theology, Temple U. Pres. Phila. Federation of Chs., 1910-14; trustee Luth. Theol. Sem., Luth. Deaconess' Motherhouse. Republican. Author: Three Vital Problems, 1909; The Need of a Re-Statement of Theology, 1911; Life of Charles S. Albert, D.D., 1912. Home: Philadelphia, Pa. Died Feb. 8, 1940.

DELLENBAUGH, Frederick Samuel, artist, author; b. McConnelsville, O., Sept. 13, 1853; s. Samuel and Elizabeth (Smith) D.; ed. Buffalo, New York, Munich, Paris; pupil of Carolus Duran and Académie Julian; m. Harriet Rogers Otis, Oct. 29, 1885 (died 1930); 1 son, Frederick Samuel. Engaged in art and literary pursuits; librarian Am. Geog. Soc., 1909-11; artist and topographer with Maj. Powell's 2d expdn. down Colo. River, 1871-73; assisted in making first map of Grand Canyon region which he carried to Salt Lake City on horseback; with Harriman expdn. to Alaska and Siberia, 1899; voyages to Iceland, Spitsbergen, Norway, West Indies and S.A., 1906; several personal expdns. to the Southwest in early days. Author: The North Americans of Yesterday, 1900; The Romance of the Colorado River, 1903; Breaking the Wilderness, 1905; A Canyon Voyage (narrative of important U.S. expdn. to complete exploration of Green and Colo. rivers and adjacent territory, 1871-73, the 2d Powell expdn., and practically a supplement to Major Powell's report), 1908, 1926; Frémont and '49, 1913; Life of Gen. George A. Custer, 1916. Home: Cragsmoor, N.Y., and New York, N.Y. Died Jan. 30, 1935.

DELLENBAUGH, Harriet Rogers Otis, actress, dramatic reader; b. Brooklyn, N.Y.; d. William H. and Elizabeth (Allen) Otis; ed. pvt. schs.; m. Frederick Samuel Dellenbaugh, Oct. 29, 1885; 1 son, Frederick Samuel. Acted with Felix Morris, Annie Russell, James K. Hackett, William H. Crane, Frances Starr and for three seasons under Belasco. One of original co. of the "New Theatre," New York. Home: Cragsmoor, N.Y., and N.Y. City. Died Nov. 15, 1930.

DEL MAR, Alexander, mining engr., author; b. New York, N.Y., Aug. 9, 1836; attended Rev. Dr. Barry's Poly., Maurice's Mil. Acad., Madrid Sch. of Mines and New York U. Edited Daily American Times, 1854, Hunt's Merchants' Magazine, 1860, Social Science Review, 1864, Financial Chronicle, 1865; organized and dir. 1865-69, U.S. Bur. of Commerce, Navigation, Emigration and Statistics (now Dept. Commerce and Labor); U.S. del. Internat. Congress, Turin, Italy, 1866, The Hague, 1868, St. Petersburg, 1872; mining commr. to U.S. Monetary Commn., 1876. Pres. Latin-Am. Chamber of Commerce. Home: New York, N.Y. Died July 2, 1926.

DELMAS, Delphin Michael, lawyer; b. France, Apr. 14, 1844; s. Antoine and Coralie D.; removed to Calif. in boyhood; A.B., Santa Clara Coll., 1862, A.M., 1863, Ph.D., 1903; LL.B., Yale, 1865; m. Pauline Hoge, Apr. 7, 1869. Admitted to Calif. bar, 1866; practiced in San Jose, Calif., 1866-83, San Francisco from 1883; later at New York; now at Los Angeles; Dist. atty. Santa Clara Co., Calif., 1868; regent U. of Calif., 1885. Catholic. Democrat. Author: Speeches and Addresses, 1901. Home: Santa Monica, Calif. Died Aug. 1, 1928.

DE LONGPRÉ, Paul, painter; b. Lyons, France, Apr. 18, 1855; s. Victor and Theresia (Pinchaud) deL.; ed. pub. sch., Paris, till 12 yrs. old; m. Josephine Estievenard, Mar., 1874. Distinguished as painter of flowers; when 12 yrs. old began to paint flowers on fans in Paris; had first oil paintings accepted at Paris Salon, 1876; failure of large Paris bank ruined him, and in 1890 came to New York; made his first exhbn. of only flower paintings at Am. Art Galleries, 1896; annual exhbns. thereafter; moved to Los Angeles, 1899, and in 1901 built residence at Hollywood, Los Angeles Co., with 3 acres of flower gardens. Catholic. Republican. Home: Hollywood, Calif. Died 1911.

De MAR, John L., cartoonist; b. Phila., Pa., Sept. 22, 1865; s. John L. and Emily E. (German) D.; pub. sch. edn., Kan., self taught in drawing; m. Cloe B. McLane, 1893; m. 2d, Lucile M. Kemper, 1917; 1 son, William MacAdam. Engaged in art dept., 1892-1903, cartoonist, 1903—, Philadelphia Record. Home: Upper Darby, Pa. Died Sept. 5, 1926.

DEMAREST, Henry Samuel, mfr. mill supplies; b. Brooklyn, N.Y., Feb. 1, 1867; s. Albert Alonzo and Constance Marie (Eakin) D.; ed. high sch.; m. Ida Read, Mar. 20, 1890 (died 1926); children—Gladys Read (Mrs. Clifford A. Seymour), Donald DeGray; m. 2d, Frieda J. Nicholas, Mar. 26, 1931. Engaged in mfg. business in N.Y. City, 1900—; pres. and treas. Greene, Tweed & Co.; dir. Union Ferry Co., New York and Brooklyn. Decorated Order Polonia Restituta. Republican. Presbyn. Home: Hempstead, N.Y. Died July 11, 1937.

DEMAREST, William Thomas; b. N.Y. City, Aug. 17, 1866; s. Garret Brinckerhoff and Mary A. (De Freest) D.; ed. Coll. City of New York (nongrad.); LL.D., Central Coll., Pella, Ia., 1922; m. Florence M. Seavey, Jan. 30, 1906 (died 1919). Commercial employment, later syndicate newspaper work; sec. Bd. of Domestic Missions Ref. Ch. in America, 1909—. Mem. bd. mgrs. Theol. Sem., New Brunswick, N.J. Republican. Home: Mamaroneck, N.Y. Died Aug. 20, 1926.

DEMBITZ, Lewis Naphtali, lawyer; b. Zirke, Posen, Feb. 3, 1833; s. Siegmund Z. and Franciska (Wehle) D.; ed. at German gymnasia; grad. gymnasium at Glogan, 1848; studied law 6 months at U. of Prague, 1848-49; m. Minna Wehle, July 13, 1858. Admitted to bar, June 23, 1853. Republican, except from 1884 to 1894; mem. Rep. Nat. Conv., Chicago, 1860; asst. city atty., Louisville, 1884-88; in 1888 was main draftsman of first Australian ballot act passed (1888) in any one of the States. Author: Kentucky Jurisprudence, 1889. Home: Louisville, Ky. Died 1907.

DE MENIL, Alexander Nicolas, editor and author; b. St. Louis, Mar. 23, 1849; s. Dr. Nicholas N. and Emelie Sophie (Chouteau) D.; desc. from the founders of St. Louis; B.S., Acad. of the Christian Brothers, 1869, M.S., 1871, A.M., 1872; LL.B., Washington U., 1871; Ph.D., Central U., 1898; LL.D., Christian Brothers' Coll., 1904; m. 2d, Bessie Bacon, Jan. 9, 1886. Practiced law, 1871-82; editor The St. Louis Mag., 1883-90; editor and pub. The Hesperian, 1894—. Elected to House of Dels., 1877, City Council, 1879. Was mem. La. Purchase Centennial Com. of 200 and a dir. La. Purchase Expn. Co. Pres. Belgian Relief Fund for Mo.; Mo. exec. officer Commn. for Relief in Belgium; hon. pres. Société Française de St. Louis. Decorated: Legion of Honor (France); King Albert Medal (Belgium). Chmn. Selective Service bds., St. Louis; service vet. of U.S. Author: Literature of the Louisiana Territory, 1904; Songs in Minority, 1905; Forest and Town (poems), 1910; Poets and Poetry; A Century of Missouri Literature, 1920; St. Louis Book of Authors, 1924. Home: St. Louis, Mo. Died Nov. 29, 1928.

DE MENT, Byron Hoover, clergyman; b. Silver Springs, Tenn., May 17, 1863; s. John Henry and Nancy Jane (Morrow) D.; grad. Peabody Coll. (then U. of Nashville), 1885 (scholarship medal); student U. of Va., 1788-90 (debater's medal); Th.D., Southern Baptist Theol. Sem., 1900; D.D., Baylor U., Waco, Tex., 1903; LL.D., Union University, Jackson, Tenn., 1927; m. Maggie Ellen Nicholas, Jan. 3, 1893; children—Elsom Nicholas (dec.), John Byron (dec.), Walter Carey, Lois Katherine (dec.), David Carroll. Ordained ministry Missionary Bapt. Ch., 1886; pastor 22d and Walnut St. Ch., Louisville, 1900-03; prof. practical theology and Hebrew, Baylor U., 1903-04; pastor 1st Ch., Waco, 1904-06 (built ch. plant); prof. S.S. pedagogy and asst. in theology and Hebrew, Southern Bapt. Theol. Sem., 1906-14; pastor 1st Ch., Greenwood, S.C., 1914-17; 1st pres. Bapt. Bible Inst., New Orleans, serving 1917-28, prof. N.T. exposition and Bible doctrines, 1928—. Wrote S.S. lesson notes for Bapt. World 6 yrs.; mem. Conservation Commn. Bapt. 75 Million Campaign; dir. Southern Baptist Assembly. Mason. Del. Bapt. World Alliance, Stockholm, Sweden, 1923. Author: Bible Readers Life of Christ, 1928. Home: New Orleans, La. Died Mar. 17, 1933.

DEMIASHKEVICH, Michael John, educator; b. Mohilev, Russia, Nov 8, 1891; s. Ivan A. and Anna S. (Isaeva) Demiashkevich; grad. Imperial Historico-Philol. and Imperial Archæol. Inst., Petrograd, 1914; Ph.D., Columbia, 1926; unmarried. Teacher Alexander I Gymnasium, 1914-17, Deutsche Hauptschule zu St. Petri, 1914-21, Navy Coll., Petrograd, 1920-23; asst. in Internat. Inst., Teachers Coll. (Columbia), 1926-27; visiting scholar univs. of Grenoble, Paris, Munich, Berlin and London, 1927-29; visiting instr. George Peabody Coll. for Teachers, Nashville, Tenn., 1929, asso. prof. edn., 1930-31, prof., 1931—; summer instr. Harvard, 1933, 35, 37. Officier d'académie, 1934. Decorated by French Govt. for contbns. to comparative edn. Mem. Greek Orthodox Church. Author: Shackled Diplomacy—Permanent Factors of Foreign Policies of Nations, 1934; Introduction to Philosophy of Education, 1935. Died Aug. 26, 1938.

DEMING, Clarence, writer; b. Litchfield, Conn., Oct. 1, 1848; s. William and Charlotte T. D.; A.B., Yale, 1872; m. Anna B. Humphrey, Nov. 10, 1879; m. 2d, Mary Bryant Whiting, June 10, 1886. Asst. editor Troy Whig, 1872-73; post-grad. student, Yale, 1873-74; night editor New Haven Palladium, 1874-75; asst. news editor and editorial writer New York Evening Post, 1875-81, traveling corr. same, 1881-84; editor New Haven (Conn.) New several yrs., and since editorial writer and asso. editor Railroad Gazette (now Railroad Age-Gazette) and general writer for newspapers and mags. Author: By-Ways of Nature and Life, 1884. Died May 8, 1913.

DEMING, Horace Edward, lawyer; b. Palmyra, N.Y., Mar. 31, 1850; s. Jeremiah P. H. and Mary (Colt) D.; A.B., Harvard, 1871; traveling in Europe and Orient, 1871-73; Harvard Grad. Sch., 1873-74. Law Sch., 1874-76; m. Caroline Springsteed, July 17, 1878; children—Eleanor, Harold Simpson, Constance, Guy Spalding, Agathe. Admitted to bar, 1877, and entered practice. A founder, 1880 (pres. and chmn. exec. com., 1880-82), Brooklyn Young Rep. Club; chmn. exec. com. Nat. Com. of Republicans and Independents, 1884; as spl. counsel of commrs. of accounts, investigated corp. counsel's office, New York, 1885; a founder and mem. exec. com. Commonwealth Club, which started ballot reform movement in N.Y., 1886-87; a founder and trustee Reform Club, 1887; chmn. gen. com. N.Y. Ballot Reform League, 1888-90; chmn. exec. com. People's Municipal League, 1891; a founder Nat. Municipal League, 1894; mem. spl. com. of municipal reform orgns. to draft proposed changes in N.Y. constitution, and of spl. com. that drafted state civil service reform clause of N.Y. constn., 1894; counsel senate com. of investigation into administration of state civil service, 1894; on spl. com. N.Y. Bar Assn. to report on proposed new charter of Greater N.Y., and represented bar assn. before mayor and gov. in opposition to proposed charter, 1897; spl. counsel for atty.-gen.'s office investigation of dist. atty.'s office in New York, 1901. Author: Government of American Cities, 1909. Joint Author: A Municipal Program, 1900. Home: New York, N.Y. Died June 11, 1930.

DEMING, Philander, lawyer; b. Carlisle, N.Y., Feb. 6, 1829; s. Rev. Rufus R. and Julia Ann (Porter) D.; A.B., U. of Vt., 1861, A.M., 1864; LL.B., Albany Law School, 1872; unmarried. Stenographic ct. reporter at Albany until 1882. Pres. N.Y. State Law Stenographers' Assn., 1878-79; pres. Alumni of U. of Vt., 1891-92. Began publication of a series of stories and sketches portraying the life of the people in Northern and Central N.Y. in Atlantic Monthly, 1873. Author: Adirondack Stories, 1880; Tompkins and Other Folks, 1885; The Story of a Pathfinder, 1907. Home: Albany, N.Y. Died Feb. 9, 1915.

DEMMON, Isaac Newton, univ. prof.; b. Northfield, O., Aug. 19, 1842; s. Leonard and Nancy (Boughey) D.; served in 132d Ind. Inf. in campaign of 1864, in Tenn. and Ala.; A.B., U. of Mich., 1868, A.M., 1871; (LL.D., U. of Nashville, 1896); m. Emma Regal, June 29, 1871. Prof. ancient langs., Hiram Coll., Ohio, 1870-72; prin. Ann Arbor High Sch., 1873-76; asst. prof. rhetoric and history, 1876-81, prof. English and rhetoric, 1881-03, prof. English, 1903—, U. of Mich. Expert bibliographer. Author: History of the University of Michigan, with late Prof. B. A. Hinsdale, 1837-1906. Died Sept. 29, 1920.

DE MOTTE, Harvey Clelland, prof. mathematics, Ill. Wesleyan U.; b. nr. Greenfield, Ill., July 17, 1838; s. John L. and Phoebe A. DeMotte; grad. Ill. Wesleyan U., 1861; Ph.D., Syracuse U. (in mathematics); admitted to bar; m. Sarah J. Kern, July 26, 1864. Prof. mathematics, Ill. Wesleyan U., 1861-84; 1st lt. Co. G, 68th Ill. vols., 1862; pres. Chaddock Coll., Quincy, Ill., 1884-87; supt. Ill. Soldiers' Orphans' Home, 1887-93; lay delegate to Gen. Conf. M.E. Ch., 1892; editor and pub. Alumni Journal 7 yrs.; editor Daily and weekly Leader, Bloomington, Ill., 1896-99. Home: Bloomington, Ill. Died 1904.

DE MOTTE, Mark L., lawyer, congressman; b. Rockville, Ind., Dec. 28, 1832; s. Rev. Daniel and Mary (Brewer) D.; ed. Ind. log sch. house until 1848; grad. Asbury (now De Pauw) U., A.B., 1853, A.M., 1856; grad. law sch. same, LL.B., 1855 (LL.D., De Pauw, 1903); m. Elizabeth Christy, Dec. 16, 1856 (died 1891); m. 2d, Clara Stephens, Jan. 12, 1893. Admitted to Ind. bar, Feb. 19, 1855; pros. atty. 31st jud. circuit, Ind., Oct. 1856—; entered Union service as ranking 1st lt., 4th Ind. battery, Aug. 1861; promoted capt. and a.q.m., May 1862. Mem. 47th Congress, 10th Ind. dist., 1881-83; mem. Ind. senate, 1886-90; dean Northern Ind. Law Sch., Valparaiso, Ind., 1879—. Methodist. Republican. Address: Valparaiso, Ind. Died 1908.

DEMPSEY, Clarence Haines, supt. of schools; b. Washington Mills, N.Y., Dec. 4, 1871; s. John Edwin and Charlotte (Carpenter) D.; A.B., Boston U., 1895, A.M., 1913; Litt.D., Norwich U., 1925; studied univs. of Munich and Berlin, 1896-98; m. Susanne Ella Goddard (A.B., Wellesley, 1895), June 28, 1902; children—John Goddard, Philip Edward. Supt. schs., Cumberland, R.I., 1898-99, St. Johnsbury, Vt., 1899-1908, Revere, Mass., 1908-10, Malden, 1910-13, Haverhill, 1913-20; commr. of edn., Vt., 1920-31; supt. schs., Arlington, Mass., 1931—. Republican. Methodist. Mason. Home: Arlington, Mass. Died June 12, 1937.

DEMPSEY, James Howard, lawyer; b. Shelby, O., Mar. 29, 1859; s. John and Martha C. (Davis) D.; A.B., Kenyon Coll., Gambier, O., 1882 (LL.D., 1912); student Columbia U. Coll. of Law, 1882, 83; m. Emma N. Bourne, Sept. 24, 1885 (died 1893). Admitted to Ohio bar, 1884, and since practiced in Cleveland; mem. Estep, Dickey & Squire, 1886-90, Squire, Sanders & Dempsey, 1890—; pres. Factory Site Co.; dir. Grasselli Chem. Co., Glidden Varnish Co., U.S. Radiator Corp., etc. Republican. Died May 2, 1920.

DEMPSIE, Ephraim, capitalist; b. Kilrea, Ireland, Oct. 25, 1854; s. Stewart D.; ed. at Kilrea and Belfast, Ireland; m. Marie E. Eaton, Feb. 12, 1900. Went to San Francisco, 1876; spent 3 yrs. in Honolulu, 1880-83; went to Spokane and entered into business, 1884; prin. owner and gen. mgr. Maple Leaf Coal Co., Bellevue, Alberta, Can., July 1907—; has other large business and mining interests. Mem. bd. regents State Normal Sch., 1894-1900; has taken active part in ednl. and municipal affairs. Home: Spokane, Wash. Died Feb. 11, 1911.

DEMPSTER, William John, clergyman; b. Newtownards, Ireland, Mar. 7, 1870; s. William and Elizabeth (Jones) D.; ed. Presbyn. Coll. (Montreal), Queen's U. (Kingston), Manitoba Coll. (Winnipeg); grad. Lane Theol. Sem. Cincinnati, 1897; D.D., Defiance Coll., 1903; m. Lucy Dell Pifer, Feb. 19, 1898. Came to America, 1889, naturalized citizen of U.S., 1898; ordained Presbyn. ministry, 1896; pastor Forest, O., 1896-98, North Baltimore, O., 1898-99, Napoleon, O., 1899-1906, Tiffin, O., 1906-09, Lima, O., 1910-12, Urbana, O., 1913-18, Crafton Ch., Pittsburgh, 1918. Prominent in brotherhood and evangelistic work in Synod of Ohio. Republican. Mason. Home: Pittsburgh, Pa. Died Mar. 17, 1932.

DENBY, Charles, lawyer, diplomat; b. Mt. Joy, Va., 1830; educated at Georgetown Univ. (LL.D.); grad. Va. Mil. Inst.; taught school 2 yrs.; located as lawyer in Ind. In Union army as lt. col., 42d Ind. vols., and later col., 80th Ind. vols., in Civil war; U.S. minister to China, 1885-98; apptd. by President, 1898, mem. of commn. to investigate conduct of war against Spain; mem. U.S. Philippines Commn., 1899. Home: Evansville, Ind. Died 1904.

DENBY, Charles, consul gen., retired; b. Evansville, Ind., Nov. 14, 1861; s. Charles and Martha (Fitch) D.; A.B., Princeton, 1882 (hon. A.M., 1895); m. Martha Dalzell Orr, Mar. 19, 1895; children—James Orr, Charles, Edwin Orr. Second sec. of legation, Peking, China, 1885-93, 1st sec., 1893-97; in business at Tientsin, China, 1897-1900; sec. gen. of provisional govt. established by allied powers, for dist. of Tientsin, 1900-02; fgn. adviser to the gov. gen. of N. China, 1902-05; chief clk. Dept. of State, 1905-07; consul gen. at Shanghai, China, 1907-09, Vienna, Austria, 1909-15; v.p. Hupp Motor Car Corp., Detroit, 1915-17; dir. Bur. of Fgn. Agents, War Trade Bd., Washington, 1917; spl. rep. of Dept. of State, in Japan and China, 1918; spl. rep. U.S. Shipping Bd., China and Japan, 1922-23. Home: Washington, D.C. Died Feb. 14, 1938.

DENBY, Edwin, sec. of the navy; b. Evansville, Ind., Feb. 18, 1870; s. Hon. Charles and Martha (Fitch) D.; bro. of Charles D.; ed. Evansville High Sch. and U. of Mich.; went to China, 1885, with father, then U.S. minister; in Chinese Imperial Maritime Customs Service, 1887-94; returned to U.S., 1894; LL.B., U. of Mich., 1896; m. Marion Bartlett Thurber, Mar. 18, 1911; children—Edwin, Marion. Admitted to bar 1896, and began practice at Detroit. Gunner's mate, U.S.S. Yosemite, during Spanish-Am. War, 1898; pvt. U.S. Marine Corps, 1917; on reserve as maj., Jan. 1, 1919. Mem. Mich. Ho. of Rep., 1903; mem. 59th to 61st Congresses (1905-11), 1st Mich. Dist.; apptd. chief probation officer Recorder's Court, City of Detroit, and Circuit Court of Wayne Co., Dec. 1920; sec. of Navy, Mar. 4, 1921-Mar. 10, 1924 (resigned). Republican. Episcopalian. Home: Detroit, Mich. Died Feb. 8, 1929.

DENCH, Edward Bradford, M.D.; b. Leedsville, N.Y., Jan. 16, 1864; s. Josiah B. and Frances M. (Lester) D.; Ph.B., Yale, 1883; M.D., Coll. Phys. and Surg. (Columbia), 1885; m. Marie Antoinette Hunt, Oct. 3, 1888; 1 dau., Mrs. Catherine Hawks. Practiced in New York from 1885; prof. otology. Univ. and Bellevue Hosp. Med. Coll., 1898-1930, emeritus. Maj. Med. R.C., Aug. 1917. Fellow A.C.S. Republican. Died Feb. 21, 1936.

DENEEN, Charles Samuel, senator, governor; b. Edwardsville, Ill., May 4, 1863; s. Samuel H. and Mary F. (Ashley) D.; A.B., McKendree Coll., 1882, A.M., LL.D. from same; m. Bina Day Maloney, May

10, 1891; children—Charles Ashley, Dorothy (Mrs. Allmand M. Blow), Frances (Mrs. Carl Birdsall), Bina Day (Mrs. Thomas W. House IV). Admitted to bar, 1886; practiced at Chicago, 1890-1904; mem. Ill. Ho. of Rep., 1892; atty. for Sanitary Dist., Chicago, 1895-96; state's atty. Cook Co., Ill., 1896-1904; gov. of Ill., 1905-09, 1909-13; resumed practice of law at Chicago; apptd. U.S. Senator, Feb. 25, 1925, to serve unexpired term of Hon. Medill McCormick, deceased, and elected to same office for term, 1925-31; resumed practice of law at Chicago. Republican. Home: Chicago, Ill. Died Feb. 5, 1940.

DENÈGRE, Walter Denis, lawyer; b. New Orleans, June 17, 1858; s. James Denis and Sylvanie (Blanc) D.; ed. Jesuits' Coll., New Orleans, 2 yrs. St. John's Coll., Fordham, N.Y.; A.B., Harvard, 1879; LL.B., Tulane U., 1881; m. Mrs. Bertha Cobb-Armour, widow William Armour and d. S. B. Cobb, of Chicago, Dec. 3, 1893; 1 dau., Elaine (Mrs. W. D. Sohier, Jr.), Admitted to bar, 1881; mem. Denègre, Blair & Denègre, from 1896; retired; was spl. counsel for U.S. before French and Am. Claims Commn., 1881. Helped suppress the "Mafia" and "black hand" in New Orleans, in 1889. "King of the Carnival" (Mardi Gras) New Orleans, 1899. Leader independent Democracy in La.; candidate for U.S. Senate, 1896, and it is claimed was elected, but S. D. McEnery was declared elected by vote of 68 to 66. Leader in campaign of 1899 which brought about the drainage and sewerage of New Orleans. Chief of Div. of Insular Possessions, Bur. of Alien Property Custodian, Washington, 1917-19. Home: Washington, D.C. Died July 28, 1934.

DENFELD, Robert Edward, educator; b. Westboro, Mass., June 29, 1853; s. Franz and Margaret (Weigand) D.; A.B., Amherst, 1876, A.M., 1879; m. Helen S. Boyd, Nov. 23, 1882. Prin. high sch., Southboro, Mass., 1876-78. Needham, 1878-81; admitted to Mass. bar, 1882; prin. high sch., Webster, Mass., 1882-83, Weymouth, 1883-84; supt. schs., Mankato, Minn., 1884-85, Duluth, 1885—. Pres. State High Sch. Bd. of Minn., 1907—. Episcopalian. Home: Duluth, Minn. Died Dec. 22, 1921.

DENHAM, Edward; b. New Bedford, Mass., Oct. 30, 1849; s. Tilson B. and Rachel G. (Leach) D., of Pilgrim, Puritan and Quaker stock; ed. pub. schs.; unmarried. Interested in hist. studies and assisting others in compiling books; his "Man in the Iron Mask," contributed to Frey's Sobriquets and Nicknames, 1888, is a complete condensed summary of that subject; compiled Vol. X, 1891, of Collections of Me. Hist. Soc., being an analytical index to the 9 preceding vols. Mason. Home: New Bedford, Mass. Died Apr. 16, 1925.

DENHARD, Charles Edward, physician; b. Schluchtern, Germany, July 15, 1840; ed. pub. schs. and Schluchtern Gymnaisum; came to U.S., 1865; grad. in pharmacy, 1871; M.D., Univ. Med. Coll. (New York U.), 1874; commr. of relief to the poor from 1875; gynecologist, German Poliklinik, 1883-88 (a founder); visiting gynecologist Assn. Hosp., 1886—; on staff's Charity, Bellevue, Park and St. Mark's hosps. Home: New York, N.Y. Deceased.

DENHARDT, Henry H., lawyer, soldier; b. Bowling Green, Ky., Mar. 8, 1876; s. William and Margaret (Denhardt) D.; student Ogden Coll., Bowling Green; LL.B., Cumberland U., 1899; student Arty. Sch. of Fire, Ft. Sill, Okla.; Army War Coll. Admitted to Ky. bar, 1899, and began practice at Bowling Green; pres. Times Journal Pub. Co. Pros. atty. City of Bowling Green, 1900-10; judge Warren County (Ky.) Court, 1910-18; del. from state at large to Dem. Nat. Conv., 1924; lt. gov. of Ky., 1923-27. Officer Ky. N.G., June 1898; maj. 3rd Ky. Inf., Mexican border service, 1916-17; maj. 3d Ky. Inf., with 139th F.A. and 319th F.A., 1917-18, lt. col. F.A., 1918-19; participated in St. Mihiel and Argonne-Meuse offensives; cited and promoted; hon. disch., Mar. 22, 1919; now brig. gen. comdg. 75th Brigade, N.G., U.S.A., comprising 149th Ky. Inf. and 150th W.Va. Inf.; comd. troops during riots at Newport, Ky., 1921-22; serving as adjutant gen. of Ky., Dec. 1931-Dec. 1935. Chmn. Ky. Disabled Ex-Service Men's Bd.; v.p. and former mem. legislative com. Nat. Guard Assn. of U.S. Former moderator Ky. Synod Cumberland Presbyn. Church. Mason. Had charge of rescue of Floyd Collins, cave explorer, 1925. Presented saddle horse by citizens of Newport, and silver service, by citizens of Ft. Thomas, for quelling riots. Home: Bowling Green, Ky. Died Sept. 20, 1937.

DENIG, Robert Gracey, commodore U.S.N.; b. Columbus, O., May 22, 1851; s. Robert McClintock and Jane (Harry) D.; grad. U.S. Naval Acad., 1873; m. Jeannie Livingston Hubbard, Apr. 11, 1878. Promoted through the various grades to commodore and retired, June 30, 1908. On board Tallapoosa, Saranac, Tuscarora, Benecia, during revolution in Panama, and in Honolulu at the time Kalakaua was elected king; aboard Huron when she was wrecked on coast of N.C., Nov. 24, 1877, and one of 29 saved; Trenton, flagship European sta.; flagship Brooklyn on tour around the world; flagship Baltimore, cruise around the world; flagship Philadelphia, Atlantic coast; gunboat Machias, U.S.S. Petrel, wintering in Manchuria during war between China and Japan; served during war with Spain on Niagara, Topeka, participating in bombardment of San Juan and battle of Nipe Bay; flagship Chicago, as fleet engr., cruise around Africa and S. America; shore duty at Mare Island, Portsmouth, N.H., U.S. Naval Acad., Naval Training Sta., Newport, R.I.; inspection duty state of Pa.; head of dept. steam engring., Phila. Navy Yard; Spl. duty, applied mathematics, Hamilton Coll. Republican. Episcopalian. Medals: Battle of Nipe Bay, Spanish-Am. War, U.S. Campaign Medal. Home: Sandusky, O. Died Apr. 9, 1924.

DENIO, Francis Brigham, theologian; b. Enosburg, Vt., May 4, 1848; s. Horace and Elzina S. (Williams) D.; A.B., Middlebury Coll., 1871; grad. Andover Theol. Sem., 1879; D.D., Middlebury, 1893; m. Julia Gertrude Holmes, Sept. 2, 1879. Ordained Congl. ministry, 1881; instr. N.T. Greek, 1879-82, prof. O. T. lang. and lit., 1882-1919 emeritus, Bangor Theol. Sem. Author: Outlines of Old Testament Theology, 1898; Supreme Leader, 1900; Supreme Need, 1913; The Literature of Greece and Israel in the Renaissance, 1925; Genealogy of Aaron Denio of Deerfield (with Herbert W. Denio), 1926. Home: Bangor, Me. Died Apr. 17, 1936.

DENISON, Charles, physician; b. Royalton, Vt., Nov. 1, 1845; s. Dr. Joseph A. D.; prep. edn. Kimball Union Acad., Lebanon, N.H.; grad. Williams Coll., 1867 (A.M., 1873); grad. med. dept. Univ. Vt., 1869; m. Ella, d. Henry Strong, Dec. 26, 1878. Went to Denver, Colo., from Hartford, Conn., 1873, because of pulmonary hemorrhage. Prof. diseases of the chest and of climatology, med. dept. U. of Denver, 14 yrs., emeritus., hon. v.p. Brit. Congress on Tuberculosis, 1901; Am. corr. mem. Internat. Central Bureau for Prevention of Tuberculosis, (Berlin) 1902. Home, Denver, Colo. Died 1909.

DENISON, Charles Simeon, engr.; b. Gambier, O., July 12, 1849; s. Rev. George and Janett Balloch (Ralston) D.; Norwich U., Northfield, Vt., 1 yr.; C.E., U. of Vt., 1871 (Sc.D., 1907); unmarried. Asst. engr. in constrn. Milwaukee & Northern R.R., 1871-72; instr. engring. from 1872, prof. stereotomy, mechanism and drawing from 1885, U. of Mich. U.S. astronomer and surveyor, locating boundary line between Wash. and Ida., part of 1873 and 1874. Republican. Episcopalian; mem. standing com. Diocese of Mich. Home: Ann Arbor, Mich. Died July 30, 1913.

DENISON, Frederic, Bapt. clergyman; b. Stonington, Conn., Sept. 28, 1819; s. Isaac and Lavina (Fish) D.; grad. Brown, 1847; m. Amey Randall Marston, Jan. 12, 1848. Pastor several Bapt. chs.; chaplain during war in Union army; pres. R.I. Vet. Citizens' Hist. Assn. Home: Providence, R.I. Died 1901.

DENISON, Henry Willard, jurist; b. Guildhall, Vt., May 11, 1846; s. Col. John Paine and Mary Shepard (Cooper) D.; acad. edn., Lancaster, N.H.; law student Columbian (now George Washington) U.; m. Helen Wilder Cross, Jan. 21, 1873. Legal adviser of the Japanese Dept. of Foreign Affairs, May 1, 1880—; represented Japan in drafting treaty of peace with Russia, at Portsmouth, N.H., 1905. Mem. Association de législation comparée, Paris; mem. Permanent Court of Arbitration of The Hague; tech. del. to Japan to the 2d Peace Conf. at The Hague. Decorations: Grand cordon (1st class) Imperial Japanese Order of the Rising Sun; Grand cordon (1st class) Japanese Order of the Sacred Treasure. Died July 3, 1914.

DENISON, John Henry, clergyman; b. Boston, Mass., Mar. 3, 1841; s. John N. and Frances (Dean) D.; A.B., Williams, 1862, later A.M. (D.D., 1884); student, Andover Theol. Sem., 1863-65; m. Caroline H., d. late Mark Hopkins, pres. Williams Coll., 1869; father of John Hopkins D. Worked among freedmen, Hampton, Va., 1866-67; ordained Congl. ministry, Jan. 30, 1870; pastor S. Williamstown, Mass., 1868-71, First Ch., New Britain, Conn., 1871-78; chaplain, Hampton (Va.) Inst., 1879-80; pastor College Ch., Williamstown, Mass., 1883-89, and prof. divinity, Williams Coll., 1884-89. Author: Christ's Idea of the Supernatural, 1895. Home: Williamstown, Mass. Died Apr. 22, 1924.

DENISON, John Henry, judge; b. Royalton, Vt., July 15, 1855; s. Dudley Chase and Eunice (Dunbar) D.; A.B., U. of Vt., 1877, LL.D., 1920; studied law, Harvard, 1879-80; m. Agnes Hawley, Oct. 22, 1884. Began practice in Vt., 1879; moved to Denver, Colo., 1881; lecturer Law Sch., U. of Colo., 1899-1903; prof. law, U. of Denver, 1900; judge Dist. Court of Denver, 1913-18; asso. justice Supreme Court of Colo., 1919-27, chief justice, 1928. Republican. Episcopalian. Home: Denver, Colo. Died Dec. 3, 1935.

DENISON, John Hopkins, clergyman; b. Westfield, Mass., Oct. 14, 1870; s. John Henry and Caroline H. (Hopkins) D.; A.B., Williams Coll., 1890 (D.D., 1915); divinity, Andover Theol. Sem.; m. Pearl L. Underwood, Dec. 30, 1902; children—Charis, John H. Ordained Congl. ministry, 1896; asst. First Congl. Ch., Kansas City, 1893, Madison Sq. Presbyn. Ch., New York, 1894-95; pastor Presbyn. Ch. of Sea and Land, New York, 1895-1903, Central Congl. Ch., Boston, 1903-10 (resigned). With Internat. Y.M.C.A. in France, 1917. Author: Beside the Bowery, 1914; Emotion as the Basis of Civilization, 1928; The Enlargement of Personality, 1930; Emotional Currents in America, 1931. Home: New York, N.Y. Died Jan. 18, 1936.

DENISON, John Ledyard, insurance; b. Stonington (Mystic), Conn., Sept. 19, 1826; s. Isaac and Levina (Fish) D.; grad. Worcester Acad., 1850, A.M., Brown Univ., 1855; m. Mary E. Burrows, May 10, 1853; m. 2d, Frances M. Breed, March 5, 1861. Reared on farm; taught 2 yrs. in dist. schools, Groton, Conn., and 1 season in Sharon, Mass.; founded, 1850, and prin., 1850-55, Mystic Acad.; entered book pub. business, 1855; editor, compiler and writer till 1872, then in insurance. Republican. Baptist lay preacher. Home: Hartford, Conn. Died 1906.

DENISON, Lindsay, newspaperman; b. Salem, Mass., Mar. 23, 1873; s. James and Elizabeth (Lindsay) D.; B.A., Yale, 1895; m. Mary Heard, Aug. 18, 1906; 1 dau., Kate (Mrs. Ralph C. Raughley, Jr.). With Cosmopolitan Mag., 1895, New York Sun, 1896-1904, Everybody's Mag., 1904-07, Evening World, New York, 1908-31. Sergt., Plattsburg (N.Y.) Training Camp, 1916; capt. Q.M.C. Reserve, U.S.A., 1917-21, with A.E.F., 1918-19; capt. Mil. Intelligence Reserve, 1921—. Author: Touchin' on and Appertainin' to Mister Deputy Commissioner Devery, 1899; Towns and Villages of New York City (with Max Fischel), 1925. Home: Great Neck, L.I., N.Y. Died Mar. 25, 1934.

DENISON, Mary Andrews, author; b. Cambridge, Mass., May 26, 1826; d. Thomas and Juliette Andrews; ed. pvt. and common schs., Boston; m. Rev. Charles Wheeler Denison, 1846. Went with him to British Guiana, where he was consul gen. until war opened. He became chaplain and she went with him to war to minister to sick and dying; since war in Washington, D.C. Author: Charles Montgomery, 1893; A Changed Life, 1895; Noble by Birth, 1899; The Yellow Violin, 1902; Her Secret, 1905; An Every Day Heroine. Home: Baltimore, Md. Died 1911.

DENISON, Robert Charles, clergyman; b. Godfrey, Ill., July 22, 1868; s. George and Emma Abbott (Webster) D.; Shurtleff Coll., Alton, Ill.; A.B., Amherst, 1889, D.D., 1919; grad. Andover Theol. Sem., 1892; m. Martha Kendrick, Oct. 31, 1894; children—George K., Mrs. Lucia D. Baylis. Ordained Congl. ministry, 1892; pastor, Little Rock, Ark., 1893-97, Janesville, Wis., 1897-1909, United Ch. on the Green, New Haven, Conn., 1909-20; head Dept. of Philosophy and lecturer on philosophy and ethics, Pomona Coll., Claremont, Calif., 1920—. Deputy commr. with rank of maj. of Am. Red Cross to Serbia, 1918; commr. Am. Red Cross to Albania, 1919. Mem. Civic Fedn., New Haven, Philos. Soc. of Southern Calif. Home: Claremont, Calif. Died Jan. 23, 1936.

DENISON, Thomas Stewart, publisher; b. Marshall Co., W.Va., Feb. 20, 1848; s. Alexander McCoy and Esther (Stewart) D.; grad. Normal Univ., Lebanon, O., 1872 (hon. A.M., 1909); unmarried. Taught sch., 1872-78; miner, 1881-82; publisher, 1878—. Author: Friday Afternoon Dialogues, 1879; An Iron Crown, 1885; The Man Behind, 1888; My Invisible Partner, 1898; Old Schoolhouse and Other Poems and Conceits in Verse, 1902; Pomes ov the Peepul, 1904; Nauatl or Mexican in Aryan Phonology, 1907; The Primitive Aryans of America, 1908; Mexican-Aryan Comparative Vocabulary, 1909, etc. Home: Chicago, Ill. Died 1911.

DENISON, Winfred Thaxter, lawyer; b. Portland, Me., June 30, 1873; s. Elias Bemis and Mary Swan (Thaxter) D.; grad. Phillips Exeter Acad., 1892; A.B., Harvard, 1896, LL.B., 1900; unmarried. Admitted to bar, 1900, and practiced at New York; asst. U.S. atty. Southern Dist. N.Y., 1906-09; spl. asst. to the atty. gen. U.S., in the sugar and other customs fraud prosecutions, 1909-10; asst. atty. gen. U.S., Jan. 1910-14; mem. Philippine Commn. and sec. of Interior, P.I., 1914-16; mem. Stetson, Jennings & Russell, N.Y. City, 1916—. Mem. Com. of 100, New York City campaign of 1909, and Fusion Com., 1917. Republican. Universalist. Home: New York, N.Y. Died Nov. 5, 1919.

DENMAN, Burt J., utility exec.; b. Toledo, O., Apr. 30, 1876; s. Charles A. and Belle (Conklin) D.; B.S. in Engring., Univ. of Mich., 1899, also E.E.; m. Fannie Louise Patrick, Feb. 20, 1900 (died 1926); children—Bernice, Dorothy, Lawrence; m. 2d, Louise Winchell Dayton, 1928. Chief electrician, Toledo & Maumee Valley Ry. Co., 1899-1901; elec. engr., Toledo, B.G.&Southern Traction Co., 1901-04; construction and operation Detroit Edison Co., 1904-13; acting asst. prof. and non-resident lecturer, U. of Mich., 1908-09; v.p. and gen. mgr. United Light & Power Co., and United Light & Rys. Co., 1913—; v.p. Am. Light & Traction Co., Northern Natural Gas Co.; and officer other corps. Trustee Northwestern Univ. Republican. Presbyn. Mason. Home: Wilmette, Ill. Died June 25, 1938.

DENMAN, Ira O., M.D., surgeon; b. Lenna, Kan., June 9, 1872; s. Francis M. and Lydia (Harding) D.; Allen Co. Normal Sch., Iola, Kan.; M.D., Hahnemann Med. Coll., Chicago, 1897; post-grad. work Chicago Post-Grad. Med. Coll.; N.Y. Eye and Ear Infirmary; Harvard Med. Coll.; univs. of Vienna and Freiburg; Morfields Hosp., London, Eng.; m. Sabra Blair, Sept. 14, 1893; children—Loraine, Ira O., Patti. Practiced general medicine and surgery, and eye, ear, nose and throat, Charleston, Ill., until close of 1907; moved to Toledo, O., Jan. 1908; practice limited to eye, ear, nose and throat. Chief of staff, Toledo Hospital, 1913—; oculist Pa. R.R., Detroit & Toledo Shore Line Railroad, Nickel Plate Railway. Chairman Bd. of Health, Charleston, Ill., 1903-07. Member Am. Bd. of Oto-Laryngology and Am. College of Physical Therapy. Republican. Mem. Christian (Disciples) Ch. Fellow A.C.S. Originated technique and designed chair for tonsilectomy under nitrous oxide and oxygen gas anesthesia. On editorial staff of Archives of Physical Therapy, X-Ray and Radium. Co-inventor of vocaphone and artificial larynx for use in talking after a laryngectomy; v.p. The Vocaphone Co. Home: Toledo, O. Died Sept. 28, 1933.

DENMAN, Leroy Gilbert, judge; b. Guadalupe Co., Tex., on farm, Oct. 31, 1855; ed. common schs. of Tex.; taught sch. 4 yrs.; B.L., U. of Va., 1880; m. Sue E. Carpenter, 1881. Practiced New Braunsfels, Tex., 2 yrs., then at San Antonio; asso. justice Supreme Ct. of Tex., 1894-99; resigned; mem. Denman, Franklin & McGowan, 1899—; pres. San Antonio Loan & Trust Co.; chmn. bd. dirs. San Antonio Nat. Bank. Home: San Antonio, Tex. Died Sept. 14, 1916.

DENNEN, Ernest Joseph, clergyman; b. Naugatuck, Conn., Sept. 6, 1866; s. Charles Oscar and Josephine (Day) D.; B.A., U. of Mich., 1893; B.D., Episcopal Theol. Sch., Cambridge, Mass., 1896; m. Anna Blake Hayden, Nov. 17, 1903; children—Anna Hayden, Elizabeth Blake, William Ives, Susan Williams. Deacon, 1895, priest, 1896, P.E. Ch.; successively asst. St. Stephen's Ch., Boston, St. John's Ch., E. Boston, and Trinity Ch., Newport, R.I., until 1905; rector St. Stephen's Ch., Lynn, Mass., 1905-14; archdeacon of Boston, 1914—; rector Christ Ch., Boston, 1927-29; on staff Cathedral Ch. of St. Paul, Boston, 1929—. Founder and supreme dir. Order of St. Galahad. Author: Introduction to the Prayer Book, 1906; The Sunday School Under Scientific Management, 1914; The Manual for Leaders (booklet for Order of Sir Galahad), 1921. Died Jan. 22, 1937.

DENNEN, Jeanne Whitney, educator; b. Watertown, Mass., Jan. 16, 1863; d. Stephen Rollins and Clara Whitney (Ludwig) D.; student Bradford Acad. Founded, with Alice K. Parsons, and conducted pvt. sch., Brooklyn, N.Y., 1885-92; founded, with same, at Los Angeles, 1892, the Girls' Collegiate Sch., removing sch. to estate of 50 acres overlooking San Gabriel Valley, in 1925. Christian Scientist. Home: Glendora, Calif. Died June 13, 1929.

DENNETT, Roger Herbert, M.D.; b. Boston, Mass., July 21, 1876; s. Herbert Enos and Alice Howard (Battles) D.; B.S., St. Lawrence U., 1898, D.Sc., 1928; M.D., Harvard U., 1902; m. Agema Wheeler, Apr. 12, 1905; children—Alice, Nancy, Sally, Roger H. Practiced Adamsville, R.I., 1903-06, New York, 1906—; apptd. instr. diseases of children, New York Post-Grad. Med. Sch., 1907; asst. attending physician and chief of clinic, N.Y. Post-Grad. Hosp., 1908; adj. prof. diseases of children, N.Y. Post-Grad. Med. Sch., 1913, now dir. dept. of pediatrics and mem. med. bd.; prof. diseases of children, N.Y. Post-Grad. Hosp., 1920—, also attending phys. in babies wards. Trustee St. Lawrence Univ. Republican. Unitarian. Fellow N.Y. Acad. Medicine, Am. Acad. Pediatrics. Author: The Healthy Baby, 1912, 1929; Simplified Infant Feeding, 1915. Died Feb. 3, 1935.

DENNEY, Joseph Villiers, univ. prof.; b. Aurora, Ill., Jan. 9, 1862; s. Thomas and Mary (Fowler) D.; A.B., U. of Mich., 1885; hon. A.M., 1910; student U. of Munich, 1907, U. of Paris, 1908; Litt.Doc., Wittenberg, 1920; m. Jane Hawkes, Aug. 30, 1893; children—Thomas Hawkes, Joseph Villiers. Journalist, 1885-87; prin. Aurora High Sch., 1888-90; instr. and grad. student, U. of Mich., 1890-91; asso. prof. rhetoric, 1891-94, prof. rhetoric and English lit., 1894-1904, dean Coll. Arts, Philosophy and Science, 1901-21, prof. English, 1904-33, prof. emeritus, 1933, acting pres., 1909, Ohio State U. Lecturer, Columbia U., summers, 1904-11. Conglist. Author: Washington, Webster, Lincoln, 1911; Argumentation and Debate (in collaboration with Duncan and McKinney), 1911; also of Paragraph Writing, 1893; Composition-Rhetoric, 1897; Elementary English Composition, 1900; Composition-Literature, 1902 (all with Fred N. Scott). Home: Columbus, O. Died June 19, 1935.

DENNING, Joseph M., diplomatic service; b. Cincinnati, O., Apr. 19, 1866; s. Joseph and Catherine D.; A.B., St. Xavier Coll., Cincinnati, 1887, A.M., 1890; student St. Mary of the West, 1887-91. Ordained priest R.C. Ch., 1891; pastor Cincinnati, Oxford, Hillsboro and Marion (O.) until 1922; apptd. diplomatic agt. and consul gen. at Tangier, Morocco, Feb. 10, 1922. Died July 26, 1927.

DENNIS, Alfred Lewis Pinneo, writer; b. Beirut, Syria, May 21, 1874 (parents were temporarily residing abroad); s. James Shepard and Mary Elizabeth (Pinneo) D.; A.B., Princeton, 1896; student Columbia, Heidelberg, Harvard, 1896-1901; Ph.D., Columbia, 1901; m. Mary Boardman, d. George W. Cable, June 7, 1899; children—Mary Elizabeth (Mrs. Alexander Standish), Louise Cable. Instr. and prof. history and polit. science, Bowdoin Coll., 1901-04; asso. prof. history, U. of Chicago, 1904-05; lecturer history, Harvard, 1905-06; prof. history, U. of Wis., 1906-20; resigned to engage in research work; prof. history and internat. relations, Clark U., Worcester, Mass., 1923—. Temp. sec. Wis. State Council Defense, 1917. Capt. Mil. Intelligence Div. Gen. Staff, 1918-19; asst. mil. attaché, Am. Embassy, London, reporting to Peace Conf., Paris, 1919. Awarded British Mil. Cross. Author: Eastern Problems at the Close of the XVIII Century, 1901; Anglo-Japanese Alliance, 1923; Foreign Policies of Soviet Russia, 1924; John Hay (in Secretaries of State Series); Adventures in American Diplomacy, 1928. Died Nov. 14, 1930.

DENNIS, Alfred Pearce, vice-chmn. U.S. Tariff Commn.; b. in Worcester Co., Md., Jan. 10, 1869; s. Samuel K. and Sally Handy (Crisfield) D.; A.B., Princeton, 1891, A.M., 1893, Ph.D., 1894; LL.D., Washington U., 1925; m. Mary Value, 1914; children—Alfred Pearce, John Value. Fellow in history and economics, Princeton, 1891-93; instr. history, Princeton, 1893-94; prof. history, Wesleyan U., Conn., 1894-95; prof. history and politics, Smith Coll., 1898-1907; resigned on account of ill health and engaged in business; commercial attaché, Am. Embassy, Rome, Italy, Dec. 1918-Jan. 1921, London, Jan.-Nov. 1921; spl. rep. Dept. of Commerce, investigations for Secretary Hoover in Central and Eastern Europe, 1922, 23; assistant to Secretary Hoover, Washington, D.C., 1924; apptd. mem. U.S. Tariff Commn., Mar. 15, 1925, and named vice-chmn., July 23, 1925. Democrat. Presbyn. Author: The Romance of World Trade. Home: Washington, D.C. Died Aug. 29, 1931.

DENNIS, David Worth, coll. prof.; b. Economy, Ind., Apr. 8, 1849; s. Nathan and Evelina (Worth) D.; A.B., Earlham Coll., 1873, A.M., 1876; Ph.D., Syracuse U., 1886; studied univs. of Bonn and Edinburgh, 1889-90; m. Martha Ann Curl, June 22, 1876 (dec.); m. 2d, Emma Zeller, June 1900; father of William Cullen D. Teacher natural science, Richmond High Sch., 1875-79; pres. Wilmington (O.) Coll., 1879-81; prin. Bloomingdale (Ind.) Acad., 1882-84; prof. biology, Earlham Coll., 1884—. Fellow A.A.A.S.; mem. Ind. Acad. Science (pres. 1901), Ind. Assn. Science Teachers (pres. 1898). Author: Key to Fossils of Richmond, Ind.; One Hundred Lessons About Plants, 1906. Home: Richmond, Ind. Died May 13, 1916.

DENNIS, Frederic Shepard, surgeon; b. Newark, N.J., Apr. 17, 1850; s. Alfred Lewis and Eliza (Shepard) D.; A.B., Yale U., 1872; M.D., Bellevue Hosp. Med. Coll. (New York U.), 1874; M.D., Royal Coll. Surgeons, Eng., 1877; m. Fannie Rockwell, Feb. 5, 1880. Visiting surgeon, St. Vincent's Hosp., 1882—; prof. surgery Bellevue Hosp. Med. Coll., 1883-98; prof. clin. surgery, Cornell U. Med. Coll., 1898-1910 (emeritus); cons. surgeon Montefiore Home, New York, 1888—; also cons. surgeon Bellevue and St. Vincent's hospitals. Fellow Royal College Surgeons, 1899, Am. Coll. Surgeons, 1925, Am. Surg. Assn. (pres. 1894). Home: New York, N.Y. Died Mar. 8, 1934.

DENNIS, Graham Barclay, mining; b. London, Eng., June 1, 1857; s. Mendenhall John and Sophia D.; bro. of William B. D.; ed. Bethany Coll.; m. Hester L. Bradley, May 20, 1879. City editor, 1875-77, business mgr., 1877-79, Dayton Journal; banker and broker, Dayton, 1879-85; publisher Farmers' Home Journal, 1880-85; published Spokane Miner, 1885-86; pres. Ross Park Electric Ry. Co., Old Dominion Mining & Milling Co., Northwest Mining Assn., Insurgent Gold Mining Co., Muscovite Mica Mining Co., Columbia Ry. & Navigation Co., Warehouse Realty Co., Knickerbocker Bldg. Co., Dennis Investment Co.; sec.-treas. Spokane Ry. & Terminal Co. Mem. Spokane City Council, 1886-88, Sch. Bd., 1888-90; chmn. publicity com. of Chamber of Commerce; v.p. Northwest Industrial Expn., 1889; rep. N.W. Mining Assn. to Parliament of British Columbia; pres. Northwest Development League; v.p. Am. Mining Congress. Home: Spokane, Wash. Died Aug. 18, 1923.

DENNIS, James Shepard, clergyman; b. Newark, N.J., Dec. 15, 1842; s. Alfred Lewis and Eliza (Shepard) D.; bro. Frederic Shepard and Samuel Shepard D.; A.B., Princeton, 1863; grad. Princeton Theol. Sem., 1867; (D.D., Princeton, 1879, U. of Aberdeen, 1906); m. Mary Elizabeth Pinneo, June 26, 1872; father of Alfred Lewis Pinneo D. (q.v.). Ordained Presbyn. ministry, 1868; missionary in Syria, 1868-91; prin. and prof. Theol. Sem., Beirut, Syria, 1873-91; hon. mem. Syria Mission, 1892—. Mem. Presbyn. Bd. Foreign Missions; sec. bd. of trustees of Syrian Protestant Coll.; mem. commn. No. I, World Missionary Conf., Edinburgh, 1910. Fellow Am. Geog. Soc. Died Mar. 21, 1914.

DENNIS, James Teackle, Egyptologist, orientalist; b. Baltimore, Oct. 6, 1865; s. James Upshur and Mary Wilson (Teackle) D.; A.B., Lafayette Coll., Pa., 1887; post-grad. Johns Hopkins; m. Ida Lee Wade. Admitted to Md. bar, 1889; state's atty., Somerset Co., Md., 1890-93; del. Internat. Congress of Orientalists, Rome, 1899, Copenhagen, 1902; field dir. excavations for Egyptian Exploration Fund, 1905, 1906. Mason. Author: On the Shores of an Inland Sea, 1895; The Burden of Isis, 1910; From Cataract to Equator, 1913. Home: Woodbrook, Md. Died Apr. 1, 1918.

DENNIS, John M(cPherson); b. Frederick, Md., Feb. 23, 1866; s. George R. and Fanny (McPherson) D.; ed. public schools; m. Mary Chiles, 1899; children—John M., Mary Frances (Mrs. Theodore Gould). With Cincinnati, Washington & Baltimore R.R., 1883-87, B.&O. R.R., 1887-90, Tate, Muller & Co. (grain export), Baltimore, Md., 1890-91; pres. Louis Muller & Co., 1891-1914; pres. Union Trust Co. of Md., 1914-1933; v.p. Belvedere Hotel Co., Claiborne-Annapolis Ferry Co.; dir. numerous cos. State treas. of Md., 1916—. Treas. and mem. bd. of regents U. of Md.; chmn. and treas. bd. trustees Teachers' Retirement System, Md.; mem. Md. State Bd. Agr., State Bd. Pub. Works; mem. advisory bd. Mt. Vernon Ladies Assn. Democrat. Episcopalian. Home: Riderwood, Md. Died Oct. 16, 1936.

DENNIS, Louis Munroe, chemist; b. Chicago, May 26, 1863; s. Joseph S. and Faustina (Munroe) D.; Ph.B., U. of Mich., 1885, B.S. (Chem.), 1886; D.Sc., Colgate, 1923; D.Sc., U. of Mich., 1926; advanced study at U. of Munich, Polytechnikum of Dresden and of Aix-la-Chapelle, and pvt. lab. of Fresenius, Wiesbaden; m. Minnie Clark, Aug. 25, 1887; children—Faustine, Clark M., Frank S. Instr. chemistry, 1887-89, asst. prof., 1891-93, asso. prof. inorganic and analyt. chemistry, 1893-1900, prof. inorganic chemistry from 1900, head dept. of chemistry, 1903-1933 (emeritus), Cornell. Mem. Com. of Nat. Research Council on design of laboratories of chemistry. Fellow A.A.A.S. Author: Elementary Chemistry (with Frank W. Clarke), 1902; Laboratory Manual of Elementary Chemistry (with same), 1902; Manual of Qualitative Analysis (with Theodore Whittlesey), 1902; Gas Analysis, 1913; Gas Analysis (with M. L. Nichols), 1929; Laboratory Manual and Problems (with A. W. Laubengayer); The Baker Laboratory of Chemistry at Cornell. Home: Ithaca, N.Y. Died Dec. 9, 1936.

DENNIS, Samuel Shepard, trustee and dir.; b. Newark, N.J., Sept. 11, 1852; s. Alfred Lewis and Eliza (Shepard) D.; bro. of James Shepard and Frederic Shepard D.; prep. edn. Phillips Acad., Andover, Mass.; entered Yale, class of 1874, but obliged to withdraw on account of ill health; m. Eliza Thomas, Apr. 15, 1884. Traveled extensively in Europe and the Orient, and on return became connected with hardware firm of Gifford & Beach, New York; retired, 1880, to devote attention to father's estate; pres. Howard Savings Instn. of Newark, United N.J. R.R. & Canal Co.; dir. numerous cos. Trustee Dennis Library (Newton, N.J.). Republican. Episcopalian. Home: Morristown, N.J. Died Apr. 12, 1924.

DENNIS, William B., mining engr.; b. Cincinnati, Dec. 8, 1865; s. Rev. Mendenhall John and Sophia D.; A.B., Central U. of Ky., 1884; m. Queen H., d. Capt. D. M. Littlefield, of Port Townsend, Wash., June 1900. Entered newspaper work at Dayton, O., as spl. corr. Dayton Daily Journal and other papers; pub. The Farmers' Home, 1885-90; editor and mgr. Port Townsend (Wash.) Leader (daily and weekly), 1890-92; was several yrs. pres. and gen. mgr. Eureka-Pacific Consol. Mining Co. of Idaho; pres. and gen. mgr. Black Butte Quicksilver Mine of Ore.; v.p., mgr. Carlton & Coast R.R. Co.; v.p., mgr. Carlton Consol. Lumber Co. Inventor of The Dennis Roasting Furnace. Chmn. Ore. State Bur Mines and Geology, 1917-25; mem. Ore. State Bd. of Engring. Examiners, 1919-31; rep. from Yamhill Co. in Ore. Ho. of Rep., 1919-20. Home: Carlton, Ore. Died Jan. 7, 1937.

DENNIS, William Henry, lawyer; b. Phila., Feb. 21, 1856; s. Edward Griscom and Katharine (Matthews) D.; A.B., Georgetown Coll., D.C., 1874, LL.B., 1876, A.M., 1882; m. Lula Lee Hughlett, June 20, 1901. Deputy register of Wills, D.C., 1876-86; asso. in practice in Washington with Enoch Totten until his death, 1898, then in gen. practice; trustee of estates. Dir. Carroll Inst., D.C.; pres. Washington Council Catholic Benevolent Legion. Author: Probate Law of District of Columbia, 1880. Home: Washington, D.C. Died Mar. 23, 1919.

DENNISON, E(dwin) Haldeman, foreign service officer; b. Columbus, O., Oct. 28, 1872; s. Neil and Mary (Haldeman) D. (grandson of William D., gov. of Ohio and postmaster gen. U.S.); educated St. Paul's Sch., Concord, N.H., 1885-91, and Sheffield Scientific Sch., Yale; m. Lucie Tessier, of Quebec, P.Q., Oct. 30, 1908. Consul at Rimouski, P.Q., Can., 1903-06; at Bombay, Nov. 1, 1906-Feb. 9, 1911; at

Dundee, Scotland, Mar. 15, 1911-Oct. 1915; consul gen. at Christiania, Norway, Oct. 1915-Apr. 1917; consul at Birmingham, Eng., Apr. 1917-Mar. 15, 1919, at Quebec, Can., Mar. 15, 1919—. Home: Columbus, O. Died Mar. 22, 1931.

DENNISON, Walter, univ. prof.; b. Saline, Mich., Aug. 9, 1869; s. James L. and Eliza J. (Flowers) D.; A.B., U. of Mich., 1893, A.M., 1894, Ph.D., 1897; studied and traveled abroad, chiefly in Italy, 1894-97; studied U. of Bonn portion of 1894-95; fellow Am. Sch. Classical Studies, Rome, 1895-97; m. Anna L. Green, Aug. 5, 1891. Instr. Latin, U. of Mich., 1897-99; prof. Latin and Roman archæology, Oberlin Coll., 1899-1902; jr. prof. Latin, U. of Mich., 1902-10; prof. Greek and Latin, Swarthmore Coll., 1910—. Prof. Latin, Am. Sch. Classical Studies in Rome, 1908-09. Author: A Junior Latin Book (with John C. Rolfe), 1898; Livy, Book I and Selections from Books II-X, 1908. Home: Swarthmore, Pa. Died Mar. 18, 1917.

DENNISTON, Henry Martyn, rear adm.; b. Washingtonville, N.Y., June 13, 1840; s. Robert and Mary (Scott) D.; ed. at home and at Yale, 1858-61, leaving in beginning of senior yr., A.B., 1862, A.M., 1892; m. Emma J. Dusenbury, Jan. 21, 1869. Entered U.S.N. pay corps, Sept. 9, 1861; promoted paymaster, Apr. 14, 1862, pay insp., Aug. 19, 1876, pay dir., July 31, 1884; retired June 13, 1902, with rank of rear admiral. Presbyn. Republican. Home: Dobbs Ferry, N.Y. Died May 23, 1922.

DENNY, Frank Lee, officer U.S. Marine Corps; b. Indianapolis, Ind., July 20, 1858; s. James Cook D. (atty. gen. Ind.) and Caroline D., d. John Wesley Davis, speaker U.S. Ho. of Rep.; m. Julia Graham, d. Gen. Innis Nelson Palmer, U.S.A., Oct. 6, 1886. Apptd. 2d lt. U.S. Marine Corps, June, 1880, 1st lt., Dec., 1884; capt. asst. q.m., Feb., 1892; maj. q.m., June, 1897; col. chief q.m., Mar., 1899. Had 6 yrs. sea service; shore service Alexandria, Egypt, 1882, after British bombardment, Isthmus Panama, 1885, Spanish-Am. War; voluntarily retired, May 1, 1913, after 30 yrs.' service. Now v.p. Real Estate Trust Co., Washington. Home: Washington, D.C. Died July 8, 1914.

DE NORMANDIE, James, clergyman; b. Newport, Bucks Co., Pa., June 9, 1836; s. Dr. James and Sarah (Yardley) D.; A.B., Antioch Coll., 1858, A.M., 1861; B.D., Harvard, 1862 (S.T.D., Harvard, 1898); m. Emily F. Jones, Oct. 27, 1864. Entered Unitarian ministry, 1862; pastor South Parish, Portsmouth, N.H., 1862-83, First Ch., Roxbury, Mass., 1883-1918 (emeritus). Editor Unitarian Review, 1879-86. Trustee, Boston Pub. Library; pres. various philanthropical orgns. Author: Life of Harriet Ryan Albee; Beauty of Wisdom. Home: Lincoln, Mass. Died Oct. 6, 1924.

DENSLOW, William Wallace, illustrator; b. Phila., Pa., May 5, 1856; s. William Wallace and Jane Eva D.; ed. New York, until 1872; studied drawing at Cooper Inst., winters of 1871-72; 2 winters Nat. Acad. Design, 1873-74; m. Mrs. Frances Doolittle, Dec. 24, 1903. Began illustrating, 1872; has traveled all over U.S. while engaged as illustrator on the prin. Am. newspapers. Has worked considerably for Elbert Hubbard of E. Aurora at "Roycroft Shop." Among his best known pictures are "What's the Use?" and "Victory"; illustrations to The Picture Gallery of the Great Lakes, 1898; illustrated An Arkansas Planter, by Opie Read; A Cruise Under the Crescent; Father Goose, His Book; The Wonderful Wizard of Oz; Denslow's Mother Goose, 1901; Denslow's Night Before Christmas, 1902; Denslow's Picture Books for Children, 18 vols., 1903; The Pearl and the Pumpkin (joint author with Paul West, and illustrator), 1904; Billy Bounce (illustrator and joint author with D. A. Bragdon); When I Grow Up, 1909. Designed costumes and scenery for plays "Wizard of Oz" and "The Pearl and The Pumpkin." His "totem" (sign) is the "Hippocampus," or sea horse. Died 1915.

DENSMORE, Emmet, physician; b. Blooming Valley, Pa., May 19, 1837; s. Joel and Sophia D.; ed. Allegheny Coll., Meadville, Pa.; M.D., Univ. Med. Coll. (New York U.), 1885; m. Elizabeth Floyd Heard, 1855; m. 2d, Helen Barnard, 1881; 3d, Mabelle Hoff, Oct., 1905. Associated with brothers in development and production of petroleum at Oil Creek, Pa., 1861-64; inventors of first tank cars by which oil was shipped to seaboard; associated with brother James in developing typewriter invented by C. Latham Scholes and afterwards known as the Remington; in 1872, introduced Remington typewriter into London; afterwards coöperated with brother Amos in development of Densmore typewriter. Principal propr. Garfield Tea Co. Author: Sex Equality. Home: New York, N.Y. Died 1911.

DENSMORE, Hiram D., botanist; b. Richmond, Wis., Jan. 20, 1862; A.B., Beloit (Wis.) Coll., 1886, M.A., 1890, D.Sc. (hon.), 1932; studied Cornell U., 1887-88, U. of Calif., 1896, Harvard, 1916; m. Effie Morse, 1889; children—Margaret, Dorothy, Janet, Theodora. Prof. botany, Beloit Coll., 1889, emeritus. Congllst. Author: General Botany (text), 1920; Laboratory and Field Exercises in Botany, 1920. Home: Beloit, Wis. Died July 18, 1940.

DENSON, Nimrod Davis, judge; b. Russell Co., Ala., June 20, 1856; s. Augustus R. and Elizabeth Ivey D.; ed. Ala. Poly. Inst.; LL.D., Howard Coll., Ala.; m. Carrie E. Vernon, Dec. 19, 1883; children—John Vernon, Nimrod Davis, Mrs. Luphelia Hine, Mrs. Mary Samford. Admitted to bar, 1876; mem. Ala. Senate, 1884-88; judge Circuit Court, 1892-1904; asso. justice Supreme Court of Ala., 1904-09; resumed practice at La Fayette, Ala., 1909; later practiced at Opelika, Ala.; judge 5th Judicial Circuit, Ala., Nov. 1924—. Democrat. Mem. Ala. Commn. for Memorial to Soldiers in World War. Home: Opelika, Ala. Died Mar. 25, 1927.

DENSON, Samuel Crawford, lawyer; b. Adams Co., Ill., Sept. 23, 1839; s. John and Emily Ann (Crawford) D.; ed. Abington (Ill.) Coll.; m. Mary M., d. Judge H. D. Beatty, of Calif., and sister of Chief Justice William H. Beatty, of Calif., July 1866 (dec.); m. 2d, Laura M. Ames, June 3, 1891. Was law partner of Hon. W. H. Beatty, and later of Hon. John J. De Haven; now head of Denson, Cooley & Denson; dir. and gen. counsel Pacific Coast Steel Co., Pacific Surety Co.; spl. counsel Merchants' Nat. Bank. Judge 6th Dist. Ct., Calif., 1876-81; judge Superior Ct., Sacramento Co., Calif., 1881-83; mem. Nev. Ho. of Rep., 1885-86; dist. atty. Ormsby Co., Nev., 1886-88. Col. and judge adv. on staff of Gov. George C. Perkins, of Calif., 1880-83. Trustee San Francisco Normal Sch., 1892-1904. Republican. Mason. Home: Easton, Calif. Died July 1917.

DENT, Marmaduke Herbert, jurist; b. Granville, W.Va., Apr. 18, 1849; s. Marshall Mortimer and Carrie (Roberts) D.; grad. W.Va. Univ., 1870; studied law, and admitted to W.Va. bar, 1875; m. Mary Jones Warder, Oct. 10, 1876. Judge Sup. Ct. of Appeals, W.Va., 1893-1904. Democrat. Presbyn. Author: Socialism Resistless. Home: Grafton, W.Va. Died 1909.

DENT, Stanley Hubert, lawyer; b. Eufaula, Ala., Aug. 16, 1869; s. Stouton Hubert and Anna Beall (Young) D.; A.B., Southern U., Greensboro, Ala., 1886; LL.B., U. of Va., 1889; m. Etta Tinsley, June 23, 1897; 1 son, William Tinsley. Practiced first at Eufaula, now at Montgomery; apptd. pros. atty. Montgomery Co., Ala., Dec. 1902, elected, 1904 (resigned, 1909); mem. 61st to 66th Congresses (1909-21), 2d Ala. Dist. Chmn. Com. on Mil. Affairs, 64th Congress, 2d session, and 65th Congress, covering the entire period of the war. Democrat. Methodist. Unanimously chosen pres. of the Constitutional Conv., Ala., for repeal of 18th amendment, 1933; apptd. by Ala. Supreme Ct. to codify laws of Ala., 1936. Home: Montgomery, Ala. Died Oct. 6, 1938.

DENTON, George Kirkpatrick, congressman; b. Webster Co., Ky., Nov. 17, 1864; s. George M. and Emma (Kirkpatrick) D.; A.B., Ohio Wesleyan U., 1891; LL.B., Boston U., 1893 (valedictorian); m. Sara L. Chick, Dec. 16, 1895. Practiced in Evansville, Ind., 1894—; gen. counsel and dir. Intermediate Life Ins. Co. Mem. 65th Congress (1917-19), 1st Ind. Dist. Democrat. Methodist. Home: Evansville, Ind. Died Jan. 4, 1926.

DENTON, James Edgar, mech. engr.; b. Piermont, N.Y., 1855; ed. pub. schs. and bus. coll.; grad. Stevens Inst. Tech., 1875. Asst. instr. and lecturer, 1875-98, prof. mech. engring. and shopwork many yrs. from 1898, Stevens Inst. Tech. (emeritus). Engaged in mfg. rock-drilling machinery, 1882-86; constructed about 3 miles of the new Croton Aqueduct tunnel. Mem. Jury Awards in engring., Chicago Expn., 1893. Home: Maplewood, N.J. Died July 1928.

DENYES, John Russell, missionary, educator; b. Brookfield, Mo., Jan. 24, 1869; s. Lawrence Stover and Mary Ann (Riggs) D.; prep. edn., normal sch. and acad.; B.A., Northwestern U., 1895; S.T.B., Garrett Bibl. Inst., 1897; D.D., Garrett Bibl. Inst., 1912; m. Mary Jane Owens, Dec. 9, 1897; children—Mary Elizabeth, Lawrence Owens, Ruth, Russell Owens. Ordained M.E. ministry, 1897; went to Singapore, 1897; founded Meth. mission work in Java, 1905; supt. Meth. missions in Java, Sumatra and Borneo, 1907-12; sent by Chinese Chamber of Commerce in Java to study ednl. work and the revolutionary movement in China, 1911; del. from Malaysia to Gen. Conf. M.E. Ch. at Minneapolis, Minn., 1912; dir. edn. for M.E. Ch. in Malaysia, 1913-16; lecturer for Bd. of Foreign Missions, 1917-19; prof. missions, Drew Theol. Sem., 1919-20; financial agt., Wesley Foundation, Madison, Wis., 1921-23; prof. religion and missions, Lawrence Coll., Appleton, Wis., Sept. 1923—. Del. from West Wis. Conf. to Gen. Conf. M.E. Church at Kansas City, 1928. Republican. Mason. Home: Appleton, Wis. Died Jan. 22, 1936.

DE PENA, Carlos Maria, diplomat; b. 1852; grad. Dr. Law and Social Sciences, U. of Montevideo, S.A., 1876; (LL.D., New York U., 1913); practiced law at Montevideo from 1876; prof. polit. economy and administrative law, 1885-1911, now hon. prof., and several yrs. dean, Sch. of Law and Social Sciences, U. of Montevideo. Mayor of Montevideo, 1889, 1890; pres. municipal census commn., 1889; was sec. of treas., Uruguay, 1890; chmn. 1st Nat. Rural Congress, 1896, and minister pub. wks., industry and pub. instrn., 1899; pres. financial commn. Montevideo harbor, to 1911; pres. commn. which organized and directed nat. census, 1907-08; spl. and confidential envoy to Brazil, 1907; del. and v.p. Uruguayan Delegation Pan-Am. Conf., Buenos Aires, 1911; E.E. and M.P. to United States, May 31, 1911. Died Apr. 30, 1918.

DEPEW, Chauncey Mitchell, senator; b. Peekskill, N.Y., Apr. 23, 1834; s. Isaac and Martha (Mitchell) D.; A.B., Yale, 1856 (LL.D., 1887); m. Elise Hegeman, Nov. 9, 1871 (died 1893); 2d, May Palmer, Dec., 1901. Admitted to bar, 1858; mem. N.Y. Assembly, 1861-62; sec. of state of N.Y., 1863; apptd. and confirmed U.S. minister to Japan, but declined. Defeated for lt. gov. N.Y. on Liberal Rep. ticket, 1872. Atty. for N.Y. & Harlem R.R., 1866; for N.Y.C.&H.R. R.R., 1869, gen. counsel, 1875, 2d v.p. same, 1882, pres. same, 1885-98; also pres., until 1898, West Shore R.R. From 1898 chmn. bd. dirs. New York Central R.R. Director Western Union Telegraph Co., West Shore R.R., C.&N.W. Railway Co., C.,St.P.,M.&O. Railway Co., C.,C.,C.&St.Louis Railway Co., Canada Southern Railway Co., and numerous railway, banking and other corps. Regent U. State of N.Y., 1877-1904; declined elections as U.S. senator, 1885; declined appmt. as Sec. of State in cabinet of Pres. Benjamin Harrison; received 99 votes for presidential nomination, Rep. Nat. Conv., 1888; del.-at-large Rep. Nat. convs., 1888, 92, 96, 1900, 04, and to all succeeding convs., including 1924 (placed Benjamin Harrison in nomination for the Presidency, 1888, and Gov. Morton, 1896); U.S. senator, 1899-1905, 1905-11. Orator at unveiling of Statue of Liberty in New York Harbor; at centennial celebration of inauguration of George Washington; at opening of Chicago Expn., 1893. Home: New York, N.Y. Died Apr. 5, 1928.

DE PEYSTER, Frederic James, lawyer; b. New York, Feb. 5, 1839; s. Capt. James Ferguson and Frances Goodhue (Ashton) DeP.; A.M., Coll. City of New York; LL.B., LL.M., Columbia Law School; m. Augusta McEvers, d. William H. Morris, Oct. 10, 1871. Pres. Archæol. Soc. from its foundation until 1889 (mem. council); treas. Am. School classical studies, 1881; lecturer on hist. and archeol. subjects; pres., 1892, St. Nicholas Soc.; New York Dispensary; Orphan Soc.; chmn. N.Y. Soc. Library; trustee Instn. for Deaf and Dumb and of the Home for Incurables. Home: Lakewood, N.J. Died 1905.

DE PEYSTER, John Watts, soldier, author; b. New York, March 9, 1821; s. Frederic de Peyster (of Holland and Huguenot descent) and Mary Justina, d. Hon. John Watts (of Scotch and Huguenot descent); ed. Columbia Univ., but was not graduated because of ill health (A.M., same, 1872; LL.D., Neb. Coll., 1870; Litt.D., 1892; LL.D., 1896; Ph.D., 1899, Franklin & Marshall Coll.); elected col. N.Y. State inf., 1846; assigned to command 22d regimental dist., N.Y., 1849; apptd. brig. gen. N.G.S.N.Y., 1851; mil. agt., State of N.Y., in Europe (endorsed by U.S.A.), 1851-53; assisted in organizing present police system, New York, and made first reports favoring paid fire dept., 1852-53; adj. gen. State of N.Y., 1855; bvtd. maj. gen. State of N.Y., "for meritorious services," by spl. act of legislature, 1866. His hundreds of published works include Life of Leonard Torstenson, Field Marshal Generalissimo of Sweden, 1855; The Dutch at the North Pole and the Dutch in Maine, 1857; Carausius, the Dutch Augustus, 1858; The Ancient, Mediæval and Modern Netherlanders, 1859; Life of Lieut. Gen. Menno, Baron Cohorn, 1860; Personal and Military History of Maj. Gen. Philip Kearny, 1869; The Pearl of Pearls (novel), 1865; Bothwell (hist. drama), 1884. Home: Tivoli, N.Y. Died 1907.

DEPONAI, John Martin, editor; b. Washington, D.C., Feb. 28, 1871; s. Martin John and Mary Agatha (von Ruhl) D.; A.B., St. John's Coll., Washington, D.C., 1888; (hon. A.M., Rock Hill Coll., Md., "for work in journalism and philanthropy"); m. May Elinor Macarthy, Aug. 27, 1898. Reporter, Gazette, Washington, D.C., 1892; local editor Nat. Democrat, 1893-94; city editor, Washington Times, 1898-99; city editor, the World, Baltimore, 1899-1900, mng. editor, 1900-03; asst. city editor, American, Baltimore, 1903-07, news editor, 1907-08; asst. mng. editor Baltimore Star, 1908-11, editor, 1911—. Mem. exec. com. Md. Home-Coming Assn., 1907; mng. dir. Star Spangled Banner Centennial, Sept., 1914 (presented silver service by City of Baltimore for "meritorious and distinguished service" in connection with this celebration); apptd. by mayor del. to New York Commercial Tercentenary, 1914. Founder Skin and Cancer Hosp., Baltimore, and 1st pres., 1912-15 (dir.). Democrat. Catholic. Home: Baltimore, Md. Died Oct. 11, 1917.

DEPUE, David A., chief justice Supreme Court, N.J., May 1, 1900—; b. Northampton Co., Pa., Oct. 27, 1826; grad. Princeton, 1846 (LL.D., Rutgers, 1874; Princeton, 1880). Admitted to bar, N.J., 1849; asso. justice Supreme Court, N.J., 1866-1900. Home: Newark, N.J. Died 1902.

DE PUY, William Harrison, M.E. clergyman; b.

Penn Yan, N.Y., Oct. 31, 1821; s. James De Puy; ed. Lima, N.Y., and grad. Genesee Coll., A.M. (D.D., Union Univ.; LL.D., Mt. Union Coll.); ordained to M.E. ministry, 1845; m. Harriet D. Adams, 1841. Asso. editor New York Christian Advocate nearly 25 yrs.; editor Methodist Year Book, 1866-89. Died 1901.

DERBY, George Strong, ophthalmologist; b. Boston, May 29, 1875; s. Hasket and Sarah (Mason) D.; A.B., Harvard, 1896; M.D., Harvard Med. Sch., 1900; surg. interne, Mass. Gen. Hosp., 1900-01; student in pathology and ophthalmology, Austria, Germany, Holland, France and England, 1901-02; m. Mary Brewster Brown, Aug. 5, 1901. Ophthalmic chief, Mass. Charitable Eye and Ear Infirmary; prof. ophthalmology, Harvard Med. Sch.; mem. advisory com. Mass. Commn. for the Blind. Served in M.C., U.S.A., May 5, 1917-Feb. 8, 1919; commd. lt. col., Oct. 1919; asst. consultant in ophthalmology, A.E.F., July 1918-Feb. 1919. Episcopalian. Home: Boston, Mass. Died Dec. 12, 1931.

DERBY, Samuel Carroll, univ. prof.; b. Dublin, N.H., March 3, 1842; s. Dexter and Julia (Piper) D.; A.B., Harvard, 1866, A.M., 1877; grad. student Harvard, 1876-77, 1892-93; at Johns Hopkins, 1880-81; Am. Sch. at Rome, 1903-04, 1913-14; m. Eunice H. Ransom, Aug. 29, 1872; 2d, Frances G. Janney, Dec. 27, 1883; 3d Margaret E. Leonard, Aug. 29, 1903. Taught in pub. and pvt. schs., 1866-70; prof. Latin lang. and lit., 1870-76, pres., 1877-81, Antioch Coll., Ohio; prof. Latin and Greek, 1881-83, prof. Latin, 1883—, dean Coll. Arts, Philosophy and Science, 1896 98, Ohio State U. Unitarian. Home: Columbus, O. Died Mar. 28, 1921.

DERCUM, Francis X., neurologist; b. Philadelphia, Pa., Aug. 10, 1856; s. Ernest and Susanna (Erhart) D.; grad. Central High Sch.; M.D., U. of Pa., 1877, Ph.D., 1877; A.M., Central High Sch., 1878; Sc.D., Jefferson Medical College, 1927; m. Elizabeth Comly, Aug. 5, 1891; children—Elizabeth Comly (Mrs. Samuel Wright Mifflin), Ernest Comly (dec.), Mary DeHaven. Began practice at Phila., 1877; prof. nervous and mental diseases, Jefferson Med. Coll., 1892-1925 (emeritus); cons. neurologist, Phila. Gen. Hosp. Mem. Med. Advisory Bd., lecturer to Army and Navy Med. Corps and mem. Med. R.C., World War. Fellow Coll. Physicians of Phila. Decorated Chevalier Legion of Honor (France). Republican. Author: Rest, Suggestion and Other Therapeutic Measures in Nervous and Mental Diseases; A Clinical Manual of Mental Diseases; Hysteria and Accident Compensation, 1916; The Biology of the Internal Secretions, 1924; The Physiology of Mind, 1925. Editor: Text book of Nervous Diseases by American Authors, 1895. Described the disease known as adiposis dolorosa (Dercum's disease). Home: Philadelphia, Pa. Died Apr. 23, 1931.

DE REMER, John A., lawyer; b. Charlton, N.Y., Oct. 14, 1835; s. William and Sarah J. (Harmon) D.; A.B., Union Coll., 1857, A.M., 1860; m. Laura C. Waring, June 12, 1888. Adj. prof. mathematics, Union Coll., 1858-66; admitted to bar, 1867; and began practice at Schenectady; pres. Mohawk Nat. Bank. Postmaster Schenectady, 1871-75 and 1881-85. Republican. Trustee Union Coll., 1885—. Home: Schenectady, N.Y. Died 1907.

DE RESZKE, Edouard, operatic singer; b. Varsovie, Poland, Dec. 22, 1853; studied under Ciaffei and Coletti; début Theatre des Italiens, Paris, as the King in "Aida," April 22, 1876; later sang at Turin, Milan and other European cities; London début as Indra in Royal Italian Opera, April 13, 1880, remaining there 4 seasons. Has appeared in grand opera, Europe and U.S., talking basso rôles. Died May 30, 1917.

DERIEUX, Samuel Arthur, writer; b. Richmond, Va., Nov. 5, 1881; s. Rev. William Thomas and Lottie (Bookhart) D.; student Wofford Coll., Spartanburg, S.C., 1897-99; B.A., Richmond (Va.) Coll., 1904; studied Johns Hopkins, 1906-08; M.A., U. of Chicago, 1910; m. Mary Ida Wiley, Aug. 23, 1911. Successively asst. prof. English, Richmond Coll., 1910-11, Mo. State Normal Sch., 1911-13. Wake Forest (N.C.) Coll., 1915-17; editorial Staff American Magazine, 1917—. Democrat. Baptist. Home: New York, N.Y. Died Feb. 26, 1922.

DERN, George Henry, secretary of war; b. Dodge Co., Neb., Sept. 8, 1872; s. John and Elizabeth (Dern) D.; grad. Fremont (Neb.) Normal Coll., 1888; student U. of Neb., 1893, 94; m. Charlotte Brown, June 7, 1899; children—Mary Joanna (Mrs. Harry Baxter), John, Louise (dec.), William Brown, Margaret (dec.), Elizabeth Ida, James George. Began mining in Utah, 1894; treas. Mercur Gold Mining & Milling Co., 1894-1900; gen. mgr. Consol. Mercur Gold Mines Co., 1900-13; mgr. various other metal mining enterprises; v.p. and gen. mgr. Holt-Christensen Process Co. (owner Holt-Dern patents). Mem. Utah Senate, 1915-23; mem. State Council of Defense, World War; gov. of Utah, 1925-32; chmn. Governors' Conf., 1929, 30; secretary of war, Mar. 4, 1933—. Democrat. Congregationalist. Mason. Joint inventor, with Theodore P. Holt, of Holt-Dern ore roaster. Was author of Workmen's Compensation Law, Corrupt Practices Act, State Mineral Land Leasing Law, etc. Home: Washington, D.C. Died Aug. 27, 1936.

DERN, John, capitalist; b. nr. Giessen, Hessen-Darmstadt, Germany, Oct. 24, 1850; s. John and Katherine M. D.; studied at Giessen; m. Elizabeth Dern, of Hessen-Darmstadt, Dec. 1870. Farming in Dodge Co., Neb., 1869-80; grain and lumber business at Scribner, Fremont, Hooper, Neb. State senator, 1889; treas. Dodge Co., 1890, 2 terms; May 1894, became mgr. Mercur Gold Mining & Milling Co., Salt Lake City; pres. Consolidated Mercur Gold Mines Co., Feb. 1902—; pres. Callaway-Hoock & Francis; v.p. of National Copper Bank, Bankers Trust Co.; pres. May Day Mining & Milling Co., Uncle Sam Consolidated Mining Co., Fremont (Neb.) Beverage Co., Gibson Commercial Co.; v.p. Dixie Power Co. Mem. State Capitol Bldg. Commn.; trustee Agrl. Coll. of Utah. Home: Salt Lake City, Utah. Died Jan. 2, 1922.

DE ROALDÈS, Arthur Washington, surgeon; b. Opelousas, St. Landry Parish, La., Jan. 25, 1849; s. Abel (M.D.) and Coralie Testas de Folmont D.; ed. by Jesuits in France; grad. in letters, 1865, in science, 1866, U. of France; M.D., U. of La., 1869, U. of Paris, 1870. Asst. surgeon 6th Internat. Ambulance Corps, Franco-German War; mentioned for bravery at Battle of Beaumont-Mouzon, for which was subsequently decorated with Cross of the Legion of Honor; surgeon Red Cross Soc. during outbreak of French Commune; returned to New Orleans, 1872; m. Laura Pandely, 1873 (died 1874); m. 2d, Annie E., d. Hon. Henry C. Miller, judge of Supreme Court of La., 1885. In charge of Charity Hosp. of La., 1880-83; founded 1889, Eye, Ear, Nose and Throat Hosp. of New Orleans, of which became trustee and surgeon-in-chief; emeritus prof. diseases ear, nose and throat, Post-Grad. Dept. Tulane U. of La. Mem. Internat. Med. congresses, Berlin, 1890, Rome, 1894, Paris, 1900, Internat. congresses Otology, Florence, 1895, London, 1899 (mem. Am. Com. of Organization 7th Otol. Congress, Bordeaux, 1904); v.p. La. State Med. Soc., 1892; pres. New Orleans Diphtheria Antitoxin Commn., 1894; fellow Am. Laryngol. Assn. (pres. 1906-07). Officer Legion d'Honneur of France, 1903, in recognition of services rendered indigent sick and med. edn. by his hosp. foundation; awarded the "Picayune Loving Cup," by the Progressive Union of New Orleans, 1905, "for the most meritorious services rendered the community during that year," the French Govt. offering at the same time a magnificent vase de Sevres to his foundation, which also received, subsequently, gifts from the govts. of Italy, Spain, Germany and Russia for gratuitous services rendered their respective indigent sick; promoted Comdr. Legion of Honor, France, 1906; Comdr. Order of St. Gregory the Great, by Pope Pius X; made Knight Order of Saints Maurice and Lazare, by King of Italy, 1909. Home: New Orleans, La. Died June 12, 1918.

DE ROSSET, Frederick Ancrum, clergyman; b. Wilmington, N.C., Apr. 13, 1856; s. Armand John (M.D.) and Eliza Jane (Lord) D.; student U. of the South, 1872-79, M.A., 1878; Gen. Theol. Sem., New York, 1879-82; m. Mary Williams Green, Oct. 10, 1882. Deacon, 1880, priest, 1882, P.E. Ch.; curate Holy Trinity Ch., Harlem, St. Thomas, New York, St. Andrew's, Harlem, St. George's, New York, 1880-81, Zion Ch., Wappinger's Falls, N.Y., 1881-83; tutored at St. John's Sch., Manlius, N.Y., and curate at Larchmont, N.Y., 1883; curate Calvary Ch., New York, 1883-84, St. Mark's, Grand Rapids, Mich., 1884-87; rector Trinity Ch., Natchez, Miss., 1887-92, Ch. of the Redeemer, Cairo, Ill., 1892-1901, and archdeacon of Cairo; rector St. Paul's pro-cathedral and archdeacon of Springfield, 1901-10; again rector Cairo, June 29, 1910-13; rector Ch. Holy Communion, Charleston, S.C., Feb. 1, 1913—. Sec. standing com. diocese of Springfield; hon. and organizing sec. for U.S.A. of the Jerusalem and the East Mission. In charge Orphanage of the Holy Child, Springfield, Ill.; treas. Province of Ill.; sec. joint commn. on ecclesiastical relations of Gen. Conv., 1898—. Mason. Home: Charleston, S.C. Died Oct. 12, 1915.

DERR, Cyrus George, lawyer; b. Lebanon, Pa., July 13, 1848; s. William M. and Caroline (Hildebrand) D.; ed. law dept. U. of Pa. and in father's law office; m. Mary Virginia, d. late Gen. John Weidman, of Lebanon, Pa., Nov. 13, 1870. Admitted to Pa. bar, 1869; atty. for Pa. R.R. Co. and many other corps.; founded Pa. Trust Co. (Reading, Pa.), Columbian Warehouse Co.; developed and controls Columbian Cutlery Co. Enlisted in Co. E, 26th Regt. Pa. Emergency Men, June 1863; taken prisoner nr. Gettysburg, Pa., June 26, 1863; paroled; reënlisted July 12, 1864, Co. G, 1st Battalion, Pa. Inf.; hon. discharged at end of service. Republican. Home: Reading, Pa. Died July 25, 1933.

DERR, Louis, physicist; b. Pottsville, Pa., Aug. 6, 1868; s. Simon and Sarah Ann (Sieger) D.; B.A., Amherst, 1889, M.A., 1892; S.B., Mass. Inst. Tech., 1892; student Harvard Grad. Sch., 1892-93; m. Jane E. Coy, June 7, 1893. Asst. in physics, 1892-93, instr., 1893-1901, asst. prof., 1901-04, asso. prof., 1904-09, prof. from 1909, Mass. Inst. Tech. Instr. physics, Boston U., 1893-98; in charge of instruction in physics, Boston Noraml Sch. of Gymnastics, 1895-1908. Fellow Am. Acad. Arts and Sciences, Royal Photo. Soc. Gt. Britain. Author: Notes on the Principles of Dynamo and Transformer Design, 1902; Photography for Students of Physics and Chemistry, 1906. Home: Brookline, Mass. Died May 11, 1923.

DE RUSSY, Isaac Denniston, brig. gen.; b. Ft. Monroe, Va., June 13, 1840; s. René Edward (U.S.A.) and Ann Alida D.; ed. Episcopal High Sch., Alexandria, Va., and Rutgers Coll.; m. Laura Lee Requa, May 19, 1891. Apptd. from N.Y., 2d lt., 1st Inf., U.S.A., Apr. 27, 1861; promoted through grades to col., 11th Inf., May 19, 1891; brig. gen., Apr. 1, 1902; retired Apr. 15, 1902, at own request, after 40 yrs.' service. Served in Puerto Rican campaign and in P.I. Bvtd. maj., Mar. 13, 1865, "for faithful and meritorious services during the war." Home: New York, N.Y. Died Feb. 16, 1923.

de SCHWEINITZ, Paul, bishop Moravian Ch.; b. Salem, N.C., Mar. 16, 1863; s. Robert de and Marie Louise von (Tschirschky) S.; A.B., Moravian Coll. and Theol. Sem., Bethlehem, Pa., 1882, B.D., 1884 (D.D., 1907); studied U. of Halle, Germany, 1885-86; m. Mary C. Daniel, Jan. 27, 1887; children—Karl, Mrs. Helena Couch, Dorothea, Mrs. Louise Darrow. Ordained Moravian ministry, 1886; home missionary, Northfield, Minn., 1886-90; pastor Nazareth, Pa., 1890-98; sec. of Missions of Moravian Ch. in America, 1898-1930. Treas. governing bd. Northern Province Moravian Ch., v.p. Bd. Ch. Extension, treas. Soc. of U.B. for Propagating the Gospel among the Heathen, treas., trustee Moravian Coll. and Theol. Sem., all 1893-1935; advisory trustee Moravian Sem. and Coll. for Women, 1898-1930; treas. of three Moravian Corporations, 1898-1937; treas. Moravian Missions, 1898-1937. Consecrated a bishop Moravian Church, Mar. 14, 1937. Trustee St. Luke's Hospital (Bethlehem, Pa.), 1915—. Vice-pres. Moravian Hist. Soc.; pres. Huguenot Soc., Pa., 1927-29; a founder Pa. German Soc. (pres. 1919-20). Del. World's Missionary Conf., New York, 1900, Missionary Conf., Edinburgh, Scotland, 1910; pres. Fgn. Missions Conf. of N.A., 1917-18; chmn. exec. bd. Fgn. Missions Conf. of N.A., 1920-22; mem. Internat. Missionary Council, 1920-28. Dir. Lehigh Valley Nat. Bank, Bethlehem, Pa., 1916; mem. bd. mgrs. Farmers' Fire Ins. Co. of Upper and Lower Saucon Townships, 1922—, pres., 1930—; also dir. sundry local corps. Republican. Home: Bethlehem, Pa. Died Feb. 8, 1940.

DESHA, Mary, teacher; b. Lexington, Ky.; d. of Dr. John Randolph and Mary Bracken (Curry) D.; ed. Sayre Inst. and Ky. State Coll., Lexington. Teacher Ky. pub. schs. 12 yrs.; in govt. employ, 1886—. Asst. dir. D.A.R. hosp. corps which furnished 1,000 trained nurses during Spanish-Am. War; one of 3 founders and hon. v.p.-gen. nat. soc. D.A.R.; pres. Albert Sidney Johnston Chapter, United Daughters of the Confederacy; parliamentarian Nat. Mary Washington Memorial Assn.; rec. sec. Pocahontas Memorial Association. Home: Washington, D.C. Died 1910.

DESHON, George, R.C. clergyman; b. New London, Conn., Jan. 30, 1823; grad. West Point, 1843 (classmate and room-mate of Gen. Grant); reached rank of capt., 1851, when he retired from army, having been converted to Catholic faith. Studied theology in Cumberland, Md.; ordained priest, 1855; joined Redemptorist order and was engaged in mission work, later pastor St. Paul's Ch., N.Y. City, being superior gen. of the Paulists. Author: Guide for Catholic Young Women; etc. Died 1903.

DESMOND, Humphrey Joseph, lawyer, author; b. Ozaukee Co., Wis., Sept. 14, 1858; s. Thomas and Joanna (Bowe) D.; B.L., U. of Wis., 1880; LL.D., Notre Dame U., 1917; m. Susie Ryan, Sept. 14, 1898; children—Dorothy L., Humphrey E., Grace E., Marion E., Thomas E., John A. Began practice, Milwaukee, 1881; mem. Milwaukee Sch. Bd., 1883-90; mem. Wis. Legislature, 1891-92; propr. Milwaukee Citizen, St. Paul Northwestern Chronicle, Washington New Century, and Memphis Journal. Author: New Laity, 1915; Curious Chapters of American History, 1924; The Ways of Courage, 1927. Home: Milwaukee, Wis. Died Feb. 16, 1932.

DE SOTO, Hernando, foreign service; b. of Am. parents Jena, Germany, Aug. 9, 1866; ed. pvt. tutelage, and coll., Paris, France, and Jena. Apptd. deputy consul, at Chemnitz, Germany, June 20, 1889; dep. consul, Dresden, 1891-92, dep. consul gen., 1892-1902; vice and dep. consul gen., St. Petersburg, Apr.-Nov. 1902; v. consul, Warsaw, 1902-03; v. and dep. consul gen., St. Petersburg, July-Nov. 1903 (retired); apptd. v. and dep. consul gen., St. Gall, Switzerland, Dec. 15, 1903; detailed to the consulate gen., Paris, 1905; dep. consul gen., Paris, 1906-07; v. consul gen., St. Gall, May-Aug. 1907; consul at Warsaw, 1907-08, Riga, 1908-10, Palermo, 1910-14, Warsaw, Apr. 27, 1914; temporarily detailed at Dept. of State, 1917; detailed to Am. Commn., Berlin, July

21, 1921; consul at Leipsic, 1921-24, foreign service officer, class 4, July 1, 1924—. Died 1928.

DESPRADELLE, Constant Désiré, architect; b. Burgoyne, France, May 20, 1862; s. Constant Antoine and Amante (Pellerin) D.; grad. École des Beaux Arts, Paris, 1882; studied architecture at same, 1882-89, student l'atelier Pascal, 1st class, 1884, diploma, 1886; classed first in the Concours de Rome with title 1st, 2d Grand Prix de Rome, 1889; Architect Diplomé du Gouvernment, 1890; Lauréat, Inst. of France; m. Leonora, d. Daniel Chamberlain and widow of W. Channing Simmons, of Boston, June 1898. Received Rougevin, Deschaumes, Ed. Labarre, Bouwens prizes and Prix de la Société Centrale des Architects Français; insp. state bldgs. and nat. palaces, France, 1889-93; Rotch prof. archtl. design, Mass. Inst. Tech., 1893—; mem. Codman & Despradelle. Received one of first 5 awards in Phoebe A. Hearst competition for U. of Calif., 1899; 1st gold medal, Salon, Paris, for design for monument, "The Beacon of Progress," to glorify the American nation (two of the drawings were purchased by French govt. for Luxembourg Gallery); apptd., 1900, mem. permanent bd. of 4 advisers to U. of Cal. (with McKim, Carrère and Howard of New York); cons. architect, Mus. Fine Arts Boston, 1906; spl. lecturer on architectural design, Harvard U., 1910—. Decorated Officier d'Académie, 1902; Officer de l'Instruction Publique, France. Home: Boston, Mass. Deceased.

De ST. AUBIN, Percival Ovide, mfg. exec.; b. Chicago, Ill., Aug. 9, 1887; s. Ovide and Corinne (Magnan) D.; ed. Chicago pub. schs. and St. Ignatius Coll.; LL.D., Providence (R.I.) Coll., 1933; m. Marion O'Hayer, Aug. 16, 1910; 1 son, Edward Ovide (dec.). Began as salesman Vesta Knitting Mill Co., 1910; treas. and dir. Vesta Underwear Co. and Vesta Corp., 1916—; dir. Industrial Trust Co., Industrial Safe Deposit Co., Narragansett Power & Light Co. Presidential elector from R.I., 1928; apptd. dir. Reemployment Service for R.I. by President Roosevelt, July 1933, resigned, July 1935; state treas. of R.I., 1936; apptd. mem. R.I. Bd. of Parole, 1937. Created Knight of St. Gregory, 1929; elected Knight of Malta, 1935. Trustee R.I. Foundation, Providence Coll.; dir. Providence Community Fund. Home: Providence, R.I. Died Nov. 1, 1940.

DESTINN, Emmy, operatic soprano; b. Prague, Bohemia, 1878; studied under Marie Loewe-Destinn; adopted stage name Emmy Destinn, real name Kittl. Début in Royal Opera House, Berlin, 1897; appeared as Senta in "Der Fliegender Hollander," upon invitation of Cosima Wagner, at Beyreuth, 1901; created rôle of Salome in Berlin and was selected to sing the part in Paris; made notable success in London in "Madame Butterfly," and as Donna Anna and Aïda, 1905; first appeared in New York, in 1908, and has since been prominently identified with the Metropolitan Opera Co.; repertoire includes over 80 operas. Died Jan. 29, 1930.

DEUTSCH, Bernard Seymour, lawyer; b. Baltimore, Md., Sept. 25, 1884; s. Leo and Annie (Steiner) D.; student Coll. City of N.Y.; LL.B., New York Law Sch., 1904; m. Frances Weinstein, Aug. 22, 1918; children—Elinor, Dorothy Edith. Admitted to N.Y. bar, 1905, and since in practice at N.Y. City; pres. Fransaro Realty Corp.; sec. Mt. Eden Estates, Popham Estates. Candidate for judge N.Y. Supreme Ct., 1932; elected pres. Board of Aldermen, on fusion ticket, 1933. Mem. N.Y. Municipal Court Commn., 1923-25; pres. Am. Jewish Congress; treas. N.Y. Conf. on Legal Edn.; v.p. Bronx C. of C. Democrat. Jewish religion. Mason. Home: Riverdale, N.Y. Died 1935.

DEUTSCH, Gotthard, college prof.; b. Kanitz, Austria, Jan. 31, 1859; s. Bernhard L. and Elise (Wiener) D.; Ph.D., U. of Vienna, 1881; m. Hermine Bacher, of Brunn, May 10, 1888. Came to U.S., 1891; prof. history, 1891—, acting pres., 1903, Hebrew Union Coll., Cincinnati. Mem. Editorial Bd. Jewish Encyclopædia. Mem. Bd. Edn., Cincinnati. Author: Symbólik in Cultus, 1886; Theory of Oral Tradition, 1895; Philosophy of Jewish History, 1897; Andere Zeiten (novel), 1897; Unloesbare fesseln (novel), 1902; Memorable Dates of Jewish History, 1904; Israel Bruna, a tragedy, 1908; History of the Jews, 1910; Der Glaube an Hobelspaene (A Survey of Modern Judaism), 1915; Scrolls, essays, 2 vols., 1917; 3d vol., 1919. Home: Cincinnati, O. Died Oct. 14, 1921.

DEVANEY, John Patrick, judge; b. Lake Mills, Ia., June 30, 1883; s. Patrick and Ellen (La Velle) D.; A.B., U. of Minn., 1905, LL.B., 1907, LL.M., 1908; LL.D., Marquette U., 1935; LL.D., De Paul U., 1936; m. Beatrice Langevin, Feb. 20, 1919; children—Patrick, Beatrice, Shiela. Admitted to Minn. bar, 1909 and in practice at Minneapolis, 1909-33; mem. Stiles & Devaney, Devaney & Edwards, and later Devaney & Gleason; chief justice Supreme Court of Minn., 1933-37. Chmn. Minn. Crime Commn. from 1934; commn. made 35 recommendations, 25 of which became laws of the state. Chmn. Industry Com., Wages and Hours Div., Dept. of Labor. Mem. President's Emergency Board in Settlement of Labor Disputes, C.G.W. Ry. and Pacific Electric Co.; pres. Radio Station WLOL, Minneapolis. Catholic. K.C. Witness for President Roosevelt's Federal Court Reform Bill before Senate Judiciary Com. Home: Minneapolis, Minn. Died Sept. 21, 1941.

DEVENDORF, Irving R., judge; b. Danube, N.Y., Nov. 2, 1856; s. Levenus and Margaret (Walrath) D.; grad. Little Falls (N.Y.) Acad., 1877; admitted to bar, 1880; m. Margaret Bellinger, 1882; children—Frederick C., Marion D. Began practice at Herkimer, 1880; dist. atty. Herkimer Co., 1889-94; co. judge and surrogate, 1896-1906; justice Supreme Court of N.Y., 5th Jud. Dist., 1906-26; official referee Supreme Court, N.Y. State, 1926—. Republican. Home: Herkimer, N.Y. Died Oct. 8, 1932.

DEVER, William Emmett, mayor; b. Woburn, Mass., Mar. 13, 1862; s. Patrick James and Mary A. (Lynch) D.; ed. pub. schs., Woburn; LL.B., Chicago Coll. of Law, 1890; LL.D., Northwestern U., 1923, Chicago Law Coll., 1924, St. Bonaventure's Coll., Allegheny, N.Y., 1925; m. Katherine E. Conway, Jan. 5, 1885. In leather mfg. business with father, at Woburn, 1881-84, and with White & Co., 1884-86, Grey, Clark & Engle, Chicago, until 1889; began practice of law, 1890. Elected alderman 17th Ward, Chicago, 5 times, 1902-10 (resigned); judge Superior Court of Cook Co., 1910-16; justice Ill. Appellate Court, 1916-23 (resigned); mayor of Chicago, term Apr. 1923-Apr. 1927. V.p. and trust officer Bank of America, 1927—. Mem. Dem. County Central Com., Cook Co.; mem. Chicago Plan Commn. Home: Chicago, Ill. Died Sept. 3, 1929.

DEVEREUX, Mary (Mrs. Mary Devereaux Watson), author; b. Marblehead, Mass.; d. Gen. J. H. and Antoinette C. (Kelsey) D.; private edn.; widow. Extensive contbr. of poems, short stories, etc., to papers and mags. Author: Betty Peach, 1896; From Kingdom to Colony, 1899; Up and Down the Sands of Gold, 1901; Lafitte of Louisiana, 1902. Home: Englewood, N.J. Died Feb. 19, 1914.

DEVINE, Thomas Hume, lawyer; b. St. Louis, Mo., Sept. 27, 1860; s. Michael and Agnes (Hume) D.; ed. pub. schs., Ill. and Mo.; m. Katherine Gregory, May 27, 1884; children—Charles Watson, Dave Gibbs. Admitted to Ill. bar, 1882, and practiced at Winchester until 1888; in gen. practice at Pueblo, Colo., 1888—; mem. Devine, Preston & Storer, 1922—; v.p. and gen. counsel Am. Beet Sugar Co.; gen. counsel Domestic Sugar Bur., Amalgamated Sugar Co.; gen. atty. for Colo.,Mo.P. R.R. Co.; Colo. counsel Southern Colo. Power Co.; local counsel Colo. Fuel & Iron Co., D.&R.G.W. R.R. Co. Republican. Mason. Died Dec. 9, 1932.

DE VINNE, Theodore Low, printer; b. Stamford, Conn., Dec. 25, 1828; s. Daniel and Joanna Augusta (Low) D.; (hon. A.M., Columbia and Yale, 1901); m. Grace Brockbank, Dec. 25, 1850 (died 1905). Learned printer's trade; employe and later partner Francis Hart; after the latter's death firm became Theodore L. De Vinne & Co., now organized as the De Vinne Press; a leader in the improvement of typography. Mem. Typothetæ (New York). Author: Printers Price List, 1869; Invention of Printing, 1876; Historic Types, 1884; Christopher Plantin, 1888; Plain Printing Types, 1900; Correct Composition, 1901; Title Pages, 1902; Book Composition, 1904; Notable Printers of Italy During the 15th Century, 1910. Home: New York. Died Feb. 16, 1914.

DEVINS, John Bancroft, editor; b. New York, N.Y., Sept. 26, 1856; s. John and Ann (Mahan) D.; A.B., New York U., 1882, A.M., 1903; grad. Union Theol. Sem., 1887; (D.D., Centre Coll., Ky., 1901; LL.D., Huron Coll., 1909); m. Charlotte Elizabeth Penfield, Oct. 18, 1883. Ordained Presbyn. ministry, 1888; pastor Hope Chapel, New York, 1888-98, Broome St. Tabernacle, New York, 1901-05. Mem. city staff New York Tribune, 1880-88; editor Christian Thought, 1890-96; mng. editor Bible Record, 1904-06; mng. editor, 1898-1902, editor, 1902—, New York Observer. Organizer, 1894, and 1st pres., Fedn. of East Side Workers; organizer, 1894, and pres. N.Y. Employment Soc.; chmn. Cooper Union Labor Bur., 1895; mem. bd. mgrs. N.Y. Assn. for Improving Conditions of the Poor, 1895—; trustee from 1905, sec. bd., 1906-08, N.Y. State Hosp. for Incipient Pulmonary Tuberculosis; trustee Industrial Christian Alliance, Evang. Alliance for U.S.A., Am. Seamen's Friend Soc.; corporate mem. China Industrial Union; chmn. com. on literature and edn. Federal Council of Chs. of Christ in America; mem. Nat. Civic Fedn., Coll. Bd. Presbyn. Ch., U.S.A., 1905-08; Nat. Vacation Bible Sch. Com., Bible Study Union, pub. lecture corps New York Bd. Edn., Child Labor Com.; 1st fraternal del. New York Presbytery to Central Federated Labor Union, 1904-08; sec. Presbyn. Union of New York, 1907—. Home: Brooklyn, N.Y. Died 1911.

DEVLIN, Robert Thomas, lawyer; b. Sacramento, Calif., June 13, 1859; s. Robert and Catharine (Otterson) D.; ed. Sacramento high schs. and by pvt. tutors; m. Mary E. Dwyer, Mar. 28, 1894. Admitted to bar, 1880; mem. State Bd. Prison Dirs., 1884-1912; was mem. State Penol. Commn. to visit and report upon reformatories in Eastern states; mem. Calif. Senate, 1900-04; U.S. atty. Northern Dist. Calif., 1905-12, when resigned. Author: A Treatise on the Law of Real Property and Deeds; The Treaty Power under the Constitution of the United States. Home: Sacramento, Calif. Died Feb. 24, 1938.

DEVOE, Frederick William, merchant, mfr.; b. New York, N.Y., Jan. 26, 1828; private edn.; clerk in stores, 1843-52; partner Raynolds & Devoe, 1852-64; F. W. Devoe & Co., 1864-90; from 1890 pres. F. W. Devoe & C. T. Raynolds Co., paint and varnish mfrs.; dir. Market & Fulton Nat. Bank. Pres. New York Bd. Edn.; pres. Bd. Commrs., Greater New York; pres. N.Y. Juvenile Asylum; mem. Council N.Y. Univ., 1903—. Died Mar. 21, 1913.

DEVOL, Carroll Augustine, army officer; b. Waterford, O., Apr. 17, 1859; s. Hiram Fosdick and Adelaide (Dyar) D.; C.E., Pa. Mil. Coll., 1878, Sc.D., 1914; m. Dora Dean Scott, Feb. 17, 1887; children—Lucile Scott (Mrs. A. G. Bates), Mary Adelaide (Mrs. George H. Brett). 2d lt. 25th Inf., Sept. 1, 1879; 1st lt., Oct. 19, 1886; capt. a.q.m., Aug. 21, 1896; maj. q.m. U.S. Vols., Oct. 17, 1898; lt. col., Feb. 6, 1899; hon. disch. from vol. service, May 1, 1901; maj. q.m., May 5, 1902; lt. col., Oct. 31, 1909; col. a.q.m. gen., Sept. 22, 1911; brig. gen. q.m. corps, Feb. 16, 1913. Served with the line of the army in Tex., S.D., Minn., Mont., Yellowstone Park and Wyo., with U. of Wis., 1896; in Philippine Islands, 1898-1900; with quarter master corps in N.Y. City, Phila., San Francisco, Washington, D.C., Tex.; chief q.m. Isthmian Canal Commn., Panama Canal, July, 1908-Apr. 1, 1913; retired with rank of maj. gen., Oct. 31, 1916. Asst. to provost marshal gen. in registration and draft office, June 24, 1917; zone supply officer and zone transportation officer, 13th Supply Zone, San Francisco, Sept. 5, 1917. Awarded D.S.M., June 6, 1919; also awarded Distinguished Service Cross. Acting chmn. and gen. mgr. Am. Nat. Red Cross. Awarded campaign badge Spanish-Am. War and Philippine Insurrection; Panama Canal Medal. Presbyn. Home: Menlo Park, Calif. Died June 3, 1930.

DE VOLL, F(rederick) Usher, artist; b. Providence, R.I., Dec. 15, 1873; s. Frederick Almy and Mary Jane McKenzie (Usher) De V.; grad. R.I. Sch. of Design; studied art under William M. Chase, Robert Henri, Charles W. Hawthorne and H. Siddons Mowbray, in U.S., and Jean Paul Laurens, Paris, France; m. Martha Elizabeth McIver, of County Tyrone, North of Ireland, Sept. 20, 1904. Landscape painter. Exhibited at Nat. Acad. Design, Carnegie Inst., Corcoran Gallery, Pa. Acad., etc. Awarded silver medal, San Francisco Expn., 1915; sr. prize, Providence Art Club. Represented in R.I. Sch. of Design; St. John's Art Club, New Brunswick, Can.; Delgado Mus., New Orleans; Milwaukee Art Museum; Newcomb Coll., New Orleans; Vanderpoel Art Assn., Chicago; Springfield (Ill.) Art Assn. Republican. Christian Scientist. Illustrated "The Regicides" (by Frederick Hull Cogswell). Specializes in New England landscapes and New York street and harbor subjects. Home: Providence, R.I. Died Mar. 13, 1941.

DE VRIES, Marion, lawyer; b. nr. Woodbridge, Calif., Aug. 15, 1865; s. William Henry and Cornelia (Crowe) De V.; Ph.B., San Joaquin Valley Coll., 1886; LL.B., U. of Mich., 1888; m. Mary L. Snead, Feb. 23, 1892 (died 1927). Admitted to Mich. bar, 1887, to Calif. bar same year and to Supreme Court of U.S., 1897; practiced at Stockton, Calif., 1889-1900; asst. dist. atty., San Joaquin Co., 1893-97; elected to 55th and 56th Congresses (1897-1901), 2d Calif. Dist.; resigned from 56th Congress, Aug. 22, 1900; mem. Bd. U.S. Gen. Appraisers (now U.S. Customs Court), New York, 1900-10 (pres. bd., 1906-10); asso. judge U.S. Court of Customs Appeals, Washington, D.C., 1910-21; presiding judge, 1921-22; resigned to resume practice, Nov. 1, 1922. Home: Lodi, Calif. Died Sept. 11, 1939.

DE VRIES, William Levering, clergyman; b. Baltimore, Md., Nov. 8, 1865; s. William Rogers and Mary Clement (Crane) De V.; A.B., Johns Hopkins, 1888, fellow, 1890, Ph.D., 1892; grad. Gen. Theol. Sem., 1894, B.D., 1897, S.T.D., 1931; D.D., St. John's Coll., Md., 1920, George Washington, 1921; unmarried. Deacon and priest P.E. Ch., 1894; missionary Howard Co., Md., 1894-96; pvt. chaplain to Bishop Satterlee, 1896-1908; rector St. Mark's, Washington, D.C., 1896-1911; canon and chancellor, Washington Cathedral, 1911-29, canon and precentor, 1929—. Trustee Washington Cathedral and its schs. for girls and boys. Mason. Author: Ethopoiia in Lysias, 1892; The Foundation Stone Book (pertaining to Washington Cathedral), 1908; also Johns Hopkins Univ. Ode, "Veritas Vos Liberabit," and the Alpha Delta Phi "Pilgrim Song." Died Mar. 14, 1937.

DEWALT, Arthur Granville, congressman; b. Bath, Pa., Oct. 11, 1854; s. Reuben and Annie E. (Dewalt) D.; grad. Keystone State Normal Sch., 1870; M.A., Lafayette Coll., Easton, Pa., 1874; married. Admitted to Pa. bar; dist. atty., Lehigh Co., Pa., 1880-83; mem. Pa. Senate, 1902-10; state chmn. Dem. Party, 1909, 1910; mem. 64th to 66th Congresses (1915-21), 13th Pa. Dist. Adj. 4th Regt.

N.G. Pa., 10 yrs. Lutheran. Mason. Home: Allentown, Pa. Died Oct. 26, 1931.

DEWART, Murray Wilder, clergyman; b. Chardon, O., Feb. 14, 1874; s. James Hartley (D.D.) and Mary (Day) D.; A.B., U. of Minn., 1897; B.D., Episcopal Theol. Sch., 1901; m. Submit T. Clarke, Apr. 30, 1906; children—Donald Day, Kenneth, Murray Wilder. Deacon, 1901, priest, 1902, P.E. Ch.; asst. St. James Ch., Roxbury, Mass., 1901-02, rector, 1902-12; rector Ch. of Epiphany, Winchester, Mass., 1912-22, Christ Ch., Baltimore, Md., 1922—. Chaplain 1st Mass. F.A., on Mexican border, 1916, 101st U.S.F.A., in France, 1917-19. Mason. Died 1927.

DEWART, William Herbert, clergyman; b. Norwood, Ont., Can., July 19, 1862; s. Rev. James Hartley (D.D.) and Mary (Day) D.; A.B., Kenyon Coll., 1887, L.H.D., 1918; B.D., Cambridge Theol. Sch., 1893; m. Elizabeth H. Russell, Oct. 4, 1899; children—Hartley, Russell, Gordon, Frances H., Wm. H., Mary, Elizabeth. Deacon, 1891, priest, 1892, P.E. Ch.; asst. rector Trinity Ch., Boston, 1893-1902; rector St. Matthew's Ch., South Boston, 1902-04, Christ Ch., Hyde Park, Boston, 1904-14, Christ Ch. ("Old North"), Boston, 1914-27 (emeritus). Republican. Home: Manchester-by-the-Sea, Mass. Died Mar. 28, 1941.

DEWEY, Charles, life underwriter; b. Montpelier, Vt., Mar. 27, 1826; s. Dr. Julius Y. and Mary (Perrin) D.; grad. Univ. of Vt., 1845; m. Betsey Tarbox, 1848. Asst. sec., 1845-50, sec., 1850-57, dir. over 30 yrs., Vt. Mut. Fire Ins. Co.; dir. from 1851, v.p., 1871-77, pres. until Jan., 1901, Nat. Life Ins. Co.; resigned. Served 3 terms in State senate; State bank examiner 2 yrs.; pres. bd. trustees Washington Co. Grammar Sch., 1879; v.p. 1878-91, pres. 1st Nat. Bank Montpelier, 1891—. Died 1905.

DEWEY, Charles Melville, painter; b. Lowville, N.Y., July 16, 1849; s. Silas Bush and Jane (Stoddard) D.; brother of Stoddard D.; ed. dist. sch.; pupil of Carolus Duran, Paris, 1876-77; m. Julia Henshaw, May 2, 1887 (died 1928). Specializes in landscapes. Represented in Corcoran and Nat. galleries, Washington; Art Inst., Brooklyn; Albright Gallery; Met. Mus.; and well known pvt. collections. N.A., 1907; mem. Nat. Inst. Arts and Letters. Home: New York, N.Y. Died Jan. 17, 1937.

DEWEY, Francis Henshaw, lawyer; b. Worcester, Mass., Mar. 23, 1856; s. Francis H. and Sarah B. (Tufts) D.; A.B., Williams Coll., 1876, A.M., 1879; LL.B., Harvard, 1878; m. Lizzie Davis Bliss, Dec. 12, 1878; children—Elizabeth Bliss, Francis Henshaw. Chmn. board Mechanics' Nat. Bank, Worcester Consol. Street Ry. Co.; trustee Worcester Mechanics' Sav. Bank, N.E. Investment & Security Co.; pres. Norwich & Worcester R.R. Co., New London Northern R.R. Co., Denholm and McKay Realty Co., Bay State House; v.p. of Worcester Morris Plan Company. Trustee, v.p. and treas. Clark U.; pres. Rufus Putnam Memorial Assn., Worcester Art Mus., Home for Aged Men.; v.p. Memorial Hosp.; dir. Associated Charities; chmn. commn. City Hosp. Funds; trustee Williams Coll., Walter E. Fernald Sch. for Feeble Minded. Home: Worcester, Mass. Died Apr. 20, 1933.

DEWEY, Frederic Perkins, chemist; b. Hartford, Conn., Oct. 4, 1855; s. Daniel S. and Elizabeth (Perkins) D.; Ph.B., Sheffield Scientific Sch. (Yale), 1876; m. Charlotte Esther Candee, Apr. 12, 1877. Asst. analytical chemistry, Lafayette Coll., 1876-77; chemist with iron and steel mfrs. until 1881; with Dr. George W. Hawes investigated the building stones of the U.S. for the 10th census, 1881; curator metallurgy, U.S. Nat. Museum, 1882-89; propr. commercial lab., 1890-1903; assayer Mint Bur., U.S. Treasury, 1903—; acting dir. Mint Bureau, 1913. Author: Descriptive Catalogue Collections in Economic Geology and Metallurgy (bull. No. 42), 1891. Deceased.

DEWEY, George, admiral; b. Montpelier, Vt., Dec. 26, 1837; s. Dr. Julius Yeamans and Mary (Perrin) D.; M.M.S., Norwich U., 1854; grad. U.S. Naval Acad., 1858; (LL.D., U. of Pa., and Princeton, 1898); m. Susie, d. Gov. Ichabod Goodwin, of N.H., Oct. 24, 1867 (died 1872); m. 2d, Mrs. Mildred (McLean) Hazen, Nov. 9, 1899. Attached to steam frigate Wabash, Mediterranean Squadron, until 1861, then to steam sloop Mississippi of West Gulf Squadron; commd. lt., Apr. 19, 1861; in Farragut's squadron which forced the passage of Fort St. Philip and Ft. Jackson, Apr. 1862, and participated in attack on Fort St. Philip and the subsequent fights with gunboats and ironclads which gave Farragut possession of New Orleans; in the smoke of the battle of Port Hudson the Mississippi lost her bearings and ran ashore under the guns of land batteries, and officers and men took to the boats after setting the vessel on fire. Was afterward on several vessels in N. Atlantic Blockading Squadron, then in European Squadron and later on various duties and at different stas.; promoted comdr., Apr. 1872; capt., Sept. 1884; commodore, Feb. 9, 1896. In Jan. 1898, assumed command of Asiatic Squadron; on May 1, 1898, in Manila Bay, he comd. that squadron in Battle of Manila Bay, annihilating the Spanish Asiatic Squadron under Admiral Montojo, destroying eleven and capturing all other vessels and all the land batteries without the loss of a man on the American side. Immediately upon receipt of official news of victory he was promoted rear admiral, and thanked by resolution of Congress; mem. U.S. Philippine Commn., 1899; promoted admiral of the navy, Mar. 2, 1899; pres. Gen. Bd., Mar. 29, 1900—. Died Jan. 16, 1917.

DEWEY, Harry Pinneo, clergyman; b. Toulon, Ill., Oct. 30, 1861; s. Samuel Mills and Cornelia (Phelps) D.; A.B., Williams Coll., 1884; B.D., Andover Theol. Sem., 1887; D.D., Dartmouth, 1898; L.H.D., Rollins College, 1934; m. Elizabeth Fearing Thatcher, June 4, 1889; children—Thatcher (dec.), Elizabeth Phelps, Eleanor Hale, Cornelia, Margaret. Ordained Congl. ministry, Oct. 12, 1887; pastor South Ch., Concord, N.H., 1887-1900, Ch. of the Pilgrims, Brooklyn, 1900-07, Plymouth Ch., Minneapolis, Minn., 1907-1935; guest preacher Community Ch. and chaplain Webber Coll., Babson Park, Fla., 1935-36. Occasional preacher at colleges, univs., and schools. Trustee Williams Coll., 1902—, Andover Theol. Sem., 1907—, Carleton Coll., 1911—; mem. com. to Federal Council Chs. of Christ in America from Nat. Council Congl. Chs., 1923-30; mem. Nat. Service Commn., of Congl. Chs., 1917-19; moderator Gen. Conf. Congl. Chs. of Minn., 1913; mem. Nat. Council Commn. on Missions, 1921-27. Dir. Northeast Neighborhood Settlement House, 1914-35, and Pillsbury Settlement House, Minneapolis, 1918-30; mem. National Councils of Com. of Twelve for Unification of Congl. Missionary Socs., 1923-37; v.p. Minneapolis Fedn. of Chs., 1929-32, pres., 1932-34; Council preacher Nat. Council of Congl. Chs., 1931; mem. advisory com. Chicago Theol. Sem., 1927—. Deceased.

DEWEY, Henry Bingham, supt. schs.; b. Niles, Mich., July 26, 1864; s. George Martin and Emma (Bingham) D.; A.B., U. of Mich., 1890; m. Harriette L. White, 1897; children—Katharine B., Elizabeth W. Co. supt. schs., Shiawassee Co., Mich., 1890-91. Pierce Co., Wash., 1898-1903, deputy asst., and state supt. pub. instrn., Wash., 1905-13. Editor and pub. Northwest Journal of Education, Seattle, 1905-08. Now mgr. ednl. dept. Houghton Mifflin Co., Boston. Republican. Episcopalian. Home: Boston, Mass. Died Oct. 30, 1931.

DEWEY, Mary Elizabeth, author; b. Gloucester, Mass., Oct. 27, 1821; d. Orville and Louisa (Farnham) D. Teaching, 1860—. Author: Life and Letters of Catherine M. Sedgwick, 1871; Autobiography and Letters of Orville Dewey, 1884. Home: Boston, Mass. Died 1910.

DEWEY, Melvil, exec. and librarian; b. Adams Center, N.Y., Dec. 10, 1851; s. Joel and Eliza (Green) D.; A.B., Amherst, 1874, A.M., 1877; (LL.D., Syracuse, and Alfred, 1902); m. Annie R. Godfrey, Oct. 19, 1878; m. 2d, Emily McKay Beal, May 28, 1924. Acting librarian, Amherst, 1874-76; started and managed 3 nat. ednl. socs. at Boston—Am. Library Assn., Metric Buro for establishing metric weights and measures, and Spelling Reform Assn., 1876-83; also Library Buro for advancing library interests, 1876-83; chief librarian and prof. of library economy, Columbia, 1883-88; dir. N.Y. State Library, 1889-1906, and of Home Edn. Dept., 1891-1906; sec. and exec. officer Univ. State of N.Y., 1889-1900; founder and dir. N.Y. State Library Sch., 1887-1906; state dir. of libraries, N.Y., 1904-06; founder, 1895, and became pres. Lake Placid Club; founder and pres. Lake Placid Club Edn. Foundation, 1922; pres. Northwood Boys' Sch.; also pres. Adirondack Music Festival; trustee Chautauqua Instn., 1907—. Author: Library School Rules, 1891; Decimal Classification and Relative Index, 1876-1929. Also numerous ednl., library, metric and spelling reform books, repts., etc. Editor: A.L.A. Catalog, 1904, The Library (London); also various jours. and reports. Founder, and editor Library Journal, 1876-81, and Library Notes, 1886-98. Founder, 1st pres. N.Y. Library Club, N.Y. State Library Assn., and library dept. N.E.A.; pres. Assn. State Librarians; trustee Carnegie Simplified Spelling Bd., pres. Efficiency Soc., 1915—; founder and pres. Lake Placid Club in Fla. Died Dec. 26, 1931.

DEWEY, Richard (Smith), psychiatrist, neurologist; b. Forestville, N.Y., Dec. 6, 1845; s. Elijah and Sophia (Smith) D.; Lit. Dept., U. of Mich., 1864-66, M.D., 1869, hon. A.M., 1900; m. Lillian Dwight, Jan. 2, 1873 (died 1880); children—Richard Dwight, Ethel Lillian, Robert Strong (dec.); m. 2d, Mary E. Brown, June 22, 1886; children—Ellinor Maria, Donald Mack. Interne Brooklyn City Hosp., 1870; vol. asst. surgeon, Franco-Prussian War, with 7th corps, field hosp., Pont à Mousson, France, and Reserve Hosp., Hesse-Cassel, Germany, 1870-71; student under Virchow, Berlin, 1871; asst. physician, State Hosp. for Insane, Elgin, Ill., 1872-99; med. supt. State Hosp. for Insane, Kankakee, Ill. (1st example in U.S. of detached ward or cottage plan of bldgs. for care of mental diseases), 1879-93; prof. mental and nervous diseases, Chicago Post-Grad. Med. Sch., 1893-1909; in charge Milwaukee Sanitarium, 1895-1921. Pres. Am. Medico-Psychol. Soc. (now Am. Psychiatric Assn.), 1896. Wrote words and music of patriotic songs, "Thou Mighty Nation" and "Starry Flag Now Bravely Borne." Home: La Cañada, Calif. Died Aug. 4, 1933.

DEWEY, Stoddard, newspaper corr.; b. New York, N.Y., Apr. 20, 1853; s. Silas Bush and Jane (Stoddard) D.; classical studies in French schs., 1870-75; philosophy and science, Belgium, 1876-77; art history, École du Louvre; unmarried. Writer (Italian matters) London Liberal weekly "The Speaker" (now "Nation"), Westminster Rev., Atlantic Monthly, New York Tribune; Paris corr. New York Evening Post, and Nation, 1892—, New York Jour. of Commerce (tariff and finance), 1895—. Sec. U.S. Treasury Commn. to France, Spain and Portugal, 1892; preparation of 105 internat. congresses of learned socs. held at Paris Expn., 1900. Chevalier de la Légion d'Honneur, 1901. Author: Tariff Relations Between France and the United States (statis. tables pub. in English and French and distributed to Congress of U.S. and French Parliament by Am. Chamber of Commerce, Paris), 1897; Four French Adventurers, 1912. Lectured 230 times in 11 Am. camps in France, 1918. Pres. Anglo-Am. Press Assn., Paris, 1920. Died July 30, 1933.

DEWEY, W(illis) A(lonzo), M.D.; b. Middlebury, Vt., Oct. 25, 1858; s. Josiah Earl and Eunice Converse (Carpenter) D.; grad. Packard's Bus. Coll., New York, 1876; M.D., New York Homœ. Coll., 1880; post-grad. work, univs. of Berlin, Vienna, Leipzig and Paris; m. Celina J. Lalande, Jan. 31, 1885 (she died Dec. 20, 1917); 1 son, Josiah Earl; m. 2d, Camille L. Roe, April 3, 1922. Prof. anatomy and materia medica, Hahnemann Med. Coll. of Pacific, 1884-93; prof. materia medica, New York Met. Post-Grad. Sch., 1893-96; prof. materia medica and therapeutics, and clin. prof. mental and nervous diseases, U. of Mich. Homœ. Coll., 1896-1922 (emeritus). Author: Boericke and Dewey's Twelve Tissue Remedies, 1888, 6th edit., 1928; Essentials of Homœpathic Materia Medica, 1894, 5th edit., 1926; Essentials of Homœopathic Therapeutics, 1895, 2d edit., 1898; Practical Homœopathic Therapeutics, 1901, 3d edit., 1933. Home: Middlebury, Vt. Died 1938.

DEWHURST, Frederic Eli, pastor University Congl. Ch., Chicago, Jan., 1900—; b. Bradford, Me., April 20, 1855; s. Eli and Diantha (Richards) D.; grad. Colby Univ., Me., 1878 (A.M., 1881); m. Oct. 9, 1883, May Taylor. Instr. history and Latin, Conn. Literary Inst., Suffield, Conn.; pastor of chs. in Quincy, Mass., and Burlington, Vt., 1882-1892; lecturer on economics and sociology, Univ. of Vt., 1889-92; pastor Plymouth Congl. Ch., Indianapolis, 1892-99. Home: Chicago, Ill. Died 1906.

DEWING, Maria Oakey, artist; b. New York, N.Y., Oct. 27, 1845; d. William Francis and Sally (Sullivan) Oakey; studied Nat. Acad. New York, and under John LaFarge and Thomas Couture; m. Thomas Wilmer Dewing, Apr. 18, 1881; 1 dau., Mrs. Elizabeth Bartol Bender. Specialties are figures and flower pieces and portraits. Died Dec. 13, 1927.

DEWING, Thomas Wilmer, artist; b. Boston, Mass., May 4, 1851; studied under Jules J. Lefebvre, 1876-79; m. Maria Richards Oakey (died 1927). Painter of portraits and figure compositions, 1879—. His picture, "The Days," gained the Clarke prize, 1887, first medal Carnegie Inst., Pittsburgh, 1908. A.N.A., 1887; N.A., 1888; mem. "Ten American Painters." Home: New York, N.Y. Died No. 6, 1938.

DE WITT, Calvin, soldier; b. Harrisburg, Pa., May 26, 1840; s. Rev. William R. (D.D.) and Mary Elizabeth (Wallace) D.; ed. Harrisburg Acad.; A.B., Princeton, 1860; A.M., 1863; M.D., Jefferson Med. Coll., Phila., 1865; m. Josephine Lesesne, 1877. Served in Army of Potomac, capt. 49th Pa. Vol. Inf., Oct. 1861-Jan. 1863. Apptd. 1st lt., asst. surg. U.S.A., May 14, 1867; advanced through grades to col. asst. surg. gen., May 7, 1901; brig. gen., U.S.A., Aug. 9, 1903; retired from active service Aug. 10, 1903. Served as med. officer U.S.A., in many mil. stas. in various parts of U.S., in several campaigns against Indians and in Cuba. Instr. in mil. hygiene, Gen. Staff Coll., Ft. Leavenworth, Kan.; prof. of mil. medicine and later pres. Army Med. Sch., Washington, D.C. Died 1908.

DE WITT, David Miller, lawyer; b. Paterson, N.J., Nov. 25, 1837; s. Moses Edwards and Lydia Ann (Miller) D.; A.B., Rutgers Coll., 1858, A.M., 1861; m. Mary Antoinette MacDonald, Apr. 10, 1867. Admitted to bar, 1858; prin. New Paltz (N.Y.) Acad., 1861-62; dist. atty. Ulster Co., N.Y., 1862-68; mem. 43d Congress (1873-75); asst. corp. counsel, Brooklyn, 1879-82; mem. N.Y. Assembly, 1883; surrogate of Ulster Co. (apptd. to fill vacancy), 1885-86. Democrat. Home: Kingston, N.Y. Died June 24, 1912.

DE WITT, George Gosman, lawyer; b. Callicoon Twp., Sullivan Co., N.Y., Apr. 9, 1845; s. George G. and Julia (Foster) D.; A.B., Columbia, 1867, LL.B., 1869, A.M., 1870; m. Ella R. Flagg, May 23, 1877. Admitted to bar, 1869, and began practice at New York; mem. De Witt, Lockman & De Witt, 1874—. Trustee Fulton Trust Co., New York Life Ins. &

Trust Co., Greenwich Savings Bank; dir. Chem. Nat. Bank. Trustee Columbia U., 1899—, Roosevelt Hosp.; gov. New York Hosp.; v.p. N.Y. Soc. Prevention of Cruelty to Children. Episcopalian. Home: New York, N.Y. Deceased.

DE WITT, John, theologian; b. Harrisburg, Pa., Oct. 10, 1842; s. William R. and Mary Elizabeth (Wallace) D.; A.B., Princeton, 1861, A.M., 1864; studied law; student Princeton Theol. Sem., 1861-64; Union Theol. Sem., 1864-65; (D.D., Princeton U., 1877; LL.D., Hanover Coll., Ind., 1888); m. Laura Aubrey Beaver, Aug. 20, 1874 (died 1892); 2d, Elinor Maclay Allen, July 26, 1894. Ordained Presbyn. ministry, 1865; pastor Irvington, N.Y., 1865-69, Boston, 1869-76, Phila., 1876-82; prof. ecclesiastical history, Lane Theol. Sem., Cincinnati, 1882-88; prof. apologetics and missions, McCormick Theol. Sem., Chicago, 1889-92; prof. ch. history, Princeton Theol. Sem., 1892-1912, and prof. emeritus, 1912—. Trustee Princeton U. Author: Sermons on the Christian Life, 1885; History of Princeton University, 1896. Home: Princeton, N.J. Died Nov. 19, 1923.

DEWITT, John Hibbett, judge; b. Sumner Co., Tenn., Sept. 21, 1872; s. Rev. Marcus Bearden (D.D.) and Mary (Hibbett) D.; A.B., Vanderbilt U., 1894; LL.B., George Washington U., 1897; LL.D., Mo. Valley Coll., 1923, Tusculum Coll., 1924; m. Rebekah Ward, Nov. 14, 1899; children—Ward, John Hibbett. Admitted to Tenn. bar, 1897; practiced, Nashville, 1897-1925; apptd. by Gov. Peay judge of Court of Appeals of Tenn., 1925, and elected to same position for 2 terms, 1926-42. Mem. Bd. of Edn., Nashville, 1906-09; chmn. Davidson County Charity Commn., 1916-25; U.S. fuel adminstr., Davidson Co., Tenn., 1917-18; chmn. Civil Service Commn. of Nashville, 1923-25; chmn. Tenn. George Washington Bi-Centennial Commn.; mem. bd. Carnegie Library; chmn. bd. commrs. Watkins Institute; trustee Vanderbilt U. Moderator Jud. Commn. General Assembly Presbyn. Ch. in U.S.A., 1923; mem. spl. commn. of 15 to study causes of unrest in the ch., 1925-27. Democrat. Mason. Home: Nashville, Tenn. Died Mar. 7, 1937.

DE WITT, Julia Woodhull (Miss), author; b. Harrisburg, Pa.; d. Rev. William Radcliff and Mary E. (Wallace) D.; ed. in schs. of Pa. Author: Life of Alexander the Great; Life of Timour the Tartar; How He Made His Fortune, 1885; Life's Battle Won, 1893. Home: Carlisle, Pa. Died 1906.

DE WITT, Lydia Maria (Mrs. Alton D. De Witt), pathologist; b. Flint, Mich., Feb. 1, 1859; d. Oscar and Elizabeth (Walton) Adams; Mich. State Normal Coll.; M.D., U. of Mich., 1898, B.S., 1899, A.M., 1914; m. Alton D. De Witt, June 22, 1878; children—Clyde A., Mrs. George B. Ritcheson. Asst. and instr. Med. Dept., U. of Mich., 1898-1910; asst. city pathologist and bacteriologist, St. Louis, 1910-12; asst. prof. pathology, U. of Chicago, 1912-18, asso. prof., 1918—; also mem. Sprague Memorial Inst. Baptist. Home: Chicago, Ill. Deceased.

DE WITT, William Hedges, mem. from Mont. Nat. Rep. Com., 1900—; b. New York, Mar. 16, 1853; s. James Robinson De W.; grad. Hamilton Coll., 1875; Columbia Coll. law school, 1878; m. Julia Child Rumley, Aug. 29, 1883. Admitted to bar, New York, May, 1878; Mont., 1879; practiced law, Helena, Mont., 1879-81; Butte, Mont., 1881-89; U.S. atty. for Mont., 1883-85; co. atty., 1886-89; justice Supreme Court, Mont., 1889-96; practiced law Butte from 1897. Home: Butte, Mont. Died 1902.

DE WOLF, John, landscape architect; b. Bristol, R.I., Mar. 26, 1850; s. Algernon Sidney and Clara (Diman) D.; ed. Bristol and Providence, R.I.; studied landscape architecture in R.I., Boston and New York, Eng. and in Europe; unmarried. Has been employed as engr. and landscape architect in all the Atlantic states; designed the Villa Maria on Lake Como, Italy; topographer and hydrographer U.S. Coast and Geod. Survey, 1871-88; landscape architect of New York, 1898-1906. Home: Bristol, R.I. Died Nov. 23, 1913.

DE WOLF, Wallace Leroy; b. Chicago, Ill., Feb. 24, 1854; s. Calvin and Frances (Kimball) D.; LL.B., Union Coll. of Law, Chicago; m. Mary Ridgely Rea, Oct. 20, 1890 (died 1915). Admitted to practice in Ill., 1876; gen. real estate business, 1894—; mem. of W. L. De Wolf & Co.; dir. Kellogg Switch & Supply Co. Painter and etcher; pictures have been exhibited in leading galleries of the country. Trustee Art Inst. Chicago, and presented to it one of the most complete collections of etchings by Zorn in the U.S. Republican. Home: Chicago, Ill. Died Dec. 25, 1930.

DeWOODY, Charles Frederick; b. Akron, O., Oct. 31, 1877; s. David Gillespie and Alice Booner (Crubaugh) D.; student Buchtel Coll., Akron, 1893-97; LL.B., Columbian U., 1906; m. Oneta Ownby, Aug. 14, 1907; 1 son, Charles Ownby. Began as law clk., atty. gen.'s office, Washington, D.C., 1901, later spl. asst. to atty. gen.; spl. investigator and prosecutor for U.S. Govt. in Ariz., Mexico and the Southwest, of violators of treaty rights with Indians; spl. examiner into fraudulent practices by officials in U.S. courts; in charge at Chicago of beef trust investigations; investigated violations of Sherman Anti-Trust Act; div. supt. N.Y. Div. Dept. of Justice in charge War Intelligence Service, 1918; resigned, Dec. 31, 1918; v.p. Nafra Co., Inc., ship owners and operators, N.Y. City; investments and practice of law, 1924—. Republican. Protestant. Home: New Port Richey, Fla., and Chicago. Died Jan. 8, 1930.

DEXTER, Edwin Grant, vocational edn.; b. Calais, Me., July 21, 1868; s. Rev. Henry Vaughan and Mary Edna (Boardman) D.; prep. edn., Worcester Acad.; Ph.B., Brown U., 1891, A.M., 1892; Ph.D., Columbia, 1899; LL.D., U. of Puerto Rico, 1912; m. Allie Martin Hodge, June 7, 1895; children—Henry Vaughan, Louise, Dwight Hodge, Edwin Boardman, William Martin. Instr. applied mathematics, Brown U., 1891-92; science master high sch., Colorado Springs, 1892-95; prof. psychology, Colo. State Normal Sch., Greeley, 1895-1900; prof. edn., U. of Ill., 1900-07; dean Sch. of Edn., same, 1903-07, dir. summer session, 1902-07; commr. of edn., Puerto Rico, and chancellor U. of P.R., 1907-12. Maj. A.R.C., 1918-20, in charge operations in Montenegro and later in S. Russia; mem. Civilian Advisory Bd. U.S. War Dept. and ednl. specialist 9th Corps Area, 1920-22; pres. U.S. Vets. Bur. Vocational School, Camp Sherman, O., 1922-24; chief of vocational Unit, U.S.V.B., 1924-25, chief of policy div. of same, 1925-30, and historian, 1930-37. Comdr. Order of St. Stanislaus (Russian); Comdr. Order of Danilo (Montenegrin); Chevalier Order of White Eagle (Serbian); Medal of Recognition, 2d class (French); Grand Cross of Red Cross (Russia, Serbia, Montenegro). Republican. Baptist. Home: Lorton, Va. Died Dec. 5, 1938.

DEXTER, Franklin, anatomist; b. Boston, Mass., May 10, 1857; M.D., Columbia, 1887. Asst. demonstrator anatomy, Columbia, 1892-93; asst. in histology, 1893-94, demonstrator anatomy, 1894-95, asst. prof., 1896-99, asso. prof., 1900—, Harvard. Home: Boston, Mass. Died 1927.

DEXTER, Franklin Bowditch, librarian; b. Fairhaven, Mass., Sept. 11, 1842; A.B., Yale, 1861, A.M., 1864 (Litt.D., 1902); m. Theodosia M. Wheeler, 1880. Tutor, 1864-67, asst. in library, 1867-69, asst. librarian, 1869-1912, emeritus, 1912, registrar, 1869-92, sec. of Corp., 1869-99. Larned prof. Am. history, 1877-88, Yale. Author: Biographical Sketches of Graduates of Yale College with Annals of the College History, 1701-1815, 6 vols., 1885-1912; Sketch of the History of Yale University, 1887. Edited the Literary Diary of Ezra Stiles, 3 vols., 1901; Historical Catalogue of First Church, New Haven, 1914; Documentary History of Yale University, 1701-45, 1916; Itineraries and Correspondence of Ezra Stiles, 1916; New Haven Town Records, 1649-84, 2 vols., 1917-18. Died Aug. 13, 1920.

DEXTER, Gordon, dir. Submarine Signal Co.; b. Beverly, Mass., Aug. 12, 1864; s. Franklin Gordon and Susan Greene (Amory) D.; A.B., Harvard, 1887; m. Annie Linzee Amory, Feb. 1, 1906 (died 1916); m. 2d, Isabella Hunnewell, Jan. 1930. Former pres. Submarine Signal Co. (dir.); clk. and dir. Hunt-Spiller Mfg. Corp.; dir. Mexican Northern Mining & Ry. Co., Submarine Signal Corp. Home: Boston, Mass. Died Mar. 10, 1937.

DEXTER, Henry, founder and pres. Am. News Co.; b. W. Cambridge, Mass., Mar. 14, 1813; s. Jonathan Marsh and Elizabeth (Balch) D.; ed. there; m. Lucretia Marquand Perry, Oct. 11, 1853. In Boston and Cambridge publishing houses until 1836; in hardware business, 1836-42; after that in wholesale trade in books, mags., periodicals and newspapers; conceived the plan and led in organization, 1864, of the Am. News Co. Life member and a founder, Met. Mus. of Art; life fellow Geog. Soc.; life dir. Am. Bible Soc., Am. Tract Soc.; life mem. and patron N.Y. Hist. Soc. Built home for N.Y. Hist. Soc., at cost of $350,000, in memory of son, Orrando Perry Dexter. Home: New York, N.Y. Died 1910.

DEXTER, (Henry) Morton, editor; b. Manchester, N.H., July 12, 1846; s. Henry Martyn (D.D., LL.D.) and Emmeline (Palmer) D.; B.A., Yale, 1867, M.A., 1870; grad. Andover Theol. Sem., 1870; m. Emily Loud Sanford, June 9, 1881. Traveled abroad, 1870-73, ordained Congl. ministry, 1873; pastor Union Ch., Taunton, Mass., 1873-88; asso. editor the Congregationalist, Boston, 1878-1901; in lit. work at Boston, 1901—. Sec. and treas. Com. of Nat. Council of Congl. Chs. of U.S., which erected memorial bronze tablet to John Robinson in Leyden, Holland, and dedicated it July 24, 1891; del. 1st Internat. Congl. Council, London, 1891, and to 2d in Boston, 1899. Independent Republican. Author: The Story of the Pilgrims, 1894; The England and Holland of the Pilgrims, 1905. Died 1910.

DEXTER, Philip, lawyer; A.B., Harvard, 1889, LL.B., 1892; in practice at Boston. Pres. Boston & Providence R.R. Corp.; trustee Provident Instn. for Savings, Albany Trust, Bedford Trust, Boston Real Estate Trust, Amoskeag Mfg. Co., Essex St. Trust, South St. Trust, Tremont Bldg. Trust; dir. Union Trust Co. of Boston, Fifty Associates, etc. Home: Boston, Mass. Died July 25, 1934.

DEXTER, Seymour, banker; b. Independence, N.Y., Mar. 20, 1841; s. Daniel and Angeline D.; prep. edn. Alfred Acad., N.Y.; grad. Alfred Univ., 1864 (A.M., Ph.D.); studied law, 1864-66; m. Ellenor Weaver, June 17, 1868. Admitted to bar, 1866, at Elmira, N.Y.; city atty., Elmira, 1872; elected mem. N.Y. assembly, 1872; county judge and surrogate, 1877, reelected, 1883; resigned, 1889; became pres. and mgr. 2d Nat. Bank of Elmira; pres. N.Y. State Bankers' Assn., 1896-97; pres. U.S. League of Local Bldg. & Loan assns., 1893-94; pres. N.Y. State League Local Bldg. & Loan assns., 1890-91; pres. Chemung Valley Mutual Loan Assn., 1875—; treas. Elmira Coll., Steel Memorial Library Assn., Elmira Building Co. Republican. A mgr. N.Y. State Reformatory, Elmira. Author: Coöperative Building and Loan Associations, 1889. Home: Elmira, N.Y. Died 1904.

DE YOUNG, Frederic Robert, judge; b. Chicago, Ill., Sept. 12, 1875; s. Peter and Effie (Van Norden) D.; B.S., Northern Ind. Normal Sch., Valparaiso, 1895; LL.B., Northwestern, 1897, LL.D., 1927; studied U. of Chicago; m. Miriam Lydia Cornell, Sept. 12, 1901; children—Herbert Cornell, Ruth Miriam. Admitted to Ill. bar, 1897, and began practice at Chicago; city atty. Harvey, Ill., 1907-19; mem. Ill. Ho. of Rep. 2 terms, 1915-18 (chmn. judiciary com., 1917); mem. Ill. Constl. Conv., 1920-22 (chmn. com. on judicial dept.); judge Circuit Court of Cook Co., by apptmt. of Gov. Lowden, to fill vacancy, 1921; elected judge Superior Court of Cook Co., Nov. 1923, term of 6 yrs., but resigned upon election as judge Supreme Court of Ill., June 2, 1924, and reëlected, 1933, for term ending June 1942. Republican. Presbyn. Home: Chicago, Ill. Died Nov. 16, 1934.

DE YOUNG, Meichel Harry, journalist; b. St. Louis, Oct. 1, 1849; s. Michel H. and Amelia (Morange) D.; removed to Calif. with parents when 5 yrs. old; with brother Charles, established The Dramatic Chronicle, 1865, later changing to the San Francisco Chronicle; upon his brother's death, 1880, Mr. De Young became sole propr. and editor-in-chief. Commr. from Calif. to Paris Expn., 1889; candidate for U.S. senator, 1892; Commr. and v.p. World's Columbian Nat. Commn., 1892-93; projector and dir. gen. Calif. Mid-winter Expn., 1893-94. Del. Rep. Nat. Convs., 1888, 1892; mem. Rep. Nat. Com., 8 years (v.chmn. 4 yrs.); pres. Internat. League of Press Clubs; dir. Asso. Press, 1882; commr. gen. from Calif., Omaha Trans-Miss. Expn., 1898; U.S. commr. and pres. U.S. Commn. Paris Expn., 1900; mem. exec. com. Relief and Red Cross Funds; v.p. and dir. of concessions Panama-Pacific Internat. Expn. Home: San Francisco. Died Feb. 15, 1925.

DIAL, Nathaniel Barksdale, senator; b. Laurens Co., S.C., Apr. 24, 1862; s. Capt. Albert and Martha Rebecca (Barksdale) D.; student Richmond Coll., 1878-79, Vanderbilt U., 1880-81; law student, U. of Va., 1882-83; m. Ruth Mitchell, Nov. 4, 1883 (died 1903); m. 2d, Josephine Minter, Oct. 17, 1906. Began practice of law, 1883; organized and was pres. Ware Shoals Mfg. Co., Georgia-Carolina Power Co., Laurens Glass Works, Laurens Oil Mills; pres. Laurens Cotton Mills, Reedy River Power Co., Home Trust Co., Sullivan Power Co. Mayor of Laurens, 1887-91 and 1895; mem. Dem. State Exec. Com., S.C., many yrs.; candidate for U.S. Senate, 1912 (defeated); elected U.S. Senate, Nov. 1918, term 1919-25; reentered law practice. Presbyn. Home: Washington, D.C., and Laurens, S.C. Died Dec. 11, 1940.

DIAZ, Abby Morton, author; d. Ichabod and Patty (Weston) Morton, of Pilgrim ancestry, Plymouth, Mass.; identified with anti-slavery work in girlhood; after brief married life, which left her with two sons to care for, became teacher in Plymouth schs. A founder and for many yrs. pres. Women's Educational and Industrial Union, Boston. Author: The William Henry Letters, 1870; Polly Cologne, 1881; Cats' Arabian Nights, 1881. Home: Belmont, Mass. Died 1904.

DIBBLE, Charles Lemuel, lawyer; b. Marshall, Mich., Nov. 30, 1881; s. William Johnson and Mollie A. (Stillwell) D.; A.B., Cornell U., 1903; LL.B., U. of Mich., 1906; D.C.L., Nashotah House, 1923; m. Louise Phillips Greene, Sept. 19, 1913; children—Charles Ralph, William James, Robert Ellis. Admitted to Ill. bar, 1906, and began practice at Chicago; moved to Kalamazoo, Mich., 1908; mem. editorial bd. Anglican Theol. Review. Pvt. inf., U.S.A., World War. Chancellor Episcopal Diocese Western Mich.; Chancellor and mem. of provincial council and court of review, Episcopal Province of Mid-West; chmn. Church Action Commn. Trustee Kalamazoo Coll., Nashotah House, Howe Sch. Author: A Grammar of Belief, 1923; When Half Gods Go, 1937. Home: Kalamazoo, Mich. Died Oct. 30, 1940.

DIBBLE, Roy Floyd, author; b. Portland, N.Y., Mar. 12, 1887; s. George E. and Miriam H. (Quilliam) D.; grad. high sch., Westfield, N.Y., 1906; A.B., Clark Coll., 1912; Ph.D., Columbia, 1921; unmarried. Instr. in English, Columbia, 1916—. Author: Albion W. Tourge, 1921; Strenuous Americans, 1923; John L. Sullivan, 1925; Mohammed, 1926. Home: New York, N.Y. Died Dec. 3, 1929.

DIBELL, Homer B(liss), judge; b. Fillmore Co., Minn., 1864; s. Elihu Lord and Elizabeth Ann (Bliss) D.; A.B., U. of Ind., 1889; LL.B., Northwestern U., 1890; unmarried. Began practice at Duluth, Minn., 1890; elected judge Dist. Court, St. Louis Co., Minn., 1898, reëlected, 1904, 10; resigned, Apr. 1913, upon appmt. as commr. Supreme Court of Minn., continued until apptd. justice Supreme Court, Oct. 12, 1918, elected justice, 1920, reëlected, 1926 and 1932. Lecturer U. of Minn. Law Sch. Home: Duluth, Minn. Died Feb. 17, 1934.

DIBRELL, James Anthony, physician; b. Van Buren, Ark., Aug. 20, 1846; s. Dr. James Anthony and Ann Eliza (Pryor) D.; ed. in neighborhood schools; became bookkeeper for James R. Berry, Auditor of State; studied medicine with his father and took course of lectures at St. Louis Med. Coll., 1867-68, and course at Univ. of Pa., med. dept.; grad., M.D., Mar. 11, 1870; took post-graduate lectures. Has practiced at Little Rock, 1870—; m. Lallie Reardon, 1876. Spent much of time, 1878-80, and in 1881, in sanitary and quarantine work. Pres. Little Rock Bd. Health; sec. State Bd. of Health; prof. anatomy, pres. and dean med. dept. Ark. Industrial Univ. Home: Little Rock, Ark. Died 1904.

DICE, Agnew Thomson, ry. official; b. Scotland, Pa., Nov. 2, 1862; s. George and Agnes Catharine (Thomson) D.; ed. Chambersburg (Pa.) Acad.; m. Margretta Boone, Feb. 3, 1887; children—Agnew Thomson, Frances, Margaret. Began as flagman with engring. corps, Pa. R.R., 1881; rodman and asst. engr., 1882-87; spl. work on signals, 1887-88; asst. supervisor, 1888-90, supervisor, 1890-91; supt. signals, N.Y.C.&H.R. R.R., 1892; asst. supt. Hudson Div., same rd., 1893-94; supt. Atlantic City R.R., 1894-97; with Phila. & Reading Ry., Phila., 1897—, as supt. Shamokin div., 1897-1903, gen. supt., 1903-10, gen. mgr., 1910-13, v.p. and gen. mgr., Jan. 1, 1913-Mar. 15, 1916, when elected pres. same road. Republican. Episcopalian. Died Mar. 25, 1932.

DICE, J(ustus) Howard, librarian; b. Pittsburgh, Pa., May 6, 1887; s. Justus and Anna J. C. (Freese) D.; A.B., U. of Pittsburgh, 1911, B.L.S., N.Y. State Library Sch., 1913; m. Helen Frost, June 23, 1920; children—Stanley Frost, Katherine Dalbey. Began as asst. librarian, Mt. Washington br., Carnegie Pub. Library, Pittsburgh, 1913; asst. reference librarian Ohio State U. Library, 1914-15, asst. librarian Ohio State Library, 1915-16; state library organizer, Ohio Bd. Library Commrs., 1916-18; asst. dir. Libraries U.S. Army, 1919-20, dir. 1920; dir. libraries and asst. prof. of bibliography, U. of Pittsburgh, 1920—. Served in U.S.A. with A.E.F., 1918-19. Methodist. Mason. Died Dec. 19, 1939.

DI CELLERE, Count V. Macchi, diplomat; b. Rome, Italy, Oct. 28, 1866; s. Count Giuseppe Macchi and Giulia (Capranica) di C.; lit. course Regio Ginnasio, Rome, and Liceo, at Sinigaglia; grad. in law, U. of Rome, 1888; (LL.D., Princeton U.); m. Dolores Cobo, of Buenos Aires, Nov. 14, 1901. Entered diplomatic service, 1889; sec. Internat. Red Cross Conf., Venice, 1892, Rome, 1892, 2d Internat. Sanitary Conf., Venice, 1897; 1st sec. Italian Legation, Buenos Aires, 1898-1903; regent Embassy, Washington, 1903-04; transferred to Petrograd, 1904; gen. sec. conf. for establishment of Internat. Inst. of Agr., Rome, 1904-05; head of cabinet of minister of foreign affairs, 1905-06; minister to Argentina, 1906-12; A.E. and P. to U.S., Nov. 6, 1913—. Died Oct. 20, 1919.

DICK, Albert Blake, mfr.; b. in Bureau Co., Ill., Apr. 16, 1856; s. Adam and Rebecca (Wible) D.; ed. pub. schs.; m. Alice S. Mathews, Jan. 25, 1881; m. 2d, Mary Henrietta Mathews, June 1, 1892. With George W. Brown & Co., mfrs. agrl. implements, Galesburg, 1872-79, Deere & Mansur Co., Moline, Ill., 1879-83; founder, 1883, and pres. A. B. Dick Co., Chicago, mfrs. labor saving devices. Republican. Home: Chicago; and Lake Forest, Ill. Died Aug. 15, 1934.

DICK, Homer T., lawyer; b. Ft. Wayne, Ind., Nov. 9, 1870; s. Daniel D.; student Chicago-Kent Coll. of Law, Chicago, 1897-1900; m. Tess A. Naughton, 1907. Entered service of Ft.W.,C.&L. Ry. (now part of Nickel Plate system) as clk., 1888; admitted to Ill. bar, 1899; dist. atty. C.&E.I. R.R., 1902-10; gen. atty., 1910-14; gen. solicitor same rd. and its successor, the C.&E.I. Ry., 1914—. Home: Chicago, Ill. Died Aug. 11, 1928.

DICK, Robert P., U.S. dist. judge, Western dist. N.C., June 7, 1872—; b. Greensboro, N.C., Oct. 5, 1823; grad. Univ. of N.C., 1843 (LL.D., 1869); admitted to bar, 1846; dist. atty., dist. of N.C., 1853-61; mem. State constl. conv., 1861 and 1865; mem. council of State, 1861-64; mem. State senate, 1864-65; asso. justice, State supreme court, 1868-72. Home: Greensboro, N.C. Died 1900.

DICK, Samuel Medary, clergyman; b. Pickaway Co., O., Apr. 4, 1857; s. Johnson and Susan R. (Green) D.; A.B., Ohio Wesleyan U., 1887, A.M., 1890; Ph.D., U. of Mich., 1891; m. Allie M. Luse, June 28, 1888. Ordained M.E. ministry, 1895; pastor Lowell, Mass., 1896-98, Providence, R.I., 1898-1903, Worcester, Mass., 1903-07, Wesley Ch., Minneapolis, 1907-12, later First M.E. Ch., Minneapolis. Won the Shearman prize of $250 given by Am. Econ. Assn., 1891, for best essay on State and Local Taxation of Personal Property in the U.S. Mem. 3d Ecumenical Meth. Conf., London, 1901; spl. rep. Bd. of Pensions and Relief of M.E. Ch. Patentee of various mech. devices; discovered new process for reduction of whole milk to a dry powder, and patentee of mechanism necessary for its production. Pres. Ever-Fresh Products Corp. Inventor Dick's universal instantaneous carbonator. Home: Pasadena, Calif. Deceased.

DICKENS, Albert, horticulturist; b. Anoka, Minn., Oct. 24, 1867; s. of William and Sarah (Ridge) D.; B.S., Kan. State Agrl. Coll., 1893, M.S., 1901; state teachers' certificate, Kan., 1895, life, 1898; m. Bertha Kimball, Jan. 1, 1898. Foreman, Munger Orchards, Eureka, Kan., 1895; instr., Ellinwood High Sch., 1897-98; asst. in horticulture, 1899-1901, actg. prof., 1901-02, prof., 1902—, Kan. State Agrl. Coll., Manhattan. Republican. Mason. Died Nov. 28, 1930.

DICKERMAN, George Sherwood, clergyman; b. Mt. Carmel, Conn., June 5, 1843; s. Ezra and Sarah (Jones) D.; grad. Williston Sem., 1861; A.B., Yale, 1865, A.M., B.D., 1868; (D.D., Bates Coll., Me., 1895); m. Elizabeth M. Street, Nov. 29, 1870. Ordained Congl. ministry, Aug. 5, 1868; pastor, Normal, Ill., 1868-69, W. Haven, Conn., 1870-73, Lewiston, Me., 1874-83, First Ch., Amherst, Mass., 1883-91, Orange Park, Fla., 1892-93; field supt., Am. Missionary Assn., 1893-95; gen. field agt., Conf. for Edn. in the South, 1899-1901; gen. field agt., Southern Edn. Bd., 1902-05, asso. sec., 1905-10; gen. field agt., John F. Slater Fund, 1907-10. Author: Families of Dickerman Ancestry, 1898; The House of Plant, 1899. Home: New Haven, Conn. Died Aug. 2, 1937.

DICKERMAN, Sherwood Owen, prof. Greek; b. Lewiston, Me., Nov. 23, 1874; s. George Sherwood and Elizabeth Mansfield (Street) D.; grad. Phillips Acad., Andover, Mass., 1892; B.A., Yale, 1896; Am. Sch. Classical Studies (Athens, Greece), 1897-99; Ph.D., U. of Halle, Germany, 1909; m. Maude Adeline Bissett, June 29, 1920; children—Margaret Huntington, Sherwood Eliot, Elizabeth. Instr. Greek, Yale, 1899-1903, 1905-06; asst. prof. Greek, Williams Coll., 1909-19, Lawrence prof., 1919—; visiting prof., Yale U., 1929-30. Conglist. Home: Williamstown, Mass. Died Sept. 20, 1930.

DICKERSON, Charles Estell, educator; b. New Germantown, N.J., Sept. 17, 1865; s. Charles E. and Elizabeth A. (Miller) D.; B.S., Lehigh U., 1889, M.S., 1905; L.H.D., Colgate, 1923; m. Emeline Marble Fletcher, Aug. 14, 1895; 1 son, Charles E. V. prin. Mt. Hermon Sch., 1890-1911; prin. The Northfield Sem., 1911-25. Republican. Conglist. Home: Oldwick, N.J. Died Jan. 16, 1939.

DICKERSON, Denver S., governor; b. Millville, Calif., Jan. 24, 1872; s. Harvey F. and Catherine M. (Bailey) D.; ed. common schs. and under pvt. tutor; m. Una L. Reilly, Apr. 23, 1904. Sergt. and 1st sergt. Troop D, 2d U.S. Vol. Cav., Spanish-Am. War, 1898; co. clk. White Pine Co., Nev., 1902-04; co. recorder, 1904-06; lt. gov. of Nev., 1906-08; succeeded as gov. upon death of Gov. Sparks, May 22, 1908, term expiring Jan. 1911. Democrat. Owner and editor White Pine News, 1904-06, since owner Ely Mining Expositor; pres. Blaine Gold Mining & Milling Co., Robinson Mining Co., White Pine County Abstract and Guarantee Co. Chmn. State Bd. of Edn., State Bd. Prison Commrs. and Insane Asylum. Mason. Home: Carson City, Nev. Died Nov. 28, 1925.

DICKERSON, James Spencer; b. Brooklyn, N.Y., Apr. 9, 1853; s. Rev. James Stokes and Julia A. (Spencer) D.; ed. Western U. of Pa., now U. of Pittsburgh; Litt.D., Denison U., Ohio, 1911; m. Fanny D. Richardson, Feb. 21, 1882; children—James Dwight, Elizabeth Richardson (Mrs. Harry Palmer), Emma G. (Mrs. Harvey B. Fuller), Willard P.; m. 2d, Leontine F. Tompson, Aug. 11, 1920. Mem. staff The Standard, 1875-92; mng. editor The Graphic (Chicago), 1892-94, The Baptist Union, 1894-95, The Standard, 1895-1914; sec. bd. of trustees of U. of Chicago, 1913-24, corr. sec., 1926— (trustee 1909-14, 1921-30; hon. trustee, 1930—); editor U. of Chicago Record, 1926—; sec. board trustees Bapt. Theol. Union, 1913-26, and Rush Med. Coll., 1913-26; trustee Frances Shimer Sch., Mt. Carroll, Ill., 1915—, pres. bd., 1927—. Treas. Eagle's Nest Assn., Oregon, Ill., 1900—, pres., 1926—. Home: Chicago, Ill. Died Sept. 5, 1933.

DICKERSON, Mary Cynthia, zoölogist; b. Hastings, Mich., Mar. 7, 1866; d. Wilbur F. and Melissa R. D.; student of U. of Mich., three years, and spent several summers at Woods Hole, Mass.; B.S., U. of Chicago, 1897; unmarried. Instr. biology, Central High Sch., Grand Rapids, Mich., 1891-94, High Sch., La Grange, Ill., 1894-95; head dept. of zoölogy and botany, R.I. Normal Sch., Providence, 1897-1905; zoölogist, instr. zoölogy, Stanford U., 1907-08; on scientific staff, Am. Mus. Natural History, New York, 1908-09, curator of dept. of woods and forestry, 1909-21, asst. curator of herpetology, 1910-13, asso. curator and curator, 1913-21. Asso. editor Am. Mus. Jour. Natural History, 1908-10, editor, 1910-21; lecturer N.Y. City Bd. Edn., 1908-17. Fellow N.Y. Acad. Sciences, Am. Mus. Natural History. Author: Moths and Butterflies, 1901; The Frog Book, 1906. Home: New York, N.Y. Died Apr. 8, 1923.

DICKEY, Adam Herbert, Christian Scientist; b. Toronto, Ont., June 26, 1864; s. Nathaniel and Elizabeth (Simpson) D.; ed. Model Sch. and Upper Can. Coll., Toronto; m. Lillian M. Selden, Nov. 16, 1887. In mfg. business, Kansas City, 1884-99; entered Christian Science practice, 1899; became sec. to Mary Baker Eddy, Feb. 1908, and remained with her 3 yrs., until her death. Trustee under the will of Mary Baker Eddy; dir. The First Ch. of Christ Scientist, in Boston. Mason. Home: Cohasset, Mass. Died Feb. 8, 1925.

DICKEY, Charles Andrews, clergyman; b. Wheeling, Va. (now W.Va.), Dec. 25, 1838; s. John R. and Margaret (De Hass) D.; grad. Washington Coll., Pa., 1858, A.M., 1861; studied U.P. Theol. Sem., Allegheny City, Pa., 1858-61; (D.D., Princeton, 1872; LL.D., Washington and Jefferson, 1902); m. Katharine Donnell, Jan. 8, 1863. Pastor Fourth U.P. Ch., Allegheny City, Pa., 1861-69, First Presbyn. Ch., St. Louis, 1869-75, Calvary Presbyn. Ch., Phila., 1875-93, Bethany Presbyn. Ch., Phila., 1893—. Pres. Presbyn. Hosp., Phila., 1883—; moderator Presbyn. Gen. Assembly, 1900; rep. of 20th Century movement, 1901; chmn. revision com., 1902, Presbyn. com. Inter-Ch. Conf. of Divorce and Re-marriage, 1903. Died 1910.

DICKEY, Charles Hadley, clergyman, writer; b. Ranger, N.C., Dec. 16, 1888; s. Allan Kilpatrick and Mary Malissa (McLeod) D.; B.A., Carson-Newman Coll., Tenn., 1915; student Southern Bapt. Theol. Sem., 1916-19; m. Billie Hall, July 22, 1919; children—Charles Hall, David Dale. Ordained Bapt. ministry, 1914; pastor Aurora, Ind., 1919-22, La Grange, Ga., 1922-25, Memorial Ch., Williamston, N.C., 1926-35; dir. publicity N.C. Bapt. Conv., 1935—. Commd. 1st lt. chaplain at Ft. Monroe (Va.) Chaplain's Sch., 1918; served with U.S. Army in machine gun batt. in Eng., France and Germany, 1918-19. Mason. Columnist Raleigh (N.C.) News and Observer. Home: Raleigh, N.C. Died Mar. 10, 1937.

DICKEY, Donald Ryder, zoölogist; b. Dubuque, Ia., Mar. 31, 1887; s. Ernest M. and Anna (Ryder) D.; B.A., Yale, 1910; hon. M.A., Occidental Coll., Los Angeles, 1925; m. Florence Van Vechten Murphy, June 15, 1921; 1 son, Donald R. Writer, lecturer and field naturalist; specializes in mammals and birds of N. and Central America; research asso. in vertebrate zoölogy, Calif. Inst. Tech., 1926—. Has collected over 50,000 specimens of birds and animals, regarded as the largest pvt. collection of the kind in U.S. Formerly mem. bd. Pasadena Br. Pacific S.W. Trust & Savings Bank. Trustee Southwest Mus., 1920-28; pres. bd. Pasadena Hosp. Assn., 1924-25, dir., 1923-27. Home: Pasadena, Calif. Died Apr. 15, 1932.

DICKEY, James Edward, bishop; b. Jeffersonville, Ga., May 11, 1864; s. Rev. James Madison and Ann Elizabeth (Thomas) D.; A.B., Emory Coll., 1891; D.D., Ky. Wesleyan U., 1903; LL.D., Emory U., 1915; m. Jessie Munroe, Sept. 9, 1891. Joined N. Ga. Conf., M.E. Ch., S., 1891; adj. prof. mental and moral science, 1891-96, prof. history and economics, 1896-99, Emory Coll.; pastor Grace Ch., Atlanta, Ga., 1899-1902; pres. Emory Coll., Oxford, Ga., 1902-15; pastor 1st Ch., Atlanta, Ga., 1915-20; sec. of edn., N. Ga. Conf., 1921; pastor 1st Ch., Griffin, Ga., 1922; elected bishop M.E. Ch., S., May 1922. Elected gen. sec. of Edn. of M.E. Ch., S., by Gen. Conf., 1910, but declined; del. 4th Ecumenical Meth. Conf., Toronto, 1911, 5th Ec. Conf., London, 1921; mem. Gen. Conf. M.E. Ch., S., 4 times, 1910-22; apptd. mem. Unification Commn. by Gen. Conf., 1918. Trustee Emory U., Atlanta, Ga. Home: Emory University, Ga. Died Apr. 17, 1928.

DICKEY, John Lindsay, M.D.; b. Wheeling, W.Va., Jan. 23, 1855; s. John R. and Elizabeth (Vance) D.; A.B., Washington and Jefferson Coll., 1876, A.M., 1879; v.-prin. Linsly Inst., Wheeling, W. Va., 1876-80; M.D., Jefferson Med. Coll., Philadelphia, 1883; m. Alice Lafon Reed, Oct. 31, 1889. Mem. W.Va. State Bd. Health, two terms, 1903-11; trustee, Washington and Jefferson Coll.; pres. Y.M.C.A., 1901—. Pres. Nat. Exchange Bank, State Bank of Elm Grove. Mem. Internat. Med. Congress, Washington, 1887, Berlin, 1890, Rome, 1894. Captain N.G., 1880. Home: Wheeling, W.Va. Died Feb. 5, 1929.

DICKEY, Lincoln Griffith, mgr. and organizer of expns.; b. Auburn, Neb., Sept. 16, 1884; s. Solomon Cravens (clergyman) and Elizabeth Augusta (Reid) D.; A.B., Lake Forest (Ill.) Coll., 1908; m. Helen Mary Cutler, May 19, 1909; children—Dr. Lincoln Cutler, Margaret Jane, Patricia Ann. Organizer, mgr. and dir. of fairs, convs., amusement enterprises, etc., 1908—; business mgr. Cleveland Symphony Orchestra, 1920-22; gen. mgr. Cleveland Public Auditorium, 1922-28; gen. mgr. Atlantic City Conv. Hall, 1928-33; exec. dir. Conv. and Visitors Bur., New York, 1933-36; gen. mgr. Great Lakes Expn., Cleveland, 1936-37; gen. mgr. Aquacade, N.Y. World's Fair, 1938-40. Dir. of programs U.S. and Allied Govt. expns., World War. Trustee and dir. Winona Instns., Winona Lake, Ind. Republican. Presbyn. Mason. Home: Cleveland, O. Died Oct. 25, 1940.

DICKEY, Solomon Cravens, clergyman; b. Columbus, Ind., June 24, 1858; s. Rev. Ninian Steele and Mary Jane (Davis) D.; grad. Wabash Coll., 1881 (D.D., 1897); m. Lizzie Augusta Reid, June 1, 1882. Ordained Presbyn. ministry by Presbytery of Nebraska City, 1882; pastor Auburn, Neb., 1882-86, Monticello, Ind., 1886-89, Peru, Ind., 1889-94; supt. home missions, Synod of Ind., 1894-96. In 1895 founded (with other dirs.) the Winona Assembly and Summer Sch., Winona Lake, Ind., of which is dir. and gen. sec. Home: Winona Lake, Ind. Died Dec. 23, 1920.

DICKEY, Walter S., mfr. and publisher; propr. W. S. Dickey Clay Mfg. Co.; pres. and treas. Kansas City Mo. River Navigation Co.; owner of Kansas City Journal, 1921—, Kansas City Post, 1922—. Was mem. Mo. Waterways Commn.; Rep. nominee for U.S. Senate, 1916; was chmn. Rep. State Com. of Mo., 1908. Apptd. v. chmn. Inland Waterways Commn. of U.S. Ry. Administration, 1917. Home: Kansas City, Mo. Died Jan. 22, 1931.

DICKEY, William Donaldson, judge; b. Newburgh, N.Y., Jan. 11, 1845; s. William and Esther (James) D.; ed. Newburgh Acad. and Mt. Retirement Sem. Deckertown, N.J.; law course in Albany Law Sch.; m. Kate W. Richmond, June 25, 1868. Served 3 yrs. in army of Potomac before 21 yrs. of age; entered as private and promoted to maj. and bvt. col.; recd. bvts. as maj., lt. col. and col. for "gallant and meritorious services"; awarded Congressional Medal of Honor. Admitted to bar; mem. N.Y. Const. Conv., 1894; justice Supreme Ct. of N.Y., Jan. 1, 1896-Dec. 31, 1909. Republican. Home: Brooklyn, N.Y. Died May 14, 1924.

DICKIE, George William, naval architect, marine engr.; b. Arbroath, Scotland, July 17, 1844; s. William and Jane (Watson) D.; ed. Tay Port, Fife, Scotland, until 1860; learned engring. business with N. British R.R. Co. and in father's shipyard; arrived in San Francisco from Scotland, 1869; m. Anna Jack, of Tay Port, Aug. 5, 1873. Engr. Risdon Iron Works, San Francisco, 1870-83; mgr. Union Iron Works, San Francisco, 1883-1905; now cons. marine and mech. engr. San Francisco. Took prominent part in steamship work on the Pacific Coast and in designing machinery for the Comstock mines, etc. Pres. and life mem. Tech. Soc. Pacific Coast. Author: Pumping and Hoisting Works, 1876. Home: San Mateo, Calif. Died Aug. 16, 1918.

DICKIE, James Francis, clergyman, author; b. Kilmarnock, Scotland, Nov. 13, 1848; s. Francis and Susan (McLelland) D.; Kilmarnock Acad.; Edinburgh U.; Berlin U.; (D.D., U. of Mich., 1892); m. Louise Beck, June 23, 1875. Ordained Presbyn. ministry, 1869; asst. pastor St. Thomas' Ch., Greenock, 1869-71; pastor St. Andrew's Ch., Berlin, Can. 1871-79, Central Ch., Detroit, 1879-94, Am. and British Union Ch., Berlin, Germany, 1894-09 (ch. edifice erected chiefly by means of funds collected by him in America). Lecturer on church history, U. of Mich., 1887-94. Died May 28, 1933.

DICKIE, Samuel, coll. pres.; b. Oxford Co., Can., June 6, 1851; s. William and Jane (McNabb) D.; B.S., Albion Coll., 1872, M.S., 1877 (LL.D., 1900); m. Mary Brockway, Dec. 22, 1872. Prof. astronomy, Albion Coll., 1877-87; engaged in mfg. business; pres. Albion Coll., Feb. 1901-June 1921. Chmn. Prohibition Nat. Conv., 1884; Prohibition candidate for gov. of Mich., 1886; mayor Albion, 1896-97; chmn. Nat. Prohibition Com., 1887-1900, vice chmn., 1900—. Home: Albion, Mich. Died Nov. 5, 1925.

DICKINS, Francis William, rear admiral; b. Beekmanville, N.Y., Nov. 2, 1844; s. George and Eunice (Pearce) D.; grad. U.S. Naval Acad., 1864; m. Edith Pratt, Apr. 9, 1902. Promoted ensign, Nov. 1, 1866; advanced through grades to rear adm., June 17, 1904. On various duties to 1873; exec. officer Monocacy, Asiatic Sta., 1873-Jan., 1875, Kearsarge, Jan.-Apr. 1875, Yantic, Apr.-July 1875; Kearsarge July 1875-Mar. 1876, Yantic, Mar.-Apr. 1876; comd. Yantic, Apr.-July 1876; leave, 1877; Naval Acad., 1878-80; exec. officer Constitution, 1881; Hydrographic Office, 1882; Kearsarge, 1882; comd. Onward, 1883-84; Tallapoosa, 1887-89; Navy Yard, Washington, head of Dept. of Yards and Docks, 1890-92; spl. duty Asiatic Sta., 1892; Navy Yard, Washington, 1892-93; spl. duty, Jan., Apr.-June, 1893; comd. Monongahela, 1893, Essex, 1894, training sta., Newport, R.I., and training-ship Constellation, 1894-96; asst. to Bur. Navigation, 1896-99; comd. Indiana, 1899-1900, Oregon, 1900-01; Brooklyn, 1901; mem. Examining Bd., 1902; comd. receiving-ship Independence, 1902-03; comdt. Navy Yard, Pensacola, 1903-04, Navy Yard, League Island, 1904-05; comd. Coast Squadron, N. Atlantic Fleet, 1905-06; spl. duty, 1906; retired, Nov. 2, 1906. Home: Washington, D.C. Died 1911.

DICKINSON, Albert, seed merchant; b. Stockbridge, Mass., Oct. 28, 1841; s. Albert F. and Ann Eliza (Anthony) D.; removed with parents to Chicago, 1855; grad. 1st Chicago High Sch., 1859; m. Dr. Emma L. Benham, Apr. 22, 1911. Engaged with father in grain and produce business, 1859-61; enlisted Apr. 1861, in Co. B, Chicago Light Arty. (Taylor's Battery), 1st Regt. Ill. Light Arty.; par-

ticipated in battles of Ft. Donelson, Shiloh, siege of Vicksburg, Battle of Missionary Ridge, etc., and Atlanta campaign; hon. disch., July 1864; spent 1 yr. at Durant, Ia., buying grain then with father again; property destroyed by Chicago fire, 1871, incurring total loss; associated with bros. and sister, Melissa, in starting anew, paying all indebtedness; firm of Albert Dickinson, 1872-88, incorporated, 1888, as The Albert Dickinson Co. of which is pres. Republican. Mem. Chicago Acad. Sciences. Home: Orange City, Fla. Died Apr. 5, 1925.

DICKINSON, Alfred Elijah, Bapt. clergyman, editor; b. Spottsylvania Co., Va., Dec. 3, 1830; ed. Richmond Coll. (A.M.) and Univ. of Va. (D.D., Furman Univ., Greenville, S.C.); held several pastorates and, 1866, became joint editor and later editor in chief of the Religious Herald. Home: Richmond, Va. Died 1906.

DICKINSON, Anna Elizabeth, author; b. Phila., Oct. 28, 1842; ed. Friends' Free Sch.; taught in Berks Co., Pa., 1859-60; employed U.S. Mint, April to Dec. 1861; lectured against slavery and for woman suffrage and other reforms; went on stage, 1876, and appeared in tragedy rôles for several yrs., returned to lecture field; retired. Author: A Paying Investment, a Plea for Education; What Answer? (novel); A Ragged Register of People, Places and Opinions; The Crown of Thorns (play); Mary Tudor (play). Died Oct. 22, 1932.

DICKINSON, Charles Henry, clergyman, educator; b. W. Springfield, Mass., Dec. 21, 1857; s. Henry Kirke White and Angeline (Dunham) D.; B.A., Amherst, 1881; B.D., Yale Div. Sch., 1884; post-grad., Yale, 1884-89; D.D., Fargo, 1903; m. Mary Lord Thorn, Jan. 20, 1886 (died 1922); children—Thorn, Sidney Edward. Ordained Congl. ministry, 1885; pastor Wallingford, Conn., 1885-93, Canandaigua, N.Y., 1894-1901, 1st Ch., Fargo, N.D., 1901-05, Middlebury, Vt., 1907-11; writer and preacher in Boston, 1911-13; in charge religious and extension work Calhoun, Ala., 1913-24 and 1932-35, v.p., 1915-24; lit. work from 1925. Corporate mem. A.B.C.F.M., 1896-1911. Trustee Fargo Coll., 1903-05. Republican. Mason. Author: The Christian Reconstruction of Modern Life, 1913; The Religion of the Social Passion, 1923; The Social Aims of Jesus, 1930. Home: Calhoun, Ala. Died Apr. 12, 1938.

DICKINSON, Charles Monroe, diplomat; b. Lowville, N.Y., Nov. 15, 1842; s. Richard and Bessie (Rea) D.; ed. Fairfield, N.Y., Sem. and Lowville Acad.; m. Bessie Virginia, d. of Hon. Giles W. and Bessie R. Hotchkiss, of Binghamton, Mar. 24, 1867; m. 2d, Alice Bond, d. Elias G. and Mary A. Minard, of Poughkeepsie, Feb. 2, 1910. Studied law with Hon. Daniel S. Dickinson; admitted to bar, 1865; practiced law in Pa., at Binghamton, N.Y., and New York City, 1865-77; abandoned profession because of broken health; editor and propr. Binghamton Republican, 1878-1911. In 1892 upon his suggestion and initiative the various news organizations of the country were combined into the present Associated Press. Presdl. elector, 1896; U.S. consul gen. to Turkey, 1897-1906; diplomatic agt. to Bulgaria, 1901-1903. While diplomatic representative to Bulgaria the Am. missionary, Ellen M. Stone, was carried off by brigands; released through his settlement and efforts; mem. bd. to draft regulations for govt. of Am. Consular service, 1906; Am. consul gen.-at-large, 1906-Oct. 1, 1908. Trustee Barlow Industrial Sch., Binghamton. Author: History of Dickinson Family, 1885; The Children and Other Verses, 1889; Political History of New York State—Cleveland to Hughes (in part), 1911; Political History of New York State, from Colonial Period (in part), 1914. Home: Binghamton, N.Y. Died July 3, 1924.

DICKINSON, Clement Cabell, congressman; b. Prince Edward Co., Va., Dec. 6, 1849; s. Asa Dupuy and Sallie Cabell (Irvine) D.; A.B., Hampden-Sydney Coll., 1869; m. Mattie Parks, Dec. 1882. Began practice of law at Clinton, Mo., 1875; sr. mem. C. C. Dickinson & Son, 1908—. Pros. atty. Henry Co., Mo., 1877-82; mem. Mo. Ho. of Rep. 1 term, Senate 1 term; presdl. elector, 1896; elected to 61st Congress, Feb. 1, 1910, from 6th Mo. Dist., for unexpired term (1910-11) of David A. DeArmond, deceased; reëlected 62d to 66th Congresses (1911-21), 68th to 70th Congresses (1923-29), 72d and 73d Congresses (1931-35), 6th Mo. Dist. Mem. bd. regents Mo. State Normal Sch., Warrensburg. Democrat. Presbyn. Died Jan. 14, 1938.

DICKINSON, Don(ald) McDonald, postmaster-gen.; b. Port Ontario, N.Y., Jan. 17, 1846; s. Col. Asa C. and Minerva H. D.; removed to Mich., 1848; ed. pub. schs. and by pvt. tutors; LL.B., U. of Mich., 1867; m. Frances L., d. Dr. Alonzo Platt. June 15, 1869. In general practice in the West, New York and Washington, 1867—; chmn. Dem. State Com., 1876; mem. Dem. Nat. Com., 1880-85; postmaster-gen. in cabinet of President Cleveland, 1887-89; chmn. Dem. Nat. Campaign Com., 1892; tendered and declined cabinet position, 1893; sr. counsel of U.S. before Internat. High Commn. on Bering Sea claims, under Fur Seal Arbitration, 1896-97; mem., with Rt. Hon. Sir Henry Strong (of

British Privy Council), and Señor Doctor Don Pacas of Salvador, of Court of Arbitration to adjust controversy between U.S. and Republic of Salvador, 1902. Pres. and trustee Detroit Mus. of Art. Home: Trenton, Mich. Died Oct. 15, 1917.

DICKINSON, Horace Danforth, judge; b. Ogdensburg, N.Y., July 25, 1866; s. William and Margaret Jane (Thompson) D.; LL.B., U. of Minn., 1890; m. Marian Elizabeth Rice, Apr. 28, 1898; 1 dau., Margaret Jane. Admitted to Minn. bar, 1890, and began practice at Minneapolis; asst. city atty., Minneapolis, 1896-1900; judge, Municipal Court, Minneapolis, 1900-05; judge, Dist. Court, Minn., 1905—. Republican. Mason. Home: Minneapolis, Minn. Died Nov. 30, 1936.

DICKINSON, Jacob McGavock, sec. of war; b. Columbus, Miss. Jan. 30, 1851; s. of Henry and Anna (McGavock) D.; A.B., U. of Nashville, 1871, A.M., 1872; studied law at Columbia Coll., New York, U. of Leipzig, and L'École de Droit, Paris, and attended lectures at Sorbonne; LL.D., Columbia, 1905, U. of Ill., 1905, Yale, 1909, Lincoln U., 1917; m. Martha Overton, Apr. 20, 1876; children—John Overton, Henry, Jacob McGavock. Admitted to bar, 1874; practiced at Nashville, 1874-99, Chicago, 1899-1909; served several times by spl. commn. on supreme bench of Tenn.; asst. atty. gen. of U.S., 1895-97; counsel for U.S. before Alaskan Boundary Tribunal, 1903; gen. solicitor I.C. R.R. Co., 1899-1901, and gen. counsel, 1901-09; sec. of war in cabinet of President Taft, Mar. 4, 1909-May 1911; receiver of Rock Island Lines, 1915-17. Home: Chicago, Ill. Died Dec. 13, 1928.

DICKINSON, James Taylor, clergyman; b. Richmond, Va., Aug. 4, 1861; s. Rev. Alfred Elijah (D.D.) and Fannie E. (Taylor) D.; Richmond Coll., Va.; U. of Va.; Grad. Southern Bapt. Theol. Sem., 1885; (D.D., Richmond Coll., 1896); m. Stella G. DeLand, Oct. 18, 1887; children—Margaret (wife of Dr. A. D. Kaiser), Helen (Mrs. W. B. Lipphard), Lois (Mrs. Leonard H. Henderson). Ordained Bapt. ministry, 1885; supply, country chs. nr. Charlottesville, Va., 1885-86; pastor North Ch., Orange, N.J., 1886-1903, 1st Ch., Rochester, N.Y., 1903-12; study, travel and sermons in Europe, Jan.-Sept. 1912; pastor 6th Av. Bapt. Ch., Brooklyn, 1913-18; gen. pulpit supply, 1918—. Convention preacher Northern Bapt. Conv., Buffalo, N.Y., 1903, also at Bapt. convs. N.J., N.Y., Conn., etc.; also college preacher. Mem. Bd. Edn., East Orange, N.J., 1898-1903; trustee Rochester Theol. Sem., Western N.Y. Instn. for Deaf Mutes; mem. Brooklyn Clerical Union, 1912-18. Mason. Author: The Preceding God, 1921. Home: Rochester, N.Y. Died Apr. 20, 1929.

DICKINSON, John Quincy, banker; b. nr. Bedford City, Va., Nov. 20, 1831; s. William and Mary Church (Grey) D.; ed. pvt. sch. and acad.; m. Mary Dickinson Lewis, Jan. 13, 1864. In banking business at Charleston, 1867—; pres. Kanawha Valley Bank; pres. J. L. Dickinson & Co. (Malden, W.Va.), Quincy (W.Va.) Coal Co., Bedford Corp., Charleston. Democrat. Presbyn. Mason. Home: Charleston, W.Va. Died Nov. 26, 1925.

DICKINSON, Marquis Fayette, lawyer; b. Amherst, Mass., Jan. 16, 1840; s. Marquis Fayette and Hannah Shepard (Williams) D.; A.B., Amherst, 1862, A.M., 1865; studied Harvard Law Sch., 1866-67; admitted to bar, 1867; m. Cecilia R. Williston, Nov. 23, 1864 (died 1904). In law practice, Boston, 1868—; mem. Dickinson & Dickinson; asst. U.S. atty., Boston, 1869-71; counsel W. End St. Ry.; dir. and counsel Met. S.S. Co. and other corps.; mem. Boston Sch. Com., 1870-71, Boston Common Council, 1871-72 (pres., 1872). Pres. bd. trustees Williston Sem.; bd. overseers Amherst Coll.; trustee Mass. Agrl. Coll.; dir. Am. Congl. Assn. Republican. Congregationalist. Home: Brookline, Mass. Died Sept. 18, 1915.

DICKINSON, Mary Low, author; b. Fitchburg, Mass., 1839; ed. common schs. and pvt. tutors; studied abroad 3 yrs.; m. John B. Dickinson (dec.). Was head asst. in Chapman Sch., Boston; taught in Hartford Female Sem.; prin. Van Norman Inst., New York. After death of her husband was prof. belles lettres, emeritus prof. and lecturer, Denver U. Sec. Female Bible Soc.; pres. Woman's Nat. Indian Assn.; pres., hon. pres. Nat. Council of Women U.S.; gen. sec. Internat. Order of The King's Daughters and Sons, 1886—, also treas. Asso. editor, with Edward Everett Hale, on Lend a Hand Magazine; editor-in-chief from its foundation, 1887. The Silver Cross Magazine; editor. 7 yrs. The Open Window, a periodical for invalids. Author: 2 vols. of poems, 6 works of fiction, illustrative of various lines of philanthropic work. Died June 1914.

DICKINSON, Oliver Booth, judge; b. Dayton, O., Sept. 25, 1857; s. Edmund W. (D.D.) and Caroline A. (Atkinson) D.; matriculated Bucknell U., Pa., class of 1877, A.M., 1903, LL.D., 1919; m. H. Evelyn Sines, Oct. 2, 1881. Admitted to Pa. bar, 1878, and practiced in Chester; del. to Dem. Co., State and Nat. convs.; judge U.S. Dist. Court, Eastern Dist. of Pa., May 4, 1914—. Trustee Pa. Mil.

Coll., Y.W.C.A. of Chester, Pa., Crozer Theol. Sem., J. Lewis Crozer Home and Hosp., A. O. Deshong Memorial. Democrat. Baptist. Home: Chester, Pa. Died Sept. 16, 1939.

DICKINSON, William Frederick, lawyer; b. Rockford, Ill., Nov. 25, 1876; s. Frederick William and Mary Margaret (Johnston) D.; A.B., U. of Wis., 1901, LL.B., 1903; m. Nannie Ruth Bray, Jan. 22, 1907; children—Frederick William, Robert James. Admitted to bar, 1903; practiced Chicago, 1903-07; with C.,R.I.&P. Ry. Co., Feb. 1, 1907—, as asst. to commerce counsel, at Chicago, 1907-09, eastern atty., at New York, Aug. 1, 1909-May 1, 1910, and gen. atty. at Chicago, in charge of all litigation arising under the Interstate Commerce Act and other federal statutory laws, 1910-18, and gen. solicitor, Aug. 1, 1918—. Editor: Hutchinson on Carriers (3d edit., with J. S. Mathews), 1906; Peirce's Digest of Decisions under Interstate Commerce Act, 1908. Republican. Episcopalian. Home: Hinsdale, Ill. Died Oct. 8, 1940.

DICKMAN, John William, univ. pres.; b. Defiance, O., Apr. 22, 1863; s. William and Martha Anna (Schott) D.; Ph.B., Upper Ia. U., 1888, LL.D., 1926; grad. study, Columbia, 1900-01; A.M., Cornell Coll., Mt. Vernon, Ia., 1904; Sc.D., Ill. Wesleyan U., Bloomington, 1907; m. Adella G. Maltbie, Aug. 22, 1889; children—Paul (dec.), John Milo, Lucile Marie. Instr. in mathematics and German, Upper Ia. U., 1888-94; with Dickman Lumber Co., 1894-98; also supt. pub. schs., Sumner, Ia., 1895-98; mem. faculty, Upper Ia. U., 1898—, treas., 1898-1928; dean of univ., 1901-28, pres., 1928—. Director of the State Bank of Fayette. Mem. Nat. Edn. Assn., Iowa State Teachers Assn. Republican. Methodist. Mason. Home: Fayette, Ia. Died Aug. 22, 1931.

DICKMAN, Joseph Theodore, army officer; b. Dayton, O., Oct. 6, 1857; s. Theodore and Mary (Weinmar) D.; grad. U.S. Mil. Acad., 1881; hon. grad. Inf. and Cav. Sch., 1883; grad. Army War Coll., Washington, 1905; (LL.D., U. of Vt.); m. Mary Rector, Sept. 26, 1882. Commd. 2d lt. 3d Cav., June 11, 1881; promoted through grades to brig. gen. U.S.A., 1917; maj. gen. N.A., Aug. 5, 1917; retired as maj. gen., Oct. 6, 1921. Awarded D.S.M. (U.S.); Croix de Guerre, Comdr. Legion of Honor (French); Knight Comdr. of the Bath (Eng.); Order of Leopold (Belgian); Grand Officer Crown of Italy, etc. Died Oct. 23, 1927.

DICKSEE, Sir Francis Bernard (Frank Dicksee), painter and illustrator; b. 1853; s. Thomas Francis D., portrait painter; brother of Margaret Isabel D., artist; studied with father and at the Royal Academy (London). Painted subjects from literature and occasionally religious subjects; in his later years he was chiefly engaged in portrait painting and illustration. Exhibited for the first time (1876) at the Royal Academy, showing: "Elijah Confronting Ahab and Jezebel in Naboth's Vineyard," which received the gold medal; "Harmony," exhibited, 1877, brought him immediate acclaim. Became member Royal Academy, 1891 (president 1924-28). Made a knight in 1925. Principal works: Mountain of the Winds; The Ideal; Dawn; Romeo and Juliet; The Passing of Arthur; Funeral of a Viking; A Reverie; Startled; (portraits) Duchess of Buckingham; Lady Aird; Mrs. Frank Shuttleworth; Lady Inverclyde; A Woman in White. Died 1928.

DICKSON, Frederick Stoever, author; b. Utica, N.Y., June 24, 1850; s. Hugh Sheridan (D.D.) and Sarah Margaret (Stoever) D.; Ph.B., Sheffield Scientific Sch. (Yale), 1871; m. Helen Hortense Hickman, Feb. 17, 1874. Admitted to Pa. bar, 1874; with John Wanamaker, Phila., 1879-84; returned to practice of law, 1884; pres. Solicitors Co., 1885-86 (resigned); chmn. bd. Abrasive Co., Phila., 1893—; pres. Cuyahoga Telephone Co., Cleveland, O., 1902; trustee bankers' com. Everett-Moore Syndicate, 1903. Originator of a plan of profit-sharing for employes of Cuyahoga Telephone Co., 1903, which attracted wide attention, a similar plan now being applied with the Abrasive Co. Republican. Author: And the Wilderness Blossomed, 1901; Bibliography of Thackeray in the United States, 1904; Bibliography of Henry Fielding, 1918; Fact and Tradition, 1925. Editor: Keightley-Fielding, 1907; An Analysis of Blackstone's Commentaries, 1872; An Analysis of Kent's Commentaries, 1874; Blackwood's History of the United States, 1896. Donated Fielding collection (about 2,000 vols.) to Yale Univ. Library, 1913. Homes: Rangeley, Me.; New York, N.Y. Died Dec. 1, 1925.

DICKSON, Samuel, lawyer; b. Newburgh, N.Y., Feb. 2, 1837; s. Samuel D. and Maria (Gillespie) D.; A.B., U. of Pa., 1855; A.M., 1857, LL.B., 1859 (LL.D., 1906); m. Fanny Hazard, 1867. Admitted to bar, 1858, and began practice at Phila.; mem. Dickson, Beitler & McCouch; dir. Reading, Lehigh Coal & Navigation, and other cos. Trustee U. of Pa., 1881—; chancellor Law Assn. Phila., 1899-1909; chmn. State Bd. Law Examiners, 1903; mem. Bd. City Trusts; mgr. Wistar Inst. Anatomy and Biology. Home: Philadelphia. Died May 28, 1915.

DICKSON, Tracy Campbell, army officer; b. Independence, Ia., Sept. 17, 1868; s. Capt. Campbell and Lucy Ellen (Tracy) D.; grad. U.S. Mil. Acad., 1892; m. Isabella Kendrick Abbott, Nov. 7, 1894. Commd. 2d lt. 2d Arty., June 11, 1892; promoted through grades to lt. col., Sept. 2, 1912; retired with rank of col., Aug. 16, 1915; recalled to active service, Mar. 7, 1917; col., Jan. 10, 1918; brig. gen., Feb. 18, 1918-May 30, 1919. Asst. to comdr. Springfield Armory, 1894-99; asst. to comdg. officer Rock Island Arsenal, 1899-1902; mem. bd. that tested and recommended magazine rifle model of 1903; recorder Bd. Ordnance and Fortification, 1903-06; asst. to chief of ordnance, 1902-06; at Sandy Hook Proving Ground, 1906-10; insp. of shops under chief engr., Panama Canal, 1910-14; pres. Ordnance Bd. and comdr. Sandy Hook Proving Ground, 1914-15; comdr. Watertown Arsenal, 1917-18; asst. to chief of ordnance, Jan.-June 1918; in charge all army work at Bethlehem Steel Co., June-Oct. 1918; comdr. Watertown Arsenal Oct. 14, 1918—. Home: Cleburne, Texas. Died May 17, 1936.

DIDAMA, Henry D., physician; grad. Albany (N.Y.) Med. Coll., M.D., 1846 (LL.D.). Chief of staff, St. Joseph's Hosp.; cons. physician, House of the Good Shepherd; emeritus prof. science and art of medicine and clinical medicine, and dean Coll. of Medicine, Syracuse Univ. Trustee Syracuse Univ. Home: Syracuse, N.Y. Died 1905.

DIDCOCT, John Joseph, educator; b. Danville, Ill., Nov. 26, 1882; s. John C. and Elizabeth (Sloan) D.; grad. Salem (O.) Acad., 1901; Ph.B., (now Coll.) of Wooster, 1905, M.S., 1908; M.A., Columbia, 1914; m. Gertrude R. Lukins, Aug. 22, 1911; children—John William, Medora Elizabeth. Asst. in biology at Wooster 3 yrs. and teacher summer sch. 8 summers; asst. high sch. visitor for U. of Ill., 1914-17; prof. secondary edn., George Peabody Coll., 1917—; asst. in edn., Teachers Coll. (Columbia), winter 1918. Mem. bd. govs. Chamber Commerce, Nashville, Tenn., 1925-28. Independent Democrat. Baptist. Co-author: Johnston's Modern High School, 1917; (Webb and Didcoct) Early Steps in Science, 1924. Home: Nashville, Tenn. Died Oct. 19, 1927.

DIEDERICH, Henry William, consul gen.; b. Pittsburgh, Nov. 13, 1845; s. Nicholas H. and Clara M. (Wessler) D.; grad. Concordia Coll., Ft. Wayne, Ind., 1866, Concordia Sem., St. Louis, 1869; post.-grad. course in Columbian Coll., Washington, 1869-70; m. Margaret Stutz, Aug. 23, 1870. Pastor St. John's Evan. Luth. Ch., New York, 1870-73; prof. English lang. and lit., Concordia Coll., Ft. Wayne, Ind.; apptd. U.S. consul to Leipzig, 1889; recalled in 1893; consul at Magdeburg, Germany, 1897-99, at Bremen, 1899-1906; consul gen. at Antwerp, 1906-17; on leave of absence, 1917, 18; consul at Sarnia, Ont., 1919—. Died Feb. 8, 1926.

DIEDERICHS, Herman, mech. engr.; b. Muenchen-Gladbach, Germany, Aug. 12, 1874; s. John Peter and Anna Marie (Kamps) D.; came to U.S., 1888, naturalized, 1893; M.E., Cornell U., 1897; unmarried. Began as instr. mech. engring., Cornell U., 1898, asst. prof., 1902, prof., 1907, dir. Sibley Sch. of Mech. Engring., 1921—, John E. Sweet prof. engring. from 1928—all of Cornell U. Author: (with R. C. Carpenter) Internal Combustion Engines, 1905; (with same) Experimental Engring, 1910; (with W. C. Andrae) Experimental Mechanical Engineering (Vol. I), 1931. Died Aug. 31, 1937.

DIEGO, José de, lawyer; b. Aguadilla, Porto Rico, Apr. 16, 1868; s. Felipe de and Elisa (Martinez) D.; grad. Poly. Coll., Logrono, Spain, 1886; student of law, U. of Barcelona, Spain; LL.B., U. of Havana, 1891; m. Mrs. Georgina Blanes, Nov. 11, 1901. Began practice, Porto Rico and Cuba, 1891; sub-sec. depts. of Interior and Justice, Porto Rico, 1898; judge Supreme Ct. of P.R., 1898-1900; chief justice Criminal Ct., Mayaguez, P.R., 1899; fiscal of Dist. Ct. of Mayaguez, 1900; mem. Exec. Council, P.R., 1900-01; mem. Ho. of Del., P.R., 1903—(speaker of House, 1907-15). V.p. bd. trustees U. of Porto Rico. Catholic. Author: La Codificación Administrativa, 1887; Los Grandes Infames, 1888; Apuntes Sobre Delincuencia y Penalidad, 1901; Pomarrosas, 1904. Home: San Juan, P.R. Died July 16, 1918.

DIEHL, Samuel Willauer Black, naval officer; b. Reading, Pa., Sept. 20, 1851; s. William W. and Jeriah C. D.; early edn. pub. schs., Reading, Pa.; grad. U.S. Naval Acad., 1873; m. Caroline Wilbank O'Connor, Apr. 4, 1892. Midshipman, U.S.N., 1869; ensign, 1874; promoted through grades to judge advocate gen. with rank of capt. U.S.N., June 4, 1904—. Served on bd. U.S.S. Alaska, Wabash Congress, Hartford, Plymouth, Marion, Boston, Detroit, Machias, Cincinnati; comd. U.S.S. Eagle, Marietta, Newport, Boston; also in Hydrographic Office; Bur. of Navigation; Bur. of Equipment; Naval Intelligence Office; supt. of compasses; judge advocate gen. Author: Practical Problems and the Compensation of the Compass, U22. Died 1909.

DIEKEMA, Gerrit John, diplomatist; b. at Holland, Mich., Mar. 27, 1859; s. W. and H. (Stegeman) D.; A.B., Hope Coll., Mich., 1881, A.M., 1884; LL.B., U. of Mich., 1883; LL.D., Hope Coll., 1913; m. Mary E. Alcott, Oct. 27, 1885; children—Marguerite Rodger, S. Marie Rodger, Willis A., Gerrit J.; m. 2d, Leona M. Belser, 1920. Admitted to bar, 1883, and began practice at Holland; mem. Diekema & Kollen, 1901-11, Diekema, Kollen & Ten Cate, 1911—; pres. First State Bank, 1902—; pres. De Pree Co., 1915—; pres. Holland, St. Louis Sugar Company, 1920—; pres. New Era Life Assn., 1925. Held various local offices; mem. Ho. of Rep., 1885-91 (speaker, 1889); pres. Mich. Municipal Commn., 1894-95; mayor, Holland, 1895; chmn. Rep. State Central Com., 1900-10 and 1927; mem. Spanish Treaty Claims Commn., 1901-07; elected to 60th Congress, Apr. 27, 1907, for unexpired term (1907-09) of William Alden Smith (elected to Senate); reëlected to 61st Congress (1909-11), 5th Mich. Dist.; mgr. speakers' bureau Rep. Nat. Com., Chicago, 1912; apptd. E.E. and M.P. to the Netherlands, Aug. 1929. Home: Holland, Mich. Died Dec. 20, 1930.

DIELMAN, Frederick, artist; b. Hanover, Germany, Dec. 25, 1847; came to U.S. in childhood; grad. Calvert Coll.; m. Lilla Marion, d. Maj. Gen. H. W. Benham, U.S. Engrs., 1883; children—F. McNiel, Lilla E. (Mrs. M. P. Corse, dec.), Ernest B. Topographer and draftsman in U.S. Engr. Dept., 1866-72; studied art under Diez at Royal Acad., Munich; opened studio in New York, 1876; illustrator and figure painter; designer of mosaic panels "Law" and "History" in Congressional Library, and of large mosaic, "Thrift," Albany Sav. Bank, and the decorations in new bldg. of the Washington Evening Star; six mosaics in State Capitol, Des Moines, Ia. N.A., 1883; pres. Nat. Acad. Design, 1889-1909; mem. Nat. Inst. Arts and Letters. Mem. Art Commn., New York, 1901-03; pres. Fine Arts Fedn. of New York, 1910-15; prof. art Coll. City of N.Y., 1903-18; art dir. Cooper Union, New York, 1905-31. Homes: New York, N.Y.; also Ridgefield, Conn. Died Aug. 15, 1935.

DIEMER, Hugo, industrial engr., author; b. Cincinnati, O., Nov. 18, 1870; s. Theodore and Bertha L. (Huene) D.; M.E. in Electrical Engring., Ohio State U., 1896; student U. of Chicago, 1900; B.A. in history and polit. science, Pa. State Coll., 1913; m. Mabel N. Hudson, June 26, 1901 (died 1934); children—Theodore Hudson, Natalie Elizabeth, Dorothy Arnold, Mary Louise. With Addyston Pipe & Steel Co., Cincinnati, 1888-92; Bullock Electric Mfg. Co. and Westinghouse Electric & Mfg. Co., 1896-1900; asst. prof. mech. engring., Mich. Agrl. Coll., 1900-01; asso. prof. mech. engring., U. of Kan., 1901-04; cons. engr., Indianapolis and Chicago, 1904-07; prof. mech. engring., in charge of dept., 1907-09, prof. industrial engring., 1909-19, Pa. State Coll. Commd. maj. ordnance dept., 1917, then lieut. col.; in charge at U.S. Cartridge Co., Lowell, Mass., 1917, Bethlehem Steel Co., 1918; personnel supt. Winchester Repeating Arms Co., 1919-20; dir. management courses and personnel, La Salle Extension U., 1920—. Summer lecturer on organization and management, University of Chicago, 1915; lecturer on industrial orgn., dept. of univ. extension Mass. State Bd. of Edn., 1917. Fellow and dir. Inst. of Management (div. of Am. Management Assn.), 1927—. Episcopalian. Mason. Author: Factory Organization and Administration, 1910, 5th edit., 1935; Modern Foremanship and Production Methods (with Meyer Bloomfield), 1921; Personnel Administration (with Daniel Bloomfield), 1921; Foremanship Training, 1927; Production Control, 1930. Home: Chicago, Ill. Died Mar. 3, 1939.

DIENST, George Elias, physician; b. Hamilton Co., Ind., Mar. 8, 1858; s. John Henry and Henrietta Wilhelmina (Goetz) D.; grad. Union Bibl. Inst., Naperville, Ill., 1883; M.D., Nat. Med. Coll., Chicago, 1898; (Ph.D.); m. Clara J. Bowman, Mar. 26, 1885. Ordained in Evang. Assn., 1883; pastor in Kan., 1883-86; missionary teacher in Theol. Sem. of the Evang. Assn., Japan, 1886-96; traveling missionary collector in America, 1896-98; practicing physician, 1898—; became Episcopalian, 1898, ordained priest P.E. Ch., 1904; rector St. John's Episcopal Ch., Naperville, 1904-08; removed to Aurora, Ill., 1908; prof. of materia medica, Hahnemann Med. Coll., Chicago, June 1908—, and Hering Med. Coll., Chicago, 1910-12. Republican. Author: What to Do for the Head, 1906; What to Do for the Stomach, 1907. Home: Aurora, Ill. Died Apr. 10, 1932.

DIES, Martin, congressman; b. Jackson Parish, La., Mar. 13, 1870; s. David Warren and Sarah Jane (Pyburn) D.; ed. pub. schs. of Tex.; m. Mrs. Olive M. Blackshear, May 15, 1892. Admitted to bar, 1892; first practiced at Woodville, then at Beaumont; elected co. judge of Tyler Co., Tex., 1894; dist. atty. 1st Jud. Dist. of Tex., 1898; mem. 61st to 65th Congresses (1909-19), 2d Tex. Dist. Democrat. Methodist. Home: Beaumont, Tex. Died July 13, 1922.

DIESEL, William F., lock mfr.; b. St. Wendel, Germany, Jan. 19, 1877; s. Louis and Eliza (Schleyer) D.; ed. in pub. and high schs. in Germany; m. Theresa B. Lettau, Sept. 28, 1899; children—Mildred

(Mrs. Myron Wilkes), Evelyn (Mrs. Luke Vail), Norman F., Richard H. Came to U.S., 1889, naturalized, 1909. Began with Sargent & Greenleaf Co., in 1891, as apprentice, successively asst. foreman, foreman, supt. and works mgr., 1891-1921; v.p., treas. and dir., 1921-33, pres. and gen. mgr., 1933—; also v.p. Sargent & Keating (New York). Republican. Catholic. Home: Rochester, N.Y. Died Oct. 10, 1939.

DIETERICH, William H., senator; b. Cooperstown, Ill., Mar. 31, 1876; s. George H. and Anna K. D.; grad. Northern Ind. Law Sch., Valparaiso; m. Nona S. Runkle; children—Mrs. Ruth D. Kalthoff, William J. Began practice at Rushville, Ill.; was city atty., Rushville, treas. Rushville Union Schs., master in chancery, later county judge, Schuyler County; spl. inheritance tax atty., 1913-17; mem. Ill. Ho. of Rep., 1917-21; mem. 72d Congress (1931-33), Ill. at large; mem. U.S. Senate, term 1933-39. Served as corpl., Co. K, Anderson's Provisional Regt., Spanish-Am. War. Home: Beardstown, Ill. Died Oct. 12, 1940.

DIETRICH, Charles Henry, senator; b. Aurora, Ill., Nov. 26, 1853; s. Leonard and Wilhelmina Carolina (Stein) D.; ed. pub. schs., Aurora, Ill., to 1868; m. Elizabeth Slaker, May 1878 (dec.); m. 2d, Margaretta Shaw Stewart, Oct. 27, 1909. Worked on farm; later in stores, St. Joseph, Mo., and Chicago; worked on plantations in South about a year; in mining and merchandising in Black Hills, 1875-76; moved to Hastings, Neb., 1878, engaged in business; pres. German Nat. Bank, Hastings. Nominated May 2, 1900, by acclamation in Rep. State Conv. for gov. of Neb.; elected gov., but resigned and was elected U.S. senator, Mar. 28, 1901, for term expiring 1905. Republican. Home: Hastings, Neb. Died Apr. 10, 1924.

DIETRICH, Frank Sigel, judge; b. Ottawa, Kan., Jan. 23, 1863; s. Jacob and Catherine (Jackel) D.; A.B., Brown U., 1887, A.M., 1890 (LL.D., 1916); m. Martha Behle, Sept. 27, 1893; children—Mrs. Margaret Ifft, Isabel, Frank S. Instr. Latin, 1887-89, history and polit. economy, 1889-91, Ottawa (Kan.) U. Admitted to bar, 1891; U.S. dist. judge, Dist. of Ida., 1907-26; U.S. circuit judge, 9th Circuit, 1926—. Home: Boise, Ida. Died Oct. 2, 1930.

DIFENDERFER, Robert E., congressman; b. Lewisburg, Pa., June 7, 1849; s. Solomon and Mary A. (Neff) D.; acad. edn.; studied dentistry, practiced dentistry at Lewisburg and at Pottsville, Pa., 14 yrs.; built and operated first woolen mill in China, at Tientsin; in wholesale lumber and contracting, Ashbourne, Pa., 1900—. Mem. 62d and 63d Congresses (1911-15), 8th Pa. Dist. Democrat. Home: Jenkintown, Pa. Died Apr. 25, 1923.

DIGGES, Walter Mitchell, judge; b. Charles Co., Md., Feb. 17, 1877; s. John Thomas (M.D.) and Catherine (Mitchell) D.; prep. edn., Charlotte Hall (Md.) Mil. Acad.; student Md. State Agrl. Coll., 1891-93, U. of Md., 1902; m. Mary Natalie Jenkins, Dec. 29, 1909; children—Eleanor Jenkins, John Dudley, Walter Mitchell, Edward Simms. Admitted to Md. bar, 1902, and began practice, La Plata, Md.; pres. Charles County Bank of Eastern Shore Trust Co., 1908-23; mem. Md. Ho. of Delegates, 1910-12; naval officer of Port of Baltimore, 1913-21; chief judge, Circuit Court, 7th Jud. Circuit, Md., 1923—; also asso. judge, Court of Appeals, Md., 1923—. Dist. chmn. Liberty Loan campaigns, 5th Md. dist., World War. Democrat. Episcopalian. Mason. Home: La Plata, Md. Died Oct. 15, 1934.

DIGGS, Annie LePorte, lecturer; b. London, Can., 1853; d. Cornelius and Ann Maria (Thomas) Le Porte; ed. pub. and pvt. schs.; engaged in newspaper work at Washington; m. A. S. Diggs. Was chmn. of delegation from D.C., Nat. People's Party Conv., Omaha, 1892. Speaker for People's Party in nearly every state and territory; state librarian of Kan., 1898-1902; asso. editor The Advocate, Topeka, Kan. Pres. Kan. State Woman Suffrage Assn.; pres. Kan. Woman's Press Assn. Delegate Internat. Coöperative Congress, Manchester, Eng., 1903, Peace Congress, Rouen, France, 1904. Author: Little Brown Brothers; Story of Jerry Simpson, 1908. Home: New York, N.Y. Died Sept. 7, 1916.

DIKE, Samuel Warren, clergyman; b. Thompson, Conn., Feb. 13, 1839; s. George and Hannah Waters (Snow) D.; A.B., Williams Coll., 1863; student Hartford Theol. Sem., 1863-65; grad. Andover Theol. Sem., 1866; (LL.D., Williams, 1888); m. Augusta M. Smith, Oct. 29, 1872. Acting-pastor Pomfret, Conn., 1866-67; ordained Congl. ministry, 1869; pastor W. Randolph, Vt., 1868-77, Royalton, Vt., 1879-82. Contbr. on marriage, divorce, the family, methods of sociol. study, statistics, polit. and religious questions. His writings and others led to organization of Divorce Reform League, 1881, then Nat. League for the Protection of the Family, of which became corr. sec. Home: Auburndale, Mass. Died Dec. 3, 1913.

DILL, Franklin Geselbracht, clergyman; by authority of Dist. Court of Kan., 1918, adopted wife's maiden name on account of its patriotic ancestral record; b. Chicago, Ill., May 27, 1876; s. of Herman and Louise (Meyer) Geselbracht; B.A., U. of Chicago, 1898; grad. McCormick Theol. Sem., 1901; M.A., Ph.D., U. of Leipzig, Germany, 1904; D.D., from U. of Tulsa, Okla., 1931; m. Emma Jane Dill, Aug. 22, 1901; 1 son, George Matthew. Ordained Presbyn. ministry, 1904; pastor Laird Memorial Ch., Chicago, 1904-07; sr. fellow in N.T., U. of Chicago, 1906-08; pastor First Ch., Albany, Ore., 1908-17, also prof. philosophy Albany Coll.; held Westminster Bible Chair, U. of Kan., 1917-19; dean, prof. Bible, head dept., U. of Tulsa, 1919-30, acting pres., 1924-27, prof. religion and Bibl. lit., 1930—. Led in erection of $50,000 ch. at Albany; moderator Synod of Oregon, 1913-14; moderator of Synod of Oklahoma, 1927-28; pres. Okla. Council of Religious Education, 1928-29. Chaplain S.A.T.C., at Barracks, U. of Kan., World War, also mem. State Com. of Am. Legion Endowment campaign. Mem. Lincoln House (U. of Chicago). Republican. Mason. Home: Tulsa, Okla. Died Feb. 2, 1936.

DILL, James Brooks, judge; b. Spencerport, N.Y., July 25, 1854; s. Rev. James H. and Catharine D. D.; A.B., Yale, 1876; LL.B., N.Y. U., 1878; admitted to bar, 1878; m. Mary W. Hansell, 1880. Judge Court of Errors and Appeals, N.J., July 1905—; term expires 1911. Republican. Author: Business Corporations; Dill on Corporations; Banking and Trust Company Laws of New Jersey. Home: East Orange, N.J. Died 1910.

DILL, Lewis, mfr.; b. Frederick, Md., Sept. 19, 1859; s. Lewis H. and Eleanor (Houck) D.; ed. Frederick Coll., Md.; m. Margaret Paxton Repp, Jan. 24, 1884; 1 son, L. Alan. In lumber business, Baltimore, 1889—; pres. Lewis Dill & Co.; chmn. bd. The James Lumber Co. (est. 1840); chmn. bd. lumber Fire Underwriters, New York. Pres. Nat. Amer. Wholesale Lumber Assn. (U.S. and Can.), 1905-07, trustee, 1903-14; pres. Baltimore Lumber Exchange, 1897-1903, trustee, 1890—; pres. Baltimore Wholesale Club, 1920; exec. com. Merchants and Mfrs.' Assn., 1915-18. Mem. Citizens' Com. for rebuilding Baltimore after the fire of 1904, treas. Patterson Memorial Assn.; mem. Am. Forestry Assn.; councillor Chamber Commerce U.S.A. Spl. rep. Ordnance Dept. U.S.A., 1917-18. Home: Baltimore, Md. Died Apr. 1929.

DILLARD, Frank Clifford, lawyer; b. Auburn, Ala.; s. George C. and Mary Frances (Williams) D.; grad. Ala. Poly. Inst., Auburn; LL.D., Austin Coll., 1924; m. Mary S. Rountree, July 10, 1894. Practiced at Sherman, Tex., 1883-1907 as Bryant & Dillard, Head & Dillard, Head, Dillard & Muse, Head, Dillard & Head; removed to Chicago, 1907, as head of dept. of legal work relating to interstate commerce, Harriman ry. lines; v.p. and gen. counsel C.,R.I.&P. Ry. Co., Apr. 1912-Apr. 1914; resigned and resumed practice at Sherman; mem. Head, Dillard, Maxey-Freeman & McReynolds. Democrat. Methodist. Home: Sherman, Tex. Died Sept. 25, 1938.

DILLARD, James Hardy, educator; b. Nansemond Co., Va., Oct. 24, 1856; s. James and Sarah Brownrigg (Cross) D.; M.A., Washington and Lee U., 1876, B.L., 1877, D.Litt., 1889; LL.D., Tulane U., 1908, Harvard, 1923, Southwestern, 1932; D.C.L., U. of the South, 1910; m. Mary Harmanson, July 5, 1882; children—James Brownrigg, Catharine Harmanson, Elisabeth Nicholson, Mary, Fay Harmanson, Lucy Tabb; m. 2d, Avarene Lippincott Budd, Nov. 18, 1899; children—George Budd, Hardy Cross, Ruth Payson, Margaret (dec.). Asst. prof. mathematics, Washington and Lee U., 1876-77; prin. Rodman Sch., Norfolk, Va., 1877-82, Norfolk Acad., 1882-87, Mary Inst., Washington U., St. Louis, 1887-91; prof. Latin, 1891-1907, dean Academic Colls., 1904-07, Tulane U.; pres. Jeanes Foundation (for Negro rural schs.), 1907-31; also director, 1910-17, and pres., 1917-31, of John F. Slater Fund; also v.p. of Phelps-Stokes Fund, 1925. Pres. Nat. Conf. Church Clubs, 1901-02. New Orleans Free Kindergarten Assn., 1896-1905, New Orleans Pub. Library, 1904-13; mem. La. State Bd. Edn., 1904-08, Southern Edn. Bd., 1908—, bd. administration Tulane U., 1909-13; mem. Gen. Edn. Bd., 1917—; trustee Gen. Theol. Sem., 1916-25; rector of William and Mary Coll., 1917. Awarded gold medal and $500, 1928, by Harmon Foundation, New York, for promoting good relations between the races and for activity in increasing educational facilities for Negroes in the South; awarded Roosevelt medal, 1937. Author: Arithmetic Exercises, 1887; Selections from Wordsworth, 1890. Editor: Fifty Letters of Cicero, 1902; Aus dem Deutschen Dichterwald (Favorite German Poems), 1903; From News Stand to Cyrano (essays for promotion of good reading), 1935. Home: Charlottesville, Va. Died Aug. 2, 1940.

DILLARD, Paul, cotton mcht.; b. Crawford, Miss., Aug. 11, 1873; s. John Woodruff and Mary (Harnesberger) D.; student Bingham Sch., Asheville, N.C., 1889-91, U. of Virginia, 1891-93; m. Julia A. Speed, Dec. 22, 1897; children—Lucy Speed (Mrs. Malcolm G. Barboro), John Speed, Ruth (Mrs. R. V. Norfleet). Began in the cotton business at Memphis, Tenn., 1893; pres. Dillard & Coffin Co., Memphis, 1905—; dir. Federal Res. Bank of St. Louis, 1926-37. A commr. Goodwyn Inst.; pres. John Gaston Hosp. Democrat. Died Nov. 10, 1938.

DILLAYE, Blanche, artist; b. Syracuse, N.Y.; d. Stephen Devolson and Charlotte (Malcolm) D.; Miss Bonney and Miss Dillaye's School (now Ogontz Sch.); studied art at Pa. Acad. Fine Arts and in Paris; etching with Stephan Parrish; unmarried. Exhibited in Paris Salons, in Eng., and in all prin. exhbns. of America; silver medals for etchings, Atlanta Expn. and Universal Expn., Lorient, France, 1903; silver medal, water color and oil, Am. Art Soc., Phila.; represented in art collection of Syracuse Museum of Fine Arts and Univ. of Syracuse. Gold medal for water color Nat. Conservation Expn., Knoxville, Tenn. Mem. Fellowship of Pa. Acad. Fine Arts, Art Alliance (Philadelphia). Home: Philadelphia, Pa. Died Dec. 20, 1932.

DILLER, Joseph Silas, geologist; b. Plainfield, Pa., Aug. 27, 1850; s. Samuel and Catharine (Bear) D.; S.B., Lawrence Scientific Sch. (Harvard), 1879; 4 yrs. in post-grad. studies, Harvard and Heidelberg; m. Laura I. Paul, June 5, 1883. Taught in State Normal Sch., Westfield, Mass., 1873-77; geologist Assos expdn., 1881-83; geologist U.S. Geol. Survey, 1883. Published many geol. papers in jours. and reports of U.S. Geol. Survey. Home: Washington, D.C. Died Nov. 13, 1928.

DILLINGHAM, Albert Caldwell, naval officer; b. Phila., June 3, 1848; s. Simeon and Mary Elizabeth (Raymond) D.; served in 7th Pa. Inf. in Civil War; grad. U.S. Naval Acad., 1869; m. Grace Gillmor, June 21, 1897. Promoted through various grades to capt., U.S.N., Feb. 19, 1906; rear adm., Dec. 10, 1910. Served on various stas. and in prin. parts of the world; was promoted for "gallant and conspicuous conduct" in battle during war with Spain; in charge of U.S. affairs in Santo Domingo waters, 1904, stopped the revolution in that republic and established a definite govt.; on diplomatic duty to Santo Domingo, 1905, and with the U.S. minister accomplished an agreement with that republic which secured uninterrupted commerce, security to lives and properties of foreign residents and a guarantee that the debt of the republic be paid, the agreement doing away with the means of revolution by placing the customs of the republic under control of the U.S. Retired by operation of law, June 3, 1910. Recalled to active duty, June 7, 1917; in charge of development of Naval Operating Base, Hampton Roads, Va. Awarded Navy Cross with citation: "for exceptionally meritorious service in a duty of great responsibility, for excellent and thorough work in charge of the development of the Naval Operating Base at Hampton Roads, Va." Home: Norfolk, Va. Died Dec. 6, 1925.

DILLINGHAM, Charles Bancroft, theatre mgr.; b. Hartford, Conn., May 30, 1868; s. Edmund Bancroft and Josephine (Potter) D.; ed. pub. schs. Produced 200 plays, mostly musical, from 1900, and managed 50 prominent stars; mgr. Globe theatre and partner of A. L. Erlanger in 20 other theatres. Commd. capt. Aviation Corps, U.S.A., 1917. Died Aug. 30, 1934.

DILLINGHAM, Frank Ayer, lawyer; b. New York City, Dec. 31, 1869; s. George W. and Helena W. (Ayer) D.; student Bahler's School, Orange, N.J.; A.B., Yale, 1891; LL.B., Columbia Law School, 1894; m. Louise Gregory Bulkley, Jan. 23, 1896; children—Louise Bulkley, Winthrop Bulkley, Dorothy Ayer (Mrs. Sherwood P. Smedley), Helena Ayer, Hope, Sherburne. Admitted to New York bar, 1894, and began practice in N.Y. City; mem. Rounds, Dillingham, Mead and Neagle; pres. South Porto Rico Sugar Co. Republican. Episcopalian. Home: Millburn, N.J. Died Aug. 21, 1941.

DILLINGHAM, John Hoag, educator, editor; b. W. Falmouth, Mass., June 1, 1839; s. Abram and Lydia Beede (Hoag) D.; A.B., Harvard, 1862, A.M., 1865; m. Mary Pim, July 20, 1871. Teacher dist. winter schs., 1855, 57, 58, 59; asst. teacher Charles A. Miles' Sch. for Boys, Brattleboro, Vt., 1862-65; proctor in Harvard Coll. a few months, 1865; librarian, tutor in Latin and Greek, 1865-69, supt. students, 1866-76, prof. moral and polit. science, 1869-78, Haverford Coll.; sr. teacher Friends' Select Sch., Phila., 1878—. Librarian Friends' Library, Phila., 1881-98; custodian Friends' records, 1881-99; editor from 1897, The Friend, denominational paper Soc. of Friends (orthodox conservative); mem., 1879—, and sec. Text-Book Assn. of Friends of Phila., to 1910. Overseer, 1873-1901, clerk 1882-86, elder 1883-89, minister, 1889—, Western Dist. Meeting of Friends, Phila.; mem. Friends' Representative Meeting of Phila., 1893—; clerk Phila. Quarterly Meeting, 1897-99. Mem. Phi Beta Kappa (Harvard), Pa. Prison Soc., Tract Assn. of Friends. Author: The Idolatry of Culture, 1884; The Society of Friends in Barnstable County, Massachusetts, 1891; What Shall I Do With My Inherited Membership (pamphlet), 1891. Deceased.

DILLINGHAM, William Paul, senator; b. Waterbury, Vt., Dec. 12, 1843; s. Gov. Paul and Julia (Carpenter) D.; bro. of Frank D.; academic edn.;

m. Mary Ellen Shipman, Dec. 24, 1874. Admitted to bar, 1867, and then in practice at Montpelier, Vt.; pres. Waterbury Nat. Bank, 1890—. State's atty., Washington Co., Vt., 1872-76; sec. civil and mil. affairs, 1866 and 1874-76; mem. Ho. of Rep., 1876, 84, Senate, 1878, 80; commr. state taxes, 1882-88; gov. of Vt., 1888-90; elected U.S. senator, Oct. 18, 1900, for unexpired term (1900-03) of Justin S. Morrill, deceased; reëlected for 4 terms, 1903-27. Republican. Chmn. U.S. Immigration Commn., 1907. Home: Montpelier, Vt. Died July 12, 1923.

DILLON, Charles Hall, judge; b. nr. Jasper, Ind., Dec. 18, 1853; s. Mathew B. and Mary A. (Stewart) D.; A.B., Ind. U., 1874, LL.B., 1876; m. Maude B. Tripp, Aug. 28, 1889 (died 1894); m. 2d, Frances D. Jolley, Sept. 26, 1900. Practiced at Jasper, Ind., 1876-80, Mitchell, S.D., 1881-93, Yankton, 1894—; dir. Dak. Nat. Bank. Mem. S.D. Senate, 1903-09; mem. 63d to 65th Congresses (1913-19), 1st S.D. Dist.; justice Supreme Court of S.D., 1922-27. Republican. Conglist. Home: Vermilion, S.D. Died Sept. 16, 1929.

DILLON, Edmond Bothwell, judge; b. Ironton, O., Feb. 9, 1869; s. Rev. John W. and Mary Catharine (Cox) D.; student Ohio Wesleyan U., 1885-89, hon. A.M., 1906; m. Marian Daisy Whitney, May 8, 1895. Practiced law, Columbus, 1891—; judge Ct. of Common Pleas, Franklin Co., 1903—; prof. law, Ohio State U., 1904—. Mem. Ohio Bd. Law Examiners, 1897-1903; mem. Columbus Civil Service Commn., 1899-1903; nominated for gov. of Ohio, 1912 (declined). Mem. Phi Kappa Psi. Methodist. Mason, Elk, K.P. Home: 83 Wilson Av. Died Nov. 11, 1919.

DILLON, John Forrest, judge; b. Montgomery Co., N.Y., Dec. 25, 1831; s. Thomas and Rosannah (Forrest) D.; went to Iowa in boyhood; M.D., Ia. U., 1850; after 6 months' med. practice began study of law; (LL.D., Ia. Coll. and Cornell Coll., Ia., 1862); m. Anna Margery Price, Nov. 10, 1853. Admitted to bar, 1852; pros. atty., 1852-58; judge 7th Jud. Dist., Ia., 1858-63; judge Supreme Ct. of Ia., 1863-69; U.S. Circuit judge, 8th Jud. Circuit, 1869-79; resigned; prof. real estate and equity jurisprudence, Columbia, 1879-82; practicing law, New York, 1882—; gen. counsel of the M.P. Ry. Co., Western Union Tel. Co., and Tex. Pacific Ry. Co. Author: Life, Character and Judicial Services of Chief Justice Marshall. Home: Far Hills, N.J. Died May 5, 1914.

DILLON, John Irving (pen names "Gray Friar," Irving Dillon), writer; b. Wilkes-Barre, Pa., Oct. 24, 1870; s. Thomas P. and Katherine E. (Considine) D.; grad. Central H. S., Philadelphia; m. Julia V. Conner, 1897 (dec.); m. 2d, Rose Adele Trafficante, Feb. 22, 1900; children—John I., Julia V. (Mrs. Paul X. Picot, dec.), Thomas E., Isabel K. (Mrs. Thomas F. Dugan). Mag. and polit. writer; editor and pub. Phila. Sunday Dispatch. Republican. Mason. Home: Philadelphia, Pa. Died Apr. 1938.

DILLON, Mary, author; b. Carlisle, Pa.; d. Herman Merrills (D.D., LL.D., pres. Dickinson Coll.) and Lucena Elizabeth (Clarke) Johnson; (hon. M.A., Dickinson Coll., 1908); m. Patrick Dillon, 1877 (died 1879). Author: The Rose of Old St. Louis, 1904; In Old Bellaire, 1906; The Leader, 1906; The Patience of John Morland, 1909; Miss Livingston's Companion, 1911; Comrades, 1917; The American, 1918; The Farmer of Roaring Run, 1920. Deceased.

DIMITRY, Charles Patton, author; b. Washington, July 31, 1837; s. Alexander (diplomat) and Mary Powell (Mills) D., d. Robert Mills (U.S. Govt. architect, and architect of Nat. Washington Monument); ed. Georgetown Coll., A.M., 1867; m. Annie Elizabeth Johnston, June 1871 (died 1880). Private C.S.A.; after war in newspaper work in Richmond, Mobile, Alexandria, Va., Washington, Baltimore, New York, Brooklyn and New Orleans. Author: Guilty or Not Guilty?; Angela's Christmas; Gold Dust and Diamonds; The House in Balfour Street; Two Knaves and a Queen; From Exile; Louisiana Families; Louisiana Story in Little Chapters; The Louisiana of the Purchase; Historical Sketches of New Orleans. Home: New Orleans, La. Died 1910.

DIMITRY, John Bull Smith, author; b. Washington, Dec. 27, 1835; s. Alexander and Mary Powell (Mills) D.; grad. Georgtown Coll., A.M., 1867; m. Adelaide Stewart, 1871. Sec. of legation to his father, who was U.S. minister to Costa Rica and Nicaragua, 1859-61; editorially connected with the press of New Orleans, Washington, New York and Phila.; prof. languages and belles-lettres, Colegio Caldas, South America, 1873-76; same Montgomery Coll., Va., 1894-95. While on New York Mail and Express, his story, Le Tombeau Blanc, won the prize of $500 offered by Storyteller Mag. for the best short story. Author: School History and Geography of Louisiana, 1877; Three Good Giants, 1887; Atahualpa's Curtain, 1889; Confederate Military History of Louisiana, 1900. Address: New Orleans, La. Died 1901.

DIMMICK, Eugene Dumont, brig. gen.; b. Athens, N.Y., July 31, 1840; s. Elnathan Ni and Emily Jane D.; ed. Athens and Hudson, N.Y.; m. Mary Caldwell, 1863 (died 1882); 2d, Mrs. Florence Palmer Hazard, 1896. Enlisted pvt. Co. G, 2d N.J. State Militia, Apr. 26, 1861; disch. July 31, 1861; 1st sergt., Co. M, 5th N.Y. Cav., Oct. 7, 1861-May 8, 1862; 2d lt. same, May 9, 1862; 1st lt., Oct. 10, 1862; capt., July 5, 1863; hon. mustered out, Nov. 6, 1863, on account of wounds; 2d lt., Vet. Reserve Corps., Feb. 3, 1864; hon. mustered out, June 30, 1866; apptd. 2d lt., 9th U.S. Cav., Aug. 9, 1867; advanced through grades to col. Cavalry, Feb. 22, 1903; retired at own request, after 40 yrs. service, Mar. 2, 1903; advanced to rank of brig. gen., retired, by act of Apr. 23, 1904. In Civil War was in actions of Harrisonburg, Culpeper; battles of Cedar Mountain (comdg. co.), 2d Bull Run (escort to Gen. Banks), South Mountain, Antietam, Brandy Sta., Chantilly; actions of Warrenton Junction, Thoroughfare Gap, Beverly Ford, Hanover Junction; battle of Gettysburg, and actions of Boonsboro and Hagerstown (severely wounded, taken prisoner and paroled). Comd. squadron D, and H. Troop, 9th Cav., at affair at Crow Agency, Mont., Nov. 5, 1887, when "Sword Bearer" was killed; in campaign against Indians under Victorio and Nana, N. Mex., Ariz. and Mexico. Bvtd. capt. for gallantry in action against Indians, Black Range Mts., N.M. Took part in Santiago campaign, and comd. 2d Cav. at Matanzas, 1898. Died Nov. 16, 1935.

DIMMOCK, George, zoölogist; b. Springfield, Mass., May 17, 1852; s. George Monroe and Elizabeth (Learned) D.; A.B., Harvard, 1877, taking spl. studies there until 1879; A.M., Ph.D., U. of Leipzig, 1881; Sorbonne, U. of Paris, 1881-82; m. Anna Katherina Hofmann, Mar. 30, 1878; 1 dau., Mrs. Anna D. Nash. Editor of Psyche, 1877-90, a jour. of entomology; engaged in anat. study of the early stages of beetles, and in compiling a history of the Dimmock family in America, 1900—. Author: The Anatomy of the Mouth-parts and of the Sucking Apparatus of Some Diptera, 1881. Home: Springfield, Mass. Died May 17, 1930.

DIMOCK, Anthony Weston, author; b. Yarmouth, N.S., Aug. 27, 1842; s. Anthony Vaughn and Susan Rathbone (Weston) D.; grad. Phillips Acad., Andover, Mass., 1859; A.M., Columbian (now George Washington) U., 1872; m. Helen Weston, 1865 (died 1901); 2d, Leila B. Allen, Feb. 6, 1909. Mem. Marquand & Dimock, bankers and brokers, New York, and later A. W. Dimock & Co.; also pres. Atlantic Mail and other steamship cos., Bankers & Merchants, Southern and other telegraph cos., 1864-84. Author: Florida Enchantments, 1908; Dick in the Everglades, 1909; Dick Among the Lumber-jacks, 1910; The Book of the Tarpon, 1911; Dick Among the Miners, 1913; Florida Enchantments, revised, 1915; Wall Street and the Wilds, 1915. Home: Peekamose, N.Y. Died Sept. 12, 1918.

DINES, Tyson S., lawyer; b. Fayette, Mo., Nov. 29, 1858; s. Tyson and Mary (Stakes) D.; A.B., Central College, Fayette, Mo., 1879, A.M., 1880; LL.D., from same, 1926; m. Katharine Mauzey, Feb. 22, 1881; children, living—Mrs. Virginia Nelson, Tyson, Cortland S., Eugene T. Assistant prin., 1880-82, prin., 1882-84, Brunswick, Mo., High Sch.; supt. schs., Chariton Co., Mo., 1884-88. Admitted to bar, 1884; practiced Brunswick, 1884, Fayette, 1887, St. Louis, 1891, Denver, 1892, later again at St. Louis; now sr. mem. Dines, Dines & Holme, Denver. Was gen.-atty. Terminal R.R. Assn., Merchants Terminal Ry. Co., Belt Line R.R., St. Louis; v.p., gen. counsel The Moffat Estate Co.; executor and trustee of Winfield Scott Stratton. Gen. counsel Colo. and Utah Coal Co., Colony Coal Co. Chairman bd. Agnes Phipps Sanatorium for Tuberculosis; pres. Central Coll. Lecturer on law of evidence, Denver U., 1898-1904. Mem. Denver sch. bd. 2 terms. Home: Denver, Colo. Died Mar. 28, 1929.

DINGLEY, Edward Nelson, writer, b. Auburn, Me., Aug. 21, 1862; s. Hon. Nelson, Jr. and Salome (McKenney) D.; student Bates Coll., Lewiston, Me., 1 yr.; A.B., Yale, 1883; LL.B., Columbian (now George Washington) U., 1885; m. Miriam Gardiner Robinson, Dec. 20, 1888. Mem. staff Boston Advertiser and Boston Record, 1886-87; part owner and one of editors Leavenworth (Kan.) Times, 1887-88; became editor and pub. Kalamazoo (Mich.) Telegraph, 1888; later editor and pub. Kalamazoo Press. Pres. Mich. League Rep. Clubs, 1895-96; clk. Com. Ways and Means, Nat. Ho. of Rep., 1897-98; mem. Mich. Ho. of Rep., 1899-1903; with Ways and Means Com. and Senate Finance Com.; also with Rep. Nat. Com. Conglist. Mason. Author: Life and Times of Nelson Dingley, Jr., 1901; Unto the Hills, 1922. Editorial writer, New York Herald, 1920-21. Economist, tariff and finance expert. Home: Chevy Chase, Md. Died Mar. 19, 1930.

DINGLEY, Frank Lambert, editor; b. Unity, Me., Feb. 7, 1840; s. Nelson and Jane (Lambert) D.; A.B., Bowdoin Coll., 1861, later A.M., Litt.D.; m. Lu Mary Greeley, Oct. 21, 1862 (died 1913). In 1861, with brother (late Nelson Dingley, Jr., M.C.), established Lewiston Journal, of which is still editor. Entire life devoted to editorial work; was spl. commr. under Harrison administration, to make investigations in regard to foreign immigration, visiting ports of embarkation in the British Isles and on the Continent of Europe, and made spl. report, published by the Dept. of State, which was made basis of the first legislation, restrictive of immigration, passed by Congress. Conglist. Progressive. Home: Auburn, Me. Died Sept. 21, 1918.

DINGS, Peter Conrad, banker; b. North Greenwich, N.Y., Mar. 10, 1870; s. John and Mathilda (Chambeau) D.; ed. pub. and high schs.; m. Alice Daiber, Nov. 13, 1895 (died Feb. 7, 1919); 1 dau., Dorothy; m. 2d, Mrs. Gertrude A. Dodson, Dec. 1924. In retail business, La Porte City, Ia., 1897-1904; in banking business, Ardmore, Okla., 1904-21; treas. North Am. Light & Power Co., Chicago, also chmn. finance com. and treas. Ill. Power & Light Corp., 1921-26; chmn. bd. Am. Nat. Bank, Ardmore, 1926—; dir. Oklahoma City Fed. Reserve Bank, Chicago Trust Co.; oil producer and refiner. Mem. Banking Bd., Okla., 4 yrs. Mem. War Petroleum Service Bd., Mid-Continent Oil Field. Republican. Mason. Home: Chicago, Ill. Died Oct. 1, 1938.

DINKEY, Alva Clymer, steel mfr.; b. Weatherly, Pa., Feb. 20, 1866; s. Reuben and Mary Elizabeth (Hamm) D.; ed. pub. schs.; m. Margaret M. Stewart, June 11, 1891; children—Robert E., Alva Charles, Leonora Stewart (Mrs. Howell L. Seiple). Entered Carnegie steel service as water boy at Edgar Thomson Steel Works, May 21, 1879; telegraph operator same works, 1885; machinist Pittsburgh Locomotive Works, Allegheny, Pa., 1885-88; expert machinist, McTighe Electric Co., Pittsburgh, 1889-93; sec. to gen. supt., 1889-93, electrician, 1893-98, supt. Electric Light and Power Plant, 1898-99, asst. to gen. supt., 1899-1901, gen. supt., 1901-03, all Homestead Works, Carnegie Steel Co.; pres. Carnegie Steel Co., 1903-15 (resigned); pres. Midvale Steel & Ordnance Co., 1915-23; pres. The Midvale Co.; dir. Am. Iron & Steel Inst. Republican. Presbyn. Home: St. Davids, Pa. Died Aug. 11, 1931.

DINKINS, James, banker; b. Madison Co., Miss., Apr. 18, 1845; s. Alexander Hamilton and Cynthia (Springs) D.; ed. country sch., 1853-60, N.C. Mil. Inst., 1860-61; m. Sue Hart, Nov. 15, 1866. Entered C.S.A. at 16; pvt. 18th Miss. Inf.; 1st lt. cav., Apr. 9, 1863; capt. Co. C, 18th Miss. Cav., Dec. 15, 1864; participated in every engagement of his command, including Leesburg, Dam No. 2, Savage Station, Malvern Hills, Harper's Ferry, Sharpsburg, Fredericksburg; served from Apr. 1863, as a.-d.-c. to Gen. J. R. Chalmers; took part in all the daring and desperate raids and campaigns of Forrest, battles of Coldwater, Okalona, West Point, Brice's Cross Roads, Ft. Pillow, Oxford, Memphis, Harrisburg, Columbia, Franklin and Nashville. Entered service I.C. R.R., 1874; served road 28 yrs. in various capacities; Jan. 1, 1903, opened Bank of Jefferson, Gretna, La., opposite New Orleans. Long edited Confederate column, New Orleans Picayune, contributing war reminiscences. Author: 1861 to 1865, by an Old Johnnie, 1897. Home: New Orleans, La. Died July 19, 1939.

DINSMORE, Charles Allen, clergyman; b. New York, Aug. 4, 1860; s. Lafayette Henry (M.D.) and Mary S. (Ladd) D.; grad. Dartmouth, 1884, A.B., 1894, D.D., 1905; B.D., Yale, 1888, D.D., 1916; m. Annie Laurie Beattie, Oct. 24, 1889; 1 dau., Rachel. Served with U.S. Engrs. in survey of Miss. River, 1881-82; ordained Congl. ministry, 1888; pastorates at Whitneyville, Conn., Willimantic, Conn., Phillips Ch., Boston; pastor First Ch., Waterbury, Conn., 1905-20; lecturer on spiritual content of literature, Yale Div. Sch., rank of prof., 1920—. Carew lecturer Hartford Theol. Sem., 1920; visiting lecturer Sch. of Religion, Athens, 1927. Author: The Teachings of Dante, 1901; Aids to the Study of Dante, 1903 (both also translated into Japanese); Atonement in Literature and Life, 1906; The New Light on the Old Truth, 1912; Life of Dante, 1919; Religious Certitude in an Age of Science, 1924; The English Bible as Literature, 1931; The Great Poets and the Meaning of Life, 1937. Alumni lecturer, Yale Div. Sch., 1904; Annie Talbot Cole lecturer, Bowdoin Coll., 1908; John Calvin MacNair lecturer, U.N.C., 1922; Samuel Harris lecturer, Bangor (Me.) Theol. Sem., 1923. Home: New Haven, Conn. Died Aug. 14, 1941.

DINSMORE, Hugh Anderson, congressman; b. Benton Co., Ark., Dec. 24, 1850; ed. pvt. schs.; studied law. Became clerk circuit ct., Benton Co., until 1874; admitted to bar, 1875; practiced in Fayetteville; pros. atty., 4th Jud. Dist., 1878-84; presdl. elector, 1884; U.S. minister resident and consul gen. in Korea, 1887-90; regent Smithsonian Instn., 1899-1903; mem. 53d to 59th Congresses (1893-1905). Democrat. Home: Fayetteville, Ark. Died May 2, 1930.

DINSMORE, John Walker, clergyman; b. Washington Co., Pa., Mar. 13, 1839; s. William and Rebecca (Anderson) D.; B.A., Washington (now Washington and Jefferson) Coll., 1859, M.A., 1862 (D.D., 1877, LL.D., 1894); grad. Presbyn. Theol. Sem., Allegheny, Pa., 1862; m. Adaline Vance, Dec. 22, 1862; m. 2d, Alice Blackford, Mar. 5, 1918. Ordained Presbyn. ministry, 1863; pastor Cambria, Wis., 1863, Prairiedu-Sac, Wis., 1864-70, Bloomington, Ill., 1870-91, San Jose, Calif., 1891-1901; retired from active pastorate, 1901. Moderator Synod of Ill., 1883, Synod of Calif., 1904; mem. 10 Presbyn. Gen. Assemblies; chmn. Gen. Assembly's spl. com. on jud. commns., which framed the constl. articles providing for the Supreme Ct. of Presbyn. Ch. in U.S.A.; was chmn. Permanent Jud. Commn.; organized the effort and secured passage of law exempting chs. of all denominations, in Calif., from taxation. An original mem. Bd. of Aid for Colls. and Acads. for Presbyn. Ch., and mem. exec. com.; dir., mem. exec. com. McCormick Theol. Sem., Chicago; pres. bd. dirs. San Francisco Theol. Sem.; mem. Rep. State Conv., Calif., 1902. Author: The Scotch-Irish in America, 1906. Home: Los Gatos, Calif. Died Apr. 2, 1922.

d'INVILLIERS, Edward Vincent, geologist, mining engr.; b. Germantown, Pa., Aug. 2, 1857; s. Camille S. and Ann S. (Maitland) d'I.; B.S., U. of Pa., 1878; (D.Sc., 1913); spl. studies in geology and mining engring.; m. Ann Maitland, June 6, 1894. Asst. geologist, 2d Geol. Survey of Pa., 1875-85; geologist and cons. engr., 1885-1919. Fellow Geol. Soc. America. Home: Germantown, Phila., Pa. Died 1928.

DINWIDDIE, Albert Bledsoe, univ. pres.; b. Lexington, Ky., Apr. 3, 1871; s. William and Emily Albertine (Bledsoe) D.; B.A., U. of Va., 1889, M.A., 1890, Ph.D., 1892; U. of Göttingen, 1902-03; LL.D., Southwestern Presbyn. U., 1911; m. Caroline Arthur, d. Rev. Dr. George Summey, of Austin, Tex., July 22, 1897; children—Emily (Mrs. Donald M. Halley), Elizabeth Worth, Albert Bledsoe (dec.), George Summey, Mary Morrison (Mrs. Andrew S. Tomb), William Courtenay. Teaching licentiate, U. of Va., 1888-91; instr. U. Sch., Charlottesville, Va., 1889-91; prin. Greenwood (Va.) Acad., 1891-93; 1st asst. Univ. Sch., Richmond, Va., 1895-96; prof. mathematics, Southwestern Presbyn. U., 1896-1906; asst. prof. applied mathematics and astronomy, 1906-08, asso. prof., 1908-10, prof., 1910—, Tulane U., also dir. of war training, 1917-18; dean Coll. of Arts and Sciences and dir. summer sch. same, 1910-18; pres. Tulane U., 1918—. Fellow Am. Geog. Soc. Trustee Carnegie Foundation for Advancement of Teaching, New Orleans Pub. Sch. Alliance (dir.), New Orleans Lyceum Assn. (pres.), La. State Bd. of Edn., Nat. Inst. Social Sciences, Am. Assn. for Med. Progress, A.A.A.S. Dir. New Orleans Assn. Commerce; v.p., New Orleans br., Italy-America Soc. since organization, 1926; mem. President's Com. of Fifty on Coll. Hygiene; mem. Nat. Com. of Awards, Prize Essay Contest of Am. Chem. Soc. Home: New Orleans, La. Died Nov. 21, 1935.

DINWIDDIE, Edwin Courtland, lecturer, minister and temperance advocate; b. Springfield, O., Sept. 29, 1867; s. John Andrew and Edith Jane (Brelsford) D.; ed. Wittenberg College, and Grove City (Pa.) Coll., A.M., 1899; D.D., Wittenberg, 1922; m. Olive Hannah Smith, Nov. 8, 1894; children—Horace Milton, Edith Rowena (Mrs. S. R. Painter). Entered Evang. Lutheran ministry, 1894; sec. Permanent Com. on Temperance, Gen. Synod Evang. Luth. Ch., 1899-1903 (chmn. 1903, till merged in United Luth. Ch., 1918); sec. Ohio Prohibition Exec. Com., 1890-92; legislative supt. Ohio Anti-Saloon League, 1893-96; state supt. Pa. Anti-Saloon League, 1897-99; first natl. legislative supt. Am. Anti-Saloon League, 1899-1907, and 1911-20. Worker in the Internat. Order of Good Templars; grand counselor, 1893-94, grand electoral supt., 1894-96, Ohio I.O.G.T.; grand chief templar of D.C. I.O.G.T., 1909-15; mem. Internat. Com. (for U.S.) on Prohibitory Liquor Legislation; nat. legislative supt., Nat. G.L. I.O.G.T., 1905—; nat. chief templar, 1922—, and international lector, 1927-30. Had charge of successful effort to prohibit army canteen, and proposed and secured appropriations by Congress of over $5,000,000 for buildings at army posts for recreative and social purposes for enlisted men; managed campaigns for statewide constl. prohibition, Okla., 1906-07, dir. campaign before Congress resulting in adoption of important amendments, 1909, in relation to interstate shipments of intoxicating liquors; also had direction of campaign before Congress resulting in passage of Webb-Kenyon interstate liquor shipment bill, 1913, over veto of President Taft; directed campaign for nat. constl. prohibition amendment before Congress, resulting in initial vote of 197 for submission to states, Dec. 1914; same for D.C. proh. law, and anti-advertising mail amendments vs. intoxicants; prohibition legislation in food and army and navy laws, 1917; directed campaign for nat. constl. proh. amendment which passed U.S. Senate and Ho. of Rep., 1917, and enforcement code, 1919; actively participated in securing legislation for increased personnel and equipment of Coast Guard, 1926-27, reorgan. of Prohibition Bur., 1927, Jones-Stalker bill for increased penalties for liquor law violations, 1929. Supt. Nat. Temp. Bur.; mem. exec. com. Nat. Temp. Council, U.S.S., 1st v.p., 1924—; mem. United Luth. Com. Moral and Social Welfare since merger United Luth. Ch., 1918; mem. Nat. Legislative Conf., 1925—; sec. Nat. Conf. orgns. supporting 18th Amendment, 1928—; asso. chmn. and exec. sec. Nat. United Com. on Dry Planks and Dry Presidential Candidates, 1928, exec. sec. bd. of strategy same, 1931-32; supt. Com. on Promotion Temperance Legislation in Nat. Congress; nat. dir. Assn. in Support of Nat. Prohibition; rep. internat. sessions I.O.G.T., Stockholm, 1902, Belfast, Ireland, 1905, Washington, 1908, London, 1923, The Hague, 1933; U.S. Govt. delegate internat. congresses against alcoholism, London, The Hague, Milan, Lausanne, Copenhagen, 1909, 11, 13, 21 and 23 resptvly.; mem. permanent internat. com. of Internat. Congress Against Alcoholism, 1911—, pres., 1920-21; mem. exec. com. World Prohibition Fedn. Mason. Home: Washington, D.C. Died May 5, 1935.

DINWIDDIE, William, newspaperman; b. Charlottesville, Va., Aug. 23, 1867; s. Maj. William A. and Hattie (Guiteau) D.; common sch. edn.; spl. courses Columbian U., 1881-83; m. Caroline Brooke, Feb. 22, 1901 (died 1928); m. 2d, Alice Brooke, Jan. 2, 1929. Asst. electrician Nat. Mus. when 14; insp. customs, Corpus Christi, Tex., when 17, and ethnophotographer; asst. archæologist, Bur. Am. Ethnology, 1886-95; in journalism, 1895—; illustrator and corr. New York Herald, 1895; photographer B.&O. R.R., 1897; corr. Cuban and Puerto Rican campaigns, 1898; corr. New York Herald and Harper's Weekly in P.I., 1899-1900; corr. S. African campaign for Harper's Weekly, 1900; Sunday editor New York Herald, 1900-01; editor Manila Cablenews, 1902; gov. Province of Lepanto-Bontoc, P.I. Corr. Russo-Japanese War for New York World, Harper's Weekly and Leslie's Weekly, 1904-05; asso. editor New York World, 1905-06. Was spl. rep. Fish-Harriman Controversy, 1908; has served as spl. rep. Rock Island-Frisco Lines, adv. and publicity mgr. Lehigh Valley R.R. Co., etc. During World War discovered Am. clays to replace German clays in mfr. of lead pencils and graphite crucibles; mfr. crucibles, 1921; asso. editor Hearst Syndicate, 1922; asso. editor New York World, 1923. Editorial writer St. Louis Post-Dispatch, 1926; mgr. personal relations Busch Estate, St. Louis, 1927-30. Author: War Sketches, in Truth; Puerto Rico and Its Possibilities, 1899; The War in the Philippines; The War in South Africa; Japanese Campaign, Japanese Situation, General Conditions, Industries, Finance. Engaged in farming. Home: Rockville, Md. Died June 17, 1934.

DIPPEL, (Johann) Andreas, operatic singer and manager; b. Cassel, Germany, Nov. 30, 1866; studied voice under Mme. Zottmayr, of the Royal Court Theatre, Cassel, at Berlin, Milan, and Vienna under Prof. Julius Hey, Alberto Leoni and Johann Ress. Made début in Bremen, 1887, as the steersman in "The Flying Dutchman;" sang at Met. Opera House, New York, season of 1890-91, and later made concert tour of U.S. under Anton Seidl, Arthur Nikisch and Theodore Thomas; with Imperial Court Opera, Vienna, 1893-98, identified with Met. Opera Co., New York, 1898-1910, administrative mgr., 1908-10; gen. mgr. Chicago Grand Opera Co., 1910-13. Died May 12, 1932.

DITHMAR, Edward Augustus, newspaperman; b. New York, May 22, 1854; s. Henry and Anna B. D.; ed. grammar schools, New York; m. Ella B. Knapp, 1882. On staff Evening Post and New York Times, 1871—; dramatic critic, 1884-1901, London corr., 1901-02, editor Saturday review of books, 1902-07, editorial writer, 1907—, New York Times. Author: John Drew—a Biographical Sketch, 1900. Died Oct. 16, 1917.

DITRICHSTEIN, Leo, actor, playwright; b. Temesvar, Hungary-Austria, 1867; s. Sigismund Ladislav and Bertha von (Etvoes) D.; ed. in Vienna; naturalized American citizen, 1897; m. Josephine Wehrle, Dec. 16, 1896. Début in America at Amberg Theatre, New York, in "Die Ehre," Mar. 12, 1890; played in "Mr. Wilkinson's Widows," 1893, later as Zou-Zou in "Trilby," as George Fisher in "Are You a Mason?", "The Business Widow," etc. Has written numerous plays, performed in U.S. and England. Progressive. Catholic. Author: Gossip (with Clyde Fitch), 1895; A Southern Romance, 1897; The Last Appeal, 1901; What's the Matter with Susan?, 1904; The Ambitious Mrs. Alcott, 1907; The Million (from the French), 1911; The Concert, 1911; Temperamental Journey, 1912; The Phantom Rival, 1914; The Great Lover, 1915. Home: Stamford, Conn. Died June 28, 1928.

DITSON, Charles Healy, music publisher; b. Boston, Mass., Aug. 11, 1845; s. Oliver and Catherine (Delano) D.; grad. English High Sch., Boston, 1862; m. Alice M. Tappin, Oct. 7, 1890. Began in music pub. business, Boston, 1865, N.Y. City, 1867; pres. Oliver Ditson Co., Boston, Chas. H. Ditson Co., New York. Trustee Oliver Ditson Soc. for Relief of Needy Musicians. Republican. Unitarian. Home: New York, N.Y. Died May 14, 1929.

DITTEMORE, John Valentine, editor; b. Indianapolis, Ind., Sept. 20, 1876; s. John W. and Mary E. (Cress) D.; Ohio Mil. Inst., College Hill, Ohio; Phillips Acad., Andover, Mass.; m. Edith L. Bingham, Feb. 16, 1898; 1 dau., Louise. In commercial pursuits, to 1908, as pres. Federal Packing Co. and v.p. Van Camp Packing Co., Indianapolis and New York, etc.; mem. bd. dirs., Christian Science Ch., 1909-19; chmn. bd. Longyear Ednl. Foundation, 1921-25, editor Progress, 1930-31. Mason. Co-author: (with Prof. Ernest Sutherland Bates) Mary Baker Eddy, The Truth and the Tradition, 1932. Died May 10, 1937.

DITTENHOEFER, Abram Jesse, lawyer; b. Charleston, S.C., Mar. 17, 1836; s. Isaac and Babetta D.; parents removed to New York when he was 4 yrs. old; A.B., Columbia Coll.; widower. Admitted to bar at 21; apptd. justice City Court to fill vacancy; later nominated for same office but declined; elected Lincoln elector, 1864; declined position of U.S. dist. judge for S.C. Chairman German Rep. Central Com., 12 terms; prominent in many corps. and commercial cases as counsel; recognized as authority on the law relating to the drama and the stage. Was counsel for the Met. Opera Co. in the suit brought by Madame Wagner, widow of Richard Wagner, to restrain the production of "Parsifal," and defeated the injunction; secured enactment of amendments to U.S. copyright law, and to the penal code of N.Y., making it a misdemeanor to pirate plays. Home: New York, N.Y. Died Feb. 23, 1919.

DIVEN, George Miles, lawyer; b. Angelica, N.Y., Aug. 28, 1835; s. Alexander S. and Amanda M. (Beers) D.; ed. acad., Elmira, N.Y., pvt. prep. sch., Geneva, N.Y.; A.B., Hamilton Coll., 1857 (A.M.); m. Lucy Minerva Brown, June 3, 1863 (died 1888). Admitted to N.Y. bar, 1860; dir. Elmira & Lake Ontario R.R. Co. Was 6 yrs. pres. Bd. of Education, Elmira; trustee Supreme Court Law Library, Elmira; one of founders (pres. 1891-92) N.Y. State Bar Assn.; trustee Hamilton Coll., 1874—. Presbyn. Republican. Home: Elmira, N.Y. Died 1909.

DIVINE, Frank Henry, clergyman; b. Kirkwood, N.Y., Mar. 19, 1865; s. Eber S. and Verona (Keyes) D.; A.B., Colgate U., 1891, A.M., 1894; grad. Hamilton Theol. Sem., 1894; D.D., Sioux Falls (S.Dak.) Coll., 1917; m. Mary Douglas, July 16, 1887; children—Walter E., May Agnes, Darwin Albert (dec.). Ordained Bapt. ministry, 1894; pastor Watervliet, N.Y., 1894-97; associational missionary Bapt. Missionary Conv. of N.Y., 1897-1902; sec. Conn. Bapt. Conv., 1902-08, also supt. missions; dist. sec. Am. Bapt. Home Mission Soc., N.Y. Dist., 1908-18; edifice sec. same, 1918-21; serving chs. as financial expert, 1921—; head of "Big Brother Financial Agency." Republican. Home: Brooklyn, N.Y. Died Apr. 1, 1941.

DIX, Edwin Asa, author; b. Newark, N.J., June 25, 1860; s. John Edwin and Mary Fisher (Joy) D.; bro. of William Frederick D.; A.B., with 1st honors and Fellowship in History, Princeton, 1881, A.M., 1884; LL.B., Columbia, 1884; m. Marion Alden Olcott, Aug. 15, 1895. Mem. N.Y. and N.J. bars; lit. editor The Churchman, New York, 1893-95. Author: Champlain—the Founder of New France, 1903; Prophet's Landing (novel), 1907; Quincy Baxter (novel), 1908. Home: East Orange, N.J. Died 1911.

DIX, John Alden, governor; b. Glens Falls, N.Y., Dec. 25, 1860; s. James Lawton and Laura (Stevens) D.; Grad. Glens Falls Acad., 1879; A.B., Cornell U., 1883; LL.D., Hamilton Coll., 1912; m. Gertrude Alden, d. Lemon Thomson, of Albany, Apr. 24, 1889. Mem. Reynolds & Dix, black marble, 1882-87, of Thomson & Dix, lumber, Thomson, N.Y., 1887-97; del. to Dem. Nat. Conv., St. Louis, 1904; Dem. nominee for lt. gov., 1908; chmn. Washington Co. Dem. Com., 1908; chmn. Dem. State Com., 1910; gov. of N.Y., term 1910-12. Trustee Cornell U. Episcopalian. Mason. Home: Santa Barbara, Calif. Died Apr. 9, 1928.

DIX, Morgan, P.E. clergyman; b. New York, Nov. 1, 1827; s. Gen. John A. and Catharine M.D.; A.B., Columbia, 1848; B.D., Gen. Theol. Sem., 1852; (S.T.D., Columbia, 1862; D.C.L., U. of South, 1885; D.D., Princeton, 1896, Oxford, England, 1900, Harvard, 1902). Deacon, 1852; priest, 1853; with Trinity Parish, New York, 1855—; asst. minister, 1855; asst. rector, 1859-62; rector, 1862—. Author: History of the Parish of Trinity Church, New York City, 1905. Died 1908.

DIXON, Amzi Clarence, clergyman; b. Shelby, N.C., July 6, 1854; s. Rev. Thomas and Amanda Elizabeth (McAfee) D.; bro. of Thomas D.; A.B., Wake Forest Coll., N.C., 1875; theol. studies Southern Bapt. Theol. Sem.; m. Mary S. Faison, July 1, 1880. Ordained Bapt. ministry, 1876; pastor Chapel Hill, N.C., 1877-80, Asheville, N.C., 1880-83, Immanuel Ch., Baltimore, 1883-1890, Hanson Place Ch., Brooklyn, 1890-96, Ruggles St. Ch., Boston, 1896-1901, Moody Ch., Chicago, 1906-11, Metropolitan Tabernacle, London, June 18, 1911-19; University Baptist Ch., Baltimore, Md., 1922. Author: Heaven on Earth, 1896; The Christian Science Delusion, 1903; Present Day Life and Religion, 1905; Young Convert's Problems, 1906; Destructive Criticism vs. Christianity; The Bright Side of Life, 1912; The Glories of the Cross, 1912; The Bright Side of Death, 1912; Through Night to Morning, 1913; Reconstruction, 1919; The Birth of Christ, the Incarnation of God, 1919; Why I Am a Christian, 1921; Higher Critic Myths and Moths, 1921. Died June 14, 1925.

DIXON, Brandt Van Blarcom, college pres.; b. Paterson, N.J., Feb. 27, 1850; s. David Ackerman

Dixon and Ann VanRiper VanBlarcom D.; student Amherst, 1866-68, Cornell, 1868-70; m. Eliza R. Carson, June 24, 1873. Principal Caledonia Collegiate Inst., 1870, Jefferson and Everett schs., St. Louis, 1870-73; asst. prin., 1873-84, prin., 1886-87, Central High Sch., St. Louis; organized Oct. 1887, and pres. H. Sophie Newcomb Memorial Coll., New Orleans (emeritus). Home: New Orleans, La. Died Sept. 6, 1941.

DIXON, Frank, lecturer; b. Shelby, N.C., Feb. 9, 1866; s. Rev. Thomas and Amanda Elizabeth (McAfee) D.; bro. of Amzi Clarence, and Thomas D.; B.A., U. of N.C., 1886; m. Launa Murray, Dec. 20, 1888. Ordained Bapt. ministry, 1888; pastor Charles Town, W.Va., 1888-89, Oakland, Calif., 1889-93, Hartford, Conn., 1893-1902; lecturer, 1902—. Observer for Am. Red Cross in France, 1918. Pres. Internat. Lyceum and Chautauqua Assn., 1923—. Home: Brooklyn, N.Y. Died May 23, 1925.

DIXON, Frederick, editor; b. London, Eng.; s. Maj. Frederick and Alice (Gray) D.; ed. Sherborne, Dorsetshire, Eng.; m. Clementina, d. Col. Thomas Milward, R.A., C.B., a.d.c., of England, July 13, 1901. Asso. editor, 1908-09, editor The Christian Science Monitor, also European mgr. same, 1909, 1914-22; editor The Internat. Interpreter, 1922—. Mem. Inst. of Journalists (British), Old Shurburnian Soc. Chevalier de l'Ordre de Leopold (Belgian). Home: New York, N.Y. Died Nov. 24, 1923.

DIXON, George Dallas, ry. official; b. Philadelphia, Mar. 28, 1857; pub. sch. edn.; m. Mary Quincy Allen; children—George Mifflin Dallas, II, Honora Allen, Mary F. Quincy. Clk. and chief rate clk. gen. freight dept. Pa. R.R., to 1894, div. freight agt., same rd., Baltimore, 1894-99; asst. gen. frt. agt., Pa. R.R., also of Phila., Wilmington & Baltimore R.R., Northern Central Ry. and West Jersey & Seashore Ry., 1899-1903; freight traffic mgr., same rys., 1903-12; v.p. in charge of traffic, Pa. R.R., 1912-25; asst. to the pres. at Phila., 1925-28; retired under rules of Pension Bd. Home: Philadelphia, Pa. Died June 5, 1937.

DIXON, George William; b. Chicago, Ill., Sept. 16, 1866; s. Arthur and Annie (Carson) D.; A.B., Northwestern U., 1889, LL.B., 1892; Doctor Humane Letters, Lincoln Memorial Univ.; m. Marion E. Martin, Mar. 2, 1903 (died 1926); children—Marion (Mrs. Stanley Zaring), George W., Jr. Active for many yrs. in Chicago business, civic and social affairs; has served as pres. Arthur Dixon Transfer Co., Colonial Land Co., and as dir. Personal Loan & Savings Bank, Central Ill. Securities Co., Grand Trunk Western R.R. (Canadian Nat.), B.&O. Chicago Terminal R.R., Butler Bros. Mem. Ill. Senate, 1st Dist., 1903-07; served on staff of Gov. Yates, rank of col.; mem. Gov. Emmerson's Commn. on Unemployment and Relief, 1930-31, vice-chmn., 1931; trustee and chmn. com. on progress through religion, Century of Progress Expn., Chicago, 1933, 34; was mem. Chicago Charter Conv. and Chicago Plan Commn.; has long served as trustee Northwestern U., American U., Ill. Wesleyan U., also as pres. Wesley Memorial Hosp., and v.p. Kobe (Japan) Coll. Corp.; officer dir. or trustee various orgns. Supt. Sunday Sch. First M.E. Ch., 38 yrs. Mason. Home: Chicago, Ill. Died Sept. 8, 1938.

DIXON, James M., tobacco mfr.; b. Memphis, Tenn., Jan. 12, 1873; s. Josiah Brown and Ida K. (Curtis) D.; ed. Drury Coll., Springfield, Mo.; m. Edythe Hall, Oct. 26, 1899. Began as bank clk., Springfield, at 15; entered employ of Am. Tobacco Co., 1890; mgr. for co. in Germany and the Levant, 1900-07; with Am. Cigar Co. (br. of Am. Tobacco Co.), 1909-12; joined staff of Tobacco Products Corp., 1913, as mgr. of its mfg. and leaf tobacco buying, pres. same co., 1919-24; closed lease of brands for 99 yrs. to Am. Tobacco Co., and retired. Chmn. bd. Am. Chamber of Commerce of the Near East. Presbyn. Mason. Home: New York, N.Y. Died Feb. 2, 1932.

DIXON, James Main, univ. prof.; b. Paisley, Scotland, Apr. 20, 1856; s. Rev. James Main and Jane (Gray) D.; honor grad. St. Andrews U., 1879; L.H.D., Dickinson Coll., 1908; m. Clara Richards, 1885 (died 1927). Fellow Royal Soc., Edinburgh, 1886; tutor in philosophy, St. Andrews U., 1879; prof. English and sec. in Imperial Coll. of Engring., Tokyo, Japan, 1879-86; prof. English, Imperial U., Japan, 1886-92; founder Ladies' Inst., Tokyo, 1887; decorated by Japanese Emperor for services to Govt., 1888; came to U.S., 1892, naturalized citizen, 1901; prof. English lit., Washington U., 1892-1901; prof. English lit., U. of Southern Calif., 1905-11, prof. Oriental studies and comparative lit., 1911-31. Author: Matthew Arnold (in Modern Poets and Christian Teaching), 1906; A Survey of Scottish Literature in the XIX Century, 1907; The Spiritual Meaning of Tennyson's In Memoriam, 1920; Manual of Modern Scots (with William Grant), 1920; Emotional Values in Australasian Verse, 1931. Home: Los Angeles, Calif. Died Sept. 27, 1933.

DIXON, Joseph Moore, governor; b. Snow Camp, N.C., July 31, 1867; s. Hugh W. and Flora (Murchison) D.; student Earlham Coll., Ind.; A.B. Guilford Coll., N.C., 1889; m. Caroline M. Worden, Mar. 12, 1896; children—Mrs. Virginia Dean, Mrs. Florence Leach, Mrs. Dorothy Allen, Mrs. Mary Joe Hills, Mrs. Betty Stearns, Frank (dec.), Peggy. Admitted to bar, 1892; pros. atty. Missoula Co., 1895-97; mem. Mont. Legislature, 1901; mem. 58th and 59th Congresses (1903-07), from Mont. at large; U.S. senator, 1907-13; chmn. Roosevelt Progressive Nat. Com., 1912; gov. of Mont., term 1921-25; first asst. sec. of Interior, 1929-33. Home: Missoula, Mont. Died May 22, 1934.

DIXON, Lincoln, tariff commr.; b. Vernon, Ind., Feb. 9, 1860; s. Samuel M. and Belinda (Foster) D.; A.B., Ind. U., 1880; m. Kate Storey, Oct. 16, 1884. Admitted to Ind. bar, 1881, and began practice at North Vernon, 1882; pros. atty. 6th Jud. Circuit, Ind., 1884-92; mem. Dem. State Com., 1897-1904; mem. 59th to 65th Congresses (1905-19), 4th Ind. Dist.; in charge Dem. campaign in the west, hdqrs. Chicago, 1924; apptd. mem. U.S. Tariff Commn., Jan. 1927, reapptd., Sept. 1930. Home: North Vernon, Ind. Died Sept. 16, 1932.

DIXON, Robert M., mech. engr.; b. East Orange, N.J., Sept. 19, 1860; M.E., Stevens Inst. Tech., 1881. Draftsman Del. Bridge Co. until 1883; with Pintsch Lighting Co., 1883-88; became engr. Safety Car Heating and Lighting Co., and mgr. Pintsch Compressing Co., 1888, later pres. both companies, also pres. Realty Security Co.; dir. Vapor Car Heating Co.; patentee of many inventions. Home: East Orange, N.J. Died Oct. 16, 1918.

DIXON, Rolland Burrage, univ. prof.; b. Worcester, Mass., Nov. 6, 1875; s. Lewis Seaver and Ellen R (Burrage) D.; A.B., Harvard, 1897, A.M., 1898, Ph.D., 1900; unmarried. Asst. in anthropology, 1897-1901, instr., 1901-06, asst. prof. 1906-15, prof. 1916—, Harvard U. Staff, Am. Commn. to Negotiate Peace, Paris, 1918-19. Fellow Am. Acad. of Arts and Sciences, Am. Philos. Soc., A.A.A.S. Author: Oceanic Mythology, 1916; Racial History of Man, 1923; The Building of Cultures, 1928. Home: Harvard, Mass. Died Dec. 19, 1934.

DIXON, Samuel Gibson, bacteriologist; b. Phila., Pa., Mar. 23, 1851; s. Isaac and Ann (Gibson) D.; grad. Mercantile Coll.; studied law, admitted to bar, 1877; M.D., with honors, U. of Pa., 1886; grad. dept. of bacteriology, King's Coll., London; studied in State Coll. of Medicine, London, and Pettenkofer's Lab. of Hygiene, Munich; (LL.D., U. of Pa., 1909); m. Fannie Gilbert. Prof. hygiene in med. and scientific depts. and dean auxiliary dept. of medicine, U. of Pa., 1888-1910; prof. bacteriology and micros. technology, 1890—, curator, 1891-92, exec. curator, 1892—, pres., 1896—, Acad. Natural Sciences, Phila. Mem. Bd. Pub. Edn., Phila., 1898; Commr. of Health, Pa., 1905—. Trustee U. of P., Wistar Inst. of Anatomy; 1st v.p. Ludwick Inst.; mgr. Grandom Instn. Author: Physiological Notes, 1886. Home: Bryn Mawr, Pa. Died Feb. 26, 1918.

DIXON, Susan Bullitt, author; b. Oxmoor, Ky., Feb. 20, 1829; d. William Christian and Mildred Ann (Fry) Bullitt; academic edn. at pvt. schs. in Louisville; m. Hon. Archibald Dixon, Oct. 29, 1853 (died 1876). Lived at Henderson, Ky., 1853-94; in New York, 1894-98; returned to Ky., 1898. Author: Repeal of Missouri Compromise, and Slavery in American Politics, 2d edit. Died 1907.

DIXON, William Palmer, lawyer; b. New York, N.Y., Mar. 17, 1847; s. Courtlandt Palmer and Hannah E (Williams) D.; A.B., Yale, 1868; LL.B., Columbia, 1870; m. Evelena F. Babcock, Apr. 26, 1871 (died 1908). Admitted to bar, 1869, and began practice in New York; sr. mem. Dixon & Holmes. Pres., trustee New York, Manhattan, Colonial and Central real est assns.; trustee Mut. Life Ins. Co. Home: New York, N.Y. Died June 24, 1927.

DIXSON, Zella Allen, librarian, author; b. Zanesville, O.; d. Josiah Buffett and Mary Caroline (Blandy) Allen; grad. Mt. Holyoke, 1880; spl. student in library science Columbia, 1885-86, British Mus., 1891, 1899, 1901; A.M., Shepardson Coll., 1892; A.M., Denison U., 1902; L.H.D., Shurtleff, 1906; m. Joseph Ehrman Dixson, 1881 (died 1885). Library asst., Columbia Coll., 1885-86; library expert, 1887-88; librarian Denison U., 1888-90, Bapt. Union Theol. Sem., 1890-91; organizer and administrative head of U. of Chicago Library, 1891-1911; lecturer and prof. library science, U. of Chicago, 1896-1911. Literary editor Bulletins Northwestern Library Assn., 1899-1900. Author: Subject Index to Prose Fiction, 1897; Children's Book-plates, 1902; Concerning Book-plates, 1903. Home: Chicago, Ill. Died Jan. 12, 1924.

DOAK, William Nuckles, secretary of labor; b. Rural Retreat, Va., Dec. 12, 1882; s. Canaro Draton and Elizabeth (Dutton) D.; ed. pub. schs. and Southern Bus. Coll., Bristol, Va.; Dr. Humanities, Lincoln Memorial U., 1931; m. Emma Marie Cricher, Oct. 15, 1908. Gen. chmn. Brotherhood R.R. Trainmen, Norfolk & Western System, 1908-16; v.p. Brotherhood R.R. Trainmen, 1916-28, Nat. legislative rep., 1916—; mem. ry. bd. of adjustment, U.S. R.R. Administration, World War; editor and mgr. The Railroad Trainmen, 1928—. U.S. sec. of labor, Dec. 8, 1930—. Republican. Mason. Home: McLean, Va. Died Oct. 23, 1933.

DOAN, Fletcher Morris, judge; b. Circleville, O., July 21, 1846; s. John and Maria D.; A.B., Ohio Wesleyan U., 1867, A.M., 1872; LL.B., Albany Law Sch., 1868; m. Anna Murray, Dec. 25, 1873. Admitted to bar, N.Y. Supreme Ct., 1868, Mo. Supreme Ct., 1869, Ariz. Supreme Ct., 1894; dist. atty., Pinal Co., Ariz., 1894-96; asso. justice Supreme Ct. and judge 2d Jud. Dist. of Ariz., July 8, 1897-Feb. 14, 1912; mem. Doan & Doan, 1912-20, Doan & Stephenson, 1921—. Home: Douglas, Ariz. Died Oct. 28, 1924.

DOAN, Frank Carleton, clergyman; b. Nelsonville, O., Feb. 13, 1877; s. Charles Henry and Hannah Virginia (Austin) D.; student Hiram Coll., 1892-95; Ph.B., Ohio State U., 1898; A.M., Harvard, 1900, Ph.D., 1904; m. Isabel Wilson, July 18, 1900; children—Pleasantine Virginia, Isabel, Alice, Daniel. Prof. psychology and edn., Ohio U., 1900-04; prof. philosophy of religion and systematic theology, Meadville Theol. Sem., 1904-13; ordained Unitarian ministry, 1914; pastor, All Souls' Ch., Summit, N.J., 1913-19, Iowa City, Ia., 1919-22, Rochester, N.Y., 1922—. Author: Religion and the Modern Mind, 1909. Home: Rochester, N.Y. Died May 14, 1927.

DOANE, William Croswell, bishop; b. Boston, Mass., Mar. 2, 1832; s. George Washington D. (2d bishop N.J.) and Eliza Greene (Callahan) D.; A.B., Burlington (N.J.) Coll., 1850, A.M., 1852; A.M., Trinity Coll., 1863; (D.D., Columbia, 1867, Trinity, 1886, Oxford, Eng., 1888, Dublin U., Ireland, 1901; S.T.D., Hobart, 1890; LL.D., Union, 1880, Cambridge, Eng., 1888, Hobart, 1890, U. of Pa., 1902; D.C.L., Union); m. Sarah Katharine Condit, Nov. 7, 1853. Deacon, 1853, priest, 1856, P.E. Ch.; rector St. Mary's Ch., Burlington, N.J., 1853-60, St. John's, Hartford, Conn., 1860-64, St. Peter's, Albany, 1867-69; consecrated bishop of Albany, Feb. 2, 1869. Adj. prof. English lit., Burlington Coll., 1854-60; lecturer English lit., Trinity, 1863-67; visitor, 1869—, trustee, 1870-79, hon. chancellor, 1889, Hobart; founded St. Agnes Sch., Albany, 1870; regent, 1892—, chancellor, till 1909, U. of State of N.Y., Albany. Died May 17, 1913.

DOBBIN, George W., M.D.; b. Baltimore, Md., Dec. 17, 1870; s. Robert A. and Elizabeth Swan (Key) D.; A.B., Johns Hopkins, 1891; M.D., U. of Md. Med. Sch., 1894; m. Beatrice Dunderdale, Oct. 10, 1900; children—Elizabeth Van C., Beatrice Dunderdale, Anna Parker, George W., Rebecca Pue. Practiced at Baltimore, 1894—; prof. obstetrics and gynecology, Coll. Phys. and Surg., Baltimore, 1900—, and U. of Md., 1914—; visiting obstetrician, Md. Lying-in Asylum (treas.), Mercy Hosp., Hosp. for Women of Md., Hebrew Hosp. and Ch. Home. Fellow Am. Coll. Surgeons, A.M.A. Democrat. Episcopalian. Home: Elk Ridge, Md. Died Oct. 15, 1928.

DOBSON, George Frederick, editor; b. Liverpool, Eng., Oct. 5, 1850; s. Henry E. and Helen D.; m. Mary Marr, Sept. 4, 1871. Associate editor-in-chief, Brooklyn (N.Y.) Daily Eagle. Pres. Harway Improvement Co.; sec. and dir. Metropolitan Jockey Club, New Montauk Theatre; dir. Long Beach Estates; sec., treas. Laurelton Land Co., etc. Died May 8, 1928.

DOBYNS, John Robert, educator; b. Columbus, Mo., March 31, 1850; s. Benjamin Franklin and Margaret Ruth (Morrow) D.; A.B., Westminster Coll., Mo., 1874, A.M., 1876 (LL.D., 1904); m. Lily Webster, June 26, 1878. Engaged in teaching deaf mutes, 1st in Instn. for Deaf, Fulton, Mo., afterward in Texas Instn. for Deaf; supt. Miss. State Instn. for Deaf, Jackson, Mar. 1, 1881-Aug. 31, 1914; pres. Southwestern Presbyn. U., Clarksville, Tenn., 1914-16; pres. Stonewall Jackson Coll., Abingdon, Va., Jan. 1, 1917-Sept. 15, 1919; supt. Ark. Deaf Mute Inst., Little Rock, Sept. 16, 1919—. V.p. Conv. Am. Instructors of the Deaf, 1908-14. Democrat. Presbyn. Deceased.

DOBYNS, William Ray, clergyman; b. Columbus, Mo., May 17, 1861; s. Benjamin Franklin (M.D.) and Margaret Ruth (Morrow) D.; Westminster Coll., Fulton, Mo.; B.D., McCormick Theol. Sem., Chicago, 1889; D.D., Westminster, 1901; LL.D., Austin Coll., Sherman, Tex., 1924; m. Mary Triplette Buckland, June 19, 1889; children—Margaret Ruth (dec.), Mary Ray. Ordained Presbyn. ministry, 1889; organizer and 1st pastor Immanuel Ch., Chicago, in "Bridgeport," 1886-90; financial sec. Westminster Coll., 1890-91; pastor 1st Ch., Marshall, Mo., 1891-99, 1st Ch., St. Joseph, Mo., 1899-1920, S. Highland Ch., Birmingham, Ala., 1920—. Chmn. exec. com. Y.M.C. Assns. of Mo.; chmn. home mission work in Mo. for 12 yrs.; founder and pres. trustees Sch. of the Ozarks, Hollister, Mo.; trustee Presbyn. Theol. Sem., Louisville, Ky., from its foundation; dir. Agnes Scott Coll. (Decatur, Ga.). Mem. World's Council of Presbyns., Liverpool, 1904; chmn. exec. com., Synod of Ala.; moderator Gen. Assembly Presbyn. Ch. in U.S., 1929. Cleveland Democrat. Mason. Camp dir. of religious work, Army Y.M.C.A., Camp Gordon, Atlanta, Ga., 1917-18. Home: Birmingham, Ala. Died Jan. 26, 1932.

DOCKERY, Alexander Monroe, governor; b. Daviess Co., Mo., Feb. 11, 1845; ed. common schs. and Macon Acad., Mo.; M.D., St. Louis Med. Coll., 1865; following winter attended lectures at Bellevue Coll.,

New York, and Jefferson Med. Coll., Phila.; LL.D., U. of Mo., 1906. Practiced medicine, Chillicothe, Mo., 1866-74; removed to Gallatin, Mo., and assisted in organizing the Farmers' Exchange Bank, of which was cashier until 1882. Pres. bd. of edn., Chillicothe, 1870-72, curator U. of Mo., 1872-82; mem. city council, 1878-81, mayor, 1881-83, Gallatin, Mo.; chmn. Dem. State Conv., 1886, 1906, mem. 48th to 55th Congresses (1882-98), 3d Mo. Dist.; gov. of Mo., 1901-05; 3rd asst. postmaster general of U.S., Mar. 17, 1913-Apr. 1, 1921. Mason. Home: Gallatin, Mo. Died Dec. 26, 1926.

DOCKING, James Tippet, univ. pres.; b. Cornwall, Eng., Jan. 29, 1861; s. Thomas and Mary (Tippet) D.; brought to America when a lad; student Albion (Mich.) Coll.; A.B., Boston U., 1886, S.T.B., 1887, Ph.D., 1890; studied in Europe; m. Lua Belle Green, May 23, 1888. Ordained M.E. ministry, 1887; pastor Asbury Ch., Des Moines, Ia., 1887-89, Boone, Ia., 1889-91, Westerly, R.I., 1892-95, Tabernacle Ch., Providence, 1895-96, West Dennis, Mass., 1897-1902, Cataumet, Mass., 1902-04; pres. Cookman Inst., Jacksonville, Fla., 1904-09; pres. Rust U., Holly Springs, Miss., 1909-15. A founder, 1889, and mem. Bd. of Control, Epworth League; organizer and conductor Epworth Pilgrimages. Prohibitionist. Author: Pulpit Bible Reading; A Study in Vocal Exegesis. Died Mar. 23, 1916.

DODD, Amzi, ins. exec.; b. Bloomfield, N.J., Mar. 2, 1823; grad. Princeton, 1841; admitted to bar, 1848; practiced at Newark; m. Jane Frame, 1852. Defeated for Congress as Republican, 1856; mem. N.J. assembly, 1863; vice chancellor of N.J., 1871-75 and 1881-82; spl. judge, Ct. of Errors and Appeals, 1872-82; pres. Mut. Benefit Life Ins. Co., 1882-1902. Home: Bloomfield, N.J. Died Jan. 22, 1913.

DODD, Charles Hastings, clergyman; b. Almond, N.Y., May 30, 1859; s. Edward and Betsy A. (Holcomb) D.; Colgate U., 1886; grad. Hamilton Theol. Sem., 1889; D.D., George Washington U., 1905; unmarried. Ordained Bapt. ministry, 1889; pastor, Weedsport, N.Y., 1889-90, 1st Ch., Mt. Vernon, N.Y., 1890-94, Peddie Memorial Ch., Newark, N.J., 1894-1905, Eutaw Place Ch., Baltimore, 1905-13, 2d Ch., Germantown, Phila., 1913-26; retired. Republican. Home: Coudersport, Pa. Died Aug. 1933.

DODD, Frank Howard, publisher; b. Bloomfield, N.J., April 12, 1844; fitted at Bloomfield Acad., for Yale, but entering his father's business temporarily, ended by remaining with him until 1870, when with Edward S. Mead, he formed Dodd & Mead and succeeded to the business of his father, M. W. Dodd (which was founded in 1839 in Brick Church Chapel, Printing House Sq.); m. Martha Bliss Parker, 1868. Now the active head of Dodd, Mead & Co. Established The Bookman, 1895, The New Internat. Ency., 1902, and other important enterprises. Pres. Riverside Assn.; v.p. Am. Publishers' Assn.; mem. Chamber of Commerce. Home: New York, N.Y. Died Jan. 10, 1916.

DODD, George Allan, army officer; b. Rose's Valley, Pa., July 26, 1852; s. of Allan Grinnell and Emily (Stiger) D.; grad. U.S. Mil. Acad., 1876; m. Agnes Clara Steele, June 1880. Commd. 2d lt. 3d Cav., June 15, 1876; advanced through grades to col. 12th Cav., Apr. 14, 1908; brig. gen., July 1, 1916, and retired by operation of law, July 26, 1916. Participated in numerous campaigns against Indians, 1876-83; introduced improved system of handling and training cavalry, 1888 and 1891-93; duty Chicago during Pullman strike, 1894; visited Eng. in connection with mil. tournaments, 1895; inaugurated U.S. mil. tournaments, Madison Sq., New York, 1896-97; duty in Cuba, 1898, in Philippines, 1899-1901; chief umpire of Div., Aug.-Sept. 1906; duty Gen. Staff, 1907-08; comd. 2d Cav. Brigade, Douglas, Ariz., 1915-16; comd. western column Mex. punitive expdn., 1916. Recommended for bvt. "for gallantry in action and returning to firing line while wounded," Battle of San Juan, Cuba, July 1, 1898; for bvts. as maj. and lt. col., by Gens. Lawton and Young, "for gallant service in attacking in the darkness, and dispersing a large force of the enemy in a most dangerous and difficult pass," 1899, later as col. for same affair; for bvts. by Gen. Wheaton, "for most gallant conduct in action." Home: Ithaca, N.Y. Died June 28, 1925.

DODD, Henry Martyn, clergyman; b. Ridgeville, O., Aug. 6, 1839; s. Rev. John and Maria Wiser (Read) D.; grad. Bridgton Acad., Me., 1858, Genesee and Wyoming Sem., N.Y., 1860; A.B., Hamilton Coll., 1863, A.M., 1866; asst. and later prin., Cortlandville Acad., Cortland, N.Y., 1863-67; grad. Theol. Sem., Auburn, N.Y., 1870; student supply, Canastota, N.Y., 1869-70; ordained Presbyn. ministry, Jan 2, 1873; m. Ella Whiting, d. David and Martha E. (Whiting) Allen, of Great Barrington, Mass., Nov. 30, 1870. Pastor-elect, Manlius, N.Y., 1870-72; pastor, Dexter and Brownville, N.Y., 1872-84, Augusta, N.Y., 1884-96, Ashland, N.Y., 1896-90; retired. Home: Clinton, N.Y. Died Nov. 13, 1920.

DODD, Lee Wilson, author, playwright; b. Franklin, Pa., July 11, 1879; s. Samuel Calvin Tate and Melvina Eliza (Smith) D.; Ph.B., Yale, 1899; LL.B., N.Y. Law Sch., 1901; admitted to bar, 1902; m. Marion Roberts Canby, Jan. 11, 1907; children—Doris, Alan. Gave up law for literature, 1907; critic, Saturday Review of Lit.; lecturer Bread Loaf Writers' Conf., Middlebury Coll., 1931-32; mem. English faculty, Sarah Lawrence Coll.; visiting lecturer English dept., Wesleyan Univ., 1923-33. Author: The Return of Eve (play), 1909; Speed (play), 1911; The Middle Miles (poems), 1915; His Majesty Bunker Bean (dramatization), 1915; Pals First (dramatization), 1917; The Book of Susan (novel), 1920; Lilia Chenoworth (novel), 1922; The Girl Next Door (novel), 1923; The Changelings (play), 1923; The Sly Giraffe (for children), 1925; The Golden Complex, 1927; The Great Enlightenment (poems), 1928. Home: New Haven, Conn. Died May 16, 1933.

DODD, Samuel C. T., lawyer; b. Franklin, Pa., Feb. 20, 1836; s. Levi L. and Julia (Parker) D.; grad. Jefferson Coll., 1857; studied law at Franklin, Pa., 1857-59; m. Mary E. Geer, July 12, 1862; 2d, Melvina Smith, March 8, 1877. Practiced law Franklin, Pa., 1859-81; gen. solicitor Standard Oil Co., Jan. 1, 1881—; mem. Constl. Conv. of Pa., 1872-73; organized Standard Oil Trust, 1882. Democrat (anti-Bryan). Home: New York, N.Y. Died 1907.

DODD, William Clifton, missionary; b. Marion, Ia., Oct. 15, 1857; s. William Wylie and Rhoda Burns (Robb) D.; A.B., Parsons Coll., Fairfield, Ia., 1883, A.M., 1886; grad. McCormick Theol. Sem., Chicago, 1886; (D.D., Parsons, 1904); m. Isabella Ruth Eakin, July 16, 1889. Ordained Presbyn. ministry, 1886; missionary to Siam, 1886—; treas. Laos Mission, 1887-90, later founded theol. sem. in connection with mission; has made extensive evangelistic tours in Siam, Burma and China; a leader in establishing missions among the Tai people in southern China and Indo-China. Home: Chiengrai, Siam. Died Oct. 18, 1919.

DODD, William Edward, univ. prof.; b. Clayton, N.C., Oct. 21, 1869; s. John D. and Evelyn (Creech) D.; B.S., Va. Poly. Inst., 1895, M.S., 1897; instr. history, same, 1895-97; Ph.D., U. of Leipzig, 1900; LL.D., Emory U., 1920, U. of Ala., 1923; m. Martha Johns, Dec. 24, 1901; children—William E., Martha Eccles. Prof. history, Randolph-Macon Coll., 1900-08; became prof. Am. history, U. of Chicago, 1908; ambassador to Germany, 1933-37. Trustee of Sweet Briar (Va.) College. Author: Jefferson's Rückkehr zur Politik (1796), 1900; Life of Nathaniel Macon, 1903; Life of Jefferson Davis, 1907; Statesmen of the Old South, 1911; Expansion and Conflict, 1915; The Cotton Kingdom (Chronicles of America Series), 1919; Woodrow Wilson and His Work, 1920; Lincoln or Lee, 1928; Textbooks on History of the United States (with E. C. Barker and W. P. Webb), 1928. Editor (with Ray Stannard Baker) of The Public Papers of Woodrow Wilson, 1924-26; Vol. I The Old South, Struggle for Democracy, 1937. Home: Round Hill, Va. Died Feb. 9, 1940.

DODDS, Alexander, editor; b. Allegheny, Pa., Apr. 5, 1874; s. Robert Carson and Alice A. H. (Gray) D.; grad. Duffs Coll., Pittsburgh, 1890; m. Gertrude Paxton Ramsay, Jan. 22, 1907. Newspaper writer and editor from 1890; asso. pub. The Builder, Pittsburgh, 1894-96; night editor Pittsburgh Dispatch, 1902; asso. pub. Telegraph, Sharon, Pa., 1902-04; New York corr., 1904, night editor, 1905-08, Gazette Times, Pittsburgh; mng. editor Christian Science Monitor, Boston, Sept., 1908-14, Los Angeles Herald, 1914-16. V.p. United Press Assn., 1909-12. Mason. Home: Hollywood, Calif. Died Nov. 30, 1920.

DODGE, Charles Richards, textile fibre expert; b. in Miss., July 17, 1847; s. Hon. Jacob Richards and Frances Gove (Buxton) D.; 2 yrs. spl. course Sheffield Scientific Sch. (Yale); m. Mira, d. Col. Josiah Reab, of New Haven, Conn., Jan. 23, 1868. Dept. Agr., 1867, asst. entomologist, and had charge Agrl. Mus. 10 yrs.; began study of fibres, 1870; spl. agt. in charge fibre investigation, Dept. Agriculture, 1890; has since published 20 spl. reports on fibres and fibre industries, including a Dictionary of the Fibre Plants of the World. Officially connected with 11 internat. expns.; dir. Agr. U.S. Commn., Paris Expn., 1900; mem. jury awards, Paris, 1889, Chicago, 1893, Atlanta, 1895, Nashville, 1897, Omaha, 1898, Paris, 1900, Buffalo, 1901, St. Louis, 1904, Jamestown Expn., 1907. Chevalier du Mérite Agricole France; Chevalier Légion d'Honneur. Home: East Haven, Conn. Deceased.

DODGE, Charles Wright, biologist; b. Cape Vincent, N.Y., Jan. 15, 1863; s. Jasper Newton and Charlotte Augusta (Wright) D.; B.S., U. of Mich., 1886, M.S., 1889; m. Louise W. Hooker, July 18, 1894; children—Charlotte Wright, Eleanor Wolcott (dec.). Instr. biology, 1890-92, prof., 1892-1931, emeritus prof., 1931—, U. of Rochester. Biologist, Rochester Health Bur., 1895-1925. Author: Introduction to Elementary Practical Biology, 1894. Reviser: Orton-Dodge General Zoölogy, 1903. Home: Rochester, N.Y. Died 1934.

DODGE, Clarence Phelps; b. Honolulu, H.T., July 26, 1877; s. David Stuart and Ellen Ada (Phelps) D.; grad. Phillips Acad., Andover, Mass., 1895; A.B., Yale, 1899; m. Regina Lunt, Jan. 1, 1900; children—Regina (Mrs. Charles William Eliot II), Clarence Phelps. Pub. Colorado Springs Gazette and pres. Gazette Pub. Co., 1904-22. Mem. Colo. Ho. of Rep., 1905; chmn. Prog. Party of Colo. Capt. O.R.C., S.S., until 1934; mem. Nat. War Work Council, Honolulu, Pacific Coast and overseas, 1917-18. Pres. Community Chest, Colorado Springs, 1925-28; pres. Labor Coll. of Colorado Springs, 1929-30; pres. Community Chest of Washington, D.C., 4 terms, 1934-38; apptd. mem. Washington-Lincoln Memorial Gettysburg Memorial Boulevard Commn., 1935; chmn. Nat. Commn. for Social Edn.; trustee and mem. exec. com. Brookings Instn. (Washington); pres. Inst. of Criminal Science, Washington, D.C.; chmn. com. on a monumental memorial in Washington for Theodore Roosevelt Island; chmn. social service com. Washington Fedn. of Chs. Fellow Roosevelt Society. Prog. Republican. Episcopalian. Home: Washington, D.C. Died July 29, 1939.

DODGE, Cleveland Hoadley, merchant; b. New York, Jan. 26, 1860; s. William Earl and Sarah (Hoadley) D.; brother of Grace Hoadley D.; A.B., Princeton, 1879, A.M., 1882; m. Grace Parish, Oct. 11, 1883. V.p., dir. Phelps Dodge Corp.; trustee Atlantic Mut. Ins. Co.; dir. Nat. City Bank, etc. V.p. Am. Mus. Natural History; pres. bd. of trustees Robert Coll., Constantinople; trustee New York Pub. Library, N.Y. Zoöl. Soc.; treas. Am. com. Near East Relief, 1917. Home: Riverdale-on-Hudson, N.Y. Died June 24, 1926.

DODGE, Daniel Kilham, univ. prof.; b. Brooklyn, June 13, 1863; s. Daniel Albert (M.D.) and Margaret Rapelje (Suydam) D.; A.B., Columbia U., 1884, Ph.D., 1886; m. Astrid Pauline Mathilde Moth, of Copenhagen, Denmark, Aug. 14, 1890 (died 1920); children—Helen Moth, Margaret Rapelje, Astrid Moth, Daniel Kilham, Elinor Nathalie Moth. Fellow, 1884-89, tutor, 1889-91, Columbia; prof. of English, U. of Ill., 1892-1928, emeritus. Contbr. to Johnson's Cyclo., 1894-95; dept. editor New Internat. Ency., 1901-04. Mem. com. on Germanic Congress, 1904; contbg. editor German-Am. Annals. Author: Lincoln—The Evolution of His Style (in U. of Ill. Studies), 1900; Abraham Lincoln, Master of Words, 1924. Editor: Lincoln's Inaugurals, Addresses and Letters (selections), 1910. Episcopalian. Democrat. Fire and police commr. of Champaign, Ill., 1916-17. Home: Pasadena, Calif. Died Oct. 13, 1933.

DODGE, David Child, capitalist; b. Shirley, Mass., Nov. 17, 1837; s. Levi and Susannah A. D.; ed. Lawrence Acad., Groton, Mass.; m. Emily K. Oatman, Nov. 15, 1859. Entered ry. service Feb., 1853, as chainman engr. corps Fox River Valley R.R.; later with Ill. & Wis., and Wis. Central roads; in engring. dept., 1856-57, gen. freight and pass. agt., and paymaster, 1857-64, Chicago, Iowa & Nebraska Ry.; gen. agt. Nevada, Ia., 1864, Denver, 1865-70, C.&N.-W. Ry.; gen. agt. Kan. Pacific Ry., Denver, 1871-72; traffic mgr., 1872-78, gen. supt., 1878-80, gen. mgr., 1880, D.&R.G. RR..; gen. mgr., 1886-1901, and 2d v.p., 1890-1901, Rio Grande Western Ry., also 1900, to 1901, 1st v.p. Colo. Midland Ry. Was also v.p. and gen. mgr. Mexican Nat. R.R., 1885-88; apptd. receiver Denver, Northwestern & Pacific R.R., 1912. Home: Denver, Colo. Died July 19, 1918.

DODGE, D(avid) Stuart, clergyman; b. New York, Sept. 22, 1836; A.B., Yale, 1857, A.M., 1864; grad. Union Theol. Sem., 1860; (D.D., Yale, 1899); m. Ellen Phelps; father of Walter Phelps D. Ordained Presbyn. ministry, Oct. 16, 1864; pres. bd. of Home Missions of Presbyn. Ch. in U.S.A., 1899-1915. Pres. bd. trustees Syrian Protestant Coll. Home: New York, N.Y. Died Dec. 17, 1921.

DODGE, Francis Safford, army officer; b. Danvers, Mass., Sept. 11, 1842; s. Francis and Rebecca Appleton (Brown) D.; grad. Danvers High Sch., 1860; attended Henniker (N.H.) Acad., 1860-61; m. Mary Hunt Weston, Dec. 3, 1878. Pvt. and corp. Co. F, 23d Mass. Inf., Oct. 9, 1861-Dec. 19, 1863; 1st lt. U.S. colored cav., Dec. 20, 1863; promoted through grades to brig. gen. p.m. gen., Jan. 23, 1904; retired by operation of law, Sept. 11, 1906. Bvtd. maj., Feb. 27, 1890, for action against Indians at Milk Creek, Colo., Sept. 29-Oct. 1, 1879; awarded medal of honor, Mar. 22, 1898, for "most distinguished gallantry" against Indians nr. White River Agency, Colo., Oct. 2, 1879. Served in N.C. and S.C., 1861-63, in Va., 1863-64, Tex., 1864-65; after the war at various posts in the west, etc. Dir. and mem. exec. com. Garfield Memorial Hosp.; dir. Am. Surety & Trust Co. Home: Washington, D.C. Died 1908.

DODGE, Frederic, judge; b. Cambridge, Mass., Apr. 1847; s. John C. and Lucy (Sherman) D.; A.B., Harvard, 1867, LL.B., 1869; m. Eugenia Louise Jackson, Sept. 20, 1877. Admitted to bar, 1869, and began practice at Boston; U.S. dist. judge, Dist. of Mass., Apr. 18, 1905-12; U.S. circuit judge, 1st Circuit, Sept. 10, 1912-June 30, 1918. Republican. Fellow Am. Acad. Arts and Sciences. Home: Belmont, Mass. Died Mar. 7, 1927.

DODGE, Grace Hoadley, educator; b. New York; d. William Earl and Sarah (Hoadley) D.; sister of

Cleveland Hoadley D.; has for 35 yrs. been active in charitable and ednl. work; apptd. mem. bd. of school commrs., New York, 1886; has been pres. Working Girls' Soc.; treas. Teachers Coll.; pres. nat. bd. of Y.W.C.A. of U.S. of America; has held responsible positions in various organizations. Died Dec. 27, 1914.

DODGE, Grenville Mellen, civil engr.; b. Danvers, Mass., Apr. 12, 1831; s. Sylvanus and Julia T. (Phillips) D.; grad. Capt. Partridge's Mil. Acad.; C.E., Norwich U., Vt., 1850 (A.M., M.M.S., LL.D., 1892; LL.D., Cornell Coll., Ia., 1904). Was engr. Ill. Central and Rock Island roads; later on U.P. R.R. survey and banker at Council Bluffs, Ia. Entered Civil War as col. 4th Inf., July 6, 1861; brig. gen. vols., Mar. 21, 1862; maj. gen. vols., June 7, 1864; resigned May 30, 1866. Chief engr. U.P. R.R. and supervised its building, 1866-70; chief engr. Tex. & Pacific Ry., 1871-81. Mem. 40th Congress (1867-69), 2d Ia. Dist. Republican. Succeeded Gen. Sherman as pres. Soc. Army of the Tenn.; comdr.-in-chief Mil. Order Loyal Legion, 1907-08. Apptd. maj. gen. U.S.V., 1898, but declined; apptd., 1898, pres. of the President's commn. to inquire into the management of the war with Spain; chmn. bd. dirs. C.&S. Ry. to Feb. 1909; dir. Ft. Worth & Denver City Ry.; v.p. Abilene & Southern Ry. Died Jan. 3, 1916.

DODGE, Henry Irving, author; b. Kasoag, N.Y., 1861; ed. pub. schs. Mem. Authors League America. Author: The Other Mr. Barclay, 1906; The Hat and the Man, 1906; Skinner's Dress Suit, 1916; Skinner's Baby, 1917; Skinner's Big Idea, 1918; The Yellow Dog, 1918; He Made His Wife His Partner, 1919; Skinner Makes It Fashionable, 1920; (plays) The Counsel for the Defense; The Higher Court; The Whirlpool; The Love Thought; The Recoil. Died July 28, 1934.

DODGE, H(enry) Percival, diplomat; b. Boston, Jan. 18, 1870; s. Henry Cleaves and Alice Almia (Lamb) D.; A.B., magna cum laude, Harvard, 1892, LL.B., 1895; admitted to bar, 1895; studied in France, Germany, and Italy, 1897-98; m. Margaret Riché Adams (died 1919); 1 dau., Alice Lamb Cleaves; m. 2d, Agnes Page-Brown, 1922. Third sec., 1899-1900, 2d sec., 1900-02, sec., 1902-06, Am. Embassy at Berlin; sec. Am. Embassy at Tokyo, 1906-07; E.E. and M.P. to Honduras and Salvador, 1907-08, to Salvador, 1908-09, to Morocco, May 12, 1909-July 1910; resident diplomatic officer of Dept. of State, and chief of Div. of Latin-Am. Affairs, 1910-11; E.E. and M.P. to Panama, July 6, 1911; apptd. chmn. com. to supervise Panamanian municipal and presdl. elections, May 12, 1912; resigned Aug. 25, 1913; May 13, 1914, apptd. sec. and diplomatic adviser to Am. Commn. to the Mediation Conf. bet. the U.S. and Mex., at Niagara Falls; Aug. 6, 1914, apptd. rep. of State Dept. on Am. Commn. for repatriation of Americans in Europe; Sept. 6, 1914, apptd. spl. agt. of State Dept. and assigned to Am. Embassy in Paris, where placed by the ambassador in charge of Austro-Hungarian and German interests in France; spl. rep. to Serbia in charge of the Am. Legation, June 10, 1917-June 17, 1919; Am. minister to Kingdom of the Serbs, Croats and Slovenes, 1919-26 (apptd. spl. ambassador to attend King's marriage), to Denmark, 1926-30; trans. to Dept. of State, 1930; retired Oct. 1, 1931. Died Oct. 16, 1936.

DODGE, Jacob Richards, statistician, Dept. Agr., 1866-93; b. New Boston, N.H., Sept. 28, 1823; s. Capt. Jacob Davis D.; academic and technical edn. (hon. A.M., Dartmouth); m. Frances Gove Buxton, Oct. 20, 1846. Teacher in Miss., 1845-49; editor in Nashua, N.H., 1850-54; editor American Ruralist, Springfield, O., 1857-61; edited reports U.S. Dept. Agr. for 24 yrs.; author of books and pamphlets on rural and political economy; one of commrs. to Vienna Expn., 1873; executed foreign commns. for Dept. Agr., 1873, 1887. From 1893 on editorial staff of Country Gentleman, Albany, N.Y. Died 1902.

DODGE, James Mapes, mech. engr.; b. Waverly, N.J., June 30, 1852; s. William and Mary (Mapes) D.; ed. Acad., Newark, N.J., Cornell U. to junior yr., and Rutgers Coll.; m. Josephine Kern, Sept. 10, 1879. Has given spl. attention to improvement and manufacture of conveying machinery and devices; now chmn. Link Belt Co. Pres. Am. Soc. M.E., 1903; v.p. Franklin Inst. Republican. Home: Germantown, Phila., Pa. Died Dec. 4, 1915.

DODGE, Josephine Marshall Jewell; b. Hartford, Conn., Feb. 11, 1855; d. Marshall and Esther (Dickinson) Jewell; student Vassar, 1870-73; m. Arthur M. Dodge, Oct. 6, 1875 (died 1894). Pres. Nat. Assn. Opposed to Woman Suffrage; pres. of Fedn. of Day Nurseries; hon. pres. N.Y. City br. Needlework Guild of America; 1st v.p. Assn. of Day Nurseries of N.Y. City; mem. Nat. Civic Fedn. (exec. com. woman's dept. of N.Y. and N.J.); dir. Pub. Edn. Assn. of New York. Presbyn. Home: New York, N.Y. Deceased.

DODGE, Joshua Eric, judge; b. W. Cambridge (now Arlington), Mass., Oct. 25, 1854; s. Joshua Giddings and Mary F. (Herrick) D.; B.S., Ia. Coll., 1875; LL.B., Boston U., 1877; (LL.D., Ia. Coll., 1906); unmarried. Practiced law, Racine, Wis., 1878-93; mem. Wis. Assembly, 1891-92; asst. atty. gen. of U.S., 1893-97; practiced at Milwaukee, 1897-98; justice Supreme Ct. of Wis., 1898-1910; resumed practice at Milwaukee. Democrat. Died May 2, 1921.

DODGE, Mary Mapes, author; b. New York; d. James Jay and Sophia Furman Mapes; m. William Dodge, lawyer, 1851 (died 1858). Was editor of home dept. Hearth and Home; from 1873 editor of St. Nicholas Mag. Author: The Irvington Stories; Hans Brinker; Rhymes and Jingles; A Few Friends; Theophilus and Others; Donald and Dorothy; Along the Way (poems); When Life Is Young (poems); The Land of Plucks. Edited: Baby Days, Baby World. Died 1905.

DODGE, Murray Witherbee, banker; b. New York, N.Y., Apr. 30, 1878; s. Arthur Murray and Josephine Marshall (Jewell) D.; A.B., Yale, 1899; m. Elsie Fordyce Barker, Feb. 6, 1900; children—Elizabeth Lee (Mrs. William H. Beers), Emily Fordyce (Mrs. W. F. C. Ewing), Alice (Mrs. James W. Husted). Became partner Bertron, Storrs & Griscom, 1907, title changed to Bertron, Griscom & Jenks, 1909, Bertron, Griscom & Co., 1912, Bertron, Griscom & Co., Inc., 1918; v.p. Chase Securities Corp., 1923; exec. v.p. Chase Harris Forbes Corp., 1931-33; dir. Continental Paper & Bag Corp. Enrolled in F.A. Central Officers' Training Sch., Nov. 1918; hon. disch., Jan. 1919. Home: Mount Kisco, N.Y. Died Dec. 6, 1937.

DODGE, Philip Tell, capitalist; b. Fond du Lac, Wis., July 1851; s. William C. and Jane (Van Patten) D.; LL.B., Columbian (now George Washington) U., 1873; m. Margaret Ball; m. 2d, Lillian Sutherland, Jan. 27, 1928. Practiced as patent lawyer, Washington, D.C., later N.Y. City; formerly pres. Mergenthaler Linotype Co.; was also dir. many corps. Republican. Protestant. Home: New York, N.Y. Died Aug. 9, 1931.

DODGE, R(obert) E(lkin) Neil, univ. prof.; b. Washington, Jan. 24, 1867; s. late Col. Theodore Ayrault (U.S.A.) and Jane Marshall (Neil) D.; A.B., Harvard, 1889, A.M., 1891; in Italy, Paris, and London, 1891-94, also in the large libraries, Bibliothèque Nationale and British Mus.; m. Katherine Eleanor Staley, June 18, 1907; children—Julia, Theodore Ayrault, Emily Pomeroy. Lecturer on Eng. lit., Barnard Coll., 1894-95; instr. in English lit., Brown U., 1895-98; instr. in English, 1898-1903; asst. prof., 1903-18, asso. prof., 1918-25, prof., 1925—, chmn. dept., 1930—, U. of Wis. Editor: Poetical Works of Edmund Spenser, 1908. Home: Madison, Wis. Died Aug. 30, 1935.

DODGE, Theodore Ayrault, army officer; military historian; b. Pittsfield, Mass., May 28, 1842; s. Nathaniel S. D.; military edn. in Berlin; grad. U. of London, Eng., 1861, LL.B., Columbian, 1865; m. Jane Marshall Neil, 1865; m. 2d, Clara Isabel Bowden, 1893. Entered Union Army, 1861, as pvt.; served in vol. forces in every regtl. rank; thrice wounded; lost right leg at Gettysburg; commd. in regular army, July 1866; served in War Dept., Chief of Bureau, 1864-70; on retired list U.S.A., 1870—. Author: History of the Art of War—Alexander, Hannibal, Cæsar, Gustavus Adolphus, Napoleon (12 vols.), 1890-1907; The Campaign of Chancellorsville, 1881; Bird'seye View of Our Civil War, 1883; Patroclus and Penelope, 1885; Great Captains, 1889; Riders of Many Lands, 1894. Home: Paris, France. Died 1909.

DODGE, William De Leftwich, artist; b. Liberty, Va., Mar. 9, 1867; s. William Miner and Mary (De Leftwich) D.; studied in Paris and Munich, 1885; entered No. 1 exam. École des Beaux Arts; m. Fanny Bland Pryor, Mar. 31, 1897; children—Roger Pryor, Sara Pryor. Awards: 2 third medals and Prix d'Atelier in Concours d'Atelier Gérôme; 2 mentions Cours Yvon; gold medal, Prize Fund Exhbn., 1887; 3d medal, David, Paris Salon, 1888; medal, Chicago Expn., 1893. Noted Works: Dome of Administration Bldg., Chicago Expn.; northwest cor. pavilion, Library of Congress, 1897; Empire Theatre, 1903; Hall of Records, New York, 1906, Acad. Music, Brooklyn, 1908; Café de l'Opera, 1909; Folies Bergères Theatre, 1910; 2 panels, 15x100 feet each, for Tower of Jewels, Panama-P.I. Expn.; Taking of the Fort de Vaux, Verdun, 1918; mural decorations for Teachers Coll., Cedar Falls, Ia., 5 panels, 1921; 12 panels for Mother's House, Rice Memorial, New York; The Signing of Peace, Versailles, 1919; 24 mural paintings for Flag Room, State Capitol, Albany, N.Y.; In Memoriam, panel for Kenosha County (Wis.) Courthouse; The Law, panel for Orlando (Fla.) County Court House; panel for Bapt. Hosp., Lynchburg, Va.; 6 panels for City Hall, Buffalo, N.Y., 1930-31, etc. Professor at Cooper Union and Art Students League; chief of color, Sesqui-centennial Expn., Phila., 1926. Home: Setauket, L.I., N.Y. Died Mar. 25, 1935.

DODGE, William Earl, mcht.; b. New York, N.Y., Feb. 15, 1832; s. late William E. D.; whom he succeeded in business of Phelps, Dodge & Co., wholesale metals; m. Sarah, d. David Hoadley, pres. Panama R.R., April 5, 1854; especially interested in mining and mfg. enterprises. Pres. Evang. Alliance; chmn. Nat. Com. of Arbitration; v.p. Am. Museum Natural History; chmn. exec. com. Met. Museum of Art; mem. exec. com. New York Botanic Garden; trustee Carnegie Inst., Washington; active in many religious and benevolent socs. Home: New York, N.Y. Died 1903.

DODSON, George Rowland, clergyman; b. Jacksonville, Mo., Aug. 20, 1865; s. Shelby Martin and Susan Eleanor (Procter) D.; A.B., U. of Mo., 1887; student Stanford U., 1894; U. of Calif., 1900-01; A.M., Harvard, 1902, Ph.D., 1903; D.D., Meadville Theol. Sem., Chicago, 1930; m. Nellie Wheeler, June 24, 1891; children—Rowland Wheeler, Virginia (dec.), Eleanor (Mrs. Malcolm C. Rees), Procter Wheeler. Ordained to Disciples of Christ ministry, Mexico, Mo., 1886; pastor 1st Unitarian Soc., Alameda, Calif., 1891-1901, Ch. of the Unity, St. Louis, Oct. 1, 1903; prof. philosophy, Washington U., until 1934 (emeritus); mem. bd. Psychiatric Child Guidance Clinic. Author: Bergson and the Modern Spirit; The Sympathy of Religion. Home: St. Louis, Mo. Died Nov. 13, 1939.

DODSON, John E., actor; b. in England; s. Henry and Elizabeth (Haslock) D.; studied law, but early took to the stage as a profession, appearing with a co. at Manchester. Supported Charles Matthews and other stars; turned his attention to comedy and character parts; came to U.S. in 1889 with Mr. and Mrs. Kendal, opening at Fifth Av. Theatre in "A Scrap of Paper"; subsequently played in "The Bauble Shop" and joined the Empire stock co. as leading comedian; originated character of Cardinal Richelieu in "Under the Red Robe"; more recently as John Weatherby, the old man, in "Because She Loved Him So"; appeared Oct. 29, 1900, at the Fifth Av. Theatre, New York, as Richelieu, in play of "Richelieu's Stratagem"; played at Drury Lane Theatre, London, 1902, as Simonides in "Ben Hur"; appeared as star in "American Invasion," Bijou Theatre, New York, Oct. 1902; played Pierre in all-star production of "Two Orphans," season 1904-05; created Stephen Roland in Clyde Fitch's comedy, "The Truth"; created star rôle, Sir John Cotswold, in "The House Next Door," at the Gaiety Theatre, New York, Apr.-Sept. 1909. Died Dec. 9, 1931.

DODSON, John Milton, M.D.; b. Berlin, Wis., Feb. 17, 1859; s. Nathan Monroe and Elizabeth Osborn (Abbot) D.; A.B., U. of Wis., 1880, A.M., 1883; Sc.D., 1925; M.D., Rush Med. Coll., Chicago, 1882, Jefferson Med. Coll., Phila., 1883; post-grad. med. study, Berlin, 1886; m. Maie Van Slyke, July 1, 1884 (died 1887); 2d, Jessie Palmer Kasson, Nov. 12, 1890 (died 1914); children—Kasson M. (dec.), Elizabeth Palmer (Mrs. Lester J. Michael); m. 3d, Mary Hyde Webb, Jan. 17, 1923. Practiced in Wis. and Chicago, Mar., 1882—; lecturer and demonstrator anatomy, 1889-92, prof. physiology and demonstrator anatomy, 1892-98, prof. pediatrics, 1899—, jr. dean, 1890-1901, dean of students, 1901-24, Rush Med. Coll.; professorial lecturer on medicine, and dean med. courses, U. of Chicago, 1901-24; dir. Bur. Health and Pub. Instrn., A.M.A.; prof. pediatrics, Northwestern U. Woman's Med. Coll., 1894-97. Maj. M.C., U.S.A., med. aide to gov. of Ill., 1918-19. Home: Chicago, Ill. Died Aug. 15, 1933.

DOE, Edward M., judge; b. Cabot, Vt., Jan. 20, 1850; s. John (M.D.) and Lemira (Damon) D.; B.S., State U. of Iowa, 1870; LL.B., 1871; married. Practiced at Iowa City, Ia., 1871-85; removed to Flagstaff, Ariz., 1887; apptd. first dist. atty. Coconino Co., Ariz., 1891, and filled same office by election, 1902-08; asso. justice Supreme Ct. of Ariz. Ty., May 1909-Jan. 1912. Resumed practice at Flagstaff upon admission of Arizona to statehood. Mem. Ariz. Constl. Conv., 1910, but refused to sign constn. on account of its radical provisions. Republican. Home: Flagstaff, Ariz. Deceased.

DOERFLER, Christian, judge; b. Milwaukee, Wis., Mar. 2, 1862; s. Christopher and Wilhelmine (Schotte) D.; grad. Normal Sch., Milwaukee, 1879; LL.B., U. of Wis., 1885; m. Julia Anderson, July 23, 1898; 1 son, Frederic Anderson (dec.). Teacher pub. schs., Milwaukee, 1880-83; admitted to Wis. bar, 1885; asst. dist. atty. Milwaukee Co., 1889-91; asso. justice Supreme Court of Wis., Apr. 1921-May 1, 1929, retired. Commr. pub. schs., Milwaukee, 1889-1900. Home: Wauwatosa, Wis. Died June 10, 1934.

DOERFLINGER, Charles Hermann, ednl. worker; b. Ettenheim, Baden, Germany, Feb. 17, 1843; s. Karl (revolutionary exile) and Theresa (Gisselbrecht) D.; came to America with parents, 1848; ed. Engelmann German-English Acad., Milwaukee; m. Augusta Barkhausen, Oct. 5, 1873. Pvt. to 1st lt. 26th Wis. Inf., 1862-63; wounded at Chancellorsville, and lost left leg by amputation, June 27, 1863; regent Wis. State Normal Sch., 1877-81; custodian Pub. Mus., Milwaukee, 1883-87; sec. and chief examiner City Civ. Service Commn., Milwaukee, 1896-1900; dir. and mgr. foreign business, Doerflinger Artificial Limb Co.; teacher, bookseller, pub. and printer; traveled extensively in Europe, U.S. and Mexico, studying ednl. systems; has been for many yrs. an active advocate of reorganization of Am. sch. system; pres. Nat. New Edn. League (inc.) and was mng. editor Nat. New Edn. (monthly). Home: Milwaukee, Wis. Died Nov. 9, 1911.

DOERMANN, Henry John, univ. pres.; b. Hickory, N.C., Oct. 20, 1890; s. Rev. Henry K. G. and Margarete (Nicol) D.; A.B., U. of Minn., 1913; A.M., Harvard, 1917, Ed.D., 1925; m. Alice Robbins Humphrey, July 2, 1921; children—Eleanor B., John H., Henry H. Supt. schools, Orion, Ia., 1917; psychol. examiner, Med. Dept. U.S.A., 1918; dir. Normal Sch. and Acad., Hampton Inst., Va., 1919-23; dean of adminstrn., U. of Porto Rico, 1925-28; pres. U. of Toledo, 1928—. Lutheran. Author: The Orientation of College Freshmen, 1926. Home: Toledo, O. Died Nov. 20, 1932.

DOGGETT, John L., lawyer; sr. partner Doggett, McCollum, Howell & Doggett, Jacksonville, Fla.; admitted to Fla. bar, 1894; once judge of criminal court of record. Home: Jacksonville, Fla. Died Oct. 10, 1937.

DOHENY, Edward Laurence, petroleum producer; b. Fond du Lac, Wis., Aug. 10, 1856; s. Patrick and Eleanor Elizabeth (Quigley) D.; grad. high sch., Fond du Lac, 1872; m. Carrie Estelle Betzold. Prospected for gold and silver 20 yrs.; prospected for and produced petroleum, 1892—; discovered several oil dists. in Calif., also petroleum fields in Mexico; chmn. bd. Petroleum Securities Co.; pres. Doheny-Stone Drill Co., Los Nietos Producing & Refining Co., Ltd. Apptd. mem. sub-com. on oil of Council Nat. Defense, July 1917. Died Sept. 8, 1935.

DOHERTY, Henry Latham, operator gas and elec. cos.; b. Columbus, O., May 15, 1870; s. Frank and Anna (McIlvaine) D.; pub. school edn.; hon. Dr. Engring., Lehigh U., 1931; m. Mrs. P. F. Eames, 1929. Office boy Columbus Gas Co. at 12, advancing through various positions until 1890; engr. or mgr. pub. utility cos., Madison, Wis., St. Paul, Minn., San Antonio, Tex., Denver, Colo., and 25 other cities until 1905; organized 1905, and since mgr. Henry L. Doherty & Co., bankers and operators of pub. utility corps.; organized, 1910, and since pres. Cities Service Co., holding co. for more than 190 pub. utility and petroleum properties with assets of more than $1,000,000,000. Recognized as one of the leaders in America in gas and electric arts and industries; leader in movement for oil conservation by means of unit operation of pools under federal control; patentee of many combustion processes and apparatus and originator of many standard practices. Awarded 1st Beall gold medal, 1898, by Am. Gas Light Assn., for paper on "Gas for Fuel"; mem. orgn. bd. World's Congress of Electricity, St. Louis, 1904; awarded Walton Clark medal, 1930, by Franklin Inst., "in consideration of his outstanding and valuable work in development of the manufactured gas industry." Died Dec. 26, 1939.

DOHERTY, Philip Joseph, lawyer; b. Charlestown, Mass., Jan. 27, 1856; s. Philip and Ellen (Munnegle) D.; LL.B., Boston U. Sch. of Law, 1876; m. Catherine A. Butler, Aug. 16, 1878 (died 1892); children—Philip J., Mary J., Eleanor M. (Mrs. William W. Wadsworth (dec.), Alice A. (Mrs. Joseph Macksey), Catherine C. (Mrs. E. A. Wahl); m. 2d, Lillian E. Cook, June 15, 1898; 1 dau., Nona L. Practiced at Boston, 1877-1908; atty., 1908-13, chief atty. div. of safety, 1913—, Interstate Commerce Commn., Washington. Mem. Mass. Ho. of Rep., 1884-86; mem. Bd. of Aldermen, Boston, 1888; examining com. Boston Pub. Library, 1888; mem. Boston Water Bd., 1889-91; dem. candidate for Congress (Lynn-Boston Dist.), 1896; chmn. Dem. State Conv., 1897; asst. dist. atty., Suffolk Co., 1907; spl. asst. to U.S. dist. atty. in each jud. dist. of U.S. in cases under safety appliance acts, and hours of service law; spl. asst. to U.S. atty.-gen. in Mondou vs. N.Y.,N.H.&H. R.R. Co., 1909, involving constitutionality of federal railroad employers' liability act; one of commn. attys. in investigation of finances of New Haven R.R., 1914; mgr. Property Protection Sect. U.S. Railroad Administration, 1918; atty. Valuation Bur. Interstate Commerce Commn., 1919—. Author: The Liability of Railroads to Interstate Employes, 1911. Died Apr. 15, 1928.

DOLAN, Francis James, college pres.; b. Jamica Plain, Mass., July 14, 1893. Ordained priest R.C. Ch.; formerly dean Coll. of the Holy Cross, Worcester, Mass., pres., 1933—. Died Sept. 6, 1939.

DOLAN, Thomas, capitalist; b. Montgomery Co., Pa., Oct. 27, 1834. Employed in retail dry goods business, 1849-55, in importing and commn. business, 1855-61; mfr. of knit goods, 1861-72, worsted goods, 1872-97, becoming one of largest producers in U.S.; became pres. The United Gas Improvement Co., Phila., and interested in various other gas, electric light, traction and other corp. Home: Philadelphia, Pa. Died June 12, 1914.

DOLBEAR, Amos Emerson, educator, inventor; b. Norwich, Conn., Nov. 10, 1837; grad. Ohio Wesleyan U., 1866 (A.M., M.E., Ph.D., all U. of Mich.; LL.D., Tufts College, 1902); from 1874 prof. physics, Tufts Coll. Invented writing telegraph, 1864; magneto telephone, 1876; static telephone, 1879; spring balance ammeter, 1889; air space telegraph cable, 1882; discovered convertibility of sound into electricity, 1873; telegraphing without wires, 1881; photographing with electric waves, 1893. Received bronze medal for acoustic apparatus, Centennial Expn., Phila., 1876, and silver medal, Paris, 1881, and gold medal, London, 1882, for static telephone. Was twice mayor Bethany, W.Va. Author: Chemical Tables; Art of Projecting; The Speaking Telephone; Matter, Ether and Motion; Modes of Motion; Natural Philosophy. Died 1910.

DOLD, Jacob C., packer; b. Buffalo, N.Y., Jan. 2, 1857; s. Jacob and Elizabeth (Scheas) D.; ed. pub. schs. and business coll.; m. Maliss Frances Means, 1890. In packing business since boyhood; pres. Jacob Dold Packing Co., Buffalo, 1910—; also pres. Dold Packing Co. (Omaha), Capital Refining Co. (Washington, D.C.), Dold Packing Co. (Wichita, Kan.); owner Wheatfield Farms. Mem. packers' advisory com. Food Administration during World War. Republican. Home: Buffalo, N.Y. Died Sept. 8, 1924.

DOLE, Charles Fletcher, clergyman; b. Brewer, Me., May 17, 1845; s. Rev. Nathan and Caroline (Fletcher) D.; A.B., Harvard, 1868, A.M., 1870; grad. Andover Theol. Sem., 1872; D.D., Bowdoin, 1906; m. Frances Drummond, Mar. 4, 1873; children—James Drummond, Katharine (dec.), Winifred, Richard Drummond (dec.). Prof. Greek, U. of Vt., 1873; minister Plymouth Ch., Portland, Me., 1874-76, First Congl. (Unitarian) Ch., Jamaica Plain, Mass., 1876-1916 (emeritus). Author: The Citizen and the Neighbor, 1884; Early Hebrew Stories, 1886; A Catechism of Liberal Faith, 1895; The Young Citizen, 1899; The Problem of Duty, 1900; The Religion of a Gentleman, 1900; Noble Womanhood, 1900; The Spirit of Democracy, 1906; The Hope of Immortality (Ingersoll lecture, Harvard), 1906; What We know About Jesus, 1908; The Burden of Poverty, 1912; The New American Citizen, 1918; A Religion for the New Day, 1920. Home: Jamaica Plain, Mass. Died Nov. 28, 1927.

DOLE, Edmund Pearson, lawyer; b. Skowhegan, Me., Feb. 28, 1850; ed. Wesleyan U., class of 1874; LL.B., Boston U. Sch. of Law, 1876. Admitted to bar, 1875; practiced at Honolulu, H. Ty.; later at Seattle, Wash. Atty.-gen. Territory of Hawaii, and ex-officio head of the police dept. and mem. bd. of health of the Territory; resigned, 1903, to argue Mankichi case before Supreme Court of U.S., case involving polit. and jud. status of Republic of Hawaii between annexation, 1898, and organization of Ty., 1900. Author: Talks About Law, 1887; The Stand-By, 1897; Hiwa, a Tale of Ancient Hawaii, 1900. Home: Alstead, N.H. Died Dec. 31, 1928.

DOLE, Nathan Haskell, author; b. Chelsea, Mass., Aug. 31, 1852; s. Rev. Nathan and Caroline (Fletcher) D.; A.B., Harvard, 1874; Litt.D., Oglethorpe U., Atlanta, Ga.; taught at DeVeaux Coll., 1874-75, Worcester High Sch., 1875-76; preceptor Derby Acad., Hingham, Mass., 1876-78; m. Helen James Bennett, June 28, 1882; children— Robert Montgomery, Arthur Alexander, Margaret Aliona (Mrs. Thomas McCall), Harold Sanford. Lit., art and mus. editor Phila. Press, 1881-87; lit. adviser, T. Y. Crowell & Co., 1887-1901; sec. dept. of publicity, D. Appleton & Co., 5 mos., 1901. President of Omar Khayyám Soc. America until 1919, Bibliophile Soc., 1901-12. Mem. adv. council Simplified Spelling Bd. Author: Famous Composers, 2 vols., 1902; revised and enlarged, 1924, 28; Omar, the Tent-Maker—A Romance of Old Persia, 1899; Peace and Progress—The Building of the Organ and Onward (poems), 1904, 1906; The Pilgrims and Other Poems, 1911; Life of Count Tolstoï, 1911; The Spell of Switzerland, 1913; America in Spitzbergen, 2 vols., 1922. Translator of works by Tolstoï, Valdès, Von Scheffel, Von Koch, Daudet, Verga and other foreign novelists; Tolstoï's Dramatic Works, 1923. Editor: Rambaud's History of Russia, 1882; The Rubáiyát of Omar Khayyám, several editions, 1896-99; The Greek Poets, 1904; The Latin Poets, 1905. Vocations, 10 vols. (with President Hyde and Caroline Ticknor), 1909-10; 10th edit. of Bartlett's Familiar Quotations with additions; Poems of Dr. Samuel S. Curry, with Biog., 1923. Home: Riverdale-on-Hudson, N.Y. Deceased.

DOLE, Sanford Ballard, judge; b. Hawaiian Islands, Apr. 23, 1844; s. Daniel and Emily (Ballard) D. (Am. missionaries); ed. Oahu Coll., and his father's school, Koloa, Hawaii, and Williams Coll., Mass.; studied law in Boston; admitted to bar there; engaged in practice in Honolulu; m. Anna P. Cate, May 19, 1873. Mem. legislature, 1884 and 1886; a leader in reform movement of 1887; judge Supreme Ct., 1887-93; placed at head of provisional govt., 1893; was pres. of Republic of Hawaii, 1894-1900. When Pres. Cleveland, Dec. 1893, through Minister Willis, demanded that he should relinquish to Queen Liliuokalani her constitutional authority, he replied, denying Cleveland's right to interfere; was strong advocate of annexation of Hawaii to U.S., and in Jan. 1898, visited U.S. in that behalf; gov. H. Ty., 1900-03; U.S. dist. judge, District of H. Ty., 1903-15. Apptd. mem. com. to recommend to Congress legislation concerning H.I. Home: Honolulu, T.H. Died June 9, 1926.

DOLGE, Alfred, mfr.; b. Chemnitz, Germany, Dec. 22, 1848; s. August and Augusta (Staib) D.; ed. common schs., Leipzig, 1855-62; m. Anna Augusta Horn, Dec. 22, 1868. Landed in New York, Sept. 1866; worked at bench as piano maker; started in business July, 1869; started first piano felt factories in America at Brooklyn, 1871; went to Herkimer Co., N.Y., and founded the town of Dolgeville, N.Y., population 3000, 1874; introduced labor pension and insurance system in his factories, 1874. Organized the Alfred Dolge Mfg. Co., and established first felt and felt shoe factories on the Pacific Coast, 1903; founded, town of Dolgeville, Calif., 7 miles east of Los Angeles. Author: Pianos and Their Makers. Home: Covina, Calif. Died Jan. 5, 1922.

DOLLAR, Robert, ship owner; b. Falkirk, Scotland, Mar. 20, 1844; s. William and Mary (Melville) D.; ed. common sch. to 11; m. Margaret Proudfoot, 1874. Began active career at 13 in lumber camp in Can.; came to U.S., 1856; naturalized citizen, 1888; settled at San Francisco, Calif., and has engaged on an extensive scale in foreign trade and lumber business; known as one of the largest operators of ocean vessels in the world; pres. Dollar Steamship Co., Robert Dollar Co., Admiral Oriental Co., Dollar Portland Lumber Co., Canadian Robert Dollar Co. Given freedom of city and keys of Falkirk, Scotland, Boston, New York and Shanghai, also medals from China. Republican. Presbyn. Author: Memoirs of Robert Dollar (3d edit.), 1925. Home: San Rafael, Calif. Died May 16, 1932.

DOLLEY, David Hough, pathologist; b. Lexington, Va., July 18, 1878; s. Rev. Saul Bland and Mary Catherine (Rodeffer) D.; A.B., Randolph-Macon Coll., 1897, A.M., 1898; M.D., Johns Hopkins, 1902; unmarried. Resident pathologist, Charity Hosp., Cleveland, O., 1902-03, Lakeside Hosp., 1903-04; prof. pathology, U. of N.C., 1906-10, U. of Mo., 1910-22, St. Louis U., 1922—. Fellow A.M.A., A.A.A.S. Home: St. Louis, Mo. Died Apr. 11, 1927.

DOLLIVER, Jonathan Prentiss, senator; b. nr. Kingwood, W.Va., Feb. 6, 1858; s. Rev. James J. and Eliza J. (Brown) D.; A.B., W.Va. U., 1875; (LL.D., Bethany Coll., 1900, Cornell Coll., Ia., 1902, Miami U., 1905); m. Louise Pearsons, Nov. 20, 1895. Admitted to bar, 1878; established practice at Fort Dodge, Iowa. Elected 51st to 56th Congresses (1889-1901), 10th Ia. Dist.; apptd. U.S. senator, Aug. 23, 1900, for unexpired term (1900-01), of John H. Gear, deceased; elected for terms, 1901-07, 1907-13. Republican. Home: Ft. Dodge, Ia. Died 1910.

DOLPH, John H., artist painter; b. Fort Ann, N.Y., April 18, 1835; s. Osmond and Olive D.; studied in Antwerp and Paris; then opened a studio in New York; academician Nat. Acad.; makes specialty figure subjects; best-known by pictures of animals, particularly dogs and cats. Died 1903.

DOMINIAN, Leon, foreign service officer; b. Constantinople, Turkey, Apr. 13, 1880; s. Joseph and Sophia (Doad) D.; B.A., Robert Coll., Constantinople, 1898; spl. courses in geography and geology, U. of Liège, Belgium, 1898-1900; m. Helen Gallagher, 1922. Traveled in Turkey, 1901-02; field asst. U.S. Geol. Survey, 1903; instr. N.M., Sch. of Mines, 1904; travel and exploration in the Southwest and Mexico, 1905-07; research and writing, N.Y. City, 1907-12; geographer and editorial writer Am. Geog. Soc., 1912-17; spl. investigations on boundary problems for Dept. of State, 1918; assisted in Honduras-Guatemala boundary mediation, 1918-20; assigned duty with Am. Peace Commn., Paris, France, Feb. 1919; apptd. spl. asst. of the Dept. of State, Aug. 1919. Lecturer in Hist. Geography, Sch. of Foreign Service, Georgetown U., 1921; apptd. consul at Rome, July 21, 1921, and detailed for economic duty in Italy; apptd. fgn. service officer, class 4, July 1, 1924; consul in charge, Rome, July 1924; consul gen. at Stuttgart, Germany, 1930—. Naturalized citizen of U.S., 1913. Author: The Frontiers of Language and Nationality in Europe, 1917, etc. Died July 25, 1935.

DOMINICK, Frank, lawyer; b. Greensboro, Ala., Apr. 22, 1885; s. Richard Bascom and Clara Geraldine (Richardson) D.; A.B., Birmingham-Southern Coll., 1906; LL.B., U. of Ala., 1910; m. Esther Elliott, Nov. 24, 1913; children—Sara Esther, Frank. Began as teacher, 1901; admitted to Ala. bar, 1910; mem. Stokely, Scrivner, Dominick & Smith, 1913—. Democrat. Methodist. Mason. Home: Birmingham, Ala. Died July 5, 1937.

DONAGHEY, Frederick, author, critic; b. Phila., Pa.; s. John Kent and Katherine Call (Dalton) D.; ed. pub. and pvt. schs., studied music under Siegfried Behrens, Phila.; student Princeton; m. Lotta Ida, d. James Alfred Watson, of Brookline, Mass., 1910. Began newspaper work in N.Y. City, 1900; editor drama, music, lit., Phila. Public Ledger, 1902-06; gen. mgr. for William A. Brady, New York and Chicago, 1906-10; Chicago mgr. successively for the Liebler Co., Geo. C. Tyler, and Klaw & Erlanger, 1910-16, also mgr. La Salle Theatre, Chicago, and wrote 2 of the plays produced there, 1910-14; music critic and spl. writer, Chicago Tribune, 1916-19; European mgr. Wolfsohn Mus. Bureau, London, 1919-22; editor "Line o' Type or Two," Chicago Tribune, 1923; drama critic, Tribune, 1923-30; dir. Dramatic League of Chicago (a subscription-theater), 1930—. Republican. Episcopalian. Mason. Adapted for Am. stage Alexandre

Bisson's "Le Mariage d'un Étoile," prod. as "The Marriage of a Star," in New York and Chicago, 1910. Author: (plays) Louisiana Lou (prod. Chicago), 1911; The Girl at the Gate (prod. Chicago), 1912; Make-Believe; Fig-Leaves; Crêpe-Hair, 1933. Home: Chicago, Ill. Died Nov. 8, 1937.

DONAGHEY, George W., gov.; b. Oakland, Union Parish, La., July 1, 1856; s. Columbus and Elizabeth (Ingram) D.; ed. common schs. and U. of Arkansas; m. Louvenia Wallace, Sept. 20, 1883. Began as carpenter and contractor; erected buildings in Arkansas, Texas, Louisiana and Oklahoma; ry. contractor on Choctaw, Okla. & Gulf R.R. 5 yrs. Gov. of Ark., 1909-11, 1911-13; built new State Capitol of Arkansas, and contractor for U.S. Govt. for $1,000,000 aviation gen. warehouse, Little Rock, World War; pres. Bd. of Control State Eleemosynary Instns., Ark., 1922-26; pres. State Bd. of Edn. Commn. 2 yrs., and pres. bd. which built two bridges across Arkansas River, at Little Rock; v.p. Bankers Trust Co., 1913-25; v.p. Beal-Burrow Dry Goods Co., 1914-24; pres. First Nat. Bank of North Little Rock, 1923-26. Democrat. Mem. M.E. Ch., S. Mason. Home: Little Rock, Ark. Died Dec. 15, 1937.

DONAHOE, Daniel Joseph, author; b. Brimfield, Mass., Feb. 27, 1853; s. Daniel and Mary (Carey) D.; ed. Wesleyan U., Conn., 1871-72; m. Margaret G. Burnes, June 21, 1877 (died 1888); children—Julia Teresa, Margert Elizabeth; m. 2d, Sarah A. D'Arcy, Oct. 7, 1891; s dau., Eleanor Clare. Admitted to Conn. bar, 1875; asso. judge Middletown City, 1887-1903; town atty., Middletown, during large part of the time, 1883—; judge Middletown City Court, 1913-15; elected by judges Supreme and Superior courts as pub. defender of Superior Court for Middlesex County, 1919. Mem. Bd. of Edn., 1889-1907 (pres. 10 yrs.). Democrat. Author: Idyls of Israel and other Poems, 1888; A Tent by the Lake and Other Poems, 1889; In Sheltered Ways, 1896; The Rescue of the Princess, 1907; Songs of the Countryside, 1914; Songs for Christmas, 1920; Songs for Easter, 1921; Gleams of Gold, 1921. Translator: Early Christian Hymns, 1908; Early Christian Hymns, Series II, 1911. Conducted "The Counselor," editorial dept. of Catholic Transcript, 1911—. Home: Middletown, Conn. Died 1930.

DONAHUE, Maurice H., judge; b. Monroe, O., May 10, 1864; s. Maurice and Louisa (O'Neill) D.; ed. pub. schs.; higher branches under pvt. tutors; m. Martina Johnson, Sept. 10, 1889. Admitted to bar, 1885, and practiced at New Lexington, O., until 1901; pros. atty., Perry Co., 1887-93; judge Circuit Ct., 5th Jud. Circuit, Ohio, 1900-10 (chief justice Circuit Cts. Ohio, 1908-10); asso. justice Supreme Ct. Ohio, 2 terms, for period 1911-23; resigned to become judge U.S. Circuit Court of Appeals, 6th Circuit, Nov. 1919—. Democrat. Home: Bexley, Columbus, O. Died Sept. 10, 1928.

DONAHUE, Patrick James, bishop; b. Malvern, Worcestershire, Eng., Apr. 15, 1849; grad. U. of London, 1869; came to U.S., 1873; LL.B., Columbian (now George Washington) U., 1876; in law practice, Washington, 1876-82; S.T.B., St. Mary's U., Md., 1884, S.T.L., 1885. Ordained R.C. ministry, 1885; chancellor archdiocese, Baltimore, 1886-91; rector Baltimore Cathedral, 1891-94; consecrated bishop of Wheeling, W.Va., Apr. 8, 1894. Died Oct. 4, 1922.

DONALDSON, Henry Herbert, neurologist; b. Yonkers, N.Y., May 12, 1857; s. John J. and Louisa Goddard (McGowan) D.; A.B., Yale, 1879; Sheffield Scientific Sch. (Yale), 1880; Coll. Phys. and Surg. (Columbia), 1881; Ph.D., Johns Hopkins, 1885; (D.Sc., Yale, 1906); m. Emma Brace, Apr. 6, 1907. Instr. biology, 1883-84, asso. prof. psychology, 1887-88, Johns Hopkins; asst. prof. neurology, Clark U., 1889-92; prof. and head of dept. of neurology, 1892-1906, dean Ogden (Grad.) Sch. Science, 1892-98, U. of Chicago; prof. neurology, Wistar Inst. Anatomy and Biology, Phila., Jan. 1906—. Author: The Growth of the Brain, 1895; The Physiology of the Central Nervous System in "An American Text-Book of Physiology," 1896; The Rat, 1924. Home: Philadelphia, Pa. Died Jan. 23, 1938.

DONALDSON, John M., architect; b. Stirling, Scotland, Jan. 17, 1854; s. John W. and Isabella (McNaughton) D.; parents removed to Detroit, Mich., 1856; grad. Detroit High Sch.; studied architect's office, Detroit, Polytechnic and Art Acad., Munich, and in Atelier "André," École des Beaux Arts, Paris; m. Mrs. C. G. (Grosvenor) Brush, Nov. 30, 1882; children—Alexander G., Bruce M. In practice with Henry T. Brush, 1876-79; mem. Donaldson & Meier, 1880—. Dir. A.I.A.; pres. Detroit Museum Art; Detroit City Plan and Improvement Commn.; mem. Nat. Council of Fine Arts, Nat. Inst. of Arts and Letters. Home: Detroit, Mich. Died Dec. 20, 1941.

DONALDSON, Robert Golden, lawyer; b. Washington, D.C., Nov. 27, 1876; s. Benjamin Sinclair and Fannie (Webster) D.; grad. Washington Business High Sch., 1892; LL.B., Georgetown U., 1895; m. Antoinette Collett, Nov. 20, 1899 (died 1927); children—Ruth (Mrs. Harold E. Irish), Robert Golden, Wyman Cleaves; m. 2d, Frances Starr, actress, Aug. 14, 1932. Admitted to Dist. of Columbia bar, 1898, to U.S. Supreme Court, 1904; in active practice of law specializing in management of estates and in administrative law before all government comms. and depts.; one of organizers and formerly chmn. bd. Mt. Vernon Savings Bank; pres. Commercial Nat. Bank, 1919-30. Mason. Home: Washington, D.C. Died Feb. 10, 1940.

DONALDSON, Thomas Quint, army officer; b. Greenville, S.C., June 26, 1864; s. T. Q. and Susan B. (Hoke) D.; grad. U.S. Mil. Acad., 1887; distinguished grad. Army Sch. of the Line, 1909; grad. Army Staff Coll., 1910; m. Mary Elizabeth Willson, Oct. 26, 1892. Commd. add. 2d lt. 3d Cav., June 12, 1887; brig. gen. (temp.), Feb. 18, 1918; brig. gen. (perm.), Jan. 16, 1925; promoted to rank of major general, Dec. 11, 1927. Participated in campaign against Sioux Indians in S.D., 1890-91; in action at Wounded Knee and White Clay Creek; prof. mil. science and tactics, Patrick Mil. Inst., Anderson, S.C., 1891-93, Clemson Agrl. Coll., Ft. Hill, S.C., 1893-95; in Cuba, 1898-99; with 8th U.S. Cav. in Philippines, 1905-07, 1910-14; assigned duty Insp. Gen.'s Dept., 1914; arrived in France, Sept. 1, 1918; insp. gen. Service of Supply, Tours, France, Sept. 1918-June 1919; retired, 1931. Decorated D.S.M.; Legion of Honor (French). Competitor div. and army cav. competitions, 1903, 1904, and also mem. Nat. Cav. Rifle Team, 1907. Methodist. Home: Greenville, S.C. Died Oct. 26, 1934.

DONALSON, John Ernest, lawyer; b. Bainbridge, Ga., Apr. 29, 1846; s. Jonathan and Caroline Jane (Williams) D.; attended several acads. in Ga. and U. of N.C., 1863, when went into C.S.A., serving in Duke's Ky. Regt. Cav., and in 1st Fla. Cav. until June, 1865; attended Mt. Zion Sch., 1866; A.B., U. of Ga., 1868, in law sch., same, 1869; m. 3 times, last to Loulie McClenden Gordon. Practiced law many yrs. from 1869; now mng. large plantations. Owned and operated, 1889-91, 3 saw mills and milling plants, 7 naval stores plants, and 7 stores; founder towns of Faceville, Miriam and Donalsonville, Ga. (latter still a flourishing town). Mayor Bainbridge, Ga., 1876-77; mem. Ga. Constl. Conv., 1877. Home: Bainbridge, Ga. Died Dec. 2, 1920.

DONEHOO, George Patterson, author, clergyman; b. Connellsville, Pa., Dec. 21, 1862; s. Rev. E. R. (D.D.) and Maria (Patterson) D.; Ph.B., U. of Pittsburgh, 1883, Ph.M., 1886; S.T.D., Western Theol. Sem., 1886; D.D., U. of Grove City, 1899, U. of Pittsburgh, 1913; m. Virginia Buttermore, M.D., Mar. 16, 1909; 1 son, George Smith. Ordained Presbyn. ministry, 1886; pastor Mt. Pleasant, Pa., until 1892, Sharon, until 1903; spl. hist. work and archæol. expdns., 1903-11; pastor Coudersport, Pa., 1911-21; state librarian, Pa., 1921-24; dir. Bureau War History, Dept. Mil. Affairs, Pa., 1927-31. Sec. Pa. Hist. Commn., 1913-24. Chaplain with rank of capt. 21st Inf., Pa. N.G., Spanish Am. War; mem. Draft Bd., World War; Chaplain Pa. Ho. of Rep., 1925-28. Republican. Author: Pennsylvania, A History, 1926; Harrisburg, the City Beautiful, 1926; History of the Indian Villages and Place Names in Pennsylvania, 1927. Wrote articles on Pa. Indian villages for Handbook of American Indians (Bur. Am. Ethnology), 1911. Home: Harrisburg, Pa. Died Jan. 11, 1934.

DONLEVY, Alice Heighes, art teacher, lecturer; b. Manchester, Eng., Jan. 7, 1846; d. John Intaglio and Alice (Heighes) D.; ed. New York; studied water color, Pleasantville, N.Y.; grad. School of Design for Women, Cooper Inst., in wood engraving and drawing and design; unmarried. Taught class in illumination at Cooper Inst.; founder, 1866, with 8 other women artists, The Ladies' Art Assn., New York; has made specialty of teaching form and color for reproductive processes; several prizes, including gold medal for tapestry, Chicago Expn., 1893; teaches and lectures on art and art industry; lecturer on Art Industry in People's Free Lecture Course, City of New York. Author: Practical Hints on the Art of Illumination, 1867. Died Mar. 5, 1929.

DONLEVY, Harriet Farley, editor, author; b. Claremont, N.H., Feb. 18, 1817; d. Rev. Stephen and Lucy (Saunders) Farley; ed. public schools, Atkinson, N.H., Acad., and Hampton Falls Acad.; was trained for teacher and taught in some country schools, but disliking the occupation went to work in cotton mills at Lowell. Edited The Lowell Offering, a mill girls' mag., 1840-48; afterward contributor, editor and later publisher New England Offering, until 1850. The quality of the work attracted wide attention at home and abroad; m. John Intaglio Donlevy, inventor, 1854 (died 1872). She edited a collection of her father's writings, 1851. Author: Shells from the Strand of the Sea of Genius (selections from Lowell Offering), 1847; Happy Hours at Hazel Nook, 1852; Christmas Stories. Died 1907.

DONLEY, William Henry, organist, conductor; b. New Haven, Conn., Apr. 20, 1863; s. Edward and Mary (Phelps) D.; ed. Western Sem., Waterloo, Ia.; studied with Edward Burnham and Otto A. Schmidt (Waterloo), A. Haverick (New York), also at N.E. Conservatory of Music; piano with Dr. Louis Maas, organ with George E. Whiting, voice with C. E. Tinney, of London, Eng., theory with S. A. Emery; m. Laura J. Wensley, Aug. 6, 1888; children—Helen Irene, Mabel Alice, Florence Eleanor. Concert organist at 19; played at Buffalo and St. Louis expns., and has given recitals throughout U.S.; as organ architect has planned about 350 organs; organist and choirmaster 1st Presbyn. Ch., Seattle, Wash., 1915—; dir. People's Chorus, Seattle, 1915-18. Fellow Coll. of Organists, London. Home: Seattle, Wash. Died Apr. 15, 1929.

DONLON, Alphonsus John, univ. pres.; b. Albany, N.Y., Oct. 30, 1867; s. Patrick and Julia (Howard) D.; A.B., Georgetown U., 1888; grad. work in philosophy, Jesuit House of Studies, Woodstock, Md., 1892-95. Prof. physics, Georgetown, 1895-1900; student theology, Woodstock, 1900-04; prof. physics, Woodstock, 1900-11; pres. Georgetown U., Jan. 23, 1912-May 1, 1918; asst. pastor Ch. of St. Francis Xavier. Home: New York, N.Y. Died Sept. 4, 1923.

DONNELL, James J., banker; b. Co. Tyrone, Ireland, Mar. 24, 1840; s. James and Mary (Rodgers) D.; came to America, 1850; pub. sch. edn.; m. Anne, d. William G. Warden, of Phila., Mar. 15, 1892 (died 1907). Entered banking business with N. Holmes & Sons, Pittsburgh, 1857; admitted to partnership, 1872; resigned, 1899, to become pres. Bank of Pittsburgh; when this bank consolidated with Mchts. and Mfrs. Bank and Iron City Bank, he retired but retained position of v.p.; an organizer and pres. Fidelity Title & Trust Co., 1908—; now chmn. bd.; one of the organizers and v.p. Citizens Ry. Co.; v.p. Union Fidelity Title Ins. Co.; dir. United Engring. & Foundry Co., Pittsburgh Steel Foundry, Pittsburgh Forge & Iron Co., etc. Mem. Sinking Fund Commn. of Pittsburgh; mem. Bd. Sinking Fund Commrs. of Allegheny Co. Home: Pittsburgh, Pa. Died Jan. 14, 1918.

DONNELLY, Arthur Barrett, army officer; b. St. Louis, Mo., May 31, 1875; s. James J. and Elizabeth (Taaffe) D.; m. Anna Pike Renick, May 10, 1898. Dept. mgr., 1901-06, asst. supt. factory, and buyer, 1906-08, Hamilton-Brown Shoe Co., St. Louis; pres. Arthur D. Donnelly & Co. (leather), Interstate Mercantile Co., Inc., Mo. Paint & Varnish Co. Enlisted in Co. F, 1st Inf., N.G. Mo., Dec. 7, 1892; promoted through grades to adj. gen. of Mo., with rank of brig. gen., Jan. 8, 1917, but granted indefinite leave of absence by gov., Mar. 25, 1917, in order to assume command 1st Mo. Inf.; apptd. brig. gen. N.A., Aug. 5, 1917. Served in Spanish-Am. War as capt. Co. F, 1st Mo. Inf., 1898; comd. regt. on Mexican border, June 18-Sept. 25, 1916; comdg. 69th Inf. Brigade, Camp Doniphan, Ft. Sill, Okla., Aug. 25, 1917. Republican. Catholic. Home: St. Louis, Mo. Died July 29, 1919.

DONNELLY, Charles, ry. official; b. Wisconsin Rapids, Wis., Nov. 9, 1869; s. Thomas F. and Catherine (Corwin) D.; LL.B., Georgetown U., 1896; m. Berthania McMichael, Nov. 6, 1894. Began practice at Washington, D.C., 1896; with N.P. Ry. Co., 1903—, successively as div. counsel, at Helena, Mont., 1903-08, asst. gen. counsel, at St. Paul, Minn., 1908-18, gen. solicitor, 1918-19, exec. v.p., 1919-20, pres., Dec. 1, 1920—. Home: St. Paul, Minn. Died Sept. 4, 1939.

DONNELLY, Dorothy Agnes, actress; b. New York; d. Thomas Lester (mgr. Grand Opera House, New York) and Sara (Williams) D.; ed. Convent of the Sacred Heart, New York; unmarried. Made first appearance at Murray Hill Theatre, New York, playing juvenile and leading rôles; created Candida in "Candida" by George Bernard Shaw, Dec. 1903; Maja in "When We Dead Awaken," by Henrik Ibsen, 1905; Jacqueline in "Madame X," by Alexander Bisson, 1909; Maria Rosa, 1914. Served overseas with A.E.F. Entertainers, 1918-19; now v.p. State Women's War Relief; dir. The Actors' Theatre. Catholic. Author: Forbidden; Blossom Time; Poppy; The Student Prince. Co-author: Florabella; Johnny Get Your Gun; Fancy-Free; The Riddle Woman. Address: New York, N.Y. Died Jan. 4, 1928.

DONNELLY, Edward Terence, army officer; b. London, Eng., Aug. 22, 1871; s. Edward C. D., of N.Y. City; ed. Manhattan Coll., Columbia U.; LL.B., New York Law Sch.; grade Sch. of Application for Cav. and Field Arty., 1905; m. Mrs. Flora Fitten Bewick, Nov. 22, 1909. Commd. capt. 8th N.Y. Inf., May 17, 1898; hon. mustered out, Nov. 3, 1898; 1st lt. 43d U.S. Inf., Aug. 17, 1899; hon. mustered out, July 5, 1901; 1st lt. Arty. Corps, Aug. 1, 1901; capt., Jan. 25, 1907; assigned to 1st Field Arty., June 6, 1907; trans. to 6th Field Arty., June 11, 1912, to 3d Field Arty., Mar. 20, 1913, to 5th Field Arty., Nov. 1, 1915; maj., July 1, 1916, later lt. col.; col. N.A., Aug. 5, 1916; brig. gen. N.A., Apr. 12, 1918. Served in Spanish-Am. War, Philippine Insurrection, and on Mexican border; comdr. 164th Brigade F.A., 89th Division, A.E.F., in France, July 1918-May 1919. Awarded Croix de Guerre (France). Catholic. Died Feb. 8, 1929.

DONNELLY, Eleanor Cecilia, author; b. Phila., Pa.; d. Dr. Philip Carroll and Catharine (Gavin) D.; acad. edn. Is foremost Catholic poetess of America and has written many stories for Catholic and secular mags. Has been several times honored by the Pope with spl. marks of approval. Author (verse): Hymns of the Sacred Heart; Children of the Golden Sheaf, and Other Poems; etc. Also (prose): Storm Bound; Girlhood's Handbook of Woman; Amy's Music Box; The Lost Christmas Tree; Thoughts on Purgatory (from the German); Life of Sister Gonzaga; Blessed Youth. Home: Philadelphia. Died Apr. 30, 1917.

DONNELLY, Frederick William, mayor; b. Trenton, N.J., Oct. 14, 1866; s. Gen. Richard A. (mayor of Trenton, 1884-86) and Susan (Davisson) D.; ed. N.J. State Model Sch., Trenton; Episcopal Coll., Burlington; bus. coll.; m. Eliza Lukens, June 25, 1896 (died 1919). Began at 17 as traveling salesman; mgr. father's store, Trenton, 1892-1907; pres. Frederick W. Donnelly Co., 1907—. Mem. Trenton Harbor Bd., 1909-11; 1st mayor under commn. form of government, 6 terms, 1911-35, resigned, 1932, after 24 years of service; chmn. Sinking Fund Commn.; Democratic candidate for U.S. senator, N.J., 1924. For many yrs. active supporter waterway projects; pres. N.J. Ship Canal Commn., N.J. Rivers and Harbors Congress, Trenton-Phila.-New York Waterways Assn.; v.p. Nat. Rivers and Harbors Congress, Atlantic Deeper Waterways Assn. Trustee Trenton Free Pub. Library, Sch. Industrial Arts. Episcopalian. Mason. Home: Trenton, N.J. Died Sept. 25, 1935.

DONNELLY, Harold Irvin, religious educator; b. Salt Lake City, Utah, Jan. 23, 1892; s. James and Charlotte (Renton) D.; B.A., Coll. of Wooster, 1911, M.A., 1912, Princeton, 1920; grad. Princeton Theol. Sem., 1916, B.D., 1921; student Sorbonne, Paris, 1 term, 1919; Ph.D., U. of Pa., 1931; m. Beatrice Irene Wetherbee, June 30, 1921; children—Harold Irvin, Frank Wetherbee, James Whitney. Instructor Wooster Acad., 1911-13; field sec. College of Wooster, 1916-17; army Y.M.C.A. sec., Montgomery, Alabama, August-Dec. 1917; student sec. Middle Atlantic States, Internat. Com. Y.M.C.A., Jan.-June 1918; student sec. Y.M.C.A., U. of Ore., 1920-21; nat. dir. boys' work, Bd. of Christian Edn., Presbyn. Ch., U.S.A., 1921-25; asst. editor intermed. and sr. publs. of Bd. of Christian Edn., 1925-27, gen. dir. dept. of ednl. research, 1927-30; prof. Christian edn., Princeton Theol. Sem., 1931—. Served as pvt. F.A., U.S.A.; with A.E.F., Sept. 1918-July 1919. Mem. bd. mgrs. Am. Sect. World S.S. Assn.; mem. Internat. Council Religious Edn., and chmn. com. on religious edn. of youth; mem. Nat. Council Com. on Work with Boys of Y.M.C.A., Nat. Council Boy Scouts of America; pres. N.J. Council Religious Education. Republican. Author; Manual for Leaders of Presbyterian Pioneers, 1923; What Shall I Do With My Life? 1924. Editor: Handbook of Presbyterian Pioneers, 1928. Home: Princeton, N.J. Died July 10, 1937.

DONNELLY, Ignatius, farmer-editor-author-orator; b. Philadelphia, Nov. 3, 1831; grad. Central High Sch., 1849; m. Katharine McCaffrey Sept. 10, 1855, (died 1894); 2d, Marian Hanson, Feb. 22, 1898. Admitted to bar, 1852; emigrated to Minn., 1856; lt. gov. and gov. Minn., 1859-63; member Congress, 1863-69; several years pres. State Farmers' Alliance of Minn.; pres. Nat. Anti-Monopoly convention that nominated Peter Cooper for President, 1872; 5 years published The Anti-Monopolist, a weekly newspaper; now editor of The Representative, a reform journal at Minneapolis; many times mem. senate and house in Minn.; nominated, Sept. 6, 1898, by People's party in Nat. conv. at Cincinnati, O., for v.p. of U.S. Author: Atlantis, the Ante-Diluvian World; Ragnarök; Caesar's Column; Doctor Huguet; The Golden Bottle; The American People's Money; etc. Home: Hastings, Minn. Died 1901.

DONNELLY, John C., lawyer; b. Plympton, Can., Nov. 27, 1850; s. William and Eleanor (Boulger) D.; ed. pub. and pvt. schs.; LL.B., Law Dept., U. of Mich., 1873; m. Anna Minton, Sept. 1875. Practiced, Detroit, 1873—; mem. Donnelly, Hally, Donnelly & Munro; has been general counsel and dir. Detroit United Ry. Co.; counsel and dir. Peninsular State Bank, etc. Mem. Mich. Ho. of Rep., 1878-80. Served as 2d lt., 1st lt. and capt. Mich. N.G., 8 yrs. Mem. Assn. Bar City of Detroit (pres.). Democrat. Catholic. Home: Bloomfield Hills, Mich. Died Aug. 6, 1924.

DONNELLY, Joseph Gordon, lawyer; b. Milwaukee, Jan. 4, 1856; s. John and Elizabeth (Grugon) D.; grad. St. Gall's Acad. (now Marquette U.), Milwaukee, 1871; m. Lois Deborah Smith, Aug. 13, 1878. Taught sch. 6 yrs.; register of probate, Milwaukee, 1877-93; admitted to bar, 1881; U.S. consul gen. to Mexico, 1893-98; in gen. practice at Milwaukee, 1898—. Dem. candidate for Congress, 1898; nominee for dist. judge, 1901; now chief judge Civil Ct., Milwaukee County. Author: Jesus Delaney (novel), 1899. Died May 10, 1915.

DONNELLY, Thomas Frederick, judge; b. New York, Dec. 13, 1863; s. Thomas Lester and Sarah (Williams) D.; LL.B., Columbia, 1884; unmarried. Admitted to N.Y. bar, 1885, and practiced in N.Y. City; mem. N.Y. Assembly, 1896, 97 98; Senate, 1899-1902; justice City Ct., New York, 1908-13; justice Supreme Ct., N.Y., 1st Dist., term 1913-26. Democrat. Home: New York, N.Y. Died Nov. 1, 1924.

DONOHO, Ruger, painter; b. Church Hill, Jefferson Co., Miss., Dec. 21, 1857; s. Robert and Julia S. (Ruger) D.; Emerson Inst., Washington; State Normal Sch., Millersville, Pa.; studied under R. Swain Gifford, New York, 1877-79; Art Students' League, New York, 1877-78; studied in Paris, 1880-87, Julien Acad., 1880-86, under Bouguereau and Fleury, also Boulanger and Lefebvre; m. Matilda Ackley, Apr. 17, 1894. Began work, Paris, 1880; silver medal, Paris Expn., 1889; Hors Concour, Paris Salon, 1890; Webb prize, Soc. Am. Artists, New York, 1892; medal, Chicago Expn., 1893; hon. mention, Carnegie Inst., 1911. Progressive. Episcopalian. Died Jan. 28, 1916.

DONOHOE, Denis, writer; b. Buffalo, Sept. 19, 1861; s. Denis (H.B.M.'s consul) and Eliza Hamilton (Ruxton) D.; ed. pvt. schs., New Orleans and Baltimore, Bishop's Coll. Sch., Lennoxville, Can., 1878-79, Imperial-Royal Frederick William U. of Bonn, 1879-80; LL.B., Columbia, 1882; m. Marie Paule Parot, June 1, 1885 (dec.). Was spl. counsel retained by British govt. to prosecute Australian murderer Butler in extradition proceedings; acted as gen. counsel of British consul-gen. at San Francisco, 1890-1900. City editor New York Star, 1886-89; from 1890 author of numerous short stories, spl. articles, etc.; financial editor N.Y. Commercial, 1904-05; mgr. of mining properties in Alaska, 1906-09; gen. mgr. Blackburn Mines Co., 1910-12; financial editor, San Francisco Examiner, 1912—. Home: San Rafael, Calif. Died Mar. 10, 1924.

DONOHOE, Thomas Joseph, lawyer; b. Sutter Co., Calif., Dec. 7, 1870; s. John Charles and Susan (Luney) D.; ed. pub. schs., Calif.; m. Rosalie Miller, Oct. 31, 1901; children—Thomas M., Ruth. Editor and pub. Willows (Calif.) Journal, 1895-96; admitted to Calif. bar, 1897; removed to Juneau, Alaska, 1898, and practiced with Judge Thomas R. Lyons until 1902; moved to Valdez, 1903, to Cordova, 1919; mem. Donohoe & Dimond. First city atty. of Juneau, 1900-01; mem. Dem. Nat. Com. for Ty. of Alaska, 1916-28. Catholic. Home: Atherton, Calif. Died Jan. 16, 1934.

DONOHUE, Charles, jurist; b. New York, Apr. 16, 1825; ed. Columbia Coll. Grammar Sch.; D.C.L., St. John's Coll.; admitted to bar; widower. Was judge N.Y. Supreme Court 14 yrs.; resumed practice. Mem. Tammany Soc., Am. Inst. Democrat. Home: New York, N.Y. Died 1910.

DONOHUE, Francis Michael, physician; b. New Brunswick, N.J., Aug. 17, 1859; s. James and Jane (Reynolds) D.; St. Francis Xavier's Coll., New York, 1873-75; M.D., Univ. Med. Coll. (New York U.), 1881; m. Elizabeth Butler, Oct. 7, 1896. In med. practice at New Brunswick, 1881—; surgeon to John Wells Memorial Hosp.; cons. surgeon to Somerset Hosp.; surgeon to Pa. R.R. Co., St. Peter's Hosp. Dir. People's Nat. Bank, New Brunswick Trust Co.; trustee New Brunswick Savings Instn. Trustee State Home for Boys. Catholic. Hon. mem. Somerset Co. Med. Soc. Home: New Brunswick, N.J. Died June 1919.

DONOVAN, Jeremiah, congressman; b. Ridgefield, Conn., 1854; ed. pub. schs. Mem. 63d Congress (1913-15), 4th Conn. Dist. Democrat. Home: South Norwalk, Conn. Died Apr. 22, 1935.

DONOVAN, John Joseph, civil engr., lumber; b. Rumney, N.H., Sept. 8, 1858; s. Patrick and Julia (O'Sullivan) D.; grad. Plymouth (N.H.) State Normal Sch., 1877; B.S. in C.E., Worcester Poly. Inst., 1882, later C.E., also D.Sc., 1932; m. Clara Isabel Nichols, Apr. 29, 1888; children—Helen Elizabeth (Mrs. Leslie Craven), John Nichols, Philip Laurence. Civ. engr. N.P. Ry., 1882-88, in charge Cascade div., 1886-87, in charge Mont. constrn., 1887-88; chief engr. and mgr. 3 rys. radiating from Bellingham and sold to G.N., N.P. and C.,M.&St.P. respectively; built and operated many miles of railroad, etc.; has been engaged in lumber business exclusively, 1906—; dir. Bloedel Donovan Lumber Mills. Mem. City Council, Fairhaven, Washington, 1890-92; developed Nooksack Falls, and sold to Stone & Webster, 1905. Trustee Bellingham State Normal Sch., 8 yrs., Bellingham Chamber Commerce (pres.), State Chamber Commerce (pres.). Republican. Catholic. Home: Bellingham, Wash. Died Jan. 9, 1937.

D'OOGE, Martin Luther, univ. prof.; b. Zonnemaire, Netherlands, July 17, 1839; s. Leonard and Johanna (Quintus) D.; A.B., U. of Mich., 1862, A.M., 1865; Ph.D., U. of Leipzig, 1872; (LL.D., U. of Mich., 1889; D.Litt., Rutgers, 1901); m. Mary Worcester, July 31, 1873. Asst. prof. ancient langs., 1867-68, acting prof. Greek lang. and lit., 1868-70, prof., 1870-1912, U. of Mich., prof. emeritus, July, 1912—. Ordained Congl. ministry, 1878; mem. mng. com. Am. Sch. Classical Studies, Athens, 1883—(dir. 1886-87). Author: The Acropolis of Athens, 1908. Prepared edit. of Demosthenes on the Crown; Antigone of Sophocles. Home: Ann Arbor, Mich. Died Sept. 12, 1915.

DOOLEY, Henry Williamson; b. Brooklyn, N.Y., Apr. 9, 1871; s. Albert Gallatin and Gertrude (Yardley) D.; ed. pub. sch.; m. Eliza Bellows King, Oct. 5, 1904; 1 dau., Mary Gertrude. Connected with Ogden & Wallace, iron and steel mchts., New York, 1886-98; resigned and served in N.Y. State Naval Battalion, Spanish-Am. War; founder, 1899, and was pres. of Dooley, Smith & Co. and Henry W. Dooley Co., till retired, 1922; now Real Estate and Investments. Apptd. by gov. of P.R. mem. Municipal Council, San Juan, 1901; candidate of Federal Party for mayor, 1901; organized Spanish Bur. Dem. Nat. Campaign Com., 1912; mem. Dem. Nat. Com., 1912-16, 1920-28. Organized, and 1st chmn. P.R. Chapter Am. Red. Cross, 1917; conducted the first Liberty Loan campaign, etc. Mem. Dem. Nat. Committee, 1920—; chmn. Woodrow Wilson Foundation. Mem. Chamber Commerce, P.R. (exec. com.), etc. Episcopalian. Home: San Juan, P.R. Died Mar. 12, 1932.

DOOLEY, Michael F., banker; b. New Britain, Conn., Dec. 1, 1852; s. Timothy and Mary (Birney) D.; A.B., Fordham U., 1872, LL.D., 1922; studied St. Sulpice, Paris, 1872-74; m. Ellen M. McManus, 1888. Chmn. Bd. of Assessors, Hartford, Conn., 1880-87; nat. bank examiner, 1887-90, for R.I. and Conn., 1893-99; receiver of First Nat. Bank of Willimantic, Conn., 1895-99; v.p. Union Trust Co. of Providence, R.I., 1899-1908; pres. Nat. Exchange Bank of Providence, 1908-25; chmn. bd., 1925-26, bank purchased, 1926, by Industrial Trust Co., of which was v.p. and dir. until early in 1934, when resigned both offices. Trustee Providence Coll., St. Joseph's Hosp.; former dir. Encyclopedia Press (Catholic Ency.); dir. Universal Foundation, Inc. (Encyclopedia), First Nat. Bank of Attleboro, Mass. Dem. presdl. elector (pres. R.I. Electoral Coll.), 1928. Iife mem. and for many years treas. gen. Am. Irish Hist. Soc. Elected Knight of Malta, 1931. Home: Providence, R.I. Deceased.

DOOLEY, William Francis, univ. pres.; b. Chicago, Ill., Mar. 30, 1872; s. John and Anna (Fleming) D.; ed. St. Ignatius Coll., Chicago; literature, Florissant, Mo., 2 yrs.; philosophy and theory, St. Louis U., 3 yrs. Joined Soc. of Jesus, 1891; prof., St. Mary's Coll., Kan., 1898-1901, Detroit U., 1901-07; dean dept. of arts and sciences, Creighton U., Omaha, Neb., 1907-11; pres. Detroit U., July 1911—. Died July 17, 1915.

DOOLIN, John B.; b. Caldwell Co., Mo., Mar. 9, 1879; s. John and Alice (Tobin) D.; grad. Cameron (Mo.) High School; m. Leo Museller, July 3, 1913; children—John B., James M. Began as farm laborer, 1900; register of deeds, Woods Co., Okla., 1902-04; pres. Schaefer-Doolin Mortgage Co., Alva, Okla., 1912—; admitted to Okla. bar, 1906; state game warden, 1910-13; has been farmer, livestock raiser and wheat grower, banker and dealer in investments; dir. Beaver, Meade & Englewood Ry. Co.; v.p. Aetna Bldg. & Loan Assn. (Topeka, Kan.), Canadian Valley Gas Co., Oklahoma City Nat. Bank. Asst. treas. Dem. Nat. Com., 1908, 1916. Compiler: (with Fred S. Bard) Field, Forest and Stream, 1911; Outdoor Oklahoma, 1912; Bird Day in Oklahoma, 1913. Home: Alva, Okla. Died Dec. 30, 1939.

DOOLING, Maurice T., judge; b. Moore's Flat, Calif., 1860; s. Timothy and Mary (Manogue) D.; A.B., St. Mary's Coll., San Francisco, 1880, A.M., 1881; (Ph.D., Santa Clara Coll., 1903; LL.D., St. Mary's, 1909); m. Ida M. Wagner, 1887. Teacher, St. Mary's Coll., 1881-83; admitted to Calif. bar, 1885; mem. Calif. Ho. of Rep., 1885-87; judge Superior Court of San Benito Co., Calif., 1897-1913; judge U.S. Dist. Court, Northern Dist. of Calif., July 28, 1913—. Catholic. Died Nov. 1924.

DOOLING, Peter J., congressman; b. New York, N.Y., 1857; ed. pub. schs. In real estate business; served as mem. State Senate, 16th Senatorial Dist., N.Y., and as county clk., City and County of New York; mem. 63d to 66th Congresses (1913-21), 16th N.Y. Dist. Democrat. Home: New York, N.Y. Died Oct. 18, 1931.

DOOLITTLE, Charles Camp, cashier Merchants' Nat. Bank of Toledo, O.; b. Burlington, Vt., March 16, 1832; ed. high school, Montreal, Can.; removed to New York, 1847; later moved to Mich.; m. Emily H. Parsons, Feb. 28, 1856. Became, May 16, 1861, 1st lt. 4th Mich. regt.; col. 18th Mich., July 22, 1862; served in Peninsular campaign in Ky., 1862-63; in Tenn., 1863-64; comd. Decatur, Ala., during 1st day's defense against Gen. Hood; led brigade at Nashville; comd. there, 1865; comd. northern dist., La., fall of 1865; brig. gen. vols., Jan. 27, 1865; bvt. maj. gen., June 13, 1865; mustered out Nov. 30, 1865. Home: Toledo, O. Died 1902.

DOOLITTLE, Charles Leander, astronomer; b. Ontario, Ind., Nov. 12, 1843; s. Charles and Celia D.; C.E., U. of Mich., 1874 (hon. Sc.D., 1897; LL.D., Lehigh U., 1912); m. Martha Cloyes Farrand, Sept. 18, 1866, m. 2d, Helen Eugenia Wolle, May 11, 1882; father of Eric D. On U.S. Boundary Survey, 1873-75; prof. mathematics and astronomy, Lehigh U., 1875-95; prof. astronomy, U. of Pa., and dir. Flower Astron. Obs., 1895-1912 (emeritus). Author: Practical Astronomy as Applied to Geodesy and Navigation; Results of Observation with Zenith Telescope, Sayre Obs., 1876-95; Results of Observation with Zenith Telescope, Flower Obs., 1894-1911. Home: Philadelphia, Pa. Died Mar. 3, 1919.

DOOLITTLE, Eric, astronomer; b. Ontario, Ind., July 26, 1869; s. Charles Leander (q.v.) and Martha Cloyes (Farrand) D.; ed. prep. sch. Lehigh U., 1883-87; C.E., Lehigh U., 1891; post-grad. work, astronomy, 1894-96; m. Sara Bitler Halliwell, Mar. 31, 1902. Instr. astronomy, Lehigh U., 1891-92, State U. of Ia., 1892-93, U. of Pa., 1896-1904; asst. prof. astronomy, U. of Pa., 1904-12; prof. astronomy and dir. Flower Astron. Obs., 1912—. Presbyn. Author: Measures of 900 Double and Multiple Stars, 1901; Measures of 1066 Double and Multiple Stars, 1905; Catalogue and Remeasurement of the 648 Hough Double Stars, 1907; Measures of 1954 Double Stars, 1914. Home: Upper Darby, Pa. Died Sept. 21, 1920.

DOOLITTLE, Roscoe Edward, chemist; b. Fowlerville, Mich., Jan. 16, 1874; s. Edward Jefferson and Caroline M. (Hoyt) D.; high schs., Howell and Morrice, Mich.; B.S., Mich. Agrl. Coll., 1896; m. Ivah May Stewart, Nov. 6, 1895; children—Stewart Edward, Kenneth Hoyt. Asst. chemist, Mich. State Dairy and Food Dept., 1896-98; state chemist, 1898-1904; asst. chemist, Bur. of Chemistry, U.S. Dept. Agr. and chief of New York Lab., 1904-11; transferred to Washington, as asso. chemist same bureau and mem. Bd. of Food and Drug Inspection, Oct. 1911; served as acting chief Bur. of Chemistry, Mar.-Dec. 1912, after resignation of Dr. H. W. Wiley; returned to former position as chief of New York Lab., 1912-17; chief eastern dist., Bur. Chemistry, Jan. 8-Oct. 1, 1917, chief central dist., Chicago, Oct. 1, 1917—. Home: Evanston, Ill. Deceased.

DOOLITTLE, Thomas Benjamin, engr., inventor; b. Woodbury, Conn., June 30, 1839; s. Benjamin and Betsey C. (More) D.; ed. Woodbury Acad.; (Sc.D., Dartmouth, 1909); m. Mary Louise Bradley, Dec. 24, 1866. In early life was a mfr. of brass articles at Bridgeport, in which he made many inventions in connection with mfr. of barbed wire; was originator of buffer platform and coupler, of which modified types are in general use on passenger cars; became connected with Bell Telephone Co. at early day; originated the first telephone switchboard, the hard drawn copper and the telephone call bell, etc.; originated and placed in use a fare registering device on street cars; retired from active service of Am. Telephone & Telegraph Co., June 1909. Received Edward Longstreth medal from Franklin Inst. of Phila., 1898, for origination of process of producing hard drawn copper wire. Home: Branford, Conn. Died Apr. 4, 1921.

DORAN, Joseph Ingersoll, lawyer; b. Phila., Pa., Jan. 17, 1844; s. Hon. Joseph M. and Ann Luker (Callahan) D.; prep. edn. at sch. of John W. Faires, Phila.; student for short period U. of Pa.; studied law in office of Hon. John C. Bullitt; m. Ida Warner Erwin, Dec. 12, 1876. Admitted to Pa. bar, 1865, Supreme Ct. of Pa., 1867, Supreme Ct. U.S., 1899; in practice with Mr. Bullitt and Samuel Dickson; dir. and gen. counsel Norfolk & Western Ry.; identified with coal and iron interests of Va. and W.Va. Home: Philadelphia, Pa. Died July 21, 1919.

DORAN, Thomas Francis, lawyer; b. Morris Co., Kan., Dec. 8, 1862; s. Francis and Mary (Clark) D.; ed. U. of Kan.; m. Mary Webb Woodward, Nov. 12, 1891; 1 dau., Josephine Woodward (Mrs. M. F. Cosgrove). Admitted to Kan. bar 1891, and began practice at Topeka; mem. Doran, Kline, Colmery & Cosgrove; devotes attention to both criminal and civil practice, but specializes in corporation law. Extensively engaged in stock raising and farming; interested in development of flowers, especially roses; chmn. bd. trustees Reinisch Rose and Rose Test Gardens, Topeka. Died Dec. 18, 1939.

DORCHESTER, Daniel, clergyman; b. Duxbury, Mass., Mar. 11, 1827; s. Daniel and Mary Otis D.; ed. pub. schs., Norwich Acad. and Wesleyan U.; m. Apr. 12, 1850, Mary Payson Davis. Entered Providence Conf. M.E. Ch., 1847; pastor Somers, Thompson, Woodstock, Eastford and Mystic, Conn.; later in Worcester, Lowell, Charleston, Salem, Lowell again, Chelsea, Springfield and Boston. Presiding elder Worcester dist. 1865, Lynn dist. 1874, N. Boston dist. 1882; retired from active ministry 1895. Commr. of Lunacy, Conn., 1855; mem. Conn. senate, 1855; supt. Indian Schs. of U.S., 1889-93. Home: West Roxbury, Mass. Died 1907.

DORE, John F., lawyer; b. Charlestown, Mass., Dec. 11, 1881; s. John F. and Mary E. (Hudson) D.; prep. edn., Boston (Mass.) Latin Sch., Seattle (Wash.) High Sch., Phillips Exeter Acad., Exeter, N.H.; student Harvard, 1901-03; m. Marian Neal, Dec. 22, 1911; children—John F., Mary E., Margaret E., Virginia A. Mem. staff Seattle Post Intelligencer, 1903-14, Seattle Times, 1904-10, Seattle Star, 1910-11; admitted to Wash. bar, 1909, and began practice at Seattle; has specialized on jury cases. Mem. Seattel Park Commn. 2 yrs.; mayor of City of Seattle, 1932-34 and 1936—. Home: Seattle, Wash. Died Apr. 18, 1938.

DOREMUS, Charles Avery, chemist; b. New York, N.Y., Sept. 6, 1851; s. Robert Ogden and Estelle Emma (Skidmore) D.; A.B., Coll. City of New York, 1870; A.M., Ph.D., U. of Heidelberg, 1873; student U. of Leipzig, 1873; (hon. M.D., U. of Buffalo, 1879); m. Elizabeth Johnson Ward (playwright), Aug. 4, 1880. Reporter on photography for U.S. govt., Vienna Expn., 1873; chemist U.S. Dairy Co., 1873; in gen. practice of chemistry, 1873—. Asst. chemistry, toxicology and med. jurisprudence, Bellevue Hosp. Med. Coll., 1874-79, adj. prof., 1879-97; prof. chemistry and toxicology, med. dept., U. of Buffalo, 1879-82; prof. chemistry, 1882-92, emeritus prof., 1892-98, Am. Veterinary Coll., New York; asst., 1882-97, asst. prof. chemistry and physics, 1897-1901, asst. prof. chemistry, 1901-03, acting prof., 1903-04, Coll. City of New York. Wrote sect. on Gaseous Poisons, Text-Book of Legal Medicine and Toxicology, 1903. Home: New York, N.Y. Died Dec. 2, 1925.

DOREMUS, Robert Ogden, chemist; b. New York, Jan. 11, 1824; grad. N.Y. Univ., 1842; med. dept., 1850 (LL.D., 1872); studied chemistry in Paris, 1847-48, establishing laboratory in New York latter yr. Has held several important chairs in collegiate instns., becoming, 1861, prof. chemistry and toxicology, Bellevue Hosp. Med. Coll.; also, 1864, prof. chemistry and physics, Coll. City of New York. In Paris, 1862-64, developing the use of compressed granulated gunpowder, which was adopted by the French govt.; has patented methods of extinguishing fires and other chem. processes. Died 1906.

DOREN, Electra Collins, librarian; b. Georgetown, O., Dec. 4, 1861; d. John Gates and Elizabeth (Bragdon) D.; ed. Dayton (O.) High Sch., Cooper Sem. and pvt. tutors; 1 yr. library study, 1 yr. abroad; unmarried. Began in library work as asst., 1879, librarian Dayton Pub. Library, 1896-1905. Engaged in planning woman's gymnasium and raising funds for same, 1891-94; organized sch. library work in Dayton, 1895; visiting English and Continental libraries, 1899, libraries of Western U.S. to San Francisco, 1900; lecturer Pittsburgh Carnegie Library Sch., 1903-05; head instr. Library Sch. of Western Reserve U., 1905-06; librarian Dayton Pub. Library, Sept. 1, 1913—. Mem. A.L.A. War Service Com. and mem. exec. bd., 1917-20; mem. Am. Library Inst. Home: Dayton, O. Died Mar. 4, 1927.

DORIA, Clara, author. See Clara Kathleen Rogers.

DORION, Eustache Charles Edouard, clergyman, editor; b. Montreal, Can., Aug. 19, 1872; s. Rev. Thomas A. and Marie Louise Elzear (DeNeault) D.; grad. high sch., Manchester, N.H., 1891; American Coll., Lowell, Mass.; spl. student, Boston U. Sch. of Theology, 1904; (D.D., Baker U., Baldwin, Kan., 1911); spl. work in philosophy, Harvard, 1913; m. Lena Bell Avery, July 18, 1906. City editor, Daily Mirror, Manchester, N.H., 1896-98; ordained M.E. ministry, 1901; stated supply, Ashland, N.H., 1898-1901; pastor, Franklin, 1902-04, Plymouth, 1905-09; asst. editor Epworth Herald, 1908-09; asso. editor, 1910-19, editor, May 1919—, Zion's Herald. Mem. Commn. on Boston Methodism, 1913; chmn. exec. com., N.E. Conv. of Meth. Men, 1914; mem. Gen. Conf. Board of Conf. Claimants, 1912—; exec. com. N.E. Home Missions Council, 1915—; bd. mgrs. N.E. Deaconess Assn., 1916—; mem. Boston Commn. on Forward Movements, 1915—. Trustee Boston U., 1916—, Tilton Sem., 1917—. Author: The Redemption of the South End, 1915. Home: Brookline, Mass. Died Jan. 29, 1920.

DORMAN, William Edwin, lawyer; b. Lynn, Mass., June 23, 1875; s. Benjamin H. and Abby C. (Duparr) D.; student Chauncy Hall Sch., Boston, 1890-92, Berkley Sch., 1892-94; A.B., Harvard, 1898, LL.B. cum laude, 1901; m. Estelle Elizabeth Herrick, Aug. 23, 1905; children—Benjamin Hallowell, Samuel Herrick, Priscilla Bradstreet (Mrs. Carl S. Marty), Lois Putnam (dec.), William Edwin. Admitted to Mass. bar, 1901; asst. instr. in history, Harvard, 1898-1903; mem. Mass. Ho. of Reps., 1907-09; lecturer on constitutional law, Northeastern U. Law Sch., Boston, 1904—; counsel to Mass. Senate, by apptmt., 1915-20, under statute, 1920— has devised and drafted laws enacted in Mass. and copied in many states; offered position as drafter of bills for U.S. Senate, 1920. Mem. Lynn Sch. Com., 1898-1901 and 1905-07 (chmn. 1905-07); trustee Walnut Hill Sch., Natick, Mass. Republican. Universalist. Mason. Home: Lynn, Mass., and Georgetown, Mass. Died Mar. 24, 1936.

DORR, Julia Caroline Ripley, author; b. Charleston, S.C., Feb. 13, 1825; d. William Young Ripley; became motherless in infancy; taken by father to Vt., 1830; ed. there; m. Seneca M. Dorr, 1847 (died 1884). Author: Bermuda, 1884; Poems Complete, 1892; In King's Houses, a Romance of the Days of Queen Anne, 1898. Home: Rutland, Vt. Died Jan. 18, 1913.

DORR, Robert East Apthœp, publisher and pres. Mail and Express, New York. Died 1900.

DORRANCE, John Thompson, pres. Campbell Soup Co.; b. Bristol, Pa., Nov. 11, 1873; s. John and Eleanor Gillingham (Thompson) D.; prep. edn., Rugby Acad., Phila.; B.S., Mass. Inst. Tech., 1895; Ph.D., U. of Göttingen, 1897; m. Ethel Mallinckrodt, Aug. 18, 1906; children—Elinor (Mrs. Nathaniel Peter Hill), Ethel Mallinckrodt, Charlotte Kelsey, Margaret Winifred, John Thompson. Originator of canned soup industry; pres. Campbell Soup Co. 1914; dir. Pa. R.R., Prudential Life Ins. Co., Guaranty Trust Co. of New York, Phila. Nat. Bank (exec. com.), etc. Mem. mus. com. Pa. Mus. and Sch. Industrial Art. Republican. Episcopalian. Home: Cinnaminson, N.J., and Radnor, Pa. Died Sept. 21, 1930.

D'ORSAY, Lawrance (Dorset William Lawrance), actor; b. in Northamptonshire, Eng.; ed. for the law; m. Marie Dagmar; m. 2d, Susan Rusholme. Début at Marylebone Theatre, 1877; toured in England 5 yrs.; played in "Still Waters Run Deep," "The Two Roses," "Prospero," etc.; made first appearance in America at Chicago, in "My Sweetheart," Oct. 1884; has been identified with Am. stage almost continuously from 1890; played in "Miss Innocence," "The Zebra," "Lights o' London"; toured in "Earl of Pawtucket," 1911. Home: New York, N.Y. Died Sept. 13, 1931.

DORSET, Marion, chemist; b. Columbia, Tenn., Dec. 14, 1872; s. Walter Clagett and Jane (Mayes) D.; B.S., U. of Tenn., 1893; M.D., Columbian (now George Washington) U., 1896; also studied at U. of Pa.; m. Emily K. Jackson, Oct. 10, 1900; children—Walter Clagett (dec.), Jane Mayes (dec.), Virgil Jackson. Has taught bacteriology and pathology; now engaged in research work on bacterial toxins, especially those of tuberculosis, etc.; asst. chemist biochemic lab., Dept. Agr., 1894-1903; chief biochemic div., 1904—. Home: Washington, D.C. Died July 15, 1935.

DORSETT, Walter Blackburn, surgeon; b. St. Louis Co., Mo., June 13, 1852; s. Henry Leonidas and George Ann (Blackburn) D.; course in civil engring., Washington U.; M.D., St. Louis Med. Coll., 1878; m. Eleanor C. French, Oct. 20, 1880. Practiced at St. Louis, 1878—; supt. and surgeon in charge of St. Louis Female Hosp., 1887-92; gynecologist Evang. Deaconess Hosp., and Mo. Bapt. Sanitarium, 1893—, prof. gynecology and pelvic surgery, Med. Dept., St Louis U. Democrat. Mason. Home: St. Louis, Mo. Died July 27, 1915.

DORSEY, Francis Oswald, physician; b. Indianapolis, Nov. 12, 1869; s. Robert Stockton and Katharine (Layman) D.; A.B., Yale, 1893; M.D., Coll. Phys. and Surg. (Columbia), 1896; resident interne, Sloane Maternity Hosp., New York, 1896-97, Presbyn. Hosp., 1897-99; m. Edith Maria Smith, Oct. 15, 1902. Practiced at Indianapolis, 1899—; asst. prof. principles and practice of medicine, 1899-1900, asst. demonstrator pathology, 1900-07, Ind. Med. Coll.; prof. materia medica and therapeutics, Ind. Dental Coll., 1900-04; cons. phys., Indianapolis Disp., 1902—; asst. attending phys., 1904-06, attending phys., 1906—, Indianapolis City Hosp.; asso. prof. medicine, Purdue U., 1907-08; asso. prof. medicine, Ind. U. Sch. of Medicine, 1908—; clinician, Bobbs Free Dispensary, 1911—; pres. Mt. Jackson Sanitarium Co.; v.p. Tucker & Dorsey Mfg. Co.; mem. Corp. Phoenix Castor Co. Republican. Presbyn. Home: Indianapolis, Ind. Died 1915.

DORSEY, George Amos, anthropologist, journalist; b. Hebron, O., Feb. 6, 1868; s. Edwin Jackson and Mary Emma (Grove) D.; A.B., Denison, 1888, LL.D., 1909; A.B., Harvard, 1890, Ph.D., 1894; m. Ida Chadsey, Dec. 8, 1892; children—Dorothy Ann, George Chadsey; m. 2d, Sue McLellan. Conducted anthrop. investigations in S. America for Chicago Expdn., 1891-92; supt. archæology, dept. anthropology, same, 1892-93; asst. in anthropology, 1894-95, instr., 1895-96, Harvard; asst. curator anthropology, 1896-98, curator, 1898-1915, Field Mus. of Natural History, Chicago; prof. comparative anatomy, Northwestern U. Dental Sch., 1898-1913; asst. prof. anthropology, 1905-08, asso. prof., 1908-15, U. of Chicago. Editor writer for Dem. Nat. Com., 1916. Lecturer on anthropology, New School for Social Research, New York, 1925—. Visited Europe, Egypt, India, Ceylon, Java, Australia, Bismarck Arch., New Guinea, P.I., China and Japan, for Field Mus., 1908; mem. edit. staff and fgn. commr. Chicago Tribune, 1909-12, investigating sources of emigration in Italy, Austria, Hungary, Roumania, Servia and Bulgaria, and studying polit. conditions in India, China, Japan, Australia and South Africa. U.S. del. Internat. Congress Anthropology and Prehistoric Archæology, Paris, 1900; mem. Jury Awards, Dept. Anthropology, St. Louis Expn., 1904. Commd. lt. U.S.N.R.F., Mar. 1918; lt. comdr., Sept. 1919; asst. naval attaché, Madrid, 1918; naval attaché, Lisbon, 1919-21; adviser on Spanish problems to Am. Commn. to Negotiate Peace, Paris. Comdr. mil. orders of Aviz and Santiago. Author: Young Low (novel), 1917, 27; Why We Behave Like Human Beings, 1925; The Nature of Man, 1927; The Evolution of Charles Darwin, 1927; Hows and Whys of Human Behavior, 1929. Home: New York, N.Y. Died Mar. 29, 1931.

DORSEY, Stephen W., senator; b. Benson, Vt., Feb. 28, 1842; s. John W. and Marie H. D.; m. Laura, d. Job P. and M. S. Bigelow, of Washington and London. Served pvt. to col. in Union Army, 1861-65. Removed to Ark.; mem. Rep. Nat. Com., 1868, 72, 76, 80; chmn. exec. com., 1876, 80; elected

U.S. senator from Ark., by combination of Democrats and Republicans, term, 1873-79. Home: Los Angeles, Calif. Died Mar. 20, 1916.

DORST, Joseph Haddox, army officer; b. Louisville, Ky., Apr. 2, 1852; s. John Henry and Catharine (Mershon) D.; grad. U.S. Mil. Acad., 1873; m. Esther J. Archer, Aug. 21, 1890. Commd. 2d lt. 4th Cav., June 13, 1873; 1st lt., Mar. 20, 1879; capt., Mar. 2, 1885; lt. col. asst. adj. gen. vols., May 9, 1898-May 12, 1899; col. 45th U.S. Inf. Vols., Aug. 17, 1899-June 3, 1901; maj. 2d U.S. Cav., Nov. 7, 1898; insp. gen., Feb. 28, 1901; lt. col. 12th Cav., June 26, 1901; col. 3d Cav., Apr. 15, 1903. Participated in campaigns against Kiowa, Comanche and Cheyenne Indians, 1874-75; Powder River expdn. against Sioux and Cheyennes, 1876-77, against Utes, 1879-81, against Apaches in Ariz., 1881, against Geronimo's band, 1885-86, against Santiago de Cuba, 1898, and against insurrectos in the Philippines, 1899-1901; retired, Aug. 10, 1911. Home: Warrenton, Va. Died 1915.

DORT, J(osiah) Dallas, mfr.; b. Inkster, Mich., Feb. 2, 1861; s. Josiah and Marcy (Jones) D.; ed. State Normal Sch., Ypsilanti, Mich.; m. Marcia Webb, May 8, 1907. Began in mfg. business at Flint, Mich., Oct. 1886; pres. Durant-Dort Carriage Co.; pres. Dort Motor Car Co.; dir. Genesee County Savings Bank (Flint), Gray-Dort Motors, Ltd. (Chatham, Ont.). Republican. Episcopalian. Mason. Home: Flint, Mich. Died May 17, 1925.

DOSKER, Henry E., theologian; b. Bunschoten, Netherlands, Feb. 5, 1855; s. Rev. Nicholas H. and Wilhelmina G. (DeRonde) D.; grad. Gymnasium, Zwolle, Netherlands, 1873; A.B., Hope Coll., Holland, Mich., 1876, A.M., 1879; grad. McCormick Theol. Sem., 1879; D.D., Rutgers, 1894; LL.D., Central U. of Ky., 1905; m. Wilhelmina Doornink, Feb. 21, 1882 (died 1923); children—Nicholas Hermanus, Amelia Alyda, Richard John, Gertrude Elizabeth, Cornelius DeRonde. Licensed by classis of Grand River, ordained by classis of Holland, clergyman of Presbyn. Ch. U.S.A., formerly in Ref. Ch. in America; pastor Ebenezer, 1879-82, Grand Haven, 1882-86; lector of theology, Holland, Mich., 1882-88; pastor Holland 3d Ch., 1889-94, elected, 1894, prof. of ch. history, Western Theol. Sem.; prof. ch. history, Louisville Presbyn. Sem., Oct. 1903—. Mem. Dutch Acad. of Leyden, 1898—. Author: De Zondagschool, 1882; Life of Doctor A. C. Van Raalte, 1893; Outline Studies in Ecclesiastical History, 1901, revised edit., 1913; The Dutch Anabaptists, 1921. Wrote series John of Barneveldt, Martyr or Traitor, Presbyterian and Reformed Review, 1898. Editorial writer Christian Observer. Home: Louisville, Ky. Died Dec. 23, 1926.

DOS PASSOS, John Randolph, lawyer; b. Phila., 1844, of Portuguese-Am. descent; ed. Phila. pub. schs.; studied law privately and in offices; attended law lectures, U. of Pa.; enlisted in Pa. militia for Civil War; widower. Admitted to practice but after admission went to New York; for yrs. engaged in banking, corporate and financial law; active in formation of large business amalgamations, including the so-called "sugar trust," Am. Thread Co., and many others. Author: A Treatise on the Law of Stock Brokers and Stock Exchanges, 2 vols., 2d edit., 1905. Home: New York, N.Y. Died Jan. 27, 1917.

DOSTER, Frank, lawyer; b. Va., Jan. 19, 1847; ed. Ind. U. and Ill. Coll. Served 2 yrs. in 11th Ind. Cav.; removed to Kan., 1871; practiced law; was judge Dist. Court 4 yrs.; then chief justice Supreme Ct. of Kan., 1897-Jan. 1903; later asst. gen. atty. Mo. Pacific Ry. Co.; retired. Home: Topeka, Kan. Died Feb. 25, 1933.

DOTY, Douglas Zabriskie, editor and publisher; b. New York, Oct. 15, 1874; s. Samuel W. and Charlotte G. (Zabriskie) D.; ed. Stevens prep. sch., Hoboken, N.J., Columbia Grammar Sch., and 2 yrs. in Sch. of Mines, Columbia U., class of '97; m. Josephine Whiting, June 25, 1903. Spl. writer Boston Journal, 1898-99; editorial staff New York Sunday Herald, 1899-1901, McClure Syndicate, 1901-02; reader and lit. adviser to the Century Co., 1902-14; editor Century Magazine and sec. of The Century Co., 1914-17; editor Cosmopolitan Mag., 1917-18; lit. adviser and mem. lit. staff Harper & Bros., 1918—. Home: New York, N.Y. Died Feb. 20, 1935.

DOTY, Paul, mech. engr.; b. Hoboken, N.J., May 30, 1869; s. William Henry Harrison and Anna (Langevin) D.; M.E., Stevens Inst. Tech., 1888; m. Mary Reddy, Apr. 8, 1913; 1 dau., Diana. Engr. with United Gas Improvement Co., Phila., 1888-95; engr. with Am. Light and Traction Co., New York, 1895-1917; v.p. and gen. mgr. St. Paul Gas Light Co., 1904-17; chmn. Minn. Bd. Registration for Architects, Engrs., and Land Surveyors, 1921—; v.p. St. Paul Trust & Savings Bank, 1921-24; regional reconditioning supervisor Home Owners' Loan Corp., Atlanta, Ga., 1934-35. Served as lt. col. Corps of Engrs., U.S.A., 1917-18; gen. staff U.S.A., constrn. adviser to Sec. of War, Washington, 1918-19. Democrat. Catholic. Home: St. Paul, Minn. Died Dec. 3, 1938.

DOUBLEDAY, Frank Nelson, publisher; b. Brooklyn, Jan. 8, 1862; s. William Edwards and Ellen M. (Dickinson) D.; ed. Brooklyn Poly. Inst.; m. Neltje De Graff, June 9, 1886 (died 1918); m. 2d, Florence Van Wyck, Nov. 27, 1918. Entered employ of Charles Scribner's Sons, 1877, and remained with that house 18 yrs.; refounded and edited The Book Buyer, 1884, and was made mgr. Scribner's Magazine when it was established, 1886; mem. Doubleday & McClure Co., pubs., 1897-1900; pres. Doubleday, Page & Co., 1900-27; chmn. bd., 1928—, Doubleday, Doran & Co., pubs. of The World's Work, Country Life, The American Home, Short Stories, West. Home: Oyster Bay, N.Y. Died Jan. 30, 1934.

DOUBLEDAY, Neltje De Graff ("Neltje Blanchan"), author; b. Chicago, Oct. 23, 1865; d. Liverius and Alice De Graff; ed. pvt. schs.; m. Frank Nelson Doubleday, June 9, 1886. Author: The Piegan Indians, 1889; Bird Neighbors, 1897; Birds that Hunt and Are Hunted, 1898; Nature's Garden; Our Wild Flowers and Their Insect Visitors, 1900; How to Attract the Birds, 1902; Birds Every Child Should Know, 1907; The American Flower Garden, 1909. Home: Oyster Bay, N.Y. Died Feb. 1918.

DOUGHERTY, Curtis, ry. official; b. Otterville, Ill., July 30, 1863; s. Henry E. and Dyantha (Curtis) D.; C.E., Washington U., St. Louis, 1885; m. Catherine Molitor, Oct. 18, 1887. In office chief engr., Wis. Central Ry., 1887-88; engr., C.&W.I. R.R., 1888-92; asst. engr., 1892-93, roadmaster Chicago div., 1893-1902, supt. Springfield div., 1902-07, I.C. R.R.; asst. chief engr., 1907-10, chief engr. maintenance of way and supplies, Nov. 1, 1910—, Cincinnati, New Orleans & Tex. Pacific Ry. (Southern Ry. System, lines west). Died Mar. 30, 1919.

DOUGHERTY, George A., clergyman; b. Baltimore, May 21, 1861; s. Michael and Margaret (Mooney) D.; A.B., St. Mary's Sem., Baltimore, 1886; S.T.L., N. Am. Coll., Rome, Italy, 1889; hon. D.D., by spl. brief of Congregation of Studies, Rome, 1909. Ordained R.C. priest, Rome, Sept. 20, 1890; pastor, Waldorf, Md., 1891-92; asst. pastor, St. Augustine's Ch., Washington, 1892-1903; pvt. sec. to rector of Catholic U. of America, 1903-05, asst. treas., 1905—, asst. sec., 1910—, vice-rector, Apr. 16. 1910—, Catholic Univ. of America; apptd. domestic prelate by Pope Benedict XV, Jan. 1921. Died Oct. 18, 1929.

DOUGHERTY, George S., detective, author; b. Cressona, Pa., Apr. 5, 1865; s. Charles A. and Ellen Jane D.; self-ed. Formerly newspaperman and printer; with Pinkerton's Nat. Detective Agency, N.Y. City, 1888-1911; dep. police commr. and chief of detectives, Police Dept., City of New York, 1911-14; partner Dougherty's Detective Bureau and Mercantile Police, N.Y. City, 1914—. Catholic. Author: In Europe, 1922, 1927; The Criminal as a Human Being, 1924. Contbr. Saturday Evening Post, Liberty, Fawcett's, etc. Known for successful detective exploits. Introduced finger print system of identification in U.S. Home: Flushing, L.I. Died July 16, 1931.

DOUGHERTY, Hugh, banker; b. Greenville, O., July 28, 1844; s. William and Margaret D.; ed. in country school nr. Greenville, O., until 1862; m. Emma Gilliland, Oct. 25, 1877. Enlisted Co. F, 94th Ohio Inf., Aug. 1862; was in battles at Richmond, Ky., Perryville and Stone River; taken prisoner at Stone River; deputy recorder Darke Co., O., 2 yrs.; asst. cashier First Nat. Bank, Bluffton, Ind., 4 yrs.; partner in private bank of John Studebaker & Co., 1869-89, when name was changed to The Studebaker Bank; pres. until July 1904, when became v.p. Fletcher Savings Trust Co., Indianapolis. Was largely interested in building Fort Wayne, Cincinnati & Louisville City R.R., and Toledo, St. Louis & Kansas City R.R. Mem. Ind. Senate, 1871-75. Dem. candidate for state treas., 1898; pres. bd. trustees De Pauw Univ. Home: Indianapolis, Ind. Died Nov. 16, 1925.

DOUGHERTY, John, congressman, lawyer; b. Platte Co., Mo., Feb. 25, 1857; attended William Jewell Coll., but was not graduated; lawyer; city atty. Liberty, Mo., 5 terms; editor and propr. Liberty Tribune, 1885-88; pros. atty. Clay Co., Mo., 3 terms; m. Annie Park. Mem. Congress 3d Mo. dist., 1899-1905. Democrat. Home: Liberty, Mo. Died 1905.

DOUGHERTY, J(ohn) Hampden, lawyer; b. N.Y. City, Dec. 17, 1849; s. Charles H. and Elizabeth (Taylor) D.; A.B., Coll. City of N.Y., 1871; LL.B., Columbia, 1874; Coll. Phys. and Surg.; m. Alice Hill, May 25, 1876. Practiced with Man & Parsons, 1874-79; mem. Prichard, Smith & Dougherty, later Smith & Dougherty, 1884-98, Dougherty, Olcott & Tenney, 1902-08; now practicing alone. Has appeared before congressional coms. in opposition to ship subsidy bills, also in various investigations; receiver D. Appleton & Co., pubs., 1900. Prominent in campaigns for reform in New York municipal elections; commr. water supply, gas, and electricity under Mayor Low; mem. N.Y. City charter revision commns., 1907, 08 and retained by city to revise charter (proposed in 1911); active in Dem. nat. and N.Y. State campaigns. Trustee Brooklyn Poly. Inst. Author: The Electoral System of the United States, 1906; Power of Federal Judiciary over Legislation, 1912; Constitutional History of New York State, 1911 and 1915. Home: New York, N.Y. Died Sept. 6, 1918.

DOUGHERTY, Raymond Philip, Assyriologist; b. Lebanon, Pa., Aug. 5, 1877; s. Joseph Brant and Mary Elizabeth (Shaeffer) D.; A.B., Lebanon Valley Coll., Pa., 1897, A.M., 1903; B.D., Bonebrake Theol. Sem., 1910; Ph.D., Yale, 1918; m. Lulu E. Landis, Oct. 4, 1910. Prin. normal dept., Leander Clark Coll., Toledo, Ia., 1900-02; ordained U.B. ministry, 1904; prin. Albert Acad., Freetown, Sierra Leone, W. Africa, 1904-14; Am. v. consul at Sierra Leone, 1905-06, 1912-13; prof. of Biblical lit., Goucher Coll., Baltimore, Md., 1918-26; William M. Laffan prof. of Assyriology and Babylonian lit. and curator of the Babylonian Collection, Yale, 1926—. Annual prof. Am. Schs. of Oriental Research, Jerusalem and Bagdad, 1925-26. Attended World's Sunday Sch. Conv., Zurich, Switzerland, 1913, Internat. Archæol. Congress, Syria and Palestine, 1926; conducted archæol. survey in southern Babylonia, 1926. Mem. exec. com. Am. Schs. of Oriental Research; mem. com. on Mediterranean antiquities of Am. Council of Learned Socs. Author: Records from Erech, Time of Nabonidus, 1920; The Shirkûtu of Babylonian Deities, 1923; Archives from Erech, Time of Nebuchadnezzar and Nabonidus, 1923; Nabonidus and Belshazzar, 1929. Home: New Haven, Conn. Died July 13, 1933.

DOUGHERTY, William Edgeworth, brig. gen. U.S.A.; b. Aranmor, Co. Roscommon, Ireland, Sept 29, 1841; s. Michael Templeton and Barbara (D'Aignon) D.; ed. pvt. schs., Eng. and Germany; m. Maria L. McCarthy, May 9, 1866. Pvt., corporal, sergt. and 1st sergt., cos. K and G, 1st U.S. Inf., Mar. 10, 1860-Mar. 17, 1863; promoted through grades to col. 8th Inf., Mar. 5, 1901; brig. gen., Jan. 24, 1904; retired at own request after over 43 yrs.' service, Jan. 25, 1904. Bvtd. 1st lt., July 4, 1863 for siege of Vicksburg. Served in Army of the Potomac, 1862-63; Vicksburg, Teche and Red River campaigns, 1863-64; provost marshal Jefferson and Orleans parishes, La., 1865-66; served on plains, 1874-82; in Cuba, 1898; in P.I., 1901-02. Home: Fruitvale, Calif. Died July 13, 1915.

DOUGHTY, Mrs. Alla, vol. observer for weather bur., 1903—. Catholic. Supplies at own expense reading matter to persons living in isolated places, garrisons, hosps., Indian police agencies, etc.; also spl. periodicals for scientific use in S. Africa and Japan. Mem. Geog. Soc. of Phila., Pa. Nat. Conservation Assn., etc. Home: Milford, Pa. Deceased.

DOUGHTY, Walter Francis, educator; b. Emory, Miss., July 22, 1873; s. Daniel Milton and Sara Elizabeth (Ray) D.; A.B., U. of Texas, 1906; A.M., U. of Chicago, 1911; m. Ettie May Adler, Mar. 22, 1897. Began as teacher country schs.; earned money to pay expenses through coll.; prin. schs., Brandon, Tex., 1898-1903; supt. schs., McGregor, 1903-05, Marlin, 1906-13; state supt. pub. instrn., Tex., 1913-19; pres. Hillsboro Junior Coll. and supt. Hillsboro City schs., 1924—; pres. Bd. of Edn., Falls Co., 1909-11, Hill Co., 1925—. Waged campaign in 1914 for new sch. laws which led to reorganization of rural schools, passage of $2,000,000 appropriation for weaker country schools, and enactment of compulsory school attendance law, and vocational edn. law. Supervised war training service for federal govt. in pub. schs. of Tex. during World War; dist. vocational officer, Federal Bd. for Vocational Edn., 1919-23; organized rehabilitation work in Dist. 14, including states of Ark., Okla. and Tex., and handled claims of more than 30,000 disabled veterans. Democrat. Mason. Presbyn. Died August 20, 1931.

DOUGHTY, William Henry, surgeon; b. Augusta, Ga., Feb. 5, 1836; academical edn.; grad. Med. Coll. of Ga., now med. dept. Univ. of Ga., 1855; began practice in Augusta. Employed exclusively in hosp. duty, March 1862 to April 1865, as surgeon in C.S.A.; prof. materia medica and therapeutics, med. dept. Univ. of Ga., 1868-75; m. Julia Sarah Felder, Oct. 11, 1855. Home: Augusta, Ga. Died 1905.

DOUGHTY, William Henry, Jr., surgeon; b. Augusta, Ga., Nov. 9, 1856; s. late Dr. William Henry and Julia Sarah (Felder) D.; B.A., U. of Ga., 1875, M.D., 1878; post-grad. study, New York; m. Mary Eleanor Gamble, 1883. In practice, Augusta, 1878—; prof. surgery and dean, med. dept. U. of Ga., with which has been connected for many yrs.; consulting surgeon University Hospital; chief surgeon Charleston & Western Carolina Ry. and Augusta and Augusta-Aiken trolley lines and Georgia & Florida Ry. Pres. Ga. State Bd. Health; trustee Augusta Orphan Asylum, Acad. of Richmond Co. Fellow Am. Acad. Medicine, Am. Coll. Surgeons. Mason. Home: Augusta, Ga. Died June 22, 1923.

DOUGLAS, Amanda Minnie, author; b. New York, July 14, 1837; d. John N. and Elizabeth (Horton) D.; ed. City Inst., New York; removed to Newark, 1853. Author: In Trust, 1866; Sydnie Adriance, 1867; Stephen Dane, 1868; Six Kathie Books, 1868-70; Claudia, 1869; Home Nook, 1870; The Old Woman Who Lived in a Shoe, 1870; Whom Kathie Married, 1871; Lost in a Great City, 1872; Seven

Daughters, 1873; Nelly Kinnard's Kingdom, 1874; Heroes of the Crusades; From Hand to Mouth, 1875; Hope Mills, 1876; A Woman's Inheritance, 1877; The Foes of Her Household, 1878; A Modern Adam and Eve., 1879; Out of the Wreck, 1880; The Fortune of the Faradays, 1881; The Heirs of Bradley House, 1882; Osborne of Arrochar, 1883; Bertha Wray's New Name, 1884; In the King's Country, 1886; Floyd Grandon's Honor, 1892; In Wild Rose Time, 1894; Her Place in the World, 1895; Sherburne Series, 6 vols., 1895-1900; Larry ($2,000 prize story, Youth's Companion), 1897; Little Girl in New York, 1897; Little Girl in Boston, 1897; Little Girl in Philadelphia, 1898; Little Girl in Washington, 1899; A Question of Silence, 1901; Almost as Good as a Boy, 1901; Little Girl in Old New Orleans, 1902; Little Girl in Old Detroit, 1903; Little Girl in Old Chicago; Little Girl in Old San Francisco; Helen Grant's School Days; Helen Grant's Friends; Helen Grant's Year at Aldred House; Helen Grant in College, 1906; A Little Girl in Old Quebec, 1906; Helen Grant, Graduate; Helen Grant, Teacher, 1909; A Little Girl in Old Pittsburgh, 1909; Helen Grant's Decision, 1910; Helen Grant's Harvest Year, 1911; Children in the Little Old Red House, 1912; Red House Children at Grafton, 1913. Home: Newark, N.J. Died July 18, 1916.

DOUGLAS, Charles A., lawyer; b. Fairfield Co., S.C., Jan. 31, 1862; s. John S. and Margaret B. D.; A.B., Erskine Coll., Due West, S.C., 1880; LL.B., Columbia, 1882; LL.D., Erskine Coll., 1920; studied constl. law, Georgetown U.; m. Augusta Aiken, 1885; children—Charles Simonton, Alexander Talley, Margaret Boyce (Mrs. Herbert Adair), Patsy Aiken. Began practice at Winnsboro, 1883, later at Columbia; settled in Washington, D.C., 1895; sr. mem. Douglas Obear & Douglas. Mem. S.C. Ho. of Rep., 1884-90; mem. law faculty Georgetown U., 1895-1915; chief counsel for John L. Phillips in war frauds lumber case; counsel for Senator Burton K. Wheeler in Govt. conspiracy prosecution; counsel for William J. and W. Sherman Burns of Burns Internat. Detective Agency in jury shadowing case; Am. counsel in negotiations for recognition of Mexican Govt. under Carranza; Am. counsel for Nicaragua, Panama and Cuba many yrs.; assisted in securing ratification by U.S. Senate of treaty involving purchase of Nicaraguan Canal route and Isle of Pines treaty with Cuba; gen. counsel for Cuban govt. Decorated by Cuban Govt. with medal of Carlos de Cespedes, rank of Comdr. Presbyn. Democrat. Author: (with John W. Daniel) Elements of Negotiable Instruments. Home: Washington, D.C. Died Oct. 31, 1939.

DOUGLAS, Davison McDowell, coll. pres.; b. Blackstock, S.C., June 20, 1869; s. Rev. James and Margaret (McDowell) D.; A.B., Davidson Coll., N.C., 1895; Louisville Theol. Sem., 1895-96; B.D., Columbia (S.C.) Theol. Sem., 1899; A.M., U. of S.C., 1899; studied Princeton, 1899-1900, Johns Hopkins, 1904-06; D.D., Davidson Coll., 1912; LL.D., Southwestern Presbyn. U., 1924; m. Lydia Welch, Sept. 16, 1903; children—Elizabeth Moffatt, Margaret McDowell. Ordained Presbyn. ministry, 1900; pastor, Brevard and Davidson River chs., N.C., 1900-04, Md. Av. Ch., Baltimore, 1904-11; pres. Presbyn. Coll. of S.C., 1911-27; pres. U. of S.C., Jan. 1927—. Moderator, Synod of S.C., 1925; trustee Columbia Theol. Sem. Home: Columbia, S.C. Died Aug. 1, 1931.

DOUGLAS, George Bruce, mfr.; b. Waterloo, Ia., Sept. 23, 1858; s. George and Margaret (Boyd) D.; Ia. State Coll. Agrl. and Mechanic Arts, 1874-76; State U. of Ia., 1876-77; m. Irene Hazeltine, June 1, 1892. Mem. Douglas & Stuart, cereal mfrs., 1875-91; organized, 1894, Douglas & Co., mfrs. linseed oil, Cedar Rapids and Minneapolis (sold out to Am. Linseed Co., 1898); organized, 1902, and pres. Douglas & Co., now Douglas Co., mfrs. of corn starch; v.p. Cedar Rapids Nat. Bank. Trustee Coe College. Prog. Republican. Presbyterian. Home: Cedar Rapids, Ia. Died Nov. 12, 1923.

DOUGLAS, George William, clergyman; b. New York, July 8, 1850; s. William Bradley and Charlotte Cornelia Dickinson (Ferris) D.; B.A., Trinity Coll., Conn., 1871, M.A., 1874; grad. Gen. Theol. Sem., 1874; Oxford, Eng., and U. of Bonn, 1874-76 (S.T.D., Hobart, 1885; D.D., Trinity, 1895, U. of the South, 1899); m. Cornelia de Koven, d. Judge Hugh T. Dickey, of New York, Sept. 3, 1884. Deacon, 1874, priest, 1878, P.E. Ch.; tutor Gen. Theol. Sem., 1877-78; asst. minister Calvary Ch., New York, 1878-79; vicar Trinity Ch., New York, 1879-86; rector St. John's Ch., Washington, D.C., and trustee of Washington Cathedral, 1888-91; rector Trinity Ch., New Haven, Conn., 1895-98; select preacher Grace Ch., New York, and instr. in Training Sch. for Deaconesses, 1898-1904; examining chaplain Diocese of New York (chmn. bd.), and sr. canon of Cathedral of St. John the Divine, 1904—. Declined presidency of Hobart Coll., Geneva, N.Y., 1885. Mem. Clerical Club, the Clericus, Churchman's Assn. Social Service Commn. of Diocese of New York; mem. general com. of Church Congress; Chapter of Cathedral of St. John the Divine. Author: Essays in Appreciation, 1912; (song) God Bless America; Christ's Challenge in this World's Crisis (advent sermons in Cathedral of St. John the Divine), 1918; Spiritual Healing and the Holy Communion, 1923, 24. Home: Tuxedo Park, N.Y. Died Oct. 20, 1926.

DOUGLAS, Henry Kyd, lawyer; b. Shepherdstown, W.Va., Sept. 29, 1840; s. Rev. Robert and Mary (Robertson) D.; grad. Franklin and Marshall Coll., 1859; grad. of Judge Brockenbrough's Law School, Lexington, Va., 1860; unmarried. Private, sergt., lt., capt., maj. col., brig.-comdr. C.S.A.; a.-d.-c. to Stonewall Jackson, asst. adj.-gen. to Gens. Edward Johnston, J. B. Gordon, Early, Pegram, Johnston, and Walker; comdr. Light Brigade from Petersburg to Appomattox, the brigade that fired the last shot at Appomattox and was last to stack arms; capt., lt. col., col., adj. gen. of Md.; maj. gen. comdg. Md. troops on strike of 1894; candidate for Congress, 6th Md. dist., 1888; judge 5th judicial circuit, Md. Gold Democrat. Home: Hagerstown, Md. Died 1903.

DOUGLAS, James, mining engr.; b. Que., Can., 1837; s. Dr. James and Elizabeth (Ferguson) D.; A.B., Queen's U., Kingston, Can., 1858; (LL.D., McGill U., 1899); m. Naomi, d. late Walter Douglas, of Glasgow, Scotland, Nov. 1860. Was prof. chemistry, Morrin Coll., Quebec; has resided in U.S., 1875—, coming to take charge of copper works at Phœnixville, Pa.; later identified with copper industry of Ariz., and Sonora and R.R. of the S. West & Northern Mexico; chmn. bd. Phelps Dodge Corp., Copper Queens Consol. Mining Co., El Paso & Southwestern Co., El Paso & Southwestern R.R. Co.; pres. Old Dominion Co. of Me., etc. With late Dr. T. Sterry Hunt did much original work in hydrometallurgy of coppers. Awarded Instn. of Mining and Metallurgy (Eng.) gold medal, 1908; John Fritz medal, 1915. Home: Spuyten Duyvil, N.Y. Died June 25, 1918.

DOUGLAS, James H., mfr.; b. Norham, Ont., Can., Dec. 15, 1858; s. Alexander and Margaret (Henderson) D.; ed. pub. schs., Can.; m. Inez Boynton, Sept. 15, 1891. With Quaker Oats Co., 1895—, 1st v.p., 1905—, also chmn. exec. com.; dir. Am. Sugar Refining Co., Armour & Co. Mem. Art Inst. Chicago, Field Mus. Natural History. Home: Lake Forest, Ill. Died Dec. 27, 1930.

DOUGLAS, John, surgeon; b. New York, N.Y., Aug. 5, 1875; s. Henry and Ella Amelia (McKee) D.; Sc.B., Coll. City of N.Y., 1894; M.D., Columbia, 1898; post-grad. study, Vienna, 1900; m. Mrs. Elizabeth Thayer Hoag (nee Ramsburg), Oct. 24, 1911; children—Elizabeth Thayer, Helen Audrey. Interne St. Luke's Hosp., N.Y. City, 1898-1900, asst. surgeon, 1903-16, asso. surgeon, 1916-27, attending surgeon, 1927—, pres. med. board, 1932-33; adjunct asst. surgeon Bellevue Hosp., 1903-07, asst. surgeon, 1907-11, visiting surgeon, 1911-27, cons. surgeon, 1927—; surgical dir. Knickerbocker Hosp., 1922-30, cons. surgeon, 1930—; asst. surgeon Gen. Memorial Hosp., 1909-10; cons. surgeon Harlem Eye and Ear Hosp., 1929—; instr. N.Y. Univ. and Bellevue Med. Coll., 1904-12, clin. prof. surgery, 1912—. Mem. Draft Bd., N.Y. City, World War. Fellow Am. Coll. Surgeons. Home: New York, N.Y. Died Dec. 4, 1938.

DOUGLAS, Julia S., educator; b. Dunkirk, N.Y., 1852; d. Joseph and Julia Blair Colman; ed. Vassar and Mich. State Normal School (Kan. Univ., A.B.); m. Selwyn Douglas, lawyer. Prin. of city high school 8 yrs.; supt. city schools 4 yrs.; pres. Okla. Ty. and Indian Ty. Federation of Women's Clubs, which she organized; has founded 4 libraries; secured donation from Hon. Andrew Carnegie for library bldg. in Oklahoma City; organized Territorial Humane Soc. Wrote: The Novel as an Educator, Quar. Rev.; The Ishmaelite of Oklahoma, same. Home: Oklahoma City, Okla. Ty. Died 1902.

DOUGLAS, Orlando Benajah, physician; b. Cornwall, Vt., Sept. 12, 1836; s. Amos and Almira (Balcom) D.; acad. edn. Brandon, Vt.; M.D., Univ. Med. Coll. (New York U.), 1877; m. Mary A. Rust, Dec. 27, 1864 (died Aug. 31, 1873); m. 2d, May L., d. Rev. A. C. Manson, Sept. 16, 1875 (died 1913). Pvt., lt. and adj. 18th Mo. Vols. and acting asst. adj. gen. in Civil War; twice wounded. Asst. surgeon, 1877-83, surgeon and dir., 1883-1902, cons. surgeon, 1902—, Manhattan Eye, Ear and Throat Hosp.; prof. diseases of nose and throat, New York Post-Grad. Med. Sch. and Hosp., 1889-1901. Pres. N.H. Orphans' Home, 1905—; mem. exec. com. Y.M.C.A. of N.H. Cons. surgeon N.H. Soldiers' Home. Mason. Home: Concord, N.H. Died Dec. 1920.

DOUGLAS, Robert Martin, judge; b. Douglas, N.C., Jan. 28, 1849; s. Stephen Arnold (U.S. senator from Ill.) and Martha Denny (Martin) D.; A.B., Georgetown U., 1867, A.M., 1870 (LL.D., 1897); m. Jessie M., d. Judge Robert P. Dick, of Greensboro, N.C., June 23, 1874; father of Robert Dick D. Pvt. sec. to gov. of N.C., 1868; col. militia, 1868-71; sec. to President Grant, 1869-73; U.S. marshal, N.C., 1873-83; standing master in chancery, U.S. Circuit Ct., 1888-96; asso. justice Supreme Ct. of N.C., 1897-1905; renominated by acclamation by Rep. State Conv., but entire ticket defeated; again nominated by acclamation, 1906, for corp. commr., and led the ticket, but defeated; again nominated by acclamation for Supreme Ct., 1910, but declined; sr. mem. Douglas & Douglas, Greensboro, N.C., 1905—. Republican, 1867—. Catholic. Home: Greensboro, N.C. Died Feb. 8, 1917.

DOUGLAS, Stephen Arnold, lawyer; b. Rockingham Co., N.C., Nov. 3, 1850; s. Stephen A. (U.S. senator from Ill.) and Martha Denny (Martin) D.; grad. Georgetown Coll., D.C.; studied law under Richmond M. Pearson, chief justice N.C.; adj. gen. N.C., 1870; master in chancery County Court, Chicago, 1880; pros. atty., Chicago, 1891; m. Agnes MacDowell, 1902. Democrat. Home: Chicago, Ill. Died 1908.

DOUGLAS, William Lewis, governor; b. Plymouth, Mass., Aug. 22, 1845; s. William and Mary C. (Vaughan) D.; ed. at brief irregular periods in pub. schs. of Mass.; (LL.D., Tufts Coll., 1905); when 5 yrs. old lost father by death; m. N. Augusta Terry, Sept. 6, 1868. At age of 7 went to work for an uncle, who set him to pegging shoes, and except for a brief return to his mother when 11 yrs. old, worked for his uncle 8 yrs.; worked in cotton mill at Plymouth at 15, and later in factory at Chiltonville, Mass.; afterward went to Hopkinton and S. Braintree, Mass., where learned bootmaking; worked as journeyman and foreman at Brockton, 1876, when began with small shop, from which has built up business with capacity of 17,600 pairs of shoes daily, and owns 117 retail shoe stores in large cities. Mem. Mass. Ho. of Rep., 1884-85, Senate, 1887; mayor of Brockton, 1890; gov. of Mass., 1905. Home: Brookline, Mass. Died Sept. 17, 1924.

DOUGLAS, William Wilberforce, judge; b. Providence, R.I., Nov. 26, 1841, s. Rev. William and Sarah (Sawyer) D.; A.M., Brown U., 1861, LL.D., 1902; served in U.S. Vols., 1861-64; 2d lt., 1st lt. and capt. 5th R.I. Vols. and 5th R.I. Heavy Arty.; with Burnside Expdn., North Carolina; LL.B., Albany Law Sch., 1866; m. Anna Jean Bennett, June 30, 1884. U.S. commr., 1874-90; mem. R.I. Ho. of Rep., 1871-73, Senate, 1890; mem. Providence Common Council, 1873-76; justice, 1891-1905, chief justice, 1905-08, Supreme Ct. of R.I. Trustee Brown U., 1902—. Div. judge advocate R.I. Militia, 1866-74; asst. adj. gen., 1881, adj. gen., 1882. Judge advocate gen. G.A.R., 1871-77. Moderator Charitable Bapt. Soc., 1900-14. Dir. Narragansett Electric Lighting Co., 1889—, v.p., 1916—. Commr. Dexter Donation, 1909-13; mem. commn. to report revised Constn. of State, 1912—. Home: Providence, R.I. Died 1929.

DOUGLASS, Andrew Ellicott, astronomer Lowell Observatory, 1894—; b. Windsor, Vt., 1867; s. of Rev. Malcolm Douglass; ed. Punchard Free (high) School, Andover, Mass., until 1884; grad. Trinity Coll., Hartford, Conn., 1889, A.B.; unmarried. Was employed in astron. work at Harvard Coll. Observatory, 1889-94, then at Lowell Observatory, Flagstaff, Ariz. Home: Flagstaff, Ariz. Died 1901.

DOUGLASS, Benjamin Wallace, writer, fruit grower; b. Indianapolis, Ind., Feb. 17, 1882; s. William Wilson and Catherine (Jackson) D.; prep. edn., Shortridge High Sch., Indianapolis, 1898-1902; student Central Coll. Phys. and Surgeons, Indianapolis, 1903-04; m. Clara Ziegler, Aug. 18, 1909. Field agt. State Bd. of Forestry, 1904-06; state entomologist, Ind., 1907-11; fruit grower and canner, 1911—, developing Hickory Hill Farmstead Community. Mem. Ind. Acad. Science, Nature Study Club of Ind. (co-founder; hon. mem.). Republican. Presbyn. Author: Orchard and Garden, 1917; Every Step in Beekeeping, 1921; Fruit Growing, 1922; The New Deal Comes to Brown County, 1936. Home: Trevlac, Ind. Died Dec. 6, 1939.

DOUGLASS, Earl, geologist, paleontologist; b. Medford, Minn., Oct. 28, 1862; s. Fernando and Abigail Louisa (Carpenter) D.; ed. U. of Dak., Vermillion, S.D., 1888; S.D. Agrl. Coll., 1889 and 1892; B.S., Ia. State Coll., 1893; M.S., U. of Mont., 1900; fellow, Princeton U., 1900-02; m. Pearl C. Goetschius, Oct. 20, 1905; 1 son, Gawin Earl. Taught sch. with interruptions, 1883-1900; prin. schs., Virginia City, Mont., 1897-98; taught geology, physical geography and physics, U. of Mont., 1899-1900; received life teacher's certificate in Mont.; asst. under Prof. William Trelease in Mo. Bot. Gardens, St. Louis, 1890-91; engaged in research work in dept. of vertebrate paleontology, Carnegie Mus., Pittsburgh, 1902-24. In charge obtaining U. of Utah collection of skeletons from the Dinosaur Nat. Monument, 1923, 24. Teaching in pub. schs., studying geol. and making collections especially of fossil vertebrates, 1894-1900; with Princeton scientific expdn. in Mont., summer 1901, collecting Cretaceous dinosaurs and marine reptiles, also made collections from Tertiary and other formations of Montana and N.D.; discovered, 1909, an immense deposit of Comanchean dinosaur skeletons near Jensen and Vernal, Utah; this region later set aside as the Dinosaur Nat. Monument. Investigating oil problems, including the origin of oilshales, asphalts, etc. Home: Salt Lake City, Utah. Died Jan. 13, 1931.

DOUGLASS, George C.; b. Granville, N.Y., June 16, 1876; s. Chester G. and Emma (Heald) D.; A.B., A.M., Williams, 1899; D.D., Syracuse, 1916; m. Mabel R. Parker, Aug. 24, 1899; children—Ruth E., Paul F., Anna F. Ordained M.E. ministry, 1903; pastor Blue Mountain Lake, N.Y., 1899, Chestertown, 1900-02, Corinth, 1903-04, Gloversville, 1904-13, Saratoga Springs, 1914-20; supt. Northern Dist. Troy Conf. N.Y., 1921-22, Central Dist. Troy conf., 1923-24; publishing agt. M.E. Ch., 1924—; treas. Methodist Book Concern (an Ohio corp.), Episcopal Fund of M.E. Ch. Mem. bd. trustees of M.E. Ch., Gammon Theol. Seminary; mem. Ecumenical M.E. Conf., 1930; mem. Federal Council Chs. of Christ in America; trustee Green Mountain Junior Coll., Union Coll. of Barbourville, Ky., Christ Hosp.; trustee Internat. Council Religious Edn.; mem. World Council of World's Sunday School Assn. Home: Cincinnati, O. Died May 21, 1940.

DOUGLASS, John Watkinson, lawyer; b. Phila., Oct. 25, 1827; s. Joseph M. and Martha D.; ed. pub. schs., Erie, Pa.; studied law in office of James Thompson, Erie. Admitted to Erie bar, 1850; collector internal revenue, 19th Pa. dist., 1862-69; 1st deputy commr. internal revenue, 1869-71; commr. internal revenue, U.S., 1871-75; in practice in D.C., 1875—; mem. 1889-93, and pres. bd. commrs., D.C. Died 1909.

DOUGLASS, Lucille Sinclair, artist, lecturer, writer; b. Tuskegee, Ala.; d. Walton Eugene and Mary (Sinclair) D.; A.B., Woman's Coll., Tuskegee, Ala.; studied with Lucien Simon and René Menard, Paris, 1909-14, and with Alexander Robinson on field trips in Europe and N. Africa. Mem. editorial staff Shanghai (China) Sunday Times, 1921-24; out-of-door painter and etcher, specializing in scenes of Far East; made etchings of ruins of temples at Angkor in jungles of Cambodia, at request of French Colonial Govt., for exhibition at French Colonial Exhbn., 1927; illustrated books on China and Angkor for Florence Ayscough and Helen Churchill Cander, 1925-32. Etchings on exhbn. in Met. Mus., Pub. Library (New York), Library of Congress, Corcoran Gallery (Washington), R.I. Sch. of Design (Providence), Mus. of Fine Arts (Minneapolis), Addison Gallery of Art (Andover, Mass.), Canadian Nat. Acad. (Montreal), British Mus. (London), Museé Guimet (Paris), L'Ecole Française d'Extremé Orient (Hanoi), and in pvt. collections in America, Europe and China. Home: New York, N.Y. Died Sept. 26, 1935.

DOUGLASS, Truman Orville, clergyman; b. Bethel, Bond Co., Ill., May 3, 1842; s. John and Jane (McCord) D.; A.B., Ill. Coll., Jacksonville, 1865; B.D., Chicago Theol. Sem., 1868; (D.D., Tabor Coll., Ia., 1893); m. Maria Greene, June 25, 1868. Mem. Co. C, 145th Ill. Inf., 100 days' service, summer of 1864. Ordained Congl. ministry, 1868; pastor, Osage, Ia., 1868-82; supt. Congl. Home Missions of Ia., 1882-1907, then hon. supt. Mem. bd. dirs. Chicago Theol. Sem., 1888-1917; trustee Ia. Coll. Republican (1st vote for Lincoln, 1864). Author: The Pilgrims of Iowa, 1911. Home: Claremont, Calif. Died Sept. 11, 1925.

DOUTRICH, Isaac H., congressman; b. Dauphin Co., Pa., Dec. 19, 1871; s. Eli and Caroline D.; grad. Keystone State Normal Sch., Kutztown, Pa.; m. Lena Erb (died 1933). Engaged in retail clothing business at Harrisburg and other towns of Pa.; pres. Doutrich and Co.'s stores in Harrisburg; mem. 70th to 74th Congresses (1927-37), 19th Pa. Dist. Republican. Home: Harrisburg, Pa. Died May 28, 1941.

DOVER, Elmer, asst. sec. U.S. treasury; b. McConnelsville, Ohio, Apr. 14, 1873; s. John Wesley and Frances (Winn) D.; public school edn., McConnelsville; m. Martha Peebles, Jan. 25, 1898 (died 1932); 1 dau., Mary Elizabeth (wife of Gerald Todd). Newspaper reporter and editor, 1889-97; sec. to late Senator M. A. Hanna, 1897-1904; sec. Rep. Nat. Com., 1904-08, Nat. Advisory Com., 1908-09. V.p. and Pacific Coast mgr. of H. M. Byllesby Co., engrs., Chicago, 1910-19; pres. Western Rubber Co., Tacoma, Wash., 1919-20; in charge presdl. campaign of Warren G. Harding on Pacific Coast, 1920; asst. sec. U.S. treasury, 1921-22; receiver First Nat. Bank, Sedro-Wooley, Wash., 1932-33. Mason. Home: Tacoma, Wash. Died Oct. 3, 1940.

DOW, Arthur Wesley, artist; b. Ipswich, Mass.; s. David F. and Mary P. (Annable) D.; ed. Ipswich High Sch., Putnam High Sch., Newburyport, Mass., and classical edn. under pvt. instrn.; studied art in Boston and at Paris, pupil of Boulanger and Lefebvre; m. M. Eleanor Pearson, 1893. Pictures in Salon, Paris, 1886-87; hon. mention, Paris, 1889; medal, Buffalo Expn. Formerly curator Japanese art, Mus. of Fine Arts, Boston; instr. art, Pratt Inst., Brooklyn, 1895-1904; instr. composition at Art Students' League, New York, 1897-1903; dir. Ipswich Summer Sch. of Art, Ipswich, Mass.; prof. fine arts, Teachers Coll., Columbia U., 1904—. Conglist. Author: Composition (7 edits.), 1898; Ipswich Prints (color prints for schs.), 1902; Along Ipswich River (color prints from wood blocks). Home: Ipswich, Mass. Died Dec. 13, 1922.

DOW, Caroline Bell, educator; b. Fowlerville, N.Y., Dec. 16, 1858; d. Benjamin Franklin and Caroline (Capron) D.; A.B., Vassar Coll., 1880; post-grad. work in music at Columbia and in Paris, France. Dean, nat. training system of Y.W.C.A., 1907-22 (retired). Dir. MacDowell Memorial Assn. Presbyn. Home: Buffalo, N.Y. Died 1935.

DOW, Charles Mason, banker; b. Randolph, N.Y., Aug. 1, 1854; s. Albert Gallatin and Lydia A. (Mason) D.; Oberlin (O.) Coll., 1869-71; studied law, Randolph, 3 yrs.; (LL.D., Bethany Coll., 1914, Niagara U., 1915); m. Eleanor Jones, Randolph, Jan. 12, 1876. Mem. A. G. Dow & Son, bankers, Randolph, 1876-79, Dow & Co., bankers, Bradford, Pa., 1879-84; v.p. Salamanca (N.Y.) Trust Co., 1880—; pres. Jamestown (N.Y.) Nat. Bank, 1888-99, Nat. Chautauqua Co. Bank, 1899—; v.p. Title Guarantee & Trust Co. of New York, 1903-04; trustee American Surety Co., New York, 1903-15; director Buffalo Br. Fed. Reserve Bank of New York, 1919—. Mem. bd. commrs. of State Reservation at Niagara, 1898-1914 (pres. 1903-14); pres. Park Bd., Jamestown, 1900—; dir. Letchworth Park and Arboretum, State of N.Y.; mem. N.Y. Constl. Conv., 1915; dir. Co. Liberty Loan campaigns; mem. Fed. Milk Commn., 1918; fed. fuel adminstr., Chautauqua Co., 1918. Republican. Presbyn. Author: A History of the State Reservation at Niagara, 1915; Bibliography and Anthology of Niagara Falls, 1919. Address: Jamestown, N.Y. Died Dec. 10, 1920.

DOW, Frederick Neal; b. Portland, Me., Dec. 23, 1840; s. Gen. Neal D.; ed. Portland Acad. and Friends' School, Providence, R.I.; LL.D., Boston U., 1929; LL.D. from Colby College, Waterville, Me., 1932; m. Julia Dana Hammond, Oct. 22, 1864. Pres. Evening Express Pub. Co., Portland Gas Light Co.; pres. Portland R.R. Co., etc.; pres. Casco Mercantile Trust Co., Union Safe Deposit & Trust Co. Served city govt. and school com.; Gov.'s Council of Me.; chmn. Rep. State Com. Collector port of Portland, 1883-85, 1890-95; mem. Me. Ho. of Rep., 1887-90 (speaker 1889-90); commr. Phila. Expn., 1876. Home: Portland, Me. Died Nov. 27, 1934.

DOW, George Francis, author, antiquarian; b. Wakefield, N.H., Jan. 7, 1868; s. George Prince and Ada Bingham (Tappan) D.; ed. pub. schs. and under pvt. tutelage; m. Alice Goldsmith Waters, June 1, 1920. In wholesale metal business, Boston, 1886-97; sec. Essex Inst., Salem, Mass., 1898-1918, also dir. its mus. and editor its publs.; curator and dir. of Soc. for Preservation of N.E. Antiquities, Boston, 1919—, also mng. editor its publs.; organized Marine Research Soc., Salem, 1922, and editor its publs. Mem. Mass. Gen. Court (legislature), 1900; chmn. bd trustees Topsfield Town Library; chmn. Topsfield Park Commn.; founder and sec. Topsfield Hist. Soc. and editor its publs. Republican. Conglist. Mason. Author: Whale Ships and Whaling, 1925; Slave Ships and Slaving, 1927; Arts and Crafts of the Eighteenth Century in New England, 1927; Sailing Ships of New England, 1928; Every Day Life in the Massachusetts Bay Colony, 1935, etc. Home: Topsfield, Mass. Died June 5, 1936.

DOW, Herbert Henry, chemist, mfr.; b. Belleville, Ont., Feb. 26, 1866; s. Joseph H. and Sarah J. (Bunnell) D.; grad. Case Sch. Applied Science, 1888, hon. D. Eng., 1924; Doctor of Engring., U. of Mich., 1929; m. Grace A. Ball, Nov. 16, 1892. Prof. chemistry and toxicology, Huron Street Hosp. Coll., Cleveland, 1888-89; mfr. chemicals, 1889—, as partner, or officer Midland Chem. Co., Inc., Dow Process Co., and Dow Chem. Co., pres. and gen. mgr. latter. Awarded Perkin medal by Soc. of Chem. Industry, 1930. Has developed many new chem. processes on which over 100 patents have been granted. Formerly member Advisory Com. of Council of Nat. Defense, The Chem. Alliance, Inc.; mem. Board Public Works, and Bd. of Edn., Midland, Mich. Trustee Case Sch. Applied Science. Presbyn. Mason. Home: Midland, Mich. Died Oct. 15, 1930.

DOW, Howard Malcolm, musician; b. Boston, Mar. 11, 1837; s. Mark and Charlotte (Parsons) D.; began study of singing and voice culture under George D. Russell, Boston, at age of 7; organ, under A. U. Hayter, at 9; piano, under Hugo Leonhard; composition, under George F. Suck; m. Mary Agnes Rice, July 19, 1864 (died 1889). Church organist at 16, and continued for 52 yrs., serving at South Congl. Ch., Arlington St. Ch., Unity Ch. (29 yrs.), Second Unitarian Ch., etc. On account of ability to interpret the most difficult scores at sight, gained wide recognition as accompanist for leading mus. artists. Won nat. reputation in Masonic fraternity as organist, composer and choir leader, his works being used in lodges all over the U.S. and Can.; retired, 1905. Mason. Author: The Masonic Orpheus, 1869; Sacred Quartettes, 1879; Dow's Responses and Sentences for Church Service, 1884; The Sacred Orpheus (for male voices), 1888. Home: New Rochelle, N.Y., and Glendale, Calif. Died June 12, 1912.

DOWD, Charles Ferdinand, educator; b. Madison, Conn., April 25, 1825; grad. Yale, 1853 (A.M., 1856); course of philosophy U. City of New York, Ph.D., 1888. Prin. and prof. several high and normal schools; later supt. public schools, Waterbury, Conn.; for years past and now prin. Temple Grove Sem. at Saratoga. Originated the idea of longitude standards for railroad time and with others secured its adoption by Am. ry. mgrs. in 1883. Home: Saratoga Springs, N.Y. Died 1904.

DOWD, Charles North, surgeon; b. New Britain, Conn., 1858; s. Charles F. and Harriet M. (North) D.; A.B., Williams, 1879, A.M., 1882, hon. Sc.D., 1924; M.D., Coll. Phys. and Surg. (Columbia), 1886; studied in London and Heidelberg; m. Eleanor R. Bliss, 1891 (died 1898); 1 dau., Constance Eleanor; m. 2d, Christiana Nostrand, 1908. Attending surgeon Gen. Memorial Hosp., 1894-1914, St. Mary's Free Hosp. for Children, 1905-14, Roosevelt Hosp., 1914-24; cons. surgeon, Roosevelt and Gen. Memorial hosps., St. Mary's Free Hosp. for Children, Richmond Memorial Hosp., Lulu Thornley Home for Crippled Children, Saratoga Hosp.; prof. clinical surgery, Columbia. Maj., M.C. U.S.A., 1917-19. Fellow Am. Coll. Surgeons, Am. Surg. Assn. Home: Saratoga Springs, N.Y. Died May 24, 1931.

DOWD, John Worthington, univ. pres.; b. Zaleski, O., Jan. 16, 1847; s. John and Olive (Fuller) D.; A.B., Ohio U., 1869, A.M., 1872, LL.D., 1903; m. Ella M. Kurtz, Aug. 31, 1871; children—Jessie (Mrs. Frederick A. Stafford), George Kurtz, Charles Fuller. Prin. Grammar Sch. and mem. Bd. of Superintendence, Chillicothe, O., 1869-74; supt. schs., Troy, 1874-80, Toledo, 1880-86; pres. Smead-Dowd Co., heating and ventilating engrs., Toronto, Can., 1886-96; mgr. Am. Warming & Ventilator Co., Toledo, 1896-1904; mem. Bd. of Elections, Toledo and Lucas County, 1904-16; prof. history and social sciences, Toledo U., 1918-25; elected pres. same univ. (in his 79th yr.), 1925. Pres. bd. of Edn., Toledo, 1900-01. Republican. Methodist. Mason. Died May 13, 1926.

DOWD, William, v.p. Mo., Kan. & Tex. Ry. Co.; was several years pres. Louisville, New Albany & Chicago Ry.; 2d v.p. Mo., Kan. & Tex. Ry., 1888-92; 3d v.p. same, 1892 and later v.p. same. Died 1900.

DOWE, Jennie Elizabeth Tupper, author; b. Wilbraham, Mass., Dec. 11, 1845; d. Edwin Lombard and Katherine (Moore) Tupper; grad. Westfield Normal Sch., 1862, and studied Wilbraham Acad.; m. William Hilton Dowe, June 29, 1864. Extensive contbr. of verse and songs to Scribner's, 1877-80, St. Nicholas, 1880-93, Century Mag., 1882—, notably 50 "Songs of Ireland," 1891-98. Author: Purty Molly Rhu, 1902; Songs of Childhood, 1904; Children's Historical Pageant, 1911; Song of the Mountain, 1913; The Minute Men, 1915. Home: Roxbury, Mass. Died Mar. 6, 1919.

DOWELL, Cassius C., congressman; b. near Summerset, Ia., Feb. 29, 1864; s. James W. and Martha (Rees) D.; ed. Bapt. Coll., Des Moines, Ia., and Simpson Coll. at Indianola, Ia.; A.B., Drake U., 1886, LL.B., 1887; m. Belle I. Riddle, Nov. 8, 1928. Admitted to Ia. bar, 1888, and began practice in Des Moines; mem. 25th, 26th and 26th extra sessions, Ia. Gen. Assembly, 1894-97, Senate, 1902-10; speaker pro tem. of House, 26th Gen. Assembly; mem. 64th to 72d Congresses (1915-33), 7th Ia. Dist., and 73d and 75th Congresses (1933-35, 1937-39), 6th Ia. District. Republican. Mem. University Ch. of Christ. Mason. Home: Des Moines, Ia. Died Feb. 4, 1940.

DOWER, Walter H., art editor; b. Syracuse, N.Y., Apr. 9, 1883; s. Philip and Mehitable Robinson (Holkings) D.; ed. high sch., Syracuse; spl. drawing and design course, Pratt Inst., Brooklyn; studied Nat. Acad. Design, New York, 1903-05; m. Nora Wade Clark, Sept. 25, 1908. Art editor Home Pattern Co., New York, 1907-15; art editor Saturday Evening Post, 1915-19, Ladies' Home Journal, 1919-27; art editor McCall's Magazine, New York, 1927—. Republican. Baptist. Deceased.

DOWLING, Alexander, judge; b. Hillsboro, Va., Dec. 19, 1839; s. Henry M. and Harriet I. D.; family removed to New Albany, Ind., 1840; ed. pub. and pvt. schs.; m. Cornelia F. Kiger, Oct. 18, 1859. Admitted to bar, 1858; elected pros. atty. for Ct. of Common Pleas, at 19; city atty., New Albany, Ind., 1860-68; refused appmt. on Supreme Ct. bench offered by Gov. Hovey, 1891; justice Supreme Ct. of Ind., 1898-1904. Republican. Home: New Albany, Ind. Died Dec. 11, 1917.

DOWLING, Austin, archbishop; b. New York, Apr. 6, 1868; s. Daniel and Mary (Santry) D.; A.B., Manhattan Coll., New York, 1887; St. John's Sem., Brighton, Boston; Catholic U., Washington, 1890-92. Ordained R.C. priest, 1891; pastor, St. Mary's Ch., Warren, R.I., 1904-05, Sts. Peter and Paul's Cathedral, 1905-12; consecrated bishop of Des Moines, Ia., Apr. 25, 1912; archbishop St. Paul, Minn. Mar. 25, 1919. Died Nov. 29, 1930.

DOWLING, John William, physician; b. New York, Sept. 24, 1864; s. John William and Frances Anne (Dowley) D.; A.B., Columbia, 1884; M.D., New York Homœ. Med. Coll., 1886; m. Alice Bliss, June 2, 1886. Practiced in New York, 1886—; prof. practice of medicine, New York Homœ. Med. Coll. and

Flower Hosp., 1892—; also sec. of faculty; visiting phys., Flower Hosp. Home: New York, N.Y. Died May 11, 1914.

DOWLING, Michael John, banker; b. Huntington, Mass., Feb. 17, 1866; s. John Jerome and Honora (Barry) D.; ed. Carleton Coll., Minn.; m. Jennie Leonora Bordewich, Oct. 2, 1895. Has lived in Minn. from boyhood; badly frozen in blizzard, 1880; dealer in real estate from 1897; pres. Olivia State Bank; sec. Nat. Rep. League, 1895-97; spl. commr. to P.I., 1900; speaker Minn. Ho. of Rep., 1901. Republican. Home: Olivia, Minn. Died Apr. 25, 1921.

DOWLING, Oscar, M.D.; b. Montgomery, Ala., Oct. 29, 1866; s. Rev. Angus and Laura L. (Boswell) D.; Athens Collegiate Inst.; M.D., Vanderbilt U., 1888; post-grad. work, New York, Chicago, and New Orleans polyclinics, New York Eye and Ear Infirmary, and clinics in London, Berlin, Paris and Mexico City; m. Mrs. Lula Tindall George, Mar. 16, 1915. County health officer, Henry Co., Ala., 1892-94. House surgeon, 1896-97, sr. resident surgeon, 1897-99, asst. to surgeon in charge, 1896-99, Eye, Ear, Nose and Throat Hosp., New Orleans; oculist and aurist State Charity Hosp., Shreveport, La., 10 yrs., also various ry. cos.; specialist in treatment of the eye, ear, nose and throat; mem. firm of Dowling & Scales, Shreveport. Mem. La. State Bd. of Health, 1906-08, and apptd. pres., 1910, reapptd., 1912, 16; term extended by legislative enactment in 1921 to 1925; reapptd. Sept. 1, 1925. Founded, 1904, and editor Medical Recorder, changed to Journal Southern Med. Assn., 1908. Mem. La. State Game Commn., 1908-10; v.p. La. State Fair Assn., 1910, 12; prof. Pub. Health, Tulane U. Home: Shreveport, La. Deceased.

DOWLING, Victor James, lawyer; b. New York, July 20, 1866; s. Denis and Eliza Fierlants (Faider) D.; A.B., Manhattan Coll., 1883, A.M., 1888; LL.B., New York U., 1887; LL.D., Manhattan Coll., 1906, New York U., 1908, Fordham U., 1912, Notre Dame, 1917, Columbia, 1930, La Salle College, Phila., 1931; m. Mary Agnes Ford, June 16, 1891 (died 1920); children—Dorothy (Mrs. Daniel L. Daly), Natalie, Victoria. Mem. New York Assembly, 1894, New York Senate, 1901-04; justice of Supreme Court of N.Y., terms 1905-18, 1919-32; reëlected 1918, receiving nomination of both Republicans and Democrats; justice Appellate Div., 1st Dept., 1911—; presiding justice Appellate Div., Jan. 1, 1927-Mar. 28, 1931, retiring to enter practice of law as member Chadbourne, Stanchfield & Levy, New York. Mem. exec. com. Tammany Hall, and leader 24th Assembly Dist., 1896, 97, 98, 1903, 04; sachem Tammany Soc., 1903-04. Created by Pope Benedict XV Knight of the Order of St. Gregory the Great, 1916; Commander Order of the Holy Sepulchre, by the Latin Patriarch of Jerusalem, 1908; Chevalier of the Legion of Honor (French), 1919, Officer, 1928; comdr. Order of the Crown (Belgian), 1919; created Papal Chamberlain of Cape and Sword, 1st class, by Pope Pius XI, July 13, 1927; comdr. Order of the Cross of Merit (Hungary), 1928; comdr. Order of the Crown (Italy), 1928; Grand Cross Order of St. Lazaire of Jerusalem, 1929; Grand Prior of America; Grand Knight Order of St. George, and of Our Lady of Mt. Carmel; Grand Cross Order of Holy Sepulchre (pres. gen. of U.S., 1930); Magistral Knight of Sovereign Mil. Order of Knights of Malta, 1931. Catholic. Home: New York, N.Y. Died Mar. 23, 1934.

DOWMAN, Charles Edward, surgeon; b. Quincy, Fla., Apr. 1, 1882; s. Charles Edward and Julia Robena (Monroe) D.; A.B., Emory U., Atlanta, Ga., 1901; M.D., Johns Hopkins, 1905; m. Caroline Westmoreland, Mar. 1908; 1 son, Charles Edward. Asst. pathol. instr., Charlottenburg Krankenhaus, Berlin, 1905-06; asst., Univ. Chirurg. Klinik, Breslau, Germany, 1906-07; clin. clk., Nat. Hosp. for Paralyzed and Epileptic, London, 1907; attending surgeon, Hillman Hosp., Birmingham, Ala., 1909-15; also prof. pathology, Birmingham Med. Coll., 1911-13, and asso. in surgery, U. of Ala., 1913-15; instr., asso. and asst. prof. surgery, Emory U., 1915-24; neurol. surgeon, Scottish Rite Hosp. for Crippled Children, Eggleston Memorial Hosp., Grady Memorial Hosp., Ga. Bapt. Hosp., Piedmont Hosp., 1918—. Served as capt., later maj., Med. Corps, U.S.A., 1917-19; chief of surg. team, mobile hosps., St. Mihiel and Argonne offensives. Fellow Am. Coll. Surgeons. Democrat. Methodist. Home: Atlanta, Ga. Died Nov. 14, 1931.

DOWNER, Charles Alfred, college prof.; b. Jersey City, N.J., May 3, 1866; s. Alfred Sayre and Caroline (de La Vere) D.; A.B., Coll. City of New York, 1886; Ph.D., Columbia, 1901; unmarried. Teacher of French, 1891—; prof. French, Coll. City of New York, 1904—; prof. Romance langs., 1909—. Decorated Chevalier de la Légion d'Honneur, 1913, Officer same, 1926; Knight Order of Crown of Italy, 1919. Author: Frédéric Mistral, Poet and Leader in Provence, 1900; A First Book in French, 1910; A First Course in French, 1922. Home: New York, N.Y. Died Aug. 14, 1930.

DOWNER, James Walker, coll. prof.; b. Orange Co., Va., June 23, 1864; s. William Walker and Lucy Mary (Reynolds) D.; A.B., U. of Va., 1895, A.M., 1897; Ph.D., U. of Pa., 1905; m. Corneille Willingham, Dec. 28, 1909. Began as teacher pub. schs., Va.; teacher high sch., Charlottesville, Va., 1895-96, McCabe's Univ. Sch., Richmond, Va., 1897-98; teacher Latin, Richmond Coll., 1898-99; prin. high sch., Clifton Forge, Va., 1899-1900; teacher Marion (Ala.) Mil. Inst., 1900-03; fellow U. of Pa., 1903-05; teacher Friends' Central Sch., Phila., 1905-08; prof. Latin, Baylor U., 1908—. Democrat. Baptist. Home: Waco, Tex. Died Mar. 19, 1932.

DOWNES, William Howe, art critic; b. Derby, Conn., Mar. 1, 1854; s. William E. and Jane Maria (Howe) D.; ed. pvt. schs. and tutors; studied German and French abroad 1 yr.; m. Helen Louise Sawyer, Sept. 28, 1875 (died 1891); children—Dorothy Helen (Mrs. Wm. Ernest Pierce), Dennis Sawyer, Barbara Howe, Carl Sawyer, Jerome Ireland Howe; m. 2d, Sarah Olive Lowell, May 16, 1892; 1 son, William Lowell. Went to Vienna Expn., 1873, as a newspaper corr.; reporter on Boston Globe several yrs., from 1874; later on Daily Advertiser; art critic Boston Evening Transcript over 30 yrs.; retired, 1922. Honorary asso. Guild of Boston Artists. Author: Life and Works of Winslow Homer, 1911; John S. Sargent, His Life and Work, 1925. Address: Boston, Mass. Died Feb. 19, 1941.

DOWNEY, David George, clergyman; b. Manor Hamilton, Co. Leitrim, Ireland, Sept. 21, 1858; s. Archibald and Mary Anne (Hawksby) D.; A.B., Wesleyan U., 1884, A.M., 1887; D.D., Wesleyan, 1899; Litt.D., Cornell Coll., Iowa, 1916; LL.D., Wesleyan U., 1920; studied Drew Theol. Sem., 1879; m. Lilian May Terrill, June 2, 1887; 1 son, Bradford. Ordained M.E. ministry, 1884; stated supply Rocky Hill, Conn., 1880-82; pastor Windsor, Conn., 1883-84, North Ch., Hartford, 1885-87, Mamaroneck, N.Y., 1888-91, Stamford, Conn., 1892-96, St. John's, Brooklyn, 1897-1907; asst. sec. Bd. Edn. and S.S., M.E. Ch., 1907; corr. sec. Bd. S.S., 1908-12; book editor M.E. Ch., 1912-28; lit. adviser Methodist Book Concern, 1928—. Chaplain Conn. Ho. Rep. and Senate, 1885-87; mem. Bd. Missions M.E. Ch.; trustee Wesleyan U. Author: Modern Poets and Christian Teaching. Home: Mt. Vernon, N.Y. Died Mar. 7, 1935.

DOWNEY, George Eddy, judge U.S. Court of Claims; b. Rising Sun, Ind., July 11, 1860; s. Alexander C. and Sophia J. (Tapley) D.; B.A., Asbury (now DePauw) U., Greencastle, Ind., 1880, M.A., 1883; m. Mary C. Wells, June 25, 1885; 1 son, Alexander C. Began practice of law at 21 at Rising Sun, Ind.; editor Franklin Democrat, Brookville, Ind., 1882-84; returned to practice, 1884; removed to Aurora, Ind., 1886; mayor of Aurora, 1894-1902; judge 7th Jud. Circuit of Ind., 1903-13 (resigned); Comptroller of the Treasury, May 15, 1913; apptd. judge of U.S. Court of Claims, Aug. 3, 1915. Democrat. Methodist. Home: Aurora, Ind. Died May 22, 1926.

DOWNEY, George Faber, army officer; b. in Ariz. Ty., July 30, 1866. Commd. maj. add. p.-m. vols., May 17, 1898; maj. p.-m., U.S.A., Feb. 2, 1901; promoted through grades to brig. gen. Apr. 27, 1921; retired. Home: Washington, D.C. Died Apr. 1, 1935.

DOWNEY, John Florin, univ. dean; b. Hiramsburg, O., Jan. 10, 1846; s. Thomas and Mary Ann (Scott) D.; served 11th Mich. Inf., Jan. 1864-Oct. 1865; B.S., Hillsdale Coll., 1870, M.S., 1873, A.M., 1877, LL.D., 1917; post-grad. U. Mich., 1871-72; C.E., State Coll. of Pa., 1877; attended lectures, univs. of Edinburgh and Göttingen, 1901-02; m. Stella Osborne, Dec. 28, 1875; children—Hal, Romeyn; m. 2d, Margaret E. Downey, Jan. 2, 1896. Instr. Hillsdale Coll., 1870-71; prin. schs., Cassopolis, Mich., 1871-72; prof. mathematics, State Coll. of Pa., 1873-80; prof. mathematics, 1880-1915, dean Coll. Science, Lit. and Arts, 1903-15, U. of Minn.; dean emeritus and prof. mathematics emeritus, 1915—; prof. mathematics and astronomy, U. of Nanking, China, 1916-18, Peking U., China, 1918-19; del. to World Edn. Conf., Edinburgh, July 1925; observer sessions League of Nations, Geneva, Sept. 1925. Author: Elements of Differentiation and Integration, 1898; Higher Algebra, 1900; The New Revelation Through the Spectroscope and the Telescope, 1914. Address: Pasadena, Calif. Died Apr. 28, 1939.

DOWNEY, June E(tta), psychologist; b. Laramie, Wyo., July 13, 1875; d. Stephen Wheeler and Evangeline (Owen) D.; A.B., U. of Wyo., 1895; A.M., U. of Chicago, 1898, Ph.D., 1907; unmarried. Prof. philosophy and psychology, U. of Wyo., 1915—. Author: The Heavenly Dykes (poems), 1904; Graphology and the Psychology of Handwriting, 1919; Plots and Personalities (with Edwin E. Slosson), 1922; The Will-Temperament and Its Testing, 1923; The Kingdom of the Mind, 1927; Creative Imagination, 1929. Home: Laramie, Wyo. Died Oct. 11, 1932.

DOWNEY, Stanley Wilson Crowell, lawyer; A.B., U. of New Brunswick, 1894, A.M., 1896; LL.B., Harvard, 1899. Admitted to Mass. bar, 1899, and began practice at Boston; pres. Babson Can Co., Bostonian Garage, Inc., C. E. Giles Co., Portland Street Garage Corp., Thompson Sq. Theatre Co.; sec., dir. Atlantic Kompost Co., Town Taxi, Inc., W. E. Betts Co.; dir. numerous cos. Died Jan. 18, 1827.

DOWNING, Augustus S., educator; b. Baltimore, Oct. 18, 1856; s. George F. and Margaret (Walter) D.; A.B., Pa. Coll., 1874, A.M., 1877; LL.D., Syracuse U., 1906, Muhlenberg, 1913; Pd.D., State Normal Coll., Albany; L.H.D., Pa. Coll., 1912; m. Louise J. Brown, July 17, 1889. Engaged in ednl. work, 1874-1927; state inst. instr., 1890-94; state supt. of insts. and training classes, 1894-98; prin. N.Y. Training Sch. for Teachers, 1898-1904; 3d asst. commr. of edn. in charge elementary schs. of the state and the instns. for the training of teachers therefor, 1904-08, asst. commr. and dir. of professional edn., in charge of higher edn., including colls., professional and tech. schs., and the administration of the laws relating thereto, 1908-26, dep. state commr. edn., 1926-Sept. 1927 (ret.). Home: Albany, N.Y. Died Feb. 1936.

DOWNING, John Franklin, banker; b. Virginia, Ill., Aug. 24, 1854; s. David Rice and Mary (Gill) D.; B.S., Ill. Coll., Jacksonville, 1879 (A.M., 1910); m. Jessie Burnham, Mar. 30, 1898. Clerk, Farmers Nat. Bank, Virginia, Ill., 1879-82; paying teller, Armour Bros. Bank, Kansas City, 1882-85; real estate and loan business, Kansas City, 1885-89; organized N.E. Safe Deposit & Trust Co., 1889, pres. Jan. 1, 1890, and elected pres., 1898, of its successor, N.E. Nat. Bank; became chmn. exec. com. Fidelity Nat. Bank & Trust Co., Jan. 1, 1929; treas. Safety Savings Assn. Treas. Fine Arts Inst., Kansas City; trustee Ill. Coll. Republican. Conglist. Home: Kansas City, Mo. Died Sept. 4, 1935.

DOWNING, John Robert, banking; b. Nicholasville, Ky., May 24, 1874; s. Robert A. and Ellen S. (Welch) D.; student Nicholasville High Sch., 1880-90; m. Evelyn S. Craig, Nov. 21, 1902; 1 son, Henry. Clk. Noland, Wilmore & Sears, 1889-97; clk. Farmers Bank of Ky., 1897-1900; successively cashier, v.p. and pres. Georgetown Nat. Bank, 1900-16; v.p. Phoenix and 3d Nat. Bank, Lexington, Ky., 1916-19; v.p. Citizens Union Nat. Bank, Louisville, 1919-30, pres., 1930—; treas. Ky. & Indiana Terminal R.R. Co.; dir. Fidelity & Columbia Trust Co. Ky. State Mgr. for 2d Red Cross War Fund Campaign, 1918. Democrat. Episcopalian. Mason. Home: Louisville, Ky. Died June 25, 1939.

DOWNS, Lawrence Aloysius, ry. official; b. Greencastle, Ind., May 9, 1872; s. James and Mary (McCarthy) D.; B.C.E., Purdue U., 1894; Doctor of Engineering, same, in 1929; LL.D., Centenary Coll., La., 1931; m. Ida May Mulligan, Nov. 27, 1901; 1 dau., Mary Katherine (Mrs. John F. Oakley). Began with Vandalia Railroad, 1895; with Illinois Central R.R., engring. party, 1896; roadmaster, 1898-1907, asst. chief engr. maintenance of way, 1907-10, div. supt. Ia., Minn. and Ky. divs., 1910-14, gen. supt. Southern lines, 1914-16, Northern lines, 1916-19, asst. gen. mgr., 1919-20—all I.C. R.R.; v.p., gen. mgr. Central of Ga. Ry., 1920-24, pres. same co. and Ocean Steamship Co. of Savannah, 1924-26, chmn. bd. both cos., 1929—; pres. Ill. Central System, 1926-38, chmn. of bd., 1938—; dir. Continental Ill. Nat. Bank and Trust Co., Ry. Express Agency, Inc.; trustee Mutual Life Ins. Co. of New York; dir. Illinois Chamber of Commerce; trustee Armour Inst. Tech. Home: Chicago, Ill. Died Aug. 10, 1940.

DOWSE, William Bradford Homer, lawyer, mfr.; b. Sherborn, Mass., Feb. 29, 1852; s. Edmund (D.D.) and Elizabeth (Bowditch) D.; A.B., Harvard, 1873; LL.B., Harvard Law Sch., 1875; post-grad. work same, 1876; m. Fanny Reed, June 20, 1883; children—Dorothy Pineo (Mrs. F. Delano Putnam), Margaret, Beatrice (Mrs. C. Sinclair Weeks). Admitted to Mass. bar, 1875; specialized in patent causes, Boston and New York, 1876-1900; since engaged in mfg.; pres. Reed & Barton Corp. (gold and silversmiths), Taunton, Mass.; pres. Theo. B. Starr, Inc. (New York), U.S. Fastener Co.; treas. Consolidated Fastener Co. Pres. Home Market Club 11 yrs.; mem. Boston Chamber Commerce. Republican. Unitarian. Home: West Newton, Mass. Died Apr. 19, 1928.

DOXTATER, Lee Walter, dentist; b. Harold, S.D., Aug. 26, 1885; s. William George and Martha Louise (Gilligan) D.; student Lowville (N.Y.) Acad., 1902-05; D.D.S., U. of Mich., 1909; m. Helen L. Simpson, Nov. 22, 1927 (died 1930). In practice of dentistry, New York, 1909—; clin. prof. denture prosthesis, New York U., 1926-29, asso. prof. crown and bridge prosthesis, 1929-30, prof. crown and bridge prosthesis, 1930-31. Fellow Am. Acad. Restorative Dentistry. Author: Procedures in Modern Crown and Bridge Work, 1931, trans. into German, 1933. Home: New York, N.Y. Died June 17, 1935.

DOYLE, Alexander, sculptor; b. Steubenville, O., Jan. 1858; s. George and Alice C. (Butler) D.; ed. in Italy and in Am. pub. schs.; qualified for Cambridge U., but did not enter; began study of sculpture in acads. of Carrara and Florence, Italy, followed by several yrs. study at Rome and Paris; m. Fannie B. Johnson, 1881. Among notable works are marble portrait and pedestal at grave of John Howard Payne at Washington; marble statues Bishop Pinkney, Margaret

Haughrey, Senator B. H. Hill, Gen. Garfield; marble portrait group of two Cupples children, St. Louis, Mo.; bronze statues Gen. Albert Sydney Johnston and Robert E. Lee, New Orleans; Sergeant Jasper, Savannah, Ga.; Gen. Philip Schuyler for Nat. Revolutionary Monument, Saratoga; Gen. James B. Steedman, Toledo, O.; Horace Greeley, New York; Admiral Semmes, Mobile, Ala.; Gen. R. H. Anderson, Savannah, Ga.; Mrs. Emma Willard, Troy, N.Y.; Gen. G. H. Ward, Worcester, Mass.; Senators Thomas H. Benton, Frank P. Blair and John E. Kenna for U.S. Capitol; Francis Scott Key, Frederick, Md.; Soldiers' Monument at New Haven; Soldiers' Monument, Montgomery, Ala. Engaged in quarrying bldg. stone in Ind., 1899-1909; resumed sculpture, 1909; has since executed statue of E. M. Stanton, Steubenville, O., equestrian statue of Gen. G. T. Beauregard for City of New Orleans. Home: Dedham, Mass. Died Dec. 21, 1922.

DOYLE, Alexander P., clergyman; b. San Francisco, Calif., Feb. 28, 1857; s. Richard and Matilda (Shea) D.; A.B., St. Mary's Coll., San Francisco, 1875, A.M., 1876; Paulist Fathers, New York, 1875-80; (LL.D., Manhattan Coll., 1906). Ordained R.C. priest, 1880; in missionary work throughout U.S., 1880-92; founder Temperance Publ. Bur., 1893; editor Temperance Truth, 1892-1903, Catholic World Mag., 1893-1904; mgr. printing dept. Paulist Fathers, 1893-1904; gen. sec. Catholic Total Abstinence Union of America, 1894-1904; founder, editor 15 yrs. of The Missionary; built and endowed Apostolic Mission House on grounds of Catholic U., for training of missionaries for the home field and rector same, 1903—; prof. homoletics and pastoral theology, dir. and sec.-treas., Catholic Missionary Union. Superior Catholic chaplains in Army and Navy. Republican. Died Aug. 9, 1912.

DOYLE, C. W., physician, author; b. Landour, India, Aug. 29, 1852; father killed in action in Sepoy war, 1858; ed. at academy at Mussoorie, nr. birthplace; won Maddock scholarship there; studied at Calcutta Univ.; studied medicine in London, Edinburgh and Aberdeen; grad. M.D., U. of Aberdeen, 1875; practiced in England, 1875-88, then in Calif. Author: The Taming of the Jungle, 1899; The Shadow of Quong Lung, 1899. Home: Santa Cruz, Calif. Died 1903.

DOYLE, Cornelius James, lawyer; b. Carlinville, Ill., Dec. 6, 1871; s. Thomas and Mary E. (Findlay) D.; ed. pub. schs.; L.H.D., Lincoln Memorial U., 1932; m. Mary Ellen Wilhite, June 15, 1904. Admitted to Ill. bar, 1906, U.S. Supreme Court, 1910; city atty. of Greenfield, Ill., 1906-08, mayor, 1908-12; atty. State of Ill. Parole Bd., 1902-04; sec. State Bd. of Arbitration, 1904-08; 1st state fire marshal, 1911-12; sec. of state of Ill., 1912-13; asso. gen. counsel Nat. Bd. of Fire Underwriters, 1913—. Chmn. Ill. Rep. State Conv., 1912, Rep. State Central Com., 1928; del. to Rep. Nat. Conv., 1932 and 1936. Dir. Ill. State Hist. Assn. Home: Springfield, Ill. Died Apr. 19, 1938.

DOYLE, Edward H., banking commr.; b. Quebec, Can., Apr. 20, 1849; s. Lawrence and Bridget (Gahan) D.; ed. pub. schs.; m. Sarah J. Walsh, Sept. 9, 1872. Began in sawmills of Bay City, Mich., continuing until 1870; connected with B. B. Buckhout, hardware, Saginaw, 1870-75; in lumber business, 1875-80; identified with banking interests of J. Seligman, Saginaw, 1880-85, and in general charge of his affairs, 1885-97; mfg. cooperage stock at Wyandotte, Mich.; was engaged in completion of Majestic Bldg., Detroit, of which is half owner; commr. of banking for Mich., 1911-15. Republican. Catholic. Home: Grosse Pointe Farms, Mich. Died Jan. 5, 1919.

DOYLE, Gregory, physician; b. Ireland, Mar. 28, 1840; s. James and Anne (Roche) D.; arrived in America, 1841; student Niagara U., 1857-60 (LL.D., 1898); M.D., Univ. Med. Coll. (New York U.), 1865; m. Urania C. Morel, Oct. 21, 1868. Practiced at Syracuse, N.Y., 1865—; health officer, Syracuse, 1870-72; health commr., 1899-1904; surgeon House of Providence and St. Vincent's Orphan Asylum, 1870-1909; pres. U.S. Pension Bd., Syracuse, 1885-89; surgeon and maj. N.G.S.N.Y., 1872-90. Democrat. Catholic. Home: Syracuse, N.Y. Died July 23, 1913.

DOYLE, John Hardy, lawyer; b. Perry Co., O., Apr. 23, 1844; parents among earliest settlers in Maumee Valley; ed. Denison U.; m. Alice Fuller Skinner, 1868. Admitted to bar, 1865; judge Ct. Common Pleas, 1879; elected judge Supreme Ct. of Ohio, 1883. Pres. National Bar Assn., 1889-90; pres. Ohio State Bar Assn., 1893. Republican. Home: Toledo, O. Died Mar. 24, 1919.

DOYLE, John T., lawyer; b. New York, N.Y., Nov. 26, 1819; s. John and Frances (Glinden) D.; grad. Georgetown (D.C.) Univ., 1838, A.M., 1840; LL.D., 1889; studied law in New York; admitted to bar, May 1842; m. Antonia Pons, May 1863. Abandoned his profession in New York, Oct. 1851, and took charge as gen. agt. of Am. Atlantic and Pacific Ship Canal Co.'s enterprise of cutting ship canal across Nicaragua (company did not obtain the money and built no canal); resigned gen. agency, removed to Calif. and resumed professional practice; retired, 1890. In 1876 recovered from Mexican Govt. $904,000 for interest on moneys held by that govt. for Catholic Ch. of Calif.; claim was first case internat. arbitration brought before the Arbitration Tribunal at the Hague, through which in Oct. 1902 he recovered $1,426,000 for subsequent interest and a decision that Mexico should hereafter pay the ch. $43,050 per annum in perpetuity. Home: Menlo Park, Calif. Died 1906.

DOYLE, Robert Morris, naval officer; b. Dyersburg, Tenn., May 5, 1853; s. James Henry and Jane (Sampson) D.; grad. U.S. Naval Acad., 1875; m. Kate Amelia, d. Dr. Thomas Snowden, of Peekskill, N.Y., Oct. 19, 1882. Promoted through the various grades to rank of rear adm., June 7, 1913; retired May 5, 1915. Navigating officer U.S.S. Dixie, during Spanish-Am. War, 1898; comd. Culgoa, Chicago; comd. Missouri on cruise of battleships around the world, 1908; comdt. Norfolk Navy Yard, 1911-13; comdr.-in-chief Pacific Reserve Fleet, 1913-15; recalled to active duty and comdt. 14th Naval Dist. and U.S. Naval Sta., Pearl Harbor, Hawaii, June 13, 1918-May 15, 1919. Episcopalian. Died Dec. 15, 1925.

DOYLE, Sarah Elizabeth, teacher; b. Providence, R.I., Mar. 23, 1830; d. Thomas and Martha Dorrance (Jones) D.; ed. pvt., pub., and high schs.; (hon. A.M., Brown U., 1894); unmarried. Prin. girls' dept., Providence High Sch., 1878-92. Retired. First pres. and a founder of R.I. Women's Club; mem. first advisory bd. Gen. Federation of Women's Clubs, 1888-90; chmn. com. to raise funds for Women's Coll., Brown U.; pres. R.I. Soc. for Collegiate Edn. of Women; chmn. advisory council of Women's Coll. in Brown U.; dir. Providence Athenæum, 1889-1903; mem. com. of 5 citizens, apptd. by mayor to investigate pub. sch. management, 1898-99; mem. com. to form assn. for maintaining the Am. Women's table at Zoöl. Sta., Naples, Italy; one of founders R.I. Sch. of Design. Unitarian. Home: Providence, R.I. Died Dec. 21, 1922.

DOYLE, Thomas Aloysius, congressman; b. Chicago, Ill., Jan. 9, 1886; s. Thomas and Julia (Egan) D.; grad. high sch., 1904; m. Emile Carstens, June 26, 1918. Real estate and ins. business, Chicago; mem. City Council, Chicago, 1914-18; mem. Ill. Ho. of Rep., 1918-23; mem. Bd. Local Improvements, Chicago, May-Dec. 1923; mem. 68th Congress (1923-25), to fill vacancy, 4th Ill. Dist., reëlected to 69th and 71st Congresses (1925-31). Democrat. Catholic. Home: Chicago, Ill. Died Jan. 29, 1935.

DRACHSLER, Julius, sociologist; b. Bella, Czechoslovakia, Sept. 5, 1889; s. Jacob and Charlotte (Neugeboren) D.; B.S., Coll. City of N.Y., 1912; M.A., Columbia, 1915, Ph.D., 1921; certificate New York Sch. of Social Work, 1915; unmarried. Came to U.S., 1903, naturalized citizen, 1913. Vol. worker in social service, 1910; asst. sec. Jewish Big Brother Assn., 1913-15; sec. of faculty, Sch. for Jewish Communal Work, 1915-18; spl. expert, Bur. War Risk Insurance, 1918-19; asst. exec. dir., Bur. Jewish Social Research, 1919-20; dir. training course for community center workers, Jewish Welfare Bd., July-Sept. 1921, 22; asst. prof. economics and sociology, Smith Coll., 1919-22; asst. prof. sociology, Coll. City of N.Y., 1922—. Consultant, Bur. Jewish Social Research, New York. Jewish religion. Author: Democracy and Assimilation, 1920; Intermarriage in New York City, 1921. Home: New York, N.Y. Died July 22, 1927.

DRAKE, Alexander Wilson, art director; b. nr. Westfield, N.J., 1843; s. Isaac and Charlotte (Osborn) D.; m. Edith True, June 27, 1901. Studied and practiced wood engraving; later drew on wood for engravers; studied oil and water color painting. Taught drawing, Cooper Inst.; in business for himself as wood engraver, 1865-70; head of art dept. of Scribner's Monthly, 1870-81, when it became The Century, then art dir. The Century and St. Nicholas; identified with many important art movements in this country for past 25 yrs. Home: New York, N.Y. Died Feb. 4, 1916.

DRAKE, C(larence) St. Clair, M.D.; b. St. Thomas, Ont., Can., Jan. 23, 1870; s. Adelbert A. and Eliza J. (McIntosh) D.; ed. in Canada; M.D., Chicago Homœ. Med. Coll., 1891; m. Alice Adams, Dec. 16, 1897; 1 son, Carlton St. Clair. Began practice in Chicago, 1891; statistician for vital statistics, Chicago Health Dept., 1895-1909; editor Weekly Bulletin, same dept., 1909-14; mem., sec. and exec. officer Ill. State Bd. of Health, Apr. 13, 1914-July 1, 1917; dir. of pub. health State of Ill., July 1, 1917-Feb. 1, 1921; ednl. field dir. Am. Pub. Health Assn., 1925-29; mng. officer Jacksonville (Ill.) State Hosp., 1929—. Ednl. dir. Chicago Pageant of Progress Exp., 1921-22; ednl. dir. Nat. Health Expn., 1923-24. Mason. Died June 2, 1935.

DRAKE, Durant, coll. prof.; b. Hartford, Conn., Dec. 18, 1878; s. James McEwen and Maria (Upham) D.; prep. edn. Boston Latin Sch., 1890-96 (won 16 prizes); A.B., summa cum laude, Harvard, 1900; studied Harvard Grad. Sch. and Harvard Div. Sch., 1901-03, A.M., in philosophy, 1902; Ph.D., Columbia, 1911; m. Anna White, June 30, 1908. Resident, Univ. Settlement, New York, N.Y., 1900-01; traveled in Eng. and France, 1901; instr. philosophy, U. of Ill., 1911-12; asso. prof. ethics and philosophy of religion, Wesleyan Univ., Conn., 1912-15; prof. philosophy and edn., Vassar Coll., 1915—. Lectured in German, Swiss, and Italian Univs., 1923-24. Conglist. Author: Problem of Things in Themselves, 1911; Problems of Conduct, 1914; Problems of Religion, 1916; Shall We Stand by the Church? 1920; Essays in Critical Realism (with others), 1921; America Faces the Future, 1922; Mind and Its Place in Nature, 1925; The New Morality, 1928. Home: Poughkeepsie, N.Y. Died Nov. 25, 1933.

DRAKE, Francis Marion, banker, gov.; b. Rushville, Ill., Dec. 30, 1830; s. John Adams and Harriet Jane (O'Neal) D.; removed to Ft. Madison, Ia., 1837; ed. there; family removed, 1846, to Davis Co., Ia., founding there the village of Drakeville; m. Mary Jane Dord, Dec. 24, 1855 (died 1883). In 1852 with company of 16 men crossed the plains with ox-teams, arriving safely after a severe but successful encounter with Pawnee Indians; again crossed, 1854, with a drove of cattle, but returning by water narrowly escaped death in the wreck of the steamer Yankee Blade, lost in the Pacific, engaged in mercantile business at Drakeville and later at Unionville, Ia. Served, 1861-65, all grades, from private to col. and bvt. brig. gen. of vols. in Union army; was severely wounded; after war practiced law and engaged in railroad and banking enterprises; now pres. Albia & Centerville Ry. Co.; pres. Centerville (Ia.) Nat. Bank, and 1st Nat. Bank of Albia; pres. bd. of trustees Drake Univ., Des Moines, which he has liberally endowed; was gov. Iowa, 1896-98. Home: Centerville, Ia. Died 1903.

DRAKE, Franklin Jeremiah, rear adm.; b. Yates, N.Y., Mar. 4, 1846; grad. U.S. Naval Acad., 1868. Promoted ensign, Apr. 19, 1869; master, July 12, 1870; lt., Nov. 15, 1872; lt. comdr., Oct. 1, 1893; comdr., Mar. 3, 1899; capt., Sept. 11, 1903; retired as rear admiral, Dec. 10, 1906. In the summer of 1863, on board the Marion, in pursuit of Confederate steamer Tacony; served on the Gettysburg, 1868-69; signal duty at Washington, 1869-70; Colorado, 1870-73; on torpedo duty, 1873-74; Portsmouth, Jamestown and Independence, 1874-75; Navy Yard, Mare Island, 1875-76; coast survey steamer Hassler, 1876-78; Ticonderoga, 1878-81; Navy Yard, New York, 1881-83; spl. duty with Rear Admiral Shufelt, 1883-85; Pensacola, 1885-88; insp. of torpedo boats, 1888; insp. ordnance, 1888-92; spl. duty at Chicago Expn., 1893; Navy Yard, Boston, 1893-94; comd. Fish Commn. (steamer Albatross, 1894-96; exec. officer Oregon, 1896-97; Navy Yard, Mare Island, 1897-1900; comd. Culgoa, 1900-01; comdt. naval station, Cavite, and comdg. Monterey, 1901-03; Navy Yard, Mare Island, 1903-05; comd. Wisconsin, 1905-06. Tech. expert, Hague Tribunal, 1913-15; operations, revision of regulations, U.S.N., 1918-19-20. Died Jan. 30, 1929.

DRAKE, Fred Raymond; b. Easton, Pa., June 12, 1865; s. Samuel and Sarah (Arndt) D.; A.B., Lafayette Coll., 1886, A.M., 1889; m. Pearce Kinkead Fox, June 15, 1911; children—Margaret Kinkead, Frederick Raymond. Entered mercantile business, 1886; pres. Drake & Co., Inc., wholesale grocers; v.p. First Nat. Bk. & Trust Co.; pres. Fire Ins. Co. of Northampton County, Jan. 5, 1925—; dir. Wahnetah Silk Co., Catasauqua, Pa. Assisted in recruiting Easton City Guard; mustered into service, Pa. N.G., July 12, 1898, for Spanish-Am. War; elected 1st lt. at muster, capt., Sept. 27, 1898; apptd. aide, brigade staff of Gen. J. P. S. Gobin, Dec. 14, 1900; aide, div. staff, rank of maj., Apr. 6, 1906; retired Jan. 5, 1912. V.p. bd. Easton Pub. Library. Mem. Bd. Trade, Easton (hon.). Home: Easton, Pa. Died July 17, 1932.

DRAKE, James Calhoun, banker; b. Cincinnati, Ark., July 26, 1858; s. Wesley and Martha (Kellum) D.; grad. U.S. Naval Acad., 1880; m. Fanny Wilcox, Apr. 23, 1893. Resigned from U.S. Navy with rank of lt., 1896, and settled in Los Angeles; pres. Los Angeles T. & S. Bank; dir. First Nat. Bank, Pacific Mut. Life Ins. Co., etc. Home: Los Angeles, Calif. Died Mar. 13, 1921.

DRAKE, James Madison, newspaper publisher; b. Somerset Co., N.J., Mar. 25, 1837; s. James S. and Eunice (Martin) D.; ed. pub. schs., Elizabeth, N.J.; m. Margaret B. Taylor, Jan. 7, 1859. Publisher Mercer Standard, Trenton, N.J., 1853-54; started Evening News, 1857; Wide Awake, 1860. Alderman, Trenton, N.J., 1860-61. Served in Union army, 1861-65; unfurled first Union flag on Virginia soil, May 24, 1861; taken prisoner, May 16, 1864, at Drury's Bluff, Va.; escaped from Charleston, S.C., Oct. 6, 1864, reaching Union lines at Knoxville, Tenn., Nov. 22, 1864; awarded Congressional Medal of Honor for distinguished gallantry; capt. 9th N.J. Veteran Vols.; bvtd. brig. gen. by spl. act of N.J. legislature. Publisher Daily Monitor, Elizabeth, N.J., 1868-81, Elizabeth Sunday Leader, 1882-87, and Elizabeth Daily Leader, 1887-1900. Historian 9th N.J. Vols., and Medal of Honor Legion. Home: Elizabeth, N.J. Died Nov. 28, 1913.

DRAKE, Samuel Adams, editor and author; b. Boston, Dec. 1833; s. Samuel G. Drake, author and publisher, Boston; ed. in public schools of Boston.

Insp. and adjt. gen. Kan. militia, 1861; col. 1st regt. same, 1863; brig. gen. same, Feb. 1864; col. 17th Kan. vol. inf., July 1864; engaged in mil. operations in Kan. and Mo. during Civil war, 1861-65. Author: The Making of New England, 1886; The Making of the Great West, 1887; Burgoyne's Invasion, 1889; The Taking of Louisburg, 1891; The Battle of Gettysburg, 1892; The Making of Virginia, 1893; The Making of the Ohio Valley States, 1894; The Campaign of Trenton, 1895; The Border Wars of New England, 1897; On Plymouth Rock, 1898; The Myths and Fables of To-day, 1900 L 6; The Young Vigilantes, 1904. Died 1905.

DRAKE, Tracy Corey, hotel propr.; b. Chicago, Ill., Sept. 12, 1864; s. John B. and Josephine C. (Corey) D.; ed. Vt. Episcopal Inst., Burlington, 1877-79, Trinity Mil. Inst., Tivoli, N.Y., 1879-82; B.S., Rensselaer Poly. Inst., 1886; m. Annie Daughaday, Jan. 12, 1893; children—Carlos Corey, Francis Augustus. Entered employ of Drake, Parker & Co., proprs. Grand Pacific Hotel, Chicago, later admitted to partnership; European and Oriental travel, 1896-98; stock and bond broker, 1898-1900; management of estate of John B. Drake until 1907; with brother, John B. Drake, organized The Drake Hotel Co. and built The Blackstone, Chicago, also the Blackstone Theatre; 1919-21 with brother, organized The Whitestone Co. and built The Drake, on Lake Shore Drive, Chicago; now pres. The Drake Hotel Co., The Whitestone Co., The Blackstone Co. Democrat. Presbyn. Home: Lake Geneva, Wis. Died Mar. 3, 1939.

DRAKE, William Henry, artist; b. New York, June 4, 1856; common sch. edn.; studied Académie Julien, Paris, under Constant and Doucet. Hon. mention, Paris Expn., 1889; exhibited Paris Expn., 1900; illustrator of Rudyard Kipling's Jungle Book and other publs. A.N.A. Died June 23, 1925.

DRAPER, Andrew Sloan, educator; b. Westford, N.Y., June 21, 1848; s. Sylvester Bigelow and Jane (Sloan) D.; grad. Albany Acad., 1866; LL.B., Albany Law Sch. (Union U.), 1871; (LL.D., Colgate, 1889, Columbia, 1903, U. of Ill., 1905); m. Abbie Louise Lyon, May 8, 1872. Practiced law at Albany till 1885; mem. Albany Bd. of Edn., 1879-81, and 1890-92; mem. N.Y. Assembly, 1881; mem. Court of Commrs. of Ala. Claims, 1885-86; state supt. pub. instrn. N.Y., 1886-92; supt. instrn., Cleveland (O.) pub. schs., 1892-94; pres. U. of Ill., 1894-1904; first commr. of edn., State of N.Y., 1904—. Elected first supt. of schs. of Greater City of New York, 1898, but declined; mem. bd. U.S. Indian Commrs., 1902—(now chmn.). Editor ednl. dept. Ency. Americana; editor-in-chief Self Culture for Young People (10 vols.). Awarded silver medal Paris Expn., 1900, for monograph on The Organization and Administration of the Am. School System; awarded gold medal and one of 2 grand prizes given at St. Louis Expn., 1904, for collaborating two or more exhibits and for unusual services in ednl. administration. Dir. Nat. Commercial Bank; a gov. Dudley Obs., Albany. Author: The Rescue of Cuba; American Education. Home: Albany, N.Y. Died Apr. 27, 1913.

DRAPER, Daniel, meteorologist; b. New York, Apr. 2, 1841; s. late Dr. John William and Antonia Cœtana de Piva Pereira (Gardner) D.; ed. New York U. Grammar School; (Ph.D., New York U., 1880); m. Ann Maury Ludlow, Apr. 28, 1887 (died 1911). Studied science under his father; was his asst. in chemistry and physiology for several yrs. and his amanuensis for his Intellectual Development of Europe and other works. Served mech. apprenticeship of 5 yrs. at Novelty Iron Works, New York; dir. New York Meteorol. Obs., 1868-July 1, 1911, retired. Designed and made the self-recording instruments there; also helped his brother, late Henry Draper, M.D., to construct the telescopes, grind the mirrors and build his observatory at Hastings-on-Hudson. Home: Hastings-on-Hudson, N.Y. Died Dec. 21, 1931.

DRAPER, Eben Sumner, governor; b. Hopedale, Mass., June 17, 1858; s. George and Hannah B. (Thwing) D.; ed. Allen's Sch., W. Newton and Mass. Inst. Tech.; studied in machine shops and cotton mills; m. Nannie Bristow, Nov. 21, 1883. Admitted into firm George Draper & Sons., 1880; when the Draper Co. was founded, 1896, became the selling agt.; pres. Manville Co.; dir. Draper Co., Milford Nat. Bank, Queen City Cotton Co. (Vt.), Old Colony Trust Co., Nat. Shawmut Bank; v.p. Mass. Hosp. Life. Ins. Co. Mem. Corp., Mass. Inst. Tech.; trustee Milford Hosp., Peter Bent Brigham Hosp.; v.p. Am. Unit. Assn. Pres. Mass. Vol. Aid Assn., which raised $200,000 for hosp. ship "Bay State," for Spanish-Am. War, 1898; chmn. Mass. delegation Nashville Expn., 1897. Chmn. Rep. State Com., 1892; chmn. Mass. delegation Rep. Nat. Conv., 1896; presdl. elector, 1900; mem. Mass. State Bd. Agr., ex-officio, 1906-07-08-09; pres. Rep. Club of Mass., 1903-04; lt. gov. of Mass., 1906-07-08; gov. 1909-10, 1910-11. Home: Hopedale, Mass. Died Apr. 9, 1914.

DRAPER, Frank Winthrop, physician; b. Wayland, Mass., Feb. 25, 1843; s. James Sumner and Emmeline Amanda (Reeves) D.; ed. Brown Univ., A.B., 1862, A.M., 1865, Harvard, M.D., 1869; m. Fanny V. (Jones) Draper, Nov. 1, 1870. Served in Civ. War as pvt. 35th Mass. Vol. Inf.; promoted capt. 39th U.S.C.T., Apr., 1864, resigned June 10, 1865. In practice of medicine from 1869; visiting physician, Boston City Hosp.; editor Mass. Registration Reports; asst. editor Boston Med. and Surg. Jour.; med. examiner, Suffolk Co., Mass.; lecturer forensic medicine, asst. prof. and now prof. legal medicine, Harvard. Fellow Am. Assn. Arts and Sciences. Mem. State Bd. of Health, and of Loyal Legion. Unitarian. Republican. Author: Legal Medicine, 1904. Home: Brookline, Mass. Died 1909.

DRAPER, George Otis, mfr.; inventor; b. Hopedale, Mass., July 14, 1867; s. William Franklin and Lydia Warren (Joy) D.; ed. W. Newton English and Classical Sch. and Mass. Inst. Tech. (non-grad.); m. Lily Duncan, Apr. 28, 1892. Learned details of mfr. of cotton machinery in father's shops; partner, George Draper & Sons, Hopedale, from 1889 to its consolidation with Draper Co., 1897; an officer in some 25 corps. connected with textile mfg., quarrying, mining and the development of patented inventions; inventor of many patented mech. devices and improved details of the Northrop loom; expert on patents, and in cotton mfr. Pres. Draper Realty Co., Draper-Hansen Co., Michener Stowage Co., Sapphire Record & Talking Machine Co., Draper-Latham Magneto Co., Scholz Fireproofing Co., Farrington Co., Phillips Mfg. Co., Hilton Mfg. Co. Author: Searching for Truth, 1902; Still on the Search, 1904, More, 1908. Home: New York, N.Y. Died Feb. 7, 1923.

DRAPER, William Franklin, diplomat; b. Lowell, Mass., Apr. 9, 1842; s. George and Hannah (Thwing) D.; ed. common schs. and 2 yrs. at acad.; m. Lydia W. Joy, 1862; 2d, Susan Preston, 1890. Enlisted, 1861, Co. B, 25th Mass.; served through war, becoming lt. col. and bvt. brig. gen. of vols. After war engaged in mfg. cotton machinery; pres. Home Market Club, Boston, 1890; mem. Congress, 1892-97; U.S. Ambassador to Italy, 1897-1900. Home: Hopedale, Mass. Died 1910.

DRAPER, William H., congressman; b. Worcester Co., Mass., June 24, 1841; moved to Troy, N.Y., 1847, and established residence there; ed. pub. schs., Troy, until 1856. Engaged in mfg. cordage and twine under firm name of Wm. H. Draper & Sons. Was trustee Lansingburg, N.Y.; commr. of jurors Rensselaer Co., N.Y., 1896-1900; mem. 57th Congress (1901-03), 19th N.Y. Dist., and 58th to 62d Congresses (1903-13), 22d Dist. Republican. Home: Troy, N.Y. Died Dec. 7, 1921.

DRAPER, William Henry, M.D.; b. Brattleborough, Vt., Oct. 14, 1830; grad. Columbia, 1851; Coll. Phys. and Surgeons, New York, 1855; studied Paris and London; in general practice in New York from 1869; member of faculty and from 1880 prof. clinical medicine Coll. Phys. and Surgeons. Home: New York, N.Y. Died 1901.

DRAPER, William Kinnicutt, M.D.; b. New York, Feb. 2, 1863; s. William Henry and Elizabeth Wald (Kinnicutt) D.; A.B., Harvard, 1885; M.D., Coll. Phys. and Surg. (Columbia), 1888; interne, Roosevelt Hosp., 1888-90; studied Munich, Dresden, Vienna and Berlin, 1890-91; m. Helen Fidelia Hoffman, Dec. 28, 1898. Practiced, New York, 1891—; prof. clin. medicine, Coll. Phys. and Surg., 1910—; attending phys. Bellevue Hosp.; cons. phys., New York Orthopedic Hosp. and Dispensary. Trustee Children's Aid Soc., New York Republican. Episcopalian. Home: New York, N.Y. Died Jan. 5, 1926.

DRAYTON, Charles O., pres. Wheat Growers Nat. Union; b. Highland, Ill., Dec. 16, 1851; s. Robert I. and Margaret Ann (Gracy) D.; ed. Ill. State Normal U., 1870-74; m. Lucy Rutherford, Sept. 25, 1877; children—Rutherford Amos, Bertha Jane, Mrs. Pauline G. Floyd, Mrs. Edna Lucy Zimmermann. Farmer, organizer, and nat. pres. Farmers' Equity Union, 1910-22; now nat. pres. Wheat Growers Nat. Union; pres. Producers Nat. Grain Co., Kansas City, Mo. Established over 560 local units of Farmers Equity Union in U.S. Prohibitionist. Presbyn. Mason. Home: Greenville, Ill. Died Nov. 14, 1928.

DRAYTON, Grace Gebbie, artist, illustrator; b. Phila., Oct. 14, 1877; d. George and Mary (Fitzgerald) Gebbie; ed. pvt. schs., Pa.; m. W. Heyward Drayton, 3d, June 23, 1911 (divorced 1923). Originated series for Sunday Phila. Press "Bobby Blake and Dolly Drake," running for 2 yrs.; formerly on staff New York Journal and Phila. Press. Illustrated Mother Goose Nursery Rhymes; series of verses by Margaret G. Hays, running for 5 yrs. in Associated Sunday Magazine, and series by same, in Sunday North America, 1909 entitled "The Terrible Tales of Kaptain Kiddo"; series of Undiscovered Beauties, in New York Herald, 1908; also prints. Writer and illustrator children's books, Bobby Blake, Dolly Drake, Tiny Tots, etc.; originator and illustrator of Campbell Soup Kids; painter of posters and designs for mag. covers; illustrator of Dolly Dingle Cut-outs in Pictorial Review, Bear Cub Series in St. Nocholas, Dimples, comic series in newspapers, Dolly Dimples and Bobby Bounce, syndicated comics. Author and Illustrator: Chickie Cheepie; Bunny's Birthday; Bettina's Bonnet; G. G. Drayton's Jumble Book; Dolly Dimples; Bobby Bounce. Home: New York, N.Y. Died Jan. 31, 1936.

DRAYTON, Henry Shipman, physician; b. Jersey City, N.J., Sept. 16, 1840; s. William R. and Mary Maranda (Shipman) D.; A.B., New York U., 1859, LL.B., 1861, A.M., 1866; M.D., Eclectic Med. Coll., 1877; M.D., N.Y. Med. Soc., 1889; m. Almira Elizabeth, d. Dr. Henry Guernsey, of New York, Sept. 21, 1864. Practiced law at New York, 1861-64; editor Am. Phrenol. Jour. and Science of Health, 1876; later also lecturer on physiology of the new system in Am. Phrenol. Inst.; was visiting phys. Bellevue Hosp., clin. lecturer State Hosp. for Insane, Ward's Isl., and conducted clinics at other New York hospitals. Home: New York, N.Y. Died Apr. 9, 1923.

DREES, Charles William, missionary; b. Xenia, O., Sept. 13, 1851; s. Tobias and Maria Susan (Hypes) D.; A.B., Ohio Wesleyan U., 1871, A.M., 1874 (D.D., 1887); S.T.B., Boston U. School of Theology, 1874; m. Mary Adaline Combs, Sept. 13, 1877. Ordained M.E. ministry, 1874; sent as missionary to Mexico, 1874; supt. Meth. missions, in Mex., 1878-85, dist. supt., 1885-86; supt. in S.A., 1887-1900; founder Meth. missions in P.R., and supt 4 yrs.; legal rep. and treas., Bd. of Foreign Missions M.E. Ch. in Mex., S.A. and P.R., successively 1878-1912: apptd. by Argentine Govt. chief of staff official translators and interpreters at Pan-Am. Conf., Buenos Aires, 1910, Internat. Law Congress, same, 1923, and Pan-Am. Red Cross Congress, 1923; apptd. by Am. Bible Society mem. of joint commn. for preparation of new Spanish version of the N.T., 1912. Founder Theol. Sem. and Meth. Inst., Puebla, Mex., 1875; prin. Theol. Sem., Buenos Aires, 1891-93; del. Gen. Conf. M.E. Ch., 1896, 1904, 16 reserve del., 1908 and 1924; del. Ecumenical Meth. Conf., 1901, 21. Retired, 1924. Home: Xenia, O. Died Aug. 31, 1926.

DREHER, Julius Daniel, Am. consul; b. Lexington Co., S.C., Oct. 28, 1846; s. John Jacob and Martha Elizabeth (Counts) D.; A.B., Roanoke Coll., 1871, A.M., 1874; (Ph.D., Williams, 1881; LL.D., Roanoke, 1905); m. Emeline Kirtland Richmond, Sept. 5, 1906. Served as pvt. and lt. C.S.A.; taught sch., 3 yrs. Asst. prof., 1871-75, financial sec., 1875-78, pres., 1878-1903, Roanoke Coll.; Am. consul at Tahiti, Society Islands, 1906-10, at Port Antonio, Jamaica, W.I., 1910-13, at Toronto, Can., 1913-15, at Colon, Panama, until July 1, 1924; retired on account of age. Home: Clearwater, Fla. Died Oct. 9, 1937.

DREHER, William Counts, newspaperman; b. Lexington Co., S.C., May 29, 1856; s. John Jacob and Martha Elizabeth (Counts) D.; A.B., Roanoke Coll., Va., 1878; studied Yale, 1881-83; studied philosophy, langs. and lit., univs. of Leipzig, Strassburg and Berlin, 1885-87; m. Georgia Chase, June 10, 1901; children—William Chase, Henry Julius. Edited tariff reform matter for country newspapers, for New York Reform Club, 1890-91; same, Dem. Nat. Com., 1892; in U.S. consular service, in Germany, 1893-97: in newspaper work at Berlin, 1897-1921, where was corr. The Annalist and The Associated Press; on editorial staff N.Y. Tribune, Sept. 1917, and Berlin corr. same, 1919-21. Home: Amherst, Mass. Died Jan. 10, 1929.

DRENNAN, Michael C., medical dir. U.S.N.; b. Easton, Pa.; m. Ellen Johnson, June 1864. Apptd. from Pa., acting asst. surgeon U.S.N., Apr. 15, 1863; asst. surgeon, June 30, 1868; passed asst. surgeon, June 13, 1870; surgeon, Apr. 20, 1879; med. insp., May 28, 1895; med. dir., Apr. 16, 1899; retired, with rank of rear adm. for services during Civil War, Oct. 24, 1899. Served on board flagship New York as surgeon of the fleet, N. Atlantic Squadron, 1895-98. Home: Easton, Pa. Died Mar. 23, 1915.

DRESEL, Ellis Loring, lawyer, diplomatist; b. Boston, Mass., Nov. 28, 1865; s. Otto and Anna (Loring) D.; ed. pvt. schs. U.S., French Switzerland and Germany, and St. Paul's Sch., Concord, N.H.; A.B., Harvard, 1887, LL.B., 1892 (hon. A.M., 1922); unmarried. Practiced at Boston, 1892-1915; attached to Am. Embassy, at Berlin, Feb. 1915; spl. rep. of State Dept. at Berlin, Dec. 1915-Feb. 1917; left Berlin on rupture of relations, also Vienna, after assignment there, Mar.-Apr. 1917; asst. to Am. Legation at Berne, June 1917, as spl. rep. State Dept.; gen. dir. and organizer Central Com. for Am. Prisoners, and Am. Red Cross rep. for Switzerland, 1917-18; rep. War Trade Bd. for Switzerland, 1917-18; hon. 1st sec. of Legation, Apr. 1918; attached to Peace Conf. at Paris, 1918-19; chief of Bur. of Diplomatic Corr., later Am. rep. on Temporary Reparation, and other coms.; assigned to Am. Embassy at Paris, with hon. rank of counsellor July 1919, but did not take up duties; apptd. Am. commr. to Germany, Nov. 1919, with hdqrs. at Berlin; signed treaty of peace with Germany as U.S. plenipotentiary, Aug. 25, 1921; chargé d'affaires at Berlin, Nov. 1921-Apr. 1922. Republican. Home: Pride's Crossing, Mass. Died Sept. 19, 1925.

DRESSER, Daniel Le Roy, mcht.; b. New York, N.Y., Dec. 13, 1866; grad. Columbia. Mem. Dresser & Co.; dir. Benedict & Burnham Mfg. Co., Am. Pin

Co., New England Watch Co. Home: Oyster Bay, L.I. Died July 10, 1915.

DRESSER, Solomon Robert, congressman; b. Litchfield, Mich., Feb. 1, 1842; s. Parker and Lydia (Cronkhite) D.; common sch. edn.; m. Vesta E. Stimson, 1863 (died 1883); m. 2d, Caroline Kirsch, Dec. 21, 1885. Engaged in mfg.; took out his 1st patent, 1880, and developed a large business; among his inventions are a packer for natural gas and oil wells, a rubber coupling to make a tight joint in natural gas pipes, and an insulating coupling to prevent leakage of electricity from conduits. Mem. 58th and 59th Congresses (1903-07), 21st Pa. Dist. Republican. Home: Bradford, Pa. Died 1911.

DRESSLAR, Fletcher Bascom, univ. prof.; b. Banta, Ind., Sept. 21, 1858; s. Archibald and Elizabeth Ann (Bromwell) D.; A.B., Indiana Univ., 1889, A.M., 1892; Ph.D., Clark Univ., Worcester, 1894; m. Cornelia Jerauld Welborn, Dec. 28, 1892 (died 1919); children—Otis Welborn, Oscar Welborn; m. 2d, Minnie Bryan Fisher, 1922. Teacher country schs., 1882-85; prin. high sch., 1889-90, supt. schs., 1890-91, Princeton, Ind.; prof. psychology and edn., State Normal Sch., Los Angeles, 1894-97; asst. prof. science and art of teaching, 1897-1906, asso. prof., 1906-09, U. of Calif.; prof. edn. and dean Sch. of Edn., U. of Ala., Jan. 1, 1909-11; specialist in sch. hygiene and sanitation, Bur. of Edn., Washington, Oct. 1911-Dec. 1912; prof. sch. hygiene, Peabody Coll. for Teachers, Nashville, Dec. 1, 1912—. Republican. Methodist. Author: Superstition and Education, 1907; School Hygiene, 1913. Editor: (with others) Moral Training in the Public Schools, 1908. Home: Nashville, Tenn. Died Jan. 19, 1930.

DRESSLER, Louis Raphael, organist; b. New York, N.Y., Dec. 8, 1861; s. William and Mary Law (Hyde) D.; grad. Lyon's Collegiate Inst., 1877; Mus.Doc., Hope Coll., Mich., 1897; m. Jeannie Eloise Ayers, Apr. 23, 1884 (died 1907); children—William Leonard (dec.), Genevieve Anna (dec.), Louis Richard. Organist and choir dir.; conductor of choral socs., glee clubs; organist and dir. All Souls' (Unitarian) Ch., New York, 16 yrs. Home: Jersey City, N.J. Deceased.

DRESSLER, Marie, actress; b. Cobourg, Can., Nov. 9, 1873; d. Alexander Rudolph and Annie (Henderson) Koerber; ed. Toronto, Can., schs. Early appearances were in various operatic rôles including tour with the Bennett and Moulton Opera Co.; appeared with Camille d'Arville, in "Madeline or the Magic Kiss"; supported Lillian Russell, in "My Lady Nicotine" at the Casino, New York, and there created the rôle of Flo Honeydew, in "The Lady Slavey"; starred in "Miss Prinnt" and took leading comedy parts in New York Theater; joined the Weber Co., New York, as leading woman, 1906; starred in "Tillie's Nightmare" on stage and in 1916 played the rôle on screen in "Tillie's Punctured Romance" with Charles Spencer Chaplin; returned to screen, 1926, and has won outstanding success in "Anna Christie," "Emma," "Caught Short," "Reducing," "Min and Bill," "Politics," "Prosperity," "Dinner at Eight," "Tugboat Annie," "The Late Christopher Bean," and others. Home: Beverly Hills, Calif. Died July 28, 1934.

DREW, Frank Gifford, pres. Winchester Repeating Arms Co.; b. Phila., Pa., Dec. 1, 1872; s. David Abbott and Elizabeth (Gifford) D.; ed. pub. schs., Phila.; m. Anne Powell Patterson, Dec. 30, 1896; children—Anne (Mrs. William A. Reynolds), Elizabeth, Frances, Ethel. In wholesale hardware business, Phila., 1887-1903; with Winchester Repeating Arms Co., New Haven, Conn., 1903—, pres., 1924—; pres. The Winchester Co.; v.p. Winchester-Simmons Co., Simmons Hardware Co. Served as capt. 1st Inf. and maj. 3d Inf., Spanish-Am. War, 1898; mem. Advisory Bd. Bridgeport Ordnance Dist., War Dept. U.S., 1927. Mem. Chamber Commerce of U.S., Conn. and New Haven. Mason. Republican. Episcopalian. Home: New Haven, Conn. Died Oct. 1928.

DREW, Franklin Mellen, lawyer; b. Turner, Me., July 19, 1837; s. Jesse and Hannah Gorham (Phillips) D.; A.B., Bowdoin Coll., 1858, A.M., 1861; admitted to bar, 1861; m. Araminta Blanche Woodman, Jan. 3, 1862. Began practice at Presque Isle, Me., 1861; served in Civil War, as capt., maj. and bvt. col., 15th Regt. Me. Vols., Oct. 22, 1861-Jan. 26, 1865; clk. Maine House of Reps., 1866-67; sec. of state of Maine, 1868-72; U.S. pension agent, Augusta, Me., 1872-77; removed to Lewiston, Me., in 1878; judge of probate, 1888-1904. Republican. V.p. Lewiston Trust and Safe Deposit Co.; treas. Bates Coll., 1893-1916. Conglist. Mason. Home: Lewiston, Me. Died Feb. 27, 1925.

DREW, Gilman Arthur, biologist; b. Newton, Ia., Nov. 15, 1868; s. Orrin Gilman and Mary Emily (Drew) D.; B.S., State U. of Ia., 1890; Ph.D., Johns Hopkins, 1898; m. Lena E. Slawson, Nov. 24, 1892. Acad. teacher, 1890-91; high sch. teacher, Oskaloosa, Ia., 1892-94; fellow, 1897-98, Bruce fellow, 1898, asst. in zoölogy, 1898-1900, Johns Hopkins; prof. biology, U. of Maine, 1900-11. Asst. dir. Marine Biol. Lab., Woods Hole, Mass., 1909-26. Fellow Am. Acad. Arts and Sciences. Home: Eagle Lake, Fla. Died Oct. 26, 1934.

DREW, Irving Webster, senator; b. Colebrook, N.H., Jan. 8, 1845; s. Amos W. and Julia Esther (Lovering) D.; A.B., Dartmouth, 1870; m. Caroline Hatch Merrill, Nov. 4, 1869. Began practice at Lancaster, N.H., 1871; mem. Drew, Shurtleff, Morris & Oakes, 1872-1919; pres. Siwooganock Guaranty Savings Bank, Upper Coos R.R.; dir. Lancaster Nat. Bank; mem. N.H. Senate, 1883-85. Republican, 1896—; mem. N.H. Constl. Conv., 1902, 12; apptd. mem. U.S. Senate to succeed Hon. Jacob H. Gallinger, deceased, holding seat Sept. 11-Nov. 1918. Protestant. Home: Lancaster, N.H. Died Apr. 10, 1922.

DREW, John, actor; b. Phila., Pa., Nov. 13, 1853; s. John (Irish comedian, died 1862) and Louisa (Lane) D. (actress, died 1897); ed. pvt. tutors and Episcopal Acad., Phila.; m. Josephine Baker, 1880 (died 1918). First appearance, Mar. 23, 1873, Arch St. Theatre, Phila., as Plumper, in "Cool as a Cucumber"; appeared in "Woman of the Day," 1871; joined Augustin Daly's Co., 5th Av. Theatre, Feb. 17, 1875, as Bob Ruggles, in "The Big Bonanza"; joined Edwin Booth, 5th Av. Theatre, 1876, in Shakespearean plays; supported Fanny Davenport, 1877-78; played Henry Beauclair, in "Diplomacy," 1878-79; leading man in Augustin Daly's Co., 1879-92, creating many rôles; starred, 1892, playing Dr. Paul Blondet, in "The Masked Ball" and Frederick Ossian, in "The Butterflies" with Maude Adams; starred in "The Bauble Shop," 1894, "Christopher, Jr." and "The Squire of Dames," 1895-96, "Rosemary," 1896-97, "Marriage of Convenience," also "One Summer's Day," 1897-98, "The Liars," 1898-99, "The Tyranny of Tears," 1899, played in "The Circle," 1921-23, and as Sir Peter Teazle in revival of "The School for Scandal," 1923, "Trelawney of the Wells," 1925. Home: East Hampton, L.I., N.Y. Died July 9, 1927.

DREWRY, William Francis, M.D.; b. Southampton Co., Va., Mar. 10, 1860; s. James David Humphrey and Martha Jane (Francis) D.; Randolph-Macon Coll., Ashland, Va., 1876-80; M.D., Med. Coll. of Va., 1884; m. Bessie Seabury, Dec. 20, 1892; children—Mrs. Elizabeth D. Gallalee (dec.), Mrs. M. Francis D. McMullen, William F., Lelia Seabury (Mrs. Lelia D. Owen), Phoebe Read. Asst. phys., 1886-96, supt., 1896-1924, Central State Hosp., Petersburg, Va.; mgr. for City of Petersburg, Va., 1924-28; dir. bur. Mental hygiene, Va. State Dept. Pub. Welfare, 1929—. Prime mover for estab. a colony for epileptics and feeble-minded in Va.; mem. Epileptic Commn., 1896-98; one of organizers State Conf. Social Work, and State Tuberculosis Assn. (pres. 1928); mem. bd. dirs. Petersburg Hospital, 1900-28; mem. State Bd. Health, 1916-24. Contract surgeon U.S.A. and psychiatrist Va. N.G., 1917; mem. Med. Advisory Bd., Dinwiddie Co., 1917-18; mem. State Civilian Commn. on Camp Activities, 1917-19; mem. exec. com. Petersburg Red Cross, 1917-19; chmn. Petersburg War History Com., 1919-24; chmn. Petersburg War Com. on law enforcement and moral welfare; etc. Visitor, U. of Virginia, 1908-16. Mem. State Bd. of Public Welfare, 1924-29; mem. State Prison Bd. of Psychiatry, 1920—. Democrat. Methodist. Died Oct. 19, 1934.

DREYER, George Peter, physiologist; b. Baltimore, Md., Sept. 22, 1866; Baltimore City Coll., 1879-84; A.B., Johns Hopkins, 1887, Ph.D., 1890; Harvard, summer 1888, Coll. Phys. and Surg., Baltimore, 1890-91; m. Aug. 1890. Teacher, acad. dept., Johns Hopkins, 1890-93, Med. Sch., same, 1893-1900; prof. physiology and head dept. of physiology and physiol. chemistry, Coll. of Med., U. of Ill., 1900—, jr. dean, 1913-15. Best known research was discovery of the secretory nerves of the suprarenal glands. Home: LaGrange, Ill. Died Feb. 27, 1931.

DREYSPRING, Adolphe, teacher of modern languages; b. Strasburg, Alsace, June 1, 1835; s. Rev. George (Luth. minister) and Caroline (Fischer) D.; ed. in Strasburg; m. Lucy Yost, 1857. Came to U.S., 1851; moved to Montgomery Co., Ala., 1857, engaged in cotton planting until 1884; removed to New York, 1884, taught pvt. sch. (Ph.D., Rutgers Coll.); now teacher in pub. sch. Author: Cumulative Method for Learning German; Easy Lessons in German; German Reader—"Rudolf"; German Verb Drill; Easy Lessons in French; French Reader; Constructive Process for Learning German. Home: New York, N.Y. Died 1906.

DRINKER, Henry Sturgis, educator; b. Hong Kong, China, Nov. 8, 1850; s. Sandwith Drinker and Susannah (Budd) D.; E.M., Lehigh U., 1871; LL.D., Lafayette, 1905, Franklin and Marshall, 1910, U. of Pa., 1911, Princeton, 1918, Moravian Coll., 1922, Lehigh, 1922; m. Aimée Ernesta Beaux, Dec. 2, 1879. Had charge of bldg. Musconetcong Tunnel for L.V. R.R., 1872-75; admitted to bar, 1878; gen. solicitor L.V. R.R., 1885-1905; pres. Lehigh U., 1905-20. Pres. Am. Forestry Assn., 1912-16, Pa. Forestry Assn., 1917-23; v.p. Nat. Conservation Congress. Pres. Nat. Reserve Corps, 1913-16; chmn. bd. Mil. Training Camps Assn., 1916-19, hon. pres., 1920. Author: Tunneling Explosive Compounds and Rock Drills, 1878. Home: Merion Station, Pa. Died July 27, 1937.

DRISCOLL, Frederick, commr. Am. Newspaper Publishers' Assn., Apr. 2, 1900—; b. Boston, July 31, 1834; acad. edn.; went to Minn., 1858; mem. State legislature, 1860; sec. Rep. State Central Com., 1867-68; chmn. same, 1869-70; pres. St. Paul Chamber of Commerce, 1890; dir. in Associated Press from 1892; dir. Am. Newspaper Publishers' Assn., 1894—; gen. mgr. Pioneer Press Co. for 36 yrs.; m. Anna L. Brown, May 31, 1858 (died 1880); m. 2d, Mrs. Lucy N. Styles, Nov. 8, 1882. Home: Chicago, Ill. Died 1907.

DRISCOLL, Michael Edward, congressman; b. Syracuse, N.Y., Feb. 9, 1851; s. Michael and Ellen (Cronin) D.; bro. of George Walter D.; A.B., with distinguished honors, Williams Coll., 1877; m. Mary McLean, 1886. Admitted to bar, 1879; mem. commn. to draft uniform charter for cities of 2d class in N.Y., 1895; counsel in examination of Equitable Life Assurance Soc., 1905; temporary chmn. Rep. State Conv., 1906; mem. 56th to 62d Congresses (1899-1913), 29th N.Y. Dist. Home: Syracuse, N.Y. Died Jan. 19, 1929.

DRIVER, James, architect; b. Bradford, Yorkshire, Eng., May 18, 1859; s. Robert and Sarah (Hopkinson) D.; ed. pvt. and tech. schs. and in office of James Young, architect, Bradford; unmarried. Came to America, 1883; practiced in Boston from 1895; mem. Hartwell, Richardson & Driver. Architect of Youth's Companion Bldg., Boston; Armory, Cambridge, Mass.; High Sch. Bldg., Springfield; 1st Parish Ch., Plymouth, etc. Conglist. Mason. Home: Wakefield, Mass. Died 1925.

DRIVER, John Merritte, clergyman; s. of James Ransom and Matilda Caroline D.; B.Sc., Ill. Agr. Coll., 1876; A.B., Boston U., 1884, S.T.B., 1885; (hon. A.M., Baker U., 1885; D.D., Rust U., 1893; Ph.D., Am. U., 1899; LL.D., Ill. Coll. of Law, 1909); m. Elsie Wiley, 1899. Ordained M.E. ministry; pastor People's Ch., Chicago, 1902-07. Home: Chicago, Ill. Died June 6, 1918.

DROMGOOLE, Will(iam) Allen (Miss), author; b. Murfreesboro, Tenn.; d. John Easter and Rebecca Mildred Dromgoole. Author: The Heart of Old Hickory; The Valley Path; The Moonshiner's Son; Cinch and Other Stories of Tennessee; The Island of Beautiful Things; Harum-Scarum Joe; Three Little Crackers from Down in Dixie; Rare Old Chums; Hero Chums; A Boy's Battle; The Farrier's Dog and His Fellow; Adventures of a Fellow; The Best of Friends (series three). Literary editor Nashville Daily Banner; mem. Banner staff and writer of original feature, "Song and Story," 1904—. Home: Nashville, Tenn. Died Sept. 1, 1934.

DRONE, Eaton Sylvester, journalist; b. Zanesville, O., Jan. 25, 1842; A.B., Harvard, 1866, A.M., 1869; admitted to New York bar, 1869; writer on New York Herald on legal subjects, 1880, editor same, 1893-1905. Author: Law of Property in Intellectual Productions, Embracing Copyright and Playright. Home: Zanesville, O. Died Feb. 2, 1917.

DROPPERS, Garrett, economist; b. Milwaukee, Wis., Apr. 12, 1860; s. John D. and Gertrude (Boyink) D.; A.B., Harvard, 1887; studies in economics and finance, Univ. of Berlin, 1887-89; m. Cora A. Rand, 1889 (died 1896); m. 2d, Jean Tewkesbury Rand, 1897; children—Seton R., Cora R., Elizabeth T., Geraldine F. Prof. polit. economy and finance at Tokyo U., Japan, 1889-98; pres. U. of S.D., 1898-1906; professorial lecturer on polit. economy, U. of Chicago, 1907; prof. economics, Williams Coll., 1908-22 (emeritus). Sec. Commn. on Commerce and Industry of Mass., 1907-08; mem. Mass. Civil Service Commn., July 1913-14; E.E. and M.P. to Greece and Montenegro, Aug. 5, 1914-July 15, 1920. Author: Economic History of the Nineteenth Century, 1923. Home: Williamstown, Mass. Died July 7, 1927.

DROSSAERTS, Arthur (Jerome), R.C. bishop; b. Breda, Holland, Sept. 11, 1862; s. Cornelius and Sophie (de Fraiture) D.; ed. Haaren Theol. Sem. Came to U.S., 1890; consecrated bishop of San Antonio (Tex.), Dec. 8, 1918. Died Sept. 8, 1940.

DROUET, Robert, actor, playwright; b. Clinton, Ia., 1870; m. Mildred, d. M. A. Loring, Oct. 1897. Joined theatrical co. at 16, and a few years later took out a co. of his own in Shakespearean repertoire; played leading parts with Robert Downing 2 years; later played General Delarouche in "Paul Kauvar"; supported Joseph Haworth and Effie Ellsler; created leading part in "Girl with Green Eyes," at the Savoy Theatre, New York; also in "A Woman in the Case," at the Herald Square Theatre, New York; later played in principal rôle in "Citizen Pierre"; John Storm in "The Christian," Viola Allen Co.; created part Col. Jack Brereton in "Janice Meredith"; leading man for Mary Mannering, Wallack's Theatre, New York; played in "Genesee of the Hills," and "The Mills of the Gods," Astor Theatre, New York, 1907; leading part in original prodn. "Madame X" in America. Author: (plays) Doris; The White Czar; Montana; Tomorrow; An Idyll of Virginia; Fra Diano; Captain Bob. Home: New York, N.Y. Died Aug. 17, 1914.

DROWN, Edward Staples, theologian; b. New Haven, Conn., Dec. 21, 1861; s. Edward Livingston and Rebecca (Staples) D.; A.B., Harvard, 1884; S.T.B., Episcopal Theol. Sch., Cambridge, Mass., 1889; D.D., Trinity Coll., 1904, Episcopal Theol. School, Cambridge, 1927; m. Mrs. Paulina Cony

(Smith) Allen, June 12, 1913. Deacon, 1889, priest, 1890, P.E. Ch.; successively instr., asst. prof. and prof. syst. divinity, Episcopal Theol. Sch., 1889—. Fellow Am. Acad. Arts and Sciences. Author: The Apostles' Creed To-day; God's Responsibility for the War; The Creative Christ, 1923; Religion or God? 1927. Home: Cambridge, Mass. Died Jan. 24, 1936.

DROWN, Thomas Messinger, pres. Lehigh Univ., 1895—; b. Phila., Mar. 19, 1842; grad. Phila. High School, 1859; M.D., med. dept., U. of Pa., 1862. Practiced medicine a short time; studied chemistry at Yale and Harvard, chemistry and metallurgy at Freiberg, Saxony, School of Mines and at Heidelberg (LL.D., Columbia, 1895); analytical chemist, Phila., several yrs.; prof. chemistry, Lafayette Coll., 1874-81; prof. chemistry, Mass. Inst. of Technology, 1885-95. Sec. Am. Inst. Mining Engrs., 1873-83; in charge chem. dept., Mass. State bd. of health, 1887—; pres. Am. Inst. Mining Engrs., 1897-98. Home: S. Bethlehem, Pa. Died 1904.

DRUM, A. L., cons. engr.; b. San Francisco, Calif., 1875; s. John Drum (maj. U.S.A.) and Margaret (Desmond) D.; B.S. in Elec. Engring., Mass. Inst. Tech., 1896; m. Jane Hunter, 1892; children—John, Charlotte, Hunter. Began engring. practice in Boston, 1896; moved to Chicago, 1904; head of A. L. Drum & Co., consulting and constructing engrs. Pres. Eastern Michigan Railways. Consulting engr. for U.S. Shipping Board and U.S. Housing Corp., World War. Fellow Am. Inst. E.E. Home: Detroit, Mich. Died Mar. 17, 1933.

DRUM, Richard Coulter, army officer; b. in Pa., May 28, 1825; s. Simon and Agnes (Lang) D.; ed. Jefferson Coll., Phila.; m. Lavinia Morgan, 1850. Enlisted as pvt. Co. K, 1st Pa. Inf., Dec. 16, 1846; participated in siege of Vera Cruz; 2d lt. inf., Feb. 18, 1847, promoted through grades to col. Arty., Feb. 22, 1869; brig. gen. adj. gen., June 15, 1880; retired May 28, 1889. Bvtd. 1st lt., Sept. 13, 1847, for battle of Chapultepec, Mex.; col., Sept. 24, 1864, for services during the war; brig. gen., Mar. 13, 1865, for services in adj. gen.'s dept. during the war. Home: Bethesda, Md. Died 1909.

DRUM, Walter, college prof.; b. Louisville, Ky., Sept. 21, 1870; s. Capt. John (killed before Santiago) and Margaret (Desmond) D.; Marquette U., Milwaukee, Wis.; Canisius Coll., Buffalo, N.Y.; A.B., Boston Coll., 1890; entered Soc. of Jesus, 1890, and studied at Frederick, Md., and Woodstock (Md.) Coll. and Jesuit univs. of Beirut, Syria, and Innsbruck, Austria. Ordained priest R.C. Ch., 1904; prof. of scripture, 1908—, librarian, 1909-18, instr. Hebrew, 1908-15, Aramaic and Syraic, 1915—, Woodstock (Md.) Coll. Editor, Homiletic and Pastoral Rev., 1920—. Author: Pastoral Medicine (Sanford and Drum), 1905; Pioneer Forecasters of Hurricanes, 1905; Divinity of Christ, 1917. Died Dec. 10, 1921.

DRUMM, Thomas W., bishop; b. Fore, Ireland, July 12, 1871; s. Thomas and Mary (Cullen) D.; came to U.S., 1888; A.B., St. Joseph's Coll., Dubuque, Ia., 1898; studied Grand Sem., Montreal, Can., Catholic U. of America. Ordained priest R.C. Ch., 1901; pastor St. Patrick's Ch., Cedar Rapids, Ia., 1915-19; consecrated bishop of Des Moines (Ia.), May 22, 1919. Pres. bd. trustees Des Moines Catholic Coll. Mem. Knights of Columbus. Died Oct. 24, 1933.

DRUMMOND, I(saac) Wyman, chemist; b. Roxbury, Mass., June 19, 1855; s. James F. and Sarah (Wyman) D.; E.M., Columbia Sch. of Mines, 1878, Ph.D., 1880; unmarried. Formerly chmn. bd. and chemist, Devoe & Raynolds Co., New York; trustee Bowery Savings Bank. Retired. Unitarian. Editor dept. of colors and dyes, Century Dictionary. Home: New York, N.Y. Died Apr. 15, 1933.

DRUMMOND, Josiah Hayden, lawyer; b. Me., 1827; admitted to bar and practiced Waterville, Me., until 1860, then practiced at Portland; m. Dec. 10, 1850. Mem. and speaker Me. Ho. Reps., 1858 and 1869; State senator, 1859; atty. gen. Me., 1860-64; dir. Me. Central R.R., 1865—; dir. Union Mut. Life Ins. Co. Prominent in Masonry; provincial grand master, Province of U.S., Royal Order of Scotland. Author: Maine Masonic Text-Book for the Use of Lodges; History of Masonic Jurisprudence. Home: Portland, Me. Died 1902.

DRUMMOND, Sara King Wiley, author; b. E. Orange, N.J., Sept. 23, 1871; d. William Halsted and Joanna King (Clarke) Wiley; ed. pvt. sch.; m. Frederic Lindsley Drummond, Jan. 24, 1906. Mem. Soc. of Nat. Art, Washington. Club: MacDowell. Author: (with W. H. Wiley), Alaska, Yosemite and the Yellowstone, 1898; Poems, Lyrical and Dramatic; Cromwell, a play, 1900; Alcestis and Other Poems, 1905; The Coming of Philibert, 1907. Home: E. Orange, N.J. Died 1909.

DRURY, Alexander Greer, M.D.; b. Covington, Ky., Feb. 3, 1844; s. Asa and Elizabeth Williams (Getchell) D.; A.B., Centre Coll., Danville, Ky., 1865, A.M., 1881; M.D., U. of Pa., 1868; M.D., ad eundem, Med. Coll. of Ohio, 1878; m. Angie Eunice Kinkead, Sept. 7, 1871; m. 2d, Louise Kieffer, June 11, 1921. In medical practice, Cincinnati, Sept. 1869—; dist. phys., 1874-75; prof. dermatology, Laura Memorial Woman's Med. Coll., 1890-1900; prof. hygiene, 1901-10, prof. emeritus, 1910—, U. of Cincinnati. Died Jan. 17, 1929.

DRURY, Augustus Waldo, theologian; b. Madison Co., Ind., Mar. 2, 1851; s. Morgan Shortridge and Elizabeth (Lambert) D.; A.B., Western Coll., Western, Ia. (now Coe Coll., Cedar Rapids, Ia.), 1872; grad. Bonebrake Theol. Sem., Dayton, O., 1877; studied U. of Berlin, summer 1886; D.D., Western, 1885; LL.D., Otterbein, 1914; m. Sophia Bookwalter, Sept. 6, 1876 (died 1922); children—Luther Edwards, Mrs. Mabel McDonald, Horace Bookwalter, Mrs. Agnes Denune, Mrs. Ruth McClure. Prof. Greek and Latin, Western Coll., 1872-73; ordained U.B. ministry, 1877; pastoral work, most of time, 1873-80; prof. ch. history, 1880-92, prof. systematic theology, 1892—, Bonebrake Theol. Sem. Trustee and pres. bd. U.B. Pub. House; sec. U.B. Hist. Soc.; pres. Dayton Bd. Edn., 1895, 96. Republican. Author: Life of Philip William Otterbein, 1884; Outlines of Doctrinal Theology, 1914, rev. edit., 1926; History of the Church of the United Brethren in Christ, 1925. Died Feb. 18, 1935.

DRURY, John Benjamin, clergyman, editor Christian Intelligencer (New York), 1887—; b. Rhinebeck, N.Y., Aug. 15, 1838; s. Alfred and Maria A. (Schultz) D.; grad. Rutgers Coll., 1858; Theol. Sem., New Brunswick, 1861 (D.D., Rutgers Coll., 1880); m. Henrietta Wynkoop Keese, Sept. 2, 1869. Licensed and ordained minister Reformed (Dutch) Ch., 1861; supplied Davenport, Ia., 1861-62; 1st Reformed Ch., Ghent, N.Y., 1864-87; pres. Gen. Synod Reformed Ch., 1886; trustee Rutgers Coll., 1887—; mem. bd. supt. Theol. Sem. at New Brunswick; Vedder lecturer Coll. and Sem. at New Brunswick, 1883; lecturer before Am. Inst. Christian Philosophy, 1885; Council of Reformed Chs. holding the Presbyn. System, London, 1888, Toronto, 1892, Washington, 1899, Liverpool, 1904. Home: New Brunswick, N.J. Died 1909.

DRURY, Marion Richardson, clergyman; b. Pendleton, Ind., Dec. 27, 1849; s. Morgan S. and Elizabeth (Lambert) D.; A.B., Western (now Coe) Coll., 1872, A.M., 1875; grad. Union Bibl. (now Bonebrake Theol.) Sem., Dayton, O., 1875; D.D., Western Coll., Westfield Coll., Ill., 1891; m. Lucinda Denny, June 20, 1872; children—Mrs. Florence Blanche Foster, Philo Walker. Ordained U.B. ministry, 1875; pastor Fayette, Ia., 1872-73, Miami Chapel, Dayton, O., 1874-75, Toledo, Ia., 1875-78, Cedar Rapids, Ia., 1878-81, Toledo, Ia., 1898-1907, Oakland, Calif., 1907-10; pres. Philomath (Ore.) Coll., 1910-13, Leander Clark Coll., Toledo, Ia., 1913-16; pastor Cedar Rapids, Ia., 1917-19; student sec. Coe Coll., 1919-22; missionary, Ponce, Porto Rico, 1922—. Asso. editor of the Religious Telescope, Dayton, O., 1881-97. Author: Handbook for Workers, 1888; After Eighty Years, 1930; Memorial Record Western College Class of 1872, 1930; Reminiscences of Early Days in Iowa, 1931; Life of Augustus Waldo Drury, D.D., LL.D., 1936. Home: Ponce, Porto Rico. Died Feb. 21, 1939.

DRURY, Samuel Smith, clergyman; b. Bristol, R.I., 1878; s. Samuel Smith (M.D.) and Hannah Wheeler (Goodwin) D.; A.B., Harvard, 1901; S.T.B., Berkeley Div. Sch., 1910; L.H.D., Trinity Coll., 1910; D.D., Dartmouth Coll., 1917, Williams Coll., 1921; Litt.D., Princeton, 1922; m. Cornelia Frothingham Wolcott, Apr. 18, 1911. Deacon, 1905, priest, 1908, P.E. Ch.; chaplain to Bishop Brent, Philippine Islands, 1905-07; rector Calvary Ch., Providence, R.I., 1908, St. Stephen's Ch., Boston, 1908-10; vice rector, 1910-11, rector, 1911—, St. Paul's Ch., Concord, N.H. Author: The Thoughts of Youth, 1922; Backbone, 1923; Schoolmastering, 1926; Fathers and Sons, 1927; In Pursuit of Pelicans, 1931; Adventures in Prayer, 1932; School, Home & Co., 1933. Home: Concord, N.H. Died Feb. 21, 1938.

DRURY, Wells, newspaperman; b. New Boston, Ill., Sept. 16, 1851; s. Squire Thompson and Rebecca (Newton) D.; ed. high sch., and Christian Coll., Monmouth, Ore.; m. Ella L. Bishop, May 23, 1888; children—Newton Bishop, Aubrey, Muriel, Lorraine. Interpreter for supt. of Indian affairs on Puget Sound, Wash., Medicine Creek treaty, 1861-65; served apprenticeship as compositor and pressman in Seattle, Wash., and Portland, Ore., 1866-69, reporter Victoria (B.C.) Colonist and Portland (Ore.) Oregonian, 1870; owner and editor, Monmouth (Ore.) Messenger, 1871-73, Carson (Nev.) Daily News, 1874-75; city editor Gold Hill Daily News, 1876-78; reporter Bodie Daily Miner, 1879; city editor Virginia City (Nev.) Chronicle, also same Daily Stage, 1879-80; city editor Daily Territorial Enterprise, Virginia City, Nev., 1881-82; deputy sec. of state of Nev., 1882-86; stumped Nevada for Blaine, 1884; mem. and speaker pro tem, Nev. Ho. of Rep., 1887-88; reporter Denver Republican, Kansas City Journal and Chicago Inter-Ocean, 1888; reporter, city editor and night editor San Francisco Examiner, 1888-90; founder and editor Daily Evening News, Sacramento, Calif., 1891-93; mng. editor San Francisco Daily Call, 1895-96, Los Angeles Daily Record, 1900-01; news editor Sacramento Union, 1902-06; city editor San Francisco Daily Examiner, 1907; mng. dir. and sec. Berkeley (Calif.) Chamber of Commerce, 1908-21, pres. 1921-22; now chmn. bd. Drury Advertising Co. Republican. Sec. local bd. for O.T.C. Assn. of U.S., 1916-18; mem. advisory council Boy Scouts of America; exec. com. Berkeley War Camp Community Service; 4 minute speaker during World War. Second and 1st lt. Co. C, 1st Regt. Nev. N.G., 1877-83; capt. and a.d.c. 1st Brigade, 1883-87. Mason. Author: Berkeley, a City of Progress, 1909; To Old Hangtown or Bust, 1912; California Tourist Guide and Handbook (with Aubrey Drury), 1913; Comstock Days—And Nights, 1931. Home: Berkeley, Calif. Died May 4, 1932.

DRUSHEL, J. Andrew, educator; b. Mt. Hope, O., Nov. 24, 1872; s. Henry and Catherine (Rowe) D.; A.B., Nat. Normal U., Lebanon, O., 1895, A.M., 1897; A.B., Yale, 1905; Ph.D., New York U., 1927; m. Hortense Wilson, Aug. 26, 1897. Teacher in Ohio pub. schs., 1890-92; instr. in mathematics, Nat. Normal U., 1893-95, in biology and geology, E. Tex. Normal Coll., Commerce, Tex., 1895-98; prin. pub. schs., Frankfort, O., 1898-1900; prof. geology and biology, Nat. Normal U., 1900-04; instr., teacher training courses, elementary science and mathematics, Harris Teachers Coll., St. Louis, 1905-24; asst. prof. of the teaching of mathematics, New York U., 1924-26, asso. prof., 1926-28, prof. edn., 1928—. Mason. Author: Arithmetical Essentials, 1922, 1923 (with J. W. Withers) Junior High School Mathematical Essentials, 1924. Home: Westfield, N.J. Died June 20, 1940.

DRYDEN, Forrest Fairchild, insurance pres.; b. Bedford, O., Dec. 26, 1864; s. John Fairfield and Cynthia J. (Fairchild) D.; Phillips Acad., Andover, Mass.; m. Grace Carleton, 1890; children—John Fairfield, Dorothy (Mrs. Newcombe C. Baker), Elizabeth Butterfield. Entered service of Prudential Ins. Co. as clk., 1882; insp., 1888, field supt., Elizabeth, N.J., 1889, dir., asst. sec. and sec., 1890, 3d v.p., 1903, 2d v.p., 1906, v.p., 1911, pres., Jan. 8, 1912-22. Was lt. col. and deputy commissary gen. N.J.N.G., resigned Feb. 11, 1913. Mem. Newark Bd. Trade, Chamber Commerce U.S.A., Chamber Commerce State of N.Y., N.J. State Chamber Commerce. Republican. Presbyn. Home: Bernardsville, N.J. Died July 19, 1932.

DRYDEN, James, poultry breeder; b. Galt, Ont., Can., Feb. 27, 1863; s. James and Mary (Swan) D.; ed. Collegiate Inst., Galt; m. Alice Keim, June 15, 1892; children—Leone (dec.), Robert James, Winfield Joseph, Horace Walter. Came to U.S., 1889, naturalized, 1892. Sec. of com. of Canadian senate, on Resources of MacKenzie River Basin, 1886; sec. to Lt. Gov. Shultz, Manitoba, 1887-88; writer Salt Lake Daily Tribune, 1889-91; instr. poultry husbandry and investigator, Utah Agrl. Coll., Logan, 1892-1907, Ore. State Agrl. Coll., Corvallis, 1907-21; pres. mgr. and chief owner, James Dryden Poultry Breeding Farm, Ltd., 1922—. Developed method of estimating laying capacity of poultry. Republican. Methodist. Woodman. Author: Poultry Breeding and Management, 1916. Home: Modesto, Calif. Died Feb. 4, 1935.

DRYDEN, John Fairfield, senator; b. on farm nr. Farmington, Me., Aug. 7, 1839; s. John and Elizabeth B. (Reynolds) D.; entered Yale, 1861, but left before graduation, because of illness (hon. A.M., 1900); m. Cynthia Fairchild, Apr. 7, 1864. Established, 1875, after comprehensive investigation, the Prudential Ins. Co. of America instn. for transaction of industrial ins.); was its sec. 1875-81, then pres.; dir. U.S. Steel Corp., 1903—; v.p. Fidelity Trust Co. (Newark); trustee Equitable Trust Co. (New York). Presdl. elector, 1896, 1900; U.S. senator, 1902-07. Republican. Home: Bernardsville, N.J. Died 1911.

DRYER, Charles Redway (Wilmarth), geographer; b. Victor, N.Y., Aug. 31, 1850; s. Daniel and Fidelia (Perry) D.; A.B., Hamilton Coll., 1871; M.D., U. of Buffalo, 1876; m. Alice Mary Peacock, 1874; children—Helen Eliza, Alice Judith, Reginald Peacock, Clare Mary. Teacher sciences, high sch., Ft. Wayne, Ind., 1877-90; prof. chemistry and toxicology, Ft. Wayne Coll. of Medicine, 1878-93; prof. geography and geology, Ind. State Normal Sch., 1893-1913. Chemist, Ft. Wayne Electric Co., 1890-93; asst. Ind. Geol. Survey, 1886-93. Author: Studies in Indiana Geography, 1897; Lessons in Physical Geography, 1901; Geography, Physical, Economic and Regional, 1911; Elementary Economic Geography, 1916. Home: Fort Wayne, Ind. Died Mar. 21, 1927.

DRYSDALE, Thomas Murray, M.D.; b. Phila., Aug. 14, 1831; grad. Pa. Med. Coll., 1852; m. Mary L., d. Dr. Washington Atlee, Oct. 1857. Prof. chemistry, Wagner Inst. of Science, 1855; lecturer on microscopy, Franklin Inst., 1862; surgeon 1st Pa. inf., 1863; specialist in surgery and gynecology; discovered and described the ovarian cell which exists in ovarian tumors; cons. gynecologist, Medico-Chirurgical Hosp.; cons. surgeon Girard Coll.; v.p., 1875, pres., 1876, Phila. Co. Med. Sec.; one of founders Am. Gynecol. Soc. 1876; mem. Internat. Med. Congress, 1876; v.p., 1881, pres., 1887-88, Phila. Obstetric Soc. Home: Philadelphia, Pa. Died 1904.

DRYSDALE, William, author; b. Lancaster, Pa., July 11, 1852; ed. by father and at Columbia Law

School; m. Adelaide L. Bigelow, 1885. City editor Phila. Times, 1876; 20 yrs. on staff of New York Times; editor and foreign corr. Author: The Princess of Montserrat; The Young Reporter; The Fast Mail; The Beach Patrol; The Young Supercargo; Cadet Standish of the St. Louis; Helps for Ambitious Boys; Helps for Ambitious Girls; The Treasury Club. Home: New Berne, N.C. Died 1901.

DUANE, Alexander, M.D., author; b. Malone, N.Y., Sept. 1, 1858; s. Gen. James Chatham (U.S.A.) and Harriet W. (Brewerton) D.; A.B., Union Coll., 1878 (Sc.D., 1919); M.D., Coll. Phys. and Surg. (Columbia), 1881; m. Susan Williams Galt, July 14, 1891; children—Alexander Galt (killed in World War), Robert Livingston, William Richard. In practice New York from 1881; served lt. (jr. grade), U.S. N., during Spanish-Am. War in charge of 2d dist. Coast Signal Service; lt. (jr. grade) on reserve list Naval Militia N.Y., 1917, acting signal officer U.S.S. Granite State, 1917-19. Trustee Union Coll., 1923—. Author: Student's Medical Dictionary, 1893, 4th edit., 1902; Fuchs' Textbook of Ophthalmology, 1892, 7th edit., 1923; Motor Anomalies of the Eye, 1897; Rules for Signaling on Land and Sea (adopted by U.S. Navy Dept. for Instrn. of Naval Militia of U.S.), 1899, 2d edit., 1901. Home: New York, N.Y. Died June 10, 1926.

DUANE, James May, banker; b. Honesdale, Pa., Aug. 21, 1851; s. Richard Bache and Margaret Anne (Tams) D.; A.B., Brown U., 1872; m. Katharine E. P. Higginson, Apr. 27, 1886. With U.S. branch of London Assurance Corp., 1872-87; with Brown Bros. & Co., 1887—, partner, Jan. 1, 1896—; mem. bd. mgrs. Lehigh Coal & Navigation Co.; dir. Lehigh & N.E. Ry. Co., Lehigh & Hudson Ry. Co., York Rys. Co. Mem. bd. trustees Brown U. Independent Democrat. Episcopalian. Home: New York, N.Y. Died Dec. 1912.

DUANE, Russell, lawyer; b. Gloucester Co., N.J., June 15, 1866; s. Rev. Charles W. and Helen F. Duane; g.g.g.gs. of Benjamin Franklin; A.B., Harvard U., 1888; LL.B., U. of Pa., 1891; m. Mary B. Morris, June 14, 1899; children—Morris, Sarah Franklin, Franklin (dec.). Admitted to bar, 1891, and began practice at Phila.; sr. mem. Duane, Morris & Heckscher. Junior counsel for U.S., Bering Sea case, 1892; lecturer on court practice, U. of Pa. Trustee Presser Foundation; pres. Osteopathic Hosp. of Phila. and Phila. Coll. of Osteopathy. Pres. Nat. Soc. Descendants of Signers of Declaration of Independence. Home: Philadelphia, Pa. Died Jan. 19, 1938.

DUANE, William, physicist; b. Phila., Pa., Feb. 17, 1872; s. Charles Williams and Emma Cushman (Lincoln) D.; A.B., U. of Pa., 1892; A.B., Harvard, 1893, A.M., 1895; univs. of Berlin and Göttingen, 1895-97, Ph.D., Berlin, 1897; hon. Sc.D., U. of Pennsylvania, 1922; hon. Sc.D., U. of Colo., 1923; m. Caroline Elise Ravenel, Dec. 28, 1899; children—William, Arthur Ravenel (dec.), John P., Margaretta C. Asst. in physics, 1893-95, Tyndall fellow, 1895-97, Harvard; prof. physics, U. of Colo., 1898-1907; research, Curie Radium Lab., U. of Paris, 1907-12; asst. prof. physics, 1913-17, prof. bio-physics, 1917—, Harvard. Mem. Am. Acad. Arts and Sciences. Episcopalian. Awarded John Scott medal and premium, 1922; Comstock prize, Nat. Acad. of Science, 1922; first Leonard prize, Am. Roentgen Ray Soc., 1923; all three prizes for researches in radioactivity and X-rays. Died Mar. 7, 1935.

DU BARRY, Beekman, brig. gen. U.S. Army, retired; b. Pa., Aug. 20, 1824; entered West Point July 1, 1845; bvt. 2d lt., July 1, 1849; commd. 2d lt. 1st art., April 1, 1850; advanced through grades to brig. gen. inspector gen., Sept. 22, 1885; retired, Aug. 20, 1888. In Civil war served as brig. gen. and bvt. maj. gen. vols. from April 1862, until mustered out of vol. service, Sept. 1, 1866; bvtd. lt. col. and col. U.S. Army, 1865, for faithful and meritorious services. Died 1901.

DUBBINK, Gerrit Hendrik, clergyman; b. Overisel, Mich., Dec. 3, 1866; s. John and Grietje (Blink) D.; A.B., Hope Coll., 1892, A.M., 1895; grad. Western Theol. Sem., 1895; (D.D., Hope, 1904); m. Margaret J. Kollen, May 29, 1895. Pastor Third Reformed Ch., Holland, Mich., 1895-1904; prof. didactic and polemic theology, Western Theol. Sem. (Reformed Ch. in Am.), Holland, Mich., 1904. Home: Holland, Mich. Died 1910.

DUBBS, Henry A(lfred), lawyer; b. Pottstown, Pa., Aug. 23, 1868; s. Joseph Henry and Mary L. (Wilson) D.; A.B., Franklin and Marshall Coll., Pa., 1887, A.M., 1890, LL.D., 1937; m. Helen Miller Wellens, Nov. 20, 1922 (died 1924); 1 son, Henry Miller. Admitted to bar, Pa., 1890, Colo., 1890. Has been counsel for various railroad companies, banks, smelters, mines, etc.; associated with development of law of irrigation in the arid West. Dir. State Hist. Soc. of Colo., pres., 1925-32. Home: Denver, Colo. Died Nov. 9, 1939.

DUBBS, Joseph Henry, coll. prof.; b. N. Whitehall, Pa., Oct. 5, 1838; s. Rev. Joseph and Eleanor (Lerch) D.; grad. Franklin and Marshall Coll., Pa.,

1856, Mercersburg Theol. Sem., 1859; (D.D., Ursinus Coll., 1878; LL.D., Heidelberg U., Ohio, 1897); m. Mary L. Wilson, Sept. 22, 1863; father of Henry Alfred D. Clergyman Ref. Ch. in U.S.; pastor at Allentown, Pottstown and Phila.; prof. history and archæology, 1875—, pres. ad interim, 1904 and 1907, Franklin and Marshall Coll. Corr. mem. Ethnographic Soc. France; fellow Royal Hist. Soc., Great Britain; pres. Pa. German Soc., 1901-02; v.p. Lancaster Co. Hist. Soc.; mem. Hist. Soc. Pa.; v.p. Pa. Federation of Hist. Socs. Author: Leaders of the Reformation, 1900; The Reformed Church in Pennsylvania, 1902; History of Franklin and Marshall Coll., 1903. Address: Lancaster, Pa. Died 1910.

DU BOIS, Augustus Jay, civil engr.; b. Newton Falls, O., Apr. 25, 1849; s. Henry Augustus and Catherine Helena (Jay) D.; Ph.B., Sheffield Scientific Sch. (Yale), 1869; C.E., 1870, Ph.D., 1873; studied mechanics 2 yrs. at Freiberg (Saxony) Mining Acad.; m. Adeline Blakesley, June 23, 1883. Prof. civ. and mech. engring., Lehigh U., 1875-77; prof. mech. engring., 1877-84, civ. engring., 1884—, Sheffield Scientific Sch. Author: Elements of Mechanics (3 vols.), 1893-95. Home: New Haven, Conn. Died Oct. 19, 1915.

DuBOIS, Charles Gilbert, businessman; b. New York City, Mar. 22, 1870; s. William H. and Anne Eliza (Gilbert) D.; A.B., Dartmouth, 1891 (specializing last 2 yrs. in physics and economics), A.M., 1923; m. Sue Sanford, June 6, 1901; children—William Sanford, Susan. Began with Western Electric Co., at New York, 1891, at Chicago, 1897, became sec. and supervisor branch houses of the co., 1902-07; comptroller Am. Telephone & Telegraph Co., 1907-18 (on leave of absence war period, as comptroller Am. Red Cross, Washington, 1917-18); v.p., 1918-19, pres., 1919-26, chmn. bd., 1926-27, Western Electric Co. Retired. Home: Englewood, N.J. Died Dec. 23, 1940.

DU BOIS, Edward Church, judge; b. London, Eng., Jan. 12, 1848; s. Edward Church and Emma Davison (in 1857, in New York, father assumed his mother's maiden name, "Du Bois," for himself, his wife and children); ed. Friends' Acad., New Bedford, Mass., 1863-65; m. Jennie Roberts, Feb. 24, 1872. Admitted to bar, Boston, 1870; clerk police court, Haverhill, Mass., 1872-77; removed to Providence, R.I., Nov. 1877; admitted to R.I. bar, 1877; atty. gen. of R.I., 1894-97; asso. justice Supreme Ct. of R.I., Mar. 3, 1899— (chief justice from Jan. 13, 1909). Republican. Home: Providence, R.I. Died Jan. 1914.

DUBOIS, Fred Thomas, senator; b. Crawford Co., Ill., May 29, 1851; s. Jesse K. (state auditor Ill.) and Adelia (Morris) D.; A.B., Yale, 1872; m. Miss Edna M. Whited, Jan. 11, 1899; children—Mrs. Elizabeth Cannon, Toussaint. Went to Ida., 1880; U.S. marshal, 1882-86; was active in the anti-Mormon agitation; del. in 50th and 51st Congresses (1887-91); instrumental in securing admission of Ida. to statehood, 1890; 1st U.S. senator from Ida., 1891-97; del. Rep. Nat. convs., 1888, 92, 96; withdrew from conv., 1896, after adoption of gold-standard platform; Silver Rep. candidate for reëlection, 1896; reëlected for term 1901-07; became Democrat after election; had charge of Champ Clark's campaign for presdl. nomination, 1912. Became v.p. First Nat. Fire Ins. Co. Pres. Capital Service and Information Bur., Washington. Apptd. civilian mem. Bd. of Ordnance and Fortification, War Dept., Mar. 1918; apptd. mem. Internat. Joint Commn., 1924; chmn. bd. Nat. U. Sch. of Law, Washington, D.C. Home: Blackfoot, Ida. Died Feb. 14, 1930.

DU BOIS, James T., diplomatist; b. Hallstead, Pa., Apr. 17, 1851; s. Joseph and Emroy D.; grad. Ithaca Acad., 1870, and took course of lectures at Cornell to prepare for journalistic career; m. Emma, d. Henry Pastor, of New York, Dec. 29, 1883. Editor National Republican, Washington, 1872-77; apptd. commercial agt., 1877, and consul, 1881, to Aix-la-Chapelle, Germany; later, in 1881, apptd. consul at Callao, Peru, which declined; apptd. consul at Leipzig, Germany, from which resigned, 1885; returned to Washington and resumed journalistic work; consul gen. at St. Gall, Switzerland, 1897-1901; editor of the laws, Dept. of State, 1901-09; consul gen. at Singapore, Straits Settlements 1909-11; M.P. and E.E. to Colombia, Aug. 21, 1911-June 15, 1913 (resigned). Author: Life of Ex-Speaker Galusha A. Grow. Home: Hallstead, Pa. Died May 27, 1920.

DuBOIS, Jean Joseph (name changed from John Joseph Tobias to ancestral name, 1927), chancellor Chicago Law Sch.; b. Vandalia, Ill.; s. Rev. S. A. and Leah Anna (Seager) Tobias; student Northwestern (now Naperville) Coll., Northwestern U., Ill. Wesleyan U., Nat. Med. Coll., U. of Chicago, Chicago Law Sch.; degrees LL.B., Ph.D. Educational work, 1892—; chancellor Chicago Law Sch., and of Chicago Seminar of Science. Grand chancellor of fraternal (law) Order of Lincoln. Mason. Author: (brochures) Common Sense Psychology; Psychology of How to Study; Legal Ethics; How and Where to Find the Law. Home: Oak Park, Ill. Died July 10, 1932.

DU BOIS, John Ezekiel; b. Tioga, N.Y., May 15, 1861; s. Ezekiel and Clarissa (Badger) Du B.; desc.

Louis du Bois, Huguenot, who settled nr. New Paltz, N.Y., 1659; m. Willie Gamble, of Va. Inherited fortune of uncle, John Du Bois, founder of Du Bois, Pa., and a large lumber operator; retired. Home: Du Bois, Pa. Died Nov. 11, 1934.

DU BOIS, Patterson, editor, literary adviser, author; b. Philadelphia, 1847; s. William Ewing D. (late curator of cabinet, U.S. Mint, Phila.) and Susanna (Eckfeldt) D.; ed. Phila. High Sch. and by pvt. tuition; student Pa. Acad. Fine Arts, and in studios of D. Ridgeway Knight and Peter Moran; m. Clara, d. Dr. Jesse C. Green, of West Chester, Pa., 1875. In assay dept., Phila. Mint, 1867, asst. assayer, 1882; asst. editor The Sunday School Times (Phila.), 1886-1900; lit. adviser F. H. Revell Co., 1901; lecturer and writer on child culture and religious and gen. edn. On com. Standard Dictionary on disputed spellings and pronunciations. Author: Beckonings from Little Hands, 1893, 1900; The Point of Contact in Teaching, 1896, 1900; Fireside Child Study, 1903; The Practice of Salvation, 1913. Home: Philadelphia, Pa. Died Aug. 8, 1917.

DU BOSE, Horace Mellard, bishop; b. Choctaw Co., Ala., Nov. 7, 1858; s. Hezekiah and Amanda (Hawkins) D.; ed. Waynesboro (Miss.) Acad.; studied langs. and classics under tutors; D.D., Emory and Henry Coll., 1892; m. Rosa Chaney, Dec. 6, 1882; m. 2d, Mrs. G. V. Amis, Dec. 20, 1899. Licensed to preach, M.E. Ch., S., Oct. 1, 1876; ordained, 1879; admitted into Miss. Conf., 1877-80; pastor Galveston, Tex., 1881-82, Huntsville, Tex., 1883-84, Houston, 1885-86, Tyler, Tex., 1887-88, Los Angeles, 1889-90; editor Pacific Meth. Advocate, San Francisco, 1890-94; pastor Tyler, Tex., 1895-96, Jackson, Miss., 1897-98; sec. Epworth League and editor Epworth Era, 1898-1910; pastor St. John's Ch., Augusta, Ga., 1910-11, First Ch., Atlanta, 1911-15; book editor M.E. Ch., S., and editor Meth. Quarterly Review, Nashville, 1915-18; elected bishop, May 1918, and stationed at Berkeley, Calif. Del. 5 Gen. Conferences; mem. Ecumenical Conf., 1901; mem. World S.S. Conv.; fraternal del. from M.E. Ch., S., to Gen. Conf. of Meth. Ch. of Can.; del. 4th Ecumenical Conf., Toronto, 1911; exec. chmn. Anti-Saloon League of Georgia, 1913-15; commr. for Ecumenical Methodist Conf., held in London, 1921; mem. commn. apptd. 1916, for unification of Methodist chs. North and South. Has done occasional work in Am. archæology, studying the habitats of the Amerinds or prehistoric races in Mexico and Western America; now collaborating with Prof. Sellin of U. of Berlin in uncovering of site of Shechem, in Palestine. Author: The Symbol of Methodism, 1907; Francis Asbury, a Biographical Study, 1909; Life of Bishop Joshua Soule, 1910; History of Methodism, 1916; Consciousness of Jesus, 1917; The Bible and the Ages, 1930; Through Two Generations, 1936. Home: Nashville, Tenn. Died Jan. 15, 1941.

DU BOSE, William Haskell, theologian; b. Abbeville, S.C., May 17, 1870; s. William Porcher and Anne (Peronneau) D.; M.A., U. of the South, 1891; grad. in divinity, same, 1898; non-collegiate student, Oxford Univ., Eng., 1½ yrs., 1896-98; D.D., Alexandria Sem., Va., 1923; m. Dean Spencer, Sept. 21, 1896; 1 son, William Haskell. Deacon, 1896, priest, 1898, P.E. Ch.; rector Christ Ch., Tracy City, Tenn., 1898-1916, Chapel of the Holy Comforter, Monteagle, Tenn., 1915-30; prof. O.T. lang. and interpretation, U. of the South, 1898—. Democrat. Home: Sewanee, Tenn. Died Oct. 15, 1936.

DU BOSE, William Porcher, theologian; b. Winnsboro, S.C., Apr. 11, 1836; s. Theodore Samuel and Jane (Porcher) D.; grad. S.C. Mil. Acad., Charleston, S.C., 1855; A.M., U. of Va., 1859; studied at Theol. Sem. of S.C.; (S.T.D., Columbia, 1875; D.C.L., U. of the South, 1907; D.D., Gen. Theol. Sem., New York, 1908); m. Anne Barnwell Peronneau, Apr. 30, 1863 (died 1873); m. 2d, Maria Louisa Yerger, Dec. 18, 1878 (died 1887). Adj. and later chaplain Kershaw's brigade, C.S.A., 1861-65. Deacon, 1864, priest, 1865, P.E. Ch.; rector St. John's, Winnsboro, 1866-67, Trinity Ch., Abbeville, S.C., 1868-71; chaplain and prof. ethics and New and O.T. lang. and interpretation, 1871-94, prof. N.T. lang. and interpretation, 1894—, dean theol. dept., 1894-1908, emeritus, U. of the South. Author: The Soteriology of the New Testament, 1892, last edition, 1906; The Ecumenical Councils, 1896; The Gospel in the Gospels, 1906; The Gospel According to St. Paul, 1907; High-Priesthood and Sacrifice, 1908; The Reason of Life, 1910; Turning Points in My Life, 1912. Died Aug. 18, 1918.

DU BOSQUE, Francis LeBrun, naval architect; b. Phila., Pa., Jan. 25, 1864; s. Francis Prosper and Viginia E. (Longmire) D.; ed. pub. schs.; m. Adele Henderson Clarke, Jan. 4, 1915; m. 2d, Ella Holland, Mar. 31, 1926. Served apprenticeship, League Island (Pa.) Navy Yard; draftsman U.S. Navy Dept.; laid out and managed Crescent Ship Yard, Elizabethport, N.J.; supt. floating equipment, design and maintenance, Pa. R.R.; retired. Republican. Home: Great Neck, L.I., and Miami Beach, Fla. Died Apr. 13, 1940.

DUCEY, Thomas James, R.C. clergyman; b. Lismore, Ireland, Feb. 4, 1843; came to U.S. when 5

yrs. old; studied at Coll. of St. Francis Xavier, New York; entered Theol. Sem., Troy, N.Y., 1864; ordained priest, 1868; after service at Ch. of Nativity and St. Michael's, founded St. Leo's Ch., 1880, becoming its pastor; prominent in movements against municipal corruption and in philanthropic enterprises. Home: New York, N.Y. Died 1909.

DU CHAILLU, Paul Belloni, explorer, author; b. New Orleans, July 31, 1838; sailed from New York to the French settlement at the mouth of the Gaboon river, W. Africa; at his own expense traveled 8,000 miles, with only native companions; covered much previously unexplored country and added 60 species of birds and 20 species of mammals (including the gorilla) to the known zoölogy of Africa. His accounts of the gorillas and Obongo dwarfs were contradicted by scientists, but have since been confirmed. Made a second exploration, 1863-65; discovered many new species of animals and birds; also traveled in Sweden, Norway, Lapland and Finland and other countries. Author: Wild Life Under the Equator; My Apingi Kingdom; The Country of the Dwarfs; Lost in the Jungle; The Land of the Long Night, 1899; The World of the Great Forest, 1900; How Animals, Birds, Reptiles and Insects Talk, Think, Work and Live, 1900. Home: New York, N.Y. Died 1903.

DUDLEY, Augustus Palmer, M.D., surgeon; b. Phippsburg, Me., July 4, 1853; ed. public school and Portland Acad.; grad. Dartmouth Med. School, 1877; practiced Portland, Me., 1877-81; New York, 1881— (except 1884-87, San Francisco); prof. diseases of women Post-Graduate Med. School and Hosp.; also in Univ. of Vt., Burlington, Vt.; surgeon to Harlem Hosp.; etc. Died 1905.

DUDLEY, Charles Benjamin, chemist; b. Oxford, N.Y., July 14, 1842; s. Daniel and Maranda (Bemis) D.; A.B., Yale, 1871, Ph.D., 1874; m. Mary V. Crawford, Apr. 17, 1906. Asst. in physics, U. of Pa., 1875, then chemist to Pa. R.R. Co.; has made noteworthy chem. researches into the quality of metals for railroad use. Home: Altoona, Pa. Died 1909.

DUDLEY, Charles Rowland, librarian; b. Easton, Conn., June 26, 1853; s. Rev. Martin and Sarah (Rowland) D.; ed. Monson (Mass.) Acad., 1869-72; LL.B., Yale, 1877; m. Rose A. Smith, Sept. 14, 1893. Practiced law, Monson, Mass., 1878-82; moved to Denver; librarian Denver Pub. Library, 1886-1911. Regent U. of Colo., 1888-1900, 1906-12, 1915—. Deceased.

DUDLEY, Edgar Swartwout, brig. gen.; b. Oppenheim, N.Y., June 14, 1845; s. James Madison and Maria (Swartwout) D.; grad. U.S. Mil. Acad., 1870; LL.B., Albany Law Sch. (Union U.), 1875; (LL.D., U. of Neb., 1904); m. Mary S. Hillabrandt, June 22, 1870. Lt. 1st N.Y. Light Arty., May 28-Nov. 28, 1864; 2d lt. 2d U.S. Arty., June 15, 1870; advanced through grades to col. judge adv., Nov. 22, 1903; brig. gen., retired at age limit, June 14, 1909. Prof. mil. science and tactics, U. of Neb., 1876-79 and 1884-88; maj. and lt. col. U.S. vols., judge adv., Div. of Cuba, and legal adviser in civ. and mil. affairs, of mil. govs. of Cuba (Gens. John R. Brooke and Leonard Wood), Dec. 1898-May 21, 1901; prof. law, U.S. Mil. Acad., July 31, 1901, until retirement. Mason. Author: Military Law and the Procedure of Courts-Martial, 1907. Home: Johnstown, N.Y. Died 1911.

DUDLEY, Emelius Clark, M.D.; b. Westfield, Mass., May 29, 1850; s. John Harmon and Marana P. (Mason) D.; A.B., Dartmouth, 1873; M.D., L.I. Coll. Hosp., 1875; (hon. A.M., Iowa College, 1892; LL.D., Grinnell College, 1917); m. Anna M. Titcomb, June 29, 1882; children—Katharine Dorothy (Mrs. H. B. Harvey), Helen, Prescott, Caroline (Mrs. Daniel J. Reagon). Engaged in practice in Chicago, 1875—; prof. gynecology, Northwestern Univ., 1882—. Commd. major O.R.C., 1917. Mem. Chicago Bd. Edn., 1901-06. Republican. Unitarian. Fellow Am. Gynecol. Assn. (pres. 1904), British Gynecol. Soc. Author: Principles and Practice of Gynecology, 1908, 6th edit., 1914. Home: Chicago, Ill. Died Dec. 1, 1928.

DUDLEY, Irving Bedell, ambassador; b. Jefferson, O., Nov. 30, 1861; s. Rev. H. C. Hamilton and Mary (Eastwood) D.; A.B., Kenyon Coll., 1882; LL.B., Columbian (now George Washington) U., 1885, LL.M., 1886 (LL.D., 1908); m. Jennie A. Kelley, Apr. 28, 1896. Admitted to bar, 1885; began practice, San Diego, Calif., 1888; judge City Ct., 1891-95; mem. Rep. State Exec. Com., Calif., 1896; E.E. and M.P. to Peru, 1897-1906; ambassador extraordinary and plenipotentiary to Brazil, Dec. 19, 1906—. Home: San Diego, Calif. Died 1911.

DUDLEY, James Benson, coll. pres.; b. Wilmington, N.C., Nov. 2, 1859; s. John B. and Annie J. D.; ed. Wilmington, N.C., and Phila.; (A.M., Livingstone Coll.; LL.D., Wilberforce U.); m. Susie W. Sampson, Feb. 23, 1882. Was editor Wilmington (N.C.) Chronicle; prin. Peabody Sch., Wilmington, 1880-96; pres. Agrl. and Tech. Coll. for the Colored Race, Greensboro, N.C., 1896—. Home: Greensboro, N.C. Died Apr. 4, 1925.

DUDLEY, Lucy (May) Bronson, author; b. Peninsula, O., May 1, 1848; d. Hiram V. and Ruth L. (Ranney) Bronson; ed. Episcopal Female Sem., Granville, O.; (M.S., Hiram Coll., 1899); m. Plimmon Henry Dudley, Dec. 12, 1871. Organist Christ Episcopal Ch., Warren, O.; Euclid Av. Congl. Ch. and Grace Episcopal Ch., Cleveland, 1866-76. Visited Panama, 1887; European tours, 1895 and 1900; received by Queen Victoria and the Prince of Wales in Windsor Castle, July 6, 1895. Author: Contributions to the Knowledge of the Termites, 1893; Letters to Ruth, 1896; A Royal Journey, 1900; A Writer's Inkhorn, 1911. Died May 1920.

DUDLEY, Nathan Augustus Monroe, brig. gen.; b. Lexington, Mass., Aug. 20, 1825; s. John and Ester Eliza (Smith) D.; ed. pub. schs. of Roxbury, Mass.; m. Elizabeth Gray Jewett (dec.). Was engaged in commercial pursuits until 1855; served 7 yrs. in Mass. Militia and was mem. Ancient and Hon. Artillery Co. of Boston, 1851-55, and served 3 yrs. as brigade and div. inspr. of Boston Troops. Apptd. from civ. life as 1st lt. 10th U.S. Inf., Mar. 3, 1855; promoted through grades to col. 1st Cav., June 6, 1885; retired by operation of law, Aug. 20, 1889; advanced to rank of brig. gen. retired, by act of Apr. 23, 1904. In Civ. War served as col. 30th Mass. Inf., Mar. 1, 1862-Feb. 16, 1865, when was hon. mustered out of vol. service. Received bvts. of maj., lt. col. and col. U.S.A. for gallant services in Civ. War, and bvtd. brig. gen. Vols., Jan. 18, 1865. Was insp. gen. Dept. of the Gulf, or chief of staff to Gen. Banks; spent 30 yrs. in campaigning against Indians on frontier, before and after Civ. War, until retired—with Harney on Sioux expdn., 1855, with Albert Sidney Johnston on Utah expdn., 1857-60; with Crook against Apaches, and comd. cav. on Buell expdn. into Mexico (coöperating with Mexican forces in killing of Victorio and capture of his band). Home: Roxbury, Mass. Died 1910.

DUDLEY, Pemberton, M.D.; b. Torresdale, Phila., Pa., Oct. 17, 1837; grad. Homœo. Med. Coll., Phila., 1861; prof. chemistry and toxicology there, 1868-69; prof. physiology and microscopic anatomy, 1876-90; prof. institutes of medicine and hygiene, Hahnemann Med. Coll., 1890—; dean same, 1896—. Gen. sec. and editor ann. Transactions, Am. Inst. Homœopathy, 1887-94; editor Hahnemannian Monthly, 1880-88; mem. State bd. of health, 1885, reapptd. 1891; m. Sarah K. Hall, Dec. 25, 1867. (LL.D., Rutherford Coll., N.C., 1899.) Home: Philadelphia, Pa. Died 1907.

DUDLEY, Plimmon Henry, civil and metall. engr.; b. Freedom, O., May 21, 1843; s. Charles and Sarah (Leete) D.; ed. Hiram (O.) Coll., Ph.D.; m. Lucy May Bronson, Dec. 12, 1871. Chief engr. Valley Ry., 1872-74; chief engr. City of Akron, O., 1866-72; now cons. engr. N.Y.C. lines. Invented dynamometer, 1874; track indicator, 1880; designed, 1883, the first 5-inch steel rail used in U.S., and in 1892 introduced the first 6-inch 100-lb. rails; invented stremmatograph for obtaining and registering strains in rails under moving trains; made first announcement, 1884, that fungi was the cause of decay in wood. Reporter for U.S. on the "Nature of the Metal for Rails" to Internat. Ry. Congress, 6th session, Paris, 1900, and on "Rails for Lines with Fast Trains," to 7th session, Washington, 1905. Died Feb. 25, 1924.

DUDLEY, Thomas Underwood, P.E. bishop; b. Richmond, Va., Sept. 26, 1837; s. Thomas Underwood and Maria (Friend) D.; grad. Univ. of Va. (A.M.), 1858; asst. prof. there until war; served in commissary dept. C.S.A., reaching rank of maj. Studied Va. Theol. Sem., Alexandria; (D.D., St. John's Coll., Md., 1874, Univ. of South, 1876; D.C.L., King's Coll., Nova Scotia; LL.D., Griswold Coll.). Ordained deacon, June 28, 1867; priest, June 26, 1868; rector Christ's Ch., Baltimore, when elected asst. bishop of Ky.; consecrated Jan. 27, 1875, and became bishop May 31, 1884; elected chmn. house of bishops, 1901. Author: A Wise Discrimination of the Church's Need; also Church Sunday School Question Books. Home: Louisville, Ky. Died 1904.

DUDLEY, William Lofland, chemist; b. Covington, Ky., Apr. 16, 1859; s. George Reed and Emma (Lofland) D.; B.S., U. of Cincinnati, 1880; (hon. M.D., Miami Med. Coll., 1885); unmarried. Demonstrator of chemistry, 1879-80, prof. chemistry and toxicology, 1880-86, Miami Med. Coll.; prof. chemistry in Vanderbilt Univ., 1866—, dean Medical Dept., 1895-1913. Commr. Cincinnati Industrial Expn., 1881-85 (2d v.p. 1884); dir. of affairs Tenn. Centennial Expn., 1897; sec. sect. inorganic chemistry, Internat. Congress Arts and Sciences, St. Louis, 1904. Devised a process for working and electro-plating with iridium which has caused its enlarged use in the arts. U.S. commr. 7th Congress Applied Chemistry, London, 1909; v.p. sect. on law and legislation as affecting chem. industry, 8th Congress Applied Chemistry, 1912; spectrographic studies on tellurium and atomic weight determinations of tellurium. Home: Nashville, Tenn. Died Sept. 8, 1914.

DUDLEY, William Russel, botanist; b. Guilford, Conn., Mar. 1, 1849; s. Samuel William and Lucy (Chittenden) D.; B.S., Cornell, 1874, M.S., 1876; studied natural history in the Agassiz School, Penikese Island, 1874, Harvard Summer Sch., 1876; studied at univs. of Strassburg and Berlin, 1887-88. Instr. botany, 1873-76, asst. prof., 1876-83, asst. prof. in charge cryptogamic botany, 1883-92, Cornell; prof. botany, Leland Stanford Jr. U., 1892—. Asso. editor Sierra Club Bull., 1898—. Author: The Cayuga Flora, 1886; Lackawanna and Wyoming Flora, 1887; Manual of Histology (with Prof. M. B. Thomas), 1894; etc. Died 1911.

DUDLEY, William Wade, lawyer; b. Weathersfield Bow, Vt., Aug. 27, 1842; ed. Phillip's Acad., Danville, Vt., and Russell's Collegiate Inst., New Haven, Conn.; removed to Richmond, Ind., 1860; engaged in milling business; became capt. City Grays there; co. enlisted July 4, 1861; mustered into U.S. service, July 29, 1861, in 19th Ind. vols.; served with distinction and became col. and bvt. brig. gen., taking part in 15 battles; wounded at Gettysburg, losing right leg; afterward served as insp. and judge adv. to close of war; m. Theresa, d. Rev. George Fiske, Richmond, Ind., 1864; m. 2d, Nannie R. Finch, 1899. Clerk of courts, Wayne Co., Ind., 1866-74; admitted to bar; cashier Richmond Savings Bank, 1875-79; U.S. marshal, dist. of Ind., 1879-81; U.S. commr. of pensions, 1881-85; in business, 1885-87; mem. law firm, 1887; became treas. Nat. Rep. Com., 1888; from 1889 in law practice at Washington. Home: Washington, D.C. Died 1909.

DUDLEY, Winfield Ware, newspaperman; b. Danvers, Mass., Aug. 23, 1879; s. George Warren and Annie Carle (Parcher) D.; ed. Shurtleff Acad. and Coll., Upper Alton, Ill.; John Marshall Law Sch., Chicago; m. Agnes May Graham, Apr. 14, 1906. Reporter, city editor and telegraph editor, St. Louis papers; assisted materially in uncovering election and pub. utility frauds in St. Louis, 1900-04; rep. in Chicago of Scripps-McRae Press Assn. (now United Press Assn.), 1904-07; with Chicago Tribune, and later with Atlanta Constitution; Sunday editor New York Herald, May 1915—. Served as officer Ill. Naval Reserve, Ga. N.G. and Colo. N.G. Home: New York, N.Y. Died May 16, 1918.

DUEL, Arthur Baldwin, surgeon; b. Granville, N.Y., Dec. 14, 1870; s. Hiram D. and Almera J. (Hicks) D.; M.D., Harvard, 1894; m. Mary Key Crawford, Dec. 11, 1907; children—Mary Hobart, Arthur B. V.p. and chmn. bd. of surgeons, Manhattan Eye, Ear and Throat Hosp., N.Y. City; cons. aural surgeon to babies, Stuyvesant Square, and New York Health Bd., and Englewood hosps.; prof. otology, N.Y. Polyclinic Med. Sch., 1908-13. Fellow Am. Coll. Surgeons. Knight Comdr. Crown of Rumania, 1927. Republican. Episcopalian. Contbr. to med. pubs. Home: Pawling, N.Y. Died Apr. 11, 1936.

DUELL, Charles Holland, lawyer; b. Cortland, N.Y., Apr. 13, 1850; s. R. Holland D. (commr. of patents, 1875) and Mary L. (Cuyler) D.; A.B., Hamilton Coll., 1871, law school same, 1872 (LL.D., 1906); m. Harriet M. Sackett, Nov. 20, 1879. Mem. N.Y. Assembly, 1878, 1880; practiced law, New York, 1873-80, 1901-04, 1906-13, 15, Syracuse, N.Y., 1880-98, as patent lawyer; U.S. commr. patents, 1898-1901; asst. treas. Rep. Nat. Com., 1904; asso. justice Court of Appeals, D.C., 1904-06; presdl. elector-at-large, N.Y., 1908; pres. N.Y. electoral coll., 1909; now sr. mem. Duell, Warfield & Duell, New York; treas. Rep. Congressional Com., 1910-11; chmn. New York City Roosevelt Com., 1912. U.S. del. Conv. for the Protection of Industrial Property, Washington, May 1911. Home: Yonkers, N.Y. Died Jan. 29, 1920.

DUFFEY, Warren Joseph, congressman; b. Toledo, O., Jan. 24, 1886; s. Joseph A. and Rose Ellen (Kavany) D.; A.B. and A.M., St. John's U., Toledo, O.; LL.B., U. of Mich.; m. Marie Louise Sawkins, Aug. 28, 1913; children—Ruth Marie, Warren Francis, Natalie Grace, Richard Comerford, Cecile Joan, John Jerome. In practice at Toledo from 1911; mem. Ohio Gen. Assembly, 1913-14, Toledo City Council, 1917-18; mem. 73d and 74th Congresses (1933-37), 9th Ohio Dist. Democrat. K.C. Home: Toledo, Ohio. Died July 7, 1936.

DUFFIELD, Edward Dickinson, ins. pres.; b. Princeton, N.J., Mar. 3, 1871; s. John Thomas and Sarah E. (Green) D.; A.B., Princeton, 1892, A.M., 1895; studied law under Frederick W. Stevens and John O. H. Pitney, 1892-95; LL.B., New York Law Sch., 1894; LL.D., Rutgers, 1932, Lafayette and Princeton, 1933, Dartmouth Coll. and N.J. Law School, 1934; m. Josephine Reade Curtis, Apr. 21, 1897 (died 1914); children—Elizabeth M. (wife of Philip Yeatman, officer U.S. Navy), Dickinson C.; m. 2d, Barbara Freeman, Oct. 12, 1916. Mng. clerk, Depew & Parker, Newark, N.J., 1895-96; atty. N.J. bar, 1895, counsellor, 1898; mem. Duffield & Kenney, 1896-1901, Colie & Duffield, 1901-05; member N.J. House of Assembly, 1904-05; asst. atty. gen. of N.J., 1905-06; apptd. gen. solicitor, 1906, elected 4th v.p. and gen. solicitor, 1913, v.p. and gen. solicitor, 1916, v.p., asso. gen. counsel, 1918, pres., Sept. 1, 1922—, Prudential Ins. Co. of America; dir. U.S. Guarantee Co., Guaranty Trust Co. of New York, etc.; mem. bd. mgrs. Howard Savings Instn.,

Newark; acting pres. Princeton U., 1932-33. Mem. Bd. of Edn., S. Orange, N.J., 1901-04; pres. Village of S. Orange, 1917-21. Former mem. bd. trustees Gen. Assembly of Presbyn. Ch. (vice moderator, 1926-27). Life trustee Princeton U. (chmn. bd.). Chmn. Com. on Credentials, Rep. Nat. Conv., 1920. Home: S. Orange, N.J. Died Sept. 17, 1938.

DUFFIELD, Henry Martyn, lawyer; b. Detroit, May 15, 1842; s. Rev. George and Isabella Graham (Bethune) D.; A.B., Williams Coll., 1861; m. Frances Pitts, Dec. 29, 1863 (died 1906); father of Pitts D. Enlisted as pvt. 9th Mich. Inf., Aug., 1861; 1st lt. and adj., Oct. 12, 1861-Oct. 14, 1864; asst. adj.-gen. 23d Brigade, Army of the Cumberland, 1862; post adj., Chattanooga, 1863; asst. and acting provost marshal gen. Army of the Cumberland. Admitted to bar, 1865; became sr. mem. H. M. & D. B. Duffield; city counsellor, 1881-87. Brig. gen. vols., May 27, 1898; hon. disch., Nov. 30, 1898. Umpire German-Venezuelan Arbitration Commn., 1903. Comdr. in chief Naval and Mil. Order of Spanish-Am. War, 1910-11. Home: Detroit, Mich. Died July 13, 1912.

DUFFIELD, Howard, clergyman; b. Princeton, N.J., Apr. 9, 1854; s. Prof. John T. and Sarah Elizabeth (Green) D.; A.B., Princeton, 1873, A.M., 1876, D.D., 1888; grad. Princeton Theol. Sem., 1877; m. Katharine Nash Greenleaf, May 24, 1877. Ordained Presbyn. ministry, 1877; pastor Leacock, Pa., 1877-80, Beverly, N.J., 1880-84, Detroit, 1884-91, "Old First" Presbyn. Ch., New York, 1891—. Trustee Sailors Snug Harbor; pres. Leake and Watts' Orphan House. Chaplain of Vet. Corps Arty., N.G.N.Y., Guilmant Organ Sch. Home: New York, N.Y. Died Jan. 5, 1941.

DUFFIELD, John Thomas, prof. mathematics in Princeton Univ., 1850—; b. McConnellsburg, Pa., Feb. 19, 1823; grad. Princeton, 1841, (D.D.; also LL.D., Lake Forest Univ.); m. Sarah Elizabeth Green, Dec. 30, 1852. Tutor of Greek at Princeton and, 1847-50, adjunct prof. mathematics. Licensed to preach, 1849; ordained to Presbyn. ministry, 1851; moderator of Synod of N.J., 1866; pres. bd. of edn. of Princeton, N.J. Author: The Princeton Pulpit. Died 1901.

DUFFIELD, William Ward, civil engr.; b. Carlisle, Pa., Nov. 19, 1823; grad. Columbia, 1841 (A.M., 1844); m. A. Louise Ladue, June 27, 1854. Lt. on staff Gen. Gideon B. Pillow in Mexican war, 1847-48; lt. col. 4th Mich. inf., 1861, in Civil War; col. 9th Mich. inf., 1862; brig. gen., April 1, 1863; bvtd. maj. gen., 1863; twice severely wounded at Murfreesboro; State senator, Mich., 1878-79; chief engr. of railways in Mich., N.Y., Ill., Texas and other states; U.S. engr. of improvements on Wabash and White rivers in Ind. and Ill., 1892-93; supt. U.S. Coast and Geodetic Survey, 1894-98. Author: School of the Brigade and Evolutions of the Line; Treatise on Logarithms—with Tables of Logarithms to Ten Places. Home: Washington, D.C. Died 1907.

DUFFY, James O. G., editor; b. Strabane, Co. Tyrone, Ireland, Jan. 4, 1864; s. Thomas P. G. and Susan (Toorish) D.; ed. pvt. tutors and travel; LL.B., Univ. of Pa., 1897; m. Florence Armstrong, June 5, 1894 (died 1931); 1 dau., Eleanora Aileen. Sunday editor, 1891-96, dramatic editor and critic, 1893-1911, lit. editor and principal reviewer, 1896-1911, asso. editor, 1911-13, dramatic and asso. editor, 1914-20, Phila. Press; editorial writer Evening Bull., Dec. 1920—. Admitted to bar, 1897; gen. counsel, 1900-12, cons. counsel, 1913-18, allied group of corps. Author: Glass and Gold (novel), 1901; Hohenzollern, play (with Cyrus Townsend Brady), 1902; The Golden Fleece (play), 1913; Brenda's Elopement (play), 1914; The Sting of Death (novel), 1916. Died Jan. 9, 1933.

DUFOURCQ, Edward Leonce, mining engr.; b. New York, Aug. 6, 1870; s. Leonce Felix and Hortense Louise (Geer) D.; Columbia, 1886-87; E.M., Sch. of Mines (Columbia), 1892; m. Ernestine King, June 29, 1896 (died 1911); m. 2d, Effie E. Mason, 1917. Assistant engr., mining, railroad and municipal work, Central America, Mexico and U.S., 1892-94; supt. Internat. Mining Co., San Miguel del Mezquital, Mexico, 1894-6; supt. Consol. Kansas City Smelting & Refining Co., Sierra Mojada, Mex., 1896-98; mem. Olcott, Fearn & Peele, cons. engrs., New York, 1898-1901; mgr. Andes Mining Co., Chimbote, Peru, 1901; gen. supt. Montezuma Lead Co., Santa Barbara, Mex., 1901-04; cons. mining engr., N.Y. City, 1904—; pres. Dufourcq & Co., Inc., export trade. Democrat. Episcopalian. Died Apr. 15, 1919.

DUGAN, Raymond Smith, prof. astronomy; b. Montague, Mass., May 30, 1878; s. Jeremiah Welby and Mary Evelyn (Smith) D.; B.A., Amherst, 1899, M.A., 1902; Ph.D., Heidelberg, 1905; m. Annette Rumford Odiorne, July 28, 1909; children—Kenneth Langdon, Hannah Priscilla. Instr. mathematics and astronomy and acting dir. obs., Syrian Protestant Coll., Beirut, Syria, 1899-1902; asst. Astrophys. Obs., Heidelberg, 1902-04; instr. astronomy, 1905-08, asst. prof., 1908-20, prof., 1920—, Princeton; exchange prof. Lowell Obs., 1929; acting dir. Princeton U. Obs., 1929-30. Mem. Lick Obs. eclipse expdn. to Spain, 1905. Republican. Presbyn. Home: Princeton, N.J. Died Aug. 31, 1940.

DUGAN, Thomas Buchanan, army officer; b. Baltimore, Md., July 27, 1858; s. Cumberland and Hariet (Buchanan) D.; grad. U.S. Mil. Acad., 1882, Army War Coll., 1913; m. Geraldine, d. Gen. Henry W. Wessells, U.S.A., Nov. 24, 1897; children—Cumberland, Thomas B., Eliza Lane. Commd. additional 2d lt. 10th Cav., June 13, 1882; 2d lt., June 26, 1882; promoted through grades to col., Dec. 9, 1915; commanding co. Apache Indian Scouts, 1884-85; brig. gen. N.A., Aug. 5, 1917; retired July 27, 1922; brig. gen. regular army, by spl. act of Congress, Feb. 28, 1927. Served in army posts in Ariz., N.M., Tex., Okla., Mo., to 1898; participated in campaign against Santiago, Cuba, 1898; Battle of San Juan, July 1-3, 1898, and siege of Santiago; in Cuba, 1901, P.I., 1905 and 1916. Comd. brigades in 86th, 85th, 35th and 5th divs., World War; comd. Brigade and Field Officers Sch., Dec. 1917-May 1918; comd. 35th Div., Dec. 1918-Mar. 1919; in Europe, July 1918-July 1919, and was with 1st Army in Meuse-Argonne offensive and with 2d Army and Army of Occupation. Campaign badges: Indian wars, Spanish-Am. War, Silver Star Citation, Cuban Occupation, Mexican Border; D.S.M.; Victory Badge with 3 clasps. Catholic. Died Apr. 27, 1940.

DUGGAN, Mell L., state supt. schs.; b. Washington Co., Ga., 1857; s. Ivy W. and Susan (Reynolds) D.; Pd.D., Mercer U., 1877; student Harvard, 1917; m. Sarah Avant, 1884; children—Nannie Sue, Lilian, Janie, Sarah Mell, James R., Ivy W., Kate. County supt. schs., Hancock Co., Ga., 1892-1909; state supervisor schs., Ga., 1909-26; state supt. schs., Ga., 1926—. Democrat. Baptist. K.P. Home: Clayton, Ga. Died Feb. 7, 1934.

DUGGAN, Walter Teeling, brig. gen.; b. Isle of Man, Apr. 11, 1843. Served as pvt. Co. B, 5th Wis. Inf., June 13, 1861-Aug. 31, 1863; hosp. steward U.S.A., Sept. 7, 1863-Mar. 23, 1867; commd. 2d lt. 10th Inf., Jan. 3, 1867; 1st lt., Nov. 13, 1874; capt., Aug. 1, 1886; maj., Mar. 2, 1899; lt. col., Mar. 2, 1901; col. 24th Inf., Oct. 3, 1902; transferred to 1st Inf., Oct. 18, 1902; brig. gen., June 26, 1906; retired by operation of law, Apr. 11, 1907. Died Jan. 2, 1915.

DUGRO, P(hilip) Henry, judge; b. New York, Oct. 2, 1855; A.B., Columbia, 1876, LL.B., 1878, A.M., 1879; admitted to bar, 1878. Mem. N.Y. Assembly, 1879; mem. 47th Congress (1881-83); nominated for comptroller, N.Y. City, 1884, but declined; justice Superior Ct. of N.Y., 1886-96, Supreme Ct., terms, 1896-1928. Democrat. Built the Hotel Savoy, Hotel Seville, and organized the Union Square Bank, New York. Died Mar. 1, 1920.

DUHRING, Louis Adolphus, dermatologist; b. Phila., Dec. 23, 1845; s. Henry and Caroline (Oberteuffer) D.; M.D., U. of Pa., 1867; resident phys. Phila. Hosp., 15 mos.; studied dermatology 2 yrs. in hosps. of Paris, London and Vienna; unmarried. Opened a dispensary for skin diseases in Phila., 1870, of which was phys., 1870-80, cons. phys., 1880—; clin. lecturer, 1871-76, prof. diseases of the skin, 1876—, U. of Pa. Author: Atlas of Skin Diseases, 1876; Practical Treatise on Diseases of the Skin, 1877 (transl. into French, Italian, and Russian); Cutaneous Medicine, 1898; also numerous other works on dermatology. Died May 8, 1913.

DUKE, Basil Wilson, lawyer; b. Scott Co., Ky., May 28, 1838; s. Nathaniel Wilson and Mary (Currie) D.; ed. Georgetown (Ky.) Coll. and Danville (Ky.) Coll.; law sch., Lexington, Ky.; m. Henrietta Hunt Morgan (sister of Gen. John H. Morgan), of Lexington, June 18, 1861 (died 1910). Served in C.S.A., 1861-65; enlisted as pvt., promoted 1st lt., lt. col., col. and brig. gen.; surrendered and paroled, May 10, 1865. Admitted to bar, 1858, and began practice at St. Louis; later at Louisville, Ky.; with law dept. L.&N. R.R. Co. more than 20 yrs. Mem. Ky. Ho. of Rep., 1861; commonwealth atty. 5th Jud. Dist. of Ky., 1875-80. Democrat. Commr. Shiloh Mil. Park, 1895—. Died Sept. 16, 1916.

DUKE, Benjamin Newton, capitalist; b. Orange (now Durham) Co., N.C., Apr. 27, 1855; s. Washington and Artelia (Roney) D.; father founder Am. Tobacco Co.; A.B., Guilford Coll., N.C.; m. Sarah Pearson Angier, Feb. 21, 1877. Pres. Durham & Southern Ry., Erwin Cotton Mills Co.; v.p. Durham Hotel Co., Southern Power Co.; dir. Durham Realty Corp. Died Jan. 8, 1929.

DUKE, Claude Walter, clergyman; b. Nansemond Co., Va., July 17, 1865; s. Abram and Sarah Louise (Daughtrey) D.; M.A., Richmond Coll. (U. of Richmond, Va.), 1893; Th.M., Southern Bapt. Theol. Sem., Louisville, Ky., 1896; D.D., Columbia Coll., Fla., 1911, John B. Stetson U., 1924, U. of Richmond, 1925; m. Estelle Butt, June 28, 1899; children—Anna Louise (Mrs. James Q. Brantley), Claude Walter, Agnes Virginia, Estelle Bruce. Made way through college by preaching in country ch. and holding revival meetings during vacations; ordained ministry Bapt. Ch., 1895; pastor successively Berkley Av. Ch., Norfolk, Va., Immanuel Ch., Baltimore, First Ch., Elizabeth City, N.C., until 1905, First Ch., Tampa, Fla., 1905—, membership growing from 346 to 2,360, and half a dozen other chs. organized out of it. Mem. City and State Mission bds.; mem. Home Mission Bd., Southern Bapt. Conv.; trustee Southern Bapt. Theol. Sem., John B. Stetson Univ. Mason. Home: Tampa, Fla. Died Sept. 3, 1936.

DUKE, James Buchanan, capitalist; b. on farm nr. Durham, N.C., 1857; s. Washington D.; ed. country schs.; m. 2d, Nannie Lee (Holt) Inman, July 23, 1907. Began in tobacco business with father and brothers, Durham, N.C., in firm of Duke Bros., acquiring an interest at 18; went to New York, 1884; organized Am. Tobacco Co., 1889, of which was pres. until 1912; was pres. Continental Tobacco Co., 1898, and Consolidated Tobacco Co., 1901; chmn. bd. dirs. British-Am. Tobacco Co., Ltd., 1912—. Dir. Union Bleaching & Finishing Co.; pres. Southern Power Co. Home: Somerville, N.J. Died Oct. 10, 1925.

DUKE, Richard Thomas Walker, Jr., lawyer; b. Charlottesville, Va., Aug. 27, 1853; s. R. T. W. and Elizabeth (Eskridge) D.; U. of Va., 1870-74; m. Edith R. Slaughter, Oct. 1, 1884 (died 1921); children—Mary, Richard Thomas Walker, III, John Flavel Slaughter, William Eskridge, Helen Risdon, Edwin Ellicott (dec.); m. 2d, Mrs. Maymee R. Slaughter, Apr. 5, 1923. Admitted to bar Oct. 1874, and began practice at Charlottesville; mem. Duke & Duke, now Duke & Duke & Gentry; pres. Kentucky Coal Co.; v.p. Nat. Bank of Charlottesville; treas. C.,C.,C.&I. Co. Judge Corporation Court, Charlottesville, 1888-1901; commonwealth atty., Albemarle County, Virginia, 1911—; Dem. presdl. elector-at-large, Va., 1912; chmn. State Library Bd.; sec., treas. Miller bd. trustees U. of Va. Mason. Presbyn. Home: Charlottesville, Va. Died Mar. 8, 1926.

DUKE, Victor LeRoy, univ. pres.; b. Rozetta, Ill., Feb. 11, 1874; s. Lewis, Jr., and Fannie King (Coghill) D.; B.A., Shurtleff Coll., 1897, M.A., 1903 (LL.D., 1917); U. of Chicago, summers, 1898-1901 and 1903; m. Louise Wempen, June 1898. Prof. mathematics, Shurtleff Coll., 1897-1909; prof. mathematics, 1909-16, dean Liberal Arts Coll., 1921-15, pres., 1915—, U. of Redlands. Dir. Internat. Bapt. Sem., Los Angeles, Calif.; pres. Southern Calif. Baptist Conv., 1920-21; pres. Bd. of Edn. of Northern Bapt. Conv., 1928-30. Republican. Home: Redlands, Calif. Died Mar. 1933.

DUKE, William Richard; b. Lewisburg, Va. (now W.Va.), July 1, 1848; s. R. T. W. and Elizabeth (Eskridge) D.; student University of Va., 1882-83; m. Edith May Coleman, June 6, 1894. Practiced law several yrs., but retired on account of ill health; mem. Va. Ho. of Delegates, 1896-1904; pres. Albemarle Mut. Home Ins. Soc. Mem. bd. of visitors U. of Va., 1922. Democrat. Home: Charlottesville, Va. Died Nov. 27, 1929.

DUKELOW, Charles Thomas, editor, pub.; b. Boston, Mass., June 14, 1865; ed. English High Sch., and classical training under pvt. tutors; m. Helen A. Wick, d. Dudley B. Wick, of Cleveland, O., Jan. 12, 1903 (died 1927); children—Helen (Mrs. William H. Clemingshaw, Jr.), Margaret (Mrs. John M. Phillips), Adele, Ruth, Charles. Employed by a Boston mercantile house, 1882-98, leaving position of mgr., 1898, to become gen. mrg. of Commercial-Financial Press Assn.; business mgr. N.Y. Daily Commercial, 1899; formed partnership, 1900, title of Dukelow & Walker, now Dukelow & Walker Co., of which is owner and treas., publishing Boston Commercial, a financial and business newspaper, also pub. Walker's Weekly Copper Letter. Elected capt. 5th Regt. Inf., M.N.G., May 17, 1901; later maj. M.N.G.; mem. staff of Gov. David I. Walsh of Mass., 1914-15. Episcopalian. Home: Brookline, Mass. Died Feb. 8, 1939.

DULANEY, Benjamin Lewis, financier, writer; b. Blountville, Tenn., Sept. 11, 1857; s. Benjamin Lewis and Rebecca Cobb (Masengill) D.; completed high sch. course, Jefferson Acad., Blountville, 1878; normal sch., Jonesboro, Tenn., 1879-80; taught high school, 2 years; m. Mary Dulaney, Oct. 10, 1881; children—Paul, Fred; m. 2d, Alice St. John, Dec. 26, 1895; children—L. C., Alice Rebecca; m. 3d, Elma Dykes, Mar. 16, 1923; 1 son, Wm. Dykes. Began development work in Va. and Tenn., 1885; built Bristol (Tenn.) Iron Furnace, and Bristol, Elizabethton & Carolina R.R., 1889-90; organized Va.&S.W. Ry. and Va. Iron, Coal & Coke Co., 1898-99; developed the Black Mountain Coal Field in Va. and Ky., 1890-1914; through a Senatorial investigation, succeeded in making Charleston, S.C., a coal loading port for all southeastern coal mines; retired. Commr. to Paris Expn., 1900, St. Louis Expn., 1904. Democrat. Unitarian. Mason. A founder of Boy Scouts of America and v.p. for 14 yrs. from its orgn. in America. Author: Cæsar's Tax, 1924. Home: Washington, D.C. Died Mar. 4, 1930.

DULANEY, Henry Stier, philanthropist; b. Baltimore, Jan. 16, 1849; s. Thomas Sim and Margaret Ellen (Stier) D.; pvt. and pub. schs. edn.; m. Amelia R. Kennedy, July 2, 1874 (died 1879); 2d, C. Estelle Kennedy, Sept. 21, 1880 (died 1925); children—Margaret Esdale, Henry Kennedy, Arthur Sim, Christiana

Young (wife of Judge George A. Solter), Miriam Cox, Ernestine Stier (wife of Dr. Elliott H. Hutchins), Emma Louise. Chief clerk accounting dept. B.&O. R.R. Co., 1880-82; mgr. proprietary medicine business, 1882-95; mem. Resinol Chem. Co., Aug. 1895—. Trustee Morgan Coll., Baltimore, First M.E. Ch., Baltimore M.E. Deaconess Home, Home of the Friendless, Moody Bible Inst.; mem. bd. mgrs. Family Welfare Assn. of Baltimore; treas. Anti-Saloon League of Md.; dir. Md. Soc. to Protect Children from Cruelty and Immorality, Baltimore. Home: Baltimore, Md. Died July 8, 1928.

DULLES, Allen Macy, theologian; b. Phila., Aug. 19, 1854; s. Rev. John Welsh and Harriet Lathrop (Winslow) D.; A.B., Princeton, 1875, A.M., 1878; grad. Princeton Theol. Sem., 1879; Leipzig and Berlin, 1879-81; D.D., Hamilton, 1901; m. Edith, d. John W. Foster, Jan. 13, 1886; children—John Foster, Mrs. Margaret Edwards, Allen Welsh, Eleanor Lansing, Nataline. Ordained Presbyn. ministry, 1881; pastor Trumbull Av. Ch., Detroit, 1881-87, First Ch., Watertown, N.Y., 1887-1904, Second Ch., Auburn, N.Y., 1904-16; prof. theology, Auburn Theol. Sem., 1904—; moderator Presbyn. Synod of New York, 1917-19. Republican. Author: The True Church, 1907; What Shall I Believe? (1912). Home: Auburn, N.Y. Died Nov. 13, 1930.

DULLES, Charles Winslow, physician; b. Madras, India, Nov. 29, 1850; s. Rev. John Welsh and Harriet Lathrop (Winslow) D.; bro. of Joseph Heatly and Allen Macy D.; acad. edn., and U. of Pa., 1866-67, M.D., 1875; studied Vienna, Paris, London, 1876-77; m. Mary Bateman, Oct. 5, 1881. Lecturer on history of medicine, U. of Pa., 1893-1908; cons. surgeon to Rush Hosp.; mgr. Univ. Hosp., 15 years. Author: Accidents and Emergencies, 7th edit., 1909; The Mechanism of Indirect Fractures of the Skull (Wm. J. Dornan, 1886). Died May 6, 1921.

DUMBA, Constantin Theodor, diplomat; b. Vienna, Austria, June 17, 1856; grad. in law, U. of Vienna, 1878; student École des Sciences Politiques et Morales, Paris, 1878-79; m. Baroness Annie von Lieven, Nov. 11, 1905. Entered Foreign Office, Vienna, 1879; apptd. privy councillor, 1908; ambassador E. & P. from Austria to U.S., Apr. 24, 1913—. Died Oct. 5, 1915.

DUMBLE, Edwin Theodore, geologist; b. Madison, Ind., Mar. 28, 1852; s. James F. and Mary A. D.; B.S., Sc.D., Washington and Lee U., Va.; m. Fanny Doswell Gray, June 15, 1876; children—Mrs. Milly Gray Mitchell, Mrs. Rosalie McCoy Davis. State geologist of Tex., 1887-96; cons. geologist and mgr. oil properties Southern Pacific Co. (Rio Bravo Oil Co., Tex., East Coast Oil Co., Mex.), 1897-1925; also cons. geologist Pacific Oil Co.; cons. practice, Houston, Tex. Fellow Geol. Soc. America, A.A.A.S., Tex. Acad. Science. Author: Brown Coal and Lignite; Geology of East Texas. Died Jan. 26, 1927.

DUMONT, Frederick Theodore Frelinghuysen, foreign service officer; b. Phillipsburg, N.J., Mar. 17, 1869; s. John Finley and Anna K. (Kline) D.; C.E., Lafayette, 1889, M.S., 1895; m. Mary Wolfe, May 16, 1900. Engineer, 1889-1900; founder and dir. of trust companies, 1901-04; cons. engr. for mining companies in Canada, Mexico, and United States, 1901-03, 1905-10; apptd. consul at Guadeloupe, W.I., Aug. 19, 1911; consul at Madrid, Spain, 1912-14, Florence, Italy, 1914-19, Dublin, Ireland, 1919-22, Frankfort-on-Main, Germany, 1923, consul gen., Frankfort, 1923-26; apptd. to Am. Foreign Service, 1924; chief of consular commercial office, Dept. of State, Washington, D.C., 1926-29; consul gen., Habana, Cuba, 1929-34, retired. Rep. of Department of State in confs. of Nat. Foreign Trade Council at Charleston, S.C., 1926, Detroit, Mich., 1927, Houston, Tex., 1928, Baltimore, Md., 1929. Del. of U.S. and chmn. Pan-Am. Commn. for the standardization and simplification of consular invoice procedure, Washington, 1927. Presbyterian. Republican. Author: Inland Waterways from New York to Key West, 1912. Home: Ronks, Pa. Died June 4, 1939.

DUMONT, Wayne, lawyer; b. Phillipsburg, N.J., Apr. 14, 1871; s. John Finley and Anne Kirkpatrick (Kline) D.; Ph.B., Lafayette Coll., Easton, Pa., 1892, A.M., M.S., 1895; LL.B., New York Law Sch., 1896, LL.M., 1897; m. Sallie Insley Hunt, Oct. 26, 1898; children—Wayne Hunt (dec.), John Finley, II, Wayne Dumont, II. Admitted to N.J. bar, 1896, N.Y., 1900; Supreme Court of U.S., 1904; practiced at Paterson, 1896—. Trustee Lafayette Coll., Blair Acad., Paterson Gen. Hosp., Charity Orgn. Soc. (Paterson), Paterson br. Am. Red Cross. Home: Elmholm, Totowa Borough, N.J. Died Apr. 7, 1929.

DUN, Edwin, diplomatic service; b. Chillicothe, O., July 1848; nephew late U.S. Senator Allen G. Thurman. Went to Japan, 1873; served chief Agrl. Bureau, colonization dept., Hokkaido, 10 yrs.; became, 1884, 2d sec. of legation, later 1st sec., and, 1893-97, U.S. minister to Japan. Died May 16, 1931.

DUN, James, civ. engr.; b. Chillicothe, O., Sept. 8, 1844; s. James and Virginia Walke D.; ed. Miami Univ., 1865-66; m. Mrs. Belle R. Otterson, Mar. 11, 1885; m. 2d, Mrs. Lucy J. Rucker, Oct. 31, 1899. Chainman with engring. corps Indianapolis & Cincinnati R.R., 1866; asst. engr. A.&P. Ry., 1867-71; asst. engr., Mo. Pacific Ry., 1871-74; engr. Union Depot Co., St. Louis, 1874-77; supt. bridges and bldgs., 1877-78, chief engr., 1878-90, S.L.&S.F. R.R.; chief engr. A.,T.&S.F. R.R. Co., and its successor, the A.,T.&S.F. Ry. Co., 1890-1900; chief engr. entire A.,T.&S.F. Ry. System, Aug. 1, 1900—. Home: Chicago, Ill. Died 1908.

DUN, Robert Graham, propr. The Mercantile Agency; b. Chillicothe, O., 1826; ed. at dist. schools and acad.; became clerk in store at 16, soon rising to a partnership; removed to New York, 1850, becoming clerk for The Mercantile Agency, then conducted by Tappan & Douglas; became partner, 1854, Tappan retiring and firm becoming B. Douglas & Co.; bought Douglas out, 1859, since being sole propr. under style of R. G. Dun & Co. Died 1900.

DUNBAR, Charles Franklin, prof. political economy, Harvard, 1871—; b. Mass., 1830; collegiate edn. (LL.D.); mem. Am. Hist. Assn. Author: Chapters on the Theory and History of Banking; Currency, Finance and Banking; etc. Died 1900.

DUNBAR, Erroll, actor; b. Baltimore; s. J. R. W. (M.D.) and Natillia B. (Hay) D.; civ. engring. course 2 yrs. Washington and Lee U.; practiced engring. several yrs. before going on the stage; m. Mary Helena Sharpsteen, of Paris, France, Oct. 8, 1905. Made début in Lester Wallack's co., and has played prominent and leading parts in support of Mrs. Fiske, Mme. Modjeska, Fanny Davenport, Mlle. Rhea, Marie Wainwright, Blanche Walsh, Fritzi Scheff, Lawrence Barrett, John McCullough, Louis James, Frederick Warde, Robert Mantell, etc. Lately under management of David Belasco. Home: New York, N.Y. Deceased.

DUNBAR, James Robert, lawyer; b. Pittsfield, Mass., Dec. 23, 1847; s. Henry W. and Elizabeth (Richards) D.; B.A., Williams Coll., 1871; studied Harvard Law Sch. short time; admitted to bar, 1874; m. Harriet P. Walton, May 15, 1875. Mem. Mass. Senate, 1885-86; chmn. Com. on Resolutions, Rep. State Conv., 1886; judge Superior Ct., Mass., 1888-98; chmn. spl. commn. on taxation, 1897; chmn. Court House Commn., Boston; now mem. Dunbar & Rackemann; dir. Boston Safe Deposit & Trust Co. Trustee Williams Coll. Conglist. Republican. Home: Brookline, Mass. Died Aug. 20, 1915.

DUNBAR, John H., lawyer; b. Goldendale, Wash., May 23, 1890; s. Ralph Oregon and Clara D.; student Whitman Coll.; LL.B., U. of Wash., 1913; m. Marie Rowe, Aug. 12, 1917; 1 dau., Dorothy; m. 2d, Lena E. Martenson, Nov. 27, 1928. Admitted to Wash. bar, 1913, and began practice at Seattle; dep. pros. atty. Chelan County, Wash., 1914-15; asst. atty. gen. State of Wash., 1920-23; atty. gen., 1923-33; has practiced in Olympia, 1933—. Served in U.S. Navy, World War. Republican. Home: Olympia, Wash. Died Mar. 6, 1936.

DUNBAR, Newell, editor, author; b. Trenton, N.J., Oct. 7, 1845; s. Hiram Pond and Martha Newell (Bird) D.; pvt. instrn.; course Yale; B.D., Harvard Div. Sch., 1875; pvt. study, 1875-80. Lit. adviser J. G. Cupples Co., Boston, 1888-95; on editorial staff Arena, 1895-96; collaborator on Charles Dudley Warner's Library of the World's Best Literature, 1897-98; on staff Anglo-American Ency., 1900-01; contbr. to Jewish Ency., J. A. Hill & Co.'s Science Library, and various mags. Author: Phillips Brooks, Bishop of Massachusetts, 1891; Phillips Brooks, Man, Preacher, Author, 1893. Home: Newark, N.J. Died Mar. 7, 1925.

DUNBAR, Paul Laurence, author; b. Dayton, O., June 27, 1872, of African descent; grad. Dayton High School, 1891; m. Alice Ruth Moore, Mar. 6, 1898; worked on newspapers; public reader of his own poems. Author: Folks from Dixie, 1898; Lyrics of the Hearthside, 1899; Poems of Cabin and Field, 1899; The Strength of Gideon, 1900; Lyrics of Love and Laughter (poems), 1903; Heart of Happy Hollow, 1904; Li'l Gal (poems), 1904; Lyrics of Sunshine and Shadow, 1905; Complete Poems (with intro. by W. D. Howells), 1913. Died 1906.

DUNBAR, Ralph O., judge; b. Schuyler Co., Ill., Apr. 26, 1845; with parents crossed plains in ox wagon, 1846; settled in Oregon; ed. Willamette U.; moved to Olympia, Wash., 1867; admitted to bar, 1869; m. Clara White, Oct. 18, 1873. Was clerk Dist. and Supreme Ct.; practiced Yakima City, 1871-77; removed to Goldendale, Wash.; several terms city atty.; one term pros. atty.; mem. Territorial Legislature, 1879 (speaker, 1885); mem. and chmn. public lands com. Constitutional Conv., 1889; asso. justice Supreme Ct. of Wash., 1889—; present term expires 1913. Republican. Home: Olympia, Wash. Died Sept. 19, 1912.

DUNBAR, Ulric Stonewall Jackson, sculptor; b. London, Ont., Can., Jan. 31, 1862; s. Alexander and Susannah (Jackson) D.; ed. common schs. in Can. and Rockwood Acad.; m. Mary John Davis, Sept. 17, 1892; children—Ulric S. J., Paul, Dorothy Davis, Erroll, Olga Marion (dec.). Professionally engaged as sculptor, 1880—; did figures for Atlanta, Buffalo and St. Louis, San Diego and San Francisco expns., for which received medals and diplomas; executed over 150 portrait busts, principally of prominent men, for U.S. Capitol and Corcoran Gallery of Art, Washington, State Capitol, St. Paul, Union Club, New York, Royal Ontario Mus. of Archæology, Toronto, Am. Mus. of Natural History, New York, Wyo. Hist. and Geol. Soc., also several monuments; bronze statue of late Gov. Alex R. Shepherd for front of new Municipal Bldg., Washington, D.C.; heroic bust of President Harding; etc. Served in Canada 3 yrs. in vol. service. Mason. Home: Washington, D.C. Died May 7, 1927.

DUNCAN, Albert Greene; b. Cleveland, O., Dec. 12, 1868; s. Rev. Samuel White and Sarah Margaret Fuller (Greene) D.; A.B., U. of Rochester, 1891; m. Mrs. Cora Moulton Hatheway, Oct. 10, 1922. Draftsman, Westinghouse, Church, Kerr & Co., Boston and New York, 1891-98; treas. Deane Steam Pump Co., Holyoke, Mass., 1898-1900; asst. treas. Dwight Mfg. Co., Boston, 1900-03; treas. Chicopee Mfg. Co., Boston, 1903-14; treas. Harmony Mills, Cohoes, N.Y., 1910-25; dir. New England Waste Co.; mem. bd. mgrs. Boston Dispensary, 1917—; v.p. John Paulding Meade Co., insurance, 1925—. Mem. exec. com., later chmn. Nat. Allied Bazaar, Boston, Dec. 1916; Boston advisory com. on purchase army supplies, Feb.-Oct. 1917; mem. Mass. Com. Pub. Safety, 1917-19; chmn. com. power plant economy N.E. Fuel Administration, 1917-19; mfrs. rep. for N.E. in U.S. Fuel Administration, 1918-19; rep. alien property custodian as pres. and dir. N.E. Waste Co., Am. Linters Co., Am. Products Co., Overseas Trading Co., W. Wolf & Sons, 1918-24. Del. Pan-Am. Financial Conf., Washington, 1915, 2d Pan-Am. Scientific Congress, Washington, 1915. Pres. Nat. Assn. Cotton Mfrs., 1914, 15; rep. same on Nat. Industrial Conf. Bd., 1915-25; dir. Textile Alliance, 1915—; treas. Nat. Indsl. Conf. Bd., 1920-22. Awarded medal by Nat. Assn. Cotton Mfrs., 1922, "for distinguished services to the cotton industry." Home: Brookline, Mass. Died Feb. 10, 1928.

DUNCAN, Charles, state health commr., pathologist; b. Chelsea, Mass., Mar. 18, 1872; s. James and Margaret (Patterson) D.; B.L., Dartmouth, 1898; M.D., Harvard, 1903; m. Charlotte Ilsley (A.B., Radcliffe), June 28, 1905; children—Laurence Ilsley, Eleanor (wife of Rev. Walter Priest Brockway), Margaret (wife of Rev. Howard E. Short). Practiced at Concord, N.H., 1903—; pathologist and bacteriologist State Bd. of Health, 1903-18, became sec., 1918, now state commr. of health; pathologist to Memorial Hosp. Republican. Congregationalist. Editor of "Health" (mag.). Home: Concord, N.H. Died Nov. 12, 1936.

DUNCAN, David Shaw, chancellor; b. Kilsythe, Scotland, Oct. 14, 1876; s. David and Margaret (Shaw) D.; brought to U.S., 1879; Ph.B., Taylor U., Upland, Ind., 1900, A.B., 1901, A.M., 1904, LL.D., 1924; Ph.D., U. of Denver, 1906; B.D., Iliff Sch. of Theology, 1913; studied United Free Ch. Coll., Glasgow, Scotland, 1902-03, Harvard, 1911; m. Laura Lovenia Walton, Dec. 24, 1903; 1 son, David Robardson. Prin., Walnut St. Night Sch., Johnstown, Pa., 1901; prof. Greek, Taylor U., 1903-05; instr. history and economics, 1906-08, asst. prof. history, 1908, prof. and head of dept., 1910—, acting dean, 1922, dean of Coll. of Liberal Arts, 1926-30, dean of Grad. Sch., 1930-33, dean emeritus and chmn. div. social sciences, 1933-35, U. of Denver, chancellor, 1935—. Mason. Home: Denver, Colo. Died Mar. 7, 1941.

DUNCAN, Edward Carlton, banker, officer; b. Beaufort, N.C., Mar. 28, 1862; s. William B. and Sarah A. (Ramsey) D.; pub. sch. edn., Beaufort, N.C. Collector of customs, port of Beaufort, N.C., 1890-94; mem. N.C. legislature, 1895, 1897; collector internal revenue, 1898-1908. Mem. Rep. State Exec. Com.; mem. Rep. Nat. Exec. Committee. Home: Raleigh, N.C. Died Aug. 30, 1920.

DUNCAN, George Martin, univ. prof.; b. Haledon, N.J., Nov. 26, 1857; s. James and Jane Martin (Torbet) D.; A.B., New York U., 1881, A.M., 1884; B.D., Yale, 1884; studied as grad. fellow in divinity and philosophy, Yale, 1884, U. of Jena, 1885, Leipzig, 1885-86, Berlin, 1886-87, Paris, 1887-88; (LL.D., New York U., 1901); m. Mary, d. Theodore R. Carter, of Montclair, N.J., Aug. 29, 1889. Instr. mental and moral philosophy, 1888-91, asst. prof., 1891-94, prof., 1894-1904, prof. logic and metaphysics, 1904-23 (emeritus), Yale U. Chairman sect. on logic, World's Congress Arts and Sciences, St. Louis, Mo., 1904. Translator from Latin and French (with notes): The Philosophical Works of Leibnitz, 1890, 1908. Home: Ridgewood, N.J. Died July 27, 1928.

DUNCAN, James, labor official; b. Kincardine Co., Scotland, May 5, 1857; s. David and Mary (Forbes) D.; ed. Aberdeen, Scotland; m. Lillian M. Holman, Jan. 1887; 1 son, Stanley Forbes (dec.). Monumental and building granite cutter from 1873, also granite statue cutter; sec. New York br., 1881, Baltimore br., 1884, president, 1895—, Granite Cutters' Internat. Assn.; successfully led ednl. campaign and ultimately the strike in the granite cutting industry for 8-hour workday, 1900; editor Granite Cutters' Journal, 1895—; elected v.p. Am. Fedn. of Labor, 1894, 1st v.p., 1902—. Represented Am. Labor movement to British Trades Congress, Bristol, Eng., 1898; rep. A.F. of L. at Internat. Secretarit Conf. of Labor,

Budapest, Hungary, 1911. Apptd. diplomatic envoy extraordinary to Russia, 1917; mem. Am. Labor Mission to Peace Conf., Paris, 1919. Presbyn. Mason. Home: Quincy, Mass. Died Sept. 14, 1928.

DUNCAN, James Cameron, clergyman; b. Scotland, July 8, 1860; s. William and Elsie (Cameron) D.; ed. Milnes Instn., Fochabers, Scotland; Meadville Theol. Sch., Pa.; Harvard Div. Sch.; Manchester Coll., Oxford, Eng.; U. of Berlin, Germany; D.D., Meadville Theol. Sch., 1928; m. Jessie Ginevra Fuller, Apr. 10, 1888; children—Robert Fuller, James Cameron. Ordained Unitarian ministry, June 17, 1886; pastor First Ch., Clinton, 1886—. Billings lecturer for Am. Unitarian Assn., Feb. and Mar. 1924. Pres. Unitarian Ministerial Union, 1924, 25; dir. Am. Unitarian Assn., 1925-26; sec. and treas. Worcester Conf. of Unitarian Chs.; pres. and treas. Weeks Inst.; moderator Worcester Ministerial Assn. Home: Clinton, Mass. Died Feb. 8, 1937.

DUNCAN, John Harris, univ. prof.; b. Columbia, Mo., Aug. 16, 1852; s. William H. and Susan W. D.; student U. of Mo., 1865-69; A.M., William Jewell Coll., Mo., 1872; M.D., U. of Mo., 1874; M.D., Bellevue Hosp. Med. Coll. (New York U.), 1875; (LL.D., William Jewell Coll., 1904); m. S. Belle Dulany, Dec. 21, 1881. Began practice at Columbia, Mo., 1875; prof. physiology, U. of Mo., 1875-83; prof. physiology and dermatology, Univ. Med. Coll. of Kansas City, 1883-93, St. Louis Coll. Phys. and Surg., 1893-94; prof. physiology, Barnes Med. Coll., St. Louis, 1898-1901; prof. diseases of the skin and syphilis, Marion Sims-Beaumont Med. Coll. (St. Louis U.), 1901—. Democrat. Baptist. Home: St. Louis, Mo. Died June 22, 1919.

DUNCAN, Joseph Wilson, army officer; b. in tent in army camp on bank Nueces River, Tex., June 29, 1853; s. Gen. Thomas (U.S.A.) and Mary Shields (Wilson) D.; ed. prep. sch., Griswold (Ia.) Coll., pub. schs., Nashville, Tenn., and Columbian Coll. (now George Washington U.); m. Catherine Amelia Keefer, Oct. 10, 1878. With Prof. F. V. Hayden on geol. survey of the Yellowstone, 1871, and latter part of same yr. was on cattle range in W. Neb.; commd. 2d lt. 21st Inf., Oct. 1, 1873; 1st lt., May 10, 1878; capt., Apr. 24, 1888; maj. 13th Inf., Mar. 2, 1899; lt. col., Oct. 16, 1901; col. 6th Inf., Aug. 9, 1903. Promoted brig. gen. U.S. Army, Jan. 4, 1911. Participated in Indian Wars (including Nez Perce, 1877, Bannock, 1878, Sioux, 1890-91) and numerous expdns. on the plains and mountains for 20 yrs.; took part in battle of San Juan Hill, and siege of Santiago de Cuba, to surrender, Spanish-Am. War; in P.I., 1899-1902, 1905-06; organized expdn. and commanded forces engaged in battle of Bud Dajo, Jolo ("battle of the Lava Cone"), with Moros, Mar. 5-8, 1906, 25 per cent of his command having been killed or wounded; detailed on gen. staff, Aug. 15, 1907—. Bvtd. 1st lt. "for gallantry in battle of Clearwater, Ida., July 11-12, 1877, Nez Perce Indian War"; recommended for maj., by bvt., "for gallantry in front of Santiago de Cuba, July 1, 1898"; recommended by comdg. gen. P.I. Div. for promotion to brig. gen. "for conduct of affairs in three days' battle against Moros." Comdg. Dept. of Texas, Jan. 1911—. Presbyn. Home: Washington, D.C. Died May 14, 1912.

DUNCAN, Louis, elec. engr.; b. Washington, D.C., Mar. 25, 1862; s. Thomas and Maria (Morris) D.; grad. U.S. Naval Acad., 1880; Ph.D., Johns Hopkins U., 1885; m. Edith McKee, 1887. Resigned from navy, 1887; maj. 1st vol. engrs., Spanish War; asso. and asso. prof. applied electricity, Johns Hopkins U., 1887-98; head dept. elec. engring., Mass. Inst. Tech., 1902-04. Fellow Am. Philos. Soc.; hon. mem. Franklin Inst. Home: Pelham Manor, N.Y. Died Feb. 13, 1916.

DUNCAN, Norman, author; b. Brantford, Ont., Can., July 2, 1871; s. Robert Augustus and Susan (Hawley) D.; bro. of Robert Kennedy D.; ed. U. of Toronto, 1891-95; (Litt.D., U. of Pittsburgh, 1912); unmarried. On staff New York Evening Post, 1897-1901; prof. rhetoric, Washington and Jefferson College, 1902-06; adj. prof. English lit., U. of Kan., 1908-10. Corr. Harper's Mag. in Syria, Palestine, Arabia, Egypt, 1907-08; in Australia, New Guinea, Dutch East Indies, Malay States, 1912-13; previously made many journeys to Newfoundland and Labrador. Author: Doctor Luke of Labrador, 1904; The Adventures of Billy Topsail, 1906; Going Down from Jerusalem, 1909; The Suitable Child, 1909; Billy Topsail & Company, 1910; The Measure of a Man, 1911; The Bird-Store Man, 1914; Harbor Tales Down North, 1918. Home: Willoughby, O. Died Oct. 18, 1916.

DUNCAN, Robert Kennedy, chemist; b. Brantford, Ont., Can., Nov. 1, 1868; s. Robert Augustus and Susan (Hawley) D.; bro. Norman D.; B.A., U. of Toronto (with 1st class honors in physics and chemistry), 1892; fellow in chemistry, Clark U., 1892-93; grad. student in chemistry, Columbia, 1897-98; m. Charlotte M., d. of George Foster, of Brantford, Ont., Dec. 27, 1899. Instr. physics and chemistry, Auburn (N.Y.) Acad. High Sch., 1893-95, Dr. Julius Sach's Collegiate Inst., New York, 1895-98, The Hill Sch., Pottstown, Pa., 1898-1901; studied abroad, 1900, 03, 04, 07; prof. chemistry, Washington and Jefferson College, 1901-06; prof. indsl. chemistry, U. of Kan., 1906—; dir. indsl. research, U. of Kan., 1910—; dir. indsl. research and prof. industrial chemistry, U. of Pittsburgh, 1910—; visiting lecturer, Clark U., 1911—. Discoverer and patentee of new process for mfg. phosphorus, of a new low-melting glass, and of processes of decorating glass; consultant in chemistry. Initiated in 1907 at U. of Kan. a new scheme of industrial fellowships which has since grown to remarkable proportions at U. of Kan. and U. of Pittsburgh. Send abroad by McClure's Mag., summer of 1901, to study radio-activity; by A. S. Barnes & Co., summer of 1903, for material for The New Knowledge; by Harper's Mag., 1905-06, to study relations of modern chemistry to industry. Author: The New Knowledge, 1905; The Chemistry of Commerce, 1907; Some Chemical Problems of Today, 1911. Died Feb. 18, 1914.

DUNCAN, Walter Jack, artist; b. Indianapolis, Ind., Jan. 1, 1881; s. James Staples and Rosalie Emily (Jack) D.; student Art Students' League, New York, 1899-1902; pupil of John Twatchman; unmarried. Began with Century Mag., 1903; sent to England by Scribner's, 1905; became connected with McClure's, 1907; with Harper's, 1912-13; illustrated books by Booth Tarkington, Robert C. Holliday, Christopher Morley, etc. Commd. capt. Engr. Corps, U.S. Army; apptd. official artist, A.E.F.; served 1 yr. and 5 mos. in France, making drawings and sketches for Official Records of the War; participated in major engagements of the Am. Army. Instr. Art Students' League, New York, 1925—. Author: First Aid to Pictorial Composition, 1939. Home: New York, N.Y. Died Apr. 11, 1941.

DUNCAN, Warren W., judge; b. in Williamson Co., Ill., Jan. 21, 1857; A.B., Ewing (Ill.) Coll., 1879, A.M., 1883; studied law under Judge W. H. Williams, of Benton, Ill., and Judge G. W. Young; LL.B., magna cum laude, St. Louis Law Sch. Began practice at Marion, Ill., 1885; elected circuit judge, 1903, reëlected, 1909; on bench of Appellate Court by apptmt. of Supreme Court of Ill., in 4th Dist., at Mt. Vernon, Ill., 1909, 10, and 1st Dist., Chicago, 1911-15; asso. justice Supreme Court of Ill., 1915-33. Home: Marion, Ill. Died Apr. 11, 1938.

DUNCAN, Watson Boone, clergyman; b. Blacksburg, S.C., Mar. 19, 1867; s. Jehu Franklin and Dulcenia (Hopper) D.; A.B., Polytechnic Coll., Ft. Worth, Tex., 1898; A.M., Erskine Coll., Due West, S.C., 1899; A.M., Wofford Coll., Spartanburg, S.C., 1902; Ph.D., Central U. at Indianapolis, Ind., 1906; D.D., Erskine Coll., 1923; m. Elizabeth Gary Huggins, Feb. 6, 1889; children—Watson Boone, Mrs. Elizabeth Gary Horne, Herman Franklin. Ordained ministry M.E. Ch., S., 1887; successively pastor 1st Ch. (Laurens), St. Johns Ch. (Rock Hill), Trinity Ch. (Sumter), Bethel Ch. (Charleston), St. Paul's Ch. (Orangeburg), Church Street Ch. (Manning), 1st Ch. (Dillon), 1st Ch., Cheraw, Main St. Ch., McColl —all of S.C. Chmn. Bd. of Christian Lit. of S.C. Conf. M.E. Ch., S.; del. Gen. Missionary Conf., New Orleans, La., 1901; pres. S.C. Legal Conf. for many years. Democrat. Mason. Author: Carlisle Memorial Volume, 1916; Ideals of American Poets, 1927. Home: Lake City, S.C. Died Mar. 16, 1930.

DUNCAN, W(illiam) Butler; b. Mar. 17, 1830; s. Alexander and Sarah (Butler) D.; ed. Edinburgh, Scotland, 1844-48; spl. student Brown U., 1849-50 (hon. A.M., 1850); m. I. Percy, d. George W. Sargent, of Natchez, Miss., Nov. 22, 1853. Banker, New York, 1851-75; pres., 1874-88, chmn. bd. dirs., 1888—, Mobile & Ohio R.R. Co. Mem. Met. Mus. of Art, Am. Mus. Natural History. Home: New York, N.Y. Died June 20, 1912.

DUNCAN, William Wallace, bishop M.E. Ch., S.; b. Boydton, Va., Dec. 20, 1839; s. Prof. David and Alice (Piemont) D.; ed. Randolph-Macon Coll. until 1854; grad. Wofford Coll., S.C., 1858; (D.D., Emory Coll., and Central Coll., Mo., 1882; LL.D., Trinity Coll., 1900); m. Medora Rice, Mar. 19, 1861. Joined Va. Conf., 1859, and filled stas. in same until 1875, except during Civil War, was chaplain C.S.A.; prof. intellectual and moral philosophy, Wofford Coll., 1875-86; del. Ecumenical Conf., London, 1881; elected bishop M.E. Ch., S., 1886. Home: Spartanburg, S.C. Died 1908.

DUNCAN-CLARK, Samuel John, editorial writer; b. Toronto, Can., Jan. 26, 1875; s. Samuel Clark and Keturah S. B. (Murray) D.; ed. U. of Toronto, 1898; LL.D., Cornell Coll., Ia., 1923; m. Blanche Goldstone Hamilton, Dec. 23, 1901; children—Laurajean, Carlyle Graeme. Pastor Christian Ch., Toronto, until 1903; editorial staff Louisville Herald, 1905-13; chief editorial writer Chicago Evening Post, 1913-31; editorial writer Chicago Daily News, 1931—. Mem. bd. dirs. Chicago Travelers' Aid Soc., Juvenile Protective Assn. Author: The Progressive Movement, 1913-21; The War at a Glance, 1916. Home: Wilmette, Ill. Died June 12, 1938.

DUNCKLEE, John Butler, civil engr.; b. Boston, July 7, 1848; s. John and Harriet (Gillmore) D.; S.B., Lawrence Scientific Sch. (Harvard), 1866; course in mining engring. Mass. Inst. Tech., 1866-68; m. Libbie S. Adams, Jan. 1875. Civil engr., 1868-74; div. engr., 1870-74, in construction of Brooklyn parks; civ. engr. connected with U.S. Engr. Dept. at Washington, on river and harbor improvements, 1874-82, and on improving Potomac River and reclaiming its flats at Washington, 1882-99; had charge construction Aqueduct bridge and Pennsylvania Av. bridge, Washington, 1901-11; consulting and bridge engineer; designed new long bridge across Potomac River, Washington. Home: S. Orange, N.J. Deceased.

DUNGLISON, Richard James, physician, author; b. Baltimore, Nov. 13, 1834; s. Dr. Robley and Hariette (Leadam) D.; grad. Univ. of Pa., 1852 (A.M., 1855); Jefferson Med. Coll., 1856; m. Aug., 1877, Mrs. Violette Fisher. Acting asst. surgeon U.S.A., on duty in mil. hosps. at Phila. during Civil war; practiced at Phila., but relinquished practice for literary work. Edited: The College and Clinical Record, 1880-99; one of original editors of The Phila. Medical Times. Author: The Practitioners' Reference Book; A Handbook of Diagnosis, Therapeutics and Dietetics; The Present Treatment of Disease; A New School Physiology and Hygiene; An Elementary Physiology and Hygiene. Home: Philadelphia. Died 1901.

DUNHAM, Arthur, organist; b. Bloomington, Ill., Mar. 8, 1875; s. John B. and Minnie (Hoyt) D.; ed. Chicago and Paris, France; studied organ with Clarence Eddy and Charles M. Widor; m. Florence A. Fairchild, June 1, 1904; children—Arthur, Leonora. Organist and dir. of music, Sinai Congregation, Chicago, 1895—; solo organist, St. Louis Expn., 1904; organist and dir. of music, First M.E. Ch. Republican. Composer: Symphonic Fantasy, for organ and orchestra, first performed by Theodore Thomas Orchestra, Chicago, Nov. 12, 1909; Symphonic Idylle, Marpessa. Home: Chicago, Ill. Died Jan. 24, 1938.

DUNHAM, Daniel H., fire insurance; b. Basking Ridge, N.J., Nov. 20, 1849; s. Robert B. and Jane (Heath) D.; ed. pub. schs.; m. Adelaide Eagles Snyder, Sept. 17, 1872. Began as office boy Fireman's Ins. Co., Newark, N.J., advancing through various positions to pres., 1896; pres. Mechanics Ins. Co., N.J. Investment Co.; v.p. Girard Fire & Marine Ins. Co., Nat. Ben Franklin Ins. Co. Trustee Newark Y.M.C.A. Republican. Mem. Ref. Ch. America. Home: East Orange, N.J. Died 1924.

DUNHAM, Edward Kellogg, pathologist; b. Newburgh, N.Y., Sept. 1, 1860; s. Carroll and Harriet E. (Kellogg) D.; Ph.B., Columbia, 1881; M.D., Harvard, 1886; m. Mary Dows, June 4, 1893. Prof. bacteriology and hygiene, 1898-1900, prof. pathology, 1898-1907, Univ. and Bellevue Hosp. Med Coll. (New York U.). Maj., Med. O.R.C., 1917; maj. Med. Corps, U.S.A., Jan. 15, 1918-June 6, 1919; lt. col., Med. O.R.C., 1919—. Home: New York, N.Y. Died Apr. 16, 1922.

DUNHAM, George Earl, newspaper editor; b. Clayville, N.Y., Apr. 5, 1859; s. Moses Earl (D.D., Ph.D.) and Harriet (Hughston) D.; A.B., Hamilton Coll., 1879, A.M., 1890 (LL.D., 1921); m. Helen L. Jones, Jan. 9, 1884. Editor Utica Daily Press, 1887—; v.p. and dir. Utica Trust & Deposit Co.; pres. Utica Chamber of Commerce, 1896-97; trustee Hamilton Coll.; pres. bd. mgrs., Utica State Hosp. for Insane. Home: Utica, N.Y. Died Oct. 29, 1922.

DUNHAM, Henry Morton, organist; b. Brockton, Mass., July 27, 1853; s. Isaac A. and Augusta L. (Packard) D.; grad. N.E. Conservatory of Music, 1873, Boston U. Coll. of Music, 1875; m. Helen Hammond, June 28, 1887. Organist, Porter Congl. Ch., Brockton, 1875-83, Ruggles St. Bapt. Ch., Boston, 1883-96, Shawmut Congl. Ch., Boston, 1896-1906, Harvard Ch., Brookline, Mass., 1906—. Prof. organ, N.E. Conservatory of Music, 1880—; dir. music sch., Lasell Sem., Auburndale, Mass., 1910. Composer of 4 sonatas for organ, 1 symphonic poem, 2 books of 12 church pieces each; "Aurora," for orchestra and organ, played by Boston Symphony Orchestra, Los Angeles Symphony Orchestra, Philharmonic Orchestra, New York. Author: Organ School, 1893; Manual and Pedal Technique; Legato Fingering and Phrasing (for the piano). Home: Brookline, Mass. Died May 4, 1929.

DUNHAM, John Dudley, M.D.; b. Columbus, O., Aug. 23, 1873; s. John Milton and Talitha Ann (Cross) D.; student Ohio State U., 1888-92; A.B., U. of Mich., 1894; M.D., Ohio Med. U., 1897; grad. study, Columbia and U. of Berlin; m. Mabel Holmes, Apr. 27, 1897; children—Lucy Bates, John Milton, Theodore Chadbourne; m. 2d, Helen Fishel, June 1, 1916; 1 dau., Nancy. Began practice at Columbus, 1897; dir. Bd. of Health Lab., Columbus, 1898-1901; prof. bacteriology, Ohio Med. U., 1898 to 1900; prof. medicine, Starling Med. Coll., Columbus, 1901-14; prof. medicine, Coll. Medicine Ohio State U., 1924-29; mem. staff Mt. Carmel, White Cross and Grant hosps.; pres. City Board of Health, Columbus, 1936-37. Served as capt., later maj. Medical Corps, U.S.A., May 1918-Apr. 1919; was chief of med. service Gen. Hosp. No. 12, Biltmore, N.C., later at U.S. Mil. Acad., West Point; lt. col.

Med. Officers Reserve. Republican. Home: Columbus, O. Deceased.

DUNHAM, Sylvester Clark, underwriter; b. Mansfield, Conn., Apr. 24, 1846; s. Jonathan Lyman and Abigail Hunt (Eldredge) D.; ed. Mt. Union Coll., Ohio; m. Mary Austin, Oct. 18, 1877. Admitted to bar, 1873; practiced at Hartford, 1873-85; gen. counsel, 1885, v.p., 1897, pres., 1901—, Travelers' Ins. Co.; pres. Travelers' Indemnity Co.; v.p. Nat. Exchange Bank; dir. numerous cos. Republican. Congregationalist. Home: Hartford, Conn. Died Oct. 26, 1915.

DUNKIN, Damon Duffield, mining engr.; b. Albia, Ia., May 10, 1875; s. John McFarland and Ida Ada (Haskell) D.; A.B., Woodland Coll., Mo., 1892; B.S., Sch. of Mines, U. of Mo., 1905; m. Dorothy Julian Perry, Aug. 10, 1910 (died 1925); m. 2d, Mertie Arnold, Mar. 4, 1928; 1 daughter, Ida Kate. Bookkeeper and credit man with wholesale house, to 1900; with bridge dept. I.C. R.R., 1902-04; supt. Midnight Mining Co., 1904-06; Moseley Lead & Zinc Co., 1906-07; supt. E. E. Dwight properties, 1907-08; prof. mining, Okla. Sch. of Mines, 1908-13; v.p. and gen. mgr., McAlester Coal & Coke Co., 1913-17; mgr. Coahuila Lead and Zinc Co., 1917-20, Standard Zinc Lead Co., 1920-21; pres. and gen. mgr. Silica Products Co., Inc., 1921—. Mem. Co. F, 3d Mo. Vols., Spanish-Am. War. Mason. Home: Harrison, Ark. Died Sept. 13, 1933.

DUNLAP, Andrew, read adm., U.S.N.; b. Ovid, N.Y., Oct. 7, 1844; s. Andrew and Hannah (Kinne) D.; grad. U.S. Naval Acad., 1867; m. Ellen Grace Derby Adams, Oct. 13, 1875. Midshipman European and Pacific stas., 1867-68; promoted through grades to capt., June 8, 1902; rear adm. and retired at own request after over 43 yrs.' service, June 27, 1905. Served on various sea and shore duties; comd. coast and geodetic steamer Blake, 1896-97; comd. ambulance and hosp. ship Solace during Spanish-Am. War, and Solace afterward as naval transport to W.I. and P.I.; light house insp., 10th Dist., Buffalo, 1900-02; comdt., Naval Sta., San Juan, P.R., 1902-06. Died Apr. 11, 1914.

DUNLAP, Boutwell; b. Sacramento, Calif., Nov. 14, 1877; s. William and Sarah Jane (Robinson) D.; B.L., U. of Calif., 1901; LL.B., Catholic U. of America, 1905, LL.M., 1910; unmarried. Admitted to Calif. bar, 1907, and practiced in San Francisco. Dem. candidate Congress, 1st Calif. Dist., 1904; consul of Argentine Republic at San Francisco, 1909-16, and honorary consul, Jan. 1, 1917—. Was chosen arbitrator by the newspaper proprs. in their dispute with the Typographical Union, San Francisco, 1914; hon. commr. of Argentine Rep. to Panama P.I. Expn., 1915; mem. Internat. Jury Award for eugenics, same; proposed, and was mem. com. orgn. of Internat. Congress of Genealogy at the Panama-P.I. Expn., 1915. Compiler: (with R. E. Cowan) Bibliography of the Chinese Question in the United States, 1909. Author: Augusta County, Virginia, in the History of the United States; The Warwicks of the West, 1921. Has made a supplementary collection of rare manuscripts on Calif. history which H. H. Bancroft, the historian, was unable to obtain for his collection. Home: San Francisco, Calif. Deceased.

DUNLAP, Charles Bates, neurologist; b. Cambridge, Mass., Aug. 24, 1863; s. Charles Henry and Martha (Smart) D.; A.B., Harvard, 1889, A.M., 1894, M.D., 1894; m. Anna Weld Carret, Sept. 23, 1902; children—Martha Weld, Ruth Weld, Charles Edward. Practiced in N.Y. City, 1902—; prof. neuropathology, Univ. and Bellevue Hosp. Med. Coll. (New York U.), 1920—. Home: Scarsdale, N.Y. Deceased.

DUNLAP, Charles Graham, univ. prof.; b. Chillicothe, O., Sept. 30, 1859; s. Joseph Levy and Ann Maria (Clingman) D.; brother of Frederick Levy D.; A.B., Ohio Wesleyan U., 1883, A.M., 1899; studied Johns Hopkins and Univ. of Berlin; Litt.D., Princeton, 1892; m. Anna March, Aug. 12, 1891 (died 1931). Asst. in English, 1887-89, asso. prof. English lit., rhetoric and belles lettres, 1889-90, prof. English lang. and lit., 1890-93, prof. English lit. and head of dept., 1893—, head dept. English lang. and lit., 1909-21, U. of Kansas. Deceased.

DUNLAP, Hiram J., consular service; b. Leyden, Ill., Feb. 8, 1841; s. Mathias L. and Emiline (Pierce) D.; common sch. edn.; m. Elizabeth E. Frith, June 25, 1895. Newspaper pub. and editor, Champaign, Ill., 1875-90; consul at Breslau, Germany, 1890-91; commercial agt., Fürth, Bavaria, 1901-03; postmaster, Kankakee, Ill., 1897-1905; consul Cologne, Germany, June 1895—. Republican. Mason. Home: Kankakee, Ill. Died Oct. 26, 1919.

DUNLAP, John Robertson, editor, pub.; b. Lexington, Ky., Apr. 11, 1857; s. Henry Clay (brig. gen. vols. Civil War) and La Belle (Boyce) D.; ed. Linsly Inst., Wheeling, W.Va.; m. Isadora Pollock, Jan. 7, 1886; children—Mortimer Pollock (dec.), La Belle Boyce (Mrs. Kenneth P. Spence), Boyce, John R.; m. 2d, Eugenia Blackmore Logan, Nov. 6, 1918. Civ. engrng. work, 1873; pres., gen. mgr. Louisville (Ky.) Daily Commercial, 1884-87; founded India Rubber World, New York, 1889, Hardware, 1890, The Engineering Magazine, 1891, The Engineering Index, 1895, Industrial Management, 1916, Industry Illustrated, 1921; later chmn. bd. Engineering Magazine Co.; business now merged with McGraw-Hill Co. Democrat. Unitarian. Wrote: Jeffersonian Democracy. Home: Upper Saranac, N.Y. Deceased.

DUNLAP, Robert, mfr.; b. New York, Oct. 17, 1834; ed. public schools; then consecutively boy, apprentice and salesman in hat trade; opened hat store of his own 1857, and a branch in Fifth Av. Hotel, 1859; later established factory in Brooklyn and branches in leading cities. Home: New York, N.Y. Died 1900.

DUNLAP, Robert Finley, lawyer; b. White Gate, Va., July 25, 1872; s. Henry and Amelia Margaret (Humphreys) D.; A.B., and B.S., Hampden-Sydney Coll., Va., 1894; studied law under pvt. tutors and in law office; m. Emma Wysor, Nov. 17, 1904; children—May Lucille (Mrs. Lawrence N. Seldomridge), Emma. Admitted to bar, Va. and W.Va., 1897; city atty., Hinton, 1901-04; pros. atty. Summers Co., W.Va., 1905-09; atty. many interests and corps.; chmn. Dem. State Exec. Com., 1920—, chmn. on orgn., 1930; adviser of special W.Va. Tax Commn.; pres. Laval Sand Co., Zenith Sand Co., Hinton Ins. Co., City Ice Co.; v.p. First Nat. Bank, Hinton Toll Bridge Co., Riverview Land Co., Hinton Holding Co., Kanawha City Oil & Gas Co. Atty. local draft bd., World War, also chmn. local food and fuel administration, Red Cross drives and bond sales. Trustee, dir. Greenbrier Coll. Presbyn. Mason. Home: Hinton, W.Va. Died Oct. 28, 1934.

DUNLAP, Roy J., editor; b. Madison, Ind., Mar. 31, 1890; s. Robert and Isabelle (Peters) D.; grad. Madison High Sch., 1908; m. Lulu M. Trunkee, June 3, 1913; children—Doris Vivian, Robert Rankin, Roy John. Began as reporter Madison Democrat, 1908; reporter for Fargo (N.D.) Daily News; sports editor Duluth (Minn.) News Tribune until 1913; reporter St. Paul Pioneer Press, 1913-14, northwest editor, 1914-17, city editor St. Paul Dispatch, 1917-18, asst. mng. editor, 1919-28, mng. editor Dispatch, also of Pioneer Press, 1928—; dir. Dispatch-Pioneer Press Co. Republican. Presbyn. Mason. Home: St. Paul, Minn. Died June 7, 1938.

DUNN, Arthur David, M.D.; b. Meadville, Pa., Nov. 1, 1873; s. Holton and Diantha M. (Curtis) D.; A.B., Allegheny Coll., Meadville, 1896; Ph.B., U. of Chicago, 1896; M.D., Rush Med. Coll. (U. of Chicago), 1902; m. Alice Gardiner Root, Aug. 11, 1904; children—Rollin (dec.), Frederick H. Began practice of medicine at Omaha, Neb., 1907; prof. internal medicine, Creighton U. Coll. of Medicine, 1910-21; prof. and head of dept. clin. investigation, U. of Neb. Coll. of Medicine, 1924—. Democrat. Home: Omaha, Neb. Died Jan. 8, 1934.

DUNN, Arthur Wallace, Washington corr.; author; b. in Meeker Co., Minn., s. James W. and Elizabeth M. (Seeley) D.; ed. Jackson (Minn.) High Sch.; m. Lillian Jay Lash, Oct. 15, 1890. Editor Grand Forks (N.D.) Plaindealer, 1883; City Editor St. Paul Pioneer Press, 1887-89; Washington corr. Pioneer Press and Portland Oregonian, 1889-93; in charge Congressional report of Associated Press, 1893-1906; Washington rep. and contbr. daily letters to Am. Press Assn., Oct. 1898—. Author: Gridiron Nights, 1915; From Harrison to Harding—a Personal Narrative of a Washington Correspondent Covering a Third of a Century; Frontier Fact and Fiction; How Presidents Are Made. Home: Washington, D.C. Died Nov. 2, 1926.

DUNN, Arthur William, educator; b. Galesburg, Ill., Mar. 12, 1868; s. William Edwin and Angelina Hager (Wyckoff) D.; A.B., Knox Coll., 1893, A.M., 1896; U. of Chicago, 1893-96, fellow in sociology, 1898-1900; m. Elizabeth Wharton Boggs, Aug. 27, 1896; children—Allison Van Vliet, Rebecca Merriam (Mrs. Henry J. Hunt, Jr.). Instr. English and lecturer in sociology, U. of Cincinnati, 1896-98; extension lecturer, 1896-1900; head dept. history and civics, Shortridge High Sch., Indianapolis, 1900-10; dir. civic edn., pub. schs., Indianapolis, 1906-10; civic sec., City Club, Phila., 1910-11; exec. sec., Pub. Edn. Assn., N.Y. City, 1911-14; specialist in civic edn., U.S. Bur. Edn., 1914-21; asso. nat. dir. Am. Jr. Red Cross, 1920-21, nat. dir. same, 1921—. Conglist. Author: The Community and the Citizen, 1907; The Teaching of Community Civics (with others), 1915; Social Studies in Secondary Education, 1916; Citizenship in School and Out (with Hannah Margaret Harris), 1920; Community Civic and Rural Life, 1920; Community Civics for City Schools, 1921. Home: Washington, D.C. Died Nov. 15, 1927.

DUNN, Charles John, judge; b. in Houghton Co., Mich., July 14, 1872; ed. Blue Hill (Me.) Acad. and at Poughkeepsie, N.Y.; LL.D. from the U. of Maine, 1920; read law in offices of Hon. E. E. Chase, Blue Hill, and Messrs. Hale & Hamlin, Ellsworth, Me.; m. Alice Isabel Ring, Dec. 16, 1896; children—Barbara (Mrs. E. R. Hitchner), Lillian (Mrs. Howard A. Sayford). Began practice at Orono, 1892. Mem. Me. Ho. of Rep., 1901-02; judge Municipal Court, Old Town, Me., 1903-11; asso. justice Supreme Judicial Court of Maine, Feb. 6, 1918-July 18, 1935, chief justice, 1935—. Universalist. Home: Orono, Me. Died Nov. 10, 1939.

DUNN, Herbert Omar, rear admiral; b. Westerly, R.I., May 29, 1857; s. Edward Maxson and Desire Anne (Gavitt) D.; grad. U.S. Naval Acad., 1877; m. Elizabeth Armada Webb, July 30, 1890 (died 1907); 1 son, Donald Omar; m. 2d, Eleanor Cameron Warwick Palmer, June 22, 1919. Ensign, Mar. 12, 1881; lt. jr. grade, July 1, 1887; lt., Feb. 17, 1893; comdr., July 1, 1905; capt., July 1909; rear admiral, Aug. 6, 1915. Served in principal stas., various parts of world; aboard Baltimore when she took Ericsson's body to Sweden; invented the Dunn anchor; aboard Terror during Spanish-Am. War, operating in West Indies; lt. comdr. Buffalo in Boxer troubles in China; exec. officer Columbia when she took body of Mexican minister to Vera Cruz, 1904, and in charge of military escort to Mexico City; spl. duty with Sec. of the Navy, 1912-13; assigned in charge Battleship Div. Five, Oct. 6, 1916; comd. Naval Base, Punta Delgada, Azores, Jan. 1918-Apr. 1919; comd. 1st Naval Dist., Boston, May 1919-21. Medals and badges; West Indies Naval Engagements, Spanish Campaign, China Relief Expdn., Philippine Campaign, Naval and Mil. Order Spanish War, Order of the Dragon, Mil. Order of the Aviz (Portugal), Order of the Rising Sun (Japan), D.S.M. (U.S.). Pres. Marine Hist. Assn. Hon. v.p. Ye Knyttes of Ye Round Table (London). Home: Westerly, R.I. Died Feb. 13, 1939.

DUNN, Jacob Piatt, author; b. Lawrenceburg, Ind., Apr. 12, 1855; s. Jacob Piatt and Harriet L. (Tate) D.; B.S., Earlham Coll., 1874, M.S., 1888; LL.B., U. of Mich., 1876; m. Charlotte Elliott Jones, Nov. 23, 1893. Sec. Ind. Hist. Soc., 1886—; State librarian of Ind., 1889-93; editorial writer, Indianapolis Sentinel, 1893-1904; city comptroller, Indianapolis, 1904-06, 1914-16. Author: Indiana (Am. Commonwealth Series), 1888; Indiana—a Redemption from Slavery, 1905; True Indian Stories, 1909; History of Indianapolis, 1910; The Unknown God, 1914; Indiana and Indianans, 1919. Private sec. to Senator S. M. Ralston, 1923—. Home: Indianapolis, Ind. Died June 6, 1924.

DUNN, James Phillip, composer; b. N.Y. City, Jan. 10, 1884; s. Thomas J. and Mary A. (O'Brien) D.; A.B., Coll. City of New York, 1903; post-grad. courses Columbia; studied music under E. A. McDowell and C. Rybner; m. Lillian E. Byrne, June 27, 1911; 1 son, Robert Lawrence. Asso. editor of "Singing" (mag.). Democrat. Composer of more than 100 compositions, including "The Galleon," grand opera, "Annabelle Lee," symphonic poem, prod. Carnegie Hall, 1913; "Lovesight," symphonic poem, prod. N.Y. Stadium, 1919; overture on Negro themes and tone-poem, "We," prod. under Damrosch, Hadley, Van Hoogstraten, and others; also songs and piano and organ pieces. Home: Jersey City, N.J. Died July 24, 1936.

DUNN, Jesse James, lawyer; b. Channahon, Ill., Oct. 2, 1867; s. James McCann and Alta F. (Lewis) D.; ed. Ill. State Normal Sch., 1886-87; grad. Garden City (Kan.) Business Coll., 1891; LL.B., U. of Kan., 1893; admitted to bar, 1893; m. Saidee A. Matson, Oct. 2, 1895; children—Claud Matson, Mrs. Alida Constance Rutherford, Dorothea Emily. Co. atty. Woods Co., Okla. Ty., 1896-1900; chmn. Dem. Territorial Com., 1904; chmn. Dem. State Com., 1906; conducted campaign for election of dels. to Constl. Conv. and wrote platform on which campaign was waged; asso. and chief justice Supreme Ct. of Okla., 1907-13; resigned. Now mem. Dunn, White & Aiken, Oakland, Calif. Mason. Died July 28, 1926.

DUNN, John Joseph, bishop; b. N.Y. City, Sept. 1, 1870; s. John and Mary (Cassidy) D.; grad. St. Charles Coll., Md., 1890, A.M., St. Joseph's Provincial Sem., Troy, N.Y., 1896, LL.D., 1918, D.D., 1922. Ordained priest R.C. Ch., 1896; founder, 1904, Soc. for R.C. Propagation of the Faith; consecrated aux. bishop of Archdiocese of New York, 1921, treas. of archdiocese, 1922—; supreme spiritual dir. Holy Name Soc. Vice-pres. Catholic Charities of N.Y. City. Home: New York, N.Y. Died Aug. 31, 1933.

DUNN, Joseph Allan, author, explorer; b. London, Eng., Jan. 21, 1872; s. Joseph Holdsworth and Elizabeth Elphinstone (Miall) D.; B.A., New Coll., Oxford, 1893; m. Loyola Lee Sanford, Oct. 30, 1936. Syndicate corr., California, Hawaii and Orient, 1900-05; corr. Spanish-American War, 1898, Russo-Japanese War, 1904; editor Sunset Magazine, 1907. Fellow Am. Geog. Society. Author: Jim Morse, South Sea Trader; Jim Morse, Adventurer; Jim Morse, Goldseeker; A Man to His Mate; The Man Trap; The Girl of Ghost Mountain; Rimrock Trail; Sea Salted, The Isle of Drums; The Water Bearer; Sanctuary Island; The Flower of Fate; The Odyssey of Boru; The Pathfinder; Lost Loot; Silver Spurs; The Sunset Trail; Barehanded Castaways. Died Mar. 25, 1941.

DUNN, Thomas B., congressman; b. Providence, R.I., Mar. 16, 1853; ed. pub. schs., Rochester, N.Y.; m. Florence L. Robinson, 1889. Mem. N.Y. State Senate, 1906-08; state treas., N.Y., 1908-10; mem. 63d to 67th Congresses (1913-23). Republican. Chief commr. N.Y. State Commn., to Jamestown Expn., 1907. Mason. Home: Rochester, N.Y. Died July 2, 1924.

DUNN, William Le Roy, M.D.; b. 1871; Ph.C., U. of Mich., 1889, M.D., 1891, B.S., 1894. Settled at Asheville, N.C., 1900; specializes in internal medicine. Home: Beaucatcher Mountain (N.C.). Died May 24, 1928.

DUNNACK, Henry E., librarian; b. Nova Scotia, May 15, 1869; s. James and Elizabeth (Usher) D.; came to U.S., 1884; grad. Bangor Theol. Seminary, 1895; A.B., Bowdoin Coll., 1897; Litt.D., U. of Maine, 1931; m. Adella Smith, 1896 (died 1913); children—Llewellyn Smith, George Bussey; m. 2d, Florence E. Merrill, Sept. 4, 1935. Ordained ministry M.E. Ch., 1897; pastor Portland, Me., 1897-1900, Augusta, 1900-17; state librarian of Me., 1914—. Trustee Kents Hill (Me.) Sem. Republican. Methodist. Mason. Author: The Maine Book, 1920; Hand Book of Maine Government, 1921; Maine Forts, 1924; Maine Methodism, 1925; Rural Maine, 1927. Home: Augusta, Me. Died Mar. 1, 1938.

DUNNE, Edmond M., bishop; b. Chicago, Feb. 2, 1864; s. Maurice and Catherine (Walsh) D.; ed. St. Ignatius Coll., Chicago; Niagara U.; Seminaire de Floreffe, Belgium; Louvain U., Belgium; D.D., Gregorian U., Rome, 1889. Ordained priest R.C. Ch., 1887; asst. pastor St. Columbkill's parish, Chicago, 1890-98; founded Guardian Angel parish (Italian) and built ch. and rectory, 1898-1905; chancellor Chicago archdiocese, 1905-09; apptd., June 29, 1909, consecrated, Sept. 1, 1909, bishop of Peoria (Ill.). Died Oct. 17, 1929.

DUNNE, Edward Fitzsimons, governor; b. Waterville, Conn., Oct. 12, 1853; s. P. W. and Delia M. (Lawler) D.; 3 yr. course Trinity Coll., Dublin U., not completed because of father's failure in business; LL.B., Union Coll. of Law, 1877; LL.D., St. Ignatius Coll.; m. Elizabeth J. Kelly, Aug. 16, 1881 (died 1928); children—Edward P. (dec.), Gerald (dec.), Charles P. (dec.), Edward F., Mrs. Eileen Corboy, Mrs. Mona Leonard, Maurice F., Dorothy (dec.), Robert Jerome, Geraldine (Mrs. Walter R. Barry), Jeannette, Richard J., Eugene. Admitted to bar, 1877; judge Circuit Court Cook Co., Ill., 1892-1905, resigned; mayor of Chicago, 1905-07; in law practice, 1907-13; gov. of Ill., 1913-17. Presdl. elector, 1900. Twice pres. Iroquois and Monticello clubs; v.p. Nat. Civic Federation; pres. League of Am. Municipalities, 1906-07. Mem. com. from Irish socs. of U.S. to present claims of Ireland for self-determination at Peace Conf., Paris, 1919; chmn. Nat. Unity Council; U.S. commr. Century of Progress Expn., 1934-35. Catholic. Author: Dunne's History of Illinois. Home: Chicago, Ill. Died May 24, 1937.

DUNNE, Edward Joseph, bishop; b. Tipperary, Ireland, Apr. 23, 1848; parents removed to Chicago, 1849; ed. Coll. St. Mary's of the Lake, theology at Sem. of St. Francis de Sales, Milwaukee, and St. Mary's of Baltimore. Ordained R.C. priest, Baltimore, June 29, 1871; served two Chicago chs. as asst. pastor All Saints' parish, Chicago, 1875-93; consecrated bishop of Dallas (Tex.), Nov. 30, 1893. Died 1910.

DUNNE, Finley Peter, author; b. Chicago, July 10, 1867; s. Peter and Ellen (Finley) D.; ed. Chicago pub. schs.; m. Margaret Abbott, Dec. 9, 1902; children—Finley Peter, Philip, David Leonard, Margaret. Entered newspaper life as reporter, 1885; served on various papers; on editorial staff Chicago Evening Post and Times-Herald, 1892-97; editor Chicago Journal, 1897-1900. Mem. Nat. Inst. Arts and Letters. Author: Mr. Dooley in Peace and in War, 1898; Mr. Dooley in the Hearts of His Countrymen, 1898; Mr. Dooley's Philosophy, 1900; Mr. Dooley's Opinions, 1901; Observations by Mr. Dooley, 1902; Dissertations by Mr. Dooley, 1906; Mr. Dooley Says, 1910, etc. Home: New York, N.Y. Died Apr. 24, 1936.

DUNNE, Peter Francis, lawyer; b. San Francisco, Dec. 29, 1860; s. Peter and Margaret (Bergin) Dunne; U. of San Francisco, 1878; LL.B., U. of Calif., 1881; m. Anne Cecelia Haehnlen, June 28, 1898. Practiced, San Francisco, 1882—; gen. atty., S.P. Co., 1902-10; mem. Dunne, Dunne & Cook. Home: San Francisco, Calif. Died Sept. 25, 1933.

DUNNELL, Elbridge Gerry, journalist; b. New York, Apr. 9, 1845; common sch. edn.; m. Marie C. Fish. Worked as a printer until 1868; began daily newspaper writing for New York Evening Post, 1873; Albany corr. same, 1875-76; on staff of New York Times, 1876-1902; Albany corr., 1879-81; transferred to Washington, Nov. 1881; in charge of bureau, 1883-1902; chmn. standing com. of press correspondents, 53d, 54th, 55th and 56th Congresses. Engaged in gen. newspaper and lit. work. Home: New York, N.Y. Died 1905.

DUNNELL, Mark Boothby, lawyer; b. Buxton, Me., June 28, 1864; s. congressman Mark Hill and Sarah A. (Parrington) D.; A.B., University of Rochester (N.Y.), 1886; m. Alice Mary Lincoln, June 15, 1935. Principal of high sch., Faribault, Minn., 1886-87; admitted to bar, 1888; U.S. deputy consul-gen., Shanghai, China, 1889-92. Author: Minnesota Practice, 1903; Minnesota Tax Law, 1904; Minnesota Digest, 1910, 27; Supplement, Minnesota Digest, 1916, 21, 30, 32, 34, 37. Minn. Probate Law, 1922. Editor Revised Laws, Minn., 1905. Home: Owatonna, Minn. Died Dec. 8, 1940.

DUNNELL, Mark Hill, lawyer; b. Buxton, Me., July 2, 1823; s. Samuel and Achsah H. D.; grad. Waterville Coll. (now Colby U.), 1849 (A.M., 1852; hon. LL.D., Shurtleff Coll., 1868; Colby Coll., 1899); m. Sarah A. Parrington, Nov. 20, 1850. Prin. Norway and Hebron Acads., 1849-54; mem. Me. legislature, 1854; State senate, 1855; State supt. common schools, Me., 1855-59; began law practice, Portland, Me., 1860; served in war, col. 5th Me. inf., 1861-62; consul at Vera Cruz, Mexico, 1862-63; went to Minn., 1865; mem. Minn. legislature, 1867; State supt. public instruction, 1867-70; mem. Congress, 1871-83 and 1889-91. Republican. Hon. mem. Soc. of Geography and Statistics, City of Mexico, 1873. Home: Owatonna, Minn. Died 1904.

DUNNETT, Alexander, lawyer; b. Peacham, Vt., Nov. 29, 1852; s. Andrew and Christiana (Galbraith) D.; ed. Newbury Sem., to 1867, McIndoes Acad., to 1869; student Randolph Normal Sch., 1872-75; (M.S., Norwich U., 1917); m. Ellen Chalmers, Apr. 29, 1889. Admitted to bar, 1877; practiced at S. Ryegate, Vt., 1877-83, St. Johnsbury, Vt., 1883—; mem. Dunnett & Slack, 1895-1913, Dunnett & Leslie, 1913-15, Dunnett & Shields, 1915-17, and of Dunnett, Shields & Conant, 1917—. Served in Vermont Militia, 1867; chmn. Rep. Co. Com., 1882-86; state's atty., Caledonia Co., 1886-90; chmn. Rep. State Conv., 1900; state senator, 1900; U.S. atty., Dist. of Vt., Oct. 20, 1906-Mar. 1915; chmn. commn. to settle boundary line with N.H., 1913; trustee Norwich U. (Northfield, Vt.). Unitarian. Mason. Home: St. Johnsbury, Vt. Died Sept. 14, 1920.

DUNNING, Albert Elijah, editor; b. Brookfield, Conn., Jan. 5, 1844; s. Elijah Starr and Abigail (Beach) D.; A.B., Yale, 1867; grad. Andover Theol. Sem., 1870; (D.D., Beloit Coll., 1889); m. Harriet W. Westbrook, Dec. 27, 1870; father of Harry Westbrook D. Ordained Congl. minister, 1870; pastor Highland Ch., Boston, 1870-81; gen. S.S. sec. for Congl. chs., 1881-89; editor-in-chief The Congregationalist, Boston, 1889-1911. Sec. Internat. S.S. Lesson Com., 1897-1902. Southworth lecturer, Andover Theol. Sem.; mem. Mass. Pilgrim Ter-Centenary Commn. Author: The Sunday School Library, 1883; Bible Studies, 1886; Congregationalists in America, 1894; Making of the Bible, 1911. Home: Brookline, Mass. Died Nov. 14, 1923.

DUNNING, Edwin James, author; b. Camillus, N.Y., July 19, 1821; ed. private school, Saratoga Springs, N.Y.; m. May 1, 1842; practiced dentistry, Ithaca and Syracuse, N.Y., 1838-44; New York, 1844-74; lost his sight in 1877 and took up literature. Author: Genesis of Shakespeare's Art. A Study of His Poems and Sonnets. Home: Cambridge, Mass. Died 1901.

DUNNING, George Freeman; b. Brunswick, Me., May 25, 1817; s. Robert Dunlap and Mary (O'Brien) D.; ed. Waterville Acad.; Bowdoin Coll. (as univ. student), 1831-33, A.M., 1861. In U.S. Mint Service, Phila. and New York, 1838-77; supt. N.Y. assay office, 1862-77; supt. Mint of Honduras, 1878-79. Home: Briarcliff Manor, N.Y. Died 1910.

DUNNING, Lehman H., surgeon; b. Edwardsburg, Mich., April 12, 1850; s. Oscar M. Dunning; grad. Rush Med. Coll., 1872; took numerous post-grad. courses in U.S. and Germany; m. Harriet J. Beauchamp, Dec. 9, 1875. Began practice of medicine at New Troy, Mich., 1872; removed to South Bend, Ind., 1878, and to Indianapolis, 1889; pension examiner 4 yrs.; mem. of numerous med. socs.; del. to 9th Internat. Med. Congress; pres. Marion Co. Med. Soc. Prof. diseases of women, Med. Coll. of Ind.; chief of staff of Deaconess Hosp. Republican. Methodist. Home: Indianapolis, Ind. Deceased.

DUNNING, William Archibald, educator; b. Plainfield, N.J.; s. John H. and Catherine D. (Trelease) D.; A.B., Columbia, 1881, A.M., 1884, Ph.D., 1885 (LL.D., 1904; Litt.D., Dartmouth, 1916); m. Charlotte E. Loomis, Apr. 18, 1888 (died 1917). Fellow, lecturer, and instr. polit. science and history, 1886-91, adj. prof. and prof. history, 1891-1903, Lieber prof. history and polit. philosophy, 1904—, Columbia. Mng. editor Polit. Science Quarterly, 1894-1903. Author: History of Political Theories, 3 vols., 1902-20; Reconstruction, Political and Economic, 1907; Carl Schurz's Political Career, 1869-1906 (with Frederic Bancroft), 1908; The British Empire and the U.S., 1914. Died Aug. 25, 1922.

DUNPHY, Charles, mining; b. Chicago, Ill., Sept. 12, 1879; s. Wm. H. and Minnie (Sloan) D.; ed. high sch., Chicago; m. Rowena Burns, Mar. 1902; children—Dana Burns, Rowena Burns. In mining business, opening mines and building mills, in Calif. and Mexico, 1897—. Home: San Francisco, Calif. Died Sept. 23, 1933.

DUNPHY, William Henry, lawyer; b. Aurora, Ill., June 29, 1860; s. Robert and Catharine D.; grad. high sch., Aurora, 1876; was locomotive engr. on C.,B.&Q. R.R. and Ore. R.R. & Navigation Co.'s R.R. until 1894; admitted to bar, 1894; in practice at Walla Walla, Wash.; m. Mary Helen Lyons, Nov. 4, 1896. Receiver public moneys, Walla Walla land office, 1894-98; mem. Dem. Nat. Com., 1900—. Died Apr. 7, 1915

DUNSCOMB, Charles Ellsworth, pub. Berkeley Daily Gazette; b. Moultrie Co., Ill., June 21, 1868; s. John Harmon and Jane Elvira (Mitchell); grad. high schs., Sullivan, Ill., 1883; m. Flora Elizabeth Damron, Apr. 3, 1893. Began with Sullivan News, 1883; with East St. Louis Journal, 1890-94; with San Bernardino Times Index, 1894-1902; owner and pub. Berkeley Daily Gazette, 1915—; mem. advisory bd. Am. Trust Co. of Calif. Republican. Mason. Home: Berkeley, Calif. Died Nov. 8, 1938.

DUNSCOMB, Samuel Whitney, Jr., lawyer; b. New York, N.Y., Jan. 11, 1868; s. Rev. Samuel W. and Mary M. (Smith) D.; A.B., Coll. City of New York, 1888; A.M., Columbia, 1891, LL.B., Ph.D., 1893; unmarried. Admitted to bar, Nov. 1893; atty. law dept. Title Guarantee & Trust Co., New York, 1899. Member Met. Mus. of Art, New York Bot. Garden; life fellow and hon. councillor N. Brit. Acad. Arts, London. Author: Bankruptcy, a Study in Comparative Legislation, 1893. Home: Yonkers, N.Y. Died April 1936.

DUNSMORE, Andrew B., lawyer; b. Tioga County, Pa., Jan. 4, 1866; s. John and Janet (Baird) D.; ed. Blossburg (Pa.) High Sch.; Mansfield (Pa.) State Teachers Coll.; m. Sarah E. Ball, May 17, 1894; 1 dau., Janet M. Began practice, Wellsboro, Pa., 1890; chmn. Rep. Com., Tioga Co., 1894, 1935-36; dist. atty. Tioga Co., 1895-1903; mem. Pa. Ho. of Rep., 3 terms, 1905-09; asst. U.S. atty. Middle Dist., Pa., 1909-11; U.S. atty., 1911-14, and 1921-34. Author of numerous bills in legislature; among them, Pa. St. R.R. Commn. bill, 2-cent R.R. fare bill, Tax Commn. bill, etc. Episcopalian. Mason. Home: Wellsboro, Pa. Died Aug. 23, 1938.

DUNTLEY, John Wheeler, mfr.; b. Wyandotte, Mich., Aug. 16, 1863; ed. public schools; married. Began as foundryman, 1878; in ry. supply business, 1884-95; founded Chicago Pneumatic Tool Co., 1895, of which was pres. until 1909; organized and was dir. Taite-Howard Pneumatic Tool Co., of London, Eng., 1898, to exploit product of the Chicago company, under its foreign patents; organized New York Air Compressor Co., 1899, at Arlington, N.J., and in 1900 merged it with Franklin (Pa.) Air Compressor Co., of which became v.p.; merged the Franklin Air Compressor Co., Chisholm & Moore Mfg. Co. (Cleveland), and the Boyer Machine Co. (Detroit) with the Chicago Pneumatic Tool Co., 1901; absorbed the Standard Pneumatic Tool Co., of Aurora, Ill., 1902, and consolidated the Taite-Howard Pneumatic Tool Co. with the Internat. Pneumatic Tool Co., of London, Eng., into the Consol. Pneumatic Tool Co., with offices at London and works at Fraserburgh, Scotland; absorbed the Phila. Pneumatic Tool Co., 1905, making it part of the Chicago Pneumatic Tool Co. From the first amalgamation of interest with the Chicago company was a mem. of the exec. bd. and a dir.; organized, 1909, and pres. Duntley Mfg. Co., mfrs. of Duntley Pneumatic Cleaners; pres. Libertad Mining and Smelting Co. (mines in Sonora, Mex.). Decorated with cross of Legion of Honor by President of France in 1900, in recognition of services in introducing pnuematic tools into gen. and practical use. Home: Chicago, Ill. Died 1921.

DUNTON, Larkin, head master Boston Normal School; b. Concord, Me., July 22, 1828; grad. Colby Univ.; prin. New Castle Acad., 2 years; Bath, Me., High School, 7 years; Lawrence School, Boston, 4 years. Home: Allston, Mass. Died 1899.

DUNTON, William Herbert, painter; b. Augusta, Me., Aug. 28, 1878; s. William Henry and Anna Katherine (Pillsbury) D.; ed. pub. schs.; art edn., Cowles Art Sch., Boston, Mass., Art Students League, New York; pupil of Leon Gaspard; m. Nellie G. Hartley, June 6, 1900; children—Vivian E., Ivan H. Represented by murals in Mo. State Capitol, Jefferson City; also in collections of Peoria (Ill.) Soc. Applied Arts, Witte Memorial Mus., San Antonio, Tex., Mus. of N.M., Santa Fe; "Fall in the Foothills" (White House, Washington, D.C.); "Portrait of Frank Riley" (Ariz. Pioneers' Historical Society, Tucson). Awarded gold medal, Nashville, Tenn., 1927; cash prize, Pacific Southwest Expn., Long Beach, Calif., 1928; cash prize, San Antonio, 1929. Home: Taos, N.M. Died May 18, 1936.

DUNWELL, Charles Tappan, congressman; b. Newark, Wayne Co., N.Y., Feb. 13, 1852; s. Almerin and Elizabeth Hill D.; removed with parents to Lyons, N.Y.; ed. Lyons Union Sch., and Cornell Univ. to end of junior yr.; grad. Columbia Coll. Law Sch., 1874, with degree of LL.B.; m. Emma B. Williams, Apr. 22, 1880. Admitted to bar, 1874; Rep. nominee for comptroller of Brooklyn, 1890; mem. Rep. State Com. of N.Y., 1891-92; mem. Congress from 3d N.Y. dist., 1903-09. Home: Brooklyn, N.Y. Died 1908.

DUNWELL, James Winslow, jurist; b. Newark, N.Y., Dec. 19, 1849; s. Almerin and Elizabeth H. D.; ed. Lyons Union Sch., Cornell Univ., 1869-71; studied law; m. Mary Ella Groat, May 22, 1878. Admitted to bar, 1873; was many yrs. counsel for N.Y. Central & Hudson River R.R. Co. and leased lines; became justice Supreme Court N.Y., elected for term from Jan. 1, 1896, to Dec. 31, 1910. Was chmn.

Rep. Co. Com. of Wayne Co., 1880. Home: Lyons, N.Y. Died 1907.

DUNWOODY, William Hood, flour mfr.; b. Westtown, Pa., Mar. 14, 1841; s. James and Hannah (Hood) D.; acad. edn. at Phila.; m. Katie L. Patten. Began business in Phila., 1864; moved to Minneapolis, Sept., 1869; was first to introduce new process for milling wheat, and to export flour from Minneapolis direct to Europe; now v.p. Washburn-Crosby Co.; pres. Northwestern Nat. Bank, St. Anthony & Dakota Elevator Co., Barnum Grain Co.; v.p. Minneapolis Trust Co., St. Anthony Elevator Co. Mem. Minneapolis and New York chambers of commerce. Home: Minneapolis, Minn. Died Feb. 8, 1914.

Du PONT, Alfred I., banking; ed. Mass. Inst. Tech.; m. Jessie D. Ball. Formerly head of E. I. du Pont de Nemours & Co.; now chmn. bd. Fla. Nat. Bank, Jacksonville. Home: San Jose, Fla. Died Apr. 27, 1935.

Du PONT, Henry Algernon, senator; b. nr. Wilmington, Del., July 30, 1838; s. Henry; g.s. of Eleuthère Irénée du Pont de Nemours; g.g.s. Pierre Samuel du Pont de Nemours, French economist and statesman (died in Del., 1817); grad. U.S. Mil. Acad., 1861; at head of class; married; children—Louise Evelina (Mrs. F. B. Crowninshield), Henry Francis. Commd. 2d lt. engrs.; 1st lt. 5th Arty., 1861; regimental adj. July 6, 1861; acting asst. adj. gen. of troops in New York harbor, 1862-63; capt. 5th Arty., Mar. 24, 1864; comd. battery at battle of Newmarket, W.Va., as chief of arty., that dept.; took part in battles of Piedmont and Lynchburg; later chief of artillery, Crook's Corps; in battles of Winchester, Sept. 19, 1864, Fisher's Hill, Sept. 22, 1864, and Cedar Creek, Oct. 19, 1964; resigned from army, Mar. 1, 1875. Bvtd. maj. "for gallant services at Winchester and Fisher's Hill"; bvtd. lt. col. Oct. 19, 1864, "for distinguished services at Cedar Creek"; awarded Congressional Medal of Honor "for extraordinary gallantry" at Cedar Creek. Received in Del. legislature May 9, 1895, 15 of the 30 votes cast for U.S. senator; election contested on question of right of ex-speaker of Del. Senate (then acting as gov.) to vote; without his vote Col. du Pont had majority of 1; U.S. Senate Com. reported in his favor, but he was not seated, not receiving unanimous party support, because of opposition to the free and unlimited coinage of silver; elected U.S. Senator for terms 1906-11, 1911-17; chmn. of Senate Mil. Com. May 1, 1911-Mar. 15, 1913. Pres. and gen. mgr., Wilmington & Norfolk R.R. Co., 1877-99. Retired. Home: Winterthur, Del. Died Dec. 31, 1926.

DU PONT, T(homas) Coleman, senator; b. Louisville, Ky., December 11, 1863; s. Antoine Bidermann and Ellen Susan (Coleman) D.; student Urbana (O.) U., Chauncy Hall Sch., Boston, and Mass. Inst. Tech.; m. Alice du Pont, Jan. 17, 1889. Surveyor Louisville & Southern Expn., and engr. Central Coal & Iron Co., 1883; gen. mgr., Johnson Co., Johnstown, Pa., 1893; has engaged extensively in coal and iron mining in Ky., 1883—, and also in constrn. and management of st. rys.; removed to Wilmington, 1900; was pres. E. I. du Pont de Nemours Powder Co., 1902-15; pres. Central Coal & Iron Co., McHenry Coal Co., Main Jellico Mountain Coal Co. (all of Ky.), Wilmington Trust Co. Mem. Corp. Mass. Inst. Tech. Mem. Rep. Nat. Com., 1908—; was chmn. Rep. State Com. of Del.; apptd. mem. U.S. Senate, July 1921, to fill vacancy, for period ending Nov. 1922; elected U.S. senator, for term 1925-31, resigned, 1928. Home: Wilmington, Del. Died Nov. 11, 1930.

DUPRE, Henry Garland, congressman; b. Opelousas, St. Landry Parish, La., July 28, 1873; A. B., Tulane U., 1892; LL.B. Asst. city atty., New Orleans, 1900-10; mem. La. Ho. of Rep., 1900-10 (speaker, 1908-10); elected to 61st Congress, Nov. 8, 1910, for unexpired term (Nov., 1910-Mar., 1911), of Samuel L. Gilmore, deceased; elected at same election mem. 62d Congress (1911-13), 2d La. Dist., reëlected to 63d to 67th Congresses (1913-23). Democrat. Home: New Orleans, La. Died Feb. 21, 1924.

DU PUY, Herbert, mfr.; A.B., Lehigh U., 1878; m. Amy Susette Hostetter. Formerly pres. and chmn. bd. Crucible Steel Co. of America. V.p. Huguenot Soc. America. Home: Pittsburgh, Pa. Died Jan. 10, 1930.

DU PUY, Raymond, civil engr.; b. Pittsburgh, Jan. 4, 1860; s. T. Haskins and Martha L. (Allen) D.; Georgetown U., D.C., 1876-77; m. Doretta Greve, Oct. 15, 1888. Began as water boy, M.,K. & T. Ry., Tex., 1877; asst. engr. same rd. and M.P. Ry., 1881; chief engr. Tioga R.R. (br. N.Y., L.E. & W. Ry.), 1881-85; gen. supt. Minn. & Northwestern Ry., 1885-87; gen. mgr. C., St. P. & K.C. Ry., 1887-88; pres. Leavenworth & St. Joseph and DeKalb & Great Western rys., to 1896; gen. supt. C.G.W. Ry., 1898-99; supt. D.L.&W. R.R., 1899-1900; v.p. and gen. mgr. St. Joseph & Grand Island Ry., 1900-05, Virginian Ry., Apr. 15, 1905—; pres. Virginian Ry. Co.; v.p. Industrial Finance Co., Norfolk (Va.) Terminal Ry. Co. Home: Norfolk, Va. Died May 14, 1933.

DU PUY, William Atherton, author; b. Palestine, Tex., Jan. 6, 1876; grad. Phoenix (Ariz.) High Sch., 1896; student U. of Ariz., 2 yrs.; m. Ada Lee Orme, June 27, 1906; children—Celene, Jacqueline. Began writing as Ariz. corr. for Pacific and eastern papers; reported legislature in Austin, Tex., 1904; worked as reporter in Houston, New Orleans, Vicksburg, St. Louis, Washington, New York and Phila.; organized, 1907, the Du Puy Syndicate with hdqrs. in Washington, supplying features on nat. affairs to newspapers; Field sec. Navy League of U.S., 1915-1916. Originator, 1916, and 1st editor of Sea Power, Capt. Mil. Intelligence Division, General Staff U.S. A., 1918. General manager Haskin Newspaper Service, 1919, Public Ledger Syndicate, 1920; editor for Internat. Labor Office, League of Nations, at Geneva, Switzerland, 1923; expert with U.S. Bur. of Efficiency investigating currency system, 1925; exec. asst. to secretary of the Interior, 1929; eastern mgr. Pan-Pacific Press Bur., 1934. One of organizers of the 1st chapter Am. Legion, Washington. Author: Uncle Sam—Wonder Worker, 1913; Uncle Sam's Modern Miracles, 1914; Uncle Sam—Detective, 1915; Uncle Sam—Fighter, 1918; Romances of Science—Our Insect Friends and Foes, 1924; Our Animal Friends and Foes, 1924; Our Bird Friends and Foes, 1925; Our Plant Friends and Foes, 1929; Wonders of the Animal World, 1929; Wonders of the Plant World, 1929. Co-author: (with Ray Lyman Wilbur) Conservation in the Department of the Interior, 1931; Hawaii and Its Race Problem, 1932; The Nation's Forests, 1938; The Green Kingdom, 1939; The Baron of the Colorados, 1940. Home: Washington, D.C. Died Aug. 11, 1941.

DURAND, Elias Judah, botanist; b. Canandaigua, N.Y., Mar. 20, 1870; s. Rufus and Ann M. (Sisson) D.; A.B., Cornell U., 1893, D.Sc., 1895; m. Anna Louise Perry, Sept. 6, 1899 (died 1901); 2d, Sue G. Stone, July 24, 1917. Fellow, Cornell U., 1893-95; asst. in botany and asst. botanist in Expt. Sta., Cornell, 1895-96; instr. botany, Cornell, 1896-1910; asst. prof. botany, 1910-11, asso. prof., 1911-18, U. of Mo.; prof. botany, U. of Minn., 1918—. Home: St. Paul, Minn. Died Oct. 29, 1922.

DURBIN, Winfield Taylor, governor; b. Lawrenceburg, Ind., May 4, 1847; ed. pub. schs.; served in Union army as pvt.; taught sch.; m. Bertha McCullough, Oct. 6, 1875. Went to Indianapolis, 1869; worked in office and traveled for wholesale dry goods house until 1879; removed to Anderson, Ind., 1879, and engaged in banking; was connected with first fuel gas co. that installed a distributing system in Anderson and a fuel supply co.; is interested in several large mfg. industries as well as electric traction lines. Col. 161st Ind. Regt. in Spanish-Am. War; several yrs. on Rep. State Com. of Ind., chmn. exec. com.; mem. Rep. Nat. Com. and also exec. com., 1896-1900; gov. of Ind., 1901-05; Rep. nominee for gov., 1912. Mason. Died Dec. 18, 1928.

DURFEE, Thomas, jurist; b. Tiverton, R.I., Feb. 6, 1826; s. Job D. (who at the time of his death was Chief Justice Supreme Court, R.I.); grad. Brown Univ., 1846 (LL.D., Brown); studied law; admitted to R.I. bar, Oct., 1848; m. Sarah J., d. John and Sarah (Tiffany) Slater. Reporter decisions Supreme Court, R.I., 1849-53; judge, 1854-60, Court of Magistrates, Providence, and, except for 1 yr., presiding judge; mem. and speaker R.I. ho. of reps., 1863-65; mem. R.I. senate, 1865; asso. justice, 1865-75; chief justice, 1875-91, Supreme Court R.I.; retired 1891; trustee from 1875, chancellor 1879-88, Brown Univ. Republican. Home: Providence, R.I. Died 1901.

DURFEE, William Franklin, civil and mech. engr.; b. New Bedford, Mass., Nov. 15, 1833; ed. at home and Lawrence Scientific School, Harvard; established as engr. and architect, 1853; city surveyor, New Bedford, 5 years; mem. Mass. legislature, 1861; examined iron ores of Lake Superior, 1862, with reference to their suitability for steel manufacture, and erected exptl. works where ingots of steel were produced from which were rolled, May 25, 1865, the first steel rails ever made in U.S.; built at Wyandotte, Mich., first analytical laboratory built as adjunct to steel works in U.S.; built at Ansonia, Conn., first successful furnaces for refining copper by gaseous fuel ever erected in U.S.; was mgr. U.S. Mitis Co.; etc. Consulting engr. and expert in patent causes. Home: West New Brighton, N.Y. Died 1899.

DURFEE, William Pitt, coll. dean; b. Livonia, Mich., Feb. 5, 1855; s. R. S. and Mary (Wightman) D.; A.B., U. of Mich., 1876; Ph.D., Johns Hopkins U., 1883; LL.D. from Hobart Coll., 1922; m. Charlotte E. Racao, Apr. 3, 1888; children—Walter Hetherington, Elizabeth Racao; m. 2d, Katharine S. Butts, June 29, 1898; 1 dau., Mary Katharine Perry. Teacher, Berkeley (Calif.) Gymnasium, 1877-81, prof. mathematics, 1884-1929, prof. of mathematics emeritus, 1929—, dean, 1888-1925, acting pres., 1897, 1901-03, 1912-13, 1917-19, Hobart Coll. (dean emeritus). Episcopalian. Republican. Author: Elements of Trigonometry, 1901. Home: Geneva, N.Y. Died Dec. 17, 1941.

DURFEE, Winthrop Carver, mfg. and cons. chemist; b. Fall River, Mass., Apr. 23, 1858; s. Walter Chaloner and Jane Frances (Alden) D.; B.Ph., Brown U., 1878; m. Sylvie Whitney, Oct. 18, 1881; children—Walter Chaloner, Pauline Elizabeth (Mrs. Harold C. Chapin), Philip Sherwood. Engaged in cotton mfg., 1878-81; salesman, 1881-85; mfg. and cons. chemist, Boston, 1885—; advanced the technique and economics of textile coloring through research. Republican. Episcopalian. Mason. Home: Jamaica Plain (Boston), Mass. Died Sept. 19, 1929.

DURHAM, (Joseph) Edward, insurance mgr., and mfr.; b. Watsontown, Pa., Oct. 22, 1857; s. Joseph Gaston and Margaret Laird (Lowry) D.; A.B., Lafayette College, Pa., 1878; m. Nellie R. Stranahan (died 1929); children—J(oseph) Edward, Fred Stranahan, Lowry (dec.), Mrs. Eleanor Lewis Male. Admitted to Pa. bar, 1882, but did not practice; gen. mgr. for Penn Mutual Life Insurance Co. of Phila. for eastern Pa. and other territory, 1883—; engaged in mfg. and other commercial enterprises; sole mem. Bourne & Durham; trustee Penn Mut.. Life Ins. Co.; pres. during corporate life of Flint Light & Power Co., Phila., also Nat. Underwriters Assn.; pres. Bonney Forge & Tool Works; dir. Nat. Bank of Germantown. Pres. Underwriters' Assn., Phila., also Nat. Underwriters' Assn. Home: Germantown, Philadelphia, Pa. Died Oct. 23, 1933.

DURHAM, John Stephens, lawyer; b. Phila., Pa., July 18, 1861; s. Samuel and Elizabeth (Stephens) D.; B.S., U. of Pa., 1886, C.E., 1889; m. Constance Mackenzie, July 1, 1897. Asso. editor Philadelphia Evening Bulletin, 1887; U.S. consul to Santo Domingo, 1890; U.S. minister to Haiti and chargé d'affaires to Santo Domingo, 1891-93; admitted to Phila. bar, 1895; in Cuba as U.S. asst. atty., preparing defenses against claims before Spanish Treaty Claims Commn. until 1905; now practicing law, representing European and Am. interests in the West Indies. Home: Philadelphia, Pa. Died Oct. 16, 1919.

DURHAM, Milton Jamison, lawyer; b. Mercer (now Boyle Co.), Ky., May 16, 1824; s. Benjamin and Margaret (Robinson) D.; A.B., Asbury (now De Pauw) U., 1844, A.M., 1847; LL.B., Louisville Law Sch., 1850; m. Martha J. Mitchell, June 16, 1850 (died 1879); m. 2d, Mrs. Margaret L. Curten, June 17, 1886. Admitted to bar, 1850; judge Circuit Ct., 1861-62; mem. 43d to 45th Congresses (1873-79); 1st comptroller of the treasury U.S., 1885-89. Democrat. Home: Lexington, Ky. Died 1911.

DURHAM, Nelson Wayne, newspaperman; b. Atchison Co., Mo., Dec. 11, 1859; s. William and Sarah Elizabeth (Shannon) D.; ed. pub. schs. Ia. and Mo.; Litt.D. from Whitworth Coll., Spokane, Wash.; m. Annie Esther McLeod, Aug. 23, 1882 (now dec.); children—Mrs. Mabel Sanders, Kenneth, Wayne, Mrs. Dorothy Taylor; m. 2d, Data Rothrock (asst. supt. schs.), June 27, 1923. News editor and spl. writer Portland Oregonian, 1883-89; mng. editor Spokane Spokesman-Review, 1889-1910; editorial writer same, 1912—. Chmn. Spokane County Council of Defense, World War. Trustee Eastern Wash. Hist. Soc., Spokane Pub. Museum; pres. Spokane Mountaineers; one of 7 who in 1887 organized Ore. Alpine Club (now the Mazamas). Home: Spokane, Wash. Died 1938.

DURHAM, Plato Tracy, clergyman, educator; b. Shelby, N.C., Sept. 10, 1873; s. Plato and Leonora Catharine (Tracy) D.; A.B., Trinity Coll., Durham, N.C., 1895 (D.D., 1913); student Yale Div. Sch., 1895-96, Christ Ch. Coll., Oxford, Eng., 1901-02; grad. Union Theol. Sem., 1899; m. Lucy Cole, Apr. 24, 1906. Licensed to preach, 1895; ordained ministry M.E. Ch., S., 1903; prof. Bibl. lit. and ch. history, Trinity Coll., N.C., 1899-1906; pastor Trinity Ch., Charlotte, N.C., 1906-08, Central Ch., Concord, N.C., 1908-11; presiding elder Winston Dist., N.C., 1911-13, Charlotte Dist., 1913-14; dean Candler sch. of Theology, Emory U., 1914-18; also prof. Ch. history, same univ., and trustee. Mem. Federal Council Chs. in America; mem. Inter-Church World Movement of N.A. Served as 1st lt. 2d Regt. N.C. Vols., Spanish-Am. War, 1898. Mason. Home: Atlanta, Ga. Died Feb. 10, 1930.

DURIER, Antoine, R.C. bishop of Natchitoches, 1885—; b. St. Bonnet des-quarts, France, Jan. 3, 1833; when preparing for priesthood at the Seminary of Lyons volunteered for missionary work in La. Arrived at U.S., 1855; completed theol. course; studied English; ordained, 1856; stationed at Chillicothe, O., until 1857; became asst. priest, Cathedral, New Orleans, and later pastor of Ch. of the Annunciation there until 1885. Died 1904.

DURKEE, Frank Williams, prof. chemistry; b. North Tunbridge, Vt., Oct. 5, 1861; s. Simeon P. and Mary E. (Smith) D.; A.B., Tufts Coll., 1888, A.M., 1889; hon. D.Sc. from same coll., 1921; m. Henrietta N. Brown, Feb. 21, 1895; children—Margaret, Robert B., Benjamin G. B. Began as instr. chemistry, Tufts Coll., 1889; prof. and head of dept., same coll., 1907—. Republican. Universalist. Home: Tufts College, Mass. Died May 21, 1939.

DURLAND, Kellogg, social worker; b. New York, N.Y., Mar. 13, 1881; s. J. H. and Eunice Lavinia (Cox) D.; ed. Harvard, 1900, U. of Edinburgh, 1900-01, École des Hautes Étude Sociale, Paris, 1901-02; unmarried. Worked as coal miner in Scotland 4 months in 1901 to study mining conditions; made spl. investigations into child labor abuses in Pa. coal mines, 1902; head of Tech. House, Boston, 1903-04; asst. head worker Univ. Settlement, New York, 1904-05; as disguised immigrant studied the Am. immigration question, 1905; traveled in Russia during the revolution of 1906 as contbr. to Collier's, Harper's Weekly, Review of Reviews, Boston Transcript, New York Evening Post; was arrested and imprisoned; writer and lecturer on events and conditions in Russia. Died 1911.

DURRETT, Reuben Thomas, lawyer; b. Henry Co., Ky., Jan. 22, 1824; s. William and Elizabeth (Rawlings) D.; student Georgetown Coll., Ky., 1844-46; A.B., Brown U., 1849, A.M., 1852; LL.B., U. of Louisville, 1850; (LL.D., Brown, 1894, Georgetown, 1895, Louisville, 1896); m. Elizabeth H. Bates, 1852. Practiced law, Louisville, 1850-80; mem. city council, 1853-54; served as park commr.; part owner and editor, 1857-59, Louisville Daily Courier; founder, 1871, and pres., 1871-80, Pub. Library of Ky.; founder, 1884, and from then pres. Filson Club, Louisville. Home: Louisville, Ky. Died Sept. 1913.

DURST, William Arthur, banker; b. Monroe, Wis., 1870; ed. pub. schs.; m. Clara J. West. Removed to Minn., 1887; with Minn. Loan & Trust Co., 1889—, later pres. until 1934; chmn. exec. com. Northwestern Nat. Bank & Trust Co., 1934—; chmn. governing com. Northwest Bancorporation; v.p. The Shawmut Co. (Duluth). Republican. Mason. Home: Minneapolis, Minn. Died Aug. 19, 1940.

DURSTON, John Hurst, editor; b. Syracuse, N.Y., Feb. 19, 1848; s. John and Sarah (Hurst) D.; ed. Yale to middle of jr. yr. in class of 1869; studied in Germany 3 yrs., Ph.D., U. of Heidelberg, 1870; studied language, civics and polit. economy, Paris, 1872-73; m. Mary Harwood, Oct. 5, 1871; children—Martha Harwood, Laura. Instr. and prof. in Syracuse U., 1871-78; editor Syracuse Standard, 1880-87; removed to Mont., 1887; editor The Anaconda Standard, 1889-1913; editor Butte Daily Post, 1913—. Home: Butte, Mont. Died Nov. 5, 1929.

DURYEA, Hiram, mfr.; b. Manhasset, L.I., N.Y., Apr. 12, 1834; pub. sch. and pvt. edn.; 1st lt. 48th N.Y. Militia, 1855; advanced through grades to col. Sept. 26, 1862; resigned Nov. 1, 1862; bvtd. brig. gen. vols., Mar. 13, 1865, for distinguished conduct at Gaines Mill, Va.; m. Laura D. Burnell, 1868. Partner, 1855, in H. V. Duryea & Son, starch mfrs., which later merged with Glen Cove Starch Mfg. Co., of which he was v.p. and later pres. until it was absorbed, 1890, by the Nat. Starch Co. of which he was pres. 18 months; now v.p. Am. Wood Working Machinery Co.; pres. Number Eighty Madison Avenue. Home: New York, N.Y. Died May 5, 1914.

DUSSER de BARENNE, Joannes Gregorius, physiologist; b. Brielle, Netherlands, June 6, 1885; s. Elize Marie and Dorothea (Vogelzang) Dusser de B.; M.D., U. of Amsterdam, 1909; hon. M.A., Yale University, 1930; m. Kate Snellen, Oct. 12, 1911 (died 1931); children—Charlotte, Dorothea Rebecca, Elizabeth Maria; m. 2d, Emily Lockwood Greene, Aug. 12, 1935; 1 dau., Marion. Instr. physiology, U. of Amsterdam, 1909-11; psychiatrist Meerenberg Asylum, 1911-14; lecturer in physiology, U. of Utrecht, 1919-30; neurologist St. Antonius Hosp., Utrecht, 1919-30; Sterling prof. physiology, Yale, 1930—. Mem. editorial board Am. Jour. Physiology; co-editor Jour. neurophysiology. Home: New Haven, Conn. Died June 9, 1940.

DUTCHER, Charles Mason, banker; b. Brooklyn, N.Y., Feb. 1, 1862; s. Charles Henry and Amanda (Story) D.; ed. Poly. Inst., Brooklyn; studied law; m. Helen Torrey Harris, M.D., Nov. 12, 1891; children—Frederick Harris, Charles Mason (dec.). With Chem. Nat. Bank, New York, 1881-83; with Greenwich Savings Bank (organized 1833), New York, 1883—, treas., 1906-20, pres., 1920—; pres. Sixth Av. Assn. Republican. Baptist. Home: Montclair, N.J. Died July 23, 1936.

DUTCHER, Silas Belden, capitalist; b. Springfield, N.Y., July 12, 1829; s. Parcefor C. and Johanna Low (Frink) D.; ed. public schools and Cazenovia Sem.; taught sch. winters, 1845-51; in railroading, 1851-55; mercantile business, New York, 1855-69; m. Rebecca J. Alwaise, Feb. 10, 1859. Supervisor city and co. of New York, 1861-62; supervisor internal revenue, 1868-72; pension agt., 1872-75; appraiser port of New York, 1877-80; supt. pub. works, N.Y., 1880-83; pres. Union Dime Savings Bank, New York, 1884-91; commr. to frame charter of Greater New York, 1896-97. Pres. Hamilton Trust Co., 1891—. Republican. Home: Brooklyn, N.Y. Died 1909.

DUTCHER, William, ornithologist; b. Stelton, N.J., Jan. 20, 1846; pub. sch. edn. Pres. Nat. Assn. of Audubon Socs.; fellow A.A.A.S., Am. Ornithologists' Union, N.Y. Acad. Sciences, N.Y. Zoöl. Soc., Royal Soc. for Protection of Birds (London). Home: Plainfield, N.J. Died July 2, 1920.

DUTTON, Benjamin F., merchant; b. Hillsboro, N.H., Oct. 14, 1831; s. Ephraim and Phœbe (Wilson) D.; ed. pub. schs. and mil. schs. at Pembroke, N.H., and Norwich, Va.; m. Harriet L. Hatch, Mar. 1852 (dec.); m. 2d, Harriet M. Conant, Mar. 1860. Began in mercantile business with father, at Hillsboro Bridge, N.H., 1852; organized B. F. Dutton & Co., which was merged into wholesale firm of Dutton & Wyman, previous to Civil War; later was mem. Brown & Dutton, burnt out at time of Boston fire; became mem. Houghton & Dutton, dept. store, 1871, incorporated, 1906, as Houghton & Dutton Co., of which is pres. Democrat. Conglist. Mason. Home: Glen Rock, Malden, Mass. Died June 2, 1915.

DUTTON, Clarence Edward, major U.S.A.; b. Wallingford, Conn., May 15, 1841; s. Samuel Henry and Emily (Curtis) D.; A.B., Yale, 1860; m. Emeline C. Babcock, Apr. 18, 1864. First lt. 21st Conn. Inf., Sept. 5, 1862; capt., Mar. 1, 1863; hon. mustered out, June 14, 1864; apptd. 2d lt. ordnance, Jan. 29, 1864; 1st lt., Mar. 7, 1867; capt., June 23, 1874; maj., May 1, 1890; retired at own request, over 30 yrs.' service, Feb. 7, 1901. Home: Englewood, N.J. Died 1912.

DUTTON, Edward Payson, publisher (E.P. Dutton & Co., pubs.); b. Keene, N.H., Jan. 4, 1831; removed to Boston, 1833; ed. Boston Latin Sch.; m. a d. of Jacob Sleeper, Boston, 1856. Mem. of Ide & Dutton, booksellers, Boston, 1852-58; bought out Ide's interest and continued, with a partner, as E. P. Dutton & Co., of which is now pres.; bought retail business of Ticknor & Fields, 1864, and of the Gen. Protestant Episcopal S.S. Union and Church Book Society of New York; finally concentrated the business in New York. Home: New York, N.Y. Died Sept. 6, 1923.

DUTTON, George Burwell, college prof.; b. Buffalo, N.Y., Mar. 24, 1881; s. West Oliver and Sarah (Bodamer) D.; grad. Central High Sch., Buffalo, 1897; B.A., Williams Coll., 1907; M.A., Harvard, 1908, Ph.D., 1910; m. Sarah Cummings, Aug. 7, 1917; 1 son, George Burwell. With Marine Bank, Buffalo, 1897-1902; instr. in English, Williams Coll., 1910-14, asst. prof., 1914-21, prof. English lit., 1921—; asst. prof. English, U. of Chicago, summer 1920; prof. English lit., U. of Buffalo, summers 1923-25 inclusive. Instr. war issues, S.A.T.C., Williams Coll., 1918. Home: Williamstown, Mass. Died Dec. 17, 1930.

DUTTON, Joseph (Ira Barnes Dutton), lay missionary; b. Stowe, Vt., Apr. 27, 1843; s. Ezra and Abigail (Barnes) D.; removed to Wis. with parents, 1847; educated under mother, Milton (Wis.) Acad. and by pvt. study. Enlisted as pvt. in Co. B, 13th Wis. Vols., summer of 1861; apptd. q.m. sergt. when regt. was being organized and served as such until Feb. 10, 1863; commd. 2d lt., Feb. 10, 1863; 1st lt., Feb. 15, 1865; apptd. regtl. q.m., Mar. 24, 1865; recommended (unknown to himself) for appmt. as capt. and a.q.m. by Maj. Gens. Thomas, Rousseau, Donaldson and Granger; assigned to staff of Gen. Granger, June 1864, later asst. to Col. Holabird, chief q.m. Dept. of Louisiana; in Govt. service for 10 yrs. after Civil War, principally in adjustment of war claims. Catholic. Lay missionary, leper settlement, Molokai, T.H., July 29, 1886—; administered estate of Father Damien, 1889; builder and in charge of the Baldwin Home (for orphan boys, helpless cases, blind—all of them lepers), where 1,284 inmates have been cared for; specially honored, July 1908, on account of services as a soldier and humanitarian, when Admiral Charles S. Sperry, in comd. of Atlantic Fleet on its tour of the world, paraded with colors flying, before the leper settlement. Mem. U.S. Catholic Hist. Soc., Am. Fedn. Catholic Socs. Died Mar. 26, 1931.

DUTTON, Samuel Train, educator; b. Hillsboro, N.H., Oct. 16, 1849; s. Jeremiah and Rebecca (Train) D.; A.B., Yale, 1873, A.M., 1890; (LL.D., Baylor U., 1912); m. Cornelia North, Oct. 8, 1874. In charge of schs., S. Norwalk, Conn., 1873-78; prin. Eaton Sch., New Haven, 1878-82; supt. schs. of New Haven, 1882-90, Brookline, Mass., 1890-1900; prof. of sch. administration, and supt. of schs., Teachers College (Columbia Univ.), 1900-15 (emeritus). Lecturer on pedagogy, Harvard, 1895-97, U. of Chicago, 1897-98, Boston U., 1898; exchange lecturer, Scandinavian univs., 1910. Hon. sec. New York Peace Soc.; chmn. exec. com. Nat. Arbitration and Peace Congress, 1907; gen. sec. World's Court League; trustee Constantinople Coll. for Women, Canton (China) Christian Coll., World Peace Foundation, Am. Scandinavian Foundation; mem. Internat. Commn. on the Balkan War, 1913. Author: Social Phases of Education; School Management. Co-author: Administration of Public Education in the United States. Editor "Historical" and "World at Work" series. Home: Hartsdale, N.Y. Died Mar. 28, 1919.

DUVAL, H. Rieman; b. Baltimore, Md., Oct. 17, 1843; s. John Rawlings and Elizabeth Warfield (Rieman) D.; ed. pvt. schs., Md.; m. Anne Gordon, d. John Hanson Thomas, of Baltimore, Feb. 1878. Served in Army of Northern Va., C.S.A.; after war, in service of B.&O. R.R. until 1873, Erie R.R., 1874, Erie Despatch Lines until 1883; receiver Florida Ry. & Navigation Co., 1884-89; pres. Fla. Central & Peninsular R.R. Co., 1889-99, South Bound R.R., 1892-99; now pres. and chmn. bd. Am. Beet Sugar Co.; trustee Mut. Life Ins. Co., of New York. Republican. Episcopalian. Died Mar. 18, 1924.

DUVAL, Isaac Harding, soldier; b. Wellsburg, W.Va., Sept. 1, 1824; common school edn.; m. Mary D. Kuhn, June 23, 1853. Was private sec. to ex-Gov. Butler of S.C.; commr. apptd. by Pres. Polk to treat with wild Indians on Texas border, 1847; comd. first co. that crossed the plains, Texas to Calif., 1849, making the trail; was in the insurrection in Cuba, 1851; served through Civil war, maj. 1st W.Va. inf. to brig. gen. and bvt. maj. gen. U.S. vols.; in 32 battles; wounded 3 times. Republican. Mem. Congress, 1869-71; served in both branches W.Va. legislature; adj. gen. State of W.Va.; collector internal revenue 14 yrs.; U.S. assessor 2 yrs., etc. Home: Wellsburg, W.Va. Died 1902.

DUVALL, Charles Raymond; b. Clarke Co., Va., Jan. 2, 1869; s. Charles Henry and Rachel Jennie (Jackson) D.; B.S., W.Va. U., 1891; grad. student in mathematics and physics, Johns Hopkins, 1892-96; m. Carrie Opie, June 6, 1900; children—Mrs. Virginia Cordani, Charles Fenton, Lindsay Opie, Raymond Opie, Edwin Leroy, William David. Computer, U.S. Coast and Geodetic Survey, 1899-1913; expert computer, Dept. Terrestrial Magnetism, Carnegie Institution, Washington, 1913-37; retired. Episcopalian. Author: (with A. L. Baldwin) Triangulation in California, Part II (Coast and Geodetic Survey), 1911. Home: Washington, D.C. Died Feb. 4, 1940.

DUVALL, William Penn, maj. gen.; b. St. Mary's Co., Md., Jan. 13, 1847; s. Robert E. and Julia (Frame) D.; ed. pvt. and pub. schs.; grad. U.S. Mil. Acad., 1869; m. Maria Cumming Lamar, Nov. 5, 1902. Commd. 2d lt. 5th U.S. Arty., June 15, 1869; 1st lt., Apr. 9, 1877; grad. Arty. Sch., 1892; capt. 1st U.S. Arty., Mar. 8, 1898; maj. insp.-gen. vols., May 12, 1898; hon. disch., July 19, 1898; lt. col. chief ordnance officer vols., July 18, 1898; hon. disch. from vol. service, May 12, 1899; lt. col. 26th U.S. Vol. Inf., July 5, 1899; col. 48th U.S. Vol. Inf., Sept. 9, 1899; hon. mustered out of vol. service, June 30, 1901; maj. Arty. Corps U.S.A., Sept. 23, 1901; lt. col., Feb. 24, 1906; brig. gen., Mar. 2, 1906; maj. gen. U.S.A., Oct. 2, 1907; asst. to the chief of staff; comdg. Philippines Div., Apr. 1909, to end of 1910; retired from active service, Jan. 13, 1911. Placed on active duty and assigned to command Southeastern Dept., Aug. 21, 1917. Home: Charleston, S.C. Died Mar. 1, 1920.

DUVENECK, Frank, artist; b. Covington, Ky., 1848; studied in Munich under Dietz and others over 10 yrs. Specialist in portraits and figure paintings, many of which are in this country; lived some yrs. in Munich and a few yrs. in Boston; from 1881 almost continuously at Florence, Italy, painting and teaching; awarded medal Chicago Expn., 1893. N.A., 1906; spl. gold medal of honor, Panama P.I. Expn., 1915. Home: Covington, Ky. Died Jan. 3, 1919.

D'VYS, George Whitefield, author; b. E. Boston, Mass., Mar. 16, 1860; s. Capt. George Cox (mariner) and Elizabeth Lucinda (Currie) D.; ed. Prescott Sch., E. Boston, Boston Latin Sch., class of 1877; accident prevented finishing course and to regain health became a deep-sea sailor; m. Frances S. Scribner, June 1, 1893. Taught sch. 2 yrs., and in various business pursuits until 1897; from 1900 in lit. and newspaper work, writing considerable verse and more than 1,000 short stories, chiefly salt sea tales, such as appear in St. Nicholas, American Boy, Classmate, young People, Boys' World, etc. Republican. Baptist. Mem. I.O.G.T. Author: On and Off Shore; The Fiji's Mate; A Sailor Boy's Log; His Third Wife; The Chanty Man (sea songs). Home: Rowe, Mass. Died May 30, 1941.

DWIGHT, Edmund; b. New York, N.Y., Nov. 23, 1856; s. Edmund and Harriet Allen (Butler) D.; ed. Coll. City of New York; Columbia Law Sch.; m. Mary F., d. Commodore Homer C. Blake, U.S.N., 1881 (dec.); 1 dau., Mary Blake, dec. (wife of Sir Alfred Booth, Bart.); m. 2d, Carolyn Allen, 1896 (died 1935); 1 daughter, Mrs. Julia Dwight Adams. Was asso. with Charles D. Hilles, as Dwight & Hilles, 1912-22 (retired); now pres. Children's Village (a training sch. for study, edn. and development of the unadjusted child). Dir. Fedn. of Protestant Welfare Agencies. Mem. Chamber Commerce State of N.Y. Republican. Episcopalian. Home: New York, N.Y. Died Dec. 16, 1938.

DWIGHT, Edwin Welles, M.D.,; b. Auburn, N.Y., Aug. 11, 1863; s. Henry Williams and Mary Jane (Winslow) D.; M.D., Harvard, 1891. Engaged in practice in Boston, 1891—; asst. commr. pub. instns., Boston, 1895-96; med. dir. N.E. Mut. Life Ins. Co.; formerly instr. legal medicine and surgery, Harvard Med. Sch., prof. legal medicine, Tufts Coll. Med. Sch., asst. visiting surgeon Boston City Hosp. Conglist. Democrat. Author: Medical Jurisprudence, 1903; Toxicology, 1904. Home: Marshfield, Mass. Died Jan. 14, 1931.

DWIGHT, Henry Otis, missionary; b. Constantinople, Turkey, June 3, 1843; s. Rev. Harrison Grey Otis and Mary (Lane) D.; prepared for coll. at home in Constantinople; entered Ohio Wesleyan U.; left coll. 1861, to enlist for mil. service; (LL.D., Amherst,

1896); m. Frances Warner Mulford, Dec. 26, 1900. Enlisted pvt. 20th O. Inf., Sept., 1861; promoted sergt., 2d lt., 1st lt., adj. and capt.; declined captaincy; a.-d.-c. to Maj. Gen. M. F. Force, comdg. 1st div. 17th Army Corps, Army of the Tenn.; mustered out, 1865. Treas. Northampton (Mass.) Street Ry. Co., 1866-67; bus. agt. at Constantinople of the mission of A.B.C.F.M., 1867-72; edited publs. in Turkish lang. of that mission, 1872-99; ordained to ministry by council of Lamoille Co. (Vt.) Assn., 1880; resigned commn. as missionary of Am. Bd., 1901; in gen. lit. and editorial work, 1901-04; recording sec. Am. Bible Soc., Jan. 1, 1907—. Mem. Manhattan Assn., Congl. Ministers' Meeting, Congl. Club, Nat. Arts Club, New York. Republican. Life work has been lit. work in Turkish language; Constantinople corr. New York Tribune, 1875-92; editor Report of Ecumenical Conf. on Foreign Missions, 1900; editor-in-chief, Ency. of Missions, 1904. Author: Treaty Rights of American Missionaries in Turkey, 1893; A Moslem Sir Galahad, 1913. Home: Roselle, N.J. Died June 19, 1917.

DWIGHT, John Wilbur, congressman; b. Dryden, N.Y., May 24, 1859; s. Jeremiah W. and Rebecca A. D.; ed. New Haven, Conn.; m. Emma Childs, 1895. Elected to the 57th Congress to fill vacancy; reëlected 58th to 62d Congresses (1903-13), 30th N.Y. Dist. Now pres. Va. Blue Ridge Ry. Home: Dryden, N.Y. Died Jan. 19, 1928.

DWIGHT, Jonathan, M.D., ornithologist; b. New York, Dec. 8, 1858; s. Jonathan and Julia Lawrence (Hasbrouck) D.; A.B., Harvard, 1880; M.D., Coll. Phys. and Surg. (Columbia), 1893; m. Georgina Gertrude Rundle, June 12, 1901 (died 1903); m. 2d, Ethel Gordon Wishart Adam, Dec. 9, 1914. Mem. 7th Regt. N.G. N.Y., 1889-96; asst. surgeon, dept. laryngology, Vanderbilt Clinic, 1894-1904. Fellow Am. Ornithologists' Union, 1886— (was treas., later pres.), N.Y. Acad. Sciences. Home: New York, N.Y. Died Feb. 22, 1929.

DWIGHT, Thomas, anatomist; b. Boston, Oct. 13, 1843; s. Thomas and May Collins (Warren) D.; A.B., Harvard, 1866, M.D., 1867, A.M., 1872; studied abroad 2 yrs.; (LL.D., Georgetown, 1889); m. Sarah C. Pasigi, Sept. 18, 1883. Instr. comparative anatomy, Harvard, 1872-73; lecturer and prof. anatomy, Bowdoin, 1872-76; instr. in histology, 1874-83, instr. topog. anatomy, 1880-83, Parkman prof. anatomy, 1883—, Harvard, succeeding Dr. Oliver Wendell Holmes. Editor Boston Med. Journal, 1873-78; gave course of lectures, Lowell Inst., on "Mechanism of the Bone and Muscle," 1884. Author: Anatomy of the Head, 1876; Variations of the Bones of the Hand and Foot, 1907. Home: Nahant, Mass. Died 1911.

DWIGHT, Timothy, educator; b. Norwich, Conn., Nov. 16, 1828; s. James and Susan (Breed) D.; g.s. Rev. Timothy D. (pres. Yale, 1795-1817); B.A., Yale, 1849, M.A., 1852; studied Yale Div. Sch., 1850-53; tutor Yale, 1851-55; studied univs. of Bonn and Berlin, 1856-58; (D.D., Chicago Theol. Sem., 1869, Yale, 1886; LL.D., Harvard, 1886, Princeton, 1888); m. Jane Wakeman, d. Roger Sherman Skinner, of New Haven, Conn., Dec. 31, 1866. Prof. of sacred lit. and N.T. Greek, Yale Theol. Sem., 1858-86. Pres. Yale U., 1886-99. Mem. of Am. com. for revision of English version of Bible. Hon. mem. Soc. of the Cincinnati. Translated and edited, with additional notes, Am. edit. Godet's Commentary on the Gospel of John, 1886. Home: New Haven, Conn. Died May 26, 1916.

DWIGHT, William Buck, geologist, educator; b. Constantinople, Turkey, May 22, 1833; s. Harrison Gray Otis (Am. missionary) and Elizabeth (Barker) D.; came to U.S. permanently, 1849; grad. Yale, A.B. 1854, A.M. 1857, B.S. 1859, Union Theol. Sem., 1857; m. Nov. 17, 1859, Eliza Howe Schneider (died 1901). Founder and prin. 1859-65; Englewood (N.J.) Female Inst.; in mining explorations Va. and Mo., 1865-67; taught at West Point, N.Y., 1867-70; asso. prin. and prof. natural sciences, State Normal Sch., New Britain, Conn., 1870-78; prof. natural history, dept. of geology and mineralogy, and curator mus., Vassar Coll. Apptd. univ. examiner in geology, State of N.Y., 1894. Invented and patented, 1891, a rock-slicing machine for scientific section of minerals; awarded bronze medal at Paris Exp'n, 1900. Fellow A.A.A.S.; original fellow Am. Soc. Naturalists and Geol. Soc. of America. Home: Poughkeepsie, N.Y. Died 1906.

DWINNELL, Clifton Howard, banker; b. Worcester, Mass., 1873; grad. Worcester Poly. Inst., 1894; m. Elisabeth Marshall; children—Sabina Adamson (Mrs. W. Edgar Crosby, Jr.), Clifton Howard, Marshall, Elisabeth, Nancy Tarbell. Began with Internat. Trust Co., Boston, 1895; became connected with Shoe & Leather Nat. Bank, 1898, and made asst. cashier, 1900; continued as asst. cashier after consolidation, 1901, of Shoe & Leather Nat. Bank with Nat. Bank of the Redemption, under latter title, and also after consolidation, 1904, with First Nat. Bank of Boston, of which was v.p. 1905-26, pres., 1926—. Treas. Trustees of Tufts Coll.; trustee and mem. finance com. Wellesley Coll.; trustee Worcester Poly. Inst. Republican. Conglist. Home: Boston, Mass. Died Mar. 13, 1928.

DWYER, Charles, editor; b. Richmond, Surrey, Eng.; s. Michael and Mary (Bateman) D.; ed. pvt. schs., Kingston and Croydon, Surrey; m. Emmeline Gertrude, d. James Simpson, of the Home Office, Whitehall, London, Mar. 7, 1888. In newspaper work in London, 1878-81; came to U.S., 1881; asst. editor The Delineator, 1881-85, editor same, 1885-1906; editor of Ladies' World, New York, 1906-13, Woman's World, Chicago, 1913—. Home: Chicago, Ill. Died Jan. 17, 1916.

DYAR, Harrison Gray, biologist; b. New York, Feb. 14, 1866; s. Harrison Gray and Eleonora Rosella (Hannum) D.; B.S., Mass. Inst. Tech., 1889; A.M., Columbia, 1894, Ph.D., 1895; m. Zella Peabody, Oct. 14, 1889; children—Dorothy, Otis Peabody; m. 2d, Wellesca Pollock Allen, Apr. 26, 1921; children—Roshan Allen, Harrison Golshan, Wallace Joshan. Asst. bacteriology, Columbia, 1895-97; custodian of lepidoptera, U.S. Nat. Mus., 1897—; entomol. asst., Bur. of Entomology, U.S. Dept. of Agriculture, 1915-17. Capt. Sanitary Dept., Organized Reserves, U.S.A., 1924. Co-author: (with L. O. Howard and the late Frederick Knab) The Mosquitoes of North and Central America and the West Indies (Carnegie Inst., Washington), 1912-17. Editor Journal of the N.Y. Entomol. Soc., 1904-07, Procs. of Entomol. Soc., Washington, 1909-12. Home: Washington, D.C. Died Jan. 19, 1929.

DYCHE, Louis Lindsay, zoölogist; b. Berkeley Springs, W.Va., Mar. 20, 1857; s. Alexander and Mary (Reilly) D.; B.A., B.S., U. of Kan., 1884, A.M., 1886, M.S., 1888. Asst. prof. zoölogy, 1885-86, prof. comparative anatomy, 1886-90, prof. zoölogy and curator of birds and mammals, 1890-1900, prof. systematic zoölogy and taxidermy and curator of birds and mammals, 1900—, U. of Kan. Has made 23 scientific expdns. and hunted all over N. America, from Mexico to Alaska and including Greenland and the arctic regions, resulting in securing for U. of Kan. one of the largest and finest collections of large N. Am. mammals in the world. State game and fish warden of Kan., Dec. 1, 1909. Home: Pratt, Kan. Died Jan. 20, 1915.

DYCHE, William Andrew, business mgr., Northwestern U.; b. Monroe, O., May 25, 1861; s. David R. (M.D.) and Mary S. (Boyd) D.; A.B., Northwestern, 1882, A.M., 1888, LL.D., 1932; grad. Chicago Coll. Pharmacy, 1886; m. May Louise Bennett, Feb. 11, 1897 (died 1923); children—David Bennett, Ruth Caroline, George Frederick. Trustee Northwestern U., 1894—, business mgr., 1903—. In drug business in Chicago, 1899; pres. State Bank of Evanston, Jan. 1909—; v.p. and chmn. bd. State Bank & Trust Co., 1919—. Mayor of Evanston, 1895-99. Dyche Stadium named in his honor, 1926, by Northwestern Univ. Home: Evanston, Ill. Died Feb. 18, 1936.

DYE, John T., lawyer; b. Mason Co., Ky., Dec. 19, 1835; s. Isaac and Martha (Fulcher) D.; grad. Bethany Coll. (Va.), 1854; studied law with James Speed, Louisville, Ky.; admitted to bar, 1857; m. Annie Glenn, d. William C. Holton, of Mason Co., Ky., Dec. 27, 1858. Gen. counsel C.,C.,C.&St.L., Ry. Co., 1889-1905. Pres. Ind. State Bar Assn., 1909-10. Author: Ideals of Democracy, 1908. Home: Castleton, Ind. Died Apr. 24, 1913.

DYER, Alexander Brydie, army officer; b. Fayetteville, N.C., Mar. 28, 1852; s. Bvt. Maj. Gen. Alexander Brydie (chief of ordnance U.S.A.) and Elizabeth B. (Allen) D.; apptd. from D.C., and grad. U.S. Mil. Acad., 1873; grad. Arty. Sch., 1878; m. Madeleine Minturn, Mar. 29, 1880. Second lt. 4th Arty., June 13, 1873; promoted through grades to col. arty. corps, Jan. 25, 1907; assigned to 4th Field Arty., June 6, 1907; retired from active service, Mar. 15, 1913. Adj., Ft. Riley, Kan., 1873-92; served in campaign against Bannock Indians, 1878; sr. instr. arty., U.S. Mil. Acad., 1892-97; chief of arty., 1st Div., 8th Army Corps, under Gens. Anderson and Lawton, in P.I.; participated in battles at Manila, Feb. 10, 1899, and San Piedro, Mar. 13, 1899; recommended for bvt. of maj.; chief of arty., 2d Div., U.S.A., under Maj. Gen. Carter, on Mexican border, 1913. Author: Handbook for Light Artillery, 1896. Home: San Francisco, Calif. Died July 9, 1920.

DYER, Catherine Cornelia, author; b. Ludlowville, N.Y.; m. Rev. Heman Dyer. Author: Henry and the Bird's Nest; Sunny Days Abroad; Brief History of the Joy Family; Records of the Dyer Family; etc. Died 1903.

DYER, David Patterson, judge; b. Henry Co., Va., Feb. 12, 1838; s. David and Nancy R. D.; moved to Mo., 1841; ed. St. Charles Coll. Admitted to bar, 1859; practiced in Pike and adjoining counties until 1875; pros. atty., 3d Jud. Circuit, 1860; recruited and comd. 49th Mo. Vol. Inf. during Civil War; mem. Mo. Ho. of Rep., 1862-65; sec. Senate, 1866; mem. 41st Congress (1869-71); removed to St. Louis, 1875; apptd. U.S. atty., 1875; prosecuted the "Whiskey Ring," 1875-76; candidate for gov. of Mo., 1880; U.S. atty. Eastern Dist. Mo., 1902-07; U.S. dist. judge same dist., Apr. 1, 1907—. Home: St. Louis, Mo. Died Apr. 29, 1924.

DYER, Elisha, gov. R.I.; b. Providence, R.I., Nov. 28, 1839; s. Gov. Elisha and Anna Jones (Hoppin) D.; ed. Brown Univ. to sophomore yr.; grad. Univ. of Giessen, Ph.D., 1860; m. a d. of Col. William and Mary Brayton (Anthony) Viall of Providence. Enlisted sergt. 1st R.I. light battery, but was severely injured on his way to Washington; col. on staff Governor Smith, 1863-66; entered Marine Corps of arty., 1860, as asst. commissary; became lt. col., 1869; resigned 1871; placed in comd. combined arty. of R.I., 1875; State senator R.I., 1878, mem. R.I. gen. assembly, 1881; adj. gen. R.I., 1882-95, retired at brig. gen. 1895, gov. R.I., 1897-1900, 3 terms. Republican. Mason. Home: Providence, R.I. Died 1906.

DYER, Francis John, Am. consul; b. Dyersville, Ia., June 21, 1864; s. William and Mary (Richards) D.; ed. high sch. and theol. prep. sch., Dubuque, Ia., Northwestern U. (non-grad.); studied Japanese lang., U. of Calif., also French, German, Spanish, private tutors; m. Lilly Ottilie Reichling, Dec. 2, 1901. Chief of staff Los Angeles Daily Journal, 1894-95; on editorial staff San Francisco Chronicle, 1895-1906; Washington corr. same, 1906-09, Los Angeles Times, San Diego Union and Albany Journal, 1909-15, Portland (Ore.) Journal, 1911-15. Contbr. to mags.; syndicated "Dyer's Washington Letter" with 193 newspapers, 1910; supplying weekly news service to large number of newspapers, 1912-13. Visited Eng., France, Belgium, 1912, and wrote series articles on polit., sociol. and general conditions. Apptd. Washington commr. Panama-Calif. Expn., 1911. Commd. Am. consul to Swansea, Wales, Apr. 3, 1915, to Ceiba, Honduras, Sept. 17, 1915; assigned to Tegucigalpa, Honduras, Mar. 20, 1917, Nogales, Mex., 1919, Coblenz, Germany, May 17, 1922—. Republican. Methodist. Mason. Home: San Francisco, Calif. Died Dec. 26, 1924.

DYER, Frank Lewis, mech. and elec. expert and inventor; b. Washington, D.C., Aug. 2, 1870; s. George Washington and Kate (Huntress) D.; ed. pub. schs., and Columbian (now George Washington) U. Law Sch.; m. Annie Augusta Wadsworth, 1892; children—John Wadsworth, Frank Wadsworth; m. 2d, Isabelle Dawson Archer, 1924; m. 3d, Eliza J. Martin, 1939. Practiced patent law, Washington, 1892-97, New York, 1897-1903; gen. counsel Edison interests, 1903-08; exec. officer T. A. Edison's indus. corps., 1908-1912; pres. Gen. Film Co., 1912-14; treas. Condensite Co. of America, 1910-20; officer and dir. numerous corps.; has secured over 100 patents in various arts, including talking books for the blind; practicing from 1914 as mech. and elec. expert. Democrat. Mason. Author: Edison—His Life and Inventions (with T. Commerford Martin), 1910-29. Home: Ventnor, N.J. Died June 4, 1941.

DYER, Frederick Rainey, lawyer; b. Oldtown, Me., Oct. 4, 1873; s. William Henry and Catherine (Noonan) D.; desc. of Thomas Dyer, Weymouth, Mass., 1632; ed. Hebron Acad., Colby College, 1 year; hon. M.A. conferred by Colby College in 1925; m. Lena H. Maxim, Oct. 27, 1900; 1 dau., Anne. Admitted to bar, 1897, and began practice at Buckfield; mem. Me. Ho. of Rep., 1907, county atty., Oxford Co., Me., 1913-15; apptd. U.S. dist. atty., Dist. of Me., July 1, 1922. Republican. Mason. Home: Portland, Me. Died Sept. 9, 1934.

DYER, George Leland, commodore U.S.N.; b. Calais, Me., Aug. 26, 1849; s. George W. and Mary (Kelley) D.; apptd. from Me., and grad. with honors, U.S. Naval Acad., 1870; m. Susan Hart, d. Gen. O. H. Palmer, Mar. 31, 1875. Ensign, July, 1871; promoted through grades to capt., Sept. 8, 1905; commodore, June 30, 1908. Served on various duties and stas.; naval attaché at Madrid at outbreak of Spanish War; comd. gunboat Stranger during war with Spain on blockade off Havana; transferred to command of gunboat Yankton, fall of 1898; detailed for patrol duty and surveying on coast of Cuba; at Naval Acad., July 1901, in charge of ships and head dept. modern languages; comd. flagship Rainbow, Asiatic sta., 1902-03, cruiser Albany, 1903-04; gov. Guam, 1904-05; comdt., Navy Yard, Charleston, S.C.; Navy Sta., Port Royal, S.C., and 6th naval dist., 1906; retired, June 30, 1908. Home: Winter Park, Fla. Died Apr. 2, 1914.

DYER, Heman, P.E. clergyman; b. Shaftsbury, Vt.; grad. Kenyon, 1833 (D.D., Trinity, 1843); entered ministry; taught in Pittsburgh, Pa., 1840-43; prof. Western Univ. of Pa., 1843-44; pres. of same, 1844-49. In 1849 entered service of Am. Sunday School Union; later became sec. and gen. mgr. Evang. Knowledge Soc. Became editor Episcopal Quarterly Review, 1854; declined bishopric of Kansas, 1862. Retired from active work, 1880. Author: Voice of the Lord Upon the Waters; Records of an Active Life (an autobiography). Home: New York, N.Y. Died 1900.

DYER, Isaac Watson, lawyer; b. Baldwin, Me., Sept. 13, 1855; s. Isaac and Martha Osgood (Porter) D.; A.B., Bowdoin Coll., 1878; Harvard U. Law Sch.; m. Mary Laura Nye, June 7, 1887; children—Laura Nye, Isaac Cabot. Asst. commr. on revision of statutes of Maine, 1883; mem. Maine Legislature, 1885; in practice at Portland, 1885—; U.S. attorney for Maine, 12 yrs., 1890-94, 1898-1906; lecturer on federal jurisdiction and procedure, and on pvt. corps., U. of Me. Republican. Conglist. Mason. Author: Maine Corporation Law, 1881 (8 edits.; now out of print); A Bibliography of Thomas Carlyle's Writings and Ana. Home: Gorhame, Me., also Portland, Me. Died Feb. 13, 1937.

DYER, Isadore, physician; b. Galveston, Tex., Nov. 2, 1865; s. Isadore and Amelia Ann (Lewis) D.; Ph.B., Sheffield Scientific Sch. (Yale), 1887; U. of Va., 1887-88, Tulane, 1888-89; M.D., Tulane, 1889; m. Mercedes Louise Percival, July 31, 1905. Interne and grad. New York Skin and Cancer Hosp., 1890-92; lecturer New York Post-Grad. Med. Sch., 1891-2; lecturer diseases of the skin, 1892-1905, asso. prof., 1905-08, prof., 1908—, asso. dean, 1907-08, dean, 1908—, Sch. of Medicine of Tulane U.; visiting dermatologist Charity Hospital and cons. dermatologist to Eye, Ear, Nose and Throat Hospital, 1892—; prof. diseases skin, 1893-1908, sec.-treas., 1895-1905, New Orleans Poly.; consultant to Presbyn. Hosp., 1916—. Editor New Orleans Med. and Surg. Journal, 1896—; founded 1894, and pres. 1st bd. of control La. Leper Home; cons. leprologist, 1902—. Lt. U.S.A. Med. R.C., July 5, 1908; maj., Apr. 9, 1917; col., June 11, 1919; pres. examining bd. Med. R.C., New Orleans, 1917-18; chmn. med. sect. of State Com. Defense, Aug. 1917-18. Mem. Nat. Bd. Med. Examiners, 1915—. Home: New Orleans, La. Died Oct. 12, 1920.

DYER, John LaFayette, lawyer; b. Waco, Tex., Apr. 17, 1873; s. John LaFayette and Roberta (Herring) D.; Baylor U., Tex.; Hampden-Sidney Coll., Va., through sophomore yr.; studied law alone; m. Annie L. Green, Oct. 14, 1897. Bookkeeper, Waco, 1891-95; practiced law, Waco, 1895-97, El Paso, 1897-1925; removed to Los Angeles, 1925; atty. Globe Grain & Milling Co., Globe Cotton Oil Mills and Globe Ice Cream Co., Los Angeles. Asst. dist. atty., 34th Jud. Dist., Tex., 1900-01; city atty., El Paso, 1901-03; mem. Sch. Bd., El Paso, 1909. Democrat. Presbyn. Home: Los Angeles, Calif. Deceased.

DYER, Louis, writer, lecturer; b. Chicago, Sept. 30, 1851; s. Charles Volney D., M.D., 6th in descent from William Dyer, 1st clerk of R.I. colony; early edn. in Chicago, Switzerland and France; grad. Harvard, 1874; Balliol Coll., Oxford, 1878; A.M., Oxford, 1893; m. Nov., 1889, Margaret, d. late Alexander Macmillan (founder, with brother Daniel, of Macmillan & Co., pubs.). Asst. prof. Greek, Harvard, 1881-87; lectured Lowell Inst., 1889, on The Gods in Greece; at Oxford, 1890—; lecturer Balliol Coll., 1893-96; acting prof. Greek, Cornell Univ., 1895-96; lectured before Royal Instn., 1899; Hearst lecturer on art, U. of Calif., 1900; repeated lectures, 1900-01, at U. of Chicago, Western Reserve, Cornell, Vassar, Harvard, Yale, Princeton, Smith, Johns Hopkins, Columbian, Bryn Mawr and Columbia, and at Metropolitan Museum, New York. Author: Plato's Apology and Crito, 1886; Studies of the Gods in Greece at Certain Sanctuaries Recently Excavated, 1891; Schiller's der Neffe als Onkel, 1895. Wrote: The Plot of the Agamemnon of Æschylus, in Vol. VII, and "The Olympian Council and Council House" in Vol. XIX, Harvard Classical Studies, 1896; Vitruvius' Account of the Greek Stage. Home: Oxford, Eng. Died 1908.

DYER, Nehemiah Mayo, naval officer; b. Provincetown, Mass., Feb. 19, 1839; s. Henry and Sally (Mayo) D.; ed. pub. schs.; followed the sea, 1854-59; mercantile employment, 1859-61; unmarried. Enlisted 13th Mass. Vols., 1861; transferred to vol. navy as acting master's mate, Apr. 4, 1862; promoted for gallant services to acting ensign, May 18, 1863; advanced through grades to capt., July 13, 1897; rear admiral, and retired, Feb. 19, 1901. Served at Navy Yard, Boston, 1862-63; Eugenie, 1863-64, Metacomet, 1864, West Gulf Blockading Squadron; participated in battle of Mobile Bay, and surrender of Ft. Morgan; on various duties and stas. to 1887; comd. Marion, 1887-90; Navy Yard, Portsmouth, 1890-93; spl. duty, 1893-94; Navy Yard, Boston, 1895-96; light-house insp. 1st dist., 1896-97; command Philadelphia, 1897, Baltimore, 1897-99; participated in battle of Manila Bay, May 1, 1898; for eminent and conspicuous conduct in this battle was advanced 7 numbers in rank; Navy Yard, Boston, 1900-01. Chmn. bd. commrs. Mass. Nautical Training Sch., 1903-04; Companion Loyal Legion. Home: Melrose, Mass. Died 1910.

DYER, Oliver, journalist, author; b. Porter, N.Y., April 26, 1824; s. Jeremiah and Mary D.; ed. Lockport and at Genesee Wesleyan Sem., Lima., N.Y.; prin. school at 17; taught 3 yrs. Determined to reform orthography of English language; studied Isaac Pitman's system of phonography, lecturer upon and teacher of same; went to Washington, 1848, as reporter U.S. senate. Studied law; admitted to bar. Abandoned practice of law, devoted himself to journalism; on reportorial staff New York Tribune, and subsequently on editorial staff New York Sun. In 1871 engaged to write exclusively for New York Ledger; ordained minister New Church (Swedenborgian), May 1876; pastor New Ch. Soc., Mt. Vernon, N.Y. (resigned). Home: Beverly Farms, Mass. Died 1907.

DYKEMAN, King, newspaper pub.; b. New Brunswick, Can., May 15, 1874; s. John and Amanda F. (Cottle) D.; LL.B., U. of Wash., 1903; m. Luella E. Hines, Aug. 22, 1906; children—John King, James Bruce, Ruth Kathleen. Came to U.S., 1891. Admitted to Wash. bar and in practice at Seattle; asst. corp. counsel, Seattle, 1906-11; apptd. judge Superior Court of Wash., 1911; elected to same office for term 1913-25; judge Juvenile Court, 1914-25; pub. Seattle Post Intelligencer. Republican. Baptist. Mason. Home: Seattle, Wash. Died Sept. 10, 1931.

DYMENT, Colin Victor, educator, pub.; b. Copetown, Can., Feb. 22, 1879; s. William and Margaret (Dodds) D.; B.A., Univ. Coll. (U. of Toronto), 1900, with honors in classics; matriculant U. of Toronto, with honors in classics, 1896; m. Paris, France, Bertha, Sabin Stuart (B.A., M.D.), Aug. 20, 1919; 1 son, Donald. With Pacific Coast newspapers, 1900-13, including the Spokesman-Review (Spokane), Daily Union (Walla Walla), Evening Telegram and Oregon Daily Journal (Portland), also newspaper corr.; prof. journalism, U. of Ore., 1913-17; dir. Sch. of Journalism, U. of Wash., 1917-19, except during war service; dean Coll. of Lit., Science and Arts, U. of Ore., 1919-26; studied in France and Italy, 1925-26; mng. editor Eugene (Ore.) Register, 1926-27; publisher Hayward (Calif.) Jour., 1928—. Naturalized citizen of U.S., 1914. Asst. dir. States Orgns., U.S. Fuel Administration, Washington, D.C., 1918; A.R.C. searcher, rank of 1st lt., 91st Div., in France and Belgium, 1918-19, at St. Mihiel, Argonne, Battle of Scheldt River in Belgium. Republican. Protestant. Home: Hayward, Calif. Died Oct. 20, 1928.

DYRENFORTH, Robert St. George, lawyer; b. Chicago, Oct. 17, 1844; s. Julius and Caroline D.; cadet at Breslau, Neisse and Berlin, Prussia, 1857-61; grad. Breslau, 1861; in U.S. army, 1861-66; M.E. Poly. Sch., Carlsruhe, Baden; Ph.D., U. of Heidelberg; M.D., Columbian (now George Washington) U., 1870, LL.B., 1875 (LL.D.); m. Jane de Lacy, 1866. Enlisted April, 1861, Schambeck dragoons, Ill., cav., serving under McClellan and Rosecrans, in W.Va.; later capt. and maj. 13th, 12th and 17th Ill. Cav.; asst. insp. gen. and signal officer in dept. of the Missouri; as acting engr. officer fortified mouth of Mo. River, in advance of Price's raid, 1864; finished service on plains in Indian campaign, 1865; several times wounded; received several brevets. Was 2d asst., 1st asst. and prin. examiner, examiner-in-chief, asst. commr., U.S. Patent Office, 1871-85; in patent practice at Washington, 1885—. Gen. and comdr.-in-chief Union Veterans' Union (5th term); comdr. Mil. Order of Merit. Home: Washington, D.C. Died 1910.

DYSON, Charles Wilson, naval officer; b. Cambridge, Md., Dec. 2, 1861; grad. U.S. Naval Acad., 1883. Promoted asst. engr., July 1, 1885; passed asst. engr., June 1, 1895; transferred to the line as lt., Mar. 3, 1899; lt. comdr., Dec. 31, 1903; comdr., May 15, 1908; capt., July 1, 1911; rear admiral, Oct. 15, 1917. Served on San Francisco, Spanish-Am. War, 1898; on Oregon, 1904-05; fleet engr Asiatic Fleet, 1905-06; duty Bur. Steam Engring., Navy Dept., 1906-13; insp. machinery, Camden, N.J., 1913-14; duty Bur. Steam Engring., in charge design of naval machinery, 1914—. Fellow Royal Soc. of Arts (British); D.S.C. Republican. Episcopalian. Home: Washington, D.C. Died Oct. 25, 1930.

E

EACHES, Owen Philips, clergyman; b. Phœnixville, Pa., Dec. 11, 1840; s. Eber and Hannah (Philips) E.; A.B., Bucknell U., Pa., 1863; 1st sergt. Co. A, 28th Regt., Pa. Vols., in Civil War; grad. Crozer Theol. Sem., Pa., 1866; m. Jennie Mount, May 14, 1879. Ordained Baptist ministry, 1870; pastor, Nicetown Ch., Phila., 1866-70, Hightstown, N.J., 1870-1913; teacher in Bapt. Inst., Phila. Trustee Peddie Inst., Crozer Theol. Sem.; pres. N.J. Bapt. Edn. Soc.; mem. Phila. Conf. Bapt. Ministers. Prohibitionist. Home: Haddonfield, N.J. Died Jan. 10, 1930.

EAGAN, Charles Patrick, brig. gen.; b. in Ireland, Jan. 16, 1841; ed. at San Francisco; m. Emma Johnson, Nov. 5, 1863. Served as 1st lt. 1st Wash. Ter. Inf., June 21, 1862-Apr. 1, 1865; apptd. from Wash., 2d lt. 9th U.S. Inf., Aug. 30, 1866; 1st lt., Jan. 2, 1869; assigned to 12th Inf., Dec. 31, 1870; capt. commissary subsistence, June 23, 1874; maj., Mar. 12, 1892; lt. col. asst. commissary gen., Jan. 26, 1897; col., Mar. 11, 1898; brig. gen. commissary gen., May 3, 1898. Brvtd. capt., Feb. 27, 1890, for gallant services in action against Indians in the Lava Beds, Cal., Apr. 17, 1873, where was wounded. Retired at own request, after 30 yrs.' service, Dec. 6, 1900. Home: New York, N.Y. Died Feb. 2, 1919.

EAGAN, John Joseph, mfr.; b. Griffin, Ga., Apr. 22, 1870; s. John Joseph and Mary Vermont (Russell) E.; high sch. edn.; m. Susan Baum Young, of Atlanta, Ga. Associated in business with uncle, William A. Russell, and succeeded by inheritance to his business and estate, 1899; Am. Cast Iron Pipe Co., Birmingham, Ala.; v. chmn. Commn. on Training Camp Activities of Navy Dept., 1917-18; mem. exec. and finance com. War Work Council of Y.M.C.A., 1917-19. Mem. Internat. Com. Y.M.C.A.; pres. Christian Council of Atlanta and chmn. Commn. on Ch. Coöperation; chmn. bd. trustees The Berry (Ga.) Schools, Mt. Berry, Ga. Democrat. Presbyterian. Home: Atlanta, Ga. Died Mar. 30, 1924.

EAGELS, Jeanne, actress; b. Kansas City, Mo., June 26, 1894; d. Edward and Julia (Sullivan) Eagels; ed. pub. schs.; m. Edward Harris Coy, Aug. 26, 1925. First appeared on stage as Puck in "A Midsummer Night's Dream," at age of 7; New York début as Miss Renault in "Jumping Jupiter," at New York Theatre, Mar. 6, 1911; played in "Mind-the-Paint Girl," the "Outcast," all star cast of "The Great Pursuit," "The Professor's Love Story," "Daddies," "The Wonderful Thing," "The Night Watch," and creator of Sadie Thompson, in "Rain," "Her Cardboard Lover." Home: Ossining, N.Y. Died Oct. 3, 1929.

EAGER, George Boardman, prof. theology; b. Jefferson Co., Miss., Feb. 22, 1847; s. Eleazer Chapin and Harriet (Ide) E.; ed. Mississippi Coll., Clinton, Miss., 1854-61; Oakland Coll., Jefferson Co., Miss., 1867-69; Mississippi Coll., 1871-73, M.A., 1873; grad. Southern Bapt. Theol. Sem., 1876; post-grad. course Washington and Lee U., Va., 1876-79; D.D., U. of Tenn., 1880, Howard Coll., Ala., 1881; LL.D., Georgetown (Ky.) Coll., 1908; m. Annie E. Coor-Pender, Feb. 20, 1880; children—W. G., Geo. B., W. H. Served in Civil War as pvt. Co. C, 16th Miss. Regt.; courier for Gen. William Mahone; sergt. maj. Power's Regt., Griffith's Brigade, Army of the Southwest. Ordained Bapt. ministry, 1873; pastor successively Lexington, Va., Knoxville, Tenn., St. Francis St. Ch., Mobile, Ala., 1st Ch., Danville, Va., Parker Memorial Ch., Anniston, Ala., until 1892, 1st Ch., Montgomery, Ala., 1892-1901; prof. Bibl. introduction and pastoral theol., Southern Bapt. Theol. Sem., 1901— (emeritus). Democrat. Mason. Awarded Cross of Honor by Albert Sidney Johnston Chapter, Daughters of Confederacy, Louisville, Ky., 1909. Home: Valdosta, Ga. Died Mar. 21, 1929.

EAGLE, James Phillip, clergyman, planter, gov.; b. Maury Co., Tenn., Aug. 10, 1837; s. James and Charity (Swaim) E.; ed. country school, Prairie Co., Ark., and 1 session Miss. Coll., 1870; served through Civil war, all grades, private to col., Confederate army; once badly wounded and once prisoner of war, confined in Camp Chase and Ft. Delaware. Since war Bapt. minister and cotton planter in Ark.; m. Mary Kavanaugh Oldham, 1882. Four times mem. Ark. legislature (once speaker); mem. constl. conv., 1874; one of 3 commrs. to adjust debt of Brooks-Baxter war over governorship, 1874; gov. Ark., 1889-93. Home: Little Rock, Ark. Died 1904.

EAGLE, Mary Kavanaugh; b. Madison Co., Ky.; d. William Kavanaugh and J. Kate (Brown) Oldham; grad. Mrs. Julia A. Tevis' School, Shelbyville, Ky.; m. James Phillip Eagle, 1882; pres. Women's Central Com. on Missions of Ark. (Bapt.), 1882—; pres. Woman's Missionary Union, Ark.; mem. Bd. Lady Mgrs., World's Columbian Expn., and chmn. Com on Congresses. Editor The Congress of Women. Home: Little Rock, Ark. Died 1903.

EAGLES, Theophilus Randolph, educator; b. Saratoga, N.C., Nov. 10, 1885; s. Theophilus Randolph and Bethia (Smith) E.; Atlantic Christian Coll., Wilson, N.C., 1902-03; A.B., U. of N.C., 1908, post-grad. work, same univ., 1910-13, A.M., 1912; m. Isabel Moore Bost, June 16, 1909; children—Manning B., Virginia B. Teacher pub. schs., Wilson Co., N.C., 1903-04; prof. mathematics, Catawba Coll., Newton, 1908-09, Bethany (W.Va.) Coll., 1909-10; instr. mathematics, U. of N.C., 1910-13; prof. mathematics, Howard Coll., 1913—, treas., 1916—, v.p., 1924—, acting pres., Feb. 1, 1931-June 1, 1932, also served as acting dean. Sec. trustees of Howard Coll., 1920—; treas. Bd. Ministerial Edn., Ala. State Conv., Bapt. Ch., 1917—. Baptist. Home: Birmingham, Ala. Died June 7, 1936.

EAGLESON, James Beaty, surgeon; s. William and Elizabeth (Hodsden) E.; commercial course, U. of Valparaiso, Ind.; ed. pvt. schs.; M.D., Coll. Phys. and Surg., Chicago, 1885; m. Blanche Mills, July 1, 1889. Practiced, U.S. Marine Hosp., Chicago, 1885-86, Port Townsend, Wash., 1886-87; with U.S.P.H.S. at Seattle, Wash., 1887-99; pvt. practice in gen. surgery, 1899—; v.p. and med. dir. Northern Life Ins. Co. Surgeon gen. N.G. Wash., 1891-96; lt., Med. R.C., 1911-17, maj. 1917, lt. col., 1919, col., 1924; organizer, comdg. officer and dir. Base Hosp. No. 50; organizer and comdg. officer U.S. Gen. Hosp. No. 50. A founder and asso. editor Northwest Medicine, 1901-17; a founder and a regent Am. Coll. Surgeons. Fellow Am. Acad. Polit. and Social Science. Home: Seattle, Wash. Died Jan. 26, 1928.

EAKIN, Robert, judge; b. Elgin, Ill., Mar. 15, 1848; s. Stewart B. and Catherine (McEldowney) E.; B.S., Willamette U., Salem, Ore., 1873; m. Mary

Walker, June 21, 1876. Admitted to bar, 1874; practiced at Union, Ore., 1875-95; judge 8th Jud. Circuit of Ore., 1895-1907; justice Supreme Ct. of Ore., terms 1907-13, 1913-18. Republican. Presbyn. Home: Salem, Ore. Died Oct. 1, 1917.

EAKINS, Thomas, artist; b. Phila., July 25, 1844; s. Benjamin and Caroline E.; grad. high school; studied art under Gérôme at École des Beaux Arts, Paris; m. Susan H. Macdowell, 1884. Has been prof. and lecturer on anatomy, painting, etc., in several schools of art; has painted many pictures of early Am. domestic life, studies of Am. sports, negroes, portraits and large composition portraits, such as Dr. Gross in his clinic, Dr. Agnew in his clinic, etc. Assisted his pupil, Samuel Murray, to model the colossal figures of the prophets which adorn the Witherspoon Bldg. in Phila.; painter of Crucifixion in Overbrook Sem., portrait of Cardinal Martinelli; etc. Awards: Chicago Expn., 1893, Paris Expn., 1900, Buffalo Expn., 1901, gold medal, St. Louis Expn., 1904; Temple gold medal, Pa. Acad. Fine Arts; Proctor prize, Nat. Acad. Design; modeled two reliefs on the Trenton Battle monument; modeled the horses ridden by Grant and Lincoln on the Soldiers' and Sailors' monument in Brooklyn. N.A., 1902. Home: Philadelphia. Died June 25, 1916.

EAKLE, Arthur Starr, mineralogist; b. Washington, July 27, 1862; s. Elias H. and Mary Frances (Byington) E.; B.S., Cornell, 1892; Ph.D., U. of Munich, 1896; m. Fannie V. Kinney, Aug. 29, 1899; 1 dau., Alice Frances. Asst. and instr. in mineralogy, Cornell, 1892-94, at Harvard, 1897-1900; instr. in mineralogy, 1900-03, asst. prof., 1903-12, asso. prof., 1912-19, and prof. mineralogy, 1919—, U. of Calif. Fellow Geol. Soc. America, Mineral. Soc. America (pres. 1925), A.A.A.S. Author: Mineral Tables for the Determination of Minerals by Their Physical Properties; California Minerals. Home: Berkeley, Calif. Died July 5, 1931.

EAMES, Hayden, industrial consultant; b. of Am. parents in Shanghai, China, Dec. 19, 1863; s. Ithama Bellows and Emma (Hayden) E.; ed. in pvt. and pub. sch. in Me.; grad. U.S. Naval Acad., 1882; m. Clare Hamilton, June 18, 1890; children—Clare Jenness (Mrs. Sidney Howard, dec.), Emma Hayden (Mrs. F. L. Yates), Julia Hamilton (dec.), Hamilton. U.S. naval officer, 1878-94; gen. mgr. Pope Tube Co., 1893-99; mgr. carriage dept., Pope Motor Co. and successors, 1895-1900; with Westinghouse Electric Co., Pittsburgh, Pa., 1900-03; propr. of orgn. distributing automobile parts, 1903-07, then stockholder same orgn. under title Am. Distributing Co.; consultant and dir. Garford Co., 1903-13; mgr. Studebaker Automobile Co., 1907-10; indsl. consultant, 1910—; mem. arbitration bd. Nat. Regional Labor Relations Bd., parts of 1934, 35. Lt. col. of ordnance in charge production of small arms, machine guns and their ammunition, World War. Home: Cleveland, O. Died Nov. 24, 1938.

EAMES, Wilberforce, bibliographer; b. Newark, N.J., Oct. 12, 1855; s. Nelson and Harriet P. (Crane) E.; ed. in Brooklyn; hon. A.M., Harvard, 1896; Litt.D., Brown U., 1924; LL.D., U. of Mich., 1924; unmarried. Asst. Lenox Library, 1885, asst. librarian, 1892, librarian, 1893, until consolidation in 1895 with the Astor Library and Tilden Trust as N.Y. Public Library. Librarian of Bibliog. Soc. of America from its origin to June 1909. Hon. officier d'Académie (ministère de l'instruct. pub. des beauxarts et des cultes, Répub. Française), 1905. Editor: Vols. 15-20, Sabin's Dictionary of Books Relating to America, 1885-92; continued his work upon Sabin Dictionary, 1927-29, his articles in that work on Bibliographies of the Bay Psalm Book, 1885, of Ptolemy's Geography, 1886, of Sir Walter Raleigh, 1886, and of Captain John Smith, 1927, have been printed separately. Wrote: List of Editions of the Margarita Philosophica, 1886; The First Year of Printing in New York, 1928; Use of Hebrew Types in English America before 1735, 1929; The Proposed Scripture Calendar, 1931; Bibliography of Amerigo Vespucci, 1935. He has made important contributions to Pilling's Indian Bibliographies, from which was reprinted Bibliographic Notes on Eliot's Indian Bible, 1890. In 1892 edited, for the Lenox Library, a comparative edition of 4 Latin texts, with new English transl. of Columbus' Letter to Sanchez on the discovery of America (revised edit., 1893). Contbd. list of catalogues, etc., pub. for the English Booktrade from 1595-1902 to Growoll's Three Centuries of English Booktrade Bibliography, 1903; compiled, for N.Y. Pub. Library, List of Maps of the World, 1904. Fellow Am. Acad. Arts and Sciences; hon. mem. Grolier Club. A vol. of bibliog. essays, including a sketch of his life, was dedicated to him, by friends and admirers, 1924. Awarded gold medal of the Bibliog. Soc. (London), 1929. Home: Brooklyn, N.Y. Died Dec. 6, 1937.

EAMES, William S., architect; b. Clinton, Mich., Aug. 4, 1857; s. William H. and Laura Maria (Scofield) E.; A.B., Washington U.; École des Beaux Arts, Paris, and pvt. study in Rome; unmarried. Engaged in practice as architect at St. Louis, 1882—; deputy commr. pub. bldgs., St. Louis, 1881-83. Mem. bd. of appeals, Bldg. Dept., St. Louis; U.S. rep.

Internat. Congress, Madrid, Spain, 1904; life mem. Am. Acad. at Rome. Mem. Am. Inst. Architects (dir. 15 yrs., pres., 1904-05). Episcopalian. Republican. Home: St. Louis, Mo. Died Mar. 5, 1915.

EARHART, Amelia, aviation; b. Atchison, Kan., July 24, 1898; d. Edwin S. and Amy (Otis) E.; grad. Hyde Park High Sch., Chicago, Ill., 1915; student Ogontz School for Girls, Rydal, Pa., Columbia U. and various colls.; m. George Palmer Putnam, Feb. 7, 1931. In charge girls' work, Denison House, Boston, Mass., 1926-28; teacher, extension course, Commonwealth of Mass., 1927-28; first woman to cross Atlantic Ocean in airplane, Trepassey Bay, Newfoundland, to Burryport, Wales, June 17, 1928; aviation editor Cosmopolitan Mag., 1928-30; v.p. Ludington Airlines, Inc., 1930-31. Vice-pres. Nat. Airways, Inc. Decorated Chevalier Legion of Honor (France), 1932; gold medal, Nat. Geog. Soc., 1932; Distinguished Flying Cross, U.S., 1932. Mem. Guggenheim Com. Aeronautical Edn.; dir. Inst. Women's Professional Relations; hon. mem. Nat. Aeronautic Assn. Mem. Nat. Women's Party. Women Geographers. Author: 20 hrs. 40 min., 1928; The Fun of It, 1931. Home: Rye, N.Y. Lost on Pacific flight, July 1937.

EARL, Edward, banker; b. Elizabeth, N.J., July 22, 1870; s. William Alexander Crane and Phœbe Magie E.; pub. sch. edn.; m. Caroline Felter. Jan. 25, 1894. Became connected, at 16, with Nassau Bank, New York, as asst. bookkeeper; was elected pres., 1908, and pres. of its successor, the Nat. Nassau Bank, 1909; v.p. Enos Richardson & Co., jewelers, New York, Richardson Mfg. Co., jewelers, Newark, N.J.; pres. Nicholas Power Co., Ilsley-Doubleday & Co. Presbyn. Mem. S.A.R. (Montclair Chapter). Mason. Died Apr. 4, 1924.

EARL, Edwin T., publisher Los Angeles Tribune and Los Angeles Herald, Los Angeles, Calif. Died Jan. 2, 1919.

EARL, Mrs. Elizabeth Claypool; b. Wayne Co., Ind., June 25, 1856; d. Austin B. and Hannah Ann (Petty) Claypool; ed. pvt. schs. and Glendale (O.) Coll.; m. Morell J. Earl. Oct. 9, 1878 (died 1879). Mem. Gen. Fedn., and Indiana State Fedn. of Women's Club; pres. Ind. Union of Literary Clubs, 1903; Indiana sec. Gen. Fedn. of Women's Clubs, 1915-16; founder, 1899, and pres. Ind. Library Commission, 1916-25; pres. Ind. Library and Hist. Dept., 1925-26. Chmn. Liberty Loan Drives, Fayette County, World War; mem. bd. Indianapolis Propylæum, 1917-25, Muncie Y.W.C.A., 1922-28. Mem. A.L.A. (first v.p. 1926), Nat. League of Library Commissions (pres. 1918), Ind. Library Assn., Ind. Library Trustees' Assn. Republican. Presbyn. Home: Muncie, Ind. Died Dec. 8, 1931.

EARL, George Goodell, civil engr.; b. Monmouth Co., N.J., Oct. 9, 1863; s. Holmes and Annie (Taylor) E.; grad. Freehold (N.J.) Inst., 1880; C.E., Lafayette Coll., Easton, Pa., 1884, D.Sc., 1918; m. Anna L. Riddell, June 1890 (died 1911); children—Anna Taylor (dec.), Ralph; m. 2d, Frances H. Fowler, Jan. 1912; 1 son, Thomas Collins. With U.S. Geol. Survey in N.J., 1884-85; r.r. location and constrn. with A.T.&S.F. R.R., in Mo., 1886-87; sewer constrn., Montgomery, Ala., 1888; gen. engring. practice, 1888-92; city engr., Americus, Ga., 1890-91; chief engr. New Orleans Sewerage Co., 1892-99; gen. supt. and chief engr., Sewerage and Water Bd., New Orleans, 1900-30, cons. engr. of same, 1931—. Has specialized in development of new methods for regulation, measurement and recording of fluid flows and pressures, especially in proportional flows, and in improvement of liquid meters to record fully on low rates of draft heretofore not recordable. Home: New Orleans, La. Died Sept. 16, 1940.

EARL, Guy Chaffee, lawyer; b. Red Bluff, Calif. May 7, 1861; s. Josiah and Adelia T. (Chaffee) E.; A.B., U. of Calif., 1883; m. Ella J. Ford, Nov. 15, 1888; children—Mrs. Alice Wilder, Mrs. Martha Graham, Mrs. Elinore Henshaw, Guy C. Admitted to bar, 1887; associated in practice at Oakland with S. P. Hall (later judge appellate ct.), 1889-95; state senator, 1893-98; with Thomas B. Bishop and Charles S. Wheeler, San Francisco, 1895-1900, then mem. Earl & Hall; pres. and gen. counsel Great Western Power Co., Calif. Electric Generating Co. Mem. Calif. Senate, 1892-96; regent U. of Calif., terms 1902-34. Republican. Conglist. Home: Oakland, Calif. Died June 25, 1935.

EARL, John Arthur, clergyman; b. Bathvale, Scotland, May 6, 1866; s. John and Mary (Gallagher) E.; came to U.S., July 1, 1883; A.B. Des Moines (Ia.) Coll., 1892, A.M., 1895; D.D., 1902; Rochester Theol. Sem., 1895; m. Jennie Lois Henley, 1890; children—Paul Judson, Ruth Anne, John Baptist (dec.), James Madison. Ordained Bapt. ministry, Dec. 10, 1887; pastor, Guthrie Center, Ia., 1887-89, Pilot Mound, Ia., 1889-91, Greece, N.Y., 1892-95, First Church, Waterloo, Ia., 1895-1906, Belden Av. Ch., Chicago, 1906-11; pres. Des Moines Coll., June 16, 1911-21; pastor First Ch., St. Paul, Minn., June 1921-23; editor "The Baptist," Nov. 1, 1923—. Home: Oak Park, Ill. Died May 4, 1929.

EARL, Robert, jurist; b. Herkimer, N.Y., Sept. 10, 1824; s. John and Margaret E.; grad. Union Coll.,

1845 (LL.D., Union; also Columbia). Admitted to bar, 1848; m. Miss Juliet Wilkerson, Oct., 1852. Held various town and village offices; judge, Herkimer Co., 1856-60; judge court of appeals, N.Y., 1870-95, retired for age, Jan. 1, 1895; engaged in farming. One of founders and now pres. Herkimer Co. Hist. Soc. Together with his wife, founded Herkimer Free Library, and gave it about $30,000 worth of property. Home: Herkimer, N.Y. Died 1902.

EARLE, Alice Morse, author; b. Worcester, Mass., Apr. 27, 1853; d. Edwin and Abby Clary Morse; grad. Worcester High Sch., 1878; m. Henry Earle, 1874. Author: China Collecting in America, 1892; Costume of Colonial Times, 1895; Colonial Dames and Goodwives, 1895; Colonial Days in Old New York, 1897; Curious Punishments of Bygone Days, 1897; Home Life in Colonial Days, 1898; Child Life in Colonial Days, 1899; Stage Coach and Tavern Days, 1900. Part author: Early Prose and Verse, 1893; Historic New York, 1897; Chap Book Essays, 1897; Old Time Gardens, 1901; Sundials and Roses of Yesterday, 1902; Two Centuries of Costume in America, 1903. Home: Brooklyn, N.Y. Died 1911.

EARLE, Franklin Sumner, botanist and agriculturist; b. Dwight, Ill., Sept. 4, 1856; s. Parker and Melanie (Tracy) E.; ed. schs., Cobden, Ill., and U. of Ill.; special studies, chiefly botany and biology, but did not graduate; M.S., Ala. Poly. Inst., 1902; m. Susan B. Skeham, 1886; children—Melanie Tracy (Mrs. William L. Keiser), Ruth Esther (Mrs. David Sturrock); m. 2d, Esther J. Skehan, 1896. Connected with U. of Ill., 1886, doing spl. mycol. work, results of which were published with title "The Erysiphaceæ of Illinois" (joint author with T. J. Burrill); connected with Miss. Agrl. Expt. Sta., 1894-95; joint author (with S. M. Tracy), "Mississippi Fungi," 1895; asst. pathologist in charge mycol. herbarium, U.S. Dept. Agr., 1895-96; horticulturist, Ala. (Coll.) Agrl. Expt. Sta., Jan. 1896; prof. biology, Ala. Poly. Inst., 1896-1901; issued "Preliminary List of Alabama Fungi" (with Dr. L. M. Underwood), 1897; asst. curator in charge mycol. collections, N.Y. Bot. Garden; sent by N.Y. Bot. Garden to Jamaica and Cuba, and by U.S. Dept. Agr. to make scientific investigations in Puerto Rico, 1903; dir. Estacion Central Agronómica of Cuba (on recommendation U.S. Dept. Agr.), 1904-06; consulting agriculturist to Cuban-Am. Sugar Co., 1908-11; pres. Cuba Fruit Exchange, 1911—. Sent to P.R. by U.S. Dept. of Agr., July 1918, to investigate serious sugar cane disease; expert in sugar cane disease Insular Govt. of P.R., July 1, 1919-Sept. 1, 1921; cons. agriculturist Aguirre Sugar Co.; dir. of agriculture Gen. Sugar Co., Havana, Cuba, 1923-24; sugar cane technologist Tropical Plant Research Foundation (in charge of work with sugar cane varieties in Cuba), 1924—. Author: "Southern Agriculture," 1907. Home: Herradura, Cuba. Died Jan. 31, 1929.

EARLE, George Howard, banker, lawyer, mfr.; b. Phila., Pa., July 6, 1856; s. George Hussey and Ellen France (von Löhr) E.; prep. edn. pvt. tutor; Harvard, 1879 (hon. A.M., 1904); m. Catharine H. French, Dec. 12, 1881. Lawyer from 1879; was v.p. Guarantee Trust and Safe Deposit Co., Phila. (resigned); now pres. Finance Co. of Pa., South Chester Tube Co., Pa. Warehousing & Safe Deposit Co., Pa. Sugar Co.; was receiver of and reorganized and is now pres. of Real Estate Trust Co. of Phila.; v.p. Market St. Nat. Bank, Tradesmens Nat. Bank; was receiver Chestnut St. Nat. Bank; assignee Chestnut St. Trust Co. Rep. nominee for mayor of Phila., 1911. Pa. commr. St. Louis Expn. Homes: Bryn Mawr, Pa., and Philadelphia. Died Feb. 19, 1928.

EARLE, Lawrence Carmichael, artist; b. New York, N.Y., Nov. 11, 1845; s. John E. and Mary M. (Dorset) E.; ed. common schools, Grand Rapids, Mich.; studied art in Munich, Florence, Rome. From 1869 steadily engaged in painting. A.N.A. Hon. mem. Art Inst. of Chicago. Home: Grand Rapids, Mich. Died Nov. 20, 1921.

EARLE, Mortimer Lamson, prof. classical philology, Columbia, 1900—; b. New York, N.Y., Oct. 14, 1864; s. Mortimer Lent and Josephine Mercy (Allen) E.; grad. Columbia Coll., 1886; grad. student in classical philology, Columbia U., 1886-87, and 1888-89 (M.A., 1887; Ph.D., 1889); m. Ethel Deodata Woodward, June 4, 1892. Fellow in Letters Columbia Univ. 1886-89; student Am. School of Classical Studies, Athens, 1887-88; instr. Greek, Barnard Coll., New York, 1889-95; assoc. prof. Greek and Latin, Bryn Mawr Coll., Pa., 1895-98; lecturer in Greek, Columbia Univ., 1898-1900. Author: An Edition of Euripides' Alcestis, 1895; An Edition of Sophocles' Œdipus Tyrannus, 1901. Home: New York, N.Y. Died 1905.

EARLE, Ralph, naval officer, educator; b. Worcester, Mass., May 3, 1874; s. Stephen Carpenter and Mary Eaton (Brown) E.; student Worcester Poly. Inst., 1892, hon. D.Sc., 1925; grad. U.S. Naval Acad., 1896; m. Janet Turner, d. of late Pay Dir. Caspar Schenck, U.S.N., Sept. 29, 1898; children—Ralph, Mary Janet. Ensign, U.S.N., May 6, 1898; lt. (jr. grade), May 6, 1901; promoted through grades to rear adm., Dec. 23, 1916, continuing during World War; capt. May 5, 1920; promoted to rank of rear adm., Sept. 1930. Served on U.S.S. Massachusetts, 1896-98; navigator and watch officer, Hornet, Apr.-Sept. 1898, participating in battles of Manzanillo, June 30 and July 18, 1898; on San Francisco, Sept. 19-25, 1898; on Essex, 1898-1901; at naval proving ground, Indian Head, 1901-02; on Lancaster, 1902-03, Yankee, May-Oct. 1903, Missouri, 1903-05; insp. of powder for East Coast, 1905-07; gunnery officer U.S.S. Maine, 1907-08, also navigator part of time; exec., navigator and gunnery officer U.S.S. Galveston, July-Oct. 1908; in charge magazine and chem. lab., P.I., 1908-10; in elec. dept., Naval Acad., 1910-11; exec. officer Iowa, May-Sept. 1911; discipline dept. Naval Acad., 1911-13; head of English dept., same, Aug.-Sept. 1912; mem. spl. bd. on naval ordnance, 1912-13; comd. Balch, Sept.-Oct. 1913, Dolphin, 1913-15, during which time (Apr. 9, 1914) occurred the "Tampico incident"; exec. officer Arkansas, June-Sept. 1915; head dept. of ordnance and gunnery, Naval Acad., 1915-16, dept. of English, June-Aug. 1916; comd. naval proving ground, Indian Head, Md., Sept.-Dec. 1916; apptd. chief Bur. of Ordnance, Navy Dept., Dec. 23, 1916; comd. U.S.S. Connecticut, May 5, 1919-Sept. 28, 1921; chief of staff of control force, U.S.S. Florida, Oct. 10, 1921-May 31, 1922; Naval War Coll., July 1, 1922-May 26, 1923; comdr. Naval Torpedo Sta., Newport, R.I., May 26, 1923-May 25, 1925; retired Aug. 25, 1925. Pres. Worcester Poly. Inst., 1925—. Mem. U.S. Naval Inst. Episcopalian. Author: Life at the U.S. Naval Academy, 1917; Makers of Naval Tradition; (brochure) Practical Interior Ballistics, 1917. Accomplished origination of and developed plans for and provided the material for the mine field across the North Sea, known as the Northern Barrage; directed making a type of mine entirely new to naval warfare; originator of the 14-inch naval ry. batteries in France. Originated plans for depth charges, and many other ordnance projects. Home: Worcester, Mass. Died Feb. 13, 1939.

EARLE, Samuel T., Jr., M.D.; b. near Centreville, Md., Dec. 2, 1849; s. Samuel T. and Mary E. (Brundige) E.; Md. Agrl. Coll., 1863; Wyer's Mil. Acad., Westchester, Pa., 1864, 65; Washington Coll., Md., 1866-67; read medicine under preceptor, 1867-68; M.D., U. of Md., 1870; m. Mary Isabel Ringgold, Jan. 2, 1872 (died 1890); children—M. Isabel, Rosetta M. (Mrs. Ellis Long); m. 2d, Dinette Tyler, Apr. 21, 1891. In practice in Md., 1870—; emeritus prof. physiology and diseases of rectum, Baltimore Med. Coll. Episcopalian. Author: Diseases of the Anus, Rectum and Sigmoid, 1911. Joint Author: (with James P. Tuttle) Surgical Diseases and Wounds of the Anus and Rectum (in Vol. VII, Am. Practice of Surgery), 1910. Home: Baltimore, Md. Died 1929.

EARLING, Albert J., ry. official; b. Richfield, Wis., Jan. 19, 1848; common sch. edn. In service of C.,M.&St.P. Ry., 1866—; telegrapher, and train dispatcher, 9 yrs., asst. supt., 4 yrs., div. supt., 1882, asst. gen. supt., 1884, gen. supt., 1888, gen. mgr., 1890, and 2d v.p., 1895, pres., 1899-1917, chmn. bd., 1917-Jan. 10, 1919. C.,M.&St.P. Ry. Home: Chicago, Ill. Died Nov. 10, 1925.

EARLY, William Wallace, consular service; b. Aulander, N.C., Dec. 2, 1867; s. Abner Williford and Eugenia (Watson) E.; M.A., Wake Forest (N.C.) Coll., 1889; M.D., U. of Pa., 1893; also studied medicine, U. of Va.; m. Rosa Elizabeth Heide McDuffie, July 18, 1902. Practiced in Mass. and N.C., 1895-1914; apptd. consular agt. Leicester, Eng., July 25, 1914; consul, Belize, British Honduras, 1919-25, San Luis Potosi, Mexico, 1925-29, Colon, Panama, 1929—. Democrat. Baptist. Home: Aulander, N.C. Died Sept. 28, 1933.

EARNSHAW, Manuel; b. Cavite, P.I., Nov. 19, 1862; s. Daniel and Gavina (Noguera) E.; ed. at Anteneo de Manila, and in engring. at works of Wilks & Earnshaw, Manila; m. Maria Villar Ubaldo, of Manila, Feb. 4, 1888. Began as marine engr., 1884; pres. The Earnshaws Slipways & Engring. Co.; dir. Manila Improvement Co., etc.; elected by Philippine legislature as resident commr. to Congress of U.S., Nov. 21, 1912, for term 1913-17; retired. Home: Manila, P.I. Died Feb. 13, 1936.

EARP, John Rosslyn, public health; b. Matlock, Eng., Sept. 5, 1891; s. John Oswald and Catherine Lavinia (Hands) E.; B.A., St. John's Coll., Cambridge, 1915, M.A., 1920; M.R.C.S., Univ. Coll. Hosp., London, 1917, L.R.C.P., 1917; Dr. P.H., Johns Hopkins, 1926; m. Kathleen May Goodliffe, Aug. 18, 1920; children—Evelyn Mary, David (dec.), Ormonde, Kenneth Roland, John Gordon. Came to U.S., 1922, naturalized, 1932. Sub-editor The Lancet, London, 1919, then editor Tubercle; asso. editor Internat. Jour. Pub. Health, 1920; dir. health dept., Antioch Coll., Yellow Springs, O., 1923-27; lecturer U. of Colo., 1928; pvt. practice, Denver, 1929; dir. pub. health, State of N.M., 1931-37; med. editor N.Y. State Health Dept., 1937—. Served with British Red Cross, Belgium, 1914-15; med. officer French Red Cross, 1917-18. Fellow A.A.A.S., A.M.A., Am. Pub. Health Assn. Author: (brochure) The Student Who Smokes, 1926. Home: Delmar, N.Y. Died May 19, 1941.

EASLEY, Ralph Montgomery, polit. economist; b. Frederick, Ill., Feb. 25, 1856; s. Charles L. and Elizabeth J. (Berry) E.; educated public schools and Johnson Coll., Quincy, Ill.; m. Nerva C. Cheney, Mar. 23, 1881 (dec.); children—Donna Rachel (Mrs. Cipriano Andrade, Jr.), Ronald Merl; m. 2d, Gertrude Brackenridge Beeks, Sept. 3, 1917. Went to Hutchinson, Kan., 1875; taught sch., 1877-78; propr. and editor Hutchinson News, 1883-91; postmaster of Hutchinson, 1882-87. Had charge politico-economic dept. Chicago Inter Ocean for three yrs.; organized and sec. Civic Federation of Chicago, 1893-1900; organized, Nov. 1900, and became chmn. exec. council, Nat. Civic Fedn. Promoted nat. confs. on primary election reform, New York, Jan. 1898; on future fgn. policy of U.S. Saratoga, N.Y., Aug. 1898; on trusts and combinations, Chicago, Sept. 1899; on taxation, Buffalo, 1901; on immigration, New York, 1905. Organized, Sept. 12, 1917, and dir. League for Nat. Unity. Republican. Wrote: Tragedy of the Worker and the Farmer Calls for Big Leadership; Let "Capitalism" Speak for Itself; Russia Is Not a Friendly Nation; Rid Methodist Church of Red Incubus; Is Communism a Menace in the U.S.?; Fish-Borah Mesalliance; We Entered the War—Why?; Communism of the C.I.O. and John L. Lewis. Home: Rye, N.Y. Died Sept. 7, 1939.

EAST, Edward Murray, biologist; b. Du Quoin, Ill., Oct. 4, 1879; s. William Harvey and Sarah Granger (Woodruff) E.; Case Sch. Applied Science, 1897-98; B.S., U. of Ill., 1900; grad. study, 1900-05, M.S., 1904, Ph.D., 1907; LL.D., Kenyon Coll., 1926; m. Mary Lawrence Boggs, Sept. 2, 1903; children—Elizabeth Woodruff, Margaret Lawrence, Edward Murray (dec.). Asst. chemist, 1900-03, 1st asst. in plant breeding, 1903-05, U. of Ill. Agrl. Expt. Sta.; agronomist Conn. Agrl. Expt. Sta., 1905-09; asst. prof. exptl. plant morphology, 1909-14, prof. exptl. plant morphology, 1914-26, prof. genetics, 1926—, Harvard U. Collaborator tobacco investigations, U.S. Dept. Agr., 1908-18. Chmn. bot. raw products com., and mem. bot. and agr. com., Nat. Research Council, 1917-18; actg. chief statistics div. U.S. Food Administration, 1918. Editorial bd. Genetics, 1916—; contbg. bd. Bot. Abstracts, 1918-22; Harvard lectureship at Yale, 1924-25; lecturer U. of Chicago, 1911, Grad. Sch. Agr., 1914; De Lamar lecturer Johns Hopkins, 1920; lecturer Cornell U., 1922; Larwill lecturer Kenyon Coll., 1927; lecturer of U. of Mich., 1930; Harvey lecturer New York U., 1931. V.p. 2d International Congress on Eugenics, 1921; hon. v.p. 6th International Botanical Congress, 1935. Fellow Am. Acad. Arts and Sciences, A.A.A.S. Author: Heterozygosis in Evolution and Plant Breeding, 1912; Inbreeding and Outbreeding, 1919; Mankind at the Crossroads, 1923; Heredity and Human Affairs, 1927. Editor: Biology in Human Affairs, 1931. Home: Boston, Mass. Died Nov. 9, 1938.

EASTER, De la Warr Benjamin, college prof.; b. Baltimore, Oct. 9, 1867; s. John, Jr., and Mary Elizabeth Cullen (Quarles) E.; A.M., Randolph-Macon Coll., Va., 1891; student in France, 1903, 06, 25; Ph.D., Johns Hopkins, 1905; m. Sarah Bayne (Ayres) Sheppard, Dec. 26, 1906. Instr., Randolph-Macon Coll., 1886-93; adj. prof. in charge of modern langs., Wofford Coll., Spartanburg, S.C., 1893-95; adj. prof. in charge of Greek and German, Randolph-Macon Coll., 1895-1900; Hopkins scholar, 1900-04, instr. in charge of undergraduate French, 1904-05, Johns Hopkins U.; prof. modern langs., Randolph-Macon Coll., 1905-10; prof. Romance langs., Washington and Lee U., 1910—; asst. dean, 1920-31. Democrat. Mem. Disciples of Christ. Author: French Composition—issued in connection with Armstrong's Syntax of the French Verb, 1910. Home: Lexington, Va. Died July 6, 1933.

EASTERBROOK, Edmund Pepperell, chief of chaplains, U.S.A.; b. Torquay, Eng., Dec. 22, 1865; s. William and Mary Jane (Pepperell) E.; student Torquay (Eng.) Public Coll., Drew U., 1889-1903; D.D., Coll. Puget Sound, 1921; LL.D., Little Rock Coll., 1929; m. Fannie Luscombe, Sept. 22, 1892; children—Arthur E., U.S.A., Gladys E. (wife of J. L. Collins, U.S.A.), Wilfred G., William, Ernest F. Ordained ministry M. E. Ch., 1889; pastor M.E. Chs., Troy Conf., 1889-98; chaplain U.S.A., Spanish-Am. War, in Cuba with Army of Occupation; commd. chaplain, U.S.A., by President McKinley, Jan. 31, 1900; on duty in Philippines during Insurrection, 1900-05; served as chaplain, U.S. Arty., World War; sr. chaplain, A.F.G., Germany, 1919-23; stationed at Fort Monroe, Va., 1923-27, Fort Sam Houston, Tex., 1927-28; chief of chaplains, U.S.A., 1928-30 (retired). Decorated Legion of Honor (France). Mason. Home: Washington, D.C. Died Jan. 18, 1933.

EASTERWOOD, William Edward, Jr., capitalist; b. Wills Point, Tex., Nov. 5, 1883; s. William Edward and Mollie (Busby) E.; ed. pub. schs., Wills Point; m. Mae Coker, Nov. 1928. Began as newsboy and became traveling man and factory rep. of large Eastern concerns; now dir. Dallas Nat. Bank, Dallas Title & Guaranty Co., U.S. Bond & Mortgage Co.; vice pres. Vanette Hosiery Mills; large property owner of Dallas. Mem. U.S. Marine Corps, World War, advancing to capt.; col. on staff 8 governors; col. Nat. Air Reserves. Especially active in promotion of aviation; has established many airports in Tex. (3 named for him); donor of $25,000 to Coste and Bellonte, French flyers, for first one-stop flight from Paris to New York and Dallas. Recipient of silver loving cups from various Tex. orgns.; decorated Legion of Honor (France), 1933. Nat. vice comdr. Am. Legion, 1933; organized Am. Legion depts. of Great Britain, Belgium and Greece, 1933. Chmn. Aviation Com. of City of Dallas, 1935-37. Mem. advisory bd. Southern Meth. Univ.; former v.p. U.S. Marine Corps League; trustee Nat. Soc. for Crippled Children of U.S.; dir. Tex. Soc. for Crippled Children. Awarded special diploma Internat. Expn. (San Francisco) as Ambassador of Good Will for State of Texas, 1939. Awarded citations from Nat. Aerographic Aviation Acad., Nat. Aeronautic Assn. Methodist. Life mem. Elks, exalted ruler, Dallas, 1936-37. Sponsor Christmas dinners to destitute children and food relief to vets. Presented with nat. citation by Am. Legion for work on Americanism, nat. defense and aviation. Home: Adolphus, Tex. Died Aug. 24, 1940.

EASTMAN, Annis Ford, independent minister; b. Peoria, Ill., Apr. 24, 1852; d. George W. and Catherine (Stehley) Ford; ed. Peoria pub. schs.; Oberlin Coll., 1872-73; m. Rev. Samuel E. Eastman, Aug. 26, 1875. Entered ministry, 1889; pastor Congl. Ch., Brookton, N.Y., 1889-91, W. Bloomfield, N.Y., 1891-93; successor to Thomas K. Beecher in Park Ch., Elmira, N.Y., 1893. Author: Have and Give (children's sermons). Home: Elmira, N.Y. Died 1910.

EASTMAN, Barrett, journalist, dramatic critic; b. Chicago, Jan. 25, 1869; s. Francis Ambrose and Gertrude (Barrett) E.; ed. acad., Utica, N.Y., The Gunnery, Washington, Conn., Racine Coll., Wis.; unmarried. Began newspaper work, 1889, as reporter Chicago Herald; later editorial writer Chicago Evening Post, Chicago Tribune, New York American and Journal, Los Angeles Tribune, Chicago Daily Journal, spl. writer, Chicago Inter Ocean, Sunday editor Chicago Tribune; dramatic critic, Chicago Tribune and Chicago Daily Journal. Episcopalian. Home: Chicago, Ill. Died 1910.

EASTMAN, Charles Rochester, geologist, palæontologist; b. Cedar Rapids, Ia., June 5, 1868; s. Austin V. and Mary (Scoville) E.; A.B., Harvard, 1890, A.M., 1891; Ph.D., Munich, 1894; m. Caroline A., d. Alvan G. Clark (famous telescope-maker), 1892. Studied natural science at Harvard, Johns Hopkins, and abroad; served on U.S., Iowa, N.Y., N.J., and other state geol. surveys; taught geology and palæontology in Harvard and Radcliffe colls.; curator at Carnegie Mus., Pittsburgh, and prof., U. of Pittsburgh, 1910-13; engaged in scientific research and editor at Am. Mus. Natural History, New York, 1913—. Editor Am. Palæontol. Soc.; translator of Von Zittel's Palæontology, 3 vols., 1900-2. Home: New York, N.Y. Died Sept. 27, 1918.

EASTMAN, Edwin Gamage, lawyer; b. Grantham, N.H., Nov. 22, 1847; s. William Henry and Paulina Sibley (Winter) E.; A.B., Dartmouth Coll., 1874, A.M.; m. Elma E. Dodge, Mar. 12, 1877; 2d, Morgie A. Follansby, Mar. 15, 1885. Began practice of law, Exeter, N.H., 1876. Mem. N.H. Ho. of Rep., 1876, Senate, 1889; mem. N.H. Constl. Conv., 1901; was solicitor Rockingham Co., 4 yrs.; atty. gen. of N.H. for 20 yrs. Conglist. Republican. Home: Exeter, N.H. Died June 20, 1916.

EASTMAN, George, mfr.; b. Waterville, N.Y., July 12, 1854; s. George W. and Maria (Kilbourn) E.; ed. Rochester, N.Y. Became an amateur photographer and experimenter and perfected a process for making dry plates; began to mfr. dry plates on small scale, 1880; originated the kodak and transparent film for use in same; chmn. bd. Eastman Kodak Co. of N.Y., and of Eastman Kodak Co. of N.J. A leader in business and philanthropic movements; donor of more than $75,000,000 to various philanthropic objects. Home: Rochester, N.Y. Died Mar. 14, 1932.

EASTMAN, John Coates, newspaper publisher; b. Eaton, O., Dec. 19, 1862; s. John and Harriet Ardella (Davis) E.; ed. Ohio State U., 1878-82; ed. as civ. engr.; m. Eva Harter, July 20, 1886. Reporter on Chicago Herald, 1890-95; business mgr. Chicago Chronicle, 1895-98; advt. mgr. New York Journal, 1898-1900; pres., treas. and business mgr. Chicago American, 1900-04; became owner of Chicago Daily Journal, Apr. 2, 1904, and pres. and treas. Chicago Journal Co. Presbyn. Home: Chicago, Ill. Died Jan. 25, 1925.

EASTMAN, John Robie, astronomer; b. Andover, N.H., July 29, 1836; s. Royal Friend and Sophronia (Mayo) E.; M.S., Dartmouth Coll., 1862; Ph.D., 1877; m. Mary J. Ambrose, Dec. 25, 1866. Asst., U.S. Naval Obs., 1861-65; prof. mathematics U.S.N., 1865—. Retired for age, July 29, 1898, with rank of capt. U.S.N., but retained on active duty till Oct. 12, 1898; promoted to rank of rear-adm. U.S.N., June 29, 1906. Engaged in astron. observations, computations and research, 1862—. Most of published work in the annual volumes of the govt. observatory. Was first pres. Washington Acad. Sciences. Was in charge of the Meridian Circle work at the observatory, 1874-91; observed total solar eclipses Aug. 7, 1869, at Des Moines, Iowa; Dec. 22, 1870, Syracuse, Sicily; July 29, 1878, at West

Las Animas, Colo., and May 28, 1900, at Barnesville, Ga. Prepared and edited the Second Washington Star Catalogue, which contains the results of nearly 80,000 observations made at the U.S. Naval Obs., 1866-91. Author: Transit Circle Observations of the Sun, Moon, Planets and Comets, 1903. Home: Andover, N.H. Died Sept. 26, 1913.

EASTMAN, Joseph, physician; b. Bleeker Mountains, N.Y., 1842; early edn. at winter schools and in home study. Learned blacksmith's trade. Enlisted 77th N.Y. regt., 1861; went to front; took part in 4 battles. Had fever after battle of Williamsburg; sent to Mt. Pleasant Hosp., Washington; placed on med. duty there; later disch. from regt.; apptd. hosp. steward U.S.A.; permitted to attend 2 courses med. lectures, U. of Georgetown; grad., 1865 (LL.D., Wabash Coll., 1891). Commissioned asst. surgeon U.S. vols. and served until May, 1866. Attended lectures Bellevue Hosp. Med. Coll., New York, 1870-71; prof. anatomy Central Coll. Phys. & Surg., Indianapolis, Ind. (pres., 1885); cons. surgeon City Hosp. and City Dispensary. Visited hosps. of London, Birmingham, Paris, Strassburg, Munich, Vienna, Leipzig, Dresden, Halle and Berlin. Home: Indianapolis, Ind. Died 1902.

EASTMAN, Julia Arabella, author; d. Rev. John and Prudence (Dole) E.; unmarried. Founder, and asso. prin., Dana Hall, Wellesley, 1881-99. Author: Kitty Kent's Troubles; Romneys of Ridgemont; School Days of Beulah Romney; Short Comings and Long Goings; Striking for the Right; Young Rick. Home: Wellesley, Mass. Died 1911.

EASTMAN, Samuel Coffin, lawyer; b. Concord, N.H., July 11, 1837; s. Seth and Sarah (Coffin) E.; A.M., Brown U., 1857; LL.B., Harvard, 1859; m. Mary Clifford Greene, July 11, 1861. Assistant librarian, Brown U., 1857-58; admitted to bar, 1859, and in practice at Concord; pres. Concord Mutual Fire Ins. Co., N.H. Savings Bank, Concord & Portsmouth R.R., and other cos. and dir. in other corps. Mem. Concord Bd. Edn. 12 yrs.; also city treas. same; mem. N.H. Ho. of Rep., 1883 (speaker), and 1893; pres. of celebration of 150th anniversary of charter of town of Concord, 1915. Republican. Author: White Mountain Guide-Book, 9 editions, 1857. Home: Concord, N.H. Died Aug. 31, 1917.

EASTMAN, Samuel Palmer, chmn. bd. Atlas Imperial Diesel Engine Co.; pres. Spring Valley Co., Southern Pacific Golden Gate Ferries, Ltd., San Francisco.; dir. Wells Fargo Bank & Union Trust Co., Fireman's Fund Indemnity Co. Died Feb. 13, 1941.

EASTON, Edward Denison, pres. Am. Graphophone Co.; b. Gloucester, Mass., Apr. 10, 1856; s. Denison Mitchel and Mary (Lyle) E.; early edn. in Bergen Co., N.J.; LL.B., Georgetown U., 1888, LL.M., 1889; m. Helen M. Jefferis, 1883. Became prominent as shorthand reporter and reported the trial of Guiteau and the two Star Route trials. Became interested in the graphophone, 1887, and became identified with its mfr. and sale; organized the Columbia Phonograph Co., 1889; now pres. Am. Graphophone Co., Columbia Phonograph Co.; pres. The Burt Co., Water Power Securities Co.; v.p. Hackensack Trust Co. Republican. Home: Arcola, N.J. Died Apr. 30, 1915.

EASTON, Morton William, philologist; b. Hartford, Conn., Aug. 18, 1841; s. Oliver Hastings and Emeline Maria (Brace) E.; A.B., Yale, 1863, Ph.D., 1872; M.D., Coll. Phys. and Surg. (Columbia), 1867; m. Maria Stillé Burton, June 15, 1875. Prof. ancient langs., 1871, later comparative philology and modern langs. to 1881, E. Tenn. U.; prof. English and comparative philology, U. of Pa., 1882-1912 (emeritus). Deceased.

EASTVOLD, Carl Johan, clergyman; b. Stavanger, Norway, Mar. 19, 1863; s. John J. and Karen H. (Ostvold) Ostvold; came to U.S., 1880; grad. Redwing (Minn.) Sem., 1891; student Chicago Theol. Sem., 1895-96; m. Sophia Nelson, June 27, 1889; children—Stella Cornelia, Joseph, Ellen Sophia (wife of Rev. Tysdol), Seth Clarance, Carl Johan, Isaac, Harold William, Marion, Esther Anseneta, Susan Madelia, Obeb Selius Ambrosius. Ordained ministry Norwegian Luth Ch., 1891; pastor Elmore, Minn., 1891-97, Jewell, Ia., 1897-1913, Dawson, Minn., 1913-17; v.p. Hauges Norw. Luth. Synod, 1903, pres., 1904-10, when resigned, reëlected, 1917; chmn. of joint com. which arranged union of United Ch. and Norwegian Luth. Synod, 1917; pres. Southern Minn. Dist., Norwegian Luth. Ch. America, 1917-27; pastor Volin, S.D., 1927—; acting pres. Jewell Luth. Coll., 1912-13. Representative of foreign mission to the ch. in China, 1916-17, mem. bd. dirs. Norwegian Luth Orient Mission Soc.; pres. bd. dirs. China mission 6 yrs.; pres. Zion Soc. for Israel; pres. "Stavangerlaget," 1910—. Home: Volin, S. Dak. Died July 23, 1929.

EATON, Amasa Mason, lawyer; b. Providence, R.I., May 31, 1841; s. Levi Curtis and Sarah Brown (Mason) E.; bro. of Charles Frederick E.; early edn. by tutors at home and 3 yrs. in Europe; A.M., Brown, 1861; LL.B., Harvard, 1878; m. Maude Dunnell, Sept. 15, 1873. Served in 1st R.I. Vols. in Civil War. Mem. and pres. Town Council, N. Providence, 1863-65; mem. R.I. Ho. of Rep., 1865-66; 1872-74; mem. Providence Common Council, 1874-75, bd. of aldermen, 1875; mem. Commn. on Uniform State Legislation, 1897 (pres. 1901-09); 1st v.p. Nat. Divorce Congress, 1906-07. Author: Constitution Making in Rhode Island, 1899; Free Trade vs. Protection, 1913. Home: Providence, R.I. Died Oct. 3, 1914.

EATON, Arthur Wentworth Hamilton, clergyman; b. Kentville, N.S.; s. William and Anna Augusta Willoughby (Hamilton) E.; A.B., Harvard, 1880; A.M., Dalhousie, N.S., 1904; (D.C.L., King's U., N.S., 1905); unmarried. Deacon, 1884, priest, 1885, P.E. Ch.; priest-in-charge of parish of Chestnut Hill, Mass., 1885-86. Author: The Church of England in Nova Scotia and the Tory Clergy of the Revolution, 1891; Tales of a Garrison Town (with Craven Langstroth Betts, q.v.), 1892; Poems of the Christian Year, 1905; The Lotus of the Nile and Other Poems, 1907; Heart of the Acadian Land, 1910; The Eaton Family of Nova Scotia, 1929. Editor: Pope's Rape of the Lock, 1901. Died July 11, 1937.

EATON, Benjamin Harrison, farmer, gov.; b. Coshocton Co., O., Dec. 15, 1833; s. Levi and Hannah E.; grad. West Bedford Acad., 1852; taught sch., 1852-54; removed to Louisa Co., Iowa; mining in Colo., 1859-61; in N. Mex., 1861-64; removed to Greeley, Colo., 1864, and became successful farmer, inaugurating thorough irrigation system on his farm. Was mem. Colo. Ho. and Senate, 1875; gov. Colo., 1885-86. Republican. Home: Eaton, Colo. Died 1904.

EATON, C. Harry, artist, illustrator; b. Akron, O., Dec. 13, 1850. Silver medal, Boston, Mass.; gold medal, Prize Fund Exhbn.; Evans prize, S.A.A., 1898. Asso. Nat. Acad. Home: Leoni, N.J. Died 1901.

EATON, Charles H., Universalist clergyman; b. Beverly, Mass., Aug. 15, 1852; s. Rev. Henry Arthur E.; grad. Tufts Coll., 1874; Tufts Coll. Div. School, 1877 (D.D., same); ordained, Palmer, Mass., 1877; succeeded Rev. E. H. Chapin, D.D., New York, 1881; m. July 31, 1895, Emily Mary Stuart. Wrote: Ideal Sunday, North Am. Review; A Decade of Magazine Literature, Forum; Pullman and Paternalism, Mag. of Civics; etc. Died 1902.

EATON, Charles Warren, artist; b. Albany, N.Y., Feb. 22, 1857; s. Daniel Oliver and Mary (Bounds) E.; pupil of Nat. Acad. Design and Art Students' League, New York; unmarried. Exhibited Royal Acad. and Grosvenor Gallery, London, Paris Expn., 1900 (hon. mention), Pan-Am. Expn. (hon. mention); Charleston Expn. (silver medal); also received Proctor prize 1901, Inness prize 1902, and Shaw prize 1903, at Salmagundi Exhbn.; gold medal, Phila. Art Club, 1903; Inness gold medal, Nat. Acad. Design, 1904; silver medal, St. Louis Expn., 1904; gold medal, Paris Salon, 1906; silver medal, Buenos Aires, 1910. A.N.A. Home: Bloomfield, N.J. Died Sept. 10, 1937.

EATON, D(aniel) Cady, coll. prof.; b. Johnstown, N.Y., June 16, 1837; s. Daniel Cady and Harriet Eliza (Cady) E.; B.A., Yale, 1860, M.A., 1863; LL.B., Albany (N.Y.) Law Sch., 1861; practiced law at New York, 1861-66; studied history of art under Prof. Friederichs, U. of Berlin, 1867-68, under Taine, Gérome and Boulanger, Paris, 1869-70; m. Alice Young, Dec. 17, 1861. Prof. history and criticism of art, 1869-76 and 1902-09, emeritus prof., 1909—, Yale U. Served in 7th N.Y. Militia, 1861-63; col. N.Y.S.M., N.Y. Militia, 1863. Democrat. Episcopalian. Author: Handbook of Greek and Roman Sculpture, 1884; Handbook of Modern French Painting, 1909. Home: New Haven, Conn. Died May 11, 1912.

EATON, Dorman Bridgeman, lawyer; b. Hardwick, Vt., June 27, 1823; grad. Univ. of Vt., 1848 (LL.D.); Harvard Law School, 1850; admitted to N.Y. bar. Traveled in Europe and investigated civil service methods and became active in civil service reform; was, 1873 and 1883-86, mem. U.S. Civil Service Commn. Author: Civil Service in Great Britain; The Independent Movement in New York. Died 1899.

EATON, Elon Howard, college prof.; b. Springville, N.Y., Oct. 8, 1866; s. Luzerne and Sophia (Newton) E.; A.B., U. of Rochester, 1890, A.M., 1893, M.Sc., 1911, Sc.D., 1927; Columbia, 1899-1900; m. Gertrude Yeames, Sept. 4, 1909; children—Elizabeth, Elon Howard; m. 2d, Esther Woodman, Sept. 1, 1915; children—Mary, Stephen Lockwood. V.prin. Canandaigua (N.Y.) High Sch., 1889-95; master of sciences, Bradstreet Sch., Rochester, N.Y., 1896-1907 (leave of absence, 1899-1900); prof. biology, Hobart Coll. and William Smith Coll., 1908—. State ornithologist, N.Y. State Mus., 1908-14; curator Hobart Coll. Mus., 1908—. Mem. Geneva (N.Y.) Bd. of Health, 1909-14 (pres. 1909-12). Fellow A.A.A.S., Rochester Acad. Science. Republican. Author: Birds of Western New York, 1901; Birds of New York (Memoir 12, N.Y. State Mus.), Vol. 1, 1910, Vol. 2, 1914; Biological Survey of Finger Lakes, 1927. Home: Geneva, N.Y. Died Mar. 27, 1934.

EATON, Fred Laurine, capitalist; b. Calais, Vt., July 10, 1859; s. Arthur Guy and Ellen May (Chase) E.; ed. pub. and high schs., Montpelier; m. Lillian Gale, Oct. 15, 1884. Clk. and teller 1st Nat. Bank, Montpelier, 1877-81; cashier Nat. Bank of Barre, Vt., 1881-85, 1st Nat. Bank, Montpelier, 1885-94; sec., treas. Sioux City Stock Yards Co., 1894-1903; pres. and gen. mgr. Sioux City Stock Yards Co., 1903—; pres. Sioux City Terminal Ry. Co., Ia. Rendering Co., Hawkeye Land Co.; v.p. Live Stock Nat. Bank, Gen. Mfg. Co.; sec., treas. Mo. River Bridge Co. Col. on staff of Gov. U. A. Woodbury, of Vt., 1894. Republican. Unitarian. Home: Sioux City, Ia. Died 1925.

EATON, Frederick Heber, mfr.; b. Berwick, Pa., Apr. 15, 1863; s. Ralph H. and Eliza Knapp (Dickerman) E.; ed. pub. schs., Berwick; m. C. Elizabeth Furman, 1881. Engaged in mfg., 1880—; pres. and dir. Am. Car & Foundry Co., 1902—; chmn. and dir. Am. Car & Fdry. Export Co.; trustee Mut. Life Ins. Co. of New York; dir. Columbia Trust Co., Seaboard Nat. Bank, Hoyt & Woodin Mfg. Co., etc. Republican; McKinley elector, Pa., 1896. Home: New York, N.Y. Died Jan. 28, 1916.

EATON, George Daniel, educator; b. Marine, Ill., June 19, 1866; s. Ephraim Marion and Mary Elizabeth (Smith) E.; grad. Manual Training Sch., Washington U., 1884; grad. Central Business Coll., St. Louis, 1891; m. Edith May Judd, June 25, 1891; children—Hazel May (Mrs. F. A. Garetson), Russell Samuel. Teacher of science, Wyman Inst., 1889-92; name changed 1892, to Western Mil. Acad., of which became part owner and prin., 1896, pres. and supt. same, 1919—. Trustee Monticello Sem., Godfrey, Ill.; dir. Alton Nat. Bank. Officer Ill. N.G. from 1893, advancing to col., 1919. Mem. Bd. Aldermen, Upper Alton, Ill., 1889-1901, mayor, 1901-03. Republican. Methodist. Mason. Home: Alton, Ill. Died Mar. 31, 1930.

EATON, Henry William, insurance mgr.; b. and ed. in Eng.; came to U.S., 1878, and soon after took out papers of citizenship; m. Mima F. Griffith, Oct. 1889. Mgr. in New York, Liverpool and London and Globe Ins. Co., of England; pres. Liverpool and London and Globe Ins. Co. of New York, Globe Indemnity Co. of New York. Elected pres. Nat. Bd. Fire Underwriters, 1897; pres. Factory Ins. Assn., 1910—. N.Y. Bd. of Fire Underwriters, 1911—. Home: Mamaroneck, N.Y. Died May 4, 1926.

EATON, Homer, pub. agent; b. Enosburg, Vt., Nov. 16, 1834; s. Rev. Bennett and Betsey Maria (Webster) E.; ed. Bakersfield (Vt.) Acad., and Theol. Sem., Concord, N.H.; (D.D., Syracuse U., 1878; LL.D., Syracuse U. and Neb. Wesleyan U., 1909); m. Hannah Saxe, Apr. 28, 1858. Entered ministry M.E. Ch., 1857; in pastorate, 1857-89; publishing agt. of Meth. Book Concern, New York, Feb. 1889—. Mem. 9 gen. confs.; fraternal del. to Gen. Conf. Meth. Ch. in Can.; del. Ecumenical Conf., London, 1881 and 1901; treas. Bd. of Foreign Missions, M.E. Ch., and trustee several univs. and theol. instns. Home: Madison, N.J. Died Feb. 9, 1913.

EATON, James Webster, lawyer; b. Albany, N.Y., May 14, 1856; s. James Webster and Eliza (Benner) E.; early edn. common school and Albany Acad.; grad. Yale, 1879; taught school, 1880-82; admitted to bar, May 1882; m. Hortense Willey Vibbard, July 17, 1894. Dist. atty. Albany Co., 1892-95; lecturer law dept. Union Univ. (Albany Law Sch.), 1891—; also, 1901, law dept. Boston U. Democrat. Author: Domestic Relations, 1888; Bankruptcy, 1900; Equity, 1901. Home: Albany, N.Y. Died 1901.

EATON, John, inspector of edn. for Puerto Rico (1899); pres. Sheldon Jackson Coll., Salt Lake City, 1895-1899; b. Sutton, N.H., Dec. 5, 1829; s. John and Janet (Andrew) E.; studied at Thetford Acad.; grad. Dartmouth, 1854 (LL.D., Ph.D., Rutgers); teacher, Cleveland, 1854-56; supt. schools, Toledo, O., 1856-59; studied at Andover Theol. Sem.; ordained and chaplain 27th Ohio vol. inf., 1862; apptd., Nov. 1862, supt. of freedmen, and later, by Sec. of War, given supervision at all military posts from Cairo to Natchez and Ft. Smith; commended by Pres. Lincoln; col. 63d U.S. colored inf., Oct. 1863; bvt. brig. gen., Mar. 1865; furnished example for Freedmen's Bureau, etc.; asst. commr., 1865-66, and mustered out; editor Memphis Post, 1866-67; State supt. schools, Tenn., 1867-69; commr. U.S. Bureau of Edn., 1870-86; pres. Marietta Coll., 1886-91. Rep. Interior Dept. at Centennial Expn.; organizer of ednl. exhibit at New Orleans; pres. Nat. Congress of Edn. Author: History of Thetford Academy; Mormons of To-day; The Freedmen in the War (report); Schools of Tennessee (report); reports of the U.S. Bur. of Edn. Home: Washington, D.C. Died 1906.

EATON, Joseph Giles, rear adm.; b. Greenville, Ala., Jan. 29, 1847; s. William Pitt and Sarah Farwell (Brazer) E.; ed. pvt. schs., Lockport, N.Y., Union Acad., Worcester Mil. Acad. and U.S. Naval Acad.; m. Mary Anne Varnum, Aug. 8, 1871. Midshipman U.S.N., 1863; ensign, 1869; master, 1870; lt., 1871; lt. comdr., 1888; comdr., 1896; capt., 1901; retired with rank of rear admiral, June 30, 1905. Comd. U.S. ships Enterprise, Resolute, Chesapeake, Oregon and Massachusetts. Has medals for battles of

Manzanillo and Santiago, war of 1898. Was engaged in interoceanic surveys, Isthmus of Panama, and Darien, 1870-74; mem. Steel Bd., 1893-95; medal of honor, Spanish-Am. War. Episcopalian. Died Mar. 8, 1913.

EATON, Joseph Oriel, mfr., banker; b. Yonkers, N.Y., July 28, 1873; s. Joseph Oriel and Emma (Goodman) E.; B.A., Williams, 1895; m. Edith Ide French, 1910; children—Mrs. Edith Dewey, Caroline Winsor French, Winsor Brown French, Edward Savage French (stepchildren), Joseph Oriel, Margaret Adams, Martha, Anne. Formerly with Am. Express Co., New York, and George P. Ide & Co., Troy; asst. gen. mgr. Empire Cream Separator Co., Bloomfield, N.J., 2 yrs.; organized, 1905, and was treas. Interstate Shirt & Collar Co., Troy; organized, 1912, and was treas., gen. mgr. and pres. Torbensen Gear & Axle Co., Newark, N.J., later the Torbensen Axle Co., Cleveland; 1st v.p. Republic Motor Truck Co., 1918; organized, 1919, and was pres. Eaton Axle Co., Cleveland, merged, 1920, with Standard Parts Co., of which was pres. and gen. mgr.; now pres. Eaton Axle & Spring Co., a merger of Eaton Axle Co., Perfection Spring Co. and Torbensen Axle Co.; mem. Otis & Co., bankers, Cleveland, Oct. 1921—. Served in Spanish-Am. War; formerly mem. N.G.N.Y., Essex Troop, N.J. Unitarian. Home: Cleveland, O. Died Nov. 23, 1926.

EATON, Lewis Tillson, educator; b. Charleston, Me., Mar. 26, 1869; s. Thomas O. and Delia Ellen (Bolster) E.; desc. John Eaton, Haverhill, Mass., 1638; prep. edn., Foxcroft (Me.) Acad., student Northern Ill. Normal Sch. 2 yrs.; M.Di., Highland Park Coll., Des Moines, Ia., 1893; M.Sc., Hopkinton, Ia., 1900; m. Mary E. Johnson, Nov. 22, 1902; 1 son, Lewis Thomas. Supt. schs., Greeley, Ia., 1891-92, Earlville, 1893-95; county supt. schs., Delaware Co., Ia., 1895-1900; prof. history and English, Highland Park Coll., 1900, dean normal dept., 1902-04; pres. Coll. of Montana, Deer Lodge, Mont., 1904-08; a founder, 1908, and thereafter ednl. dir. Billings Poly. Inst. Republican. Conglist. Home: Billings, Mont. Died Mar. 14, 1934.

EATON, Marquis, lawyer; b. Mattawan, Mich., Apr. 5, 1876; s. Gen. Charles L. and Nellie (Joiner) E.; ed. U. of Mich., 1893-95; m. Jacquette Hunter, June 8, 1904. Admitted to practice in Mich., 1898, Ill., 1901, U.S. Sup. Ct., 1903; asst. reporter Mich. Sup. Ct., 1898-1901; mem. Cody & Eaton, 1901-09; became mem. Defrees, Buckingham, Ritter, Campbell & Eaton, Jan. 1, 1910, title later, Defrees, Buckingham & Eaton; official atty. for city treas., Chicago, 1909-10. Mem. state bd. examiners in accountancy, 1912-15. Dir. Chicago Trust Co., U. State Bank. Originator, 1908, and thereafter pres. Sane Fourth Assn. (first organized expression of movement for constructive celebration of Independence Day). Chmn. Chicago Chapter Am. Red Cross, 1917—; dir. United Charities of Chicago. Infant Welfare Soc. Decorated Commendatore Italian Crown for war services. Consul general for Bulgaria. Republican. Conglist. Mem. Chicago Congl. Brotherhood (pres. 1910), Chicago Congl. Club (pres. 1914-15). Mason. Author: The Lawyer and the Trust Company, 1911. Home: Chicago, Ill. Died Sept. 19, 1925.

EATON, Seymour, author; b. Epping, Ont., Can., 1859; taught dist. sch. 7 yrs.; m. Jennie V. Adair, Jan. 15, 1884. Resident Boston, 1886-92. Founder Booklovers and Tabard Inn libraries in U.S. and Great Britain and of The Booklovers' Magazine. For 5 yrs. dir. Drexel Inst.; daily contbr. Chicago Record, 4 yrs. Author: The Roosevelt Bears; The Teddy Bears Musical Comedy; Traveling Bears, 1927. On staff of the New York Times. Home: Lansdowne, Pa. Died Mar. 13, 1916.

EATON, Thomas Treadwell, Bapt. clergyman; b. Murfreesborough, Tenn., Nov. 16, 1845; s. Joseph H. and Esther M.E.; grad. Washington and Lee Univ., 1867 (D.D., Washington and Lee Univ.; LL.D., Southwestern Bapt. Univ., Jackson, Tenn.); ordained ministry, 1870; m. Alice Roberts, June 1872. Held pastorates at Lebanon and Chattanooga, Tenn., and Petersburg, Va.; now pastor Walnut St. Bapt. Ch., Louisville, Ky. Trustee Georgetown Coll., Southern Bapt. Theol. Sem.; mem. Am. Soc. Religious Edn., Am. Sunday Assn.; moderator Ky. Bapt. Gen. Assn., 1901-03. Editor The Western Recorder (religious weekly), 1887—. Home: Louisville, Ky. Died 1907.

EATON, William Colgate, commodore U.S.N.; b. Hamilton, N.Y., Feb. 4, 1851; s. George W. (D.D., LL.D.) and Eliza H. (Boardman) E.; A.B., Colgate U., 1869, A.M., 1872, Ph.D., 1881; grad. U.S. Naval Acad., 1874; m. Lizzie Blish, Sept. 6, 1890 (died 1929); 1 son, William W. Commd. chief engr., U.S.N., June 1, 1895, capt., Nov. 18, 1907. Served as fleet engineer Pacific Squadron, 1899-1900; detailed as head dept. of engring., Colgate U., 1888-90; apptd. by Viceroy Li Hung Chang, examiner of naval engring. graduates, Imperial U., Tientsin, China, 1892; retired as commodore at own request, June 30, 1908. On war duty as inspr. engring. material, Cincinnati, 1917-19. Home: Hamilton, N.Y. Died June 1, 1936.

EAVES, George, clergyman; b. Stratford-on-Avon, Eng., July 30, 1858; s. William Barnes and Aminda (Bennett) E.; ed. Bristol Coll. (Bapt. Sem.) and Univ. Coll., Bristol, 1879-84; D.D., Rollins Coll., Fla., 1911; m. Clare Vaughan Curtis, of Southampton, Eng., Nov. 29, 1897. Missionary, Japan, of (English) Bapt. Missionary Soc., 1884-89; came to U.S., Dec. 1889; founded church in S. Denver, Colo., 1891; founded Baptist Record, 1892. Joined Congl. Ch., Denver, 1894; served mountain parishes (Creede, Silverton) until removal to Tex., 1903; built Central Ch., Dallas, 1903; pastor Pilgrim Ch., Birmingham, Ala., 1907-12. Founder, 1910, sec., 1912—, Anti-Tuberculosis Assn., Birmingham; pres. Ala. Sociol. Congress, 1913-14; sec. Ala. Anti-Tuberculosis League, 1914-18. Mgr. welfare dept. Southern States Life Ins. Co. Home: Birmingham, Ala. Died Nov. 26, 1926.

EBERLE, Edward Walter, naval officer; b. Denton, Tex., Aug. 17, 1864; s. Joseph and Mary E.; grad. U.S. Naval Acad., 1885; m. Tazie Harrison, Oct. 24, 1889; 1 son, Edward Randolph. Ensign, June 12, 1896; promoted through grades to rear admiral, Feb. 1, 1918. Served on Oregon, Spanish-Am. War, 1898, and in Philippine insurrection, 1899; Asiatic Fleet, 1899, and Atlantic Fleet, 1903-05; Naval War Coll., 1905; Bd. of Inspection and Survey, Navy Dept., 1905-07; exec. officer Louisiana, 1907-08; comd. Naval Training Sta., San Francisco, Calif., 1908-10; comd. Milwaukee, 1910, Wheeling, 1910-11; comd. Atlantic Torpedo Fleet, 1911-13; at Naval War College, Newport, R.I., 1913-14; comd. U.S.S. Washington and Naval force in Santo Domingo, 1914; comdg. Navy Yard and Naval Gun Factory, Washington, 1914-15; supt. U.S. Naval Acad., 1915-19; comd. Battleship Div. Five, Atlantic Fleet, 1919-20; comdr. Battleship Div. 7, Atlantic Fleet, 1920-21; comdr. in chief Pacific Fleet with rank of Admiral, 1921-22; comdr. in chief Battle Fleet, 1922-23; chief of naval operations, Navy Dept., 1923—. Home: Washington, D.C. Died July 6, 1929.

EBERSOLE, Ezra Christian, lawyer; b. Mt. Pleasant, Pa., Oct. 18, 1840; s. Jacob and Catherine (Keister) E.; A.B., Amherst, 1862, A.M., 1875; (LL.D., Western [now Leander Clark] Coll., 1894); m. Emma Smith, July 10, 1895. Prof. mathematics and astronomy, 1863-65, pres., 1867-68, Western Coll.; adj. prof. Latin and Greek, State U. of Ia., 1868-70; admitted to bar, 1870; in practice at Toledo, Ia., 1873-1912. Atty. for Tama Co., 1874-82; Ia. Supreme Ct. reporter, 1882-90; editor Ia. Code of 1897, by unanimous vote of Legislature; mem. Ia. State Bd. of Law Examiners, 1901-12. Republican. Author: Encyclopædia of Iowa Law, 1900; Negotiable Instruments Law of Iowa, 1903. Retired. Home: Toledo, Ia. Died July 14, 1919.

ECCLES, Robert G(ibson), M.D.; b. Scotland, Jan. 1, 1848; s. David and Isabella E.; ed. in schools in Scotland, Ireland, Mo., Kan., etc.; M.D., L.I. Coll., 1881; Pharm.D., Scio Coll., 1903; m. Mary Hance, Sept. 1876; 1 son, David Charles. Was chemist U.S. Dept. Indian Affairs, prof. and dean Brooklyn Coll. of Pharmacy, eidtor Merck's Archives, and mem. com. of revision of U.S. Pharmacopœia. Discoverer of the alkaloids calycanthine, glaucosine, etc., and of calycanthic acid; devised the 1900 ofcl. method of assaying pepsin; investigator of effects of drugs on peptic digestion. Fellow A.A.A.S., New York Acad. Sciences. Author: Food Preservatives, 1905; Darwinism and Diabetes, 1908; Letters from Foreign Lands, 1908; Darwinism and Malaria, 1909; Parasitism and Natural Selection, 1909; Touring the Lands Where Medical Science Evolved, 1909; Darwinism and Anaphylaxis, 1911. Home: Brooklyn, N.Y. Died June 9, 1934.

ECHOLS, Charles Patton, army officer; b. Huntsville, Ala., Sept. 6, 1867; s. William Holding and Mary Beirne (Patton) E.; grad. U.S. Mil. Acad., 1891; unmarried. Commd. additional 2d lt. engrs., June 12, 1891; 2d lt., Oct. 4, 1894; 1st lt., Jan. 6, 1896; in command of A Co. U.S. Engrs. in 3d expdn. to Philippines in War with Spain, 1898; asso. prof. mathematics, U.S. Mil. Acad., Nov. 1898, prof., 1904—; on detached service visiting foreign schools, July 1905-June 1906; lt. col., 1904; col., 1914; observer with Allied Armies in France, July-Sept. 1918; retired from active service Sept. 1931. Home: Englewood, N.J. Died May 21, 1940.

ECHOLS, John Warnock, lawyer; b. Clarksville, Pa., May 13, 1849; s. James and Mary E.; ed. Westminster Coll. and Lafayette Coll.; traveling salesman for wholesale drug houses, 1870-73; mem. Echols & Co., cotton factors, Augusta, Ga., 1873-77; studied law with Gen. Robert Toombs, 1877-79; admitted to Supreme Court U.S., also Pa., Ga., Va. and D.C. bars; m. Mary Lou, d. Hon. Joseph H. Echols, Dec. 1874; children—Robert Bonner, Helen (dec.), John (dec.), Joseph (dec.); m. 2d, Katrina, d. late Maj. O. E. Hine, of Vienna, Va., Oct. 10, 1906; 1 son, Warnock (dec.). Practiced Lexington, Ga., 1879-88, Pittsburgh, 1888-92, Atlanta, Ga., 1892-96, then in Washington, D.C., and Virginia. Supreme pres. Am. Protective Assn., 1896-97; propr. The Republic, published weekly in Washington, 1896-99; mem. exec. com. Scotch-Irish Soc. of America several yrs. and managed its congresses at Pittsburgh, 1890, and Atlanta, 1892. Asst. librarian, A.L.A. War Service Library, Camp Meade, Md., Sept. 1918-Feb. 1919, Camp Hancock, Ga., Feb.-April 1919; librarian, Camp Gordon, Ga., Apr. 1919-June 1, 1920. Unitarian. Democrat. Mason. Home: Vienna, Va. Died Mar. 31, 1932.

ECHOLS, William Holding, Jr., univ. prof.; b. San Antonio, Tex., Dec. 2, 1859; s. William Holding and Mary Beirne (Patton) E.; B.S., C.E., U. of Va., 1882; m. Mary Elizabeth Blakey, Sept. 9, 1885 (died 1894); children—Jane Johnston, William Holding (dec.), Angus Blakey, Oliver Patton, George Blakey; m. 2d, Elizabeth Mitchell Harrison, June 15, 1897; children—Lelia Harrison (dec.), Marion Patton, Constance Tucker (dec.), Gessner Harrison, Robert Lewis. Asst. engr. in constrn. Vicksburg, Shreveport & Pacific Ry., 1882; resident engr., location, constrn. and bridgework, Louisville, New Orleans & Tex. Ry., 1883; mining engr. and supt. N. & O. Mining Co., Colo., 1884; 1st resident engr. Memphis & Birmingham Ry., Ala., 1886; prof. applied mathematics, 1887-91, dir. 1888-91, Mo. Sch. of Mines; adj. prof. mathematics, 1891-96, prof., 1896—, U. of Va. Democrat. Episcopalian. Author: Differential and Integral Calculus, 1902, 1908. Died Sept. 25, 1934.

ECHOLS, William Joseph, banker; b. Tate Co., Miss., Aug. 3, 1872; s. William Joseph and Elizabeth Trader (Carter) E.; prep. edn. Pantops Acad., Charlottesville, Va.; U. of Va., 1891-93; m. Fannie Sandels, July 1901. Pres. Merchants Nat. Bank, Ft. Smith, 1904—; v.p. William Echols Dry Goods Co., Ark. Warehouse Co. Democrat. Mem. Christian (Disciples) Ch. Home: Fort Smith, Ark. Died Sept. 1933.

ECKARD, Leighton Wilson, clergyman; b. Savannah, Ga., Sept. 23, 1845; s. Rev. James Read and Margaret (Bayard) E.; A.B., Lafayette Coll., 1866, later A.M. (D.D., 1891); grad. Princeton Theol. Sem., 1869; master orator, 1869; m. Elizabeth Abbott Longstreth, June 3, 1869. Ordained Presbyn. ministry, 1869; missionary Shantung, China, 1869-75; pastor, Abington, Pa., 1875-91, Easton, Pa., 1891-1906; sec. Atlantic agency, Am. Bible Soc., 1906—. Author: A History of Abington Church, 1714 to 1876. Home: Philadelphia, Pa. Died Nov. 16, 1925.

ECKELS, James Herron, comptroller of currency, U.S., 1893-97; b. Princeton, Ill., Nov. 22, 1858; ed. in city public and high schools, graduating 1876; grad. Albany (N.Y.) Law School, 1880; practiced law at Ottawa, Ill., 1881-93; apptd., April 3, 1893, comptroller of currency. Democrat. Made many speeches on currency question and became prominent as gold-standard advocate; in 1896 affiliated with Nat. (gold-standard) Democrats. Remained in office until end of 1897, becoming, Jan. 1, 1898, pres. Commercial Nat. Bank, Chicago. Died 1907.

ECKERSALL, Walter H., newspaperman; b. Chicago, Ill., June 17, 1887; s. Walter and Mary (Killerlain) E.; ed. Hyde Park High Sch., Chicago, and U. of Chicago. Began as sports writer, Chicago Tribune, 1907; now football expert same paper, chooses All-American football team annually. Home: Chicago, Ill. Died Mar. 24, 1930.

ECKERT, Thomas Thompson, chmn. bd. Western Union Telegraph Co.; b. St. Clairsville, O., Apr. 23, 1825; learned telegraphy; supervised construction, 1852, and became supt. of line, Pittsburgh to Chicago, so remaining, with extended jurisdiction, when line became part of Western Union Telegraph Co.; resigned, 1859, becoming supt. of a gold mining co. in N.C. until Civil War broke out, when he went to Cincinnati. Supt. mil. telegraph, Dept. of Potomac, with rank of capt.; later gen. supt. mil. telegraph, with rank of maj.; bvtd. lt. col., col. and brig. gen. vols., Mar. 13, 1865, "for meritorious and distinguished services." Asst. Sec. of War, July 27, 1866-Feb. 28, 1867. Gen. supt. eastern div., Western Union Telegraph Co., 1866-75; pres. Atlantic & Pacific Telegraph Co., 1875-81; pres. Am. Union Telegraph Co., 1880-81; v.p. and gen. mgr. Western Union Telegraph Co., 1881-92, and pres. from 1892, later chmn. bd. Home: New York, N.Y. Died 1910.

ECKFELDT, Thomas Hooper, head master; b. Phila., May 5, 1853; s. Adam and Sarah Malvina (Hooper) E.; A.B., Wesleyan U., Conn., 1881; student Am. Sch. Classical Studies, Athens, Greece, 1884-85, U. of Munich, 1885-86; A.M., Harvard, 1897; m. Grace Blanchard Weed, June 17, 1889. Asst. prin. Middletown (Conn.) High Sch., 1881-83; tutor in Greek, Wesleyan U., 1883-84; head master Friends' Acad., New Bedford, Mass., 1887-1900, Concord (Mass.) Sch., 1900-07, St. Andrew's Sch., Concord, Mass., 1907-14. Home: Cambridge, Mass. Died Apr. 22, 1923.

ECKHART, Bernard Albert, mfr.; b. Alsace, France, 1852; s. Jacob and Eva (Root) E.; arrived with parents in U.S., in infancy; grad. from a coll. at Milwaukee, 1868; m. Katie L. Johnston, Dec. 25, 1874. Chicago rep. of Eagle Milling Co., Milwaukee, 1870-74; founded firm of Eckhart & Swan, which later became Eckhart & Swan Milling Co., of which was pres.; became pres. B. A. Eckhart Milling Co.; dir. Continental Ill. Bank & Trust Co., Continental Ill. Co., Harris Trust & Savings Bank, Chicago Title & Trust Co., Armour & Co., Montgomery Ward & Co., etc. Mem. Ill. Senate, 35th and 36th Gen. Assemblies (1887-89); trustee Sanitary Dist. of Chicago, 1891-1900 (pres. bd. 1896-1900); pres. bd. West Chicago Park Commrs., 1905-08; del. and chmn. Com. on Rules, Procedure and Gen. Plans Chicago Charter Conv., 1905. Assisted in organizing and officer 1st Regt. Ill. N.G.; a.d.c. with rank of col. on staff of Gov. Deneen, 1906-13. Dir. Chicago Bd. Trade, 1888-91; 1st pres. Millers' Nat. Fedn., 1902-04; pres. Ill. Mfrs.' Assn., 1903; v.p. Nat. Council of Commerce, 1908. U.S. del. Internat. Congress Edn., Vienna, 1910; v.p., treas. Lewis Inst. Tech., Chicago; trustee Shedd Aquarium Soc.; life gov. mem. Art Inst. Chicago; mem. Ill. State R.R. and Warehouse Commn., 1907-13; chmn. Ill.-Wis. Milling Div. of U.S. Food Administration; dir. and mem. exec. com. Citizens War Bd. of Chicago. Asst. treas. Rep. Nat. Com. Mem. exec. com. capital issues com. of Federal Reserve Bank of 7th Dist. Home: Lake Forest, Ill., and Chicago. Died May 11, 1931.

ECKLES, Clarence Henry, prof. dairy husbandry; b. Marshall County, Ia., Apr. 14, 1875; s. Charles and Elvira A. (Powers) E.; B.S. in Agr., Ia. State Coll. 1895, M.Sc., 1897 (D.Sc., 1916); univs. of Wisconsin 1897-98, Göttingen, 1904-05, Berne, Switzerland, 1905; m. Alice L. Smith, Dec. 14, 1898; children—Doris L., Charles E., Ruth L., Rachel (dec.). Asst. in dairy husbandry, Ia. State Coll., 1901; prof. dairy husbandry, U. of Mo., 1901-19; chief dairy husbandry div. U. of Minn., 1919—. Conglist. Author: Dairy Cattle and Milk Production, 1911; Dairy Farming, 1916; Milk and Milk Products, 1929. Home: St. Paul, Minn. Died 1933.

ECKLEY, William Thomas, anatomist; b. Lancaster, Ia., Sept. 8, 1855; s. Thomas R. and Honora Demming (Hart) E.; ed. lit. dept., U. of Iowa; grad., M.D., U. of Iowa, 1884; m. Mary E. Woodbridge; m. 2d, Corrinne Buford Cheek. Prof. anatomy, Coll. Phys. and Surg., Keokuk, Ia., 1890-94; later prof. anatomy, North Western Univ. Dental Sch.; prof. anatomy, Woman's Med. Coll.; demonstrator anatomy, Coll. Phys. and Surg., Chicago, and prof. anatomy, Chicago Post-Grad. Med. Sch.; became prof. anatomy, Chicago Clin. Sch., Chicago Sch. Anatomy and Physiology, and in med. and dental depts. U. of Ill. Was in charge anat. and pathol. exhibits at St. Paul, 1901, Saratoga, 1902, New Orleans, 1903, and at La. Purchase Expn., 1904. Republican. Author: Practical Anatomy, 1899, 1903; Anatomy of Head and Neck, 1890; Anatomical Nomenclature. Died 1908.

ECKMAN, George Peck, clergyman; b. Gouldsboro, Pa., Jan. 8, 1860; s. John G. and Margaret L. (Hile) E.; student Wesleyan U., Conn., class of 1884, A.M., 1891; B.D., Drew Theol. Sem., N.J., 1886; Ph.D., New York U., 1897; (D.D., Syracuse, 1902, Wesleyan, 1906; LL.D., Syracuse U., 1913); m. May Townley, Oct. 7, 1891. Ordained M.E. ministry, 1886; pastor, Metuchen, N.J., 1886-87, South Orange, 1888-90, First Ch., Orange, 1891-93, Morristown, 1894-96, St. Paul's Ch., New York, 1897-1912; editor Christian Advocate, New York, 1912-15; pastor Elm Park Ch., Scranton, Pa., 1915—. Trustee Drew Theol. Sem. Mem. Bd. of Foreign Missions M.E. Ch. Republican. Author: Passion Week Sermons, 1909; The Literary Primacy of the Bible, 1915; When Christ Comes Again, 1917. Home: Scranton, Pa. Died June 28, 1920.

ECKOFF, William Julius, educator, author; b. Hamburg, Germany, Mar. 24, 1853; s. Henry and Angelica (Schroeder) E.; grad. Lehrerseminar, Hamburg, 1873, Sch. of Pedagogy, U. City of New York, Pd.D., 1891, Ph.D., Columbia Univ., 1894; m. Alice Mary Lockwood, 1892. Engaged in teaching, 1873—; dir. del Colegio Nacional, Granada, Nicaragua, 1883; prof. philosophy and pedagogy U. of Colo., 1893; prof. pedagogy U. of Ill., 1894; prin. Herbart Prep. Sch., Suffern, N.Y., 1895; prin. Woodycliff Sch., South Orange, N.J., 1902. Author: Kant's Inaugural Dissertation (trans. with introduction), 1894; Herbart's A B C of Sense-Perception (edit. of graded series of essays of Herbart), 1896. Home: Newark, N.J. Died 1908.

ECKSTEIN, Louis, businessman; b. Milwaukee, Wis., Feb. 10, 1865; s. Samuel E. and Anna (Bloch) E.; ed. pub. schs.; m. Elsie Snydacker, 1900. Was in ry. service with Wis. Central R.R. for 10 yrs. until entering firm of Stumer, Rosenthal & Eckstein, millinery; firm later changed into various corps.; now pres. Buck & Rayner, North Am. Bldg. Restaurant Co., The Ravinia Co.; one of owners North Am. Bldg. and Metropolitan Bldg. Home: Chicago, Ill. Died Nov. 21, 1935.

EDDINGER, Wallace, actor; b. Albany, N.Y., July 14, 1881; s. Lawrence and May E.; prep. edn. Columbia Inst. and Hamilton Inst., N.Y. City; matriculated at Columbia U. On stage from childhood. Star of many New York productions. Died Jan. 8, 1929.

"EDDINGTON, Jane" (Caroline Maddocks Beard), writer; b. East Eddington, Me., Apr. 2, 1866; d. John and Eliza Anne (Thomas) Maddocks; A.B., Wellesley, 1892; A.M., U. of Chicago, 1895; post-grad. study same, 1899-1900. Dean of women, Washburn Coll., Topeka, Kan., 1896-1899; writer for Chicago Tribune,

1910-30; free lance writer, 1930—. Hon. mem. Colonial Coverlet Guild of America. Protestant. Author: The Tribune Cook Book (syndicated as The Cook Book). Home: E. Holden, and Bangor, Me. Died Apr. 5, 1938.

EDDY, Alfred Delavan, lawyer; b. Bellona, N.Y., June 3, 1846; s. Rev. Alfred (Presbyn. clergyman) and Catherine H. (Wilcox) E.; removed to Ill., 1856; served 6 mos. in Co. D, 134th Ill. Inf., 1864; student U. of Chicago; LL.B., Union Coll. of Law, Chicago, 1879; m. Caroline H. Silvey, Oct. 7, 1869. In practice at Chicago, 1878—. Republican. Home: Chicago, Ill. Died Oct. 3, 1918.

EDDY, Arthur Jerome, lawyer; b. Flint, Mich., Nov. 5, 1859; s. Jerome and Ellen M. E.; studied law at Harvard; m. Lucy C. Orrell, June 3, 1890. Admitted to Ill. bar, 1890, and began practice at Chicago. Gold Democrat. Author: Delight, the Soul of Art; Recollections of James McNeill Whistler; The New Competition, 1912; Cubists, and Post-Impressionism, 1914; Property, 1921. Home: Chicago, Ill. Died July 21, 1920.

EDDY, Clarence, organist; b. Greenfield, Mass., June 23, 1851; s. George Sanger and Silence (Cheney) E.; began musical edn. at age of 11; studied under Dudley Buck at Hartford, Conn., 1867; organist Bethany Ch., Montpelier, Vt., 1868-71; studied piano under Loeschorn and organ under August Haupt, Berlin, 1871-74; married. Organist First Congl. Ch., Chicago, 1874-76; afterward organist and choirmaster First Presbyn. Ch., 17 yrs., and became dir. Hershey Sch. of Musical Art, 1875. Played at Vienna Expn., 1873, Centennial Expn., 1876, Paris Expn., 1889, Chicago Expn., 1893, Pan-Am. Expn., 1901, St. Louis Expn., 1904, Panama P.I. Expn., 1915. Author of organ works: The Church and Concert Organist (3 vols.); The Organ in Church, and Concert Pieces for the Organ; Pipe Organ Method (6 vols.). Home: Winnetka, Ill. Died Jan. 10, 1937.

EDDY, Forrest Greenwood, dentist; b. Providence, R.I., Sept. 8, 1853; s. Thomas Whitman and Sarah Maria Gano (Smith) E.; ed. Univ. Grammar Sch. and Brown U., 1870-72 (A.B., 1907); D.M.D., Harvard, 1875; m. Elenora Frances Greene, Dec. 29, 1875; 1 dau., Lillian May (Mrs. S. Harold Greene). In practice as dentist, Providence, 1875-79, at Lancaster, Wis., 1882-84, at Providence, 1884—. Instr. operative dentistry, Harvard Dental Dept., Oct. 1888-1916, and asst. prof., 1916—. Appointed to R.I. State Bd. of Registration in Dentistry, 1905, and elected pres. of same. Fellow Am. Coll. Dentists. Republican. Conglist. Home: Buttonwood, R.I. Died May 17, 1939.

EDDY, Frank Woodman, merchant, mfr.; b. Warsaw, N.Y., July 29, 1851; s. Rev. Zachary (D.D.) and Malvina R. (Cochran) E.; Collegiate and Poly. Inst., Brooklyn; Williams Coll., Mass.; m. Florence Taylor, Sept. 10, 1879. Began in employ of wholesale hardware firm of Mulford & Sprague, New York; went to Calif., 1873; located in Detroit, 1875; mem. H. D. Edwards & Co., rubber goods, mill supplies and marine hardware, 1876—; pres. Nat. Can Co.; v.p. Detroit Trust Co.; treas. H. V. Hartz Co. (Cleveland). Trustee Detroit Gen. Hosp. Republican. Conglist. Home: Grosse Pointe, Mich. Died June 12, 1914.

EDDY, Harrison Prescott, civil engr.; b. Millbury, Mass., Apr. 29, 1870; s. William Justus and Martha Augusta (Prescott) E.; B.S. Worcester Poly. Inst., 1891, hon. D.Engring. 1930; m. Minnie Locke Jones, June 1, 1892; children—Willard Jones (dec.), Harrison Prescott, Randolph Locke, Charlotte Frances. Supt. sewage treatment works, Worcester, 1891-92; supt. sewer dept., 1892-1907; mem. Metcalf & Eddy, May 1907—; has been cons. engr. on sewage, drainage, etc., to cities of Boston, Louisville, Milwaukee, New York, Dayton (O), Cincinnati, Pittsburgh, Portland, Ore., San Francisco, Cleveland, Chicago. Mason. Author: (with Leonard Metcalf) American Sewerage Practice, Vol. I, Design of Sewers, 1914, Vol. II, Construction of Sewers, 1915, Vol. III, Disposal of Sewage, 1915; Sewerage and Sewage Disposal (with Leonard Metcalf), 1922. Home: Newton Centre, Mass. Died June 15, 1937.

EDDY, Henry Turner, univ. dean; b. Stoughton, Mass., June 9, 1844; s. Rev. Henry and Sarah Hayward (Torrey) E.; A.B., Yale, 1867, Ph.B., Sheffield Scientific Sch., 1868, A.M. 1870; C.E., Cornell, 1870, Ph.D., 1872; studied at U. of Berlin and Physikalische Inst., Berlin, 1879; Sorbonne and Collége de France, Paris, 1880; (LL.D., Center Coll., 1892; Sc.D., Yale, 1912); m. Sebella Elizabeth Taylor, Jan. 4, 1870. Instr. in field work, Sheffield Scientific Sch., 1867-68; instr. Latin and mathematics, U. of Tenn., 1868-69; asst. prof. mathematics and civ. engring., Cornell, 1869-73; adj. prof. mathematics, Princeton, 1873-74; prof. mathematics and astronomy and civ. engring. 1874-90, dean academic faculty, 1874-77, 1884-89, acting pres. and pres.-elect, 1890, U. of Cincinnati; pres. Rose Poly. Inst., 1891-94; prof. engring. and mechanics, 1894-1907, head prof. mathematics and mechanics Coll. Engring., 1907-12, dean Grad. Sch., 1906-12, prof. and

dean emeritus, 1912—, U. of Minn. Author: Concrete Steel Construction (with C. A. P. Turner), 1914, new edit., 1919. Home: Minneapolis, Minn. Died 1921.

EDDY, Mary Baker Glover, discoverer and founder of Christian Science; b. Bow, N.H., July 16, 1821; d. (youngest child) Mark and Abigail Barnard (Ambrose) Baker; (father died 1865, mother died 1849); ed. Ipswich (N.H.) Sem. and by pvt. tutors; studied natural philosophy, chemistry, astronomy, etc., and Latin, Greek, Hebrew and French languages; m. George Washington Glover, Dec. 1843 (died 1844); 2d, Dr. Daniel Patterson, 1853 (divorced 1873, died 1896); 3d, Asa Gilbert Eddy, Jan. 1, 1877 (died 1883). Baptized a Congregationalist and remained mem. Congl. Ch. until 1879; discovered Christian Science, 1866; began to teach the "Science of Mind Healing," 1867; established Mass. Metaphysical Coll., Boston, 1881 (had about 4,000 students from 1881 until it closed, 1889); founded the first Christian Science Assn., 1876, the Nat. Christian Science Assn., 1886; preached in Bapt. Tabernacle, Boston, 1878; organized The First Church of Christ, Scientist, Boston, 1879; presented a lot in Boston to the ch. and an edifice was erected thereon, 1894, costing $200,000, known as the "Mother Church," of which she was made pastor emeritus; also presented to Concord, N.H., a ch. costing $200,000. Established Christian Science Journal, 1883, and was editor several yrs., Christian Science Sentinel, 1898, and Der Herold der Christian Science, 1902. Awarded grand prize and a diploma of honor by French govt. as founder of Christian Science movement; also decorated Officier d'Academie, Nov. 1907. Author: Science and Health with Key to the Scriptures (the text-book of Christian Science), 1875 (many edits.); Christian Healing, 1886; People's Idea of God, 1886; Unity of Good, 1891; Rudimental Divine Science, 1891; No and Yes, 1891; Retrospection and Introspection, 1892; Communion Hymn; Feed My Sheep; Miscellaneous Writings, 1896; Christ and Christmas, 1897; Pulpit and Press, 1898; Christian Science versus Pantheism, 1898; Message to the Mother Church, 1900; Our Leader's Message, 1901; Truth versus Error, 1905. Died 1910.

EDDY, Richard, Universalist minister; b. Providence, R.I., June 21, 1828; s. Richard and Martha (James) E.; academic edn. Clinton, N.Y. (S.T.D., Tufts Coll.); chaplain 60th N.Y. vols., 1861-63; pres. Universalist Hist. Soc., 1877—; editor Universalist Quarterly Review, 1884-91; editor Universalist Register, 1887—; Prohibitionist. Was pastor Universalist Ch. at Gloucester, Mass.; retired. Author: History of Universalism in America, 1636-1886 (2 vols.), 1884, 1886; History of Universalism, A.D. 120-1890 (in vol. X, Am. Ch. Hist. series), 1894. Died 1906.

EDDY, Spencer, diplomatist; b. Chicago, Ill., June 18, 1874; s. of Augustus and Abby Louise (Spencer) E.; A.B., Harvard, 1896; post-grad. studies univs. of Berlin and Heidelberg; m. Lurline Elizabeth Spreckels, Apr. 28, 1906. Pvt. sec. to late Hon. John Hay, while ambassador to Great Britain, 1897-98; clerk, Dept. of State, 1898-99; 3d sec. Am. Embassy, London, 1899; 2d sec., Paris, 1899-1901; 1st sec. Constantinople, 1901-03 (chargé d'affaires, 1 yr.), St. Petersburg, 1903-06 (chargé d'affaires, 1 yr.), Berlin, 1906-07; E.E. and M.P. to Argentine Republic, 1908-09, to Roumania, Servia and Bulgaria, Jan.-Sept. 1909; resigned Lt. comdr. U.S.N.R.F., Mar. 6, 1917, in active service, later promoted comdr. Died Oct. 7, 1939.

EDDY, William Abner, expert in kite photography; b. New York, Jan. 28, 1850; s. Rev. H. J. (D.D.) and Amanda (Doubleday) E.; boyhood at Belvidere, Ill.; grad. Belvidere High Sch., prep. course Chicago Univ.; m. Cynthia S. Huggins, Apr. 21, 1887. Engaged in business as accountant, 1869—. Began aerial and kite experiments in July, 1890; took mid-air kite photograph in Western Hemisphere, May 30, 1895; mid-air temperature in the world, from kites, taken Feb. 4, 1891. Experimented extensively with atmospheric electricity drawn from kite sustained wire, and with flying machine aeroplanes dismissed from kites' lines in mid-air. Home: Bayonne, N.J. Died 1909.

EDEBOHLS, George Michael, surgeon; b. New York, May 8, 1853; s. Henry and Catherine (Brull) E.; grad. A.B., 1871, A.M., 1886, LL.D., 1903, St. Johns Coll., Fordham, N.Y.; M.D., Coll. Phys. and Surg. (Columbia U.), 1875; m. Barbara Leyendecker, Sept. 19, 1882. House physician and surgeon St. Francis Hosp., New York, 1875-79, gynecologist same, 1887-1903; cons. surg., 1903—. Prof. diseases of women, N.Y. Post-Grad. Med. Sch. and Hosp., 1893—; cons. gynecologist St. John's Hosp. and Nyack Hosp. Fellow New York Acad. Medicine, Am. Gynecol. Soc. Catholic. Author: The Surgical Treatment of Bright's Disease, 1904. Died 1908.

EDELHERTZ, Bernard, lawyer; b. Kharkoff, Russia, Feb. 17, 1880; s. Mordecai and Rebecca (Rubenstein) E.; brought to U.S., 1893; prep. edn. Gymnasium, Kharkoff; LL.B., New York U., 1900, LL.M., 1901; m. Clara Greenberg, May 1, 1904; children—

Mildred Evelyn (Mrs. Mitchell Salem Fisher), Helen Ruth. Admitted to N.Y. bar, 1901, and began practice in N.Y. City; asst. to atty. gen. of U.S., 1917-22; under leave of absence, visited Poland, 1919, to investigate outrages committed on Jews in that country and while there joined Am. Anti-Typhus Commn.; on return, contributed series of articles describing conditions in Poland; visited Russia, 1927, to study Jewish agrl. colonies. Purchased controlling interest, 1916, of Am. Hebrew Magazine, published by The Am. Hebrew Pub. Co. of which is dir., sec. and treas.; pres., treas. Cyclopedia Judaica, Inc.; dir., sec., treas. Independent Am. Jewish Pub. Co. Identified with motion pictures from 1921 and a leader in securing the uniform contract and the arbitration boards, serving as chmn. Uniform Contract Com. and Arbitration Bd. Com. Died July 17, 1931.

EDENBORN, William, capitalist; b. Westphalia, Prussia, Mar. 20, 1848; s. John J. and Antinette (Hessmer) E.; ed. in Prussia; came to U.S., 1867; m. Sarah Drain, Oct. 5, 1876. Mechanic, St. Louis, 1869-71; pres. St. Louis Wire Mill Co., 1877-82; later pres. Consolidated Steel & Wire Co., until 1898; v.p. and mem. exec. com. Am. Steel & Wire Co., 1898-1901; mem. exec. and advisory coms. U.S. Steel Corp., 1901-04; pres. La. Ry. & Navigation Co., New Orleans, 1903—; pres. Pittsburgh & Southern Coal Co. Died May 14, 1926.

EDES, Henry Herbert, mgr. Conveyancers Title Ins. Co., of Boston, 1889—; b. Charlestown, Mass., Mar. 29, 1849; s. Henry Augustus and Sarah Louisa (Lincoln) E.; ed. Charlestown grammar and high schs.; hon. member Harvard chapter Phi Beta Kappa, 1898; A.M., causa honoris, Harvard, 1906; mem. Visiting Com., history, Harvard, 1907—; editor-in-chief of the Harvard Quinquennial catalogue, 1916-1921; in commercial life, Boston, 1865-89; m. Grace, d. William Cross Williamson, of Boston, Dec. 2, 1896. Fellow Am. Acad. Arts and Sciences (council, treas.). He has arranged and bound under municipal contract the MS. records and archives of Charlestown (1630-1847) in more than 100 vols. Editor: Wyman's Genealogies and Estates of Charlestown (2 vols.), 1879; Vol. II, Foote's Annals of King's Chapel, Boston, 1896. Unitarian. Mugwump. Home: Cambridge, Mass. Died Oct. 13, 1922.

EDES, Robert Thaxter, physician; b. Eastport, Me., Sept. 23, 1838; s. Richard S. and Mary (Cushing) E.; A.B., Harvard, 1858, M.D., 1861; m. Elizabeth T. Clarke, Apr. 30, 1867; m. 2d, Anna C. Richardson, Dec. 20, 1881. Asst. surgeon and passed asst. surgeon U.S.N., 1861-65; prof. materia medica, 1870-84, clin. medicine, 1884-86, Harvard Med. Sch.; phys. Boston City Hosp., 1872-86, Garfield Memorial Hosp., Washington, 1889-91; resident phys. Adams Nervine Asylum, 1891-97. Fellow Am. Acad. Arts and Sciences. Companion Mil. Order Loyal Legion. Home: Springfield, Mass. Died Jan. 12, 1923.

EDES, William Cushing, civil engr.; b. Bolton, Mass., Jan. 14, 1856; s. Richard S. and Mary (Cushing) E.; B.S. in Civ. Engring., Mass. Inst. Tech., 1875; m. Mary Burnham, Jan. 1901. Began in employ of Mass. Census Bur., 1875; with Spring Valley Water Co., Calif., 1876-77; surveys for S.P. R.R., in Ariz., N.M. and Tex., 1877-81; gen. engring. practice, in Mass., 1882-86; asst. engr., S.P. and A.,T.&S.F. rys., in Cal., 1886-1907; chief engr. Northwestern Pacific R.R., 1907-14; chmn. Alaskan Engring. Commn., in charge of U.S. Govt. ry. in Alaska, May 1914-Aug. 1919; cons. engr. Alaskan Engring. Commn., Aug. 1919-20; gen. practice as cons. engr., 1920—. Unitarian. Home: San Rafael, Calif. Died June 25, 1922.

EDESON, Robert, actor; b. New Orleans, 1868; s. George R. and Marion (Taliferro) E.; ed. Brooklyn pub. schs.; m. Ellen Burg, actress (died 1906); m. 2d, Georgie Eliot, d. Linn Boyd Porter, July 8, 1908. First appearance, in "Fascination," Park Theatre, New York, 1887; later appeared in "A Night Off," "The Dark Secret," "Incog."; appeared in "Under the Red Robe," 1906; leading man in "The Climbers"; starred in "Soldiers of Fortune," 1902-04; "Ransom's Folly," "Strongheart," 1905-07; "Classmates," 1907; "The Call of the North," 1908; "The Noble Spaniard," 1909; "Fine Feathers," 1913; with Famous Players-Lasky Corp. (moving pictures), 1921—. Home: Hollywood, Calif. Died Mar. 24, 1931.

EDGAR, Charles Bloomfield, newspaperman; b. St. Louis, April 2, 1847; s. Joseph Crowell and Lucy (Dorey) E.; grad. Ky. U., 1872; m. Aurora Drescher, May 24, 1882. Became editor and pub. St. Joseph (Mo.) News, 1894; acquired control of St. Joseph Daily Gazette-Herald, 1900, which he published 2 yrs. in connection with the News; sold the News, 1906; half owner and pub. Lincoln (Neb.) Star, 1906-10; became sole owner Oklahoma City Times, May 1911, and later bought and consolidated with the Times the Daily Pointer and the Free Press; disposed of the Times, 1914, and returned to St. Joseph, Mo., where established The Weekly Review, 1917. Retired 1918. Home: St. Joseph, Mo. Died Dec. 30, 1923.

EDGAR, Charles Leavitt, electrical engr.; b. Griggstown, N.J., Dec. 23, 1860; s. Thomas and Annie (Veghte) E.; A.B., Rutgers Coll., 1882, E.E., 1887, D.Sc., 1927; also LL.D., Tufts College, 1927; m. Annette M. Duclos, June 16, 1886. In employ of Edison Electric Light Co., New York, 1883-87; gen. supt., 1887-90, v.p. and gen. mgr., 1890-1900, pres. and gen. mgr., 1900—, Edison Electric Illuminating Co. of Boston; chmn. bd. N.E. Power Assn. Trustee Rutgers U., Employers Group Associates, Mass. Utilities Associates (exec. com.); dir. Life Extension Inst. Republican. Episcopalian. Home: Brookline, Mass. Died Apr. 14, 1932.

EDGAR, J(ames) Clifton, obstetrician; b. N.Y. City, June 14, 1859; s. James Alexander and Eliza Maria (Coe) E.; Ph.B., Lafayette Coll., 1882, A.M., 1884; M.D., U. Med. Coll. (New York U.), 1885; post-grad. and interne, Royal Frauenklinik, Munich, 1888; m. Ellen Muriel Beatrice Soutter, May 29, 1899. Interne, asst. curator and attending phys. diseases of women, Bellevue Hosp., 1885-87; instr. pathology, 1887-88, lecturer obstetrics, 1888-89, adj. prof., 1889-1900, New York U.; prof. obstetrics and clin. midwifery, Cornell U. Med. Coll., 1900 (emeritus); cons. obstetrician, Bellevue Hosp.; obstet. surgeon, Manhattan Maternity Hosp. and Dispensary. Fellow Am. Coll. Surgeons, N.Y. Acad. Medicine. Club: University. Author: The Practice of Obstetrics, 1903. Home: Greenwich, Conn. Died Apr. 7, 1939.

EDGAR, Randolph, writer; b. Minneapolis, Minn., Aug. 31, 1884; s. William Crowell and Anne Randolph Page (Robinson) E.; ed. Lawrenceville and Harvard; m. Grace Mary Wainwright, Dec. 20, 1915. Contbr. to The Bellman, 1906-19, also to Vanity Fair, The Theatre Magazine, etc.; mem. editorial staff Literary Digest, 1910-11; contbr. Am. pubis. from London, Eng., 1911, 26; dramatic critic and daily column writer St. Paul Pioneer Press, 1924; publicity agt., Minneapolis Symphony Orchestra, 1925-26; with Boston Sunday Advertiser, 1927. Wrote: Frank Norris, 1905; "Iron" (in Bellman Book of Fiction), 1921; Mr. Yeates at Petitpas', 1923; A Record of Old Boats, 1926. Home: Boston, Mass. Died July 10, 1931.

EDGAR, Thomas Delbert, clergyman; b. Coulterville, Ill., Mar. 26, 1868; s. Robert Sinclair (M.D.) and Sarah Jane (Alexander) E.; prep. edn., Coulterville Acad.; student Monmouth (Ill.) Coll., 1889-90; grad. Xenia Theol. Sem., 1897; D.D., Muskingum Coll., 1912; m. Nancy Jane Caruth, Sept. 6, 1892; children—Robert McNeill (dec.), Helen Caruth, Alexander Willis, Thomas Delbert, Ralph Caruth. Ordained ministry U.P. Ch., 1897; pastor successively Morning Sun., O., First Ch., Cambridge, O., until 1905, Second Ch., Wilkinsburg, Pa., 1905—. Mem. Board of Am. Missions U.P. Ch.; rec. sec. Bd. of Ch. Extension; chmn. Evangelistic Com. U.P. Ch., also of Pa. Council of Chs.; mem. Commn. on Evangelism and Life Service of Fed. Council Chs.; dir. Nat. Reform Assn. (ex-pres.); recording sec. Bd. of Administration U.P. Ch. Republican. Rotarian. Home: Wilkinsburg, Pa. Died Feb. 1932.

EDGAR, William Crowell, journalist; b. at La-Crosse, Wis., Dec. 21, 1856; s. Joseph C. and Lucy (Dorey) E.; high sch. edn., St. Louis; m. Anne Randolph Page Robinson, June 6, 1883; children—Randolph, Marjorie. In St. Louis business house, 1874-82; became mgr. Northwestern Miller, Minneapolis, 1882, and its editor, 1886-1924; established The Bellman, 1906, was its editor and mgr. until 1919, when discontinued its publication. Pres. Miller Pub. Co. until retirement, 1924. In 1891, organized movement through which Am. millers gave shipload of flour for the relief of Russian peasants; personally superintended its collection, shipment and distribution; received gold flagon from Emperor of Russia in recognition of services; in 1914, directed Millers' Belgian relief movement, chartered S.S. South Point and therein carried cargo of flour, valued at $500,000, to Rotterdam, when it was delivered to Belgium, personally accompanied this contribution to destination and inspected method of distribution, coöperating with Commission for Relief in Belgium; in 1917, assisted Herbert Hoover, food administrator, in perfecting orgn., regulating and controlling Am. milling industry during the war. In 1918, at request of British Ministry of Information, went to Great Britain, where he made addresses and wrote articles concerning the war spirit of the Northwest. Chevalier de l'Ordre de la Couronne (Belgium); Officier de l'Instruction Publique, France; received bronze medallion from Comité National de Secours et d'Alimentation, Brussels, in recognition of relief work. Mem. Commn. for Relief, Belgium, 1914—. Democrat. Episcopalian. Author: Story of a Grain of Wheat, 1903; The Medal of Gold, 1925; At Christmas Time, 1925; Judson Moss Bemis, Pioneer, 1926; Christmas at Dingley Dell, 1926. Home: Marine-on-St. Croix, Minn. Died Dec. 2, 1932.

EDGERLY, Winfield Scott, brig. gen.; b. Farmington, N.H., May 29, 1846; s. Josiah Bartlett and Cordelia (Waldron) E.; ed. pub. schs., Farmington, Effingham Inst., Phillips Exeter Acad.; grad. U.S. Mil. Acad., 1870; m. Grace Cory Blum, Oct. 27, 1875. Apptd. 2d lt. 7th Cav., U.S.A., June 15, 1870; 1st lt., June 25, 1876; capt., Sept. 22, 1883; maj. 6th Cav., July 9, 1898; transferred to 7th Cav., Jan. 5, 1899; lt. col. 10th Cav., Feb. 19, 1901; transferred to 7th Cav., Mar. 20, 1901; col. 2d Cav., Feb. 17, 1903; brig. gen., June 23, 1905; retired, Dec. 29, 1909. Served in Indian wars, in Spanish-Am. War and in the Philippines; comdg. Dept. of the Gulf, 1907. Republican. Died Sept. 10, 1927.

EDGERTON, Charles Eugene, economist; b. Nineveh, N.Y., Dec. 25, 1861; s. Franklin and Julia (Taggart) E.; A.B., Hamilton Coll., 1882; grad. student, economics and statistics, Columbia and Cornell, 1897-98, and 1900; m. Annie Benedict White, Oct. 9, 1884; children—Franklin, Henry White, William Franklin. Banking and mfg., 1882-96; taught economics, Smith Coll., 1898-99; expert agt. U.S. Industrial Commn., 1900-01; asst. sec. Immigration Restriction League, and sec. Nat. Fedn. for Majority Rule, 1901-03; statis. investigator for Bur. of Statistics, Dept. of Agr., 1903-05; spl. examiner for Bur. of Corps., 1905-15, for Federal Trade Commn., 1915-18. Home: Ithaca, N.Y. Died Sept. 24, 1932.

EDGERTON, Hiram H., mayor; b. Belfast, N.Y., Apr. 19, 1847; s. Ralph H. and Octavia C. Penhollow) E.; ed. pub. schs., Rochester Free Acad., Rochester Bus. Inst.; m. Medora L. DeWitt, 1868. Contractor, Rochester, 1868—; has erected many chs. and pub. bldgs., business blks., N.Y. and other states. Mem. Bd. of Edn., Rochester, 1872-76 (twice pres.); pres. Commn. in charge of constrn. East Side Sewer; pres. Common Council, 1900-08; mayor of Rochester, 1908—. Trustee Rochester Public Library; hon. pres. Rochester Expn. Assn. Republican. Presbyn. Mason. Home: Rochester, N.Y. Died June 18, 1922.

EDGERTON, James Arthur, author; b. Plantsville, O., Jan. 30, 1869; s. Richard and Tamar (Vernon) E.; grad. Normal U., Lebanon, O., 1887, A.M., 1895; 1 year's post-grad. work, Marietta (O.) Coll.; m. Blanche Edgerton (2d cousin), Mar. 21, 1895; children—James Clark, Joseph Selby, Mrs. George Lacy, John Eldon, Justin Lincoln, Elizabeth. Editor county and state papers several yrs.; on editorial staff Denver News, 1899-1903, Am. Press Assn., New York, 1904, Watson's Mag., 1905; editorial writer New York American, 1907, Am. Press Assn., 1908-13; purchasing agt. Post Office Dept., 1913-20; member of War Industries Board, 1917-19; federal prohibition dir., New Jersey, 1920, now mfrs.' agt. Chmn. Populist State Com., Neb., 1895-96; sec. Populist Nat. Com., 1896-1904; mem. Populist Nat. Exec. Com., 1904-08; sec. State Labor Bur., Neb., 1895-99; received party vote for clerk U.S. Ho. of Rep., 1897. Gen. organizer Independence League, 1906; pres. Nat. New Thought Alliance, 1909-14, Internat. New Thought Alliance, 1914-24, 34. Prohibition nominee for vice-pres. of U.S., 1928. Author: Glimpses of the Real, 1903; In the Gardens of the God, 1904; The Philosophy of Jesus, 1928; Invading the Invisible, 1930. Home: Alexandria, Va. Died Dec. 3, 1938.

EDGERTON, John Emmett, woolen mfr.; b. Johnston Co., N.C., Oct. 2, 1879; s. Gabriel Griffin and Harriet (Copeland) E.; B.A., Vanderbilt, 1902, M.A., 1903; m. Harriet Figuers, Dec. 15, 1909; 1 dau., Harriet Figuers. Cofounder, and prin. 7 yrs., Columbia (Tenn.) Mil. Acad.; pres. Lebanon (Tenn.) Woolen Mills, 1912—; pres. of Nat. Boston Montana Mines Corp., Natural Gas Corp. of Tenn. Chmn. War Resources Com. for Tennessee, World War; also mem. Federal Fuel and Food administrations for Tenn.; state chmn. United War Work Campaign; mem. state exec. com. War Savings Campaign. Mem. President Harding's Conf. on Unemployment, 1921; mem. Nat. Com. on Unemployment Relief; pres. Southern States Industrial Council (Nashville). Sec. and mem. bd. of trustees Vanderbilt U.; treas. Fifty Million Dollar Fund, Southern Meth. Ch. Democrat. Mem. M.E. Ch., S. Home: Lebanon, Tenn. Died Aug. 4, 1938.

EDGERTON, John Warren, prof. law; b. Middletown, Conn., Feb. 20, 1875; s. Francis Daniel and Amelia Dupont (Cruger) E.; B.A., Trinity Coll., Conn., 1894; M.A., Yale, 1896, LL.B., 1900; m. Marion Gallaudet, Nov. 5, 1905. Admitted to Conn. bar, 1899, and practiced at New Haven; sec. law faculty, 1903—, and prof. mercantile law, 1911—, Yale. Republican. Episcopalian. Mason. Home: Pine Orchard, Conn. Died July 3, 1920.

EDGINGTON, Thomas Benton, lawyer; b. Ontario, O., Apr. 23, 1837; s. Jesse and Hannah (Mitchell) E.; student Baldwin U., Berea, O., until sophomore yr.; A.B., Ohio Wesleyan U., 1859, A.M., 1862, LL.D., 1905; m. Catherine Vose Baxter, Apr. 5, 1865; children—Hugh, Irving H., Jesse, Katherine B. (wife of Dr. R. B. Underwood, dec.), Mary Rose. Admitted to bar, 1861; mustered into Union Army as 1st sergt., Co. A, 12th Ia. Inf., Oct. 17, 1861; participated in siege of Ft. Henry, battles of Ft. Donelson and Shiloh; comd. co. in latter battle, was wounded and taken prisoner; remained prisoner of war about 7 months; 1st lt., Apr. 9, 1862-Apr. 4, 1863, resigned on account of ill health; aided in organizing Union Mil. forces in W. Tenn., and became maj. 4th regt.,

1863. Now senior mem. Edington & Edington. Episcopalian. Democrat. Author: The Monroe Doctrine, 1904. One of speeches, The Race Question, in opposition to the Force Bill, was published (1889) and attracted wide attention; The Waves of Kosmos, 1920; Electronomy, 1923, revised and enlarged, 1924. Home: Memphis, Tenn. Died Jan. 4, 1929.

EDGREN, John Alexis, clergyman; b. Vermland, Sweden, Feb. 20, 1839; s. A. H. E.; grad. Navigation School, Stockholm, Sweden, as capt., 1859; Astron. Observatory, as teacher navigation, 1862; studied theology, Princeton, Hamilton and Chicago; B.D., Bapt. Union. Theol. Sem., 1872; D.D., Univ. of Chicago, 1880; m. Anna Chapman, April 10, 1866. Went to sea, 1852; sailed before mast until 1859, then as 2d and 1st mate to 1862; passed examination and apptd. acting ensign, U.S.N., 1862; served as sailing-master U.S.S. "Young Rover"; commdr. U.S.S. "Catalpa" and "Transport"; served at naval battery, Morris Island; took part in several engagements on land with naval brigade, late in 1864, between Charleston and Savannah. Ordained minister of Gospel, 1866; served in Bethel Sem., Stockholm, Sweden, 1866-69, as pastor two churches; as instr. and later prof. Scandinavian dept., Bapt. Union Theol. Sem., Chicago, 1871-84; prin. Swedish-Am. Bible Sem., St. Paul, 1884-85; Central Bible Sem., Stromsburg, Neb., 1885-87; later doing lit. work in Calif. Home: Oakland, Calif. Died 1908.

EDIE, Guy Lewis, surgeon U.S.A.; b. in Va., June 18, 1858; M.D., U. of Va., 1879. Apptd. asst. surgeon U.S.A., Dec. 3, 1883; capt. asst. surgeon, Dec. 3, 1888; maj. brigade surgeon vols., June 4, 1898; vacated Feb. 2, 1901; maj. surgeon U.S.A., Feb. 2, 1901; maj. Med. Corps, Feb. 2, 1901; lt. col., Jan. 1, 1909; col., Aug. 6, 1912. At Presidio, San Francisco, 1916. Died Apr. 9, 1930.

EDISON, Thomas A(lva), inventor; b. Milan, O., Feb. 11, 1847; s. Samuel and Nancy E.; received some instruction from his mother; (hon. Ph.D., Union Coll., 1878; D.Sc., Princeton U., 1915; LL.D., Univ. of the State of N.Y., 1916); m. Mary G. Stillwell, 1873; children—Marion Estelle, Thomas A., William L.; m. 2d, Mina Miller, 1886; children—Madeleine, Charles Theodore. At 12 years of age became newsboy on the Grand Trunk Ry.; later learned telegraphy; worked as operator at various places in U.S. and Canada; invented many telegraphic appliances, including automatic repeater, quadruplex telegraph, printing telegraph, etc. Established workshop at Newark, N.J., removing to Menlo Park, N.J., 1876, and later (1887) to West Orange, N.J. Invented machines for quadruplex and sextuplex telegraphic transmission; the electric pen and mimeograph; the carbon telephone transmitter; the microphone; the microtasimeter for detection of small changes in temperature; the megaphone; the phonograph; the incandescent lamp and light system; the electric valve, (at first called the "Edison effect"), now fundamentally essential in wireless telegraphy; a system of wireless telegraphy to and from moving railway trains; motion pictures; the telescribe; alkaline storage battery; since commencement of European War, 1914, designed, built and operated successfully several benzol plants; also 2 carbolic acid plants; also other chemical plants for making myrbane aniline oil, aniline salt, and paraphenylenediamine; has received patents for more than 1,000 inventions. Was made Chevalier, Officer, and afterwards Comdr. Legion of Honor, by French Govt.; apptd. 1903, hon. chief consulting engr., St. Louis Expn., 1904. Awarded John Fritz medal, 1908; Rathenau medal (German), Am. Mus. of Safety, 1914; congressional gold medal, 1928, "for development and application of inventions that have revolutionized civilization in the last century." Pres. Naval Consulting Bd., July 1915—. Made many war inventions for U.S. Govt. Home: West Orange, N.J. Died Oct. 18, 1931.

EDMANDS, John, librarian; b. Framingham, Mass., Feb. 1, 1820; s. Jonathan and Lucy (Nourse) E.; B.A., Yale, 1847; studied Yale Div. Sch., 1848-51; m. Abigail Jane Lloyd, Aug. 1, 1854; 2d, Ellen Elizabeth Metcalf, June 17, 1889; 3d, Clara Augusta Roberts, Aug. 23, 1893. Librarian, Soc. of Brothers in Unity, Yale, 1846-47; asst. Yale Coll. Library, 1851-56; librarian Mercantile Library, Phila., 1856-1901, emeritus. Deacon and clerk Central Congl. Ch., Phila., 1864—. Published, 1847, Subjects for Debate, with References to Authorities, which is the germ of Poole's Index; devised, 1877, a system of library classification and numbering scheme. Home: Philadelphia, Pa. Died Oct. 17, 1915.

EDMANDS, Samuel Sumner, engr., educator; b. Kalamazoo, Mich., Apr. 30, 1877; s. John and Maria Clara (Goodwin) E.; B.S. in E.E., 1899, D.Eng., 1930, Worcester Poly. Inst.; m. Althea Florence Miller, Nov. 28, 1916; 1 dau., Patricia. With Am. Tel. & Tel. Co., Providence, R.I., 1899-1900; instr. elec. engring., Ohio State U., 1900-01; teacher and head of dept. elec. engring., 1901-10, dir. Sch. of Science and Technology, 1910—, Pratt Inst., Brooklyn, N.Y. Died May 24, 1938.

EDMONDS, George Washington, congressman; b. Pottsville, Pa., Feb. 22, 1864; s. Henry R. and Catherine Ann (Huntzinger) E.; Central High Sch., Phila.; Ph.G., Phila. Coll. of Pharmacy, 1885; m. Julia H. Riley, June 14, 1899. In retail drug business until 1887; an organizer of Black Diamond Coal Co., 1887; subsequently partner in coal firms of George Warner (later Warner, Shuster & Co.), G. W. Edmonds & Co., 1892, until merged with George B. Newton Coal Co. in 1912; mem. Edmonds & Heidler, wholesale coal and lumber, 1925-36; dir. George B. Newton Coal Co. Mgr. Port of Phila. Ocean Traffic Bureau, 1927-32. Mem. Common Council, Phila., 3 terms of two yrs. each; mem. 63d to 68th and 73d Congresses (1913-25 and 1933-35), 4th Pa. Dist. Progressive Republican. Episcopalian. Mason. Home: Philadelphia, Pa. Died Sept. 28, 1939.

EDMONDS, Richard Hathaway, editor; b. Norfolk, Va., 1857; s. late Rev. Richard H. and Mary E. E.; went to Baltimore, 1871; attended pub. sch., 1874, later clk.; served as asst. editor of Journal of Commerce, Baltimore, 1878-82; D.C.L., Univ. of the South, 1926; m. Addie L. Field, 1881. Founder, 1882, of The Manufacturers' Record, of which is editor and chmn. of board, publication devoted to industrial and commercial interests of the country with special reference to utilization of resources of the South. Served as trustee Southern Bapt. Theol. Sem., Louisville. Has pub. numerous pamphlets about South and its resources; also "Facts About the South"—hist. review of business conditions of South before and after the war. Active in advocating nat. preparedness; mem. bd. trustees Am. Defense Society. Author: National Insuredness through National Preparedness, 1916; America's Relation to the World War; Shall This Nation Live or Perish? Home: Baltimore, Md. Died Oct. 4, 1930.

EDMONDSON, Thomas William, univ. prof.; b. Skipton-in-Craven, Yorkshire, Eng., June 26, 1869; s. Thomas and Sarah (Dodgson) E.; B.A., London U., 1888; B.A., Cambridge, Eng., 1891; Ph.D., Clark U., Worcester, Mass., 1896; m. Minnie Ramsden, Perth, Ont., 1897. Math. scholar, Pembroke Coll., Cambridge, Eng., 1888-91, Akroyd scholar, 1888-90; fellow in physics, Clark U., 1894-1906; asst. prof. physics, 1896-1903, asso. prof., 1903-05, prof. mathematics, 1905-34 (emeritus), acting dean Graduate School, 1916-21, New York University. Author: Worked Examples in Coördinate Geometry, 1891; Mensuration and Spherical Geometry (with W. Briggs), 1893; Deductions in Euclid, 1901. Home: Mt. Vernon, N.Y. Died Nov. 4, 1938.

EDMUNDS, Albert Joseph, librarian; b. Tottenham, Middlesex, Eng., Nov. 21, 1857; s. Thomas and Rebecca (Hallat) E.; ed. Friends' Sch., Croydon, and Flounders Inst., Ackworth; matriculated U. of London, 1877; pvt. student of N.T., James Rendel Harris, 1890-95; (hon. A.M., U. of Pa., 1907); fellow U. of Pa., 1914; unmarried. Sec. to T. W. Backhouse, astronomer, 1879-83; emigrated to U.S., 1885, asst. librarian, Haverford Coll., 1887-89; classifier Phila. Library, 1889-90; cataloguer Hist. Soc. of Pa., 1891-1936. Prepared Catalogue Sunderland (Eng.) Library, 1881-84. Author: Hymns of the Faith (Dhammapada), 1902; Buddhist and Christian Gospels, 1902, 3d edit., Tokyo, 1905, 4th edit., Phila., 1908-09, with postscripts, 1912, 14, 21, 26, 28, 35, 37, 38; A Dialogue Between Two Saviors, 5th edit., 1931; Lucy Edmunds (1859-1935) in The Two Worlds, 1935; Leaves from the Gospel of Mark, 1936. Home: Cheltenham, Pa. Died Dec. 17, 1941.

EDMUNDS, Charles Wallis, medical educator; b. Bridport, Dorset, Eng., Feb. 22, 1873; s. Thomas Hallett and Caroline (Wallis) E.; Ind. U., 1895-96; M.D., U. of Mich., 1901, A.B., 1904; post-grad. work Univ. Coll., London; Mass. Gen. Hosp. and Johns Hopkins Hosp.; m. Lilian Virginia Kaminski, Sept. 15, 1909; children—Ann, Charles Wallis. Came to U.S., 1883; with U. of Mich. Med. Sch., 1902—, prof. materia medica and therapeutics, 1907—, sec., 1911-21, asst. dean, 1918-21, mem. exec. committee of Medical School (1935-39) and Grad. Sch., U. of Mich. Mem. Com. for Revision U.S. Pharmacopœia, 1910-20, 1920-30, 1930-40, 2d vice chmn. and chmn. com. on bioassays, chmn. advisory board for antianemic preparations; mem. internat. com. on drug standardization, Health Com. of League of Nations, Geneva, 1925; mem. exec. com. National Research Council, 1939; mem. com. on study of drug addiction, Nat. Research Council, 1930—. Republican. Episcopalian. Author: (with Arthur R. Cushny, M.D.), Laboratory Guide in Pharmacology, 1909, 18, 24, 39. Reviser (with Prof. J. A. Gunn, Oxford, Eng.) Cushny's text book, Pharmacology and Therapeutics, 1928, 34, 36, 40. Home: Ann Arbor, Mich. Died Mar. 1, 1941.

EDMUNDS, George Franklin, senator; b. Richmond, Vt., Feb. 1, 1828; s. Ebenezer and Naomi (Briggs) E.; ed. in common schs. and with pvt. tutor; (hon. A.M., U. of Vt., 1855; LL.D., Middlebury, 1869, U. of Vt., 1879, Trinity, 1887, Dartmouth, 1890). Began law practice, 1849; removed to Burlington, Vt., 1851. Mem. Vt. Ho. of Rep., 1854-59 (speaker, 1856-59); mem. and pres. pro tem Vt. Senate, 1861-62; U.S. senator, 1866-91; resigned. Mem. Electoral Commn., 1877; author of Act of Mar. 22, 1882, for suppression of polygamy in Utah and disfranchisement of those who practice it, known as Edmunds Act; also of the anti-trust law of 1890; pres. pro tem of U.S. Senate during presidency of Gen. Arthur; was a leader in Senate on Republican side; received 34 votes for presdl. nomination Nat. Rep. Conv., 1880, and 93 votes, 1884; notable as a constl. lawyer. In 1897 became chmn. of the Monetary Commn. apptd. by exec. com. of the Indianapolis Monetary Conf. Address: Pasadena, Calif. Died Feb. 27, 1919.

EDMUNDS, Harry Nicholas, law sch. dean; b. Ridgeway, S.C., Jan. 25, 1876; s. Robert Henry and Mattie Peay (Lamar) E.; A.B., U. of S.C., 1896, LL.B., 1898; m. Gulielma Pitts Marks, June 20, 1931. In practice of law as mem. Logan & Edmunds, Columbia, S.C., 1898-1914; city atty., Columbia, 1902-04, 1911-14; acting asso. justice Supreme Court of S.C., 1916; referee in bankruptcy, Eastern S.C. Dist., 1918-28; prof. law, U. of S.C., 1920-28; prof. law and dean of Law Sch., U. of Ga., 1928—. Chmn. County Dem. Orgn., Richland Co., S.C., 1910-14; sec. S.C. State Dem. Exec. Com., 1918-28. Presbyn. Home: Athens, Ga. Died Nov. 1934.

EDMUNDS, Samuel Henry, supt. schs.; b. Millgrove, S.C., May 28, 1870; s. Nicholas William (D.D.) and Mary Claudia (Leland) E.; A.B., Davidson Coll., 1890, also A.M.; studied Columbia U. and U. of Chicago; Litt.D., Wofford, 1917, Presbyn. Coll. of S.C., 1918; m. Eliza Champion Davis, Dec. 1896; children—Mrs. J. E. Hunter (dec.), Leland Nicholas, Samuel Henry, DeSaussure Davis, Champion Moore, Thomas Frederick. Supt. schs. Sumter, S.C., 1895—. Mem. State Bd. of Edn., Commn. to Revise School Laws, Illiteracy Commn. of Edn. Trustee Presbyn. Theol. Sem., Columbia, S.C. Democrat. Mason. Home: Sumter, S.C. Died Sept. 14, 1935.

EDMUNDSON, James Depew, capitalist; b. Des Moines Co., Ia., Nov. 23, 1838; s. William and Priscilla (Depew) E.; (family name originally Edmiston); ed. common sch. and acad.; m. Jennie Way Hart, May 25, 1871 (died 1890); m. 2d, Mrs. Laura B. Kirby, Jan. 1, 1894 (died 1908). Admitted to bar, 1860; practiced at Glenwood, Ia., 1861-66; removed to Council Bluffs, 1866; dealt extensively in Ia. farm lands; organized, 1882, and pres., 1882, Citizens' State Bank and its successor, the First Nat. Bank, until removed to Des Moines, 1900; an organizer and was dir. State Savings Bank, Council Bluffs. Deputy provost marshal, deputy internal revenue collector and asst. assessor internal revenue, all for southwestern Ia., 1863-66; mem. bd. trustees Free Pub. Library, Council Bluffs, for many yrs.; mem. bd. trustees Home for the Aged, Des Moines. Erected the Jennie Edmundson Memorial Hosp. at Council Bluffs, in memory of his first wife; presented statue of Mahaska (Indian chief), Oskaloosa, Mahaska County, 1909. Home: Des Moines, Ia. Died Apr. 1933.

EDRINGTON, William Reynolds, capitalist; b. Madison Parish, La., Feb. 22, 1872; s. Henry Clay and Virginia (Clarke) E.; ed. Agrl. and Mech. Coll. of Tex., U. of Tex. and U. of Va.; m. Frances Feild, Oct. 24, 1893; children—Henry Clay, Florence (Mrs. Geo. B. Ismay), Olive (Mrs. Evans S. Pillsbury II). Began in investment business, Ft. Worth, 1897; pres. Edrington-Minot Corp., Edrington Investment Co.; v.p. Minot Holding Corp. Democrat. Baptist. Mason (Shriner). Home: New York, N.Y. Died Nov. 6, 1932.

EDSALL, Samuel Cook, bishop; b. Dixon, Ill., Mar. 4, 1860; s. James K. and Caroline Florella (More) E.; ed. Racine Coll.; read law, and admitted to bar, 1882; studied Western Theol. Sem.; (A.M., Racine, 1888; D.D., Ill. Coll., 1898; S.T.D., Western Theol. Sem., 1900); m. Grace Harmon, Apr. 11, 1883 (died 1913). Deacon, 1888, priest, 1889, P.E. Ch.; founded St. Peter's Mission, Chicago, 1887, lay reader, 1887-89; rector St. Peter's Ch., Chicago, 1889-99; missionary bishop of N.D., 1899-1901; elected coadjutor bishop of Minn., June 6, 1901; translated as bishop, Oct. 3, 1901. State chaplain Soc. Colonial War, 1906-09, 1912-15. Mason. Author: Prayer Book Preparation for Confirmation, 1898. Died Feb. 17, 1917.

EDSON, Andrew Wheatley, supt. schs.; b. Montello, Wis., Dec. 26, 1851; s. Jerah and Mary H. (Wheatley) E.; grad. Randolph (Vt.) State Normal Sch., 1870, Montpelier (Vt.) Sem., 1874; A.B., Dartmouth, 1878, A.M., 1881 (Pd.D., 1916); m. Cynthia F. Paine, Aug. 20, 1878. Prin. high sch., W. Randolph, Vt., 1878-79, State Normal Sch., Randolph, 1879-84; supt. schs., Attleboro, Mass., 1884-85, Jersey City, N.J., 1885-87; agt., State Bd. Edn., Mass., 1887-97; asst. supt. schs., New York, 1897, and now asso. supt. same. Home: New York, N.Y. Died Feb. 1, 1924.

EDSON, Carroll Everett, M.D.; b. Roxbury, Mass., Oct. 14, 1866; s. Ptolemy O'Meara and Mary Augusta (Young) E.; A.B., Harvard, 1888, A.M. and M.D., 1892; unmarried. Began practice at Boston, 1892; moved to Colo., 1894; prof. therapeutics, U. of Denver, 1897-1906; prof. theory and practice of medicine, U. of Colo., 1906-10. Acting asst. surgeon U.S.A., Spanish-Am. War; mem. Dist. Bd., Selective Service,

1917-18. Republican. Unitarian. Home: Denver, Colo. Died Jan. 18, 1930.

EDSON, Cyrus, physician; b. Albany, N.Y., Sept. 8, 1857; s. Franklin E., ex-mayor of New York; ed. Columbia Coll.; grad. Coll. Phys. & Surg., 1881; became asst. sanitary insp., 1882, and promoted through grades to commr. of health of New York; 3 terms pres. Bd. of Pharmacy, city and Co. of New York; apptd. commr. of health of State of N.Y., 1893; was surgeon and lt. col. N.Y. Nat. Guard; has served in various other positions; inventor of many useful surg. instruments; m. Virginia Churchill Page (died 1889); m. 2d, Mary E. Quick. Home: New York, N.Y. Died 1903.

EDSON, Franklin, mcht., mayor; b. Chester, Vt., Apr. 5, 1832; s. Ophir and Seviah (Williams) E.; ed. common schools; m. Fanny Cameron Wood, 1856, g.d. Jethro Wood, inventor cast-iron plow. Was, 1851-65, asso. with a brother in a distillery at Albany; then became grain commn. mcht. in New York, 1866; pres. Produce Exchange, 1873, 1874 and 1878. Affiliating with the County Democracy, was elected mayor of New York, 1882. Home: New York, N.Y. Died 1904.

EDSON, Job Adolphus, ry. pres.; b. Sylvania, O., Feb. 14, 1854; s. Charles and Mary E. E.; pub. sch. edn.; m. Margaret Gilroy, Nov. 1880. Telegraph operator L.S.&M.S. Ry., 1867-72; operator, train dispatcher, chief dispatcher, and train master, U.P. Ry., 1872-86; chief dispatcher I.&D. div., C.,M.&St. P. Ry., 1886-87; div. supt. Mo. Pac. Ry., Atchison, Kan., 1887-89; supt., gen. supt., gen. mgr. and v.p., entire line, Cotton Belt Rd., 1889-99; gen. mgr. for receivers, Kansas City, Pittsburg & Gulf R.R., 1899-1903; mgr. D.&R.G. and R.G. Western rys., 1903-04; gen. mgr. C.H.&D. Ry., 1904-05; elected pres. Kansas City Southern Ry. Co., June 1, 1905; federal mgr. Kansas City, Mexico & Orient R.R., K.C.S. R.R., Midland Valley R.R., June 1918-Feb. 29, 1920; pres. K.C.S. Ry. Co., 1920-28, retired; also pres. Tex. & Ft. Smith Ry. Co.; v.p. Ark. Western Ry. Co. Died July 30, 1928.

EDSON, John Joy, banker; b. Jefferson, O., May 17, 1846; served in 61st N.Y. Vols., 1861-63; ed. Ohio pub. schs.; LL.B., Columbian (now George Washington) U., 1868; married; children—John Joy (dec.), Elizabeth, Frederick Wade (dec.). Admitted to bar, 1869; clerk Treasury Dept., 1863-1875; patent atty., 1875-81; organized, 1879, sec. 1879-98, pres., 1898—, Equitable Bldg. Assn.; treas. exec. com. Am. Red Cross, Spanish-Am. War; pres., 1894-1917, chmn. bd. Washington Loan & Trust Co.; pres. Washington Sanitary Improvement Co. Chmn. Citizens' Exec. Com., 1892, to receive and entertain G.A.R. first reunion at Washington; mem. board Columbia Hist. Soc., 1916—; chmn. McKinley 2d inaugural com., 1901. Pres. Nat. Homœ. Hosp., 1889-95, Civil Service Reform Assn. of D.C., 1895-1907, Bd. of Trade, 1900-01; pres. and mem. govt. bd. charities, 1900-26; chmn. and mem. new Bd. of Pub. Welfare for Washington; treas. George Washington U., 1903-05, and trustee 1917-29; treas. Associated Charities, 1897-1929, Nat. Geog. Soc., 1900—, also trustee of Nat. Geog. Society; dir. Chamber of Commerce U.S.A. Mem. Prison Commn. under act of Congress, making their report Jan. 1, 1909, still mem. Mem. bd., treas. Nat. Assn. for Constl. Govt.; del. Pan-Am. Financial Congress, Washington, 1915, 19; chmn. Selective Service Appeal Bd., 1917-18, also chmn. Capital Issue Com., D.C., during the war. Mem. bd. and treas. Nat. Press Bldg. Corp. for the Nat. Press Club, Washington. Republican. Declined appointment to Bd. Commrs. of D.C., 1893, and 1901. Home: Washington, D.C. Died July 15, 1935.

EDSON, Katherine Philips; b. Kenton, O., Jan. 12, 1870; d. William H. (M.D.) and Harriet J. (Carlin) Philips; ed. Convent of the Sacred Heart, Clifton, Cincinnati, and Glendale Female Sem.; m. Charles Farwell Edson, Oct. 8, 1890; children—Katharine, Philips Josiah, Charles Farwell. Interested in constructive philanthropy, public health and industrial problems; active worker for woman suffrage; mem. Progressive Party State Central Com., Calif., 1912-16; mem. exec. com. Rep. State Com., 1916-20; mem. exec. com. Rep. Nat. Com., 1920-24; mem. state bd. Calif. Fedn. Women's Clubs, 1910-16; mem. Charter Revision Commn. of Los Angeles, 1912; mem. exec. com. Nat. Municipal League; exec. com. Nat. League for Woman's Service; chmn. women in industry com. Calif. Council of Defense; chmn. com. on Women in Industry and mem. bd. dirs. Calif. League of Woman Voters, 1922—; mem. and exec. officer Indsl. Welfare Commn., Calif.; chief of Div. of Indsl. Welfare of State Dept. of Indsl. Relations, 1927-31. Del. Pan-Pacific Conf. of Women, Honolulu, 1928. Author of minimum wage bill, enacted by Calif. legislature, 1913. Apptd. mem. advisory com. of Conf. on Limitation of Armament, Nov. 1921. Home: Pasadena, Calif. Died Nov. 5, 1933.

EDSTROM, David, sculptor; b. Hvetlanda, Sweden, Mar. 27, 1873; s. John Peter and Charlotte (Gustaveson) E.; grad. Poly. Sch., Stockholm, Sweden, 1896, Royal Acad. Fine Arts, Stockholm, 1899; studied Florence, Italy, 1900-02, in Paris, France, with Injalbert, 1905; Doctor of Arts, Chicago Law Sch., 1920; m. Anna Levertin, of Stockholm, 1902; m. 2d, Cora Evelyn Downer, 1909 (died 1921). Came to U.S., 1880; began as newsboy, at Ottumwa, Ia., at 13; later employed in factories; started for Europe to study art at 21; tramped to New York, crossed ocean as coal stoker, and worked way through tech. schs. and Royal Acad. of Fine Arts, Stockholm; propr. pvt. sch. for sculpture, in Paris, France, 1907-09; employed by City of Gothenburg on plans for pub. square, 1914-15. Lectured at Upsala (Sweden) Univ., spring 1924. Has made portrait busts of many noted personages, including Crown Prince and Princess of Sweden; Princess Patricia of Connaught; Dr. Ludvig Looström, dir. Nat. Gallery, Stockholm; Ellen Key; etc. Psychol. sculptures: "Fear," "Pride," "Envy," "Caliban," "The Cry of Poverty," etc.; made war memorial, Montreal, Can.; statue of Samuel P. Cochran, Dallas; heroic bust of Lincoln in marble, E. P. Clark Collection; statue of M. H. Whittier, Los Angeles; memorial to Florence Nightingale, Los Angeles. 35 of his sculptures bought for Ia. State Univ. Silver medal, St. Louis Expn., 1904. Mem. Company G, 2d Regt., Iowa N.G., 1892-94. Episcopalian. Author: The Testament of Caliban (autobiography). Home: Los Angeles, Calif. Died Aug. 12, 1938.

EDWARDS, Alanson W., journalist, consul; b. in Lorain Co., O., Aug. 27, 1840; s. Milton W. and Esther (Powers) E.; ed. McKendree Coll., 1856-59, scientific course; m. Elizabeth Robertson, June, 1869. Enlisted in 122d Ill. Inf., 1862, as pvt.; served to end of war; was with Sherman from Atlanta to the sea, and from Savannah, Ga., to Washington, at final review; became capt. 1st Ala. Union Cav. with Kilpatrick; mustered out as capt. and a. a. gen. with Corse at end of war, 4th div., 15th corps; bvtd. maj. After war in newspaper work with Carlinville (Ill.) Democrat, and Chicago Evening Post. In 1878 founded Fargo (N. Dak.) Daily Argus, and became editor of that paper and its successor, the present Fargo Forum; pres. Forum Printing Co. Was warden Ill. Penitentiary, 1870-73; dir. Dak. (territorial) Penitentiary and chmn. bd. Republican. Am. consul gen. at Montreal, Can., 1902-06. Methodist. Home: Fargo, N. Dak. Died 1908.

EDWARDS, Arthur Robin, M.D.; b. Chicago, June 26, 1867; s. Arthur (D.D.) and Caroline M. (Whitehead) E.; A.B., Northwestern U., 1888, A.M., 1891; M.D., Chicago Med. Coll. (Northwestern U.), 1891; m. Susannah Taylor Harrison, Feb. 15, 1900; 1 son, Arthur. Interne Cook Co. (Ill.) Hosp., 1891-92; in med. practice from 1892; prof. principles and practice of medicine and clin. medicine, 1897-1917, later dean Northwestern U. Med. Sch. Was attending phys. to Cook Co., Mercy, Michael Reese and St. Luke's hosps., Chicago; retired. Author: Principles and Practice of Medicine. Died May 17, 1936.

EDWARDS, Benjamin D.; b. Churchill, Trumbull Co., O., Apr. 10, 1881; s. David B. and Rachel Bynon (Davis) E.; Ph.B., Mount Union Coll., 1910; student Detroit Coll. of Law, 1 yr.; Dr. Bus. Administration, Mount Union Coll., 1922; m. Maud Muack Grove, June 17, 1911; children—Benjamin David, John Todd. Prin., Detroit Tech. Inst., 1910-11, and chancellor of its successor, Detroit Inst. Tech., 1911-1923, also chancellor Detroit Coll. of Law, 1915-23; organizer and chancellor Hudson Sch., 1911-23 (all these instns. identified with Detroit Y.M.C.A.); gen. sec. Y.M.C.A., Oklahoma City, 1923-25; metropolitan sec. Duluth Y.M.C.A., 1925-28. Past pres. Nat. Assn. Ednl. Secretaries of N.A.; mem. bd. govs. United Y.M.C.A. Schs.; mem. Nat. Council Y.M.C.A., 1919-26; chief probation officer Champaign County, O.; sr. mem. Am. Assn. Social Workers. Republican. Methodist. Mason. Home: Urbana, O. Died Sept. 7, 1930.

EDWARDS, Charles Gordon, congressman; b. Tattnall Co., Ga., July 2, 1878; s. Thomas Jefferson and Ann (Conley) E.; ed. Gordon Inst., Barnesville, Ga., U. of Fla., Lake City, Fla.; LL.B., U. of Ga., 1898; m. Ora Beach, Dec. 17, 1902; 1 son, Charles Beach. Mem. 60th to 64th, 69th to 71st Congresses (1907-17, 1925-31), 1st Ga. Dist. Democrat. Home: Savannah, Ga. Died July 13, 1931.

EDWARDS, Charles Lincoln, nature-study dir.; b. Oquawka, Ill., Dec. 8, 1863; s. John and Nancy (Stockton) E.; B.S., Lombard U., 1884; B.S., Indiana U., 1886, A.M., 1887; Johns Hopkins U., 1886-89; Ph.D., U. of Leipzig, 1890; fellow in morphology, Clark U., 1890-92; m. Jessie Safford, June 5, 1889; children—John Robert, Richard Safford, Charles Stockton. Asst. prof. biology, 1892-93, adj. prof., 1893-94, U. of Tex.; prof. biology, U. of Cincinnati, 1894-1900; prof. natural history, Trinity Coll., 1900-10; Kristineberg, Sweden, Zoöl. Sta., 1909; Smithsonian table, Naples Zoöl. Sta., and U. of Würzburg, 1910; lecturer under Bd. of Edn. New York, 1910-11; asso. prof. biology and asso. dir. Venice Marine Biol. Sta., 1911-12, prof. embryology and histology, 1912-13, U. of Southern Calif.; naturalist, park dept., Los Angeles, 1912; dir. dept. nature-study, Los Angeles schs., 1912, until retired. Zoöl. investigations, Bahama Is., 1888, 1891, 93, Tex. coast, 1892, Fla. Keys, 1896, Calif. coast, 1911-13. Author: Bahama Songs and Stories (vol. 3, Memoirs Am. Folk-Lore Soc.), 1895; Nature-study, Part 1, 1924, Part 2, 1926; Jim and Tim and other stories. Home: West Los Angeles, Calif. Died May 4, 1937.

EDWARDS, Clarence Ransom, army officer; b. Cleveland, O., Jan. 1, 1860; s. William and Lucia (Ransom) E.; grad. U.S. Mil. Acad., 1883; hon. A.M., St. John's Coll., Fordham, N.Y., 1893; LL.D., Fordham U., New York, 1909, Middlebury Coll., 1919, Trinity Coll., Conn., 1919, Boston Coll., 1923, University of Me., 1923; m. Bessie Rochester Porter, June 11, 1889 (died 1929). Second lieutenant 23d Infantry, June 13, 1883; promoted through grades to brig. gen. U.S.A., June 30, 1906; maj. gen., Aug. 5, 1917. Assigned to staff of Gen. Lawton as adj-gen., Jan. 6, 1899, and served until Gen. Lawton's death, Dec. 19, 1899; chief of Bur. of Insular Affairs, Washington, July 1, 1902; transferred to line, May 12, 1912; later comd. 6th Brigade, 2d Div., Texas City, Tex., and 1st Hawaiian Brigade, Honolulu and Schofield Barracks, H.T.; comd. U.S. troops, Panama Canal Zone, 1915-17; comd. newly created Dept. of the Northeast (N.E. States), May-Sept. 1917; organized 26th Div., U.S.A., Aug. 1917; sailed to France, Sept. 1917; ten months' front line duty; returned to U.S., Nov. 1918; comdg. Northeastern Dept., Dec. 1918-20; assigned to 1st Div. Sept. 1, 1920; promoted maj. gen., Mar. 5, 1921; assigned to comd. 1st Corps Area, hdqrs., Army Base, Boston, Mass., July 1, 1921; retired Nov. 1, 1922. Home: Westwood, Mass. Died Feb. 14, 1931.

EDWARDS, David Morton, univ. pres.; b. Earlham, Ia., Oct. 6, 1871; s. Ira Wilson and Naomi (Lindley) E.; A.B., Penn Coll., Ia., 1900; U. of Chicago, summers 1900-02; Boston U., 1905-08, Ph.D., 1908; m. Della Russell, Mar. 29, 1903; m. 2d, Elizabeth Way, Aug. 12, 1914. Began teaching at Dexter, 1889; pres. Penn Coll., Oskaloosa, Ia., 1910-17, Earlham Coll., Richmond, Ind., 1917-29; spent 2 years travel in Europe and 8 months study in Library of British Mus.; pres. Friends Univ., Wichita, Kan., 1934—. Chmn. Bd. of Edn. of Five Year Meeting of Soc. of Friends in America; mem. Commn. on Institutions of Higher Edn. of the North Central Assn. of Colleges and Secondary Schs.; pres. Wayne Co. Social Service Bureau. Home: Wichita, Kan. Died Aug. 19, 1939.

EDWARDS, Don Calvin, congressman; b. Appanoose Co., Ia., July 13, 1861; s. Lewis Edwards and Jane (Saylor) E.; reared on farms in Ia. and Kan.; ed. common schs. of Ia. and Kan., and Campbell Normal U., Holton, Kan.; m. Lida Hodge, Feb. 11, 1904. Moved to Laurel Co., Ky., 1892; mfr. of rough lumber, 1892—; pres. Nat. Bank of London, 1903—. Clerk Circuit Ct., Laurel Co., Ky., 1898-1904; mem. 59th to 61st Congresses (1905-11), 11th Ky. Dist. Chmn. Ky. State Rep. Conv., 1908. Was mem. State Council Defense, chmn. 5 Liberty Loan campaigns and fuel administrator for Laurel Co., 1917-18; chmn. Am. Red Cross relief work for Laurel Co. Home: London, Ky. Died Sept. 19, 1938.

EDWARDS, Edward Irving, senator; b. Jersey City, N.J., Dec. 1, 1863; s. William W. and Emma J. (Nation) E.; student New York U., 1880-1882; m. Jule Blanche Smith, Nov. 14, 1888 (died 1928); children—Edward Irving, Elizabeth Jule. Connected with First Nat. Bank, Jersey City, 1882—; asst. to pres., 1903, later cashier, pres., 1916-25, now chmn. bd.; dir. Nat. Paper & Type Co., Raritan River R.R. Co., Stand. Motor Constrn. Co. State comptroller, N.J., 1911-17; mem. State Senate from Hudson Co., 1919 (resigned); gov. of N.J., Jan. 1920-Jan., 1923; mem. U.S. Senate, term 1923-29. Democrat. Episcopalian. Mason. Home: Jersey City, N.J. Died Jan. 26, 1931.

EDWARDS, George Porter, publisher; b. Dunkirk, N.Y., June 15, 1878; s. Francis Smith and Eliza Mary (Hatch) E.; ed. pub. schs., Dunkirk, and normal schs. at Buffalo and Fredonia, N.Y.; m. Emilie Louise Kohler, Apr. 7, 1907; children—Dorothy Buell, Patricia Eugenie, Constance Hunt, Jacqueline Porter, Barbara Grace, George Porter, Betty Standish, Frank Buell, Robert Kohler (dec.). Founder of "Money," financial jour., Pittsburgh, Pa., 1902, "Finance," Cleveland, O., 1900; moved to Calif., 1906; organizer and formerly pres. Bank of Balboa, Calif.; founder 1907, and pub. Coast Banker, San Francisco, 1908-39, founder and pub. Coast Investor, 1926; founder Pacific Banker, 1932, merged it, with Coast Banker under name of Coast Banker, continuing as publisher; organized Coast Foundation, Inc., of Nev., Coast Foundation, Inc., of San Francisco. Past pres. Oakland Campfire Girls. Home: Berkeley, Calif. Died July 12, 1941.

EDWARDS, George Thornton, author, composer; b. Annapolis, Md., May 6, 1868; s. Thomas and Mary J. (Peirce) E.; ed. pub. schs., Portland, Me.; studied music under George W. Marston, a pupil of Buonamici and Raff; m. Carol Content Sackett, Feb. 14, 1893. Treas. Underwood Spring Corp.; pres. Fessenden Park Co., Geo. T. Edwards Real Estate Co. Republican. Conglist. Dir. General State Liberty Chorus of Me.; mem. Nat. Community Music Assn., Mus. Alliance U.S.; mem. com. of dept.

nat. community music of Nat. Alliance de Edn. Societe et Civique. Mem. publicity com. War and Navy Depts. Commn. on Training Camp Activities. Conductor People's Community Chorus, Portland, Me. Author: The Youthful Haunts of Longfellow, 1907; The Appeal of Liberty. Composer: "America, My America," a nat. peace anthem; "State of Maine, My State of Maine," which has been adopted as the soc. song by State of Me. socs. in many states; has set several of Longfellow's poems to music, including "The Rainy Day," "My Lost Youth," etc.; "My Heart's in Tipperary Where the River Shannon Flows" and the "Soldier's Parting Song," sung by soldiers in Europe before U.S. entered the war, the latter having been translated into French, Italian and German; other songs: "Liberty, Sweet Liberty," "America, My Country," "Their Golden Wedding Song," "The New Hymn of Maryland," "Hark the Call of Liberty," "The New Dixie," "The Land of Sweet Adventure," etc. Author and editor in chief Music and Musicians of Maine, 1920; composed vocal arrangement and words for Italian nat. hymn, "Marcia Reale." State musical dir., also song leader during war period; organized Liberty choruses of Me. into Centennial Chorus for Me. Centennial Celebration, 1920. Died Mar. 21, 1932.

EDWARDS, Harry Stillwell, author; b. Macon, Ga., Apr. 23, 1855; B.L., Mercer U., Macon, 1877, also LL.D.; hon. P.B.K., U. of Ga.; m. Mary Roxie Lane, Jan. 13, 1881; children—Jackson Lane, Frances Brooking (dec.), Roxilane, Prentiss Stillwell, Virginia Lane (dec.), Fender. Asst. editor and editor Macon Telegraph, 1881-87, Evening News and Sunday Times, 1887-88, postmaster Macon, 1900-13. Del.-at-large Rep. Nat. Conv., Chicago, 1904, and seconded nomination of Theodore Roosevelt for the South; referee, Ga., for Roosevelt administrations, 7 yrs.; independent candidate for U.S. Senate, 1920. Originated Stone Mountain Memorial half dollar and secured its issue, 1925. Mem. Nat. Inst. Arts and Letters. Author: Sons and Fathers ($10,000 prize from the Chicago Record in contest open to the world—817 competitors); The Marbeau Cousins; Fifth Dimension ($500 prize), 1912; Two Runaways, and Other Stories; His Defense, and Other Stories; Just Sweethearts, 1919; Æneas Africanus, 1919; Æneas Africanus, Defendant, 1921; Little Legends of the Land (verse), 1930; etc. Awarded 2d prize, Life's short story contest, for "The Answer," 1916. Home: Macon, Ga. Died Oct. 22, 1938.

EDWARDS, Howard, college pres.; b. Fauquier Co., Va., Nov. 7, 1854; s. Francis Marion and Frances Lawson (Bland) E.; M.A., Randolph-Macon Coll., Va., 1876; student U. of Leipzig, 1877-78, the Sorbonne, Paris, 1891-92; LL.D., U. of Ark., 1891, Brown U., 1914; LL.D., Mich. State Coll., 1927; Litt.D., R.I. Normal Coll., 1927; m. Elizabeth M. Smith, Jan. 5, 1881; children—Marion Norman (dec.), Thomas Howard (dec.), Clarence Bland, Mildred Elizabeth (dec.). Asso. prin. Bethel Mil. Acad., 1878-80; teacher Bingham Sch., N.C., 1880-82; prin. Bethel (Va.) Acad., 1882-84, acad. at Tuscumbia, Ala., 1884-85; prof. English and modern langs., U. of Ark., 1885-90, Mich. Agrl. Coll., 1890-1906; pres. R.I. State Coll., July 1, 1906—. Pres. Nat. Assn. Land-Grant Colls., 1923. Home: Kingston, R.I. Died Apr. 9, 1930.

EDWARDS, James Thomas, educator; b. Barnegat, N.J., Jan. 6, 1838; s. Rev. Job and Susannah (Haywood) E.; A.B., Wesleyan U. 1860, A.M.; (D.D., and LL.D., Allegheny Coll.); m. Emma A. Baker, July 10, 1862. Lt. and adj. U.S.A., 1862-63. Prin. E. Greenwich Sem., R.I., 1864-70, Chamberlain Inst., N.Y., 1870-92; field sec. Chautauqua System of Edn., 1892-93; prin. McDonogh Sch., nr. Baltimore, 1893-98. Mem. R.I. Senate, 1865-69; presdl. elector, 1868; mem. N.Y. Senate, 1892-93; author University bill and Library and Traveling Library bills. Dir. dept. physics and chemistry, Chautauqua U. (summer schs.), 1883-93; v.p. Chautauqua bd. trustees; mem. Congress of Religions, 1893; pres. Western N.Y. Agrl. Soc. Home: Randolph, N.Y. Died Aug. 20, 1914.

EDWARDS, John Richard, naval officer; b. Pottsville, Pa., July 9, 1853; grad. U.S. Naval Acad., 1874. Promoted asst. engr., Feb. 26, 1875; passed asst. engr., Sept. 11, 1881; chief engr., Nov. 5, 1895; transferred to the line as lt. comdr., Mar. 3, 1899; promoted comdr., Sept. 23, 1903; capt. Jan. 3, 1908; rear admiral, Sept. 11, 1911. Served on Puritan during Spanish-Am. War; detailed Bur. Steam Engring., 1895-97, 1900-04; chief engr. officer, Navy Yard, Portsmouth, N.H., 1904-08; insp. machinery, works of Wm. Cramp & Sons Co., Phila., 1908-11; gen. insp. machy. for Navy, 1911-12; pres. Bd. Inspection and Survey for shore stations, 1912-14; comdt. Navy Yard, Charleston, S.C., 1914-15; retired on account of age, July 9, 1915. Sr. mem. Naval Liquid Fuel Bd., 1901-04; chmn. Am. delegation to Internat. Radio-telegraphic Conf., London, 1912; sr. mem. Naval Fuel Oil Bd., 1915; comdt. U.S. Naval Unit, Brown U., 1918; spl. duty Naval Training Sta., Newport, R.I., 1918-19. Home: Bristol, R.I. Died Dec. 2, 1922.

EDWARDS, Julian, composer; b. Manchester, Eng., Dec. 11, 1855; ed. there; student of music under Sir Herbert Oakeley, Edinburgh, and Sir George Macfarran, London; m. Philippine Siedle, Jan. 9, 1889. Composed several operettas played in British provinces; became conductor Royal English Opera Co.; came to U.S., July 1888. Composer: Jupiter (comic opera), prod. 1892; Friend Fritz (musical comedy), 1893; King Rene's Daughter (lyrical drama), 1893; Goddess of Truth (comic opera), 1896; Brian Boru, 1893; music to Quo Vadis. Cantatas: The Redeemer; Lazarus; Mary Magdalene; The Lord of Light and Love; The Mermaid. Songs: When Johnny Comes Marching Home; Princess Chic; Wedding Day; Belle of London Towne; Gay Musician; Gentleman from France; Palace of the King; Maid of Plymouth; On a Balcony; Land of Heart's Desire. Author: Sunlight and Shadow (song collection). Home: Yonkers, N.Y. Died 1910.

EDWARDS, Landon Brame, physician, editor; b. Prince Edward Co., Va., Sept. 20, 1845; s. Rev. John Ellis and Elizabeth Agnes (Clark) E.; ed. private schools, Lynchburg Mil. Coll., Randolph-Macon Coll.; M.D., U. City of New York, 1867; m. Nannie Pettyjohn Rucker, Jan. 17, 1871. House phys. Blackwell's Island, New York, 1867-68; practiced Lynchburg, Va., 1869-72; removed to Richmond, 1872; founded, 1874, and since editor and propr. Va. Med. Monthly (changed to Va. Med. Semi-Monthly, 1896). Mem. Va. State Bd. Health, 1872-1908; lecturer Med. Coll. of Va., 1874-77; prof. 1893-1907, clinical prof. and chmn. med. faculty, 1900-07, Univ. Coll. of Medicine, Richmond. Del. 9th Internat. Med. Congress, 1887; mem. Pan-Am. Med. Congress, 1893; del. Internat. Med. Press Congress, Paris, 1900. Charter fellow and recording sec., 1870— (except 1883), Med. Soc. of Va., hon. fellow of same; also of W.Va. State Med. Assn. Home: Richmond, Va. Died 1910.

EDWARDS, Louise Betts, author, journalist; b. Phila., Pa., ed. pvt. schs., Friends Sch.; connected with Phila. Press, several yrs., and with Curtis Pub. Co., Phila., 1910-17, as mgr. "Girls' Club" of The Ladies' Home Journal, then engaged in publicity work, etc. Author: The Tu-Tze's Tower (novel); A Friend of Cara's; A Woman for Nothing. Home: Philadelphia, Pa. Died Jan. 8, 1928.

EDWARDS, Nathaniel Marsh, civil engr.; b. Haverhill, Mass., July 5, 1837; s. John and Mary (Marsh) E.; grad. Union, C.E., 1859; served in Civil war, all grades private to capt., 5th Mass. vols. and 1st N.Y. Vol. Engrs. after capture Charleston, S.C., was chief engr. in charge of its fortifications; engr. and supt. Green Bay and Mississippi Canal Co., 1866-71; in charge under U.S. engrs., of Fox and Wisconsin rivers improvements, 1871-76; in practice as civil and hydraulic engr. Home: Appleton, Wis. Died 1908.

EDWARDS, Ogden Matthias, Jr., M.D.; b. Pittsburgh, Pa., Dec. 23, 1869; s. Ogden M. and Sara (Herron) E.; B.S., Princeton, 1893; M.D., Coll. Phys. and Surg. (Columbia), 1896; m. Lela Harkness, Nov. 28, 1898; children—Martha Harkness (Mrs. John M. Lazear), Lela Harkness (Mrs. Harry Cook), Harkness, Katherine Harkness (Mrs. H. Willis Nichols, Jr.). Began practice in Pittsburgh, 1897; prof. of pediatrics, 1909-17, actg. dean, 1917-19, Sch. of Medicine U. of Pittsburgh; retired from practice, 1917. Trustee Shady Side Academy, U. of Pittsburgh, Presbyn. Hospital. Presbyterian. Home: Pittsburgh, Pa. Died Dec. 28, 1940.

EDWARDS, Richard, educator; b. Cardiganshire, Wales, Dec. 23, 1822; s. Richard and Anne (Jones) E.; came to U.S., 1833; grad. State Normal Sch., Bridgewater, Mass., 1845; C.E., B.S., 1848, Rensselaer Poly. Inst.; (A.M., Harvard, 1863; LL.D., Shurtleff Coll., 1867; D.D., Blackburn Coll., Ill., 1890); m. Betsey Josselyn Samson, July 5, 1849. Prin. State Normal Sch., Salem, Mass., 1854-57, St. Louis City Normal Sch., 1857-62; pres. State Normal Univ., Ill., 1862-76; pastor 1st Congl. Ch., Princeton, Ill., 1876-85; agt. Knox Coll., Ill., 1885-87; state supt. pub. instrn., Ill., 1887-91; prof. Wesleyan Univ., Bloomington, Ill., 1894-97. Republican. Presbyn. Home: Bloomington, Ill. Died 1908.

EDWARDS, Samuel, judge; b. Glenville, N.Y., Apr. 24, 1839; s. Samuel B. and Ruth L. (Rogers) E.; grad. Union Coll., 1862; studied law; m. Harriet A. Mellen, Oct. 2, 1867 (died 1891); m. 2d, Emma W. Peck, Feb. 1, 1898. Justice Supreme Ct. of N.Y., Jan. 1887 to Dec. 31, 1901; was a mem. of the Appellate Div. when term expired. Home: Hudson, N.Y. Died 1912.

EDWARDS, Stephen Ostrom, lawyer; b. Glen, N.Y., Jan. 22, 1855; s. William Henry and Eleanor Schenck (Mount) E.; A.B., Brown U., 1879, A.M., 1882; studied Boston U. Law Sch., 1882-83; m. Ellen A. Chace, June 30, 1887. Admitted to bar, Feb. 1884; instr. mathematics and logic, Brown U., 1886-87; clerk R.I. Ho. of Rep., 1889-91; sr. mem. Edwards & Angell, May 1, 1894—; pres. Providence & Worcester R.R. Co.; dir. Providence Journal Co., R.I. Hosp. Trust Co., Providence Lying-in Hospital, Providence Soc. for Organizing Charities; pres. Providence Working Men's Loan Assn. Mem. commn. on revision of jud. system of R.I., 1904-05; mem. com. of management, John Carter Brown Library; trustee Brown U., 1889—, and mem. advisory and exec. com.; trustee Ann Mary Brown Memorial. Home: Providence, R.I. Died Jan. 22, 1916.

EDWARDS, Thomas Cynonfardd, clergyman; b. Swansea, Wales, Dec. 6, 1848; s. Richard and Mary (Owen) E.; ed. Nat. Sch., Cwmbach, Wales, 1855-62, British Sch., Aberdare, Wales, 1865-66; Tydvil Sch., Merthyr, as student and asst. master, 1866-67; Carmarthen Presbyn. Coll., 1868-70; Nat. Sch. Oratory, Phila., 1879-81, degree Master of Oratory, 1899; D.D., Marietta Coll., Ohio, 1891; m. Elizabeth, d. Rev. Jonah Morgan, Cwmbach, Wales, May 4, 1871; children—Gwendolen Cynon, Annie Mary, Morgan Owen, Frances Morgan, Lillian Sylva, Cromwell (dec.), Oliver M. (dec.). Congl. clergyman, Jan. 1, 1871—; pastor of largest Welsh Congl. ch. in U.S., at Edwardsville, Pa., Jan. 1, 1878—. Prof. elocution, Wyoming Sem., Kingston, Pa., 1880-90. Is frequently called to Wales to conduct the great Nat. Eisteddfod (assemblies of 12,000 to 20,000 people); elected arch-druid of America, 1913. Republican. Author: The Mayflower, and Other Poems, 1877; Darllen a Siarad, 1891; Elocution, 1893; last 2 pub. in Wales. Edited Welsh Congregational mag., The Missionary, several yrs., the new Congregational Hymnal, Welsh-English hymns and tunes, 1917. V.p. Kingston Deposit & Savings Bank, 1915—. Home: Kingston, Pa. Died Mar. 13, 1927.

EDWARDS, Victor Everett, mech. engr.; b. North Chelmsford, Mass., Sept. 4, 1862; s. Nathan Brown and Sibbyl Robbins (Hutchins) E.; B.S., Worcester Poly. Inst., 1883, D.Engring., same, 1927; m. Janet Gage, Oct. 6, 1896. Asst. chief engr., Merrimack Mfg. Co., Lowell, Mass., 1883-84; later with Washburn & Moen, Worcester, Otis Steel Co., Cleveland, and Charles H. Morgan, Worcester, Mass.; v.p. Morgan Constrn. Co., 1891—; maj. ordnance engring., 1918; maj. Ordnance R.C. Home: West Boylston, Mass. Deceased.

EDWARDS, William Augustus, architect; b. Darlington, S.C., Dec. 8, 1866; s. Augustus Fulton and Elizabeth Sarah (Hart) E.; prep. edn., St. Davids Acad., Society Hill, S.C.; student Richmond (Va.) Coll. 1 yr.; B.S. in Mech. Engring., U. of S.C., 1889; m. India Pearl Brown, Dec. 21, 1898; children—William Augustus, Mary Wilson (dec.), Araminta (Mrs. Ralph Copeland Pate), Harrison Griffith. Began practice as mem. firm Wilson & Edwards, Roanoke, Va., 1893, at Columbia, S.C., 1896-1902; mem. Edwards & Walter, at Columbia, 1902-08, at Atlanta, 1908-10; practiced alone, Atlanta, 1910-15, mem. Edwards & Sayward, 1915—. Firm architects for U. of Florida at Gainesville, State Coll. for Women, Tallahassee, Ga. State Woman's Coll., Valdosta, Ga., Columbia Theol. Sem., Decatur, Ga., Winthrop Coll., Rock Hill, S.C.; post office and court house, Columbus, Ga.; Pub. Works Administration univ. housing project for Negroes, Atlanta, Ga.; Agnes Scott Coll. library building, Decatur, Ga.; Teachers College, Statesboro, Ga., etc.; also architects for 9 court houses in South Carolina, 2 in Florida, 2 in Ga., Hotel Candler, Decatur, Ga., Hotel Thomas, Gainesville, Fla., etc. Mem. Am. Inst. Architects. Democrat. Unitarian. Home: Atlanta, Ga. Died Mar. 30, 1939.

EDWARDS, William Henry, naturalist; b. Hunter, N.Y., Mar. 15, 1822; s. William W. and Helen Ann Mann E.; grad. Williams, 1842; admitted to New York bar, 1847; made a voyage up the River Amazon, 1846, collecting objects of natural history; has lived for some yrs. in W.Va.; m. Catherine Colt Tappan, May 29, 1851. Author: The Butterflies of North America (3 series), 1879, 1884 and 1897. Home: Coalburgh, W.Va. Died 1909.

EDWARDS, William Seymour, lawyer; b. New York, Sept. 14, 1856; s. William H. and Catherine Colt (Tappan) E.; B.S., Cornell, 1879; LL.B. (cum laude), Columbia, 1882; admitted to bar, 1883; m. Hope M. Christensen, July 5, 1902. Engaged in law practice; also pres. Hamilton Gas Co., Vespertine Oil Co., Coalburg-Kanawha Coal Co., Gallatin Mining Co. Mem. W.Va. House of Dels., 1892-95 (speaker, 1894-95); Rep. candidate for Congress, 3d W.Va. Dist., 1898; chmn. W.Va. delegation Rep. Nat. Conv., Chicago, 1908; mem. Rep. Nat. Com. for W.Va., 1912—; candidate Progressive and Roosevelt Republicans for the U.S. Senate, 1913. Author: Coals and Cokes in West Virginia, 1892; Into the Yukon, 1904; Through Scandinavia to Moscow, 1906; On the Mexican Highlands, 1906-07. Home: Coalburg, W.Va. Died Dec. 26, 1915.

EELLS, Dan Parmelee, banker; b. Westmoreland, N.Y., Apr. 16, 1825; s. Rev. James and Hetty (Parmelee) E.; grad. Hamilton Coll., 1848; connected with commercial branch State Bank of Ohio and its successor, the Commercial Nat. Bank of Cleveland, Mar. 1, 1849, to July 1, 1897; cashier, 1857-65; v.p., 1865-68; pres., 1868-97. Dir. U.S. Express Co., and, until recent retirement from business on account of failing health, identified with many corporations, and with many ednl. and charitable enterprises. Home: Cleveland, O. Died 1903.

EELLS, Howard Parmelee, real estate; b. Cleveland, O., June 16, 1855; s. Dan Parmelee and Mary (Howard) E.; A.B., Hamilton Coll., N.Y., 1876; A.B., Harvard, 1877; m. Alice Maude Overton, Apr. 20, 1881 (died 1885); m. 2d, Maud Stager, Nov. 11,

1889. Chmn. of bd., Bucyrus Co., mfrs. excavating machy., etc., South Milwaukee, Wis.; also pres. Atchison & Eastern Bridge Co., Dolomite Products Co., Howard Realty Co. Trustee Western Reserve U., Cleveland Sch. of Art, Home for Aged Women, Second Presbyn. Church, East End Sch. Assn.; treas., Cleveland Protestant Orphan Asylum, Cleveland Humane Soc. Mem. Cleveland Chamber Commerce. Republican. Home: Euclid Heights, Cleveland, O. Died Feb. 11, 1919.

EELLS, Myron, Congl. clergyman; b. Walker's Prairie, Wash., Oct. 7, 1843; s. Rev. Cushing and Myra F. E.; ed. in Ore.; grad. Pacific Univ., Ore., 1866 (A.M.); grad. Hartford Theol. Sem., 1871 (D.D., Whitman Coll.); m. Sarah M. Crosby, Jan. 18, 1874. Ordained Hartford, Conn., 1871; pastor Boise City, Ida., 1872-74; from 1874, missionary Am. Missionary Assn. among Indians at Skokomish, Wash.; from 1876 also pastor Skokomish Congl. Ch. and serves 4 other Congl. chs. in Wash. Trustee Pacific Univ. and Whitman Coll. Supt., 1893, ethnol. exhibit of Wash., World's Columbian Expn. Author: History of Indian Missions on the Pacific Coast, 1882; Ten Years at Skokomish, 1886. Has furnished Smithsonian Instn. with Vocabularies of the Chemakum, Clallum and Twana languages; Skwaksin dialect of the Niskwalli language; Lower and Upper Chehalis languages and Chinook jargon. Home: Twana, Wash. Died 1907.

EELLS, Stillman Witt, foreign service officer; b. Cleveland, O., Apr. 24, 1873; s. Dan P. and Mary (Witt) E.; prep. edn., Brook's Mil. Acad., Cleveland Manual Training Sch. (Cleveland) and Taft's Sch. for Boys, Pelham Manor, N.Y.; B.A., Yale, 1895; m. Helene Florence Waterman, Sept. 4, 1895. Began as sec. Chicago Drop Forge & Foundry Co., 1896; pres. Wheeler Mfg. Co. and the Alignum Co., New York, 1896-1903, also dir. Sandusky Portland Cement Co., Cleveland, Ohio; retired from active business, 1904; moved to Bermuda, 1909; apptd. vice-consul to Hamilton, Bermuda, Mar. 20, 1916, consul, 1918; consul, Mombassa, Brit. East Africa, 1918, Nairobi, Kenya Colony, 1918-21, Funchal, Madeira, 1921-25, Leeds, Eng., 1925-28, Colombo, Ceylon, 1928-31, Cardiff, Wales, 1931-34, Valencia, Spain, 1934-35; retired. Decorated Cavalieri del Ordine della Corona d'Italia, 1922. Mason. Home: Larchmont, N.Y. Died May 12, 1937.

EFFINGER, John Robert, prof. French; b. Keokuk, Ia., July 3, 1869; s. John Robert and Lucretia (Knowles) E.; Ph.B., U. of Mich., 1891, Ph.M., 1894, Ph.D., 1898; Litt.D. from Kalamazoo (Mich.) Coll., 1927; studied in Paris, France; m. Margaret Thain, June 24, 1903; children—Margaret Knowles, John Robert. Instr. in French, 1892-98, asst. prof., 1898-1906, jr. prof., 1906-12, prof., 1912—, U. of Mich.; dean summer session, U. of Mich., 1908-12, acting dean, Col. of Lit., Science and Arts, same, 1912-15, dean, 1915—. Mem. Commn. on Higher Edn., N. Central Assn. of Colls. and Secondary Schs., 1923—; pres. Assn. of Am. Colls., 1926—; chmn. Com. of Selection Rhodes Scholars for Mich.; mem com. on Classification of Colleges, Assn. of Am. Univs., 1926—; mem. bd. visitors Kalamazoo Coll. Republican. Unitarian. Author: A French Grammar (with H. P. Thieme), 1908. Editor: Selected Essays from Ste. Beuve, 1895; Hugo's Préface de Cromwell and Hernani, 1899; Labiche's Voyage de M. Perrichon, 1905; Molière's Précieuses Ridicules and Femmes Savantes, 1912. Died June 7, 1933.

EGAN, Martin; b. Martinez, Calif., June 18, 1872; s. James and Mary (Canty) E.; ed. pub. schs.; studied law; m. Eleanor Franklin, July 19, 1905 (died 1925); m. 2d, Cornelia Cousins, Nov. 19, 1927. Admitted to Calif. bar, 1898; writer for newspapers and mags., U.S. and Can., and with Associated Press in New York, London, Tokyo, Peking and Manila; corr. during Spanish-Am. War, Philippine Insurrection, Boxer uprising and Russo-Japanese War; editor Manila Times, 1908-13; mem. staff of J. P. Morgan & Co., New York, 1914—. Personal asst. to H. P. Davison, chmn. Am. Red Cross War Council, 1917, and civilian aide to Gen. Pershing, 1918. Home: New York, N.Y. Died Dec. 7, 1938.

EGAN, Maurice Francis, diplomat; b. Phila., May 24, 1852; s. Maurice and Margaret (MacMullen) E.; A.B., LaSalle Coll., 1873, A.M.; entered Georgetown (D.C.) Coll., 1875; (A.M., Notre Dame, 1878; LL.D., Georgetown, 1879; J.U.D., Ottawa U., 1891; Ph.D., Villanova, Pa., 1907; Litt.D., Columbia, 1919; LL.D., St. John's, Brooklyn, 1920); m. Katharine Mullin, 1880 (died 1921). Sub-editor McGee's Illus. Weekly, 1877-79, Catholic Review, 1879-80; asso. editor and editor Freeman's Journal, 1880-88; prof. English lit., U. of Notre Dame, 1888-95; prof. English lang. and lit., Catholic U. of America, 1895-1907; E.E. and M.P. from U.S. to Denmark, 1907-18. Author: The Life Around Us; Jack Chumleigh at Boarding School; The Disappearance of John Longworthy; Chatelaine of the Roses; Jasper Thorne; In a Brazilian Forest; The Leopard of Lancianus; Studies in Literature; The Watson Girls; Belinda; Belinda's Cousins; The Wiles of Sexton Maginnis; Everybody's St. Francis; Ten Years on the German Frontier, 1919. Translator: (for Augustin Daly) Coppée's Pater; Sonnets of José de Hérédia (in World's Best Literature). One of the editors of the World's Best Literature, Ency. of Irish Literature, etc. Decorated by King of Belgium, 1906; awarded Lætare Medal for poetry, 1911. Lecturer, Johns Hopkins, on Percy Turnbull Foundation, 1911. Mem. Indian Commn., 1906-07. Comdr. Order of the Dannebrog, 1919. Mem. Nat. Inst. Arts and Letters, Am. Acad. Arts and Letters. Lecturer Harvard U., 1914. Spl. book reviewer for New York Times; mem. Knights of Columbus hist. commn. for examining sources of Am. history. The Danish West Indies were bought by the U.S. during his term of office; served under 3 presdl. administrations; was slated by Pres. Cleveland for mission to Athens, Greece, but declined, the diplomatic crisis having passed; declined ambassadorship to Vienna tendered by Presidents Taft and Wilson. Died Jan. 15, 1924.

EGBERT, Seneca, M.D.; b. Petroleum Centre, Pa., Feb. 17, 1863; s. Albert G. and Eliza (Phipps) E.; A.B., Princeton, 1884, A.M., 1887; M.D., U. of Pa., 1888, Dr. P.H., 1921; m. Nancy McClellan Bredin, Sept. 26, 1888; children—Victor Egbert, Mrs. Catherine Bredin Sparks. Lecturer on hygiene at U. of Pa., 1890-92, at P.E. Ch. Training Sch., 1891-1931; prof. hygiene, 1893-1916, dean, 1898-1916, Medico-Chirurg. College, Temple Coll., Phila., 1896-99; prof. of hygiene, U. of Pa. Medical Sch., 1916-31 (emeritus). Major Medical O.R.C., 1917-18. Author: A Manual of Hygiene and Sanitation, 1898, 8th edit., 1926; Personal Hygiene for Nurses, 1930. Home: Wayne, Pa. Died Dec. 6, 1939.

EGBERT, W(illiam) Grant, musician; b. Danby, N.Y., Dec. 28, 1869; s. William Lewis and Esther Roper (Grant) E.; ed. pub. schs., Syracuse U. and under pvt. tutors; student Joachin Royal Hochschule für Musik, Berlin, 1890-92; studied with Prof. O. Sevcik, Prague, 1903-06, and other European masters; hon. M.A. in Music, Syracuse U., 1904; m. Mabelle Chamberlaine Greene, June 27, 1914 (died 1918); children—Gladys Adelle, William Grant. Début at 8 as violinist; toured U.S., and played in the capitals of Europe; concertmeister and asst. conductor Sevcik Orchestra, Prague, 3 yrs.; founder, 1892, and musical dir. Ithaca Conservatory of Music and affiliated schs., 18 yrs., resigned; brought Cèsar Thomson and Sevcik to U.S. as teachers. Diamond medal (Anglo-Am.), Prague, for distinguished services, 1906. Republican. Methodist. Mason. Home: Ithaca, N.Y. Deceased.

EGERTON, Graham, lawyer; b. nr. Bombay, India, May 6, 1861; s. Philip Henry and Mary (Marjoribanks) E.; ed. Rossall Coll., Eng., Edinburgh U., Scotland; LL.B., Cumberland U., Tenn., 1889; m. Julia Donegan Easley, Feb. 13, 1887. Came to U.S., 1881, naturalized citizen, 1887; admitted to Tenn. bar, 1888, and practiced at Dickson; apptd. spl. judge 9th Jud. Circuit, 1911; solicitor for Navy Dept., Sept. 13, 1913-Dec. 1, 1921; law practice, Washington, 1921—. Democrat. Mem. Ch. of Christ (Disciples). Compiler: The Eight Hour Law (Govt. publ.), 1918. Home: Washington, D.C. Died Mar. 1922.

EGGERT, Charles Augustus, coll. prof.; b. Magdeburg, Prussia; s. Charles Augustus and Sophia (Siegfried) E.; A.M., Princeton; A.M., Ph.D., U. of Heidelberg; LL.B., State U. of Iowa, 1889; fellow in Romance philology, Johns Hopkins, 1892-93; widower; father of Carl Edgar E. Prof. of modern langs., State U. of Ia., 1878-89; practiced law in Salt Lake City, 1889-91; prof. Romance langs., Vanderbilt U., 1892-95; prof. modern langs., U. of S.D., 1895-97; prof. French and history, Ill. Wesleyan U., Sept., 1908-11. Republican. Conglist. Author: The School and the Farm, 1902. Editor: Racine's Athalie, 1894; Molière's Le Misanthrope, 1899; Goethe's Iphigenie, 1899; Goethe's Das Märchen, 1900; Schiller's Wallenstein's Tod., 1901; Scribe's Le Verre d'Eau, 1901; Von Wildenbruch's Harold, 1901; Voltaire's Zaïre et Epîtres, 1902; Von Wildenbruch's Das Edle Blut, 1904; Scribe's Bataille de Dames, 1908; Molière's Les Femmes Savantes, 1910. Died Feb. 1931.

EGGLESTON, Edward, author; b. Vevay, Ind., Dec. 10, 1837; s. Joseph Cary and Mary Jane E.; ed. in country and village schools in Ind., and at boarding school in Amelia Co., Va. (hon. degrees A.M., S.T.D., L.H.D.); m. 2d, Frances E. Goode, Sept. 14, 1891. Entered M.E. ministry, 1857, traveling circuit in Southeast Ind., and later for 9 yrs. in Minn.; asso. editor Little Corporal, Chicago, 1866-67; chief editor Nat. Sunday School Teacher, 1867-70; editor Independent, New York, 1870-72; Hearth and Home, New York, 1871-72; pastor Ch. of Christian Endeavor, Brooklyn, 1874-79; retired from ministry and devoted to literature; pres. Am. Hist. Soc. Author: The Hoosier Schoolmaster, 1871; The End of the World, 1872; The Mystery of Metropolisville, 1873; The Circuit Rider, 1874; Roxy, 1878; The Hoosier School-Boy, 1883; The Graysons, 1888; History of the United States and Its People, for the Use of Schools, 1888; First Book in American History, 1889; Stories of Great Americans for Little Americans; Stories of American Life and Adventure; The Beginners of a Nation, 1896; The Transit of Civilization from England to America, 1900. Editor: Christ in Art, 1874; Christ in Literature, 1875. Homes: Lake George, N.Y., and N.Y. City. Died 1902.

EGGLESTON, George Cary, author; b. Vevay, Ind., Nov. 26, 1839; s. Joseph Cary and Mary Jane (Craig) E.; ed. Ind. Asbury (now De Pauw) U. and Richmond Coll., Va.; practiced law in Va.; served in C.S.A. during Civil War; m. Marion Craggs, Sept. 9, 1868. After war filled important newspaper positions in New York among them lit. editor of Evening Post for 6 yrs., and editor-in-chief of Hearth and Home; editor Commercial Advertiser, 1884-89; editorial writer World, 1889-1900. Author: The Big Brother, 1875; Captain Sam, 1876; The Signal Boys, 1877; The Wreck of the Red Bird, 1882; The Last of the Flatboats, 1900; A Carolina Cavalier, 1901; Camp Venture, 1901; Dorothy South, 1902; American Immortals, 1902; The Bale Marked Circle X, 1902; The Master of Warlock, 1903; Evelyn Byrd, 1904; A Daughter of the South, 1905; Jack Shelby, 1906; Love is the Sum of it All, 1907; Long Knives, 1907; Two Gentlemen of Virginia, 1908; The Warrens of Virginia, 1908; Irene of the Mountains, 1909. Died 1911.

EGLE, William Henry, State librarian of Pa., 1887—; b. Harrisburg, Pa., Sept. 17, 1830; ed. public schools; m. Eliza White Beatty, 1860. Engaged in printing and newspaper work, but later studied medicine; grad. med. dept. U. of Pa., 1859; settled in Harrisburg. Served through Civil War as surgeon of vols.; from 1871 engaged in historical research. Member of learned societies in U.S., France and England, and of various hereditary societies. Author: History of Pennsylvania; Pennsylvania Genealogies, Scotch-Irish and German; Pennsylvania in the Revolution; Notes and Queries, Historical, Biographical, and Genealogical (10 vols.). Edited Pa. Archives (2d series, vols. 1-19; 3d series, vols. 1-30). Home: Harrisburg, Pa. Died 1901.

EGLESTON, Thomas, mining engr. and metallurgist; b. New York, Dec. 9, 1832; grad. Yale, 1854 (A.M., 1857); grad. Ecole des Mines, Paris, E.M., 1860 (Ph.D., Princeton, 1874; LL.D., Trinity, 1874); chevalier, 1890; officer, 1895, Legion of Honor of France; m. Augusti McVickar (died 1895), May 2, 1865. In charge mineral and metallurgical products, Smithsonian Instn., 1861-64. Founded, 1864, School of Mines, Columbia; prof. mineralogy and metallurgy there, 1864-97, emeritus. Author: Lectures on Mineralogy (4 vols.); Metallurgy of Silver; Metallurgy of Gold; Tables for Determination of Weights, Measures and Coins in the Metric and English Systems. Died 1900.

EGLIN, William Charles Lawson, elec. engr.; b. Glasgow, Scotland, July 14, 1870; s. William and Mary Porter (Meikle) E.; ed. Andersonian University, Glasgow, and U. of Glasgow; unmarried. With Edison Electric Light Co., Philadelphia, 1889—; 2d v.p. and chief engr. Phila. Electric Co., which has leased all the electric lighting plants in the city; has designed many of the co.'s plants, notably the modern main generating sta. at Christian St. Home: Philadelphia, Pa. Died Feb. 7, 1928.

EHRENFELD, Charles Hatch, chemist, educator; b. Shippensburg, Pa., Mar. 12, 1864; s. Charles Lewis and Helen Margaret (Hatch) E.; A.B., Wittenberg Coll., Ohio, 1886, A.M., 1889; Ph.D., U. of Pa., 1894; Sc.D., Wittenberg, 1916; Litt. D., Gettysburg, 1926; m. Bertha K. Spahr, Apr. 16, 1891; children—Helen (Mrs. Lewis C. Spencer), Walter Spahr. Assistant in chem. laboratory, Wittenberg Coll., 1886-87; professor chemistry and physics, York (Pa.) Collegiate Inst., 1887-1916; pres. same, Jan. 31, 1916-July 1, 1928; chief chemist York Mfg. Co. (refrigeration machinery), 1903-16; cons. chemist same, 1923-28, mgr. of chem. and testing materials dept., 1928-31; with editorial dept., The Science Press, Lancaster, Pa., 1931; York County supervisor Civil Works Adminstrn. and State Emergency Relief Bd., 1933-35; supervisor census of business, U.S. Dept. Commerce (22d Congressional Dist. Pa.), 1935-36; editorial columnist York Gazette and Daily, 1935—. Mem. City Council, 1906-13 (pres. 1908-13); pres. health dept., York, 1907-08. Apptd. by U.S. Dept. of Labor industrial adviser to Draft Bd. for the Middle Dist. of Pa., 1918, and by the U.S. Employment Service, chmn. Community Labor Bd., No. 34, of Pa. Author: (with R. E. Gibbs) Water for Ice-Making and Refrigeration, 1928. Home: York, Pa. Died Sept. 25, 1937.

EHRENFELD, Charles Lewis, clergyman, teacher; b. Mifflin Co., Pa., June 15, 1832; s. Augustus Clemens and Charlotte Catharine (Stitzer) E.; A.B., Wittenberg Coll., Springfield, O., 1856, A.M., 1859, Ph.D., 1878; m. Helen Margaret Hatch, Oct. 3, 1860. Ordained Luth. ministry, 1860; pastor Altoona, Shippensburg and Hollidaysburg, Pa., 1860-71; elected head of Southwestern Normal Coll., California, Pa., 1871 (instn. obtained recognition by state as one of its normal schs., 1874); resigned, 1877, to become financial sec. Dept. of Pub. Instrn. of Pa.; state librarian of Pa., 1878-82, resigned; prof. Latin and English, Wittenberg Coll., 1882-92; with Southwestern State Normal Sch., 1892—, becoming asso. prof. German and English. Ind. Republican. Chmn. com. apptd., 1876, by Pa. State Teachers' Assn. to devise plan for better orgn. of state normal schs. Home: York, Pa. Died Jan. 31, 1914.

EHRHARDT, Julius George, oculist and aurist; b. Beardstown, Ill., Oct. 21, 1849; s. Dr. Frederick and Caroline E.; ed. in pub. schs. and by pvt. tutors; M.D., St. Louis Med. Coll., 1869; studied univs. Göttingen, Berlin, and at Paris, Vienna, studying ophthalmology and otology; m. Fannie Eggers. Practiced in Beardstown, 1872-75, then in St. Louis. Mem. 10th Internat. Med. Congress, Berlin, 1890, 8th Internat. Ophthalmol. Congress, Edinburgh, 1894. Home: St. Louis, Mo. Died Sept. 3, 1922.

EHRHORN, Edward Macfarlane, entomologist; b. San Francisco, Calif., Jan. 24, 1862; s. Adolphus and Louisa Maria E.; ed. Hamburg, Germany, 1871-78, Grenchen, Switzerland, 1878-79, Brighton (Eng.) Coll., 1879-80; spl. student entomology, Stanford U., 1891; hon. M.S., U. of Hawaii, 1932; married. Assistant entomologist and deputy quarantine officer State Bd. Horticulture, Calif., 1890-91; co. entomologist and hort. commr., Santa Clara Co., Calif., 1892-1904; 1st deputy state commr. horticulture and horticultural quarantine officer, Calif., 1904-09; supt. entomology of Bd. of Agr. and Forestry of Hawaii, Oct. 1, 1909; chief plant insp. same, 1916, retired from active duty Aug. 1, 1926; cons. entomologist for termite eradication for Bishop Trust Co., Honolulu, 1926—. Honorary cons. entomologist Board of Agr. and Forestry of Hawaii, 1928; lecturer in horticulture, U. of Hawaii, 1932-33. Agent of Territorial Board of Health (hon.), Oct. 1, 1917. Home: Honolulu, T.H. Died Feb. 10, 1941.

EHRICH, Harold Louis, art dealer; b. N.Y. City, Jan. 9, 1880; s. Louis R. and Henriette (Minzie) E.; student Yale, 1902; unmarried. Pres. The Ehrich Galleries, New York. Author: One Hundred Early American Paintings (with Walter L. Ehrich), 1918. Home: New York, N.Y. Died Mar. 28, 1932.

EHRICH, Louis R., antique paintings; b. Albany, N.Y., Jan. 23, 1849; s. Joseph and Rebecca (Sporborg) E.; A.B., Yale, 1869, A.M., 1872; student U. of Berlin, 1869-70; m. Henriette Minzesheimer, Jan. 14, 1874. Only del. from Rocky Mountain region to Palmer and Buckner conv., 1896; mem. of Nat. Com. for Colo. of Good Democrat Party; mem. exec. com., Anti-Imperialist League; temporary chmn. of Third Party conv., Indianapolis, 1900; independent in politics. Author: The Question of Silver. Died 1911.

EHRMAN, Mary Bartholomew, composer; b. Cincinnati, O.; d. George Kellam and Eliza Jane (Briggs) Bartholomew; grad. Bartholomew English and Classical Sch., Cincinnati; traveled and studied in Europe 2 yrs.; m. Dr. George Bigler Ehrman, Dec. 27, 1893; children—Mrs. Ernest Meeves (dec.), George Bartholomew, Albert Hoyt, Robert Briggs. Composer: The Child's Song Garden, 1908; The Child's Song Treasury, 1909; Sleepy Songs for Sleepy Eyes, 1910; Little Songs for Little Folks, 1911; Fairy Songs from Fairyland, 1912; Songs of Happiness, 1912; Melodies in Verse, 1918. Wrote: The Lure of Miami (short poems), 1933. Home: Miami Beach, Fla. Died Mar. 2, 1939.

EICKEMEYER, Rudolf, photographer; b. Yonkers, N.Y., Aug. 7, 1862; s. Rudolf and Mary True (Tarbell) E.; ed. pub. sch., Yonkers, and Hoboken Academy; m. Isabelle Hicks, Oct. 7, 1891; m. 2d, Florence Brevoort, June 1, 1918. Began photographic work as amateur, 1893; asso. with James L. Breese at Carbon Studio, 1895-1900; art mgr. Campbell Studio, 1900-05; partner Charles H. Davis (Davis & Sanford Studio), Oct. 1905-09, Campbell Studio, 538 5th Av., New York, 1911-15. Mem. Yonkers Bd. Edn., 1895-1919; chmn. 1st Municipal Art Commn., Yonkers, 1910—; comr. Yonkers Museum of Science and Art. Received medal, Royal Photog. Soc., England; Viceroy medal, Calcutta Internat. Exhbn.; gold medal, St. Louis Expn.; spl. gold medal, Hamburg Senate; about 75 other medals and diplomas. Mem. the Linked Ring, London, London Salon of Photography, and of New York Camera Club, art dir. Salon Club of America. Mason. Illustrator: In and Out of the Nursery; Nature and Culture (Hamilton Wright Mabie), 1904; The Four Seasons (lecture). Author: How to Make a Picture, 1898; Down South, 1901; The Old Farm, 1902; Winter, 1904. U.S. Govt. acquired 83 of his photographs for permanent exhibition at the National Mus., Washington, D.C., 1930. Home: Yonkers, N.Y. Died Apr. 25, 1932.

EIDLITZ, Charles Leo, elec. engr.; b. New York, Sept. 3, 1866; s. Marc and Mathilde (Sohr) E.; bro. of Otto Marc E.; ed. Columbia Grammar Sch. and Columbia U.; m. Margretta Ruth Lydon, Sept. 25, 1889. With Edison Electric Co., 1888-89; organized, 1889, and became pres., Charles L. Eidlitz Co., Atlantic Elec. Goods Co., R. B. Corey Co.; treas. and dir. Eastave Realty Co. Organized 1903, pres., 1903-05, Building Trades Employers' Assn.; 1st pres. Nat. Elec. Contractors' Assn., 1901-03; mem. sch. bd. Gen. Soc. Mechanics and Tradesmen. Home: New York, N.Y. Died Sept. 5, 1921.

EIDLITZ, Otto Marc, builder; b. New York, Sept. 18, 1860; s. Marc and Mathilde (Sohr) E.; bro. of Charles Leo E.; ed. Coll. City of New York, 1875-77; B.C.E., Cornell Univ., 1881, C.E., 1890; m. Anna May Thomas. Entered employ of father, 1881; became sr. partner, Marc Eidlitz & Son, 1892, on death of father, inc., now pres.; trustee Bank for Savings. Appointed Tenement House commr., 1900; mem. commn. to investigate question of employers' liability, safety appliances and the causes and effects of unemployment in the state of N.Y., 1909; mem. bd. arbitration in controversy bet. 52 rys. east of Chicago and Brotherhood of Locomotive Engrs., 1912. Apptd. chmn. com. on housing, for industrial war workers, Oct. 18, 1917; apptd. dir. Bur. of Housing and Transportation of Dept. Labor, Mar. 18, 1918, and pres. U.S. Housing Corp., July 2, 1918; about 60 projects started and 27 completed upon or after the armistice, including about 6,000 houses and other bldgs. Pres. Mason Bldrs.' Assn. of N.Y., 1900-04; chmn. bd. of govs., Bldg. Trades Employers' Assn., 1903-05. Home: New York, N.Y. Died Oct. 30, 1928.

EIDMANN, Frank Lewis, prof. mech. engring.; b. Kingston, N.Y., Dec. 20, 1887; s. John Frederick and Susanna (Reinmuth) E.; prep. edn. Stevens Prep. Sch., 1902-05; M.E., Stevens Inst. of Tech., 1909; m. Ethel Irene Fischbeck, 1924; 1 son, John Frank. Began as instr., Stevens Inst. Tech., 1909; with engring. dept. Olds Gas Power Co. and Seager Engine Works, Lansing, Mich., 1909-13; instr. in gas engines, Y.M.C.A. Evening Sch., Lansing, 1910-13; instr. in mech. engring., Rensselaer Poly. Inst., 1913-15; instr. in gas engines, Albany (N.Y.) Evening Schs., 1914-15; engr. for developing mfg. processes, Am. LaFrance Fire Engine Co., Elmira, N.Y., 1915-16; plant engr. Heald Machine Co., Worcester, Mass., 1916-17; factory mgr. and chief engr. Cowan Truck Co., Holyoke, Mass., 1917-18, 1919-20; travel around the world, 1921-22; cons. engr. Barrett-Cravens Co., Chicago, and Revolvator Co., Jersey City, N.J., 1922-23; asso. prof. of machine design and industrial practice, Princeton U., 1923-30; prof. mech. engring., Columbia, 1930—; dir. research lab., Gen. Time Instruments Corp., New York, 1931—. Served as lt. j.g., U.S. Naval Aviation, 1918-19. Republican. Presbyterian. Author: Economic Control of Engineering and Manufacturing, 1931. Editor: Aircraft Engine Manual, 1919. Home: Princeton, N.J. Died Sept. 4, 1941.

EIGENMANN, Carl H., zoölogist; b. Flehingen, Germany, 1863; s. Philip and Margaretha (Lieb) E.; A.B., Ind. U., 1886, A.M., 1887, Ph.D., 1889; m. Rosa Smith, Aug. 20, 1887; children—Lucretia Margaretha, Charlotte Elizabeth, Theodore Smith, Adele Rosa E. (Mrs. John O. Eiler), Thora Marie. Prof. zoölogy, 1891—, dean Grad. Sch., 1908—, Ind. U.; curator of fishes, Carnegie Mus., Pittsburgh, 1909-18. Founder and dir. biol. sta., Ind. U., 1895-1920. Explorations in Calif., Ore., Ida., Mont., Dak. and Western Can., 1890-92, Cuba, 1902-04, British Guiana, 1908, Colombia, 1911-12, Peru and Bolivia, 1918, Chile, 1919. Author: Cave Vertebrates of North America, The Archiplata-Archhelenis Theory, The American Characidæ, The Fresh-water Fishes of British Guiana, The Fishes of Western South America, and The Doradidæ. Home: Bloomington, Ind. Died Apr. 24, 1927.

EIKENBARY, Charles Franklin, orthopedic surgeon; b. Eaton, O., Jan. 30, 1877; s. Peter S. and Calista Elizabeth (Crandall) E.; student Miami U., 1897-98; M.D., U. of Chicago, 1903; m. Edna Florence Fisher, Oct. 5, 1904. Began practice in N.Y. Hosp. for the Ruptured and Crippled, 1903; moved to Spokane, Wash., 1907; was orthopedic surgeon St. Luke's, Sacred Heart and Deaconess hosps.; settled at Seattle, 1926; chief of staff Children's Orthopædic Hosp. Served 4 mos. in orthopedic surgery for British Govt., 1917; trans. to France with 2d Div. U.S.A., later with 89th Div.; served at Château-Thierry, Belleau Wood, Verdun, and beginning of St. Mihiel drive; hon. disch., May 1919. Mem. Bd. of Edn., Spokane. Fellow Am. Coll. Surgeons. Republican. Presbyn. Mason. Home: Seattle, Wash. Died Dec. 31, 1933.

EILENBERGER, Clinton B., 3d asst. postmaster general; b. nr. Shawnee on Delaware, Pa., Jan. 25, 1876; s. John M. and Catharine V. (Bush) E.; student East Stroudsburg (Pa.) State Normal Sch., 1896, Drexel Inst., Phila., 1899; m. Florence Savacool, Mar. 7, 1906. Teacher pub. schs., 1895 and 1896; dep. co. treas., Monroe Co., Pa., 1900-09; with Stroudsburg Nat. Bank, 1901-20; treas. Stroudsburg Trust Co., 1920-33; v.p. Stroudsburg Security Trust Co.; 3d asst. postmaster gen. of U.S., Mar. 6, 1933—. Dem. candidate for auditor gen. of Pa., 1928; treas. Pa. Motor Fedn.; pres. Monroe Co. Automobile Club; mem. Bd. of Edn. of Stroudsburg. Democrat. Presbyn. Mason. Home: Stroudsburg, Pa. Died Aug. 28, 1937.

EILERS (Frederic) Anton, mining engr., metallurgist; b. Nassau, Germany, Jan. 14, 1839; s. E. J. A. Frederic and Elizabeth E.; ed. Mining School, Clausthal, and U. of Göttingen; m. Elizabeth Emrich, May 3, 1863. Came to U.S., 1859; asst. to Adelberg and Raymond, mining engrs., 1863-66; in charge mines and copper smelting works, W.Va., 1866-69; deputy U.S. commr. mining statistics, 1869-76; part owner and mgr. Germania Smelting & Refining Works, Salt Lake City, 1876-79; in smelting business (Billing & Eilers), Leadville, Colo., 1879-82; pres. The Colorado Smelting Co. of Pueblo, Colo., 1883-99; dir. and gen. mgr. United S. & R. Co. of Mont. and Chicago, 1890-99; dir. and tech. mem. of exec. com. of Am. Smelting & Refining Co., and of Am. Smelters' Securities Co., 1899-1910, when retired from active business. V.p. Last Dollar Gold Mining Co.; pres. Colo. Mines Exploring Co. Homes: Brooklyn, and Sea Cliff, L.I., N.Y. Died Apr. 22, 1917.

EILERS, Karl (Emrich) metallurgist; b. near Marietta, O., Nov. 20, 1865; s. F. Anton and Elizabeth (Emrich) E.; grad. in arts, Poly. Inst. Brooklyn, 1884; E.M., Sch. of Mines (Columbia), 1889; post-grad. work, U. of Berlin, 1889, until spring of 1891; France and Spain 4 mos. each; m. Leonie Jeannette Wurlitzer, Oct. 19, 1896; children—Marguerite E., K. Fritz, F. Farny. Successively assayer Colo. Smelting Co., Pueblo, Colo., St. Louis Smelting & Refining Co., St. Louis, United Smelting & Refining Co., Chicago, until 1893; supt. Colo. Smelting Co., Pueblo, 1893-98; manager, 1899, dir. and mem. exec. com., 1906-20, v.p., 1916-20, Am. Smelting & Refining Co.; cons. practice, N.Y. City, Apr. 1920—; pres. Colo. Mines Exploring Co. Home: Sea Cliff, L.I., N.Y. Died Aug. 18, 1941.

EILSHEMIUS, Louis Michel, artist; b. Laurel Manor, N.J., Feb. 4, 1864; s. Henry Gotfried and Cecile Eugene (Robert) E.; student Cornell U., 1882-84, Acad., N.Y. City, 1883-86, Julian Acad., Paris, 1886-89; unmarried. Represented in Phillips Memorial Gallery, Washington, D.C., Metropolitan Mus. of Art, Mus. of Modern Art, Whitney Mus. of Art, N.Y. City; Detroit Inst. of Art; Cleveland Mus.; Luxembourg Mus., Paris; Museum of Fine Arts, Boston. Home: New York, N.Y. Died Dec. 29, 1941.

EISELEN, Frederick Carl, educator; b. Mundelsheim, Germany, Nov. 25, 1872; s. Christian and Elizabeth (Veigel) E.; prep. edn., Gymnasium Landsberg, Germany; A.M., New York U., 1899; B.D., Drew Theol. Sem., 1900; student U. of Pa., 1901-02; Ph.D., Columbia, 1907; U. of Berlin, 1908; D.D., Cornell Coll., Ia., 1906, Garrett Bibl. Inst., 1932; LL.D., Lawrence Coll., 1922; m. Lillian R. Robinson, Oct. 23, 1901; children—Malcolm Rogers, Elizabeth. Prof. Semitic langs., Garrett Bibl. Inst., 1902-32, dean, 1919-24, pres., 1924-32; prof. Bibl. lit. Northwestern U., 1918-24; corr. sec. Board of Edn. of M.E. Ch., 1932—. Mem. University Senate of M.E. Ch., 1920-24; mem. Candidates Com. (Chicago) Bd. of Foreign Missions M.E. Ch., 1922, chmn., 1924—; mem. Bur. of Bilingual Work, Bd. of Home Missions, 1924-32; mem. Joint Com. on Religious Edn. in Foreign Fields, 1924—; mem. Wesley Foundations Joint Com., 1924-32; mem. Bd. of Edn., M.E. Ch., 1924-32; mem. Internat. S.S. Lesson Com., 1908-28, and of its successor, the Ednl. Commn. of Internat. Council of Religious Education, 1928—; mem. Standard Bible Com., 1929—, and sec. O.T. Sect., 1930—. Author: Sidon—A Study in Oriental History, 1907; A Commentary on the Minor Prophets, 1907; Prophecy and the Prophets, 1909; The Worker and His Bible (with W. C. Barclay), 1909; The Christian View of the Old Testament, 1912; Books of the Pentateuch, 1916; The Psalms and Other Sacred Writings, 1918; The Prophetic Books of the Old Testament (2 vols.), 1923. Co-editor (with Edwin Lewis and David G. Downey) of The Abingdon Bible Commentary. Home: Evanston, Ill. Died May 5, 1937.

EISEN, Gustavus A(ugustus), biologist, archeologist; b. Stockholm, Sweden, Aug. 2, 1847; s. Frans August and Amalia (Markander) E.; Ph.D., U. of Upsala, Sweden, 1873; came to U.S., Oct. 1873, naturalized, 1887; unmarried. Known specially for researches in Oligochæta (earthworms) of America, researches in the elements of blood of batrachians and man, and the amœba of carcinoma. Publns. on antique glass, antique beads and antique bronzes; author of "The Fig," and "The Raisin Industry," articles, the biol. nature of caprification, explorations in Lower Calif., Mexico, Central Am. republics (1880-1903); archeol. explorations, especially Christian archeology and antique glass (1903-15), in Spain, Italy, Algiers, Tunis, Morocco and Egypt; studies in the principal museums of Europe, 1910-15. One time docent in zoölogy, University Upsala, and collaborator, U.S. Dept. Agriculture; late curator Calif. Acad. Sciences. Pres. San Francisco Micros. Soc. Comdr. Order of North Star (Sweden), 1935; Knight of the Gothic Golden Griffin, 1939. Originator of Sequoia Nat. Park in Calif., 1890. Described and classified the Gellatly and Freer Museum collections of antique glass, Smithsonian Inst. Wrote: (monograph) The Great Chalice of Antioch, 1924; Glass—Antique Glass—Its History and Classification (monographs), 2 vols., 1927. Died Oct. 29, 1940.

EISENDRATH, Daniel Nathan, surgeon; b. Chicago, Nov. 8, 1867; s. Nathan and Helen (Felheimer) E.; A.B., Johns Hopkins, 1889; M.D., Northwestern U. Med. Sch., 1891; was 1½ yrs. on Cook Co. Hosp. house staff; studied abroad 2½ yrs., serving 1 yr. as asst. surgeon in Hamburg Gen. Hosp.; m. Maude Rosenbaum, Feb. 15, 1898. Former asst. clin. prof. surgery (genito-urinary), Rush Med. Coll. (U. of Chicago) and attending urologist Michael Reese Hosp.; cons. urologist Am. Hosp., Paris, France. Fellow

Chicago Surg. and Urological Soc. Republican. Author: A Text Book of Clinical Anatomy, 1903; Text Book on Surgical Diagnosis; Clinical Urology (with H. C. Rolnick), 1928. Died May 30, 1939.

EITEL, George Gotthilf, surgeon; b. Chanhassen, Minn., Sept. 28, 1858; s. John George and Mary (Ulmer) E.; M.D., Minn. Hosp. Coll., 1888, U. of Pa., 1891, U. of Berlin, 1901; m. Jeannette E. Larsen, Feb. 1, 1908. Interne St. Barnabas Hosp., 1888; practiced at Centralia, Wash., 1891-93, at Minneapolis, 1893—; staff surgeon, Asbury Hosp., 1893-1902, St. Barnabas and City hosps., 1902-12; founder, 1912, and propr. Eitel Hosp. Fellow Am. Coll. Surgeons. Rationalist. Mason. Home: Minneapolis, Minn. Died Feb. 8, 1928.

EKENGREN, Wilhelm August Ferdinand, diplomat; b. Stockholm, Sweden, Nov. 10, 1861; s. Wilhelm Alfred Ferdinand and Augusta Josefina Bernhardina (Backert) E.; ed. Royal U. of Upsala, 1883-95; (final degree in jurisprudence); m. Laura Wolcott Jackson, Mar. 6, 1909. Apptd. vice-consul, Rouen, France, 1896, Bordeaux, 1897, Havre, 1898, New York, 1899; actg. consul gen., Lubeck, Germany, 1902; vice-consul, New York, 1902; in Royal Foreign Office, Stockholm, 1903-06; apptd. second sec. in the Foreign Office, 1905; actg. chief of Consular Bur., 1906; apptd. sec. of Legation of Sweden, Washington, Sept. 28, 1906; counselor of Legation, 1910; E.E. and M.P. to the U.S., Mar. 22, 1912—. In charge of Austro-Hungarian affairs during the period of broken diplomatic relations and war. Lutheran. Home: Washington, D.C. Died Nov. 26, 1920.

ELA, John Whittier, lawyer; b. Meredith, N.H., Sept. 26, 1838; s. Joseph and Sally (Miller) E.; ed. at Northfield Acad.; attended Harvard Law School; practiced law in Chicago, 1864—; pres. Chicago Civil Service Reform Assn., 1894-95; drafted Ill. civil service law and led in movement which resulted in its passage by legislature and adoption by Chicago; pres. Chicago police commn. (1894), which applied the reform to Chicago police force; defended law before Supreme Court; atty. for Chicago Times-Herald in its fight on alleged corrupt legislation in Ill. legislature, 1895; dir. Ill. State Reformatory, 1892-95; mem. Civil Service Commn. of Chicago, 1900. Home: Chicago, Ill. Died 1902.

ELAM, Emma Lee, college pres.; b. Franklin Co., Ind.; d. John Runion and Cyrene Jane (Davis) Lee; B.A., Oxford (Ohio) Coll., 1873; m. John B. Elam, July 22, 1875. Mem. Bd. of State Charities, Ind.; organizer, Needlework Guild America (hon. pres.); pres. Indianapolis Orphan Asylum; trustee Indianapolis Free Kindergarten and Children's Aid Soc., Teachers' Coll. of Indianapolis, Oxford Coll.; charter mem., became pres. Marion Co. Bd. of Charities and Correction; apptd. by gov., 1901, mem. bd. mgrs. Ind. Industrial Sch. for Girls and Woman's Prison. Pres. Woman's Union of Plymouth (now 1st Congl.) Ch. for past 30 yrs. Pres. Oxford (O.) Coll. for Women, Nov. 1917—. Died 1919.

ELAM, John Babb, lawyer; b. Spring Valley, O., Dec. 16, 1845; s. Ambrose and Susan (Babb) E.; pvt. Co. D, 110th Ohio Inf., 1864-65; A.B. (with honors), Miami U., 1870, A.M., 1873; LL.B., U. of Mich., 1872; m. Emma Lee, July 22, 1875. Admitted to bar, 1872; was law partner of (President) Benjamin Harrison, 1883-88; pros. atty. Marion Co., Ind., 1878-82; police commr. Indianapolis, 1887-91; mem. Ind. Insane Hosp. Bd., 1881-82; atty. for C.,H.&D. R.R.; dir. and atty. Indianapolis Telephone Co.; mem. Elam, Fesler, Elam & Young. Republican. Conglist. Home: Indianapolis, Ind. Died Mar. 27, 1916.

ELDEN, John Aten, lawyer; b. East Liverpool, O., Apr. 3, 1891; s. Enoch and Mary (Aten) E.; prep. edn. Va. Mil. Inst.; A.B., Adelbert Coll. (Western Reserve U.), Cleveland, O., 1912; LL.B., Western Reserve, 1914; post-grad. work, Columbia U., George Washington U., and Cleveland Law Sch., M.A., from latter, 1928; m. 2d, Ruth Knox; children—Betty Jane (by first marriage), John A. Admitted to Ohio bar, 1914, then practiced at Cleveland; head of John A. Elden; chmn. advisory bd. Lake Erie Trust Co.; pres. Economy Mortgage Co.; v.p. Franklin Savings & Loan Co., D. C. Pierce, Inc., brokers. Mem. Bd. of Bar Examiners for State of Ohio, term 1926-31; asst. atty. gen. State of Ohio, 1927-28. Served as capt. Gas Service, U.S.A., World War, now O.R.C. Republican. Presbyn. Mason. Author: Here and There, 1928. Home: Cleveland, O. Died Jan. 1, 1935.

ELDER, Cyrus, lawyer, author; b. Somerset, Pa., June 16, 1833; s. Clifford and Rosanna (Benford) E.; ed. pub. and pvt. schs., Utica, O., and Forensic and Lit. Circle, Phila.; m. Nancy Jane Swank, Mar. 22, 1859 (died 1889). Admitted to bar, 1856; served as 1st lt. and a.-q.-m. 10th Pa. Res. Vol. Corps, 1861-62; settled in law practice at Johnstown, 1863; solicitor and gen. agt. Cambria Iron (now Steel) Co., until 1901, when retired from business. Organized Bessemer Steel Co., Ltd.; organized, and was solicitor Johnstown Savings Bank, Cambria (Pa.) Mut. Benefit Assn.; organized, and was pres. Cambria Pub. Library, Union Benevolent Assn., Johnstown; was sec. Johnstown Flood Finance Com. Was sec. Industrial League, and editor of its bull.; editor Farmers' and Mechanics' Almanak (protectionist). Mem. commn. to revise tax laws of Pa. Republican. Swedenborgian. Author: My Gift (poems); Dream of a Free Trade Paradise; Man and Labor; Poems. Home: Philadelphia. Died Dec. 14, 1912.

ELDER, Joseph Freeman, clergyman; b. Portland, Me., Mar. 10, 1839; s. Samuel and Sarah (Ayers) E.; A.B., Waterville (now Colby) Coll., 1860; grad. Rochester Theol. Sem., 1867; (D.D., Colgate, 1875); m. Martha E. Kimball, Jan. 4, 1864. Ordained Bapt. ministry, 1867; pastor N. Orange, N.J., 1867-70, Ch. of the Epiphany, New York, 1870-90, Calvary Ch., Albany, 1890-1902; mem. exec. com. Am. Bapt. Missionary Union, 1895—. Home: New York, N.Y. Died 1910.

ELDER, Samuel James, lawyer; b. Hopeville, R.I., Jan. 4, 1850; s. James and Deborah (Keen) E.; A.B., Yale, 1873 (LL.D., 1908); m. Lilla S. Thomas, May 10, 1876 (died Aug. 13, 1907). Admitted to bar, 1875 and began practice at Boston; mem. firm Elder, Whitman & Barnum. One of sr. counsel for U.S. before The Hague Tribunal in the N. Atlantic Fisheries Arbitration with Great Britain, 1910. Mem. Mass. Ho. Rep., 1885. Pres. Boston Bar Assn. Home: Winchester, Mass. Died Jan. 22, 1918.

ELDER, William Henry, R.C. archbishop of Cincinnati; b. Baltimore, March 22, 1819; s. Basil Spalding and Elizabeth Miles (Snowden) E.; ed. Mt. St. Mary's Coll., Emmittsburg, Md., and Coll. of the Propaganda, Rome (D.D.); ordained priest, March 29, 1846; apptd. dir. of Ecclesiastical Sem. and prof. theology, Mt. St. Mary's, 1846, consecrated bishop of Natchez (Miss.), May 3, 1857; coadjutor to the archbishop of Cincinnati, April 18, 1880; after death of Archbishop Purcell, 1883, became archbishop Dec. 13, 1883. Died 1904.

ELDER, William Line; b. Indianapolis, July 31, 1855; s. John Ritchey and Amelia Ann (Line) E.; grad. high sch., Indianapolis; m. Laura Bowman, Oct. 21, 1885; 1 son, Bowman. Cashier Bank of Commerce, Indianapolis, 1877-82; paymaster Indianapolis, Decatur & Springfield R.R., 1883-87; v.p. Indianapolis Street Ry. Co., 1893-97; mem. William L. Elder and Bowman Elder, real estate, Indianapolis, 1900—; v.p. Crown Hill Cemetery. Chmn. Ind. Tax Commn., 1915-17; collector internal revenue, Dist. of Ind., 1919-21; pres. Indianapolis Real Estate Board, 1919; controller of City of Indianapolis, 1930-33. Mem. Indianapolis Chamber of Commerce. Democrat. Presbyn. Home: Indianapolis, Ind. Died Feb. 8, 1940.

ELDREDGE, Arch Bishop, ry. pres.; b. Fond du Lac, Wis., May 12, 1853; s. Chas. A. and Maria (Bishop) E.; student Princeton U., 1872-74; A.B., Racine Coll., Wis., 1875; m. Jeanie H. Rose, June 22, 1882. Admitted to Wis. bar, 1877; atty. for Mich., C.&N.-W. Ry., 1882-90; gen. atty. at Marquette, Mich., 1890-1910, v.p., 1910-11, pres. and gen. counsel, Dec. 1, 1911—, Duluth, South Shore & Atlantic Ry. Republican. Died Sept. 9, 1919.

ELDREDGE, Charles Henry, rear adm.; b. Dedham, Mass., Sept. 21, 1839; s. Nathaniel T. and Mary H. (Haven) E.; m. Genevieve Redfield, Feb. 2, 1881. Apptd. from N.Y. asst. p.-m. U.S.N., July 10, 1861; promoted p.-m., Feb. 16, 1862; pay insp., July 3, 1871; pay dir., Aug. 31, 1881; retired with rank of rear adm., Sept. 21, 1901, for services during Civil War. Served on various vessels and at various stas. during Civil War. Home: Norfolk, Va. Died July 16, 1916.

ELDREDGE, Joseph U., Jr., publisher; b. Utah, Dec. 18, 1874; s. Joseph U. and Vienna (Pratt) E.; student U. of Utah; m. Maude Jenkins, Oct. 27, 1894; children—J. Wayne, Vernon J., Harry J., Mary J. County and dist. clk., Salt Lake Co., 1904-08; supt. Salt Lake City assay office, 1908-13; pub. Ogden Examiner, 1912-20; consolidated Examiner with Ogden Standard as Ogden Standard-Examiner, 1920 and became pub. and gen. mgr.; pres. Alhambra Theatre Co.; v.p. Glasmann Investment Co. Chmn. Rep. Com., Salt Lake County, 1903-10; mem. U.S. Assay Commn., 1922-27. Republican. Mormon. Home: Ogden, Utah. Died Jan. 20, 1933.

ELDREDGE, Zoeth Skinner, banker; b. Buffalo, N.Y., Oct. 13, 1846; s. Zoeth and Elizabeth (Curry) E.; pub. sch. edn.; m. Frances Maria Webster, Oct. 18, 1892. Sec. Virginia Savings Bank, Nev., 1878-79; cashier Pacific Bank, San Francisco, Calif., 1879-83; Nat. bank examiner, San Francisco, 1893-1900; bank commr., Calif., 1904-05; pres. Nat. Bank of the Pacific, 1905-09. Democrat. Presbyn. Author: March of Portola, 1909; Beginnings of San Francisco, 1912; History of California, 1915. Deceased.

ELDRIDGE, Frank Harold, commodore U.S.N.; b. Columbus, O., July 14, 1852; s. Charles and Catherine Taylor (Nelson) E.; grad. U.S. Naval Acad., 1875; m. Lucy Ramsden, of Yorkshire, Eng., Dec. 5, 1883. Promoted through the various grades to commodore and retired, June 30, 1909. Instr. and head of dept. steam engring. and naval constrn., U.S. Naval Acad., 1900-02; prof. engring., Ohio State U., 1882-85; served in Spanish-Am. War and in P.I. Returned to active service, Aug. 23, 1917-Sept. 29, 1919. Died Dec. 1921.

ELDRIDGE, Frederick William, editor; b. Alexandria, Va., Aug. 10, 1877; s. Manchester and Sybil (Hewlett) E.; ed. pub. and pvt. schs., Baltimore, and high sch., Alexandria; m. Isabelle Murphy, Apr. 1899 (died 1919); children—James (dec.), Frederick Wm. Night editor Phila. Inquirer, 1904; mng. editor New York Evening Journal, 1904-05; city editor and mng. editor New York American, 1905-08; mng. editor Los Angeles Examiner, 1908—, also editor and v.p. of same, and during period 1924-27 supervising editor Ft. Worth Record, Seattle Post-Intelligencer, Chicago Herald and Examiner and New York American; now supervising editor Hearst Pacific Coast morning newspapers. Organizer Los Angeles Crime Commn. Presbyn. Author: The Social Cockatrice; (comedy drama) The Eternal Triangle, prod. 1910. Home: Los Angeles, Calif. Died Aug. 9, 1937.

ELDRIDGE, George Homans, geologist, b. Yarmouth, Mass., Dec. 25, 1854; s. Ellery and Sarah (Matthews) E.; grad. Harvard, 1876; spl. studies in geology; m. Jessie Newlands, Oct. 31, 1898. Engaged in geology and teaching, 1876-79; spl. expert, coal and base metals, 10th Census U.S., 1879-81; geologist Northern Transcontinental Survey (econ. survey Northern Pacific R.R.), 1881-84; in charge Rocky Mountain Div.; geologist U.S. Geol. Survey, 1884—. Author: Report on Montana Coal Fields and on The Industries of the Base Metals (lead, zinc and copper), Tenth Census, 1880. Home: Chevy Chase, Md. Died 1905.

ELIOT, Charles William, educator; b. Boston, Mar. 20, 1834; s. Samuel Atkins and Mary (Lyman) E.; fitted for coll. at Boston Latin Sch.; A.B., Harvard, 1853, A.M., 1856, LL.D. and hon. M.D., 1909; LL.D., Williams and Princeton, 1869, Yale, 1870, Johns Hopkins, 1902, Tulane, U. of Mo., and Dartmouth, 1909, Brown, 1914, Boston U., 1923, U. State of N.Y., 1924; Ph.D., Breslau, 1911; m. Ellen Derby Peabody, Oct. 27, 1858 (died 1869); children—Charles (dec.), Samuel Atkins; m. 2d, Grace Mellen Hopkinson, Oct. 30, 1877. Tutor in mathematics, Harvard, and student in chemistry with Prof. Josiah P. Cooke, 1854-58; asst. prof. mathematics and chemistry, Lawrence Scientific Sch. (Harvard), 1858-63; studied chemistry and investigated ednl. methods in Europe, 1863-65; prof. analyt. chemistry, Mass. Inst. Tech., 1865-69; in France, 1867-68; pres., 1869-1909 (emeritus), Harvard. Commandeur Légion d'Honneur (France); Grand Officer of the Crown of Italy, 1908; Imperial Order of the Rising Sun of 1st class (Japan), 1909; Royal Prussian Order of the Crown (1st class), 1909; Order of the Crown of Belgium, 1919; Grand Cordon of the Order of St. Sava, 1923. Awarded 1st gold medal, Am. Acad. Arts and Letters as a recognition of "special distinction," 1915. Fellow Am. Acad. of Arts and Sciences; mem. Gen. Edn. Bd., 1908-17, Rockefeller Foundation, 1914-17, and Internat. Health Bd., 1913-17. Author: Manual of Qualitative Chemical Analysis (with Francis H. Storer); Manual of Inorganic Chemistry (with same); Five American Contributions to Civilization, and Other Essays; Educational Reform; Charles Eliot—Landscape Architect, 1902; Annual Reports of the President of Harvard University, 1869-1909; More Money for the Public Schools, 1903; John Gilley, 1904; The Happy Life, new edit., 1905; Four American Leaders, 1906; The Durable Satisfactions of Life, 1910; The Road Toward Peace, 1915. Home: Cambridge, Mass. Died Aug. 22, 1926.

ELIOT, Edward Cranch, lawyer; b. St. Louis, July 3, 1858; s. William G. (D.D.) and Abby Adams (Cranch) E.; bro. of Thomas Lamb E.; A.B., Washington U., St. Louis, 1878, A.M., 1881; LL.B., St. Louis Law Sch., 1880; m. Mary A. Munroe, Nov. 1, 1883 (died 1911); children—Edward M., Frank M., Mrs. Alice Martin, William C., John G. Admitted to Mo. bar, 1880; mem. Eliot, Blayney & Bedal, St. Louis. Lecturer on internat. law, St. Louis Law Sch., 1907-23. Pres. bd. Mo. Bot. Garden, 1926—. Mem. St. Louis Bd. of Edn., 1897-1903 (pres. 1898-99); pres. Bellefontaine Cemetery Assn., 1924—. Pres. Civic Improvement League, 1903-04, N.E. Soc., 1907. Pres. Soldiers' Orphans' Home. Unitarian. Home: St. Louis, Mo. Died Apr. 2, 1928.

ELIOT, Thomas Lamb, clergyman; b. St. Louis, Oct. 13, 1841; s. William G. (D.D.) and Abby Adams (Cranch) E.; A.B., Washington U., 1862, A.M., 1866, LL.D., 1912; grad. Harvard Div. Sch., 1865, S.T.D., 1889; Litt.D., Reed Coll., 1915; m. Henrietta R. Mack, Nov. 28, 1865; children—William G., Mrs. Dorothea Wilbur, Mrs. Ellen Weil, Mrs. Grace Scott, Henrietta M., Samuel E., Thomas D. Entered Unitarian ministry, 1865; asso. pastor Ch. of the Messiah, St. Louis, 1865-67; minister First Ch., Portland, Ore., 1867-93 (emeritus). Dir. Am. Unit. Assn. (Boston), 1890-1899 (commr. to Japan, 1903); trustee Pacific Unit. Sch., 1906-18. Supt. pub. schs., Portland, 1872-76; Ore. commr. on prisons, to Europe, 1876; mem. Park Commn., 1900-06. Trustee Reed Inst., Portland, 1904-25 (pres. 1904-20); mem. provisional com. Am. Red Cross work, 1917-18. V.p., dir. Art

Assn. Portland, 1892-1917, Library Assn. Portland, 1896-1916. Home: Portland, Ore. Deceased.

ELIOT, Walter Graeme, civil engr.; b. New York, Nov. 16, 1857; s. Augustus G. (M.D.) and Elizabeth (Proctor) E.; E.M., Ph.B., Columbia, 1878, C.E., 1879, Ph.D., 1882; LL.D., St. Francis Xavier Coll., 1892; admitted to senior class, Harvard; m. Maud Stoutenburgh, Feb. 4, 1892; children—Marion Elinor Viola (wife of Lt. Carlton James), Amory Vivion (U.S.A.), Van Cortlandt Stoutenburgh, Priscilla Alden. Insp. tenements, N.Y. Health Dept., 1877-78; judge, municipal, competitions, 1878-80; sanitary engr. of health dept., New York, 1880-81; engring. expert on water supply, 10th Census, 1881; gen. mgr. Am. Photo Litho. Co., 1881-82; sec., auditor Westcott Express Co., 1884-87; editor and a propr. University Magazine, 1890-94; asst. chemist, and insp. foods, health dept., 1896-98. Active for 4 yrs. in orgn. of milk interests of New York; on tech. staff. dept. taxes and assessments, New York, 1898-1902; asst. engr. topog. bur., Borough of Queens, New York, 1902-10, engr. in charge, 1910; commr. parks, Borough of Queens, New York, 1911-14. Author of 1st bill to license professional engrs.; apptd. mem. N.Y. State Board of Licensing for Professional Engrs., term 1921-30 (chmn. 1925). Member Co. K, 7th Regt., N.G. N.Y. and of its victorious rifle teams of 1904, 05, 06; 1st lt. Co. A, 71st Inf., N.G.N.Y., Oct. 1907-09; maj. Coast Arty. Corps, N.G.N.Y., 1911-13; lt. col. Inf., 1918. Trustee New York Coll. Dentistry, 1903-25. Pres. Technical League of Engrs., 1908-11; a founder and mem. Soc. Municipal Engrs., New York. Episcopalian. Author: Sketch of the Eliot Family, 1889; History of the Stoutenburgh Family, 1905. Home: Hyde Park-on-Hudson, N.Y. Deceased.

ELKIN, John Pratt, judge; b. Indiana Co., Pa., Jan. 11, 1860; s. Francis and Elizabeth (Pratt) E.; ed. Indiana (Pa.) State Normal Sch.; LL.B., U. of Mich., 1884; (hon. A.M., Lafayette, 1892); m. Adda Prothew, June 17, 1884. Admitted to bar, 1884; mem. Pa. Ho. of Rep., 1885, 1887; deputy atty. gen. of Pa., 1895-99, atty. gen., 1899-1903; Rep. candidate for gov., 1902; asso. justice Supreme Ct. of Pa., Jan. 1, 1905—. Has been chmn. Rep. State Com. of Pa. Pres. Farmers' Bank of Indiana, Pa.; pres. sch. bd., 10 yrs.; trustee State Normal Sch. Home: Indiana, Pa. Died Oct. 3, 1915.

ELKIN, William Lewis, astronomer; b. New Orleans, Apr. 29, 1855; s. Lewis and Jane (Fitch) E.; C.E., Royal Poly. Sch., Stuttgart, 1876; Ph.D., U. of Strassburg, 1880; (hon. M.A., Yale, 1893, Ph.D., Christiania, 1911). Associated with Sir David Gill, Royal Obs., Cape of Good Hope, investigating parallaxes of southern stars, 1881-83; astronomer, 1884-96, dir., 1896-1910 (emeritus), Yale Obs. Lalande prize, Paris Acad. Sciences, 1908. Home: New Haven, Conn. Died May 30, 1933.

ELKINS, George W., capitalist; b. Phila., Sept. 26, 1858; s. William L. and Louise (Broomell) E.; ed. pub. and pvt. schs.; m. Stella McIntire, Nov. 17, 1881 (died 1913); m. 2d, Mrs. A. L. Cummer, June 19, 1917. V.p. Vulcanite Portland Cement Co.; dir. Huston Mfg. Co. (Chester, Pa.), Land Title & Trust Co., etc. Trustee Hahnemann Hosp., Phila. Home: Abington, Pa. Died Oct. 23, 1919.

ELKINS, Stephen Benton, senator; b. Perry Co., O., Sept. 26, 1841; s. Col. Philip Duncan and Sarah Pickett (Withers) E.; A.B., U. of Mo., 1860, A.M., 1868; m. Sallie Jacobs, June 10, 1866; 2d, Hallie, d. Senator Henry Gassaway Davis, Apr. 14, 1875. Admitted to bar, 1864; went to N.M., 1864; mem. territorial legislature, 1864-65; later territorial dist. atty., atty. gen., 1868-69, and U.S. dist. atty., 1870-72; del. in 43d and 44th Congresses, from N.M., 1873-77; removed to W.Va. Became largely interested in coal mining and railroads; founded town of Elkins, W.Va. Sec. of War in cabinet of President Harrison, 1891-93; U.S. senator from W.Va., 1895-1901, 1901-07, 1907-13. Home: Elkins, W.Va. Died 1911.

ELKINS, William Lukens, capitalist; b. W.Va., May 2, 1832; removed to Phila., 1840; public school edn.; clerk in a store, 1849-52; produce mcht., 1852-61; oil producer, 1861-75; partner in Standard Oil Co., 1875-80; sold out oil interests to that co. Acquired large interests in gas plants through U.S.; organized and is dir. in The United Gas and Improvement Co.; one of organizers of the Phila. Traction Co., and acquired large st. ry. interests in Chicago, New York, Baltimore and Pittsburgh, in conjunction with P.A.B. Widener and others. Home: Philadelphia. Died 1903.

ELLEGOOD, Robert Griffith, M.D.; b. Concord, Del., March 16, 1828; s. Joshua Adkinson and Ann Houston (Griffith) E.; ed. common schools and Laurel Acad.; grad. Pa. Med. Coll., 1852; began practice at Concord; m. Elizabeth Cannon (dec.), July 28, 1858. Has been pres. Del. State Med. Soc.; mem. Del. Gen. Assembly; 6 yrs. State Auditor; mem. State Bd. of health. Home: Concord, Del. Deceased.

ELLERBE, William Haselden, gov. S.C., 1896—; b. Marion Co., S.C., April 7, 1862; prepared for college at Pine Hill Acad., Marion Co.; attended Wofford Coll., Spartanburg, S.C., 1880-82, then went to Vanderbilt Univ., but soon left on account of bad health; m. Henrietta Rogers, June 1887. Farmer, 1882—. Elected comptroller-gen. of S.C., at age of 28; in 1896 was elected gov. Home: Marion, S.C. Died 1899.

ELLERMAN, Ferdinand, astronomer; b. Centralia, Ill., May 13, 1869; s. Mathias and Rosa Augusta (Fleischbein) E.; ed. high sch., Belleville, Ill., and special studies U. of Chicago; hon. A.M., Occidental College, 1927; m. Hermine Louise Hoenny, May 16, 1895; children—Leola, Louise. In mercantile business, 1885-92; asst., Kenwood Obs., 1892-95, Yerkes Obs., 1895-1901; instr. in astrophysics, 1901-04, asst. astronomer, 1905-15, astronomer, 1915-37, Mt. Wilson Obs. of Carnegie Instn., Washington, D.C. Presbyn. Home: Pasadena, Calif. Died Mar. 20, 1940.

ELLING, Henry, banker-merchant; b. Germany, Dec. 9, 1842; emigrated to U.S., 1858; engaged in store-keeping, Lexington, Mo.; crossed plains to Colo., thence to Mont.; in clothing business, 1864—; m. 1870; started private bank, 1873. Pres. Union Bank & Trust Co., Helena; Commercial Nat. Bank, Bozeman; Carbon Co. Bank, Red Lodge, Mont.; interested in mining; part owner in stores, Madison Co. Home: Virginia City, Mont. Died 1900.

ELLINGHAM, Lewis Glendale, newspaper pub.; b. Bluffton, Ind., Feb. 23, 1868; s. Charles and Hanna (Scotton) E.; ed. pub. schs.; m. Nellie Miller, Jan. 2, 1895; children—Winifred Margaret (Mrs. James Ewing Bond), Martin Miller. In newspaper business successively in Geneva, Winchester and Decatur, Ind.; pub. Ft. Wayne (Ind.) Journal-Gazette, 1916-34; postmaster Fort Wayne, Ind. Sec. State of Ind., 1910-14. Democrat. Presbyn. Mason. Home: Ft. Wayne, Ind. Died Mar. 1939.

ELLINGWOOD, Albert Russell, coll. prof.; b. Cedar Rapids, Ia., June 22, 1887; s. Francis L. and Amanda Priscilla (Russell) E.; B.A., Colorado Coll., 1910; B.C.L., Oxford U., Eng., 1913; Ph.D., U. of Pa., 1918; m. Rea Schimpeler, June 11, 1914; children—Robert Whitcomb, Donald. Instr. and asst. prof. polit. science, Colorado Coll., 1914-19; prof. polit. and social sciences, Lake Forest (Ill.) Coll., 1919-27, also dean dept. business administration, 1921-25; asso. prof. polit. science, Northwestern U., 1927-30, prof., 1930—, also asst. dean, 1931—; prof. polit. science, Univ. of Ill., summer 1919, Northwestern U., summer 1923, 26, U. of Southern Calif., summer 1928. Mem. Chicago Govt. Planning Commn. Presbyn. Author: Departmental Coöperation in State Government, 1918. Co-author (with Whitney Coombs): The Government and Labor, 1926; The Government and Railroad Transportation, 1929. Home: Evanston, Ill. Died May 12, 1934.

ELLINGWOOD, Finley, physician; b. Manchester, Ind., Sept. 12, 1852; s. Elijah and Mary Abigail (Rice) E.; acad. edn.; M.D., Bennett Med. Coll., Chicago, 1878; m. Jennie S. Elliott, Sept. 1, 1880. Practiced medicine at Braidwood, Ill., 1876-77, in Kankakee Co., Ill., 1878-84, at Chicago, 1884—; prof. chemistry, 1884-1900, materia medica and therapeutics, 1900-07, Bennett Med. Coll. Editor Chicago Med. Times, 1884-1906, Eclectic Med. Annual, 1889-91, and Ellingwood's Therapeutist, 1906—. Democrat. Methodist. Hon. mem. 22 State eclectic assns.; sec. Nat. Eclectic Med. Assn., 1903-07 (pres. 1919); 1st v.p. World's Eclectic Med. Congress, 1903. Author: Ellingwood's Materia Medica (8 edits.), 1899; Ellingwood's Practice of Medicine, 1910; Ellingwood's Pregnancy and Labor, 1912; Ellingwood's New American Materia Medica, 1915. Home: Evanston, Ill. Died June 29, 1920.

ELLINWOOD, Frank Field, Prsbyn. clergyman; b. Clinton, N.Y., June 20, 1826; s. Eli and Sophia (Gridley) E.; grad. Hamilton Coll., 1849; studied Auburn Theol. Sem., 1851-52, Princeton, 1852-53; (D.D., U. City of New York, 1865; LL.D., N.Y. Univ.); m. Rowana Hurd, June 26, 1853; m. 2d, Laura Hurd, Apr. 15, 1867. Ordained, June 21, 1853; pastor Belvidere, N.J., 1853-54, Rochester, N.Y., 1854-65; sec. Presbyn. bd. of ch. erection, 1866-70, memorial fund com., 1870-71; corr. sec. Bd. Foreign Missions, 1871-1905; prof. comparative religion, Univ. City of New York, 1887—. Author: Oriental Religions and Christianity, 1892; Questions and Phases of Modern Missions, 1899. Home: Cornwall, Conn. Died 1908.

ELLINWOOD, Ralph Everett, newspaper editor; b. Flagstaff, Ariz., Aug. 9, 1893; s. Everett E. and Minnie Lucinda (Walkley) E.; student Phillips Exeter Acad., Exeter, N.H., 1909-11, Montclair (N.J.) Acad., 1911-14; A.B., honoris causa, Amherst, 1917; B.Litt., Columbia, 1921; m. Clare Betsey Rounsevell, June 22, 1921; children—Thomas Rounsevell, Betsey Phelps, John Cole. Began with Ariz. Daily Star, Tucson, 1921, editor, 1924—; pres. State Consolidated Pub. Co. Served with U.S. Ambulance Corps, in France, World War; prisoner in Germany. Democrat. Presbyn. Author: Behind the German Lines, 1919. Home: Tucson, Ariz. Died Aug. 30, 1930.

ELLINWOOD, Truman Jeremiah; b. Smithfield, N.Y., June 11, 1830; s. George W. and Cyrina P. E.; reared on farm; ed. Oneida Acad., Cazenovia Sem. and N.Y. Central Coll.; m. Sarah M. Thompson, 1854 (died 1900); m. 2d, Elizabeth S. Jennings, 1902. Taught in dist. schs.; later instr. and part owner of Adelphi Acad., Brooklyn; taught in Boys' High Sch., Y.M.C.A., and his own shorthand acad., Brooklyn; one of founders, officer and teacher, Martha's Vineyard Summer Inst.; for 12 yrs. pres. Cottage City Rural Improvement Soc. and Free Public Library Assn. Private stenographer for Henry Ward Beecher, 1858 until latter's death, 1887, and furnished reports of his sermons and addresses to various periodicals. Trustee Oak Bluffs Free Pub. Library. Compiler (from his stenographic notes and reports) of works from Mr. Beecher's discourses. Co-editor: A Treasury of Illustration, by Henry Ward Beecher, 1904; Sermon Briefs, by same, 1905. Home: Oak Bluffs, Mass. Died June 29, 1921.

ELLIOT, Daniel Giraud, zoölogist; b. New York, Mar. 7, 1835; s. George Thompson and Rebecca Giraud (Foster) E.; acad. edn.; studied zoölogy; (Sc.D., Columbia, 1906); m. A. E. Henderson, 1858 (died 1905). Traveled in Europe, Africa, Palestine and Asia Minor, 1856-78; later in greater part of U.S., Can., Alaska, S. America; hon. and supervisory curator zoölogy, Field Mus. of Natural History, Chicago, 1895—. Led expdn. into interior of E. Africa, 1896, and into the recesses of the Olympic Mountains, 1898, being first naturalist to penetrate that little-known range. Fellow Royal Soc. Edinburgh; decorated 10 times by European govts. for labors in natural science. Author: Shore Birds of North America, 1895; Gallinaceous Game Birds; Wild Fowl of the United States and the British Possessions, 1898; Synopsis of the Mammals of North America and the Adjacent Seas, 1901; Land and Sea Mammals of Middle America and West Indies (2 vols.), 1894, and many others. Part author The Deer Family, 1902; Check List Mammals N. American Continent and W. Indies, 1905; Catalogue Mammals in Field Columbian Museum, 1906. Died Dec. 22, 1915.

ELLIOT, George Thomson, dermatologist; b. New Orleans, Dec. 20, 1855; s. Andrew Foster and M. A. O. (de Buys) E.; A.B., Yale, 1877; M.D., U. of La. (now Tulane U.), 1881; interne Charity Hosp., New Orleans, 2 yrs.; studied dermatology in Europe, 1881-84; m. Miss E. M. Briggs, Nov. 8, 1892. In practice of medicine (specialist in dermatology), New York, 1884—; prof. dermatology, N.Y. Post-Grad. Med. Sch., 1896-98, Cornell U. Med. Coll., 1898-1920, emeritus; retired from practice, 1921; asst. visiting physician and pathologist, N.Y. Skin and Cancer Hosp., 1884-1904; dermatologist, Demilt Dispensary, New York, 1886-96; cons. dermatologist, St. Luke's, Columbus, New York Lying-In, New York Skin and Cancer hosps., and New York Eye and Ear Infirmary. Episcopalian. Home: Otisfield, Me. Died Sept. 14, 1931.

ELLIOT, Henry Rutherford, editor The Church Economist; b. Woodbridge, Conn., April 21, 1849; s. Samuel Hayes and M. L. E.; grad. Yale, 1871; m. Elizabeth Johnston, 1887. Since graduation engaged in journalism; taught 2 yrs. in Japan under engagement with Japanese Govt.; Washington corr. New York Evening Post for 6 yrs.; sec. Textile Pub. Co., New York, and editor Dry Goods Economist several yrs.; pres. Church Economist Pub. Co. Author: The Bassett Claim, 1887; The Common Chord, 1888. Home: New York, N.Y. Died 1906.

ELLIOT, John Wheelock, surgeon; b. Keene, N.H., Oct. 1852; s. John Henry and Emily Ann (Wheelock) E.; A.B., Harvard, 1874, M.D., 1878; house pupil Mass. Gen. Hosp., 1878; studied medicine Vienna, Dresden, Berlin, Paris and London, 1879-80; began practice, Boston, 1881; m. Mary Lee Morse, May 8, 1883. Phys. to Boston Dispensary, 1882; asst. surgeon, Free Hosp. for Women, 1883-87; surgeon to out patients, 1886-94, surgeon, 1894-1907, Mass. Gen. Hosp.; clin. instr. gynecology, 1888-89, lecturer on surgery, 1900-05, Harvard Med. Sch.; retired from practice, 1913. Dir. Sullivan Machinery Co. Chmn. N.E. Surg. Dressings Com. Auxiliary of Am. Red Cross, 1917. Fellow Am. Surg. Assn., etc. Home: Boston, Mass. Died Sept. 17, 1925.

ELLIOTT, A(aron) Marshall, philologist; b. Wilmington, N.C., Jan. 24, 1844; s. Aaron and Rhoda (Mendenhall) E.; A.B., Haverford, 1866, A.M., 1878; A.B., Harvard, 1868; studied College de France, École des Hautes Études, Paris, 1868-71, Istituto degli Studii Superiori, Florence, 1871-72, U. of Madrid, 1873, univs. of Munich, Tübingen, Vienna, 1874-76; (Ph.D., Princeton, 1877; LL.D., Wake Forest, 1891, Haverford, 1908); m. Lily Tyson Manly, d. James E. Tyson, June 14, 1905. Asso. in Romance langs., 1876-84, asso. prof., 1884-92, prof., 1892—, Johns Hopkins. Editor Modern Lang. Notes, now in 5th vol. Del. to Paris Expn., 1900; membre de la Légion d'Honneur, France, 1907. Home: Baltimore, Md. Died 1910.

ELLIOTT, Byron Kosciusko, lawyer; b. Hamilton, O., Sept. 4, 1835; s. William J. and Mary L. E.; ed. Hamilton (O.) Acad., Furman's Acad., Marion Co. Sem.; admitted to bar, Feb. 8, 1858; m. Harriet A. Talbott, Sept. 5, 1855. Elected city atty., Indianapolis, 1859; served as capt. 132d Ind. Vols.;

detailed for duty on staff of Maj. Gen. Milroy, 1864; city atty., 1865, 1867, 1869; judge Criminal Circuit Ct., 1870; city solicitor, 1872; city atty., 1873; elected judge Superior Court of Ind., 1876; judge Supreme Court, 1881-93. Republican. Author: Work of the Advocate (subsequently enlarged into 2 vols. and given the title of "General Practice"); Appellate Procedure; The Law of Roads and Streets; The Law of Railroads; Treatise on the Law of Evidence, 4 vols., vol. 2, 1905. Home: Indianapolis, Ind. Died Apr. 19, 1913.

ELLIOTT, Charles Addison, M.D.; b. Lincoln, Neb., Mar. 6, 1873; s. Simon C. and Franc (Roads) E.; B.S., U. of Neb., 1895; M.D., Northwestern U. Med. Sch., 1898; studied U. of Vienna, 1904-05; m. Genevieve Cole, Dec. 20, 1911; children—Frank Roads, Margaret, Ernest Charles. Practiced at Chicago, 1900—, specializing in internal medicine; asso. with Dr. Walter H. Nadler, 1917—, and Dr. Paul Starr, 1924—; prof. medicine Northwestern U. Med. Sch., 1919—; attending phys. Passavant Memorial Hosp. Mem. Yellow Fever Commn. sent to Ecuador, 1918; mem. Nat. Board of Med. Examiners. Protestant. Home: Chicago, Ill. Died June 26, 1939.

ELLIOTT, Charles Burke, lawyer, author; b. Morgan Co., O., Jan. 6, 1861; s. Edward and Angeline E.; ed. at public sch. and Marietta Coll.; LL.B., State Univ. of Ia., 1881, LL.D., 1895; Ph.D., U. of Minn., 1888; LL.D., Marietta Coll., 1904; m. Edith Winslow, May 13, 1884; children—Charles Winslow, Edwin Eugene, Ethel (Mrs. V. C. Benton), Walter A., Philip Clarkson. Practiced law, Minneapolis; judge Municipal Ct., 1890-93; judge Dist. Ct., 4th Dist., 1893-1904; asso. justice Supreme Ct. of Minn., 1904-09; asso. justice Supreme Ct. of P.I., Sept. 1, 1909-Feb. 1910; mem. Philippine Commn. and sec. Dept. Commerce and Police, Feb. 1910-Dec. 4, 1912. Republican. Prof. corp. and internat. law, U. of Minn., 1890-99; professorial-lecturer on constl. law, U. of the Philippines, 1911-12. Pres. Philippine Carnival Assn., 1910, Philippine Industrial Expn., 1911. Author: Minnesota Practice, 1900, new edit., 2 vols., 1923. Home: Minneapolis, Minn. Died Sept. 18, 1935.

ELLIOTT, Charles Gleason, drainage engr.; b. La Salle Co., Ill., June 8, 1850; s. John B. and Elizabeth (Searles) E.; B.S., U. of Ill., 1877, C.E., 1893; m. Lura M. Bullock, Jan. 1, 1879; children—Merton Melville (dec.), Herman Randolph, Mrs. Marion Morehouse. Engaged in civ. engring., 1878—; editor Drainage Jour., Indianapolis, 1901-02; chief of drainage investigations, U.S. Dept. Agriculture, 1902-13; mem. Elliott & Harman Engring. Co., Peoria, Ill., and Washington, D.C., 1916—. Author: Practical Farm Drainage, 1882, 1908; Engineering for Land Drainage, 1903, 1911, revised 1919; Drainage of Farm Lands Bull. 187, U.S. Dept. Agr., 1904. Home: Washington, D.C. Died Sept. 14, 1926.

ELLIOTT, Ernest Eugene; b. Indianapolis, Ind., Oct. 15, 1878; s. James Perry and Frances (Dwinnell) E.; ed. pub. schs. and 1 term (summer), U. of Chicago; m. Bessie M. Estes, Jan. 4, 1900; children—Estes Eugene, Ashley Dwinnell. Messenger to asst. gen. mgr. Ill. Car Service Assn. and its successor, Ill. and Ia. Demurrage Bur., Peoria, Ill., 1898-1909; nat. sec. Brotherhood of Disciples of Christ, Kansas City, Mo., 1909-14; transportation and publicity sec. Internat. Conv. of Disciples of Christ, 1914-20, also duties with various bds. and socs. Editor Christian Men Mag., 1909-14; business and editorial staff Christian Board of Publ., St. Louis, 1914-16; staff corr. Christian Evangelist, St. Louis, and other publs. Chmn. publicity commn. Kansas City Council of Chs., 1923-24; mem. exec. com. Men and Religion Forward Movement, 1911-12; dir. Near East Relief for Mo., 1918-19; transportation sec. Christian Missionary socs. of Mo., Kans., and Oklahoma, 1920-30. Vice-president Publishers' Adjusting Assn. and Physicians and Surgeons' Adjusting Assn., Kansas City, 1916-25; spl. rep. and writer financial advertising agencies and bank publs., 1925—; spl. corr. and contbr. feature articles and children's stories, The Kansas City Star and other newspapers. Republican. Winner $1,000 letter writing contest for best sales letters, 1919 and 26. Home: Kansas City, Mo. Deceased.

ELLIOTT, Francis Perry, author; b. Nashville, Tenn., July 29, 1861; s. William Francis and Mary E.; ed. pub. schs., Montgomery Bell Acad. and Vanderbilt U., Nashville; English lit., classics and rhetoric under specialists; m. Winifred McKenzie Payne, Sept. 22, 1897. Teacher and supt. in pub. sch. systems in Tenn. and Miss., 1883-90; prof. English lit., Belmont Coll., Nashville, 1880-86; head master, The Castle, Tarrytown-on-Hudson, N.Y., 1896-98; with Harper & Bros., New York, 1898-1900; mng. editor Home Mag., New York, 1900-03, The New Age, Washington, 1903-04, The Great Southwest, Denver, 1906-08. Democrat. Episcopalian. Mason. Author: Pals First, 1915; Lend Me Your Name, 1916; The Shadow Girl, 1919. Home: Nashville, Tenn. Died Aug. 13, 1924.

ELLIOTT, George, clergyman; b. Licking Co., O., Dec. 14, 1851; s. Rev. Alexander C. and Margaret A. E.; student Otterbein U.; B.S., Cornell Coll., Ia., 1872, M.S., 1875, D.D., 1894, LL.D., 1904; LL.D., Albion Coll., 1902; m. Anna Margaret Corfield, Nov. 12, 1875; children—George (dec.), Philip (dec.), Mary, Margaret. Pastor, Baltimore, 1884, Washington, 1887, Phila., 1894; Central M.E. Ch., Detroit, 1900-07, field sec. Bd. of Home Missions, M.E. Ch., Chicago, 1907-10; pastor Madison Av. Ch., Bay City, Mich., 1910-14, Mt. Clemens, Mich., 1914-18; preacher at large, Detroit Episcopal area of M.E. Ch., 1918-20; editor Methodist Review, 1920—. Mem. Federal Council Chs. of Christ in America. Author: The Abiding Sabbath, 1884; The Beauty of Jesus, 1904; Biblical Criticism and Preaching, 1913; The Christmas Canticles, 1922. Home: New York, N.Y. Died Nov. 2, 1930.

ELLIOTT, George Frank, major gen. U.S. Marine Corps.; b. in Ala., Nov. 30, 1846. Entered U.S. Marine Corps, Oct. 12, 1870; promoted 1st lt., Mar. 30, 1878; capt., June 15, 1892; maj., Mar. 3, 1899; lt. col., Sept. 11, 1899; col., Mar. 3, 1903; comdt. U.S. Marine Corps with rank of brig. gen., Oct. 3, 1903; maj. gen., May 13, 1908. Made Arctic cruise of 2 yrs. and 10 months while comdg. marine guard of U.S.S. Alliance; comd. marine guard in protection of Am. Legation, Seoul, Korea, 1894, and served in China, guarding Am. interests during war between China and Japan; comd. Co. C, 1st Battalion of Marines, organized for service in Cuba during Spanish-Am. War, Apr. 22-Sept. 22, 1898; advanced three numbers in his grade for eminent and conspicuous conduct in battle nr. Guantanamo, June 14, 1898; served in P.I., Sept. 21, 1899-Mar. 22, 1900; comd. marines in the engagement at Novaleta, P.I., Oct. 8, 1899; comd. an expeditionary brigade of marines on the Isthmus of Panama, Dec. 1903-Mar. 1904. Retired. Home: Washington, D.C. Died Nov. 4, 1931.

ELLIOTT, Howard, ry. president; b. New York, Dec. 6, 1860; s. Charles Wyllys and Mary (White) E.; C.E., Lawrence Scientific Sch. (Harvard), 1881; LL.D., Middlebury (Vt.) Coll., 1916; LL.D., Trinity Coll., 1924, Carleton Coll., 1927; m. Janet, d. D. A. January of St. Louis, Oct. 12, 1892 (died 1925); children—Janet (Mrs. Frederick Roelker Wulsin), Edith January (Mrs. Edmund P. Rogers, dec.), Howard. Served as rodman with engring corps on C.,B.&Q. R.R., 1880; clerk in office of v.p. same road, 1881-82, clerk in office of auditor and asst. treas., and auditor and asst. auditor, 1882-87, gen. freight and pass. agt., 1887-90, St. Louis, Keokuk & Northwestern R.R. Co., gen. freight agt. of 4 roads of Burlington System—the Hannibal & St. Joseph R.R., St. Louis, Keokuk & Northwestern Ry., Kansas City, St. Joseph & Council Bluffs R.R., and Chicago, Burlington & Kansas City Ry., 1891-96; gen. mgr. same roads, 1896-1902; 2d v.p. C.,B.&Q. Ry. Co., 1902-03; pres. Northern Pacific Ry. Co., Oct. 21, 1903-13; pres. N.Y.,N.H.&H. R.R. Co., 1913, and chmn. bd. dirs. same; resigned Apr. 1917, and was chmn. com. on intercorporate relations of the New Haven system until 1922; pres. N.P. Ry. until 1920; chmn. same, Mar. 1, 1920—. Mem. Railroads' War Bd. of Am. Ry. Assn., 1917. Was mem. exec. com. La. Purchase Expn., St. Louis. Mem. Bd. of Overseers, Harvard, 1909-15, 1916-22, and 1924— (pres. 1925-27); pres. Harvard Alumni Assn., 1917. Home: New York, N.Y. Died July 8, 1928.

ELLIOTT, James Douglas, judge; b. Mt. Sterling, Ill., Oct. 7, 1859; s. William and Mary (McPhail) E.; educated in high school and under private tutelage; taught school, 1878-81; read law in the office of Gamble Bros., Yankton, S.D.; LL.D., Yankton Coll., 1927; m. Agnes S. Stilwill, May 29, 1890; children—Marion Agnes (Mrs. Willard Johnson), Douglas S., Mary Helen (Mrs. Homer D. Cogdell). Was admitted to South Dakota bar, April 1884, and practiced at Tyndall, 1884-1910; counsel for C.,M.& St.P. R.R. for N. and S.D., Aberdeen, 1910-11. State's atty., Bon Homme Co., S.D., 1887-91; chmn. Rep. State Central Com., 1896; U.S. atty Dist. of S.D., 1897-1907; U.S. dist. judge, Dist. of S.D., 1911—. Mason. Home: Sioux Falls, S.D. Died Jan. 30, 1933.

ELLIOTT, John, artist; b. in Eng., Apr. 22, 1858; pvt. edn. in gen. branches; student in Julien's Acad., pupil of Carolus Duran, Paris, José di Villegas at Rome; m. Maud, d. Samuel Gridley and Julia (Ward) Howe, Feb. 7, 1887. Subjects chiefly portraits and mural decorations, some of more notable in America being "The Vintage," frieze and ceiling in house of Mrs. Potter Palmer, Chicago; "The Triumph of Time," ceiling decoration in Boston Public Library; "Diana of the Tides," mural painting, National Museum, Washington. Represented in permanent collection Met. Mus. of Art, New York, Old State House, Boston, collection of H. M. the Dowager Queen of Italy. Served with Am. Red Cross Assn. relief expdn. on cruise of S.S. Bayern in aid of sufferers Messina earthquake, Dec. 28, 1908. Architect Am. village, Messina, Villaggio Regina Elena, etc., built by naval relief expdn. in Sicily and Calabria, 1909. Presented with the freedom of the city of Messina. Medal of merit, Am. Red Cross; silver medal, Italian Red Cross; diploma, Spanish Red Cross; silver medal, Italian Govt., silver medal and Order of the Crown of Italy, conferred by King Victor Emanuel III; comdr. Royal Order of Isabella the Catholic. Awarded People's prize, annual exhbn. Art Assn. of Newport, R.I., 1917, 18. Home: Newport, R.I. Died May 26, 1925.

ELLIOTT, John Asbury, plant pathologist; b. Ness City, Kan., Dec. 1, 1887; s. George Athey and Adelaide (Parker) E.; B.A., Fairmount Coll., Wichita, Kan., 1913; M.A., U. of Kan., 1914; Ph.D., U. of Ill., 1916; m. Margaret Elizabeth Allen, June 10, 1916. Asst. plant pathologist, Delaware Coll., Newark, Del., 1916-17; plant pathologist, Ark. Expt. Sta., and prof. plant pathology, U. of Ark., July 1917—. Methodist. Home: Fayetteville, Ark. Died Jan. 18, 1923.

ELLIOTT, John Mackay, banker; b. Pendleton, S.C., Oct. 6, 1844; s. Dr. Ralph Emms and Margaret Couper (Mackay) E.; student Ga. Mil. Inst., Marietta, 1861-62; pvt. 54th Ga. Regt., C.S.A., 1863-65; m. Alice Ingram Peel, Dec. 31, 1873 (died 1902); children—Mrs. Mary Richards, Robert Peel. Began as receiving teller, Central Rail Road Bank, Savannah, Ga., 1866; removed to Calif., 1870; cashier Los Angeles Co. Bank, 1874-80; asst. cashier, First Nat. Bank of Las Angeles (now Los Angeles-First Nat. Trust & Savings Bank), 1881-84, cashier, 1884-92, pres. 1892-1917, now chmn. bd.; pres. Los Angeles Cemetery Assn. Mem. Sch. Bd., 1884-85, Water Bd., 1901-07, Los Angeles; trustee Whittier State Sch., 1892-94. Republican. Episcopalian. Home: Los Angeles, Calif. Died 1929.

ELLIOTT, Maxine, actress; b. (Jessie Dermot) Rockland, Me., Feb. 5, 1873; d. Thomas and Mary Adelaide (Hall) Dermot; sister of Gertrude E.; convent edn.; m. George A. McDermott; 2d, Nathaniel C. Goodwin, Feb. 20, 1898. Made début with E. S. Willard in small parts, 1890; engaged by Rose Coghlan, 1894, as leading lady and played with her in "Diplomacy," "Forget Me Not," and in "London Assurance"; with Augustin Daly's co., 1895-97, in "Two Gentlemen of Verona," "A Midsummer Night's Dream," and "Twelfth Night"; co-star with N. C. Goodwin in Eng. and America, 1898-1903, in "Nathan Hale," and in "An American Citizen," "The Cowboy and the Lady," "When We Were Twenty-One"; starred in "Her Own Way," 1903-05, "Her Great Match," 1905-07, "Under the Greenwood Tree," 1907, "Myself—Bettina," 1908; owner and mgr. of her own, Maxine Elliott's Theatre, New York, 1908—, where she has since starred in "The Chaperon," "Deborah of Tods," etc. Died Mar. 5, 1940.

ELLIOTT, Milton Courtright, lawyer; b. Norfolk, Va., Dec. 28, 1879; s. Warren Grice and Margaret (Blow) E.; ed. U. of N.C., 1895-98; U. of Va. Law Sch., 1900-02; m. Lucy Hamilton Cocke, Dec. 29, 1906; children—Warren Grice, John Page. Admitted to Va. bar, 1902, Pa. bar, 1909, U.S. Supreme Ct., 1916, Supreme Ct. D.C., 1919; began practice in Richmond; removed to Norfolk, 1903; counsel to comptroller of currency, 1907, and 1913; practiced in Phila., 1909-10; in Charlottesville, Va., 1911-13; apptd. sec. and counsel to Reserve Bank Orgn. Com. Jan. 1914; counsel to Federal Reserve Bd., Sept. 14, 1914-Mar. 1, 1919; cons. counsel to War Finance Corp., 1919-23; mem. Ry. Loan Advisory Com. to Federal Reserve Bd., 1921. Del. to 1st and 2d Pan Am. and Financial Conf., mem. permanent group com. for Cuba. Pres. Alumni Assn. of Va., 1923-24. Mason. Democrat. Episcopalian. Home: Washington, D.C. Died Dec. 14, 1928.

ELLIOTT, Oliver Morton, educator; b. White Water, Ind., Feb. 11, 1867; d. Daniel Thomas and Sarah (Moon) E.; B.A., Marietta (O.) Coll., 1890; M.A., State U. of Ia., 1907; m. Frances M. Conner, 1890. Teacher, Ia., 1890-1903; supt. schs., Sheldon, Ia., 1903-09, Twin Falls, Ida., 1909-14, Salem, Ore., 1914-16; pres. Lewiston State Normal Sch, 1916—. Conglist. Home: Lewiston, Ida. Died Dec. 15, 1925.

ELLIOTT, Orrin Leslie, author; b. Centerville, N.Y., Mar. 8, 1860; s. Chauncey Harrison and Lovina Lucelia (Dunshee) E.; Ph.B., Cornell, 1885, Ph.D., 1890; m. Ellen Coit Brown, Dec. 28, 1886; children—Louis Dunshee, Christabel, David Coit. Instr. English, Cornell, 1886-91; registrar of Stanford U., 1891-1925, emeritus. Author: The Tariff Controversy in the United States to 1833, 1892; Stanford University and Thereabouts, 1896; The Things That Abide, 1903; Stanford University—the First Twenty-five Years, 1937. Died Aug. 28, 1940.

ELLIOTT, Sarah Barnwell, author; d. Bishop Stephen and Charlotte Bull (Barnwell) E. (D.C.L., U. of the South, 1913). Mem. Soc. Colonial Dames S.C., Hist. Soc. S.C., U.D.C., Descendants of Colonial Governors of S.C.; pres. Tenn. Equal Suffrage Assn.; v.p. Southern States Woman's Suffrage Conference. Author: The Felmeres, 1880; A Simple Heart, 1886; Jerry, 1889; John Paget, 1893; The Durket Sperret, 1897; An Incident, and Other Happenings, 1899; Sam Houston, 1900; The Making of Jane, 1901. Plays: His Majesty's Servant. Died Aug. 30, 1928.

ELLIOTT, Walter, clergyman; b. Detroit, Mich., Jan. 6, 1842; s. Robert T. and Frances (O'Shea) E.; ed. Christian Bros. Coll., Notre Dame U.; sergt. Co.

K, 5th O. Vol. Inf., Union Army, 1861-64. Ordained R.C. priest, of the Paulist Congregation, 1872; rector Apostolic Mission House, Washington, 1912; rector emeritus. Dir. Catholic Missionary Union. Author: Life of Isaac T. Hecker, 1894; Life of Jesus Christ, 1897; (translation) Tauler's Sermons, 1910; Parish Sermons, 1913; Spiritual Life, 1913; Manual of Missions, 1923; Retreat for Priests, 1924. Retreat for Nuns, 1926; Mission Sermons, 1927. Died Apr. 18, 1928.

ELLIOTT, William, congressman, lawyer; b. Beaufort, S.C., Sept. 3, 1838; ed. at Beaufort Coll., Harvard, and U. of Va.; admitted to bar in Charleston, April, 1861; officer in C.S.A. during Civil war. Elected, 1866, mem. of legislature and intendant of Beaufort; presdl. elector, 1880; mem. Congress, 1887-1903, 1st S.C. dist. Democrat. Home: Columbia, S.C. Died 1907.

ELLIOTT, William Arthur, coll. prof.; b. Hillier, Ont., Can., Mar. 27, 1866; s. George and Eliza (Orr) E.; A.B., Allegheny Coll., 1889, A.M., 1892; studied in Germany and at Am. Sch. of Classical Studies, Athens, 1894-95; (hon. L.H.D., Dickinson, 1902); m. Ella Wade Miller, Aug. 19, 1896; children—Ruth Anna, Ernest Sawyer (dec.). Instr. Greek and Latin, Allegheny Coll., 1889; prin. Allegheny Coll. Prep. Sch., 1890; prof. Greek, 1892—, v.p., 1907-09, Allegheny Coll. Has traveled in Greece, Asia Minor, Sicily, Italy. Contbr. to mags. and revs. Methodist. Mem. of University Senate of M.E. Ch., 1920-28; mem. Joint Commn. on Unification of M.E. Ch. and M.E. Ch., S., 1924-28. Home: Meadville, Pa. Died Aug. 27, 1935.

ELLIOTT, William Henry, newspaperman; b. New Castle, Ind., July 4, 1844; s. Jehu T. E. (judge Supreme Court of Ind.); grad. U.S. Naval Acad., 1865; m. Emma E. Conner, Oct. 20, 1876. Ensign U.S.N., Dec. 1866; master, 1868; lt., Oct. 1869; resigned Apr. 20, 1870. Studied and practiced law, New Castle, Ind.; owner and pub. new Castle Courier, 1877-99, and, 1904—. Mem. of original G.A.R. com. that planned and secured erection of Soldiers' and Sailors' Monument at Indianapolis; filled numerous official places; vol. in war with Spain; apptd. lt. in the Navy; served as 2d in command of the Leonidas, vessel that won notoriety as the "Fire ship" on account of a fire in the coal stored in the forehold, which was extinguished after 30 days of hard fighting and the consumption of 730 tons of coal, without material injury to the ship. Organized postal system of Puerto Rico, Jan. 1899, to June 6, 1900; commr. of interior, P.R., June 6, 1900-Dec. 1, 1904. Home: New Castle, Ind. Died 1914.

ELLIOTT, William Swan, engineer, mfr.; b. Wellsville, O., Oct. 18, 1863; s. John and Katherine (Adams) E.; M.E., Cornell U., 1887; m. Anna M. Leyden, Feb. 18, 1901; children—George Frederick, Margaret Alexander, William Adams, Gilbert Leyden. With Sprague Electric and Ry. Motor Co., 1887-90; dept. mgr. Edison Electric Co., Chicago, 1890-92; mgr. of sales, Stirling Boiler Co., 1892-95; pres. Elliott Co., mfrs. electric, steam and hydraulic power plant apparatus, 1905—; pres. Kerr Turbine Co., Liberty Mfg. Co.; v.p. Lagonda Mfg. Co. Republican. Presbyn. Mason. Home: Pittsburgh, Pa. Died Feb. 21, 1934.

ELLIS, Alston, univ. pres.; b. Kenton Co., Ky., Jan. 26, 1847; s. Absalom and Mary E.; B.S., Miami U., 1865, A.B., 1867, A.M., 1872; (hon. Ph.D., U. of Wooster, 1879, Ohio State U., 1887; LL.D., Ohio State, 1890, Miami, 1894); m. Katherine Anne Cox, July 23, 1867. Prin. 3d dist. sch., 1867-68, Cabot St. Sch., Newport, Ky., 1868-71; supt. pub. schs., Hamilton, O., 1871-79, 1887-92, pub. schs., Sandusky, O., 1880-87; pres. State Agrl. Coll., Fort Collins, Colo., 1892-1900; dir. Colo. Expt. Sta., 1893-1900; pres. Ohio U., Athens, O., July 18, 1901—. Mem. bd. trustees Ohio State Univ., 1878-83, Oxford (Ohio) Female Coll., 1874-87. Col. on staff of gov. of Colo. Life mem. Victoria Inst., Philos. Soc. of Great Britain. Mem. Ohio State Bd. of Sch. Examiners, 1875-79 and 1887-92. Author: History of the Ungraded Schools of Ohio. Home: Athens, O. Died Nov. 14, 1920.

ELLIS, Anna M. B. ("Max Eliot"), critic, journalist; b. Dayton, O.; m. Granville Alden Ellis, 1876. Removed to Boston; while still at sch. contributed letters to Dayton Journal on the Centennial Expn.; spl. corr. Cincinnati Times, 1879-81; Boston Herald, spl., 1882; on editorial staff, same, 1884, and on regular staff ever since; acted during the theatrical season as spl. dramatic critic for all important New York prodns., 1884-91; European corr. in summer, and founded and edited (till removing to London) the dept. in the Boston Herald, "Personal and Social Gossip"; author of "Chats About Folks," appearing consecutively in the same paper's Sunday edition, 1885-90; was Boston corr. New York World, and later on New York Herald; and spl. London corr. Paris edition New York Herald. Founded Boston Amusement Gazette and edited it 1st yr.; removed to London, 1891, and became spl. London corr., Boston Herald; also spl. London critic New York Dramatic News. Author: Bermula Romance; A Tragic Marriage; Part of a Summer; New Edinburgh Notes; Actors at Home. Home: London, Eng. Died 1911.

ELLIS, Arthur McDonald, lawyer; b. Linn Creek, Mo., Sept. 13, 1875; s. William David and Malinda Elizabeth (McDonald) E.; father a Calif. pioneer of 1852; B.Litt., U. of Calif., 1899; m. Bessie Bailey, Aug. 6, 1913; children—Mildred Walton, Herbert Bailey. Admitted to Calif. bar, 1903, then practiced at Los Angeles. Mem. State of Calif. Geog. Bd.; trustee Southwest Mus. Mem. Los Angeles Chamber of Commerce. Republican. Home: Los Angeles, Calif. Died Apr. 17, 1932.

ELLIS CARLETON, research chemist, author; b. Keene, N.H., Sept. 20, 1876; s. Marcus and Catharine (Goodnow) E.; B.Sc., Massachusetts Institute of Technology, 1900; m. Birdella M. Wood, Nov. 28, 1901. Instr. M.I.T., 1900-02; has worked extensively in field of edible oils, fats, waxes, synthetic resins, paints, varnishes, petroleum products, and gasoline mfr.; has taken out about 750 patents; dir. Ellis-Foster Company. Gold medal for inventions at Jamestown Expn., 1907; Edward Longstreth medal, Franklin Institute, 1916. Selected as a "modern pioneer" by a committee of which Karl Compton is the chairman. Author: Hydrogenation of Organic Substances, 3d edit., 1930; Synthetic Resins and Their Plastics, 1923; 2d edit., 1935; Chemistry of Petroleum Derivatives, 1934; Vol. 2, 1937; Chemistry of Printing Ink, 1939. Co-author: The Vital Factors of Foods; Ultra Violet Light; Soilless Growth, etc. Home: Montclair, N.J. Died Jan. 13, 1941.

ELLIS, David Abram, lawyer; b. Buffalo, N.Y., Feb. 20, 1873; s. William David and Bertha (Strass) E.; A.B., Harvard, 1894; LL.B., Harvard Law Sch., 1896; m. Amy Friedman, Oct. 6, 1898; children—Margaret Constance (dec.), Mildred Elna. Admitted to Suffolk Co. bar, Mass., 1895; with Warren & Brandeis, and Brandeis, Dunbar & Nutter to 1900; practiced alone until Jan. 1, 1914; then firm of Ellis & Balch; mem. exec. com. and trustee Home Savings Bank, Boston; mem. Boston Transit Commn., 1913-18; commr. Mass. Dept. Public Utilities, 1919-26, with Fed. Fuel Adm., Boston, World War. Mem. Sch. Com., Boston, 1903-13 (chmn. 1909-13). Mem. Visiting Coms. Harvard; lecturer on municipal govt. at Harvard U. Trustee Jewish Theol. Sem. America, Am. Jewish Com., Jewish Welfare Bd., Federated Jewish Charities, Franklin Foundation, Old South Meeting House. Mason. Home: Boston, Mass. Died July 27, 1929.

ELLIS, Edward Sylvester, author; b. Geneva, O., Apr. 11, 1840; s. Sylvester and Mary (Alberty) E.; ed. N.J. State Normal Sch.; (hon. A.M., Princeton, 1887); m. Annie M. Deane, Dec. 25, 1862; m. 2d, Clara Spalding Brown, Nov. 20, 1900. Engaged in teaching; became prin. Trenton High Sch., later was trustee and supt. schs., Trenton, N.J.; entire time devoted to lit. work, 1876—. Author: History of Our Country, 1896; Standard History of the United States, 1898; The Story of the World's Greatest Nations; Low Twelve, 1908; High Twelve; History of New York; History of New Jersey. Also Deerfoot Series of Juveniles, and many other juveniles, since 1885. Home: Upper Montclair, N.J. Died June 20, 1916.

ELLIS, Edwin Erastus, steel exec.; b. Hinsdale, Ill., Mar. 8, 1883; s. John and Ella Harriet (Gary) E.; A.B., Northwestern U., 1904; grad. study, U. of Wis., 1904-05; m. Alice Scott, Dec. 25, 1909; children—Scott, Alice Edwina, Gary. With Wis. Geol. Survey, 1902-03, U.S. Geol. Survey, 1904-05; asst. geologist Oliver Iron Mining Co., 1905-08; with Tenn. Coal, Iron & R.R. Co., 1908-32, as geologist, 1908-10, asst. mgr. land dept., 1910-17, mgr., 1917-25, land and tax commr. same, 1917-32; pres. Ceylon (mining) Co., 1916-27; pres. Universal Exploration Co., 1925—; v.p. U.S. Steel Corp., 1932—; pres. Ion Corp. (elect. physics research and patent dev.), 1935—; pres. Lake Superior Consol. Iron Mines, Piloto Mining Co. Republican. Died March 10, 1936.

ELLIS, George Washington, investigator, writer; b. Weston, Mo., May 4, 1875; s. George and Amanda Jane (Drace) E.; LL.B., U. of Kan., 1893; studied 4 yrs. collegiate dept., U. of Kan., while practicing law; took U.S. Census examination and apptd. clerk in Census Dept., Washington, 1900; post-grad. studies, philosophy and psychology, 2 yrs., Howard U., Washington; grad. Gunton's Inst. Economics and Sociology, New York, 1900; widower. Sec. of Am. Legation to Republic of Liberia, 1902-10; mem. Ellis & Westbrooks, Chicago; asst. corp. counsel of Chicago. Studied social conditions in Africa, collecting folk-lore stories and African proverbs; contbg. editor Jour. of Race Development of Clark U., The Citizen, Boston, etc.; addresses on Africa and race question. Has large collection of ethnol. specimens loaned to Nat. Mus., Washington; campaign speaker and dir. of the colored western bur. of Nat. Progressive hdqrs., 1912; Progressive Republican. Mem. gen. financial bd. of A.M.E. Ch., 1912-16. Fellow Royal Geog. Society Great Britain. Decorated Knight Comdr. of Order of African Redemption. Author: Negro Culture in West Africa; The Leopard's Claw; Negro Achievements in Social Progress. Home: Chicago, Ill. Died Nov. 26, 1919.

ELLIS, H. Bert, physician; b. Lincoln Centre, Me., May 17, 1863; s. James Henry and Annie M. (Bullard) E.; A.B., Acadia Coll., Wolfville, N.S., 1884; M.D., Los Angeles Dept. Coll. of Medicine of U. of Calif., 1888; post-grad. work univs. of Göttingen and Vienna; m. Florence E. Chandler, May 27, 1907. Practiced in Los Angeles, 1889—; practice confined to diseases of the eye, ear, nose and throat; prof. ophthalmology, Los Angeles Dept. Coll. Medicine of U. of Calif., 1896-1915. Retired. Home: Los Angeles, Calif. Died Apr. 15, 1922.

ELLIS, Harvey, artist; b. Rochester, N.Y., 1852; pupil of Edwin White, N. A. Exhibited at Paris Expn., 1900. Mem. New York Water Color Club; pres. Rochester Soc. of Arts and Crafts. Is also an architect. Home: Rochester, N.Y. Died 1904.

ELLIS, Horace, educator; b. Decatur, Ill., July 9, 1861; s. Ira and Mary Frances (Ferguson) E.; reared on farm; A.B., Ind. U., 1896; A.M., U. of Indianapolis, 1897; Ph.D., Am. U., 1903; m. Grace V. Mapes, 1886; children—Max Mapes, Ira Howell. Taught country schs. to 1882; supt. Indianapolis suburban schs., 1885-92; then re-entered Ind. U.; taught at Lafayette, Ind., and N. Vernon, Ind., 1896-98; supt. pub. schs., Franklin, Ind., 1898-1902; pres. Idaho State Normal Sch., 1902-04; pres. Vincennes (Ind.) U., 1904-16; state supt. pub. instrn. of Ind., 1916-19; dir. western area, all states west of Pittsburgh, for Rep. Nat. Com., 1919-24; rep. Rep. Nat. Com., 1919-31. Mem. M.E. Ch. Mason. Author and pub. lecturer on "The Scientific Approach to Political Problems," etc. Home: Indianapolis, Ind. Died Dec. 30, 1932.

ELLIS, Job Bicknell, mycologist; b. Potsdam, N.Y., Jan. 21, 1829; s. Freeman and Sarah E.; worked his way through sch. and coll., first on farm, afterward by teaching; grad. Union Coll., 1851; m. Arvilla J. Bacon, Apr. 19, 1856. Filled several edni. positions as teacher classics, etc., at Germantown, Pa., Albany, N.Y., Acad., and schs. at Poughkeepsie, N.Y., Alexander, Ga., Canton, N.Y., Acad., Potsdam, N.Y.; served in U.S. Navy, 1864-65; located in Newfield, N.J., 1865; from 1878 devoted entirely to mycol. research and the preparation and sale in sets of collections of N. Am. fungi, and 2d edit. under title of "Fungi Columbiani." Author: (with B. M. Everhart) North American Pyrenomycetes. Home: Newfield, N.J. Died 1905.

ELLIS, John William, clergyman; b. Carthage, Ill., Dec. 29, 1839; s. Timothy and Olivia (Evans) E.; A.B., Georgetown (Ky.) Coll., 1860, A.M., 1863; (hon. Ph.D., Chautauqua U., 1888; LL.D., U. of Chicago, 1889); m. Sallie Breckenridge, Dec. 29, 1863; father of J(ohn) Breckenridge and Perry Canby E. Admitted to Ky. bar, 1862; Mo. bar, 1869; practiced law St. Louis, 1869; ordained Christian (Disciples) ministry, 1874; pres. Plattsburg (Mo.) Coll., 1880-97; pres. Central Christian Coll., Albany, Mo., 1900-02; elder Christian Ch., Plattsburg, Mo.; pastor Bentonville, Ark. Democrat. Author: Life Mission, 1876; Transl. of Antigone of Sophocles into English verse, 1879; Song of Songs, 1897. Home: Plattsburg, Mo. Died 1910.

ELLIS, Mary, teacher; b. Holden, Mass., Sept. 21, 1834; d. Charles and Ruth (Stearns) E.; grad. Mt. Holyoke Sem., S. Hadley, Mass., 1855; (hon. M.A., Ia. [now Grinnell] Coll., 1877). Teacher, 1855-58, 1859-72, asso. prin., 1867-72, acting prin., 1871-72, Mt. Holyoke Sem.; abroad, 1869-70 (also 1872-74); lady prin. and teacher, Iowa (now Grinnell) Coll.; prof. English, Smith Coll., short time, 1883; resigned on account of ill health; invalid, 1883-90; teacher, Mills Coll., Calif., 1892-1903, and 6 months, 1905; retired. Home: Northampton, Mass. Died May 20, 1917.

ELLIS, Overton Gentry, judge; b. Nodaway Co., Mo., Oct. 26, 1860; s. Thomas Cowle (M.D.) and Jane Harris (Gentry) E.; B.Litt., U. of Mo., 1883; Law Sch., U. of Va., 1884-85; read law in office of Edwards & Ellison, Maryville, Mo.; m. Jennie Wilhite, Aug. 29, 1894; children—Overton Gentry, Presley Wilhite. Admitted to Mo. bar, 1886, and practiced at Maryville, 1886-87; title atty. Lombard Investment Co., Kansas City, Mo., 1887-89, trial atty., 1889-92; removed to Tacoma, Wash., 1892; mem. Ellis & Fletcher, 1901-08, Ellis, Fletcher & Evans, 1908-10; apptd. by Gov. Hay as asso. judge Supreme Ct. of Wash., May 10, 1910, to fill unexpired term of Frank H. Rudkin, resigned; elected, Nov. 1912; chief justice, 1917-19, resigned; then mem. Ellis & Evans; then in practice alone. Assistant prosecuting attorney Nodaway County, Mo., 1886-87, resigned; city attorney, Tacoma, 1904-06, resigned; mem. commn. of 15 to draft new charter for Tacoma, which reported commn. plan of govt. adopted by vote of electors Oct. 16, 1909; formerly mem. Judicial Council of State of Washington. Democrat. Pres. of Wash. State Soc. S.A.R. 2 terms; v.p. Gen. Mountain and Pacific dist. S.A.R. Home: Tacoma, Wash. Died Nov. 9, 1940.

ELLIS, Perry Canby, editor, publicist; b. in Boone Co., Ky., Aug. 21, 1867; s. John William and

Sallie (Breckenridge) E.; bro. of J(ohn) Breckenridge E.; A.B., A.M., Plattsburg (Mo.) Coll., 1885; unmarried. On staff Kansas City Times, 1886-90, Journal, 1890-93, World, 1893-96,, St. Louis Post-Dispatch, 1896, Star, 1897-99; editor Quincy (Ill.) Whig, 1899-1911; editor of Adams County Farmer. Chmn. Rep. Senatorial Com., 36th Ill. Dist., 1904-08; presdl. elector, Ill., 1904; mem. Rep. State Com., 1908-10; chmn. Supreme Court Jud. Com. 4th Dist., Ill., 1908-20; del. Deep Waterways convs., Memphis, 1906, New Orleans, 1909. Mem. Nat. Publicity Com. on Training Camp Activities; supt. Ill. State Free Employment Bur., 1921—. Mason. Home: Quincy, Ill. Deceased.

ELLIS, Robert Walpole, prof. geology; b. Nevinville, Ia., July 16, 1868; s. Joseph Loran and Theresa Margaret (Trask) E.; Tabor (Ia.) Coll., 1893-95; B.Sc., U. of S. Dak., 1897; studied U. of Chicago, summer 1899; M.A., U. of Wis., 1910; m. Bess M. Olds, Aug. 4, 1914; children—Jean Harrison, Margaret Elizabeth. Prin. and teacher secondary schs. until 1913; instr. geology, U. of Neb., 1913-18; prof. geology, U. of N.M., 1918—; acting state geologist, 1918-27. Field work, summers, various states. Republican. Conglist. Home: Albuquerque, N.M. Died Mar. 10, 1937.

ELLIS, Rudolph, banker; b. Elkton, Md., Nov. 20, 1837; son of Francis A. and Eliza (Howard) E.; ed. Elkton; m. Helen Struthers, Apr. 26, 1866. Served pvt. 1st troop Phila. City Cav., May 13, 1861; 1st lt. and adj. 6th Pa. Cav., Nov. 20, 1862; capt., Apr. 11, 1864; hon. mustered out, Dec. 27, 1864. Pres. Fidelity Trust Co.; dir. Pa. R.R. Co., Fourth St. Nat. Bank (Phila.), Am. Telegraph & Telephone Co. Commercial Trust Co. of Phila., Manhattan Trust Co. (New York). Commr. Tp. of Radnor, Delaware Co., Pa. Mem. Loyal Legion (Pa. Commandery). Pres. Radnor Hunt Club. Home: Bryn Mawr, Pa. Died Sept. 21, 1915.

ELLIS, Seth H., farmer; b. nr. Martinsville, O., Jan. 3, 1830; s. Robert and Anna Hockett (Moon) E.; ed. common schools, Clinton and Warren counties, O.; m. Rebecca J. Tressler, Aug. 21, 1851. Was master Ohio State Grange from organization April 9, 1873 to 1879; chmn. exec. com. same, 1879-88; again master same, 1888-92, 1896-1900, and again chmn. exec. com., 1892-96, and Dec. 1900—; chaplain Nat. Grange 4 yrs.; mem. exec. com. Nat. Grange 2 yrs.; trustee Ohio State Univ., 9 yrs.; mem. bd. control, Ohio Agrl. Expt. Sta., Wooster, O., 12 yrs.; Prohibition candidate for Gov. Ohio, 1892; candidate, 1900, for president of U.S. of Union Reform Party—first candidate ever placed in nomination for president by direct vote of people. In religion mem. Orthodox Friends (Quaker). Home: Waynesville, O. Deceased.

ELLIS, Theodore Thaddeus, newspaper pub. mfr.; b. St. Louis, Mo., Apr. 25, 1867; s. John and Mary (Bentley) E.; ed. pub. schs.; m. Mary Ellis. Chmn. bd. Royal Worcester Corset Co.; pres. and treas. N.E. Woolen Fabric Co., N.E. Fibre Blanket Co.; v.p. and half owner Chicago Daily News; v.p. and dir. Daneco Corp. (Del.); former owner Worcester Telegram Gazette. Served in U.S. Navy, in China, under Adm. Hugh Rodman. Owner of a notable herd of purebred cattle, among them "Green Meadow Lustre," world champion Guernsey cow. Art collector and owner of one of the most valuable collections of pictures in America. Identified with many philanthropies. Home: Worcester, Mass. Died Jan. 6, 1934.

ELLIS, William Russell, congressman; b. nr. Waveland, Ind., Apr. 23, 1850; s. James and Susan (Stone) E.; removed to Guthrie Co., Ia., 1855; worked on farm and attended sch.; later farmed, taught sch. and attended Ia. State Agrl. Coll.; LL.B., State U. of Ia., 1874; m. Jennie B. Edwards, Mar. 31, 1880 (died 1882); 2d, Mrs. Ida J. Scott, June 16, 1885. Practiced law and did newspaper work at Hamburg, Ia.; 2 yrs. city atty. and 1 term mayor there. Removed to Ore., 1883; supt. schs. Morrow Co., 1884-85; dist. atty. 7th Jud. Dist., 3 terms, 1885-90; mem. 53d to 55th Congresses (1893-99); judge 6th Jud. Dist., 1900-06; mem. 60th and 61st Congresses (1907-11), 2d Ore. Dist. Republican. Home: Pendleton, Ore. Died Jan. 18, 1915.

ELLISON, Everett Monroe, M.D.; b. Parrottsville, Tenn., Mar. 2, 1879; s. John Ford and Laura Elizabeth (Ottinger) E.; A.B., U.S. Grant U., Tenn., 1901, A.M., 1903; M.D., George Washington U., 1912, Ph.D., 1925; spl. courses New York Post-Grad. Med. Sch., 1915; grad. Med. Field Service Sch., Carlisle Barracks, Pa., 1926; m. Alberta Bayne Huntt, Dec. 30, 1916 (died 1926); children—Alice Elizabeth, Margaret Isabel, Nancy Doris; m. 2d, Fannie May Huff, Aug. 15, 1930. Teacher in prep. schools, Tenn., 1896-1901; pres. Powells Valley Sem., Well Spring, Tenn., 1901-03; teacher, later prin. Bataan High Sch., nr. Manila, P.I., 1904-07; mem. house staff Garfield Memorial Hosp., Washington, 1911-13; personal physician to Hon. Levi P. Morton, v.p. of U.S., 1913-14; dir. of clinics, Emergency Hosp., Washington, 1915-20; attending physician, Tuberculosis Clinic, D.C. Health Dept., 1917—; mem. visiting staffs Gallinger

Municipal and George Washington University hosps., 1916-30, Children's and Sibley Memorial hosp., 1917—; cons. in tuberculosis, U.S. Vets. Bureau, 1920-23; clin. asso. in medicine, George Washington U., 1918-32. Mem. Citizens Com. of One Thousand, N.Y. City; pres. Citizens' Service Assn. for Law and Order, D.C.; mem. bd. mgrs. Washington Y.M.C.A.; mem. Official Bd. Foundry M.E. Ch.; pres. United Dry Forces (D.C.). Mem. med. dept. D.C.N.G., 1907-12, Vol. Med. Service Corps, World War; maj. Med. R.C. Trustee Southeastern U., D.C., Tenn. Wesleyan Coll. Republican. Methodist. Mason. Home: Washington, D.C. Died July 24, 1939.

ELLISON, Thomas Emmet, lawyer; b. La Grange Ind., Aug. 12, 1852; s. Andrew and Susan Miranda (Tuttle) E.; student Notre Dame Coll., Ind.; spl. student lit. dept. U. of Mich., LL.B., 1874; m. Emma S. Stockbridge, Jan. 10, 1878 (died Mar. 1884); m. 2d, Hannah Hall, Dec. 14, 1887. Admitted to bar, Dec. 23, 1873, and U.S. Supreme Court bar; mem. Bd. State Charities, Ind., 1892-99; mem. Ind. Senate, 1895-99; drew present law as to care of dependent children, also remolding penal system, establishment parole system and indeterminate sentence law, etc.; first pres. Ind. Reformatory. Mem., v.p., Nat. Conference. Ind. Democrat. Prominent in promoting constrn. of Lakes Erie and Mich. Canal by U.S. Govt. Home: Ft. Wayne, Ind. Died Dec. 18, 1925.

ELLISON, William Bruce, lawyer; b. St. Thomas, Ont., Can., July 17, 1857; s. Richard and Sarah Eleanor (Arthurs) E.; ed. Ont. pub. schs.; m. May Alma Jackson, Sept. 5, 1883. Admitted to Canadian bar, 1880, New York bar, 1882; mem. N.Y. Legislature, 1893; commr. water, gas and electricity, New York, 1906; corp. counsel, 1907; commr. to revise laws affecting fire ins. in N.Y. State, 1913. Democrat. Episcopalian. Mason. Author: The Canadian-American Fisheries; Insurance Companies Before the Courts; etc. Home: New York, N.Y. Died Dec. 6, 1924.

ELLSLER, Effie, actress; b. Phila., 1858; her father, John Ellsler, veteran actor, became mgr. of a Cleveland, O., theatre at which she made her first appearance in child parts; gained local fame and went to Madison Sq. Theatre, New York, then to Union Sq. Co.; was the original Hazel Kirke in play of that name, and played other stage heroines; has played leading parts in her own co., 1886—; m. Frank Weston, actor. Died Dec. 12, 1918.

ELLSWORTH, James Drummond; b. Milford, Mass., Oct. 14, 1863; s. Alfred Augustus and Agelina Grimke Clementine (Cook) E.; prep. edn., Knox Acad., Galesburg, Ill.; Colorado Coll., Colorado Springs, 1880-84; m. Mabel Silsby Morrison, June 1, 1893; children—Elizabeth, Elmer Morrison, Mrs. Fanny Goulding Scannell. Editor Coal Creek (Colo.) Enterprise, 1884; reporter, Denver Republican, 1885-89, Boston Herald and New York Recorder, 1890-97; corr. New York Herald, 1898-99; with Publicity Bur., Boston, 1900-07; publicity mgr., 1908-24, asst. v.p., 1924-27, asst. to pres., 1927-30, Am. Telephone & Telegraph Co. Trustee Am. Defense Soc. Republican. Episcopalian. Home: Boston, Mass. Died June 13, 1940.

ELLSWORTH, James William, capitalist; b. Hudson, O., Oct. 13, 1849; s. Edgar Birge and Mary H. (Dawes) E.; ed. pub. schs., Hudson, and Western Reserve Prep. Sch.; LL.D., Kenyon College, 1918; m. Eva, d. Oliver M. Butler, of Chicago, Nov. 4, 1874 (died 1888); m. 2d, Mrs. Julia M. Fincke, d. Benjamin G. Clarke, of New York, April 22, 1895 (died 1921). Owner and operator of coal mines; dir. Postal Telegraph-Cable Co., Baltimore & Ohio & Chicago Railway. Mem. Bd. South Park Commrs., Chicago, 1889-99; mem. bd. dirs. Chicago Expn., 1892-94 (chmn. com. on liberal arts—was also on exec. com. and com. on finance). Known as bibliophile; connoisseur in Chinese porcelains, ancient Greek statuettes, oriental rugs. Comdr. Order of Crown of Italy. Home: New York, N.Y. Died June 3, 1925.

ELLSWORTH, William Webster, publisher; b. Hartford, Conn., Oct. 30, 1855; s. Oliver and Caroline Cleveland (Smith) E.; (great g.s. of Chief Justice Oliver Ellsworth and of Noah Webster); ed. pvt. schs., Boston; m. Helen Yale Smith, June 4, 1878; children—Lucy Morris (Mrs. George M. Creevey), Bradford, Helen Adelaide (Mrs. M. C. C. Van Loben Sels), Elizabeth (Mrs. F. S. Gaucher, dec.). Sec. the Century Co., publishers, N.Y. City, 1881-1913, and pres., 1913-16; retired. Lecturer on literary topics. Author: A Golden Age of Authors, 1919; Creative Writing, 1929. Home: New Hartford, Conn. Died Dec. 18, 1936.

ELLWANGER, George Herman, author; b. Rochester, N.Y., July 10, 1848; s. George and Cornelia (Brooks) E.; ed. in Europe (A.M., Rochester Univ.). Formerly engaged in journalism; now mem. and sec. Ellwanger & Barry, horticulturists. Editor: The Rose, by H. B. Ellwanger, 1893; Love's Demesne, a Garland of Contemporary Love Poems (with critical introduction), 1896; Love's Old Sweet Song, 1903. Home: Rochester, N.Y. Died 1906.

ELLWANGER, William De Lancey, author; b. Rochester, N.Y., Sept. 27, 1855; s. George and Cornelia (Brooks) E.; A.B., Yale, 1876; admitted to

bar, 1878; m. Laura Selden, May 10, 1887. Author: A Summer Snowflake and Drift of Other Verse and Song, 1902; The Oriental Rug, 1903; Snuff Box Full of Trees and some Apocryphal Essays, 1909. Home: Rochester, N.Y. Died Feb. 16, 1913.

ELLWOOD, Isaac Leonard, capitalist; b. Salt Springville, N.Y., Aug. 3, 1833; s. Abram and Sarah (DeLong) E.; m. Harriet Miller, Jan. 27, 1859. In the early seventies became interested, with J. F. Glidden, in the mfr. and sale of barbed wire; Glidden sold interest, 1876, to Washburn & Moen Mfg. Co.; business afterward carried on under name I. L. Ellwood & Co. Became the mng. partner, and later became sole owner large mfg. establishments at De Kalb, under names I. L. Ellwood Mfg. Co., and Ellwood Wire & Nail Co. (both plants sold to Am. Steel & Wire Co. when organized in 1898, in the management of which he held responsible position). Home: De Kalb, Ill. Died 1910.

ELLYSON, J(ames) Taylor, business man; b. Richmond, Va., May 20, 1847; s. Henry K. and Elizabeth P. E.; student Columbia Coll., Richmond Coll.; grad. U. of Va., 1869; m. Lora E. Hotchkiss, 1869. Served in C.S.A., as mem. 2d co., Richmond Howitzers, surrendering with co. at Appomattox and resuming coll. work; after leaving univ. engaged in commercial business in Richmond; has been pres. city council, pres. bd. of pub. interests, state senator, 1885-88, and 3 terms mayor of Richmond, beginning, 1888; lt. gov. of Va. 3 terms, 1906-18. For past 25 yrs. chmn. Dem. State Com. of Va., also Va. mem. Dem. Nat. Com. Active mem. R. E. Lee and George E. Pickett camps of U.C.V.; chmn. city sch. bd., 16 yrs.; mem. and pres. bd. trustees Richmond Coll.; 40 yrs. exec. officer Ednl. Bd. of Bapt. Gen. Assn. of Va.; has been pres. State Bapt. Assn., v.p. Southern Bapt. Conv. and a rep. on State Mission Bd., the Orphanage Bd. and Edn. Bd.; pres. Bapt. Conv. N. Am., Gov. Div. of History, Edn. and Social Economy, Jamestown Expn. Home: Richmond, Va. Died Mar. 18, 1919.

ELMENDORF, Dwight Lathrop, lecturer; b. Brooklyn, Mar. 13, 1859; s. John Augustus and Frances Richards (Lathrop) E.; A.B., Princeton, 1882, A.M., 1885; unmarried. For 15 yrs. teacher of the deaf; lecturer, 1897—. Pres. New York Microscopic Soc. Author: Lantern Slides, How to Make and Color Them, 1894; A Camera Crusade, 1912. Died May 7, 1929.

ELMENDORF, Henry Livingston, supt. Buffalo Pub. Library, 1897—; b. Brooklyn, Oct. 10, 1852; s. Anthony and Sarah C. E.; ed. Brooklyn Poly. Inst.; m. Theresa West, Oct. 3, 1896. Asst. Gardner Sage Library, New Brunswick, N.J., 1877; librarian Public Library, St. Joseph, Mo., 1891-96; sec. Am. Library Assn., 1895-96; v.p., 1896-97. Past pres. Buffalo Library Club, N.Y. State Library Assn. Writer on libraries in Library Jour. and Proc. Nat. Endl. Assn. Home: Buffalo, N.Y. Died 1906.

ELMENDORF, Joachim, clergyman; b. Rochester, N.Y., Mar. 26, 1827; s. Levi and Salise (De Puy) E.; grad. Rutgers Coll.; 1850; (D.D., Union Coll.; 1865;) ordained Ref. Ch., 1853; m. Sarah Bull, Oct. 5, 1854. Pres. Gen. Synod Ref. Ch. 1871; pres. bd. of edn.; trustee Rutgers and Vassar. Pres. Quill Club, New York. Home: Saratoga Springs, N.Y. Died 1908.

ELMENDORF, Theresa Hubbell, librarian; b. Pardeeville, Wis., Nov. 1, 1855; d. Hubbell and Helen (Roberts) West; grad. Miss Wheelock's Sem., Milwaukee, 1874; m. Henry Livingston Elmendorf, Oct. 3, 1896 (died 1906). Deputy librarian, 1880-92, librarian, 1892-96, Milwaukee Pub. Library; vice-librarian of Buffalo Public Library, 1906-26. Editor for selection of A.L.A. Catalog, 1904. First woman pres. A.L.A. (1911-12), mem. A.L.A. Council, A.L.A. Inst.; pres. N.Y. Library Assn., 1903-04. Died Sept. 4, 1932.

ELMER, Henry Whiteley, M.D.; b. Bridgeton, N.J., April 26, 1847; s. William and Eliza R. E.; grad. Princeton, 1866; M.D., Univ. of Pa., 1869. Mem. Cumberland Co. Med. Soc.; 1st v.p. Med. Soc. of N.J.; mem. State bd. of health. Home: Bridgeton, N.J. Died 1907.

ELMER, William, M.D.; b. Bridgeton, N.J., Dec. 14, 1840; s. William and Eliza (Robeson) E.; grad. Princeton, 1861 (A.M., 1864); M.D., Univ. of Pa., 1864; m. Sept. 29, 1869, Alice Gray (died Nov. 17, 1888); 2d, Dec. 25, 1899, Emma Burke. Has practiced at Trenton from 1869; pres. N.J. State Med. Soc.; v.p. Am. Acad. of Medicine; med. dir. Mercer Hosp. Home: Trenton, N.J. Died 1908.

ELMORE, Jefferson, univ. prof.; b. Ashley, Mo., Oct. 1, 1862; s. James Calvin and Lucinda Rogers (Pritchett) E.; A.B., Leland Stanford Jr. U., 1895, A.M., 1895, Ph.D., 1901; univs. of Bonn and Berlin, 1900-01; m. Margaret Hilliard Robb, May 29, 1890; 1 son, Garrett Henry. Vice prin. Laurel Hall Sch., San Mateo, Calif., 1888-91; prin. Madero (Calif.) Acad., 1891-93, Merced Co. (Calif.) High Sch., 1895-97; instr. Latin, 1899-1902, asst. prof., 1902-10, asso. prof., 1910-24, prof. classical literature, 1925—, Stanford U. Democrat. Unitarian. Author: Syntax of Certain Latin Verbs of Desire, 1901; Book of Latin

Prose Composition for Use in Colleges, 1909; A French Grammar (with O. M. Johnston), 1926. Deceased.

ELMORE, Samuel Edward, banker; b. South Windsor, Conn., Nov. 3, 1833; s. Harvey and Clarissa (Burnham) E.; prep. edn. Williston Sem. and Hinsdale Acad., Mass.; A.B., Williams Coll., 1857; m. Mary A. Burnham, Nov. 1, 1864 (died 1878). Teacher, Great Barrington, Mass., 1857-58, Stowe, Vt., 1859; in office of state treas., Hartford, 1860-64; founder, 1864, sec. and pres., 1864-73, Continental Life Ins. Co.; pres. Conn. River Banking Co., 1874-1913 (retired); pres. Dwight State Machine Co.; pres. and treas. E. Haddam Electric Light Co.; dir. and treas. J. R. Montgomery Co., Windsor Locks, Conn. Mem. Conn. Ho. of Rep., 1860 and 1864 (chmn. mil. com.); spl. state agt. to enlist troops, 1862. Mem. Hartford Bd. Trade. Republican. Conglist. Home: Hartford, Conn. Died Apr. 8, 1919.

ELMORE, Wilber Theodore, clergyman, educator; b. St. Charles, Ill., July 29, 1871; s. Jerome H. and Emeline S. (Hall) E.; A.B., U. of Neb., 1896, A.M., 1897, Ph.D., 1914; B.D., Rochester Theol. Sem., 1900; D.D., Colgate, 1923; m. Maude Poucher Johnson, Oct. 25, 1900; children—Wilber Jerome (dec.), Rachel Emeline, Donald Theodore (dec.), Robert Hall. Ordained Bapt. ministry, 1900; missionary among the Telugus, in S. India, 1900-14, also mem. faculty Ramapatnam Theol. Sem.; pastor First Ch., Hamilton, N.Y., 1915-18, First Ch., Lincoln, Neb., 1918-25; prof. comparative religions and Christian missions, Eastern Bapt. Theol. Sem., Phila., 1925—. With Y.M.C.A., World War. Author: The Dravidian Gods of Modern Hinduism, 1915. Home: Wayne, Pa. Died Nov. 27, 1935.

ELROD, Samuel Harrison, governor; b. nr. Coatesville, Ind., May 1, 1856; s. Jesse F. and Lydia (Pursel) E.; A.B., DePauw U., 1882, A.M., 1885 (worked way through univ. by doing janitor work); m. Mary Ellen Masten, Nov. 11, 1884. Admitted to bar, 1882, and began practice at Clark, S.D. Mem. Sioux Falls (Dak. Ty.) Conv.; was county atty. Clark Co.; postmaster Clark; later probate judge; state's atty. 10 years; U.S. Indian disbursing agt.; gov. of S.D., 1905-07. Republican. Methodist. Home: Clark, S.D. Died July 13, 1935.

ELSER, Frank B(all), newspaperman; b. Ft. Worth, Tex., Jan. 9, 1885; s. Maximilian and Elizabeth (Loving) E.; grad. Mercersburg (Pa.) Acad., 1902; student Cornell U., 1902-04; m. Rebecca Elsbre Mix, Dec. 28, 1910; 1 son, Robert Fielding. Began as reporter Ft. Worth Star-Telegram, 1904; mem. staff New York Evening Sun, 1906-08; city editor Associated Press, New York, 1908-14; spl. corr. Associated Press with British Army in France, 1915, later on staff, London; at Queenstown, Ireland, covered sinking of Lusitania, later the sinking of the Titanic, at Halifax; went to Can. for Associated Press in pursuit of Harry Thaw; with Pershing in Mexico as spl. corr. New York Times, 4 mos., 1916; night city editor New York Times, 1916-17; resigned to engage in spl. writing. Ind. Democrat. Episcopalian. Author: The Keen Desire (novel), 1926; Mr. Gilhooley (play from novel of Liam O'Flaherty), prod., 1930; Low Bridge (play in 3 acts, from novel of Walter D. Edmonds), 1932; The Farmer Takes a Wife (play in collaboration with Marc Connelly), 1934. Died Feb. 1, 1935.

ELSNER, Henry Leopold, physician; b. Syracuse, N.Y., Aug. 15, 1855; s. Leopold and Hanschen (Sulzbacher) E.; M.D., Coll. Phys. & Surg., Columbia, 1877; post-grad. work, Vienna, Austria, 1878; m. Pauline D. Rosenberg, Jan. 5, 1881. Connected with Med. Dept., Syracuse U., 1881—, now prof. medicine; cons. phys., Women's and Children's Hosp., Syracuse, etc. Republican. Jewish religion. Home: Syracuse, N.Y. Died Feb. 17, 1916.

ELSON, Arthur, musical critic; b. Boston, Nov. 18, 1873; s. Louis Charles and Bertha (Lissner) E.; Harvard, 1892-95; S.B., Mass. Institute Tech., 1897; unmarried. Author: A Critical History of Opera, 1901; Orchestral Instruments and Their Use, 1902; Woman's Work in Music, 1903; Modern Composers of Europe, 1904; Music Club Programs from All Nations, 1907; The Musician's Guide, 1913; The Book of Musical Knowledge, 1915. Home: Boston, Mass. Died Mar. 1, 1940.

ELSON, Louis Charles, music teacher, lecturer; b. Boston, Apr. 17, 1848; s. Julius and Rosalie E.; ed. Brimmer and Mayhew schs., Boston; studied music with Aug. Kreissmann and Carl Gloggner Castelli, Leipzig; m. Bertha Lissner, 1873. Teacher and lecturer on music, 1876—; was prof. Boston U.; editor "Vox Humana," 1880; editor Musical Herald, 1880; European corr. Boston Transcript, 1883-84; music editor Boston Daily Advertiser, 1888—; teacher and lecturer N.E. Conservatory, 1880—. Contbr. European letters to New York Tribune, New York Evening Post, and Boston Transcript, 1884; Boston corr. of "Die Musik," Berlin, and Revue Musicale, Paris. Lecturer at Lowell Inst., Boston (2 series) and has lectured at Harvard, Cornell, Yale Graduates Club, etc.; city lecturer (Boston) on music, 1907—, giving about 40 lectures annually. Author: European Reminiscences, 1893; Great Composers, 1897; Shakespeare in Music, 1900; History of American Music, 1904, revised, 1914; Folksongs of Many Nations, 1905; Elson's Music Dictionary, 1906; Elson's Pocket Dictionary of Music. Editor-in-chief University Ency. of Music (10 vols.), 1911; Women in Music, 1918; Children in Music, 1918. Wrote History of Music, in New Standard Ency. and in Ency. Americana, 1905-06. Home: Boston, Mass. Died Feb. 14, 1920.

ELSON, William Harris, author; b. Carrollton, O., Nov. 22, 1856; s. Thomas and Hannah Brown (Alexander) E.; A.B., Ind. U., Bloomington, Ind., 1895; m. Martha Ellen Welch, 1879; children—Carl W. (dec.), Frank W. Began as teacher rural schs.; county supt. schs., Parke Co., Ind., 1881-91; acting supt. schs., LaPorte, Ind., 1892; supervisor schs., Indianapolis, 1893; supt. schs., Superior, Wis., 1895-1900, Grand Rapids, Mich., 1900-06, Cleveland, O., 1906-12. Lecturer on edn., Cornell U., 1912-13. Fellow Am. Geog. Soc. Republican. Conglist. Mason. Author: The Elson Readers (9 books), 1909; Good English (3 books), 1917; Junior High School Literature (3 books), 1919-20; Child-Library Readers (9 books), 1923-24; The Elson Basic Readers (9 books), 1931; Literature and Life (Book I); Elson Junior Literature (2 books), 1932. Home: Chicago, Ill. Died Feb. 2, 1935.

ELSTON, Isaac Compton, banker; b. Crawfordsville, Ind., Feb. 5, 1836; s. Isaac Compton and Maria E. (Aiken) E.; student Wabash Coll., Crawfordsville, 1849-53; U. of Mich., 1854-55; m. Sarah S. Mills, Aug. 7, 1862. Enlisted in 11th Ind. Regt. Vols., Apr., 1861, and elected lt. Co. I; promoted capt.; major, Jan., 1862; apptd. a.-d.-c. on staff of Maj. Gen. Wool, with rank of lt. col., and chief of staff to Gen. Lew Wallace, with rank of col.; participated in capture of Ft. Henry, siege of Ft. Donelson, Battle of Shiloh, and other important engagements. Established 1st Nat. Bank of Memphis (Tenn.), 1864; in brokerage business, Cincinnati, 1866; with brothers-in-law, Henry S. Lane and Gen. Lew Wallace, founded Elston & Co., bankers, Crawsfordsville, 1868; mgr. same till 1905; then pres. of its successor, the Elston Nat. Bank; dir. Union Trust Co. (Indianapolis). Republican. Presbyn. Home: Crawfordsville, Ind. Died July 2, 1925.

ELSTON, John Arthur, congressman; b. Woodland, Calif., Feb. 10, 1875; s. Allen Mandeville and Ada Florence (Elliott) E.; B.S., Hesperian Coll., Woodland, Calif., 1891; Ph.B., U. of Calif., 1897; m. Tallulah LeConte, g.d. John LeConte, 1st pres. U. of Calif., May 15, 1911. Admitted to Calif. bar, 1899, and began practice at Berkeley. Sec. to Gov. Pardee, of Calif., 1903-07; atty. for Calif. State Bd. of Health, 1907-09; trustee Calif. Instn. for Deaf and Blind, Berkeley, 1911-14; mem. 64th to 66th Congresses (1915-21), 6th Calif. Dist. Republican. Home: Berkeley, Calif. Died Dec. 15, 1921.

ELSWORTH, Edward, banker; b. New York, N.Y., Jan. 6, 1840; s. John and Martha (Van Varick) E.; ed. Rutgers Grammar Sch., New York, Dutchess Co. Acad., N.Y. State and Nat. Law Sch.; (A.M., Rutgers, 1892); m. Mary Johnston, Dec. 26, 1867; m. 2d, Mary Louise Armstrong, Aug. 29, 1906. Admitted to bar, 1861; practiced law in New York, 1861-63, in Rockland Co., 1864-65, in Poughkeepsie, 1865-67; engaged in bus., Poughkeepsie, 1868-91; pres. Fallkill Nat. Bank, Poughkeepsie, 1891-1903 (dir.); pres. Poughkeepsie Savings Bank, 1903—. Maj. and judge advocate 8th brigade, N.G.S.N.Y., 1875-82; mem. bd. of edn., City of Poughkeepsie, 1880-87; mayor, 1887-88 and 1891-92. Trustee and treas. Vassar Coll. Democrat. Home: Poughkeepsie, N.Y. Died 1911.

ELTINGE, Julian, actor; b. Boston, Mass., May 14, 1883; s. Joseph Dalton and Julia Edna (Baker) E.; ed. pub. schs. of Los Angeles, Calif., Butte, Mont., San Francisco and Boston. Began professional career at Keith's Theatre, Boston. Mason. Died Mar. 7, 1941.

ELTINGE, LeRoy, army officer; b. South Woodstock, N.Y., Sept. 17, 1872; s. Lamont Eltinge and Arvelia (Lake) E.; grad. U.S. Mil. Acad., 1896, honor grad. Army Sch. of the Line, 1908; grad. Army Staff Coll., 1909; m. Effée B. Trotter, Dec. 3, 1897; 1 dau., Margaret (Mrs. James L. Bolt). Commd. 2d lt. 4th Cav., June 12, 1896; promoted through grades to rank brig. gen., July 19, 1924. In Philippines, 1898-99 and 1901-03; with Army Cuban Pacification, 1906-07; on Mexican border, 1914, again, 1916, crossing into Mexico after bandits; arrived in France, July 28, 1917; in operations sect. of gen. staff, Gen. Hdqrs., till Apr. 30, 1918; dep. chief of staff at Gen. Hdqrs., May 1, 1918-June 30, 1919; asst. chief of staff Philippine Dept., 1921-23; asst. chief of staff War Plans Div., Washington. Decorated D.S.M., Croix de Guerre with palm and Comdr. Legion of Honor (French); Comdr. Order of the Crown (Belgian); Comdr. Order of the Crown (Italian); Companion Order of the Bath (British); Order of Solidaridad (Panamanian). Baptist. Died May 13, 1931.

ELTON, James Samuel, mfr., banker; b. Waterbury, Conn., Nov. 7, 1838; s. John Prince and Olive Margaret (Hall) E.; ed. Everest's Sch., Hamden, Conn., and Russell's Mil. Acad., New Haven; m. Charlotte Augusta Steele, Oct. 28, 1863 (died 1899). Entered employ Waterbury Brass Co., 1863, of which was pres., 1874, until it was merged into Am. Brass Co., 1900; pres. Waterbury Nat. Bank, 1896-1916; dir. Am. Hardware Co. Mem. Conn. Senate, 1882-83. Dir. Waterbury Hosp., Silas Bronson Library, the Westover Sch. Corp. Republican. Episcopalian. Home: Waterbury, Conn. Died Nov. 10, 1923.

ELTZHOLTZ, Carl Frederick, clergyman; b. Brahetrolleborg, Denmark, Oct. 10, 1840; s. Johan C. and Tobia M. (Lange) E.; ed. pub. sch., Denmark, and later as a nautical inst., Svendborg, Denmark, from which grad.; sailor several yrs.; 2d officer; participated in Danish-German war, 1864; war-medal; m. Isabella Williams, June 15, 1872 (died 1917). Clergyman M.E. Ch., 1867—, serving churches at Coon Prairie, Wis., Ashippun, Wis., Racine, Wis., Cambridge, Wis., Chicago, LaCrosse, Wis., Evanston, Ill., Milwaukee, Oakland, Calif., Veile, Denmark, Copenhagen, Denmark, and Horsens, Denmark; pastor First Norwegian and Danish M.E. Ch., Cambridge, Wis., 1906-12. Dist. supt. among the Norwegian and Danish people 6 yrs.; editor Den Kristelige Talsmand, Norwegian and Danish Methodist paper, 7 yrs. On Dec. 12, 1878, started the Danish Temperance Movement, now having about 200,000 members. Author: The Child—Its Relation to God and the Church. Home: Los Angeles, Calif. Died Apr. 17, 1929.

ELVERSON, James, newspaper pub.; b. in Eng., 1838; came to U.S., 1847; ed. Newark (N.J.) pub. schs. Telegraph messenger boy, operator and later mgr. consolidated offices in Newark, N.J., and agt. Associated Press; mgr. Am. Telegraph office, Washington, 1861-65; one of founders, 1865, and 1879—, sole propr. Phila. Saturday Night; established, 1880, Golden Days, a weekly publ. for boys and girls; propr. Philadelphia Inquirer, 1889—. Home: Philadelphia, Pa. Died 1911.

ELWELL, Charles Clement, civil engr.; b. Belfast, Me., July 16, 1855; s. Benjamin Tyler and Martha (Wilson) E.; B.C.E., U. of Me., 1878, C.E., 1890, D.Engring., 1927; m. Nancy Bolton, Mar. 25, 1885; children—Francis Bolton, Charles Clement. Supt. constrn. and repairs, Southern Coast, U.S. Light House Engring. Dept., 1878-82; asst. engr., constrn. and maintenance, N.Y.&N.E. Ry., 1882-85; asst. engr. and roadmaster, Wilmington & Northern R.R., 1885-91; engr. maintenance of way, B.&O. R.R. Co., 1891-93; roadmaster, in charge 4-track constrn., N.Y.,N.H. &H. R.R., 1893-95, supt., 1895-1908, in charge Shore Line, Air Line, Northampton, Norwich and Worcester divs., and chief engr. trolley lines of same co., in N.Y. and Conn., 1908-11; chief engr. Pub. Utilities Commn., Com., 1911-15, mem. Commn., 1915—. Republican. Conglist. Mason. Home: New Haven, Conn. Died May 21, 1931.

ELWELL, Francis Edwin, sculptor; b. Concord, Mass., June 15, 1858; s. John W. and Clara (Farrar) E.; ed. Concord pub. schs.; studied sculpture first under May Alcott, at Concord, Mass., and at École des Beaux Arts, Paris, and finally under Jean Alexandre Falguiere; m. Annie Marion Benjamin. Was the first American sculptor to model a statue in America that was erected in Europe. Received medal, Chicago Expn., 1893; gold medal twice, Art Club Phila.; medal from King of Belgium for study in architecture. Among his better known works are: monument, "Death of Strength," Edam, Holland; bust of Lord Provost of Aberdeen, at Aberdeen; statue of "Awakening of Egypt," Paris; equestrian statue of Gen. Hancock, Gettysburg; monument to Edwin Booth, Mt. Auburn, Cambridge; The two fountains of "Kronos" and "Ceres," Buffalo Expn., 1901; "Dickens and Little Nell," Phila.; statue of "New Life," Lowell (Mass.) Cemetery; statue of "Intelligence"; busts of Levi P. Morton and Garret A. Hobart, senate chamber, Washington; statue in stone, "Classic Art," Art Palace, St. Louis Expn., 1904; marble statues of "Greece and Rome," N.Y. Custom House, 1904; marble bust of Col. R. T. Van Horn, Journal office, Kansas City, Mo., 1904; monument to Gen. L. P. di Cesnola, Kensico Cemetery, N.Y., 1903; "Dispatch Rider" of the Am. Revolution, Orange, N.J.; "The Flag," 7th R.I. Inf., monument at Vicksburg, Miss.; Dante and Shakespeare for Scranton Memorial Library (in marble); statue of "Kronos," Harvard Univ.; "The Orchid Dance," Gorham & Co.; statue of Lincoln, E. Orange Parkway, N.J.; bust of Hon. Robert Miller Walmsley, New Orleans; bust of Morris Pattan; statue of Rear Admiral Charles H. Davis, for U.S. naval monument, Vicksburg, Miss., 1910; statue of Gen. Frederick Steele, for Nat. Mil. Park, Vicksburg, 1911; "Acrosteria" for Agrl. Bldg., Panama Expn., 1915; bust of Marion Elwell; heroic marble "Genius of Memory," Lowell, Mass., 1915; heroic bust, in marble of Amzi L. Dodd, for Mut. Benefit Life Ins. Co., Newark, N.J., 1915. Late curator of ancient and modern sculpture, Met. Mus. of Art, New York; lecturer at Harvard U., etc. Medal, Buffalo Expn., 1901. Hon. col. 7th R.I. Infantry. Del. Atlantic Congress for the League of Nations and speaker for same, actively in war work during the war. Home: Weehawken, N.J. Died Jan. 23, 1922.

ELWELL, Levi Henry, coll. prof.; b. Northampton, Mass., Mar. 22, 1854; s. Levi Henry and Harriet Addaline (Ross) E.; B.A., Amherst, 1875, M.A., 1878; studied Yale, 1876-77; m. Abbie Miner Nickerson, Dec. 20, 1883. Teacher at Poughkeepsie, N.Y., 1875-76; instr. Latin, 1877-78, Greek, 1878-90, Sanskrit, 1881—, asst. and asso. prof. Greek, 1890—, Amherst Coll. Sec. trustee Amherst Acad.; historian Northampton High Sch. Alumni Assn.; founded, 1893, and endowed, 1900, Classical Prize Fund, Northampton High Sch. Conglist. Editor: Nine Jatakas (first Pali text book issued in America), 1886; The Gravestone Records of Shaftsbury, Bennington County, Vermont, 1911; The Gravestone Inscriptions of Rupert, 1913. Home: Amherst, Mass. Died Dec. 27, 1916.

ELY, Albert Heman, gynecologist; b. Elyria, O., Nov. 22, 1860; s. Heman and Mary (Day) E.; B.A., Yale, 1885; M.D., Coll. Phys. and Surg. (Columbia), 1888; post-grad. work, Vienna, Berlin, Dublin; m. Maude L. Merchant, Oct. 7, 1891; children—Albert Heman, Francis Sherburne (dec.). Practiced at N.Y. City, 1890—; associated with St. Luke's, Roosevelt, and City hosps.; consulting surgeon Southampton Hosp. Republican. Episcopalian. Mason. Home: New York, N.Y. Deceased.

ELY, Charles Russell, teacher of deaf; b. Columbus, O., Feb. 20, 1870; s. Charles Wright and Mary (Darling) E.; A.B., Yale, 1891, A.M., 1897; A.M., Gallaudet Coll., Washington, D.C., 1892; Ph.D., George Washington U., 1900; m. Louise Day Crane, Dec. 25, 1897; children—Elizabeth Day, Grace Darling, Sylvia Louise. Instr., natural science, 1892-96, asst. prof., 1896-99, prof., 1899-1912, Gallaudet Coll.; prin. Md. Sch. for the Deaf, Frederick, Md., 1912-13; prof. natural science, Gallaudet, 1913—, now v.p. Mem. Selective Service Bd. Dist. 11, Washington, 1917-18. Republican. Unitarian. Collaborator on forest insect investigations (micro-lepidoptera), U.S. Dept. Agr. Home: Washington, D.C. Died Feb. 22, 1939.

ELY, Charles Wright, teacher of deaf; b. Madison, Conn., Mar. 14, 1839; s. Elias Sanford and Hester Maria (Wright) E.; A.B., Yale, 1862, A.M., 1865; (L.H.D., Gallaudet Coll., 1908); m. Mary Grace Darling, Oct. 24, 1867. Second lt. 27th Conn. Vol. Inf., 2d Corps, Army Potomac, 1862-63. Teacher, Ohio Sch. for Deaf, Columbus, 1863-70; prin. Md. Sch. for Deaf, Frederick, 1871—. Pres. 1st Bd. Health, Frederick; dir. Frederick Coll., Y.M.C.A. Republican. Presbyn. (elder). Home: Frederick, Md. Died Oct. 1, 1912.

ELY, Frederick David, judge; b. Wrentham, Mass., Sept. 24, 1838; s. Nathan and Amelia Maria (Partridge) E.; M.A., Brown U., 1859; m. Eliza B. Whittier, Dec. 6, 1866; m. 2d, Anna Emerson, Aug. 10, 1885 (both dec.). Admitted to bar, 1862; began practice at Dedham; v.p., trustee Dedham Instn. for Savings; dir. Dedham Mut. Fire Ins. Co. Mem. Mass. Ho. of Rep., 1873, Senate, 1878, 1879; mem. 49th Congress (1885-87); asso. justice Municipal Ct. of Boston, 1888-1914; trial justice Norfolk County, Mass., 1867-84; mem. Sch. Com., Dedham, 12 yrs. Republican. Episcopalian. Mason. Home: Dedham, Mass. Died Aug. 6, 1921.

ELY, John Hugh, clergyman, educator; b. Chillicothe, O., July 21, 1846; s. Seneca W. and Mary (Delano) E.; grad. Kenyon Coll., 1871, M.A., 1901; m. Mary Darwin Stanton, Jan. 2, 1873. In wholesale hardware house, 1860-64; served 1st sergt. 137th Ohio Vol. Inf., May to Aug., 1864—hon. discharge; master's mate in Mississippi Squadron, U.S.N., Sept. 7, 1864; served on U.S.S. Chillicothe until July 19, 1865. Clerk in Freedman's Bureau, at hdqrs. Ky., 6 mos., in U.S. Treasurer's office, Washington, 2 yrs. Ordered deacon, June 1871, priest, 1872, P.E. Ch.; rector St Mary's, Hillsboro, O., 1871-75; archdeacon, diocese of Southern Ohio, 1875-77; from 1877 rector Grace Ch., College Hill, Cincinnati. Also during same period in charge St. Philip's Ch., 1877-79, and from 1879 founded Holy Trinity Ch., Hartwell, and had charge till 1891. Mem. Gen. Convs., P.E. Ch., in Minneapolis, Washington, and San Francisco; sec. diocese of Southern Ohio, 1891—; trustee Kenyon Coll., 1891—; regent and in full charge of Ohio Mil. Inst., College Hill, since 1897. Mem. Standing Com. Southern Ohio, 1895—. Was chaplain 1st regt. Ohio Nat. Guard 5 yrs.; pres. sch. bd., College Hill, 5 yrs.; dir. Young Men's Mercantile Library, Cincinnati. Republican. Died 1906.

ELY, John Slade, prof. theory and practice of medicine, med. dept. Yale, 1897—; b. New York, Dec. 4, 1860; s. John Cole and Lucy Lord (Slade) E.; grad. Sheffield Scientific Sch., Yale, 1881; post-grad. Yale and Johns Hopkins, M.D., Coll. Phys. & Surg., N.Y., 1886; M.A., Yale, 1897; m. Grace G. Taylor, 1893. Interne Bellevue Hosp., New York, 1886-87; studied in Germany and France, 1887-88; asst. in pathology, Coll. Phys. & Surg., N.Y., 1888-97; prof. pathology, Woman's Med. Coll., New York Infirmary, 1890-98. Home: New Haven, Conn. Deceased.

ELY, Smith, mayor New York; b. Hanover, Morris Co., N.J., Apr. 17, 1825; LL.B., New York U., 1862. Engaged in mercantile business until 1878; since devoted attention to care of property interest and investments. Sch. trustee, 1856-60; mem. N.Y. Senate, 1857; co. supervisor, 1860-68; Brooklyn Bridge commr., 1875; elected to 42d Congress (1871-73) and 44th Congress (1875-77); resigned from 44th Congress, Dec. 12, 1876; mayor of New York, 1877-78; presdl. elector, 1880; Central Park commr., 1897-98. Democrat. Presbyn. Home: New York. Died 1911.

ELY, Theodore Newel, engr.; b. Watertown, N.Y., June 23, 1846; s. Adriel and Evelina (Foster) E.; C.E., Rensselaer Poly. Inst., 1866; (hon. M.A., Yale, 1897; Sc.D., Hamilton, 1904). In engring. dept. Pa. R.R. System, 1868-1910; chief of motive power, lines east and west of Pittsburgh and Erie, 1893-1910; retired, July 1, 1911. Dir. Pa. Steel Co., Cambria Steel Co. Dir. Pa. Acad. Fine Arts; trustee Drexel Inst., Phila. Commercial Mus. Mem. permanent commission Internat. Ry. Congress; pres. Eastern R.R. Assn.; v.p. Am. Acad. in Rome; hon. mem. A.I.A. Home: Bryn Mawr, Pa. Died Oct. 28, 1916.

ELZAS, Barnett Abraham, rabbi; b. Eydkuhnen, Germany, Dec. 7, 1867; s. Abraham and Hinda (Lewinthal) E.; studied Jews' and Univ. colls., London, Eng.; came to America, 1890; B.A., with honors, U. of Toronto, 1893, M.D., Med. Coll. of State of S.C., 1900; LL.D., U. of S.C., 1905; m. Annie Samuel, of London, June 25, 1890; 1 dau., Sybil Edna (Mrs. Lewis T. Mann). Ordained rabbi, 1890; rabbi, Toronto, Can., 1890-93, Sacramento, Calif., 1893-94, Beth Elohim, Charleston, S.C., 1894-1910; minister to the Jewish deaf of New York, 1910—; rabbi Congregation Beth Miriam, Long Branch, N.J., 1912—. Author: The Sabbath School Companion, 1895-96; Judaism—An Exposition, 1896; The Old Jewish Cemeteries of Charleston, 1903; The Jews of South Carolina, from the Earliest Times to the Present Day, 1905; Leaves from My Historical Scrap Book, 1907-08; The Jewish Cemeteries of South Carolina, 1910-11. Home: New York, N.Y. Died Oct. 18, 1936.

ELZNER, Alfred Oscar, architect; b. Cincinnati, Dec. 12, 1862; s. Herman August and Marie Sidonia (Hecker) E.; ed. pub. and high schs., Cincinnati; office of Jas. W. McLaughlin, architect, Cincinnati; spl. course in architecture, Mass. Inst. Tech.; office of H. H. Richardson, architect, Brookline, Mass.; m. Jennie Ellis Sanford, Oct. 28, 1894. Practiced, Cincinnati, 1887—; mem. Elzner & Anderson. Fellow A.I.A., 1889. Pres. Home for Colored Girls. Republican. Episcopalian. Home: Cincinnati, O. Died Nov. 29, 1933.

EMBER, Aaron, Egyptologist; b. Tulnas, Lithuania, Dec. 25, 1878; s. Mendel and Rebekah (Quitz) E.; came to U.S., 1891; A.B., Johns Hopkins, 1901, Ph.D., 1904; m. Regina Mandelstamm, of Fraustadt, Germany, Apr. 28, 1911; children—Theodore, Ruth, Robert. With Johns Hopkins, 1907—, prof. Egyptology, 1924—. Jewish religion. Editor of The Paul Haupt Memorial Volume (Leipzig), 1925. Established the close kinship between the Old Egyptian and Semitic langs. Home: Baltimore, Md. Died June 1, 1926.

EMBODY, George Charles, prof. aquiculture; b. Auburn, N.Y., Nov. 23, 1876; s. Daniel A. and Emma (Washburn) E.; B.S., Colgate, 1900, M.S., 1901, Sc.D., 1924; Johns Hopkins, 1906-07; Ph.D., Cornell U., 1910; m. Mary Madelene Riceman, Oct. 9, 1909 (died 1931); 1 son, Daniel Robert; m. 2d, Flora B. Taylor, Jan. 29, 1935. Teacher of science, Delaware Literary Inst., Franklin, N.Y., 1901-02, high sch., Bradford, Pa., 1902-03; prof. science, Bethel Coll., Russellville, Ky., 1903-06; prof. biology, Randolph-Macon (Va.) Coll., 1907; instr. zoölogy, Cornell U., 1909-10; prof. biology, Butler Coll., Indianapolis, 1910; instr. in aquiculture, Cornell U., 1911, asst. prof., 1912-20, prof., 1920—. Cons. biologist, N.J. Fish Commn., 1918-24; biologist and adviser in fish culture, N.Y. State Conservation Dept., 1926-35; biologist in charge Calif. trout investigations, 1932. Republican. Mason. Home: Ithaca, N.Y. Died Feb. 17, 1939.

EMBREE, Charles Fleming, author; b. Princeton, Ind., Oct. 1, 1874; s. D. F. and Mary (Fleming) E.; now Mrs. M. V. Witherspoon; ed. public schools, Princeton, Ind., 1880-92, Wabash Coll., 1892-95; m. Virginia Broadwell, Jan. 18, 1898. Author: For the Love of Tonita, 1897; A Dream of a Throne, 1900. Home: Santa Ana, Calif. Died 1905.

EMERICK, Charles Franklin, educator; b. on a farm, nr. Dayton, O., Nov. 17, 1867; s. Simon and Mary Ann C. (Kumler) E.; Antioch Coll., O., 1885-87; A.B., Wittenberg Coll., O., 1889, A.M., 1891; M.S., Mich. Agrl. Coll., 1891; prof. history and economics, Avalon Coll., Trenton, Mo., 1891-94; Ph.M., U. of Mich., 1895; Ph.D., Columbia, 1897; m. Ruth W. Butterworth, June 18, 1901. Asst., 1897-98, instr., 1898-99, Vanderbilt U.; asso. prof., 1899-1903, prof. economics and sociology, 1903—, Smith Coll. Ind. Republican. Home: Northampton, Mass. Died Mar. 22, 1920.

EMERSON, Benjamin Kendall, geologist; b. Nashua, N.H., Dec. 20, 1843; s. Benjamin F. and Elisazeth (Kendall) E.; A.B., Amherst, 1865 (LL.D., 1914); univs. of Göttingen and Berlin; Ph.D., Göttingen, 1870; m. Mary Annette Hopkins, Apr. 2, 1873 (died 1895); m. 2d, Anna H. Seelye, Sept. 4, 1901. Instr. geology, 1870-72, prof. geology and mineralogy, 1872-1917, prof. emeritus, 1917—, Amherst College; prof. same, Smith College, 1878-1912. Asst. geologist, 1890-96, geologist, 1896—, U.S. Geol. Survey. Mem. Internat. Geol. Congress, St. Petersburg, 1897 (v.p.). Fellow Am. Acad. Arts and Sciences. Home: Leonia, N.J. Died Apr. 7, 1932.

EMERSON, Charles Franklin, college dean; b. Chelmsford, Mass., Sept. 28, 1843; s. Owen and Louisa (Butterfield) E.; A.B., Dartmouth, 1868, A.M., 1871; m. Caroline Flagg, Jan. 20, 1875. Instr. mathematics, N.H. Coll. Agr. and Mech. Arts, 1868-74; tutor Dartmouth Coll., 1868-72, asso. prof. mathematics and natural philosophy, 1872-78, instr. astronomy, 1878-92, prof. natural philosophy, 1878-99, dean academic faculty, 1893-1913, dean emeritus, July 1, 1913—, Dartmouth Coll. Mem. N.H. Ho. of Rep., 1915-16, 1917-18. Home: Hanover, N.H. Died Dec. 1, 1922.

EMERSON, Charles Phillips, M.D.; b. Methuen, Mass., Sept. 4, 1872; s. Jacob and Josephine (Davis) Emerson; A.B., Amherst College, 1894, Sc.D., 1934; M.D., Johns Hopkins U., 1899; studied univs. of Strassburg, 1900, Basel, 1901, Paris, 1903; m. Effie Gilmour Perry, Apr. 14, 1909; children—Phoebe, Charles Phillips, James Perry, Marjorie Gilmour, Alice Woodbury. Formerly asso. in medicine Johns Hopkins and resident phys., Johns Hopkins Hosp.; supt. Clifton Springs (N.Y.) Sanitarium, 1908-11; asst. prof. medicine, Cornell U., 1909-10; prof. medicine and dean, Ind. U. Sch. of Medicine, Indianapolis, 1911-32, research prof. of medicine, 1932—. Commr. to the Orient, Laymen's Foreign Mission Inquiry, 1931-32. Republican. Presbyn. Author: Clinical Diagnosis, 1906; Essentials of Medicine, 1908. Joint author: Emerson and Betts Physiology and Hygiene, 1920; Physical Diagnosis, 1928; The Nervous Patient, 1935; Text Book of Medicine, 1936. Home: Indianapolis, Ind. Died Sept. 26, 1938.

EMERSON, Charles Wesley, pres. Emerson Coll. Oratory, 1880-1902; b. Pittsfield, Vt., Nov. 30, 1837; s. Thomas and Mary (Hewitt) E.; ed. common schools and acad. there; later took theol. course in Vt. and law and med. courses in Boston and Phila.; entered ministry at early age; preached for many yrs.; founded Emerson Coll. of Oratory, 1880, resigned, 1902. Home: Millis, Mass. Died 1908.

EMERSON, Edward Randolph, wine grower; b. New York, N.Y., Oct. 22, 1856; s. Jesse Milton and Sophia Thankful (Pierson) E.; ed. pub. schs. and by pvt. tutor; m. Idanthea de Lacey, June 20, 1874. Pres. Brotherhood Wine Co., 1885—; pres. First Nat. Bank, Washingtonville, N.Y.; pres. of Brotherhood Corp., Washingtonville; pres. Am. Wine Growers' Assn.; mem. Old Time Telegraphers and Military Corps. Conglist. Mason. Author: Story of the Vine, 1901; Lay Theses on Bible Wines, 1902; Beverages, Past and Present, 2 vols., 1908. Home: Washingtonville, N.Y. Died Dec. 27, 1924.

EMERSON, Edward Waldo, M.D.; b. Concord, Mass., July 10, 1844; s. Ralph Waldo and Lidian (Jackson) E.; A.B., Harvard, 1866, M.D., 1874; married; 1 son, Raymond Emerson. Fellow Am. Acad. Arts and Sciences. Author: Emerson in Concord, 1888; Early History of the Saturday Club of Boston. Editor: Correspondence of John Sterling and Ralph Waldo Emerson, with sketch of Sterling's Life, 1897; Centenary Edition of Works of Ralph Waldo Emerson (annotated), 1903; Life and Letters of General Charles Russell Lowell, 1907; Emerson's Journals (with W. E. Forbes), 1909. Co-author (with M. Storey): Life of E. R. Hoar, 1911. Home: Concord, Mass. Died Jan. 27, 1930.

EMERSON, Ellen Russell, author; b. New Sharon, Me., Jan. 16, 1837; d. Dr. Leonard White and F. F. (Lovejoy) Russell; ed. Mt. Vernon Sem., Boston; m. 1862, Edwin R. Emerson. Medal conferred by the Junta Directiva, Columbian Hist. Expn., Madrid, Spain, 1893; hon. mem. Société Americaine, France, 1887. Author: Indian Myths, Legends and Traditions compared with those of other countries, 1885; Masks, Heads and Faces, with some consideration Respecting Art, 1894; Nature and Human Nature, 1901. Home: Cambridge, Mass. Died 1907.

EMERSON, Frank Collins, governor; b. Saginaw, Mich., May 26, 1882; s. Byron Delbridge and Anne Collins (Pendell) E.; B.S. in C.E., U. of Mich., 1904; m. Zennia Jean Reynders, Jan. 17, 1910; children—Frank Collins, David Williams, Eugene Reynders. Gen. engring. practice in Wyo., 1904-07; chief engr. Wyo. Land & Irrigation Co., and Wyo. Irrigation Co., 1907-15; supt. Big Horn Canal Assn., and Lower Hanover Canal Assn., 1915-19, also engr. Wyo. Sugar Co.; state engr. Wyo., 1919-27; pres. Farmers' Coop. Lumber Co., Worland, Wyo. Gov. of Wyo., term 1927-30 inclusive. Republican. Baptist. Mason. Home: Cheyenne, Wyo. Died Feb. 18, 1931.

EMERSON, Harrington, efficiency engr.; b. Trenton, N.J., Aug. 2, 1853; s. Edwin and Mary Louise (Ingham) E.; ed. Royal Bavarian Polytechnic, 1872-75; univs. in Italy and Greece, 1875-76; m. June 9, 1879; children—Raffe, Eugene, Eleanor; m. 2d, Mary Crawford Suplee, Feb. 5, 1895; children—Isabel, Margot, Louise. Prof. modern langs., U. of Neb., 1876-82; in banking and land business, 1882-96; pres. Emerson Engineers, efficiency engrs., 1900-23. As

U.S. rep. of British syndicate examined many industrial plants and mines in U.S., Mex. and Can., 1896-98; put into operation some of first long distance mail routes in Alaska and down the Yukon, 1898-1901; reported on all the known coal deposits of N. Am. western coast, and reported on northern submarine cable route to Asia which was largely followed by the War Dept. in laying its Alaskan cables; gained recognition on account of results obtained by efficiency methods installed on the Santa Fé System. Author: Efficiency as Basis for Operation and Wages, 1909; also The Twelve Principles of Efficiency. Apptd., 1921, mem. Herbert Hoover's Com. for Elimination of Waste in Industry, of Federated Am. Engring. Socs. (assigned to investigate and report on railroads and bituminous coal mining). Home: New York, N.Y. Died May 23, 1931.

EMERSON, Henry Pendexter, supt. edn.; b. Lynnfield, Mass., Jan. 11, 1846; s. Oliver and Eliza (Weston) E.; A.B., U. of Rochester, 1871, A.M., 1874 (LL.D., 1911); m. Mary A. Estey, Aug. 4, 1874. Teacher State Normal Sch., Potsdam, N.Y., 1871-74; teacher Latin and Greek, 1874-83, prin., 1883-93, Buffalo Central High School; supt. of education, Buffalo, 1893-1918. Pres. council of sch. supts. of N.Y.; pres. N.Y. State Teachers' Assn., 1901-02; pres. dept. of Superintendence of N.E.A., 1904. Author: Latin in High Schools, 1881; A Summer in Europe, 1891; A course in English for Schools, 1905. Home: Middleton, Mass. Deceased.

EMERSON, James Ezekiel, retired machinist; b. Norridgewock, Me., Nov. 2, 1823; ed. at Bangor, Me., 1829-39; m. Mary Shepherd, 1849; 2d, Mary Belle Woods, 1878. Was farmer, carpenter, saw-mill worker; mfr. wood-work. machinery, Lewiston, Me., 1850-52; went to Calif., 1852; engaged in saw-mill enterprises; visited Europe, 1869. Invented inserted tooth circular and band saws and many other devices. Manufactured edge tools at Trenton, N.J., and during Civil war, cavalry sabres; later supt. Am. Saw Co.; and then pres. and supt. Emerson Smith & Co. Saw Works, Beaver Falls, Pa.; retired. Home: Columbus, O. Died 1900.

EMERSON, Luther Orlando, composer; b. Parsonsfield, Me., Aug. 3, 1820; ed. Parsonsfield Sem. and Effingham Acad.; (Mus.D., Findlay College, Ohio, 1891); m. Mary J. Gove, Mar. 4, 1847 (died 1902). Studied music and became teacher and choir master 8 yrs. at Salem, Mass.; afterward organist and musical dir. 4 yrs. at Bullfinch St. Ch., Boston; has directed about 300 musical festivals and convs. Has made over 70 collections of ch. and other music; composed about 80 songs, quartets and piano pieces, 3 masses, and many ch. anthems. Composed the music for the war song: We Are Coming Father Abraham, written by William Cullen Bryant. Home: Hyde Park, Mass. Died Sept. 29, 1915.

EMERSON, Nathaniel Bright, physician; b. Waialua, Oahu, Hawaii, July 1, 1839; s. Rev. John S. and Ursula Sophia (Newell) E.; bro. of Justin Edwards E.; ed. Punahou Sch., and Oahu Coll., Honolulu, 1850-61; Williams Coll., Mass., 1861-62; enlisted 1st Mass. Inf., 1862; disch. May 25, 1864; wounded Fredericksburg, Va., Dec. 13, 1862, Chancellorsville, May 1, 1863. A.B., Williams Coll., 1865, A.M., 1868; Harvard Med. Sch., 1865-68; M.D., Coll. Phys. and Surg. (Columbia), 1869; m. Sarah Eliza Peirce, M.D., d. Capt. A. W. Peirce, of Mass., Jan. 22, 1885. Practiced medicine at New York, 1869-78; med. supt., leper settlement, Kalawao Isl. of Molokai, 1878-80; pres. Hawaiian Bd. Health, 1887-90; police surgeon, many yrs., etc. Trustee Oahu Coll., 17 yrs., Honolulu Library, several yrs. Republican. Author: Unwritten Literature of Hawaii; The Long Voyages of Ancient Hawaii. Contbr. to mags. on Hawaiian life and history. Translator, from Hawaiian of David Malo, of Hawaiian Antiquities, 1903. Home: Honolulu, T.H. Died July 15, 1915.

EMERSON, Nathaniel Waldo, surgeon; b. Boston, Mass., Mar. 6, 1854; s. Joseph Barrett and Sarah (Weston) E.; student Bowdoin Coll., A.M.; M.D., Boston U. Med. Sch., 1881; m. Carlotta Adams Bond, Sept. 20, 1905. Practiced, Boston, 1880—; formerly demonstrator anatomy, lecturer in surgery, asso. prof. surgery, now emeritus prof. gynecology, Boston U. Med. Sch.; founder, owner, now sr. surgeon, Emerson Hosp., Forest Hills, Mass.; sr. surgeon Tuell Hosp., Biddeford, Me.; cons. surgeon to Henry Haywood Memorial Hosp. (Gardner, Mass.), Wasson Memorial Hosp. (Springfield, Mass.), Melrose (Mass.) Hosp., Bath (Me.) City Hosp., etc. Home: Jamaica Plain, Mass. Died Dec. 20, 1930.

EMERSON, Oliver Farrar, univ. prof.; b. nr. Traer, Ia., May 24, 1860; s. Oliver and Maria (Farrar) E.; A.B., Iowa Coll., 1882, A.M., 1885, Litt.D., 1912; Ph.D., Cornell U., 1891; m. Annie L. Logan, Sept. 24, 1891, children—Harold Logan, Olive Logan. Supt. schs., Grinnell, Ia., 1882-84, Muscatine, Ia., 1884-85; prin. Acad. of Iowa Coll., 1885-88; Goldwin Smith fellow in English, 1888-89, instr. in English, 1889-91, asst. prof. rhetoric and English philology, 1892-96, Cornell U.; prof. English, Western Reserve U., 1896—. Author: History of the English Language, 1894; A Brief History of the English Language, 1896; Middle English Reader, 1905; Outline History of the English Language, 1906. Editor: Johnson's Rasselas, 1895; Memoirs of the Life and Writings of Edward Gibbon, 1898; Poems of Chaucer, 1911. Home: Cleveland, O. Died Mar. 13, 1927.

EMERSON, Paul, prof. soils; b. Wilmington, Del., July 6, 1887; B.S., U. of Del., 1914, M.S., 1915; grad. study, U. of Pa., half-time 1914-15; Ph.D., Ia. State Coll., 1917; m. Grace Reynolds, July 22, 1916; children—Paul, Reynolds Llewellyn. Asst. in soil investigations, U. of Md., 1917; acting bacteriologist, U. of Ida., 1918; asst. chief in soil bacteriology, Ia. State Coll., Ames, 1919—, asso. prof. soils, 1922-32; cons. soils expert for The Grace Co., 1932—. Apptd. chief soil expert, Soil Conservation Service, S.D., N.D. and Mont. area, 1935. Episcopalian. Author: Soil Characteristics, 1925; Principles of Soil Technology, 1930. Died Sept. 17, 1937.

EMERSON, Ralph, mfr.; b. Andover, Mass., May 3, 1831; s. Rev. Ralph (D.D., prof. in Andover Theol. Sem.) and Eliza (Rockwell) E.; ed. Phillips Acad., Andover; studied law under pvt. instruction, but, by advice of Abraham Lincoln (who was his intimate friend) dropped the law for business career; m. Adaline Elizabeth, d. Hon. Wait and Elizabeth (Norton) Talcott, of Rockford, Ill., Sept. 7, 1858. Inventor and one of the pioneers in west in wholesale manufacture of agrl. implements; also inventor of certain kinds of seamless hosiery, now in world wide use. Former propr. of two Rep. newspapers; originator of City Electric Lighting works; one of organizers and officer of two nat. banks; pres. two ins. cos.; now pres., dir. or trustee of numerous mfg. cos., notably the Emerson-Brantingham Co., and Burson Knitting Co., of Rockford, Ill. Published a Genealogy of the Emerson Family. Founder Emerson Normal and Industrial Inst., Mobile, Ala. Home: Rockford, Ill. Died Aug. 19, 1914.

EMERSON, Robert Stephen, lawyer; b. Pawtucket, R.I., Sept. 1, 1876; s. Charles Albert and Elizabeth Gould (Price) E.; A.B., Brown Univ., 1897; LL.B., summa cum laude, New York Law Sch., 1903; m. Marian Butterworth, of Feb. 7, 1905. Admitted to R.I. bar, 1903, and began practice of law at Providence; now mem. Emerson & Mason; pres. Narragansett Rubber Co., Bristol, R.I., 1914-19, Tilden-Thurber Corp., Providence, 1915-19, Narragansett Fish Co., 1916-26; pres. and dir. Cadillac Automobile Co. of R.I., 1920-28; sec. and dir. Pawtucket Glazed Paper Co., 1921-33; pres. and dir. Henry L. Scott Co.; sec. and dir. The Meiklejohn Co., Webster Co., Shaw Paper Box Co., A. H. Barney Stable, Inc., Gledhill Co., Emerson Apparatus Co., Transparent Cellulose Printing Corp.; treas. Derwil Realty Co. Clk and asso. justice 10th Jud. Dist. Ct., R.I., 1905-14; judge of probate, Pawtucket Dist., 1915-26. Govt. appeal agt., Draft Bd., Pawtucket Dist., World War. Republican. Baptist. Mason. Home: Pawtucket, R.I. Died Jan. 23, 1937.

EMERSON, Samuel Franklin, coll. prof.; b. Norwich, Vt., Aug. 26, 1850; s. Edward Brown and Ann (Lummus) E.; A.B., Yale, 1872. Head of private sch. for boys, Stratford, Conn., 1872-75; grad. Union Theol. Sem., 1878; post-grad. work, Tübingen and Berlin, 1878-80; (hon. Ph.D., Amherst Coll., 1885); m. Mary Brayton Hitchcock, Dec. 28, 1881. Prof. Greek, 1881-89, history and sociology, 1889—, U. of Vt. Conglist. Home: Burlington, Vt. Died Apr. 5, 1939.

EMERSON, Willis George, author; b. near Blakesburg, Ia., Mar. 28, 1856; s. Rev. Stephen L. and Mary L. (Peck) E.; Knox Coll., Ill., 1876-77; (LL.D., Northern Ohio U., 1900); m. Bonnie O'Neal, June 4, 1907. Admitted to bar, 1886; removed to Kan., 1886; engaged in banking; now pres. Emerson Realty Co., Los Angeles. Presdl. elector, 1888; commr. Paris Expn., 1900, St. Louis Expn., 1904. Vice-chmn. Speakers' Bur., Rep. Nat. Com., campaign 1900; his speech replying to "Coin" Harvey's Financial Sch. was issued as a Republican campaign document, 1896, and in 1900 over half a million copies of his speech on sound money were circulated throughout the country. Author: American Valor (speech at Gettysburg, 1911); The Treasure of Hidden Valley, 1915; A Vendetta of the Hills, 1916; The Man Who Discovered Himself, 1917. Home: Denver, Colo. Died Dec. 11, 1918.

EMERTON, Ephraim, univ. prof.; b. Salem, Mass., Feb. 18, 1851; s. James and Martha (West) E.; A.B., Harvard, 1871; Ph.D., Leipzig, 1876; m. Sibyl M. Clark, Apr. 18, 1877; 1 dau., Clara Browning (dec.). Instr. history and German, 1876-78, instr. history, 1878-82, Winn prof. eccles. history, 1882-1918 (emeritus), Harvard. Fellow Am. Acad. Arts and Sciences. Author: Introduction to the Study of the Middle Ages; Synopsis of the History of Continental Europe, Mediæval Europe, 814-1300; Desiderius Erasmus; Unitarian Thought, 1911; Beginnings of Modern Europe, 1917; The Defensor Pacis of Marsiglio of Padua, 1920; Learning and Living (academic essays), 1921; Humanism and Tyranny—Studies in the Italian Trecento, 1925. Translator: Correspondence of Pope Gregory VII, 1931; Correspondence of St. Boniface, 1934. Home: Cambridge, Mass. Died Mar. 3, 1935.

EMERTON, James H., naturalist, illustrator; b. Salem, Mass., 1847. Student of Am. spiders. Illustrator of zööl. publs. Illustrations in Packard's Guide to the Study of Insects; Scudder's Butterflies of North America; A. E. Verrill's papers in Reports of U.S. Fish Commn., 1874-84; C.S. Minot's text-book of Embryology. Made models of large octopus and squid in museums at Cambridge, New Haven, New York and Washington; anatomical models in med. museums of Harvard, U. of Pa., and Army Med. Mus., Washington. Author: The Structure and Habits of Spiders, 1878; Common Spiders of the United States, 1902; also The New England Spiders, 11 papers in Trans. Conn. Acad., New Haven, 1882-1915. Address: Boston, Mass. Died Dec. 5, 1930.

EMERY, Albert Hamilton, civil and mech. engr.; b. Mexico, N.Y., June 21, 1834; s. Samuel and Catherine S. E.; ed. Mexico Acad.; C.E., Rensselaer Poly. Inst., 1858; m. Mrs. F. B. Myers, Mar. 3, 1875; 1 son, Albert Hamilton. Invented and designed the well-known testing machine at Watertown Arsenal, as well as several others including two installed at Bur. of Standards, Washington, one of 230,000 lbs. capacity for tension and compression, and one of 1,150,000 lbs. capacity for tension, and 2,300,000 lbs. for compression on specimens of all lengths up to 33 ft. Invented and developed the method of constructing guns by hydraulic radial expansion. Home: Stamford, Conn. Died Dec. 2, 1926.

EMERY, Edward Kellogg, judge; b. E. Aurora, N.Y., July 29, 1851; s. Josiah and Elizabeth C. E.; acad. edn., E. Aurora; read law at Buffalo, N.Y.; m. Clara B. Darbee, Oct. 7, 1886. Admitted to bar, 1877, and practiced at Buffalo. Mem. N.Y. Assembly, 1887, 1888; judge Co. Ct., Erie Co., N.Y., 1896-1906; justice Supreme Ct. of N.Y., term Jan. 1, 1907-Dec. 31, 1920. Republican. Home: Buffalo, N.Y. Died Nov. 10, 1919.

EMERY, Fred Parker, college prof.; b. Pembroke, N.H., Apr. 11, 1865; s. Natt B. and Abbie H. (Sargent) E.; A.B., Dartmouth, 1887, A.M., 1890; U. of Paris, 1891-92; U. of Berlin, 1892-93; m. Mary E. Chesley, June 26, 1889. Instr. English, Mass. Inst. Tech., 1887-91; asst. prof. English, Pa. State Coll., 1893-94; asst. prof. rhetoric and oratory, 1894, prof., 1895—, Dartmouth. Author: Notes on English Literature, 1891. Editor of Shakespeare plays. Home: Hanover, N.H. Died Jan. 16, 1927.

EMERY, Grenville C., schoolmaster; b. Ripley, Me., July 19, 1843; s. John G. and Mary (Stanley) E.; A.B., Bates Coll., Lewiston, Me., 1868, A.M., 1869, hon. Litt.D., 1904; m. Ella Rhoda Emery; children—Ellen Rosalind, Mary Rhoda (dec.), Bertrand Grenville (dec.), Laura Johnson, Ella Pike (dec.), John (dec.), Grenville Pike (dec.); m. 2d, Mrs. Katherine D. Monroe, Dec. 22, 1920; 1 stepson, Charles Mattison Monroe. Instr. Me. State Sem., 1868-69; prin. high sch. and supt. schs., Auburn, Me., 1869-71; prin. high sch., Grand Rapids, Mich., 1872; with Lawrence Grammar Sch., Boston, 1872-81; master in Boston Latin Sch., 1882-97; founder (with wife Ella R. Emery) and head master, Harvard Sch., Los Angeles, Calif., 1900-12; founder (with wife, Katherine D. Emery), Seale Acad. (now West Coast Mil. Acad.), Palo Alto, Calif., and head master, 1920—. Republican. Episcopalian. Author: The Academic Algebra (with William F. Bradbury), 1889; Algebra for Beginners (with same), 1894. Died May 1927.

EMERY, Henry Crosby, economist; b. Ellsworth, Me., Dec. 21, 1872; s. Lucilius Alonzo and Annie S. (Crosby) E.; A.B., Bowdoin, 1892; A.M., Harvard, 1893; Ph.D., Columbia, 1896; U. of Berlin, 1896-97; (hon. A.M., Yale, 1900; LL.D., Bowdoin, 1911); m. Susanne C. Allinson, 1917. Instr. and prof. polit. economy, Bowdoin, 1894-1900; prof. polit. economy, Yale, 1900-15; chmn. U.S. Tariff Bd., 1909-13; fgn. rep. of Guaranty Trust Co. of New York, 1916; now mgr. Asia Banking Corp., hdqrs. New York. Author: Speculation on the Stock and Produce Exchanges of the United States, 1896; Politician, Party and People, 1913. Home: Peking, China. Died Feb. 6, 1924.

EMERY, Ina Capitola, author; b. Bethel, Vt., Feb. 25, 1868; d. George S. and Abbie Adelia (Moxley) E.; sister of Fred A. Emery; ed. Washington High Sch. Society editor Washington Evening News, 1894-95; contbr. to mags. and other publs., 1895-1902; lit. critic and instr. in short story writing, Nat. Corr. Inst., 1899-1905; pres. Nat. Lit. Bur., 1906-10; dir. Florence Crittenden Assn.; dir. Intercontinental Univ., Washington, D.C., 1911-13. Author: Emery's Courses in Short Story Writing and Scenarios, 1899; Emery's Constructive English (text book), 1915. Publisher of Washington Monument Guide, 1902—, Emery's Washington Guide, 1909, Emery's Magazine, 1911. Home: Washington, D.C. Died July 25, 1941.

EMERY, John Runkle, judge; b. Flemington, N.J., July 6, 1842; s. William P. and Ann (Runkle) E.; A.B., Princeton, 1861, A.M., 1864; Harvard Law Sch., 1863-64; (LL.D., Princeton, 1901); m. Alla MacKie, Oct. 6, 1885. Second lt. 15th N.J. Vols., Aug. 1862-Feb. 1863, hon. disch.; admitted to N.J. bar, 1865; vice chancellor of N.J., Jan. 1895—; term expires, 1916. Republican. Episcopalian. Home: Morristown, N.J. Died Jan. 29, 1916.

EMERY, Lewis, Jr., mfr.; b. Chautauqua Co., N.Y., Aug. 10, 1839; s. Lewis and Marie (Gilson) E.; Hillsdale (Mich.) Coll.; m. Elizabeth A. Caldwell, Dec. 29, 1863 (dec.). Operating in oil, 1865—, also large mfr. chemicals; dir. 1st Nat. Bank, Bradford, Pa. Was mem. Pa. Ho. of Rep. and Senate; was nominee of Lincoln and Dem. parties for gov. of Pa. Pres. Northwestern Anti-Tuberculosis League. Home: Bradford, Pa. Died Nov. 19, 1924.

EMERY, Lucilius Alonzo, judge; b. Carmel, Me., July 27, 1840; s. James S. and Eliza A. (Wing) E.; A.B., Bowdoin, 1861, A.M., 1864 (LL.D., 1898); m. Annie S. Crosby, Nov. 9, 1864; father of Henry Crosby E., and Annie Crosby Emery Allinson. Admitted to bar, 1863, and practiced at Ellsworth, Me.; co. atty. Hancock Co., Me., 1867-71; mem. Me. Senate, 1874, 75, 81; atty. gen., 1876-79; justice Supreme Jud. Ct. of Me., 1883-1911 (chief justice, Dec. 17, 1906-July 26, 1911), resigned. Republican. Prof. med. jurisprudence, Med. Sch. of Me. (Bowdoin), 1889-12; lecturer Roman Law, U. of Me., 1896—. Overseer, 1874-1907, trustee, 1907—, Bowdoin. Lecturer on probate law, Boston U. Law Sch., 1913. Conglist. Author: Concerning Justice, 1914. Home: Ellsworth, Me. Died Aug. 26, 1920.

EMERY, Matthew Gault; b. Pembroke, N.H., Sept. 28, 1818; s. Jacob E.; ed. Pembroke, N.H.; left home and went to Baltimore at 18 yrs. of age; apprenticed himself to a stone cutter. In 1840 received 1st govt. contract, cutting of stone in the quarry for P.O. dept. bldg., Washington. Removed to Washington, 1842; did much stone work on Capitol; cut and laid cornerstone for its extension; prepared, cut and squared, and on July 4, 1848, laid cornerstone of Washington Monument. Organized and became capt. of militia co., May 16, 1861. Took charge of sick and disabled soldiers from his State in Washington, and gave up his residence at Brightwood for that purpose. Treas. N.H. Soldiers' Aid Assn., Washington; was mem. bd. aldermen, Washington, and its mayor, 1870, holding position until territorial govt. adopted by Congress for dist. abolished office of mayor. Sold his interest in business, 1872. Has been regent Smithsonian Instn.; trustee Dickinson Coll., Pa.; regent and vice chancellor Nat. Univ.; regent and treas. Am. Univ.; pres. bd. of trustees Metropolitan Meth. Ch. Identified, 1845—, as incorporator, dir. or officer in nearly all fire and life ins. cos. organized in Washington, as well as banks, trust cos., market cos., gas and electric light cos., etc.; pres. 2d Nat. Bank. Home: Washington, D. C. Died 1901.

EMERY, Natt Morrill, educator; b. Suncook, N.H., Apr. 16, 1873; s. Natt B. and Abbie H. (Sargent) E.; A.B., Dartmouth Coll., 1895; M.A., Lehigh Univ., 1899; (Litt.D., Ursinus College, 1916); m. Bertha Elizabeth Snyder, June 23, 1904; children—Natt M., Martha. Instr., Tilton Sem., Tilton, N.H., 1895-96; instr. in English, 1896-1902, registrar, 1899-1912, asst. to pres., 1907-10, v.p., 1910—, v.p. and comptroller, 1922—, Lehigh U. Home: Bethlehem, Pa. Died Oct. 31, 1935.

EMERY, Sarah Anna, author; b. Newburyport, Mass., Nov. 9, 1821; d. David and Sarah (Smith) E.; ed. at home; unmarried. Taught pvt. sch., 1841-54; afterward gave lessons in drawing, etc. Author: Three Generations (a novel); My Generation (novel). Edited: Reminiscences of a Nonogenarian (her mother's recollections). Home: Newburyport, Mass. Died 1907.

EMERY, Susan L., editor; b. Dorchester, Mass., Sept. 26, 1846; d. Charles and Susan Hilton (Kelly) E.; grad. high sch., Dorchester, Mass., 1864; then to Miss Stone's Boarding Sch., Greenfield, Mass., 1865-66. Was Episcopalian until 1875, then became Roman Catholic. Asst. editor The Young Christian Soldier, New York, 1871-74; on staff The Sacred Heart Review, Boston, 1891—. Author: Uncle Rod's Pet, 1869; Noël, 1892; Thoughts for Every Day in the Year—from Spiritual Writings of St. John of the Cross, 1891; Inner Life of the Soul, 1903. Translator: (into English verse) The Poems of Soeur Thérèse de l'Enfant Jésus (Petals of a Little Flower), 1907; A Catholic Stronghold and Its Making, 1910. Deceased.

EMERY, Z(achary) Taylor, physician; b. Novi, Oakland Co., Mich., Feb. 22, 1847; s. John C. and Mary (Yerkes) E.; student U. of Mich., 1870-71, med. dept. same, 1872-73; M.D., Detroit Med. Coll. (now Detroit Coll. Medicine), 1874, and L.I. Coll. Hosp., Brooklyn, 1874; m. Georgina Colville, Jan. 17, 1889. Interne, U.S. Marine Hosp., Detroit, 1873-74; practiced in Brooklyn, 1874-1905; commr. of health, Brooklyn, 1894-97; med. dir. Manhattan Life Ins. Co., New York, 1895—, also dir.; trustee Manhattan Savings Instn. Republican. Presbyn. Home: White Plains, N.Y. Died Oct. 7, 1924.

EMMERSON, Louis Lincoln, governor; b. Albion, Ill., Dec. 27, 1863; s. Jesse E.; ed. high sch.; LL.D., James Millikin U., 1930; m. Anna Mathews, 1887; children—Mrs. Aline Ward, Mrs. Dorothy Watson. Began in mercantile business, Mt. Vernon, Ill., 1883; organized, 1901, and pres. Third Nat. Bank, Mt. Vernon. Was chmn. Rep. County Central Com., Jefferson Co., and chmn. State Central Com.; was mem. State Bd. of Equalization and mem. bd. commrs. Southern Ill. Penitentiary; elected sec. of state of Ill., 1916, reëlected, 1920 and 1924; gov. of Ill., term 1929-33. Mason. Home: Mt. Vernon, Ill. Died Feb. 4, 1941.

EMMET, Grenville Temple, lawyer; b. New Rochelle, N.Y., Aug. 2, 1877; s. Richard Stockton and Katharine (Temple) E.; student St. Paul's Sch., Concord, N.H., 1888-94; A.B., Harvard, 1898; student N.Y. Law Sch., 1900-01; m. Pauline A. Ferguson, Sept. 18, 1905; children—Pauline Anne, Grenville Temple, Elizabeth Patricia. Admitted to N.Y. bar, 1901; mem. firm Emmet & Robinson, N.Y. City, 1903-1906, Emmet & Parish, 1912-20; formed firm Emmet, Marvin & Roosevelt which changed to Emmet, Marvin & Martin when Franklin D. Roosevelt retired in 1923. E.E. and M.P. to The Netherlands, 1934—. Served in Spanish-Am. War, 1898. Trustee and treas. Home for Incurables and Braker Memorial Home, N.Y. City. Democrat. Episcopalian. Home: New York, N.Y. Died Sept. 26, 1937.

EMMET, Thomas Addis, physician; b. Charlottesville, Va., May 29, 1828; s. Prof. John Patten, of U. of Va.; ed. Charlottesville, Va., St. Thomas Hall, Flushing, L.I., and 1845-46, U. of Va.; M.D., Jefferson Med. Coll., Phila., 1850; married. Apptd. visiting phys. to Emigrant Refuge Hosp., Ward's Island, 1851; asst. surgeon Woman's Hosp., May, 1855; surgeon-in-chief, same, 1861-72; since then visiting surgeon; cons. phys. or surgeon to several public hosps. in New York; specialist in women's diseases; has introduced new operations and methods of treatment. Author: Principles and Practice of Gynecology. Died Mar. 1, 1919.

EMMET, William LeRoy, electrical engr.; b. New Rochelle, N.Y., July 10, 1859; s. William J. and Julia Colt (Pierson) E.; grad. U.S. Naval Acad., 1881; Sc.D., Union Coll., 1910, Trinity Coll., Hartford, Conn., 1925. D.Eng., Stevens Inst. of Technology, 1939; unmarried. Left navy, 1883; elec. engr., 1887—; in service Gen. Elec. Co., 1892—; reëntered navy during Spanish-Am. War; most important work has been in steam turbine inventions and developments, and invention of mercury vapor power process. Awarded Edison medal, 1919, Elliott Cresson medal, 1920; gold medal from Am. Society M.E.; David W. Tayloe medal from Am. Soc. of Naval Architects and Marine Engrs., 1938. Author: Alternating Current Wiring and Distribution, 1894; The Autobiography of an Engineer, 1931. Mem. Naval Consulting Bd., 1915, and chmn. com. on submarines. Home: Schenectady, N.Y. Died Sept. 26, 1941.

EMMET, William Temple, lawyer; b. New Rochelle, N.Y., July 28, 1869; s. Richard Stockton and Katharine (Temple) E.; prep. edn. St. Paul's Sch., Concord, N.H.; student Columbia, 1887-89; Columbia Law Sch., 1889-90; m. Cornelia Zabriskie, June 16, 1896. Admitted to N.Y. bar, 1890; mem. N.Y. State Constl. Conv., 1894; mem. Bd. of Edn., N.Y. City, 1899-1901; supt. ins., State of N.Y., 1912-14; pub. service commr., N.Y., April 2, 1941—. Dir. Met. Life Ins. Co. Home: South Salem, N.Y. Died Feb. 14, 1918.

EMMONS, Charles Demoss, transportation official; b. LaFayette, Ind., Feb. 13, 1871; s. Charles Cadwell and Martha Jennie (Briney) E.; C.E., Western U. of Pa. (now U. of Pittsburgh), 1892; m. Bertha E. Ewart, May 1, 1894; children—Samuel Ewart, Mrs. Martha Cooke, Charles DeMoss, Mrs. Edith E. Pennoyer, Mrs. Cornelia Hicks, Charles Cadwell; m. 2d, Mrs. Sadie Ramsey Ferree, Apr. 15, 1922; 1 son, Robert B. Ferree. With Engineering Dept. Pa. R.R. Co. East of Pittsburgh, 1892-1901; gen. supt. LaFayette (Ind.) St. Ry. Co., 1901-03; gen. mgr. Ft. Wayne & Wabash Valley St. Ry. Co., 1903-11; Chicago, South Bend & Northern Ind. Ry. Co., 1912-16; 2d v.p. and gen. mgr. Boston & Worcester St. Ry. Co., 1916-18; gen. mgr. Boston Elevated Ry. Co., 1918-19; became president United Rys. & Electric Co. of Baltimore, 1919; now pres. Hudson & Manhattan R.R.; pres. Baltimore Coach Co., Baltimore, Halethorpe & Elkridge Ry. Co., Md. Electric Ry. Co.; v.p. Riverview Co., Catonsville Short Line R.R. Co.; mem. bd. trustees Savings Bank of Baltimore, also of Brown Memorial Ch. Republican. Presbyn. Died Feb. 2, 1933.

EMMONS, Samuel Franklin, geologist; b. Boston, Mar. 29, 1841; s. Nathaniel H. and Elizabeth (Wales) E.; A.B., Harvard, 1861, A.M., 1866; studied at École Impériale des Mines, Paris, 1862-64, Bergakademie, Freiburg, 1864-65; (Sc.D., Columbia and Harvard, 1909); m. Waltha Anita Steeves, Aug. 5, 1876; 2d, Sophie Dallas Markoe, Feb. 14, 1889 (died 1896); 3d, Suzanne Earle Ogden-Jones, of Dinard, France, Aug. 4, 1903. Geologist, U.S. Geol. Survey, exploration 40th parallel, 1867-77; conducted cattle ranch in Wyo., 1877-79; geologist U.S. Geol. Survey, 1879—. Fellow Am. Acad. Arts and Sciences, London Geol. Soc., A.A.A.S. Author: Geological Distribution of the Useful Metals in the United States, 1893; Progress of the Precious Metal Industry in the United States, 1893; Geology of the Denver Basin in Colorado, 1896; Died 1911.

EMORY, Frederic, chief Bur. Trade Relations, U.S. Dept. of State, 1903-05; b. Centreville, Md., Sept. 18, 1853; s. Blanchard and Mary Bourke E.; ed. by private instrs. and at Centreville, Md., Acad., until Oct., 1868, St. John's Coll., Annapolis, Md., Oct. 1868, to May 1872; married. Until Mar. 1893, on staffs Baltimore Sun, Philadelphia Ledger, etc.; apptd. sec. Bur. Am. Republics, March 22, 1893; chief Bur. of Statistics (later Bur. Foreign Commerce), Dept. of State, April 17, 1894; was also dir. Bur. of Am. Republics, Feb. 1898-May 1899. Editor: Commercial Relations of the United States, 1894, 1903; United States Consular Reports, 1894, 1903. Resigned as chief of Bur. of Trade Relations, 1905. Home: Queenstown, Md. Died 1908.

EMORY, Frederick Lincoln, univ. prof.; b. Lunenberg, Mass., Apr. 10, 1867; s. Edward Franklin and Mary M. (Colby) E.; B.S., Worcester Poly. Inst., 1887, M.E., 1899; M.M.E., Cornell, 1896; m. Mary M., d. Judge John A. Dille, of Morgantown, W.Va., Mar. 1893. Established mech. dept. Washington (D.C.) High Sch., 1887-89; established and superintended the Trades Schs., Mass. Reformatory, 1889-90; prof. mech. engring. and mechanic arts, W.Va. U., 1890-92; established and directed Industrial Training and Tech. High Sch. for the city of Indianapolis, 1892-95; prof. mechanics and applied mathematics, W.Va. U., 1897— (as supt. bldgs. and grounds, built the armory, library, mechanical hall, president's house and central heating plant). Mem. bd. sch. commrs., Morgantown, etc. Translator (with F. W. Truscott): Philosophical Essay on Probabilities (La place), 1902. Home: Morgantown, W.Va. Died Dec. 31, 1921.

EMORY, William Hemsley, rear adm.; b. Washington, Dec. 17, 1846; grad. U.S. Naval Acad, 1866; promoted ensign, U.S.N., Mar. 12, 1868; master, Mar. 26, 1869; lt., Mar. 21, 1870; lt. comdr., May 26, 1887; comdr., Dec. 29, 1895; capt., Apr. 14, 1901; rear adm., Nov. 2, 1906. Summer of 1863 on the Macedonian in pursuit of Confederate cruiser Tacony; served on Iroquois, 1866-70; Naval Obs., 1870-71; Relief and Constellation, 1871; Asiatic sta., 1872-74; European sta., 1874-76; Naval Acad., 1876-79; Trenton, 1880-81; spl. duty with Admiral Porter, 1881-84; comd. Bear, 1884, Despatch, 1885-86, Thetis, 1887-89; naval attaché, Am. Embassy, London, 1889-92; comd. Petrel, 1894-96; mem. Bd. Inspection and Survey, 1897-98, 1898-1900; comd. Yosemite during Spanish War; Navy Yard, New York, and comdt. Naval Sta., Key West, 1900; comd. Monongahela, 1901, Indiana, 1901-02; insp. merchant vessels, New York, 1902; comd. Indiana, 1902-03, Hancock, 1904-06; comdg. Second Squadron, Atlantic Fleet, 1907; retired by operation of law, Dec. 17, 1908. July 15, 1917.

EMRICH, Frederick Ernest, clergyman; b. New York, Aug. 25, 1848; s. Philip and Anna F. (Ganss) E.; A.B., Bates Coll., Me., 1876, A.M., 1879, D.D., 1894; Bangor (Me.) Theol. Sem., 1871-72; grad. Cobb Div. Sch., 1877; D.D., Amherst, 1911; m. Olive Emma Chandler, Feb. 24, 1869 (died 1884); children—Frederick Ernest (dec.), John P. Chandler (dec.), Thomas Rich (dec.), Richard S. M. (dec.), Melvin Eveleth (dec.); m. 2d, Clara R. Denison, Aug. 8, 1885; children—Katharine Denison (wife of Rev. Harry S. Lowd), Hilda W. Ordained Congl. ministry, Sept. 1875; pastor, Mechanic Falls, Me., 1874-82, Tabernacle Ch., Chicago, 1882-89, Grace Ch., S., Framingham, Mass., 1889-1903; sec. Mass. Home Missionary Soc., Boston, 1903-23, emeritus. Mem. corp. Am. Internat. Coll. Home: Jamaica Plain, Mass. Died Feb. 5, 1933.

ENANDER, John Alfred, journalist; b. Westgothia, Sweden, May 22, 1842; s. Johannes Johnson and Gustava (Glad) E.; grad. Venersborg Coll., 1868; came to U.S., 1869 (LL.D., Augustana Coll., Ill.); m. Malinda Lawson, 1872. Editor of Swedish-Am. papers, Dec. 1869—; now editor Hemlandet, Chicago. Prof. Swedish lang. and lit., Augustana Coll., 1890-93. Mem. Ill. State Bd. Edn., 1879-83; apptd. U.S. minister to Denmark, 1889, but resigned before entering upon duties because of illness; speaker for Rep. Nat. Com. (in Swedish lang.) in campaigns of 1884, 88, 92, 96, 1900, 04. Mem. numerous Swedish clubs and socs.; hon. mem. Polish Nat. Alliance; v.p. Swedish dept. Germanic Congress, 1904, 1905. Decorated with Order Literis et Artibus by King Oscar II of Sweden and Norway, 1905. Home: Chicago, Ill. Died 1910.

ENDICOTT, Henry, mfr.; b. Canton, Mass., Nov. 14, 1824; s. Elijah and Cynthia (Child) E.; desc. of Gilbert E., who settled in Wells, Me., 1648, and afterwards in Canton, Mass.; ed. pub. schs.; m. Abigail Hastings Browning, Sept. 2, 1851; father of Emma Endicott Marean (q.v.). Formerly mem. Allen & Endicott, mfrs. steam engines, boilers, etc., Cambridge, Mass.; pres. Allen & Endicott Bldg. Co., Hittinger Fruit Co., Cambridgeport Savings Bank. Mason. Home: Cambridge, Mass. Died Nov. 8, 1913.

ENDICOTT, Mordecai Thomas, rear adm.; b. May's Landing, N.J., Nov. 26, 1844; s. Thomas Doughty and Ann (Pennington) E.; prep. edn. parochial sch. of Presbyn. ch.; C.E., Rensselaer Poly. Inst., 1868; m. Elizabeth Adams, May 29, 1872. In practice from July 1868 as civil engr. and in mining until apptd. civil engr., U.S.N., July 14, 1874. Duty at various navy yards and in navy dept. at Washington as consulting engr.; apptd. mem. Nicaragua Canal Commn., 1895; mem. U.S. Naval Armor factory bd., 1897; apptd. chief Bureau Yards and Docks, Navy Dept., Apr. 7, 1898, with rank of commodore; later advanced to rank of rear adm.; reappointed Apr. 7, 1902, and Apr. 7, 1906; apptd. mem. Isthmian Canal Commn., 1905; rear adm. and retired, Nov. 26, 1906, but continued upon active duties until June 30, 1909. Recalled to active duty in Navy Dept., Oct. 12, 1917. Home: Washington, D.C. Died Mar. 6, 1926.

ENDICOTT, William, banker; s. William and Annie Thorndike (Rand) E.; desc. of Gov. Endicott, 1628 (gov. of Mass., 1629-30); A.B., Harvard, 1887; m. Helen Southworth Shaw, June 11, 1889 (dec.); m. 2d, Ellice Mack, of London, Mar. 27, 1919. Connected with Kidder, Peabody & Co., bankers, from 1887, mem. of firm, 1897-1929; pres. Boston & Albany R.R.; chmn. bd. New Eng. Trust Co.; dir. Bigelow-Sanford Carpet Co. Overseer Harvard Coll., 1907-13, 1914-17; Am. Red Cross commr. for Great Britain, Oct. 1916-Mar. 1919. Dir. Employers' Group Associates; mem. finance com. Employers' Liability & Assurance Corp. Home: Boston, Mass. Died Aug. 25, 1941.

ENDICOTT, William Crowninshield, sec. of war, U.S.; b. Salem, Mass., Nov. 19, 1826; prepared for college in Salem Latin School; grad. Harvard, 1847; studied law in office and at Harvard Law School; admitted to bar, 1850; began practice in Salem, 1851; m. Ellen, dau. George Peabody, of Salem, Dec. 13, 1859. Member, 1852, and later pres., Salem common council; city solicitor, 1857-64. Democratic nominee for atty. gen. of Mass., 1871, 72, 73; for Congress, 1870; for gov. of Mass., 1884. Judge supreme court, Mass., 1873-83; resigned. Sec. of war, U.S., 1885-89. Pres. Peabody Acad. of Science, Salem, 1863—. Home: Danvers Centre, Mass. Died 1900.

ENDICOTT, William Crowninshield, lawyer; b. Salem, Mass., Sept. 28, 1860; s. William Crowninshield (sec. of war, 1885-89) and Ellen (Peabody) E.; lineal desc. in the 9th generation from Gov. John E., 1st gov. of Mass. Colony; A.B., Harvard, 1883; studied law at Harvard Law Sch. and in an office in Salem; m. Marie Louise Thoron, Oct. 3, 1889. Admitted to Essex bar, 1886, and since in practice at Boston and Washington. Vice-pres. and trustee Peabody Mus. (Salem); treas. and trustee Humane Soc. of the Commonwealth of Mass.; trustee Peabody Inst., Mass. Soc. for Promoting Agriculture, Boston Library Soc., Mass. Hort. Soc.; v.p. Isabella Stewart Gardner Mus.; pres. Mass. Hist. Soc. Trustee Suffolk Savings Bank for Seamen and Others; pres. Essex Inst. Democrat. Episcopalian. Home: Boston, Mass. Died Nov. 28, 1936.

ENDLICH, Gustav Adolf; judge; b. Alsace Tp., Berks Co., Pa., Jan. 29, 1856; s. Hon. John and Emma N. (Miller) E.; ed. Stuttgart, Tübingen, Darmstadt, 1867-72; A.B., Princeton, 1875, A.M., 1878; studied law in office of George F. Baer, 1875-77; LL.D., Muhlenberg, 1898, Dickinson, 1903; m. Amy H. Duffield, Dec. 12, 1883. Admitted to bar, 1877; judge 23d Dist. of Pa., 1890-1908, pres. judge, 1908-25. Mem. U.S. Assay Commn., 1897; pres. bd. trustees Muhlenberg Coll., 1906-10. Democrat. Author: The Law of Building Associations, 1882, 1895. Address: Reading, Pa. Died Feb. 11, 1929.

ENELOW, Heman Gerson, rabbi; b. Russia, Oct. 26, 1877; s. Leopold and Matilda (Marver) E.; U. of Chicago, 1894-95; B.A., U. of Cincinnati, 1897; fellow in English, 1897-98; grad. Hebrew Union Coll., Cincinnati, as rabbi, 1898, D.D., 1900, D.H.L., 1925; unmarried. Rabbi Temple Israel, Paducah, Ky., 1898-1901, Temple Adath Israel, Louisville, 1901-12, Temple Emanu-El, New York, 1912—. Pres. Ky. State Conf. Charities and Corrections, 1910-11; pres. Conf. of Social Workers, Louisville, 1910-11; a founder, and mem. exec. com. Fedn. of Jewish Charities, Louisville, 1908-11; etc. Mem. Central Conf. Am. Rabbis (pres. 1927-29). Author: Aspects of the Bible, 1911; The Effects of Religion, 1917; The Varied Beauty of the Psalms, 1917; The Faith of Israel, 1917; The Allied Countries and the Jews, 1918; A Jewish View of Jesus, 1920; The Adequacy of Judaism, 1920; The Jew and the World, 1921; The Diverse Elements of Religion, 1924. Editor: Yahwism, 1903; Origins of Synagogue and Church, 1929; Al-Nakawa's Menorat Ha-Maor, 1929-31. Served in France as overseas commr. and gen. field sec., Jewish Welfare Bd., July 1918-Apr. 1919; Army Ednl. Corps, Apr.-June 1919. Home: New York, N.Y. Died Feb. 6, 1934.

ENGBERG, Carl Christian, mathematician; b. Hytton, Sweden, Nov. 3, 1872; s. Carl August and Ida Charlotta (Lundin) E.; came to U.S., 1888; B.Sc., U. of Neb., 1895, A.M., 1897, Ph.D., 1899; m. Anne Eliza Borland, June 19, 1901; children—one died in infancy and Charlotte Edith. Began teaching, U. of Neb., 1896; prof. mathematics, 1911—, also exec. dean of the univ., 1913—. Republican. Conglist. Home: Lincoln, Neb. Died Sept. 21, 1929.

ENGEL, Peter, abbot; b. St. Nicholas, Wis., Feb. 3, 1856; s. Jacob and Margaret E.; early edn. at St. Michael, Minn.; grad. St. John's U., Collegeville, Minn., 1874. Took orders and entered Order of St. Benedict, advancing until he became a mitred abbot with the title of "Right Reverend." Home: (St. John's Abbey) Collegeville, Minn. Died Nov. 27, 1921.

ENGELHARDT, Zephyrin, clergyman, author; b. Bilshausen, Hanover, Germany, Nov. 13, 1851; s. Anthony and Elisabeth E.; arrived at New York, Dec. 8, 1852; ed. in classics, St. Francis Seraph Coll., Cincinnati; in philosophy, Franciscan Monastery, Quincy, Ill.; in theology, Franciscan Monastery, St. Louis. Joined Order of St. Francis, 1872; ordained priest, R.C. Ch., 1878; missionary among Indians and head of 3 Indian boarding schs., 1880-1900; writing history exclusively, 1903—. Author: The Franciscans in California, 1897; The Franciscans in Arizona, 1899; The Missions and Missionaries of California, 5 vols., 1908-16; San Diego Mission, 1920; San Luis Rey Mission, 1921; San Juan Capistrano Mission, 1922; Santa Barbara Mission, 1923; Mission Dolores and the Beginnings of San Francisco, 1925; San Gabriel Mission and the Beginnings of Los Angeles, 1927; San Fernando Mission, 1927; San Miguel, San Antonio and Soledad Missions, 1929; San Buenaventura Mission, 1930; San Juan Bautista Mission, 1931; Missions Santa Inés and Purisima Concepcion, 1932; Mission San Luis Obispo, 1933. Home: Santa Barbara, Calif. Died Apr. 27, 1934.

ENGELMANN, George Julius, gynecologist; b. St. Louis, Mo., July 2, 1847; s. Dr. George and Dora (Horstman) E.; grad. Washington Univ., 1867, A.M., 1870; studied medicine in Europe, 1867-73, at univs. of Tübingen, Berlin (M.D., 1871), and Vienna (Master in Obstetrics, 1872); m. Emily Engelmann, 1879 (died 1890); m. 2d, Loula H. Clark. Surgeon Franco-Prussian war, 1870-71; practiced St. Louis, 1873-95; practicing at Boston, 1895—. Extensive traveler; sought recreation in ethnol. and archæol. researches. His collection of Missouri flints and pottery is now in Peabody Archæol. Museum, Cambridge, Mass., with parts in Washington, Berlin, Vienna. Prof. diseases of women, St. Louis. Post-grad. Sch. Medicine and Mo. Med. Coll. until 1894; was founder and pres. St. Louis Obstet. Soc.; founder and pres. Am. Gynecol. Soc., 1900, hon. pres. gynecol. sect., Internat. Med. Congress, 1884; hon. pres. Internat. Congress of Obstetrics and Gynecology, Brussels, 1892; Amsterdam, 1899; Rome, 1902; trustee Mo. Bot. Garden, St. Louis, 1890-94; fellow Washington Acad. Sciences; fellow in many Am. and foreign socs. Writer on med. topics. Home: Boston, Mass. Died 1903.

ENGERUD, Edward, lawyer; b. Racine, Wis., Feb. 13, 1868; s. Lars and Christine M. (Bakke) E.; student Beloit Coll., 1882-87; studied law with Clapp & Haupt, Fergus Falls, Minn., 1887-89; admitted to bar, 1889; m. Clara J. Jacobsen, July 22, 1890. City atty. Lisbon, N.D., 1896; state's atty. Ransom Co., N.D., 1897; resigned on removal to Fargo; asst. state's atty. Cass Co., N.D., 1897-1901; asst. U.S. atty. Dist. of N.D., 1902-04; apptd. judge Supreme Ct. of N.D., Aug. 10, 1904; elected, Nov. 1904; resigned, Jan. 10, 1907, to practice law; sr. mem. Engerud, Holt & Frame. U.S. atty. for N.D., Feb. 6, 1911—. Conglist. Home: Fargo, N.D. Deceased.

ENGLAND, George Allan; b. Fort McPherson, Neb., Feb. 9, 1877; s. Rev. George Allen and Hannah Pearl (Lyon) E.; father chaplain 9th Inf. Regt., U.S. Army; A.B., Harvard, 1902, A.M., 1903; married; 1 dau., Isabelle Pearl. Author: Cursed, 1919; Keep Off the Grass, 1919; Their Son, and The Necklace (Spanish transls.), 1919; The Flying Legion, 1920; The White Wilderness, 1922; Dialect Dictionary of Newfoundland, and Vikings of the Ice, 1923; Adventure Isle, 1925; Isle of Romance, 1929. Home: Bradford, N.H. Died June 26, 1936.

ENGLER, Edmund Arthur, educator; b. St. Louis, Mo., Dec. 23, 1856; s. Jacob and Augustina (Knecht) E.; A.B., Washington U., 1876, Ph.B., 1877, A.M., 1879, Ph.D., 1892 (LL.D., 1901); m. Catherine A. Ashbrook, June 17, 1886. Prof. mathematics, 1881-1901, dean Sch. Engring., 1896-1901, Washington U.; pres. Worcester (Mass.) Poly. Inst., 1901-11; sec. and treas., Washington U., July 1, 1911—. Mem. Washington U. eclipse party at Norman, Calif., 1889; chmn. of jury dept. mfrs., Buffalo Expn., 1901; chmn. Internat. Jury on instruments of precision, St. Louis Expn., 1904. Home: St. Louis, Mo. Deceased.

ENGLIS, Charles Mortimer, shipbuilder; b. Long Island City, N.Y., Dec. 14, 1857; s. John and Jeannette A. (Carrick) E.; grad. Mt. Washington Inst., N.Y. City, 1873; student New York U., 1873-74; m. Maude Louise Pratt, 1895. Learned shipbuilding business in father's shipyard, Brooklyn; became mem. John Englis & Sons, 1882, sole propr., 1892—; pres. N.Y. & Hudson Steamboat Co. Mem. 7th Regt., N.G.N.Y., 12 yrs. Republican. Presbyn. Home: New York, N.Y. Died Jan. 15, 1926.

ENGLISH, David Combs, physician; b. New Brunswick, N.J., Mar. 2, 1842; acad. edn.; M.D., Coll. Phys. and Surg. (Columbia), 1868; m. Susan Cary, d. Hon. Harrison Blake, of Me., 1870. Alderman New Brunswick, 1867-68; on staff Wells Memorial (now Middlesex) Hosp., 1893—; del. to Pan-Am. Med. Congress; fellow and trustee N.J. State Med. Soc. (pres. 1897-98, and editor of its journal, 1905—); treas. Middlesex Co. Med. Soc., 1877— (ex-pres.); fellow A.M.A., mem., 1870—. Mem. Vol. Med. Service Corps U.S. Elder First Presbyn. Ch., New Brunswick, 1873—; del. to 3 Presbyn. Gen. Assemblies; trustee N.J. Presbyn. Home. Home: New Brunswick, N.J. Died Sept. 19, 1924.

ENGLISH, Harry David Williams, underwriter; b. Sabbath Rest, Pa., Dec. 21, 1855; s. Rev. George W. and Lydia (Hildebrand) E.; ed. mil. acad., Milroy, Pa., and Duff's Business Coll., Pittsburgh; m. Jennie McLean Sellers, June 10, 1896. In newspaper business until 1876, then became life ins. agt. Mem. English & Furey, ins., 1905—. Pres. Pittsburgh Chamber Commerce; chmn. Pittsburgh Civic Commn.; pres., trustee Kingsley Assn. (social settlement). Pres. Allegheny County (Pa.) Sabbath Sch. Assn.; pres. of Brotherhood of St. Andrew in U.S.; chmn. Social Service Council Chs. of Christ; mem. Bd. Religious Edn. U. of Pittsburgh. Republican. Episcopalian. Mason. Home: Pittsburgh, Pa. Died Mar. 28, 1926.

ENGLISH, John Mahan, theologian; b. Tullytown, Pa., Oct. 20, 1845; s. Abram G. and Caroline L. E.; A.B., Brown U., 1870; grad. Newton Theol. Instn., 1875; D.D., Brown, 1891; m. Frances, dau. Wilson T. Drake, May 22, 1877; children—Lida Suydam, Howard La Rue (dec.), Everett Wilson (dec.). Teacher Latin, Suffield Acad., Conn., 1870-72; teacher Greek, Denison U., 1874; ordained Bapt. ministry, 1875; pastor First Ch., Gloucester, Mass., 1875-82, Dudley St. Ch., Boston, 1882; prof. homiletics and pastoral duties, Newton Theol. Instn., 1882-1918, emeritus. Lecturer on homiletics, Andover Theol. Sem., 1895-96, Hartford Theol. Sem., 1922-23. Trustee Brown U. Republican. Author: For Pulpit and Platform; The Minister and His Ministry. Home: Newton Centre, Mass. Died May 17, 1927.

ENGLISH, Thomas Dunn, M.D., author; b. Phila., June 29, 1819; grad. Univ. of Pa., M.D., 1839; later studied law; admitted to Phila. bar, 1842; in journalism in New York, 1844-59; from 1859 in med. practice at Newark; mem. N.J. legislature, 1863-64. Wrote Ben Bolt, long a popular ballad. Author: Poems; American Ballads; Book of Battle Lyrics; Walter Woolfe; Jacob Schuyler's Millions; Ambrose Fecit, or the Peer and the Painter; etc. Home: Newark, N.J. Died 1902.

ENGLISH, William Eastin, congressman; b. at Englishton Park, Ind., Nov. 3, 1854; s. William H. E. (Dem. candidate for v.p. U.S., 1880) and Emma Mardulia (Jackson) E.; ed. Northwestern Christian (now Butler) U.; LL.B., same, 1877; m. Helen Orr, Jan. 5, 1898; 1 dau., Rosalind Orr. Practiced law at Indianapolis until 1882; always active and prominent in politics, and mem. state, co. and city coms. (chmn. two latter, 1878); mem. Ind. Ho. of Rep., 1879-80; mem. 48th Congress (1883-85), declined reelection; pres. bd. of park commrs., 1898-99, bd. police and fire commrs., 1901-02, Indianapolis; mem. Ind. State Senate, 1916-28; in practice with daughter under firm name English & English, 1925—. Spent several yrs. in foreign travel; apptd., 1898, capt. U.S. Vols., served a.d.c. on staff Gen. Joseph Wheeler during campaign in Cuba; seriously injured during battle before Santiago, July 1, 1898; col. and p.m. gen. on staff gov. of Ind., 1899-1900, col. and insp. gen., 1900-04, and col. and a.d.c., 1901-20. Has large property interests. Owner English's block, English's Opera House, Hotel English, etc. Vice-pres. Ind. Hist. Soc., Western Geneal. Soc.; past comdr. in chief Nat. Assn. United Spanish War Veterans. Mason. Author: History of Masonry; Letters from Europe, etc. Republican. Home: Indianapolis, Ind. Died Apr. 29, 1926.

ENLOE, Benjamin Augustine, congressman; b. Clarksburg, Tenn., Jan. 18, 1848; s. Benjamin S. and Nancy O. E.; ed. Bethel Coll., Tenn., 1867-69, Cumberland U., 1869; LL.B., Cumberland, 1873; m. Fannie Howard Ashworth, Apr. 5, 1870. Mem. Tenn. Ho. of Rep., 1869-72; admitted to bar, 1873; editor Jackson (Tenn.) Tribune and Sun, 1874-86; commr. to negotiate settlement of state debt, 1872; mem. Dem. State Exec. Com., 1878-80; mem. 50th to 53d Congresses (1887-95). Exec. commr. for Tenn., St. Louis Expn., 1904; mem. Tenn. R.R. Commn., 1905—, chmn., 1906—. Home: Jackson, Tenn. Died July 9, 1922.

ENNEKING, John Joseph, artist; b. Minister, O., Oct. 4, 1840; s. Joseph and Margeretha (Bramlage) E.; ed. Mt. St. Mary's Coll., Cincinnati; studied art in Munich, and Paris, pupil of Bonnât and D'Aubigny; m. Mary E. Elliott, Oct. 14, 1864. Landscape and figure painter; awarded 4 medals Charitable Mechanics' Expn., Boston; hon. mention, Paris Expn., 1900; silver medal, St. Louis Expn., 1904. Home: Hyde Park, Mass. Died Nov. 17, 1916.

ENNIS, George Pearse, painter; b. St. Louis, Mo., July 21, 1884; s. Allen Rucker and Lillie Webber (Pearse) E.; ed. Art Sch. of Washington U., Holmes Art Sch., Chicago, and Chase Sch., New York, under William M. Chase; m. Gladys Atwood. Landscape and mural painter. Prin. works: stained glass windows, N.Y. Athletic Club, Ch. of All Nations, New York; victory windows, Military Chapel, N.Y. Military Acad.; mural decorations and stained glass windows, Unitarian Ch., Eastport, Me., First Bapt. Ch., Jamaica, L.I., Presbyn. Ch., Cornwall, N.Y.; 4 figure medallion windows and one figure window, M.E. Ch. Home of New York, Inc.; wind-swept birches collection U. of Ark.; Estey's head Syracuse Mus.; 31 pencil drawings and 15 oils for the making of big guns, 1918, authorized by the U.S. Ordnance Dept.; also sketches for the U.S. Air Service; stained glass window for Washington Hall, U.S. Mil. Acad. Awarded the Shaw prize by Salmagundi Club, New York, 1922; William Church Osborn prize, 1926; Gallatin prize for landscape, 1927; Isador prizes in water color and pencil drawing, 1924; Kramer prize, Art Inst. Chicago, 1922; Phila. Water Color prize, 1930, also Dana gold medal; Wilmington Soc. Fine Arts purchase prize, 1931; Mrs. Carll Tucker prize ($200), N.Y. Water Color Club, 1932. Works on exhbn. in Nat. Acad. Design, New York, Pa. Acad. Fine Arts, Phila., Art Inst. Chicago, Albright Gallery, Buffalo. Held commn. Air Service, U.S.A., World War. Fellow Am. Geog. Soc. Dir. Eastport (Me.) Summer Sch. of Art and Geo. Pearse Ennis Sch. of Painting (New York). Wrote: Making Water Colour, 1933. Home: New York, N.Y. Died Aug. 28, 1936.

ENNIS, Luna May, author; b. Martinsville, Ind.; d. late Judge Alfred and Almarinda (Baldridge) E.; of Scotch-English descent; ed. N.E. Conservatory of Music, Boston; Art Inst. Chicago, U. of Chicago; grad. Dearborn Sem., Chicago, Miss Anne Brown's Sch., New York. Mem. Soc. Midland Authors, Woman's City Club, Poetry Lovers of America. Episcopalian. Author: Music in Art, 1903; Our Little Danish Cousin, 1912; Our Little Boer Cousin, 1915. Home: Chicago, Ill. Deceased.

ENSIGN, Josiah Davis, lawyer; b. Boston, N.Y., May 14, 1833; s. Reuben S. and Mary Griffin (Hamburg) E.; ed. acads., Ashtabula and Trumbull cos., Ohio; m. Kate A. Jones, Sept. 4, 1858 (died 1868); m. 2d, Rose Watrous, Dec. 19, 1872. Admitted to Ohio bar, 1864; practiced at Jefferson, 6 yrs.; located in Duluth, Minn., 1870; served as co. auditor, clk. of court and pros. atty. in Ohio; mayor of Duluth, 2 terms; co. atty., St. Louis Co., Minn., 1 term; apptd. judge Dist. Ct., Apr. 28, 1889, and elected 5 times; last term expired Jan. 1, 1921. Republican. Unitarian. Home: Duluth, Minn. Died Nov. 24, 1923.

ENSIGN, Orville Hiram, electrical mech. engr.; b. Ithaca, N.Y., July 8, 1863; s. Hoffman W. and Jennie (Chambers) E.; ed. pub. and high schs., Ithaca, N.Y., and 2 yrs.' course in mech. arts, Cornell U.; m. Jennie Kirtland, Aug. 15, 1888. Machinist, Ithaca, N.Y., 1882-83; with Schenectady Locomotive Works, 1883-87; with Edison United Co., New York, in charge power plant construction for N.Y., 1887-89; with Gen. Elec. Co., Schenectady, N.Y., in charge of tests, 1889-90, chief insp. factory, 1890-93; consulting engr. Redlands (Calif.) Electric Light & Power Co., and in other miscellaneous pvt. work on telephone patents; elec. and mech. engr. on construction and operation of power plants, Pasadena & Los Angeles Elec. Ry. and Los Angeles, Santa Monica Ry., 1894-95; supt. and chief engr. Redlands Electric Light & Power Co., 1896; supt. and chief engr., 1897, of Southern Calif. Power Co., planning and constructing 30,000-volt long distance transmission line, and when this, with other cos., was consolidated as Edison Electric Co. of Los Angeles, became supt. and chief elec. and mech. engr. until 1904; was chief elec. and mech. engr. U.S. Reclamation Service, in charge of hydroelectric power and pumping problems; now cons. engr. U.S. Reclamation Service and of Los Angeles Aqueduct Power; mfr. of carburetors. Republican. Methodist. Home: Pasadena, Calif. Died June 1, 1935.

ENTWISTLE, James, rear adm.; b. Paterson, N.J., 1937; ed. pub. schs.; entered U.S. Navy in engr. service, Oct. 1861; commd. lt., July 26, 1866; lt. comdr., Mar. 21, 1873; comdr. Jan. 31, 1888; capt., Apr. 1899; rear admiral, Apr. 1899, and retired, having reached age limit. First sea service on gunboat Aroostook in the Western Gulf Squadron under Farragut; afterward served on 21 vessels in all parts of the world; wrecked on Ashuelot in China waters, 1883; was inspector of machinery at Bath (Me.) Iron Works, 1890-95, during construction of harbor defense ram Katahdin, and gunboats Machias and Castine; asst. to gen. insp. at Morgan Iron Works, New York, during the completion of the Atlanta, Boston, Chicago and Dolphin; then at Mare Island Navy Yard, 1895; joined Asiatic Squadron at Yokohama, 1895; apptd. fleet engr., 1887, and assigned to Olympia; took part in Battle of Manila, May 1, 1898, and was highly commended by Admiral Dewey; awarded Dewey medal and recommended by Sec. of Navy and bd. of officers for advancement in numbers for meritorious services at Manila. Home: Paterson, N.J. Died 1910.

EPES, Louis Spencer, judge; b. Greenwich, Va., Jan. 12, 1882; s. Theodorick Pryor (D.D.) and Joanna Tyler (Spencer) E.; A.B., Hampden-Sydney (Va.) Coll., 1900, B.S. and A.M., 1901; LL.B., Washington and Lee U., 1908; m. Julia Pegram Bagley, Nov. 5, 1914; 1 dau., Julia Bagley. Teacher, Horner Mil. Sch., Oxford, N.C., 1901-03, West Ky. Coll., Mayfield, 1903-04, Collegiate Prep. Sch., Helena, Ark., 1904-06; admitted to Va. bar, 1907, and began practice at Lexington; practiced at Blackstone, Va., 1908-25; mayor of Blackstone, 1911-18; mem. Va. State Senate, 1920-25; mem. Va. State Corp. Commn., 1925-29; asso. justice Supreme Court of Va., 1929—, for term 1929-37. Served as pvt. U.S.A., assigned to F.A. Res. Officers Training Sch., Camp Zachary Taylor, Louisville, Ky., Nov. 5-Dec. 6, 1918. Trustee Washington and Lee U. Democrat. Presbyn. Home: Blackstone, Va. Died Feb. 14, 1935.

EPES, Sydney P., congressman; b. Nottoway Co., Va., Aug. 20, 1865; moved to Ky. when 14 years old; returned to Va., 1884, and engaged in journalism; newspaper editor and publisher several years; was chmn. Dem. County Committee, Nottoway Co.; mem. State and congl. committees; mem. gen. assembly, 1891; register land office, Va., 1895-97; member Congress, 1897—, from 4th Va. dist.; present term expiring 1901. Democrat. Home: Blackstone, Va. Died 1900.

ERB, Newman, ry. pres.; b. Breslau, Germany, June 16, 1850; s. Adolphus L. and Esther (Peck) E.; came to America, 1853; ed. pvt. and pub. schs. St. Louis, and St. Louis High Sch. Admitted to bar, 1872; practiced until 1902. Receiver Memphis, Selma & Brunswick R.R. Co. (now part of Frisco System), 1885-86; gen. atty. for Ark., Tenn. and Miss., of Kansas City, Fort Scott & Memphis R.R., 1881-86; pres. Western Telegraph Co. (absorbed by W.U. Tel. Co.), 1886-98; pres. and receiver Kansas City, Wyandotte & Northwestern R.R. Co., Kansas City & Beatrice R.R. Co. (now part of M.P. Ry.), 1887-92; receiver Chattanooga Southern R.R. Co.; v.p. Meridan & Conn. R.R. Co. (now part of N.Y.,N.H.&H. R.R Co.), 1892; v.p. Pere Marquette R.R. Co., Detroit, 1895-98; pres. and constructed St. Louis, Memphis & Southeastern R.R. (now part of Frisco System), 1896-98; pres. and dir. Wis. Central Ry. Co., Dec. 1908-Apr. 1909; pres. Ann Arbor R.R. Co., Manistique & Lake Superior R.R. Co., R.R. Securities Co.; chmn. Middletown & Unionville R.R. Co.; v.p. New Dominion Copper Co. Home: New York, N.Y. Died Mar. 25, 1925.

ERICKSON, Alfred William, advertising; b. Farmers Mills, N.Y., Oct. 15, 1876; s. John and Marie Louise (Eken) E.; grad. high sch., Brooklyn, N.Y.; m. Anna Edith McGrann, Sept. 7, 1900. In advertising dept., Cleveland Baking Powder Co., 1890-99, Royal Baking Powder Co., 1899-1900; advt. mgr. Jas. McCutchen Co., 1900-02; established Erickson Advt. Agency, 1902, merged with H. K. McCann Co., 1930; chmn. McCann-Erickson, Inc., 1930—; chmn. bd. Congoleum-Nairn, Inc.; chmn. exec. com. Technicolor, Inc.; mem. exec. com. Bon Ami Co. Founder and now chmn. Desert Sanatorium and Inst. of Research, Tucson, Ariz.; business mgr. Vigilantes; trustee Roosevelt Memorial Assn. Republican. Conglist. Home: New York, N.Y. Died Nov. 2, 1936.

ERICSON, Charles John Alfred, banker; b. nr. Vimmerby, province of Kalmer, Sweden, Mar. 8, 1840; s. Erik Nelson and Carrie Clemetson (Nelson) E.; ed. in common schs. of Sweden and U.S.; (LL.D., Augustana Coll., 1902); m. Nellie Linderblood, Nov. 8, 1873 (died 1899). Came to U.S., 1852; resided in Rock Island and Knox cos., Ill., 1852-59, removing to Boone Co., Ia., 1859, engaging in merchandising and live stock business at Mineral Ridge, until 1870, then in business at Boone, Ia.; pres. City Bank of Boone, Ia. In 1901 built memorial library and presented to city of Boone; was instrumental in securing large park for Augustana Coll., Rock Island, Ill., named Ericson Park. Mem. Ia. Ho. of Rep., 14th Legislature; Senate, 26th, 27th, 30th, 31st and 32d Gen. Assemblies (now serving). Pres. bd. trustees Ericson Memorial Library. Presbyn. Home: Boone, Ia. Died 1910.

ERICSON, John Ernst, engineer; b. Stockholm Co., Sweden, Oct. 21, 1858; s. Andrew and Sophia (Lind) E.; C.E., Royal Poly. Inst., Stockholm, 1880; m. Inez Malmgren, July 11, 1888 (died 1893); m. 2d, Esther Malmgren, June 30, 1896; 1 dau., Mildred D. (Mrs. Ralph Haven Quinlan). Bridge constr. in Stockholm, 1880-81; came to U.S., 1881; resident engineer, T.,C.&St.L. (Clover Leaf) R.R. until Apr. 1882; designer Hopkins & Co., bridge builders, St. Louis, summer of 1882; on U.S. Govt. canal surveys (Ill. and Miss. Canal) until summer of 1883; draftsman, City Hall, Chicago, 1884-86; asst. engr., 1886-89; asst. chief engr., designing $2,000,000 water works for Seattle, Wash., 1889-90; asst. engr., Sanitary Dist. of Chicago, 1890-92; asst. engr., tunnel work, etc., City of Chicago, 1892-93; first asst. city engr., 1893-97, city engr., July 6, 1897—. Mem. Bd. Local Improvements, Chicago, July 1, 1903-Apr. 12, 1904, having leave of absence as city engr.; chmn. Chicago Subway and Harbor Commn. Decorated Royal Order of Vasa, Sweden, 1909. Progressive Democrat. Mason. Home: Chicago, Ill. Died Apr. 16, 1927.

ERIKSSON, Erik McKinley, prof. history; b. Odebolt, Ia., Apr. 21, 1896; s. Erik and Maria (Matson) E.; A.B., State U. of Ia., 1920, A.M., 1921, Ph.D., 1922 (jr. fellow in history); m. Minnie Louise Reuber, June 16, 1921; children—Lois Minnie, Margaret Helen, Robert McKinley, Mary Louise. Prof. history and head of dept., Lombard Coll., Galesburg, Ill., 1922-25; instr. Am. history, Ia. State Teachers' Coll., Cedar Falls, summer, 1922; research asso. State Hist. Soc. of Ia., summers 1923-24; lecturer Am. history, State U. of Ia., summer 1925; prof. Am. history and head of dept., Coe Coll., Cedar Rapids, Ia., 1925-29; asso. prof. history, U. of Southern Calif., 1929-37, prof., 1937—. Historian of Coe Coll., 1927-29. Capt. Inactive Reserve, U.S. Army. Presbyterian. Mason. Author: Official Newspaper Organs and the Presidential Elections of 1828, 1832 and 1836, 1925; Federal Civil Service Under President Jackson, 1927; Founders of Coe College—Dr. E. R. Burkhalter, 1927; History of Scottish Rite Masonry in Cedar Rapids, 1928; (with J. Hugo Tatsch) Morgan Affair and Anti-Masonry, 1928; Cedar Rapids Collegiate Institute, 1928; Parsons Seminary, 1929; Coe Collegiate Institute, 1930; American Constitutional History (with D. N. Rowe), 1933; Constitutional Basis for Judging the New Deal (with T. H. Steele), 1936; The Supreme Court and the New Deal, 1940. Syndicate writer "You and Your Nation's Affairs," 287 daily newspapers, 1936-39, radio commentator "Government in Action," 1936-37. Died May 22, 1941.

ERLANGER, Abraham Lincoln, theatrical mgr.; b. Buffalo, May 4, 1860; s. Leopold and Regina E.; ed. Cleveland pub. schs. Mem. Klaw & Erlanger; pres. Los Angeles-Biltmore Amusement Corp.; v.p. East River Safe Deposit Co.; dir. Broadway Assn. Died Mar. 7, 1930.

ERLANGER, Mitchell Louis, judge; b. Buffalo, N.Y.; s. Leopold and Regina E.; pub. sch. edn., self-taught in classics; LL.B., Columbia; unmarried. Sheriff New York Co., 1904, 05, effecting many reforms and secured release of many prisoners; justice Supreme Ct., N.Y., 1st Dist., terms 1907-27, retired Dec. 31, 1927, and apptd. official referee for life. Democrat. Home: New York, N.Y. Died Aug. 30, 1940.

ERMENTROUT, Daniel, congressman, lawyer; b. Reading, Pa., Jan. 24, 1837; ed. public schools, Franklin and Marshall Coll., and Elmwood Inst., (Norristown, Pa.); admitted to Pa. bar, 1859; dist. atty. Berks Co., Pa., 1862-65; city solicitor, Reading, 1867-70; State senator, 1873-80; mem. bd. of school control, Reading, for many years; mem. Pa. statuary commn., 1877; member Congress, 1881-89, and 1897—; term expiring 1901. Democrat. Home: Reading, Pa. Died 1899.

ERNSBERGER, Millard Clayton, mechanical engr.; b. Varick, N.Y., June 12, 1862; s. Daniel W. and Hannah (Warne) E.; A.B., U. of Rochester, 1888; M.E., Sibley Coll. (Cornell U.), 1908; unmarried. Admitted to N.Y. bar, 1891, and practiced at N.Y. City until 1897; mgr. illustrating depts. New York Tribune 2 yrs.; draftsman and designing engr. with MacIntosh, Seymour & Co., steam engines, Auburn, N.Y., 1899-1906; asst. and instr. in power engring., Sibley Coll. until 1909; prof. mech. engring., U. of Rochester, 1909-21; prof. heat-power engring., Sibley Sch. Mech. Engring., Apr. 30, 1921—. Home: Ithaca, N.Y. Died Jan. 25, 1940.

ERNST, Bernard Morris Lee, lawyer; b. Uniontown, Ala., Mar. 17, 1879; s. Moritz Leopold and Cornelia (Pake) E.; student Coll. City of New York, 1893-97; A.B., Columbia, 1899; LL.B., Columbia Law Sch., 1903; mem. University debating teams 5 yrs.; m. Roberta Christine Claus, Aug. 4, 1908; children—Cornelia Pake, Eleanor, Richard Charles. Began as clk. in law office of James, Schell & Elkus, N.Y. City, 1903; member Ernst, Cane & Berner; has specialized in law of copyright; pres. Sphinx Publishing Corp., Peter Minuit Corp., Hale Realty Corp., Canebrake Realty Co. Chmn. Legal Draft Bd., World War; mem. mayor's com. to welcome distinguished visitors. Trustee Fedn. of Jewish Philanthropic Socs., City of New York; sec. and trustee Ednl. Alliance, and chmn. nominating com. Surprise Lake Camp (philanthropic instns.); mem. council Met. League of Jewish Community Assns. Life mem., pres. Soc. of Am. Magicians, 1926—, succeeding Houdini; owner of Houdini's pvt. papers and correspondence; has given over 50 performances in magic; collector of books, periodicals, etc., on magic; mem. various Am. and European magical socs. Republican. Jewish religion. Co-author: Houdini's Magic, 1932; Houdini's Diaries, 1932. Editor: Houdini-Doyle Correspondence, 1932. Home: New York, N.Y. Died Nov. 28, 1938.

ERNST, George Alexander Otis, lawyer; b. Cincinnati, O., Nov. 8, 1850; s. Andrew Henry and Sarah H. (Otis) E.; bro. of Oswald Herbert and Harold Clarence E.; A.B., Harvard, 1871, LL.B., 1873; m. Jeanie C. Bynner, Dec. 11, 1879. Mem. Mass. Ho. of Rep., 1883-84, Boston Sch. Bd., 1901-03, Boston Finance Commn., 1907-08, which drafted the new Boston charter; dir. municipal research for present Boston Finance Commn., June, 1910—. Republican. Unitarian. Author: Law of Married Women in Massachusetts, 1897. Home: Jamaica Plain, Mass. Died June 13, 1912.

ERNST, Harold Clarence, bacteriologist; b. Cincinnati, O., July 31, 1856; s. Andrew Henry and Sarah H. (Otis) E.; bro. of Oswald Herbert and George Alexander Otis E.; A.B., Harvard, 1876, M.D.,

1880, A.M., 1884; m. Ellen Lunt Frothingham, Sept. 20, 1883. Demonstrator bacteriology, 1885-89, instr., 1889-91, asst. prof., 1891-95, prof., 1895—, Harvard; chmn. of visiting staff Children's Hospital. Editor Jour. of Med. Research, 1896—. Fellow Am. Acad. Arts and Sciences (councilor), Assn. Am. Pathologists and Bacteriologists (sec. 1901-08 and 1909—, pres. 1908-09), Mass. Med. Soc. Author: Infectiousness of Milk, 1896; Infection and Immunity, 1898; Animal Experimentation, 1902; Modern Theories of Bacterial Immunity, 1902. Home: Boston, Mass. Died Sept. 7, 1922.

ERNST, Henry, theologian; b. Anspach-Uringen, Germany, May 17, 1842; s. John and Katharine (Henrioi) E.; ed. Anspach-Uringen, Germany, 1848-56; acad. edn., Frankfort, Germany, and Ft. Wayne, Ind., 1856-62; grad. Concordia Sem., St. Louis; (D.D., Capital U., of Columbus, O.); m. Albertine Krahn, Feb. 23, 1868. Entered Lutheran ministry, 1865; mem. Mo. Synod until 1881; Synod of Ohio, 1881-84; pres. and prof. theology, Lutheran Sem., St. Paul, Jan. 5, 1885, dean theol. dept. Home: St. Paul, Minn. Died Aug. 9, 1929.

ERNST, Oswald Herbert, major general U.S. Army; b. near Cincinnati, O., June 27, 1842; s. Andrew Henry and Sarah H. (Otis) E.; attended Harvard, 1858-60; grad. U.S. Mil. Acad., 1864; m. Elizabeth Amory, d. W. R. Lee, of Roxbury, Mass., Nov. 3, 1866; children—Helen Amory, Mrs. Elizabeth Lee Grinnell. First lt. engrs., June 13, 1864; promoted through grades to rank of maj. gen., Aug. 29, 1916. Brevetted captain, Mar. 13, 1865, for faithful and meritorious services. Served asst. chief engr. Army of Tenn., to close of Atlanta campaign; asst. engr. on fortifications Pacific Coast, 1864-68; astronomer with U.S. commn. to observe solar eclipse in Spain, 1870; instr. practical mil. engring., mil. signaling and telegraphy, West Point, 1871-78; engr. in charge of Western river improvements, 1878-86; in charge of harbor improvements on Tex. coast, 1886-89, where he inaugurated the great work which resulted in deepening the channel at the entrance to Galveston harbor from 12 to 26 feet; engr. on numerous bds., 1880-1906; in charge pub. bldgs. and grounds, Washington, 1889-93; supt. U.S. Mil. Acad., 1893-98; served in war against Spain, going to P.R., July 1898; had immediate command of the troops in the affair of Coamo, Aug. 9; mem. Isthmian Canal Commn., 1899-1901, and 1905, 1906; pres. Miss. River Commn., 1903-06; mem. Internat. Commn. upon the condition and use of waters adjacent to boundary lines between U.S. and Can., 1903-15; retired, June 27, 1906. Author: Manual of Practical Military Engineering, etc. Home: Washington, D.C. Died Mar. 21, 1926.

ERNST, Richard Pretlow, senator; b. Covington, Ky., Feb. 28, 1858; s. William and Sarah (Butler) E.; Covington and Chickerings acads., Cincinnati; B.A., Centre Coll., 1878, later LL.D.; LL.B., U. of Cincinnati, 1880; m. Susan Brent, 1886; children—Sarah (Mrs. John Palmer Darnall), William. Admitted to bar, 1880, and entered practice at Covington and Cincinnati; U.S. senator from Ky., 1921-27. Republican. Long active in ednl. and ch. work; trustee Centre Coll., Pikeville Coll., Chicago, Lane, Cincinnati, Louisville Presbyn. theol. sems. Elder First Presbyn. Church, Covington, Kentucky. Died April 13, 1934.

ERSKINE, Albert Russel, pres. Studebaker Corp.; b. Huntsville, Ala., Jan. 24, 1871; s. William Michael and Ursula Dudley (Ragland) E.; ed. pub. and private schs.; C.P.A., Conn., 1908, LL.D., U. of Notre Dame, 1924; m. Annie Lyell Garland, 1903; 1 son, Albert Russel. With American Cotton Co., St. Louis, later New York, as general auditor and manager operating depts., supervising 300 cotton gins in the South, 1898-1904; treas. Yale & Towne Mfg. Co., 1904-10; v.p. Underwood Typewriter Co., 1910-11; joined Studebaker Corp. as treas. and mem. exec. com., 1911, 1st v.p., 1913, pres. 1915—; pres. Studebaker Corp. America, Studebaker Corp. of Can.; chmn. bd. and pres. Pierce Arrow Motor Car Co. Pres. bd. lay trustees U. of Notre Dame; dir. and chmn. of War Chest, South Bend, Ind., 1917-19; pres. South Bend Council of Boy Scouts of America, 1924; mem. City Plan Commn., South Bend, 1922-26. Presbyn. Home: South Bend, Ind. Died July 1, 1933.

ERSKINE, Ebenezer, Presbyn. clergyman; b. Ridley Park, Pa., Jan. 31, 1821; grad. Jefferson Coll., 1843; Princeton Theol. Sem., 1848 (D.D., Centre Coll., 1869); held pastorates at Phila., 1849-51; Columbia, Pa., 1851-57; Sterling, Ill., 1858-64; edited Northwestern Presbyterian, Chicago, 1865-69; pastor Big Spring Presbyn. Ch., Newville, Pa., 1870—; dir. of McCormick Theol. Sem., Chicago, 1864-69; from 1878 a dir. Princeton Theol. Sem. Mem. of com. of conf. with Southern Presbyn. Ch., 1873; chmn. of com. on revision in Assembly of 1890; mem. of revision com., 1890-93. Moderator Synod of Harrisburg and Synod of Pa. Home: Newville, Pa. Died 1902.

ERSKINE, Emma Payne, author; b. Racine, Wis., May 10, 1854; d. Alfred and Olive (Child) Payne; ed. at home; m. Charles Edwin Erskine, Apr. 8, 1873 (died 1908). Now engaged in designing and home-building on own land at Tryon, N.C.; pres. Holly Co. Episcopalian. Author: The Mountain Girl (novel), 1912; Joyful Heatherby (novel), 1913; The Eye of Dread (novel), 1913; A Girl of the Blue Ridge, 1914. Address: Tryon, N.C. Died Mar. 5, 1924.

ERVING, William Gage, surgeon; b. Hartford, Conn., Aug. 11, 1877; s. Henry Wood and Mary Ella (Gage) E.; B.A., Yale, 1898; M.D., Johns Hopkins, 1902; m. Emma Lootz, Sept. 19, 1903. Practiced, Washington, 1904—; prof. orthopedic surgery, Howard U., and Georgetown U.; attending orthopedic surgeon to Providence, Children's and Georgetown University hospitals. Major M.C. U.S. Army, on active service, May 1917-Apr. 1919. Fellow Royal Geog. Soc. England, Am. Coll. Surgeons. Home: Washington, D.C. Died May 10, 1923.

ERWIN, Guy Burton, lawyer; b. Mt. Pleasant, Minn., June 20, 1872; s. Richard R. and Margaret Isabelle (Reading) E.; high sch. and business coll., student Chicago Sch. of Law, 1903-04; m. Lillian M. Coyle, Oct. 16, 1895. Began practice at Fairbanks, Alaska, 1905; U.S. commr. and probate judge, 1906-08; U.S. dist. atty., Div. 4, Alaska, 1921-24. Mem. Minn. N.G. 6 yrs.; mem. advisory bd. Selective Service and four-minute man, World War. Republican. Christian Scientist. Mason. Home: Fairbanks, Alaska. Died May 15, 1929.

ERWIN, James Brailsford, army officer; b. Savannah, Ga., July 11, 1856; s. Robert and Mary Ann (Gallaudet) E.; student Trinity Coll., Hartford, Conn., 1872-75 (B.S., 1917); grad. U.S. Military Academy, 1880; hon. grad. Inf. and Cav. Sch., Fort Leavenworth, Kan., 1883; m. Isabel Doan, June 27, 1883. Commd. 2d lt. 4th Cav., June 12, 1880; promoted through grades to brig. gen., N.A., Aug. 20, 1917. Participated in Indian campaigns, 1885-86; supt. Yellowstone Nat. Park, 1897-98; in P.I., 1898-1903; in charge relief work, Oakland, Calif., after San Francisco earthquake, 1906; adj. gen., Sept. 1915-Aug. 1916; comdg. 9th Cav., Aug. 19-Dec. 27, 1916; comdg. 7th Cav., Dec. 27, 1916-Aug. 1917, and in punitive expdn. in Mexico; comdg. 157th Depot Brigade, Camp Gordon, Ga., Aug. 25-Nov. 16, 1917; comdg. 82d Div., Nov. 17-Dec. 27, 1917; assigned to 12th Brigade, 6th Div., Dec. 27, 1917; comdg. U.S. troops, Ft. Oglethorpe and Chickamauga Park, Ga., and 6th (regular) Div., Dec. 28, 1917; comd. 6th Div., A.E.F., France, until Sept. 1918; comd. 12th Brig., 6th Div., until Dec. 15, 1918, taking part in two major offensives; comd. 92d Div., Dec. 15, 1918, to its demobilization, Feb. 1919; comd. El Paso Dist., Mar. 27-Sept. 1, 1919, and ordered troops across boundary, attacking Villistas to protect lives and property of citizens of El Paso, June 15-16, 1919; remanded to regular rank of col. of cav. and assigned to 6th Cav., Sept. 7, 1919. Episcopalian. Mason. Died July 10, 1924.

ERWIN, Richard Kenney, judge; b. Adams County, Ind., July 11, 1860; s. David and Mary Ellen (Need) E.; ed. dist. sch. and one term at Methodist Coll., Ft. Wayne, Ind.; m. Luella A. Wass, Jan. 17, 1883. Admitted to Ind. bar, 1886; mem. Ind. Ho. of Rep. 2 terms, 1891, 93 (Dem. caucus chmn. last session); county atty., Adams County, Ind., 1889-97; judge 26th Jud. Circuit, Ind., 1901-07; elected justice Sup. Ct., Nov., 1912, by 120,330 plurality (largest plurality ever given any man in Ind.); term expired 1919. Democrat. Methodist. Mason. Home: Fort Wayne, Ind. Died Oct. 4, 1917.

ERWIN, Robert Gallaudet, ry. official, lawyer; pres. Atlantic Coast Line R.R. Co. (formerly Plant system of rys. and steamships); pres. Winston & Bone Valley Ry. Co.; dir. Louisville & Nashville R.R. Co., Charleston Terminal Co., Belt Line Ry. (Montgomery, Ala.), Peninsular & Occidental Steamship Co. Died 1906.

ESBERG, Milton Herman; b. San Francisco, Calif., May 17, 1875; s. Mendel and Matilda (Hirschfeld) E.; B.Litt., U. of Calif., 1896; m. Caroline Sloss Lilienthal, May 1, 1901; children—Milton Henry, Ernest L. Vice-pres. Gen. Cigar Co., New York; dir. Pacific Lighting Corp., Southern Calif. Gas Corp., Pacific Portland Cement Co., Southern Pacific Golden Gate Ferries, Investment Properties Corp. Chmn. purchase bd. Q.M. Dept., San Francisco div., and mem. bd. contract rev., Q.M.C., 1917-18. Mem. exec. com. Golden Gate Internat. Expn. (1939). Cavaliere, Order Crown of Italy. Republican. Home: San Francisco, Calif. Died July 19, 1939.

ESCH, John Jacob, congressman, Interstate Commerce commr.; b. Norwalk, Wis., Mar. 20, 1861; s. Henry and Matilda E.; A.B., U. of Wis., 1882, LL.B., 1887; m. Anna Herbst, Dec. 24, 1889; children—Irene (Mrs. V. K. Tremblett), Marie (Mrs. Donald Moore), Ruth (Mrs. Paul Gatterdam), Anna (Mrs. Harold R. Hall), John, Mark, Margaret (Mrs. John O. Weaver). Admitted to bar, 1887, and began practice at La Crosse, Wis.; mem. Esch, Kerr, Taylor & Shipe, Washington, until 1938. Was capt. Cos. I and M, 3d Wis. N.G.; judge-advocate-gen., with rank of col., 1894-96. Mem. 56th to 66th Congresses (1899-1921), 7th Wis. Dist.; mem. Interstate Commerce Commn., 1921-28; joint author with Sen. Cummins of Iowa of "Transportation Act, 1920." Pres. Assn. Practitioners Before Interstate Commerce Commn., 1931; pres. Am. Peace Soc., 1930-38. Republican. Home: La Crosse, Wis. Died Apr. 27, 1941.

ESCHWEILER, Franz Chadbourne, judge; b. Houghton, Mich., Sept. 6, 1863; s. Carl Ferdinand and Hannah Lincoln (Chadbourne) E.; student State U. of Ia., 1881-83; student U. of Mich. 6 mos., 1885-86; m. Ida C. Kindt, June 12, 1895; children—Elaine K., John (dec.), Paul C., Mary. Admitted to Wis. bar, 1889, and practiced in Milwaukee; judge Circuit Court, Milwaukee County, 1910-16; justice Supreme Court of Wis., 1916—. Catholic. Home: Madison, Wis. Died Nov. 14, 1929.

ESHLEMAN, John Morton, lawyer; b. Villa Ridge, Ill., June 14, 1876; s. William J. and Rachel Elizabeth (Kelly) E.; A.B., U. of Cal., 1902, A.M., 1903; m. Elizabeth Ledgett, Sept. 5, 1906. Admitted to bar, 1905; mem. Legislature, Calif., 1907; dist. atty., Imperial County, Calif., 1907-10; pres. R.R. Commission, Calif., 1911-14. Progressive. Mason. Home: El Centro, Calif. Died Feb. 29, 1916.

ESKRIDGE, J. T., physician; grad. Jefferson Med. Coll., 1875; was post-grad. instr. nervous diseases in same; consulting alienist and neurologist, Arapahoe County Hosp.; neurologist St. Luke's Hosp., Denver; pres. Colo. State Bd. Commrs. for the Insane. Home: Denver, Colo. Died 1902.

ESLICK, Edward Everett, congressman; b. Giles County, Tenn., April 19, 1872; s. Merritt and Martha Virginia (Abernathy) E.; ed. Bethel Coll., Russellville, Ky.; m. Willa McCord Blake, June 6, 1906. Lawyer; mem. 69th to 72d Congresses (1925-33), 7th Tenn. Dist. Democrat. Home: Pulaski, Tenn. Died June 14, 1932.

ESLING, Charles Henry Augustine, lawyer, author; b. Philadelphia, Pa., 1845; s. Joseph Jeremiah and Mary Anna (Holahan) E.; ed. St. Joseph's Coll., Phila. and Georgetown Univ., D.C.; grad. law dept., Univ. of Pa., 1882 (A.M., Georgetown, 1889, LL.D., St. Joseph's Coll., 1901); m. Elizabeth, d. Charles Baeder, Jenkintown, Pa., Apr. 10, 1890. Admitted to bar, 1869; represented archbishop of Baltimore and the Catholic laity of U.S. at Golden Jubilee of Pope Pius IX, 1877, and received bronze jubilee medal. Del. to Lay Catholic Congresses of U.S., Baltimore, 1889, and Chicago, 1893. Extensive traveler in America and in Europe, where he has resided, 1896—; foreign mem. of Royal Court of Saxony; lecturer. Treas. Law Alumni Soc., Univ. of Pa., 1894-96; founder and 1st pres. De Sales Inst., Phila. Author: Melodies of Mood and Tense, 1894. Translator: Life of St. Germaine Cousin, Shepherdess of Pibrac (from Italian); Legends of the Madonna (from French). Died 1907.

ESTABROOK, Arthur F., banker; b. Boston, Mass., May 17, 1847; s. James A. and Louisa (Hill) E.; ed. at Belmont, Mass.; m. Ida Fletcher, Oct. 8, 1874. Sr. mem. Estabrook & Company, bankers. V.p. Real Estate Exchange and Auction Bd., N.E. Conservatory of Music; trustee Clark U., Worcester, Mass., Brewster Free Acad. (Wolfboro, N.H.), Mass. Gen. Theol. Library (treas.); member corp. Mass. Inst. Tech.; treas. Homœ. Hosp. Republican. Unitarian. Home: Swampscott, Mass., and Boston, Mass. Died July 27, 1919.

ESTABROOK, Fred Watson, capitalist; b. Grafton, Mass., Sept. 23, 1852; s. John Watson and Julia Ann (Howe) E.; ed. pub. schs., Grafton and Marlboro, Mass., Bryant and Stratton Business Coll., Boston; m. Alice Sawyer, Nov. 5, 1879 (dec.). V.p. Sioux City (Ia.) Stock Yards Co. Mem. Rep. Nat. Com., 1908-28. Home: Nashua, N.H. Died Aug. 19, 1939.

ESTABROOK, Henry Dodge, lawyer; b. Alden, N.Y., Oct. 23, 1854; s. Experience and Caroline Augusta (Maxwell) E.; removed to Neb. (of which Territory his father was apptd. atty.-gen.) 1855; ed. Omaha pub. schs.; LL.B., Washington U., 1875; m. Clara Campbell, Oct. 23, 1880. Practiced at Omaha, 1875-96, Chicago, 1896-1902; mem. Lowden, Estabrook & Davis; solicitor Western Union Telegraph Co., at New York, Sept. 1902-Feb. 1911; became mem. Noble, Estabrook & McHarg. Republican. Home: Tarrytown, N.Y. Died Dec. 22, 1917.

ESTABROOK, Leon Moyer, statistician; b. Rockford, Ill., Mar. 24, 1869; s. John Otis and Emma (Brown) E.; grad. N. Tex. Business Coll., 1890; student Berlitz Sch. of Langs. and Corcoran Scientific Sch. (George Washington U.), Washington, D.C.; LL.B., Georgetown Law Sch., 1897; m. Nellie Louise Melling, June 7, 1902; children—Thelma Lee, Otis Woodrow (adopted). Farmer, teacher and stenographer; clk. War Dept., 1895-1903; stenographer Bur. Plant Industry, Dept. of Agr., 1904-05; organized central accounting office same, 1905, and in charge records, 1905-08; asst. in charge office of seed distribution, 1909-13; chief clk. Dept. of Agr., July-Sept. 1913; statistician and chief Bur. of Crop Estimates, 1913-21; became asso. chief Bur. Agrl. Economics, 1921, U.S. Dept. Agr.; reorganizing agrl.

dept., Argentina, 1923-24; dir. of World Agrl. Census, Internat. Inst. of Agr., Rome; asst. to dir. of scientific work, U.S. Dept. of Agr., 1930-31; retired. U.S. del. to Gen. Assembly, Internat. Inst. of Agr. at Rome, Nov. 1920; sec. gen. Inter-Am. Conf. on Agr., Forestry and Animal Industry, Washington, D.C., 1930. Home: Frederick, Md. Died 1937.

ESTEE, James Borden, investments, lawyer; b. Milton, Wis., Feb. 8, 1856; s. Henry and Lucretia (Green) E.; grad. Peoria County (Ill.) Normal Sch., 1875, and State Normal Univ., Normal, Ill., 1881; granted life teacher's certificate Wis., 1880, Ill., 1881; studied at U. of Valparaiso, Ind., and Milton (Wis.) Coll.; LL.B., Am. Extension U., 1926, Nat. U. Law Sch., 1927, LL.M., 1928, J.D. and S.J.D., 1929; A.B., Nat. Univ. Sch. of Economics and Govt., 1929; m. Adelaide Gillan, Aug. 16, 1883; children—Rush Gillan, Wanda Elizabeth, Loraine Borden, Marjora Adelaide. Was teacher, prin. and supt. schs. in Ill., 1874-82; life ins. business, Madison, Wis., 1882-84; real estate business, and pres. Citizens Bank, Woonsocket, S.D., 1884; apptd. clk. Dist. Court and U.S. court commr., 1884; elected dir. and supt. agencies Iowa Life Ins. Co., June 1888; gen. mgr. for Wis. for Nat. Life Ins. Co. of Vt., 1891, supt. agencies, 1898, dir., 1901, and 2d v.p. same, 1902-11. Has been chmn. Rep. Co. Central Com. and mem. Rep. State Central Com.; supt. U.S. Census returns in S.D.; mayor of Montpelier, Vt., 2 terms, 1912-14; apptd. mem. Vt. Ednl. Commn., 1912, Vt. State Fair Commn., 1914 (pres. 1914-24); practices in Montpelier and Washington, D.C.; exec. com. Montpelier Pub. Safety Com., 1917-18; pres. Montpelier Bd. Trade, 1916, 17. Mem. Vt. Legislature, 1919-21, Vt. Senate, 1921-23. Mason. Home: Montpelier, Vt. Died July 11, 1933.

ESTEE, Morris M., lawyer, author; long active in Calif. politics; Rep. candidate for gov. Calif., 1882; defeated by Gen. George Stoneman; candidate for U.S. senator, 1899; permanent chmn. Nat. Rep. Conv., Chicago, 1888. Author: Estee's Pleadings and Forms, etc. Home: San Francisco, Calif. Died 1903.

ESTERLINE, Blackburn, lawyer; b. Clark County, O., Aug. 5, 1877; s. Adam and Mary Lavina (Winget) E.; ed. high sch. and pvt. sch., Springfield, O.; LL.B., Nat. Law Sch., Washington, D.C., 1902; spl. courses in internat. and constl. law, Columbian (now George Washington) U., 1902-04; unmarried. Admitted to D.C. bar, 1902, Ill. bar, 1904; practiced in office of Frederick S. Winston and John Barton Payne, Chicago; apptd. spl. asst. to atty. gen. of U.S., 1911, and assigned to enforcement of acts to regulate commerce; apptd. asst. solicitor gen. of U.S., Oct. 1921. In handling 172 Government equity cases in three-judge Federal courts, has personally appeared and argued before 149 circuit and district judges throughout U.S.; appeared in 119 cases before Supreme Court of U.S. Chief counsel for U.S. Govt. in suit brought, 1922, at Chicago vs. 400,000 striking railroad shopmen and their officers who were enjoined by Judge Wilkerson from conspiring to hinder and obstruct commerce and carriage of mails. Republican. Presbyn. Home: Washington, D.C. Died Oct. 21, 1928.

ESTERLY, Calvin Olin, prof. zoology; b. Fort Stockton, Tex., Aug. 1, 1879; s. Calvin and Alice Medora (Olin) E.; A.B., U. of Calif., 1902; A.M., 1904, Le Conte fellow, 1904-05; Ph.D., Harvard, 1907; m. Ruth Elizabeth Orgren, July 15, 1909. Asst. in zoology, Harvard, 1906-07; prof. zoology, Occidental Coll., Los Angeles, Calif., 1907—; zoologist, Scripps Instn. for Biol. Research and Scripps Instn. of Oceanography, U. of Calif., 1910—. Baptist. Home: Los Angeles, Calif. Died Aug. 10, 1928.

ESTES, Dana, publisher; b. Gorham, Me., Mar. 4, 1840; ed. in public schs. (A.M., Bowdoin, 1898); m. Grace D. Coues Page, Nov. 10, 1884. Clerk in gen. store, Augusta, Me., 1855-59; in book business with Henry D. Degen & Son, Boston, 1859-61. In Union army from April 1861, until 2d battle of Bull Run, where he was 3 times wounded and disabled from further service. Re-entered book business as clerk, later as mem. Degen, Estes & Co., then with Lee & Shepard until 1872, when became partner in Estes & Lauriat, succeeded, 1898, by Dana Estes & Co., of which was head. Home: Brookline, Mass. Died 1909.

ESTES, David Foster, theologian; b. Auburn, Me., Oct. 18, 1851; s. Hiram C. (D.D.) and Sophia B. (Foster) E.; A.B., U. of Vt., 1871, A.M., 1874; grad. Newton Theol. Instn., 1874; studied U. of Göttingen, 1878-79; (D.D., U. of Vt., 1896); m. Effigene L. Galusha, May 12, 1880; 1 son, Walter Dalton. Ordained Bapt. ministry, 1874; pastor Manchester, Vt., 1874-76, Belfast, Me., 1876-78, Vergennes, Vt., 1880-83; prof. and acting pres. Atlanta Bapt. Coll., 1883-86; pastor Holden, Mass., 1886-91; prof. N.T. interpretation, Colgate U., 1891-1920, librarian, 1898-1921, retired. Author: History of Holden, Mass., 1894 (printed by town); An Outline of New Testament Theology, 1900. Home: Los Angeles, Calif. Died Feb. 19, 1926.

ESTES, Webster Cummings, mfr.; b. Port Kent, N.Y., Oct. 19, 1855; s. Elihu Beech and Hannah Smith (Meeker) E.; ed. pub. and pvt. schs.; m. Jennie Belle Carman, Dec. 5, 1883. Treas. E. B. Estes & Sons, mfrs. turned and shaped wooden work. Mem. Kings County Rep. Gen. Com. Episcopalian. Home: New York, N.Y. Deceased.

ESTES, William Lawrence, surgeon; b. on plantation near Brownsville, Tenn., Nov. 28, 1855; s. Albert Monroe and Marcia Burton Owen E.; ed. Bethel Coll., Ky., 1872-74; M.D., U. of Va., 1877; M.D., Univ. Med. Coll. (New York U.), 1878; (hon. A.M., Bethel Coll., 1893); Sc.D., Lehigh U., 1934; m. Jeanne Wynne, Oct. 5, 1881 (died 1903). Emeritus surgeon in chief, St. Luke's Hosp., Bethlehem, Pa.; lecturer on physiology and hygiene, Lehigh U., 1883-1923; chief surgeon, Lehigh Valley R.R., 1886-1904. Fellow Internat. Surg. Assn., Am. Surg. Assn., N.Y. Acad. Medicine, A.C.S. Baptist. Author: Treatment of Fractures, 1900. Home: Bethlehem, Pa. Died Oct. 20, 1940.

ESTES, William Lee, judge; b. Boston, Tex., Oct. 18, 1870; s. Benjamin Thomas and Jessie (Hicks) E.; grad. Wytheville (Va.) Mil. Acad., 1888; A.B., Hampden-Sydney Coll., Va., 1891; LL.B., Univ. of Tex., 1893; LL.D., Hampden-Sydney Coll., Va., 1926; m. Annie Poindexter Dunn, Dec. 9, 1903; children—Evelyn, Annie Dunn, Leigh (dec.). Began practice at Texarkana, Tex., 1894; mem. Hudgins & Estes, later Glass, Estes & King; dir. Texarkana Nat. Bank, etc.; U.S. Dist. judge Eastern Dist. of Tex., Feb. 18, 1920—. Formerly press. Bd. of Edn., Texarkana. Trustee of William Buchanan Foundation, Texarkana. Democrat. Presbyn. Mason. Home: Texarkana, Tex. Died June 14, 1930.

ESTEY, Stephen Sewall, clergyman; b. Calais, Me., May 20, 1861; s. R. B. and Jane E.; A.B., Oberlin, 1883, A.M., 1888; Ph.D., Wooster, 1901; spl. work in sociology, U. of Chicago; D.D., Park Coll., Parkville, Mo., 1905; LL.D. from Washburn Coll., Topeka, Kan., 1928; m. Helen Miller Rolland, Aug. 23, 1888; 1 dau., Mrs. William Macferran, Jr. Supt. pub. schs., Edgerton, O., and Humboldt, Kan., to 1895; ordained Presbyn. ministry, 1895; pastor successively 1st Ch., Independence, Kan., 1st Ch., Salina, Kan., to 1904, 1st Ch., Topeka, 1904-29 (emeritus). Trustee Emporia Coll. (Kan.), Oswego Coll., Omaha Theol. Sem.; mem. Gen. Council Presbyn. Ch., 1922-26. Republican. Mason. Home: Topeka, Kan. Died Apr. 28, 1932.

ESTILL, John Holbrook, editor and propr. Savannah Morning News, 1867—; b. Charleston, S.C., Oct. 28, 1840; ed. Savannah schs. Printer by trade. Published Savannah Evening Express, 1859. Served in Confederate army during Civil war. Married. Home: Savannah, Ga. Died 1907.

ESTOPINAL, Albert, congressman; b. Parish of St. Bernard, La., Jan. 30, 1845; ed. pub. and pvt. schs.; served in 28th and 22d La. regts., C.S.A., Jan. 1862-Mar. 1865; m. Eliska Legier, Feb. 1868. Sheriff St. Bernard Parish, 1872-76; mem. La. Ho. of Rep., 1876-1880, Senate, 1880-1900; mem. La. Constl. Conv., 1879 and 1898; lt. gov. of La., 1900-04; elected to 60th Congress to fill vacancy caused by death of Adolph Meyer; reëlected 61st to 65th Congresses (1909-19), 1st La. Dist. Democrat. Home: St. Bernard, La. Died Apr. 28, 1919.

ESTY, William, electrical engr.; b. Amherst, Mass., July 9, 1868; s. William Cole (q.v.) and Martha Ann (Cushing) E.; A.B., Amherst, 1889, A.M., 1893; B.S., Mass. Inst. Tech., 1893; m. Julia Louise Coy, June 14, 1894; children—William Cole, Lucien Coy, John Cushing. With Thomson-Houston Electric Co., Lynn, Mass., 1892-93; instr., asst. prof. and asso. prof. elec. engring., U. of Ill., 1893-1901; asst. prof., 1901-03, prof. elec. engring., 1903—, Lehigh U. Fellow Am. Inst. Elec. Engrs., A.A.A.S. Author: Alternating Current Machinery, 1911, new edit., 1920; Elements of Electrical Engineering, 2 vols. (with W. S. Franklin), 1906-07; Dynamo Laboratory Manual; Dynamos and Motors, 1909. Home: Bethlehem, Pa. Died July 6, 1928.

ESTY, William Cole, educator; b. Westmoreland (now Park Hill), N.H., Apr. 8, 1838; s. Isaac and Anna (Cole) E.; A.B., Amherst, 1860 (LL.D., 1888); Harvard, 1860-61; m. Martha Ann Cushing, July 18, 1867 (died 1887); father of William E. Teacher high sch., Salem, Mass., 1861-62; instr., 1862-65, prof. mathematics, 1865-1905, emeritus prof. mathematics and astronomy, 1905, Amherst. Republican. Conglist. Home: Worcester, Mass. Died July 26, 1916.

ETHERIDGE, Emerson, lawyer; b. Currituck County, N.C., Sept. 28, 1819; ed. at primitive school in N.C.; m. Fanny Bell, Oct. 17, 1849 (died 1854). Became a lawyer in Tenn., 1840; mem. Tenn. legislature, 1845; mem. Congress, 1853-57 and 1859-61; clerk 37th Congress, 1861-63; last Whig mem. Congress, being the only mem. of 36th Congress whose politics is given in the Congressional Globe as a "Whig;" Republican since conclusion of Civil war; defeated for gov. Tenn., 1867, by Gov. Brownlow; mem. State senate, 1869; defeated for U.S. senator, 1869; surveyor of customs at Memphis, 1891-94; resigned. Home: Dresden, Tenn. Died 1902.

EUSTIS, James, U.S. senator; b. New Orleans, La., Aug. 27, 1834; classical edn.; grad. Harvard Law School, 1854; practiced at New Orleans; served as judge-advocate Confederate army, under Gens. Magruder and Joseph E. Johnston, 1861-65; served in La. house, 1872, and senate, 1874-78; U.S. senator, 1877-79, and 1885-91; prof. civil law, Univ. of La., 1879-84; U.S. minister to France, 1893-97. Home: New Orleans, La. Died 1899.

EUSTIS, John Edward, lawyer; b. Limerick, N.Y., Jan. 17, 1847; s. Tobias and Mary (Markwick) E.; served in Co. M. 20th N.Y. Cav., 1864-65, B.S., Wesleyan Univ., Conn., 1874, LL.D., 1910; LL.B., Dwight Law Sch., New York, 1877; m. Minnie Rutty, Sept. 21, 1881 (died Jan. 6, 1892); children—John R., Mary, Sarah E., Helen F., Constance, Edwin M.; m. 2d, Permelia A. Quackenbos, May 31, 1894; children—Elmer T., Richard C. In law practice at New York from 1877; mem. Eustis, Foster & Coleman, 1891-1900, Eustis & Foster, 1900-09; mem. Eustis & Carrington, 1920-22, J. E. and E. S. Eustis, 1923—; sec., dir. Babcock & Wilcox Co., Pelham Hod Elevating Co.; dir. Manhattan Mortgage Co. School trustee 24th Ward, New York, 1882-95; sch. insp., 1895-96; sch. commr., 1896-99; park commr. Bronx Borough, 1902-04; public service commr., 1st Dist., N.Y., July 1, 1907-June 1914. Republican. Methodist. Trustee New York Skin and Cancer Hosp., Wesleyan Univ. Mason. Republican. Home: New York, N.Y. Died June 21, 1929.

EUSTIS, William H., lawyer; b. Oxbow, N.Y., July 17, 1845; s. Tobias and Mary (Marwick) E.; A.B., Wesleyan U., Conn., 1873; LL.B., Columbia Law Sch., 1874; unmarried. Practiced at Saratoga Springs, N.Y., 6 yrs.; settled in Minneapolis, Minn., 1881; one of founders, dir. and sec. North Am. Telegraph Co.; mayor of Minneapolis, 1892; del. Rep. Nat. Conv., 1892; candidate for gov. of Minn., 1898; spl. U.S. commr. to Hawaiian Islands, 1902. Methodist. Created $2,000,000 trust to be known as the Minn. Hosp. and Home for Crippled Children, for well-being of needy crippled children. Died Nov. 29, 1928.

EVANS, Alvin, congressman, lawyer; b. Ebensburg, Pa., Oct. 4, 1845; pub. sch. edn.; admitted to Pa. bar, 1873; m. Nov. 17, 1875, Kate E. Shryock (dec.). Mem. Congress, 1901-03, 20th Pa. dist., and 1903-05, 19th dist. Republican. Home: Ebensburg, Pa. Died 1906.

EVANS, Arthur Grant, univ. pres.; b. Madras, India, Sept. 9, 1858; s. Edward Josiah and Caroline (Taylor) E.; A.B., Borough Rd. Coll., London, Eng., 1879; (D.D., Henry Kendall Coll., Okla.; LL.D., U. of Okla.); m. Katherine Robb, Apr. 23, 1891. Prin. pub. schs., Earls Barton, Eng., 1879-93; came to America, 1883; prof. Cherokee Male Sem., Tahlequah, Ind. Ty., 1884-85; in charge of sch. and mission work of Presbyn. Ch. in Cherokee Nation, 1885-89; ordained Presbyn. ministry, 1887; pastor, Oswego, Kan., 1889-91, Pendleton, Ore., 1891-92; prin. Salida (Colo.) Acad., 1892-95; pastor Leadville, Colo., 1895-98; pres. Henry Kendall Coll., Muskogee, Okla., 1898-1908; pres. State U. of Okla., June, 1908-12. Del. Gen. Assembly Presbyn. Ch. in U.S., 1895, 1904, Pan-Presbyn. Council, Liverpool, 1904. Democrat. Home: Long Beach, Calif. Died Nov. 30, 1928.

EVANS, Aurelius Augustus, lawyer; b. Russell County, Ala., Dec. 24, 1862; s. John Quincy and Frances Elizabeth (Collier) E.; A.B., U. of Ala., 1885, A.M., 1892; read law at Clayton, Ala.; m. Lessie Victoria Waddell, Dec. 27, 1888. Prin. Clayton (Ala.) Male Acad., 1885-89; admitted to bar, 1889; practiced at Clayton, 1889-1898, Montgomery, 1909—. Mayor of Clayton, 1895-98; judge Circuit Ct., 3d Circuit, Ala., 1898-1909; justice Supreme Court of Ala., 1909-11; sr. mem. Evans & Friedman, 1915. Mem. State Tax Commn. of Ala., 1911-15 and 1919-23; spl. asst. atty. gen. State of Ala., 1923-27, became 1st asst. atty. gen. 1927. Home: Montgomery, Ala. Deceased.

EVANS, Beverly Daniel, judge; b. Sandersville, Ga., May 21, 1865; s. Beverly D. and Sallie (Smith) E.; A.B., Mercer U., Macon, Ga., 1881, A.M., 1882; (LL.D., 1920); studied law, Yale U., 1883-84; m. Bessie Warthen, Nov. 15, 1886 (died 1892); 2d, Jennie Irwin, July 11, 1894. Admitted to bar, 1884, and was continuously in practice until 1899. Mem. Ga. legislature, 1886-87; solicitor gen., Middle Jud. Circuit, Ga., 1890-97, judge, same circuit, 1899-1904; justice Supreme Ct. of Ga., 1904-17 (presiding justice 1907-17); resigned Aug. 31, 1917; U.S. dist. judge, Southern Dist. of Ga., Sept. 1, 1917—. Baptist. Democrat. Home: Savannah, Ga. Died May 7, 1922.

EVANS, Britton Duroc, physician; b. Bridgetown, Md., Oct. 1, 1858; s. Dr. Louis W. E.; M.D., Coll. Phys. and Surgeons, Baltimore, 1885. Med. dir. N.J. State Hosp., Morris Plains; expert in mental diseases and the medico-legal aspects of insanity. Mem. Med. and Chirurgical Faculty of Md. Died Jan. 14, 1920.

EVANS, Charles, librarian, bibliographer; b. Boston, Mass., Nov. 13, 1850; s. Charles P. and Mary (Ewing) E.; ed. Boston pub. schs.; m. Lena Young, Apr. 8, 1883; children—Gertrude (Mrs. Donald

Jones), Eliot Howland, Charles, Constance (dec.). Asst. Boston Athenæum Library, 1866-72; organized, and was librarian, Pub. Library of Indianapolis, 1872-80 and 1889-92; organized Enoch Pratt Free Library, Baltimore, and 4 of its branches, 1884-87; reorganized Omaha Pub. Library, 1887-88; classified the Newberry Library, Chicago, 1892-95; organized the Virginia Library of the McCormick Theol. Sem., Chicago, 1895-96. Author: American Bibliography, a chronol. dictionary of all books, pamphlets and period. publs. printed in U.S. of America from 1639 to 1820, of which 11 quarto vols., bringing the record down to 1798, have been issued; Oaths of Allegiance in Colonial New England, 1921. Home: Chicago, Ill. Died Feb. 8, 1935.

EVANS, Charles Rountree, lawyer; b. Lancaster, Wis., Apr. 4, 1863; s. Jonathan H. and Sarah (Kilbourne) E.; A.B., U. of Wis., 1881 (hon. A.M., 1907); admitted to bar, 1884. Located in Chattanooga, Tenn., 1885; city atty., 1887, 88, 91; Rep. candidate for judge 4th Jud. Circuit of Tenn., 1892; prof. law, 1899-1900, dean, 1901—, Chattanooga Coll. of Law. Commr. registration, 1894-95; county atty., Hamilton County, 1894-98. In Spanish-Am. War in P.R. as capt. 6th U.S. Vol. Inf., June 20, 1898; promoted maj., Jan. 7, 1899; judge-adv. of gen. court-martial P.R. and Vieques; mem. mil. court, province of Arecibo; hon. disch., Mar. 15, 1899. Rep. candidate for presdl. elector-at-large, 1900, for 62d Congress, 3d Tenn. Dist., 1910; judge 6th Jud. Circuit of Tenn., 1911-12. Judge adv. gen. State of Tenn., with rank of brig. gen., 1913-14. Died Oct. 3, 1920.

EVANS, Clement Anselm, lawyer; b. Stewart County, Ga., 1833; s. Anselm L. and Sarah Hinton (Bryan) E.; ed. pub. schs., Lumpkin, Ga.; LL.B., Ga. Law Sch., Augusta, 1853. Admitted to bar, 1853, and practiced at Lumpkin; judge County Court of Stewart County, 1855; mem. Ga. Senate, 1859-60. Served in C.S.A. as maj., col., brig. gen. and acting maj. gen., Army of Northern Va. and surrrendered with Lee. Devoted principally to lit. work. Democrat. State comdr. of Ga. Div. U.C.V. 12 yrs., dept. comdr. 3 yrs.; comdr.-in-chief U.C.V., 1909. Editor: Confederate Military History (12 vols.). Author: Military History of Georgia, 1895. Home: Atlanta, Ga. Died 1911.

EVANS, Clinton Buswell, editor, pub.; b. Fryeburg, Me., Aug. 3, 1848; s. John and Mary A. (Adams) E.; A.B., Dartmouth, 1873; m. Emma Rose Townsend, June 3, 1886. Reporter and night editor Springfield (Mass.) Republican, 1873-83; financial editor Chicago Tribune, 1883-88; established the Economist, a weekly, Oct. 20, 1888, and became pres., Economist Pub. Co. Writer for Ledger Syndicate, Phila. Republican. Presbyn. Home: Chicago, Ill. Died Mar. 21, 1923.

EVANS, Dafydd Joshua, prof. Latin; b. near Oak Hill, O., Aug. 22, 1846; s. Joshua and Margaret (Evans) E.; A.B., Ohio U., Athens, 1871, A.M., 1874; (LL.D., Lenox Coll., Hopkinton, Ia., 1914); m. Lydia Margaret Lash, Oct. 22, 1872. Prof. Latin, Union Christian Coll., Merom, Ind., 1873-80; prin. Putnam Collegiate Inst., Zanesville, O., 1880-82; prof. Latin, Ohio U., 1882-1921 (resigned). Presbyterian. Mason. Home: Athens, O. Died Jan. 4, 1926.

EVANS, Donald, author; b. Phila., Pa., July 24, 1884; s. William Penn and Anne (Idell) E.; student Haverford (Pa.) Coll., 1906; m. Esther E. Porter, Jan. 9, 1918. Asst. editor Phila. Inquirer, 1905-12, New York Times, 1912-15, Phila. Inquirer, 1915-17, True Story Magazine, 1919; mng. editor, Daily Garment News. With Med. Dept., U.S. Army, 1917-19. Republican. Episcopalian. Author: (poems) Discords, 1912; Sonnets from the Patagonian, New York, 1914, 2d edit., 1918; Two Deaths in the Bronx, 1916; Nine Poems from a Valetudinarium, 1917; Ironica, 1919. Home: New York, N.Y. Died May 26, 1921.

EVANS, Dudley; b. Morgantown, W.Va., Jan. 27, 1838; s. Rawley and Clarissa (Cox) E.; A.B., Washington (now Washington and Jefferson) Coll., 1859; capt. 20th Va. Cav., C.S.A., 1862; lt. col., 1863-65; mem. Va. Ho. of Rep., 1863-65; m. Nellie Seelye, Sept. 17, 1878. Gen. express agt. Wells Fargo & Co., Portland, Ore., 1872-82; supt. Portland office, 1882-88; v.p., 1892-1902, pres., 1902—, Wells Fargo & Co.; pres. Wells Fargo & Co.'s Bank, New York. Home: Englewood, N.J. Died 1910.

EVANS, Earle Wood, lawyer; b. near Wellington, Kan., Feb. 20, 1873; s. Frank Edward and Emma (Wood) E.; student Garfield U., Wichita, Kan., 1888-90; m. Madge Balfour, Oct. 10, 1900 (died 1915); children—Bruce Balfour, Earle W.; m. 2d, Mary Cooper, Nov. 30, 1917; 1 dau., Elizabeth. Admitted to Kan. bar, 1894, and began practice at Wichita; mem. Vermilion, Evans, Carey & Lilleston; dir. First Nat. Bank in Wichita, Chandler Nat. Bank (Lyons, Kan.), A.,T.&S.F. Ry., etc. Pres. Wichita Community Chest, 1931-32; dir. Internat. Society for Crippled Children, Kansas Soc. for Crippled Children, Wichita League for Social Work. Republican. Presbyterian. Mason. Home: Wichita, Kan. Died July 30, 1940.

EVANS, Edward, surgeon; b. Seaforth, Ont., Can., Mar. 7, 1860; s. Joseph and Mary (Doyle) E., M.D. gold medalist, McGill U., Montreal, Can., 1887; m. Sarah Thompson, Oct. 6, 1892; children—Mary Frances (dec., Mrs. Warren D. Leary), James A., Arthur R., Edward T., Jessie T., Joseph P. Began practice at Seaforth; now in practice at LaCrosse; chief of Evans Clinic; chief of staff, St. Frances Hosp.; preceptor, U. of Wis. Med. Sch. Chmn. City Bd. of Health, LaCrosse; mem. Bd. of Edn. Served as capt., Am. Red Cross, surgeon in France, 1918. Regent U. of Wis., 1902-14. Fellow Am. Coll. Surgeons, A.M.A., K.C. Democrat. Catholic. Home: LaCrosse, Wis. Died June 2, 1932.

EVANS, Elizabeth Edson, author; b. Newport, N.H., Mar. 8, 1832; d. Dr. Willard Putnam and Lucia Field (Williams) Gibson; removed to Ann Arbor, Mich., 1841; ed. in pvt. sch. Began early to write both prose and verse for newspapers; m. Edward Payson Evans, 1868. Has resided in Europe, 1870—. Author: The Abuse of Maternity, 1875; Laura, an American Girl (novel), 1884; A History of Religions, 1892; The Story of Kaspar Hauser, 1892; The Story of Louis XVII of France, 1893; Transplanted Manners (novel), 1895; Confession (novel), 1895; Ferdinand Lassalle and Helene von Dönniges, a Modern Tragedy, 1897; The Christ Myth, 1900. Died 1911.

EVANS, George Ballentine, surgeon; b. Franklin, O., Apr. 1, 1855; s. Otho and Jane E.; A.M., Hanover (Ind.) Coll.; M.D., Ohio Medical Coll. (Univ. of Cincinnati), 1878; m. Sannie Beaver, June 8, 1880. Practiced in Dayton, O., 1880—; visiting urologist and proctologist, St. Elizabeth's Hosp. Fellow Am. Coll. Surgeons. Republican. Presbyn. Home: Dayton, O. Deceased.

EVANS, George E., ry. official; b. Cambridge, O., May 2, 1856; ed. pub. schs. Began as telegraph operator B.&O. R.R., at Cambridge, 1871; with L.&N. R.R., 1873—, respectively as telegraph operator and train dispatcher till 1880, chief operator and train dispatcher Louisville div., 1880-82, master of trains, same div., 1882-85, and supt. same div., 1885-86, supt. transportation, 1886-1900, gen. mgr., 1900-05, v.p. in charge of operation, 1905—, exec. v.p., 1926—. Home: Louisville, Ky. Died Jan. 7, 1931.

EVANS, Harry Carroll; b. Bloomfield, Ia., July 14, 1858; s. Joseph Vance and Nancy Ellen (Childers) E.; student Southern Ia. Normal Sch., Bloomfield; LL.D., Columbian (now George Washington) U., 1896; m. Susan, dau. of Gen. James B. Weaver, Aug. 12, 1890; children—Alice (Mrs. M. T. Dannreuther), Clara (Mrs. R. H. Gallaher). Began newspaper work at Bloomfield, 1882; postmaster, Bloomfield, 1885-89; chief of div., U.S. Treasury Dept., 1893-97; editor Bloomfield Democrat, 1883-91; supreme officer Brotherhood of Am. Yeoman and editor Yeoman Shield, 1901—. War corr., Germany, 1916, France and Italy, 1918. Y.M.C.A. service in France, 1917-18; dir. same, Italy, 1918-19. Mem. Bd. of Edn., Des Moines, Ia., 1919-26 (pres. 1926); mem. Federal Commn. to study methods of caring for indigent poor in Europe, 1927. Dem. candidate for Congress, 1916-18. Chmn. com. on conservation of child life, Nat. Fraternal Congress, 1922-27; commr. of conciliation, U.S. Dept. of Labor, 1926. Methodist. Mason. Author: The American Poorfarm and Its Inmates, 1926; The Pioneers and Politics of Southern Iowa, 1929. Directed survey of county poor farms in U.S. Home: Des Moines, Ia. Died Apr. 1932.

EVANS, Harry G., banker; b. Baltimore, Md., Apr. 13, 1862; s. John and Mary L. (Clackner) E.; ed. pub. schs., Baltimore; m. Julia H. Ludington, Nov. 16, 1888; 1 dau., Helen L. (wife of Dr. Robert M. Lewis). Pres. Central Savings Bank of Baltimore; dir. Md. Casualty Co. (mem. exec. com.), Baltimore Equitable Soc. (mem. investing com.). Pres. bd. trustees Samuel Ready Sch. for Female Orphans. Republican. Presbyn. Home: Baltimore, Md. Died Sept. 13, 1930.

EVANS, Henry, fire ins.; b. Houston, Tex., Apr. 14, 1860; s. Col. Joseph Henry (C.S.A.) and Cora Wilbur (Taylor) E.; father died in army, Feb. 3, 1863; after war brought North; ed. pvt. sch., Brooklyn, boarding sch., Norwalk, Conn., and Sch. of Mines, Columbia Coll.; m. Mary Roland Lopez, June 21, 1892. Began in office of Continental Fire Ins. Co., Mar. 1, 1878, as minor clerk; elected sec. agency dept., May 1888, 2d, v.p., 1889, 1st v.p., 1892, pres. Jan. 15, 1903; chmn. bd. Jan. 1, 1921; also chmn. bd. Fidelity-Phoenix Fire Ins. Co., Am. Eagle Fire Ins. Co., Farmers Ins. Co.; dir., exec. com. Sloss Sheffield Coal & Iron Co.; trustee Central Union Trust Co. Home: New York, N.Y. Died Aug. 29, 1924.

EVANS, H(enry) Clay, mfr.; b. Juniata County, Pa., June 18, 1843; s. Jesse B. and Anna (Single) E.; academy edn.; (LL.D., U. of Chattanooga); enlisted 41st Wis. Inf., May 1864; m. Adelaide Durand, Feb. 18, 1869. Located at Chattanooga, Tenn., as iron and ry. car mfr. Chmn. bd. of edn. and twice mayor Chattanooga; mem. 51st Congress (1889-91), 3d Tenn. Dist.; 1st asst. postmaster gen., 1893; elected gov. Tenn., 1894, on face of returns, but a recount by legislature resulted in rejection of certain returns for alleged irregularities, and Turney, Democrat, was declared elected. Del.-at-large Rep. National Conventions, 1892-1916; was second in the balloting for v.p. of U.S., 1896; U.S. commr. of pensions, 1897-1902; Am. consul general at London, 1902-05. Trustee U. of Tenn. and Chattanooga U. Home: Chattanooga, Tenn. Died Dec. 12, 1921.

EVANS, Hiram Kinsman, congressman; b. Walnut Twp., Ia., Mar. 17, 1863; s. Hiram and Sarah Jane (Robison) E.; ed. Allerton (Ia.) High Sch.; LL.B., U. of Ia., 1886; m. Harriet Belvel, Jan. 1, 1891; children—Portia (Mrs. James D. Cooney), Genevieve (Mrs. V. Starzinger). Admitted to Ia. bar, 1886; mem. Freeland & Evans, 1891-1904; county atty. Wayne County, Ia., 1891-95; mem. Ia. Ho. of Rep., 1896-98; mayor of Corydon, 1901-03; judge 3d jud. dist., Ia., 1904-23; elected to 68th Congress (1923-1925), 8th Ia. Dist., and spl. election, June 1923, to fill vacancy; chmn. State Bd. of Parole, term 1927-33. In gen. practice of law at Corydon with his wife Harriet B. Evans. Regent State U. of Ia., 1897-1904. Republican. Methodist. Home: Corydon, Ia. Died July 9, 1941.

EVANS, Ira Hobart; b. Piermont, N.H., Apr. 11, 1844; s. Dr. Ira and Emeline (Hobart) E.; grad. Barre (Vt.) Acad., 1862; m. Frances A. Hurlbut, July 13, 1871; m. 2d, Jessie M. Stewart, Oct. 14, 1920. Enlisted as pvt. Co. B, 10th Vt. Vols., July 28, 1862; promoted 1st lt., capt. and bvt. maj. U.S. Vols.; awarded Medal of Honor by Congress "for distinguished bravery" at Hatchers Run, Va., Apr. 2, 1865; hon. mustered out Jan. 31, 1867. Asst. assessor and dep. collector U.S. internal revenue, 2d Dist., Tex., 1868, 1869; mem. and speaker Tex. Ho. of Rep., 1870, 1871; gen. mgr. Tex. Land Co., 1872-80; sec. Houston & Gt. Northern R.R. Co., 1873-74, I.&G.N. R.R. Co., 1874-80; pres. N.Y. and Tex. Land Co., Ltd., 1880-1906; agt. for sale of land formerly owned by I.&G.N. R.R. Co., 1906-21; dir. Austin Nat. Bank, 1890—; dir. I.&G.N. R.R. Co., 1875-1908; receiver Austin Rapid Transit Ry. Co., Feb. 20, 1897-May 1902; dir. and pres. Austin Electric Ry. Co., May 17, 1902-Nov. 30, 1903; has been actively identified with many other corps. in Texas. President bd. trustees Tillotson Coll., Austin, 1909-21; dir. Austin United Charities Assn., 1910-21. Moderator N. Tex. Congl. Assn., 1883-86, Lone Star Congl. Assn., 1907; 1st asst. moderator Nat. Congl. Council, 1889; pres. bd. trustees 1st Congl. Ch., Austin, 1909-21; v.p. Am. Missionary Assn., 1917-21; mem. Nat. Service Commission of the Congl. Chs., 1917-19. Republican. Home: San Diego, Calif. Died Apr. 19, 1923.

EVANS, Isaac Blair, lawyer; b. Ogden, Utah, May 22, 1885; s. Thomas Benjamin and Ruth (Blair) E.; A.B., Harvard, 1908, LL.B., 1913; m. Grace Grant, June 30, 1909; children—Mary Wells, Ruth Louise, Robert Blair. Asst. prof. history and head of dept., Utah Agrl. Coll., Logan, 1908-10; began practice at Salt Lake City, 1913; mem. Evans and Boyle, Pasadena, Calif.; asst. dist. attorney, 3d Jud. Dist., Utah, 1917-18; asst. U.S. atty. for Utah, 1918-1919; U.S. atty., 1920-21. Served as legal adviser to draft boards, as four-minute man, on Liberty Bond coms., etc. Democrat. Mason. Author: The Thomson Masonic Fraud, 1922. Home: Pasadena, Calif. Died May 7, 1941.

EVANS, James, M.D.; b. Marion, S.C., Sept. 12, 1931; s. Thomas and Jane B. E.; was in the class of 1854 at S. C. Mil. Acad., 3½ yrs., ending in 1853, but class never graduated; m. Miss M. A. Powell, 1865. Went to Ark. and was State civil engr.; served on Mississippi 5 yrs.; M.D., Univ. of Pa., 1861; surgeon 3d S.C. regt., C.S.A., 1861-65; began practice in S.C.; now sec. State bd. of health; hon. mem. Pan-Am. Med. Congress, etc. Home: Florence, S.C. Died 1909.

EVANS, Jervice Gaylord, pres. Hedding Coll., 1872-78, 1889-98—resigned; b. Wenona, Ill., Dec. 19, 1833; s. Joshua and Elizabeth Radcliffe E.; ed. at Peoria Wesleyan Sem., Judson Coll. and Onio Wesleyan Univ. (A.M., Quincy Coll.; D.D., Chaddock Coll.; LL.D. on Thesis, Chicago Coll. Sci.); m. Nettie G. Gardner, June 14, 1857. United with M. E. Ch. in 1849; in ministry, 1854—; 5 times del. to gen. conf. M. E. Ch. Mem. Centennial, Canada, 1884. Worker and writer in temperance, equal suffrage and reform movements; supt. Nat. Sociol. convocation; chmn. permanent com. of M. E. Ch. on Temperance and Prohibition. Home: Grant Park, Ill. Died 1910.

EVANS, Lawrence Boyd, lawyer, writer; b. Radnor, O., Feb. 3, 1870; nephew and adopted son of Edward Payson and Elizabeth Edson (Gibson) E.; Ph.B., U. of Mich., 1894; Ph.D., U. of Chicago, 1897; Harvard Law Sch., 1911-14; unmarried. Prof. history, Tufts Coll., 1900-12; mem. and v. chmn. commission on information for Constl. Conv. of Mass., and technical adviser to conv., 1917-19; state librarian of Mass., 1917-19; counsel to Brazilian Embassy, Washington, D.C., 1918—. Spl. counsel U.S. Shipping Bd. for codification of U.S. navigation laws, 1920-23. Pres. N.E. History Teachers' Assn., 1909-10. Nat. Conf. Church Clubs, 1912-13. Republican.

Episcopalian. Editor: Leading Cases on American Constitutional Law, 1915; Leading Cases on International Law, 1917. Died Oct. 30, 1928.

EVANS, Lawton Bryan, educator, author; b. Lumpkin, Ga., Oct. 27, 1862; s. Clement Anselm and Mary Allen (Walton) E.; grad. Richmond Acad., Augusta, Ga., 1878; student Emory Coll., Oxford, Ga., 1878-80; A.M., U. of Ga., 1881 (Phi Beta Kappa), LL.D., 1930; Pd.D., Oglethorpe Coll., 1927; LL.D. from Emory U., 1933; m. Florence Eve Campbell, Feb. 15, 1887. Teacher Richmond Acad., 1881; supt. schs., Augusta and Richmond County, Ga., Nov. 11, 1882—. Trustee Carnegie Endowment for Internat. Peace. Democrat. Methodist. Author: History of Georgia, 1898; Elements of English Language, 1908; English Grammar, 1908; Essential Facts of American History, 1923; First Lessons in American History, 1924; Our Old World Beginnings, 1927; also (juvenile books) Worth While Stories, 1916; America First, 1919; Old Time Tales, 1921; Heroes of Israel, 1922; Heroes of Troy, 1923; The Trail Blazers, 1924; The Pirate of Barataria, 1925; With Whip and Spur, 1927; With Wind and Tide, 1928; With Pack and Saddle, 1929. Awarded medal for distinguished service, Columbia University, 1933. Home: Augusta, Ga. Died Apr. 6, 1934.

EVANS, Lewis Orvis, lawyer; b. Utica, N.Y.; s. Owen and Emily Jane (Church) E.; student Cazenovia (N.Y.) Sem. 2 yrs.; studied law in office; m. Martha Nichols, Nov. 16, 1903; children—Lewis Nichols, Richard O., Elizabeth Warren. Admitted to Mont. bar, 1894, and began practice at Helena; settled in Butte, 1895; mem. Farbis & Evans, 1897-1910, alone, 1910—; gen. counsel Anaconda Copper Mining Co., Chile Copper Co., Andes Mining Co., Inspiration Consol. Copper Co., and other corps.; counsel for Montana Power Co. Republican. Methodist. Mason. Home: Butte, Mont. Died May 30, 1931.

EVANS, Milton G., theologian; b. on farm near Ebensburg, Pa., Dec. 7, 1862; s. Rev. John William and Rebecca (Bowen) E.; A.B., Bucknell U., Pa., 1882, A.M., 1885, D.D., 1895; grad. Crozer Theol. Seminary, 1890; LL.D., 1914; m. Josephine W. Rivenburg, June 24, 1890. Teacher Keystone Acad., Factoryville, Pa., 1883-87; instr. in Hebrew, 1890-95, prof. Bibl. theology, 1895-1907, prof. Christian theology, 1907-09, dean of faculty, 1906-09, pres. and prof. comparative theology, 1909-34, Crozer Theol. Sem. Home: Chester, Pa. Died Sept. 17, 1939.

EVANS, Nelson Wiley, lawyer; b. Sardinia, O., June 4, 1842; s. Edward Patton and Amanda J. (King) E.; A.B., Miami U., 1864 (hon. A.M., 1883); m. Elizabeth Henderson, Sept. 9, 1868. First lt. Co. G, 129th and 1st lt. and capt., 173d Ohio Vol. Inf., and acting asst. adj. gen., Civil War. Practiced law in Portsmouth, O., 1866—. Republican. Episcopalian. Author: History of Adams County, O., 1900; History of Scioto County, O., 1903; History of Taxation in Ohio, 1906. Home: Portsmouth, O. Died May 27, 1913.

EVANS, Richard Joseph, civil engr.; b. Washington, D.C., July 14, 1837; s. Dr. John and Sarah Zane (Mills) E.; ed. Rittenhouse Acad.; studied architecture and building under his grandfather, Robert Mills, govt. architect; m. Anais D. Lagarde, Feb. 4, 1861. Served several yrs. as aide in U.S. Coast Survey; removed to New Orleans during mil. occupation of that city; apptd. engr. New Orleans, Carrollton & Lake Pontchartrain Ry.; later chief engr. New Orleans, Opelousas & Great Western Ry.; afterward in employ of the Morgan Co. (steamship and ry. lines); devised adaptation of stern wheel steamboats for transferring loaded freight cars over Mississippi River; one of 3 engrs. apptd. to pass upon plans for the drainage of New Orleans and its protection from overflow; built and superintended Gulf, Western Tex. & Pacific Ry. to Cuero; in Bur. of Steam Engring., Navy Dept., 1875-77; took charge of engring. of terminals, New Orleans Pacific Ry., 1877; later chief engr. Memphis, Selma & Brunswick Ry.; supt. Brunswick & Western Ry. of Ga.; chief engr., 1885, v.p. and gen. mgr., 1888 to 1894, Tex., Sabine Valley & N.W. R.R.; in constrn. drainage, sewerage and water system of New Orleans, 1898—. Home: New Orleans, La. Died Dec. 30, 1916.

EVANS, Robert Emory, congressman; b. Coalmont, Pa., July 15, 1856; s. Levi and Mary (Keith) E.; student State Normal Sch., Millersville, Pa., 1876, Indiana (Pa.) Normal Sch., 1883-84; LL.B., U. of Mich., 1886; m. Annie M. Burket, Jan. 27, 1887. Learned machinist's trade; lived in Colo., 1877-83; admitted to bar in Mich., 1886, Pa., 1886, Neb., 1888, later to practice in U.S. courts; settled in Dakota City, Neb., 1887; supt. Winnegago Industrial Sch., 1889-91; county atty., Dakota County, Neb., 1895 (resigned); Judge of 8th Jud. Dist. of Neb., 1895-99; mem. 66th and 67th Congresses (1919-23), 3d Neb. Dist. Methodist. Mason. Home: Dakota City, Neb. Died July 8, 1925.

EVANS, Robert Kennon, brig. gen.; b. Jackson, Miss., Nov. 19, 1852; s. Samuel Wildes and Mary (Kennon) E.; grad. U.S. Mil. Acad., 1875; s. Jane Findlay Shunk, Nov. 11, 1880. Commd. 2d lt. 12th Inf., June 16, 1875; promoted through grades to brig. gen. Jan. 30, 1911. Served in Nez Percé and Bannock Indian campaigns, 1877-78; mil. attaché, Am. Embassy, Berlin, 1892-96; in Cuba during Spanish-Am. War and later in Philippine insurrection; chief, div. mil. affairs and asst. to the chief of staff U.S. Army 1911-12; comdg. gen. Dept. of the Gulf, Atlanta, Ga., Oct. 1, 1912-14, and comdr. 2d Brigade, 1st div., Jan. 1913-14, comdr. Dept. of the East, 1914-15, 2d Brigade, Laredo, Tex., 1915-16; retired, Nov. 19, 1916. Was exec. officer Nat. and Internat. matches, Camp Perry, Ohio, Aug. 15-Sept. 10, 1913. Ordered on active duty and comd. Philippine Dept., Manila, June 30, 1917-Sept. 5, 1918. Episcopalian. Died July 31, 1926.

EVANS, Robley Dunglison, rear adm.; b. Floyd County, Va., Aug. 18, 1846; s. Dr. Samuel Andrew Jackson E.; ed. pub. schs. of Washington; apptd. from Utah, and grad. U.S. Naval Acad., 1863; m. Charlotte, d. Franck Taylor, of Washington, 1871. Ensign, Oct. 1, 1863; lt., July 25, 1866; lt. comdr., Mar. 12, 1868; comdr., July, 1878; capt., June 27, 1893; rear adm., Feb. 11, 1901. Participated in both attacks on Ft. Fisher, Jan. 15, 1865, and in land attack received 4 severe rifle-shot wounds; when in command of the Yorktown at Valparaiso, Chile, 1891, during period of strained relations between Chile and U.S., his actions in connection with various incidents earned him name of "Fighting Bob." In war with Spain comd. Iowa in Sampson's fleet off Santiago, taking active part in battle with Cervera's fleet, July 3, 1898; was pres. Bd. of Inspection and Survey; comdr.-in-chief Asiatic Sta., Oct. 1902-04; comdg. Atlantic Fleet, 1905-07; comdr.-in-chief Atlantic Fleet, on tour of the world, 1907-08; retired Aug. 18, 1908. Author: A Sailor's Log, 1901. Home: Washington, D.C. Died 1912.

EVANS, Walter, judge; b. Barren County, Ky., Sept. 18, 1842; s. Joseph Warder and Matilda (Ritter) E.; self ed.; entered Union Army, 1861; admitted to bar, 1864; m. Louise Gowen, June 9, 1868; m. 2d, Louise Wood, Aug. 25, 1915. Mem. Ky. Ho. of Rep., 1871, Senate, 1873; removed to Louisville, 1874; Rep. candidate for Congress, 1876, for gov., 1879; commr. of internal revenue of U.S., 1883-85; mem. 54th and 55th Congresses (1895-99); U.S. dist. judge, Dist. of Ky., Mar. 6, 1899—. Died Dec. 30, 1923.

EVANS, William D., judge; b. Marquette County, Wis., May 10, 1852; s. Evan J. and Ann (Davis) E.; A.B., State U. of Ia., 1878, LL.B., 1879, A.M., 1890; LL.D., Grinnell (Ia.) Coll., 1916; m. Julia Stark, Oct. 29, 1879; children—Evan Stark, William Donald, Julia Gwendolen, Alice Adelaide, John Stark, David Benjamin. Practiced, Hampton, Ia., 1879-1903; judge 11th Jud. Dist. of Ia., 1903-08; justice Supreme Court of Ia., Sept. 17, 1908—. Republican. Conglist. Home: Hampton, Ia. Died May 4, 1936.

EVANS, William Frank, lawyer; b. Monroe County, Ia., Nov. 17, 1859; s. William and Margaret J. (Vestal) E.; ed. pub. schs.; unmarried. Admitted to bar, 1884, and began practice at Centerville, Ia.; was asst. gen. atty., 1892-1902 (moving to St. Louis in 1901), gen. atty., 1902-07, C.,R.I.&P. Ry.; asst. gen. solicitor, 1904-07, gen. solicitor, 1907—, St.L.& S.F. Ry. Co. Home: St. Louis, Mo. Deceased.

EVANS, William Gray; b. Evanston, Ill., Dec. 16, 1855; s. John and Margaret P.E.; B.S., Northwestern U., 1877; m. Cornelia L. Gray, Dec. 12, 1883. One of organizers Denver Electric & Cable Ry. Co., 1885, and its 1st sec.; actively identified with street rys. in Denver, many yrs.; pres. Denver City Tramway Co., 1902-12; chmn. State R.R. Commn. of Colo., 1919-21; pres. Evans Investment Co., June 1921—. Republican. Home: Denver, Colo. Died Oct. 21, 1924.

EVANS, Wilmot Roby, banker; b. Everett, Mass., Mar. 18, 1878; s. Wilmot Roby and Florence Carleton (Fowler) E.; student Harvard, 1896-1900; LL.B., Boston U., 1903; m. Susan McPherson Kramer, 1901. Admitted to Mass. bar, 1903, and practiced at Boston; mem. Mass. Ho. of Rep., 1905, 06, Senate, 1909, 10, 11; lecturer Suffolk Law Sch.; U.S. commr. for Dist. of Mass., 1924—; pres. Boston Five Cents Savings Bank, 1926—; pres. Lawyers Title Ins. Co., Lawyers Mortgage Investment Corp. Mem. First Motor Corps, Mass., World War. Trustee Suffolk Law Sch., Tufts Coll., Thayer Acad., New England Deaconess Hosp.; mem. bd. Boston Home for Incurables. Republican. Conglist. Home: Boston, Mass. Deceased.

EVARTS, Allen Wardner, lawyer; b. New York, N.Y., Dec. 10, 1848; s. William Maxwell and Helen Minerva (Wardner) E.; bro. of Maxwell E.; B.A., Yale Univ., 1869, M.A., 1872; Columbia Law Sch., 1871; unmarried. Practiced law in New York, 1873—; mem. Evarts, Southmayd & Choate, 1874-84, Evarts, Choate & Beaman, 1884-1901, Evarts, Choate & Sherman, 1908-19, Evarts, Choate, Sherman & Léon, 1919-34, Evarts, Choate, Curtin & Léon, 1934—. Died May 30, 1939.

EVARTS, Edward Mark, lawyer; b. Moscow, Russia, Oct. 12, 1888; s. Mark and Ida (Hoffman) E.; brought to U.S., 1889; A.B., Harvard, 1909; LL.B., Nat. Univ. Law Sch., Washington, D.C., 1915; postgrad. work in patent law, George Washington U., 1915-16; m. Anna M. Evarts, Feb. 11, 1911; 1 dau., Marjorie Ida. Asst. at U.S. Naval Obs., Washington, 1909-10; asst. examiner patents, U.S. Patent Office, 1910-17; patent counsel Barrett Co., New York, Feb.-Oct. 1917; asso. in practice with Emery, Booth, Janney & Varney, New York, 1917-21; mem. Evarts & Zalla, 1921-22; practicing alone, patent, trademark and copyright law, 1922—; rep. alien property custodian in connection with seizure of enemy-owned patents and trademarks during World War; pres. Pawling Development Corp.; sec., dir. Turl Iron & Car Co., Suchar Process Corp. of N.Y., also of Del. Home: New York, N.Y. Died Oct. 11, 1933.

EVARTS, Hal G., author; b. Topeka, Kan., Aug. 24, 1887; s. George Alfred and Emma E.; high sch., Topeka, 2 yrs.; m. Sylvia Abraham, Dec. 31, 1911; 1 son, Hal George. Was surveyor, Indian Territory; rancher, trapper and licensed guide, Wyo., also raising fur-bearing animals in captivity. Mem. O.T.C., Camp Pike, Ark., 1918; commd. 2d lt. but discharged at Armistice. Republican. Mason. Author: Passing of the Old West, 1921; The Yellow Horde, 1921; The Settling of the Sage, 1922; Fur Sign, 1922; Tumbleweeds, 1923; Spanish Acres, 1925; The Painted Stallion, 1926; The Moccasin Telegraph, 1927; Fur Brigade, 1928; Tomahawk Rights, 1929; The Shaggy Legion, 1930; Shortgrass, 1932. Home: Los Angeles, Calif. Died Oct. 18, 1934.

EVARTS, Maxwell, lawyer; s. William Maxwell and Helen Minerva (Wardner) E.; bro. of Allen Wardner E.; A.B., Yale, 1884. Pres. State Nat. Bank (Windsor, Vt.); dir. Southern Pacific R.R. Co. of Mex., Ore. Short Line R.R. Co, Pacific Mail Steamship Co., Union Pacific Land Co.; v.p. Windsor (Vt.) Machine Co. Died Oct. 7, 1913.

EVARTS, William Maxwell, lawyer; b. Boston, Mass., Feb. 6, 1818; grad. Yale, 1837; studied, Harvard Law School (hon. LL.D., Union, Harvard, and Yale). Began law practice, New York, 1841; asst. dist. atty., 1849-53; was counsel for defense for Pres. Johnson on impeachment trial, 1868; rep. U.S. in Alabama Claims case; chief counsel for Henry Ward Beecher in case with Theodore Tilton; for Rep. party in Hayes-Tilden contest; atty. gen. U.S., July 1868-March 1869; U.S. Sec. of State, 1877-81; U.S. senator (Rep.) from N.Y., 1885-91. Died 1901.

EVELAND, Samuel S., capitalist; b. Phila., Pa.; s. J. Samuel and Eleanor (Loosley) E.; m. Helen Miller, Apr. 12, 1893. Founder and pres. Standard Roller Bearing Co. (capital, $5,000,000), Standard Real Estate Improvement Co., Ball Bearing Co., Boston; pres. and owner Standard Gas & Electric Power Co., Phila. Truck Co., Eveland Engring. & Mfg. Co.; v.p. Puritan Mortgage Corp., also of Dahlberg Corp. of America, etc.; v.p., gen. mgr. and dir. Universal Fibre Corp. Inventor Eveland roller bearings now in use in revolving light houses U.S. Govt., electric self-starter for automobiles, electric lighting device, electric riveter, etc.; holds over 100 U.S. patents. Republican. Presbyn. Home: Philadelphia, Pa. Died Jan. 22, 1932.

EVELAND, William Perry, missionary bishop; b. Harrisburg, Pa., Feb. 12, 1864; s. John C. and Mary (MacAleer) E.; ed. Pennington Sem., N.J., 1886-88; A.B., Dickinson Coll., Carlisle, Pa., 1892, A.M., 1893, Ph.D., 1896 (D.D., 1906); m. Rosalie C. Mullin, Oct. 12, 1893. Began in ministry while in sem., at Yardley, Pa., 1888; preacher at Shippensburg, Pa., for 2 yrs. while coll. student; became mem. Central Pa. Conference M.E. Ch., 1891; pastor Shippensburg, 1890-95, Danville, Pa., 1895-96; dir. Jacob Tome Inst., Port Deposit, Md., 1896-98; pastor York, Pa., 1899-1900, Chambersburg, 1900-02, Bloomsburg, Pa., 1902-05; pres. Williamsport Dickinson Sem., 1905-May 1912; missionary bishop for southeastern Asia, May 1912—. Home: Williamsport, Pa. Died July 24, 1916.

EVEREST, Frank Fort, corp. officer; b. Sparland, Ill., May 1, 1869; s. Asa Elmore and Anna Mary (Fort) E.; Peddie Sch., Hightstown, N.J., Ia. Coll. Acad.; Ph.D., Grinnell Coll., 1893; m. Florence Folsom, Jan. 1, 1894; children—George Folsom, Frances (dec.), Edward Asa (dec.), Frank Fort, Charles Blake, Jack Mason (dec.). Real estate and loan business, Council Bluffs, 1895-99; partner in Greenshields & Everest Co., 1900—, pres., 1920—; incorporator Interstate Realty Co., 1900; organizer McClelland Savings Bank, 1903, v.p., 1905—; consolidated Council Bluffs abstract cos., 1904; receiver Union Transfer Co., 1907, Lee Light & Power Co., 1933; reorganizer Mondamin Savings Bank, 1923; apptd. mem. advisory com. for Ia. of Reconstruction Finance Corp., Feb. 1932; dir. Omaha br. Regional Agrl. Credit Corp. Bank, 1933. Chmn. Rep. County Central Com., 1898-99; supervisor census, 9th congl. dist., 1900; city assessor, Council Bluffs, 1901-04; mem. sch. bd., Council Bluffs, 1918-22. Mem. Ia. State Council Defense, 1917-20. Presdl. elector 9th congl. dist., 1920. Trustee Grinnell Coll., 1920. Conglist. Mason, Elk. Home: Council Bluffs, Ia. Died Aug. 31, 1939.

EVERETT, Arthur Greene, architect; b. Roxbury, Mass., Aug. 14, 1855; s. Thomas Blake and Sarah Elizabeth (Greene) E.; ed. pvt. and pub. schs., Boston and New York, Mass. Inst. Tech.; m. Georgiana F. Hughes, Sept. 6, 1886. Practiced, Boston, 1877—; was with Bradley Winslow & Westerell, and McKim, Mead & White; later mem. Cabot, Everett & Mead, later Everett & Mead; then alone. Sec. Bd. of Appeal from Bldg. Commr., 1892-1907; bldg. commr., May 1, 1908-Feb. 1, 1914. Fellow A.I.A., Boston Soc. Architects. Unitarian. Home: Boston, Mass. Died Oct. 5, 1925.

EVERETT, Charles Carroll, dean Harvard Div. Sch., 1878—; b. Brunswick, Me., June 19, 1829; grad. Bowdoin, 1850 (A.M., D.D., LL.D.); studied at Univ. Berlin, Germany; m. 1859. Returned to Bowdoin, where he was 2 years tutor and 2 years prof. of modern langs.; during these 4 years he was also college librarian; then grad. Harvard Divinity Sch., 1859 (D.D.); pastor, 1859-69, Independent Congl. (Unitarian) Ch., Bangor, Me.; prof. theology, Harvard, 1869—. Author: Poetry, Comedy and Duty; Religions Before Christianity; Ethics for Young People; The Gospel of Paul; Fichte's Science of Knowledge, a Critical Exposition; The Science of Thought; etc. Home: Cambridge, Mass. Died 1900.

EVERETT, Henry A., capitalist; b. Cleveland, O., Oct. 16, 1856; s. Dr. Azariah and Emily (Burnham) E.; ed. private and pub. schs., Cleveland; m. Josephine Pettengill, 1886. Electric ry. and independent telephone promoter, constructor and operator; selected by Toronto City Council, as expert, to supervise conversion of the then existing horse-car st. rys. into modern electric rys., 1892, and was v.p. and mng. dir. Toronto Ry. Co.; also supervised changing Montreal st. rys. from horse-car lines into electric roads; also supervised many other electric lines and telephone and telegraph lines, etc., in Can.; pres. Northern Ohio Traction & Light Co., London (Can.) Street Ry. Co. Home: Willoughby, O. Deceased.

EVERETT, Herbert Edward, univ. prof.; b. Worcester, Mass., Feb. 16, 1863; s. Edward S. and Ellen M. E.; ed. Worcester High Sch., Harvard U.; art edn. Boston Mus. Fine Arts, Julian Acad., Paris, Pa. Acad. Fine Arts, Phila.; hon. A.E.D., U. of Pa., 1921; m. Catherine Arms Childs; children—Jane Hamlin, Catherine Arms. Prof. history of art, U. of Pa., 1892—. Lecturer on History of Ornament, Cornell U., 1900-1901, History of Art, Smith Coll., 1900-05. Fellow in medieval archæology, Am. Sch. of Archæology at Rome. Home: Philadelphia, Pa. Died Dec. 10, 1932.

EVERETT, Walter Goodnow, univ. prof.; b. Rowe, Mass., Aug. 21, 1860; s. Samuel P. and Alcesta (Goodnow) E.; A.B., Brown U., 1885, A.M., 1888, Ph.D., 1895; studied univs. of Berlin and Strassburg, 1895-96; m. Harriet M. Cleveland, Dec. 25, 1885 (died 1910); m. 2d, Elizabeth Comstock, Dec. 11, 1918. Tutor, Providence, 1885-89; instr. Greek and Latin, Brown U., 1889-94; asso. prof. philosophy, 1894-96, philosophy and natural theology, 1896-99, prof., 1899—, acting pres., 1912-13, Brown U. Trustee Butler Hosp., Providence, 1913—. Am. del. Allied Congress of Philosophy, Paris, 1921; pres. Am. Philos. Assn. (eastern div.), 1922. Author: Moral Values, 1918. Address: Providence, R.I. Deceased.

EVERETT, William, teacher, author; b. Watertown, Mass., Oct. 10, 1839; s. Hon. Edward E.; grad. Harvard, 1859 (Ph.D., 1875; hon. LL.D., Williams, 1893, Dartmouth, 1901); B.A., Trinity Coll., Cambridge, Eng., 1863, M.A., 1869. Tutor and asst. prof. Latin, Harvard, 1870-77; master Adams Acad., Quincy, Mass., 1877-93, and from 1897; has license to preach from Boston Ministers' Assn. (Unitarian). Active in politics; Republican until 1884; after that acted with Democrats as civil service and tariff reformer; mem. Congress, 1893-95; unmarried. Author: College Essays; School Sermons; Hesione, or Europe Unchained (poem); also juvenile books: Chancing Base; Double Play; Thine, Not Mine. Home: Quincy, Mass. Died 1910.

EVERETT, William Henry, rear adm.; b. New York, N.Y., Mar. 6, 1847; s. William Moore and Charlotte M. E.; apptd. from Conn. and grad. U.S. Naval Acad., June 1868; m. Bessie Bell Hackett, Aug. 6, 1885. Promoted ensign, U.S. Navy, Apr. 19, 1869; master, July 12, 1870; lt., Dec. 12, 1873; lt. comdr., Dec. 6, 1894; comdr., Mar. 3, 1899; capt., Feb. 17, 1904; advanced to rear admiral, Oct. 9, 1906, and retired at own request. Home: Newport, R.I. Died June 10, 1912.

EVERHART, Benjamin Matlack, mycologist; b. West Whiteland Tp., Chester County, Pa., Apr. 26, 1818; s .William and Hannah (Matlack) E.; ed. schs. of Chester County; unmarried. Was associated for years with his father in conducting largest gen. mdse. store in Chester County; visited Eng. in 1884-85; for 50 yrs. has devoted time to scientific research; has collected and arranged large collection of lichens, mosses, ferns, algæ, liverworts and fungi. Asso. editor Jour. of Mycology, 1885-88 (4 vols.); contbr. to 5th and 6th vols. same issued by Dept. of Agr. Compiled index to Ellis' North American Fungi. Author: (with J. B. Ellis) The North American Pyromycetes, 1892. Home: West Chester, Pa. Died 1904.

EVERITT, George Bain, corp. officer; b. Mitchell, S.D., May 25, 1885; s. George Bain and Martha Smyth (Davis) E.; ed. Central High Sch., Philadelphia, Pa.; m. Lois E. Richter, Oct. 19, 1912; children—George Bain, Mary Louise. Gen. accounting work until 1910; served as dept. head, office mgr., system mgr., Nat. Cloak & Suit Co., New York, 1910-16; gen. mgr. Ency. Britannica Corp., New York, 1916-18; asst. to operating v.p. Am. Internat. Corp., later assigned to Amsinck & Co., New York, 1918-19; sec. and treas. European Textile Corp., 1919-21; successively asst. to pres., operating v.p., v.p. and gen. mgr., Montgomery Ward & Co., Chicago, 1921-26, pres. until 1932; chmn. bd. Merchandise Nat. Bank. Republican. Conglist. Home: Winnetka, Ill. Died Aug. 2, 1941.

EVERMANN, Barton Warren, naturalist; b. Monroe County, Ia., Oct. 24, 1853; s. Andrew and Nety (Gardner) E.; B.S., Indiana Univ., 1886, A.M., 1888, Ph.D., 1891; LL.D., Univ. of Utah, 1922, and of Indiana U., 1927; m. Meadie Hawkins, Oct. 24, 1875; children—Toxaway Bronté, Edith (Mrs. Wm. E. Humphrey). For 10 yrs. teacher and supt. of schs. in Ind. and Calif.; prof. biology, Ind. State Normal Sch., 1886-91; asst. ichthyologist, 1888-91, ichthyologist, 1891-1914, chief Div. Statistics and Methods of Fisheries, 1902-03, asst. in charge of scientific inquiry, 1903-10, chief Alaska Fisheries Service, July 1, 1910-14, U.S. Bur. of Fisheries. U.S. fur seal commr., 1892; spl. lecturer, Stanford U., 1893-94 and 1926—; lecturer on fish and game protection, Cornell, 1900-03, Yale, 1903-06; chmn. fur seal bd., 1908-14; v.p. Bd. of Edn., D.C., 1906-10; dir. Museum Calif. Acad. Sciences, 1914—, and of Steinhart Aquarium, 1922—. Editor Proc. Washington Acad. Sciences, 1904-11, Calif. Acad. Sciences, 1914—. Chmn. com. on zoöl. investigations of State Council of Defense, and mem. exec. com. Calif. Research Conf. of same, 1917-19; mem. com. Pacific investigation, Nat. Research Council, and chmn. Com. on Conservation of Marine Life of the Pacific. Author: The Fishes of North and Middle America, 4 vols. (with Dr. David Starr Jordan), 1896, 1900; American Food and Game Fishes, 1902; The Aquatic Resources of the Hawaiian Islands (with David Starr Jordan); The Alaska Salmon Fisheries; Fishes of the Philippines, 1906; The Golden Trout of the Southern High Sierras, 1906; The Fishes of Alaska, 1907; The Fishes of Peru, 1915; A Review of the Giant Mackerel-like Fishes, Tunnies, Spearfishes, and Swordfishes (with David Starr Jordan); etc. Home: Berkeley, Calif. Died Sept. 27, 1932.

EVERTS, Orpheus, M.D.; b. Union County, Ind., Dec. 18, 1826; s. Dr. Sylvanus and Elizabeth (Heywood) E.; common school edn.; grad., M.D., Med. Coll. Ind., 1846; same degree, U. of Mich., 1865-66; Rush Med. Coll., 1867. Surgeon 20th regt. Ind. vols., 1861-65, in the field; supt. Ind. Hosp. for Insane, 1868-79; supt. Cincinnati Sanitarium (private hosp.), 1880—, making 33 yrs.' service in med. care and treatment of the insane. Died 1903.

EVINS, Robert Benson, lawyer; b. Perry County, Ala., Mar. 31, 1875; s. Robert Hamilton and Martha Amelia (Thompson) E.; student Marion (Ala.) Mil. Inst.; grad. Eastman Coll., Poughkeepsie, N.Y., 1891; m. Florence Elizabeth Mann, Nov. 12, 1913. Admitted to Ala. bar, 1895; legal adviser to gov. of Ala. and spl. counsel to the State, 1911-15; declined appmt. to Court of Appeals of Ala.; mem. Ala. Senate, 1919-23. Chmn. Four-Minute Men and all other war campaigns in Hale County, Ala., during war period; chmn. Ala. Dem. Exec. Com., 1923. Democrat. Episcopalian. Mason. Home: Birmingham, Ala. Died Nov. 28, 1933.

EVJEN, John Oluf, church historian; b. Ishpeming, Mich., Dec. 13, 1874; s. John and Anne (Kleven) E.; B.A., Augsburg Sem., Minneapolis, 1895; grad. Theol. Dept., same, 1898; grad. study, Univ. of Leipzig, 1899-1903, Ph.D., 1903; Th.D., Carthage (Ill.) Coll.; m. Selma Ottilie Kretschmann, Aug. 10, 1904; children—Siegfried Albert, Victor Harald, Rudolph Norman, Margaret Elizabeth, Henry Oscar, Myrtle Marie. Taught sch. in Dak., Wis., Minn. and Mich.; ordained Luth. ministry, 1903; pastor, Muskegon and Grand Rapids, Mich., 1903; acting prof. ch. history, United Ch. Theol. Sem., St. Paul, 1903-05; prof. bibl. history, Pa. Coll., Gettysburg, 1905-09; prof. theology, Augsburg Sem., Minneapolis, 1909-19; pres. State Normal Sch., N.D., 1919-23; prof. history and modern lang., Carthage (Ill.) Coll., 1923-24; prof. theology, Hamma Div. Sch., Wittenberg Coll., 1924-30; prof. philosophy of history, Carthage Coll., 1930—, dean, 1933—. Republican. Author: Scandinavian Immigrants in New York, 1630-1674, 1916; Luther and the Reformation, 1916; Life of J. H. W. Stuckenberg (book), 1938. Contbr. to work, Danske i Amerika (Minneapolis), Schaff-Herzog Ency., Herzog-Haucks Protestantische Realencyclopädie (Leipzig), Dr. Ruoff's Volume Library, Ferm's "What Is Lutheranism?," Norlie's "The Translated Bible," Dictionary of Am. Biography. Home: Carthage, Ill. Died Jan. 4, 1942.

EWART, Hamilton Glover, judge; b. Columbia, S.C., Oct. 23, 1849; s. James B. and Mary Ann E.; ed. schs. of Columbia, S.C.; LL.B., U. of S.C., 1876; m Sarah C. Ripley, Apr. 8, 1875. Admitted to bar, 1876, and engaged in practice at Hendersonville; mayor, 1878-79; presdl. elector, 1876; mem. N.C. Ho. of Rep., 1887, 1894; mem. 51st Congress (1889-91); judge Criminal Ct., 1895-97, Circuit Ct., 1897-98; U.S. dist. judge, Western Dist. of N.C., 1898—. Republican. Home: Hendersonville, N.C. Died Apr. 28, 1918.

EWELL, Ervin Edgar, chemist; b. Washington, Mich., Oct. 22, 1867; s. Samuel Day Edgar E.; grad. Sch. of Pharmacy, U. of Mich., 1888; B.S., Univ. of Mich., 1900; m. Alice Priest, Aug. 19, 1896. Asst. to prof. qualitative analysis, U. of Mich., 1888-90; asst. chemist, div. chemistry, U.S. Dept. Agr., 1890-93; chemist for Magnolia Sugar and R.R. Co., Lawrence, La., 1893-94; asst. chemist, 1894-97, and asst. chief Bur. of Chemistry, 1897-1903, U.S. Dept. Agr.; mgr. Atlanta office German Kali Works, 1903—. Home: Atlanta, Ga. Died 1904.

EWELL, Marshall Davis, lawyer; b. Oxford, Mich., Aug. 18, 1844; s. Edmund C. and Frances E. (Davis) E.; grad. Mich. State Normal Sch., 1864; LL.B., U. of Mich., 1868 (LL.D., 1879; A.M., Northwestern U., 1879; M.D., Chicago Med. Coll., 1884); m. Abbie L. Walker, 1870; m. 2d, Nellie C. Bigelow, 1919. Was prof. common law, Union Coll. of Law, Chicago, from 1877 until founded Kent Coll. of Law, of which he became prof. common law, pres. and dean. Lecturer on med. jurisprudence, U. of Mich., 1890-96. Microscopist and handwriting expert. Pres. Am. Micros. Soc. 1893, 1906, Ill. Micros. Soc., 1909, 1911; hon. fellow Royal Micros. Soc., London. Author: Essentials of the Law, 1882, 2d edit., 1915. Home: Osprey, Fla. Died Oct. 4, 1928.

EWEN, John Meiggs, engr.; b. Newtown, N.Y., Sept. 3, 1859; s. Warren and Sarah (Faulkner) E.; grad. Stevens Inst. Tech., 1880; m. Grace Patterson, Mar. 29, 1889. Asst. engr. J. B. and J. M. Cornell, iron works, New York, 1884-86; archtl. engr. W. L. B. Jenny, Chicago, 1886-90; engr. and gen. mgr. Burnham & Root, architects, 4 yrs.; v.p. and gen. mgr. (4 yrs. in London, Eng.) and western contracting agent George A. Fuller & Co., Chicago, 1890-1902; v.p. and western rep. Thompson-Starrett Co., bldg. contractors, New York, 1902-04; now pres. John M. Ewen Co., engrs. and builders, Chicago. Republican. Presbyn. Home: Evanston, Ill. Died Dec. 19, 1933.

EWER, Warren Baxter, editor; b. Windsor, Vt., Apr. 22, 1814; s. Seth E., Bapt. minister; fitted for college at South Reading, Mass.; entered Brown Univ., class of 1834, but left at close of 1st yr. because of ill health (hon. A.M., Colby Univ.); m. (4th wife) Ora Smith Healey, Feb. 4, 1900. Began editorial work in 1836 in Dedham, Mass., and continued until 1895; allowing for intermissions, 56 yrs. of actual editorial work; over 30 yrs. chief editor of The Mining and Scientific Press, San Francisco, in which he had one-third interest; retired from editorial chair, 1895. Published campaign paper in Boston in interest of William Henry Harrison, 1840. Home: Piedmont, Calif. Died 1906.

EWERS, Ezra Philetus, brig. gen. U.S. Army; b. Wayneport, N.Y., Apr. 13, 1837. Pvt., sergt. and 1st sergt. Co. E, 1st Battalion, 19th Inf., Jan. 18, 1862-Dec. 4, 1863; commd. 2d lt., 19th Inf., Oct. 31, 1863; 1st lt., Mar. 16, 1864; transferred to 37th Inf., Sept. 21, 1866; capt., Sept. 12, 1866; transferred to 5th Inf., May 19, 1869; maj., 9th Inf., Mar. 7, 1893; lt. col., Apr. 30, 1897; brig. gen. vols., July 12, 1898; hon. disch. from vol. service, Apr. 20, 1899; col. 10th U.S. Inf., May 16, 1899; retired by operation of law, Apr. 13, 1901; advanced to rank of brig. gen. retired, by act of Apr. 23, 1904. Bvtd. 1st lt., June 26, 1863, for action at Hoovers Gap, Tenn.; capt., Nov. 25, 1863, for battle of Chattanooga, Tenn.; maj., Feb. 27, 1890, for action against Indians at Tongue River, Mont., Jan. 8, 1877. Died Jan. 16, 1912.

EWING, Arthur Eugene, M.D.; b. near Cartersville, Ga., Apr. 26, 1855; s. Whitley Thomas (M.D.) and Hannah Jane (Pettingill) E.; A.B., Dartmouth, 1878; admitted to Ala. bar, 1879; M.D., St. Louis Med. Coll., 1883; studied at Koenigliche Christian-Albrecht's U., Kiel, Germany, 1886-88; A.M., Washington U., 1912; D.Sc. from same univ., 1926; m. Josephine Willard, Jan. 15, 1891; children—Margaret Frances, Charlotte Eugenia. Practiced in St. Louis, 1883—; clin. lecturer on ophthalmology, 1895-1902, clin. prof. ophthalmology, 1902-21 (emeritus), Washington U. Med. Sch. Republican. Baptist. Author of Visual Test-Types and articles on ophthalmic subjects; co-author of Optotypes, Test Letters and Pictographs. Home: St. Louis, Mo. Died Jan. 26, 1929.

EWING, Arthur Henry, missionary; b. Saltsburg, Pa., Oct. 18, 1864; s. James Henry and Eleanor Jane

(Rhea) E.; B.A., Washington and Jefferson Coll., 1887; grad. Western Theol. Sem., Pa., 1890; Ph.D., Johns Hopkins, 1901; (D.D., Washington and Jefferson); m. Estelle Field Loomis, Sept. 19, 1890. Ordained Presbyn. ministry, Sept. 9, 1890; prin. Christian Boys' Boarding Sch., Ludhiana, Punjab, India, 1891-98; prin. Allahabad Christian Coll., 1901-09. Fellow U. of Allahabad, 1902—, syndic, 1905—, also acting registrar same; treas. North India Mission, 1902—, hon. sec. North India Christian Book and Tract Soc., 1905-06; hon. sec. Christian Lit. Soc. (United Provinces Branch); chmn. United Council on Work Among Young People in India, 1907—. Mem. bd. dirs. Theol. Sem., Saharanpur, India, Allahabad Christian Coll. Died Sept. 13, 1912.

EWING, Charles H., ry. official; b. Chester Co., Pa., May 28, 1866; s. James and Maria (Potts) E.; ed. high sch. and in civ. engring. under pvt. tutor; m. Sarah Newlin, Nov. 24, 1892; 1 son, George N. Rodman, asst. engr. and supervisor P.&R. Ry., 1883-92; div. engr. and chief engr. Central N.E. Ry., 1892-1902; div. engr. and engr. maintenance of way, P.&R. Ry., 1902-10; supt. Atlantic City R.R., 1910-12; gen. supt. P.&R. Ry., 1913-16, gen. mgr. 1916-17, v.p., 1917-18; federal mgr. same rd. and Central R.R. of N.J., 1918-20; v.p. P.&R. Ry., 1920-23; v.p. Reading Co., 1924-32, pres. Apr. 28, 1932—; pres. Central R.R. Co. of N.J., June 1933—. Home: Melrose Park, Pa. Died Dec. 8, 1935.

EWING, David L., traffic official; b. Muscatine, Ia., Apr. 5, 1877; s. William Wallace and Alice (Bumbarger) E.; ed. pub. schs.; m. Luella Crawford McLain, June 14, 1913. Began as office boy with K.C., Ft. Scott & Memphis R.R., 1893; became connected with St.L.&S.F. Ry. Co. as traveling frt. agt., 1901, advancing to asst. gen. frt. agt., 1911; apptd. dir. traffic U.S. Shipping Bd., May 8, 1917, and asst. dir. operations, Nov. 20, 1917; v.p. France & Canada Steamship Corp., Dec. 1, 1918-Jan. 26, 1921. Democrat. Home: New York, N.Y. Died Jan. 1923.

EWING, Hugh Boyle, soldier, lawyer; b. Lancaster, O., Oct. 31, 1826; s. Thomas E.; ed. by private tutor and at U.S. Mil. Acad.; went to Calif., 1849, on expdn. sent by his father (then Sec. of the Interior) to the high Sierras to rescue emigrants from snows; returned, 1852. Practiced law, St. Louis, 1854-56, Leavenworth, Kan., 1856-58; in charge of salt works in Ohio, 1858-61; m. Henrietta Young, 1858. Served through war, 1861-65, maj. to brig. gen., and bvt. maj. gen.; comd. brigade at Antietam and Vicksburg, and a division at Chickamauga, U.S. minister to The Hague, 1866-70; retired. Home: Lancaster, O. Died 1905.

EWING, James Caruthers Rhea, college pres.; b. Rural Valley, Pa., June 23, 1854; s. James Henry and Eleanor Jane (Rhea) E.; B.A., Washington and Jefferson Coll., Pa., 1876, M.A., 1879; grad. Western Theol. Sem., Pa., 1879; (D.D., Washington and Jefferson, 1887, LL.D., 1908; D.Litt., U. of Punjab, 1917); m. Jane Hindman Sherrard, June 24, 1879. Ordained Presbyn. ministry, 1879; went to India as missionary, 1879; prof. in Theol. Sem. in India, 1884-88; pres. Forman Christian Coll., Lahore, India, 1888-1918; sec. India Council of the Presbyn. Ch. U.S.A., 1918-22. Dean faculty of arts, U. of Punjab, 1890-1907, vice chancellor, 1910-17. Received from King Edward VII of Eng. decoration of Kaiser-i-Hind Gold Medal, 1907; from King George V. C.I.E. (Companion of the Indian Empire), 1915, Knight-Comdr. of Indian Empire, 1923. Home: Princeton, N.J. Died Aug. 20, 1925.

EWING, James Stevenson, lawyer; b. McLean County, Ill., July 19, 1835; s. John W. and Maria M. (Stevenson) E.; ed. Ill. Wesleyan Coll.; grad. Centre Coll., Danville, Ky., 1858; read law in office of John C. Bullitt, Phila.; m. Katherine Spencer, June 28, 1866. Admitted to bar, 1859, and entered practice at Bloomington, with Adlai E. Stevenson, as Stevenson & Ewing; U.S. minister to Belgium, 1893-97. Democrat. Home: Bloomington, Ill. Died Feb. 7, 1918.

EWING, John, diplomatic service; b. Mobile, Ala., June 24, 1857; s. James Lindsay and Margaret Ann (Hunter) E.; ed. pvt. schs., Mobile; studied law; m. Helen Toulmin, Dec. 22, 1880. Dep. register of chancery, Mobile, 1878-92; dep. collector of customs, Mobile, 1894-1906; customs broker, land agt., 1906-09; with Daily States, New Orleans, 1909-13; E.E. and M.P. to Honduras, Sept. 1913-May 1918. Democrat. Episcopalian. Died June 24, 1923.

EWING, John Thomas, prof. classics; b. Sparta, Ill., Oct. 29, 1856; s. Joseph Wier and Catherine (Gregg) E.; A.B., U. of Mich., 1880; A.M., Wooster, 1891, Litt.D., 1913, L.H.D., Alma Coll., 1925; studied U. of Chicago, summer quarter, 1899, Columbia, 1916-17; m. Mary M. Potter, July 3, 1883; children—Herbert, Ernest, William—all dec. Supt. schs., Petoskey, Mich., 1882-87; prin. prep. dept. and asst. in Greek, U. of Wooster, 1887-90; prof. Greek, 1890-1906; prof. classics, 1906—, Alma Coll., also registrar, 1891—; also sec. of faculty. Repub-

lican. Presbyn. Home: Alma, Mich. Died Oct. 31, 1926.

EWING, Nathaniel, judge; b. Uniontown, Pa., June 17, 1848; s. Judge John Kennedy and Ellen Louisa (Willson) E.; A.B., Coll. of N.J. (now Princeton), with honor, 1869, A.M., 1872; m. Sallie E. Mitchell, Oct. 22, 1878. Admitted to bar, 1871; apptd. judge 14th Jud. Dist., Pa., Aug. 1887, elected, Nov. 1887, for 10 yrs.; counsel for W. J. Rainey and the H. C. Frick Coke Co., and other corps.; was counsel Pa. R.R. Co. until elevated to bench. Pres. Nat. Bank of Fayette Co.; dir. Finance Co. of Pa., Pittsburgh Life & Trust Co. U.S. dist. judge, Western Dist. of Pa., 1906-08, resigned; chmn. Pa. State R.R. Commn., Jan. 1908-July 1913; chmn. Pub. Service Commn. of Pa., Aug. 1913—. Trustee Princeton, 1904-07. Republican. Presbyn. Home: Uniontown, Pa. Died Mar. 28, 1914.

EWING, Presley Kittredge, lawyer; b. La Fourche, La., July 21, 1860; s. Fayette Clay (M.D.) and Eliza Josephine (Kittredge) E.; Bro. of Fayette Clay and Quincy E.; Ph.B., U. of Miss., 1881, LL.B. (first honor), 1881; m. Mary Ellen Williams, Feb. 10, 1885 (died 1919); children—Vesta (Mrs. W. Veatch), Gladys (Mrs. Abbott C. Combes); m. 2d, June Throckmorton, June 12, 1923; prac. law in Houston, Tex., 1882—; enrolled atty. Supreme Ct. of U.S.; represented before Trans-Miss. Com. Congress at Wichita, Kan., May 1899, the plan of govt. appropriation for deep-water gulf outlet from Houston. Commd. Chief Justice Supreme Ct. Tex., Apr. 1905; campaigned in the East in successive presdl. campaigns for Dem. Nat. Com. Mason. Home: Houston, Tex. Died Feb. 4, 1927.

EWING, Robert, newspaper pub.; b. Mobile, Ala., Sept. 27, 1859; s. James Lindsay and Martha Ann (Hunter) E.; ed. pvt. schs., Mobile; m. May Dunbrack, Nov. 17, 1888 (died 1904); children—James Lindsay, John Dunbrack, Esther (Mrs. E. G. Brown), Toulmin Hunter, Robert, Wilson; m. 2d, Grace Nolan Mackay, Sept. 1, 1917. Engaged in telegraph service as messenger, operator and mgr., Mobile and New Orleans, 1871-87; telegraph editor Daily States, New Orleans, 1887, becoming asst. bus. mgr., 1893, business mgr., 1898, and pub. and owner, 1900—; also pub. Shreveport Times (morning paper), 1908—. Supt. fire alarm system and city electrician, New Orleans, 1888-92; state tax collector, 4th Municipal Dist., 1900-08; La. mem. Dem. Nat. Com., 1908-19, and of exec. com., 1908-19, and chmn. press contributions bur.; elected del. at large, mem. Platform Com. and chmn. La. delegation to Dem. Nat. Conv., Houston, 1928; mem. La. Constl. Conv., 1898. Episcopalian. Mason. Home: New Orleans, La. Died Apr. 27, 1931.

EWING, Robert Legan, sec. N.Y. City Y.M.C.A.; b. Arcola, Ill., Aug. 18, 1878; s. Joseph Henry and Ann Louisa (McDonald) E.; student Ohio Wesleyan U., and U. of Wash.; B.A., Oberlin Coll., 1904; M.A., U. of Chicago, 1913; m. Georgia Mathilda Carrothers, Aug. 22, 1905; children—Robert Legan (dec.), Thomas Carrothers (dec.), Helen Elizabeth. Sec. Y.M.C.A. at U. of Wash., 1901-03, Oberlin Coll., 1905. Madras, India, 1905-12. U. of Neb., 1913-15; sr. sec. Am. Y.M.C.A. in Eng., in charge 700 secretaries, also of Y.M.C.A. work for prisoners of war, 1915-19; sec. Nat. Council Y.M.C.A., 1919-30; dir. of activities, William Sloan House, New York, Jan. 1, 1930—. Mem. Bd. of Education, Mt. Vernon, N.Y., 1926-31. Awarded Delhi Durbar Medal, 1911 (British). Conglist. Author: (with Arthur Davies) Three Hundred Anglo-Indians (sociol. study), 1912; How to Conduct Forums and Discussions. Editor: Forum Bulletin, 1922-29, Discussion Outlines on International Questions, 1924-29. Home: Mt. Vernon, N.Y. Died Dec. 10, 1934.

EXALL, Henry, agriculturist; b. Richmond, Va., Aug. 30, 1848; s. Rev. George G. and Angeline (Pierce) E.; ed. in father's pvt. sch.; twice married; m. 2d, May Dickson, Nov. 1887. Served in 10th Va. Cav., C.S.A., spring 1863, to close of war; went to Ky., 1869, to Tex., 1877; del. New Orleans Cotton Expn., 1884; col. and q.-m. Texas state troops, 1884-85; del. Dem. Nat. Conv., 1884; chmn. Dem. State Exec. Com., Tex., 1886-88; del. New York centennial of inauguration of first president, 1889; pres. Texas State Fair, 1889; commr.-at-large Chicago Expn., 1893; pres. Texas Indsl. Congress. Engaged in breeding fine horses and in farming. Home: Dallas, Tex. Died Dec. 29, 1913.

EXCELL, Edwin Othello, song composer; b. Uniontown, O., Dec. 13, 1851; s. Rev. J. J. and Emily (Hess) E.; ed. pub. schs. of Ohio and Pa.; studied music; m. Eliza Jane Bell, June 6, 1871. Was for 20 yrs. associated with the Georgia evangelist, Rev. Sam P. Jones, as gospel singer; pub. of ch. and S.S. music books, 1881—; composer of many gospel songs, and musical dir. gospel meetings. Methodist. Prohibitionist. Home: Chicago, Ill. Died June 10, 1921.

EYCLESHYMER, Albert Chauncey, anatomist; b. Cambridge, N.Y., June 16, 1867; s. David C. and Anna M. (Perry) E.; B.S., U. of Mich., 1891; fellow, Princeton, 1891, Clark U., 1892. U. of Chicago,

1893, Ph.D., latter, 1895; student, U. of Cambridge, Eng., 1895-96; Austin fellow, Harvard U., 1901; M.D., St. Louis U., 1909; m. Mary Elizabeth Donovan, Sept. 23, 1895. Asst. prof. human embryology, Rush Med. Coll., Chicago, 1897-99; asst. prof. human anatomy, U. of Chicago, 1903; dir. of anatom. dept., 1903-13, acting dean Coll. of Medicine, 1913, St. Louis U.; prof. and head of dept. anatomy, 1913—, and dean of faculty, 1917—, Coll. Medicine of U. of Ill., Chicago. Member Nat. Board of Medical Examiners. Received grand prize for embryol. work from La. Purchase Expn., 1904. Author: Manual of Surgical Anatomy for U.S. Army and Navy, 1919. Home: Oak Park, Ill. Died Dec. 30, 1925.

EYMAN, Henry C., alienist; b. Lancaster, O., Apr. 13, 1856; s. Henry Brian and Mary (Baker) E.; ed. Southern Ohio Normal Sch.; M.D., Columbus Med. Coll. (now Med. Dept. Ohio State U.), 1880; m. Celestia Dern, Sept. 12, 1880 (died 1908). Began practice in Tarlton, O., 1880; asst. phys., Athens State Hosp., 1884-87; asst. supt. Toledo State Hosp., 1887-91; supt. Cleveland State Hosp., 1891-99, Massillon State Hosp., 1899-1918; prof. nervous and mental diseases, Coll. of Wooster Med. Dept., 1891-1905. Methodist. Retired Nov. 1, 1918. Home: Massillon, O. Died Oct. 8, 1925.

EYTINGE, Rose, actress, teacher, writer; b. Phila., Nov. 21, 1838; ed. at home; has traveled much; lived in various parts of America, Europe and Africa —the latter in Alexandria and Cairo, as the wife of the consul-gen. to that country. As actress has played many of Shakespeare's heroines, notably, Hermione in Winter's Tale; Cleopatra in Antony and Cleopatra; Lady Macbeth, etc. Has created many parts, including Rose Michel, Amande Chandoce in Led Astray; Felicia, etc. Author: It Happened This Way (novel); Golden Chains (play). Home: New York, N.Y. Died 1911.

EZEKIEL, Moses, sculptor; b. Richmond, Va., Oct. 28, 1844; s. Jacob and Catherine (de Castro) E.; after service with corps of cadets in C.S.A.; grad. Va. Mil. Inst., 1866; studied anatomy Med. Coll. of Va.; removed to Cincinnati, 1868; visited Berlin, Germany, 1869, where he studied at Royal Acad. Art and under Prof. Albert Wolf. Admitted into Soc. of Artists, Berlin, on the merits of his colossal bust of Washington, and was 1st foreigner to win the Prize of Rome. Jewish order, Sons of the Covenant, commissioned him, 1874, to execute marble group representing Religious Liberty, for Centennial Exhbn., now in Fairmount Park, Phila.; monument to Jessie Seligmann for orphan asylum, New York. After 1886 his work became largely ideal. Among his productions are busts of Liszt and Cardinal Hohenlöhe, Eve, Homer, David, Judith, Christ in the Tomb, statue of Mrs. Andrew D. White for Cornell U.; Faith, Cemetery Rome; Madonna, for Ch. in Tivoli; Apollo and Mercury, in Berlin; Robert E. Lee; Pan and Amor; The Fountain of Neptune, for City of Netturno, Italy; bust of Lord Sherbrooke, for St. Margaret, Westminster, London, and scores of busts and reliefs, and Jefferson Monument, for Louisville, Ky.; Homer group for U. of Va.; Virginia Mourning Her Dead at Lexington, Va.; Napoleon I at St. Helena; Jefferson monument, U. of Va.; monument to Senator Daniel, Lynchburg, Va.; Confederate Soldiers' monument, Nat. Cemetery, Arlington, Va. Died Mar. 27, 1917.

F

FABER, William Frederic, bishop; b. Buffalo, N.Y., Feb. 27, 1860; s. Theobald and Caroline W. (Schoenthal) F.; A.B., U. of Rochester, 1880, D.D., 1905; grad. Auburn Theol. Sem., 1883; A.M., Hobart Coll., 1898; m. Dorothea J. Kniest, June 26, 1883 (died 1895); children—Harold Kniest, Dorothy Elizabeth. Ordained Presbyn. ministry, 1883; pastor First Ch., Westfield, N.Y., 1883-92; entered P.E. Ch., 1892; asst. St. Peter's Church, Geneva, N.Y., 1893; rector Grace Ch., Lockport, N.Y., 1893-1905, St. John's Ch., Detroit, 1905-14; consecrated coadjutor-bishop of Diocese of Montana, Nov. 10, 1914; became bishop, 1916. Author: Nobiscum Deus, 1893; Henry VIII and the Reformation in Relation to the Church of England, 1897; Stained Glass Windows, 1900; Fifty Years—A History of Saint John's Church in Detroit, Michigan. Home: Helena, Mont. Died July 20, 1934.

FABYAN, George; b. Boston, Mass., Mar. 15, 1867; s. George Francis and Isabella Frances (Littlefield) F.; ed. pub. schs.; m. Nellie Wright, 1887. Settled in Chicago, 1883; with Kirby-Carpenter Co., lumber, 5 yrs.; spent 5 yrs. in the West; became identified, 1893, with Bliss, Fabyan & Co., dry goods commn. mchts., of which is now resident partner. Organized, 1903, the Riverbank Labs., Geneva, Ill., and associated with a number of scientists, inheriting the work of the late Wallace Clement Sabine, an authority on archtl. acoustics; labs. noted for work on sound and cryptography. Republican. Home: Geneva, Ill. Died May 17, 1936.

FACCIOLI, Giuseppe, elec. engr.; b. Rome, Italy, Apr. 7, 1877; s. Col. Luigi and Flora (Garbochi) F.;

grad. as elec. and industrial engr., Royal Poly. Inst., Milan, 1899; unmarried. Came to U.S., 1902, naturalized citizen, 1914. With Lab. of New York Edison Co., 1902; in employ Interborough Rapid Transit Co., 1903; designer of alternating current machines, Crocker-Wheeler Co., 1904; asst. to Wm. Stanley, Gt. Barrington, Mass., 1905-07; with ry. dept. Gen. Electric Co., Schenectady, N.Y., 1907, and continued with same co. at Pittsfield, Mass., serving as works engr., 1913-27, asso. mgr. and works engr., 1927-30. Fellow Am. Inst. E.E., Am. Phys. Soc., British Instn. E.E., Associazione Elettrotecnica Italiana. Known for investigations in connection with transmission of power at high voltage and for constrn. of high voltage elec. apparatus. Home: Pittsfield, Mass. Died Jan. 13, 1934.

FACKENTHAL, Benjamin Franklin, Jr., iron mfr.; b. Doylestown, Pa., June 2, 1851; s. Benjamin Franklin and Catharine (Dennis) F.; ed. public schs., and special course in chemistry and metallurgy, Lafayette College, 1874-75; hon. A.M., from same, 1897, Sc.D., 1911, and LL.D., 1929; m. Sarah J. Riegel, July 15, 1875 (died 1925). With Durham Iron Works, of Cooper & Hewitt, 1866-92, becoming supt. works and mines, 1876-92; also gen. mgr. Cooper & Hewitt's blast furnaces and mines, Ringwood and Pequest, N.J., and Riegelsville, Pa., 1879-92; pres. Thomas Iron Co., 1893-1913; pres. Ironton R.R. Co., 1893-1914; pres. Clymer Power Co., 1905-26; pres. Taylor, Stiles & Co., knife works, 1926-37; v.p. and chmn. exec. com. Easton Trust Co., 1893-1938; dir. Lehigh Portland Cement Co. Receiver Consol. Lake Superior Co., Sault Ste. Marie, 1902-03. Trustee Franklin and Marshall Coll., 1899—, pres. bd., 1915—; endowed chair biology and geology, 1910, and erected Fackenthal Labs., 1929, for chem. biol. depts., also indoor swimming pool, 1930, and a library, 1937. Mem. Washington Crossing Park Commn., 1922-24. Republican. Mason. Home: Riegelsville, Pa. Died Oct. 10, 1941.

FACKLER, David Parks, actuary; b. Kempsville, Va., Apr. 4, 1841; s. Rev. David Morris and Susan Stith (Satchell) F.; A.B., Coll. City of New York, 1859, A.M., 1891; m. Elizabeth Leverett Davenport, Nov. 17, 1875. Proposed, 1862, the method of dividing surplus now used by all U.S. life ins. cos.; 1872, asked by 20 cos. (N.Y. Life, Equitable, etc.), for an opinion; 1877, apptd. actuary to com. of policy holders examining Equitable Life Assurance Soc.; 1889, brought about the formation of the Actuarial Soc.; 1900, employed as its cons. actuary by one of the depts. of the U.S. Govt.; actuary of the N.J. Senate com. to investigate life ins., 1906, and, 1909-11, by a joint commn. of Congress. Author of Agents' Tables and Explanations, 1868-70. Home: Montclair, N.J. Died Oct. 30, 1924.

FAELTEN, Carl, pianist, teacher; b. Ilmenau, Thuringia, Dec. 21, 1846; s. Carl G. and Frederika (Moller) F.; ed. Latin School at Weimar; in music chiefly self-taught, but studied with Montag at Weimar and with Schoch at Frankfort-on-the-Main; studied violin and other orchestra instruments at Arnstadt; m. Adele Schloesser, of Lubeck, Germany, 1877. Taught, Frankfort-on-the-Main, 1868-82 (1878-82 in Dr. Hoch's Conservatory), Peabody Inst., Baltimore, 1882-85, NE. Conservatory of Music, Boston, 1885-97. Founder, 1897, and from then dir. Faelten Pianoforte Sch., Boston. Concert pianist. Has compiled numerous instruction books, including (with his brother) The Faelten System of Fundamental Training. Home: Holliston, Mass. Died July 20, 1925.

FAGAN, Charles Aloysius, lawyer; b. Pittsburgh, July 11, 1859; s. Thomas Jefferson and Mary (McLaughlin) F.; ed. Pittsburgh Catholic Inst. and Ewalt Coll.; m. Mary Kane, Feb. 11, 1888. In law practice at Pittsburgh, 1887—; mem. Fagan & Magee (William A.), 1896-1908, Fagan & McElroy, 1908—. V.p. German Nat. Bank of Pittsburgh, Iron City Sanitary Mfg. Co., Post Pub. Co., Pittsburgh Sun Pub. Co.; pres. Wheatley Hills Land Co. (New York). Asst. dist. atty., Allegheny Co., 1888-95; Dem. presdl. elector, 1892; chmn. Dem. Co. Com., 1894-96. Pres. Pittsburgh Hosp.; dir. Allegheny Co. Juvenile Court Home. Catholic. Home: Pittsburgh, Pa. Died Nov. 5, 1925.

FAGAN, James J., banking; m. Alice Bennett; children—Harold, James J., Paul I., Doris (Mrs. Edward T. Harrison). Formerly exec. v.p., now dir. Crocker First Nat. Bank of San Francisco; dir. Crocker First Federal Trust Co. Home: Woodside Calif. Died Jan. 25, 1935.

FAGG, John Gerardus, clergyman; b. Bethlehem, Wis., Feb. 21, 1860; s. Peter and Mary (Tillema) F.; A.B., Hope Coll., Holland, Mich., 1881; grad. New Brunswick (N.J.) Theol. Sem., 1885; (D.D., New York U., 1892); m. Margaret Watson Gillespie, Sept. 1889. Licensed to preach by Classis of Wis., Ref. Ch. in America, 1885; pastor Lawyersville and Cobleskill, N.Y., 1885-87; missionary, Amoy, China, 1888-94; pastor New Paltz, N.Y., 1894-95; stationed in N.Y. City, 1896—; pres. Gen. Synod Ref. Ch. in America and Bd. Foreign Missions. Author: Forty Years in South China (life John Van Nest Talmage), 1896. Home: New York, N.Y. Died May 3, 1917.

FAGNANI, Charles Prospero, theologian; b. New York, N.Y., Oct. 29, 1854; s. Giuseppe and Harriet Emma (Goodwin) F.; A.B. and B.S., Coll. City of New York, 1873; LL.B., Columbia, 1875; grad. Union Theol. Sem., 1882; D.D., Western Reserve, 1898; m. Flora Carleton, 1883 (died 1907); 2d, Alice Mary Le Gras, 1913. Teacher pub. schs., New York, 1873-79, Union Theol. Sem., New York, 1879-82; ordained Presbyn. ministry, 1882; chapel minister Grace Mission of 4th Av. Ch., 1882-85; pastor Westminster Ch., Yonkers, N.Y., 1885-86; in Europe, 1886-91; apptd. instr., Harvard Div. Sch., 1891 but could not serve owing to ill health; instr. Hebrew, 1892-99, asso. prof. O.T. lang. and lit., 1899-1915, prof. O.T. Literature and Exegesis, 1915-26 (emeritus), Union Theol. Sem. Deported from Munich by order from Berlin, Sept. 1921; for pro-allied activity during World War. Decorated Knight of the Legion of Honor (France), 1924. Author: A Primer of Hebrew, 1903; Notes on Hebrew Text of Book of Zephaniah in William R. Harper Memorial Volumes; Genesis I-XI, The Beginnings of History according to the Jews, 1925. Published The Art Life of a XIXth Century Portrait Painter, Fagnani; Some Facts Regarding the Biblical Narrative of the Creation, 1937. Home: Paris, France. Died Nov. 25, 1940.

FAHNESTOCK, Harris Charles, banker; b. Harrisburg, Pa., Feb. 27, 1835; s. Adam K. and Sibyl T. F.; ed. at Harrisburg; m. Miss M. A. McKinley, Oct. 16, 1856. V.p. First Nat. Bank, East Jersey Water Co.; dir. Am. Cotton Oil Co., Central R.R. Co. of N.J., Montclair Water Co., Southern Ry. Co., Western Union Telegraph Co.; trustee Bankers' Safe Deposit Co., N.J. Junction R.R. Co.; mem. bd. mgrs. D.,L.&W. R.R., Tidewater Pipe Co., Ltd. Home: New York, N.Y. Died June 4, 1914.

FAHNESTOCK, James Frederick, ry. official; b. Gettysburg, Pa., Oct. 16, 1859; s. James F. and Sarah Gates (Lord) F.; desc. from William Brewster, of the Mayflower; A.B., Phila. High Sch., 1879; m. Mary Elsinore McClure, Oct. 21, 1890. Began, 1879, in employ of Peter Wright & Sons, gen. agts. Am. Line of Steamships and Internat. Navigation Co.; inaugurated voucher system, 1884; was in charge of adjustment of through freights between ocean carriers and rys.; apptd. asst. treas. Internat. Navigation Co., Jan. 1892; asst. treas. Internat. Mercantile Marine Co., 1902-07, treas., 1907-08; apptd. asst. treas., Pa. R.R. Co., Dec. 9, 1908, elected treas., Mar. 23, 1909; also treas. L.I. R.R. Home: Philadelphia, Pa. Died June 7, 1924.

FAHNESTOCK, William, capitalist; b. Harrisburg, Pa., Sept. 2, 1857; s. Harris C. and Margaret (McKinley) F.; ed. pub. schs.; m. Julia Goetchius, Nov. 10, 1898; 1 son, William. Head of N.Y. Stock Exchange firm of Fahnestock & Co.; dir. Del., Lackawanna & Western Railroad Co., Gold Dust Corp., Lackawanna Securities Co., N.J. Gen. Security Co. Dir. New York Post-Grad. Med. Sch. and Hosp.; mem. bd. mgrs. St. Luke's Hosp. Republican. Episcopalian. Home: Katonah, N.Y., and New York, N.Y. Died July 5, 1936.

FAHS, David Wesley, clergyman; b. Germantown, Pa., Mar. 18, 1856; s. Tobias and Araminta (Willard) F.; A.B., Wabash Coll., 1877; grad. McCormick Theol. Sem., Chicago, 1880; (D.D., Lenox Coll., Hopkinton, Ia., 1877); m. Jennie M. Kerr, May 6, 1880. Ordained Presbyn. ministry, 1879; pastor Sandwich, Ill., 1880-84, Le Mars, Ia., 1884-94, Independence, 1894-1907, Cedar Falls, May 1, 1907—. Trustee Lenox Coll., Presbyn. Hosp., Waterloo, Ia. Moderator Ia. Synod of Presbyn. Ch., 1895; pres. Ia. Christian Endeavor Union, 1893-94. Republican. Home: Cedar Falls, Ia. Deceased.

FAIR, Eugene, college pres.; b. nr. Gilman City, Mo., Oct. 19, 1877; s. Joel J. and Sarah Jane (Brown) F.; Avalon Coll., Trenton, Mo.; B.S.D., State Normal Sch., Kirksville, Mo., 1901; A.B., U. of Mo., 1904, A.M., 1909; Ph.D., Columbia, 1923; m. Alta Mona Lorenz, Aug. 1903; children—Elizabeth June, Robert Eugene, Sarah Eleanor. Teacher rural schs., and Twp. High Sch., Murphysboro, Ill., until 1905; asst. prof. history, 1905-08, prof. Am. history, 1909-16, prof. polit. science, 1916-25, pres., 1925—, State Teachers Coll., Kirksville. Teacher George Peabody Coll. for Teachers, Nashville, Tenn., summer 1916; acting prof. polit. science, U. of Mo., 6 mos., 1918; mem. Mo. Ho. of Rep., 1920-21. Mgr. War Savings Certificate drive, Adair Co., Mo., 1918. Republican. Presbyn. Rotarian. Author: (brochures) Outline of Oriental History, 1908; Government and Politics in Missouri, 1922; Public Administration in Missouri, 1923. Home: Kirksville, Mo. Died Oct. 13, 1937.

FAIRBAIRN, Henry Arnold, physician; b. Catskill, N.Y., May 5, 1855; s. Rev. Robert Brinckerhoff (D.D., LL.D.) and Juliet (Arnold) F.; B.A., St. Stephen's College, Annandale, New York, 1875, M.A., 1878 (Litt.D., 1910); M.D., U. of Virginia, 1877; M.D., Coll. of Physicians and Surgeons (Columbia), New York, 1878; interne for several years at St. John's Hospital, Brooklyn; m. Alice LeFevre, Feb. 7, 1888. Practicing medicine in Brooklyn since graduation; attending phys. to St. John's Hosp.; cons. phys. to Brooklyn, L.I. Coll., L.I. State and Swedish hosps.; regent L.I. Coll. Hosp. Fellow N.Y. Acad. Medicine, Am. Coll. Physicians. Republican. Episcopalian. Mem. bd. mgrs. Ch. Charity Foundation, L.I. Home: Brooklyn, N.Y. Died June 11, 1925.

FAIRBANK, Arthur Boyce, lawyer; b. Ft. Wayne, Ind., Oct. 31, 1873; s. John Barnard and Ruth (Boyce) F.; A.B., Ill. Coll., Jacksonville, 1896, A.M., 1925; LL.B., Washington U., 1901; m. Lorena King, Apr. 15, 1906; 1 son, John King. Began practice at Huron, S.D., 1902; city atty., Huron, 1903-10; moved to Sioux Falls, 1912; mem. Boyce, Warren & Fairbank, 1912—; dir. Girton, Adams Ice Co.; treas. Sioux Falls Constrn. Co. Republican. Conglist. Mason. Home: Sioux Falls, S.D. Died Sept. 13, 1936.

FAIRBANK, Kellogg, lawyer; b. Chicago, Ill., 1869; s. Nathaniel K. and Helen L. (Graham) F.; A.B., Harvard, 1890, LL.B., 1893; m. Janet, d. Benjamin F. Ayer, May 29, 1900; children—Janet, Kellogg, Jr., Benjamin Ayer. Admitted to Ill. bar, 1893, and began practice at Chicago. Home: Chicago, Ill. Died Feb. 18, 1939.

FAIRBANKS, Charles Warren, 26th Vice-President of the United States; b. on farm nr. Unionville Center, O., May 11, 1852; s. Loriston M. and Mary A. (Smith) F.; A.B., Ohio Wesleyan U., 1872, A.M., 1875 (LL.D., 1901; LL.D., Baker U., 1903, Ia. State U., 1903, Northwestern, 1907); was agent for the Associated Press at Pittsburgh and Cleveland, 1872-74; admitted to Ohio bar, 1874, and established practice at Indianapolis; m. Cornelia Cole, d. of Judge P. B. Cole, of Marysville, O., 1874 (died 1913). Chmn. Ind. Rep. State convs., 1892, 98, 1914; del.-at-large Rep. Nat. convs., St. Louis, 1896 (temporary chmn.), Phila., 1900 (chmn. com. on resolutions), Chicago, 1904 (unanimously nominated for Vice-President), Chicago, 1912 (chmn. com. on resolutions); Rep. caucus nominee for U.S. senator, 1893, but defeated by David Turpie, Democrat; elected U.S. senator from Ind., for terms 1897-1903, 1903-09; resigned Mar. 4, 1905; elected Vice-President of the United States, on the ticket with Theodore Roosevelt, Nov. 1904, receiving 337 of the 476 electoral votes, to 139 for Henry Gassaway Davis, of W.Va., the Dem. candidate; term expired Mar. 4, 1909. Unanimously nominated for Vice-President of the U.S. at Rep. Nat. Conv., Chicago, 1916, with Charles E. Hughes, candidate for President; ticket defeated by narrow margin. Mem. Joint High British-Am. Commn., 1898, and chmn. Am. commrs. U.S. rep. Tercentenary Celebration at Quebec, 1908. Trustee Ohio Wesleyan U., American U. (Washington), De Pauw U.; regent Smithsonian Instn. Pres. Meth. Hosp. of Ind. Forestry Assn. Made tour of the world, 1909-10. Home: Indianapolis, Ind. Died June 4, 1918.

FAIRBANKS, Cornelia Cole; d. Judge P. B. Cole; A.B., Ohio Wesleyan U., 1872; m. Charles Warren Fairbanks, 1874. Pres. gen. of D.A.R., 1901-05; also active in Nat. Fedn. of Women's Clubs and other orgns.; one of the promoters of the "Junior Republic." Made tour of the world, 1909-10. Home: Indianapolis. Died Oct. 24, 1913.

FAIRBANKS, Douglas, actor; b. Denver, May 23, 1883; Jarvis Mil. Acad., Denver; East Denver High Sch.; Colo. Sch. of Mines; m. Anna Beth Sully, July 11, 1907 (divorced 1918); m. 2d, Mary Pickford, actress, Mar. 28, 1920 (divorced 1935); m. 3d, the former Sylvia, Lady Ashley, Mar. 7, 1936. Made his first stage appearance in New York City, 1901; starred in Hawthorne of the U.S.A., Frenzied Finance, All for a Girl, A Gentleman from Mississippi, The Cub, Gentleman of Leisure, Comes up Smiling, Henrietta, Show Shop. Starred in motion pictures, and head of own producing co., 1916—; later productions: His Majesty the American; When the Clouds Roll By; The Mollycoddle; The Mark of Zorro; The Nut; The Three Musketeers; Robin Hood; The Thief of Bagdad; Don Q, Son of Zorro; The Black Pirate; The Gaucho; The Iron Mask; The Taming of the Shrew, etc. Home: Beverly Hills, Calif. Died Dec. 11, 1939.

FAIRBANKS, Edward Taylor, clergyman; b. St. Johnsbury, Vt., May 12, 1836; s. Joseph Paddock and Almira (Taylor) Fairbanks; St. Johnsbury Acad. and Phillips Acad., Andover, Mass.; A.B., Yale, 1859; Andover Theol. Sem., 1861-62; studied abroad, 1863-64; (D.D., U. of Vt., 1892); m. Emma C. Taplin, July 9, 1862. Ordained Congl. ministry, 1868; pastor First and South Chs., St. Johnsbury, Vt., 1868-1902; librarian and dir. St. Johnsbury Athenæum, 1902—. Trustee, sec. and treas. St. Johnsbury Acad. Mem. Vt. State Senate, 1908-09. Republican. Died Jan. 12, 1919.

FAIRBANKS, Frank Perley, artist; b. Boston, Mass., July 17, 1875; s. Jonathan Robinson and Wilma (Hutchins) F.; ed. English High Sch., Boston; studied art in Sch. of Drawing and Painting, of Boston Mus. Fine Arts, Am. Acad. in Rome; m. Sophie Grace Griswold François, Oct. 19, 1912; children—David, Barbara. Has exhibited at Paris Salon, Royal Academy, London, and in United States; prin. work: decorations, Pub. Library, St. Paul, Minn.; The U.S. Supreme Court Building and Scottish Rite Temple, Washington, D.C.; Comptroller's Suite, Municipal Bldg., New York; Am. Acad. in Rome, etc. Annual prof. Sch. of Fine Arts, Am. Acad. in Rome, 1919-21, prof. in charge Sch. of Fine Arts, 1922-32; mem. firm Paris & Wiley, 522 5th Av., New York, N.Y. Capt. Am. Red Cross, civilian relief, on the Piave, Italy, World War. Decorated Order Cavaliere della Corona d'Italia, D.S.M., Italian Red Cross. Died Aug. 8, 1939.

FAIRBANKS, Frederick Cole, publisher; b. Indianapolis, Ind., June 14, 1881; s. Charles Warren (Vice-President U.S., 1905-09) and Cornelia (Cole) F.; prep. edn. Lawrenceville (N.J.) Sch., Phillips Exeter Acad.; A.B., Princeton, 1903; student U. of Southern Calif. Law Sch.; m. Helen Scott, Oct. 10, 1906; children—Charles Warren, 3d, Cornelia Scott (Mrs. David L. Stone, Jr.); m. 2d, Dorothy Kernochan, Dec. 22, 1938. Admitted to Calif. bar, 1910, and practiced in Los Angeles, 1910-18; then engaged in orange growing, farming and gen. business, Calif.; pres. and pub. The Iidianapolis News Pub. Co., 1937—. Republican. Methodist. Mason. Home: Indianapolis, Ind. Died May 22, 1940.

FAIRBANKS, Henry, inventor, mfr.; b. St. Johnsbury, Vt., May 6, 1830; s. late Thaddeus (inventor of scales) and Lucy P. (Barker) F.; A.B., Dartmouth, 1853, A.M., 1856 (Ph.D., 1880); grad. Andover Theol. Sem., 1857; m. Annie S. Noyes, Apr. 30, 1862 (died 1872); m. 2d, Ruthy Page, May 5, 1874; father of Arthur F. Ordained Congl. ministry, 1857; in pastorates, 1857-60; prof. natural philosophy, 1859-65, natural history, 1865-68, Dartmouth. Identified with E. & T. Fairbanks & Co., mfrs. of scales, etc., 1868—; has received more than 30 patents on various devices. Trustee Dartmouth Coll., 1870-96; pres. St. Johnsbury Acad.; mem. Nat. and Internat. Congl. councils. Home: St. Johnsbury, Vt. Died June 7, 1918.

FAIRBANKS, Warren Charles, newspaper pub.; b. Indianapolis, Ind., Apr. 25, 1878; s. Charles Warren and Cornelia (Cole) F.; A.B., Ohio Wesleyan U., 1898; m. Ethel Cassidy, Jan. 14, 1904; children—Edith Anne (wife of Count Ruggero Visconti di Modrone), Cornelia Warren (wife of Frederick A. Poole, Jr.). With Standard Mfg. Co., Springfield, O., 1898-1901, sec., 1898-1901; sec. Oliver Typewriter Co., Chicago, Ill., 1901-04; pres. and pub. Indianapolis News Publishing Co., Indianapolis, Ind., 1922—; president Indianapolis Switch & Frog Co.; director Pure Oil Company. State director President Hoover's Unemployment Relief. Capt. U.S. Vols., 1898. Trustee McKinley Nat. Memorial Assn., M.E. Hosp. (Indianapolis). Republican. Methodist. Home: Indianapolis, Ind. Died July 27, 1938.

FAIRCHILD, Charles Stebbins, sec. of the treasury; b. Cazenovia, N.Y., Apr. 30, 1842; s. Sidney T. and Helen (Childs) F.; A.B., Harvard, 1863, LL.B., 1865; (LL.D., Columbian, 1888, Harvard, 1888); m. Helen Lincklaen, June 1, 1871. Admitted to bar, 1865, and began practice at Albany; deputy atty. gen. of N.Y., 1874, atty. gen. of N.Y., 1876-77; spent two years in Europe; removed to New York, 1880; asst. sec., 1885-87, sec. of the treasury in cabinet of President Cleveland, 1887-89. Democrat (gold standard). Pres. N.Y. Security & Trust Co., 1889-1904; now pres. Atlanta & Charlotte Air Line R.R. Co.; dir. Erie & Pitts. R.R. Co. Pres. and treas. State Charities Aid Assn.; v.p. Charity Organization Soc. of N.Y., was several yrs. pres. Reform Club. Mem. Monetary Commn., apptd. by exec. com. of Indianapolis Monetary Conf. of 1897. Home: Cazenovia, N.Y. Died Nov. 24, 1924.

FAIRCHILD, David Sturges, surgeon, editor; b. Fairfield, Vt., Sept. 16, 1847; s. Eli and Grace Dimond (Sturges) F.; student U. of Mich., 1866-68; M.D., Albany Med. Coll. (Union U.), 1868; m. Wilhelmina Conrad Tattersall, May 1, 1870; children—David Sturges (lt. col. Med. Corps, U.S.A.), Mrs. A. W. Brown, Mrs. H. R. Reynolds. Began practice, High Forest, 1869; prof. physiology and comparative anatomy, Ia. State Coll., 1879-93; prof. surg. pathology, Drake U. Coll. of Medicine, 1882-1909, dean, 1903-09; div. surgeon C.&N.W. Ry., 1883—. Editor Journal Ia. State Med. Soc. Mem. Sch. Bd., Ames, Ia., 9 yrs. (pres. 6 yrs.). Fellow Am. Coll. Surgeons (gov.). Episcopalian. Mason. Author: Pioneer Practice, 1914. Home: Clinton, Ia. Died 1930.

FAIRCHILD, Edward Thomson, coll. pres.; b. Doylestown, O., Oct. 30, 1854; s. Samuel and Eliza Jane (Huestis) F.; ed. Ohio Wesleyan U., Wooster U.; (hon. A.M., Kan. State Agrl. Coll.; Pd.D., Baker U., 1908); m. Frances L. Postlewait, Oct. 10, 1883. Began teaching in Ohio, 1872; removed to Kan., 1885; regent Kan. State Agrl. Coll., 1889-1907; state supt. pub. instrn. of Kan., 1907-12; pres. N.H. Coll., Durham, 1912—. Life mem. N.E.A.; mem. Nat. Council of Edn. Republican. Methodist. Home: Durham, N.H. Died Jan. 23, 1917.

FAIRCHILD, George Thompson, v.p. and prof. English literature, Berea Coll., 1898—; b. Brownhelm, O., Oct. 6, 1838; s. Grandison and Nancy (Harris) F.; grad. Oberlin, 1862 (A.M., 1865; LL.D., 1893); Oberlin Theol. School, 1865; m. Charlotte Pearl Halsted, Nov. 25, 1863. Reared on father's farm; prof. English literature, Mich. Agrl. Coll., 1865-79; pres. Kan. State Agrl. Coll., 1879-97. Ordained Congl. minister at Lansing, Mich., 1871; pres. Am. Assn. of Agrl. Colls. and Expt. Stas., 1897. Home: Berea, Ky. Died 1901.

FAIRCHILD, George Winthrop, congressman; b. Oneonta, N.Y., May 6, 1854; s. Jesse F.; ed. dist. schs. until 13; m. Josephine Mills Sherman, 1891. Learned printer's trade; v.p. and chmn. bd. Computing-Tabulating-Recording Co., New York; pres. Internat. Time Recording Co. (Endicott, N.Y.), White Plains Development Co., Ry. Improvement Co. (New York); dir. Peoples Trust Co. (Binghamton), Citizens Nat. Bank (Oneonta), Internat. Business Machines Co., of Can. Mem. 60th to 66th Congresses (1907-19), 34th N.Y. Dist. Mem. Sulgrave Instn. Homes: Oneonta, N.Y., and New York, N.Y. Died Dec. 31, 1924.

FAIRCHILD, James Harris, Congl. clergyman, educator; b. Stockbridge, Mass., Nov. 25, 1817; moved to Brownhelm, O., 1818; grad. Oberlin Coll., 1838 (D.D., LL.D.); ordained to ministry, 1841. Tutor, 1838-42; prof. langs., 1842-47; prof. mathematics, 1847-58; prof. moral philosophy and theology, 1858; pres., 1866-89, Oberlin Coll.; resigned, 1889; was Finney prof. from 1898, now prof. emeritus theology, Oberlin Theol. Sem. Traveled in Europe, Asia and Africa, 1870-71; in Hawaiian Islands, 1884. Author: Moral Philosophy; Needed Phases of Christianity; Oberlin: The Colony and the College; Elements of Theology; Woman's Right to the Ballot. Home: Oberlin, O. Died 1902.

FAIRCHILD, Julian D., banker; b. Stratford, Conn., Apr. 17, 1850; s. Douglas and Lydia (Hawley) F.; pub. sch. edn.; m. Florence I. Bradley, Jan. 9, 1879; children—Florence Esther Read, Julian P. Office boy in mfg. house of New Haven at 13; sec. Quinnipiac Fertilizer Co., 1871-74; identified with Coe Fertilizing Co., New York, 1874-94. Pres. Kings Co. Trust Co., Brooklyn, 1893—; v.p. Mortgage Bond Co.; Eagle Warehouse Co. Declined Dem. nomination for mayor of Brooklyn, 1894, and comptrollership Greater City of New York, 1896; mem. and treas. commn. for constrn. of Williamsburg Bridge, 1896-1900. Trustee Brooklyn Inst. Arts and Sciences. Mem. N.Y. Chamber of Commerce, N.Y. Produce Exchange. Home: Brooklyn, N.Y. Died Feb. 21, 1926.

FAIRCHILD, (Edwin) Milton, educationist; b. East Lansing, Mich., Nov. 7, 1865; s. George T. and Charlotte Pearl (Halsted) F.; student Kan. State Coll.; A.B., Oberlin, 1890; grad. Andover Theol. Sem., 1893; m. (Mary) Salome Cutler, July 1, 1897 (died 1921). Chmn. Character Edn. Instn., Washington, D.C., 1911—; chmn. exec. com. Nat. Morality Codes Competition, for prize of $5,000, 1915; and $20,000, for Best Method of Character Education, 1919. Compiler of "five point plan" for character edn. in schs., 1927; also author, editor or compiler of the "Character Graph," "Characteristics of Human Beings," "Science Thinking Graph," "List of Varieties of Thinking," "The Scientific Method," "Self-Character Education Plan" for high schools; "Objectives of Human Life"; "Graph of the Urges." Author: (brochures) Marriage Service, 1897; Commandments Father Wisdom Taught the Child He Loved, 1897. Home: Washington, D.C. Died Dec. 26, 1939.

FAIRCHILD, (Mary) Salome Cutler, library lecturer; b. Dalton, Mass., June 21, 1855; d. Artemus Hubbard and Lydia (Wakefield) Cutler; grad. Mt. Holyoke Sem., 1875; B.L.S., U. State of N.Y., 1891; m. (Edwin) Milton Fairchild, July 1, 1897. Cataloguer, Columbia Coll. Library, 1884-89; instr., Columbia Coll. Library Sch., 1887-89; vice-dir. N.Y. State Library Sch., 1889-1905; lecturer on Am. libraries and selection of books, 1906—. Chmn. com. in charge library exhibit Chicago Expn. which issued Catalog of A.L.A. Library. Wrote: Children's Home Libraries, 1894; Function of the Library, 1901. Address: Washington, D.C. Died Dec. 20, 1921.

FAIRCHILD, Thomas Everett, educator, clergyman; b. Milford, Calif., Apr. 8, 1894; s. Thomas Manley and Emma Jane (Maxwell) F.; B.S., U. of Me., 1916, M.S., 1917; S.T.B., Boston U. Sch. of Theology, 1927, also student Sch. of Edn., 1928; student U. of Chicago, 1931; m. Ruth Eyelyn March, July 30, 1918; children—Thomas Leonard, Rowena Evelyn. Ordained to ministry M.E. Ch., 1917; pastor various chs. in Me., 1915-28; prin. East Corinth (Me.) Acad., 1917-18; dir. Wesley Foundation, Orono, Me., 1921-24; asst. to pres. Boston U., 1928—; dir. Boston U. Summer Sch., 1932—. Mem. Me. Conf. of M.E. Ch. Republican. Mason. Home: West Somerville, Mass. Died Apr. 19, 1934.

FAIRCLOTH, William Tyson; chief justice Supreme Court, N.C., Raleigh, N.C. Died 1900.

FAIRCLOUGH, Henry Rushton, philologist; b. nr. Barrie, Ont., Can., July 15, 1862; s. James and Elizabeth (Erving) F.; A.B., U. of Toronto, 1883, A.M., 1886, Litt.D., 1922; Ph.D., Johns Hopkins, 1896; m. Frederica, d. Rev. J. A. Allen, of Kingston, Ont., Aug. 25, 1888 (died 1927); 1 dau., Kathrine Rushton (Mrs. Rufus Hatch Kimball); m. 2d, Mary Charlotte Holly, Sept. 24, 1930. Fellow in classics, 1883-84, lecturer in Greek, 1887-93, U. Coll., Toronto; asso. prof. of Greek and Latin, 1893-97, prof. classical lit., 1897-1902, and 1922—, also prof. Latin, 1902-22 (emeritus, 1927), Stanford University. Professor Latin, summer session, U. of Wisconsin, 1906, Columbia U., 1908, U. of Chicago, 1910; prof. in Am. Sch. of Classical Studies, Rome, 1910-11; prof. Latin, summer, U. of Calif., 1921; prof. N.T. lit. Church Div. Sch. of Pacific, San Francisco, 1921-27; visiting lecturer on Greek and Latin, Harvard, 1925-26; visiting prof. of Greek and Latin, Amherst College, 1927-29; prof. of Greek, U. of Chicago, summer session, 1928; lecturer on archæology, U. of N.M., summer 1935. Del. centennial celebration, U. of Berlin, 1910; del. Toronto U. Centenary, 1927, Internat. Congress Anthropol. Sciences, 1934. With Swiss commn. at Berne, in charge of Belgian and Am. Relief for Am. Red Cross, 1918-19; lt. col. Am. Red Cross, and commr. to Montenegro, 1919-20. Decorated by Serbian Red Cross and by Crown Prince Alexander with Order of White Eagle, Class IV; Comdr. Order of St. Sava III (Serbia); comdr. Order of Danilo (Montenegro); Officier de l'Ordre de la Couronne (Belgium), 1920. Author: The Classics and our Twentieth Century Poets, 1927; Love of Nature among the Greeks and Romans, 1930; Aspects of Horace, 1935; Some Aspects of Nature, 1935. Translator: Antigone of Sophocles, 1903; Virgil's Æneid (with S. L. Brown) 1908; Phormio of Terence (with L. J. Richardson), 1908; Trinummus of Plautus, 1909. Editor Students' Series Latin Classics; dir. and editor of Art and Archæology, 1925, now asso. editor. Editor complete works of Virgil, and of Satires and Epistles of Horace in the Loeb classics; The Andria of Terence, 1901. Died Feb. 12, 1938.

FAIRFIELD, Edward George, newspaper editor; b. LaCrosse, Wis., May 15, 1890; s. George and Anna (Finn) F.; student Columbia Acad., Dubuque, Ia., 1905-08; A.B., Columbia Coll., Dubuque, 1910; m. Maude Ethel Allen, Sept. 23, 1912; children—Allen Edward, Lois Anna, Thomas Allen, Joan Adele, Edward George, Anna May, David Bruce. Began as reporter Times-Journal, Dubuque, 1910, Des Moines (Ia.) Capital, 1912-13; city editor Times-Journal, 1913-17, editor, 1920-27; editor Dubuque Herald & Times-Journal (consolidated), 1927—. Sec. Liberty Loan and Am. Red Cross campaign Plymouth Co., Ia., 1917, Muscatine Co., 1918-19. Republican. Catholic. Home: Dubuque, Ia. Died Feb. 4, 1933.

FAIRFIELD, Louis W., congressman; b. nr. Wapakoneta, O., Oct. 15, 1858; s. George and Clarissa (Gardiner) F.; student Ohio Northern U., Ada, 1876-82; (M.S., Tri-State Coll., 1902); m. Ina Maude Howe, 1884 (dec.); m. 2d, Marie Almond, June 28, 1891. Editor Hardin Co. (Ohio) Republican, 1881-82; began teaching at Angola, Ind., 1885; prof. physics and philosophy, Tri-State Coll., 1885-1917, also trustee and v.p. Mem. 65th to 68th Congresses (1917-25), 12th Ind. Dist. Republican. Mem. Christian (Disciples) Ch. Mason. Home: Angola, Ind. Died Feb. 20, 1930.

FAIRLAMB, James Remington, organist-composer; b. Phila., Jan. 23, 1838; s. Col. Jonas P. and Hannah (Kennedy) F.; ed. in grammar and Central High Schools there; organist Western M.E. Ch., Phila., at 14. Went abroad at 21; studied under Prudent, Marmontel, Danhauser, Masset, and Mabellini; later U.S. consul at Zurich, Switzerland; decorated by King of Würtemberg with "Great Gold Medal of Art and Science," and received numerous prizes for compositions; has composed many songs, an oratorio, two operas, an operetta, church music, etc. Organist and choirmaster, 7 yrs., St. Ignatius (Episcopal) Ch., N.Y. City; 5 yrs. Rutgers Riverside Presbyn. Ch.; now at Ch. of the Messiah, and instr. in music, De Witt Clinton High School, New York. Former chmn. Music Com., The Manuscript Soc. of New York; m. Marian Kerr, d. Judge David Higgins of O.; m. 2d, Melusina Therese, d. George Fred Muller, Pittsburgh. Home: New York, N.Y. Died 1908.

FAIRLEIGH, David William, lawyer; b. Cloverport, Ky., Nov. 28, 1853; s. James La Rue and Jane (Murray) F.; ed. pvt. schs., Brandenburg, Ky., to 18; LL.B., Law Dept., U. of Louisville, 1874 (LL.D., 1912); m. Emma Ditto, May 28, 1878. Practiced in partnership with James W. Lewis, as Lewis & Fairleigh, Brandenburg, 1875-87; removed to Louisville, 1887, and formed partnership with Frank P. Straus, as Fairleigh & Straus; son James F. admitted to firm, 1903, and title became Fairleigh, Straus & Fairleigh; retired, 1919. Pres. Bd. of Trustees, U. of Louisville. Republican. Presbyn. Dir. Masonic Widows' and Orphans' Home of Ky., Louisville. Home: Louisville, Ky. Died 1924.

FAIRLEY, Edwin, clergyman; b. at March, Cambridgeshire, Eng., Feb. 7, 1864; s. Rev. Samuel and Caroline (Cole) F.; A.B., Amherst, 1886; grad. Union Theol. Sem., 1892; grad. study English, Columbia, 1904-06; m. Phebe Parsils Hall, June 30, 1898 (died 1899); m. 2d, Jessie Waldo Stebbins, Jan. 16, 1901;

children—Arthur Samuel, Donald Cole (dec.), Frances (Mrs. Edward M. Collins), Margaret Ostrander (Mrs. Alex. S. Traub, Jr.), William Edwin. Teacher of Latin, Holbrook's School, Ossining, New York, 1886-89; pastor, Roseland (N.J.) Presbyn. Ch., 1891-1902; teacher of English Boys' High Sch., Brooklyn, 1902-09; head English dept., Jamaica (N.Y.) High Sch., 1909-21; ednl. sec. Am. Unitarian Assn., 1921-33; minister Unitarian Ch., Flushing, N.Y., 1920-29; minister in charge Flushing Unitarian Ch., 1933-35, minister emeritus, 1932—; minister Unitarian Ch., Barneveld, N.Y., 1936—. Pres. Mohawk Valley Conf. Unitarian Chs., 1939. Mem. of College Conf. on Uniform Entrance Requirements in English, 1918-20. Lecturer New York Bd. Edn., 1904-17; extension lecturer in English, Columbia, 1909-10. Mem. Amherst Alumni Council, 1926-31. Editor: Selections from the Spectator, 1911; Dickens' David Copperfield, 1911; Homer's Odyssey, 1911; Stevenson's Treasure Island, 1912; Eliot's Silas Marner, 1913. Author: (with Clarence H. Wilson), Talks to Young People on Ethics, 1924. Corr. editor, English Journal, 1912-22; Am. corr. Inquirer, London, 1932-40. Unitarian. Home: Barneveld, N.Y. Died May 16, 1941.

FAIRLEY, William, high sch. prin.; b. Hexham, Eng., Aug. 26, 1857; s. Rev. Samuel and Elizabeth Anna (Barrett) F.; A.B., Amherst, 1878, A.M., 1883; (D.D., Beloit, 1896; Ph.D., U. of Pa., 1897); m. Sherah R. Spike, Jan. 26, 1888. Ordained R.E. ministry, 1880; rector Peoria, Ill., 1884-94; prof. ch. history, R.E. Theol. Sem., Phila., 1894-98; head of history dept., Brooklyn Commercial High Sch., 1904-10, prin. same, 1910—. Author: Monumentum Ancyranum, or Deeds of Augustus, 1897; Notitia Dignitatum, or Register of Dignitaries of Roman Empire, 1898. Home: Brooklyn, N.Y. Died July 8, 1918.

FAISON, John Miller, congressman; b. near Faison, N.C., Apr. 17, 1862; s. Dr. Henry and Martha (Hicks) F.; B.S., Davidson Coll., N.C., 1883; M.D., U. of Va., 1884; attended New York Polyclinic, 6 months, 1884-85; m. Eliza F. DeVane, Dec. 17, 1887. In med. and surg. practice at Faison, 1885—; also farmer; dir. Bank of Faison. Mem. Dem. State Exec. Com., 1894-98; mem. N.C. Jamestown Expn. Commn., 1907; chmn. bd. commrs., Duplin Co., 1908-10; mem. 62d and 63d Congresses (1911-15), 3d N.C. Dist. Presbyn. Chmn. trustees Faison Male Acad. Home: Faison, N.C. Deceased.

FAISON, Samson Lane, army officer; b. in N.C., Nov. 29, 1860; grad. U.S. Mil. Acad., June 13, 1883; Army War Coll., 1911. Commd. 2d lt. 1st Inf., June 13, 1883; promoted through grades to Col. Inf., Oct. 2, 1915; brig. gen. N.A., Aug. 5, 1917. Comd. company in engagement with Filipino insurgents, Guadaloupe Ridge, P.I., June 10, 1899; running engagement of 3 days with insurgents, Cavite to San Francisco de Malabon; served as judge Provost Court and judge adv. of Mil. Commn., Manila; mem. Gen. Court Martial at Manila, Apr.-May 1901; again in P.I., in command Camp Downs, Leyte, 1907-08; at Schofield Barracks, H.T., 1916. Brig. gen. N.A., Aug. 5, 1917, and assigned to comd. 60th Inf. Brig., 30th Div., Sept. 1917; comd. 30th Div., Dec. 22, 1917-July 20, 1918; comd. 60th Inf. Brig., Sept. 1917-Apr. 1919, when it was demobilized. Reverted to reg. rank of col. U.S.A., July 15, 1919, comdg. 43d Inf., Camp Lee, Va. Took part in Canal Sector, Belgium, defensive, July and Aug. 1918; Ypres-Lys offensive, Aug. 31 and Sept. 1, 1918, and Somme offensive, Sept. 24-Oct. 20, 1918. Awarded D.S.M.; French Legion of Honor, with rank of Officer, and Croix de Guerre, with Palm. Died Oct. 17, 1940.

FAITHORN, John Nicholson, ry. official; b. London, Eng., Mar. 21, 1852; s. John Nicholson and Caroline Elizabeth F.; ed. St. Mark's Coll., London; m. Sarah Levett, of London, Eng., Jan. 1, 1873. Entered ry. service, 1872; clerk C.&A. Ry., 1872-82; auditor Southwestern Ry. Assn., 1882-85; commr. Western Ry. and Northwestern Freight Assn., 1885-87; commr. same and chmn. Western Freight Assn., 1887-90; chmn. Southwestern Ry. & Steamship Assn. and commr. Western Freight Assn., 1890-92; v.p. and gen. mgr. Street's Western Stable Car Co., 1893-98; gen. mgr. Wis. & Mich. Ry., 1895-96; pres. and gen. mgr. St. Louis, Peoria & Northern Ry., 1898-99; v.p. C.&A. Ry., 1902-04; pres. and gen. mgr. Chicago Terminal Transfer R.R. from Aug. 1, 1899, also receiver same, Apr. 16, 1906-11; retired from active business, 1911. Home: Winnetka, Ill. Died Mar. 28, 1914.

FALCONER, John Ironside, rural economist; b. Mason, N.H., Jan. 13, 1888; s. George and Annie (Watson) F.; B.S., New Hampshire Coll., Durham, N.H., 1909; M.S., U. of Wis., 1912, Ph.D., 1914; unmarried. Asst. in agronomy, R.I., Agrl. Expt. Sta., 1909-11; asst. prof. rural economics, 1914-17, prof. and head of dept., 1917—, Ohio State U.; chief Dept. Rural Economics Ohio State Agrl. Expt. Sta., 1925—. Apptd. by sec. of agr., Mar. 1919, as mem. com. to make studies and report on cost of farm products in U.S. Republican. Presbyn. Mason. Home: Columbus, O. Deceased.

FALCONER, John Mackie, artist; b. Edinburgh, Scotland, May 22, 1820; s. Hugh M. and Catherine (Stewart) F.; high school edn.; came to U.S., 1836; studied art at Nat. Acad. and other schools in New York and Brooklyn, and at the Louvre in Paris. Paintings principally of historic buildings in America and Europe, in oil, water colors, and enamel on porcelain; also etchings on copper. Lately has made a specialty of conservation and restoration of paintings. Hon. mem. Nat. Acad. Design; fellow Royal Soc. Painter Etchers, 1888. Home: Brooklyn, N.Y. Deceased.

FALCONER, Robert Clemons, civil engr.; b. St. Mary's, Pa., Mar. 21, 1874; s. Nathaniel Sill and Elizabeth (Clemons) F.; B.S., in C.E., U. of Wis., 1895; m. Clara Eliza McLain, Oct. 25, 1906; children—Clara Evans, Elizabeth, Robert McLain. With Purdy & Henderson, New York, 1895-97, Cambria Steel Co., Johnstown, Pa., 1897-98, Pa. Lines West of Pittsburgh, 1898-1901; sales engr. Am. Bridge Co., Pittsburgh, 1901-02; prospecting for Pittsburgh Zinc Co., 1902-03; designer, Walton Iron Co., Cincinnati, 1903-04; designer and estimator McClintock-Marshall Constrn. Co., Pittsburgh, 1904-05; with Erie R.R., 1905—, advancing through various positions in engineering dept. to asst. v.p. and chief engr., and asst. v.p. in charge of engrng.; also dir. Paterson & Ramapo, Paterson, Newark and New York. Home: Cleveland, O. Died Feb. 20, 1941.

FALCONER, William Armistead, prof. law; b. Charleston, Ark., June 16, 1869; s. Col. John Peregrine and Fannie Taliaferro (Armistead) F.; ed. U. of Va.; D.C.L., U. of the South, 1922; LL.D., U. of Ark., 1925; m. Anna Lyons, d. Prof. James H. Gilmore of U. of Va., Oct. 24, 1894. Admitted to Ark. bar, 1894; judge of County Court and Probate Court, Sebastian Co., Ark., 1902-08; mem. Ark. Ry. Commn., 1909-11 (chmn. 1910-11); chancellor 10th Circuit, Ark., 1913-19; gen. practice at Ft. Smith, Ark., 1919-25, prof. of law, U. of Ark., 1925—. Democrat. Episcopalian. Transl.: Cicero's De Senectute, De Amicitia, De Divinatione (Loeb Classical Library), 1922. Home: Fayetteville, Ark. Died 1927.

FALCONIO, Diomede, cardinal; b. Pescocostanzo, in the Abruzzi, Italy, 1842; entered Franciscan Order, Sept. 2, 1860; on completion of studies, Nov. 1865, sent as missionary to the U.S.; was ordained priest Jan. 4, 1866, by Bishop Timon, of Buffalo. Prof. philosophy and v.p. St. Bonaventure's Coll., Allegany, N.Y., 1866; prof. theology and sec. Franciscan Province the Immaculate Conception, 1867; pres. Coll. and Sem. of St. Bonaventure, 1868; became citizen of U.S., 1868; sec. and adminstr. of Cathedral at Harbor Grace, Newfoundland, 1872-82; in U.S., 1882-83; returned to Italy, 1883, and elected Provincial of Franciscans in the Abruzzi, later reëlected and was also commissary and visitor-gen. Province of Naples, 1888; synodial examiner, Diocese of Aquila; commissary and visitor-gen. Franciscan Province in Puglia, 1889; procurator-gen. Franciscan Order and visitor-gen. in various Provinces of the Order, 1889-92. Consecrated, July 17, 1892, bishop of Lacedonia, and was raised, Nov. 29, 1895, to be archbishop of Acerenza and Matera, in Basilicata; apostolic delegate to Canada, 1899-1902; apostolic del. to U.S., Sept. 30, 1902-Nov. 1911; elevated to the cardinalate, Nov. 27, 1911. Died Feb. 7, 1917.

FALK, Louis, organist, musical theorist; b. Unter Ostern, Germany, Dec. 11, 1848; s. John A. and Wilhelmina Francesca (Roessing) F.; ed. Rochester, N.Y., 1856-62; pvt. pupil of Dr. William Volckmar, in Hesse Cassel, 1865-67; grad. Conservatory, Leipzig, 1869; (Dr. of Music, Chicago Mus. Coll., 1896); m. Cara Dayton Dickinson, Mar. 11, 1875. Prof. organ theory, Chicago Mus. Coll., 1869—. Organist Union Park Congl. Ch., Chicago, 1872-97; concert organist, orchestral and choral conductor; composer. Home: Chicago, Ill. Died May 26, 1925.

FALK, Otto Herbert, soldier, mfr.; b. Milwaukee, June 18, 1865; s. Franz and Louise (Wahl) F.; ed. German-English Academy, Milwaukee; Northwestern Coll., Watertown, Wis.; grad. as capt., Allen Mil. Acad., Chicago, 1884; m. Elizabeth A. Vogel, Dec. 10, 1901; children—Mrs. Elisabeth Eberbach, Otto Herbert. Identified with financial interests of Falk family since beginning of active career, now v.p. The Falk Co., mfrs. steel castings; apptd. receiver Allis-Chalmers Co., 1912, and pres. reorganized co., 1913-32, chmn. bd., 1932—; pres. Allis-Chalmers-Rumely, Ltd., Canada; director Harnischfeger Corporation, First Wis. Nat. Bank, First Wis. Trust Co., Wis. Telephone Co., etc. Chmn. bd. govs. Marquette U. Commd. adj. 4th Batt., Wis. N.G., Mar. 1886; col. and a.-d.-c. to Gov. Rusk, Aug. 1887; lt. col., comdg. 4th Inf., Oct. 1887; q.-m. gen., Jan. 1891; adj. gen., Dec. 1893; commd. maj. and chief q.-m. U.S. Vols., Spanish-Am. War, June 1898; assigned to 1st Div., 3d Army Corps, Chickamauga Park, Ga., apptd. chief q. m. 3d Army Corps, U.S. Army, Oct. 1898, services Cuba and Puerto Rico; hon. discharged from vol. service, June 20, 1899; col. comdg. 1st Regt. Inf., Wis. N.G., June 1899; transferred to gen. staff as chief engr., 1906; retired with rank of brig. gen., Jan. 1911; was in active duty in riots at Milwaukee, 1886, Ashland, 1893, Merrill, 1893, Spooner, 1894, Kenosha, 1909; in charge of relief expedition sent to give aid to starving miners in northern Wis. and Mich., winter of 1893. Dir. Milwaukee Assn. of Commerce (pres. 1909-12) Wis. Mfrs.' Assn. Presented with loving cup as "Milwaukee's foremost citizen," 1924. Home: Milwaukee, Wis. Died May 21, 1940.

FALKNER, Roland Post, statistician; b. Bridgeport, Conn., Apr. 14, 1866; s. Rev. John B. and Helen (Butler) F.; Ph.B., U. of Pa., 1885; studied economics at Berlin, Leipzig and Halle-on-Saale, Ph.D., Halle, 1888; m. Agnes I. Hamilton, Apr. 14, 1898; children—Charles Hamilton (dec.), Elizabeth Helen (Mrs. Harold F. Schmehl), Helen Butler (Mrs. William H. Sargeant), Francis Howard (capt. U.S.A.). Instr. in accounting and statistics, Wharton School of Finance and Economy, U. of Pa., 1888-91; asso. prof. statistics, 1891-1900; chief div. of documents, Library of Congress, 1900-04; commr. of edn., Puerto Rico, 1904-07; statistician in charge of sch. inquiries for U.S. Immigration Commn., 1908-11; asst. dir. U.S. Census, 1911-12; mem. Joint Land Commn., U.S. and Panama, 1913; editor, 1915-23, dir. of research, 1923-26, Alexander Hamilton Inst., New York; research staff Nat. Industrial Conf. Bd., 1926—. Statistician, U.S. Senate Com. of Finance, 1891; sec. U.S. del. Internat. Monetary Conf., 1892, and sec. of conf.; chmn. U.S. commn. to Republic of Liberia, 1909. Translator: The History, Theory and Technique of Statistics, by August Meitzen, 1891. Editor, Annals Am. Acad. of Polit. and Social Science, 1890-1900; Report of Statistician on Wholesale Prices and Wages, Aldrich Report, 1892. Home: East Orange, N.J. Died Nov. 27, 1940.

FALL, Charles Gershom, lawyer; b. Malden, Mass., June 22, 1845; s. Gershom Lord and Rowena (Moody) F.; A.B., Harvard, 1868, A.M.; LL.B., Harvard Law Sch., 1871; m. Emily Bentham Fabian, Feb. 16, 1887. Admitted to Mass. bar, 1869; retired from practice, 1894. "Father" of first employers' liability act in Mass., 1887 (now adopted in all states of U.S. and the basis of the workman's compensation acts); also of first bd. of arbitration in Mass. for settlement of strikes and labor disputes, 1885 (system now in force in many states). Republican. Episcopalian. Home: Boston, Mass. Died Jan. 22, 1932.

FALL, Clifford Pervines, M.D., surgeon; b. Thorntown, Ind., Feb. 9, 1863; s. David and Annie (Kernodle) F.; Danville Central Normal Coll.; M.D., Coll. of Phys. & Surg., Chicago, 1888; m. Annie Kemper, June 16, 1885; children—Hazel Hellen (Mrs. C. F. Shaffer), Frederic K. Practiced, Beatrice, Neb., 1888—; owner Beatrice Sanitarium; supt. Neb. Instn. for Feeble Minded Youth, 1897; spl. contract surgeon, rank of lt., Spanish-Am. War. Pres. Neb. State Board of Health, 1909-11, later sec. Democrat. Mason. Home: Beatrice, Neb. Died July 26, 1941.

FALL, Delos, educator; b. Ann Arbor, Mich., Jan. 29, 1848; s. Benjamin F. and Ann M. F.; B.S., U. of Mich., 1875, M.S., 1882; (Sc.D., Albion, 1898, LL.D., 1908); m. Ida J. Andrews, July 21, 1877; father of Frank Andrews F. Prin. Flint High Sch., 1875-78; prof. science, 1878-88, chemistry, 1888—, Albion (Mich.) Coll. Mem. Mich. State Bd. Health, 1889-1901; state supt. pub. instrn., 1901-05; mem. Albion Bd. Edn.; mem. Mich. Constl. Conv., 1907-08 (chmn. com. edn.). Author: Science for Beginners; The Young Scientist and His Environment. Chmn. Albion City Charter Revision Commn., 1915. Home: Albion, Mich. Died Feb. 19, 1921.

FALL, Henry Clinton, entomologist; b. Farmington, N.H., Dec. 25, 1862; s. Orrin T. and Annie (Hayes) E.; B.S., Dartmouth, 1884, Sc.D., 1929; unmarried. Teacher; investigator of Coleoptera, Acmæodera, Apion, etc., shown in lists, revisions and articles contributed to transactions of entomol. socs. and entomol. mags. Fellow Entomol. Soc. America (v.p. and asso. editor Annals), A.A.A.S.; mem. Permanent Com. of Internat. Entomol. Congress. Home: Tyngsboro, Mass. Died Nov. 14, 1939.

FALLIGANT, Robert, judge of Superior Court of Eastern jud. circuit of Ga., 1889—; b. Savannah, Ga., Jan. 12, 1839; g.s. Alexander Raiford (soldier in war of 1812); ed. Cherokee Bapt. Coll., nr. Cassville, Ga., then at Univ. of Va., till war broke out; joined "Southern guard"; was one of party that seized Harper's Ferry. Remained in army of Northern Va. until end of war; promoted lt. after Antietam by special order Gen. R. E. Lee. Studied law in office of William Law. Mem. State legislature, 1882, State senator, 1884; comd. Oglethorpe Light Inf., 18 yrs. Home: Savannah, Ga. Died 1902.

FALLOWS, Alice Katharine, author; b. Milwaukee; d. Right Rev. Samuel and Lucy Bethia (Huntington) F.; sister of Edward Huntington F.; A.B., Smith Coll., 1897; unmarried. Began writing while in coll., later writer for New York Sun, Evening Post, Mail and Express, etc.; assisted father in psycho-therapeutic works in Chicago, winter, 1908; studied psychotherapeutics, London and on Continent, 1909-10. Reformed Episcopalian. Author: Everybody's Bishop, the Life and Times of the Rt. Rev. Samuel Fallows, D.D., 1927. Died Jan. 9, 1932.

FALLOWS, Edward Huntington, lawyer; b. Appleton, Wis., 1865; s. Samuel and Lucy Bethia (Huntington) F.; A.B., summa cum laude, Amherst, 1886, A.M., 1890; grad. student, Yale, 1890; studied law, Columbia, 1892; m. Julia Haughton Kittredge, 1893; 1 dau., Annette Richards. In practice at New York, 1892—. Mem. N.Y. Assembly, 1898-1900; transfer tax atty. for state comptroller, N.Y., 1902-12; pres. Grandanor Corp., Falvan Corp.; v.p. Holding Investments, Inc. V.p. Huntington Family Assn. Republican. Author: Collateral Inheritance and Transfer Tax, 1902. Episcopalian. Home: Norfolk, Conn. Died Jan. 12, 1940.

FALLOWS, Samuel, bishop; b. Pendleton, Lancashire, Eng., Dec. 13, 1835; s. Thomas and Anne (Ashworth) F.; removed to Wis., 1848; A.B., U. of Wis., 1859, A.M., 1862 (LL.D., 1894; D.D., Lawrence U., 1873, Marietta Coll., 1903); m. Lucy Bethia Huntington, Apr. 9, 1860 (died 1916). V.p. Galesville U., 1859-61; chaplain 32d Wis. Inf., Sept. 25, 1862; resigned June 29, 1863; lt. col., 40th Wis. Inf., May 20, 1864; col. 49th Wisconsin Infantry, Jan. 28, 1865; bvtd. brig. gen. vols., Oct. 24, 1865, "for meritorious services"; hon. mustered out, Nov. 1, 1865. In M.E. ministry, 1859-75; rector St. Paul's R.E. Ch., Chicago, 1875—; bishop R.E. Ch., 1876—; elected presiding bishop 8 times. Regent U. of Wis., 1866-74; state supt. public instrn., Wis., 1871-74; pres. Ill. Wesleyan U., 1874-75; pres. bd. of mgrs. Ill. State Reformatory, 1891-1912; chmn. gen. ednl. commn., World's Congress Auxiliary, 1893; chancellor Univ. Assn.; chaplain-in-chief G.A.R., 1907-08; nat. patriotic instr. G.A.R., 1908-09; dept. comdr. of Ill., G.A.R., 1913-14; chaplain 2d Regt. Illinois N.G., 1890-1916; comdr. Military Order Loyal Legion, Dept. of Ill., 1907. Author: The Bible Looking Glass, 1898; Story of the American Flag, 1903; Complete Dictionary of Synonyms and Antonyms, 1925. Editor-in-chief the Human Interest Library. Pres. Ill. Commn. to Conduct Half-Century Anniversary of Negro Freedom in 1915; chmn. Grant Memorial Commn.; pres. Chicago Sch. for Home Nursing, 1919—. Pres. Soc. Army of the Tennessee, 1917. Died Sept. 5, 1922.

FALLS, DeWitt Clinton, artist, author; b. New York, Sept. 29, 1864; s. DeWitt Clinton and Georgiana Feltus (Gassner) F.; ed. pvt. schs., New York; m. Mary Augusta Lahens, Apr. 27, 1905. Began work in New York about 1885. Enlisted in Co. K, 7th Inf., N.G.S.N.Y., 1886; brigade staff, Spanish War, 1898; regtl. adj., 7th Inf., 1899; bvt. maj., 1910; aide on staff of Gov. John A. Dix, 1911-12; maj. 7th Inf., 1916; service on Mexican border, 1916; col. 7th Inf. N.Y.G., 1917; maj. U.S.A. and assigned to insp. gen.'s dept., 1918; transferred to duty with Gen. Staff; promoted lt. col., and trans. to R.C., 1919; brig. gen. and retired, 1928. State decoration for long and faithful service of over 25 years; 7th Regt. Cross of Honor. Rep. N.G. of U.S. at Centennial Celebration of the Vols. of Eng., 1899; range officer for Am. Rifle Team which won the Palma trophy at Bisley, Eng., 1903; spl. duty with Russian Army during the Russo-Japanese War, 1904; spl. duty in connection with the late war with mil. attaché, Am. Embassy, London, and Am. Legation, Brussels, 1914. Republican. Episcopalian. Author: Army and Navy Information, 1917. Illustrator of various books. Home: New York, N.Y. Died Sept. 7, 1937.

FANCHER, Bertram Hull, banker; b. New Canaan, Conn., Dec. 15, 1865; s. George N. and Adaline T. (Hull) F.; ed. pub. schs., Pound Ridge, N.Y., and Bedford (N.Y.) Acad.; m. Annie Williams, Sept. 29, 1887; 1 son, G. Carlton. Began in employ Fifth Av. Bank, N.Y. City, 1884, v.p., 1910-28; pres. Industrial Banking Corp. of America, 1929—; dir. Am. Reserve Ins. Co., Fire Re-assurance Corp. of New York, Lincoln Fire Ins. Co. of New York. Treas. Internat. Y.M.C.A.; trustee Westchester County Hist. Soc. Conglist. Home: Pound Ridge, N.Y. Died Apr. 9, 1932.

FANCHER, Elvadore R., banker; b. Bloomer Center, Mich., Oct. 17, 1864; family removed from Mich. to Lorain, O., 1873; grad. high sch., Lorain, 1879; m. Harriet S. Schroder, Feb. 16, 1893. Bookkeeper, 1885-96, asst. cashier, 1896-1904, cashier, 1904-09, v.p., 1909-14, pres., Oct. 1-Nov. 2, 1914, Union Nat. Bank, Cleveland; resigned to become gov. Federal Reserve Bank of Cleveland, Nov. 2, 1914. Republican. Home: Cleveland, O. Died Jan. 16, 1935.

FANCIULLI, Francesco, musical dir.; b. Port St. Stephen, Tuscany, 1853; s. Alexander and Julia (Lubrano) F.; ed. Florence, where he afterward conducted grand opera; settled in U.S., 1876; m. Amanda Schile, 1882. Occupied himself as teacher, organist and composer; succeeded Sousa as conductor Marine Band, Washington, 1893-98; bandmaster 71st Regt. N.G.S.N.Y., 1898-1904; organized, 1904, and thereafter dir. of his own band. Home: New York, N.Y. Died July 17, 1915.

FANNING, Cecil, concert baritone; b. Columbus, O., Nov. 28, 1883; s. Capt. Richard J. and Cecilia (Miller) F.; pupil in voice of H. B. Turpon, Columbus; unmarried. Began as concert singer in 1906; début in London, Eng., 1908, Berlin, 1912, recital début, New York, Dec. 1916; has appeared as soloist with musical orgns. throughout U.S. Decorated by War Camp Community Service for work in organizing concerts for soldiers, and community singing. Catholic. Author: (poems) The Flower-Strewn Threshold, 1912; also librettos for cantatas, lyrics, etc. Home: Columbus, O. Died Dec. 7, 1931.

FANNING, John Thomas, civil engr.; b. Norwich, Conn., Dec. 31, 1837; s. John Howard and Elizabeth (Pridde) F.; acad. and normal sch. edn.; m. M. Louise Bensley, June 14, 1865. Studied architecture and civil engring. until 1861; served during Civil War, lt. to lt. col., 3d Conn. S.M. After war became prominent in engring., particularly in planning and constructing pub. water works and water powers in N.E., and later in the West, notably on the power of the Miss. River at Minneapolis, of the Spokane River in Washington, and Missouri River nr. Helena and at Great Falls, Mont., and on the Weenatahee River in Wash. for the electrification of the G.N. Ry.'s cascade tunnel; was cons. engr. St. Paul, Minneapolis & Manitoba R.R. and G.N. Ry., and v.p. Minneapolis Union Ry. Home: Minneapolis, Minn. Died 1911.

FANT, John Clayton, college pres.; b. nr. Macon, Miss., Jan. 15, 1870; s. Joshua C. and Anne Eliza (Connor) F.; A.B., Emory and Henry Coll., Va., 1889, A.M., 1892; Pd.M., New York U., 1895; A.M., U. of Miss., 1912; Pd.D., New York U., 1913; m. Mabel Beckett, July 2, 1903; 1 son, Richard Beckett. Prin. sch., Newton, Miss., 1889-93; supt. schs., Water Valley, Miss., 1895-96, Meridian, Miss., 1896-1910; prof. secondary edn. for Miss., 1910-20, also dean Sch. of Edn., U. of Miss.; pres. Miss. State Coll., 1920—. Mem. State Bd. of Examiners, of Miss., 1897-99; trustee State Teachers' Coll., 1910. Democrat. Methodist. Mason. Home: Columbus, Miss. Died Nov. 8, 1929.

FARABEE, Samuel Howard, editor, pub.; b. Clemmons, N.C., Apr. 11, 1882; s. John Anderson and Elizabeth Caroline (Inscore) F.; student Univ. of N.C., 1903-07; m. Jennie Mabel Powell, Nov. 24, 1908; children—Jean Powell (Mrs. Myron M. Varn), Carol Elizabeth (Mrs. John Paul Payne), Sarah Willard. Began as reporter in Raleigh, N.C., 1907; founder Daily Record, Hickory, N.C., 1915; founder Lakeland (Fla.) Ledger, 1924, and since editor; pres. Ledger Pub. Co. Democrat. Methodist. Mason. Home: Lakeland, Fla. Died Nov. 21, 1939.

FARABEE, William Curtis, anthropologist; b. Washington, Pa., Feb. 7, 1865; s. Samuel N. and Susannah (Henkins) F.; Calif. (Pa.) State Normal Sch., 1885-87; A.B., Waynesburg Coll., Pa., 1894; A.M., 1900, Ph.D., 1903, Harvard; m. Sylvia Manilla Holdren, Mar. 12, 1897. Teacher and prin. pub. schs., Pa., 5 yrs.; prin. Jackson Acad., Jackson Centre, Pa., 1896-99; Austin teaching fellow, 1901-03, instr. anthropology, 1903-13, Harvard U.; curator, museum of U. of Pa., 1913—. In charge of DeMilhan-Harvard S. Am. expdn., S. Am. expdn. U. of Pa., 1913-16, 1921-23. Hon. mem. Faculty of Science, San Marcos U., Lima, Peru. Presbyn. Fellow Am. Acad. Arts and Sciences, A.A.A.S., Royal Geog. Soc., hon. mem. Am. Geog. Soc. Ethnographer Am. Commn. to Negotiate Peace, Paris, 1918-19; mem. spl. diplomatic mission to Peru; mem. Ancient Order El Sol, Lima, Peru. Home: Philadelphia, Pa. Died June 24, 1925.

FARENHOLT, Oscar Walter, rear-admiral U.S.N.; b. nr. San Antonio, Tex., May 2, 1845; ed. in schs. of San Antonio, New Orleans, La., and Pittsburgh, Pa. Entered navy at New York as seaman, Apr. 18, 1861; served on frigate Wabash; participated in engagements and battles at Ft. Hatteras, N.C., Port Royal, S.C., Ft. Pulaski, Ga., etc.; severely wounded at battle of Pocotaligo, S.C., Oct. 22, 1862; sent to Naval Hosp., New York, and discharged from navy. Recovered from wounds; reëntered navy Feb. 1863, on monitor Catskill; was in almost daily engagements with defences of Charleston, S.C., Apr. 1863-Apr. 1864; participated in unsuccessful storming party of Ft. Sumter, Sept. 1863; promoted acting ensign Aug. 1864, comd. schooner Henry James attached to squadron in Sounds of N.C., participated in recapture of Plymouth and several engagements on Roanoke, Chowan and Black Water rivers, and capture of Ft. Fisher, N.C. After war on various duties; commd. ensign, Mar. 12, 1868; master, Dec. 18, 1868; lt., Mar. 21, 1870; lt. comdr., May 11, 1882; comdr., June 19, 1892; capt., Sept. 1900; rear admiral, Sept. 1, 1901, and voluntarily retired from active service after 40 yrs.' service. Served on many stations and in varied duties; during Spanish-Am. War stationed at Shanghai, China, as Admiral Dewey's base of supplies and information; at Boston Navy Yard and Naval War Coll., Feb. 1899; comdt. navy yard Cavite, P.I., 1900, comd. monitor Monadnock, Asiatic station, 1901. Died June 30, 1920.

FARGO, Charles; b. Pompey, N.Y., Apr. 15, 1831. Entered express business at Detroit, 1851; took charge of Toledo office, Am. Express Co., 1853; Detroit office, 1856, and in 1866 became asst. gen. supt. with general management of Chicago office; second v.p. and general Western mgr., 1881—. Home: Chicago, Ill. Died 1900.

FARGO, James Congdel; b. Pompey, N.Y., May 5, 1829. In 1844 entered employ of Wells & Co. (in which his brother, William George F., was a partner, at Buffalo); afterward at Detroit and Chicago, where he became agt. and mgr. of the firm's successor, the Am. Express Co.; went, in 1866, to New York as gen. supt. and mgr., and in 1881 became pres. of the co.; also pres. Westcott Express Co. and Nat. Express Co.; dir. C.&N.W. Ry. Co., Nat. Express Co. Died Feb. 8, 1915.

FARIS, Charles Breckenridge, judge; b. nr. Charleston, Mo., Oct. 3, 1864; s. James White and Willie Anne (Stovall) F.; B.L. and B.Pd., U. of Mo., 1889, LL.D., 1922; student St. Louis Law School (Washington U.), 1891; m. Anna L. McClanahan, Aug. 22, 1894; children—James Claiborn (dec.), Adalyn (Mrs. Harold Moore), Charles Breckenridge (dec.), Mary Lee, James White, William Breckenridge. Admitted to Mo. bar, 1891, and practiced in Caruthersville; city atty., 1892-93; pros. atty., Pemiscot Co., 1893-99; pres. Bank of Caruthersville, 1898-1910; mem. Mo. Ho. of Rep., 36th Gen. Assembly; judge 28th Jud. Circuit, 1910-12; judge Supreme Ct. of Mo. for term 1912-22, resigned, Oct. 31, 1919, to become U.S. dist. judge for Eastern Dist. of Mo., serving until Feb. 6, 1935; circuit judge 8th Circuit, Feb. 6-Dec. 1, 1935. Mem. bd. curators U. of Mo., 1903-09 (pres. 1907-09); mem. bd. control Cottey Coll. for Young Women, Nevada, Mo., 1916-19. Democrat. Presbyn. Mason. Home: St. Louis, Mo. Died Dec. 18, 1938.

FARIS, George Washington, congressman; b. on farm, Jasper Co., Ind., June 9, 1854; s. James Collins and Margaret M. (Brown) F.; A.B., Asbury (now DePauw) U., 1877, A.M., 1880; m. Anna C., d. late Judge Solomon Claypool, May 28, 1878. Admitted to bar, 1880, and since in practice at Terre Haute, Ind. Mem. 54th to 56th Congresses (1895-1901); declined renomination. Republican. Home: Terre Haute, Ind. Died Apr. 17, 1914.

FARIS, Herman Preston, prohibitionist; b. nr. Bellefontaine, O., Dec. 25, 1858; s. Samuel Davies and Sarah Plumer (Preston) F.; removed with parents to Kan.; ed. pub. schs.; m. Adda Winters, Apr. 26, 1880 (died 1909); children—Sarah Olivia (Mrs. Paul McGeehan), Florence Julia (Mrs. G. C. Lingle), Adda Winters (Mrs. H. F. Finks); m. 2d, Mrs. Sallie A. Lewis, Feb. 6, 1911. Began in printing office, Clinton, Mo., at age of 13, later office boy, Brinkerhoff & Smith, Clinton; acting dep. clk. Dist. Court, Trinidad, Colo., 1878; returned to Clinton, 1879; pres., treas. and mgr. Brinkerhoff-Faris Trust and Savings Co., 1887—; v.p. Clinton Realty Co., Benton Land Co. Prohibition candidate for sec. of State of Mo., 1888, for gov. 3 times and for President of U.S., 1924. Pres. Y.M.C.A., Clinton. Presbyn. Home: Clinton, Mo. Died Mar. 20, 1936.

FARIS, Robert Lee, civil engr.; b. Caruthersville, Mo., Jan. 13, 1868; s. James White and Willie Ann (Stovall) F.; C.E., U. of Mo., 1890; spl. course in mathematics, Columbian (now George Washington) U., 1893; m. Carrie Elizabeth Hellen, June 8, 1897; children—Robert Lee, Hellen Mills, Carolyn, Elizabeth R., Charles William. U.S. asst. engr., survey Mo. River, 1890-91; recorder, 1891, aid, 1893, asst., 1895—. Coast and Geod. Survey; assisted in survey Yukon delta and N. Coast Behring Sea, Alaska, etc.; comd. coast survey steamers at P.R. and on East Coast, U.S., 5 yrs.; insp. magnetic work and chief of div. of Terrestrial Magnetism, Sept. 1906-Nov. 1914; asst. insp. hydrography and topography, Nov. 1914-Mar. 1915; asst. dir. Coast and Geod. Survey, Mar. 1915—. Mem. com. on navigation and nautical instruments of Nat. Research Council, 1917; mem. Miss. River Commn.; mem. Federal Bd. on Surveys and Maps. Home: Washington, D.C. Died Oct. 5, 1932.

FARLEY, John Murphy, cardinal; b. Newton Hamilton, county Armagh, Ireland, Apr. 20, 1842; s. Philip and Catherine (Murphy) F.; ed. St. Marcartan's Coll., Monaghan; St. John's Coll., Fordham, and St. Joseph's Sem., Troy, N.Y.; studied 4 yrs. in Am. Coll., Rome; ordained priest in Rome, June 11, 1870. Asst. rector St. Peter's, New Brighton, S.I., 1870-72; sec. to Archbishop McCloskey, 1872-84; pvt. chamberlain to Pope Leo XIII, with title of monsignore, 1884; vicar-gen. Archdiocese of New York, 1891; domestic prelate of Pope Leo XIII, 1892; prothonotary apostolic, 1895; apptd. auxiliary bishop of New York, 1895; consecrated, Dec. 21, 1895, titular bishop of Zeugma; on death of Archbishop Corrigan, May 5, 1902, apptd. adminstr. of New York; Sept. 15, 1902, became the fourth Archbishop of New York; elevated to the cardinalate, Nov. 27, 1911. Author: Life of Cardinal McCloskey (serially in Hist. Records and Studies, New York), 1899-1900; History of St. Patrick's Cathedral. Died Sept. 17, 1918.

FARLEY, Joseph Pearson, brig. gen.; b. Washington, Mar. 2, 1839; s. Capt. John (U.S.A.) and Anna Maria (Pearson) F.; grad. U.S. Mil. Acad., 1861; m. Miss F. E. Brinley, Apr. 6, 1864. Bvt. 2d lt. and commd. 2d lt. 2d Arty., June 24, 1861; transferred to ordnance, Oct. 24, 1861; 1st lt., Mar. 3, 1863; capt., Apr. 6, 1866; maj., Mar. 25, 1876; lt. col., Feb. 28, 1889; col., July 7, 1898; brig. gen. U.S.A., Feb. 17, 1903; retired at own request over 40 yrs.' service, Feb. 18, 1903. Bvtd. capt., Mar. 13, 1865, "for meritorious services in ordnance dept. during the war." Asst. prof. drawing West Point, 1865-67; mem. various statutory bds., ordnance bds., gun-testing bds.; has comd. various arsenals and in the field during Civil War. Author: West Point in the Early Sixties, 1902; Three Rivers, a Retrospect of War and Peace, 1910. Died Apr. 6, 1912.

FARLEY, Michael F., congressman; b. Birr, Ireland. Engaged in business in N.Y. City; mem. 64th Congress (1915-17), 14th N.Y. Dist. Republican. Home: New York, N.Y. Died Oct. 8, 1921.

FARLEY, Robert E(mmet), lawyer, suburban developer; b. Ft. Plain, N.Y., Sept. 28, 1871; s. Worthington S. and Helen Hall (Moyer) F.; grad. Clinton (N.Y.) Liberal Inst., 1888; A.B., Rutgers Coll., 1892, A.M., 1895; LL.B., cum laude, N.Y. Law Sch., 1894; m. Grace Hazard Colvin, Dec. 1, 1897; children—Colvin, Theodore S., Helen E., Grace H. Admitted to N.Y. bar, 1894, and began practice at N.Y. City and White Plains; organizer and 1st pres., Gramatan Nat. Bank (Bronxville, N.Y.), Gedney Farm Co.; pres. Robert E. Farley Orgn., Scarsdale Estates, Eastern Mill & Material Co., Estates of Tappan Zee, Middlesex Manors, Inc. Pres. Rutgers Associates, Inc.; mem. exec. com. World Alliance Internat. Friendship, Citizens Com. of 1,000; mem. advisory council Regional Plan of New York; dir. Westchester Co. Conservation Assn., N.Y. City Y.M.C.A.; chmn. Fort Jay Y.M.C.A. Republican. Presbyn. Mason. Home: White Plains, N.Y. Died Sept. 28, 1933.

FARLOW, Alfred, writer; b. Knoxville, Ill.; s. William and Paulina J. (McGrew) F.; grad. Mass. Metaphysical Coll., 1887; unmarried. Christian Science teacher and lecturer, since 1888; located Christian Science inst. at Topeka, 1889, removed to Kansas City, 1894; pastor and reader Christian Science Ch.; mgr. com. on publ. Christian Science Ch., Boston, 1898-1914. Home: Los Angeles, Calif. Died Sept. 1919.

FARLOW, William Gilson, botanist; b. Boston, Dec. 17, 1844; s. John Smith and Nancy White (Blanchard) F.; A.B., Harvard, 1866, A.M., 1869, M.D., 1870; studied botany in Europe several yrs.; (LL.D., Harvard, 1896, U. of Glasgow, 1901, U. of Wis., 1904; Ph.D., Upsala, 1907); m. Lillian, d. E. N. Horsford, of Cambridge, Jan. 10, 1900. Asst. prof. botany, 1874-79, prof. cryptogamic botany, 1879—, Harvard. Fellow A.A.A.S. (v.p. 1887, 1898, pres. 1905), Am. Acad. Arts and Sciences. Author: The Gymnosporangia, or Cedar; Apples of the United States, 1880; Marine Algæ of New England, 1881; The Potato Rot; Index of Fungi; etc. Home: Cambridge, Mass. Died June 3, 1919.

FARMAN, Elbert Eli, judge; b. New Haven, N.Y., Apr. 23, 1831; s. Zadok and Martha (Dix) F.; A.B., Amherst Coll., 1855, A.M., 1858 (LL.D., 1882, same); m. Lois Parker, Dec. 24, 1855 (died 1881); 2d, Adelaide Frisbie, Oct. 8, 1883. Admitted to bar, 1858, to U.S. courts, 1862; one of pubs. of Western New Yorker, 1859-61; traveled in Europe and studied langs. and internat. law, univs. of Berlin and Heidelberg, 1865-67; dist. atty., Wyo. Co., N.Y., 1868-75; U.S. diplomatic agt. and consul-gen. at Cairo, Egypt, 1876-81; accompanied Gen. Grant in voyage up Nile, 1878; mem. on part of U.S. of Internat. Commn. to revise jud. codes of Egypt for use of mixed tribunals (Internat. courts), 1880-81; judge mixed tribunals of Egypt, 1881-84; U.S. mem. International Commn., 1883-84, which examined the claims (over 10,000) and determined the amounts to be paid ($20,000,000) to inhabitants of Alexandria for losess arising from bombardment and burning of city in 1882; secured the obelisk, "Cleopatra's Needle," as a gift of Khedive to New York, 1879; made large collections of ancient coins and Egyptian antiquities, now in Met. Mus. of Art, New York; delivered polit. addresses in presdl. campaigns, 1856-88; in Europe in lit. work during winters 1894-1900. Decorated by the Khedive, Grand Officer Imperial Order of the Medjidieh. Home: Warsaw, N.Y. Died 1911.

FARMER, Fannie Merritt, author; b. Boston, Mar. 23, 1857; d. John Franklin and Mary (Watson) Farmer; ed. Medford High Sch. and Boston Cooking Sch.; unmarried. Prin. Miss Farmer's Sch. of Cookery, Boston, 1892—. Author: The Boston Cooking School Cook Book, 1902; Chafing-Dish Possibilities, 1898; Food and Cookery for the Sick and Convalescent, 1904; What to Have for Dinner, 1905; Catering for Special Occasions, 1910; A New Book of Cookery, 1912. Died Jan. 15, 1915.

FARMER, Harry, clergyman; b. West Bend, Wis., Apr. 18, 1872; s. Thomas and Mary Catharine (Clow) F.; B.S., George Washington U., 1898; B.D., Garrett Bibl. Inst., 1902, D.D., 1917; m. Olive Esther Osborn, Oct. 16, 1902; children—John Albert, Grace Esther (Mrs. Charles G. Apgar), Paul Osborn, Frances. Employed in railroad office, surgeon gen.'s office, Washington, D.C., and at Paris Expn. until 1900; missionary in Philippines, 1904-16; a founder Union Theol. Sch., Manila; asso. sec. Bd. of Foreign Missions M.E. Ch., 1916-24; gen. sec. Am. Mission to Lepers, 1924-26; now pastor First M.E. Ch., Lake Worth, Fla. Democrat. Mason. Home: Lake Worth, Fla. Died Sept. 27, 1932.

FARMER, Leslie P., commr. passenger dept., Trunk Line Assn., Aug. 1, 1890—; b. Ellington, Conn., Dec. 22, 1848; clerk treasurer's office, 1863-64; clerk gen. ticket office, 1864-68, Bellefontaine R.R., Indianapolis; chief clerk, gen. ticket office, I.&St.L. R.R., 1868-71; asst. gen. passenger agt., 1871-72, Mo. Pacific R.R.; asst. gen. passenger agt., 1872-77; gen. passenger agt., 1877-81, New Eng. passenger agt., 1882-86, Pennsylvania R.R.; gen. passenger agt., 1887-90, N.Y., Lake Erie & Western R.R. Died 1908.

FARMER, Lydia Hoyt, author; b. (Hoyt) Cleveland, O.; m. E. J. Farmer. Book reviewer Boston Ideas and other journals. Author: Boys' Book of Famous Rulers; Girls' Book of Famous Queens. Home: Cleveland, O. Died 1903.

FARMER, Sarah Jane; b. Dover, N.H., July 22, 1847; d. Prof. Moses Gerrish and Hannah Tobey (Shapleigh) F.; grad. Salem (Mass.) High Sch., 1868; pvt. tutors, 1868-81, and European travel, 1886, 1893, 1900; unmarried. Founded, 1894, Green Acre Confs. at Eliot, Me., and in 1896 the associated Monsalvat Sch. for Comparative Study of Religion, with an annual assembly for lectures, etc., by leaders of advanced thought, Am., European and Oriental. Home: Eliot, Me. Died Nov. 23, 1916.

FARMER, Silas, publisher; b. Detroit, June 6, 1839; s. John F., map maker, to whose business he succeeded; is also antiquarian; m. Orpha C. Littlefield, June 18, 1868. Author: History of Detroit and Michigan; Champions of Christianity. Elected city historiographer of Detroit (Mich.), 1882. Died 1902.

FARMER, William Burton, ch. official; b. Bloomington, Ind., Nov. 28, 1872; s. Rev. William M. and Agnes Roberts F.; A.B., Ind. U., 1899; S.T.B., Garrett Bibl. Inst., 1901, D.D., 1919; D.D., DePauw U., 1912; m. Mary Elizabeth Brown, May 1, 1902; 1 dau., Mary Louise. Ordained ministry M.E. Ch., 1900; pastor successively, Indianapolis, Poseyville, Liberty, Evansville, Indianapolis and Columbus, Ind., 1896-1924; exec. sec. Preachers' Aid Soc., Ind. Conf., 1924-28; sec. Bd. Pensions and Relief, Gen. Conf., M.E. Ch., 1928—; dean of Ind. Sch. Ministerial Training, 1900—. Mem. Com. of 25 on Post Centenary Program of M.E. Ch., exec. com. World Service Commn., M.E. Ch.; chmn. Gen. Conf. Com. on Temporal Economy, 1924, 28, 32; mem. Meth. Ecumenical Conf., 1931. Dir. Anti-Saloon League America (exec. com.); chmn. state exec. com. Ind. Anti-Saloon League; mem. exec. com. Federal Council Chs. Christ in America. Home: Evanston, Ill. Died Jan. 12, 1938.

FARMER, William M., judge; b. Fayette Co., Ill., June 5, 1853; s. William and Margaret (Wright) F.; ed. McKendree Coll., Lebanon, Ill.; LL.B., Union Coll. of Law (now Northwestern Law Sch.), 1876; m. Miss Illinois V. Henninger, Dec. 23, 1875; children—Virginia, Gwendolen. Began practice at Vandalia, Ill., 1876; elected state's atty., 1880; mem. Ill. Ho. of Rep., 1888-90, Senate, 1890-94; judge Circuit Ct., 1897-1906; justice Supreme Ct. of Ill., 1907—, chief justice 4 times to 1930. Democrat. Home: Vandalia, Ill. Died Aug. 28, 1931.

FARNAM, Henry Walcott, polit. economist; b. at New Haven, Conn., Nov. 6, 1853; s. Henry and Ann Sophia (Whitman) F.; A.B., Yale, 1874, A.M., 1876, LL.D., 1923; studied at Berlin, Göttingen, and Strassburg U., receiving degree R.P.D., 1878; m. Elizabeth U. Kingsley, June 26, 1890; children—Louise Whitman, Katharine Kingsley (wife of Dr. Samuel Clarke Harvey), Henry Walcott. Tutor, 1878-80, prof. economics, 1880-1918, now emeritus, Yale (same at Sheffield Scientific Sch., 1881-1903). Apptd. Roosevelt prof. in Berlin, 1914-15, but prevented by war from going to Germany. Chmn. New Haven Civil Service Bd., 1898-99, State Commn. of Sculpture, 1887-1909; pres. Conn. Civil Service Assn., 1901-23. Editor, as mem. of Com. of Fifty, of Economic Aspects of the Liquor Problem, by John Koren, 1899; mem. supervisory bd. Am. Year Book, 1910-30. Collaborator. dept. of economics and sociology, Carnegie Instn. Washington, 1903-16 (chmn. 1909-16). Fellow Am. Acad. Arts and Sciences. Mem. publicity com. Conn. State Council Defense, 1917; exec. com. New Haven War Bur., 1917-19; chmn. Community Labor Bd., 1918-19. Author: The Economic Utilization of History, 1913; Shakespeare's Economics, 1931. Home: New Haven, Conn. Died Sept. 5, 1933.

FARNAM, William Whitman, treasurer Yale U.; b. New Haven, Conn., Apr. 6, 1844; s. Henry and Ann Sophia (Whitman) F.; A.B., Yale, 1866, A.M., 1869; J.U.D., Heidelberg, 1868; LL.B., Columbia, 1871; m. Susan Frances, d. Gen. William K. Strong, of New York, June 4, 1873 (died 1917); m. 2d, Anna Heaton, d. John Brewster Fitch, New Haven, Conn., June 8, 1918. Fellow, 1885-89, treas., 1888-99, Yale U. Mem. New Haven Commn. of Pub. Parks, 1880-1914. Home: New Haven, Conn. Died June 28, 1929.

FARNHAM, Charles Chittenden, physician; b. Clinton, Conn., Nov. 4, 1838; s. John Redfield and Artimesia Hand (Chittenden) F.; A.B., U. of Rochester; Yale Med. Sch.; M.D., Coll. Phys. and Surg., Boston, 1882; m. Annie Tolman Howard, Oct. 8, 1874. Practiced in Randolph, Mass., 1874—; specializes in treatment of kidney diseases; pres. Coll. Phys. and Surg., Boston, 1916—. Dir. Randolph Nat. Bank. Librarian Turner Library, Randolph, 41 yrs., resigned 1917, now librarian emeritus. Sec. and dir. Old Stoughton Musical Soc. (oldest mus. orgn. in America). Democrat. Baptist. Home: Randolph, Mass. Died Mar. 8, 1925.

FARNHAM, Charles Wells, lawyer, lecturer; b. Buffalo, N.Y., June 4, 1867; s. Horatio Nelson, Jr., and Maria Love (Shiels) F.; ed. Griswold Coll., Davenport, Ia.; LL.B., Law Sch., U. of Minn., 1895, LL.M., 1896; m. Kate Humbird, Sept. 25, 1900; children—John D., Charles Wells, Mrs. Caroline Davidson. Pres. Patriotic League of St. Paul, 1917—. Republican. Episcopalian. Home: St. Paul, Minn. Deceased.

FARNHAM, Roswell, lawyer, gov. Vt.; b. Boston, July 23, 1827; s. Roswell and Nancy (Bixby) F.; family removed to Bradford, Vt., 1840; grad. Univ. of Vt., 1849 (A.M., 1852); m. Mary Elizabeth Johnson, Dec. 25, 1849. Admitted to bar, 1857; State's atty., 1859-62; served in army, lt. 1st Vt. regt. to lt. col. 12th Vt. regt., in Civil war; State senator, 1869-70; Presidential elector, 1876; gov. Vt., 1880-82. Republican. Home: Bradford, Vt. Died 1903.

FARNSWORTH, Frederick Eugene, assn. sec.; b. Detroit, Dec. 2, 1852; s. Leander L. and Frances (Higgins) F.; pub. sch. edn.; m. Henrietta Bloomfield Clarkson, Dec. 2, 1891; children—Frederick Clarkson, Clarkson Lewis (dec.). In shoe business, Detroit, 1867-83; cashier Union Nat. Bank, Detroit, 1898-1903; gen. mgr. Great Northern Portland Cement Co., Marlborough, Mich., 1903-07; gen. sec., Am. Bankers' Assn., Oct. 1, 1907-19. City assessor, City of Detroit, 1891-97; officer Detroit Light Guard; on staff of Gen. I. C. Smith, comdg. Mich. N.G., rank of capt.; on staff of Gov. Cyrus G. Luce of Mich., 1887-91, rank of col. Corporator Detroit Museum of Art, and 25 yrs. its sec., until 1907; sec. Mich. (Rep.) Club, 1887-97. Mason. Home: Huntington, L.I., N.Y. Died Nov. 10, 1930.

FARNSWORTH, Louis Henderson, banker; b. Provo City, Utah, Sept. 1, 1859; s. Moses Franklin and Elizabeth Jane (Duzette) F.; ed. night sch. and home study; m. Agnes Wilkinson Forsythe, of Glasgow, Scotland, June 10, 1884; children—Louis Duzette, Edna Irene (Mrs. Glenwood E. Traul), Earle Forsythe, Ruth Agnes (Mrs. Charles A. Barker, Jr.). With Walker Brothers, bankers, Salt Lake City, Utah, 1870—, chmn. bd., 1920—; v.p., treas. Independent Coal & Coke Co.; treas., dir., M. H. Walker Realty Co. Chmn. Council of Defense, State of Utah, World War. Republican. Christian Scientist. Mason. Home: Cottonwood, Utah. Died Nov. 15, 1930.

FARNSWORTH, Wilson Amos, missionary; b. Greene, N.Y., Aug. 29, 1822; s. Isaac and Eunice (Page) F.; A.B., Middlebury Coll., 1848, A.M., 1851 (D.D., 1877); grad. Andover Theol. Sem., 1852; m. Caroline Elizabeth Palmer, Oct. 21, 1852. Ordained Congl. ministry, 1852; missionary A.B.C.F.M., in Asia Minor more than 50 yrs. Home: Glen Ridge, N.J. Died June 5, 1912.

FARNUM, Dustin, actor; b. Hampton Beach, N.H., May 27, 1876; s. Greenleaf D. and Clara A. F.; m. Mary Elizabeth Conwell; 1 dau., Estelle; m. 2d, Winifred Kingston, 1924. Début with Ethel Tucker Co., 1897; later with Margaret Mather and 2 seasons with Chauncey Olcott; appeared in "The Virginian," "The Ranger," "The Rector's Garden," etc.; toured as Jim Carston in "The Squaw Man" and as Lt. Col. Morrison in "The Littlest Rebel." Died July 3, 1929.

FARNUM, Loring Nelson; retired engr.; b. North Andover, Mass., Feb. 2, 1868; s. Jacob Loring and Julia (Kimball) F.; B.S., Worcester Poly. Inst., 1890; m. Evelyn Bunting, 1898. Engaged in practice as engr. and contractor in hydraulic work and rys., 1890-1907; v.p. J. G. White & Co., engring., N.Y. City, 1907-11, asso. with same, 1911-30; cons. engr. and exec. of various indsl. concerns, 1911-30; retired. Home: Pelham Manor, N.Y. Died Nov. 13, 1941.

FARNY, Henry F., artist; b. 1847. Formerly illustrated exclusively for Harper's; now painter of Indians and Western life. Home: Clifton Heights, Cincinnati, O. Died Dec. 24, 1916.

FARQUHAR, Arthur B., mfr., polit. economist; b. Sandy Spring, Md., Sept. 28, 1838; s. William Henry and Margaret (Briggs) F.; ed. Hallowells Sch. for Boys, Alexandria, Va.; (LL.D., Kenyon Coll., 1902); m. Elizabeth, d. Edward Jessop, of Baltimore, 1860. Managed father's farm 1 yr.; removed to York, Pa., to learn machinists' trade, 1856; became partner, 1858; bought firm's interest, 1862; from 1889 pres. A. B. Farquhar Co., Ltd., conducting Pa. Agrl. Works; was some yrs. propr. York Gazette; has large property interests. Pres. York Hosp., York Municipal League, York Oratorio Soc. State Commr. from Pa. (and apptd. commr. to Europe) World's Columbian Expn., 1892-93; was elected pres. Nat. Assn. Exec. Commrs.; apptd., 1897, del. from Pa. to Coast Defense Conv., at Tampa, Fla.; Pa. del. 1st Nat. Conservation Congress, Seattle, Wash., 1909; dir. Nat. Conservation Assn.; pres. Pa. Conservation Assn.; v.p. and dir. Chamber of Commerce U.S.; chmn. City Planning Commission and Tree Commn. of York, Pa.; pres. State Housing and Town Planning Assn.; mem. Am. Industrial Commn. to France, 1916; apptd. mem. of Pa. defense orgns., 1917. Episcopalian. Home: York, Pa. Died Mar. 5, 1925.

FARQUHAR, Edward, asst. librarian U.S. Patent Office, 1865—; b. Sandy Spring, Md., Sept. 2, 1843; s. William H. and Margaret (Briggs) F.; lived on farm until grown; ed. in common schools, but principally at home (Ph.D., Columbian U.); m. Mary W. Milam, May 29, 1902. Instr. English literature, 1893, then prof. history till 1903, Columbian Univ.; sec. Washington Soc. for Philos. Inquiry. Died 1905.

FARQUHAR, Henry, writer; b. Sandy Spring, Md., Aug. 27, 1851; s. William Henry and Margaret (Briggs) F.; brother of Arthur Briggs F.; attended Cornell, but was not graduated; m. Isabel Robbins, 1881. Employed as teacher; then on U.S. Coast Survey; later as editorial writer; in statis. work for Dept. Agr. and Census Bur., 1900-21; retired by operation of law. Unitarian. Author: Economic and Industrial Delusions (with A. B. Farquhar), 1891. Home: Washington, D.C. Died Oct. 1925.

FARQUHAR, John McCreath, congressman; b. Scotland, Apr. 17, 1832; s. John and Marion (McCreath) F.; ed. Ayr Acad., Scotland; m. Jane Wood, Sept. 11, 1862. Pres. Internat. Typographical Union, 1860-62. Served throughout Civil War, Army of the Cumberland, pvt. to maj., acting as judge advocate and insp. on staff duty. Awarded Congressional Medal of Honor for bravery at battle Stone River, Tenn. Mem. 49th to 51st Congresses (1885-91); mem. U.S. Industrial Commn., 1898-1902. Republican. Elder emeritus, Calvary Presbyn. Ch., Buffalo. Home: Buffalo, N.Y. Deceased.

FARQUHAR, Norman von Heldreich, rear admiral U.S.N.; b. Pottsville, Pa., Apr. 11, 1840; s. George W. and Amilie (von Schrader) F.; grad. U.S. Naval Acad., 1859; m. Addie W. Pope, Apr. 26, 1862. With squadron, coast Africa, for suppression slave trade, midshipman and acting master, 1859-61; brought to U.S. captured salver, the Triton, with crew 10 men and no other officer; commd. lt., Aug. 31, 1861; served in N. Atlantic blockading squadron; was present at both attacks on Fort Fisher; lt. comdr. Aug. 5, 1865; comdr., Dec. 12, 1872; commodore, 1897. Served in various stations; comd. the Trenton, Pacific sta., when wrecked in great hurricane at Apia, Samoa, March 16, 1889, but saved from drowning the crew of 450 officers and men. Mem. Light House Bd., Oct. 1889; chief bureau yards and docks, Navy Dept., March 6, 1890, later becoming comdt., Norfolk Navy Yard; comdr.-in-chief N. Atlantic sta., Oct. 1899—; chmn. Light House Bd., 1901-02; retired on account of age, 1902. Hon. mem. and prize essayist U.S. Naval Inst. Died 1907.

FARR, Albert George, banker; b. Brandon, Vt., Dec. 3, 1851; s. Flavius Josephus and Chastina Eliza Buck (Parkhurst) F.; Brandon Sem., 1861-68; grad. Columbus (O.) High Sch., 1870 (first honors); m. Alice Parkhurst, July 23, 1873 (died 1888); 2d, Lottie Snow, April 30, 1890 (died 1911). Teacher and prin., high sch., Columbus, O., 1871-81; admitted to Ill. bar, 1882; atty., 1882-91, partner N. W. Harris & Co., bankers, Chicago, New York and Boston, 1891; dir. Harris Trust & Savings Bank, Chicago, 1907 (1st v.p. 1912—); dir. Harris, Forbes & Co., New York, and N. W. Harris & Co., Inc., Boston, 1911—, chmn. bd. dirs., 1910-12, dir. and mem. exec. com. Mich. State Telephone Co., 1894. Trustee and treas. Ripon (Wis.) Coll. Independent Republican. Home: Chicago, Ill. Died Dec. 22, 1913.

FARR, Finis King, theologian; b. College Mound, Mo., Nov. 11, 1870; s. William Benton and Louvenia Adelaide (Holloway) F.; A.B. and C.E., Cumberland U., Tenn., 1889, B.D., 1894; U. of Chicago, 1894-97, A.M., 1911; D.D., Mo. Valley Coll., 1907; m. Ethel Riley, June 5, 1901; children—Finis King, Rosemary. Ordained Presbyn. ministry, 1895; prof. Hebrew Dept., Cumberland U., 1895-1909; same chair, Presbyn. Theol. Sem. of the South, Lebanon, Tenn., 1909-10; prof. ch. history and missions same sem., allied with Lane Sem., Cincinnati, 1910-13; prof. N.T. Greek and Exegesis, 1913-15, of Hebrew and O.T. Lit., 1915—, and librarian, Lane Sem. Lecturer in Biblical Lit. U. of Cincinnati, 1921—. Author: Westminster Handbooks on the Sunday School Lessons, 1910-13. Died July 29, 1929.

FARR, Frederic William, clergyman; b. Litchfield, Me., Mar. 16, 1860; s. Moses Wadsworth and Lucinda White (Cram) F.; grad. Colby Coll., 1882; A.B., Newton Theol. Sem., 1886; LL.D., Los Angeles Bapt. Theol. Sem., 1932; m. Susie Agnes Coltman, May 27, 1886 (died 1903); 1 dau., Margaret Elizabeth; m. 2d, Katherine Eden, Apr. 24, 1905; children—Felicia Frances, Dorothea Lucile. Ordained ministry Bapt. Ch.; dean Los Angeles Bapt. Theol. Sem., 1926—; pastor Calvary Ch., Los Angeles, 1915—. Republican. Author: The Representative Christ; Manual of Christian Theology; Manual of Christian Evidences. Home: Los Angeles, Calif. Died June 24, 1939.

FARR, John Richard, congressman; b. Scranton, Pa., July 18, 1857; s. Edward and Elizabeth F.; attended Phillips Acad., Andover, Mass., and Lafayette Coll., Easton, Pa.; m. Justine Levy, Feb. 20, 1884. Real estate business, Scranton, 1899—. Mem. Scranton Sch. Bd., 4 yrs.; mem. Pa. Ho. of Rep., 5 terms, 1891-1901 (speaker, 1899); mem. 62d to 65th Congresses (1911-19), 10th Pa. Dist. Republican. Home: Scranton, Pa. Died Dec. 11, 1933.

FARRAND, Livingston, educator; b. Newark, N.J., June 14, 1867; s. Samuel A. and Louise (Wilson) F.; A.B., Princeton, 1888, A.M., 1891; M.D., Coll. of Phys. and Surg. (Columbia), 1891; studied Cambridge, Eng., 1891-92, Berlin, 1892-93; LL.D., Colo. Coll., 1914, U. of Denver, 1914, U. of Mich., 1917, U. of Colo., 1919, Union U., Princeton, Colgate, 1922, Yale, 1923, U. of Pa., 1925, Dartmouth Coll., 1925, U. of Toronto, 1927, Columbia U., 1929, Syracuse U., 1934, Lafayette Coll., 1935, Williams Coll., 1937; L.H.D., Hobart Coll., 1922; hon. Ph.D., Rensselaer Poly. Inst., 1924; m. Margaret K. Carleton, Feb. 1, 1901; children—Margaret Propert, Louisa Wilson, John, Mary Dalton, Robert Kitchell. Instr. psychology, 1893-1901, adj. prof. same, 1901-03, prof. anthropology, 1903-14, Columbia; pres. U. of Colo., Jan. 1, 1914-Mar. 1, 1919; chmn. Central Com. of Am. Red Cross, Mar. 1919-Oct. 1921; pres. Cornell U., 1921-37 (emeritus). Dir. tuberculosis work in France of Internat. Health Bd., 1917-18; Officer Legion of Honor (France). Exec. sec. Nat. Assn. for Study and Prevention of Tuberculosis, 1905-14; treas. Am. Pub. Health Assn., 1912-14. Author: Basis of American History, 1904. Home: Brewster, N.Y. Died Nov. 8, 1939.

FARRAND, Wilson, headmaster; b. Newark, N.J., Sept. 22, 1862; s. Samuel Ashbel and Louise (Wilson) F.; grad. Newark Acad., 1878; A.B., Princeton, 1886, A.M., 1889; hon. A.M., Columbia, 1907; L.H.D., Hamilton Coll., 1918; Litt.D., Princeton Univ., 1935; L.H.D., Rutgers U., 1936; LL.D., U. of Newark, 1940; m. Margaret Washburne Walker, Nov. 23, 1889; children—Margaret L. Katharine (dec.), Dorothy W. Asst. editor Scribner's Magazine, 1886-87; master, Newark (N.J.) Acad., 1887-89, asso. headmaster, 1889-1901, headmaster, 1901-35, emeritus, 1935—. Mem. College Entrance Examination Bd., 1900—. Mem. Schoolmasters' Assn. of New York (pres., 1895-96), Middle States Assn. Colls. and Prep. Schs. (pres. 1902), Head Masters Assn. of U.S. (pres. 1911), New Eng. Soc. of Orange (pres. 1906-08); pres. Princeton Alumni Fedn. of N.J., 1909-11. Alumni trustee Princeton U., 1909-19, life trustee and clerk bd., 1919—; mem. Commn. on Higher Institutions, Middle States Assn. Presbyn. Editor: Carlyle's "Essay on Burns," 1896; Tennyson's "Princess," 1898. Home: Princeton, N.J. Died Nov. 4, 1942.

FARRAR, Edgar Howard, lawyer; b. Concordia Parish, La., June 20, 1849; s. Thomas Prince and Anna Girault F.; A.M., U. of Va., 1871; studied law U. of La.; m. Lucinda Davis Stamps, 1878. Admitted to bar, 1872; asst. corp. counsel, 1878-80; corp. counsel, 1880; selected, 1822, by Paul Tulane, one of trustees of fund of over $1,000,000 to found what became Tulane U. Was for yrs. chmn. exec. com. of 100 to reform municipal govt. of New Orleans; chmn. of com. of safety formed to prosecute Mafia assassins of chief of police; led campaign which defeated proposition to extend charter of La. Lottery. One of organizers of Nat. Democracy in 1896; sr. mem. Farrar, Goldberg & Dufour. Home: New Orleans, La. Died Jan. 6, 1922.

FARRAR, James McNall, clergyman, author; b. Candor, Pa., June 16, 1853; s. James and Jane (McNall) F.; A.B., Westminster Coll., Pa., 1875, A.M., 1904; grad. Princeton Theol. Sem., 1878; (LL.D., Ursinus Coll., 1909); m. Ella J. Merrick, Oct. 22, 1879. Ordained United Presbyn. ministry, Dec. 10, 1878; pastor, Harrisville, O., 1879-84, 4th Ch., Phila., 1884-89, 1st Reformed Ch., Brooklyn, 1889—. Pres. Gen. Synod Ref. Ch. in America, 1905-06; pres. Bd. Domestic Missions Reformed Ch. in America; v.p. Seney Hosp.; dir. Bible Training Sch., New York; mem. Fed. Council Chs. of Christ in Am. Author: A Junior Congregation, 1908; Little Talks to Little People, 1910; Chats with Children of the Church, 1912. Home: Brooklyn, N.Y. Died June 22, 1921.

FARRAR, William Edmund, educator; b. Lynchburg, Va., Aug. 13, 1866; s. John Micou and Annie Carter (Bickers) F.; A.B., Richmond (Va.) Coll., 1890; U. of Va., 1890-92; (M.A., Bethel Coll., Ky., 1901); m. Clara Taylor Bond, Dec. 19, 1895. Licentiate instr., U. of Va., 1892; prof. Greek and Latin, Union U., Jackson, Tenn., 1892-97 and 1912-13; same, Bethel Coll., 1897-1909, dean and prof., 1910-12 and 1913-18, elected pres., 1918; dean and prof. Latin and Greek, Mercer U., 1918-19, dean and prof. Greek, 1919—; dean Coll. of Arts and Sciences, 1923—. Mem. Accredited Commn. Ga. High Schs. Democrat. Baptist. Home: Macon, Ga. Died May 9, 1925.

FARRELL, Charles LeRoy, banker; b. Bristol, Ind., Nov. 14, 1874; s. John W. and Mary Josephine (Maffitt) F.; student Transylvania U., Ky.; m. Nellie May Richards, Oct. 12, 1898 (died 1939). Began as bookkeeper State Bank of Ind., Indianapolis, 1894; asst. cashier Capitol Nat. Bank, Indianapolis, 1898-1903; v.p. Ft. Dearborn Nat. Bank, Chicago, 1903-06; v.p. Irving Nat. Bank, New York, 1906-09; pres. Essex County Nat. Bank, Newark, N.J., 1909-18, when the bank consolidated with the Nat. Newark Banking Co., forming the Nat. Newark & Essex Banking Co., of which is pres.; also pres. Newark & Essex Securities Corp. Treas. Trustees of State Assn. Y.M.C.A.'s of N.J.; pres. Babies Hosp.; trustee Marcus L. Ward Home, Newark. Republican. Methodist. Home: Newark, N.J. Died Aug. 25, 1940.

FARRELL, James Charles, capitalist; b. Albany, N.Y., Mar. 24, 1870; s. John Henry and Mary V. (Gibbons) F.; m. Margaret R., d. Anthony N. Brady, Apr. 15, 1893. Dir. in various corps. Home: Albany, N.Y. Died Dec. 28, 1918.

FARRELL, J(ohn) Fletcher, petroleum producer; b. Paris, Mo., Aug. 19, 1878; s. William Martin and Susan (Weatherford) F.; ed. pub. schs.; m. Nellie West Curtright, June 17, 1901; children—Esther (Mrs. Wardell Wilkinson, dec.), William Fletcher. Asst. state treas., Mo., 1901-03; asst. cashier Third Nat. Bank, St. Louis, Mo., 1904-10; v.p. Fort Dearborn Trust & Savings Bank, Chicago, 1910-16; v.p. and treas. Consol. Oil Corp., 1916—; v.p. and dir. Penn Mex. Fuel Co.; v.p., treas. and dir. Mexican Sinclair Petroleum Corp., Sinclair Coal Co., Sinclair Navigation Co.; v.p. Pierce Oil Co., S.A., Sinclair Cuba Oil Co. Democrat. Mem. Ref. Ch. Home: Bronxville, N.Y. Died Sept. 25, 1938.

FARRELLY, John P., bishop; b. Memphis, Tenn., Mar. 15, 1856; s. John P. and Martha (Clay) F.; ed. Georgetown Coll., D.C.; N.D. de la Paix, Namur, Belgium, and Am. Coll., Rome. Ordained priest R.C. Ch., 1880; spiritual dir., Am. Coll., Rome, 1893-1909; consecrated bishop of Cleveland (O.), May 1, 1909. Died Feb. 12, 1921.

FARRER, Henry, artist; b. London, England, Mar. 23, 1844; g.s. Thomas Farrer, well-known miniature painter of London, 1770-1850; came to New York, 1863, first becoming known by his water colors, and later as a landscape painter, his specialties being scenes found near the coast, especially on Long Island, but most widely known as an etcher. In 1879 became sec. Am. Water Color Soc., and 1881, pres. New York Etching Club; 1882 elected fellow Royal Soc. of Painter-Etchers. Home: Brooklyn, N.Y. Died 1903.

FARRINGTON, Edward Holyoke, prof. dairy husbandry; b. Brewer, Me., Dec. 20, 1860; s. Joseph Rider and Ellen Elisabeth (Holyoke) F.; B.S., M.S., U. of Me.; M.S., Sheffield Scientific Sch., Yale, 1882; m. Margaret Tate, June 1, 1898. Chemist Conn. Agrl. Expt. Sta., New Haven, Conn., 1883-89; in office Expt. Stas., U.S. Dept. Agr., Washington, 1889-90; chemist Ill. Agrl. Expt. Sta., Champaign, 1890-94; prof. dairy husbandry, Univ. of Wis., 1894-1927. Chemist World's Fair Dairy Tests, Chicago, 1893, St. Louis, 1904. Alderman, City of Madison, Wis., 1910-12. Mason. Progressive. Conglist. Author: Testing Milk and Its Products, 1896; Dairy Products, 1927. Originated: Alkaline Tablet Test for acidity in dairy products; High Pressure Oven Test for water in dairy products; Milk Sediment Test; Butter Test for fat per cent. Home: Madison, Wis. Died 1934.

FARRINGTON, Edward Silsby, judge; b. Yreka, Calif., Sept. 6, 1856; s. Daniel and Elizabeth Ann (Silsby) F.; A.B., Amherst Coll., 1880; student Hastings Law Sch., San Francisco, 1885-86; LL.D., U. of Nev., 1908; m. Celia Taber, Aug. 14, 1892. Prin. Nev. State U., 1883-84; admitted to Nev. bar, 1886; Rep. nominee for Congress, 1900, 1902; U.S. dist. judge, Dist. of Nev., Feb. 4, 1907—. Home: Carson City, Nev. Died Aug. 31, 1929.

FARRINGTON, Ernest Albert, psychologist; b. Phila., Pa., July 25, 1880; s. Ernest Albert (M.D.) and Elizabeth (Aitken) F.; B.S., Bryn Athyn Acad., 1898; M.D., Dunham Med. Coll., Chicago, 1902, Hahnemann Med. Coll., Phila., 1909; m. Mary S. Cooper, May 26, 1903; children—Robert Grant, Ernest Albert, George Dudley, Mary Elizabeth (Mrs. J. Edward Mitchell). Practiced in Chicago and Phila. until 1907; lecturer in chemistry, Hering Med. Coll., Chicago, 1901-04, asst. prof. chemistry and toxicology, 1904-05; lecturer in physiology, Hahnemann Med. Coll., Phila., 1905-09; psychologist Bancroft Sch. for Retarded Children, Haddonfield, N.J., 1907—, pres., supt. and trustee, 1912—. Republican. Presbyn. Home: Haddonfield, N.J. Died April 5, 1937.

FARRINGTON, Frank George, judge; b. Augusta, Me., Sept. 11, 1872; s. Franklin L. and Cordelia (Wilson) F.; A.B., Bowdoin Coll., 1894; student Harvard Law Sch., 1900-02; m. Martha Blanche French, Sept. 5, 1894; children—Mildred Blanche (dec.; Mrs. Raymond Whitney Swift), Frank Alden. Prin. high sch., Machias, Me., 1894-96, Skowhegan, Me., 1897-99; admitted to Me. bar, 1902, and began practice at Augusta; asst. sec. Me. State Senate, 1903-05.

sec., 1907-09; city clk., Augusta, 1903-06; U.S. commr., 1913-16; mem. Me. Ho. of Rep., 1917-21 (Rep. floor leader; speaker 1919); mem. Me. State Senate, 1921-25 (pres. 1923); asso. justice Supreme Jud. Court of Me., 1929-33; v.p. Augusta Savings Bank, Overseer Bowdoin Coll.; trustee Lithgow Pub. Library. Conglist. Mason. Home: Augusta, Me. Died Sept. 3, 1933.

FARRINGTON, Frederic Ernest, educator; b. Waltham, Mass., Dec. 15, 1872; s. John Henry and Mary Ellen (Hildreth) F.; A.B., Harvard, 1894; A.M., Columbia, 1902; student, Jena, 1902, Paris, 1903; Ph.D., Columbia, 1904, also doctor's diploma, Teachers Coll.; m. Isabelle Scudder, Nov. 23, 1898. Instr. Waltham (Mass.) High Sch., 1894-97; instr. mathematics, Collegiate Sch., New York, 1897-1901; fellow in edn., Teachers Coll., Columbia, 1901-02; internat. fellow for study in France, 1902-03; dir. neighborhood work, Speyer School (Teachers Coll.), 1903-04; asst. prof. edn., U. of Calif., 1904-08; asso. prof. observation and practice, U. of Tex., 1908-10; asso. prof. ednl. adminstrn. (comparative edn.) Teachers Coll. (Columbia U.), 1910-15; spl. collaborator, U.S. Bur. Edn., Washington, 1914-19; headmaster, Chevy Chase Sch., Washington, 1917-27, pres., 1927—; pres. Chevy Chase Savings Bank. Asso. prof. edn., summer sessions, Columbia U., 1909, U. of Chicago, 1910; lecturer on edn., Yale U., and Conn. State high sch. insp., 1914-15. Exec. sec. N.E.A. com. on Internat. Congress on Edn., Oakland, Calif., 1915; investigator San Francisco school survey, 1916. Mem. Dutch Reformed Ch. Author: The Public Primary School System of France, 1906; French Secondary Schools, 1910 (2d edit. 1915); Commercial Education in Germany, 1914; Public Facilities for Educating the Alien, U.S. Bur. Edn., Bull. 1916, No. 18. Editor: French Educational Ideals of Today (with F. Buisson), 1919. Died June 1930.

FARRINGTON, Harry Webb, clergyman, author; b. Nassau, B.W.I., July 14, 1880; s. William Gilliland and Emma Russell Farrington; lost mother in infancy and was early thrown on own resources; worked way through schools; ed. Darlington (Md.) Acad.; grad. Dickinson Sem., 1903; A.B., Syracuse U., 1907; S.T.B., Boston Theol. Sem.; A.M., Harvard; m. Dora W. Davis, June 24, 1920. Asst. in psychology and tutor in Logic, Syracuse U., 1908; asst. and spl. lecturer in philosophy, Harvard, 1913; inaugurated for M.E. denomination Week Day Ch. School, at Gary, Ind., 1914-16; continued same N.Y. City, 1916-18; went to France for Foyers du Soldat and given hon. life commn. in 7th and 10th Cuirassiers, 1918-19. Mem. N.Y. East Conf., M.E. Ch. Author: Poems from France, 1920; Rough and Brown (verse), 1921; Faith of Franklin, 1922; Cher Ami (Dear Friend), prose and verse, 1923; Washington the Servant, 1924; The Liberty of Lincoln, 1924; Roosevelt the Righteous, 1924; Walls of America (The House of Uncle Sam) prose and verse, 1925. Home: New York, N.Y. Died Oct. 25, 1931.

FARRINGTON, Oliver Cummings, geologist; b. Brewer, Me., Oct. 9, 1864; s. Joseph Rider and Ellen E. (Holyoke) F.; B.S., U. of Me., 1881, M.S., 1888; Ph.D., Yale, 1891; m. Clara A. Bradley, Aug. 3, 1896. Teacher of science in acads., 1882-87; lab. asst. Yale, 1890-91; asst. U.S. Nat. Mus., 1893; curator geology, Field Mus. of Natural History, Chicago, 1894—. Lecturer on mineralogy, U. of Chicago, 1894-1904. Collaborator, mines and metallurgy, Paris Expn., 1900; mem. Internat. Jury of Awards, St. Louis Expn., 1904. Pres. Am. Assn. of Museums, 1915-16. Fellow Geol. Soc. America, A.A.A.S. Mem. Field Museum Expedn. to Brazil, 1922-23. Conglist. Author: Gems and Gem Minerals, 1903; Meteorites, 1915. Home: Chicago, Ill. Died Nov. 2, 1933.

FARRINGTON, Wallace Rider, gov.; b. Orono, Me., May 3, 1871; s. Joseph Rider and Ellen E. (Holyoke) F.; B.S., Univ. of Me., 1891, LL.D., 1931; m. Catharine McAlpine Crane, Oct. 26, 1896; children—Joseph R., Ruth (Mrs. Edmond H. Levy), Frances (Mrs. John R. Whittemore). Began newspaper work, 1891, as reporter, and later night editor Bangor (Me.) Daily News; reporter Kennebec Journal, Augusta, Me., and 1892-93, asst. editor on publs. of Phelps Pub. Co., Springfield, Mass.; mng. editor and one of founders Rockland (Me.) Daily Star; editor Pacific Commercial Advertiser and pres. Hawaiian Gazette Co., Honolulu, 1894-96; editor Evening Bulletin and Pres. Bulletin Pub. Co., Ltd., June 1898-July 1912; v.p. and gen. bus. mgr. Honolulu Star-Bulletin, Ltd. Served on Territorial Bd. of Edn.; also on Rep. Territorial Com., 1906-07; chmn. Territorial Sch. Fund Commn., 1909-11; hon. pres. Honolulu Ad Club. Wrote: Review of the Revolt of 1895 (appendix to Alexander's History of the Hawaiian Revolution). Chmn. bd. of regents Coll. of Hawaii; gov. of Hawaii 2 terms, 1921-29; now pres. and pub. Honolulu Star Bulletin, Ltd. Pres. Pan Pacific Union. Died Oct. 6, 1933.

FARRINGTON, William George, clergyman; b. New York, Dec. 15, 1832; s. John G. and Louisa (Brady) F.; A.B., Columbia, 1853, A.M., 1856; grad. Gen. Theol. Sem., 1856; (D.D., William and Mary Coll., 1872); m. Anna Wilson, d. Leonard W. Kip, Jan. 14, 1865. Deacon and priest P.E. Ch., 1856; rector St. John's Ch., Huntington, L.I., 1856-58; asst. Trinity parish, New York, 1858-62; rector Christ Church, Hackensack, N.J., which he founded, 1863-70; rector Christ Ch., Bloomfield, N.J., 1877-89; mem. editorial staff The Churchman, 1889-1904. Sec. bd. trustees Gen. Theol. Sem., 1867-83. Home: Orange, N.J. Died Mar. 13, 1913.

FARRIS, Robert Perry, Presbyn. clergyman; b. St. Louis, Mo., Sept. 6, 1826; s. Robert P. and Catherine A. (Cross) F.; grad. Yale, 1847, Princeton Theol. Sem., 1850 (D.D., Westminster Coll., Mo., 1867); m. Eliza S. Bowen, Aug. 3, 1848. Ordained to ministry, 1851; editor St. Louis Presbyterian, 1866-95; moderator, 1881, "Gen. Assembly Presbyn. Ch. in the U.S." or Southern Presbyn. Ch.; permanent clerk of same, 1885—. Home: St. Louis, Mo. Died 1903.

FARRISS, Charles Sherwood, educator; b. Warrenton, N.C., June 1, 1856; s. Charles Maurice and Julia Ann (Carter) F.; A.B., Wake Forest (N.C.) Coll., 1880, D.D., 1894; student Southern Bapt. Theol. Sem., 1881-82, 1886-87; U. of Va., 1892; U. of Chicago, 1900-01; LL.D., Stetson U., DeLand, Fla., 1927; m. Alma Richardson, Dec. 25, 1889; 1 son, Carl Vernon. Began teaching, 1892; editor Bibl. Recorder, Raleigh, N.C., 1881-87, The Baptist Witness, 1892-1904; acting pres. Stetson U., 1904 and 1933, v.p., 1904-32, 1933—. Democrat. Baptist. Author: The American Soul, 1920; Robert E. Lee (drama), 1924. Home: DeLand, Fla. Died April 14, 1938.

FARROW, Edward Samuel, cons. engr.; b. Snow Hill, Md., Apr. 20, 1855; s. William H. and Catherine A. F.; A.B., Baltimore City Coll., 1872; grad. U.S. Mil. Acad., 1876; m. Elizabeth E. Downing, 1897. Commd. 2d lt., 21st Inf., June 15, 1876; 1st lt., Sept. 17, 1883; instr. tactics, U.S. Mil. Acad., 1880-85; resigned from army, Feb. 24, 1892. Served against Indians in Ore., Mont., Dak. and Wash. Ty.; captured the hostile Sheep-Eater Indians, in Salmon Mountains, Ida., 1879, and was recommended for brevets "for conspicuous bravery, energy and soldierly conduct" in Nez Perce, Bannock, Piute and other Indian campaigns. Engring. operations include exploration of mining dists. in eastern Ore. and northwestern Ida.; ry. constn. and timber operations in Adirondacks; surveys and reports on Appalachian fields of Va.; exams. and reports on gold and copper deposits in Black Hills of S.D., mica deposits of Me., arsenical ore deposits in Putnam Co., N.Y., mineral deposits in Bland Co., Va., also reports on Panama Canal and Canal Zone, etc. Founder of Farrow Pub. Library, Pinewald, and Pinewald Mil. Camp of Instrn. Episcopalian. Author: American Small Arms, 1904; West Point and the Military Academy, 1900; Camping on the Trail, 1902; Dictionary of Military Terms, 1917; Farrow's Manual of Military Training, 1919; Riots and Riot Duty, 1919; Gas Warfare, 1919; American Guns in the War with Germany, 1919. Compiler: Farrow's Military Ency. (3 vols.), 1885; owner and editor Pinewald Bull. (newspaper advocating peace). Inventor of toxic gases and gas grenade; discoverer of gravity control by intensification of Hertsian waves. Home: Pinewald, N.J. Died Sept. 25, 1926.

FARSON, John, banker, lawyer; b. Union City, Ind., Oct. 8, 1855; s. Rev. John T. Farson (M.E. clergyman) and Harriet C. (Page) F.; ed. public schools, Champaign, Ill., and Univ. of Ill., 1874-76; studied law, Chicago, in office of J. R. Doolittle, U.S. senator from Wis.; admitted to bar, 1880; m. Mamie A. Ashworth, Sept. 1, 1881. Banker, 1881—; organized Farson, Leach & Co., 1889, which was succeeded by Farson, Son & Co., 1906; pres. Calumet Electric St. Ry. Co., Chicago; v.p. and dir. Rockford & Interurban Ry. Co. Trustee Am. Univ., Washington; v.p. New York and Chicago Road Assn.; pres. Am. Automobile Assn., 1906, Oak Park (Ill.) Horse Show Assn. Home: Oak Park, Ill. Died 1910.

FARWELL, Arthur Burrage; b. North Leominster, Mass., Oct. 2, 1852; s. Peter and Elizabeth Smith (Burrage) F.; ed. pub. schs., Leominster; m. Floretta Woodbery, Dec. 25, 1882; children—Stanley P., Burrage (dec.), Florence (Mrs. Myron S. Strong, dec.), Elizabeth (Mrs. Edward P. Farwell), Louise, Dorothy (Mrs. Luther H. Barber). With Babcock Fire Extinguisher Co., 1869-70; stockman and salesman, John V. Farwell & Co., 1870-76; salesman, C. M. Henderson & Co., boots and shoes, 1876-1901, Watson-Plummer Shoe Co., 1901-07; has devoted entire time from 1907 to such work as that of the Chicago Law and Order League (pres.); dir. Ill. Vigilance Assn. (pres., 1910-14), Hyde Park Protective Assn. (chmn. finance com. or sec.), Ill. Anti-Saloon League, etc. Republican. Was one of the charter members of Kenwood Evang. (Union) Ch., 1885. Home: Glencoe, Ill. Died Sept. 18, 1936.

FARWELL, Charles Benjamin, merchant, senator; b. Painted Post, N.Y., July 1, 1823; s. Henry and Nancy (Jackson) F.; ed. in dist. schools until 1838; removed to Ogle Co., Ill.; worked at farming and on Govt. surveys until 1844, when he went to Chicago on a load of wheat with $10 in his pocket. Secured employment in county clerk's office; later teller in a bank; county clerk Cook Co., Ill., 1854-62; joined his brother, John V. Farwell in firm of John V. Farwell & Co., wholesale dry goods, and, 1891, became pres. The John V. Farwell Co. With his brother built, 1887, the Texas State capitol, receiving 3,000,000 acres of land therefor. They now have a ranch there, stocked with 150,000 cattle; was mem. State bd. of equalization, 1867; chmn. bd. of supervisors, Cook Co., Ill., 1868; Nat. bank examiner, 1869; mem. Congress, 1871-76 and 1881-87; U.S. senator, 1887-91. Republican. Home: Chicago, Ill. Died 1903.

FARWELL, John Villiers, sr. mem. J. V. Farwell Co., wholesale dry goods merchants; b. Painted Post, N.Y., July 29, 1825; s. Henry and Nancy (Jackson) F.; removed to Ogle Co., Ill., 1838; ed. Mt. Morris (Ill.) Sem., 1841-45; m. Abigail G. Taylor, Apr. 16, 1849; m. 2d, Emeret C. Cooley, Mar. 8, 1854. Was employed by the oldest wholesale dry goods house in 1849; in 3 yrs. was made a partner, and the concern is now the John V. Farwell Co. Presdl. elector on Lincoln ticket, 1860; one of U.S. Christian Commn. during Civil War; Indian commr. during Pres. Grant's first term; donated to Y.M.C.A. his first residence lot in Chicago, upon which the Association Bldg. now stands. Largely interested in all of Mr. Moody's enterprises. Home: Lake Forest, Ill. Died 1908.

FARWELL, John W., cotton goods mfr.; b. Waltham, Mass., Apr. 17, 1843; s. Nathaniel and Eliza (Fletcher) F.; ed. pub. schs.; m. Ruby F. Howe, May 8, 1870. In cotton mfg. business, 1860—; pres. Nyanza Mills, Cabot Mfg. Co., Boston Storage Warehouse; treas. Farwell Bleachery, Farwell Mills. Trustee of a Republican Instn. in the Town of Boston. Republican. Home: Boston, and Cohasset, Mass. Died Oct. 7, 1929.

FARWELL, Thomas Abbot, author; b. Belfast, Ireland, July 6, 1842; s. Thomas William and Edith (Abbot) F.; educated at Oxford Univ., England. Author: Can All This Grandeur Perish, 1872; Fellow Countrymen, 1875; Gas-house McGinty, 1876; Judgement Day, 1880; Literary Criticisms, 1882; The American Saddle Horse, 1885; Winds of Chance, 1889; Voices from the Dust, 1893. Home: Boston, Mass. Died January 17, 1904.

FASSETT, Charles Marvin; b. Elmira, N.Y., Dec. 23, 1858; s. Samuel Montague and Ruth Clara (Marvin) F.; ed. Elmira Free Acad.; m. Edith May Benham, Jan. 1, 1884. Settled in Nev., 1879; mem. Nev. Ho. of Rep., 1885; propr. chem. lab. in Reno, Nev., 1885-89; moved to Spokane, Wash., 1889; designed and built several mining and metal extraction plants, including 1st gold cyanide mill in Asia, in Northern Korea, 1900. Mem. Charter Commn., Spokane; one of 1st commrs. of Spokane under commn. form of govt.; commr. pub. utilities, Spokane, 1911-19; mayor of Spokane, two terms, 1915, 1918-19; now professorial lecturer and consultant in municipal govt., Dept. of Polit. Science, U. of Kan. Pres. Chamber of Commerce, Spokane; mem. Bd. of Edn., Library Bd., Park Bd. Mem. Nev. N.G. 5 yrs., advancing to capt. Home: Lawrence, Kan. Died Aug. 10, 1923.

FASSETT, Jacob Sloat, congressman; b. Elmira, N.Y., Nov. 13, 1853; s. Newton P. and Martha E. (Sloat) F.; A.B., U. of Rochester, 1875, A.M.; adm. to bar, 1878; studied law and polit. economy, U. of Heidelberg, 1880-81; (LL.D., Colgate, 1901); m. Jennie L., d. of late Judge E. B. Crocker, of Sacramento, Calif., Feb. 13, 1879. In practice at Elmira, 1878—; propr. Elmira Daily Advertiser, 1879-96; v.p. Second Nat. Bank. Dist. atty. Chemung Co., 1878-80; mem. N.Y. Senate, 1884-91 (temporary pres., 1889, 1890, 1891); sec. Rep. Nat. Com., 1888-92; Rep. nominee for gov. N.Y., 1891; mem. 59th to 61st Congresses (1905-11), 33d N.Y. Dist. Temporary and permanent chmn. N.Y. State Rep. Advisory Conv., Saratoga, 1918. Home: Elmira, N.Y. Died Apr. 21, 1924.

FASSETT, James Hiram, author; b. Nashua, N.H., Jan. 11, 1869; s. James Boutelle and Ellen Maria (Morrill) F.; A.B., Dartmouth, 1890; m. Bertha Chester Smith, June 23, 1897 (died 1921); 1 son, James Adams; m. 2d, Isabella Deshler Stahl, Jan. 15, 1923. Principal Mt. Pleasant Grammar Sch., Nashua, 1890-93; supt. sch., Nashua, 1893-1920. Trustee N.H. State Normal Sch. Republican. Unitarian. Mason. Author: Colonial Life in New Hampshire, 1899; History of Education in New Hampshire, 1900; The Beacon Series of School Readers, 1914. Home: Orlando, Fla. Died Nov. 9, 1930.

FASSIG, Oliver Lanard, meteorologist; b. Columbus, O., Apr. 5, 1860; s. Mathias and Elizabeth (Lanard) F.; B.S., Ohio State U., 1882; studied Yale and U. of Berlin; Ph.D., Johns Hopkins, 1899; m. Ann Green McCoy, Sept. 14, 1898. With U.S. Weather Bureau, 1883—. Instructor meteorology, 1897-1901, asso., 1901-19, Johns Hopkins Univ.; meteorologist, Md. State Weather Service, 1900-09 and 1912-19; chief instr. Sch. of Meteorology, Signal Corps U.S.A., Coll. Station, Tex., 1918; in charge West Indies and Caribbean service, U.S. Weather Bur., 1919-30. Lecturer on climatology, Sch. of Tropical Medicine, U. of P.R., 1926-30; chief of div. of climatology, U.S. Weather Bureau, 1930-32; research asso. Blue Hill Obs., Harvard, 1932—. Mem. Ziegler Arctic Relief Expedition, 1905. Editor: A Bibliography of Meteorology (U.S. Weather Bur.), 4 vols., 1889-91; Report of the Chicago Meteorological

Congress, 1893 (U.S. Weather Bur.), 1894-96; A Report on the Climate and Weather of Baltimore, 1904-07; Reports on the Climate of Puerto Rico, 1910-30. Died Dec. 6, 1936.

FAULKNER, Charles James, senator; b. Martinsburg, W.Va., Sept. 21, 1847; s. Hon. Charles James (minister to France) and Mary Wagner (Boyd) F.; early edn. in France and Switzerland; entered Va. Mil. Inst., Lexington, 1862; served with cadets at battle of New Market and afterwards as aide to Gens. Breckenridge and Wise in C.S.A., to end of war; grad. U. of Va., 1868; admitted to W.Va. bar, 1868. Judge 13th Jud. Circuit, W.Va., 1880-87; U.S. senator, 1887-99; mem. British-Am. Joint High Commn., 1898. Permanent chmn. Dem. State convs., 1888-92; chmn. Dem. Congressional Com., 1894, 96, 98. Mason. Home: Martinsburg, W.Va. Died Jan. 13, 1929.

FAULKNER, Herbert Waldron, artist; b. Stamford, Conn., Oct. 8, 1860; s. James W. and Sarah E. (Breasted) F.; Ph.B., Sheffield Scientific Sch. (Yale), 1882, M.E., 1884; studied art, Art Students' League (New York), École des Beaux Arts, École R. Collin, Paris, France; m. Mary John, of St. Ives, Cornwall, Eng., Sept. 12, 1895; children—Waldron, Louis M. Hon. mention, Buffalo Expn., 1901; pictures purchased by St. Louis Mus., Dallas (Tex.) Art Assn., Nashville Mus., John Herron Art Assn. (Indianapolis), etc. Mem. Syndicat de la Presse Artistique, Paris. Author: The Mysteries of the Flowers; Wood Carving as a Hobby; Designs for Wood-Carving; Decorative Plant Forms. Home: Washington, Conn. Died Mar. 27, 1940.

FAULKNER, John Alfred, theologian; b. Grand Pré, N.S., July 14, 1857; s. John L. and Elizabeth (Armstrong) F.; A.B., Acadia Coll., N.S., 1878, M.A., 1890; B.D., Drew Theol. Sem., 1881; studied Andover Theol. Sem., 1881-82, U. of Leipzig, 1902-03, U. of Bonn, 1904; D.D., Wesleyan, 1897, Acadia, 1902; LL.D., Pa. Coll., 1919; m. Helen Underwood, July 28, 1887; children—Harold Underwood, John Arthur, Helen Katharine. Ordained M.E. ministry, 1883; pastor Beach Lake, Yatesville, Scranton, Taylor and Great Bend, Pa., 1883-94, Binghamton, N.Y., 1894-97; prof. church history, Drew Theol. Sem., 1897—. Stone lecturer, Princeton Theol. Sem., 1923. Author: The Methodists, in the Story of the Churches series, 1903; Cyprian; the Churchman, in Men of the Kingdom series, 1906; Erasmus—the Scholar, in same series, 1908; Crises in the Early Church, 1912; Wesley as Sociologist, Theologian, Churchman, 1918; Value of Study of Church History, 1920; Modernism and the Christian Faith, 1921; Miraculous Birth of Our Lord, 1924; Burning Questions in Historic Christianity, 1930; also large portion of Hurst's History of the Christian Church, 1897-1900; article "Methodism" in New International Ency. Home: Madison, N.J. Died Sept. 6, 1931.

FAUNCE, Daniel Worcester, clergyman; b. Plymouth, Mass., Jan. 3, 1829; s. Peleg and Olive (Finney) F.; A.B., Amherst, 1850 (D.D., 1880); Newton Theol. Instn., 1850-53; m. Mary P. Perry, Aug. 15, 1853; m. 2d, Mrs. Mary E. Tucker, 1891; father of William Herbert Perry F. Ordained Bapt. ministry, 1853; pastor Somerville, Mass., 1853-54, Worcester, Mass., 1854-60, Malden, Mass., 1860-66, Concord, N.H., 1866-75, Lynn, Mass., 1875-81, Washington, D.C., 1881-89, W. Newton, Mass., 1889-93, Pawtucket, R.I., 1894-99. Mem. bd. mgrs., Am. Bapt. Missionary Union. Author: A Young Man's Difficulties with His Bible, 1877; Prayer as a Theory and a Fact (which also received Fletcher prize), 1890; Inspiration Considered as Trend, 1896; Shall We Believe in a Divine Providence?, 1900. Home: Providence, R.I. Died 1911.

FAUNCE, William Herbert Perry, univ. pres.; b. Worcester, Mass., Jan. 15, 1859; s. Rev. Daniel Worcester and Mary P. (Perry) F.; A.B., Brown, 1880, A.M., 1883, D.D., 1895; instr. mathematics, Brown, 1881-82; grad. Newton Theol. Instn., 1884; D.D., Brown, 1895, Yale, 1901, Harvard, 1904; LL.D., Baylor, 1904, Alabama, 1905, Dartmouth, 1909, Wesleyan, 1909, Denison, 1914, Amherst, 1915, McMaster, 1923; m. Sarah R. Edson, June 18, 1884; 1 son, Perry Edson (dec.). Pastor State St. Ch., Springfield, Mass., 1884-89, Fifth Av. Ch., New York, 1889-99; pres. Brown U., June 1899—. President of World Peace Foundation. Lecturer U. of Chicago, 1897; trustee Newton Theol. Instn., Worcester Acad., R.I. Sch. Design. Author: The Educational Ideal in the Ministry, 1908; What Does Christianity Mean?, 1912; Social Aspects of Foreign Missions, 1914; Religion and War, 1918; The New Horizon of State and Church, 1918. Home: Providence, R.I. Died Jan. 31, 1930.

FAUST, Charles Lee, congressman; b. near Bellefontaine, O., Apr. 24, 1879; s. Wilson S. and Ellen May F.; student Highland (Kan.) U.; LL.B., U. of Kan., 1903. Began practice at St. Joseph, Mo., 1903; city counselor, St. Joseph, 1915-19; mem. 67th to 70th Congresses (1921-29), 4th Mo. Dist. Republican. Home: St. Joseph, Mo. Died Dec. 17, 1928.

FAUST, Samuel D., clergyman, educator; b. nr. Roxbury, Pa., Nov. 24, 1852; s. Samuel and Elizabeth (Detweiler) F.; B.A., Lebanon Valley Coll., Annville, Pa., 1889, A.M., 1892, D.D., 1894, LL.D., 1916; grad. Bonebrake Theol. Sem., Dayton, O., 1884; m. Lizzie J. Mower, June 17, 1884; 1 dau., Grace Lenore (Mrs. H. C. Cridland). Ordained ministry U.B. in Christ, 1888; pastor Intercourse, Pa., 1884-85, Harrisburg, Pa., 1889-92, Hygiene, Colo., 1893; prof. ch. history, Bonebrake Theol. Sem., 1893—, emeritus. Trustee Lebanon Valley Coll., 1889-1902, U.B. Printing Establishment, 1899-1909; sec. Bd. of Edn. U.B. in Christ, 1894-1909. Author: Regeneration, 1902. Died July 12, 1929.

FAVERSHAM, William, actor; b. in Eng., Feb. 12, 1868; ed. Chigwell Grammar Sch., Essex, Eng., and Hillmartin Coll., London; served in the English yeomanry; twice married; m. 2d, Julie Opp, actress, 1902. First appearance on stage, 1887; came to America, 1888; supported Mrs. Fiske 2 yrs.; under Frohman's management was leading man at Empire Theatre, New York, 6 yrs.; 9 yrs. mem. of co.; played rôle of Jim Carson in "The Squaw Man," 1905-06; later appeared in motion pictures. Died Apr. 7, 1940.

FAVILL, Henry Baird, physician; b. Madison, Wis., Aug. 14, 1860; s. John and Louise (Baird) F.; A.B., U. of Wis., 1880; M.D., Rush Med. Coll., Chicago, 1883; m. Susan Cleveland Pratt, June 1885. In practice of medicine at Chicago, 1893—; prof. medicine, Chicago Policlinic, 1893—; prof. therapeutics, Rush Med. Coll., 1898—; phys. to St. Luke's, Passavant, and Augustana hosps. Apptd. 1st lt. U.S.A. Med. Reserve Corps, 1908. Trustee Chicago Bur. Pub. Efficiency. Home: Chicago, Ill. Died Feb. 20, 1916.

FAVILLE, John, clergyman; b. Milford, Wis., July 7, 1847; s. Elijah and Eliza (Ostrom) F.; B.S., Lawrence Coll., 1871, M.S., 1874, D.D., 1896; A.B., Boston U., 1896, Ph.D., 1896; B.D., Boston U. Sch. of Theology, 1876; m. Louise G. Thayer, Oct. 26, 1876; children—Henry Thayer (dec.), Mildred, John. Ordained M.E. ministry, 1876. Pastorates of nine years in M.E. Church; pastor 1st Congl. Ch., Appleton, Wis., 1886-89, 1st Ch., Peoria, Ill., 1899-1907, again 1st Ch., Appleton, 1907-17. Chmn. com. on temperance Nat. Council Congl. Chs., 1910-13; pres. Wis. Anti-Saloon League, 1895-96. Trustee Milwaukee-Downer Coll., Chicago Theol. Sem., Northland Coll., Lawrence Coll. Elected mayor of Appleton, Wis., 1917. Author: Problem of Authority in Religion; I Believe in God, the Father. Home: Lake Mills, Wis. Died Sept. 6, 1927.

FAVOUR, Alpheus Hoyt, lawyer; b. Natick, Mass., Oct. 8, 1880; s. Richmond and Josephine (Temple) F.; B.S., Amherst Coll., 1903; LL.B., New York Law Sch., 1905; m. Ethel Lambert, Sept. 25, 1907 (died 1917); children—Catharine (Mrs. Henry A. Merchant), Mary Temple (Mrs. Sherman Hazeltine Prescott), Alpheus Lambert; m. 2d, Eva McLean, June 26, 1919; 1 son, John McLean. Began as social settlement and boy club worker, N.Y. City, 1903; resident East Side Settlement House, 1903; in charge Christy Street House, 1904; asst. worker Gordon House, 1905; in charge boys' work, Madison Sq. Church House, 1906-09; admitted to N.Y. bar, 1905 and practiced in N.Y. City until 1916, Prescott, Ariz., 1916—; sr. partner Favour & Baker; mem. Ariz. State Senate, 1924-32; mem. Legislative Commn. revising Ariz. laws, 1927-28, and of Ariz.-Colo. River Commn., 1927-29 and 1933-35; v.p., dir., Bank of Ariz. (oldest bank in Ariz.). Democrat. Conglist. Mason. Home: Prescott, Ariz. Died Dec. 30, 1939.

FAVROT, Charles Allen, architect; b. West Baton Rouge, La., May 22, 1866; s. Henry Mortimer and Celestine (Dubroca) F.; student La. State U., 1880-85, M.E., 1885; student in office of James Freret, architect, New Orleans, 1885-88; post-grad. work in architecture, Cornell U., 1888-89; m. Marie Beatrice Freret, Jan. 8, 1891; children—Olga F., (Mrs. C. B. Read), Carmen F., Henri Mortimer, Gervais F., Clifford F. Practiced in New Orleans, 1889—; sec. State Bd. Archtl. Examiners, 1910—. Mem. Bd. of Trade and Assn. of Commerce, New Orleans; mgr. Industrial Bur., Assn. of Commerce, 1914; mem. Bd. of Finance, same, 1915-18; chmn. City Planning Commn., 1922-31; treas. Govtl. Research Bureau of New Orleans. Trustee Tulane University. Mem. Am. Inst. Architects (bd. dirs., 1914-18; 1st v.p., 1918-19). Democrat. Roman Catholic. Home: New Orleans, La. Died Mar. 10, 1939.

FAVROT, George Kent, judge; b. at Baton Rouge, La., Nov. 26, 1868; grad. La. State U., 1888; LL.B., Tulane, 1890. Dist. atty. 22d Jud. Dist. of La., 1892-96, 1900-04; dist. judge, 1904-07; del. at large La. Constl. Conv., 1898; mem. 60th Congress (1907-09), 67th and 68th Congresses (1921-25), 6th La. Dist.; mem. La. Ho. of Rep., 1912-16; now judge, 19th Judicial Dist. of La. Democrat. Home: Baton Rouge, La. Died Dec. 26, 1934.

FAWCETT, Angelo Vance, mayor; b. Knox Co., O., Mar. 6, 1846; s. Phillip and Martha Ellen (Vance) F.; left Wesleyan U., Bloomington, Ill., to serve in 7th Ill. Inf., Civil War; m. 4th, Margaret J. Smith, 1896. Wounded in Battle of Altoona Pass, Ga., Oct. 1864 (46 out of 51 men in his co. being killed and only three returning unharmed). Began with Kingman & Co., Peoria, Ill., farm machinery, 1877; moved to Tacoma, Wash., 1883, and engaged in same line of business and made $500,000 in 10 yrs.; fortune nearly all swept away in panic of 1893; was head of Fawcett Bros., farm machinery and seeds, Tacoma, also Fawcett Bros., North Yakima and Bellingham, Wash.; pres. Fawcett Wagon Co., Tacoma. County commr. Pierce Co., Wash., 1 term; state senator, 1917-21; has been mayor of Tacoma many terms; secured Cushman Power Plant for city. Republican. Home: Fort Lewis, Wash. Deceased.

FAWCETT, Edgar, author; b. New York, May 26, 1847; grad. Columbia, 1867 (A.M.); since then engaged in literature; traveled in Europe; has lately resided in London, Eng. Not married. Author: The Confessions of Claud; The Adventures of a Widow; Song and Story (poems); Romance and Revery (poems). Died 1904.

FAWCETT, George D., actor; b. Va., Aug. 25, 1861; s. Asbury Francis and Ann Eliza (Means) F.; student U. of Va. 4 yrs.; m. Percy Haswell, June 2, 1895. Début, Manhattan Theatre, N.Y. City, 1886; supported Tomasso Salvini, 1890; with Alexander Salvini, 1894; in repertoire with Nat Goodwin, 1895-96; with Maude Adams, 1897-99; many productions with Fawcett Stock Co., 1900; played title rôle in Great John Ganton, Aldwych Theatre, London, 1917; subsequently in vaudeville, later in motion pictures. Trustee Actors' Fund of America. Democrat. Died June 6, 1939.

FAWCETT, M. Edward, bishop; b. New Hartford, Ia., Nov. 1, 1865; s. William (D.D.) and Sarah (Houghton) F.; A.B., Upper Ia. U., 1886, A.M., 1889, Ph.D., 1893; div. studies at Garrett Biblical Inst., S.T.D., Nashotah House, Wis., 1904; m. Esther L. Faul, Nov. 3, 1887; children—Sarah (dec.), Lewis (dec.), Suzanne. Deacon and priest, P.E. Ch., 1897; rector Ch. of the Redeemer, Elgin, Ill., 1897-1901, St. Bartholomew's Ch., Chicago, 1901-04; elected 3d bishop of Quincy, Ill., May 20, 1903, consecrated Jan. 20, 1904. Capt. and chaplain 5th Ill. Inf.; divisional chaplain 33d Div. U.S.A., Oct. 12, 1917—. Pres. Quincy Chamber Commerce, 1919; v.p. Ill. State Chamber Commerce, 1919; v.p. Nat. Research Forum. Home: Quincy, Ill. Died Sept. 17, 1935.

FAWCETT, Owen, actor; b. London, England, Nov. 21, 1838; s. Charles and Mary Fawcett; landed in New York, Nov. 1840, on the election day when William Henry Harrison was elected president. First appearance on stage, Dec. 7, 1853; was 20 yrs. with Edwin Booth and has supported every star of prominence for past 40 yrs.; has created many important character rôles in modern drama. Home: Flat Rock, Mich. Died 1904.

FAXON, Charles Edward, botanical artist; b. Roxbury, Mass., Jan. 21, 1846; s. Elisha and Hannah Mann (Whiting) F.; bro. of Walter Faxon; S.B., Lawrence Scientific Sch., Harvard, 1867 (hon. A.M., 1897). Instr. of botany, Harvard, 1879-84; asst. dir. Arnold Arboretum, Jamaica Plain, 1882—. Best known as bot. artist; drew all the plates for Sargent's Silva of North America, Eaton's Ferns of North American Garden and Forest, Sargent's Forest Flora of Japan, Sargent's Manual of the Trees of North America; Trees and Shrubs, and numerous plates in leading bot. jours. Fellow Am. Acad. Arts and Sciences. Home: Jamaica Plain, Mass. Died Feb. 6, 1918.

FAXON, Frederick Winthrop, bibliographer; b. W. Roxbury, Mass., Aug. 24, 1866; s. Marcus and Augusta Chalmers (Fernald) F.; A.B., Harvard, 1889; m. Adeline True Thompson, May 16, 1900 (died 1929). Proprietor of the F. W. Faxon Company. Treasurer of the Bibliog. Soc. America; life mem. Am. Library Assn. (travel sec. 1896, 99, 1900, gen. sec. 1900-03, chmn. travel com. 1902-34); mem. Special Libraries Assn., Mass. Library Club (pres. 1931-32), N.J. and N.Y. library assns.; mem. bd. dirs. New-Church Theol. School. Editor, Bulletin of Bibliography, Boston, 1897—. Wrote: Bibliography of Literary Annuals and Gift Books, 1912. Originator and editor Dramatic Index (ann.), 1909—, compiler Magazine Subject-Index, vol. 1, 1907, 08, 09; editor same, 1910—. Home: Roslindale, Mass. Died Aug. 31, 1936.

FAXON, Walter, naturalist; b. Roxbury, Mass., Feb. 4, 1848; s. Elisha and Hannah Mann (Whiting) F.; bro. of Charles Edward F.; A.B., Harvard, 1871; S.B., 1872, Sc.D., 1878. Curator in invertebrate dept., Mus. of Comparative Zoölogy, 1874—; asst. in charge mus., 1892-96; asst. prof. zoölogy, Harvard, 1880-85. Fellow Am. Acad. Arts and Sciences, Am. Ornithologists Union. Author scientific memoirs and papers, published by Mus. Comparative Zoölogy, Cambridge, U.S. Nat. Mus., Am. Ornithologists' Union, etc. Home: Lexington, Mass. Died 1920.

FAXON, William Bailey, artist; b. Hartford, Conn. A.N.A., 1906; mem. Am. Fine Arts Soc. (pres. 1906-21), Artists' Aid Soc. (treas. 1895-1920). Home: New York, N.Y. Died Aug. 13, 1941.

FAY, Albert Hill, mining engr.; b. Appleton City, Mo., Mar. 12, 1871; s. L. Lankton and Adeline (Hill) F.; B.S., Mo. Sch. of Mines, 1902, E.M., 1905; A.M.,

Columbia, 1907; m. Clara Louise Constable, Nov. 4, 1908; 1 son, Albert Hill. Engr. with Greene Consolidated Copper Co., Cananea, Mex., 1903-05; prospecting and development, Bartel's Tin Mining Co., Alaska, 1906-07; mining engr. with John T. Williams & Son, Bristol, Tenn., 1907-08; editorial staff Engineering and Mining Journal, New York, 1908-11; editor Mineral Industry, 1911; with U.S. Bur. Mines, 1911-20; valuation engr. and head of natural resources div., Income Tax Unit, Internal Revenue Bur., Treas. Dept., specializing in petroleum, 1920-23; cons. mining engr., 1923-25; asst. editor Engineering Mining Journal-Press, New York, 1925-27; cons. engr. U.S.S.R., 1929-30; now cons. mining engr. and asst. prof. mining engring., Lafayette Coll., Easton, Pa. Sec. mining sect. Pan-Am. Scientific Congress, Washington, 1915. Republican. Conglist. Author: Glossary of the Mining and Mineral Industry (20,000 terms and words), 1920. Home: Easton, Pa. Died Aug. 7, 1937.

FAY, Charles Ernest, college prof.; b. Roxbury (Boston), Mass., Mar. 10, 1846; s. Rev. Cyrus Hyde F.; A.B., Tufts Coll., 1868, A.M., 1872, Litt.D., 1900 and LL.D. from same college in 1928; m. Mary W. Lincoln, Nov. 22, 1870; children—Mary DeWolf (dec.), Lincoln (dec.), Ethel, Margaret Lincoln, Harold. Instructor mathematics, 1868, modern langs., 1869, in Europe on leave of absence, 1869-70, Wade prof. modern langs., 1871-1928, and dean Grad. Sch., 1912-23, Tufts Coll. Lecturer on literary and geog. topics. Bore a part in founding Modern Lang. Assn. America, 1883 (pres. pedag. sect., 1890), N.E. Assn. of Colleges and Prep. Schs., 1885 (pres. 1888-89), Appalachian Mountain Club, 1876 (pres. 1878, 1881, 1893, 1905), Round Table (Boston), 1885 (v.p. 1900); a pioneer in the development of mountaineering in the Canadian Rockies and the Selkirks, from 1890. Officer of the Order of St. Charles, Monaco, 1921. Fellow Harvard Travelers' Club (v.p. 1911-12, gold medalist, 1922). Editor Appalachia, 1879-1920; has written for it many papers on mountain exploration in the Canadian Alps and elsewhere; editor Alpina Americana, 1907-14. Died Jan. 25, 1931.

FAY, Edward Allen, educator; b. Morristown, N.J., Nov. 22, 1843; s. Barnabas Maynard and Louise (Mills) F.; A.B., U. of Mich., 1862, A.M., 1865; Ph.D., Johns Hopkins, 1881; (Sc.D., U. of Mich., 1912; Litt.D., Gallaudet Coll., 1916); m. Mary Bradshaw, July 6, 1871; father of Sidney Bradshaw F. Instr., N.Y. Instn. for the Deaf, 1862-65; prof., 1866-1920, v.p., 1885-1920, emeritus. Gallaudet Coll. Editor Am. Annals of the Deaf, 1870-1920. Author: Concordance of the Divina Commedia, 1888. Home: Washington, D.C., and Nantucket, Mass. Died July 14, 1923.

FAY, Edwin Whitfield, univ. prof.; b. Minden, La., Jan. 1, 1865; s. Edwin Hedge and Sarah Elizabeth (Shields) F.; A.M., Southwestern Presbyn. U., 1883; Ph.D., Johns Hopkins, 1890; student in Leipzig, 1891-92; m. Lucy B. Hemphill, Dec. 20, 1904. Instr. Sanskrit and classics, U. of Mich., 1890-91; acting asso. prof. Latin, U. of Tex., 1892-93; prof. Latin, Washington and Lee U., 1893-99; prof. Latin, U. of Tex., 1899—. Author: The Mostellaria of Plautus, 1902. Home: Austin, Tex. Died Feb. 17, 1920.

FAY, Irving Wetherbee, prof. chemistry; b. Natick, Mass., Nov. 3, 1861; s. Gilbert Park and Laura Sophia (Brigham) F.; A.B., magna cum laude, Harvard, 1886; Ph.D., U. of Berlin, 1897; m. Elizabeth Webster Schwefel, Aug. 18, 1897; 1 dau., Ernestine (Mrs. Herbert Thompson Scott). Instr. in sciences, Montpelier (Vt.) Sem., 1886-87; instr. in chemistry and physics, Belmont (Calif.) Sch., 1887-93; prof. chemistry, Ohio U., 1896-97; prof. chemistry, Poly. Inst. of Brooklyn, 1897—. Fellow Brooklyn Inst. Arts and Sciences (pres. dept. chemistry). Republican. Conglist. Author: Coal Tar Dyes, 1910. Home: Brooklyn, N.Y. Died 1936.

FEAGIN, Noah Baxter, lawyer, humanitarian; b. Midway, Barbour Co., Ala., July 7, 1843; s. James Madison and Almira (Cole) F.; Nashville (Tenn.) Mil. Inst., 1860-61; B.L., Washington Coll. (now Washington and Lee U.), 1870; m. Annie Martin Phillips, Feb. 9, 1876. Pvt. to capt., 15th Ala. Inf., 1861-65; called "boy captain" of his regt.; wounded 5 times; served under "Stonewall" Jackson in 1st Shenandoah Valley campaign, under Gen. Longstreet at Chickamauga, and under Gen. Lee in Va. campaigns. In law practice, 1870—; editor Union Springs (Ala.) Times, 1870-71; mayor, Union Springs, 1875, Anniston, 1886. Apptd. judge Inferior Criminal Ct., Birmingham, Ala., Apr. 1895; elected to same by legislature 3 times; under recent act elected to same by city council as "recorder"; last term expired Nov. 1910. Established, 1898, without legal enactment, a juvenile ct. for city of Birmingham after model instituted in Chicago by Judge Hurd; movement resulted in adoption of juvenile ct. law by legislature of Ala., 1908. Upon invitation of President Roosevelt attended Children's Conf., Washington, Jan. 1909; made argument before com. of Congress, 1909, for establishment of a Children's Bur. by Nat. Govt. Home: Birmingham, Ala. Deceased.

FEARING, Daniel Butler, mayor; b. Newport, R.I., Aug. 14, 1859; s. Henry Seymour and Serena Mason (Jones) F.; ed. St. Mark's Sch., Southboro, Mass., and Harvard, class of 1882 (hon. A.M., 1911); m. Henrietta Strong, Jan. 12, 1887 (died 1908); m. 2d, Charlotte, d. late Benj. Woodhull and Frances (Hoffman) Strong, of New York, June 22, 1912. School commr., Newport, 1891, alderman, 1892, 1893, mayor, 1894, and mem. council from 4th ward, 1909-12. Democrat. Trustee St. Mark's Sch.; pres. Redwood Library, Newport, 1909-10, 1911-12. Mem. R.I. Inland Fish Commn., 1910— (v.p. 1912-17, pres. 1917—). Episcopalian. Mason. Home: Newport, R.I. Died May 26, 1918.

FECHNER, Robert; b. Chattanooga, Tenn., Mar. 22, 1876; s. Charles and Virginia (Roberts) F.; student high sch., Griffin, Ga., 1891-92; m. Clare Dickey, Oct. 25, 1902. Machinist, foreman and master mechanic, 1896-1912; exec. officer Internat. Assn. of Machinists, 1913-33; dir. Civilian Conservation Corps, U.S. Govt., 1933—. Served in 2d Ga. Inf., Spanish-Am. War. Mason, K.P., Eagle, Elk. Lectured at Harvard Grad. Sch. of Business Administration, Dartmouth, Simmons and various other colls. Home: Wollaston, Mass. Died Dec. 31, 1939.

FECHTELER, Augustus Francis, naval officer; b. Paderborn, Prussia, Sept. 1, 1857; s. Joseph and Elizabeth (Lücken) F.; brought to U.S., 1865; grad. De La Salle Inst., New York, 1873, U.S. Naval Acad., 1877; m. Maud, d. U.S. Circuit Judge W. W. Morrow, of San Rafael, Calif., Oct. 16, 1893. Ensign, Nov. 23, 1880; promoted through grades to rear adm., U.S.N., July 11, 1915. Made first cruise on flagship Trenton to the Mediterranean, later on Shenandoah to the S. Atlantic; duty on Coast Survey, 1882-85; cruise around the world through Suez Canal, 1886-89; with Office of Naval Intelligence, Washington, 1889-92; in Behring Sea, protection of seal herds, 1892-94; in charge hydrographic office, San Francisco, 1894-96; on the Monterey, participating in taking of Manila, then navigator of the Concord, later of the Solace, 1896-99; aide to comdt., Mare Island Navy Yard, 1899 to 1901; navigator and later exec. Iowa, cruising in Pacific and the Atlantic, 1901-03; at Union Iron Works, San Francisco, 1903-04; at office of Naval Intelligence, 1904-05; in comd. cruiser Dubuque, 1905-06; mem. Bd. of Inspection and Survey, Washington, 1906-10; comdr. battleship South Carolina, 1910-11, cruising to English Channel and the Baltic; pres. Bd. of Inspection, 1911-13; aid for inspection to Sec. of Navy, 1913-14; comdg. div. of battleships in Atlantic Fleet, July 1915; comdt. Navy Yard, Norfolk, Va., Jan. 1918, 5th Naval Dist., Apr. 1919. Died May 26, 1921.

FECHTER, Oscar Augustus, banker; b. Manitowoc, Wis., Sept. 2, 1864; s. George W. and Clara (Schmidt) F.; student U. of Wis., 1880-83, LL.B., 1887; m. Gertrude Bartholet, Sept. 2, 1890; m. 2d, Maud Nash Allen, Aug. 22, 1917. Engaged in real estate business, N. Yakima, Wash., 1888-1904; pres. Yakima Valley Bank, Nov. 17, 1904—; pres. Yakima Valley Bank & Trust Co., First Nat. Bank of Kennewick. Mayor of N. Yakima, Wash., 8 terms; chmn. Yakima County Council Defense, 1917. Mem. bd. of regents U. of Wash., 1914-25. Republican. Translator: The Silesian Horseherd (from German of Max Muller), 1903. Home: Yakima, Wash. Died Feb. 24, 1935.

FEDIGAN, John J., provincial, Order St. Augustine in U.S., July 1898—; b. Ireland, Apr. 27, 1842; s. James and Ann (McGovern) F., of County Meath, Ireland; came to U.S. in childhood; ed. in Westchester, Pa., and Wilmington, Del., 1850-60; grad. St. Mary's Coll., 1864; went to Ghent, Belgium, and entered novitiaite of Augustinian Fathers; made full ecclesiastical course there; ordained priest Oct. 24, 1868, at Phila., by Bishop Jeremiah Shannahan, of Harrisburg; pastor successively at St. Denis Ch., W. Haverford, Pa., 1868-69; Cambridge, N.Y., 1869-73 (also attending Salem and Greenwich); Carthage, N.Y., 1873-78; pres. Villanova Coll., 1878-80; pastor Atlantic City, N.J., 1880-98. Elected, 1898, provincial of Order of St. Augustine, with residence at Bryn Mawr, Pa. Went to Villanova, bldg. new monastery and coll. at cost of $300,000, and having finished and paid for them returned to Bryn Mawr. In 1899 opened houses of order on Staten Island, N.Y., at Lawrence, Mass., and Havana, Cuba. Died 1908.

FEE, Charles S., ry. official; b. Laurel, O., Sept. 24, 1853; ed. pub. schs. Sec. to gen. supt. M.C. R.R., 1873-75; chief clk. to gen. mgr. Hannibal & St. Joseph R.R., 1875-77; chief clk. to gen. mgr., 1877-83, gen. pass. and tkt. agt., 1883-1904, N.P. Ry.; pass. traffic mgr. S.P. Co., 1904—. Died Sept. 25, 1923.

FEE (MacFee), William Thomas, consul; b. Niles, O., May 6, 1854; s. Dr. William Miller and Mary (Bernheisel) F.; Ph.B., Lafayette Coll., 1876, and LL.D., 1909; M.D., Western Reserve U., 1891; post-grad. study U. of Göttingen; studied law in office of Hon. Marriott Brosius, Lancaster, Pa.; m. Margaret Drake Semple, Mar. 1, 1882. Admitted to Ohio bar, 1879; practiced law at Warren, O.; city solicitor, Niles, O., 1879-80; mayor of Warren, O., 2 terms; pres. and mem. Warren Bd. of Health, 5 yrs.; Am. consul at Cienfuegos, Cuba, Mar. 1, 1898, at Bombay, India, 1899-1906, at Bremen, Germany, June 22, 1906-Feb. 3, 1917 (recalled on account of breaking off of diplomatic relations wtih Germany); consul at Guatemala City, C.A., July 6, 1917—. Officer independent mil. co., Spanish-Am. War, 1898; chmn. Americo-Indian Relief Commn., 1899-1900, which distributed contributions among the famine sufferers in India. Mason. Home: Warren, O. Died Apr. 1, 1919.

FEEHAN, Daniel F., bishop; b. Athol, Mass., Sept. 24, 1855; s. William and Johanna (Foley) F.; ed. St. Mary's Coll., Montreal, Can., St. Joseph's Sem., Troy, N.Y.; asst. St. Bernard's Ch., Fitchburg, Mass.; pastor St. Luke's Ch., West Boylston, Mass., St. Bernard's Ch., Fitchburg, Mass.; consecrated bishop of Fall River (Roman Catholic), Sept. 19, 1907. Home: Fall River, Mass. Died July 19, 1934.

FEEHAN, Patrick A., R.C. archbishop; b. Tipperary, Ireland, 1829; ed. Maynooth Coll., Kildare; came to U.S., 1852; became pres. of Sem. of Carondelet and pastor Ch. of the Immaculate Conception, St. Louis; consecrated bishop of Nashville, Tenn., 1865; in 1880, when Chicago was made an archiepiscopal see, was consecrated its 1st archbishop. Died 1902.

FEELY, John Joseph, congressman, 2d dist. Ill. for term 1901-03; b. Will Co., Ill., Aug. 1, 1875; s. John B. and Winifred F.; ed. dist. school, Will Co., Ill., and high school, Joliet, Ill.; grad. Niagara Univ., 1895; Yale Law School, 1897; unmarried. Moved to Chicago, 1894. Democrat. Home: Chicago, Ill. Died 1905.

FEHLANDT, August Frederick, clergyman, educator; b. Mazomanie, Wis., July 4, 1869; s. Carl and Maria (Niebuhr) F.; grad. high sch., Mazomanie, 1887; A.B., U. of Wis., 1891; student Princeton Coll. and Theol. Sem., 1891-92; B.D., Yale U., 1894; studied summers, U. of Chicago, U. of Wis.; m. Luella Belle Knapp, Nov. 26, 1896; children—Helen Bradley, Philip Raymer, Carl Harvey, Theodore Frederick, Ruth Adaline. Ordained Congl. ministry, 1894; pastor LeMars, Ia., 1896-97, Creston, Ill., 1897-1901, Lone Rock, Wis., 1901-04, West Salem, Wis., 1904-09, Grand Forks, N.D., 1909-10, Michigan, N.D., 1910-14, Green Lake, Wis., 1914—; prof. economics and sociology, Ripon, Coll., 1914-37, emeritus. Author: A Century of Drink Reform in the United States, 1904. Home: Ripon, Wis. Died Oct. 26, 1939.

FEHR, Harrison Robert, cons. engr.; b. Nazareth, Pa., Mar. 20, 1863; s. Michael M. and Anna Caroline (Edmonds) F.; ed. pub. schs. and Moravian parochial sch.; m. Achshaw Walter. Teacher, 1880-83; civil engring. dept. L.V. R.R., 1883-89, bridge engr., 1890-91; civil engr., Easton, Pa., 1891-99; chief engr. Easton Transit Co., 1892-1900, Trenton & New Brunswick R.R., 1901-02; contracting engr., 1902-04; pres., gen. mgr. Easton Transit Co., 1904-13; pres., gen. mgr. Lehigh Valley Transit Co., 1913-20; cons. practice, 1920—. Promoter constrn. of William Penn Highway, bet. Easton and Allentown, Pa.; pres. Pa. St. Ry. Assn., 1912-13. Republican. Presbyn. Mason. Home: Allentown, Pa. Died May 30, 1930.

FELAND, Logan, officer U.S.M.C.; b. Hopkinsville, Ky., Aug. 18, 1869; s. John and Sarah F.; B.S. in Architecture, Mass. Inst. Tech., 1892; m. Katherine Cordner, Feb. 14, 1907. Capt. comdg. Co. F, 3d Ky. Inf., Spanish-Am. War, May 31, 1898; hon. mustered out, May 16, 1899; apptd. 1st lt. U.S.M.C., July 1, 1899; capt., Mar. 3, 1903; maj., Aug. 29, 1916; lt. col., Mar. 26, 1917; col. (temp.), July 1, 1918; brig. gen. (temp.), Mar. 9, 1919, apptmt. permanent, July 1, 1920; maj. gen., Nov. 12, 1919—. Served in Cuba, the Philippines, Panama, Santo Domingo and various periods at sea; arrived in France, June 13, 1917. Awarded D.S.C. "for energy, courage and disregard of personal safety" in leading troops into action; D.S.M. "for exceptionally meritorious and distinguished service during the World War"; received six awards of the Croix de Guerre, among them one with bronze star, "for generously contributing" to the success of the 116th French Inf., one with palm "for remarkable ardor and tenacity in driving the enemy back for a distance of 11 kilometers," Croix de Guerre with palm "for coolness and skill in command of troops in the Bois de Belleau," Croix de Guerre with palm "for glorious part taken by his regiment in attack in the Champagne, between Blanc Mont and Medeah Farm"; made Officer Legion of Honor, and awarded Croix de Guerre with gold star, "for services in attack South of Soissons," July 18, 1918; awarded Navy D.S.M. for "distinguished and gallant services"; cited six times in divisional orders for gallantry. Comdg. 5th Regt. U.S. Marines, July 17-Nov. 11, 1918; comdg. 2d Brig., U.S. Marines, San Domingo, Dec. 4, 1919-Oct. 24, 1920. Comdg. Am. forces on shore in Nicaragua, 1927-29; retired as maj. gen., Sept. 1, 1933. Methodist. Home: Columbus, Ohio. Died July 17, 1936.

FELKEL, Herbert, editor; b. De Funiak Springs, Fla., June 23, 1889; s. Henry Noel and Safronia (Hoag) F.; Fla. State Coll., Tallahassee, 2 yrs.; U. of Chattanooga, 1 year; student U. of Florida, 1907-08, B.Sc. as of 1908; m. Myrtie Warren, 1916; children—Jeanne, Warren. Began on Chattanooga News, 1907; later owner controlling interest Pensacola News and mng. editor same; editor Florida Record, Tallahassee, 1915-17; mng. editor, 1917-20, editor, 1921—, St. Augustine Evening Record; also v.p. and gen. mgr. Record Pub. & Printing Co., Jan. 1, 1921—. Chmn. campaign com. State Dem. Exec. Com.; apptd. collector of internal revenue for Fla., 1933, and confirmed by Senate same day, declined apptmt. to remain in newspaper and pub. business. Appt. mem. gov.'s personal staff rank of lt. col., 1923, again, 1925 and 1929, being only Floridian ever serving on staff under three successive govs. Episcopalian (vestryman Trinity Ch.). Editor, Sunshine, Fla. Mag., 1923—. Home: St. Augustine, Fla. Died Mar. 26, 1934.

FELKER, Samuel Demeritt, governor; b. Rochester, N.H., Apr. 16, 1859; s. William H. and Deborah (Demeritt) F.; A.B., Dartmouth, 1882, A.M., 1887; LL.B., Boston U. Law Sch., 1887; (LL.D., N.H. State Coll., May, 1913); m. Mary J. Dudley (A.B., Wellesley, 1883), June 26, 1900. Practiced, Rochester, N.H., 1887—; mem. State Constl. Conv., 1889; mem. N.H. State Senate, 1891, 1892; mayor of Rochester, 1896, 1897; city solicitor, 1898-1915; mem. N.H. Ho. of Rep., 1909-11; gov. of N.H., 1913-15; judge Rochester Municipal Court, July 1915—. Democrat. Conglist. Home: Rochester, N.H. Died Nov. 14, 1932.

FELL, Alpheus Gilbert, mayor; b. Prescott, Ont., Can., Mar. 13, 1846; s. James and Sarah F.; ed. Iroquois High Sch., Ontario; m. Annie Marigold Grier, Oct. 13, 1870; children—Carrie Mabel, Eliza Winifred, Daisy Alberta (dec.), Gilberta Marie, Anna Marigold, Arthur Grier (dec.). Telegraph operator, 1863-64, train dispatcher, 1864-67, Grand Trunk R.R., Can.; freight agt. and dispatcher, U.P. Co., 1 yr.; chief train dispatcher Central Pacific R.R. Co., of Calif., and later S.P. Co., of Calif. (same rd.), 1868-79; supt. Salt Lake div. S.P. Co., 1879-88; also engaged for a number of yrs. in wool growing, banking and real estate business; mayor-commr. of Ogden, Jan. 1, 1912-Dec. 31, 1915. Republican. Now v.p. Commercial Nat. Bank, Murphy Wholesale Grocery Co., Ogden. Methodist. Discovered at Ogden a subterranean deposit of pure water which has been developed to extent of 16,0000,000 gallons daily, providing one of the finest artesian water supplies in America. Home: Ogden, Utah. Deceased.

FELL, D(avid) Newlin, judge; b. Buckingham, Pa., Nov. 4, 1840; grad. Pa. State Normal Sch., 1862; served in 122d Pa. Vols. during Civil War. Admitted to bar in Phila.; practiced there until 1877; judge Ct. of Common Pleas, Phila., 1877-94; asso. justice Supreme Ct. of Pa., 1894— (chief justice, 1910—). Republican. Home: Philadelphia, Pa. Died Sept. 22, 1919.

FELL, George Edward, surgeon; b. Chippewa, Ont., July 10, 1850; s. James Wilkins and Ann Elizabeth (Hoffman) F.; ed. high sch.; M.D., U. of Buffalo, 1882; ad eundum degree, Niagara U., 1886; m. Annie Argo Duthie, Oct. 15, 1872; 2d, Gertrude Luella Axtell, May 20, 1912. Prof. physiology and microscopy, Med. Dept., Niagara U., also phys. Buffalo Hosp. Sisters of Charity, 1885-95; surgeon Charity, Eye, Ear, Nose and Throat Hosp., Buffalo, 1910-16. Pres. Buffalo Cuban Am. Junta, 1897-98. Invented first successful apparatus to induce artificial mechanical respiration in cases of drowning, asphyxiation, etc., 1887, by which thousands of lives have been saved and thoracic surgery attained. Republican. Episcopalian. Home: Chicago, Ill. Died July 29, 1918.

FELLAND, Ole Gunderson, clergyman, educator; b. Utica, Wis., Oct. 10, 1853; s. Gunder G. and Tone (Nevestveit) F.; A.B., Luther Coll., Decorah, Ia., 1874; A.M., Northwestern Coll., Watertown, Wis., 1876; grad. Concordia Sem., Mo., 1879; m. Thea Johanna Midboe, May 11, 1883 (died 1905); children—Thonny Genevieve, Gunnar Hermo, Elsa Bianca, Signy Valborg, Osmond Adolph, Nordis Adelheid. Ordained Luth. ministry, 1879; pastor in Minn., 1879-81; apptd. prof. in St. Olaf Coll., Northfield, Minn., 1881; head of dept. of Semitic langs., 1910-23, also librarian from 1891 and head librarian (emeritus, 1926). Democrat. Wrote: History of St. Olaf Coll., 1899. Home: Northfield, Minn. Died June 10, 1938.

FELLOWS, C(harles) Gurnee, M.D.; b. Milwaukee, Wis., Apr. 27, 1863; s. George and Emeline Electa (Gurnee) F.; A.B., Lawrence Coll., Wis., 1883; A.M., 1886; M.D., Hahnemann Med. Coll., Chicago, 1885; post-grad. work in New York, Vienna, Paris and London; m. Angie Woodward, Apr. 27, 1886; children—Mrs. Margaret May Hart, Woodward. Practiced in New Orleans, 1885-88, Chicago, 1889—; formerly sr. prof. ophthalmology and otology, Hahnemann Med. College; sr. attending surgeon, eye and ear dept., same. Fellow Am. Coll. Surgeons. Republican. Episcopalian. Home: Chicago, Ill. Died Feb. 2, 1929.

FELLOWS, (Jennie) Dorkas, library work; b. Griswold, Conn., Apr. 4, 1873; d. Franklin Ebenezer and Jane Eliza (Stiles) F.; grad. Norwich (Conn.) Free Acad., 1892; diploma N.Y. State Library Sch., Albany, 1905. Asst. Peck Library, Norwich, 1892-95; cataloger Free Pub. Library, Worcester, Mass., 1897-99; asst. N.Y. State Library, 1899-1925; instr. N.Y. State Library Sch., 1911-18, 1922-26, Chautauqua Sch. for Librarians, 1919, 23, 24; editor Dewey Decimal Classification and Relative Index, 1921—. Republican. Author: Cataloging Rules (2d edit.), 1922. Died Oct. 10, 1938.

FELLOWS, George Emory, univ. prof.; b. Beaver Dam, Wis., June 9, 1858; s. Rev. George and Emeline E. F.; A.B., Lawrence U., Wis., 1879, L.H.D., 1902; studied U. of Munich, 1888-89, Edinburgh U., summer 1889, Berne, 1890, Ph.D.; Paris, 1898, 99; LL.D., Bowdoin, 1902, U. of Me., 1926; m. Lucia Russell, 1881; children—Gladys Ethel (Mrs. G. F. Wittig), Dorothy R. B. (dec.), Donald R. H. Taught 10 yrs. in high schs., Appleton, Wis., New Orleans, La., and Aurora, Ill.; prof. European history, Ind. U., 1891-95; asst. prof. history, U. of Chicago, 1895-1902; pres. U. of Me., 1902-11; pres. Decatur Coll. of James Millikin U., 1913-15; head dept. history, polit. science, U. of Utah, 1915-35, emeritus. Author: Outlines of 16th Century, 1895; Recent European History, 1902. Home: Great Neck, N.Y. Died Jan. 14, 1942.

FELLOWS, Grant, judge; b. Hudson, Mich., Apr. 13, 1865; s. Nelson H. and Sarah M. (Perry) F.; ed. Hudson High Sch.; unmarried. Admitted to Mich. bar, Dec. 11, 1886; mem. Fellows & Chandler, Hudson, Mich., 1890-1916. Atty.-gen. of Mich., Jan. 1, 1913-Jan. 1, 1917; justice Supreme Ct. Mich., 1917-23, reëlected for term, 1924-31 inclusive, chief justice, 1922. Republican. Mason. Home: Hudson, Mich. Died July 16, 1929.

FELLOWS, Oscar F., lawyer; b. Bristol, N.H., Sept. 10, 1857; s. Milo and Susan D. (Locke) F.; ed. New Hampton (N.H.) Lit. Inst.; admitted to bar, 1881; m. Eva M., d. Hon. L. W. Fling, of Bristol, May 24, 1883. Mem. Me. Ho. of Rep., 1901-03 (speaker 1903); collector customs port of Bucksport, 4 yrs.; co. atty. Hancock Co., 4 yrs.; counsel for U.S. of Internat. St. John River Commn. Republican. Methodist. Home: Bucksport, Me. Died Dec. 28, 1921.

FELLOWS, William Bainbridge, lawyer; b. Sandwich, N.H., July 5, 1858; s. Enoch Q. and Mary E. (Quimby) F.; A.B., Dartmouth, 1880; m. Ida Grace Scribner, Nov. 1, 1881 (died 1908); m. 2d, Clara Douglas Merrimam, Aug. 24, 1909. Admitted to N.H. bar, 1883; pvt. sec. to U.S. Senator A. F. Pike, and later to U.S. Senator P. C. Cheney; clk. Com. on Claims, U.S. Senate, 1885-87; solicitor Belknap Co., N.H., 1891-97; judge of probate, same co., 1895-1909; sec. N.H. Bd. of Equalization, 1901-08; chmn. N.H. Spl. Tax Commn., 1908; state auditor, 1909-11; sec. N.H. State Tax Commn., 1911—. Republican. Methodist. Home: Tilton, N.H. Died May 2, 1921.

FELMLEY, David, normal sch. pres.; b. nr. Somerville, N.J., Apr. 24, 1857; s. John S. and Ellen (Voorhees) F.; student Blackburn U., 1873-76, U. of Mich., 1876-78, 1880-81, B.A., 1881, L.H.D., 1906; LL.D., U. of Ill., 1905; m. Auta Stout, July 6, 1887; children—Ruth (Mrs. Alva Brace Meek), Mildred Helen, John Benjamin; m. 2d, Jenny Green, 1928. Supt. schs., Carrollton, 1882-90; prof. mathematics, 1890-1900, pres. 1900—, Ill. State Normal U., Normal, Ill. Mem. Ill. State Ednl. Commn., 1911-13. Rotarian. Home: Normal, Ill. Died Jan. 24, 1930.

FELS, Joseph, mfr.; b. Halifax C.H., Va., Dec. 16, 1854; s. Lazarus and Susannah (Freiberg) F.; ed. pvt. schs., Yanceyville, N.C., Richmond, Va., and Baltimore; left sch. at 17; m. Mollie Fels, Nov. 16, 1891. Began business as traveling salesman for toilet soap mfrs., Baltimore, 1870; engaged in soap mfg. with his father, at Baltimore, 1874, Fels & Co., 1894—; established a selling branch in Eng., 1901, and since resides there part of each year. Became deeply interested in the single-tax propaganda, 1905, and has since given large amounts and much time to the cause. Founded the Joseph Fels Fund of America, to which contributes $25,000 annually for 5 yrs. and has founded similar funds in almost every country of the globe. Purchased 1,300 acres at Hollesley Bay, Eng., to form a labor colony for unemployed, which has since been taken over by the government; also purchased 600 acres at Maylands, Essex, Eng., which was put under cultivation by small holders. One of chief supporters of vacant lot cultivation activities at Phila., supporter of Fairhope Single Tax Colony, Mobile Bay, Ala., and another at Arden, Del.; extended propaganda work for econ. philosophy of Henry George into all civilized countries. Mem. United Com. Taxation of Land Values in London. Homes: Philadelphia, and Regents Park, London. Died Feb. 22, 1914.

FELT, Charles Frederick Wilson, civil engr.; b. Salem, Mass., Apr. 29, 1864; s. Charles Wilson and Martha Seeth (Ropes) F.; B.S., Mass. Agrl. Coll., 1886; m. Clara C. Root, Apr. 6, 1904. Axman, rodman and bridge engr., A.,T.&S.F. Ry., 1886-88; levelman, D.&R.G. Ry., Feb.-May 1888; instrument-man, Ariz. & Southeastern R.R., 1888-89; transitman, Topolobampo Ry., Mex., 1889-90; resident engr., Gulf, Colo. & Santa Fe Ry., at Cleburne, Tex., 1890-92; office engr. Rio Grande Southern Ry., 1892-93; div. engr. Gulf, Colo. & Santa Fe Ry., Feb.-May 1893; resident engr. same rd., Galveston, Tex., 1893-96, chief engr., 1896-1909; chief engr., A.,T.&S.F. Ry., 1909-13, and of entire system, 1913—. Home: Chicago, Ill. Died Feb. 4, 1928.

FELT, Dorr Eugene, inventor; b. Beloit, Wis., Mar. 18, 1862; s. Eugene Kincaid and Elizabeth (Morris) F.; ed. pub. schs., Beloit; m. Agnes McNulty, Jan. 15, 1891; children—Virginia, Elizabeth, Constance, Dorothea. Inventor first key operator calculating machines, also first practical adding and listing machines; organized firm Felt & Tarrant, 1886, to manufacture his inventions, and in 1887 inc. Felt & Tarrant Mfg. Co., of which is pres. Regional adviser War Industries Bd., for Ill., Ind. and Ia. (Region No. 9), 1918; mem. Employers' Commn., by appmt. of Sec. of Labor William B. Wilson, and sent to Eng. to study and report on labor conditions and governmental policies in Great Britain, 1919. Dir. Chicago Assn. of Commerce; mem. Chamber of Commerce U.S.A. Republican. Baptist. Home: Chicago, Ill. Died Aug. 7, 1930.

FELT, Edward Webster, judge; b. Allegheny Co., Va., Nov. 7, 1859; s. Sylvester Wakefield and Rebecca Jane (Latshaw) F.; grad. Central Normal Coll., Danville, Ind., 1884; teacher pub. schs., 7 yrs.; m. Mattie L. Thomas, Apr. 17, 1885; children—Mable M. (Mrs. Clifford H. Browder), Elsie Rebecca (Mrs. Howard Caldwell), Truman T. Admitted to Ind. bar, 1887; practiced law at Greenfield, Ind.; removed to Indianapolis, 1909; pros. atty. 18th Jud. Circuit of Ind., 1891-95; county atty. Hancock Co., Ind., 1896-98; judge 18th Jud. Circuit, 1901-06, inclusive; judge Appelate Ct. of Ind. for terms 1911-15, and 1915-19; practiced law in Indianapolis, 1919-26; apptd. Judge Municipal Court, term 1926-30. Chmn. Dem. County Central Com., Hancock Co., Ind., 1894, 98. Methodist. Home: Indianapolis, Ind. Died June 1926.

FELTER, Harvey Wickes, M.D.; b. Rensselaerville, N.Y., June 15, 1865; s. Andrew Jay and Elizabeth (Nichols) F.; ed. Lansingburgh Acad. and spl. work in U. of Cincinnati; M.D., Eclectic Med. Inst., Cincinnati, 1888; m. Martha Reyburn Caldwell, Jan. 1, 1890; children—Lloyd King, Mrs. Dorah Helen Elmore. Practiced medicine, Troy, N.Y., 1888-89, at Cincinnati, 1889—. Demonstrator anatomy, 1891-97, prof. anatomy, 1892, and again, 1899-1908, quizmaster in chemistry, 1895-97, prof. chemistry and toxicology, 1897-1904, demonstrator of chem. lab., 1898-99, Eclectic Med. Inst., Cincinnati; prof. med. history, 1908-09, med. history, materia medica and therapeutics, 1909—. Pres. Cincinnati Chapter, Wild Flower Preservation Soc.; founder and editor Wild Flower; also editor Eclectic Med. Gleaner, 1904-13; many yrs. asst. and from Jan. 1, 1913, editor Eclectic Med. Jour. Editor: Locke's Syllabus of Eclectic Materia Medica and Therapeutics, 1895. Author: Eclectic Materia Medica and Therapeutics, 1922. Home: Cincinnati, O. Died Oct. 27, 1927.

FELTON, Charles, senator; b. Erie Co., N.Y., 1832; acad. edn.; went to Calif. Under sheriff Yuba Co., Calif., 1857; later tax collector; mem. Calif. Ho. of Rep., 2 terms; asst. treas. and treas. U.S. Mint San Francisco, 6 yrs.; mem. 49th and 50th Congresses (1885-89); U.S. senator to fill vacancy, 1891-93; voted for in Calif. Legislature, 1899, for U.S. senator. Republican. Home: Menlo Park, Calif. Died Sept. 13, 1914.

FELTON, Edgar Conway, steel mfr.; b. Thurlow, Pa., Apr. 13, 1858; s. Samuel Morse and Maria Low (Lippitt) F.; A.B., Harvard, 1879; m. Alice Bent, June 2, 1884; children—Margaret, Eleanor, Samuel Morse, Cornelius Conway, Edgar Conway, Winslow Bent. Traveled in Europe 1 yr.; with Pa. Steel Co. from 1880, beginning in chem. lab. at Steelton, Pa., becoming asst. supt. and supt. works, 1884-93, gen. mgr., 1893-96, pres., 1896; now retired from active business; mgr. Girard Trust Co., Western Savings Fund. Overseer Harvard; trustee Drexel Inst.; pres. pub. schs., Steelton and Haverford. Republican. Unitarian. Home: Haverford, Pa. Died Sept. 18, 1937.

FELTON, Rebecca Latimer, writer, speaker; b. De Kalb Co., Ga., June 10, 1835; d. Charles and Eleanor Ann (Swift) Latimer; grad. Madison (Ga.) Female Coll., 1852; D.Litt., U. of Ga., 1922; m. W. H. Felton (mem. Congress, 1875-81), Oct. 11, 1853. For many yrs. newspaper writer, suffrage and temperance advocate; apptd. to U.S. Senate to fill vacancy occasioned by death of Thomas E. Watson, being the first woman senator; sat for two days, Nov. 21, 22, 1922, and was succeeded by Walter F. George, who was regularly elected. State dir. Ga. Training Sch. for Girls. Mem. Bd. Lady Mgrs. Chicago Expn., 1893 (temp. pres.); juror at St. Louis Expn., 1904; chmn. Woman's Exec. Bd., Atlanta Expn. Author: Country Life in Georgia in Days of My Youth, 1918. Home. Cartersville, Ga. Died Jan. 24, 1930.

FELTON, Samuel Morse, ry. pres.; b. Phila., Feb. 3, 1853; s. Samuel Morse and Maria Low (Lippitt) F.; ed. Mass. Inst. Tech.; (LL.D., 1919); m. Dora Hamilton, 1880 (died 1923); children—Mrs. Hadasah F. Posey, Mrs. Ruth F. Sowers, Mrs. Dorothy F. Rogers, Samuel Morse. Began railway service 1868, rodman Chester Creek R.R.; leveler and asst. engr. Lancaster R.R., 1870-71; chief engr. Chester & Del. River R.R., 1873-74; gen. supt., P.,C.&St.L., 1874-

82; gen. supt. Little Miami and C.&M. rys., 1881-82; gen. mgr. N.Y.&N.E. R.R., 1882-84; asst. to pres. Erie R.R., 1884; gen. mgr. N.Y.,P.&O. R.R., 1884-85; v.p. Erie R.R., 1885-90; pres. E. Tenn., Va. & Ga. Ry., 1890-92; pres. Louisville Southern R.R. and Ala. Great Southern R.R., 1891-93; v.p. Memphis & Charleston R.R. and Mobile & Birmingham Ry., 1891-92; pres. and receiver Cincinnati, New Orleans & Tex. Pacific Ry., 1890-99; receiver Columbus, Sandusky & Hocking Ry., 1897-99, Ky. & Ind. Bridge Co., 1893-1900; pres. C.&A. R.R. Co., Sept. 1899-Nov. 1907; pres. Mexicad Central Ry. Co., Nov. 1907-Mar. 1909; chmn. bd. dirs. Tenn. Central R.R., June 9, 1909-Sept. 1909; pres. C.G.W. R.R., 1909-25. One of receivers P.M. R.R., Aug. 1912-June 1914. Apptd. dir. gen. mil. rys., July 1917; v.chmn. Port and Harbor Facilities Commn. of U.S. Shipping Bd., May 1918-Jan. 1919, acting chmn. to Feb. 15, 1919. D.S.M., 1919 "for especially meritorious and conspicuous service" as dir. gen. of mil. rys.; awarded Cross Legion of Honor (French). Home: Chicago, Ill. Died Mar. 11, 1930.

FELTON, William Hamilton, lawyer; b. Macon, Co., Ga., Sept. 19, 1860; s. Leroy Munroe and Mary (Lowe) F.; student Mercer U., Macon, Ga.; studied law, U. of Va.; m. Mary Ellen Johnston, Nov. 28, 1888. Began practice at Macon, 1880; mem. Ga. Ho. of Rep.; solicitor gen. Macon Circuit; judge Superior Court of Macon Circuit; lecturer on evidence, criminal law and Constitution of State of Ga., Mercer U., 1901—; mem. Bd. of Edn., Bibb Co., 16 yrs.; chmn. Dist. Exemption Bd., 1917-18. Pres. Central Ga. Power Co., Macon Ry. & Light Co., Macon Gas Co. Democrat. Episcopalian. Home: Macon, Ga. Deceased.

FENGER, Christian, surgeon; b. Copenhagen, Denmark, 1840; ed. there; grad. Univ. of Copenhagen, M.D., 1867; private and hosp. practice there until Franco-German war, in which was surgeon in Internat. Ambulance Assn.; afterward 3 yrs. prosector at City Hosp., Copenhagen; lecturer, Univ. of Copenhagen, 1874, later in Egypt, where was apptd. by Khedive med. officer of Khalifa Quarter, Cairo; in Chicago, 1877—. Was many yrs. prof. principles and practice of surgery, until he resigned, 1899, to become prof. clinical surgery, Rush Med. Coll. Has also been prof. principles of surgery and clinical surgery, Coll. of Phys. & Surg., and later Chicago Med. Coll.; prof. surgery, Chicago Polyclinic; surgeon-in-chief, German Hosp.; is surgeon Passavant Memorial, Tabitha, and Presbyn. hosps.; pres. Chicago Med. Soc. Died 1902.

FENLEY, Oscar, banker; b. Jefferson Co., Ky., June 1855; s. John N. and Mary Elizabeth (Carr) F.; ed. pub. schs.; m. Mary Johnston Woolley, June 1897. Began in banking business, in Louisville, 1871; pres. Nat. Bank of Ky., 1896-1921. Dir. Federal Reserve Bank of St. Louis. Home: Louisville, Ky. Died June 28, 1931.

FENN, E(dward) Hart, congressman; b. Hartford, Conn., Sept. 12, 1856; s. Edward Hart and Frances Pitkin (Talcott) F.; desc. Benjamin Fenn, a founder New Haven, Conn., 1638, John Talcott, a founder Hartford, Conn., 1636, William Pynchon and Elizur Holyoke, founders Springfield, Mass., 1636; student Yale 3 years; m. Margaret Bacon Clark, Jan. 30, 1902; 2 children. For many yrs. city editor Hartford Post; formerly state editor, Hartford Courant; mem. Conn. Ho. of Rep., 1907, Senate, 1909-13; mem. 67th to 71st Congresses (1921-31), 1st Conn. Dist.; commr. of fisheries and game, Conn., 1909-14. Mem. Co. F, 1st Regt., C.N.G. 5 yrs. Republican. Conglist. Mason. Home: Wethersfield, Conn. Died Feb. 23, 1939.

FENN, Harry, artist; b. Richmond, Surrey, Eng., Sept. 14, 1838; s. James and Alice C. (Gibbs) F.; came to U.S., 1857; m. Marian Tompson, 1862. Painter of water colors; illustrator, notably of the books "Picturesque Europe," "Picturesque America," "Picturesque Palestine," "Sinai and Egypt." Lecturer on Oriental subjects. Home: Upper Montclair, N.J. Died 1911.

FENN, William Wallace, theologian; b. Boston, Feb. 12, 1862; s. William Wallace and Hannah Morrill (Osgood) F.; A.B., Harvard, 1884, A.M., 1887, S.T.B., 1887, S.T.D., 1908; m. Faith Huntington Fisher, May 28, 1891; children—Dorothy, Wallace Osgood, Roger Carlisle, Donald Fisher, Dan Huntington. Unitarian ministry, 1887—; minister Unity Ch., Pittsfield, Mass., 1887-91, First Unitarian Soc., Chicago, 1891-1901; Shaw lecturer bibl. lit., Meadville Theol. Sch., 1892-1901, 1905-07; preacher to Harvard, 1896-98, 1902-05; Bussey prof. systematic theology, 1901—, dean, 1906-22, Harvard Div. Sch. Fellow Am. Acad. Arts and Sciences. Author: Lessons on Acts, 1894; Theism and Immortality, 1921. Home: Cambridge, Mass. Died Mar. 9, 1932.

FENNELL, William George, clergyman; b. Goshen, Conn., Nov. 15, 1859; s. Enoch and Eliza (Pierce) F.; grad. Conn. Instn., 1880; A.B., Madison (now Colgate) U., 1885, A.M., 1888; student Hamilton Theol. Sem., 1886-87; studied Yale Summer Sch., New York U., Hartford Theol. Sem.; (D.D., Colgate, 1908); m. Inez C. Warner, June 30, 1885. Ordained Bapt. ministry, 1887; pastor 1st Ch., Middletown, Conn., 1887-92, 1st Ch., Meriden, 1892-1900, South Ch., Newark, N.J., 1900-08, Asylum Av. Ch., Hartford, Conn., 1908—. Instr. Hartford Sch. of Missions; lecturer on Bibl. topics. Trustee Conn. Literary Instn., Conn. Bapt. Conv.; sec. Conn. Bapt. Edn. Soc. Home: Hartford, Conn. Died Feb. 26, 1917.

FENNER, Burt L., architect; b. Rochester, N.Y., Sept. 5, 1869; s. Edward B. and Margaret Virginia (Taylor) F.; U. of Rochester, 1888-89; Mass. Inst. Tech., 1890-91; (hon. M.A., U. of Rochester, 1911); m. Louise McKittrick, Dec. 9, 1896. Practiced in Rochester, 1889-90; entered office of McKim, Mead & White, New York, Sept. 1891, mem. of firm, Jan. 1, 1906—. Recent bldgs. designed by firm: Municipal Bldg., Post Office Bldg., Bellevue Hosp., Columbia Coll. bldgs., Met. Mus. of Art, J. P. Morgan Library Bldg., Pa. R.R. Station, Hotel Pennsylvania, all in New York; gen. mgr. U.S. Housing Corp. of U.S. Dept. of Labor, during the war. Fellow Brooklyn Inst. of Arts and Sciences, A.I.A. Home: Croton-on-Hudson, N.Y. Died Jan. 25, 1926.

FENNER, Charles Erasmus, judge; b. Jackson, Tenn., Feb. 14, 1834; s. Dr. Erasmus Darwin and Annie America (Callier) F.; ed. New Orleans schs., Western Mil. Inst. of Ky., and U. of Va.; law at U. of Va. and U. of La.; (LL.D., U. of the South); m. Carrie Payne, Oct. 16, 1866. Admitted to La. bar, 1855; capt. Fenner's La. battery, light arty., C.S.A., during Civil War; justice Supreme Ct. of La., 1880-94; Democrat. Episcopalian. Pres. Administrators of Tulane U. of La.; trustee Peabody Edn. Fund. Home: New Orleans, La. Died 1911.

FENNER, Charles Payne, lawyer; b. New Orleans, La., Oct. 26, 1867; s. Judge Charles Erasmus and Carrie (Payne) F.; grad. Va. Mil. Inst., 1888; LL.B., U. of Va., 1890; LL.D., Washington and Lee U., 1921; m. Eveline M. Gasquet, Jan. 27, 1898. Began practice at New Orleans, 1890; mem. La. Senate, 1896-1900; dean Tulane U. Law Sch., 1914-21. Trustee Carnegie Instn., Washington, D.C. Democrat. Protestant. Home: New Orleans, La. Died Oct. 10, 1927.

FENNER, Hiram Walter, M.D.; b. Bucyrus, O., Feb. 3, 1859; s. Hiram and Elizabeth (Myers) F., M.D., Med. Coll. of Ohio, 1881; m. Laura Ida Hemme, Oct. 16, 1889. Practiced in Ariz., 1881—; dean staff of St. Mary's Hosp. Sanatorium and Training Sch. for Nurses, Tucson; consulting surgeon S.P. Co.; has made extensive investigations in tuberculosis. Chmn. trustees Pub. Library Tucson. Republican. Mason. Home: Tucson, Ariz., and Carmel, Calif. Died May 5, 1929.

FENOLLOSA, Ernest Francisco, educator; b. Salem, Mass., Feb. 18, 1853; s. Manuel and Mary (Silsbee) F.; ed. Harvard B.A.; grad. with highest honors in philosophy, 1874; m. Mary McNeill, Dec. 28, 1895. Prof. political economy and philosophy, Tokio Univ., Japan, 1878-80, philosophy and logic, same, 1880-86; Imperial fine arts commr. to Japanese govt., 1886-87; prof. æsthetics, and mgr. Tokio Fine Arts Acad., and mgr. art dept. Imperial Museum, Tokio, 1887-90; curator dept. of oriental art, Museum of Fine Arts, Boston, 1890-96; prof. of English literature, Imperial Normal Sch., Tokio, 1897-1900; lecturer on oriental subjects in America, 1901-03. Decorated by H. I. M., the Mikado, with 4th class "Rising Sun," 1886; 3d class "Rising Sun," 1890; 3d class "Sacred Mirror," 1890. Author: Epochs of Chinese and Japanese Art (2 vols.), 1911. Home: Spring Hill, Ala. Died 1908.

FENSHAM, Florence (Amanda), educator; b. E. Douglas, Mass., May 25, 1861; d. Hon. John and Sarah Alice F.; B.D., Chicago Theol. Sem., 1902; studied in Mansfield Coll., Oxford, Eng., 1885-86; at Cambridge and Edinburgh—summer courses; unmarried. Entered Am. Coll. for Girls, Constantinople, Turkey, as teacher, Sept. 1883; prof. Bibl. literature and dean until 1905; instr. in Christian Inst. of Chicago Theol. Sem., Chicago, 1906-09; dean Congl. Training Sch. for Women, Chicago, Oct., 1909—. Died 1912.

FENTON, Hector Tyndale, lawyer; b. Phila., Aug. 6, 1850; s. Thomas H. and Caroline (Kummer) F.; ed. by pvt. tutors and at Boys' High Sch., Phila., and later in various scientific and law schs.; widower. Admitted to practice in co. courts in Phila., 1870, to Supreme Ct. of Pa., 1872; later to federal courts and in 1881 to Supreme Ct. of U.S.; partner with late Furman Sheppard in practice of law, 1870-80; from 1885 has given spl. attention to federal court practice, especially copyright and patent causes. Mem. Franklin Inst. Was active in politics and chmn. various polit. organizations, 1875-85. Republican. Episcopalian. Home: Philadelphia, Pa. Deceased.

FENTON, Lucien Jerome, banker; b. nr. Winchester, O., May 7, 1844; s. Benjamin and Elizabeth (Smith) F.; ed. Lebanon Normal and Ohio U.; m. Belle Manker, May 22, 1872. Enlisted in 91st Ohio Regt., Aug. 14, 1862; permanently disabled by gunshot wound at battle of Winchester, Va., Sept. 19, 1864; teacher and supt. pub. schs. in Ohio several yrs.; awarded high sch. life certificate by Ohio State Bd. of Sch. Examiners, 1878; apptd. to position in custom house, New Orleans, 1880, and in U.S. Treas. Dept., Washington, 1881; organized Winchester Bank, 1884. Apptd. trustee Ohio U., 1892; mem. Ohio Centennial Commn., 1898; mem. 54th and 55th Congresses (1895-99), 10th Ohio Dist.; served on House Com. on Mil. Affairs during Spanish-American War. Pres. trustees Wilson Children's Home, West Union, O., 1912; pres. Co. Bd. Edn., 1914. Home: Winchester, O. Died June 28, 1922.

FENTON, William David, lawyer; b. Scotland Co., Mo., June 29, 1853; s. James Davis and Margaret Ann (Pinkerton) F.; A.B., Christian Coll. (now State Normal), Monmouth, Ore., 1872, later A.M.; m. Katherine L. Lucas, Oct. 16, 1879. Read law, Salem, Ore., 1874-75; admitted to bar, 1875; engaged in corp. and gen. practice; counsel for S.P. Co. Lines in Ore., 1891-1917; retired from active practice. Mem. Ore. Ho. of Rep., 1876; Dem. nominee for Congress, 1882; Dem. presdl. elector, 1884. Home: Portland, Ore. Died May 15, 1925.

FERGUSON, Alexander Hugh, surgeon; b. Ontario Co., Ont., Can., Feb. 27, 1853; s. Alexander and Annie (McFadyen) F.; ed. Rockwood Acad. and Manitoba Coll.; honor grad., M.B., Med. Coll. of Trinity U., Toronto, 1881, later in same year an honor grad., M.D., C.M.; visited Am. hosps., 1881, London, Edinburgh, Glasgow and Berlin hosps., 1889; was student at Koch's lab., Berlin; m. Sarah Jane Thomas, of Nassagaweya, Ont., Can., Apr. 7, 1882. Practiced at Winnipeg, Can., 1882-94; founded Manitoba Med. Coll., in which was 3 yrs. prof. of physiology and histology, and prof. surgery, 1886-94; was mem. gen. staff of Winnipeg Gen. Hosp.; surgeon-in-chief St. Boniface Hosp. and chief operator at Brandon and Mordon hosps., Manitoba; mem. Provincial Bd. of Health; prof. clin. surgery, Coll. Phys. and Surg., Chicago, 1900—; prof. surgery, Chicago Post-Grad. Med. Sch. and Hosp., 1894—; surgeon to Post-Grad. Hosp.; surgeon-in-chief to the Chicago Hosp.; surgeon to Cook Co. Hosp. for the Insane. Fellow Am. Surg. Assn., Chicago Acad. Medicine, Am. Assn. of Obstetricians and Gynecologists, Southern Surg. and Gynecol. Assn., Western Surg. and Gynecol. Soc. (pres.), Royal Geog. Soc., etc. Presbyn. Mason. Comdr. Order of Christ of Portugal. Home: Chicago, Ill. Died 1911.

FERGUSON, Edmund Sheppard, M.D.; b. Port Stanley, Ont., Can., June 13, 1871; s. Dugald and Sarah (Shearer) F.; teachers certificate St. Thomas Collegiate Inst., 1890; M.D., Detroit Coll. of Medicine and Surgery (now a dept. of Wayne U.), 1895; post grad. work N.Y. Eye and Ear Infirmary, 1900-01, U. of Vienna, 1910; m. Marie Haven, 1884 (died 1934); children—Edmund Gordon, John Haven. Came to U.S. 1892, naturalized 1901. Began practice of medicine in Oklahoma City, Okla., 1895, mem. Ferguson & Wails; practice limited to eye, ear, nose and throat; prof. and head dept. of ophthalmology, U. of Oklahoma, 1911-38, emeritus; ophthalmologist and otolaryngologist University, St. Anthony's, Okla. General and Wesley hosps. Fellow Am. Coll. Surgeons. A.M.A. Democrat. Presbyn. Mason. Died June 28, 1941.

FERGUSON, Emma Henry, author, composer; b. Red Hill, Va., 1840; d. John and Elvira (McClelland) Henry; g.d. of Patrick Henry; ed. under pvt. tutors; grad. in music at Conservatoire, Paris, 1867; m. Maj. James B. Ferguson (dec.), Dec. 22, 1858. Author: Courage and Loyalty (novel), 1898. Composer: Monogram, Initial and Signature Waltzes, etc. Home: Balham, Goochland Co., Va. Died 1905.

FERGUSON, Everard D., physician; b. Moscow, 1843; s. Smith and Emily F.; grad. Bellevue Med. Coll., M.D., 1868; m. Marian A. Farley, Jan. 1, 1865. Attending surgeon to Samaritan Hosp., Troy, N.Y. Mem. Am. Med. Assn.; treas. N.Y. State Med. Assn. Home: Troy, N.Y. Died 1906.

FERGUSON, Finlay Forbes, architect; b. Norfolk, Va., Nov. 16, 1875; s. Charles Martin and Mary (Fitzgerald) F.; A.B. and B.S., Hampden-Sydney Coll., 1895; B.S. in Architecture, Mass. Inst. Tech., 1898; m. Helen Atkinson Evans, Nov. 25, 1902; children—Finlay Forbes, Frances. Practiced at Norfolk, 1899—; mem. Peebles & Ferguson, 1917—; specializes in ch. and sch. bldgs.; architect of Ghent M.E. Ch., Ch. of the Sacred Heart, First Presbyn. Ch. and Ohef Sholom Synagogue, Norfolk; Grace Covenant Presbyn. Ch., Richmond, Va.; Phi Beta Kappa Memorial Hall, Williamsburg, Va.; Virginia Museum of Fine Arts, Richmond. Mem. bd. Public Library, Norfolk; former mem. Advisory Com. of Architects on restoration work at Williamsburg; trustee Norfolk Academy. Democrat. Presbyn. Mason. Home: Norfolk, Va. Died Oct. 7, 1936.

FERGUSON, Frank William, architect; b. Portsmouth, N.H., Nov. 3, 1861; s. Stephen and Martha M. (Marden) F.; student Scientific Dept., Dartmouth (class of 1887); m. Elizabeth Clark Gardner, Oct. 28, 1891 (died 1896); 1 son, Donald Gardner. Mem. Cram & Ferguson, architects of buildings at U.S. Military Acad. ($7,000,000); St. Thomas Ch., New York; Cathedral of St. John the Divine, New York; Rice Inst., Tex.; Princeton Univ.; Williams Coll.; Richmond Coll., etc.; also firm cons. architects of

St. Alban's Cathedral, Washington, D.C. Fellow Am. Inst. Architects, 1910. Home: Boston, Mass. Died Oct. 4, 1926.

FERGUSON, George Albert, chemist; b. Brooklyn, Aug. 31, 1868; s. David W. and Ellen T. F.; Ph.B., Columbia Sch. Mines, 1890; m. Elsie Loeb, 1893. Examiner med. supplies, etc., U.S. Interior Dept., 1893—; asst. instr., demonstrator, chem. laboratory, prof. analytical chemistry and mathematics, New York Coll. of Pharmacy, 1896—; chemist N.Y. State Bd. of Pharmacy, 1898—; expert in clin. chemistry and toxicology, United Labs. Co., of New York; sr. mem. Ferguson-Hancock Labs., Blue Point, L.I., N.Y.; dir. Ferguson Labs., New York; official chemist Internal Revenue Service, Treas. Dept. Author: Elliott and Ferguson's Qualitative Chemical Analysis. Home: Brooklyn, N.Y. Deceased.

FERGUSON, Henry, clergyman, educator; b. Stamford, Conn., 1848; s. John and Helen (Morewood) F.; A.B., Trinity, 1868, A.M., 1875 (LL.D., 1900); m. Emma J. Gardiner, Oct. 15, 1873. Deacon, 1872, priest, 1873, P.E. Ch.; rector Christ Ch., Exeter, N.H., 1872-78; Trinity Ch., Claremont, N.H., 1878-80; prof. history and polit. science, Trinity Coll., 1883-1906; rector St. Paul's Sch., Concord, N.H., 1906-11. Author: Four Periods in the Life of the Church, 1885; Essays in American History, 1895. Home: Hartford, Conn. Died Mar. 31, 1917.

FERGUSON, Henry A., artist; b. Glens Falls, N.Y.; self-taught in painting; ed. Trinity Coll., A.N.A. Home: New York, N.Y. Died 1911.

FERGUSON, John William, corp. official; b. Tiffin, O., Dec. 19, 1857; s. Peter and Jeanette (Bixby) F.; prep. edn. pub. schs. and high sch., New Haven, Conn.; m. Jennie Beam Cooke, May 25, 1892; children—John William (dec.), Arthur Donald, Jean B. (Mrs. L. L. Buck). Began engring. career with Lehigh & Wilkes-Barre Coal Co., 1875; with Boston & N.Y. Air Line R.R., 1875-77; in engring. dept., N.Y., Lake Erie & Western R.R., through grades to asst. chief engr., 1878-91; entered business for self in engring. and bldg. constrn., 1892; pres. John W. Ferguson Co., Inc., 1895—; hon. pres. Mfrs. Assn. of N.J. and affiliates, Alexander Hamilton Hotel Corp.; v.p. Cedar Lawn Cemetery Co. Home: Paterson, N.J. Died Feb. 4, 1942.

FERGUSON, Louis Aloysius, electrical engr.; b. Dorchester, Mass., Aug. 19, 1867; s. Denis and Louisa (Doherty) F.; B.S., Mass. Inst. Tech., 1888; m. Martha Sargent Jenkins, June 21, 1892. Joined staff Chicago Edison Co., Aug. 1888, as engr. underground dept., promoted asst. elec. engr. constrn. dept., 1889, elec. engr. of co. 1890, gen. supt. Chicago Edison Co., 1897-1902, and of Commonwealth Elec. Co., 1898-1902; 2d v.p. Chicago Edison Co., and Commonwealth Elec. Co., 1902-07; 2d v.p. Commonwealth Edison Co., 1907-14, v.p., 1914-36. Has done much notable work in central station practice. Apptd. 1895 on staff of lecturers U. of Wis. Catholic. Home: Evanston, Ill. Died Aug. 25, 1940.

FERGUSON, Robert Gracey, educator; b. Dry Run, Pa., Feb. 16, 1842; s. James and Mary Ann (Doyle) F.; A.B., Jefferson (now Washington and Jefferson) Coll., Pa., 1862; grad. U.P. Theol. Sem., Allegheny, Pa., 1866; D.D., 1885, LL.D., 1902, Washington and Jefferson; LL.D., Monmouth, 1906; m. Emma M., d. Dr. H. S. Huber, Jan. 28, 1868 (died Sept. 7, 1922). 2d lt., 21st Pa. Cav., 1863-64; ordained United Presbyn. ministry, 1866; pastor Mercersburg and Cove, Pa., 1866-74, Butler, Pa., 1874-84; pres., 1884-1906, prof. Bibl. lit., 1907-14, prof. emeritus, 1915—, Westminster Coll., Pa. Dir. Allegheny Theol. Sem., 1889—; moderator U.P. Gen. Assembly, 1898. Home: Mt. Lebanon, Pa. Died Nov. 8, 1926.

FERGUSON, Samuel David, bishop; b. Charleston, S.C., Jan. 1, 1842; s. Edward and Roseine Elizabeth F.; m. Mary Leonora Montgomery, Apr. 1863 (dec.); 2d, Sarah Elizabeth Brown, July 1879. Emigrated with parents to Liberia, Africa, 1848; ed. in mission schs. there; (D.D., Kenyon, 1885; D.C.L., Liberia Coll., 1893). Apptd. teacher, 1862; deacon, 1865; priest, 1868; elected missionary bishop of Cape Palmas and parts adjacent by the Ho. of Bishops assembled in New York in 1884, and consecrated in Grace Ch., New York, June 24, 1885. Is the first African to be raised to the episcopate of P.E. Ch. of America. Died Aug. 3, 1916.

FERGUSON, Thompson B., governor; b. nr. Des Moines, Ia., 1857; ed. Emporia (Kan.) State Normal Sch. Postmaster Watonga, Okla. Ty., 1897-1900; chmn. Rep. Territorial Com., 1900-02; gov. of Okla. Ty., 1901-06. Republican. Home: Watonga, Okla. Died Feb. 14, 1921.

FERGUSON, Walter, banker; b. Wauneta, Kan., Mar. 28, 1886; s. Gov. Thompson B. and Elva U. (Shartel) F.; prep. edn., Wentworth Mil. Acad., Lexington, Mo.; student Oklahoma U., 1904-07; m. Lucia Loomis (newspaper syndicate writer), Nov. 7, 1908; children—Loomis Benton, Ruth Elva, Thomas Bruce. Editor Cherokee (Okla.) Republican 10 yrs.; exec. v.p. Mid-Continent Oil and Gas Assn.-Okla.-Kan. Div.; mem. State Senate, Okla., 1916-18. Mason. Home: Tulsa, Okla. Died March 1936.

FERGUSON, William J., actor; born of N.E. parentage. Appeared in minor parts for several yrs.; first notable success as Capt. Redfern, the detective, in "Jim, the Penman," under A. M. Palmer's management; joined Mansfield's co. and played character rôles, such as the valet in "Beau Brummel." Since then, leading man in prominent cos.; lately as Champalier in "The Turtle." Died May 5, 1930.

FERGUSON, William Porter Frisbee, editor; b. Delhi, N.Y., Dec. 13, 1861; s. P. Rice and Electa A. (Frisbee) F.; grad. Walton (N.Y.) Acad., 1884; B.D., Drew Theol. Sem., 1887; A.B., Tex. Wesleyan U., Ft. Worth, 1889; (declined degree LL.D. on finding that the univ. offering it owned saloon property); m. L(ena) Grace Hathaway, Apr. 5, 1887; children—Horace Porter Frisbee, Josiah Deming, Dorothy Hilda. Served in M.E. fgn. mission service (Mexico) and as pastor several churches (Meth., Presbyn. and Universalist) in U.S. Devoted to Prohibition movement, 1896-1918; edited Prohibition papers, Voice, New Voice (New York and Chicago), Citizen (Harriman, Tenn.), Defender (New York), Nat. Prohibitionist (Chicago), Vindicator (Franklin, Pa.); editor Venango Daily Herald, Franklin, Pa., 1912-19, News-Herald, Franklin, Pa., 1919—. Spoke in 40 states and Can. on prohibition. Student, explorer and lecturer American archæology. Discovered, in 1922, on Isle Royale in Lake Superior, prehistoric stone-age city; financed and led Franklin-Isle Royale Expdn. which made extensive excavations on site of that town, 1923; conducted preliminary survey of Michipicoten Island (Lake Superior) with view to exploration for prehistoric work, 1924. Universalist. Home: Franklin, Pa. Died June 23, 1929.

FERGUSSON, Arthur Walsh, insular official; b. Benicia, Calif., Dec. 4, 1859; s. of Col. David and Emily Amelia (Walsh) F.; spent from second to tenth year of age in Mexico; grad. St. Augustine Coll., Calif., 1877; grad. Georgetown U. Law Sch., 1885, LL.M., 1886; m. Mary Stanton Williams, Feb. 1, 1887. Owned, edited and published, 1879-82, Benicia New Era, weekly newspaper. When Internat. Am. Conf. met at Washington, 1889, was apptd. official interpreter and has ever since been connected with movement inaugurated by J. G. Blaine. Sec. Internat. Am. Monetary Commn., 1891; official interpreter Intercontinental Ry. Commn., 1891; sec. U.S. Chilian Claims Commn., 1893; sec. U.S. and Venezuelan Claims Commn., 1894; chief transl. Bur. Am. Republics, 1897-1900; Official Interpreter Am. and Spanish Peace Commn., Paris, 1898. Spanish sec. U.S. Philippine Commn., April 1, 1900; chief sec. July 6, 1900-01; exec. sec. for the Philippine Islands, July 16, 1901—. Home: Washington, D.C. Died 1908.

FERGUSSON, E(dmund) Morris, Sunday school writer; b. Phila., Sept. 7, 1864; s. Alexander C. and Mary A. (Morris) F.; A.B., U. of Pa., 1883, A.M., 1886; grad. Princeton Theol. Sem., 1886; D.D., Park Coll., 1914; m. Mary Fry Huber, May 26, 1898; children—Edmund M. (dec.), Martha H. (dec.). Ordained Presbyn. ministry, 1886; pastor, Absecon, N.J., 1886-87, Phillipsburg, N.J., 1889-92; asst. editor Sunday School Times, 1887-89; gen. sec. N.J.S.S. Assn., 1892-1909; ednl. supt. Presbyn. Board of Pubn. and S.S. Work, Phila., 1909-16; gen. sec. Md. S.S. Assn., 1916-19, Mass. S.S. Assn., 1920-21; spl. prof., Boston U. Sch. of Religious Edn., 1919, 1923-25; prof. Tennent Coll. of Christian Edn., 1929—. Active in work of Internat. S.S. Assn.; established the first summer sch. for S.S. teachers, 1894. Author: How to Run a Little Sunday School, 1916; Church-School Administration, 1922; Piloting the Sunday School, 1925; Teaching Christianity, 1929. Home: Swarthmore, Pa. Died Mar. 14, 1934.

FERGUSSON, Frank Kerby, army officer; b. Riddleton, Tenn., Feb. 18, 1874; s. W. W. and Medora C. (Kerby) F.; grad. U.S. Mil. Acad., 1896, Sch. of Submarine Defense, 1906; Army War Coll., 1912; general staff Coll., Washington, D.C., 1920; m. Ocie Hardesty Sheppard, Apr. 1922; 1 dau., (adopted), Dora Margaret (by wife's 1st marriage). Add. 2d lt. 3d Arty., June 12, 1896; promoted through grades to brig. gen. (temp.), Aug. 8, 1918; col. C.A.C., June 1920; col. gen. staff, Sept. 1920. At various posts, 1896-98; in Galveston, Tex., and on recruiting service, 1898; comd. U.S. Army mine planter, Colonel George Armistead, 1906; duty in submarine mine instrn., 1906-08; comd. Armistead, to Pacific Coast via Straits of Magellan, Dec. 1908-Apr. 1909; a.-d.-c. to Maj. Gen. Barry, 1909-10; coast defense officer, Dept. of Calif., 1910-11; duty at Army War Coll., 1911-12; mem. Ordnance Bd. of the Army, 1912-14; in Philippines, 1914-17; comdr. 8th Regt. C.A.C. (R.R. Arty.), Newport, R.I., and in France, July-Oct. 1917; comdr. Trench Mortar Sch. and on staff at Hdqrs. A.E.F., France, Oct. 1917-Mar. 1918; comdr. Coast Arty. Training Center, Ft. Monroe and Camp Eustis, Va., Apr. 1, 1918-Feb. 1919; comdr. S. Pacific Coast Arty. Dist., to June 1919; at Gen. Staff Coll., Washington, D.C., 1919; Chief of Staff, 3d Corps Area, Baltimore, Md., Sept. 1920-Apr. 1922; Chief of Staff Philippine Div., Manila, June 1922-24; comdg. 11th Coast Arty. and Coast Defenses, L.I. Sound, Ft. H. G. Wright, N.Y., 1924-28; comdg. 2d Coast Arty. Dist., Ft. Totten, N.Y., 1929; comdg. harbor defenses of Cristobal, Forts DeLesseps and Sherman, Canal Zone, 1930-31, apptd. exec. officer, 2d Coast Arty. Dist., N.Y. City, 1931-34; comdg. 62d Reg Coast Arty. (Anti-Aircraft), harbor defenses of Eastern New York and the 5th dist. Civilian Conservation Corps, Ft. Totten, N.Y., 1934-35. Awarded D.S.M. "for conspicuous and specially meritorious service" while comdg. gen. of Coast Arty. Training Center. Died July 18, 1937.

FERGUSSON, Harvey Butler, congressman; b. in Ala., Sept. 9, 1848; A.M., Washington and Lee U., 1873, B.L., 1874. Instr. Greek and modern langs., Washington and Lee U., 1873-74; admitted to bar, 1874; practiced in Wheeling, W.Va., until 1882; at Albuquerque, N.M., 1884—. Del. to 55th Congress (1897-99); mem. 62d and 63d Congresses (1911-15), State of N.M. Ex-mem. Dem. Nat. Com. Home: Albuquerque, N.M. Died June 10, 1915.

FERNALD, Bert M., senator; b. West Poland, Me., Apr. 3, 1858; s. James H. and Betsy S. (Libby) F.; ed. pub. schs., Hebron Acad., Boston business and prep. schs.; m. Annie Keene, Nov. 18, 1877; children—James Henley, Mrs. Mellie Eveleth. Packer of canned goods, 1888—; dir. Fidelity Trust Co. (Portland). Exec. com. Nat. Canners' Assn. (pres. 1910). Has held various local and state offices; mem. Me. Ho. of Rep.; state senator 2 terms; gov. of Me., 1909-11; elected U.S. senator, Sept. 1916, for unexpired term (1916-19) of Edwin C. Burleigh, deceased; reëlected for terms 1919-31. Republican. Home: West Poland, Me. Died Aug. 23, 1926.

FERNALD, Charles Henry, zoölogist; b. at Mt. Desert, Me., Mar. 16, 1838; s. Eben and Sophronia (Wasgatt) F.; ed. at Me. Wesleyan Sem.; (hon. A.M., Bowdoin, 1871; Ph.D., Me. State Coll., 1886); m. Maria Elizabeth Smith, Aug. 24, 1862; father of Henry Torsey F. Served during Civil War as acting ensign U.S.N.; prin. Litchfield Acad., 1865, Houlton Acad., 1866-71; prof. natural history, Me. State Coll., 1871-86; prof. zoölogy, Mass. Agrl. Coll., and dir. Grad. Sch., 1886-1910. Entomologist to State Bd. of Agriculture. Mem. many scientific socs. U.S. and Europe. Home: Amherst, Mass. Died Feb. 22, 1921.

FERNALD, Chester Bailey, author; b. Boston, Mar. 18, 1869; s. Frank Lysander and Mary Elizabeth (Remick) F.; ed. Episcopal Acad., Phila., Washington (D.C.) High Sch., Somerville (Mass.) High Sch., and pvt. tutoring; m. Josephine Harker, June 12, 1896; children—Van Dyke (killed in the World War), John Bailey; m. 2d, Margaret Mary Hood, Mar. 29, 1934. Traveled extensively in the United States; moved to California, 1889; 4 yrs. asst. draftsman in the Navy Dept. in connection with building war vessels at San Francisco; Washington corr. San Francisco Chronicle, 1893-94; visited Alaska, China and Japan; lived abroad, 1898-1904 and 1907—. Mem. of Nat. Inst. of Arts and Letters; associate Royal Academy of Dramatic Art. Author: The Cat and the Cherub, and Other Stories, 1896; Chinatown Stories, 1899; Under the Jackstaff, 1903; John Kendry's Idea, 1907; The White Umbrella, 1919. Plays: The Cat and the Cherub. Died Apr. 10, 1938.

FERNALD, Frank Lysander, capt. U.S.N.; b. Kittery, Me., Nov. 11, 1835; s. William Salisbury and Sarah A. (Hanscom) F.; pub. sch. edn. to 1853; m. Mary Elizabeth Remick, Jan. 8, 1857; father of Chester Bailey F. Served several years in shipbuilding; entered naval service, 1854; apptd. chief draftsman at Navy Yard, Boston, 1868; asst. naval constr., May 4, 1871; constr., with rank of capt., Mar. 12, 1875. In Eng., France and Germany on spl. duty, 1875-79; mem. naval advisory bd. designing and supervising building of Chicago, Boston, Atlanta and Dolphin, 1887-91; supt. building of first Charleston, San Francisco and Monterey at Union Iron Works, San Francisco, 1891-95; in charge of constrn. dept. at Navy Yard, New York, built (old) Maine and Cincinnati; on spl. duty in Eng., 1895-97, and then in China and Burma and at Baltimore, Wilmington and New York superintending new work; retired, Nov. 11, 1897. Home: South Eliot, Me. Deceased.

FERNALD, Gustavus Stockman, lawyer; b. Otisfield, Me., Nov. 11, 1857; s. Osborne and Hannah E. (Stockman) F.; acad. edn., Oxford Normal Inst., Paris, Me.; read law in office of Gen. Charles P. Mattocks, Portland, Me.; m. Gertrude Whittier Bucknam, Sept. 24, 1878. Admitted to bar, 1882, and began practice at Brainerd, Minn.; atty., 1886-90, tax commr., 1890-1905, N.P. Ry.; spl. counsel for receivers, same, 1893-96; moved to Chicago, 1905; asst. gen. solicitor, 1905-09, gen. atty., 1909-18, gen. counsel, 1918—, The Pullman Co. Republican. Episcopalian. Home: Chicago, Ill. Died Apr. 7, 1925.

FERNALD, James Champlin, clergyman, author, editor; b. Portland, Me., Aug. 18, 1838; s. Henry B. and Mabel C. F.; A.B., Harvard, 1860; grad. Newton Theol. Instn., 1863; (L.H.D., Denison, 1904); m. Mary B. Griggs, Apr. 29, 1869 (died 1870); 2d, Nettie S. Barker, June 18, 1873. Ordained Bapt. ministry, 1864; pastor Rutland, Vt., 1862-65, Waterville, Me., 1865-66; in Europe, 1866-67; pastor, Granville, O., 1869-72; in govt. service, Washington, 1872-76; pastor in Ohio, at McConnelsville, 1876-77, Clyde, 1877-79, Galion, 1879-80, Springfield, 1881-85, Garrettsville, 1885-89; on staff Funk & Wagnalls Co., 1889—. Dean dept. English, Intercontinental U., Dec. 1905-09. Editor-in-chief Students' Standard Dictionary, and other abridgments; The Classic Speller; Scientific Side-Lights, 1901; for a time editor Homiletic Review. Author: Synonyms, Antonyms and Prepositions of the English Language, 1896; Connectives of English Speech, 1904; A Working Grammar of the English Language, 1907; English Grammar Simplified, 1915; Effective English, 1918. Home: Upper Montclair, N.J. Died Nov. 10, 1918.

FERNALD, Merritt Caldwell, univ. pres.; b. S. Levant, Me., May 26, 1838; s. Robert and Roxana (Buswell) F.; A.B., Bowdoin, 1861, A.M., 1864 (hon. Ph.D., 1881, LL.D., 1902); m. Mary Lovejoy Heywood, Aug. 24, 1865; father of Robert Heywood and Merritt Lyndon F. Prin. Gould's Acad., Bethel, Me., 1863-64; scientific studies at Harvard, 1864-65; prin. Houlton (Me.) Acad., 1865-66, Foxcroft (Me.) Acad., 1866-68; prof. mathematics and physics, 1871-79, acting pres., 1868-71, pres., 1879-93, emeritus prof. philosophy, 1898—, Me. State Coll. (now U. of Me.) Home: Orono, Me. Died Jan. 8, 1916.

FERNALD, Robert Heywood, engineer; b. Orono, Me., Dec. 19, 1871; s. Merritt Caldwell and Mary Lovejoy (Heywood) F.; B.M.E., Me. State Coll., 1892; Mass. Inst. Tech., 1892-93; M.E., Case Sch. Applied Science, 1918; A.M., Columbia, 1901, Ph.D., 1902; Sc.D., U. of Pa., 1924; m. Catherine Mason Coupland, June 27, 1905; children—Merritt Caldwell, Frances Mason (dec.), Mason. Instr., 1893-96, asst. prof., 1896-1901, Case Sch. Applied Science, dir. dept. mech. engr., 1907-12; dir. dept. mech. engring., Washington U., 1902-07; Whitney prof. dynamical engring., and dir. dept. mech. engring., U. of Pa., 1912—, dean Towne Scientific Sch. same univ., 1930—. Conducted investigations for U.S. Geol. Survey and Bur. of Mines in U.S. and Europe; engr. in charge technologic branch, U.S. Geol. Survey, Sept. 1, 1904-July 1, 1910; cons. engr. Pub. Service Commn. of Pa., 1913-15; cons. engr., fuel div. Bureau of Mines, 1910-20. Formulated rules and regulations for gas, heating and water utilities of Pa., 1914. President Cleveland Engring. Soc., 1912; mem. bd. dirs. Sesquicentennial Internat. Expn. at Phila.; engr. mem. Giant Power Survey Bd. of Pa.; mem. science advisory com. (mech. engring. dir.), Century of Progress Expn., Chicago; mem. exec. com. Traffic Commn. of Phila., 1930—; engring. mem. advisory com., Phila. Agency of Reconstruction Finance Corp., 1932—; mem. exec. com. 3d World Power Conf., 1935-36; chmn. exec. com. Tech. Advisory Council affiliated with Phila. Chamber of Commerce, Jan. 1936—. Author: Engineering of Power Plants (with George A. Orrok), 1916, 3d edit., 1927. Home: Haverford, Pa. Died April 24, 1937.

FERNALD, Walter Elmore, psychiatrist; b. Kittery, Me., Feb. 11, 1859; s. William A. and Margery C. F.; prep. edn. New Hampton (N.H.) Lit. Instn.; M.D., Med. Sch. of Me. (Bowdoin), 1881; hon. M.A. from Harvard U., 1913; m. Kate M. Nolan, Oct. 5, 1887. Asst. phys., State Insane Hosp., Mendota, Wis., 1882-87; supt. of Mass. Sch. for Feeble Minded, 1887—; asso. prof. mental diseases, Tufts Coll.; lecturer on mental diseases of children, Harvard Grad. Sch. of Edn. Home: Waverly, Mass. Died Nov. 27, 1924.

FERNOW, Bernhard Eduard, forester; b. Inowraclaw, Posen, Prussia, Jan. 7, 1851; s. Eduard and Clara (Nordmann) F.; ed. at gymnasium, Bromberg, Forest Acad., Muenden, and U. of Königsberg; (LL.D., U. of Wis., 1897, Queen's Univ. of Canada, 1902, U. of Toronto, 1919); m. Olivia Reynolds, 1879. Came to U.S., 1876; engaged in metall. business; chief div. of forestry, U.S. Dept. Agr., 1886-98; dir. and dean N.Y. State Coll. of Forestry, Cornell U., 1898-1903; prof. forestry, State Coll. of Pa., 1907; dean faculty of forestry, U. of Toronto, 1907-19 (prof. emeritus). Editor Journal of Forestry. Author: The Care of Trees, 1911. Edited Annual Reports and Bulletins, Div. of Forestry, U.S. Dept. Agr., 1886-98. Mem. Canadian Commn. of Conservation. Died Feb. 6, 1923.

FERNOW, Berthold, author, editor; b. Inowraclaw, Prussian Poland, Nov. 28, 1837; s. Edward F. (landrath of County of Inowraclaw) and Bertha (von Jachman) F.; ed. by private tutors and at Gymnasium of Our Lady, Magdeburg, Prussian Saxony, 1849-59; lt. of the reserve, Prussian army, 1860; private 4th Mo. cav., 1862; lt. 3d U. S. Inf., colored troops, 1863; topog. engr., coast div., Dept. of the South, 1864; State archivist, N.Y., Albany, 1876-89. Author: Ohio Valley in Colonial Days, 1889. Editor and translator: Documents Relating to Colonial History of N.Y. (vols. XII, XIII, XIV); New York in the Revolution, 1887; Records of New Amsterdam, 1897. Companion Mil. Order Loyal Legion. Deceased.

FERNSTROM, Henning, civil engr.; b. Orebro, Sweden, Jan. 26, 1857; tech. edn. in Sweden; m. M. Louise Dickson, 1886 (died 1920); 1 son, Karl D.; m. 2d, Cornelia D. Hodgman, 1923. Came to U.S., 1880, naturalized citizen. Draftsman in engineer's office, Boston, Mass., 1880-81; in engring. dept. various rys. and asst. engr. Minn. & N.W. Ry. bridge across Miss. River, at St. Paul, Minn., 1881-85; chief engr. C.G.W. Ry. and its predecessors, 1885-1900; chief engr. St.J.&G.I. R.R. and K.C.&O. Ry., 1900-01; prin. asst. engr. and asst. chief engr. N.Y.C.& H.R. R.R., 1901-03; chief engr. same rd., 1903-05; chief engr. Virginian Ry. Co. and its predecessors, 1905-27, retired. Vice Consul for Sweden at Norfolk, 1905-17. Decorated Order of North Star, 1st class, by King of Sweden, 1905. Fellow Am. Geog. Society. Home: Norfolk, Va. Died Feb. 26, 1932.

FERRARI-FONTANA, Edoardo, tenor; b. Rome, Italy, July 8, 1878; s. Edoardo Ferrari-Fontana and Giuseppa (Fornari) Fontana; ed. Gymnasium Coll. of Rome; U. of Rome, 1892-1901; m. 2d, Edith Tallez, 1919. Adopted stage career, 1902; début at Royal Theatre, Turin, 1910; engaged for season at the Grand Expn., Rome, 1911; later appeared at La Scala Theatre, Milan, Colon Theatre, Buenos Ayres; joined Met. Opera Co., New York, 1913; with Chicago Grand Opera Co., 1915-16; sang at Paris Opera House, season of 1913-14. Hon. mem. Circolo Monarchio Romano; Knight of the Italian Crown. Died July 4, 1936.

FERRATA, Giuseppe, prof. music; b. Gradoli, Italy, 1865; s. Paolo and Lucia (Donati) F.; grad. with highest honors and grand prize of Ministry of Pub. Instr., Royal Acad. Music, Rome, 1885; Dr. Mus., Univ. State of N.Y., 1900; m. Alice Lagarde, 1893. Came to U.S., 1892, naturalized citizen, 1916. Début as pianist at Costanzi Theatre, Rome, 1883; gave many concerts in Italy; head of piano dept. and prof. composition and instrumentation, Newcomb Coll., New Orleans, 1908—. Decorated, 1885, by King of Portugal, and twice by King of Italy, with Knighthood and as Comdr. Order of the Crown. Catholic. Winner of nat. and internat. competitions. Composer of 3 operas, 3 string quartettes, a symphony, piano concertos, sonata, and 4 masses. Home: New Orleans, La. Died Mar. 28, 1928.

FERREE, Barr, editor, author; b. Phila.; s. Samuel Patterson and Annie Appleton (Drown) F.; grad. U. of Pa., 1884. Hon. and corr. mem. Royal Inst. British Architects; corr. mem. Academie d'Aix-en-Provence, France; corr. mem. Société Archéologique du Midi de la France, Toulouse; corr. mem. Am. Inst. of Architects; pres. dept. architecture, Brooklyn Inst. of Arts and Sciences, etc.; founder and present sec. Pa. Soc. of New York. Author: Pennsylvania: A Primer, 1904. Editor Year Book of Pa. Soc. Died Oct. 14, 1924.

FERRELL, Chiles Clifton, editor, author; b. nr. Greenville, S.C., Aug. 20, 1865; s. James Overton and Elizabeth Ann (Austin) F.; early edn. in father's pvt. sch., Hopkinsville, Ky., 1875-80; A.B., Vanderbilt U., 1885, A.M., 1886; fellow and instr. Greek, Vanderbilt, 1885-89; student U. of Leipzig, 1889-92, Ph.D., 1892; traveled in Great Britain, Germany, Switzerland, Austria, Italy; student Paris (summer), 1894, U. of Berlin, summer semester, 1902; m. Tenney Marr Taliaferro, Aug. 16, 1899. Prof. modern langs., 1893-1905, Germanic langs., 1905-08, U. of Miss.; engaged in lit. work, 1908—. Author: Teutonic Antiquities in the Anglo-Saxon Genesis, 1893 (Halle). Edited (with intro. and notes), Sappho-Trauerspiel in fünf Aufzügen von Franz Grillparzer, 1899. Home: Birmingham, Ala. Died May 1, 1915.

FERRELL, John Appley, lawyer; b. Lanes Prairie, Maries Co., Mo., Sept. 23, 1865; s. John M. and Elvira F.; grad. Northern Ind. Normal Sch., Valparaiso, Ind., business course, 1885, teacher's course, 1886, scientific course, 1887, C.E., 1897; m. Emma Lugabill, June 8, 1887. Admitted to bar, 1896, at Sedan, Kan.; taught in pvt. normal sch., steelville, Mo., 4 yrs., Ft. Scott, Kan., 1 yr.; prof. mathematics, Southwestern State Normal Sch., Okla., 3 yrs. Now practicing law at Sedan, Kan. Home: Sedan, Kan. Deceased.

FERRERO, Edward, soldier; b. Granada, Spain, of Italian parentage; came to U.S. in infancy. Conducted a dancing school, New York, and taught dancing at Military Acad., West Point; became lt. col. 11th N.Y. militia; in 1861 raised 51st N.Y. regt. and became its col.; commd. brig. gen., Sept. 1862; bvtd. maj. gen., Dec. 1864; mustered out, Aug. 1865. During Grant's final campaign commanded colored div. of 9th corps. Died 1899.

FERRIS, Albert Warren, M.D.; b. Brooklyn, Dec. 3, 1856; s. Richard B. and Sarah A. (Demarest) F.; A.B., New York U., 1878, A.M., 1885; M.D., Coll. Phys. and Surg. (Columbia), 1882; m. Juliet A. Gavette, Sept. 29, 1897 (died 1923). Interne Kings Co. Hosp., Brooklyn, 1883-85; asst. resident phys., Sanford Hall, Flushing, N.Y., 1885-91; physician-in-charge Dr. Choate's House, Pleasantville, N.Y., 1893-94, 1896, and of Dr. Bond's House, Yonkers, N.Y., 1904-05, 1907; in practice of medicine, New York, 1892-1912; pres. N.Y. State Commn. in Lunacy, 1907-11; sr. resident phys., The Glen Springs, Watkins, N.Y., 1912-13, 1917-30; med. expert and dir. Saratoga Springs State Reservation Commn., 1913-16. Asst. in medicine, Vanderbilt Clinic, New York, 1892-95; asst. in neurology, Columbia, 1893-1901; asst., principles and practice of medicine, Univ. and Bellevue Hosp. Med. Coll., 1898-1907. Consulting phys. Manhattan and Binghamton State hosps.; declined election as supt. Danvers (Mass.) State Hosp., 1911. Mem. Am. Congress on Internal Medicine. Trustee and treas. Rutgers Female Coll., N.Y., 1891-92; incorporator, dir. and financial sec., Pringle Memorial Home, Poughkeepsie, N.Y., 1899-1908. Fellow Am. Coll. Physicians. Chmn. Home Defense Com., Saratoga Co., 1917; "Four Minute" war campaigns speaker, 1917-18, Red Cross, 1919. Mason. Republican. Home: East Orange, N.J. Died Oct. 4, 1937.

FERRIS, David, retired farmer; b. in the house where he died, Wilmington, Del., July 16, 1821; ed. at Smith's Acad., Wilmington; m. April 12, 1849, Sarah A. Underwood (dec.); mem. Society of Friends and Universal Peace Union; sec. Del. Peace Soc. Writer of articles advocating peace and against late war with Spain. Died 1907.

FERRIS, George Hooper, clergyman; b. Lamartine, Wis., June 5, 1867; s. George Horace and Annette (Stowe) F.; grad. Wayland Acad., Beaver Dam, Wis., 1887; B.A., Brown U., 1891, M.A., 1893; grad. Union Theol. Sem., 1896; (D.D., Brown U., 1907); m. Carrie Sivyer, Jan. 1, 1892. Ordained Bapt. ministry, 1896; pastor 1st Ch., Tarrytown, N.Y., 1896-99, Calvary Ch., New Haven, Conn., 1899-05, 1st Ch., Phila., 1905—. Mem. Commn. on Municipal Charities, 1910, and of Vice Commn., 1911; exec. com. Soc. for Organizing Charity; mem. Pub. Service Commn. of 100; mem. exec. com. N. Bapt. Conv. Republican. Author: The Formation of the New Testament, 1907; The Elements of Spirituality; or, The Spiritual Man, 1912. Home: Philadelphia, Pa. Died Sept. 16, 1917.

FERRIS, Harry Burr, prof. anatomy; b. Old Greenwich, Conn., May 21, 1865; s. Samuel Holmes and Mary F. (Clark) F.; B.A. Yale, 1887, M.D., 1890; m. Helen Whiting, June 23, 1892; children—Helen Millington (Mrs. Davenport Hooker), Henry Whiting. Instr. in anatomy, 1891, asst. prof. 1892, prof. of anatomy, 1895-1933, Yale U., prof. emeritus, 1933—. Conglist. Author: The Indians of Cuczo and the Apurimac, 1916; The Quichua and Machiganga Indians, 1921. Home: New Haven, Conn. Died Oct. 12, 1940.

FERRIS, Jean Léon Gérome, painter; b. Phila., Aug. 8, 1863; s. Stephen James (portrait painter) and Elizabeth Anastasia (Moran) F.; mother a sister of Thomas Moran, the artist; studied under S. J. Ferris and Christian Schuessele, in Phila., 1878-83; at Académie Julien, Paris, under W. Bouguereau, 1884; pvt. pupil of J. L. Gérome; South Kensington Museum, London, 1888; m. Annette S. Ryder, May 17, 1894; 1 dau., Elizabeth Mary (dec.). Has devoted attention from 1900 to production of series of paintings of Am. history, covering period from 1492-1865; in 1917 the city of Phila. built a gallery in Congress Hall for accommodation of the entire collection, numbering over 70 subjects, where they now hang. Has made a special study of early types of Am. vehicles, ships, and ordnance, models of same being now in Congress Hall Mus., Phila., and data filed with Nat. Mus., Washington, and N.Y. Hist. Soc.; presented to the Nat. Museum (Washington), 1927, a collection of over 3,000 etchings, line engravings, mezzotints and lithographs, of the 16th, 17th, 18th and 19th centuries. Sec.-treas. Artists' Fund Soc., Phila. Home: Philadelphia, Pa. Died Mar. 18, 1930.

FERRIS, John Mason, clergyman; b. Albany, N.Y., Jan. 17, 1825; s. Rev. Isaac and Catharine Ann (Burchan) F.; A.B., New York U., 1843, A.M., 1846; studied New Brunswick Theol. Sem., 1846-49; (D.D., Rutgers, 1867); m. Mary E. Schoonmaker, Sept. 10, 1850; 2d, Anna M. Martense, Apr. 13, 1871. Ordained Dutch Reformed ministry, 1849; pastor Tarrytown, N.Y., 1851-54, Chicago, 1854-62, Grand Rapids, Mich., 1862-65; prof. Western Theol. Sem., Holland, Mich., 1864-65; corr. sec. Bd. Foreign Missions, Reformed Dutch Ch., New York, 1865-83, treas., 1886; editor Christian Intelligencer, 1881—. Home: Brooklyn, N.Y. Died 1911.

FERRIS, Mary Lanman Douw, author; b. Poughkeepsie, N.Y., May 22, 1855; d. Col. John de Peyster and Marianne Chandler (Lanman) Douw; grad. Cook's Collegiate Inst., Poughkeepsie, N.Y., 1874; m. Morris Patterson Ferris, Sept. 4, 1879 (died 1918); children—Mary Van Rensselaer, Morris Douw, Van Wyck. Engaged in geneal. and hist. work since 1876. A founder of Daughters of the Cincinnati; in charge of the restoration of Van Cortlandt Mansion, Van Cortlandt Park, N.Y. Editor: The American Author. Wrote: (brochures) Dutch Nursery Rhymes of Colonial Times; Random Rhymes of Old Dutch Times; History of Fort Crailo; The Van Cortlandt Mansion, Colonial Dames; Legend of New Year's Eve; etc. Home: Hempstead, N.Y. Died Mar. 31, 1932.

FERRIS, Morris Patterson, lawyer; b. New York, Oct. 3, 1855; s. Isaac F. (D.D., LL.D., 3d chancellor of the U. of New York) and Letitia (Storm) F.;

acad. edn., U. of New York; LL.B., same, 1876; m. Mary Lanman Douw, Sept. 4, 1879. In law practice at New York, 1876—. An organizer Brooklyn Young Republican Club, mem. exec. com., corr. sec., 1881-84; treas. Soc. Am. Authors, 1898-1906; sec. S.R., 1899-1906; mem. council N.Y. Soc. Colonial Wars, 1903-05; mem. council Order Foreign Wars, 1899-1902, 1904-07; registrar and commissary Vet. Corps of Arty., Soc. War of 1812, 1895-1906; charter mem. and 1st atty. gen. Order Founders and Patriots of America; founder, and sec. N.Y. State Hist. Assn., 1899-1903, trustee, 1899—. Mem. advisory council Daughters of the Cincinnati; pres. Yonkers Hist. and Library Assn.; founder and 1st pres. Garden City Club. Published, Records of Dutch Church of Sleepy Hollow, Tarrytown, N.Y. Home: Garden City, N.Y. Died Oct. 26, 1918.

FERRIS, Woodbridge Nathan, senator; b. Spencer, N.Y., Jan. 6, 1853; s. John, Jr. and Estella (Reed) F.; ed. acads., and Oswego (N.Y.) Normal and Training Sch., 1870-73, med. dept. U. of Mich., 1873-74; m. Helen F. Gillespie, 1874. Prin. of a business coll. and acad., Freeport, Ill., 1875-76; prof. Rock River U., Dixon, Ill., 1876-77; prin. Dixon (Ill.) Business Coll. and Acad., 1878-79; supt. schs., Pittsfield, Ill., 1879-84; founded, 1884, pres., Ferris Inst., 1884—. Pres. Big Rapids (Mich.) Savings Bank. Dem. candidate for Congress, 1892, for gov. of Mich., 1904; elected gov. for terms 1913-14 and 1915-16. U.S. senator, term 1923-29. Home: Big Rapids, Mich. Died Mar. 23, 1928.

FERRISS, Franklin, lawyer; b. Peru, N.Y., Sept. 22, 1849; s. Charles and Mercy (Macomber) F.; B.S., Cornell U., 1873; student St. Louis Law Sch., 1875; m. Elizabeth Simon, Feb. 10, 1880; children—Henry T., Hugh, Margery Semple. Began in practice of law in St. Louis, 1875; mem. Rowell & Ferriss; mem. City Council, St. Louis, 1893-97; judge, 8th Jud. Circuit, Mo., 1898-1903, resigned to accept appmt. as gen. counsel La. Purchase Expn. Co.; also dir. of same co. Mem. Ferriss, Zumbalen & Ferriss, until Jan. 1, 1911, when apptd. asso. justice Supreme Court of Mo. by Gov. Hadley to fill an unexpired term of 2 yrs.; reëlected judge 8th Circuit; retired Jan. 1, 1923. Republican. Home: St. Louis, Mo. Died Nov. 10, 1933.

FERRISS, James Henry, newspaperman; b. Yorkville, Ill., Nov. 18, 1849; s. William H. F.; ed. Bristol, Ill.; m. Olive E. Hunt, June 30, 1880. Commenced editorial and reform work on the Yorkville News, 1876; editor Joliet Daily News, 1876—, except 2 yrs. on papers at Portland and Chase's Mills, Me. Chmn. Nat. Com. People's Party; candidate lt. gov. of Ill., 1900; presdl. elector, 1908. Pres. Fern Soc. U.S. and Canada 4 yrs. Home: Joliet, Ill. Died 1926.

FERRY, Dexter Mason, seed mcht.; b. Lowville, N.Y., Aug. 8, 1833; s. Joseph N. and Lucy D. F.; grew up on a farm; ed. Rochester, N.Y.; went to Detroit, Mich., 1852; clerked in stationery store, 1852-56; one of organizers of M. T. Gardner & Co., seedsmen, 1856; organized, 1867, D. M. Ferry & Co., now conducting largest seed enterprise in U.S. Is pres. First Nat. Bank, Union Trust Co., Standard Life and Accident Ins. Co., Mich. Fire and Marine Ins. Co., etc. Died 1907.

FERRY, E. Hayward, banker; b. Peterborough, N.H., June 14, 1864; s. Charles Brace and Ellen (Hayward) F.; A.B., Harvard, 1886; m. Amelia Parsons, Feb. 14, 1889; 1 dau., Harriet (Mrs. William De Forest Manice). With Nat. Bank of Redemption (Boston), 1886-87; sec. Bay State Trust Co. (Boston), 1887-1900; v.p. Nat. Shawmut Bank (Boston), 1900-07; v.p. Hanover Nat. Bank (New York), 1907-29; retired. Republican. Home: New York, N.Y. Died Apr. 4, 1940.

FERRY, George Bowman, architect; b. Springfield, Mass., Feb. 7, 1851; s. Robert Spencer and Almira Tirzah F.; studied architecture at Mass. Inst. Tech., 1871-72; m. Cora Frances Phillips, Jan. 7, 1880. Architect Pub. Library, Milwaukee; library, Hist. Soc. of Wis., Madison; Pub. Library, Jackson, Mich.; Wis. Bldg., St. Louis Expn., 1904; Northwestern Nat. Ins. Co., and Auditorium, Milwaukee. Consulting architect, U. of Wis. Fellow A.I.A.; pres. Art Commn. Died Jan. 29, 1918.

FERRY, William Mont(ague); b. Grand Haven, Mich., Mar. 12, 1871; s. Edward P. and Clara (White) F.; B.S., Olivet (Mich.) Coll., 1891; studied State Sch. of Mines, Golden, Colo.; m. Ednah Truman, June 3, 1896; children—(twins) William and Sanford Truman. Engaged in mining in Utah, 1891—; settled in Salt Lake City, 1898; v.p. and mng. dir. Silver King Coalition Mines Co. Mem. City Council, Salt Lake City, 1905-11; pres. Utah State Senate, 1911-15; mayor Salt Lake City, 1915-19. Republican. Conglist. Home: Salt Lake City, Utah. Died Jan. 11, 1938.

FESS, Simeon D., senator; b. on farm, Allen Co., O., Dec. 11, 1861; s. Henry and Barbara (Herring) F.; A.B., Ohio Northern U., Ada, O., 1889, A.M., 1891, LL.B., 1896, LL.D., 1900; LL.D. from Wilberforce U. (Ohio), 1927; m. Eva C. Thomas, Mar. 1890 (died 1925); children—Hamilton L., Thomas L., Charles S. Prof. Am. history, 1889-96, head of Coll. of Law, 1896-1900, v.p. 1900-02, Ohio Northern U.; grad. student and lecturer, U. of Chicago, 1902-07; pres. Antioch Coll., Yellow Springs, O., 1907-17. Del. and v.p. Ohio Constl. Conv., 1912; chmn. edn. com. and author of amendment creating dept. of state supt. pub. instrn., etc. Mem. 63d Congress (1913-15), 6th Ohio Dist., and 64th to 67th Congresses (1915-23), 7th Dist.; chmn. Com. on Edn. Chmn. Rep. Nat. Congressional Campaign Com., 1918, 20, 22; mem. U.S. Senate, 2 terms, 1923-35; temporary chmn. and keynoter, Rep. Nat. Conv., 1928; chmn. Rep. Nat. Com., 1930-31. Methodist. Mason. Home: Yellow Springs, O. Died Dec. 23, 1936.

FESSENDEN, Francis, soldier; b. Portland, Me., March 18, 1839; s. William Pitt F., sec. of Treasury; grad. Bowdoin, 1858; studied law, Harvard; m. Ellen Winslow Fox, Aug. 26, 1863 (died 1886). Apptd. capt. 19th U.S. inf., May 14, 1861; severely wounded at Shiloh; col. 25th Me. inf., Sept., 1862; col. 30th Me. vet. inf., 1864; brig. gen., May 1864; and maj. gen. vols., Nov. 1865; bvt. maj. gen. U.S.A., 1865; lost a leg at Monetts Bluff, La., 1864; afterward served until Nov. 1, 1866; retired with rank of brig. gen. U.S.A. Was mayor of Portland, 1876. Home: Portland, Me. Died 1906.

FESSENDEN, Franklin Goodridge, judge; b. Fitchburg, Mass., June 20, 1849; s. Charles and Martha Elizabeth (Newton) F.; Fitchburg High Sch.; LL.B., Harvard U. Law Sch., 1872; studied in Paris, France, 1872; m. Mary J. Rowley, Oct. 3, 1878. Practiced, Greenfield, Mass., 1874-91; served as dist. atty. temporarily justice Superior Court of Mass. Aug. 19, 1891—. V.p. Franklin Savings Instn., Greenfield. Capt. Co. L, 2d Regt., Mass. Vol. Militia, later col. and asst. insp. gen. Democrat. Unitarian. Home: Greenfield, Mass. Died Mar. 16, 1931.

FESSENDEN, Reginald Aubrey, physicist, engr.; b. of New England parentage at Milton, P.Q., Can., Oct. 6, 1866; s. Rev. E. J. and Clementina (Trenholme) F.; ed. Bishop's Coll., P.Q.; m. Helen May Trott, 1889; 1 son, Reginald Kenneley. Prin. Whitney Inst., Bermuda, 1885-86; insp. engr. Edison Machine Works, 1886-87; head chemist Edison Lab., 1887-90; electrician Westinghouse Electric & Mfg. Co., 1890-91; prof. elec. engring., Purdue U., 1892-93; prof. same, Western U. of Pa. (U. of Pittsburgh), 1893-1900; spl. agt. U.S. Weather Bur., 1900-02; gen. mgr. Nat. Elec. Signaling Co., 1902-10; cons. engr. Submarine Signal Co., 1910. Home: North Newton, Mass. Died July 22, 1932.

FESSENDEN, Samuel, lawyer; b. Rockland, Me., April 12, 1847; s. Samuel C. and Mary A. G. (Abbe) F.; common school and academic edn.; grad. Harvard Law School, 1871; m. Helen M. Davenport, June 18, 1873. Served, April 1864, to close of war, private, sergt. maj. and 2d lt. in 7th Me. battery, 1st regt., Me. light arty. Since 1871 engaged in practice of law at Stamford, Conn. Mem. Conn. Ho. of Reps., 1874, 1879, 1895 (speaker, 1895); state's atty., 1880—. Mem. Rep. Nat. Com., 1884-1900. Mem. Conn. senate, 1905, 1906 (pres. pro-tem). Home: Stamford, Conn. Died 1908.

FETHERS, Ogden Hoffman, lawyer; b. Sharon, N.Y., Sept. 20, 1845; s. Daniel and Laura (Adams) F.; grad. Ft. Edward Collegiate Inst., June 1863; (A.M., Coll. Christian Brothers, St. Louis, 1872; LL.D., St. Lawrence U., N.Y., 1895); admitted to bar, 1867; m. Frances Conkey, July 15, 1868. Wis. commr. to Centennial Celebration of Founding of the Federal Govt., New York, 1889; U.S. commr., Paris Expn., 1900, and v.p. Bd. of Commrs. Republican. Past Supreme Chancellor Knights of Pythias. Home: Janesville, Wis. Died 1911.

FETTEROLF, Adam H., coll. pres.; b. Perkiomen, Pa., Nov. 24, 1841; s. Gideon and Elizabeth (Hunsicker) F.; ed. Freeland Sem., now Ursinus Coll.; A.M., Lafayette Coll., 1865, Ph.D., 1878; (LL.D., Delaware Coll., 1886); m. Annie Hengesheimer, Oct. 1865; 2d, Laura Mangam, Oct. 1883. V.p., 1880-82, pres., 1882-Jan. 1910, Girard Coll., Phila. Home: Philadelphia, Pa. Died Dec. 2, 1912.

FEUSTEL, Robert M., consulting engr.; b. Fort Wayne, Ind., Aug. 5, 1884; s. August Frederick and Sophia Dorothy (Kiefer) F.; B.S. in C.E., Purdue U., 1905, C.E., 1909; m. Esther Gertrude Griffiths, Sept. 7, 1909; children—David Feustel (dec.), Robert G., Jean E. Constrn. engr. interurban and city ry. properties, Northern Ind., 1905-07; asst. chief engr. R.R. Commn. of Wis., 1907-13; chief engr. Pub. Utilities Commn. of Ill., 1914-15; pres. and mgr., 1916—, Ind. Service Corp., operating 300 miles city and interurban lines and light and power business in Northern Ind.; vice chmn. Interstate Pub. Service Co.; pres. Midland United Co.; v.p. Central Ind. Power Co., Northern Ind. Public Service Co. V.p. Ft. Wayne Chamber of Commerce; pres. Ft. Wayne Art Sch. Mason. Home: Ft. Wayne, Ind. Died 1932.

FEW, William Preston, univ. pres.; b. Greenville, S.C., Dec. 29, 1867; s. Benjamin Franklin and Rachel (Kendrick) F.; A.B., Wofford Coll., Spartanburg, S.C., 1889, LL.D., 1911; A.M., Harvard U., 1893, Ph.D., 1896; LL.D., Southwestern, 1912, Allegheny Coll., 1915, Syracuse Univ. and Ohio Wesleyan, 1928, Univ. of N.C., 1932; Litt.D., Birmingham-Southern, 1930; LL.D., Davidson (N.C.) College, 1935; Ed.D., Southern College, Fla., 1935; m. Mary Reamey Thomas, Aug. 17, 1911; children—William, Lyne Starling, Kendrick Sheffield, Randolph Reamey, Yancey Preston. Prof. English, 1896-1910, dean, 1902-10, pres. 1910-24, Trinity Coll., Durham, N.C.; pres. Duke U. (including Trinity Coll.), 1924—. Joint editor South Atlantic Quarterly, 1909-19. Mem. bd. of dirs. of Southern Edn. Foundation. Trustee Jeanes Foundation. Democrat. Methodist. Died Oct. 16, 1940.

FEWKES, J(esse) Walter, ethnologist; b. Newton, Mass., Nov. 14, 1850; s. Jesse and Susan E. (Jewett) F.; A.B., Harvard, 1875, A.M., Ph.D., 1877; student of Louis and Alexander Agassiz, student of zoölogy, U. of Leipzig, Germany, 1878-1880; LL.D., U. of Ariz., 1915; m. Harriett O. Cutler, Apr. 4, 1893. Asst. in Mus. Comparative Zoölogy, Harvard, 1881-89; editor Journal of Ethnology and Archæology, 1890-94; field dir. Hemenway Southwestern Archæol. Expdn. field work in Ariz., 1891-94; ethnologist Bur. Am. Ethnology, 1895-1918; chief Bur. Am. Ethnology, 1918-28. Mem. for 30 yrs. of Com. of the Overseers to visit Peabody Mus. of Harvard Coll. In charge excavation and repair Casa Grande, Ariz., Spruce Tree House, Cliff Palace, Sun Temple, Fire Temple, Far View House, Pipe Shrine House, Mesa Verde Nat. Park, Colo., Wupatki, Elden, Pueblo, Ariz., Weden Island near Tampa, Fla., 1908-26. Fellow Am. Acad. Arts and Sciences, A.A.A.S. (v.p. 1911-12), Am. Anthrop. Soc. (pres. 1911, 12), Anthrop. Soc. Washington (pres. 1909, 10), Am. Folk-Lore Soc. (v.p.), Washington Acad. Sciences. Knight Order of Isabella the Catholic, Spain, 1892. Author: Snake Ceremonials at Walpi, 1894; Archæological Expedition to Arizona in 1895; Two Summers' Work in Pueblo Ruins, 1897; Aborigines of Puerto Rico and Neighboring Islands, 1907; Casa Grande, Arizona, 1913. Home: Forest Glen, Md. Died May 31, 1930.

FFOULKE, Charles Mather, mfr., collector of tapestries; b. Quakertown, Pa., July 25, 1841; s. Benjamin Green and Jane (Mather) Ffoulke; ed. Friends' schs. in Quakertown, Gwynedd, and Phila.; m. Sarah A. Cushing, Dec. 10, 1872. Teacher, Friends' Sch., Phila., later prin. Friends' sch., Quakertown. In wool business, Phila., 1861-72, retired; studied art abroad, 1872-74, and 1885-90, and on many shorter visits. Owns one of the largest and most varied collections of antique tapestries in the world, including the famous collection of the Barberini family, bought in 1888. Dir. Fletcher Mfg. Co., Providence, R.I., and interested in several other cos. Pres. Nat. Soc. of Fine Arts. Home: Washington, D.C. Died 1909.

FICK, Henry H., teacher; b. Luebeck, Germany, Aug. 16, 1849; s. H. F. C. and Sophie (Trost) F.; came to America, 1864; Ph.D., Ohio U., Athens, O., 1891; m. Clementine Barna, July 25, 1872. Teacher pub. schs., Cincinnati, 1870—; prin. 6th Dist. Sch., 1892-1901, asst. supt. pub. schs., 1901-03, supervisor of German, Sept. 1903—. Trustee Nat. German-Am. Teachers' Sem. Author: Pencil and Brush, 1884; The Dance of Death, 1885; Dies und Das, 1908; Neu und Alt, 1911; Hin und Her, 1913; Ich und Du, 1916; Hier und Dort, 1916; In Freud und Leid (coll. poems), 1914. Home: Cincinnati, O. Died Mar. 23, 1935.

FICKEN, H(enry) Edwards, architect; b. London, Eng.; s. Martin and Emily (Coles) F.; ed. Greenock (Scotland) Acad. and under pvt. tutors; studied art in Europe; m. Josephine Hubbard, 1881; children—Margery (Mrs. W. B. Prescott), Dorothy (Mrs. F. W. Gwynne). Came to America, 1869; practiced in N.Y. City, 1878—; supervising architect and engr., Woodlawn Cemetery, 1913—. Architect of Sigma Delta Chi Bldg., Yale; Ferguson Memorial Bldg., Stamford, Conn.; Birmingham (Conn.) Town Hall; also many bldgs. in N.Y. City and throughout the country. Awarded 1st premium, competition of jr. members, A.I.A., 1877, for pub. library design. Mem. Troop A, and Squadron A, N.G.N.Y., 15 yrs.; resigned 1st lt., 1905; rejoined Squadron A, 1916, promoted sergt. maj., 1917; commd. 1st lt. insp. gen.'s dept., Feb. 1, 1918, capt., May 14, and maj., Nov. 26, 1918. Champion (amateur) in running high jump, and 120 yd. hurdle race, 1876, 77, 78. Home: New York, N.Y. Died Jan. 16, 1929.

FICKLEN, John Rose, prof. history and polit. science, Tulane U., 1893—; b. Falmouth, Va., Dec. 14, 1858; s. J. B. and Ann E. F.; ed. Univ. of Va. Was prof. history and rhetoric, Tulane Univ., several yrs. before taking present chair. Author: "A History of Louisiana" (with Grace Elizabeth King), 1892; An Outline History of Greece, 1894; The Civil Government of Louisiana, 1901. Home: New Orleans, N.Y. Died 1907.

FIDLER, Harry L.; b. Dayton, O., July 14, 1870; s. George F. and Margaret (Robinson) F.; grad. high sch., Urbana, O.; m. Bertha M. Schram, Nov. 1912; children—Gertrude M., Frederick H. Passenger engineman, Pa. R.R., 20 yrs.; gen. sec. and treas.

Brotherhood Locomotive Engrs., Pa. Lines W. of Pittsburgh, 19 yrs., later pres. Ins. Assn., B.L.E.; became pres. Locomotive Engrs. and Conductors' Mutual Protective Assn., Detroit, Mich.; mem. Federal Bd. Vocational Edn., 1921-29; engaged in real estate and hardware business. Mem. Ind. State Bd. Edn., 1920-24; mem. Herbert Hoover's Pre-convention Campaign Com. Republican. Methodist. Mason. Home: Miami, Fla. Died Sept. 12, 1934.

FIEBEGER, Gustav Joseph, army officer; b. Akron, O., May 9, 1858; s. Joseph and Rosalie (May) F.; grad. U.S. Mil. Acad., 1879; m. Anna Perkins Upson, June 29, 1887; 1 dau., Julia Ford. Additional 2d lt. engrs., June 13, 1879; 2d lt., Oct. 31, 1879; 1st lt., June 15, 1882; capt., Feb. 22, 1891; prof. with rank of col., May 4, 1896. Officer corps engrs. U.S.A., 1879-96, and engr. in charge of improvement of rivers and harbors of Va. and N.C. and of city of Washington; prof. civ. and mil. engring., U.S. Mil. Acad., 1896-1922; retired. Author: Civil Engineering, 1905; Strategy. Awarded D.S.M. Home: Washington, D.C. Died Oct. 18, 1939.

FIELD, B(enjamin) Rush, physician; b. Easton, Pa., Nov. 3, 1861; s. Dr. C. C. and Susan (Freeman) F.; ed. pub. schs. and Lafayette Coll.; M.D., U. of Pa., 1883; m. Nan Edna Rounsavell, Apr. 9, 1902; 1 son, B. Rush. Official phys. Northampton Co., Pa., prison; 10 yrs. phys. for coronor. Mem. and pres. civic council, 1890-93, mayor Easton, 1893-96, and 1899-1902; commr. of Public Safety, 1914-20; chmn. med. board Easton Hospital; also supt. of Easton Hospital, 1926-29. Co-chmn. Civic Assn. of Northampton County; chmn. taxation com. of Easton Board of Trade. Democrat. Capt. Co. E and maj. 2d battalion 11th Pa. Vols., 1898; after Spanish-Am. War, on consolidation of 11th and 13th regts., maj. 13th regt. Pa. N.G., lt. col., 1904; retired at own request, 1908. Trustee Easton Pub. Library, 1902—; trustee, 1915, hon. v.p., 1919, League of Cities of the Third Class in Pa. Chmn. Northampton Co. mil. sect. of Pa. Com. Pub. Safety, 1917; mem. War History Commn. of Pa.; mem. County Com. Citizens' Mil. Training Camp.; mem. Internat. Kiwanis Conv., 1919. Author: Medical Thoughts of Shakespeare, 1884, 3d edit., 1905. Editor: Romeo and Juliet (Vol. 5, Bankside Edit. of Shakespeare), 1889. Home: Easton, Pa. Died May 1, 1935.

FIELD, Caroline Leslie, author; b. Milton, Mass.; d. late Seth D. and Mrs. A. D. T. Whitney (author); m. James A. Field (died 1884); lived some yrs. at Guilford, Conn.; now at Milton, Mass. Author: High-Lights (novel), 1886; The Unseen King and Other Verses, 1887; Nannie's Happy Childhood, 1899. Died 1902.

FIELD, Cortlandt de Peyster, mcht.; b. New York, Dec. 28, 1839; s. Benjamin Hazard and Catharine M. Van Cortlandt (de Peyster) F.; A.B., Columbia, 1859, A.M., 1862, followed by 2 yrs. post-grad. study. Mcht. and banker, 1861—; gave pub. library to Peekskill, N.Y., as memorial of his mother; founded and endowed, 1887, Field Home for Aged, Infirm and Respectable Poor Persons, at Fieldhome, Yorktown, N.Y.; founded St. Catharine's Ch., 1888. Home: New York, N.Y. Died Aug. 9, 1918.

FIELD, Daniel F., mem. Rep. Nat. Com.; b. Phillips, Me., July 7, 1872; s. Elias and Mary (Hamlin) F.; A.B., Bates Coll., 1894; m. Clare Hinkley, July 7, 1896 (died 1925); 1 son, Richard H. Asst. cashier Phillips Nat. Bank, 1900, pres., 1920; pres. Field Pulpwood Co., 1917—, Kennebago Bus Co., 1933—; also pres. Ed. Grant & Son Co. Chmn. Me. Rep. State Com., 1926-34; mem. Rep. Nat. Com. for Me., 1934—. Mason. Home: Phillips, Me. Died Apr. 26, 1937.

FIELD, E(dward) B(ell), telephone official; b. Chelsea, Mass., Sept. 4, 1850; s. James Barker and Eliza Ann (Bell) F.; grad. Chelsea Grade Sch., 1865; requested Rev. C. H. Leonard, pastor, Chelsea, to outline a course of reading and study, and followed same; m. Mary Alice Legge, Jan. 22, 1873 (died 1916); m. 2d, Miss Anna J. Henry, Sept. 25, 1917. Was connected with wholesale woolen business, Boston, 1865-79; removed to Colo. on account of ill health, and started there as telephone operator; apptd. mgr. operating dept. Colo. Telephone Co., 1881; successively gen. supt., 1885, v.p. and gen. mgr., 1890, pres., 1898; organized various cos. and became pres. The Mountain States Telephone & Telegraph Co. (8 states), A.D.T. Co., Tri-State Telephone Co. Mem. advisory bd. of Gov. Henry A. Buchtel, 1907. Trustee Denver U. two yrs. Pres. Denver Philharmonic Assn. Republican. Dir. and treas. Denver Chamber of Commerce, 1897; mem. Chamber Commerce U.S.A. Mason. Home: Denver, Colo. Died Feb. 21, 1919.

FIELD, Elisha C., lawyer; b. Valparaiso, Ind., Apr. 9, 1842; s. Thomas J. and Antoinette L. F.; ed. Valparaiso Coll.; LL.B., Law Dept., U. of Mich., 1865; m. Mary E. Jackman, Sept. 1, 1864. Admitted to bar, 1865; judge Circuit Ct., Ind., 1879-89; gen. solicitor Louisville, New Albany & Chicago Ry. and its successor, the Chicago, Indianapolis & Louisville Ry., 1889—; also v.p. latter; v.p. Ind. Stone R.R. Co. Home: Chicago, Ill. Died Apr. 2, 1916.

FIELD, Hamilton Easter, artist; b. Brooklyn, N. Y., Apr. 21, 1873; s. Aaron and Lydia Seaman (Haviland) F.; ed. Brooklyn Poly. Inst., Columbia U., Harvard, and École des Beaux Arts, Paris, France; studied under Raphael Collin and Fantin-Latour. Unmarried. Dir. Thurnscoe Sch., of Modern Art, Ogunquit, Me., 1911—, Ardsley Sch. of Modern Art, Brooklyn, 1916—, Ardsley Studios, Brooklyn, 1916—. Art editor Brooklyn Daily Eagle, 1919—; editor Arts and Decoration, 1919-20; editor and owner The Arts, 1920—, The Touchstone Mag. and Am. Art Student, 1921—. Macsoud gold medal, Brooklyn Soc. Artists, 1919. Home: Brooklyn, N.Y. Died Apr. 9, 1922.

FIELD, Harry Ashby, naval officer; b. Baltimore, Md., July 2, 1862; s. John Albert and Susan R. M. (Easter) F.; grad. U.S. Naval Acad., 1883; m. Julia Sewall Waters, Apr. 25, 1900. Ensign, July 1, 1885; lt. jr. grade, Apr. 23, 1895; lt., May 1, 1898; lt. comdr., Jan. 1, 1904; comdr., July 1, 1908; capt., July 1, 1911; rear adm. (temp.), July 1919. Served on the Alert, Independence and Phila., Spanish-Am. War, 1898; insp. equipment, Gen. Electric Co., Schenectady, N.Y., 1904-06; exec. officer Tennessee, 1906-08; comd. Yorktown, 1908-09; in charge 6th Light House Dist., 1910-12; comd. Tennessee, 1912-13, Louisiana, 1913-14; capt. of yard, Navy Yard, Portsmouth, N.H., 1914-15; at Naval War Coll., 1915; comd. North Dakota, 1915-16; apptd. mem. Naval Exam. and Retiring Bd., Sept. 1916; comdt. Puget Sound Navy Yard, 1918-21; comdr. train, Pacific fleet, Apr.-July 1921; pres. bd. of Inspn., Pacific coast, July 1921—. Presbyn. Home: Baltimore, Md. Died July 1, 1936.

FIELD, Henry Martyn, minister, editor, and author; b. Stockbridge, Mass., April 3, 1822; s. Rev. David Dudley F.; grad. Williams, 1838; studied theology; pastor of a Presbyn. ch., St. Louis, 1842-47; resigned to go abroad; visited Ireland in the year of the famine; spent winter in Paris and saw revolution of 1848. On return settled in West Springfield, Mass., in 1850; removed to New York, 1854, to become partner, and later sole owner and editor of The Evangelist, in which he remained 44 yrs. In 1875-76 made the circuit of the globe, which he described in 2 vols.: From the Lakes of Killarney to the Golden Horn, and from Egypt to Japan (20 editions). In 1882 went to the East, across the desert of Mt. Sinai, thence to the Holy Land and Constantinople, and described his journey in 3 books: On the Desert; Among the Holy Hills, and The Greek Islands. In 1886-87, went again to the Mediterranean, and wrote on Spain, Gibraltar and The Barbary Coast. Home: Stockbridge, Mass. Died 1907.

FIELD, Herbert Haviland, zoölogist; b. Brooklyn, Apr. 25, 1868; s. Aaron and Lydia Seaman (Haviland) F.; Poly. Inst. Brooklyn, 1882-85; A.B., Harvard, 1888, A.M., 1890, Ph.D., 1891; univs. of Frieburg, Leipzig and Paris, 1891-95; m. Nina Eschwege, of London, Eng., Apr. 25, 1903. Founder, and dir. Concilium Bibliographicum, Zürich, Switzerland, 1895—. Hon. asst., Mus. Comparative Zoölogy, Harvard, 1902—; an editor Zoölogischer Anzeiger, Leipzig, 1903—. Trustee Internationale de Bibliographie, Brussels; hon. mem. Leipzig Naturalists' Soc. Died Apr. 5, 1921.

FIELD, Isaac S., publisher; b. Baltimore, Md., Nov. 20, 1860; s. Abiathar William and Penelope Jane (Healey) F.; ed. pub. schs. and City Coll., Baltimore; m. Rose Ellen Parsons, Dec. 21, 1881 (dec.); children—A. William, Mrs. Rose Ellen Wood, Mrs. Marie Field Jones (dec.). Became v.p. Mfrs.' Record (weekly), 1882, retired; dir. and mem. exec. com. Real Estate Trust Co., Baltimore. Pres. Bd. Sch. Commrs., Baltimore, for 6 yrs.; asso. judge of The Orphans Court of Baltimore City; pres. Montrose Sch. for Girls; pres. Md. Soc. to Protect Children from Cruelty and Immorality; pres. Children's Fresh Air Soc. of Baltimore; mem. Md. com. Nat. Golden Rule Foundation. Republican. Baptist. Mason. Home: Baltimore, Md. Died May 12, 1941.

FIELD, James Alfred, economist; b. Milton, Mass., May 26, 1880; s. James Alfred and Caroline Leslie (Whitney) F.; A.B., Harvard, 1903; post-grad. work, Harvard, 1903-05, U. of Berlin, 1905-06; m. Amy Morehead Walker, Sept. 17, 1914; children—James Alfred, Charles Walker. Asst. in economics, 1903-04, Austin teaching fellow in economics, 1904-05, instr., 1906-08, Harvard; instr. in economics, Radcliffe Coll., 1906-07; instr. polit. economy, 1908-10, asst. prof., 1910-13, asso. prof., 1913-18, prof., 1918—, dean Colls. of Arts and Literature, 1923-24, U. of Chicago. Asso. editor, Jour. Polit. Economy. Spl. investigator Div. of Statistics of Council Nat. Defense, 1917; chief statistician, American Shipping Mission, Allied Maritime Transport Council, London, 1918-19. Fellow Am. Statis. Assn. Author: The Progress of Eugenics, 1911. Joint Author: Outlines of Economics, 1910; Materials for the Study of Elementary Economics, 1913. Home: Chicago, Ill. Died July 15, 1927.

FIELD, James Gaven, lawyer; b. Walnut, Va., Feb. 24, 1826; classical edn.; went to Calif., in pay-dept., U.S.A., in 1848; one of secs. Calif. Constl. Conv., 1850; returned to Va., Oct. 1850; admitted to bar, 1852; commonwealth's atty. Culpeper Co., Va., 1859-61; private to maj. C. S. A., 1861-65, on staff Gen. A. P. Hill; wounded at Cold Harbor; lost leg at Slaughter's Mountain (Cedar Creek); atty. gen. Va., 1877-82; retired to farm in Albemarle Co.; People's Party candidate for Vice President U.S., 1892; m. Miss Cowherd, 1854; m. 2d, Miss Logwood, 1882. Address: Gordonsville, Va. Died 1901.

FIELD, Marshall, merchant; b. Conway, Mass., 1835; s. John and Fidelia (Nash) F.; spent boyhood on farm; studied at acad. until 1852; dry goods clerk, Pittsfield, Mass., 1852-56; in Chicago, 1856-60; jr. partner, 1860-65, then sr. partner in house, which became, 1865, Field, Palmer & Leiter; Potter Palmer retired, 1867, and Levi Z. Leiter, 1881, Mr. Field becoming head of Marshall Field & Co., wholesale and retail dry goods business. Founded, with gift of $1,000,000, the Field Columbian Museum of Chicago; gave money and land to the amount of $450,000 to U. of Chicago. Twice married; 2d, London, Sept. 5, 1905, Mrs. Delia Spencer Caton. Home: Chicago, Ill. Died 1906.

FIELD, Neill Brooks, lawyer; b. Louisville, Ky., Feb. 6, 1854; s. Charles Withers and Rebecca (Greenfield) F.; pub. schs. and Forest Acad., Louisville; studied law while in office of clerk of Circuit Ct. of Jefferson Co., Ky.; admitted to Ky. bar, 1874; m. Mary Agnes Lester, June 16, 1886. Went to N.M., 1882; conducted foreclosure and reorganization proceedings in N.M., Ariz. and Calif. for bondholders of A.&P. R.R. Co., 1893-96; also rebate case of Caledonian Coal Co. vs. A.,T.&S.F. R.R. Co. and Colo. Fuel & Iron Co.; retired, 1927. Democrat. Mayor of Albuquerque, 1893-94. Home: Albuquerque, N.M. Died Oct. 28, 1932.

FIELD, Roswell Martin, author; b. St. Louis, Sept. 1, 1851; s. Roswell Martin and Frances (Reed) F.; ed. Phillips Exeter Acad., class of 1869; grad. U. of Mo.; m. Henrietta Dexter, Oct. 28, 1885. Employed in journalistic work in San Francisco, St. Louis, Kansas City, New York and Chicago. Author: The Bondage of Ballinger, 1903; Little Miss Dee, 1904; Madeline, 1906, etc. Home: Morristown, N.J. Died Jan. 10, 1919.

FIELD, Stephen Dudley, inventor; b. Stockbridge, Mass., Jan. 31, 1846; s. Jonathan Edwards and Mary Ann (Stuart) F.; nephew of late Cyrus W. F. and David Dudley F.; ed. Williams Acad. and Reid Hoffman's Sch., Stockbridge, and Dutchess Co. Acad., Poughkeepsie, N.Y.; m. Celestine Butters, Sept. 30, 1871. Invented multiple call dist. telegraph box, 1874, electric elevator, 1878; pioneer of modern trolley ry., 1878-79; made 1st application of dynamo machines to telegraphy, 1879; invented dynamo quadruplex telegraph, 1880, fast stock ticker, 1884; made 1st application of quadruplex telegraph on ocean cable (Key West to Havana), 1909. Home: Stockbridge, Mass. Died May 18, 1913.

FIELD, Theron Rockwell, banker; b. Southwick, Mass., June 27, 1869; s. Heman and Martha (Rockwell) F.; Ph.B., Yale, 1889; m. Amelia Rausch, Dec. 9, 1895; 1 dau., Mary Rockwell (dec.). With Colo. Nat. Bank, Denver, 1890—, cashier, 1919-31, v.p., 1931-39, chmn. of the bd., 1939—. Mem. Yale Advisory Bd., 1923—; mem. Yale Scholarship Com. for Colo.; v.p., Colo. Hist. Soc. Republican. Episcopalian (jr. warden St. John's Episcopal Cathedral, 1922—). Home: Denver, Colo. Died July 22, 1940.

FIELD, Walbridge Abner, chief justice supreme judicial court, Mass., 1890—; b. Springfield, Vt., April 26, 1833; grad. Dartmouth Coll., 1855 (LL.D., 1888; also, Harvard, 1886); admitted to bar, Boston, 1860; asst. U.S. atty. for Mass., 1865-69; Asst. Atty. Gen. U.S., 1869-70; member Congress, 1879-81; asso. justice supreme judicial court, 1881-90. Republican. Home: Boston, Mass. Died 1899.

FIELD, Walter Taylor, author; b. Galesburg, Ill., Feb. 21, 1861; s. Horatio Nelson and Charity Lamoreux (Taylor) F.; prep. edn., Denmark (Ia.) Acad., 1876-78; student Dartmouth, 1879-81; A.B., Amherst, 1883, hon. A.M., 1918; m. Sara Lounsberry Peck, Dec. 6, 1892; children—Walter Donald (dec.), Ruth Alden (dec.), John Stanley. Editorial dept. S. C. Griggs & Co., pubs., Chicago, 1883-86; asso. editor The Advance, Chicago, 1886-87; connected with Harper & Bros., pubs., 1887-90; studied and traveled in Italy, 1890; with Chicago house of Ginn & Co., pubs., 1890—; treas. Soc. Midland Authors, 1919-23; mem. Authors' League America. Author: Children's Books—Their Selection and Their Influence, 1901; Rome (2 vols.), 1904; What Is Success?, 1910; The Quest of the Four-leaved Clover, 1911; (with Mrs. Ella Flagg Young) Young and Field Literary Readers, 1914-15. Editor of The Abbey Classics, 1907-10; Readings from English and American Literature, 1919; The Field Readers, 1920-25; (with Katherine Martin) The Field-Martin Primer, 1925; (with Cornelius H. Patton) Eight O'Clock Chapel—a Study of New England College Life in the Eighties, 1927; A Guide to Literature for Children, 1928; Finding the New World, 1935; Psalms of the Modern Life, 1937. Home: Hinsdale, Ill. Died Aug. 18, 1939.

FIELD, Wells Laflin, rear-admiral U.S.N.; b. St. Louis, Jan. 31, 1846; s. Matthew D. and Clarissa (Laflin) F.; grad. U.S. Naval Acad., 1867; m. Ruth Dunning Clark, Nov. 8, 1894. Promoted ensign, 1868; master, 1870; lt., 1871; lt. comdr., 1892; comdr., Apr. 1898; capt., June 16, 1902; rear admiral and retired, Nov. 20, 1902, after 40 yrs'. service in varied sea and shore duties. Died Nov. 27, 1914.

FIELD, William Henry, newspaper mgr.; b. Rutland, Vt., Apr. 18, 1877; s. Henry Francis and Annie Louisa (Howe) F.; B.A., Yale, 1899; m. Ethel Scovil Clement, Sept. 8, 1903 (died July 28, 1932); children—Lindsay Clement, Elizabeth Clement, William. With Frank A. Munsey Co., New York, until 1909; 2d v.p. and business mgr. The Tribune Co. (pubs. Chicago Tribune), until 1919; gen. eastern rep. of Chicago Tribune, and a founder New York Daily News, 1919-27; owner Rutland (Vt.) Herald, 1927—. Republican. Conglist. Home: Rutland, Vt. Died Mar. 15, 1935.

FIELD, William Hildreth, lawyer; b. New York, Apr. 16, 1843; grad. Union, 1863; Columbia Law School, 1865; entered practice at New York. Edited (with late Judge John W. Edmonds) Statutes at Large of the State of New York. Past pres. Catholic Club, New York. Died 1900.

FIELDE, Adele Marion, author; b. E. Rodman, N.Y., Mar. 30, 1839; d. Leighton and Sophia (Tiffany) F.; grad. Albany Normal Coll., 1860; unmarried. Missionary in Siam and China, 1865-90; lecturer at League for Polit. Edn., New York, 1894-1907; traveling, 1907—; toured Alaska and Yukon Ty., 1908, Arizona, 1911-12; has toured the world 3 times. Lecturer Marine Biol. Lab., Woods Hole, Mass., 1901-07. Author: Chinese Fairy Tales, 1912; A Corner of Cathay, 1894; Parliamentary Procedure, 1898; Political Primer for New York City and State, 1900; also several books in Chinese, pub. 1873-89, by Bapt. Mission, China. Home: Seattle, Wash. Died Feb. 3, 1916.

FIELDER, William, educator, clergyman; b. Northiam, Sussex, Eng., Oct. 13, 1852; s. Isaac and Susan A. F.; ed. pub. and pvt. schs., Eng.; D.D., Dak. Wesleyan, 1900; married; children—Charles W., Susan A., Marguerite B., Bertha Elizabeth. Came to U.S., 1876; ordained M.E. ministry, 1879; pastor Sioux Falls, S.D., 1876-79, Central City, Black Hills, 1879-81, Watertown, S.D., 1881-83; presiding elder S.D., 1883-89; pres. S.D. Prohibition Alliance, 1889-92, and author of state prohibitory law passed 1889; pastor Brookings, S.D., 1892-94, First Ch., Minneapolis, 1894-99; presiding elder Minneapolis, 1899-1905; pres. Ft. Worth (Tex.) U., 1905-11; actg. chancellor Meth. U., Guthrie Okla., 1911-14; pres. John H. Snead Sem., Boaz, Ala., 1914-31. Pres. Minn. Anti-Saloon League, 1897-1900; chmn. bd. Florence Crittendon Home, Minneapolis, 1898-1901, one of founders and pres. Ministers' Casualty Union; one of founders Dak. Wesleyan U. Home: Birmingham, Ala. Died Oct. 31, 1936.

FIELDING, Mantle, architect; b. N.Y. City, Sept. 20, 1865; s. Mantle and Anna M. (Stone) F.; grad. Germantown Acad., 1883; student Boston Sch. of Tech. 1 yr.; m. Amy Reeve Williams, 1898; children—Richard M., Frances. Practiced at Phila., 1889—; architect of Page Memorial Chapel, Oswego, N.Y.; Terry Office Building, Roanoke, Va.; also many residences. Republican. Episcopalian. Author: Life and Works of Thomas Sully (with Edward Biddle), 1922; Gilbert Stuart and His Portraits of Washington, 1923; Dictionary of American Painters, Sculptors and Engravers; Life Portraits of George Washington and their Replicas by Mantle Fielding (with John Hill Morgan). Home: Chestnut Hill, Philadelphia, Pa. Died Mar. 27, 1941.

FIELDS, John, farmer; b. nr. Davenport, Ia., July 29, 1871; s. David T. and Sara (Mosser) F.; B.S., Pa. State Coll., 1891; m. Caro Chamberlain Emerson, July 14, 1900. Asst. chemist, Pa. Agrl. Expt. Sta., 1891, tech. expert, New York, 1895; asst. chemist, 1896-97, asso. chemist, 1898-99, dir. and chemist, 1899-1906, Okla. Agrl. Expt. Sta.; asso. prof. chemistry, Okla. Agrl. and Mech. Coll., 1898-99; business agt. same, 1900-06. Editor Oklahoma Farmer, 1902-24; v.p. Farmers Nat. Bank, 1924-26; v.p. The Federal Land Bank and Federal Intermediate Credit Bank, both of Wichita, 1926-28, pres., 1929-33; v.p. and dir. Union Nat. Bank of Wichita, 1934—; pres. Times Co., pubs. Okla. (daily) Times, 1915, Okla. State Fair, 1909-12. Rep. candidate for gov., 1914; Rep. candidate for gov., 1922. Home: Wichita, Kan. Died Apr. 17, 1934.

FIELDS, Lew (Lewis Maurice Fields), actor; b. New York, Jan. 1, 1867; s. Samuel and Sarah F.; ed. Allen pub. sch., New York; m. Rose Harris. Began stage career, 1877, with Joseph Weber, in juvenile Dutch sketches; assisted in organizing Weber & Fields Co., 1885, proprs. Broadway Music Hall, 1895; became mem. Hamlin, Mitchell & Fields, 1904; opened Lew Fields' Theatre, New York, Dec. 5, 1904; acquired Herald Sq. Theatre, 1906; toured with Joseph Weber, 1914. Produced musical comedy "Zuzi," 1915, Bosom Friends, 1916. Died July 20, 1941.

FIERO, J(ames) Newton, lawyer; b. Saugerties, N.Y., May 23, 1847; s. Col. Christopher and Margaret (Backer) F.; A.B., Union Coll., 1867 (LL.D., 1899); read law in office of Judge William Murray, Delhi, N.Y.; m. Jeanette S. McCall, Apr. 28, 1870. Admitted to bar, 1869; dean Albany Law Sch., 1895-1924; mem. Constl. Commn., N.Y., 1890; state reporter, Jan. 1909—. Author: Special Actions, 1897, 1908, 12; Special Proceedings, 1899, 1911; Torts, 1903. Home: Albany, N.Y. Died Apr. 13, 1931.

FIFE, George Buchanan, editor; b. Charlestown, Mass., Aug. 9, 1869; s. late Dr. George Storrs (U.S.N.) and Letitia McKean (Buchanan) F.; midshipman U.S. Naval Acad., 1885-86; Lehigh U., 1887-88; m. Elizabeth, dau. Hon. William H. Welsh, of Baltimore and Washington, Apr. 21, 1898 (died June 24, 1909); m. 2d, Viola, dau. of late Carl E. Vetter, of New York, Sept. 26, 1916; m. 3d, Judith, dau. of late Thomas F. Delaney, of New York, June 23, 1931. On editorial staff New York Sun, 1893-94; asst. city editor New York Mail and Express, 1895-96; on editorial staff New York Evening Journal, 1896-1901, New York Evening Post, 1901-05; mng. editor Harper's Weekly, 1906-11; mem. of editorial party visiting Mexico as guests of President Diaz, 1910; lit. editor New York Times, 1911; editorial staff New York Evening World, 1912-17; traveling corr. Am. Red Cross in England, France, Italy, 1917-19; special aide to military attaché U.S. Legation, Berne, Switzerland, for six months preceding World War Armistice; returned to editorial staff Evening World, 1920, remaining until its sale in 1931. Author: The Passing Legions, 1920; Lindbergh, The Lone Eagle, 1927; Ask Your Wife (play), 1929. Home: New York, N.Y. Died Mar. 12, 1939.

FIFER, Joseph Wilson, governor; b. Staunton, Va., Oct. 28, 1840; s. John and Mary F.; ed. dist. schs., McLean Co., Ill.; pvt. 33d Ill. Vol. Inf., 1861-64; participated in Vicksburg campaign, 1863; wounded in battle, Jackson, Miss., July 13, 1863; B.S., Ill. Wesleyan U., 1868 (LL.D., 1892); m. Gertrude Lewis, June 15, 1870; children—Herman W., Mrs. Florence Bohrer. Admitted to bar, 1869, and began practice at Bloomington. Corp. counsel, Bloomington, 1871; state's atty., McLean Co., 1872-79; mem. Ill. Senate, 1880-84; gov. of Ill., 1889-93; candidate for reëlection, 1892; candidate for vice-presdl. nomination before Rep. Nat. Conv., 1896; mem. Interstate Commerce Commn., 1899-1906. Republican. Home: Bloomington, Ill. Died Aug. 6, 1938.

FIFIELD, Benjamin F., lawyer; b. Orange, Vt., Nov. 18, 1832; s. Orange and Melissa N. F.; A.B., U. of Vt., 1855, later A.M. (LL.D., 1906); m. Lucy Hubbard, Jan. 1865. Admitted to bar, 1858; gen. counsel Central Vt. R.R., many years; U.S. atty. for Vt., 1869-80; mem. Vt. Ho. of Rep., 1880; commr. to Chicago Expn., from Vt., 1893; del. Rep. Nat. Conv., 1884; declined appmt. to U.S. Senate to fill vacancy caused by death of Senator Morrill, 1899 (retired). Home: Montpelier, Vt. Died July 23, 1911.

FIFIELD, Lawrence Wendell, clergyman; b. Berrien Springs, Mich., June 10, 1891; s. James William and Mary Irene (Stoddard) F.; A.B., Oberlin (O.) Coll., 1913; B.D., Chicago Theol. Sem., 1916; D.D., Yankton (S.D.) Coll., 1925; m. Juanita Elizabeth Sloan, July 15, 1914; children—William Leroy, Robert Edwin. Prof. Bible and pub. speaking, Yankton Coll., 1916-18; pastor First Congl. Ch., Sioux Falls, S.D., 1917-27, Plymouth Congl. Ch., Seattle, Wash., 1927—. Pres. Wash. State Conf. Congl. Ch. Mason. Author: How to Use the Bible, 1920. Home: Seattle, Wash. Died Mar. 10, 1935.

FIFIELD, Samuel Stillman, postmaster; b. Corinna, Me., June 24, 1839; s. Samuel Stillman and Naoma (Pease) F.; ed. grammar schs. and in printing office; m. Stella Grimes, Sept. 24, 1862. Went to Wis., 1854; pub. and editor Polk Co. Press, Osceola, Wis., 1861-70; established Bayfield Co. (Wis.) Press, 1870, Ashland (Wis.) Press, 1872, Daily Press, 1882; retired 1889. Mem. Wis. Assembly, 1874, 75, 76 (speaker, 1876), Senate, 1877, 80, 81; lt. gov. Wis., 1882-87; postmaster, Ashland, Wis., 1889—. Republican. Pres. Vaughn Pub. Library, Ashland. Presbyn. Mason (33°, Past Master, Past Comdr., etc.), Elk. Home: Ashland, Wis. Died Feb. 17, 1915.

FIGUERAS CHIQUÉS, José Maria, jurist; b. San Juan, P.R., Jan. 30, 1851; s. Santiago Figueras and Catalina Chiqués; ed. Jesuit Coll., P.R., and Inst. of Pontevedra, Galicia, Spain; grad. U. of Santiago de Galicia, Spain; before going to Spain served in head office of the Pub. Treasury, San Juan, P.R.; licentiate civil and canonical law, Madrid, Aug. 1, 1879; m. Gloria Suro y Navedo, May 16, 1887. Practiced law, San Juan, 1879-92; sec. Audencia Territorial, 1892-94; asst. pros. atty. Audencia Territorial, Santiago de Cuba, 1894-95; judge of 1st Instance, Mayaguez, 1895-97; asst. pros. atty. Audencia de Havana, May-June 1897; judge Audencia de lo Criminal, Mayaguez, 1897-98; apptd. pros. atty., Audencia Mayaguez, by Maj.-Gen. James H. Wilson; justice, Supreme Ct. of Justice, P.R., under mil. appmt., Nov. 1897, to Aug. 1898; asso. justice under provisional govt., 1898, 1900; under presdl. appmt., June 1900—. Home: San Juan, P.R. Died 1910.

FILBERT, Ludwig S., pres. Vulcanite Paving Co.; b. Berks Co., Pa., March 12, 1825; academic edn.; grad. Pa. Med. Coll., Phila., 1848; m. Annie C. Nagle, Dec. 21, 1848. Practiced medicine 18 yrs.; quarantine physician for port of Phila., 1858-61; gave up med. practice, 1870; organized, 1871, and became pres. Vulcanite Paving Co. Home: Philadelphia, Pa. Died 1903.

FILENE, Edward A., merchant; pres., chmn. finance com. Wm. Filene's Sons Co.; b. Salem, Mass.; s. William and Clara (Ballin) F.; pub. and high sch. edn.; LL.D., Lehigh U., 1931, Rollins Coll., 1932, Tulane U., 1935; planner and co-organizer Boston Chamber of Commerce, Chamber of Commerce of U.S. and Internat. Chamber of Commerce; pioneer in applying scientific methods and efficient organization in retail distribution; active in promotion of better organization of prodn. and distbn. in U.S. and Europe, "in order to lower costs, eliminate waste, increase wages and profits and raise the general standard of living"; founder and pres. Twentieth Century Fund, organized to study and advance the next steps forward in the social and economic life of the people; organizer of credit union movement in U.S., 1909; founder Credit Union Nat. Extension Bur., 1921, directing organization of coöperative credit assns. throughout U.S.; first pres. Credit Union Nat. Assn., 1934; founder and pres. Consumer Distribution Corp., the central orgn. for a nat. league of coöperative dept. stores, 1935; v.p. Am. Assn. for Labor Legislation; chmn. Met. Planning Commn. of Boston; coörganizer and pres. Pub. Franchise League of Boston; chmn. Mass. State Recovery Bd., 1933-34; was chmn. War Shipping Com. and mem. U.S. Chamber of Commerce Com. for Financing War; served as vice-chmn. exec. com. and chmn. finance com. League to Enforce Peace; organized and financed European Peace awards in Gt. Britain, France, Germany and Italy. Officer Legion of Honor (France); le Cavaliere, Order of the Crown (Italy); Comdr. Order of the White Lion (Czechoslovakia); Great Gold Cross of Merit (Austria). Author: The Way Out, 1924; More Profits from Merchandising, 1925; The Model Stock Plan, 1930 (all in Am. and foreign edits.); Successful Living in this Machine Age, 1931 (Am. and fgn. edits.). Died Sept. 26, 1937.

FILER, Herbert Augustus; b. Gaines, N.Y., June 7, 1870; s. Alexander D. and Ruth (Ennis) F.; ed. common and high schs.; read law 3 yrs.; m. Anna M. Springer, Oct. 18, 1892; 1 dau., Laura Marie (Mrs. William R. Langdon). Law clk., North Tonawanda, N.Y., 1890-93; sales mgr. D. M. Osborne & Co., Chicago, 1894-98; apptd. clk. U.S. Civil Commn., Washington, D.C., 1898, and promoted through grades until apptd. chief examiner by President Wilson, May 25, 1920. Pres. Kensington Home School and Community Assn. Republican. Presbyn. Mason; pres. Kensington Masonic Temple Assn. Home: Kensington, Md. Died Feb. 10, 1927.

FILLEBROWN, Charles Bowdoin, single-tax propagandist; b. Winthrop, Me., Dec. 26, 1842; s. James Bowdoin and Almira (Butler) F.; ed. Kent's Hill, Me., 1858-61; Phillips Acad., Exeter, N.H., 1862; Mass. Inst. Tech., 1866-67; m. Mary Louise Hall, Oct. 9, 1873 (died 1887). In Union Army, 1862-66; in 24th Me. Inf., 9 months; 29th Me. Inf., 3 yrs.; a.-d.-c., 1st brigade, 1st div., 19th Army Corps; brigade staff Bank's 2d Red River Expdn.; div. staff Sheridan's Shenandoah Valley campaign. Pres. and gen. mgr. Glenark Knitting Co., Woonsocket, R.I., 1881-1903. Treas. Mass. Single Tax League, 1892, pres., 1899-1909; active as single tax propagandist from 1895. Died Dec. 1917.

FILLER, Mervin Grant, educator; b. Boiling Springs, Pa., Oct. 9, 1873; s. Peter Paul and Elizabeth (Shuh) F.; A.B., Dickinson Coll., 1893, A.M., 1895; post-grad. work univs. of Chicago and Pa.; Litt.D., Neb. Wesleyan U., 1915; LL.D., Ohio Wesleyan U. and Bucknell U., 1929; m. Mildred E. Beitzell, June 12, 1895; children—Donald Beitzell, Mildred Clare, Mary Elizabeth. Prof. Latin, Dickinson Coll., 1899-1914, dean, 1914-28, pres., 1928—. Chautauqua work, 1900-12 (chancellor Pa. Chautauqua, 1908-12); in charge dept. of Latin, U. of Pa. Summer Sch., 1916. Asso. sec. War Personnel Bd. of Internat. Y.M.C.A., Washington, 1917-18. Methodist. Mason. Home: Carlisle, Pa. Died Mar. 28, 1931.

FILLEY, Chauncey Ives; b. Lansingburg, N.Y., Oct. 17, 1829; s. Augustus and Amelia (Filley) F.; pvt. sch. and acad. edn.; tendered appmt. to U.S. Mil. Acad. (declined); arrived at St. Louis, Sept. 16, 1850; m. Anna E. Adams, June 28, 1855 (died 1896). Entered commercial career as clerk; co-partner, 1855; visited Staffordshire (Eng.) potteries, 1858, and designed and controlled own patterns, becoming largest importer and distributor of queensware in Miss. Valley. Rep. nominee for mayor of St. Louis, 1863 (declination refused), and elected for term of 2 yrs.; proposed and secured an act providing for bonds and city ownership of St. Louis Gas Co.; proposed and secured an act for construction, bonds, and bd. of commrs., eventuating in present water system of St. Louis; mem. State Constl. Conv. which (1865) abolished slavery in Mo., and revised state constn.; drafted bill, 1868, making St. Louis direct port of entry, act approved July 14, 1870; pres. Miss. Valley Commercial and Deep Waterway Conv., New Orleans, 1869; postmaster of St. Louis, 1873-78; secured, 1874, div. of 16 states and tys., 4th div. Ry. Mail Service, creation new 7th div. at St. Louis, resulting in local and gateway record dispatch of mail matter; managed city, congressional and state campaign, 1894, resulting in election of the entire Republican state ticket, 12 out of 15 congressmen, and secured Filley Election Law for "honest elections." Presdl. elector, 1868, and thereafter del. to every Rep. nat. and state conv. up to and including 1896; one of the "306"; originated slogan "Stand up for Missouri"; mem. Rep. Nat. Com., 1876-92; twice declined Garfield's tender of Berlin mission, 1881, and portfolio of postmaster-gen. in President McKinley's cabinet. Was mem. and promoter of Merchants' Exchange reorganization, St. Louis, 1862; pres. St. Louis Bd. Trade, 1876-79; charter mem. Mo. Hist. Soc., 1864. Was the originator, promoter and securer, 1897-98, of the 50-yr. charter of the Good Govt. Rep. League Club. Home: St. Louis, Mo. Died Sept. 24, 1923.

FINCH, Francis Miles, lawyer; b. Ithaca, N.Y., June 9, 1827; s. Miles Finch; prep. edn. at Ithaca Acad.; grad. Yale, 1849 (LL.D., Hamilton, 1880, Yale, 1889); studied law at Ithaca; m. Elizabeth A. Brooke, May 25, 1853 (died 1892). Internal revenue collector, 26th dist., N.Y., 1869; hon. mem. Army of Potomac, 1879; asso. judge, N.Y. Court of Appeals, 1880-96; dir. and dean Cornell Coll. of Law, 1896. Republican. Wrote: Nathan Hale, The Blue and the Gray, etc. Home: Ithaca, N.Y. Died 1907.

FINCH, John Aylard, mine operator; b. Cambridgeshire, Eng., May 12, 1854; s. William and Sophia (Aylard) F.; was brought to America, 1856; ed. pub. schs., Cleveland; m. Charlotte R. Swingler, Sept. 3, 1896. In iron business at Cleveland, 1874-80; in iron mills, Youngstown, O., 1880-81; engaged in mining at Leadville, Colo., 1881-82; iron business, Chicago, 1883-87; removed to Coeur d'Alene dist., Idaho, 1887, and became mgr. Milwaukee Mining Co., Standard Mining Co., Hecla Mining Co.; now pres. and part owner Standard Lead Silver Mining Co., of British Columbia; pres. Blalock Fruit Co., Walla Walla, Coeur d'Alene Hardware Co., Nat. Lumber & Box Co. of Washington, etc. Mem. Bd. Overseers Whitman Coll.; mem. Senate, 1st session, Ida., 1891, 1892. Republican. Episcopalian. Home: Spokane, Wash. Died June 20, 1915.

FINCH, William Albert, univ. prof.; b. Newark, N.J., June 8, 1855; s. Gold A. and Anna Mary (Woodruff) F.; A.B., Cornell U., 1880; unmarried. Admitted to bar, 1880, and practiced at Ithaca, N.Y., 1880-91; prof. law, Cornell, 1891—. Editor Finch's Selected Cases on the Law of Property in Land, 2d edit.; The Law of Property in Land—A Syllabus, 1900. Home: Ithaca, N.Y. Died Mar. 31, 1912.

FINCH, William Rufus, newspaperman; b. Walworth Co., Wis., Dec. 14, 1847; s. John Reynolds and Lydia Ann (Rogers) F.; pub. sch. edn.; m. Lillie M. Law, Nov. 2, 1897. Editor and pub. La Crosse Republican and Leader. E.E. and M.P. to Paraguay and Uruguay, 1897-1905. Republican. Home: La Crosse, Wis. Died Aug. 9, 1913.

FINCK, Henry Theophilus, author; b. Bethel, Mo., Sept. 22, 1854; s. Henry C. and Beatrice (Fink) F., of Würtemberg, Germany; A.B., Harvard, 1876; resident grad., Cambridge, 1877-78, studying sociology; received Harris fellowship and studied psychology at Berlin, Heidelberg, Vienna, 1878-81; m. Abbie Helen Cushman, 1890. Musical critic and gen. editorial writer, New York Evening Post, 1881-1923. As musical critic, special champion of Wagner, Chopin, Liszt, Grieg, MacDowell. Originator of theory that romantic love is a modern sentiment unknown to savages and the ancient civilized nations. Author: Pacific Coast Scenic Tours, 1890; Spain and Morocco, 1891; Lotos Time in Japan, 1898; Songs and Song Writers, 1900; Fifty Mastersongs, 1902; Success in Music and How It Is Won, 1909; Food and Flavor, 1913; Gardening with Brains, 1922; Girth Control, 1923; Musical Progress, 1923; Musical Laughs, 1924. Home: Bethel, Me. Died Oct. 1, 1926.

FINCKEL, Martin Luther, capitalist; b. Germantown, Pa., Dec. 4, 1842; s. Samuel De Vin and Harriet (Keller) F.; ed. private schs., Washington, D.C.; m. Mary L. Royal, May 16, 1865 (died 1914). Mfr. of hosiery and knit goods, title of Conyers, Button & Co., Germantown, 33 yrs., retiring 1900; pres. Ivy Hill Cemetery Co. Was connected with Union Army in various capacities during Civil War. Past pres. Am. S.S. Union. Republican. Lutheran. Home: Germantown, Pa. Died Aug. 25, 1926.

FINDLAY, John Van Lear, lawyer; b. nr. Williamsport, Md., Dec. 21, 1839; grad. Princeton, 1858; established law practice at Baltimore; mem. Congress, 1883-87. Republican. Third arbitrator U.S. and Venezuela Commn., 1890. Well known as an orator. Home: Baltimore, Md. Died 1907.

FINDLEY, Alvin Irwin, editor; b. Monmouth, Ill., June 29, 1859; s. Samuel and Mary Ann (Hardie) F.; Buchtel Coll., Akron, O., 1875-77; B.A., Wooster, 1881, M.A., 1886; m. Belle Holloway, May 28, 1884. City editor Akron Daily Beacon, 1877-79; staff Chicago Interior, 1881, Phila. Press, 1882; editor Akron Daily Beacon, 1883-90; spl. corr., Akron, 1890-92; editor Iron Trade Rev., Cleveland, and v.p. Iron Trade Rev. Co., 1892-1905; editor Iron Age, 1905-10, editor-in-chief, 1910-30, emeritus; dir. Iron Age Pub. Co.; v.p. Montclair Nat. Bank, 1922-24, and dir. 1922-35. Vice-pres. Am. Foundrymen's Assn., 1902-03; trustee Biblical Sem. in N.Y., 1907-35; v.p. Nat. Fgn. Trade Conv., 1920. Home: Montclair, N.J. Died Dec. 12, 1940.

FINE, Henry Burchard, univ. dean; b. Chambersburg, Pa., Sept. 14, 1858; s. Lambert Suydam and Mary Ely (Burchard) F.; A.B., Princeton, 1880, A.M., 1883; Ph.D., U. of Leipzig, 1885; LL.D., Williams, 1909; m. Philena Fobes, Sept. 6, 1888; children—John (dec.), Susan Breese Packard (dec.), Philena Fobes (Mrs. Bradford B. Locke). Tutor, 1881-84, asst. prof., 1885-90, Dod prof. mathematics, 1891—, dean faculty, 1903-12, dean dept. science, 1911—, Princeton U. Author: The Number System of Algebra, 1891; A College Algebra, 1905; Coördinate Geometry (with Henry Dallas Thompson), 1909; Calculus, 1927. Home: Princeton, N.J. Died Dec. 22, 1928.

FINEGAN, James Emmet, lawyer; b. Chico, Calif., Nov. 21, 1876; s. Patrick and Anna Rose (McCoy) F.; Ph.B., Phi Beta Kappa Union Coll., 1902; M.A., Columbia Univ., 1904, LL.B., 1905; hon. fellow in govt., Union College, Aug. 1934; L.H.D., from Union Coll., 1937; m. Lena Merle Barton, Sept. 18, 1906; children—James Emmet, Edward Scott, Thomas Patrick, Laura Elizabeth. Admitted to N.Y. bar, 1904, began practice at New York; instr. Fordham U. Sch. of Social Service, 1918-23; anti-Tammany candidate for comptroller N.Y. City on fusion Republican and citizens tickets, 1925; has been active in politics opposing machine bosses; pres. Municipal Civ. Service Commn., N.Y. City, 1934—. Served as State Dept., K.C., collecting over $1,000,000, World War. Chmn. Gov's. Com. Eastern Dist., Brooklyn, on Inventory of Wealth and Property, 1915-16; Borough of Brooklyn Commr. Boy Scouts of America, 1925—. Awarded Silver Beaver by Boy Scouts of America, 1932; medal for distinguished alumni service to Columbia, 1933. Democrat. Catholic. K.C. Author: Tammany at Bay. Home: Brooklyn, N.Y. Died Feb. 10, 1940.

FINEGAN, Thomas Edward, educator; b. W. Fulton, N.Y., Sept. 28, 1866; s. Michael and Ann (Welch) F.; grad. State Coll. for Teachers, Albany, N.Y., 1889; admitted to N.Y. bar, 1894; M.A., Hamilton Coll., 1894, LL.D., 1917; Pd.D., State Coll. for Teachers, 1909; LL.D., Colgate, 1912, U. of Me., 1918, Temple U., Grove City Coll., Dartmouth, 1921; Litt.D., U. of Pa., 1920; L.H.D. from Susquehanna U., 1922; m. Grace E. Browne, Dec. 10, 1894; 1 son, Edmund Randolph. Teacher in pub. schs. of N.Y., 6 yrs.; prin. pub. schs., W. Fulton, 1889-90; sch. commr. Schoharie Co., N.Y., 1891-92; supervisor of exams. N.Y. State Dept. Pub. Instrn., 1892-1904; chief of law div., N.Y. State Edn. Dept., 1904-08; asst. commr. for elementary edn., N.Y., Oct. 1, 1908-Apr. 1915; dep. commr. of edn., N.Y., Apr. 1, 1915-June 1, 1919; state supt. pub. instrn., for Pa., 1919-23; reorganized state dept. edn., also state school system; declined reappointment; dir. surveys sch. systems of Buffalo, 1917, Phila., 1922, Washington, D.C., the latter on request coms. of U.S. Senate and House, report submitted to Senate, 1923; chmn. com. surveying schs. of Pittsburgh, 1927; mem. Nat. Ednl. Finance Inquiry, 1921-23, President's Advisory Com. on Edn., 1929-31; mem. and v.p. Nat. Com. on Edn. and Business, 1931. Education dir. Eastman Kodak Co., directing exptl. program in developing motion pictures for regular work of class room in pub. schs., 1927-28; pres. Eastman Teaching Films, Inc. Democrat. Presbyn. Author: Text-Book on New York School Law, Judicial Decisions in Education; Teacher Training Agencies; Free Schools; The Township System. Home: Rochester, N.Y. Died Nov. 25, 1932.

FINERTY, John Frederick, editor The Chicago Citizen, 1882—; b. Galway, Ireland, Sept. 10, 1846; ed. national schools in Ireland, 1863, followed by academic studies with private tutors. Came to U.S., 1864; served in Union army; m. Sadie I. Hennessy, 1882. Reporter, 1868-71, city editor, 1871-72, Chicago Republican; reporter Chicago Tribune, 1872-75; war corr. (for Indian wars), Chicago Times, 1876-82; mem. Congress from Chicago, 1883-85, as Independent; advocated increase of navy and fortification. Supported Blaine in 1884; since up to 1900 Republican. Pres. (7 times) United Irish Socs. of Chicago; pres. United Irish League of Am. 3 terms. Supported Bryan on anti-imperialistic issue, 1900. Author: Warpath and Bivouac, 1890. Wrote: The People's History of Ireland, 1904. Home: Chicago, Ill. Died 1908.

FINGER, Charles Joseph, writer, editor; b. Willesden, Eng., Dec. 25, 1869; s. Charles H. and Julia (Connolly) F.; ed. private school; D.Litt., Knox College, 1921; LL.D., University of Arkansas, 1931; m. Nellie B. Ferguson, June 7, 1902; children—Hubert Philip, Julia Louise, Charles J., Helen Grace, Herbert Eric. Came to U.S., 1887; traveled in S. America and Africa; served before the mast; guide to ornithol. expdn. in Tierra del Fuego; on the Klondike gold fields, 1905, also in Mexico; dir. Conservatory of Music, San Angelo, Tex., 1903-06; gen. mgr. group of rys. in Ohio, 1906-20; receiver for several railroads; editor Reedy's Mirror, 1919; editor and propr. All's Well (mag.), 1920—. Author: In Lawless Lands, 1923; Highwaymen, 1923; Bushrangers, 1924; Tales from Silver Lands, 1924-25; Spreading Stain (a romance), 1927; Life of David Livingstone, 1927; Frontier Ballads, 1927; Tales Worth Telling, 1927; Romantic Rascals, 1927; A Man for a' That, 1929; Courageous Companions, 1929; Adventures Under Sapphire Skies, 1930; Paul Bunyan Geography, 1931; Foot Loose in the West, 1931; Magic Tower, 1933; After the Great Companions, 1934; A Dog at His Heel, 1935; Our Navy—Boys' History of the U.S. Navy, 1935; Guns Thundered at Tripoli, 1937; Give a Man a Horse, 1937; Bobbie and Jock and the Mailman, 1938; Cape Horn Snorter, 1939; Golden Tales from Far and Near, 1939; Fighting for Fur, 1940. Winner of Newbury medal for most distinguished contribution to juvenile lit. and Longmans Green & Co. prize for best adventure story, 1929. Mng. editor for Bellows-Reeve Co. Home: Fayetteville, Ark. Died Jan. 8, 1941.

FINK, Bruce, botanist; b. Blackberry, Ill., Dec. 22, 1861; s. Reuben and Mary Elizabeth (Day) F.; B.S., U. of Ill., 1887, M.S., 1894; A.M., Harvard, 1896; Ph.D., U. of Minn., 1899; studied U. of Chicago, 1903; m. Ida May Hammond, Jan. 9, 1888; children—Mrs. Lois Honberger, Hugh Willard, Ruth Elizabeth. Principal of high schools, 1887-92; prof. biology, Upper Iowa University, 1892-1903; prof. botany, Grinnell Coll., 1903-06; prof. botany, Miami U., 1906—. Mem. Minn. Bot. Survey, 1896-1903; in charge of botany, U. of Wash. Marine Sta., 1906. Asso. editor Micologia, 1908—. Author: Tobacco, a book on the tobacco problems, 4 revised edits.; The Lichens of Minnesota, 1910; Laboratory Exercises in Plant Physiology and Ecology, 1911. Mem. Ohio Biol. Survey Bd. Bot. editor Ohio Jour. of Science. Taxonomic studies of lichens. Home: Oxford, O. Died July 10, 1927.

FINK, Henry, ry. official; b. Germany, Nov. 29, 1831; ed. polytechnic sch., Darmstadt. Entered ry. service, 1851; held numerous positions on various rys. until 1876, when became receiver and gen. mgr., Atlantic, Miss. & Ohio R.R., until 1881; 2d v.p. and gen. mgr. Norfolk & Western R.R., 1881-83; v.p. and gen. mgr. E. Tenn., Va. & Ga. Ry., and gen. mgr. Memphis & Charleston Road, Nov. 1881-Jan. 1885; gen. mgr. Va., Tenn. & Ga. Air Line, Nov. 1881-Oct. 1888; receiver E. Tenn., Va. & Ga. Ry., Jan. 7, 1885-June 30, 1886, v.p. same, June 30, 1886-June 24, 1892; v.p. Richmond & Danville R.R., April-Dec. 1887; v.p. Memphis & Charleston R.R., 1887-92; v.p. Cincinnati, New Orleans & Tex. Pacific Ry., 1890-93; receiver E. Tenn., Va. & Georgia Ry., 1892-95, Memphis & Charleston Rd., 1892-98, Norfolk & Western Rd., Feb. 1895-Oct. 1896, pres. reorganized co., Norfolk & Western Ry., Oct. 1896, chmn. bd. same, Mar. 5, 1902—. Home: New York, N.Y. Died July 15, 1912.

FINK, Louis Maria, R.C. bishop of Leavenworth, Kan.; b. Triftersberg, Bavaria, 1834; studied in Latin school and gymnasium at Ratisbon; came to U.S., 1852; joined order of St. Benedict and made his profession at St. Vincent's Abbey, Pa., 1854; finished his theol. studies, 1857, and ordained priest; was stationed at Bellefonte, Pa.; Newark, N.J., and Covington, Ky., where he established a convent and built a church; then pastor St. Joseph's, Chicago; later prior, Benedictine monastery, Leavenworth, Kan., and vicar-gen. of Kan.; consecrated bishop, 1871. Died 1904.

FINKELNBURG, G. A., lawyer; b. nr. Cologne, Prussia, April 6, 1837; ed. in Germany and at St. Charles, Mo.; attended St. Charles Coll., Mo., and grad. Cincinnati Law Coll.; admitted to Mo. bar, 1860; mem. Mo. legislature, 1864-68; mem. Congress, 1868-72; Republican nominee for gov. Mo., 1876; defeated; same for supreme judge, 1898; defeated. Republican. Author: Practice in Supreme Court and the Courts of Appeals in Missouri, 1894. Judge U.S. Dist. Ct., eastern dist. Mo., 1905-07; resigned. Home: St. Louis, Mo. Died 1908.

FINLAY, Charles John, physician; b. Puerto Principe, Cuba, Dec. 3, 1833; s. Dr. Edward and Isabel (de Barrès) F.; coll. edn. partly at Lycée de Rouen, France; M.D., Jefferson Med. Coll., Phila., 1855; (hon. D.Sc.); m. Adele Shine, Oct. 16, 1865. Del. of Cuba to Internat. Sanitary Conf., Washington, 1881; chief sanitary officer of Cuba, 1902-08; del. of Cuba to Sanitary Congress, Washington, 1903; hon. pres. Junta Nacional de Sanidad y Beneficencia, 1909—. Fellow Soc. Tropical Medicine and Hygiene, England; hon. mem. Am. Soc. Tropical Medicine, Société de Médicine Tropicale, Paris. Founder of doctrine mosquito-borne diseases, which he has maintained, with respect to yellow fever, 1881—. Home: Havana, Cuba. Died Aug. 20, 1915.

FINLAY, Kirkman George, bishop; b. Greenville, S.C., Oct. 1, 1877; s. James Alexander and Marian Ponsonby (Gun) F.; B.Litt., Furman U., Greenville, 1899; G.D., U. of the South, 1902; D.D., U. of S.C., 1920; m. Lucy Reed, Apr. 22, 1903. Deacon, 1902, priest, 1903, P.E. Ch.; missionary in charge Trinity Chapel, Clemson (S.C.) Coll., 1902-07; rector Trinity Ch., Columbia, S.C., 1907-21; consecrated bishop coadjutor Diocese of S.C., Jan. 20, 1921; bishop Diocese of Upper S.C., since Oct. 10, 1922. Y.M.C.A. sec. with A.E.F. in France, 1918-19. Trustee Florence (S.C.) Industrial School, Porter Mil. Acad. (Charleston, S.C.), St. Mary's Colored Sch. (Columbia, S.C.); dir. Rescue Orphanage, Columbia. Mem. of State Relief Council of Reconstruction Finance Corp. Democrat. Mason. Home: Columbia, S.C. Died Aug. 27, 1938.

FINLEY, Charles, congressman; b. Williamsburg, Ky., Mar. 26, 1865; s. Hugh Frank and Jennie Renfro (Moss) F.; ed. Milligan (Tenn.) Coll.; unmarried. Pres. Proctor Coal Co., 1909-30, now director; pres. Farmers Bank & Trust Co., Williamsburg, 1925-30; pres. Whitley Republican Co.; sec. Interstate Grocery Co. Mem. Ky. Ho. of Rep., 1893-95; elected sec. of State of Ky., 1895; chmn. Rep. Dist. Com., 11th Congl. Dist., 1916-28; elected mem. 71st Congress to fill vacancy, Feb. 1930, and reëlected for full term, 72d Congress (1931-33), 11th Ky. Dist. Republican. Mem. Christian (Disciples) Ch. Mason (Shriner). Home: Williamsburg, Ky. Died Mar. 18, 1941.

FINLEY, David Edward, congressman; b. Trenton, Ark., Feb. 28, 1861; s. David Miller and Elizabeth (McIlwain) F.; ed. pub. schs.; grad. S.C. U. Law Sch.; m. Elizabeth Lewis Gist, Oct. 9, 1889. In law practice, 1886—. Mem. S.C. Ho. of Rep., 1890-91 (chmn. com. ways and means); mem. S.C. Senate, 1892-96 (chmn. finance com.); mem. 56th to 64th Congresses (1899-1917), 5th S.C. Dist. Democrat. Home: Yorkville, S.C. Died Jan. 26, 1917.

FINLEY, John Huston, editor, educator, author; b. Grand Ridge, Ill., Oct. 19, 1863; s. James Gibson and Lydia Margaret (McCombs) F.; A.B., Knox Coll., 1887, A.M., 1890; Johns Hopkins, 1887-89; LL.D., Park Coll., 1895, Knox Coll., 1899, U. of Wis., 1904, Princeton, 1905, Tulane, 1906, Williams, 1908, Dartmouth, 1909, Hobart, 1913, Columbia, 1914, Brown U., 1915, U. of State of N.Y. 1921, U. of Mich., 1925, Miami U., 1927, Hamilton Coll., 1927, U. of Toronto, 1927, McGill, 1932, Colby, 1932, Middlebury, 1933, Marietta Coll., 1935, U. of Calif., 1936, Johns Hopkins, 1938; L.H.D., Colgate, 1914, New York Univ., 1915, Univ. of Vt., 1925, Yeshiva, 1933, Trinity, 1933, St. Lawrence U., 1935; J.U.D., Univ. of Pa., 1927; Litt.D., Lafayette, 1930, U. of Rochester, 1931, Butler, 1932; m. Martha Ford Boyden, June 29, 1892; children—Ellen Boyden, Margaret Boyden (deceased), Robert Lawrence, John Huston. Secretary State Charities Aid Assn., N.Y., and editor Charities Rev., 1889-92. Pres. Knox Coll., 1892-99; editor Harper's Weekly, 1899; prof. politics, Princeton, 1900-03; pres. Coll. City of New York, 1903-13; commr. of edn., State of N.Y., and pres. U. of the State of New York, 1913-21; asso. editor New York Times, 1921-37, editor-in-chief, 1937-38, emeritus. Dir. Hall of Fame, New York U., 1938—. Harvard exchange lecturer on the Hyde Foundation, at The Sorbonne, Paris, 1910-11; lecturer on the Weil Foundation, U. of North Carolina, 1922, on Page-Barbour Foundation, Univ. of Va., 1924, on Watson Foundation, U. of Edinburgh, 1929, on the Evangeline Wilbour Blashfield Foundation, Am. Acad. of Arts and Letters, 1930, on Earl Foundation, Pacific School of Religion, 1931; Phi Beta Kappa orator, Harvard, 1925; Laureate Chapter Kappa Delta Pi, 1935. Member bd. arbitration in eastern ry. controversy, 1913-14; chmn. N.Y. State Commn. for the Blind, 1913; pres. N.Y. Assn. for the Blind; mem. N.Y. State Constl. Conv. Commn., 1914-15; dir. N.Y. Life Ins. Co., 1910-22; trustee, majority stock of Equitable Life Ins. Co., 1919-25; trustee Sage Foundation, Knox Coll., Berea Coll.; also trustee of New York Public Library; special rep. of Regents of U. State Am. of N.Y. on ednl. mission to France, 1917; mem. Am. Army Edn. Com. in France, 1918; head of Am. Red Cross in Palestine and Near East, 1918-19. Decorated Order Rising Sun (Japanese); Officer Legion of Honor (French); Comdr. Order of Crown of Italy; Knight of the Holy Sepulchre; Comdr. Order of St. Sava (Serbian); Comdr. Polonia Restituta (Polish); Comdr. Order of White Rose (Finnish); Order of St. Olaf (Norwegian); Knight of Dannebrog (Danish); Knight of Gediminas (Lithuanian); Comdr. Order of the Savior (Greek); Comdr. Order of the White Lion (Czechoslovakia); Comd. Order of the Royal North Star (Sweden); Book on French in America crowned by Académie Française and awarded gold medal Geographic Soc., Paris. Mem. National Inst. Arts and Letters (v.p.); mem. Am. Acad. Arts and Letters, 1927. Mem. Nat. Council of Boy Scouts; hon. v.p. Boy Scouts of Scotland. Author: Taxation in Am. States and Cities (with Richard T. Ely), 1889; The Am. Exec. and Executive Methods (with John F. Sanderson), 1908; The French in the Heart of America, 1914; French Schools in War Time, 1917; A Pilgrim in Palestine, 1918; The Debt Eternal, 1923; The Mystery of the Mind's Desire, 1936. Editor Nelson's Ency. Home: New York, N.Y. Died Mar. 7, 1940.

FINLEY, Martha ("Martha Farquharson"), author; b. Chillicothe, O., April 26, 1828; d. Dr. James Brown and Maria Theresa (Brown) F.; ed. in select schools in Phila. and South Bend; taught school; wrote for the press; lived in Phila. several yrs., writing Sunday-school books, etc. Author ("Elsie Books"): Elsie Dinsmore, 1868; Elsie's Holidays, 1869; Elsie's Girlhood, 1872; Elsie's Womanhood, 1875; Elsie's Motherhood, 1876; Elsie's Children, 1877; Elsie's Widowhood, 1880; Grandmother Elsie, 1882; Elsie's New Relations, 1883; Elsie at Nantucket, 1884; The Two Elsies, 1885; Elsie's Kith and Kin, 1886; Elsie's Friends at Woodburn, 1887; Christmas with Grandma Elsie, 1888; Elsie and the Raymonds, 1889; Elsie Yatching with the Raymonds, 1890; Elsie's Vacation, 1891; Elsie at Viamede, 1892; Elsie at Ion, 1893; Elsie at the World's Fair, 1894; Elsie's Journey on Inland Waters, 1894; Elsie at Home, 1897; Elsie on the Hudson, 1898; Elsie in the South, 1899; Elsie's Young Folks, 1900; Elsie's Winter Trip, 1902. ("Mildred Books"); Mildred Keith, 1878; Mildred at Roselands, 1879; Mildred and Elsie, 1881; Mildred's Married Life, 1882; Mildred at Home, 1884, Mildred's Boys and Girls, 1886; Mildred's New Daughter, 1894. Also: Cassella, 1867; Old-Fashioned Boy, 1870; Our Fred, 1874; Wanted—A Pedigree, 1870; Signing the Contract and What It Cost, 1878; The Thorn in the Nest, 1880; The Tragedy of Wild River Valley, 1893; Twiddledetwit, 1898; Elsie and Her Loved Ones, 1903; Elsie and Her Namesakes, 1905. Home: Elkton, Md. Died 1909.

FINLEY, William Henry, civil engr.; b. Delaware City, Del., Jan. 22, 1862; s. William F. and Mary (McDonough) F.; ed. pub. schs. and by pvt. tutelage; m. Sarah H. Furry. Worked in office of Delaware Gazette, 1878-82; engring. dept. Edge Moor Iron Co., 1882-87; in engring. dept., C.,M.&St.P. Ry., 1887-92; entered service of C.&N.W. Ry. Co., May 1892; engr. of bridges, 1892-1900, prin. asst. engr., 1900-05, same rd. v.p. and mgr. Widell-Finley Co., engrs. and contractors, 1905-06; asst. chief engr. C.&N.W. Ry., 1906-13, chief engr., 1913-18, and pres., June 1918—, also pres. C.,St.P.,M.&O. Ry. Co., Sept. 19, 1922—. Home: Wheaton, Ill. Died Mar. 17, 1926.

FINLEY, William Wilson, ry. pres.; b. Pass Christian, Miss., Sept. 2, 1853; (LL.D., Tulane U. of La., 1910, State U. of Ky., 1910). Served from v.p.'s stenographer to asst. gen. freight agt., New Orleans, Jackson & Great Northern, and Chicago, St. Louis & New Orleans rys., 1873-83; asst. gen. freight agt. Tex. & Pacific Ry., 1883-85; asst. gen. freight agt. for the receiver of Tex. & Pacific Ry., 1885-86; gen. freight agt., Tex. & Pacific Ry., 1886-88, "Pan-Handle Route," 1888-89; chmn. Trans.-Mo. Traffic Assn., at Kansas City, 1889-90, Western Pass. Assn., 1890-92; gen. traffic mgr. G.N. & Mont. Central R.R., 1892-95; commr. Southern States Pass. Assn., Apr.-Oct., 1895; 3d v.p. Southern Ry., Oct. 1, 1895-May 1896; 2d v.p. G.N. Ry., May-Sept. 15, 1896; 2d v.p. Southern Ry., 1896-1906, pres. same, Dec. 1906—; also pres. Mobile & Ohio R.R., Southern Ry. in Miss., Ala. Great Southern R.R., Cincinnati, New Orleans & Tex. Pacific Ry., Ga. Southern & Fla. Ry., Va. & Southwestern Ry., and Northern Ala. Ry. Died Nov. 25, 1913.

FINN, Francis James, clergyman; b. St. Louis, Oct. 4, 1859; s. John and Mary (Whyte) F.; ed. pvt. sch. and St. Louis Univ.; grad. Sacred Heart Coll., Woodstock, Md. (3 yrs. philosophy, 4 yrs. theology); entered Jesuit order, 1879; ordained priest, June 29, 1891; dir. St. Xavier Sch., Cincinnati. Editor St. Xavier Calendar, 1907—. Founder of "Little Flower Library," 1924. Author: Percy Wynn, 1890; Tom Playfair, 1890; Henry Dee, 1891; Claude Lightfoot, 1892; New Faces and Old, 1894; Ada Merton, 1894; The Best Foot Forward, 1898; Facing Danger, 1919; Bobby in Movieland, 1921; On the Run, 1922; Lord Bountiful, 1923; The Story of Jesus, 1924; Sunshine and Freckles, 1925; Candles' Beams, 1926. Home: Cincinnati, O. Died Nov. 2, 1928.

FINNEY, Frederick Norton, retired; b. Boston, Mar. 7, 1832; s. Rev. Charles Grandison and Lydia R. (Andrews) F.; ed. Oberlin Coll.; m. Willieanna W. Clarke, Dec. 29, 1863 (died 1899). Admitted to bar, 1857; practiced at Oshkosh, Wis., 1857-60; engr. constrn. C.&N.-W. Ry., 1860-62; city engr., Toledo, O., 1862-64; 1st asst. engr. Mountain div. U.P. R.R., 1864; resident engr. and supt. Jamestown div., L.S.&M.S. R.R., 1864-67; chief engr. and supt. Erie & Pittsburgh R.R., 1867-70. As chief engr. and gen. supt. located, built and operated Canada Southern Ry. (now Mich. Central R.R.), 1870-74; chief engr. and supt. Toledo, Peoria & Warsaw Ry., 1874-78; gen. mgr. Wis. Central R.R., 1878-89; pres. M.,St.P.&St.M. Ry., 1889-91; supt. constrn. M.,K.&T. Ry., 1893-1902; pres. Mo., Kan. & Okla. R.R. Co., 1902-04; pres. Texas & Okla. R.R. Co., constructing 389 miles ry. in Okla. and Ind. Ter., 1902-04; pres. M.,K.&T. Ry., Oct. 1, 1904-Dec. 1, 1906. Died Mar. 18, 1916.

FINNEY, James Imboden, editor; b. West Carroll Parish, La., May 31, 1877; s. Samuel Greenway and Cornelia (Imboden) F.; ed. pub. schs., McMinnville, Tenn.; m. Herminie Jeanmaire, Sept. 12, 1899; children—John Wesley, James I., Louis Jeanmaire. Editor McMinnville New Era, 1900-04; polit. writer Nashville American, 1904-07; editor and part owner Columbia Daily Herald, 1907-26 (still part owner, editor in chief Nashville Tennessean, 1926—; pres. Columbia Herald Co. Served as pvt. 1st Tenn. Inf., Spanish-Am. War, 1898; O.T.C., 1917; asst. state federal food adminstr., Tenn., 1917-19; mem. bd. trustees U. of Tenn.; pres. Tenn. Press Assn., 1912-13. Democrat. Methodist. Home: Culleoka, Tenn. Died Aug. 5, 1931.

FINNEY, Ross Lee, ednl. sociologist; b. Postville, Ia., Aug. 8, 1875; s. Solon B. and Ellen (Bike) F.; Ph.B., Upper Ia. U., 1896; student Northwestern U. and U. of Chicago; S.T.B., Boston U., 1902, A.M., 1907, Ph.D., 1911; studied Teachers Coll. (Columbia); m. Carrie Mitchell, 1898; children—Theodore M., Nathanael S., Ross L. Ordained M.E. ministry, 1902; pastor in Minn., 1902-09; prof. philosophy and economics, Ill. Wesleyan U., 1909-14; prof. edn., State Normal School, Valley City, N.D., 1914-19; asso. prof. ednl. sociology, U. of Minn., 1919—. Author: (with A. L. Schafer) Administration of Village and Consolidated Schools, 1920; The American Public School, 1921; Elementary Sociology, 1923; General Social Science for the Junior High School Grades, 1926; A Sociological Philosophy of Education, 1927. Home: Minneapolis, Minn. Died Feb. 24, 1934.

FINNIGAN, George Joseph, bishop; b. Potsdam, N.Y., Feb. 22, 1885; s. John Henry and Louise Frances (Canton) F.; Litt.B., Notre Dame U., 1910; Ph.D., Gregorian U., Rome, 1912, S.T.L., 1915; S.T.D., Laval U., Quebec, Can., 1916. Ordained priest R.C. Ch., 1915; mem. Holy Cross Mission Band, 1916-18; rector Holy Cross Sem., 1919-25; v.p. Notre Dame U., 1925-26; provincial superior Congregation of Holy Cross in America, 1926-27; apptd. bishop of Helena, Mont., May 20, 1927, consecrated, Aug. 1, 1927. Commd. 1st lt. chaplain, U.S.A., Jan. 13, 1918; capt., May 2, 1919; served with 137th and 80th F.A., A.E.F., Oct. 1918-June 1919. Died Aug. 14, 1932.

FINTY, Tom, Jr., editorial exec.; b. Xenia, Ill., Oct. 1, 1867; s. John and Honora (Doolin) F.; ed. pub. schs.; m. Georgie Bonner, Sept. 14, 1892; 1 dau., Evelyn. Clk. and bookkeeper, gen. store, 1880-85; telegraph operator, station agt. and business solicitor various rys., 1885-89; bank accountant, 1889-92; court stenographer and law student, 1892-94; admitted to bar, 1894; reporter, city editor, Galveston Tribune, 1894-97; city editor Galveston News, 1897-1901; polit. editor Galveston News and Dallas News, 1901-14; editorial exec. and legal counsel A. H. Belo Corp. (pubs. Dallas News, Dallas Journal, Dallas Semi-Weekly Farm News and Texas Almanac) and editor Dallas Journal, 1914—, also dir. corp., 1919—. Mem., sec. Tex. (State) Ednl. Survey Commn., 1923—. Democrat. K.P. Home: Dallas, Tex. Died Apr. 25, 1929.

FIRESTONE, Harvey Samuel, mfr.; b. Columbiana Co., O., Dec. 20, 1868; s. Benjamin and Catherine (Flickinger) F.; ed. high sch. and business coll.; hon. Dr. Business Administration, Mt. Union Coll., Alliance, O.; scroll of distinction, Spencerian Sch. of Commercial Accounts and Finance, Cleveland, O.; hon. LL.D., Kenyon College, Gambier, Ohio, 1934; m. Idabelle Smith, Nov. 20, 1895; children—Harvey Samuel, Russell Allen, Leonard Kimball, Raymond Christy, Roger Stanley, Elizabeth Idabelle. Pres. Firestone Rubber Co., Chicago, 1896-1900; organized Firestone Tire & Rubber Co., Akron, O., 1900, beginning with 17 employes, growing to 40,000 in 1935; president Firestone Tire & Rubber Co. of U.S.A., 1903-32, chmn. bd., 1932—; chmn. bd. Firestone Steel Products Co., Firestone Park Trust & Savings Bank, and officer or director many other subsidiary cos.; also mfr. batteries, spark plugs, brake lining and several thousand mechanical rubber goods and rubber automobile parts; operating several hundred auto supply and service stores. Largely instrumental in investigation of rubber growing possibilities of Philippines and S. American countries and in encouragement of investment of American capital in rubber-growing countries; obtained lease in 1926 for 1,000,000 acres of land in Liberia for development of rubber plantations; opened up 100,000 acres and planted 60,000 acres by 1936. Member Ohio Council Nat. Defense, World War, also instrumental in organizing rubber div. of War Industries Bd.; pres. Rubber Assn. America, 1916-18, organizing its activities for war work. Pres. Ohio Fedn. of Churches, 1922-23. Republican. Episcopalian. Author: Rubber, Its History and Development, 1922; Men and Rubber (with Samuel Crowther), 1926. Donor, from 1920-27, of yearly scholarship providing expenses for 4 years' coll. edn. to high sch. student writing best essay on good roads and highway transportation. Home: Akron, O. Died Feb. 7, 1938.

FIRKINS, Oscar W.; b. Minneapolis, Minn.; s. Otis W. and Mary O. (Ten-Eyck) F.; B.A., U. of Minn., 1884, M.A., 1898; unmarried. Prof. comparative lit., U. of Minn. Mem. Nat. Inst. Arts and Letters. Author: Ralph Waldo Emerson, 1915; Jane Austen,

1920; William Dean Howells—A Critical Biography, 1924; Cyrus Northrop—A Memoir, 1925; Two Passengers for Chelsea and Other Plays, 1928. Contbr. Atlantic Monthly, North Am. Rev., Yale Rev., etc.; reviewer of poetry for the Nation, 1915-18. Dramatic critic Weekly Rev., New York, 1919-21. Home: 1528 4th St. S.E., Minneapolis, Minn. Died Mar. 7, 1932.

FISCHEL, Washington Emil, physician; b. St. Louis, Mo., May 29, 1850; s. Ephraim and Babette (Taussig) F.; high sch. edn.; M.D., St. Louis Med. Coll., 1871; univs. Prague, Vienna, Berlin, 1872-74; m. Martha Ellis, Mar. 28, 1876. Prof. clin. medicine, Washington U., 1887—; pres. med. staff, The Barnard Free Skin and Cancer Hosp. Home: St. Louis, Mo. Died Sept. 15, 1914.

FISCHER, Ernst Georg, mech. engr.; b. Baltimore, Md., Aug. 6, 1852; s. Georg Ernst and Caroline (Schmidt) F.; ed. Zschogg's Real Schule, Dresden, Germany, 1865-67; Engring. Works of Moritz Kleber, Dresden, 1867-70; subsequently under pvt. tutors; m. Julia Frances Lawson, Apr. 26, 1876 (died 1915). With U.S. Coast and Geod. Survey, June 1, 1887—, chief of Instrument Div., Mar. 1, 1898—. Has made many improvements in the instrumental equipment and devised and constructed new apparatus and instruments as follows: Improvements in plane table alidade; base bars; spring balance for base tape measurement; tape stretching apparatus; tide gauge and tide indicator; photographic camera; compass declinometer; interferometer for measuring flexure of gravity pendulum supports; electric signal lamp for triangulation; magnetometer; transit micrometer; pendulum apparatus for determination of gravity; plane table; direction theodolite for primary triangulation; astronomical transit. Designed and constructed, after principles taken from Sir William Thomson and Dr. William Ferrel, U.S. Coast and Geod. Survey tide predicting machine No. 2, the geodetic or precise level, geodetic invar level rod, a new tyye of pressure sounding tube, a new artificial horizon for sextants, etc. Retired Aug. 22, 1922. Home: Washington, D.C. Died Sept. 1935.

FISCHER, George Alexander, author; b. Troy, N.Y.; s. Albert and Margaret (Raab) F.; ed. in pub. schs.; unmarried. Author: Beethoven—A Character Study, 1905; This Labyrinthine Life, 1907. Home: Los Angeles, Calif. Died May 17, 1922.

FISCHER, Louis Albert, physicist; b. Washington, D.C., Jan. 4, 1865; s. Frederick G. and Anna (Cox) F.; B.S., Columbian (now George Washington) U., 1864; m. Marion G. Harvey, Aug. 6, 1888. In Office of Weights and Measures, U.S. Coast and Geod. Survey, 1891-1901; chief of weights and measures div., Bur. of Standards, with title of asso. physicist, 1901-10, physicist, 1910-17; major, Ordnance, U.S.A., Aug. 6, 1917-Jan. 30, 1919. Asst. in physics, George Washington U., 1906. Author: Recomparison of United States Prototype Meter, 1904; History of Weights and Measures, 1905. Compiler: Laws Relating to Weights and Measures in United States, 1904. Home: Washington, D.C. Died July 25, 1921.

FISH, Carl Russell, univ. prof.; b. Central Falls, R.I., Oct. 17, 1876; s. Frederick Elihu and Louisiana Nixon (Oliver) F.; A.B., Brown, 1897; A.M., Harvard, 1898, Ph.D., 1900; m. Jeanne, dau. of Louis and Stella (Edwards) l'Hommedieu. Instr., asst. prof., asso. prof. and prof. Am. history, U. of Wis., 1900—; prof. Am. history, summer schs., Harvard, 1914, Washington, 1923, Stanford, 1925, 27, 30. Research asso. Carnegie Instn., 1908-09; dir. British Br. Am. Univ. Union, 1919. Author: The Civil Service and the Patronage, 1904; Guide to Materials for American History in Roman and Other Italian Archives, 1911; Development of American Nationality, 1913; American Diplomacy, 1915; The Path of Empire, 1919; Guide to the Study of American Diplomacy, 1919; History of America, 1925; Rise of the Common Man. Home: Madison, Wis. Died July 10, 1932.

FISH, Daniel, lawyer; b. Cherry Valley, Ill., Jan. 31, 1848; s. Daniel and Parmelia (Adams) F.; ed. pub. schs., Winnebago Co., Ill.; m. Elizabeth Meigs Porter, August 21, 1873. Enlisted as private Co. G, 45th Illinois Infantry, January 4, 1864; mustered out, July 12, 1865; adj. gen. G.A.R., 1887-88; asst adj. gen. Minn. G.A.R., 1886, judge advocate, 1887. Removed to Iowa at close of war; admitted to bar, 1871; removed to Delano, Minn., 1871; established and edited Delano Eagle, 1872; probate judge, Wright Co., Minn., 1876-77 and 1879; removed to Minneapolis, 1880; alternate del. Rep. Nat. Conv., 1880; 1st atty. city park commn., 1883-87; also atty. state park commn., atty. of Court House and City Hall Commn., 1887—; counsel and trust officer Minn. Title Ins. & Trust Co., 1889-94; apptd. court receiver of Northern Trust Co., 1897; commr. to revise and codify the gen. laws of Minn., Apr. 16, 1901; chmn. commn. after Mar. 1904; report adopted and went into effect Mar. 1, 1906; city atty. of Minneapolis, 1911-14; resigned and apptd. judge 4th Jud. Dist.; elected to same for term ending Jan. 1921; declined reëlection. Republican. Author: Lincoln Bibliography, 1906. Home: Minneapolis, Minn. Died Feb. 9, 1924.

FISH, Frank Leslie, jurist; b. Newfane, Vt., Sept. 17, 1863; s. Frederick Appleton and Sarah Moore (Gates) F.; ed. Leland and Gray Sem., Townshend, Vt., and Vt. Acad., Saxtons River, Vt.; m. Mary Jane Lyon, Mar. 15, 1892; children—Sarah Katherine (Mrs. Wm. Atherton Knight), Frederick Lyon, Prudence Hopkins. Supt. schs., Newfane, 1881-86; admitted to Vt. bar, 1889, and began practice at Vergennes, 1890; states atty. Addison Co., Vt., 1892-1900; nat. bank examiner, 1900-08; tax collector, Vergennes, 1901-05; judge Superior Court, 1912-25; justice Supreme Court of Vt., 1927—. Trustee Middlebury Coll., Vt. Acad. Republican. Conglist. Mason. Author: The Vermont Bench and Bar (5th vol. The Green Mountain State, by Walter H. Crockett), 1923. Home: Vergennes, Vt. Died Sept. 7, 1927.

FISH, Frederick Perry, lawyer; b. Taunton, Mass., Jan. 13, 1855; s. Frederick L. and Mary Jarvis (Perry) F.; A.B., Harvard, 1875; Harvard Law Sch., 1875-76; m. Clara P. Livermore, Apr. 7, 1880 (dec.); children—Margaret, Erland F. Practiced law, New York and Boston, until July 1, 1901; pres. Am. Bell Telephone Co. and Am. Telephone & Telegraph Co., 1901-07; resumed practice, May 1, 1907; mem. Fish, Richardson & Neave. Dir. N.E. Trust Co. Mem. corp. Mass. Inst. Tech.; asso. Radcliffe Coll. Fellow Am. Acad. Arts and Sciences. Home: Brookline, Mass. Died Nov. 6, 1930.

FISH, Frederick Samuel, retired corp. official; b. Newark, N.J., Feb. 5, 1852; s. Henry Clay (D.D.) and Clara (Jones) F.; A.B., U. of Rochester, 1873; m. Grace A. Studebaker, June 16, 1887. Admitted to N.J. bar, 1876, and practiced at Newark and N.Y. City, 1876-90; removed to South Bend, Ind., and became dir. and gen. counsel Studebaker Brothers Mfg. Co., chmn. exec. com., 1897-1911; chmn. exec. com. Studebaker Corp., 1911, pres., 1911-15, became chmn. bd., 1915; now retired. City atty. Newark, 1880-84; mem. N.J. Gen. Assembly, 1884-85. N.J. Senate, 1875-87 (pres. 1887). Republican. Baptist. Home: New York, N.Y. Died Aug. 13, 1936.

FISH, Horace (Francis Xavier), writer; b. Richmond Hill, L.I., N.Y., Oct. 25, 1885; s. of James Horace and Isabella Van Veghten (Coggeshall) F.; ed. Trinity Sch., New York; unmarried. With Evening Sun, New York, 1902-04; credit investigator, later head of credit dept. Nat. Bank of Commerce, New York, 1905-11; spl. writer New York Herald and New York Herald Sunday Book Rev. Catholic. Author: The Great Way (novel—dramatized and prod. New York, Nov. 7, 1921), 1921; Terassa of Spain (short story collection), 1923; The Saint's Theatre (novel), 1923; The Wrists on The Door (dramatized and prod. New York, 1924), 1924. Died 1929.

FISH, Nicholas, banker; b. New York, Feb. 19, 1848; e.s. Hamilton F.; grad. Columbia Coll., 1867; grad. Dean Law School, of Harvard, 1869; 2d sec. U.S. legation, Berlin, 1871, becoming 1st sec., 1874; charge d'affaires to the Swiss Confederation, 1877-81; U.S. minister to Belgium, 1882-86; engaged in banking in New York, 1887—; m. Clemence S. Bryce. His town house is at Irvington Pl. and country residence is "Wahnfried," in Tuxedo. Died 1902.

FISH, Pierre Augustine, univ. prof.; b. Chatham, N.Y., Feb. 17, 1865; s. Irvin A. and Margaret (Shufelt) F.; B.S., Cornell, 1890, D.Sc., 1894; D.V.M., N.Y. State Veterinary Coll., 1899; m. Arethusa Poff, Aug. 25, 1897; children—Elinor Mary, Margaret Arethusa, Katherine, William Cornelius, Elizabeth Shufelt. Instr. physiology, vertebrate zoölogy and neurology, Cornell, 1890-95; instr. Woods Hole, Mass., 1891-95; asst. Bur. Animal Industry, Dept. Agr., 1895-96; asst. prof. comparative physiology and pharmacology, 1896-1902, prof., 1902—, now prof. vet. physiology, Cornell. Maj., U.S.A. Vet. Corps, 1918-19. Author: Book of Veterinary Doses, Therapeutic Terms and Prescription Writing, 1904; Examination of the Urine of the Horse and Man, 1906; Exercises in Physiology, 1906. Home: Ithaca, N.Y. Died Feb. 19, 1931.

FISH, Stuyvesant, banker, ry. official; b. New York, June 24, 1851; s. Hamilton (sec. of state in cabinet of President Grant) and Julia (Kean) F.; brother of Hamilton F.; A.B., Columbia, 1871, A.M., 1874; m. Marion Graves Anthon, June 1, 1876. In Oct. 1871, became clerk in New York office of I.C. R.R., sec. to pres., 1872; clerk Morton, Bliss & Co., New York, and Morton, Rose & Co., London, 1872-77; became dir. I.C. R.R. Co., Mar. 16, 1877; also treas. and agent for purchasing com., New Orleans, Jackson & Great Northern R.R.; 1877-82, sec., and 1882-84, v.p. Chicago, St. Louis & New Orleans R.R.; 2d v.p., 1883-84, v.p., 1884-87; pres. May 18, 1887-Nov. 7, 1906, I.C. R.R.; trustee Mut. Life Ins. Co. of N.Y., 1883-1906; trustee N.Y. Life Ins. & Trust Co.; v.p. and dir. Nat. Park Bank, and dir. in other corps. Mem. Monetary Commn. created by Indianapolis Monetary Conf., 1897; pres. Am. Ry. Assn., 1904-06; chmn. 7th Internat. Ry. Congress, Washington, 1905. Died Apr. 11, 1923.

FISH, William Hansell, judge; b. Macon, Ga., May 12, 1849; s. Judge George W. and Martha E. (Hansell) F.; A.B., U. of Ga, 1869; LL.D., 1920; grad. law student at U. of Va., 1869-71; m. Mary P. Hines, 1876; 1 dau., Mrs. Nina McCleskey. Engaged in practice in Ga. and was circuit judge, 1891-96; asso. justice, 1897-1905, chief justice, 1905-23, Supreme Ct. of Ga.; dean Law Sch., Mercer U., Macon, Ga., 1923—. Trustee U. of Ga., 1893-1905, Wesleyan Female Coll., Ga., 1895-1915. Mem. M.E. Ch., S., for 40 yrs. Home: Macon, Ga. Deceased.

FISH, William Henry, clergyman; b. Millville, Mass., Mar. 1, 1844; s. William Henry and Anne E. (Wright) F.; A.B., Harvard, 1865; grad. Harvard Div. Sch., 1869; at U. of Berlin, 6 months, 1869-70, Rome, Athens, Constantinople, London, Paris, etc., spring and summer of 1870; m. Helen A., d. Everett Case, of Vernon, N.Y., June 12, 1872. Minister Unitarian Ch., Northampton, Mass., 1871-73; in charge Carter Lane Mission to the Poor, London, Eng., 1873-74; minister New Meeting, Kidderminster, Eng., 1874-76; minister First Unitarian Ch., Troy, N.Y., 1877-85, Kidderminster, Eng., 1885-86, Lebanon and Hanover, N.H., 1886-88, First Ch., Dedham, Mass., 1889-97, Colorado Springs, 1897-1901, Salt Lake City, 1903-04; minister Independent Congl. Ch., Meadville, Pa., Mar. 1, 1905—. Home: Meadville, Pa. Deceased.

FISH, Williston, lawyer, author; b. Berlin Heights, O., Jan. 15, 1858; s. Job and Annie E. (Peabody) F.; entered Oberlin Coll., 1876; grad. U.S. Mil. Acad., 1881; m. Gertrude Cameron, Sept. 22, 1881; children—Cameron, Hamilton (dec.), Gertrude Cameron, Josephine Cameron, Margaret (dec.). Admitted to bar, 1893; with S. Chicago City Ry. Co., 1890-99; with Chicago Union Traction Co., 1899-1908; asst. to pres., 1908-12, v.p., gen. mgr., 1912-14, Chicago Rys. Co.; v.p. West Penn Rys. Co., Pittsburgh, 1914-20; gen. mgr Chicago Surface Lines, 1920-23. Author: A Last Will (many edits.), Short Rations, 1900. Home: Western Springs, Ill. Died Dec. 19, 1939.

FISHBACK, William Meade, lawyer, gov.; b. Jeffersonton, Va., Nov. 5, 1831; s. Frederick and Sophia Ann (Yates) F.; grad. Univ. of Va., 1855; read law in Richmond, Va.; settled in Ft. Smith, Ark., 1858; mem. Constl. Conv., 1861. Elected U.S. senator, 1864, by Union legislature; seat refused because State was not "reconstructed." Mem. Constl. Conv., Ark., 1874; mem. legislature, 1877, 1879 and 1885; gov. Ark., 1893-95. Author of "Fishback Amendment" to Constitution, forbidding legislature ever to pay fraudulent bonds. Pres. of Southern Governors' Conv. at Richmond, Va., Apr. 1893. Home: Fort Smith, Ark. Died 1903.

FISHBERG, Maurice, M.D.; b. Kamenetz-Podolsk, Russia, Aug. 16, 1872; s. Philip and Kate (Moverman) F.; came to America, 1890; M.D., New York U., 1897; m. Bertha Cantor, Nov. 5, 1896; children—Arthur Maurice, Ella Harriet. Began practice in New York, 1897; traveled in Europe, 1905, for Bur. of Immigration, investigating certain aspects of immigration problem; report pub. by U.S. Govt. Clin. prof. medicine, Univ. and Bellevue Hosp. Med. Coll., 1915-28; chief physician, Montefiore Hosp. and Bedford Sanatorium. Fellow A.M.A., N.Y. Acad. Sciences (v.p., 1909-10), A.A.A.S., N.Y. Acad. Medicine. Author: The Jews—A Study of Race and Environment, 1910; Zür Anthropologie der Juden, 1911; Rassenmerkmale der Juden, 1912. Treatise on Pulmonary Tuberculosis, 4th edit., 1932. Edited Am. edit. of Gley's Internal Secretions, 1917. Died 1934.

FISHBURN, John Eugene, banker; b. Joliet, Ill., Sept. 13, 1859; s. Daniel G. and Ellen (Burson) F.; student U. of Notre Dame, U. of Mich.; LL.B., U. of Mich., 1879; m. Gertrude E. Toles, Sept. 5, 1900; children—John E.; Doris C. Bookkeeper Crete (Neb.) State Bank, 1881 to 1883; removed to Calif., 1887; cashier 1st Nat. Bank of San Diego, 1889-98; asst. cashier Calif. Bank, Los Angeles, 1898; cashier Nat. Bank of Calif., 1898-1912, pres. 1912-17; pres. Merchants Nat. Bank, 1917-23, chmn. bd., 1923—. Republican. Mason. Home: Los Angeles, Calif. Died May 8, 1929.

FISHBURN, Randolph Eugene, cons. engr.; b. Rockford, Ill., June 8, 1862; s. Eugene Heald and Susan Wiggins (Moore) F.; prep. edn., Peekskill (N.Y.) Mil. Acad.; student Sch. of Mines (Columbia), 1880-84; m. Carmen M. Robles, June 12, 1913; children—Randolph Eugene, Mayhew Wainwright. Gen. engring. work, U.S., Australia, B.C. and Mexico; formerly cons. engr. Internat. Boundary Commn., U.S. and Mexico. Served as 1st lt. 2d U.S. Engrs., Spanish-Am. War. Mem. City Council, Tucson, 2 terms; chmn. Pima Co. (Ariz.) Highway Commn., 1919-22. Republican. Presbyn. Mason. Home: Tucson, Ariz. Died Nov. 1, 1929.

FISHBURNE, John Wood, congressman; b. Albemarle Co., Va., Mar. 8, 1868; s. Clement Daniel and Elizabeth (Wood) F.; student Washington and Lee U., 1885-86; LL.B., U. of Va., 1890; m. Mary Norwood Lyons, Sept. 15, 1898; children—Mary Norwood, Eleanor Snowden (Mrs. Gray Williams), Katharine Barton (Mrs. A. Hewson Michie), John Wood, Lucy Lyons, Thomas Lyons, Junius Rodes. Began practice at Charlottesville, 1890; mem. Va. Ho. of Rep., 1895-96; apptd. judge 8th Jud. Circuit, 1913, and elected for 3 terms by state legislature, serving until 1930;

mem. 72d Congress (1931-33), 7th Va. Dist. Democrat. Presbyn. Mason, Elk. Home: Charlottesville, Va. Died June 26, 1937.

FISHER, Cassius Asa, geologist; b. Fremont, Neb., Feb. 15, 1872; s. Marcius Clay and Nellie (LePrand) F.; grad. Fremont Normal Sch., 1892; B.A., U. of Neb., 1898, M.A., 1900; Sc.D. from same univ., 1927; post-grad. work Yale, 1902-03; m. Evangeline Hazlewood, Aug. 22, 1900; children—Eleonora H., Maurice H., Robert V. Fellow in geology, U. of Neb., 1898-1902; asst. instr. in geology, Yale, 1902-03; asst. geologist, 1896-1909, geologist, 1909-10, also asst. chief of Fuel Sect., U.S. Geol. Survey; cons. geologist and engr., splty. fuels, 1910—; mem. Fisher & Lowrie. Consulting mining engr., Bur. of Mines, 1911-12; in charge of U.S. Navy fuel expdn. Alaska, 1912; geologist and cons. engr. in development of Salt Creek oil field, Wyo., 1910-13. Universalist. Fellow Geol. Soc. America. One of the 3 originators of the former method of valuation by U.S. Govt. of coal lands on the public domain; co-author Manual for the Oil and Gas Industry, pub. by Treas. Dept. for use in appraising oil properties as basis for taxation; has made extensive studies of coal and oil fields in U.S., Central and South America, Alaska, Canada and Europe; del. representing petroleum interests of U.S. at Internat. Chamber of Commerce Conv., London, 1921. Home: Denver, Colo. Died Nov. 4, 1930.

FISHER, Charles A., banker; b. Union City, Pa., Sept. 9, 1875; s. Samuel J. and Caroline (Stranahan) F.; ed. Pittsburgh High Sch.; m. Ritchie Newell, Oct. 20, 1897; (now dec.); children—Howard R., Henry C., Charles N. Bookkeeper, Oliver Wire Co., 1894-98; with Jones & Laughlin Steel Corp., Pittsburgh, 1898-1928, advancing from bookkeeper to pres.; pres. Pitt. Nat. Bank, Pittsburgh, 1933—. Vice-pres. Pittsburgh Park and Playground Soc., Bd. of Edn., Pittsburgh. Home: Pittsburgh, Pa. Died Jan. 5, 1940.

FISHER, Clarence Stanley, historical architect; b. Phila., Pa., Aug. 17, 1876; s. F. Theodore and Emily M. (Shewell) F.; B.S., U. of Pa., in architecture, 1897; m. Florie M., d. Rev. E. R. Carswell, of Augusta, Ga., Nov. 14, 1907. In office of J. L. Mauran, architect, St. Louis, 1897-98; architect of Babylonian Expdn. to Nippur, 1898-1900; at Mus. of U. of Pa., 1900-02; research fellow in Babylonian architecture, U. of Pa., 1903-05; dir. Carswell Inst., Phila., 1907—. Architect of Harvard Palestinian expdn., excavating at Samaria, 1908-10; also architect and field dir. of Harvard U.—Boston Mus. of Fine Arts expdn., carrying on excavation in Egypt, at Valley Temple of Mykerinos at Gizeh, pre-Dynastic cemetery at Girgeh, and oldest known pyramid at Zawiet-el-Aryan. Mem. Am. Inst. Architects. Author: Excavations at Nippur (to be issued in 6 parts), Part 1, 1905, Part 2, 1907. Home: Philadelphia, Pa. Died July 20, 1941.

FISHER, Daniel Webster, coll. pres.; b. Huntingdon Co., Pa., Jan. 17, 1838; s. Daniel and Martha (Middlesworth) F.; A.B., Jefferson Coll., 1857; B.D., Western Theol. Sem., 1860; (D.D., Muskingum Coll., 1874; LL.D., U. of Wooster, 1887, also Washington and Jefferson); m. Amanda D. Kouns, Apr. 15, 1860; father of Walter Lowrie F. Ordained Presbyn. ministry, 1860; pastor Thalia St. Ch., New Orleans, 1860-61, First Ch., Wheeling, W.Va., 1861-76, Madison, Ind., 1877-79; pres. Hanover Coll., 1879-1907. Chmn. Com. of Presbyn. Assembly on orgn. of union chs. in foreign lands; mem. both revision coms. of Presbyn. Ch. on confession of faith and new statement. V.p. bd. dirs. McCormick Theol. Sem.; lecturer on anthropology, same. Was examiner of U.S. Mint, 1889-93. Author: A Human Life (autobiography), 1909; The Unification of the Churches; Calvin W. Mateer, or Forty-five Years in Shantung. Died Jan. 28, 1913.

FISHER, Elam, lawyer; b. on farm, nr. Eaton, O., July 26, 1846; s. Joseph and Christina (Harter) F.; A.B., 2d honor, Miami U., Oxford, O., 1870, A.M., 1886; LL.B., U. of Michigan, 1872; (LL.D., Ohio U., 1917); m. Maria Still, of London, Eng., May 9, 1872. Began law practice, Eaton, 1872; counsel C.,H.&D. R.R. Co.; dir. and counsel Eaton Nat. Bank; pres. Eaton Lighting Co.; dir. and treas. Eaton Telephone Co.; officer or dir. many corps. Mem. Ohio Ho. of Rep., 1891-93; mem. Torrens Land Commn., 1894-96; judge Ct. of Common Pleas, 2d Jud. Dist. of Ohio, 1894-11. Pvt. Co. D, 156th O.V.I., Civil War. Trustee Miami U., 1887—, Oxford Coll. for Women, 1908—. Republican. Methodist. Mason. Died May 9, 1923.

FISHER, Frederic John, mfr. Fisher Bodies; b. Sandusky, O., Jan. 2, 1878; s. Lawrence and Margaret (Theisen) F.; ed. parochial schs. and bus. coll.; LL.D., U. of Detroit; D.Eng., U. of Notre Dame, 1939; m. Burtha Meyers, June 1908. Organizer Fisher Body Co., 1908, Fisher Closed Body Co., 1910; pres. and gen. mgr. both cos. until merger, 1916, as Fisher Body Corp., continuing as pres. and gen. mgr. same until 1924; v.p. and mem. exec. and finance coms. Gen. Motors Corp., 1924-34; now chmn. Fisher & Co.; pres. Senior Investment Corp.; dir. many companies. Trustee U. of Notre Dame, Detroit Symphony Soc., Detroit Community Fund. With wife, donor of Burtha M. Fisher Home for the Aged Poor, Detroit (in charge of Little Sisters of the Poor), 1928, Burtha M. Fisher Nurses Home of the House of Providence Hospital, Detroit, 1927. Republican. Catholic. Home: Detroit, Mich. Died July 14, 1941.

FISHER, Frederick Bohn, bishop; b. Greencastle, Pa., Feb. 14, 1882; s. James Edward and Josephine (Bohn-Shirey) F.; B.Sc., Asbury Coll., 1902, B.A., 1903, D.D., 1916; Boston U. and Harvard, 1906-09, 1920; S.T.B., Boston U., Ph.D., 1909, S.T.D., 1930; D.D., De Pauw U., 1920; LL.D., Wesleyan U., 1924; L.H.D., Hillsdale Coll., 1932; m. Edith Jackson, Feb. 4, 1903 (died 1921); m. 2d, Welthy Honsinger, June 18, 1924. Deacon M.E. Ch., 1903; pastor, Kokomo, Ind., 1903; missionary in India, 1904-06; student pastor N. Cohasset, Mass., 1907; First Ch., Boston, 1908-10; sec. Foreign Missions M.E. Ch., and Laymen's Missionary Movement, 1910-20; bishop M.E. Ch., official residence at Calcutta, India, 1920-30; minister First M.E. Ch., Ann Arbor, Mich., 1930-34, minister Central Ch., Detroit, 1934—. Fondren lecturer Southern Methodist Univ. (Dallas, Tex.), 1931; Earl lecturer Pacific Sch. of Religion (U. of Calif.), 1932; Beemer lecturer De Pauw Univ., 1932; special lecturer Boston U., 1924, 28, 30, Syracuse U., 1933, Morningside Coll., 1934; Adams lecturer Indiana Univ., 1936; Cole lecturer Vanderbilt Univ., 1937. Del. to World Missionary Conf., Edinburgh, Scotland, 1910; missionary tour of India, Japan and China, 1917-18; dir. industrial relations dept. Interchurch World Movement (which apptd. interchurch commn. of inquiry and publ. "Report on Steel Strike of 1919"), 1919; del. to World Conf. on Faith and Order, Lausanne, Switzerland, 1927; pres. Free Ch. Fellowship of America; pres. Internat. Soc. of Theta Phi. Fellow Am. Geog. Soc., Royal Geog. Soc. (mem. continuation and exec. com.). Mason. Author: The Way to Win (with others), 1915; Gifts from the Desert, 1916; India's Silent Revolution (with Gertrude Marvin Williams), 1919; Garments of Power, 1920; Which Road Shall We Take?, 1923; Building the Indian Church (with Walter Brooks Foley), 1929; Personology, 1930; That Strange Little Brown Man Gandhi, 1932; Can I Know God?, 1934. Home: Detroit, Mich. Died Apr. 15, 1938.

FISHER, George Egbert, college prof.; b. Westerlo, N.Y., Apr. 20, 1863; s. Farley Broadstreet and Harriett Matilda (Sloan) F.; Union Coll., N.Y., 1880-82; A.B., Cornell, 1887; A.M., U. of Pa., 1893; Ph.D., 1895; m. Martha Elizabeth Plack, July 29, 1890. Instr. mathematics, Cornell, 1887-89; asst. prof. mathematics, 1889-1908, prof., 1908—, U. of Pa. Translator: Durége's Elements of the Theory of Functions, 1896. Author: Text Book of Algebra, Part I, 1898; Elements of Algebra, 1899; School Algebra, 1899; Complete Secondary Algebra, 1901; Higher Algebra, 1901; Quadrates as Beyond, 1901; Rudiments of Algebra, 1901. Home: Philadelphia, Pa. Died Mar. 28, 1920.

FISHER, George Park, prof. divinity (coll. preacher and pastor), 1854-61, and prof. ecclesiastical history, Yale, 1861—; b. Wrentham, Mass., Aug. 10, 1827; s. Lewis Whiting F.; grad. Brown, 1847; studied theology, Yale Div. Sch., and at Andover and in Germany; (D.D., Harvard, Brown, 1866, Edinburgh, 1886, Princeton, 1896; LL.D., Yale, 1891, Princeton, 1896). Author: History of the Reformation, 1873; The Beginnings of Christianity, 1877; The Christian Religion, 1882; The Grounds of Theistic and Christian Belief, 1883; History of the Christian Church, 1888; Manual of Christian Evidences, 1890; Manual of Natural Theology, 1893; History of Christian Doctrine, 1896. Home: New Haven, Conn. Died 1909.

FISHER, Harrison, artist; b. Brooklyn, N.Y., July 22, 1877; s. Hugo A. F.; ed. in San Francisco, Eng. and France; unmarried. Has illustrated numerous books, also short stories for Saturday Evening Post, Scribner's, Ladies' Home Jour., McClure's, Life, Puck, Cosmopolitan, etc.; also portrait painter and etcher. Now painting covers, and making pen and ink drawings for Cosmopolitan. Author: The Harrison Fisher Book (drawings). Died Jan. 19, 1934.

FISHER, Henry C., army officer; b. Montgomery Co., Md., May 20, 1867; s. Milton Lyles and Mary Ann (Jones) F.; M.D., Georgetown U., 1891, hon. A.M., 1925; m. Jessie T. Noerr, June 30, 1892. Apptd. 1st lt. and asst. surgeon, U.S.A., Oct. 31, 1891, and advanced through grades to col., May 15, 1917; brig. gen., asst. surgeon gen., Oct. 11, 1929; retired May 31, 1931. Served in Spanish-Am. War, Philippine Insurrection, World War. Comdr. Army and Navy Gen. Hosp., Hot Springs, Ark., 1913, Walter Reed Gen. Hosp., 1913; in charge supply div., Surgeon General's Office, 1913-17; gen. med. insp., A.E.F., 1917-19; chief health officer, Panama Canal, 1919-24; comdt. Army Med. Sch., Washington, 1924-29. Fellow Am. Coll. Surgeons. D.S.M.; silver star citation "for gallantry in action" at Battle of Santiago de Cuba; awarded the Victory Medal for service in France; Officer Legion of Honor (France). Methodist. Mason. Home: Arlington, Va. Died Dec. 18, 1936.

FISHER, Henry Wright, elec. engr.; b. Youghal, Ireland, Jan. 31, 1861; s. Abraham and Sarah (Wright) F.; came to U.S., 1874; M.E., Cornell U., 1888; m. Harriette Prentice Wixom, Oct. 16, 1889; children—Harold Wright (dec.), Kenneth Dudley, Leicester Wright. With Bergmann & Co., also C. & C. Motor, New York, 1888; entered service of Standard Underground Cable Co., 1888, chief elec. engr., 1889-1915; chief elec. engr. and mgr., Lead Cable & Rubber Works, 1915-23, tech. dir. electrical engring. and mgr. same, 1923-28; cons. engr., 1928-30. Fellow Am. Inst. E.E. Republican. Mason. Died Oct. 1937.

FISHER, Hubert Frederick, congressman; b. Milton, Fla., Oct. 6, 1877; s. Frederick and Mary Anne (McCarter) F.; A.B., U. of Miss., 1898, LL.B., 1904 A.M., Princeton, 1901; m. Louise Sanford, Nov. 6 1909; children—Hubert Frederick, Adrian Sanford Practiced law in Memphis, Tenn., 1904—. Del. Dem Nat. Conv., Baltimore, 1912; mem. Tenn. Senate 1913-14; U.S. atty. for Western Dist. of Tenn., 1914 17; mem. 65th to 71st Congresses (1917-31), 10th Tenn. District. Presbyn. Home: Germantown, Tenn Died June 16, 1941.

FISHER, John Frederick, clergyman, educator; b Jefferson Co., O., Oct. 15, 1859; s. Joseph Andrew and Mary Jane (Risher) F.; Ph.B., Mt. Union Coll., Alliance, O., 1887, D.D., 1897; studied Drew Theol. Sem., Western Reserve U.; m. Emma P. Burt, Nov. 27, 1884 (died 1893); 1 son, Eugene Burt; m. 2d, Lena A. Leonard, Apr. 22, 1896; 1 dau., Leonarda (wife of Alan Kemp Laing). Ordained M.E. ministry, 1884; pastor North Bloomfield, O., 1884-86, Windsor, 1887, Bedford, 1888-90, Mt. Union, 1891, Geneva, 1892-94; presiding elder Akron and Cleveland dists., 1895-99; supt. Children's Aid Soc., Cleveland, 1900-05; dean Sch. of Religion, U. of Southern Calif., Sept. 1921—. Republican. Mason. Home: Los Angeles, Calif. Deceased.

FISHER, John S., lawyer, gov.; b. South Mahoning Twp., Pa., May 25, 1867; s. Samuel Royer and Mariah (McGaughey) F.; grad. Indiana State Normal Sch. of Pa., 1886; LL.D., Lafayette, Franklin and Marshall, Westminster and Juniata colls., U. of Pa., Pa. Mil. Coll. and Temple Univ.; m. Hapsie Miller, Oct. 11, 1893; children—Robert M., Mrs. Mary F. Brown. Admitted to Pa. bar, 1893, and practiced at Indiana as mem. Cunningham & Fisher until assuming duties as gov.; now chmn. bd. Nat. Union Fire Ins. Co.; chmn. Capitol Investigating Commn. which exposed the frauds in connection with furnishing of State Capitol at Harrisburg; apptd. state commr. of banking, 1919; also mem. Commn. on Constl. Amendment and Revision, Pa.; gov. of Pa., term 1927-31, retiring from all business connections and trusteeships while in office. United Presbyn. Home: Indiana, Pa. Died June 25, 1940.

FISHER, Lewis Beals, college dean; b. Charlotte, Me., Apr. 30, 1857; s. Daniel J. and Caroline (Lincoln) F.; ed. Phillips Acad., Mass., St. Lawrence U., and Canton Theol. Sem., N.Y.; (D.D., St. Lawrence, 1901; LL.D., Buchtel, 1907); m. Fannie Shaw, 1886. Ordained Universalist ministry, 1881; pastor Rochester, N.Y., 1882-86; Bridgeport, Conn., 1886-91; prof. pastoral theology and sociology, Canton Theol. Sem., 1891-1905; pres. Lombard Coll. and Rider Divinity Sch., Galesburg, Ill., June 1905-June 1911; dean Ryder Div. Sch., affiliated with U. of Chicago, 1911—; minister Ch. of Redeemer, Chicago, 1923. Author: Prayers for the Home, 1890; History of the Universalist Church, 1897; The Story of a Down East Plantation, 1915. Home: Chicago, Ill. Died Mar. 22, 1936.

FISHER, Lucius George, mfr.; b. Beloit, Wis., Nov. 27, 1843; s. Lucius George and Caroline S. (Field) F.; ed. pvt. and high schs.; freighted with ox-team across plains in 1860; pvt. and color sergt. 84th N.Y. Vols., in Civil War; served through campaign in Shenandoah Valley; in p.m. dept. U.S.N. on bd. U.S.S. Wyandank, until close of war; m. Katharine Louise Eddy, Apr. 20, 1870 (died 1910). Interested in Wheeler & Hinman, mfrs. of paper bags, firm changing to Wheeler, Fisher & Co., of which became mgr.; inc. Jan. 1875, as Union Bag & Paper Co., of which became pres.; organized N.J. corp. of same name, Mar. 1899, with capital stock of $27,000,000, of which was pres. until 1908, resigning to become chmn. bd. dirs. In 1875 organized and put in successful working order a company to mfr. paper plates, then sold it; in 1877 with Frank Davis, of Beloit, organized company to mfr. paper pails; sold it in 1879; organized Exhaust Ventilator Co., 1881, and soon after another of same name in London; afterwards sold it. Has large real estate interests in Chicago, including the 18-story Fisher Bldg., built in 1897; large interests in mines, western real estate, and irrigation projects. Republican. Presbyn. Home: Chicago, Ill. Died Mar. 20, 1916.

FISHER, Oscar Louis, pres. Fort Worth U., 1891-1903; b. Stephenson Co., Ill., Aug. 12, 1841; s. Geo. Wilt and Barbara H. Fisher; academic edn. at Rock River Sem., Mt. Morris, Ill.; grad. Garrett Bibl. Inst., 1871; A.M., Denver U., 1886 (D.D., 1892); m. Charlotte E. Smith, Oct. 17, 1881. Since 1871 in ministry of M.E. Ch. as pastor, presiding elder and supt. of ch. extension; 2 yrs. in Iowa and 17 yrs. in Colo. (most of the time in Denver). Vice-chancellor U. of Denver, June 1904—. Died 1907.

FISHER, Richard Thornton, forester; b. Brooklyn, Nov. 9, 1876; s. Edward Thornton and Ellen Bowditch (Thayer) F.; A.B., Harvard, 1898; Yale Forest Sch., 1901-02, M.F., 1902; hon. M.S., Yale U., 1929; studied forestry in Germany, May-Sept. 1903; m. Georgina Paine, July 1913; children—Richard Thornton, Anne, Faith, Charles Paine, John Bryant. Field collector for U.S. Biol. Survey, 1898; attached to U.S. Bur. of Forestry (now U.S. Forest Service), 1899-1901; with U.S. Forest Service, 1902-03, Sept. 1903-Feb. 1904; chmn. Dept. of Forestry, Harvard, 1904—; dir. Harvard Forest, 1908—. Fellow Soc. Am. Foresters, A.A.A.S. Home: Petersham, Mass. Died June 9, 1934.

FISHER, Robert (Strettle) Jones, lawyer; b. York, Pa., July 25, 1847; s. Robert Strettle Jones and Catherine Jameson F.; A.B., Pa. Coll., 1867, A.M., 1870; LL.B., Albany Law Sch., 1869; m. Harriet S. Tyler, Feb. 7, 1876; m. 2d, Louise Martin, Jan. 15, 1907. Admitted to bar, 1869; examiner, examiner-in-chief and asst. commr. U.S. Patent Office, 1876-91; gen. counsel Eastern R.R. Assn., 1891-1927, cons. counsel, 1927—. Home: Washington, D.C. Died Nov. 10, 1932.

FISHER, Robert Joseph, mfr., inventor; b. Athens, Tenn., Jan. 23, 1857; s. Richard M. and Ann M. (Gettys) F.; ed. E. Tenn. Wesleyan U.; m. Alice M. Gauche, June 9, 1892. Teller Cleveland (Tenn.) Nat. Bank, 1880-83; organized First Nat. Bank, Athens, Tenn., and cashier same, 1884-96. Inventor Fisher Book Typewriter (N.Y. and Pa.), and has taken out numerous patents; awarded John Scott Medal by City of Phila. on recommendation of Franklin Inst. for meritorious invention, 1899. Home: Athens, Tenn. Died May 1, 1932.

FISHER, Robert Welles, M.D.; b. Seaford, Del., Oct. 10, 1863; s. Isaac M. and Sarah J. (Vaughan) F.; grad. Phila. Coll. Pharmacy, 1887; M.D., Jefferson Med. Coll., 1890 (Bartholow prize); m. Margaret Van B. Terry, 1892; children—Vaughan Terry, Anna Bathsheba, Margaret Louise, Robert Welles. Practiced in Salt Lake City from 1890; physician to St. Mark's Hosp., 1893-1917; prof. materia medica and pharmacy, med. dept. U. of Utah, 1899-1914; sec. State Bd. Med. Examiners, 1901-09; mem. Bd. of Health, Salt Lake City, 1892-1916. Commd. capt. M.R.C., June 15, 1917; served in Base Hosp. 131, France; commd. maj. M.R.C., May 29, 1919. Republican. Home: Salt Lake City, Utah. Died Jan. 16, 1927.

FISHER, Samuel Brownlee, civil engr.; b. Cherry Fork, O., Oct. 24, 1846; s. Rev. Jacob Piper and Jane Thompson (Brownlee) F.; B.S., Washington and Jefferson Coll., 1868, M.S., 1871 (D.Sc., 1909); m. Agnes Crooks, Feb. 8, 1881 (died 1906); children—Brownlee, Ann Palmer. With Rogers Locomotive Works, Paterson, N.J., 1869-71; engring. dept. Pa. lines Pittsburgh, from chainman to asst. engr., 1873-85; chief engr. Milwaukee & Northern R.R., 1885-90, Minneapolis, St. Paul & Sault Ste. Marie Ry., 1890-92, Everett & Monte Cristo Ry., Everett, Wash., 1893-94, M.,K.&T. Ry., 1895-1913; chmn. valuation com., M.,K.&T. Ry., 1913-16, cons. engr. same, 1916—. Republican. Presbyn. Home: Parsons, Kan. Died July 9, 1926.

FISHER, Samuel Jackson, clergyman, educator; b. Cincinnati, O., Sept. 9, 1847; s. Rev. Samuel Ware (D.D., LL.D.) and Jane (Jackson) F.; A.B., Hamilton Coll., 1867, D.D., 1892; grad. Auburn Theol. Sem., 1870; D.D., U. of Pittsburgh, 1892; m. Mary Anna Shreve, Oct. 20, 1870. Ordained Presbyn. ministry, 1870; pastor Swissvale, Pa., 1870-1905; prof. mental and moral sci., Pa. Coll. for Women, 1879—. Lecturer and librarian, trustee, rec. sec., Western Theol. Sem. Pres. Presbyn. Bd. of Missions for Freedmen. Author: The American Negro, 1908; The Negro, an American Asset, 1909; The Negro Boy and Girl, 1920. Home: Pittsburgh, Pa. Died May 21, 1928.

FISHER, Stokely S., clergyman, educator; b. nr. Graysville, O., Aug. 8, 1865; s. Simon A. and Maria W. (Westbrook) F.; student Adrian (Mich.) Coll. until 1885, leaving coll. to become pastor of ch. at Wellsville, O.; (hon. A.M., West Lafayette [O.] Coll., 1903, Sc.D., 1904; D.D., Kansas City U., 1904); m. Alwilda A. Smith, July 1, 1886. Admitted to Muskingum (O.) Conf., 1883; pastor Mt. Zion, 1883-84, Wellsville, 1886-88, Smithfield, 1888-90, York, 1890-93, Empire, 1893-96, Attica, 1896-99, McConnelsville, 1899, Cambridge, 1900-04; pres. West Lafayette Coll., 1904-06; pastor, Coshocton, O., 1907-12, Univ. Ch., Kansas City, Kan., 1912-15; 1st pres. Kansas City U. Assn., 1912-16, prof. English, 1913—, dean of the University, 1922—, also v.p. bd. trustees. Head of ednl. dept. Kan. Authors' Club. Mem. Gen. Conf. M.P. Ch. 3 times. Republican. Mason. Author: Poems, 1884; Lela and Other Poems, 1885; Fanny and Other Poems, 1885. Home: Kansas City, Kan. Died May 30, 1924.

FISHER, Sydney George, lawyer, author; b. Phila., Sept. 11, 1856; s. Sidney George and Elizabeth (Ingersoll) F.; A.B., Trinity Coll., 1879; law student Harvard, 2 yrs.; L.H.D., Western U. of Pa., 1897; LL.D., Trinity, 1902; U. of Pa., 1914; admitted to Pa. bar, 1883; unmarried. Trustee of Trinity Coll., Pa. Instn. for Edn. of the Blind, and Library Co. of Phila. Has written many mag. articles, including the letter to the New York Nation, July 30, 1880, which began the movement which established the various civil service reform societies throughout the country; also notable article in Forum, Jan. 1894, entitled, "Has Immigration Dried Up Our Literature?" and other articles on immigration. Author: The Making of Pennsylvania, 1896; Pennsylvania—Colony and Commonwealth, 1897; The Evolution of the Constitution, 1887; Men, Women and Manners in Colonial Times, 1898; The True Benjamin Franklin, 1899; The True William Penn, 1900; The True History of the American Revolution, 1902; The Struggle for American Independence, 1908; The True Daniel Webster, 1911; American Education, 1917; The Quaker Colonies, 1918. Home: Essington, Pa. Died Feb. 22, 1927.

FISHER, Walter L., secretary of the interior; b. Wheeling, Va. (now W.Va.), July 4, 1862; s. Daniel Webster and Amanda D. (Kouns) F.; student Marietta (O.) Coll., 1878-79; Hanover (Ind.) Coll., 1879-83, LL.D., 1913; m. Mabel Taylor, Apr. 22, 1891. Admitted to bar, 1888, and practiced at Chicago, 1888, 1911, and 1913; mem. Fisher, Boyden, Bell, Boyd & Marshall. Sec. of Interior, cabinet of President Taft, Mar. 13, 1911-Mar. 5, 1913. Spl. assessment atty., Chicago, 1888-89; special counsel for City of Chicago in local transportation, ry. terminal and other matters, 1906-11 and 1914—; mem. exec. com. Municipal Voters' League (sec. 1901-06, pres. 1906); pres. Conservation League America, 1908-09; v.p. Nat. Conservation Assn., 1910-11; mem. Ry. Securities Commn. (U.S.), 1910-11. Home: Hubbard Woods, Ill. Died Nov. 9, 1935.

FISHER, Willard Clark, prof. economics; b. Westerlo, N.Y., Mar. 4, 1865; s. Farley and Harriet (Sloan) F.; A.B., Cornell U., 1888; fellow in history and polit. economy, same, 1888-89, 1891-92. Instr. economics and finance, Brown U., 1890-91; asso. prof. economics and social science, 1892-96, prof. 1896-1913, Wesleyan U., Middletown, Conn. Lecturer on economics, Harvard, 1913-14; prof. economics, New York U., 1916-27. Councilman, City of Middletown, 1903-04, mayor, 1906-08, 1910-12. Home: Middletown, Conn. Deceased.

FISHER, William Cummings, orthodontist; b. Washington, D.C., July 14, 1876; s. Henry W. and Mary (Snyder) F.; grad. Washington High Sch., 1895; D.D.S., George Washington U., 1899; m. Adelaide Jacques, of Paris, France, Oct. 9, 1907. Practiced Washington, 1899-1901, in New York, 1901—; dental surgeon U.S.A., 1901-04. Maj. Dental Corps U.S.A., during the war; now col. Dental R.C. Clubs: New York, Pelham Country. Home: Bronxville, N.Y. Deceased.

FISHER, Willis Richardson, leather mfr.; b. Boston, Mass., Feb. 13, 1875; s. Theodore Willis and Ella Gertrude (Richardson) F.; A.B., Harvard, 1899 as of 1897; m. Alice Chester Nichols, June 19, 1902; 1 son, Richard. Began with A. C. Lawrence Leather Co. of which has been pres., 1923—; also pres. Nat. Leather Co. Unitarian. Home: Waban, Mass. Deceased.

FISK, Charles Henry, lawyer; b. Fiskburg, Ky., Aug. 31, 1843; s. John Flavel and Elizabeth Sarah (Johnson) F.; A.B., Miami U., 1863 (valedictorian), A.M., 1868, LL.D., 1904; LL.B., Cincinnati Law Sch., 1864; m. Margaret A. Emmal, Oct. 23, 1866. Capt. Co. A, 1st Regt., "Squirrel Hunters," Ohio Vol. Inf., during Kirby Smith's raid, 1862; admitted to Ky. bar, 1864; practiced, Lexington, 1865, Covington, 1865—; mem. John F. & Charles H. Fisk, 1868-90, then privately; practiced U.S. mil. courts, Lexington, 1865. Sec. Covington & Cincinnati Bridge Co.; 1st pres. Masonic Temple Assn. of Covington; trustee and treas., K.T. & M.M. Aid Assn., Cincinnati. Republican. Mem. Christian (Disciples) Ch.; supt. S.S. for nearly 35 yrs. Mason. Home: Covington, Ky. Died Oct. 20, 1930.

FISK, Charles Joseph, judge; b. Whiteside Co., Ill., Mar. 11, 1862; s. Clark S. and Adelia E. (Reynolds) F.; ed. common schs. and Northern Ill. Coll., Fulton; m. Ida M. Myers, Oct. 20, 1886. Admitted to N.D. bar, 1886; practiced at Larimore and Grand Forks, N.D.; sec. commn. to revise the 7 codes of the state, 1893-95; city atty. Grand Forks, 1893-95; judge 1st Jud. Dist. of N.D., 1897-1907; judge Supreme Court of N.D., 1907-17; resumed practice at Minot, Jan. 1917; later referee of N.D. State Guaranty Commn., to hear claims of depositors in closed state banks. Democrat. Home: Minot, N.D. Died May 8, 1932.

FISK, Eugene Lyman, M.D.; b. Brooklyn, N.Y., Jan. 1, 1867; s. Samuel Nelson and Marie Louise (Johnson) F.; prep. edn. Trinity Sch., New York; M.D., Univ. Med. Coll. (New York U.), 1888; m. Emma Louise Sweet, June 3, 1889; children—Ruth Sterling (Mrs. Oliver Alden III), Marie Louise (Mrs. Jean A. Toulemonde). He became connected with the medical dept. of Equitable Life Assurance Soc. of U.S., 1890; in charge western depts. same, until 1898; med. dir. Provident Savings Life Assn., New York, 1898-1910, Postal Life Ins. Co., 1910-13, Life Extension Inst., 1913—, now v.p. Fellow A.M.A., Am. Public Health Assn. Republican. Episcopalian. Author: (with Prof. Irving Fisher) How to Live, 1915; Alcohol—Its Relation to Human Efficiency and Longevity, 1916; Food—Fuel for the Human Engine, 1916; (with Prof. Fisher) Health for the Soldier and Sailor, 1918; Health Building and Life Extension, 1923; How to Make the Periodic Health Examination, 1927. Home: New York, N.Y. Died July 5, 1931.

FISK, Everett Olin; b. Marlboro, Mass., Aug. 1, 1850; s. Rev. Franklin and Chloe Catherine (Stone) F.; A.B., Wesleyan U., Conn., 1873, A.M., 1876; LL.D., Olivet, 1915; m. Helen Chase Steele, Sept. 12, 1882 (died 1901); 1 dau., Harriet Storer; m. 2d, Louisa Holman Richardson, June 16, 1915. Taught sch. in Wallingford and Enfield, Conn., 1873-75; N.E. agt. for Ginn & Co., pubs., 1875-85; founder, 1885, and pres. of Fisk Teachers' Agencies. Mem. M.E. Gen. Confs., 1892 and 1916; pres. N.E. Conf. Missionary Soc., 1893-95; pres. Boston Missionary and Ch. Extension Soc., 1894-96, and 1912-30; pres. Preachers' Aid Soc. of New England Conf., 1907—. Trustee Holman Institute (Agra, India), New England Home for Little Wanderers; trustee Wesleyan Bldg. (Boston), N.E. Deaconess Hosp., Morgan Memorial Industries, First M.E. Ch. Republican. Methodist. Home: Brookline, Mass. Died Nov. 3, 1934.

FISK, Harlan Wilbur, magnetician; b. Geneva, Kan., Sept. 25, 1869; s. Wilbur and Angelina Sarah (Drew) F.; B.S., Carleton Coll., Northfield, Minn., 1896; m. Louie B. Hubbell, June 30, 1897; children—Clarence Wilbur, Marion Sarah, Willis Hubbell, Ernest Harlan. Prin. pub. schs., Grand Meadow, Minn., 1896-99; prof. mathematics, Fargo (N.D.) Coll., 1899-1906, acting dean, 1904-06; magnetician dept. Terrestrial Magnetism, Carnegie Instn. of Washington, 1906—; now chief of sect. of land magnetic survey. Made magnetic surveys of Bermuda Islands, 1907 and 1922; led magnetic survey expdn. Brit., Dutch and French Guiana, 1908. Home: Kensington, Md. Died 1932.

FISK, Herbert Franklin, educator; b. Stoughton, Mass., Sept. 25, 1840; s. Rev. Franklin and Chloe Catherine (Stone) F.; brother of Everett Olin F.; A.B., Wesleyan U., 1860, A.M., 1863 (D.D., 1888; LL.D., Allegheny Coll., 1899, Northwestern U., 1904); m. Anna Green, July 11, 1866 (died 1908); m. 2d, Carla Fern Sargent, Feb. 15, 1912; father-in-law of Charles Zueblin. Teacher in various schs., 1855-61; prin. Shelburne (Vt.) Acad., 1861-63; teacher Latin and Greek, Cazenovia (N.Y.) Sem., 1863-67, Wesleyan Acad., Mass., 1867-68; prin. Genesee Wesleyan Sem., N.Y., 1868-73, Evanston Acad. of Northwestern U., 1873-1904; prof. edn., Northwestern U., 1888—. Licensed as local preacher, M.E. Ch., 1859, ordained deacon, Ithaca, N.Y., 1866, elder, Cazenovia, N.Y., 1868; mem. Oneida Ann. Conf. M.E. Ch., 1866-78, Rock River Conf., 1878—; pastor for brief periods at Middlebury, Vt., 1862, Oneida, N.Y., 1866, Wilbraham, Mass., 1867, Evanston, Ill., 1876. Propr. and mgr. Chicago office of Fisk Teachers' Agencies, Chicago, 1905—. Home: Evanston, Ill. Died Dec. 19, 1916.

FISK, Samuel Augustus, physician; b. Feb. 9, 1856; s. Robert Farris and Narcissa Perry (Whittemore) F.; A.B., Yale, 1877, A.M., 1884; M.D., Harvard, 1880; m. Clara W. Crumb, Feb. 22, 1906. Prof. medicine, 1884-99, sec., 1884-95, dean, 1895-99, Med. Dept., U. of Denver; removed to Brimfield, Mass., 1905; retired; mem. 1st bd. mgrs. The Home for Consumptives; on the staffs of County, St. Luke's, and Deaconesses' hosps. Mem. 6th Internat. Congress on Tuberculosis. Author articles on climate of Colo., Calif., Nassau and various med. subjects. Home: Brimfield, Mass. Died Jan. 1915.

FISKE, Amos Kidder, author; b. Whitefield, N.H., May 12, 1842; s. Henry and Lucinda (Keyes) F.; A.B., Harvard, 1866, A.M., 1869; m. Caroline Child, Oct. 27, 1870. Admitted to bar, New York, 1868; asso. with late George Ticknor Curtis in the preparation of the Life of Daniel Webster; contbr. to Am. Cyclo.; on editorial staff New York Times 22 yrs., on staff New York Mail and Express, 1900-02; asso. editor New York Jour. of Commerce and Commercial Bulletin, 1903—. Author: The Modern Bank, 1904; Honest Business, 1914. Home: New York, N.Y. Died Sept. 18, 1921.

FISKE, Charles, P.E. bishop; b. New Brunswick, N.J., Mar. 16, 1868; s. William H. and Mary Elizabeth (Houghton) F.; A.B., St. Stephen's Coll., Annandale, N.Y., 1893, D.D., 1912; B.D., Gen. Theol. Sem., 1896, also S.T.D.; LL.D., Syracuse U., 1916, Litt.D., 1930; D.D., Hamilton Coll., 1921; L.H.D., Hobart Coll., 1926; m. Bessie Curlett Crampton, 1901. Deacon, 1896, priest, 1897, P.E. Ch.; asso. missionary Trenton, N.J., 1896-97; rector Westfield, N.J., 1897-1900; asst. Mt. Calvary Ch., Baltimore, 1900-01; rector Ch. of the Transfiguration, Phila., 1901-02, Somerville, N.J., 1902-08, St. John's Ch., Norristown, Pa., 1908-10, St. Michael and All Angels, Baltimore, 1910-15; consecrated bishop coadjutor of Central N.Y., 1915, bishop, 1923. Declined election as bishop coadjutor of Dallas, 1913; retired, May 1936; since then spl. lecturer at Coll. of Preachers,

Washington, at Phila. Divinity Sch., etc. Author: The Perils of Respectability; The Experiment of Faith; The Faith by Which We Live; The Christ We Know; The Confessions of a Puzzled Parson, 1928; Calvary Today, 1929; The Real Jesus (with Prof. B. S. Easton), 1929; From Skepticism to Faith, 1934. Died Jan. 8, 1941.

FISKE, Edmund Walter, lawyer; b. of Am. parents, London, Ont., Can., Apr. 12, 1874; first ancestor in America settled in Mass., 1638; s. Romanzo Eliot and Mary Ann (Lince) F.; ed. Redfield (S.D.) and Olivet (Mich.) colls.; m. Martha Thomas, Dec. 11, 1901; one son, Thomas E. (lawyer). Admitted to bar of State of South Dakota, 1901, and began practice at Redfield; city atty., Redfield, 6 yrs.; Dem. candidate for Congress, and for atty. gen. of S.D.; asst. U.S. atty., S.D., 1913-19; U.S. atty., term Aug. 1919-Aug. 1923. Conglist. Mason. Home: Sioux Falls, S.D. Died Feb. 19, 1940.

FISKE, Eugene Allen, lawyer; b. Manchester, N.H., Jan. 17, 1848; s. Allen and Mercie Rogers (Parmenter) F.; 2d lt. U.S. Vols., Hancock's corps; severely wounded; B.L., Columbian (now George Washington) U., 1868; m. Josie A. Frantz, Sept. 27, 1888. Admitted to bar, 1868; to Supreme Ct. of U.S., 1890; apptd. asst. sec. to sign land patents to President Grant, Sept. 5, 1870; apptd. chief pvt. land claims, Gen. Land Office, Mar. 9, 1876; in practice Santa Fé, N.M., 1876—; U.S. atty. for N.M., 1889-93. Republican. Home: Santa Fé, N.M. Deceased.

FISKE, Haley, insurance; b. New Brunswick, N.J., Mar. 18, 1852; s. William H. and Sarah (Blakeney) F.; A.B., Rutgers, 1871, A.M., 1874, LL.D., 1921; studied law in offices of Arnoux, Ritch & Woodford, with whom he later became partner; practiced until 1891; m. Marione Cowles Cushman, Apr. 27, 1887; children—Mrs. Helen Evans, Archibald Falconer Cushman, Mrs. Marione Virginia Johnson, Haley, Katherine Cushman, Mrs. Margaret Lois Walker. 3d. V.p. Met. Life Ins. Co., 1891, pres. 1919; dir. Chatham and Phenix Nat. Bank and Trust Co., Victor Chem. Wks., Nat. Surety Co., Met. Life Ins. Co., Great Am. Ins. Co., Great Am. Indemnity Co., Am. Alliance Ins. Co.; mem. advisory com. Met. Branch, Chase Nat. Bank. Trustee Rutgers Coll., St. Stephen's Coll., New York P.E. City Mission Soc., House of the Holy Comforter, Ch. of St. Mary the Virgin, Cathedral of St. John the Divine. Home: New York, N.Y., and Bernardsville, N.J. Died Mar. 2, 1929.

FISKE, Horace Spencer, editor, author; b. Dexter, Mich., Nov. 4, 1859; s. Rev. John Billings and Mary (Gregory) F.; A.B., Beloit College, 1882, A.M., 1885; A.M., U. of Mich., 1885; m. Ida Peck Nettleton, June 22, 1889. Instr. Greek, Latin and English lit., Beloit Coll. Acad., 1886-87; prof. polit. economy and civics, Wis. State Normal Sch., 1887-93; elected to fellowship in English, U. of Wis., 1892; student univs. of Oxford and Cambridge, Eng., and Trinity Coll., Dublin, 1893-94; lecturer on English literature, extension div., U. of Chicago, 1894-1912. Represented Wis. in Inter-State Oratorical Contest, Indianapolis, 1882; joint editor State Readers of Indiana, 1899; lit. editor The World Review, Chicago, 1901-02; asst. recorder U. of Chicago, 1903-12; editor University Record, 1903-14; asso. editor U. of Chicago Magazine, 1908-14; publication dept., U. of Chicago Press, 1912-24; Public Relations Office, U. of Chicago, 1924-30. Trustee Eagle's Nest Camp Assn., Oregon, Ill. (organization of artists and authors). Author: The Ballad of Manila Bay and Other Verse, 1900; Provincial Types in American Fiction, 1903; Chicago in Picture and Poetry, 1903; Poems on the University of Chicago, 1914; In Stratford and the Plays, 1917; Ballads of Peace and War, 1918, Poems on Chicago and Illinois, 1927. Contbr. to various anthologies. Founded The John Billings Fiske prize in poetry, at U. of Chicago, 1919. Died June 22, 1940.

FISKE, James Porter, surgeon; b. New York, N.Y., Nov. 22, 1866; s. Thomas Scott and Clara (Pittman) F.; ed. pvt. instrn.; M.D., Coll. Phys. and Surg. (Columbia), 1891; m. Amy Treadwell, June 14, 1906. Surgeon Charity Hosp. and New York Maternity Hosp., 1891-92; obstetric surgeon Church Hosp. and attending surgeon St. Elizabeth's Hosp., 1893—; attending phys. North Western Dispensary, 1895-97; orthopedic surgeon New York Post-Grad. Hosp., 1895-99; lecturer on surgery, New York Post-Grad. Med. Sch., 1895-99; orthopedic surgeon Roosevelt Hosp., 1893-1901; asst. surgeon and lecturer on surgery, Cornell, 1901-03; asst. surgeon Bellevue Hosp., 1899-1900; orthopedic surgeon New York Hosp., 1904—. Specialty, deformities and errors of development; introduced into U.S. at Roosevelt Hosp., 1893, the ambulatory treatment of fractures of the leg. Pres. Guild for Crippled Children of the Poor of New York City, 1905-07; attending surgeon Free Sch. for Crippled Children, 1901-13; charter mem. W. H. Davis Sch. for Crippled Children; mgr. N.Y. State Hosp. for Crippled and Deformed Children, 1908—. Sec. Am. Posture League, New York, 1922—. Fellow New York Acad. Medicine. Commd. capt. and surgeon, Med. R.C., Aug. 5, 1917; maj., Med. Corps U.S.A., Aug. 15, 1918; lt. col., M.O.R.C., 1924; was cons. orthopedic surgeon at various camps and at Washington, D.C. Comdr. European Commandery, Mil. Order of Foreign Wars, 1927-28; vice comdr. gen. Mil. Order of Foreign Wars of U.S., 1932-35; del. at Geneva, Les Amities Internationales, 1930. Died Oct. 24, 1941.

FISKE, John, author (name originally Edmund Fiske Green); b. Hartford, Conn., March 30, 1842; s. Edmund Brewster and Mary Fiske (Bound) Green; at the age of 13 took the name of maternal g.g., John Fiske, of Middletown; grad. Harvard, 1863; admitted to Suffolk bar, 1864; grad. Harvard Law School, 1865, but never practiced; m. Abby M. Brooks, Sept. 6, 1864. Univ. lecturer on philosophy, 1869-71; asst. librarian, 1872-79; mem. bd. of overseers, Harvard, 1879—. Lecturer and writer on philosophy and history; has done much to develop doctrine of evolution. Author: Myths and Mythmakers, 1872; Outlines of Cosmic Philosophy, 2 vols., 1874; The Unseen World, 1876; Excursions of an Evolutionist, 1883; The Destiny of Man, 1884; The Idea of God, 1885; American Political Ideas, 1885; The Critical Period of American History, 1888; The War of Independence, 1889; The Beginnings of New England, 1889-98; Civil Government in the United States, 1890; The American Revolution, 2 vols., 1891 (illus. edn. 1896); The Discovery of America, 2 vols., 1892; History of the United States for Schools, 1894; Edward Livingston Youmans, 1894; Old Virginia and Her Neighbors, 2 vols., 1897 (illus. edn. 1901); The Dutch and Quaker Colonies in America, 2 vols., 1899; Through Nature to God, 1899; A Century of Science, 1900; The Mississippi Valley in the Civil War, 1900. Editor: (with James Grant Wilson) Appleton's Cyclopædia of Am. Biography. Home: Cambridge, Mass. Died 1901.

FISKE, Lewis Ransom, clergyman, educator, author; b. Penfield, N.Y., Dec. 24, 1825; s. James and Eleanor (Ransom) F.; grad. U. of Mich., 1850 (A.M., LL.D., U. of Mich.; D.D., Albion Coll.). Entered ministry M.E. Ch.; held pastorates in Jackson, Ann Arbor and Detroit; held professorships in Mich. State Normal Sch., Mich. State Agrl. Coll.; pres. Albion Coll., 20½ yrs., up to Jan. 1898; emeritus prof. of philosophy, same. Editor Mich. Christian Advocate, 1875-79; mem. Nat. Bd. of Edn. of M.E. Ch. Home: Albion, Mich. Died 1901.

FISKE, Minnie Maddern, actress; b. New Orleans, La.; d. Thomas W. and Elizabeth (Maddern) Davey, a theatrical mgr.; appeared in child's part when 3 yrs. old; at 12 was alternately playing leading rôles and old women parts, and at 15 became a star, under name of Minnie Maddern; m. Harrison Grey Fiske, Mar. 19, 1890. Has starred in numerous plays and is identified especially with "Tess of the D'Urbervilles," "Becky Sharp," "The Rivals," and Ibsen dramas. LL.D. from U. of Wis., 1927. Home: Big Moose, N.Y. Died Feb. 16, 1932.

FISKE, Stephen, dramatic editor; b. New Brunswick, N.J., Nov. 22, 1840; ed. Rutgers Coll., 1862. Connected with New York Herald as editorial writer and spl. corr.; accompanied Japanese Princes, President-elect Lincoln and the Prince of Wales on Am. tours; called from seat of war, 1862, to become dramatic critic of the Herald; sailed for England, 1866, in the Henrietta yacht race; with Garibaldi in his last campaign against Rome; managed St. James Theatre and Royal English Opera Co., London, and 5th Av. Theatre, New York; first introduced Modjeska and Mary Anderson. Home: New York, N.Y. Died Apr. 27, 1916.

FISKE, William Mead Lindsley, M.D., surgeon; b. New York, N.Y., May 10, 1841; s. Almond Dunbar F.; studied New York Med. and Bellevue Hosp. colls.; grad. from latter, after serving in the war, in 1863; grad. New York Homœ. Coll., 1864; studied meteorology and established the meteorol. sta. at San Mateo, Fla.; elected pres. Brooklyn Homœ. Hosp., 1882; one of the founders of the Brooklyn Homœ. Dispensary; 1891 attended the Berlin congress as a rep. of the Kings Co. and N.Y. State socs. as ex-pres. of each. Home: Brooklyn, N.Y. Died 1904.

FITCH, Ashbel Parmelee, lawyer; b. Mooers, N.Y., Oct. 8, 1848; ed. in public schools of New York, Williston Sem., Easthampton, Mass., and Univs. of Jena and Berlin; studied at Columbia Law School; admitted to bar, 1869; a corp. lawyer, 1869—. Originally a Republican, but declined nomination for Congress, 1884, because not in favor of high protection; in 1886 ran as low-tariff Republican, defeating Gen. Egbert Viele, high-protection Democrat. Left Republican party on tariff issue and was re-elected 3 times as Democrat, serving in Congress, 1887-93; advocate of internat. copyright; opponent of free coinage of silver, ship subsidy, and McKinley tariff bills. Comptroller of New York, 1893-97, as Democrat, but being a strong gold-standard man ran for re-election on Republican ticket, 1897, and was defeated; pres. The Trust Co. of Am., July 1, 1899—. Died 1904.

FITCH, Charles Elliott, journalist; b. Syracuse, N.Y., Dec. 3, 1835; s. Thomas Brockway (banker in Syracuse for 40 yrs) and Ursula (Elliott) F.; A.B., Williams, 1855; LL.B., Albany Law Sch., 1857; A.M., ad eundem, Syracuse U., 1875; (L.H.D., Hamilton, 1895); m. Louise Lawrence Smith, July 21, 1870. Clerk provost ct., Newbern, N.C., 1864-65; practiced law, Syracuse, N.Y., and Newbern, N.C., 1857-66; editor-in-chief Syracuse Daily Standard, 1866-73, Rochester Democrat and Chronicle, 1873-90; collector U.S. internal revenue, 1890-04; state lecturer N.Y. Dept. Pub. Instrn., 1895-1904; chief div. of records, Edn. Dept., New York, 1904-06; chief div. of sch. libraries, 1906-12. Supervisor U.S. census, 1880; chmn. Rep. State Conv., 1888; sec. N.Y. Constl. Conv., 1894; regent U. State of N.Y., 1877-1904. Editor: Recollections of Abraham Lansing; Political New York from Cleveland to Hughes; New York—Political and Governmental; Encyclopedia of Biography of New York. Home: Syracuse, N.Y. Died Jan. 16, 1918.

FITCH, Clifford Penny, veterinarian; b. Sauquoit, N.Y., July 1, 1884; s. Menzo and Cora Lilian (Penny) F.; B.S., Hamilton Coll., Clinton, N.Y., 1906, M.S., 1909; D.V.M., Cornell U., 1911; D.S.C. from Iowa State Coll., 1929; m. Florence Lily Adams, July 15, 1911; children—Alva Farnham, James Adams. Asst. in bacteriology, N.Y. State Vet. Coll. (Cornell U.), 1909-11; instr. bacteriology, 1911-13, asst. prof., 1914-16, prof.; 1916-17, prof. animal pathology and bacteriology and chief div. of vet. medicine, U. of Minn., 1917—. Republican. Conglist. Author: (with V. A. Moore) Bacteriology and Diagnosis, 1914. Home: St. Paul, Minn. Died Jan. 11, 1940.

FITCH, (William) Clyde, author and playwright; b. New York, N.Y., May 2, 1865; s. William Goodwin and Alice (Clarke) F.; grad. Amherst, 1886 (A.M., 1902). Author: Nathan Hale, 1899; Barbara Frietchie, 1900; Captain Jinks of the Horse Marines, 1902. Original Plays: Beau Brummell; The Moth and the Flame; Nathan Hale; Barbara Frietchie; The Cowboy and The Lady; The Climbers; Capt. Jinks of the Horse Marines; The Stubbornness of Geraldine; The Girl with the Green Eyes; Her Own Way; Glad of It; The Truth, 1906, and many others. Adaptations: The Masked Ball; Bohemia; The Frisky Mrs. Johnson; The Head of the Family; Granny; Cousin Billy; The House of Mirth, 1906. Died 1909.

FITCH, Ezra Charles, mfr.; b. Bremen, Germany, July 19, 1847; s. Ezra and Auguste A. C. (Fedeler) F.; father a native of Conn. and a sea captain; ed. pub. schs., Worcester, Mass.; m. Helen Louise Stevens; children—Mary A. (Mrs. Frank Northen), Conover (dec.), Ezra Charles (dec.), Mrs. Helen Louise Fairchild (dec.). Has been connected with the Waltham Watch Co. since boyhood; became mgr. New York office, 1872; was placed in charge of mfg. plant at Waltham, Mass., 1883; pres. Waltham Watch Co., 40 yrs., then chmn. bd. and now v.p. of the co. Home: Brookline, Boston, Mass. Died Feb. 3, 1932.

FITCH, George, author; b. Galva, Ill., June 5, 1877; s. Elmer Eli and Rachel (Helgesen) F.; B.S., Knox Coll., Ill., 1897; m. Clara Gattrell Lynn, Oct. 5, 1904. Began as newspaper writer at Galva, 1897; spl. writer Council Bluffs (Ia.) Nonpariel, 1902-05; editor Peoria (Ill.) Herald-Transcript, 1905-11. Mem. Ill. Ho. Rep., 1912; Progressive, Pres. Am. Press Humorists. Conglist. Author: The Big Strike at Siwash, 1909; At Good Old Siwash, 1911; My Demon Motor Boat, 1912. Home: Peoria, Ill. Died Aug. 9, 1915.

FITCH, Grant, banker; b. Milwaukee, Wis., Sept. 22, 1859; s. William Grant and Martha E. (Curtis) F.; grad. Milwaukee Acad., 1877; B.A., Yale, 1881; m. Eliza Eliot, Dec. 7, 1887. Asst. cashier, 1886-88, cashier 1888-1906, v.p., 1906-25, pres., 1925-29, chmn. bd., 1929-30, Nat. Exchange Bank of Milwaukee which consolidated with Marine Nat. Bank forming Marine Nat. Exchange Bank of which is dir.; dir. Wis. Securities Co. Republican. Episcopalian. Home: Milwaukee, Wis. Died Feb. 23, 1940.

FITCH, Thomas Davis, M.D.; b. Troy, Pa., July 14, 1829, removing to Ill., 1846; ed. Knox Coll.; grad. Rush Med. Coll., Chicago, 1854; located at Kewanee, Ill.; m. Harriet Winslow Skinner, April 6, 1852. Surg., 42d Ill. regt., U.S. vols., 1861-63; located in Chicago, 1864; has been surg. and lecturer on obstetrics in various Chicago hospitals; one of originators, 1870, of Woman's Med. Coll., and prof. there. Home: Quincy, Ill. Died 1901.

FITCH, Walter, mining exec.; b. London, Eng., Jan. 20, 1854; s. Alfred and Rebecca (Glover) F.; ed. pvt. schs.; m. Exilda Marcotte, May 5, 1879; children—Lilian Charlotte (Mrs. J. Fred Johnson), Howard, Maud (Mrs. Paul Hilsdale), Cecil, Walter. Came to United States, 1874, naturalized, 1880. Began mining in Mich., 1881, superintending operation of iron mines, subsequently copper mines; for last 25 years operating in Utah, organizing in 1909 the Chief Consol. Mining Co., as its pres., in Tintic mining dist. Republican. Catholic. Home: Eureka, Utah. Died April 23, 1937.

FITCH, William Foresman, ry. official; b. Circleville, O., June 28, 1839. Began as clk. in office of gen. mgr. C.&N.W. Ry., 1871, advancing to supt. Peninsular div. same rd.; gen. mgr. Fremont Elkhorn & Mo. Valley and Sioux City & Pacific rys., 1866-88; gen. mgr. Duluth, S. Shore & Atlantic Ry., 1888-1911, also 2d v.p. same rd., 1888-1902, and pres., 1902-11; was pres. and receiver Duluth & Winnipeg R.R. and pres. reorganized rd., the Duluth, Superior & Western Ry.; was also pres. Mineral Range R.R., gen. mgr. Hancock & Calumet R.R., and pres. Lake Superior Terminal & Transfer Ry.; v.p. Wis. Central Ry.

1912—; v.p. Western Express Co. Home: Marquette, Mich. Died Sept. 16, 1915.

FITHIAN, Edward, naval officer; b. N.J., Dec. 13, 1820. Apptd. 3d asst. engr. U.S.N., Oct. 31, 1848; promoted 2d asst. engr., Feb. 26, 1851; chief engr., Oct. 23, 1859; retired, Dec. 13, 1882; advanced to rank of rear admiral retired, June 29, 1906, for services during Civil War. Served on Roanoke and at New York during Civil War. Home: Bridgeton, N.J. Died 1908.

FITKIN, Abraham Edward, investment securities; b. Brooklyn, N.Y., Sept. 18, 1878; s. Thomas Furlong and Mary (Vought) F.; ed. pub. schs.; m. Susan Norris, May 14, 1895; children—A. Raleigh (dec.), Mary Louise, Willis Carridine, Ralph M. Began as bookkeeper Pelser Walker Co., New York, 1900, later mgr.; asso. with W. C. Harty in pub. utilities investments, 1908-26, since in own name; chmn. bd. A. E. Fitkin & Co., Ltd., United Am. Utilities, Inc. Mason. Republican. Home: Allenhurst, N.J. Died Mar. 18, 1933.

FITTS, George Henry, judge; b. Cohoes, N.Y., Sept. 29, 1851; s. Lucien and Lemira M. (Slocum) F.; A.B., Dartmouth, 1873; LL.B., Albany Law Sch., 1874; m. Clara B. Bogue, June 4, 1896. City atty., Cohoes, 1888-95; surrogate, Albany Co., N.Y., 1896-1905; justice Supreme Ct. of N.Y., 3d Jud. Dist., 1906-20. Republican. Trustee and v.p. Mechanics Savings Bank; pres. Masonic Temple Assn., Cohoes. Home: Cohoes, N.Y. Died 1909.

FITZ, Reginald Heber, physician; b. Chelsea, Mass., May 5, 1843; s. Albert and Eliza Roberts (Nye) F.; A.B., Harvard, 1864, A.M., 1867, M.D., 1868 (LL.D., 1905); m. Elizabeth L. Clarke, June 12, 1879. Instr. pathol. anatomy, 1870-73, asst. prof., 1873-78, prof., 1878-79, Shattuck prof. same, 1879-92, Hersey prof. theory and practice of physic, 1892-1908, emeritus prof., 1908—, Harvard. Fellow Am. Acad. Arts and Sciences. Author: (with Dr. Horatio C. Wood) The Practice of Medicine, 1897. Died Sept. 30, 1913.

FITZ-GERALD, Aaron Ogden, mfr.; b. Newark, N.J., Sept. 14, 1845; s. John Driscoll and Osee Melinda (Boylan) F.-G.; ed. pub. schs. and pvt. tutors; m. Harriet Minerva Haines, May 20, 1869; children—John Driscoll, Charles Stuart Haines, Osee Clare (dec.), Aaron Boylan, Mary. Admitted, 1870, to partnership with father in mfr. of varnish firm Fitz-Gerald & Co.; pres., treas., 1893-1927, The Fitz-Gerald Co. Sergt. Co. A, 1st Regt. N.J. Rifle Corps, 1865-67. In philanthropic and religious work; trustee and sec. Home for Friendless, 1896-1929, v.p., 1929—; trustee, 1898—, sec., 1913-20, pres., 1920—, Central M.E. Ch., Newark; trustee Centenary Fund Newark Conf.; pres. Mt. Tabor Bd. Health, 1915-27. Mason. Formerly prominent in baseball matters (non-professional); pres. Nat. Assn. Junior Baseball Players, 1866-67. Home: Newark, N.J. Died Nov. 2, 1932.

FITZGERALD, Desmond, civil engr.; b. Nassau, New Providence, May 20, 1846; s. Capt. Lionel C. W. H. and Caroline (Brown) F.; ed. Phillips Acad., Andover, Mass.; m. Elizabeth P. C. Salisbury, June 21, 1870. For 40 yrs. practice as hydraulic engr., principally in connection with construction maintenance of Boston water-supply system. Dept. engr. Met. Water Bd., Boston; was chmn. of the Topographical Survey Commn. of Mass.; chmn. Brookline Park Commn.; mem. Met. Improvement Commn. of Mass.; cons. engr., water supply and sewage systems, Manila, P.I., 1904. Fellow Am. Acad. Arts and Sciences. Home: Brookline, Mass. Died Jan. 12, 1928.

FITZGERALD, Edward, R.C. bishop of Little Rock (Ark.), 1867—; b. Limerick, Ireland, 1833; came to U.S., 1849; entered Coll. of the Barrens, Mo., 1850; finished ecclesiastical studies in Mt. St. Mary's Coll., Emmitsburg, Md.; ordained priest, 1857; pastor at Columbus, O., until 1867. Died 1907.

FITZGERALD, Francis Alexander James, consulting engr.; b. Dublin, Ireland, June 1, 1870; s. Charles Edward (M.D.) and Isabel (Clarke) F.; B.A., Trinity Coll., Dublin U., 1892; S.B., Mass. Inst. Tech., 1895; m. Frances Mary Winifred Knox, of Dublin, Oct. 1, 1910. Chemist Carborundum Co., Niagara Falls, N.Y., 1895-1900; research chemist Internat. Acheson Graphite Co., Niagara Falls, 1900-08; consulting practice and research, 1903—. Fellow A.A.A.S. Home: Niagara Falls, N.Y. Died 1929.

FITZGERALD, Francis Scott Key, author; b. St. Paul, Minn., Sept. 24, 1896; s. Edward and Mary (McQuillan) F.; student Newman School, Lakewood, N.J., Princeton Univ., 1913-17; left coll. to join army; m. Zelda Sayre, Apr. 3, 1920; 1 dau., Frances Scott. Commd. 2d lt. 45th Inf., Nov. 1917; 1st lt. 67th Inf., July 1918; served as a.-d.-c. to Brig. Gen. J. A. Ryan, Dec. 1918-Feb. 1919. Author: This Side of Paradise, 1920; Flappers and Philosophers, 1920; The Beautiful and Damned, 1921; Tales of the Jazz Age, 1922; The Vegetable (play), 1923; The Great Gatsby, 1925; All the Sad Young Men, 1926; Tender Is the Night, 1934; Taps at Reveille, 1935; The Last Tycoon (an unfinished novel, together with The Great Gatsby and selected stories), 1941. Died Dec. 21, 1940.

FITZGERALD, Frank Dwight, gov.; b. Grand Ledge, Mich., Jan. 27, 1885; s. John Wesley and Carrie G. (Foreman) F.; ed. pub. schs. (Grand Ledge) and Ferris Inst. (Big Rapids, Mich.); m. Queena M. Warner, June 28, 1909; 1 son, John Warner. Committee clk. Mich. Senate, 1913; proofreader Ho. of Rep., 1915, bill clk., 1917; also served as clk. in office of sec. of state and as exec. sec. Mich. Federal Food Administration; apptd. dep. sec. of state, 1919; business mgr. Mich. State Highway Dept., 1923-31; sec. of state, Mich., 1931-34; gov. of Mich., 1935-36; pres. Loan & Deposit State Bank. Mem. Eaton County Rep. Com. many yrs. (chmn. 2 terms); mem. Rep. State Central Com., 1925-26, sec., 1929-30. Conglist. Mason. Home: Grand Ledge, Mich. Died Mar. 16, 1939.

FITZGERALD, Harrington, editor, artist; b. Phila., Apr. 5, 1847; s. Thomas and Sarah Levering (Riter) F.; acad. edn., Phila.; m. Mary Dager Wills, May 4, 1881 (died 1909); children—Mrs. Sarah Riter Hobart, Mrs. Mary Hitner Watt, Mrs. Helen Levering Brookfield, Mrs. Alice Leinster Taubel (dec.), Harrington. Began business career as cashier for Jay Cooke & Co. for 4 yrs. until failing eyesight compelled a year's rest; then bus. mgr. and mng. editor The Philadelphia Item for 30 yrs. Became interested in art, as a relaxation, in early '60s, and studied under George W. Nicholson, and John S. Sargent, Phila., and in Paris, under Gérôme and Fortuny; has exhibited pictures in Phila., Chicago, New York, Detroit, Pittsburgh, Buffalo Expn., 1901, the two Omaha Expns. and Charleston Expn., where received medal, also at St. Louis Expn., 1904; also gold medal at exhbn. of Am. Art Soc., Phila.; has large and valuable art collection. Represented in permanent collections of Nat. Gallery, Smithsonian Instn., Washington, Albright Gallery, Buffalo, Mus. of Art, Detroit, and Phila. Mus. of Art. Inventor, holds U.S. patents. Episcopalian. Republican. Home Philadelphia, Pa. Died Sept. 16, 1930.

FITZ GERALD, James, judge; b. Ireland, Oct. 28, 1851; ed. pub. schs. and Cooper Inst., New York; grad. Columbia Law Sch., 1880; m. Anna Tynan, Apr. 14, 1884. Mem. N.Y. Assembly 1878, Senate, 1882; asst. dist. atty., 1884; judge Ct. of Gen. Sessions, 1890-98; judge Supreme Ct. N.Y., 1888-1912. Democrat. Home: New York, N.Y. Died Dec. 17, 1922.

FITZGERALD, James Merlin, vocational counselor; b. Springfield, Ill., Apr. 1, 1870; s. John J. and Mary E. (Cunningham) F.; student Valparaiso (Ind.) U., 1890-93, Harvey Med. Coll., Chicago, 1904-06; M.D., Jenner Med. Coll., Chicago, 1908; m. Marie Alice Ringle, May 15, 1902; children—James La-Fayette, Mary Cunningham. Vocational counselor, Chicago, 1898—; prof. mental physiology, Bennett Med. Coll., 1903-10; counselor to J. J. McManamann, chief probation officer and atty. of Juvenile Court, Chicago, 1902-10; asso. lecturer on psychology to late Bishop Samuel Fallows of Chicago. Home: Oak Park, Ill. Died Aug. 16, 1939.

FITZ GERALD, James Newbury, M.E. bishop, 1888—; b. Newark, N.J., July 27, 1837; s. John D. and Osee M. (Boylan) F.; admitted to N.J. bar, 1858; joined Newark Conference, 1862; m. Mary Eliza, d. Dr. J. D. Annin, Jan. 1864. Mem. General Conference, 1876, 1880, 84 and 88; rec. sec. Missionary Soc., M.E. Ch., 1880-88; received degrees D.D., Wesleyan Univ., 1880; LL.D., Hamline Univ., 1889. Was presiding elder dists. of Newton, Newark and Jersey City. Died 1907.

FITZGERALD, Joseph, editor, author; b. Limerick, Ireland, Jan. 6, 1837; s. James and Joanna (Pratt) F.; grad. Mt. St. Mary's, Emmittsburg, Md., 1856; m. Julia E. Knox, 1873. Asst. editor Popular Science Monthly, 1872-79; publisher Humboldt Library, 1879-89; was asst. editor North Am. Review and later 4 yrs. on Forum; sub-editor Columbian Cyclo., Ency. Americana, Dictionary Cyclo.; 1 yr. editor The Twentieth Century (weekly). Author: Caseine—being Rural Meditations, 1869; Word and Phrase—True and False Use in English, 1901. Home: Mamaroneck, N.Y. Died 1908.

FITZGERALD, Louis, pres. Mercantile Trust Co. of New York; b. New York, May 31, 1838; ed. there and engaged in business; became mem. 7th N.Y. regt., 1857; marched with it to defense of Washington; later lt. 11th N.Y. inf.; served through Civil war, becoming col. 1st Miss. regt. On return to New York re-entered 7th N.Y. regt., becoming lt. col., and, 1882-98, brig. gen., resigning Jan. 1898. Active in important railroad reorganizations and financial operations; retired. Home: Garrison, N.Y. Died 1908.

FITZGERALD, Oscar Penn, bishop; b. in N.C., Aug. 24, 1829; ed. common schs. in N.C. and in a printing office in Va.; (D.D., U. of the South); m. Sarah Banks, Feb. 16, 1855. Entered M.E. Ch., S., ministry in Ga., 1853; went to Calif., 1855; was editor Pacific Methodist and Christian Spectator; supt. of pub. instrn. for Calif., 1867-71, and ex-officio editor Calif. School Journal; elected editor of the Nashville Christian Advocate, 1878; elected bishop, 1890. Author: California Sketches; Glimpses of Truth; Daily Bread; Sunset Views, 1900; Upper Room Meditations, 1902. Home: Nashville, Tenn. Died 1911.

FITZGERALD, Robert Mullins, lawyer; b. San Francisco, Jan. 7, 1858; s. Edward and Catherine (Mullins) F.; grad. Oakland (Calif.) High Sch., 1879; LL.B., U. of Calif., 1883; m. Laura M. Crellin, Dec. 23, 1902. Began practice Oakland, 1883; mem. Fitzgerald, Abbott & Beardsley; pres. Archon Co.; v.p. Central Nat. Bank, Central Savings Bank. Mem. 1st Bd. Pub. Works, Oakland, 1889; mem. State Bd. Prison Dirs., 1895-1905. Catholic. Home: Oakland, Calif. Died Jan. 3, 1934.

FITZGERALD, William A., editor; b. Stockton, Calif., Nov. 23, 1874; s. Michael and Bridget (Slattery) F.; grad. high sch., Stockton, 1893; m. Minnie Randolph Rutherford, Dec. 25, 1901 (died 1931). Mng. editor Fresno (Calif.) Republican, 1898-1903; recorder, Calif. R.R. Commn., 1921-23; pub. and editor Stockton Independent, 1923-33; asso. editor San Francisco Chronicle, 1933—. Republican. Died Oct. 26, 1936.

FITZ GERALD, William Sinton, lawyer; b. Washington, D.C., Oct. 6, 1880; s. David and Esther (Sinton) F.; grad. high sch., Washington; LL.M., George Washington U., 1903. Began practice at Washington, 1903; moved to Cleveland, O., 1905; dir. of law, City of Cleveland, 1916-20; mayor of Cleveland, term May 1, 1920-Dec. 31, 1921; mem. Cleveland Civil Service Commn., 1922-28. Republican. Mason. Home: Cleveland, O. Died Oct. 3, 1937.

FITZGIBBONS, John; b. Glenmore, N.Y., July 10, 1868; s. John and Mary (Gubbins) F.; ed. pub. schs.; m. Nellie M. Stone, Jan. 24, 1900. Legislative rep. Brotherhood of Railroad Trainmen of N.Y. State, for over 25 years; deputy compensation commr. of N.Y. State, May 1914-Feb. 1915; alderman Fourth Ward, Oswego, N.Y., Apr. 1908-Dec. 1909; mayor of Oswego, 1910-11 and 1918-21; mem. 73d Congress (1933-35), N.Y. at large. Democrat. Home: Oswego, N.Y. Died Aug. 4, 1941.

FITZHENRY, Louis, judge; b. Bloomington, Ill., June 13, 1870; LL.B. and LL.D., Ill. Wesleyan U., Bloomington; m. Lottie B. Rankin, 1909. Admitted to Ill. bar, 1897; city atty., Bloomington, 1907-11; mem. 63d Congress (1913-15), 17th Ill. Dist.; U.S. dist. judge, Southern Dist. of Ill., 1918-33; judge U.S. Circuit Court of Appeals, June 16, 1933—. Mason. Home: Bloomington, Ill. Died Nov. 18, 1935.

FITZHUGH, Guston Thomas, lawyer; b. in Smith Co., Miss., Aug. 31, 1866; s. Lewis Thomas and Julie (Delony) F.; B.A., U. of Miss., 1886 (1st honor); LL.B., Law Dept., same univ., 1889; m. Josie Millsaps, Apr. 17, 1901; children—Millsaps, Guston T., Mary, Alice (dec.), Julie (dec.). Admitted to bar of Tenn., 1889; counsel Memphis Commercial Appeal, WMC, Inc.; dir. Internat. Vegetable Oil Co., Maury-Cole Co. Capt. Co. L 4th Tenn., Spanish-Am. War. Trustee Emory U., Methodist Hosp. (Memphis), Hermitage Assn. (Andrew Jackson's home); mem. Laymen's Advisory Com. of Nat. Conf. of Jews and Christians, Citizens Advisory Com. of Southwestern U., State Council of Nat. Econ. League. Fellow Am. Geog. Society. Mem. M.E. Ch., South. Home: Memphis, Tenn. Died Jan. 16, 1940.

FITZ-PATRICK, Gilbert, obstetrician; b. Columbiana Co., O., Jan. 19, 1873; s. Thomas C. and Mary J. (Gilbert) F.; ed. Ohio Northern U., Ada; M.D., Chicago Homœ. Med. Coll., 1896; m. Elizabeth Sanford, May 1913. Interne Silver Cross Hosp., Joliet, Ill., 1897; house surgeon, Garfield Park Hosp., Chicago, 1898-99, Rotunda Hosp., Dublin, Ireland, 1902, Sloane Maternity Hosp., New York, 1903; formerly head dept. of obstetrics, Hahnemann Med. Coll. and Hosp., and attdg. obstetrician Cook Co. Hosp.; cons. obstetrician, Ill. Masonic Hosp.; attdg. obstetrician Chicago Polyclinic and Henrotin hosps.; mem. visiting staff Passavant Hosp.; trustee Ill. Masonic Hosp. Mem. Ill. State Med. Exam. Bd. Mem. bd. Gorgas Memorial Inst. of Tropical Medicine; fellow and gov. Am. Coll. Surgeons; chmn. Ill. Cancer Committee. Colonel Med. R.C., U.S.A.; chief of surgery, Base Hosp., Camp Gordon, Atlanta, Ga., World War; now comdg. officer U.S. Gen. Hosp. No. 110; del. from Assn. Mil. Surgeons, U.S.A., to Royal Inst. of Pub. Health, Ghent, Belgium, 1927; U.S. del. to 1st Internat. Congress of Pub. Health and Hygiene, Cairo, Egypt, 1928. Republican. Mason. Home: Chicago, Ill. Died Nov. 15, 1936.

FITZPATRICK, John Clement, historian and archivist; b. Washington, D.C., Aug. 10, 1876; s. James Nicholas and Elizabeth A. (Combs) Fitzpatrick; ed. high and private schs.; A.M., St. Mary's Coll., Pa., 1918; L.H.D., George Washington U., 1926; Litt.D., Washington and Lee U., 1932; m. Elizabeth V. Kelly, 1922 (died 1933); 1 dau., Elizabeth Lavery. With Library of Congress, 1897-1928, asst. chief manuscript div., 1902-28; resigned to engage in editorial and hist. work. Mem. Pub. Archives Commn., 1916-17. Editor, compiler Complete Diaries of George Washington, 1925; Journals Continental Congress, U.S. Washington Bicentennial edit., writings of Washington; etc. Author: Washington's Expenses as Commander in Chief, 1917; The Spirit of the Revolution, 1924; George Washington, Colonial Traveler, 1927; George Washington, Himself, 1933. Home: Washington, D.C. Died Feb. 10, 1940.

FITZPATRICK, John Tracy, editor, author; b. Washington, D.C., Jan. 6, 1878; s. James Charles and Marion Aurelia (Mattoon) F.; A.B., Cornell U., 1900; student Albany Law Sch. (Union U.) 1903; m. Marcella Lucida Coughlin, Sept. 28, 1918; children—Marcella Catherine (dec.), John Tracy. Admitted to N.Y. bar, 1903; asst. in sociology, N.Y. State Library, 1907; legislative reference librarian, same library, 1913; law librarian, same library, 1915-30; first deputy Supreme Court reporter, 1930—; lecturer N.Y. State Library Sch., 1913-26, Albany Law Sch., 1915—. Commd. 1st lt. Ordnance Dept., U.S. Army, Aug. 20, 1918; chief of communications sect. of administration div., Office of Chief of Ordnance, Oct. 2, 1918-Jan. 23, 1919; 1st lt. Reserve List, N.G.N.Y., June 30, 1919. Republican. Catholic. Editor: Parsons' Practice Manual of New York, 1921 (2d edit., 1922); Gilbert's Civil Practice, 1922 (supplement, 1923, 24, 25); Gilbert-Bliss Civil Practice, 1925, 26 (supplement, 1927, 28, 29, 30, 31); Practice Manual of New York, 1924, 26, 27, 28, 29, 30, 31. Editor: Official Edition N.Y. State Session Laws (ann.), 1909-29; Parsons' New York Code of Civil Procedure (40th-43d, 45th edits.), 1915-18, 1920; Penal Law and Code of Criminal Procedure of New York (7th-33d edits.), 1915-31; Cook's Criminal Code of New York (27th-30th edits.), 1915-18, Supplements to Bliss' Code of Civil Procedure, 1917, 19; Selected Statutes of State of N.Y. (9th-14th edits.), 1916-27; Tax Law of the State of N.Y. (ann.), 1915-31; New York Village Laws, 1923 (supplement, 1925), 2d edit., 1927; Laws of State of N.Y. Relating to Spanish War Veterans, 1926; N.Y. State Veterans' Laws, 1929, 31. Home: Albany, N.Y. Died May 16, 1933.

FITZPATRICK, Paul Edward, wholesale dry goods; b. West Newton, Mass., Sept. 2, 1879; s. Thomas Bernard and Sarah Mary (Gleason) F.; A.B., Harvard, 1902; m. Alice Marie Wilcok, Oct. 22, 1907; children—Paul Wilcok, Elizabeth Hyland O'Neill, Donald Gleason, Edwin Newman. With Brown, Durrell Co. (of which father was pres.) since 1902; now pres. Mem. Corp. Peter Bent Brigham Hosp. Mem. Boston Chamber Commerce. Home: Brookline, Mass. Died Feb. 22, 1940.

FITZPATRICK, Thomas Vanhook, M.D.; b. Nicholsville, O., Apr. 9, 1855; s. Solomon and Zerilda (Vanhook) F.; ed. common schs., Nicholsville, and Hughes High Sch., Cincinnati; M.D., Cincinnati Coll. Medicine and Surgery, 1875; studied at Post-Grad. Med. Sch., New York; studied abroad, 1895; (Ph.D., Twin Valley College); married; children—Earle Verne, Thomas Vanhook. Distinguished as aurist and laryngologist. Fellow Am. Coll. Surgeons. Republican. Home: Cincinnati, O. Died 1934.

FITZSIMONS, Charles, soldier, contractor; b. New York, Dec. 26, 1835; removed with parents to Rochester; ed. common schs. and later studied engring. Entered Union army, 1861, as capt. 3d N.Y. cav.; promoted maj., May 1862; wounded June 1862, and obliged to resign early in 1863 because of wound; after few months' rest re-entered service as lt. col.; went to front Oct. 1863, with 21st N.Y. cav.; took part in engagements Shenandoah Valley; wounded Ashley's Gap, July 19, 1864; later comd. "remount" camp of cav., Pleasant Valley, Md.; commd. col., June, 1865; served on Western plains until mustered out, Denver, Colo., July 26, 1866, with bvt. rank brig. gen. Entered contracting business, sr. mem. Fitz Simons & Connell Co., contractors; constructed substructure of all modern, wide bridges in Chicago, tunnels, cribs and other important works; col. 1st regt. Ill. Nat. Guard, 1882, and same yr. apptd. by Gov. Cullom brig. gen. 1st brigade; apptd. and confirmed brig. gen., U.S.V., June, 1898, but soon after resigned. Home: Chicago, Ill. Died 1905.

FLACK, William Henry, congressman, mfr.; b. Franklin Falls, N.Y., Mar. 22, 1861; s. Daniel W. and Jane B. F.; ed. pub. schs.; m. Katherine M. Lynch, Oct. 7, 1882. Became interested in lumbering and tanning; was supervisor, town of Waverly, 10 yrs., and chmn. of the bd., 2 yrs.; co. clerk Franklin Co., 1897-1903; mem. Congress, 26th N.Y. dist., 1903-07. Was chmn. Rep. Co. Com., 1898-1902; was trustee village of Malone, and elected its pres., 1902. Home: Malone, N.Y. Died 1907.

FLAGG, Charles Allcott, librarian; b. Sandwich, Mass., Oct. 1, 1870; s. Samuel Benjamin and Anna Bigelow (Allcott) F.; A.B., Bowdoin, 1894; B.L.S., N.Y. State Library Sch., 1899; M.A., George Washington U., 1902; m. Ethel M. Flinder, Feb. 18, 1909. Prin. High Sch., Hopedale, Mass., 1894-95; asst. and later sub-librarian in charge of history and genealogy, N.Y. State Library, 1896-1900; specialist in Am. history, Library of Congress, 1900-13; librarian Bangor Pub. Library, 1913—. Mem. Me. Library Commn., 1915—. Republican. Unitarian. Author: Reference List on Connecticut Local History, 1900; Bibliography of New York Colonial History, 1901; A Guide to Massachusetts Local History, 1907; An Index of Pioneers from Massachusetts, 1915. Home: Bangor, Me. Died Mar. 28, 1920.

FLAGG, Charles Noël, artist; b. Brooklyn, Dec. 25, 1848; s. Rev. Jared Bradley and Louisa (Hart) F.; bro. of Ernest F.; ed. Hopkins Grammar Sch., New Haven; pupil in art of L. Jacquesson de la Chevreuse; m. Ellen F. Earle, Apr. 23, 1874. Founded 1888, at Hartford, the Conn. League of Art Students (now Flagg Night Sch. of Drawing for Men), in which he is dir. instr.; mem. Conn. State Capitol Commn. of Sculpture; awarded Thomas R. Proctor prize for portrait, Nat. Acad. Design, 1908, A.N.A., 1909; pres. Conn. Acad. Fine Arts, Municipal Art Soc. Hartford. Author: The Evolution of an Equestrian Statue, 1909. Home: Hartford, Conn. Died Nov. 10, 1916.

FLAGG, Edward Octavus, clergyman; b. Georgetown, S.C., Dec. 13, 1824; s. Henry C. and Martha F.; studied civil engring.; A.B., Trinity Coll., Conn., 1848; (D.D., New York U., 1866; LL.D., St. John's Coll., Md., 1898); m. Eliza W. McNiel; m. 2d, Mary L. Ferris. Deacon, 1848, priest, 1849, P.E. Ch.; held several pastorates; was rector of All Saints Ch. and Ch. of the Resurrection, New York, and asst. in Grace Ch., New York, nearly 6 yrs.; chaplain 9th Regt. N.G.S.N.Y.; also of the Prince of Orange Masonic Lodge, New York; retired from active ministry. Author: Earlier and Later Poems, 1906. Died 1911.

FLAGG, Jared Bradley, artist-clergyman; b. New Haven, Conn., June 16, 1820; ed. Lancasterian School and Trinity Coll., Hartford (non-grad.); (A.M., Trinity, 1861; S.T.D., Columbia, 1863). Studied painting with his brother, George Whiting Flagg, and his uncle, Washington Allston; located in New York; mem. Nat. Acad., 1849—. Entered ministry P.E. Church, 1854; rector St. James, Birmingham, Conn., 9 months; Grace Ch., Brooklyn Heights, N.Y., 8 years. Resigned and returned to practice of art. Principally portrait painter, but has also painted ideal figure pieces, notably "Hester Prynne in Prison." Author: Life and Letters of Washington Allston. Died 1899.

FLAGG, Josiah Foster, civil engr.; b. Dedham, Mass., Sept. 4, 1835; s. Josiah Foster and Mary (Wait) F.; ed. in common, high and Latin schs., Boston; S.B., summa cum laude, Harvard, 1854; m. Emma A. Wiggin, Apr. 13, 1858 (died 1888); m. 2d, Florence N. Dukes, Dec. 3, 1903. Had charge of important engring. works in Mexico, S. America and the W.I., as well as in New York, and other parts of U.S. Home: Santa Barbara, Calif. Died Apr. 13, 1928.

FLAGG, Montague, painter; b. Hartford, Conn., 1842; s. Jared Bradley (N.A.) and Sarah (Montague) F.; studied painting under Jacquesson de la Chevreuse, Paris; married. Proctor prize, Nat. Acad. Design, 1909; silver medal, St. Louis Expn., 1904; N.A., 1910. Died Dec. 24, 1915.

FLAGG, Rufus Cushman, clergyman; b. Hubbardton, Vt., Aug. 3, 1846; s. Amasa Wesson and Electa Lyman (Cushman) F.; A.B., Middlebury Coll., 1869 (D.D., 1891); grad. Andover Theol. Sem., 1872; m. Martha Brooks Rowley, July 10, 1872. Ordained Congl. ministry, 1872; pastor N. Andover, Mass., 1872-77, Westford, Mass., 1877-79, Fair Haven, Vt., 1880-89, Wells River, Vt., 1889-92; pres. Ripon (Wis.) Coll., 1892-1901; pastor Berlin, N.H., 1901-05, Newport, Vt., 1905-10; asso. pastor Federated First Chs. of Burlington and Winooski, Vt., 1911—. Home: Burlington, Vt. Died May 18, 1922.

FLAGLER, Clement Alexander Finley, army officer; b. in Ga., Aug. 17, 1867; B.S., Griswold Coll., Ia., 1885; grad. U.S. Mil. Acad., 1889, Engring. Sch. of Application, 1892; Army War Coll., 1914. Apptd. add. 2d lt. engrs., June 12, 1889; promoted through grades to brig. gen., Jan. 4, 1918. Instr. civ. and mil. engring., U.S. Mil. Acad., 1894-95; on staff Maj. Gen. J. H. Wilson, Chickamauga Park, Ga., Charleston, S.C., and in Puerto Rico, 1898; engr. officer, Dept. of the East, 1900-02; apptd. mem. Chesapeake & Del. Canal Commn., 1906; on staff Gen. Frederick Funston, Vera Cruz expdn., 1914; instr. Army War Coll., 1914-15; duty at Washington, 1916; comd. arty. of 5th Div. at St. Mihiel; promoted maj. gen. and comd. arty., 3d Corps in the Argonne-Meuse; comd. 42d (Rainbow) Div. in the Army of the Rhine, Nov. 21, 1918-Apr. 6, 1919; comdt. Engr. Sch., Camp Humphreys, Va., 1919; dept. engr., Honolulu, 1920; div. engr., Baltimore, 1921. Died May 7, 1922.

FLAGLER, Henry M., capitalist; b. Canandaigua, N.Y., 1830. Became clerk in country store; went to Saginaw, Mich., and became salt mfr.; removed to Cleveland, becoming partner in Rockefeller, Andrews & Flagler, oil refiners, who were succeeded by the Standard Oil Co., with management of which he was continuously connected. Owner Ponce de Leon and Alcazar hotels, Fla., which he built at a cost of $3,000,000; also owns about 600 miles of railroad in Fla. V.p. and dir. Standard Oil Co. of N.J. to June 1908, and dir. to Dec. 4, 1911, when resigned; chmn. bd. dirs. Fla. East Coast Ry. Home: Palm Beach, Fla., and N.Y. City. Died May 20, 1913.

FLAGLER, Isaac Van Vleck, composer, organist and music publ.; b. Albany, N.Y., 1848; s. John O. and Christina F.; ed. Albany and Kinderhook acads.; studied music Paris and Germany; unmarried. Organist and musical lecturer, Chautauqua Assembly, Chautauqua, N.Y.; one of founders Am. Guild of Organists. Is organist 1st Presbyn. Ch., Auburn, N.Y. Composer and editor: Five New Collections of Organ Music; Organists' Treasury; New Collection of Choir Music; New Era of Song; Songs of Praise and Devotion. Home: Auburn, N.Y. Died 1909.

FLAGLER, John Haldane, capitalist; b. Coldspring, N.Y., about 1838; s. Harvey K. and Sarah J. (Haldane) F.; acad. edn., Paterson, N.J.; m. Anna H. Converse, 1856; m. 2d, Alice Mandelick, 1898; m. 3d, Beatrice Frances Wenneker. Entered employ of Haldane & Co., iron, New York, 1854, and was mgr. Boston branch, same, several yrs.; organized John H. Flagler & Co., iron and steel, Boston, Nat. Tube Works, E. Boston, Nat. Tube Co., McKeesport, Pa., being pres. of latter until it was merged into U.S. Steel Corp. Home: New York, N.Y. Died Sept. 8, 1922.

FLAHERTY, Frederick H., surgeon; b. Chittenango, N.Y., Apr. 21, 1873; s. Patrick J. and Harriet (Vosburgh) F.; Syracuse U., 1891-92; M.D., Coll. of Medicine, Syracuse U., 1896; studied U. of Berlin, Germany, 1898; m. Kate Luddington, Jan. 4, 1898; children—Mrs. Helen Denison, Mrs. Elizabeth J. Brown, Mrs. Harriet A. Grove, Frederick. Clin. prof. surgery, Syracuse U.; surgeon St. Joseph's Hosp., Syracuse Free Dispensary, Syracuse Memorial Hosp. Trustee St. Joseph's Hosp. Fellow Am. Coll. Surgeons. Republican. Home: Syracuse, N.Y. Died Sept. 7, 1938.

FLAHERTY, Lawrence J., congressman; b. San Mateo, Calif., July 4, 1878; ed. pub. schs. Cement mason; served on Bd. Police Commrs., San Francisco; mem. Calif. Ho. of Rep. 8 yrs.; U.S. surveyor customs, San Francisco, 1923-25; mem. 69th Congress (1925-27), 5th Calif. Dist. Formerly pres. San Francisco Building Trades. Republican. Home: San Francisco, Calif. Died June 13, 1926.

FLANAGAN, Webster, lawyer, stockman; b. Cloverport, Ky., Jan. 9, 1832; s. James W. F.; moved to Tex., 1843. Held several local offices before joining C.S.A. as brig. gen.; after war an active Republican; apptd. judge 5th Jud. Dist., Tex., 1865; mem. Tex. Constl. convs., 1869, 1875; lt. gov., 1871-73; mem. Tex. Senate, 1875; pres. Henderson & Overton R.R., 1876-82; collector internal revenue 4th Tex. Dist., 1884-85; collector of customs at El Paso, Tex., 1891-93; apptd. collector of internal revenue, 3d Tex. Dist.; candidate for gov., 1890. Home: Henderson, Tex. Died May 5, 1924.

FLANDERS, Henry, lawyer; b. Sullivan Co., N.H., Feb. 13, 1826; s. Charles (grad. Harvard, 1808) and Lucretia (Kingsbury) F.; ed. Kimball Acad., N.H., and Newbury, Vt., Sem.; (hon. A.M., Dartmouth Coll., 1856); m. Elizabeth O. Barnwell, 1847. In law practice at Phila., 1850—. Lecturer, law dept., U. of Pa.; mem. Commn. for Collation and Publication of the Acts of Assembly of Pa. from 1700 to 1800. Author: Adventures of a Virginian, 1881. Home: Philadelphia. Died 1911.

FLANDERS, James Greeley, lawyer; b. New London, N.H., Dec. 13, 1844; s. Walter Powers and Susan Everett (Greeley) F.; A.B., Yale, 1867; Columbia Law Sch., 1869; m. Mary C. Haney, June 18, 1873. Mem. Milwaukee Sch. Bd., 1875-77; mem. Wis. Assembly, 1877; del.-at-large Dem. Nat. Conv., 1896, Chicago, and Democratic Nat. Conv. (gold Democrats), Sept. 1896. Home: Milwaukee, Wis. Died Jan. 1, 1920.

FLANDRAU, Charles Eugene, lawyer; b. New York, July 15, 1828; s. Thomas H. and Elizabeth (Macomb) F.; ed. Georgetown, D.C.; sailor before the mast, 1841-44; worked as sawyer of mahogany veneers, 1845-47; studied law in his father's office, Whitesboro, N.Y.; admitted to N.Y. bar, 1851; settled in practice, St. Paul, Minn., 1853; m. Isabella R. Dinsmore of Ky., Aug. 10, 1859 (died 1867); m. 2d, Mrs. Rebecca B. (McClure) Riddle, Feb. 28, 1871. Served as mem. Territorial Council; Indian agt., Sioux Nation, 1856; mem. constl. conv., 1857; asso. justice, Minn. Ty. and State, 1857-64. Was comdr.-in-chief of vol. forces resisting uprising of Sioux, whom he defeated at defense of New Ulm, Aug. 18, 1862, after desperate battle for 40 hours. Resigned from Supreme Court, 1864; practiced at Carson City, Nev., and later in St. Louis, but returned to Minn.; practiced Minneapolis, and was city atty. and, 1867, 1st pres. Minneapolis Bd. of Trade; again practicing at St. Paul, 1870—. Chmn. State Dem. Exec. Com., 1868-69; once nominated for gov., another time for chief justice Supreme Court; opposed Bryan on stump in 1896. Home: St. Paul, N.Y. Died 1903.

FLANIGAN, Edward Joseph (Ruane), judge; b. San Francisco, Calif., Oct. 19, 1874; s. Edward and Margaret (Wallace) F.; grad. high sch. course, St. Mary's Coll., Oakland, 1890; m. Georgie Hull, May 5, 1905; children—Charles Meacham, John Henry, Martha Anne. Admitted to Calif. bar, 1898; moved to Bisbee, Ariz., 1902; city atty., Bisbee, 3 terms, 1911-17; mem. firm Williams & Flanigan, 1911-18, Flanigan & Murry, 1918-21; Rep. candidate for justice Supreme court of Ariz., 1920; apptd. asso. justice Supreme Court of Ariz., Oct. 1, 1921, to fill vacancy occasioned by death of Hon. Albert C. Baker, term expired Jan. 1, 1923; mem. Flanigan & Fields, 1923—. Home: Phoenix, Ariz. Deceased.

FLANNIGAN, Richard Charles, judge; b. Ontonagon, Mich., Dec. 12, 1857; s. James and Ellen (Sullivan) F.; pub. schs., Ontonagon and Marquette, Mich.; student junior yr., Law Dept., U. of Mich., class of 1879, LL.B., as of class of 1879, 1923; m. Anna Haessly, Nov. 11, 1884. Admitted to Mich. bar, 1879; began practice, Norway, Mich., 1880; pros. atty., Menominee Co. (in which Norway was then situated), 1881-82 and 1885-86; 1st mayor City of Norway, 1891; mem. Mich. Constl. Conv., 1908-09; nominated by all polit. parties for judge 25th Jud. Circuit and apptd. by Gov. Warner, 1909; elected to same office at spl. election, without opposition, Apr. 1910, reëlected without opposition, 1923, term expires 1929; presiding judge, Roosevelt libel case, 1913. Republican. Catholic. Home: Norway, Mich. Died Feb. 17, 1927.

FLATHER, John Joseph, mech. engr.; b. Phila., June 9, 1862; s. Henry and Sarah S. (Hockensmith) F.; Ph.B., Sheffield Scientific Sch. (Yale), 1885; M.M.E., Cornell, 1890; several yrs.' practical experience in European and Am. machine shops, as supt. and mech. engr.; m. Harriet F. Lum, June 18, 1890 (died 1917); m. 2d, Florence Evelyn Foster, Feb. 23, 1925. Instr. mech. engring. Lehigh U., 1888-91; prof. mech. engring., Purdue U., 1891-98; head of dept. of mech. engring., U. of Minn., 1898—. Fellow A.A.A.S. (v.p., 1901-02). Joint author: Thermodynamics. 1915. Home: Minneapolis, Minn. Died May 14, 1926.

FLATTERY, M(aurice) Douglas, lawyer, financier; b. Dungarvan, Ireland, Feb. 6, 1870; s. Michael Angelo and Catherine (O'Brien) F.; came to U.S., 1893; ed. in Ireland and at Centre Coll., Ky.; student Harvard Law Sch., 1901-02; m. Georgina A. Mackie, of London, Eng., Aug. 18, 1897; prof. physiology, Nebr. U., 1894, Centre Coll., 1895-98; practiced law at Boston, later devoted attention principally to business affairs; pres. Globe Enterprises; now chmn. bd. Murray & Tregurta Corp. (mfrs. marine engines), Old Colony Woolen Mills Co.; mng. dir. Loew's Theatres Co., State Theatre Co., Globe Vaudeville Co., Columbia Amusement Co., State Theatre Co. Endowed radium clinic at Carney Hosp., also donated Lab. Bldg.; endowed fellowship in research medicine, Harvard Med. Sch.; endowed fund of $500 yearly, and gold medal, Harvard, for most important discovery in any part of the world, in preservation of health, or prevention of disease; endowed fund for Boston Theatre employees, etc. Served with Leinster Regt., British Army; pvt., 1885, corpl., instr. in sch., sergt., chief instr. gymnastics and fencing, instr. Sch. of Musketry; passed for capt. with honors. Awarded medal by Brit. Humane Soc., for saving life of drowning soldier off Sandgate, 1889; medal, Mass. Humane Soc. for saving life, 1907. Vol. mgr. Industrial Survey, Washington, D.C., 1918, World War; mem. Harvard Cancer Commn., 1919, established M. Douglas Flattery Foundation, for research work in preventive medicine at U. of Lyons, France, 1920; reported, for Pres. Harding, plan to organize research workers in medicine at U.S. univ. centers; mem. vocational advisory bd. Boston U., chmn. Boston Conservation Bureau; chmn. Spl. Com. on Med. Research. Republican. Author: The Subterfuge, 1903; The Conspirators; Annie Laurie, 1906; Duchess of Dublin, 1914. Home: Boston, Mass. Died Nov. 25, 1925.

FLECK, Henry Thomas, prof. music; b. Buffalo, N.Y., Apr. 28, 1863; s. George H. and Sarah M. (Carney) F.; A.B., Upper Canada Coll., Toronto, Can., 1883; LL.D., Lincoln Memorial U.; m. Katherine Deegan; children—Marie A., Harry Deegan, Donald F. Pres. Peekskill Conservatory of Music since 1894; prof. music Hunter Coll., 1900-1933; originated and organized Jr. Philharmonic Soc. for young people's concerts, 1893, conductor 1st concert, 1895; founder Haarlem Philharmonic Soc., founder free concert system in pub. schs. of N.Y. City and State. Served as pub. commr. and trustee of Commercial Tercentenary of N.Y. City (1614-1914), under Mayors McClellan, Gaynor and Mitchel; apptd. chmn. Safe and Sane Fourth by Mayors Gaynor and Hylan; apptd. commr. and trustee for Shakespeare Tercentenary Celebration, 1916, also N.Y. State Aqueduct Commn., 1917; chmn. N.Y. State Liberty Loan Ednl. Dept. Composer: String Quartette; Overture in D minor; also anthems, masses, songs, etc. Established Adolph Lewisohn Chamber Music Coll. Course, free to public, every Wednesday night throughout academic yr. Home: New York, N.Y. Died Sept. 6, 1937.

FLEET, Alexander Frederick, educator; b. King and Queen Co., Va., June 6, 1843; s. Benjamin (M.D.) and Maria Louisa (Wacker) F.; ed. Fleetwood Acad., Va., and U. of Va.; 1 yr. in medicine, U. of Va.; studied in Greece, 1887-88; (hon. A.M., Columbian, 1869; LL.D., Richmond Coll., 1889); m. Belle Seddon, July 6, 1871. Officer C.S.A., 1861-65; surrendered at Appomattox as adj. gen., H. A. Wise's Brigade. Prof. Greek, William Jewell College, Mo., 1868-73; pres. Lexington (Mo.) Female Coll., 1873-79; prof. Greek, U. of Mo., 1879-90; founder, and supt. Mo. Mil. Acad., 1890-96; supt. Culver Mil. Acad., 1896—. Home: Culver, Ind. Died 1911.

FLEETWOOD, Benjamin Franklin, clergyman; b. New York, Feb. 20, 1845; s. Stanley Hall and Mary Jane (Finley) F.; A.B., Racine (Wis.) Coll., 1863, A.M., 1866 (S.T.D., 1888); B.D., Nashotah Theol. Sem., Wis., 1867; m. Josephine E. Fake, Jan. 14, 1880. Deacon, 1867; priest, 1869, P.E. Ch.; asst. minister St. James', Chicago, 1867; rector Christ Ch., Adrian, Mich., 1868-73, St. Paul's, Marquette, Mich., 1873-77, St. Mark's, Chicago, 1877-89; rector Waterman Hall, The Chicago Diocesan Sch. for Girls, Sycamore, Ill., 1889-1918. Dean, Northern Deanery, Diocese of Chicago, 1894-1919. Home: Sycamore, Ill. Died Feb. 24, 1923.

FLEETWOOD, Frederick Gleed, congressman; b. St. Johnsbury, Vt., Sept. 27, 1868; s. Henry W. and Laura J. (Kenney) F.; grad. St. Johnsbury Acad., 1886; student U. of Vt., 1887, 88; A.B., Harvard, 1891; unmarried. Admitted to Vt. bar, 1894; town clk. and treas. Morrisville; presdl. elector and messenger, 1900; mem. Vt. Ho. of Rep., 1900-02; sec. of state and ins. commr. of Vt., 1902-06; mem. 68th Congress (1923-25), 1st Vt. Dist. Republican. Episcopalian. Home: Morrisville, Vt. Died Jan. 28, 1938.

FLEISCHMANN, Julius, mayor; b. June 8, 1872; s. of Charles and Henriette (Robertson) F.; m. Lily Ackerland; m. 2d, Mrs. Laura Heminway, Jan. 25, 1920. Pres. The Fleischmann Co. Mayor of Cincinnati, 2 terms. Mem. Bd. Pk. Commrs., 1908-12. Republican. Home: New York, N.Y. Died Feb. 5, 1925.

FLEISCHMANN, Simon, lawyer; b. Iowa City, Ia., Sept. 11, 1859; s. Emanuel and Eliza (Dessauer) F.; grad. Central High Sch., Buffalo, 1879; studied law in office of Grover Cleveland and Wilson S. Bissell, Buffalo; m. Laura G. Justice, June 29, 1898. Admitted to bar, 1882; supervisor, Buffalo, 1898-99, councilman for city at-large, 1900-03, pres. Bd. of Councilmen, 1902-03, Buffalo. Trustee and pres. Erie Co. Bar Assn. Jewish religion. Ind. Republican. Home: Buffalo, N.Y. Died Sept. 1, 1930.

FLEMING, Adrian Sebastian, army officer; b. Midway, Ky., Dec. 6, 1872; s. William B. F.; grad. U.S. Mil. Acad., 1895, Sch. of Submarine Defense, 1905; Field Officers' Course, Army Sch. of the Line, 1912; General Staff Col., 1920; m. Mabel V. Gassen, June 17, 1902. Commd. add. 2d lt. 5th Arty., June 12, 1895; promoted through grades to col., May 15, 1917; brig. gen. N.A., Apr. 12, 1918; brig. gen. O.R.C., July 12, 1921; brig. gen. retired, June 21, 1930. Accompanied Light Battery D, 6th Arty., to Philippines, 1898; in Philippine Rebellion from outbreak, Feb.-July 1898, in numerous engagements on Island of Luzon; cited for gallantry in action against insurgent forces nr. Manila, Feb. 5, 1899, and for gallantry in action at Calumpit River, Luzon, Apr. 25, 1899; comdt. School of Fire for Field Arty., Sept. 1917-May 1918; apptd. comdr. 158th Brigade, F.A., 83d Div., 4th Army Corps, A.E.F., May 1918; with A.E.F., June 1918-May 1919, serving in action during Meuse-Argonne Offensive, with 17th French Corps and 29th, 32d and 91st U.S. divs.; Gen. Staff Corps, Aug. 25, 1920; retired at own request after 30 yrs.' service, June 17, 1921. Vice pres. Columbia River Paper Co., Columbia River Paper Mills, Oregon Pulp & Paper Co., Calif.-Oregon Paper Mills. D.S.M.; awarded two oak leaves; Officier Légion d'Honneur (France). Presbyterian. Home: Portland, Ore. Died Dec. 1, 1940.

FLEMING, Aretas Brooks, governor; b. Fairmont, W.Va., Oct. 15, 1839; s. Benjamin F. and Rhoda (Brooks) F.; ed. acad., Fairmont, and law dept., U. of Va., 1859-60; (LL.D., W.Va. U., 1891); m. Carrie Watson, Sept. 7, 1865. Admitted to bar, 1862; pros. atty., 1863-68; mem. W.Va. Ho. of Rep., 1872-73, 1875-76; judge Circuit Ct., 2d Jud. Circuit, 1877-88; gov. of W.Va., 1889-93. Democrat. Home: Fairmont, W.Va. Died Oct. 13, 1923.

FLEMING, Arthur Henry, lumber mfr.; b. Halton Co., Ont., Can., Apr. 3, 1856; s. Samuel and Sophia (Harwood) F.; ed. common schs.; m. Clara H. Fowler, Nov. 30, 1892 (died 1904); 1 dau., Marjorie (Mrs. Wilton Lloyd-Smith). Came to U.S., 1879, naturalized citizen, 1886. Practiced law in Detroit, 1886-96; moved to California in 1896, and engaged in lumber business; also pres. Johnson Connector Co. (owning an automatic electric safety connector for all standard ry. cars). Pres. emeritus bd. trustees Calif. Inst. Tech., Pasadena, Calif. Donor of over $5,000,000 founding Calif. Inst. Tech., to be known as the Clara H. Fleming Memorial. Decorated Legion of Honor (France). Republican. Presbyn. Home: Pasadena, Calif. Died Aug. 11, 1940.

FLEMING, Burton Percival, civil and mech. engr.; b. Valley, Neb., Aug. 7, 1881; s. Allan Maris and Edith (Clark) F.; B.S. in C.E., Utah Agrl. Coll., 1900; Lawrence Scientific Sch. (Harvard), 1900-01; M.E., Cornell, 1906; m. Florence Foster, June 29, 1909; children—Allaire, Allan, Foster; m. 2d, Ethel Arnold, 1934. Dep. co. surveyor, Cache Co., Utah, 1899-1900, irrigation engr. Wyo. Expt. Sta., 1901-04; with U.S. Dept. Agr., 1906-07; hydraulic engr., Calif. Development Co., 1907; irrigation engr., N.M. Expt. Sta., 1907-09; prof. steam engring. and head of dept. mech. engr., U. of Ia., 1909-29; gen. mgr. Elephant Butte Irrig. Dist., N.M., 1929-32; dean of engring. N.M. State College, 1932-35; cons. engr. Iowa State Bd. Edn., 1923-32; chief engr. U.S. Soil Conservation Service, 1933-35. Capt. Co. M, 34th Engineers, A.E.F., in France, 1918-19; major Engr. R.C., 1919. Episcopalian. Mason. Author: Irrigation and Pumping, 1915. Home: Las Cruces, N.M. Died May 26, 1936.

FLEMING, Charles A., mayor; b. Eau Claire, Wis., Mar. 21, 1868; s. Michael and Catherine (O'Reilley) F.; ed. pub. schs. and business coll., Eau Claire; studied law in office of H. H. Hayden; m. Cora A. Thompson, Dec. 27, 1893; children—Albert Thompson, George Bernard. Admitted to Wis. bar, 1895, and began practice at Eau Claire; moved to Spokane, Wash., 1897, and practiced until 1903; city clk. of Spokane, 1903-13; elected commr. of Spokane, 1912, and has held that office by successive reëlections since Jan. 1, 1913, also mayor, 1913—; Dem. candidate for Congress, 1924. Catholic. Home: Spokane, Wash. Died Nov. 5, 1929.

FLEMING, Francis Philip, lawyer, gov.; b. Panama, Fla., Sept. 28, 1841; s. Lewis and Margaret (Seton) F.; ed. by private tutors; in C.S.A., July 1861, to May 1865; private 2d Fla. inf. and lt., 1st Fla. cav.; m. May 23, 1871, Floride Lydia Pearson. Admitted to Fla. bar, May, 1868; established practice at Jacksonville; gov., Fla., 1889-93. Democrat. Home: Jacksonville, Fla. Died 1908.

FLEMING, Fred W., life ins.; b. New Brunswick, Can., Aug. 9, 1866; s. Robert and Lucy S. (Hovey) F.; grad. Ricker Classical Inst., Houlton, Me., 1885; m. Alice Ogden Fleming, Dec. 22, 1896; children—Mrs. Wingate Bixby, Mrs. Marion Goodwin, Kathleen. Bookkeeper and accountant, Kansas City; real estate and loan business on own account, 1887-94; job printing and pub., 1894-1900; sec. and mgr., 1904-11, v.p., 1911-15, chmn. bd., 1915-17, Kansas City Life Ins. Co. Receiver of Kansas City Rys. Co.; pres. Central Surety & Ins. Corp. Vice chmn. Federal Reserve Bank of Kansas City. Col. 3d Regt. N.G. Mo., 1898-1901; served as maj. 3d Mo. Inf. U.S.V., Spanish-Am. War and filled every position in the Nat. Guard from enlisted man to colonel. State oil insp., 1894-97; pres. Dem. Club, 1888-90; del. Dem. Nat. Conv., 1904, 08, 12. Pres. Trans-Miss. Commercial Congress, 1911-13; 1st v.p. Nat. Irrigation Congress, 1911-13. Campaign chmn. Red Cross war fund; pres. Navy League of Kansas City; mem. Mo. Council Defense; federal dir. Nat. War Savings Campaign, 1917. Trustee Y.M.C.A., Christian Coll., Columbia, Mo., Christian Ch. Hosp., Kansas City; treas. Internat. Conv. Disciples of Christ; trustee Horner Inst. Conservatory of Music. Home: Kansas City, Mo. Died Nov. 14, 1929.

FLEMING, Henry Stuart, cons. engr.; b. Philadelphia, July 21, 1863; s. Joseph and Emma (Scherzer) F.; spl. student U. of Pa., 1881-83; m. Caroline M. Pelgram, 1905 (died 1927); children—Raoul Pelgram, Elizabeth; m. 2d, Thelma Cecelia Jacobsen Odegaarden, Sept. 29, 1933. Engaged in examination and rehabilitation of mining, mfg. and indsl. operations, 1884—; pres. La. Southern Ry.; voting trustee, dir. and mem. exec. com. Middle States Petroleum Corp. Episcopalian. Home: Bronxville, N.Y. Died Oct. 19, 1938.

FLEMING, James Wheeler, banker; b. Troy, N.Y., Feb. 15, 1867; s. James and Mary (Wheeler) F.; prep. edn., Troy Acad.; student Rensselaer Poly. Inst., 1886-89; m. Ann M. Carbrey, Sept. 1, 1904. V.p. Mfrs. Nat. Bank; dir. Securities Corp., Troy Gas Co., Lake Placid Nat. Bank; conservation commr. State of N.Y., 1911-13, inclusive; mayor of Troy, 1920-23, inclusive; comptroller State of N.Y., 1923-24. Democrat. Catholic. Home: Troy, N.Y. Died Apr. 27, 1928.

FLEMING, John Donaldson, prof. law; b. Elizaville, Ky., Sept. 16, 1851; s. John Faris and Amelia Perrin (Anderson) F.; A.B., Centre Coll., Ky., 1875, LL.D., 1910; LL.B., U. of Louisville, 1879; spl. course in law, U. of Va., 1879; m. Elizabeth Keith Stodghill, Aug. 27, 1890; children—William Donaldson, Marjorie Elizabeth, Nancy Amelia. Began practice at Leadville, Colo., 1879; financial mgr. Robert E. Lee Mining Co., 1880-82 (resigned); mayor of Leadville, 1882-83; city solicitor, Leadville, 1885-86; U.S. atty. for Colo., 1889-93; resumed pvt. practice at Denver, 1893; chmn. Arapahoe (Denver) Silver-Republican Co. Central Com., 1898-1900; dean Law Sch., U. of Colo., 1903—, also Thompson prof. of law, 1913—. Apptd. insp. law schs. having units of S.A.T.C., Oct. 26, 1918. Home: Boulder, Colo. Died Aug. 8, 1927.

FLEMING, Rufus, consul; b. W. Lebanon, Ind., Jan. 11, 1853; s. Dr. Jackson and Mary (Jamieson) F.; ed. lit. dept. U. of Mich., 1869-71, LL.B., 1873; m. Annabel Lee, d. Carleton B. Hutchins, of Ann Arbor, Mich., Mar. 1875. Reporter on Missouri Republican, St. Louis, 1877-78; mng. editor Cincinnati Times-Star, 1882-97; Am. Consul at Edinburgh, Oct. 5, 1897—. Home: Cincinnati, O. Died Apr. 3, 1920.

FLEMING, Walter Lynwood, college prof.; b. Brundidge, Ala., Apr. 8, 1874; s. William Le Roy and Mary Love (Edwards) F.; B.S. Ala. Poly. Inst., 1896, M.S., 1897; A.M., Columbia, 1901, Ph.D., 1904; m. Mary Wright Boyd, Sept. 17, 1902; children—Esther, William Le Roy, Mary Boyd, Eleanor. Farmer to 1894; taught sch., 1894-96, when not in coll.; instr. history, English and mathematics, 1896-97, asst. librarian, 1897-98, 1899-1900, Ala. Poly. Inst.; lecturer in history Columbia U., 1902-03; prof. history, W.Va. U., 1903-07, La. State U., 1907-17; prof. history, 1917—, dean Coll. of Arts and Sciences, 1923-29, also dir. of graduate work during same period, Vanderbilt U., Nashville, Tenn. Was officer 3d Alabama Vol. Inf., 1898-99, in war with Spain; q.-m., field hosp., 2d Div., 4th Army Corps, 1899. Democrat. One of editors Historians' History of the World. Editor: Lester and Wilson's History of Ku Klux Klan, 1905; Documentary History of Reconstruction (2 vols.), 1906, 1907. Editor-in-chief of sect. VI of The South in the Building of the Nation, 12 vols. Now engaged in research in Am. social and economic history, especially of the Southern States. Author: Reconstruction of the Seceded States, 1905; Civil War and Reconstruction in Alabama, 1905; William Tecumseh Sherman as College President, 1912; The Sequel of Appomattox, 1919; The Freedmen's Savings Bank, 1927. Mem. bd. editors Miss. Valley Hist. Review, 1914-22. Died Aug. 3, 1932.

FLEMING, William Bowyer, lawyer; b. Woodford Co., Ky., Apr. 3, 1845; s. William Bowyer and Agnita C. (Van De Graff) F.; Centre Coll., Ky.; matriculated at Yale; B.A., U. of Toronto, 1865, M.A., 1866; studied law State U. of Ky., Lexington, Ky.; univs. of Göttingen and Berlin; m. Susan Armstrong Harris, Apr. 12, 1871. Began practice in Ky., 1870; represented State of Ky. in noted Lottery Case, 1892; mem. Ky. Ho. of Rep., 1880-82; Dem. presdl. elector-at-large, Ky., 1884; justice U.S. Ct. of New Mexico, 1885-86; mem. Bd. of Aldermen, Louisville, Ky., 1886-88; railroad commr., State of Ky., 1888-92; law officer, U.S. Treasury Dept., 1893-96; apptd. foreign trade adviser, State Dept., Washington, Oct. 1, 1913. One of chief organizers Am. Anti-Trust Conf., Chicago, 1900. Presbyn. Deceased.

FLEMING, William Hansell, author; b. Phila., Aug. 23, 1844; s. George Matthews and Sarah Forde (Hansell) F.; ed. Central High Sch., Phila., and Princeton U. (A.M., causa honoris, Princeton, 1900); unmarried. Lecturer for Bd. Edn. Greater New York, also for Am. Soc. for Extension of Univ. Teaching, and Free Library of Phila., on Shakespearean literature. Edited The Looker-On 2 yrs. Author: How to Study Shakespeare (4 vols), 1897-1904; Shakespeare's Plots, A Study in Dramatic Construction, 1902. Edited, with critical introductions, 3 vols. Bankside Shakespeare. Wrote: A Bibliography of Shakespeare First Folios in New York City. Home: New York, N.Y. Died Oct. 1, 1915.

FLEMING, Williamina Paton, astronomer; b. Dundee, Scotland, May 15, 1857; d. Robert and Mary (Walker) Stevens; ed. there; married. Taught at Dundee, 1871-76; asst. Harvard Coll. Obs., 1879—; apptd. 1898, curator astron. photographs. Has charge of Astrophotographic Bldg., Harvard, and is assisted by more than a dozen women computers; known to astronomers as a discoverer of new stars, variables, etc. Hon. mem. Royal Astron. Soc. (London), 1906; hon. asso. in astronomy, Wellesley Coll., 1906. Home: Cambridge, Mass. Died 1911.

FLETCHER, Alice Cunningham, ethnologist; b. Boston, 1845; ed. pvt. schs. Devised system for loaning of small sums of money to aid Indians to buy land and build houses for themselves; instrumental in securing land in severalty to Omaha tribe by Act of Aug. 7, 1882, and apptd. spl. agt. to allot the Omaha tribe, 1883-84; apptd. spl. agt. under Severalty Act of Feb. 1887; allotted the Winnebago tribe, 1887-88, Nez Perces tribe, 1889-92; connected with anthrop. dept. of Chicago Expn., 1893. Asst. in ethnology, Peabody Mus. Am. Archæology and Ethnology, 1882—; holder Thaw Fellowship, 1891—. Author: Indian Story and Song from North America, 1900. Home: Washington, D.C. Died Apr. 1923.

FLETCHER, Andrew, mfr.; b. N.Y. City, June 8, 1864; s. Andrew Fletcher and Mary A. (Pollock) F.; ed. Coll. of the City of New York, also as naval architect and marine engr.; m. Jean L. Drummond, April 10, 1894. Pres. Am. Locomotive Co., Am. Locomotive Sales Corp., Montreal Locomotive Works, Richmond Locomotive Works; pres. and treas. W. & A. Fletcher Co., Consol. Iron Works, North River Derrick Co.; dir. numerous cos.; mem. exec. com. Atlantic Gulf & West Indies Co.; trustee Am. Surety Co. Republican. Presbyn. Home: New York, N.Y. Died Nov. 29, 1925.

FLETCHER, Austin Barclay, lawyer; b. Mendon, Mass., Mar. 13, 1852; s. Asa A. and Harriet (Durkee) F.; A.B., Tufts Coll., 1876 (LL.D., 1899); LL.B., Boston U., 1879, A.M., 1880; m. Hortense M.

Follett, Jan. 26, 1882 (died 1905). Prof. oratory, Boston and Brown univs., 1878-81; in practice as bank and corp. lawyer; dir. Irving Nat. and Bowery Savings banks of N.Y. City, also various banks, corps., rys., etc.; trustee several large estates. Pres. trustees Tufts Coll.; trustee Boston U. and Dean Academy. Mason. Died July 5, 1923.

FLETCHER, Austin Bradstreet, civil engr.; b. Cambridge, Mass., Jan. 19, 1872; s. Ruel Haseltine and Rebecca Caroline (Wyman) F.; student Lawrence Scientific Sch., 1889-93; S.B. in C.E., Harvard, 1893; m. Ethel Hovey, Mar. 1, 1894; children—Dorothy (Mrs. Laurence H. Chapman), Norman (dec.). Sec. and exec. officer Mass. Highway Commn., 1893-1910; sec. and engr. San Diego County (Calif.) Highway Commn., 1910-11; state highway engr. of Calif., 1911-23; highway engr. Joint N.E. R.R. Com., Jan.-May 1923; cons. highway engr. U.S. Dept. Agr., Bur. of Pub. Roads, 1923—. Acting chief engr. U.S. Bur. of Pub. Roads, assisting in formulation of new federal aid road policies, duirng leave of absence, 1916. Pres. State Reclamation Bd., Calif., 1917-23; dir. State Dept. of Pub. Works, Calif., 1921-23. Del. from Mass. to 1st Internat. Road Congress, 1908, del. from Calif. to 3d congress, 1913; pres. 4th Nat. Road Congress, 1914. Mem. exec. com. State Council of Defense, Calif., World War. Fellow Am. Geog. Society. Republican. Conglist. Home: Chevy Chase, Md. Died Mar. 8, 1928.

FLETCHER, Duncan Upshaw, senator; b. Sumter Co., Ga., Jan. 6, 1859; s. Capt. Thomas Jefferson and Rebecca Ellen (McCowen) F.; B.S. Vanderbilt U., Tenn., 1880; studied law at Vanderbilt U.; LL.D., John B. Stetson U.; m. Anna Louise Paine, June 20, 1883; children—Ellen A. (Mrs. Lionel Smith-Gordon), Louise Chapin (Mrs. Thomas J. Kemp). Admitted to bar, 1881, and began practice at Jacksonville, Fla. Mem. Fla. Ho. of Reps., 1893; mayor of Jacksonville, 1893-95, and 1901-03; chmn. Bd. of Pub. Instrn., Duval Co., Fla., 1900-06; chmn. Dem. State Com., 1905-08; nominated at primary election June 16, 1908, and apptd. by gov. as U.S. senator; took seat, Mar. 4, 1909; elected by legislature, Apr. 1909, term, 1909-15; reëlected, 4 terms, 1915-39; mem. Senate Com. on Commerce, Joint Com. on Printing (chmn.), Military Affairs, Banking and Currency (chmn.), and Sub. Com. on Appropriations. Mem. U.S. Sect. Internat. High Commn.; chmn. U.S. Commn. on Rural Credits. Trustee John B. Stetson Univ., De Land, Fla., St. Luke's Hospital Assn. (Jacksonville); v.p. Children's Home Soc. of Fla. Unitarian. Home: Jacksonville, Fla.; also Washington, D.C. Died June 17, 1936.

FLETCHER, Frank Friday, admiral U.S.N.; b. at Oskaloosa, Ia., Nov. 23, 1855; s. James Duncan and Nancy Powers (Jack) F.; grad. U.S. Naval Acad., 1875; m. Susan Hunt Stetson, Feb. 1895; children—Sybil Avery, Alice Stetson. Commd. ensign, July 1876; promoted through the various grades to rank of rear admiral, Oct. 1911. Has comd. torpedo boat Cushing, gunboats Kanawha and Eagle, cruiser Raleigh and battleship Vermont; aid to Sec. Navy for div. of material, 1910; comdg. 3d div. Atlantic Fleet, 1913, then 2d div. and later 1st div.; comd. naval force on West Coast of Mex., Feb. 1913-Apr. 1914, and Apr. 1921, seized and occupied City of Vera Cruz; comdr.-in-chief Atlantic Fleet, Sept. 1914, and promoted to rank of admiral, Mar. 1915. Mem. War Industries Bd. of Council of Nat. Defense, 1917, and mem. Gen. Bd. of the Navy and Joint Army and Navy Bd.; mem. President's Air Craft Bd., 1925. Inventor of the Fletcher breech mechanism and gun mounts. Awarded medal of honor for distinguished conduct in battle, D.S.M. (Army and Navy). Died Nov. 28, 1928.

FLETCHER, Horace, author, lecturer; b. Lawrence, Mass., Aug. 10, 1849; s. Isaac and Mary Blake F.; ed. Dartmouth (hon. A.M.); m. Grace A. Marsh. A traveler in all parts of the world from 1865, and engaged in numerous occupations. From 1895 has devoted his attention to sociology, and especially to scientific research in human nutrition, in chem.-physiol. labs. of U. of Cambridge, Eng., and Yale U.; originator of "Fletcherism," mastication of food. Pres. Nat. Mouth Hygiene Assn. America; mem. Com. of 100 on Nat. Health, Nat. Com. of Mental Hygiene; v.p. Food Reform Society, Eng.; fellow A.A.A.S. Author: Menticulture; Happiness; That Last Waif, or Social Quarantine; Glutton or Epicure; A B-Z Our Own Nutrition; Optimism—A Real Remedy; Fletcherism, What It Is. Engaged as food economist of Commn. for Relief in Belgium and in research work connected with nutrition and child-conservation. Died Jan. 13, 1919.

FLETCHER, Loren, congressman; b. Mt. Vernon, Me., Apr. 10, 1833; ed. in pub. schs. and Me. Wesleyan Sem.; removed to Bangor, 1853, and was clerk for a mercantile and lumber co. Removed to Minneapolis, 1856; has since been engaged in mercantile and mfg. pursuits there, largely as mfr. of lumber and flour. Mem. Minn. Ho. of Rep., 8 terms from 1872 (speaker, 3 yrs.); mem. 53d to 57th Congresses (1893-1903) and 59th Congress (1905-07), 5th Minn. Dist. Republican. Home: Minneapolis, Minn. Deceased.

FLETCHER, Montgomery, naval officer; b. in Va., Feb. 15, 1830; s. Charles and Sarah (Marshall) F.; unmarried. Apptd. from Pa., 3d asst. engr. U.S.N., June 24, 1850; 2d asst. engr., Feb. 26, 1851; 1st asst. engr., June 20, 1856; chief engr. with rank of capt., Oct. 25, 1859; retired with rank of commodore, Feb. 15, 1892; advanced to rank of rear-admiral, 1906. On Steamer Walker, coast survey, 1850-51; Alleghany, 1851-53; Saranac, 1853-56; Bur. of Steam Engineering, 1856-57; Wabash, 1857-59, Saranac, 1861-65; spl. duty, New York, 1855-56; Navy Dept., Mare Island, 1866-71; fleet engr., Pacific Squadron, 1861-63; insp. of machinery afloat at Mare Island, 1873-76; Navy Yard, Mare Island, 1877-83; mem. Bd. of Inspection, Calif., 1884-90; Bur. of Steam Engineering, 1890-92. Home: Washington, D.C. Died 1908.

FLETCHER, Mordecai Hiatt, physician; b. Richmond, Ind., Sept. 18, 1849; s. Francis Nixon and Elizabeth Dix (Hiatt) F.; D.D.S. Ohio Dental Coll., Cincinnati, 1880; M.D., Miami Med. Coll. (now a dept. U. of Cincinnati), 1884; M.S., Earlham Coll., 1893; E.E., Nat. Elec. Coll., Cincinnati, 1895; m. Anna E. Perry, Apr. 2, 1884. Practiced, Cincinnati, 1880—; specializes in treatment of diseases of the mouth; mem. Ohio State Bd. Dental Exmnrs., 1898-1904. Chairman stomatol. sect. Pan-Am. Med. Congress, 1893. Republican. Presbyn. Home: Avondale, O. Died Mar. 26, 1914.

FLETCHER, Orlin Ottman, clergyman, educator; b. Scotland, Ont., Can., July 29, 1847; s. David Calvin and Margaret (Smith) F.; ed. under pvt. tutors; B.D., and B.A., Chicago U. (now U. of Chicago), 1883; M.A., Colgate, 1886; D.D., Shurtleff Coll., Upper Alton, Ill., 1889; m. Lillian Reynolds, July 1873 (died 1874); m. 2d, Eva Emery, Mar. 28, 1877. Ordained Bapt. ministry, 1876; pastor Spring Lake, Mich., 1876, Allegan, 1877, Caro, 1880, Ottawa, Ill., 1882, Aurora, 1886, Springfield, 1888; sec. Bapt. Missionary Union, 1892; pastor Suffield, Conn., 1899, Chicopee Falls, Mass., 1903; prof. philosophy and polit. science, Furman U., Greenville, S.C., 1908—; lecturer on philosophy, Grove City (Pa.) Coll., summers 1913-17, also at Southern Bapt. Theol. Sem., 1916. Democrat. Author: Resurrection of Jesus, 1905; Introduction to Philosophy, 1913. Died 1937.

FLETCHER, Robert, engr.; b. New York, Aug. 23, 1847; s. Edward H. and Mary (Hill) F.; student Coll. City of New York, 3 yrs.; grad. U.S. Mil. Acad., 1868; hon. A.M., 1871, Ph.D., 1881, D.Sc., 1918, Dartmouth Coll.; m. Ellen M. Huntington, July 2, 1872. Commd. 2d lt., 1st U.S. Arty., June 1868; instr. mathematics, U.S. Mil. Acad., Sept. 1869-Dec. 31, 1870; sr. prof. and dir., Thayer Sch. of Civ. Engring., Dartmouth Coll., Jan. 1871-July 1918, dir. emeritus and overseer, 1918—. Cons. engr. for steel bridges over White River, at Hartford, N.H.; engr. Enfield (N.H.) Waterworks, 1902; pres. and engr. Hanover Water Works Co.; served many yrs. as mem. and pres. N.H. Bd. of Health, also in charge N.H.-Vt. boundary survey. Republican. Baptist. Home: Hanover, N.H. Died Jan. 7, 1936.

FLETCHER, William Baldwin, physician; b. Indianapolis, Ind., Aug. 18, 1837; grad. N.Y. Coll. of Phys. & Surg., 1859; served in scout service at beginning of Civil war; was imprisoned 9 months; later, on med. staff Union army; practiced medicine since war; mem. State senate, 1882-83; supt., 1883-88, Ind. Hosp. for the Insane. In 1888 established private infirmary for treatment and care of insane; is emeritus prof., diseases of brain, Med. Coll. of Ind. Home: Indianapolis, Ind. Died 1907.

FLETCHER, William Isaac, librarian; b. Burlington, Vt., Apr. 28, 1844; s. Stillman and Elizabeth (Severance) F.; ed. Winchester (Mass.) common schs., 1850-61; (hon. A.M., Amherst, 1884); m. Annie Le Barron Richmond, 1869. Librarian, Amherst Coll., 1883-1911; teacher library economy, Amherst Summer Sch., 1891-1905. Author: Public Libraries in America, 1895. Joint-editor Poole's Index to Periodical Literature and editor of continuations of same, 1882-1911. Home: Amherst, Mass. Died June 15, 1917.

FLICK, Lawrence F., M.D.; b. Carrolltown, Pa., Aug. 10, 1856; s. John and Elizabeth (Schabache) F.; prep. edn., St. Vincent Coll., Pa.; M.D., Jefferson Med. Coll., 1879, LL.D., 1929; LL.D., Catholic U. of America, 1915, Villanova Coll., 1916, St. Vincent Coll.-, Pa., 1925; m. Ella Stone, May 26, 1885; children—Lawrence Francis Patrick, Ella Mary Elizabeth, Seton Mary Mercedes, John Bernard Las Casas, Cecelia Mary Veronica, Thomas Walter George, Joseph Samuel Aloysius. Engaged in med. practice in Phila., 1879—; specialist in the pathology and treatment of tuberculosis. Med. dir. Henry Phipps Inst. Received Laetare medal, Univ. of Notre Dame, 1920. Catholic. Author: Consumption, a Curable and Preventable Disease, 1903; The Development of our Knowledge of Tuberculosis, 1925; Tuberculosis—A Book of Practical Knowledge to Guide the General Practitioner of Medicine, 1937. Home: Philadelphia, Pa. Died July 7, 1938.

FLICKINGER, Daniel Kumler, bishop; b. Sevenmile, O., May 25, 1824; acad. edn.; corr. sec. U.B.

Ch. Missionary Soc., 1857-85; foreign missionary bishop U.B. Ch., 1885—. Has made 12 missionary tours in Africa. Author: The Church's Marching Orders; Our Missionary Work from 1853 to 1889; Fifty-five Years of Ministerial Life, 1907. Home: Hamilton, Ind. Died 1911.

FLICKINGER, Samuel Jacob, editor; b. Millville, O., Feb. 14, 1848; s. Daniel Kumler and Mary (Lintner) F.; A.B., Otterbein Coll., Westerville, Ohio, 1872, A.M., 1875; post-grad. study Cornell, 1875-76; unmarried. Reporter Dayton (O.) Journal, 1876-78; Columbus corr. of the Cincinnati Enquirer, 6 yrs.; part owner Ohio State Journal, 1878-81, mng. editor, dir. and sec., 1884-93; corr. Associated Press, Cincinnati, 1893-1904; editor, dir. and sec. Dayton Journal, 1904-06; sec. to Gov. A. L. Harris, of Ohio, 1906-09; editor Dayton (O.) Daily Herald, 1909-12; editor Durham (N.C.) Sun, 1912-15; editorial writer Hamilton News, 1922—. Trustee Otterbein U. Home: Hamilton, O. Died Apr. 1929.

FLICKINGER, Smith M., wholesale grocer; b. Sardinia, N.Y.; s. Michael and Mary (Siebel) F.; ed. pub. schs.; m. Louise M. Nassal, 1893; children—Burt P., Glenn W. Organized and operated firm of S. M. Flickinger Co., wholesale grocers, Buffalo, N.Y., 1902—; established Flickinger Stores, 1916; formed Red and White Stores, Wholesaler sponsored group, 1921; organized Flickinger Coöp. Plan on partnership basis with store mgrs., 1923; disposed of stores to mgrs. to be operated as ind. Red and White Stores, 1934. Mem. Buffalo Chamber of Commerce (pres. 1935-36); chmn. City Planning Com. (1936-37). Republican. Universalist. Home: Buffalo, N.Y. Died Apr. 2, 1939.

FLICKWIR, David Williamson, ry. official; b. Phila., Pa., Sept. 26, 1852; s. Joseph Williamson and Rebecca (Barton) F.; ed. pub. and pvt. schs.; m. Mildred Elder, May 2, 1925. Began as rodman ry. engring. corps, 1871; asst. engr. Centennial Bldgs., Phila., 1875; engr. on constrn. Shenandoah Valley R.R., 1879-83, supt. and engr. same rd., 1883-90; gen. supt. Norfolk & Western Ry. Co., 1890-95; gen. contractor, 1896-1915; chmn. exec. com. Norfolk & Western Ry. Co., 1916—; v.p. First Nat. Exchange Bank, 1926—. Mem. Select Council Roanoke. Mem. Dist. Exemption Bd., 1917-18, World War. Republican. Episcopalian. Died Oct. 31, 1935.

FLING, Fred Morrow, univ. prof.; b. Portland, Me., 1860; s. Charles H. and Cynthia E. (Davis) F.; A.B., Bowdoin Coll., 1883; A.M., Ph.D., U. of Leipzig, 1890; m. Helene A. Dresser, July 26, 1893. Prof. European history, U. of Neb., 1891—. Founded Assn. of Neb. Teachers of History, 1897. One of the 100 electors to Hall of Fame. Author: A Source Book of Greek History, 1907; The Writing of History, 1920. Commd. maj. U.S.A., and was chief of sect. of diplomatic history of hist. branch of Gen. Staff; in Paris, during Peace Conference, as rep. of the hist. branch, collecting material for a history of the Peace Conf.; del. to 6th Internat. Congress of Hist. Sciences, Oslo, Norway, 1928; and to the 7th Congress, Warsaw, Poland, 1933. Home: Lincoln, Neb. Died June 8, 1934.

FLINN, Alfred Douglas, civil engr.; b. New Berlin, Pa., Aug. 4, 1869; s. Matthew Bonner and Sarah Jane (Jones) F.; B.S., Worcester Poly. Inst., 1893; Dr. of Applied Science, Univ. of Louvain, 1927; Dr. of Eng., Worcester Poly. Inst., 1932; m. Mary Brownell Davis, Nov. 1, 1900. Engr. with Met. Water Works, Boston, 1895-1902; mng. editor Engring. Record, New York, 1902-04; engr. Croton Aqueduct Commn., 1904-05; dep. engr. and dep. chief engr. Bd. of Water Supply of N.Y. City (Catskill Aqueduct), 1905-18; sec. United Engring. Trustees, Inc., 1918-34; sec. Engring. Council, 1918-21; sec., 1918—, dir., 1922, Engring. Foundation; mem. Nat. Research Council, 1918-23 (chmn. Div. of Engring., 1920-23). Knight Order of the White Lion (Czechoslovakia). Republican. Protestant. Compiler: (with R. S. Weston and C. L. Bogert) Waterworks Handbook, 1916. Home: Scarsdale, N.Y. Died Mar. 14, 1937.

FLINN, John Joseph, lecturer, editor; b. Clonmel, Ireland, Dec. 5, 1851; s. James and Margaret (Cunningham) F.; ed. pub. sch. and newspaper offices; began work as reporter at 21; m. Mary Talbot Cole, Oct. 9, 1877; children—Clara Cole, Melville Stone, Mrs. D. W. Roche, John Cunningham, Mrs. Lucius Smith, James Miller. Night editor St. Louis Globe, 1873; afterward staff corr. in legislature and constl. conv. for Globe-Democrat; became asso. editor of Chicago Daily News a few months after founding of that paper and remained with it 7 yrs.; later was mng. editor Chicago Mail and the Chicago Times; editorial writer on Chicago Inter Ocean, 1898-1908; editorial writer Christian Science Monitor from its founding, 1908-19. Compiled The Standard Guide to Chicago. Appointed U.S. consul to Chemnitz, Saxony, 1882, and during 2 yrs. abroad contributed series of humorous letters to Chicago Morning News. First reader, First Ch. of Christ, Scientist, Winchester, Mass. (1911-14). Alderman, Evanston, Ill., 3 terms. Apptd. mem. Christian Science Bd. of Lectureship, June 1921. Home: Glencoe, Ill. Died Nov. 27, 1929.

FLINT, Albert Stowell, astronomer; b. Salem, Mass., Sept. 12, 1853; s. Simeon and Ellen Rebecca (Pollard) F.; A.B., Harvard, 1875; A.M., U. of Cincinnati, 1880; m. Helen A. Thomas, Oct. 22, 1884. Computer U.S. Naval Obs., 1881-83, 1888-89; asst., U.S. Transit of Venus Commn., 1883-88; asst. astronomer, 1889, astron., 1904-19 (emeritus), Washburn Obs., U. of Wis. Coöperated with the dir. of the obs. and others in producing several of the publs. of The Washburn Obs. Fellow A.A.A.S. Author: Meridian Observations for Stellar Parallax, 1st series (Vol. XI, Publ. Washburn Obs.), 1902; 2d series, Vol XIII, Part I, 1919. Home: Madison, Wis. Died Feb. 22, 1923.

FLINT, Austin, physician; b. Northampton, Mass., Mar. 28, 1836; s. Austin (physician) and Anne (Skillings) F.; ed. pvt. schs., Buffalo, and Harvard, 1852-53; studied medicine in office, and med. dept. U. of Louisville, 1854-56; M.D., Jefferson Med. Coll., 1857 (LL.D., 1885; hon. A.M., Princeton, 1894); m. Elizabeth B. McMaster, Dec. 23, 1862. Practiced in Buffalo, 1857-59; editor Buffalo Med. Journal, 1857-60; prof. physiology, med. dept., U. of Buffalo, 1858-59; visiting surgeon, Buffalo Gen. Hosp., 1858; removed to New York, 1859; prof. physiology, N.Y. Med. Coll., 1859-60, New Orleans Sch. of Medicine, 1860-61; acting asst. surgeon, U.S.A., at Gen. Hosp., New York, 1862-65; a founder and prof. physiology, 1861-98, Bellevue Hosp. Med. Coll.; prof. physiology, L.I. Coll. Hosp., 1862-68, Cornell U. Med. Coll., 1898—(emeritus prof.). Visiting phys. 1869, cons. phys., 1896, visiting phys. Insane Pavilion, 1896, Bellevue Hosp.; surgeon-gen. N.Y., 1874-78; cons. phys. Manhattan State Hosp. for Insane, 1896 (pres. cons. bd., 1899). Decorated 3d class Order of Bolivar, Venezuela, 1891. Mem. exec. com. N.Y. Prison Assn., 1896. Author: Text-Book of Human Physiology (4 edits.), 1875-88. Died Sept. 23, 1915.

FLINT, Charles Ranlett, merchant, banker; b. Thomaston, Me., Jan. 24, 1850; s. Benjamin and Sarah (Tobey) F.; grad. Polytechnic Inst., Brooklyn, 1868; m. E. Kate Simmons, 1883; m. 2d, Charlotte Reeves, July 28, 1927. Partner Gilchrist, Flint & Co., 1871, and W. R. Grace & Co., 1872, in San Francisco, Chile and Peru; Chilean consul, N.Y., 1877-79; later consul-gen. of Nicaragua and Costa Rica to U.S.; in 1885 joined Flint & Co., ship owners, lumber and gen. merchandise (founded by his father and uncle in 1837). Mem. Internat. Conf. Am. Republics, 1889-90; represented U.S. on banking com. and formulated recommendation of an Internat. Am. Bank, reported on Unification of Customs Regulations, and recommended establishing of Bur. of Am. Republics; fitted out fleet of war vessels for Brazilian Republic, 1893; purchased Esmeralda cruiser from Chile and delivered to Japan during China-Japan war, 1895; established Pacific Coast Clipper Line between New York and San Francisco, 1896; chmn. reorganization com. which consolidated st. rys. of Syracuse, N.Y., 1897; confidential agt. of U.S. in negotiating for war vessels, 1898; sold Russian Govt. 20 submarine and torpedo boats and went to Turkey and other countries in its interest, 1904-05. Acted as organizer in the formation of Am. Chicle Co., Computing-Tabulating-Recording Co. (now Internat. Business Machines Corp.), U.S. Rubber Co., and many others. Widely known as the "father of trusts." Author: Memories of an Active Life, 1923. Home: New York, N.Y. Died Feb. 13, 1934.

FLINT, Frank Putnam, senator; b. N. Reading, Mass., July 15, 1862; s. Francis Eaton and Althea (Hewes) F.; removed with parents to San Francisco, 1869, and ed. in pub. schs. there; moved to Orange Co., Calif., 1886; m. Katharine J. Bloss, Feb. 25, 1890. Began study of law before leaving San Francisco; clerk in U.S. marshal's office, Los Angeles, 1888-92, and admitted to bar; asst. U.S. atty., Los Angeles, 1892-93; practiced law as partner with Judge M. T. Allen, 1893-95; U.S. atty., Southern Dist. of Calif., 1897-1901; U.S. senator, 1905-11; mem. Flint & MacKay. Republican. Home: Los Angeles, Calif. Died Feb. 11, 1929.

FLINT, James Milton, medical dir. U.S.N.; b. Hillsborough, N.H., Feb. 7, 1838; s. Amos and Mary (Stickney) F.; ed. common schs. and Pembroke Acad.; M.D., Harvard, 1860; m. Caroline H. Conant, June 27, 1871 (died 1901). Asst. surgeon, U.S.N., Apr. 14, 1862; surgeon, 1874; med. insp., 1893; med. dir., 1897; retired with rank of rear admiral, Feb. 7, 1900. Connected with U.S. Fish Commn., 1884-87, and at 3 different periods, in all about 20 yrs., with Smithsonian Instn. as curator, div. of medicine, U.S. Nat. Mus. Has written reps. and bulls. U.S. Nat. Museum. Died Nov. 21, 1919.

FLINT, Weston, lawyer and librarian; b. Pike, N.Y., July 4, 1835; s. Nicholas and Phebe Burt (Willoughby) F.; ed. Chamberlain Inst., N.Y., Alfred Acad., N.Y.; grad. Union Coll., 1860, A.M., 1863; (Ph.D., Alfred U., 1888, LL.D., 1900); grad. Columbian U. Law Sch., 1877, LL.M., 1878; m. Lucy Romilda Brown, 1883. Ednl. work, 1860-63; Ohio State Mil. agt., 1863-66; practiced law, 1866-69; sec. Southern Loyalist Conv., 1866; editor and pub. Daily Tribune, St. Louis, 1869-70; sec. 2d Geol. Survey, Mo., 1868-71; U.S. consul to China, 1871-74; librarian Scientific Library, U.S. Patent Office, 1877-87; acting chmn. Bd. U.S. Civ. Service Examiners, 1884-87; sec. Nat. Statist. Assn., 1895-98; statistician U.S. Bur. Edn., 1889-95. Trustee, 1897-98, librarian, 1898-1904, Public Library, D.C. Republican. Author: Catalogue of the Library of the U.S. Patent Office, 1878; Catalogue of Additions to the Library of the U.S. Patent Office, 1878-82; Statistics of Libraries in the U.S. and Canada, Washington, 1893. Died 1906.

FLIPPIN, James Carroll, dean, prof. medicine; b. Lunenburg, Va., Jan. 26, 1878; s. John James and Lucie Frances (Haskins) F.; M.D., U. of Va., 1901; m. Isabel Anderson, Dec. 19, 1905; children—Harrison Fitzgerald, Isabel Anderson, Lucie Armistead. With U. of Va., 1902—, sucessively instr. in med. biology until 1905, adj. prof. bacteriology, 1905-15, prof. clin. medicine, 1915—, dean dept. of medicine, 1924—. Past pres. Med. Soc. of Va. Democrat. Home: University, Va. Died Feb. 16, 1939.

FLOOD, Henry Delaware, congressman; b. Appomattox Co., Va., Sept. 2, 1865; s. J. W. and Ella W. F.; ed. Washington and Lee U. and Univ. of Va., LL.B., 1886; married. Admitted to bar, Sept. 15, 1886; elected to Va. Ho. of Dels., 1887, 1889, Senate, 1891, 1895 and 1899; atty. for the Commonwealth for Appomattox Co., 1891, 1895, 1899; presdl. elector, 10th Congl. Dist., Va., 1892; Dem. candidate for Congress, 1896; mem. 57th to 66th Congresses (1901-21), 10th Va. Dist. Author of the bill calling the constl. conv. in Va., and mem. Va. Constl. Conv., 1901-02; mem. bd. of visitors U. of Va., 1906-14. Home: Appomattox, Va. Died Dec. 8, 1921.

FLOOD, Ned Arden, industrial banker; b. New Market, N.H., Sept. 12, 1870; s. Theodore L. and Anna Catherine (Black) F.; A.B., Johns Hopkins, 1890; A.M., Allegheny Coll., 1892; studied law, U. of Mich. and in offices of late Judge John J. Henderson, of the Superior Court of Pa.; m. Anna Davis, 1892; 1 dau., Josephine. Was editor of Chautauqua Daily Herald, 1889-98, also asso. editor Chautauquan Mag., 1890-98; mng. dir. Chautauqua-Century Press, official pubs. Chautauqua Instn., 1890-98; mng. dir. University Press Div. of U. of Chicago, 1898-1900; practiced law in Pa., 1900-10; asso. of banking group comprising Lehman Bros., New York, and Kleinwort Sons & Co., London, 1910-17; in France representing U.S. War Dept., 1917-18; v.p. and dir. Dept. of Finance of B. F. Keith Theatres Co., 1918-19. Negotiated following sales—Mishawaka Woolen Mfg. Co. to U.S. Rubber Co., 1903, South Bend (Ind.) Gas Co. to N.Y. interests, 1906, The Hemingray Glass Co. to Owens-Ill. Glass Co., 1933, etc.; participant in orgn. of F. W. Woolworth Co. and Merger of B. F. Goodrich and Diamond Rubber Cos.; an incorporator and dir. Cluett, Peabody & Co., 1912-18; consultant in reorganization and recapitalization of Burroughs Calculating Machine Co., 1922; consultant in merger of Owens Bottle Co. and Ill. Glass Co., 1930. A.d.c., rank lt. col., staffs of Govs. Stone, Pennypacker and Stuart, of Pa. Trustee State Hosp. for Insane, Warren, Pa., 1899-1919. Died Nov. 8, 1938.

FLORANCE, Ernest Touro, lawyer; b. Pass Christian, Miss., July 30, 1854; s. Benjamin and Rebecca (Kursheedt) F.; ed. Northwick Coll., London, Lusher's Acad., New Orleans; unmarried. Admitted to bar, 1875. Pres. Commercial Law League of America. Dir. pub. schs., New Orleans, 1892-98; mem. New Orleans Sewerage and Water Bd., 1916—. Southern Democrat. Jewish religion. Home: New Orleans, La. Died July 1918.

FLORENCE, Mrs. William J., actress (b. Malvina Pray); noted as a danseuse when a young girl; m. W. J. Florence, Jan. 1, 1853 (died 1892). The Florences made a name in The Yankee Housekeeper, and subsequently in many other plays in U.S., Can. and England, notably The Mighty Dollar. Retired. Died 1906.

FLORIDIA, Pietro (hereditary Baron Napolino), composer, pianist; b. Modica, Sicily, May 5, 1860; s. Francesco and Anna Maria (Napolino) F.; studied piano under Beniamino Cesi, at the Conservatory of S. Pietro a Majella, Naples, and composition of Lauro Rossi; m. Lina Bickel, of Zurich, Switzerland, Apr. 24, 1890; 1 dau., Perla (Mrs. G. V. Sumner). Published many piano compositions while pupil, and in 1889 gained first prize of Società del Quartetto of Milan, by a symphony which was played in 1904 at Zurich as the representative Italian symphony in series of internat. concerts. In 1882 produced successful comic opera, "Carlotta Clepier," at Naples, but burned score and retired for 3 yrs. to Sicily for study; toured as pianist, 1885, 86, 88, 90; became prof. of piano at Palermo Conservatory; declined offer of Frau Cosima Wagner to become prof. in her sch. of music at Bayreuth, 1892; del. extraordinary with Boito for judging candidates for Conservatory diplomas, 3 yrs. Produced opera, "Maruzza," at Venice, 1894 (of which wrote both text and music), and the opera "La Colonia Libera" (based on Bret Harte's "M'Liss"), at the Costanzi Theatre, Rome, May 1899. Declined directorship of Conservatory of Bergamo, 1897, and of Benedetto Marcello Conservatory, Venice, 1902; came to U.S., 1904; pianist, teacher and composer, New York, 1904-06 and 1908—; mem. faculty Cincinnati Coll. of Music, 1906-08. Wrote grand opera "Paoletta," prod. Cincinnati, Aug. 1910.

Conductor Italian Symphony Orchestra of New York, 1913—. Home: New York, N.Y. Deceased.

FLORIO, Caryl (family name William J. Robjohn), organist; b. Tavistock, Devonshire, Eng., Nov. 2, 1843; ed. at home; self-taught in music, owing to parental opposition; unmarried. First boy soloist Trinity Ch., New York, 1858-60; actor, 1861-67, returned to New York, 1869; engaged as teacher, pianist, conductor, organist, composer; brought out Gertrude Corbett in grand opera, Acad. of Music, New York, June 1875; condr. opera troupe, Havana, Cuba, 1878; produced his own opera, "Uncle Tom," Phila., 1881; has given concerts of own compositions—one with Thomas orchestra, New York, 1888; after which concert Thomas requested the score and parts of his 2d symphony for use in his concerts; later was requested to send the symphony to Antwerp for performance there. Organized Palestrina Choir, chorus of 100 voices for prodn. of mediæval music, 1886; mus. dir. Wells Coll., Aurora, N.Y., 1889-91; had charge of George W. Vanderbilt's mus. affairs, Biltmore, N.C., 1896-1901. Home: Asheville, N.C. Deceased.

FLORY, George Daniel, banker; b. Four Locks, Md., Oct. 31, 1867; s. Alexander Murphy and Mary Elizabeth (Jacques) F.; ed. pub. schs.; unmarried. Began with Pacific Express Co., at El Paso, Tex., 1888; with Wells Fargo & Co., El Paso, 1893-96; with State Nat. Bank, El Paso, 1896—, v.p., 1920—; dir. El Paso Br. Federal Res. Bank of Dallas. Home: El Paso, Tex. Died June 14, 1932.

FLORY, Joseph, expn. official; b. on farm, nr. Logansport, Ind., June 19, 1856; s. Nathan and Elizabeth (Cuppy) F.; ed. common schs., Logansport; m. Emma Johnson, June 30, 1876. Removed to Mo.; engaged in railroad business; elected State R.R. Commr. of Mo., 1894, for 6 yrs.; Rep. nominee for gov. Mo., 1900; now sec. La. Purchase Expn. Commn. Home: St. Louis, Mo. Died Apr. 3, 1925.

FLOURNOY, Parke Poindexter, clergyman; b. Chesterfield C. H., Va., Sept. 25, 1839; s. Richard Wilson and Sarah Parke (Poindexter) F.; A.B., Hampden-Sydney Coll., Va., 1861; D.D., 1896, Litt.D., 1924; m. Mary Moore Smith, d. Rev. Prof. B. M. Smith, D.D., Union Theol. Sem. Va., Aug. 30, 1866 (died 1897). Enlisted in the "Hampden-Sydney Boys," 20th Va. Regt. C.S.A., in May 1861; taken prisoner at Battle of Rich Mountain, Va.; paroled by Gen. George B. McClellan in July 1861; exchanged in Aug. 1862; joined the Otey Battery, 13th Va. Battalion of Arty. and served in it until close of war. Ordained Presbyn. ministry, 1869; pastorates: Elizabethtown, Ky., 1869-75, Springfield, Md., 1882-90, Bethesda, Md., 1875-82, and 1890-1922. Elected mem. Victoria Inst., London, 1897 (Gunning Prizeman, 1912, 27), and Life Asso. of Victoria Inst., 1927. Author: New Light on the New Testament, 1903. Home: Washington, D.C. Died June 14, 1935.

FLOWER, Anson Ranney, banker; b. Theresa, N.Y., 1843; s. Nathan M. and Mary Ann F.; high sch. edn.; m. Ida M. Babcock, Dec. 31, 1878. Spl. mem. Flower & Co.; dir. Brooklyn Rapid Transit Co., People's Gas Co., Internat. Paper Co., Colonial Trust Co., Corn Exchange Bank, etc.; trustee Trust Co. of America. Pres. bd. trustees N.Y. Homœopathic Med. Coll. and Hosp. Home: New York, N.Y. Died 1909.

FLOWER, Benjamin Orange, editor; b. Albion, Ill., Oct. 19, 1858; s. Rev. Alfred and Elizabeth (Orange) F.; ed. Ky. U., Lexington; m. Hattie Cloud, Sept. 10, 1885. Editor The American Sentinel, social and lit. weekly, Albion, Ill., until 1880; went to Phila., and later to Boston; established The Am. Spectator, which subsequently was merged into The Arena, which he founded; remained at its head until the end of 1896; one of editors The New Time, Chicago, short time, 1897-98; editor The Coming Age, until it was merged into The Arena, which was purchased by Albert Brandt, Mar. 1904, when he again became editor The Arena, 1904-09; editor Twentieth Century Mag., Boston, 1909-Nov. 1911; became pres. Menace Pub. Co., Aurora, Mo. Author: Christian Science as a Religious Belief and a Therapeutic Agent, 1910; Patriot's Manual, 1915; Righting the People's Wrongs, 1917. Died Dec. 24, 1918.

FLOWER, Elliott; b. Madison, Wis., Aug. 2, 1863; s. James M. and Lucy L. F.; ed. Phillips Acad., Andover, Mass., and with tutor at Keene, N.H.; m. Laura Durlin, Dec. 27, 1887. Editor The Rambler, 1885-86; night city editor, Chicago Tribune, 1892-93; editorial writer, Chicago Evening Post, 1895-99; in lit. work, 1899—. Home: Coronado, Calif. Died July 3, 1920.

FLOWER, Frank Abial, author; b. Cottage, N.Y., May 11, 1854; s. Lothrop T. and Sarah M. (Titus) F.; ed. N.Y. State Normal Sch., Fredonia; studied law, but practiced less than a year, renouncing it for journalism; m. Mabel Claire Powers, May 15, 1892. Commr. statistics, Wis., 1884-89; statistician and fiscal agt. of city of Superior, Wis.; propr. Lake Superior Leader, 1889-98; pres. Internat. Traffic Assn.; exec. sec. and mem. Exec. Bd. Internat. Deep Waterways Assn.; editor and interpreter 12th Census; attaché to U.S. Commn. to investigate conditions in Liberia, Africa, 1909. Republican. Author: Outline History of Wisconsin; Industrial Wisconsin; Eye of the Northwest (hist. and statis., Superior, Wis., 2 vols.); Plan of International Coöperation; International Deep Waterways. Died 1911.

FLOWER, Walter C., mayor of New Orleans; b. parish of East Feliciana, La., Aug. 6, 1850; grad. Pass Christian (Miss.) Coll., 1872 (A.M., 1873); grad. law dept., Univ. of La., 1876; practiced law in New Orleans 10 years; atty. of police bd. 4 years; upon death of his father, a cotton merchant, gave up practice to take charge of the business; pres. New Orleans Cotton Exchange two terms; retired from business, 1895; elected mayor April 1896 for term expiring April 5, 1900, on a citizens' movement. Died 1900.

FLOWERS, Allen Gilbert, prof. law; b. Sumter, S.C., Dec. 31, 1869; s. Thomas Evans and Matilda Ann (Mack) F.; ed. Y.M.C.A. night sch., Washington, D.C.; LL.B., George Washington U., 1906, LL.M., 1907; m. Sue Duncan Hall, Nov. 4, 1908. Learned printer's trade, beginning at age of 10; mem. Bd. of Aldermen, Sumter, 1894-96; with Govt. Printing Office, Washington, D.C., 1900-11; admitted to D.C. bar, 1908; chmn. Washington delegation, Internat. Typographical Conv., Minneapolis, 1910; editor and pub. Arkansas Sentinel, Fayetteville, 1911-13; dep. pros. atty. Washington Co., Ark., 1912-19; lecturer dept. of economics, U. of Ark., 1916; prof. law and dean Law Sch., Baylor U., 1920— (graduates of this sch. admitted to practice in Tex. without examination). Maj. Home Guards, State of Ark., 1918; rep. of adj. gen. of Ark., Selective Service bds. Democrat. Baptist. Mason. Home: Waco, Tex. Died May 11, 1935.

FLOWERS, Herbert Baker, pub. utility exec.; b. Detroit, Mich., July 14, 1881; s. Charles and Mary (deNormandie) F.; ed. Detroit Univ. Sch. and U. of Mich.; m. Marcella Hamilton Goodrich, Apr. 21, 1909; children—Hamilton Goodrich, Phoebe deNormandie. With Detroit United Rys., 1902-12; v.p. and gen. mgr. United Rys. & Electric Co., Baltimore, 1912-23; pres. New Orleans Pub. Service, Inc., 1923—. Mason. Home: New Orleans, La. Deceased.

FLOWERS, Montaville, lecturer, educator, publicist; b. Cincinnati, O., Jan. 7, 1868; s. Wilson Hosea and Martha (Dean) Flowers; A.B., Ohio Northern U., Ada, Ohio, 1890; grad. Cincinnati Coll. of Music, Voice and Oratory, 1894; A.M., Ohio U., 1905; m. Eva Belle Keller, July 17, 1890; children—Mary LaBelle (Mrs. Otis D. Dolan), Montaville Dean, Evelyn Grace (Mrs. J. P. Sykes), Esther May (Mrs. H. G. Hubbard). Superintendent of Norwood (O.) public schs., 1890-96; dir. univ. extension, U. of Cincinnati, 1891-94; pres. and treas. Interstate Lyceum Bur., 1896-1903; pres. Flowers Acad. of Music and Dramatic Arts, 1903-07; pres. Internat. Lyceum Assn., 1910-12 and 1917-18. Lecturer on dramatic lit., education, Oriental problems, world problems; spl. lecturer extension div., univs. of Wis., Minn., N.D. and Ind. Methodist. Mason. Was head of speakers bureau Prog. Nat. hdqrs., New York, 1913-14. Rep. nominee for Congress, Los Angeles, 1918. Mem. advisory com. of Com. on Pub. Information, Washington; pres. Taxpayers Central Council of Los Angeles County, Special Assessment Relief Assn. of Calif. Home: Pasadena, Calif. Died Nov. 10, 1934.

FLOY, Henry, engr.; b. Elizabeth, N.J., Sept. 19, 1866; s. James and Sarah A. F.; A.B., Wesleyan U., 1889, A.M., 1892; M.E., Cornell U., 1891; m. Alice Van Benschoten, 1895. Engaged as consulting engr. with office in New York, spl. reputation as elec. engr. in connection with hydraulic and high tension long-distance transmission work, valuation of utility properties. Mem. Internat. Com. of Awards, and elec. juror, St. Louis Expn., 1904. Spl. engr., Dept. of the Interior; appraiser, apptd. by U.S. Circuit Ct. Fellow Am. Inst. Elec. Engrs. Republican. Author: Valuation of Public Utility Properties. Died May 5, 1916.

FLOYD, Charles Miller, governor; b. Derry, N.H., June 5, 1861; s. Sewall and Sarah J. (Sleeper) F.; acad. edn. Derry, N.H.; m. Carrie E. Atwood, June 16, 1886. In clothing business at Manchester, N.H., 1888—. Member N.H. Senate, 1901-02; mem. Governor's Council, 1904; gov. of N.H., 1907-09. Conglist. Home: Manchester, N.H. Died Feb. 1923.

FLOYD, David Bittle, clergyman, educator; b. Middletown, Md., Mar. 15, 1846; s. Hezekiah and Lydia (Bittle) F.; A.B., Roanoke Coll., Salem, Va., 1872 (2d honor), M.A., 1879; med. dept. U. of Mich., 1866-67; student Bellevue Med. Coll. and Hosp., New York, 1872-73; grad. Luth. Theol. Sem., Gettysburg, Pa., 1876; (D.D., Roanoke Coll. and Susquehanna U., 1906); studied Bible history in Greece, Palestine and Egypt, 1910; m. Mary Elizabeth Cutting, Feb. 15, 1877. Ordained Evang. Luth. ministry, 1876; pastor Uniontown, Md., 1876-82, Boonsboro, 1882-85, Newville, Pa., 1885-99, Funkstown, Md., 1900-1904, Washington, D.C., 1905; prof. Hebrew and Greek langs., Bibl. criticism, Christian ethics and ch. polity, Susquehanna U., 1905—. Served as corpl., sergt. and lt., Co. I, 75th Ind. Regt. Vols., Civil War, 1862-65; fought under Gen. Thomas at Chickamauga, and Gen. Grant at Chattanooga, and participated under Gen. Sherman in the March to the Sea. Mem. Com. on 100th Anniversary Luth. Gen. Synod; mem. Exam. Com. Md. Synod. Home: Selinsgrove, Pa. Died Jan. 23, 1922.

FLOYD, John Charles, congressman; b. Sparta, Tenn., Apr. 14, 1858; s. John Wesley and Eliza Jane (Snodgrass) F.; A.B., U. of Ark., 1879; m. Sarah Virginia Berry, Nov. 24, 1887; children—Nina Berry, Rector Hamilton, James Berry. Admitted to bar, 1882, and entered law practice. Elected to Ark. legislature, 1888, and served in session of 1889; pros. atty., 14th Ark. Circuit, 1890-94; mem. 59th to 63d Congresses (1905-15), 3d Ark. Dist.; mem. Floyd & Floyd, 1923—. Democrat. Resumed law practice. Methodist. Home: Yellville, Ark. Died Nov. 5, 1930.

FLOYD-JONES, De Lancey, soldier; b. Queens Co., N.Y., Jan. 20, 1826; s. Hon. Henry and Helen Watts (De Lancey) F.-J.; grad. U.S. Mil. Acad. and commd. 2d lt., 7th inf., July 1, 1846; m. Laura Jane Whitney, 1852. Served during Mexican war; took part in siege of Vera Cruz, battles of Cerro Gordo and Molino del Rey, and capture of City of Mexico; bvt. 1st lt. for gallant and meritorious conduct in battle of Molino del Rey; capt. 4th inf., July 31, 1854; served during Civil war, 1861-65, as maj. 11th U.S. inf.; engaged in battles of Yorktown, Gaines' Mill and Malvern Hill; bvt. lt.-col., July 4, 1862, for gallant and meritorious service during peninsular campaign; engaged in battles of Manassas, Antietam, Sharpsburg, Chancellorsville and Gettysburg; bvt. col., July 2, 1863; lt. col. 19th inf., 1863; served on the plains, 1868-79; col., 3d inf., Jan. 2, 1873; retired from active service, March 1879. Died 1902.

FLÜGEL, Ewald, philologist; b. Leipzig, Germany, Aug. 4, 1863; s. Dr. Felix (author of the Universal Dictionary) and Pauline (Mencken) F.; student univs. of Freiburg and Leipzig, 1882-85; Ph.D., Leipzig, 1885; m. Helene Burchardt, of Magdeburg, Germany. Privat docent of English philology, U. of Leipzig, 1888-92; prof. English philology, Leland Stanford Jr. U., 1892—. Orator at German Day, Midwinter Fair, San Francisco, 1894, at unveiling of Goethe-Schiller monument, San Francisco, 1901. Hon. mem. Akadem Neuphilologische Verein, Leipzig, Verein für Neuere Philologie, Dresden. Died Nov. 15, 1914.

FLYNN, Dennis Joseph, college pres.; b. Louisville, Ky., 1856; s. Daniel and Mary (Linehan) F.; A.B., Mt. St. Mary's Coll., 1880, A.M., 1882 (LL.D., same, 1897, Georgetown U., 1906). Ordained R.C. priest, 1883; mem. faculty, 1899, v.p. and treas., 1904, pres., June 1905—, Mt. St. Mary's Coll. Home: Emmitsburg, Md. Died 1911.

FLYNN, Dennis T., lawyer; b. Phoenixville, Pa., Feb. 13, 1861; s. Dennis T. and Margaret (Clancy) F.; ed. pub. schs.; m. Addie M. Blanton, 1887; children—Streeter Blanton, Olney Foster. Admitted to Okla. bar, 1890, began practice at Guthrie; dir. First Nat. Bank & Trust Co., Okla. City Hardware Co. Mem. Rep. Nat. Com., Ty. of Okla., 1890-92; del. in Congress from Ty. of Okla., 1892-1902. Catholic. Knight of St. Gregory. Home: Oklahoma City, Okla. Died June 19, 1939.

FLYNN, William James, chief U.S. Secret Service; b. New York, Nov. 18, 1867; s. Michael and Elizabeth (Stanion) F.; ed. pub. schs.; m. Ann E. Mackey, Sept. 11, 1895; children—William W., Veronica E., Gerard M., Kathleen C., Elmer M., Jane M. With U.S. Secret Service, 1897—, except 8 mos., 1910-11, when reorganized New York detective bureau; chief U.S. Secret Service, 1912-17. Apptd. chief of secret service of U.S.R.R. Administration, Sept. 7, 1918; dir. Bur. Investigation, Dept. of Justice, July 1, 1919-Aug. 1921 (resigned). Mem. 9th Regt. N.G.N.Y., 12 yrs. Editor of Flynn's Weekly. Home: Larchmont, N.Y. Died Oct. 13, 1928.

FLYNT, Charles Fremont, newspaper pub.; b. Abbot, Me., Mar. 19, 1857; s. Daniel Damon and Narcissa Jane (Crocket) F.; grad. high sch., Dexter, Me., 1874; m. Ida M. Horton, June 21, 1880; children—Roy H., Bertha M., Charles W., Leigh D. Began with Dexter Gazette, 1874; with Portland (Me.) Press, 1878-80; with Kennebec Journal, Augusta, 1880, part owner and gen. mgr., 1887-1922, prin. owner, pres. and gen. mgr., 1922-29, retired. Republican. Universalist. Mason. Home: Augusta, Me. Died Sept. 1933.

FOCHT, Benjamin K., editor, publisher, congressman; b. New Bloomfield, Pa., Mar. 12, 1863; educated Bucknell U., Pa. State Coll. and Susquehanna U.; hon. A.M., 1908; m. Edith Wolf; children—Ellen, Brown, Edith (dec.). Editor and propr. Saturday News, Lewisburg, Pa., since 18 yrs. of age; now pres. Saturday News Pub. Co. Active in politics, 1882—; mem. Pa. Assembly 3 terms; Senate 4 years; water supply commr. Pa., 1913-14; mem. 60th to

FOCHT, John Brown, clergyman; b. Chambersburg, Pa., July 20, 1851; s. Rev. David Henlein and Susan 62d and 64th to 67th Congresses (1907-13 and 1915-23), 17th Pa. Dist. and 73d and 74th Congresses (1933-37), 18th Pa. Dist.; deputy sec. Commonwealth of Pa. Republican. Home: Lewisburg, Pa. Died Mar. 27, 1937.

(Brown) F.; A.B., Pa. Coll., Gettysburg, Pa., 1874 (D.D., 1897); grad. Luth. Theol. Sem., Gettysburg, 1877; m. Elizabeth Born, June 27, 1878. Ordained

Evang. Luth. ministry, 1876; teacher Pa. State Coll., 1876-77, Missionary Inst., Selinsgrove, 1877-82, Pa. Coll., 1882-87; pastor Lewistown, Pa., 1887-94, Barren Hill, 1894-99, Selinsgrove, 1899-1904; pres. Susquehanna U., 1904-05; pastor Southington, Conn., 1907-17, Selinsgrove, Pa., 1917; prof. of practical theology, Susquehanna Univ., 1921—. Republican. Home: Selinsgrove, Pa. Died Mar. 10, 1924.

FOELL, Charles Michael, judge; b. Taylor Twp., Ia., Nov. 21, 1870; s. George M. and Caroline (Kanthlener) F.; Ph.B., Cornell Coll., Ia., 1894; LL.B., Northwestern U., 1896. Began practice in Chicago, 1896; formed partnership, 1897, with W. N. Gemmill (now judge Municipal Court); judge Superior Court of Cook County, Ill., 1911—. Capt. provisional regt. (Chicago Reserves), 1898. Republican. Mason. Home: Chicago, Ill. Died July 23, 1937.

FOELLINGER, Oscar G., newspaper pub.; b. Fort Wayne, Ind., Apr. 11, 1885; s. Martin C. and Christina (Stellhorn) F.; ed. Luth. parochial schs., Ft. Wayne; m. Esther Anna Deuter, Nov. 16, 1909; children—Helene Ruth, Loretta Esther. Asst. cashier Citizens Trust Co., Ft. Wayne, 1901-05; business mgr. Journal-Gazette Co., 1905-10; same, News Pub. Co., pubs. Ft. Wayne News-Sentinel, 1912-19, pres. and gen. mgr., 1919—. Served as 1st lt. Ind. N.G., 1903-06. Dir. Ind. State and Fort Wayne anti-tuberculosis leagues. Republican. Lutheran. Mason. Home: Fort Wayne, Ind. Died Oct. 8, 1936.

FOERSTE, August Frederick, paleontologist; b. Dayton, O., May 7, 1862; A.B., Denison U., 1887, D.Sc., 1927; A.M., Harvard, 1888, Ph.D., 1890; studied Heidelberg and Paris, 1890-92; unmarried. Asst. U.S. Geol. Survey, 1887-91, 1895; with Ohio Geol. Survey, 1892, 1908-10, 1917-19; Ind. Geol. Survey, 1896, 97, 99, Ky. Geol. Survey, 1904-12, Geol. Survey of Can., 1911-12; asso. in paleontology, U.S. Nat. Museum, 1932—; Marsh fund grant of Nat. Acad., 1928. Rep. of Paleontol. Soc. in Nat. Research Council, 1932-35. Specializes in Ordovician and Silurian paleontology, with particular reference to the Cincinnatian and Silurian faunas of the Central States; also in Ordovician and Silurian Cystids and in Ordovician and Silurian Cephalopods of North America, especially of Arctic areas. Author of reports pub. by surveys of U.S., Canada, Ohio, Ind., Ky., Iowa, also in bulls. of Denison U., Ohio Jour. of Science, and contbr. from Museum of Paleontology, U. of Mich. Home: Washington, D.C. Died Apr. 23, 1936.

FOERSTER, Adolph Martin, musician; b. Pittsburgh, Pa., Feb. 2, 1854; s. Emil and Elise Marie (Noll) F.; ed. pub. schs., Allegheny and Pittsburgh; grad. Conservatory of Music, Leipzig, 1875; m. Henrietta M. Reineman. Choral condr., Symphonic Soc. (orchestra). Orchestral works: Festival, dedication march, Am. Ode, prelude to Goethe's Faust, suites, arias with orchestra, etc., chamber music, songs, piano, organ, and church music; especially successful, Ave Maria with violin obl.; album of 14 selected songs. Home: Pittsburgh, Pa. Died Aug. 10, 1927.

FOERSTER, Robert Franz, economist; b. Pittsburgh, Pa., July 8, 1883; s. Adolph Martin and Henrietta Margaret (Reineman) F.; A.B., Harvard, 1905 as of 1906, Ph.D., 1909, studied Harvard, Berlin and Paris; m. Lilian Hillyer, d. Theobald Smith, of Boston, June 5, 1916; children—Lilian Egleston, Margaret Dorothea. Instr., 1909-13, asst. prof. social ethics, 1913-21, Harvard; prof. economics and dir. industrial relations sect., Princeton, 1922-26. Dir. Social Research Council, Boston, 1911-13; chmn. commn. on support of dependent children of widows, Mass., 1912; mem. spl. com. of Boston Chamber Commerce on Social Insurance, 1916-17; mem. Am. Management Assn. Com. on Personnel Administration, 1925—. Author: The Italian Emigration of Our Times, 1919; also (report to Secretary of Labor) The Racial Problems Involved in Immigration from Latin America and the West Indies to the United States, 1925; Employee Stock Ownership in the United States (in collaboration), 1926. Home: Princeton, N.J. Died July 29, 1941.

FOGARTY, Thomas, illustrator; b. New York, 1873; s. Andrew and Margaret (Barrett) F.; studied drawing and painting at Art Students' League, New York, under H. Siddons Mowbray and Carroll Beckwith; m. Helen Arden Huggins, Feb. 1907; children—Alexander Roux, Thomas. Took up illustrating in mags.; has done work on leading periodicals; first book illus. was Crockett's Cleg Kelly, 1896; also illus. Sailing Alone Around the World, 1900; Riis' The Making of an American, 1901, and Battle with the Slum, 1902; The Forest, 1903; Tommy & Co., 1904; Blazed Trail, 1907; Adventures in Contentment, 1907; Adventures in Friendship, 1911. Teacher of illustration at Art Students' League, 1903-22. Died Aug. 11, 1938.

FOGG, Lawrence Daniel, author, editor; b. Sheffield, Eng., Apr. 9, 1879; s. Isaac and Rosina Glossop (Goodinson) F.; came to U.S., 1886; spl. studies Trinity Coll., 1895-97. Reporter Meriden (Conn.) Journal, 1896; editor Windham Co. (Conn.) Observer, 1898, New York School Journal, 1900-01; suburban editor, Asbury Park (N.J.) Journal, 1902-04; editor Ocean Grove (N.J.) Times, 1905; telegraph editor Eau Claire (Wis.) Leader, 1906; asst. editor Springfield (Mass.) Union, 1907-13; now editor Tale-Teller, New York. Corr. Asso. Press, New York Herald, New York World; dept. editor Home and Flowers, Springfield, O., 1900-05. Author: Confessions of a Male Flirt, 1904; Wedded by Wire, 1904; Man Proposes, but Woman Disposes, 1905. Home: Springfield, Mass. Died Feb. 12, 1914.

FOIK, Paul Joseph, clergyman, librarian; b. Stratford, Ont., Can., Aug. 14, 1880; s. John and Joanna (Dameck) F.; Ph. B., U. of Notre Dame, 1907; grad. Holy Cross Coll., 1911; Ph.D., Catholic Univ. of America, 1912. Came to the U.S. in 1900. Librarian in chief U. of Notre Dame, 1912-24, also archivist Catholic Archives of America; librarian in chief St. Edward's U., Austin, Tex., 1924—, also head dept. foreign langs., prof. German and of Am. history, dean Grad. Sch. Mem. Congregation of Holy Cross. Founder Irish Nat. Library Foundation, Catholic Laymen's Library Aid Soc.; co-founder and v.p. Catholic Library Assn. Founder of library sect. N.C.E.A.; founder and pres. Tex. Catholic Hist. Soc.; chmn. Tex. K. of C. Hist. Com. Library editor of Catholic School Interests; asso. editor Mid-America; chmn. editorial bd. Catholic Periodical Index. Fellow Tex. Hist. Assn. (v.p.), Am. Geog. Soc.; mem. A.L.A. Wrote: The Catholic Press in America (in Ency. Americana), 1918; Pioneer Catholic Journalism; Martyrs of the Southwest; Early Catholic Explorers of the Southwest; Fray Juan de Padilla. Editor: Our Catholic Heritage in Texas (7 vols.). Mem. advisory board Commn. of Control for Tex. Centennial Celebrations, 1936. Home: Austin, Tex. Died Mar. 1, 1941.

FOKKER, Anthony H(erman) G(erard), airplane designer and mfr.; b. of Dutch parents, Kediri, Dutch East Indies, Apr. 6, 1890; ed. Haarlem, Holland; m. Viola Lawrence, Feb. 8, 1929 (died 1929). Began flying, 1911; head of important aircraft concerns in Germany during World War; came to U.S., 1922. Former pres. Fokker Aircraft Corp. of America. Home: Alpine, N.J. Died Dec. 23, 1939.

FOLDS, Charles Weston, banker; b. Oshkosh, Wis., Aug. 23, 1870; s. William B. and Mary D. (Jenkins) F.; high sch. and evening classes, U. of Minn.; m. Florence Symonds, May 24, 1893; children—Weston Symonds, Mrs. Elizabeth F. Eggleston, Mrs. Florence F. Gregg, George R. Messenger in Northwestern Nat. Bank, Minneapolis, 1889; apptd. mgr. Chicago office of Charles Hathaway & Co., brokers, 1899; admitted to partnership, 1904; firm name changed, 1910, to Hathaway, Smith, Folds & Co., now Hathaway & Co.; pres. Charles W. Folds & Co., 1923, now Folds, Buck & Co.; chmn. bd. First Nat. Bank of Lake Forest, Ill.; v.p. Commercial Credit Co. of Baltimore. Chmn. exec. com. Izaak Walton League of America. Republican. Episcopalian. Home: Chicago; and Lake Forest, Ill. Died Apr. 24, 1928.

FOLEY, George Cadwalader, theologian; b. Phila., Pa., June 29, 1851; s. David Francis and Elizabeth (Freeland) F.; A.B., Griswold Coll., 1872; grad. Phila. Div. Sch., 1875, D.D., 1899, on examination and thesis; m. Jennie B. Witmer, Jan. 8, 1880. Deacon, 1874, priest, 1875, P.E. Ch.; rector St. James' Ch., Pittston, Pa., 1875-79; Trinity Ch., Williamsport, Pa., 1879-1905; became prof. homiletics and pastoral care, Phila. Div. Sch., 1905; prof. systematic divinity, 1915. Editor The Church Standard, 1907-08. Home: Philadelphia, Pa. Died May 8, 1935.

FOLEY, James William, Jr., newspaperman; b. St. Louis, Mo., Feb. 4, 1874; s. James William and Rachel Aston (Shryock) F.; ed. U. of S.D.; m. Edith Deborah Skeels, Dec. 1, 1900. Began newspaper work on the Tribune, Bismarck, 1892; asso. editor Evening Post, Pasadena, 1919-29; editor A. E. Little Co., Los Angeles, 1924-32; spl. writer Pasadena Star-News and Long Beach Press-Telegram. Mason. Author: Boys and Girls, Plains and Prairie, Life and Laughter—Complete Verses, 1911; Old Friends in Joyous Verses, 1912; The Way of Smiles, 1913; Tales of the Trail, 1914; The Letters of William Green, 1914; Friendship Series, including 10 subjects, 1915; The Voices of Song, 1916; The Brothers (outdoor play prod. by Uplifters, Los Angeles), 1925; outdoor play, In Old Virginia, prod. by Uplifters, 1928; With Happiness to You, 1928; Cheer Up and Hang On, 1929; White Gods and Red, outdoor play, prod. by Uplifters, 1932. Birthday celebrated by all public schools of N.Dak. on his fiftieth birthday, 1924, by order of State Dept. of Pub. Instrn., to be continued yearly. Mason. Home: Pasadena, Calif. Died May 17, 1939.

FOLEY, John Burton; b. Chicago, Ill., Dec. 19, 1857; s. John and Sarah (Whittaker) F.; ed. pvt. sch. and pub. high sch., Steubenville, O.; m. Anna Shaw McCloskey, Jan. 1, 1889. Drug clk., Steubenville, 1872-78; bookkeeper, Clinton Paper Mills, Steubenville, 1878-81; in wholesale drug business, 1881-88; moved to Chicago, 1888, and engaged in the mfr. of proprietary medicines and toilet preparations; pres. Foley & Co., printers, lithographers and engravers, 1911—; pres. Magnolia Springs Land Co., 1905—. Founder of town of Foley, Ala. Republican. Presbyn. Home: Chicago, Ill. Died Feb. 4, 1925.

FOLEY, John Samuel, bishop; b. Baltimore, Md., Nov. 5, 1833; grad. St. Mary's Coll., 1850; studied in St. Mary's Ecclesiastical Sem., Baltimore, and at the Roman Sem. Ordained R.C. priest, 1856; first was rector St. Bridget's, Baltimore, Ellicott City, Md., 6 yrs.; then asst. pastor St. Peter's, Baltimore; founder, and pastor St. Martin's, Baltimore; consecrated bishop of Detroit (Mich.), Nov. 4, 1888. Died Jan. 5, 1918.

FOLEY, Thomas J., ry. mgr.; b. Convoy, O., Aug. 26, 1866; s. John and Bridget (Sullivan) F.; ed. pub. schs., Convoy; unmarried. Began with Pa. R.R., as telegraph operator, 1878-80; train dispatcher, 1880-93, chief dispatcher, 1893-97, asst. trainmaster, 1897-98; transportation insp., 1898-1901, same rd.; asst. to gen. mgr., 1901-02, supt., 1903-04, gen. supt., 1904-05, B.&O. R.R.; chief dispatcher, 1906-07, asst. supt., 1907-10, U.P. Ry.; asst. gen. mgr., 1910-12, gen. mgr., 1912-17, v.p. in charge operation, maintenance and constrn., 1917—, I.C. R.R., at Chicago. Died Dec. 9, 1918.

FOLGER, Henry Clay, capitalist; b. New York, N.Y., June 18, 1857; s. Henry C. and Eliza J. (Clark) F.; A.B., Amherst Coll., 1879; A.M., 1881; LL.B., cum laude, Columbia, 1881; (Litt.D., Amherst, 1914); m. Emily C. Jordan, Oct. 6, 1885. With Standard Oil Co. of N.J., 1879-1911; became pres. Standard Oil Co. of N.Y., Dec. 4, 1911, later chmn. bd.; dir. Seaboard Nat. Bank of N.Y. City. Conglist. Died June 11, 1930.

FOLGER, William Mayhew, rear-admiral U.S.N.; b. Massillon, O., May 19, 1844; s. Robert and Amelia (Hayden) F.; apptd. from Ohio, and grad. U.S. Naval Acad., 1864. Ensign, Nov. 1, 1866; promoted through grades to rear admiral, June 1, 1904. Served receiving-ship North Carolina, 1864-65; sch.-ship Sabine, New London, to July 1865; Hartford, Asiatic Squadron, 1865-68; Franklin, 1868-72; ordnance duty, 1872-75; leave in Europe, 1875; Marion, 1876-77; ordnance duty, Navy Yard, Washington, 1878; Naval Acad., 1878-79; Swatara, 1879-82; Bur. of Ordnance, 1882; ordnance duty, Naval Acad., 1882-85; insp. ordnance, Navy Yard, Washington, 1886-87; comd. Quinnebaug, 1887-88; insp. ordnance, Navy Yard, Washington, 1888-90; chief Bur. of Ordnance with rank of commodore, 1890-93; comd. Yorktown, 1894-95; light house insp., 11th dist., 1896-98, 3d dist., Jan.-Apr. 1898; comd. New Orleans, 1898-99; gen. insp. Kearsarge, 1899-1900; comd. Kearsarge, 1900-01; light house insp., 3d dist., 1901-04; comd. Philippine Squadron, Asiatic Fleet, Apr.-Sept. 1898; comd. Cruiser Squadron, Asiatic Fleet, to Mar. 1905; comd. Asiatic Fleet, until Mar. 30, 1905; retired, June 30, 1905. Home: Windsor, Vt. Died July 22, 1928.

FOLIN, Otto, chemist; b. Asheda, Sweden, Apr. 4, 1867; s. Nils Magnus and Eva (Olson) F.; came to America, 1882; B.S., U. of Minn., 1892; Ph.D., U. of Chicago, 1898, Sc.D., 1916; univs. in Sweden and Germany, 1897, 1898; M.D., U. of Lund (Sweden), 1918; Sc.D., Washington U., 1915; m. Laura Churchill Grant, Sept. 11, 1899; children—Joanna (dec.), Grant, Teresa. Asst. prof. physiol. chemistry, U. of W.Va., 1899-1900; research chemist, McLean Hosp., Waverley, Mass., 1900-08; prof. biol. chemistry, Harvard Med. Sch., 1907—. Home: Brookline, Mass. Died Oct. 25, 1934.

FOLK, Edgar Estes, clergyman; b. Haywood Co., Tenn., Sept. 6, 1856; s. Henry B. and Mattie C. (Estes) F.; A.M., Wake Forest Coll., N.C., 1877 (D.D., 1895); grad. Southern Bapt. Theol. Sem., 1882; m. Lizzie Handly, Mar. 6, 1888. Ordained Bapt. ministry, 1882; pastor, Murfreesboro, Tenn., 1882-85; Millersburg, Ky., 1886, Albany, Ga., 1887-88; editor Baptist Reflector, 1888-89, Baptist and Reflector, 1889—. Pres. S.S. Bd. Southern Bapt. Conv., 1895—; pres. Anti-Saloon League of Tenn., 1899-1911, Tenn. Bapt. Conv., 1912, 13, 14. Author: Plan of Salvation, 1907. Home: Nashville, Tenn. Died Feb. 27, 1917.

FOLK, Joseph Wingate, governor, lawyer; b. Brownsville, Tenn., Oct. 28, 1869; s. of Henry B. and Martha (Estes) F.; LL.B., Vanderbilt U., 1890; (LL.D., U. of Mo., 1905, William Jewell Coll., 1906, Drury Coll., 1907, Westminster Coll., Fulton, Mo., 1907, Southwestern Baptist Univ., Tenn., 1908, and Baylor U., Texas, 1919); m. Gertrude Glass, Nov. 10, 1896. Admitted to bar 1890; practiced, Brownsville, 4 yrs.; moved to St. Louis, Mo., 1894; circuit atty., City of St. Louis, 1900-04; exposed vast amount of polit. and official corruption and prosecuted numerous bribery cases which attracted wide attention; Gov. of Mo., 1905-09, carrying the State on Dem. ticket by majority of 30,000, although Rep. nat. ticket, headed by Theodore Roosevelt, carried the State by 25,000; author of Missouri anti-lobby law; state-wide primary law; initiative and referendum law; the child labor law; compulsory education law; public utility commns. for cities. Made lecture tour of U.S., 1909-10; apptd. solicitor for U.S. Dept. of State, Sept. 22, 1913; chief counsel for Interstate Commerce Commn., 1914-18. Conducted investigations of New Haven, the L.&N., and Rock Island rys.; now practicing law in Washington and St. Louis. Homes: St. Louis, Mo., and Washington, D.C. Died May 28, 1923.

FOLKMAR, Daniel, statistician, anthropologist; b. Roxbury, Wis., Oct. 28, 1861; s. Rev. M. and Ragnbild (Anderson) F.; A.B., Leander Clark Coll., Ia., 1884, A.M., 1888; studied Harvard U., Clark U., U. of Chicago, U. of Paris, Berlin and Brussels; certificate École d'Anthropologie, Paris, 1899; D.Sc. Sociales, U. Nouvelle, Brussels, 1899; Docteur de U. Paris, 1900; m. Dr. Elnora Cuddeback, Aug. 20, 1895. Prof. psychology and social science, and pres. Ind. Normal U., 1890-92; prof. in commercial dept. and pres. West Mich. Coll., 1892-93; prof. psychology, Milwaukee State Normal Sch., 1895-98; prof. anthropology, New Univ., Brussels, 1898-1901; anthropologist and lt.-gov. Philippine Civ. Service, 1903-07; spl. agt. U.S. Immigration Commn., 1908-09; spl. agt. U.S. Census, 1910-14; on editorial staff, U.S. Dept. Commerce, 1914-17; statistician, War Dept., 1918-19 (anthropologist in charge of measuring soldiers, 1919); in U.S. Census, 1919-31. Author: Dictionary of Races (Vol. 5, Immigration Commn. Repts.), 1911; Mother Tongue of Foreign Stocks (U.S. Census of 1910). Died 1932.

FOLLANSBEE, George Alanson, lawyer; b. in Cook Co., Ill., Feb. 26, 1843; s. Horatio N. and Emeline (Sherman) F.; A.B., Lawrence U., Appleton, Wis., 1865; LL.B., Harvard, 1867; m. Susan D. Davis, Apr. 14, 1869. Admitted to the bar, Mar. 17, 1867; now counsel, Adams, Follansbee, Hawley & Shorey. Republican. Home: Winnetka, Ill. Died Mar. 14, 1920.

FOLLANSBEE, Mitchell Davis, lawyer; b. Chicago, Jan. 23, 1870; s. George Alanson and Susie Dana (Davis) F.; A.B., Harvard, 1892; LL.B., Northwestern U., 1894, LL.D., 1915; m. Julia Rogers McConnell, Apr. 14, 1903; children—Eleanor (Mrs. Helmut von Erffa), Mitchell Davis, Jr., Rogers, Susan (Mrs. Robert J. Cameron-Smith), Julie. Admitted Illinois bar, 1894, and began practice at Chicago; mem. Follansbee, Shorey & Schupp; dir. Erie Railroad, Bucyrus-Erie Co., Met. Life Ins. Co. Pres. Asso. Harvard Clubs. Republican. Unitarian. Home: Chicago, Ill. Died Jan. 26, 1941.

FOLLETT, Martin Dewey, judge; b. Enosburg, Vt., 1826; s. John Fassett and Sarah Lemira (Woodworth) F.; A.B., Marietta Coll. (with highest honors), 1853, A.M., 1856; m. Harriet L. Shipman, 1856; m. 2d, Abbie M. Bailey, 1875. Admitted to bar, 1858; elected judge Supreme Ct. of Ohio, 1883. Dem. nominee for Congress, 1866, 1868; del. Internat. Prison Congress, Brussels, 1900. Home: Marietta, O. Died 1911.

FOLLETT, William W., civil engr.; b. New Sharon, Me., Sept. 22, 1856; s. William T. and Julia (Merrill) F.; C.E., U. of Mich., 1881 (M.Engring., 1914); m. Helen Jordan, June 13, 1888. In practice as civil engr., 1881—; cons. engr. Internat. Boundary Commn. U.S. and Mexico, 1897-1900, and again, Feb. 1, 1902-July 1, 1914; cons. engr. to U.S. Reclamation Service in the drainage of the Rio Grande, Apr. 1906-Nov. 1914; also cons. engr. for some pvt. irrigation projects. Home: El Paso, Texas. Died Dec. 28, 1915.

FOLLMER, Harold Newton, theologian; b. Milton, Pa., June 11, 1861; s. William G. and Esther (Hoy) F.; student Missionary Inst., Selinsgrove, Pa.; A.B., Wittenberg Coll., Ohio, 1885, A.M., 1888, D.D., 1915; grad. Theol. Sem., Susquehanna U., 1887; m. Anna Maude Schoch, Sept. 6, 1887; children—E. Louise (dec.), Frank S., Harold W. Ordained Evang. Luth. ministry, 1887; pastor Yeagertown, Pa., 1887-93, Pittsburgh, 1893-1901, Huntingdon, 1901-09; prof., Susquehanna U., 1909—, prof. economics and sociology in coll. of same univ. Republican. Home: Selinsgrove, Pa. Died May 20, 1933.

FOLSOM, Benjamin, lawyer; b. Folsomdale, N.Y., Dec. 5, 1847; s. Benjamin R. and Mary (Rathbone) F.; A.B., U. of Rochester, 1871, A.M., 1888; m. Ella Blanchard Howard, of Rochester, N.Y., Oct. 11, 1893. Journalist and corr., 1871-73; admitted to N.Y. bar, 1875; U.S. consul at Sheffield, Eng., 1886-93; practicing law, Buffalo, N.Y., 1893-1902, at Pasadena, Calif., 1903—. Episcopalian. Home: Pasadena, Calif. Died Aug. 17, 1922.

FOLSOM, Charles Follen, physician; b. Haverhill, Mass., Apr. 3, 1842; s. Nathaniel S. and Ann Wendell (Penhallow) F.; A.B., Harvard, 1862; in Freedmen's Bur. in South, 1862-65; returned to Mass.; grad. Harvard Med. Sch., 1870; student Vienna and Berlin, 1873-74; Munich, 1879; m. Martha Tucker Washburn, May 12, 1886. Lecturer on hygiene, Harvard, 1877-82; lecturer and asst. prof. mental diseases, same, 1879-88. Formerly visiting physician, then cons. physician, Boston City Hosp. Mem. Am. Acad. Arts and Sciences. Home: Boston, Mass. Died 1907.

FOLSOM, Justus Watson, entomologist; b. Cambridge, Mass., Sept. 2, 1871; s. James Nelson and Charlotte Elizabeth (Watson) F.; Sc.B., Harvard, 1895, Sc.D., 1899; unmarried. Won Bowdoin prize and was lab. asst. in botany and zoölogy, at Harvard; prof. natural sciences and physiology, Antioch Coll., O., 1899-1900; instr., 1900-06, asso., 1906-08, asst. prof. entomology, 1908-23, U. of Ill.; asso. entomologist, 1925-27, entomologist, 1927-28, sr. entomologist, 1928—, U.S. Bureau of Entomology. Fellow A.A.A.S., Entomol. Soc. America (pres. 1931). Republican. Author: Entomology, with Special Reference to Its Biological and Economic Aspects, 1906. Home: Tallulah, La. Deceased.

FOLWELL, William Watts, univ. prof.; b. Romulus, N.Y., Feb. 14, 1833; s. Thomas J. and Joan (Bainbridge) F.; A.B., Hobart Coll., 1857, A.M., 1860, LL.D., 1878; LL.D., Racine, 1870, U. of Minn., 1925; m. Sarah Hubbard Heywood, Mar. 13, 1863. Teacher langs., Ovid Acad., N.Y., 1857-58; adj. prof. mathematics, Hobart, 1858-60; student in Berlin, 1860-61; 1st lt. to maj. and bvt. lt. col., 50th N.Y. Engrs., 1862-65; in business in Ohio, 1865-69; prof. mathematics, Kenyon Coll., 1869; pres., 1869-84, prof. polit. science, 1875-1907, pres. emeritus, 1907—, U. of Minn. Mem. Minn. Centennial Commn., 1876; mem. Bd. Park Commrs., Minneapolis, 1889-1907 (pres. 1894-1900); chmn. State Bd. of Charities and Correction, 1895-1901. Author: Minnesota, the North Star State; Economic Addresses; University Addresses; History of Minnesota, 4 vols. Home: Minneapolis, Minn. Died Sept. 18, 1929.

FONTAINE, William Morris, univ. prof.; b. in Louisa Co., Va., Dec. 1, 1835; s. James and Juliet (Morris) F.; A.M., U. of Va., 1859; Royal Sch. of Mines, Freiberg, Saxony, 1869-70; unmarried. Served in Civ. War as 2d lt. of arty., C.S.A., until 1862, then 1st lt. of ordnance till Apr. 9, 1865; prof. chemistry and geology, W.Va. U., 1873-78; prof. geology and natural history, U. of Va., 1878-1911. Fellow Geol. Soc. of America. Episcopalian. Democrat. Author: Resources of West Virginia (with Prof. M. F. Maury), 1876; Report of Second Pa. Geol. Survey (with I. C. White), 1880; Monograph VI, 1883, and Monograph XV, 1889, U.S. Geol. Survey, and bull. of same on The Potomac Formation. Retired Sept. 1, 1910, and placed on Carnegie Foundation for Advancement of Teaching. Home: Charlottesville, Va. Died Apr. 29, 1913.

FOOTE, Arthur, musician; b. Salem, Mass., Mar. 5, 1853; s. Caleb and Mary Wilder (White) F.; A.B., Harvard, 1874, A.M., 1875; mus. edn. under Prof. John K. Paine and B. J. Lang; Mus.D., Trinity Coll., 1919, Dartmouth, 1925; m. Kate G. Knowlton, July 7, 1880; 1 dau., Katharine. Organist and teacher of pianoforte playing; organist at First Unitarian Ch., Boston, 1878-1910. Has composed and published suites, etc., for orchestra; trios, quartets, etc., for chamber music; cantatas for chorus and orchestra; songs, part-songs, anthems, organ and pianoforte pieces, etc. Mem. Nat. Inst. Arts and Letters. Home: Newton Centre, Mass. Died Apr. 8, 1937.

FOOTE, Dellizon Arthur, M.D., surgeon; b. Leroy, O., Apr. 14, 1860; s. Seth and Amorette E. (Rich) F.; A.B., Upper Ia. U., Fayette, Ia., 1882, A.M., 1883; M.D., Chicago Homœ. Med. Coll., 1887; post-grad. study, Vienna and Berlin, 1891; m. Milla Harriet Baird, Sept. 24, 1891; children—Mrs. Marjorie Baird McCament, Arthur Newman, Mrs. Mildred Amorette Robbins. Practiced Omaha, 1888—. Trustee Upper Ia. U. Pres. Nat. Obstet. Soc., 1904-05; pres. Mo. Valley Homœ. Med. Soc., 1898-99, Neb. State Homœ. Med. Soc., 1900-01, Omaha Med. Soc., 1891-92; v.p. Physicians' Casualty Assn.; fellow Am. Coll. surgeons. Republican. Methodist. Home: Omaha, Neb. Died Aug. 25, 1935.

FOOTE, Edward Bliss, M.D.; b. Cleveland, O., Feb. 20, 1829. Well known as author of Medical Common Sense; Plain Home Talk; Science in Story, and Dr. Foote's Home Cyclopædia of Medical and Social Science. Home: Larchmont, N.Y. Died 1906.

FOOTE, Harry Ward, chemist; b. Guilford, Conn., Mar. 21, 1875; s. Christopher Spencer and Hannah Jane (Hubbard) F.; Ph.B., Yale, 1895, Ph.D., 1898; studied in Leipsic and Munich, 1899-1900; m. Martha Babcock Jenkins, June 22, 1904; children—William Jenkins, Mary, Margaret Spencer. Instr. in chemistry, 1898-1904, asst. prof., 1904-12, prof. physical chemistry, 1912—, Sheffield Scientific Sch., Yale. Episcopalian. Fellow Royal Geog. Society. Home: New Haven, Conn. Died Jan. 14, 1942.

FOOTE, John A., M.D.; b. Archbald, Pa., June 9, 1874; s. John (M.D.) and Margaret (McAndrew) F.; Georgetown Coll., 1900-04; M.D., Georgetown U., Washington, 1906; post-grad. work, Berlin, 1913; m. Lois Gibson Dyer, Oct. 12, 1910; children—Mary Virginia, William Dyer. Practiced in Washington, 1906—; asst. prof. therapeutics and materia medica, 1906-08, asst. prof. anatomy, 1908-10, asso. prof. therapeutics and pharmacology, 1911-17, asso. prof. clin. medicine and diseases of children, 1917-20, prof. diseases of children, 1920—, Georgetown U., also dean of faculty of medicine, 1929—; pediatrist to Providence and Children's hosps.; cons. pediatrist to Foundling and Gallinger hosps. Mem. sub-com. to Gen. Med. Bd., Council Nat. Defense; also lecturer on social hygiene for Bur. of Training Camp Activities and U.S. Pub. Health Service, 1918. Del. Internat. Med. Congress, London, 1913; trustee Nat. Geog. Soc., 1924—. Author: Essentials of Materia Medica and Therapeutics, 1910; State Board Questions for Nurses, 1916; Diseases of the New-Born, 1925; Diseases of Bones and Joints in Childhood, 1926. Official del. from U.S. to Pan Am. Child Conf., Havana, 1927. Home: Washington, D.C. Died Apr. 12, 1931.

FOOTE, Lucius Harwood, diplomat; b. Winfield, N.Y., Apr. 10, 1826; s. Rev. Lucius and Electa (Harwood) F.; A.B., Western Reserve, 1850, A.M., 1853; (hon. A.M., Knox Coll., 1875); m. Rose Frost Carter, 1862 (died 1885). Crossed plains to Calif., 1853; admitted to bar, 1856; municipal judge, Sacramento, 1856-60; collector port of Sacramento, 1861-65; adj. gen. Calif., 1872-76; consul to Valparaiso, Chili, 1878-81; chargé d'affaires, Chili, 1881; on spl. diplomatic mission in Central America, 1882; E.E. and M.P. to Corea, 1882; distinguished himself in protection of Japanese and other foreigners in nationalist revolt of 1883 at Seoul; received thanks of Emperor of Japan and freedom of City of Tokio; thanks of govt. of China, and an autograph letter of thanks from the Emperor of Corea; resigned, 1884; sec. and treas. Calif. Acad. of Sciences, 1890—. Died June 4, 1913.

FOOTE, Mary Hallock, author; b. Milton, N.Y., Nov. 19, 1847; m. Arthur De Wint Foote, civil engr., Feb. 9, 1876. Lived for some yrs. in Colo., Calif. and Ida. Studied art in New York; has done much work in black and white for mags. and book illustration. Author: The Led Horse Claim, 1883; The Last Assembly Ball, 1889; In Exile and Other Stories, 1894; Cœur d'Alène, 1894; The Prodigal, 1900; A Picked Company, 1912; The Valley Road, 1915; Edith Bonham, 1917; The Ground Swell, 1919. Died June 25, 1938.

FOOTE, Morris Cooper, brig. gen. U.S. Army, retired; b. Madison Barracks, Sackett's Harbor, N.Y., Sept. 16, 1843; s. Lyman (surgeon U.S.A.) and Mary Morris (Cooper) F.; ed. pub. schs., Cooperstown, N.Y., and acad. at Plattsburg, N.Y.; grad. Commercial Coll., Syracuse, N.Y.; m. Annie, d. D. F. Murphy, official reporter to U.S. Senate, Apr. 29, 1891. Entered vol. service as pvt. 44th N.Y. vols., Sept. 1861; served through Civil war as 2d lt., 1st lt. and bvt. capt. N.Y. vols. Entered regular army May 1866, as 2d lt., 9th U.S. Inf.; served as 2d lt., 1st lt., capt., maj. and lt. col. 9th inf.; col. 28th Inf., Apr. 15, 1902; brig. gen. Feb. 18, 1903; retired Feb. 19, 1903. After Civil War served through various Indian campaigns, through the Santiago campaign and battle of San Juan Hill, Cuba, 1898; through the entire campaign for the relief of Peking, China, 1900. Mem. Provisional govt. of Tien-tsin, China, winter of 1900-01; served in the Philippines, summer of 1901 and winter of 1902-03. Home: Cooperstown, N.Y. Died 1905.

FORAKER, Burch, telephone exec.; b. Hillsboro, O., Feb. 17, 1872; s. Burch and Emily (Rockhold) F.; ed. pub. schs., Ohio Wesleyan U. and Cornell U.; m. Carrie E. Jellig, July 26, 1900. Began with New York Telephone Co., 1893, div. plant supt. for Manhattan, the Bronx and Westchester County, 1912-24, gen. mgr. upstate area, 1925; pres. Mich. Bell Telephone Co., 1926—. Republican. Methodist. Home: Detroit, Mich. Died Mar. 29, 1935.

FORAKER, Joseph Benson, senator; b. on farm nr. Rainsboro, O., July 5, 1846; enlisted July 14, 1862, as pvt. 89th Ohio Inf., and served to end of war, becoming 1st lt. and bvt. capt.; grad. Cornell, 1869; m. Julia, d. Hon. H. S. Bundy, Oct. 4, 1870. Admitted to bar and began practice at Cincinnati, 1869; judge Superior Ct., Cincinnati, 1879-82; resigned on account of ill health; Rep. candidate for gov. Ohio, 1883; defeated, but elected gov. in 1885 and 1887; again defeated, 1889, for same office; U.S. senator, 1897-1903, 1903-09. Chmn. Rep. State convs., Ohio, 1886, 1890, 1896, 1900; del.-at-large (O.) Rep. Nat. Convs., 1884, 88, 92, 96, 1900, 04; presented name of William McKinley to the convs. of 1896 and 1900 for nomination to the presidency. Author: Notes of a Busy Life, 1916. Home: Cincinnati, O. Died May 10, 1917.

FORBES, Allen Boyd, banker; b. Cleveland, O.; s. Alexander and Catharine Cleaver (Boyd) F.; LL.B., Northwestern U., 1886, Yale, 1888; m. Laura Wells Hately, Sept. 25, 1899. Head of Harris, Forbes & Co., New York; dir. Bankers Trust Co., U.S. Mortgage & Trust Co., Mercantile Safe Deposit Co. (New York), Harris Trust & Savings Bank, Harris Safe Deposit Co. (Chicago); trustee Carnegie Foundation Teachers' Ins. Co., N.Y. Sch. of Applied Design. Home: Greenwich, Conn. Died Sept. 27, 1923.

FORBES, Charles Henry, academy prof.; b. Providence, R.I., Mar. 27, 1866; s. Kenneth David and Jane (Dunlap) F.; A.B., Brown U., 1900, hon. A.M., same, 1915, Yale U., 1926; studied U. of Berlin, 1897-98, Paris, Rome, 1908-09, 1922-23; L.H.D., Amherst, 1930; m. Georgianna Snow, July 25, 1894 (died 1907); m. 2d, Ellen Snow, Jan. 3, 1914. Instructor in Latin, 1891-94, prof., 1894—, acting prin., 1912-13, elected to Alfred L. Ripley Foundation, 1927, Phillips Acad., Andover, acting headmaster, 1931-32. Mem. bd. visitors, Brown U., Harvard. Co-editor: (Harkness and Forbes) Cæsar's Gallic War, 1901. Editor: Eight Orations of Cicero, 1903; A School Cicero, 1905. Author: Sham Argument Against Latin, 1917; Chapel Prayers, 1920; Verba Transversa, 1926; Catalogue of the Charles H. Forbes Collection of Vergiliana in the Oliver Wendell Holmes Library, 1931. Home: Andover, Mass. Died Mar. 12, 1933.

FORBES, Elmer Severance, editor; b. Westboro, Mass., Sept. 12, 1860; s. Baxter and Caroline Hannah (Severance) F.; B.S., Amherst, 1881; m. Sallie Latou Flemming, June 3, 1890; children—Alice Caroline (Mrs. Harold B. Hayden), Robert Latou. Deacon, 1890, priest, 1891, P.E. Ch.; rector St. Mary's Ch., Haledon, N.J., 1890-93; successively asst., vicar, and rector, St. John's Ch., Jersey City, 1893-1908 (resigned 1908), and withdrew from Episcopal Ch.; sec. dept. of community service of Am. Unitarian Assn., 1908-29. Unitarian. Home: Weston, Mass. Died July 2, 1933.

FORBES, Frederick Faber, newspaperman; b. Wilkes-Barre, Pa.; s. John J. and Anna (Kelly) F.; ed. pub. and pvt. schs. in Pa.; m. Anna Emily Moon. Read law with Judge James J. O'Neill, of Lackawanna County (Pa.). Editor Scranton (Pa.) Republican, 1900; asst. mng. editor Philadelphia North American, 1905, chief editorial writer, 1912, mng. editor, 1913, directing editor, 1924; joined editorial staff The Chronicle, San Francisco (Calif.), 1926. Home: Berkeley, Calif. Died Nov. 17, 1933.

FORBES, Frederick Levi, clergyman; b. Elkhart, Ind., May 27, 1854; s. Frederick Lotan and Harriet (Farnham) F.; student Ind. State Normal Sch., Terre Haute, 1873-74; grad. State Normal and Training Sch., Brockport, N.Y., 1878; Ph.B., Lake Forest (Ill.) Coll., 1880, hon. M.Ph., 1885; B.D., McCormick Theol. Sem., 1885; D.D., Grove City (Pa.) Coll., 1899; m. Carrie F. Barstow, Aug. 23, 1880 (died 1913); children—Ethel Forbes (Mrs. Louis Lomax Harding), Frederick Barstow (dec.); m. 2d, Mary M. Clark, Jan. 10, 1921. Ordained ministry Presbyn. Ch., 1885; pastor in Ill. and Mich., 1884-93; supt. missions for Northern Mich., 1893-96; prin. Pendleton (Ore.) Acad., 1896-1903; pastor Lane St. Ch., Seattle, Wash., 1903-05; asst. pastor First Presbyn. Ch., Seattle, 1905-17 and 1920—; supt. Federal Schs., Yukon Dist., Alaska, 1917-20; stated clk., Eastern Ore. Presbytery, 1899-1903, Seattle Presbytery, 1912-17 and 1923—; moderator Synod of Ore., 1901-02, Synod of Wash., 1926-27. Republican. Died Apr. 4, 1940.

FORBES, George Mather, univ. prof.; b. Middlesex, N.Y., June 13, 1853; s. Merrill and Maria (Palmer) F.; A.B., U. of Rochester, 1878, A.M., 1881; studied Luisen-Städtischen Realschule, Berlin, also U. of Berlin, 1874-75; LL.D., Colgate U., N.Y., 1909; married; children—Gordon Merrill (dec.), Mrs. Florence Killam. Asso. prin. Genesee and Wyoming Sem., Alexander, N.Y., 1872-73; prin. Arcade (N.Y.) Union Sch. and Acad., 1873-76; asso. prin. Overhiser Sch., Brooklyn, 1878-81; prof. Greek, 1881-90, philosophy and edn., 1890—, U. of Rochester. Commr. of schs. at-large, 1900-06; pres. Bd. of Edn., Rochester, to 1912. Home: Rochester, N.Y. Died Oct. 29, 1934.

FORBES, Gerrit Angelo, jurist; b. Clockville, N.Y., May 30, 1836; s. Isaac J. and Abigail (Sayles) F.; ed. pub. schs. of Clockville; studied law; m. Ellen Brooks, July 10, 1862. Admitted to bar May 13, 1863; dist. atty. Madison Co., Jan. 1, 1871, to Dec. 31, 1874; justice Supreme Court N.Y., 1888—; now in 2d term, expiring Dec. 31, 1906. Republican. Mem. N.Y. State and Madison Co. bar assns. Home: Canastota, N.Y. Died 1906.

FORBES, Henry Prentiss, theologian; b. Paris, Me., July 4, 1849; s. Elbridge and Julia (Prentiss) F.; grad. St. Lawrence U. Theol. Sch., N.Y., 1873; student U. of Leipzig, 1874-75; (D.D., Buchtel Coll., 1890); m. Harriet E. Wood, Sept. 12, 1876. Ordained Universalist ministry, 1874; pastor Danvers, Mass., 1875-80; prof. bibl. lang. and lit., 1880—, dean, 1899—, Theol. Sch. St. Lawrence U. Home: Canton, N.Y. Died Oct. 2, 1913.

FORBES, James, playwright; b. Salem, Ont., Can.; s. James Reid and Clementina (Erskine) F.; ed. Collegiate Inst., Galt., Ont.; m. Ada Eugenie Fischer, Sept. 21, 1901; 1 son, Anthony. Came to U.S., 1884; naturalized citizen, 1892; actor, 1894-96; dramatic critic Pittsburgh Dispatch and asst. dramatic editor New York World, 1897-98; press rep. various orgns., 1898-1902; gen. mgr. Henry B. Harris enterprises, 1902-06; playwriting, 1906—. Organized and directed formation of groups of professionals, sent to Europe to entertain the A.E.F., during the war; also first stock co. of actors to play in repertoire in France, known as the James Forbes Stock Co.; originated plan of organizing other actors who were serving in the army into stock companies. Mem. Nat. Inst. Arts and Letters. Democrat. Author: The Chorus Lady, produced at the Savoy Theatre, New York, 1906; The Traveling Salesman, 1908; The Commuters, 1910; A Rich Man's Son, 1912; The Show Shop, 1914; The Famous Mrs. Fair, 1919—The Famous Mrs. Fair, The Traveling Salesman, The Commuters, The Show Shop and The Chorus Lady also appeared in bookform. Home: New York, N.Y. Died May 26, 1938.

FORBES, Jesse Franklin, clergyman; b. Hartford, Conn., Dec. 19, 1847; s. Franklin Joshua and Elizabeth (Carpenter) F.; A.B., Amherst, 1874; A.M., 1884; grad. Union Theol. Sem., 1877; Ph.D., New York U., 1894; (D.D., Bellevue Coll., Neb., 1906); m. Jennie Crane Savage, Sept. 20, 1877. Ordained Congl. ministry, 1878; pastor First Ch., Warren, Mass., 1878-85, Adams Memorial Presbyn. Ch., New York, 1886-1911; sec. Ch. Extension Com. Presbytery of New York, June 15, 1911—. Moderator 3 times, stated clerk and mem. Moderator's Council, Presbytery of New York. Presbyn. Republican. Home: New York, N.Y. Died July 8, 1922.

FORBES, Richard Tasker, banker; b. Port Lavaca, Tex., Mar. 4, 1868; s. Robert Mitchell and Mary (Read) F.; ed. pvt. sch. and Hobbs Sch., Dallas, Tex.; m. May Coudrey Palmer, June 28, 1910. Began as messenger Am. Nat. Bank, Dallas, 1884; bookkeeper Nat. Bank of Commerce, Kansas City, Mo., 1887-89; teller First Nat. Bank, Las Vegas, N.M., 1889-91; pres. Stephens Lithographing & Engraving Co., St. Louis, 1891-96; cashier Am. Trust & Savings Bank, Cedar Rapids, Ia., 1898-1905, pres. same, 1907; v.p. and cashier Citizens Nat. Bank, Cedar Rapids, 1905-07; v.p. Drovers Deposit Nat. Bank, Chicago, 1907-08, pres., 1908-10; pres. First Nat. Bank, St. Joseph, Mo., 1910-20, chmn. bd.; v.p. Ft. Dearborn Nat. Bank, Chicago, 1920-21; v.p. Continental & Commercial Nat. Bank, which absorbed Ft. Dearborn Nat. Bank, 1922—. First lt. 5th Battery, Ia. Vol. Light Arty., Spanish-Am. War. Pres. Ia. Soc. S.R., 1905; mem. Mil. Order Spanish-Am. War; chmn. St. Joseph Br. Nat. Security League, 1915. Episcopalian. Mason. Died Mar. 1926.

FORBES, Robert, clergyman; b. Stoneham, P.Q., Can., Nov. 13, 1844; s. Alexander and Margaret (Dundass) F.; ed. in Can.; (D.D., Hamline U., Minn., 1888); m. Sarah E. Savage, May 15, 1866. Ordained M.E. ministry, 1870; pastor Byron, Minn., 1870-73, Kasson, Minn., 1873-76, Waseca, Minn., 1876-79, Faribault, Minn., 1879-81, First Ch., Minneapolis, 1881-84, Jackson St. Ch., St. Paul, 1884-87, Bates Av., 1888; presiding elder St. Paul Dist., 1889-92; pastor Asbury Ch., Duluth, 1892-97; presiding elder Duluth Dist., 1897-1903; asst. corr. sec. 1903-07, corr. sec. from Nov. 1907, Bd. of Home Missions and Ch. Extension, M.E. Ch. Editor The Christian Republic (monthly); chaplain Minn. Ho. of Rep., 2 terms, Senate, 2 terms. Trustee Hamline U. for many yrs. Republican. Author: The Changeless Christ, 1905. Wrote 1st chapter of "Methodism and the Republic"; chapter on Thoburn in India. Home: Philadelphia. Died Oct. 25, 1913.

FORBES, Stephen Alfred, naturalist; b. Silver Creek, Ill., May 29, 1844; s. Isaac Sawyer and Agnes (Van Hoesen) F.; ed. at Beloit Acad. and Rush Med. Coll.; Ph.D., on exam. and thesis, Ind. U., 1884; (LL.D., U. of Ill., 1905); m. Clara Shaw Gaston, Dec. 25, 1873; children—Bertha Van Hoesen, Ernest Browning, Winifred, Ethel Clara, Richard Edwin (dec.). Capt. 7th Ill. Vol. Cav. in Civil War; prisoner 4 months; curator Mus. of Ill. State Natural History Soc., 1872-77; taught zoölogy, Ill. State Normal U., 1875-78; founded, 1877, and dir. Ill. State Lab. of Natural History to 1917; since chief of natural history survey of Ill.; state entomologist, 1882-1917; prof. zoölogy, 1884-1909, prof. of entomology, Sept. 1, 1909-21, dean Coll. of Science, 1888-1905, Univ. of Ill. Awarded first class medal of Société d'Acclimatation de France for scientific publs., 1886; organized Internat. Congress Zoölogists, Chicago Expn., 1893; dir. aquarium of U.S. Fish Commn. and prepared natural history exhibit of Ill. at same. Was founder of and has been editor and contbr. to Bulletins of Illinois State Lab. of Natural History, 1877— (now Bulletin Ill. State Nat. Hist. Survey). Author: Biennial Reports as State Entomologist, 1883-1916; Studies of the Food of Birds, Fishes and Insects; Contagious Diseases of Insects. Final Report on the Fishes of Illinois and Studies on the Biology of the Illinois River (with R. E. Richardson). Home: Urbana, Ill. Died Mar. 13, 1930.

FORBES, Theodore Frelinghuysen, soldier; b. in Hawaii, July 13, 1840; s. Cochran and Rebecca Denman (Smith) F.; acad. edn.; m. Mrs. Henrietta A. Woodward, June 19, 1900. Enlisted pvt. 102d N.Y. Vols., Nov. 9, 1861; apptd. corporal same month; severely wounded in battle of Cedar Mountain, Va., Aug. 9, 1862, and in hosp. on account of wounds until Feb. 1863; apptd. 2d lt. 102d N.Y. Vols., Aug. 9, 1862; mustered out on account of disability, Mar. 7, 1863; apptd. 2d lt. Vet. Reserve Corps, Aug. 19, 1863, 2d lt. 42d Inf. (Vet. Reserve Corps), July 28, 1866; transferred to 5th Inf., Nov. 15, 1869; promoted 1st lt., Aug. 31, 1875; capt., Oct. 8, 1885; maj. 5th Inf., Feb. 27, 1899; lt. col. 29th Inf., Feb. 28, 1901; col. 27th Inf., July 14, 1902; brig. gen., Aug. 14, 1903, and retired from active service, Aug. 15, 1903. Died Mar. 9, 1917.

FORBES, W(illiam) O(scar), clergyman; b. Berrien Springs, Mich., Sept. 2, 1852; s. Rev. Frederick Levi and Harriet (Farnham) F.; direct desc. Rev. John Forbes, D.D., moderator Gen. Assembly Scottist Ch.; grad. Warsaw Collegiate Inst., 1873, Brockport (N.Y.) State Normal Sch., 1876; Ph.B., Lake Forest (Ill.) U., 1880, M.A., 1884, D.D., 1924; B.D., Princeton (N.J.) Theol. Sem., 1883; hon. alumnus Whitworth College, Tacoma, 1908; D.D., Jamestown (N.D.) Coll., 1910; m. Alice Cary Platt, Aug. 3, 1881 (died 1905); children—Edith Emily (dec.), Alice Maude Mary (Mrs. Lorne P. King); m. 2d, Mrs. Nellie Frazer Arnold, Oct. 10, 1910; stepson—Frazer Arnold. Ordained ministry, Presbyn. Ch., 1884; pastor Forbes Ch., Portland, Ore., 1883-93, 1897-1901; field missionary and synodical supt. of Ore., 1893-97; S.S. missionary Wash. and Ida., 1901-10; supt. North Pacific Synods (including Alaska) and dist. field sec., Pacific Coast Synods (Ida., Wash., Ore., Calif., Nev., Ariz., Alaska), Presbyn. Ch. in U.S.A. (organizer Sunday schs. and chs.), 1910-30; dist. sec. emeritus. Moderator Synod of Ore., 1895; twice vice moderator Synod of Wash. Corporate dir. Patton Home, Portland, Ore.; founder Portland-Seamen's Inst., also Forbes and Westminster chs., Portland. Awarded gold service pin (47 years as missionary), Nat. Gen. Assembly Presbyn. Ch. in U.S.A., 1927. Republican. Home: Hollywood, Calif. Died Nov. 1937.

FORBES, William Trowbridge; b. Westborough, Mass., May 24, 1850; s. Ephraim Trowbridge and Catharine (White) F.; B.A., Amherst, 1871; m. Harriette Merrifield, Feb. 6, 1884. Instr. in mathematics, Robert Coll., Constantinople, Turkey, 1871-74; judge, 1st Dist. Court, East Worcester, Mass., 1875-79; mem. Mass. Ho. of Rep., 1881-82, Senate, 1886, 87; judge of probate and insolvency, 1888-1925, retired. Mem. Sch. Com., Westborough, 6 yrs.; commr. of parks, Worcester; v.p. Peoples Savings Bank, etc. Chmn. Mass. Minimum Wage Bd. Pres. bd. trustees Bancroft Sch., Worcester; pres. Worcester Pub. Library; v.p. Mass. Soc. for Prevention of Cruelty to Animals; clk. Memorial Home for the Blind; trustee Old Men's Home; dir. Asso. Charities, Worcester Art Museum. Trustee Worcester Natural History Soc.; pres. Amherst Assn. of Central Mass., Westborough Hist. Soc.; Mass. state historian of S.R. Mem. Worcester Rotary Edn. Fund, Inc. Republican. Home: Worcester, Mass. Died Nov. 8, 1931.

FORBES-ROBERTSON, Johnston, actor; b. London, Eng., Jan. 16, 1853; s. John and Frances Forbes-Robertson; ed. Charterhouse, Eng.; studied painting art schs. in France and Royal Acad. Sch., London; m. Gertrude Elliott, Dec. 22, 1900. Début as Chastelard, in "Mary Stuart," London, 1874; appeared with the Bancrofts, Mme. Modjeska, Irving, Mary Anderson, Sir John Hare, 1880-95; opened Lyceum Theatre, London, under own management, 1895; first toured America with Mary Anderson, 1885; again in 1889, 1902, 1905, 1909-10. Played with Henry Irving, in "Much Ado About Nothing," 1882, and commd. by him to paint the church scene now in The Players, New York; with Mary Anderson, in "The Winter's Tale," 1885; with Irving, in "Henry VIII," 1889; with Hare, in revival of "Diplomacy," 1893; last appeared with Irving in "King Arthur," 1895; produced several plays in the Lyceum, London, 1895, ending with "Hamlet," with which and "Macbeth," toured Germany and Holland; produced "Cæsar" and "Cleopatra," 1906, and revived "Merchant of Venice," "Othello," and "Hamlet"; appeared "Passing of the Third Floor Back," London and America, 1908-11. Home: London, England. Died Nov. 6, 1937.

FORBUSH, Edward Howe, ornithologist; b. Quincy, Mass., Apr. 24, 1858; s. Leander Pomeroy and Ruth Hudson (Carr) F.; m. Etta L. Hill, June 28, 1882; children—Myrtice Elizabeth, Erwin Hill, Lewis Edward, Etta Lorenda. Dir. div. of ornithology Mass. Dept. Agr., 1893-1908, 1921; state ornithologist, 1908—. Life mem. Worcester Natural History Soc.; fellow Am. Ornithologists' Union; founder Mass. Audubon Society. Author: Birds of Massachusetts and other New England States, Vol. 1; Water Birds, Marsh Birds and Shore Birds, 1925; Vol. 2, Land Birds, from Bob-White to Grackels, 1927. Home: Westboro, Mass. Died Mar. 7, 1929.

FORBUSH, William Byron, author; b. Springfield, Vt., Feb. 20, 1868; s. Rufus O. and Eliza Ann (Spencer) F.; A.B., Dartmouth, 1888; Union Theol. Sem., 1892; Ph.D., New York U., 1892; Litt.D., Hanover Coll., 1895; m. Maud Muller Barden, Nov. 29, 1890; children—Arthur Rex, Dascomb, Bliss. Ordained Congl. ministry, 1892; pastor Warren, Mass., 1896-98; Winthrop Ch., Boston, 1898-1905, North Ch., Detroit, 1906-13; gen. editor the University Society, N.Y. City, 1918-24; cons. editor John C. Winston Co., 1924—. Lecturer Brown U., 1893-94, Hartford Theol. Sem., 1901-04, Chautauqua, 1903-07. Founded, 1893, Internat. Order Knights of King Arthur, the largest fraternity of ch. boys. Author: The Boy Problem, 1901; The Boys' Life of Christ, 1905; Ecclesiastes in the Metre of Omar, 1906; Guide Book to Childhood, 1913; Manual of Play, 1914; Manuel of Stories, 1914; Boy Problem in the Home, 1916; Young Folks' Book of Ideals, 1917; The Home Education of Children, 1919; The Character Training of Children, 1919; Be Square, 1924; The Book of Games, 1927; Myths and Hero Tales, 1928. Edited: The Young Folks' Treasury, 12 vols., 1919; The Boys' and Girls' Bookshelf, 17 vols., 1920; The Home Kindergarten Manual, 3 vols., 1921. Home: Media, Pa. Died Oct. 23, 1927.

FORCE, Manning Ferguson, comdt. Ohio Soldiers' and Sailors' Home, 1889—; b. Washington, Dec. 17, 1824; grad. Harvard, 1845 (LL.B., Harvard; LL.D., Marietta Coll.). Admitted to bar, Cincinnati, 1850; apptd. maj. 20th O. vol. Inf., Aug. 1861; served through Civil War; mustered out as brig. gen. and bvt. maj. gen., Jackson, Miss., Jan. 1866. Judge of common pleas, Hamilton Co., O., 1867-77; judge superior court, Cincinnati, 1877-87; prof. equity and criminal law, Cincinnati Law School, 1878-88. Author: From Fort Henry to Corinth; General Sherman (Great Comdrs. Series), 1899. Died 1899.

FORCHHEIMER, Frederick, physician; b. Cincinnati, Sept. 25, 1853; s. M. S. and Fanny F.; ed. Woodward High Sch., Cincinnati, and univs. of Strassburg and Würzburg; M.D., Coll. Phys. and Surg. (Columbia), 1873; m. Edith S. Perry, June 22, 1885. Prof. theory and practice of medicine, Med. Coll., U. of Cincinnati, 1895—. Home: Cincinnati, O. Died June 1, 1913.

FORD, Arthur Hillyer, prof. elec. engring.; b. Chicago, Feb. 6, 1874; s. Charles Henry and Edna Coe (Hillyer) F.; B.S. in E.E., U. of Wis., 1895, E.E., 1896, fellow, 1895-97; fellow Columbia, 1897-98; m. Sadie Murray Hess, June 18, 1908; children—Ellen, Edwin Hillyer, Robert Murray. Engr. with Western Electric Co., Chicago, 1899-1900; acting prof. elec. engring., U. of Colo., 1900-01; prof. same, Ga. Sch. of Tech., 1901-05, State U. of Ia., Sept. 1905—. Fellow Am. Inst. Elec. Engrs., 1912. Congregationalist. Home: Iowa City, Ia. Died Feb. 16, 1930.

FORD, Arthur Younger, univ. pres.; b. Parkville, Mo., Nov. 11, 1861; s. Salem Holland and Sarah (Beauchamp) F.; student Center Coll., Danville, Ky., 2 yrs.; A.B., Brown U., 1884, A.M.; LL.D., U. of Louisville, 1923; m. Esther Brown, Jan. 3, 1887. Established Inquirer (daily and weekly newspaper), Owensboro, Ky., 1884; editorial writer, later mng. editor Louisville Courier-Journal, 1890-1905; treas. Columbia Trust Co., 1906-09, v.p., 1909-13; pres. Goodwin Preserving Co., 1913-22; pres. bd. of trustees, U. of Louisville, 1914-22; pres. U. of Louisville, 1922—. Pres. Ky. World's Fair Commn. to St. Louis, 1903-04; trustee Georgetown (Ky.) Coll., 1904-14; chmn. com. on tax reform of Louisville Bd. of Trade, 1907-18, and pres. of its successor, the Ky. Tax Reform Assn., 1918—; mem. State Tax Commn., 1908-09; dir. and hon. life mem. Louisville Bd. of Trade. Mem. Louisville Health and Hosp. Council. Trustee and mem. exec. com. Southern Bapt. Theol. Sem.; mem. advisory bd. Simmons U. Died June 8, 1926.

FORD, Charles Halsey Lindsley, clergyman, educator; b. Binghamton, N.Y., Dec. 10, 1887; s. Charles Lindsley and Sarah Townsend (Miller) F.; B.A., St. Stephen's Coll., Annandale, N.Y., 1910; grad. Gen. Theol. Sem., 1913; studied Syracuse U., 1920-21; studied N.Y. Univ. Sch. of Edn., 1926-27; m. Frances N. Alley (B.S., Simmons Coll.), Oct. 4, 1916. Deacon, 1913, priest, 1914, P.E. Ch.; in charge Zion Ch., Windsor, N.Y., 1913-15; rector Grace Ch., Cortland, N.Y., 1915-18; chaplain St. John's Mil. Sch., Manlius, N.Y., 1919-21; head of Jr. House and instr. history and Latin, Howe Sch., 1921-23; prin. St. Faith's Sch., Saratoga Springs, N.Y., 1923-32; rector Trinity Ch., Gloversville, Oct. 1, 1932—. Y.M.C.A. dir. religious work, Camp Wadsworth, S.C., 1917-18; grad. Army Chaplains' Sch., 1918; sr. chaplain Coast Defenses, Boston, Mass., 1918; chaplain 4th Antiaircraft Sector, C.A.C., A.E.F., 1918-19; capt. chaplain O.R.C.; also maj. chaplain 105th Inf., N.G., N.Y. Trustee St. Stephen's Coll. Alumni Assn. Republican. Mason. Home: Gloversville, N.Y. Died Mar. 13, 1939.

FORD, Clyde Ellsworth, M.D.; b. Leetonia, O., Mar. 26, 1874; s. Homer J. and Emma J. (Berry) F.; ed. Lewis Acad., Wichita, Kan.; M.D., Cleveland Coll. Phys. and Surg. (Ohio Wesleyan U., merged with Western Reserve Medical Coll.), 1902; m. Florence R. Biddle, Apr. 29, 1909. Practiced, Cleveland, 1902. Commr. of Health, Cleveland, 1910-16; med. dir. Gen. Chem. Co., N.Y. City, 1916-24. Home: Cleveland Heights, Cleveland, O. Died Feb. 19, 1927.

FORD, Daniel Sharp, publisher; b. Cambridgeport, Mass., April 5, 1822; ed. there and in Boston; learned printer's trade; became a partner with his employer as asst. editor and publisher of The Watchman and Reflector. In 1856 he bought from N. R. Willis, the father of N. P. Willis (poet), The Youth's Companion, which has ever since been published under firm name of Perry Mason & Co. Died 1899.

FORD, Francis Chipman, anatomist; b. Niles, Mich., June 26, 1865; s. Henry Allen and Emily F. (Chipman) F.; desc. on mother's side of four Mayflower passengers; A.B., U. of Mich., 1888; M.D., Homœ. Med. Dept., U. of Mich., 1890; m. Ida Harriet Larimore, July 15, 1890. Practiced, Niles, Mich., 1890-91, Chicago, 1891-93, Los Angeles and Pasadena, Calif., 1893-96; removed to Chicago, 1897; anatomist in Chicago med. colls., 1897-1906; prof. and head dept. of anatomy, Hahnemann Med. Coll., Chicago, 1906—; chmn. com. of management, Hahnemann dept., Chicago Y.M.C.A. Mem. Vol. Med. Service Corps, 1918-19. Republican. Presbyn. Home: Chicago, Ill. Died May 9, 1922.

FORD, Frank Richards, cons. engr.; b. Phila., Pa., 1871; s. Henry C. and Emilie C. (Richards) F.; B.S. and M.E., U. of Pa., 1890; m. Sunshine H. Donaldson, 1898 (died 1923); 4 children; m. 2d, Ethelwyn Linnell, 1927. Mem. Ford, Bacon & Davis, cons. engrs., 1894—. Dir. L. C. Smith & Corona Typewriters, Inc., Lackawanna & Wyo. Valley R.R. Corp., Syracuse Washing Machine Corp. Mem. New York, New Jersey Port and Harbor Development Commn., 1917-21; mem. Port of New York Authority, 1921-23. Trustee Washington Square Assn. Republican. Episcopalian. Homes: Roseland, N.J., and New York City. Died Sept. 17, 1930.

FORD, George Burdett, city planning; b. Clinton, Mass., June 24, 1879; s. Andrew Elmer and Ellen Louise (Burdett) F.; A.B., Harvard, 1899; S.B., Mass. Inst. Tech., 1900, M.S., 1901; École des Beaux Arts, Paris, 1903-07; diplôme par le gouvernement français, 1907; m. Harriet Chalmers Bliss, June 15, 1912. With George B. Post & Sons, architects, New York, 1907-17; v.p. Tech. Advisory Corp., City Planning Consultant to the U.S. War Dept. Consultant to commn. on city plan of Bd. of Estimate and Apportionment and to commn. on bldg. dists. and restrictions, New York; advisor to Russell Sage Foundation Regional Plan of New York and Environs and to Regional Planning Fedn. of the Phila. Tri-State Dist.; city planner to Trenton, Newark, Jersey City, Elizabeth, and East Orange, N.J., Omaha, Neb., Louisville and Lexington, Ky., Richmond and Norfolk, Va., Savannah, Ga., Charleston, S.C., Port Chester, New Rochelle and Elmira, N.Y., Chester, Pa., New Britain and New Haven, Conn., Wilmington, Del., Cincinnati, Dayton and Mansfield, O., Worcester, Somerville and Springfield, Mass.; zoning consultant 94 cities and towns; consultant to French Govt. for replanning Rheims, Soissons, etc., 1919-20; consultant to Philippine Govt. for replanning of Manila and environs, 1929. Deputy commr. Am. Red Cross in France, June 1917; mem. housing com. of Council Nat. Defense; mem. Am. Industrial Commn. to France, 1916; fgn. rep. of Nat. Information Bur., 1919-20. U.S. del. 9th Internat. Housing Congress, Vienna, 1910; town planning lecturer, Columbia U., 1914-16, to U.S. Army Ednl. Corps, France, 1919, to Harvard U. Sch. of City and Regional Planning, 1929. Chevalier de la Légion d'Honneur. Mem. Am. Inst. Architects. Author: City Planning Progress, 1917; Out of the Ruins, 1919; Urbanisme en Pratique, 1919. Home: Lake Mahopac, N.Y. Died Aug. 15, 1930.

FORD, George Michael, state supt. schs.; b. Kasson, W.Va., Jan. 7, 1871; s. Frederic G. W. and Jemima Elizabeth (Hebb) F.; student Fairmont (W.Va.) State Normal Sch., 1887; A.B., W.Va. U., 1892, LL.B., 1896; m. Annie L. Linn, Keyser, W.Va., Dec. 22, 1897; children—Margaret Buchanan (Mrs. Harry W. Hall), Jemima Elizabeth (Mrs. Silas E. Richmond), Annie Laurie Linn, Frederick Wayne. Began as teacher pub. schs., 1892; traveling rep. Ginn & Co., pubs., 1900-03; served as prin. schs., Terra Alta, high schs., Grafton and Benwood; pres. Concord State Normal Sch.; head dept. economics and Am. history, Marshall Coll.; supt. schs., Bluefield, Brown's Creek Sch. Dist., pub. schs., Dunbar; state supt. schs., W.Va., Mar. 1922—, 2d term ending 1929. Commd. capt. 2d Inf., W.Va. N.G., May 12, 1911; maj. 1914; served as capt. on Mexican border, 1916-17, and overseas 6 mos. with 150th U.S. Inf., 38th Div., 358th Inf., 90th Div., and 145th Inf., 37th Div.; hon. disch. Apr. 25, 1919; lt. col. 398th Inf. (Res.). Life mem. N.E.A. Methodist. Mason. Home: Dunbar, W.Va. Died Aug. 21, 1941.

FORD, Henry Clinton, educator; b. Charlotte Co., Va., Dec. 12, 1867; s. Luther Rice and Pernette (Smith) F.; student Va. Poly. Inst., 1884-85; B.S., Va. Mil. Inst., 1889; Ph.D., U. of Va., 1899; m. Agnes Palmer, Jan. 10, 1900 (died 1902); children—Thomas Lewis (dec.), Mary Lewis; m. 2d, Elizabeth Walker, July 12, 1905; children—Virginia Easton, Henry Clinton, Medora Beall. Instr. in French, English and tactics, Va. Mil. Inst., 1889-90; comdt. cadets and instr., Wentworth Mil. Acad., Lexington, Mo., 1890-93; asst. prof. modern langs. and tactics, Va. Mil. Inst., 1895-96; master St. Albans' Sch., Radford, Va., 1896-98; adjunct prof. Latin, English and history, Va. Mil. Inst., 1899-1902, comdt. of cadets, 1901-03, prof. Latin, English and history, 1902-10, prof. history, 1910—. Mem. Va. State Bd. of Edn., 1911-23, 1927-30; mem. Town Council, Lexington, 1913-19. Col. and chief of engrs., staff of Gov. James Hodge Tyler, 1898-1902. Episcopalian. Home: Lexington, Va. Deceased.

FORD, Henry Jones, univ. prof.; b. Baltimore, Aug. 25, 1851; s. Franklin and Annie Elizabeth (Jones) F.; grad. Baltimore City Coll., 1868 (LL.D., U. of Maryland, 1918). Editorial writer on Baltimore American, 1872; has been city editor Baltimore Sun; mng. editor Baltimore American, 1875-79; editorial writer New York Sun, 1879-83; on staff Baltimore Sun, 1883-85; mng. editor Pittsburgh Commercial Gazette, 1885-95; mng. editor Pittsburgh Chronicle Telegraph, 1895-1901; editor Pittsburgh Gazette, 1901-05; lecturer on polit. science, Johns Hopkins, 1906, 1907; prof. politics, Princeton, June 1908—. Commr. of banking and ins. of N.J., 1912; mem. of Interstate Commerce Commn., 1920-21. Author: The Natural History of the State, 1915; Alexander Hamilton, 1920; Representative Government, 1923. Home: Washington, D.C. Died Aug. 29, 1925.

FORD, Henry P., mayor, Pittsburgh; b. Hudson, N.Y., Oct. 15, 1837; parents moved to Pittsburgh, 1840; ed. in public and select school, and bus. coll.; m. Rebecca Gillespie, June 1870. Took position as clerk at 16; soon made reputation as accountant; bookkeeper for local ins. cos. until 1861; in charge accounting depts. Singer, Nimick & Co., 1861-71; partner Emerson, Ford & Co., saw mfrs., Beaver Falls, Pa., 1871-76; later became sec. and treas. Crescent Tube Co. and bookkeeper for successor, the Pa. Tube Co.; retired from business, 1881; mem. select council, 1881-96; mayor, 1896-99. Republican. Home: Pittsburgh, Pa. Died 1905.

FORD, H(oratio) Clark, lawyer, banker; b. Cleveland, O., Aug. 25, 1853; s. Horatio Cyrus and Martha C. (Cozad) F.; Oberlin Coll., 1870-72; B.S., U. of Mich., 1875; m. Ida M. Thorp, Oct. 17, 1877. In law practice, Cleveland, 1878—; sr. mem. Ford, Snyder & Tilden; also pres. Garfield Savings Bank, 1892—; pres. Williamson Co. Mem. City Council, 1879-85 (part of time v.-p.). Trustee Oberlin Coll.; v.-p. Congl. Bldg. Soc.; dir. Congl. Bd. Ministerial Relief. Home: Cleveland, Ohio. Died Aug. 25, 1915.

FORD, Isaac Nelson, newspaper corr.; b. Buffalo, N.Y., June 11, 1848; s. Hon. Elijah and Louisa Jane (Merrick) F.; A.B., Brown U., 1870 (L.H.D., 1903); m. Sevilla, d. James S. Hawley, M.D., of Brooklyn, Sept. 25, 1879. Entered journalism under Horace Greeley and Whitelaw Reid, Oct., 1870, as reporter on staff New York Tribune, and has since remained in service of that journal as news editor, editorial writer, book reviewer and corr.; made repeated journeys in Can., U.S., W.I., Mex., Central and S. America; became London corr. New York Tribune, 1895. Traveled extensively in France, Switzerland, Italy, Germany, Austria-Hungary, Russia, Sweden, Norway, Holland and Belgium. Republican. Author: Tropical America, 1893. Home: London, Eng. Died Aug. 7, 1912.

FORD, James Lauren, author; b. St. Louis, Mo., July 25, 1854; s. James K. and Louisa (Livermore) F. Author: The Brazen Calf; Waitful Watching, 1916; Forty Odd Years in the Literary Shops, 1921; Hot Corn Ike, 1923, etc. Editor The Porcupine, 1917-18. Home: Brookhaven, L.I., N.Y. Died Feb. 26, 1928.

FORD, John, judge; b. Knowlesville, N.Y., July 28, 1862; s. Michael and Sarah (O'Malley) F.; A.B., Cornell, 1890; m. Lulu Fairchild Van Aken, Sept. 16, 1891; children—Esther, Edith. Member New York Senate, 19th New York Dist., 1896-1901; framed, introduced and put through legislature the Franchise Tax Law, now in operation in N.Y.; candidate for comptroller, New York, 1905; justice Supreme Court of New York, 1st Dist., 1906-20; reëlected for 2d term, 1920; official referee Supreme Court since retirement, 1932. Author: Criminal Obscenity—A Plea for Its Suppression, 1926. Home: New York, N.Y. Died July 25, 1941.

FORD, John Donaldson, rear adm.; b. Baltimore, May 19, 1840; s. Thomas C. and Isabella (Logie) F.; grad. Md. Inst. Sch. of Design, 1861, receiving Peabody prize; grad. Potts Sch. of Mech. Engring., 1862; m. Laura Jane Darling, Apr. 30, 1866. Entered U.S.N. as 3d asst. engr., July 30, 1862; promoted 2d asst. engr., Feb. 13, 1864; 1st asst. engr., June 6, 1868; passed asst. engr., Feb. 24, 1874; chief engr., Dec. 27, 1890. During Civil War took part in recapture of Baton Rouge, La., Mar., 1863, battles of Mobile Bay, 1864; was on Arizona, destroyed by fire off Poverty Point, Mississippi River, Feb. 27, 1865, etc.; was wrecked, in the Sacramento, on Coramandel coast of India, June, 1867; served on many expdns. and stas.; detached and ordered to start Baltimore Manual Training Sch., Mar. 13, 1884; at Md. Agrl. and Mech. Coll., 1894-96; on U.S.S. Brooklyn, 1896-98 (relative rank of comdr., 1897); U.S.S. Baltimore (flagship), Jan. 25, 1898; and fleet engr., Pacific Sta.; joined Asiatic fleet; took part in the actions of May 1 and Aug. 13, 1898; the destruction of the Spanish fleet off Cavite; the destruction of the batteries at Cavite and at Sangley Point, and the capture of the forts at Corregidor and the capture of Manila; commd. comdr. Mar. 3, 1899, and later advanced in that grade for "eminent and conspicuous conduct in battle"; promoted capt., Mar. 5, 1902, rear adm. and retired, May 19, 1902, but continued on duty as insp. machinery and ordnance at Baltimore and Sparrow's Point, Md., until Dec. 25, 1908. Home: Baltimore, Md. Died Apr. 8, 1918.

FORD, Patrick, editor; b. Galway, Ireland, Apr. 12, 1835; s. Edward and Anne (Ford) F.; was brought to America, 1842; ed. Boston pub. schs. and Latin Sch.; m. Odele McDonald, Mar. 11, 1863. Served apprenticeship in printing office of William Lloyd Garrison, Boston; began writing for newspapers, 1855; editor and pub. Boston Sunday Times, 1859-60,

Charleston (S.C.) Gazette, 1864-66; founded The Irish World, Sept. 10, 1870. Raised $343,072 for Land League Fund (Ireland), 1880-81, and has sent to Ireland more than $600,000, 1880—; printed a spl. issue of 1,650,000 The Irish World, Jan. 11, 1879. Served in Civ. War with 9th Mass. Regt.; one of founders of Greenback-Labor Party, 1874; organized the Land League (Irish) in U.S., 1880-81. Catholic. Home: Brooklyn, N.Y. Died Sept. 23, 1913.

FORD, Paul Leicester, author, historian; b. Brooklyn, 1865; s. Gordon Lester and Emily Ellsworth (Fowler) F.; private edn.; edited Writings of Thomas Jefferson (10 vols.); Writings of John Dickinson (3 vols.); and numerous other works relating to American history and bibliography; m. Mary Grace Kidder, 1900. Author: The Honorable Peter Stirling; The Great K. & A. Train Robbery; The Story of an Untold Love; The True George Washington; The Many-Sided Franklin (serially in the Century, 1898-99); Tattle Tales of Cupid; A Collection of Short Stories; Janice Meredith (serially in The Bookman, 1899); etc. Died 1902.

FORD, Samuel Howard, Bapt. clergyman; b. 1819; grad. Mo. State Univ. (LL.D., William Jewell Coll., Liberty, Mo.). At one time editor and propr. Western Recorder, Louisville, and editor Mo. Baptist, St. Louis. Since 1853 editor of Christian Repository and Home Circle. Has been pastor in Louisville, Memphis and St. Louis; m. 1855, Sallie Rochester. Author: Baptist Waymarks. Home: St. Louis, Mo. Died 1905.

FORD, Simeon, hotel propr.; b. Lafayette, Ind., Aug. 31, 1855; ed. pub. schs. Propr. Grand Union Hotel; mem. firm Ford & Shaw; pres. Official Hotel Red Book & Directory Co., Zeeland Realty Co., and Apollinaris Agency Co.; dir. Rye Land & Improvement Co., Columbia Bank, Henry Morgenthau Co.; trustee Franklin Savings Bank. Home: New York, N.Y. Died Aug. 30, 1933.

FORD, Smith Thomas, clergyman; b. Camden, N.Y., Feb. 3, 1851; s. Rev. William and Susannah (Hedge) F.; A.B., Colgate U., Hamilton; N.Y., 1878, A.M., 1881, D.D., 1900; grad. Hamilton Theol. Sem., 1881; m. Mary H. Grant, Feb. 19, 1879 (died 1889); 1 son, Grant; m. 2d, Myra Louella Palmer, July 6, 1891; 1 son, Montague. Ordained Bapt. ministry, 1879; pastor Greene, N.Y., 1878-81, Waverly, N.Y., 1881-84, First Ch., Albany, N.Y., 1884-86, Central Ch., Syracuse, N.Y., 1886-96, First Ch., Lowell, Mass., 1896-1905, Englewood Ch., Chicago, 1905-19, First Ch., Wheaton, Ill., 1919-26; prof. pastoral theology, Northern Bapt. Theol. Sem., 1923-26, retired. Pres. Chicago Fedn. of Chs., 1908-10; v.p. Baptist Old People's Home; pres. Central Baptist Children's Home; v.p. Chicago Bapt. Theol. Union. Home: Newton Centre, Mass. Died May 27, 1929.

FORD, Tirey Lafayette, lawyer; b. Monroe Co., Mo., Dec. 29, 1857; s. Jacob Harrison and Mary Winn (Abernathy) F.; ed. pub. schs.; m. Emma Byington, Feb. 1, 1888 (dec.); children—Relda (Mrs. Samuel F. B. Morse), Byington, Tirey Lafayette. Removed to Calif., 1877; admitted to bar, 1882; dist. atty., Sierra Co., 1888-92; state senator, 1892-96; atty. State Harbor Commn., 1894-98; atty. gen., 1898-1902; mem. Calif. State Bd. of Prison Dirs., 1905-14. Author: Dawn and the Dons—the Romance of Monterey (a history). Home: San Francisco, Calif. Deceased.

FORD, William Ebenezer, mineralogist; b. Westville, Conn., Feb. 18, 1878; s. William Elbert and Caroline Aby (Bishop) F.; Ph.B., Yale, 1899, Ph.D., 1903; m. Mary Treat Jennings, 1920. Asst. in mineralogy, 1899-1903, instr., 1903-06, asst. prof., 1906-20, prof., 1920—, Sheffield Scientific Sch., Yale. Fellow Am. Acad. Arts and Sciences. Editor: Second and Third Appendices to Dana's System of Mineralogy, 1909 and 1915; New Edition of Dana's Manual of Mineralogy, 1912, 29; Dana's Text Book of Mineralogy (new edits.), 1921, 32. Home: New Haven, Conn. Died Mar. 23, 1939.

FORD, William Miller, surgeon; b. Brooklyn, N.Y., Nov. 30, 1878; s. A. William and Evelyn M. (Miller) F.; M.D., U. of Va., 1899; grad. St. Vincent's Hosp., 1901, Woman's Hosp., N.Y. City, 1902; m. Theresa E. Dunne, Aug. 30, 1910; children—William Miller, Anne Evelyn, Laurence Maunsell. Junior attending surgeon, Woman's Hosp., 1907-17; attending surgeon, St. Vincent's Hosp., 1905-26, dir. gynecology, 1927-31; attending surgeon, Manhattan Maternity Hosp., 1908—; cons. gynecologist, N.Y. Hosp. for Ruptured and Crippled, 1921—; chief surgeon and dir., Manhattan Maternity Hosp., 1928—; cons. gynecologist, St. Clare's Hosp., N.Y. City, 1935—; pres. med. board, St. Vincent's Hosp., N.Y. City, 1935—; clin. prof. obstetrics, New York U., 1920-33, Capt. N.Y.N.G., 1903-16, on Mexican border, 1916; maj. Medical Corps U.S.A., World War. Fellow Am. Coll. Surgeons. Democrat. Catholic. Home: New York, N.Y. Died Nov. 26, 1938.

FORD, William Webber, bacteriologist; b. Norwalk, Ohio, Dec. 15, 1871; s. James B. and Cornelia (Cook) F.; A.B., Western Reserve U., 1893; M.D., Johns Hopkins U., 1898; fellow, McGill U., 1899-1901, Rockefeller Inst., New York, 1901-02; D.P.H., McGill U., 1902. Instr. bacteriology, 1903-05, asso., 1905-06, asso. prof. hygiene and bacteriology and lecturer on legal medicine, 1906-16, Johns Hopkins Med. Sch.; prof. bacteriology, School of Hygiene and Pub. Health and lecturer on hygiene, Medical Sch. Johns Hopkins U., 1917-37. Home: Baltimore County, Md., and Boston, Mass. Died Feb. 10, 1941.

FORD, Worthington Chauncey, editor; b. Brooklyn, Feb. 16, 1858; s. Gordon Lester and Emily Ellsworth (Fowler) F.; ed. Brooklyn Poly. Inst. and Columbia U.; hon. A.M., Harvard, 1907; hon. Litt.D., Brown, 1919; LL.D., U. of Mich., 1920; m. Bettina Fillmore Quin, Oct. 1899; children—Crimora Chauncey, Emily Ellsworth. Chief of Bur. of Statistics, Dept. of State, 1885-89, of Bur. of Statistics, Treasury Dept., 1893-98; connected with Boston Pub. Library, 1897-1902; chief div. of manuscripts, Library of Congress, 1902-09; editor Mass. Hist. Soc., 1909-29; dir. European mission of Library of Congress, 1929-35. Lecturer on statistics, U. of Chicago, 1901, on hist. manuscripts, Harvard, 1901-29, on history, U. of Mich., 1921-26. Fellow Am. Acad. Arts and Sciences; mem. Am. Inst. Arts and Letters, Am. Philos. Soc. Author: American Citizen's Manual, 1883; The Standard Silver Dollar, 1884; George Washington, 1899; etc. Home: Cambridge, Mass. Died Mar. 7, 1941.

FORDNEY, Joseph Warren, congressman; b. Blackford Co., Ind., Nov. 5, 1853; common sch. edn., Ind.; m. Cathern Haren, 1873. Went to Saginaw, Mich., 1869, and engaged in lumber woods; since extensively engaged in lumber business. Alderman, Saginaw, 1895-99; mem. 56th to 67th Congresses (1899-1923), 8th Mich. Dist. Republican. Home: Saginaw West Side, Mich. Died Jan. 8, 1932.

FORDYCE, Charles, educator; b. Bloomington, Ill., Feb. 7, 1857; s. Lebbeus and Martha Ellen (Stephens) F.; diploma, Ill. State Normal U., 1882; A.M., Neb. Wesleyan U., 1893; B.Sc., U. of Neb., 1896, A.M., 1898, Ph.D., 1900; grad. student De Pauw U., 1892, U. of Chicago, 1904, Columbia, summers, 1910, 1912, 2r semester, 1913, Harvard, summer 1929; m. Marie Gray, June 8, 1882; children—Claude P., Glenn G., Mildred Marie (dec.). Supt. schs., McLean, Ill., 1882-84, Lena, 1884-85, Brownville, Neb., 1885-87, Auburn, 1887-93; prof. edn. and zoölogy, 1893-98, dean Coll. Liberal Arts, 1896-1908, Neb. Wesleyan U.; dean Coll. Edn., and prof. of education, U. of Neb., 1908-21; head of dept. of Ednl. Measurements and Research, U. of Neb., 1921—; dir. Neb. Bur. of Measurements and Research, 1916—. Mem. staff and specialist in Cladocera, Biol. Survey of Great Lakes, by U.S. Fish Commn., 1898. Lecturer under Fosdick com. among S.A.T.C. of Southern colls. and univs., 1918; mem. Nat. Assn. Dirs. of Ednl. Research; chmn. of research, personnel division of National Council of Y.M.C.A. Republican. Methodist. Rotarian. Home: Lincoln, Neb. Died Sept. 30, 1936.

FORDYCE, John Addison, physician; b. Guernsey Co., O., Feb. 16, 1858; s. John and Mary A. F.; bro. of Samuel Wesley F.; A.B., Adrian Coll., 1878, A.M., 1889 (hon. Ph.D., 1901); M.D., Chicago Med. Coll., 1881, U. of Berlin, 1888; m. Alice Dean Smith, June 29, 1886. Prof. dermatology and syphilology, Columbia U.; visiting dermatologist, City Hosp.; cons. dermatologist, Presbyn. and Women's hosps. and Neurol. Inst. Editor Jour. of Cutaneous and Genito-Urinary Diseases, 1888-96. Home: New York, N.Y. Died June 4, 1925.

FORDYCE, Samuel Wesley, capitalist; b. Guernsey Co., O., Feb. 7, 1840; s. John and Mary A. F.; bro. of John Addison F.; ed. Madison Coll., Pa., and North Ill. U., Ill.; m. Susan E. Chadwick, 1866. Enlisted in Co. B, 1st Ohio Cav., 1861, serving throughout Civil War; became capt. of cav. and insp. gen. of cav., Army of the Cumberland; at close of war located in Huntsville, Ala.; mem. Dem. State Central Com., Ala., 1874; removed to Arkansas, 1876; became v.p. and treas., 1881, of Tex. & St. Louis R.R., of which was apptd. receiver, 1885, and when road was reorganized as the St. Louis, Ark. & Tex. Ry. Co. was made its pres.; again apptd. receiver, 1889, and in 1891 road was reorganized as the St. Louis Southwestern Ry., of which was pres., 1891-99; pres. Houston Oil Co., of Tex.; v.p. Jefferson Hotel Co., St. Louis, Eastman and Arlington Hotel cos., Hot Springs, and other corps. Democrat; mem. Dem. Nat. Com. (Ark.), 1884-88. Home: St. Louis, Mo. Died Aug. 3, 1919.

FOREMAN, Henry Gerhard; b. Chicago, Aug. 22, 1857; s. Gerhard and Hannah (Greenebaum) F.; ed. pub. schs. and business coll.; m. Lottie, d. Charles H. Schwab, Apr. 28, 1885. Received commercial and financial training in First Nat. Bank, Chicago; has devoted attention chiefly to real estate and financial operations. One of organizers Chicago Stock Exchange, Chicago Title & Trust Co. and Chicago Real Estate Bd. Pres. Board Commrs. of Cook Co., 1902-04; mem. Bd. South Park Commrs., 1902-13 (pres. bd., 1903-05 and 1907-13); apptd. commr., 1904, to create outer belt of parks to circle Chicago (known as Forest Preserve of Cook County), and complete outdoor recreation system. Home: Chicago, Ill. Died July 25, 1932.

FOREMAN, Milton J., lawyer; b. Chicago, Ill., Jan. 26, 1863; s. Joseph and Mary (Hoffman) F.; ed. pub. schs. and Chicago Coll. of Law (night); LL.D., Knox Coll., Ill., 1930; unmarried. Began in employ of Keith Bros. & Co., wholesale hats, Chicago, at 12 and continued 23 yrs.; admitted to Ill. bar, 1899; now mem. Foreman, Bluford, Krinsley & Schultz. Mem. City Council, Chicago, 1899-1911; chmn. Street Ry. Commn., 1900-02; chmn. on Local Transportation, 1907-11, chmn. Chicago Charter Conv., 1905-06; mem. Ill. Liquor Control Commn., 1934—. Enlisted in Ill. N.G., 1895; capt. 1st Ill. Cav., Spanish-Am. War, 1898; col. 1st Cav., Ill. N.G., 1906-17; col. 122d F.A., A.E.F., 1917-19; brig. gen. 33d Div., 1920; apptd. maj. gen. comdg. 33d Div., 1921; retired with rank of lt. gen., 1931. Awarded D.S.C., D.S.M. and Silver Star Decoration with two clusters (U.S.); Comdr. Legion of Honor (French); Comdr. Order of Crown (Belgian); hon. citizen City of Tarbes, France, Village of Bourseche, France; hon. life mem. Nat. Guard Assn. of U.S.; past nat. comdr. Am. Legion; past comdr. in chief Mil. and Naval Order Spanish-Am. War. Republican. Home: Chicago, Ill. Died Oct. 16, 1935.

FOREMAN, Oscar G., banker; b. Chicago, Ill., Nov. 1, 1863; s. Gerhard and Hannah (Greenebaum) F.; ed. pub. schs.; m. Fannie Mandel, Sept. 28, 1893; children—Gerhard, Madeleine. Began, 1881, with the Nat. Bank of Ill., and in 1883 entered the banking house of his father, who retired in 1885, after transferring his banking business to his sons; business carried on as Foreman Bros. until incorporated, 1897, as Foreman Bros. Banking Co., of which was v.p. until 1915, pres., 1915-23; chmn. bd., 1923-29 Foreman Nat. Bank and Foreman Trust and Savings Bank, successors to Foreman Bros. Banking Co.; chmn. of exec. com., successor banks, Foreman State Nat. Bank and Foreman State Trust & Savings Bank, 1929-31. Home: Glencoe, Ill. Died Mar. 6, 1933.

FOREST, John Anthony, bishop; b. St. Martin's, St. Germain, France, Dec. 25, 1838; ed. for priesthood in France; advanced to diaconate. Emigrated to diocese of Galveston, Tex., 1863; stationed at St. Mary's Settlement, Lavaca Co., Tex., later pastor Sacred Heart, Hallettsville, Tex.; consecrated bishop of San Antonio, Oct. 28, 1895. Died 1911.

FORGAN, David Robertson, banker; b. St. Andrews, Scotland, Apr. 16, 1862; s. Robert and Elizabeth (Berwick) F.; bro. of James Berwick F.; common sch. edn.; (hon. M.A., Ill. Coll., 1903); m. Agnes Kerr, of Winnipeg, Manitoba, June 9, 1885. At 15 entered Clydesdale Bank as messenger; emigrated to Halifax, N.S., 1880, and secured position in Bank of N.S.; was mgr. of its branch at Fredericton, N.B., 1883-88; asst. cashier Am. Exchange Bank, Duluth, Minn., 1888-90; cashier Northwestern Nat. Bank, Minneapolis, 1890-95; v.p., 1896-98, pres. 1898-1900, Union Nat. Bank, which was merged into First Nat. Bank of Chicago, of which his brother was pres.; organized, 1907, and pres. Nat. City Bank of Chicago, until Nat. City Bank was merged, 1925, with Nat. Bank of the Republic, of which is v. chairman. Home: Evanston, Ill. Died Dec. 26, 1931.

FORGAN, James Berwick, banker; b. St. Andrews, Scotland, Apr. 11, 1852; s. Robert and Elizabeth (Berwick) F.; bro. of David Robertson F.; ed. Madras Coll., St. Andrews, Scotland, and Forres Acad., Forres, Scotland; m. Mary Ellen Murray, of Halifax, N.S., Oct. 19, 1875. First engagement was with the Royal Bank of Scotland, for about 3 yrs.; later with Bank of British N. America, with assignments to Montreal, New York and Halifax; later paying teller, afterward inspector of agencies, Bank of N.S.; established agency in Minneapolis, of which was mgr. for 3 yrs.; about 1888 became cashier and mgr. of the Northwestern Nat. Bank; v.p. First Nat. Bank, Chicago, 1892, and succeeded Lyman J. Gage as pres., 1900; chmn. bd. Jan. 1, 1916—. Decorated Order of St. Sava, Serbia, 1918, for work in raising funds for relief of destitute Serbians; Officer Legion of Honor, by Pres. of France, May 1921, for services to French cause during the war. Pres. Fed. Advisory Council, Fed. Reserve Bd., Washington, D.C., 6 yrs. Home: Chicago, Ill. Died Oct. 28, 1924.

FORMAN, Allan, editor; b. Mattituck, L.I., N.Y., Sept. 27, 1860; s. Alexander and Amelia (Cox) F.; ed. private school and tutors in Brooklyn, and spl. course in English lit. and economics at Williams Coll.; m. Xesia Carlstedt, June 2, 1900. Started Brooklyn Advance, 1881; wrote for 5 yrs. as dramatic critic on various papers; established The Journalist, 1884, and with exception of 3 yrs.' travel in the Old World, conducted it until 1908, when retired to a farm. Home: Mattituck, L.I., N.Y. Died Mar. 15, 1914.

FORMAN, Justus Miles, author; b. Le Roy, N.Y., Nov. 1, 1875; s. J. M. and Mary (Cole) F.; A.B., Yale, 1898; student of painting in Ateliers Julian under Bougureau, Bashchet, etc., 1898-1901. Author: The Garden of Lies, 1902; Journey's End, 1903; Monsigny, 1904; Tommy Carteret, 1905; Buchanan's Wife, 1906; The Stumbling Block, 1907; Jason, 1909; Bianca's Daughter, 1910; The Unknown Lady, 1911; The Opening Door, 1913; The Blind Spot, 1914. Also dramatization (with Sydney Grundy) of Garden of Lies, played by George Alexander, London, 1904-05. Fellow Royal Geog. Society. Died May 7, 1915.

FORMAN, William St. John, lawyer, congressman; b. Natchez, Miss., Jan. 20, 1847; ed. nr. Nashville, Ill., and, 1867-69, at Washington Sem., Richview, Ill.; admitted to bar; Ill. State senator, 1885-89; mem. Congress, 1889-95; Commr. of Internal Revenue, 1896-98. Democrat. Gold Dem. candidate for gov. Ill., 1896. Home: East St. Louis, Ill. Died 1908.

FORMENTO, Felix, surgeon; b. New Orleans, La., March 16, 1837; s. physician same name; ed. Jefferson College, La.; grad. Royal Univ. of Turin, Italy; grad. in sciences and letters in 1857, and in medicine in 1858; took post-grad. med. course in Paris; m. Celestine Voorhies, 1861 (died 1875); m. 2d, Louise Chiapella, 1878. Was surgeon in the Franco-Sardinian army, 1859; chief surgeon La. (Confederate) Hosp., Richmond, Va., during war. Mem. and pres. Am. Public Health Assn.; mem. many Am. and foreign socs.; pres. Conf. of State and Provincial Bds. of Health of N. Am.; mem. La. State bd. of health, 1880-04, and 1890-97; surgeon La. Soldiers' Home, Nov. 1898—. Officer of the Order SS. Mauritius and Lazarus. Home: New Orleans, La. Died 1907.

FORNES, Charles Vincent, congressman; b. Erie Co., N.Y., Jan. 22, 1846; s. John and Rosina (Krumholz) F.; grad. Lockport (N.Y.) State Normal Sch., 1864; prin. pub. sch., Buffalo, 3 yrs.; m. Eda Lyde, Nov. 16, 1898. Sr. mem. C. V. Fornes & Co., 1877-1914. Director Columbian Nat. Life Ins. Co.; trustee Emigrant Industrial Savings Bank. President Bd. of Aldermen, New York, 1902-07; mem. 60th, 61st, 62d Congresses (1907-13), 11th N.Y. Dist. Home: New York, N.Y. Died May 22, 1929.

FORNEY, James, brig. gen. U.S. Marine Corps; b. Lancaster, Pa., Jan. 17, 1844; s. John W. (journalist) and Matilda (Reitzel) F.; ed. Georgetown U., D.C.; m. Jane R. Richardson, Dec. 1, 1886. Entered U.S. Marine Corps at 2d lt., Mar. 1, 1861; promoted through grades to brig. gen., June 5, 1904; retired, July 1904. Began service on frigate Roanoke, Sept. 1, 1861; was on Brooklyn, Mex. Gulf Squadron, in battles of Ft. St. Philip, Fts. Jackson and Chalmette, and capture of New Orleans, in two attacks at Vicksburg, Baton Rouge, Galveston; landed brigade at Havre de Grace, Md., 1864; comd. marines, Formosa, 1867, and in labor riots, 1877; in Europe on spl. duty, 1873, afterward on various duties, fleet marine office, N. Pacific Squadron, 1876; grad. Torpedo Sch., Newport, R.I., 1879; comd. recruiting rendezvous, Phila., 1879-81; and comd. marines on various stas. and duties; during Spanish-American War commanded the Spanish Camp, consisting of 1,700 prisoners from Admiral Cervera's fleet; comd. 1st brigade, U.S. marines, P.I., 1901-02. Home: Philadelphia, Pa. Died Feb. 2, 1921.

FORNEY, John H., civil engr.; b. Lincoln Co., N.C., Aug. 12, 1829; s. Jacob and Sabina Swope (Hoke) F.; moved to Jacksonville, Ala., 1835; apptd. cadet, U.S. Mil. Acad., June 1848; bvt. 2d lt., 1852; 1st lt., 1855; staff officer to Col. Charles F. Smith on exploring expdn. to Pembina, 1855; comd. pioneer corps with Gen. A. S. Johnson in Utah Campaign, 1857; instr. West Point, 1860; 1st lt. 10th inf.; resigned to accept service as col. and aide to gov. Ala., Jan. 23, 1861; apptd. col. arty., Army of Ala., March 1861, comdg. at Pensacola, Fla.; resigned to accept capt. arty., C.S. army and insp. gen. with Gen. Bragg; apptd. col. 10th Ala. regt.; mustered for war June 4, 1861; brig. gen., C.S.A., March 10, 1862, comdg. Dept. Gulf, hdqrs. Mobile; maj. gen., Oct. 27, 1862, comdg. dist. of Vicksburg; comd. parole camp, Enterprise, Miss., July 1863; ordered July 1864 to Trans-Mississippi Dept. to bring East a div. of troops; 4 large brigades were concentrated at Hempstead, Tex., preparatory to running blockade from Galveston to St. Mark's, Fla., when Gen. Lee surrendered; paroled at Galveston, and returned to home in Ala.; m. Septima Sexta Middleton Rutledge, great g.d. Edward Rutledge, Feb. 5, 1863. Home: Jacksonville, Ala. Died 1902.

FORNIA, Rita, dramatic soprano; b. San Francisco, Calif., July 17, 1876; d. Joseph and Sophie Newman; in early girlhood heard Patti sing and decided on a musical career; studied in New York, later in Paris and Berlin; m. James P. Labey, of Jersey, England, May 21, 1910. Début as Eudoxia, in "La Juive," Hamburg, Germany; sang with Henry Savage English Opera Co., New York, 1906; appeared with Met. Opera Co., 1909, as Leonora, in "Il Trovatore," being suddenly called on account of illness of Emma Eames. Died Oct. 27, 1922.

FORREST, Jacob Dorsey, corp. mgr.; b. Baltimore, Md., July 21, 1866; s. Andrew Jackson and Emily Louise (Dorsey) F.; A.B., A.M., Hiram Coll., 1892; grad. student, Ohio State U., 1893-94; grad. student, 1894-95, fellow in sociology, 1895-97, univ. extension lecturer sociology, 1896-99, Ph.D., 1900, U. of Chicago; m. Albertina May Allen, Aug. 17, 1893 (died 1904); m. 2d, Cordelia Kautz, 1915. Prof. sociology and economics, Butler Coll., 1897-1909. One of promoters, 1907, of Citizens Gas Co. of Indianapolis, which he afterwards organized and has since managed; also pres. Milburn By-Products Coal Co. of W.Va.; operates a farm near Warrentown, Va. During World War converted Citizens Gas Co. into producer of high explosives, first for the Allies and later for the U.S. Mem. coke com. of Council Nat. Defense until that com. was superseded by the Fuel Administration. Author: The Development of Western Civilization, 1907. Home: Indianapolis, Ind. Died Nov. 7, 1930.

FORRESTER, James Joseph, statistical and research expert; b. near Wauseon, Fulton County, Ohio, Oct. 28, 1867; s. Patrick and Ann (McDaunald) F.; ed. Ohio pub. schs., Fayette (Ohio) Normal Sch., Northwestern Ohio Normal Univ. and Collegiate Inst., Wauseon, Ohio (now defunct); studied law in pvt. office, Wauseon; m. Rose A. Yates, Feb. 12, 1919. Clk. L.S.&M.S. R.R., 1881; letter carrier, Toledo, O., 1888-99; ry. and express clerical work, Toledo, Columbus and elsewhere, 1899-1904; asst. yardmaster, yardmaster and chief clk. in charge stas., also in operative dept. until 1908; v.p., 1908-09, dep. grand pres., 1909-15, grand pres., 1915-20, Brotherhood of Ry. Clerks; mem. pub. group, President Wilson's first Industrial Conf., 1919; mem. U.S.R.R. Labor Bd., Apr. 3, 1920-Apr. 16, 1921; nat. legislative rep. Brotherhood of Ry. and Steamship Clerks, Freight Handlers, etc., 1921-25; del. Am. Fed. Labor to British Trade Union Congress, 1921; envoy of Am. Labor to Ireland, 1921; organized labor representative, 1925-28; statis. expert Wilson-Vare senatorial contest, 1929; research expert Hoover Law Observance Enforcement Commn., 1930; spl. investigator Immigration Bur., U.S. Dept. Labor, Feb. 1931-May 1933; labor research and statistical expert various agencies. Fellow Am. Geog. Soc. Democrat. Catholic. K.P. Died May 1, 1939.

FORSANDER, Nils, theologian; b. Gladsax, Sweden, Sept. 11, 1846; grad. Augustana Coll. and Theol. Sem., Paxton, Ill., 1872, D.D., 1894; m. Johanna Charlotta Ahlgren, Jan. 6, 1875 (died 1909). Clergyman in Evang. Luth. Ch.; prof. theology Augustana Theol. Sem., 1899—. Editor Augustana Theol. Quarterly, 1900-12; contbr. to Korsbaneret and other Swedish Evang. Luth. periodicals. Decorated by King Oscar II of Sweden, Knight Royal Order of the North Star, 1907. Author: Augsburgiska Bekännelsen, 1899, 1902; Life Pictures from Swedish Church History, 1913; Olavus Petri, 1918; The Marburg Colloquy, 1919; Lifsbilder ur Augustana Synodens historia, Vol. I, 1915, Vol. II, 1925. Home: Rock Island, Ill. Died Aug. 21, 1926.

FORSE, Charles Thomas, rear adm.; b. Pittsburgh, Dec. 29, 1846; s. William and Mariamne (Boyer) F.; apptd. to U.S. Naval Acad. from Ky., Sept. 24, 1863; grad. June 2, 1868; unmarried. Promoted ensign, 1869, master, 1870, commd. lt., 1873, lt. comdr., June 1894, comdr., Mar. 3, 1899; light house insp., 4th dist., Mar. 13, 1900; comdg. Celtic, 1900; promoted capt., Oct. 11, 1903, rear adm., U.S.N., Dec. 26, 1903, and retired. Home: Pittsburgh, Pa. Died Apr. 14, 1925.

FORSYTH, David Dryden, clergyman; b. Dane Co., Wis., Mar. 5, 1864; s. James Riddell and Ann Elizabeth (Dryden) F.; A.B., U. of Neb., 1889; student Garrett Bibl. Inst., 1890-91; D.D., Denver U., 1905; m. Myra Elizabeth Clark, Sept. 20, 1892; children—Margaret, James C. Ordained M.E. ministry, 1894; pastor Calloway, Neb., 1889-90, Gothenburg, 1891-94, Cozad, 1894-97, Kearney, 1897-1901, 1st Ch., Cheyenne, Wyo., 1901-03, Delta, Colo., 1903-04, Grand Junction, 1904-09; dist. supt., Denver Dist., Colo., 1909-15; sec. Bd. of Edn. M.E. Ch., 1915-16; corr. sec. Bd. of Home Missions and Ch. Extension M.E. Ch., May 1916—. Trustee Denver U. Home: Philadelphia, Pa. Died Nov. 8, 1926.

FORSYTH, George Alexander, colonel; b. Muncy, Pa., Nov. 7, 1837; s. Orrin and Elizabeth (Frederick) F.; ed. Canandaigua, N.Y., Acad.; m. Natalie S., d. Col. E. B. Beaumont, U.S.A., 1885. Pvt. Chicago Dragoons, Apr. 19-Aug. 18, 1861; 1st lt. 8th Ill. Cav., Sept. 18, 1861; capt., Feb. 12, 1862; maj., Sept. 1, 1863; hon. mustered out of vol. service, Feb. 1, 1866; maj. 9th U.S. Cav., July 28, 1866; lt. col. 4th Cav., June 26, 1881; retired, Mar. 25, 1890; advanced to rank of col. retired, by act of Apr. 23, 1904. Bvtd.: col. vols., Oct. 19, 1864, for gallant and meritorious services at Opequan and Winchester; brig. gen. vols., Mar. 13, 1865, for distinguished services and conspicuous gallantry; lt. col. U.S.A., Mar. 2, 1867, for gallantry at Dinwiddie C.H.; col. U.S.A., for services at battle of Five Forks, Va.; brig. gen. U.S.A., Sept. 17, 1868, for gallant conduct in engagement with hostile Indians, in which he was 3 times wounded. Served through Civil War with Army of W.Va., Army of the Potomac, Army of the Shenandoah; took part in 16 pitched battles, 2 sieges and over 60 minor engagements; wounded 4 times in service in Civil War; mil. sec. to Lt. Gen. Sheridan, 1869-73; a.d.c. to same, 1878-81; mem. bd. of officers to inspect the armies of Europe and Asia, 1875-76; on staff and frontier service, 1866-90. Author: Thrilling Days in Army Life, 1900; The Story of the Soldier, 1900. Home: Rockport, Mass. Died Sept. 12, 1915.

FORSYTH, Henry Hazlett, clergyman; b. Sewickley, Pa., June 14, 1877; s. William Riddle and Jeannette Stirling (Black) F.; A.B., Western U. (now U. of Pittsburgh), 1898; grad. Princeton Theol. Sem., 1902; studied New Coll., Edinburgh, Scotland; D.D., Westminster Coll., Mo., 1920; LL.D., Mo. Valley Coll., 1923; m. Ethel Pierson, July 16, 1908 (died 1919); children—Jeannette Stirling, Anne Pierson, Margaret Black, Henry Hazlett. Ordained Presbyn. ministry, 1903; pastor Ben Avon, Pa., 1903-22, Kingshighway Ch., St. Louis, Mo., 1922-26, Sixth Ch., Pittsburgh, 1926—. Republican. Home: Pittsburgh, Pa. Died June 11, 1934.

FORSYTH, James McQueen, rear adm. U.S.N.; b. Long Island, Bahamas, British W.I., Jan. 1, 1842; s. James and Catherine Ann (Taylor) F.; came to U.S., Sept. 1853; grad. Central High Sch., Phila., Feb. 1858 (hon. M.A., 1886); m. Mary J. M. Perkins, Aug. 1, 1871 (dec.); m. 2d, Caroline A. Helfenstein, Oct. 7, 1903. Went to sea as sailor before mast, 1858-61, when he entered vol. navy; apptd., Sept. 25, 1861, acting master's mate, serving through Civil War; took part in capture Fts. Clarke and Hatteras, Aug. 27, 1861; engagements under Farragut on the Miss.; engagement with the rebal ram, Arkansas; engagement with Sumter, Moultrie and other fortifications in Charleston harbor. Promoted acting ensign, Sept. 5, 1862; acting master, Aug. 1, 1864; entered competitive exam. for regular navy; passed No. 23 of 65 admitted out of 900 competing; commd. master Mar. 12, 1868; promoted through grades to capt., Mar. 3, 1899; placed on retired list, Sept. 25, 1901, at his own request, on 40 yrs.' service, with rank of rear adm. Comd. at various times U. S.S. Tallapoosa, U.S. protected cruiser Baltimore, U.S. armored cruiser Brooklyn and U.S. battleship Indiana; comd. naval sta., Key West, Fla., during Spanish-Am. War; commended for efficient service; chief of staff to Rear Admiral J. C. Watson, comdg. Philippine fleet, 1899-1900. Mason. Home: Shanokin, Pa. Died Aug. 3, 1915.

FORSYTH, James W., maj. gen. U.S.A., retired; b. in Ohio, Aug. 26, 1836; grad. West Point, 1856; assigned to inf.; promoted to 1st lt., Mar. 15, 1861; capt., Oct. 24, 1861. On Gen. McClellan's staff during Peninsular and Md. campaigns; bvtd. maj., Sept. 30, 1863, for gallantry at Chickamauga; in 1864-65, asst. adj. gen. of vols. and chief of staff to Gen. Sheridan; reached rank of brig. gen. vols. and bvtd. brig. gen. regular army; asst. insp. gen. Dept. of the Gulf, 1866-67; aide to Gen. Sheridan, 1869-73; later on frontier and garrison service; became col. 7th cav., 1886; brig. gen., 1894, until retirement, 1897, with rank of maj. gen. Home: Columbus, O. Died 1906.

FORSYTH, Robert, cons. engr.; b. Troy, N.Y., Sept. 28, 1849; s. James and Sarah (Tibbits) F.; C.E., Rensselaer Poly. Inst., 1869; unmarried. Professional experience entirely in connection with design, constrn. and operation of iron and steel works; supt. Steel Works, North Chicago Rolling Mill Co., 1871-83; mgr. Union Steel Co., 1884-89; chief engr. and 2d v.p. Ill. Steel Co., 1889-96; cons. engr. in iron and steel matters, 1896—. Mem. bd. dirs. John Crerar Library. Republican. Home: Chicago, Ill. Died Sept. 11, 1927.

FORSYTH, William, artist; b. Hamilton Co., O.; s. Elijah J. and Mary M. (Hackett) F.; ed. pub. schs., Ohio and Ind.; Ind. Sch. of Art; Royal Acad. of Art, Munich, Bavaria, Germany; m. Alice Atkinson, Oct. 14, 1897; children—Dorothy Alice, Constance Elizabeth, Evelyn Mary. Instr. life classes, John Herron Art Inst., Indianapolis. Awarded medal, Royal Acad. of Art, Munich, 1885, silver and bronze medals, St. Louis Expn., 1904; Fine Arts Prize ($500) Soc. Western Artists, 1910; bronze medal, Universal Expn., Buenos Aires, Argentina, and Santiago, Chile, 1910; Foulke Prize, Richmond, Ind., 1906 and 1912; silver and bronze medals, Panama Expn., San Francisco, 1915; Halcomb prize, 1919 and 1924, Jessie Landon prize, 1925, Indianapolis Art Assn. Episcopalian. Home: Indianapolis, Ind. Died Mar. 29, 1935.

FORSYTHE, Robert Stanley, bibliographer; b. Lincoln, Ill., Oct. 6, 1886; s. Robert Nelson and Anna (Potter) F.; B.L., Lincoln (Ill.) Coll., 1908, Litt.D., 1929; A.M., Columbia, 1909, fellow, 1912-13, Ph.D., 1914; student U. of Ill., summer 1911, U. of Wis., summer 1912; m. Nelle R. Lucas, Aug. 24, 1915 (died 1937). Served as instr. in rhetoric, University of Kan., 1909-11; instr. in English, Western Res. U., 1914-17, asst. prof., 1917-18; same, Northwestern U., 1918-26; also lecturer in English, Sch. of Commerce, same U., 1920-23, 1924-26, and spl. bibliographer, Newberry Library, Chicago, 1926; prof. English, U. of N.D., 1926-33; head dept. of book selection, Newberry Library, Chicago, 1933—; exchange lecturer, U. of Manitoba, 1926-27; visiting instr. Harvard U. Summer Sch., 1931, 33. Asso. editor Quarterly Jour. of U. of N.D., 1929-32; mem. advisory bd. Am. Literature, 1932—, advisory board The Living Age, 1932—, advisory council, Scholars' Facsimiles Assn., 1937—. Mem. spl. rep. of War Dept. in France, 1918-19; civilian aide to Gen. Pershing in France, 1919: under sec. gen. of League of Nations, 1919-20.

Pres. and trustee of Rockefeller Foundation and General Edn. Board. Awarded D.S.M. (U.S.), Comdr. Legion of Honor (France). Author: European Police Systems, 1915; Keeping Our Fighters Fit (with E. F. Allen), 1918; American Police Systems, 1920; The Old Savage in the New Civilization, 1928; Toward Liquor Control (with Albert L. Scott), 1933. Home: New York, N.Y. Died June 5, 1941.

FORT, Franklin William, congressman; b. Newark, N.J., Mar. 30, 1880; s. John Franklin (gov. of N.J., 1908-10) and Charlotte Elizabeth (Stainsby) F.; grad. Lawrenceville Sch., 1897; A.B., Princeton, 1901; attended New York Law Sch., 1901-03; m. Emita H. Ryan, Jan. 25, 1904; children—Franklin Ryan, Barbara, Elizabeth Delano, William Stainsby. Admitted as atty., bar of N.J., 1903, counsellor, 1906; recorder East Orange, 1907-08; mem. MacLear & Fort, Newark, 1908-11, Fort & Fort, 1911-19; pres. Lincoln Nat. Bank (Newark), Sussex Fire Ins. Co.; organizer, v.p., mgr. and counsel, Eagle Fire Ins. Co. (the first Am. reinsurance co.); mgr. for U.S. of Baltica Ins. Co., Ltd., of Copenhagen; receiver and chmn. reorganization com., Botany Consol. Mills; dir. Central R.R. of N.J., Am. Hide & Leather Co., Savings Investment & Trust Co. (East Orange), The Freehold Trust Co.; mem. 69th to 71st Congresses (1925-31), 9th N.J. Dist.; organizer and chmn. N.J. Building & Loan Finance Com., 1932; chmn. of first Federal Home Loan Bank Board, 1932-33. Mem. U.S. Food Administration, 1917-19. Presbyn. Compiler: Labor Laws of New Jersey, 1903. Home: East Orange, N.J. Died June 20, 1937.

FORT, J(ohn) Franklin, governor; b. Pemberton, N.J., Mar. 20, 1852; s. Andrew H. and Hannah Ann (Brown) F.; prep. edn. Mt. Holly, N.J., Inst.; grad. Pennington Sem., N.J.; LL.B., Albany Law Sch., 1872; (LL.D., Dickinson, Union, and Seton Hall, 1908, Rutgers, New York U., and Middlebury, 1909, Lafayette, 1910); m. Charlotte E. Stainsby, Apr. 20, 1876. Admitted to bar, 1873; asst. journal clerk, N.J. Legislature, 1873-74; judge Dist. Ct. Newark, 1878-86; pres. judge Common Pleas, Essex Co., N.J., 1896-1900; justice Supreme Ct., N.J., 1900-07; gov. of N.J., 1908-11. Spl. envoy U.S. to Dominican Republic, Aug. 1914, and to Haiti, Mar. 1915. Mem. Federal Trade Commn., Mar. 20, 1917-Nov. 30, 1919. Home: South Orange, N.J. Died Nov. 17, 1920.

FORTIER, Alcée, univ. prof.; b. St. James Parish, La., June 5, 1856; s. Florent and Edwige (Aime) F.; acad. edn. U. of Va. and at New Orleans under pvt. tutors; studied phonetics under Prof. Passy, Paris; (Litt.D., Washington and Lee, 1894, Laval U., 1908); m. Marie Lanauze, 1881. Prof. of Romance langs., Tulane Univ. of La., 1880—. Mem. faculty summer sessions at univs. of Chicago, Tenn., Calif., Wis., Colo., Kan., Harvard; lecturer at many chautauquas, univs., etc. Mem. La. State Bd. Edn., 1888-96; v.p. bd. civ. service commrs., 1897-1901; pres. Catholic Winter Sch. of America, 1897-1902; mem. advisory council, Warner Library; chmn. history jury, St. Louis Expn., 1904. Officier d'Académie; officier d. l'Instruction Publique; chevalier de la Légion d'Honneur; pres. Fedn. Alliance Française aux Etats Unis et au Canada, 1906-07; pres. Athénée Louisianais, 1892—; mem. Académie de Macon. Author: Histoire de la Littérature Française, 1893; Louisiana Studies, 1894; Louisiana Folk Tales, 1894; Voyage en Europe en 1895, 1895; Précis de l'Histoire de France, 1899; History of Louisiana, 1904; History of Mexico, 1907; etc. Home: New Orleans, La. Died Feb. 14, 1914.

FORTIER, Samuel, engineer; b. Leeds, P.Q., Can., Apr. 24, 1855; s. Leandre and Ann (Reid) F.; grad. McGill Normal Sch., Montreal, Can., 1880; B.Sc., McGill U., 1885, M.E., 1896, D.Sc., 1907; m. S. B. Helena Macleay, of Danville, P.Q., Oct. 17, 1888; children—Roy Macleay, Winifred R., Ernest Cleveland. First asst. engr., Denver Water Co., 1886-90; chief engr. and supt. Ogden Water Works and Bear River Canal & Irrigation Co., 1890-93; prof. civ. and hydraulic engring., Agrl. Coll. of Utah, 1893-97, also acting as hydrographer U.S. Geol. Survey and cons. engr. for irrigation enterprises; dir. Montana Expt. Station, 1899-1903, also resident hydrographer of U.S. Geol. Survey in Mont., and irrigation engr. U.S. Dept. Agr.; in charge Pacific Coast Dist. of irrigation investigations of U.S. Office of Expt. Stas., 1903-07, and delivered lectures on irrigation, U. of Calif.; chief of irrigation investigations, 1907-15; adviser to govt. of B.C. on irrigation law and its administration, 1912; chief of division of irrigation investigations, U.S. Bureau Public Roads, 1915-22; asso. chief Div. Agrl. Engring., 1922-24, sr. irrigation engr., 1924-27, prin. irrigation engr., 1927-30; retired 1930. Awarded Gowski medal, 1896, by Canadian Soc. C.E., for paper on storage of water. Author: Use of Water in Irrigation. Home: Berkeley, Calif. Died Aug. 17, 1933.

FORTUNE, William; b. Boonville, Ind., May 27, 1863; s. William H. and Mary (St. Clair) F.; honorary LL.D., Indiana Univ., 1938; m. May Knubbe, Nov. 25, 1884 (died 1898); children—Russell, Evelyn (Mrs. Frederic Clay Bartlett), Madeline (Mrs. Bowman Elder). City editor Indianapolis Journal, 1886-1888; editorial writer Indianapolis News, 1888-90; founder Municipal Engineering Magazine, 1890; pres. Indianapolis Telephone Co., 1908-23; served as chmn. finance com. and dir. Eli Lilly & Co., 1913-27; pres. New Long Distance Tel. Co., also several other phone cos.; pres. Interstate Life Assurance Co., 1908-09. Originator of Commercial Club, 1890, which marked a new era in development of Indianapolis (sec. 1890-95, v.p. 1895-97, pres. 1897-98); exec. dir. G.A.R. Nat. Encampment, Indianapolis, 1893; originator, 1892, Indiana Good Roads Movement; mem. com. of 3 that had charge of relief of over 5,000 unemployed in Indianapolis, winter of 1894; originator Ind. State Board of Commerce, 1894 (pres., 1897, 1898, 1899); chmn. Chamber of Commerce Elevated R.R. Commn., 1898-1916, which secured abolition of grade crossings in Indianapolis, etc. Chmn. exec. com. for reorganization of county and twp. governments in Ind. in 1899, reducing expenses $3,000,000 first yr.; presented with loving cup, 1898, by 100 citizens of Indianapolis, headed by Benjamin Harrison, "in recognition of services in promoting the general welfare of the city." Chairman com. in charge of dinner given by friends throughout the country in honor of James Whitcomb Riley in last year of poet's life; purchased James Whitcomb Riley's old home, on Lockerbie Street, Indianapolis, Apr. 1920, as a memorial to the poet until the property could be taken over by the James Whitcomb Riley Memorial Association. Decorated Order of the Double Dragon, by Emperor of China, also mandarin rank, 1904; awarded medal of merit, Nat. Council of Am. Red Cross, 1916. First pres. Indianapolis Chapter Am. Red Cross, and since continuously reëlected; chmn. exec. com. which raised half million dollars for Red Cross war fund, 1917. First pres. Indianapolis Chamber of Commerce under reorganization, 1917-18; at head of orgns. which raised over $4,000,000 in Indianapolis for war relief and charities, 1916-19; originator and pres. Indianapolis War Chest, 1918-19; chmn. com. on state and local taxation, U.S. Chamber Commerce, 1926-28, 1939-40, and continuously mem; pres. George Rogers Clark Memorial Commn., 1927-28. Commended for outstanding public service as citizen, in letters from President Coolidge and Pres. O'Leary of U.S. Chamber Commerce, read at dinner given in his honor by 200 fellow citizens, July 1926, also presented with medal "in recognition of notable service to humanity in time of war and peace"; honored by pub. homecoming, Boonville, Oct. 23, 1929. Commd. hon. col. on staff of gov. of Tenn., 1930. Mem. Am. Red Cross Tornado Relief Com. for Ind., Ill., and Mo., for administration of relief fund of $3,000,000, 1925; hon. nat. rep. of Am. Red Cross accompanying Am. Legion to France, 1927; elected, 1927, life mem. Gen. Bd. of Incorporators of Am. Nat. Red Cross; mem. of Nat. Central Com., Am. Red. Cross, 1932—, and mem. exec. com. and nat. chairman's advisory com.; chmn. Indianapolis Community Welfare Bd. (created by legislature as exec. dep. of municipal govt.), 1919—; life dir. Indianapolis Chamber of Commerce; dir. U.S. Chamber of Commerce; hon. dir. Boys' Club (Indianapolis). Fellow Royal Society of Arts (London, England), Am. Geog. Society. Elected Nov. 1928, successor to Senator Theodore E. Burton as 16th nat. pres. Am. Peace Soc., founded in 1828. Donor of 30-acre site in Riverside Park for U.S. Vets. Hosp., Indianapolis, 1930. First to receive annual citation by Indianapolis Kiwanis Club "for distinguished services as a citizen," 1931; one of ten elected to charter membership of Staff of Honor of Indianapolis by Chamber of Commerce and other civic organizations, with citations and medal for public service at banquet, Feb. 1939. Home: Indianapolis, Ind. Died Jan. 28, 1942.

FORWOOD, William Henry, brig. gen. U.S.A.; b. Brandywine Hundred, Del., Sept. 7, 1838; s. Robert and Rachel Way (Larkin) F.; grad. Crozier Acad., Chester, Pa., 1856; M.D., U. of Pa., 1861; (LL.D., Georgetown U., 1897); m. Mary A. Y. Osborne, Sept. 28, 1870. Apptd. from Pa., asst. surgeon U.S.A., Aug. 5, 1861; capt. asst. surgeon, July 28, 1866; maj. surgeon, June 26, 1876; lt. col. dep. surgeon gen., June 15, 1891; col. asst. surgeon gen., May 3, 1897; brig. gen. surgeon gen., June 8, 1902. Bvtd. capt. and maj., Mar. 13, 1865, for faithful and meritorious services during the war. Severely wounded in battle, Oct. 1863; in comd. Whitehall Gen. Hosp.; 2,000 beds, 1864-65; served in Indian campaigns; surgeon and naturalist Sheridan's exploring expdns., 1880-82; pres. army exam. bds.; pres. Army Med. Sch.; built Montauk hosp., 1898; retired, Sept. 7, 1902. Prof. surg. pathology, Georgetown Med. Coll.; prof. mil. surgery, Army Med. Sch., etc. Died May 11, 1915.

FOSDICK, Charles Austin ("Harry Castlemon"), author; b. Randolph, N.Y., Sept. 6, 1842; ed. Central High Sch., Buffalo; when war broke out shipped as landsman in Mississippi Squadron; passed through all intermediate grades and came out receiver and supt. coal for the squadron. Author: Frank, the Young Naturalist; Frank on a Gunboat; Frank in the Woods; Frank Before Vicksburg; Frank on the Lower Mississippi; Frank on the Prairie; Frank Among the Rancheros; Frank in the Mountains; Frank in the Forecastle; The Buried Treasure; The Boy Trapper; The Mail Carrier; George in Camp; George at the Wheel; George at the Fort; Don Gordon's Shooting Box; The Young Wild Fowlers; Go-Ahead; No Moss; True to His Colors; Marcy the Blockade Runner; Marcy the Refugee; Sailor Jack the Trader; Rebellion in Dixie; A Sailor in Spite of Himself; The Ten-Ton Cutter; The Pony Express Rider; The White Beaver; Carl the Trailer. Home: Westfield, N.Y. Died Aug. 22, 1915.

FOSDICK, James William, artist; b. Charlestown, Mass., Feb. 13, 1858; s. William and Elizabeth T. (Peirce) F.; ed. Boston pub. schs.; studied sch. of Boston Mus. Fine Arts; studied drawing and painting, Paris, 1881-88, under Boulanger, Lefebvre, Colin and others; m. Gertrude, d. Judge Joseph Christian, of Richmond, Va., Oct. 22, 1890. Mural painter; founder of art of fire etching in America; decorations in homes of the Goulds, Havemeyers, Lewisohns, etc.; also in Pa. Acad. Fine Arts, St. Louis Mus., etc. His principal works are The Veneration of St. Jeanne d'Arc, Nat. Gallery of Fine Arts, Washington, Evans Collection; The 14 Stations of the Cross, Ch. Immaculate Conception, Waterbury, Conn.; reredos, Ch. of St. Joan of Arc, Jackson Heights, L.I. Grand gold medal for mural decoration, "The Field of the Cloth of Gold," Atlanta Expdn. Secretary Nat. Soc. Mural Painters; pres. Am. Alumni of Julian Academy (Paris); v.p. Nat. Society of Craftsmen. Author: The Honor of the Braxtons, 1902. Died Sept. 14, 1937.

FOSHAY, James A., educator; b. Cold Spring, N.Y., Nov. 25, 1856; s. Andrew J. and Emeline (Griffin) F.; grad. State Normal Sch., Albany, N.Y., 1879; Pd.D., State Normal Coll., Albany, N.Y., 1898; (hon. A.M., U. of Southern Calif., 1898); m. Phebe Powell Miller, Mar. 18, 1885. Taught pub. schs., Putnam Co., N.Y., 1879-82; sch. commr., 1881-87; sec. N.Y. Assn. School Commrs. and Supts., 1884-86; removed to Calif., 1887; mem. Sch. Examining Bd., Los Angeles Co., 1889-95; deputy supt. schs., 1893-95, supt. schs., Los Angeles, 1895-1906. Mem. Nat. Council of Edn., Calif. Council of Edn.; chmn. exec. com. Southwest Soc. of Archæol. Inst. America. Republican. Home: Los Angeles, Calif. Died Jan. 14, 1914.

FOSS, Claude William, college prof.; b. Geneva, Ill., Aug. 28, 1855; s. Charles John and Charlotte Christine (Erickson) F.; A.B., Augustana Coll., Ill., 1883, A.M., 1889, Ph.D., 1900; m. S. Margaret Shuey, Aug. 2, 1887. Prof. history, Augustana College, 1884-1932, now prof. emeritus; v.p. 1888-99, acting pres., 1899-1901, Augustana Coll. and Theol. Seminary. Mem. various historical associations. Republican. Lutheran. Sent as commr. to inspect mission field of Gen. Council of Evang. Luth. Ch. of N. America, and traveled extensively in South India, 1908-09; also as commr. of Augustana Synod, traveled in southern Russia, Asia Minor and southern and central Europe, 1909. Author: Glimpses of Three Continents; also juvenile lit. Home: Rock Island, Ill. Died Feb. 8, 1935.

FOSS, Cyrus David, M.E. bishop, May 1880—; b. Kingston, N.Y., Jan. 17, 1834; s. itinerant Methodist minister; grad. Wesleyan Univ., 1854 (D.D., Wesleyan Univ., 1870; LL.D., Cornell Coll., Ia., 1879; Univ. of Pa., 1889), instr. and later prin. Amenia Seminary, N.Y., 1854-57; entered itinerant ministry in N.Y. conf., 1857; stationed at Chester, N.Y., 1857-59; transferred to N.Y. East conf.; pastor in Brooklyn, 1859-65; in New York chs., 1865-75; pres. Wesleyan U., 1875-80. Fraternal del. to the Gen. Conf. M.E. Ch. South, 1878, and to the British Wesleyan Conf. in 1886; officially visited the M.E. Missions in Europe, 1886; in Mexico, 1893; in India and Malaysia, 1897-98; tour of missionary observation around the world, 1906-07. Home: Philadelphia, Pa. Died 1910.

FOSS, Eugene Noble, governor; b. West Berkshire, Vt., Sept. 24, 1858; s. George Edmund and Marcia Cordelia (Noble) F.; brother of George Edmund F.; U. of Vt., 1877-79 (A.B., 1901, LL.D., 1912); m. Lilla Sturtevant, June 12, 1884. Entered mfg. at Boston, 1882; became pres. B. F. Sturtevant Co.; officer in other corps. Prominent from 1902 in advocacy of tariff revisions and reciprocity. Elected to 61st Congress, Mar. 22, 1910, for unexpired term (1910-11) of William C. Lovering, deceased; gov. of Mass. terms 1910-11, 1911-12, 1912-13; defeated for reëlection, 1913. Democrat. Baptist. Home: Jamaica Plain, Mass. Died Sept. 13, 1939.

FOSS, George Edmund, congressman; b. Berkshire, Vt., July 2, 1863; s. George Edmund and Marcia Cordelia (Noble) F.; A.B., Harvard, 1885; Columbia Law School, N.Y., 1888; LL.B., Union Coll. of Law, Chicago, 1899; m. Georgia L. Fritze (died 1929); children—Katherine, Marcia Noble, Constance. Was admitted to bar, 1889, and began practice at Chicago. Mem. 54th to 57th Congresses (1895-1903), 7th Ill. Dist., 58th to 62d Congresses (1903-13), and 64th and 65th Congresses (1915-19), 10th Dist.; candidate for nomination U.S. Senate, 1918. Republican. Chmn. Com. Naval Affairs, 56th to 61st Congresses; mem. Com. on Foreign Affairs, 64th and 65th Congresses. Home: Chicago, Ill. Died Mar. 15, 1936.

FOSS, Sam Walter, librarian; b. Candia, N.H., June 19, 1858; s. Dyer and Polly (Hardy) F.; A.B., Brown, 1882 (hon. A.M., 1907); m. Carrie M., d. Rev. Henry W. Conant, of Providence, R.I., July 13, 1887. Editor Saturday Union, 1883-87, Yankee Blade, 1887-94, Lynn, Mass.; gen. writer, 1894-98; editorial writer Boston Globe, 1888-95; librarian Somerville Pub. Library, 1898—. Author: Back Country Poems,

1894; Whiffs from Wild Meadows, 1895; Dreams in Homespun, 1897; Songs of War and Peace, 1898; Songs of the Average Man, 1907. Home: Somerville, Mass. Died 1911.

FOSSLER, Laurence, univ. prof.; b. Würtemberg, Germany, Mar. 12, 1857; s. J. J. and Maria (Erchinger) F.; came to U.S., 1872; A.B., U. of Neb., 1881, A.M., 1890; student at Paris and Leipzig; m. Ida E. Sundean, 1885; children—Lynn S., Lois B., Shirley A. (dec.). Teacher, asst. prin. and prin., Lincoln High Sch., 1883-89; adj. prof. modern langs., 1889-94, prof. Germanic langs. and lit., 1894—, U. of Neb. Author: A Brief German Grammar (with A. H. Edgren), 1896; Practical German Conversation, 1905. Home: Lincoln, Neb. Died Jan. 7, 1933.

FOSTER, Addison Gardner, senator; b. Belchertown, Mass., Jan. 28, 1837; s. Samuel and Mary (Walker) F.; ed. common schs., Oswego, Ill.; m. Martha Wetherbee, Mar. 19, 1863. Taught sch.; removed to Wabasha, Minn.; in grain and real estate business, 1859-75; 1 term co. auditor and 1 term surveyor, Minn.; removed to St. Paul; 12 yrs. later to Tacoma; v.p. St. Paul & Tacoma Lumber Co.; active in development of coal mines and in ry. bldg.; pres. Consolidated Lumber Co. U.S. senator from Wash., 1899-1905. Republican. Retired 1914. Home: Tacoma, Wash. Died Jan. 16, 1917.

FOSTER, Agnes Greene, author, lecturer; b. Athens, Ala.; d. of John and Mary Greene, and g.d. of Lady Agness Stuart; ed. in high school and the college of oratory and in Woman's Dept. of Belles Lettres, Trinity Coll., Dublin, and Mlle. Piquot's finishing school, Blois, France; m. William Clarence Foster. Author: Your Happy Way, 1923; Vision, 1926. Home: Washington, D.C. Died Sept. 12, 1933.

FOSTER, Alfred Dwight, insurance pres.; b. Worcester, Mass., Apr. 27, 1852; s. Dwight and Henrietta Perkins (Baldwin) F.; A.B., Harvard, 1873; LL.B., Boston U. Law Sch., 1875; m. Evelyn M. Samborne, of Bath, Eng., Nov. 17, 1892; children—Margaret, Dwight, Francis Baring, Hilda Samborne, Evelyn Lucy. Practiced law, Boston, 1875-93; v.p. N.E. Mut. Life Ins. Co., 1893-1908, pres., 1908-24, chmn. bd., 1924—. Episcopalian. Home: Milton, Mass. Died Oct. 29, 1932.

FOSTER, Allyn King, clergyman; b. Baltimore, Md., Apr. 14, 1868; s. Robert Edward and Josephine (Wilkinson) F.; grad. Baltimore City Coll., 1886; spl. course, Johns Hopkins, 1886-89; Th.M., Southern Bapt. Theol. Sem., 1894; M.A., Yale, 1901; D.D., Brown, 1916; m. Emily Howard Foley, Oct. 28, 1902; children—Allyn King, Cicely. Ordained Bapt. ministry, 1894; pastor Olivet Ch., New Haven, Conn., 1895-1901; founder, 1901, headmaster Foster Sch., 1901-07; acting pastor Lafayette Av. Presbyn. Ch., Brooklyn, N.Y., 1908-09; pastor First Ch., Worcester, Mass., 1909-16, Washington Av. Ch., Brooklyn, 1916-17; Y.M.C.A. sec. in U.S., France and Germany, World War; sec. dept. student work, Bapt. Bd. of Edn., 1920—. Author: The Coming Revival of Religion, 1929; New Dimensions of Religion, 1931. Home: Chicago, Ill. Died Nov. 10, 1934.

FOSTER, Ben, painter; b. N. Anson, Me.; s. Paulinus Mayhew and Lydia (Hutchins) F.; pupil of Abbott Thayer, New York, and Luc Oliver Merson and Aimé Morot, Paris. Awarded medal, Chicago Expn., 1893; 2d prize for water colors, Cleveland, 1895; bronze medal, Paris Expn., 1900; silver medal, Internat. Exhbn., Carnegie Inst., Pittsburgh, 1900; Webb prize, Soc. Am. Artists, New York, 1901; silver medal, Buffalo Expn., 1901, St. Louis Expn., 1904; Carnegie prize, N.A.D., 1906; Inness gold medal, same, 1908; gold medal, Nat. Arts Club, 1917; Altman prize, N.A.D., 1917. Exhibited at Paris Expn., 1900. N.A., 1904; mem. Nat. Inst. Arts and Letters. Home: New York, N.Y. Died Jan. 28, 1926.

FOSTER, Cassius G., U.S. judge, dist. of Kan., March 10, 1874—; b. Monroe Co., N.Y., Jan. 22, 1837; academic edn. at Adrian, Mich.; studied law at Rochester, N.Y.; admitted to N.Y. bar, March 1859; removed to Kan., June 1859, and established practice at Atchison. State senator, 1863-64; mayor of Atchison, 1867. Founder and pres. Foster Humane Society. Home: Topeka, Kan. Died 1899.

FOSTER, Charles, sec. treasury; b. nr. Tiffin, O., Apr. 12, 1828; ed. pub. schs., Norwalk (O.) Acad. and pvt. studies. Partner in father's gen. store at 18; entire charge at 19. Mem. Congress 9th Ohio dist., 1871-73, 10th dist., 1873-79; on com. to make examination of La. affairs, 1874, visiting New Orleans as chmn. sub.-com.; gov. Ohio, 1880-84; apptd. by President Harrison chmn. commn. to negotiate treaty with Sioux Indians; Rep. nominee for U.S. senator, 1890; candidate for Congress, 1890; sec. of the Treasury, U.S., 1891-93. Long identified with business interests of town of Fostoria, founded by his father. Pres. bd. trustees State Hosp., Toledo, 1887—; pres. Assn. Trustees and Officers of Hosps. for the Insane, 1895—. Home: Fostoria, O. Died 1904.

FOSTER, Charles Elwood, lawyer; b. Phila., Sept. 9, 1841; s. Charles B. and Anna Maria (Worrall) F.; common sch. edn.; m. Rose Adelaide Rehn, June 4, 1872. Began as patent atty. and mech. expert, 1876; admitted to bar, 1905; sr. mem. Foster, Freeman, Watson & Coit. An organizer of Asso. Charities of D.C.; pres. Y.M.C.A. of D.C.; pres. Industrial Home; dir. Sanitary Improvement Assn. Independent Republican. Presbyn. Mason. Home: Gloucester, Mass. Deceased.

FOSTER, Charles Richard, asso. supt.; b. Oil City, Pa., Feb. 3, 1879; s. William James and Ellen Karnes (Cherry) F.; grad. Clarion (Pa.) State Normal Sch., 1896; A.B., U. of Pittsburgh, 1911, A.M., 1914, LL.D., 1925; m. Ella May Weible, Feb. 9, 1900; 1 son, Charles Richard. Rural teacher, elementary sch. prin. and high sch. prin., 1896-1923; asso. supt. schs., Pittsburgh, Pa., 1923-25, first asso. supt., 1925-27, asso. supt. in charge secondary edn., 1936—; pres. State Teachers Coll., Indiana, Pa., 1927-36. Republican. Presbyn. Mason. Author: Extra-Curricular Activities in the High School, 1925. Home: Pittsburgh, Pa. Died Dec. 14, 1937.

FOSTER, David Johnson, congressman; b. Barnet, Vt., June 27, 1857; s. Jacob Prentiss and Matilda (Cahoon) F.; A.B., Dartmouth, 1880; m. Mabel M. Allen, Oct. 4, 1883. Admitted to bar, 1883, and began practice at Burlington, Vt. State's atty., Chittenden Co., Vt., 1886-90; mem. Vt. Senate, 1892-94; commr. state taxes, 1894-98; chmn. Bd. R.R. Commrs., 1898-1900; mem. 57th to 62d Congresses (1901-13), 1st Vt. Dist. Republican. Chmn. delegation representing U.S. at Centennial Celebration of Republic of Mexico, City of Mexico, Sept. 1910; chmn. delegation from U.S. to Gen. Assembly of Internat. Inst. of Agr., Rome, May 1911. Home: Burlington, Vt. Died Mar. 21, 1912.

FOSTER, David Nathaniel, merchant; b. Coldenham, N.Y., Apr. 24, 1841; s. Dr. John Lyman and Harriet (Scott) F.; ed. pub. schs. and academy, Montgomery, N.Y.; m. Garetta Lambert Reger, Feb. 20, 1865 (died 1867); 1 son, Frederick Reger (dec.); m. 2d, Arrietta Smedes Blauvelt, June 1869 (died 1875); 1 son, Albert Zabriskie (dec.); m. 3d, Sara J. Pyne, Jan. 10, 1878 (died 1912); children—Pearl (Mrs. Frank J. Rahe), Florence (Mrs. Harvey Hall). Began as "bundle boy," later clk., in dry goods store of Wm. E. Lawrence, N.Y. City; organizer with brother Scott, 1859, Foster Bros., dry goods, N.Y. City; established stores at 8th Av., N.Y. City, 1865, Fort Wayne, Ind., 1868, Terre Haute, 1870, Evansville, 1871, Grand Rapids, Mich., 1872; sold interest in firm, 1873, and established Grand Rapids Saturday Evening Post, sold, 1877; mem. Foster Brothers, 1877—. One of organizers Tri-State Loan & Trust Co. (dir.), Wayne Knitting Mills, Fort Wayne Hotel Co. and many others; pres. Foster-Rahe Furniture Co., Fort Wayne Land & Improvement Co., Fort Wayne & Lake Erie Ry. Served as pvt., later capt., U.S.A., Civil War. Pres. Fort Wayne Bd. Park Commrs., 1905—. Donor, with brother, Samuel M. Foster, of Foster Park to Fort Wayne. Dir. Pixley Relief Home, Allen County-Fort Wayne Hist. Soc. Home: Fort Wayne, Ind. Died Sept. 13, 1934.

FOSTER, David Skaats, author, mcht.; b. Utica, N.Y., Jan. 23, 1862; s. Thomas and Eliza Pearson (Skaats) F.; pub. sch. edn., Utica; widower. Head of David S. Foster, Sons & Co., iron and coal mchts., Utica. Master of half a dozen langs. Author: The Romance of the Unexpected (poems); Rebecca the Witch (poems); Elinor Fenton (novel); Spanish Castles by the Rhine; The Road to London; The Divided Medal; Our Uncle William; Nate Sawyer; The Lady of Castle Queer; Mademoiselle of Cambria. Home: Syracuse, N.Y. Died June 23, 1920.

FOSTER, Ellsworth D(ecatur), ency. editor; b. Clayton, Mich., Oct. 2, 1869; s. Spencer Herbert and Louisa (Benedict) F.; 3½ years coll. work; m. Martha E. Clodfelter, Jan. 2, 1893 (died 1932); m. 2d, Mabel E. Cumley, Instructor in history and economics, Benton Harbor Coll., 1891-94; supt. schs., Coloma, Mich., 1894-98; in introductory dept., Ginn & Co., sch. textbook pubs., 1898-1901; sec. Interstate Sch. of Corr., 1901-06; in editorial work, 1906—; asso. editor New Practical Reference Library, 1907-14; editor The World Book (ency.), 1914-18 and 1920-31; chief editor Volume Library (ency.), 1931-34; editor in chief The Am. Educator (ency.), 1935—; contbg. editor Book of Rural Life (ency.), 1924-25. Republican. Methodist. Mason. Author: Cyclopedia of Civil Government, 1908. Home: Chicago, Ill. Died Nov. 7, 1936.

FOSTER, Enoch, judge; b. Newry, Me., May 10, 1839; s. Enoch and Persis (Swan) F.; 2d and 1st lt., Co. H, 13th Me. Vols., 1861-64; was in Dept. of the Gulf and in Butler's expdn. in the capture of New Orleans, and in Banks' expdn. to Texas and Red River; A.M., Bowdoin, 1864; LL.B., Albany Law Sch., 1865; m. Adeline O. Lowe, June 3, 1864 (died 1872); m. 2d, Sarah W. Chapman, June 6, 1873. Admitted to bar, 1865; practiced at Bethel, Me., 1865-84; justice Supreme Jud. Ct. of Me., 1884-98; in practice at Portland, 1898—; now sr. mem. Foster & Foster. Co. atty., 1868-74; mem. Me. Senate, 1874-75. Republican. Overseer Bowdoin Coll. Home: Portland, Me. Died Nov. 15, 1913.

FOSTER, Eugene Clifford, Y.M.C.A. official; b. Phila., Pa., Sept. 8, 1867; s. Whilldin and Jennie (Baker) F.; B.S., in chemistry, Lafayette Coll., Pa., 1893, M.S., 1896; m. Rosa Lee Doby, June 21, 1900; children—Eugene W., Gordon L., Dorothy M. Prof. physics and chemistry, Temple Coll., Phila., 1894-1900; scientific lab. work and pub. lectures, 1900-02; mgr. book dept. S.S. Times Co., 1902-09; city sec. for boys, Detroit Y.M.C.A., 1909-16; boys' work sec., in charge editorial work and research, Internat. Com. Y.M.C. Assns., 1916-19; city sec. for boys, Y.M.C.A. of New York City, 1919-24; dir. of boys' work course Internat. Y.M.C.A. Coll., Springfield, Mass., 1924—; editor The Intermediate Quarterly, Am. S.S. Union. Conglist. Author: The Boy and the Church, 1906; Starting to Teach, 1910; The Intermediate Department (Sunday School), 1917; Problems of the Intermediate and Senior Teacher, 1917; Making Life Count, 1918. Home: Springfield, Mass. Died Nov. 4, 1927.

FOSTER, Frank Hugh, clergyman; b. Springfield, Mass., June 18, 1851; s. William and Mary Flagg (Miller) F.; A.B., Harvard, 1873; grad. Andover Theol. Sem., 1877; Parker fellow of Harvard, 1881-82; Ph.D., U. of Leipzig, 1882; D.D., Chicago Theol. Sem., 1894, Olivet Coll., 1909; S.T.D., Harvard, 1932; m. Eliza C. Grout, Aug. 20, 1877 (died 1912); children—Frederick Montague, Harold Park, Katharine Rose; m. 2d, Margaret Tracy Algoe, Nov. 26, 1913 (died 1920). Ordained Congl. ministry, 1877; prof. philosophy, Middlebury, 1882-84; prof. ch. history, Oberlin Theol. Sem., 1884-92; prof. systematic theology, Pacific Sem. (Calif.), 1892-1902; pastor Coll. and village church, Olivet, Mich., 1904-07; prof. hist., 1907-16, prof. of philosophy, 1914-16 (emeritus prof. history), Olivet (Mich.) Coll.; non-resident prof. Bibl. lit., Lake Erie Coll., Painesville, O., 1919; instr. Hebrew and Grek langs., Oberlin Grad. Sch. of Theology, 1926-33. Contbr., 1878—, and some time editor, Bibliotheca Sacra, Oberlin, O. Author: Fundamental Ideas of the Roman Catholic Church, 1899; Christian Life and Theology, 1900; A Genetic History of the New England Theology, 1907. Home: Oberlin, O. Died Oct. 20, 1935.

FOSTER, Frank Keyes, printer, lecturer; b. Palmer, Mass., Dec. 19, 1854; s. Charles Dwight and Jane Elizabeth (Burgess) F.; ed. pub. schs., Palmer, Mass., and Monson Acad.; m. Lucretia Ella Ladd, May 22, 1879. Began as printer, 1874; edited Daily Laborer, Haverhill, Mass., 1883-86; editor and publisher Liberator (monthly), 1886—. Has lectured on social and econ. topics in 23 States; Labor Day orator at Phila., Cincinnati, Baltimore, Portland (Me.), Lynn, Atlanta, Syracuse, etc. Dem. nominee for lt. gov. Mass., 1886; mem. bd. mgrs. Franklin Fund (jud. appmt.), 1904; mem. exam. com. Boston Pub. Library, 1904-06; mem. Com. 100, Boston, Boston Chamber of Commerce, New Eng. Civic Fedn. Ind. Democrat. Author: The Evolution of a Trade Unionist, 1901; The Karma of Labor (verse), 1903. Died 1909.

FOSTER, Frank Pierce, physician; b. Concord, N.H., Nov. 26, 1841; ed. Concord High Sch.; M.D., Coll. Phys. and Surg. (Columbia), 1862; took hosp. course 2 yrs.; acting asst. surgeon U.S.A., 1865; m. Georgiana Molleson, Oct. 18, 1869. In gen. practice at New York; editor N.Y. Medical Journal. Co-author Illustrated Encyclopædic Medical Dictionary. Died 1911.

FOSTER, George Burman, theologian; b. Alderson, W.Va., Apr. 2, 1858; s. Oliver Harrison and Helen Louise (Skaggs) F.; ed. Shelton Coll., W.Va., 1876-79; A.B., W.Va. U., 1883, A.M., 1884; grad. Rochester Theol. Sem., 1887; univs. Göttingen and Berlin, 1891-92; (hon. Ph.D., Denison U., 1892); m. Mary, d. Prof. Franklin Lyon, of W.Va. U., Aug. 6, 1884. Ordained Baptist ministry, 1879; pastor Saratoga Springs, N.Y., 1887-91; prof. philosophy, McMaster U., 1892-95; asso. prof., 1895-97, prof. systematic theology, 1897-1905, prof. philosophy of religion, 1905—, U. of Chicago. Author: The Finality of the Christian Religion, 1906; The Function of Religion in Man's Struggle for Existence, 1909; The Function of Death in Human Experience, 1917. Joint author: A Guide to the Study of the Christian Religion. Died Dec. 22, 1918.

FOSTER, Harry LaTourette, author; b. Brooklyn, N.Y., Oct. 31, 1894; s. Alonzo and Mary Emily (LaTourette) F.; prep. edn., Newton (N.J.) Acad.; student Lafayette Coll., Easton, Pa., 1912-16; unmarried. Newspaper reporter, free lance corr. in Mexico, miner, tourist-guide, attaché U.S. Embassy, Lima, Peru, etc. Student 1st R.O.T.C., Madison Barracks, N.Y., 1917; commd. 2d lt. inf., U.S.A.; served with 78th Div. in France; 1st lt. and instr. in modern warfare; with 25th U.S. Inf. on Mexican border, 1918-19. Author: The Adventures of a Tropical Tramp, 1922; A Beachcomber in the Orient, 1923; A Gringo in Mañana-Land, 1924; A Tropical Tramp with the Tourists, 1925; A Vagabond in Fiji, 1927; Combing the Caribbees, 1929; A Vagabond in Barbary, 1930. Co-author of drama, "Savages Under the Skin," prod. on Broadway, 1927. Editor of guide-book to South America, 1927. Died Mar. 15, 1932.

FOSTER, Herbert Darling, college prof.; b. W. Newbury, Mass., June 22, 1863; s. Davis (D.D.) and Harriet Louisa (Darling) F.; A.B., Dartmouth, 1885;

A.M., Harvard, 1892; fellow in history, Harvard Grad. Sch., 1891-93; grad. work and research in Cambridge (Eng.), Berlin, Geneva, Paris, and London; Litt.D., U. of Geneva, Switzerland, 1909; m. Lillian Darlington Smith, July 7, 1897. Taught English and history, 1885-88, and organized dept. of history, 1888-91, Worcester (Mass.) Acad.; prof. history, Dartmouth, 1893—. In ednl. work with A.E.F. in France and Germany, Feb.-June 1919, successively as actg. dir. Coll. of Letters and Sciences, head of dept. of history, A.E.F., Univ., Beaune, France, and dir. instrn. in history, A.E.F. Editor: A Syllabus of Modern European History, 1500-1920 A.D. (with others), 10th edit., 1925. Home: Hanover, N.H. Died Dec. 28, 1927.

FOSTER, Horatio Alvah, electrical engr.; b. Phila., Pa., Jan. 12, 1858; s. Edward Vose and Martha Allis (Smith) F.; ed. Northampton (Mass.) High Sch.; m. Florence Louise Root, Dec. 22, 1893. Installed first commercially operated electric ry. in U.S., in Baltimore, 1885; engr. for Thomson-Houston Electric Co., 1886-91, and of Central Sta., New York, for same co., 1890-91; elec. expert for U.S. Census Office, 1891-92; editor "Electrical Industries," Chicago, during World's Fair; 1st asst. to Prof. George Forbes, of London; elec. consulting engr., Niagara Falls Power Co., 1895-1900; federal receiver Consumers Brewing Co., Phila., 1901-06; with L. B. Stillwell, engrs., 1906-08; with Bion J. Arnold, Chicago, 1908-11; J. G. White & Co., New York, 1912—. Fellow Am. Inst. Elec. Engrs., 1912. Republican. Unitarian. Author: Electrical Engineers' Pocket Book, 1901; Engineering Valuation of Public Utilities and Factories, 1912. Home: Yonkers, N.Y. Deceased.

FOSTER, Irving Lysander, prof. Romance languages; b. Washington, D.C., July 6, 1870; s. Publius Darwin and Amanda Elizabeth (Warren) F.; B.A., Brown U., 1893, M.A., 1894; studied U. of Leipzig, and the Sorbonne, Paris; hon. Litt.D., Susquehanna U., Selin's Grove, Pa., 1915; m. Nellie Olive Patterson, June 9, 1898. Teacher dist. sch., Conn., 1888-89; instr. in French, Brown U., 1893-94; instr. modern langs., Pa. State Coll., 1895; successively instr. and asst. prof. Romance langs., same coll., prof., 1905—; spl. teacher in English, U. of Porto Rico, summer 1924. Dir. First Nat. Bank (State College), Mount Nittany Building & Loan Assn. Y.M.C.A. ednl. secretary, Camp Hancock, Ga., 1917-18. Director Camp Kanesetake. V.p. S.S. Assn. of Center Co., Pa. Republican. Presbyn. Part author: Foundations of French, 1900; A French Reader, 1903; Practical French (war manual), 1917; Elementary French (revised), 1922. Editor: Les Américains chez nous (Brieux), 1925. Home: State College, Pa. Died June 1, 1929.

FOSTER, John Early, judge; b. N.Y. City, Sept. 22, 1864; LL.B., Columbia Law Sch., 1886. Admitted to N.J. bar as atty., 1886, counselor 1889; prosecutor of pleas, Monmouth Co., N.J., 1900-04; law judge of Monmouth Co., 1904-15 (resigned); v. chancelor of N.J. by appmt. of Chancellor Walker, Jan. 15, 1916—, term of 7 yrs., reappointed Jan. 15, 1923. Republican. Home: Atlantic Highlands, N.J. Died Apr. 21, 1925.

FOSTER, John Gilman, consul-gen.; b. Derby Line, Vt., Mar. 9, 1859; s. Austin T. and Sarah H. (Gilman) F.; A.B., Tufts Coll., 1880; m. Clara, d. Judge Amos Lee Merriman, June 9, 1886; children—Katherine Reed (Mrs. C. C. Aikins), Austin T., Stephen M. Admitted to Vt. bar, 1881; engaged in management of trust estates and banking at Derby Line, Vt., 1881-97; v.p. Nat. Bank of Derby Line; pres. Massawippi Valley Ry. Co. Mem. Vt. Ho. of Rep., 1892; col. on staff Gov. Levi K. Fuller of Vt., 1892-94; U.S. consul-gen. at Halifax, N.S., 1897-1903, at Ottawa, Ont., 1903-27 (ret.). Apptd. mem. Internat. Commn. for Advancement of Peace, Mar. 6, 1928. Home: Derby Line, Vt. Died Jan. 6, 1931.

FOSTER, John Hopkins, congressman; b. Evansville, Ind., Jan. 31, 1862; s. Alexander H. and Martha (Hopkins) F.; A.B., Ind. U., 1882; LL.B., Columbian (now George Washington) U., 1884; admitted to bar, 1885; m. Josephine Piper, Dec. 28, 1887. Mem. Ind. Ho. of Rep., 1893-94; judge Superior Ct., Vanderburg Co., Ind., 1894-1906; elected to 59th Congress, at spl. election, May 16, 1905, to fill unexpired term of James A. Hemenway (elected to U.S. Senate); reëlected to 60th Congress (1907-09), 1st Ind. Dist. Republican. Home: Evansville, Ind. Died Sept. 5, 1917.

FOSTER, John McGaw, clergyman; b. Bangor, Me., Feb. 4, 1860; s. John B. and Catharine (McGaw) F.; A.B., Harvard, 1882; grad. Andover Theol. Sem., 1885; m. Grace G. Eames, Jan. 4, 1887; children—Katharine McGaw (dec.), Duncan Graham. Deacon, 1885, priest, 1886, P.E. Ch.; curate St. Anne's Ch., Lowell, Mass., 1885; rector St. John's Ch., Bangor, Me., 1886-98, Ch. of the Messiah, Boston, 1898-1922; rector honorarius of same church, 1922—. Dep. to Gen. Conv. P.E. Ch., 1892; hon. canon, Cathedral, Portland, Me., 1895-99. Examining chaplain to bishop of Mass., 1901-08; mem. and pres. standing com., diocese of Mass., 1904-22. Author: The White Stone, 1901; To Know and Believe, 1908; The Crowded Inn, 1918. Home: Cambridge, Mass. Died Oct. 30, 1928.

FOSTER, John Pierrepont Codrington, physician; b. New Haven, Conn., Mar. 2, 1847; s. Eleazer Kingsbury and Mary (Codrington) F.; bro. of William Edward F.; B.A., Yale, 1869, M.D., 1875 (hon. M.A., 1909); m. Josephine Bicknell, July 1, 1875. In med. practice at New Haven, 1875—; has been largely identified with state and nat. work for prevention and treatment of tuberculosis; acting asst. surgeon, U.S. Marine Hosp. Service. Chairman Conn. Tuberculosis Commn.; exec. chmn. Gaylord Farm Sanatorium, Wallingford, Conn. Republican. Episcopalian. Home: New Haven, Conn. Died 1910.

FOSTER, John Watson, secretary of state; b. Pike Co., Ind., Mar. 2, 1836; s. Judge Matthew Watson and Eleanor (Johnson) F.; A.B., Ind. U., 1855, A.M., 1858; student 1 yr. Harvard Law Sch.; (LL.D., Princeton, 1895, Wabash Coll., 1895, Yale, 1896, U. of Pa., 1907); admitted to Ind. bar and practiced at Evansville, 1857-61; m. Mary Parke McFerson, 1859. Entered Union Army, 1861, as maj. 25th Ind. Vols.; promoted lt. col. at Ft. Donelson, col. at Shiloh; editor Evansville Daily Journal, 1865-69; postmaster, Evansville, 1869-73; chmn. Rep. State Central Com., 1872; minister to Mexico, 1873-80, to Russia, 1880-81; established, 1881, in practice in internat. cases in Washington, representing foreign legations before commns., arbitration bds., etc. Minister to Spain, 1883-85; spl. plenipotentiary to negotiate reciprocity treaties with Brazil, Spain, Germany, British W.I., etc., 1891; sec. of state, in cabinet of President Harrison, 1892-93; agt. U.S. in Bering Sea Arbitration, at Paris, 1893; invited by Emperor of China and participated in peace negotiations with Japan; ambassador on spl. mission to Great Britain and Russia, 1897; mem. Anglo-Canadian Commn., 1898; agt. U.S. Alaskan Boundary Tribunal, London, 1903; rep. of China to 2d Hague Conf., 1907. Author: A Century of American Diplomacy, 1900; American Diplomacy in the Orient, 1903; Arbitration and The Hague Court, 1904; The Practice of Diplomacy, 1906. Died Nov. 15, 1917.

FOSTER, Joseph, rear adm. (retired); b. Gloucester, Mass., June 17, 1841; s. Joseph and Adelaide Coues (Spalding) F.; ed. pub. and pvt. schs., Portsmouth, N.H.; m. Helen Dickey, Oct. 7, 1875 (died 1904); children—Joseph, Beatrice (dec.), Dorothy (Mrs. L. S. Stewart), Isabel; m. 2d, Josephine Hunt, of Broxbourne, Hertfordshire, Eng., Mar. 17, 1906. Entered U.S.N., Oct. 3, 1862; apptd. actg. asst. p.-m., Oct. 19, 1863; transferred to regular navy, Aug. 10, 1866; advanced through various grades and commd. pay dir., with rank of capt., Aug. 27, 1901; advanced to rank of rear admiral and retired at own request after 40 yrs.' service, Dec. 9, 1902. Served during Civil War in S. Atlantic Blockading Squadron, most of the time off Charleston. Mem. bd. of instrn. pub. schs., Portsmouth, N.H., 1909-13. Republican. Theist. Author: The Graves We Decorate, Storer Post G.A.R., Portsmouth, N.H., edits., 1893, 1907, 15, 17, 21, 23; Soldiers' Memorial, Portsmouth, N.H., 1893-1921, tercentenary edit., 1893-1923. Died May 17, 1930.

FOSTER, Judith Ellen Horton, lecturer; b. Lowell, Mass., Nov. 3, 1840; r. Rev. Jotham and Judith (Delano) Horton; ed. N.E. schs. and Genesee Wesleyan Sem., Lima, N.Y., 1855-56; removed to Clinton, Ia.; m. E. C. Foster, lawyer, 1869. Studied law; admitted to Iowa bar, 1872, and practiced law. Became prominent in W.C.T.U.; was supt. legislative dept. and popular lecturer. When the W.C.T.U. affiliated with the Prohibition party, she united with the Non-Partisan W.C.T.U. Author: The Crime Against Ireland, 1883. Died 1910.

FOSTER, Martin D., congressman; b. Edwards Co., Ill., Sept. 3, 1861; s. Elashel and Emily (Housler) F.; ed. Eureka (Ill.) Coll., 2 yrs.; M.D., Eclectic Med. Inst., Cincinnati, 1882; M.D., Hahnemann Med. Coll., Chicago, 1894; m. Lula Cliffe, Oct. 27, 1891. Practicing medicine, Olney, Ill., 1882—; mem. Bd. U.S. Examining Surgeons, 1885-89, 1893-97. Mayor of Olney, 1895, 1902; mem. 60th to 65th Congresses (1907-19), 23d Ill. Dist. Democrat. Home: Olney, Ill. Died 1919.

FOSTER, Murphy James, senator; b. Franklin, La., Jan. 12, 1849; studied at Washington and Lee U., 1867-68; grad. Cumberland U., 1870; LL.B., Tulane U., 1871; engaged in law practice, Franklin, La.; married. Mem. La. Senate, 1880-92 (pres. 1888-90); led and won fight against La. state lottery; gov. of La., 1892-1900; U.S. senator, La., 1901-13; resumed practice of law; now U.S. collector of customs. Democrat. Home: Franklin, La. Died June 12, 1921.

FOSTER, Nellis Barnes, M.D.; b. Durhamville, N.Y., July 18, 1875; s. Theodore and Loretta (Barnes) F.; A.B., Amherst, 1898; M.D., Johns Hopkins, 1902; post-grad. work European univs.; hon. Sc.D., Amherst College, 1926; m. Julia Catharine Morris, Oct. 26, 1904. Instr. and asso. in biol. chemistry, Columbia U., 1906-12; asso. phys. to New York Hosp., 1907-16; instr. medicine, 1913-14, asst. prof., 1914-17, Cornell Med. Coll. of New York; prof. medicine, U. of Mich. and dir. med. clinic Univ. Hosp., 1917-18. Maj., Med. R.C., 1917, and chief of med. service, Base Hosp., Camp Meade, Md.; lt. col. M.C., 1919; dir. School of Mil. Medicine, Ft. Oglethorpe, Ga.; asso. prof. medicine, Cornell Med. Coll., New York, and asso. phys. to New York Hosp., 1919—. Democrat. Home: New York, N.Y. Died Aug. 20, 1933.

FOSTER, Percy Semple, musical dir.; b. Richmond, Va., Sept. 15, 1863; s. Robert Edward and Josephine (Wilkinson) F.; ed. Baltimore City Coll.; m. Loulie Wescott, Oct. 19, 1882; children—Norman Percy, Ethel Louise (Mrs. Herbert T. Shannon). Began as stenographer and ch. organist; with Standard Oil Co., Washington, D.C.; various lines of business and owner Percy S. Foster Piano Co. and bank pres.; now in investment business. Musical dir. civic and religious convs. in Washington, D.C., and throughout U.S., including Internat. Christian Endeavor Convs., 1892—, World's S.S. gatherings, Moody, Gypsy Smith and Billy Sunday meetings, etc.; dir. vocal music at presdl. inaugurations, 1897—. Baptist; a founder and trustee Nat. Bapt. Memorial Ch.; trustee at large and life mem. Internat. Christian Endeavor; charter mem. World Christian Endeavor. Mason. Home: Washington, D.C. Deceased.

FOSTER, Randolph Sinks, M.E. bishop, 1872—; b. Williamsburg, O., Feb. 22, 1820; ed. Augusta Coll., Ky.; entered itinerant ministry M.E. Ch., 1837, in Ky. conf.; later transferred to Ohio, and in 1850 to New York, remaining until 1857; pres. Northwestern Univ., 1857-60; again in pastorates, New York and Sing Sing, 1860-68; 1868 prof. systematic theology, 1868-69 and 1869-72; pres. Drew Theol. Sem., Madison, N.J. Home: Roxbury, Boston. Died 1903.

FOSTER, Robert Sandford, mcht., soldier; b. Vernon, Ind., Jan. 27, 1834; s. Riley S. and Sarah J. F.; ed. in common school there. Fought through the Civil war with Ind. troops, becoming brig. gen. of vols., 1863, and bvt. maj. gen., 1865. Has resided in Indianapolis since the war; city treas., 1867-72; U.S. marshal for dist. of Ind., 1881-85; now a broker and commission mcht.; unmarried. Home: Indianapolis, Ind. Died 1903.

FOSTER, Robert Verrell, theologian; b. Wilson Co., Tenn., Aug. 12, 1845; s. Rufus Harrison and Sarah (Spain) F.; A.B., Cumberland U., 1870; grad. Union Theol. Sem., 1877; (D.D., Trinity U., Tex., 1884; LL.D., Washington and Jefferson, 1906); m. Belle Braden, Nov. 7, 1882. Ordained Cumberland Presbyn. ministry, 1879; prof. Hebrew and N.T. Greek, 1877-93, systematic theology, 1893—, Cumberland Presbyn. Theol. Seminary. Author: Old Testament Theology, 1890. Editor: Theological Quarterly Review, 1891, 1892; A Study of the Lord's Prayer; The Systems of Doctrine. Home: Lebanon, Tenn. Died Jan. 27, 1914.

FOSTER, Roger, lawyer, legal writer; b. Worcester, Mass., 1857; s. Dwight F. (judge Supreme Ct., Mass.) and Henrietta, d. Gov. and U.S. Senator Roger S. Baldwin, of Conn.; ed. Boston Latin School, U. of Marburg, Germany, 1873-74; A.B., Yale U., 1878, A.M., 1881; LL.B., Columbia, 1880; m. Laura Pugh, d. Prof. William R. Moxley, Feb. 22, 1921. Admitted to N.Y. bar, 1880; apptd. tenement house commr. by Gov. Flower, 1894; spl. counsel bd. of health, New York, 1896, 1897, 1898; counsel for Caro heirs in first case that established liability of elevated ry. cos. to abutters in New York, 1882. Drafted tenement house laws of 1895, and prosecuted proceedings which established constitutionality of one of these laws and resulted in destruction of more than 70 tenements; secured appointment of receivers of Bay State Gas Co., 1896; was counsel for Senator W. A. Clark in the Montana election case before the U.S. Senate, 1900. Author: A Treatise on the Federal Judiciary Acts of 1875 and 1887; A Treatise on Federal Practice, 1890, 6th edit., 1921. Home: New York, N.Y. Died Feb. 22, 1924.

FOSTER, Samuel Monell, banking, ins.; b. Coldenham, N.Y., Dec. 12, 1851; s. John L. (M.D.) and Harriett (Scott) F.; A.B., Yale, 1879; m. Margaret Harrison, June 12, 1881; 1 dau., Alice (Mrs. Alice Foster McCulloch). First pres. Lincoln National Bank, 1905-23, chmn. of the board; 1st pres. Lincoln Nat. Life Ins. Co., 1905-23, since chmn. bd.; pres. Samuel M. Foster Co.; treas. Fort Wayne Hotel Co., Fort Wayne Land & Improvement Co. Trustee Purdue U., 1911-17. Democrat. Mason. Home: Fort Wayne, Ind. Died Apr. 4, 1935.

FOSTER, Volney William, contractor; b. Aztalan, Wis., Feb. 27, 1848; s. Volney and Marrianne (Torrey) F.; ed. Portage City, Wis., Jefferson Inst. and Milton Coll.; m. Aug. 9, 1876, Eva Adelle Hill (died 1887). Has been engaged in gen. contracting; until recently pres. Western Paving & Supply Co.; pres. U.S. Silica Co.; v.p. Bonded Warehouses of Mexico & Vera Cruz; pres. U.S. Repair & Guaranty Co., The Foster Contracting Co. Pres. Sheridan Road Assn., 1887—; treas. Nat. Rep. Campaign Com. in Chicago, 1900; treas. Back Lot Studies Soc.; del. to Internat. Conf. Am. Republics, 1901-02, City of Mexico; deputy gov. Soc. Mayflower Descendants. Home: Evanston, Ill. Died 1904.

FOSTER, William, chemist; b. Hartford, Ky., May 15, 1869; s. William and Sarah Jane (Carson) F.; A.B., Hartford Coll., 1892; B.S., Vanderbilt U., 1893; A.M., Princeton, 1896, Ph.D., 1899; m. Helen Dunham Stewart, Sept. 3, 1902; children—Katharine Sutliff, Helen Stewart, Wilhelmina. Prof. chemistry, Central U. of Ky., 1899-1900; instr. chemistry, 1900-05, asst. prof., 1905-10, prof., 1910—, Princeton. Formerly chief examiner in chemistry, Co'l. Entrance

Examination Bd. Fellow A.A.A.S. Democrat. Presbyn. Author: A Laboratory Manual in General Chemistry, 1905; Introduction to General Chemistry, 1922, 31; The Elements of Chemistry, 1925, 32; Experiments in General Chemistry (with H. W. Heath), 1925; The Romance of Chemistry, 1927, German edit. of same as Welt und Wunder der Chemie, 1931; Inorganic Chemistry for Colleges, 1929; A Laboratory Course of General Chemistry, 1930. Home: Princeton, N.J. Died May 24, 1937.

FOSTER, William Davis, surgeon; b. Van Buren Co., Ia., Sept. 7, 1841; s. Joseph and Elizabeth Kummler (Griffith) F.; ed. pub. schs. and Birmingham, Ia., Acad.; med. study began with Dr. David Prince, Jacksonville, Ill., 1857; hosp. steward 7th Mo. Cav., Oct. 3, 1861; asst. surgeon, July 2, 1863-June 5, 1865; M.D., Homœ. Med. Coll. of Mo., St. Louis, 1869; m. Mrs. Christie K. Farwell, Oct. 16, 1878. Prof. surgery, 1889-1901, dean faculty, 1897-99, Kansas City Homœ. Med. Coll.; chief surgeon Kansas City, Osceola & Southern R.R., 1893-98. Sr. mem. Am. Inst. Homœopathy (pres. 1908-09); del. Internat. Homœ. Med. Congress, Basle, Switzerland, 1886. Fellow Am. Coll. Surgeons. Dean and prof. surgery, Southwest Sch. of Medicine and Hosp. Home: Kansas City, Mo. Died Feb. 5, 1925.

FOSTER, William Eaton, librarian; b. Brattleboro, Vt., June 2, 1851; s. Joseph Coggin and Abigail Ann (Eaton) F.; A.B., Brown U., 1873, A.M., 1876, Litt.D., 1901; m. Julia Appleton, Mar. 2, 1886. Librarian Hyde Park (Mass.) Pub. Library, 1873-76; cataloguer Turner Free Library, Randolph, Mass., 1876-77; librarian Providence Pub. Library, 1877-1930. Author: The Civil Service Reform Movement, 1881; The Literature of Civil Service Reform in the United States, 1881; Libraries and Readers, 1883; The Point of View in History, 1906; Five Men of '76, 1926; The First Fifty Years of the Providence Public Library, 1928. Home: Providence, R.I. Died Sept. 10, 1930.

FOSTER, William Edward, editor; b. New Haven, Conn., 1839; s. Eleazer Kingsbury and Mary (Codrington) F.; bro. of John Pierrepont Codrington F.; A.B., Yale, 1860; admitted to Conn. bar and U.S. Court, New Haven, 1866; m. S. E. Betts. Acting p.m. U.S.N., in Civil War; editor and part propr. Lynchburg (Va.) Republican, 1867-70; mng. editor Buffalo Commercial, 1870-1911. Home: Buffalo, N.Y. Died Aug. 25, 1915.

FOSTER, William Edward; b. Thomaston, Me., Sept. 26, 1864; s. Benjamin T. and Susan (Harrington) F.; ed. pub. schs.; m. Rebecca Clarendon, June 19, 1900; children—Madeleine (Mrs. Charles H. Conklin), Jane (dec.). Began as office boy Am. Sugar Refining Co., N.Y. City, 1883, auditor, 1901-11, comptroller, 1911-13, treas., 1913-20, v.p., 1920-25, pres., 1925-29, vice-chmn. bd., 1929—; dir. Hackensack Trust Co., Preferred-Havana Tobacco Co., M. E. Clarendon Sons Co. Chmn. Liberty Loan and Am. Red Cross drives, Hackensack, World War. Gov. Hackensack Hosp., Hackensack Y.M.C.A.; mem. Hackensack Sinking Fund Commn. Mem. N.Y. Chamber Commerce. Mem. Bd. of Foreign Missions and Board of Direction, Dutch Ref. Ch. in America. Republican. Home: Hackensack, N.J. Died Aug. 8, 1940.

FOSTER, William Wilson, Jr., coll. pres.; b. Moriah, N.Y., July 27, 1849; s. William W. and Frances (Wheelock) F.; prep. edn. Ft. Edward (N.Y.) Collegiate Inst.; student Drew Theol. Sem., 1870-71; S.T.D., Boston U. Sch. of Theology, 1873; D.D., Moores Hill (Ind.) Coll., 1894; m. Mary J. Chisholm, Dec. 11, 1872; 1 dau., Constance. Ordained M.E. ministry, 1873; pastor Pittsford, Vt., 1873-75, Castleton, Vt., 1876-78, Ft. Edward, N.Y., 1879-80, Central Ch., Lowell, Mass., 1880-82, Bennington, Vt., 1883-84, St. Luke's Ch., Albany, N.Y., 1885-87, North Adams, Mass., 1888-92, 1st Ch., Amsterdam, N.Y., 1893-97; pres. Rust U., Holly Springs, Miss., 1898-1909, Beaver (Pa.) Coll., 1909-10; pastor Johnstown, N.Y., 1910; dist. supt. Albany dist., 1912; pres. Clark U., Atlanta, Ga., 1912-18; pastor Embury M.E. Ch., Cambridge, N.Y., 1918-21, retired. Trustee Rust U., Beaver Coll., Clark U., Troy Conf. Edn. Bd. Mason. Home: 11 S. Pine Av., Albany, N.Y. Died Feb. 22, 1933.

FOUGNER, G. Selmer, newspaperman; b. Chicago, Ill., Aug. 24, 1884; s. Albert C. and Mathilde (Selmer) F.; Bach ès Lettres, Sorbonne, Paris, France, 1905; m. Vera Byrtha Ellon, June 2, 1911; 1 son, Robert Selmer. Mem. editorial staff New York Herald, New York and Paris, 1906-09, New York Press, 1909-12, New York Sun, 1912-17; rep. New York Sun and Chicago Tribune at mediation conf. between U.S. and Mexico, Niagara Falls, Can., May-July 1914; sent to Europe, 1915, as chief London corr. and gen. European mgr. New York Sun; spent much time at British and French fronts as spl. war corr. Sun, also contbg. to London Times, London Daily Mail and London Evening News; returned to U.S., Mar. 1917; with U.S. Treas., 1917-20, as mgr. Press Bureau of New York liberty loans; directed all newspaper publicity for 2d, 3d, 4th and 5th loans, also war savings stamp campaign; dir. publicity of Community Councils of Nat. Defense, Nat. Social Unit Orgn., Nat. Com. on Prisons and Prison Labor, Nat. Birthday Com. (Serbian Child Welfare Assn.), Boy Scouts America (1919 New York campaign), Actors Nat. Memorial (July-Oct. 1919), Pres. Wilson's Address on the League of Nations on the eve of his departure for Europe, Metr. Opera House, Apr. 1919, Capital vs. Labor debate between Samuel Gompers and Henry Allen, Carnegie Hall, May 1920, Nat. Budget Com., and Honest Ballot Assn.; dir. Panthéon de la Guerre, Paris, France, 1923; directed West Coast of Fla. publicity campaign, 1924-25; dir. publicity Rep. gubernatorial campaign, N.Y., 1926; also dir. publicity Internat. League of Aviators (Paris) and United Air Force (Geneva, Madrid and Paris); dir. Aero News (Paris), G. Selmer Fougner Syndicate. Editor of "Paper," The Publishers Guide, L'Exportateur Américain. Chevalier Legion of Honor (France); Officer Order of the Crown of Italy. Author: Along The Wine Trail, 1935; A Good Living Tour Through Italy, 1935; Dining Out in New York and What to Order, 1939. Translator: René Benjamin's Gaspard, 1916. Has written extensively under pseudonym of Baron Fougner; conductor from 1933 of daily column, "Along the Wine Trail," in New York Sun and syndicated newspapers. Address: New York, N.Y. Died Apr. 2, 1941.

FOUKE, William Hargrave, bishop; b. Shepherdstown, W.Va., Oct. 30, 1851; s. William Henry and Mahala Ann (Chaplain) F.; ed. common schs., Dixon, Ill.; took conf. course of 4 yrs. after entering the ministry; (D.D., Dallas Coll., Ore., 1911); m. Mary M. Tobias, Mar. 1877. Licensed to preach, 1876; deacon, 1878, elder, 1880, Evang. Assn. Ch.; pastor in Ill., at Shannon, 1876, Cedarville, 1877-78, S. Chicago, 1879-81, Freeport, 1882-83, Adams St. Ch., Chicago, 1884-87, Freeport, 1888-90, Shannon, 1891; United Evang. Ch., Adams St. Ch., Chicago, 1892-95; presiding elder Freeport Dist., 1896-99; pastor Naperville, 1900-02; bishop Oct. 1910-18. Pres. Ill. Conf. Missionary Soc., 1893. Asso. editor Evangelical, 1918. Home: Harrisburg, Pa. Died Feb. 6, 1923.

FOULKE, William Dudley, author; b. New York, N.Y., Nov. 20, 1848; s. Thomas and Hannah (Shoemaker) F.; A.B., Columbia, 1869, LL.B., 1871, A.M., 1872; LL.D., Earlham, 1906; m. Mary Taylor Reeves, 1872; children—Caroline (wife of John F. Urie), Lydia (Mrs. Stanley C. Hughes, dec.), Mary (Mrs. James W. Morrisson), Arthur Dudley (dec.), Lucy Dudley (dec.), Gwendolen (Mrs. Dudley Cates). Admitted to bar, 1870; removed to Ind., 1876; mem. Ind. Senate, 1883-85; mem. U.S. Civ. Service Commn., 1901-03; editor Evening Item, Richmond, Ind., 1909-12. Chmn. Suffrage Congress, Chicago Expn., 1893; formerly pres. Am. Woman's Suffrage Assn. up to 1890; conducted investigations of the civil service as chmn. spl. com. of Nat. Civil Service Reform League. Pres. Nat. Municipal League, 1910-15; mem. platform com. Progressive Party, 1912; pres. Nat. Civil Service Reform League, 1923-24. Author: Life of Oliver P. Morton, 1899; Fighting the Spoilsman, 1919; To-Day and Yesterday (poems), 1920; A Hoosier Autobiography, 1922; Is Our Civilization Really Declining?, 1923; A Random Record of Travel During Fifty Years, 1925; Roosevelt and the Spoilsmen, 1925; Songs of Eventide, 1928; Earth's Generations Pass (verse), 1930; Lucius B. Swift, American Citizen—A Biography, 1930. Home: Richmond, Ind. Died May 30, 1935.

FOULKROD, William W., congressman; b. Frankford, Phila., Nov. 22, 1846; ed. pub. and pvt. schs., Phila.; m. Mary C. Buckius. Pres. Frankford Hosiery Mills Co., Frankford Fire Ins. Co. One of organizers Phila. Trades League (pres. 12 yrs.); trustee Phila. Commercial Mus., T. W. Evans Mus. and Inst. Soc.; mem. Citizens' Permanent Relief Com., Phila.; acting pres. Nat. Export Exhbn. Co., Phila., 1899. Mem. 60th and 61st Congresses (1907-11), 5th Pa. Dist. Republican. Member Hist. Soc. Pa. Home: Frankford, Phila., Pa. Died 1910.

FOUNTAIN, Samuel Warren, brig. gen.; b. Parkersburg, W.Va., Dec. 13, 1846; s. Chauncy and Ruhama (Ogle) F.; grad. U.S. Mil. Acad., 1870; m. Emily M. Kauffman, 1879 (died 1885); m. 2d, Katherine G. McGrath, Jan. 11, 1888. Enlisted as pvt. Co. K, 140th Ohio Vol. Inf., May 2, 1864; disch., Sept. 3, 1864; commd. 2d lt. 8th U.S. Cav., June 15, 1870; 1st lt., Oct. 22, 1878; capt., Apr. 11, 1889; maj. 9th Cav., Feb. 2, 1901; asst. adj. gen., Feb. 28, 1901; lt. col. 13th Cav., Aug. 26, 1903; transferred to 4th Cav., Aug. 28, 1903; brig. gen., Apr. 10, 1905; retired, at own request, over 30 yrs.' service, Apr. 11, 1905. Served in campaigns against Geronimo, 1885-86; against the Sioux Indians, 1890-91; in Cuba during Spanish-Am. War and as adj. gen. dept. of Mindanao and Jolo, P.I.; comd. Jefferson Guards at St. Louis Expn., 1904. Catholic. Home: Devon, Pa. Died Nov. 15, 1920.

FOUSE, Levi Garner, life underwriter; b. Clover Creek, Pa., Oct. 21, 1850; s. Adam and Susannah (Garner) F.; ed. Juniata Collegiate Inst., 1866, Heidelberg Coll., Tiffin, O., 1867, Mercersburg Coll., 1869; spl. studies in actuarial science; m. Mary B. Hause, Jan. 10, 1870. Founded, 1878, and has since been pres. Fidelity Mutual Life Ins. Co.; dir. Third Nat. Bank, and Central Trust Co., Philadelphia, Pa. Died Jan. 16, 1914.

FOWKE, Gerard, archeologist; b. Maysville, Ky., June 25, 1855; s. John D. and Sibella (Mitchell) Smith; present name adopted; unmarried. Was engaged in explorations and surveys of aboriginal remains in eastern half of U.S. in connection with Bur. of Am. Ethnology, 1885-88, and 1891-93; also under other auspices at various times; excavations among Norse remains near Boston, 1894 and 1896; explorations on Vancouver Island, B.C., and lower Amoor River in Siberia, for Am. Mus. Natural History, New York, 1898; examinations at Kimmswick, Mo., and Lansing, Kan., of geol. deposits containing prehistoric human remains of aboriginal flint quarries and of caves for early human remains, in Ky., Ind., Ill., Mo., Tenn., and Ala., 1902-04; geol. and archæol. investigations in Mo., 1905-08; investigated glacial deposits and traced pre-glacial channels, in entire length of Ohio valley, within above dates, and later; with Mo. Hist. Soc., St. Louis, 1911-16. Explored caves in Ozark mountain region for Bur. of Ethnology, 1918-23; preliminary ethnologic examination of Hawaiian Island group, 1920; mound explorations around Portsmouth, O., 1921, mound explorations vicinity of Muscle Shoals, 1924; investigation of mounds and village-sites along Red River in La. and in western Ark., and examination of flint quarries in S.W. Mo., 1925; archæol. work in La. and Mexico, 1926; in Ohio and Ky., 1927; with Mo. Hist. Soc., 1930; investigations in Ohio Valley, Cincinnati to Cairo, 1931. Author: Archæological History of Ohio (Ohio Archæol. and Hist. Soc.), 1902. Home: Madison, Ind. Died 1933.

FOWLER, Benjamin Austin, rancher; b. Stoneham, Mass., Dec. 14, 1843; s. Benjamin Coleman and Sophia Cowdrey (Stevens) F.; grad. Phillips Acad., Andover, Mass., 1862; served in signal corps, 50th Mass. Vols., 9 mos., 1862-63, under Gen. Banks, participating in siege of Port Hudson; B.A., Yale, 1868; studied law 1 yr. at Boston; m. Ella Frances Quinby, Oct. 17, 1888. Subscription and pub. bus., Boston, New York, Chicago, 1872-99, ten yrs. of which were with Dodd, Mead & Co., New York; ranching nr. Phoenix, Ariz., Mar. 1899-1916; dir. Phoenix Title & Trust Co. Mem. Ariz. Legislature, 1901; spent part of two winters, 1900-01, 1901-02, in Washington, working for passage of Nat. Irrigation Act; Rep. nominee for del. to Congress, 1904. Past pres. Ariz. Agrl. Assn., Phoenix Bd. Trade, Salt River Valley Water Users' Assn., Associated Charities, Phoenix, Phoenix Y.M.C.A. Mem. Nat. Irrigation Congress (exec. com. 1900-07, sec. 16th and 17th Congresses, 1908, 09, pres. 18th and 19th Congresses, 1910, 11). Home: Long Beach, Calif. Died Apr. 11, 1921.

FOWLER, Charles Henry, M.E. bishop; b. Burford, Ont., Aug. 11, 1837, of English-Scotch ancestry; grad. (valedictorian) Genesee Coll., 1859; Garrett Biblical Inst., 1861; (D.D., Garrett Bibl. Inst.; LL.D., Syracuse U. and Wesleyan U.); studied law, Chicago, 1859, but never practiced; m. Myra A., d. Rev. Luke Hitchcock, D.D., of Chicago, 1868. Pastor 11 yrs. in Chicago; pres. Northwestern Univ., 1872-76; sent to Gen. Conf., 1872, 1876, 1880, 1884; presented to Rock River Conf. plan to pool interests of chs. after Chicago fire, 1871; apptd. by gov. of Ill. to deliver oration at Centennial Expn., Phila., 1876; elected editor New York Christian Advocate, 1876; elected corr. sec. Missionary Soc., 1880; elected bishop, May 1884; visited S. America, 1885; resumed work in U.S., 1886; visited Japan, Corea and China, 1888; organized Pekin and Nankin univs., Central China; organized 1st M.E. Ch., St. Petersburg, Russia; made trip around the world visiting missions in Malaysia and India, and holding confs. in Europe; worked 8 yrs. on Pacific coast; established Maclay Coll. of Theology in Southern Calif.; asst. in founding Neb. Wesleyan U., Lincoln; sent as fraternal del. to Wesleyan Conf., Great Britain, 1898 and from Gen. Conf. M.E. Ch. to M.E. Ch., S., at Louisville, Ky.; 1st delegation since division of church in 1844. Died 1908.

FOWLER, Charles Newell, congressman; b. Lena, Ill., Nov. 2, 1852; A.B., Yale, 1876; LL.B., Chicago Law Sch., 1878. Removed to Elizabeth, N.J.; banker. Mem. 54th to 57th Congresses (1895-1903), 8th N.J. Dist., and 58th to 61st Congresses (1903-11), 5th Dist.; chmn. Com. on Banking and Currency many yrs. Mem.-at-large Rep. State Com., 1898-1907. Author of Seventeen Talks on the Banking Question, National Issues of 1916, United States Reserve Bank. Home: Elizabeth, N.J. Died Mar. 27, 1932.

FOWLER, David, judge; b. Washington Co., Md., Oct. 21, 1836; s. Robert and Susan F.; grad. Coll. of St. James, Washington Co., Md., 1858; m. Mary B. Brinkley, Nov. 23, 1875. Admitted to Md. bar, 1861; practiced law Baltimore until 1882; asso. judge 3d Jud. Dist., Md., 1882-89; asso. justice Ct. of Appeals, Md., 1889-1906; resigned; mem. Whitelock & Fowler until Nov. 1, 1909, retired. Democrat. Home: Baltimore, Md. Died 1911.

FOWLER, Elbert Hazelton, banker; b. Watford, Ont., Can., Dec. 31, 1883; s. Henry John and Elizabeth Ellen (Hazelton) F.; came with parents to U.S., 1892; student U. of Mich., 1901-10; m. Fanny Livingston Ptolemy, Mich., 1908. children—Hugh Stratton, Ruth Elizabeth, Marian Louise, Janet Helena. Admitted to Mich. bar, 1910, and practiced at Detroit until 1921; chmn. bd. Commonwealth-Commercial State Bank of Detroit; pres. Berkley (Mich.) State Bank, Detroit Investment Co.; treas. Mich. Home & Realty Co. Methodist. Mason. Home: Detroit, Mich. Deceased.

FOWLER, Elting Alexander, newspaper corr.; b. Caledonia, N.Y., Nov. 20, 1879; s. Archibald Kennedy and Jennie Belle (Fraser) F.; A.B., Princeton, 1902; unmarried. Became connected with New York Sun, 1903, Washington corr. same, Feb. 12, 1910—. Home: Washington, D.C. Died Oct. 31, 1916.

FOWLER, Frank, painter; b. Brooklyn, July 12, 1852; s. late John and Margaret (Westervelt) F.; ed. by pvt. tutors and Adelphi Acad., Brooklyn; studied 2 yrs. at Florence with late Edwin White, N.A.; 6 yrs. at Paris under Carolus Duran and at École des Beaux Arts; m. Mary B. Odenheimer, d. late bishop of N.J., 1878. Established in New York, 1880; painted portraits of Govs. Samuel J. Tilden and Roswell P. Flower (N.Y.); also portraits of late Gov. Greenhalge of Mass., Mme. Modjeska, Charles A. Dana, Archbishop Corrigan, Pres. Hadley of Yale, William Dean Howells; also many officers of the U.S. Mil. Acad., etc. Medal, Paris, 1889, Atlanta, 1895, Buffalo, 1901, Charleston, 1901. N.A., 1899. Author: Oil Painting; Drawing in Charcoal and Crayon; Portrait and Figure Painting. Home: New York, N.Y. Died 1910.

FOWLER, George Little, mech. engr.; b. Cherry Valley, N.Y., Aug. 9, 1855; s. Jonathan A. and Eliza O. F.; A.B., Amherst, 1877; m. Harriet F. Goldie, Oct. 17, 1882. In practice as consulting mech. engr., 1899—, previous to that in ry. service. U.S. commr. to Ry. Expn., Paris, 1887. Author of a number of books on engring. matters. Editor Locomotive Dictionary; asso. editor Railway & Locomotive Engineering. Home: New York, N.Y. Died July 2, 1926.

FOWLER, George Ryerson, M.D., surgeon; b. New York, Dec. 25, 1848; s. Thomas W. and Sarah Jane F.; ed. public schools, Jamaica, L.I.; grad. Bellevue Hosp. Med. Coll., 1871; m. Louise R. Wells, 1873. Surgeon M.E. Hosp.; surgeon-in-chief Brooklyn Hosp.; sr. surgeon German, cons. surgeon, St. Mary's hosps.; cons. surgeon Relief (E. dist.) Norwegian, and Nassau hosps.; late prof. surgery N.Y. Polyclinic. Fellow Acad. of Medicine; examiner in surgery N.Y. State Bd. of Med. Examiners. Served in war, 1898, as chief surgeon, 3d div., 7th army corps, with Gen. Fitzhugh Lee; later cons. surgeon and chief of operating staff, 7th army corps, accompanying Gen. Lee to Havana, where he organized hosps.; disch., Jan. 31, 1899. Author: Appendicitis, 1894 (enlarged edit., 1900). Home: Brooklyn, N.Y. Died 1906.

FOWLER, H. Robert, congressman; b. Pope Co., Ill.; grad. Ill. Normal U., Normal, Ill., 1877; prin. pub. schs., Cave-in-Cave, Ill., 1877-82, Elizabethtown, Ill., 1882-84; LL.B., U. of Mich., 1885; m. Mary E. Griffith, 1892. In law practice at Elizabethtown, Ill.; state's atty., Hardin Co., Ill., 1888-92; mem. Ill. Ho. of Rep., 1892-94, Senate, 1900-04; mem. 62d and 63d Congresses (1911-15), 24th Ill. Dist. Democrat. Mason. Home: Elizabethtown, Ill. Died Jan. 5, 1925.

FOWLER, Jessie Allen; b. New York, July 11, 1856; d. Lorenzo Niles (phrenologist) and Lydia (Folger) F.; studied brain dissection in Med. Sch. for Women, London, Eng., 1884; student summer sch., Columbia U., 1901; grad. Women's Law class, New York U., 1901; unmarried. Became identified with father's phrenol. work, 1879; lectured on phrenology and physical culture, in Australia, 1887-89; assumed editorial charge of Phrenological Magazine, London, 1889; returned to U.S., 1896; editor in chief Phrenological Jour., 1897—; v.p. Am. Inst. Phrenology until 1927. Conglist. Author: (with father) Phrenological Dictionary, 1895; Manual on Mental Science for Teachers and Students, 1897. Home: New York, N.Y. Died Oct. 15, 1932.

FOWLER, John, consul; b. Boston, May 9, 1858; s. John Henry and Julia A. (Brown) F.; ed. Phillips Acad., Exeter, N.H., class of '79; m. Lydia Marie Loureiro, Mar. 18, 1891 (died 1901). Entered govt. service Apr. 1879; in Naval Rendezvous, Washington, until 1881; then on U.S.S. Tallapoosa until that vessel was wrecked, Aug. 1885. Clerk to capt., to Sec. of the Navy, and to the President. Cruised around the world, 1886-89; U.S. consul at Ningpo, China, 1890-96, at Chefoo, China, 1896-1912, Foochow, China, July 1, 1912-14, at Rimouski, Can., Dec. 29, 1914-Oct. 21, 1915; resigned. Appointed consul-general, Feb. 2, 1904, reappointed consul, June 10, 1908; apptd. consul at Riviere du Loup, Can., Mar. 12, 1915, but declined. Decorated Order Double Dragon, 1st class, 3d div. and also 2d div., 1908, and 2d class 2d div. by the Emperor of China. Order Sacred Treasure, 3d class (Japan), 1907; also received thanks from Japanese Govt. for services in China-Japan War, 1895; presented with silver loving cup and address by entire native city of Chefoo for services to it in Boxer War; also with an address and silver punch bowl by foreign community of Chefoo; also an address from the Chinese authorities for services in the Russo-Japanese War, and thanks of Russian and Japanese authorities, and many resolutions, addresses, etc., Europe, Eng., Can. and U.S. for services in Boxer War; presented with an address and pair of vases by entire Am. community of Foochow, China, 1915. Home: Winchester, Mass. Died Dec. 30, 1923.

FOWLER, Joseph Smith, lawyer, U.S. senator; b. Steubenville, O., Aug. 31, 1820; parents removed to country two yrs. later; brought up on a farm; attended dist. schools, Island Creek Acad., Grove Acad., Steubenville and Franklin Coll., New Athens, O., spending most of time teaching to pay his way at school. Went to Ky., taught school and studied law; went to Tenn., 1844; prof. mathematics Franklin Coll., Tenn., 4 yrs.; pres. Howard Female Coll., Gallatin, Tenn., 1856-61. Under Mr. Davis' 40-day proclamation, went with family to Ill., remaining until Federal army took possession of Nashville; returned to Tenn. and was apptd. State comptroller under Andrew Johnson, mil. gov.; legislature which met March 1865, chose him U.S. senator for the long term, but he was not admitted to seat until July, 1866; made strong opposition to impeachment proceedings against President Johnson; opposed the 15th amendment to the constitution; supported Grant, 1868, but was Greeley elector, 1872 (electors voted for Thomas A. Hendricks of Ind., Greeley having died). Was mem. Baltimore conv. of 1864, that nominated Lincoln and Johnson; mem. Southern Loyalist Conv., Phila., 1866. Has practiced law in Washington, 1871—. Died 1902.

FOWLER, Nathaniel Clark, Jr., author, business adviser; b. Yarmouth, Mass., Jan. 21, 1858; s. Nathaniel Clark and Elizabeth Ann (Ellis) F.; ed. Roxbury Latin Sch., Boston; m. Fannie Alice Foote, Apr. 27, 1882. On staffs of Boston Traveller, 1876-78, Boston Commercial Bulletin, 1879; founder, 1880, pub. and editor Pittsfield (Mass.) Daily Journal; later Worcester, Mass., Light; founder, 1892, and mgr. Fowler Sch. of Advertising. Instr. advertising, salesmanship, printing, etc., Boston pub. high schs. and elsewhere; lecturer on publicity, business methods and human betterment subjects; planned publicity and selling campaigns for over 50 large Am. business houses. Conducted syndicates of publicity, business and salesmanship articles, 25 years aggregating over 10,000 newspapers and business and trade jours.; syndicate of "Success for Boys" in over 12,000 newspapers; established lab. of business method of teaching. Mason. Author: Practical Publicity, 1896; Fowler's Publicity—Starting in Life, 1906; Practical Salesmanship, 1911; How to Save Money, 1912; How to Get Your Pay Raised, 1912; The Art of Letter-Writing, 1913; The Art of Story-Writing, 1913; How to Obtain Citizenship (in 5 langs.), 1913; One Thousand Things Worth Knowing, 1913; The Art of Speech Making, 1915; Getting a Start, 1915; Beginning Right, 1916; Grasping Opportunity, 1917. Home: Winter Hill, Mass. Died Nov. 25, 1918.

FOWLER, Robert Ludlow, lawyer; b. Newburgh, N.Y., Apr. 15, 1849; s. I. Sebring and Mary (Ludlow) F.; LL.B., Columbia, 1870; (A.M., Brown U., 1895); m. Miss Groesbeck, June 1, 1876. Practiced in N.Y. City, 1870—; surrogate N.Y. Co. Pres. N.Y. Law Inst.; trustee St. Luke's Home; vestryman Trinity Ch. Author: Law of Charitable Uses, Trusts and Donations in New York, 1896; Real Property Law of the State of New York, 3d edit., 1909; Personal Property Law of the State of New York, 2d edit., 1909; History of the Law of Real Property in New York; Decedent Estates of the State of New York, 1911. Home: New York, N.Y. Died July 13, 1936.

FOWLER, Thomas Powell, ry. pres.; b. Newburgh, N.Y., Oct. 26, 1851; LL.B., Columbia, 1874; entered practice in New York. Pres. New York, Ont. & Western Ry., 1886-1902; dir. A.,T.&S.F. Ry. Co., Cal. Eastern Ry., Gulf, Colo. & Santa Fé Ry., Lehigh & Hudson River Ry. Co., Santa Fé, Prescott & Phœnix Ry. Co. Home: New York, N.Y. Died Oct. 12, 1915.

FOWLER, William Charles, M.D.; b. Washington, D.C., Nov. 24, 1864; s. Thomas Walter and Virginia (Wall) F.; M.D., Georgetown U. Med. Sch., 1888; m. Minnie Chauncey, Feb. 10, 1891; 1 dau., Minnie Chauncey (dec.); m. 2d, Laura Jaques, Aug. 27, 1932. Practiced in Washington, D.C.; health officer Dist. of Columbia, 1918-34. Mason. Methodist. Home: Washington, D.C. Died Nov. 19, 1937.

FOX, Albert Charles, clergyman, educator; b. Cincinnati, O., Sept. 9, 1878; s. Peter James and Mary Josephine (Quinn) F.; A.B., St. Xavier's Coll., Cincinnati, 1898, LL.D., 1922; M.A., St. Louis U., 1903; LL.D., Columbia U., 1928. Joined Soc. of Jesus (Jesuits), 1898; ordained priest R.C. Ch., 1910; v.p. St. Xavier's Coll., Cincinnati, 1913-18; pres. Campion Coll., Prairie du Chien, Wis., 1918-22; pres. Marquette U., 1922-28; dean John Carroll U., Cleveland, Aug. 1928—. Pres. Dept. Colls. and Secondary Schs. of Catholic Ednl. Assn.; chmn. Commn. on Standards, same assn.; mem. Nat. Com. on Coll. Standards of Am. Council on Edn.; mem. Com. on Revision of Standards of North Central Assn.; mem. Com. of Fifteen of Liberal Arts Coll. Movement; pres. Ohio Poetry Soc.; mem. Internat. Writers' League (life). Effected adoption of regional standards by all Catholic cols. of U.S. Rotarian. Died Sept. 8, 1934.

FOX, Austen George, lawyer; b. N.Y. City, Sept. 7, 1849; s. George Henry and Hannah C. (Austen) F.; A.B., Harvard, 1869, LL.B., 1871; m. Alice Hoppin, 1877. Admitted to N.Y. bar, 1872; spl. asst. dist. atty. in prosecution police officials after Lexow com. investigation, New York, 1894-96; counsel for defense, Sulzer Impeachment Trial, 1913; counsel opposing confirmation of apptmt. of Louis D. Brandeis to Supreme Court of U.S., 1916; Citizens' Union nominee for dist. atty., 1897; mem. Com. of 15, 1901; chmn. Com. of 9, police problem, 1905. Vice chmn. Anti-Imperialistic League, 1899; v.p. Assn. Opposed to 18th Amendment; mem. N.Y. State Bd. Law Examiners (past pres.). Home: Wickford, R.I. Died May 15, 1937.

FOX, Charles Eben, naval officer; b. Chelsea, Mass., Sept. 20, 1851; s. John Lawrence (surgeon U.S.N.) and Elizabeth Amory (Morris) F.; apptd. at-large, and grad. U.S. Naval Acad., 1872; m. Nelly Beckwith, June 10, 1884. Promoted ensign, 1873; master, 1879; lt., Aug. 1884; lt. comdr., Mar. 1899; comdr., Apr. 1902; capt., Aug. 5, 1906; rear-admiral, Sept. 16, 1910; retired, on own application, Aug. 1911. Homes: Washington, D.C., and Cazenovia, N.Y. Died Feb. 12, 1916.

FOX, Charles Eli, architect; b. Reading, Pa., July 1, 1870; s. William M. and Martha E. (McCauley) F.; entered for course in civ. engring., Lafayette Coll., Easton, Pa.; architectural course class of 1891, Mass. Inst. Tech.; unmarried. With Holabird & Roche, architects, Chicago, 1891-1904; mem. Marshall & Fox, 1904—; firm architects of Blackstone Hotel, Morrison Hotel, Lytton Bldg., and many Chicago skyscrapers; firm drew plans for colossal Victory Memorial as Chicago's tribute to heroes of World War. Mem. German Ref. Ch. Home: Chicago, Ill. Died Oct. 31, 1926.

FOX, Charles Shattuck, univ. prof.; b. Oil City, Pa., Nov. 8, 1868; s. William F. and Mary (Shattuck) F.; A.B., U. of Rochester, 1891; LL.B., Albany Law Sch., 1893; studied univs. Göttingen, Berlin, Chicago; A.M., Harvard, 1903, Ph.D., 1907; m. Bertha Sprague, Feb. 23, 1907; children—Beatrice Sprague, Norman. Instr. Morgan Park (Ill.) Acad., 1900-02; instr. modern langs., 1905-08, asst. prof., 1908-09, asst. prof. Romance langs., 1909-10, prof., 1910—, Lehigh U. Moravian. Author: Drill Book in Spanish Grammar, 1925. Home: Bethlehem, Pa. Died July 5, 1939.

FOX, Della, actress; b. St. Louis, Oct. 13, 1872; d. A. J. F.; first appearance, when 9 yrs. old, in child parts; later with James O'Neil and Marie Prescott; joined Bennett & Moulton Opera Co., then soubrette with Conried Opera Co. Played leading comedy parts in De Wolf Hopper Co. and Lillian Russell Opera Co.; starred in "The Little Trooper," 1894; and later in "Fleur-de-Lis"; appeared in "The Wedding Day," 1897; "The Little Host," 1898; appearing chiefly in vaudeville, 1900—; m. Jacob D. Levy, Dec. 26, 1900. Died June 16, 1913.

FOX, Edward J., lawyer; b. Easton, Pa., Apr. 3, 1858; s. Edward J. and Mary (Wilson) F.; brother of John F.; A.B., Lafayette Coll., 1878, A.M., 1881; LL.D., U. of Pa., Feb. 22, 1920; m. Cora L. Marsh, Oct. 9, 1888; children—Dorothy Rodman (dec.), Louis Rodman, Edward Jay. Admitted to bar, 1880; partner with father from 1882, until his death, 1889; with James W. Fox, 1896-1924; now with Edward J. Fox, Jr. President Easton Trust Company; dir. Lehigh & N.E. Railroad Co. and Lehigh Coal and Navigation Co. Delegate to Universal Congress Lawyers and Jurists, St. Louis, Mo., 1904. Trustee Lafayette Coll. Presbyterian. Democrat. Apptd. asso. justice Supreme Ct. of Pa., June 23, 1918, to fill vacancy caused by death of S. Leslie Mestrezat, term expiring Jan. 6, 1919. Home: Easton, Pa. Died Feb. 5, 1937.

FOX, George Henry, dermatologist; b. Ballston Spa, N.Y., Oct. 8, 1846; s. Rev. Norman and Jane (Freeman) F.; A.B., U. of Rochester, 1867, A.M., 1870; M.D., U. of Pa., 1869; univs., Berlin, Paris, Vienna and London, 1870-73; m. Harriet Gibbs, Aug. 29, 1872; children—Howard, Adaline (Mrs. Henry R. Russell), Alanson Gibbs, Helen (Mrs. Mason Trowbridge). Surgeon N.Y. Dispensary, 1873-75; clin. prof. diseases of the skin, Woman's Med. Coll. of N.Y. Infirmary, 1875-79; clin. prof. dermatology, Starling Med. Coll., Columbus, O., 1879; clin. prof. diseases of the skin, 1881-1904, prof. dermatology, 1904-07, Coll. Phys. and Surg. (Columbia); prof. skin diseases, Post-Grad. Med. Sch., 1890-95; cons. dermatologist, New York Bd. Health. Author: Photographic Atlas of Diseases of the Skin, 1900; Reminiscences, 1926; The Lineage of One Hundred American Physicians Named Fox, 1927. Home: New York, N.Y. Died May 3, 1937.

FOX, George Levi, educator; b. New Haven, Conn., Nov. 16, 1852; s. Levi G. and Elizabeth Hamlin (Bodfish) F.; A.B., Yale, 1874, LL.B., 1877, A.M., 1885; unmarried. Head classical dept., Hillhouse High Sch., New Haven, 1877-85; rector Hopkins Grammar Sch., New Haven, 1885-1901; established Univ. Sch., New Haven, 1901. Delivered course of 12 lectures on English Pub. Schs. before Lowell Inst.; lecturer on comparative municipal govt., Yale, 1896-1901. Mem. com. of 7 of Am. Hist. Assn., on teaching history. Visited Eng., Dec. 1909, to assist the Liberals in the campaign for the Budget and against the unconstitutional action of the House of Lords, and again, Dec. 1910, to campaign for the Liberals in the gen. election. Mem. Conn. Commn. on Arbitration and Mediation, 1917-20. Home: New Haven, Conn. Died Aug. 6, 1931.

FOX, Jabez, judge; b. Taunton, Mass., Apr. 10, 1850; s. Henry Hodges and Sarah Ann (Burt) F.; A.B., Harvard, 1871; LL.B., Harvard U. Law Sch., 1875; m. Susan E. Thayer, June 18, 1879. Admitted to Suffolk bar, 1876; in practice with late Charles Allen, 1878-82; justice Superior Ct. of Mass., Sept 1900-20. Active in formation of new Tariff Reform League, 1884, also civ. service reform clubs. Trustee Cambridge Pub. Library, 1893-1900; mem. Mass. State Bd. of Charity, 1896-1900; mem. State Bd. Bar Examiners, 1897-1900. Lecturer on Evidence, Boston U. Law Sch., 1896-1900. Conglist. Home: Cambridge, Mass. Deceased.

FOX, James D., judge; b. Fredericktown, Mo., Jan. 22, 1847; s. David M. and Elijah P. F.; ed. Fredericktown pub. schs., and St. Louis U., 1864-65; m. Laura A. Frazer, June 28, 1870. Admitted to bar, Fredericktown, in 20th year; circuit judge, 27th Jud. Circuit, Mo., 1880-1902; asso. justice Supreme Ct. of Mo., 1903—. Democrat. Home: Jefferson City, Mo. Died 1910.

FOX, John, clergyman; b. Doylestown, Pa., Feb. 13, 1853; s. Edward J. and Mary (Wilson) F.; bro. of Edward J. F.; A.B., Lafayette Coll., 1872, later A.M. (D.D., 1891, LL.D., 1912); grad. Princeton Theol. Sem., 1876; m. Margaret B. Kinkead, July 28, 1886. Ordained Presbyn. ministry, 1877; pastor Hampden Ch., Baltimore, 1877-82, North Ch., Allegheny, Pa., 1882-93, Second Ch., Brooklyn, N.Y., 1893-98; corr. sec. Am. Bible Soc., New York, 1898-1918. Mem. bd. dirs. and bd. trustees Princeton Theol. Sem. Home: Easton, Pa. Died Dec. 23, 1924.

FOX, John (William), Jr., author; b. Bourbon County, Ky., 1863; prep. edn. Transylvania Univ., Ky.; A.B., Harvard Univ., 1883. Member Nat. Inst. of Arts and Letters. Author: A Mountain Europa, 1894; A Cumberland Vendetta, 1895; Hell-for-Sartain, 1896; The Kentuckians, 1897; Crittenden, 1900; Bluegrass and Rhododendron, 1901; The Little Shepherd of Kingdom Come, 1903; Christmas Eve on Lonesome, 1904; Following The Sun Flag, 1905; Knight of the Cumberland, 1906; Trail of the Lonesome Pine, 1908; The Heart of the Hills, 1913. Home: Big Stone Gap, Va. Died July 8, 1919.

FOX, John McDill, lawyer; b. Milwaukee, Wis., Jan. 3, 1891; s. William (M.D.) and Narcissa (McDill) F.; A.B., Notre Dame, 1909; LL.B., Harvard, 1914; m. Elsa Sonnemann, June 27, 1914; children—Narcissa, Elinor, Eileen. Began law practice at Boston, Mass., with Whipple, Sears & Ogden, 1914; in ind. practice, Boston, 1914-16, at Milwaukee, Wis., 1916-30; instr. in law, Marquette U., 1918-30; dean of Sch. of Law, Catholic U. of America, 1930-35; sr. atty. for Registration Division of Securities and Exchange Commn., 1936-37; atty. for Consumers' Counsel Nat. Bituminous Coal Commn., 1937—. Republican. K.C. Mem. Mass., Wis., D.C. and U.S. Supreme Court bar. Home: Washington, D.C. Died Apr. 18, 1940.

FOX, Joseph John, bishop; b. Green Bay, Wis., Aug. 2, 1855; s. Paul and Frances (Bartel) F.; elementary edn. at Cathedral Sch., Green Bay; classics at St. Francis Sem., Milwaukee; philosophy and theology at Am. Coll. and U. of Louvain, Belgium, 1875-79 (D.D.). Ordained R.C. priest, June 7, 1879; first pastoral work at New Franken, Brown Co., Wis., then for 3 yrs. in charge St. John's Ch., Green Bay, also serving as sec. to Bishop Krautbauer, then bishop of Green Bay; rector Our Lady of Lourdes Ch., Marinette, Wis., 1883-94; vicar-gen. diocese of Green Bay, 1894-1904; apptd. domestic prelate to Pope Leo XIII, 1898; bishop of Green Bay, July 25, 1904—. Died Mar. 14, 1915.

FOX, L(awrance) Webster, ophthalmologist; b. Hummelstown, Pa., Mar. 19, 1853; s. Thomas G. and D. (Hershey) F.; student Pa. State Normal Sch., 1872-75; M.D., Jefferson Med. Coll., 1878; hon. A.M., Lafayette Coll., 1894; LL.D., Dickinson Coll., 1908; m. C. Beatrice Bickerton, of Liverpool, Eng., Sept. 4, 1889. Asst. ophthalmologist, Jefferson Med. Coll., 1882-85; ophthalmic surgeon Germantown Hosp., 1883-93; prof. ophthalmology, Medico-Chirurg. Coll., Phila., 1893—; also prof. ophthalmology, Grad. Sch. of Medicine, U. of Pa. Mem. Army Reserve Corps. Address: Philadelphia, Pa. Died June 4, 1931.

FOX, Norman, Bapt. clergyman; b. Glens Falls, N.Y., Feb. 13, 1836; s. Rev. Norman and Jane (Freeman) F.; grad. U. of Rochester, 1855 (D.D.); Rochester Theol. Sem., 1857. Pastor Bapt. ch., Whitehall, N.Y., 1859-62; chaplain 77th N.Y. vols., 1862-65; editor Central Baptist, St. Louis, 1868-70; prof. School of Theology, William Jewell Coll., Mo., 1870-73; spl. literary and religious work, 1873—; m. Julia T. McKnight, 1868 (died 1869); 2d. Jane B. Bleecker, 1874 (died 1880). Apptd. mem. Bd. of Excise Commrs., Morristown, N.J., 1898; elected mayor same, 1900. Apptd. 1901, mem. bd. mgrs. N.J. State Village for Epileptics. Home: Morristown, N.J. Died 1907.

FOX, Oscar Chapman, prin. examiner class of Tillage, U.S. Patent Office, July 1, 1873—; b. Pitcher, N.Y., Aug. 23, 1830; s. Daniel and Harriet Amanda (Chapman) F.; grad. Nat. Univ., law dept., 1876; m. Abbie Galt, Sept. 11, 1866. Capt. (bvt. maj.) 76th N.Y. vols.; disch. for wounds, Dec. 1862. Prin. Nelson Acad., Ohio, 3 yrs. Admitted to bar, 1876. Home: Washington, Ill. Died 1902.

FOX, Walter Dennis; b. nr. Murfreesboro, Tenn., July 4, 1867; s. William and Tennessee (Rowton) F. (of Irish descent); educated Ky. U., class of 1888; business course in Jennings' Business Coll., Nashville; m. Josie Williams Ewing, May 17, 1892 (died 1895); 2d, Sara Antoinette Bell, June 12, 1900. Grand Keeper of Records and Seal, Knights of Pythias, Tenn., 1904—. Founder of "Ovoca," a home and assembly grounds, nr. Tullahoma, Tenn. Gold Democrat. Home: Tullahoma, Tenn. Died Dec. 8, 1912.

FOX, William Freeman, supt. state forests, N.Y.; b. Ballston Spa, N.Y., Jan. 11, 1840; s. Rev. Norman and Jane (Freeman) F.; ed. Union Classical School, Schenectady, and Union Coll., class of 1860; served in Civil War as capt., maj. and lt. col. 107th N.Y. vols.; wounded at Antietam, Chancellorsville and Resaca; m. Mary Ann Shattuck, Sept. 28, 1865. For past 22 yrs. with State Forestry Dept. Mem. Soc. Am. Foresters; companion Mil. Order Loyal Legion; mem. N.Y. Hist. Soc.; pres. Chi Psi Alumni Assn., New York; corr. sec., Soc. Army of the Potomac; pres. Soc. Twelfth Army Corps. Author: Forest Tree Nurseries and Nursery Methods in Europe, 1905. Home: Albany, N.Y. Died 1909.

FOX, Williams Carlton, diplomatist; b. St. Louis, May 20, 1855; s. Elias Williams and Eusebia (Johnson) F.; ed. Washington U., St. Louis, and Pa. Mil. Coll., Chester; m. Louise Ludewig, of Brunswick, Germany, May 1, 1880. Am. consul at Brunswick, Germany, 1876-88; vice-consul-gen. Teheran, Persia, 1891-92; was in charge Am. legation there, and during cholera epidemic of 1892 he organized and financed the Am. Missionary Hosp. and Dispensary; received thanks of Shah of Persia and of Am. Bd. of Foreign Missions for this work; sec. to Am. minister to Greece, Roumania and Servia, 1892-93. Established, 1895, and carried on for some time only strictly diplomatic and consular jour. ever attempted in U.S. Chief clerk Bur. of Am. Republics, 1898-1905, dir. same, 1905-07; E.E. and M.P. to Ecuador, Jan. 10, 1907-Aug. 18, 1911; retired. Arbitrator in controversy between Govt. of Ecuador and The Guayaquil & Quito Ry. Co., 1907. Represented Internat. Union Am. Republics at 2d Internat. Am. Conf., Mexico, 1901-02, and at 3d Conf., Rio de Janeiro, 1906. Mem. Govt. Bd. of Management, Buffalo Expn., 1901, St. Louis Expn., 1904, Lewis and Clark Expn., 1905. Home: New York, N.Y. Died Jan. 20, 1924.

FOXCROFT, Frank, editor; b. Boston, Jan. 21, 1850; s. George A. and Harriet Elizabeth (Goodrich) F.; A.B., Williams Coll., 1871; m. Elizabeth D. Howard, Sept. 11, 1872 (died 1888); 2d, Lily Sherman Rice, Sept. 9, 1891. Asst. editor Boston Journal, 1871-1904; dept. editor The Youth's Companion, 1895-1911; editor of (Littell's) Living Age, 1896-1918. Civ. service commr. of Mass., 1904-13. Author: Transcript Pieces (original verse), 1868. Editor: Resurgit—A Collection of Hymns and Songs of the Resurrection, 1879; War Verse, 1918. Home: Cambridge, Mass. Died Dec. 10, 1921.

FOY, Eddie (Edward Fitzgerald), actor; b. N.Y. City, Mar. 9, 1857; s. Richard and Ellen (Hennessy) F.; m. Madeline Morando; m. Marie Combs, Jan. 9, 1923. Made début in Chicago, 1869; played in variety theatres in all parts of U.S.; toured in "The Tigers," "Jack-in-the-Box," "Over the Garden Wall," etc.; played in "Sindbad," "Ali Baba," "Cinderella," "Bluebeard," etc.; starred as Jim Cheese in "The Earl and the Girl," 1905-06, as Momus in "Up and Down Broadway," 1910, etc.; starred with family in "That Casey Girl," 1923. Home: New Rochelle, N.Y. Died Feb. 16, 1928.

FOYE, Andrew Jay Coleman, mcht., mfr.; b. Northumberland Co., Pa., Dec. 23, 1833; moved in childhood to Morrow Co., O.; grad. high school, Mt. Gilead, O.; in business there until 1859; consecutively clerk, traveler and partner in dry-goods trade, New York, 1859-71; traveled in America and Europe 5 yrs.; has been for many yrs. dir. and New York mgr. Joseph Dixon Crucible Co.; is now pres. the Standard Graphite Co.; has other business interests; m. Katherine Sophia House, Feb. 12, 1862. Home: New York, N.Y. Died 1905.

FOYE, Wilbur Garland, prof. geology; b. Brockton, Mass., Feb. 8, 1886; s. Josiah Williams and Helen (Howard) F.; A.B., Colby Coll., 1909; A.M., Harvard Univ., 1912, Ph.D., 1915; M.A., Wesleyan Univ., Conn., 1925; m. Evelyn Louise Ryder, Aug. 9, 1916; children—Howard Ryder, William Dean. Austin teaching fellow, Harvard, 1912-15, Sheldon traveling fellow, 1915-16; asst. prof. geology, Middlebury Coll., 1916-18; asso. prof. geology, Wesleyan U., Conn., 1918-24, prof., 1924—. Fellow Geol. Soc. America, Am. Geog. Soc., A.A.A.S. Republican. Baptist. Author: (with William N. Rice) The Geology of Middletown, Conn. (Conn. Geol. and Natural History Survey), 1927. Home: Middletown, Conn. Died Jan. 9, 1935.

FRACHTENBERG, Leo Joachim, anthropologist; b. Czernautz, Austria, Feb. 24, 1883; s. Abraham and Jeanette (Rottenstreich) F.; grad. Imperial Royal Gymnasium, Przemysl, Austria, 1904; studied Cornell U., 1904-05; M.A., Columbia, 1906, Ph.D., 1910; m. Claudia E. McDonald, May 22, 1913; children—Margaret Janet, Maurice James, Richard (dec.). Asst. supt. Ednl. Alliance, N.Y. City, 1907-09; expert to Commn. on Crime and Dependency, N.J., 1909; asst. U.S. Immigration Commn., 1909-10; chief of fgn. population, U.S. Census for N.Y. City, 1910; lecturer on anthropology, Columbia, 1910-12; ethnologist, Bur. of Am. Ethnology, 1913-17; translator, Dept. of Justice (war work), Com. on Pub. Information, 1917-18; head worker Jewish Welfare Bd., at Camp Humphreys, Va., and Camp Funston, Kan., 1918-19; dir. service clubs, rank of capt., and supervisor service clubs, rank of lt. col., for Central Dept., U.S.A., 1919-20; hon. disch. from army, Nov. 7, 1920; gen. sec. Y.M. Hebrew Assn., Troy, N.Y., June 1921; regional dir. Palestine Foundation Fund, 1922-23, nat. field dir., 1923—, exec. dir. region 4, 1922-27, region 10, 1927—. Researches among Indians of N. America, especially those living on Pacific Coast, seeking establishment of genetic relationships between several langs. spoken by Indians of Northwest Coast. Fellow Am. Ethnological Soc., Am. Geog. Society. Democrat. Author: Coos Texts, 1913; Coos, an Illustrative Sketch, 1914; Lower Umpqua Texts, 1914; Siuslawan, an Illustrative Sketch, 1917; Alsea Texts and Myths, 1919. Home: Chicago, Ill. Died Nov. 26, 1930.

FRADENBURGH, Adelbert Grant, college prof.; b. Pt. Peninsula, N.Y., Sept. 15, 1868; s. Jason Nelson and Lucetta (Minor) F.; B.A., Allegheny Coll., Pa., 1890; Johns Hopkins, 1891-92; Ph.D., U. of Wis., 1894; m. Julia Edson, June 18, 1895; children—Miriam, Adelbert. Instr. in economics, Lake Forest (Ill.) U., 1894-96; asst. prof. history and politics, Adelphi Coll., Brooklyn, 1896-1900, prof., 1900-26; dean Coll. City N.Y., Brooklyn Coll. Center, 1926-30; dean Brooklyn Coll., 1930—. Mem. city com., Citizens' Union, N.Y. City. Democrat. Congregationalist. Home: Brooklyn, N.Y. Died July 2, 1936.

FRAILEY, Leonard August, rear adm.; b. Washington, Aug. 8, 1843; s. Charles S. and Caroline M. B. F.; ed. Union Acad., Gonzaga Coll. and Young Commercial Coll.; m. Helen Watson Freeman, Sept. 28, 1869. Apptd. acting asst. p.-m. U.S.N., Aug. 20, 1864; passed asst. p.-m., July 23, 1866; p.-m., Jan. 29, 1869; pay insp., May 24, 1894; pay dir., Aug. 29, 1899; retired at own request after 40 yrs'. service, Feb. 17, 1905, with rank of rear admiral, for services during Civil War. Home: Washington, D.C. Died Dec. 31, 1913.

FRAME, Alice Browne, educator; b. of Am. parents, Harpoot, Turkey, Oct. 29, 1878; d. John Kittredge and Leila (Kendall) Browne; B.A., Mt. Holyoke Coll., 1900 (Phi Beta Kappa), hon. Litt.D., 1925; B.D., Hartford Theol. Sem., 1903; studied Columbia, 1913, Union Theol. Sem., 1921; m. Rev. Murray Scott Frame, Oct. 10, 1913 (died 1918); children—Frances Kendall (dec.), Murray S. (dec.), Rosamond. Sec. Young People's Work, Women's Bd. of Missions (Congl. Ch.), Boston, 1903-05; prin. Fu Yu Girls' Sch., Tungchou, China, 1906-10; teacher N. China Union Women's Coll., 1912; with Yenching Coll., Peiping, from 1918, dean, 1922-31; acting dean of residence at Mt. Holyoke Coll., 1928-29; became gen. sec. of North China Kunghimi, Pekin, China. Republican. Conglist. Home: Peking, China. Died Aug. 16, 1941.

FRAME, Andrew Jay, banker; b. Waukesha, Wis., Feb. 19, 1844; s. Maxwell and Jane (Aitken) F.; ed. pub. schs., Waukesha; LL.D., Carroll Coll., Waukesha, 1908; m. Emma J. Richardson, Aug. 25, 1869. Office boy Waukesha Co. Bank, 1862; asst. cashier, 1865, cashier, 1866-80, became pres. 1880, Waukesha Nat. Bank (chmn. bd.); organized Waukesha Malleable Iron Co., 1894, Waukesha Springs Sanitarium, 1902 (chmn. bd.); trustee Northwestern Mut. Life Ins. Co., Milwaukee. Authority on financial subjects. Trustee Carroll Coll., 41 yrs., and treas.; mem. sch. bd., Waukesha, 27 yrs. (pres. 3 yrs.). Republican. Baptist. Mason. Appeared on invitation of chairmen of coms. of Ho. of Rep. and of Senate com. on banking and currency, as an expert in formulating Glass-Owen bill. Home: Waukesha, Wis. Died Oct. 4, 1932.

FRANCE, Evalyn Smith, philanthropist; b. Port Deposit, Md.; d. Henry Clay and Hannah (Elizabeth) Nesbitt; M.E.L., Wesleyan Coll., Del., 1873; m. Jacob Tome, 1884, and founder with him of The Jacob Tome Inst. (he died 1898); m. 2d, Hon. Joseph I. France, June 24, 1903. Pres. bd. trustees Jacob

Tome Inst., 1894-1903; pres. Cecil Nat. Bank, Port Deposit, 1898-1905, Nat. Bank of Elton, Md., 1898-1904; now dir. various corps. Homes: Port Deposit, and Baltimore, Md. Died Apr. 22, 1927.

FRANCE, Joseph Irwin, M.D., senator; b. Oct. 11, 1873; s. Joseph Henry (A.B., LL.B., D.D.) and Hannah Fletcher (James) F.; A.B., Hamilton Coll., Clinton, N.Y., 1895 (Elihu Root foreign fellowship); U. of Leipzig; Clark U.; M.D., Coll. Phys. and Surg., Baltimore, 1903; m. Evalyn S. (Nesbitt) Tome, June 24, 1903 (died 1927); m. 2d, Tatiana Vladimirovna Dechtereva, Paris, France, July 13, 1927. Practiced medicine in Baltimore, Md.; sec. Medical and Chirurg. Faculty of Md., 1916-17; mem. Md. Senate, 1905-09; del. Rep. Nat. Conv., 1908; finance and business, 1906—; U.S. senator from Md., term 1917-23. Special student of Russian economic conditions. Renominated for U.S. Senate, 1922; candidate against Herbert Hoover, 1931-32, for Rep. presidential nomination; engaged in internat. trade; pres. Republic Internat. Corp.; mem. State Planning Commn. of Maryland; mem. Md. State Board of Health; v.p. bd. trustees Jacob Tome Inst. of Port Deposit, Md. Mason. Presbyn. Home: Port Deposit, Md. Died Jan. 26, 1939.

FRANCE, Lewis B., lawyer, author; b. Washington, Aug. 8, 1833; academic edn. in Georgetown (D.C.) Coll.; practices law in Colo. Author: Rod and Line, 1884; Mountain Trails and Parks in Colorado, 1886; Mr. Dide, His Vacation, 1890; Over the Old Trail, 1894; Pine Valley, 1897; Scraps, 1899. Prepared vols. 3 to 11, Reports of Supreme Court of Colo., etc. Home: Denver, Colo. Died 1907.

FRANCINE, Albert Philip, physician; b. at Phila., Dec. 8, 1873; s. Albert Philip and Anna French (Hollingshead) F.; A.B., U. of Pa. 1894; A.M., Harvard, 1895; M.D., U. of Pa., 1898; m. Emilie D. Ehret, Apr. 27, 1912. Formerly asso. prof. medicine, Post-Grad. Sch. of Medicine, U. of Pa.; chief of the Div. of Tuberculosis, Pa. State Dept. of Health, Harrisburg. Now clinical dir. of tuberculosis, U.S. Veterans' Bur., Washington, D.C. Lt. col. M.O.R.C., U.S.A. Republican. Episcopalian. Home: Philadelphia, Pa. Deceased.

FRANCIS, Charles Edward, dentist; b. Hartford, Conn., Jan. 24, 1828; s. George F.; ed. there; studied medicine under preceptor and took partial med. course Univ. Med. Coll., New York; grad. Pa. Coll. of Dentistry, D.D.S., 1867 (M.D.S., Regents' Univ. of N.Y.); m. Abbie H. Sutherland, 1852. One of the original corporators N.Y. Coll. of Dentistry; a founder and 1st pres. N.Y. Odontol. Soc.; a founder and pres. 1st Dist. Dental Soc. of N.Y. State; pres. Dental Soc. State of N.Y.; emeritus prof. dental dept. U. of Buffalo, N.Y.; retired from practice, 1901. Home: Stamford, Conn. Died 1905.

FRANCIS, Charles Spencer, ambassador; b. Troy, N.Y., June 17, 1853; s. John Morgan (diplomatist and founder Troy Times) and Harriet E. (Tucker) F.; prep. edn. Troy Acad.; grad. Cornell, 1877; m. Alice d. late Prof. Evan Evans, of Cornell U., May 23, 1878. Repeatedly won single scull and long-distance running championships of univ.; won inter-collegiate single scull championship, Saratoga Lake, 1876 (time: 2 miles in 13 minutes and 42¾ seconds). Successively reporter, city editor and mgr., Troy Times; acquired interest, 1881, equal partner with father, 1887, and on latter's death, 1897, succeeded to editorial direction and sole ownership. Was sec. to his father during the latter's 3 yrs'. residence at Athens as U.S. minister to Greece; E.E. and M.P. to Greece, Roumania and Servia, 1900-02; ambassador extraordinary and plenipotentiary to Austria-Hungary, Mar. 22, 1906-10 (both posts previously held by his father). Republican. Was officer on staff of Gov. Alonzo B. Cornell, of N.Y. and Maj. Gen. J. B. Carr, N.G.S.N.Y.; twice elected alumni trustee Cornell U.; twice elected by legislature regent U. State of N.Y., 1903-06. Vice pres. N.Y. Soc. for Preservation of Scenic and Historic Places and Objects. Home: Troy, N.Y. Died 1911.

FRANCIS, David Rowland, secretary the interior; b. Richmond, Ky., Oct. 1, 1850; s. John B. and Eliza (Rowland) F.; went to St. Louis, 1866; A.B., Washington U., 1870; LL.D., U. of Mo., 1892, Shurtleff Coll., 1903, St. Louis U., 1904, Washington U., 1905; m. Jane Perry, 1876. Became clerk and afterward partner in a commn. house; in 1877 established what became Francis Bro. & Co., and D. R. Francis & Bro. Commn. Co., grain mchts., of which he is pres.; v.p. Merchants-Laclede Nat. Bank; pres. Madison Co. Ferry Co.; trustee N.Y. Life Ins. Co. Mayor St. Louis, 1885-89; gov. of Mo., 1889-93; Sec. of the Interior, in cabinet of President Cleveland, 1896-97; pres. La. Purchase Centennial Expn. of 1904; apptd. A.E. and M.P. to Russia, Mar. 6, 1916. Pres. Merchants' Exchange, St. Louis, 1884; pres. Bd. of Curators of U. of Mo., Hosp. Saturday and Sunday Assn. (St. Louis), Mo. Hist. Soc.; dir. St. Louis Art Mus. Democrat. Home: St. Louis, Mo. Died Jan. 15, 1927.

FRANCIS, George Blinn, civil engr.; b. W. Hartford, Conn., Jan. 31, 1857; s. Blinn and Lucy (Hart) F.; ed. Hartford High Sch.; (hon. A.M., Brown U., 1905); m. Florence Louise Green, Apr. 11, 1882. Began civ. engring. in 1874; identified with numerous important works; in st. ry. engring. and other railroad work. Mason. Home: New York. Died June 9, 1913.

FRANCIS, James A., clergyman; b. Upper Stewiacke, N.S., Mar. 20, 1864; s. Daniel (M.D.) and Crystie Ann (Tupper) F.; ed. common schs. and home study; D.D., Denison U., Granville, O.; m. Nellie Stewart, Nov. 2, 1891. Clk. in Boston, 1884-87; sec. branch Y.M.C.A., Boston, 1887-88; ordained Bapt. ministry, 1888; pastor Peterboro, N.H., 1888-91, Riverside Ch., New York, 1891-98, 2d Av. Ch., New York, 1898-1902, Clarendon St. Ch., Boston, 1902-03; evangelist Am. Bapt. Home Mission Soc., 1905-09; again pastor Clarendon St. Ch., Boston, 1909-14, 1st Ch., Los Angeles, Calif., Dec. 1, 1914—. Spl. speaker for Y.M.C.A. in the cantonments of the Pacific Coast and Tex., July 4-Dec. 25, 1917 and with A.E.F. in camps in Eng., Ireland, Scotland, France and Germany, July 1918-Jan. 1919; speaker for League to Enforce Peace, 1919. Pres. Calif. State Fedn. of Chs. Author: The Real Jesus, and Other Sermons, 1926. Home: Los Angeles, Calif. Died June 30, 1928.

FRANCIS, John Haywood, supt. schs.; b. Preble Co., O., May 18, 1867; s. George and Mary (Fall) F.; A.B., Otterbein U., Westerville, O. (LL.D., 1917); A.B., A.M., San Joaquin Valley Coll., Woodbridge, Calif, 1892; m. Lou L. Hott, June 4, 1892. Teacher and prin. schs., Los Angeles, Calif., 1896-1910, supt. schs., 1910-16; supt. schs., Columbus, O., 1916—. Home: Columbus, O. Deceased.

FRANCIS, John Miller, chemist; b. Jacksonville, Ala., Oct. 25, 1867; s. Miller W. and Julia (Clark) F.; M.A., U. of Ala., 1887; grad. work in organic chemistry Johns Hopkins University, 1889-90; m. Evie E. Harris, 1891. Adj. prof. chemistry, U. of Ala., 1887-92; chemist, Parke, Davis & Co., Detroit, Mich., 1892—, chief chemist, Aug. 1904—. Mem. Com. Revision U.S. Pharmacopœia. Republican. Presbyn. Home: Detroit, Mich. Died Jan. 8, 1924.

FRANCIS, John Morgan, editor, pub.; b. Troy, N.Y., Apr. 30, 1879; s. Charles Spencer and Alice (Evans) F.; B.A., Cornell U., 1902; m. Florence Hastings Lovell, Apr. 16, 1903. One of proprs. Troy Times. Has written several plays which have been published. Republican. Mason. Attended Central O.T. Sch., Camp Zachary Taylor, Ky., 1918. Home: Troy, N.Y. Died Oct. 25, 1925.

FRANCIS, Joseph Marshall, bishop; b. Eaglesmere, Pa., Apr. 6, 1862; s. James B. and Charlotte A. (Marshall) F.; ed. Racine Coll. and Oxford U., Eng.; D.D., Nashotah, 1899, Hobart Coll., 1901; m. Kate Stevens, 1887. Deacon, 1884, priest, 1886, P.E. Ch.; pastorates at Milwaukee and Greenfield, Wis., 1884-85; canon of Cathedral, Milwaukee, 1886-87; rector, Whitewater, Wis., 1887-88; went to Japan as missionary and became priest in charge of cathedral at Tokyo, and prof. in Trinity Divinity Sch. there; returned from Japan, 1897; rector St. Paul's Ch., Evansville, Ind., Jan. 1898; consecrated bishop of Ind., Sept. 21, 1899. Chaplain, Base Hosp. No. 32, in France, 1917. Mem. Domestic and Foreign Missionary Soc. (now the Nat. Council), 1904-34; vice chmn. House of Bishops, 1934. Decorated Officer, Order of the Crown (Belgium). Died Feb. 13, 1939.

FRANCIS, Mark, veterinarian; b. Shandon, O., Mar. 19, 1863; s. Abner and Martha Ann (Vaughan) F.; D.V.M., Ohio State U., 1887; 1 yr. at Am. Vet. Coll., New York; some time at U. of Mich.; Berlin and Munich, 1904; LL.D., Miami U., 1929; m. Anna J. Scott, Sept. 10, 1890; children—Andrew Jones (dec.), William Bebb. Professor veterinary science from 1888, dean Sch. Vet. Medicine, 1916—, Agrl. and Mech. Coll. of Texas. Veterinarian to Tex. Expt. Sta. and introduced methods of producing immunity to Texas fever by subcutaneous injections with infected cattle blood. Home: College Station, Texas. Died June 28, 1936.

FRANCISCO, John Bond, painter, violinist; b. Cincinnati, O., Dec. 14, 1863; s. Andrew Wiggins and Ella (Clark) F.; ed. Ohio State U.; studied painting in Munich and Berlin, and at Julian and Colorossi acads., Paris; pupil of Fechner, Nauen, Bouguereau, Robert-Fleury and Coutoir; studied violin with Wirth, Berlin, Walter, Munich, Leonard, Paris; m. Nanette Louise, d. Judge Louis Gottschalk, formerly of St. Louis, June 6, 1894; children—Yvette (dec.), Mrs. Nanette Louise McGaffey, Jack Bond. Traveled and sketched in Switzerland, the Tyrol, Germany and France; settled at Los Angeles, 1887; conducted art sch. until 1901; painter of figures and landscapes, especially of Calif. mountains and trees; mem. jury Dept. of Fine Arts, Chicago Expn. Republican. Episcopalian. Mason. Home: Los Angeles, Calif. Died Jan. 8, 1931.

FRANCKE, Kuno, univ. prof.; b. Kiel, Germany, Sept. 27, 1855; s. Judge August Wilhelm S. and Katharine Marie (Jensen) F.; grad. Gymnasium, Kiel, 1873; Ph.D., U. of Munich, 1878 (honorary, 1928); LL.D., U. of Wisconsin, 1904; Litt.D., Harvard, 1912; m. Katharine Gilbert, June 27, 1889; children—K. Marie (Mrs. Elliott Dunlap Smith), H. Gilbert, Hugo (dec.). Instructor, 1884-87, asst. prof. German, 1887-92, asst. prof. German lit., 1892-96, prof. history of German culture, 1896-1917, curator Germanic Mus., 1902-17, prof. emeritus and hon. curator, 1917, Harvard. Chevalier Royal Prussian Order Red Eagle, and Order of Crown. Fellow Am. Acad. Arts and Sciences, Am. Philos. Soc., Mediæval Acad. of America. Author: History of German Literature, 1901; Handbook of the Germanic Museum, 1906; German Ideals of To-day, 1907; Die Kulturwerte der deutschen Literatur des Mittelalters, 1910; A German-American's Confession of Faith, 1915; The German Spirit, 1916; Personality in German Literature before Luther, 1916; Die Kulturwerte der deutschen Literatur von der Reformation bis zur Aufklärung, 1923; Deutsches Schicksal, 1923; Kant and Art, 1925; German After-War Problems, 1927; Weltbuergertum, 1928; Deutsche Arbeit in Amerika, 1930. Editor in chief German Classics of the XIX and XX Centuries. Home: Cambridge, Mass., and Gilbertsville, N.Y. Died June 25, 1930.

FRANK, Abraham, hotelman; b. Chicago, Ill., April 13, 1871; s. of Jacob and Rose (Tobias) F.; ed. pub. schs.; m. Anna Barker, Nov. 18, 1890; children—Benjamin L., Lester E., Louisa A. Began as clk. in ry. ticket office; asso. with Fred Harvey in establishing on the A.,T.&S.F. R.R. the Fred Harvey dining system, of which was supt., 1888-1903; managing dir. and part owner Sherman Hotel, Chicago, 1903-08; also mgr. Rector's, College Inn and North American restaurants, Chicago; managing owner Oliver Hotel, South Bend, Ind., to 1920; v.p. and gen. mgr. Ambassador Hotel Corp., 1921—. Republican. Jewish religion. Mason. Home: Los Angeles, Calif. Died Sept. 17, 1932.

FRANK, Fritz John, publisher; b. Emporium, Pa., Sept. 9, 1871; s. Joseph Warren and Eliza (Campbell) F.; A.B., Rollins Coll., Winter Park, Fla., 1896; m. Anna Raynor Bush, Mar. 11, 1909. Advertising mgr. Mines and Minerals (mag.), 1898-1907; pres. Savage Safety Brake Co., 1907-09; pres. Iron Age Pub. Co.; exec. v.p. Chilton Co.; dir. Robbins Pub. Co. Trustee Rollins Coll. Home: Madison, N.J. Died Dec. 8, 1939.

FRANK, Glenn, publicist, editor; b. in Queen City, Mo., Oct. 1, 1887; s. Gordon and Nancy Elizabeth (Hombs) F.; spl. student Kirksville (Mo.) State Normal Sch., 3 yrs.; B.A., Northwestern U., 1912, M.A., 1921; Litt.D., Lincoln Memorial U., 1922, DePauw U., 1923; L.H.D., U. of Mich., 1924; LL.D., Northwestern U., 1926, Temple Univ., 1934, Lake Forest U., 1937, Rollins Coll., 1938; m. Mary Smith, June 2, 1917; 1 son, Glenn. Asst. to president Northwestern U., 1912-16; in business research and orgn., 1916-19; asso. editor Century Magazine, 1919-21, editor in chief, May 1921-Sept. 1, 1925; pres. U. of Wis., Sept. 1, 1925-July 1, 1937; editor and pub., July 1, 1937—. Lecturer in U.S. and Canada, 1912—. Chairman Rep. Program Committee, 1938-40. Methodist. Author: The Politics of Industry, 1919; An American Looks at His World, 1923; Thunder and Dawn—Studies in the Outlook for Western Civilization, 1932; America's Hour of Decision, 1934. Part author: Stakes of the War, 1918; The League of Nations—The Principle and the Practice, 1919. Writer of a daily editorial syndicated in Am. newspapers, 1925—. Home: Madison, Wis. Died Sept. 15, 1940.

FRANK, Henry, lecturer, author; b. Lafayette, Ind., Dec. 21, 1854; s. Jacob H. and Henrietta (Auerbach) F.; grad. Phillips Acad., Andover, Mass., 1874, student Harvard U., 1874; m. Carrie Cleveland, 1876 (dec.); m. 2d, Alice R. Field, Jan. 14, 1886; 1 son, Crosby Field. Prof. of lit. and history, Cornell Coll., Mt. Vernon, Ia., 1876-77; was M.E. minister, then pastor Congl. Ch., Jamestown, N.Y., 1886; renounced orthodoxy and originated Independent Congl. (New Theology) Ch., Jamestown, 1888; founded, 1897, and lecturer Met. (Ethical Religious) Soc., New York; called to San Francisco, 1917, to succeed Dr. Charles Aked; founded and was leader People's Liberal Ch., San Francisco. Author: Doom of Dogma and Dawn of Truth, 1901; Modern Light on Immortality, 1909, 2d ed., 1912; The Tragedy of Hamlet, 1910; Psychic Phenomena, Science and Immortality, 1911, 16; The Story of America, 1912; The Clash of Thrones (sonnets on the Great War), 1915; The Challenge of the War—Can Science Answer Riddle of the Grave? 1919; The Last Enigma (British and Am. edits.), 1924, 27; Jesus, A Modern Critical Study, 1930. Home: San Diego, Calif. Died July 31, 1933.

FRANK, Isaac William, machinery mfg.; b. Pittsburgh, Pa., Dec. 2, 1855; s. William and Paulina (Womser) F.; prep. edn., Newell Inst., Pittsburgh; C.E., Rensselaer Poly. Inst., 1876; m. Tinnie Klee, Nov. 15, 1883; children—Mrs. Bessie Anathan, William K., Robert J. Draftsman Keystone Bridge Co., 1876-77; insp. materials New York Elevated R.R. Co., 1877; asst. engr. on Mississippi River improvement, 1878; dep. U.S. mineral surveyor, 1879-80; sec. and engr. Lewis Foundry & Machine Co., of Pittsburgh,

1880-92; organizer 1892, and pres. Frank-Kneeland Machinery Co., 1892-1901; organizer, 1901, and thereafter pres. United Engring., 1921—. Trustee, Rensselaer Poly. Inst., U. of Pittsburgh. Mem. Rodolf Shalom Congregation, Y.M. and Y.W. Hebrew Assn., etc. Republican. Home: Pittsburgh, Pa. Died Dec. 1, 1930.

FRANK, Nathan, lawyer; b. Peoria, Ill., Feb. 23, 1852; s. Abraham and Branette (Weil) F.; ed. St. Louis High Sch.; Washington U.; LL.B., Harvard, 1872; unmarried. Practiced in St. Louis from 1874, making specialty of corp. law. Unsuccessfully contested election of John F. Glover to 50th Congress; mem. 51st Congress (1889-91), 12th Mo. Dist., chmn. Rep. State Exec. Com. during McKinley campaign of 1896. V.p. and later mem. exec. com. La. Purchase Expn., 1904. Founder of St. Louis Star. Home: St. Louis, Mo. Died Apr. 5, 1931.

FRANK, Royal Thaxter, army officer; b. Gray, Me., May 6, 1836; s. Alpheus and Nioma (Stimson) F.; grad. U.S. Mil. Acad., 1858. Bvt. 2d lt. 5th Inf., July 1, 1858; 2d lt. 8th Inf., Oct. 19, 1858; 1st lt., May 14, 1861; capt., Feb. 27, 1862; transferred to 1st Arty., Dec. 15, 1870; maj. Jan. 2, 1881; lt. col. 2d Arty., Jan. 25, 1889; col. 1st Arty., Oct. 25, 1894; brig. gen. vols., May 4, 1898; hon. disch. from vol. service, May 12, 1899; brig. gen. U.S.A., Oct. 17, 1899; retired at own request after 40 yrs.' service, Oct. 18, 1899. Bvtd. maj., July 3, 1862, for gallant and meritorious services in peninsular campaign; lt. col., Dec. 13, 1862, for same in battle of Fredericksburg, Va. Home: Washington, D.C. Died 1908.

FRANK, Tenney, univ. prof.; b. Clay Center, Kan., May 19, 1876; s. Oliver and Caroline (Danielson) F.; A.B., U. of Kan., 1898, A.M., 1899; Ph.D., U. of Chicago, 1903; studied U. of Göttingen, 1910, U. of Berlin, 1910-11; m. Grace Edith Mayer, 1907. Instr. Latin, U. of Chicago, 1901-04; asso. and prof. Latin, Bryn Mawr, 1904-19; prof. Latin, Johns Hopkins U., 1919—; Horace White lecturer, Bryn Mawr (Pa.) Coll., 1929; Sather lecturer, U. of Calif., 1929-30; Martin lecturer, Oberlin Coll., 1931; lecturer on Hertz Foundation, British Acad., 1931-32; George Eastman visiting prof., Oxford, Eng., 1938-39; annual prof., 1916-17, prof. in charge, 1922-23 and 1924-25, Classical Sch., Am. Acad. in Rome; Am. del. to Union Acad. Internationale, 1925. Fellow British Acad., Swedish Royal Soc. of Letters, Am. Acad. Arts and Sciences. Author: Roman Imperialism, 1914; Economic History of Rome, 1920, revised 1927; Vergil, a Biography, 1922; A History of Rome, 1923; Roman Buildings of the Republic, 1924; Catullus and Horace, 1928; Life and Literature of the Roman Republic, 1930; Aspects of Social Behavior in Ancient Rome, 1931; Cicero (lecture), 1932; An Economic Survey of Ancient Rome (Vol. I), 1933; Chapters in Cambridge Ancient History, Vols. VII, VIII, and Encyclopædia of Social Sciences, Vol. I. Translator: Bynkershoek's Quaestiones Juris Publici, 1931. Home: Baltimore, Md. Died Apr. 3, 1939.

FRANKEL, Lee Kaufer, insurance; b. Phila., Aug. 13, 1867; s. Louis and Aurelia (Lobenburg) F.; B.S., U. of Pa., 1887, Ph.D., 1891; m. Alice Reizenstein, Apr. 18, 1898. Instr. chemistry, U. of Pa., 1888-93; cons. chemist, Phila., 1893-99; v.p. and pres. Chem. Sect., Franklin Inst., 1895-98; mgr. United Hebrew Charities, New York, 1899-1908; spl. investigator Russell Sage Foundation, 1908; with Met. Life Ins. Co., 1909—, now 2d v.p. Was mem. Ellis Island Commn., 1903; commr. State Bd. of Charities; welfare dir. P.O. Dept., 1921-22. Dir. Nat. Assn. for Study and Prevention of Tuberculosis (v.p. 1914), Am. Pub. Health Assn. (treas.; pres. 1919), Nat. Conf. Jewish Charities (pres. 1912), Survey Associates (nat. council), Life Extension Inst. (hygiene reference bd.); pres. N.Y. State Conf. Charities and Correction, 1917; chmn. spl. European commn. Am. Jewish Relief Com., 1922; chmn. Nat. Health Council, 1923-25; v.p. Nat. Conf. of Social Work, 1923-24; chmn. Commn. of Experts making survey of Palestine under auspices of Jewish Agency, 1927. Author: Workingmen's Insurance in Europe, 1911; The Human Factor in Industry, 1920; The Health of the Worker, 1924; Ency. of Health, 1925. Home: New York, N.Y. Died July 25, 1931.

FRANKENFIELD, Harry Crawford, meteorologist; b. Easton, Pa., Nov. 24, 1862; s. David Daniel and Susan (Eichman) F.; A.B., Lafayette Coll., 1881, A.M., 1884; M.D., Howard U., 1886; m. Katharine Presley, d. Judge Anthony Thornton, of Shelbyville, Ill., Nov. 24, 1891. In charge U.S. Weather Bur. office, Chicago, 1887-94, St. Louis, 1894-98; forecaster and prof. meteorology, U.S. Weather Bur., 1898-1920. Also in charge of river and flood service, mountain snowfall investigations and coöperative meteorol. forest expt. stas., 1898-1912, 1921-27. Wrote Bulletins F, M, and Y, Weather Bureau—Report on Kite Observations, 1899; Report on Spring Floods of 1903, and Report on Floods of 1912 and 1922. Died July 29, 1929.

FRANKLAND, Frederick William; b. Manchester, Eng., Apr. 18, 1854; s. late Sir Edward (K.C.B.), and Sophie Jeannette Christiana (Fick) F.; attended U. of London, 1870; m. Miriam Symons of Foxton, New Zealand, Apr. 30, 1879. Entered New Zealand civil service, 1876; govt. ins. commr., 1889; del. from New Zealand Govt. to Internat. Congress of Hygiene and Demography, 1891; later asso. actuary N.Y. Life Ins. Co.; retired and apptd. justice of the peace in New Zealand, 1907. Fellow Inst. Actuaries Great Britain and Ireland, Actuarial Soc. America, Am. Math. Soc., A.A.A.S. Traveled, 1903 and 1910, during latter year arranging with Am. capitalists for purchase of large lumber interests in New Zealand, and with English capitalists for purchase of water powers. Died July 24, 1916.

FRANKLIN, Benjamin A.; b. Northumberland County, Va., Oct. 15, 1869; s. Benjamin A. and Placidia (Cralle) F.; student Johns Hopkins, 1887-1889; hon. Master Humanics, Internat. Y.M.C.A. Coll., 1924; m. Jeanette Haslett, of England, Apr. 25, 1896; children—Benjamin Allan, Paul Lawrence. With Midvale Steel Co., Phila., 1889-1902; organizer, 1902, Miller, Franklin & Co., efficiency engrs., N.Y. City (of which was treas.), now Miller & Franklin Co.; with Strathmore Paper Co., Springfield, Mass., 1909-32, v.p., 1911-32. Industrial eng. and bus. counsel; sec.-treas. Specialty Paper and Board Affiliates; chmn. bd. Perkins Machine and Gear Co.; trustee Internat. Y.M.C.A. Coll., Springfield branch Northeastern University; chmn. board Am. Youth Council, Inc. Maj., lt. col. and col. Ordnance Dept., U.S.A.; chief Hartford Ordnance District. Distinguished Service Medal, 1919. Republican. Episcopalian. Author: Cost Reports for Executives, 1913; Experiences in Efficiency, 1915; The Industrial Executive, 1925; Banners in the Wind (a personal philosophy), 1940. Home: Springfield, Mass. Died June 17, 1940.

FRANKLIN, Edward Curtis, chemist; b. Geary City, Kan., Mar. 1, 1862; s. Thomas Henry and Cynthia Ann (Curtis) F.; B.S., U. of Kan., 1888, M.S., 1890; student U. of Berlin, 1890-91; Ph.D., Johns Hopkins, 1894; D.Sc., Northwestern, 1923; D.Sc. from Western Reserve U., 1926; LL.D., Wittenberg Coll., O., 1927; m. Effie June Scott, July 22, 1897; children—Mrs. Anna Comstock Barnett, Charles Scott (dec.), John Curtis. Assistant in chemistry, 1888-93, asso. prof., 1893-99, prof. physical chemistry, 1899-1903, U. of Kan.; asso. prof., 1903-06, prof. organic chemistry, 1906-29 (emeritus), Stanford Univ. Professor chemistry and chief div. chemistry, U.S. Pub. Health Service, 1911-13. Mem. U.S. Assay Commn., 1906. Mem. Advisory bd. U.S. Bur. Mines, 1917-18; phys. chemist U.S. Bur. Standards, 1918; consulting chemist Ordnance Bur., U.S.A., 1918. Fellow A.A.A.S., Am. Acad. Arts and Sciences. Was guest British Assn. Advancement Science, Capetown and Johannesburg, 1929. Awarded Nichols medal, 1924; Willard Gibbs medal, 1931. Home: Stanford University, Calif. Died Feb. 13, 1937.

FRANKLIN, Fabian, writer; b. Eger, Hungary, Jan. 18, 1853; s. Morris J. and Sarah (Heilprin) F.; Ph.B., Columbian (now George Washington) U., 1869, LL.D., 1904; civ. engr. and surveyor, 1869-77; fellow Johns Hopkins, 1877-79, Ph.D., 1880; m. Christine Ladd, Aug. 24, 1882; 1 dau., Margaret Ladd. Asso. prof. and prof. mathematics, Johns Hopkins, 1879-95; editor Baltimore News, 1895-1908; asso. editor New York Evening Post, 1909-Feb. 1917. Author: People and Problems, 1908; Life of Daniel Coit Gilman, 1910; Cost of Living, 1915; What Prohibition Has Done to America, 1922; Plain Talks on Economics, 1924; The A B C of Prohibition, 1927; Nuggets from the Wickersham Report, 1931. Editor (with Harold de Wolf Fuller) of The Review, polit. and lit. weekly (title changed to The Independent and The Review), 1919-22. Home: New York, N.Y. Died Jan. 9, 1939.

FRANKLIN, Melvin M., M.D.; b. Phila., Pa., Aug. 13, 1874; s. Marcus (M.D.) and Matilda (Morris) F.; ed. Pa. Mil. Coll., Columbia U.; B.Sc., Temple U., Phila., 1894; A.M., LaSalle Coll., 1900; M.D., U. of Pa., 1895; LL.D., Villa Nova, 1910; m. Elsie N. Franklin, Nov. 8, 1899; children—Melvin M., Horace A., Courtney V. Visiting orthopedic surgeon St. Joseph's Hosp.; cons. surgeon to St. Joseph's, Mercy and Jewish hosps., Bamberger Memorial Hosp (N.J.), Paul Kimball Hosp. (Lakewood, N.J.). Col. M.C. (R.) U.S.A. Fellow Am. Coll. Surgeons, Internat. Coll. of Surgeons; fellow in surgery N.Y. Acad. Medicine; hon, fellow Acad. Phys. Medicine. Home: Philadelphia, Pa. Died July 31, 1938.

FRANKLIN, Philip Albright Small, pres. Internat. Mercantile Marine Co.; b. Ashland, Md., Feb. 1, 1871; s. Col. Walter S. and Mary C. (Small) F.; ed. pub. and pvt. schs.; m. Laura F. Merryman. Began as office boy, Atlantic Transport Co., later traffic solicitor, mgr. and gen. mgr., and was made pres. same co., 1902, when it became affiliated with Internat. Mercantile Marine Co.; v.p. Internat. Mercantile Marine Co., 1916, pres, 1921—; pres. Atlantic Transport Co. of W.Va.; chmn. bd. Roosevelt Steamship Co., Inc. Chmn. Shipping Control Com. at New York, a joint creation of War Dept. and U.S. Shipping Bd., Feb. 17-Dec. 31, 1918. Awarded D.S.M. (U.S.), Chevalier Legion of Honor (France). Home: New York, N.Y. Died Aug. 14, 1939.

FRANKLIN, Samuel Rhoads, rear admiral U.S.N., retired Aug. 1887; b. York, Pa., Aug. 25, 1825; apptd. midshipman, Feb. 18, 1841; passed midshipman, Aug. 10, 1847; promoted through grades to rear admiral, Jan. 24, 1885; m. dau. of Rear Admiral B. F. Sands, Jan. 10, 1883. A large share of his 46 yrs. of service was passed at sea and included naval operations and actions in the Mexican and Civil Wars. Supt. U.S. Naval Observatory, 1884-85; comdr.-in-chief European sta., 1885-87. Author: Memories of a Rear Admiral. Died 1909.

FRANKLIN, Thomas Levering, P.E. clergyman; b. Philadelphia, April 10, 1822; grad. Trinity, 1841 (D.D., Hobart, 1871); deacon, 1844; priest, 1845; held several pastorates; became rector Ch. of the Evangelists, Philadelphia. Founded Jane Grey School, Mount Morris, N.Y., 1866; was its rector until 1870; was 6 years editor Episcopal Register. Author: The Creed; several tracts on Divorce. Home: Philadelphia, Pa. Died 1899.

FRANKLIN, Walter Simonds, civil engr.; b. York, Pa., Mar. 1, 1836; s. Walter Simonds and Sarah (Buel) F.; B.S., summa cum laude, Lawrence Scientific Sch. (Harvard), 1857; m. Mary Campbell Small, Dec. 13, 1866. Began work in wholesale store in New York, 1850; chainman and rodman in engring. party of Pa. R.R., 1852; studied, 1854; entered engring. sch., Harvard; on Fernandina & Cedar Keys R.R., Fla., 1857-88; in Europe, 1859; apptd. 1st lt. 12th U.S. Inf., May 1861; served in Army of the Potomac in McClellan's campaign; afterward under Sheridan in Shenandoah Valley, and with Grant until surrender of Lee; on staff of Gen. Sedgwick until he was killed, then with Wright as insp.-gen. 6th Army Corps, with rank of lt. col.; bvtd. maj. and lt. col. U.S.A., and col. U.S.V.; returned to regt. as capt., 1865, and resigned, 1870. Gen. mgr. Ashland Iron Co., Md., till 1887, then with Md. Steel Co. till 1894 (dir.); pres. Baltimore City Passenger R.R. till consolidation of all the roads; v.p. of the consolidated roads till 1903; retired. Mem. U.S. Lighthouse Bd., 1884—. Presbyn. Democrat. Home: Baltimore, Md. Died 1911.

FRANKLIN, William Buel, engr., soldier; b. York, Pa., Feb. 27, 1823; s. Walter Simonds and Sarah (Buel) F.; grad. West Point, 1843; m. Anna L. Clarke, July 7, 1852 (died 1900). Assigned to topog. engrs.; served through Mexican war and engaged in engring. service, becoming col. 12th inf., May 14, 1861; brig. gen. vols., May 17, 1861; maj. gen. vols., July 4, 1862, and afterwards received bvt. rank of brig. gen. and maj. gen. U.S. Army; resigned March 15, 1866; became v.p. Colts Patent Fire Arms Mfg. Co., Hartford; widower. Was pres. of commn. for laying out Long Island City, 1871-72; pres. of commn. for building new State house at Hartford, Conn., 1872-73; cons. engr. of same, 1874; U.S. commr. gen. for Paris Expn., 1889; grand officer French Legion of Honor, Oct. 1889; pres. Bd. Mgrs. Nat. Soldiers' Home until 1899. Hartford, Conn. Died 1903.

FRANKLIN, William Suddards, physicist; b. Geary City, Kan., Oct. 27, 1863; s. Thomas Henry and Cynthia Ann (Curtis) F.; B.S., U. of Kan., 1887, M.S., 1888; student Cornell, winters 1892-96, D.Sc., 1901; student U. of Berlin, 1890-91; holder Morgan fellowship, Harvard, 1891-92; m. Hattie F. Titus, Aug. 14, 1888; children—Curtis, Kellogg. Asst. prof. physics, U. of Kan., 1887-90; prof. physics and elec. engring., Ia. State Coll., 1892-97, Lehigh U., 1897-1903; prof. physics, Lehigh, 1903-15; prof. physics, Mass. Inst. Tech., 1917-29; prof. physics, Rollins Coll., Winter Park, Fla., 1929—. Hon. mem. Kan. Acad. Sciences. Joint author: Elements of Physics, 3 vols.; Elements of Alternating Currents; Elements of Electrical Engineering, 2 vols., 1906; Dynamo Laboratory Manual; Elements of Electricity and Magnetism; Practical Physics, 3 vols.; Electric Waves. Died June 6, 1930.

FRANKS, Robert A., capitalist; b. Liverpool, Eng., Oct. 27, 1861; s. William and Isabella (Evans) F.; ed. at Southport, Lancashire; m. Thetta Quay, Feb. 18, 1890; children—Jerome A. Q., Robert A., Ralph C. In steel mfg. business many yrs.; retired. Pres. and dir. Home Trust Co. Trustee and treas. Carnegie Foundation for Advancement of Teaching; life trustee Carnegie Corp. of New York (v. chmn. and treas.). Home: Orange, N.J. Died Sept. 1, 1935.

FRANTZ, Frank, governor; b. Roanoke, Ill., May 7, 1872; s. Henry J. and Maria (Gish) F.; ed. 2 yrs. Eureka (Ill.) Coll.; m. Matilda Evans, Apr. 9, 1900; children—Frank, Louise, Matie, Virginia. First lt. 1st U.S. Vol. Cavalry ("Roosevelt's Rough Riders"), May 1, 1898; capt., July 1, 1898; participated in Cuban campaign and Battle of San Juan Hill, July 3, 4, 1898; mustered out, Sept. 15, 1898. Postmaster Enid, Okla., 1901-03; U.S. Indian agt. for Osage Indians, 1903-04; gov. of Okla., 1905-07. Republican. Real estate broker, 1908-13; petroleum producer, 1913—; became chmn. bd. and gen. mgr. Franko Co.; pres. Roanoke Oil Co. Presbyn. Mason. Home: Wichita, Kan. Died Mar. 9, 1941.

FRANTZ, Joseph Henry, rolling mills; b. Cincinnati, O., Jan. 24, 1864; s. John H. and Eliza

(Meyer) F.; ed. pub. schs., Cincinnati; m. Jessie Guthrie, Sept. 11, 1889; 1 dau., Gretchen (Mrs. Harry M. Runkle). Began with Cincinnati Corrugating Co., 1884; sec. Piqua Rolling Mill Co., 1889-1900; v.p. Columbus Iron and Steel Co., 1902-17; v.p. Am. Rolling Mill Co., 1917-30, vice chmn. bd., 1930—. Fuel administrator, Ohio, World War. Republican. Presbyn. Home: Columbus, O. Died Aug. 19, 1938.

FRANZ, Shepherd Ivory, psychologist; b. Jersey City, N.J., May 27, 1874; s. D. M. William and Frances Elvira (Stoddard) F.; A.B., Columbia, 1894, Ph.D., 1899; U. of Leipzig, 1896; hon. M.D., George Washington U., 1915; LL.D., Waynesburg Coll., 1915; m. Lucie Mary Niven, of London, Ont., Can., June 18, 1902; children—Theodora Niven, Elizabeth Knox, Patricia Wilderspin. Asst. in psychology, Columbia, 1897-99; asst. in physiology, Harvard, 1899-1901; instr. physiology, Dartmouth Med. Sch., 1901-04; pathol. psychologist, McLean Hosp., Waverley, Mass., 1904-06; prof. physiology, 1906-21, exptl. psychology, 1906-24, George Washington U.; psychologist, 1907-24, scientific dir., 1910-19, dir. labs., 1919-24, St. Elizabeth's Hosp. (govt. hosp. for insane), Washington, D.C.; instr. in neurology, Naval Med. Sch., 1920-24; lecturer psychology, U. of Calif. at Los Angeles, 1924-25, prof., 1925—, research lecturer, 1926; chief of psychol. and ednl. clinic, Children's Hosp., Hollywood, 1924—. Lecturer in psychology, U. of Chicago, 1922, Johns Hopkins, 1922-23. Editor Psychol. Bull., 1912-24, Psychol. Monographs, 1924-27. Awarded Butler medal, Columbia University, 1924. Author: Handbook of Mental Examination Method, 1912, 2d edit. 1919; Nervous and Mental Re-education, 1923. Died Oct. 14, 1933.

FRANZEN, August, portrait painter; b. Norrköping, Sweden, 1863; pupil of Dagnan-Bouveret, Paris. Rep. in various museums of U.S.; awarded several medals. N.A., 1920; mem. Century Club, Lotos Club (New York), Union Interalliée (Paris). Died 1938.

FRASER, Abel McIver, clergyman, educator; b. Sumter, S.C., June 14, 1856; s. Thomas Boone and Sarah Margaret (McIver) F.; A.B., Davidson (N.C.) Coll., 1876; grad. Columbia (S.C.) Theol. Sem., 1880; D.D., Davidson, and Central U. of Ky., 1896; LL.D., Hampden-Sydney Coll., 1921; m. Octavia Blanding, July 14, 1881; children—Nora Blanding (dec.), Margaret McIver, Thomas Boone (dec.), Douglas de Saussure, Abel McIver (dec.), Jean Blanding (wife of Prof. Freeman H. Hart). Ordained ministry Presbyn. Ch. in U.S., 1881; pastor successively Mt. Horeb Ch., Fayette Co., Ky., Walnut Hill and Bethel, same county, until 1893, First Ch., Staunton, Va., 1893-1929 (emeritus); pres. Mary Baldwin Coll., 1923-29. Elected pres. Columbia Theol. Sem. 3 times (declined); moderator Synod of Va., 1903, Gen. Assembly Presbyn. Ch. in U.S., 1919; chmn. Com. of Presbyn. Ch. in U.S. on Closer Relations with Other Chs., 1919-22; chmn. of Conf. of Committees of Presbyn. Chs. on Closer Relations, 1919-22. Democrat. Home: Staunton, Va. Died Nov. 18, 1933.

FRASER, Daniel (real name Donald, but popularly known as Daniel), lawyer; b. Ramsey, near Montreal, Can., July 14, 1855; s. James and Sareph (Robertson) F.; ed. pvt. tutelage and Lewiston Acad.; unmarried. Practiced, Fowler, Ind., 1876—; has been identified with many important causes. Rep. presdl. elector, 1908. Home: Fowler, Ind. Deceased.

FRASER, Elisha Alexander, lawyer; b. Bowmanville, Ont., Can., Mar. 13, 1837; s. Rev. Niram A. and Elizabeth (Fletcher) F.; student Oberlin Coll., 1853-56; A.B., U. of Mich., 1863, A.M., 1866; m. Maud J. Lymburner, Dec. 24, 1863. Supt. pub. schs., Kalamazoo, Mich., 1864-73; admitted to bar, 1873; practiced at Battle Creek, Mich., 1873-76, Detroit, 1876—. City atty., Battle Creek, 1875-76; prof. Detroit Coll. of Law, 1892—, lecturing on contracts, constl. law and internat. law. Republican. Ruling elder Fort St. Presbyn. Ch., Detroit, 1877—; mem. com. selected to revise the creed, 1900-04; represented Presbyn. Ch. U.S.A. at Pan-Presbyn. Alliance, Liverpool, Eng., 1904, and by spl. request delivered address on "Christianity and National Expansion"; mem. Council of Reformed Chs. in America holding Presbyn. System, 1911-14 (v.p. 1912-14). Home: Detroit, Mich. Died July 10, 1916.

FRASER, Melvin, missionary; b. Lyndon, N.Y., Mar. 7, 1858; s. Robert and Eliza Jane (Dales) F.; Lake Forest (Ill.) Coll., 1878-81; B.A., Lafayette Coll., 1882, M.A., 1885, D.D., 1912; grad. McCormick Theol. Sem., 1887; m. Margarette W. Snodgrass, May 1, 1884 (died 1894); 1 dau., Elizabeth S. (Mrs. W. F. Hatch). Ordained Presbyn. ministry, 1885; pastor Iron Mountain, Mich., 1885-86; stated supply, Pingree Grove, Ill., 1887-88; pastor Mt. Pleasant, Mich., 1888-89; stated supply, Pipestone, Minn., and gen. supply, 1889-94; for Bd. Foreign Missions Presbyn. Ch. U.S.A., in Cameroun, W. Africa, 1894-1929. Moderator of the Synod of New Jersey, 1900; foreign pastor House of Hope, Elgin, Ill., 1922—, and hon. resident missionary House of Hope, 1929—. Honorary life mem. Am. Bible Society. Compiler and co-translator of Bulu Hymn Book. Home: New York, N.Y. Died Dec. 15, 1936.

FRASER, Thomas Boone, judge; b. Sumter, S.C., June 21, 1860; s. Judge Thomas Boone and Sarah Margaret (McIver) F.; A.B., Davidson Coll., N.C., 1881; read law under father; m. Emma Edmunds, Dec. 16, 1886. Admitted to S.C. bar, 1883; mem. S.C. Ho. of Rep., 1901-12 (chmn. judiciary com., 5 yrs.); asso. justice Supreme Ct. of S.C., 1912—. Democrat. Presbyn. Home: Sumter, S.C. Died May 21, 1925.

FRASER, William Alexander, ins. exec.; b. Woodside, Scotland, Jan. 29, 1869; s. Duncan Fraser and Marjory (McBain) F.; ed. pub. schs. and Dallas Bus. Coll.; m. Isabel Quillman, 1911; children—William Alexander II, George Duncan. Began with Woodmen of the World Life Ins. Assn., Dallas, Tex., 1892; city electrician, Dallas, 1905-09; pres. Woodmen of the World Life Ins. Assn., 1913—; pres. Globe Ins. Co., 1927—; dir. Omaha Nat. Bank. Apptd. an organizer and advisory mgr. Bur. War Risk Ins., World War. Mayor of Highland Park, Tex., 1913. Pres. Nat. Fraternal Congress, Am. Fraternal Congress, Texas Fraternal Congress. Trustee and treas. Brownell Hall Sch. for Girls, Omaha, Neb.; mem. Greater Omaha Com. Democrat. Episcopalian. Mason. Home: Omaha, Neb. Died Nov. 6, 1932.

FRASER, William Lewis, artist, art manager of Century Magazine, Century Dictionary, etc.; born London, England, Nov. 5, 1841; s. John Fraser, Lovat Highlander (newspaperman and song-writer, Chartist leader in early '40s); came with parents to U.S., 1856; ed. in English private acads.; studied art; m. Sarah Hannah Fraser, of Montreal, Can., 1867. Mem. Players, Grolier and Salmagundi clubs (pres. latter, 1896); v.p. Black and White Club; mem. Metropolitan Museum, Municipal Art League, Archtl. League, etc.; writer and lecturer on art. Died 1905.

FRAYNE, Hugh, labor official; b. Scranton, Pa., Nov. 8, 1869; s. Michael and Grace (Decon) F.; m. Mary E. Cawley, Nov. 8, 1888. Began at 8 as breaker boy in anthracite mine of Pa.; learned sheet metal trade; gen. v.p. Sheet Metal Workers' Union, 1901-04; apptd. a gen. organizer Am. Fed. of Labor, 1901; in charge of New York office of the Fed., 1910—. Rep. of labor on War Industries Bd., July 1917, and served as chmn. Labor Div. until bd. was dissolved, 1919; mem. General and Reception coms., N.Y. City, during war period. Mem. Nat. Com. on Prisons and Prison Labor, etc. Gold medal, 1920, by Nat. Com. on Prisons and Prison Labor in recognition of his work in prison reform; D.S.M. (U.S.), 1923, in recognition of war service. Mem. advisory com., Federation Bank and Trust Co. of New York. Home: Scranton, Pa. Died July 13, 1934.

FRAZEE, Harry Herbert, theatrical mgr.; b. Peoria, Ill., June 29, 1880; s. William Byron and Margaret A. (Teal) F.; ed. pub. schs., Peoria; m. Elsie Clisbee, Dec. 1901. Went on road as advance theatrical agt. at 16; first production on road was "Uncle Josh Perkins," 1902-03; launched a number of mus. comedy successes, 1904-07; financed and built the Cort Theatre, Chicago, 1907, Longacre Theatre, New York, 1913. Producer of "Madame Sherry," "Ready Money," "Fine Feathers," "A Pair of Sixes," "Nothing but the Truth," "My Lady Friends," New York, 1919, "No, No, Nanette," New York, 1924, London, 1925; "Yes, Yes, Yvette," New York, 1927; purchased Frazee Theatre, New York, 1920; leased Lyric Theatre, New York, 1921. Owner and pres. Boston Am. League Baseball Club. Home: New York, N.Y. Died June 4, 1929.

FRAZER, David Ruddach, clergyman; b. Baltimore, July 10, 1837; s. William R. and Eliza J. (Armitage) F.; A.B., Princeton, 1861, A.M., 1864 (D.D., 1880); grad. Union Theol. Sem., New York, 1864; m. Rose Thompson, July 2, 1866. Ordained Presbyn. ministry, 1865; pastor First Ch., Cliffton, S.I., 1865-67, Hudson, N.Y., 1867-72, Buffalo, N.Y., 1872-80, Classon Av. Ch., Brooklyn, N.Y., 1880-83, First Ch., Newark, N.J., 1883-1909; retired. Trustee Princeton U., 1887—; dir. Bloomfield (N.J.) Theol. Sem., 1886—, Union Theol. Sem., New York, 1888—, Bloomfield Sem. (pres. 1902); mem. Bd. of Ch. Erection Presbyn. Ch. 34 yrs., serving 28 yrs. as rec. sec.; resigned 1913. Home: Short Hills, N.J. Died Jan. 23, 1916.

FRAZER, John Stanley, clergyman; b. Clarke Co., Ala., Jan. 24, 1849; s. William Emsley and Satira (Cassity) F.; ed. Summerfield (Ala.) Inst.; D.D., Southern U., Greensboro, Ala., 1900; m. Mary Ella Chapman, Feb. 10, 1874; children—Daisy (Mrs. W. F. Betts), Maggie (Mrs. M. F. Washington), Jessie (dec.), Mary (Mrs. D. H. McNeal), John W., Lucile (Mrs. L. L. Shertzer), K. C., G. S., Leila Dumas (Mrs. Hubert Baughn). Licensed to preach, M.E. Ch., S., 1870; in charge various circuits, Ala., 1873-81; presiding elder (districts), Marianna, 1882, Pensacola, 1883-85, Union Springs, 1886, Montgomery, 1887-89, Selma, 1890-93, Mobile, 1894-97, Eufala Sta., 1898, Pensacola, 1899-1900, Montgomery, 1901-04, Mobile, 1905-08, Pensacola, 1909; conf. missionary sec., 1910; commr. edn., 1911-12; presiding elder Mobile Dist., 1913-15; commr. Emory U., 1915-20; sec. Christian Edn. Movement for Ala. Conf., 1920—. Mem. Gen. Conf. 4 times, Ecumenical Conf., 1901; mem. Federal Council Chs. of Christ in America, 1906-14; mem. Book Com., M.E. Ch., S., 1909—; was presiding elder Selma Dist. M.E. Ch., S.; now presiding elder Pensacola, Fla., Dist. Trustee Ala. Poly. Inst., Southern U. Democrat. Mason. Home: Evergreen, Ala. Died July 2, 1927.

FRAZER, Persifor, geologist, chemist, bibliote; b. in Philadelphia, July 24, 1844; s. John Fries (LL.D.), and Charlotte (Cave) F.; grad. Univ. of Pa., 1862 (A.M., 1865); was aide U.S. Coast Survey in S. Atlantic squadron, 1862-63; then in the cav. through Gettysburg campaign, 1863; actg. ensign U.S.N., in Mississippi squadron till hon. disch., Nov. 1865; studied Saxon Sch. Mines, Freiberg, Germany, 1866-69; mineralogist and metallurgist U.S. Geol. Survey, 1869-70; instr. and prof. chemistry, Univ. of Pa., 1870-74; asst. geol. survey, Pa., 1874-82; received degree of Docteur és-Sciences Naturelles, Université de France, being the first, not a native of France, to whom this degree was ever awarded; m. Isabella Nevins Whelen. Fellow Geol. Soc. of America, A.A.A.S. Officer de l'Instruction Publique (France); corr. k. k. Reichsanstalt, Vienna. Author: Tables for the Determination of Minerals (5 edits.), 1874-1901; Reports of Sub-com. of the Am. Committee, Internat. Geol. Congress, 1888; Bibliotics, or the Study of Documents (3 edits.), 1894-1901. Received from City of Phila. the John Scott legacy medal "for his system of colorimetry and contbns. to the science of Bibliotics," 1905. Home: Philadelphia, Pa. Died 1909.

FRAZER, Robert Sellers, judge; b. Fayette City, Pa.; s. Caleb T. and Sarah J. (Baker) F.; ed. pub. and pvt. schs. and West Chester (Pa.) Mil. Acad.; LL.D., U. of Pittsburgh, 1924, Lafayette Coll., 1931, Temple U., 1932, Univ. of Pa., 1935. Admitted to Pa. bar, Mar. 29, 1873, and began practice at Pittsburgh; mem. Pa. Ho. of Rep., 1877, 78, 79; elected judge Ct. of Common Pleas of Allegheny Co., Pa., 1896; reëlected, 1906; president judge 5th Jud. Dist. of Pa., Nov. 5, 1900-Dec. 31, 1914; justice Supreme Ct. of Pa. for term 1915-36, then chief justice. Republican. Presbyn. Home: Pittsburgh, Pa. Died July 31, 1936.

FRAZIER, Benjamin West, educator; b. Phila., Oct. 3, 1841; s. Benjamin West and Isabella (Zimmermann) F.; grad. Univ. of Pa., 1859, A.M., 1862, Sc.D., 1899; student École des Mines, Paris, 1866-68, Bergakademie, Freiburg, Saxony, 1868-69; m. Alice Clark, Apr. 9, 1866. Prof. mineralogy and metallurgy, Lehigh Univ., 1871—. Died 1905.

FRAZIER, Charles Harrison, surgeon; b. Germantown, Phila., Apr. 19, 1870; s. William W. and Harriet (Harrison) F.; A.B., U. of Pa., 1889, M.D., 1892; post-grad. studies, Berlin, 1895; m. Mary Spring Gardiner, Aug. 19, 1901. Prof. clin. surgery, 1900-22, dean med. dept., 1902-09, John Rhea Barton prof. surgery, 1922—, U. of Pa.; on staff University Hosp. Fellow Am. Coll. Surgeons. Home: Philadelphia, Pa. Died Aug. 26, 1936.

FRAZIER, George Harrison, financier; b. Phila., Pa., 1867; s. William W. and Harriet (Morgan) F.; A.B., U. of Pa., 1887; m. Cornelia Sibley, Nov. 1889. Dir. Pa. Fire Ins. Co., Campbell Hall Connecting R.R. Co., Elmira & Williamsport R.R. Co., Guarantee Co. of N. America, Interstate R.R. Co., Lehigh & Hudson River Ry. Co., Lehigh and New England R.R. Co., Pa. Co. for Ins. on Lives and Granting Annuities, Lehigh Power Securities Corp., Provident Trust Co. of Phila., etc. Trustee U. of Pa.; treas. Episcopal Hosp. (Phila.). Republican. Episcopalian. Home: Philadelphia, Pa. Died Jan. 9, 1934.

FRAZIER, James B., senator; b. Pikeville, Tenn., Oct. 18, 1856; s. Thomas N. and Margaret (McReynolds) F.; A.B., U. of Tenn., 1878, also grad. law dept.; m. Louise Douglas Keith, Jan. 10, 1883; children—Annie Keith (Mrs. R. N. Somerville), James B., Thomas A., Louise Douglas (Mrs. John P. Fort). Admitted to bar, 1881, and began practice at Chattanooga, Tenn. Presdl. elector-at-large, 1900 and 1920; gov. of Tenn., terms, 1902-04, 1904-06; elected U.S. senator, Mar. 21, 1905, to fill unexpired term (1905-11) of William B. Bate, and resigned as gov., Mar. 27, 1905. Democrat. Home: Chattanooga, Tenn. Died Mar. 28, 1937.

FRAZIER, Robert Thomas, first asst. commr. patents; b. Pulaski, Tenn., Apr. 27, 1863; s. Robert Thomas and Susan Rebecca (Harmon) F.; grad. U.S. Naval Acad., 1883; hon. disch. from naval service, 1885; LL.B., Nat. U. Law Sch., Washington, 1895; m. Corinne Reid Frazier, Sept. 26, 1888. Examiner in Patent Office, Washington, 1887-93; mgr. in Phila., New York and Washington, for Howson & Howson, patent lawyers, 1893-1901, partner, 1901-06; mem. Smith & Frazier, 1906-10; mem. Patent Office examining corps by apptmt. of Pres. Taft, 1910-13; apptd. 1st asst. commr. of patents, June 1913. Mason. Home: Washington, D.C. Died Apr. 19, 1914.

FREAR, James A., congressman; b. Hudson, Wis., Oct. 24, 1861; s. Aaron H. and Margaret J. F.;

served in U.S. Signal Corps 5 yrs.; LL.B., Nat. Law U., 1884; married. Practiced law at Hudson, 1884—; city atty. several terms; apptd. dist. atty., St. Croix Co., Wis., 1896, and elected for 3 terms, 1897-1901; elected mem. Wis. Ho. of Rep., 1902, Senate, 1904; chmn. Wis., legislative ins. investigation, 1906; Sec. of State, Wis., 1907-13; mem. 63d to 72d Congresses (1913-33), 10th Wis. Dist., and 73d Congress (1933-35), 9th Wis. Dist. Republican. Home: Hudson, Wis. Died June 4, 1939.

FREAR, William, chemist; b. Reading, Pa., Mar. 24, 1860; s. Rev. George and Malvina (Rowland) F.; A.B., U. of Lewisburg (now Bucknell U.), 1881; Ph.D., Ill. Wesleyan U., 1883; m. Julia Reno, July 18, 1900. Asst. in sciences, Bucknell U., 1881-83, asst. chemist U.S. Dept. of Agr., 1883; prof. agrl. chemistry, 1885-1907, exptl. agrl. chemistry, 1907—, Pa. State Coll. Vice-dir. and chemist Pa. Agrl. Expt. Sta., 1887—; chemist to Pa. State Bd. Agr., 1888-1919; chemist Pa. Dept. of Agr., 1895-1916; spl. agt., U.S. Dept. of Agr., 1900—; chief chemist, Pa. Bur. of Foods. Writing exclusively communications to scientific periodicals and expt. station and state reports. Editor and prop. of "Agricultural Science," 1892-94. Pres. Assn. of Official Agrl. Chemists of U.S.; pres. Soc. for Promotion Agrl. Science; fellow A.A.A.S.; chmn. Nat. Food Standards Commn., 1902-07; mem. Joint Com. on Food Definitions and Standards, 1914—; mem. Assn. Am. Dairy Food and Drug Officials (pres. chem. sect. 1911-13), Franklin Inst., Washington Acad. Sciences. Mason. Dir. First Nat. Bank. Died Jan. 7, 1922.

FREAS, Thomas Bruce, prof. chemistry; b. nr. Newark, O., Nov. 2, 1868; s. Andrew and Mary (Bruce) F.; A.B., Stanford, 1896; Ph.D., U. of Chicago, 1911; m. Mary Kuhn, Dec. 28, 1898; children—Royal Bruce, Joseph Kuhn (dec.). Prin. high sch., Hiawatha, Kan., 1896-97; chemist, Western Electric Co., Chicago, 1897-98; asst. in chemistry and grad. student, U. of Chicago, 1898-1903; mgr. Ernst Leitz apparatus house, Chicago, 1903-04; instr. chemistry, U. of Chicago, 1904-11; successively asst. prof., asso. prof. and prof. chemistry, Columbia, 1911—; pres. Thermo Electric Instrument Co., Irvington, N.J. Fellow A.A.A.S., Am. Geog. Soc., N.Y. Acad. of Sciences. Republican. Presbyn. Home: Leonia, N.J. Died Mar. 15, 1928.

FREAS, William Streeper, minister; b. Marble Hall, Pa., May 11, 1848; s. Jesse W. and Ann Catharine F.; A.B., Pa. Coll., Gettysburg, 1873, A.M., 1876; grad. Theol. Sem., Gettysburg, 1876; (D.D., Wittenberg Coll., 1891); m. Ella A. Streeper, June 5, 1878. Instr. Lutherville Sem., Md., 1876; Evang. Luth. clergyman; pastor Everett, Hughesville, Carlisle, and York, Pa., and Baltimore; supt. instruction Deaconess Motherhouse, Baltimore, 1905—. Sec. Alleghany Synod, 1878-80; dir. Sem., Gettysburg; sec. Gen. Synod, 1887-99; pres. same, 1901-03 and 1905. Mem., 1886—, pres., 1891—, Bd. Ch. Extension; mem. Com. to Revise Book of Worship, 1893-97; pres. W.Pa. Synod, 1894-97. Home: Baltimore, Md. Died 1911.

FREDERICK, George Aloysius, architect; b. Baltimore, Dec. 16, 1842; s. John M. and Anne Margaret (Hild) F.; ed. Christian Bros.' Acad., Baltimore; studied architecture in office of Lind & Murdoch, 4 years; m. Mary Elenor Everist, 1865. Designer and architect City Hall, Baltimore, 1866-75 (then considered finest municipal building in the country); architect U.S. Marine Hosp., 1st Nat. Bank, Chesapeake & Potomac Telephone Exchange, Baltimore; in charge of design of all city parks, Baltimore, 1864-96; etc. Fellow A.I.A. Catholic. Home: Baltimore, Md. Died Aug. 17, 1924.

FREDERICK, Pauline, actress; b. Boston, Mass., Aug. 12, 1885; d. Richard O. and Loretta E. (Fisher) Libby; ed. Boston, Mass.; m. 5th, Colonel Joseph A. Marmon, U.S. Army, Jan. 1934 (died 1934). Début with the Rogers Brothers, in "Harvard," at Knickerbocker Theatre, New York, Sept. 1, 1902; played Titiana, in "A Princess of Kensington," Broadway Theatre, 1903; later starred in "It Happened in Nordland"; star, in "The Little Gray Lady"; lead in "Samson" with Wm. Gillette; star in "The Fourth Estate," "Joseph and His Brethren," 1913. "Innocent," 1914-15. Screen début in "The Eternal City"; later appeared in "Zaza," "La Tosca," "The Woman on the Index," "Bonds of Love," "The Paliser Case," "Madame X," "The Glory of Clementina," etc. Home: Beverly Hills, Calif. Died Aug. 19, 1938.

FREDRICK, Leopold, capitalist; b. Polstrau (Sredisce), Jugo-Slavia, Jan. 1, 1876; s. Sigmund and Emilie (Neuwirth) F.; ed. Realschule and High Sch. of Commerce, Marburg (Maribor), Jugo-Slavia; m. Millie Bruhl, Sept. 21, 1915. Became connected with Ministry of Finance, of Austria-Hungary, 1897, and apptd. sec. to Paris Expn., 1909; with foreign dept. of Nat. City Bank of New York, 1902-07; mgr. foreign dept. Nat. Bank of Commerce, New York, 1907-11; dir., treas. Am. Smelting & Refining Co., 1911-20; treas. of Yukon Gold Co.; treas. Chile Exploration Co., Chile Copper Co., Braden Copper Co., Braden Mines Co.; dir., treas. Chile Steamship Co., Sherman Steamship Co.; dir., mem. exec. com. New River Collieries Co., Chesapeake & Ohio Coal & Coke Co., 1911-23. Decorated by French Govt. Home: New York, N.Y. Died July 1936.

FREE, Edward Elway, chemist; b. Dagus Mines, Pa., May 3, 1883; s. Spencer Michael (M.D.) and May Irene (Elway) F.; grad. Bellefonte (Pa.) Acad., 1902; A.B., Cornell U., 1906; Ph.D., Johns Hopkins, 1917; m. Marion Allen, Apr. 28, 1922. Asst. chemist Agrl. Expt. Sta., U. of Ariz., 1906-07; physicist and scientist U.S. Dept. Agr., Washington, D.C., 1907-12; cons. chemist, and physicist, 1912—, head E.E. Free Laboratories, New York. Editor Scientific American, 1924-25; owner and editor "The Week's Science" (a news service). Lecturer on Outlines of Science, New York U., 1926-34. Served as capt. Ordnance Dept., U.S.A., 1917-18; maj. C.W.S., 1918-19. Fellow A.A.A.S., Wash. Acad. of Science, Acoustical Soc. America (treas. 1930-34). Died Nov. 24, 1939.

FREE, Spencer Michael, surgeon; b. New Freedom, York Co., Pa., Sept. 19, 1856; s. Eli Wesley and Virginia Ann (Michael) F.; B.A., Ohio Wesleyan U., 1877, M.A., 1880; M.D., Coll. Phys. and Surg., Baltimore, 1880; post-grad., Johns Hopkins, 1885-87; m. May Irene Elway, Feb. 8, 1882 (died 1909); children—Edward Elway, Rohe Chambers (dec.), Virginia Michael (dec.), Spencer M. Practiced in DuBois, Pa., 1892—; insp. for State Bd. of Health, Pa., 1887-1905; surgeon Du Bois Hosp.; sr. surgeon Adrian Hosp., Punxsutawney, Pa.; formerly lecturer on med. ethics and economics, Coll. Phys. and Surg., Baltimore. Fellow Am. Coll. Surgeons, A.M.A. Mason. Republican. Author: Human Touch and Other Poems, 1925; Shawnee Cabin and Other Poems, 1931. Home: Du Bois, Pa. Died May 16, 1938.

FREED, Charles Abram, pres. theol. sem.; b. Waynesboro, Va., Aug. 23, 1868; s. William Abram and Martha Ellen (Harner) F.; A.B., Roanoke Coll., Salem, Va., 1890; student Luth. Theol. Sem., Mt. Airy, Pa., 1890-93; post grad. study, U. of Pa., 1891-92; D.D., Newberry (S.C.) Coll., 1911; m. Ada Grove, Sept. 25, 1895; children—Dr. Charles Conrad, Janet Grove, Elizabeth (Mrs. Ward Thresh), Joe Edward. Ordained Luth. ministry, 1893; pastor Middlebrook, Va., 1893-1903, Ebenezer Ch., Columbia, S.C., 1903-21, Ch. of the Redeemer, Newberry, S.C., 1921-25, Grace Ch., Winchester, Va., 1925-29, Ch. of the Ascension, Columbia, S.C., 1929-32; pres. Luth. Theol. Southern Sem., Columbia, 1932—. Asst. editor Lutheran Ch. Visitor, 1904-06; chaplain S.C. State Senate, 1913-21; v.p. bd. of trustees Luth. Theol. Southern Sem., 1908-32; mem. Nat. Luth. Council, 1920—; pres. S.C. Luth. Synod, 1932. Democrat. Kiwanian. Home: Columbia, S.C. Died Apr. 1938.

FREEDLEY, Angelo Tillinghast, lawyer; b. Cincinnati, Nov. 12, 1850; s. E. T. and Anna (Tillinghast) F.; studied law with William Henry Rawle; admitted to bar, 1871; m. Ida Welles Vinton, June 24, 1890. Counsel for Pa. senate investigating com., 1895; now counsel for Phila. Clearing House, and for several banks, members thereof. Republican. Author: The General Corporation Law of Pennsylvania, 1880, 1890; Limited Partnership Association Laws of Pennsylvania, 1884. Home: Philadelphia, Pa. Died 1907.

FREEDLEY, Edwin Troxell, author; b. Phila., July 28, 1827; academic edn.; studied law at Harvard, 1845; in marble business Cincinnati, 1847-51, then in Phila. Author (and compiler): Practical Treatise on Business; Philadelphia and Its Manufactures; Business Man's Legal Adviser; Common Sense in Business; Opportunities for Industry; History of American Manufactures; etc. Founded Manufacturers' Gazette and The Journalist. Twice married and has 3 children. Home: Philadelphia, Pa. Died 1904.

FREEDMAN, Andrew, capitalist; b. New York, Sept. 1, 1860; s. Joseph and Elizabeth (Davies) F.; ed. City Coll.; unmarried. V.p. and dir. Wright Co.; dir. N.Y. Transportation Co., Fifth Av. Coach Co., Interborough Met. Co., Interborough Rapid Transit Co., etc. Treas. Dem. campaign, 1897. Home: New York, N.Y. Died Dec. 4, 1915.

FREEDMAN, John Joseph, judge; b. Nüremberg, Germany, Oct. 7, 1835; ed. Germany; came to U.S. at 16; admitted to bar, 1860; m. Agnes Roessel; father of William Horatio F. Judge Superior Ct. of N.Y., 1869-96, Supreme Ct., 1896-1904. Home: New York, N.Y. Died Oct. 31, 1921.

FREEDMAN, William Horatio, elec. expert; b. New York, Dec. 28, 1867; s. John Joseph and Agnes (Roessel) F.; ed. Coll. City of New York, 1882-85; C.E., Columbia Sch. of Mines, 1889, E.E., 1891; post-grad. physics and mathematics, and fellow Columbia, 1891-92; M.S., U. of Vt., 1908; m. Lillian Augusta Wilson, Jan. 30, 1895. Instr. elec. engring., Columbia, 1892-99; prof. elec. engring., U. of Vt., 1899-1910; head of dept. applied electricity, Pratt Inst., Brooklyn, 1910-13; prof. elec. engring., U. of Vt., 1913-20; tech. employment rep. Am. Telephone & Telegraph Co., Apr. 1, 1920-Sept. 1, 1922; research dept. Bonded Products Corp., 1923. Ednl. dir. U.S. Signal Corps schs. at U. of Vt., Sept. 1917-Jan. 1919. Fellow A.A.A.S., Am. Inst. E.E. Home: Nyack, N.Y. Died Dec. 11, 1940.

FREEMAN, Abraham Clark, lawyer, author; b. Hancock Co., Ill., May 15, 1843; s. Obadiah Schenck and Nancy (Clark) F.; ed. dist. schs.; removed to Calif. with father 1861; taught dist. sch. in Joaquin Co. 2 yrs.; studied law; m. Josephine B. Foulks, Sept. 7, 1867. Admitted to bar, 1864; mem. Constl. Conv., 1878-79, and of com. to propose such amendments as were required to harmonize the codes of the state with its new constitution. Became editor Am. Decisions 1879, Am. State Reports 1888. Mem. and pres. of common. to revise and reform the laws of Calif., 1899-1903. Author: Law of Judgments, 1873; Cotenancy and Partition, 1874; Executions, 1876; Void Judicial States, 1877. Home: San Francisco, Calif. Died 1911.

FREEMAN, Clarence Campbell, college prof.; b. Shelby Co., Ky., July 1, 1862; s. John Chandler and Nancy (King) F.; A.B., Transylvania Coll., Ky., 1883, A.M., 1888, LL.D., 1928; grad. student, Johns Hopkins U., 1888-90, U. of Chicago, summers, 1906, 14; m. Mary Dale, June 21, 1893. Prin. prep. dept. Georgetown (Ky.) Coll., 1886-88; prof. English, Union U., Jackson, Tenn., 1890-92, Transylvania Coll., 1892-1905, Georgetown (Ky.) Coll., 1905-09; Morrison prof. English, and head of dept., Transylvania Coll., 1909—, dean, 1904-05; prof. English, U. of Ky., summer 1923. Democrat. Baptist. Home: Lexington, Ky. Died May 13, 1935.

FREEMAN, George Fouche, plant geneticist; b. Maple Grove, Ala., Nov. 4, 1876; s. George W. and Laura C. (Nuckols) F.; B.S., Ala. Polytechnic, 1903; Sc.D., Harvard, 1917; m. L. Adelle Blachly, Kan., 1906; children—Eleanor Adelle (Mrs. G. C. Wilson), George Donald. Principal Downer Inst., Beech Island, S.C., 1899-1901; asst. instr. in botany, Mass. Coll. of Agr., 1903-04; asso. botanist, Kan. State Agr. Coll., 1904-06; plant breeder, Ariz. Agr. Expt. Sta., 1906-18; acting dean, Coll. of Agr. and dir. Expt. Sta., Ariz., 1915-16; chief plant breeding, Soc. Sultanienne d'Agr., Cairo, Egypt, 1918-22; chief Dept. of Cotton Breeding, Tex. Agrl. Expt. Sta., 1922-23; official agriculturist and economist mission for French Govt. to Indo-China, 1923; dir. gen. Service Technique d'Agriculture et de l'Enseignement Professionnel, Republic of Haiti, 1923—. Mason. Home: Tucson, Ariz. Died 1930.

FREEMAN, Henry Blanchard, brig. gen.; b. Mt. Vernon, O., Jan. 17, 1837; s. Luther and Charlotte (Blanchard) F.; Puritan ancestry; ed. pub. schs., Sloans Acad., Mt. Vernon, O.; m. Sarah E. Darlington, Apr. 26, 1866. Pvt. Co. G, 10th Inf., July 16, 1855-Feb. 5, 1856; promoted through the various grades to col. 24th Inf., Oct. 4, 1898; brig. gen. U.S.A., Jan. 16, 1901; retired by operation of law, Jan. 17, 1901. Bvtd.: capt., Dec. 31, 1862, "for gallant and meritorious services in battle of Murfreesboro, Tenn."; maj., Sept. 20, 1863, for same in battle of Chickamauga, Ga. Awarded Congressional Medal of Honor, Feb. 17, 1894, "for distinguished gallantry in battle of Stone River." Was taken prisoner of war, Chickamauga; escaped from Libby; was recaptured and again escaped; acting asst. adj. gen. 17th Corps; served on frontier in Sioux war, 1867-68, Powder River and Fort Phil. Kearney, in Cheyenne war; in Kan., 1868-69; in Sioux war, 1876, Yellowstone and Custer; in Ute war in Colo., 1879; served in Cuba and P.I. Home: Washington, D.C. Died Oct. 16, 1915.

FREEMAN, Henry Raymond, clergyman; b. New York, Mar. 10, 1860; s. Henry and Mary A. (Fee) F.; advanced study under pvt. tutors; student Gen. Theol. Sem., 1885-88; D.D., St. Stephen's Coll., 1915; m. Fannie E. H. Herendeen, Jan. 22, 1890. Deacon, 1884, priest, 1889, P.E. Ch.; curate Ch. of Holy Spirit, New York, 1886-89; rector St. Mark's Ch., Islip, L.I., N.Y., 1889-92; became rector of St. John's Ch., Troy, 1892, emeritus. Past pres. Standing Committee, Diocese of Albany; chaplain, Citizens' Corps of Troy, 1896—. Republican. Mason. Home: Troy, N.Y. Died Aug. 17, 1936.

FREEMAN, Henry Varnum, judge; b. Bridgeton, N.J., Dec. 20, 1842, of Pilgrim ancestry; s. Henry and Mary (Bangs) F.; A.B., Yale, 1869, A.M., 1874; studied law, New Haven, Conn., and Chicago; admitted to bar, 1872; m. Mary L. Curtis, Oct. 16, 1873. Enlisted Company K, 74th Ill. Inf., Aug. 6, 1862, and made 1st sergt.; capt. 12th U.S. Colored Inf., Aug. 24, 1863; hon. disch., July, 1865; practiced law in Chicago, 1873-93; elected judge Superior Ct., Nov. 1893; reëlected, 1898, 1904, 1911; apptd. justice Appellate Ct., Feb. 1898; presiding justice June, 1898. Republican. Professorial lecturer legal ethics and med. jurisprudence, U. of Chicago, and lecturer on legal ethics, law dept. same. Home: Chicago, Ill. Died Sept. 16, 1916.

FREEMAN, James Midwinter ("Robin Ranger"), clergyman-author; b. New York, Jan. 29, 1827; ed. New York public schs.; trained for teacher and taught several years (A.M., Wesleyan, Conn., 1866; D.D., Mt. Union, Ohio, Coll., 1875); joined N.J. conference, M.E. Church, 1850; stationed at Newark, Paterson, Jersey City, Orange, Haverstraw, N.Y., and various other places; from 1872 asst. editor Sunday school and tract publs. of M.E. Ch. Author: A Short

History of the English Bible; Handbook of Bible Manners and Customs; also about 30 books for children, under pen-name "Robin Ranger." Homes: Morristown, N.J., and N.Y. City. Died 1900.

FREEMAN, John Charles, univ. prof.; b. Lisle, N.Y., Feb. 14, 1842; s. Charles Waldo and Charlotte (Brockway) F.; A.B., U. of Mich., 1868, A.M., 1871; B.D., Union Theol. Sem., 1872; (LL.D., U. of Chicago, 1880); m Emma Belden, 1870. Served in Civil War, 27th and 168th N.Y. Vol. Inf., 1862-63; capt., 1st N.Y. Vet. Cav., 1864; asst. insp. gen. cav. corps; comd. expdn. to Lewisburg and the Greenbrier, Apr. 1865. Asst. prof. Greek, U. of Chicago, 1868-74; prof. Latin, 1874-78, English lit., 1879—, U. of Wis. Republican. U.S. consul at Copenhagen, 1900; U.S. chargé d'affaires to Denmark, 1901. Editor of Xenophon's Memorabilia and of Dialogues of Lucian; History of American Literature. Home: Madison, Wis. Died 1911.

FREEMAN, John Ripley, civil and mech. engr.; b. W. Bridgeton, Me., July 27, 1855; s. Nathaniel D. and Mary Elizabeth (Morse) F.; B.S., Mass. Inst. Tech., 1876; hon. Sc.D., Brown U., 1904, Tufts, 1905, Sachs Tech. Hochschule, 1926, U. of Pa., 1927, Yale, 1931; m. Elizabeth Farwell Clark, Dec. 27, 1887. Prin. asst. engr. Water Power Co., Lawrence, Mass., 1876-86; prin. asst. to Hiram F. Mills, consulting engr., 1878-86; chief engr. Associated Factory Mut. Ins. Cos., 1886- 96; cons. engr. on water power and mill construction to sundry large mfg. corps., 1886—. Made extensive studies of water supply for Greater New York, for finance dept., 1899-1900; chief engr. investigations, Charles River Dam, Boston Harbor, 1903; cons. engr. Boston Met. Park Commn. on sanitary and drainage problems, 1903-04. Water Commr., Winchester, Mass., 1882-86; engr. mem. Mass. Met. Water Bd., 1895-96; mem. R.I. Met. Park Commn., 1904; mem. spl. commn. additional water supply, New York. Was civilian engr. mem. spl. bd., gun carriage tests, War Dept., 1902. Pres. Mfrs., R.I. Mechanics, State, Enterprise and Am. Factory Mut. Ins. cos. Planned water power developments Feather River, Calif., 1904-05, St. Lawrence River, Long Sault, 1905, regulation of Great Lakes, 1924-26; cons. engr. water supplies of Nashua, Los Angeles, San Diego, Baltimore, City of Mexico; cons. engr. New York Bd. of Water Supply since 1905; in charge water power investigations N.Y. State Water Supply Commn., 1906-07; cons. engr. on Isthmian Canal locks and dams, 1907 and 1909; cons. engr. San Francisco water supply, 1910— (planned Hetch Hetchy water supply now bldg.); to Canadian Govt. on water power conservation, etc., 1910. Trustee of Mass. Inst. Tech., 1895—. Twice received Normal medal, Am. Soc. C.E., for best engring. paper contributed to its Transactions during year. Fellow Am. Acad. Arts and Sciences. Chmn. Nat. Advisory Com. for Aeronautics, 1918-19; cons. engr. for Chinese Govt., Grand Canal Improvement Bd., 1917—. Unitarian. Republican. Home: Providence, R.I. Died Oct. 6, 1932.

FREEMAN, John William, M.D.; b. Virden, Ill., Dec. 13, 1853; s. Peter S. and Elizabeth Pierce (Warriner) F.; Blackburn U., Ill., 1 yr.; Miami Med. Coll., Cincinnati, 1876-78; M.D., U. Med. Coll. (New York U.), 1879; studied N.Y. Polyclinic, 1893; m. Hattie V. Dickinson, Sept. 5, 1885. Asst. Jacksonville (Ill.) Sanitarium, 1879-81; actg. asst. surgeon U.S.A., 1881-83; with hosp. dept., Homestake Mining Co., 1884—, chief surgeon, 1904-19. V.p. First Nat. Bank, Lead. Mem. Bd. Med. Examiners, S.D., 1903-05; health officer of Lead, S.D., 1910-17; pres. State Bd. Med. Examiners and Bd. of Health, 1919-23; med. mem. Exemption Bd., Selective Service, Dist. 25, S.D., 1917, 18; mem. Bd. of Edn., Lead, 9 yrs. Fellow Am. Coll. Surgeons. Republican. Episcopalian. Mason. Home: Lead, S.D. Died Feb. 2, 1926.

FREEMAN, Julia S. Wheelock; b. Lorain Co., O., Oct. 7, 1833; reared in Erie Co., Pa.; ed. Kalamazoo Coll., Mich.; taught school. In 1862 entered Union army as visiting and distributing agent for the Mich. Soldiers' Relief Assn., and remained to close of war; clerk Treasury Dept., Washington, 1865-73, resigned; m. Porter C. Freeman, 1873. In 1881 removed to Springfield, Mo. Author: Boys in White (a history of her war experiences). Home: Springfield, Mo. Died 1900.

FREEMAN, Leonard, surgeon; b. Cincinnati, Dec. 16, 1860; s. Zoeth and Ellen (Ricker) F.; B.S., U. of Cincinnati, 1882; M.D., Med. Coll. of Ohio, 1886; univs. of Göttingen, Berlin and Vienna; (hon. M.A., U. of Denver, 1901); m. Amanda Frank, 1894 (dec.); m. 2d, Jeanne Wright, July 27, 1905; children—Frank, Paul R. (dec.), Leonard. Prof. surgery, Med. Dept. U. of Colo.; surgeon St. Joseph's Hospital, Denver. Fellow Am. Coll. Surgeons, A.M.A., Am. Surgical Assn. Author: Skin Grafting, 1912. Home: Denver, Colo. Died Dec. 27, 1935.

FREEMAN, Mary E. Wilkins, author; b. Randolph, Mass., 1862. Writer for mags.—poems, short stories; m. Dr. Charles M. Freeman, Jan. 1, 1902. Author: A Humble Romance, 1887; A New England Nun, 1891; Young Lucretia, 1892; Giles Corey, 1893; Pembroke, 1894; Portion of Labor, 1901; Green Door, 1910; Copy-Cat and Other Stories, 1914; A New England Nun and Other Stories, 1920; also The Jamesons, and People of Our Neighborhood (serially in Ladies' Home Journal). Home: Metuchen, N.J. Died Mar. 14, 1930.

FREEMAN, Robert, clergyman; b. Edinburgh, Scotland, Aug. 4, 1878; s. Robert and Jemima (Rivles) F.; came to America, 1896; George Heriot's School and Heriot-Watt Coll., Edinburgh; A.B., Allegheny Coll., 1904, D.D., 1912; grad. Princeton Theol. Sem., 1907; M.A., Princeton, 1907, D.D., 1922; Litt.D., College of Wooster, 1928; m. Margery Fulton (A.B., Vassar, 1909), July 14, 1909; children—Robert Gowans, Bertrice, Margaret, Fulton, David Guthrie. In mission work, McKeesport, Pa., and Binghamton and Buffalo, N.Y., 1896-1900; ordained Bapt. ministry, 1900; preached in Bapt. Ch., Springboro, Pa., 1900-02, Presbyn. Ch., Erie, 1902-04, Lafayette Presbyn. Ch., Buffalo, during course at Princeton, and as pastor until 1910; pastor Pasadena Presbyn Ch., 1911-40, pastor emeritus. Trustee Occidental Coll.; moderator Synod of Calif., 1920-21, and of Los Angeles Presbytery, 1931; mem. Board of Nat. Missions of the Presbyn. Ch., Nat. Council Boy Scouts; pres. Monte Vista Grove Homes, Pasadena. Republican. On leave in France as dir. 1st expeditionary div. of Y.M.C.A. and dir. religious work in France, July 1917-July 1918. Author: The Land I Live In (poems), 1921, 24, 28; New Every Morning, 1927; What About the Twelve?, 1929; Castles in the Air, 1935. Home: Pasadena, Calif. Died June 28, 1940.

FREEMAN, Thomas J. A., S. J., clergyman, prof. physics and chemistry, St. Peter's Coll., Jersey City, N.J., 1900—; b. Colchester Co., Nova Scotia, April 5, 1841; s. James and Mary (Marr) F.; student Montreal Coll., 1859-63; taught there, 1863-65; made a yr. of divinity studies in Montreal Sem.; entered Jesuit novitiate at Sault-au-Récollet, nr. Montreal, Sept. 1866; treas. St. Francis Xavier's Coll., New York, 1868-70; one year's spl. study, chemistry, Columbia Coll.; studied divinity 2 yrs. at Louvain, Belgium; has been prof. physics and chemistry St. Francis Xavier's Coll., and St. John's Coll., Fordham, N.Y., and Woodstock Coll., Md.; treas. St. John's Coll., 1899-1900; was prof. physics, Boston Coll. Home: Jersey City, N.J. Died 1907.

FREEMAN, Thomas Jones, lawyer; b. Trenton, Tenn., Nov. 29, 1859; student U. of Tenn., 1877-78; LL.B., Law Dept., Cumberland U., Lebanon, Tenn., 1880. Admitted to Tenn. bar, 1880; asst. gen. atty., 1891-92; gen. atty., 1892-1908, 1st v.p., 1911-13, gen. counsel, 1913-14, and now gen. solicitor for Tex. & Pacific Ry. Receiver Internat. & Great Northern Ry., 1908-11; made pres. the reorganized rd., the Internat. & Great Northern Ry., Sept. 1911; gen. counsel Weatherford Mineral Wells & Northwestern Ry., Tex. Pacific and Mo. Pacific Terminal R.R. of New Orleans. Home: New Orleans, La. Died Oct. 29, 1933.

FREEMAN, Walker Burford; b. Bedford Co., Va., Aug. 28, 1843; s. Garland Hurt and Thermuthis (Burford) F.; ed. pvt. schs.; m. Bettie Allen Hamner, Jan. 8, 1874 (died 1909); children—Hamner G., Walker B. (dec.), Allen W., Douglas S. Mercantile business, 1869-87; gen. agt. New York Life Ins. Co., Richmond, Va., 1877—; mem. W. B. Freeman & Son, 1900—. Enlisted in Confederate Army, June 1861; served as pvt. and spl. brigade courier, 34th Va. Inf., in S.C. and with Army of Northern Va.; surrendered at Appomattox, Apr. 9, 1865. Active in affairs of U.C.V.; mem. R. E. Lee Camp No. 1; brig. gen. U.C.V., 1912; maj. gen. comdg. Va. Div., 1915-25; elected gen. and comdr. in chief U.C.V., 1925. Trustee Lee Camp Soldiers' Home (Richmond), Stone Mountain Memorial Assn. (Atlanta, Ga.). Life mem. Underwriters' Assn. of Richmond. Democrat. Baptist. Mason. Home: Richmond, Va. Died Feb. 9, 1935.

FREEMAN, Winfield, lawyer; b. London, O., Jan. 3, 1848; s. James F. and Eleanor (Dawson) F.; ed. common schs., Winchester, O.; read law in office of Hon. A. Stiver, Winchester; admitted to Ohio bar, 1869; m. Reba Silver, July 6, 1876 (died 1921); children—Frank, Mrs. Nellie F. Griest (both adopted); m. 2d, Mrs. Mary Judy Flickinger, June 24, 1922. Pros. atty. Preble Co., O., 1878-79; asst. atty. Solomon Valley R.R. Co., Kan., 1880-84; mayor of Minneapolis, Kan., 1881; atty. and one of promoters Kansas City Elevated R.R. Co., 1884-88; councilman, 1887-89, city counselor, 1880-92, Kansas City, Kan.; county atty. Wyandotte Co., Kan., 1893; probate judge Wyandotte Co., 1903-07; mem. 38th Gen. Assembly of Kan.; librarian Kan. State Library, 1919—. Lecturer on med. jurisprudence, Coll. of Phys. and Surg., Kansas City, Kan., 1893, 1902. Rep. campaign speaker, 1880—. Methodist. Made trip around the world, 1907-08, and delivered addresses at prin. missionary centres. Wrote: The Battle of Arickaree, in 6th Vol. Kansas History; The Prodigal Son, 1921; A Short Story About Leprosy, 1923. Home: Kansas City, Kan. Died July 1926.

FREER, Charles Lang, capitalist; b. Kingston, N.Y., 1856; s. Jacob R. and Phoebe Jane (Townsend) F.; ed. pub. schs., Ulster Co., N.Y.; (hon. A.M., U. of Mich.); unmarried. Was engaged in ry. service and mfg. in Detroit; now retired. Connoisseur of art; presented his art collection to Smithsonian Instn., Washington; also presented $1,000,000 for bldg. for same. Home: Detroit, Mich. Died Sept. 25, 1919.

FREER, Frederick Warren, artist, painter; b. Chicago, June 16, 1849; s. Dr. Joseph Warren and Katherine (Gatter) F.; ed. in pub. schs.; attended Royal Acad., Munich, Bavaria; spent several yrs. in Europe; m. Margaret Cecilia Keenan, June 16, 1886. Lived in New York, 1880-90; is asso. Nat. Acad. of Design. Received medal at World's Columbian Expn., 1893; bronze medal, Pan-Am. Expn., Buffalo, 1901; silver medal, Charleston Expn., 1902; Martin B. Cohn prize, Art Inst., Chicago, 1902; Artist's prize and medal, Chicago, 1903; bronze medal, St. Louis Expn., 1904. His principal works are: A Lady in Black; Consolation; The Old Letter; In Ambush; Sympathy. Teaches at Chicago Art Inst. Home: Chicago, Ill. Died 1908.

FREER, Hamline Hurlburt, college dean; b. Ellsworth, Ohio, Sept. 9, 1845; s. Sweeny Chauncey and Louisa (Hurlburt) F.; B.S., Cornell Coll., Ia., 1869, M.S., 1878, A.B., 1880, A.M., 1883 (LL.D., 1911); sr. fellow, U. of Chicago, 1892-93; m. Mary Louisa Markle, Dec. 22, 1871. Prin. schs., Chariton, Ia., 1869-70; teacher acad. Cornell Coll., 1870-72; prin. prep. and normal dept., 1872-87, prof. science and art of teaching and polit. economy, 1887-1902, dean, and David Joyce prof. polit. economy and sociology, 1902-19, emeritus, Cornell College, Mt. Vernon, Ia. Mem. Iowa State Bd. Ednl. Examiners, 1898-1902. Acting pres. Cornell Coll., 1914-15. Republican. Methodist. Died Aug. 26, 1920.

FREER, Otto (Tiger), laryngologist; b. Chicago, Aug. 8, 1857; s. Joseph Warren (M.D.) and Catharine (Gatter) F.; M.D., Rush Med. Coll., Chicago, 1879, followed by a semester each in the univs. of Munich, Vienna and Heidelberg; interne in Cook Co. Hosp., 1879-80; m. Agnes (Rand) Lee, May 18, 1911. Specialist in diseases of the nose, throat and ear; attending laryngologist to Henrotin Memorial Hosp., Chicago; prof. laryngology, Chicago Policlinic, emeritus. Republican. Home: Chicago, Ill. Died April 21, 1932.

FREER, Paul Caspar, chemist; b. Chicago, Mar. 27, 1862; s. Joseph Warren (M.D.) and Catharine (Gatter) F.; bro. of Otto Tiger F.; M.D., Rush Med. Coll., Chicago, 1882; Ph.D., U. of Munich, 1887; m. Agnes May Leas, June 1891. Asst., with Dr. Perkin, in Owens Coll., Manchester, 1887; asst. and instr. Tufts Coll., 1887-89; lecturer, 1889-90, prof. gen. chemistry, 1889-1903, U. of Mich.; supt. Govt. Laboratories, Manila, P.I., 1901-05; dir. Bur. Science, Manila, P.I., 1905—; dean P.I. Med. Sch. (now Coll. Medicine and Surgery), 1906—; prof. chemistry, U. of Philippines; editor Philippine Jour. of Science. Author: A General Inorganic Descriptive Chemistry, 1895; The Elements of Chemistry, 1896. Home: Manila, P.I. Died Apr. 17, 1912.

FREER, William Davis, water works exec.; b. Cortland, O., July 30, 1880; s. Frank Fletcher and Sarah E. (Davis) F.; student Ohio State U.; m. Ida L. Hess, June 23, 1904; 1 dau., Audrey Lee (Mrs. C. Carroll Simmonds). Pres. Alton (Ill.) Water Co., East St. Louis (Ill.) & Interurban Water Co., Peoria (Ill.) Water Works Co., Cairo (Ill.) Water Co., City Water Co. of Chattanooga (Tenn.), Birmingham (Ala.) Water Works Co., New Rochelle (N.Y.) Water Co., Port Chester (N.Y.) Water Co., Greenwich (Conn.) Water Co., Noroton Water Co. of Darien, Conn. Home: New York, N.Y. Died Oct. 11, 1940.

FREIBERG, Albert Henry, orthopedic surgeon; b. Cincinnati, Aug. 17, 1868; s. Joseph and Amalia F.; U. of Cincinnati; M.D., Med. Coll. of O. (U. of Cincinnati), 1890; univs. Würzburg, Strassburg, Berlin and Vienna; LL.D., Cedarville Coll., 1915; m. Jeannette Freiberg, Dec. 1, 1897; children—Joseph A., Albert M. Practiced at Cincinnati, 1893; prof. orthopedic surgery, med. dept. U. of Cincinnati, 1902-38, emeritus. Cons. orthopedic surgeon, Cincinnati and Children's hosps.; dir. orthopedic service, Jewish Hospital. Was mem. advisory bd. on orthopedics, and maj., M.C., U.S.A. Fellow Am. Coll. Surgeons, Am. Acad. Orthopedic Surgery; mem. Advisory Com. on Crippled Children, to Children's Bureau, U.S. Dept. of Labor. Mem. bd. of govs. Hebrew Union Coll.; mem. bd. of trustees, Cincinnati, O. Died July 14, 1940.

FREIBERG, Maurice (Julius), merchant, mfr.; b. Cincinnati, O., Jan. 7, 1861; s. Julius and Duffie (Workum) F.; ed. high sch., Cincinnati; m. Martha Pritz, Apr. 19, 1892 (died 1919); children—Duffie W. (Mrs. Benj. F. Stein), Caroline (Mrs. Marcus Fechheimer). Began as mem. Freiberg & Workum Co. (in liquidation); v.p. Morris Plan Bank (Cincinnati); treas. Cincinnati R.R. Terminal Development Co. Pres. Cincinnati union bd. high schs.; mem. Bd. Sinking Fund Trustees, Cincinnati; sec., v.p. and pres. Cincinnati Chamber Commerce, 1895-96; v.p. bd. trustees, commrs. new waterworks, Cincinnati, 1895-99. Treas. Cincinnati Community Chest,

Cincinnati Inst. Fine Arts; v.p. Cincinnati Museum Assn., Jewish Hosp. Assn. Democrat. Jewish religion. Mason. Home: Cincinnati, O. Died Dec. 30, 1936.

FRÉMONT, Jessie Benton, author; b. Va., 1824; d. Senator Thomas H. Benton of Mo.; m. Lt. (afterward Gen.) John C. Frémont, Oct. 19, 1841 (died 1890). Author: Story of the Guard; A Year of American Travel; Far West Sketches; Souvenirs of My Time; Sketch of Senator Benton; Will and the Way Stories. Home: Los Angeles, Calif. Died 1902.

FRÉMONT, John Charles, naval officer; b. San Francisco, Apr. 19, 1849; s. Maj. Gen. John Charles (U.S.A.) and Jessie (Benton) F.; grad. U.S. Naval Acad., 1872; adding expert studies in torpedoes, elec. science and ordnance; m. Sally Anderson, May 27, 1877. Promoted through various grades to rank of capt., Oct. 10, 1906. Comd. U.S.S. Pinta, 1875-77 (suppressed riots Baltimore, 1877); U.S.S. Drift, 1883-85; torpedo boat Porter in Spanish-Am. War; comdt. Cavite Navy Yard, 1899-1901; U.S.S. Calgoa, 1902-03; was comdg. U.S. monitor Florida, June 1903; 6 months' spl. duty as expert on searchlights on army bd. for coast fortification, 1902; naval attaché Paris and St. Petersburg, 1906-07; comdg. Mississippi, 1908-09. Died 1911.

FRENCH, Alice ("Octave Thanet"), author; b. Andover, Mass., Mar. 19, 1850; d. Hon. George Henry F.; ed. Abbott Acad., Andover; Litt.D., State U. of Ia., 1911. Author: Knitters in the Sun, 1887; Stories of a Western Town, 1893; The Heart of Toil, 1898; A Slave to Duty, 1900; Man of the Hour, 1905; The Lion's Share, 1907; By Inheritance, 1910; Stories That End Well, 1911; A Step on the Stair, 1913; And the Captain Answered, 1917. Home: Davenport, Ia. Died Jan. 9, 1934.

FRENCH, Amos Tuck, banker; b. Boston, Mass., July 20, 1863; s. Francis Ormond and Ellen (Tuck) F.; A.B., Harvard, 1885; m. Pauline Le Roy, Dec. 2, 1885. Mem. N.Y. Stock Exchange, 1887-91; treas., 1888, sec., 1891, v.p. and dir., 1893-1908, Manhattan Trust Co.; retired. Dir. Northern Securities Co., C.,B.&Q. Ry. Co., N.P. Ry. Co., Lying In Hosp. Republican. Gov. Breeders Club of N.H. Home: Tuxedo Park, N.Y., and Chester, N.H. Died Nov. 15, 1941.

FRENCH, Anne Warner, author; b. St. Paul, Minn.; Oct. 14, 1869; d. William P. and Anne Elizabeth (Richmond) Warner; ed. at home; m. Charles Ellis French, Sept. 12, 1888. Author: Susan Clegg and Her Friend, Mrs. Lathrop, 1904; The Rejuvenation of Aunt Mary, 1905; Susan Clegg and Her Neighbor's Affairs, 1906, and many others. Home: Dorset, England. Died Feb. 1, 1913.

FRENCH, Asa Palmer, lawyer; b. Braintree, Mass., Jan. 29, 1860; s. Asa and Sophia Briggs (Palmer) F.; A.B., Yale, 1882; instr. Latin and French, Thayer Acad., 1 yr.; LL.B., Boston U.; admitted to bar, 1885; clk. to judges, Ct. Commrs. Ala. Claims, Washington, 2 yrs.; m. Elisabeth Ombrose Wales, Dec. 13, 1887. Began practice at Boston, 1887; dist. atty. Southeastern Dist. of Mass., 1901-06; U.S. atty. for Dist. of Mass., 1906-14; del. Mass. Constl. Conv., 1917-18. Republican. Pres. Randolph Savings Bank. Counselor gen. Soc. of Mayflower Descendants. Home: Randolph, Mass. Died Sept. 17, 1935.

FRENCH, Calvin Hervey, educator; b. Williamsburg, O., June 13, 1862; s. Charles Porter and Mary (Brown) F.; A.B., Lake Forest U., 1888, A.M., 1891, D.D., 1928; grad. Union Theol. Sem., 1891; D.D., Coll. of Wooster, 1900; LL.D., Huron (S.D.) Coll., 1913; m. Anna Long, July 28, 1897; children—Robert Calvin, Ralph Voorhees, Charles Louis. Ordained Presbyn. ministry, 1891; pastor Scotland, S.D., 1891-98; prin. Scotland Acad., 1897-98, pres. Huron Coll., S.D., 1898-1913; asso. sec. Coll. Bd. of Presbyn. Ch. in U.S.A., New York, 1913-17; pres. Rollins Coll., Winter Park, Fla., Sept. 1, 1917-May 1, 1919; mgr. of survey of denominational and independent colleges and univs. for Interchurch World Movement of N. America, New York, 1919-20; pres. Hastings (Neb.) College, 1920—. Decorated Royal Order of St. Sava (Servia). Died Nov. 21, 1934.

FRENCH, Charles Wallace, teacher; b. Woodstock, Vt., Apr. 5, 1858; s. Charles W. and Anne M. F.; A.B., Dartmouth Coll., 1879, A.M., 1882; m. Mary L. Heart, July 17, 1889; 2d, Fannie K. Bartlett, June 28, 1900. Prin. Hyde Park High Sch., Chicago, 1891-1905; v.prin. Chicago Normal School, 1906-10; prin. Parker Practice Sch., Chicago, 1910-17; principal Parker High School, 1917. Member joint committee on English requirements for admission to college, 1896-1905; pres. Chicago Christian Endeavor Union, 1886-88. Author: Life of Lincoln (Am. Reformer's Series), 1889; Words of Lincoln, 1890; Introduction to the Study of Browning, 1892. Editor: Burke's Conciliation, 1900; Lights of Literature for the 7th and 8th Grades, 1900; Macaulay's Essays on Milton, Addison, Macbeth, 1898; Rab and His Friends, 1899; Black Beauty, 1900; The Sketch Book, 1901; Idylls of the King. Home: Chicago, Ill. Deceased.

FRENCH, Daniel Chester, sculptor; b. Exeter, N.H., Apr. 20, 1850; s. Hon. Henry Flagg and Anne (Richardson) F.; Mass. Inst. Tech., 1 yr.; under Dr. William Rimmer, Boston, Thomas Ball, Florence; hon. A.M., Dartmouth, 1898, Yale, 1913, Harvard, 1917; Litt.D., Columbia, 1913; m. Mary French, 1888; 1 dau., Margaret. Had studio in Washington, 1876-78; in Boston and Concord, Mass., 1878-87, in New York, 1887—. Among his best known works are: "The Minute Man of Concord," at Concord, Mass.; a statue of Gen. Cass, in the Capitol at Washington; statue of Rufus Choate, Boston Ct. House; John Harvard, at Cambridge, Mass., and Thomas Starr King statue; "Dr. Gallaudet and His First Deaf-Mute Pupil," the Milmore Memorial (3d class medal at Paris Salon, 1892); and colossal "Statue of the Republic," at Chicago Expn.; bronze doors, Boston Pub. Library; statue of Alma Mater, Columbia Coll.; 4 groups—Europe, Asia, Africa and America—in front of New York Custom House; statue of George F. Hoar, Worcester, 1908; statue of Governor James Oglethorpe, Savannah, Ga., 1910; statue of Abraham Lincoln, Lincoln, Neb., 1912; statue of Abraham Lincoln, Lincoln Memorial, Washington, D.C., 1920; etc. Mem. Nat. Commn. Fine Arts, 1910-15 (chmn. 1912-15). Medal of honor, Paris Exposition, 1900. N.A. 1902; trustee Metropolitan Museum of Art; fellow Am. Acad. Arts and Sciences. Home: Stockbridge, Mass. Died Oct. 7, 1931.

FRENCH, Edwin Davis, designer, engraver; b. N. Attleborough, Mass., Jan. 19, 1851; s. Ebenezer and Ann Maria (Norton) F.; prep. edn. Conn. Lit. Inst., Suffield, Conn., and 2 yrs. Brown Univ.; studied drawing at Art Students League under William Sartain; m. Mary Olivia Brainerd, Nov. 18, 1873. From 1894 has made specialty of book-plates. Pres. Art Students League of New York, 1889-91; mem. Am. Fine Arts Soc. (trustee 1891-96); mem. Ex-Libris Soc., London, Ex-Libris Verein zu Berlin. Home: Saranac Lake, N.Y. Died 1906.

FRENCH, Ferdinand Courtney, univ. prof.; b. Berkley, Mass., Dec. 14, 1861; s. Cicero R. C. and Harriet (Crane) F.; A.B., Brown U., 1885 A.M., 1888; Ph.D., Cornell, 1892; m. Caroline Mott West, July 1, 1896; children—Rodney West, Katharine. Prin. High Sch., Westminster, Mass., 1885-86, Johnston, R.I., 1886-88; studied univs. Berlin and Strassburg, 1888-90; instr. mathematics and psychology, Brown U., 1890-91; fellow Sage Sch. of Philosophy, Cornell, 1891-92; pro. philosophy, Colgate U., 1892-94, Vassar Coll., 1894-1901; hon. fellow Cornell, 1901-02; lecturer in philosophy of religion, Colgate U., 1902-03; prof. philosophy, U. of Neb., 1903-10, Colgate U., 1910—. Home: Hamilton, N.Y. Died Mar. 15, 1927.

FRENCH, Frances Graham, translator; b. Bangor, Me.; d. Hon. Augustus S. and Caro (Meade-Whitney) F.; ed. in Germany, France and Italy. Translator, essayist and editorial writer for publs. at home and abroad; spl. corr. at Chicago and Atlanta Expns. U.S. del. Internat. Congresses of Charities, Corrections and the Protection of Children, Switzerland, 1896; del. Internat. Congress of Women, Berlin, 1896; delivered papers at those congresses; del. Gen. Fedn. of Women's Clubs, Nashville and Denver; Internat. League of Press Clubs, New York and Stockholm; del. congresses, Brussels and Paris, 1899, 1900. Corr. sec. Internat. Press Union. Mem. Women's Federated Council on Employment for D.C.; member U.S. Food Administration. Died May 19, 1919.

FRENCH, Francis Henry, army officer; b. in Indiana, Sept. 27, 1857; grad. U.S. Mil. Acad., 1879, Army War Coll., 1912. Commd. 2d lt., June 13, 1879; 1st lt., Mar. 24, 1888; capt., Nov. 26, 1894; maj. 16th Inf., Feb. 28, 1901; lt. col., 12th Inf., June 25, 1906; assigned to 11th Inf., Jan. 13, 1911; col. 28th Inf., Feb. 15, 1911; assigned to 2d Inf., Nov. 23, 1912, to 21st Inf., Oct. 1, 1915; brig. gen., Sept. 30, 1916; maj. gen. N.A., Aug. 5, 1917. Duty on Mexican border, 1916, 17; apptd. comdr. Camp Jackson, Columbus, S.C., 1917; hon. disch. as maj. gen., Mar. 27, 1918. Died Mar. 10, 1921.

FRENCH, Frank, artist; b. London, N.H., May 22, 1850; s. Hiram W. and Lydia W. F.; m. Alice Hendricks, Apr. 22, 1875; children—Frank Allison, Mabel Edna. Medal Chicago Expn., 1893; Buffalo Expn., 1901; gold medal, St. Louis Expn., 1904; splty. is portrait painting. Mem. jury of selection for art, Chicago, Buffalo, and St. Louis expns. A.N.A. Home: Reeds Ferry, N.H. Died Feb. 19, 1933.

FRENCH, George, writer; b. N. Clarendon, Vt., June 4, 1853; s. Josiah Adams and Emeline L. (Nourse) F.; ed. common schs.; m. Inez Gertrude DeLand, Nov. 2, 1880. Author: How to Advertise, 1917; Advertising Fundamentals (with Harry Tipper), 1921; Advertising Campaigns (with Harry Tipper), 1923; Twentieth Century Advertising, 1925; and other business books. Home; Montclair, N.J. Died Mar. 20, 1935.

FRENCH, Harlan Page, educator; b. Cambridge, Vt., Sept. 29, 1843; s. Christopher and Persis (Lyon) F.; A.B., Amherst, 1868, A.M., 1871; m. M. Augusta Bowers, Aug. 22, 1872. Vice prin. high sch., Princeton, Ill., 1868-70; prin. high sch., Sterling, Ill., 1870-73; mfr. and dealer in sch. and office furniture, Albany, N.Y., 1873-80; mcht., New York, 1880-86; propr. Albany Teachers' Agency, 1890-1912; Albany Teachers' Agency, Inc., 1912—. Pres. and business mgr. N.Y. Education Co., Pubs. of Am. Education, 1899-1906. Mem. Bd. Public Instrn., Albany, N.Y., 1895-1902. Congregationalist, moderator annual meeting N.Y. State Assn. of Congl. Chs., 1900; trustee N.Y. Home Missionary Soc., 1898-1904. Republican. Home: Albany, N.Y. Died June 4, 1921.

FRENCH, Hollis, consulting engr.; b. Boston, Mass., June 26, 1868; s. John James and Frances M. (Stratton) F.; B.S., Mass. Inst. Tech., 1889; m. Helen Goodwin, June 3, 1896; children—Alden, Stanley Goodwin, Hollis Stratton, Rue Elizabeth. Cons. engr., alone, 1895-98; mem. Hollis French & Allen Hubbard, 1898-1930; office of Hollis French, 1931—; v.p. Exolon Co. Episcopalian. Author: American Silversmiths and Their Marks, 1917; The Thatcher Magoun, An American Clipper Ship, 1934; Jacob Hurd and His Sons, 1939. Home: Boston, Mass. Died Nov. 21, 1940.

FRENCH, Howard Barclay, mfr.; b. Salem, O., Sept. 3, 1848; s. Samuel H. and Angelina (Dunseth) F.; 6th in descent from Thomas F., Burlington, N.J., 1680; Friends' Schs.; grad. Phila. Coll. Pharmacy, 1870; entered Jefferson Med. Coll., 1879, but later yielded to wishes of father and withdrew; m. Ida Colket, Nov. 9, 1882. Began, in 1870, in father's firm, French, Richards & Co., wholesale druggists and paint mfrs.; became mem. Samuel H. French & Co., 1883, and sole propr., 1901—; pres. Samuel H. French & Co., Inc.; pres. Equitable Trust Co. of Phila., 1902-12 (dir.). Trustee Phila. Coll. Pharmacy, (pres.). Active worker in numerous leading orgns., city, state and nat. Pres. Phila. Chamber Commerce, formerly Trades League, of which is dir.; 1st v.p. Pa. State Chamber Com.; mem. exec. com. Tenn. Centennial Commn. Phila.; was sec. Union Com. on transportation, mfg. and commercial interests of Phila.; was chmn. joint com., also of subcom., on selection of site for U.S. Mint, Phila., 1893-94; mem. spl. com. on Transportation and R.R. Terminals, 1909-11; mem. com. of Organizing Commn. for 12th Congress of Permanent Internat. Assn. of Navigation Congs. Manager of Home Missionary Soc.; mgr. and trustee So. Home Destitute Children. Chmn. Citizens' Com. of 95 for Good City Government. Chmn. Phila. war shipping com. Chamber of Commerce U.S.A. Mem. bd. dirs. and chmn. Com. on Grounds and Buildings of Sesqui-Centennial; acting chmn. com. having charge of Independence Hall and adjoining building. Home: Radnor, Pa., and Philadelphia. Died Oct. 16, 1924.

FRENCH, James Adolphus, clergyman; b. Ballsville, Va.; s. of John W. and Judith (Blanton) F.; spl. course, with medals, Richmond (Va.) Coll., 1871-74; grad. Southern Bapt. Theol. Sem., Louisville, 1877; studied U. of Va., 1877-78; (D.D., Howard Coll., 1893); m. Fannie T. Madison, grandniece Pres. Madison, May 25, 1880. Ordained Bapt. ministry, 1876; pastor Orange and Gordonsville, Va., jointly, 1877-82, Paris, Ky., 1882-85, Shelbyville, Ky., 1885-90, Talladega, Ala., 1890-96, First Ch., Austin, Tex., 1896-1908, First Ch., Eufaula, Ala., 1908-13, First Ch., Columbia, Ala., Dec. 1, 1913—. Pres. of Texas Baptist S.S. Conv., 3 yrs.; trustee Tex. Instn. for Deaf and Dumb, 8 yrs., Howard Coll., Birmingham, Ala.; mem. Bapt. Mission Bds. of Ky. and Ala., Tex. Bapt. Edn. Commn.; quasi chaplain U. of Tex. 12 yrs. Home: Columbia, S.C. Died June 1916.

FRENCH, Joseph Lewis, author, editor; b. N.Y. City, Aug. 16, 1858; s. Creighton Brewer and Caroline (Baldwin) F.; student Geneva Coll., West Geneva, O., 1872-73; unmarried. Founder The New West (monthly mag.), Kansas City, Mo., 1887; co-founder The Wave (weekly), San Francisco, 1890; newspaperwork at Rochester, N.Y., 1879, later in Colo., and at Chicago, Kansas City, San Francisco, returning east, 1894. Author or compiler: Christ in Art, 1899; Great Ghost Stories, 1918; The Best Ghost Stories, 1919; Great Sea Stories, 1921; Masterpieces of Mystery (4 vols.), 1921; Great Pirate Stories, 1922; Thrilling Escapes, 1923; The Pioneer West, 1923; Sixty Years of American Humor, 1924; Great Detective Stories (3 vols.), 1924; Sagas of the Seas, 1924; Great Sea Stories (2d series), 1925; Great Pirate Stories (2d series), 1925; Tales of Terror, 1925; The Book of the Rogue, 1926; The Book of Chinese and Japanese Verse, 1926; These Splendid Women, 1926; These Splendid Rulers, 1926; The Jolly Roger (pirate-stories for boys), 1927; Big Aviation Book for Boys, 1929; Pioneers All, 1929; Great Detective Stories of the World, 1929; Gray Shadows, 1931; Ghost Story Omnibus, 1933. Editor: Aces of the Air, 1930; Gallery of Old Rogues, 1931; Wings Over the World, 1931; Conquerors of the Sky, 1932. Died Dec. 14, 1936.

FRENCH, Nathaniel Stowers, educator, author; b. Prospect, Me., 1854; s. Robert and Frances (Stowers) F.; grad. Boston Univ., 1881, Ph.D., 1894; m. Myra Putnam, Apr. 3, 1882. Teacher, 1875—, Roxbury High Sch., Boston. Author: Animal Activities, 1902; also Laboratory Experiment Blanks for Chemistry and Physics, and Experiments with Alcohol. Home: Sandy Point, Me. Died 1905.

FRENCH, Samuel Gibbs, soldier; b. Gloucester Co., N.J., Nov. 22, 1818; s. Samuel F.; grad. U.S. Mil. Acad., 1843; in U.S.A. until May 1856, when he resigned, having reached grade of capt.; served in Mexican War and took part in battles of Palo Alto, Resaca de la Palma, Monterey and Buena Vista (severely wounded); m. E. Matilda Roberts; m. 2d, Mary E. Abercrombie. Cotton planter, Greenville, Miss., 1856-78; col. and chief of ordnance, Army of State of Miss., before he joined the Confederacy; commd. brig. gen. C.S.A., Oct. 23, 1861; maj. gen., Aug. 31, 1862; served in Army of Northern Va., Oct. 1861, to June 1863; comd. Dept. of N.C. and Southern Va., July 1862 to June 1863, when he was sent to join Gen. Joseph E. Johnston in Miss.; served in the West on the Dalton and Atlanta campaign; took part in many battles, blockaded the Potomac at Evansport, 1861-62; comd. the troops at Harrison's Landing on the James River (where he shelled McClellan's army from midnight to dawn, July 31, 1862, with 45 pieces of artillery), Kingstown, Whitehall, Rome, Tilton; fought the battle of Allatoona, Kenesaw Mountain, defeating Gen. McPherson's assault, and Jackson, Miss., on the Meridian campaign. Home: Pensacola, Fla. Died 1910.

FRENCH, William John, cattle raiser; b. Frenchpark, Co. Roscommon, Ireland, Apr. 21, 1854; s. Charles (Lord De Freyne) and Catherine (Maree) (Lady De Freyne) F.; ed. Beaumont Coll., Berkshire, Eng., Trinity Coll., Dublin, Ireland; m. Mary Josephine Beirne, July 10, 1900; children—Charles William, Miss M. J. (Wockie), Arthur Valentine, Gwendolen Frances, Richard John, Robert Dermot, Laura Elizabeth, Evelyn Agnes. Served as 1st and 2d lt. and capt., in 3d Batt., Royal Irish Regt., 1876-83; came to U.S., 1883, naturalized citizen, 1895; formerly mgr. and dir. W.S. Land & Cattle Co., N.M. Home: Los Angeles, Calif. Died Dec. 6, 1928.

FRENCH, William Merchant Richardson, art dir.; b. Exeter, N.H., Oct. 1, 1843; s. Henry Flagg and Anne (Richardson) F.; bro. of Daniel Chester F.; A.B., Harvard, 1864; m. Sarah M. Lovejoy, Sept. 9, 1879 (died 1881); m. 2d, Alice Helm, Mar. 28, 1890. Practiced civ. engring. and landscape gardening, 1865-77; became connected, 1877, with the Sch. and Mus. of Art in Chicago; dir. Art Inst. of Chicago, 1879—. Pres. Am. Assn. of Museums, 1907-08. Home: Chicago, Ill. Died June 3, 1914.

FRETTER, Frank B., oil producer, refiner; b. Cleveland, O., Oct. 2, 1864; s. Nathaniel and Barbara (Kirch) F.; ed. pub. schs.; m. Margaret A. Hurlbut, 1892; 1 dau., Margaret (Mrs. Walker H. Nye). Connected with Nat. Refining Co., 1887—, pres., 1920—; pres. Canadian Oil Cos., Ltd. Clubs: Union, Mayfield Country. Home: Cleveland Heights, O. Died Apr. 14, 1935.

FREUND, Ernst, univ. prof.; b. New York, N.Y., Jan. 30, 1864; s. Ludwig A. and Nannie (Bayer) F.; ed. Kreuzschule, Dresden, Gymnasium, Frankfort-on-Main, univs. of Berlin and Heidelberg, J.U.D., 1884, Columbia U. Law Sch. and Sch. of Polit. Science, Ph.D., 1897; LL.D., U. of Mich., 1931; m. Harriet Walton, May 13, 1916. Acting prof. administrative law, Columbia, 1892-93; instr., asst. prof., asso. prof., 1894-1902, prof. jurisprudence and pub. law, 1902—, U. of Chicago. Commr. Uniform State Laws for Ill. Author: Police Power, 1904; Standards of American Legislation, 1917; Administrative Powers Over Persons and Property, 1928. Home: Chicago, Ill. Died Oct. 20, 1932.

FREW, Walter Edwin, banker; b. Brooklyn, N.Y., July 18, 1864; s. George Edward and Amanda (Crooker) F.; m. Ella Louise Carman, July 28, 1888; 1 dau., Mrs. Helen Peters. Began as clk. in office of Shepherd, Knapp & Co., stock brokers, 1880; chmn. Corn Exchange Bank Trust Co., New York City; pres. Corn Exchange Safe Deposit Co.; dir. Woodlawn Cemetery Co., Ingersoll-Rand Co. Republican. Mem. Dutch Ref. Ch. Home: New York, N.Y. Died May 19, 1941.

FREW, William Nimick, lawyer; b. Pittsburgh, Pa., July 10, 1854; s. William and Martha E. (Long) F.; A.B., Yale, 1876; m. Emily W. Berry, Jan. 13, 1881. Admitted to bar, 1879; mem. select council, Pittsburgh, 1885-89. Pres. bd. trustees Carnegie Library, controlling free library system of Pittsburgh; pres. bd. trustees Carnegie Inst., comprising 3 depts. of art, science and tech. schs.; pres. Pittsburgh Orchestra Com., 1897-1902; mem. bd. trustees Carnegie Instn. of Washington, Carnegie Corp. of New York, Carnegie Hero Fund Commn., Pa. Coll. for Women, State Library Commn. of Pa. Dir. Union Trust Co., Mellon Nat. Bank, Union Savings Bank, City Deposit Bank of Pittsburgh. Republican. Home: Pittsburgh, Pa. Died Oct. 28, 1915.

FREY, Oliver W., congressman; b. Bucks Co., Pa., Sept. 7, 1890; A.B., Coll. of William and Mary, Williamsburg, Va., 1915; LL.B., U. of Pa., 1920; m. Jessie M. Straub, June 28, 1928. Admitted to Pa. bar, 1920, and began practice at Allentown; elected to 73d Congress, Nov. 7, 1933, and reëlected to 74th and 75th Congresses (1935-39), 9th Pa. Dist. Served as commd. officer U.S. Army, 1917-19. Democrat. Home: Allentown, Pa. Died Aug. 26, 1939.

FRICK, Frank, mcht.; b. Baltimore, Md., Jan. 3, 1828; s. Judge William F., whose German ancestors settled in Md. early in 18th century; grad. St. Mary's Coll., Baltimore, 1845; m. Fanny L. Lürman (dec.). Engaged in commercial life; for 25 yrs. mem. firm of C. Morton Stewart & Co.; at one time pres. Baltimore Bd. of Trade; pres. Auditorium Co. Music Hall, and other financial, charitable and ednl. instns.; led in reorganizing sugar refining interests in Baltimore. Takes much interest in promoting the prosperity of his native city and development of art and high class music. Home: Baltimore, Md. Deceased.

FRICK, Henry Clay, mfr.; b. W. Overton, Pa., Dec. 19, 1849; s. John W. and Elizabeth (Overholt) F.; began business life as a clerk for his grandfather, a flour mcht. and distiller; later embarked in coke business; m. Adelaide Howard, d. late Asa P. Childs, of Pittsburgh, Dec. 15, 1881. Was pres. and from 1897, chmn. bd. dirs. H. C. Frick Coke Co. Came into pub. notice by his vigorous management during the famous strike at Homestead, 1892. Chmn. bd. Carnegie Bros., 1889-92, and later chmn. bd. mgrs. Carnegie Steel Co. Home: New York, N.Y. Died Dec. 2, 1919.

FRICK, Joseph E., judge; b. Tiffin, O., Aug. 6, 1848; s. Michael and Mary Ann (Kuen) F.; ed. common schs.; read law at Toledo, Ia.; m. Catharine L. Kunz, Dec. 25, 1872; children—Frank T. (dec.), Laura E. (dec.), Frederick O., Etta L. Admitted to bar, 1880, and began practice at Toledo, Ia., but soon removed to Fremont, Neb.; went to Utah, 1897. Justice Supreme Ct. of Utah, Oct. 1, 1906—(chief justice, Jan. 1, 1911-13, 1917-18); present term expires Jan. 1931. Home: Salt Lake City, Utah. Died Feb. 12, 1927.

FRICK, William Keller, clergyman; b. Lancaster, Pa., Feb. 1, 1850; s. William and Maria Barbara (Keller) F.; A.B., Muhlenberg Coll., Pa., 1870, A.M., 1873 (D.D., 1902); m. Louisa Frederica Klump, Oct. 7, 1873. Ordained Luth. ministry, 1873; 1st pastor St. Paul's Ch., Phila., 1873-83; prof. English, Gustavus Adolphus Coll., Minn., 1883-89; missionary in Wash. and Ore., summer of 1889; a founder of English Luth. work in Wis., and 1st pastor Ch. of the Redeemer, Milwaukee, 1889—. Organizer of a number of chs. in Wis.; 1st sec., 1891-93, pres., 1894-1901, English Evang. Luth. Synod of the Northwest; rec. sec. Gen. Council Evang. Luth. Ch. in N. America, 1895-1901, 1905—; trustee and sec. bd. dirs. Chicago Luth. Theol. Sem. Author: Henry Melchior Muhlenberg, Patriarch of the Lutheran Church in America, 1902. Home: Milwaukee, Wis. Died Aug. 20, 1918.

FRIEDEN, John Pierre, univ. pres.; b. Luxembourg, Nov. 18, 1844; student high sch., normal sch. and coll., Luxembourg; entered Society of Jesus and came to America, 1869; student St. Stanislaus Sem., Florissant, Mo., 1869-71; instr. in lit., St. Louis U., 1871-74; took complete courses in philosophy, science and divinity, at Woodstock Coll., Md., 1874-81. Ordained priest R.C. Ch., 1880; prof. philosophy, dir. of studies, and pres., Detroit Coll., 1881-89; provincial superior, Jesuit instns. in Middle West, 1889-94; spiritual dir. St. Stanislaus Sem., 1894-96; gen. superior Jesuit instns. in Calif., and pres. St. Ignatius Coll., San Francisco, 1896-1907; pres. St. Louis U., Feb. 10, 1908—. Home: St. Louis, Mo. Died 1911.

FRIEDENWALD, Julius, M.D.; b. Baltimore, Md., Dec. 20, 1866; s. Dr. Aaron and Bertha (Bamberger) F.; A.B., Johns Hopkins, 1887; M.D., Coll. Phys. and Surg. (now U. of Md.), Baltimore, 1890; student Berlin, Vienna, Paris, London, 1891-93; hon. A.M., Loyola Coll., Baltimore, 1898; m. Esther Lee Rohr, Oct. 24, 1900. Practicing medicine in Baltimore, 1890—. Prof. emeritus gastro-enterology, U. of Md. Sch. of Medicine and Coll. Phys. and Surg., Baltimore; visiting gastro-enterologist to Mercy Hosp.; consultant in digestive diseases to Union Memorial Hospital, Ch. Home and Infirmary, Sinai and Woman's hosps.; advisor Am. Board Internal Medicine. Trustee Inst. for Advanced Study, Princeton, N.J. Fellow A.M.A. (chmn. sect. on gastro-enterology, 1930), Am. Coll. Physicians. Author: Guide to Clinical Laboratory Diagnosis (with Drs. Beck and Knapp), edits., 1901-04; Diet in Health and Disease (with Dr. John Ruhrah), 6 edits., 1905-25; Dietetics for Nurses (with same), 5 edits., 1905-24; Secondary Gastro-Intestinal Disorders (with T. H. and Samuel Morrison), 1938. Home: Baltimore, Md. Died June 8, 1941.

FRIEDLAENDER, Israel, college prof.; b. Russia, Sept. 8, 1876; s. Pinkus and Gitel (Ehrlich) F.; Berlin U. and Rabbinier Seminar, 1896-1900; Ph.D., U. of Strassburg, 1901, admitted as privatdozent for Semitic langs., 1902; m. Lilian Ruth Bentwich, of London, Eng., Sept. 26, 1905. Sabato Morias prof. Bibl. lit. and Exegesis, Jewish Theol. Sem. of America, New York, Oct. 1903—. Mem. exec. com. Jewish Community of N.Y. City, United Synagogue America; mem. Am. Jewish Com.; trustee Ednl. Alliance, New York; mem. publ. com. Jewish Publ. Soc. America; mem. joint distbn. com. of Am. Funds for Jewish War Sufferers. Editor: The Jews of Russia and Poland, 1915; S. M. Dubnow, History of the Jews in Russia and Poland, from the Earliest Times Until the Present Day (transl. from the Russian), 1916, 2d vol., 1918; Past and Present (Jewish essays), 1919. Home: New York, N.Y. Died July 5, 1920.

FRIEDLANDER, Alfred, M.D., educator; b. Cincinnati, Ohio, July 5, 1871; s. Abraham Joseph and Lisette (Friedman) F.; A.B., Harvard, 1892; M.D., U. of Cincinnati, 1895; grad. study, Strassburg, Berlin, Vienna, Erlangen; m. Gertrude Hyman, Apr. 17, 1900; children—Alfred Joseph, Susie, Peggy. Began practice at Cincinnati, 1898; asso. prof. pediatrics, U. of Cincinnati, 1910-17, prof. medicine, 1919—, also dean College of Medicine. Was maj. Med. Corps, U.S.A., 1917-19; lt. col. Med. O.R.C. Jewish religion. Author: Hypotension, 1927. Home: Cincinnati, O. Died May 28, 1939.

FRIEDMAN, Isaac Kahn, author; b. Chicago, Ill., Nov. 3, 1870; s. Jacob and Henrietta (Kahn) F.; bro. of Herbert Jacob F.; Ph.B., U. of Mich., 1893; spl. studies in polit. economy and philosophy; later took part of post-grad. course in philosophy and English, U. of Chicago; m. Mrs. Sara M. Gimbel, Jan. 9, 1909. In florist bus. with bro. 3 yrs., then became spl. writer on Chicago newspapers and for mags.; traveled extensively in Japan, China and Korea, 1908, as corr. for Chicago Daily News on financial, econ. and sociol. topics. Author: The Lucky Number, 1896; Poor People, 1900; By Bread Alone; The Autobiography of a Beggar; The Radical, 1907. Home: Winnetka, Ill. Died Sept. 22, 1931.

FRIEDSAM, Michael, merchant; b. N.Y. City; s. Morris and Barbara F.; ed. Weston Mil. Acad.; hon. Dr. Commercial Science, New York U., 1921; hon. LL.D., Fordham U., 1925; unmarried. Long with B. Altman & Co., dry goods mchts., becoming pres. of the company; pres. Altman Foundation, Fifth Av. Assn.; dir. Bankers Trust Co., Bank of Manhattan Co.; trustee Franklin Savings Bank. Decorated Comdr. Legion of Honor (French). Republican. Home: New York, N.Y. Died Apr. 6, 1931.

FRIEND, Emil, newspaperman; b. Prague, Austria, Dec. 25, 1863; s. Adolph and Katherine (Brandeis) F.; grad. U. of Vienna; m. Frieda Meyer, Jan. 9, 1899. Began newspaper work on staff of Fremdenblatt, Vienna, Austria; came to U.S., 1886, and was on staff of German press at New York, subsequently on English literary, musical and dramatic papers, New York; removed to Chicago, 1898; on staff Chicago Daily News, 1898-1908; financial editor Chicago Examiner, then Herald-Examiner, 1908—. Writes under nom de plume of "Boersianer." Home: Hinsdale, Ill. Died Oct. 27, 1921.

FRIES, Archibald, ry. official; b. Cincinnati, O., Feb. 27, 1864; s. John and Martha Ann (Harper) F.; ed. pub. and high schs., Cincinnati, and spl. coll. course; m. Elizabeth Johnson. Clk. and cashier, Ohio & Miss. Ry., Storrs, O.; chief rate and claim clk., Continental Line, 1890, later accountant, chief clk. and acting mgr., and afterwards chief clerk gen. frt. office B.&O. R.R. Co., later made gen. agt. and asst. gen. frt. agt. at Cincinnati; trans. to Pittsburgh as gen. frt. agt., 1913, and made gen. traffic mgr. B.&O. Eastern Lines, hdqrs. Baltimore, 1916, jurisdiction extended over entire B.&O. System, 1918; served as traffic mgr. frt. and pass. traffic under Railroad Administration, during war period, of B.&O. Eastern Lines and various rys. in Allegheny region; made gen. traffic mgr. B.&O. System Corporate Co., Jan. 1, 1920; v.p. in charge traffic and commercial development B.&O. System, Feb. 25, 1920—. Was mem. Freight Traffic Com. in control export and domestic traffic, Boston to Norfolk and Newport News inclusive, during early part of war period. Presbyn. Home: Severna Park, Md. Died June 9, 1939.

FRIES, Francis Henry, banker; b. Salem, N.C., Feb. 1, 1855; s. Francis and Lisette M. (Volger) F.; A.B., Davidson (N.C.) Coll., 1873; m. Anna de Schweinitz, Aug. 19, 1886; 1 dau., Mrs. Eleanor Fries Wellingham. Began as mem. F. & H. Fries, cotton mfrs., 1875; supt. of Arista Mills, 1881, later director; builder Roanoke & Southern Ry., and president 1887 until its absorption by Norfolk & Western Ry. in 1893; president Wachovia Bank & Trust Co., Washington Mills; v.p. Oakdale Cotton Mills, Indera Mills, N.C. Granite Corp. Dir. War Savings, State of N.C., 1918. Mem. staff Gov. Scales of N.C., title of col. Trustee Salem Acad. and Coll. Democrat. Moravian. Home: Winston-Salem, N.C. Died June 5, 1931.

FRIES, J(oens) Elias, engr.; b. Frinnaryd, Sweden, Apr. 6, 1876; E.E. and M.E., Kongl. Tekniska Hogskolan, Stockholm, 1898; m. Annerika Bjerkander, Vestergotl, Sweden; 1 son, Erik Fritiof Bjerkander. Came to U.S. 1903; with Westinghouse, Church, Kerr & Co., New York, 1903-05, Allis-Chalmers Co., 1905-07, Canadian Gen. Electric Co., 1907-08, Crocker-Wheeler Co., advancing to asst. chief engr., 1908-16; chief elec. engr., Tenn. Coal, Iron & R.R. Co., 1916-20; chief engr. same, 1920—, and Chickasaw Shipbuilding & Car Co. Fellow Am. Inst. E.E., A.A.A.S. Unitarian. Author: Einstein's Theory of Relativity, 1921. Translator: Death and Resurrection (by G. Bjorklund), 1910; The Destinies of the Stars (by Arrhenius), 1918. Home: Birmingham, Ala. Died Jan. 23, 1932.

FRIES, John William, mfr., banker; b. Salem, N.C., Nov. 7, 1846; s. Francis and L. M. (Vogler) F.; ed. University of N.C.; LL.D. from U. of N.C., 1926; m. Agnes S., d. Bishop E. A. de Schweinitz, Oct. 25, 1870. Has been justice of the peace, presiding judge of co. ct. and co. commr. Has been cotton and woolen mfr.; inventor machines and processes for dyeing yarns and cloth; pres. People's Nat. Bank, Winston, N.C. Trustee U. of N.C., Salem Acad. and Coll.; mem. gov. bd. Southern province, Moravian Ch. Mem. of Monetary Commn. to propose a plan of currency reform. Home: Winston-Salem, N.C. Died Nov. 21, 1927.

FRIES, William Otterbein, clergyman, editor; b. Winchester, Va., Nov. 17, 1860; s. William and Mary Jane (Fulkerson) F.; prep. edn. Shenandoah Sem., Va.; A.B., Lebanon Valley Coll., Annville, Pa., 1882, A.M., 1885; grad. Bonebrake Theol. Sem., 1884; (D.D., Otterbein U., 1903); m. Fannie Coe Nelson, Feb. 18, 1886. Ordained U.B. ministry, 1884; pastor Hagerstown, Md., 1884-86; prin. W.Va. Acad., Buckhannon, W.Va., 1886-89; pastor Fostoria, O., 1889-93, Otterbein U., 1893-97, Van Buren, O., 1897-99; supt. Sandusky (O.) Conf., 1899-1905; editor S.S. lit., U.B. Ch., 1905—. Trustee Otterbein U. Hon. mem. Philophronean Soc. (Otterbein U.). Trustee Bonebrake Theol. Sem. Home: Dayton, O. Died Oct. 15, 1925.

FRIESEKE, Frederick Carl, artist; b. Owosso, Mich., Apr. 7, 1874; s. Herman Carl and Eva (Graham) F.; Art Inst. of Chicago; Art Students' League, New York; Julian Acad. and Whistler Sch., Paris; studied under Constant Laurens and Whistler; m. Sarah A. O'Bryan, Oct. 31, 1905. Pictures in Gallerie-Moderne, Venice; Luxembourg Gallerie, Paris; Museum, Odessa, Russia; Telfair Acad., Ga.; Art Inst. of Chicago, 1912; Met. Mus.; Minneapolis Inst. Art; City Art Mus., St. Louis; Cincinnati Mus.; Toledo Mus.; Detroit Mus.; Corcoran Art Gallery, Washington; Harrison Gallery; Los Angeles Mus. of History, Science and Art; John Herron Art Inst., Indianapolis; U. of Illinois, Urbana; Addison Gallery of Am. Art, Andover, Mass., etc. Mural decorations: Hotel Sherbourne, Atlantic City; Wanamaker Auditorium, New York. Awarded gold medal, Munich, 1904; silver medal, St. Louis Expn., 1904; 4th W. A. Clark prize ($500) Corcoran Art Gallery, 1908; Temple gold medal, Pa. Acad. Fine Arts, 1913; grand prize for painting, Panama P.I. Expn., 1915; Harris silver medal and prize, Art Inst. Chicago, 1916; Palmer gold medal and French medal, Art Inst. Chicago, 1920; Edward B. Butler prize, Art Inst. Chicago, 1920; Gold medal, Art Club, Philadelphia, 1922. N.A., 1914. Decorated Chevalier Legion of Honor (French). Died Aug. 27, 1939.

FRINK, Fred Goodrich, civil engr.; b. Pilot Grove, Ill., Apr. 16, 1862; s. Morey French and Ellen E. (Goodrich) F.; B.S. in Civ. Engring., U. of Mich., 1886; M.S., U. of Chicago, 1902; spl. student in sanitary engring., Mass. Inst. Tech., 1900-01; m. Mae Beadle, July 10, 1888. Asst. engr. Big 4, C.&A. and C.&N.W. rys., 1886-88; computer and supt. Vierling & McDowell, and Snead & Co. iron works, Chicago, 1888-90; instr. archtl. drawing, Manual Training High Sch., Chicago, 1890-97; in charge drawing, Chicago Athenæum, 1893-97; prof. civ. engring., U. of Ida., 1897-1900; in pvt. bus., 1900-02; taught engring. classes of the late Dean C. E. Greene, U. of Mich., 1902-04; asst. prof. civ. engring., U. of Ill., 1904-06; pres. Lake Constrn. Co., Hammond, Ind., 1906-08; prof. of engring., U. of Ore., 1908-15; cons. practice, 1915—. Republican. Episcopalian. Mason. Author: Trigonometry (Hall and Frink), 1909. Home: Palo Alto, Calif. Died Sept. 30, 1929.

FRINK, John Samuel Hatch, lawyer, banker; b. Newington, N.H., Nov. 9, 1832; s. Simes and Sarah (Hatch) F.; prep. edn. Hampton Acad.; grad. Bowdoin Coll., 1851; m. Lucretia Morse Pickering, 1860. Admitted to bar, 1855; atty. for Rockingham Co., N.H., 1871-75; apptd. judge Supreme Court N.H., 1871 and 1878, but declined both apptmts.; U.S. dist. atty., N.H., 1885-90; Palmer Democrat. Pres. Portsmouth Savings Bank. Home: Greenland, N.H. Died 1905.

FRISBIE, Alvan Lillie, clergyman; b. Thompkins, N.Y., Oct. 22, 1830; s. Daniel G. and Bernice (Lowrey) F.; student Oberlin Coll., 1852-53; A.B., Amherst Coll., 1857; theol. studies Yale Div. Sch. and Andover Theol. Sem.; (D.D., Amherst, 1882); m. Jerusha R. Slocomb, July 22, 1859; 2d, Martha J. Crosby, July 29, 1873; father of William Albert F. Ordained Congl. ministry, 1860; pastor Ansonia, Conn., 1860-65, First Ch., Danbury, Conn., 1865-71, Plymouth Ch., Des Moines, Ia., 1871-98; pastor emeritus, 1898—. Chaplain 20th Conn. Inf., 1863-64. Trustee Ia. Coll., 1889—; chmn. State Bd. Home Missions for Ia. 20 yrs. Republican. Address: Des Moines, Ia. Died Dec. 17, 1917.

FRISBY, Edgar, astronomer; b. Great Easton, Leicestershire, Eng., May 22, 1837; s. Thomas and Noah F.; B.A., U. of Toronto, 1863, M.A., 1864; m. Laura Virginia Ebert, Aug. 6, 1872. Taught in Canada, 1863-67; afterward acting prof. mathematics, Northwestern U.; later asst. astronomer U.S. Naval Obs., Washington, and prof. mathematics U.S.N., June 11, 1878; present relative rank of comdr.; retired, May 22, 1899. Observed for Govt. several eclipses and made noteworthy computation of orbit of comet of 1882. Home: Washington, D.C. Died Jan. 7, 1927.

FRISCH, William, newspaper editor; b. Austria, 1854; s. Siegfried and Sophia F.; located in Baltimore with parents, 1865; acad. and business coll. edn.; worked as bookkeeper and in printing a short time; unmarried. Reporter, 1872-79, polit. editor, and Washington corr., 1879-81, mng. editor, 1881—. Baltimore American. During a trip to Europe, 1896, he had lengthy conversations with Gladstone and Salisbury in Eng., Profs. Momsen and Herman Grimm in Germany, and Verdi and Pope Leo XIII in Italy; visited southern and northern Spain, southern France, Italy, Sicily, Egypt, Palestine and Syria, Turkey and Greece, 1909. Home: Baltimore, Md. Died 19—.

FRISSELL, Algernon Sydney, banker; b. S. Amenia, N.Y., Feb. 1, 1845; s. Rev. Amasa Cogswell and Lavinia (Barker) F.; ed. Amenia Sem. and pvt. sch., Poughkeepsie, N.Y.; m. Susan Brinckerhoff Varick, May 12, 1870 (died 1885). Began employment in City Bank, Poughkeepsie, 1862; asst. cashier Nat. Bank of the Metropolis, Washington, D.C., 1865-66; went to New York City, 1867; clerk Importers & Traders Nat. Bank, and afterwards loan clerk there several yrs.; cashier, 1875-85, pres., 1885-1916, chmn. bd. Fith Avenue Bank, 1916—. Mem. com. apptd. to report on improvements in banking laws of N.Y.; mem. N.Y. Bd. of Edn., 1901-05. Treas. Civ. Service Reform Assn., Hampton Assn. Presbyn. Home: New York, N.Y. Died Dec. 19, 1932.

FRISSELL, Hollis Burke, educator; b. Amenia, N.Y., July 14, 1851; s. Rev. Amasa Cogswell and Lavinia (Barker) F.; bro. of Algernon Sydney F.; A.B., Yale, 1874; grad. Union Theol. Sem., New York, 1879; (D.D., Howard, 1893; S.T.D., Harvard, 1900; LL.D., Yale, 1901, Richmond, 1909); m. Julia F. Dodd, Nov., 1883. Ordained Persbyn. ministry, 1880; asst. pastor Madison Av. Ch., New York, 1880; chaplain, 1880-93, prin., 1893—, Hampton Inst., a famous sch. for Indians and colored youth of both sexes. Mem. Southern Edn. Bd. (an organizer), Gen. Edn. Bd., Negro Rural Sch. Fund, Anna T. Jeanes Foundation; chmn. trustees Calhoun Colored Sch., and Penn N., A. and I.; trustee Va. Manual Labor Sch. of the Negro Reformatory Assn. of Va., 1900—; pres. N.Y. State Colonization Soc., 1914. Home: Hampton, Va. Died Aug. 5, 1917.

FRITZ, John, mech. engr.; b. Chester Co., Pa., Aug. 21, 1822; ed. common schs.; (hon. A.M., Columbia, 1898; Sc.D., U. of Pa., 1906; Temple U., 1911; D.Eng., Stevens Inst. Tech., 1907). Apprenticed to blacksmith trade, 1838; employed in Norristown (Pa.) Iron Works, where soon became mill foreman; with others started small machine shop, 1852; made gen. supt. Cambria Iron Works, Johnstown, Pa., 1854; entered service of Bethlehem Iron Co. as gen. supt. and engr., 1860, and built works of co.; retired in 1892. Received complimentary resolution from Am. Soc. Mech. Engrs., 1892 (hon. mem.); elected, 1893, hon. mem. Iron and Steel Inst. of Great Britain, from which received Bessemer gold medal for services in advancement of steel mfrs. (hon. v.p. same, 1909). Selected by Armor Plate Bd., 1897, to make plans and estimates for a Govt. armor plate works. Republican; presdl. elector, 1896. Mem. Group I, Centennial Expn., Phila., 1876; hon. expert on iron and steel, St. Louis Expn., 1904; awarded John Fritz medal, United Engring. Socs., 1902; Elliott Cresson medal, Franklin Inst., 1910. Home: Bethlehem, Pa. Died Feb. 13, 1913.

FRIZELL, Joseph Palmer, civil engr.; b. Barford, Quebec, Mar. 13, 1832; s. Oliver and Mary S. (Beach) F.; ed. in Can.; spl. studies in civ. engring.; m. Julia A. Bowes, Oct. 1864. Was engaged in constrn. of fortifications on Gulf Coast during Civil War; later employed in pub. service in improvement of rivers and harbors; especially in charge system of reservoirs on head waters of the Mississippi; chief engr. bd. pub. works, Austin, Tex., 1890; from 1892 in Boston engaged in hydraulic engring., mainly in line of water power. Home: Boston, Mass. Died May 4, 1910.

FRIZZELL, Albert Burnett, publisher; b. Minneapolis, Minn., Jan. 16, 1891; s. Charles William and Annie (Sweeney) F.; m. Anna Johnston, Sept. 17, 1919; 1 dau., Marilyn Ann. Began as advertising solicitor Minneapolis Daily News, 1912; purchased the L. K. Lee Advertising Agency, 1919, and has since conducted it as the Frizzell Advt. Agency; purchased Farm, Stock & Home mag., 1923, later merged with Northwest Farmstead, and pub. as Farm, Stock & Home and Northwest Farmstead, now pub. as Farm, Stock & Home; owner controlling interest, 1924—, and pub. The Minneapolis Star (daily newspaper). Home: Minneapolis, Minn. Died Jan. 17, 1934.

FROELICHER, Hans, coll. prof.; b. Solothurn, Switzerland; s. Joseph Felix and Anna (Buchser) F.; grad. Gymasium, Solothurn, 1885; student Germanic Philology, univs. of Zurich and Munich, 1885-88, Ph.D., Zurich, 1888; m. Frances Henrietta Mitchell, Ph.D., Sept. 5, 1888; children—Charles (dec.), Hans, Francis. Came to U.S., 1888, naturalized citizen, 1896. With Woman's Coll. of Baltimore (now Goucher Coll.), 1888—, successively asso. prof. French lang. and lit. until 1890, German lang. and lit., 1890-93, prof., 1893—, also prof. of art, 1895—; instr. German, Pa. State Summer Sch., 1905-08, Johns Hopkins Coll. for Teachers, Summer Sch., 1911, Johns Hopkins U. Coll. Courses for Teachers, 1913-19, history of art, same, 1916-21, 1927-28. Mem. Bd. Sch. Commrs, Baltimore City, 1909-11; mem. Mayor's Art Survey Com., 1924; pres. bd. trustees Park Sch., Baltimore; mem. bd. dirs. Baltimore Mus. of Art; mem. exec. com. Baltimore Reform League; etc. Democrat. Home: Baltimore, Md. Died Jan. 17, 1930.

FROHMAN, Charles, theatrical mgr. b. Sandusky, O., June 17, 1860; bro. of Daniel F.; ed. pub. schs., New York; unmarried. Was employed in office Daily Graphic, New York, and sold tickets evenings at Hooley's Theater, Brooklyn; in 1877 took charge of company that was sent West to play "Our boys"; was with Wm. Haverly (Haverly's Mastodon Minstrels), 1879-80, in U.S. and Europe; went on road with "Lady Clare" and "Victor Durand," 1881, but tour was a failure; on Nov. 18, 1888, saw "Shenandoah" at Boston Museum; organized a company and bought rights to that play outside of Boston; made great success with that and succeeding ventures; organized Charles Frohman Stock Co., 1890; now propr. and mgr. Empire Theater, Criterion, Lyceum, Garrick, Savoy and Knickerbocker theaters, New York, and Duke of York's, Comedy, Globe and Adelphi theaters, London; also joint mgr. Vaudeville Theater, London. Home: New York, N.Y. Died May 7, 1915.

FROHMAN, Daniel, theatrical mgr.; b. Sandusky, O., 1851; common school edn. Became office boy, New York Tribune, 1866; remained in newspaper business 5 yrs.; then mgr. of traveling theatrical cos. through U.S.; mgr. 5th Av. Theatre and Madison Sq. Theatre, New York, 1879-85; mgr. Lyceum Theatre, 1885—, also pres. of company; mgr. Daly's Theatre, New York, with the Daniel Frohman Stock Co. Also mgr. of English and American stars and theatrical companies and part owner New Lyceum Theatre, New York. Pres. Actors' Fund of America. Home: New York, N.Y. Died Dec. 26, 1940.

FROMKES, Maurice portrait painter; b. Poland, Feb. 19, 1872; s. Solon and Esther (Kaplan) F.; brought to America, 1880; ed. pub. schs. New York; entered Cooper Union, 1888, Nat. Acad. Design, 1890, and won prizes in drawing in both instns. first yr. of entry; studied Holland and France, 1899; m. Eva Maryan Halle, Aug. 17, 1910. Traveled in Italy, 1904, and painted Cardinal Merry del Val, Papal sec. of state (canvas in Vatican), also Sir Edward Elgar, Maurice Renaud in "Thaïs." Portrait prize Salmagundi Club, 1908; diploma of honor from Internat. Exhibitors of Fine Arts, Bordeaux, France, 1927. Works in permanent collections: Nat. Mus. Modern Art, Madrid, Spain; Delgado Mus., New Orleans; Sophie Newcombe Coll., New Orleans; Albright Art Gallery, Buffalo, N.Y.; R.I. Sch. of Design, Providence; Duncan Phillips Memorial Gallery, Washington; Lynchburg (Va.) Art Assn. Mem. Allied Artists of America, Artists Fund Soc. A.N.A., 1927. Spent 4 yrs. in Spain, 1920-24. Home: New York, N.Y. Died Sept. 17, 1931.

FROST, Albert Ellis, univ. prof.; b. St. Johnsbury, Vt., Aug. 9, 1851; s. Selim and Emily Sophia (Ellis) F.; A.B., Dartmouth, 1872, A.M., 1877 (Sc.D., 1897); m. Addie Mary Dalbey, July 20, 1882. Asst. to Prof. S. P. Langley, Allegheny Obs., 1872-75; prof. physics, Pittsburgh Central High Sch., 1875-85; prof. physics, U. of Pittsburgh (formerly Western U. of Pa.), 1885-1908; registrar, 1887—, treas., 1892-1909, acting dean and prof. mathematics, 1908-10, Coll. and Engring. Sch. U. of Pittsburgh; prof. mathematics and registrar, U. of Pittsburgh, 1910-12. Treas. Engrs. Soc. of Western Pa., 1880—; pres. Acad. Science and Arts, Pittsburgh, 1903-05; mem. council Univ. Extension Soc. Ind. Republican. Episcopalian. Home: Pittsburgh, Pa. Died May 1917.

FROST, Alfred Sidney, soldier; b. Chicago, Feb. 5, 1858; s. Thomas and Mary (Stickley) F.; ed. pub. schs., Syracuse, N.Y.; grad. U.S. Inf. and Cav. Sch., Ft. Leavenworth, Kan., 1891; studied law and admitted to bar, 1893, Supreme Ct. of U.S., 1900; m. Florence E. Mann, Dec. 31, 1884. Pvt., corporal and sergt., Co. A, 11th Inf., Sept. 13, 1881-Aug. 6, 1884; 2. lt., 25th Inf., Aug. 4, 1884; 1st lt., 7th Inf., July 10, 1891; transferred to 25th Inf., July 20, 1891; col. 1st S.D. Inf., May 19, 1898. Served with that regt. in Philippine insurrection and was recommended for bvts. of maj. and lt. col. U.S.A., and brig. gen., U.S.V., for gallantry in action; hon. mustered out of vol. service with regt. Oct. 5, 1899. Recd. captaincy, U.S.A., while col. of vols., Jan. 1, 1899; maj., Jan. 20, 1900; retired for disability in line of duty, Feb. 14, 1900. Chief of police, Evanston, Ill., 1905-07; candidate for mayor, Evanston, 1907. On duty with organized militia of S.D., 1909-10; recruiting officer U.S.A., Memphis dist., July 1, 1914-Oct. 31, 1918; comdg. officer S.A.T.C., U. of Tenn., Nov. 1, 1918-Feb. 5, 1919; prof. mil. science and tactics, city high schs., Memphis, Feb. 6-Aug. 31, 1919, and from Apr. 7, 1921; lt. col., July 10, 1918, in active service, Sept. 1, 1919; recruiting duty Nashville Dist. May 23, 1920-Apr. 1, 1921. Comdr.-in-chief Soc. Army of the Philippines, 1905. Republican. Died Oct. 15, 1922.

FROST, Arthur Burdett, illustrator, author; b. Philadelphia, 1851; self-taught in art; exhibited at

Paris Expn., 1900. Author: Bull Calf and Other Tales; Golfer's Alphabet; Stuff and Nonsense; Sports and Games in the Open, 1899; Book of Drawings, 1905; Carlo, 1913. Home: Pasadena, Calif. Died June 22, 1928.

FROST, Charles Sumner, architect; b. Lewiston, Me., May 31, 1856; s. Albert and Eunice (Jones) F.; ed. pub. schs.; studied architecture in offices 3 yrs.; spl. course Mass. Inst. Tech.; m. Mary, d. Marvin Hughitt, Jan. 7, 1885. Draftsman in Boston 3 yrs.; removed to Chicago, 1882, and practiced with Henry Ives Cobb under firm of Cobb & Frost, 1882-89; afterward practiced alone for several yrs.; sr. mem. Frost & Granger until Jan. 1, 1911. Fellow Am. Inst. Architects. Home: Lake Forest, Ill. Died Dec. 11, 1931.

FROST, Edwin Brant, astronomer; b. Brattleboro, Vt., July 14, 1866; s. Carlton P. and Eliza A. (DuBois) F.; A.B., Dartmouth, 1886, A.M., 1889, D.Sc., 1911; hon. D.Sc. Cantab., 1912; studied physics and astronomy, Princeton, Strassburg (Germany), and Astrophys. Observ., Potsdam, Germany; m. Mary E. Hazard, Nov. 19, 1896; children—Katharine Brant, Frederick Hazard, Benjamin DuBois. Instr. physics and astronomy, 1887-90, asst. prof. astronomy and dir. of obs., 1892-95, prof. astronomy, 1895-98, nonresident instr. 1898-1902, Dartmouth; prof. astrophysics, 1898—, dir. Yerkes Observatory, 1905-32, director emeritus, U. of Chicago. Assistant editor, 1895-1901, editor, 1902, Astrophysical Journal. Fellow Am. Acad. Arts and Sciences, A.A.A.S. Translated, revised and enlarged, A Treatise on Astronomical Spectroscopy, by Dr. J. Scheiner, 1894. Author: An Anstronomer's Life, 1933. Died May 14, 1935.

FROST, Eliott Park, psychologist; b. Oxford, Mass., Jan. 9, 1884; s. George Benjamin and Amelia Adelaide F.; B.A., Dartmouth, 1905, M.A., 1906; Ph.D., Harvard, 1908; studied at U. of Berlin, 1908-09; m. Elizabeth Hollister, June 3, 1916; 1 son, Granger Hollister. Teacher of psychology, Princeton, 1909-10, Yale, 1910-14; head dept. of psychology and chmn. athletic council, U. of Tenn., 1914-18; dir. Industrial Management Council and Mfrs.' Council, Rochester, N.Y., 1919-22; head dept. psychology and edn., 1922—. U. of Rochester, also dir. extension div. and summer sch.; dir. Hollister Lumber Co., Hollister Real Estate Co. Enlisted in U.S. Army, Mar. 19, 1918, as psychol. expert; mil. training at Ft. Oglethorpe, Ga.; apptd. 1st mil. morale officer, June 1918, at Camp Greenleaf, Ga.; inaugurated the morale work subsequently established throughout the Army; transferred to newly created morale branch of the Gen. Staff, Washington, D.C., Oct. 19, 1918, rank of capt.; hon. disch., May 17, 1919. Sec. bd. of governors Rochester Homœ. Hosp.; phes. Social Welfare League, Tuberculosis Assn. Republican. Conglist. Home: Rochester, N.Y. Died Sept. 3, 1926.

FROST, Fredric Worthen, lawyer; b. Franklin Falls, N.H., Jan. 8, 1870; s. Lorenzo L. and Harriet L. (Hayward) F.; A.B., cum laude, Wesleyan U., Conn., 1894; student Columbia Law Sch., 1897; LL.B., New York Law Sch., 1898; m. Christine K. Glover, Oct. 25, 1899; children—Fredric Worthen, Constance Hopkins. Teacher of English and French, Shady Side Acad., Pittsburgh, Pa., 1894-96; pvt. tutor, Europe, 1896; admitted to N.Y. bar, 1898, and began practice at N.Y. City; asst. atty. Third Av. Ry. System, New York, 1924-35, v.p., 1933-35; pres. Cuban Land & Steamship Co., Piloto Land Co. (Cuba); v.p. and gen. counsel Pittsburgh, Shawmut & Northern R.R.; trustee Manhattan Savings Institution. Trustee Tilton (N.H.) Sch., Wesleyan University, Chappaqua Pub. Library. Republican. Home: Chappaqua, N.Y. Died Oct. 27, 1938.

FROST, George Henry, publisher; b. Ontario, Can., July 9, 1838; s. Ebenezer and Caroline (Harwood) F., of Vt., of Puritan descent; C.E., McGill U., Montreal, 1860; m. Louisa Hunt, Dec. 3, 1868. Was land surveyor and ry. engr. in Chicago before establishing in New York in 1878; founded, 1874, and pub. the Engineering News to Aug. 31, 1911, when it was sold; pres. Courier-News Pub. Co., Plainfield, N.J. Republican. Home: Plainfield, N.J. Died Mar. 15, 1917.

FROST, James Marion, corr. sec. and treas. S.S. Bd. of Southern Bapt. Conv. Author: Moral Dignity of Baptism, 1905; Memorial Supper of Our Lord, 1908; Our Church Life, 1909; School of the Church, 1911; Pedobaptism; also various brochures, etc. Home: Nashville, Tenn. Died Oct. 31, 1917.

FROST, John, artist; b. Phila., Pa., May 14, 1890; s. Arthur Burdett and Emily Louise Levis (Phillips) F.; ed. Morris Acad., Morristown, N.J.; studied art, Académie Julian, Paris, France; m. Priscilla Geiger, d. Wilbert Morgrage, of Pasadena, Calif., May 20, 1922; children—John, Priscilla Emily. Landscape painter. Home: Bryn Mawr, Pa. Died June 5, 1937.

FROST, John Edward, dealer in lands; b. Rome, N.Y., Apr. 22, 1849; s. Thomas Gold and Elizabeth Anna (Bancroft) F.; Knox Coll., Galesburg, Ill.; Hamilton Coll., N.Y., 1869-71, A.B., 1871 (hon. A.M., 1906, LL.D., 1908); m. Margaret Elizabeth Kitchell, Oct. 10, 1871. Read law, Galesburg, 1871-72; in employ land dept. A.,T.&S.F. Ry., directing immigration to Kan., from 1872; removed to Topeka, 1882, in same line of work successively as gen. agent and chief clerk of "Santa Fe" Land Dept. until 1890, when was apptd. land commr. of the co.; resigned, Nov. 1, 1898; became engaged in sale and care of proprietary lands. Pres. Rocky Ford (Colo.) Town & Investment Co., 1886-90, Newton Land & Investment Co., 1887-1911; v.p. and dir. Morris Plan Co., Topeka, 1918—; v.p. Morris Plan Bank, Topeka. Pres. Exhibitors' Assn. of Internat. Cotton Expn., Atlanta, Ga., 1881; pres. Nat. Irrigation Congress, Albuquerque, N.M., 1895; v.p., treas. Kansas com. to Trans-Miss. and Internat. Expn., Omaha, 1898-99; chmn. exec. com. for 11th Internat. Conf. Y.M.C.A., 1903, and chmn. com. on reception to President Roosevelt, at laying of cornerstone of R.R. Y.M.C.A. Bldg. in Topeka; pres. 26th ann. conv. Kan. State Y.M.C.A., Wichita, Feb., 1908; mem. Governors' Conf. at White House, May 12-14, 1908, upon invitation of President Roosevelt, etc.; mem. exec. com. Y.M.C.A. of Kan. Republican. Presbyn. Home: Topeka, Kan. Died Nov. 19, 1921.

FROST, Timothy Prescott, clergyman; b. Mt. Holly, Vt., June 26, 1850; s. Timothy Moors and Mary Gray (Prescott) F.; Montpelier (Vt.) Sem.; Wesleyan U., 3 yrs., class of 1876, hon. A.M., 1890, D.D., 1895; D.D., Middlebury Coll., 1910; LL.D., Northwestern U., 1911; m. Carrie Maria Holt, Jan. 23, 1876; children—Philip Prescott, Florence Virtine. Ordained M.E. ministry, 1877; pastor in Vt., 1875-89, Summerfield Ch., Brooklyn, 1889-93, First Ch., Baltimore, 1893-98, St. Paul's Ch., Newark, N.J., 1898-1903, First Ch. Evanston, Ill., 1903-17; lecturer on Christian ethics, Garrett Bibl. Inst., Evanston, 1917-18; retired. Pres. Frost Family Assn. of America, 1922-26. Author: Tragedy and Triumph, 1926. Home: Bradford, Vt. Died July 5, 1937.

FROST, Wade Hampton, sanitarian; b. Marshall, Va., Mar. 3, 1880; s. Henry and Sabra J. (Walker) F.; student Randolph-Macon Coll., 1896-97; A.B., U. of Va., 1901, M.D., 1903; m. Susan Noland Haxall, Feb. 10, 1915; 1 dau., Susan Haxall. Apptd. asst. surgeon U.S.P.H.S., 1905; passed asst. surgeon, 1909; surgeon, 1917-29. At Hygienic Lab., Washington, 1908-13; in charge stream pollution studies, U.S.P.H.S., Cincinnati, 1913-29; dir. Bur. Sanitary Service, Am. Red Cross, Washington, D.C., 1917; in charge statis. studies of influenza epidemic for U.S.P.H.S., 1918, 19; resident lecturer in epidemiology, 1919-21, prof. epidemiology, 1921—, dean, 1931-34, Johns Hopkins U. Sch. of Hygiene and Public Health. Home: Baltimore, Md. Died May 1, 1938.

FROST, William Goodell; b. Le Roy, N.Y., July 2, 1854; s. Rev. Lewis P. and Maria (Goodell) F.; reared on farm; studied Milton and Beloit colls., Wis.; A.B., Oberlin Coll., 1876, A.M., 1879, B.D., 1879, D.D., 1894, LL.D., 1908; studied univs. of Wooster, Harvard, Göttingen (Germany), also abroad, 1904, 1910-11; Ph.D., Wooster, 1891; D.D., Harvard, 1907; LL.D., Georgetown (Ky.) Coll., 1913, Ky. State U., 1916; m. Louise Raney, 1876; children—Stanley, Wesley, Norman; m. 2d, Eleanor Marsh, 1891; children—Edith (Mrs. Ernest Colbert), Cleveland C. (killed in World War). Instr. Greek, 1877-79, prof. Greek lang. and lit., 1879-92, Oberlin Coll.; pres. Berea Coll., 1892-1920, winning as supporters: D. K. Pearsons, C. M. Hall, et al.; lit. work since 1920. Distinctive work at Berea Coll., of adapting ednl. methods to conditions in the Southern mountains. Author: Greek Primer, 1887; Inductive Studies in Oratory, 1890; For the Mountains, an Autobiography, 1937. Home: Berea, Ky. Died Sept. 11, 1938.

FROST, William Henry, editor, author; b. North Providence, R.I., Mar. 18, 1863; s. John Dudley and Frances Caroline F.; grad. Brown Univ., A.B., 1886, A.M., 1889; unmarried. On editorial staff New York Tribune, 1887—. Author: The Wagner Story Book, 1894; The Court of King Arthur, 1896; The Knights of the Round Table, 1897; Fairies and Folk of Ireland, 1900. Died 1902.

FROTHINGHAM, Arthur Lincoln, archeologist; b. Boston, June 21, 1859; s. Arthur Lincoln and Jessie (Peabody) F.; bro. of Jessie Peabody F.; early edn. Acad. Christian Bros., Rome, Italy, 1868-73; spl. courses in Oriental langs., Catholic Sem., S. Apollinare and Royal U., Rome, 1875-81; A.M., Ph.D., U. of Leipzig, 1883; (hon. A.M., Princeton U., 1896); m. Helen Bulkley Post, Jan. 27, 1897. Fellow in Semitic langs., and lecturer in archæology, Johns Hopkins, 1882-86; prof. archæology and history of art, 1887-98, ancient history and archæology, 1898-1906, Princeton. Founded, 1885, editor and propr., 1885-96, Am. Jour. of Archæology; founded Princeton College Bulletin; asso. dir. Am. Sch. Classical Studies, Rome, 1895-96. Author: A History of Sculpture; Mediæval Art Inventories of the Vatican; Monuments of Christian Rome, 1908; Roman Cities of Italy and Dalmatia, 1910; A History of Architecture, III-IV (sequel to vols. I-II by Russell Sturgis), 1915; Handbook of War Facts and Peace Problems; Simplified Italian Manual, etc., 1918-19. Co-Author (with A. E. Stevenson) of 4 vols. Report on Revolutionary Radicalism of the Joint Legislative Com. of State of N.Y. (Lusk Com.), 1921. Home: Princeton, N.J. Died July 28, 1923.

FROTHINGHAM, Ellen, translator; b. Boston, Mar. 25, 1835; d. Rev. Dr. N. L. and Anne Gorham (Brooks) F. Translated Lessing's Nathan der Weise, 1867; Goethe's Herman und Dorothea, 1870; Grillparzer's Sappho; Auerbach's Edelweiss, 1871; Lessing's Laocoon, 1873. Home: Boston, Mass. Died 1902.

FROTHINGHAM, James, clergyman; b. Johnstown, N.Y., Sept. 21, 1834; s. John and Jane Ann (Dodge) F.; ed. Johnstown (N.Y.) Acad., 1846-51, Union Coll., N.Y., 1851-53, Princeton (N.J.) Theol. Sem., 1854-57; m. Chloe D. Hazeltine, July 23, 1857. Ordained Presbyn. ministry, 1857; in charge of Spencer Acad., Indian Territory, 1857-59; pastor, Caledonia, Minn., 1860-64, Lansing, Ia., 1864-78, Manchester, Ia., 1878-80, Morrison, Ill., 1880-84, Waukegan, Ill., 1884-88, Ninth Ch., Chicago, 1888-92, Harvey, Ill., 1899-1903. Stated clk. of the Presbytery of Chicago, 1891-1917; asso. in pastoral work, Hyde Park Presbyn. Ch., Chicago, 1917—. Home: Chicago, Ill. Died Dec. 7, 1920.

FROTHINGHAM, Louis Adams, lawyer; b. Jamaica Plain, Mass., July 13, 1871; s. Thomas B. and Anne Pearson (Lunt) F.; A.B., Harvard U., 1893, LL.B., 1896; m. Mary S. Ames. Admitted to bar, 1896; 2d lt. U.S. Marine Corps, serving in the Atlantic Squadron during Spanish War, 1898; resumed practice of law, Boston, 1899. Mem. Mass. Ho. of Rep., 1901-05 (speaker 1904-05); Rep. candidate for mayor of Boston, 1905; elected lt.-gov. of Mass., Nov. 1908; Rep. nominee for governor of Mass., 1911; mem. of 67th to 70th Congresses (1921-29), 14th Mass. Dist. Overseer, Harvard, 1904-10, 1912-18, 1920-26. Lecturer on Mass. govt., Harvard, 1913-15. Col. 13th Regt. Mass. State Guard, 1917; maj. U.S.A., 1918. Unitarian. Author: Brief History of the Constitution and Government of Massachusetts. Home: N. Easton, Mass. Died Aug. 23, 1928.

FROTHINGHAM, Paul Revere, clergyman; b. Jamaica Plain, Mass., July 6, 1864; s. Thomas B. and Annie Pearson (Lunt) F.; A.B., Harvard, 1886, A.M., S.T.B., 1889, D.D., 1915; m. Anna C. Clapp, June 14, 1892. Minister First Congl. Soc., New Bedford, Mass., 1889-1900, Arlington St. Ch. (Unitarian), Boston, 1900—. Preacher to Harvard U., 1899-1902, 1909-10 and from 1914 (acting chmn. bd. preachers, 1919-20); overseer, Harvard, 1904-10, 1913-24; trustee Perkins Instn. and Mass. Sch. for the Blind; pres. Mass. Cremation Soc. Fellow Am. Acad. Arts and Sciences. Author: William Ellery Channing; His Messages from the Spirit; The Temple of Virtue, 1907; A Confusion of Tongues, 1917; We Believe, 1917; Edward Everett, Orator and Statesman, 1925. Home: Boston, Mass. Died Nov. 27, 1926.

FROTHINGHAM, Robert, author, compiler; b. Galesville, Wis., Mar. 22, 1865; s. Rev. John (Princeton Theol. Sem.) and Margaret (Hurley) F.; collateral desc. of Washington Irving; ed. pub. schs.; m. Minnie Yerdon, Sept. 22, 1886; children—Donald, Roy, Dorothy, Robert. Began as telegraph operator; reporter on Brooklyn Eagle and New York Sun, 1890-95; active in advertising and periodical publication field for 20 yrs., notably with "Life" and Everybody's Mag.; specialized in poster advertising, 1914-25; retired from business to lit. work. Lecturer and writer on outdoor life; world-traveler and big game hunter. Compiler: (anthologies) Songs of Men, 1918; Songs of Dogs, 1920; Songs of Horses, 1920; Songs of Challenge, 1922; Songs of the Sea and Sailors' Chanteys, 1924; Songs of Adventure, 1926. Author: The Pioneer (a biography), 1920; Around the World, 1925; Arctic Walrus Hunting with the Eskimos, 1931; Trails Through the Golden West, 1932. Home: Mayfield, N.Y. Died Dec. 7, 1937.

FRUEAUFF, Frank W., operator gas and elec. cos.; b. Columbia, Pa., Mar. 29, 1874; s. John F. and Annie Day (Taggart) F.; grad. high sch., Denver, 1891; m. Antoinette Perry, Nov. 30, 1909. Began as meter reader, Denver Gas & Electric Co., 1891, and was pres. same, 1907-10; pres. Denver Gas & Electric Light Co., 1910—; mem. Henry L. Doherty & Co., owners and operators pub. utility properties, since orgn., 1906. Home: New York, N.Y. Died July 1, 1922.

FRUITNIGHT, John Henry, M.D.; b. New York, Nov. 9, 1851; grad. Coll. City of New York, 1872 (A.M., 1875); Bellevue Hospital Med. Coll., 1875, and began practice in New York; specialist in diseases of children; m. Mary A. Stewart, May 17, 1881. Member 9th Internat. Med. Congress, Washington, 1887; fellow Am. Acad. Medicine, Am. Pædiatric Soc., New York, Acad. of Medicine and many other prominent med. societies. Died 1900.

FRY, Alfred Brooks, engineer; b. New York, Mar. 3, 1860; s. Maj. Thomas William Gardiner (U.S.V.) and Frances (Olney) F.; g.g.s. Capt. Benj. F., Continental Army; ed. pvt. schs. and Morse's Sch., New York; engring. sch. Columbia Coll.; m. Emma V., d. Brig. Gen. George A. Sheridan, U.S.V., 1890; 1 son, Sheridan Brooks. Marine and mech. engr., 1879-86; acting asst. engr. U.S. Treasury service, 1886, advanced through grades to supervising chief engr., supervising engr., duty at Port of New York, 1924-26;

chief inspection engr. for supervising architect U.S. pub. bldgs., etc., on Pacific Coast, Aug. 1926-Mar. 1927; consulting engr., 1927—; engr. lt. and engr. lt. comdr. naval militia, 1892-1910; comdr. and chief of staff, naval militia, New York, 1910—; acting chief engr. U.S.N., Spanish-Am. War, 1898; chief engr. and supt. constrn., etc., U.S. pub. bldgs., New York, 1899-1917; engr. aide to Admiral Burd, industrial mgr. Navy Yard N.Y., and 3d Naval Dist., Mar. 1917. Capt. U.S. N.N.V., 1917; capt., U.S.N.R., July 1, 1918; duty in Navy Yard, New York, at sea and French and English ports. Mem. bd. consulting engrs. for improvement of state canals, 1904-11; consulting engr. to Assn. for Protection of the Adirondacks, 1908—, Congressional Commn. of 1913 on mech. transmission of mails; mem. com. on waterways Merchants' Assn., New York; cons. engineer, Dept. Water Supply, Gas and Electricity, City of New York, 1914; mem. com. of engrs. representing Nat. Engring. Socs. at N.Y. Constl. Conv., 1915; mem. Special Panama Canal Commn., 1921; cons. engr. U.S.A., transport service, 1922. Commodore, comdg. Naval Militia, N.Y., 1923; retired as rear adm. Feb. 27, 1924. Mem. Harbor Com. of San Diego Chamber of Commerce, 1929; mem. City Council, Coronado, Calif., 1929-30, mayor pro tem., 1930-31; elected mayor for term, 1932-34. Pres. San Diego County League of Municipalities, 1932-33; mem. Engrs. Employment Com. of Southern Calif., 1931. Home: Coronado, Calif. Died Dec. 4, 1933.

FRY, C(harles) Luther, prof. sociology; b. Philadelphia, Mar. 16, 1894; s. Charles Livingston and Laura Frick (Housekeeper) F.; A.B., Muhlenberg Coll., Pa., 1916, A.M., Columbia, 1917, Ph.D., 1924; m. Marion Boyd Warren, Sept. 3, 1921; children—Charles Luther, Jr., Clementine Antoinette. Study of the prices of explosives for War Industries Board, 1919; study of migratory laborers for Interchurch World Movement, 1919-20, with Industrial Bur., Merchants Assn., New York, 1920-22; dir. Bur. Standards, Inst. Social and Religious Research, 1922-23; prof. sociology, U. of Rochester, 1933—. Served as pvt., later 2d lt., U.S.A., World War. Asso. dir. Near East Survey, 1926-27; dir. India Fact-Finding Commission of Laymen's Foreign Missions Inquiry, 1930-31; investigator Hoover Study of Recent Social Trends, 1932; impartial vice chmn. Regional Labor Board for the 3d Dist., 1935. Author: The New and Old Immigrant on the Land, 1922; Diagnosing the Rural Church, 1924; A Census Analysis of American Villages, 1925; American Villagers, 1926; The Near East and American Philanthropy (with others), 1929; The U.S. Looks at Its Churches, 1930; also the text of summary volume of 1926 Federal Census of Religious Bodies; chapter "Changes in Religious Organizations" in Recent Social Trends, 1933; preface and summary of India-Burma, report of Fact-Finding Commn. of Laymen's Foreign Missions Inquiry, 1933; The Technique of Social Investigation, 1934; Studies of the Rochester Community. Home: Rochester, N.Y. Died Apr. 12, 1938.

FRY, Franklin Foster, clergyman; b. Carlisle, Pa., Nov. 1, 1864; s. Jacob and Eliza Jane (Wattles) F.; A.B., Muhlenberg Coll., 1885, D.D.; grad. Phila. Theol. Sem., 1888; m. Minnie C. McKeown, June 14, 1898; 1 son, Franklin Clark. Ordained Luth. ministry, 1888; pastor Grace Ch., Bethlehem, Pa., 1890-1901, Ch. of the Reformation, Rochester, N.Y., 1901-27; exec. sec. Bd. Am. Missions United Luth. Ch. in America, Jan. 1927—. A leader in organizing United Luth. Ch. in America; has been pres. Luth. Synod of N.Y. and pres. Rochester Fedn. of Chs.; official del. First World Conv. of Lutherans, at Eisenach, Germany, 1923; chmn. 150th Anniversary of Lutheranism in N.Y. and N.E. Trustee Phila. Theol. Sem. Republican. Home: New York, N.Y. Died Dec. 13, 1933.

FRY, Henry Davidson, physician; b. Richmond, Va., Apr. 11, 1853; s. Hugh Walker and Mary (Davidson) F.; ed. Richmond, Va., and Columbian (now George Washington) U.; M.D., U. of Md., 1876 (Sc.D., 1907); twice married; m. 2d, Mrs. Annabel Lee (Squire) Atkins, Sept. 16, 1908. Prof. obstetrics and clin. prof. gynecology, Georgetown U., from 1895 (emeritus); was also prof. obstetrics, Washington Post-Grad. Med. Sch., gynecologist to Garfield Memorial Hosp., and obstetrician to Columbia Lying-in and Georgetown U. hosps. several yrs. Fellow Am. Coll. Surgeons. Author: Maternity, 1907. Home: Washington, D.C. Died May 12, 1919.

FRY, Jacob, theologian; b. Trappe, Pa., Feb. 9, 1834; s. Hon. Jacob and Mary (Gross) F.; A.B., Union Coll., 1851; grad. Luth. Theol. Sem., Gettysburg, Pa., 1853; (D.D., 1873, L.H.D., 1911, Union Coll.; LL.D., Muhlenberg Coll., 1911); m. Eliza J. Wattles, Sept. 13, 1855. Ordained Luth. ministry, 1853; pastor, Carlisle, Pa., 1854-65, Trinity Ch., Reading, Pa., 1865-96; prof. homiletics and sacred oratory, Luth. Theol. Sem., Phila., 1891—; removed to Phila., 1896. Pres. Luth. Mission and Ch. Extension Soc. Author: Elementary Homiletics, 1897; The Pastor's Guide, 1915. Home: Philadelphia, Pa. Died Feb. 19, 1920.

FRY, Wilfred Washington, advertising; b. Mt. Vision, N.Y., Aug. 14, 1875; s. Rev. Walter and Eleanor A. (Kemp) F.; prep. edn., Mt. Hermon (Mass.) Boys Sch.; LL.D., Colgate, 1927; m. Anna Gilman Ayer, 1904; children—Mrs. Dena Fry Bree, Wayland Ayer, Eleanor Kemp. Asst. sec. Bedford Br. Y.M.C.A., Brooklyn, N.Y., 1896-98; gen. sec. Y.M.C.A., New Brunswick, N.J., 1898-1901, Trenton, N.J., 1901-07, Pittsburgh, Pa., 1907-09; asso. with N. W. Ayer & Son, Phila., from Apr. 16, 1909, admitted to firm, 1911, mng. partner 1916, head of firm from decease of F. W. Ayer (founder) in 1923, pres. from incorporation, 1929; governing dir. N. W. Ayer & Son, Ltd. (London); pres. Meridale Dairies, Inc., and master Meridale Farms (Jersey breeding). Pres. Religious Press Assn. (Phila.); chmn. Internat. Com. of Y.M.C.A.'s; trustee Colgate U., Brown U.; v.p. bd. trustees Crozer Theol. Sem.; pres. bd. trustees Jefferson Med. Coll. and Hosp. (Phila.), also of Northfield Schools; mem. bd. mgrs. Franklin Inst. Republican. Baptist. Home: Camden, N.J. Died July 27, 1936.

FRYBERGER, Agnes Moore, instructor music; b. Madison, Ind., May 30, 1868; d. Benjamin Franklin and Florence Virginia (Wilber) Moore; student U. of Minn., Northwestern U. and Teachers' Coll. (Columbia); grad. Northwestern Conservatory of Music, Minneapolis, 1888; grad. Am. Inst. Normal Methods, Evanston, Ill., 1916; student at Sorbonne, Paris, France, 1930; m. Dr. W. O. Fryberger, 1891 (died 1921). Asst. supervisor of music, pub. schs., Minneapolis, Minn., 1911-20; instr. in sch. music, McPhail Music Sch., Minneapolis, 1916-20; instr. in music appreciation, Coll. of Edn., U. of Minn., 1918-20; music dir. State Teachers Coll., San Diego, Calif., 1920-21; ednl. dir. Minneapolis Symphony Orchestra, 1924-25, St. Louis Symphony Orchestra, 1926-30; instr. music appreciation, Eastman Sch. of Music, Rochester, N.Y., summers, 1926-30; instr. College Liberal Arts, U. of Louisville, 1932—. Republican. Unitarian. Author: Listening Lessons in Music, 1916, 25; Kiddie Canticles, 1925; also (serial) Creative Listening, 1932. Home: Louisville, Ky. Deceased.

FRYE, Alexis Everett, educator; b. N. Haven, Me., Nov. 2, 1859; s. Capt. E. S. and Jane (King) F.; grad. English High Sch., Boston, 1878, Cook Co. Normal Sch., Chicago, 1885; LL.B., Harvard, 1890, A.M., 1897; LL.D., U. of Redlands, Calif., 1929; m. Teresa Arruebarrena, Havana, Cuba, Jan. 1, 1901; children—Pearl Eliot (dec.), Frank Brewster, Charles (dec.), Carmen, Pearl. Teacher of methods and practice in teaching, Chicago Normal Sch., 1883-86; delivered over 1,500 ednl. lectures, 1886-90; admitted to Mass. bar, 1890; supt. schs., San Bernardino, Calif., 1891-93. Traveled extensively in Europe, Asia, Africa, 1897; supt. schs. of Cuba, 1899-1901; organized and equipped pub. sch. system of Cuba; organized and conducted Cuban teachers' expdn., bringing 1,284 native teachers to U.S., 1900. Medal of Legion of Honor of Cuba, 1900; medal of La. Purchase Expn., awarded by Pres. Taft commn., for Philippine Is. textbooks, 1903. Pres. Nat. Teachers' Assn. of Cuba, 1904-06. Capt. Co. E. 7th Calif. N.G., 1893; helped organize Harvard U. Batt., and capt. Harvard Graduates' Co., 1898; lt. Co. K, 1st Mass. Arty., 1898-99. Life fellow Am. Geog. Society. Author: Child and Nature, 1888; Brooks and Brook Basins, 1891; Geografia Elemental (Spanish), 1899; Manual para Maestros, 1899; School Law of Cuba, 1899; Grammar School Geography, 1901; First Steps in Geography, 1903; Home Geography, 1911; New Geography, Book One, 1917; The Brooklet's Story, 1927. Home: Redlands, Calif. Died July 1, 1936.

FRYE, James Albert, author; b. Boston, May 5, 1863; s. James Nichols and Sabina (Bacheler) F.; grad. Boston Latin Sch., 1882; A.B., Harvard, 1886; spl. course Harvard Law Sch., 1886-89; m. Kate, d. Hon. Horatio Colony, of Kenne, N.H., Oct. 29, 1891. Served on staffs Govs. Wolcott, Crane and Guild of Mass.; maj. arty., U.S.V., at Ft. Warren, Mass., Apr. 26-Nov. 14, 1898; col. comdg. corps coast arty., 1900-06; comd. Ft. Rodman, Mass., in U.S. Army and Navy combined maneuvers, 1902; acting chief of staff arty., Dist. of Portland, Me., U.S.A. and Navy maneuvers, 1903; mem. nat. bd. (War Dept.) on small arms practice, 1903—; adj. gen., Mass., 1906-07; retired as maj. gen., Mass. Vol. Militia, Mar. 15, 1907. Author: From Headquarters, 1893; Fables of Field and Staff, 1894; History of First Massachusetts Artillery, 1899. Home: Keene, N.H. Deceased.

FRYE, Prosser Hall, univ. prof.; b. New York, Nov. 1, 1866; s. Charles H. and Frances A. (Hall) F.; B.S., Trinity Coll., Conn., 1889; post-grad. Harvard U. and U. of Strassburg; m. Ellen Theresa Leinbach, Aug. 7, 1899. Instr. English, Lehigh U., 1891-96; instr., adj. prof., asst. prof., asso. prof. English, prof. and head prof. of rhetoric, prof. English, U. of Neb., 1896—. Editor Mid-West Quarterly. Author: Romance and Tragedy, 1922; Visions and Chimeras, 1929. Home: Lincoln, Neb. Died June 3, 1934.

FRYE, William Pierce, senator; b. Lewiston, Me., Sept. 2, 1831; s. Col. John M. and Alice M. (Davis) F.; A.B., Bowdoin Coll., 1850, A.M., 1853; (LL.D., Bates, 1881, Bowdoin, 1889); studied and practiced law; m. Caroline Spear (died, 1900). Mem. Me. legislature, 1861, 1862, 1867; mayor of Lewiston, 1866-67; atty. gen. Me., 1867-69; presdl. elector, 1864; mem. 42d to 46th Congresses (1871-81); elected U.S. senator, Mar. 15, 1881, succeeding James G. Blaine; reëlected, 1883, 1888, 1895, 1901, 1907; present term expires, 1913; elected pres. pro tem. of the Senate, Feb. 7, 1896, reëlected Dec. 4, 1899, serving until Mar. 4, 1900 and reëlected Mar. 7, 1901. Mem. Rep. Nat. Exec. Com., 1872-80. Home: Lewiston, Me. Died 1911.

FRYER, Robert Livingston, banker; b. Albany, N.Y.; s. William J. and Margaret (Livingston) F.; m. Melissa Dodge Pratt, Dec. 7, 1882. Began at Albany in wholesale lumber business, with extensive timber lands and saw mills in Mich. and La.; became pres. Manufacturers and Traders Nat. Bank, Fidelity Trust Co., H. O. Co., all of Buffalo; v.p. Buffalo Gas Co. Trustee Am. Scenic and Preservation Soc. of New York, Buffalo State Normal Sch. Episcopalian. Home: Buffalo, N.Y. Died Oct. 20, 1915.

FTELEY, Alphonse, civil engr.; b. Paris, France, April, 1837; several yrs. in engring. offices in Europe; came to U.S., 1865; was draftsman and asst. until 1870, then in general practice. In 1873-80 resident engr. in charge of investigation and construction for Sudbury River Water Works system, at Boston; chief asst. city engr., Boston, 1880-84; principal asst. engr., 1884-86; consulting engr., 1886-88, and chief engr. Aqueduct Commn. of New York, 1888-1900. Identified with many water supply, sewerage, rapid transit and other engring. projects. Died 1903.

FUCHS, Emil, painter, sculptor; b. Vienna, Austria, Aug. 9, 1866; s. Leopold and Josephine F.; ed. Imperial Acad. of Fine Arts, Vienna, and Berlin; unmarried. Came to U.S., 1905, naturalized citizen, 1924. Teacher Royal Acad. (London), Salon (Paris), Berlin, Munich, Vienna, Rome. Exhibited Nat. Acad. Design, New York. Awarded gold medal, Munich, 1896; hon. mention, Paris, 1907; $1,000 prize for the best head of a girl, Brown and Bigelow Competition, New York, 1925. Represented in Met. Mus., Cleveland Mus., Brooklyn Mus., New York Pub. Library, Congressional Library, Washington. Author: With Pencil, Brush and Chisel (The Life of an Artist), 1925. Home: New York, N.Y. Died Jan. 13, 1929.

FUERTES, Estevan Antonio, dir. Coll. Civ. Engineering and prof. sanitary engring., Cornell, 1890—; b. San Juan, Puerto Rico, May 10, 1838; s. Estevan and Demetria (Charbonnier) F.; academic edn. (Ph. D., C.E.); asst. engr., 1861-62, dir. western dist., 1862-63, public works, Island of Puerto Rico; asst. engr., 1863-64, engr., 1864-69, Croton Aqueduct Bd., New York; engr. in chief U.S. ship canal expdn. to Tehuantepec and Nicaragua, 1870-71; cons. engr., New York, 1871-73; dean dept. civ. engring. Cornell, 1873-90. Home: Ithaca, N.Y. Died 1903.

FUERTES, James Hillhouse, engineer; b. Ponce, Puerto Rico, Aug. 10, 1863; s. Prof. Estevan Antonio and Mary Stone (Perry) F.; grad. Cornell, 1883; m. Mary Hill Cable, Jan. 10, 1895 (died 1921). Has designed and constructed numerous works for the sewerage, drainage, refuse disposal, water purification and water supply of cities in U.S., Canada, H.I. and Brazil; consulting engr. for various municipalities and corps. Author: Water Filtration Works, 1901; Water and Public Health, 1897; European Sanitary Engineering Series in Engineering Record. Home: Brooklyn, N.Y. Deceased.

FUERTES, Louis Agassiz, painter, naturalist; b. Ithaca, N.Y., Feb. 7, 1874; s. Estevan Antonio and Mary Stone (Perry) F.; A.B., Cornell, 1897; m. Margaret F. Sumner, 1904; children—Louis Sumner, Moz. Painter of birds, 1896—. Illustrated Upland Game Birds, 1902, and companion vol., Waterfowl, 1903; Birds of New York, 1910; several series in Nat. Geog. Mag., 1914-19. Burgess's Bird Book for Children, 1919; Burgess's Animal Book for Children, 1920. Permanent work, Habitat groups, Am. Mus. Natural History, New York; 25 decorative panels for F. F. Brewster, New Haven, Conn.; birds of New York at State Mus., Albany; murals in Flamingo Hotel, Miami, Fla.; paintings for N.Y. Zoöl. Soc., Bronx, N.Y. Lecturer in Ornithology, Cornell U. Home: Ithaca, N.Y. Died Aug. 22, 1927.

FUESSLE, Newton Augustus, author; b. Chicago, Ill., Oct. 16, 1883; s. Rev. Carl August and Elizabeth (Schaefle) F.; Ph.B., U. of Chicago, 1906; m. Helen Louise Hessong, Jan. 3, 1912. Began as reporter Idaho Statesman, 1906, later with Seattle Star, Post-Intelligencer, Times, Chicago Inter-Ocean, Sioux City Tribune, Omaha News, United Press, New York; editor The Mediator, Cleveland, O., 1910-14; writing staff, The Nat. City Bank of New York, 1919; on the staff of The Outlook, 1920—. Author: Flesh and Phantasy (short stories), 1919. Home: New York, N.Y. Died Mar. 18, 1924.

FULLAM, William Freeland, naval officer; b. Monroe Co., N.Y., Oct. 20, 1855; s. N. S. and Rhoda F.; grad. U.S. Naval Acad., 1877 (head of class); m. Mariana Winder, d. late Chief Justice Robinson, Md. Court of Appeals, of Eastern Shore, Md., Apr. 15, 1885. Promoted ensign, 1880, advanced through the ranks to rear admiral, Dec. 15, 1914. Served on Trenton and Marion, European sta.; Swatara, China sta.; instr. in different depts. and head of dept. of ordnance, U.S. Naval Acad., 1883-1904; on Boston,

Yorktown, Chicago, Vesuvius, Raleigh, Miantonomah and Lancaster; on bd. New Orleans in war with Spain; comd. Chesapeake and Terror, practice ships, and Marietta in W.I.; comdt. Naval Training Sta., Newport, R.I., 1907-09; comdg. Battleship Mississippi, 1910; comdt. Naval Training, Great Lakes, Ill., 1912; aid for inspections to Sec. of Navy Meyer, 1913, and for personnel to Sec. Daniels, 1914; supt. Naval Acad., Annapolis, Feb. 7, 1914; comdr.-in-chief Pacific Reserve Fleet, Oct. 15, 1915; comdr. Patrol Force, Pacific Fleet, 1916-17; comdr. 2d Div., Pacific Fleet, and sr. officer in command in the Pacific, 1917-19; retired Oct. 20, 1919. Santiago (Sampson) medal; West India Campaign medal; Cuban Pacification medal, 1906; Mexican Service medal, 1916; Order of Rising Sun (Japan); also Victory medal and Navy Cross from U.S. Author: Hand-Book of Infantry and Artillery, U.S.N., 1899; Text-Book of Ordnance and Gunnery, 1902; Recruits' Hand-Book. Home: Washington, D.C. Died Sept. 23, 1927.

FULLER, Anna, author; b. Cambridge, Mass., Nov. 9, 1853; d. Robert Henry and Mary Lucretia (Bent) F.; grad. Abbot Acad., Andover, Mass.; unmarried. Author: Pratt Portraits; A Literary Courtship, 1893; Peak and Prairie, 1894; A Bookful of Girls, 1905; Later Pratt Portraits, 1911. Home: New York, N.Y. Died July 11, 1916.

FULLER, Ben Hebard, officer U.S.M.C.; b. Big Rapids, Mich., Feb. 27, 1870; s. Ceylon C. and Frances (Morrison) F.; ed. U.S. Naval Acad.; m. Katharine Offley, Oct. 26, 1892. Apptd. naval cadet, May 25, 1885; trans. to U.S.M.C. and commd. 2d lt., July 1, 1891; advanced through grades to col., Aug. 29, 1916; brig. gen. (temp.) July 1, 1918; brig. gen., Feb. 8, 1924. Served on U.S.S. Columbia, Spanish-Am. War; in Philippines, 1899-1901; with Boxer Relief Expdn. to Peking, 1900; comd. 2d Brigade, U.S. Marines in Santo Domingo, Nov. 1918-Dec. 1919, 1st Brigade, Haiti, 1924-25; apptd. maj. gen., comdt. U.S. Marine Corps, Aug. 5, 1930; retired, Mar. 1, 1934. Commended by Dept. "for gallant, meritorious and courageous conduct" in Battle of Tientsin, July 13, 1900. Home: Hamilton, Va. Died June 8, 1937.

FULLER, Charles E., congressman; b. Boone Co., Ill., Mar. 31, 1849; s. Seymour and Eliza A. (Mordoff) F.; ed. Wheaton Coll.; m. Sarah A. Mackay, Apr. 24, 1873. Admitted to bar, 1870, and began practice at Belvidere, Ill.; city atty., 4 yrs.; state's atty., Boone Co., 4 yrs.; mem. Ho. of Rep., 3 terms, and Senate, 2 terms, 1879-1893; judge Circuit Ct., 17th Jud. Circuit, 1897-1903; mem. 58th to 62d Congresses (1903-13) and 64th to 66th Congresses (1915-21), 68th and 69th Congresses (1923-27), 12th Ill. Dist.; chmn. Com. on Invalid Pensions, 66th and 67th Congresses. V.p. Peoples Bank of Belvidere. Raised a regt., Spanish-Am. War and commd. col., 1898. Home: Belvidere, Ill. Died June 25, 1926.

FULLER, Charles Gordon, oculist, aurist; b. Jamestown, N.Y., Apr. 9, 1856; s. Frederick Augustus and Emeline Rathbone Fuller; ed. pub. schs. and Jamestown Collegiate Inst., 1874; spl. studies Columbia Coll.; M.D., Chicago Homœ. Med. Coll.; spl. studies Coll. Phys. and Surg. (Columbia), New York Ophthal. Hosp. Coll. (O.A.Ch.), New York Ophthal. and Aural Inst.; m. Isabella Hunt White, June 30, 1885; children—Elizabeth Barret (Mrs. Charles Barnet Goodspeed), Dorothy Rathbone (Mrs. William Arthur Vawter, II). Maj. and surgeon 1st Inf., Ill. N.G.; asst. surgeon to N.Y. Ophthal. Hosp. Fellow Royal Micros. Soc., England. Home: Chicago, Ill. Deceased.

FULLER, Edward, newspaperman; b. Syracuse, N.Y., June 30, 1860; s. George and Mary (Griffiths) F.; A.B., Harvard, 1882; m. Anne Devens Robinson, July 3, 1885. Editorial writer, Boston Advertiser, 1883-85; dramatic critic Boston Post, 1885-91; editorial writer and lit. editor, 1891-1906; leading editorial writer in charge of editorial page, 1906-14, Providence Journal; editorial writer on Phila. Public Ledger, 1914-19; asso. editor, Phila. Inquirer, 1919-36, retired. Author: Fellow Travelers, 1886; The Dramatic Year, 1888; The Complaining Millions of Men, 1893; John Malcolm, 1902. Home: Philadelphia, Pa. Deceased.

FULLER, Edward Hawley Laton, capitalist; b. Hanley, Pa., Oct. 10, 1851; s. Edward Charles and Ellen (Ruthven) F.; ed. pub. schs. and Scranton (Pa.) High Sch.; m. Helen M. Silkman. Was partner Hunt Bros. & Co., hardware, Scranton, 8 yrs.; then in anthracite coal business, becoming connected with several mining and coal ry. co's, salt and other enterprises. Pres. Avery Rock Salt Co., Internat. Salt Co., Retsof Mining Co., Genesee and Wyoming R.R., Greigsville & Pearl Creek R.R., Livonia & Lake Conesus R.R., Wyoming Shovel Co., etc. Identified with Mr. George Gould's interests in coal regions. Died 1909.

FULLER, Eugene, surgeon; b. Wayland, Mass., May 8, 1858; s. Richard F. and Addie (Reeves) F.; A.B., Harvard, 1880, M.D., 1884; m. Margaret E. MacTavish, Apr. 23, 1890; children—Dorothy Margaret (dec.), Duncan MacTavish (dec.), Eugenia M., Richard Eugene. Formerly prof. venereal and genitourinary surgery, New York Post-Grad. Med. Sch.; visiting genito-urinary surgeon, City and Post-Grad. hosps. Author: Diseases of the Genito-Urinary System, 1901. Died June 4, 1930.

FULLER, George R(iley), telephone official; b. Massena, N.Y., Apr. 7, 1850; s. Wyman M. and Olive (Densmore) F.; ed. pub. schs.; m. Helen Gregg, June 3, 1885; children—George Gregg, Helene Densmore (Mrs. David Mitchell Hough). Formerly in service N.Y.C. Ry. Co.; with Rochester Telephone Co., 1899—, pres., 1905—; pres. George R. Fuller Co.; treas., dir. Reserve Mortgage Bond Co. Mem. U.S. Independent Telephone Assn. (dir.), Up-State Telephone Assn. of N.Y. (pres.). Presbyn. Mason. Home: Rochester, N.Y. Died May 7, 1927.

FULLER, George Warren, engineer; b. Franklin, Mass., Dec. 21, 1868; s. George Newell and Harriet (Craig) F.; S.B., Mass. Inst. Tech., 1890; post-grad. course U. of Berlin; m. Miss Goodloe, Nov. 1899 (died 1907); m. 2d, Mrs. Charlotte Bell Todd, June 1913 (divorced 1918); m. 3d, Mrs. Eleanor Todd Burt, Oct., 1918. With Mass. State Board of Health, at Lawrence Expt. Sta., 1890-95 (in charge 1893-95); in charge of elaborate tests for cities of Louisville, Ky., and Cincinnati, O., on most feasible method of purifying water, 1895-99; in pvt. practice, 1899—, as hydraulic and sanitary engr. Has been expert adviser for filtration plants for New York, Baltimore, Washington, New Orleans, Montreal, etc. Home: New York, N.Y. Died June 1934.

FULLER, George Washington, librarian; b. Charlestown (Boston), Mass., Nov. 17, 1876; s. George W. and Catherine C. (Toole) F.; grad. Boston Latin Sch., 1895; S.T.B., Tufts Coll., 1901; matriculated Harvard, 1895; m. Genevieve Forrest, Mar. 11, 1902. News editor, Bangor (Me.) Daily News, 1896-98; ordained Unitarian ministry, 1902; pastor Ch. of Our Father, Spencer, Mass., 1901-02; asso. pastor with Benjamin Fay Mills, 1st Ch., Oakland, Calif., 1902-03; pastor 1st Ch., Pomona, Calif., 1903-06; field agt. Am. Unitarian Assn., in Ida. and Mont., 1906; pastor 1st Ch., Spokane, Wash., 1907-11; librarian, Spokane Pub. Library, Sept. 1, 1911-Sept. 1, 1936. Chmn. Bd. of Theatre Censorship (municipal), Spokane, 1910-11; sec. Social Service Bur. of Spokane, 1907-25, pres., 1925-34. Camp librarian, Camp Funston, Kan., 1918. Pres. N. Pacific Conf. Unitarian Chs., 1911-12, Pacific Northwest Library Assn., 1914-15; sec. Eastern Wash. State Hist. Soc., 1916-23 and 1928-35. Author: Bibliography of Bookplate Literature, 1926; The Inland Empire, 3 vols., 1928; History of the Pacific Northwest, 1931. Home: Spokane, Wash. Died Oct. 24, 1940.

FULLER, Henry Amzi, judge; b. Wilkes-Barre, Pa., Jan. 15, 1855; s. Henry Mills and Harriet Irwin (Tharp) F.; A.M., Princeton, 1874; LL.D., Lafayette Coll., 1920; m. Ruth H. Parrish, Nov. 20, 1879. Began practice of law at Wilkes-Barre, 1877; asst. dist. atty. Luzerne Co., Pa., 1876-79, 1879-82, 1883 and 1885-88; apptd. by gov. law judge same county, Apr. 15, 1907, and elected Nov. 1907, for term 1907-17; reëlected for term 1917-27. Republican. Episcopalian. Home: Wilkes-Barre, Pa. Died Dec. 11, 1931.

FULLER, Henry Blake, author; b. Chicago, Ill., Jan. 9, 1857. Author: The Chevalier of Pensieri-Vani, 1891; The Châtelaine of La Trinité, 1892; The Cliff-Dwellers, 1893; With the Procession, 1895; The Puppet-Booth (dramatic sketches), 1896; From the Other Side (short stories), 1898; The Last Refuge, 1900; Under the Skylights, 1901; Waldo Trench and Others, 1908; Lines Long and Short (verse), 1917; On the Stairs, 1918; Bertram Cope's Year, 1919. Address: Chicago, Ill. Died July 28, 1929.

FULLER, Henry Brown, artist; b. Deerfield, Mass., Oct. 3, 1867; s. George and Agnes Gordon (Higginson) F.; prep. edn. St. Mark's Sch.; studied art at Cowles Art Sch., Art Students' League and Sch. of Raphael Colin, Paris; m. Lucia Fairchild, Oct. 25, 1893 (dec.); children—Clara Fairchild, Charles. Painter of subject pictures and decorations; best known works: Illusions, Life Disarming Death; bronze medal, Buffalo Expn., 1901; Carnegie prize, Nat. Acad. Design, 1908; silver medal, San Francisco, 1915. A.N.A. Originated mellow-tint etching. Home: Deerfield, Mass. Died July 1934.

FULLER, Howard G., justice of Supreme Court of S.Dak., Jan. 1, 1903—; b. Glens Falls, N.Y., Jan. 5, 1851; ed. common schools at Maquoketa, Ia.; academic edn. at Eldora, Ia.; m. Marie E. Leonard, April 1876. Taught in common schools of Iowa 6 yrs.; prin. graded schools, Union, Ia., 4 yrs.; co. supt. Hardin Co., Ia., 1882-86. Practiced law in Dakota Ty., 1886-89; elected circuit judge on admission of S.Dak. into Union, 1889; reëlected 1893, resigned; asso. justice Supreme Court of S.Dak., 1894-99, chief justice, 1900-02, and from 1906, term expiring, 1913. Home: Pierre, S.Dak. Died 1908.

FULLER, Leslie Elmer, theologian; b. Los Angeles, Dec. 28, 1882; s. Henry and Helen (Day) F.; B.S., Pomona Coll., Calif., 1907, D.D., 1927; B.D., Drew Theol. Sem., 1910; M.A., Columbia, 1910; Ph.D., U. of Berne (Switzerland), 1912; m. Mabel B. Gore, Sept. 2, 1908; children—John Leslie, Thomas Charles. Ordained ministry, M.E. Ch., 1912; pastor Pacific Beach, Calif., 1912-13; asst. prof. O.T. interpretation Garrett Bibl. Inst., Evanston, Ill., 1913-24, asso. prof., 1924-27, prof., 1927—; also prof. Bibl. lit., Northwestern U., 1921—. Mem. Soc. Bibl. Lit. and Exegesis, Am. Oriental Soc., Chicago Soc. Bibl. Research. Methodist. Home: Evanston, Ill. Died Aug. 8, 1936.

FULLER, Loie, soubrette, dancer; b. on farm nr. Chicago, Ill. Began stage career in child parts, Acad. Music, Chicago; appeared in many rôles and became a farce comedy soubrette. Invention of the "Serpentine" dance won her fame as a danseuse; appeared in this specialty in U.S. and Europe; has resided in Paris several yrs., performing at the Folies Bergères. Died Jan. 2, 1928.

FULLER, Lucia Fairchild, artist; b. Boston, Mass., Dec. 6, 1872; d. Charles and Elizabeth (Nelson) Fairchild; ed. Mrs. Shaw's (pvt.) Sch., Boston, Cowles Art Sch., under Dennis M. Bunker, Art Students' League, New York, under William M. Chase and H. Siddons Mowbray; m. Henry Brown Fuller, Oct. 25, 1893. Engaged professionally as painter, 1889—, chiefly of miniatures; bronze medal, Paris Expn., 1900; silver medal, Buffalo Expn., 1901; gold medal, St. Louis Expn., 1904. A.N.A., 1906. Home: Madison, Wis. Died May 20, 1924.

FULLER, Marcellus Bunyan, clergyman; b. Troy, O., June 12, 1868; s. Robert and Elija (Robinson) F.; A.B., Ohio Wesleyan U., 1890; D.D., Moores Hill Coll., Evansville, Ind., 1905, Ohio Wesleyan, 1908; m. Gertrude McKnight, Sept. 9, 1891; children—Glenn Vincent, Mark Adin. Ordained ministry M.E. Ch., 1891; pastor successively in Ohio at Manchester, Georgetown, First Ch., Urbana, Trinity Ch., Cincinnati, Grace Ch., Dayton, Trinity Ch., Lima, until 1917, Lakewood Ch., Cleveland, 1917-31, Emory Ch., Pittsburgh, 1931—. Trustee St. Luke's Hosp., Cleveland, Superannuated Fund Assn. Home: Pittsburgh, Pa. Died July 21, 1935.

FULLER, Melville Weston, chief justice of the U.S.; b. Augusta, Me., Feb. 11, 1833; s. Frederick Augustus and Catherine M. (Weston) F.; A.B., Bowdoin Coll., 1853, A.M., 1856; attended a course of lectures at Harvard Law Sch.; (LL.D., Northwestern, and Bowdoin, 1888, Harvard, 1891, Yale, Dartmouth, 1901); m. Calista O., d. Eri Reynolds, of Chicago, June 28, 1858; m. 2d, Mary E., d. William F. Coolbaugh, of Chicago, May 30, 1866. Admitted to bar, 1855; practiced at Augusta, Me., 1855-56; pres. Common Council and city solicitor, 1856; asso. editor The Age (Dem. paper), 1855-56; practiced at Chicago, 1856-88; apptd., Apr. 30, confirmed, July 20, and sworn in Oct. 8, 1888, chief justice of the United States. Mem. Ill. Ho. of Rep., 1863-65. Chancellor Smithsonian Instn.; chmn. trustees Peabody Edn. Fund; trustee Bowdoin Coll. Mem. arbitrators to settle boundary dispute between Venezuela and British Guiana, Paris, 1899; mem. Permanent Ct. of Arbitration, The Hague; mem. arbitral tribunal in matter of Muscat Downs, The Hague, 1905; received thanks of Congress, Dec. 1889. Fellow Am. Acad. Arts and Sciences, etc. Home: Washington, D.C. (Legal residence, Chicago.) Died 1910.

FULLER, Robert Higginson, newspaperman; b. Deerfield, Mass., Sept. 18, 1864; s. George and Agnes Gordon (Higginson) F.; brother of Henry Brown F.; A.B., Harvard, 1888; m. Elizabeth Adams Clagett, June 13, 1895. Began newspaper work on Worcester Spy, 1888; asso. editor Evening Journal, Albany, N.Y., 1889-95; polit. reporter and Albany legislative corr. New York Herald, 1895-1907; sec. to Gov. Charles E. Hughes, of N.Y., Jan. 1, 1907-July 1, 1910; mem. State Water Supply Commn., to July 22, 1911; asso. editor Knickerbocker Press, Albany, N.Y., July 1911—. Republican. Author: The Golden Hope, 1905; Government by the People, 1907. Home: Brookline, Mass. Died Dec. 23, 1927.

FULLER, Stuart Jamieson, diplomatist; b. Keokuk, Ia., May 4, 1880; s. George and Mary (Jamieson) F.; student U. of Minn., 1896-98; Litt.B., U. of Wis., 1903; m. Anne Howe Regan, Jan. 4, 1915; children—Stuart J., Regan. In ry. and mercantile business until 1906; Am. vice consul gen., later acting consul gen., Hongkong, 1906-10; in charge consulate at Naples, Italy, through cholera epidemic, 1910-11; consul at Gothenburg, Sweden, 1911-12, at Iquitos, Peru, 1912-13 (investigated Putumayo rubber atrocities in upper Amazon region), at Durban, Natal, Sept.-Nov. 1913; consul gen. at large for British and French N. America and Mexico to Mar. 1915, for Eastern Asia, Australasia and the islands of the Pacific, 1915-19; consul gen. at Tientsin, China, 1919-23; in business in Calcutta, 1924-26, Far East, 1927-30; divisional asst. Dept. of State, Washington, D.C., 1930-31; asst. chief Div. of Far Eastern Affairs, 1931—. Mem. Haiho Conservancy Commn., 1922-23, Am. Soc. Internat. Law; Am. rep. 15th to 24th sessions of League of Nations Advisory Com. on Traffic in Opium and Other Dangerous Drugs; del. of U.S. to Conf. to Conclude a Conv. for the Suppression of the Illicit Traffic in Narcotic Drugs, Geneva, 1936; adviser 20th session Internat. Labor Conf., Geneva, 1936. Home: Washington, D.C. Died Feb. 2, 1941.

FULLER, Thomas Staples, lawyer; b. Raleigh, N.C., Feb. 9, 1881; s. Williamson W. and Annie Margaret (Staples) F.; student U. of Va., 1901; LL.B., U. of

N.C., 1903; m. Pearle Penn, Feb. 17, 1904; children—Annie Margaret, Williamson W.; m. 2d, Mrs. Candida Milholland, Apr. 9, 1925; 1 dau., Candida Baie. Practiced at Raleigh, N.C., 1903-07; removed to New York, 1907; was mem. Nicoll, Anable, Fuller & Sullivan; now mem. Jackson, Fuller, Nash & Brophy. Presbyn. Home: Briarcliff Manor, N.Y. Died Mar. 5, 1940.

FULLER, William Elijah, lawyer; b. Howard, Pa., Mar. 30, 1846; s. Levi (M.D.) and J. E. (Tipton) F.; went to Iowa in childhood; ed. State U. of Ia., and Upper Ia. U.; LL.B., State U. of Ia., 1870; m. Lou J. Harper, Jan. 1, 1868; m. 2d, Clara H. Manning, Dec. 10, 1903. Admitted to bar, June 1870; mem. Ia. Ho. of Rep., 1876-77; mem. 49th and 50th Congresses (1885-89), 4th Ia. Dist. (judiciary com.); asst. atty. gen. U.S., 1901-07. Republican. V.p. Fayette Co. Nat. Bank. Home: West Union, Ia. Died Apr. 23, 1918.

FULLER, William Oliver, newspaperman; b. Rockland, Me., Feb. 3, 1856; s. William O. and Bethiah (Snow) F.; grad. Rockland High Sch., 1874; M.Litt., Colby College, 1929; m. Elizabeth N. Jones, Oct. 25, 1882; children—Douglas Wardwell, Donald Hills, Elizabeth Jones; m. 2d, Kathleen Stephens, Mar. 29, 1892; 1 son, Richard Stearns. Editor Rockland Courier-Gazette, 1874—. Postmaster of Rockland, Me., 1902-14. Republican. Lecturer. Author: What Happened to Wigglesworth, 1901; An Old Town by the Sea, 1910; A Night with Sherlock Holmes, 1929. Contbd. to New York World, 1899, humorous sketches "Unknown Husbands of Well-Known Wives"; etc. Awarded silver plaque by Me. Press Assn. as oldest editor in point of service (63 yrs.), 1937. Home: Rockland, Me. Died Sept. 21, 1941.

FULLER, Williamson Whitehead, lawyer; b. Fayetteville, N.C., Aug. 28, 1858; s. Thomas C. and Caroline D. (Whitehead) F.; grad. U. of Va., 1878; studied law Dick & Dillard's Law Sch., Greensboro, N.C., 1879; m. Annie M. Staples, Feb. 19, 1880. Admitted to bar, 1880; gen. counsel Am. Tobacco Co., and many other corps. until 1912; retired from business 1912, to devote himself to farming and country life. Home: Briarcliff Manor, N.Y. Died Aug. 23, 1934.

FULLERTON, Baxter P., clergyman; b. Pleasant Hope, Mo., Mar. 20, 1851; s. Andrew Washington and Harriet Elizabeth (Gilbreath) F.; A.B., Drury Coll., Mo., 1876; B.D., Cumberland U., Tenn., 1879; D.D., Drury, 1887; LL.D., Central U. of Ky., 1908; m. Callie L. Mitchell, Dec. 14, 1881. Ordained Cumberland Presbyn. ministry, 1879; pastor, Kansas City, Mo., 1879-91, Lucas Av. Ch., St. Louis, 1891-1906; field sec., Dist. of South and Southwest, Presbyn. Bd. of Home Missions of U.S., 1906-14; sec. Bd. of Home Missions, 1914—. Pres. Cumberland Presbyn. Bd. of Missions, 1894-1906; editor Missionary Record, 1899-1907; moderator Presbyn. Gen. Assembly, 1908. Trustee Mo. Valley Coll., Drury Coll. Was mem. Bd. of Freeholders, 1885, that made present charter of Kansas City. Died June 26, 1933.

FULLERTON, Edith Loring, author; b. Brooklyn, N.Y., Oct. 24, 1876; d. John A. and Eleanor Louise (Switzer) Jones; ed. Friends' Sch., Phila., and Pratt Inst., Brooklyn; m. Hal B. Fullerton, June 3, 1898; children—Mrs. Hope Tuttle, Mrs. Eleanor Frances Ferguson, Loring. Actively identified with agrl. development of Long Island; director of agriculture for Long Island R.R.; winner of 4 medals as butter maker, at N.Y. State Fair, and Nat. Dairy Show; hon. mem. Suffolk County Home Bureau. Awarded 1600-hour medal, Am. Red Cross. Republican. Unitarian. Author: The Book of the Home Garden, 1919. Home: East Setauket, L.I., N.Y. Died Aug. 9, 1931.

FULLERTON, George Stuart, prof. philosophy, author; b. Fatehgarh, India, Aug. 18, 1859; s. Rev. Robert Stewart and Martha (White) F.; A.B., U. of Pa., 1879, A.M., 1882; B.D., Yale, 1883; (Ph.D., Muhlenberg, 1892, LL.D., 1900); m. Rebekah Daingerfield Smith, Jan. 26, 1884 (died 1892); m. 2d, Julia Winslow Dickerson, Mar. 8, 1897. Instr., 1883-85, adj. prof., 1885-87, prof. philosophy, 1887-1904, U. of Pa.; prof. philosophy, Columbia, 1904-17. Am. exchange prof. to Vienna and other Austrian univs., 1913-14; apptd. hon. prof., U. of Vienna by Emperor Francis Joseph, 1914. Author: The Philosophy of Spinoza, 1894; On Spinozistic Immortality, 1899; A System of Metaphysics, 1904; An Introduction to Philosophy, 1906; The World We Live In, 1912; Die Amerikanischen Hochschulen, 1914; Germany of Today, 1915; A Handbook of Ethical Theory, 1922. Died Mar. 23, 1925.

FULLERTON, Kemper, college prof.; b. Cincinnati, O., Nov. 29, 1865; s. Thomas and Lina Hall (Kemper) F.; A.B., Princeton, 1888, M.A., 1894; grad. Union Theol. Sem., New York, 1891; fellow Union Theol. Sem. at U. of Berlin, 1891-93; hon. D.Th., U. of Tübingen, 1927; D.D., Princeton, 1932; D.D., Oberlin College, 1936; m. Kate Spencer, Dec. 19, 1905; children—Spencer, Katharine Palmer. Instr. in Hebrew, Lane Theol. Sem., Cincinnati, 1893-1904; Finney prof. Old Testament, lang. and lit., Oberlin Graduate School of Theology, 1904-34, prof. emeritus. Author: Prophecy and Authority, 1918; Essays and Sketches (Oberlin 1904-1934), 1938. Home: Oberlin, O. Died Mar. 24, 1940.

FULLERTON, Mark A., judge; b. Salem, Ore., Nov. 13, 1858; ed. Willamette U., 1875-78; admitted to bar, Oct. 1883; m. Ella Ione Rounds, June 8, 1887. Judge Supreme Ct. of Wash., 1898—. Republican. Home: Olympia, Wash. Died Sept. 15, 1931.

FULMER, Clark Adelbert, educator; b. Marcellus, N.Y., Apr. 22, 1867; s. David Morgan and Ellen Elizabeth (Longstreet) F.; grad. (higher course) Fremont (Neb.) Normal Sch., 1892; Ph.B., Neb. Wesleyan U., 1898; M.A., U. of Neb., 1910; LL.D., Grand Island College, 1914; D.Edn., Neb. Wesleyan U., 1934; m. Evalena Anna Ingham, June 23, 1887; children—Elbert (dec.), Ellis Ingham, Miriam, Pauline. Prin. pub. schs., Gibbon, 1888-92; supt. schs., Edgar, Neb., 1892-98, Pawnee City, Neb., 1898-1903, Beatrice, Neb., 1903-08; dean, Coll. Liberal Arts, 1908-11, acting-chancellor, 1910-11, chancellor, 1911-17, Neb. Wesleyan U.; state dir. of vocational edn. of Neb., Jan. 1, 1918—. Pres. Neb. State Teachers' Assn., 1903, S.E. Neb. Ednl. Assn., 1904, State Bd. of Examiners for State Professional Certificates, 1906-08; treas. Neb. Teachers' Reading Circle Bd., 1899-1903. Republican. Methodist. Rotarian. Author: Fulmer's Civil Government of Nebraska, 1909; Whither? The Choice of a Life Work, 1936. Home: Lincoln, Neb. Died Sept. 11, 1940.

FULMER, (Henry) Elton, chemist; b. Marcellus, N.Y., Feb. 6, 1864; s. David Morgan and Ellen Elizabeth (Longstreet) F.; bro. of Clark Adelbert F.; B.S., U. of Neb., 1887, A.M., 1889; m. Helen Barbara Aughey, Dec. 25, 1889. Instr. chemistry, U. of Neb., 1888-93; prof. chemistry, 1893—, dean of faculty, 1908—, State Coll. of Wash. State chemist of Wash., 1900—. Republican. Methodist. Home: Pullman, Wash. Died 1916.

FULTON, Charles William, senator; b. Lima, O., Aug. 24, 1853; s. Jacob and Eliza A. F.; ed. Magnolia, Ia., up to 1870, Pawnee City, Neb., 1870-73; read law in office of A. H. Babcock, Pawnee City; m. Ada M. Hobson, Sept. 5, 1878. Admitted to bar, 1875, and since in practice at Astoria, Ore. Elected Ore. Senate, 1878, 1890, 1898, 1902 (pres. 1893, 1901); presdl. elector, 1888; U.S. senator, 1903-09. Republican. Home: Astoria, Ore. Died Jan. 27, 1918.

FULTON, John, P.E. clergyman; b. Glasgow, Scotland, Apr. 2, 1834; ed. at Aberdeen; came to U.S. and engaged in ministry; ordained priest at New Orleans, 1857 (D.D., Univ. of Ga.; LL.D., U. of Ala.; D.C.L., U. of the South). Prof. canon law, Divinity Sch., Phila.; editor of The Church Standard. Author: Letters on Christian Unity, 1868; Index Canonum, 1873; Laws of Marriage, 1883; The Chalcedonian Decree, 1890; Palestine. Home: Philadelphia, Pa. Died 1907.

FULTON, John Allen, mining engr.; b. Reno, Nev., Sept. 24, 1878; s. Robert Lardin and Mary Alice (Bragg) F.; B.Sc., U. of Nev., 1898, E.M., Columbia, 1900; m. Maria Anita Bertheau, Aug. 20, 1914; children—Mary Anita, Helene, Robert Bertheau, John Allen, Margaret. Engr. Selukwe Gold Mines Co., Ltd., Rhodesia, S. Africa, 1901-03; engr., later asst. underground mgr. East Rand Proprietary Mines, Ltd., Transvaal, 1903-06; pvt. practice, 1906-09; mgr. Fairview Eagle Mining Co., Nev., 1909-10; engr. for George Wingfield, in Nev. and Ont., Can., 1910-11; supt. Melones (Calif.) Mining Co., 1911-17, acting mgr., 1917-19; gen. mgr. Ida.-Md. Mines Co., Grass Valley, Calif., 1919-24; dir. Mackay Sch. of Mines, Reno, Nev., Sept. 1924—, also pvt. practice. Fuel adminstr. Calaveras County, Calif., 1917-18. Exec. sec. Nevada State Planning Board; v.chmn. State Bd. of Registered Professional Engineers. Republican. Episcopalian. Home: Reno, Nev. Died Oct. 9, 1939.

FULTON, John Hamilton, banker; b. Cote des Neiges, Montreal, Can., Nov. 12, 1869; s. John and Janet Hume (Brown) F.; ed. high sch., Montreal; m. Jean Montgomery Thomson, Sept. 17, 1895. Began with Merchants Bank of Can., Montreal, 1883; entered employ of Canadian Bank of Commerce, Montreal, 1887; acountant for same bank, New York, 1894, mgr. New Orleans agency, 1898-1901; became mgr. Commercial Nat. Bank, New Orleans, 1901; organized Commercial T. & S. Bank, 1902, and was mgr. both banks more than 10 yrs. and then pres. several yrs.; also organized and was pres. First Nat. Bank, McComb, Miss.; v.p. Jan. 1916, one of exec. mgrs., 1918, also sr. v.p. Nat. City Bank of New York; pres. Nat. Park Bank, 1922—. Was organizer and 1st pres. Morris Plan Bank of New Orleans; trustee Morris Plan Trustees Assn. Presbyn. Home: N.Y. City and Essex, N.Y. Died Sept. 25, 1927.

FULTON, John Samuel, physician; b. Fremont, O., 1859; s. Rev. William and Nancy (Organ) F.; A.B., St. John's Coll., Md., 1876; M.D., U. of Maryland, 1881; m. Nancy Helen White, Oct. 25, 1888. Prof. state medicine, U. of Md.; sec. State Bd. of Health of Md. Pres. of Conf. of State and Provincial Bds. of Health of N. America, 1905. Home: Baltimore, Md. Died Aug. 12, 1931.

FULTON, Justin Dewey, Baptist clergyman; b. Earlville, N.Y., Mar. 1, 1828; grad. U. of Rochester, 1851 (D.D., 1871); studied 1 year in Rochester Theol. Sem.; held pastorates in St. Louis; Sandusky, O.; Albany, N.Y.; Tremont Temple, Boston, Mass.; Brooklyn, N.Y., and Somerville, Mass. Author: Why Priests Should Wed. Home: Somerville, Mass. Died 1901.

FULTON, Robert Burwell, educator; b. Sumter Co., Ala., Apr. 8, 1849; s. William F. and Elizabeth K. (Frierson) F.; A.B., 1st honors of class, U. of Miss., 1869, A.M., 1873; (LL.D., U. of Nashville, 1873, S.C. Coll., 1905, U. of Ala., 1906, U. of Miss., 1909); m. Annie Rose Garland, 1871 (died 1893); m. 2d, Florence Thompson, Apr. 2, 1903. Taught in high schs., 1869-70, at Pleasant Ridge, Ala., and in New Orleans, 1870-71; asst. prof., 1871-72, adj. prof. physics and astronomy, 1872-75, prof., 1875-1906, chancellor, 1892-1906, U. of Miss.; supt. Miller Sch. (tech.), Va., 1906—. Trustee Miller Fund of U. of Va., 1914. Died May 29, 1919.

FULTON, Robert Irving, univ. dean; b. Leesburg, Va., Mar. 19, 1855; s. William and Martha Ann (Hawling) F.; grad. Bethel Mil. Acad., Va., 1876; studied elocution and oratory under James E. Murdoch and other eminent teachers; law student, U. of Va., 1877; A.M., Ohio Wesleyan U., 1887; m. Clara J. Buxton, June 2, 1882. Supt. pub. schs., Berlin, Ill., 1877-78; asso. prin., 1878-81, dir., 1884-92, Sch. of Oratory, Kansas City; asst. prof. English, Kan. State U., 1891; prof. elocution and oratory, Ohio State U., 1892-99; prof. elocution and oratory, 1890—, founder and dean Sch. of Oratory, Ohio Wesleyan U. Instr. elocution, Ohio Wesleyan, Mo. State and Ky. State univs., 1882-90. Author: (with Thomas Clarkson Trueblood) Standard Selections, 1907; Choice Readings, 1883; Patriotic Eloquence, 1900; Practical Elocution, 1893; Essentials of Public Speaking, 1909; British and American Eloquence, 1911. Also (alone) The Speaker's Prompt Box of Parliamentary Usage, 1915. Home: Delaware, O. Died July 2, 1916.

FULTON, William Pomeroy, clergyman; b. Florence, Pa., Oct. 4, 1856; s. David Campbell and Nancy (Mayhew) F.; A.B., Ohio Wesleyan U., 1881; supt. pub. schs., Thornville, O., 1881-84; grad. Princeton Theol. Sem., 1887; D.D., Heidelberg U., Ohio, 1903; m. Osmie Yost, July 27, 1887; children—David Irvin, Francis Merle. Ordained Presbyn. ministry, Oct. 13, 1887; pastor, Huntingdon Valley, Pa., 1887-90, Ninth Ch., Phila., 1890-1908; supt. City Missions and Ch. Extension in Phila., 1905—. Mem. legal, exec. and evangelistic coms. of Gen. Assembly; moderator Synod of Pa., 1905; permanent clk. Presbytery of Phila., 1904-19, stated clk., 1919-29; stated clk. Gen. Council Reformed Chs. in America; pres. Presbyn. Ministers' Fund, 1900-09; pres. Log Coll. Assembly, Hartsville, Pa., 1910-16; moderator of Presbytery of Phila., 1931; asso. sec. Western Sect. World Presbyn. Alliance. Mason. Ind. Republican. Home: Philadelphia, Pa. Died Dec. 16, 1936.

FULTON, William Stewart, surgeon; M.D., Ohio Med. U., Columbus, 1898. Practiced at Wheeling, W.Va., 1898—; now mem. surg. staff Ohio Valley Gen. Hosp.; cons. surgeon Wheeling Hosp.; visiting surgeon Reynolds Memorial Hosp., Glendale, W.Va.; mem. surg. staff Barnesville (Ohio) Gen. Hosp.; founder and dir. Wheeling Clinic. Mem. W.Va. State Advisory Bd. of Pub. Assistance. Gov. Am. Coll. Surgeons. Mason. Home: Wheeling, W.Va. Deceased.

FUNK, Clarence Sidney; b. Scales Mound, Ill., Aug. 14, 1866; s. Sidney B. and Frances A. (Cowen) F.; ed. common schs., bus. coll. and law study at home; m. Kathryn Frances Meeker, Dec. 22, 1895. Began as clerk, Warder, Bushnell & Glessner, mfrs. of harvesting machinery, Springfield, O., and Chicago, 1885, and advanced through various dept. until became sales mgr., 1901; business was purchased, 1902, by Internat. Harvester Co. and was made asst. to pres.; gen. mgr. same, 1906-13; pres. M. Rumely Co., Laporte, Ind., 1913-16. Republican. Trustee First Congl. Ch., Oak Park, Ill. Home: Oak Park, Ill. Died Jan. 6, 1930.

FUNK, Frank Hamilton, congressman; b. Bloomington, Ill., Apr. 5, 1869; s. Benjamin Franklin and Sarah J. (Hamilton) F.; Ph.B., Yale, 1891. Farmer and stock raiser, on family farm, "Funk's Grove," McLean Co., Ill., 1891—. Mem. Rep. State Com., 1906-08; mem. Ill. Senate, 1908-12; Prog. party nominee for gov. of Ill., 1912; mem. Ill. R.R. and Warehouse Commn., 1913; Prog. party nominee for U.S. senator, 1913; mem. Pub. Utilities Commn., Ill., 1914-21; mem. 67th to 69th Congresses (1921-27), 17th Ill. District. Mason. Home: Bloomington, Ill. Died Nov. 24, 1940.

FUNK, Henry Daniel, prof. history; b. Schapsville, Ill., Nov. 5, 1875; s. John Emanuel and Sophia (Kortemeyer) F.; B.A., Macalester Coll., 1901, M.A., U. of Minn., 1903; studied U. of Minn., U. of Chicago and Harvard; D.D., U. of Dubuque, 1922; m. Lydia Christina Loetscher, Mar. 16, 1898; children—Victor Karl, Esther Helen, Henry Daniel, Harold Loetcher. With Macalester Coll., 1901—, prof. history, 1911—, also clergyman Presbyn. Ch. Mason. Home: St. Paul, Minn. Died June 2, 1925.

FUNK, Isaac Kaufman, author, pub.; b. Clifton, O., Sept. 10, 1839; A.B., Wittenberg Coll., 1860, later A.M.; grad. Wittenberg Theol. Sem., 1861 (D.D., LL.D., 1896); m. Eliza Thompson, 1864. Ordained Luth. ministry, 1861; in pastorates, 1867-72. Entered pub. business, 1876; in 1878 took A. W. Wagnalls in as partner; the firm became the Funk & Wagnalls Co., 1890, of which became pres.; treas. Nat. Prohibition Park Co. Editor-in-chief various periodicals of Funk & Wagnalls Co., Standard Dictionary, new edit., revised, 1903, 1911-12; chmn. ed. bd. that produced Jewish Encyclopedia; founder-editor Metropolitan Pulpit (now Homiletic Review), 1876; in connection with his house founded The Voice, 1880, Missionary Review, 1888, Literary Digest, 1889. Author: The Next Step in Evolution, 1902; The Widow's Mite, and Other Psychic Phenomena, 1904; The Psychic Riddle, 1907. Home: Montclair, N.J. Died Apr. 4, 1912.

FUNK, William R., publishing agent; b. West Newton, Pa., Aug. 1, 1861; s. Abraham and Catharine (Zumbro) F.; Otterbein Coll., O., 1879-82 (D.D.); Bonebrake Theol. Sem., 1882-86; m. Lottie M. Hamlin, Aug. 3, 1882; children—Nellis R., M. Adrienne (Mrs. F. J. Hughes), Alford Z., James Leland (dec.). Ordained U.B. ministry, 1883; pastorates: Industry, Owensville, Scottdale, and Greensburg, Pa.; pub. agt. for U.B. Ch., 1897-1933. Chmn. Com. of Otterbein Home, U.B. Ch. Mason. Author: Book on Africa; Life of Dr. I. L. Kephart; Life of Bishop J. S. Mills. Home: Dayton, O. Died Nov. 2, 1935.

FUNKHOUSER, George A., clergyman, educator; b. Mt. Jackson, Va., June 7, 1841; s. Andrew and Elizabeth (Rinker) F.; A.B., Otterbein U., O., 1868, A.M., 1871 (D.D., 1881, LL.D., 1908); grad. Western Theol. Sem., Pittsburgh, 1871; m. Susie M. Kumler, Oct. 26, 1871. Served in Co. A, 95th Ohio Vol. Inf., Aug. 5, 1862-Aug. 16, 1865; wounded and taken prisoner, Aug. 30, 1862; participated in siege of Vicksburg and numerous battles. Ordained U.B. ministry, 1870; a founder of Bonebrake Theol. Sem., Dayton, O., and prof. Greek exegesis 42 yrs.; prof. emeritus and dir. of seminary extension, 1913—. Republican. Elected bishop, 1893, but declined. Home: Dayton, O. Died July 30, 1927.

FUNSTEN, James Bowen, bishop; b. Clarke Co., Va., July 23, 1856; s. Col. Oliver Ridgeway and Mary (Bowen) F.; grad. Va. Mil. Inst., 1875; LL.B., U. of Va., 1878; practiced law; grad. Va. Theol. Sem., 1882; (D.D., U. of the South, 1902); m. Ida Vivian Pratt, 1886. Deacon, 1882, priest, 1883, P.E. Ch.; minister Bristol, Tenn., 1882-84; rector, Christ Ch., Richmond, Va., 1884-90; gen. missionary in Va., 1890-92; rector Portsmouth, Va., 1892-99; elected, 1898, consecrated, July 13, 1899, 1st missionary bishop of Boisé; bishop in charge of Wyo., 1907-09; 1st bishop of Ida., 1907. Pres. St. Luke's Hosp., 1900-07, St. Margaret's Hall. Chaplain 2d Regt. Ida. N.G., 5 yrs. Home: Boisé, Ida. Died Dec. 2, 1918.

FUNSTON, Edward Hogue, congressman; b. Bethel Twp., O., Sept. 16, 1836; s. Frederick and Julia (Stafford) F.; ed. pub. schs., New Carlisle Acad. and Marietta Coll.; m. Ann Eliza Mitchell; father of Frederick F. Entered army as lt. 16th Ohio Battery; took part in principal engagements along the Mississippi; mustered out 1865; removed, 1867, to prairie farm in township of Carlyle, Kan.; mem. Kan. Ho. of Rep., 1873, 1874, 1875 (speaker 1875), Senate, 1880-84 (pres. pro tem); telected to 48th Congress, Mar. 1, 1884, for unexpired term (1884-85) of D. C. Haskell, deceased; reëlected 49th to 52d Congresses (1885-93); reëlected to 53d Congress but unseated after a contest, Aug. 2, 1894. Republican. Home: Iola, Kan. Died 1911.

FUNSTON, Frederick, army officer; b. New Carlisle, O., Nov. 9, 1865; s. Edward Hoge and Ann Eliza (Mitchell) F.; grew up on farm in Kan.; student U. of Kan. 2½ yrs.; m. Eda Blankart, Oct. 25, 1898. Apptd. spl. agt. U.S. Dept. Agr., 1890, and as such took part in Death Valley Expdn., 1891; in Alaska and adjacent portions of British Northwest, 1892-94; crossed Alaska to Arctic Ocean and traveled from McKenzie River to Bering Sea, total journey of 3,500 miles; camped on the Klondike, winter of 1893-94; floated down Yukon alone in a canoe; resigned from Dept. of Agr. and traveled in Mexico; entered Cuban insurgent army as capt. of arty., 1896, and promoted to maj. and lt. col., participating in campaigns of Maximo Gomez and Calixto Garcia. Returned to U.S. at outbreak of Spanish-Am. War and was commd. col. 20th Kan. Vol. Inf., May 13, 1898; sent with regt. to Philippines and participated in Northern Luzon campaign of General MacArthur; for crossing Rio Grande River at Calumpit, Apr. 26, 1899, on small bamboo raft in face of heavy fire, and establishing rope ferry by means of which U.S. troops were enabled to cross and win battle, was promoted to brig. gen. vols., May 1, 1899, and awarded Congressional Medal of Honor, Feb. 14, 1900; continued in campaign at head of a brigade; wounded at Santo Tomas; assigned to comd. 4th Dist., Dept. of Northern Luzon, Jan. 1900; organized and comd. expdn. resulting in capture of Aguinaldo, the insurgent leader, Mar. 23, 1901; brig. gen. U.S.A., Apr. 1, 1901; returned to U.S., 1901, and comd. in succession Depts. of the Colo., the Columbia, the Lakes, Southwestern Div. and Dept. of Calif., and Army Service schs.; comd. Dept. of Luzon, 1911-13, Hawaiian Dept., 1913-14; apptd. comdr. 2d Div. U.S.A., at Texas City, Tex., Jan. 1914; comd. expdn. to Vera Cruz, Apr. 1914, and was mil. gov. of the city until Nov. 1914; maj. gen., Nov. 17, 1914; apptd. comdr. Southern Dept., Feb. 1915; placed in gen. command of U.S. forces along Mexican border, 1916, and also of movements of U.S. troops in Mexico, in pursuit of Villa. Home: Iola, Kan. Died Feb. 19, 1917.

FUQUA, Henry, governor; b. Baton Rouge, La., Nov. 8, 1865; s. James Overton and Jeannette M. (Fowles) F.; prep. edn., Magruder's Collegiate Inst., Baton Rouge; student La. State U.; m. Laura Matta, June 24, 1890; children—Matta (Mrs. Walter Scott), Henry. Began with corps of engrs. on constrn. of what is now the Yazoo & Miss. Valley R.R., later engaged in bridge building, same rd.; in hardware business, Baton Rouge, as clk. and traveling man, 9 yrs.; organizer and mgr. Fuqua Hardware Co., 1892-1916; warden, State Prison of La., 1916-24, also including management of three large plantations owned by the State; gov. of La., term May 1924-May 1928. Democrat. Episcopalian. Mason. Home: Baton Rouge, La. Died Oct. 11, 1926.

FURBUSH, Charles Lincoln, physician; b. New York, Dec. 2, 1863; s. Silas Smith and Henrietta (Hatfield) F.; pvt. and high schs., New York; M.D., Medico-Chirurgical Coll., Phila., 1893; univs. of Berlin and Heidelberg, semesters, 1893, 94, 95; m. Persis Burnham, Oct. 19, 1904. Began practice, Phila., 1893; apptd. acting asst. surgeon U.S.A. hosp. ship Missouri, July 27, 1898; chief surgeon's office, headquarters Dept. of Havana, Cuba, May 4, 1899; dir. Dept. of Charities and Hosp., Havana, May 11, 1899; capt. and asst. surgeon U.S. vols., Aug. 21, 1899; maj. and surgeon, Mar. 16, 1901; acting chief sanitary officer, Havana, Dec. 19, 1901; chief sanitary officer, May 20, 1902. Served in Philippine Islands, 1900, 1901. Resumed practice, Phila., Oct. 1, 1902. Chmn. Phila. Milk Commn., 1911—; del. Internat. Hygiene Expn., Dresden, Germany, 1911; dir. Pa. Soc. for Prevention of Tuberculosis; fellow Coll. of Physicians, Phila. Republican. Apptd. 1st lt. Med. R.C., U.S.A., Jan. 29, 1912; apptd. Oct. 1, 1916, spl. asst. to the Am. ambassador (Gerard) to Germany. Maj., asst. surgeon Med. R.C., May 10, 1917; lt. col., M.C.U.S.A., Jan. 29, 1918; col., Apr. 30, 1918; mil. observer with A.E.F., in France, Sept. 8, 1918; hon. disch., Dec. 10, 1918; col., Med. Sect. O.R.C., Jan. 28, 1919. Mem. yellow fever commn. of Rockefeller Foundation, to Central America, Dec. 12, 1918. Companion Order St. Michael and St. George (C.M.G.), hon. mem. Mil. Order 3d Class, Eng., July 18, 1919. Dir. Dept. of Pub. Health and pres. Board of Health, Phila., 1919—. Home: Philadelphia, Pa. Died June 26, 1923.

FURCHES, David Moffatt, jurist; b. Davie Co., N.C., Apr. 21, 1832; s. Stephen Lewis and Mary Howell F.; ed. in Union Acad. there; read law with Chief Justice Pearson; admitted to N.C. bar, 1857, locating at Mocksville, Davie Co. Was co. atty., 1858; Republican candidate for Congress, 1872; apptd. judge superior court, 1875; Republican candidate for supreme court judge, 1888; and for gov., 1892; asso. justice Supreme Court, N.C., 1894-1900; chief justice, 1901-02. Home: Statesville, N.C. Died 1908.

FUREY, John Vincent, brig. gen.; b. Brooklyn, May 22, 1839; s. Robert and Mary F.; ed. at Brooklyn; m. Georgianna G. Grosholz, Dec. 23, 1868. Pvt. Co. C, 84th N.Y. Inf., Apr. 18, 1861-Sept. 28, 1862; capt. asst. q.m. vols., Apr. 7, 1864; capt. asst. q.m. U.S.A., Jan. 18, 1867; maj. q.m., Nov. 11, 1887; lt. col. deputy q.m. gen., Aug. 21, 1896; col. q.m. vols., July 12-Mar. 2, 1899; col. asst. q.m. gen., Aug. 12, 1900; brig. gen. U.S.A., Feb. 25, 1903; retired, Feb. 26, 1903. Home: Brooklyn, N.Y. Died Dec. 17, 1914.

FURLOW, Floyd Charles, pres. Otis Elevator Co.; b. Americus, Ga., Apr. 9, 1877; s. Charles Timothy and Carrie V. (Meriwether) F.; B.S., Ga. Sch. Tech., 1897; post-grad. work, Worcester Poly. Inst., and in Europe; m. Nellie Johnson, Dec. 26, 1898. Cons. engr. and lecturer in exptl. engring., Ga. Sch. Tech., 1900-02; chief engr. Plunger Elevator Co., Worcester, Mass., 1902-04; v.p. same co., New York, 1904-05; with Otis Elevator Co., 1905—, pres., 1918—; also dir. Otis Elevator Co. of N.J., Ill., Tex., Mo., also of Otis-Fensom Elevator Co., Ltd. (Toronto). Inventor automatic self-leveling elevator; designer electric and hydraulic elevators; one of first experimentors in X-ray photography in America; specialist in metallurgy (iron and steel). Trustee Ga. Sch. Tech. Home: New York, N.Y. Died Apr. 26, 1923.

FURMAN, John Myers, clergyman; b. Schenectady, N.Y., Sept. 30, 1866; s. Henry Alonzo and Catharine (Myers) F.; A.B., Union Coll., 1889, A.M., 1892, L.H.D., 1921; m. Anna Cuyler Rector, Sept. 5, 1889. Deacon, 1919, priest, 1921, P.E. Ch. Began teaching at Cambridge, N.Y., 1889; owner and headmaster Irving Sch. (for boys), Tarrytown, N.Y., 1891—. Republican. Home: Tarrytown, N.Y. Died Jan. 24, 1933.

FURNAS, Elwood, pres. Nat. Farmers' Alliance, 1894—; b. Vandalia, O., Feb. 22, 1840; s. Benjamin and Mary Patty F.; common school edn.; m. Mary E. Sunderland, great-g.d. Capt. R. Sunderland of Revolutionary fame, 1859. Has been justice in Story Co., Ia., 1872—; defeated by 2 votes for representative in State legislature, 1892. Republican. Organized, 1892, and from then pres. Farmers' Inst. of Story Co., Ia. Pres. Story Co. Farmers' Alliance, 1889-92; del. to State Alliance, 1888-93; del. to Nat. Alliance, 1891-92; chmn. of its ednl. bd., 1893; was a del. to the Farmers' Nat. Congress held at Fort Worth, Tex., 1898, Boston, 1899, and Colorado Springs, 1900. Home: Nevada, Ia. Died 1902.

FURNAS, Robert Wilkinson, farmer, gov.; b. Miami Co., O., May 5, 1824; s. William and Martha (Jenkins) F.; m. Mary E. McComas, Oct. 29, 1845 (died); celebrated golden wedding before wife's death; m. 2d, Mrs. Susannah (Emswiler) Jameson. Practical printer and editor; resident Neb., 1855—; col. 2d Neb. cav. in Civil war; gov. Neb., 1873-75. Republican. Presbyterian. U.S. commr. to expns. at Phila., New Orleans, Chicago; pres. Neb. State Bd. Agr. Mason. On retiring from public life engaged in farming and tree culture. Home: Brownville, Neb. Deceased.

FURNESS, Caroline Ellen, prof. astronomy; b. Cleveland, O., June 24, 1869; d. Henry Benjamin and Caroline Sarah (Baker) F.; A.B., Vassar, 1891; Ph.D., Columbia, 1900. Began as asst., Vassar Coll. Obs., promoted instr., asso. prof., and has been Alumnae Maria Mitchell prof., 1915—. Vol. research asst., Yerkes Obs., and research worker, Groningen, Holland. Unitarian. Author: Catalog of Stars Within 1° of North Pole, 1900; Catalog of Stars Within 2° of North Pole, 1906; Introduction to Study of Variable Stars, 1915. Editor Observations of Variable Stars Made at Vassar College (1901-12), 1913. Visited Japan, 1918-19, in interest of Am. and Japanese women, and organized Japan br. Asso. Coll. Alumnae. Travelled around world, 1926-27, visiting oriental scientific instns. Del. 3d Pan-Pacific Congress in Japan, 1926. Home: Poughkeepsie, N.Y. Died Feb. 9, 1936.

FURNESS, Horace Howard, editor; b. Phila., Nov. 2, 1833; s. Rev. William Henry and Annis P. (Jenks) F.; A.B., Harvard, 1854, A.M., 1858; (hon. A.M., Harvard, 1877; Ph.D., Halle, 1878; LL.D., U. of Pa., 1879, Harvard, 1894, Yale, 1901; L.H.D., Columbia, 1887; Litt.D., Cambridge, Eng., 1899); in Europe, 1855-56; studied law in Phila.; admitted to bar, 1859; m. Helen Kate Rogers, June 12, 1860 (died 1883); father of Horace Howard, Jr., William Henry, III, and Caroline Furness Jayne. Acting chmn. of Seybert Commn. for Investigating Modern Spiritualism. Fellow Am. Acad. Arts and Sciences. Editor: (Variorum edit.) Romeo and Juliet, 1871; Macbeth, 1873; Hamlet, 2 vols., 1877; King Lear, 1880; Othello, 1886; Merchant of Venice, 1888; As You Like It, 1890; The Tempest, 1892; Midsummer Night's Dream, 1895; The Winter's Tale, 1898; Much Ado About Nothing, 1899; Twelfth Night, 1901; Love's Labors Lost, 1904; Anthony and Cleopatra, 1907. Home: Wallingford, Pa. Died Aug. 13, 1912.

FURNESS, Horace Howard, Jr., editor; b. Phila., Jan. 24, 1865; s. Horace Howard and Helen Kate (Rogers) F.; A.B., Harvard, 1888; Litt.D., U. of Pa., 1916; m. Louise B. Winsor, May 3, 1890. Instr. physics, Episcopal Acad., Phila., 1891-1901; after latter date began to work with father as co-worker on Variorum Shakespeare, his work henceforth to be devoted to editing the hist. plays. Fellow Am. Acad. Arts and Sciences. Unitarian. Republican. Editor: Macbeth (revised edit. of Variorum edit.), 1903; Richard III, 1908; Julius Cæsar, 1913; King John, 1919. Died Apr. 15, 1930.

FURNESS, William Henry, 3d, physician; traveler; b. Wallingford, Pa., Aug. 18, 1866; s. Horace Howard and Helen Kate (Rogers) F.; bro. Horace Howard F., Jr., and Caroline Furness Jayne; A.B., Harvard, 1888; M.D., U. of Pa., 1891; unmarried. Extensive traveler. Fellow Royal Geog. Soc., Anthrop. Inst. Great Britain. Was sec. and curator Free Mus. of Science and Arts, U. of Pa., from 1904. Author: Home Life of Borneo Head Hunters, Its Festival and Folklore, 1902; Uap, the Island of Stone Money, 1910. Commd. capt., Med. R.C., Apr. 1917. Home: Wallingford, Pa. Died Aug. 11, 1920.

FURNISS, Henry Dawson, gynecologist; b. Selma, Ala., Mar. 25, 1878; s. John Perkins and Elizabeth Matthews (Dawson) F.; student U. of Ala., 1894-96, LL.D., 1928; M.D., U. of Va., 1899; m. Ruth Kellogg Pine, Nov. 18, 1912; children—Henry Dawson, James Pine, Warren Todd. Interne N.Y. Post-Grad. Hosp., 1894-1901; in practice of gynecology and urology, 1903—; prof. gynecology, N.Y. Post-Grad. Med. Sch., 1917-27; attending gynecologist N.Y. Post-Grad. Hosp., 1917-27, cons. gynecologist, 1927—; cons. gynecologist Broad St. Hosp., N.Y. City, St. Luke's Hosp., Newburgh, N.Y., Holy Name Hosp., Teaneck, N.J., Hackensack (N.J.) Hosp., All Souls Hosp., Morristown, N.J.; cons. cystoscopist N.Y. Infirmary for Women and Children; surgeon Flower-Fifth Av. and Metropolitan hosps., N.Y. City. Served as capt. Med. Corps, U.S. Army; chief surgeon Camp Hancock, 1918. Fellow Am. Coll. Surgeons. Home: New York, N.Y. Died Jan. 25, 1942.

FURST, Clyde (Bowman), educator; b. Williamsport, Pa., Aug. 29, 1873; s. Rev. Samuel and Alice (Bowman) F.; Ph.B., Dickinson Coll., 1893, M.A., 1895, Litt.D., 1911; student Johns Hopkins, 1893-97, Oxford, 1897, Columbia U., 1899-1900; LL.D., Southwestern U., 1929; m. Mary Louise O'Neil, June

12, 1900 (died 1925); children—Lowry, Breading. Asst. Johns Hopkins, 1894-97; lecturer, Am. Soc. Extension of Univ. Teaching, 1897-99; dir. secondary sch., 1900-02; sec. Teachers Coll., Columbia U., 1902-11; lecturer and asso. prof. English, same, 1903-11; sec. Carnegie Foundation for Advancement of Teaching, 1911—. Adviser, War Dept. Com. on Edn., 1917-18; sec. Teachers Ins. and Annuity Assn., 1918—; lecturer Columbia U., 1925—. Trustee, Harmon Assn. Advancement Nursing, Spence School Retirement Fund. Mem. 2d Pan-Am. Scientific Congress, Nat. Conf. Com. on standards of Colls. and Secondary Schs., Am. Council on Edn., Coll. Entrance Exam. Bd., Boy Scouts Nat. Council and Nat. Com. on Education. Republican. Episcopalian. Author: A Group of Old Authors, 1900; American Literature, 1911; The Observations of Professor Maturin, 1917; Survey of College Entrance Examination Board, 1923. Joint author: The Efficient College, 1927. Home: New York, N.Y. Died Mar. 6, 1931.

FURUSETH, Andrew; b. Norway, Mar. 12, 1854; s. Andreas Nielsen and Martha (Jensdatter) F.; ed. common schs. Went to sea, 1873, and followed same many yrs.; first came to U.S., 1880; pres. Internat. Seamen's Union of America, 1908—; official sec. Sailors' Union of the Pacific. Recognized as an authority on Am. merchant marine. Protestant. Home: San Francisco, Calif. Died Jan. 22, 1938.

FUSSELL, Lewis, prof. electric engring.; b. Media, Pa., Apr. 22, 1882; s. Henry Moore and Mary (Townsend) F.; grad. Friends' Central Sch., Phila., 1899; B.S., Swarthmore Coll., 1902, M.S., 1903; E.E., and Ph.D., U. of Wis., 1907; m. Margaret Hardy Lewis, Dec. 28, 1907; children—Lewis, Morris Hardy. Joshua Lippincott fellow, Swarthmore Coll., 1905-06; with Swarthmore Coll., 1907—, prof. electric engring. and head of dept., 1920—; has served, summers and part time, with Gen. Electric Co., Bell Telephone Co. of Pa., Phila. Electric Co., Westinghouse Electric & Mfg. Co., United Gas Improvement Co., R.C.A. Victor Co., electrolysis surveys, cons. elec. engineer. Republican. Mem. Soc. of Friends. Author: The Self Excited Polyphase Asynchronous Generator, 1907. Home: Swarthmore, Pa. Died July 15, 1935.

FUSSELL, M(ilton) Howard, physician; b. Belvidere, Pa., Nov. 24, 1855; s. Milton and Tamar (Haldeman) F.; ed. Friends' Central Sch., Phila., until 1872; U. of Pa. med. dept., 1875-76; taught pub. sch., Radnor, Pa., 1876-81; U. of Pa., 1881-84, grad. M.D., 1884; m. Sarah E. Entwisle, May 3, 1884. Entered pvt. practice, Manayunk, Phila., July 1884; in fall of 1884, apptd. asst. in med. dispensary, U. of Pa., later instr. clin. medicine and phys.-in-chief, med. dispensary, and asst. phys. to hosp., and asst. prof. medicine, 1901—, consultant to med. dispensary, 1909—, phys. to hosp., and asst. prof. medicine, 1901, consultant to medical dispensary, 1909—; mem. council of Med. School, U. of Pa., 1904—; prof. applied therapeutics, June 1911—, U. of Pa. Phys. and dir. pathol. lab., St. Thimothy's Hosp.; phys. to Episcopal and Chestnut Hill hosps. Mem. Soc. of Friends. Republican. Editor: Tyson's Practice of Medicine. Author of Differential Diagnosis of Internal Diseases, in Monographic Medicine. Home: Philadelphia, Pa. Died Oct. 15, 1921.

FUTCHER, Thomas Barnes, M.D.; b. St. Thomas, Ont., Jan 1, 1871; s. Thomas and Susan (Northwood) F.; ed. Ontario pub. schs.; grad. U. of Toronto Med. Sch., 1893; house officer, Toronto Gen. Hosp., 1893-94; asst. resident physician, 1894-98, resident physician, 1898-1901, Johns Hopkins Hosp., Baltimore; student U. of Graz, Austria, 1896, U. of Strassburg, 1898; m. Gwendolyn Marjorie Howard, Nov. 24, 1909. Instr. medicine, 1896-97, asso., 1897-1901, asso. prof. medicine, 1901-14, asso. prof. clinical medicine, 1914-32, asso. prof. medicine, 1932—, Johns Hopkins U.; visiting physician, Johns Hopkins Hospital; chief consultant in medicine, Johns Hopkins Dispensary; cons. practice in internal medicine, Baltimore. Episcopalian. Lt. col. Canadian Army Med. Corps and in charge of med. div. of No. 16, Canadian Gen. Hosp., Orpington, Kent, Eng., Sept. 1917-Apr. 1918. Home: Guilford, Baltimore, Md. Died Feb. 25, 1938.

FUTRALL, John Clinton, univ. pres.; b. Jackson, Tenn., Mar. 9, 1873; s. Thomas Andrew and Emma (Headen) F.; B.A., M.A., U. of Va., 1894; post-grad., U. of Chicago, Johns Hopkins, and univs. of Bonn and Halle, Germany; LL.D., Tulane U., 1920, U. of New Mexico, 1926; m. Annie Gaines Duke, June 15, 1898; children—Clinton D. (dec.), Helen (Mrs. D. B. Stough), Emily (Mrs. J. K. Donaldson). Prof. Latin, 1894-95, Latin and Greek, 1895-1913, acting pres., 1913-14, pres., Mar. 6, 1914—, U. of Ark. Mem. Ark. State Bd. Edn., 1914-24. Democrat. Mem. M.E. Ch., S. Home: Fayetteville, Ark. Died Sept. 12, 1939.

FUTRELLE, Jacques, author; b. Pike Co., Ga., Apr. 9, 1875; s. Wiley H. H. and Linnie (Bevill) F.; ed. pub. and pvt. schs.; m. L. May Peel, July 17, 1895. In newspaper work, 1890-1902; theatrical mgr., 1902-04; in editorial dept. Boston American, 1904-06. Author: The Chase of the Golden Plate, 1906; The Thinking Machine, 1907; The Simple Case of Susan, 1908; The Thinking Machine on the Case, 1908; Elusive Isabel, 1909; The Diamond-Master, 1909; The High Hand, 1910; also writer of short stories. Home: Scituate, Mass. Died Apr. 15, 1912.

FYLES, Franklin, author, critic; s. Frederick and Mary F. Dramatic critic New York Sun, 1886-1903. Author: Cumberland '61; The Girl I Left Behind Me; The Governor of Kentucky; The Theatre and Its People; A Ward of France; Drusa Wayne, etc. Home: New York, N.Y. Died 1911.

G

GABBERT, William Henry, judge; b. on farm, Scott Co., Ia., Oct. 12, 1849; s. Henry and Eliza J. (McGarvey) G.; ed. dist. and high sch., Davenport, Ia.; m. Mrs. Eva Adams, Dec. 19, 1883. Began law practice at Davenport, 1870; moved to Colo., 1879, settled at Telluride, 1882; judge 7th dist., Colo., 1893-97; asso. justice Supreme Ct. Colo., 1898-1917 (chief justice, 1904-07 and 1915-16); resumed practice at Denver. Home: Denver, Colo. Deceased.

GABLE, George Daniel, univ. prof.; b. Cherryville, Pa., June 10, 1863; s. Edwin and Mary Anna (App) G.; A.B., Lafayette Coll., 1886, A.M., 1889, Ph.D., 1891; U. of Chicago, summers, 1900, 1901; m. Nellie Selima Rexford, Aug. 20, 1889. Teacher of Greek, French and mathematics, Delaware Acad., Delhi, N.Y., 1886-87; instr. mathematics and Latin, Lafayette Coll., Pa., 1887-95; prof. mathematics, and sec. of faculty, Parsons Coll., Ia., 1895-1907; Johnson professor mathematics and astronomy, U. of Wooster, July 1, 1907—. On editorial staff Standard Dictionary (etymol. dept.), 1890-95; assisted in revision of March's Thesaurus Dictionary of the English Language, 1903. Republican. Presbyn. Home: Wooster, O. Died 1911.

GABLE, Morgan Edwards, editor; b. Strasburg, Pa., Apr. 18, 1862; s. William Henry and Sarah Auten (Morgan) G.; ed. pub. schs.; m. Susan Ellen Fowler, June 9, 1906. Printer and asst. editor Tamaqua (Pa.) Courier, 1876-81; mng. editor Reading (Pa.) Herald, 1881-87; telegraph and city editor Pittsburgh Commercial Gazette, 1887-89; spl. corr., 1889-91; city editor, mng. editor and editor, Pittsburg Times, 1891-1906; chief editorial writer Pittsburgh Gazette Times, May 1, 1906—. Republican. Presbyn. Deceased.

GABRIELS, Henry, bishop; b. Wannegem, Belgium, Oct. 6, 1838; s. Leopold and Rosalie (Moerman) G.; common school edn., 1845-52, in Belgium; academic edn., Audenarde, Belgium, 1852-57, St. Nicholas, 1857-58, Ghent, 1858-60; S.T.L., Louvain, 1864 (hon. Doctor in Theology, same, 1882). Taught theology in St. Joseph's Sem., Troy, N.Y., 1864-92; pres. same, 1871-92; apptd. bishop of Ogdensburg, N.Y., Dec. 20, 1891, consecrated, May 5, 1892. Apptd. Officer Order of Leopold by King of Belgium, Oct. 1904. Author of book on Rubrics and transl. of "Rudiments of Hebrew." Died Apr. 23, 1921.

GABRILOWITSCH, Ossip, pianist, orchestral dir.; b. St. Petersburg, Russia, Feb. 7, 1878; ed. Conservatory of Music, St. Petersburg, pupil of Tolstoff, Liadov and Glazunov; winner Rubinstein prize, 1894; later studied piano with Leschetizky and composition with Navratil, Vienna; m. Clara Clemens, d. "Mark Twain," 1909; 1 dau., Nina. Has made many tours in U.S., 1900—, playing in recitals and with leading orchestras; dir. Detroit Symphony Orchestra, 1918—. Died Sept. 14, 1936.

GADSKI, Madame Johanna (Madame H. Tauscher), opera and concert singer; b. Anclam, Prussia, Germany, June 15, 1872; d. Julius and Bertha (Degner) G.; grad. pvt. sch., Stettin, Prussia, 1888; singing lessons from Madame Schroeder-Chaloupka, of Stettin; m. Hans Tauscher, of Berlin, Germany, Nov. 11, 1892. Début as "Undine" in Lortzing's opera of that name, Kroll's Theatre, Berlin, at age of 17, and was at once engaged for all seasons to 1893 inclusive; made tour through Holland and Germany, 1894, also sang in Royal Opera House, Berlin; Am. début under Walter Damrosch, at Met. Opera House, New York, as "Elsa" in "Lohengrin," 1895; became mem. Met. Opera Co., 1898, later alternating between Covent Garden, London, and New York; has appeared in all prin. cities, Europe and America. Repertoire includes leading soprano parts in all the standard operas; regarded as especially effective in Wagnerian rôles. Awarded gold medal for art and sciences, Kingdom of Bavaria; Am. gold medal for art and sciences presented by President Taft; gold medal Nat. Inst. Social Science. Retired from stage 1917; reappeared Oct. 30, 1921, at Carnegie Hall, in Wagner program with N.Y. Philharmonic Orchestra. Home: New York, N.Y. Died Feb. 23, 1932.

GAENSLEN, Frederick Julius, orthopedic surgeon; b. Milwaukee, Wis., Dec. 7, 1877; s. Julius and Mathilda (Hummel) G.; B.S., U. of Wis., 1899; M.D., Johns Hopkins, 1903; student summer sch., Harvard, 1901; m. Clara F. Schock, June 17, 1909; children—Eleanor Flora, Gustave Frederick. Interne, German Hosp. (now Lennox Hill Hosp.), N.Y. City, 1903-06; gen. practice, Milwaukee, 1906-12; specializing in orthopedic surgery, 1912—; orthopedic surgeon Milwaukee Children's Hosp., Milwaukee Hosp., Columbia Hosp.; asso. prof. orthopedic surgery, Marquette U., 1918; prof. orthopedic surgery, U. of Wis., 1925—. Home: Milwaukee, Wis. Died Mar. 11, 1937.

GAGE, Alfred Payson, educator; b. Hopkinton, N.H., April 15, 1836; s. Sewall and Eliza A. G.; grad. Dartmouth, 1859 (A.M., Ph.D.); m. Mary E. Prescott. Prof. English, High School, Boston. Author: Elements of Physics, 1882; Introduction to Physical Science, 1887; Principles of Physics, 1895. Home: Arlington, Mass. Died 1903.

GAGE, George Williams, judge; b. Meadow Woods, S.C., Feb. 4, 1856; s. Robert James and Martha Ann (Williams) G.; A.B., Wofford Coll., Spartanburg, S.C., 1875; LL.B., Vanderbilt U., 1880 (Founders' Medal for Law); m. Janie Gaston, Dec. 21, 1881. Admitted to S.C. bar, 1881; practiced at Chester, 1881-98; mem. Chester City Council, 1884; Dem. presdl. elector, 1888; mem. S.C. State Constl. Conv., 1895; mem. S.C. Ho. of Rep., 1897; judge South Carolina Circuit Court, 1898-1914; asst. justice S.C. Supreme Court, Jan. 1914—. Home: Chester, S.C. Deceased.

GAGE, Henry Tifft, governor; b. nr. Geneva, N.Y., Nov. 25, 1852; ed. pub. schs. in Mich., and under pvt. tutors. Practiced law at Los Angeles; gov. of Calif., 1899-1903; E.E. and M.P. to Portugal, Dec. 21, 1909-11. Republican. Counsel for Southern Pacific Co. and other corporations. Died Aug. 28, 1924.

GAGE, Homer, surgeon; b. Worcester, Mass., Oct. 18, 1861; s. Thomas Hovey and Annie M. (Lane) G.; A.B., Harvard U., 1882, A.M., M.D., 1887; Dr. Engring., Worcester Poly. Inst., 1929; LL.D., Clark U., 1937; m. Mabel Reynolds Knowles, June 15, 1893. Cons. surgeon Worcester City and St. Vincent's hosps.; retired. Pres. Crompton & Knowles Loom Works. Commd. major, Med. R.C., 1917, lt. col., 1919. Trustee and treas. Worcester Poly. Inst.; pres. bd. trustees Memorial Hosp.; pres. Community Chest of Worcester. Fellow Am. Surg. Assn., Am. Coll. of Surgeons. Comdr. Legion of Honor (France); v.p. Conseil d'Administration de Foñdation des Etats Unis, U. of Paris. Home: Worcester, Mass. Died July 3, 1938.

GAGE, Lyman Judson, sec. of the treasury; b. De Ruyter, N.Y., June 28, 1836; s. Eli A. and Mary (Judson) G.; removed to Rome, N.Y., 1848; ed. Rome Acad.; LL.D., Beloit, 1897, New York U., 1903; m. Sarah, d. Dr. F. B. Etheridge, 1864 (died 1874); m. 2d, Mrs. Cornelia Washburn Gage, June 7, 1887; m. 3d, Mrs. Frances Ada Ballou, Nov. 25, 1909. At 17 entered Oneida Central Bank; served as office boy and junior clerk until 1855, when he went to Chicago; clerk in planing mill until 1858; bookkeeper, 1858-61, and cashier, 1861-68, Merchants' Loan & Trust Co.; became, in 1868, cashier, in 1882, v.p., and in 1891, pres., First Nat. Bank of Chicago; sec. of the treasury in cabinet of Presidents McKinley and Roosevelt, 1897-1902; pres. U.S. Trust Co., New York, 1902-06; retired, 1906. Was 1st pres. bd. of dirs., Chicago Expn.; 3 times pres. Am. Bankers' Assn.; 1st pres. Chicago Bankers' Club; twice pres. Civic Fedn. of Chicago. Trustee Carnegie Instn., Washington. Home: San Diego, Calif. Died Jan. 26, 1927.

GAGE, Susanna Phelps, writer; b. Morrisville, N.Y., Dec. 26, 1857; d. Henry S. and Mary (Austin) Phelps; Ph.B., Cornell, 1880; m. Simon Henry Gage, Dec. 15, 1881. Has written numerous scientific articles, published in transactions of scientific socs. and jours.; has illustrated scientific papers for Prof. Gage and Dr. Burt G. Wilder. Trustee George Washington Memorial Assn.; fellow A.A.A.S. Home: Ithaca, N.Y. Died Oct. 5, 1915.

GAGE, Thomas Hovey, lawyer; b. Worcester, Mass., Jan. 13, 1865; s. Thomas Hovey and Anna M. (Lane) G.; A.B., Harvard, 1886, A.M. and LL.B., 1889; m. Alice Chase, June 8, 1898; 1 dau., Mary Hovey. Admitted to Mass. bar, 1890, and began practice at Worcester; mem. Gage, Hamilton, June & White, 1924—; trustee Worcester County Inst. Savings. U.S. fuel adminstr., Worcester, also with U.S. Food Administration, World War. Chmn. Jud. Council of Mass. Pres. Worcester Art Museum; trustee Memorial Hosp. Fellow Am. Acad. Arts and Sciences. Republican. Unitarian. Home: Worcester, Mass. Died July 15, 1938.

GAGE-DAY, Mary, M.D.; b. Worcester, N.Y.; d. Henry Van Tassel and Lucy (Grover) Gage; spl. scientific study, Cornell U., 1 yr.; M.D., Med. Dept. U. of Mich., 1888; post-grad. work N.Y. Post-Grad. Med. Sch. and Hosp. Resident phys. State Pub. Sch., Coldwater, Mich., 10 mos.; practiced at Wichita, Kan., 6 yrs., at Kingston-on-Hudson, N.Y., 1897—; attending gynecologist, Benedictine Sanitarium, and Hosp.; mem. bd. mgrs. Ulster Co. Tuberculosis Hosp. Episcopalian. Collaborator for Practical Therapeutics (Foster's). Home: Kingston, N.Y. Died Mar. 7, 1935.

GAGEL, Edward, civil engr.; b. Mt. Hope, N.Y., Oct. 25, 1858; s. Christian J. and Anna M. (Aulinger) G.; ed. Cooper Inst., New York; m. Jennie Field Smith, Oct. 14, 1885. Began with Dennis & Mairs, civ. engrs., New York, 1876; draftsman and engr. in charge constrn., Brooklyn, Flatbush & Coney Island R.R., 1877-79; draftsman and asst. engr. in charge constrn., Met. Elevated R.R., N.Y. City, 1879-80; draftsman West Side & Yonkers Ry., Jan.-Mar. 1880; leveler, draftsman and on constrn. extension to Hudson River, of N.Y.&N.E. R.R., 1880-82; transit man on location Erie & Wyo. Valley R.R., Jan.-July 1882; contractor's engr. on constrn. Pittsburgh, McKeesport & Youghiogheny R.R., July-Sept. 1882; draftsman, N.Y.C.&H.R. R.R., Sept.-Dec. 1882; with N.Y.,N.H. &H. R.R., 1882-1929, successively draftsman, engr. in charge constrn., div. engr., prin. asst. engr., dist. engr. and chief engr., 1905-29. Conglist. Home: West Haven, Conn. Died Feb. 11, 1931.

GAGER, Edwin Baker, judge; b. Scotland, Conn., Aug. 30, 1852; s. Lewis and Harriet (Jennings) G.; B.A., Yale, 1877 (hon. M.A., 1907); m. Nellie A. Cotter, Oct. 15, 1885. Prin. Ansonia schs., 1877-1881; admitted to bar, 1881; mem. Wooster, Torrance & Gager, 1882-85, Wooster, Williams & Gager, 1885-1900, Williams & Gager, 1900-01; judge Superior Ct. of Conn., 1901—, and asso. justice Supreme Ct. of Errors, from Aug. 30, 1918. Mem. State Bar Examining Com., 1890— (chmn. 1919—); instr. Yale Law Sch., 1892-1903; lecturer on jurisprudence, 1895-98, prof. gen. jurisprudence, 1903—, Yale. Pres. Derby Pub. Library; chmn. New Haven Co. Bar Library Committee. Pres. Fountain Water Co., Derby Textile Co. Republican. Conglist. Home: Derby, Conn. Died Apr. 28, 1922.

GAILLARD, David Du Bose, soldier; b. Fulton P.O., S.C., Sept. 4, 1859; s. Samuel Isaac and Susan Richardson (Du Bose) G.; ed. pvt. country sch., Clarendon Co., S.C., and Mt. Zion Sch., Winnsboro, S.C., 1872-74; apptd. from S.C. and grad. U.S. Mil. Acad., 1884, Engr. Sch. of Application, 1887; m. Katherine Ross Davis, Oct. 6, 1887. Apptd. 2d lt. engrs., June 15, 1884; 1st lt., Oct. 27, 1887; capt., Oct. 25, 1895; col. 3d U.S.V. engrs., June 7, 1898; hon. mustered out, May 17, 1899; maj., Apr. 23, 1904; lt. col., Apr. 11, 1909. Asst. to Capt. W. M. Black, and in charge various surveys and harbor improvements at St. Augustine and Tampa and Withlacoochee River, Fla., 1887-91; mem. Internat. Boundary Commn., U.S. and Mex., 1891-94; in charge Washington Aqueduct, etc., 1895-98; on staff Maj. Gen. J. F. Wade, U.S.V., Apr.-June, 1898; served in U.S. and Cuba, June 1898-May 1899; chief engr. Dept. of Santa Clara, Cuba, Feb.-Apr. 1899; asst. to engr. commr. of D.C., 1899-1901; in charge all river and harbor improvement of Lake Superior, 1901-03; mem. gen. staff corps and engr. officer Northern Div., 1903-04; on duty at Army War Coll., 1904-06; chief mil. information div., army of Cuban pacification at Marianao, Cuba, Oct. 1906-Feb. 1907; mem. Isthmian Canal Common. and dir. Panama R.R. Co., Mar. 16, 1907—. Supervising engr. in charge of dredging in harbors, building breakwaters, etc., Apr. 1, 1907-July 1, 1908; div. engr. Central Div., Gatun to Pedro Miguel, July 1, 1908—. Author: Wave Action in Relation to Engineering Structures, 1904. Died Dec. 5, 1913.

GAILLARD, Edwin White, librarian; b. Louisville, Ky., June 14, 1872; s. Edwin Samuel and Mary Elizabeth (Gibson) G.; ed. by tutors, in Trinity and in New York night schs.; m. Clara H. Sackett, Apr. 12, 1902; children—Edwin Gibson, Francis Gurney, Catherine Eyre. Editorial staff The Independent, 1888-95; engaged in lit. and scientific (coal-tar preparations) pursuits; has traveled extensively in N.S., Western U.S., Mex., W.I. and islands of S. Pacific; was spl. corr. from Tahiti and the Marquesas Islands for Harper's Weekly, The Independent, New York Evening Post. Librarian Webster Free Circulating Library, New York, 1897-1904; supervisor pub. edn. dept., N.Y. Pub. Library, 1904-13; spl. investigator N.Y. Pub. Library, 1913—. Pres. Pt. Washington Free Library, 1913-14; pres. N.Y. Pub. Library Staff Assn.; trustee East Side House Settlement. Mem. 7th Inf. N.Y. Guard, 1918-21. Publicity dir. U.S. Food Adminstrn., 1918-19. Awarded medal Order of the White Lion, 1st Class, by Czechoslovakian Republic, 1927. Home: Mt. Kisco, N.Y. Died Oct. 27, 1928.

GAILOR, Thomas Frank, bishop; b. Jackson, Miss., Sept. 17, 1856; s. Frank M. and Charlotte M. G.; A.B., Racine (Wis.) Coll., 1876, A.M., 1879; S.T.B., Gen. Theol. Sem., New York, 1879, S.T.D., 1893; S.T.D., Columbia, 1891; D.D., Trinity Coll., 1892, U. of the South, 1894, Oxford, England, 1920; LL.D., Oglethorpe, 1921; m. Ellen Douglas, d. G. W. Cunningham, of Nashville, Tenn., Nov. 11, 1885; children—Nannie Cunningham (Mrs. R. W. Daniel, dec.), Charlotte Moffett, Frank Hoyt, Ellen Douglas (Mrs. Richard F. Cleveland). Deacon, 1879, priest, 1880, P.E. Ch.; rector Ch. of the Messiah, Pulaski, Tenn., 1879-82; prof. eccles. history, 1882-90, chaplain, 1883-90, v.-chancellor, 1890-93, U. of the South; coadjutor bishop, 1893-98, succeeding to bishopric on death of Bishop Quintard, Feb. 1898. Declined bishopric of Ga., 1890; chancellor and pres. bd. trustees, U. of the South, 1908—; chmn. of Ho. of Bishops, P.E. Church, 1916-22; Presiding Bishop and Council, 1919-25; pres. of National Council, 1922-25. Author: The Christian Church and Education (Bedell lectures), 1910; The Episcopal Church, 1914. Home: Memphis, Tenn. Died Oct. 3, 1935.

GAINES, Frank Henry, coll. pres.; b. Tellico Plains, Tenn., July 25, 1852; s. John Rhea and Sarah (Rice) G.; A.B., Cumberland U., Tenn., 1870; B.D., Union Theol. Sem., Va., 1876; (D.D., Davidson Coll., N.C.; also LL.D., same, 1911); m. Mary Louise Lewis, May 17, 1877. Ordained Presbyn. ministry, 1876; pastor, Hopewell and Clintonville, Ky., 1876-78, Hebron Ch., Augusta Co., Va., 1878-84, Falling Spring Ch., Rockbridge Co., Va., 1884-88, Decatur, Ga., 1888-96; pres. Agnes Scott Inst. (now Agnes Scott Coll.), 1896—. Author: Bible Course, Outline and Notes (3 vols.), 1895. Home: Decatur, Ga. Died Oct. 5, 1923.

GAINES, John Wesley, congressman; b. Davidson Co., Tenn., Aug. 24, 1861; s. Dr. John Wesley and Maria (Wair) G.; ed. country schools; taught school; grad. U. of Nashville; M.D., Vanderbilt U., 1882. Never practiced medicine, but in law practice, Nashville, 1884—; presdl. elector on Cleveland ticket, 1892; mem. 55th to 60th Congresses (1897-1909), 6th Tenn. Dist. Democrat. Home: Nashville, Tenn. Died July 4, 1926.

GAINES, Lewis McFarland, M.D.; b. Staunton, Va., May 16, 1878; s. Frank Henry and Mary Louise (Lewis) G.; A.B. and B.S., Hampden-Sydney (Va.) Coll., 1898; post-grad. study, U. of Va., 1898-99; M.D., Johns Hopkins, 1903; m. Virginia Ethel Alexander, June 12, 1906; children—Mary Eloise, Alexander, Virginia Ethel. Prof. anatomy and physiology, dept. medicine, Wake Forest (N.C.) Coll., 1904-07; prof. neurology, Atlanta Sch. of Medicine, 1911-12; prof. nervous and mental diseases, Med. Dept. Emory U., 1913-26; phys. to Ga. Bapt. and Wesley Memorial hosps., Atlanta. Democrat. Presbyn. Home: Atlanta, Ga. Died May 24, 1937.

GAINES, Reuben Reid, judge; b. Sumter Co., Ala., Oct. 30, 1836; s. Jacob and Lucinda (McDavid) G.; A.B., U. of Ala., 1855; LL.B., Cumberland U., 1857; m. Louisa Shortridge, Mar. 1859. Adj. 3d Ala. Cav. C.S.A., 1862-63; asst. adj. Gen. Morgan's brigade, Allen's div., 1863-64; asst. adj. gen., Allen's cav. div., 1864-65. Judge 6th Jud. Dist., Tex., 1876-85; asso. justice, 1885-94, chief justice, 1894-1911, Supreme Ct. of Tex. Democrat. Retired, Jan. 5, 1911. Home: Austin, Tex. Died Oct. 13, 1914.

GAINES, Wesley John, bishop; born a slave, Wilkes Co., Ga., Oct. 4, 1840; received theol. edn. from a P.E. clergyman at Athens, Ga.; m. Julia A. Camper, Aug. 30, 1863. Became minister M.E. Ch., S., 1860; united with A.M.E. Ch., 1865; consecutively pastor, presiding elder, mission sec.; elected bishop, May 1888. Built Bethel Ch., Atlanta, largest colored ch. in South; founded Morris Brown Coll., Atlanta; trustee Wilberforce U., Ohio; v.p. Payne Theol. Sem.; pres. bd. trustees Edward Waters Coll., Jacksonville, Fla.; pres. financial bd. A.M.E. Ch. Home: Atlanta, Ga. Deceased.

GAIR, George West, chmn. bd. Robert Gair Co.; b. Jersey City, N.J., Aug. 10, 1872; s. Robert and Emma (Eyre) G.; ed. pub. and private schs. and Columbia Inst., New York; m. Helen Fitz Maurice, Dec. 31, 1910; 1 son, George West. With Robert Gair Co., Inc., paper products, New York, 1886—, v.p., 1903-20, pres., 1920-27, pres. and chmn. of bd., 1927-31, chmn. of bd., 1931—; pres. and dir. Gair Realty Corp., Gair Properties, Inc. Dir. Westport Y.M.C.A. Mem. Anglican Church. Home: Greens Farms, Conn. Died July 21, 1940.

GAITSKILL, Bennett S., lawyer; b. Montgomery Co., Ky., Nov. 12, 1858; s. Henry and Catherine T. (Branham) G.; student Georgetown (Ky.) Coll., 1876-78; read law with Morton & Parker, Lexington, Ky., 1878-79; student U. of Va. Law Sch., 1878-81; m. Belle Ennis, July 12, 1892. Practiced in Girard, 1882—; county atty. Crawford Co., Kan., 3 terms, 1888-92 and 1898-1900. Baptist. Mason. Home: Girard, Kan. Deceased.

GALBRAITH, Anna Mary, physician, author; b. Carlisle, Pa.; d. Thompson Moore and Elizabeth (Woods) G.; student Vassar Coll., 1875-79; M.D., Woman's Med. Coll., Pa., 1884; post. grad. work, Vienna Hosp., 1884-86, Woman's Hosp., Munich, 1886; unmarried. Gynecol. clinician and asst. to gynecol. staff, Woman's Hosp., Phila., 1886-88; attending med. clinician and instr. clin. medicine, Woman's Med. Coll. of N.Y. Infirmary, 1889-94; attending phys. neurol. dept., N.Y. Orthopædic Hosp. and Dispensary, 1889-1908; med. examiner Presbyn. Bd. Foreign Missions, 1912-18. Fellow N.Y. Acad. Medicine, A.M.A. Author: The Four Epochs of Woman's Life, 1901; Personal Hygiene and Physical Training for Woman, 1911. Home: Carlisle, Pa. Deceased.

GALBRAITH, Clinton Alexander, lawyer; b. Hartsville, Ind., Mar. 6, 1860; s. Joseph William and Elizabeth G.; grad. Hartsville Coll., 1883; law student U. of Mich., 1884-85; (LL.D., Huntington [Ind.] Coll., 1918); m. Nova J. Hartman, Dec. 22, 1886. Admitted to bar, 1885; atty. gen. Okla. Ty., 1893-97; moved to Hilo, H.I., Apr. 1898; asso. justice Supreme Court of H.I., 1900-04; returned to Okla.; Supreme Court commr., Okla., 1913-18; presiding judge, Div. No. 2, 1915-18. Democrat. Mason. Home: Ada, Okla. Died May 27, 1923.

GALBREATH, Charles Burleigh, librarian; b. on farm nr. Leetonia, O., Feb. 25, 1858; s. Edward Paxon and Jane Minerva (Shaw) G.; grad. Lisbon (O.) High Sch., 1879; Ph.B., Mt. Union Coll., O., 1882, B.C.S., A.B. (with honors), 1883, M.A., 1894; m. Ida Kelly, July 29, 1882; 1 son, Albert W. Supt. schs., Wilmot, O., 1884-86, E. Palestine, 1886-93; co. sch. examiner, 1886-93; taught in Ohio Normal U., Ada, summers, 1891, 1892; v.p. 1893-95, pres., 1896, Mt. Hope College, Rogers, Ohio.; state librarian of Ohio, May 25, 1896-July 1, 1911; again elected and served, 1915, 1918 and temp. 1927; spl. research asst. of joint legislative com. on administrative reorganization of Ohio, July 9, 1919-20. Holds life certificate from State Bd. of Examiners of Ohio; organized a system of traveling libraries in the state, including, in 1911, about 1,200 of them, aggregating over 56,000 vols.—Ohio then leading in number of traveling libraries. Sec. 4th Constl. Conv. of Ohio, 1912-13. Mem. Soc. of Friends. Author: Story of Ohio, 1913; Story of the Aeroplane, 1915; This Crimson Flower, answer to "In Flanders Fields," and other verse, 1919; Visit of Lafayette to Ohio Valley States, 1920; Expedition of Celoron to the Ohio Country, 1921; History of Ohio, 1925. Home: Columbus, O. Died Feb. 23, 1934.

GALBREATH, John Morrison, college prof.; b. Dublin, Md., Dec. 24, 1848; s. Alexander and Catharine (Ramsey) G.; U. of Va., 1866-69; grad. Western Theol. Sem., 1874; m. Jeanie M. Scott, Oct. 7, 1879. Ordained Presbyn. ministry, 1874; pastor Chestnut Level, Pa., 1875-1901; prof. English Bible, Lincoln U. (Pa.), 1901—, also trustee. Democrat. Died July 15, 1915.

GALE, Stephen Henry, shoe mfr.; b. East Kingston, N.H., Mar. 23, 1846; s. Elbridge Gerry and Ann Maria (Barnes) G.; ed. East Kingston village schs., Kingston Acad. and Boston Commercial Coll.; m. Anna M. Brown, Nov. 22, 1866. Started mfg. shoes, 1864, cutting them out himself and sending them to farmers in adjoining towns to be made up; became mem. Gale & Blaisdell; was pres. and treas. Gale Bros. until retired. Chairman com. asso. shareholders Pere Marquette R.R. Co. Mem. Haverhill City Council, 1874, Haverhill Rep. City Com.; commissary gen. of N.H., staff of Gov. John B. Smith, 1893-95; mem. N.H. Senate, 1895-97; alternate del. Rep. Nat. Conv., St. Louis, 1896; mem. Governor's Council (Gov. Frank W. Follins), 1898-1900; mem. N.H. Ho. of Rep., 1905-09. Conglist. Home: Exeter, N.H. Died Feb. 19, 1920.

GALE, William Holt, consul gen.; b. New York, N.Y., Jan. 26, 1864; s. William and Elisabeth Varian (Naylor) G.; Ph.B., Sheffield Scientific Sch. (Yale), 1885; studied law and diplomacy, George Washington U., 1900-01; m. Corinne Blackburn, Aug. 5, 1905. Served through Spanish-Am. War in 71st N.Y. Vols. Asst. sec. of P.R., 1902-04; Am. consul at Puerto Plata, Dominican Republic, 1906-07, at Malta, Maltese Islands, 1907-10; consul gen. at Athens, Greece, 1910-14; consul, Colon, Panama, 1914-15; consul gen., Munich, Germany, 1915-17, Copenhagen, Denmark, 1917; commercial adviser to Am. Legation, Denmark, to rank with but after counselor of Legation, 1918; consul gen., Hongkong, 1920-24, Amsterdam, Netherlands, 1924, now Budapest, Hungary. Home: Washington, D.C. Died Apr. 25, 1932.

GALE, Zona, writer; b. Portage, Wis., Aug. 26, 1874; d. Charles Franklin and Eliza (Beers) G.; B.L., U. of Wis., 1895, M.L., 1899, Litt.D., 1929; D. Humanities, Rollins College, Florida, 1932; Litt.D., Wooster (Ohio) College, 1935; m. William Llewelyn Breese, June 12, 1928; children—(by adoption) Juliette Blackman (Mrs. Cecil Bennett) and Leslyn Beers. On staffs Milwaukee papers until 1901; on staff New York World and writer for newspapers and mags., 1901-04. Member board regents U. of Wis., 1923-29; mem. Wisconsin Free Library Commn., 1923—. Author: The Loves of Pelleas and Etarre, 1907; Friendship Village, 1908; Friendship Village Love Stories, 1909; When I Was a Little Girl, 1913; Neighborhood Stories, 1914; Heart's Kindred, 1915; Birth, 1918; Peace in Friendship Village, 1919; Miss Lulu Bett, 1920; The Secret Way (verse), 1921; Faint Perfume, 1923; Preface to a Life, 1926; Yellow Gentians and Blue, 1927; Portage, Wisconsin, and Other Essays, 1928; Borgia, 1929; Bridal Pond, 1930; Old-Fashioned Tales, 1933; Papa La Fleur, 1933; Light Woman, 1937; (plays) The Neighbors (one act); Uncle Jimmy (one act); Miss Lulu Bett (awarded Pulitzer prize), prod. 1920; Mister Pitt (dramatization of Birth), prod. 1924; Evening Clothes (one act), 1932; The Clouds (one act). Home: Portage, Wis. Died Dec. 27, 1938.

GALEN, Albert John, judge; b. on ranch near Three Forks, Mont., Jan. 16, 1876; s. Hugh F. and Matilda (Gillogly) G.; student Manhattan Coll., New York, 1892-93; LL.B., U. of Notre Dame, Ind., 1896; LL.B., U. of Mich., 1897; m. Ethelene Bennett, Feb. 22, 1898. Admitted to Mont. bar, 1897; mem. Galen & Moore, 1897-99, Galen & Beattie, 1899-1901, Galen & Mettler, 1905-21. Atty. gen. of Mont. 2 terms, 1905-13. Served on Mont. Capitol Commn. until new bldg. was completed, 1912. Chmn. Selective Service Board, Division 1, Montana, 1917. Commd. maj., judge adv. U.S.A., Jan. 5, 1918; judge adv. 8th (regular) Div. Camp Fremont Calif., Jan.-Aug. 1918; judge adv. gen. of A.E.F., Siberia, Aug. 1918-June 1919; lt. col., Mar. 28, 1919; hon. disch., July 25, 1919; lt. col. O.R.C. Asso. justice Supreme Court of Mont., 2 terms, 1921-27 and 1927-33; resumed practice at Helena. Awarded D.S.M. (U.S.). Republican. Catholic. Home: Helena, Mont. Died May 16, 1936.

GALLAGHER, Charles Theodore, lawyer; b. Boston, Mass., May 21, 1851; s. William and Emily (Davenport) G.; LL.B., Boston U., 1875; (hon. A.M., Dartmouth, 1894); m. Nellie W. Allen, Feb. 19, 1880. Served 3 mos. in 1st Unattached Co. of Mass. Inf., 1864, Civ. War, and in Mass. State Militia, 1867; admitted to Suffolk bar, and began practice, 1875; officer or dir. various corps. Mem. Mass. Senate, 1882; mem. Boston Sch. Com., 1880-92 (pres. 4 yrs.); mem. Boston Art Commn.; trustee Benjamin Franklin Will and Fund, Roxbury Latin Sch., Boston U., Farm and Trades Sch., S. Boston Sch. of Art; dir. Legal Aid Soc.; v.p. Dartmouth Ednl. Assn. Mason. Home: Roxbury, Mass. Died Sept. 28, 1919.

GALLAGHER, Charles Wesley, coll. pres.; b. Boston, Mass., Feb. 3, 1846; s. Samuel Chartres and Roxby Moody (Foster) G.; served in Mass. Inf. in Civil War; A.B., Wesleyan U., Conn., 1870, A.M., 1873 (D.D., 1887); m. Emily Eliza Hubbard, Sept. 13, 1876 (died 1890); m. 2d, Eva Corscaden, Aug. 21, 1893 (died 1914). Ordained M.E. ministry, 1870; pastor N.Y. East and N.E. Southern Confs., 1870-87; dist. supt., New Bedford Dist., 1887-89; pres. Lawrence U., Wis., 1889-93, Me. Wesleyan Sem. and Coll., 1893-97; asso. prin. Laselle Sem., 1897-1901; pres. Nat. Training Sch., Washington, 1901-08, Md. Coll. for Women, Lutherville, June 1908—. Del. Gen. Conf. M.E. Ch., 1888-92. Republican. Author: Theism, or God Revealed, 1899. Died Dec. 14, 1916.

GALLAGHER, Hugh Clifford, mfr.; b. Sackville, N.B., Can., Aug. 25, 1855; s. Hugh and Alice (Truman) G.; ed. Sackville (N.B.) Acad.; m. Edith W. Everett, Sept. 22, 1880. Pres. Walter Baker & Co., Ltd., chocolate mfrs., 1903-25, chmn. bd. of dirs., 1925-29; was also pres. Milton Savings Bank; dir. Milton Building Associates. Trustees Boston U. Republican. Methodist. Mason. Resided at Milton, Mass. Died May 3, 1931.

GALLAGHER, Michael James, bishop; b. Auburn, Mich., Nov. 18, 1866; s. James and Mary (Toomey) G.; student Assumption Coll., Sandwich, Ont., 1884-85; Mungret Coll., Limerick, Ireland, 1885-89; U. of Innsbruck, Austria, 1889-94. Ordained priest R.C. Ch., 1893; pastorates Carrollton, Hemlock, Mich., and St. Andrew's Cathedral, Grand Rapids; bishop's sec., 1895; chancellor, Diocese of Grand Rapids, 1900-12, vicar gen., 1912-16; consecrated coadjutor bishop of Grand Rapids, Sept. 8, 1915; succeeded as bishop of Grand Rapids, Dec. 26, 1916; transferred to See of Detroit, July 18, 1918. Died Jan. 20, 1937.

GALLAGHER, Nicholas Aloysius, bishop; b. Temperanceville, O., Feb. 19, 1846; s. John and Mary Ann (Brinton) G.; grad. Mt. St. Mary's Sem., Cincinnati, 1868; ordained R.C. priest, Dec. 25, 1868. Asst. priest, St. Patrick's Ch., Columbus, O., 1869-71; pres. St. Aloysius Sem., Columbus, 1871-76; pastor St. Patrick's Ch., Columbus, 1876-78; administrator Diocese of Columbus, 1878-80; pastor St. Patrick's and vicar gen., Diocese of Columbus, 1880-82; apptd. bishop of Canopus and administrator of Galveston, Tex., Jan. 10, 1882; consecrated Apr. 30, 1882; made bishop of Galveston, Dec. 16, 1892. Died Jan. 21, 1918.

GALLAGHER, Thomas, congressman; b. Concord, N.H., July 6, 1850; s. John and Margaret (Tighe) G.; went to Chicago, 1866; ed. pub. schs.; m. Mrs. Margaretta Borsh, Oct. 12, 1886. Engaged in hat business, Chicago, 1878-1911. Mem. City Council, 1893-97; mem. Chicago Bd. Edn., 1897-1903 (v.p. 3 yrs.); pres. Cook Co. Democracy; chmn. Cook Co. Central Com.; mem. 61st to 66th Congresses (1909-21), 8th Ill. Dist. Catholic. Home: Chicago, Ill. Died Feb. 24, 1930.

GALLAGHER, William, headmaster; b. Boston, Mass., Jan. 6, 1849; s. William and Emily (Collins) G.; A.B., Harvard, 1869, hon. A.M., 1872; grad. Chicago Theol. Sem., 1874; Ph.D., Amherst, 1899; m. Frances Harriet McCulloch, Oct. 21, 1874; m. 2d, Ella Williams Sheppard. Licensed to preach, 1874; master Boston Latin Sch., 1877-85, Girls' Latin Sch., Boston, 1885-86; prin. Williston Seminary, Easthampton, Mass., 1886-96; headmaster, Thayer Acad., South Braintree, Mass., 1896-1920 (emeritus). Republican. Conglist. Home: Brookline, Mass. Died Feb. 3, 1922.

GALLANT, Albert Ernest, surgeon; b. June 27, 1861; s. Rev. Walter and Sarah (Horsley) G.; common sch., edn.; M.D., Coll. Phys. and Surg. (Columbia), 1890; interne Sloane Maternity Hosp., 1891, New York Cancer Hosp., 1892; m. Eudora Milroy Elliott, Jan. 1, 1895; m. 2d, Mary Claire Parsons, June 14, 1920. Instr. surgery, N.Y. Post-Grad. Med. Sch., 1894-96, N.Y. Polyclinic Med. Sch. and Hosp., 1897-99; asst. surgeon, Lebanon Hosp., 1894-95; med. dir. Miss Helen Gould's War Relief Assn. and Soldiers' Comfort Com., 1898; prof. gynecology, N.Y. Sch. Clin. Medicine, 1901-06; was attending gynecologist, McDougal Mem. Hosp., Metropolitan Hosp. and Dispensary, and cons. surgeon Bapt. Deaconess Home and Training Sch., Jamaica Hosp., and Eastern L.I. Hosp.; asst. surgeon, Med. Reserve Corps U.S.N.; operating surgeon 1st Gen. (mil.) Hosp., Birmingham, Eng., 1917-18. Republican. Home: Sarasota, Fla. Deceased.

GALLATIN, Francis Dawson, lawyer; b. N.Y. City, Sept. 2, 1870; s. James and Elizabeth (Dawson) G.; g.g.s. Albert Gallatin, sec. U.S. Treasury under President Madison and President Jefferson; prep. edn. Berkeley Sch.; A.B., Columbia, 1891; student Columbia Law Sch. and N.Y. Law Sch.; m. Harriet L. Bogert, 1892 (divorced 1908); children—Lucile, Theodore; m. 2d, Dorothy C. Brady, Aug. 20, 1926. Admitted to N.Y. bar, 1909; mem. Fay, Rubin & Gallatin; formerly city magistrate; commr. of parks, Borough of Manhattan, 1919-27; pres. Park Bd., City of New York, 1919-27. Enlisted in Co. K, 7th Regt., N.Y.N.G., 1888; 2d lt. Co. H, 12th Regt., 1891. During incumbency as park commr. suggested and organized Museum of the City of New York. Home: New York, N.Y. Died Dec. 23, 1933.

GALLAUDET, Bern Budd, surgeon; b. New York, N.Y., Feb. 11, 1860; s. Thomas (D.D.) and Elizabeth (Budd) G.; A.B., Trinity Coll., Conn., 1880, A.M., 1883; M.D., Coll. Phys. and Surg. (Columbia), 1884; interne New York Hosp., 1884-86; student medicine, Vienna, 1886-87; m. Elise G., d. late Col. William A. Elderkin, U.S.A., June 4, 1894. Engaged in practice of surgery, 1887-1909; surgeon to Vanderbilt clinic, 1888-90; asst. demonstrator anatomy, 1887-91, clin. lecturer on surgery, 1890-97, demonstrator anatomy, 1891-1905, instr. surgery, 1897-1909, asst. prof. anatomy, 1905-29, asso. prof., 1929—, Coll. Phys. and Surg.; visiting surgeon, 1890-1909, cons. surgeon, 1909—, Bellevue Hosp., N.Y. City. Author: Surgery, Quiz Compends, 1892. Editor: Gray's Anatomy, 1897. Died Mar. 30, 1934.

GALLAUDET, Edward Miner, college pres.; b. Hartford, Conn., Feb. 5, 1837; s. late Thomas Hopkins G.; B.S., Trinity Coll., 1856 (LL.D., 1869; also LL.D., Yale, 1895; Ph.D., Columbian, 1869). Taught in his father's instn. for deaf mutes at Hartford, 1856-57; organized, 1857, Columbia Instn. for Deaf, Dumb and Blind, at Washington; developed from it the Gallaudet Coll. for the Deaf, founded 1864 (still the only coll. for deaf in the world), of which was pres. until May 1911 (emeritus). Pres. conv. of Am. Instns. for the Deaf; at invitation of British govt., appeared before Royal Commn. in interest of deaf-mute edn., 1886. Author: Popular Manual of International Law; Life of Thomas Hopkins Gallaudet. Home: Hartford, Conn. Died Sept. 26, 1917.

GALLAUDET, Thomas, P.E. clergyman; b. Hartford, Conn., June 3, 1822; s. late Thomas Hopkins, educator of deaf mutes, and Sophia (Fowler) G.; grad. Trinity Coll., 1842; (A.M., 1845; D.D., 1862); m. Elizabeth R. Budd, July 15, 1845. Ordered deacon, 1850; ordained priest, 1851; taught in New York Instn. for Deaf Mutes, 1843-58; asst. minister, St. Stephen's Ch., New York, 1850; St. Paul's Morrisiania, N.Y., 1851-52; organized, 1852, St. Ann's Ch., New York, providing services for deaf-mutes; rector emeritus St. Matthew's Ch., and vicar of St. Ann's Ch., built and supported by St. Matthew's, exclusively for deaf mutes. General mgr. Church Mission to Deaf Mutes, 1872—; founded, 1885, Gallaudet Home for Deaf Mutes, nr. Poughkeepsie. Died 1902.

GALLAWAY, Robert Macy, banker; b. New York, N.Y., Aug. 4, 1837; A.B., Yale, 1858, A.M., 1868; m. Elizabeth A. Williams, 1868. Vice-pres., 1891-92, pres., 1892—, Merchants' Nat. Bank, New York; dir. N.Y. Mut. Gas Light Co.; v.p., dir. and mem. exec. com., Manhattan Ry. Co. Home: New York, N.Y. Died Nov. 13, 1917.

GALLIHER, William Thompson, banker, lumber mcht.; b. Port Deposit, Md., July 29, 1856; s. Joseph Wesley and Agnes (Thompson) G.; ed. pub. schs., finishing in 8th grade; m. A. Laura, McIntire, Oct. 2, 1877. Dir. Am. Nat. Bank, Washington, D.C., at orgn., 1903, v.p., 1908-10, pres., 1910-22, and chmn. bd. Federal-Am. Nat. Bank following merger of Am. Nat. Bank and Fed. Nat. Bank, Nov. 1922; pres. W. T. Galliher & Bro., Inc., lumber (estab. 1889); pres. Home Building Assn.; v.p. Nat. Union Fire Ins. Co.; treas. Rosslyn Steel & Cement Co. Pres. Lumber Exchange of D.C., 1900-22 inclusive; pres. Washington Bd. of Trade, 1918; pres. D.C. Bankers Assn.; mem. Washington Chamber Commerce. Chmn. Inauguration Com. (Coolidge and Dawes), Mar. 4, 1925. Formerly maj. and brigade q.m. D.C.N.G. Chmn. Rep. Com., D.C., 1916-24. Trustee Am. Univ., Swartzell Home for Children; mem. Bd. of Charities, D.C. Methodist. Trustee and treas. Bd. of Temperance, Prohibition and Pub. Morals of M.E. Ch. Mason. Home: Washington, D.C. Died June 30, 1929.

GALLINGER, Jacob H., U.S. senator; b. Cornwall, Ont., Mar. 28, 1837; s. Jacob and Catharine (Cook) G.; academic edn.; M.D., Med. Institute, Cincinnati, 1858; M.D., N.Y. Homœo. Med. Coll., 1868; (hon. A.M., Dartmouth, 1885); m. Mary Anna Bailey, Aug. 1860. Engaged in med. practice Concord, N.H., 1862-85; surgeon gen. N.H. with rank of brig. gen., 1879-80. Mem. N.H. Ho. of Rep., 1872-73, 1891, Senate, 1878, 1879, 1880 (pres., 1879, 80); mem. Constl. Conv., 1876; chmn. Rep. State Com., 1882-90, and 1898-1907; chmn. N.H. delegation Rep. Nat. convs., 1888, 1900, 1904, 1908 (made speech seconding nomination of Benjamin Harrison, 1888); mem. Rep. Nat. Com., 1902-04; mem. 49th and 50th Congresses (1885-89); declined renomination; U.S. senator for terms, 1891-97, 1897-1903, 1903-09, 1909-15, 1915-21; minority leader. Home: Concord, N.H. Died Aug. 17, 1918.

GALLISON, Henry Hammond, artist; b. Boston, Mass., May 20, 1850; s. Joseph H. and Lavinia G.; pupil of Bonnefoy, Paris; m. Marie Reuter, of Lübeck, Germany, June 1886. Exhibited in London, Paris, Turin, and Paris Expn., 1900; spl. mention, Turin; hon. mention, Paris; picture, Rising Mists, exhibited in exhbn., Turin, Italy, 1902, purchased by the Italian Govt. for the Nat. Mus., being the first American artist to be so honored; medal, St. Louis Expn., 1904. Home: Cambridge, Mass. Died 1910.

GALLIVAN, James Ambrose, congressman; b. Boston, Mass., Oct. 22, 1866; s. James S. and Mary (Flynn) G.; grad. Boston Latin Sch., 1884 (Benjamin Franklin Medal); A.B., Harvard, 1888; m. Louise A. Burke, Feb. 21, 1898. Entered newspaper work, Boston, 1888; mem. Mass. Ho. of Rep., 1895, 1896, Senate, 1897, 1898; street commr., Boston, 1901-14; elected mem. 63d Congress, 12th Mass. Dist., Apr. 12, 1914; reëlected 64th to 66th Congresses (1915-21), and 68th and 69th Congresses (1923-27). Democrat. Mason. Home: Boston, Mass. Died Apr. 3, 1928.

GALLIVER, George Alfred, financier; b. Ingersoll, Canada; s. Henry and Mary J. (Luscombe) G.; student Albion (Mich.) Coll.; M.D., Harvey Med. Coll., Chicago, Ill.; m. Lillian Campbell, July 7, 1901. Various positions, P.M. R.R., sales mgr. U.S. Graphite Co., Saginaw, Mich., 1890-92; sec.-treas. Chicago Paint Co., 1892-93; pres. Merkel & Co., produce commn. mchts., Chicago, 1893-95; supt., then sales mgr., Monarch Cycle Mfg. Co. and Chicago Sewing Machine Co., Chicago, 1895-98; scientific rep. Parke, Davis & Company, pharmaceuticals, Detroit, 1898; sales mgr. Am. Bicycle Mfg. Co., Chicago, 1900-02; gen. mgr., Stearns & Culver Lumber Co., Bagdad, Fla., 1902-05; gen. mgr., Domestic Sewing Machine Co. and Nat. Sweeper Co., Newark, N.J., 1906-09; with Harrison Williams and associates, pub. utilities and investment bankers, 1909-17, as pres. Central States Electric Corp., v.p. Federal Utilities, Inc., also Republic Ry. & Light Co., Mahoning & Shenango Ry. & Light Co., pres. Electric Investment Corp., also Utilities Securities Corp., Gen. Internat. Co., Inc. (New York); v.p. The Flintlock Co. (Detroit); became pres. Am. Writing Paper Co., 1918; mem. Schott & Galliver, members N.Y. Stock Exchange, brokers and investment bankers; mem. Galliver & Rockefeller, financing, brokers; dir. Eastern States Agr. and Indsl. League; trustee Holyoke City Hospital. Republican. Methodist. Home: Orange, N.J.; Tavares, Fla. Died June 22, 1932.

GALLIZIER, Nathan, author; b. Ludwigsburg, Germany, Feb. 8, 1866; grad. Royal Coll., Ludwigsburg; unmarried. Came to U.S., 1882. Author: Castel Del Monte, 1905; The Sorceress of Rome, 1907; The Court of Lucifer, 1911; The Hill of Venus, 1913; The Crimson Gondola, 1915; Under the Witches' Moon, 1917; The Leopard Prince, 1920; The Lotus Woman, 1922; The Wand of Circe, 1924; The Red Confessor, 1926. Home: Cincinnati, O. Died Jan. 14, 1927.

GALLOWAY, Beverly Thomas, botanist; b. Millersburg, Mo., Oct. 16, 1863; s. Robert M. and Jane (McCray) G.; B.Agr.Sc., U. of Mo., 1884, LL.D., 1902; m. Agnes S. Rankin, Sept. 5, 1888; children—Robert Rankin, Alexander Gordon, Beverly Stewart. Asst. in hort. dept., U. of Mo., 1884-86; asst. pathologist, 1887-88, pathologist and chief Div. Vegetable Pathology and Physiology, 1888-1900, chief Bur. Plant Industry, 1901-12; asst. sec. of agr., U.S., 1913-14; dean State Coll. Agr., Cornell U., 1914-16; pathologist, Office Foreign Plant Introduction of U.S. Dept. Agr., 1916-33; now collaborator U.S. Dept. of Agriculture. Home: Takoma Park, D.C. Died June 13, 1938.

GALLOWAY, Charles Betts, bishop M.E. Ch., S., 1886—; b. Kosciusko, Miss., Sept. 1, 1849; grad. Univ. of Miss., 1868 (D.D., 1882; LL.D., Northwestern U., Tulane U.); m. Miss H. E. Willis, Sept. 1, 1869. Entered Miss. Conf., M.E. Ch., S., 1868; served numerous chs. in Miss.; had yellow fever in Vicksburg, 1878, reported dead, obituary written. Editor New Orleans Christian Advocate, 1882-86; many yrs. pres. Prohibition exec. com., Miss.; fraternal messenger to Gen. Conf., Methodist Ch. of Canada, 1886; to Wesleyan Conf., England, 1892; mem. Ecumenical Methodist Conf., Washington, 1891; officially visited missions in Japan, China and Korea, 3 times, twice to Brazil Mission Conf.; preached opening sermon at Ecumenical Conf., London, 1901; pres. Bd. of Edn. of M.E. Ch., S. Mem. bd. trustees John F. Slater Fund; pres. bd. trustees Millsaps Coll. and Vanderbilt Univ.; mem. Miss. Historic Commn. Author: A Circuit of the Globe; Modern Missions—Their Evidential Value; Christianity and the American Commonwealth. Home: Jackson, Miss. Died 1909.

GALLOWAY, Charles William, ry. official; b. Baltimore, Md., Dec. 11, 1868; s. Charles Barton and Susan Jane (Smith) G.; ed. pub. schs.; m. Margaret B. Leiritz, Nov. 10, 1890; 1 dau., Mrs. Margaret Jane Dickey. Began as messenger telegraph dept., B.&O. R.R. Co., 1883; clk., stenographer, etc., same rd., until 1897; trainmaster Baltimore div., 1897-99, asst. supt. main line, 1st div., 1899-1901; supt. Cumberland div., 1901-03, Baltimore div., 1903-06; supt. transportation, at Baltimore, 1906-10, all with B.&O. R.R. Co.; gen. supt. transportation, same rd. and B.&O.S.W. R.R., July-Sept. 1910; gen.-supt. B.&O.S.W. R.R. Co., at Cincinnati, O., 1910-12; gen. mgr. B.&O. R.R., 1912-16; v.p. and gen. mgr. B.&O.S.W. R.R. and B.&O. R.R. Western Lines, 1916-18; federal mgr. U.S. R.R. Adminstration, over B.&O. Western Lines, Dayton & Union Railroad and Dayton Union Railway, 1918-19, and of B.&O. Eastern Lines, Coal & Coke, Railroad, Morgantown & Kingwood Railroad, Western Maryland Railway, Cumberland Valley R.R. and Cumberland & Pa. R.R., 1919-20, and B.&O. System, S.I. Rapid Transit Ry., and Baltimore & New York, Coal & Coke, Morgantown & Kingwood, Dayton Union and Dayton & Union Railroads, Jan. 15-Mar. 1, 1920; v.p. operation and maintenance, B.&O. System, Baltimore, 1920—. Died Dec. 13, 1940.

GALLOWAY, Thomas Walton, biologist; b. Columbia, Tenn., Nov. 2, 1866; s. William T. and Elizabeth Rebecca (Smith) G.; A.B., Cumberland U., Tenn., 1887, A.M., 1889, Ph.D., 1892; A.M., Harvard, 1890; m. Mary L. Armstrong, Dec. 22, 1892; 1 dau., Mrs. Elizabeth Joan Woods. Prof. natural history, Baird Coll., Clinton, Mo., 1887-89; grad. student, Harvard, 1889-91; prof. biology, 1891-1902, dean, 1899-1902, Mo. Valley Coll.; prof. biology James Millikin U., Decatur, Ill., 1902-15; prof. zoölogy, Beloit (Wis.) Coll., 1915-19; asso. dir. Dept. of Edn., Am. Social Hygiene Assn., 1919—. On leave of absence at Harvard, 1897-98, won Bowdoin prize. Sec. Am. Micros. Soc. and editor Quarterly Transactions; fellow A.A.A.S. Author: Biology of Sex for Parents and Teachers; Reproduction, 1916; Motivation in Moral Education; Sex and Life, 1919; Sex Factor in Human Life; The Father and His Boy; The Dramatic Instinct in Religious Education; Sex and Social Health; Love and Marriage; Parenthood and the Character Education of Children, etc. Home: New York, N.Y. Died July 16, 1929.

GALLUP, William Arthur, mfr.; b. Adams (now North Adams), Mass., Oct. 28, 1851; s. William Witherell and Eugenia Olive (Smith) G.; 8th descent from John Gallup, Nantasket, Mass., 1630; ed. pub. sch. and Drury Acad.; m. 2d, Florence L. Houghton, Sept. 20, 1893. Began as jr. clk. in office of Harvey Arnold & Co., Jan. 3, 1870; name later changed to Arnold Print Works, finishers of textile fabrics, of which was for many yrs. dir. and treas.; clk. North Adams Nat. Bank, later dir., v.p. and president. Republican. Mem. Gen. Com. Mass. Bay Tercentenary (1930), and of Pilgrim Tercentenary of the N.E. Hist.-Geneal. Soc.; mem. exec. com. Mass. Bible Soc., 1904—. Mem. U.S. Chamber Commerce, Boston Chamber Commerce (life). Episcopalian. Home: Boston, Mass. Died Aug. 9, 1930.

GALPIN, Kate Tupper, teacher; b. on farm nr. Brighton, Ia., Aug. 3, 1855; d. Allen and Ellen (Smith) Tupper; ed. at home by mother, 9 months in Brighton (Ia.) pub. sch.; Iowa State Coll., B.S., 1874; m. Cromwell Galpin, Aug. 16, 1890. Taught in vacations throughout coll. course, and afterward in country schs., high schs., normal schs. and U. of Nevada; teaching classes in Shakespeare, 1893—, 200 women now studying with her, including the "Galpin Shakespeare Club" of 89 mems., all holding her certificate of having critically studied 20 of Shakespeare's plays. Mem. faculty and v.p. Cumnock Sch. of Expression. Home: Los Angeles, Calif. Died 1906.

GALPIN, Stanley Leman, college prof.; b. Cleveland, O., Jan. 6, 1878; s. William Adams and Sarah Adams (Burns) G.; A.B., Western Reserve U., 1901; A.M., Yale, 1902, Ph.D., 1904; m. Winifred Worswick Stowe, Dec. 18, 1901; 1 dau., Marjorie. Instr. Romance langs., Amherst, 1904-08; asso. prof. Romance langs., 1908-13, prof., 1913—, Trinity Coll., Conn. Home: Berlin, Conn. Died Apr. 1, 1934.

GALT, Herbert Randolph, editor; b. Upperville, Va., Apr. 27, 1881; s. Francis Land and Lucy (Randolph) G.; ed. Marston's Univ. Sch., Baltimore, Md., and Episcopal High Sch., Alexandria, Va.; m. Elsie Robinson Andrews, Oct. 12, 1908; children—John Randolph, Elizabeth Andrews. On editorial staff Baltimore American, 1900-02; with Baltimore News, 1902-09; connected with St. Paul Dispatch and Pioneer Press, 1909—, editor, 1913—. Episcopalian. Home: St. Paul, Minn. Died Dec. 19, 1926.

GALT, John Randolph, banker; b. Newburgh, N.Y., June 5, 1867; s. John and Anne Eveline (Roberts) G.; A.B., Yale, 1889; m. Agnes Carter, of Honolulu, May 18, 1892 (died 1927); children—John (dec.), Charles Lunt Carter; m. 2d, Lucy Keeff, of Honolulu, Feb. 13, 1937. Began with Galt Bros. & Co., Seattle, Wash., 1890; with Pope Mfg. Co., Hartford, Conn., 1896-99; became sec. Hawaiian Trust Co., 1899, treas. and mgr., 1903, v.p., 1918, pres., 1928, now chmn. bd. Was Hawaiian consul, Seattle, 1893-96. Served as capt., Q.M.C.R., and disbursing officer Omaha area, 1918-19. Pres. Social Service Bur., Palama Settlement; hon. pres. United Welfare Fund. Mem. Honolulu Chamber Commerce (pres. 1925). Republican. Home: Honolulu, H.T. Died Aug. 3, 1941.

GALVIN, John, mayor; b. Cincinnati, O., June 13, 1862; s. Maurice and Ellen G.; grad. Covington (Ky.) High Sch.; LL.B., Cincinnati Law Sch., 1883; m. Julie Edair Cusson, Feb. 28, 1889. Began law practice in office of C. B. Simrall, Cincinnati; asst. city solicitor, 1887-94; Rep. candidate for judge Superior Court, 1898; pres. City Council and vice-mayor of Cincinnati, 1908-09; mayor, July 28, 1909-Jan. 1, 1910, and 1918-21 inclusive. Grand Exalted Ruler B.P.O.E. of the U.S., 1908-09. Home: Cincinnati, O. Died Mar. 1, 1922.

GALVIN, John Francis; b. New York, N.Y., May 17, 1859; s. Jeremiah and Katherine (Connor) G.; A.M., St. Francis Xavier Coll., New York, 1875; m. Margaret Agatha Murphy, June 4, 1885; children—Katherine (Mrs. Parker C. Kalloch, Jr.), Agatha (Mrs. Matthew T. Murray, Jr.), John F., Paul, Walter, Frank, Joseph. Began as a bank clk., 1875; mem. Albert Haug & Co., 1885-89; pres. Metal Stamping Co., 1889-1933. Queens chmn. commrs. Port of New York Authority. Home: New York, N.Y. Deceased.

GAMA, Domicio da; b. Rio de Janeiro, Brazil, 1862; m. Mrs. Arthur Hearn, of N.Y. City, Nov. 1913. Began diplomatic service as sec. Brazilian Legation at Washington, D.C., 1893; later sec. at Paris, Berne, London, and in foreign office, Rio de Janeiro; served successively as minister to Colombia, to Peru, Argentina and Chile, until 1911; A.E. and P. to U.S., 1911—. Was mem. Mediation Conf. between U.S. and Mexico, 1916. Died Nov. 8, 1925.

GAMBLE, Eleanor Acheson McCulloch, psychologist; b. Cincinnati, Mar. 2, 1868; d. late Joseph and Mary (McGill) G.; g.d. late Alexander T. McGill, D.D., of Princeton Theol. Sem.; A.B., Wellesley Coll., 1889; Ph.D., Cornell U., 1898; studied U. of Göttingen, Germany, 1906-07; unmarried. Began teaching, Wellesley Coll., 1898, asso. prof. psychology, 1903-10, prof., 1910—. Episcopalian. Author: Study in Memorizing Various Materials by the Reconstruction Method, 1909. Editor: Wellesley College Studies in Psychology, No. 2. Home: Wellesley, Mass. Died Aug. 30, 1933.

GAMBLE, James Norris, mfr.; b. Cincinnati, Aug. 9, 1836; s. James and Elizabeth Ann (Norris) G.; A.B., Kenyon Coll., O., 1854, A.M., 1857; spl. course in chemistry, U. of Baltimore; m. Margaret Penrose, of Corduff, Co. Leitrim, Ireland, Apr. 1862. Mem. Procter & Gamble, mfrs. soap, candles and oils, 1862-90; v.p. Procter & Gamble Co., 1890—. Mayor of Westwood, 1895. Home: Westwood, O. Died July 2, 1932.

GAMBLE, Robert Bruce, surgeon; b. Mosiertown, Pa., June 28, 1871; s. William J. and Helen (Beebee) G.; A.B., Allegheny Coll., Pa., 1893, A.M., 1896; M.D., U. of Buffalo Med. Dept., 1896; m. Nella M. White, July 5, 1900. House surgeon, City Hosp., Rochester, N.Y., 1896-97; settled in Meadville, Pa., 1897; surgeon City Hosp.; dir. First Nat. Bank, Meadville. Capt. 15th Pa. Vol. Inf., Spanish-Am. War, later lt. col. 16th Inf., N.G. Pa.; lt. col. of the 112th Inf., 1917; with A.E.F., 15 months. Chevalier Legion of Honor (France). Trustee Allegheny College. Fellow Am. Coll. of Surgeons. Republican. Episcopalian. Mason. Home: Meadville, Pa. Died July 11, 1940.

GAMBLE, Robert Jackson, senator; b. Genesee Co., N.Y., Feb. 7, 1851; s. Robert and Jennie A. (Abernethy) G.; A.B., Lawrence U., Wis., 1874 (LL.D., 1909); m. Carrie S. Osborn, Mar. 26, 1884. Admitted to bar, 1875; practiced at Yankton, S.D., until 1915; since at Sioux Falls, S.D.; was mem. Gamble Bros., 1876-91 (John R. Gamble elected to Congress, 1890, but died 1891, before taking seat). Dist. atty., 2d Jud. Dist., Dak. Ty., 1880; city atty., Yankton, 1881-82; mem. S.D. Senate, 1885; chmn. Rep. State Conv., 1892-1893; mem. 54th and 56th Congresses (1895-97, 1899-1901); U.S. senator for terms, 1901-07, 1907-13. Republican. Chmn. S.D. br. and mem. nat. exec. com. League to Enforce Peace, 1916-19 (resigned). Dir. for S.D. of Am. Red Cross, 1917-19. Trustee Yankton Coll., 1890-1900. Mason. Home: Sioux Falls, S.D. Died Sept. 22, 1924.

GAMBLE, Samuel Walter, clergyman; b. Worthington, Pa., Nov. 15, 1852; s. Samuel B. and Eliza S. G.; ed. chiefly in pub. schs., Woodhull, Ill.; m. Ethel R. Dysert, Apr. 30, 1890; children—Ira Samuel, Mrs. May Adelia Glover, Mrs. Sadie Belle Crary, Mrs. Agnes Verna Stokes (all by previous marriages), Carroll Milton, Verne Dysert (dec.), Mrs. Olla Barbara Dean. Entered M.E. ministry, 1881; in pastoral work until 1899. Became known for research in the ancient lit., enabling him to reproduce the long-lost Hebrew Calendar, upon which he bases arguments to prove that Sunday and not Saturday was the ancient and the true Sabbath. Selected by internat. com. for the World's Sunday Rest Congress to lecture at St. Louis Expn., 1904, on "the transfer of the Sabbath from the Jewish to the Christian Sabbath"; delivered 900 addresses in Can. for the Lord's Day Alliance of Can. Editor of The Toiler's Friend, and The True Sabbath (mags.). Field sec. Nat. Reform Assn. for Calif., on the Sabbath dept., 1917-21. Author: Sunday the True Sabbath of God, 1900; A Brief Statement of Sabbath Truth, 1918. Exposed the so-called Religious Liberty Assn., 1923. Was selected by Internat. Lord's Day Congress to lecture at the Panama P.I. Expn., July 1915. Home: Long Beach, Calif. Died Dec. 29, 1932.

GAMBRELL, James Bruton, clergyman; b. Anderson, S.C., Aug. 21, 1841; s. Joel Bruton and Jane (Williams) G.; ed. Orizaba and Cherry Creek, Miss., and U. of Miss.; (D.D., Furman U., 1884; LL.D., Wake Forest, 1895, also Baylor U.); m. Mary Tom Corbell, Jan. 13, 1864. Capt. C.S.A., 1861-65; ordained Bapt. ministry, 1867; pastor West Point, Oxford, and Clinton, Miss.; editor Bapt. Record, 15 yrs.; pres. Mercer U., Ga., 3 yrs.; supt. Bapt. Mission in Texas; corr. sec. Bapt. Gen. Conv. of Tex.; pres. Texas Bapt. Edn. Commn., Am. Bapt. Edn. Soc.; became prof. Southwestern Bapt. Theol. Sem., Ft. Worth, Tex. Pres. Southern Bapt. Conv. Editor Baptist Standard 3 yrs. Died June 10, 1921.

GAMBRELL, Joel Halbert, clergyman; b. Tippah Co., Miss. May 7, 1855; s. Joel Bruton and Jane (Williams) G.; ed. pub. schs. and pvt. tutors; liberal arts and law course, U. of Miss., 1872-76; ancient langs., Miss. Coll., Clinton, 1879-80 (D.D., 1905); m. Victoria Pickens, Dec. 23, 1883. Licensed Bapt. ministry, 1879; teacher, Granada, Miss., 1877-78; state prohibition organizer of Miss., 1880-90; editor Sword and Shield, Clinton and Jackson, Miss, 1881-85; ordained ministry, 1890; pastor Lincoln Co., Miss., 1890-94, First Ch., Greensboro, Ga., 1894-98, First Ch., Tyler, Tex., 1898-1904; editor Baptist Standard, Dallas Tex., 1904-08; asso. supt. Anti-Saloon League of Tex., 1908; pastor First Ch., Marlin, Tex., 1908-10; founder and editor Christian Patriot, 1909-10; supt. Anti-Saloon League of Tex., 1910-15; asso. editor The Californian, 1915-16; gen. missionary, Bapt. Gen. Conv. of Tex., 1916—. Trustee Rusk (Tex.) Coll., 1898-1904, Baylor Coll. for Women, about 8 yrs. Mason. Democrat. Home: Dallas, Tex., and El Paso, Tex. Died Jan. 30, 1923.

GAMBRILL, Stephen Warfield, congressman; b. Howard Co., Md., Oct. 2, 1873; s. Stephen and Kate (Gorman) G.; student Md. Agrl. Coll.; LL.B., Columbian (now George Washington) U., 1897; m. Haddie D. Gorman, 1900 (died 1923). Admitted to Md. bar, 1897, and began practice at Baltimore; mem. Ho. of Rep., Md., 1920, 22, Senate, 1924; elected to 68th Congress to fill vacancy caused by death of Sidney E. Mudd; also reëlected 69th to 75th Congresses (1925-39), 5th Md. Dist. Democrat. Episcopalian. Home: Laurel, Md. Died Dec. 19, 1938.

GAME, Josiah Bethea, coll. prof.; b. Mullins, S.C., Aug. 14, 1869; s. Robert Bethea and Elizabeth (Campbell) G.; A.M., U. of S.C., 1895; M.S., Erskine Coll., 1898, Litt.D., 1922; M.A., Yale, 1906, Ph.D., 1909; m. Agnes Irene Hughes, Feb. 15, 1892; children—Josiah Bethea, Ralph Hughes (dec.), Robert Gilmore (dec.), Agnes Hughes (Mrs. J. C. Greenfield, Jr.), Mildred G. Rector, Cokesbury Conf. Sch., S.C., 1895-98; prof. Latin and Greek, Wesleyan Coll., 1898-99; pastor 1st Meth. Ch., Brunswick, Ga., 1899-1902; at Central Coll., Fayette, Mo., 1902-05; univ. scholar, Yale Grad. Sch., 1905-06; univ. fellow same school, 1906-07; prof. Latin and Greek, State Normal Sch., Cape Girardeau, Mo., 1907-11; prof. Latin, State Normal Coll., Florence, Ala., 1911-14, also dean, 1912-14; prof. classics and gen. lit., Fla. State Coll. for Women, Tallahassee, Fla., 1914—. Sec., treas. Tallahassee Nat. Farm Loan Assn. (of Columbia Federal Loan Bank), 1917—; pres. Fla. Nat. Farm Loan Assns., 1924-28. Chaplain Pat Houston Camp, Sons Confederate Vets. Dir. and sec. Fla. Meth. Foundation; chmn. State Library Board, 1932—. Mason. Democrat. Author: Teaching High School Latin, 1916, revised edit., 1925; (with Charles Upson Clark) Clark and Game's First Latin, 1917; Clark and Game's Second Latin, 1924; Game's General Literature; Myth, Epic, and Drama, 1924. Editor: Clark and Game's Medieval and Late Latin Selections, 1925. Died Mar. 4, 1935.

GAMERTSFELDER, Solomon Jacob, theologian; b. Jefferson Tp., O., Oct. 10, 1851; s. Carl Jacob and Anna (King) G.; A.B., Northwestern Coll., Ill., 1878, A.M., 1881; grad. Evang. Theol. Sem., Naperville, 1881 (D.D., 1900); Ph.D., Coll. of Wooster, 1903; m. Emma D. Spreng, May 30, 1883. Ordained ministry Evang. Assn., 1881; pastor Cleveland, 1879-80, Napoleon, O., 1881-83, West Salem, O., 1883-85, Circleville, O., 1885-87; asso. editor Evang. Messenger, Cleveland, 1887-95; prof. systematic theology, 1895—, pres., 1911-19, pres. emeritus, Evang. Theol. Sem., Naperville, Ill. Author: A Bible Study on Prayer, 1907. Died Aug. 6, 1925.

GAMMACK, James, clergyman; b. Turriff, Scotland, Apr. 23, 1837; s. Alexander and Elizabeth (Robertson) G.; M.A., Marischal Coll., Scotland, 1857; studied Trinity Coll., Glenalmond, Scotland; (LL.D., Aberdeen U., 1887); m. Jane Anne Wilson, Apr. 29, 1862; father of Arthur James G. (q.v.). Deacon, 1859, priest, 1861, Scotland Episcopal Ch.; served in various parishes, Scotland, 1861-89; rector E. Toronto, Ont., 1889-92, St. Peter's Plymouth, Conn., 1893-95, St. James', West Hartford, Conn., Nov. 1895-1911; rector emeritus. Home: West Hartford, Conn. Died Feb. 17, 1923.

GAMMELL, Robert Ives, financier; b. Providence, R.I., Dec. 30, 1852; s. William and Elizabeth Amory (Ives) G.; A.B., Brown U., 1872, A.M., 1875; m. Eliza A. Hoppin, Feb. 28, 1878. Mem. Goddard Bros., and Brown & Ives, cotton mfrs.; pres. Providence, Nat. Bank; treas. Lonsdale Co., Blackstone Mfg. Co.; dir. numerous fire ins. cos. Trustee Brown U., 1890—; pres. R.I. Hosp. Independent Republican. Episcopalian. Home: Providence, R.I. Died Jan. 8, 1915.

GANDY, Charles Moore, army officer; b. Ocean View, N.J., Nov. 6, 1857; s. Lewis Corson and Eliza A. (Smith) G.; prep. edn. S.Jersey Inst., Bridgeton, N.J.; M.D., Jefferson Med. Coll., Phila., 1879; m. Emma R. Graham, Nov. 6, 1884; children—Charles Lewis, Lila Marguerite. Apptd. asst. surgeon, Dec. 3, 1883; capt. asst. surgeon, Dec. 3, 1888; maj. brigade surgeon vols., June 4, 1898; maj. chief surgeon, Jan. 7, 1899; hon. disch. from vols., Mar. 22, 1899; maj. surgeon U.S.A., Feb. 2, 1901; maj. med. corps, Feb. 2, 1901; lt. col., Jan. 1, 1909; col. Apr. 16, 1913. Acting chief surgeon 4th Army Corps, Oct. and Nov., 1898; surgeon and prof. mil. hygiene, U.S. Mil. Acad., 1906-10; chief surgeon Western Dept., 1910-11; asst. surgeon gen.'s office, Washington, 1912-14; chief surgeon Philippine Dept., 1915-16; comdg. Army and Navy Gen. Hosp., Hot Springs, Ark., Feb. 20, 1917-May 26, 1919; chief surgeon, Eastern Dept., Governors Island, N.Y., 1919-21; retired Nov. 6, 1921. Mason. Home: Ocean View, N.J. Died Jan. 8, 1937.

GANFIELD, William Arthur, educator; b. Dubuque Co., Ia., Sept. 3, 1873; s. Samuel and Mary Jane (Patterson) G.; A.B., Cornell Coll., Ia., 1898, A.M., 1901; grad. McCormick Theol. Sem., 1901; studied U. of Chicago, 1904; D.D., Carroll, 1912; LL.D., Univ. of Ky., 1916; m. Clara Evelyn Boardman, Aug. 27, 1901; children—Dorothy Evelyn, Arthur Boardman, Elizabeth Anne, Ruth Winifred, Eleanor Jane. Ordained Presbyn. ministry, 1901; pastor Green Bay, Wis., 1901-04; prof. history and polit. science, Carroll Coll., Waukesha, Wis., 1904-15; pres. Centre Coll., Danville, Ky., 1915-21; pres. Carroll Coll., 1921-39. Chmn. Ky. Sch. Survey Commn.; mem. exec. com. Internat. S.S. Assn.; mem. bd. dirs. Wis. S.S.Assn.; Moderator Presbyn. Synod of Wis., 1922-23. Mem. bd. dirs. Nat. Reform Assn., Wis. State Chamber of Commerce. Mason. Rep. candidate for U.S. senator, 1922. Mem. advisory council Living Age. Home: Waukesha, Wis. Died Oct. 18, 1940.

GANIERE, George Etienne, sculptor; b. Chicago, Ill., s. John George and Margaret (Weiand) G.; studied art at the Art Institute Chicago; m. Ann Esther Varney. Exhibited at the Buffalo Exposition, 1901; St. Louis Expn., 1904; San Francisco Exposition, 1915. Highest award for ideal sculpture, Art Inst. Chicago, 1909. Principal works: Statues of Lincoln, Burlington, Wis., and Webster City, Ia.; Lincoln tablet, Starved Rock, Ill.; Gen. Anthony Wayne equestrian statue, Ft. Wayne, Ind.; statuette "The Bather," De Land, Fla.; etc. Designed fountain for Arché Club, at intersection of Lincoln Highway and Dixie Trail, Chicago Heights, Ill.; Dr. Frank W. Gunsaulus memorial at Armour Inst. Tech., Chicago; Hately memorial, Highland Park, Ill. Formerly instr. sculpture, Art Inst. Chicago; now dir. Dept. of Sculpture, John B. Stetson U., De Land, Fla., also dir. dept. of sculpture, Rollins Coll., Winter Park, Fla.; official sculptor, State of Fla., at A Century of Progress Expn., Chicago, 1933. Mem. 1st Regt. Cavalry, I.N.G., 5 yrs. Address: De Land, Fla. Died July 29, 1935.

GANLY, James Vincent, congressman; b. N.Y. City, Sept. 13, 1878; ed. pub. schs. and business coll.; m. Mary R. Leddy, June 14, 1911. Pres. Motor Mercantile Co., Inc.; mem. N.Y. Assembly, 1907; first county clk. of Bronx Co., 1914-18; mem. 66th Congress (1919-21), 24th N.Y. Dist. Democrat. Home: New York, N.Y. Died Sept. 7, 1923.

GANN, Edward Everett, lawyer; b. Monticello, Ky., Oct. 12, 1880; s. William Kendrick (M.D.) and Mary Jane (Daugherty) G.; LL.B., Jefferson Sch. of Law, Louisville, Ky., 1908; m. Dolly Curtis, June 12, 1915. Admitted to Ky. bar, 1908; began practice, Louisville, 1908, Washington, 1920; atty. and examiner, Interstate Commerce Commn., 1910-14; spl. asst. to atty. gen. of U.S., 1914-21; became eastern counsel N.Y.,C.&St.L. R.R. Co.; counsel for Mid-Continent Oil & Gas Assn., Legation of El Salvador Legation of Dominican Republic. Democrat. Presbyn. Home: Washington, D.C. Died Oct. 2, 1936.

GANNETT, Henry, geographer; b. Bath, Me., Aug. 24, 1846; s. Michael Farley and Hannah (Church) G.; S.B., Lawrence Scientific Sch. (Harvard), 1869; M.E., Hooper Mining Sch. (Harvard), 1870; (LL.D., Bowdoin, 1899); m. Mary E. Chase, Nov. 24, 1874. Asst. Harvard Obs., 1870-71; topographer, Hayden Survey, 1872-79; geographer, U.S. Geol. Survey, 1882—. Geographer 10th, 11th and 12th censuses; asst. dir. of census of P.I., 1902, of Cuba, 1907-08; geographer, Conservation Commn., 1908-09; asso. editor Bulletin Am. Geog. Soc.; chmn. U.S. Geog. Bd. Pres. Nat. Geog. Society. Author: Manual of Topographic Surveying; Statistical Atlases 10th, 11th and 12th Censuses; Commercial Geography; Dictionary of Altitudes: Stanford Compendium of Geography; Census of Cuba (part); Census of Porto Rico (part); Census of Philippine Islands (part); The Contour Map of U.S.; Magnetic Declination in U.S. Died Nov. 5, 1914.

GANNETT, Thomas Brattle, banker; b. Cambridge, Mass., Feb. 28, 1876; s. Thomas B. and Edith (Bates) G.; A.B., Harvard, 1897; m. Dorothy Draper, Nov. 21, 1911; children—Thomas Brattle, John Draper, Robert Tileston, Dorothy, William Bristow. Began in bond and stock bus., Boston, 1897; mem. Parkinson & Burr, 1905—; dir. Androscoggin Pulp Co., Galveston Electric Co., Galveston-Houston Electric Co., etc. Trustee Mass. Gen. Hosp.; treas. Boston Provident Assn.; pres. Infants' Hosp. Home: Hyde Park, Mass. Died May 6, 1931.

GANNETT, William Channing, clergyman; b. Boston, Mar. 13, 1840; s. Rev. Ezra Stiles and Anna (Tilden) G.; A.B., Harvard, 1860, A.M., 1863; grad. Harvard Div. Sch., 1868 (D.D., 1908); m. Mary Thorn Lewis, Nov. 3, 1887. Entered Unitarian ministry, 1868, ordained 1879; pastor, Milwaukee, 1868-70, E. Lexington, Mass., 1871-72, St. Paul, 1877-83, Hinsdale, Ill., 1887-89, Rochester, N.Y., 1889-1908 (pastor emeritus). Author: Of Making One's Self Beautiful, 1899; A Wicket Gate to the Bible, 1907. One of editors of Unity Hymns and Chorals, 1880, rev. and enlarged, 1911. Died Dec. 15, 1923.

GANNON, Frank Stanislaus, ry. pres.; b. Spring Valley, N.Y., Sept. 16, 1851; s. John and Mary (Clancey) G.; ed. pub. schs., Port Jervis, N.Y.; m. Marietta Burrows, Sept. 24, 1874. Began ry. service as telegraph operator on Erie Ry., 1868-70; on N.J. Midland R.R. (now N.Y., Susquehanna & Western), clerk terminal agt. and train dispatcher, 1870-75; train dispatcher, master transportation L.I. R.R., 1875-81; supervisor trains B.&O. R.R., 1881; gen. supt. New York City & Northern R.R., 1881-86; gen. supt., 1886-94, gen. mgr., 1894-96, S.I. Rapid Transit R.R.; also gen. supt. N.Y. div. B.&O. R.R., 1890-96, also pres. S.I. Railway, 1893-96; 3d v.p. and gen. mgr. Southern Ry., 1897-1902; v.p. N.Y. City Ry. Co., 1903-06; pres. Norfolk & Southern R.R. Co., Atlantic & N.C. Co., Raleigh & Pamlico Sound R.R. Co., Va. & Carolina Coast R.R. Co., May 1-Nov. 28, 1906, when these cos. were merged into Norfolk & Southern Ry. Co., of which was pres. until 1909; pres. Mont., Wyoming & Southern R.R., 1909—; trustee Emigrant Industrial Savs. Bank. Home: West Brighton, S.I. Died Nov. 8, 1922.

GANNON, Thomas Joseph, educator; b. Cambridge, Mass., July 14, 1853; s. Patrick and Martha (Walley) G.; ed. Boston Coll., which he left in 1872 to become a mem. of the Soc. of Jesus. Taught classics Holy Cross Coll., Worcester, Mass.; also chief disciplinarian; lecturer logic and gen. metaphysics, Boston Coll., and Jesuit House of Studies, Woodstock, Md.; pvt. sec. to the Very Rev. Provincial of the Md.-N.Y. province of the Soc. of Jesus, 1890-91, 1896-1901; pres. St. John's Coll., New York, 1891-96; provincial of the Md.-N.Y. province, 1901-06; mem. Missionary Band, Mar. 25, 1906—; instr. of the Fathers in 3d yr. of probation, July 1907-Jan. 1915; Am. asst. to the Gen. of Soc. of Jesus, Rome, Italy, 1915—. Died Jan. 29, 1918.

GANONG, William Francis, botanist; b. St. John, N.B., Can., Feb. 19, 1864; s. James H. and Susan E. (Brittain) G.; A.B., U. of N.B., 1884, A.M., 1886; A.B., Harvard, 1887; Ph.D., U. of Munich, 1894; Ph.D., ad eundem, U. of N.B., 1898, LL.D., 1920; m. Jean M. Carman, Apr. 4, 1888 (died 1920); m. 2d, Anna Hobbet, June 20, 1923; children—William Francis, Ann Hobbet. Asst. and instr. botany, Harvard, 1887-93; prof. botany and dir. Bot. Garden, Smith Coll., 1894-1932; prof. emeritus. Author: The Teaching Botanist, 1899, 2d edit., 1910; Laboratory Course in Plant Physiology, 1901, 2d edit., 1908; The Living Plant, 1913, 23; Textbook of Botany for Colleges, 1917. Home: Northampton, Mass. Died Sept. 7, 1941.

GANTENBEIN, Calvin Ursinus, judge; b. Phila., Pa., Mar. 22, 1865; s. John (D.D., M.D.) and Mary (Schwaeble) G.; grad. Royal Charles Gymnasium, Stuttgart, Germany, 1885; post-grad. work, Collège de France, Paris, 4 mos., 1885; LL.B., U. of Ore., 1891; m. Winifred Watson, d. of James Finley Watson, of Roseburg, Ore., Oct. 18, 1899. Prof. ancient and modern langs., West Chester (Pa.) State Normal Sch., 1885-88; instr. German and Latin, Portland (Ore.) High Sch., 1888-92; admitted to Ore. bar, 1892, and began practice at Portland; judge Circuit Court, 4th Jud. Dist., 1906-13, and 1915—; declined appmt. as justice Supreme Court of P.I., 1899; judge Juvenile Court, Multnomah Co., Ore., 1907-09, 1909-11; dean Sch. of Law, U. of Ore., 1903-15; dean Northwestern Coll. of Law, Portland, Ore., Oct. 1915—. Private and advanced to lt. col. Oregon N.G., 1891-98; maj. 2d Oregon U.S. Vol. Inf., 1898-99; adj. gen. State of Ore., 1899-1903; col. 3d Inf., Ore. N.G., 1903-06; v.p. Interstate N.G. Assn., 1902; commd. col. of infantry, O.R.C., 1917. Was mem. 1st Mil. Commn. in Philippines, also of Bd. of Liquidation, etc. Mem. Portland Chamber of Commerce. Republican. Mem. German Reformed Ch. Scottish Rite Mason. Author: Oregon Volunteers in Spanish War and Philippine Insurrection, 1902. Home. Portland, Ore. Died Nov. 19, 1919.

GANTT, James Britton, judge; b. Putnam Co., Ga., Oct. 26, 1845; s. Henry and Sarah G.; B.L., U. of Va., 1868; (LL.D., U. of Mo., 1908). Admitted to bar, St. Louis, 1868; practiced in Henry and Pettis counties, Mo. Circuit judge, Henry Circuit, Mo., 1880-86; curator Warrensburg Normal, 1885-86; elected presiding judge, div. No. 2, Supreme Ct., 1891; elected chief justice, Feb. 1898, reëlected Jan. 2, 1907; present term expires 1910. Served in 12th Ga. Inf.; Stonewall Jackson's corps, C.S.A., and was thrice wounded. Home: Jefferson City, Mo. Died May 28, 1912.

GANTVOORT, Arnold Johann, musician, educator; b. Amsterdam, Holland, Dec. 6, 1857; s. Martienus Johannes and Jansie (Voogt) G.; pvt. sch. and gymnasium, Amsterdam; studied music under Joseph Coenen and others; came to America, 1876; m. Nettie M. Looker, Aug. 29, 1881. Teacher and mgr. Coll. of Music, Cincinnati, until 1921; lecturer on music U. of Calif. at Los Angeles, 1924-32; dean Zoellner Conservatory, Los Angeles. U.S. del. Internat. Mus. Congress, Rome, Italy, 1911. Chmn. N.E.A. com. for revision of nat. songs; mem. Congressional Com. for revision of "Star Spangled Banner." Mason. Author: The High School Ideal, 1893; The Model Music Course (with J. A. Broekhoven), 1894; Gantvoort's Shorter Music Course, 1907; Progressive Harmony; Familiar Talks on the History of Music. Home: Los Angeles, Calif. Died May 18, 1937.

GANZ, Albert Frederick, educator, electrical engr.; b. Elberfeld, Germany, Apr. 25, 1872; s. Albert and Helene Theresa (Brinkmann) G.; ed. Coll. City of New York, 1886-87; Cooper Inst. Night Sch., New York, 1887-91; M.E., Stevens Inst. Tech., 1895; m. Antonia Christina Stursberg, June 21, 1902. Instr. gen. physics and applied electricity, 1895-97, asst. prof., 1897-1902, prof. elec. engring., and head dept. of elec. engring., 1902—, Stevens Inst. Tech. Patent expert and cons. engr., specializing in electric lighting and investigation of and remedies for electrolysis from stray electric currents. Fellow Am. Inst. Elec. Engrs., A.A.A.S. Home: Hoboken, N.J. Died July 27, 1917.

GARBER, John Palmer, educator; b. White House, Pa., Jan. 16, 1858; s. Peter and Sarah (Foreman) G.; B.E., Cumberland Valley (Pa.) State Normal Sch., 1879; Ph.D., U. of Pa., 1897; summer course, U. of Jena, Germany; m. Emma B. Stone, June 5, 1883; children—John Hubert (dec.), Dorothy Stone Miller. Teacher in rural schs., 1876-78; prin. schs., Leiperville, Pa., 1879-80; supt. schs., New Castle, Del., 1881-84; supervising prin., Kenderton Sch., Phila., 1886-97; associate supt. schs., Phila., 1897-1915, supt. schools, 1915-20 (ret.). Baptist. Author: Annals of Educational Progress, 1911. Home: Philadelphia, Pa. Died Dec. 16, 1936.

GARCELON, Alonzo, M.D., gov.; b. Me., 1813; grad. Med. Coll. Ohio, Cincinnati, 1839; served Me. legislature; surgeon-gen. on governor's staff, Me., during Civil War; candidate for Congress, 1868, defeated; was candidate for gov., 1878, and no candidate having majority was elected by legislature, serving until 1880. Democrat. Home: Lewiston, Me. Died 1906.

GARD, Warren, congressman; b. Hamilton, O., July 2, 1873; s. Samuel Z. and Mary (Duke) G.; ed. Hamilton High Sch.; grad. Cincinnati Law Sch., 1894; m. Pearl Woods, June 22, 1910. Pros. atty., Butler Co., O., 1898-1903 inclusive; judge Ct. of Common Pleas, 1st Subdivision, 2d Jud. Dist. of Ohio, 1907-13; mem. 63d to 66th Congresses (1913-21), 3d Ohio Dist. Democrat. Home: Hamilton, O. Died Nov. 1, 1929.

GARD, Willis Lloyd, coll. prof.; b. Owen Co., Ind., Aug. 22, 1869; s. Jacob Nelson and Sarah Ellen (Anderson) G.; Union Christian Coll., Merom, Ind., 1888-92; A.B., Ind. U., 1896, A.M., 1907; Ph.D., Clark U., 1908; m. Olive D. Chamberlain, July 21, 1898; 1 son, Leavitt Nelson. Was teacher in pub. schs. of Ind. until 1906; prof. history and principles of edn., Ohio U., 1908—; exchange prof. education, U. of Florida, summer, 1935; fellow Clark U., 1906-08. Home: Athens, O. Died May 12, 1936.

GARDENER, Cornelius, army officer; b. in Netherlands, Sept. 4, 1849; s. Rev. Wynand and Barendina (Visser) G.; grad. Holland (Mich.) Acad., 1865; student Hope Coll., 1865-66 (A.M., 1892); grad. U.S. Mil. Acad., 1873; m. Bessie E. Patton, Oct. 1901. Commd. 2d lt. 19th Inf., June 13, 1873; 1st lt., June 19, 1879; capt., Feb. 24, 1891; col. 31st Mich. Inf., May 11, 1898; hon. mustered out of vol. service, May 17, 1899; col. 30th U.S.V. Inf., July 5, 1899; hon. disch., Apr. 3, 1901; major 13th U.S. Inf., Sept. 16, 1899; lt. col., 21st Inf., Feb. 18, 1903; colonel 16th Inf., Dec. 26, 1905. Served in Indian wars, 1874-80; on Rio Grande, 1881-90; Ft. Wayne, Detroit, 1891-96; instr. Mich. N.G., 1897-98; in charge Pingree potato farms, Detroit, 3 yrs.; col. 31st Mich. Vols. in U.S. and Cuba, Spanish War; in Philippines as col. 30th U.S. Vols., Oct. 1899, to Apr. 1901; gov. of Tayabas, Luzon, P.I., Mar. 1901-Mar. 1902; retired, Sept. 4, 1913, after 44½ yrs.' service. Home: Claremont, Calif. Died Jan. 2. 1921.

GARDENER, Helen Hamilton, author; b. Winchester, Va.; d. Rev. Alfred Griffith Chenoweth and Katherine A. (Peel) Chenoweth; grad. Ohio State Normal Sch., 1872; post-grad. work in biology, medicine and other branches in New York; m. 2d, Col. Selden Allen Day, U.S.A., 1901. Prin. Ohio Branch State Normal Sch., 1873, 74; lecturer on sociology, Brooklyn Inst. Arts and Sciences, and univ. extension centers; first woman mem. U.S. Civ. Service Commn., apptd. Apr. 13, 1920. Active in movements for progress and development of women and for social and ethical reform; mem. exec. bd., v.p. and v. chmn., Congressional Com. of Nat. Am. Woman Suffrage Assn. Author: Facts and Fictions of Life, 1893; An Unofficial Patriot, 1894. Home: Washington, D.C. Died July 26, 1925.

GARDENHIRE, Samuel Major, lawyer, author; b. Fayette, Mo., Nov. 23, 1855; s. James B. and Sarah (Major) G.; ed. Central Coll., Fayette, Mo.; m. Mary Jetmore, Dec. 24, 1881. Practiced law at St. Louis, 1875-80, Topeka, Kan., 1880-85, during which period also operated daily paper; was sec. to Gov. John P. St. John, maj. on his staff, clerk dist. and circuit courts, municipal judge and mem. Kan. legislature; in practice at New York, 1895—. Author: The Long Arm, 1906; Purple and Homespn, 1908; Cinderella of the Circus, 1911. Home: Richmond Hill, N.Y. Died Feb. 27, 1923.

GARDINER, Asa Bird, army officer; lawyer; b. New York, Sept. 30, 1839; s. Asa and Rebekah Willard (Bentley) G.; A.B., Coll. City of New York, 1859, A.M., 1862; LL.B., New York U., 1860; (hon. A.M., Dartmouth, 1864, Columbia, 1869; LL.D., New York U., 1875; L.H.D., Hobart, 1896); m. Mary Austen, Oct. 18, 1865 (died 1900); 2d, Harriet Isabella Lindsay, Nov. 5, 1902. 1st lt. 31st N.Y. Vol. Inf., May 14, 1861; capt. 22d N.Y. Vols., May 31, 1862; 1st lt. U.S. Vet. Reserve Corps, Feb. 11, 1865, and adj.; bvt. capt. U.S. vols., May 13, 1865, for gallant and meritorious services during the war; hon. mustered out of vol. service, Aug. 13, 1866; 2d lt. 9th U.S. Inf., July 20, 1866; 1st lt., Feb. 14, 1868; transferred to 1st Arty., April 3, 1869; maj. judge advocate U.S.A., Aug. 13, 1873; awarded Congressional Medal of Honor, Sept. 23, 1872, "for conspicuous bravery and distinguished conduct during the Gettysburg Campaign, particularly in the action at Sporting Hill, Pa., June 30, 1863, and in the defense of Carlisle, Pa., July 1-2, 1863," where wounded; retired Dec. 8, 1888; lt. col. U.S.A. retired, Apr. 23, 1904. Served during Civil War in 6th Corps, Army of the Potomac, and in 8th and 23d Army Corps; participated in fight at Union Mills, nr. Fairfax C.H., Va.; battles of Blackburn's Ford and Bull Run; skirmish at Winchester, Va., Aug. 30, 1862; etc. Acting adj. gen., recruiting service U.S.A., 1866-68; a.-d.-c. to Maj. Gen. McDowell, and chief signal officer Dept. of the East, 1869-72; judge advocate and acting adj. gen. Mil. Div. of South, 1871-73; judge adv. Mil. Div. of the Atlantic, 1878-87; prof. law, U.S. Mil. Acad., 1874-78; acting asst. sec. of war, 1887-88; dist. atty. N.Y. Co., 1897-1900. Counsel for Generals Grant and Sheridan in the Gen. G. K. Warren court of inquiry; counsel for govt. in Freedman's Bur. investigation, and Gen. Fitz John Porter and colored cadet Whittaker cases, and in many habeas corpus damage actions and criminal causes affecting army or navy. Commandant Vet. Corps Arty. State N.Y., and bvtd. maj. gen., mil. forces of State of N.Y., under concurrent resolution of legislature of N.Y., "for gallant conduct in Gettysburg Campaign and gallant and meritorious services during the war." Trustee Am. Coll. Musicians; sachem Tammany Soc., New York; deputy Gen. Conv. P.E. Ch., 1892, 1910; deputy P.E. Conv. Diocese L.I., 1885—; mem. P.E. Gen. Conv. Standing Commn. on Archives, 1892—. Author: The Writ of Habeas Corpus as Affecting the Army and Navy, 1874; Practice and Proceedings of Courts-Martial, 1878; The Rhode Island Continental Line of the Revolution, 1885; The Order of the Cincinnati in France, 1905. Died May 28, 1919.

GARDINER, Charles Alexander, lawyer; b. Canada, Sept. 2, 1855; s. Peter and Amelia (Leishman) G.; grad. Hamilton Coll., N.Y., 1880, Columbia Law Sch., 1884; (A.M., Hamilton; Ph.D., D.C.L., Syracuse U.; L.H.D., Western Reserve U.; LL.D., New York U.); m. Alice May Driggs, June 1890. Admitted to bar, 1885; gen. atty. for elevated and subway systems of New York; counsel and dir. various other ry. and financial corps. Trustee New York Univ., 1898, Hamilton Coll., 1900; regent Univ. State of N.Y., 1903. Author: The Constitution and our New Possessions, 1900; Constitutional Solution of Negro Problem, 1903; Constitutional Powers of the President, 1905. Home: New York, N.Y. Died 1909.

GARDINER, Frederic, secretary; b. Gardiner, Me., Apr. 5, 1858; s. Frederic and Caroline (Vaughan) G.; A.B., Harvard, 1880, post-grad., 1880-83, A.M., 1890; Berkeley Div. Sch., 1885; (L.H.D., St. John's Coll., 1911); m. Sallie Merrick, 1885. Deacon, 1885, priest, 1886, P.E. Ch.; dean Calvary Cathedral, Sioux Falls, S.D., 1885-89; rector, All Saints' Ch., Pomfret, Conn., 1889-99; instr. biology and geology, Trinity Coll., Conn., 1890-93; asso. master, 1893-98, head master, 1898, Pomfret Sch.; head master Yeates Sch., Lancaster, Pa., 1899-1915; field sec. Bd. of Rel. Edn. Prov. of Washington, for schools and colls., 1915—. Died 1917.

GARDINER, George Schuyler, lumber mfr.; b. Penn Yan, N.Y., Apr. 12, 1854; s. Stimson B. and Nancy (Bonney) G.; ed. pub. schs., Penn Yan, and Clinton, Ia.; m. Catherine Marshall, Apr. 24, 1877. Pres. Eastman, Gardiner & Co. Introduced many improvements in methods of lumbering and caring for employés. Mem. Ia. Ho. of Rep., 1890. Democrat. Episcopalian. Lived at Laurel, Miss. Died May 29, 1921.

GARDINER, Harry Norman, college prof.; b. Norwich, Eng., Nov. 6, 1855; s. Hezekiah and Sophia (Savage) G.; came to U.S., 1874; A.B., Amherst Coll., 1878, A.M., 1885; Union Theol. Sem., 1879-82; studied Göttingen, 1882, Leipzig, 1883-84, Heidelberg, 1884; L.H.D., Smith Coll., 1924. Unmarried. Teacher Glens Falls (N.Y.) Academy, 1878-79; instr. psychology, Amherst Coll., 1891-92; instr. and later prof. Philosophy, Smith Coll., 1884-1924, emeritus. Author: Outlines of Modern Philosophy, 1892. Editor: Jonathan Edwards—A Retrospect, 1901; Selected Sermons of Jonathan Edwards, 1904. Home: Northampton, Mass. Died Dec. 29, 1927.

GARDINER, James Terry, civil engr.; b. Troy, N.Y., May 6, 1842; ed. Rensselaer Poly Inst. and Sheffield Scientific Sch.; (hon. Ph.B., Yale, 1868); m. a d. of William Croswell Doane. Became subasst. engr. Brooklyn Water Works; insp. U.S. ordnance corps, 1861-62; constructing earthworks around harbor, San Francisco, 1863-64; topog. asst. geol. survey of Calif., 1864-67; with Clarence King, 1867-72, and 1872-75 under Ferdinand V. Hayden, in U.S. Geol. Survey; dir. state survey of N.Y., 1876-86; mem. State Bd. of Health, 1880-86; afterward in practice as cons. engr.; pres. St. R.R. and Lighting Co., St. Joseph, Mo., 1892-95; v.p. coal cos. of Erie R.R. Co., 1895; pres. Mexican Coal & Coke Co., 1899—, Coahuila Coal Ry., Northeast Harbor Water Co. Home: New York, N.Y. Died Sept. 1912.

GARDINER, Robert Hallowell, trustee; b. Ft. Tejon, Calif., Sept. 9, 1855; s. John William Tudor and Annie E. (Hays) G.; A.B., Harvard, 1876; Harvard Law Sch., 1878-80; admitted to bar, 1880; m. Alice Bangs, June 23, 1881. Practiced law at Boston, 1880—; dir. Arlington Mills, Webster and Atlas Nat. Bank, Boston & Albany R.R., etc.; trustee Gardiner Real Estate Assn., Boston Real Estate Trust, Hotel Trust, School Street Trust, Trimountain Trust, etc. One of founders and formerly chmn. exec. com. Republican Club of Mass. Episcopalian. Pres. Brotherhood of St. Andrew, 1904-10; mem. standing com. P.E. Ch. for Diocese of Me.; sec. World Conf. on Faith and Order; exec. and administrative com. Fed. Council of Chs.; trustee Gen. Theol. Sem.; treas. Foreign Policy Assn. Pres. trustees Roxbury Latin Sch. Home: Gardiner, Me. Died June 15, 1924.

GARDINER, T(heodore) Momolu, bishop; b. Dearlah, Cape Mount, Liberia, Jan. 30, 1870; s. Momolu Fiker and Guarnyar (Tarweh) G.; grad. Cuttington Collegiate and Divinity Sch., Cape Palmas, Liberia, 1892; B.D., Liberia Coll., 1912, D.D., 1916; m. Miss F. R. Neal, May 3, 1897; m. 2d, Danielette F. Wilson, May 13, 1903. Dean, 1896, priest, 1906, P.E. Ch.; was prof. history and asst. tutor in theology, Cuttington Coll. and Div. Sch.; rector Mt. Vaughan Ch., Cape Palmas, 1902-13; served as asst. curate St. Mark's Ch., Harper, Cape Palmas, 1896-1905, and as asst. sec. and sec. Gen. Conv. Missionary Dist. of Liberia, 1905-13; consecrated suffragan bishop of Liberia, at Ch. of the Incarnation, N.Y. City, June 23, 1921. Pres. Council of Advice, 1911-21, Dist. of Liberia. Decorated Knight Comdr. African Redemption, 1918. Home: The Bishop's Lodge, West Africa. Died Apr. 3, 1941.

GARDNER, Augustus Peabody, congressman; b. Nov. 5, 1865; s. Joseph Peabody and Harriet (Amory) G.; A.B., Harvard, 1886; studied Harvard Law Sch.; m. Constance, d. Henry Cabot Lodge, June 14, 1892. Mem. Mass. Senate, 1899-1901; elected to 57th Congress, 1902, for unexpired term (1902-03) of William H. Moody, resigned; reëlected 58th to 64th Congresses (1903-17), 6th Mass. Dist.; Rep. nominee for gov. of Mass., 1913. Served as capt. and asst. adj. gen. on staff Gen. James H. Wilson during Spanish-Am. War. Home: Hamilton, Mass. Died Jan. 14, 1918.

GARDNER, Eugene C., architect; b. Ashfield, Mass., Mar. 28, 1836; s. Bela and Lucy (Barber) G.; ed. pub. schs., and Ashfield and Conway acads.; m. Harriet B., d. John Hubbard, of New Ipswich, N.H., Sept. 7, 1858. Prin. of an acad., Tallmadge, O., 1858-62; practiced architecture, Northampton, Mass., 1863-68, then at Springfield; sr. mem. E. C. & G. C. Gardner. Mem. Mass. Ho. of Rep., 1901. Edited The Builder, Holyoke, Mass., 1885-87. Author: House that Jill Built. Home: Springfield, Mass. Died Feb. 7, 1915.

GARDNER, Frank Saltus; b. New York, Mar. 29, 1852; s. William and Mary Cole (Wright) G.; ed. Coll. City of N.Y., 1867-69; m. Hattie Merrill, June 22, 1881. In mercantile bus. until 1876; asst. sec. and sec. New York Bd. of Trade and Transportation, 1877—, also hon. v.p. (office created for him alone); exec. com. N.Y. State Waterways Assn. (1st sec.); dir. and sec. Canal Assn. of Greater New York, 1902-12; sec. Anti-monopoly League, N.Y., 1879-83, Union for Improvement of Canals, N.Y., 1885-92, N.Y. State Commerce Conv., 1899-1903 inclusive, N.Y. State Com. on Canal Referendum, 1915, etc. Mem. 7th Regt., N.Y.S.N.G., 1870-77. Republican. Presbyn. Decorated Chevalier Royal Order of the Savior by King George of Greece, 1895. Drafted law of N.Y., 1885, creating N.Y. State Forest Commn. (the second State forest commn. in U.S.); drafted provision of N.Y. State Constitution relating to forest preserve, 1894, etc. Home: Brooklyn, N.Y. Died July 8, 1927.

GARDNER, Frederick Dozier, governor; b. Hickman, Ky., Nov. 6, 1869; s. William H. and Mary Ellen (Dozier) G.; ed. pub. schs. of Ky. and Tenn.; m. Jeannette Vosburgh, Oct. 10, 1894; children—William King, Dozier Lee, Janet. Removed to St. Louis at 17 and entered employ of St. Louis Coffin Co.; now sole owner of the business. Mem. Bd. of Freeholders, St. Louis, 1913-15, and assisted in drafting charter of St. Louis; gov. of Mo., term 1917-21. Democrat. Methodist. Home: St. Louis, Mo. Died Dec. 18, 1933.

GARDNER, George Peabody, corp. official; b. Boston, Nov. 19, 1855; s. George Augustus and Eliza Endicott (Peabody) G.; B.A., Harvard U., 1877; m. Esther Burnett, June 11, 1884; children—Catharine, George Peabody, Jr. Pres. Provident Instn. for Savings; pres. and trustee Amoskeag Co.; dir. State St. Exchange, Am. Telephone & Telegraph Co., Union Freight R.R. Co., etc. Mem. bd. of mgrs. Mass. Eye and Ear Infirmary; trustee Mus. Fine Arts; treas. Soc. for the Relief of Aged and Disabled Episcopal Clergymen. Hon. pres. Children's Hosp. Mem. 1st Corps Cadets; capt. and a.-d.-c. 2d Brig. staff, M.V.M. Home: Boston, Mass. Died June 6, 1939.

GARDNER, George W., mfr., banker; b. Pittsfield, Mass., 1834; s. James and Caroline Griscilda (Porter) G.; has lived in Cleveland from 1837; grad. Cleveland High Sch.; m. d. late Gen. O. M. Oviatt of Cleveland, but is now a widower. Was a sailor boy in early youth; 40 yrs. in grain elevator and flour mill business, 5 yrs. in banking; pres. Sagertown (Pa.) Mineral Springs Co.; v.p. since organization Cleveland & Buffalo Steamship Line. Pres. and charter mem. Cleveland Bd. of Trade; pres. for 5 yrs., bd. trustees Ohio State Industrial Sch.; mem. city council 10 yrs.; mayor of Cleveland 1885-86 and 1889-90; dir. municipal govt., 1892-93. Commodore for life, Cleveland Yacht Club; life mem. Cleveland Chamber of Commerce. Republican. Home: Cleveland, O. Died Dec. 18, 1911.

GARDNER, Gilson, newspaperman; b. Chicago, Mar. 16, 1869; s. Charles and Louise (Crapo) G.; B.A., Williams Coll., 1892; B.L., Northwestern U., 1894; admitted to Ill. bar, 1894; m. Matilda Campbell Hall, Nov. 3, 1900. Reporter, telegraph editor, editorial writer, Chicago Daily News, 1893-95; reporter, dramatic critic, municipal reporter, editorial writer, city editor, mng. editor, polit. editor, Springfield (Ill.) corr., Washington corr., Chicago Journal, 1895-1905; Washington corr. Newspaper Enterprise Assn. Mem. editorial bd. Scripps newspapers. With President Roosevelt from Khartum to New York. Author: A New Robinson Crusoe, 1920; Lusty Scripps (biography), 1932; Life of William Kent. Home: Alexandria, Va. Died Aug. 16, 1935.

GARDNER, Henry Brayton, univ. prof.; b. Providence, R.I., Mar. 26, 1863; s. Henry Wood and Mary (Rathbone) G.; A.B., Brown, 1884, A.M., 1887; Johns Hopkins, 1884-88, Ph.D., 1890; m. Mabel Richmond, June 9, 1890. Instr. political economy, 1888-90, associate prof., 1890-98, prof., 1898—, Brown University. Wrote: Statistics of Municipal Finance, in pubs. of Am. Statis. Assn., New Series, No. 6, 1889; same title, in pubs. Am. Economic Assn., New Series, No. 2, 1899. Home: Providence, R.I. Died Apr. 22, 1939.

GARDNER, Horace Chase, engineer, architect; b. Bentonsport, Ia., Oct. 3, 1856; s. David Noble and Susan (Kuhn) G.; ed. pub. sch.; studied engring. under father; m. Nellie Gray, Jan. 5, 1888; 1 dau., Ruth (Mrs. Robert M. See). Came to Chicago in 1884 and entered employ of Swift & Co., later becoming mgr. constrn. and mech. depts.; began practice as architect, 1897; mem. Gardner & Lindberg, indsl. engrs. and architects, 1913-31, retired. Republican. Conglist. Home: Evanston, Ill. Died Sept. 20, 1936.

GARDNER, Isabella Stewart; b. New York; d. David Stewart, of New York; m. John Lowell Gardner (dec.). Owns one of the finest private art galleries in the world, which has been opened to the public. Episcopalian. Home: Boston, Mass. Died July 17, 1924.

GARDNER, James Augustus, surgeon; b. Poughkeepsie, N.Y., Oct. 28, 1870; s. La Vergne F. and Frances (McNutt) G.; student New York U., leaving in sophomore yr.; M.D., Coll. Phys. and Surg. (Columbia), 1895; m. Mary Louise Everett, Jan. 21, 1898; children—Helen Louise, James MacDowell. Intern, Bellevue Hosp., New York, 1895-98; practiced at Buffalo, 1898—; cons. urologist, Millard Fillmore

Memorial Hosp. Fellow Am. Coll. Surgeons. Republican. Mason. Writer on prostatechtomy, post-operative treatment of same, and kindred topics. Home: Buffalo, N.Y. Died Sept. 13, 1926.

GARDNER, John J., congressman; b. Atlantic Co., N.J., Oct. 17, 1845; brought up as waterman until 16 yrs. of age; served in 6th N.J. Vols., 1862-65; then enlisted in U.S. Veteran Vols. Engaged in real estate and ins. business. Alderman, Atlantic City, 1867; mayor, 1868, 69, 70, 73, 74; mem. Common Council and one of coroners, 1875; mem. N.J. Senate, 1878-93 (pres. 1883, and longest service of any senator in N.J.); mem. 53d to 62d Congresses (1893-1913), 2d N.J. Dist. Home: Atlantic City, N.J. Died Feb. 7, 1921.

GARDNER, Obadiah, senator; b. Port Huron, Mich., Sept. 13, 1852; s. John and Mary (Strevils) G.; Eastman's Business Coll., Poughkeepsie, N.Y., and Coburn Classical Inst., Waterville, Maine; m. Corrinna A. Sherer, Nov. 28, 1875. Farmer, Rockland, 1872—; also in lumber and lime business. Master State Grange, 1897-1907. Dem. candidate for gov., Me., 1908, for U.S. senator, 1911; apptd. assessor for State of Me., Apr. 1911; apptd U.S. senator, Sept. 23, 1911, for unexpired term (1911-13) of William P. Frye, deceased. Became mem. Internat. Joint Commn. for settlement of questions arising on the boundary waters between U.S. and Can., Oct. 1, 1913 (chmn. U.S. commn.). Universalist. Home: Rockland, Me. Died July 24, 1938.

GARDNER, Rathbone, lawyer; b. Providence, R.I., Feb. 18, 1856; s. Henry Wood and Mary Brown (Rathbone) G.; A.B., Brown U., 1877, A.M., 1880; m. Sophie L. Gardner, Jan. 1, 1880 (died 1912); children—Henry B., Marianna Taft; m. 2d, Karine Marine Froberg, Jan. 14, 1914; 1 dau., Ellen R. Admitted to bar, 1879; chmn. bd. R.I. Co. (operating electric rys., 1914-20. Pres. Common Council, Providence, 1885-86; U.S. dist. atty. for R.I., 1889-93; mem. R.I. Ho. of Rep., 1897, Senate, 1907-08. Pres. Butler Hosp. Republican. Episcopalian. Home: Providence, R.I. Died June 22, 1931.

GARDNER, Robert Waterman, architect; b. Jackson, Miss., Nov. 17, 1866; s. Hezekiah Ripley and Eliza (Wheeler) G.; grad. Central High Sch., Buffalo, N.Y., 1886; studied architecture with Vaux and Radford and with Clarence Luce, both of New York, 1887-91; m. Eleanor O'Neill, Oct. 19, 1893 (died 1925); 1 dau., Persis Brooks (dec.); m. 2d, Elizabeth Randolph Royce, Apr. 20, 1926. Began practice in N.Y. City, 1905, specializing in residential work; lecturer on reinforced concrete, New York U. Maj. Ordnance Dept., U.S. Aux. Res.; mem. N.Y. State Vet. Corps Arty. Trustee Staten Island Inst. Arts and Sciences. Episcopalian. Author: The Parthenon—Its Science of Forms, 1925. Home: Hampton Bays, L.I., N.Y. Died Aug. 6, 1937.

GARDNER, Walter Edwin, newspaperman; b. Watertown, N.Y., Aug. 7, 1849; s. Henry Shaaf and Hannah Martha G.; ed. Oswego, N.Y.; m. Mary Dunbar, Jan. 20, 1874. Associate editor Evening Wisconsin, Milwaukee, 1882-89; U.S. consul at Rotterdam, Holland, 1889-93; editor and owner Green Bay (Wis.) Gazette, 1894-98; editor and pub. Syracuse Post-Standard, 1898—. Republican. Home: Syracuse, N.Y. Died July 8, 1927.

GARDNER, Washington, congressman; b. Morrow Co., O., Feb. 16, 1845; s. John L. and Sarah (Goodin) G.; pvt. 65th Ohio Vol. Inf., 1861-65, severely wounded; A.B., Ohio Wesleyan, 1870; LL.B., Albany Law Sch., 1876; LL.D., Albion Coll. and Ohio Wesleyan U.; m. Anna Powers, 1871; children—Grace Bartlett (dec.), Mary Theodosia, Carleton Frederick, Elton Goldthwaite (dec.), Raymond Huntington, Lucy Reed, Helen Louise. Practiced at Grand Rapids, Mich., 1 yr.; prof. in Albion Coll., 1889-94; sec. of state, Mich., 1894-99; mem. 56th to 61st Congresses (1899-1911), 3d Mich. Dist.; mem. Com. Appropriations. Commr. of Pensions, 1921-25. Republican. Comdr. in chief G.A.R., 1913-14. Home: Albion, Mich. Died Mar. 31, 1928.

GARDNER, William A., ry. pres.; b. Gardner, Ill., Mar. 1859. Learned telegraphy and began as operator on C.&A. R.R. at Lemont, Ill., 1872; entered the service of C.&N.W. Ry., 1878, with which he has since been connected in various positions until 1885, asst. supt. Wis. div., 1885-90, supt. Wis. div., 1890-96, asst. gen. supt., 1896-99, gen. mgr., 1899-1906, v.p., Jan. 23, 1906-10, pres., Oct. 1910—, C.&N.W. Ry.; also pres. C.,St.P.,M.&O. Ry., 1907; v.p. Superior Coal Co. Republican. Home: Evanston, Ill. Died May 11, 1916.

GARDNER, William Henry, song writer; b. Boston, Oct. 28, 1865; s. Charles Russell and Hannah E. (French) G.; ed. Dudley Grammar Sch. and Roxbury High Sch.; m. Marion B. Hodgson, Oct. 10, 1900 (died 1914); children—Donald Hodgson, Ruth, Edwin Russell. Head of W. H. Gardner & Co., mfrs. cotton goods, 1898—. As a pastime is a lyric author. Best known classical song is "Thy Beaming Eyes" (music by E. A. MacDowell); and best known popular song, Can't Yo' Heah Me Callin', Caroline (music by Mme. Roma); has written 6 songs with Sir Alexander C. Mackenzie, Royal Acad. Music, London, also with Otto Cantor; with Arthur Penn, composer "Smilin' Through," with Reginald DeKoven, composer "Robin Hood"; author words "Ring Out, Sweet Bells of Peace" (music by Mme. Roma), "peace" song of the World War. Author: Little Songs for Little Singers; Children's Treasury of Sacred Song (with Jessie M. Ball); Books of Song Cycles (with others); operetta, The Debutante (with George Lowell Tracy); oratorio, The Lord of Glory (with Dr. Adam Geibel); sacred cantata, The Lord of Light and Love (with Julian Edwards). Wrote librettos for comic operas, "The Omos of Omona"; "The Lark of the Larks," and "Atlantis"; Irish and Scotch Character Songs, music by Clara Lane Murray. Conductor newspaper Column under nom de plume of "Old Timer." Home: Winthrop, Mass. Died Mar. 12, 1932.

GARFIELD, Charles Fowler, investor; b. Holley, N.Y., Oct. 10, 1872; s. George and Sarah A. (Fowler) G.; ed. Holley High Sch., Brockport (N.Y.) Normal School, Bryant and Stratton Business Coll.; m. Myra A. Shipley, Aug. 23, 1894 (died 1925); m. 2d, Helen Arnold Martin, March 1931. President of Garfield Real Estate Co., 1893-1918, Bank of Williamson, 1905-12; v.p. Nat. Bank Commerce, Rochester, 1907-18; pres. several corps. Advocate of economic homes for wage-earners, and co-operative development, agricultural, commercially and industrially; has published pamphlets along those lines. Pres. Rochester Chamber of Commerce, 1908. Republican. Presbyn. Homes: Williamson, N.Y., and Beverly Hills, Calif. Died July 8, 1933.

GARFIELD, Charles William, banker; b. Milwaukee, Mar. 14, 1848; s. Samuel Marshall and Harriet Eliza (Brown) G.; B.S., Mich. State Agrl. Coll., 1870, and M.S., 1873, LL.D., 1917; m. Jessie Robertson Smith, of Scotland, Nov. 24, 1897; 1 dau., Deborah (wife of Prof. A. J. Decker). Teacher, Mich. Agrl. Coll., 1873-77, since farmer, teacher of agr., horticulture and forestry, business man. Chmn. exec. com. Grand Rapids Savings Bank; pres. Grand Rapids Calendar Co.; hon. chmn. Grand Rapids City Planning Commn. Mem. Mich. Ho. of Rep., 1881-82, State Bd. Agr., 12 yrs.; pres. Mich. Forestry Commn., 9 yrs.; trustee Mich. Agrl. Coll. Pres. Mich. Forestry Assn., Grand Rapids Playground Assn.; treas. Mich. Civ. Service League, sec. Mich. Hort. Soc. 10 yrs. Republican. Conglist. Home: Grand Rapids, Mich. Died Sept. 9, 1934.

GARFIELD, Lucretia Rudolph; b. Hiram, O., Apr. 19, 1832; d. of a farmer named Rudolph. First met James Abram Garfield when both were students at Hiram Coll.; married him Nov. 11, 1858; soon after he became pres. of the college. After President Garfield was assassinated a popular subscription for his widow and children realized $360,000, the income to go to Mrs. Garfield during her life, after which the principal is to be divided among her four sons and one daughter. Homes: Mentor, O., and Pasadena, Calif. Died Mar. 13, 1918.

GARFORD, Arthur L., mfr.; b. Elyria, O., Aug. 4, 1858; s. George and Hannah (Lovett) G.; ed. pub. schs.; m. Miss Nelson, Dec. 14, 1881. Pres. Cleveland (O.) Automatic Machine Co., Am. Lace Mfg. Co. (Elyria); chmn. bd. Savings Deposit Bank & Trust Co. (Elyria); dir. Standard Trust Bank (Cleveland), Perry Fay Co. (Elyria). Progressive Party candidate for gov. of Ohio, 1912. Home: Elyria, O. Died Jan. 23, 1933.

GARLAND, Daniel Frank, welfare worker; b. Perry County, Pa., July 10, 1864; s. Daniel Minnick and Elizabeth (Kistler) G.; A.B., Pa. Coll., Gettysburg, 1888, A.M., 1891, D.D., 1906; grad. Gettysburg Theol. Sem., 1891; m. Anna Jane Comfort, Oct. 29, 1891; 1 son, Charles Comfort. Ordained Luth. ministry, 1891; pastor Ch. of Reformation, Baltimore, Md., 1891-96, Trinity Ch., Taneytown, Md., 1896-99, First Ch., Dayton, O., 1899-1914; dir. of public welfare, Dayton, 1914-21; welfare dir. Nat. Cash Register Co., 1921—. Trustee Feghtly Home and District Tuberculosis hospitals. Home: Dayton, O. Died Mar. 9, 1928.

GARLAND, Hamlin, novelist, dramatist; b. West Salem, Wis., Sept. 14, 1860; s. Richard Hays and Isabelle (McClintock) G.; grad. in lit. course, Cedar Valley Sem., Osage, Ia., 1881; m. Zulime Taft, Nov. 1899; children—Mary Isabelle, Constance Hamlin. Worked on farm when not at sch.; taught sch. in Ill., 1882-83; took up claim in McPherson Co., Dak., but soon after went to Boston and began to write stories; returned to the West, 1893. Founder and first pres. Cliff Dwellers Club (Chicago). Author: Main-Traveled Roads, 1890-98; Rose of Dutchers Coolly, 1895-98; Ulysses Grant (biography), 1898; The Eagle's Heart, 1900; Her Mountain Lover, 1901; The Captain of the Gray Horse Troop, 1902; Hesper, 1903; The Tyranny of the Dark, 1905; The Long Trail, 1907; Boy Life on the Prairie, 1907; The Shadow World, 1908; Cavanagh Forest Ranger, 1909; Other Main Traveled Roads, 1913; A Son of the Middle Border, 1917; A Daughter of the Middle Border, 1921; The Book of the American Indian, 1923; The Trail Makers, 1926; Back Trailers of the Middle Border, 1928; Roadside Meetings, 1930; Companions on the Trail, 1931; My Friendly Contemporaries, 1932; Afternoon Neighbors, 1934; Forty Years of Psychic Research, 1936; The Mystery of The Buried Crosses, 1939. Mem. Am. Acad. Arts and Letters. Home: Hollywood, Calif. Died Mar. 4, 1940.

GARLAND, James A., editor; b. New York, Nov. 25, 1870; s. James A. and Anna Louisa (Tuller) G.; grad. Harvard, 1893; m. Marie L. Tudor, Sept. 20, 1893. Was editor New England Mag.; also a well-known horseman. Trustee James A. Garland estate. Author: The Private Stable—Its Establishment, Management and Appointments. Home: New York, N.Y. Died 1906.

GARLAND, Mahlon M., congressman; b. Pittsburgh, Pa., May 1856; largely self-ed.; began work at 9; m. Mary C. Brown, 1888. Learned trade of puddling and heating; joined Amalgamated Assn. of Iron, Steel and Tin Workers, of which was pres., 1891-98; apptd. U.S. collector of customs, Pittsburgh, 1898, and twice reappointed (resigned 1915); mem. Select Council, City of Pittsburgh, 2 terms; mem. Pittsburgh Sch. Bd. 4 yrs.; mem. Borough Council, Edgewood, Pa., 6 yrs.; mem. 64th to 66th Congresses (1915-21), Pa. at-large. Republican. Was v.p. A. F. of L.; Supreme Dictator, 1914-15, Gen. Dictator, 1915-19, L.O.M. of the World. Home: Edgewood, Pa. Died Nov. 19, 1920.

GARLAND, Mary J., prin. of Kindergarten Normal Class; b. Machias, Me., March 16, 1834; ed. private schools and acads.; unmarried. First teaching experience in Me.; in 1861 went to Montreal and was 9 yrs. there as teacher in girls' boarding school; in 1870 went to Vassar for 1 yr.; in 1871 to Boston and took course in kindergarten training with Mme. Mathilde Kriege, of Germany; opened private kindergarten, Boston, 1872, from which a plan for connecting and school classes was developed which was continued until 1892. Later a normal class for the training of kindergartners was instituted. Died 1901.

GARLAND, Thomas James, bishop; b. Ireland, Oct. 25, 1866; s. Robert and Eliza (Atwell) G.; A.B., St. Bees' Coll., Eng., 1891; B.D., Phila. Div. Sch., 1903; D.D., U. of Pittsburgh, 1911; D.C.L., Phila. Div. Shc., 1912; LL.D., U. of Pa., 1925; m. Miss McKibbin, 1892. Deacon, 1891, priest, 1892, P.E. Ch.; asst. St. Peter's Ch., Pittsburgh, 1892; rector All Saints' Ch., Johnstown, Pa., 1892-94, Trinity Ch., Coatesville, Pa., 1894-98 (ch. erected during rectorship), St. David's Ch., Lorain, O., 1898-1900, St. Paul's Ch., Bristol, Pa., 1900-03; asst. editor Church Standard, 1903-05; sec. Diocese of Pa.; sec. 3d Missionary Dept.; consecrated bishop suffragan of Pa., Oct. 28, 1911; elected as bishop of Pa., 1923. Home: Philadelphia, Pa. Died Mar. 1, 1931.

GARLICK, Henry M., banker; b. Youngstown, O., Dec. 28, 1848; s. Richard and Caroline Lord (Manning) G.; ed. pub. sch.; m. Sarah Stambaugh Ford, Apr. 5, 1870; children—Richard, Mrs. Julia Bonnell. Connected with banking business at Youngstown, 1874—, chmn. bd. First Nat. Bank, 1915—, also chmn. bd. Dollar Savings & Trust Co.; mem. bd. dirs. Standard Textile Products Co. Pres. Community Chest of Youngstown, Mahoning Cemetery Assn. Republican. Presbyn. Home: Youngstown, O. Died 1928.

GARLINGTON, Ernest Albert, brig. gen.; b. Newberry C.H., S.C., Feb. 20, 1853; s. Albert Creswell and Sally Lark (Moon) G.; collegiate edn. at U. of Ga., 1869-72; apptd. from Ga., and grad. U.S. Mil. Acad., 1876; m. Anna, d. T. J. and Grace Bowers Buford, of Rock Island, Ill., Aug. 17, 1886. Second lt. 7th Cav., June 15, 1876; promoted through grades to brig. gen. insp. gen. U.S.A., Oct. 1, 1906. Comd. Greely Relief Expdn., 1883; severely wounded in battle with hostile Indians at Wounded Knee P.O., Dec. 29, 1890; awarded Congressional Medal of Honor for distinguished gallantry in that action; mem. bd. to revise cav. drill regulations, 1894; insp. gen. cav. div., in Cuba, 1898; present at battle, siege and surrender of Santiago de Cuba; insp. gen. Div. of the Philippines, 1899-1901, and May 2, 1905-June 6, 1906; gen. staff U.S.A., June 6, 1906; brig. gen. and insp. gen. U.S.A., Oct. 1, 1906. Author: Historical Sketches of the Seventh Cavalry Regiment—A Catechism; Cavalry Outposts, Advance and Rear Guards, Reconnoissance, etc. Died Oct. 16, 1934.

GARMAN, Charles Edward, prof. mental and moral philosophy, Amherst Coll.; b. Limington, Me., Dec. 18, 1850; s. John Harper G.; grad. Amherst Coll., 1872; Yale Divinity Sch., 1879 (A.M., 1880, D.D., 1896, Amherst); m. Eliza N. Miner, Aug. 24, 1882. Died 1907.

GARMAN, Samuel, naturalist; b. Indiana Co., Pa., June 5, 1843; s. Benjamin and Sarah Ann (Griffith) G.; grad. Ill. State Normal U., 1870; hon. S.B., Harvard, 1898, A.M., 1899; m. Florence, d. R. Sands Armstrong (barrister and M.P.), of St. John, N.B., Sept. 2, 1895. Prin. Miss. State Normal Sch., 1870-71; prof. natural sciences, Ferry Hall Sem., Lake Forest, Ill., 1871-72; spl. pupil of Louis Agassiz in natural history, 1872-73; asst. in herpetology and ichthyology, Mus. of Comparative Zoölogy, Harvard, 1873—. Was with Major Powell's 1st expdn. in Colo.; with Alexander Agassiz in South Am expdns. Author: Deep Sea Fishes, 1899; The Chimæroids,

Chismopnea, 1904; New Plagiostomia, 1906; New Plagiostomia and Chismopnea, 1907; The Reptiles of Easter Island, 1908; Plagiostomia (sharks, skates and rays), 1913. Home: Arlington Heights, Mass. Died Sept. 30, 1927.

GARNER, James Wilford, univ. prof.; b. Pike Co., Miss., Nov. 22, 1871; s. W. O. and Martha A. G.; B.S., Miss. Agrl. and Mech. Coll., 1892; Ph.M., U. of Chicago, 1900; univ. fellow in polit. science and pub. law, 1900-01, George William Curtis fellow, 1901-02, Ph.D., 1902, lecturer in history, 1902-03, Columbia; m. Therese Leggett, Dec. 24, 1895. Instr. polit. science, U. of Pa., 1903-04; prof. polit. science, U. of Ill., 1904—. Am. collaborator for the French Revue Politique et Parlementaire, 1903-14. Editor-in-chief, Am. Jour. of Criminal Law and Criminology, 1910-11; asso. editor Am. Jour. Internat. Law, 1924—; pres. Institut Internat. de Droit Public, 1935-36. Pres. Am. Polit. Science Assn., 1924. Chevalier Legion of Honor (French), 1925. Hyde lecturer in French univs., 1921; Tagore lecturer Univ. of Calcutta, 1922; Stokes lecturer New York U., 1926; prof. in Institut des Hautes Etudes Internationales, Geneva, 1928-29; visiting prof. Carnegie Endowment for Internat. Peace at various English and French univs., 1929; lecturer The Hague Acad. Internat. Law, 1923 and 1931. Author: History of the United States (with Senator Henry Cabot Lodge), 4 vols., 1906; Introduction to Political Science, 1910; American Government, 1911; Civil Government for Indian Students, 1920; Idées et Institutions Politiques Américaines, 1921; International Law and the World War, 2 vols., 1920; Recent Developments in International Law, 1925; Prize Law During the World War, 1927; American Foreign Policies, 1927; Political Science and Government, 1927; Law of Treaties, 1935. Home: Urbana, Ill. Died Dec. 9, 1938.

GARNETT, James Mercer, teacher; b. Aldie, Va., Apr. 24, 1840; s. Theodore Stanford and Florentina Isidora (Moreno) G.; bro. of Theodore Stanford G.; A.M., U. of Va., 1859; (LL.D., St. John's Coll., Md., 1874); served in C.S. Army, 1861-65, becoming capt. of arty.; taught in several schools and colls., 1865-82; studied Berlin and Leipzig, 1869-70; m. Kate H., d. Maj. Burr P. Noland, of Middleburg, Va., Apr. 19, 1871. Prin. St. John's Coll., Annapolis, 1870-80; prof. English lang. and lit., U. of Va., 1882-96; acting prof. English lit., Woman's Coll. of Baltimore, 1896-97; pvt. teacher, 1897-1909. Author: Translation of Beowulf, 1882, 1904; Elene and Other Anglo-Saxon Poems, 1889, 1900; History of University of Virginia, 1904. Editor: Burke's Speech on Conciliation with America, 1901. Home: Baltimore, Md. Died Feb. 18, 1916.

GARNETT, Judith Livingston Cox, author; b. of Colonial ancestry in Nottaway Co., Va., Jan. 19, 1862; d. George William and Laura Maria (Speir) G.; g.g.d. Capts. Booker and Garnett, of the Revolutionary Army; desc. on maternal side of the Speirs of Scotland and Adm. Fleetwood of Eng.; father and 6 bros. in Confederate Army, Civil War; ed. under pvt. tutors at home. Engaged in philanthropic work and in spreading the doctrine of peace and brotherhood. Mem. nat. campaign com. to build Fundamentalist univ. at Dayton, Tenn.; apptd. by Gov. Byrd mem. Narcotic Conf., Phila., 1926. Life dir. Am. Bible Soc. Mem. Disciples of Christ. Author: A Point of Honor, Misunderstod, 1927. Awarded blue ribbon for display of fruit, Essex Fair, 1927. Home: Richmond, Va. Deceased.

GARNETT, Louise Ayres, author, composer; b. Plymouth, Ind.; d. Lafayette and Sallie (Munday) Ayres; grad. Dearborn Sem., Chicago; m. Eugene H. Garnett, June 14, 1900; children—Gordon Munday, Virginia Ayres (dec.), Gloria Louise. Eiscopalian. Author: The Muffin Shop, 1908; The Merrymakers, 1918; Three to Make Ready (3 plays for children with the incidental music), 1922; text and music for Creature Songs, 1912; music for A Forest Rondo (cantata, Shakespeare's text); Eve Walks in Her Garden (poetry), 1926; The Joyous Pretender (novel), 1928; Adeste Fideles, a Christmas processional, 1936; and the texts for The New Earth (oratorio), Resurgam (oratorio), Mirtil in Arcadia (lyric drama), Belshazzar (oratorio), and A Fairy Wedding (cantata for children)—all set to music by Henry Hadley. Home: Evanston, Ill. Died Oct. 31, 1937.

GARNETT, Theodore Stanford, lawyer; b. Richmond, Va., Oct. 28, 1844; s. Theodore Stanford and Florentina Isidora (Moreno) G., bro. of James Mercer G.; ed. Episcopal High Sch., nr. Alexandria, 1854-61; pvt. to Capt. Army of Northern Va., C.S.A., 1861-65; a.-d.-c. on staffs Gens. J. E. B. Stuart and W. H. F. Lee; a.-a.g. on staff of Gen. Wm. P. Roberts, N.C. cav. brigade; LL.B., U. of Va., 1867; m. Emily Eyre Baker, Oct. 23, 1873; 2d, Louisa Bowdoin, July 25, 1885. In practice at Norfolk, Va., 1873—. Maj. gen. comdg. Va. Div., U.C.V., 1900-06; comdg. Army of Northern Va. Dept., U.C.V., 1912. Mem. Bd. Trustees P.E. Theol. Sem. and High Sch. in Va. Democrat. Home: Norfolk, Va. Died Apr. 27, 1915.

GARRARD, Jeptha, lawyer; b. in Ohio; A.B., Yale, 1858; LL.B., U. of Cincinnati, 1859; m. Anna Knapp, Oct. 4, 1864. Admitted to bar, 1859, and began practice at Cincinnati. Capt. 3d N.Y. Cav., Sept. 18, 1861; maj., Sept. 27, 1862; col. 1st U.S. Colored Cav., Dec. 7, 1863; bvtd. brig. gen. vols., Mar. 13, 1865, "for gallant and meritorious services"; resigned, Apr. 25, 1865. Died Dec. 16, 1915.

GARRETSON, Abram Quick, jurist; b. Somerset Co., N.J., Mar. 11, 1842; s. Martin S. and Ann Beekman (Quick) G.; grad. Rutgers Coll., 1862, Harvard Law Sch., 1865; m. Josephine Boker, Nov. 12, 1879. Admitted to bar, 1865; practiced Jersey City until 1900; has been dir. of many corps., but resigned from all on being apptd., July, 1900, justice Supreme Court, N.J. Home: Morristown, N.J. Died 1907.

GARRETSON, Austin Bruce, labor union pres.; b. Winterset, Ia., Sept. 14, 1856; s. Nathan and Hannah G. (both Quakers); ed. high sch., Osceola, Ia.; m. Marie Ream, Sept. 2, 1878. Conductor Des Moines, Osceola & Southern, M.K.&T., Mexican Nat. and Mexican Central rys. until 1889; v.p., 1889-1906, pres., 1906-19, Order of Ry. Conductors; was also editor-in-chief The Railway Conductor (monthly mag.). Mem. Federal Commn. on Industrial Relations, 1912-15. Republican. Home: Cedar Rapids, Ia. Died Feb. 27, 1931.

GARRETSON, Garret James, judge; b. Newtown, N.Y., July 16, 1847; s. Rev. Garret I. and Catherine (Rapalie) G.; ed. Flushing Inst., L.I., N.Y.; admitted to bar, 1869; m. Eliza L. Eastman, Sept. 20, 1876 (died, Dec. 17, 1888); m. 2d, Sara Wilson, June 30, 1897. Was many yrs. pres. Newtown, N.Y., bd. of edn.; school commr. Queens Co., N.Y., 1873-75; surrogate, 1880; co. judge, 1885-96; justice of Supreme Ct. of N.Y., 1896-1917. Mem. commn. apptd. by Gov. Morton to frame Greater New York charter, 1896. Home: Elmhurst, N.Y. Died July 9, 1922.

GARRETSON, George Armstrong, banker; b. Columbiana Co., O., Jan. 30, 1844; s. Hiram and Margaret King (Armstrong) G.; grad. U.S. Mil. Acad., 1867; m. Anna Scowden, 1870 (died 1886); m. 2d, Emma R. Ely, Dec. 5, 1888. Enlisted Co. E, 84th Ohio Vol. Inf., May 26, 1862; served in W.Va. and Md.; hon. disch., Sept. 20, 1862; 2d lt. 4th U.S. Arty., 1867-Jan. 1, 1870 (resigned); capt. 1st Cleveland Troop (Troop A, O.N.G.), 1887-92 (resigned); brig. gen. vols., May 27, 1898; hon. disch., Nov. 30, 1898. Pres. Bank of Commerce, Cleveland, 1890—. Republican. Presbyn. Home: Cleveland, O. Died Dec. 8, 1916.

GARRETSON, Joseph, editor; b. Cincinnati, O., Dec. 16, 1874; s. George C. and Katherine (Schaefer) G.; ed. Woodward High Sch., Cincinnati; m. Aline Hibbard, Aug. 18, 1895. City editor Cincinnati Commercial-Gazette, 1891-93, Cincinnati Post, 1894; city editor Cincinnati Times-Star, 1895-99, mng. editor 1899-23 (retired because of sickness). Republican. Episcopalian. Home: Terrace Park, Cincinnati, O. Died Oct. 26, 1931.

GARRETT, Alexander Charles, bishop; b. Ballymot, Co. Sligo, Ireland, Nov. 4, 1832; s. Rev. John G. (rector of Ballymot) and Elizabeth (Fry) G.; grad. Trinity Coll., Dublin U., 1855 (D.D., 1882; D.D., Neb. Coll.; LL.D., U. of Miss., 1876). Deacon, 1856, priest, 1857, P.E. Ch.; curate E. Worldham, Hampshire, Eng., 1856-59; missionary in British Columbia, 1859-69; rector St. James' Ch., San Francisco, 1870-72; dean Trinity Cathedral, Omaha, 1872-74; elected missionary bishop of Northern Tex. and consecrated Dec. 20, 1874, and when diocese of Dallas was created remained its bishop. Died Feb. 18, 1924.

GARRETT, Daniel Edward, congressman; b. Springfield, Tenn., Apr. 28, 1869; s. Edward C. and Susan Olive (Haddox) G.; ed. common schs.; m. Ida Jones, Dec. 7, 1893. Began practice of law at Springfield, Tenn., 1893; mem. Tenn. Ho. of Rep., 1892-96, Senate, 1902-06; removed to Houston, Tex., 1906; mem. 63d Congress (1913-15) and 65th Congress (1917-19), Tex. at large; mem. 67th and 69th to 72d Congresses (1921-23, 1925-33), 8th Tex. Dist. Democrat. Baptist. Home: Houston, Tex. Died Dec. 13, 1932.

GARRETT, David Claiborne, clergyman; b. Burlington, Ia., Dec. 23, 1857; s. William and Martha (Rorer) G.; A.B., Griswold Coll., Davenport, Ia., 1880, A.M., 1881; European corr. Living Church, 1880; spl. student Episcopal Theol. Sch., Cambridge, Mass., 1881-82; A.B., Harvard, 1882; B.D., Griswold Theol. Sem., 1883; m. Lily Selmes, Sept. 1, 1883; children—Lucy May, Claiborne Mauro, Jackson Russell. Deacon, 1880, priest, 1883, P.E. Ch.; rector united parishes Trinity and Christ Ch., Davenport, Ia., 1883-90, St. Mark's Ch., Seattle, Wash., 1890-97, Trinity Ch., Portland, Ore., 1897-99, St. Luke's Ch., San Francisco, 1899-1900, Zion Ch., Oconomowoc, Wis., 1900-03, Ch. of the Redeemer, Chestnut Hill, Mass., 1903-06, St. Peter's Ch., St. Louis, 1906-12, Trinity Ch., and student-pastor Episcopal Ch. U. of Ia., Iowa City, Ia., 1913-17; special preacher St. Michael's Ch., Marblehead, Mass., Feb. 1, 1918-May 1, 1919, St. Peter's Ch., Cambridge, May-Nov. 1919, Dept. Gen. Conv. P.E. Ch., 1895, 98, 1910; mem. Gen. Com. of Ch. Congress, P.E. Ch., 1907—. Chaplain 1st Regt. Ore. N.G., 1897-98; vet. N.G. rank of capt. Organizer, and pres. Bur. of Charities, Seattle, 1891-97; mem. Pub. Library Commn., Seattle, 1895-96 (chmn. 1897); pres. Dickens Fellowship, St. Louis, 1911-12. Republican. Home: Concord, Mass. Died Aug. 17, 1930.

GARRETT, Edmund Henry, artist, author; b. Albany, N.Y., Oct. 19, 1853; s. Anthony and Eliza A. (Miers) G.; ed. Boston, and Académie Julien, Paris; pupil of Jean Paul Laurens, Boulanger, and Lefèbvre; m. Marietta Goldsmith, 1877; children—Frank Bertram (dec.), Edmund Anthony, Julian. Medal at Boston, 1890; exhibitor at Paris Salon and principal exhibitions in America. Lecturer. Author: Elizabethan Songs, 1891; Three Heroines of New England Romance, 1894; Victorian Songs, 1895; Carmen—transl. from Prosper Mérimée, 1896, 97; The Romance and Reality of the Puritan Coast, 1897; The Pilgrim Shore, 1900. Home: Needham, Mass. Died Apr. 2, 1929.

GARRETT, John Biddle; b. Phila., Dec. 30, 1836; s. Thomas C. and Frances Biddle G.; A.B., Haverford Coll., 1854; m. Hannah Rhoads Haines, Sept. 6, 1866. Mcht. and mfr., 1854-74; entered service Lehigh Valley R.R., 1874; 3d v.p., 1887, 2d v.p., 1898, v.p., 1899; successively treas., v.p. and pres. Girard Trust Co., 1879-87. Mgr. Haverford Coll., 1872-1914 (pres. pro tem. 1890-91); mgr. Pa. Hosp., 1879-1909; trustee Bryn Mawr Coll., 1885-1902. Apptd. commr. to locate Osage Indians by President Johnson, 1866; chmn. 1st Mohonk Internat. Arbitration Conf., 1895. Home: Rosemont, Pa. Died Feb. 16, 1924.

GARRETT, J(oshua) Tracy, newspaperman; b. Burlington, Ia., Mar. 18, 1881; s. Henry Cook and Nellie (Tracy) G.; ed. public schools; m. Kathleen Tibbitts, May 1, 1907; 1 son, George Tracy. Began newspaper work in Burlington, 1900; editor and mgr. Creston (Ia.) Gazette, 1901-02; on various newspapers, New York, Chicago and Ia., until 1905; became connected with Des Moines Register, 1904, resigned on account of ill health, 1910, and ranched and in coal mining business in N.M., until 1917; connected with the Burlington Hawk-Eye, 1917—, editor, publisher, 1927-33; editor and publisher of The Daily Hawk-Eye Gazette (consolidation), 1933—; postmaster Burlington, 1923, 1936. Pres. bd. trustees Burlington Library; pres. Social Service League; v.p. Old Des Moines Hist. Soc. Episcopalian. Mason. Home: Burlington, Ia. Died Apr. 4, 1941.

GARRETT, Philip C., mfr.; b. Phila., 1834; s. Thomas C. and Frances (Biddle) G.; grad. Haverford Coll., 1851; m. Elizabeth W. Cope, May 18, 1865; was mfr. textile fabrics, 1854-78; retired. Chmn. Reform Com. of 100, Phila., 1881-83; offered Independent Rep. nomination gov. of Pa., 1883; mem. and pres. Bd. of Public Charities of Pa.; pres. State Lunacy Commn., Pa.; apptd. on Bd. Indian Commrs.; apptd. spl. commr. to Senecas, 1885; pres. Nat. Conf. Charities and Corrections, 1885; pres. Mohonk Nat. Indian Conf., 1898; apptd. chmn. commn. on N.Y. Indians, 1900. Republican. Home: Philadelphia, Pa., Died 1905.

GARRETT, William Abner, ry. vice-pres.; b. Canton, Miss., Aug. 18, 1861; s. Hibbard and Hannah (Griffith) G.; ed. pub. schs., St. Louis; m. Cornelia Cheyney, Feb. 7, 1889. Supt. in charge St. Louis Union Station during planning, and opening, Sept. 1894; supt. various divs. Wabash Ry., 1896-99; gen. supt. Philadelphia & Reading Railway, 1899-1903; gen. mgr. Queen & Crescent Ry., 1903-06; pres. Seaboard Airline Ry., 1906-09; chmn. Gen. Mgrs. Assn. of Chicago, Oct. 2, 1911-Sept. 1912; v.p. C.&G.W. Ry., Chicago, Sept. 1912—. U.S. Govt. del. to Internat. Ry. Congress, Berne, Switzerland, 1910. Episcopalian. Died Oct. 10, 1924.

GARRETT, William Robertson, educator; b. Williamsburg, Va., Apr. 12, 1839; s. Dr. Robert M. and Susan (Winder) G.; ed. Williamsburg Mil. Acad.; grad. William and Mary Coll., A.M., 1858; studied law 1 yr., 1858-59, Univ. of Va.; hon. Ph.D., U. of Nashville, 1891; capt. Co. F 1st Va. regt. arty., 1861-62; adjt. 11th Tenn. cav., 1862-65; capt. Co. B, same, in Forrest's cav., 1865; m. Julia Flournoy Batte, Nov. 12, 1868. Master grammar school, William and Mary Coll., 1866-67; moved to Pulaski, Tenn., 1868; pres. Giles Coll., 1868-73; co. supt. schools, Giles Co., 1873-75; asso. prin. Montgomery Bell. Acad., Nashville, 1875-91; State supt. public instn., Tenn., 1891-93; prin. Mil. Acad., 1893-95; supt. Watkins Inst. night schs., 1887—; prof. Am. history, Peabody Normal Coll., 1895—; dean of coll., 1899—. Author: The South as a Factor in the Territorial Expansion of the United States (200 pp. in "Confederate Military History," 12 vols.); Garrett & Goodpasture's History of Tennessee, 1900; Geography of Tennessee (Supplement to Frye's Geography). Editor: Am. Hist. Mag. of Peabody Normal Coll. (quarterly), 1895-1900; etc. Home: Nashville, Tenn. Died 1904.

GARRIGAN, Philip Joseph, bishop; b. in Ireland in early 40's; s. Philip and Alice G.; ed. pub. schs., Mass., and St. Charles Coll., Md.; philol. and theol. studies in St. Joseph's Provincial Sem. (then at Troy, N.Y.). Ordained R.C. priest, June 11, 1870; dir. Troy Sem., 1872-75; pastor St. Bernard's Ch., Fitchburg, 1875-88; then called to assist as vice-rector in establishing Catholic Univ., Washington, the duties of which he discharged until promoted to new diocese of Sioux City, Ia.; consecrated bishop, May 25, 1902. Died Oct. 14, 1919.

GARRIGUES, Henry Jacques, physician; b. Copenhagen, Denmark, June 6, 1831; s. Jacques Louis and Cecelia Olivia (Duntzfelt) G.; A.B., Metropolitan Coll., Copenhagen, 1850, A.M., 1863; M.D., U. of Copenhagen, 1869; m. Louise Riemer, 1868. In U.S., 1875—; obstetric surgeon N.Y. Maternity Hosp., 1881, Infant Asylum, 1884; gynecologist to German Hosp., 1885; prof. obstetrics, Post-Grad. Med. Sch. and Hosp., 1886; gynecologist St. Mark's Hosp., 1890; cons. surgeon Maternity Hosp., 1892; prof. gynecology and obstetrics, Sch. of Clin. Medicine, 1898. Hon. fellow Am. Gynecol. Society, 1901, Obstet. Soc. (Edinburgh), 1902. Author: Text-Book of Obstetrics, 1902, 1907; Gynecology, Medical and Surgical, 1905. Died Aug. 1913.

GARRIOTT, Edward Bennett, meteorologist; b. Lockland, O., Mar. 17, 1853; ed. pub. schs. and Washington U., St. Louis; m. Gertrude L. Dewey, Jan. 12, 1882. Asst. observer, 1874-75, observer, 1876-87, meteorol. clerk, 1888-91, chief Div. Meteorology, 1892-93, forecaster, 1893-94, supervising forecaster and prof. meteorology, 1895—, U.S. Weather Bureau, Washington, D.C. Writer and lecturer on meteorology. Died 1910.

GARRISON, Charles Grant, judge; b. Swedesboro, N.J., Aug. 3, 1849; s. Rev. Joseph Fithian and Elizabeth Vanarsdale (Grant) G.; acad. edn. Princeton and Phila.; M.D., U. of Pa., 1872; practiced medicine at Swedesboro, 1872-76; m. Anna Hoffman Miller, Mar. 4, 1880. Admitted to bar, 1878; practiced law, 1878-88; justice Supreme Ct. of N.J., 1888-1920 (retired). Democrat. Chancellor P.E. Diocese of N.J., 1882-88; judge adv. gen. of N.J., 1884-88. Home: Merchantville, N.J. Died Apr. 22, 1924.

GARRISON, Daniel Mershon, naval officer; b. Bordentown, N.J., May 3, 1874; s. Samuel and Hannah Gary (Mershon) G.; grad. Bordentown Mil. Inst., 1891; grad. U.S. Naval Acad., 1895; hon. D.Sc., St. John's Coll., 1923; m. Jessie Croft Kelly, Sept. 26, 1901; children—Jessie Croft (Mrs. G. F. Good), Daniel Mershon. Promoted asst. engr., July 1, 1897; ensign, Mar. 3, 1899; lt. (jr. grade), July 1, 1900; lt., July 4, 1902; commd. prof. mathematics, Oct. 27, 1906; captain, Sept. 18, 1918; head dept. of mathematics, U.S. Naval Acad., 1918-23, retired; head dept. of mathematics, St. John's Coll., Annapolis, Md., 1923—. Served on board Indiana during Spanish-Am. War; took part in bombardments of San Juan, P.R., and Santiago, Cuba; awarded Congressional Medal for battle of July 3, 1898; chief engr. Pacific Submarine Telegraph Survey which surveyed route for cable across Pacific, 1899-1900; served on Cincinnati, on guard duty at Chemulpo, Korea, and Chefo, China, during Russo-Japanese War. Episcopalian. Died Dec. 30, 1927.

GARRISON, Fielding Hudson, col. U.S.A.; b. Washington, D.C., Nov. 5, 1870; s. John Rowzee and Jennie (Davis) G.; A.B., Johns Hopkins, 1890; M.D., Georgetown U., 1893; m. Clara Augusta Brown, Apr. 26, 1909. Asst. librarian, Surgeon General's Office, Washington, D.C., 1889-1922. Editor Index Medicus, 1903-1927; asso. editor of the Quarterly Cumulative Index Medicus, 1927-29. Commd. maj. Med. Reserve Corps, 1917; lt. colonel M.C.U.S.A., 1918; lt. col., M.C. regular army, July 1, 1920; lt. col. retired, May 19, 1930. Librarian Welch Med. Library, Baltimore, 1930—. Author: An Introduction to the History of Medicine, 1913, 4th edit., 1928; A Physician's Anthology (with Casey A. Wood), 1920; The Principles of Anatomic Illustration before Vesalius, 1925; Medicine in Space, 1934. Died Apr. 18, 1935.

GARRISON, Francis Jackson, author; b. Boston, Mass., Oct. 29, 1848; s. late William Lloyd and Helen E. (Benson) G.; grad. Boston Latin Sch., 1865; m. Mary Pratt, 1879 (died 1882); m. 2d, Theresa Holmes, 1891 (died 1915). With Riverside Press and its allied publishing house, Houghton, Mifflin Co., 1871—. Author: Anna Phillips, Wife of Wendell Phillips, A Memorial Sketch. Joint author: William Lloyd Garrison, 1805-1879—The Story of His Life Told by His Children. Home: Newtonville, Mass. Deceased.

GARRISON, George Pierce, univ. prof.; b. Carrollton, Ga., Dec. 19, 1853; s. P. G. and Mary Ann (Curtiss) G.; L.A. (Literate in Arts), U. of Edinburgh, 1881; Ph.D., U. of Chicago, 1896; m. Annie Perkins, Nov. 6, 1881. Instr. English and history, U. of Tex., 1884-88; a student of the univ., 1884-86, asst. prof. history, 1888-89; adj. prof., 1889-91, asso. prof., 1891-97, prof. Am. history, 1897-1909, U. of Tex. Author: The Civil Government of Texas, 1898; Texas (Am. Commonwealth series), 1903; Westward Extension (The Am. Nation, Vol. XVII), 1906. Editor: Diplomatic Correspondence of the Republic of Texas. Home: Austin, Tex. Died 1910.

GARRISON, James Carr, publisher; b. St. Paul, Minn., Sept. 19, 1870; s. Thomas Jasper and Maria (Mooney) G.; ed. by father and pvt. and pub. schs.; m. Gertrude Emilie Strain, June 3, 1904. Editor Ashland (Wis.) Daily News, 1888-89; staff of Milwaukee Evening Wisconsin and Milwaukee Sentinel, 1889-94; asso. editor, mng. editor, New York Press, 1895-1913; staff of New York World; Albany corr. New York Evening Mail, 1913; editorial staff Providence Journal, 1914-17; became publisher and v.p. Providence News, 1918; now living in New York. Died Feb. 9, 1929.

GARRISON, John R., treasury official; b. nr. Garrisonville, Va., Aug. 27, 1838; s. John R. and Frances (Hudson) G.; ed. West River Classical Inst., Md., Union Acad., D.C., Dickinson Coll., Pa.; grad. LL.B., law dept., Columbian Univ., D.C. (LL.M.); mem. bar Supreme Court, D.C., U.S. Court of Claims, Supreme Court U.S., and Supreme Court of Puerto Rico; m. Jennie Davis, Sept. 9, 1869. Entered First Comptroller's office, Treasury Dept., clerk class 1, 1863; promoted grade by grade to chief div. of diplomatic and consular accounts, 1884-85; deputy 1st comptroller Treasury, 1885-93; auditor under mil. govt. 1899-1900, under civil govt. 1900-03, Puerto Rico; was chief, Customs Div., U.S. Treasury Dept.; auditor D.C., Aug. 1903—. Republican. Home: Washington, D.C. Died 1908.

GARRISON, Lindley Miller, secretary of war; b. Camden, N.J., Nov. 28, 1864; s. Rev. Joseph Fithian and Elizabeth Vanarsdale (Grant) G.; bro. of Charles Grant G.; ed. pub. schs.; P.E. Acad., Phila., 2 years; Phillips Exeter Acad., 1 yr.; spl. student, Harvard, 1 yr.; LL.B., U. of Pa., 1885; LL.D., New York U., 1914, Rutgers, 1915, Kenyon, 1916, Brown, 1917; m. Margaret Hildeburn, June 30, 1900. Studied law in offices of Redding, Jones & Carson, Phila.; admitted to Pa. bar, 1886; practiced with preceptors, and successors, Jones & Carson, 1883-88; admitted to N.J. bar, 1888, and practiced at Camden, N.J., until Dec. 1898; mem. Garrison, McManus & Enright, Jersey City, 1899-1904; vice chancellor of N.J., June 15, 1904-Mar. 5, 1913; sec. of war in cabinet of President Wilson, Mar. 5, 1913-Feb. 10, 1916 (resigned). Democrat. Episcopalian. Home: New York, N.Y. Died Oct. 19, 1932.

GARRISON, Wendell Phillips, literary editor The Nation, July, 1865—; b. Cambridgeport, Mass., June 4, 1840; s. William Lloyd and Helen Eliza (Benson) G.; grad. Harvard, 1861, A.M., 1895; m. 1865, Lucy McKim; 2d, 1891, Annie McKim Dennis. Mem. bd. dirs., geol. survey of N.J. Author: Parables for School and Home, 1897; Sonnets and Lyrics of the Ever-Womanly, 1898; The New Gulliver, 1898. Home: Orange, N.J. Died 1907.

GARRISON, William Lloyd, publicist; b. Boston, Jan. 21, 1838; s. late William Lloyd and Helen Eliza (Benson) G.; ed. Boston pub. schs.; m. Ellen Wright, Sept. 14, 1864. Bank cashier, Dorchester, Mass., 1862-64; wool merchant, Boston, 1866-83; dealer in investment securities, 1883-1902; now sec. Am. Free Trade League; has spoken and written frequently on questions of civil polity of reformatory character; warm advocate of the single tax theory as propounded by Henry George and of free trade; Woman Suffragist; Anti-Imperialist; opponent of restriction laws against the Chinese in this country. Home: Lexington, Mass. Died 1909.

GARST, Perry, rear admiral U.S.N.; b. Dayton, O., July 11, 1848; apptd. from Ill. and grad. U.S. Naval Acad., 1868. Ensign, Apr. 19, 1869; promoted through grades to capt., June 17, 1904; retired as rear adm. June 30, 1907. Service during Civil War on bd. the Marion in summer of 1864; served successively in Pacific Squadron, the Terror, Potomac, Frolic, on Asiatic sta., Palos, and receiving ship Franklin, 1868-79; coast survey, 1879-82; Franklin and Shenandoah, 1882-86; Navy Yard, Washington 1886-88; Navy Department, 1888-90; Jamestown, 1890-92; Naval Acad., 1892-96; exec. officer Newark and Raleigh, 1896-97, Terror, 1897-98; Naval Academy, 1898-1900; comdr. Isla de Cuba, 1900-02; inspector 10th light house district, 1902-04; capt. of yard, Navy Yard, Portsmouth, 1904-05; comd. Rhode Island, 1906; mem. bd., Naval Acad., 1907. Home: Bradenton, Fla. Died Aug. 29, 1939.

GARST, Warren, governor; b. Dayton, O., Dec. 4, 1850; s. Michael and Maria Lauri (Morrison) G.; self educated; m. Clara H. Clark, Nov. 27, 1889. Removed with parents to Ill., 1858; entered mercantile business at Boone, Ia., 1869, and later at Coon Rapids; also farmer and banker; mem. Ia. Senate, 25th to 31st Gen. Assemblies (chmn. appropriation com. for 5 sessions); elected lt. gov. of Ia., Nov. 1906, and became gov., Nov. 25, 1908, on account of resignation of Gov. Cummings (elected to U.S. Senate); term expired Jan. 1, 1909. Republican. Home: Coon Rapids, Ia. Died Oct. 5, 1924.

GARTH, Thomas Russell, psychologist; b. Paducah, Ky., Dec. 24, 1872; s. Robert and Jane Elizabeth (Campbell) G.; B.A., U. of Denver, 1909, M.A., 1910; Ph.D., Columbia U., 1917; m. Ethel Nadine Tucker, 1909; children—Thomas Russell, Francis Marion, and Ethel Nadine (adopted). Psychologist N.Y. Post-Grad. Sch., 1912-13; asst. in edn., State Normal Sch., Farmville, Va., 1913-15; asst. prin. N.Y. Parental Sch., 1915-16; prin. Barton Heights Sch., Richmond, Va., 1916-17; head dept. of edn., State Normal Sch., Canyon, Tex., 1917-19; adj. prof. psychology, U. of Tex., 1919-22; prof. edn., U. of Denver, 1922-29, prof. ednl. psychology, 1929-30, prof. exptl. psychology, 1930—; prof. in Summer Sch., U. of Colo., 1922, U. of Tex., 1923. Asst. Rockefeller Hookworm Investigation, 1912; mem. Univ. Race Commn., 1920. Head expdn. to study color blindness of Indians, 1930-31, to study foster Indian child in white homes, 1935-37, also with various other expdns. to study psychology of the Indian, 1919—; specialist with U.S. Govt. in Indian Service School, 1936, 37. Democrat. Presbyn. Author: Mental Fatigue During Continuous Exercise, 1918; Race Psychology, 1931; Educational Psychology, 1937; Life of Henry Augustus Buchtel, 1937. Home: Denver, Colo. Died Apr. 20, 1939.

GARTHE, Louis, newspaper corr.; b. Baltimore, Sept. 10, 1861; s. August and Marie Christine (Pilert) G.; A.B. (with honors), Baltimore City Coll., 1879; A.B., Johns Hopkins U., 1882; m. Emma Francis Berry, 1912. Reporter on the Baltimore Sun 1884-87; established New York bur. of Baltimore American, 1888; spent 6 mos. in Europe for American, 1888; in charge of American's Washington bur., 1889—. Frequently detached for newspaper work in Cuba, S.A., and polit. work in nat. campaigns; a voluminous writer on politics, news and editorial. Republican. Lutheran. Home: Washington, D.C. Died Sept. 8, 1920.

GARVAN, Francis Patrick, lawyer; b. East Hartford, Conn., June 13, 1875; s. Patrick and Mary (Carroll) G.; A.B., Yale, 1897; LL.B., New York Law Sch., 1899; studied Catholic U., 1898; LL.D., Fordham, 1919; A.M., Yale, 1922; LL.D., Trinity Coll., 1935; m. Mabel Brady, June 9, 1910. Began practice in N.Y. City, 1899, asst. dist. atty., 1900-10; dir. Bur. of Investigation, U.S., and mgr. New York office of alien property custodian, Nov. 1917-Mar. 1919; apptd. alien property custodian, Mar. 4, 1919; also asst. atty. gen. of U.S. Dean Fordham Law Sch., 1919-23; trustee Catholic U. Democrat. Catholic. Home: New York, N.Y. Died Nov. 7, 1937.

GARVER, Austin Samuel, clergyman; b. Scotland, Pa., Dec. 12, 1847; s. Samuel and Sarah (Coldsmith) G.; student Pa. Coll., 1865-67, A.M., 1890; grad. Andover Theol. Sem., 1871; m. Sarah C. Brackett, Aug. 2, 1881. Ordained Congl. ministry, 1872; pastor, Hingham, Mass., 1872-75, Greenwood, 1875-80, Hopedale (Unitarian), 1880-85, Second Parish Ch., Worcester, 1885-1910, minister emeritus. Mem. School Bd., Worcester, 1888-1901; trustee Clark Univ., Worcester Poly. Inst.; v.p. Leicester Acad.; pres. Worcester Art Mus., 1885-13, Worcester Art Soc., 1894-14. Has taught classes in art for many years. Home: Worcester, Mass. Died June 20, 1918.

GARVER, John Anson, lawyer; b. Scotland, Pa., July 11, 1854; s. Samuel and Sarah (Goldsmith) G.; B.A., Yale, 1875; LL.B., Columbia U. Law Sch., 1877; m. Rebecca C. Brewster, Oct. 5, 1882. Admitted to N.Y. bar, 1877, and since practiced in N.Y. City, and before state and federal courts and U.S. Supreme Court; mem. from 1884, of Shearman & Sterling (founded 1873), now sr. mem.; officer or dir. many corps. Died Oct. 23, 1936.

GARVEY, Eugene A., bishop; b. Carbondale, Pa., Oct. 6, 1845; s. Michael and Catherine (Boylan) G.; student St. Charles' Coll., Ellicott City, Md.; grad. St. Charles' Sem., Phila. (D.D.). Ordained R.C. priesthood; asst. pastor, Hawley, Pa., 1870; pastor Athens, Pa., 1871, Williamsport, Pa., 1871-99, Pittston, Pa., 1899-1901; consecrated bishop of Altoona, Pa., Sept. 8, 1901. Died Oct. 22, 1920.

GARVIN, Lucius Fayette Clark, governor; b. Knoxville, Tenn., Nov. 13, 1841; s. James and Sarah Ann (Gunn) G.; A.B., Amherst, 1862; M.D., Harvard, 1867; m. Lucy Waterman Southmayd, Dec. 23, 1869 (dec.); m. 2d, Sarah Emma Tomlinson, Apr. 2, 1907. Pvt. 51st Mass. Vols. in Civil War. Has resided in R.I., 1864—, studying and practicing medicine; elected to R.I. legislature 16 times from 1883; Dem. candidate for Congress, 1894, 96, 98, 1900, 06, 2d R.I. Dist.; Dem. candidate for gov., 1901, elected gov. of R.I., Nov. 1902, 1903; defeated, 1904 and 1905; elected state senator, 1920, serving 4th term. Home: Lonsdale, R.I. Died Oct. 2, 1922.

GARWOOD, Hiram Morgan, lawyer; b. Bastrop, Tex., Jan. 1, 1864; s. Calvin Baxter and Frances (Walker) G.; B.S., U. of the South, Sewanee, Tenn., 1882, D.C.L., 1922; m. Hettie Page, 1890; children—Calvin B., St. John, Louise; m. 2d, Huberta R. Nunn, 1921. Admitted to Tex. bar, 1885, and began practice at Bastrop; moved to Houston, 1901; mem. Baker, Botts, Parker & Garwood; v.p. 2d Nat. Bank, Houston. Mem. Tex. Ho. of Rep., 1886-88, Tex. State Senate, 1890-92; county judge, Bastrop Co., Tex., 1888-90. Regent, U. of Tex., 1894-96. Democrat. Episcopalian. Mason. Home: Houston, Tex. Died May 15, 1930.

GARWOOD, Sterling Marion; b. Cartersville, Ga., Dec. 27, 1893; s. Oscar Lee and Cora (Roberts) G.; ed. pub. and pvt. schs. Atlanta, Ga., 1900-15; m. Helen Leedham, June 6, 1921; children—Sterling Marion, Emily Joan. With engring. dept., City of Atlanta, 1915-17; with M. W. Elkins Co., investments,

Little Rock, Ark., 1920-27; v.p. W. B. Wortham Co., investments, 1927-30; v.p. Bankers Trust Co. and v.p. and mgr. Nat. Securities Co., Little Rock, 1930-32; production credit commr., Farm Credit Adminstrn., 1933-39. Second lt. (pilot), U.S. Air Service, 1917-18. Was sec. Ark. Agrl. Credit Bd. Democrat. Mason. Home: Columbia, S.C. Died Jan. 2, 1941.

GARY, Elbert Henry, chmn. and chief exec. officer, U.S. Steel Corp.; b. on father's farm nr. Wheaton, Ill.; s. Erastus and Susan A. (Vallette) G.; ed. in pub. schs., Wheaton Coll. and U. of Chicago; LL.B., U. of Chicago, 1867; LL.D., McKendree Coll., 1906, Lafayette Coll., 1915, Lincoln Memorial U., 1919, Trinity Coll., 1919, Syracuse U., 1921, Northwestern U., 1922; Sc.D., U. of Pittsburgh, 1915; D.C.S., New York U., 1925; m. Julia E. Graves, June 23, 1869 (died 1902); children—Mrs. Gertrude Sutcliffe, Mrs. Bertha Campbell; m. 2d, Emma T. Townsend, Dec. 2, 1905. Admitted to Ill. bar, 1867, bar of Supreme Court of U.S., 1882. Pres. Town of Wheaton, 3 terms; first mayor City of Wheaton, 2 terms; county judge, DuPage Co., Ill., 2 terms; in gen. practice of law, Chicago, 25 yrs.; connected with organization Federal Steel Co. and retired from law practice to become its pres.; prominently identified with organization U.S. Steel Corp., of which is chmn. bd., chmn. finance com., and chief exec. officer in gen. charge of affairs. Mem. U.S. sect. Internat. High Commn., 1917 (resigned). Pres. Am. Iron and Steel Inst. from its beginning, 1909; chmn. advisory bd., N.Y. Ordnance Dist.; trustee Northwestern U., Syracuse U. Second Class Order of the Sacred Treasure (Japan), 1918; Grand Cordon Order of Leopold II (Belgium), 1920; Grand Officer Order of Ouissan Alaouite Cherifien (Morocco), 1920; Officer Legion of Honor (France), 1920; Golden Cross of the Commandership of the Royal Battalion of George I (Greece), 1921; Grand Cross Knight of the Crown of Italy, 1922. Home: New York, N.Y. Died Aug. 15, 1927.

GARY, Eugene Blackburn, judge; b. Cokesbury, S.C., Aug. 22, 1854; s. Dr. Franklin F. and Mary Caroline (Blackburn) G.; A.B., S.C. Coll., 1872; LL.D., U. of S.C., 1915; studied law; admitted to bar. Mem. S.C. legislature, 1889; lt.-gov., 1890-93; elected asso. justice Supreme Court of S.C., Dec. 1893; elected chief justice, Jan. 10, 1912, reëlected Jan. 1914, for term expiring Aug. 1, 1924. Home: Abbeville, S.C. Deceased.

GARY, Frank Boyd, senator; b. Cokesbury, S.C., Mar. 9, 1860; s. Dr. Franklin F. and Mary Caroline (Blackburn) G.; bro. of Eugene Blackburn G.; ed. Cokesbury Conf. Sch. and Union Coll., Schenectady, N.Y. (withdrew in sr. yr. on account of ill health); m. Maria Lee Evans, Jan. 7, 1897. Admitted to bar, 1881, and since in practice at Abbeville, S.C. Mem. S.C. Ho. of Rep., 1890-1900 and 1906 (speaker 1895-1900); mem. Constl. Conv., 1895; presided at trial of James H. Tillman for killing of Editor Gonzales; elected U.S. senator, Mar. 6, 1908, for unexpired term (1908-09) of A. C. Latimer, deceased; apptd. judge 8th Circuit, S.C. Methodist. Home: Abbeville, S.C. Died Dec. 7, 1922.

GARY, James Albert, postmaster general; b. Uncasville, Conn., Oct. 22, 1833; ed. Rockhill Inst., Md., and Allegheny Coll., Pa.; m. Lavina Corrie, Nov. 1856. Removed to Md. 1840; became, 1861, partner with his father in firm of James S. Gary & Son, cotton duck mfrs.; head of firm, 1870—. Was the Whig nominee for Md. Senate, 1858; was one of 3 delegates from his co. to Union Conv., 1861, at Md. Inst.; Rep. candidate for Congress, 1872. Postmaster gen. in cabinet of President McKinley, Mar. 1897, to May 1898. Home: Baltimore, Md. Died Oct. 31, 1920.

GARY, Joseph Easton, judge Superior Court of Cook Co., Ill., 1863—; b. Potsdam, N.Y., July 9, 1821; common school edn.; m. Elizabeth Jane Swelting, Nov. 28, 1855. Went to St. Louis, 1843; read law, admitted to bar, 1844; practiced at Springfield, Mo., 1844-49; then at Las Vegas, N.Mex., and San Francisco, until 1856; practiced in Chicago, 1856-63. Presided in celebrated Anarchist trial, and wrote article concerning it in Century Magazine, April 1893. Died 1906.

GASKILL, Francis Almon, justice Superior Court of Mass., 1895—; b. Blackstone, Mass., Jan. 3, 1846; s. Albert and Anna S. G.; grad. Brown Univ., 1866 (LL.D., 1899); studied in Harvard Law School; admitted to bar, 1869; dist. atty. Middle dist. of Mass., 1887-95; m. Katharine Mortimer Whitaker, Oct. 20, 1869; m. 2d, Josephine L. Abbott, July 12, 1892. Wrote: Civic History of Worcester, Mass. Home: Worcester, Mass. Died 1909.

GASQUE, Allard Henry, congressman; b. Florence Co., S.C., Mar. 8, 1873; s. Wesley and Martha Washington (Kirton) G.; B.A., U. of S.C.; m. Bessie M. Hawley, Mar. 5, 1908; children—Martha Elizabeth, Doris, John Allard, Thomas Nelson. Formerly teacher pub. schs.; county supt. schs., Florence Co., S.C., 1903-23; mem. Dem. State Exec. Com., 1912-20; chmn. Dem. County Com., 1919-23; mem. 68th to 75th Congresses (1923-39), 6th S.C. Dist. (chmn. com. on pensions). Baptist. Mason. Home: Florence, S. C. Died June 17, 1938.

GASS, Howard Allan, educator; b. Audrain Co., Mo., Aug. 22, 1852; s. Samuel B. and Mary Anne (Pearson) G.; ed. pub. and pvt. schs.; m. Alice Josephine Shell, Dec. 25, 1876. Sch. commr., Audrain Co., Mo., 1885, 1887; chief clk. in office of state supt. pub. schs., Mo., 13½ yrs. in all; state supt. pub. schs., 1907-11, 1915-19; editor Mo. School Journal, 1887—, and pres. Mo. Sch. Jour. Pub. Co., mem. (ex-officio) 5 state normal sch. bds. of Mo., and Lincoln Inst., also State Bd. of Agr., etc. Pres. Merchants Bank, Jefferson City, 1911, 1912. Democrat. Missionary Bapt. Mason. Home: Jefferson City, Mo. Died 1916.

GASSAWAY, Percy Lee, congressman; b. Waco, Tex., Aug. 30, 1885; s. Rev. B. F. and Elizabeth Caroline (Scoggins) G.; ed. 15 mos. in schs. of Indian Ty.; m. Lillian Fooshee, Oct. 30, 1920; children—Betty Jo, Peggy Jane, Jim. Moved with parents to Ft. Sill, Okla. (then Indian Ty.) early in life; admitted to Okla. bar, 1919; apptd. county judge of Coal Co., 1923; elected county atty., 1924; dist. judge, 26th Jud. Dist., Okla., 1926-34; mem. 74th Congress (1935-36), 4th Okla. Dist. Democrat. Mem. M.E. Ch. S. Mason. Home: Coalgate, Okla. Died May 15, 1937.

GASSON, Thomas Ignatius, clergyman, educator; b. Sevenoaks, Kent, Eng., Sept. 23, 1859; s. Henry and Arabella (Quinnell) G.; ed. St. Stephen's Sch., London, under tutors in Phila., at Frederick, Md., and Woodstock Coll., Md., and Royal U., Innsbruck, Austria; entered Soc. of Jesus, 1875. Ordained R.C. priest by Prince-Bishop of Brixen, 1891; has been prof. of poetry, rhetoric, mental philosophy, ethics and economics; pres. Boston Coll. and rector Ch. of the Immaculate Conception, 1907-14; dean of grad. dept. and prof. sociology, Georgetown U., 1914-23; supt. Retreat House, Mt. Manresa, Ft. Wadsworth, S.I., 1923—. Died Feb. 28, 1930.

GAST, Charles E., lawyer; b. Lancaster, Pa., Dec. 12, 1848; s. Christian and Maria (Eckert) G.; grad. Franklin and Marshall Coll., A.B., 1868 (later A.M.), Albany Law Sch., LL.B.; m. Elizabeth S. Shaeffer, June 10, 1875. Admitted to bar, 1870; practiced at Lancaster, Pa., few yrs.; removed to Pueblo, Colo., 1873; solicitor in Colo., Atchison, Topeka & Santa Fé Ry. Co., 1876—. Republican. Home: Pueblo, Colo. Died 1908.

GAST, Frederick Augustus, theologian; b. Lancaster, Pa., Oct. 17, 1835; s. Christian and Maria (Eckert) G.; A.B., Franklin and Marshall Coll., 1856, A.M., 1859; (D.D., Waynesburg Coll., 1877; LL.D., Franklin and Marshall, 1906); m. Adaline Frey, Dec. 24, 1857 (died 1901). Ordained in ministry of Reformed Ch. in U.S. (German), 1859; held two pastoral charges, and was chaplain 45th Pa. Vols. during Civil War. Tutor, 1872-74, prof. Hebrew and O.T. theology, 1874-1909, prof. emeritus, Theol. Sem., Lancaster, Pa. Asso. editor Reformed Church Review. Died Feb. 11, 1917.

GASTON, Ernest B., single tax advocate; b. Henderson, Ill., Nov. 21, 1861; s. James E. and Catherine (Estep) G.; student Drake U., 1885-87 (grad. commercial dept.); m. Clara Leah Mershon, Nov. 24, 1887; children—Frances Lily (widow of Henry Crawford), James Ernest, Cornelius A. (M.D.), Leah Catherine (Mrs. Max P. McGill), Arthur Fairhope. Real estate business, University Place (suburb of Des Moines), 1887-89; served as justice of the peace, town recorder and as mem. Town Council; editor Suburban Advocate, 1889, 90; connected with The Tribune (later The Farmers Tribune), Des Moines, 1891-94; became interested in Farmers Alliance and Peoples Party movements; organizer, 1893, and made sec. Fairhope Industrial Assn. for promotion of single-tax and other reforms; led party of colonists to eastern shore of Mobile Bay, 1894; the assn. reorganized, 1904, under title of Fairhope Single Tax Corp., of which was sec., also editor and pub. The Fairhope Courier, 1894—. Ind. Democrat. Home: Fairhope, Ala. Died Dec. 21, 1937.

GASTON, James McFadden, physician; b. nr. Chester, S.C., Dec. 27, 1824; s. John Brown and Polly (McFadden) G.; grad. S.C. Coll., 1843; M.D., same, 1846; (M.D. ad eundem Univ. of Brazil, 1854); m. Sue G. Brumby, Nov. 2, 1852. Practiced Chester dist., S.C., 1846-52, Columbia, S.C., 1852-61; surgeon and med. director C.S. army, 1861-65; practiced in province of São Paulo, Brazil, 1867-73, Campinas, Brazil, 1874-83; at Atlanta, Ga., 1883—. Prof. principles and practice of surgery, Southern Med. Coll., Atlanta, 1884—. Honorary mem. Am. Assn. Obstetricians and Gynecologists, Southern Surg. and Gynecol. Assn. Asso. editor Annual of the Universal Medical Sciences and Sajous' Annual and Analytical Cyclopædia of Practical Medicine. Home: Atlanta, Ga. Died 1903.

GASTON, Joseph Alfred, army officer; b. Honey Brook, Pa., Sept. 2, 1856; s. Joseph (M.D.) and Agnes (Greenbank) G.; prep. edn. Wyoming (Pa.) Sem. and Commercial Coll.; grad. U.S. Mil. Acad., 1881; grad. Army War Coll., 1912; m. Lavinia, d. Brig. Gen. William L. Haskin (U.S.A.), May 16, 1903. Commd. 2d lt. 8th Cav., June 11, 1881; promoted through grades to brig. gen. N.A. (temp.), Aug. 5, 1917. Engaged against Apache Indians, 1885-86, against Sioux Indians, 1890-91; served in Cuba, 1899-1902, P.I., 1908-10; supt. permanent camps, relief work, San Francisco, 1906; commandant Ft. Riley, Kan., 1913-14; on Mexican border, 1914-17; comd. 6th Cav., with punitive expdn., Mexico, 1916; brig. gen. N.A., Aug. 5, 1917; comdg. 165th Depot Brigade, Camp Travis, Tex., until Nov. 22, 1917, 90th Div., Nov. 23-Dec. 27, 1917, 11th Brigade, 6th Div., Camp Forrest, Ga., Dec. 30, 1917; trans. to 37th Div., Camp Sheridan, Ala., Mar. 1918, which comd. about 2 weeks; comdg. Camp Meade, Md., June 29, 1918-Feb. 5, 1919; resumed rank of col. of cav., U.S.A., Feb. 5, 1919; recruiting duty, Phila., Feb. 1919-20; retired Sept. 2, 1920. Died Mar. 31, 1937.

GASTON, Lucy Page, reformer; b. Delaware, O., 1860; d. Alexander H. and Henrietta (Page) G.; sister of Edward Page G.; ed. Lacon, Ill., and State Normal Sch. Founder and supt. Anti-Cigarette League America; was active in W.C.T.U. under Frances E. Willard; led long series of test fights in the courts on validity of prohibition law at Harvey, Ill., while editing The Citizen there; has directed many prosecutions of cigarette dealers in Chicago and elsewhere; agitated, with frequent success, for anti-cigarette legislation in various states and cities, has extended the work abroad; editor of Anti-Cigarette Herald and other reform publication. Home: Chicago, Ill. Died Aug. 20, 1924.

GASTON, William Alexander, lawyer, banker; b. Boston, May 1, 1859; s. William and Louisa Augusta (Beecher) G.; A.B., Harvard, 1880; Harvard Law Sch., 1881-82; m. May Davidson Lockwood, Apr. 9, 1892. Admitted to Suffolk bar, 1883; mem. Gaston, Snow, Saltonstall & Hunt; mem. exec. com. Nat. Shawmut Bank; pres. Boylston Market Assn., Killingly Trust Co.; dir. 2d Nat. Bank (Barre, Mass.), Windham County Nat. Bank (Danielson, Conn.), Gillette Safety Razor Co., etc. Col. on staff Governor William E. Russell of Mass., 1890-1902; Dem. candidate for gov. of Mass., 1902, 1903; Dem. nominee for U.S. Senate, 1905; mem. Dem. Nat. Com., Dem. State Committee. Episcopalian. Home: Boston, Mass. Died July 17, 1927.

GATCH, Thomas Milton, educator; b. Milford, O., Jan. 29, 1833; s. Gen. Thomas and Lucinda E. (McCormick) G.; A.B., Ohio Wesleyan U., 1855, A.M., 1860; Ph.D., Asbury (now DePauw) U., 1874; m. Orytha Bennett, Sept. 9, 1858. Prof. natural science, U. of the Pacific, 1856; prin. Santa Cruz pub. schs., 1857; prof. mathematics, U. of the Pacific, 1858; prof. ancient langs, 1860, pres., 1860-65, Willamette U.; prin. Santa Cruz pub. schs., 1866; prin. Portland Acad., 1867-70; pres. Willamette U., 1870-80; prof. history and English lit., U. of Ore., 1880; prin. Wasco Acad., 1881-87; pres., 1887-95, prof. polit. and social science, 1895-97, U. of Wash.; pres. Ore. Agrl. Coll., 1897-1907; retired under Carnegie Foundation, 1907, "in view of long service to education in the Northwest." Elected pres. U. of Wash. at organization, 1862, and of U. of Ore. at organization, 1876, but declined both. Home: Seattle, Wash. Died Apr. 22, 1913.

GATCHELL, George Washington, army officer; b. in R.I., Feb. 22, 1865; s. James Lawrence and Mary E. (Jones) G.; grad. U.S. Mil. Acad., 1887, Arty. Sch., 1898. Commd. add. 2d lt. 5th Arty., 1887; promoted through grades to brig. gen. N.A. (temp.), Dec. 17, 1917. Participated in campaign against Sioux Indians, 1890-91; prof. mil. science and tactics, Vermont Acad., Saxtons River, 1891-95; with siege arty. at Ybor City, Fla., May-Aug. 1898, Spanish-Am. War; duty with tests of mortar fire at Portland, Me., 1901-02; on march with 6th Battery, Field Arty., from Ft. Riley, Kan., to Ft. Sam Houston, Tex., Nov. 1905-Jan. 1906; comd. Ft. Rosecrans and Arty. Dist. of San Diego, 1907; comdg. Ft. Strong, Mass., 1910; insp. instr. R.I.N.G., 1911-15; comdg. Ft. Williams, Me., and coast defenses, Portland, 1915-Feb. 1918; comd. 31st Heavy Arty. Brig., A.E.F., Feb.-Aug. 1918; chief of arty., 3d Army Corps., A.E.F., Aug.-Oct. 1918; remanded to regular rank of col. after the armistice; comd. Camp de Souge, later Embarkation Camp, Pauillac, France, Nov. 1918-Feb. 1919; comd. Ft. Howard, Md. and coast defenses, Baltimore, Apr.-Dec. 1919; retired Dec. 6, 1919. Participated in Marne-Aisne, Oise-Aisne and Meuse-Argonne offensives. Home: San Diego, Calif. Died Feb. 4, 1939.

GATES, Charles Gilbert, broker; b. Turner Junction (now West Chicago), Ill., May 21, 1876; s. John W. and Dellora R. (Baker) G.; ed. Smith Acad., St. Louis, and at Lake Forest, Ill.; m. Mary W. Edgar, Nov. 22, 1898. Became clerk (1893) and later (1895) asst. to pres. of Consol. Steel & Wire Co.; partner in Baldwin, Gurney & Co., stock and comm. brokers, Chicago, 1897-99; organized (1899) First Nat. Bank, Port Arthur, Tex., Port Arthur Rice Milling Co., and Port Arthur Light & Power Co.; has been sec. and treas. Omaha, Kansas City & Eastern, Kansas City & Northern Connecting, and Davenport, Rock Island and Northwestern rys. Home: New York, N.Y. Died Oct. 28, 1913.

GATES, Charles Winslow, governor; b. Franklin, Vt., Jan. 12, 1856; s. Harrison and Loena Rebecca

(Shedd) G.; grad. St. Johnsbury (Vt.) Acad., 1880; m. Mary Elisabeth Mayden, Apr. 9, 1890 (died 1913); children—Mrs. Edith Rebecca Davis, Paul Hayden, Winslow Harrison; m. 2d, Mary Ellen Ide, 1924. Engaged in farming since boyhood, and lives on farm where was born; teacher, Franklin (Vt.) Acad., 1880-84; mcht., Franklin, 1884-1913; now pres. Franklin Telephone Co. Mem. Vt. Ho. of Rep., 1898-99, Senate, 1900-01; state highway commr., 1904-15; gov. of Vt., 1915-17. Trustee Haston Library, Franklin, St. Johnsbury Academy (pres. bd.); pres. Franklin County Fair Assn. 18 yrs.; chmn. State Highway Board. Republican. Conglist. Home: Franklin, Vt. Died July 1, 1927.

GATES, Ellen M. Huntington, author; b. Torrington, Conn. (youngest sister late Collis P. Huntington); m. Isaac E. Gates. Writer of hymns: The Home of the Soul; Eternity; The Prodigal Child; Slumber Song; etc.; also of The Body to the Soul (Harper's Mag., Aug., 1899), and much other verse in magazines. Author: Treasures of Kurium (collected poems), 1897; The Dark; To the Unborn Peoples (collected poems), 1910. Died Oct. 23, 1920.

GATES, Elmer, psychologist; b. nr. Dayton, O., 1859; s. Jacob and Phoebe Goetz; ed. in common and normal schools, but mostly by pvt. tutors, followed by spl. courses in several colleges; m. Phebe Edson, 1895. Evolved a practical art of brain or mind-building by systematic means, which causes an increase in the structural elements of the brain-cells, fibers and whole nervous system, increases mental capacity and skill; has made numerous other discoveries in exptl. psychology out of which he has evolved an art of using the mind more efficiently in the processes of discovery, invention, etc.; has done original work in electric meteorology, higher temperatures, and made a number of successful electric mining inventions; has laboratories for experimental research in psychology, psychurgy, and in the other sciences. Prof. psychology, Pa. Sch. Industrial Art, Phila. Mus. Author: Psychurgy, or The Art of Using the Mind; Art of Mind-Building, etc. Died Dec. 3, 1923.

GATES, Fanny Cook, prof. physics; b. Waterloo, Ia., Apr. 26, 1872; d. John Cook and Adelia (St. John) G.; B.S., Northwestern U., 1894, M.S., 1895; grad. scholar in mathematics, Bryn Mawr Coll., 1895-96, grad. fellow, 1896-97; European fellow Asso. Coll. Alumnæ, at U. of Göttingen, and Zurich Polytechnic, 1897-98; studied U. of Chicago, McGill U., U. of Cambridge, U. of Pa., Ph.D., 1909; unmarried. Head Dept. of Physics, Woman's Coll. of Baltimore (now Goucher Coll.), 1898-1911; prof. physics and dean of women, Grinnell (Ia.) Coll., 1913-16; dean of women, U. of Ill., 1916-18; gen. sec. Y.W.C.A., N.Y. City, 1918-19; head mistress, Model School of Bryn Mawr Coll., 1922-23; spl. teacher physics, Lincoln and Brearley Schs., N.Y. City, 1920-22 and 1923-28. Was chmn. edn. com. Md. State Fedn. of Women's Clubs, 1909-11. Home: New York, N.Y. Died Feb. 24, 1931.

GATES, Frederick Taylor, business mgr.; b. Maine, N.Y., July 2, 1853; s. Rev. Granville and Sara J. (Bowers) G.; A.B., U. of Rochester, 1877, A.M., 1879; grad. Rochester Theol. Sem., 1880; LL.D., U. of Chicago, 1911; m. Emma L. Cahoone, Mar. 3, 1886. Ordained Bapt. ministry, 1880; pastor Central Ch., Minneapolis, 1880-88; corr. sec. Am. Bapt. Edn. Soc., 1888-93; engaged as business and benevolent representative of John D. Rockefeller, 1893-1912. Chmn. trustees Rockefeller Inst. for Med. Research; dir. Rockefeller Foundation, Gen. Edn. Bd., Internat. Health Bd., Western Md. R.R. Home: Montclair, N.J. Died Feb. 6, 1929.

GATES, George Augustus, univ. pres.; b. Topsham, Vt., Jan. 24, 1851; A.B., Dartmouth, 1873; studied in Germany, 1878-80; grad. Andover Theol. Sem., 1880; (D.D., Dartmouth, 1892; LL.D., U. of Neb., 1893); m. Isabelle Augusta Smith, Dec. 14, 1882. Ordained Congl. ministry, 1880; pastor Upper Montclair, N.J., 1880-87; pres. Ia. Coll., 1887-1901; pastor First Ch., Cheyenne, Wyo., Jan.-Nov. 1901; pres. Pomona Coll., 1902-09; pres. Fisk U., Nashville, Tenn., 1909—. Died Nov. 20, 1912.

GATES, Isaac Edgar, clergyman; b. Mart, Tex., June 26, 1874; s. William Collier and Nancy Caroline (Fowler) G.; A.B., Baylor U., 1903, D.D., 1921; student Baylor Theol. Sem. 4 yrs.; m. Stella Wood, Feb. 26, 1893; children—Pauline, Collier Wood (dec.), Kathleen (Mrs. D. D. Wallen), Stanton E., Annie Jo (Mrs. Ted Sykes). Began preaching, 1897; ordained ministry Missionary Bapt. Ch., 1897; pastor Mart, Tex., 4 yrs., Caldwell, 2 yrs.; gen. missionary in Tex., 1904-05; ednl. sec. Bapt. State Bd. of Ark., 1906-07; financial sec. Southwestern Bapt. Theol. Sem., 1908-09; founder, 1910, pres. until 1916 Wayland Coll., Plainview, Tex.; pastor First Bapt. Ch., Plainview, 3 yrs., First Bapt. Church, Amarillo, 1 yr., First Bapt. Ch., San Antonio, 1920— (built $275,000 ch. auditorium). Mem. bd. dirs. Baptist State Bd. of Tex., Bapt. Standard; trustee Bapt. Acad., San Marcos. Democrat. Mason. Author: Vital Themes, 1914; Watching the World Go By, 1930. Home: San Antonio, Tex. Died July 17, 1933.

GATES, John Howard, judge; b. Waterloo, Ia., Oct. 26, 1865; s. John Cook and Adelia (St. John) G.; Ph.B., State U. of Ia., 1888; student Columbia Law Sch., New York, 1889-90; m. Mary Edna Carter, Nov. 13, 1899; children—Beatrice (Mrs. Frank K. Shuttleworth), John Carter, Hobart Hare. Admitted to S.D. bar, 1890, and practiced at Sioux Falls; mem. Davis, Lyon & Gates; city atty., 1893-94; asso. judge Supreme Court of S.D., Jan. 7, 1913—, presiding judge, 1917, 1922 and 1926. Mem. Bd. of Edn., Sioux Falls, 1906-08; trustee of All Saints Sch.; chancellor Missionary Dist. of S.D., P.E. Ch., 1905—, and mem. Court of Review, Province of the Northwest; lay deputy, Triennial Conv. P.E. Ch., many times. Republican. Mason. Author: Annotations South Dakota Constitution, 1915, 17, 21, 23, 25, and Revised Code, 1919; Annotations Dakota Code of 1877, 1918. Home: Sioux Falls, S.D. Died Nov. 8, 1927.

GATES, John Warne, capitalist; b. on farm nr. Turner Junction (now West Chicago), Ill., 1855; s. Asel A. and Mary G.; ed. in country schs.; m. Dellora R. Baker, Feb. 25, 1874; father of Charles Gilbert G. Conducted small hardware store at Turner Junction, Ill.; became salesman in Texas, introducing barbed wire for I. L. Ellwood; built up large business; established for himself in St. Louis; organized Southern Wire Co., 1880; later in Braddock Wire Co., nr. Pittsburgh; absorbed two other cos., 1892, in Consol. Steel & Wire Co.; sold it to Federal Steel Co., 1898; organized Am. Steel & Wire Co. (now part of U.S. Steel Corp.), 1897; identified with numerous large interests in ry. and industrial stock. Was col. Ill. militia, 1897-1901. Died 1911.

GATES, Josephine Scribner, author; b. Mt. Vernon, O., Sept. 12, 1859; d. Charles H. and Mary E. (Morehouse) Scribner; grad. pub. schs., Toledo, O., 1879; m. Charles H. Gates, Oct. 12, 1881; children—Alice (dec.), Jessie, Charlotte. Author: The Story of Live Dolls, 1901; More About Live Dolls, 1903; Little Girl Blue, 1910; The Turkey Doll, 1912; Nannette and the Baby Monkey; Nannette Goes to Visit Her Grandmother; The Secret of Live Dolls, 1924. Home: Ottawa Hills, Toledo, O. Died Aug. 21, 1930.

GATES, Merrill Edwards, educator, lecturer, author; b. Warsaw, N.Y., Apr. 6, 1848; s. Seth M. (late congressman and anti-slavery leader) and Fanny Jeanette (Parsons) Gates; bro. of Lewis Edwards G.; A.B., U. of Rochester, 1870, A.M., 1873; Ph.D., U. State of N.Y., 1880; (LL.D., Princeton and Rochester, 1882, Columbia, 1891, Williams, 1893; L.H.D., Columbia, 1887); m. Mary C., d. William S. Bishop, of Rochester, N.Y., Apr. 10, 1873 (died 1905); m. 2d, Elizabeth Palmer, d. Franklin H. Head, of Chicago, June 14, 1913. Principal of Albany Boys' Acad., 1870-82; pres. Rutgers Coll., 1882-90; pres. Amherst Coll., 1890-99; mem., 1884—, chmn., 1890-99, sec., 1899-1912, U.S. Bd. of Indian Commrs. Licensed preacher Congl. Ch., 1899—; pres. Am. Missionary Assn., 1892-98; pres. Lake Mohonk Indian Conf., 8 yrs.; mem. Internat. Com. Y.M.C.A., 1882-1902; v.p. Am. Bible Soc., Am. Tract Society. Author: International Arbitration, 1897; Highest Use of Wealth, 1901, etc. Home: Washington, D.C. Died Aug. 11, 1922.

GATES, Milo Hudson, clergyman; b. Gardner, Mass., June 29, 1866; s. Samuel Gerry and Eliza (Ray) G.; A.B., Amherst College, 1886, D.D., 1930; B.D., Gen. Theol. Sem., 1889; D.D., U. of the South, 1910; S.T.D., St. Stephen's Coll., 1910, Columbia U., 1930; m. Pauline Gavit, Oct. 4, 1892. Deacon, 1889, priest, 1890, P.E. Ch.; asst. minister Ch. Ascension, New York, 1889-92; rector Ch. Ascension, Ipswich, Mass., 1892-99, St. Stephen's, Cohasset, Mass., 1899-1904, Ch. Intercession, New York, 1904-07; vicar Chapel Intercession, Trinity Parish, N.Y., 1907-29; dean Cathedral of St. John the Divine, N.Y. City, 1930—. Dir. Church Life Ins. Corp., Church Hymnal Corp. Chaplain 8th Regt. Inf. Mass. Vol. Militia, 1897-1902, 22d Regt. Engrs., 1917—. Trustee P.E. Pub. Sch. Corp., Home for Old Men and Aged Couples, St. Luke's Home, House of the Holy Comforter. Fellow Am. Geog. Society. Died Nov. 27, 1939.

GATES, Owen Hamilton, librarian; b. Tinmouth, Vt., Oct. 18, 1862; s. Rev. Matthew Alonzo and Dency L. (Ward) G.; A.B., Dartmouth, 1883, Ph.D., 1887; studied U. of Leipzig, 1883-84; grad. Union Theol. Sem., 1889; fellow of same in Univ. at Berlin, 1889-91; m. Henrietta Middlekauff, Aug. 3, 1891 (died 1931); children—Gaylord Merritt, Harold Emery. Ordained Congl. ministry, 1891; instr. Latin, Dartmouth, 1884-85; instr. Hebrew, Union Theol. Sem., 1891-92; prof. O.T. lang. and lit., Oberlin Theol. Sem., 1892-99; instr. Hebrew, 1902-08, asst. librarian, 1903-05, librarian, 1908-11, Andover Theol. Sem.; librarian, Andover-Harvard Theol. Library, 1911-36. Home: New Castle, N.H. Died Jan. 1940.

GATES, Philetus Warren, mfr.; b. Chicago, June 23, 1857; s. Philetus W. and Abigail E. (Scoville) G.; ed. acads. Lake Geneva, Wis., and Woodstock, Ill.; m. Phimelia Winter, July 31, 1880. Mgr., 1875-87, then propr. of the Gault House, which was built by his father; supt. of the Gates Iron Works, 1887-94, and v.p. and pres. until 1901, when the business was purchased by Allis-Chalmers Co.; became mgr. of the Gates plant of Allis-Chalmers Co. and later elected 3d v.p. and gen. supt. of Allis-Chalmers Co., and had charge of the operating of its plants until Apr. 1904 (resigned); pres. Hanna Engring. Works, 1908-22, dir., 1904—. Home: Evanston, Ill. Died Nov. 7, 1933.

GATES, Susa Young, author; b. Salt Lake City, Utah, Mar. 18, 1856; d. Brigham and Lucy (Bigelow) Young; attended father's pvt. sch.; grad. Brigham Young U., Provo, Utah; m. Jacob F. Gates, Jan. 5, 1880; children—Brigham Cecil, Harvey H., Franklin Young, Mrs. Leah D. Widtsoe, Mrs. Lucy Bowen. Organized music dept., 1878-79, domestic science dept., 1897-98, of Brigham Young U., and now trustee same. Founded, 1889, and was editor and owner for 11 yrs. of The Young Woman's Journal, Salt Lake City, and after it was successfully established presented it to the Young Ladies' Mutual Improvement Assn., which now publishes it. Mem. bd. Y.L.M.I.A., 1889-1911; editor Relief Society Mag., 1914-21; mem. bd. State Agrl. Coll., 1905-11. Latter Day Saint. Republican. Author: Lydia Knight's History, 1885; Life Story of Brigham Young (with Leah D. Widtsoe), 1931. Genealogist of Young Family; editor geneal. dept. Deseret News. Home: Salt Lake City, Utah. Died May 27, 1933.

GATEWOOD, James Duncan, officer Med. Corps, U.S.N.; b. Halifax Co., Va., May 24, 1857; s. Robert (D.D.) and Harriet Elizabeth (Duncan) G.; ed. Norfolk Acad. (father prin.); B.S., Va. Mil. Inst., 1876; M.D., U. of Va., 1879 (spl. certificate in chemistry); post-grad. work, N.Y. Univ. and Bellevue Hosp. Medical Coll.; (hon. M.A., Va. Mil. Inst., 1916); m. Anne Wythe Mallory Critcher, June 12, 1883. Commd. asst. surgeon U.S. Navy, July 6, 1880; promoted passed asst. surgeon, July 6, 1883; surgeon, Jan. 28, 1896; med. insp., Sept. 19, 1908; med. dir., July 12, 1911. Served on Franklin, New Hampshire, Kearsarge, Dispatch (when she was lost in 1891), Dolphin, Puritan, Lancaster, Yankee, Tennessee, California; asst. to Bur. Medicine and Surgery, 1900-02; instr. naval hygiene, U.S. Naval Med. Sch., Washington, 1905-09; fleet surgeon Pacific fleet, 1909-10; pres. Naval Examining Bd., 1910-12; in command Naval Med. Sch. and Naval Hosp., Washington, 1912-16; Naval Examining Bds., 1916-17; in command Naval Hosp., Gulfport, Miss., 1917-21. Mem. mil. com. Nat. Research Council, 1917. Holds Cuban campaign medal and badge, and Victory medal. Fellow Am. Coll. Surgeons. Author: Naval Hygiene, 1909. Retired with rank of commodore, 1921. Died Feb. 27, 1924.

GATLEY, George Grant, army officer; b. Portland, Me., Sept. 10, 1868; grad. U.S. Mil. Acad., 1890; m. Bessie W. Crabb, Feb. 10, 1896. Commd. additional 2d lt. 5th Arty., June 12, 1890; 2d lt. 3d Arty., July 31, 1891; transferred to 5th Arty., Aug. 12, 1891; 1st lt. 2d Arty., Mar. 21, 1898; transferred to 5th Arty., May 4, 1898; capt. Arty. Corps, May 8, 1901; assigned to 3d Field Arty., June 6, 1907; maj. 2d Field Arty., Mar. 11, 1911, to 4th Field Arty., July 21, 1913; col., May 15, 1917; brig. gen. N.A., Aug. 5, 1917. With Siege Battery K, 5th Arty., Tampa, Fla., July-Aug., 1898; organized 17th Battery, and served with same in P.I., 1903-05; participated in various expdns. against the Moros and battery mentioned for "distinguished service"; in Cuba throughout 2d intervention 1906-09; organized and instructed Cuban field arty., 1909-13; Mexican border, 1913-15; Ordance Bd., 1915-17; apptd. comdr. 55th Field Arty Brigade, Camp Sevier, Greenville, S.C., Sept. 1917; trans. to 67th F.A. Brig., 42d (Rainbow) Div., July 1, 1918, and comd. same in Champagne-Marne defensive, and Aisne-Marne, San Mihiel, Meuse-Argonne offensive and occupation of Germany; Camp Dix, N.J., demobilization duty, May 1-Aug. 13th, 1919; comdg. 8th F.A. Brig., and Camp Knox, Ky., Aug. 1919—. Died Jan. 9, 1931.

GATLEY, H(oward) Prescott, lawyer; b. Washington, D.C., Mar. 23, 1875; s. William Albert and Mary Greenleaf (Goodrich) G.; LL.B., George Washington U., 1895, LL.M., 1896; m. Maybelle Hermann, Dec. 17, 1902; children—Helen H., H. Prescott. Resigned as asst. clk. Supreme Court of D.C., 1900; practiced in Washington, 1900-34; pres. and dir. Nat. Savings and Trust Co. Republican. Presbyn. Home: Chevy Chase, Md. Died July 5, 1940.

GATLING, Richard Jordan, inventor; b. Hertford Co., N.C., Sept. 12, 1818. As a boy assisted his father in perfecting machine for sowing cotton-seed; later invented machine for sowing rice; adapted it to sowing wheat and patented it. Grad. Ohio Med. Coll., 1850, but never practiced. Invented, 1862, the revolving gun known as the "Gatling gun"; invented, 1886, a new gun metal, composed of steel and aluminum. Congress voted him $40,000 for proof experiments in a new method of casting cannon. Also invented hemp-breaking machine, a steam plow, etc. Home: Hartford, Conn. Died 1903.

GATSCHET, Albert Samuel, linguist Bur. of Am. Ethnology, Smithsonian Instn.; b. Berne, Switzerland, Oct. 3, 1832; studied at Berne, 1846-52; univs. of Berne and Berlin, 1852-58; (Ph.D., Berne, 1892); m. 1892. Gave spl. attention to linguistics, continuing studies until 1868, when he settled in New York. Since 1874 has made spl. study of languages of Am. Indians; apptd. ethnologist U.S. Geol. Survey, 1877, becoming connected with Bureau of Am. Ethnology, 1879. Home: Washington, D.C. Died 1907.

GATTI-CASAZZA, Giulio, operatic mgr.; b. Udine, Italy, Feb. 3, 1869; s. Senator Stefano and Ernestina Gatti-Casazza; grad. naval engineer, Poly. College, Genoa, Italy, 1890; m. Frances Alda, operatic soprano, Apr. 4, 1910 (divorced 1928); m. 2d, Rosina Galli, June 18, 1930. Dir. Ferrara (Italy) Municipal Theatre, 1892-98, Teatro Alla Scala, Milan, 1898-1908; gen. dir. Metropolitan Opera House, New York, 1908—. Mem. Faculty Council Inst. of Musical Art, New York. Grand Officer Order Crown of Italy; Officer Order SS. Maurizio e Lazzaro; etc. Died Sept. 2, 1940.

GAUGENGIGL, Ignaz Marcel, painter; b. Passau, Bavaria, 1855; s. Ignaz and Barbara (von Hauser Schreiner) G.; grad. Munich Gymasium, 1871, Acad. of Fine Arts, Munich, 1878; unmarried. Came to U.S., 1880; settled in Boston. Received gold medal New Orleans Expn. Represented at Boston Mus. of Fine Arts, Metropolitan Mus. (New York). Mem. council for sch., Boston Mus. Fine Arts. Home: Boston, Mass. Died Aug. 3, 1932.

GAUL, Gilbert William, artist; b. Jersey City, N.J., Mar. 31, 1855; s. George W. and Cornelia A. (Gilbert) G.; studied art under John G. Brown and L. E. Wilmarth, 1872-76; m. Marian, d. Vice Admiral G. A. Halstead, R.N., Eng., Sept. 16, 1898. Splty. hist. and genre paintings; medal, Am. Art Assn., 1882; medal, Paris Expn., 1889; 2 bronze medals, Chicago Expn., 1893; medal, Buffalo Expn., 1901; gold medal, Appalachian Exhbn., Knoxville, 1910. A.N.A., 1880, N.A., 1882. Home: Ridgefield Park, N.J. Died Dec. 21, 1919.

GAULT, Franklin Benjamin, educator, lecturer; b. Wooster, O., May 2, 1851; s. Joseph and Caroline (Zinn) G.; B.S., Cornell Coll., Ia., 1877, M.S., 1880; A.M., 1897; Ph.D., U. of Wooster, 1901; m. Jennie F. Perrett, June 29, 1886. Supt. schs., Tama, Ia., 1877-81, Mason City, Ia., 1881-83, Pueblo, Colo., 1883-88; organized Tacoma (Wash.) sch. system, 1888-92; organized U. of Idaho and was its pres., 1892-98, reorganized Whitworth Coll., Tacoma, 1899, and was its pres., 1899-1906; pres. U. of S.D., 1906-13. Mem. Wash. State Bd. Edn., 1891-92; pres. Ida. State Teachers' Assn., 1893; mem. bd. of visitors, U.S. Naval Acad., 1902. Mason. Home: Sumner, Wash. Died Mar. 16, 1918.

GAUS, Charles H., mayor of Albany, N.Y.; present term expires, Dec. 31, 1907. Republican. Home: Albany, N.Y. Died 1909.

GAUT, John McReynolds, lawyer; b. Cleveland, Tenn., Oct. 1, 1841; s. John Conaway and Sarah Ann (McReynolds) G.; A.B., Rutgers, 1866, A.M., 1869; (LL.D., Mo. Valley Coll., 1906, Rutgers, 1908); m. Michael M. Harris, May 5, 1870 (died 1871); m. 2d, Sallie Crutchfield, Oct. 25, 1876. In practice at Nashville, Dec., 1867—; gen. counsel, Presbyn. Ch. U.S.A., 1906—; atty. Am. Nat. Bank, Nashville, 1883—. Mem. City Council, 1873-74; spl. judge Supreme Ct., Tenn., 1881. Democrat. Mem., pres., and gen. mgr., Bd. Publ. Cumberland Presbyn Ch., 1870-1901; mem. Jud. Commn. Presbyn. Ch. U.S.A., 1908-11; trustee U. of Nashville. Home: Nashville, Tenn. Died Dec. 19, 1918.

GAVIN, Frank Stanton Burns, clergyman, educator; b. Cincinnati, O., Oct. 31, 1890; s. William James (M.D.) and Laura Adelaide (Burns) G.; A.B., U. of Cincinnati, 1912; studied Hebrew Union Coll., Cincinnati, 1908-12, B.H.L., 1918; M.A., Columbia, 1915; Ph.D., 1922; S.T.B., Gen. Theol. Sem., 1915; S.T.M., Harvard, 1917, Th.D., 1919; m. Eula Christian Groenier, June 22, 1921; children—William Francis, James Louis, Peter Michael, Mary Elizabeth Christian, Jane. University fellow in Semitics, Columbia Univ., 1913-14; deacon, 1914, priest, 1915, P.E. Ch.; rector St. Luke's Ch., Cincinnati, 1915-17; asst. Ch. of St. John the Evangelist, Boston, 1917-18; warden collegiate dept. Nashotah House, Wis., 1919-20; prof. New Testament, Nashotah House, 1921-23; Hale lecturer, Chicago, 1921-22; prof. ecclesiastical history, Gen. Theol. Sem., 1923—; Chapman lecturer, London, 1927. Mem. Theol. Com. of World Conf. on Faith and Order. Decorated by King of Rumania as comdr. Order of the Star, also as Patriarch with the Patriarchal Cross of Miron Cristea. Author: Some Aspects of Contemporary Greek Orthodox Thought, 1922; The Ideas of the Old Testament, 1923; Aphraates and the Jews, 1923; The Jewish Antecedents of the Christian Sacraments, 1928; Selfhood and Sacrifice, 1932. Home: New York, N.Y. Died Mar. 20, 1938.

GAVISK, Francis Henry, clergyman; b. Evansville, Ind., Apr. 6, 1856; s. Michael and Mary (Tierney) G.; ed. St. Meinrad's (Ind.) Coll. and Sem.; (LL.D., Notre Dame, 1914). Reporter and editor Evansville Courier, 1874-80; ordained priest R.C. Ch., 1885; asst. rector St. John's Ch., Indianapolis, 1885-90, rector, 1890—; chancellor of Diocese of Indianapolis, 1899—. Vicar Gen., 1918; apptd. Prothonotary Apostolic by Pope Benedict, 1919. Mem. Nat. Conf. Charities and Correction (v.p. 1910-15, pres. 1915-16); mem. Bd. of State Charities of Ind., 1907—; dir. Family Welfare Soc., Indianapolis; v.p. Ind. Chapter Am. Red Cross. Trustee of Indianapolis Foundation. Mem. Indianapolis Chamber of Commerce, Indianapolis Art Assn. Died Oct. 22, 1932.

GAWTRY, Harrison E., capitalist. Chmn. trustees Consolidated Gas Co. of New York; v.p. Astoria Light, Heat & Power Co., N.Y., Mut. Gas Light Co.; dir. Central Union Gas Co., Consol. Telegraph & Elec. Subway Co., N.Y. & Queens Electric Light & Power Co., N.Y. & Queens Gas Co., etc. Died Jan. 29, 1919.

GAY, Edward, painter; b. Dublin, Ireland, Apr. 23, 1837; s. Richard and Ellen (Kilduff) G.; came to U.S., 1848; began to study art in studios in Albany, N.Y., 1854; went abroad, 1862, to study art under Lessing and Schirmer at Carlsruhe, Germany; m. Martha Fearey, of Bedford, Eng., 1864. Splty. landscapes: took Metropolitan prize of $2,000 in 1887 for the picture "Broad Acres," presented to the Met. Mus. of Art, New York; later large canvases are: "Washed by the Sea"; "Atlantis"; "The Suburbs," in Tewksberry Collection, New York; "Where Sea and Meadow Meet" (Governor's Mansion, Albany, N.Y.); "The Waving Grain" (Minneapolis Gallery of Fine Arts); "Happy Summer Fields," etc., bought by various public galleries. Received Shaw prize, Soc. Am. Artists, 1903; Inness gold medal, Nat. Acad. Design, 1905. A.N.A., 1868, N.A., 1907. Home: Mt. Vernon, N.Y. Died Mar. 21, 1928.

GAY, Frank Butler, librarian; b. Granby (now East Granby), Conn., Nov. 15, 1856; s. Alfred and Jane Skinner (Thrall) G.; ed. pub. and pvt. schs.; hon. M.A., Trinity Coll., Conn., 1917; m. Jennie H., d. Maj. Seth E. Marsh, of Hartford, Nov. 22, 1893; children—Constance Marsh, Mrs. Eleanor Marsh Wiley. Asst. Hartford Pub. Library, 1877-83; asst., 1883-90, librarian, 1890—; Watkinson Library of Reference, Hartford. Exec. head Wadsworth Athenæum, 1884-1911, trustee and dir. emeritus. Mem. A.L.A., Conn. Library Assn. (a founder and pres.). Republican. Episcopalian. Home: West Hartford, Conn. Died June 15, 1934.

GAY, Frederick Lewis, antiquary; b. Boston, Mass., Oct. 28, 1856; s. George Henry and Elizabeth Greenough (Lewis) G.; A.B., Harvard, 1878; m. Josephine Spencer, June 5, 1889. Trustee of estates. V.p. Prince Soc.; registrar Colonial Soc. of Mass.; dir. Bunker Hill Monument Assn. Trustee Brookline Pub. Library, 1906-09. Editor: A Descriptive Catalogue of the Massachusetts Exhibit of Colonial Books, at the Jamestown Tercentennial Exposition, 1907. Home: Brookline, Mass. Died Mar. 3, 1916.

GAY, Frederick Parker, pathologist, bacteriologist; b. Boston, Mass., July 22, 1874; s. George Frederick and Louisa Maria (Parker) G.; A.B., Harvard, 1897; M.D., Johns Hopkins, 1901; Sc.D. from George Washington U., 1932; m Catherine Mills Jones, Oct. 18, 1904; children—Louisa Parker, Lucia Chapman, Frederick P. (dec.), William. Asst. on Johns Hopkins Med. Commn. to Philippines, 1899; asst. demonstrator pathology U. of Pa., 1901-03; fellow, Rockefeller Inst. for Med. Research, 1901-03; research student Pasteur Institute, Brussels, 1903-06; bacteriologist, Danvers Insane Hosp., 1906-07; asst. and instr. in pathology, Harvard Med. Sch., 1907-10; prof. pathology U. of Calif., July 1910-21, prof. bacteriology, 1921-23; prof. bacteriology, Columbia, 1923—. Maj., M.C., U.S.A., 1918-19; mem. med. sect. Nat. Research Council, 1917-24, chmn., 1922-23, chmn. Med. Fellowship Bd., 1922-26; C.R.B. exchange prof. to Belgian univs., 1926-27. Comdr. Order of Crown of Belgium. Republican. Author: Studies in Immunity, 1909; Typhoid Fever, 1918; Agents of Disease and Host Resistance (with others), 1935; The Open Mind—a Life of Elmer Ernest Southard. Home New Hartford, Conn. Died July 14, 1939.

GAY, George Washington, surgeon; b. Swanzey, N.H., Jan. 14, 1842; s. Willard and Fanny (Wright) G.; acad. edn., Swanzey, N.H., and Bernardston, Mass.; M.D., Harvard, 1868; hon. A.M., Dartmouth, 1895; m. Mary E. Hutchinson, Nov. 1868 (died 1873); m. 2d, Grace Greenleaf Hathorne, Nov. 1875. Surgeon Boston City Hosp. many years; instr. clin. surgery, 1888-1900, lecturer, 1900-07, Harvard Med. School. Trustee Wrentham State Sch. for the Feeble Minded. Retired after practicing 55 yrs. Home: Chestnut Hill, Mass. Died May 30, 1931.

GAY, H(arry) Nelson, author; b. Newton, Mass., Aug. 4, 1870; s. L. Bachelor and Antoinette A. (Kenny) G.; A.B., Amherst, 1891; A.M., Harvard, 1896; fellow of Harvard, 1900-03; m. Eugenie Guthrie, Apr. 23, 1896. V.p. exec. com. Keats-Shelley Memorial Assn., Rome; v. chmn. bd. trustees Library for Am. Studies in Italy, pres. Phi Beta Kappa Assn. of Italy, and chmn. Roosevelt Memorial Assn. in Italy; hon. sec. Am. Relief Com., Rome, for earthquake sufferers in Sicily and Calabria, and conducted Am. relief expdn. into Calabria, 1909; rep. in Italy, Am. Poets' Ambulances, 1917-18; gen. rep. Italian War Relief Fund of America, 1918-22. Collected noted library upon history of Italy, 1815-70. Comdr. Order St. Maurice and St. Lazaraus, and Comdr. Order Crown of Italy. Founding mem. Nat. Soc. for Modern Italian History; mem. Royal Italian Commn. for Nat. History. Author: Abramo Lincoln (in Americani Illustri series); Cavour e l'Incognita; Strenuous Italy, 1927. Editor: Italy's Great War and Her National Aspirations; Americani Illustri; (with Sir Rennell Rodd) Bulletin of the Keats-Shelley Memorial. Collaborator on "The Inquiry," directed by Col. House, 1918-19, to obtain data for the Peace Conference. Died Aug. 13, 1932.

GAY, Walter, artist; b. Hingham, Mass., Jan. 22, 1856; s. Ebenezer and Ellen Blake (Blood) G.; ed. Roxbury Latin Sch.; m. Matilda E. Travers, 1889. Began to paint flower subjects, 1873; went to Paris, 1876, to study art; pupil of Bonnât. Constant exhibitor at Paris Salon; painted the large picture "Benedicite," now in Museum at Amiens, France; "Las Cigarreras," in the Luxembourg, Paris; also pictures in London, Met. Mus. of Art, New York, and Mus. Fine Arts, Boston; represented in Mus. of Brussels, Pinakothecq Mus., Munich, Carnegie Inst., Pittsburgh, Pa. Acad. Fine Arts. Gold medals at Antwerp, Vienna, Berlin, Munich, Paris, and Hors Concours, Paris. Life fellow Met. Mus. of Art, New York; created Chevalier Legion of Honor, 1894; officer Legion of Honor, 1906, comdr., 1927. Mem. Nat. Inst. Arts and Letters. Died July 14, 1937.

GAY, W(inckworth) Allan, painter; b. W. Hingham, Mass., Aug. 18, 1821; s. Ebenezer and Mary Allyn (Otis) G.; common school edn.; began study of art at age of 17, under Robert W. Weir, prof. drawing at U.S. Mil. Acad.; went to Europe, 1847, studied under Troyon at Paris, visited Italy, Switzerland, etc., returning to U.S., 1850; unmarried. Opened studio in Boston; splty. landscapes; spent winter of 1874 on the Nile; went to Japan, 1877, staying 3 yrs.; passed 1 winter in China and 1 in India; returned through Europe, passing 2 yrs. in Paris; returned to U.S.; living in retirement at native place. Died 1910.

GAYLEY, Charles Mills, univ. prof.; b. Shanghai, China, Feb. 22, 1858; s. Rev. Samuel Rankin and Sarah S. (Mills) G.; student Blackheath, Eng., 1867-74, Royal Acad. Instn., Belfast, 1874-75; B.A., U. of Mich., 1878; student Giessen and Halle, 1886-87; Litt.D., Kenyon, 1900; LL.D., Glasgow, 1901, U. of Mich., 1904, U. of Calif., 1923; m. Sallie Pickett, d. late Rt. Rev. Samuel S. Harris, of Mich., Dec. 17, 1891; children—Mary Harris (dec.), Elizabeth Pickett. Instr. Latin, 1880-84, asst. prof. Latin, 1884-86, asst. prof. English, 1887-89, U. of Mich.; prof. English, 1889-1923, dean faculties, 1918-20, and co-administrator of presidency, 1919, research lecturer, 1921 (prof. emeritus), U. of Calif. Chevalier Legion of Honor (France), 1921. Turnbull lecturer on poetry, Johns Hopkins U., 1921. Dir. Am. Univ. Union (London), 1924-25. Asso. Nat. Inst. Arts and Letters, 1900; pres. Pacific Coast div. Am. Philol. Assn., 1902-03; gov. Calif. Soc. Mayflower Descendants (deputy gov. nat. soc.); hon. mem. Elizabethan Club, Yale; v.p. Shakespeare Assns. of America and London, Irish Texts Soc., Internat. Soc. Apocrypha; hon. pres., English-Speaking Union, Calif.; trustee Am. Field Service Fellowships for France; mem. advisory bd. Berkeley Branches Am. Trust Co. Author: A Guide to the Literature of Aesthetics (with F. N. Scott), 1890; Classic Myths in English Literature, 1893; English in Secondary Schools, 1894; Methods and Materials of Literary Criticism (with F. N. Scott), 1899; Representative English Comedies (4 vols.), vol. I, 1903, vol. II, 1913, vol. III, 1914; The Poetry of the People (with M. C. Flaherty), 1903; R. E. Gibbs' Songs of Contents (edited with intro.), 1903; The Principles and Progress of English Poetry (with C. C. Young), 1904; Plays of Our Forefathers, 1907; Lyric Epic, and Allied Forms of Poetry (with B. P. Kurtz), 1919; The Gayley Anniversary Papers (dedicatory vol.), 1922. Home: Berkeley, Calif. Died July 26, 1932.

GAYLEY, James, mfr.; b. Lock Haven, Pa., Oct. 11, 1855; s. Samuel Alexander (D.D.) and Agnes (Malcolm) G.; M.E., Lafayette Coll., 1876; (Sc.D., Univ. of Pa., and Lehigh U.); m. Julia Thurston Gardiner, Feb. 1884. Chemist for Crane Iron Works, Catasauqua, Pa., 1877-80, Mo. Furnace Co., St. Louis, 1880-82; E. & G. Brooke Iron Co., Birdsboro, Pa., 1882-85; supt. blast furnaces of the Edgar Thomson Steel Works of Carnegie Steel Co., was promoted to mgr. Edgar Thomson plant and later to a mng. dir. Carnegie Steel Co., until Apr. 1901; 1st v.p. U.S. Steel Corp., 1901-09; in charge ore mining, shipping, transportation. Invented a bronze cooling-plate for blast furnace walls, an auxiliary casting-stand for Bessemer steel plants, etc.; received Elliott Cresson medal, Franklin Inst., Phila., for invention of dry air blast. Pres., dir. Sheffield Iron Corp., Am. Ore Reclamation Co. Trustee Lafayette Coll., Tome Inst., Md. Pres. bd. dirs. Am. Inst. Mining Engrs.; mem. Iron and Steel Inst. Great Britain. Home: New York, N.Y. Died Feb. 25, 1920.

GAYLORD, Harvey Russell, med. scientist; b. Saginaw, Mich., Oct. 4, 1872; s. Augustine S. and Ellen Emaline (Warren) G.; ed. Cheltenham Acad., Ogontz, Pa.; M.D., U. of Pa., 1893; m. Bessie May Ketcham, Oct. 4, 1893. Interne Phila. Hosp., 1893; asst. in pathology, U. of Göttingen, 1895-98; dir. State Inst. for Study of Malignant Disease, Buffalo, 1899—; prof. surg. pathology, U. of Buffalo, 1899-1906; surgeon to Erie Co. Hosp., 1900. Republican. Joint author: Gaylord and Aschoff's Pathological Histology, 1901. Maj., M.C. U.S.A., May 20, 1917-Dec. 24, 1918, div. surgeon 99th Div. Home: Eggertsville, N.Y. Died June 21, 1924.

GAYLORD, Truman Penfield, electrical engr.; b. Shelby, Mich., Feb. 15, 1871; s. Edward B. and Maranda G.; prep. edn. Allen Acad., Chicago, 1886-89; studied U. Mich., 1889-92; B.S. in Elec. Engring., Armour Inst. Tech., 1894; m. Helen Ross-Lewin, 1903; children—Katharine (dec.), Marion Helen. Asst. prof. of elec. engring., Armour Inst. Tech., 1894-98; engr., Commonwealth Edison Co., 1898-1900; engr. sales, later acting v.p., Westinghouse Electric & Mfg. Co., 1900-29, v.p., 1929—; v.p. Interboro Improvement Co. Mem. Pittsburgh Chamber Commerce (pres.), Pa. State Chamber Commerce (dir.). Republican. Presbyn. Home: Pittsburgh, Pa. Died July 5, 1931.

GAYNOR, Frank R., judge; b. Hamilton, Ont., Sept. 2, 1852; s. Christopher and Sarah Jane (Stoney) G.; brought to U.S. at age of 3; student Griswold Coll., Davenport, Ia.; A.B., State U. of Ia., 1877; m. Annie C. Judd, Nov. 29, 1877. Admitted to Ia. bar, 1878; practiced with Judge John F. Talbott, 1878-85; resided in Marshalltown, Ia., 1885-86; practiced at Le Mars, with Ira T. Martin, 1886-90; judge Dist. Court, 4th Jud. Dist. of Ia., 1890-1912; justice Supreme Court of Ia., 1912—. Republican. Episcopalian. Mason. Home: Des Moines, Ia. Died 1920.

GAYNOR, Jessie Smith, writer of music; b. St. Louis, Mo., Feb. 17, 1863; d. Henry W. and Susan Fenimore (Taylor) Smith; grad. Pritchett Sch. Inst., Glasgow, Mo., 1881; studied music, St. Louis and Boston; m. Thomas Wellington Gaynor, Jan. 18, 1886. Teacher music, schs. and conservatories, Chicago, St. Joseph, Mo., and St. Louis. Episcopalian. Author: Songs of the Child World (I and II); Lilts and Lyrics; Playtime Songs; Elements of Musical Expression; First Pedal Studies; Songs of the Child World, No. 3; Songs to Little Folks; Five Love Songs; cantata "Return of Proserpina"; Ballad Book, for girls' voices; Miniature Melodies, vols. 1 and 2; Miniature Duets, sacret songs for children. Home: Webster Groves, Mo. Died Feb. 20, 1921.

GAYNOR, William Jay, mayor; b. Whitestown, N.Y., 1851; ed. Whitestown Sem. and in Boston; went to Brooklyn, 1873; worked on New York and Brooklyn newspapers while studying law. Admitted to bar, 1875, and began practice; writer on legal subjects; judge adv. on staff Gen. McLeer, 2d Brigade, N.G.S.N.Y., 1890; became nationally known for his work in breaking up rings within the Democratic party; elected judge Supreme Ct. of N.Y. for terms 1893-1907, 1907-21; elected mayor of New York, 1909. Twice declined Dem. nomination for gov. and also for judge of the Ct. of Appeals, and for mayor of Brooklyn, 1896. Home: Brooklyn, N.Y. Died Sept. 10, 1913.

GAZZAM, Joseph M., lawyer; b. Pittsburgh, Dec. 2, 1842; s. Edward D. and Elizabeth Antoinette de Beelen de Berthoff G.; ed. Univ. of Pa.; admitted to bar, 1864; m. Anna Reading; 1 dau., Antoinette E.; m. 2d, Nellie M. Andrews, 1893; children—Joseph M., Olivia Mary de Beelen. Pres. Rees Welsh Digest & Law Pub. Co. (Phila.), Ames-Bonner Co. (Toledo, O.); v.p. Dent's Run Coal Co.; chmn. of bd. Peale, Peacock & Kerr, Inc. Was mem. council in Pittsburgh and state senator. Republican. Home: Philadelphia, Pa. Died Sept. 25, 1927.

GEAR, John Henry, U.S. senator from Iowa for term 1895-1901; b. Ithaca, N.Y., Apr. 7, 1825; common school edn.; removed to Galena, Ill., 1836; to Fort Snelling, Iowa Ter., 1838; to Burlington, 1843, engaging in merchandising. Mayor of Burlington, 1863; mem. Ia. legislature 6 years and speaker 4 years; gov. Ia., 1878-82; mem. Congress, 1887-91; asst. sec. of treasury, U.S., 1892-93; mem. Congress, 1893-95; elected to the senate, 1894. Republican. Home: Burlington, Ia. Died 1900.

GEARE, Randolph Iltyd, museum official; b. Abingdon, Eng., Feb. 13, 1854; s. Rev. Edward and Ann Jane (Payne) G.; ed. The Derby Sch., Eng.; came to U.S., 1872; m. Mae Julia Cooper, Feb. 28, 1881. Traveled in West, 1872-75; taught in schs., Baltimore, 1875-78; prin. St. Paul's Sch., Baltimore, 1879-80; connected with U.S. Fish Commn. as sec. to Commr. Baird, 1881-82; chief of div. of corr. and documents, U.S. Nat. Museum, 1883—. Compiled a list of Dr. G. Brown Goode's writings, which was published in Vol. II of the Report of the U.S. Nat. Mus., 1897; also a list of the publs. of the U.S. Nat. Mus. up to 1900, and a supplement including the publs. of the Nat. Mus., 1901-06. Episcopalian. Dir. Washington Boys' Club Assn. Home: Washington, D.C. Died Apr. 11, 1917.

GEARIN, John M., senator; b. Umatilla Co., Ore., Aug. 15, 1851; s. John and Ellen (Burns) G.; grad. Notre Dame (Ind.) U., 1871 (LL.D., 1903); admitted to Ore. bar, 1873. Mem. Ore. Legislature, 1874; city atty., Portland, 1875; Dem. candidate for Congress, 1878; dist. atty., Multnomah Co., Ore., 1884-86; apptd. spl. prosecutor for govt. in opium fraud cases, 1893; apptd. U.S. senator, Dec. 13, 1905, for unexpired term (1905-07) of John H. Mitchell. Democrat. Home: Portland, Ore. Died Nov. 12, 1930.

GEDDES, Frederick Lyman, lawyer; b. Adrian, Mich., Nov. 10, 1850; s. Norman and Laura (Casey) G.; A.B., U. of Mich., 1872, A.M., 1875; m. Kate A. Rosebrugh, Dec. 24, 1879. Admitted to bar, 1875; in partnership with Barton Smith, 1875-81, with Clarence Brown, 1882, until the latter's death, 1918; present firm, Geddes, Schmettau, Williams, Eversman & Morgan. Exclusively engaged in recent years in organization and conduct of corps.; dir. Toledo Trust Co., Toledo Glass Co., Owens European Bottle-Machine Co., Toledo Scale Co., etc. Trustee Toledo Mus. of Art. Republican. Unitarian. Mason. Home: Toledo, O. Died Oct. 9, 1931.

GEDDES, Williamson Nevin, editor; b. Newville, Pa., Dec. 28, 1836; s. John Peebles (M.D.) and Catherine I. (Maclay) G.; A.B., Jefferson (now Washington and Jefferson) Coll., 1854, A.M., 1857; teacher, 1854-58; grad. Princeton Theol. Sem., 1861; (Ph.D., Franklin and Marshall Coll., 1887); unmarried. Teacher, in Pa., Ohio, Mass., W.Va., 1861-71; ordained Presbyn. ministry, 1871; pastor Waynesboro, Pa., 9 mos., 1871; in charge Prep. Dept., Hanover Coll., Ind., 1872-73; prof. mathematics, mech. philosophy and astronomy, 1873-76; in charge pvt. sch. Williamsport, Pa., 1881-85; editor bot. dept. Standard Dictionary, 1891-94; prepared all bot. matter for "Addenda," same, 1901-02, and for flora of "Botany All the Year Round," 1903-04; editorial writer with Funk & Wagnalls Co., 1909-10. Home: Williamsport, Pa. Died May 6, 1913.

GEE, Nathaniel Gist, educator; b. Union, S.C., Apr. 20, 1876; s. Reuben Thompson and Gertrude (Gist) G.; A.B. and A.M., Wofford Coll., Spartanburg, N.C., 1896, LL.D., 1926; grad. study Harvard, summer, 1899, U. of Chicago, summer, 1901, Columbia, summer, 1923; m. Christine N. South, June 23, 1923; children—Charles M., Gertrude G., Drucilla E., Claribel. Prin. Jordan (S.C.) Acad., 1896-98, high sch., Marion, S.C., 1 term 1898; prof. natural sciences, Columbia (S.C.) Coll., 1898-1901; same, Soochow (China) U., 1901-20, also head of Dept. of Biology, 1915-20; supt. pub. schs., Summerton, S.C., 1920-21; prof. biology, Winthrop Coll. Summer Sch. for Teachers, Rock Hill, S.C., 1921; rep. of Spencer Lens Co. in Far East, 1921-22; adviser on pre-med. edn., China Med. Bd., Rockefeller Foundation, 1922-25, asst. resident dir., 1926-29; field dir. Div. Med. Edn., Rockefeller Foundation, 1927-28, adviser for China in natural sciences, 1928-32; v.p. Yenching U., Peiping, China, 1932-36; prof. biology Lander Coll., Greenwood, S.C., 1935—. Del. to 3d Pan-Pacific Science Congress, Japan, 1926. Mem. M.E. Ch., South. Author: Chinese Birds (with others), 1926. Home: Greenwood, S.C. Died Dec. 18, 1937.

GEER, Curtis Manning, theologian; b. Hadlyme, Conn., Aug. 11, 1864; s. John A. and Lucretia (Rogers) G.; A.B., Williams Coll., 1887; grad. Hartford Theol. Sem., 1890; A.M., Ph.D., U. of Leipzig, 1894; m. Mary L. Gillette, Sept. 9, 1890; children—Dorothy, Russel Mortimer, Alice, David Livingstone (dec.). Ordained Congl. ministry, 1890; pastor East Windsor, Conn., 1890-92; fellow Hartford Sem., at Leipzig, 1892-94; pastor Danvers, Mass., 1895-97; prof. history and economics, Bates Coll., 1897-1901; asso. prof. ch. history, 1901-06, prof., 1906-22, prof. social service, 1922-33, now emeritus, Hartford Theol. Sem., acting dean, 1928. Lecturer Hartford School of Sociology, 1894-95. Pres. Conn. Consumers League, 1930-33. Home: West Hartford, Conn. Died Aug. 2, 1938.

GEER, Walter, author; b. Williamstown, Mass., Aug. 19, 1857; s. Asahel Clarke and Helen Augusta (Danforth) G.; A.B., Williams Coll., 1878; A.M., 1881; LL.B., Nat. U., Washington, D.C., 1881, LL.M., 1882; m. Mary Potter, Sept. 26, 1883 (died 1931); children—Olin Potter, Walter, Joseph White, Helen Danforth (Mrs. Eugene S. Coler); m. 2d, Mrs. Beatrice Mac Williams Parslow, July 1, 1932. Asst. mgr. Walter A. Wood Mowing & Reaping Machine Co., 1882-86; pres. N.Y. Archtl. Terra Cotta Co., 1886-1918, later chmn. bd.; chmn. bd. Terra Cotta Products Corp.; dir. Chem. Products Corp.; v.p. New York Knife Co. Democrat. Episcopalian. Author: Story of Terra Cotta, 1919; Napoleon the Third, 1920; Napoleon the First, 1921; The French Revolution, 1922; The Geer Genealogy, 1923; Napoleon and Josephine, 1924; Napoleon and Marie-Louise, 1925; Campaigns of the Civil War, 1926; Napoleon and His Family (3 vols.), 1927-29. Translator: Recollections of the French Revolution and the Empire (from the French), 1920. Home: Long Beach, N.Y. Died Feb. 23, 1937.

GEER, William Henry, dir. physical edn.; b. Alexandria, Minn., Jan. 30, 1885; s. Franklin Taylor and Mary Elizabeth (Van Loon) G.; S.B., Carleton Coll. Northfield, Minn., 1908; B.P.E., Internat. Y.M.C.A. Coll., Springfield, Mass., 1913; extension courses, New York U., 1916-17; m. Ruth Edna Wilson, July 30, 1912. Asst. in chemistry, Carleton Coll., 1906-08; science instr. and athletic dir. high sch., Austin, Minn., 1908-09; sec. and recreational dir. Government Club House, Canal Zone, Panama, 1910-12; instr. mathematics, Internat. Y.M.C.A. Coll., 1912-13; dir. physical edn. and supervisor playgrounds, Mt. Vernon, N.Y., 1913-17; asst. insp. phys. training, Mil. Training Commn., State of N.Y., 1917-19. Supervisor physical edn., State of N.Y., July-Sept. 1919; dir. phys. edn. and mem. faculty arts and sciences, Harvard, Aug. 1919—; dir. Summer Sch. of Physical Edn., Harvard; lecturer and mem. faculty Harvard Grad. Sch. Education. Awarded Roosevelt medal for service on Panama Canal. Republican. Unitarian. Organized Dept. of Physical Edn., at Harvard. Home: Cambridge, Mass. Died Apr. 1, 1925.

GEER, William Montague, clergyman; b. Balston, N.Y., Apr. 9, 1848; s. Rev. George Jarvis and Isabelle (Montague) G.; A.B., Columbia, 1869, A.M., 1872, S.T.D., 1914; admitted to N.Y. bar, 1875; grad. Gen. Theol. Sem., 1878; m. Katharine Gridley Throop, Apr. 8, 1880 (died 1906): children—Isabel Montague (Mrs. Elliot H. Goodwin) (dec.), Enos Throop, William Montague, Garrow Throop, Katharine Throop (dec.), Francis Hunt, Cornelia Throop (Mrs. Martin Le Boutillier), Gertrude Marshall (Mrs. Hooker Talcott). Deacon, 1878, priest, 1879, P.E. Ch.; asst. to Rev. Henry Y. Satterlee, Wappingers Falls, N.Y., 1878-79; rector at St. John's, N. Adams, Mass., 1879-80, Christ Ch., Oyster Bay, L.I., N.Y., 1880-88; asst. minister St. Paul's Chapel, Trinity Parish, N.Y. City, 1888-94, vicar, 1894-1918, emeritus. Inaugurated noonday services, and midnight services for night workers, in St. Paul's Chapel, and pastoral work for seamen on steamers and on docks near St. Paul's Chapel, also work for army nurses during World War. Pres. bd. trustees Trinity and St. Agatha's schs., 1920-25; v.p. Soc. Promotion of Religion and Learning; pres. N.Y. Churchman's Assn., 1898; trustee Gen. Theol. Sem., 1892-1913. Home: New York, N.Y. Died Apr. 1935.

GEHRING, Albert, author; b. Cleveland, Mar. 21, 1870; s. Charles E. and Anna Barbara (Fornoff) G.; A.B., Harvard, 1894, A.M., 1895; m. Irma Mueller, Feb. 10, 1898; children—Ilse M., Waldo E., Hermine B. Spl. lecturer, Coll. for Women, Cleveland, 1900-02. Mem. Cleveland Sch. Council, 1902-04 (pres. 1903-04). Author: The Religion of Thirty Great Thinkers, 1925. Home: Cleveland, O. Died Feb. 25, 1926.

GEHRING, John George, M.D.; b. Cleveland, O., July 4, 1857; s. Karl August and Wilhelmina (Vetter) G.; M.D., Western Reserve U. Sch. of Medicine, 1885, D.Sc., 1913; post-grad. work, U. of Berlin, 1891; LL.D., Bates Coll., 1923; m. Marian True Farnsworth, Oct. 20, 1888. Began practice at Cleveland, 1885, practiced at Bethel, Me., specializing in functional nervous diseases, 1895—; dir. Bethel Nat. Bank; pres. Gould's Acad., Bethel. Author: The Hope of the Variant, 1923. In recognition of his work in neurology, a gift of $200,000 was made by William Bingham, II, of Bethel, Me., in 1927, for the construction of one of the two large wards in the New Neurol. Inst. of New York, 168th St. and Broadway, and named "The Gehring Ward and Rooms." Home: Bethel, Me. Died Sept. 1, 1932.

GEHRMANN, Adolph, hygienist, bacteriologist; b. Decatur, Ill., July 19, 1868; s. Theodore A. and Emelie (Jehnke) G.; M.D., Chicago Med. Coll., 1890; m. Albertina Marianne Weinstein, Dec. 24, 1910. Interne Cook Co., Hosp., 1890-92; established Chicago Bur. of Food Inspection, 1893; apptd. prof. bacteriology and hygiene, Coll. Phys. and Surg. (U. of Ill.), 1894 (emeritus); supt. food inspection, and bacteriologist Health Dept., City of Chicago, 1884-1903; organizer and pres. Columbus Med. Laboratory. Presbyn. Home: Chicago, Ill. Died Oct. 3, 1920.

GEHRS, John Henry, author, educator; b. Versailles, Mo., Feb. 2, 1882; s. Judge Henry and Anna (Hirschvogel) G.; grad. Warrensburg (Mo.) State Normal Sch., 1907; B.S., U. of Mo., 1912; M.S., U. of Wis., 1915; grad. work U. of Chicago, U. of Wis. and U. of Minn.; m. Amelia L. Luetjen, Aug. 1, 1905 (dec.); children—Perl Stella, Milton J. H.; m. 2d, Lilly E. Brucher, 1928. Teacher rural schools, 3 yrs.; prin. high school, Pleasant Hill, Mo., 1907-08, Calif., Mo., 1908-11; supt. schs., Pleasant Hill, 1911-14; asst. in agr., State Normal Sch., Warrensburg, Mo., 1914-18; head Dept. of Agr. State Teachers Coll., Cape Girardeau, Mo., 1918—. Active in Red Cross drives, World War. Republican. Methodist. Mason. Author: One Hundred Exercises in Agriculture (with J. A. James), 1915; Productive Agriculture, 1917; Principles of Agriculture, 1919; Live Stock and Farm Mechanics, 1922; Soils and Crops, 1924; Agricultural Nature Study (Books I and II), 1929. Home: Cape Girardeau, Mo. Died June 4, 1939.

GEIBEL, Adam, composer, organist; b. nr. Frankfort-on-the-Main, Germany, Sept. 15, 1855; s. Adam Henry and Louisa (Frey) G.; came to America with parents, 1862; became blind at age of 9 days, through physician's mistake; grad. Pa. Inst. for Instrn. of the Blind, 1874; studied harmony, counterpoint, orchestration and composition under Dr. David D. Wood, of Phila.; Mus.D., Temple Univ., 1911; m. Kate Anna Rinck, Nov. 24, 1881 (died 1906); 1 dau., Kathryn (Mrs. Clifford R. Skinner). Began as organist in ch. position, 1873; organist John B. Stetson Mission, 1885—, and teacher of Bible class; asso. with Dr. Wood at the Temple, 1891-96. First composition published, 1874; organized Geibel & Lehman, 1897 (dissolved); became pres. Adam Geibel Music Co., 1906. Presbyn. Author: Geibel's Collection of Part Songs (for men's voices), 1906; Geibel's Collection of Part Songs (for women's voices), 1906; The Incarnation (Christmas cantata), 1907; Light Out of Darkness (Easter cantata), 1910; Immanuel (Christmas

cantata), 1910; The Lord of Glory (Christmas cantata), 1911; The Light of Life (Christmas cantata), 1914; Resurrexit (Easter cantata), 1917; Heavenly Story (Christmas cantata), 1917; Light and Glory (Christmas cantata), 1923; Sesquicentennial Ode (orchestra, organ and chorus), 1926. Also Sunday-school songs, "Stand Up, Stand Up, for Jesus," "Let the Gospel Light Shine Out," etc. Home: Philadelphia, Pa. Died Aug. 3, 1933.

GEIER, Frederick August, mfr.; b. Cincinnati, June 23, 1866; s. Philip and Sophia L. (Otten) G.; grad. Woodward High Sch., Cincinnati, 1884; m. Juliet Esselborn, Nov. 24, 1904. Engaged in mfg. machinery, 1887—; pres. Cincinnati Milling Machine Co., Cincinnati Rubber Mfg. Co., Factory Power Co., Factory Colony Co. Dir. Ohio Mechanics Inst., Children's Home; former trustee U. of Cincinnati. Republican. Presbyn. Home: Cincinnati, O. Died Mar. 27, 1934.

GEIGER, Ferdinand A., judge; b. Cassville, Wis., Oct. 15, 1867; s. John and Josephine (Scholz) G.; ed. pub. schs.; m. Kathryn L. Mayhew, June 8, 1897. Admitted to Wis. bar, 1890; practiced in Milwaukee; apptd. U.S. dist. judge, Eastern Dis. Wis., Mar. 20, 1912. Home: Milwaukee, Wis. Died July 31, 1939.

GEIGER, Jacob, surgeon; b. Württemberg, Germany, July 25, 1848; s. Anton and Marie Gliova (Eberhart) G.; brought to America, 1856; M.D., U. of Louisville, 1872; (LL.D., Park Coll., Mo., 1907); m. Louise Kollaz, Apr. 13, 1888. Practiced in St. Joseph, Mo., 1870—; dean and prof. surgery, Ensworth Med. Coll., St. Joseph, 1883-1914; prof. surgery, St. Louis U., 1890-1910; pres. bd. mgrs. State Hosp. No. 2, 1910-14; pres. City Council, St. Joseph, 1886-88; pres. Am. Exchange Bank; owner St. Francis Hotel, Leader Dept. Store Bldg. Republican. Presbyn. Mason. Home: St. Joseph, Mo. Died Dec. 8, 1934.

GEIL, William Edgar, explorer, author; b. nr. Doylestown, Pa.; s. Samuel and Elizabeth (Seese) G.; Doylestown pub. schs., Doylestown Sem.; student Lafayette College, Easton, Pa. Received several hon. degrees from colleges; spent 6 months making archæol. studies in Western Asia, 1896; m. L. Constance (B.A.), d. Hon. E. O. Emerson. In 1901 started on journey for comparative study of primitive races and independent observation of the missions of the world; crossed China and Africa; went farther into pigmy forest than Stanley, journey required 4 yrs. Explored the Great Wall of China; visited all the 19 capitals of China, traveled 120,000 miles. Lectured in Australia, Japan, China, India, Great Britain and U.S. Life fellow Royal Geog. Society, Royal Astron. Society. Author: A Yankee on the Yangtze, 1904; The Man of Galilee, 1904, 1906; A Yankee in Pigmyland, 1905; The Men on the Mount, 1905; The Automatic Calf, 1905; The Great Wall of China, 1909-1911; Eighteen Capitals of China, 1911; Adventures in the African Jungle Hunting Pigmies, 1917. Explored the Wu Yo or 5 Sacred Mountains of China, 1919. Home: Doylestown, Pa. Died Apr. 1925.

GEISEL, Carolyn, physician, lecturer; unmarried. Lecturer on general health topics before colleges and chautauquas, 1898—. Mem. health com. Gen. Fedn. Woman's Clubs; chmn. health com. Mich. Fedn. of Woman's Clubs; asso. supt. health and heredity dept. of Nat. W.C.T.U.; nat. lecturer for Med. Temperance Anti-cigarette League, etc. Home: Battle Creek, Mich. Died Sept. 1932.

GEISSINGER, James Allen, clergyman; b. Burbank, O., Oct. 14, 1873; s. James and Henrietta A. (Dorsey) G.; student Ohio Wesleyan U., 1891-92; spl. work in German, Capital U., Columbus, 1894; B.A., Ohio State U., 1895; student in economics, U. of Cincinnati, 1897-1900; D.D., U. of Southern Calif., 1914; m. Effie E. Bryan, June 12, 1895; children—Wayland B., Paul Maurice (dec.), Roger J. Ordained M.E. ministry, 1895; pastor Brosebeck, O., 1895, Finley Chapel, Cincinnati, 1896-98, Ripley, 1899-1900, Mt. Auburn (Cincinnati), 1900-04, Oxford, 1905, El Paso, Tex., 1906, Phoenix, Ariz., 1907-08, University Ch., Los Angeles, Calif., 1909-15, Boyle Heights Ch., 1915-16, First Ch., Long Beach, Calif., 1916-19; exec. sec. San Francisco area, Centenary Conservation Com., M.E., Ch., Sept. 1919-20. Pastor White Temple, Anaheim, Calif., 1920-25, Holliston Av. Ch., Pasadena, 1925-29; supt. San Diego Dist. M.E. Ch., 1929—. Author: Programs and Pointers, 1901; Heart Problems and World Issues, 1914; The Democracy of Methodism, 1920. Died Oct. 21, 1935.

GEISSLER, Ludwig Reinhold, prof. psychology; b. Leipsic, Germany, Sept. 22, 1879; s. Frederick William (M.D.) and Frederica (Dietzmann) G.; Litt.B., U. of Tex., 1905; Ph.D., Cornell U., 1909; m. Sarah Maria Steel, of Ont., Can., June 17, 1909; children—Felix D., Carolyn V. Came to U.S., 1902, naturalized citizen, 1912. Asst. in psychology, Cornell U., 1905-09, instr. 1909-11; research psychologist Nela Research Lab., 1911-12; asso. prof. psychology and dir. Psychol. Lab., U. of Ga., 1912-16; asst. prof. psychology, Clark Coll., Worcester, Mass., 1916-20; non-resident lecturer, Wellesley Coll., 1917-19; asso. prof. and prof. psychology, Randolph-Macon Woman's Coll., 1920—. State mental examiner for Va. Founder, Jour. Applied Psychology, 1916, editor until 1920. Mem. Nat. Research Council, World War. Presbyn. Home: Lynchburg, Va. Died Dec. 14, 1932.

GEIST, Clarence Henry, pub. utilities; b. La Porte, Ind., 1874; s. Ezra and Eloise (Bradley) G.; ed. Valparaiso (Ind.) Normal Sch.; m. Florence Hewitt, 1906; 3 daughters. Pres. C. H. Geist Co., Inc., Phila. Suburban Water Co., Indianapolis Water Co., Am. Pipe & Construction Co.; dir. United Gas Improvement Co., Lehigh Coal & Navigation Co., Lehigh & N.E. R.R. Co. Republican. Presbyn. Home: Villanova, Pa. Died June 12, 1938.

GEIST, Emil Sebastian, orthopedic surgeon; b. St. Paul, Minn., May 9, 1878; s. Emil and Anna (Erd) G.; ed. U. of Minn., M.D., same, 1900; interne, St. Joseph's Hosp., 1900-01; post-grad. work, Paris, Breslau, Vienna, 1901-04; m. Augusta Ohage, May 9, 1911. Practiced, Minneapolis, 1904—; asst. prof. orthopedic surgery, U. of Minn.; orthopedic surgeon, St. Mary's, St. Barnabas, Abbott, Asbury, Swedish, Northwestern hosps.; cons. orthopedist, Minn. State Hosp. for Crippled Children. Fellow Am. College Surgeons, Minn. Acad. Medicine. Maj. Med. R.C., U.S.A., 1915-18. Home: Minneapolis, Minn. Died May 14, 1933.

GELERT, Johannes Sophus, sculptor; b. Schleswig, Denmark, Dec. 10, 1852; s. Ludwig C. F. and Constance A. F. (Pedersen) G.; m. Georgine Betsy Sundberg, Oct. 28, 1896. Apprenticed to a wood carver at Copenhagen, 1867; student Royal Acad. of Fine Arts, 1870-75. Exhibited in the Salon of 1878; came to U.S., 1887, and became citizen, 1892. Exhibited and was mem. Internat. Jury of Award, Chicago Expn., 1893; hon. mention, Paris Expn., 1900. Awarded gold medal at Nashville Centennial Expn., 1897; also from Phila. Art Club; hon. mention and gold medal, Am. Art Soc. Works: Hans Christian Andersen and Beethoven statues in Lincoln Park, Haymarket monument, Chicago; hist. bas-relief, MacVicker's Theatre, and on exterior of the Herald Building, Chicago; also Gen. U. S. Grant's statue at Galena, Ill.; statue of Emperior Napoleon at St. Louis Expn., statue of Denmark for U.S. Custom House, New York; series of statues representing the Roman Civilization, for Brooklyn Inst. of Arts and Sciences; portrait-statue for the Vanderbilt U.; statue of Col. J. F. Stevens, founder of Minneapolis; decoration of Bergen Co. courthouse, Hackensack, N.J., with 9 symbolic statues and a frieze around exterior of dome; for Earnshaw mausoleum, Cincinnati, 6 symbolical statues; portrait statue of C. W. Post, Battle Creek, Mich.; statue rep. the Divine Wisdom, or God Creating the World. Home: New York, N.Y. Died Nov. 4, 1923.

GELLHORN, George, gynecologist; b. Breslau, Germany, Nov. 7, 1870; s. Adolph and Rosalie (Pincus) G.; ed. Gymnasium, Ohlau, Germany, 1876-90; M.D., U. of Würzburg, 1894; m. Edna Fischel, Oct. 21, 1903; children—George, Walter F., Martha E., Alfred A. Asst. in clinics at univs. of Berlin, Jena and Vienna, 1895-99; came to America, 1899; practiced, St. Louis, 1900—; prof. of gynecology and obstetrics, and dir. of dept., St. Louis U. Sch. of Medicine, 1922-32; professor clin. obstetrics and gynecology, Washington U. Sch. of Medicine, 1932—; gynecologist, Barnard Free Skin and Cancer Hosp.; gynecologist and obstetrician, St. Luke's and City hosps., asso. gynecologist and obstetrician, Barnes and St. Louis Maternity hosps.; cons. gynecologist and obstetrician, Jewish and St. Louis County hosps. Home: St. Louis, Mo. Died Jan. 25, 1936.

GEMMELL, Robert Campbell, mining engr.; b. Port Matilda, Pa., July 5, 1863; s. Robert Brown and Anna Eliza (Campbell) G.; B.S. in Civ. Engring., U. of Mich., 1884, C.E., 1895, Master Engring., 1913; m. Belle E. Anderson, Oct. 17, 1888. Engr. surveys and constrn., A.,T.&S.F., R.R., 1884-90; civ. and mining engr. in Ore., Wash. and Utah, 1890-96; mining engr. in Utah, Nev., Ida. and Calif., and engr. of De La-Mar's mines, 1896-1901; mgr. Mexican Mining Syndicate, Mex., 1901-03; supt. of mines for Guggenheim Exploration Co., in Mexico, 1903-05; examining mines in Spain, 1905; gen. supt., 1906-09, asst. gen. mgr., 1909-13, gen. mgr., 1913—, Utah Copper Co.; gen. mgr. Bingham & Garfield Ry. Co.; from Aug. 1, 1919, asst. mng. dir. Utah, Chino, Ray Consol. and Nevada Concol. copper cos. Republican. Presbyn. Home: Salt Lake City, Utah. Died Oct. 25, 1922.

GEMMILL, Benjamin McKee, clergyman; b. New Park, Pa., Oct. 24, 1866; s. John Brown and Agnes Mary (Workman) G.; A.B., Lafayette Coll., 1889, D.D., 1922; McCormick Theol. Sem., 1889-90; grad. Princeton Theol. Sem., 1892; Ph.D., Blue Ridge Coll., New Windsor, Md., 1895; m. Clara Marie Genso, June 1, 1898; children—Charlotte Eleanor, Chalmers Laughlin, Kenneth Wilfred, Janet Muriel. Ordained Presbyn. ministry, 1892; pastor Anacortes, Wash., 1892-93, 1st Ch., Cresson, Pa., 1893-1905; asst. pres. Kendall Coll., Muskogee, Ind. Ty., 1905; connected with The Presbyterian, Phila., 1905-06; pastor Hartsville, Pa., 1908—; also prof. of Bible and philosophy, Beaver College for Women, Jenkintown, Pa. Stated clerk Synod of Pa., permanent clerk 17 years; member Permanent Judicial Com. of Gen. Assembly Presbyn. Ch. in U.S.A.; moderator Phila. North Presbytery; secretary of The Curran Foundation. Democrat. Author: Manual of Parliamentary Practice for Church Courts; Faith for a Bewildered World; Psychology of the Will of God; The Problems of Youth. Home: Hartsville, Pa. Died Mar. 5, 1940.

GEMMILL, Willard Beharrell, lawyer; b. Rigdon, Ind., Aug. 7, 1875; s. Andrew and Maria (Covalt) G.; Ph.B., De Pauw U., 1898; LL.B., Ind. Law Sch., Indianapolis, 1902; m. Florence B. Jones, June 9, 1909; 1 son, Robert Andrew. Admitted to Ind. bar, 1902, and practiced at Marion until 1918; mem. Ind. Ho. of Rep., 1909-11, Senate, 1914-18; city atty. Marion, 1918; spl. dep. atty. gen. of Ind., 1918-20; again in practice at Marion, 1920-25; judge, Supreme Court of Ind. (chief justice part of time), 1925-30; mem. Gemmill, Browne & Campbell, Marion, 1931—. Republican. Mason. Home: Marion, Ind. Died May 24, 1935.

GEMMILL, William Nelson, judge; b. Shannon, Ill., Dec. 29, 1860; s. William and Susan G.; Ph.B., Cornell Coll., Ia., 1886 (LL.D., 1916); m. Edna E. Billings, 1893; children—Jeanette, William B. Supt. pub. schs., Marion, Ia., 1889-90; removed to Chicago, 1891; admitted to bar, 1892; judge Municipal Court, 1906-23; elected judge Superior Court of Cook Co., 1923 for term ending in 1929. Republican. Methodist. Mason. Author: The Witches of Salem; Romantic America; The Kingdom of Hearts; Origin and Romances of Place Names; Jesus at the Bar. Home: Chicago, Ill. Died Mar. 31, 1930.

GENTH, Frederick Augustus, Jr., chemist; b. Phila., Pa., Feb. 12, 1855; s. Frederick A. and Minna P. (Fischer) G.; B.S., U. of Pa., 1876, M.S., 1878; (Pharm. Dr. Medico-Chirurg. Coll., Phila., 1909); m. Louise Thekle Raht, Sept. 8, 1881 (died 1889); m. 2d, Miriam Stoddart Du Bois, Apr. 30, 1890. Asst. in chemistry, Pa. Geol. Survey, 1877-80; instr., 1881-83, asst. prof. chemistry, 1883-88, U. of Pa.; chemist of Dairy and Food Commn., Dept. of Agr. of Pa., 1897-1903; state pharm. examining bd. of Pa., 1901-03; prof. mineralogy and assaying, dept. pharm. chemistry, Medico-Chirurg. Coll., Pa., 1908—; also in gen. practice as analytical and expert chemist. Home: Lansdowne, Pa. Deceased.

GENUNG, George Frederick, clergyman; b. Willseyville, N.Y., Jan. 27, 1850; s. Abram C. and Martha (Dye) G.; A.B., Union Coll., N.Y., 1870, D.D., 1895; also hon. A.M. from Union College, 1922; m. Harriet Elizabeth Bronson, Aug. 3, 1875; 1 dau., Mrs. Sarah Elizabeth Minott. Ordained Bapt. ministry, 1875; pastor Camillus, N.Y., 1875-78, Baldwinsville, N.Y., 1878-81, Amherst, Mass., 1881-84, Huntington St. Ch., New London, Conn., 1885-87; prof. Benedict Inst., Columbia, S.C., 1887-89; pastor Suffield, Conn., 1890-98; prof., 1898-99, dean, 1889-1901, Richmond (Va.) Theol. Sem.; chaplain Conn. State Prison, 1902-03; pastor Brooklyn, Conn., 1905-19, N. Sunderland, Mass., 1919—. Editor Senior Quarterly (Am. Bapt. Pub. Soc.). Author: The Fourfold Story, 1891; Magna Charta of the Kingdom of God, 1900. Died Jan. 6, 1935.

GENUNG John Franklin, college prof.; b. Willseyville, N.Y., Jan. 27, 1850; s. Abram C. and Martha (Dye) G.; A.B., Union Coll., 1870; grad. Rochester Theol. Sem., 1875; A.M., Ph.D., U. of Leipzig, 1881; (D.D., Yale, 1905; L.H.D., Union U., 1913); m. Florence M. Sprague, May 15, 1880. Ordained Bapt. ministry, 1875; pastor Baldwinsville, N.Y., 1875-78, Am. Chapel, Leipzig, 1879-81, Westport, N.Y., 1881-82; instr. English lang., 1882-84, asso. prof. rhetoric, oratory and English lit., 1884-89, prof. rhetoric and English lit., 1889-1906, prof. lit. and Bibl. interpretation, 1906—, Amherst. Author: Practical Elements of Rhetoric, 1886; The Epic of the Inner Life, being the Book of Job, 1891; Outlines of Rhetoric, 1893; The Working Principles of Rhetoric, 1901; Hebrew Literature of Wisdom in the Light of Today, 1906; Outlines of Composition and Rhetoric (with C. L. Hanson), 1915. Died Oct. 1, 1919.

GEORGE, Andrew Jackson, head English dept. Newton (Mass.) High School; b. Goffstown, N.H., Feb. 16, 1855; s. Amos and Dorothy (Turner) G.; grad. Amherst, 1876 (A.M., 1881; Litt.D., 1903); m. Alice Nelson Vant, July 11, 1888. Editor: Coleridge's Ancient Mariner, Critical Essays; Webster's Great Orations; Burke's American Orations; Select Poems of Burns; Tennyson's Princess; Carlyle's Essay on Burns; Burke's Speech on Conciliation; Milton's Comus, Lycidas, etc; From Chaucer to Arnold; Byron's Childe Harold; Select Poems of Coleridge; Wordsworth's Complete Poetical Works; Select Poems of Browning; Lyrical Poems of Browning; Hudson's Essays on English Studies. Home: Brookline Mass. Died 1907.

GEORGE, Charles Carlton, real estate; b. Galesburg, Ill., Mar. 21, 1863; s. John Wesley and Mary Elizabeth (Younger) G.; B.S., Knox Coll., 1885, M.S., 1888, LL.D., 1935; m. Idella Louise Hamlin (A.B., Radcliffe), Dec. 14, 1905; 1 dau., Mary. Began as clk. in real estate office, Omaha, 1885; mem. Potter & George Co., 1890; became pres. George & Co., Dundee Realty Co. Charter mem., pres. Omaha Chamber Commerce; dir. Chamber of Commerce of U.S., 1919-23. Republican. Episcopalian. Home: Omaha, Neb. Died Feb. 18, 1940.

GEORGE, Edgar Jesse, M.D.; b. Fairfield, Ia., May 17, 1863; s. Charles F. and Esther A. (Mendenhall) G.; ed. pub. and pvt. schs., Fairfield; M.D., Chicago Homœ. Med. Coll., 1891. Specialist in diseases of the eye; prof. ophthalmology and otology Gen. Med. Foundation. Fellow Am. Coll. Surgeons. Democrat. Home: Chicago, Ill. Died Oct. 21, 1930.

GEORGE, Harold Coulter, engineer; b. Oil City, Pa., May 24, 1881; s. Wesley and Belle (Coulter) G.; B.S. in Mining, Pa. State Coll., 1904; E.M., U. of Pittsburgh, 1906; m. Laura Holland Painter, June 25, 1908; children—Richard Painter, Julia Elizabeth. Instr. in mining and metallurgy, U. of Pittsburgh, 1904-07; mgr. Columbia Mining Co., Platteville, Wis., 1907-08; dir. Wis. State Mining Sch., 1908-11; chief engr. Wis. Zinc Co., Platteville, 1911-16 and 1918-21, gen. mgr., 1916-17; pres. Platteville Gas Co., 1913-20; cons. practice, 1917-18; oil recovery engr., U.S. Bur. Mines, San Francisco, 1921-23, petroleum engr. in charge Ardmore (Okla.) office, 1923-24; dir. Sch. of Petroleum Engring., U. of Okla., 1924-33; head dept. of oil and gas production, U. of Pittsburgh, 1933—; cons. petroleum engr., U.S. Bur. Mines. Mem. com. which drew up Brief of Zinc Producers of U.S., 1913; com. which drew up Safety Rules for Wis. Zinc Mines, 1915; com. which drew up Safety Orders for Drilling and Production in Oil Fields of Calif., 1924. Author: Oil Well Completion and Operation, 1931. Home: Pittsburgh, Pa. Died Sept. 23, 1937.

GEORGE, Henry, congressman; b. Sacramento, Calif., Nov. 3, 1862; s. Henry G. (polit. economist); ed. pub. schs.; in printing office at 16; m. Marie M. Hitch, Dec. 2, 1897. In newspaper work, 1881—; accompanied his father, 1883, on lecturing tour in Great Britain as sec.; on his father's sudden death during mayoralty campaign, 1897, was nominated to succeed his father as candidate of Jeffersonian party for mayor of Greater New York, but was defeated. Corr. for a syndicate of newspapers and several mags. in Japan, 1906; corr. for Collier's Weekly and other periodicals in Japan and around the world, 1909; campaigned in British Budget gen. election, 1909. Mem. 62d Congress (1911-13), 17th N.Y. Dist., and 63d Congress (1913-15), 21st Dist. Author: Life of Henry George, 1900; The Menace of Privilege, 1905; The Romance of John Bainbridge, 1906. Home: New York, N.Y. Died Nov. 14, 1916.

GEORGE, Joseph Henry, college pres.; b. Cobourg, Ont., May 3, 1852; s. Joseph and Margaret (Armstrong) G.; A.B., Victoria U., Toronto, 1880, A.M., 1882; Ph.D., Boston U., 1884; (D.D., Congl. Coll., Montreal); m. Blanche H. Northrup, June 12, 1889. Pastor Presbyn. Ch., Belleville, Ont., 1884-90, First Congl. Ch., St. Louis, 1891-97; prin. Congl. Coll., Montreal, 1897-01; pres. and prof. homiletics, Chicago Theol. Sem., 1901-06; pastor First Congl. Church, Burlington, Vt., 1906-07; pres. and prof. philosophy, 1907-13, pres. emeritus and prof. ethics and Christian edn., 1913-17, Drury Coll.; retired under Carnegie Foundation as pres. emeritus, 1918. Ad interim pastor First Congl. Ch., St. Louis, 1918-21; pres. Industrial Loan & Investment Co., Springfield, Mo., 1922—. Mem. Springfield Chamber of Commerce. Home: Springfield, Mo. Died Dec. 15, 1923.

GEORGE, Robert James, clergyman; b. Venice, Pa., July 15, 1844; s. John and Jane (Slater) G.; A.B., Westminster Coll., Pa., 1866; grad. Ref. Presbyn. Theol. Sem., Allegheny, Pa., 1870; (D.D., Westminster, and Lenox Coll., Ia., 1892); m. Margaret R. Hamilton, Oct. 28, 1868. Ordained R.P. ministry, 1870; pastor Poland and N. Jackson, O., 1870-75, Beaver Falls, Pa., 1875-92; prof. theology, R.P. Theol. Sem., 1892. Aided in locating and building up Geneva Coll., Beaver Falls, Pa.; sec. bd. of corporators same, 1880-1909; mem. Central Bd. Missions R.P. Ch. Home: Pittsburgh, Pa. Died 1911.

GEORGE, Vesper Lincoln, artist, teacher, b. Boston, Mass., June 4, 1865; s. Alvin and Mary Jane (Benner) G.; ed. pub. schs., Boston; art edn., Art Students' League, New York, 1888-89, Julian Acad., Paris, under Jules Lefebvre and Benjamin Constant, 1889-92; m. Mary Emma Hills, Oct. 20, 1892; children—Dorothy Hills, Eleanor Benner (dec.), Alan Whitman (dec.), Barbara Leland, Elsa Benner (dec.). In dept. of design, Lowell (Mass.) Textile Sch., 1897-1906; head of dept. of design, Mass. Normal Art Sch., Boston, 1901-27; owner and dir. Vesper George Sch. of Art, Inc., Boston, 1924—. Prin. works (murals): Lowell Pub. Library, Bristol (Conn.) Trust Co., McClain High Sch., Greenfield, O. Home: Boston, Mass. Deceased.

GEORGE, William Reuben, founder George Junior Republic; b. West Dryden, N.Y., June 4, 1866; s. John Francis and Eleanor (Baker) G.; common school edn.; removed from his country home to New York, 1880, and engaged in business; m. Esther Brewster, Nov. 12, 1896; children— Eleanor Miller, George Tyson (dec.), Esther Armington, Edith Van Etten. Became interested in boys and girls of the poorer class; during 1890-94 he took parties of 200 to the country for 2 weeks to a month to spend their vacation with him. Appalled at the large number endeavoring to live on charity in 1894 he conceived plan of requiring payment in labor for everything the children received and in addition instituted self-government. From these reforms came the idea of the "Junior Republic," put into operation in 1895, arousing interest as an effectual method in the training of youth in citizenship; he also founded the "Junior Municipality," and the "Social Sanitarium" (prison reform); gen. dir. Nat. Assn. of Junior Republic of America. Author: The Junior Republic, Its History and Ideals. Collaborator, with Lyman Beecher Stowe, Citizens Made and Remade. Home: Freeville, N.Y. Died Apr. 25, 1936.

GEORGESON, Charles Christian, agriculturist; b. on Island of Langeland, Denmark, June 26, 1851; s. J. C. and Jórgine (Hansen) G.; early edn. in pub. and pvt. schs. in Denmark; student of agr. on large estates in Denmark, 1867-72; came to U.S., 1873; B.S., Mich. State Coll. Agr., 1878, M.S., 1882, D.Sc., 1916; m. Margaret Thompson Lovett, Jan. 2, 1882; children—Dagmar, Rosemary, Valdemar. Asst. editor, Rural New Yorker, 1878-80; prof. agr. and horticulture, Texas State Agrl. and Mech. Coll., 1880-83; prof. agr., Coll. of Agr., Imperial U., Tokio, 1885-89; prof. agr., Kan. State Agrl. Coll., 1890-97; was spl. agt. U.S. Dept. Agr. and sent to investigate dairy industry of Denmark, 1893; spl. agt. U.S. Dept. of Agr. in charge of Alaska investigations with headqrs. at Sitka, 1898; agronomist in charge of Alaska Expt. Stas., 1915-28, dir. 1923-28 (retired), disbursing agt. appropriations made for same, 1902—; established and supervised development of 7 agrl. expt. stas. in Alaska. Home: Seattle, Wash. Died Apr. 1, 1931.

GERAGHTY, James M., judge; b. Ireland; s. Patrick and Bridget (Haley) Geraghty; came with parents to United States, 1880; educated in common schools; studied law at Georgetown U., 1 year; m. Nora Toolen, Nov. 16, 1898 (died 1930); children—Thomas, Nora, Helen, Anna, James, John, Patrick, Cecil, Sheila. Admitted to Washington bar, 1897, and began practice at Spokane. Was mem. Wash. House of Reps., 1897; chmn. Wash. del., Dem. Nat. Conv., 1928; corp. counsel, Spokane, 18 years; apptd. dir. of efficiency, Gov. Martin's cabinet, Jan. 1933; apptd. justice Sup. Ct., Wash., Aug. 1933. Home: Olympia, Wash. Died Apr. 29, 1940.

GERAGHTY, Martin John, clergyman; b. Carthage, N.Y., Nov. 11, 1867; classical and scientific edn., Villanova Coll., 1882-85; entered Augustinian Novitiate, 1885 (D.D., degree of Master of Sacred Theology, 1906). Ordained priest R.C. Church, May 31, 1890; pastor Chestnut Hill, Phila.; chosen Master of Novices and Sub-Prior Monastery at Villanova, the mother house of Augustinian Order in America; rector of Augustinian Mission Band. Visited Rome, Italy, to attend middle chapter of the Order; prior provincial of the Order in the U.S., 1902. Founder of Saint Rita's Hall, Villanova. Commissary Gen. over the Italian Augustinian Fathers in Phila., Aug. 1909—. Died Sept. 28, 1914.

GERARD, James Watson, lawyer; b. New York, 1822; grad. Columbia, 1843; practiced law until 1880. Long trustee and inspector public schools; State senator, N.Y., 1876-77. Author: The Pelican Papers, a Satire: Titles to Real Estate in New York City; Title of the Corporation and Others to the Streets, Wharves, Lands and Franchises in New York City; The Peace of Utrecht; Aquarelles (verse); Ostrea (verse); etc. Home: New York, N.Y. Died 1900.

GERBERDING, George Henry, theologian; b. Pittsburgh, Aug. 21, 1847; s. Henry and Josephine (Lustenberger) G.; grad. Thiel Coll., Greenville, Pa., 1873; A.B., A.M., Muhlenberg College, Pa., 1873; D.D., Muhlenberg, 1894; LL.D., Lenoir Coll., 1915; m. Annie Danver, Oct. 31, 1876 (died 1900); children—Esther May, Gus M. (dec.), Mary Emma, Josephine H. (dec.), Annie Comfort (dec.), Ruth Danver, Richard H., William P.; m. 2d, Dorothy Welty, Aug. 4, 1904. Ordained Luth. ministry, 1876; pastor McKees Rocks and Mt. Zion, Allegheny City, Pa., 1876-81, Jewett, O., 1881-87, Fargo, N.D., 1887-94; prof. practical theology, Luth. Theol. Sem., Chicago (now Maywood, Ill.), 1894-1921, Northwestern Luth. Theol. Sem., 1921—. Author: The Way of Salvation in the Lutheran Church, 1887; New Testament Conversions, 1889; The Lutheran Pastor, 1902; The Lutheran Catechist, 1910; Problems and Possibilities, 1914; The Lutheran Church in the Country, 1916. Home: Minneapolis, Minn. Died Mar. 27, 1927.

GERDINE, Thomas Golding, engineer; b. West Point, Miss., June 2, 1872; s. John and Susan (Golding) G.; B.E., U. of Ga., 1891; m. Frances E. Bishop, 1907; m. 2d, Marguerite N. Rowell. Topographic engr. U.S. Geol. Survey, 1893-1907; geographer in charge Pacific div. topographic survey, 1907-11, Northwestern div., 1912-16; major Eng. O.R.C., in charge mil. mapping Tex. and N.M., 1917; geographer in charge Northwestern and Rocky Mountain divs., topographic surveys, 1917-19; topographic engr. in charge Rocky Mountain Div. Topographic Surveys, 1920-21, in charge Pacific Div., Sacramento, Calif., 1922—. Author many maps published by the Survey. Deceased.

GERE, Charles Henry, founder and editor, 1867—, Neb. State Journal; b. Gainsville, N.Y., Feb. 18, 1838; s. Horatio Nelson and Julia Delay (Grant) G.; grad. Dickinson Coll., A.M.; (A.M., U. of Neb.); m. Mariel E. Clapham, Sept. 19, 1871. Private Co. B, 10th Md. inf., during Civil war. Admitted to bar, Baltimore, 1865; moved to Neb.; atty. for Pawnee Co., Neb., 1865-66; mem. legislature, 1866; gov.'s private sec., 1867-68; moved to Lincoln, 1868; State senator, 1869-70, 1881-82; chmn. State central com. 4 terms; mem. State constl. conv., 1875; pres. bd. regents, U. of Neb., 1881-91; postmaster Lincoln, 1891-95; pres. State Journal Co. Home: Lincoln, Neb. Died 1904.

GERHARD, William Paul, sanitary engr.; b. Hamburg, Germany, July 30, 1854; s. Bernhard and Mathilda (Hühn) G.; grad. Poly. Sch., Carlsruhe, Baden, 1875; served as 1-yr. vol. in railroad regt., Berlin, 1875-76; passed exam. as lt. of the reserve; worked 6 weeks at the Gen. Staff under Gen. Helmuth Moltke; civil engr. in Hamburg, 1876-77; came to U.S., 1877, settling in St. Louis; hon.D. Engring., Tech. U., Darmstadt, 1911; m. Selma Weiskirch, May 10, 1881 (dec.); children—Hans W., Norman P. Asst. engr. Dept. Pub. Works, St. Louis, 1877-79; in Capt. James B. Eads' office, 1880; chief asst. engr. to Col. George E. Waring, Newport, R.I., 1881-83; engaged in New York as cons. sanitary expert. Editor Building (archtl. jour.), 1885-86; sanitary engr. on staff state architect of N.Y., 1892-99. Author: Recent Practice in Sanitary Drainage of Buildings, 1890; Gas Lighting and Gas Fitting, 1894; Sanitary Engineering, 1898; Sanitary Engineering of Buildings, 1899; Theatres—Their Safety from Fire and Panic, 1900; The Superintendence of Piping Installations in Buildings, 1907; The Sanitation of Public Buildings, 1907; American Practice of Gas Piping and Gas Lighting in Buildings, 1908; Guide to Sanitary Inspections, 4th edit., 1909; The Sanitation, Water Supply and Sewage Disposal of Country Houses, 1909, 2d edit., 1914; Sanitation and Sanitary Engineering, 1909; The Water Supply, Sewerage and Plumbing of Modern City Buildings, 1909. Naturalized citizen of U.S. Home: Scarsdale, N.Y. Died July 8, 1927.

GERHART, Emanuel Vogel, clergyman (German) Reformed Ch. in the U.S.; b. Freeburg, Pa., June 13, 1817; s. Rev. Isaac and Sarah (Vogel) G.; grad. Marshall Coll., Pa., 1838 (D.D.); ordained to ministry, Aug. 1842; pres. Heidelberg Coll., Tiffin, O., and prof. in Theol. Sem., 1851-55; pres. Franklin and Marshall Coll., 1855-66; prof. systematic and practical theology, Reformed Ch. Sem., Lancaster, Pa., 1868. Author: Institutes of the Christian Religion, 2 vols., 1891; Junior Heidelberg Catechism; etc. Died 1904.

GERICKE, Wilhelm, condr. Boston Symphony Orchestra; b. Graz, Styria, April 18, 1845; ed. Real School, Graz; and at Vienna Conservatorium, for composition under Dessoff, 1862-65; conductor of theatres in different cities, 1865-74, devoting himself to composition; condr., 1874-84, Vienna Hofoper; 1880-84, condr. Gesellshafts Concerte, Vienna; condr. Boston Symphony Orchestra, 1884-89, but returned to Europe because of impaired health; resumed same position on his return, 1898. Hon mem. Gesellschaft der Musikfreunde of Vienna. Composer of many songs, choruses and orchestral works. Home: Brookline, Mass. Died Oct. 28, 1925.

GERLACH, John Joseph, banker, merchant; b. Virden, Ill., June 7, 1865; s. Frantz Joseph and Mary (Gilmartin) G.; pub. sch. edn.; m. Margaret Moody, Jan. 14, 1894; children—Alice Marie (wife of Dr. Joseph C. Stephenson), Margaret Louise (Mrs. Joshua B. Lee), John Joseph (dec.). Moved to Larned, Kan., 1880, Hemphill Co., Tex., 1883, to Canadian, Tex., 1887, to Okla. at opening of Cherokee Outlet, Sept. 1893. Opened large gen. mercantile store, with brother George, at Canadian, 1887, at Woodward, Okla., 1893; sec. and treas. Gerlach-Hopkins Mercantile Co., Woodward. Treas. Hemphill Co., Tex., 1887-94; treas. Woodward Co., Okla., 1899-1901; mem. State Banking Bd., 1914-18; apptd. mem. Coal Commn. (to settle strike of miners), 1919. Chmn. County Council of Defense, World War. Chmn. Okla. Commn. for Adult Blind. Democrat. Baptist. Home: Woodward, Okla. Died Dec. 16, 1931.

GERRISH, Frederic Henry, surgeon; b. Portland, Me., Mar. 21, 1845; s. Oliver and Sarah (Little) G.; A.B., Bowdoin, 1866, A.M., 1869, M.D., 1869; (LL.D., U. of Mich., 1904, Bowdoin, 1905); m. Emily Manning Swan, Dec. 31, 1879. Lecturer therapeutics, materia medica and physiology, 1873-74, prof., 1874-75, U. of Mich.; prof. materia medica and therapeutics, 1873-82, anatomy, 1882-1904, surgery, 1904-11, medical ethics, 1911-15, emeritus prof. surgery, 1911—, Bowdoin Coll. Pres. Me. State Bd. of Health, 1885-89; Shattuck lecturer, Mass. Med. Soc., 1910; cons. surgeon and dir. Me. Gen. Hosp. Fellow Am. Surg. Assn., Am. Acad. Medicine (pres. 1887-88), Am. Coll. Surgeons. Governor State of Me. Soc. Colonial Wars, 1916—. Author: Prescription Writing, 1878. Home: Portland, Me. Died Sept. 8, 1920.

GERRY, Elbridge Thomas, lawyer; b. New York, Dec. 25, 1837; s. Thomas R. G. (formerly U.S.N.) and Hannah G. Goelet, y.d. of Peter P. Goelet; g.s. Elbridge Gerry, V.P. of U.S. and signer Declaration of Independence; A.B., Columbia, 1857, A.M., 1858; LL.D., Nashotah, 1910; m. Louisa M., o.d. Robert J.

and Louisa M. (Storm) Livingston, 1867. Admitted to bar, 1860; mem. N.Y. Constl. Conv., 1867; pres. N.Y. Soc. for Prevention of Cruelty to Children, 1876-1901; v.p. Am. Soc. for Prevention of Cruelty to Animals until 1899; gov. N.Y. Hosp., 1878-1912; commodore N.Y. Yacht Club, 1886-93; chmn. N.Y. State Commn. on Capital Punishment (which substituted electrocution for hanging), 1886-88; chmn. Exec. Com. Centennial Inauguration of George Washington, 1889; pres. Annual Conv. N.Y. Socs. for Prevention of Cruelty, 1889-1903; trustee Gen. Theol. Sem., 1877-1913, Am. Mus. Natural History, 1895-1902; chmn. N.Y. City Commn. on Insanity, 1892. Has pvt. law library of 30,000 vols. Home: Newport, R.I. Died Feb. 18, 1927.

GERSHWIN, George, composer; b. Brooklyn, N.Y., Sept. 26, 1898; s. Morris and Rose (Bruskin) G.; ed. pub. and high schs.; studied piano with Charles Hambitzer, harmony with Edward Kilenyi and Rubin Goldmark; unmarried. Writer of musical comedies and orchestral works. Hebrew. Composer: (musical comedy) La La Lucille, 1919; all music for G. White's Scandals, 1920-24; Our Nell, 1923; Sweet Little Devil, 1923; Lady, Be Good! 1924; Primrose, Rainbow, Stop Flirting, all prod. in London; Tip-Toes, Blue Monday (one act opera), 1922; Rhapsody in Blue, 1923; Concerto in F written for the New York Symphony Soc., 1925; Song of the Flame, Tell Me More, prod. 1925; Oh Kay, prod. 1926; Strike Up the Band, prod. 1927; Funny Face, prod. 1927; musical comedy, Treasure Girl, prod. 1928; Show Girl, 1929; Symphonic Music, An American in Paris, 1928; Girl Crazy, 1930; Delicious (Fox musical picture); Second Rhapsody, 1931; Of Thee I Sing (Pulitzer Prize), 1931; Cuban Overture for Philharmonic Orchestra, 1932; Let 'Em Eat Cake, 1933; Porgy and Bess (opera), 1935; also many songs. Home: New York, N.Y. Died July 11, 1937.

GERSTER, Arpad Geyza (Charles), surgeon; b. Kassa, Hungary, Dec. 22, 1848; s. Nicholas and Caroline (Schmidt-Adamkovich) G.; grad. Acad. Kassa; grad. in medicine, U. of Vienna, 1872; m. Anna Barnard Wynne, Dec. 14, 1875. Asst. surgeon, Austrian Army, 1872-73; surgeon Lenox Hill Hosp., 1878—, Mt. Sinai Hosp., 1879—, New York; prof. surgery, N.Y. Polyclinic, 1882-94, emeritus; former prof. clin. surgery, Columbia U. Author: Recollections of a New York Surgeon, 1917. Died Mar. 11, 1923.

GESNER, Anthon Temple, clergyman, educator; b. Le Roy, N.Y., July 20, 1865; s. Rev. Abraham Herbert and Helen Catlin (Dickinson) G.; ed. St. Stephen's Coll., Annandale, N.Y.; B.A., Trinity Coll., Conn., 1890, M.A., 1894; grad. Brekeley Div. Sch., Middletown, Conn., 1893; m. Blanche Louise Pinniger, of Chippenham, Wiltshire, Eng., June 14, 1893; children—Helen Sargent, Dorothy Dickinson, Conrad Herbert, Harriett Davis. Deacon, 1893, priest, 1894, P.E. Ch.; rector St. Luke's Ch., Detroit, Minn., 1893-95, St. Peter's Ch., St. Paul, 1895-97, St. Paul's Ch., Grand Forks, N.D., 1897-1900, St. Luke's Ch., Billings, Mont., 1900-02; v.-rector Shattuck Mil. Sch., Faribault, Minn., 1902-07; prof. ethics and apologetics, Seabury Div. Sch., and chaplain St. Mary's Hall, Faribault, 1904-10; prof. ethics and evidences of Christianity, Berkeley Div. Sch., 1910-17; rector All Souls Ch., Waterbury, Conn., 1917-30, Christ Ch., Roxbury, Conn., 1931-33. Author: The Gesner Family of New York and Nova Scotia, 1912; The Dickinson Family of Milton and Litchfield, 1913. Home: Roxbury, Conn. Died Jan. 14, 1939.

GESSLER, Theodore, A. K., clergyman; b. Phila., Pa., Oct. 16, 1841; s. Christian H. and Christina (Schaeffer) G.; A.B., Bucknell U., Lewisburg, Pa., 1864, A.M., 1867; Bucknell Theol. Sem., 1863-64; (D.D., Bucknell, 1883); m. Annie L. Sherborne, 1863 (died 1880); m. 2d, Georgie M. Edwards, Dec. 1883. Ordained Bapt. ministry, 1864; pastor Pilgrim Ch., New York, 1864-68, 1st Ch., Elizabeth, N.J., 1868-79, Central Ch., Brooklyn, 1880-86, Grace Ch., New York, 1886-97; retired, but friends erected a ch. at Lake Hopatcong, N.J., and pastor same, Oct. 1910—. Pres. Bd. of Council, Borough of Hopatcong, 1897-1913. Pvt. Co. A, 28th Regt. Pa. Vols., during emergency of Lee's invasion. Pres. N.J. Bapt. S.S. Union, 1870-79; sec. Bapt. Congress, 1895-1912. Chaplain Crescent Lodge F.&A.M., New York, 1880—. Republican. Died Dec. 4, 1925.

GEST, John Marshall, judge; b. Phila., Pa., Mar. 17, 1859; s. John Barnard and Elizabeth Ann (Purves) G.; A.B., U. of Pa., 1879, A.M., LL.B., 1882, LL.D., 1930; m. Emily Judson Baugh, Apr. 17, 1888; children—Sydney Grier, Margaret Ralston. Admitted to Pa. bar, 1882; practiced in Phila., 1882-1911; judge of Orphans' Court, Phila., 3 terms, 1911-41. Vice-provost Law Acad., 1911, provost, 1932; trustee Free Library of Phila.; trustee U. of Pa., 1919-27, Presbyn. Hosp., 1896-1916. Chairman commn. to codify and revise the law of decedents' estates, 1915-17; the commn. reported 7 acts which were adopted by the legislature and approved by the gov., June 7, 1917. Republican. Author: Drawing Wills and Settlement of Estates in Pennsylvania, 1910; The Lawyer in Literature, 1913; The Old Yellow Book—Source of Browning's The Ring and the Book, 1925. Home: Overbrook, Pa. Died Nov. 30, 1934.

GEST, Joseph Henry, museum dir.; b. Cincinnati, O., Apr. 24, 1859; s. Joseph John and Susannah (Bailey) G.; A.B., Harvard, 1880; L.H.D., U. of Cincinnati, 1922; m. Lillie Schultze, 1887 (died 1925); children—Susannah (Mrs. Philip Hinkle), Frederick Schultze (dec.), Elizabeth Harriet (dec.), Henry. Asst. to the dir., 1888-89, asst. dir. and sec., 1889-1902, dir. and sec., 1902-29, dir. emeritus, Cincinnati Museum Assn. (mus. of art and archeology and art acad.). Vice-pres. Rookwood Pottery, 1902, pres., 1914. Sec. Municipal Art Soc., 1894-1915. Mem. Nat. Gallery of Art Commn., 1921. Home: Cincinnati, O. Died June 26, 1935.

GEST, William Purves, banker; b. Phila., Pa., Feb. 27, 1861; s. John Barnard and Elizabeth Ann (Purves) G.; A.B., U. of Pa., 1880, A.M., 1883, LL.B., 1883, and LL.D. from same U., 1932; m. Isabel Thorn Howell, Nov. 15, 1894; children—Mrs. Isabel Rotan, Lillian. Admitted to Pa. bar, 1883; practiced with bro. John Marshall G., until 1889; with Fidelity Trust Co. from 1889, pres., 1915-26, and chmn. bd. Fidelity-Phila. Trust Co., from consolidation of Fidelity Trust Co. and Phila. Trust Co., July 8, 1926; mem. bd. dirs. First Nat. Bank, Lehigh Coal and Navigation Co., Lehigh&N.E. R.R. Co., Phila. Traction Co., etc. Republican. Presby. Home: Merion, Pa. Died Jan. 12, 1939.

GESTEFELD, Ursula Newell, author; b. Augusta, Me. Founder of system of thought known as the Science of Being; instr. for Exodus Club organized in Chicago, 1897, which later became Ch. of the New Thought and Coll. of the Science of Being (both incorporated); 1st pastor of the ch. and head of the coll. Author: The Metaphysics of Balzac, 1898; The Builder and the Plan, 1898; Reincarnation or Immortality, 1899; The Science of The Larger Life, 1905; The Master of the Man, 1907. Died Oct. 22, 1921.

GETCHELL, J(ohn) Stirling, advertising; b. New York, N.Y., July 7, 1899; s. John Burt and Edna (Locke) G.; student Peddie Inst., 1916-17; m. Marjorie Lillian Jelliff, Sept. 2, 1919 (divorced 1936); 1 son, John Stirling; m. 2d, Sarah Paschall Davis, Dec. 21, 1936; 1 son, David Paschall. Began as advertising writer, 1919; asso. with various advt. agencies, including Lord & Thomas, Frank Seaman, Inc., J. Walter Thompson, George Batten Co., 1919-31; formed own agency, J. Stirling Getchell, Inc., 1931, becoming pres. Served with Machine Gun Troop, Squadron A, Nat. Guard, and Air Service U.S. Army, 1917-18. Republican. Home: Greenwich, Conn. Died Dec. 17, 1940.

GETTEMY, Charles Ferris, statistician; b. Chicago, Ill., Mar. 12, 1868; s. Robert H. and Mary E. (Ferris) G.; A.B., Knox Coll., 1890, A.M., 1893; A.B., Harvard, 1891; m. Hattie Brockway, Dec. 28, 1897; children—Catharine Ellen, Richardson; m. 2d, Bertha R. Cheney, Jan. 1, 1932. Served as reporter and Washington corr. Boston Daily Advertiser, 1891-99, Boston Herald, 1899-1905; sec. to Gov. Curtis Guild, Jr., of Mass., 1905-07; dir. Mass. Bur. of Statistics, 1907-19; asst. federal reserve agt., Fed. Reserve Bank of Boston, 1919-37. Supervisor 13th U.S. Census, for Mass. Dir. mil. enrollment for Mass. under Selective Draft Act, 1917; chmn. Mass. Homestead Commn., 1911-19. Fellow Am. Statis. Assn. Author: Memoir and Genealogy of Silvanus Ferris, 1935. Home: Dorchester, Mass. Died 1939.

GETTY, Robert N., army officer; b. Ft. Hamilton, N.Y., Jan. 17, 1855; s. Gen. C. W. and Elizabeth Graham (Stevenson) G.; grad. U.S. Mil. Acad., 1878; m. Cornelia T. Colegate, Oct. 14, 1885. Additional 2d lt. 22d Inf., June 14, 1878; promoted through grades to brig. gen., Aug. 5, 1917. Served with Casey's scouts against Sioux Indians, 1890-91, with 5th Army Corps in Cuba, 1898, participating in battles of El Caney and San Juan, and in siege of Santiago; in P.I., 1900-03, 1906-07, 1908-11; comd. Recruit Depot, Ft. Logan, Colo., 1914-17; apptd. comdr. 175th Inf. Brigade, Camp Dodge, Ia., Sept., 1917. Home: Warrenton, Va. Died Apr. 15, 1941.

GETZ, George Fulmer, coal operator; b. Mechanicsburg, Pa., Dec. 26, 1865; s. John and Amanda G.; ed. dist. sch.; m. Susan D. Rankin, Dec. 7, 1904; children—George Fulmer, James Rankin. Came to Chicago, Ill., at 14; with B.&O. R.R. until 1885, Weaver, Tod & Co., coal, until 1890; mem. Weaver, Getz & Co., 1890-95; in business on own account, 1895—; chmn. bd. Globe Coal Co.; receiver Goodrich Transit Co., Miami Coal Co.; dir. and mem. finance com. Consumers Co. (Chicago); dir. and mem. exec. com. City Nat. Bank & Trust Co. Treasurer Republican Nat. Com., 1933—. Hon. vice chmn. Governor's Commn. on Unemployment and Relief; gen. chmn. Sports Com. of Century of Progress Expn., Chicago, 1933, also a founder and trustee; dir. Chicago Boys Clubs; state chmn. Navy Day; trustee Policemen's Annuity and Benefit Fund (Chicago). Mem. Ill. State Athletic Commn., 1929—. In charge gen. relief work as asso. dir. Am. Red Cross, in France, rank of maj., 1917-18. Republican. Baptist. Home: Chicago, Ill. Died Feb. 11, 1938.

GEYER, Lee Edward, congressman; b. Wetmore, Kan., Sept. 9, 1888; s. Jacob and Mary Helena (Zabel) G.; A.B., Baker U., Kan., 1922; student U. of Wis., summer of 1927, U. of Southern Calif., 1923-24; m. Nellie Lucille Cordts, Dec. 11, 1920; children—Robert Lee, John J. Teacher rural schools of Kansas, 1908-12; prin. Hamlin (Kan.) High Sch., 1916-18, Corning (Kan.) High Sch., 1919-23, Duncan (Ariz.) High Sch., 1925-27; teacher of social sciences, Los Angeles City High Schools, 1927-38; mem. 76th Congress (1939-41), 17th Calif. Dist.; mem. Calif. State Assembly, 1935-36. Served in O.T.C., 1917-18. Methodist. Mason. Home: Gardena, Calif. Died Oct. 11, 1941.

GHEEN, Edward Hickman, rear admiral; b. Delaware Co., Pa., Dec. 11, 1845; s. Edward and Phebe (Hickman) G.; grad. U.S. Naval Acad., 1867; m. Florence, d. Delos A. and Mary Edgerton Monfort, Oct. 17, 1883. Promoted ensign, Dec. 18, 1868; master, Mar. 21, 1870; lt., Mar. 21, 1871; comdr., Mar. 28, 1898; capt., June 14, 1902; retired at his own request, after 40 yrs.' service, as rear admiral, Dec. 1, 1902. Flagship "Delaware," Asiatic Sta., Oct. 10, 1867, to Nov. 28, 1870; signal duty, Washington, Mar. 15 to July 1, 1871; at different stations and on various duties to 1890; steel inspection, Pittsburgh and Thurlow, Pa., Oct. 6, 1890, to May 9, 1891; branch Hydrographic Office, Phila., May 9, 1891, to May 31, 1892; Navy Yard, Phila., Apr. 1, 1893, to Sept. 17, 1894; "Minneapolis," North Atlantic and European Stas., Dec. 13, 1894, to Oct. 27, 1896; Hydrographic Office, Washington, Jan. 5, 1897, to June 20, 1898; comdg. "Frolic," June 23 to Sept. 27, 1898; Hydrographic Office, Washington, Sept. 27, 1898, to June 18, 1899; comdg. "Marietta," Asiatic Sta., June 20, 1899, to Apr. 29, 1901; "Petrel," May 4 to Sept. 7, 1901; inspector 11th Light House Dist., Detroit, Feb. 12, 1902, to Sept. 15, 1902; naval recruiting office, Chicago, Sept. 19, 1902, to Feb. 24, 1903. Died Aug. 10, 1920.

GHERARDI, Bancroft, rear admiral.; b. Jackson, La., Nov. 10, 1832; entered navy from Mass. as midshipman, June 29, 1846; served on Ohio, Pacific squadron, until 1850; entered Naval Acad.; passed midshipman, June 8, 1852; master and lt., 1855; lt. comdr., July 16, 1862; comdr., July 25, 1866; capt., Nov. 9, 1874; commodore, Nov. 1884; rear admiral, Aug. 1887; retired, Nov. 10, 1894. In numerous engagements in Civil war; took especially prominent part in battle of Mobile Bay. Vice-comdr. for N.Y. Mil. Order of Foreign Wars. Home: Stratford, Conn. Died 1903.

GHERARDI, Bancroft, telephone engr.; b. San Francisco, Apr. 6, 1873; s. Bancroft (rear adm. U.S.N.) and Anna Talbot (Rockwell) G.; B.Sc., Poly. Inst. Brooklyn, 1891, Dr. Engring. from same institute, 1933; M.E., Cornell U., 1893, M.M.E., 1894; m. Mary Hornblower Butler, June 15, 1898. Began as engr. asst., N.Y. Telephone Co., 1895; traffic engr. same, 1900; chief engr. New York and New Jersey Telephone Co., 1901-06; asst. chief engr. N.Y. Telephone Co., and N.Y. and N.J. Telephone Co., 1906-07; equipment engr. Am. Telephone & Telegraph Co., 1907-09, engr. of plant same, 1909-18; acting chief engr. same co., 1918-19, chief engr., 1919-20, v.p., chief engr., 1920-38, retired. Trustee Cornell U. Republican. Episcopalian. Awarded Edison Medal, 1932, "for contributions to the art of telephone engineering and the development of electrical communication." Home: Short Hills, N.J. Died Aug. 14, 1941.

GHERARDI, Walter Rockwell, naval officer; b. Honolulu, H.I., Aug. 9, 1875; s. Bancroft (rear adm. U.S.N.) and Anna Talbot (Rockwell) G.; grad. U.S. Naval Acad., 1895; m. Neville Sims Taylor, June 4, 1904; children—Walter Rockwell, Harry Taylor, Neville Taylor, Bancroft II (dec.). Ensign U.S.N., July 1897; promoted through grades to rear adm., May 10, 1930. Served in Atlantic, Pacific and Asiatic waters; on U.S.S. Marblehead, Santiago Campaign, Spanish-Am. War, 1898; on U.S.S. Annapolis, Philippine Insurrection, 1900-02; naval attaché, Am. Embassy, Berlin, 1913-17; comdr. U.S.S. De Kalb and U.S.S. New Jersey, World War; attached to Am. conf. to negotiate peace, Paris, Dec. 1918-Mar. 1919; comdr. Aircraft Squadrons, Scouting Fleet, 1922-24; hydrographer of Navy, 1930-35; comdt. First Naval Dist. and Navy Yard, Boston, June 5, 1935—. Fellow Am. Geog. Society. Episcopalian. Died July 24, 1939.

GIAUQUE, Florien, law author; b. on farm nr. Berlin, O., May 11, 1843, of Swiss descent; s. Augustus and Sophia (Guillaume) G.; served in Federal armies in Civil War, 1862-65; A.B., Kenyon Coll., 1869, A.M., 1872 (LL.D., 1898); m. Mary Miller, Nov. 18, 1884 (died 1912); m. 2d, Elisabeth Trisler, Jan. 8, 1918. Supt. schs., Glendale, O., 1869-75; studied law under late Justice Stanley Mathews; admitted to bar, 1875, and began practice at Cincinnati. Author: Revised Statutes of Ohio (8 edits., and various supplements thereto); Raff's Guide for Executors, etc. (2 edits.), 1879; Manual for Road Supervisors (7 edits.), 1879; U.S. Election and Naturalization Laws, 1879; Manual for Guardians and Trustees (6 edits.), 1881; Manual for Assignees (6 edits.), 1882; Notary's and Conveyancer's Manual (4 edits.), 1888; Manual for Constables, Marshals, etc. (5 edits.), 1891; Settlement of Decedents' Estates (8 edits.), 1907; Present Value Tables (for value of dower damages, etc.—2 edits.), 1894; Road and Bridge Laws of Ohio, 1894; Drainage Laws of Ohio, 1896. Long a trustee Kenyon Coll. Home: Glendale, O. Died May 8, 1921.

GIAVER, Joachim G., civil engr.; b. in Norway, Aug. 15, 1856; s. Jens H. and Hanna Birgitte (Holmboe) G.; came to America, 1882; C.E., Throndhjems Tech. Coll., Throndhjem, Norway, 1881; m. Louise C. Schmedling, Throndhjem, Norway, Sept. 3, 1885. Draftsman bridge dept. N.P. R.R., St. Paul, Minn., 1882-83; draftsman, 1883-85, chief engr., 1885-90, Shiffler Bridge Co., Pittsburgh; asst. chief engr. World's Columbian Expn., Chicago, 1891-93; gen. contracting, 1893-96; bridge designer for Sanitary Dist., Chicago, 1896-98; chief engr., D. H. Burnham & Co., Chicago, 1898-1915; cons. engr., Chicago, 1915—; mem. Giaver & Dinkelberg. Trustee Norwegian Am. Hosp. Decorated by the King of Norway with Order of St. Olaf, first grade, 1921. Home: Chicago, Ill. Died May 29, 1925.

GIBBES, Heneage, physician, pathologist; b. Berrow, Somerset, Eng.; s. Rev. Heneage and g.s. Sir G. S. G.; M.D., F.R.S. (physician to Queen Charlotte); prep. edn. pvt. tutors; M.B., C.M., U. of Aberdeen, 1879, M.D., 1881; licentiate Royal Coll. Phys., 1879; m. Jessie Emily Swinhoer, niece of Sir Walter Carew, of Devonshire, Eng. Curator Anat. Mus., King's Coll., London, 1879; lecturer physiology, normal and morbid histology, Westminster Med. Sch., London, 1880-87; cholera commr. to India for British Govt., 1884; came to America, 1888; prof. pathology, U. of Mich., 1887-95; prof. theory and practice of medicine and pathology, Mich. Coll. of Medicine, 1897—; health officer, City of Detroit, 1897—. Editor: Practical Histology, 1880; Practical Pathology and Morbid Histology, 1891. Died July 18, 1912.

GIBBON, Thomas Edward, lawyer; b. near Devall Bluff, Ark., May 28, 1860; s. William Richard and Mary Jane (Wilie) G.; ed. principally at home; m. Ellen Rose, Dec. 9, 1891. Admitted to Ark. bar, 1883; removed to Los Angeles, Calif., 1888; organized Los Angeles Terminal Ry. Co., 1891, and was v.p. and gen. atty. until 1901; organized San Pedro, Los Angeles & Salt Lake Ry. Co., 1901, and was 2d v.p. and gen. counsel until 1905. Mem. Ark. House of Rep., 1884-85; mem. of Police Commission, Los Angeles, 1897-98; mem. Harbor Commn., Los Angeles, 1910-14, and chmn. com. to plan system of Municipal Terminal Ry. Democrat. Methodist. Home: Los Angeles, Calif. Died June 23, 1921.

GIBBONS, Floyd (Phillips), war corr.; b. Washington, D.C., July 16, 1887; s. Edward Thomas and Emma Theresa (Phillips) G.; ed. Gonzaga Coll. and Georgetown (D.C.) Univ. Began newspaper work on Minneapolis Daily News, 1907; later on Milwaukee Free Press and Minneapolis Tribune; on staff Chicago Tribune, 1912—. Began as war corr. at Battle of Naco on Arizona-Sonora frontier, Dec. 1914; with Francisco Villa in Mexican revolution as corr., 1915; instrumental in preliminaries that brought about Pan-Am. Conf. on Mexican question; joined with Washington bureau of Chicago Tribune; reported Villa's raid on Columbus, N.M., Mar. 1916, and accompanied Gen. Pershing on dash into Mexico, later accredited by War Dept. as corr. with punitive expdn. in Mexico; wrote widely pub. series of articles exposing conditions of poorly equipped state troops on Mexican border, quoted extensively in campaign for universal mil. training in U.S.; accompanied Gen. Funston on his last inspection of Am. militia and regulars on border and in Mexico; London corr., Chicago Tribune, 1917. Was a passenger on S.S. Laconia, torpedoed and sunk night Feb. 25, 1917, 200 miles off Irish coast; rescued after night in small boat, and cabled 4,000-word account of disaster in which Americans lost lives. War corr. in France, 1918; wounded at Battle of Château-Thierry, losing sight of one eye; was foreign dir. Chicago Tribune and editor European edit., pub. in Paris, 1918-27. Awarded French and Italian Croix de Guerre with palm; Officer Legion of Honor (France), 1923. Mem. Congressional Press Gallery, Washington, D.C. Author: How the Laconia Sank; Militia Mobilization on the Mexican Border, 1917; And They Thought We Wouldn't Fight, 1918; The Red Knight of Germany, 1927; The Red Napoleon, 1929. Died Sept. 24, 1939.

GIBBONS, Henry, college prof.; b. Luzerne Twp., Pa., Sept. 3, 1849; s. Joshua Vernon and Maria Louisa (Oliphant) G.; A.B., Amherst, 1873; studied Göttingen, 1877, U. of Leipzig, 1889-90, 1893-94; m. Mary Elizabeth Scovel, Dec. 19, 1878. Head of classical dept. Central High Sch., Pittsburgh, Pa., 1873-80; prof. Greek, Western U. of Pa. (now U. of Pittsburgh), 1880-89, Amherst Coll., 1890-92; prof. Latin lit., 1894-1915, prof. emeritus, U. of Pa. Mem. mng. com. Am. Sch. Classical Studies at Athens, Greece, 1890—. Presbyn. Home: Narberth, Pa. Died 1926.

GIBBONS, Henry, Jr., physician; b. Wilmington, Del., Sept. 24, 1840; s. Dr. Henry and Martha (Poole) G.; ed. pub. and pvt. schs., San Francisco; M.D., U. of the Pacific, 1863 (hon. A.M., 1884); m. Marie Conger Raymond, Dec. 18, 1871. Acting asst. surgeon U.S.A. Gen. Hosp., Washington, 1863-65; dean med. dept., 1870—, prof. materia medica, 1873-76, prof. obstetrics and diseases of women and children, 1882—, U. of the Pacific (now Cooper Med. Coll.). Health officer, San Francisco, 1870-73; mem. San Francisco Bd. of Health, 1880-83, Bd. of edn., 1889-90. Pres. Med. Soc. State of Calif. Home: San Francisco, Calif. Died Sept. 1911.

GIBBONS, Herbert Adams, author; b. Annapolis, Md., Apr. 9, 1880; s. Hughes Oliphant and Cora Ida (Johns) G.; grad. William Penn Charter Sch., Phila., 1897; A.B., U. of Pa., 1902; M.A., Princeton, 1907, Ph.D., 1913; B.D., Princeton Theol. Sem., 1908; hon. Litt.D., U. of Pa., 1920; m. Helen Davenport Brown, June 3, 1908; children—Christine Este, Lloyd Irving, Mimi, Hope Delarue. Ordained Presbyn. ministry, 1908; corr. New York Herald in Turkey, Egypt, Balkan States and France, 1908-18; corr. Century and Harper's in Europe, 1914-19; staff corr. Century, 1919-21; corr. Harper's, at Conf. on Disarmament, 1921, Christian Sc. Monitor in Europe, 1922; editorial adviser Century Co., 1925-33. Prof. history and polit. economy, Robert Coll., Constantinople, 1910-13; faculty, Chautauqua Summer School, 1915-16, 20, U. of Southern Calif., 1926; Am. lecturer for French foreign affairs ministry, in France, 1917-18; Spencer Trask lecturer, Princeton, 1919; hon. asso. prof. Army War Coll., Washington, D.C., 1919—; with 308th Ammunition Train 32d Div., A.E.F. Officer Legion of Honor (France); gold medal Société de Géographie de Paris, for work in Alsace-Lorraine during the war; silver medal City of Paris, 1927; was made honorary citizen of Le Touquet, France. Mem. advisory bd. All-America Standards Council, Albanian-Am. Agr. School; corr. member Institut Historique de France; president Persia Society of America. Member board governors, Brooks-Bryce Foundation (New York and London). Mason. Managed transatlantic flight of Byrd. Author: The New Map of Europe, 1914; Paris Reborn, 1915; The Foundation of the Ottoman Empire, 1915; The New Map of Africa, 1916; Reconstruction of Poland and the Near East, 1917; The New Map of Asia, 1919; France and Ourselves, 1920; Riviera Towns (with Lester G. Hornby), 1920; Venizelos (Modern Statesmen Series), 1920; An Introduction to World Politics, 1922; Europe Since 1918, 1923; America's Place in the World, 1924; Ports of France, 1926; Life of John Wanamaker, 1926; Europe of To-Day, 1927; The New Map of South America, 1929; Nationalism and Internationalism, 1929; Contemporary World History, 1934. Compiler: Songs From the Trenches, 1918. Received Albert Kahn Around-the-World fellowship, 1930; special corr. N.Y. Times in China and Manchuria, 1930. Made two trips to China and two to Africa, 1930, 31. Home: Princeton, N.J. Died Aug. 7, 1934.

GIBBONS, James; cardinal; b. Baltimore, July 23, 1834; at early age taken by parents to their former home in Ireland; began his edn. there; returned to U.S., and resided in New Orleans with his family, 1848; entered St. Charles' Coll., Md., 1855; transferred, 1857, to St. Mary's Sem. Baltimore. Ordained R.C. priest, June 30, 1861; asst. St. Patrick's, Baltimore, for a few months; then pastor St. Bridget's, Canton (surburb of Baltimore); later pvt. sec. to Archbishop Spalding and chancellor of the arch-diocese; asst. chancellor, Second Plenary Council of Am. R.C. Ch., Baltimore, Oct. 1866; vicar apostolic N.C., with rank and title of bishop, 1868; coadjutor archbishop of Baltimore, May 20, 1877; succeeded to the see, Oct. 3, 1877; presided at 3d Nat. Council at Baltimore, Nov. 1884; was nominated as cardinal; invested with the princely insignia, June 30, 1886. Author: The Faith of Our Fathers; Our Christian Heritage; The Ambassador of Christ; A Retrospect of Fifty Years, 1917. Made Grand Officer Legion of Honor (French), 1918. Died Mar. 24, 1921.

GIBBONS, John, judge; b. Ruhan Fanad, Co. Donegal, Ireland, Mar. 28, 1848; s. John and Cecilia (Carr) G.; came to U.S., 1866; graduated Notre Dame U., 1877; (LL.D. from several colls.); m. Mrs. R. B. Fuller, Apr. 20, 1892. Admitted to Ia. bar, 1870; city atty., Keokuk, Ia., 1871-76; mem. Ia. Ho. of Rep., 1876; removed to Chicago and admitted to Ill. bar, 1880; judge of the Circuit Ct. of Cook Co., 1893—; present term expiring 1921. Author: Tenure and Toil, or, The Rights and Wrongs of Property and Labor, 1889; American Criminal Reports, 1886-93. Died Feb. 11, 1917.

GIBBS, Alfred Wolcott, mech. engr.; b. Fort Fillmore, N.M., Oct. 27, 1856; s. Gen. Alfred Gibbs (U.S.A.) and Peggy F. (Blair) G.; student Rutgers Coll., 1873-74; M.E., Stevens Inst. Tech., 1878. Apprentice in Altoona shop of Pa. R.R., 1879-81; draftsman, 1881-86; master mechanic, 1886-90, 1892-93, Richmond & Danville R.R.; supt. motive power, Central of Ga. Ry., 1890-92, 1893-1902; asst. mech. engr., Pa. R.R., and supt. motive power, Phila., Wilmington & Baltimore R.R., 1902-03; gen. supt. motive power, 1903-11, chief mech. engineer, July 1, 1911—, Pa. R.R. Mem. bd. of mgrs. Franklin Inst., Phila. Home: Wayne, Pa. Died May 19, 1922.

GIBBS, Edwin C(lark); b. Cincinnati, O., May 7, 1859; s. Ira B. and Margaret (Clark) G.; ed. public schools; m. Corinne Neare, Jan. 3, 1883 (died 1932); 1 dau., Louise (Mrs. Cecil H. Gamble). Was in marine ins. business, firm of George W. Neare, Gibbs & Co., Cincinnati, 1884-1915 (retired). Regional advisor War Industries Bd., World War. Actively interested in improvement of water ways. Pres. Cincinnati Chamber of Commerce several terms; chmn. exec. com. Ohio Valley Improvement Assn.; dir. Chamber of Commerce of U.S. Fellow Am. Geog. Soc.; hon. mem. Cincinnati Chamber of Commerce. Republican. Presbyn. Mason. Home: Avondale, Cincinnati, O. Died April 1936.

GIBBS, Frederick Seymour, pres. Metropolitan Water Co.; b. Seneca Falls, N.Y., Mar. 22, 1845; enlisted in 1862 in the 148th N.Y. vols., and served until the close of the war, when he was bvtd. 1st lt.; m. June 20, 1867, Carrie A., d. Charles D. Mynderse, Seneca Falls, N.Y.; m. 2d, Sept. 5, 1895; Daisy M., d. Judge Clarence W. Meade, New York. Has served as State senator; Rep. candidate for mayor of New York, 1884; mem. Rep. Nat. Com., 1896—, and mem. Exec. Com. of Rep. Nat. Com., 1900. Died 1903.

GIBBS, George, consulting engr.; b. Chicago, Apr. 19, 1861; s. Francis S. and Eliza G. (Hosmer) G.; grad. Stevens Inst. Tech., 1882, Dr. Engineering, 1931. Engineer of tests and chemist, C.,M.&S.P. Ry., 1888-97; mech. engr. same road and Milwaukee & Northern Railroad; cons. engr. Baldwin Locomotive Works and Westinghouse Electric & Mfg. Co., 1897-1902, also chief engr. Brit. Westinghouse Electric & Mfg. Co., and Continental Westinghouse cos.; 1st v.p. Westinghouse, Church, Kerr & Co., 1901-05; cons. engr. Interborough Rapid Transit Co., Pa. R.R., and elec. engr. L.I. R.R.; mem. elec. traction commn. N.Y.C.&H.R. R.R., 1902-05; chief engr. electric traction and sta. constrn. Pa. R.R., N.Y. terminal, 1905-12; chief engr. electric traction L.I. R.R., 1912—, also cons. elec. engr. Pa. R.R.; cons. engr. Chicago Assn. Commerce Com. on Smoke Abatement and Electrification of Ry. Terminals, N.Y. Connecting R.R., N.&W. Ry., Pa. R.R., Pub. Service Commn. 1st Dist. State of N.Y., I.C. R.R., Transit Commn. State of N.Y., D.,L.&W. R.R., N.Y.,N.H.&H. R.R., Virginia Ry. Confidential adviser on engineering, Carnegie Instn. of Washington, D.C. Mem. U.S. Govt. Commn. of Ry. Experts to Russia, 1917. Trustee Stevens Inst. Tech., Presbyn. and Woman's hosps., New York. Fellow Am. Institute Electrical Engineers. Reporter on electric traction to Internat. Railway Congress, session, 1910, and pres. at Rome session, 1922. Awarded Norman medal, Am. Soc. C.E., 1911; Wellington prize, 1930. Home: New York, N.Y. Died May 19, 1940.

GIBBS, Harry Drake, chemist; b. Cincinnati, Mar. 10, 1872; s. William Henry and Emma A. (Drake) G.; student Rose Poly. Inst., Terre Haute, Ind., 1890; B.S., Cornell, 1894; Ph.D., Stanford, 1913; m. Camille Lafayette Hopper, Nov. 1, 1909; children—Edward H. D., Emma Carroll, Helen Barbara, William Eric. Asst. prof. chemistry, Ore. Agrl. Coll., 1901-03; research asst., Stanford U., 1904; chief chemist, San Francisco Bd. of Health, 1905-07; chief, div. of organic chemistry, Bur. of Science, Manila, 1907-14, also chief, Food and Drug Inspection Lab. and asst. to dir. of bur.; asso. prof. chemistry, 1910-12; chief Dept. of Chemistry, 1912-14, U. of Philippines; asst. chief eastern food inspection dist. Bur. of Chemistry, 1914-15, and chemist in charge of color lab., 1915-19; head of chem. dept. science and research div. of Bur. of Aircraft Production, 1918; mem. Nat. Research Council, 1918; chemist E. I. duPont de Nemours & Co., 1919-22; senior chemist Hygienic Lab., U.S. Pub. Health Service, 1922-29; cons. chem. engr. Presbyn. Home: Hyattsville, Md. Died Dec. 28, 1934.

GIBBS, Josiah Willard, prof. mathematical physics, Yale, 1871—; b. New Haven, Conn., Feb. 11, 1839; s. Prof. Josiah Willard and Mary Anna (Van Cleve) G.; grad. Yale, 1858 (Ph.D., 1863; also Erlangen, 1893; LL.D., Williams, 1893; also Princeton, 1896); studied at univs. of Paris, Berlin, and Heidelberg. Mem. Nat. Acad. Sciences, Royal Soc. of London, and other learned socs. Died 1903.

GIBBS, Willis Benjamin, congressman; b. Dupont, Ga., Apr. 15, 1889; s. Willis Bartow and Lilla (Johnson) G.; ed. public schools and business coll.; student Mercer U., 1910-11; m. Florence Adel Reville, Jan. 1, 1912; children—Warner Benjamin, Betty (Mrs. Joseph A. Leaphart). Admitted to Ga. bar, 1911, and began practice in Jesup; solicitor City Court (pros. atty.), 1913-24; solicitor Gen. Brunswick Judicial Circuit (superior court pros. atty.), 1924-39; mem. 76th Congress (1939-41), 8th Ga. Dist. Mem. Ga. State Bd. of Control for Eleemosynary Instns., 1931-37. Democrat. Methodist. Mason. Home: Jesup, Ga. Died Aug. 7, 1940.

GIBBS, Winifred Stuart, home economist; b. New York, Oct. 6, 1871; d. George Holman and Catherine Stuart (Karnes) G.; Chicago high schs.; U. of Rochester; diploma Rochester Mechanics Inst., 1901; unmarried. Founded home economy dept. of New York Assn. for Improving the Condition of the Poor; began work at Teachers Coll. (Columbia) for purpose of training home economic students to use specialty in social service; adviser to workers in similar fields in Providence, Boston, Chicago, St. Louis, etc. Del. Congress, Brussels, Belgium, to consider questions of home edn., 1909. Consultant to Nat. War Labor Bd. Organizer original projects, Home Representation in Industry; supervisor of Nutrition, Fedn. for Child

Study, 1919-22; editor Am. Food Journal; The Home Economist, 1922—. Episcopalian. Author: Minimum Cost of Living; The Children's Book of Food Verses, etc. Home: New York, N.Y. Died Feb. 8, 1928.

GIBBS, (Oliver) Wolcott, chemist; b. New York, Feb. 21. 1822; s. George and Laura (Wolcott) G.; A.B., 1841, A.M., 1844, Columbia; M.D., Coll. Phys. & Surg., New York, 1843; studied at Univ. of Berlin and under Liebig at Giessen, and at Coll. of France, Paris; (LL.D., Columbia, 1873, Harvard, 1888, Columbian, 1895; U. of Toronto, 1897, U. of Pa., 1902). Delivered lectures at Delaware Coll., Newark; prof. physics and chemistry, Coll. City of New York, 1849-63; Rumford prof. and lecturer on the application of science to the useful arts, 1863-87, prof. emeritus, Harvard. Mem. exec. com. U.S. Sanitary Commn., New York, during Civil War; U.S. commr. Vienna Expn., 1873. Home: Newport, R.I. Died 1908.

GIBIER, Paul, M.D.-biologist-author; grad. Faculty of Medicine, Paris, France, 1884; was house physician to hospitals in Paris; came to U.S., becoming med. director Pasteur Inst.; founder private sanitarium. Author: (in French) Spiritisme; Analyse des Choses (also published in English as Psychism: Analysis of Things Existing). Home: New York, N.Y. Died 1900.

GIBNEY, Virgil Pendleton, surgeon; b. Jessamine Co., Ky., Sept. 29, 1847; s. Dr. Robert A. and Amanda (Weagley) G.; A.B., Ky. U., 1869, A.M., 1872, LL.D., 1899; M.D., Bellevue Hosp. Med. Coll. (New York U.), 1871; m. Charlotte L. Chapin, Dec. 1883; m. 2d, Julia Trubee, June 20, 1893. Asst. phys., 1871, resident house surgeon, 1871-84, surgeon-in-chief, 1887—, Hosp. for Ruptured and Crippled; prof. orthopedic surgery, N.Y. Polyclinic, 1882-94; clin. lecturer orthopedic surgery, 1894-95, clinical prof., 1895-1904, prof., 1904-17, Coll. of Phys. and Surg. (Columbia). Fellow Am. Coll. Surgeons. Democrat. Author: The Hip and Its Diseases, 1884. Died June 16, 1927.

GIBSON, Axel Emil; b. Stockholm, Sweden, Oct. 20, 1863; s. Lars Z. and Karna (Anderson) Jepson; grad. Royal Tech. Inst., Gothenburg, 1900; grad. Pacific Coll. Surgery and Osteopathy, Los Angeles, 1905; m. Margaret H. Harper, June 15, 1907; children—John Oscar, Paul Wesley, Kathryn Mathilde. Came to U.S., 1895, naturalized citizen, 1900. Head of Gibson Health Concern Pub. Co., Los Angeles, also of Gibson Recreation Farm, Beaumont, Calif. Theosophist. Author: Blood and Nerve Diseases, 1922; New Light on Living, 1922; Vital Engineering, 1929; Voice Magic—Functional Control through the Human Voice, 1931; Immortality in the Light of Reason, 1933; Why Men Drink, 1934; The Psychology of Suicide, 1934; What Becomes of the Dead, 1935; Capital Punishment, 1935; Jazz Salads and Their Digestive Discards, 1935; The Moral Value of Lee Katz Murals, 1936. Home: Los Angeles, Calif. Deceased.

GIBSON, Carleton Bartlett, supt. of schs.; b. Mobile, Ala., Sept. 18, 1863; s. James Spalding and Julia A. (Powers) G.; A.B., U. of Ala., 1884, A.M., 1885, LL.D., 1914; U. of Chicago, summers, 1898, 99, 1900; m. Martha Goodwin Newcomb, Jan. 7, 1888. Prin. pub. sch., Mulberry, Ala., 1884-85; pres. State Normal Sch., Jacksonville, Ala., 1885-91; founder and prin. Univ. Mil. Sch., Mobile, 1892-93; pres. Central Female Coll., Tuscaloosa, Ala., 1893-94; prin. high sch., Columbus, Ga., 1894-95; supt. schs., Columbus, 1896-1909; pres. Mechanics Inst., Rochester, N.Y., 1910-16; supt. of schools, Savannah, Ga., 1916—. Democrat. Baptist. Director Y.M.C.A., Columbus, 1900-04. Associated Charities, 1907-09. Mason. Home: 108 Bull St., Savannah, Ga. Died May 1927.

GIBSON, Charles Hopper, lawyer, senator; b. Queen Anne Co., Md., Jan. 19, 1842; grad. Washington Coll., Chestertown, Md.; admitted to bar, 1864; practiced at Easton, Md.; State's atty., Talbot Co., Md., 1870-79; member Congress, 1885-91; U.S. senator from Md., Jan. 1892 to March 3, 1897. Democrat. Home: Easton, Md. Died 1900.

GIBSON, Edgar J., newspaperman; b. Smithville, N.Y.; s. Rev. John and Sarah (Merchant) G.; m. Cora L. Taft. Editorial writer and corr. New York Tribune, 10 yrs.; editor and mgr. Oswego (N.Y.) Times; business mgr. Wheeling (W.Va.) Standard; mng. editor Baltimore News; has written letters from various parts of the world for The Phila. Press; war corr. in Cuab, 1898; mgr. Washington bur. and editorial writer Phila. Press; was asst. chief, Bur. of Manufacturers; expert spl. agt., U.S. Census, Washington, Jan. 18, 1911—. Deceased.

GIBSON, Ernest Willard, U.S. senator; b. Londonderry, Vt., Dec. 29, 1871; s. William L. and Saville (Stowell) G.; B.S., Norwich U., 1894, A.M., 1896; studied law, U. of Mich., 1898-99; m. Grace Hadley, Nov. 25, 1896 (died 1925); children—Frank Hadley (dec.), Ernest William, Doris, Preston Fullerton. Prin. Chester High Sch., 1894-98; practiced at Brattleboro, 1899—; register of probate and deputy clk. U.S. Dist. Court; mem. Vt. Ho. of Rep., 1906, Senate 1908 (pres. of Senate); del. Rep. Nat. Conv., 1912; state's atty., 1919-21; sec. civil and mil. affairs, Vt., 1921-22; mem. 68th to 73d Congresses (1923-35), 2d Vt. Dist.; apptd. mem. U.S. Senate Nov. 22, 1933, to fill vacancy occasioned by death of Hon. Porter H. Dale, elected to same office, Jan. 16, 1934, reëlected, 1938. Enlisted in Vt. N.G., 1899, retired, 1908; col. insp. rifle practice, staff of Gov. Fletcher D. Proctor; returned to service, 1915, as capt. inf.; served on Mexican border and over seas; col. 172d Inf., Aug. 5, 1921-Nov. 5, 1923. Republican. Episcopalian. Trustee Diocese of Vt. Home: Brattleboro, Vt. Died June 20, 1940.

GIBSON, Eva Katherine Clapp, author; b. Bradford, Ill.; d. Henry and Ann (Ely) Clapp; acad. edn.; m. Dr. Charles Brockway Gibson, June 29, 1891. Most of her books were published under her maiden name; in lit. work, 1880—. Author: Her Bright Future, 1884-88; A Lucky Mishap, 1886; Songs of Red Rose Land (poems), 1901; Famous Lovers (historical sketches), 1901; Zauberlinda, the Wise Witch, 1902. Songs: The Anthem of the Free, Our Old Commander. Home: Chicago, Ill. Deceased.

GIBSON, Frank Markey, clergyman; b. Bedford Springs, Pa., Jan. 16, 1857; s. Alexander Early (M.D., D.D.) and Mary (Markey) G.; A.B., Dickinson, 1877, A.M., 1880; LL.B., U. of Md., 1879; Ph.D., St. John's, Md., 1893; m. Mary, d. William Walker Plummer, Nov. 10, 1891; 1 son, Alexander Stuart. Admitted to bar, 1879, and practiced, 1879-83; deacon, 1883, priest, 1884, P.E. Ch.; curate Emanuel Ch., Baltimore, 1883-85; rector Ch. of Holy Innocents, Baltimore, 1885-86, Elkridge, Md., 1886-93; curate St. Paul's 1893-96, St. Andrew's, 1896-97, Trinity, 1897-1904, Washington; rector Westminster, Md., 1904-12. Librarian Md. Diocesan Library. Editor Md. Churchman, 1912-14. Examining chaplain diocese Md. and Washington, 1890-99; mem. ecclesiastical court, 1897-98. Mason. Home: Baltimore, Md. Died Sept. 24, 1929.

GIBSON, George Miles, clergyman; b. Tazewell Co., Va., Dec. 7, 1860; s. Wesley and Jane (Ward) G.; A.B., Emory and Henry Coll., Va., 1887, A.M., 1890 (D.D. same, 1914); m. Florence Allen, Oct. 14, 1891 (died 1913); children—Mrs. W. F. Carruthers, Mrs. R. K. Withrow, George M.; m. 2d, Mrs. Leila Allen, July 1915. Professor Latin and Greek, St. Charles College, Missouri, 1887-88; ordained ministry M.E. Ch., S., 1888; pastor Troy, Mo., 1888-90, Albany, Mo., 1890-91, St. Joseph, Mo., 1891-93, Glasgow, Mo., 1893-95, Macon, Mo., 1895-98, Fayette, Mo., 1898-1901, Richmond, Mo., 1901-04, Trinity Ch., El Paso, Tex., 1904-08; pres. Central Coll. for Women, Lexington, Mo., 1908-10; pastor 1st Ch., Dallas, Tex., Dec. 1910-14, St. Mark's Ch., Dallas, 1915-22, Munger Place Church, Dallas, 1922-26; dir. of religious edn., North Texas Conf., 1926-29; asst. pastor First Ch., Dallas, Tex., 1929—. Mason. Author: A History of New Testament Times, 1925; The Evangelization of Children, 1929. Died Mar. 30, 1932.

GIBSON, Henry Richard, congressman; b. Kent, Island, Md., 1837; s. Woolman and Catherine (Carter) G.; A.B., Hobart, 1862, A.M., 1865, LL.D., 1892; served in commissary dept. Union Army, 1863-65; studied in Albany (N.Y.) Law Sch.; m. 1st Frances M. Reed, Sept. 1863 (died 1918); children—Helen, Frances; m. 2d, Lizzie R. Clark, July 1920. Admitted to bar, 1865; removed to Tenn., 1866; commr. of claims, 1868-69; del. Constl. Conv., 1870; mem. Senate, 1871-72; Rep. nominee for presdl. elector, 1872 and 1880; mem. Ho. of Rep., 1875-76; founded, and editor, Knoxville Republican, 1879-81; postoffice insp., 1881-82; editor Knoxville Daily Chronicle, 1882-84; U.S. pension agt., 1883-85; chancellor, 2d Div. of Tenn., 1886-94; mem. 54th to 58th Congresses (1895-1905), 2d Tenn. Dist. Home: Washington, D.C. Died May 25, 1938.

GIBSON, Horatio Gates, brig. gen. U.S.A.; b. Baltimore, Md., May 22, 1827; s. Rev. John and Elizabeth (Jameson) G.; grad. U.S. Mil. Acad., 1847; m. Harriet L. Atkinson, Mar. 16, 1863. Bvtd. 2d lt., 2d Arty., July 1, 1847; served in war with Mexico, 1847-48, Vera Cruz, Puebla and City of Mexico; 2d lt., 3d Arty., Sept. 8, 1847, 1st lt., May 26, 1851, capt., May 14, 1861; lt. col., 2d Ohio Arty., Aug. 1, 1863; col., Aug. 15, 1863; hon. mustered out of vol. service, Aug. 23, 1865; maj. 3d Arty., Feb. 5, 1867; lt. col. 2d Arty., Apr. 19, 1882; col. 3d Arty., Dec. 1, 1883; retired, May 22, 1891; advanced to rank of brig. gen. retired, by act of Apr. 23, 1904. Bvtd.: maj., May 5, 1862, "for gallant and meritorious services in battle of Williamsburg, Va."; lt. col., Sept. 17, 1862, for same at Antietam, Md.; col., Mar. 13, 1865, for same in the field during the warfil brig. gen. vols., Mar. 13, 1865, for same during the war. Died Apr. 12, 1924.

GIBSON, James Alexander, lawyer; b. Boston, Mass., Aug. 21, 1852; s. Thomas and Mary (Berry) G.; ed. pub. schs.; m. Sarah Waterman, June 21, 1882 (died 1888); m. 2d, Gertrude Van Norman, July 18, 1894. Admitted to Calif. bar, 1879, and began practice in San Bernardino; judge Superior Court of San Bernardino Co., 1885-89; mem. Supreme Court Commn., 1889-91; practiced in San Diego, 1891-97, then in Los Angeles; mem. Gibson, Dunn & Crutcher. Home: Los Angeles, Calif. Died Aug. 3, 1922.

GIBSON, Joseph Thompson, clergyman; b. Jefferson Co., Pa., Feb. 13, 1844; s. Andrew and Jane (McSparren) G.; A.B., Washington and Jefferson Coll., Pa., 1869; grad. Western Theol. Sem., Pa., 1872; (D.D., Grove City Coll., Pa., 1893, Washington and Jefferson Coll., 1895); m. Isabel B. Brown, May 21, 1872. Sergt. 78th Pa. Inf., 1861-64; was in battles of Missionary Ridge, Stone River, Chickamauga and Lookout Mountain, etc.; wounded at battle of New Hope Ch., nr. Atlanta, Ga. Supt. pub. schs., Indiana Co., Pa., 1869-71; ordained Presbyn. ministry, 1872; pastor Govanstown, Md., 1872-80, Sharpsburg, Pa., 1880-87; sec. Synodical Sustentation Presbyn. Ch., 1887-90; sec. and treas. Bd. of Missions for Freedmen, 1884-94; editor Presbyn. Messenger, 1894-98; asso. editor Presbyn. Banner, 1898-99, editor same, 1917—, and president of the Presbyn. Banner Pub. Co. Acting pastor of the East Liberty Ch., Pa., 1901. Trustee Western Theol. Sem., Grove City Coll., Presbyn. Hosp., Pittsburgh. Mem. Chickamauga Nat. Mil. Park Commn. for Pa., 1894-99; chaplain-in-chief Union Vet. Legion U.S. Republican. Home: Pittsburgh, Pa. Died July 17, 1922.

GIBSON, Lorenzo P., physician; b. Little Rock, Ark., Aug. 18, 1855; s. Lorenzo and Caroline Louisa (Thomas) G.; Ph.B., St. John's Coll., Little Rock, 1875; M.D., Jefferson Med. Coll., Phila., 1877; m. Mary Johnson Jordan, Apr. 18, 1883. In practice at Little Rock, Ark., 1877—; demonstrator anatomy U. of Ark., 1878-1903; acting asst. surgeon, U.S. Pub. Health Service, 1882—. Chief med. staff, St. Vincent's Infirmary. Sec. Ark. State Bd. Health. Editor Journal Ark. Med. Soc., 1890-95. Died Dec. 31, 1919.

GIBSON, Louis Henry, architect; b. Aurora, Ind., 1854; ed. Mass. Inst. Technology; spl. course at École des Beaux Arts, Paris; m. Emily S. Gilbert, 1879. Engaged in practice at Indianapolis; contbr. to mags. and newspapers on artistic and tech. topics. Author: Convenient Houses, 1889; Beautiful Houses, 1895; etc. Home: Indianapolis, Ind. Deceased.

GIBSON, Paris, senator; b. Brownfield, Me., July 1, 1830; s. Abel and Ann (Howard) G.; A.B., Bowdoin Coll., 1851 (LL.D., 1901); m. Valeria G. Sweat, Aug. 23, 1858 (died 1900). Mem. Ho. of Rep., 1854; went to Minneapolis, 1858; with W. W. Eastman, built the first flour mill and first woolen mill in Minneapolis; settled in Fort Benton, Mont., 1879; first examined Falls of the Missouri, 1882, and at once founded city of Great Falls; mem. Constl. Conv., 1889; mem. Mont. Senate, 1891; U.S. senator, 1901-05, for unexpired term of William A. Clark, resigned. Democrat. In real estate and farming. Home: Great Falls, Mont. Died Dec. 16, 1920.

GIBSON, Preston, playwright; b. Washington, D.C., Mar. 13, 1879; s. late Randall Lee (U.S. senator from La.) and Mary (Montgomery) G.; nephew Edward D. White; ed. Yale, 1897-1900; m. Minna Field, d. Mrs. Thomas Nelson Page and niece of Marshall Field, of Chicago, Jan. 27, 1900; 2d, Grace McMillan Jarvis, g.d. late Senator James McMillan, of Mich., Feb. 29, 1908; m. 3d, Mrs. Beatrice Rogers Benjamin Pratt, of New York, g.d. late H. H. Rogers, Oct. 17, 1919. Contbr. Sunday stories and news articles, Chicago Tribune, 1902-03, also writing mag. stories; contbr. daily and Sunday articles Washington Post, 1908-09. Democrat. Mem. Bezerlius Soc. (Yale). Author (plays): Mrs. Erskine's Devotion, prod. Davidson Theatre, Milwaukee, 1904; Fate, prod. Ill. Theatre, Chicago, 1905; Cupid's Trick, Ill. Theatre, 1905, Success, Belasco Theatre, Washington, 1908; The Vacuum, Belasco Theatre, 1908; The Turning Point, Hackett Theatre, New York, 1909; Derelicts, Ben Greet Players, Belasco Theatre, Washington, 1909; Drifting, Nazimova Theatre, 1910; also The Secret Way, Magnolia, Treason, Adelia, The Missing Inventor, and Lola Montez; The Vale of Content. A volunteer in the Norton-Harjes Ambulance Corps and decorated for bravery under fire, with the Croix de Guerre by French Govt.; returned to U.S. and enlisted as pvt. in U.S.M.C.; temporarily assigned on recruiting duty and enrolled 3,200 vols.; commd. lt.; hon. discharged. Descendant of Patrick Henry. Died Feb. 15, 1937.

GIBSON, Robert Atkinson, bishop; b. Petersburg, Va., July 9, 1846; s. Rev. Churchill J. and Lucy Fitzhugh (Atkinson) G.; served in Rockbridge battery, 1st Va. Arty., Army of Northern Va., C.S.A., 1864-65; A.B., Hampden-Sidney Coll., 1867; grad. Va. Theol. Sem., 1870; (D.D., U. of the South and Kenyon Coll., 1897); m. Susan Baldwin Stuart, Nov. 12, 1872. Deacon, 1870, priest, 1871, P.E. Ch.; missionary in Southern Va., 1870-72; asst. in St. James Ch., and in charge of Moore Memorial Chapel, Richmond, 1872-78; rector Trinity Ch., Parkersburg, W.Va., 1878-87, Christ Ch., Cincinnati, 1887-97; consecrated coadjutor bishop of Va., Nov. 3, 1897, bishop of Va., June 1902. Home: Richmond, Va. Died Feb. 17, 1919.

GIBSON, Robert Williams, architect; b. Essex, Eng., Nov. 17, 1854; s. Samuel Lodwick and Eliza (Williams) G.; ed. at Ingress House Schs., Gravesend, Eng.; entered Royal Acad. of Arts, 1875; grad. at London, 1879; m. Caroline J. Hammond, 1890; children—Mrs. Lydia G. Minor, Robert H., Katherine G. (Mrs. A. Van Cortland, Jr.), Hester G. (Mrs. Ellery C. Huntington, Jr.). Passed arit. exam. Royal Inst. British Architects; came to New York, 1881, and began practice; retired; architect of Albany

Cathedral, U.S. Trust Co.'s Bank Clearing House, Greenwich Savings Bank, Coffee Exchange, Bot. Mus., New York; bank bldgs. at Buffalo, Albany, Utica and Syracuse, N.Y., Minneapolis, Minn., Providence, R.I., and elsewhere. Mason. Author: The Morality of Nature—a Philosophy of Evolution, 1923. Home: Woodbury, L.I., N.Y. Died Aug. 17, 1927.

GIBSON, William Campbell, rear admiral; b. Albany, N.Y., July 23, 1838; s. Joseph and Marion (Campbell) G.; ed. Albany, N.Y., 1838-47, Sand Lake Acad., N.Y., 1847-52; m. Aurelia A. Holbrook, Aug. 5, 1875. Clerk in hardware business, Albany, N.Y., 1853-54; went to sea in merchant service, 1855; enlisted in U.S.N., Aug. 1861; apptd. acting mate, Dec. 1862, acting ensign, Aug. 1863; promoted through grades to capt., Feb. 1900; rear admiral and retired, July 23, 1900. Served on Potomac flotilla and North and South Atlantic blockading squadrons during Civil War; subsequently served on the European, North Atlantic, Pacific and South Atlantic stations. During the Spanish-Am. war comd. Str. City of Peking, which carried part of 1st mil. expdn. to Manila, arriving there June 30, 1898; last duty, command battleship Texas, North Atlantic Station. Died 1911.

GIBSON, William Meredith, physician; b. Waterville, N.Y., May 12, 1856; s. Rev. William T. and Martha (Field) G.; prep. edn. Utica Free Acad.; M.D., Univ. Med. Coll. (New York U.), 1878; m. Mary F. Burr, June 28, 1888. Health commr., Utica, 1884-89; mgr. N.Y. State Hosp. for Insane, 1894-95; sch. commr., Utica, 1898-1904; phys. to St. Luke's and St. Elizabeth hosps. Episcopalian. Home: Cazenovia, N.Y. Died May 18, 1925.

GIBSON, William Richie, army officer; b. Ontario, O., June 3, 1877; s. Andrew Rae and Margaret Lemon (Richie) G.; grad. Inf. and Cav. Sch., 1904; grad. Army War Coll., 1925; m. Louise G. Beatley, June 13, 1911. Cadet U.S. Mil. Acad., June 15, 1896; commd. 2d lt. inf., June 1, 1899; promoted through grades to brig. gen. regular army, and asst. to q.-m. gen., Mar. 1, 1934; retired, July 31, 1937. Served as capt. 51st Ia. Inf., Spanish-Am. War; lt. col. inf., N.A., Aug. 5, 1917, col., July 30, 1918; hon. disch. from N.A., Mar. 15, 1920. Home: Pasadena, Calif. Died Oct. 29, 1940.

GIDDINGS, Franklin Henry, sociologist; b. Sherman, Conn., Mar. 23, 1855; s. Rev. Edward J. and Rebecca Jane (Fuller) G.; A.B., Union Coll., 1877, A.M., 1899, hon. Ph.D., 1897; LL.D., Columbia, 1929; m. Elizabeth P. Hawes, Nov. 8, 1876. Engaged in journalism, 1877-83; prof. Bryn Mawr Coll., 1888-94; lecturer sociology, 1891-94, prof. sociology, 1894-1906, sociology and history of civilization, 1906—, Columbia. Fellow Am. Statis. Assn.; mem. Nat. Inst. of Arts and Letters. Trustee Union Coll.; mem. Bd. of Edn., N.Y. City, 1915-17. Author: The Modern Distributive Process (with J. B. Clark), 1888; The Theory of Sociology, 1894; The Principles of Sociology, 1896 (also French, German, Russian, Spanish, Hebrew, Czech and Japanese transls.); The Theory of Socialization, 1897 (Italian translation, 1898); The Elements of Sociology, 1898; The Western Hemisphere in the World of Tomorrow, 1915; The Responsible State, 1918; Studies in the Theory of Human Society, 1922; The Scientific Study of Human Society, 1924; The Mighty Medicine—Superstition and Its Antidote, 1929. Home: Scarsdale, N.Y. Died June 11, 1931.

GIDLEY, James Williams, vertebrate paleontologist; b. Springwater, Ia., Jan. 7, 1866; s. Isaac Mosier and Rebecca Penrose (Williams) G.; B.S., Princeton, 1898, M.S., 1901; Ph.D., George Washington U., 1922; m. Florence Emily Martin, Apr. 4, 1900. With Am. Mus. Natural History, New York, 1899-1905, U.S. Nat. Mus., 1905—; asst. curator of fossil mammals, U.S. Nat. Mus., 1911—. Has conducted various expdns. for Am. Mus. Natural History, and Nat. Mus., Washington, D.C., in fossil localities of U.S. Republican. Conglist. Home: Washington, D.C. Died Sept. 26, 1931.

GIEGERICH, Leonard Anthony, judge; b. Rötz, Bavaria, May 20, 1855; s. Leonhard and Barbara G.; brought to U.S. when 1 yr. old; ed. pub. and parochial schs. and De La Salle Inst.; (LL.D., Manhattan Coll., 1903, St. Francis Xavier Coll., 1909). Admitted to bar, 1877; mem. N.Y. Assembly, 1887; collector internal revenue, N.Y., 1887-90; judge City Ct., 1890; co. clerk, 1891; judge Ct. of Common Pleas, 1891-95; justice Supreme Ct., 1st Dist. of N.Y., 1896—. Democrat. Home: Riverdale-on-Hudson, N.Y. Died Dec. 20, 1927.

GIELOW, Martha Sawyer, lecturer, author; b. Greensboro, Ala.; d. Capt. Enoch and Sophie E. (Barkley) Sawyer; widow; children — Una (Mrs. Charles Willis Fisher), Roland Sawyer. Reader and lecturer; founder and v.p. Southern Industrial Ednl. Assn. (Washington, D.C.), to promote industrial edn. among the Anglo-Saxon children of the Southern Appalachian Mountains. Author: Mammy's Reminiscences, 1898; Old Plantation Days, 1902; Old Andy the Moonshiner, 1910; Uncle Sam, 1913; The Light on the Hill, 1915. Home: Greensboro, Ala. Died Jan. 30, 1933.

GIERING, Eugene Thomas, newspaper editor; b. Emaus, Pa., Apr. 9, 1867; s. James Oliver and Matilda (Stahler) G.; ed. pub. schs.; m. Agnes May Fleming, Dec. 15, 1898; children—James Herbert, Eugene Thomas, Frances Claire (wife of Dr. Emmett Stanley Burke), John Fleming. Began with Wilkes-Barre (Pa.) Record, 1888, editor, 1906—. Mem. sch. bd., Wilkes-Barre. Pres. Luzerne County Sch. for Boys; v.p. United Charities, Community Welfare Fedn.; dir. Wilkes-Barre Gen. Hosp. Mem. Greater Wilkes-Barre Chamber Commerce (pres.). Trustee Wyoming Hist. and Geol. Soc. Republican. Rotarian. Home: Wilkes-Barre, Pa. Died Apr. 9, 1934.

GIFFEN, James Kelly, clergyman, educator; b. St. Clairsville, O., Feb. 11, 1885; s. Robert Emmett and Anna Margaret (Bentley) G.; A.B., Muskingum Coll., O., 1910; student Xenia Theol. Sem., 1910-13, Northwestern U., summer, 1926, 28, 29; m. Mary Adelia Lorimer, June 26, 1913; children—Lowell Lorimer, Helen Loraine, John Kelly (dec.), James Kelly (dec.). Ordained ministry United Presbyn. Ch., 1918; asst. pres. Muskingum Coll., 1913-15; pastor Moundsville, W.Va., 1915-17; prin. Stanton (Ky.) Acad., 1917-18; pres. Knoxville Coll., Aug. 1918—. Home: Knoxville, Tenn. Died Feb. 4, 1937.

GIFFEN, John Kelly, missionary; b. St. Clairsville, O., June 3, 1853; s. Morrison and Margaret (Taggart) G.; A.B., Franklin Coll., O., 1879; grad. U. P. Theol. Sem., Allegheny, Pa., 1881; D.D., Tarkio (Mo.) Coll., 1904; m. Grace Henderson, July 12, 1881; children—Margaret Harvey, Morrison Beal. Ordained U.P. ministry, 1881; sent as missionary to Egypt and Soudan; asst. in Training Coll., 1881-88; evangelistic supt. in Upper Egypt, 1888-91, supt. various dists. in Africa, 1891—. Sec. Assn. (mission) in Egypt, 1883-91, to Soudan, 1900; gen. sec. and treas. Am. Mission, Soudan, 1905—. Del. World's Missionary Conf., Edinburgh, 1910; moderator Gen. Assembly U.P. Ch., 1922. Author: The Egyptian Soudan, 1905. Died Apr. 6, 1932.

GIFFORD, Augusta Hale, author; b. Turner, Me., Feb. 19, 1842; d. James S. and Betsey (Staples) Hale; prep. edn. in Turner, Me.; classical course, Oberlin Coll.; m. George Gifford, who has been for many yrs. U.S. consul at Basel, Switzerland, Aug. 8, 1869. Went abroad first time, 1877; nearly half of life spent abroad since then; extensive foreign correspondence with N.E. journals. Author: Germany, Her People and Their Story, 1899; Italy, Her People and Their Story, 1905; New Italy, 1909. Home: Portland, Me. Died Feb. 9, 1915.

GIFFORD, George, consul; b. Hallowell (now Manchester), Me., Nov. 19, 1842; s. Ichabod Clark and Sarah Jane (McFadden) G.; A.B., Colby Coll., Waterville, Me., 1862, A.M., 1864 (LL.D., 1911); m. Augusta Hale. Admitted to bar, 1864; editor-in-chief Portland Daily Press, 1867-71; mem. Me. Ho. of Rep., 1874; agt. U.S. Treasury Dept., London, Eng., 1877; attaché to commr. Paris Expn., 1878; commercial agt., at Nantes, May 31, 1878; consul La Rochelle, Feb. 24, 1882; apptd. consul, Cognac, May 9, 1883 (declined); consul Basel, Switzerland, from Jan. 1884 to July 1913, when resigned on account of ill health. Longest term of service of any Am. consul. Home: Portland, Me. Died Oct. 6, 1924.

GIFFORD, Harold, ophthalmic surgeon; b. Milwaukee, Oct. 18, 1858; s. Charles and Mary Caroline (Child) G.; B.Sc., Cornell, 1879; M.D., U. of Mich., 1882, hon. M.A. from same univ., 1912; LL.D., U. of Neb., 1918; post-grad. studies, New York, Erlangen, Vienna, Zurich; m. Mary Louise Millard, Dec. 30, 1890. Began practice as ophthalmic and aural surgeon, Omaha, 1886; prof. emeritus of ophthalmology, U. of Neb.; ophthalmic and aural surgeon to Methodist Hosp. Home: Omaha, Neb. Died Nov. 28, 1929.

GIFFORD, James Meacham, lawyer; b. Monkton, Vt., Mar. 19, 1856; s. Henry Oscar and Avis Josephine (Eaton) G.; A.B., Middlebury (Vt.) Coll., 1877; A.M., Syracuse U., 1880; teacher, Mechanicsville (N.Y.) Acad., 1877-78; prin. Mexico Acad., 1878-81; LL.B., Columbia, 1883; (LL.D., Middlebury, 1897); m. Harriet R. Brangan, June 28, 1883. In practice at New York, 1883—; instr. Columbia Law Sch., 1883-86; now sr. mem. Gifford, Woody, Carter & Hays; dir. DeHaven Razor Corp., North Am. Clay Co. Trustee Middlebury Coll., 1900—. Home: New York, N.Y. Died Oct. 21, 1938.

GIFFORD, Livingston, patent lawyer; b. Jersey City, N.J., Sept. 8, 1855; s. George and Eleanor C. (Van Ranst) G.; Ph.B., Yale, 1875; LL.B., Columbia, 1877; m. Marie Louise Davis, June 10, 1885; 1 dau., Evelyn G. (Mrs. Henry A. Gardner). Practiced in New York, 1877—; mem. Gifford, Scull & Burgess. Home: New York, N.Y. Died Feb. 11, 1937.

GIFFORD, Orrin Philip, clergyman; b. Montague, Mass., Apr. 15, 1847; s. P. R. and Parthenia (Perkins) G.; A.B., Brown U., 1874; grad. Rochester Theol. Sem., 1877; D.D., U. of Rochester, 1896; m. Florence N. Lamson, June 26, 1877; children—Flora, Mary (Mrs. Geo. Rolfe), Orrin Philip, Paul Lamson. Ordained Bapt. ministry, 1877; pastor successively Pittsfield, Mass., Warren Av. Ch., Boston, Brookline, Mass., Chicago, Del. Av. Ch., Buffalo, and Brookline, Mass., until 1918 (emeritus); moved to Pasadena, Calif., 1921. Republican. Author: Sermons, 1880, 1925, 26. Home: Pasadena, Calif. Died Feb. 1, 1932.

GIFFORD, Ralph Waldo, prof. of law; b. West Dedham (now Westwood), Mass., Oct. 15, 1867; s. Elisha and Louisa Jane (Knapp) G.; A.B., Harvard, 1892, LL.B., 1901; (hon. A.M., Yale U., 1912; LL.D., Fordham U., 1912); m. Sarah Lowell Parsons, June 30, 1892. Asst. Harvard Coll. Obs., 1886-88; admitted to N.Y. bar, 1902; clk. in law office, 1902-04; asso. in practice, 1903, with Sherman Cox, title of Gifford & Cox; retired from practice, 1907; prof. of law, Fordham, 1906-12; Lines prof. testamentary law, Yale, 1912-15; prof. law, Columbia, July 1914—. Republican. Unitarian. Home: New York, N.Y. Died Dec. 2, 1925.

GIFFORD, Robert Swain, artist; b. Naushon Island, Mass., Dec. 23, 1840; ed. in pub. schs., New Bedford, Mass.; studied painting under Albert Van Beest, Rotterdam, Holland; is a painter of landscapes and coast scenes; m. Frances Eliot. Received medals at Centennial Expn., 1876, and Internat. Expn., Paris, 1889; $2,500 prize from Am. Art Assn., New York, 1885; silver medal Pan-Am. Expn.; gold medal Charleston Expn. Mem. of art jury of awards, World's Columbian Expn. Home: New York, N.Y. Died 1905.

GIFFORD, Seth Kelley, school prin.; b. W. Falmouth, Mass., July 29, 1854; s. Azariah Shove and Lois (Bean) G.; A.B., Haverford Coll., Pa., 1876, A.M., 1877; studied Berlin, Bonn and Munich, 1883-85, Halle, 1901-02, Ph.D., 1902; m. S. Elma Winslow, June 15, 1878; m. 2d, Mary Amy Collins, June 28, 1883; children—Margaret Amy, Philip Collins. Teacher Greek and Latin, Friends' Sch., Providence, 1876-82; asst. prof. Greek and Latin, 1882-83, prof. German and Latin, 1885-86, Greek and German, 1886-88, Greek, 1888-1904, Haverford Coll.; prin. Moses Brown Sch., Providence, 1904-24. Mem. bd. of mgrs. Haverford Coll., 1905-24. Home: Providence, R.I. Died Sept. 2, 1933.

GIGOT, Francis Ernest, theologian; b. Lhuant (Indre), France, Aug. 21, 1859; s. Denis Wenceslas and Madeline (Pelletier) G.; college at Le Dorat (Haute-Vienne), France; theol. sem., Limoges (Haute-Vienne), France; A.B., U. of France, 1879; S.T.L., Catholic Inst. of Paris, 1884; (D.D., St. Mary's U., Baltimore, 1903). Ordained R.C. priest, 1883; prof. dogmatic theology, 1885-86, prof. philosophy, 1886-87, prof. Scripture, 1888-99, St. John's Sem., Boston; prof. Scripture, St. Mary's Sem., Baltimore, 1899-1904, St. Joseph's Sem., Yonkers, N.Y., Sept. 1904—. Trustee Soc. Propagation of the Faith. Author: Outlines of Jewish History from Abraham to Our Lord, 1897; Outlines of New Testament History, 1898; General Introduction to the Study of the Holy Scriptures, 1899, 1904; Special Introduction to the Study of the Old Testament, Part I, 1901, Part II, 1906; Christ's Teaching Concerning Divorce in the New Testament, 1912. Home: Yonkers, N.Y. Deceased.

GIHON, Albert Leary, med. dir. U.S.N., retired; b. Phila., Sept. 28, 1833; A.B., Phila. High School, 1850; M.D., Coll. of Medicine and Surgery, 1852; A.M., Princeton, 1884; m. Clara Montfort Campfield, Apr. 3, 1860. Prof. chemistry and toxicology, Phila. Coll. Medicine and Surgery, 1853-54; asst. surgeon U.S.N., May 1, 1855; served at attack and capture barrier forts, nr. Canton, China, Nov., 1856; on Paraguay expdn., 1858-59; during Civil war, 1861-65; received thanks of British govt. of comdr.-in-chief French Asiatic squadron, and made Knight of the Portuguese Mil. Order of Christ, for services to British, French and Portuguese men-of-war while senior med. officer of Idaho (1st hosp. ship in U.S.N.); sr. med. dir., U.S.N., May 1, 1895; retired by operation of law, Sept. 28, 1895, with rank of commodore. Fellow and pres. Am. Acad. of Medicine. Was editor Annual of the Medical Sciences 6 yrs. Died 1901.

GILBERT, Arthur Witter, commr. agr.; b. West Brookfield, Mass., Apr. 20, 1882; s. Lewis Abbott and Louise (Brigham) G.; grad. Mass. Agrl. Coll., 1904; B.S., Boston U., 1904; M.S. in Agr., Cornell, 1905, Ph.D., 1909; m. Susan Grace Cooper, June 8, 1910. Instr. in agr., 1905-06, asst. prof. agronomy, 1906-07, U. of Me., also supervisor agrl. extension courses during same period; asst. prof., plant breeding, 1909-11, prof., 1911-17, Cornell U.; grad. studies in economics, Harvard, 1917; agrl. sec. of Boston Chamber of Commerce, 1917-19; commr. Agriculture Mass., 1919-36; advisor on state relations Agrl. Adjustment Administration, Washington, Jan. 1936—. Teacher of agr., Chautauqua Summer Sch., 1911; dir. Chautauqua Sch. of Practical Agr., 1912-13. Sec. Federal Milk Commn. during the war. Mem. bd. dirs. N.E. Council, Boston Chamber Commerce; chmn. Am. com. Internat. Inst. of Agriculture (Rome); mem. Economics Com. League of Nations, 1926; pres. Regional Agrl. Credit Corp. of Albany, N.Y., 1932—. Republican. Conglist. Author: Plant Breeding (with L. H. Bailey), 1914; The Potato (with others), 1917. Editor of Food Supply of New England, 1923. Home: Belmont, Mass. Died Dec. 7, 1936.

GILBERT, Cass, architect; b. Zanesville, O., Nov. 24, 1859; s. Gen. Samuel Augustus (U.S. Coast Survey and U.S.V.) and Elizabeth Fulton (Wheeler) G.; ed. pub. schs., Zanesville, St. Paul, and Mass. Inst. Tech.; LL.D., U. of Mich., Oberlin and Middlebury colls.; Dr. Fine Arts, New York Univ., 1931; D.Litt.,

Columbia U., 1931; m. Julia T. Finch, Nov. 29, 1887. Architect the Capitol and other bldgs., St. Paul; Essex Co. court-house, Newark, N.J.; Agriculture Bldg., Omaha Expn., 1897; Broadway-Chambers, West Street, Woolworth bldgs., and U.S. Custom House, New York; Art Building and Festival Hall, St. Louis Expn.; Central Pub. Library, St. Louis; Detroit Pub. Library; gen. plan, U. of Minn., U. of Tex., and for completion Ark. Capitol, Little Rock; U.S. Treasury Annex, Washington; Army Supply Base, Brooklyn; Federal Reserve Bank, Minneapolis; W.Va. State Capitol; U.S. Chamber of Commerce, Washington; City Hall, Waterbury, Conn.; one of architects new Union Club, New York; Union Central Life Ins. Bldg., Cincinnati; Gibraltar Bldg., for Prudential Life Ins. Co., Newark, N.J.; N.Y. Life Ins. Co. Bldg., New York; cons. architect for Port of New York. Authority on Hudson River Bridge and Kill Van Kull Bridge, Supreme Court Bldg. (Washington), U.S. Court House (New York), Seaside Tuberculosis Hosp. (Niantic, Conn.). Chairman Council of the Fine Arts; mem. Commn. of Fine Arts; mem. Nat. Jury of Fine Arts, Chicago Expn.; mem. Nat. Jury for Architecture, Paris Expn., 1900; mem. commn. for selecting design for reconstruction of U.S. Mil. Acad. One of founders Archtl. League New York (pres. 1913-14); N.A., 1908; pres. Nat. Inst. Arts and Letters, 1919; pres. A.I.A., 1908-09; mem. Am. Acad. Arts and Letters, Nat. Acad. Design (pres. 1926-30), S.R.; hon. corr. mem. Royal Inst. Brit. Architects; hon. mem. Royal Archtl. Inst. of Can., Archtl. Soc. U. of Liverpool, Eng.; hon. foreign mem. Royal Acad. of Arts. Mem. Legion of Honor. Awarded gold medal by Acad. Arts and Sciences. Home: Ridgefield, Conn. Died May 17, 1934.

GILBERT, Charles Allan, painter; b. Hartford, Conn., Sept. 9, 1873; s. Charles E. and Virginia E. G.; ed. pub. schs., Hartford; studied at Art Students' League, New York, and Julian Acad., Paris; unmarried. Has furnished illustrations to leading mags.; exhibited landscapes and figures in leading exhbns. Publications (drawings): Overheard in the Whittington Family; Portfolio of Heads; Collection of Heads in Color; Separate Drawings in Color; Women of Fiction; All Is Vanity; A Message from Mars; The Honeymoon. Invented and patented new form of motion pictures, combination of living actors and animated drawings. Ship camoufleur, 1917-18. Home: New York, N.Y. Died Apr. 20, 1929.

GILBERT, Charles Benajah, educator; b. Wilton, Conn., Mar. 9, 1855; s. Benajah and Fannie M. (Keeler) G.; A.B., Williams Coll., 1876; m. Jennie Weed, Aug. 8, 1885. Prin. high schs., Mankato and Winona, Minn., Beaver Dam and Oshkosh, Wis., 1878-83; prin. St. Paul High Sch., 1883-89; supt. schs. St. Paul, 1889-96, Newark, N.J., 1896-1900; Rochester, N.Y., 1900-03; editor-in-chief, ednl. dept., D. Appleton & Co., 1903-04; lecturer on edn., Western Reserve U., 1906—. Lecturer Teachers Coll., Columbia, 1897-1900. Pres. Nat. Assn. Sch. Supts., 1897. Author: Stepping Stones to Literature (with Sarah Louise Arnold), 8 vols.; A Graded List of Stories and Poems (with Ada Van Stone Harris); The School and its Life, 1906. Editor and part author: Stories of Heroes (6 vols.); Guide Books to English (with Ada Van Stone Harris), 2 vols.; The Gilbert Arithmetics (with C. H. Gleason), 3 vols.; The American School Readers (with K. F. Oswell), 7 vols. Associated editorially with the Macmillan Co. Home: New York, N.Y. Died Aug. 26, 1913.

GILBERT, Charles Henry, zoölogist; b. Rockford, Ill., Dec. 5, 1859; s. Edward and Sarah (Bean) G.; B.S., Butler U., 1879; M.S., Ind. U., 1882, Ph.D., 1883; m. Julia R. Hughes, Aug. 7, 1883. Asst. in natural sciences and modern langs., Ind. U., 1880-84; prof. natural hist., U. of Cincinnati, 1884-89; prof. zoölogy, Ind. U., 1889-91; prof. zoölogy, Stanford, 1891—. Asst. to U.S. Fish Commn., 1880-98; naturalist in charge U.S. Fish Commn. steamer Albatross, 1889-90; naturalist in charge Hawaiian Explorations of U.S. Fish Commn. steamer Albatross, 1902, and explorations in northwest Pacific and Japan, 1906; asst., Internat. Fisheries Commn., 1909; in charge expert salmon investigations for U.S. Bur. of Fisheries and British Columbia Fisheries Dept., 1909-27. Author: Synopsis of the Fishes of North America (with David Starr Jordan), 1882; The Deep-Sea Fishes (of the Hawaiian Islands), 1905. Home: Stanford University, Calif. Died Apr. 20, 1928.

GILBERT, Clinton Wallace, newspaper corr.; b. Long Island, N.Y., July 25, 1871; s. Edgar Lathrop and Susan (McCalvey) G.; A.B., U. of Rochester, 1891. Began as reporter New York Press, 1891, later with various New York newspapers; asso. editor New York Tribune, 1913-18; Washington corr. Evening Pub. Ledger, Phila., 1918—. Officier de l'Instruction Publique (France). Author: The Mirrors of Washington (in part), 1921, 1925; Behind the Mirrors, 1922; You Takes Your Choice, 1924. Home: Washington, D.C. Died May 17, 1933.

GILBERT, Frank Bixby, lawyer; b. Bainbridge, N.Y., Mar. 10, 1867; s. Don A. and Amelia (Bixby) G.; A.B., Hamilton, 1889, LL.D., 1920; m. Frances Freiot, Oct. 9, 1895. Admitted to bar, 1892; asst. to commrs. of statutory revision, N.Y. State, 1893-1901; atty. designated by state Legislature to draft legislative bills, 1901-05; N.Y. state law librarian, 1906-08; counsel N.Y. State Edn. Dept., 1908-19—; deputy commr. of edn. and counsel to State Edn. Dept., 1919—; acting commr. edn., N.Y., Jan.-Sept. 1921. Lecturer on constl. law and statutes and statutory construction, Albany Law Sch. Trustee Hamilton Coll., 1923—. Compiler: Law of Domestic Relations, 1898; Lien Laws of New York, 1900; Official Court Rules, N.Y., 1900, 06; N.Y. State Code of Civil Procedure, with Annotations, 1905, 2d edit., 1910; Town and County Officers Manual, N.Y. State, 1912. Co-editor: General Law of State of New York, Annotated, 1901, Supplement, 1901-06, 1906; Annotated Consolidated Laws of the State of New York, 1909, 2d edit., 1917, supplements, 1919-23. Home: Castleton, N.Y. Died Aug. 28, 1927.

GILBERT, George Gilmore, congressman, lawyer; b. Spencer Co., Ky., 1850; grad. Cecilian Coll., Ky., 1866; Lyndland Inst., Ky., 1870; (LL.B., Univ. Louisville, 1873); m. Lizzie W. Hinkle, Nov. 4, 1875. Atty. Spencer Co., 1876; mem. State senate, 1886-88; mem. Congress, 1899-1907, 8th Ky. dist. Democrat. Home: Shelbyville, Ky. Died 1909.

GILBERT, Mrs. George Henry, actress; b. Rochdale, Lancashire, Eng., Oct. 21, 1821; 1st appearance was as dancer in the Norwich circuit, 1846; m. George Henry Gilbert, dancer, 1846 (died 1866). They came to U.S., 1849, and she continued as dancer until 1857, when she began playing leading "old woman" characters, in which she has ever since been a recognized leader; after 1869 in Augustin Daly's company until his death; since then with Charles Frohman. Author: Mrs. Gilbert's Reminiscences, 1901. Died 1904.

GILBERT, George Holley, theologian; b. Cavendish, Vt., Nov. 4, 1854; s. Oliver C. and Harriet E. G.; A.B., Dartmouth, 1878, D.D., 1894; grad. Union Theol. Sem., 1883; Ph.D., U. of Leipzig, 1885; m. Flora L. Gates, June 1886. Ordained Congl. ministry, 1886; acting prof. N.T. lit., 1886-87, prof. 1887-1901, Chicago Theol. Sem. Author: The Student's Life of Jesus, 1899; The Student's Life of Paul, 1899; A Short History of Christianity in the Apostolic Age, 1906; A Commentary on Acts, 1908; Jesus, 1912; The Bible and Universal Peace, 1914; Jesus for the Men of Today, 1917; Jesus and His Bible, 1926. Home: Dorset, Vt. Died Feb. 11, 1930.

GILBERT, Grove Karl, geologist; b. Rochester, N.Y., May 6, 1843; s. Grove Sheldon and Eliza (Stanley) G.; A.B., U. of Rochester, 1862, A.M., 1872 (LL.D., 1898, U. of Wis., 1904, U. of Pa., 1907); m. Fannie L. Porter, Nov. 10, 1874. Asst. in Ward Mus., Rochester, 1863-68; geologist in Ohio survey, 1868-70, Wheeler survey, 1871-74, Powell survey, 1875-79, U.S. Geol. Survey, 1879—(chief geologist, 1889-92). Spl. lecturer, Cornell, 1886, Columbia, 1892, Johns Hopkins, 1895 and 1896. Walker grand prize, Boston Soc. Natural History, 1908. Editor geol. and phys. geography depts., Johnson's Encyclopædia. Author: Introduction to Physical Geography, 1902; Glaciers and Glaciation, vol. 3, Harriman Alaska Expdn., 1904. Died May 1, 1918.

GILBERT, Henry Franklin Belknap, composer; b. Somerville, Mass., Sept. 26, 1868; s. Benjamin Franklin and Therese Angeline (Gilson) G.; studied harmony N.E. Conservatory, 1888, composition with Edward MacDowell, Boston, 1889-92; m. Helen Kalischer, of Jassy, Roumania, June 4, 1906; children—Isolde Therese, Elizabeth Yolande. With Prof. J. D. Whitney of Harvard, gave a series of concerts illustrating modern Slavic tendencies in musical composition. Composer: A Group of Songs, 1891; Two Episodes (orchestra), 1897; Salammbô's Invocation to Tanith, Pirate Song, 1902; Zephyrus, The Lament of Deirdré (vocal), 1903; Mazurka, Negro Episode, Scherzo (piano), 1903; Two Verlaine Moods, The Island of the Fay (piano and orchestra), 1904; Croon of the Dew, 1904; Rain Song, Two Wind Songs, Sleep and Poetry, 1904; Fairy Song, 1904; Celtic Studies (4 songs), 1905; Two South American Gypsy Songs, 1906; Summerday Fantasie, American Humoresque, Comedy Overture on Negro Themes (orchestra), 1906; Orlamonde (vocal), 1907; Americanesque (orchestra), 1907; One Hundred Folksongs (edited), 1909; American Dances (orchestra), 1911; symphonic poem—The Dance in Place Congo (after Geo. W. Cable, orchestra, prod. as ballet by Met. Opera Co., New York and Boston, 1918); Negro Rhapsody, (orchestra), written for the Norfolk (Conn.) Festival of 1913; symphonic prologue, Riders to the Sea, 1914; hymn To America (chorus and orchestra), 1914; Indian Sketches (orchestra), 1914; 1-act opera Fantasy in Delft (libretto by Thomas P. Robinson); Symphonic Piece, 1926, and Nocturne, 1927; etc. Composed the Prelude, Norse Scene, and music for various pantomimes in Pilgrim Tercentenary Memorial Pageant (Plymouth, Mass.), 1921. Pres. Composer's Club of Boston. Lecturer at Harvard and Columbia univs. Home: Cambridge, Mass. Died May 19, 1928.

GILBERT, Hiram Thornton, lawyer; b. Troy Grove, Ill., May 9, 1850; s. Dr. Alson I. and Mary C. (Hapeman) G.; ed. Cornell U., 1869-71; U. of Leipzig, Germany, 1871-73; m. Georgiana J. Leland, Oct. 16, 1877; children—Helen S., Georgiana W. (Mrs. John S. Hess). Admitted to bar, Sept. 1875, and practiced at Ottawa until 1888, then at Chicago. County judge of La Salle Co., 1882-86. Author Municipal Court Act under which Municipal Court of Chicago was organized; was mem. 47th Gen. Assembly of Illinois. Home: Chicago, Ill. Died Nov. 29, 1939.

GILBERT, Horace Mark, orchardist; b. Geneseo, Ill., Oct. 22, 1862; s. Nathaniel Carpenter and Francelia (Amsden) G.; A.B., Knox Coll., Ill., 1885, A.M., 1889; m. Marion Hamilton Richey, Feb. 15, 1893; children—Curtiss Richey, Lois Marion (Mrs. Nelson R. Anderson), Elon James, Margaret Guida (Mrs. Luke L. Benz), Horace Nathaniel, Dorothy Marcia (Mrs. V. R. Boaz), Evelyn Luella. Pres. and mgr. Richey & Gilbert Co., fruit and cold storage, 1904—; grower of 800 acres of orchard, mostly apples; pres. H. M. Gilbert Co., First Fruit Credit Corp. of Yakima; trustee Liberty Savings & Loan Assn. Mem. Washington State Irrigation Inst., State Hort. Assn. (pres.), Tieten Water Users Assn. (pres. 1912-29, now pres.). Mem. bd. trustees Whitman Coll. Mem. Chamber Commerce U.S.A. (nat. councillor), Wash. State Chamber Commerce. Republican. Conglist. Rotarian. Home: Yakima, Wash. Died 1934.

GILBERT, James Eleazer, clergyman; b. Alexander, N.Y., Dec. 20, 1839; s. David and Amanda (Crawford) G.; ed. Genesee Coll., N.Y. (D.D., Cornell, 1884, L.L.D., Am. Univ. of Harriman, 1896); m. Sarah J. Thompson, June 11, 1866. Was deputy to U.S. commr. for Western N.Y., city editor Buffalo Courier, asso. editor Buffalo Christian Advocate, editor Sunday School Standard, prin. pub. sch., Buffalo and Dayton, O., prin. acad., Lancaster, N.Y.; entered ministry M.E. Ch., 1872; pastor Cincinnati, Lexington, Ky., Topeka, Kan., Milwaukee, Grand Rapids, Indianapolis. While at Buffalo, prepared the curriculum of pub. schs., originated system of language lessons, etc.; while in Topeka founded Kan. Methodist, was sec. Kan. Christian Temperance Union, Kan. Relief Soc.; in Milwaukee founded Teachers' Normal Coll. and is still pres.; organizer, 1889, and sec. Am. Soc. Religious Edn.; editor Jour. of Religious Edn. Prepared weekly expositions of internat. S. S. lessons for many secular papers, 1894—. Home: Washington, D.C. Died 1909.

GILBERT, John, actor; b. Logan, Utah, July 10, 1897; s. Walter B. and Sarah Ida (Apperley) G.; ed. grammar schs. and at Hitchcock Mil. Acad., San Rafael, Calif.; m. Leatrice Joy (divorced); 1 dau., Leatrice Joy; m. 2d, Ina Claire (divorced); m. 3d, Virginia Bruce, Aug. 10, 1932. 1 dau. Identified with stage since early childhood; writer, dir., cutter of motion pictures; actor; a leading character in "Big Parade"; "Merry Widow," etc. Mason. Home: Beverly Hills, Calif. Died Jan. 9, 1936.

GILBERT, John Ingersoll, lawyer; b. Pittsford, Vt., Oct. 11, 1837; s. Simeon and Margaret (Ingersoll) G.; grad. Univ. of Vt., 1859, A.M., 1862, LL.D., 1884; m. Katharine Fessenden, June 20, 1870. Admitted to bar, 1869; mem. Assembly, 1876-78; declined re-election, 1879; mem. N.Y. Senate, 1884-85; chmn. judiciary com. Assembly, 1878; chmn. select com. to investigate N.Y. State Normal Schs., 1878—report, which was widely circulated in this country and abroad, submitted to legislature, 1879; chmn. select senate com. to investigate Consolidated Gas Co. of N.Y. City, 1885; Rep. candidate sec. of state, 1889; del. at large N.Y. Constl. Conv., 1894; mem. bd. trustees State Normal Sch., Potsdam, N.Y., 1869—. Editor (with Louis W. Pratt) Revised Edition (with notes), first 10 vols. N.Y. Court of Appeals Report, 1887 (Albany). Home: Malone, N.Y. Died 1904.

GILBERT, Levi, editor; b. Brooklyn, Aug. 23, 1852; s. Thomas and Mary (Keymer) G.; A.B., Wesleyan U., 1874, A.M., 1876; student Drew Theol. Sem., 1875; (D.D., Hamline, 1888, Wesleyan, 1900; B.D., Drew Theol. Sem., 1902; LL.D., Moores Hill Coll., 1905; Litt.D., Ohio Wesleyan, 1907); m. Annie Louise Murphy, Aug. 4, 1875 (died 1885); m. 2d, Jennie, d. Dr. J. M. Cole, of Winona, Minn., Feb. 9, 1887. Ordained M.E. ministry, 1878; pastor in Minn., Lansing and Brownsdale, 1875-76, Kasson, 1876-79, Waseca, 1879-80, Northfield, 1881-82, Duluth, 1883-85, Winona, 1885-90, Seattle, Wash., 1890-82, Cleveland, O., 1892-97, New Haven, Conn., 1897-1900; editor of Daily Christian Advocate, 1900, Western Christian Advocate, 1900—; lecturer on social and patriotic subjects. Del. Gen. Confs., 1904, 1908; del. Fed. Council of Federated Chs. of Christ in America, 1908, 1912, Meth. Ecumenical Conf., Toronto, 1911; mem. exec. com. Fedn. for Social Service, Freedmen's Aid Soc. M.E. Ch. Mason. Home: Cincinnati (Madisonville), O. Died Dec. 24, 1917.

GILBERT, Lyman D., lawyer; b. Harrisburg, Pa., Aug. 17, 1845; grad. Yale, 1865; studied law in office of John C. Kunkel. In 1871 became partner of Hon. Wayne MacVeagh and John B. McPherson, firm becoming Gilbert & McPherson after removal of Mr. MacVeagh to Phila. Apptd. deputy atty. gen. of Pa., 1873, and after death of Hon. S. E. Dimmick, served several months as atty. gen., resigning 1882, and engaging in private practice with John H. Weiss as partner until 1898; became counsel for Pa. R.R. and other large interests. Home: Harrisburg, Pa. Died May 4, 1914.

GILBERT, Mahlon Norris, coadjutor P.E. bishop of Minn.; consecrated Oct. 17, 1886; b. Laurens, N.Y., Mar. 23, 1848; ed. Fairfield Sem., and Hobart Coll.; (A.M., D.D., LL.D.); left before end of course because of sickness; grad. Seabury Div. Sch., Minn., 1875; (D.D.; also D.D., Racine Coll.); m. Fannie Pierpoint Carvill, 1880. Before entering Seabury was in charge School of the Good Shepherd, Ogden, Utah. Ordered deacon, June 1875; ordained priest, Oct. 1875; rector St. James, Deer Lodge, Mont., 1873-78; St. Peters, Helena, Mont., 1878-81; rector Christ Ch., St. Paul, Minn., 1881-86. Died 1900.

GILBERT, Matthew William, clergyman; b. Mechanicsville, S.C., July 25, 1862; s. Rev. Mark and Mary (Rembert) G.; A.B., Colgate U., Hamilton, N.Y., 1887; B.D., Union Theol. Sem., New York, 1907; (D.D., Guadaloupe Coll., 1896); m. Agnes Boozer, May 15, 1882. Ordained Bapt. ministry, 1882; pastor Nashville, Tenn., 1887-90, Jacksonville, Fla., 1890-92; prin. at Live Oak and Jacksonville, Fla., 1892-94; pastor Savannah, Ga., 1894-97, Charleston, S.C., 1899-1902; prof. in Benedict Coll., Columbia, S.C., 1902-04; pastor Mt. Olivet Ch., New York, 1904-11; pres. Selma (Ala.) Univ., June 1911—. Member Fed. Council of Chs. of Christ in America, bd. of mgrs. Bapt. City Mission Soc. of New York; corr. sec. Am. Nat. Baptist Conv.; recording sec. Permanent Council of Baptists of New York. Trustee Women's Training Sch. (Washington), Voorhees Normal Sch. (Denmark, S.C.). Republican. Home: Selma, Ala. Died Mar. 8, 1917.

GILBERT, Newton Whiting, lawyer; b. Worthington, O., May 24, 1862; s. Theodore R. and Ellen L. G.; ed. Ohio State U. (non-grad.); admitted to bar, 1885; LL.D., Iowa Wesleyan and U. of Philippines, 1913; m. Martha Edna Berge, Aug. 8, 1906; 1 dau., Viola. Practiced at Angola, Ind.; mem. Ind. Senate, 1896-1900; lt. gov. of Ind., 1900-04; mem. 59th Congress (1905-07), 12th Ind. Dist.; capt. Co. H, 157th Ind. Vol. Inf., May-Nov. 1898; judge Court of 1st Instance, Manila, P.I., 1906-08; mem. Philippine Commn., 1908-09; apptd. sec. pub. instrn. of P.I., 1909, and v. gov., 1909-13 (acting gov. gen. 1912-13); del. Rep. Nat. Conv., 1916. In New York, 1916—. Pres. bd. regents Philippine U., 1908-13. Fellow Royal Geog. Soc., London. Mason. Episcopalian. Home: Santa Ana, Calif. Died July 5, 1939.

GILBERT, Prentiss Bailey; b. Rochester, N.Y., Oct. 3, 1883; s. Lt. Col. William Wallace (U.S.A.) and Mary Elizabeth (Chapman) G.; Ph.B., Univ. of Rochester, 1906, A.M., 1916; A.B., Yale Univ., 1907; studied Columbia, and El Colejio de San Carlos, Cebu, P.I.; grad. U.S. Army War Coll., 1924; m. Charlotte Jeannette Gilder, Nov. 9, 1918. Mine supt., 1907-10; travel and study in Europe, Orient, Australasia, Oceania, and Central America, 1911-16; organizer, and first dir. Sch. of Extension Teaching, U. of Rochester, 1916. Spl. aide U.S.A., in Philippines, Spanish-Am. War; 1st lt., capt. and maj., Gen. Staff U.S.A., World War; was chief of Combat Sect., Div. of Mil. Intelligence; chief Div. of Polit. and Econ. Intelligence, 1919-24; chief Div. of Western European Affairs, Dept. of State, Washington, 1924-29; 1st sec. Am. Embassy, Paris, 1930; U.S. consul, Geneva, 1930-37; counselor Am. Embassy, Berlin, 1937—. First rep. of U.S. on Council of League of Nations; rep. of U.S. at Congress of Internat. Chamber of Commerce, Stockholm, 1927, Amsterdam, 1929; rep. of U.S. Govt. on Com. for Tech. Assistance to China. Commd. lt. col. O.R.C., U.S.A., July 31, 1923. Author: A Maid of Honor (play), adapted (from the German): Der Gute König, by Raoul Aurenheimer, play, presented by Philadelphia Civic Theatre, 1930. Home: Berlin, Germany. Died Feb. 24, 1939.

GILBERT, Ralph, state senator; b. Taylorville, Ky., Jan. 17, 1882; s. George G.; student U. of Va.; LL.B., U. of Louisville, 1901; m. Jane Thompson (died 1933); children—Jane E., Dorothy, Betsy; m. 2d, Victoria M. Vodila, Aug. 20, 1935. Practiced law in Shelby County; judge Shelby County Court, 1910-17 (resigned); mem. 67th to 70th and 72d Congresses (1921-29, 1931-33), 8th Ky. Dist.; now mem. Ky. State Senate (majority leader). Democrat. Home: Shelbyville, Ky. Died July 30, 1939.

GILBERT, Seymour Parker, banker; b. Bloomfield, N.J., Oct. 13, 1892; s. Seymour Parker and Carrie Jennings (Cooper) G.; A.B., Rutgers Coll., 1912, A.M., 1916, hon. M.Sc., 1922; LL.B., cum laude, Harvard, 1915, LL.D., same and Columbia, Rutgers, Lehigh; m. Louise Ross Todd, Oct. 8, 1924; children—S. Parker III, Louise Todd. With Cravath & Henderson, New York, 1915-18; mem. War Loan Staff, office sec. of Treasury, as counsel in war loan matters, 1918-20; asst. sec. of Treasury, in charge fiscal affairs, June 1920-June 30, 1921; under-sec. of the Treasury, in charge fiscal affairs, July 1, 1921-Nov. 17, 1923; mem. Cravath, Henderson and de Gersdorff, New York, 1923-24; agent gen. for reparation payments in Germany, Oct. 30, 1924-May 17, 1930; partner J. P. Morgan & Co., 1931—; dir. Bankers Trust Co. Decorated Grand Officer Legion of Honor (France), 1930; Grand Officer Order of Leopold (Belgium), 1930; Grand Officer Order Saints Maurizio and Lazzaro (Italy), 1930. Republican. Home: Southampton, N.Y., and N.Y. City. Died Feb. 23, 1938.

GILBERT, William Ball, judge; b. Fairfax Co., Va., July 4, 1847; s. John and Sarah Catherine (Ball) G.; A.B., Williams Coll., 1868, LL.D., 1898; LL.B., U. of Mich., 1872; m. Julia W. Lindsley, Sept. 3, 1873. In practice at Portland, Ore., 1872-92; U.S. circuit judge, 9th Circuit, 1892-1911; judge U.S. Circuit Ct. of Appeals, Jan. 1, 1912—. Republican. Home: Portland, Ore. Died Apr. 27, 1931.

GILBRETH, Frank Bunker, cons. engineer; b. Fairfield, Me., July 7, 1868; s. John Hiram and Martha (Bunker) G.; grad. English High Sch., Boston, 1885; LL.D., U. of Me., 1920; m. Lillian Evelyn Moller (B.L., M.L., U. of Calif.; Ph.D., Brown U.), Oct. 19, 1904. Contracting engr., Boston, 1895-1904, New York, 1904-11; consulting engr., 1911—; pres. Frank B. Gilberth (Inc.). Commd. maj., Engrs., July 1917; on active duty Gen. Staff Coll., Washington, Dec. 1917. Lecturer at 20 Am. and European univs.; dir. Summer Sch. of Management for Professors of Engineering, Psychology and Economics; organized Soc. Promotion Science of Management (afterwards Taylor Soc., the first of its kind); founder internat. museums for elimination of unnecessary fatigue of workers in the industries; inventor of the micro-motion and chronocyclegraph processes for determining fundamental units and methods of industrial edn., and of methods for fitting crippled soldiers for industrial life. Author: Field System, 1908; Concrete System, 1908; Bricklaying System, 1909; Motion Study, 1911; Primer of Scientific Management, 1911; also with wife, Time Study; Fatigue Study, 1916; Applied Motion Study, 1917; Motion Study for the Handicapped, 1919. Home: Montclair, N.J. Died June 14, 1924.

GILCHRIST, Albert Waller, governor; b. (during temporary absence of mother from Florida) at Greenwood, S.C., Jan. 15, 1858; s. Gen. William E. (planter, slave owner, state senator) and Rhoda Elizabeth (Waller) G.; desc. of Col. Joseph Ball, g.f. George Washington, and Col. Edwin Conway, g.f. James Madison; grad. Carolina Mil. Inst., Charlotte, N.C.; cadet U.S. Mil. Acad. 3 yrs., class of '82. Civ. engr., real estate dealer, orange grower. Mem. Fla. Ho. of Rep., 1893, 95, 1903, 05 (speaker 1905); gov. of Fla., 1909-13. Democrat. Resigned as brig. gen., Fla. Militia, June 1898, and enlisted as pvt. Co. C, 3d U.S. Vol. Inf.; served in Santiago, Cuba; mustered out with rank of capt., 1899. Mason. Mem. bd. visitors U.S. Mil. Acad., 1896. Home: Punta Gorda, Fla. Died May 16, 1926.

GILCHRIST, Alexander, gen. sec. bd. of home missions U. P. Ch., 1899—; b. West Hebron, N.Y., Mar. 25, 1856; s. Joseph and Martha Jane G.; ed. pub. schs. Waterman, Ill., 1865-70, Monmouth, Ill., Coll.; grad. Univ. of Wooster, 1879; studied Allegheny U. P. Theol. Sem., Pa., 1879-82 (D.D., 1894); m. Cora Seaton, Oct. 22, 1885. In U. P. pastorates 1882-99. Republican. Home: Pittsburgh, Pa. Died 1907.

GILCHRIST, Donald Bean, librarian; b. Franklin, N.H., Jan. 11, 1892; s. Harry W. and Martha (Bean) G.; A.B., Dartmouth, 1913; B.L.S., N.Y. State Library Sch., 1915; m. Ella Trowbridge, June 26, 1918; 1 son, David Trowbridge. Dept. head, U. of Minn. Library, 1915-16; librarian U. of Rochester, 1919—. Served on Mexican border, 1916-17; capt. 339th F.A., U.S.A., Aug. 1917-Dec. 1918; librarian Am. Commn. to Negotiate Peace, Paris, France, 1918-19. Sec. Assn. Research Libraries. Protestant. Editor: Doctoral Dissertations Accepted by American Universities, 1933-35. Home: Rochester, N.Y. Died Aug. 4, 1939.

GILCHRIST, T(homas) Caspar, M.D.; b. Crewe Cheshire, Eng., June 15, 1862; s. Robert and Emma (Weiss) G.; ed. Owen's Coll. (Victoria U.), Eng.; intermediate M.B., U. of London, 1886; M.R.C.S., London, 1887; licentiate in medicine, surgery and midwifery, London, 1887; hon. M.D., U. of Md., 1907; m. Annie McKerrow Hall, 1894. Came to America, 1890; clin. prof. dermatology, U. of Md., 1897—; clin. prof. dermatology, Johns Hopkins U. and dermatologist, Johns Hopkins Hosp., 1898—. Presbyn. Home: Roland Park, Md. Died Nov. 14, 1927.

GILCHRIST, William Wallace, composer; b. Jersey City, N.J., 1846; s. W. W. and R. A. G.; studied music under Prof. Clarke, U. of Pa.; organist in Cincinnati, 1872-73. Conductor Phila. Festival Chorus, Mendelssohn Club, Philadelphia, Harrisburg Choral Soc., Symphony Soc. and other ch. socs. and orchestra. Organizer, and pres. Manuscript Soc.; pres. Musical Art Club; mem. Nat. Inst. Arts and Letters. Composer: 46th Psalm (chorus and orchestra); Easter Idyl (chorus and orchestra); Christmas Oratorio (chorus and orchestra); Symphony in D, also C, Nonet in G minor, Quintett in C minor, also one in F, trio in G minor. Three suites, violin and piano. also much church music and many songs, part-songs, etc. Home: Philadelphia, Pa. Died Dec. 20, 1916.

GILDER, Jeannette Leonard, journalist, critic; b. St. Thomas Hall (woman's coll., conducted by her father), Flushing, N.Y., Oct. 3, 1849; d. late Rev. William H. and Jane (Nutt) G.; sister of Richard Watson, Robert Fletcher and Joseph B. G.; at 18 became writer on Newark (N.J.) Morning Register, and Newark reporter for New York Tribune; was asso. with her brother R. W. Gilder, in editorial dept. Scribner's Monthly (later The Century); lit. editor and afterward musical and dramatic editor New York Herald, 1875-80; with brother, Joseph B. Gilder, started Jan. 1881, The Critic (later Putnam's Mag.), of which was asso. editor; was 18 yrs., over pen-name "Brunswick," New York corr. Boston Saturday Evening Gazette and Boston Evening Transcript; was corr. London Acad. and for some time New York corr. Philadelphia Press and Record; now regular corr. Chicago Tribune. Author: The Autobiography of a Tomboy, 1900; The Tomboy at Work, 1904. Edited: Essays from the Critic (with Joseph B. Gilder), 1882; also (with Helen Gray Cone, q.v.) Pen Portraits of Literary Women, 1887; Authors at Home (with J. B. Gilder), 1889. Home: New York, N.Y. Died Jan. 17, 1916.

GILDER, John Francis, pianist and composer; b. Phila., Apr. 3, 1837; s. Rev. William H. Gilder; unmarried. Has traveled throughout U.S. and Canada on concert tours; was in San Francisco, 1873-75, and gave many concerts there and in that section; brother of Richard Watson Gilder, editor of The Century, and of Joseph B. and Jeannette L. Gilder, editor of Putnam's Monthly. Composer of about 75 pieces for piano and 12 vocal. Home: New York, N.Y. Died 1908.

GILDER, Joseph B., journalist; b. St. Thomas's Hall (woman's coll., conducted by father), Flushing, N.Y., June 29, 1858; s. late Rev. William H. and Jane (Nutt) G.; brother of Jeannette Leonard, Robert Fletcher and Richard Watson Gilder; entered the U.S. Naval Acad., 1872, resigned, 1874; married May 7, 1892. Reporter, Newark, N.J., 1874-77; wrote New York letters to Boston Advertiser, Buffalo Courier, etc.; reporter and asst. city editor New York Herald, 1877-80; with sister Jeannette L., started The Critic (later Putnam's Mag.), Jan. 1881; (co-editor, 28 yrs.); pres. The Critic Co., 1893-1901. Treas. Am. Copyright League, 1886; an organizer and 1st sec. of Univ. Settlement Soc. of New York; lit. adviser to The Century Co., 1895-1902; U.S. Govt. despatch agt. at London, 1902-04; editor New York Times Review of Books, 1910-11; in banking business, 1911-14; sec. Industrial Finance Corp., 1914-29, Morris Plan Ins. Soc., 1917-29; travel in Europe, 1928-35. Editor: J. R. Lowell's Impressions of Spain, 1899; Andrew Carnegie's Gospel of Wealth, 1900; The American Idea, 1902; Addresses of John Hay, 1906; also (with Jeannette L. Gilder), Essays from The Critic, 1882; Authors at Home, 1889. Home: New York, N.Y. Died Dec. 9, 1936.

GILDER, Richard Watson, editor The Century; b Bordentown, N.J., Feb. 8, 1844; s. Rev. William H. and Jane (Nutt) G.; ed. at father's sem., Flushing, L.I.; (LL.D., Dickinson Coll., 1883; A.M., Harvard, 1890; L.H.D., Princeton, 1896, Yale, 1901; LL.D., Wesleyan, 1903); m. Helena, d. Commodore George de Kay, and g.d. Joseph Rodman Drake, June 3, 1874. Private Landis' Phila. battery, in Emergency campaign in Pa., 1863; in railroad service, 1864-65; corr., and later mng. editor Newark (N.J.) Advertiser; later (with Newton Crane) established Newark Register; then edited Hours at Home, a New York monthly; mng. editor Scribner's Monthly, 1870; editor-in-chief, 1881, under its later name of The Century. Pres. Public Art. League of U.S.; mem. Council Nat. Civil Service Reform League; mem. Nat. Inst. Arts and Letters; an organizer Internat. Copyright League. Was chmn. N.Y. Tenement House Commn., 1894; also 1st pres. New York Kindergarten Assn.; v.p. and acting pres. City Club. Author: (of poems): The New Day, 1875-76; The Celestial Passion; Lyrics; Two Worlds; etc.; A Book of Music (collection), 1906. Home: New York, N.Y. Died 1909.

GILDER, Robert Fletcher, newspaperman; b. Flushing, N.Y., Oct. 6, 1856; s. late Rev. William H. and Jane (Nutt) G.; ed. pub. schs. of Newark, N.J., and The Gunnery School, Washington, Conn.; studied art in New York and Omaha; Sc.D., U. of Neb., 1917. With Omaha World-Herald, 27 years. Discoverer prehistoric flint quarries in eastern Wyo., 1904; discoverer Neb. Loess man, oldest human remains found in Am. up to that time; of a prehistoric culture in Eastern Neb.; discoverer, with Prof. C. J. Sarle, 47 pueblo ruins in southern Ariz. Desert. Landscape painter. Author of monographs, newspaper and mag. articles on archæology of Valley of Mo. River, Wyo., Neb., Western Ia. and Ariz.; archæologist, U. of Neb. Museum 12 years. Home: Omaha, Neb. Died Mar. 7, 1940.

GILDERSLEEVE, Basil Lanneau, philologist; b. Charleston, S.C., Oct. 23, 1831; s. Rev. Benjamin and Emma Louisa (Lanneau) G.; A.B., Princeton.

1849, A.M., 1852; studied in univs. of Berlin, Bonn and Göttingen, Ph.D., Göttingen, 1853; (LL.D., William and Mary, 1869, Harvard, 1886, Yale, 1901, U. of Chicago 1901, U. of Pa., 1911; D.C.L., U. of the South, 1884; L.H.D., Princeton, 1899; D.Litt., Cambridge, 1905, Oxon, 1905); m. Eliza Fisher Colston, Sept. 18, 1866. Prof. Greek, 1856-76, and of Latin, 1861-66, Univ. of Va.; prof. Greek, Johns Hopkins U., Baltimore, 1876-1915, when retired. Founder and editor Am. Journal of Philology, 1880—. Fellow Am. Acad. Arts and Sciences; mem. Am. Acad. Arts and Letters, etc. Author: Latin Grammar, 1867-94; Latin Series (primer, reader, school Latin grammar, Latin composition, etc.), 1875; Greek Syntax, 1900; Creed of the Old South, 1915. Editor: Persius, 1875; Justin Martyr, 1877; Odes of Pindar, 1885. Died Jan. 9, 1924.

GILDERSLEEVE, Ferdinand, merchant, banker; b. Gildersleeve, Conn., Aug. 20, 1840; s. Sylvester and Emily Shepard (Cornwall) G.; ed. in pub. and pvt. schs., and 6 mos. in Europe, 1864; m. Adelaide Edna Smith, Oct. 29, 1879 (died 1880); m. 2d, Harriet Elizabeth Northam, Sept. 12, 1883. Sr. partner S. Gildersleeve & Sons, mchts. and formerly shipbuilders, established 1821; pres. First Nat. Bank, Portland, Conn. (organized, 1865), 1894—; treas. Freestone Savings Bank, Portland, 1902— (pres., 1887-02); dir. and sec. Portland Water Co., owner large farm at Gildersleeve; trustee Conn. Hosp. for Insane (finance com.); mem. Portland Town Sch. Com.; established postoffice at Gildersleeve, 1872, and p.m. until 1916; corporator Middlesex Hosp.; vestryman Trinity Ch. (Episcopal), Portland, 1865—, now jr. warden. Home: Gildersleeve, Conn. Died June 27, 1919.

GILDERSLEEVE, Henry Alger, lawyer; b. Dutchess Co., N.Y., Aug. 1, 1840; s. Smith James and Rachel (Alger) G.; ed. College Hill, Poughkeepsie, N.Y., and Columbia U. Law Sch.; m. Virginia Crocheron, Apr. 14, 1868. Admitted to bar, 1866; served capt. and maj. during Civil War and was bvtd. lt. col. for gallant and meritorious services in Georgia and Carolina campaigns. Judge Ct. of General Sessions, 1876-89; judge Superior Ct., 1891-94; justice Supreme Ct. of N.Y., 1894-1909, resigned. Democrat. Mem. N.G.N.Y.; capt. of co. of Am. riflemen sent to Ireland, 1875. Home: New York, N.Y. Died Feb. 27, 1923.

GILDERSLEEVE, Oliver, shipbuilder; b. Portland (now Gildersleeve), Conn., Mar. 6, 1844; s. Henry and Emily (Finette) G.; and descendant of a noted line of ancestors and shipbuilders, extending in America to Richard Gildersleeve, Wethersfield, Conn., 1636; high sch. edn.; m. Mary Ellen Hall, Nov. 8, 1871. Apprenticed in father's shipyard at 17; in shipping commn. business with bro., Sylvester, New York, 1881-84, and actively identified for many yrs. with S. Gildersleeve & Sons; has organized and conducted many large business enterprises; pres. Portland (Conn.) Water Co., 1889—, Portland St. Ry. Co., 1893-96, Portland Electric Light Co., 1890-92, Middletown St. Ry. Co., 1902-05, Gildersleeve & Cromwell Ferry Co., 1887-91, Middlesex Quarry Co., 1904—, Phœnix Lead Mining Co., Sliver Cliff, Colo., 1900—, Brown Wire Gun Co., New York, 1903-05, Gildersleeve Shipbuilding Co., 1909—, Oliver Gildersleeve & Son, 1909—; pres. treas. Portland Mfg. Co., organized 1908; v.p. and treas. Me. Produce Co., 1905—; trustee Freestone Savings Bank, Portland, Conn., 1887—, etc. An incorporator and trustee Conn. Coll. for Women, New London; mem. Rivers, Harbors and Bridges Commn. of Conn.; candidate for Congress, 1900. Democrat. Episcopalian; del. Annual Diocesan Episcopal Conv., 1884—, and prominent in many philanthropic enterprises of the ch.; established Memorial Fund, Trinity Ch., Portland. Home: Gildersleeve, Conn. Died July 26, 1912.

GILE, John Martin, physician; b. Pembroke, N.H., Mar. 8, 1864; s. Brainerd and Mary (Kimball) G.; A.B. Dartmouth, 1887; M.D., 1890; m. Vesta Grace Fowler, June 8, 1892. Began practice at Tewksbury, Mass., 1890; prof. practice of medicine, 1896-1910, dean and prof. clin. surgery, 1910—, Dartmouth Med. Sch. Fellow Am. Coll. Surgeons. Member Governor's Council, 4th dist., 1911, 1912. Commd. lt. Med. R.C., and med. aide to the gov., 1917-18. Trustee Dartmouth Coll. Home: Hanover, N.H. Died July 15, 1925.

GILE, M(oses) Clement, college prof.; b. Haverhill, Mass., Dec. 4, 1858; s. Moses and Elizabeth (Kelly) G.; grad. Phillips Acad., Andover, Mass., 1879; A.B., Brown U., 1883, A.M., 1886; (hon. Litt.D., Brown, 1913, Colo. Coll., 1913); m. Josephine E. Richards, June 29, 1886. Instr. Latin and Greek, Phillips Acad., 1883-92; asst. prof. Greek, U. of Chicago, 1892; prof. Greek, 1892-96, prof. classical langs., 1896—, Colorado Coll., Colorado Springs. Republican. Baptist. Died 1916.

GILES, William Alexander, retired; b. in Mass., 1836; ed. New Salem Acad.; taught in high sch.; m. Elizabeth H. Harper, 1857. Went to Chicago, 1862, and engaged in wholesale jewelry business; retired 1882. Pres. N.E. Soc. of Chicago several yrs. Asso. mem. Chicago Real Estate Bd. Prominent in sociol. and economic affairs; has lectured at U. of Chicago, Northwestern U., Ill. Coll. Home: Chicago, Ill. Died Dec. 17, 1913.

GILL, Adam Capen, univ. prof.; b. Chesterville, Me., Aug. 22, 1863; s. Elisha and Huldah (Capen) G.; A.B., Amherst, 1884; Ph.D., Munich, 1893; m. Ella E. Eaton, Oct. 2, 1896. Asst. prof. mineralogy and petrography, 1894-1910, prof., 1910—, Cornell U. Author of Tables for Determination of the Common Minerals. Chromite of Kenai Peninsula, Alaska. Home: Ithaca, N.Y. Died Nov. 9, 1932.

GILL, Augustus Herman, prof. chemistry; b. Canton, Mass., Aug. 1, 1864; s. Augustus and Hannah P. (Drake) G.; S.B., Mass. Inst. Tech., 1884; Ph.D., U. of Leipzig, 1890; Sc.D., Rhode Island State Coll., 1923; m. Mabel F. Shepard, Sept. 2, 1897; children—Helen (Mrs. Charles McKay Welling), Paul Herman. Became assistant, 1884, instr., 1886-87, and 1890-94, asst. prof. gas analysis, 1894-1906, asso. prof. tech. analysis, 1906-09, prof., 1909-34, professor emeritus, Mass. Inst. of Technology. Lecturer Wellesley Coll., 1892-93. Unitarian. Republican. Mason. Author: Gas and Fuel Analysis for Engineers, 1896; A Short Handbook of Oil Analysis, 1897; Engineroom Chemistry, 1907; Automobile Gasoline, 1923; Power Plant Chemistry, 1935. Home: Belmont, Mass. Died Nov. 11, 1936.

GILL, Benjamin, college prof.; b. Holmfirth, Yorkshire, Eng., July 11, 1843; s. Mark and Amelia (Kaye) G.; grad. Wesleyan Acad., Wilbraham, Mass., 1866; A.B., Wesleyan U., Middletown, Conn., 1870, A.M., 1873 (D.D., 1904) m. Lucy Eleanor Whitman, Apr. 26, 1870 (died 1897); 2d, Ellen Urania Clark, June 19, 1907. Mem. N.E. Conf. M.E. Ch., 1870—; ordained elder, 1876; instr., 1872-76, prof. Greek and history, 1876-92, Wesleyan Acad.; prof. Latin and instr. German, 1892-94, prof. Greek and Latin, 1894-1908, dean Sch. Lang. and Lit., 1895-1908, in charge dept. history, 1897-99, chaplain, 1899—, Pa. State College. Republican. Chmn. sch. bd., Wilbraham, Mass., 1881-84. Died Feb. 11, 1912.

GILL, Bennett Lloyd, banker; b. Huntsville, Ala., Oct. 9, 1862; s. Charles Alexander and Antoinette (Lloyd) G.; ed. pub. sch.; m. Rena Childress, Jan. 26, 1887; children—Kate Antoinette (wife of Dr. Harry P. Harber), Brice (Mrs. James T. Marriott), Lloyd Childress, Bennett Lloyd. Began as laborer in planing mill; clk. in grocery and feed store 3 yrs., in dry goods store 2 yrs.; began in banking business with Bivins & Corley, 1883, later with Am. Nat. Bank, Terrell, chmn. bd., 1922—; v.p. 1st Nat. Bank, Terrell, 1890-1911, later served as chmn. bd.; v.p. dir. Seaboard Nat. Bank, New York, 1913-22. Commr. ins. and banking, Tex.; v.p. Tex. State Fair Assn.; pres. N. Tex. Hosp. for Insane; mem. Sch. Bd. and Library Bd., Terrell. Democrat. Episcopalian. Home: Terrell, Tex. Died Sept. 30, 1935.

GILL, Henry Z., physician; b. on farm, Richboro, Pa., Oct. 6, 1831; s. Henry and Mary (Fretz) G.; ed. in public schools and private acad. (A.M., McKendree Coll., 1875; LL.D., U. of Wooster, 1885); taught school, 1853-54; read medicine under physicians and at Starling Med. Coll., Columbus, O.; grad. Jefferson Med. Coll., Phila., 1857; m. Mattie W., d. Timothy R. Carpenter, Columbus, O., April 21, 1869. Practiced at Columbus, O., until 1861; asst. surgeon 11th regt., 1861, and later surgeon 95th regt., Ohio vols.; surgeon U.S. vols. from June, 1864-65 (surgeon-in-chief 1st div., 20th army corps, during Atlanta, Savannah and Carolina campaigns); 2 yrs. in European hosps.; later 3 yrs. asst. St. Louis Eye and Ear Infirmary; lecturer on pathology, St. Louis Med. Coll.; asso. editor and prop. St. Louis Med. and Surg. Jour.; pres. St. Louis Micros. Soc.; physician Southern Ill. penitentiary, 1881-83; prof. operative and clinical surgery, med. dept. Wooster Univ., 1883-86; resigned and removed to Kan.; some time prof. histology, microscopy and bacteriology, Kan. Med. Coll., Topeka; sec. State bd. of health, Kan., 1897-99. Author: Gill's Sanné on Diphtheria, Croup and Tracheotomy. Home: Long Beach, Calif. Died 1907.

GILL, John Jr., congressman; b. Baltimore, June 9, 1850; s. George M. and Ann (McKim) G.; acad. edn. Hampden-Sidney Coll., Va.; studied law, U. of Md.; married. Admitted to bar, 1871, and began practice at Baltimore; mem. Gill, Preston & Field. One of legal advisers City of Baltimore; police commissioner, 9 yrs.; mem. Md. Ho. of Dels., 1874-77. Senate, 1882-84, 1904-06, resigned; mem. 59th to 61st Congresses (1905-11), 4th Md. Dist.; Democrat. Officer 5th Regt. Md. N.G., 1877-78. Home: Baltimore, Md. Died Jan. 27, 1918.

GILL, John Edward, educator; b. Quincy, Ill., June 19, 1872; s. John Edward and Mary (Jochem) G.; ed. pub. schs. and Gem City Coll.; grad. M. Accts., 1893; m. Nellie M. Goodner, Jan. 28, 1899; children—Helen Mary (Mrs. Alexander C. Oliphant), John Goodner, Alice Margaret (Mrs. R. Victor Kuser, Jr.). Vice president and dean of Rider College, Trenton, N.J., 1901—; member N.J. Assembly 1912, and 1917, 18; trustee N.J. State Home for Boys 6 yrs.; trustee N.J. State Hosp.; mem. bd. N.J. Crippled Children's Commn. Pres. Trenton Chamber Commerce, City Rescue Mission. Mem. Nat. Assn. Commercial Teachers, Eastern Commercial Teachers' Assn. (pres.); hon. mem. N.J. Soc. Accountants. Republican. Presbyn. Mason. Lt. gov. N.J. Kiwanis, 1925. Home: Trenton, N.J. Died Jan. 15, 1934.

GILL, Joseph A., judge; b. Wheeling W.Va., Feb. 17, 1854; s. John W. and Rhoda S. G.; ed. Springfield, Ill.) pub. schs. and Ill. Industrial U., Champaign; m. Nannie, d. Hon. M. Donahue, of Clinton, Ill., Dec. 27, 1887; children—Mrs. Edna G. McClintock, Mrs. Rose M. Border, Joseph A. Teacher several years; admitted to bar, Springfield, Ill., 1880; practiced law there, 1880-83, Astoria, Ore., 1883-87, Colby, Kan., 1887-99; U.S. dist. judge, Northern Dist. of Ind. Ty. and chief justice Ind. Ty. Court of Appeals, 1899-1908. Republican. One of 3 commrs. on organization of Indian Ty. as part of State of Okla. Mem. Missionary Bapt. Ch. Mason. Edited Pacific Journal, Pacific Co., Wash. Ty., and Thomas Co. Cat, Colby. Home: Tulsa, Okla. Died Mar. 23, 1933.

GILL, Joseph Kaye, bookseller; b. Holmfirth, Yorkshire, Eng., Aug. 13, 1841; s. Mark and Amelia (Kaye) G.; ed. Worcester (Mass.) Acad., Wilbraham (Mass.) Acad.; m. Frances A. Willson, Aug. 17, 1866 (dec.). Came to U.S. 1854; entered book and stationery business, Salem, Ore., 1867; moved to Portland, Ore., 1871; pres. and treas. The J. K. Gill Co., Inc. (Portland), J. K. Gill & Co. (Salem). Republican. Methodist. Home: Portland, Ore. Died Oct. 1, 1931.

GILL, Laura Drake, educator; b. Chesterville, Me., Aug. 24, 1860; d. Elisha and Huldah (Capen) G.; sister of Adam Capen G.; A.B., Smith Coll., 1881, A.M., 1885; studied mathematics, univs. of Leipzig, 1890-92, Geneva 1892, Sorbonne, Paris, 1892-93; (D.C.L., U. of the South, 1907); unmarried. Teacher of mathematics in Miss Capen's Sch., Northampton, Mass., 1881-98; in exec. work in connection with placing nurses in Spanish-Am. War, 1898; edni. and relief work for Cuban orphans, for Cuban Orphan Soc., 1899-1901; dean of Barnard Coll., New York, 1901-08. Pres. Assn. of Collegiate Alumnæ; chmn. edn. for Gen. Fedn. of Women's Clubs, 1907-11; organizer first Vocation Bureau for Coll. Women. Women's Edn. and Ind. Union, Boston, 1909-11; organization work U. of the South, Sewanee, Tenn., 1911-14, Trinity Coll., Durham, N.C., 1914-15; training sect. of U.S. Employment Service, Dept. of Labor, Washington, 1918-19; worker Pine Mt. Settlement, Ky., 1921-22, Berea Coll., Ky., 1922—. Died Feb. 3, 1926.

GILL, Patrick Francis, congressman; b. Independence, Mo., Aug. 16, 1868; s. Thomas and Rose (Murphy) G.; ed. parochial schs. and St. Louis U.; m. Alicia McCarran, Sept. 24, 1902. In grocery business, and clk. Circuit Ct., 4 yrs.; mem. 61st, 62d, 63d Congresses (1909-15), 11th Dist., Mo. (won seat in contest against Theron E. Catlin, 1912). Democrat. Catholic. Home: St. Louis, Mo. Died May 21, 1923.

GILL, Paul Ludwig, artist; b. Auburn, N.Y., Mar. 14, 1894; s. Arthur J. and Amelia (Huebner) G.; B.F.A., Syracuse U., 1916; student Pa. Acad. of Fine Arts, 1920-24, Pa. Acad. of Fine Arts Summer Sch., 1921; m. Sue May Gill, Feb. 17, 1928; stepdaughter, Mary Sue Wescott. European traveling scholarship, Pa. Acad. Fine Arts, 1922, 23. Exhibited Pa. Acad., Art Inst. Chicago, Brooklyn Mus., Am. Fedn. Arts, Toledo Mus. of Art, New York and Am. Water Color Soc. exhbns. in N.Y. City, etc.; represented in permanent collections of Brooklyn Mus., La France Inst. (Phila.), Canajoharie (N.Y.) Art Gallery, Hackley Art Gallery (Muskegon, Mich.), Soc. of Fine Arts and History (Evansville, Ind.), and in pvt. collections. Awards: silver medal, Sesquicentennial, Phila., 1926; Baltimore Water Color prize, 1926; Tuttle Purchase prize, Art Inst. Chicago; Phila. Water Color prize, 1927; N.Y. Water Color prize, 1928; William Church Osborne prize, Am. Water Color Soc., 1929; William Adams Delano prize, same, 1932; 1st prize, Mr. and Mrs. Exhbn., N.Y. City, 1933; and others. Instr. Moore Inst. of Art, Science and Industry (Phila. Sch. of Design for Women). Served in U.S. Army, 1917-20. Home: Wynnewood, Pa. Died May 30, 1938.

GILL, Theodore Nicholas, zoölogist; b. New York, N.Y., Mar. 21, 1837; s. James Darrell and Elizabeth (Vosburgh) G.; ed. in pvt. schs. and under spl. tutors; (hon. A.M., Columbian [now George Washington U.], 1865, M.D., 1866, Ph.D., 1870, LL.D., 1895); unmarried. Adj. prof. physics and natural history, 1860-61, lecturer on natural history, 1864-66 and 1873-84, prof. zoölogy, 1884-1910, emeritus, George Washington U. Librarian, Smithsonian Instn., 1865-67; asst. librarian, Library of Congress, 1866-75; asso. in zoölogy, U.S. Nat. Mus. Pres. A.A.A.S., 1897. Author: Parental Care Among Fresh-Water Fishes, 1906; contributions to the Life-histories of Fishes, Vol. I, 1909. Asso. editor Johnson's New Univ. Ency., Century Dictionary and Standard Dictionary. Home: Washington, D.C. Deceased.

GILL, Thomas Augustus, rear admiral U.S.N.; b. Philadelphia, Pa., Feb. 8, 1840; s. John S. and Sarah B. G.; A.B., Bucknell U., 1865, A.M., 1868, B.D.,

Theol. Sem., 1867, D.D., 1893; m. Miss M. A. Nevin, Apr. 8, 1875 (died 1878); m. 2d, Miss R. H. Souder, June 19, 1883. During coll. course served 2 enlistments in vol. army during Civil War; pastor Phila., 1868-71; apptd. chaplain U.S.N., from Pa. by President Grant, and commd. Dec. 22, 1874; served on various vessels, and at various stas. during period of active service; retired—pursuant to personnel act of Mar. 3, 1890—with rank of rear admiral, Feb. 8, 1902. Home: Brookline, Mass. Died Aug. 2, 1926.

GILL, Waltus Hughes, lawyer; b. Allensville, Ky., Nov. 25, 1860; s. William Sherwood and Sarah Frances (Hughes) G.; grad. Eastman Business Coll., Poughkeepsie, N.Y., 1879; LL.B., Tenn. Law Sch., Lebanon, Tenn., 1882; m. Mrs. Caroline Arnold Mangum, Aug. 28, 1890. Began practice, Palestine, 1882; city atty., Palestine, 1884-86; county atty., Anderson Co., Tex., 1886-88; dist. atty., Anderson, Henderson and Houston counties, 1888-92; partner of S. A. Means, Palestine, 1892-96; dist. judge, 1896-99; judge Appellate Court, Galveston, 1899-1907 (resigned as chief justice); mem. Gill, Jones & Tyler. Head of Bd. Penitentiary Commrs., Tex., 1907-10. Democrat. Mason. Home: Houston, Tex. Deceased.

GILL, William Andrew, naval officer; b. Tamaqua, Pa., June 8, 1859; grad. U.S. Naval Acad., 1879. Ensign jr. grade, Mar. 3, 1883; ensign, June 26, 1884; lt. jr. grade, June 25, 1891; lt., Oct. 10, 1895; lt. comdr., Oct. 9, 1901; comdr., Aug. 5, 1906; capt., July 1, 1910. Served on Miantonomoh, Spanish-Am. War, 1898; exec. officer Celtic, 1902-03; insp. duty, Bur. of Equipment, 1903-05; exec. officer Cleveland, 1905, Maryland, 1905-06; insp. ordnance, Midvale Steel Co., 1906-08; comd. Solace, 1908; duty Navy Yard, Mare Island, 1908-09, Navy Yard, New York, 1909; comd. receiving ship Texas, 1909-10; comd. Colorado, 1910-12; supervisor Naval Auxiliaries, 1913-14; mem. Naval Examining Bd., Washington, 1914-15; comd. Delaware, 1915-16; apptd. pres. Bd. of Inspection and Survey, Navy Dept., May 30, 1916. Home: Washington, D.C. Died Oct. 10, 1918.

GILL, William Fearing, author; b. Boston, Mass., Sept. 1844; s. Thomas and Catherine (Lebeau) G.; m. Edith O. Gwynne, Nov. 12, 1888. Was the poet of centennial of the Boston Tea Party, 1873; editorially connected with prominent New York newspapers from 1878; rescued the Poe cottage at Fordham, N.Y., from threatened destruction, 1889, and the Poe Park at Fordham resulted; projected the idea of an American poet's corner (temple of fame), and of a nat. gallery of sculpture. Organized a peace congress of leading socs. of Europe, Paris, 1898; founded the Washington and Lafayette Soc., Paris, 1898, to perpetuate friendly feeling between France and the U.S.; founded Edgar Poe Soc., 1903. Author: Life of Edgar Allan Poe; The Evolution of the Peace Movement; Dr. Jekyll and Mr. Hyde (dramatization). Coined the phrase, "The Sixth Sense," N.Y. Graphic, 1880. Died Oct. 18, 1917.

GILL, William Francis, prof. Latin; b. Henderson, N.C., Oct. 5, 1874; s. Robert Jones and Annie Mary (Fuller) G.; A.B., Trinity College, Durham, N.C., 1894; studied Johns Hopkins, 1894-98, Rome and Athens, 1902; unmarried. With Trinity Coll., 1898—, prof. Latin, in charge of dept., 19—. Democrat. Methodist. Mason. Home: Durham, N.C. Died Oct. 18, 1917.

GILL, William Hugh, Presbyn. clergyman; b. in Ireland, Feb. 27, 1841; s. Hugh and Elizabeth (Davidson) G.; grad. Jefferson Coll., 1864 (A.M.); studied Princeton Sem., junior year, and Allegheny, middle and senior, where graduated (D.D., Washington and Jefferson Coll., 1892); m. Kate Russell, June 23, 1868. Successively pastor 1st Presbyn. Ch., Greensburg, Pa.; the 6th St. Ch., St. Joseph, Mo.; Central Ch., Allegheny, Pa.; Westfield, N.J.; Owego, N.Y., and the Evangel, Phila. Led in investigation of Western Pa. Reform School at Pittsburg, 1874, which resulted in its reformation and discontinuance of the contract system in such institutions throughout country; conducts Sunday school dept. Presbyn. Journal. Died 1904.

GILL, Wilson Lindsley, educator; b. Columbus, O., Sept. 12, 1851; s. John Loriman and Mary Smith (Waters) G.; 8th generation from Gov. Wm. Bradford; mem. 1st kindergarten class in America, taught by Caroline Frankenberg, Froebel's first kindergarten teacher; Dartmouth Coll.; Sheffield Scientific Sch. (Yale); LL.B., Yale Law Sch. (pres. of class), 1874; post-graduate study social and polit. sciences, Yale; m. Florence Lydia Henry, 1882 (dec.); 1 son, Bradford; m. 2d, Abbie McClennen, Mar. 1895; children—Mary Allis Patience (Mrs. William Calvin Stamm), Constance (Mrs. Ray Wilbert Strong). Gen. mgr. Gill Car & Car Wheel Works, Columbus, 1874-84, also of various mercantile and mfg. concerns; editor "Our Country" (mag.), 1895-1901; projector and engr. tunnel under 42d St. New York and East River. Was gen. supervisor moral and civic training, Island of Cuba, during 1st Am. occupation, to introduce method he had successfully applied in N.Y. City public schools, 1897; U.S. supervisor at large of Indian schools, Department of Interior, charged especially to organize each Govt. Indian Sch. as a democracy for moral and civic training. President Am. Patriotic League, Mount Airy, Phila.; dir. Nat. Soc. for Improving Methods of Sch. Discipline in Great Britain and Ireland. Originator and architect of Children's Bldg., Chicago World's Fair, 1893, and St. Louis latter. Mem. nat. advisory com. of 100, Jamestown Tercentenary World's Fair. Pres. from 1908 of Children's Internat. State, founded by commrs. from govts. of Sweden, Germany, Argentine and Japan, for promotion of efficient citizenship and internat. friendship. Recipient Elliott Cresson gold medal, Franklin Inst., for originating the School Republic method of moral and civic training; wrote constitutions of the two national societies of the Sons and Daughters of American Revolution. Presbyterian. Author: Children and the Constitution, 1928; Manual of the School Republic, 1932; also writer of monographs on social topics. Secured enactment of law in Mass., 1917, requiring training in the duties of citizenship in all pub. schs., the 1st of its kind in U.S.; ednl. dir. Constitutional League America, 1920—; organized all pub. schs. in Washington, D.C., as Sch. Republics, 1925, and Madison, Wis., 1931. Home: Philadelphia, Pa. Died Sept. 12, 1941.

GILLESPIE, Barnes, lawyer; b. Tazewell Co., Va., Oct. 2, 1871; s. George William and Barbara (Emmons) Gillespie; Milligan (Tenn.) Coll., 1886-88; A.B., cum laude, Bethany (W.Va.) Coll., 1892; LL.B., U. of Va., 1894; m. Ruth McDowell Pepper, June 5, 1901; children—Charles Pepper, George William, Barnes. Practiced, Tazewell, 1894—; mem. Greever & Gillespie; pres. Hall Mining Co.; v.p. Yukon Pocahontas Coal Co.; sec. treas. Big Sandy Coal & Coke Co., etc. Commonwealth's atty., Tazewell Co., Va., 1901-04; U.S. atty. Western Dist. of Va., 1910-14. Republican. Mem. Christian (Disciples) Ch. Home: Tazewell, Va. Died Apr. 20, 1932.

GILLESPIE, Charles Bowen, editor; b. Forney, Tex., Dec. 17, 1872; s. Rufus Calvin and Annie Elizabeth (Walker) G.; ed. pvt. and pub. schs.; m. Frances Elizabeth Eldridge, Mar. 30, 1902; children—Ina Elizabeth, Charles Love. Began as reporter Rockwall (Tex.) News, 1892; city editor Houston Chronicle, 1901-04, mng. editor, 1904-20, v.p. and mng. editor, 1923-26, v.p. and editor, 1926—; v.p. Sugarland R.R., 1920-23; dir. Gulf Coast Lines, M.P.R.R. Dollar a year man, World War; 1st lt., U.S.N.R. Tex. commr. to Rio de Janeiro World's Fair. Trustee Laura Eldridge Memorial Hosp., Sugarland, Tex. Democrat. Methodist. Home: Houston, Tex. Died Feb. 7, 1929.

GILLESPIE, George De Normandie, P.E. bishop of Western Mich., Feb. 24, 1875—; b. Goshen, N.Y., June 14, 1819; s. John De Normandie and Susan (Bedford) G.; grad. Gen. Theol. Sem., New York, 1840 (D.D., Hobart Coll., 1875); deacon, 1840; priest, 1843; m. Rebecca P. Lathrop (dec.), May 26, 1845. Held pastorates at St. Mark's Ch., Leroy, N.Y.; St. Paul's, Cincinnati; Zion Ch., Palmyra, N.Y.; then rector St. Andrew's Ch., Ann Arbor, Mich., until 1875. Has been chmn. Mich. State Bd. Corrections and Charities, 1876—. Home: Grand Rapids, Mich. Died 1909.

GILLESPIE, George Lewis, maj. gen.; b. Kingston, Tenn., Oct. 7, 1841; grad. U.S. Mil. Acad., 1862. Second lt. engrs., June 17, 1862; promoted through grades to maj. gen. U.S.A., Jan. 23, 1904. Breveted: maj., Aug. 1, 1864, for gallant and meritorious services during campaign before Richmond; lt. col., Apr. 9, 1865, for same in campaign from Winchester to Appomattox C.H., Va.; awarded Congressional Medal of Honor, Oct. 27, 1897, for most distinguished gallantry in action near Bethesda Ch., Va., May 31, 1864. Engr. officer on staff gen. comdg. Army of Potomac, 1862-64, participating in all the battles of that army; then chief engr. Army of Shenandoah, Gen. Sheridan commanding; present at Lee's surrender at Appomattox; was with Sheridan in New Orleans, 1865, and as chief engr. took part in reconstruction of Gulf States and the restoration of the Republic of Mexico; pres. Miss. River Commn., 1885; later mem. bd. of engrs., U.S.A., New York; mem. Lighthouse Bd., Washington; div. engr., N.E. div., Atlantic Coast from British boundary to Barnegat, N.J.; during war with Spain, 1898, assigned to command of Dept. of East for the defense of the Atlantic Coast; mem. bd. of officers to visit Puerto Rico, 1900, to set apart from the late crown lands those needed for mil. and naval purposes of U.S.; mem. bd. of ordnance and fortification of Army War Coll. Bd. and mem. joint Army and Navy Bds.; retired, June 17, 1905. Home: Washington, D.C. Died Sept. 27, 1913.

GILLESPIE, Julian Edgeworth, commercial attaché; b. Brownwood, Tex., June 20, 1893; s. James and Ethel (Muse) G.; prep. edn., high sch., Dallas, Tex.; A.B., U. of Tex., 1914; student law dept. U. of Chicago; LL.B., Georgetown (D.C.) U., 1915; m. Adrian Inez Posey, Mar. 20, 1924; children—Mary Howard, Ann Muse, Julian E. Admitted to Tex. bar, 1915, and practiced at Dallas; 1st lt. and capt. with A.E.F., 1917-20; asst. trade commr. U.S. Dept. Commerce, to near East and Balkans, 1920-22 (hdqrs. Constantinople), trade commr., 1922-26; commercial attaché to Turkey, Dec. 1, 1926—. Served as economic and financial adviser to Am. observers, Allied and Turkish Peace Conf., Lausanne, Switzerland, 1922-23; to Am. delegation, Internat. Economic Conf., Geneva, May-June, 1927; del. to negotiate treaty of commerce and navigation between Turkey and U.S., at Angora, 1929. Baptist. Home: LaPlata, Md. Died June 23, 1939.

GILLESPIE, Richard Thomas, clergyman, educator; b. Tirzah, S.C., Oct. 23, 1879; s. Richard T., Sr. and Minnie (Bryan) G.; A.B., Davidson (N.C.) Coll., 1904; B.D., Columbia (Ga.) Theol. Sem., 1908; D.D., Centre Coll., Ky., 1921; LL.D., Presbyterian Coll. (S.C.) in 1925; m. Elizabeth L. Hall, June 25, 1908; children—Richard Thomas, Robert Hall, Mary Caroline. Ordained Presbyn. ministry, 1908; pastor First Ch., Florence, S.C., 1908-16, Maxwell St. Ch., Lexington, Ky., 1917-21, First Ch., Louisville, 1922-24; pres. Columbia Theol. Sem., Jan. 1, 1925—. Served as chmn. Com. on Schs. and Colleges, Synod of Ky.; chmn. on Joint Commn. on Schs. and Colleges, Synods of Ky., U.S. and U.S.A.; mem. Southern Presbyn. Gen. Assembly's Com. of Christian Edn. and Ministerial Relief, and Com. on Men's Work. Democrat. Home: Decatur, Ga. Died May 30, 1930.

GILLESPIE, Thomas A., contractor, mfr.; b. Pittsburgh, Pa., July 1, 1852; s. James and Diana (Mitchell) G.; ed. pub. schs., Pittsburgh; m. Julia B. Wall, Jan. 7, 1875; children—Thomas H., Henry Lloyd, Jean (Mrs. H. Seaver Jones), James Parke. Formerly gen. supt. Phila. Co. (natural gas); engaged in contracting and in mfr. "Lock-Bar" steel pipe for water mains; now chmn. bd. T. A. Gillespie Co., East Jersey Pipe Co.; pres. and chmn. bd. Dey Street Realty Corp.; dir. Equitable Life Assurance Soc.; trustee N.Y. Trust Co. Built Pittsburgh Filtration Plant; aqueduct tunnel under Hudson River, at Storm King; built 3d tracks on New York elevated lines. Engaged in mfr. and loading of high explosive shells for U.S. Govt. and allies, World War. Republican. Presbyn. Home: West Orange, N.J. Died Jan. 27, 1926.

GILLET, Charles William, congressman; b. Addison, N.Y., Nov. 26, 1840; A.B., Union Coll., 1861; pvt. and adj. 86th N.Y. Vols., 1861-63; disch., Nov. 1863, for disabilities. Mem. 53d to 58th Congresses (1893-1905). Republican. Home: Addison, N.Y. Died 1908.

GILLETT, Arthur Lincoln, clergyman; b. Westfield, Mass., Jan. 5, 1859; s. Edward Bates and Lucy Douglas (Fowler) G.; A.B., Amherst Coll., 1880, A.M., 1884, D.D., 1901; grad. Hartford Theol. Sem., 1883, post-grad. study same, 1883-84, univs. of Berlin and Tübingen, 1889-91; m. Mary Bradford Swift, June 22, 1887 (died 1901); children—Edward Bates (dec.), Robert Swift (dec.), Frederick Webster; m. 2d, Sara Phillips Colton, June 10, 1911. Pastor's asst. Plymouth Ch., Milwaukee, 1884-85; pastor Plymouth Ch., Grand Forks, N.D., 1885-88; instr., 1888-90, asso. prof., 1890-95, prof. apologetics, 1895-1924, philosophy of religion, 1924-28 (emeritus), Hartford Theol. Seminary. Conglist. Republican. Home: Hartford, Conn. Died Sept. 9, 1938.

GILLETT, Frederick Huntington, lawyer; b. Westfield, Mass., Oct. 16, 1851; s. Edward Bates and Lucy Douglas (Fowler) G.; A.B., Amherst, 1874, A.M., 1877, LL.D., 1906; LL.B., Harvard, 1877; m. Christine Rice Hoar (widow of late Congressman Rockwood Hoar), Nov. 25, 1915. In law practice at Springfield, Mass., 1877—. Asst. atty. gen. of Mass., 1879-82; mem. Mass. Ho. of Rep., 1890, 91; mem. 53d to 68th Congresses (1893-1925), 2d Mass. Dist.; Speaker of House 1919-25; elected U.S. senator, term 1925-31. Home: Springfield, Mass. Died July 31, 1935.

GILLETT, James Norris, gov., lawyer; b. Viroqua, Wis., Sept. 20, 1860; s. Cyrus L. and Sarah J. G.; ed. high sch., Sparta, Wis.; m. Isabella Erzgraber, May 8, 1898. Admitted to bar, 1881; mem. Calif. Senate, 1897-99; mem. 57th and 58th Congresses (1903-07), 1st Calif. Dist.; gov. of Calif., 1907-11; resumed practice of law; retired. Republican. Home: Berkeley, Calif. Died Apr. 20, 1937.

GILLETT, John Henry, lawyer; b. Medina, N.Y., Sept. 18, 1860; s. Hiram A. and Helen L. (Stitt) G.; ed. pub. schs., Valparaiso, Ind.; m. Agnes O. Ackerman, Apr. 23, 1884. Admitted to Ind. bar, 1881; practiced at Hammond, Ind.; asst. atty. gen. Ind., 1886-90; judge Circuit Ct., 1892-1902; apptd. judge Supreme Ct., Ind., 1902, elected Nov. 1902, for term 1902-08 (chief justice 1903-08). Republican. Home: Hammond, Ind. Died Mar. 16, 1920.

GILLETT, Philip Goode, educator of the deaf; b. Madison, Ind., Mar. 24, 1833; s. Samuel Trumbull and Harriet (Goode) G.; A.B., Ind. Asbury (now DePauw) U., 1852, A.M., 1855 (LL.D., 1871); m. Ellen Maria Phipps, 1854. Teacher Ind. Inst. for Deaf and Dumb, 1852-56; supt. Ill. Instn. for Edn. of Deaf and Dumb, 1856-93. Pres., 1886-90, mem. exec. com., 1880-95, conv. Am. Instrs. of the Deaf; mem. bd. dirs., 1880-90, pres. and gen. mgr., 1893-99, Am. Assn. to Promote Teaching of Speech to the Deaf. Pres. Internat. S.S. Conv., 1872-75; mem. Internat. S.S. Lesson Com., 1872-96; mem. Gen. Conf., 1880, 84, 88, book com., 1880-84, M.E. Ch.;

pres. Ill. State S.S. Conv. Home: Jacksonville, Ill. Deceased.

GILLETT, William Kendall, univ. prof.; b. New York, May 16, 1860; s. Ezra Hall (D.D.) and Mary Jane (Kendall) G.; bro. of Charles Ripley G.; A.B., New York U., 1880, A.M., 1883; student Columbia Law Sch., 1880-81, U. of Berlin, 1881-83, U. of Paris, 1884, 1889-90; pvt. study Paris, Geneva, Florence, 1883, 1884, Madrid and Seville, 1888-89; (L.H.D., Huron Coll., 1913); unmarried. Instr. German and French, Lehigh U., 1885-88; prof. Romance langs., undergraduate and grad. faculties, 1890—, sec. faculty, same, 1891-98, chmn. com. on coll. orgns., 1902-09, New York U. Curator N.Y. Univ. Hist. Soc., 1900—. Village trustee Pelham Manor, N.Y., 1893-99; sch. trustee Town of Pelham, 1900-06. Home: Pelham Manor, N.Y. Died Sept. 28, 1914.

GILLETTE, Clarence Preston, entomologist; b. Lyons, Mich., Apr. 7, 1859; s. William Henry and Larissa Esther (Preston) G.; B.S., Mich. Agrl. Coll., 1884, M.S., 1887; spl. work in entomology, U. of Ill., 1885, D.Sc., 1917; embryology, Woods Hole, Mass., 1900; m. Clara M. Smith, Mar. 3, 1886. Asst. entomologist and physiologist, Mich. Agrl. Coll., 1886-87; entomologist, State Expt. Sta., Ames, Ia., 1888-90; head dept. of zoölogy and entomology, and entomologist, Expt. Sta., Colo. Agrl. Coll., 1891-1933; dir. Colo. Expt. Sta., July 1, 1910-33; prof. and dir. emeritus, 1933—. Expert entomologist, St. Louis Expn., 1904. Presbyn. Home: Ft. Collins, Colo. Died Jan. 4, 1941.

GILLETTE, Edward Hooker, farmer; b. Bloomfield, Conn., Oct. 1, 1840; s. Francis G. (U.S. senator from Conn.) and Elizabeth Daggett (Hooker) G.; bro. of William G.; ed. Hartford (Conn.) High Sch., and N.Y. State Agrl. Coll.; m. Sophie T. Stoddard, June 26, 1866; 2d, Mrs. Jennie Isabel (Grove) Apple, of Springfield, O., Feb. 28, 1907. Went to Des Moines, Ia., 1863; engaged in farming and mfg. Mem. 46th Congress (1879-81); editor Ia. Tribune, 1881-91. Chmn. Nat. Com. Union Labor (afterward Populist) party for yrs. Home: Valley Junction, Ia. Died Aug. 14, 1918.

GILLETTE, King Camp, mfr.; b. Fond du Lac, Wis., Jan. 5, 1855; s. George Wolcott and Fanny Lamira (Camp) G.; mother author of the White House Cook Book; ed. public schools, Chicago; m. Alanta Ella Gaines, July 2, 1890; 1 son, King G. Inventor Gillette razor; organizer Gillette Safety Razor Co., 1901, pres. until 1931, now dir. Republican. Mason. Address: Los Angeles, Calif. Died July 9, 1932.

GILLETTE, Lewis Singer, capitalist, mfr.; b. Niles, Mich., May 9, 1854; s. Mahlon Bainbridge and Nancy Mary (Rees) G.; B.S. and B.E., U. of Minn., 1876, C.E., 1889; m. Louise E. Perkins, Dec. 18, 1877. Right of way agt. G.N. Ry., 1881-84; purchased half interest, 1884, in Herzog Mfg. Co., Minneapolis, later the Gillette-Herzog Mfg. Co., skeleton steel constrn.; an organizer Minn. Malleable Iron Co., 1895, also of Am. Bridge Co., later absorbed by U.S. Steel Corp.; a founder of Red Wing Malting Plant, and various other commercial enterprises; formerly v.p. Metropolitan Bank and dir. Northwestern Nat. Bank, and Minn. Loan & Trust Co.; now pres. L. S. Gillette Co., Chippewa Land & Pastures Co. and Plymouth Investment Co. Prominent in forwarding plans for the greater U. of Minn., and many other pub. enterprises; hon. v.p. and chmn. bldg. com. Chamber Commerce of U.S., mem. Internat. Chamber Commerce, Minneapolis Civic Commn. Mem. bd. trustees Carleton Coll., bd. edn. Northern Bapt. Conv., Gen. Bd. of Edn.; trustee Pillsbury Acad., Owatonna, Minn. Active in war service and awarded silver medal by French govt. Baptist. Republican. Home: Minneapolis, Minn. Died Mar. 30, 1924.

GILLETTE, Walter Robarts, insurance, physician; b. Phila., 1840; s. Rev. Abram D. and Hannah (Jenkins) G.; grad. Madison Univ., A.B., 1861, A.M., 1864, Coll. Phys. & Surg., New York, 1863; m. Annie Curtenius, 1871. Served in Civil War as acting asst. surgeon. Now vice-pres. The Mutual Life Ins. Co., of N.Y. Consulting physician Bellevue, St. Francis and Maternity hosps.; mgr. State Asylum for Insane. Home: New York. Died 1908.

GILLETTE, William, actor, playwright; b. Hartford, Conn., July 24, 1855; s. Francis G. (U.S. senator from Conn.) and Elizabeth Daggett (Hooker) G.; acad. edn.; spl. courses at U. of New York, Mass. Inst. Tech., Boston U., while playing in stock companies in New York and Boston; unmarried. Began theatrical work, 1877; with stock cos. successively at New Orleans, New York, Boston, Cincinnati and Louisville; traveled for a season with John T. Raymond Co.; since then has played his own pieces almost exclusively, though appeared in "Samson," "Diplomacy," "The Admirable Crichton," "A Successful Calamity," "Dear Brutus," etc. Author of plays (unpublished): The Professor; The Private Secretary; Esmeralda; A Legal Wreck; Held by the Enemy; Too Much Johnson; Mr. Wilkinson's Widows; All the Comforts of Home; A Maid of All Work; The Red Owl; Because She Loved Him So; Settled Out of Court; Clarice; Secret Service; Sherlock Holmes; The Astounding Crime on Torrington Road. Mem. Am. Acad. Arts and Letters. Home: Hadlyme, Conn. Died April 29, 1937.

GILLHAM, Robert, civil engr.; b. New York, Sept. 25, 1854; ed. Classical and Math. Inst., Hackensack, N.J.; studied engineering; engaged in practice at Hackensack; invented furnace for desulphurizing zinc ores; constructed cable road in Kansas City; became v.p. and chief engr. Kansas City Elevated Ry.; constructed cable railways in Omaha, Denver and Cleveland, O.; afterward with numerous companies; now gen. mgr. and chief engr. Kansas City, Pittsburgh and Gulf Ry. Home: Kansas City, Mo. Died 1899.

GILLIG, Edward M., state seed commr.; b. Big River, Wis., Feb. 25, 1894; s. Peter and Mary (Nachazel) G.; B.S., in agr., U. of Minn., 1917; m. Emma R. Rost, Sept. 5, 1918; children—Edward Charles, Roy Wilfred, John Peter. Teacher vocational agr. in Minn., 1917-27; engaged in growing and marketing certified seed potatoes, Minn. and N.D., 1927-29; N.D. state seed commr., 1929—. Home: Fargo, N.D. Died Dec. 10, 1938.

GILLILAND, Clarence Vosburgh, prof. history; b. Linesville, Pa., Sept. 9, 1866; s. Samuel Amos and Eliza Almeta (Vosburgh) G.; A.B., Cornell Coll., 1900, A.M., 1904; S.T.B., Garrett Bibl. Inst., 1907; D.D., Dakota Wesleyan U., 1911; A.M., U. of Chicago, 1920; D.D. from Garrett Bibl. Inst., 1929; m. Carrie Stewart Collins, 1891; children—Grace Eliza, Floyd (dec.), Glen Clarence, Roy Collins, Miles Thompson. Minister of M.E. Ch.; prof. Bibl. lit., Dak. Wesleyan U., 1906-11; pres. Carleton Coll., Farmington, Mo., 1911-13; dean Coll. of Liberal Arts and prof. history, Dak. Wesleyan U., 1913-19; prof. history, U. of Southern Calif., 1919—. Home: Los Angeles, Calif. Died Jan. 30, 1939.

GILLIS, James Henry, commodore U.S.N.; b. Ridgway, Pa., May 14, 1831; s. James L. and Cecilia Ann (Berray) G.; grad. Naval Acad., 1854; m. Lydia A. Alexander, Sept. 21, 1854 (died 1893); 2d, Ursula Z. Canfield, Mar. 17, 1903. Passed midshipman, June 15, 1854; promoted through grades to commodore, Jan. 29, 1887. Rescued master and three of crew of an Argentine vessel that had foundered outside of the harbor of Montevideo during a terrific "pampero," Mar. 1, 1859 (received thanks from Argentine minister and many testimonials from citizens of Montevideo; also medal from citizens of Buenos Aires and officers of Argentine Navy); took part in sinking Confederate privateer Petrel, July 1861; served N. Atlantic blockading squadron, 1862; after capture of Confederate battery at junction of Dawho and S. Edisto Rivers, was ambushed at Slamm's bluff by a battery and 2 regts. of infantry, but drove them off; comd. Commodore Morris in battle of Jamestown Island, S.C., June 1862; engagement with battery, Taylor's Landing, Pamunkey River, Apr. 16, 1863; was up Red River with Admiral Porter; comd. iron-clad Milwaukee until it was sunk by torpedo during engagement with Spanish Fort, Mobile Bay, March 28, 1865; then comd. naval battery on shore at siege of fort until it fell; afterward on various stations and duties; comd. the Wateree, S. Pacific squadron, which was carried half a mile inland by tidal wave at Arica, Peru (received thanks of British govt. for assistance rendered British subjects on this occasion); comd. S. Atlantic sta. as rear admiral, 1888-90; retired May 14, 1893. Home: Melbourne Beach, Fla. Died 1910.

GILLIS, James Louis, librarian; b. Richmond, Ia., Oct. 3, 1857; s. Charles and Emily Eliza (Gelatt) G.; ed. pub. schs., Sacramento, Calif.; m. Kate Petree, Dec. 25, 1881. Began as messenger with Sacramento Valley R.R. Co., 1872; retired from ry. service as asst. supt., 1894; keeper of archives, sec. of state's office, Calif., 1895-99; clerk Com. on Ways and Means, Gen. Assembly, sessions, 1895, 97, 99; state librarian of Calif., Apr. 1, 1899—. Pres. Calif. Library Assn., 1906-09 and 1911-15. Republican. Home: Sacramento, Calif. Died July 27, 1917.

GILLMAN, Henry, scientist; b. Kinsale, Ireland, Nov. 16, 1833; s. Edward and Eleanor Mandeville (Hackett) G.; desc. from Adam Winthrop, lord of the manor, of Groton, Suffolk, grandfather of Gov. Winthrop of Mass., 1630; acad. edn.; m. Mary Julia, d. Hiram Reeve Johnson, of Detroit, Dec. 7, 1858. Came with his parents to Detroit, 1850; was 1st asst. U.S. Geod. Survey of Great Lakes, in charge of a topog. and hydrographical party, 1851-69; asst. supt. construction 10th and 11th lighthouse dists. on Northern lakes, 1870-76; supt. and librarian Detroit Pub. Library, 1880-85; U.S. consul, Jerusalem, 1886-91. Took such a stand against expulsion of Jews from Palestine by Turks that his position was upheld by several European powers and exclusion laws were modified by the sultan. Known for his researches in archeology and botany and his procurement and publication of photograph fac-similes of texts of early Christian MSS., including the Didache. Home: Detroit, Mich. Died July 30, 1915.

GILLMER, Gipson P(erry), lawyer; b. Newton Falls, O., July 31, 1872; s. James Alexander and Laura (Byers) G.; student Mount Union Coll., Alliance, O., 1897-98; B.S., Northern Ind. U., 1899; grad. study Waynesburg (Pa.) Coll., 1900-01; m. Maud Ella Kern, Aug. 22, 1900. Teacher pub. schs. in Trumbull Co., 1891-96; prin. high sch., Gustavus, O., 1896-98; teacher, Niles, O., 1898-99; supt. schs., Waynesburg, Pa., 1900-02; admitted to Ohio bar, 1903, and in practice at Niles, O., 1903-09; partner of Thomas H. Gillmer, 1909-12; sr. mem. Gillmer, Gillmer, Stevens & Patchin, 1918-27; sr. mem. Gillmer, Gillmer & Anderson, 1927-34; sr. mem. G. P. & M. E. Gillmer, 1934—; chmn. bd. The Taylor-Winfield Corp.; treas. and dir. Pa. Tank Line, Inc. City solicitor, Niles, 1907-09; pros. atty., Trumbull Co., O., 1909-13; spl. U.S. atty., Housing Corp., 1917-21. Trustee Lakeside (O.) Assn., Warren Community Chest Corp., Warren City Hosp., Warren Y.M.C.A. Republican. Methodist. Mason. Home: Warren, O. Died Oct. 23, 1936.

GILLMORE, James Clarkson, commodore U.S.N.; b. Phila., July 10, 1854; s. James Clarkson and Josephine Augusta (Hagner) G.; Pa. Mil. Acad., Chester; grad. U.S. Naval Acad., 1876; m. Mary Stuart Ball, May 12, 1882 (dec.). Promoted ensign, 1879; lt., jr. grade, 1890; lt., sr. grade, 1893; lt. comdr., 1900; comdr., 1904; capt., 1909; promoted commodore and retired at own request after 40 yrs.' service, July 1, 1911. Served as midshipman aboard Hartford, N. Atlantic Sta., Monongahela, China Sta.; returned home in Alert from China, 1879; served on Jamestown in Alaska, 1879-82, Iroquois, Pacific Sta., 1882-85, comdg. gatling co. at Panama, in landing force, 1885; aboard Marion, Asiatic Sta., 1887-90, Machias, Atlantic Sta., Vesuvius, and again Machias, Asiatic Sta., 1893-97; during war with Spain was navigator U.S.S. St. Paul; comd. torpedo boat Porter; exec. officer Scorpion; navigator Solace, sailing for Manila, 1899; navigator U.S.S. Yorktown; captured by Filipinos and prisoner 8½ mos.; exec. officer Franklin, Norfolk, Va., 1900-01; exec. officer, Cincinnati, 1901-04, N. Atlantic, European and Asiatic Stas.; comdr. Navy Yard, New York; Asiatic Sta., 1905-07; capt. Cavite Navy Yard, P.I., and comdg. Helena; in charge naval recruiting sta., New York, 1907-09; comdg. battleship Illinois; comdg. Maryland, Pacific Sta., 1909-11. Esoteric Buddhist. Sampson medal, Philippine War medal, Congressional medal for Spanish-Am. War. Mason. Died June 14, 1927.

GILLMORE, Rufus (Hamilton), author; b. Chelsea, Mass., Apr. 30, 1879; s. Robert Burns and Charlotte Annie (Gould) G.; ed. pub. schs., Boston; m. Louise Wolfe, Oct. 28, 1921. Began with weekly commercial newspaper, Boston, of which became gen. mgr., 1903; resigned, 1907. Republican. Conglist. Author: The Mystery of the Second Shot, 1912; The Opal Pin, 1914; The Alster Case, 1914. Home: New York, N.Y. Died Jan. 1935.

GILLON, John William, Baptist clergyman; b. Providence, Miss., Aug. 26, 1867; s. John Jerome and Elizabeth (Hughes) G.; Mississippi Coll., Clinton; Southern Bapt. Theol. Sem., Louisville, 1893, 94; D.D., Carson and Newman Coll., Tenn., 1913; m. Lucie Conner, July 20, 1898; children—John William, Harvey E., Verser C., Lucie Kate. Ordained Bapt. ministry, 1891; pastor, Okolona, Miss., 1892-93, Milan, Tenn., 1894-95, Orlando, Fla., 1896, Union City, Tenn., 1897-98, in Tex. at Sherman, 1899-1901, Broadway Ch., Ft. Worth, 1902-05, Mineral Wells, 1906, Gaston Av. Ch., Dallas, 1907-08, La Belle Pl. Ch., Memphis, Tenn., 1909-10; corr. sec. and treas. Bapt. Mission Bd. of Tenn., 1910-20; pastor Mayfield, Ky., 1920-22; became pastor Winchester, Ky., 1922, later pastor First Ch., Shawnee, Okla. Mason. Home: Shawnee, Okla. Died Dec. 23, 1931.

GILMAN, Arthur, educator, author; b. Alton, Ill., June 22, 1837; s. Winthrop Sargent G., of New York; ed. in St. Louis and New York; (A.M., Williams, 1867, Harvard, 1904); m. 1st, Amy Cooke Ball; m. 2d, Stella Scott. Banker, New York, 1857-62; retired to Berkshire Co., Mass., because of ill health; removed to Cambridge, 1870. Originated Harvard Annex; was its exec. officer, and when it became Radcliffe Coll. its regent. Mem. Corporation (and finance com.) Radcliffe Coll. Author: Magna Charta Stories, 1882; The Story of Rome, 1886; Short Stories from the Dictionary; The Colonization of America, 1887; The Making of the American Nation, 1887. Editor: Dryden's Palamon and Arcite, 1898. Founder of the Gilman Sch. Hon. mem. Harvard Hist. Soc. Home: Cambridge, Mass. Died 1909.

GILMAN, Benjamin Ives, essayist; b. New York, Feb. 19, 1852; s. Winthrop Sargent and Abia Swift (Lippincott) Gilman; A.B., Williams Coll., 1872; fellow in logic, Johns Hopkins, 1881-82, hon. A.M., 1901; grad. student in psychology, Harvard U., 1883-85, Univ. of Berlin, 1882, and Paris, 1886; m. Cornelia Moore Dunbar, Sept. 14, 1892; children—Edith Dunbar (Mrs. William Adams Brown, Jr.), Alice Ives. Lecturer Princeton, Columbia, Harvard, 1890-91; instr. psychology, Clark U., 1892-93; sec. Mus. of Fine Arts, Boston, 1893-1925, retired. Author: Manual of Italian Renaissance Sculpture, 1904;

Hopi Melodies, 1908; Museum Ideals, 1918. Home: Boston, Mass. Died Mar. 18, 1933.

GILMAN, Bradley, clergyman; b. Boston, Jan. 22, 1857; s. Thomas R. and Ruth (Mathews) G.; A.B., Harvard, 1880, S.T.B., 1884; m. Mary Rebecca Foster, 1886; 1 dau., Dorothy Foster. Ordained Unitarian ministry, 1886; pastor Belmont and Waverley, Mass., 1884-86, Concord, N.H., 1886-92, Third Congl. Soc., Springfield, 1892-1903, First Congl. Parish, Canton, Mass., 1903-17, Unitarian Ch., Palo Alto, Calif., 1917-19. Author: The Parsonage Porch, 1900; Back to the Soil, 1901; Ronald Carnaquay, 1903; The Open Secret of Nazareth, 1906; A Son of the Desert (juvenile), 1909; The Sultan's Rival (juvenile); Life of Robert E. Lee; Roosevelt the Happy Warrior, a biography, 1921. Address: Boston, Mass. Died June 19, 1932.

GILMAN, Charlotte Perkins, author, lecturer; b. Hartford, Conn., July 3, 1860; d. Frederic Beecher and Mary A. Fitch (Westcott) Perkins; g.g.d. Lyman Beecher; m. C. W. Stetson, 1884; 1 dau., Katharine Beecher Stetson; m. 2d, George H. Gilman, June 11, 1900. Began public work in 1890, lecturing on ethics, economics and sociology. Specially identified with labor and woman movements; sole editor of The Forerunner magazine, 1909-16. Visited Europe as public speaker, 1896, 99, 1904, 05, 13. Author: His Religion and Hers, 1923. Home: Norwichtown, Conn. Died Aug. 11, 1935.

GILMAN, Daniel Coit, educator; b. Norwich, Conn., July 6, 1831; s. Wm. C. and Eliza (Coit) G.; desc. Councillor John Gilman, of Exeter, N.H., emigrant from Eng., 1638; grad. Yale, 1852 (A.M., 1855); continued studies in Cambridge, New Haven and Berlin; (LL.D., Harvard, 1876, St. John's, Md., 1876, Columbia, 1887, Yale, 1889, Univ. of N.C., 1889, Princeton, 1896, Univ. of Toronto, 1903, Univ. of Wis., 1904, Clark, 1905, William and Mary, 1906); m. Mary, d. T. Ketcham, 1861 (died 1869); m. 2d, Elizabeth Dwight, d. John M. Woolsey, 1877. Librarian, sec. Sheffield Scientific Sch., and prof. phys. and polit. geography, Yale, 1856-72; pres. U. of Calif., 1872-75; first pres. Johns Hopkins U., 1875-1901, emeritus; first pres. Carnegie Instn., Washington, 1901-04. Member U.S. Commn. on boundary line between Venezuela and British Guiana, 1896-97; mem. commn. to draft new charter for City of Baltimore, 1897; mem. bd. school commrs., 1900; v.p. Archæol. Inst. of America; commr. awards, Atlanta Expn., 1895; pres. John F. Slater Fund for Edn. of Freedmen; v.p. Peabody Edn. Fund; mem. Gen. Edn. Bd.; trustee Russell Sage Foundation; pres. Nat. Civil Service Reform League, 1901-07; trustee Carnegie Instn. Author: Life of James Monroe, 1883, 1898; University Problems, 1888; Introduction to De Tocqueville's Democracy in America; Life of James D. Dana, geologist, 1899; Science and Letters in Yale, 1901; Launching of a University, 1906. Editor-in-chief New Internat. Ency. Home: Baltimore, Md. Died 1908.

GILMAN, John E.; b. S. Boston, Mass., Dec. 22, 1844; s. John and Margaret (Crowley) G.; ed. pub. schs., Quincy and Boston; m. Mary E. Lynch, Nov. 8, 1870. Enlisted in 12th Mass. Inf., Aug. 5, 1862; participated in battles of Rappahannock Sta., Thoroughfare Gap, 2d Bull Run, Chantilly, South Mountain, Antietam, Fredericksburg, Chancellorsville and Gettysburg (lost right arm); hon. disch. Oct. 28, 1863. Mass. State govt. employe, 1864-83; employe and later chief settlement div., bd. dirs. of pub. instns., Boston, 1883-1901; commr. soldiers' relief dept., Boston, 1901—. Mem. Post 26 G.A.R., past post comdr., dept. insp., jr. vice-comdr., sr. vice comdr., comdr. Dept. Mass., adj. gen., 1904-05, and comdr.-in-chief, 1910-11. Home: Roxbury, Mass. Died Feb. 21, 1921.

GILMAN, John Ellis, physician; b. Harmar, suburb of Marietta, O., July 24, 1841; s. Dr. John Salvin and Elizabeth C. (Fay) G.; ed. schs. of Marietta; student medicine and surgery under his father and brother, and Dr. George Hartwell, of Toledo, O.; M.D., Hahnemann Med. Coll., Chicago, 1871; m. Mary D., d. William Johnson, 1860. Was the first physician to offer his services for relief of sufferers at time of Chicago Fire, 1871, and apptd. by the Relief and Aid Soc. as sec. of its com. on sick and hosps.; prof. physiology, sanitary science and hygiene, and later prof. materia medica, Hahnemann Med. Coll., Chicago, 1884-1904 (emeritus). Introduced X-ray in therapeutic use, 1906; afterwards used it in treating cancers. Home: Chicago, Ill. Died June 21, 1916.

GILMAN, Lawrence, critic, author, editor; b. Flushing, N.Y., July 5, 1878; s. Arthur C. and Bessie (Lawrence) G.; ed. N.Y. pub. schs. and Collins St. Classical Sch., Hartford, Conn.; studied painting with William M. Chase, and illustration at Art Students' League; on staff N.Y. Herald, 1896-98; self-taught in musical theory, composition, orchestration, organ and piano; m. Elizabeth Wright Walter, Aug. 1, 1904. Music critic Harper's Weekly, 1901-13, asst. editor, 1903-11, mng. editor, 1911-13; on editorial staff Harper's Mag., 1913-15; musical, dramatic, and literary critic, North Am. Review, 1915-23; music critic N.Y. Herald-Tribune, 1923—, succeeding Henry Edward Krehbiel. Program annotator for Philharmonic Soc., N.Y., and Philadelphia Orchestra, 1921—. Radio commentator for Sunday broadcasts of the New York Philharmonic-Symphony Concerts during closing years of Toscanini's conductorship of Orchestra, 1933-36. Mem. National Institute Arts and Letters. Author: Stories of Symphonic Music, 1907; A Guide to Debussy's "Pelléas et Mélisande," 1907; Edward MacDowell—A Study (revised and enlarged edit.), 1909; Nature in Music, 1914; A Christmas Meditation, 1916; Music and the Cultivated Man, 1929; Aspects of Wagner's Operas, 1937. Composer: A Dream of Death, 1903; The Heart of the Woman, 1903; The Curlew, 1904 (3 settings for voice and piano of poems by W. B. Yeats). Died Sept. 8, 1939.

GILMAN, Nicholas Paine, educator; b. Quincy, Ill., Dec. 21, 1849; s. Charles and Annette Maria (Dearborn) G.; acad. edn.; grad. Harvard Div. Sch., 1871; m. Mary Sherwood Stubbs, June 20, 1895. Settled as Unitarian clergyman over 3 parishes in Mass., 1872-84; prof. in Antioch Coll., O., 1878-81; editor Literary World, Boston, 1888-95; prof. sociology and ethics, Meadville Theol. Sch., 1895—; editor The New World, 1892-1900. Author: Profit Sharing Between Employer and Employee, 1889; A Dividend to Labor, 1899. Home: Meadville, Pa. Died Jan. 23, 1912.

GILMAN, Samuel P., lawyer; b. Troy, N.Y., Mar. 13, 1877; s. Charles J. and Anne (Blatt) G.; Ph.B., St. Francis Xavier Coll., N.Y. City, 1895; LL.B., New York U., 1898; m. Josephine Rosenbaum, June 5, 1907; children—Doris, Richard. Admitted to N.Y. bar, 1898, and began practice at N.Y. City; dir. and gen. counsel Standard Commercial Tobacco Corp., German Am. Tobacco Co.; gen. counsel New York Bd. Trade, 1932-38. Mason. Home: New York, N.Y. Died Mar. 17, 1941.

GILMAN, Stephen Warren, college prof.; b. nr. Jacksonville, Ill., July 11, 1857; s. Henry and Arminda A. (Holmes) G.; LL.B., U. of Wis., 1899; LL.D., Franklin Coll., 1925; C.P.A., Wis., 1913; m. Frances Fraser, June 21, 1882; 1 son, Stephen. In business, management of corps., Chicago, 1879-96; mem. legal firm of Bird & Gilman, 1902-08; mem. commn. to simplify accounting system of state of Wis., 1899; prof. business administration, U. of Wis., 1908—. Consulting accountant President Taft's inquiry into efficiency and economy in U.S. Govt. business, 1910; consulting accountant Bur. of Efficiency and Economy, Milwaukee, 1911; mem. Wis. Board Accountance, 1913-17; mem. State Bd. of Conciliation, 1919—. Republican. Presbyn. Home: Madison, Wis. Died June 2, 1930.

GILMAN, Theodore; b. Alton, Ill., Jan. 2, 1841; s. Winthrop Sargent and Abia Swift (Lippincott) G.; A.B., Williams Coll., 1862, A.M., 1865; m. Elizabeth Drinker Paxson, Oct. 22, 1863; children now Living—Frances Paxson, Theodore, Helen Ives, Robbins. Began in banking business on Wall St., New York, 1862, and became connected with many corps. Chmn. New York Sabbath Com., 1915-27. Fellow Nat. Acad. Design. Home: Yonkers, N.Y. Died Aug. 9, 1930.

GILMER, Thomas Lewis, M.D., D.D.S.; b. Lincoln Co., Mo., Feb. 19, 1849; s. Dr. F. G. and Sarah Jane (Loving) G.; acad. edn. in Mo. and Ill.; D.D.S., Mo. Dental Coll. (dental dept. Washington Univ.), St. Louis, 1881; St. Louis Med. Coll., 1870-71, 1881-82; M.D., Quincy (Ill.) Coll. of Medicine, 1885; (Sc.D., Northwestern, 1912); m. Ella M. Bostick, Sept. 29, 1868; children—Mrs. Virginia Gilmer Ames, Frank Bostick. Practiced Chicago, 1889—; emeritus dean, prof. oral surgery, Northwestern U. Dental Sch., 1891—; oral surgeon to St. Luke's Hosp. Mem. U.S. Advisory Bd. Fellow Am. Coll. Surgeons, A.M.A., Inst. Medicine Chicago. Home: Chicago, Ill. Died Dec. 28, 1931.

GILMORE, George William, theologian; b. London, Eng., May 12, 1858; s. George William and Mary (Mansfield) G.; A.B., Princeton, 1883, A.M., 1889; grad. Union Theol. Sem., 1886; m. Emily C. Van Mater Lake, Apr. 18, 1886; 1 son D(avid) Percy. Apptd. 1886, by U.S. commr. edn., in response to request of King of Korea, to go to Seoul, to found and teach in Royal Korean Coll.; remained until 1889; engaged in lit. work and teaching, Brooklyn Poly. Inst., 1889-93; instr. English Bible, 1893-95, prof. bibl. history and lecturer on comparative religion, 1895-99, Bangor Theol. Sem.; prof. O.T. lang and lit., and history of religion in Meadville Theol. Sch., 1899-1906; bibliographer, asso. editor, indexer and writer for the New Schaff-Herzog Ency. of Religious Knowledge, 1905-14; asso. editor Homiletic Review, 1911—. Conglist. Author: Animism—Thought Currents of Primitive Peoples, 1919; translated from German, Jesus as Problem, Teacher, Personality and Force, by Bornemann, Veit, Schuster, and Foerster, 1910; The Apostles' Creed and the New Testament, by Johannes Kunze, 1912. Editor (with Robert Scott) of The Church, the People, and the Age, 1913; Selections from the Classics of Devotion, 1916. Editor of Cobern's Archæological Discoveries, 1922, 24, archæol. supplement, 1929; Tax Talks, 1925. Home: Brooklyn, N.Y. Died Aug. 22, 1933.

GILMORE, James Roberts ("Edmund Kirke"), author; b. Boston, Sept. 10, 1822; m. d. Judge John W. Edmonds. Engaged as shipping mcht. in New York until 1857; wrote several novels of Southern life during Civil War under pen-name; founded Continental Monthly magazine; again in mercantile business, 1873-83; resumed writing. Gave a course of lectures before Lowell Inst., Boston, 1889, and Peabody Inst., Baltimore, 1890. Author: The Rear Guard of the Revolution; John Sevier as a Commonwealth Builder; The Advance Guard of Western Civilization; The Last of the Thorndikes; Personal Recollections of Abraham Lincoln. Died 1903.

GILMORE, John Curtis, brig. gen.; b. in Can., Apr. 18, 1837; s. James and Mary G.; when 6 months old went with family to Louisville, N.Y.; ed. there; LL.B., Albany (N.Y.) Law School. Capt. 16th N.Y. Inf., May 15, 1861; maj., Sept. 29, 1862; lt. col. 193d N.Y. Inf., Mar. 28, 1865; bvtd. col. vols., Nov. 14, 1865; hon. mustered out of vol. service, Jan. 18, 1866; bvtd. maj., Mar. 2, 1867, for gallant and meritorious services at Antietam; lt. col., Mar. 2, 1867, for same, at Fredericksburg; Congressional Medal of Honor, Oct. 10, 1892, for distinguished conduct at Salem Heights, Va., May 3, 1863. Apptd. 2d lt., 12th U.S. Inf., May 11, 1866; capt. 38th Inf., Jan. 22, 1867; maj. a.-a.-g., Aug. 14, 1890; lt. col. a.-a.-g., Nov. 15, 1896; brig. gen. vols., May 27, 1898-June 12, 1899; col. a.-a.-g., Apr. 28, 1900; retired, Apr. 18, 1901; brig. gen. retired, by act of Apr. 23, 1904. Chief of staff and adj. gen. to Gen. Miles, headquarters of the army in Cuba and Puerto Rico, during summer of 1898 and until retired; as mem. bd. of officers took part in preparing Infantry, Cavalry and Light Artillery Drill Regulations and Manual of Guard Duty. Home: Washington, D.C. Died Dec. 22, 1922.

GILMORE, Joseph Henry, univ. prof.; b. Boston, Apr. 29, 1834; s. Joseph Albree (gov. of N.H.) and Ann (Whipple) G.; A.B., Brown U., 1858, A.M., 1861 (hon. Ph.D., 1892); grad. Newton Theol. Instn., 1861; m. Mary Josephine Parkhurst, May 10, 1861; 2d, Lucy Ann Brown, Sept. 21, 1865. Ordained Bapt. ministry, 1862; pastor Fisherville, N.H., 1862-64; pvt. sec. to his father, and editor Concord (N.H.) Daily Monitor, 1864-65; pastor Second Ch., Rochester, N.Y., 1865-67; acting prof. Hebrew, Rochester Theol. Sem., 1867-68; prof. rhetoric, logic and English, Univ. of Rochester, 1868-1908; retired on the Carnegie Foundation. Author: Familiar Chats About Books and Reading, 1892. Home: Rochester, N.Y. Died July 23, 1918.

GILMORE, Melvin Randolph, ethnobotanist; b. Valley, Neb., Mar. 11, 1868; s. Capt. John Randolph and Mary Louisa (Concannon) G.; A.B., Cotner Coll., Neb., 1904; M.A., U. of Neb., 1909, Ph.D., 1914; unmarried. Prof. biol. sciences, Cotner Coll., 1905-11; curator Mus. Neb. State Hist. Soc., 1911-16; curator State Hist. Soc., N. Dak., 1916-23; mem. scientific staff Mus. of Am. Indian, Heye Foundation, New York, 1923-28; curator of ethnology, Mus. of Anthropology, U. of Mich., 1929—. Mem. teaching staff, Am. Sch. of Wild Life Protection, McGregor, Ia., 1922—, Nature Training Sch., Gardner Lake, Conn., 1929. Rep. of gov. of N.D. on Nat. Conf. on State Parks, Des Moines, Ia., 1921; conducted expdn. of Mus. Am. Indian to record ancient ritualistic ceremonies of Arikara tribe, 1924; originated proposed project of Am. Ethnobotanical Garden of Mus. of Am. Indian; established, 1931, Ethnobot. Lab., Mus. of Anthropology, U. of Mich. Fellow Am. Geog. Soc. Author of "Uses of Plants by Indians of the Missouri River Region" in Annual Rept. Bur. of Am. Ethnology, Washington, 1919. Died July 25, 1940.

GILMORE, Samuel Louis, congressman; b. New Orleans, July 30, 1859; s. Thomas and Elizabeth Agnes G.; A.B., Seton Hall Coll., S. Orange, N.J., 1877, A.M., 1879; LL.B., Tulane U., 1879; m. Martha Frazer, d. late Capt. John T. Nolan, C.S.A., of St. Elizabeth Plantation, Ascension Parish, La., Nov. 3, 1887. Asst. city atty. of New Orleans, 1889-1902; corp. counsel, 1906-09; mem. 61st Congress (1909-11), 2d La. Dist. Democrat. Catholic. Home: New Orleans, La. Died 1910.

GILMORE, Thomas Mador, editor; b. Columbus, Ga., Sept. 4, 1858; s. Thomas Kervin and Ann Eliza (Forster) G.; mainly self-educated; m. Julia C. Forster, Dec. 16, 1880; 2d, Mary McGowan, June 25, 1909. Publisher of Bonfort's Wine and Spirit Circular, New York. Originator and pres. Nat. Model License League; writer and speaker on saloon reform. Ind. Democrat. Episcopalian. Home: Louisville, Ky. Died June 5, 1921.

GILPIN, Charles Sidney, actor; b. Richmond, Va., Nov. 20, 1878; s. Peter and Caroline (White) G.; ed. St. Francis Sch., Richmond. Began with Canadian Jubilee Singers, Hamilton, Ont., 1903; appeared with Williams and Walker's "Abyssinia" co., and Gus Hill's "Smart Set" co., 1905-06, Pekin Stock Co., Chicago, 1907-08, Pan-Am. Octette, 1911-13, "Old Man's Boy," 1913-14. Entered vaudeville, 1914; head of 1st negro dramatic stock company, New York, 1916; creator of William Custis, Negro clergyman, in Drinkwater's "Abraham Lincoln," 1919; starred in Eugene O'Neill's "Emperor Jones," 1920-21. Republican. Catholic. Home: New York, N.Y. Died May 6, 1930.

GILPIN, Joseph Elliott, prof. chemistry; b. Baltimore, Md., Nov. 21, 1866; s. Albert G. and Fannie (Elliott) G.; A.B., Johns Hopkins, 1889, Ph.D., 1892; m. Katharine Pleasant, 1895 (died 1903); m. 2d, Olive Russell, Nov. 18, 1904. Instr. chemistry, 1892-95, associate, 1895-1911, asso. prof., 1911-13, collegiate prof., 1913—, Johns Hopkins. Christian Scientist. Died Aug. 25, 1924.

GILROY, Thomas F., mayor of New York, 1893-95; b. in Ireland, June 3, 1840; came to U.S., 1847; ed. New York public schools; learned printer's trade; several yrs. clerk Supreme Court; 1885-88, co. clerk, city and co. of New York; undersheriff, 1888; commr. public works, 1889-92; now engaged as builder and real estate operator. Mem. Tammany Soc.; chmn. "com. of twenty-four," grand sachem, 1891. Home: New York, N.Y. Died 1911.

GILSON, Roy Rolfe, author; b. Clinton, Ia., Aug. 12, 1875; s. Frank Rindge G. (editor) and Marian (Roff) G.; grad. Benton Harbor (Mich.) Coll., 1895; m. Mary Walker McGrath, Jan. 30, 1902; children—Edward McGrath, Dorothy Jean, Robert. Served in various capacities on staffs of Grand Rapids (Mich.) Herald, Detroit Tribune and News, New York Commercial Advertiser. Ordained deacon, P.E. Ch., Sept. 28, 1913; priest, June 21, 1914; rector parishes in N.H. and Me.; now rector St. Peter's Church, Salisbury, Md. Author: The Flower of Youth, 1904; Miss Primrose, 1906; Katrina, 1906; The Wistful Years, 1909; Ember Light, 1911; The Legend of Jerry Ladd, 1913. Home: Salisbury, Md. Died Aug. 2, 1933.

GILTNER, Frank Carlton, live stock; b. Eminence, Ky., July 20, 1876; s. William Spencer and Elizabeth (Raines) G.; A.B., Eminence Coll., 1894; m. Mary D. Tanner, Apr. 30, 1913; 1 dau., Martha Elizabeth. Builder, 1895, mgr. until 1920, Eminence Milling Co.; engaged in export live stock trade, mem. Giltner Bros., 1897—; with Farmers & Drovers Bank, 1904, became pres., 1918; now appraiser Federal Land Bank, Louisville. Sec. and treas. Old Odd Fellows and Rebekahs Home, Eminence, Ky. Holstein Cattle Club. Democrat. Mem. Christian (Disciples) Ch. Home: Eminence, Ky. Died Feb. 25, 1935.

GIMBEL, Charles, mcht.; b. Vincennes, Ind.; s. Adam and Fredolyn G.; ed. pub. schs., Philadelphia, Pa.; m. Ella Long, Jan. 15, 1889. Chmn. bd. Gimbel Bros. Home: Philadelphia, Pa. Died Sept. 9, 1932.

GINN, Edwin, publisher; b. Orland, Me., Feb. 14, 1838; s. James and Sarah (Blood) G.; A.B., Tufts Coll., 1862, A.M., 1865 (Litt.D., 1902); m. Clara A. Glover, 1869; 2d, M. Francesca Grébe, 1894. Engaged in pub. business; head of Ginn & Co., publishers of sch. and coll. text-books; 1st book, Allen's Latin Grammar, published in 1868; business now second to no other single house in America. Especially interested in housing of the poor and promoting better conditions between labor and capital; also in movement favoring universal peace among nations; founder, World Peace Foundation. Home: Winchester, Mass. Died Jan. 21, 1914.

GINN, Frank Hadley, lawyer; b. Fremont, O., Feb. 25, 1868; s. Francis Marion and Millicent Ophelia (Pope) G.; Ph.B., Kenyon Coll., Gambier, O., 1890, LL.D., 1925; m. Cornelia Root, June 25, 1899; children—Francis, Marian Root (Mrs. W. P. Jones), Alexander, Barbara Root. Admitted to bar of State of Ohio, 1892, and began practice at Cleveland; pres. Ohio and Pa. Coal Co.; dir. many companies. Home: Gates Mills, O. Died Feb. 6, 1938.

GIRARD, Alfred Conrad, brig. gen.; b. Switzerland, July 31, 1841; s. Prof. C. F. (of U. of Basel) and J. (Blumer) G.; grad. U. of Würzburg, Germany, 1864; m. Annie R., d. J. P. M. Epping, U.S. marshal, of Charleston, S.C., Mar. 3, 1868. Acting asst. surgeon, Jan. 1865-67; asst. surgeon U.S.A., May 14, 1867; advanced through grades to col.; asst. surgeon-gen., June 28, 1902; brig. gen., Apr. 6, 1905; retired at own request, Apr. 7, 1905. Served in depts. of La. and Tex., 1867-82; visited hosps. in Europe and published report advocating antiseptic surgery; then served 8 yrs. on frontier in campaigns against Indians, and after another trip to Europe published an atlas of clinical microscopy; just before Spanish-Am. War represented U.S. at an internat. congress, Madrid; chief surgeon, 2d Army Corps, during Spanish-Am. War; at its close equipped Gen. Hosp. at the Presidio, Calif., where he took care of 19,000 patients in 3 yrs., mostly invalids from P.I.; chief surgeon Dept. Luzon, 1 yr., then chief surgeon Dept. Calif.; med. reference librarian, John Crerar Library, Chicago, 1907-; now representing same at Washington. Died Jan. 31, 1914.

GIRARD, Joseph Basil, army surgeon; b. Courpiere, Puy-de-Dome, France, Dec. 26, 1846; s. Michael and Genevieve (Navarron) G.; ed. pvt. schs., France and Can.; M.D., U. of Mich., 1867; m. Louise Oury, May 17, 1875 (died 1899). Entered U.S.A. as asst. surgeon with rank of 1st lt., May 14, 1867; capt. asst. surgeon, May 14, 1870; maj. surgeon, Mar. 22, 1888; lt. col. deputy surgeon gen., Feb. 2, 1901; col. asst. surgeon gen., Sept. 7, 1902. Service has been chiefly on western plains, H.I. and P.I., where was chief surgeon Div. of the Philippines, 1904-06; chief surgeon Dept. of Tex., 1907-10; retired for age, Dec. 26, 1910. Home: San Antonio, Tex. Died Aug. 25, 1918.

GIRTY, George Herbert, paleontologist; b. Cleveland, O., Dec. 30, 1869; s. Alfred P. and Emma (Hopkins) G.; A.B., Yale, 1892, Ph.D., 1894; married. Stratigraphic paleontologist, 1895—, now geologist, U.S. Geol. Survey. Fellow A.A.A.S. Home: Washington, D.C. Died Jan. 27, 1939.

GIVAGO-GRISHINA, Nadeshda, author, illustrator; b. Moscow, Russia; d. Ivan and Sophia (Fleroff) Givago; ed. at home and in art schs. and colls., Moscow, France and Germany; m. Vladimir Grishin, Sept. 17, 1903 (dec.); 1 son, George. Came to U.S., 1923, naturalized citizen, 1930. Interpreter and family case work, Internat. Inst. Y.W.C.A., Los Angeles, Calif., 1924—; lecturer; story teller to children. Mem. Russian Orthodox Ch. Author and illustrator: Shorty, 1924; Peter Pea, 1926; Sparrow House, 1928; Grisha and His Clay Pig, 1930; The Magic Squirrel, 1933. Deceased.

GIVEN, Josiah, justice Supreme Court Iowa; b. Westmoreland Co., Pa., Aug. 31, 1828; s. Josiah and Jane (Glendening) G.; common school edn. Holmes Co., O., 1838-51; m. Elizabeth Armour, Oct. 6, 1852 (dec.). Admitted to bar, 1851; served 2 terms as State's atty. and for 24 yrs. on nisi prius and supreme bench of Iowa; also 1 term in Iowa Ho. Reps. and 1 term postmaster Ho. Reps., 39th Congress; dep. commr. internal revenue during Grant's 1st administration. Served as drummer, private and corporal in war with Mexico, and capt., lt. col., col. and bvt. brig. gen. in the Union army. Republican. Home: Des Moines, Ia. Deceased.

GJERSET, Knut, educator, author; b. Romsdal, Norway, Sept. 15, 1865; s. Ole S. and Karen Marie (Eidem) G.; brought to U.S., 1871; B.L., U. of Minn., 1893; post-grad. work, Johns Hopkins; Ph.D., Heidelberg Univ., 1898; studied univs. of Oslo and Berlin; Litt.D., St. Olaf Coll., Northfield, Minn., 1925; m. Helen Baumgarten, 1894. Prin. St. Ansgar (Ia.) Sem., 1893-95, Glenwood (Minn.) Acad., 1900-02; prof. history, Luther College, Decorah, Ia., 1902-16; pres. Park Region Luther Coll., Fergus Falls, Minn., 1916-17; head of depts. of history and Norse, Luther Coll., 1917-23, head dept. of history and curator of the Norwegian Am. Hist. Museum, 1923—. One of founders of the Norwegian-Am. Hist. Assn.; vice-pres. Ia. Hist. Assn., 1933, pres. 1934. Decorated Knight of 1st Class, Order of St. Olaf, by King of Norway, 1916; Knight Order of the Falcon (Iceland), 1927. Republican. Lutheran. Author: English Grammar, 1908; History of the Norwegian People (2 vols.), 1915; History of Iceland, 1923; Norwegian Sailors on the Great Lakes—A Study in American Inland Transportation, 1927; Norwegian Sailors in American Waters—A Study in the History of Maritime Activity on the Eastern Seaboard, 1933. Home: Decorah, Ia. Died Oct. 29, 1936.

GLACKENS, William J., artist; b. Phila., Mar. 13, 1870; s. Samuel and Elizabeth (Finn) G.; ed. pub. schs.; pupil Pa. Acad. Fine Arts, and studied in Europe; m. Edith Dimock, Feb. 16, 1904; children—Ira D., Lenna D. Rep. by paintings Art Inst. of Chicago, Columbus (O.) Gallery of Fine Arts, Detroit Inst. of Arts, Museum of History, Science & Art (Los Angeles), Metropolitan Mus. of Art (N.Y. City), Whitney Mus. of Am. Art (N.Y. City), Newark (N.J.) Mus., Pa. State Coll. (Dept. of Architecture), Phillips Memorial Gallery, Corcoran Gallery of Art (Washington, D.C.), Addison Gallery of Am. Art (Andover, Mass.), Albright Art Gallery (Buffalo). Exhibited at Paris Salon, 1896, Paris Expn., 1900; gold medal, Buffalo Expn., 1901; silver and bronze medals, St. Louis Expn., 1904; Temple gold medal, 1924; second prize, Carnegie Inst. Internat. Exhbn., 1929; Carol H. Beck gold medal, 1933; Jennie Sesnan medal, 131st Annual Exhbn., Pa. Acad. of Fine Arts, Phila., 1936; Garden Club prize, Internat. Exhbn. of Paintings, Carnegie Inst., Pittsburgh, 1936. A.N.A., 1906; N.A., 1933; mem. Nat. Inst. of Arts and Letters. Home: New York, N.Y. Died May 22, 1938.

GLADDEN, George, editor; b. N. Adams, Mass., Oct. 13, 1867; s. Washington and Jennie (Cohoon) G.; spl. courses in arts, polit. science and economies, Cornell U.; unmarried. In newspaper work, Columbus, O., 1889-91, Pittsburgh, 1891-93, Springfield, Mass. (The Republican), 1894-98, New York, 1898-1901; editor biography, New Internat. Ency., 1901-04 (same revision, 1906-07; contbr. to 2d edition, 1914-16); asso. editor Current Literature, 1904-05; editor, biography, Nelson's Ency., 1905-07; New Internat. Year Book, 1907, 08; in 1908-09 contbr. of Am. biography, geography and history to Ency. Britannica, 11th edit., 1910; "Conservation of Wild Life" to Am. Year Book, 1913; asst. corr. dept., Cambridge Univ. Press (Ency. Britannica), 1910-12; asst. in wild-life protection work to Dr. W. T. Hornaday, 1912-13. Planned Birds of America, 3 vols. (1916-17) and wrote 200 of 500 characterizations of species, and most of introductions to generic groups; asso. editor, Mother Nature's News, bi-weekly, 1917-18; editor and writer of ednl. pamphlets for Boy Scouts of America, 1918-19. Mem. Exec. Com. Manhattan Council, Boy Scouts of America; founded Nat. History Group of same, 1918; mem. Linnæan Soc. (N.Y. Acad. Sciences). Home: New York, N.Y. Died Mar. 11, 1924.

GLADDEN, Washington, author, clergyman; b. Pottsgrove, Pa., Feb. 11, 1836; s. Solomon and Amanda (Daniels) G.; A.B., Williams, 1859; (LL.D., U. of Wis., 1881, U. of Notre Dame, 1895; D.D., Roanoke Coll., 1882); m. Jennie Cohoon, Dec. 5, 1860 (died 1909); father of George G. Ordained Congl. ministry, 1860; pastor Brooklyn, N.Y., 1860-61, Morrisania, N.Y., 1861-66, N. Adams, Mass., 1866-71; on editorial staff of The Independent, 1871-74; pastor North Ch., Springfield, Mass., 1874-82; pastor First Congl. Ch., Columbus, O., 1882-14, pastor emeritus. Author: The Lord's Prayer, 1880; Santa Claus on a Lark, 1890; Who Wrote the Bible, 1891; Tools and the Man, 1893; Ruling Ideas of the Present Age, 1895; Seven Puzzling Bible Books, 1897; Social Salvation, 1901; Witnesses of the Light, 1903; Where Does the Sky Begin?, 1904; The Church and Modern Life, 1908; Recollections, 1909; Present Day Theology, 1913; Live and Learn, 1914. Home: Columbus, O. Died July 2, 1918.

GLADDING, Albert F., judge; b. Pharsalia, N.Y., Dec. 9, 1843; s. James C. and Mary Ann (Fargo) G.; ed. Norwich Acad.; read law with Judge David L. Follett, and admitted to bar, 1869; m. Grace V. E. Randall, Mar. 16, 1881 (dec.). Co. judge and surrogate, Chenango Co., N.Y., 1889-1906; justice Supreme Ct. of N.Y., 6th Dist., 1907-20. Republican. Mem. N.Y. State Constl. Conv., 1915. Pres. Chenango Nat. Bank of Norwich, N.Y., 1905—. Home: Norwich, N.Y. Died May 29, 1922.

GLADWIN, Mary Elizabeth, teacher of nursing; b. Stoke-upon-Trent, Staffordshire, Eng., Dec. 24, 1861; d. Francis and Sarah (Cooper) G.; brought to U.S. in childhood; Ph.B., Buchtel (O.) Coll., 1887; grad. cum laude, Boston City Hosp. Sch. of Nursing, 1903; LL.D., U. of Akron (O.), 1920; unmarried. Teacher of physics, chemistry, Norwalk, O., schs., 1887-93; pupil in Boston City Hosp., 9 months, 1896; chief nurse U.S. Army, 1898, Am. Red Cross, Manila, P.I., 1899; supt. Beverly (Mass.) Hosp., 1903-04, and 1905-07; Red Cross nurse, Japanese hosp., Hiroshima, Russo-Japanese War, 6 months of 1904; supt. of nurses, Women's Hosp., N.Y. City, 1907-08; organized and directed Sch. and Visiting Nursing Assn., Akron, O., 1912-14; chief nurse Am. Red Cross, Dayton, O., floods, 1913, Belgrade, Serbia and Saloniki, Greece, 1914-19; teacher Akron Red Cross, 1919-20; lecturer Ohio Red Cross, 1921; dir. nursing edn., Indiana, 1922-23, Minnesota, 1923-28; dir. Sch. of Nursing, Rochester, Minn., 1928-29; lecturer on nursing edn., 1930—. Awarded Japanese Order of the Crown, Port Arthur medal; Serbian Royal Red Cross, Order of St. Sava, La Croix de Charité; Russian Imperial Medal and Ribbon of St. Anne; Internat. Florence Nightingale medal. Episcopalian. Home: Akron, O. Died Nov. 22, 1939.

GLADWIN, William Zachary, author. See Gulielma Zollinger.

GLAENZER, Richard Butler, editor, author; b. Paris, France, Dec. 15, 1876; s. Georges A. and Alice Cary (Butler) G.; prep. edn., École Monge, Paris, Friends Seminary, pub. schs., N.Y. City, and Hill School; A.B., Yale, 1898; m. Anita Gibson, June 3, 1903 (divorced 1915); children—Marion, Doris; m. 2d, Sophie E. Basham, Aug. 18, 1915 (died July 7, 1935). Engaged in arts, 1900-11; freelance writer, 1906-27; editor Decorative Art in America, 1907; screen writer for Goldwyn, Asso. Producers, 1921-22; publ. dir. Robert M. McBridge & Co., 1927-28, editor, 1929-34. Fellow Metropolitan Mus. of Art. Episcopalian. Author: Beggar and King (verse), 1917; Literary Snapshots, 1920. Home: New York, N.Y. Died April 15, 1937.

GLASCOCK, Hugh Grundy, educator; b. Ralls Co., Mo., Feb. 14, 1865; s. French and Lucy (Muldrow) G.; grad. Strother (Mo.) Acad., 1881; student Westminster Coll., Fulton, Mo., 1881-83; B.S., Ind. Normal Sch., 1887; studied U. of Chicago, 1894-95; m. Ella Bodine Woods, June 15, 1897. Taught in Paris (Mo.) High Sch., 1890-94; headmaster, Missouri Mil. Acad., 1894-96, Culver Mil. Acad., 1896-1929 (emeritus). Presbyterian. Home: Culver, Ind. Died July 25, 1934.

GLASGOW, William Anderson, Jr., lawyer; b. Fincastle, Va., Apr. 29, 1865; s. William Anderson and Grace Ellen (Shanks) G.; B.L., Washington and Lee, 1886; LL.D., 1918; LL.D., Temple U., 1920; m. Jean Cresswell Macara, July 8, 1897. Admitted to Va. bar, 1886, Pa. bar, 1904; practiced in Fincastle and Roanoke, Va., 1886-1904; removed to Philadelphia, 1904. Episcopalian. Deceased.

GLASS, Franklin Potts, newspaperman; b. Centreville, Ala., June 7, 1858; s. Benjamin F. and Caroline (Potts) G.; A.B., Princeton, 1877, A.M., 1880; m. Mattie Byrd Purnell, Apr. 2, 1884; children—Franklin Purnell, John Purnell, Christine, Evelyn Byrd (Mrs. E. E. McCoy), Louise (Mrs. P. B. Marzoni), Hugh Bryson. Founded Bibb Blade, Bibb Co., Ala., 1880; bought Selma Daily Times, 1881, and moved to Selma; bought half interest in Montgomery Advertiser, 1886, of which was gen. mgr. until Aug. 1915; editor-in-chief Birmingham (Ala.) News, 1910-20, and was v.p. of the co.; sold interest in News, 1920; editorial dir., St. Louis Star, 1923-25; pres. and pub. The Advertiser Co., Montgomery, Ala., 1927—. Apptd., 1913, to vacancy in U.S. Senate caused by death of Senator Joseph F. Johnston; seat denied by Senate, Feb. 4, 1914, by vote 32 to 31, on constrn. of 17th Amendment, denying the governor right of appmt. under existing statutes of Ala. Democrat. Home: Montgomery, Ala. Died Jan. 10, 1934.

GLASS, Gilbert, clergyman, editor; b. Harrodsburg, Ky., Jan. 24, 1875; s. Harvey (D.D.) and Susan (Downton) G.; B.A., Central U., Richmond, Ky., 1895; B.D., Presbyn. Theol. Sem., Louisville, Ky., 1898; D.D., King Coll., Bristol, Tenn., 1915; m. Mary Grandin Orr, Dec. 21, 1911; children—Margaret Downton, James Harvey. Ordained ministry Presbyn. Ch. in U.S.A., 1898; pastor Broadwell, Glasgow, Munfordville, Stanford, Covington (all of Ky.), Johnson City, Tenn., until 1916; gen. supt. Sunday School and Young Peoples Work, 1916-24; editor in chief Presbyn. S.S. Publs., Apr. 1924—. Mem. Nat. Council Boy Scouts of America; mem. bd. United Soc. Christian Endeavor. Home: Richmond, Va. Died Mar. 19, 1934.

GLASS, Henry, naval officer; b. Hopkinsville, Ky., Jan. 7, 1844; s. Henry and Martha K. G.; grad. U.S. Naval Acad., 1863; m. Ella M. Johnson, Mar. 15, 1881. Promoted ensign, May 28, 1863; advanced through grades to rear admiral, Oct. 9, 1901. Served in Canandaigua, S. Atlantic Blockading Squadron, 1863, Pawnee, 1863-65; participated in all gen. engagements with forts and batteries in Charleston Harbor, July-Sept., 1863; engagements with batteries in Stono River, S.C., Dec. 28, 1863, and July 3 to 11, inclusive, 1864; engagements with batteries in North Edisto River, Feb. 9, 1865; capture of Georgetown, S.C., Feb. 5, 1865; served in Powhatan and Dacotah, Pacific Squadron, 1865-68; Tuscarora, 1869; Navy Yard, Phila., 1869-70; Mohican, 1870; comd. Nyack, 1870; California, 1871-72; chief of staff Iroquois and Hartford, 1873-74; comd. nautical sch.-ship Jamestown, 1874, 1876-78; exec. officer receiving-ship Independence, 1875; spl. duty San Francisco, 1879; comd. Jamestown, 1880-81, Wachusett, 1881-82; Navy Yard, Mare Island, 1883-86; comd. Monocacy, 1886-88; Naval Acad., 1889-91; mem. Examining and Retiring Bds., 1891-92; Navy Yard, Mare Island, 1893-94; comd. Cincinnati, 1894-95, Texas, 1895-97; capt. of yard, Navy Yard, Mare Island, 1897-98; comd. Pensacola, April, 1898; Charleston, May-Dec. 1898, capture of Ladrone Islands, May 1898, taking of Manila, Aug. 1898, capt. of port, Manila, Aug.-Oct. 1898, while comdg. Charleston; comd. Pensacola and comdt. naval training sta., San Francisco, 1899-1902; comdr.-in-chief Pacific Sta., 1903-04; comdt. Pacific Naval Dist., 1904-08; retired, Jan. 7, 1906. Author: Marine International Law, 1885. Home: Berkeley, Calif. Died 1908.

GLASS, Hiram, lawyer; b. nr. Mt. Vernon, Tex., June 25, 1859; s. Alexander and Jane (Blake) G.; Mt. Vernon Inst., Tex., 1879-82; Cumberland U. Law Sch., Lebanon, Tenn., 1882-83; m. Henrietta P. Dodson, Dec. 15, 1885. Admitted to Tex. bar, 1883; practiced, Mt. Vernon, Tex., 1883-95; dist. atty. 5th Jud. Dist., Tex., 1892-96; mem. Todd & Glass, Texarkana, Tex., 1895-1900, Glass, Estes, King & Burford, 1900-10; engaged as Tex. atty. for prin. Tex. rys. at Austin, Tex., 1910—. Democrat. Baptist. Mason. Home: Austin, Tex. Died June 14, 1919.

GLASS, James H., surgeon; b. Mohawk, N.Y., June 15, 1854; s. Robert and Emily Lowell (Merrill) G.; student U. of Mich., 1874-75; M.D., Bellevue Med. Coll. (New York U.), 1877; (hon. A.M., Hamilton); m. Anna Wells, May 31, 1882. Attending surgeon, St. Luke's Hosp., Utica, N.Y., 1882-90; phys. and surgeon in charge Utica City Hosp., 1886-91; attending surgeon St. Elizabeth's Hosp., 1890-93; surgeon in charge Faxton Hosp., 1893-1922; consulting surgeon Utica State Hosp., Rome City Hosp. many yrs.; pres. bd. trustees Utica City Dispensary from 1895; retired. Trustee Hamilton Coll. Home: Trenton Falls, N.Y., and Benson Springs, Fla. Died Aug. 4, 1931.

GLASS, Joseph Sarsfield, R.C. bishop; b. Bushnell, Ill., Mar. 13, 1874; s. James and Mary Edith (Kelly) G.; grad. St. Vincent's Coll., 1889; joined Congregation of the Mission, founded by St. Vincent de Paul; theol. studies at St. Mary's Sem., Barrens, Perryville, Mo., and grad. Pontifical Coll. of St. Thomas de Urbe (Minerva), Rome, Italy, 1899 (D.D.). Prof. dogmatic theology, St. Mary's Sem., 1899-1901; pres. St. Vincent's Coll., Los Angeles, 1901-11; pastor St. Vincent's Ch., 1901-15; consecrated bishop of Salt Lake, Aug. 24, 1915. Mem. Utah State Council of Defense, 1917; mem. Nat. Catholic War Council. Died Jan. 26, 1926.

GLASS, Montague (Marsden), author; b. Manchester, Eng., July 23, 1877; s. James David and Amelia (Marsden) G.; came to U.S., in 1890; ed. Coll. City of New York, and New York U.; m. Caroline Patterson, Feb. 14, 1907; children—James Montague (dec.), Elizabeth Mary. Hebrew. Republican. Author: Potash and Perlmutter, 1910; Abe and Mawruss, 1911; Elkan Lubliner—American, 1912; Object: Matrimony, 1912; Competitive Nephew, 1915; Worrying Won't Win, 1918; Potash and Perlmutter Settle Things, 1919; Y' Understand, 1925. Plays: Potash and Perlmutter (with Charles Klein), 1913; Abe and Mawruss (with R. C. Megrue), 1915; (and with J. E. Goodman) Object: Matrimony, 1916; Business Before Pleasure, 1917; Land of Joy, 1917; Why Worry? 1918; His Honor Abe Potash, 1919; (with J. E. Goodman) Partners Again, 1921; Present Company Excepted, 1921; (with J. E. Goodman) It's Never Too Late, 1923; Potash & Perlmutter—Detectives, 1926; Lucky Numbers, 1927; Pleasure Bound, 1927; You Can't Learn Them Nothing, 1929. Died Feb. 3, 1934.

GLASSCOCK, William Ellsworth, governor; b. nr. Arnettsville, W.Va., Dec. 13, 1862; s. Daniel and Prudence (Michael) G.; ed. pub. schs. and W.Va. U.; admitted to bar, 1902; m. Mary Alice Miller, Aug. 15, 1888. Taught school in Ia., Neb. and W.Va.; co. supt. free schs. Monongalia Co., 1887-90; mem. Rep. State Central Com., 1900-08 (chmn. and sec. at various times); U.S. collector internal revenue for Dist. of W.Va., 1905-08, resigned; gov. of W.Va., 1909-13. Methodist. Home: Morgantown, W.Va. Died Apr. 12, 1925.

GLASSIE, Henry Haywood, spl. asst. atty. gen. U.S.; b. Nashville, Tenn., Aug. 12, 1871; s. Col. Daniel W. and Minna Haywood (Nash) G.; A.B., Johns Hopkins, 1892; student law dept. Columbian (now George Washington) U.; hon. LL.M., Nat. Univ. Law Sch.; m. Gertrude, d. late Senator Donelson Caffery, of Franklin, La.; children—Donelson Caffery, Gertrude Caffery, Henry Haywood. Admitted to bar, 1894; asst. U.S. atty. Dist. of Columbia, 1902-03; spl. asst. to atty. gen. in cases involving 2d class mailing privilege, 1903-07; sec. Joint Congl. Com. on 2d Class Mail Matter, 1906; counsel Joint Congl. Commn. for Codification of Postal Laws, 1908; atty. in charge condemnations and land litigations in D.C., 1914; spl. asst. to atty. gen., 1921; mem. U.S. Tariff Commn., by appmt. of President, Mar. 8, 1923-Mar. 4, 1927; counsel for U.S. before Virginia-District of Columbia Boundary Commn., 1934-35; now special asst. atty. general of U.S. Democrat. Episcopalian. Home: Chevy Chase, Md. Died Jan. 26, 1938.

GLATFELTER, Samuel F., congressman; b. York Co., Pa., Apr. 7, 1858; s. Isaac K. and Sarah (Feiser) G.; desc. Casper Glatfelter, 1743; prep. edn., York County Acad.; student Pa. Coll., Gettysburg, Pa.; m. Ida Gilbert, 1880. Formerly teacher pub. schs.; building contractor; pres. Hartley Mut. Fire Ins. Co.; mem. 68th Congress (1923-25), 22d Pa. Dist. Democrat. Protestant. Home: York, Pa. Died Apr. 23, 1927.

GLATFELTER William Lincoln, paper mfr., banker; b. Spring Forge (now Spring Grove), Pa., Apr. 27, 1865; s. Philip Henry and Amanda Emma (Loucks) G.; ed. York Co. (Pa.) Acad., Gettysburg (Pa.) Acad. and Eastman Nat. Business Coll., Poughkeepsie, N.Y.; m. Katharine Rebecca Hollinger, Sept. 15, 1887; 1 son, Philip Hollinger. Began in paper mfg. business, Spring Grove, 1886; pres. P. H. Glatfelter Co., paper mfrs., Hanover Wire Cloth Co., 1st Nat. Bank. Served as chief burgess, also sch. dir. of Spring Grove. Republican. Lutheran. Home: Spring Grove, Pa. Died Apr. 20, 1930.

GLAZEBROOK, Otis Allan, consular service; b. Richmond, Va., Oct. 13, 1845; s. Larkin White and America Henley (Bullington) G.; ed. Randolph-Macon Coll., Va. Mil. Inst., Episcopal Theol. Sem. in Va.; D.D., Adrian (Mich.) Coll. Deacon, 1868, priest, 1869, P.E. Ch.; served in missionary fields in Va. 7 yrs.; rector in Baltimore, 4 yrs., Macon, 3 yrs.; chaplain U. of Va. 2 yrs.; rector St. John's Ch., Elizabeth, N.J., 1885-1912; clerical dep. from N.J. to Gen. Conv. P.E. Ch. 8 times. Consul at Jerusalem, 1914-20, Nice, France, Dec. 2, 1920—. Served as chaplain 3d Regt., N.J., Spanish-Am. War, and also as chaplain Grand Lodge of Masons of N.J., Mil. Order Foreign Wars (N.J. Commandery), 5th Regt. of Baltimore and Southern Soc. of N.Y. City; now hon. chaplain No. 3 Riviera Post Am. Legion. Decorated Knight of the Holy Sepulchre. Died Apr. 26, 1931.

GLAZIER, Willard, soldier, explorer; b. Fowler, N.Y., Aug. 22, 1841; s. Ward and Mehitable (Bolton) W.; worked on farm summers, attended dist. sch. winters; at 15 a trapper in the woods, earning means for higher edn.; 2 yrs. at Gouverneur Wesleyan Sem.; later at State Normal Coll., Albany; teaching sch. at intervals; m. Harriet Ayres, 1868. Served 1861-65, pvt. to 1st lt. and bvt. capt., Harris Light (2d N.Y.) and 26th N.Y. cav.; took part in over 60 battles and engagements; 14 months in Confederate prisons, 1863-64, escaped, was recaptured and escaped a 3d time and reached Union line at Savannah after trial as spy. Toured U.S. and Can., 1865-75, gathering lit. material; rode horseback, Boston to San Francisco, 1876; located 1881, and verified on 2d expdn., 1891, true source of Mississippi, in a lake beyond Itasca, now known as Lake Glazier. Organized and was col. provisional regt., Ill. vols., for the Spanish war, 1898. Visited Southern States and W. Indies, 1899; explored coast and interior of Labrador, 1902. Lecturer. Author: Ocean to Ocean on Horseback, 1896. Home: Albany, N.Y. Died 1905.

GLEASON, Arthur Huntington, writer; b. Newark, N.J., Dec. 14, 1878; s. William Henry and Leila (Seward) G.; B.A., Yale, 1901; m. Helen Hayes, Oct. 5, 1912. Reporter, New York Tribune, 1901-03; manuscript editor, The Cosmopolitan, 1903; asst. editor, Country Life in America, 1904-07, The Survey, 1907; asso. editor, Collier's Weekly, Jan. 1, 1908-13; Red Cross worker in Hector Munro ambulance corps with the Belgian Army, Sept. 1914-Sept. 1915; corr. in Europe of the New York Tribune and Century Magazine, 1916-17; corr. in England of The Survey, 1919. Awarded the Mons Star and Ribbon, 1919. Socialist. Author: British Labor and the War (with Paul V. Kellogg); What the Workers Want, 1920; Workers' Education (Bur. Industrial Research), 1921. Home: New York, N.Y. Died Dec. 30, 1923.

GLEASON, Carlisle Joyslin, lawyer; b. Montpelier, Vt., Oct. 27, 1874; s. Louis Pomeroy and Anne Louise (Timothy) G.; student Vermont Episcopal Inst., Burlington, 1890-92; B.S., Amherst, 1896; LL.B., Harvard, 1899; m. Ellen L. Fifield, Oct. 18, 1902; children—Louise Fifield (Mrs. Frederic S. Withington), Elizabeth Fifield (Mrs. James A. Moffett, II). Admitted to New York bar, 1899; dir. numerous corps. Episcopalian. Home: New York, N.Y. Died Apr. 29, 1940.

GLEASON, Daniel Angell, treas. Fitchburg R.R. Co., 1887—; b. Worcester, Mass., May 9, 1836; s. John Fiske and Maria (Tourtelotte) G.; grad. Harvard Coll., 1856; grad. in law, Harvard, 1860; m. Annie Louisa Hall, Jan. 7, 1863. Asst. to atty. gen. of Mass., 1862-63; tax commr. and commr. of corps. of Mass., 1864-81; treas. of Mass., 1881-86; held various town offices between 1864-92. Republican. Editor of Bouvier's Law Dictionary, 1865; Bouvier's Institutes; Phillips on Insurance; etc. Pres. Medford Savings Bank. Home: Medford, Mass. Died 1908.

GLEASON, Edward Baldwin, physician; b. Phila., Oct. 13, 1854; s. Dr. Cloyes W. and Margaretta (Baldwin) G.; S.B., U. of Pa., 1875, M.D., 1878; M.D., in course, Medico-Chirurg. Coll., 1899; LL.D., Villanova Coll., Pa., 1905; m. Marion E. Currie, 1887. Prof. otology, Grad. Sch. of Medicine, Univ. of Pa., and pres. of the otolaryngological faculty; prof. otology, Medico-Chirurg. College; visiting laryngologist, Phila. Hosp.; surgeon in charge of nose, throat and ear dept., Northern Dispensary. Fellow Coll. Physicians, Phila., Am. Acad. Medicine. Republican. Author: Manual of Diseases of the Nose, Throat and Ear, 1907 (5 edits.). Home: Philadelphia, Pa. Died Nov. 30, 1934.

GLEASON, Elliott Perry, mfr., inventor; b. Westmoreland, N.H., June 27, 1821; common school edn.; one of the pioneers in the mfr. of gas burners in early stages of the industry; inventor of regulating argand burner and many other standard devices; also identified with development of electric lighting. Pres. and prin. owner E. P. Gleason Mfg. Co., New York, mfrs. gas and electric lighting appliances, also Gleason & Bailey Mfg. Co., Seneca Falls, N.Y., mfrs. fire dept. rolling stock. Home: Brooklyn, N.Y. Died 1901.

GLEASON, Frederic Grant, composer, music teacher, dir. Chicago Auditorium Conservatory; b. Hartford, Conn., Dec. 18, 1849; s. Frederic Lathrop G.; studied under Dudley Buck; went to Europe, 1869; studied under Moscheles and Richter, Leipzig; Weitzmann, Raif, Haupt and Loeschhorn, Berlin; and Oscar Beringer, London; m. Mabel Blanche Kennicott, 1888. Returned to U.S., first locating in Hartford, and since 1876 in Chicago. Was musical critic of the Tribune, 1887-91; composed 2 operas, Otho Visconti and Montezuma, symphonic works, etc. Fellow Am. Coll. Musicians. Received diploma and gold medal from Associazione dei Benemeriti Italiana of Palermo, Sicily, "for distinguished services in the cause of art." Home: Chicago, Ill. Died 1903.

GLEASON, Kate, mech. engr.; b. Rochester, N.Y., Nov. 25, 1865; d. William and Ellen (McDermot) G.; ed. Nazareth Convent, Rochester, N.Y., and high sch., Rochester; student Cornell U.; studied under father. Sec. and treas. Gleason Works, mfrs. machine tools, Rochester, 1890-1913; 1st woman receiver in bankruptcy in N.Y. State, 1914; pres. 1st Nat. Bank, East Rochester, 1917-19 (1st woman pres. of a nat. bank); mfr. of fireproof houses by unskilled labor, using standardized designs and assembly methods, 1920—; engaged in restoration work in Sea Islands off coast of S.C. where there are remains of pre-revolutionary art and culture dating back to 1690. Home: Rochester, N.Y. Died Jan. 9, 1933.

GLEASON, Lafayette B(lanchard), lawyer; b. Delhi, N.Y., May 30, 1863; s. William and Caroline (Blanchard) G.; prep. edn., Delaware Acad., Delhi; A.B., Yale, 1885; m. Frances Rich McEntee, Mar. 14, 1908; 1 son, Gordon P. Admitted to N.Y. bar, 1887, and began practice at Delhi; mem. William and Lafayette Gleason, 1887-91; in practice at N.Y. City, 1891—; atty. for State of N.Y. in collection of inheritance taxes, 1915-23. Clk. of N.Y. State Senate, 1905-11. Sec. Rep. State Com., 1906—; Rep. Nat. Conv., 1912, 16, 20, 24, 28, 32. Co-author: Inheritance Taxation (with Alexander Otis), 1925. Home: Delhi, N.Y. Died Oct. 24, 1937.

GLEASON, William Palmer, steel mfr.; b. Chicago, Ill., Feb. 12, 1865; s. Martin Francis and Alice (Simmes) G.; ed. pub. schs., Joliet, Ill.; m. Elizabeth Harvey, 1890 (died 1895); 1 dau., Mary Louise (dec.); m. 2d, Ann Knowlton, 1898; 1 dau., Eleanor May. Began as chem. apprentice Ill. Steel Works, 1880, foreman machine shop, 1887; master mechanic Joliet Works, same co., 1892-1900; master mechanic Colo. Fuel & Iron Works, Pueblo, Colo., 1900-01; asst. mgr. Clairton Works of Carnegie Steel Co., 1901-06; gen. supt., gen. mgr. constrn. Gary Works, U.S. Steel Corporation, 1906-08, gen. mgr., 1908-35, retired; dir. Gary State Bank, Ind. Steel Co. Mem. bd. trustees Ind. World War Memorial; mem. Nat. Council Boy Scouts America; dir. Ind. Tuberculosis Assn.; pres. Lake County Tuberculosis Assn.; v.p., bd. mgrs., Lake County Tuberculosis Sanatorium (Crown Point, Ind.); chmn. Gary Chapter, Am. Red Cross; pres. W. P. Gleason Welfare Center. Republican. Catholic. Home: Gary, Ind. Died June 14, 1936.

GLEAVES, Albert, naval officer; b. Nashville, Tenn., Jan. 1, 1858; s. Henry Albert and Eliza (Tannehill) G.; ed. U.S. Naval Acad.; m. Evelina M. Heap, June 12, 1889; children—Mrs. Anne Heap Van Metre, Mrs. Evelina Porter Cohen. Commissioned ensign U.S. Navy, Jan. 1, 1881; promoted through various grades to rear admiral, July 29, 1915; temp. vice adm. and adm. World War; reverted to rank of rear admiral after the war and later advanced to admiral on the retired list. Served in Hartford, S. Atlantic Station, in Plymouth and Texas on N. Atlantic, Nipsic on European Sta., Trenton and Monocacy on Asiatic Sta.; comd. torpedo-boat Cushing during Spanish-Am. War; served as navigator battleships Indiana and Alabama, 1900-01; comd. Dolphin and Mayflower, spl. service, 1901-04; in charge of Torpedo Sta., Newport, R.I., 1904-08; spl. service in Europe, 1907; comdg. U.S.S. St. Louis, Pacific Fleet, 1908-09; aid to asst. sec. of the Navy and mem. Gen. Bd., until July 1910; comdg. U.S.S. North Dakota, July 1910-Nov. 1911; comdt. Naval Sta., Narragansett Bay, Nov. 1911-May 1912, Navy Yard and Naval Sta., New York, June 1912-Sept. 28, 1914; comd. U.S.S. Utah, Sept. 28, 1914-July 28, 1915; comdg. destroyer Force, Atlantic Fleet, Nov. 22, 1915-July 16, 1917; comdr. convoy operations in Atlantic, May 29, 1917, and convoyed the 1st A.E.F. to France, June 1917; comdg. cruiser and transport force, Atlantic Fleet, July 16, 1917-Sept. 1, 1919; comdg. Asiatic Sta., Sept. 1, 1919-21; spl. duty, Washington, D.C., Mar.-May 1921; comdt. 1st Naval Dist. and Navy Yard, Boston; retired Jan. 1922; gov. of U.S. Naval Home, Phila., Pa., 1928-31. While in command of Dolphin discovered greatest depth in North Atlantic Ocean. Established 1st govt. torpedo factory, 1908. Awarded Victory Medal with star, and D.S.M. (both Navy and army); Mil. Medal (Czecho-Slovakian); Order of Sacred Treasure, 1st Class (Japanese); Order of Weng Hu, 1st Class (Chinese); Commander Legion of Honor (French). Presented with gold and jeweled sword by citizens of Nashville, 1919; LL.D., Jefferson Coll., Pa., 1919; gold watch, Hoboken (N.J.) Chamber of Commerce, 1919. Mem. board of Mgrs. Naval History Soc., 1934—. Episcopalian. Author: Captain James Lawrence, U.S.N., 1904; History of the Cruiser and Transport Force, 1921; Life of An American Sailor—William Hemsley Emory, Rear Admiral, U.S.N., 1923; Life and Letters of Rear Admiral S. B. Luce, U.S. Navy, 1925. Home: Haverford, Pa. Died Jan. 6, 1937.

GLEED, Charles Sumner, lawyer; b. Morrisville, Vt., Mar. 23, 1856; s. Thomas and Cornelia (Fisk) G.; bro. of James Willis G.; A.B., U. of Kan., 1880; student U. of Kan. Law Sch.; admitted to bar, 1884; m. Mabel Gore, June 28, 1888. Dir. A.,T.& S.F. Ry. Co. and several other ry. and banking cos.; in traffic or law depts. Kan. Pacific, U.P. and A.,T. &S.F. cos., 1880-84; editor Denver Daily Tribune, 1884; pres. Kan. City Daily Journal; v.p. Pioneer Trust Co.; dir. Southwestern Bell Telephone group, Guaranty Trust Co. (Kansas City), Central Nat. Bank, Topeka Ry. Co. (Topeka), etc. Trustee U. of Kan. 12 yrs. Republican. Home: Topeka, Kan. Died July 25, 1920.

GLEED, James Willis, lawyer; b. Morrisville, Vt., Mar. 8, 1859; s. Thomas and Cornelia (Fisk) G.; A.B., U. of Kan., 1879, A.M., 1882; LL.B., Columbia, 1884; LL.D., Columbia, 1904, Baker U., 1909; m. Grace Greer, Aug. 25, 1886; children—Mary Elizabeth (Mrs. John P. Coe), Dorothy Cornelia (Mrs. Pendleton A. Miller), Jeannette (Mrs. Francis C. King). Tutor Latin and Greek, 1879-82, prof. in charge of Greek chair, 1882-83, prof. of law of real property, 1887-1900, U. of Kan.; in active practice of law, 1884—; gen. atty. for Southwestern Bell Telephone Co.; regent U. of Kan.; trustee Washburn Coll. Republican. Home: Topeka, Kan. Died Oct. 12, 1926.

GLEESON, Joseph Michael, artist; b. Dracut, Mass., Jan. 8, 1861; s. Jeremiah and Jane G.; went to Munich to study art, 1885, and afterward made many trips to Europe, studying in France and Italy; m. Florence Helene Stebbins, 1902. Settled in New York as painter and illustrator of animal life. Died Sept. 1917.

GLEISS, Henry Crete, clergyman; b. Greenvine, Tex., Mar. 12, 1870; s. Frank Julius and Marie (Moegelin) G.; Ph.B., Baylor U., 1890, D.D., 1920; grad. Rochester Theol. Sem., 1893; m. Lottie Wagner, Sept. 11, 1894; children—George Herman, Mary Margaret (Mrs. F. B. Sack), Winnefred Minerva (Mrs. R. G. Williams), Ruth Mildred (Mrs. Oswald C. White), Esther Elizabeth (Mrs. Willard O. Moore), Henry Osgood, Grace Sarah (Mrs. Paul Parker). Was ordained to Baptist ministry, 1893; pastor in Houston, Texas, 1893-97, in Dallas, Tex., 1897-98, Pittsburgh, Pa., 1898-1906; gen. supt. Detroit Bapt. Union (97 churches), Oct. 1917-Sept. 1938. Corr. sec. German Baptist Orphans' and Children's Home, now at St. Joseph, Mich., 1898-1918; corr. sec. Pittsburgh Bapt. Assn. 11 yrs.; pres. Orphanage and Home Soc. of Western Pa. 5 yrs.; an organizer of advisory council Detroit Bapt. Union and of Bapt. Children's Home, Detroit, etc. Mem. Mich. Bapt. Conv., Detroit Council of Chs., Mich. Anti Saloon League. Republican. Home: Detroit, Mich. Died Oct. 17, 1939.

GLEISSNER, John M., newspaperman; b. Abilene, Kan., Oct. 25, 1893; s. of John M. and Kate (Northcraft) G.; A.B., U. of Kan., 1916; unmarried. Began as reporter Cleveland (O.) Press, 1916; with United Press Assn., 1919-22; mng. editor Baltimore (Md.) Post, 1923; editor Washington (D.C.) Daily News, 1923-27; later mng. editor Scripps-Howard Newspaper Alliance; news mgr. Washington City News Service, 1933—. Served from pvt. to 2d lt. U.S.A., World War. Died Feb. 27, 1941.

GLEN, Irving Mackey, musical director; b. Brooklyn, Feb. 14, 1871; s. John and Lucy Maria G.; grad. State Normal Sch., Cal. Sch. of Elocution and Oratory, Elwood Sch. of Music (all at San Jose, Cal.), 1890; A.B., U. of Ore., 1894, A.M., 1897; Johns Hopkins U., 1894-96; m. Julia Grace Veazie, Aug. 30, 1897. Prof. English and Latin, McMinnville (Ore.) Coll., 1896-97; prof. English lang. and lit., 1897-1911, dean Sch. of Music, 1901-11, U. of Ore., prof. music and musical dir., 1911—, dir. fine arts, 1912—, dean College of Fine Arts, 1915—, U. of Wash.; music dir. Willamette Valley Mus. Festival, 1903, 07, 09, Gladstone Park, and Ashland Chautauquas, during various seasons. Methodist. Home: Seattle, Wash. Died Feb. 18, 1931.

GLENDINNING, Robert, banker; b. Philadelphia, Pa., Aug. 10, 1867; s. Robert and Ellen E. (Butcher) G.; prep. edn. Cheltenham Acad.; A.B., U. of Pa., 1888; m. Elizabeth Rodman Fisher Carpenter, Sept. 17, 1894. Mem. Robert Glendinning & Co., bankers, Phila. Served through P.R. campaign in 1st Troop, Phila. City Cav., Spanish-Am. War, 1898; founded the aviation sch. at Essington, Pa., 1917; served as lt. col. U.S. Air Service, A.E.F., for 19 mos. from June 1917. Decorated D.S.M.; Officer Crown of Italy. Home: Philadelphia, Pa. Died Apr. 19, 1936.

GLENN, Edwin Forbes, army officer; b. nr. Greensboro, N.C., Jan. 10, 1857; s. Robert Washington (M.D.) and Julia (Gilmer) G.; Lenoir Sch. for Boys, Caldwell Co., N.C., Dr. Simon's Prep. Sch., Sing Sing, N.Y.; grad. U.S. Mil. Acad., 1877; LL.B., U. of Minn., 1890; grad. War Coll., Washington, 1914; hon. degrees Union and Kenyon colls. and Ohio, DePauw and Vt. univs.; m. Louise, d. Henry Murney Smyth, of St. Paul, Minn., Apr. 29, 1886. Second lt. 25th Inf., June 15, 1877; promoted through grades to brig. gen., May 15, 1917; maj. gen. N.A., Aug. 5, 1917. Instituted mil. training and was asst. prof. mathematics, U. of Minn., 1888; admitted to Minn. bar and was mem. Stephens, O'Brien & Glenn; judge advocate Dept. Dak., later Dept. Columbia, 1896-98; comd. exploring and relief expdns. to Alaska, 1898-99; judge advocate Dept. Visayas, P.I., 1900; comd. Columbus (O.) Barracks, 1905-07; again in P.I. with 23d Inf.; comd. Ft. McIntosh, Tex., 1910; col. 23d Inf., 1911-13; War Coll., 1913-14; chief of staff Dept. of East, 1914-16; comd. 18th Inf. and 1st Separate Brig., Deming, N.M., 1916-17; organized Camp Sherman, O., and 83d Div., Aug. 1917-Jan. 1918; overseas for observation at various fronts, Jan.-Apr. 1918; comd. 83d Div. A.E.F., June 1918, also organized and comd. 2d Replacement Depot and Training Centre, Le Mans, Sarthe, France, and Am. Embarkation Centre there, also most extensive small arms target facilities, comd. demobilization at Camp Sherman, Feb. 1919; retired at own request, Dec. 1919. Comdr. Legion of Honor (French). Author: Glenn's International Law, 1895; Rules of Land Warfare (pub. auspices Gen. Staff), 1914. Pres. Inf. Assn., 1913-20. Home: Glendon, N.C. Died Aug. 5, 1926.

GLENN, J(ohn) Lyles, lawyer, banker; b. Lowryville, S.C., Apr. 26, 1858; s. Ephraim Lyles (M.D.) and Louise (Carter) G.; ed. Wofford Coll., Spartanburg, S.C., and law dept. Vanderbilt U.; m. Alice Hall, 1882; children—Louise (Mrs. W. H. McNairy), Kate (Mrs. E. K. Hardin), Rebecca (dec.), James H., J. Lyles, Thomas Hall. Admitted to S.C. bar, 1881, and began practice at Chester; served as dist. counsel Seaboard Air Line Ry.; mem. Constl. Conv., S.C., 1895; mem. S.C. Senate, 1896-1900; pres. Nat. Exchange Bank, Chester, 1900—. Food Administrator Chester Co., World War. Democrat. Methodist. Home: Chester, S.C. Died June 21, 1927.

GLENN, John McGaw, secretary Ill. Mfrs. Assn.; b. Fort Wayne, Ind., Nov. 14, 1859; s. Judge John J. and Mary Jane Patterson (McGaw) G.; A.M., Monmouth (Ill.) Coll., 1883; m. Jeanie M., d. N. A. Chapin, May 24, 1888; children—Mary Chapin, Mrs. T. J. Bryce, John J., Robert. Began on staff of Monmouth Atlas, 1883; staff Chicago Inter-Ocean, Tribune, and Times-Herald, until 1897; sec. Ill. Mfrs'. Assn., Feb. 28, 1898—; also sec. Nat. Conf. State Mfrs'. Assn.; pub. Manufacturers' News. Sec. civil service commn., Chicago, 1897-98. Mem. Indiana Soc. of Chicago, Art. Inst. Dir. Assn. Arts and Industries. Republican. Presbyn. Home: Evanston, Ill. Died Apr. 22, 1928.

GLENN, Mary Willcox; b. Baltimore, Md., Dec. 14, 1869; d. J. Willcox and Turner (Macfarland) Brown; ed. pvt. sch., Baltimore; m. John M. Glenn, May 21, 1902. Teacher in pvt. schs.; exec. sec. Henry Watson Children's Aid Soc., Baltimore, 1897-1900; gen. sec. Charity Orgn. Soc. of Baltimore, 1900-01; pres. Nat. Conf. Charities and Correction, 1915; mem. bd. Community Service Soc. of N.Y.; pres. Nat. Council Ch. Mission of Help, 1919-37, Family Welfare Assn. of America, 1920-37; chmn. home service sect. N.Y. and Bronx Co. chapters Am. Red Cross, 1917-20; chmn. Com. of Nat. Conf. Social Work for 2d Internat. Conf. Social Work, Frankfort, July 1932. Episcopalian. Home: New York, N.Y. Died Nov. 3, 1940.

GLENN, Robert Brodnax, governor; b. in Rockingham Co., N.C., Aug. 11, 1854; s. Chalmers L. and Annie S. (Dodge) G.; ed. Davidson Coll., N.C., U. of Va., and Pearson's Law Sch., Richmond Hill, N.C.; m. Nina Deaderick, Jan. 8, 1878. Engaged in gen. law practice, first at Danbury, N.C., 1878; in 1886 with W. B. Glenn and in 1891 with Manly & Hendren; was asst. div. counsel for Southern Ry., atty. for Western Union Telegraph Co., etc. Was mem. legislature, 1881; solicitor for state, 1886; elector for Cleveland, 1884, 1892; U.S. dist. atty., 1893-97; gov. of N.C., 1905-09. Democrat. Presbyn. Was capt. and maj. Nat. State Guard, 1890-93. Home: Winston-Salem, N.C. Died May 16, 1920.

GLENN, William Schaeffer, physician; b. Pine Grove Mills, Pa., Apr. 4, 1858; s. Ephraim and Elizabeth (Meek) G.; ed. acads. and normal schs., Pa.; M.D., Eclectic Med. Coll., Cincinnati, O., 1883; m. Nannie M. Sloane, M.D., Sept. 16, 1906; children—Robert Olin, Harold Gray, Elizabeth Breckenridge (Mrs. John P. Kottcamp), Grover Cleveland, William Schaeffer, Anna Mary. Practiced at State College, Pa., 1883—; mem. Bd. of Health, State Coll. Burough, 1897—, health officer, 1897-1911; mem. Bd. of Edn., 1901—, etc. Pres. Bd. of Trustees, M.E. Ch., State College, 1909—. Democrat. Home: State College, Pa. Died Jan. 14, 1931.

GLENNON, James Henry, naval officer; b. French Gulch, Calif., Feb. 11, 1857; grad. U.S. Naval Acad., 1878; m. Susan Davenport Blair, Aug. 12, 1884; children—Isabel Harrison (wife of M. A. Cross, U.S.A.), James Blair, Randolph Harrison (dec.), Harrison Randolph, Philip Thompson (dec.). Ensign, Feb. 4, 1882; promoted through grades to rear admiral, Aug. 10, 1916. Served on Massachusetts, Spanish-Am. War, 1898; actg. capt. of port, Havana, 1899; exec. officer and navigator Vicksburg, 1900-02; comd. General Alava, 1902; in charge Nautical Sch., Manila, P.I., 1902; exec. officer and navigator Monterey, 1902-03; exec. officer Independence, 1904; duty Bur. of Ordnance, Navy Dept., 1905-07; comd. Yorktown, 1907-08; Navy Yard, New York, 1909; comd. Virginia, 1910-11; pres. Bd. on Naval Ordnance and Joint Army and Navy Bd. on smokeless powder, 1912-13; comd. Florida, 1913, Wyoming, 1913-15; mem. Panama Fortifications Bd., pres. Bd. on Naval Ordnance and Joint Army and Navy Bd. on gun forgings, 1915; comd. Navy Yard, and supt. Naval Gun Factory, Washington, 1915-17; naval rep. Pres. of U.S. Am. spl. mission to Russia, 1917; comdr. Squadron One, Battleship Force, Atlantic Fleet, Sept. 1917; comdr. 5th Div. Atlantic Fleet, 1918; comdt. 13th Naval Dist., 1918-19, 3d Dist., 1919; retired Feb. 11, 1921. Died Dec. 24, 1927.

GLESSNER, John Jacob, mfr.; b. Zanesville, O., Jan. 1843; s. Jacob and Mary (Laughlin) G.; ed. pub. schs.; m. Frances, d. of James R. Macbeth; children—John G. M., Frances (Mrs. F. G. Lee). Director International Harvester Co. Pres. Citizens' Association; dir. Chicago Relief and Aid Soc., 15 yrs.; pres. trustees Rush Med. Coll.; trustee Chicago Orphan Asylum, Chicago Orchestral Assn., Art Inst. Homes: Littleton, N.H., and Chicago, Ill. Died Jan. 20, 1936.

GLICK, George Washington, governor; b. Fairfield Co., O., July 4, 1827; s. Isaac and Mary Vickers (Sanders) G.; ed. Central Coll., Ohio; m. Elizabeth Ryder, Sept. 17, 1857. Admitted to bar, 1850, and practiced in Ohio, 1850-59; apptd. col. and judge advocate gen. 17th Regt. Ohio Militia by Gov. S. P. Chase, 1857; enlisted for Mexican War, but saw no active service; went to Kan., 1859; served in Civil War short time; atty., central branch, U.P. R.R., 1867-74; engaged in farming and stock raising, 1874-1903; now retired. Mem. Kansas legislature, 1863-64-65-66-68, 76, 82; gov. of Kan., 1883-85; U.S. pension agt., Topeka agency, 1885-92; mem. Kan. State Bd. Agr. past 32 yrs. (pres. 1902-03). Democrat. Commr. Centennial, Chicago and St. Louis expns. Mason. Home: Atchison, Kan. Died 1911.

GLIDDEN, Charles Jasper, financier, automobilist; b. Lowell, Mass., Aug. 29, 1857; s. Nathaniel Ames and Laura Ellen (Clark) G.; ed. pub. schs., Lowell; m. Lucy Emma, d. James Cleworth, July 10, 1878. Mgr. Atlantic Pacific Telegraph Co., 1873-77; became interested in the telephone, 1876 and conducted experiments with Prof. A. Graham Bell, from Boston to Manchester, N.H., built pvt. lines in Mass. and N.H.; secured the first subscriber to an exchange system in the world, at Lowell, 1877; built 1st long distance line from Lowell to Boston, 1879; organized and was pres. and treas. several N.E. and Western telephone cos., 1876-1900; at one time controlled one-sixth of the Bell system in U.S.; retired, 1900. Interested in development of the automobile and aerial navigation; first to tour around the world in an automobile, touring 46,528 miles in 39 countries, 1901-08; pres. Aerial Navigation Co. to operate a line of airships bet. Boston and New York (1st co. of the kind); has made 42 balloon ascensions in U.S., 3 in France and 4 in Eng. After completion of cable from Vancouver to Australia sent 1st telegram around the world, from Boston to Boston, etc. Commd. 1st lt., Aviation Sect., Signal O.R.C., June 12, 1917; capt., Signal Corps U.S.A., Feb. 20, 1918; hon. disch., Aug. 19, 1919; maj., Aviation Sect., O.R.C., Oct. 3, 1919. Made 3d tour of world, Oct. 1919-June 1920, as exec. sec. of commn. which organized the 1st aerial derby around the world. Elected pres. World's Bd. Aeronautical Commrs., Inc., Mar. 24, 1921; pres. Aeronautical Digest Pub. Corp. Col. Police Reserve of N.Y. Home: New York, N.Y. Died Sept. 11, 1927.

GLOGAUER, Fritz, newspaperman; b. Germany, July 15, 1857; collegiate edn.; came to U.S., 1877; m. Carrie Seibel, 1885. Connected with German-Am. newspapers, 1879—; established the Abendpost, Chicago, 1889, of which was editor for many years. Home: Munich, Germany. Died Mar. 23, 1926.

GLORIEUX, Alphonsus Joseph, bishop; b. Dottignies, Belgium, Feb. 1, 1844; ed. there, 1852-57, and at Courtrai, Belgium, 1857-63, graduating latter yr.; Louvain U., 1863-67; (D.D.). Prin. St. Michael's Coll., Portland, Ore., 1871-84; consecrated titular bishop of Apoelollonia, Apr. 19, 1885; transferred to See of Boisé (Ida.), Aug. 26, 1893. Died Aug. 25, 1917.

GLOTZBACH, William Edward, mem. Dem. Nat. Com.; b. Natrona, Pa.; s. John and Mary (Kissler) G.; ed. pub. and parochial schs., Pa. and Minn. and Sch. of Pharmacy, St. Paul; unmarried. Druggist at Anamoose, N.Dak., 1905—, also owns and operates farm lands. Mem. Dem. State and Exec. Com., N.Dak., 25 yrs.; treas. Dem. State Conv., 10 yrs.; mem. Dem. Nat. Com., 1934—. Catholic. Home: Anamoose, N.Dak. Deceased.

GLOVER, Charles, mfr.; b. Nottingham, England, June 16, 1847; s. George and Rebecca (Wood) G.; brought to U.S. in infancy; ed. dist. sch., Enfield, Conn., and by home study; m. Margaret S. Wainwright, 1867. Was farm hand and machinist several yrs.; entered employ of P. & F. Corbin, New Britain, Conn., 1876; upon consolidation of various companies as The Corbin Screw Corp., was elected pres. and gen. mgr.; also pres. and treas. Corbin Screw Corp., Chicago; pres. Corbin Motor Vehicle Corp., D. C. Judd Co. (New Britain), Skinner Chuck Co., H. R. Walker Co.; 1st v.p. Am. Hardware Corp. Republican. Mason. Home: New Britain, Conn. Died Oct. 25, 1922.

GLOVER, Charles Carroll, financier; b. on farm, N.C., Nov. 24, 1846; s. Charles and Caroline (Piercy) G.; ed. Rittenhouse Acad., Washington; m. Annie C., d. Rear Admiral Poor, U.S.N., Jan. 10, 1878. Clerk in book store 3 yrs. prior to entering, at age of 19, employ of Riggs & Co., bankers, as clerk; became partner in firm, 1873, and from its orgn., July 1, 1896 to June 13, 1921, was pres. Riggs Nat. Bank, then became chmn. board. Inaugurated and successfully carried through Congress projects for establishing of Rock Creek, Potomac and Zoölogical parks, the erection of the P.E. Cathedral, the American U. bldgs., the new Corcoran Art Gallery and other important projects. Home: Washington, D.C. Died Feb. 25, 1936.

GLOVER, James Waterman, educator; b. at Clio, Mich., July 24, 1868; s. James Polk and Emerette (Neff) G.; B.L., U. of Mich., 1892; A.B., Harvard, 1893, A.M., 1894, Ph.D., 1895; m. Alice Durfee Webber, Aug. 29, 1900; children—James Webber, Sanford Webber (dec.). Instr. mathematics, 1895-1903, estab. courses in financial, statis. and ins. mathematics, 1902, asst. prof. mathematics and lecturer on ins., 1903-06, jr. prof. mathematics and ins., 1906-11, prof., 1911-30 and 1932-38, U. of Mich.; pres. Teachers Ins. and Annuity Assn. America, 1930-32. Expert Royal Commission on Insurance, Canada, 1906; cons. actuary, Wisconsin Legislative Ins. Investigation Com., 1906, Wis. Legislative Joint Com. on Banks and Ins., 1907; expert spl. agt. U.S. Census Bur., 1910-29; cons. statistician office of Pub. Roads, Dept. of Agr., 1913-16; mem. advisory statis. com. Children's Bur., Dept. Labor, 1916-17; mem. advisory bd. Bur. War Risk Ins., Treas. Dept., 1917-18; actuary, Mich. Teachers' Retirement Fund Bd., 1918-31; trustee Teachers Ins. and Annuity Assn. of America, 1919-32; chmn. Actuarial Com. on Econ. Security, 1934-35. Fellow Am. Inst. Actuaries, Casualty Actuarial Soc. Home: Ann Arbor, Mich. Died July 15, 1941.

GLOVER, Lyman Beecher, theatrical mgr.; b. Ann Arbor, Mich., Feb. 10, 1846; s. Rev. Livingston M. G.; A.B., Wabash Coll., 1867, later A.M.; m. Louise Thompson, Oct. 25, 1876. Gen. agt. Am. Press Assn. (United Press) for some yrs.; was the founder and editor Chicago Saturday Evening Herald, 1886; joined staff of the daily Herald, which was successively merged with the Times into the Times-Herald, and then with the Record, later known as the Record-Herald; was also 4 years its lit. critic, and dramatic and musical critic, 1886-1902; mgr. Richard Mansfield Co., 1902-04; mgr. Majestic Theatre and gen. mgr. Kohl-Castle theatres, Chicago. Trustee Wabash Coll., 1901-02. Home: Chicago, Ill. Died Apr. 6, 1915.

GLUCK, Alma, soprano singer; b. Bucharest, Roumania, 1884; maiden name Reba Fiersohn; brought to America, 1890; ed. pub. schs. and Normal Coll., New York; Union Coll., Schenectady, N.Y.; studied music under Signor Buzzi-Peccia, New York; m. Efrem Zimbalist, violinist, June 15, 1914; children—Maria Virginia (Mrs. Ogden Goelet), Efrem. Debut, New York in "Werther," 1909, and during season sang 11 different rôles, only 2 of which she had previously studied; noteworthy as one who gained recognition in opera and on the concert stage, without European training. Died Oct. 27, 1938.

GLYNN, James P., congressman; b. Winsted, Conn., Nov. 12, 1867; s. Dennis and Mary J. (Geraghty) G.; ed. pub. schs.; m. Katherine J. Meade, Oct. 14, 1903. Admitted to Conn. bar, 1895; pros. atty., Town of Winchester, 1899-1902; postmaster, Winsted, 1902-14; mem. 64th to 67th, 69th and 70th Congresses (1915-23, 1925-29), 5th Conn. Dist. Republican. Home: Winsted, Conn. Died Mar. 6, 1930.

GLYNN, Martin H., governor, editor; b. Kinderhook, N.Y., Sept. 27, 1871; s. Martin and Ann G.; A.B., St. John's Coll., Fordham, N.Y., 1894, A.M., 1898; (LL.D., Fordham, Georgetown, Syracuse and Union univs.); m. Mary C. E. Magrane, Jan. 2, 1901. Editor and pub. the Times-Union, Albany, N.Y., 1895—. Admitted to bar, 1897. Mem. 56th Congress (1899-1901), 20th N.Y. Dist.; v.p. Nat. Commn. La. Purchase Expn., 1901-05; comptroller, N.Y. State, 1907-08; elected lt. gov. of N.Y., Nov. 1912; became gov. Aug. 14, 1913, for term expiring Dec. 31, 1914; temporary chmn. Dem. Nat. Conv., St. Louis, 1916, making the keynote speech; mem. President's Industrial Commn., 1919-20. Prominent in initiation of conferences between De Valera and Lloyd George to Settle Irish question in 1921. Home: Albany, N.Y. Died Dec. 14, 1924.

GMEINER, John, clergyman; b. Baernau, Bavaria, Dec. 5, 1847; s. Sebastian and Caroline (Fritsch) G.; came to Milwaukee, 1849; entered St. Francis Sem. there, 1859; ordained R.C. priest, 1870. Editor Columbia, Milwaukee, over 3 yrs.; prof. at St. Francis Sem., Milwaukee, and St. Thomas Sem., St. Paul, about 7 yrs., then in pastoral duties; rector St. Raphael Ch., Springfield, Minn., 1902—. At World's Parliament of Religions, 1893, delivered address on "The Primitive and Prospective Religious Unity of Mankind." Died Feb. 17, 1915.

GOBIN, Hillary Asbury, univ. prof.; b. Terre Haute, Ind., Mar. 25, 1842; s. Calvin and Jane E. (Gray) G.; served in Union army, 1862-65; A.B., Ind. Asbury Coll. (now DePauw U.), 1870, A.M., 1873; (D.D., Ind. Asbury U., 1880; LL.D., Baker U., 1903, DePauw, 1909); m. Florence A. Orrill, Nov. 8, 1871 (died 1891); m. 2d, Clara L. Beals, July 11, 1895. Became pastor in Northwest Ind. Conf., M.E. Ch., 1869; pastor Bainbridge, Ind., 1869-70, Remington and Goodland, Ind., 1870-73, S. Bend, Ind., 1873-76, Lafayette, Ind., 1876-79, S. Bend, 1879-80; Robert Stockwell prof. Greek lang. and lit., 1880-86, sec. faculty, 1881-86, DePauw U.; pres. Baker U., Kan., 1886-90; dean Sch. Theology, 1890, v.p., 1894-95, acting pres., 1895-96, pres., 1896-1903, v.p. and prof. bibl. science, 1903, DePauw U. Mem. Gen. Conf., M.E. Ch., 1892, 96, 1900, 12, and Eumenical Meth. Conf., London, 1901. Pres. Preachers' Aid Soc., 1898-1913; pres. DePauw Alumni Assn., 1914-17; mem. Beta Theta Phi, Phi Beta Kappa. Address: Greencastle, Ind. Died Mar. 18, 1923.

GOBIN, John Peter Shindel, lawyer; b. Sunbury, Pa., Jan. 26, 1837; s. Samuel S. and Susan (Shindel) G.; acad. edn.; LL.D., Susquehanna U.; m. Annie M. Howe, 1866. Served in Union Army, attaining rank of bvt. brig. gen.; practiced law at Lebanon, Pa.; dir. in various industrial instns. Mem. Pa. Senate, 1884-98; comdr. a div. of Pa. N.G.; served as birg. gen. U.S.V. in war with Spain; elected lt. gov. of Pa., 1898; comd. Pa. N.G. during coal strike, 1902. Comdr.-in-chief G.A.R., 1897-98; past grand master Knights Templar U.S. Address: Lebanon, Pa. Died 1910.

GODARD, George Seymour, librarian; b. Granby, Conn., June 17, 1865; s. Harvy and Sabra Lavinia (Beach) G.; A.B., Wesleyan U., 1892; B.D., Yale, 1895; hon. M.A., Wesleyan, 1916, Trinity, 1919; m. Kate Estelle Dewey, June 23, 1897; children—George Dewey, Paul Beach, Mary Katharine (Mrs. Earl H. Dresser). Asst. librarian, 1898-1900, librarian, 1900—, Conn. State Library. Editor Conn. State Records, 1901—; custodian State Library and Supreme Court Bldg., 1910—; in charge of Conn. State Military Census, 1917—; chmn. com. on hist. records, Conn. State Council Defense, 1918-19; dir. Conn. Dept. War Records, 1919—. Pres. Nat. Assn. State Libraries, 1904-05, Conn. Library Assn., 1906-07, Am. Assn. Law Libraries, 1909-11; chmn. joint com. Nat. Assn. State Libraries and A.L.A., on nat. legislative information service, 1909—, etc. Mem. publication com. "Index Legal Periodicals and Law Library Journal," 1908—. Public Affairs Information Service, 1913—. Trustee Wesleyan U. (sec. 1920-25); pres. bd. Frederick H. Cossett Library (N. Granby). Fellow Am. Geog. Soc. Chmn. Conn. Sesquicentennial Commn., Phila., 1926; chmn. State Capitol G.A.R. and Associated Orgns., 1933-34. Mason (32°, K.T.). Conglist. Home: Hartford, Conn. Died Feb. 12, 1936.

GODBEY, John Emory, clergyman; b. Casey County, Ky., Aug. 11, 1839; s. Josiah and Sena (Kelly) G.; ed. St. Charles (Mo.) Coll.; D.D., Emory Coll., Ga.; m. Mary S. Holloway, Nov. 2, 1865 (died 1911); m. 2d, Martha Virginia Dunnovant, Dec. 23, 1911. Ordained M.E. Ch., S., ministry, 1861; pastor 1st Ch., St. Louis, 1877-78, Page Av. Ch., St. Louis, 1879-82; editor Southwestern Methodist, 1882-90; presiding elder, Kansas City Dist., 1890-94; editor Ark. Methodist, Little Rock, 1894-1905; pastoral work, 1905-08; prof. philosophy, Hendrix Coll., Ark., 1908-11; pastor Christy Memorial Ch., St. Louis, 1912-13, Scruggs Memorial 1st Ch., St. Louis, 1913—. Del. Gen. Confs., M.E. Ch., S., Richmond, Va., 1866, Memphis, 1894, Dallas, Tex., 1902, Birmingham, Ala., 1906. Served on joint commn. M.E. Ch. and M.E. Ch., S., to establish common catechism and common order of worship. Democrat. Author: Light and Darkness, or Missions and Missionary Heroes, 1885; Methodist Church Members' Manual, 1886; Foundation of Faith, 1902; Lights and Shadows of Seventy Years, 1913; Pioneer Methodism in Missouri, 1929. Home: Kirkwood, Mo. Died Feb. 29, 1932.

GODBOLD, Norman Dosier, judge; b. Bethel, Ala., Apr. 1, 1877; s. Leonard William and Alice (Ratcliffe) G.; grad. Florence (Ala.) State Normal Coll., 1891-94; LL.B., U. of Ala., 1895; m. Irene Alford, June 25, 1902; children—Evelyn (wife of Harry Sanders, U.S.N.), Norman Dosier, Wilford Darrington. Admitted to Ala. bar, 1895; in practice in Ala., 1895-1919 and Honolulu, H.T., 1919-33; solicitor Washington County, Ala., 1896-97, Wilcox County, 1904-07; mayor Camden, Ala., 1903-05; mem. Ala. State Senate, 1911-15; asst. U.S. atty., Honolulu, 1919-23, asst. city and county atty., 1924-26; apptd. first judge, 1st Circuit Ct. of H.T., 1933. Del. Nat. Dem. Conv., New York, 1924. Mason (past W.M. and H.P.), K.P. (past C.C.). Democrat. Presbyn. Home: Honolulu, H.T. Died July 17, 1936.

GODDARD, Harry Williams, mfr.; b. Holyoke, Mass., Sept. 14, 1863; s. Dorrance Sibley and Mary Howe (Williams) G.; ed. pub. schs. of Worcester, and 1 yr. at Wilbraham Acad.; m. Grace Watson, Dec. 14, 1887. In employ of Spencer Wire Co., 1881-84, sec. and supt., 1884-95, pres. and chief owner, 1895-1925; pres. Charlton Woolen Co.; dir. Mechanics

Nat. Bank; trustee Peoples Savings Bank. Home: Wooster and Auburn, Mass. Died Sept. 8, 1927.

GODDARD, Leroy Albert, banker; b. Marion, Ill., June 22, 1854; s. James T. and Winifred (Spiller) G.; ed. pub. schs. and 1 term Ill. State Normal Sch.; m. Anna Breidenthal, Nov. 14, 1888. Mcht. and banker at Marion, 1875-90; organized, and pres. First Nat. Bank, Mt. Carmel, Ill., 1890-92; cashier Ft. Dearborn Nat. Bank, Chicago, 1892-1903, pres., 1903-08; v.p. State Bank of Chicago, 1908-09, pres., 1909-19, chmn. bd., 1919-29; retired Jan. 1931. Pres. Chicago Clearing House Assn., 1911-12; treas. Chicago Stock Exchange 2 yrs.; mem. Normal Sch. Bd. of Ill. many yrs.; declined position on Federal Reserve Bd. offered by Pres. Harding. Elected city treas. of Marion at age of 21, mayor at 23, and reëlected for 2d term; erected and presented memorial chapel in cemetery established under his mayoralty. Mem. bd. dirs. and finance com. Destitute Crippled Children's Home. Treas. Supreme Council 33° Masons, Northern Jurisdiction U.S.A., 1912—, and one of five delegates to Internat. Conf., Lausanne, Switzerland, 1922; Grand Master Masons Ill., 1894, 95, Grand Treas., 1903—. Home: Chicago, Ill. Died Jan. 22, 1936.

GODDARD, Luther M., judge; b. Palmyra, N.Y., Oct. 27, 1840; ed. Hedding Coll., Ill.; LL.B., Chicago Law School, 1866. Mem. Kan. Ho. of Rep., 1872; removed to Leadville, Colo., 1878; elected judge 5th Jud. Dist., Colo., 1882, reëlected 1888; elected justice Supreme Ct. for term expiring 1901; apptd. justice Supreme Ct., 1905-09. Republican. Address: Denver, Colo. Died May 20, 1917.

GODDARD, Morrill, editor writer; b. Portland, Me., Oct. 7, 1866; s. Judge Charles W. and Rowena C. (Morrill) G.; A.B., Dartmouth, 1885; m. Jessamine Rugg, Dec. 28, 1899; children—Morrill, DeWitt R., Mary R., Jessamine, Rowena. Began newspaper work as editor, foreign and war corr., 1885—; later editor of American Weekly Magazine. Traveler; magazine writer. Author: What Interests People and Why, 1935. Home: New York, N.. Died July 1, 1937.

GODDARD, Pliny Earle, anthropologist; b. Lewiston, Me., Aug. 24, 1869; s. Charles W. and Elmira A. (Nichols) G.; A.B., Earlham Coll., Ind., 1892, A.M., 1896; Ph.D., U. of Calif., 1904; m. Alice C. Rockwell, Dec. 28, 1893; children—Mrs. Myra H. Marini, Frances Emma, Charles Lawrence (dec.), Pliny Earle, David Rockwell, Mildred Alice. Instr. anthropology, U. of Calif., 1901-06, asst. prof., 1906-09; asst. curator of anthropology, Am. Mus. Natural History, New York, 1909-10, asso. curator, 1910-14, curator of ethnology, 1914—. Lecturer anthropology, Columbia U., 1915—. Fellow Am. Acad. Arts and Sciences. Author: Life and Culture of the Hupa, 1903; Hupa Texts, 1904; The Morphology of the Hupa Language, 1905; The Phonology of the Hupa Language, 1907; Kato Texts, 1909; Indians of the Southwest, 1913; Indians of the Northwest Coast, 1924. Home: Leonia, N.J. Died July 12, 1928.

GODDARD, Ralph Bartlett, sculptor; b. Meadville, Pa., June 18, 1861; s. Frederick Bartlett and Lydia Jane (Mason) G.; ed. Brooklyn pub. schs., Nat. Acad. Design, Art Students' League, New York, Académie Julian, Paris; m. Louise Reynolds Holly; children—Anna Louise, Madeline Holly. Early years devoted to execution of bronze bas-relief portraits of noted men, including series of 12 of the foremost authors and poets of modern English literature for reproduction in bronze; made splty. of portrait busts; statue, the "Première Épreuve," now in Detroit Mus. of Fine Arts, exhibited in Paris Salon, 1897; completed for Robert Hoe the bronze heroic statue of Gutenberg erected at Grand and Sheriff Sts., New York; finished ideal statue, "Invictus," 1890. Mem. Nat. Sculpture Soc. Home: New York, N.Y. Died Apr. 25, 1936.

GODDARD, Ralph Willis, educator; b. Waltham, Mass., Apr. 20, 1887; s. Frederic Emerson and Kate Perry (Woodberry) G.; grad. English High Sch., Worcester, Mass., 1907; B.S. in E.E., Worcester Poly Inst., 1911; m. Frances Margaret Gascoigne, Aug. 14, 1911; children—Kenneth Ralph, Raymond Francis, Earl Gascoigne, Roy Franklin. Estimator on bldg. constrn. for Gascoigne & Shattuck, Boston, 1911-13; instr. elec. engring., U. of Neb., 1913-14; prof. elec. engring., N.M. Coll. Agr. and Mech. Arts, 1914-17, 1919-20, dean of engring, 1920—. Civilian dir. instrn. Elec. Div. U.S.A., Training Detachment at State Coll., N.M., 1918; capt. U.S. Signal Corps, O.R.C. Pres. bd. schs. and Las Cruces Union High Sch. Dist. Republican. Mason (K.T., Shriner). Author: Electrical Laboratory Manual, 1915. Inventor of motorcycle side car, etc. Home: Mesilla Park, N.M. Died Dec. 31, 1929.

GODDARD, Robert Hale Ives, mfr.; b. Providence, R.I., Sept. 21, 1837; s. William Giles and Charlotte (Ives) G.; A.M., Brown U., 1858; m. Rebekah B. Grosbeck. Served pvt. 1st R.I. Inf., May 2-Aug. 2, 1861; lt. and vol. a.-d.-c. to Gen. Burnside, Sept. 23, 1862; capt. a.-d.-c. vols., Mar. 11, 1863; bvtd. maj. vols., Aug. 1, 1864, for gallant and meritorious services during campaign in E. Tenn. and at siege of Knoxville; lt. col. vols., Apr. 2, 1865, for same at Ft. Steedman and in assault before Ft. Sedgwick, Va.; resigned July 3, 1865. Mem. firms Goddard Bros., and Brown & Ives, cotton mfrs.; pres. Lonsdale Co.; treas. Berkeley Co., and Hope Co.; dir. R.I. Hospital Trust Co. Rep. presdl. elector, 1896; mem. R.I. Senate, 1897-98; mem. State Bd. Charities and Correction; commr. Providence parks; nominated for U.S. senator by Dem. State Conv., 1907. Mem. bd. fellows, Brown U., 1893—. Home: Providence, R.I. Died Apr. 22, 1916.

GODDARD, William, banker, mcht.; b. Warwick, R.I., Dec. 25, 1825; s. William Giles and Charlotte (Ives) G.; grad. Brown U., 1846; m. Mary Edith Jenckes, Feb. 19, 1867. After graduation studied law; traveled extensively; engaged in mercantile and mfg. business; mem. Providence Common Council, 1852-55; was mem. 1st light inf.; maj. 1st regt. R.I. detached militia; commissioned col. vols. for gallantry at battle of Bull Run, a.d.c. on Gen. Burnside's staff before Fredericksburg, Dec. 11, 1862. Head of firm of Brown & Ives, mchts., founded in 18th century; mem. firm of Goddard Bros., and pres. Providence Nat. Bank. Trustee Brown U., 1857—, chancellor, 1888—. Home: Providence, and Warwick, R.I. Died 1907.

GODDING, John Granville, pharmacist; b. Gardiner, Me., Mar. 28, 1853; s. Nathaniel and Rachel H. (Motherwell) G.; Ph.G., Mass. Coll. of Pharmacy, Boston, 1874, hon. Pharm.D., 1924; m. Adelaide M. Smith, Sept. 1, 1880. Propr. J. G. Godding & Co., apothecaries. Trustee, 1885—, treas., 1890—, and chmn. com. on edn., 1910—, Mass. Coll. of Pharmacy. Pres. Am. Pharmaceutical Assn., 1911-12. Republican. Conglist. Mason (K.T.). Home: Newton, Mass. Died Apr. 7, 1929.

GODDING, William Whitney, physician; supt. Govt. Hospital for Insane; grad. Dartmouth Coll., 1854; Castleton (Vt.) Med. Coll., 1857 (LL.D., Dartmouth); prominent as an alienist. Address: Washington, D.C. Died 1899.

GODFREY, Edward Settle, army officer; b. Kalida, O., Oct. 9, 1843; s. Dr. Charles Moore and Mary (Chambers) G.; ed. public sch. in Ohio, and Vermilion Inst.; pvt. Co. D, 21st Ohio Inf., Apr. 12, 1861; grad. U.S. Mil. Acad., 1867; m. Mary Pocock, June 15, 1869; children—Guy C. M., Edward S., Mary, David Ewing; m. 2d, Ida D. Emley, Oct. 6, 1892. Second lt. 7th Cav., June 17, 1867; promoted through grades to brig. gen., Jan. 17, 1907. Bvtd. maj., Feb. 27, 1890, and awarded Congressional Medal of Honor for "most distinguished gallantry" at Bear Paw Mts. against Chief Joseph and Nez Percé Indians, Sept. 30, 1877. In all the campaigns and Indian fights of his regiment, under General Custer, until Custer's death; originated "Cossack" and "Rough Riding" for Army; mem. bd. of officers that devised drill regulations for inf., cav. and arty. for the Army; served in Cuba and P.I.; retired by operation of law, Oct. 9, 1907. Former sr. vice commander-in-chief Military Order Loyal Legion U.S. (mem. Council-in-Chief). Mason (32°, K.T.). Home: Cookstown, N.J. Died Apr. 1, 1932.

GODFREY, Hollis, engr., teacher; b. Lynn, Mass., Apr. 27, 1874; s. Andrew Hollis and Anna S. (Alexander) G.; Ph.B., Tufts, 1895; Harvard, 1896, 1905-06; Mass. Inst. Technology, 1898 and in Europe; Sc.D., Tufts; Eng.D., U. of Vt.; LL.D., Miami U., Queen's U.; D.C.L., Bishop's College; m. Mary Lawrence, Sept. 11, 1895. Engaged in teaching, writing and engring., 1898-1905; head of dept. of science, Sch. of Practical Arts, Boston, 1906-10; consulting engr. to Ia. Survey, to cities of Phila., Atlantic City, and pvt. corps., also research worker, 1910-17; chief bur. of gas, Phila., 1912-13; pres. Drexel Inst., 1913-21; chmn. bd. and pres. Engring. Economics Foundation, 1921-31; consulting engineer, 1932-34. Created with Elihu Root, Leonard Wood and Howard Coffin, Council of Nat. Defense of U.S.; served as federal commr. of advisory com. of Council Nat. Defense, and in charge of its sect. of engring. and edn., 1916-Dec. 1, 1918; mem. Nat. Research Council and of its engring. research com.; mem. Commercial Economy Bd. of the U.S., 1917-18. Formerly mem. Bd. of Visitors Tufts Coll., of Alumni Council Mass. Inst. Tech.; trustee Drexel Inst. Mason. Author: The Man Who Ended War, 1908; The Norton Name, 1908; Elementary Chemistry, 1909; The Health of the City, 1910; Juveniles, 1911, 12; Creating Wealth, 1927; Stable Profits, 1933; The Plea for the Citizen and the Constitution, 1935. Contbr. to mags. Home: Duxbury, Mass. Died Jan. 17, 1936.

GODFREY, Lincoln, merchant; b. Phila., Pa., May 17, 1850; s. Benjamin Granger and Emeline Maxwell (Field) G.; ed. private schs.; m. Mary Simpson, Oct. 17, 1872. Began career with father's firm, B. G. Godfrey & Co., dry goods; mem. William Simpson Sons & Co., 1893—; v.p. and dir. Phila. Nat. Bank; dir. Pa. R.R. Co., Pa. Trust, Safe Deposit & Ins. Co., Argo Mills Co., Mut. Fire & Inland Ins. Co., Ins. Co. of N. America, Wm. Cramp & Sons' Ship & Engine Building Co.; mem. bd. mgrs. Western Savings Fund, Merchants' Fund Assn. Republican. Episcopalian. Home: Philadelphia, Pa. Died Feb. 8, 1916.

GODING, Frederic Webster, consular service; b. Hyde Park, Mass., May 9, 1858; s. Alphonso Landon and Lydia Mehitable (Chandler) G.; M.D., Northwestern U., 1882; Ph.D., Bethel Coll., Tenn., 1890; m. Ella Blanche Phelps, June 8, 1880; children—Hazle Vera (Mrs. H. B. Ames), Frederic Landon; m. 2d, Jessie E. Ayre, May 12, 1913 (died 1918). Taught in pub. schs., Ill., 5 yrs.; prof. science, Loudon (Tenn.) Coll., 1 yr.; practiced medicine, 1882-98; mayor of Rutland, Ill., 10 yrs.; del. Ill. Rep. State convs., 1886-96; consul at Newcastle, N.S.W., 1898-1908; coal inspector for U.S. Army, Newcastle, 1905-08; consul at Montevideo, Uruguay, 1908-13; in charge of American Legation in Montevideo, June-Sept. 1911; consul gen. at Guayaquil, Ecuador, 1913-24. Mem. First Ecuadorian Med. Congress, Med. Surg. Soc. of Guayaquil. Author of Genealogy of the Goding Family, and many articles and monographs on entomology and biology, ethnology, and of commercial reports; published classification and monograph of the Membracidæ of the World. Home: Livermore Falls, Me. Died May 5, 1933.

GODKIN, Edwin Lawrence, editor New York Evening Post and The Nation; b. Moyne, County Wicklow, Ireland, Oct. 2, 1831; ed. at grammar school nr. Wakefield, Eng.; grad. Queen's Coll., Belfast, 1851 (A.M., Harvard; D.C.L., Oxford). Became corr. London News in the Crimea, and later in U.S. Studied law; practiced at New York, 1857-65; corr. London News and editorial writer New York Times, 1862-65. Established The Nation, 1865; merged it with the New York Evening Post, 1882, becoming editor of both. Author: History of Hungary; Reflections and Comments; Problems of Democracy; Unforeseen Tendencies of Democracy; etc. Home: New York, N.Y. Died 1902.

GODOWSKY, Leopold, pianist and composer; b. Wilna, Russia, Feb. 13, 1870; s. Dr. Mathew and Anna (Lewin) G.; studied at Berlin Hochschule, 1884, and later with Saint-Saëns, Paris, France; hon. Dr. Music, Curtis Inst. of Phila., 1934; m. Frieda Saxe, Apr. 30, 1891 (died 1933). First played in public at the age of 9; toured in Russia, Poland, and Germany; first Am. tour, 1884-86; dir. piano dept. Chicago Conservatory Music, 1895-1900; Berlin debut, 1900, also London and all capitals of Europe; apptd. by Emperor dir. Imperial Royal Meisterschule for Piano at Imperial Royal Acad. Music, Vienna, 1909—, and created imperial royal prof. of highest rank. Editor-in-chief, Art Publication Soc., St. Louis, 1912—. Composer of 53 studies on Chopin Études; "Renaissance" (24 pieces); Walzermasken (24 compositions); sonata in E minor, 3 symphonic metamorphoses, 12 compositions for the violin; Triakontameron (30 pieces) for piano; Phonoramas (Java cycle of 12 compositions); Transcriptions for piano of sonatas and suites for violin and violoncello, of J. S. Bach; Transcriptions for piano of 12 Schubert songs; Passacaglia; 46 Miniatures for four hands; for the left hand alone, a prelude and fugue, suite, six waltz-poems, capriccio, elegy, meditation, impromptu, intermezzo, etude macabre and symphonic valse paraphrase; also many other piano compositions. Toured through Europe, U.S., Can., Mexico, Cuba, Japan, China, Java, Philippines, Hawaii, S. America, etc. Home: New York, N.Y. Died Nov. 21, 1938.

GODWIN, Edward Allison, army officer; b. Kingwood, W.Va., May 18, 1850; s. Joseph Madison and Elizabeth (Royse) G.; grad. U.S. Mil. Acad., 1870; m. Elizabeth Jackson Clark, June 30, 1870. Pvt. Co. A, 1st W.Va. Cav., Feb. 13-July 8, 1865; apptd. cadet at West Point, from 2d Dist. W.Va., Oct. 17, 1865; 2d lt. 8th Cav., June 15, 1870; 1st lt., Oct. 3, 1876; capt., July 5, 1886; col. 7th U.S. Vol. Inf., May 24, 1898; hon. mustered out Feb. 28, 1899, maj. 7th Cav., July 1, 1899; col. 40th U.S. Vol. Inf., Aug. 17, 1899; hon. mustered out June 24, 1901; transferred to 10th Cav., Oct. 2, 1902; lt. col. 9th Cav., Jan. 16, 1903; col. 14th cav., June 22, 1905; brig. gen. and retired, Nov. 15, 1908, after more than 43 yrs.' service. Died July 13, 1923.

GODWIN, Harold, editor; b. May 21, 1857; s. Parke and Fanny (Bryant) G.; A.B., Princeton, 1879; after graduation fellow in history same. Asst. New York Evening Post, 1880; later art critic of New York Mail and Express; afterward art critic New York Commercial Advertiser; mng. editor same, 1890; then editor and part owner of Current Literature, and Short Stories. Home: Roslyn, L.I., N.Y. Died May 8, 1931.

GODWIN, Parke, author; b. Paterson, N.J., Feb. 25, 1816; grad. Princeton, 1834 (LL.D.); studied law in N.J., but never practiced; m. Fanny Bryant, 1842. An editor New York Evening Post, 1836-86; contributor to Democratic Review, Putnam's Monthly and the Atlantic. Author: Pacific and Constructive Democracy; A Popular View of Fourier; History of France; Dictionary of Biography; Political Essays; Out of the Past; Life and Works of William Cullen Bryant (4 vols.); Commemorative Addresses. Translator, from German, Goethe's Autobiography; Zshokke's Tales; A New Study of Shakespeare's Sonnets, 1900. Home: New York, N.Y. Died 1904.

GOEBEL, Herman Philip, congressman; b. Cincinnati, Apr. 5, 1853; s. Christian and Elizabeth G.; ed.

pub. schs., Cincinnati; LL.B., Cincinnati Law Sch. at 18; admitted to bar on coming of age, and practiced at Cincinnati; m. Florence G. Voight, Nov. 26, 1903. Mem. Ohio Ho. of Rep., 1875; probate judge, Hamilton County, 1884-91; mem. 58th to 61st Congresses (1903-11), 2d Ohio Dist. Republican. Home: Cincinnati, O. Died May 5, 1930.

GOEBEL, Julius, univ. prof.; b. Frankfort-on-the-Main, Germany, May 23, 1857; s. Ludwig and Christine M. G.; student U. of Leipzig, 1879-81; Ph.D., U. of Tübingen, 1882; came to U.S., 1882; m. K. I. Vreeland, 1888; children—Marie Christina, Louise Kathryn, Julius Ludwig, Irma Gretchen, Anna Vreeland, Walther Frederick, Eunice Cooksey. Instr. German, Johns Hopkins, 1885-88; prof. Germanic philology and lit., Leland Stanford Jr. U., 1892-1905; lecturer Germanic philology, Harvard, 1905-08; prof. Germanic langs., U. of Ill., 1908-26 (emeritus). Editor Bellettristisches Jour., 1888-92, Jour. of English and Germanic Philology, 1909-26; editor German part of Modern Lang. Notes, 1886-89. Author: Über die Zukunft unseres Volkes in Amerika, 1883; Über tragische Schuld und Sühne, 1884; Gedichte, 1895; Das Deutschtum in den Vereinigten Staaten, 1904; Der Kampf um deutsche Kultur in Amerika, 1914. Editor: Goethe's Poems, 1901; Goethe's Faust, 1907; Schiller's Poems, 1903. Gen. editor German Classics, Oxford U. Press, 1909—, Year Book German American Hist. Society, 1912—, German Literature and Culture, Oxford Univ. Press, 1913—; Chr. von Graffenried's Account of the Founding of New Bern, N.C. (N.C. Hist. Commn.), 1920. Contbr. to Am. Journal Philology, Modern Language Notes, Anglia, Goethe-Jahrbuch, etc. Home: Urbana, Ill. Died Mar. 28, 1931.

GOEBEL, Peter W., banker; b. Germany, 1859; ed. pub. schs. Came to U.S., 1873; cashier Bank of Louisburg, Kan., 1882-98; organizer, 1897, and many yrs. pres. Commercial State Bank and of its successor the Commercial Nat. Bank; pres. Fidelity Savings Trust Co., Kansas City. Was mem. Kan. Ho. of Rep.; apptd. by Pres. Wilson, June 1917, mem. U.S. sect. Internat. High Commn.; apptd. state dir. War Savings, 1918. Home: Kansas City, Mo. Died Feb. 2, 1934.

GOEKE, John Henry, lawyer; b. nr. Minster, O., Oct. 28, 1869; s. Mathias and Bernardine (Rumping) G.; grad. Pio Nono Coll., St. Francis, Wis., 1888; LL.B., Cincinnati Law Sch., 1891; m. Katherine Nichols, Sept. 11, 1907; children—Mary Jane, Kathryn. Admitted to Ohio bar, 1891, and practiced at Wapakoneta; pros. atty. Auglaize County, O., 1894-1900; chmn. Dem. State Conv., 1903; mem. 62d and 63d Congresses (1911-15), 4th Ohio Dist.; partner firm Goeke, Parmenter & Reid; gen. counsel, dir. Lima Trust Co., City Loan & Savings Co. (Lima), First Nat. Bank (Wapakoneta); officer or dir. various cos. Democrat. Catholic. Home: Lima, O. Died Mar. 25, 1930.

GOELET, Augustin Hardin, gynecologist; b. Wilmington, N.C., Apr. 1, 1854; s. Edward H. and Virginia (Lane) G.; ed. Cape Fear Mil. Acad., 1870-72, U. of Va., 1872-73; M.D., Bellevue Hosp. Med. Coll. (New York U.), 1874; m. Elaine Goodnow, 1897. Engaged in practice of medicine and surgery in New York; prof. diseases of women, New York Sch. of Clin. Medicine (post-grad. sch.) from its organization, 1895, and pres. faculty same, Oct. 1902-Oct. 1904; gynecol. surgeon to Met. Hosp. for Women, etc. Founder and pres. Am. Electro-therapeutic Soc. Episcopalian. Democrat. Author: Electro-therapeutics of Gynecology, 1892; Technique of Surgical Gynecology, 1902. Contbr. to med. journals. Home: New York, N.Y. Died 1910.

GOELET, Robert Walton, real estate; b. New York, Mar. 19, 1880; s. Robert and Harriette Louise (Warren) G.; A.B., Harvard U., 1902, A.M., 1903; m. Anne Marie Guestier, Jan. 1921. Dir. U.P. R.R. Co., Chem Bank and Trust Co., Guaranty Trust Company, Air Reduction Co., Goelet Realty Co.; chmn. bd. Ritz-Carlton Hotel Corp. Address: New York, N.Y. Died May 2, 1941.

GOEPP, Philip Henry, musician; b. New York, June 23, 1864; s. Charles and Martha Neal C. G.; ed. classical schools Stuttgart and Esslingen, Germany, 1872-77; A.B., Harvard, 1884; LL.B., U. of Pa., 1888; Mus. Doc., Temple U., 1919. Admitted Phila. bar, 1888; adopted music as a profession, 1891; teacher, composer, organist, choirmaster; prof. theory of music Temple U. A founder and pres. Manuscript Music Soc., Phila.; hon. mem. Harvard Mus. Club. Composer of a fairy opera, "The Lost Prince" (words by John Jay Chapman), and numerous songs, anthems, part-songs and instrumental music, including a sonata for piano and violin in D, a quintet for piano and strings, a tone-poem "King Cole" and a Hindu suite for orchestra; also writer for years of descriptive notes in programs for symphony concerts of Philadelphia Orchestra. Author: Symphonies and Their Meaning (3 vols.), 1898, 1902, 13. Editor: Annals of Music in Philadelphia, 1896. Contbr. to Atlantic Monthly. Prof. of music, Ursinus Coll. and instr. in theory of music, Temple U. Home: Philadelphia, Pa. Died Aug. 26, 1936.

GOESSMANN, Charles Anthony, chemist; b. Naumburg, Germany, June 13, 1827; prepared in gymnasium, Fritzlar, Germany; Ph.D., U. of Göttingen, 1853; LL.D., Amherst, 1899. Asst. in lab., Göttingen, 1853-57; came to U.S., 1857; m. Miss M. A. Kinny, 1862. Chemist and mgr. sugar refinery, Phila., 1857-61; chemist Onondaga (N.Y.) Salt Co., 1862-69; prof. chemistry, Rensselaer Poly. Inst., 1866-68; prof. chemistry, Mass. Agrl. Coll., 1869—. Chemist to Mass. State Bd. Agr.; analyst to Mass. State Bd. Health; dir. Mass. Agrl. Expt. Sta.; made hon. dir. Hatch Expt. Sta., 1895; hon. representative of Dept. of Agr. to study certain scientific matters in Germany, France, etc., 1899. Author many reports, monographs and papers on chem. subjects. Home: Amherst, Mass. Died 1910.

GOETCHIUS, Henry Richard, lawyer; b. Columbus, Ga., June 13, 1852; s. Richard Rose and Mary Anne (Bennett) G.; A.B., U. of Ga., 1871; attended law lectures, U. of Va., 1876; m. Mary Ross Russell, May 30, 1885. Admitted to Ga. bar, and practiced at Columbus; mem. firm Goetchius & Chappell, 30 yrs., later practicing alone; apptd. master in chancery U.S. Court, 1901; mem. State Bd. Bar Examiners, Ga. Trustee Bd. of Edn., Columbia, 13 yrs. (pres. 8 yrs.); trustee U. of Ga. Democrat. Home: Columbus, Ga. Died Oct. 1925.

GOETHALS, George Washington, army engr.; b. Brooklyn, June 29, 1858; student Coll. City of New York, 1873-76; grad. U.S. Mil. Acad., 1880; LL.D., U. of Pa., 1913, Princeton U., 1915. Apptd. 2d lt. engrs., June 12, 1880; 1st lt., June 15, 1882; capt., Dec. 14, 1891; lt. col. chief engr. vols., May 9, 1898; hon. discharged from vol. service, Dec. 31, 1898; maj. engr. corps, Feb. 7, 1909; grad. Army War Coll., 1905; lt. col. engrs., Mar. 2, 1907; col., Dec. 3, 1909; major general, March 4, 1915; retired, Nov. 15, 1916. Instr. in civil and mil. engring., U.S. Mil. Acad., several yrs. until 1888; in charge of Muscle Shoals Canal constrn., on Tenn. River; chief of engrs. during Spanish-Am. War; mem. Bd. of Fortifications (coast and harbor defense); chief engr. Panama Canal, Feb. 26, 1907-14; 1st civil gov. Panama Canal Zone, 1914-16; chmn. bd. apptd. to report on Adamson 8-hour law, 1916; apptd. state engr., N.J., 1917; gen. mgr. Emergency Fleet Corp., Apr.-July 1917 (resigned); apptd. acting q.-m. gen. U.S.A., Dec. 18, 1917; apptd. chief Div. of Storage and Traffic of General Staff, Feb. 1918, and chief of Div. of Purchase, Storage and Traffic, Apr. 1918; was also mem. War Industries Bd.; relieved from active duty at own request, Mar. 1919. Received thanks of Congress, Mar. 4, 1915, for "distinguished service in constructing Panama Canal"; awarded D.S.M., 1918, "for especially meritorious and conspicuous service" in reorganizing Q.-M. Dept.; Comdr. Legion of Honor (France), 1919; medals, Nat. Geog. Soc., Civic Forum and Nat. Inst. Social Sciences. Address: New York, N.Y. Died Jan. 21, 1928.

GOFF, Frederick Harris, banker; b. Blackbury, Ill., Dec. 15, 1858; s. Frederick C. and Catharine J. (Brown) G.; Ph.B., U. of Mich., 1881; m. Frances Southworth, Oct. 16, 1894. Admitted to bar, 1884; practiced in Cleveland; mem. law firm Carr & Goff, 1884-90, Estep, Dickey, Carr & Goff, 1890-96, Kline, Tolles & Goff, 1896-June 8, 1908; pres. Cleveland Trust Co.; v.p. Cleveland, Terminal & Valley R.R., Cleveland, Loraine & Wheeling R.R. Chmn. bd. Chicago, Lake Shore & S. Bend Ry. Co.; dir. many corps. Trustee Western Reserve U.; founded Cleveland Foundation, Jan. 2, 1914. V. chmn. capital issues com. of War Finance Corp., Apr. 1918-Aug. 30, 1919. Republican. Unitarian. Home: Cleveland, O. Died Mar. 14, 1923.

GOFF, Guy Despard, senator; b. Clarksburg, W.Va., 1867; s. Nathan and Laura E. (Despard) G.; grad. Kenyon Mil. Acad., Gambier, O., Sept. 8, 1906. Began practice in Boston, 1891; moved to Milwaukee, Wis.; U.S. dist. atty., Eastern Dist. of Wis., 1911-15; served as mem. and gen. counsel U.S. Shipping Bd., also as asst. to atty. gen. of U.S.; mem. U.S. Senate from W.Va., term, 1925-31. Republican. Episcopalian. Home: Clarksburg, W.Va. Died Jan. 7, 1933.

GOFF, Harold, editor; b. West Jordan, Utah, June 13, 1884; s. Hyrum and Maria T. (Arnold) G.; grad. Utah State Normal Sch., 1902; A.B., U. of Utah, 1917; grad. study Columbia, U. of Chicago and Chautauqua Summer Sch.; m. Lulu Ormsby, Aug. 16, 1911 (died 1927). Teacher grade sch., Midvale, Utah, 1903-05; teacher Ricks Normal Coll., Rexburg, Ida., 1905-08; instr. in English and oral expression, U. of Utah, 1909-13; began as reporter, West Jordan (Utah) Journal, 1898; later with Intermountain Republican, Salt Lake City, Salt Lake Herald and Salt Lake Herald-Republican; with Deseret News, Salt Lake City, 1913—, editor in chief and mng. editor, 1922—. Mem. Bd. Regents, U. of Utah. Republican. Mormon. Home: Salt Lake City, Utah. Died 1928.

GOFF, John W., judge; b. Wexford, Ireland, Jan. 1, 1848; came to U.S. in childhood; ed. Cooper Union, New York; read law in offices of Hon. S. G. Courtney, and admitted to bar, 1870; m. Catherine O'Keefe, May 26, 1881. Asst. dist. atty., N.Y., under Col. J. Fellow, 1888-91; counsel for law association in the investigating and prosecution of election frauds in New York; counsel for celebrated Lexow senatorial com. in the investigation of the administration of police affairs in New York; recorder of City of New York, 1894-1906; justice Supreme Ct. of N.Y., 1st Dist., 1907-18. Home: New York, N.Y. Died Nov. 9, 1924.

GOFF, Nathan, senator; b. Clarksburg, W.Va., Feb. 9, 1843; s. Nathan G.; ed. Northwestern (Va.) Acad., Georgetown Coll., and U. of City of New York; (LL.D., Georgetown, 1889; m. Catherine Penny, Aug. 28, 1919. Served in Union Army, lt. to maj., 1861-65; admitted to bar, 1866; mem. W.Va. Ho. of Rep., 1867; U.S. atty., Dist. W.Va., 1868-81; Rep. candidate for Congress, 1870, 1874, for gov., 1876; Sec. of the Navy in cabinet of President Hayes, 1881; again U.S. dist. atty., 1881-82; mem. 48th to 50th Congresses (1883-89); elected gov. W.Va., 1888, on the face of returns by plurality of 130 votes, but election was contested by the Dem. candidate, who was seated by a majority vote of the legislature; U.S. circuit judge, 4th Circuit, 1892-1911; judge U.S. Circuit Ct. of Appeals, Jan. 1912-13; U.S. senator, 1913-19. Address: Clarksburg, W.Va. Died Apr. 24, 1920.

GOFFE, J(ames) Riddle, surgeon; b. Kenosha, Wis., Aug. 10, 1851; s. William and Betsy D. (Riddle) G.; Ph.B., U. of Mich., 1873, Ph.M., 1876, A.M., 1916; M.D., Bellevue Hosp. Med. Coll. (New York, U.), 1881; Woman's Hosp., N.Y., 1883; studied Paris and Vienna; m. Eleanor Taylor, Sept. 29, 1890 (died 1908). Attending surgeon Polyclinic Hosp., 1894—, Woman's Hosp., 1902—; consulting surgeon, St. Joseph's Hosp., Yonkers, N.Y., Mt. Vernon (N.Y.) Hosp., New York City Hosp., Lawrence Hosp., Bronxville. Prof. diseases of women, New York Polyclinic Med. Sch. and Hosp., Dartmouth Med. Sch. Trustee New York Polyclinic Med. Sch. and Hosp. Republican. Home: New York, N.Y. Died Dec. 24, 1931.

GOING, (Ellen) Maud ("E. M. Hardinge"), author; b. Westchester (now N.Y. City); d. Charles Henry and Eliza (Buxton) G.; ed. normal coll. and partial course at McGill U. Author: With the Wild Flowers, 1894; Field, Forest and Wayside Flowers, 1899; With the Trees, 1903; Our Field and Forest Trees, 1915. Home: Montreal, Can. Died Feb. 17, 1925.

GOLD, William Jason, warden Western Theol. Sem., Chicago; b. Washington, D.C., June 17, 1845; s. Daniel and Mary Ann (Kendall) G.; prep. edn. Columbian Coll. (now Univ.) Washington, D.C., 1858-61; grad. Harvard Coll., 1865, Gen. Theol Sem., 1865-67, Seabury Hall, Faribault, Minn., 1867-68 (D.D., Racine Coll., 1885); ordained to P.E. ministry, 1868; m. Kate D. Eaton, 1868. Prof. exegesis, Seabury Hall (Divinity School), 1873-76; instr. classical languages Racine Coll., Wis., 1877-80; prof. Greek, same, 1880-85; instr. exegesis and liturgics, Western Theol. Sem., Chicago, 1895—; examining chaplain, diocese of Chicago, 1885—; deputy to Gen. Conv. P.E. Ch., 5 successive times, beginning 1886. Address: Chicago, Ill. Died 1903.

GOLDBECK, Edward, writer; b. Berlin, Germany, Apr. 21, 1866; s. Carl and Luise (Bollert) G.; ed. U. of Berlin; m. Lina Abarbanell (actress and singer), Oct. 10, 1900. Officer in Prussian Army 7 yrs.; came to U.S., 1911; contbr. special articles to Chicago Tribune. Author: Krieg in Sicht, 1906; Deutschland's Zukunft Nationaldemokratie, 1907; Briefe an den Deutschen Kronprinzen, 1907; Politische Plaudereien, 1908; Seine Hoheit der Bastard; Die Bazillenkutsche. Home: Evanston, Ill. Died Apr. 25, 1934.

GOLDBECK, Robert pianist, composer; b. Potsdam, Prussia, Apr. 19, 1839; grad. Potsdam gymnasium; pupil in pianoforte and harmony of Louis Köhler, his mother's brother; also in pianoforte and composition of Litoff, Brunswick, and for a short time with Liszt at Weimar; m. Elise Frederica Haenschen, June 22, 1880. Was in Paris, 1852-56, went to London, 1856, to New York, 1861; founded a conservatory in Boston, another at Chicago, 1868, living there 1864-71; resided in St. Louis, 1871-78 and was one of dirs. Beethoven Conservatory and conductor St. Louis Harmonic Soc.; lived in New York, 1880-85, in Germany, 1886-91, St. Louis, 1891-94, Chicago, 1894-99, London, 1899-1903. Engaged in teaching, piano recitals, conducting, composition, gave concerts at Devonshire House (the duke's residence), London, in 1863 and again in 1888. Author: Encyclopedia of Musical Education (3 vols.), 1903. Address: London, Eng. Died 1908.

GOLDBERG, Isaac, author, critic; b. Boston, Mass., Nov. 1, 1887; s. Simon Mordechai and Ida (Silverman) G.; A.B., Harvard U., summa cum laude, 1910, A.M., 1911, Ph.D., 1912; m. Elsie Frieda Horvick, Sept. 6, 1914. Lt. editor American Freeman, 1923-32. Instrumental in introducing to English readers the modern lit. of Spanish and Portuguese America, also the modern literature of Yiddish. Author: Sir William G. Gilbert—A Study in Modern Satire and the Gilbert-Sullivan Operas, 1913; Studies in Spanish-American Literature, 1920; Brazilian Literature, 1922; The Drama of Transition, 1922; The Man Meneken, 1925; Havelock Ellis, 1926; The Theatre of George Jean Nathan, 1926; Panorama—A Book of Critical Sexual and Aesthetic Views (monograph), 1927; The Sexual Life of Man, Woman and Child (monograph), 1927; The Story of Gilbert & Sullivan, 1928; The Fine Art of Living, 1929; Tin Pan Alley—A Chronicle of the American Music Racket, 1930; Sexarians (short tales), 1931; George Gershwin—A Study in American Music, 1931; Madame Sex (short tales), 1932; The German Jew—His Share in Modern Culture (with Dr. A. Myerson), 1933; Queen of Hearts—The Passionate Pilgrimage of Lola Montez, 1936; Dictatorship Over the Intellect, 1935; Backsliders to God, 1936; Major Noah: American Jewish Pioneer, 1937; Music for the Layman, 1938; What Makes You Laugh—And Why, 1938. Translations of plays, novels, tales, criticism from the Yiddish, Spanish, French, German, Italian and Portuguese; also numerous monographs in the Haldeman-Julius Blue Book Series, and articles in mags. Special lecturer at Harvard U. on Hispano-American literature. Staff reviewer for American Mercury, of music and books on music, 1930-32; editor and founder Panorama (survey of people and ideas, now appearing as weekly column of Jewish Telegraphic Agency Syndicate). Contbr. articles on Latin-Am. lit. to Collier's Nat. Ency. Home: Brookline, Mass. Died **July 14, 1938.**

GOLDBERGER, Joseph, medical research; b. Austria-Hungary, July 16, 1874; s. Samuel and Sarah (Gutman) G.; ed. Coll. City of New York, 1890-92; M.D., Bellevue Hosp. Med. Coll. (New York U.), 1895; m. Mary Humphreys Farrar, Apr. 19, 1906; children—E. Farrar, Joseph H., B. Humphreys, Mary Humphreys. Resident physician Bellevue Hosp., 1895-97; pvt. practice, Wilkes-Barre, Pa., 1897-99; commd. asst. surgeon U.S. Pub. Health Service, 1899; passed asst. surgeon, 1904; surgeon, 1912. Chief work, research in preventive medicine, infectious diseases; now dir. field nutrition investigations. Mason. Contbr. results of original investigations of trematodes, the straw itch, yellow fever, dengue fever, measles, typhus fever, cholera media, diphtheria carriers and pellagra. Home: Washington, D.C. Died Jan. 17, 1929.

GOLDEN, Richard, actor; b. Bangor, Me., July 6, 1854; s. Patrick and Matilda G.; ed. in common school and by private tutor, Penobscot County, Me.; m. Katherine Kittleman. Began career as actor in comedy, "Fashion," 1867. Produced Old Jed Prouty, of which he is co-author, 1889, several thousand performances having been given; also appeared in numerous rôles. Home: Port Washington, N.Y. Died 1909.

GOLDEN, S(amuel) Herbert, mcht., philanthropist; b. Sept. 15, 1875; s. Berrah and Miriam (Skoll) G.; ed. pub. schs.; m. Rebecca Harris, Oct. 20, 1908; children—William Theodore, Barry Z. Began as textile salesman, 1895; in textile business, 1901—; commercial banker, 1907—. Pres. United Synagogue of America; mem. League for Abolition of Capital Punishment (mem. advisory com.), Fed. for Jewish Philanthropic Socs., Acad. Polit. Science, Metropolitan Mus. Art, Art Centre of New York; dir. Hebrew Free Loan Soc., Nat. Conf. of Jewish Congregational Orgns.; treas. Am. Pro-Falasha Com.; mem. exec. com. Jewish Theol. Sem. Endowment Fund, Alliance Isralite Universelle; exec. mem. Com. of Jewish Exhibits, N.Y. World's Fair 1939; mem. Municipal Com. for Relief of Home Owners; former pres. United Synagogues America; v.p. Hebrew Free Loan Soc.; mem. Nat. Conf. of Christians and Jews; organizer New Era Boys Club; former mem. exec. com. Y.M.H.A., Washington Heights branch; treas. Synagogue Council of America. Home: New York, N.Y. Died Jan. 1, 1941.

GOLDENWEISER, Alexander, anthropologist, sociologist; b. Kiev, Russia, Jan. 29, 1880; s. Alexander S. and Sofia G. (Munstein) G.; Kiev Gymnasium, 1896-1900; Harvard, 1900-01; A.B., Columbia, 1902, A.M., 1904, Ph.D., 1910; m. Anna Hallow, July 31, 1906; 1 dau., Alice Rosalind; m. 2d, Ethel Cantor, Jan. 31, 1930. Lectured on anthropology, Columbia, 1910-19; lecturer on anthropology and sociology, New Sch. for Social Research, New York, 1919-26; lecturer on anthropology and psychology, Rand School of Social Science, 1915-29; prof. thought and culture, Ore. State System of Higher Edn., Portland Extension, 1930—; visiting prof. sociology, Reed Coll., Ore., 1933-39; visiting prof. anthropology, U. of Wis., 1937-38; prof. anthropology, U. of Wash., summer 1923; prof. sociology, U. of Ore., summer 1925; prof. sociology, Stanford U., summer 1935, U. of Buffalo, summer 1936; public lecturer. On editorial staff, Encyclopedia of the Social Sciences, 1927-28. Editor: (with W. F. Ogburn) The Social Sciences and Their Inter-relations, 1927. Author: Totemism, an Analytical Study, 1910; Early Civilization, 1922; Robots or Gods, 1932; History, Psychology and Culture, 1933; Anthropology, an Introduction to Primitive Culture, 1937; (co-author) American Indian Life, 1924; Our Changing Morality, 1924; Political Theories—Recent Times, 1925; History and Prospects of the Social Sciences, 1925; Population Problems, 1925; Sex in Civilization, 1929. Address: Portland, Ore. **Died July 6, 1940.**

GOLDER, Frank Alfred, prof. history; b. Russia, Aug. 11, 1877; came to U.S., 1880; A.B., Harvard, 1903, Ph.D., 1909; studied Paris and Berlin; unmarried. Instr. history, U. of Mo., 1908-09, history and economics, Boston U., 1909, history, U. of Chicago, 1910; asst. prof. and prof. history, State Coll. of Wash., 1910-14; investigations in Russian archives for Carnegie Instn. of Washington, 1914-15; prof. history, State Coll. of Wash., 1915-20. Investigations in Russian archives for Carnegie Instn. and Am. Geog. Soc., 1917; on staff Col. House commn. of inquiry, 1917-19; mem. Am. Relief Adm., spl. work in Europe, 1920-23; asso. prof. modern history, Stanford U., 1921-24, prof., 1924—; dir. Hoover War Library, Stanford, 1924—. Unitarian. Author: Russian Expansion on the Pacific, 1914; Guide to the Materials for American History in Russian Archives, 1917; Bering's Voyages, 1922; John Paul Jones in Russia, 1927; (with L. Hutchinson) On the Trail of the Russian Famine, 1927. Home: Stanford University, Calif. Died Jan. 7, 1929.

GOLDFOGLE, Henry M., congressman; b. N.Y. City, May 23, 1856; s. Mayer G.; ed. Townsend Coll.; unmarried. Admitted to N.Y. bar at 21; judge Municipal Court, New York, 1888-1900; 3 times del. and twice alternate to Dem. nat. convs.; mem. 57th to 62d Congresses (1901-13), 9th N.Y. Dist., and 63d and 66th Congresses (1913-15, and 1919-21), 12th N.Y. Dist.; accomplished abrogation of treaty of 1833 with Russia; counsel of U.S. Ho. of Rep. in successful proceedings to punish a U.S. dist. atty. for contempt; pres. City of N.Y. Dept. of Taxes and Assessments, Borough of Manhattan, 1921—; dir. Howard L. Curry Co., Inc. Pres. Jewish Temple, Congregation Rodeph Sholom, New York. Democrat. Address: New York, N.Y. Died June 1, 1929.

GOLDING, Frank Henry, pub. utilities; b. Hartford, Conn., June 21, 1875; s. Martin Henry and Mary Jane (Bolger) G.; prep. edn., high sch., Hartford; spl. student Trinity Coll., Hartford; m. Anna Bell Crouch, Feb. 3, 1897; 1 son, Charles Paget. Supt. Branford (Conn.) Lighting & Water Co., 1895-1905; asst. gen. mgr. Dayton (O.) Lighting Co., 1905-07; successively v.p., gen. mgr. Rockford (Ill.) Electric Co., Atlantic City (N.J.) Electric Co., Ohio Power Co. until 1920; gen. mgr. Holmes Automobile Co., Canton, O., 1920-21; treas., gen. mgr. Fox Motor Car Co., 1921-23, Cambridge Electric Light Co., 1923-27; pres. N.E. Gas & Electric Assn. and subsidiaries, 1927-38, chmn. bd., 1938—; pres. Cambridgeport Savings Bank, 1936-39; v.p. and dir. Harvard Trust Co., 1940. Republican. Episcopalian. Mason. Home: Cambridge, Mass. Died Feb. 3, 1941.

GOLDMAN, Mayer C., lawyer; b. New Orleans, La., Sept. 2, 1874; s. David and Selma (Franko) G.; ed. pub. schs. and Central Evening High Sch., New York; LL.B., New York U., 1895; m. Mattie Marcosson, June 17, 1902; children—Helen May, Allan David. Began practice in New York, 1895; leader of movement throughout U.S. to establish office of public defender in criminal cases. Mem. Am. Inst. Criminal Law and Criminology (pub. defender com.), American Bar Assn. (mem. com. on legal aid work), N.Y. State Bar Assn. (chairman com. on pub. defender; mem. com. on professional economics), Nat. Lawyers' Guild (chmn. com. on pub. defender of N.Y. City chapter). Apptd. col. staff of gov. of Ky., July 8, 1935. Democrat. Author: The Public Defender, 1917; also of pub. defender bills introduced in New York legislature, 1915-31. Co-author motion picture play, "The Public Defender." Contbr. to mags. and periodicals. Lecturer on "The Public Defender." Home: New York, N.Y. **Died Nov. 24, 1939.**

GOLDMARK, Rubin, composer; b. New York, N.Y., Aug. 15, 1872; s. Leo and Augusta (Stern) G.; student Coll. City of New York 3 yrs.; attended lectures of philos. faculty, U. of Vienna, for short time; hon. A.M., Colo. Coll., 1900; student Vienna Conservatory of Music, 1889-91; while there pupil of Door (piano), and Fuchs (composition); subsequently pupil of Rafael Joseffy (piano), and Antonin Dvořák (composition); unmarried. Instr. piano and theory, Nat. Conservatory of Music, New York, 1891-93; dir. Colo. Coll. Conservatory of Music, 1895-1901; returned to New York, 1902; in charge dept. of composition Juilliard Graduate School, 1924; has given about 500 lecture recitals in U.S. and Canada. Pres. the Bohemians (New York musicians' club), 1907-10, 26. Recd. Paderewski prize for chamber music, 1910. Composer: Trio for piano, violin and cello, Sonata for piano and violin; songs; piano compositions; quartet for piano, violin, viola, cello; symphonic poem, Samson; overture, Hiawatha; tone poem, Gettysburg Requiem for Orchestra; A Negro Rhapsody; etc. Address: **New York,** N.Y. Died March 6, 1936.

GOLDSBOROUGH, Richard Francis, lawyer; b. Baltimore, Md., Mar. 31, 1871; s. Richard H. and Henrietta Maria Frances (Martin) G.; grad. U. of Va., 1889; A.B., Princeton, 1891; read law in office of Henry Wise Garnett (Washington); Law Sch. U. of Va., 1892-93, Harvard Law Sch., 1893-94 (spl. course arranged by Woodrow Wilson, of Princeton); m. Anna Girault Farrar, Dec. 31, 1905. Admitted to Va. bar, 1893, N.Y., 1894, La., 1909; in office of Henry Wise **Garnett, Washington, 1894,** Hornblower, Byrne, Taylor & Miller, New York, 1894-98; practiced alone and with others, finally sr. of Goldsborough, Warner & Sykes, 1904-06; retired, 1906-09, account of ill health; mem. Farrar, Jonas, Goldsborough & Goldberg, New Orleans, 1909—, also practiced portion of each yr. in New York. Democrat. Episcopalian. Mason. Home: New Orleans, La. Died Mar. 6, 1931.

GOLDSBOROUGH, Worthington, naval officer; b. Cambridge, Md., Oct. 9, 1834. Apptd. acting asst. p.m. in vol. navy, Sept. 30, 1862; apptd. asst. p.m. in regular service, July 2, 1864; promoted p.m., May 4, 1866; pay insp., Nov. 24, 1891; retired, Oct. 9, 1896; advanced one grade and promoted pay dir. retired, with rank of capt., for service during Civil War, June 29, 1906. Served during the Civil War, on the Southfield and St. Lawrence, 1862-65; Shamrock, 1866-68; Naval Acad., 1868-71; Omaha, 1872-75; accounts of vessels at Naval Acad., 1876; coast survey, 1876-80; Brooklyn, 1881-84; Navy Yard, League Island, 1885-88; navy pay office, San Francisco, 1888-90; San Francisco, 1890-91; Charleston, as fleet p.m. Asiatic sta., 1891-92; San Francisco, fleet p.m. Pacific sta., 1892-93; Naval Acad., 1893-96; during the Spanish War was on duty at Navy Yard, Norfolk, 1898; Naval Acad., 1901-03. Home: Cambridge, Md. Died Apr. 23, 1918.

GOLDSCHMIDT, Samuel Anthony, chemist; b. New York, N.Y., Sept. 17, 1848; s. John and Celestine (Judah) G.; A.B., Coll. City of New York, 1868, A.M., 1890; E.M., Columbia Sch. of Mines, 1871; Ph.D., Emory Coll., Ga., 1875; m. Ellen C. Chesebrough, Oct. 23, 1879. Pres., 1890-1915, chmn. bd., 1915—, Columbia Chem. Works, now Parsons Ammonia Co. Wrote article on Offensive Trades, in the Reference Handbook of Medical Literature, 1888; Reports on Gas Works and other mfg. establishments, Board of Health Reports, 1873, 1875, 1878, 1883. Home: New York, N.Y. Died 1933.

GOLDSMITH, Robert, writer, lecturer; b. Kingston, N.Y., May 24, 1882; s. Abraham Marshall and Sarah Jane (Tootill) G.; ed. Mt. Hermon (Mass.) Sch. and Phillips Acad., Andover, Mass.; m. Edith Darrow, Dec. 25, 1907. Began as credit mgr., Harper & Brothers; asst. editor Collier's Weekly, 1907-08; pastor Coll. Ch. (Independent Conglist.), East Lansing, Mich., 1909-11; founder, Civic Ch., Little Rock, Ark., 1912; pastor Mapleton Park Congl. Ch., Brooklyn, N.Y., 1914-16; staff lecturer League for Polit. Edn., N.Y. City, 1915; spl. editor Russell Sage Foundation, 1916; asso. sec. League to Enforce Peace, 1916-18; spl. editor Rockefeller Foundation, 1918-19; dir. lecture dept. of Interch. World Movement, 1920; editorial writer New York World, 1921; dir. Bur. of Polit. Research, Dem. Nat. Com., 1921—. Democrat. Author: A League to Enforce Peace, 1917. Address: Ridgewood, N.J. Died Feb. 24, 1924.

GOLDSPOHN, Albert, physician; b. Dane County, Wis., Sept. 23, 1851; B.S., Northwestern Coll., Naperville, Ill., 1875; M.D., Rush Med. Coll., Chicago, 1878; studied in Germany 2 yrs.; m. Cornelia E. Walz, 1887 (died 1901). Resident physician and surgeon, Cook County Hosp., Chicago, 1878-79; practiced at Des Plaines 6 yrs.; settled in Chicago; attending surgeon former German Hosp., 1888-1904; prof. diseases of women and abdominal surgery, Post-Grad. Med. Sch. and Hosp., 1890-1922; surgeon in chief Evang. Deaconess Hosp. Trustee Northwestern Coll., 1889— (donated abt. $40,000 to this instn.). Republican. Mem. Evangelical Ch. Devised a fundamental operation for injuries sustained during childbirth, and two major operations for displacements and prolapse of the womb. Home: Naperville, Ill. **Died Sept. 1, 1929.**

GOLDSTEIN, Max Aaron, M.D., oto-laryngologist; b. St. Louis, Mo., Apr. 19, 1870; s. William and Hulda (Loewenthal) G.; M.D., Mo. Med. Coll., 1892; LL.D.; study in oto-laryngology, Strassburg, Berlin, Vienna and London, 1893; m. Leonore Weiner, June 4, 1895; 1 dau., Helen (Mrs. Norman C. Wolff). Began practice oto-laryngology, St. Louis, 1894; prof. otology and laryngology, Beaumont Hosp. Med. Coll., 1896-1900, St. Louis U., 1900-12; founder, 1914, and dir. Central Inst. for Deaf, St. Louis; dir. dept. otology and laryngology, Jewish Hosp. of St. Louis. Founder, 1896, and editor The Laryngoscope (monthly mag.); founder, 1922, and editor Oralism and Auralism (semi-annual jour.). Served as maj., Med. Corps, U.S. Army, World War; head of dept. head surgery, Camp Dodge, Ia.; mem. com. on reconstrn. for deaf and defective speech soldiers. Democrat. Mem. Jewish Ref. Ch. Author: Problems of the Deaf; The Acoustic Method for Training the Deaf and Hard of Hearing Child, 1939. Home: Clayton, Mo. Died July 27, 1941.

GOLER, George W., physician; b. Brooklyn, Aug. 24, 1864; s. Louis E. and Sarah H. (Keyes) G.; ed. Brooklyn pub. schs.; M.D., U. of Buffalo, 1889; hon. D.Sc., U. of Rochester, 1925; m. Lena L. Dodge, June 4, 1895; 1 dau., Marie (wife of Prof. William Franklin Spafford). House physician, 1888-89, asst. physician, 1891-93, attending physician, 1894-97, Infants' Hosp., Charlotte, N.Y.; med. insp. Rochester Bd. Health, 1892-96, health officer, 1896-1932; established first Am. municipal milk depots, 1897; established, 1904, and attending physician, Rochester Hosp.

for Infectious Diseases. Mem. bd. mgrs. N.Y. State Industrial Sch., Rochester, 1896-1902. Fellow Rochester Acad. Medicine; hon. pres. 4th sect. Internat. Congress Child Hygiene, Berlin, 1911; mem. council, med. sect. N.Y. State Com. Defense, 1917. Author of papers on hygiene and sanitary science. Lecturer on preventive medicine, Med. Sch. of U. of Rochester. Home: (winter) Beaufort, S.C.; (summer) Sodus, N.Y. Died Sept. 18, 1940.

GOLTMAN, Maximilian, surgeon; b. Glasgow, Scotland, May 24, 1867; s. Solomon and Cecelia (Tobias) G.; brought to Can., 1875; C.M., M.D., Bishops U., Montreal, Can., 1892, McGill, 1916; post-grad. work, London, Edinburgh, Glasgow, Boston, Baltimore, New York, etc.; m. Mollie Sternberg, Dec. 12, 1895; children—Dr. A. M., Mrs. J. D. Shroder, Dr. Jack S., Dr. David W., Mrs. Maurice Caheen. Began practice in Montreal, 1892; settled in Memphis, 1897; pres. Dept. of Health, 1910-14; sr. prof. surgery, U. of Tenn., also prof. gen. surgery, dental department, same; surgeon to Memphis General and Bapt. hosps.; physician in chief, Associated Charities. Jewish religion. Mason. Home: Memphis, Tenn. Died June 17, 1933.

GOLTRA, Edward Field, iron metallurgy; b. Jacksonville, Ill., Dec. 29, 1862; s. Moore Compton and Evelina (Parsons) G.; Ill. Coll.; A.B., Princeton, 1887; m. Kate Mary Brown, May 31, 1888. Began in iron business at St. Louis, 1889; organized and operated various iron and steel properties. Mem. Dem. Nat. Com. for Mo., 1911—; chmn. Municipal Commn. on Tuberculosis, St. Louis; mem. Bd. of Edn., St. Louis; trustee Ill. Coll. Address: St. Louis, Mo. Died Apr. 2, 1939.

GOMPERS, Samuel, pres. Am. Federation of Labor; b. England, Jan. 27, 1850; s. Solomon and Sarah (Root) G.; m. Sophia Julian, Jan. 27, 1867 (died 1920); m. 2d, Gertrude Gleaves Neuscheler, Apr. 16, 1921. Cigarmaker by trade; has been advocate of the rights of labor, and connected with the efforts to organize the working people since his 14th yr.; helped develop the Cigarmakers Internat. Union, becoming an officer, 1887; one of the founders of the Federation of Trades and Labor Unions, organized in 1881, of which was pres. 3 yrs.; one of founders Am. Federation of Labor, 1886, and has continuously served as pres. excepting 1895, also editor of the American Federationist; has written a number of pamphlets on the labor question and the labor movement; 1st v.p. Nat. Civic Federation; mem. Advisory Com. Council Nat. Defense, 1917-19; rep. of A. F. of L. at Peace Conf., Paris, France, 1918-19; pres. Internat. Commn. on Labor Legislation, at the Peace Congress; chmn. delegates from A. F. of L. to Conv. of Internat. Federation of Trades Unions, Amsterdam, 1919; mem. President's First Industrial Conf., 1919, President's Unemployment Conf., 1921, President's Advisory Disarmament Com., 1921—, President's Agricultural Conference, 1921. Pres. Pan-Am. Federation of Labor; member of Sulgrave Inst. Author: Labor in Europe and America; American Labor and the War; Labor and the Common Welfare; Labor and the Employer; Out of Their Own Mouths. Home: New York, N.Y. Died Dec. 13, 1924.

GONZALES, Ambrose Elliott, newspaper pub.; b. Adams Run, S.C., May 29, 1857; s. Ambrosio Jose and Harriet Rutledge (Elliott) G.; ed. pvt. schs.; LL.D., U. of S.C., 1923; unmarried. Telegraph operator in S.C., 1874-78, in New York and New Orleans, 1881-85; traveling agent and corr. Charleston (S.C.) News and Courier, 1885-89; with his brother, N. G. Gonzales, founded The State (daily), Columbia, S.C., Feb. 18, 1891, becoming its pres. and publisher, Mar. 1893. Democrat. Episcopalian. Capt., U.S. Vols., Spanish-Am. War, 1898-99; service at Santiago, Cuba. Author: The Black Border: Gullah Stories of the Carolina Coast, 1922; With Aesop Along the Black Border, 1924; The Captain: Stories of the Black Border, 1924; Laguerre—A Gascon of the Black Border, 1924; all pub. by The State Company, Columbia, S.C. Address: Columbia, S.C. Died July 11, 1926.

GONZALES, William Elliott, editor, publisher; b. Charleston, S.C., Apr. 24, 1866; s. Ambrosio José and Harriet Rutledge (Elliott) G.; ed. King's Mountain Mil. Sch., S.C.; m. Sarah C. Shiver, Feb. 2, 1887 (died 1932); children—Robert Elliott (dec.), Alida (wife of R. K. McMaster, U.S.A.). Asst. corr. News and Courier bureau, Columbia, 1884-88; private sec. to Gov. J. P. Richardson, of S.C., 1888-90; telegraph and news editor The State, Columbia, 1891-1903, editor-in-chief, 1903-13 and 1922—; also pres. The State Co. E.E. and M.P. to Cuba, June 21, 1913-Dec. 1, 1919; first American ambassador to Peru, 1919-22. Adj. Independent Batln. S.C. Vols. and capt. 2d S.C. Vols., Spanish-Am. War, 1898-99, service in Cuba. Chief commr. of S.C. at Jamestown Expn., 1907. "Distinguished Public Service Award" by Am. Legion, Dept. of S.C. Democrat. Episcopalian. Home: Columbia, S.C. Died Oct. 20, 1937.

GOOCH, Frank Austin, chemist; b. Watertown, Mass., May 2, 1852; s. Joshua Goodale and Sarah Gates (Coolidge) G.; A.B., Harvard, 1872, A.M., Ph.D., 1877; hon. M.A., Yale, 1887; m. Sarah Elisabeth Wyman, Aug. 12, 1880; 1 dau., Meredyth (Mrs. John Downes Whiting). Asst. in chem. lab. under Prof. Josiah P. Cooke until 1875; studied with Prof. Wolcott Gibbs, and in Europe until 1878; engaged in analytical work at Newport for U.S. 10th Census, 1879-81; chemist on Northern Transcontinental Survey, 1881-84, and U.S. Geol. Survey, 1884-86; prof. chemistry, Yale, 1885-1918, and dir. Kent Chem. Lab.; emeritus. Investigator of inorganic and analytical chemistry. Author: Analyses of Waters of the Yellowstone Park (with J. E. Whitfield), 1888; Research Papers from the Kent Chemical Laboratory of Yale Univ. (2 vols.), 1901; Outlines of Inorganic Chemistry (with C. F. Walker), 1905; Laboratory Experiments (with C. F. Walker), 1905; Outlines of Qualitative Chemical Analysis (with P. E. Browning), 1906; Methods in Chemical Analysis, 1912; Representative Procedures in Quantitative Chemical Analysis, 1915. Home: New Haven, Conn. Died Aug. 12, 1929.

GOOD, Edward Ellsworth, judge; b. Bloomfield, Ia., May 13, 1862; s. William Henry Calvin and Mary Anne (McCullough) G.; ed. high sch. and Southern Ia. Normal Sch.; LL.B., State U. of Ia., 1885; m. Orpha J. Gillilan, July 8, 1885. Admitted to Neb. bar, 1885, and began practice at Wahoo; jr. mem. firm Good & Good, 1885-1900; sr. mem. Good & Slama, 1900-02; mem. Simpson & Good, 1902-08 and 1909-12. County atty. Saunders Co., Neb., 1895-96; commr. Supreme Court of Neb., 1908-09; elected judge Dist. Court, 5th Jud. Dist. of Neb., Nov. 1911, reëlected, 1916, 20; justice Supreme Court of Neb., 1923—. Mem. bd. First Nat. Bank of Wahoo. Republican. Conglist. Mason (K.T., 32°, Shriner); K.P., Elk, Woodman; mem. O.E.S. Home: Wahoo, Neb. Died Aug. 4, 1937.

GOOD, James Isaac, theologian; b. York, Pa., Dec. 31, 1850; s. William A. and Susan B. G.; A.B., Lafayette Coll., 1872, A.M., 1875; grad. Union Theol. Sem., 1875; D.D., Ursinus Coll., 1887, Lafayette Coll., 1912; LL.D., Ursinus Coll., 1911; unmarried. Ordained German Reformed ministry, 1875; pastor, York, Pa., 1875-77; Philadelphia, 1877-90, Reading, Pa., 1890-1905; prof. church history, 1890-93, dogmatics and pastoral theology and dean of school of theology, 1893-1907, Ursinus Coll., Phila.; prof. Reformed Church history and liturgics, Central Theol. Sem., Dayton, O., 1907. Pres. Gen. Synod Ref. Ch. in U.S., 1911-14, Am. sect. Alliance of Reformed Chs.; v.p. World Alliance of Ref. and Presbyn. Chs. Author: Origin of the Reformed Church of Germany; History of the Reformed Church of Germany; Rambles Around Reformed Lands; History of the Reformed Church in the United States; Famous Women of the Reformed Church; Famous Missionaries of the Reformed Church; Famous Places of the Reformed Churches, 1910; History of the Reformed Church in the U.S. in the Nineteenth Century, 1911; History of the Swiss Reformed Church Since the Reformation, 1913; The Heidelberg Catechism in its Newest Light, 1914; Famous Reformers of the Reformed and Presbyterian Churches, 1916; The Reformed Reformation, 1917. Address: Philadelphia, Pa. Died Jan. 22, 1924.

GOOD, James William, congressman; b. Cedar Rapids, Ia., Sept. 24, 1866; s. Henry and Margaret Elizabeth (Combs) G.; B.S., Coe Coll., Ia., 1892; LL.B., U. of Mich., 1893; m. Lucy Deacon, Oct. 4, 1894; children—James W., Robert Edmund. City atty., Cedar Rapids., 1906-08; mem. 61st to 67th Congresses (1909-23), 5th Ia. Dist.; resigned from Congress, June 1921, to engage in practice of law at Chicago; mem. firm Good, Childs, Bobb & Wescott. Republican. Presbyn. Mason (32°). Home: Evanston, Ill. Died Nov. 11, 1929.

GOODALE, Charles Warren, mining engr.; b. Honolulu, Hawaii, Sept. 6, 1854; s. Warren and Ellen R. (Whitmore) G.; grad. English High Sch., Boston, 1871; S.B., Mass. Inst. Tech., 1875; unmarried. With the Boston & Colorado Smelting Co., at Boston, 1875-76, at Black Hawk, Colo., 1876-80; supt. and mgr. Boston & Ariz. Smelting & Reduction Co., Tombstone, Ariz., 1880-85; supt. mining dept., Colo. Smelting & Mining Co., at Butte, 1885-98; with Boston & Mont. Consolidated Copper & Silver Mining Co. (now Boston and Mont. dept. of Anaconda Copper Mining Co.), 1898-1914, Great Falls, Mont., 1898-1901, asst. mgr. and mgr. at Butte, 1901-18; chmn. bur. of safety Anaconda Copper Mining Co., 1914-20. Alderman, 2d Ward, City of Butte, 1888-90. Republican. Episcopalian. Home: Butte, Mont. Died Apr. 11, 1929.

GOODALE, George Lincoln, botanist; b. Saco, Me., Aug. 3, 1839; s. Stephen Lincoln and Prudence Aiken (Nourse) G.; A.B., Amherst, 1860, A.M., 1866; M.D., Harvard, 1863; Bowdoin, 1863; hon. A.M., Bowdoin, 1869; LL.D., Amherst, 1890, Bowdoin, 1894, Princeton, 1896; m. Henrietta Juel Hobson, 1866; 1 son, Joseph Lincoln. Practiced medicine, Portland, Me., 3 yrs.; Josiah Little prof. natural science and prof. mineralogy, botany and applied chemistry, Bowdoin, 1868-72; instr. botany and lecturer on vegetable physiology, 1872-73, asst. prof., 1873-78, prof. botany, 1878-88, Fisher prof. botany, 1888-1909, Fisher prof. natural history emeritus, 1909, curator Bot. Mus., 1879-1909, hon. curator, 1909—, Harvard. Home: Cambridge, Mass. Died Apr. 12, 1923.

GOODALE, George Pomeroy, dramatic critic; b. Orleans, N.Y., Aug. 12, 1843; s. Elijah and Mary E. (Palmer) G.; common school edn.; m. Josephine Gardner, Nov. 30, 1864; 2d Katherine Brigham Molony, Dec. 1, 1902. Worked in printing office when a boy; for many yrs. city editor of Detroit Free Press, also writing dramatic criticisms; dramatic editor same, 1865—; pres. Detroit Free Press Prtg. Co. Author: Signor Max papers (essays, several hundred in number); The Kaleidoscope, editorials; several series of papers entitled "Picked Up in New York." Address: Detroit, Mich. Died May 7, 1919.

GOODALE, Greenleaf Austin, army officer; b. Orrington, Me., July 4, 1839; s. Ephraim, Jr. and Lucinda Larned (Martin) G.; ed. E. Me. Conf. Sem., Bucksport; m. Fidelia S. Beach, June 1, 1870; 2d, Margaret Montgomery, Sept. 1, 1886. Pvt., corporal and sergt. Co. E, 6th Me. Inf., May 7, 1861-Jan. 2, 1864; 1st lt., 77th U.S.C.T., Jan. 2, 1864; capt., May 24, 1864; hon. mustered out of vol. service, Nov. 14, 1866; 1st lt., 23d U.S. Inf., July 28, 1866; capt., June 25, 1878; maj., Apr. 26, 1898; lt. col. 3d Inf., July 19, 1899; col. 17th Inf., Apr. 1, 1901; brig. gen., Feb. 23, 1903. Bvtd.; maj., Mar. 13, 1865, for faithful and meritorious services during the war; capt., Mar. 2, 1867, for gallant and meritorious services in battle of Gettysburg. Served in Army of Potomac, 1861-63, Dept. of Gulf, 1864-66, frontier and Indian country, 1867-98; Philippines, 1898-1901; retired after 42 yrs.' service, Feb. 24, 1903. Home: Wakefield, Mass. Died Feb. 17, 1915.

GOODALL, Louis Bertrand, congressman; b. Winchester, N.H., Sept. 23, 1851; s. Thomas and Ruth (Waterhouse) G.; ed. Kimball Union Acad., Meriden, N.H.; m. Rose V. Goodwin, July 21, 1877 (died 1894); children—Lela Helen, Mildred Vaughn (Mrs. William N. Campell), Thomas Milton. Began in wool mfg. (Mousam River Mills), 1874; dir. Sanford Mills (consolidation various concerns), 1886—, pres. many years, later chmn. bd.; organizer, 1899; and treas. and agt. Goodall Worsted Co., later chmn. bd. Chmn. Me. Commn. to St. Louis Expn., 1904; lt. col. on staff Gov. Fernald, 1909. Mem. 65th and 66th Congresses (1917-21), 1st Me. Dist. Republican. Unitarian. Home: Sanford, Me. Died June 26, 1935.

GOODCHILD, Frank Marsden, clergyman; b. Philadelphia, Pa., Dec. 26, 1860; s. Robert Guest and Elizabeth (Williams) G.; A.B., Bucknell U., 1884, A.M., 1887, D.D., 1904; grad. Crozer Theol. Sem., Upland, Pa., 1887; m. Clara H. Myers, Feb. 8, 1888; 1 son, Franklin Myers. Ordained Bapt. ministry, 1888; pastor Amenia, N.Y., 1887-90, Spruce St. Ch., Phila., Pa., 1890-95, Central Ch., N.Y. City, 1895-1924. Pres. Am. and Foreign Bible Soc.; v.p. Bapt. Union for Ministerial Edn.; pres. Ministers' Home Soc.; chmn. bd. mgrs. Am. Bapt. Home Mission Soc.; mem. bd. mgrs. Ministers' and Missionaries' Benefit Bd., Bd. of Edn. of Northern Bapt. Conv., N.Y. City Bapt. Mission Soc., Am. Tract Soc., Am. Bible Union. Trustee Northern Bapt. Theol. Sem. (Chicago), Gordon Bible Coll. (Boston), Phila. Bapt. Inst. for Christian Workers. Leader of fundamentalists of Northern Bapt. Conv. Republican. Mason. Made tour of the world, 1913-14; visited the Indians of western Okla., 1920, and was adopted by the Cheyennes and given the name of their favorite chief, Whirlwind. Author: Can We Believe?, 1926; Around the Lord's Table, 1927; also numerous monographs. Contbg. editor The Watchman Examiner, New York. Home: New York, N.Y. Died Feb. 18, 1928.

GOODE, John, lawyer; b. Bedford County, Va., May 27, 1829; s. John and Ann M. G.; grad. Emory and Henry Coll., Va., 1848 (LL.D.); admitted to bar, 1851; mem. Va. house of delegates, 1852-63 and 1866-67; mem. Va. (secession) Conv., 1861; Confederate Congress, 1862-65; during recesses of that body vol. aide on staff Gen. Jubal A. Early; after war practiced law, Norfolk, Va. Mem. U.S. Congress, 1875-81; presidential elector, 1852, 1856 and 1884; solicitor gen. U.S., May, 1885, to Aug., 1886; mem. Chilean Claims Commn., 1893-94. Practiced law in Washington. Lecturer on criminal law, Nat. Law U.; mem. Dem. Nat. Com., 8 yrs.; mem. bd. of visitors, William and Mary Coll., U. of Va., and Va. Agrl. and Mech Coll.; pres. Va. Constitutional Conv., 1901-02. Address: Washington, D.C. Died 1909.

GOODE, J(ohn) Paul, univ. prof.; b. Stewartville, Minn., Nov. 21, 1862; s. Abraham John and Huldah Jane (Van Valkenburgh) G.; B.S., U. of Minn., 1889; grad. student Harvard, 1894; grad. student, 1895-99, fellow in geology, U. of Chicago; grad. student, 1900-01, Ph.D., 1901, U. of Pa.; m. Ida Katherine Hancock, Sept. 12, 1901; 1 son, Kenneth Hancock. Prof. science, State Normal Sch., Moorhead, Minn., 1889-98; prof. physics and geography, State Normal Sch., Charleston, Ill., 1898-1901; instr. geography, U. of Penn., 1901-03; instr. physiography and meteorology, summers, 1897-1900, 02, asso. prof. geography, 1903-17, prof., 1917-28, U. of Chicago, emeritus. Expert Chicago Harbor Commn. on development of great ports of Europe, report pub. 1908. Apptd. by President Taft to aid in entertainment of the hon. commercial commrs. of Japan, in their trans-continental tour, 1909; lecturer for Philippine govt. at the Baguio Assembly, 1911. Chmn. local draft bd. for div. 16, Chicago, 1917-18. Author of a series of Physical Wall Maps, Polit. Wall Maps, geog. globes, series of base maps, series of lantern slide maps, and of a School Atlas, 1923, 4th edition, 1931, also The Geographic Background of Chicago; inventor of the interrupted homolographic map projection, 1916, the homolosine projection, 1923, polar equal area projection, 1928. Fellow, dir. and pres. Geog. Soc. Chicago (Helen Culver gold medal, 1923, for distinguished achievement in cartography). Home: Chicago, Ill. Died Aug. 5, 1932.

GOODE, Richard Livingston, judge; b. Henry County, Ky., Feb. 4, 1855; s. William Thomas and Martitia Elizabeth (Guthrie) G.; student Drury Coll., Springfield, Mo., 1875-76, M.A., 1880, LL.D., 1901; studied law with Jere C. Cravens, Springfield; m. Estelle B. Maurer, Apr. 22, 1885; children—Mrs. Grace Clarke, Mrs. Kathryn Moss. Admitted to Mo. bar, 1879, and practiced in Springfield; was partner with Jere C. Cravens 20 yrs.; city atty. 1 yr.; pres. Sch. Bd. 6 yrs.; atty. of K.C., Ft. Scott & Memphis Ry. Co., 1896-1901; judge Court of Appeals, St. Louis, 1901-10; prof. equity, 1906-10, prof. law and dean law sch., 1915-19 and 1921—, Washington U.; justice Supreme Court State of Mo., 1919-21; counsel Mercantile Trust Co., Mercantile Nat. Bank, etc. Democrat. Home: St. Louis, Mo. Died Mar. 4, 1927.

GOODE, Richard Urquhart, geographer; b. Bedford, Va., Dec. 8, 1858; s. John and Sally (Urquhart) G.; student Norfolk, Va., Hanover Acad. Va., and U. of Va.; m. Sophie J. Parks, Jan. 2, 1889. Asst. engr. army engr. corps, 1877-78; topographer U.S. Geol. Survey, 1879-82; engr. and topographer Northern Transcontinental Survey, 1882-84; engr. and astronomer Panama Canal Co., 1888; geographer U.S. Geol. Survey, 1889—. Lecturer. Home: Washington, D.C. Died 1903.

GOODELL, Charles Elmer, educator; b. Washburn, Ill., Mar. 17, 1862; s. Harrison and Mary (Taylor) G.; A.B., Franklin (Ind.) Coll., 1888, A.M., 1891; post-grad. work, Cornell U., 1890-92, U. of Chicago, 1898-1900; LL.D., Colgate U., 1918; m. Laura B. Ogle, Aug. 6, 1890 (died 1921); children—Charles Lawrence, Robert Taylor; m. 2d, Bertha M. Smith, Aug. 24, 1923. Prin. high sch., Mankato, Minn., 1892-94; prof. history and polit. science, Franklin Coll., 1894-1900; fellow polit. science, U. of Chicago, 1898-1900, Kan. State Agrl. Coll., 1900-03; head history and polit. science dept., registrar and dir. summer sch., Denison U., Granville, O., 1903-17; pres. Franklin Coll., 1917-26 (resigned); pres. Am. Coll. Bur. and Fisk Teachers' Agency, Chicago, 1927—. Baptist. Editor College Bulletin. Home: Chicago, Ill. Died June 10, 1931.

GOODELL, Charles Le Roy, clergyman; b. Dudley, Mass., July 31, 1854; s. Warren and Clarinda (Healy) G.; A.B., Boston U., 1877; A.M., New York U., 1900; D.D., Wesleyan U., 1906; m. Mary F. Blair, June 3, 1896; children—Lucius Le Roy, Earl Warren, Charles Edwin (dec.), Francis Dudley Blair, Mary Clarinda, Chester Corbin. Entered N.E. Southern Conf., M.E. Ch., serving ch. at Acushnet, 1879; pastor Broadway Ch., Providence, 1880-82, Chestnut St. Ch., Providence, 1883-85, Trinity, Providence, 1886-88; N.E. Conf., Winthrop St. Ch., Boston, 1885-93, First Ch., Boston, 1894-96; New York East Conf., Hanson Place Ch., Brooklyn, 1897-1903, Calvary Ch., New York, 1904-13, St. Paul's, New York, 1913-18; in charge religious work, Camp Meade, Md., 1918; exec. sec. Commn. on Evangelism, Federal Council Chs. of Christ, 1918. Republican. Author: My Mother's Bible, 1891; The Drill Master of Methodism, 1902; The Price of Winning Souls, 1906; Pathways to the Best, 1907; Pastoral and Personal Evangelism, 1907; The Old Darnman; Followers of the Gleam, 1911; Heralds of a Passion, 1921; Pastor and Evangelist, 1922; What Are You Worth?, 1923; Motives and Methods of Modern Evangelism, 1925; The Book We Love, 1929; Twilight Reveries, 1929; Life Reveries, 1930; Soul Reveries, 1931; Prayers of Sabbath Reveries, 1931; Black Tavern Tales, 1932; Radiant Reveries. Address: New York, N.Y. Died April 27, 1937.

GOODELL, David Harvey, governor; b. Hillsboro, N.H., May 6, 1834; s. Deacon Jesse Raymond and Olive Atwood (Wright) G.; grad. Francestown Acad., 1852; student Brown U., 1852-53; hon. A.M., Brown, and Dartmouth, 1889; m. Hannah Jane Plumer, Sept. 1, 1857. Taught sch. and farmed for several yrs.; treas., bookkeeper and gen. agt. Antrim Shovel Co., and its successor, Treadwell & Co., 1857-64; in company with George R. Carter, began mfr. of apple parers, of which was inventor under firm name of D. H. Goodell & Co., the business now conducted as the Goodell Co. Mem. N.H. Ho. of Rep., 1876-78; mem. State Bd. of Agr., 1876-83; mem. Governor's Council, 1883-85; gov. of N.H., 1889-91. Republican. Trustee Colby Acad., New London, N.H. Pres. N.H. Anti-Saloon League. Address: Antrim, N.H. Died Jan. 22, 1915.

GOODELL, Henry Hill, pres. Mass. Agrl. Coll.; b. Constantinople, Turkey, May 20, 1839; s. Rev. William G., missionary; grad. Amherst, 1862 (A.M., 1865; LL.D., 1891); m. Helen E. Stanton, Dec. 10, 1873. Served in Union army, 1862-63, a.d.c. on staff of Col. Bissell of 19th army corps. Prof. modern languages, Williston Sem., Easthampton, Mass., 1864-67; prof. Mass. Agrl. Coll., 1867-86, pres., 1886—. Home: Amherst, Mass. Died 1905.

GOODELL, Roswell Eaton, pres. Denver Stock Exchange; b. Abington, Conn., Oct. 21, 1825; s. Roswell and Olive Goodell; came to Ill., 1834; attended school, Ottawa, Ill., in winters and worked on farm summers to age of 15. Clerked in gen. store in Chicago; returned to Ottawa and became deputy county recorder. Served in Judge T. Lyle Dickey's company, in Mexican war, 1846-47; deputy sheriff La Salle Co., Ill., 1848; sheriff, 1850; sec. Ill. State senate, 1853-54; sec. Ill. Canal Commn., 1854; cashier Merchants' and Drovers' Bank, Joliet, Ill., 1854; treas. and dir. Chicago & Alton R.R., 1854-59; supt., 1858; gave George M. Pullman 1st order for palace coach; Ill. mem. bd. visitors to West Point, 1858; organized 20th Ill. Inf., 1861; interested in govt. contracts for war supplies, 1861-65; removed to Chicago, 1871; pres. 4th Nat. Bank, 1874-75; later city marshal Chicago; acting chmn. Dem. State Central Com. of Ill., 1876; chmn. city and county Dem. coms., Chicago, 1877; removed to Colo., 1878; postmaster Leadville, 1886-90; secured govt. fish hatchery at base of Mt. Massive, Leadville, Colo.; one of World's Columbian Commn., 1890-93; largely interested in mining enterprises. Democrat. Home: Denver, Colo. Died 1903.

GOODELL, Thomas Dwight, univ. prof.; b. Ellington, Conn., Nov. 8, 1854; s. Francis and Sophia Louisa (Burpee) G.; A.B., Yale, 1877, Ph.D., 1884; studied in Europe, 1886-87; m. J. Harriet Andross, May 9, 1878. Classical teacher High Sch., Hartford, 1877-88; asst. prof. Greek, 1888-93, prof. Greek lang. and lit., 1893—, Yale. Prof. same, Am. Sch. Classical Studies, Athens, 1894-95 (mem. mng. com. same, 1908—). Author: The Greek in English, 1886; Greek Lessons, 1892; Chapters on Greek Metric, 1901; Greek Festival Hymn for Yale U. (music by Horatio W. Parker), 1901; School Grammar of Attic Greek, 1902. Home: New Haven, Conn. Died July 7, 1920.

GOODENOUGH, George Alfred, college prof.; b. Davison, Mich., May 3, 1868; s. James Webster and Eliza (Gifford) G.; B.S., Mich. Agrl. Coll., 1891; grad. student, U. of Mich., 1892-93; M.E., U. of Ill., 1900; m. Elizabeth Clara Kitzmiller, Sept. 27, 1894. Instr. mechanics, Mich. Agrl. Coll.; 1891-93; text book writer, Internat. Corr. Schs., Scranton, Pa., 1893-95; instr. mech. engring., U. of Ill., 1895-97; editor, Internat. Corr. Schs., 1897-99; asst. prof. mech. engring., 1899-1906, asso. prof., 1906-11, prof. thermodynamics, 1911—, U. of Ill. Author: First Course in Calculus, 1908; Essentials of Calculus (with E. J. Townsend), 1910; Principles of Thermodynamics, 1911; Properties of Steam and Ammonia, 1915. Home: Urbana, Ill. Died Sept. 29, 1929.

GOODFELLOW, Edward, scientist; b. Philadelphia, Pa., Feb. 23, 1828; grad. U. of Pa., 1848; m. Julia C. Smiley, 1871. Entered service of U.S. Coast Survey as aid; in 1860 became asst. in U.S. Coast and Geodetic Survey and executive asst. in 1861-62, and again from 1875-82; then became editor of the Annual Reports of the Survey and other publications relating thereto. Home: Washington, D.C. Died 1899.

GOODHUE, Bertram Grosvenor, architect; b. Pomfret, Conn., Apr. 28, 1869; s. Charles Wells and Helen Grosvenor (Eldredge) G.; ed. Russell's Collegiate and Commercial Inst., New Haven, Conn.; hon. Sc.D., Trinity Coll., 1911; m. Lydia T. Bryant, Apr. 8, 1902. Studied architecture for 6½ yrs. under Renwick; became partner Cram & Wentworth, Nov. 1891, Cram, Goodhue & Ferguson until 1914; private practice, 1914—. Fellow Am. Inst. Architects; A.N.A., 1917, N.A., 1923; mem. Nat. Inst. Arts and Letters. Author: Mexican Memories. Address: New York, N.Y. Died Apr. 23, 1924.

GOODING, Frank R., U.S. senator; b. in England; came to U.S. with parents, 1867; educated pub. schs., Paw Paw, Mich.; went to California at 15, and to Idaho at 21. For many years a contractor for mining companies, and actively engaged in the stock and farming business, 20 yrs., being one of the largest owners of sheep in the state, and farming several thousand acres of land. Was mem. Ida. Senate; chmn. Rep. State Central Com., 4 yrs.; gov. of Ida., 1905-07; apptd. U.S. senator to fill unexpired term of John F. Nugent, Jan. 15, 1921, elected for terms, 1921-27 and 1927-33. Home: Gooding, Ida. Died June 24, 1928.

GOODKIND, Maurice Louis, M.D.; b. Chicago, Ill., Nov. 14, 1867; s. Louis G.; Williams Coll., 1885-86; M.D., Coll. Phys. and Surg. (Columbia), 1889; post-grad. work, Vienna and Munich; m. Rose S. Snydacker, 1896; children—G. L., Ruth, M. Lewis. Attending physician Cook County Hosp., 14 yrs., Michael Reese Hosp., 29 yrs.; prof. clin. medicine, U. of Ill. Coll. of Medicine; specializes in internal medicine. Was chief of med. service, Base Hospital 53, U.S. Army, Langres, France; col. Med. R.C. Officier the French Acad., silver palm, for services during war. Republican. Mason. Home: Chicago, Ill. Died Jan. 4, 1939.

GOODKNIGHT, James Lincoln, church sec.; b. Mt. Aeriel, Ky., Aug. 24, 1846; s. Isaac and Lucinda (Billingsley) G.; A.B., Cumberland U., 1871, A.M., 1896; Union Theol. Sem., 1879; post-grad. studies and first honors in philosophy, U. of Edinburgh, 1889-90; U. of Jena, 1890-91; (D.D., Waynesburg Coll., 1890; LL.D., Cumberland U., 1903); traveled extensively in Europe, Egypt, Palestine, Syria, Turkey, Greece; m. Chattie Williams, May 1881 (died 1882); m. 2d, Alice Cleaver, Dec. 1884 (died 1886); m. 3d, Mrs. Estelle Biddle Elliott, June 1889 (died 1911); m. 4th, Mrs. Edna Whitaker Perry, July 8, 1913. Ordained Cumberland Presbyn. ministry, 1872; pastor, Little Muddy, Pilot Knob and Casper River, Ky., 1871-76, Covington, O., 1879-89, Waynesburg, Pa., 1891-95; pres. W.Va. U., 1895-97; farmer, 1897-1900; organizer and cashier Citizens' Nat. Bank, Covington, O., 1900; pres. Lincoln (Ill.) U., 1900-04; half owner and business mgr. The Courier Co. (newspapers), 1904-11. Stated clk. and treas. Gen. Assembly Cumberland Presbyn. Ch., and gen. traveling sec., 1907—. Prominent opposer of merging the Cumberland Presbyn. Ch. into Presbyn. Ch. U.S.A., 1906. Home: Lincoln, Ill. Died Oct. 2, 1914.

GOODMAN, Mrs. Jean R.; b. Wayne County, Ind., Feb. 2, 1870; d. William and Esther (Starbuck) Strawbridge; grad. South Div. High Sch., Chicago, Ill., 1886; student U. of Chicago, 1893-94; m. Herbert E. Goodman, Oct. 3, 1893 (dec.); children—William E., Howard, Grace. Mem. bd. mgrs. Woman's Bapt. Foreign Mission Soc. of West, 1900-14; mem. bd. mgrs. Woman's Am. Bapt. Foreign Mission Soc., 1914-24, pres., 1924-33. Attended Bapt. World Alliance, Stockholm, Sweden, 1923, Jerusalem Conf., 1928. Has visited mission field in Japan, China, Philippine Islands, Burma, India, Egypt and the Holy Land, 1926, Africa, from Belgian Congo to Cape Town (2000 miles by airplane), 1928. Home: Chicago, Ill. Died July 31, 1934.

GOODMAN, William Owen, lumberman; b. Wellsboro, Pa., Sept. 24, 1848; s. Owen Bruner and Susan (Barber) G.; 1st maternal ancestor Barber came to Pa. with William Penn, 1682; parents died when he was very young, and was put under care of grandparents and aunts at Columbia, Pa.; ed. Columbian Inst. and later at Athens, Pa.; m. Erna M. Sawyer, Oct. 31, 1878; 1 son, Kenneth Sawyer (died 1918). In 1866 entered employ of uncle, Gen. Williston, lumber dealer at Athens, Pa.; removed to Chicago, 1868, and became bookkeeper, and, in 1869, salesman for Spalding & Porter, lumber; soon after represented interests of Hon. Philetus Sawyer and also began investing in lumber business on own account at various points in Ill., Ia. and Neb.; with others organized firm of Sawyer, Goodman & Co., 1878, inc., 1880, as Sawyer-Goodman Co., of which was pres.; v.p. Goodman (Wis.) Lumber Co. Founder Goodman Theatre (Chicago)—in memory of son Kenneth Sawyer Goodman; pres. Friends of Am. Art, Art Assn. of Old Lyme, Conn.; v.p. Am. Federation of Art (hon.); trustee and governing life mem. and hon. v.p. Art Inst. Chicago; trustee Chicago Orchestra Assn. Republican. Died Mar. 22, 1936.

GOODNIGHT, Cloyd, coll. pres.; b. Michigantown, Ind., Dec. 2, 1881; s. John and Ida Layton G.; B.A., Butler Coll., Indianapolis, 1906, M.A., 1907; studied U. of Chicago, 1912; D.D., U. of Pittsburgh, 1921; LL.D., Butler U., 1929; m. Anna Hussey, Nov. 20, 1907; children—John Thomas, Ida Frances. Ordained ministry Christian (Disciples) Ch., 1907; pastor Danville, Ind., 1907-09, Shelbyville, 1910-13, Uniontown, Pa., 1913-19; pres. Bethany Coll., 1919—. Home: Bethany, W.Va. Died Oct. 15, 1932.

GOODNIGHT, Isaac Herschel, circuit judge of 7th Ky. dist., Jan. 1898, to Jan. 1904; b. Allen County, Ky., Jan. 31, 1849; s. Isaac and Lucinda (Billingsley) G.; prep. edn., Franklin, Ky.; grad. Cumberland U., Lebanon, Tenn.; studied law, same; admitted to bar, Mar. 1874; m. Ella Hoy, Franklin, Ky., Mar. 12, 1879. Served in Ky. legislature, 1877-78; mem. Congress, 1889-95 (mem. com. on invalid pensions and judiciary); pres. The J. A. McGoodwin Banking Co., Franklin, Ky. Democrat. Home: Franklin, Ky. Died 1901.

GOODNOW, Charles Allen, ry. official; b. Baldwinsville, Mass., Dec. 22, 1853; s. Josiah B. and Abigail R. (Wheeler) G.; ed. pub. schs.; m. Josephine A. B. Gleason, Oct. 3, 1876. Entered ry. service, 1868, and was consecutively with Vt. & Mass. R.R., Fitchburg, Troy & Greenfield Ry. and Hoosac Tunnel N.Y.,W.S.&B. as trainmaster and train dispatcher; with C.,M.&St.P. Ry. as supt. of constrn., div. supt., asst. gen. supt. and gen. supt., 1884-1902; gen. mgr. C.,R.I.&P. Ry., 1902-03; gen. mgr. C.&A. Ry., 1903-08; asst. to the pres. C.,M.& Puget Sound Ry., 1908-13; asst. to the pres., 1913-17, v.p., 1917—, C.,M.&St.P. Ry.; pres. Gallatin Valley Ry. Co.; v.p. Puget Sound & Willapa Harbor Ry. Co. Republican. Home: Evanston, Ill. Died July 27, 1918.

GOODNOW, Frank Johnson, univ. pres.; b. Brooklyn, Jan. 18, 1859; s. Abel F. and Jane M. (Root) G.; A.B., Amherst, 1879, A.M., 1887; LL.B., Columbia, 1882; studied École Libre des Sciences Politiques, Paris, and U. of Berlin; LL.D., Amherst, 1897, Columbia, 1904, Harvard, 1909, Brown, 1914, Princeton,

1917, Johns Hopkins, 1930; J.D., U. of Louvain, 1927; m. Elizabeth Lyall, June 2, 1886. Instr. history and lecturer administrative law of U.S., 1883-87, adj. prof. same, 1887-91, prof. administrative law, 1891-1903, Eaton prof. administrative law and municipal science, 1903, acting dean of polit. science, 1906-07, Columbia. Legal adviser to Chinese Govt., Mar. 13, 1913-14; pres. Johns Hopkins U., 1914-29, emeritus. Author: Comparative Administrative Law, 1893; Municipal Home Rule, 1895; Municipal Problems, 1897; Politics and Administration, 1900; City Government in the United States, 1904; Principles of the Administrative Law of the United States, 1905; Municipal Government, 1910; Social Reform and the Constitution, 1911; Principles of Constitutional Government, 1916. Editor: Selected Cases on the Law of Taxation, 1905; Selected Cases on Government and Administration, 1906; Selected Cases on the Law of Officers, 1906; Principles of Constitutional Government, 1916; China, an Analysis, 1926. Address: Baltimore, Md. Died Nov. 15, 1939.

GOODNOW, John, U.S. consul general at Shanghai, 1897—; b. Greensburg, Ind., June 29, 1858; s. James Goodnow, lt. col. 12th Ind. vols.; grad. U. of Minn., 1879; m. Elizabeth Beaver, Dec. 7, 1897. Republican. Lived in Minneapolis until apptd. consul gen. Apptd. commr. to negotiate treaty with China, 1902. Address: Shanghai, China. Died 1907.

GOODRELL, Mancil Clay, brig. gen. U.S. Marine Corps; b. Cambridge, O., Nov. 9, 1843; s. Stewart and Jane Priscilla (Israel) G.; ed. pub. schs. and Dr. Nash's Acad., Des Moines, Ia.; m. Emily Truxtun Read, Nov. 14, 1872. Served during Civil War in 15th Ia. Vols., Army of the Tenn.; apptd. from Ia. 2d lt. U.S. Marine Corps, Mar. 9, 1865; promoted 1st lt., Apr. 21, 1870; capt., Aug. 16, 1886; maj., Mar. 3, 1889; lt. col., Mar. 3, 1899; col., Mar. 3, 1903; brig. gen. and retired, Jan. 31, 1906. Served on flagship New York during war with Spain and later in P.I. Died May 23, 1925.

GOODRICH, Arthur (Frederick), author; b. New Britain, Conn., Feb. 18, 1878; s. Fred and Eva (Emmons) G.; Ph.B., Wesleyan U., Middletown, Conn., 1899, hon. M.A., 1927; univ. scholar in English, Columbia, 1899-1900; m. Alice Elizabeth Dougherty, May 15, 1907 (died 1920); children—Evelyn Hampden, Eleanor Wells, Elizabeth Ocain. With Doubleday, Page & Co., publishers, 1900-01; managing editor, The World's Work, 1901-03; asso. editor, The Outing Magazine, 1903-04; foreign editorial rep., with residence in London, of Outing Mag. and American Mag., 1904-05; editorial staff, Outing Pub. Co., 1905-06; mfr., 1906-14. Capt. U.S.A., 1918; capt. Gen. Staff, U.S.A., 1919; maj. R.C., U.S.A., 1919-29. Trustee Wesleyan U., 1923-35. Republican. Methodist. Author: The Story of the Welsh Revival, 1905; The Balance of Power, 1906; Gleam o' Dawn, 1908; The Lady Without Jewels, 1909; The Yardstick Man, 1910; The Man with an Honest Face, 1911; The Sign of Freedom, 1916; Yes or No (play), prod. 1917; So This Is London! (play) prod. 1922; The Ring of Truth (play), prod. 1923; The Joker (play), prod. 1925; You Don't Understand (play), prod. 1926; Caponsacchi (play, winning Theatre Club gold medal for best play of the year), prod. 1926, pub. 1927; The Plutocrat (play), prod. 1929; Richelieu (play), prod. 1930, pub., 1931; The Perfect Marriage (play), prod. 1932; (grand opera libretto) Tragedy in Arezzo, prod. in Germany, 1932, and at Metropolitan Opera House, New York, under title "Caponsacchi," 1937; Mr. Grant (play), 1934; A Journey by Night (play) prod. 1935; You Wouldn't Believe It, 1936; I Can't Help It (play), prod. 1938. Address: New York, N.Y. Died June 26, 1941.

GOODRICH, Caspar Frederick, naval officer; b. Phila., Jan. 7, 1847; s. William and Sarah A. (Bearden) G.; grad. U.S. Naval Acad., 1864; hon. A.M., Yale, 1888; D.Sc., Princeton, 1919; m. Eleanor Milnor, Sept. 4, 1873; m. 2d, Sarah M. Hays. Ensign, Nov. 1, 1866; master, Dec. 1, 1866; lt., Mar. 12, 1868; lt. comdr., Mar. 26, 1869; comdr., Sept. 27, 1884; capt., Sept. 16, 1897; rear adm., Feb. 17, 1904; retired, Jan. 7, 1909. Commandant Naval Unit, Princeton U., 1918, and officer Material Sch. for the Pay Corps, Princeton, N.J., 1918-19. Naval del. to Historical Conv., Saragossa, Spain, 1908. Gold medalist, U.S. Naval Inst.; pres. Naval History Soc., 1914-16. Home: Princeton, N.J. Died Dec. 26, 1925.

GOODRICH, Chauncey, missionary; b. Hinsdale, Mass., June 4, 1836; s. Elijah Hubbard and Mary Northrop (Washburn) G.; A.B., Williams, 1861; student Union Theol. Sem., 1862; grad. Andover Theol. Sem., 1864; D.D., Williams, 1891, L.H.D., 1917; Litt.D., Peking (China) U., 1917; m. Sarah Boardman Clapp, May 13, 1880. Missionary A.B.C.F.M. in China, 1865—; teacher in Gordon Miss. Theol. Sem., 1873-1911, dean 25 yrs.; prof. astronomy and Christian evidences, N. China Coll. Engaged as chmn. of com. of 5 in translating the Bible into the colloquial language of China, the book to be known as the Universal Mandarin Colloquial Bible (language spoken by ¾ of the people of China). Wrote: Pocket Chinese-English Dictionary (10,400 characters); A Character Study of Mandarin Colloquial, 39,000 sentences. Joint editor (with Henry Blodget) of Chinese hymnal, and mus. editor of same; translator and composer of many Chinese hymns. Address: Peking, China. Died Sept. 29, 1925.

GOODRICH, Frank, college prof.; b. Dryden, N.Y., Apr. 21, 1856; s. Milo and Eunice Amanda (Eastman) G.; B.A., Yale, 1880; studied univs. of Leipzig, Heidelberg, Berlin and Halle, 1882-83, 1892-93; Ph.D., Halle, 1893; m. Kate M. Hara, Aug. 16, 1881; children—Dorothy Allen, Charlotte Phelps. Teacher Latin and Greek, Auburn (N.Y.) High Sch., 1880-81; prin. N. Adams (Mass.) High Sch., 1884-87; instr. German, Yale, 1887-91, 1893-94; prof. German and European history, 1894-1903, prof. European history, 1904-24, Williams Coll. Editor: Freytag's Dokter Luther, 1894; Goethe's Götz von Berlichingen, 1896. Home: New York, N.Y. Died Apr. 29, 1929.

GOODRICH, James Putnam, governor; b. Winchester, Ind., Feb. 18, 1864; s. John Bell and Elizabeth Putnam (Edger) Goodrich; ed. DePauw U.; LL.D., Wabash Coll., U. of Notre Dame; Sc.D., Hanover College; m. Cora Frist, 1888. Admitted to Indiana bar, 1886, and practiced in Winchester and Indianapolis; receiver Chicago, Cincinnati & Louisville R.R.; pres. Peoples Loan & Trust Co. Chmn. Rep. State Central Com., 10 yrs.; mem. Rep. Nat. Exec. Com., 8 yrs.; gov. of Ind., 1917-21. Mem. exec. com. Gt. Lakes-St. Lawrence Tide Water Assn.; chmn. Indiana-St. Lawrence Waterways Com.; mem. Internat. St. Lawrence Waterways Commn. by apptmt. of President; mem. Nat. Conservation Commn., by apptmt. of President Hoover; trustee Roosevelt Memorial Commn., Am. Child Welfare Assn.; mem. and trustee Am. Relief Adminstrn.; mem. Russian Relief Commn. by apptmt. of President making 4 trips to Russia; v.p. and mem. exec. com. Civil Legion of America. Trustee Wabash Coll. (pres. bd.), Presbyn. Theol. Sem., Chicago. Presbyn. Mason. Home: Winchester, Ind. Died Aug. 15, 1940.

GOODRICH, John Ellsworth, univ. prof.; b. Hinsdale, Mass., Jan. 19, 1831; s. Elijah Hubbard and Mary Northrop (Washburn) G.; A.B., U. of Vt., 1853, A.M., 1856; grad. Andover Theol. Sem., 1860; D.D., U. of Vt., 1897; m. Ellen Miranda Moody, Feb. 8, 1869. Chaplain 1st Vt. Cav., 1864-65; prin. of acads., Mass., Vt., N.H., between 1853 and 1872; supt. Burlington (Vt.) schs., 1868-70; prof. rhetoric and Latin, 1872-77, Greek and Latin, 1877-89, Latin, 1889-1907, prof. emeritus, 1907, librarian, 1873-86, dean dept. of arts, 1903-07, U. of Vt. Home: Burlington, Vt. Died Feb. 24, 1915.

GOODRICH, Joseph King, author; b. Phila., Jan. 13, 1850; s. William and Sarah Ann (Bearden) G.; ed. Hopkins Grammar Sch., New Haven, Conn.; Del. Lit. Inst., Franklin, N.Y.; m. Jennie Turner Sponsler, Oct. 25, 1897. Organized dept. of ethnology, U.S. Nat. Museum, Washington, 1881-84; asst. editor Smithsonian Instn., 1884-86; prof. English, Imperial Govt. Coll., Osaka, and later Kyoto, Japan, 1886-1910. Republican. Episcopalian. Author: The Coming China, 1911; Africa of Today, 1912; Russia in Europe and Asia, 1912; The Coming Mexico, 1913; Our Neighbors: The Japanese, 1913. Home: Brooklyn, N.Y. Died Aug. 13, 1921.

GOODRICH, William W., jurist; b. Havana, N.Y., Aug. 23, 1833; s. David and Mary Wenton G.; ed. Amherst Coll., LL.D., and Albany Law School, LL.B., 1853; m. Frances A. Wickes, Sept. 10, 1857. Admitted to the bar, 1854. Maj. N.G.S.N.Y.; was chmn. Bd. of Edn.; del. to Internat. Maritime Conf., Washington, 1889; pres. Rep. gen. com., 1886-87; mem. assembly, 1866-70. Pres. justice appellate div. Supreme Court, N.Y., 1896-1904; del. diplomatic conf. at Brussels to formulate treaty on Maritime Law. Also counsel for Justice Warren B. Hooker in proceedings for impeachment or removal. Home: Brooklyn, N.Y. Died 1906.

GOODSELL, Charles True, coll. prof.; b. Medina, N.Y., Mar. 2, 1886; s. William Edward and Josephine (Chase) G.; A.B., U. of Rochester (N.Y.), 1909; D.B., Colgate-Rochester Divinity School, 1912; A.M., U. of Chicago, 1924; LL.D., Kalamazoo Coll., 1936; m. Frances Elizabeth Comee, Sept. 10, 1920; children—Betty Jo, Barbara Jean, Charles True. Ordained Bapt. ministry, 1912; pastor Emmanuel Ch., Sparks, Nev., 1912-18, Central Ch., Olympia, Wash., 1918-21, First Ch., Mendota, Ill., 1921-24, First Ch., Lafayette, Ind., 1924-28; head of history dept., Kalamazoo (Mich.) Coll., 1928—, v.p., 1933-35, actg. pres., 1935-36. Served with Y.M.C.A., A.E.F., 1917-18. Mason, Odd Fellow, K.P. Author: (with W. F. Dunbar) A Centennial History of Kalamazoo College, 1933. Home: Kalamazoo, Mich. Died Nov. 25, 1941.

GOODSELL, Daniel Ayres, M.E. bishop, 1888—; b. Newburg, N.Y., Nov. 5, 1840; prepared at Clinton Acad.; grad. Univ. City of New York, 1859 (S.T.D., Wesleyan, Conn.; D.D., New York U.; LL.D., Dickinson, Pa.); entered ministry, M.E. Ch., 1859; m. S. F. Loweree, June 5, 1860. Lit. editor Christian Advocate, New York, 1880-88; sec. bd. of edn., M.E. Ch., 1888. Has officially visited China, Japan, Korea, Italy, Bulgaria, Switzerland, Germany, Scandinavia, Finland, and nearly the entire U.S. Author: Nature and Character at Granite Bay, 1901 M4; The Things Which Remain, 1904. Home: Brookline, Mass. Died 1909.

GOODSPEED, Frank Lincoln, clergyman; b. Moretown, Vt., Mar. 15, 1861; s. Hiram and Rebecca V. (Blackstone) G.; A.B., Harvard, 1890; S.T.B., Boston U., 1891; D.D., Fairmount Coll., 1905; m. Cora Belle Spaulding, June 29, 1884. Ordained Congl. ministry, 1887; pastor Mattapoisett, Mass., 1887-90, Amherst, Mass., 1891-94, First Ch., Springfield, Mass., 1894-1908, First Presbyn. Ch., Oakland, Calif., 1908—. Coll. preacher at Amherst, Williams, Vassar, etc.; preached London, 6 summers. Corporate mem. A.B.C.F.M.; mem. exec. com. Nat. Congl. Home Missionary Soc.; pres. Mass. C.E. Union, 1896; pres. Conn. Valley Congl. Club, 1896; asst. moderator Nat. Congl. Council, 1907; del. Internat. Congl. Council, Edinburgh, 1908; commr. to Presbyn. Gen. Assembly, 1911. Author: Palestine—A Fifth Gospel, 1902. Address: Oakland, Calif. Died July 20, 1941.

GOODSPEED, George Stephen, theologian, educator; b. Janesville, Wis., Jan. 14, 1860; s. Edgar Johnson and Caroline (Raymond) G.; grad. Brown Univ. 1880, A.M. 1883; studied Rochester Theol. Sem., 1881; Bapt. Union Theol. Sem., Chicago, 1881-83, B.D., 1883; Yale U., 1888-91, Ph.D., 1891; student Freiburg in Baden, 1891-92; m. Florence D. Mills, Aug. 7, 1884. Pastor Bapt. chs. Sonora, Calif., 1884-86; Springfield, Mass., 1886-88; recorder U. of Chicago, 1895-1901; prof. comparative religion and ancient history, 1892—. Asso. editor Biblical World and Am. Journal of Theology. Author: Outlines of Lectures on the History of the Hebrews, 1898; Israel's Messianic Hope, 1900; History of the Babylonians and Assyrians, 1902. Home: Chicago, Ill. Died 1905.

GOODSPEED, Thomas Wakefield; b. Glens Falls, N.Y., Sept. 4, 1842; s. Stephen and Jane (Johnson) G.; studied Prep. Sch. of Knox Coll., 1857; U. of Chicago, 1859-62; A.B., U. of Rochester, 1863; grad. Rochester Theol. Sem., 1866; D.D., U. of Chicago, 1885; LL.D., U. of Rochester, 1913; m. Mary Ellen Ten Broeke, Sept. 4, 1866 (died 1921); children—Charles Ten Broeke, Edgar Johnson. Was ordained to ministry, 1865; pastoral supply, North Ch., Chicago, 1865; pastor Vermont St. Ch., Quincy, Ill., 1866-72; asso. pastor Second Ch., Chicago, 1872-76; pastor Morgan Park Ch., Chicago, 1877-80; sec. Bapt. Union Theol. Sem., Chicago, 1876-89; assisted, 1889-90, in raising the funds, $1,000,000, for founding new U. of Chicago; sec. bd. trustees, 1890-1913, registrar, 1897-1913, corr. sec., 1913—, U. of Chicago. Sec. and mem. bd. trustees Bapt. Theol. Union, 1894—, Francis Shimer Acad., 1895-1914, Chicago Manual Training Assn., 1897-1913; mem. bd. trustees Chicago Bapt. Hosp., 1895-1900; sec. Rush Med. Coll. Bd., 1898-1913; pres. U. of Rochester Central Alumni Assn., 1904-05. Pres. Village of Morgan Park, Ill., 1889; trustee U. of Chicago, 1906-13. Author: A History of the University of Chicago, 1916; The University of Chicago Biographical Sketches, Vol. I, 1922, Vol. II, 1925; The Story of The University of Chicago, 1925. Home: Chicago, Ill. Died Dec. 16, 1927.

GOODWILLIE, David Lincoln, mfr.; b. Chicago, Ill., July 21, 1863; s. David and Cecilia C. G.; ed. Lake View High Sch., Chicago; unmarried. Succeeded, with brothers, to lumber and box mfg. business estab. by father in 1857, mills at Wausau, Wis., and Manistique, Mich.; mem. firm Goodwillie Bros.; organizer and pres. Goodwillie Green Box Co. Organized 1st Batt., 2d Reserve Regt., Ill. N.G., 1918, also band, hosp. and motor corps for same. Chmn. Chicago Zoning Conf., 1919. Home: Chicago, Ill. Died Dec. 16, 1924.

GOODWIN, Arthur C., artist; b. Portsmouth, N.H., Sept. 12, 1874; s. Joseph W. and Annie M. (Briggs) G.; self-taught; married. Landscape and figure painter; exhibited at Carnegie Inst., Pa. Acad. Fine Arts, Art Inst. Chicago, Nat. Acad. Design; represented in Union and St. Botolph Clubs, Boston, and in many pvt. collections. Address: New York, N.Y. Deceased.

GOODWIN, Charles Jaques, prof. Greek; b. Farmington, Me., Mar. 13, 1866; s. Benjamin and Nancy Lander (Durrell) G.; A.B., Bowdoin, 1887, A.M., 1890; Ph.D., Johns Hopkins, 1890; studied U. of Berlin, 1896; m. Ellen Converse Blagden, Oct. 23, 1902 (died 1904). Prof. Greek, Cornell Coll., 1890-92; instr. Greek, Wesleyan U., Conn., 1892-95; prof. Greek, St. Stephen's Coll., 1898-99, Lehigh U., 1899—. Episcopalian. Author: The Rose and the Thorn, 1900. Home: Bethlehem, Pa. Died Sept. 19, 1935.

GOODWIN, Daniel, clergyman; b. Sutton, Mass., Mar. 10, 1835; s. Daniel Le Baron and Rebecca (Wilkinson) G.; A.M., Brown U., 1857, Ph.D., 1895, D.D., 1903; grad. General Theol. Sem., New York, 1862; m. Hannah Allen Eldred, June 1, 1875; m. 2d, Adeline Ellis Vaughan, Feb. 17, 1886. Deacon, 1862, priest, 1863, P.E. Ch.; rector St. John's, Bangor, Me., 1862-69, St. Paul's, Wickford, R.I., 1869-74, St. Paul's, Dedham, Mass., 1874-79, St. Luke's, East Greenwich, R.I., 1879-92. Editor: The Mac Sparran Diary, 1899; History of the Narragansett Church, 1907; The Gardiners of Narragansett, 1919. Wrote The History of Religions in Rhode Island in new "History of Rhode Island to the Close of the 19th Century," 1902. Address: East Greenwich, R.I. Died Aug. 28, 1922.

GOODWIN, Edward C., lawyer, librarian; b. St. Albans, Me.; ed. pub. schs. and Classical Inst., Waterville, Me.; m. Mabel Hall, Apr. 24, 1895; 1 dau., Mabel Hall; m. 2d, Grace Louise White, Apr. 28, 1906. In employ U.S. Senate, 1887-1921 and 1923—; clk. Com. on the Judiciary and other Senate coms., 1887-1904; sec. to late U.S. Senator George F. Hoar, 1893-1904; actg. librarian, 1904-05, librarian, 1906-21 and 1923—, U.S. Senate. Mem. of Mass. bar, Circuit Ct. of U.S., Dist. of Mass., and Supreme Ct. of U.S.; asso. with law firm Baker & Baker, Washington, D.C. Joint compiler of Consolidated Index to U.S. Statutes at Large, 1789-1903. Address: Washington, D.C. Died Nov. 26, 1930.

GOODWIN, Edward Jasper, educator; b. Sanford, Me., May 6, 1848; s. Charles E. and Dorcas P. (Libby) G.; A.B., Bates Coll., Me., 1872, Litt.D., 1895; L.H.D., Amherst, 1905; m. Ida I. Nute, July 15, 1874. Prin. high schs., Farmington, N.H., 1872-81, Portsmouth, N.H., 1881-84, Nashua, N.H., 1884-87, Newton, Mass., 1887-97, Morris High Sch., New York, 1897-1904; asst. commr. of edn. for State of N.Y., 1904-08; prin. Packer Collegiate Inst., Brooklyn, 1908-18. Home: Pine Point, Me. Died Apr. 29, 1931.

GOODWIN, Edward Jewett, M.D.; b. Washington, Mo., Aug. 3, 1864; s. Robert Allan and Harriet Amanda (Perryman) G.; prep. edn. pub. schs. and Smith Acad., St. Louis, Mo.; M.D., Washington U. Medical Dept., 1894. Began practice in St. Louis, 1894. Editor Journal of Mo. State Med. Assn., 1904-38, sec.-editor emeritus, 1938; asso. editor Interstate Med. Jour., St. Louis, 1903-10. Democrat. Baptist. Home: St. Louis, Mo. Died Feb. 18, 1941.

GOODWIN, E(dward) McKee, supt. school for the deaf; b. Wake County, N.C., Apr. 12, 1859; s. S. P. and Delia (Yates) G.; prep. edn., Raleigh Male Acad.; L.I., U. of Nashville (now Peabody Teachers Coll.), 1884; M.A., Peabody, 1896; L.H.D., Wake Forest (N.C.) Coll., 1932; Litt.D., Gallaudet Coll., 1935; m. Maude Fuller Broadaway, June 1894; children—Louise Winston (Mrs. Carl E. Rankin), Miriam Fuller, Maude Broadaway (Mrs. Leonhard Nurk), Edith Adele. Supt. Kinston (N.C.) Schs., 1884-85; teacher N.C. Sch. for Deaf and Blind, Raleigh, 1885-86, Iowa Sch. for the Deaf, Council Bluffs, 1886-88; engaged in propaganda for ednl. legislation and for establishing N.C. Sch. for the Deaf, 1889-91; founder, and pres. N.C. Sch. for the Deaf, laying first brick at Morganton, 1891; alderman, City of Raleigh, 1887; N.C. commr. to Paris Expn., 1889. Del. to World S.S. Conv., London, 1889; trustee N.C. State Normal Coll. for Women, 1891-94; trustee Meredith Coll. for Women, 1893—; dir. Am. Assn. to Promote Teaching of Speech to the Deaf, 1903—; v.p. and acting pres. Assn. of Am. Instructors of the Deaf, 1908; pres. Conf. of Executives of Am. Schs. for Deaf, 1926; mem. Com. on Melville Bell Memorial Citation by spl. joint act of Gen. Assembly of N.C., "for fifty years of distinguished service to the state in education of the deaf," 1935. Baptist. Mason. Home: Morganton, N.C. Died July 18, 1937.

GOODWIN, Elliot H.; b. Cambridge, Mass., Jan. 6, 1874; s. Hersey Bradford and Ellen Christina (Hopkinson) G.; A.B., Harvard, 1895, A.M., 1896; Ph.D., U. of Leipzig, 1900; m. Isabel M. Geer, Feb. 19, 1914; children—Katharine Throop, Eliot Hersey. Asst. sec. and sec. Nat. Civil Service Reform League, 1902-12; gen. sec. Chamber of Commerce, U.S.A., Aug. 1912-20, resident v.p. 1920-26; commr. of civil service, State of Mass., 1927—. Home: Cambridge, Mass. Died Feb. 15, 1931.

GOODWIN, Godfrey G., congressman; b. Nicollet County, Minn., Jan. 11, 1873; s. Gustavus and Cecilia G.; B.A., U. of Minn., 1895, LL.B., 1896; m. Geneva E. J. Gouldberg, June 5, 1905; children—Alden N., Margery Anne, Lois Geneva, Eleanore Elaine. Admitted to Minn. bar, 1896, and began practice at Cambridge; county atty. Isanti County, Minn., 20 yrs.; dir. First Nat. Bank, Cambridge; pres. Bd. of Edn. 17 yrs.; pres. Common Council, Cambridge, 1 yr.; U.S. Govt. appeal agt., World War; mem. 69th to 72d Congresses (1925-33), 10th Minn. Dist. Republican. Lutheran. Mason (32°, Shriner). Home: Cambridge, Minn. Died Feb. 16, 1933.

GOODWIN, Harold, lawyer; b. Brunswick, Me., Nov. 15, 1850; s. Daniel Raynes (D.D.) and Mary R. (Merrick) G.; A.B., U. of Pa., 1870, A.M., 1873, LL.B., 1873; m. Julia Murray McIlvaine, June 17, 1884 (died 1896); children—Mary Merrick (wife of Rev. Charles L. Storrs), Harold, Margaret Shippen, Daniel Rodman; m. 2d, Mary Shippen (McIlvaine) Spencer, Aug. 22, 1901 (died 1918). Practiced law in Phila. Republican. Home: Philadelphia, Pa. Died Aug. 17, 1935.

GOODWIN, John Benjamin, lawyer; b. Cobb County, Ga., Sept. 22, 1850; s. Williamson Harvey and Lucinda (Page) G.; ed. in pvt. grammar and high schs. of Ga.; m. Emma A. McAfee, Sept. 20, 1877 (died 1915); m. 2d, A. J. Norton, Feb. 22, 1916. Admitted to Ga. bar, 1871; reporter Daily Atlanta Herald, 1871-72; in gen. practice of law at Atlanta, 1874-1905; retired. Mem. gen. council, City of Atlanta, 1874-81; mayor of Atlanta, pro tempore, 1881; mayor, 1883-84 and 1893-94; city atty., Atlanta, 1885-93; mem. Ga. Ho. of Rep., 1890-91; chmn. of commn. to treat with Indians in Utah, Idaho, Ore., Wash. and Mont., 1896-97; mem. bd. commrs., Fulton County, Ga., 1903-04, chmn., 1905. Active in Odd Fellowship, Grand Master Grand Lodge, Ga., 1879-80, representative to Sovereign Grand Lodge, 1880-1900, Deputy Grand Sire, 1900-02, Grand Sire Sovereign Grand Lodge, I.O.O.F., 1902-04; Grand Sec. Sovereign Grand Lodge, I.O.O.F., 1905—. Home: Baltimore, Md. Died May 12, 1921.

GOODWIN, James Junius, capitalist; b. Hartford, Conn., Sept. 16, 1835; s. James and Lucy (Morgan) G.; ed. pvt. schs. and Hartford High Sch.; m. Josephine S. Lippincott, June 19, 1873. Dir. Erie R.R. Co., Conn. Mutual Life Ins. Co., Hartford Fire Ins. Co., Holyoke Water Power Co.; trustee Conn. Trust & Safe Deposit Co., Hartford. Address: Hartford, Conn. Died June 24, 1915.

GOODWIN, J(ohn) Cheever, dramatic author; b. Boston, July 14, 1850; s. E. Stone and A. Jane G.; A.B., Harvard, 1873; m. Ida B. Driggs, 1878. Reporter on Boston Traveler, 1873-74, pvt. sec. to comptroller New York, 1886-91; is "mugwump." Wrote plays (about 40) beginning with "Evangeline," 1874, down to "The Monks of Malabar," 1900. Leading plays: "Evangeline," "Wang," "The Merry Monarch," "Panjandrum," "Dr. Syntax," "The Lion Tamer," "Lost, Strayed or Stolen," etc. Home: New York, N.Y. Died Dec. 18, 1912.

GOODWIN, Lavinia Stella, author; b. St. Johnsbury, Vt.; d. James P. and Philura (Crocker) Tyler; ed. pub. and pvt. schs. and State Sem., Derby, Vt.; m. E. W. Goodwin (dec.). Teacher pub. schs.; connected with the press; asso. editor The Watchman and corr. for it and other journals at Centennial and Paris expns.; also as traveler in Europe and on Pacific Coast to the tropics; on editorial staff Journal of Education. Author: Little Folks' Own (collection of stories and verse); The Little Helper (biography); also The Mysterious Miner; Quicksands; The Light of Home; Wings, Legs and Voices; etc. Home: Boston, Mass. Died 1911.

GOODWIN, Maud Wilder, author; b. Ballston Spa, N.Y., June 5, 1856; d. John N. and Delia A. Wilder; m. Almon Goodwin, 1879. Author: The Colonial Cavalier; The Head of a Hundred; White Aprons; Flint, 1897; Sir Christopher, 1901; Life of Dolly Madison; Claims and Counter Claims, 1905; Veronica Playfair, 1909; Dutch and English on the Hudson (in Chronicles of America Series). Co-Editor: Open Sesame; Historic New York; Four Roads to Paradise, 1904. Home: New York, N.Y. Died Feb. 5, 1935.

GOODWIN Nat(haniel) C(arl), actor; b. Boston, July 25, 1857; s. Nathaniel C. and Caroline R. G.; ed. pub. and pvt. schs.; m. Eliza Weathersby, actress (died 1887); m. 2d, Maxine Elliott, Feb. 20, 1898; m. 4th at Boston, Edna Goodrich, actress, Nov. 8, 1908. Made début with Stuart Robson, Howard Athenæum, Boston, Mar. 5, 1873, in "The Law in New York"; played comedy parts until 1879; appeared as Modus in "The Hunchback" and as a grave digger in "Hamlet," Am. Dramatic Festival, Cincinnati, 1883; at Bijou Theatre, New York, 1885; played in "A Gold Mine" and "The Bookmaker," London, and in "The Nominee," 1890; later starred as Capt. Crostree, in "Black Eyed Susan," Rice's "Evangeline," "Hobbies," "The Member from Slocum," "In Mizzoura," "Nathan Hale," "The Skating Rink," "Cruets," "Confusion," "Turned Up," "A Gilded Fool," "David Garrick"; starred in "The Rivals," and "An American Citizen," 1896; "Nathan Hale," 1898; "The Cowboy and the Lady," 1899; "When We Were Twenty-One," 1900; played Shylock, in "The Merchant of Venice," 1901; appeared in "The Altar of Friendship," 1902; "The Usurper," 1903; played Bottom, in "A Midsummer Night's Dream," 1904; starred in "The Beauty and the Barge," 1905; "Wolfville," and "The Genius," 1906; "What Would a Gentleman Do," "The Master Hand," "The Easterner," 1908-09. Owner of restaurant, Ocean Park. Home: Boston, Mass. Died Jan. 31, 1919.

GOODWIN, Philip Arnold, congressman; b. Athens, N.Y., Jan. 20, 1882; s. John H. and Mary F. (Tolley) G.; grad. high sch. Coxsackie, 1900, Albany Bus. Coll., 1902; m. Eva M. Jeune, June 27, 1916; children—John H., Jean Elizabeth. Began as mgr.'s asst., Am. Bridge Co., 1902; contract agt. United Constrn. Co., 1904-18; prop. J. H. Goodwin & Son, lumber, 1917—; v.p. Coxsackie Milling & Supply Co., 1924-28; pres. Nat. Bank of Coxsackie, 1925—; pres. Goodwin-Griswold, Inc., 1928-32. Mem. 73d and 74th Congresses (1933-36), 27th N.Y. Dist. Republican. Methodist. Mason (32°), Odd Fellow, Granger. Home: Coxsackie, N.Y. Died June 6, 1937.

GOODWIN, Russell Parker, lawyer; b. Du Page County, Ill., Dec. 24, 1851; s. Jeremiah and Mary D. (Sedgwick) G.; ed. Jennings Sem., Aurora, Ill.; m. Nellia A. Ames, Aug. 1890. Admitted to Ill. bar, 1876; pub. administrator, Kane County, Ill., 1878-91; city atty., Aurora, 1886-89; mem. bd. of edn., Aurora, 1887-93; judge city courts of Aurora and Elgin, 1891-1903; presided over courts in Chicago at frequent intervals, 1898-1903; asst. atty. gen. for P.O. Dept., 1904-13. Republican. Conglist. Home: Washington, D.C. Died Dec. 2, 1916.

GOODWIN, William Archer Rutherfoord, clergyman, educator; b. Richmond, Va., June 18, 1869; s. John Frances and Lettie (Rutherfoord) G.; B.A. and M.A., Roanoke College, Salem, Va., 1889, D.D., 1907, LL.D., 1929; post-graduate study Richmond Coll., 1890; B.D., Va. Theol. Sem., 1893; m. Evelyn Tannor, 1895 (died 1915); children—Evelyn Withers (Mrs. Barclay Harding Farr), Katherine (Mrs. George C. Buell), T. Rutherfoord; m. 2d, Ethel Howard, June 1918; children—Edward Howard, William Archer Rutherfoord, John Seaton. Became deacon, 1893, priest, 1894, P.E. Church; was rector St. John's Church, Petersburg, 1893-1903; prof. Bishop Payne Div. Sch., 1893-1903; rector Bruton Parish, Williamsburg, 1903-09, St. Paul's Ch., Rochester, N.Y., 1909-23; head Dept. Bibl. Lit. and Religious Edn., Coll. William and Mary, 1923—, also rector Bruton Parish Ch., 1926-37. Restorer of Bruton Parish Ch., Williamsburg, 1907; George Wythe House, 1926; dir. Rockefeller restoration of historic Williamsburg, capital of colonial Va.; pres. Yorktown Sesquicentennial Assn., 1931. Author: History Bruton Parish Church, 1903; Bruton Parish Church Restored, 1907; The Church Enchained, 1916; The Parish, 1920; History Virginia Theological Seminary (2 vols.), 1923. Home: Williamsburg, Pa. Died Sept. 7, 1939.

GOODWIN, William Hall, surgeon; b. Lexington, Ky., Feb. 3, 1882; s. William Moore and Katherine (Hall) G.; B.A., Transylvania U., Ky., 1904; M.D., U. of Va., 1908; m. Mary Stuart Cocke, Dec. 27, 1921. Interne U. of Va. Hosp., 1908-09; mem. house staff, Bellevue Hosp., New York, 1909-10; recalled to U. of Va. as house surgeon of hosp., 1910, later prof. clinical surgery and gynecology. Commd. maj. Med. Corps, U.S.A., Sept. 6, 1917; lt. col., June 27, 1918; hon. discharged, Apr. 23, 1919; was organizer and chief of surg. service, Base Hosp. 41, A.E.F., at Saint Denis, France. Citation by Gen. John J. Pershing, Apr. 19, 1919. Democrat. Presbyterian. Home: University, Va. Deceased.

GOODWIN, William Watson, educator; b. Concord, Mass., May 9, 1831; s. Hersey Bradford and Lucretia Ann (Watson) G.; A.B., Harvard, 1851; studied at univs. of Göttingen, Berlin, and Bonn; Ph.D., Göttingen, 1855 (LL.D., Amherst, 1881, Cambridge, Eng., 1883, Columbia, 1887, Edinburgh, 1890, Harvard, 1891, Chicago, 1901, Yale, 1901; D.C.L., Oxford, Eng., 1890; hon. Ph.D., Göttingen, 1905. Tutor, 1856-60, prof. Greek lit., 1860-1901, prof. emeritus, 1901, Harvard. First dir. Am. Sch. of Classical Studies, Athens, Greece, 1882-83; Knight Greek Order of the Redeemer. Overseer Harvard, 1903-09. Author: Syntax of the Moods and Tenses of the Greek Verb; Greek Grammar. Editor: Demosthenes on the Crown and Against Midias. Home: Cambridge, Mass. Died June 16, 1912.

GOODYEAR, Charles Waterhouse, ry. pres.; b. Cortland, N.Y., Oct. 15, 1846; s. Bradley and Esther P. (Kinne) G.; ed. Wyo. Acad.; admitted to bar, 1871; m. Ella P. Conger, Mar. 23, 1876. Apptd. asst. dist. atty., 1875, dist. atty., 1876; mem. firm Bissell Sicard & Goodyear, Buffalo, N.Y.; abandoned law practice, 1887; pres. Buffalo & Susquehanna Ry. Co., Goodyear Lumber Co., Buffalo & Susquehanna Coal & Coke Co., Great Southern Lumber Co., New Orleans Great Northern R.R. Co.; dir. Marine Nat. Bank, Gen. Ry. Signal Co., Western New York Water Co. Trustee Buffalo Hist. Soc., State Normal Sch. Home: Buffalo, N.Y. Died 1911.

GOODYEAR, William Henry, curator; b. New Haven, Conn., Apr. 21, 1846; s. Charles G.; A.B., Yale, 1867, hon. A.M., 1904; studied gen. history and history of art, Heidelberg and Berlin (under Prof. Carl Friedrichs), 1867-70. Visited Cyprus, Syria, Greece and Italy, 1869-70; curator Metropolitan Museum of Art, 1882-88; curator of fine arts, Museum of the Brooklyn Institute of Arts and Sciences, 1899—. Visited Egypt in 1891 for studies of lotus ornament, and again in 1914 for architectural studies; surveyed many cathedrals in Italy and Northern Europe, 1895-1901, 1903, 1905, 1907, 1910, 1914, for studies of architectural refinements. Home: Brooklyn, N.Y. Died Feb. 19, 1923.

GOOLD, Marshall Newton, author; b. Montrose, Scotland, Mar. 3, 1881; s. John and Chrissie (Duncan) G.; M.A., Glasgow U., 1900; m. Mary Haskell Wyman, 1911. Came to U.S., 1911, naturalized citizen, 1925. With British Army, 1915-19, World War. Republican. Conglist. Author: The Sea Sphinx, 1911; Spindrift and Sand-drift, 1911; The Ship of Destiny, 1924; Saint Claudia (play), 1925; Heather Heretics, 1926; The Quest Divine and The Shepherds (plays), 1926; Paul and Thekla (play), 1927; Miriam (play), 1928. Home: Leicester, Mass. Died Oct. 25, 1935.

GORDIN, Harry Mann, chemist; b. in Russia, Aug. 16, 1855; ed. Gymnasium; grad. in pharmacy at U. of Moscow; came to U.S., 1882; engaged in drug business at San Francisco till 1893; studied chemistry in France, Germany and Switzerland; Ph.D., U.

of Berne, 1897. Research chemist for U.S. Pharmacopœia at U. of Mich., 1897-1900; head chemist William S. Merrell Chem. Co., Cincinnati, 1900-02; prof. chemistry, schs. of dentistry and pharmacy, Northwestern U., 1902—. Spl. subjects alkaloids and drug assaying. Home: Chicago, Ill. Died July 5, 1923.

GORDON, Anna Adams, temperance worker; b. Boston, Mass., July 21, 1853; d. James M. and Mary E. (Clarkson) Gordon; ed. Newton (Mass.) High Sch. and at Mt. Holyoke Coll.; hon. Dr. Humane Letters, Northwestern U., 1924. Private sec. to late Frances E. Willard 21 yrs.; pres. World's W.C.T.U.; hon. pres. Nat. W.C.T.U.; one of 4 presidents of World League Against Alcoholism. As an internat. officer has visited Europe, South America and Mexico. Author: Marching Songs; Songs for Young Americans; Everybody Sing; Questions Answered on Juvenile Work; The Life of Frances E. Willard; What Frances E. Willard Said, 1905; Toots, and Other Stories (juvenile). Home: Evanston, Ill. Died June 15, 1931.

GORDON, Armistead Churchill, lawyer, author; b. Albemarle County, Va., Dec. 20, 1855; s. George Loyall and Mary (Daniel) G.; attended U. of Va., 1873-75; LL.D., William and Mary Coll., Va., 1906; Litt.D., Washington and Lee U., 1923; admitted to bar, 1879; m. Maria Breckinridge Catlett, Oct. 17, 1883; children—Margaret Douglas, Mary Daniel, James Lindsay, Armistead Churchill, George Loyall (dec.). Mayor of Staunton, 1884-86; has been city atty. and commonwealth atty.; visitor U. of Va., 1894-98, 1906-18, rector of same, 1897-98, 1906-18; visitor Coll. of William and Mary, 1898-1906; State visitor to Mount Vernon, 1895-96; chmn. State Library Bd., Va., 1903-19. Author: Befo' de War, Echoes in Negro Dialect (with Thomas Nelson Page), 1888; Ommirandy—Plantation Life at Kingsmill, 1917; Jefferson Davis, 1918; Gordons in Virginia, 1918; The Balwearie Mystery, 1920; Thomas Nelson Page—An Appreciation, 1923; Men and Events—Chapters of Virginia History, 1923; Virginian Portraits—Essays in Biography, 1924; Memories and Memorials of William Gordon McCabe (2 vols.), 1925; Allegra—The Story of Byron and Miss Clairmont, 1926; The Western Front (poems), 1928; also many previous books. Home: Staunton, Va. Dec. 21, 1931.

GORDON, Arthur Horace, physician; b. Calais, Me., Oct. 23, 1863; s. David and Mary Brooks (Keen) G.; ed. Calais Acad.; M.D., Hahnemann Med. Coll., Chicago, 1887; m. Julia Agnes Cavanaugh, Dec. 30, 1891; 1 dau., Jewel M. Practiced, Chicago, 1887—; prof. internal medicine Hahnemann Med. Coll., 1898-1922; head of dept., 1921-22; attending physician same hosp., 1902-22; prof. internal medicine, Gen. Med. Coll., 1922-24; mem. gen. staff Ill. Masonic Hosp.; mem. staff Edgewater Hosp.; pres. Hahnemann Instns., Inc., 1928—. State med. examiner, The Maccabees; trustee New York Homœ. Med. Coll. and Flower Hosp., 1928-29; mem. exec. com. Med. Interfraternity Congress, 1928-30, vice-chmn., 1932-34. Mason (32°, Shriner). Home: Chicago, Ill. Died Dec. 2, 1938.

GORDON, Charles Henry, geologist; b. Caledonia, N.Y., May 10, 1857; s. John and Ann (McKinnon) G.; B.S., Albion Coll., 1886, M.S., 1890; fellow, U. of Chicago, 1893-95, Ph.D., 1895; U. of Heidelberg, 1897-98; m. Mary E. Hydorn, June 22, 1887; children —Irene Hydorn (Mrs. Burton Ashton Gaskill), Helen Garnett (Mrs. Don Carlos Ellis), Isabel (Mrs. Hugh Sevier Carter). Instr. high sch., Keokuk, Ia., 1886-87; prin. Wells Sch., Keokuk, 1887-90; instr. natural history, Northwestern U., Ill., 1890-93; supt. schs., Beloit, Wis., 1895-97, Lincoln, Neb., 1899-1903; lecturer, U. of Neb., 1901-03; acting prof. geology, U. of Wash., 1903-04; prof. geology and mineralogy, N.M. Sch. of Mines, 1904-05; field asst., 1905-06, asst. geologist, 1906-13, U.S. Geol. Survey; prof. geology, U. of Tenn., 1907-31, emeritus, 1931. Asso. state geologist, Tenn., 1910-14; dir. and supt. Dept. of Minerals, Nat. Conservation Expn., Knoxville, 1913. Home: Anna Maria, Fla. Died June 12, 1934.

GORDON, David Stuart, army officer; b. Franklin County, Pa., May 23, 1832; s. Alexander and Hannah (Ely) G.; ed. pub. and pvt. schs. in country and Commercial Sch., Baltimore; m. Ann E. Hughes; m. 2d, Mrs. Bell (Vedder) Fleming; step-children—Robert Vedder Fleming, Mrs. Louis F. Corea. Apptd. from Kan. 2d lt. 2d Dragoons, Apr. 10, 1861; 1st lt. 2d Cav., June 1861; capt., Apr. 25, 1863; maj., June 25, 1877; lt. col., Nov. 20, 1889; col., 6th Cav., July 28, 1892; retired May 23, 1896; advanced to rank of brig. gen. retired, by act of Apr. 23, 1904. Bvtd. maj., July 3, 1863, "for gallant and meritorious services in Gettysburg campaign"; lt. col., Feb. 27, 1890, "for gallant services in action against Indians at Miners Delight, Wyo., May 4, 1870." In Civil War served in Army of Potomac and engaged at first battle of Bull Run; taken prisoner and confined in Libby Prison, Richmond, Va., Castle Pinckney, Charleston and Columbia jails, S.C., and Salisbury, N.C.; exchanged Aug. 1862; took part in many other battles of Civ. War, including Manassas Gap, Todd's Tavern, Cold Harbor, Hawes Shop, Trevillian Sta., etc.; after war engaged in frontier service and battles with Indians as well as various other branches of service until retired. Presbyn. Home: Washington, D.C. Died Jan. 28, 1930.

GORDON, Edward Clifford, clergyman; b. Richmond, Va., Sept. 1, 1842; s. John Newton and Louisiana (Coleman) G.; ed. U. of Va.; 1st lt. arty., C.S.A., 1862-65; grad. Union Theol. Sem., Va., 1872; D.D., Hampden-Sidney Coll., 1886; student in mathematics, proctor, sec. of faculty and treasurer, Washington Coll. (now Washington and Lee U.), 1867-69; m. Mary Frances Bell, Nov. 12, 1873. Ordained Presbyn. ministry, 1872; pastor, Lebanon, Va., 1872, Savannah, Ga., 1874-80, Salem, Va., 1880-88; prof. Bibl. history, 1892-98, pres., 1894-98, Westminster Coll.; pastor Lexington, Mo., 1898-1910; sec. and treas. Home Missions, Synod of Mo., Presbyn. Ch. in U.S., 1911-15, treas., 1915—. Address: St. Louis, Mo. Died Jan. 26, 1922.

GORDON, Edwin Seamer, architect; b. Rochester, N.Y., Mar. 28, 1867; s. Henry Robert and Mary Jane (Benton) G.; grad. architectural course, Rochester Athenaeum and Mechanics Inst., 1891; m. Mary Larke, Sept. 12, 1885; children—Stewart, Constance (Mrs. Eugene Vincent), Grace Gordon (Mrs. Frank Willems, dec.), Ruth. With James G. Cutler, architect, Rochester, 1887-91; mem. firm Gordon, Bragdon & Orchard, 1891-95; with J. Foster Warner, 1895-1903; mem. Gordon & Madden, 1903-18, Gordon & Kaelber, 1918—. Architect with others of Rochester Dental Dispensary, Jefferson, Madison and Monroe junior high schs., Benjamin Franklin High Sch., Bapt. Temple, First Ch. of Christ and Second Ch. of Christ, Scientist, Eastman Theatre and Sch. of Music, U. of Rochester Med. Sch., Men's Coll. and Hosp., etc. Mem. bd. trustees Rochester Athenaeum and Mechanics Inst. Home: Rochester, N.Y. Died Apr. 5, 1932.

GORDON, Eleanor Kinzie; b. Chicago, Ill., June 18, 1835; d. John Harris and Juliette Augusta (Magill) Kinzie; ed. Chicago and N.Y. City; m. William Washington Gordon, Dec. 21, 1857. Organizer, 1894, and 1st pres. Ga. br. Soc. Colonial Dames of America, and served 6 yrs.; 2d v.p. Nat. Soc. Colonial Dames of America, 1899-1903; organizer, 1906, Ga. Soc. Am. Red Cross; hon. state regent D.A.R., for Ga. one term. Equipped and conducted convalescent hosp., at Miami, Fla., during Spanish-Am. War, 1898, for soldiers of 1st Brigade, under Gen. Lloyd Wheaton, and of 2d Brigade, under her husband, Gen. W. W. Gordon. Hon. mem. Ellsworth's Zouaves, Chicago, 1852. Episcopalian. Author: (poems) Rosemary and Rue, 1906; Life of John Kinzie, the Father of Chicago, 1906; Lieutenant Helm's Account of the Massacre at Fort Dearborn, 1912. Home: Savannah, Ga. Died Feb. 22, 1917.

GORDON, Elizabeth (Mrs. George Edwin Canfield), author; b. Winn, Me., Feb. 2, 1865; d. William H. and Ellen Lucinda (Royal) G.; ed. pub. schs., Me., and spl. studies, U. of Minn.; m. John Priest, July 1, 1881 (died 1885); m. 2d, George Edwin Canfield, Sept. 1, 1891. Began writing as contrb. spl. articles from the West, to Portland (Me.) Transcript, Bangor (Me.) Courier, etc.; editor Children's Tribune, Minneapolis, 1901-04, also asst. lit. critic Cumulative Index; mem. League Am. Pen Women, Story Tellers' League (Los Angeles and Chicago), Southern California Women's Press Club, Illinois Women's Press Association, Midland Authors. Author: Flower Children, 1910; Bird Children, 1912; Four Footed Folk, 1913; Book of Bow Wows, 1913; Mother Earth's Children, 1914; Butter Fly Babies, 1914; Watermelon Pete and Grand Dad Coco-Nut's Party, 1914; Dolly and Molly Series, 1914; Loraine and The Little People, 1915; What We Saw at Madame World's Fair, 1915; A Sheaf of Roses, 1916; I Wonder Why, 1916; King Gum Drop, 1917; Loraine and the Little People of Spring, 1918; Wild Flower Children, 1918; Billy Bunny's Fortune, 1919; Johnny Mouse's Trip to the Moon, 1920; Loraine and the Little People of Summer, 1920; The Turned Into's, 1920; "Babyland" department Junior Instructor Magazine, 1920-21. Home: Chicago, Ill. Died Apr. 2, 1922.

GORDON, Francis, clergyman; b. Tryszczn, Poland, Aug. 29, 1860; s. Thomas and Anna (de Rozycki) G.; ed. in Poland; A.M., St. Mary's Coll., Marion Co., Ky.; student philosophy and theology, Gregorian U., Rome. Came to U.S., 1881. Ordained priest R C Ch., 1889; rector St. Stanislaus Sch. and mgr. Polish Pub. Co., Chicago, 1889-92; prof. Coll. of Resurrection Fathers, Adrianople, Turkey, 1893-94; acting procurator gen. at mother house of Resurrection Fathers, Rome, 1895-96; superior at St. Stanislaus House, 1896-99; founder St. Mary's of the Angels parish, 1899, Polish Daily News, Chicago, 1890, Macierz Polska, The Young Men's Catholic Assn. of N. America, 1897; del. general of the Congregation of the Resurrection for U.S. and Can., 1918. Democrat. Received 1,132,524 votes (plurality of 138,354) in Chicago Examiner contest, 1906, for most popular clergyman in Chicago, and made trip, 1907-08 to Germany, Austria, Poland, Russia, Italy, Egypt, Holy Land and Turkey. Home: Chicago, Ill. Died Feb. 13, 1931.

GORDON, Frederick Charles, artist; b. Cobourg, Ont., Can., June 30, 1856; s. George Nelson and Sophia (Webster) G.; pub. and high sch. edn.; studied Art Students' League, New York, and Julien and Colorossi acads., Paris; unmarried. Began work, 1882, at Toronto, Can.; came to U.S., 1886; painter of portraits, landscapes, genre, etc., but during recent yrs. has devoted attention chiefly to decorative draw-

ings for publication. Address: Westfield, N.J. Died Mar. 20, 1924.

GORDON, George Angier, clergyman; b. Scotland, Jan. 2, 1853; s. George and Catherine (Hutcheon) G.; ed. common schs., Insch, Scotland; came to U.S., 1871; grad. Bangor Theol. Sem., 1877; A.B., Harvard, 1881; D.D., Bowdoin, 1893, Yale, 1893; S.T.D., Harvard, 1895, Columbia, 1903; LL.D., Western Reserve U., 1912; D.D., Brown U., 1914; D.D., Williams Coll., 1922; LL.D., Boston U., 1923; m. Susan Huntington Manning, June 3, 1890. Ordained Congl. ministry, 1877; pastor Temple, Me., 1877-78, Greenwich, Conn., 1881-83, Old South Ch., Boston, 1884-1927. University preacher to Harvard, 1886-90 and 1906-09, Yale, 1888-1916; Ingersoll lecturer, Harvard, 1896; lecturer, Lowell Inst., 1900; Lyman Beecher lecturer, Yale, 1901; Nathaniel W. Taylor lecturer, Yale, 1908; overseer, Harvard U., 1897-1916 and 1925—. Author: The Witness to Immortality, 1893; The Christ of Today, 1895; Immortality and the New Theodicy, 1897; The New Epoch for Faith, 1901; Ultimate Conceptions of Faith, 1903; Through Man to God, 1906; Religion and Miracle, 1909, revised edit., 1910; Revelation and the Ideal, 1913; Aspects of the Infinite Mystery, 1916; Humanism in New England Theology, 1920; My Education and Religion, 1925. Home: Brookline, Mass. Died Oct. 25, 1929.

GORDON, George Breed, lawyer; b. Edgewood Borough, Pa., Aug. 1, 1860; s. Alexander and Catherine (Edwards) G.; ed. Western U. of Pa.; LL.B., Columbia, 1883; m. Mary Edwards Boorum, June 4, 1889. Practiced in Pittsburgh; sr. mem. firm Gordon, Smith, Buchanan & Scott, 1924—. Home: Pittsburgh, Pa. Died Sept. 8, 1927.

GORDON, George Byron, museum dir.; b. P.E.I., Can., Aug. 4, 1870; s. James and Jane (Maclaren) G.; student U. of S.C., 1888-89, Harvard, 1890-94, Sc.D., 1894; unmarried. Chief of Harvard U. Expdn. to Central America, 1894-1900; asst. curator anthropology, 1903-04, curator, 1904-10, lecturer on anthropology, 1904-07, asst. prof., 1907-15, U. of Pa.; dir. U. of Pa. Mus., 1910—. Author: Prehistoric Ruins of Copan, 1896; Researches in the Uloa Valley, 1898; Caverns of Copan, 1898; The Hieroglyphic Stairway at Copan, 1902; The Serpent Motive in Ancient Art, 1906; The Book of Chilam Balam of Chumayel, 1913; In the Alaskan Wilderness, 1917; Baalbek, 1919; The Walls of Constantinople, 1921; Ancient London, 1923; Rambles in Old London, 1924. Home: Philadelphia, Pa. Died Jan. 30, 1927.

GORDON, George Washington, congressman; b. Giles County, Tenn., Oct. 5, 1836; s. Andrew and Eliza K. G.; grad. Western Mil. Inst., 1859; m. Ora S. Paine, Sept. 5, 1876. Practiced civ. engring. till outbreak of Civil War; enlisted in mil. service of Tenn. as drill master 11th Inf.; transferred to mil. service of C.S.A.; promoted capt., lt. col., col.; in 1864 made brig. gen.; participated in every engagement fought by his command with exception of Bentonville, N.C., being a prisoner until Aug. 1865, at Ft. Warren, Boston Harbor. Studied law Lebanon, Tenn.; practiced at Pulaski and Memphis until 1883; apptd. one of ry. commrs. of state; received apptmt. in Interior Dept., U.S., 1885; served 4 yrs. in Indian country and territories west of Rocky Mountains. Resumed practice of law Memphis until 1892; supt. city schools of Memphis, 1892-1907; mem. 60th and 61st Congresses (1907-11), 10th Tenn. Dist. Democrat. Maj. gen. comdg. Tenn. div. U.C.V. Address: Memphis, Tenn. Died 1911.

GORDON, James, senator; b. Monroe County, Miss., Dec. 6, 1833; s. Robert and Mary Elizabeth (Walton) G.; A.B., U. of Miss., 1855; m. Carolina Virginia Wiley, Feb. 7, 1856; m. 2d, Ella Narcissa Neilson, Apr. 28, 1904. Capt. Co. B, Jeff Davis Legion, under Gen. J. E. B. Stuart, Army of Va., C.S.A.; later col. 4th Miss. Cav. Cotton planter. Appointed U.S. senator, Dec. 27, 1909, and served until Feb. 22, 1910, when legislature elected a successor to Anselm J. McLaurin, deceased. Author: The Old Plantation, and Other Poems. For many yrs. contbr. to mags., especially field notes to Forest and Stream, American Field, London Field, etc. Home: Okolona, Miss. Died Nov. 28, 1912.

GORDON, James Herndon, judge; b. Locust Dale, Va., Oct. 3, 1868; s. Andrew James and Lucy Herndon (Willis) G.; A.B., U. of Va., 1887, B.L., 1890; m. Bertha L. Frederick, Apr. 4, 1900; children—Margaret Frederick, Andrew James. Settled at McAlester, I.Ty., 1890; apptd. master in chancery, U.S. Court, 1895; formed partnership with C. B. Stuart, as Stuart & Gordon, 1895; began practicing alone, 1918, specializing in corp. law; apptd. asso. justice Supreme Court of Okla., May 1, 1924, for period ending Jan. 8, 1925; associated in practice with son, A. James, 1933—. Dir., atty. First Nat. Bank of McAlester (pres. 2 terms). Apptd. mem. bd. govs., State Bar of Okla., 1929. State chmn. 3d Liberty Loan Campaign. Chmn. County Bd., Salvation Army. Democrat. Mem. M.E. Ch., S. Mason (33°, Shriner), Elk. Home: McAlester, Okla. Died Oct. 23, 1936.

GORDON, James Logan, minister; b. Phila., Pa., Mar. 28, 1858; s. John Robert and Margaret (Logan) G.; ed. under pvt. tutors; m. Lillian Hoffman James, June 15, 1887. Ordained Congl. ministry, 1898; pastor

St. John, N.B., 1898-1900, Toronto, Ont., 1900-05, Winnipeg, Man., 1905-14, Washington, D.C., 1915-19, First Ch., San Francisco, 1920—. Republican. Mason, Odd Fellow. Author: The Young Man and His Problems, 1911; All's Love Yet All's Law, 1914; The Weight of a Word, 1925. Home: San Francisco, Calif. Died Oct. 11, 1930.

GORDON, John, univ. pres.; b. Pittsburgh, Pa., Mar. 10, 1850; s. Alexander and Catherine (Edwards) G.; A.M., Western U. of Pa., 1866; studied Auburn Theol. Sem., 1868-70, Union Theol. Sem., 1870-71; hon. A.M., Yale, 1901; D.D., Western U. of Pa., 1889; m. Emma Ward Bacon, May 31, 1877. Ordained Presbyn. ministry, 1872; pastor Rensselaerville, N.Y., 1871-79, First Ch., Lincoln, Neb., 1880-82, Fourth Church, Pittsburgh, 1884-86, Westminster Church, Omaha, 1887-97; prof. ecclesiastical history, Omaha Theol. Sem., 1891-99; prof. history, 1900-01, pres., 1901-03, Tabor Coll., Ia.; pres. Howard U., Washington, 1903-06. Lecturer on ednl. and hist. subjects. Author: History of Presbyterian Church, Rensselaerville, N.Y., 1876; The Bulls Distributing America, 1892; Three Children of Galilee, 1895; What Christian Science Really Is, 1898. Home: Rensselaerville, N.Y. Died Feb. 9, 1923.

GORDON, John Brown, gov.; b. Upson County, Ga., Feb. 6, 1832; ed. U. of Ga.; admitted to bar; m. Fanny Haralson, 1854. Served in C.S.A., capt. to lt. gen.; shot 8 times; severely wounded at Antietam; Dem. candidate for gov. of Ga., 1868, and claimed election, but his Rep. opponent, Rufus B. Bullock, obtained the office; U.S. senator, 1873-80, and 1891-97; gov. Ga., 1887-90; comdr.-in-chief United Confederate Veterans. Home: Atlanta, Ga. Died 1904.

GORDON, Joseph Claybaugh, supt. Ill. Instn. for Edn. of the Deaf, 1897—; b. Piqua, O., March 9, 1842; s. Rev. John McDaniel and Elizabeth (Fisher) G.; moved to Ill., 1850; grad. Monmouth (Ill.) Coll., 1866 (Ph.D.); m. Aug. 1, 1878, Anna Sibyl Wadsworth. Pioneer in oral edn. of the deaf in America, organizing oral dept., Ind. Instn. for the Deaf, 1869; prof. mathematics and chemistry, Gallaudet Coll. (for the deaf), Washington, 1873-97; 1st pres. oral sect., Assn. Am. Educators of the Deaf; 1st pres. XVI sect. (dept. for the deaf), Nat. Ednl. Assn. Author: Education of Deaf Children; Notes and Observations on the Education of the Deaf; etc. Home: Jacksonville, Ill. Died 1903.

GORDON, Julien (Julie Grinnell Chance), novelist; b. (Storrow) Paris, France, of Am. parents; m. Col. S. Van Rensselaer Cruger (dec.); m. 2d, Wade Chance, 1908. Author: A Wedding and Other Stories; A Diplomat's Diary; Poppæa; A Successful Man; Eat Not Thy Heart; Mademoiselle Réséda; A Puritan Pagan; Mrs. Clyde, 1901; The Wage of Character, 1901; World's People, 1902; Poems, 1905. Address: New York, N.Y. Died July 12, 1920.

GORDON, M. Lafayette, missionary-educator; b. Waynesburg, Pa., July 18, 1843; grad. Waynesburg Coll., 1867; New York Coll. Phys. and Surg., 1870; Andover Theol. Sem., 1871; soon after went to Japan as a missionary and later became prof. homiletics and pastoral theology in theol. dept., Doshisha, U. of Kyoto. Author: An American Missionary in Japan. Address: Kyoto, Japan. Died 1900.

GORDON, S(amuel) D(ickey), author, lecturer; b. Phila., Pa., Aug. 12, 1859; s. John R. and Margaret (Logan) G.; ed. pub. schs.; m. Mary Kilgore, June 5, 1902. Asst. sec. Y.M.C.A., Phila., 1884-86; state sec. Y.M.C.A. of Ohio, 1886-95; pub. speaker, 1895—; spent 4 yrs. on speaking journey in Orient and Europe. Author: Quiet Talks on Power, 1901; Quiet Talks on Prayer, 1904; Quiet Talks on Service, 1906; Quiet Talks About Jesus, 1906; Quiet Talks on Personal Problems, 1907; Quiet Talks with World Winners, 1908; Quiet Talks on Home Ideals (with wife), 1909; Quiet Talks About the Tempter, 1910; Quiet Talks on Our Lord's Return, 1912; Quiet Talks on Following the Christ, 1913; Quiet Talks About the Crowned Christ, 1914; Quiet Talks on John's Gospel, 1915; Quiet Talks on the Deeper Meaning of the War, 1919; Quiet Talks on Life After Death, 1920; Quiet Talks on Simple Essentials, 1924; Quiet Talks on The Healing Christ, 1924; Quiet Talks on The Crisis and After, 1926; Quiet Talks on How to Pray, 1929; Quiet Talks on Difficult Questions, 1931; The Quiet Corner, 1932; Bent Knee Time, 1932; Quiet Talks on the New Order of Things, 1933; Quiet Talks with Eager Youth, 1934; Prayer and the Bible, 1935; Quiet Talk About the Old Book, 1937; also booklets on similar topics. Died June 26, 1936.

GORDON, Seth Chase, physician; b. Fryeburg, Me., Aug. 17, 1830; s. Stephen and Lydia (Chase) G.; ed. Fryeburg Acad.; M.D., Bowdoin, 1855; LL.D., Dartmouth, 1905. Practiced at Gorham, Me., 1855-61, Portland, Me., 1865—; served as asst. surgeon, 13th Me. Vols., and surgeon, 1st La. Vol. Inf. in Union Army; has been mem. common council, and of sch. com., Portland; mem. Dem. Nat. Com. for Me., 1896-1900. Surgeon Me. Gen. Hosp., 1874-94. Home: Portland, Me. Died June 22, 1921.

GORDON, Walter Henry, army officer; b. Artonish, Miss., June 24, 1863; s. William Crawford and Mary (Lewis) G.; grad. U.S. Mil. Acad., 1886, Sch. of Submarine Mining, Willits Point, N.Y., 1891, grad. Army War Coll., Washington, 1914; m. Laura A. Doan, Feb. 17, 1896. Commd. 2d lt. 12th Inf., July 1, 1886; 1st lt. 18th Inf., Nov. 30, 1892; maj. 1st Del. Inf., June 29, 1898; col., Sept. 21, 1898; hon. mustered out vol. service, Nov. 16, 1898; capt. U.S. Army, Mar. 2, 1899; promoted through grades to major gen., Nov. 7, 1923; retired, Jan. 18, 1924. Died Apr. 26, 1924.

GORDON, William, lawyer; b. Oak Harbor, O., Dec. 15, 1862; s. Washington and Margaret (Rymers) G.; LL.B., U. of Mich., 1893; m. Elizabeth M. Gernhard, Sept. 12, 1893. Began practice, Oak Harbor, 1893; pres. Gordon Lumber, Basket & Mfg. Co. Mem. county bd. sch. examiners, Ottawa County, 1890-96; deputy county treas., under father, 1887-91; pros. atty., Ottawa County, 1894-1900; mem. 63d to 65th Congresses (1913-19), 20th Ohio Dist. Trustee Andrews Inst. for Girls, Willoughby, O. Democrat. Mason (K.T., Shriner). Home: Cleveland, O. Died Jan. 16, 1942.

GORDON, William St. Clair, physician; b. Raleigh, N.C., Mar. 28, 1858; s. James and Mary St. Clair (Cooke) G.; prep. edn. University Sch., Richmond, Va.; M.D., Med. Coll. of Va., 1879; spl. courses, Jefferson Med. Coll., Phila., and med. dept., U. of Pa.; m. Kate Blanks Gordon, Oct. 16, 1890. Practiced at Richmond, Va.; a founder University Coll. of Medicine, Richmond, 1893, and prof. physiology, later asso. prof. clin. medicine, same; prof. medicine, Med. Coll. of Va., 1913-14, emeritus; physician and mem. bd. dirs. Laurel (Va.) Reformatory. Democrat. Presbyn. Author: Recollections of the Old Quarters (dialect, prose and verse), 1902. Investigated outbreak of typhoid in Richmond, 1884, and subsequently, and submitted extensive rept. on same, 1893. Home: Richmond, Va. Died Apr. 24, 1924.

GORDON, William W., merchant; b. Savannah, Ga., Oct. 14, 1834; s. William Washington G. and Sarah Anderson (Stites) G.; A.B., Yale, 1854; m. Eleanor Lytle Kinzie, Dec. 21, 1857. Second lt. Ga. Hussars, J. E. B. Stuart's Cav., C.S.A.; capt. and insp. Mercer's brigade of inf.; capt. and adj. Anderson's brigade, Wheeler's cav.; wounded at Lovejoy's Sta., Ga.; placed upon the Roll of Honor for gallantry at Frederick City, Md. After war served in Ga. cav.; 4 times in command of troops for riot duty. Engaged in cotton business, Savannah, Ga., 1854—; sr. partner W. W. Gordon & Co.; v.p. Merchants Nat. Bank, 1894-98; pres. Savannah Cotton Exchange, 1876-79, Savannah Benevolent Assn., 1890-91. Mem. Ga. Ho. of Rep., 1884-90. Brig. gen. U.S.V., May 27, 1898-Mar. 24, 1899, Spanish-Am. War; mem. Puerto Rican Evacuation Commn., Aug.-Oct., 1898. Home: Savannah, Ga. Died Sept. 11, 1912.

GORDY, J. P., educator; b. Md., 1851; academic edn. (Ph.D., Leipzig, 1884; LL.D., Western U. of Pa.); prof. edn., Ohio U., 1886-96; Ohio State U., 1896-1900; prof. history of edn., New York U., 1901—. Translator Kuno Fischer's Descartes. Author: The Growth and Development of the Normal School Idea in the United States; Text-Book on Psychology; History of Political Parties in the United States; A Liberal Education in the Elementary School. Home: New York, N.Y. Died 1908.

GORDY, Wilbur Fisk, educator; b. nr. Salisbury, Md., June 14, 1854; s. Elijah Melson and Martha Ellen G.; A.B., Wesleyan U., 1880; m. Isabel Drummond Hunter, July 9, 1889. Vice pres. high sch., Middletown, Conn., 1880-81; supt. schs., Ansonia, Conn., 1881-84; supervising prin. pub. schs., Hartford, Conn., 1884-1904; supt. schs., Springfield, Mass., 1904-11. Mem. Com. of Eight, 1904-08; pres. Hartford Bd. Edn.; pres. trustees Hartford Pub. Library; dir. Conn. Humane Soc. Lecturer on sch. topics and contbr. to ednl. jours. Author: A School History of the United States, 1897; American Leaders and Heroes, 1901; Stories of American Explorers, 1906; Colonial Days, 1907; Elementary History of the United States, 1910; American Beginnings in Europe, 1911; Stories of Early American History, 1913; Stories of Later American History, 1915; Abraham Lincoln, 1917; Causes and Meaning of the Great War, 1919; History of the United States, 1922; Leaders in Making America, 1923. Co-Author: A Pathfinder in American History, 1892; Language Lessons, 1903; Grammar Lessons, 1903. Home: Hartford, Conn. Died Dec. 23, 1929.

GORE, Joshua Walker, university prof.; b. Frederick County, Va., Jan. 10, 1852; s. Mahlon and Sidney Sophia (Cather) G.; student Richmond Coll., 1871-73; C.E., U. of Va., 1875; fellow in mathematics, Johns Hopkins, 1876-78; m. Margaret Corinthia Williams, Nov. 9, 1883. Prof. physics and chemistry, Southwestern Bapt. U., Jackson, Tenn., 1881; asst. in mathematics, U. of Va., 1881-82; prof. physics, U. of N.C., 1882—. Democrat. Baptist. Home: Chapel Hill, N.C. Deceased.

GORE, W. A., ry. official; b. Knoxville, Tenn., Aug. 31, 1874; ed. high sch. Began as telegraph operator E. Tenn., Va. & Ga. Ry., 1889; chief dispatcher S. Atlantic & Ohio Ry., 1896-97; dispatcher Southern Ry., at Knoxville, Tenn., 1897-98; operator and dispatcher, L.&N. R.R., at East Nashville and for I.C. R.R., at McComb, Miss., 1898-99; trainmaster Chicago & Southeastern R.R., 1899-1901; chief dispatcher L.E.&W. R.R., at Lima, O., 1901-02; chief clk. to asst. supt. U.P. R.R., at Evanston, Wyo., 1902-03, and dispatcher same rd.; chief dispatcher Seaboard Air Line, at Raleigh, N.C., 1903-04, continuing as trainmaster 2d div., same rd., 1904-07, supt. 3d div., 1907-10, 2d div., 1910-13; supt. Carolina, Atlantic & Western Ry., 1913-14; receiver Orangeburg Ry., 1914-17; gen. supt. Vaughan Constrn. Co., Jan.-Nov. 1918; supt. Norfolk & Portsmouth Belt Line R.R., 1918-19; with Virginian Ry., successive supt. Norfolk div., 1919-20, New River div., 1920-21, gen. mgr., 1921—. Address: Norfolk, Va. Died Feb. 4, 1928.

GORGAS, William Crawford, surgeon gen. U.S. Army; b. Mobile, Ala., Oct. 3, 1854; s. Gen. Josiah (C.S.A.) and Amelia (Gayle) G.; A.B., U. of the South, 1875; M.D., Bellevue Hosp. Medical College (New York U.), 1879; interne, Bellevue Hosp., 1878-80; hon. Sc.D., U. of Pa., 1903, U. of the South, 1904, Harvard, 1908, Brown, 1909, Jefferson Med. Coll. 1909; LL.D., U. of Ala., 1910, Tulane, 1911; m. Marie Cook Doughty, Sept. 15, 1885. Apptd. surgeon U.S. Army, June 16, 1880; capt. asst. surgeon, June 16, 1885; maj. brigade surgeon vols., June 4-July 6, 1898; maj. surgeon, July 6, 1898; chief sanitary officer of Havana and in charge of sanitary work there, 1898-1902; applied methods of combating yellow fever which eliminated that disease in Havana; col. asst. surgeon gen., by spl. act of Congress, for yellow fever work at Havana, Mar. 9, 1903; surgeon gen. U.S. Army, with rank of brig. gen., Jan. 16, 1914; major gen., surgeon gen., U.S. Army, Mar. 4, 1915; retired, Dec. 1, 1918; director yellow fever research, Rockefeller Foundation. Apptd. chief sanitary officer Panama Canal, Mar. 1, 1904; mem. Isthmian Canal Commn., Mar. 4, 1907—; permanent dir. Internat. Health Board of Rockefeller Foundation. Recipient of Mary Kingsley medal from Liverpool School of Tropical Medicine, May 27, 1907; gold medal Am. Museum of Safety, 1914. Awarded D.S.M., 1918; comdr. Legion of Honor (French), 1919; Grand Officer Order of the Crown of Italy, 1918. Died July 4, 1920.

GORHAM, Frederic Poole, biologist; b. Providence, R.I., Apr. 29, 1871; s. Samuel and Abby Harding (Fish) G.; A.B., Brown U., 1893, A.M., 1894; spl. studies in bacteriology, Harvard Med. Sch.; m. Emma Mary Lapham, June 24, 1897 (died 1913); children—Mary Emma, Sayles, Nancy, Hope; m. 2d, Ruth Elizabeth Björkdahl, Jan. 1, 1917; 1 dau., Ruth. Instr. biology, 1893-99, asst. prof., 1899-1901, asso. prof., 1901-13, prof. bacteriology, 1913—, Brown U. Bacteriologist, Providence Health Dept., 1899; bacteriologist and biologist, R.I. Shellfish Commn., 1913—; deputy insp. milk, City of Providence, 1914—. Sec. trustees R.I. State Sanatorium, 1908—. Author: Laboratory Guide to the Dissection of the Cat (with R. W. Tower), 1895; Laboratory Course in Bacteriology, 1897, 1901. Home: Providence, R.I. Died June 4, 1933.

GORHAM, George Congdon, sec. U.S. Senate; b. Greenport, N.Y., July 5, 1832; s. George Gorham; ed. New London, Conn.; emigrated to Calif., arriving Dec. 20, 1849; clerk to Stephen J. Field, alcalde of Marysville, Calif. (afterward justice U.S. Supreme Court), 1850; elected city clerk, Marysville, 1856; asst. editor Sacramento Daily Standard, 1859; editor San Francisco Daily Nation (Douglas Democratic paper), 1860; editor Marysville Democrat (unconditional Union), 1861; asst. editor Sacramento Daily Union, 1861-62; actively participated in forming Union Party (fusion of Republicans and Union Democrats), 1862; clerk U.S. Circuit Court, San Francisco, 1863-67; nominated for gov. Calif. by Republican Party, 1867; sec. U.S. senate, 1868-79; represented Calif. on Rep. Nat. Com., 1868-80; editor Daily National Republican, Washington, D.C., 1880-84. Author: Life of Edwin M. Stanton, 1899. Home: Washington, D.C. Died 1909.

GORIN, Orville B., banker; b. Taylorville, Ill., Jan. 25, 1849; s. Jerome Rinaldo and Eleanor Elizabeth Douglas (Fawcett) G.; ed. pub. schs., Decatur, Ill.; m. Ella McClellan, Nov. 26, 1872 (died 1920); 1 dau., Gussie Judith. Pres. The Millikin Nat. Bank, Decatur, 1865—; also pres. Union Iron Works, Mut. Home & Savings Assn., Millikin Trust Co. Trustee Millikin estate. Republican. Persbyn. Mason (K.T.), K.P. Home: Decatur, Ill. Died June 19, 1935.

GORMAN, Arthur Pue, U.S. senator; b. Howard County, Md., Mar. 11, 1839; ed. public schools; apptd. page in U.S. Senate, 1852, serving until 1866. Collector internal revenue, 5th dist., Md., 1866-69. In 1869 was apptd. dir. Chesapeake & Ohio Canal Co., pres., 1872—. Mem. Md. House of Delegates, 1869-75 (speaker, 1873-75); State senator, 1875-81; U.S. senator, Md., 1881-99 and 1903—. Democrat. Home: Laurel, Md. Died 1906.

GORMAN, Arthur Pue, Jr., lawyer; b. Howard County, Md., Mar. 27, 1873; s. Arthur Pue and Hannah (Donnegan) G.; ed. Columbian U., Washington, and U. of Md.; m. Grace James Norris, Nov. 27,

1900. Practiced at Baltimore; dir. Citizens Nat. Bank, Laurel, Md. Mem. staffs Gov. John Walter Smith, rank of col., 1900-04, Gov. Austin L. Crothers, rank of brig. gen., 1908-12; mem. Md. State Senate, 3 terms, 1904-10 (pres. of Senate, 1910); Dem. candidate for gov. of Md., 1911 (defeated); apptd. 1914, chmn. Md. State Tax Commn., term 6 yrs. Presbyn. Home: Howard Co., Md. Died Sept. 3, 1919.

GORMAN, Charles Edmund, lawyer; b. Boston, July 26, 1844; s. Charles and Sarah J. (Woodbury) G.; ed. pub. schs., Providence, R.I.; employed in stores from age of 12 to 18; studied law with Richard Ward Greene, Providence; admitted to bar, 1865; LL.D., Georgetown U., 1896; m. Josephine C. Dietrich, July 8, 1874. Mem. City Council and Bd. Aldermen, Providence, many yrs.; mem. R.I. Ho. of Rep., 1870, 85, 87 (speaker 1887); presented silver tea service by citizens of R.I. for labors in securing constl. amendment repealing property qualifications of voters, 1887; Dem. presdl. elector, 1900; candidate for mayor of Providence, 1885, for lt. gov., R.I., 1892, and for Congress, 1900; U.S. atty., Dist. of R.I., 1893-97; mem. commn. to revise constn. of R.I., 1897, and to revise judicial system, 1904; prof. law of domestic relations and wills, R.I. Law Coll. Address: Providence, R.I. Died Feb. 16, 1917.

GORMAN, Daniel M., bishop; b. Wyoming, Ia.; s. John and Mary (Rooney) G.; ed. Wyoming High Sch.; St. Joseph's Coll., Dubuque; St. Francis Sem., Milwaukee, Wis.; LL.D., St. Mary's Coll., Emmitsburg, Md., 1906. Ordained priest R.C. Ch., 1893; became associated as prof. with St. Joseph's Coll., now Dubuque Coll., Sept. 1894; pres. Dubuque (Ia.) Coll., 1904-18; apptd., Feb. 4, 1918, consecrated, May 1, 1918, bishop of Boise. Prothonotary Apostolic conferred by Pope Benedict XV, Feb. 26, 1917. Home: Boise, Ida. Died June 9, 1927.

GORMAN, George Edmond, congressman; b. Chicago, Apr. 13, 1873; s. Patrick and Mary (McInirney) G.; LL.B., Georgetown (D.C.) U., 1895; m. Marguerite O'Connor, June 27, 1900. Practiced, Chicago, 1896—; mem. firm of Gorman, Pollock, Sullivan & Livingston. Asst. city atty., Chicago, 1897-1900; mem. 63d Congress (1913-15), 3d Illinois Dist. Democrat. Catholic. Home: Chicago, Ill. Died Jan. 13, 1935.

GORTON, Eliot, physician; b. Newburgh, N.Y., July 26, 1863; s. David Allyn and Maria Frances (Graham) G.; ed. White Plains Mil. Inst. and Norwich U.; M.D., L.I. Med. Coll., 1888; m. Bertha Fonda, Sept. 12, 1888. Owner and resident physician Fair Oaks Sanitarium, Summit, N.J., 1902—. Home: Summit, N.J. Died Mar. 3, 1917.

GOSHEN, Elmer Isaac, clergyman; b. Farmington, Ill., Feb. 16, 1872; s. Levi and Harriet (Thornton) G.; A.B., Northwestern U., 1894; Northwestern Law Sch., 1894-96; B.D., Chicago Theol. Sem., 1899; m. Jené Melvin, Nov. 25, 1909. Ordained Congl. ministry, 1899; pastor Ogden Ch., 1899-1902, 1st Ch., Salt Lake City, 1902—. Instituted "habit cure" for treatment of persons addicted to use of alcohol, morphine, etc. Pres. bd. trustees, Salt Lake Coll., Salt Lake Symphony Orchestra. Mason (K.C.C.H., Scottish Rite, 33°). Commr. in Utah under NRA; U.S. conciliation commr. for State of Utah. Author of 17 books. Address: San Francisco, Calif. Died Dec. 18, 1941.

GOSHORN, Alfred Traber; b. Cincinnati, 1833; grad., A.B., Marietta Coll. (LL.D.); pres. Cincinnati Industrial Expns. (annual), 1869-72; dir. gen. Centennial Expn., Phila., 1873-77; one of organizers, 1881, Cincinnati Museum Assn., dir. from orgn. Home: Cincinnati, O. Died 1902.

GOSLEE, Hart John, dental surgeon; b. St. Joseph, Mo., Apr. 30, 1871; s. James Wilder and Katherine Ryland (Todhunter) G.; D.D.S., Chicago Coll. Dental Surgery, 1895; B.S., Marquette U., 1910; m. Edith Pearl Blakemore, Nov. 26, 1891. Practiced at Chicago. Fellow Am. Coll. Dentists. Republican. Episcopalian. Author: Principles and Practice of Crowning Teeth, 1903; Principles and Practice of Crown and Bridgework, 1907, 5th edit., 1925. Home: Chicago, Ill. Died May 31, 1930.

GOSLING, Thomas Warrington, educator; b. Cincinnati, O., Sept. 15, 1872; s. Flavius Josephus and Elizabeth (Bates) G.; B.A., Yale U., 1894, M.A., 1904; Ph.D., U. of Cincinnati, 1911; m. Laura Louise Feid, Dec. 22, 1906 (died 1937); children—Arthur Warrington, Jane Frances; m. 2d, Emily Elizabeth Tandy Ford, Sept. 9, 1939. Teacher, Hughes High Sch., Cincinnati, 1894-1915; prin. 27th Dist. Elementary Sch., Cincinnati, 1915, Lafayette Bloom Jr. High Sch., Cincinnati, 1915-18; supervisor high schs., Wis. State Dept. Pub. Instrn., 1918-21; supt. schs., Madison, Wis., 1921-28, Akron, O., 1928-34; nat. dir. Am. Jr. Red Cross, Washington, 1934-38; asst. supt. D.C. Pub. Schs. in charge of white senior high schools and Wilson Teachers College, 1938-39; ednl. cons. Nat. Congress of Parents and Teachers, 1939—. Adj. prof. of edn., George Washington U., 1938—. Teacher, summer sessions Miami U., 1907, Johns Hopkins, 1917, U. of Calif. (Southern Branch), 1920, U. of Wyo., 1921, 30, U. of Wis., 1922, 24, 25, 26, New York U., 1923, Ohio State U., 1927, 31, U. of Chicago, 1928, 29. Del. of U.S. to 4th Internat. Conf. on Pub. Instrn., Geneva, Switzerland, 1935, to 5th Internat. Conf. on Family Edn., Brussels, 1935; del. of N.E.A. to World Fed. of Edn. Assn., Oxford, Eng., 1935; del. of Am. Red Cross to 3d Pan-Am. Red Cross Conf., Rio de Janeiro, Brazil, 1935. Capt. Ohio N.G., 1913; capt. Cincinnati Home Guards, 1917-18; chmn. Akron and Summit County Chapter Am. Red Cross (chmn. drought relief campaign), 1931. Trustee and mem. bd. of control Akron Art Inst.; dir. Akron Chamber Commn., 1929-31. Mem. Nat. Safety Council (vice-chmn. ednl. sect.; chmn. child education section), mem. Gen. Advisory Com. on Survey of Secondary Edn., Office of Edn., Dept. of Interior; offices many ednl. assns. Republican. Episcopalian. Mason (32°). Mem. consulting editorial board The Nations Schools. Home: Washington, D.C. Died Sept. 30, 1940.

GOSS, Charles A., judge; b. Edinburg, O., Dec. 10, 1863; s. Alfred Ruggles and Martha (Carr) G.; A.B., Mt. Union Coll., O., 1885, A.M., 1888, LL.D., 1935; m. Carrie Shimp, 1890 (died 1936); 1 dau., Catherine (Mrs. J. D. Pollock). Admitted to bar, 1887, and in practice at Omaha until 1920. Mem. Neb. Ho. of Rep., 1893; U.S. atty., 1906-10; judge 4th Dist., 1920-27; chief justice Supreme Court of Neb., 1927-39. Methodist. Mason (32°), Elk. Address: Lincoln, Neb. Died Aug. 13, 1938.

GOSS, Charles Frederic, clergyman; b. Meridian, N.Y., June 14, 1852; s. Simon Sartwell and Mary Catharine (Weaver) G.; A.B., Hamilton Coll., 1873, D.D., 1898; grad. Auburn Theol. Sem., 1876; m. Rosa E. Houghton, Aug. 30, 1876. Ordained Presbyterian ministry, 1876; pastor Weatherford, Tex., 1876-78, Limestone, N.Y., and Kendall Creek, Pa., 1878-81, Utica, N.Y., 1881-85, Moody Ch., Chicago, 1885-90; spent 2 yrs. recovering health at Kettle Falls, Wash.; asso. pastor Madison Av. Ch., New York, 1892-94; pastor Avondale Presbyn. Ch., Cincinnati, 1894-1912. Author: The Optimist, 1897; The Philopolist, 1898; Hits and Misses, 1899; The Redemption of David Corson, 1901; The Loom of Life, 1902; Little Saint Sunshine, 1902; Just a Minute, 1904; Husband, Wife and Home, 1905; That Other Hand Upon the Helm, 1910; History of Cincinnati, 1912. Editorial writer for Cincinnati Enquirer, 1917. Home: Cincinnati, O. Deceased.

GOSS, Chauncey Porter, brass mfr.; b. Rochester, N.Y., Aug. 5, 1838; s. Ephraim and Margaret (Porter) G.; ed. pub. schs.; m. Caroline Amelia Ketcham, Feb. 23, 1864. Clk. in gen. store, Pittsford, N.Y., 3 yrs.; entered employ of Scovill Mfg. Co., as asst. bookkeeper, 1862; promoted through various offices, pres. and treas., 1900—. Republican. Conglist. K.T. Home: Waterbury, Conn. Died July 19, 1918.

GOSS, Edward Otis, pres. Scovill Mfg. Co.; b. Waterbury, Conn., Sept. 29, 1865; s. Chauncey Porter and Caroline (Ketcham) G.; M.E., Mass. Inst. Tech., 1887; m. Harriet Wheeler, Sept. 15, 1891; children—Edward Wheeler, William M., Eliot P. Became draftsman Scovill Mfg. Co., 1888, dir., 1898, asst. treas., 1900, gen. mgr., 1911, v.p. and treas., 1918, pres., 1920—; dir. N.Y.,N.H.&H. R.R., The Connecticut Co., Citizens and Mfrs. National Bank. Formerly pres. Bd. of Aldermen; mem. Bd. Pub. Works, and mem. Bd. of Edn., Waterbury. Home: Waterbury, Conn. Died July 4, 1938.

GOSS, Elbridge Henry, author, banker; b. Boston, Dec. 22, 1830; s. Henry and Betsey (Kendall) G.; common school edn.; m. Hannah Jane Baker, Dec. 22, 1853. Settled in Melrose, Mass., where he has been auditor, water registrar, trustee, 1870—, and many yrs. chmn. public library; alderman; mem. Mass. legislature; treas. Melrose Savings Bank. Author: The Melrose Memorial (local history), 1868; Early Bells of Massachusetts, 1874; Centennial Fourth Address, 1876; Bibliography of Melrose, 1889; Life of Colonel Paul Revere (2 vols.), 1891; History of Melrose, 1902. Home: Melrose, Massachusetts. Died 1908.

GOSS, Evan Benson, judge; b. Rockford, Mich., Dec. 8, 1872; s. Benson O. and Hope A. G.; LL.B., U. of Mich., 1894, LL.M., 1895; m. Louisa Wright, Nov. 24, 1898; 1 dau., Marion E. Practiced at Bottineau, N.D., 1895-1904, Minot, N.D., from Jan. 1, 1905. State's atty., Bottineau County, 1896-99; dist. judge, 8th Jud. Dist., N.D., 1905-10; asso. justice Supreme Ct., N.D., term 1911-16; resumed practice in firm of McGee & Goss, 1917. Republican. Mason (K.T., Shriner), Elk. Home: Minot, N.D. Died Mar. 23, 1930.

GOSS, Francis Webster, physician; b. Salem, Mass., July 3, 1842; s. Ezekiel and Almira Dwelley (Hatch) G.; A.B., Harvard, 1862, A.M., 1865, M.D., 1869; m. Maria L. Draper (died 1875); m. 2d, Mrs. Helen L. Young, Jan. 10, 1878 (died 1914). Practiced in Roxbury (Boston), 1869-1914; removed to Calif., 1914. Sec. Mass. Med. Soc., 1875-1909; v.p., 1912-13. Home: Sacramento, Calif. Died July 10, 1923.

GOSS, Warren Lee, author; b. Brewster, Mass., Aug. 19, 1835; s. William W. and Hannah (Foster) G.; ed. Pierce Acad., Middleboro, Mass., and (1860-61) Harvard Law Sch.; pvt. in U.S. engrs., 1861-62; reënlisted, Nov. 1863, sergt. Co. H, 2nd Mass. Regt.; was prisoner of war at Libby, Belle Isle, Va., and Andersonville, Ga.; also at Charleston Fair Ground and Florence, S.C.; discharged, Nov. 1865; m. Emily A. Torbush, 1871; 1 son, Harry T. Largely engaged as editor and mag. writer; pres., 1873-76, and historian, 1890, Nat. Union of Ex-Prisoners of War; was for 5 yrs. on staff of comdr.-in-chief G.A.R., 2 yrs. as nat. patriotic instr. Author: The Soldier's Story of Captivity at Andersonville, 1866; Jed, 1889; Tom Clifton, 1892; Jack Alden, 1895; The Recollections of a Private, 1890 (1st 8 chapters previously published in Century War Series, 1887, and in "Battles and Leaders of the Civil War," 1888); In the Navy, 1898; Boys' and Girls' Life of Grant, 1911; The Boy's Life of General Sheridan, 1913; Jed's Boy, 1919; Jack Gregory. Home: Rutherford, N.J. Died Nov. 20, 1925.

GOSS, William Freeman Myrick, engineer; b. Barnstable, Mass., Oct. 7, 1859; s. Frank B. and Mary Gorham (Parker) G.; Mass. Inst. Tech., Boston, 1877-79; M.S., Wabash, 1888; D.Engring., U. of Ill., 1904; m. Edna D. Baker, Aug. 22, 1884. Organized dept. of practical mechanics, Purdue U., 1879; instr. practical mechanics, 1879-83, prof., 1883-90, prof. exptl. engring., dean schs. of engring. and dir. engring. lab., 1890-1907, Purdue U.; dean Coll. of Engring., dir. Sch. of Ry. Engring. and Adminstrn., and prof. ry. engring., U. of Ill., 1907-17, and dir. Engring. Expt. Sta., 1909-17; pres. Railway Car Mfrs. Assn., New York, 1917-25. Mem. Jury of Awards, Chicago Expn., 1893; chmn. advisory com. of Pa. Ry Co., charged with testing locomotives, St. Louis Expn., 1904; chief engr., com. of investigation on somke abatement and electrification of ry. terminals, Chicago, 1913-15. Author: Bench Work in Wood, 1890; Locomotive Sparks, 1902; Locomotive Performance, 1907; High Steam Pressures in Locomotive Service, 1907; Superheated Steam in Locomotive Service, 1910. Home: Barnstable, Mass. Died Mar. 23, 1928.

GOSSARD, George Daniel, college pres.; b. Greencastle, Pa., Nov. 26, 1868; s. Hilary and Anna Mary Rebecca (Zentmyer) G.; grad. W.Va. Normal and Classical Acad., Buckhannon, W.Va., 1890; A.B., Otterbein U., 1892; B.D., Union Bibl. Sem., Dayton, O., 1896; student Johns Hopkins, 1911-12; D.D., Lebanon Valley Coll., 1910; Litt.D., Susquehanna U., 1927; LL.D., Otterbein and Albright colleges, 1927; m. Florence Elizabeth Huber, Dec. 31, 1902 (died 1904); m. 2d, Ella Augusta Plitt, Feb. 2, 1910; 1 dau., Mary Elizabeth. Ordained ministry U.B. Ch., 1897; pastor Marion (Pa.) Circuit, 1897-99, Shippensburg, Pa., 1899-1902, Baltimore, Md., 1902-12; pres. Lebanon Valley Coll., 1912. Died April 17, 1932.

GOTSHALL, William Charles, engineer and scientist; b. St. Louis, May 9, 1875; s. Daniel H. and Minnie Wortmann Gotshall. Began as an elec. expert with Mo. Electric Light & Power Co.; U.S. Govt. engr. in charge of work of riprapping and protecting banks of 150 miles of Mississippi River; in charge location St. Louis & Eastern R.R.; rebuilt and operated Cairo (Ill.) Electric Ry.; built Belleville (Ill.) Electric Ry.; built Marshalltown (Ia.) ry. and lighting plant, Muncie (Ind.) Electric Ry., Grand Av. Ry., St. Louis; apptd. chief engr. Union Depot Ry. Co., St. Louis, and rehabilitated entire system and made pioneer introduction of and operated 3-wire system on electric rys.; converted 2d Av. (horse) Ry., New York, into a conduit electric ry., 1897-98; was pres. and chief engr. New York & Portchester R.R. Co., in the development of which the pioneer work in the design and development of high-speed electric traction was done—first high speed electric ry. in U.S. located entirely on a private right of way, with no grade crossings whatever, and cost about $25,000,000. Now engaged in design and development of new and in purchase and rehabilitation of existing railroads in U.S., Europe, the Near and Far East and Africa. Commd., Engr. R.C., 1917, and in active service. Author: Electric Railway Economics (text-book), 1914. Active in organizing and directing Near East archæol. excavations. Address: New York, N.Y. Died Aug. 20, 1935.

GOTT, Charles, educator; b. Arlington, Mass., Sept. 29, 1887; s. Charles and Bessie (Elwell) G.; A.B., Tufts Coll., 1911; A.M., Harvard U., 1914, Ph.D., 1919; m. Gladys Louise Baker, June 10, 1915; children—Marjorie Louise, Helen Elwell. Instr. in English, Tufts Coll., 1911-14; asst. Harvard U., 1914-18; asst. prof. Carnegie Inst. Tech., 1919-23, asso. prof., 1923-25, prof. English and head dept., Tufts Coll., 1925—, dean Grad. Sch., 1935—. Mem. bd. of visitors Harvard U. Republican. Universalist. Co-author: (with J. A. Behnke) A Preface to College Prose, 1935. Home: West Medford, Mass. Died Feb. 18, 1938.

GOTT, William Thomas, M.D.; b. Montgomery County, Ind., Mar. 18, 1855; s. William and Rhoda A. (Mount Schwindler) G.; ed. Ladoga (Ind.) Acad.; M.D., Eclectic Med. Coll., Cincinnati, O., 1878; post-grad. deg., N.Y. Polyclinic, 1884-88; m. Mary M. Allen, May 19, 1886; 1 son (dec.). Pres. U.S. Examining Bd. of Surgeons, Crawfordsville, Ind., 1885-89 and 1897; mem. Ind. Bd. Med. Registration and Examination, 1897— (pres. 1898 and 1901, sec., 1903—). V.p. Ind. and Ohio Live Stock Insurance

Co., Crawfordsville Trust Co. Mem. med. exec. com. Ind. Council Nat. Defense, 1917-18. Home: Crawfordsville, Ind. Died Feb. 24, 1933.

GOTTHEIL, Gustave, rabbi Temple Emanuel, New York, 1873—; b. Pinne, Prussia, May 28, 1827, of Jewish parentage; ed. according to rabbinical code; attended lectures in U. of Berlin and at the Inst. for Hebrew Literature; asst. to Dr. Samuel Holdheim, of Berlin Reform Temple, 1855-60; rabbi at Manchester, England, 1860-73. Liberal in opinions, and a leader in Reform branch of Hebrew ch. Address: New York, N.Y. Died 1903.

GOTTHEIL, Richard James Horatio, univ. prof.; b. Manchester, Eng., Oct. 13, 1862; s. Gustave (rabbi, New York) and Rosalie (Wollmann) G.; A.B., Columbia, 1881; Litt.D., 1929; studied at univs. of Berlin, Tübingen, Leipzig (Ph.D. summa cum laude, 1904), Hochschule für die Wissenschaft des Judenthums, and Veitel-Heine-Ephraimsche Beth Hamidrash, in Berlin; m. Emma R. Léon, Sept. 16, 1891. Lecturer Syriac lang. and lit., 1886-87, prof. Semitic langs., 1897—, Columbia U. Exchange prof. U. of Strasbourg, 1920-21. Head of Oriental dept., New York Pub. Library, 1896—; in charge Am. Sch. of Archæology at Jerusalem, 1909-10. Chevalier Legion of Honor, 1919; grand officier de l'Odre du Ouissam Alaouite Chérifien. Author: The Syriac Grammar of Mar Elia of Zobha, Berlin, 1887; Selections from the Syriac Julian Romance, with a full glossary in German and English, Leyden, 1906; The Syriac-Arabic Glosses of Isha bar Ali, Rome, 1910-27; Zionism, 1914; The Belmont-Belmonte Family, N.Y., 1917. Editor: Fragments from the Cairo Genizah, N.Y., 1927. One of editors of the Jewish Ency., 1901—. Rep. of Columbia Univ. at 400th anniversary of founding of U. of Grenada, 1933. Home: New York, N.Y. Died May 22, 1936.

GOTTSCHALK, Alfred L. Moreau, consul gen.; b. New York, Feb. 8, 1873; s. Gaston and Louise de L. Boucher G.; ed. New York City Coll., 1888-89, Packard's Bus. Coll., 1890, Kenyon Coll., 1891-94, New York U., 1895-96, and abroad. Attached to Gen. Brooke's div., P.R. campaign, 1898, as corr. New York Herald and London Telegraph; engaged in sugar growing, Santo Domingo and Hayti, 1899; apptd. collector of customs, Monte Cristi, Santo Domingo; U.S. consul at San Juan del Norte, Nicaraugua, 1902, at Callao, Peru, 1903; consul gen. Callao, 1905-06, City of Mexico, 1906-08; apptd. consul gen.-at-large, and inspector, 1908, in the District of Middle East and Africa; detailed to assist at the Am. Consulate Gen. at London on work in connection with European war, July-Nov. 1914; consul gen. at Rio de Janeiro, Brazil, 1914—. Detailed to West Africa by President Roosevelt to write spl. reports on Liberian situation, 1908. Home: New York, N.Y. Died Mar. 1, 1918.

GOUCHER, John Franklin, educator; b. Waynesburg, Pa., June 7, 1845; s. John (M.D.) and Eleanor (Townsend) G.; A.B., Dickinson Coll., 1868, A.M., 1872, D.D., 1885, LL.D., 1899; m. Mary C. Fisher, Dec. 24, 1877 (dec.). Entered M.E. ministry in Baltimore Conf., 1869; pastor in various churches in Baltimore; pres., 1889-1908, pres. emeritus, 1908, The Woman's Coll. of Baltimore (now Goucher College). Projected and built Harlem Park and Strawbridge chs. and the new First Ch. of Baltimore; pres. trustees, Centenary Bibl. Inst. (now Morgan Coll.), Baltimore, 1883—; projector, benefactor Princess Anne Training Sch.; lifted debt of Martin Mission Inst., Frankfort-on-the-Main, Germany; projected and directed organization of Anglo-Japanese College, Tokyo, 1882; founded West China Mission and Korean Mission M.E. Ch.; inspected by appointment Bd. of Missions M.E. Ch., their missions in Italy, 1886; Mexico, 1892; India, 1897-98; India, Java, China, Korea and Japan, 1906-07; projected and supported a system of over 120 primary and secondary vernacular schs. in India, 1883-1908; mem. Bd. Foreign Missions, M.E. Ch. (chmn. com. on edn.), 1884—. Trustee U. of Peking, China; pres. bd. of govs. West China Union U., Chentu. Del. to General Conferences, 1888—; fraternal del. to M.E. Church, South, 1894; mem. business com. of World Missionary Conf., Edin-Mission Field, 1910-20; inspected edni. instns. in Japan, Korea, China, 1910-11, 13, 14-15, 19, 20-21; a founder, 1902, mem. exec. com., 1902-09, Young Peoples Missionary movement; founder Pai Chai (1st Christian sch. in Korea), Seoul, 1883; mem. Joint Commn. Unification Am. Methodism, 1912-20. Pres. Md. Bible Soc., 1909. Trustee Fukien Christian Univ. (Foochow, China), Chosen Christian Coll. (Seoul), Union M.E. Theol. Sem. (Seoul). Decorated Order of Rising Sun, Japan, 3d Class, 1920; awarded Chia-ho Decoration, China, 3d Class, 1921. Author: Young People and the World's Evangelization; The Sunday School and Missions; Christianity and the United States, 1908; Growth in the Missionary Concept; Principles of Stewardship. Home: Pikesville, Md. Died July 19, 1922.

GOUDY, Franklin Curtis, lawyer; b. Hayesville, O.; s. Abel Curtis and Scinaette (Vantilburg) G.; ed. Baldwin U., Berea, O., Oberlin Coll. and U. of Mich.; m. Ida J. Gephart, Dec. 10, 1879. Admitted to Kan. bar, 1878, Colo. bar, 1879; attorney for Travelers Ins. Co. of Hartford, Conn.; mem. firm of Goudy & Goudy, Denver; also pres. Colorado Valley Land Co., Rio Grande Reservoir & Ditch Co., etc. Dist. atty. 7th Dist. of Colo., 1881-83; Rep. presidential elector, 1884; county atty. Arapahoe Co., Colo., 1895; Rep. nominee for gov. of Colorado; campaign speaker. Grand Sire, 1916-18, I.O.O.F. Methodist. Home: Denver, Colo. Died Mar. 28, 1924.

GOUGAR, Helen M., author, lecturer; b. Hillsdale, Mich., July 18, 1843; d. William Jackson and Clarissa Dresser Jackson; A.M., Hillsdale Coll., Mich., 1862; m. John D. Gougar, Dec. 10, 1863. Mem. of Ind. bar; author of the municipal woman suffrage law of Kansas, and has been instrumental in securing sch. suffrage for women in several states. Advocate of woman suffrage and prohibition; pres. Woman Suffrage Assn. of Ind., 23 yrs. Author: Strange Incidents in One Life; Forty Thousand Miles of World Wandering. Home: LaFayette, Ind. Died 1907.

GOULD, Ashley Mulgrave, judge; b. Lower Horton, N.S., Oct. 8, 1859; s. Charles Edward and Mary Jane (Fuller) G.; A.B., Amherst, 1881; LL.B., Georgetown U., 1884; m. Margaret Gray, Nov. 22, 1888. Admitted to bar, 1884; mem. Md. Ho. of Dels., 1898 (Rep. caucus nominee for speaker); U.S. atty. for D.C., 1901-02; asso. justice Supreme Ct. of D.C., 1902—. Prof. law of contracts, domestic relations and ins., Georgetown U., 1901—. Home: Washington, D.C. Died May 20, 1921.

GOULD, Carl Frelinghuysen, architect; b. N.Y. City, Nov. 24, 1873; s. Charles Judson and Annie L. (Westbrook) G.; grad. Phillips Exeter Acad., 1894; A.B., Harvard, 1898; studied École des Beaux Arts, Paris, 1899-1903; m. Dorothy Wheaton Fay, June 22, 1915; children—Carl Frelinghuysen, Anne Westbrook, John Bradford Van Wyck Fay. In offices of McKim, Mead & White, New York, 1905-06; then with George B. Post, in charge Madison State Capitol competition, and asst. in D. H. Burnham San Francisco plan; mem. firm Carpenter, Blair & Gould, New York, 1906-07; moved to Seattle, Wash., 1908; associated with Charles H. Bebb, 1914—. Established Dept. of Architecture, U. of Wash., 1914, and prof. in charge, 1914-26, author of adopted Campus Plan, 1915-37, architect for Main Library bldgs., Art Gallery, Gymnasium and swimming pools, class room bldgs.; supervising architect grounds and buildings, and asso. Chemistry Bldg., Woman's Dormitory; architect group plan for U.S. Govt. Locks, Ballard; architect Pacific Telephone & Telegraph Co. bldgs., Tacoma, Bremerton, Longview, Yakima, Olympia; supervising architect State Capitol bldgs., Olympia; author of program and tech. adviser for Ore. State Capitol Commn. in selection of architect. Mem. Civic Planning Commission, Seattle, 1925-30; author of ordinance creating Zoning Commission of Seattle. Fellow A.I.A. (president Washington state chapter). Architect of spruce production, etc., World War. Home: Seattle, Wash. Died Jan. 4, 1939.

GOULD, Charles Winthrop, lawyer; b. N.Y. City, Aug. 19, 1849; s. Charles and Henrietta Saltonstall (Mumford) G.; B.A., Yale, 1870, M.A., 1873; LL.B., Columbia, 1872; m. Louise Adele Dickerson, Jan. 20, 1881 (died 1883). Practiced at N.Y. City, 1872-1916; counsel to commn. for Spanish evacuation of Cuba at close of Spanish-Am. War. Trustee Met. Mus. Art. Republican. Episcopalian. Home: New York, N.Y. Died Mar. 18, 1931.

GOULD, Edward Sherman, civ. engr.; b. New York, Aug. 13, 1837; s. Edward Sherman and Mary Elizabeth (Du Bois) G.; ed. pvt. tutors and pvt. schs., New York; École des Mines, St. Etienne, France; m. Arabella Duncan Ludlow, 1868. Sec. to Hon. John Bigelow, U.S. Consul Gen. at Paris, France, 1862-65. Began practice, 1865; asst. engr. U.S. Corps of Engrs., 1872-76; asst. engr. Croton Aqueduct, div. engr. New Croton Aqueduct, 1879-86; built Scranton, Pa., water works, 1886-90, Havana (Cuba) water works, 1890-94, etc. Received Venezuelan decoration "El Busto del Libertador." Author: Practical Hydraulic Formulæ, 1889; Elements of Water Supply Engineering (3d edit.) 1899; Arithmetic of the Steam Engine, 1897. Home: Yonkers, N.Y. Died 1905.

GOULD, Edwin; b. New York, Feb. 25, 1866; s. Jay and Helen Day (Miller) G.; student Columbia, class of '88; m. Sarah Cantine, d. Dr. George F. Shrady, Oct. 27, 1892. Was mem. Troop A, and later capt. and insp. of rifle practice, 71st Regt. N.G.N.Y.; supply sergt. Troop A, Squadron A, N.Y.G., 1917-18; maj. ordnance officer, 1st Brigade, N.Y.G., 1918. Sec. St. Louis, Ark. & Tex. Ry., 1888, until reorganized, 1891, as the St. Louis Southwestern, of which was vice-pres., later pres. and chmn. bd., then sr. v.p.; organized in 1894, the Continental Match Co., which was consolidated with the Diamond Match Co., 1899; pres. Bowling Green Trust Co. of New York until merged with the Equitable Trust Co.; dir. Pine Bluff, Ark., River Ry., Paragould Southeastern Ry. Home: New York, N.Y. Died July 11, 1933.

GOULD, Edwin Sprague, clergyman; b. New Braintree, Mass., Feb. 20, 1844; s. Rufus and Mary (Henry) G.; ed. Williston Sem., Easthampton, Mass., 1861; Phillips Acad., Andover, Mass., 1862 and 1865; Hartford Theol. Sem., 1870-72; grad. Andover Theol. Sem., 1873; m. Phebe S. Gladding, Oct. 20, 1875 (died 1899). Ordained Congl. ministry, 1873; pastor Free Evangelical Ch., Providence, R.I., 1873-76, West Brookfield, Mass., 1877-81, Carthage, Mo., 1882-83, Globe Ch., Woonsocket, R.I., 1886-89, Athol, Mass., 1890-96. Served as corporal 51st and 60th Mass. regts., Civil War; editor Hartford and Worcester daily papers 4 yrs. Progressive Republican. Chaplain G.A.R., Dept. of R.I. Address: Providence, R.I. Deceased.

GOULD, Elgin Ralston Lovell, pres. of City and Suburban Homes Co., New York; b. Oshawa, Ont., Aug. 15, 1860; s. John T. and Emily Adelaide G.; A.B., U. of Toronto, 1881; Ph.D., Johns Hopkins U., 1886; (LL.D., U. of Toronto, 1911); m. Mary Hurst Purnell, Sept. 27, 1887. Fellow, 1882-84, lecturer, 1892-97, Johns Hopkins; prof. U. of Chicago, 1895-96; pres. City and Suburban Homes Co., New York, 1896—. Lecturer polit. economy, Columbia, 1901-02; city chamberlain, New York, 1902-04; vice chmn. New York City Charter Revision Commn., 1907, 08. Active in financial, philanthropical and ch. affairs and reform movements in New York. Author: Housing of Working People; Popular Control of the Liquor Traffic; The Gothenburg System of Liquor Traffic; The Social Condition of Labor. Home: New York, N.Y. Died Aug. 18, 1915.

GOULD, Elizabeth Lincoln, author; b. Boston, Mass.; d. Charles Duren and Sarah Bell (Wheeler) G.; ed. Boston pub. schs.; unmarried. Weekly contbr. to the Youth's Companion. Author: Play from Louisa M. Alcott's "Little Men," 1900; Play from Louisa M. Alcott's "Little Women," 1900; Little Polly Prentiss, 1902; A Rose of Holly Court, 1903; The Admiral's Granddaughter, 1907; Felicia, 1908; Felicia's Friends, 1909; Felicia Visits, 1910; The Admiral's Little Housekeeper, 1910; Felicia's Folks, 1911; The Admiral's Little Secretary, 1911; Grandma, 1911; The Admiral's Little Companion, 1912; Polly Prentiss Goes to School, 1912; Polly Prentiss Goes A-Visiting, 1913. Died Dec. 1914.

GOULD, Ezra Palmer, clergyman; b. Boston, 1841; grad. Harvard, 1861 (S.T.D., Columbia); served private 24th Mass. vols., 1861-63; lt. 55th Mass., 1863-64; capt. and maj. 59th Mass., 1864-65; prof. New Testament interpretation, Theol. Inst., Newton Centre, Mass., 1868-82; pastor Burlington, Vt., 1884-88; prof. New Testament literature, Philadelphia Episcopal Divinity School, 1889-98; asst. St. George's Ch., New York, 1898—. Author: Commentary on Corinthians; Commentary on St. Mark; Biblical Theology of the New Testament. Home: Brooklyn, N.Y. Died 1900.

GOULD, Frank Horace, lawyer; b. Fayette County, Ia., Aug. 29, 1856; s. Albert Langdon and Jane Augusta (Holbrook) G.; State Normal Sch., San José, Calif.; LL.B., Law Dept., U. of Ala., 1887; m. Hester A. Farnsworth, Jan. 16, 1878 (died 1894); m. 2d, Mrs. Nettie Eaton, Dec. 16, 1897. Practiced, Merced, Calif., 1887-93, Stockton, 1893-97, San Francisco, 1897—. Mem. Calif. Ho. of Rep., 1890-95 (speaker House, 1893-94); regent U. of Calif., 1893-95; building and loan commr., 1897-1901; chmn. Dem. State Conv., 1896 and 1904. Universalist. Mason. Home: San Francisco, Calif. Died Jan. 26, 1918.

GOULD, George Jay, capitalist; b. New York, Feb. 6, 1864; s. Jay and Helen Day (Miller) G.; pvt. edn.; m. Edith M. Kingdon, Sept. 14, 1886 (died 1921). Became clerk in the banking house of W. E. Connor & Co., New York, and succeeded his father as partner, Dec. 1885; became mem. New York Stock Exchange, Feb. 1886; entered ry. service, Apr. 26, 1888, as pres. Little Rock & Ft. Smith Ry.; pres. Manhattan Ry., 1888-1913; 1st v.p., 1888-93, pres. until 1913, Tex. & Pacific Ry.; pres. and dir., 1893-1911, and chmn. bd. until 1917, M.P. Ry.; pres. and dir., 1902-11, St. Louis, Iron Mountain and Southern Ry.; pres. Internat. & Great Northern Ry., 1893-1911; chmn. bd. dirs. Wabash R.R., 1903-05; v.p. Western Union Telegraph Co., 1901-10. Home: New York, N.Y. Died May 16, 1923.

GOULD, George Milbry, physician; b. Auburn, Me., Nov. 8, 1848; s. George Thomas and Eliza A. (Lapham) G.; drummer boy, 63d Ohio Vols., 1861-62; enlisted in 141st Ohio Vols., 1864-65; A.B., Ohio Wesleyan U., 1873, A.M., 1892; Harvard Div. Sch., 1873; M.D., Jefferson Med. Coll., Phila., 1888; m. Harriet Fletcher Cartwright, Oct. 15, 1876; m. 2d, Laura Stedman, Oct. 3, 1917. Began practice, Phila., 1888, splty. ophthalmology; ophthalmologist, Phila., Almshouse, 1892-94. Editor Medical News, 1891-95, Philadelphia Medical Journal, 1898-1900, American Medicine, 1901-06. Speaker Congress Arts and Sciences, St. Louis Exposition, 1904. Received first Doyne medal, Ophthalmological Congress, at Oxford, England. Author (in collaboration) of many med. books and dictionaries. Address: Atlantic City, N.J. Died Aug. 8, 1922.

GOULD, Howard, actor; b. Minneapolis, Minn., Mar. 19, 1867; s. Dr. H. W. and E. I. Gould; ed. grammar and high schs., Boston; m. Lena M. Bugbee. Began theatrical career, 1882, as call boy at old Boston Museum; afterward acted with James

O'Neil, Maggie Mitchell, E. H. Sothern, and starred 4 yrs. in Prisoner of Zenda, 1 yr. in A Colonial Girl; leading support to Mrs. Patrick Campbell, Mary Mannering and Viola Allen, 1901-07; starred in Witching Hour, 1908-10; leading man in Madame X, 1910-11; in Garden of Allah, 1915-18; one of title rôles in Three Wise Fools, 1919-21; leading man in "Welcome Stranger," 1921-22. Died Feb. 3, 1938.

GOULD, Laura Stedman (Mrs. George M. Gould), author; b. New York, Feb. 18, 1881; d. Frederick Stuart and Ellen (Douglas) Stedman; ed. Miss Brackett's Sch., New York; m. Dr. George Milbury Gould, Oct. 3, 1917 (died 1922). Lit. asst. to E. C. Stedman, 1898-1908; and to George M. Gould, M.D., 1906-22; literary executor to both. Author: Bibliography of Lafcadio Hearn, 1908. Asso. editor of Stedman's Complete Poems, 1908; Life and Letters of Edmund Clarence Stedman, 1910; Genius and Other Essays (by E. C. Stedman), 1911; Mrs. Kinney's Italian Reminiscences, 1913. Home: Atlantic City, N.J. Deceased.

GOULD, Samuel Wadsworth, congressman; b. Porter, Me., Jan. 1, 1852; s. Elias and Ruth (Clemons) G.; A.B., U. of Me., 1877; m. Nellie L. Winslow, Dec. 1879; 1 son, Champ Clark; m. 2d, Grace Cain, Aug. 1, 1922. Practiced law, Skowhegan, Me.; postmaster, Skowhegan, 1896-1900; Dem. candidate for gov. Me., 1902. Pres. Skowhegan Water Co.; dir. Milburn Co., Somerset Traction Co., Lakeside Worsted Mills, Bloomfield Acad., Somerset Loan Assn.; pres. and gen. counsel Dirigo Mut. Fire Ins. Co. Dem. candidate for 61st Congress, 3d Me. Dist., 1908; elected to 62d Congress (1911-13), 3d Me. Dist. Pres. bd. trustees U. of Me., Bloomfield Acad. Home: Skowhegan, Me. Deceased.

GOULDEN, Joseph Augustus, congressman; b. Adams County, Pa., Aug. 1, 1844; s. William and Mary A. (Wivell) G.; served in navy, May 1864-66; m. Isabelle Allwein, Dec. 1867. Engaged in ins. business; state mgr. Pa. Reformatory, 1884-88; sch. commr., New York City, 1893-98; state trustee Soldiers' and Sailors' Home, Bath, N.Y.; chmn. memorial com., G.A.R., New York, 1896-1902, and a mem. and sec. of the commn. that erected the Soldiers' and Sailors' Memorial monument in New York; mem. 58th to 61st Congresses (1903-11), 18th N.Y. Dist., and 63d Congress (1913-15), 23d Dist. Democrat. Home: New York, N.Y. Died May 3, 1915.

GOULDER, Harvey Danforth, lawyer; b. Cleveland, O., Mar. 7, 1853; s. Christopher and Barbara (Freeland) G.; grad. Cleveland High Sch. Admitted to bar, 1875, and began practice at Cleveland; prominent in maritime, ins. and corp. law; gen. counsel Great Lakes Protective Assn., Am. Bur. of Shipping (New York). Active in connection with legislation for improvement of channels on Great Lakes and tributaries and rehabilitating U.S. merchant marine. Home: Cleveland, O. Died June 14, 1928.

GOURLEY, William B., lawyer; b. Mar. 2, 1856; s. Henry G. and Catherine (Boyle) G.; LL.D., Seton Hall College, N.J., 1915. Admitted to bar as atty., 1880, counsellor-at-law, 1883; practiced at Paterson, N.J. Mem. N.J. Assembly, 1886; prosecutor of the pleas, 1886-96; chmn. Dem. State Com., 1898-1908; mem. Dem. Nat. Com., 1900-08. Trustee Rutgers U. Home: Clifton, N.J. Died Oct. 19, 1935.

GOUVERNEUR, Marian (Campbell), author; b. Jamaica, L.I., N.Y.; d. James and Marianne (Hazard) Campbell; ed. pvt. schs., New York; m. Samuel L. Gouverneur, Jr., Mar. 5, 1855 (dec.). Author: As I Remember—Recollections of American Society During the 19th Century, 1911. Home: Washington, D.C. Died Mar. 12, 1913.

GOVE, Aaron, educator; b. Hampton Falls, N.H., Sept. 26, 1839; s. John Francis and Sarah Jane (Wadleigh) G.; grad. Ill. Normal U., 1861; hon. A.M., Dartmouth, 1878; LL.D., U. of Colo., 1888; m. Caroline Spofford, Feb. 13, 1865. Entered Union Army as pvt., Sept. 1861, elected 1st lt. 33d Ill. Inf.; left service honorably as adj., bvt. maj., Aug. 1864. In charge of schools at Normal, Ill., 1864-74; supt. schs., Denver, 1874-1904; rep. of the beet sugar industry in the arid states, 1905—. Mason. Conglist. Republican. Address: Denver, Colo. Died Aug. 1, 1919.

GOVE, Charles Augustus, naval officer; b. Concord, N. H., July 5, 1854; s. Colonel Jesse Augustus and Maria Louise (Sherburne) G.; grad. U.S. Naval Acad., 1876; m. Minnie Webster, May 23, 1887. Ensign, Mar. 29, 1879; promoted through grades to rear adm., July 11, 1914. Served on all the principal stations, and 21 yrs. and 6 mos. at sea; on U.S.S. Topeka during Spanish-Am. War, 1898; commandant of midshipmen, U.S. Naval Acad., 1908-09; comd. the new dreadnaught Delaware, 1910, making trip around Cape Horn, and later in comd. same ship at coronation of King George V, naval review off Spithead, the Delaware being the largest of all the war ships there; comd. U.S. Naval Training Sta., San Francisco, 1912-13; retired 1914. Episcopalian. Mason. Comdt. U.S. Naval Unit U. of Calif., 1918. Home: San Francisco, Calif. Died Sept. 11, 1933.

GOVIN, Rafael R., publisher; b. N.Y. City, Aug. 31, 1868; s. Rafael R. and Rosa (de Tejada) G.; ed. pvt. schs. and tutors, New York, Havana, Madrid; LL.B., Columbia, 1889; m. May Medina, Feb. 10, 1898. Practiced law at N.Y. City in firm of Eustis, Jones & Govin; newspaper work, 1896—, later pub. and mgr., Journal of Commerce (New York), El Mundo, and La Prensa (Havana). Home: Claryville, N.Y. Died Feb. 14, 1926.

GOW, John Russell, clergyman; b. Waterville, Me., Oct. 20, 1855; s. George Boardman and Lucy Ann (Marston) G.; A.B., Brown U., 1877; grad. Newton Theol. Instn., 1882; D.D., Colby, 1908; m. Harriet Lee Hovey, Sept. 10, 1884 (died 1904); m. 2d, Rosa Howes Bevins, Mar. 22, 1909. Ordained Bapt. ministry, 1882; pastor Fairhaven, Vt., 1882-86, Bridgeport, Conn., 1886-91, Hyde Park Ch., Chicago, 1891-95, Somerville, Mass., 1895-1908, Brattleboro, Vt., 1908-13, Olivet Ch., Minneapolis, 1914—. Trustee Newton Theol. Instn., Vt. Acad. Home: Minneapolis, Minn. Deceased.

GOWDY, John Kennedy, consul gen.; b. Arlington, Ind., Aug. 23, 1843; s. A. M. C. and Nancy (Oliver) G.; ed. pub. schs., Rush County, Ind.; m. Eve Gordon, Jan. 24, 1867. Pvt. Co. L, 5th Ind. Cav., Sept. 1, 1862-Oct. 5, 1865; with regt. in pursuit through Ky., Ind. and Ohio and capture of John Morgan; served under Gen. Burnside, winter, 1863-64; under Gen. Sherman in Ga. campaign. Sheriff, 1871-75, auditor, 1883-91, Rush County, Ind.; chmn. Rush County Rep. Central Com., 1880-90; chmn. Ind. Rep. State Central Com., 1891-97; Am. consul general at Paris, France, 1897-1905. Decorated with Cross of Legion of Honor, 1905. Home: Rushville, Ind. Died June 26, 1918.

GOWDY, Roy Cotsworth, civil engr.; b. Washington, Ia., Sept. 3, 1878; s. L. H. and Anna L. (Reid) G.; ed. pub. and high schs., Colorado Springs, Colo.; Colo. Coll., 1 yr.; m. Emma L. Malden, June 27, 1905; 1 son, Joseph Scott. Rodman and asst. engr. on location and constrn., Colo. Springs & Cripple Creek Dist. Ry., 1899-1900; draftsman and instrument man, Denver & Northwestern Ry. (Moffatt Line), 1902-03, draftsman and clk. to E. C. von Diest, Colorado Springs, 1905-06; resident engr. and later chief engr., Ft. Worth & Denver City Ry., and Wichita Valley Lines, 1906-18; corporate chief engineer, C.&S. Ry. Co., Fort Worth & Denver City Ry. Co., and Wichita Valley Lines, 1918-20; chief engr. C.&S. Ry. Co., Fort Worth & Denver City Ry. Co., and Wichita Valley Ry. Co., 1920—. Home: Denver, Colo. Died June 10, 1939.

GOWEN, Francis Innes, lawyer; b. Germantown, Phila., Aug. 17, 1855; student U. of Pa., class of 1875, A.B., 1906; read law in father's office; m. Alice Robinson. Admitted to Pa. bar, 1877; was counsel at Phila. for Lehigh Valley Ry.; asst. gen. solicitor Phila. and Reading Ry. until 1902; gen. solicitor, Pa. R.R., Dec. 1902-12, gen. counsel, 1912-21, v.p. and gen. counsel, 1921—. Home: Philadelphia, Pa. Died Apr. 8, 1927.

GOWEN, Isaac William, clergyman; b. New Brunswick, N.J., Dec. 29, 1858; s. Henry and Margaret (Hopper) G.; A.B., Rutgers, 1879, A.M., 1883 (D.D.); grad. New Brunswick Theol. Sem., 1883; LL.D., Central Coll., Ia., 1925; m. Emma Elwell O'Brien, Oct. 15, 1885; children—Wilber Thomas, Hazel Margaret (Mrs. John Borg), May Christine (wife of Rev. Francis E. Wilber), William Winthrop (dec.). Ordained ministry Ref. Ch. in America, 1883; pastor Cold Spring, N.Y., 1883-85, Grove Church, North Bergen, 1885—. Pres. Gen. Synod Ref. Ch. of America, 1915; corr. sec. Ref. Ch., Bd. of Publ.; mem. bd. of suprs., New Brunswick Theol. Sem.; mem. exec. and administrative coms. of Federal Council of Chs. of Christ in America; mem. exec. com. Lord's Day Alliance of U.S.; mem. Internat. Com. of Sunday Schs.; mem. bd. dirs. Am. Tract Soc.; mem. council Hope Coll., Holland, Mich.; mem. bd. supts. Theol. Sem., Holland, Mich. Home: North Bergen, N.J. Died Feb. 28, 1929.

GRABER, Edward Darwin, educator; b. Wooster, O., Mar. 17, 1862; s. Philip and Pauline (de la Guerne) G.; student Mt. Union (Ohio) Coll., 1884-86; B.S., Nat. Normal U., Lebanon, O., 1887, M.S., 1891, Ph.D., 1896; post-grad. work in higher mathematics, Washington U., St. Louis, Mo., and Harvard, 1891-92; m. Antoinette Akers, July 5, 1888. Supt. pub. schs., Gunnison, Colo., 1887-91; prof. higher mathematics and astronomy, Highland Park Coll., Des Moines, Ia., 1892-95; prof. mathematics, logic and methods, N.Y. State Normal Sch., Geneseo, [illegible] 1895-1907; prin. Greenwich (Conn.) High Sch., 1907-13; asso. principal Mt. Pleasant Acad., Ossining-on-Hudson, N.Y., 1913—. Institute lecturer, N.Y. Democrat. Episcopalian. Home: Ossining-on-Hudson, N.Y. Died July 17, 1926.

GRABFELDER, Samuel; b. Bavaria, Germany, Sept. 2, 1844; s. Emanuel and Regina (Dreyfus) G.; came to America, 1858; ed. boarding sch., Hardinsburg, Ky.; m. Delia Griff, Feb. 13, 1870. In distilling business, Louisville, Ky., 1867-1903; devoted attention to charitable work. Pres. Nat. Jewish Hosp. for Consumptives, Denver (donated $40,000 to this instn., 1913); officer various other instns. Republican. Jewish religion. Home: Philadelphia, Pa. Deceased.

GRACE, Francis Mitchell, clergyman M.E. Ch. South; b. Elyton, Ala. (now Birmingham), Feb. 28, 1832; s. Baylis Earle and Ann (Mitchell) G.; prepared at Elyton Acad., 1837-46; grad. East Tenn. Univ., 1849 (A.M., same, D.D., Hiwassee Coll.); m. 1st, Mary J. Borden, Apr. 3, 1854; m. 2d, Kitty Greene, Aug. 1872; m. 3d, Ida F. Hoskins, June 1894. Ordained to ministry, M.E. Ch. South, serving as pastor at Newbern, Ala., 1853; Eufaula, Ala., 1854; Demopolis, Ala., 1855-56; Talladega, Ala., 1857-58; Tuskaloosa, Ala., 1859-60; Newbern, Ala., 1861-65; edited Daily Messenger, Selma, Ala., 1866; prof. U. of Tenn., Knoxville, 1867-70; pres. Hiwassee Coll., 1871-72; pres. Mansfield Female Coll., La., 1883-88; prof. Hiwassee Coll., Tenn., 1890-99; prof. North Ala. Conf. Coll. Contributor to religious and gen. periodicals. Home: Birmingham, Ala. Died 1904.

GRACE, Thomas, bishop; b. Wexford, Ireland, Aug. 2, 1841; ed. St. Peter's Coll., Wexford; ecclesiastical studies All Hallows Coll., Dublin; (D.D.). Ordained R.C. priest, June 11, 1867; first parochial work at Red Bluff, later at Eureka, Humboldt and Carson, Nev.; afterward rector cathedral at Marysville 8 yrs.; pastor Sacramento Cathedral, 1881-96; preconized bishop Feb. 27, 1896; consecrated bishop of Sacramento, June 16, 1896. Address: Sacramento, Calif. Died Dec. 27, 1921.

GRACE, William, contractor; b. Hull, Eng., Sept. 11, 1847; s. William Evans and Mary (Bodell) G.; ed. St. Charles' Sch., Hull; m. Mary Booth, 1868. Came to America, 1871; engaged in building in Chicago and other cities; pres. William Grace Co.; rebuilt N.Y.C. Depot, New York; builder La Salle St. Sta., 1906, Court House, Chicago, 1907, etc. Home: Barrington, Ill. Died Nov. 7, 1921.

GRACE, William Russell, mayor; b. Queenstown, Cork, Ireland, May 10, 1832; s. James and Ellen Mary (Russell) G.; ran away from school at 14; worked his way on a sailing vessel to New York; employed there for 2 yrs., returned to Ireland on a visit; m. Lillius Gilchrist, Sept. 11, 1859. Went to Callao, Peru, 1850; became clerk, and, in 1852, partner in firm of Bryce & Co., which later became Bryce, Grace & Co., and afterward Grace Bros. & Co. Came to New York, 1865; organized W. R. Grace & Co.; in 1891 established the New York and Pacific Steamship Co., Ltd. Mayor of New York, 1881-82 and 1885-86. In 1897 founded Grace Inst. for affording women and girls a practical edn. in stenography, dressmaking, millinery, domestic science, etc. Democrat. Home: New York, N.Y. Died 1904.

GRACEY, Samuel Levis, consul; b. Phila., Sept. 8, 1835; s. John and Ann B. (Leech) G.; S.T.B., Boston U., 1858; m. Leonora Thompson, Nov. 21, 1860 (died 1897); m. 2d, Corda E. Pratt, Jan. 15, 1900; 1 son, Wilbur Tirrell G. Ordained M.E. ministry, 1858; pastor Phila., 1857; enlisted as pvt. 16th Pa. Regt., 1862; commd. chaplain 6th Pa. Cav., 1862; served in Sheridan's Cav., Army of the Potomac, 3 yrs.; pastor Smyrna, Del., 1866-69, Pawtucket, 1871-73, Fall River, 1873, Weymouth, 1874, Westfield, 1878-80, Chelsea, 1882-84, Cambridge, 1884-85, Salem, 1886-88, Natick, 1889-90, Lynn, Mass., 1896-97. Consul at Foochow, 1890-93 and 1897—. Received decoration Double Dragon from Chinese Govt. for services in Boxer uprising, 1900. Home: Boston, Mass. Died 1911.

GRADLE, Henry, ophthalmologist; b. Frankfurt, Germany, Aug. 17, 1855; s. Bernard G. and Rosa (Schottenfels) G.; ed. Chicago; M.D., Chicago Med. Coll., 1874; studied also at Vienna, Heidelberg, Leipzig, Paris; m. Fanny Searls, Aug. 31, 1881. Prof. physiology, 1879-83, diseases of the eye and ear, 1898—, Northwestern U. Med. Sch. Author: Bacteria and the Germ Theory of Disease, 1883; Text-book of Diseases of the Nose, Pharynx and Ear, 1901. Home: Chicago, Ill. Died 1911.

GRAFF, George E., newspaper pub.; b. Williamsport, Pa., Sept. 1, 1865; s. Frederick and Mary (Fritz) G.; grad. high sch., Williamsport, 1884; m. Flora Scott, Jan. 31, 1889. Reporter Williamsport Sun, 1889, bus. mgr., 1893-1904; court reporter, Lycoming County, Pa., 1892-1904; pub. Williamsport Sun, 1904—, Williamsport Gazette and Bulletin, 1926—; pres. The Sun-Gazette Co. Pres. and dir. Williamsport Chamber of Commerce, 1933. Republican. Presbyn. Mason. Home: Williamsport, Pa. Died Nov. 12, 1935.

GRAFF, Joseph Verdi, congressman; b. Terre Haute, Ind., July 1, 1854; s. Jacob K. and Mary J. (Miller) G.; grad. Terre Haute High Sch.; student 1 yr. at Wabash Coll.; m. Mary B. Crane, Oct. 5, 1882. Admitted to bar, 1879; practiced at Pekin, Ill., and was pres. bd. edn. there; practiced law at Peoria, Ill. Mem. 54th to 57th Congresses (1895-1900), 14th Ill. Dist., and 58th to 61st Congresses (1903-11), 16th Dist. Home: Peoria, Ill. Died Nov. 10, 1921.

GRAFLY, Charles, sculptor; b. Phila., Dec. 3, 1862; s. Charles and Elizabeth (Simmons) G.; pupil Pa. Acad. Fine Arts and Chapu and Dampt, Paris; m. Frances Sekeles, June 7, 1895; 1 dau., Dorothy. Hon. mention salon of 1891; Temple Trust Fund, Phila., 1892; medal Chicago Expn., 1893; silver medal, Atlanta Expn., 1895; Converse gold medal, Pa. Acad. Fine Arts, 1899; gold medal, Paris Expn., 1900, Charleston Expn., 1901, Buffalo Expn., 1901; mem. Internat. Jury of Awards, St. Louis Expn., 1904; instr. sculpture, Pa. Acad. Fine Arts, 1892—. Represented in permanent collections of Pa. Acad. Fine Arts, Detroit Art Mus., St. Louis Mus., Carnegie Inst., Pittsburgh, Boston Mus., Cincinnati Mus., Peabody Institute, Baltimore, Maryland. Mem. of Municipal Art Jury, Philadelphia, N.A., 1906; mem. Nat. Inst. Arts and Letters. Was awarded George D. Widener gold medal, 1913; Watrous gold medal, N.A., 1918; medal of honor, Concord Art Asso., 1922. Mem. Internat. Jury of Awards, Panama Expn., 1915. Instr. Sch. of Boston Museum of Fine Arts, 1917—. Home: Philadelphia, Pa. Died May 5, 1929.

GRAFTON, Charles Chapman, bishop; b. Boston, Apr. 12, 1830; s. Joseph and Anna Maria (Gurley) G.; ed. Boston Latin Sch.; LL.B., Harvard, 1853; studied div. under Bishop Whittingham, of Md.; D.D., Racine Coll., 1889; LL.D., Lawrence U., 1909. Deacon, 1855, priest, 1858, P.E. Ch.; asst. at Reisterstown, Md.; then missionary, Baltimore; asst. minister, St. Paul's Ch., Baltimore, and chaplain Md. Deaconesses; rector Ch. of the Advent, Boston, 1872-88; consecrated bishop of Fond du Lac, Wis., Apr. 25, 1889. Organized in Eng., 1865 (with Rev. R. M. Benson), the Soc. of St. John the Evangelist, a religious brotherhood (known as "Cowley Fathers"); established an affiliated house of The St. Margaret's Sisterhood, Eng., in Boston, founded in 1888; mother house of Sisters of the Holy Nativity, at Providenve, R.I.; founded Grafton Hall, for young ladies, Fond du Lac. Author: Vocation, or Call of the Divine Master to a Sister's Life; Plain Suggestions for a Reverent Celebration of the Holy Communion; Fond du Lac Tracts; Christian and Catholic, 1905; Catholic Atlas. Address: Fond du Lac, Wis. Died Aug. 30, 1912.

GRAFTON, Robert Wadsworth, artist; b. Chicago, Ill., Dec. 19, 1876; s. George and Delia Irene (Oviatt) G.; ed. Art Inst., Chicago, Julian Acad., Paris, France; studied in Holland and Eng.; Dr. of Fine Arts, Kan. Wesleyan U., 1933; m. Elinda M. Oppermann, July 27, 1908; 1 dau., Elinda Patricia. Has exhibited in New York, Boston, Phila., Chicago and other cities; awarded Mary T. R. Foulks prize, Richmond (Ind.) Art Assn., 1910, 19; Leroy Goddard prize, Hoosier Salon, 1925. Mural panels, First Nat. Bank and Anthony Hotel, Ft. Wayne, Ind.; State House, Springfield, Ill.; "End of French Market," Delgado Mus., New Orleans, La.; "St. Louis Cathedral," Richmond Pub. Art Mus.; "Oyster Shuckers," Lafayette (Ind.) Art Assn.; "Northwestern Station," Union League Club, Chicago; mural, "Coming of the Pioneer," Kan. Wesleyan Univ., Salina, Kan.; portrait of President Calvin Coolidge, painted at the White House, for Saddle and Sirloin Club of Chicago; official portrait of Secretary Jardine for Dept. of Agriculture; portraits of Governor Jackson, Governor McCray and Governor Leslie for Indiana State Capitol; of Governor Chase Osborn for Michigan State Capitol; of Governor Fred Green of Michigan; of Howard Vanderslice of Kansas City Art Inst.; Cardinal Mundelein at Mundelein Sem.; Ex-President Hoover, Arthur M. Hyde and Frank O. Lowden for Saddle and Sirloin Club; also portraits at Northwestern, Purdue and Tulane univs., U. of Wis. and Earlham College, and of Ambassador Charles Faulkner, for Am. Embassy, Paris. Dir. fine arts Kan. Wesleyan U. Republican. Episcopalian. Home: Michigan City, Ind. Died Dec. 17, 1936.

GRAHAM, Allen Jordan, cotton mfr.; b. Asheville, N.C., Mar. 30, 1884; s. Charles Edgar and Susan (Jordan) G.; M.A., Furman U., 1902; m. Mabel Kirkpatrick, Dec. 29, 1909; children—Susan, Allen J., Thomas K. Began as sec. and treas. Camperdown Mills, 1902, pres., 1922—; pres. and treas. Alice Mills (Easley, S.C.), Enoree (S. Carolina) Mills; pres. Gramath Realty Co.; dir. Glenwood Cotton Mills, Peoples Nat. Bank, Am. Bank & Trust Co., Easley Cotton Mills. Mem. Draft Bd., Greenville County, S.C., World War; v.p. Chamber of Commerce, Greenville. Trustee Central Y.M.C.A., Greenville Community Fund; chmn. bd. govs. City Hosp. Democrat. Presbyn. Home: Greenville, S.C. Died Nov. 29, 1931.

GRAHAM, David Wilson, surgeon; b. Biggsville, Ill., June 11, 1843; s. Andrew and Rachel (Davis) G.; A.B., Monmouth Coll., Ill., 1870, A.M., 1873, LL.D., 1910; M.D., Bellevue Hosp. Med. Coll., 1872; served in 83d Ill. Inf., 1862-65; m. Ida A. Barned, July 12, 1877. Demonstrator anatomy, 1874-77, prof., 1877-82, prof. surgery, 1883-98, Woman's Med. Coll., Chicago; surgeon, Central Free Dispensary, 1874-91, Presbyn. Hosp., 1883—, Cook County (Ill.) Hosp., 1888-89; prof. clin. surgery, Rush Med. Coll. (U. of Chicago), 1891—; consulting surgeon, Evanston Hosp., and chief surgeon, Ill. Naval Reserves, 1905-1911. Editor Chicago Medical Register, 1882-85. Home: Chicago, Ill. Died Feb. 9, 1925.

GRAHAM, Edward Kidder, college pres.; b. Charlotte, N.C., Oct. 11, 1876; s. Archibald and Eliza Owen (Barry) G.; Ph.B., U. of N.C., 1898; M.A., Columbia, 1902, graduate student, 1903-04; D.C.L., U. of South, 1914; LL.D., Erskine, 1914, Wake Forest, 1915, Lafayette, 1915; m. Susan Williams Moses, June 25, 1908. Prof. English and dean, Coll. Liberal Arts, 1908-14, acting pres., 1913-14, pres., 1914—, U. of N.C. Democrat. Presbyn. Home: Chapel Hill, N.C. Died Oct. 26. 1918.

GRAHAM, Edwin R., publishing agt.; b. Upper Sandusky, O., May 7, 1854; s. Rev. John and Jane Glasgow (McKee) G.; B.S., Baldwin U., 1874, Litt.D., 1915; m. Mary Hawthorne Dolliver, Nov. 14, 1888. Engaged in mercantile pursuits until 1881; western representative of Houghton, Mifflin & Co., Boston, 1893-1904; publishing agt. of The Methodist Book Concern, at Chicago, 1904-16, at New York, 1916—. Trustee Baldwin-Wallace Coll., 1911. Home: New York, N.Y. Died Feb. 20, 1920.

GRAHAM, Ernest Robert, architect; b. Lowell, Mich., Aug. 22, 1868; s. Robert and Emma (Post) G.; ed. pub. schs.; LL.D., U. of Notre Dame and Coe Coll.; m. Carlotta Hall, 1894 (died 1923); m. 2d, Ruby Leffingwell, Dec. 1925. Practiced at Chicago; asst. dir. of works during constrn. and operation of Chicago Expn.; partner D. H. Burnham & Co., 1904-12; sr. partner Graham, Burnham & Co., 1912-17, of Graham, Anderson, Probst & White, 1917; architect of many noteworthy structures, including Equitable Bldg., Flatiron, Chase Nat. Bank Bldg., and Eighty Maiden Lane (N.Y. City), Union Station and General Post Office (Washington), Union Trust Bldg., Union Station and Terminal Tower Bldg. (Cleveland), Field Museum of Natural History, John G. Shedd Aquarium, Continental-Ill. Bank Bldg., 208 S. La Salle Street Bldg., Union Station, Marshall Field & Co. stores, Straus Bldg., New Post Office, Field Bldg., Pittsfield Bldg., Wrigley Bldg., State Bank of Chicago, 20 Wacker Drive Bldg., The Merchandise Mart (Chicago); Pennsylvania Sta. (Philadelphia), Selfridge & Co. Store (London, Eng.). Home: Chicago, Ill. Died Nov. 22, 1936.

GRAHAM, George Scott, congressman; b. Phila., Sept. 13, 1850; ed. pub. schs. and pvt. tutors; LL.B., U. of Pa.; LL.D., Lafayette Coll., 1889; m. Emma Ellis, Dec. 14, 1870; children—Adele (dec.), George Ellis, (dec.), Ethel Scott (Mrs. C. P. Wentz), Blanche (Mrs. Erskine Bains); m. 2d, Pauline M. Wall, June 1898; 1 dau., Marion Hollister (Mrs. Graham Williams). Admitted to bar, 1870; mem. select council of Phila., 1877-80; dist. atty., Phila. County, Pa., 1880-99, being elected for 6 consecutive terms of 3 yrs. each, and 4 times upon all tickets, without opposition; declined reëlection and retired to pvt. practice, Phila., Jan. 1, 1899; mem. firm of Graham and Gilfillan, Phila., also mem. firm of Graham & L'Amoreaux, New York. Prof. criminal law, U. of Pa., 11 yrs. Mem. 63d to 71st Congresses (1913-31), 2d Pa. Dist. Address: Philadelphia, Pa. Died July 4, 1931.

GRAHAM, Horace French, gov.; b. N.Y. City, Feb. 7, 1862; s. Samuel H. and Lucy F. (Swett) G.; prep. edn. Craftsbury (Vt.) Acad.; LL.B., cum laude, Columbia Law Sch., 1888 (also course in polit. science); unmarried. Practiced at Craftsbury; state's atty., Orleans County, Vt., 1898-1902; mem. Vt. Ho. of Rep., 1892 and 1900; Rep. presdl. elector, 1900; auditor of accounts for Vt., 1902-17; gov. of Vt., 1917-19. Home: Craftsbury, Vt. Died Nov. 23, 1941.

GRAHAM, Hoyt Conlin, coll. pres.; b. Eldorado, Ark., Nov. 25, 1899; s. Albert Wesley and Sallie Amelia (Thompson) G.; B.S., Ouachita Coll., Arkadelphia, 1922; M.S., State U. of Ia., Ph.D., 1927; m. Alice Marion Millett, Aug. 22, 1927. Asst. in physics and chemistry, Ouachita Coll., 1919-22; teacher physics, high sch., Winterset, Ia., 1922-24; grad. asst. in chemistry dept., State U. of Ia., 1924-27; head of chemistry dept., Eastern State Teachers Coll., Madison, S.D., 1927-28; head of chemistry dept., N.M. State Teachers Coll., Silver City, N.M., 1928-33, pres., 1933—. Served as sergeant, World War. Mason. Address: Silver City, N.M. Died June 21, 1936.

GRAHAM, Jonathan Thomas, lawyer; b. Oil City, Pa., Dec. 11, 1865; s. William T. and Lucy Ann (Rodgers) G.; ed. pub. and pvt. schs.; studied law in office of H. C. Graham and Wm. J. Breene, 1888-92; m. Mary L. Chapman, Jan. 5, 1895 (died 1932); 1 son—William Carl; m. 2d, Ruby Heinz, Aug. 3, 1935. Admitted to Pa. bar, 1892, and began practice at Oil City; moved to W.Va., 1892, to Huntington, W.Va., 1901; mem. firm Scott, Graham & Wiswell, 1923—. Pros. atty., Wayne County, W.Va., 1895-96; judge Circuit Court, 6th Jud. Circuit of W.Va., 1913-23; chmn. Rep. State Com., 1924-28. Republican. Mason. Home: Huntington, W.Va. Died Nov. 7, 1938.

GRAHAM, Lawrence Pike, brig. gen. vols., Col. U.S. Army; b. Amelia County, Va., 1815; apptd. 2d lt., 2d dragoons, 1837; later becoming 1st lt. and capt.; served in campaign against Seminoles, 1842; bvtd. maj. for gallantry in Mexican War; promoted maj., June 14, 1858; lt. col., 5th cav., Oct. 1861; col., 14th cav., May 1864; bvtd. brig. gen. for meritorious services in Civil War, March 1865. Commissioned brig. gen. vols., Aug. 1861; raised, 1862, and comd. cav. brigade in Army of Potomac; mustered out of vol. service, Aug. 1865; retired as col., Dec. 1870. Home: Washington, D.C. Died 1905.

GRAHAM, Margaret Collier, author; b. Van Buren County, Ia., Sept. 29, 1850; d. David and Lydia A. (Lindsay) Collier; common school edn. at Keokuk, Ia.; grad. Monmouth (Ill.) Coll., 1869; m. Donald M. Graham, Oct. 21, 1873. Author: Stories of the Foot-Hills; The Wizard's Daughter, 1905; Gifts and Givers, 1906. Contbr. to mags. Home: South Pasadena, Calif. Died 1910.

GRAHAM, Ray Austin, mfr.; b. Washington, Ind., May 28, 1887; s. Ziba Foote and Margaret (Cabel) G.; prep. edn., St. Simon's Acad., Washington, Ind.; student St. Mary's (Kan.) Coll., 1900-04; B.S., U. of Ill., 1908; m. Eugenia Winston, Apr. 18, 1911; children—Laura Margaret, Ray Austin, John Winston, Barbara Ann. Mgr. Graham Farms, Washington, Ind., 1908-11; sec.-treas. Graham Glass Co., Evansville, Ind., 1911-16; sec.-treas. Graham Bros., Inc., truck mfrs., Detroit, Mich., 1916-26; gen. mgr. Dodge Bros., 1925-26; pres. Graham Bros. Corp., 1927—; sec.-treas. Graham-Paige Motors Corp., 1927—. Decorated Knight of St. Gregory (papal), 1928. Catholic. Homes: New York, N.Y., and Roslyn, L.I., N.Y. Died Aug. 13, 1932.

GRAHAM, Robert Orlando, univ. dean; b. Butler, Pa., Jan. 10, 1853; s. Malcolm and Mary (Boggs) G.; A.B., Amherst, 1877, A.M., 1882; Ph.D., Johns Hopkins, 1888; m. Eleanor S. Campbell, June 23, 1881. Prof. chemistry, Westminster Coll., Pa., 1878-86; prof. chemistry, 1888—, acting pres., 1897-98, dean, 1898—, Ill. Wesleyan U. Chemist Funk Corn Breeding Co.; formerly water analyst C.&A. Ry. Mem. city council, 1897-1903, and acting mayor, 1897-99, Bloomington; mem. city library bd., 1896—. Active horticulturist; pres. Ill. State Hort. Soc. and mem. State Hort. Advisory Bd., 1907—. Home: Bloomington, Ill. Died 1911.

GRAHAM, William Johnson, judge; b. New Castle, Pa., Feb. 7, 1872; s. Richard Johnson and Caroline (Mundwiler) G.; B.L., U. of Ill., 1893; studied law in office of James M. Brock, Aledo, Ill.; m. Olive Whan, Nov. 8, 1899 (died 1911); m. 2d, Edna Robey, Nov. 9, 1912. Admitted to Ill. bar, 1895, and practiced at Aledo. Republican campaign speaker, 1892—; state's attorney, Mercer County, Ill., 1901-09; mem. Ill. Ho. of Rep., 1915, 16; mem. 65th to 68th Congresses (1917-25), 14th Ill. Dist.; nominated 69th Congress, and resigned June 7, 1924; presiding judge, U.S. Court of Customs and Patent Appeals, Washington, D.C., 1924—. Presbyn. Mason. Home: Washington, D.C. Died Nov. 10, 1936.

GRAHAM, William Montrose, army officer; b. Washington, Sept. 28, 1834; s. Col. James Duncan and Charlotte (Meade) G. Apptd. from D.C., 2d lt. 1st Arty., June 7, 1855; promoted through grades to brig. gen., 5th Arty., May 26, 1897; maj. gen. vols., May 4, 1898; retired, Sept. 28, 1898; hon. discharged from vol. service, Nov. 30, 1898. Bvtd.: maj., July 1, 1862, "for gallant and meritorious services during Peninsular campaign"; lt. col., Sept. 17, 1862, for same in battle of Antietam; col., July 3, 1863, for same in battle of Gettysburg; brig. gen., Mar. 13, 1865, for same in the field during the war. Comd. Dept. of Texas, 1897; organized and comd. Dept. of the Gulf until apptd. maj. gen. of vols., May 4, 1898; organized and comd. 2d Army Corps for service in Spanish War. Mem. bd. of officers apptd. by Sec. of War to locate positions of the regular batteries of Arty. on the battlefield of Gettysburg and to prepare the inscriptions on the tablets erected to mark the same. Died Jan. 17, 1916.

GRAMMER, Elijah Sherman, senator; b. Hickory County, Mo., Apr. 3, 1868; s. John W. and Sarah F. G.; ed. Bentonville (Ark.) Coll.; m. Emma Kindley, Jan. 21, 1904. Logger, later gen. mgr. lumber camps, Washington; in charge constrn. tramway, Chilcoot Pass, Alaska; owner logger successively of Scott & Grammer, Sisco, Wash., Grammer's Camp, Montborne, Brown's Bay Logging Co., Seattle, Admiralty Logging Co., Seattle; later v.p. and treas. Flora Logging Co., Portland, Ore.; pres. and mgr. Grammer Investment Co.; v.p. and treas. Carlton & Coast Ry. Co. Served as maj. U.S. Army, assigned to Spruce Production Div., 1918. Apptd. mem. U.S. Senate to fill unexpired term of Senator Wesley L. Jones, dec., Nov. 22, 1932, term expiring Mar. 4, 1933. Republican. Presbyn. Mason. Home: Seattle, Wash. Died Nov. 21, 1936.

GRAMMER, Jacob, editor; b. Velburg, Bavaria, Germany, May 22, 1871; s. Franz Xaver and Julia (Liebler) G.; ed. in Germany until 12; came to U.S., 1883; m. Charlotte Hils, July 15, 1896; children—Edward August (dec.), Carolyn Julia, Elsie Charlotte. Learned printer's trade; joined staff

Brooklyn Freie Presse, 1890, city editor, 1898-1904, mng. editor, 1904-12; legislative corr. New York Staats Zeitung, 1912-14; asst. managing editor, Staats Zeitung, 1914-20, mng. editor, 1920—. Presbyterian. Home: Brooklyn, N.Y. Died Nov. 3, 1931.

GRANBERY, John Cowper, bishop M.E. Church South; b. Norfolk, Va., Dec. 5, 1829; s. Richard Allen and Ann (Leslie) G.; grad. Randolph-Macon Coll., 1848, D.D., 1870. Became preacher in M.E. Ch. South, in Va. conference, 1848; chaplain C.S.A., 1861-65; prof. moral philosophy and practical theology, Vanderbilt U., 1875-82; bisohp M.E. Ch., S., 1892; m. 1st, Jennie Massie, 1858 (died 1859); m. 2d, Ella Winston, 1862. Author: Bible Dictionary, 1885; Twelve Sermons, 1896; Experience the Crowning Evidence of the Christian Religion, 1900. Home: Ashland, Va. Died 1907.

GRANGER, Alfred Hoyt, architect; b. Zanesville, O., May 31, 1867; s. Judge Moses Moorhead and Mary Hoyt (Reese) G.; A.B., Kenyon Coll., Gambier, O., 1887, D.Sc., 1932; grad. Mass. Inst. Tech., 1889; student École des Beaux Arts, Paris, Atelier Pascal; m. Belle Hughitt, Oct. 4, 1893; children—Mrs. Elisabeth Granger Brown, Mrs. Chester D. Shepard, Mrs. Martha Granger Blair. Spent several yrs. as draftsman in offices of Shepley, Rutan & Coolidge, Boston and Chicago, and with Jenney & Mundie, Chicago; began practice for self at Cleveland, O., 1893, planned laying out of Euclid Heights; formed partnership with Charles S. Frost, Chicago, 1898; designed La Salle St. and C.&N.W. Ry. terminals, Northern Trust Bank Bldg., St. Luke's Hosp., Home for Incurables, James C. King Home for Aged Men (Chicago); Union Sta. (Omaha); C.,M.,&St.P. Sta. (Minneapolis). Commd. capt., Corps of Engrs. U.S. Army, Nov. 8, 1917; mem. com. on emergency constrn. until Aug. 1, 1918; capt. Co. C, 78th Engrs. until Dec. 1, 1918; hon. disch. as maj. engrs.; designed Hosp. Bldg. for Soldiers Home, Washington, D.C.; formed firm of Granger and Bollenbacher, Chicago, Dec. 1919; designed Union and Adminstrn. bldgs., Ind. U., Medical and Dental bldgs. (U. of Ill.), Peirce Hall (Kenyon Coll.), Chicago Club, Winnebago County Courthouse (Oshkosh, Wis.). Fellow Am. Inst. Architects (pres. Chicago Chapter). Republican. Episcopalian. Author: Charles Follen McKim; England's World Empire; Spirit of Vienna, 1936. Home: Roxbury, Conn. Died Dec. 3, 1939.

GRANGER, Arthur Otis, mfr.; b. Providence, R.I., Feb. 14, 1846; s. Rev. Arthur and Sarah Alcorn (Rowan) G.; ed. pub. schs., Phila.; m. Caroline Dickson Gregory, Aug. 15, 1870. Began business career as cash boy in dry goods store, Phila., 1858, at 16, enlisted pvt. 15th Pa. Cav., Sept. 8, 1862; clerk cav. hdqrs., Army of the Cumberland, 1863; confidential clerk, Sherman's hdqrs., Mil. Div. of the Miss., Atlanta campaign, March to the Sea, and campaign of the Carolinas, 1864-65; mil. secretary to Gen. Sherman, 1865-66. Head of A. O. Granger & Co., engrs. and contractors, 1876; pres. Granger Water Gas Co., 1880; gen. mgr. United Gas Improvement Co., 1886; pres. Welsbach Light Co., 1888, Chautauqua Lake R.R. Co., 1889, Etowah Iron Co., 1889; pres. Am. Gold Dredging Co., Caribbean Co., Auer Incandescent Light Co., Marles Carved Molding Co. Presbyn. Republican. Author: Water Gas—What Is It? 1884. Home: Cartersville, Ga. Died July 30, 1914.

GRANGER, Barlow, farmer; b. Tioga County, N.Y., May 31, 1816; s. Erastus G.; ed. public schs. Elmira and Rochester, N.Y.; has been occupied as printer, lawyer, land agent, farmer and editor; m. Lucinda L. Rush, Oct. 7, 1856. Learned printing in office of Cortland Advocate, Cortland, N.Y., and worked till 1835; admitted to the bar of Iowa, 1848; located at Des Moines same year; established The Iowa Star, 1st paper published at Des Moines, 1849; pros. atty., 1854; mayor of Des Moines, 1855; acting county judge, 1855; was 1st mayor of Sevastopol, Ia.; farming, 1856—. Home: Des Moines, Ia. Died 1905.

GRANGER, Charles Trumbull, lawyer; b. Monroe County, N.Y., Oct. 9, 1835; acad. edn. at Waukegan, Ill. Taught sch. until Aug. 1862; was supt. schs., Mitchell County, Ia., 1861-62; admitted to bar, 1860, at Waukon, Ia. Twice married; now widower. Recruited, Aug. 1862, Co. K, 27th Ia. Inf.; was its capt. to close of war. After war practiced law; dist. atty., 10th Jud. Dist., Ia., 1869-72; circuit judge, 1872-86; dist. judge after change of jud. system, 1886-89; judge Supreme Ct. of Ia., 1889-1900. Address: Waukon, Ia. Died Oct. 26, 1915.

GRANGER, Daniel Larned Davis, congressman, lawyer; b. Providence, May 30, 1852; s. Rev. James N. (D.D.) and Anna Brown (Davis) G.; grad. Brown U., A.B., 1874, A.M., 1902; Boston U., LL.B., 1877; unmarried. Admitted to R.I. bar, 1877, and practiced in Providence; admitted to practice, U.S. bar, 1882; twice elected reading clerk Ho. Reps., R.I.; city treas. Providence, 1890-1900; mayor Providence 1900, 1901; congressman 1st R.I. dist., 1903-09. Democrat. Mem. Standing Com. diocese of R.I. (P.E. Ch.); v.p. Am. Group Inter-Parliamentary Union for Promotion of Internat. Arbitration and Am. v.p. of the Union. Treas. Dorilton Corp. (New York). Home: Providence, R.I. Died 1909.

GRANGER, Frank Butler, M.D., b. Belmont, Nev., Aug. 22, 1875; s. Frank Clark and Alice M. (Butler) G.; A.B., Harvard, 1899, M.D., 1902; m. Clara Talbot Davis, Oct. 29, 1902. Instr. physical therapeutics, Harvard Grad. Sch. of Medicine, 1911—; lecturer on same, Tufts Coll. Sch. of Medicine, 1906-10; physician for physical therapeutics, Boston City Hosp.; neurologist Boston Dispensary. Commd. capt. Med. Corps, U.S. Army, May 17, 1918; major, September 5, 1918; honorably discharged, rank lieutenant colonel, December 5, 1919; organizer and dir. dept. of physiotherapy, Div. of Physical Reconstruction, Office of Surgeon Gen., Washington; counsellor med. council, U.S. Vets.' Bur. Pres. Am. Coll. Physiotherapy. Progressive Rep. Episcopalian. Mason. Author: Technic of Physiotherapy, 1920. Home: Allston, Mass. Died Oct. 23, 1928.

GRANGER, Moses Moorhead, judge; b. Zanesville, O., Oct. 22, 1831; s. James and Matilda Vance (Moorhead) G.; A.B., Kenyon Coll., 1850, A.M., 1853, LL.D., 1880; m. Mary Hoyt, d. Gen. William J. Reese, Dec. 29, 1858. Practiced law at Zanesville, 1853-61 and 1865—; capt. 18th U.S. Inf., May 14, 1861; maj. 122d Ohio Inf., Sept. 10, 1862; lt. col., May 1, 1863; bvtd. col. vols., Oct. 19, 1864, for gallant and meritorious services in campaign before Richmond, Va., and in Shenandoah Valley; resigned Dec. 16, 1864. City solicitor, Zanesville, O., 1865-66; pros. atty., 1866; judge Ct. Common Pleas, 8th Jud. Dist., from 1866; chief judge Ohio Supreme Ct. Commn., 1883-85. Author: The Battle of Cedar Creek, 1890; Washington versus Jefferson, The Case Tried by Battle, 1861-65, 1898; Ohio Judiciary, 1803-1903, in Ohio Centennial Celebration, 1903; A Fair Answer to the Confederate Appeal at Richmond, Va., 1907. Home: Zanesville, O. Died Apr. 29, 1913.

GRANGER, Walter, museum curator; b. Middletown, Vt., Nov. 7, 1872; s. Charles H. and Ada Byron (Haynes) G.; student high sch., Rutland, Vt., 1888-90; hon. D.Sc., Middlebury College, 1932; m. Anna Dean Granger, Apr. 7, 1904. With Am. Mus. of Natural History, 1890—, serving successively as asst. in taxidermy, field collector in zoölogy, asst. curator, asso. curator, 1927—, as curator of fossil mammals; palæontologist and 2d in command of Central Asiatic Expdn., 1921-31. Mason. Home: New York, N.Y. Died Sept. 6, 1941.

GRANGER, William Alexander, clergyman; b. Cambridgeshire, Eng., Mar. 22, 1850; s. Thomas and Lydia (Lowe) G.; A.B., Colgate, 1874, A.M., 1877, D.D., 1896; m. Elizabeth A. Smith, Aug. 16, 1876. Ordained Bapt. ministry, 1874; pastor, successively, at Long Island City, N.Y., Brewster and Mt. Vernon. Trustee Colgate U., Hamilton Theol. Sem. Home: Mt. Vernon, N.Y. Died Sept. 10, 1922.

GRANNIS, Elizabeth Bartlett, humanitarian; b. Hartford, Conn., Mar. 27, 1840; d. Edward P. and Melinda (Howard) Bartlett; ed. pub. and pvt. schs. and Lake Erie Coll., Painesville, O.; m. Col. Fred W. Grannis, July 20, 1865. Teacher pub. schs., later head of pvt. sch.; editor and propr. The Church Union (Evangelical) 23 yrs., also of Children's Friend and Kindergarten Magazine; founder, 1887, and pres. Nat. Christian League for Promotion of Purity; del. and speaker many times, Nat. and Internat. Council of Women. Active in securing legislation for sterilization of habitual criminals and mental defectives, against infidelity in wedlock, etc. Mem. Christian Ch. Home: New York, N.Y. Died Mar. 22, 1926.

GRANNISS, Robert Andrews, life underwriter; b. Brooklyn, July 28, 1840; s. George Benjamin and Laura Ann (Dunham) G.; ed. Churchill's Mil. Acad., Sing Sing, 1854, Brooklyn Poly. Inst., to 1856; m. Florence Peters, Oct. 27, 1870. Sec. Metropolitan Life Ins. Co., 1872; 2d v.p. The Mutual Life Ins. Co. of New York, 1877-85, v.p. same, 1885-1907. Dir. U.S. Mortgage & Trust Co. Home: Morris Plains, N.J. Died Dec. 26, 1917.

GRANT, Abraham, bishop; b. Lake City, Fla., Aug. 25, 1848; was a slave and was sold at Columbus, Ga., for $6,000 Confed. money; after war returned to Fla., clerked in grocery store of former owner and spent few hours daily in a missionary school; later steward in hotels at Lake City and Jacksonville, Fla.; attended night school at Cookman Inst. a short time; m. Mrs. L. R. Armstrong, Oct. 23, 1902. Licensed to preach, A.M.E. Ch., Apr. 3, 1873; ordained deacon, Dec. 1873, elder, Mar. 4, 1876; while in Jacksonville was insp. of customs, and apptd. by Gov. Stearns co. commr. Duval Co. Transferred to Tex., 1878; pastor at San Antonia and Austin; became presiding elder and v.p. Paul Quinn Coll., Waco, Tex.; elected bishop, May 24, 1888. Was bishop consecutively of 9th, 1st and 4th dists.; then in charge 5th dist.; was pres. of bd. trustees Wilberforce U.; pres. bd. trustees Western U.; pres., 4 yrs., bd. publication A.M.E. Ch. (Phila.); pres. ch. extension bd. A.M.E. Ch., 12 yrs.; pres. financial bd., Washington. Mem. Ecumenical Meth. Conf., Washington, 1891; presided over confs. at Freetown, Sierra Leone and Monrovia, Liberia, West Coast Africa, Feb. 1899; mem. Ecumenical Missionary Conf., New York, 1900, Ecumenical Meth. Conf., London, 1900. Address: Kansas City, Kan. Died 1911.

GRANT, Albert Weston, naval officer; b. E. Benton, Me., Apr. 14, 1856; grad. U.S. Naval Acad., 1877; married; children—Albert Weston, Charles Sharp, Richard Southall. Ensign, May 17, 1881; lt. jr. grade, Nov. 1, 1887; lt., May 9, 1893; promoted through grades to rear adm., Sept. 7, 1915. Served on Massachusetts, Spanish-Am. War, 1898; duty U.S. Naval Acad., 1894-97, 1900-02, 1905-07; exec. officer Oregon, 1902-03; comd. Frolic, 1903-05; comd. U.S.S. Arethusa, 1907-08; chief of staff Atlantic Fleet during cruise battleships around world, 1908-09; comd. Connecticut, 1909-10, Navy Yard, Phila., 1910-13; duty in connection with building of Texas, 1913-14; comd. Texas, 1914-15; comd. Submarine Force, Atlantic Fleet, 1915-17; apptd. comdr. Battleship Force One, Atlantic Fleet, July 1917, with rank of vice admiral, and comd. U.S. Fleet in Western Atlantic, 1918-19; Navy Yard, Washington, D.C., 1919-20; retired, 1920. Address: Philadelphia, Pa. Died Sept. 30, 1930.

GRANT, Charles Henry, marine artist; b. Oswego, N.Y., Feb. 6, 1866; s. James MacDonald and Christina (Trotier) G.; ed. Nat. Acad. Design, New York; San Francisco Art Inst.; pupil of M. F. H. De Haas, formerly court painter to Queen of Holland; widower. Exhibited in leading cities, also San Francisco Expn., 1915; prin. works: "Will the Anchors Hold?" (owned by R. A. C. Smith, New York); "Ship Off the Starboard Bow"; "Nearing Port"; "At the Mercy of Neptune"; "Under Sealed Orders"; "Arrival of the Atlantic Battle Ship Fleet at the Golden Gate, 1908" (owned by City of San Francisco and in Golden Gate Park Mus.); "The Salute to the Flag" (owned by City of Oswego, N.Y.); "Ship Ahoy"; "They Made the World Safe for Democracy" (owned by Bohemian Club, San Francisco); "The Arrival of the Pacific Battleship Fleet in San Francisco Bay, Sept. 1, 1919," owned by Bohemian Club; commissioned to paint picture presented to Vice Adm. Frederick Field of British Navy on occasion of visit of British Fleet to San Francisco (only Am. port of call), June 1924; also commissioned to paint picture presented to Vice Adm. Hyakutake on visit of Japanese Fleet to San Francisco (only Am. port of call), Jan. 1924; official artist with Am. fleet on Australian cruise, 1925; painting "Sail on Columbus Ships" purchased by Bohemian Club, 1933. Republican. Odd Fellow. Home: San Francisco, Calif. Died Jan. 21, 1939.

GRANT, Claudius Buchanan, judge; b. Lebanon, Me., Oct. 25, 1835; s. Joseph and Mary (Merrill) G.; A.B., U. of Mich., 1859, A.M., 1862, LL.D., 1891; teacher and prin., Ann Arbor High Sch., 1859-62; m. Caroline L. Felch, June 13, 1863. Served in Civil War, capt. to col., 20th Mich. Vols., 1862-65; studied law, U. of Mich., 1865-66; admitted to bar, 1866; recorder and postmaster, Ann Arbor, 1867-70; mem. Mich. Ho. of Rep., 1870-74 (speaker pro tem.); regent U. of Mich., 1872-80; practiced law, Houghton, Mich., 1873-82; pros. atty., Houghton County, 1876-77; judge Circuit Ct., 1881-89; justice, 1889-1909, chief justice, 1888, 1889 and 1908, Supreme Ct. of Mich. Republican. Retired from the bench Jan. 1, 1910, and engaged in practice of law as gen. counsel the law firm of Warren, Cady & Ladd, Detroit. Address: Detroit, Mich. Died 1921.

GRANT, Frederick Dent, army officer; b. St. Louis, May 30, 1850; s. President Ulysses S. and Julia (Dent) G.; apptd. at-large, and grad. U.S. Mil. Acad., 1871; m. Ida M. Honoré, Oct. 20, 1874. Commd. 2d lt. 4th Cav., June 12, 1871; 1st lt., June 28, 1876; lt. col. a.-d.-c. to Lt. Gen. Sheridan, Mar. 17, 1873-June 1, 1881; engr. on U.P. and Colo. Central rys., 1871; served on frontier, 1873-81; resigned Oct. 1, 1881. U.S. minister to Austria, 1889-93; police commr. of New York, 1894-98; apptd. col. 14th N.Y. Inf., May 2, 1898; apptd. brig. gen. vols., May 27, 1898; hon. discharged, Apr. 15, 1899; apptd. brig. gen. vols., Apr. 15, 1899, brig. gen. U.S. Army, Feb. 18, 1901; maj. gen. U.S. Army, Feb. 6, 1906. Served in P.R. 1 yr., and after war comd. mil. dist. of San Juan; comd. 2d Brigade, 1st Div., 8th Army Corps in P.I., Apr.-Nov. 1899, 2d Brigade, 2d Div., Nov. 1899-Jan. 1900; comd. 5th dist. Northern Luzon, Jan. 1900-Apr. 1901, Southern Luzon, Oct. 1901-Apr. 1902; comd. Dept. of Tex., 1902-04, Dept. of the Lakes, Jan.-Sept. 1904, Dept. of the East, 1904-08, Dept. of the Lakes, 1908-10, Dept. of the East, July 25, 1910-July 1, 1911, Eastern Div., July 1, 1911—. Died Apr. 11, 1912.

GRANT, Henry Horace, surgeon; b. Petersburg, Ky., Dec. 12, 1853; s. Dr. Elijah Lane and Jane Rebecca (Prest) G.; A.B., Centre Coll., Danville, Ky., 1875, A.M., 1884; M.D., Jefferson Med. Coll., Phila., 1878; m. Leila Owsley, Aug. 3, 1886. Prof. surgery, Hosp. Coll. of Medicine, 1893-1909; prof. principles of surgery and oral surgery, Louisville Coll. Dentistry, 1893—; prof. surgery, med. dept. U. of

Louisville, 1909—. Author: Principles of Surgery and Diseases of the Mouth and Jaws, 1902. Editor of Louisville Monthly Journal of Medicine and Surgery. Home: Louisville, Ky. Died Jan. 1921.

GRANT, James Benton, gov., b. Russell County, Ala., Jan. 2, 1848; s. Thomas McDonough and Mary (Benton) G.; served as boy of 16 for 1 yr. in C.S.A.; went to Ia. after war; ed. Ia. Agrl. Coll., Cornell, and Sch. of Mines, Freiburg, Saxony; m. Mary Matteson Goodell, Jan. 19, 1881. Settled in Denver, 1876; became interested in mines and smelting furnaces in Gilpin Co., and at Leadville; in 1882 joined his business with that of another co. as the Omaha & Grant Smelting Co., which was afterwards consolidated with other smelting cos. under the name of Am. Smelting & Refining Co. of which became mem. exec. com.; v.p. Denver Nat. Bank. Gov. of Colo., 1883-85. Democrat. Home: Denver, Colo. Died 1911.

GRANT, John Cowles, teacher; b. Avon, Conn., Apr. 21, 1848; s. Rev. Joel and Abigail F. (Cowles) G.; B.A., Yale, 1869, M.A., 1872; LL.D., Fargo (N.D.) Coll., 1897; m. Susan R. Henry, July 14, 1878 (died 1883); m. 2d, Anna F. Coffin, Aug. 11, 1886. Teacher, Lake Forest (Ill.) Acad., 1869-74, Allen Acad., Chicago, 1874-79; in Europe, 1879, 1880; prin. of The Harvard (pvt.) School, Chicago, 1880—. Trustee Tuskegee (Ala.) Inst. Republican. Presbyn. Mason. Author: Historical Sketch of the Second Presbyterian Church of Chicago. Home: Chicago, Ill. Died Mar. 21, 1914.

GRANT, John Henry, lawyer; b. Burlington, Ind., Sept. 22, 1857; s. John M. and Catharine (Spangler) G.; A.B., U. of Mich., 1882, LL.B., 1883; m. Henrietta Mason, Apr. 5, 1883. In practice at Manistee, Mich., 1883—; mem. firm McAlvay & Grant, 1887-1902, Grant & Neal, 1905-Feb. 1911; dir. Manistee Co. Savings Bank, Northern Assurance Co. Probate judge, Manistee County, 1894—; mem. bd. edn., Manistee, 1887-93, 1899-1908; city atty., 1905-08; regent, U. of Mich., 1909—. Republican. Methodist. Pres. Mich. State Epworth League, 1896-98; Epworth Assembly, Ludington, Mich, 1900—, Mich. Conf. Brotherhood, 1908-10, Mich. State S.S. Assn., 1908—. Mason. Home: Manistee, Mich. Died Jan. 26, 1913.

GRANT, John MacGregor, banker; b. Grantown-on-Spey, Scotland, Sept. 6, 1874; s. William Stewart and Elsie (Robertson) G.; student Cromdale Sch., Scotland, 1879-88, Kingussie Sch., Scotland, 1888-91; m. Fanny Sarah Etheridge, 1900; children—Etheridge, Clinton Furbish; m. 2d, Edith Crowell Montanye, Oct. 19, 1919. Came to U.S., 1895, naturalized, 1903. With Caledonian Bank of Scotland, Ltd., 1891-95, Merchants Loan & Trust Co., Chicago, 1896-1902; European mgr. Am. Express Co. at London and New York, 1902-15; U.S. mgr. Second Russian Ins. Co., New York, 1916-21; v.p. Mercantile Trust Co., San Francisco, 1921-25; v.p. Bank of America, San Francisco, 1925-28; v.p. Transamerica Corp., San Francisco and London, 1928-32, pres. and dir., 1932—; dir. Occidental Life Ins. Co., Banca d'America e'd Italia, Milan, Italy. Presbyterian. Home: San Francisco, Calif. Died Mar. 25, 1941.

GRANT, Joseph Henry, lawyer; b. Clarkesville, Ga., Mar. 27, 1869; s. William Daniel and Samentha Jane (Holland) G.; ed. pub. sch., Clarkesville, Ga.; m. Lily May Fant, Sept. 20, 1899; children—Mary Ermita (Mrs. William B. Krepps), George William, Catherine Elizabeth, Joseph Fant. Admitted to Ga. bar, 1891, and began practice at Clarkesville; moved to Oklahoma City, Okla., 1903; mem. firm Grant & Grant; atty., Okla., for St.L.&S.F. R.R., 1909-22; sec. and gen. counsel Tom Slick, Inc., oil producers, and affiliated cos.; dir. and gen. counsel Miami Mineral Belt R.R. Co., Okla. Southwestern Ry. Co., Okla. Union Ry. Co., Union Transportation Co. Served as regtl. adj., U.S. Vols., 1898, capt., 1899-1901. Civil gov., Province of Leyte, P.I., 1901-03. Democrat. Bapist. Home: Oklahoma City, Okla. Died Jan. 6, 1933.

GRANT, Julia Dent; b. St. Louis, Feb. 16, 1826; d. Frederick and Ellen Bray (Wrenshall) Dent; m. Lt. U. S. Grant, Aug. 22, 1848, afterward Gen. Grant, and President of the U.S.; after his death Congress passed a bill giving her a pension of $5,000 a year. Address: Washington, D.C. Died 1902.

GRANT, Lewis Addison, soldier, lawyer; b. Bennington County, Vt., Jan. 17, 1829; s. James and Elizabeth (Wyman) G.; ed. Townshend and Chester, Vt.; taught sch. in Vt., N.J., and Mass., 1848-53; m. S. Augusta Hartwell, Mar. 11, 1857 (died 1859); m. 2d, Mary Helen Pierce, Sept. 9, 1863; father of Ulysses Sherman G. Admitted to bar, 1855, and engaged in practice at Bellows Falls, Vt. Maj. 5th Vt. Inf., Aug. 15, 1861; lt. col., Sept. 25, 1861; col., Sept. 16, 1862; brig. gen. vols., Apr. 27, 1864; bvtd. maj. gen. vols., Oct. 19, 1864, "for gallant and meritorious services in campaign before Richmond and in Shenandoah Valley"; hon. mustered out, Aug. 24, 1865; Congressional Medal of Honor, May 11, 1893, for Battle of Salem Heights, Va.; wounded at battle of Fredericksburg, Dec. 14, 1862, and at battle of Petersburg, Apr. 2, 1865; apptd. lt. col. 36th Inf., U.S.A., July 1866, but declined; asst. sec. of war, Apr. 5, 1890-Dec. 15, 1893. Republican. Home: Minneapolis, Minn. Died Mar. 20, 1918.

GRANT, Madison, lawyer; b. New York, Nov. 18, 1865; s. Gabriel and Caroline (Manice) G.; A.B., Yale, 1887; LL.B., Columbia, 1890; unmarried. Admitted to bar, 1889. Pres. N.Y. Zoöl. Soc.; v.p. Immigration Restriction League, Nat. Inst. Social Sciences, Am. Bison Soc., Soc. for Preservation of Fauna of British Empire; trustee Am. Mus. Natural History, Am. Defense Soc., Am. Geog. Soc., Eugenics Research Assn., Save the Redwoods League, Am. Coalition; mem. Taconic Park Commn. Traveler, hunter, explorer, etc. Author: The Passing of the Great Race, 1916; The Founders of the Republic; The Conquest of a Continent, 1933; also various works on zoöl. subjects. Home: New York, N.Y. Died May 30, 1937.

GRANT, Percy Stickney, clergyman; b. Boston, May 13, 1860; s. Stephen Mason and Annie (Stickney) G.; B.A., Harvard, 1883, M.A., 1886; B.D., Episcopal Theol. Sch., 1886; S.T.D., Hobart. Deacon, 1886, priest, 1887, P.E. Ch.; asst. minister Ch. of the Ascension, Fall River, Mass., 1886; minister St. Mark's, Fall River, 1887-93; also rector Swansea, Mass., 1890-93; rector Ch. of the Ascension, New York, 1893-1924. Author: Ad Matrem, 1905; The Search of Belisarius, 1907; Observations in Asia, 1908; Socialism and Christianity, 1910; The Return of Odysseus, 1912; Fair Play for the Worker, 1918; Essays, 1922; Poems, 1922; The Religion of Main Street, 1923. Home: Bedford Hills, N.Y. Died Feb. 13, 1927.

GRANT, Robert, author; b. Boston, Jan. 24, 1852; s. Patrick and Charlotte Bordman (Rice) G.; A.B., Harvard, 1873, Ph.D., 1876, LL.B., 1879, Litt.D., 1922; Litt.D., Columbia, 1921; m. Amy Gordon, d. Sir Alexander Tilloch Galt, G.C.M.G., July 3, 1883; children—Robert, Alexander Galt, Patrick, Gordon. Water commr., Boston, 1888-93 (chmn. of bd., 1889-93); judge Probate Ct. and Ct. of Insolvency for Suffolk County, 1893-1923. Overseer of Harvard, 1895-1921; mem. Sacco-Venzetti Commission, 1927. Author: Jack Hall, 1887; Jack in the Bush, 1888; The Reflections of a Married Man, 1892; The Opinions of a Philosopher, 1893; The Art of Living, 1895; Search-Light Letters, 1899; Unleavened Bread, 1900; The Orchid, 1905; The Law-breakers, 1906; The Chippendales, 1909; The Convictions of a Grandfather, 1912; The High Priestess, 1915; Law and the Family, 1919; The Bishop's Granddaughter, 1925; Occasional Verses, 1926; The Dark Horse, 1931; Fourscore—An Autobiography, 1934. Home: Boston, Mass. Died May 19, 1940.

GRANT, Rollin P., banker; b. Westfield, N.J., Jan. 6, 1870; s. Anson F. and Elizabeth P. G.; ed. pub. schs. Began as bank messenger, 1888, later with wholesale shoe house of Morse & Rogers; paying teller New York Nat. Exchange Bank, 1898-1901; was made cashier, 1901, of Irving Nat. Exchange Bank, title later changed to Am. Exchange Irving Trust Co., of which was pres., 1912-19, vice chmn., 1919-29; later asso. with Tobey & Kirk, mems. N.Y. Stock Exchange; dir. Diamond Match Co., Electric Power & Light Corp., Pa. Securities Corp., Globe & Republic Ins. Co., Bankers-Commercial Security Co. (chmn. finance com.). Home: New York, N.Y. Died Jan. 17, 1936.

GRANT, Ulysses S., Jr., lawyer; b. Bethel, O., July 22, 1852; s. President Ulysses S. and Julia (Dent) G.; A.B., Harvard, 1874; LL.B., Columbia, 1876; m. Josephine Chaffee, Nov. 1, 1880; children—Miriam (Mrs. John Rice), Chaffee, Julia Dent (Mrs. Edmund C. King), Fannie Chaffee (Mrs. Isaac Hart Purdy), Ulysses S.; m. 2d, Mrs. America Will, July 12, 1913. Admitted to bar, 1876 and practiced at San Diego, Calif.; was sec. to his father last year and half of his presidency. Del.-at-large, Rep. Nat. convs., 1896, 1900; presdl. elector-at-large, 1904, 1908. Home: San Diego, Calif. Died Sept. 25, 1929.

GRANT, Ulysses Sherman, geologist; b. Moline, Ill., Feb. 14, 1867; s. Gen. Lewis Addison G. and Mary Helen (Pierce) G.; B.S., U. of Minn., 1888; Ph.D., Johns Hopkins, 1893; m. Avis Winchell, Oct. 1, 1891; children—Addison Winchell, Lois, Avis Harriet (Mrs. E. E. Swick), Willard Winchell. Asst. state geologist, Minn., 1893-99; instr. geology, U. of Minn., 1897-98; prof. geology and curator of Mus., 1899—; acting dean Coll. Liberal Arts, 1907-08 and 1916-19, Northwestern U. Geologist on Geol. and Natural History Survey of Wis., 1899-1907, U.S. Geol. Survey, 1904-25, Ill. Geol. Survey, 1906-20, Ore. Bur. Mines and Geology, 1913-15. Asso. editor Am. Geologist, 1897-1906. Author: Preliminary Report on the Copper-bearing Rocks of Douglas County, Wis., 1900, 2d edit., 1901; Vols. IV and V, Final Report of the Geol. and Natural History Survey of Minn. (with N. H. Winchell), 1899-1900; Report on the Lead and Zinc Deposits of Wis., 1906; Copper and Other Mineral Resources of Prince William Sound, Alaska, 1906, 1910; Description of the Lancaster and Mineral Point Quadrangles, Wis., 1907; Glaciers of Prince William Sound and Kenai Peninsula, Alaska, 1910-12; Mineral Resources of Kenai Peninsula, Alaska, 1910-12. Address: Evanston, Ill. Died Sept. 22, 1932.

GRANT, Walter Bruce, lawyer; b. Milwaukee, Wis., Mar. 21, 1859; s. Albert and Harriet N. (Taylor) G.; student Columbian (now George Washington) U., 1876-80; LL.B., Columbian Law Sch., 1884, LL.M., 1885; m. Lucinda E. Tripp, Aug. 28, 1889 (dec.). Admitted to D.C. bar, 1885, to bar U.S. Supreme Court, 1889, Mass. bar, 1891; practiced in Boston; chief counsel for U.S. in Chamizal case (Mex. boundary), apptd. under treaty between U.S. and Mexico, dated June 24, 1910; pres. Am. Tube Works. Trustee Lincoln Memorial U., Cumberland Gap, Tenn. Republican. Unitarian. Mason. Chmn. Draft and Exemption Bd., dist. 20, Boston, 1917. Home: Boston, Mass. Died Feb. 15, 1939.

GRANT, Whit McDonough, lawyer; b. Seale, Ala., Apr. 26, 1851; s. Thomas McDonough and Mary J. (Benton) G.; grad. State U. of Iowa, 1873; m. Kate L. Weagley, Oct. 9, 1878 (dec.); children—Alice Cory (dec.), Katie Weagley, Marguerite Whitaker. Practiced law, Davenport, Ia., 1873-87; mem. Ia. Legislature, 1884-85; U.S. atty. for Alaska, 1887-89, closing up the sealing cases so long in dispute between U.S. and Great Britain; in practice in Okla., 1893—. First mayor of Oklahoma City, under new charter (commn. form of govt.), term 1911-15. Mem. Dem. Nat. Com., 1896-99. Address: Oklahoma City, Okla. Died Dec. 10, 1927.

GRANT, William West, surgeon; b. Russell County, Ala., Nov. 15, 1846; s. Dr. Thomas McDonough and Mary J. (Benton) G.; served in C.S.A. 16 mos.; prep. edn. pvt. schs.; Jeff. Med. Coll.; Bellevue Hosp. Med. Coll.; M.D., L.I. Med. Coll., 1868; hosps. Berlin, Vienna, London; m. Mary A. Mosely, 1878 (died 1888); m. 2d, Nanny Craig Green, 1895. Practiced at Davenport, Ia., 1870-88; post surgeon Rock Island (Ill.) Arsenal, 1885-88; Europe, 1888-89; Denver, 1890—. Pres. surg. staff of St. Joseph's Hosp.; surgeon St. Luke's Hosp.; local surgeon, C.,R.I.&P. Ry. at Denver, 1890—; surgeon gen., Colo., 1899-1903. First complete operation for facial paralysis by anastomosis of facial and spinal accessory nerves; originator of standard operation for diseases and deformity of the mouth; first operation for appendicitis, Jan. 4, 1885. Mem. Med. R.C. U.S.A., 1911-19; maj., M.C. U.S.A., active service, Sept. 1917-May 3, 1919. Home: Denver, Colo. Died Jan. 8, 1934.

GRANTHAM, Edwin Lincoln, lawyer; b. Daviess County, Mo., Jan. 23, 1866; s. John E. and Roxanna (Austin) G.; studied law in office of Hicklin & Yates, Gallatin, Mo., and with Ed. E. Aleshire, Stanberry, Mo.; m. Ida Morris, Sept. 4, 1889 (dec.); children—Durand (dec.), Beryl, Madge Amanda. Formerly court reporter; admitted to S.D. bar, 1899, and practiced at Custer until 1911; represented Westinghouse Electric & Mfg. Co., operating mica mines at Custer; apptd. asst. solicitor C.,M.&St.P. Ry. Co., 1911, solicitor, in charge legal dept. for N. and So. Dak., 1918-27. Republican. Episcopalian. Mason. Compiled Statutes of South Dakota, approved by legislature, 1899. Home: Aberdeen, S.D. Deceased.

GRANVILLE-SMITH, W(alter), artist; born in N.Y., 1870. Works on exhbn. Smithsonian Instn., Washington; Butler Art Inst., Youngstown, O.; Toledo (O.) Mus.; etc. Nat. Academician, 1915. Address: New York, N.Y. Died Dec. 7, 1938.

GRASSELLI, Caesar Augustin, mfg. chemist; b. Cincinnati, O., Nov. 7, 1850; s. Eugene R. and Frederica (Eisenbarth) G.; Sc.D., Mt. St. Mary's Coll., Emmitsburg, Md., 1904; m. Johanna Ireland, Aug. 1, 1871. Pres. The Grasselli Chem. Co. (founded by Eugene R. Grasselli, at Cincinnati, O., 1839) many yrs. from 1885, then chmn. bd. of dirs.; also pres. Woodland Av. Savings & Trust Co., Cleveland, 1887-1921, Broadway Savings & Trust Co., 1893-1921, dir. Union Nat. Bank—all of which were merged with Union Trust Company, 1921, apptd. dir.; also dir. Akron & Chicago Junction R.R., B.&O. System. Decorated Knight Order of Golden Crown of Italy by Victor Emanuel III, 1910; Commander same order, 1921; decorated by Pope Pius XI as Comdr. Order of St. Gregory the Great, 1923. Fellow Cleveland Museum of Natural History; mem. Cleveland Inst. of Music (one of founders), Cleveland Museum of Art. Founder Grasselli House (for the blind), Cleveland; Rose Mary, the Johanna Grasselli Home for Crippled Children. Republican. Catholic. Home: Cleveland, O. Died July 28, 1927.

GRASTY, Charles Henry, newspaper propr.; b. Fincastle, Va., Mar. 3, 1863; s. John Sharshall (D.D.) and Ella Giles (Pettus) G.; ed. U. of Mo. (non-grad.); Litt.D., Washington and Lee U.; m. Leota Tootle Perrin, May 29, 1889. Mng. editor, Kansas City Times, 1884-89; editor and propr., Baltimore Evening News, 1892-1908; editor and controlling owner, St. Paul Dispatch, and Pioneer Press, 1908-09, and of The Sun, Baltimore, 1910-14; war corr. Associated Press, New York Times and Kansas City Star, in Europe, 1915; treas. New York Times, 1916-20. Editorial staff corr. New York Times, European War, 1916-21. Dir. Associated Press, 1900-10.

Democrat. Home: Pikesville, Md. Died Jan. 19, 1924.

GRASTY, John Sharshall, geologist, mining engr.; b. Versailles, Ky., Mar. 15, 1880; s. Thomas Percy and Mattie Virginia (White) G.; A.B., Johns Hopkins, 1902, Ph.D., 1908; studied Washington and Lee U. and Mass. Inst. Tech.; Sc.D., Washington Coll., Md., 1912; m. Elizabeth Montgomery Cochran, Nov. 9, 1909; children—Thomas P., John Sharshall. Asst., U.S. Geol. Survey, 1905; geologist, Md. Geol. Survey, 1906-08; asst. state geologist, Va., 1909-16; adj. prof. econ. geology, 1908-13, asso. prof., 1913-16, U. of Va.; prof. mining geology, Washington and Lee U., 1916-18 (on leave); investigations for B.&O. Ry., Southern Ry. and C.&O. Ry.; spl. geologist, Ala. Geol. Survey; chem. engr. Ordnance Dept., U.S. Army, 1918; oil geology, Mid-Continent Fields, 1919-20. Inventor "fire sentinel" apparatus; specialist on rock slides and foundations. Author: Limestones of Maryland, 1909; The Slate Deposits of Virginia, 1917; Origin of Caverns in Relation to Structure, 1925. Home: Charlottesville, Va. Died June 5, 1930.

GRATACAP, Louis Pope, curator, author; b. Brooklyn, Nov. 1, 1851; s. John L. and Lucinda (Benton) G.; A.B., Coll. City of New York, 1869, A.M., 1880; Ph.B., Columbia Sch. of Mines, 1876. Engaged in investigations in geology and mineralogy, 1876—; asst. curator, Am. Mus. Natural History, 1881—. Author: Philosophy of Ritualism, or Apologia pro Ritu, 1887; Analytics of a Belief in a Future State, 1888; Political Mission of a Tammany Hall, 1892; Protection, a Reasonable Doctrine, 1892; As to the Public Schools, 1893; The Silver Catchechism, 1894; Political Mission of Reform, 1895; Centralization, the Cure for Political Corruption, 1896; Geology of the City of New York, 1901, 3d edit., 1909; The Certainty of a Future Life in Mars (scientific romance), 1903; Vade Mecum Guide to Mineral Collections, 1903; The World as Intention, 1905; The Museum, 1905; A Woman of the Ice Age, 1906; The Substance of Literature, 1907; The Evacuation of England, 1909; The Mayor of New York, 1910; Popular Mineralogy, a Guide to Collections, 1911; Benjamin the Jew, 1913; Why the Democrats Must Go, 1914; The New Northland, 1915; The World's Prayer, 1915; Europe's Handicap, 1915. Home: West New Brighton, S.I., N.Y. Died Dec. 23, 1917.

GRAU, Maurice, operatic mgr.; b. Brunn, Austria, 1849; came to New York with parents when 5 yrs. old; grad. Free Acad., New York, 1867; attended Columbia Law School; was 2 yrs. in law office; in 1872, with a partner, became mgr. for Aimée, opera bouffe prima donna, until 1875, also managed Rubinstein, pianist, the Clara Louise Kellogg Opera Co., Salvini, the Italian tragedian, and many others; afterward partner with Henry Abbey and managed Sara Bernhardt's tours; then as partner in Abbey, Shoeffel & Grau, mng. Patti, Sara Bernhardt, Henry Irving and Ellen Terry, Coquelin, Jane Harding, Mounet-Sully and Mme. Réjane; later mng. dir. Maurice Grau Opera Co.; lessee Metropolitan Opera House, New York. Address: Croissy, France. Died 1907.

GRAUSTEIN, William Caspar, mathematician; b. Cambridge, Mass., Nov. 15, 1888; s. Adolf Henry and Julia (Caspar) G.; A.B., Harvard, 1910, A.M., 1911; traveling fellow Harvard; Ph.D., Bonn, 1913; m. Mary Florence Curtis, June 10, 1921. Instr. mathematics, Harvard, 1913-14; instr. same, Rice Inst., Houston, Tex., 1914-15, asst. prof., 1915-18; lecturer in mathematics, Harvard, 1919, asst. prof., 1919-26, asso. prof., 1926-33, prof., 1933—. With Ordnance Dept., U.S. Army, Aberdeen Proving Grounds, Md., May-Dec. 1918; commd. 1st lt. O.R.C. Baptist. Author: (with Prof. William F. Osgood) Plane and Solid Analytic Geometry, 1921; Introduction to Higher Geometry, 1930; Differential Geometry, 1935. Editor of Trans. of Am. Math. Soc., 1936—. Home: Cambridge, Mass. Died Jan. 22, 1941.

GRAVES, Abbott Fuller, painter; b. Weymouth, Mass., Apr. 15, 1859; s. James Griswold and Eliza Nicholls (Fuller) G.; ed. Mass. Inst. Tech.; studied, 1888, under Georges Jeannin, Paris; pupil of Cormon 3 yrs.; m. Montie Mayo, d. Louis Aldrich (actor), Sept. 30, 1886; children—Enid, Louis T. (dec.). Has done notable decorative work and executed much work in flower and figure paintings; specializes in Colonial doorways and gardens. A.N.A., 1926. Home: Kennebunkport, Me. Died July 15, 1936.

GRAVES, Anson Rogers, bishop; b. Wells, Rutland Co., Vt., Apr. 13, 1842; s. Daniel and Almira (Rogers) G.; A.B., Hobart Coll., 1866, A.M., 1869; Gen. Theol. Sem., 1870; S.T.D., Racine Coll., 1890; LL.D., Hobart, 1890; m. Mary Totten Watrous, April 3, 1877; children—Frederick Daniel, Margaret (wife of Bishop Bennett), Eliot Varnum, Mrs. Gertrude Martin, David Watrous Paul. Deacon, 1870, priest, 1871, P.E. Ch.; asst. Grace Ch., Brooklyn, 1870-71; rector Plattsmouth, Neb., 1873; asst. Gethsemane Ch., Minneapolis, 1874-75; rector All Saints', Northfield, Minn., 1876; missionary in N.H., 1877-80; rector St. Peter's, Bennington, Vt., 1880-83, Gethsemane, Minneapolis, 1883-89; consecrated missionary bishop of the Platte (now dist. of W. Neb.), Jan. 1, 1890; resigned Oct. 1910. Author: The Farmer Boy Who Became a Bishop (autobiography); Sermons for Lay-Readers. Has written various tracts. Home: La Mesa, Calif. Died Jan. 1, 1932.

GRAVES, Charles Alfred prof. law; b. Albemarle County, Va., Oct. 20, 1850; s. William and Elizabeth (Dawson) G.; M.A., Washington Coll. (now Washington and Lee U.), Lexington, Va., 1869, LL.B., 1873; LL.D., Davidson Coll., N.C., 1894, Washington and Lee U., 1911; m. Elizabeth Turner Kirkpatrick, Aug. 28, 1877; m. 2d, Catherine Rebecca Lipop, Dec. 26, 1925. Prof. law, Washington and Lee U., 1873-99, U. of Va., 1899-1927. Democrat. Presbyterian. Author: Summary of Personal Property, 1893; Notes on Real Property, 1912. Co-founded, 1895, and asso. editor, 1895-97, Virginia Law Register. Home: Charlottesville, Va. Died Nov. 10, 1928.

GRAVES, Charles Burleigh, judge; b. Richmond, Ind., Nov. 13, 1841; s. Pusey and Jane (Witchell) G.; reared on farm; ed. pub. and pvt. schs., Vt., and Bushnell, Ill.; m. Hattie S. Hawkins, Nov. 10, 1872. Served in Co. F, 9th Kan. Cav., Nov. 15, 1861-Feb. 15, 1865; mustered out as 1st sergt.; engaged in sawmill business in Leavenworth County and at Trading Post, Kan., 1865-67; admitted to Kan. bar, 1869; city atty. and justice of the peace at Neosho Falls, Kan.; county atty. Coffey County, Kan., 1876; district judge, 5th Judicial Dist., 1881-93; city atty. Emporia, Kan., 1893; pres. bd. edn., Emporia, 1893-99; asso. justice Supreme Ct. of Kan., 1905-11. Republican. Home: Emporia, Kan. Died Mar. 25, 1912.

GRAVES, Charles Hinman, diplomat; b. Springfield, Mass., Aug. 14, 1839; s. Rev. Hiram Atwell and Mary (Hinman) G.; ed. pub. schs., Boston, and Litchfield, Conn.; m. Grace Totten, May 20, 1873; m. 2d, Alice K. Trippe, Apr. 25, 1905. Sergt. 40th N.Y. Inf., June 27, 1861; 2d lt., Nov. 4, 1861; 1st lt., July 8, 1862; capt. a.-a.-g. vols., Feb. 29, 1864; maj. a.-a.-g. vols., Jan. 15, 1865; bvtd. lt. col. and col. vols., Mar. 13, 1865, for faithful and efficient services during the war, and gallant conduct in the field; bvtd. maj., U.S.A., Mar. 2, 1867, for gallant and meritorious services at Gettysburg; lt. col. U.S. Army, Mar. 2, 1867, for same at Ft. Fisher; hon. mustered out of vol. service, Sept. 1, 1866; apptd. 1st lt. 14th U.S. Inf., Nov. 29, 1865; capt. 34th Inf., July 28, 1866; hon. discharged at own request, Dec. 29, 1870. Officer on staffs, Gens. Phil. Kearney, Birney, Stoneman, A. H. Terry; served in all operations and battles Army of Potomac. Settled in Minn.; pioneer in many of the important business enterprises of Duluth. Mem. Minn. Senate, 1875-78, Ho. of Rep., 1889-91 (speaker); mayor of Duluth, 1881-83; state capitol commr., Minn., 1893-1905; U.S. minister to Sweden and Norway, Mar. 1905-June 1906, to Sweden, 1906-14. Pres. Cottage Hosp., Santa Barbara. Republican. Companion Loyal Legion. Episcopalian. Home: Santa Barbara, Calif. Died Oct. 7, 1928.

GRAVES, Frederick Rogers, bishop; b. Auburn, N.Y., Oct. 24, 1858; s. Samuel Seabury and Elizabeth Anna (Wilson) G.; A.B., Hobart, 1878, A.M., 1881; grad. Gen. Theol. Sem., 1881, D.D., 1893; D.D., Oxford, 1908; m. Miss J. H. Roberts, Jan. 27, 1883; children—Elizabeth Woodward, Frederick Rogers, Lucy Josephine, Josephine Marion. Deacon, 1881, priest, 1882, P.E. Ch.; missionary at Wu-Chang, 1881-83, 1884-85; prof. Theol. Sch., St. John's Coll., Shanghai, 1885-87; prof. Theol. Sch., Wu-Chang, 1887-93; consecrated bishop of Shanghai, June 14, 1893; retired 1937. Author of various works in Chinese. Address: Shanghai, China. Died May 17, 1940.

GRAVES, Herbert Cornelius, civil engr.; b. Alexandria, Va., Aug. 17, 1869; s. Willard Purdy and Lucy Malvina (Libby) G.; C.E., U. of Va., 1889; m. Clara Edith Walter, Sept. 4, 1894. Railroad surveyor, N.C., 1889-90; railroad, land and townsite surveys, Va., 1890-91; city surveyor, Alexandria, Va., 1891-95; nautical expert, Hydrographic Office, U.S. Navy, Cleveland, O., 1895-98; nautical expert and asst., 1898-1917; apptd. chief Div. of Hydrography and Topography, U.S. Coast and Geodetic Survey, 1915. Compiler of "Coast Pilots," relative to coasts of U.S. and Alaska (pub. by Coast and Geodetic Survey). Home: Washington, D.C. Died July 26, 1919.

GRAVES, Jackson Alpheus, banker; b. Hauntown, Ia., Dec. 5, 1852; s. John Q. and Katherine Jane (Haun) G.; A.B., St. Mary's Coll., San Francisco, 1872, A.M., 1873, LL.D., 1912; m. Alice H. Griffith, Oct. 23, 1879. Admitted to Calif. bar, 1876; practiced in Los Angeles, 1876-1904; became v.p. Farmers & Merchants Bank, 1903, later pres.; largely interested in oil production and orange growing. Republican. Home: Alhambra, Calif. Died Feb. 13, 1933.

GRAVES, John Temple, journalist and orator; b. Willington Church, S.C., Nov. 9, 1856; s. Gen. James Porterfield and Katherine Floride (Calhoun) G.; student U. of Ga., class of '75; m. Mattie E. Simpson, Apr. 17, 1878; m. 2d, Annie E. Cothran, Dec. 30, 1890. Editor Daily Florida Union, Jacksonville, 1881-83, Atlanta (Ga.) Daily Journal, 1887-88, Tribune of Rome (Ga.), 1888-90; editor-in-chief and co-propr. Atlanta Daily Georgian, 1905-07; editor-in-chief N.Y. American, 1907-15; editorial rep. 12 daily Hearst newspapers, 1915—. Presidential elector-at-large from Fla., 1884, from Ga., 1888; candidate for U.S. senator from Ga., 1905, but withdrew candidacy on account of ill health; candidate of Nat. Independence Party for Vice-Pres., 1908. Orator and leader of progressive and patriotic sentiment in South; author of the movement of 1907 for another "Era of Good Feeling," which began with his speech at the Bryan banquet, Chattanooga, at which he urged upon Bryan who was present that as representative of the Dem. party he should renominate Roosevelt as the candidate of both parties to carry to a successful conclusion the fight in behalf of the people against predatory wealth. Orator on many notable occasions. Was col. on staff Gov. Northen of Ga. Independent Democrat. Author: History of Florida of To-Day; History of Colleton, S.C.; Twelve Standard Lectures; Platform of To-Day; Speeches and Selections for Schools; The Negro. Address: Washington, D.C. Died Aug. 8, 1925.

GRAVES, Ralph A., editor; b. Bainbridge, Ga., May 15, 1882; s. James Ralph and Agnes (Donalson) G.; A.B., U. of Ga., 1902; George Washington U.; m. Elizabeth H. Evans, Oct. 4, 1923; children—Ralph A., William P. E. Teacher English, West Tex. Mil. Coll., 1904-05; editor and owner Bainbridge (Ga.) Argus, 1902-03; editor Brunswick (Ga.) Journal, 1903-04; successively city editor, Sunday editor, dramatic editor and news editor, Washington, D.C. Times, until 1908; gen. mgr. New Britain (Conn.) Herald, 1908-09; Sunday and dramatic editor Washington Post, 1909-16; with Nat. Geog. Mag., 1916—, becoming asst. editor. Democrat. Presbyn. Home: Washington, D.C. Died Sept. 17, 1932.

GRAVES, Ralph H., editor; b. Chapel Hill, N.C., July 11, 1878; s. Ralph H. and Julia C. (Hooper) G.; A.B., U. of N.C., 1897, A.M., 1898; m. Frances Morgan Griffith, Jan. 20, 1906. On staffs New York Times and New York Evening Post, 1899-1923; city editor, 1915-17, Sunday editor, 1917-23, New York Times. On editorial staff Red Cross Mag., Sept. 1918-Jan. 1919; editor Syndicate of Doubleday, Doran & Co., Garden City, N.Y., 1923-36; mng. editor World's Work Mag., 1924-25; editor his own syndicate, 1936—. Home: Garden City, N.Y. Died Dec. 1, 1939.

GRAVES, Schuyler Colfax, surgeon; b. Kalamazoo, Mich., Mar. 6, 1858; s. Samuel (D.D.) and Mary Colfax (Baldwin) G.; M.D., U. of Mich., 1881; m. Annie M. Dryden, Oct. 9, 1883; m. 2d, Caroline Elizabeth Launt, Apr. 16, 1906. Maj. and brigade surgeon in Spanish-Am. War (chief surgeon 1st Brigade, 3d Div., 4th Corps). Home: Grand Rapids, Mich. Died July 14, 1941.

GRAVES, Waller W., judge; b. Lafayette Co., Mo., Dec. 17, 1860; s. Abram L. and Martha E. (Pollard) G.; ed. Mo. State U.; admitted to Mo. bar, 1885; m. Alice M. Ludwick, June 30, 1892. City atty., Butler, 1892-94; judge 29th Jud. Circuit, Mo., 1898-1904; justice Supreme Ct. of Mo., 1906—. Democrat. Address: Jefferson City, Mo. Died June 17, 1928.

GRAVES, William Blair, educator; b. W. Fairlee, Vt., Feb. 3, 1834; s. Cyrus and Lucena G.; A.B., Amherst, 1862, A.M., 1865; hon. A.M., Yale, 1902; m. Luranah H. Copeland, Aug. 26, 1863. Instr. mathematics, Amherst, 1865; instr. Phillips Acad., 1866-70; prof. natural sciences, Marietta (O.) Coll., 1870-74; prof. mathematics and civil engring., Mass. Agrl. Coll., 1874-81; prof. natural sciences, Phillips Acad., 1881-1909, prof. emeritus, 1909—. Elected mem. bd. overseers Charitable Fund of Amherst Coll., 1878. Home: Andover, Mass. Died May 6, 1915.

GRAVES, William Phillips, M.D.; b. Andover, Mass., Jan. 29, 1870; s. William Blair and Luranah Hodges (Copeland) G.; grad. Phillips Acad., Andover, 1887; A.B., Yale, 1891; M.D., Harvard, 1899; m. Alice M. Chase, Oct. 10, 1900; children—Sidney C., William P., Alice. Teacher, Hill Sch., Pottstown, Pa., 1891-95; in med. practice at Boston, 1900—; surgeon-in-chief Free Hosp. for Women, 1907—; prof. gynecology, Harvard Medical Sch., 1911—. Consulting gynecologist, Boston Lying-in Hosp. Conglist. Author: Graves' Gynecology, 5 edits., 1916; Female Sex-Hormonology, 1931. Home: Boston, Mass. Died Jan. 25, 1933.

GRAVES, William Sidney, army officer; b. Mt. Calm, Tex., Mar. 27, 1865; s. Andrew C. and Evelyn (Bennett) G.; grad. U.S. Mil. Acad., 1889; m. Katherine Boyd, Feb. 9, 1891; children—Sidney C., Dorothy (wife of Wm. R. Orton, U.S.A.). Commd. 2d lt. 7th Inf., June 12, 1889; promoted through grades to maj. gen. July 11, 1925. Instr. small arms practice, Dept. of Columbia, 1897-99; also acting judge advocate, 1898-99; same, Dept. of Colo., 1899; ordered to P.I., 1899, participating in various campaigns; received thanks of Gen. J. F. Bell for gallantry in action against insurgents at Caloocan, Dec. 31, 1901; again in P.I., 1904-06; at San Francisco, Apr.-May 1906, after earthquake; duty Gen. Staff, 1909-11; sec. Gen. Staff Corps, Jan. 1911-July 1912, and Sept. 3, 1914-Feb. 6, 1918; comdr. A.E.F. in Siberia, 1918-20; comdr. Ft. William McKinley, P.I., Apr.-Oct. 1920, 1st Brigade of 1st Div., Dec. 1920-Apr. 1, 1925; comdr. 1st Div., Apr. 1-July 10, 1925; comdr. 6th Corps Area, Chicago, July 11, 1925-Oct. 26, 1926; comdr. Panama Canal Div., Dec. 14, 1926-Oct. 1, 1927; comdr. Panama Canal Dept., Oct. 1, 1927; retired, 1928. Awarded D.S.M., 1919; Order of Rising Sun, 2d Class, Japan; Order of the Wen Hu (Striped Tiger), China; War Cross, Czechoslovakia; Comdr. Order of Crown of Italy. Home: Shrewsbury, N.J. Died Feb. 27, 1940.

GRAY, Alexander, engineer; b. Edinburgh, Scotland, Mar. 9, 1882; s. James and Christina (Seton) G.; diploma in engring., Heriot Watt Coll. (night sch.), Edinburgh, 1904; B.Sc. in Engring., Edinburgh U., 1904; B.Sc. in Elec. Engring., McGill U., Montreal, Can., 1906, M.Sc., 1916; m. Margaret Annandale Low, Oct. 11, 1906. Machinist, 1897-1900; draftsman and erection engr., Edinburgh, 1900-04; elec. designer with Bullock Elec. Co. and Allis-Chalmers Co., 1905-10; asst. prof. elec. engring., McGill U., 1910-15; head of elec. engring. dept., Cornell U., 1915—. Presbyn. Author: Electrical Machine Design, 1913; Principles and Practice of Electrical Engineering, 1914. Wrote Sect. 8 of Standard Handbook for Electrical Engineers. Home: Ithaca, N.Y. Died Oct. 13, 1921.

GRAY, Alfred Leftwich, Roentgenologist; b. Palmyra, Va., Oct. 2, 1873; s. Alphonso Alexander and Bettie Ann (Leftwich) G.; student U. of Va. 3 yrs. until 1894, M.D., 1897; m. Alice Lear Clark, Dec. 23, 1903; children—Alfred Leftwich, Ernest Emery, John Newton. Undergraduate asst. in pathology, etc., U. of Va., 1896-97; interne, short time, Pa. Hosp., Phila., 1898; instr. anatomy and orthopedic surgery, Univ. Coll. of Medicine, Richmond, 1899-1901; prof. physiology same, 1901 until it was merged with Med. Coll. of Va., 1913, and then was continued in same chair; resigned 1916; prof. Roentgenology, Med. Coll. of Va., 1916—; dean Sch. of Medicine, same, until resignation, 1920; dean med. dept. Univ. Coll. of Medicine, 1909-13; Roentgenologist, Memorial Hosp., St. Luke's Hosp., McGuire Clinic, St. Philip Hosp., Pine Camp Hosp. Maj. Med. O.R.C., May 19, 1917, and placed in charge Richmond Sch. of Mil. Roentgenology, training X-ray specialists for army service. Democrat. Baptist. Author: Lectures on Physiology, 1911. Home: Richmond, Va. Died Oct. 13, 1932.

GRAY, Alfred Walter, lawyer; b. Heuvelton, N.Y., Dec. 21, 1868; s. Walter Rutherford and Mary Jane (Chambers) G.; grad. Ogdensburg (N.Y.) Acad., 1887; A.B., Hamilton Coll., 1892; LL.D., Tusculum Coll., 1920; m. Frances Foster Newman, Oct. 19, 1899 (died 1933); children—Mary Orrea (Mrs. Foster Parmelee), Clinton Newman; m. 2d, Cecilia M. Ryan, Nov. 21, 1934. Admitted to N.Y. bar, 1896, and began practice at Buffalo; mem. Dudley, Gray, Phelps & Gray; dir. and gen. counsel United Hotels Co. of America, Inc.; sec., treas., gen. counsel Lewiston Heights Co.; sec. and treas. Mountain View Development Co.; dir. and gen. counsel Roosevelt Hotel, Inc., N.Y., Niagara Alkali Co., Niagara Falls Hotel Corp., Niagara Searchlight Co. Mem. Bd. of Edn., Niagara Falls, 1917-24; pres. Niagara Falls Y.M.C.A.; mem. zoning commn., Niagara Falls, 1920; appointed by Niagara Falls to draft new city charter. Dir. Memorial Hosp. Republican. Presbyn. Home: Niagara Falls, N.Y. Died Aug. 30, 1941.

GRAY, Andrew Caldwell, lawyer; b. New Castle, Del., Oct. 13, 1871; s. George and Harriet Lawrence (Black) G.; A.B., Princeton, 1892, A.M., 1895; student Harvard Law Sch., 1894-95; unmarried. Practiced at Wilmington, Del., 1895—; mem. firm, Gray, Southerland, Hughes, Berl & Ward; dir. Wilmington Trust Co. Judge advocate gen. State of Del., 1897-1900; atty. gen. of Del., 1909-13; mem. Dem. Nat. Com., 1921—. Presbyn. Home: Wilmington, Del. Died Dec. 15, 1929.

GRAY, Arthur Romeyn, ednl. sec.; b. Bergen Point, N.J., Dec. 30, 1875; s. George Zabriskie and Kate (Forrest) G.; Columbia U., 3 yrs.; Oxford U., Eng., 1½ yrs.; m. Laura Ferguson, Mar. 10, 1898. Deacon, 1900, priest, 1901, P.E. Ch.; instr. and prof. apologetics, U. of the South, 1901-11, chaplain, 1908-11; ednl. sec. Domestic and Foreign Missionary Soc. P.E. Ch., 1911-17, and sec. for Latin America, 1917-30; mem. staff of Cathedral of St. John the Divine, New York, 1930—. Home: New York, N.Y. Died Jan. 11, 1923.

GRAY, Bowman, tobacco; grad. U. of N.C., 1892; m. Nathalie F. Lyons; children—Bowman, Gordon. Chmn. bd. R. J. Reynolds Tobacco Co. Home: Winston-Salem, N.C. Died July 7, 1935.

GRAY, Carl Raymond, ry. pres.; b. Princeton, Ark., Sept. 28, 1867; s. Col. O. C. and Virginia L. (Davis) G.; ed. prep. dept. U. of Ark., LL.D., 1929; LL.D., U. of Md., 1916, Washington and Jefferson Coll., 1937; m. Harriette Flora, Dec. 6, 1886; children—Carl Raymond, Russell Davis, Howard Kramer. Began ry. service Mar. 20, 1883, and has served with St.L.&S.F. R.R. as telegraph operator and sta. agt., 1883-86, chief clk. to gen. western agt., Wichita, Kan., 1886-87, commercial agt., 1887-90, dist. freight agt., 1890-96, div. freight agt., 1896-97, div. supt., 1897-1900, supt. transportation, 1900-04, gen. mgr., Apr.-Oct., 1904, 2d v.p. and gen. mgr., Oct. 30, 1904-July 31, 1906, 2d v.p. in charge of operation, Aug. 1, 1906, and sr. v.p., 1909-11; also gen. mgr. C.&E.I. R.R., Apr.-Oct. 1904; pres. Spokane, Portland & Seattle, Ore., Electric Rys., 1911; pres. G.N. Ry., 1912-14; pres. Western Md. Ry., 1914-18, and chmn. Wheeling & L.E. Ry., 1917-18; dir. div. of operation under the dir.-gen. of rys., 1918-19; pres. Western Md. Ry. and chmn. Wheeling & L.E. Ry., Jan.-Dec. 1919; pres. U.P. System, 1920-37, vice chmn. of bd., 1937—. Address: New York, N.Y. Died May 9, 1939.

GRAY, Charlotte Elvira, author; b. Reading, Mich.; d. George and Elvira Eliza (Gaskill) Gray; ed. high sch., Monticello, Minn., and Munson Business Coll., Minneapolis; unmarried. Bookkeeper and stenographer, 1898-1905. Methodist. Author: Experimental Object Lessons, 1910; Out of the Mire, 1911; The Jericho Road, 1912; The Inn by the Sea, 1914; As His Mother Saw Him, 1917; Illustrative Object Lessons, 1923. Home: Minneapolis, Minn. Died Oct. 3, 1926.

GRAY, Clifton Merritt, clergyman; b. Cape Rosier, Me., Sept. 10, 1873; s. Martin Seymour and Ella Sarah (Dyer) G.; prep. edn., Castine (Me.) Normal Sch.; grad. Meadville (Pa.) Theol. Sch., 1898; grad. study Harvard Div. Sch., 1899, Coll. of Charleston (S.C.); m. Sallie Savage, Oct. 6, 1901. Ordained ministry Unitarian Ch., 1899; minister Millbury, Mass., 1899-1901, Charleston, S.C., 1901-21, Topeka, Kan., 1921—. Chmn. and dist. organizer of 4-minute men, publicity chmn. War Camp Community Service and denominational chaplain Camp Jackson, World War. Mason (32°, Shriner). Home: Topeka, Kan. Died May 2, 1933.

GRAY, Cyrus S., banker; b. Plum Township, Allegheny County, Pa., Mar. 23, 1854; s. James and Rachel (Hughey) G.; ed. pub. schs. and Eastman Business Coll., Poughkeepsie, N.Y.; m. Margaret J. Wilson, May 4, 1873. Clk. Orphans' Court, Allegheny Co., Pa., 1877-94 (resigned); began as trust officer, Fidelity Title & Trust Co., Pittsburgh, 1894, pres., 1909—. Home: Pittsburgh, Pa. Died Jan. 1918.

GRAY, David L.; ry. official; b. New York, N.Y., Oct. 1, 1870. Began as clerk, office of pres. Erie R.R. Co., 1886; in freight dept., same rd., 1891-1904, div. freight agent, Elmira, N.Y., 1904-05, asst. gen. freight agent, N.Y. City, 1905-09, asst. freight traffic mgr., N.Y. City, 1909-15, asst. gen. traffic mgr., N.Y. City, 1915-18; became asst. traffic mgr. N.Y. Central R.R. and West Shore R.R., 1920-25; v.p. in charge traffic Erie R.R. Co., 1925-39; consulting v.p. Erie R.R. and affiliated lines, 1939—. Mgr. Inland Traffic U.S. Shipping Board, Emergency Fleet Corp., Washington, D.C., 1918; staff asst. U.S. R.R. Administration, N.Y. City, 1918-19, traffic asst., regional dir. Eastern Region, same, 1919-20. Home: Scarsdale, N.Y. Died Feb. 11, 1941.

GRAY, Dudley Guy, ry. official; b. Columbus, O., May 15, 1868; s. William Ritchie and Virginia Jane (Beckwith) G.; student Ohio State U.; m. Katherine Leonard, Feb. 23, 1895. Began as messenger B.&O. R.R., 1887, later chief clk. div. freight office, at Columbus; chief clk. gen. freight office same rd., Pittsburgh, 1897-1902, div. freight agt., Columbus, 1902-05, Pittsburgh, 1905-10; gen. freight agt., Pittsburgh, 1910-12; gen. western freight agt. Western Md. Ry., Pittsburgh, Jan.-Nov. 1913, continuing with same rd. as gen. freight agt., Baltimore, Md., 1913-16, freight traffic mgr., 1916-19, gen. traffic mgr., 1919-20, v.p. in charge of traffic, 1920—. Mason. Democrat. Address: Baltimore, Md. Died Sept. 23, 1930.

GRAY, Elisha, electrician, inventor; b. nr. Barnesville, O., Aug. 2, 1835; m. M. Delia Shepard, 1862. Learned blacksmithing, carpentry and boat-building; then pursued special studies in physical science at Oberlin Coll., supporting himself by working at his trade. Invented, 1867, a self-adjusting telegraph relay; established as mfr. of electric apparatus at Cleveland, 1869; perfected the type-writing telegraph, the telegraph repeater, telegraphic switch, annunciator, etc. Organized, 1872, Western Electric Mfg. Co., but retired from it in 1874. Invented the speaking telephone, 1876; telautograph, 1893; established the Gray Electric Co., Highland Park. Organized the Congress of Electricians, in connection with World's Columbian Expn., 1893, and was its chmn. Author: Experimental Researches in Electro-Harmonic Telegraphy and Telephony; Elementary Talks on Science. Home: Highland Park, Ill. Died 1901.

GRAY, George, judge; b. New Castle, Del., May 4, 1840; s. Andrew C. and Elizabeth M. S.; A.B., Princeton, 1859, A.M., 1863; studied law at Harvard; LL.D., Princeton, 1889, Yale, 1903; m. Harriet L. Black, 1870; m. 2d, Margaret J. Black, 1882. Admitted to bar, 1863; practiced at New Castle, 1863-69, afterward at Wilmington. Atty. gen. of Delaware, 1879-85; elected U.S. senator as a Democrat, for unexpired term (1885-87) of Thomas F. Bayard (apptd. Sec. of State); reëlected for terms 1887-93, 1893-99; U.S. circuit judge, 3d Jud. Circuit, 1899-1914. Affiliated with the Nat. (gold-standard) Democrats in the presdl. election, 1896; mem. Peace Commn., Paris, 1898; apptd. by the Pres. mem. of the Joint High Commn. at Quebec, 1898, and mem. of the Internat. Permanent Court of Arbitration under the Hague Conv., Nov. 1900; chmn. anthracite coal strike commn., 1902; apptd. by President Roosevelt as umpire in U.S.-San Domingo Arbitration, 1903; mem. Tribunal of the N. Atlantic Coast Fisheries Arbitration, at The Hague, 1910; apptd. peace commr. with Great Britain, May 17, 1915; apptd. chmn. U.S. delegation to Pan-Am. Scientific Congress, 1915; apptd. mem. American-Mexican Commn., 1916. Regent and chmn. exec. com. Smithsonian Instn.; trustee and v.p. Carnegie Endowment for Internat. Peace. Home: Wilmington, Del. Died Aug. 7, 1925.

GRAY, Horace, asso. justice Supreme Court U.S., 1882—; b. Boston, Mass., 1828; grad. Harvard, 1845; Harvard Law School, 1849; admitted to Mass. bar, 1851; reporter Supreme Jud. Court, Mass., 1854-61; asso. justice, 1864-73, chief justice, 1873-82, Supreme Jud. Court, Mass. Address: Washington, D.C. Died 1902.

GRAY, James, editor; b. Falkirk, Scotland, Feb. 18, 1862; s. John and Elizabeth (Ronald) G.; brought to U.S., 1866; B.Sc., U. of Minn., 1885; m. Grace Orpha Farrington, Oct. 25, 1893. Reporter and city editor, Minneapolis Times, 1885-98, and sec. and dir. Times Newspaper Co., 1895-99; editorial writer Minneapolis Journal, 1904-14; later Washington corr. same. Mayor of Minneapolis, 1899-1900; Dem. nominee for gov. of Minn., 1910. Address: Washington, D.C. Died Sept. 8, 1916.

GRAY, James M., clergyman; b. 1851; pres. and trustee Moody Bible Inst., Chicago. Author: Antidote to Christian Science, 1907; How to Master the English Bible, 1909; Great Epochs of Sacred History, 1910; Progress in Life to Come, 1910; Bible Problems Explained, 1913; Christian Workers' Commentary on the Old and New Testaments, 1915; Picture of the Resurrection, 1917; Prophecy and the Lord's Return, 1917; Textbook on Prophecy, 1918; Primer of Faith; Synthetic Bible Studies; Spiritism and The Fallen Angels, 1920; My Faith in Jesus Christ, 1928; Steps on the Ladder of Faith, 1930. Home: Chicago, Ill. Died Sept. 21, 1935.

GRAY, James Richard, newspaper man; b. Adairsville, Ga., Sept. 20, 1859; s. John William and Sarah Jane (Venable) G.; grad. N. Ga. Agril. Coll., 1878; m. May Inman, Nov. 16, 1881. Admitted to bar, 1879; in law practice, 1879-1901; became editor-in-chief and general mgr. Atlanta Journal, Dec. 1901. Democrat. Home: Atlanta, Ga. Died June 25, 1917.

GRAY, John Chipman, lawyer; b. Brighton, Mass., July 14, 1839; s. Horace and Sarah Russell (Gardner) G.; A.B., Harvard, 1859, LL.B., 1861; (LL.D., Yale, 1894, Harvard, 1895); m. Anna Lyman (Mason), 1873. Admitted to bar, 1862; served in Civil War, 1862-65; 2d lt., 3d Mass. Vol. Cav., a.d.c. to Gen. George H. Gordon; maj. and judge-advocate, U.S.V.; in practice of law in Boston, 1865—. Lecturer, 1869-71, Story prof. law, 1875-83, Royall prof. law, 1883-1913, Harvard Law Sch. Author: Restraints on Alienation, 1883, 1905; The Rule Against Perpetuities, 1886, 1906; Select Cases and Other Authorities on the Law of Property, 6 vols., 1888-92 (2d edit., 1905-08). Home: Boston, Mass. Died Feb. 25, 1915.

GRAY, John Clinton, judge; b. New York, Dec. 4, 1843; s. John A. C. and Susan Maria (Zabriskie) G.; student U. of Berlin, 1860-61; A.B., New York U., 1865, A.M., 1868; LL.B., Harvard, 1866, LL.D., 1913. In practice at New York, 1866-88; judge Ct. of Appeals of N.Y. for terms 1888-1902, 1902-16; retired, Nov. 1913. Democrat. Died June 28, 1915.

GRAY, John Pinkham, lawyer; b. Boise, Ida., Mar. 17, 1880; s. John Strickland and Alice G.; grad. high sch., Boise; LL.B., George Washington U., 1898, LL.M., 1899, D.C.L., 1900; m. Stella Lee, June 11, 1904; children—Katherine, Mary Lee. Admitted to Ida. bar, 1901, and began practice at Wallace; moved to Coeur d'Alene, 1911; practiced in mining dists. of Ida., Mont., Utah, Ariz., Wash. and Alaska. Lecturer on mining law U. of Ida. and U. of Wis. Del. Rep. Nat. Conv., 1920. Republican. Home: Coeur d'Alene, Ida. Died Jan. 6, 1939.

GRAY, Joseph Preston, dentist; b. Pettus, County, Mo., Jan. 20, 1855; s. Sidney C. and Margaret L. G.; M.D., U. of Tenn., 1890, D.D.S., 1891; m. Ella Duncan, 1898. Practiced dentistry at Nashville; prof. prosthetic and oral surgery, U. of Tenn., 1890—; prof. prosthetic dentistry and mgr. and sec. dept. dentistry, Vanderbilt U., 1905—. Pres. Nashville Bd. Edn., 1903. Mem. 4th Internat. Dental Congress, 1904 (chmn. com. on clinics). Home: Nashville, Tenn. Died 1910.

GRAY, Morris, lawyer; b. Boston, Mar. 7, 1856; s. Francis H. and H. Regina (Shober) G.; A.B., Harvard, 1877, LL.B., 1880; m. Flora Grant, Sept.

15, 1883; children—Morris, Elizabeth, Francis C. Admitted to bar, 1880. Pres. Boston Mus. of Fine Arts, 1914-24, later trustee. Author: Treatise on the Law of Communication by Telegraph, 1885; The City's Voice (poems), 1923. Home: Boston, Mass. Died Jan. 12, 1931.

GRAY, Prentiss Nathaniel, banker; b. Oakland, Calif., July 2, 1884; s. George D. and Susan (Thayer) G.; B.A., U. of Calif., 1906; m. Laura Sherman, May 27, 1908; children—Barbara, Sherman; m. 2d, Dale Hartley McLeod, Oct. 29, 1932. Mgr. Calif. & Ore. Coast S.S. Co., 1910-14; pres. P. N. Gray, Inc., grain exporters, New York, 1919-23; pres. J. Henry Schroder Banking Corp., 1922—. Dir. Commn. for Relief in Belgium, 1917; chief of Marine Transportation Div., U.S. Food Administration, 1917-18; dir. Am. Relief Administration, 1918-19. Decorated Officier de l'Ordre de la Couronne (Belgian); Chevalier de la Légion d'Honneur (French). Republican. Presbyn. Editor of Records of North American Big Game. Home: New York, N.Y. Died Jan. 30, 1935.

GRAY, Thomas, dir. dept. mech. and elec. engineering, Rose Polytechnic Inst.; b. Lochgelly, Scotland, Feb. 4, 1850; grad. Glasgow (Scotland) U., 1878; taught electrical engring. in Imperial Coll. of Engring., Tokio, Japan, 1879-81; asst. in elec. engring. work to Lord Kelvin, 1881-88; represented him and Prof. Fleming Jenkin during mfr. and laying of the Mackay-Bennett system of Transatlantic cable. Author of Directions for Seismological Observations in the British Admiralty Manual of Scientific Enquiry; of articles on Telegraphs and Telephones in Encyclopædia Britannica; of the Smithsonian Physical Tables. Mem. expert staff of the Century Dictionary in dept. of electricity. Home: Terre Haute, Ind. Died 1908.

GRAY, William C., editor The Interior, 1871—; b. Butler County, O., Oct. 17, 1830; s. Jonathan and Mary (Woods) G.; Belmont Coll., 1849; Ph.D., Wooster U.; LL.D., Knox Coll.; admitted to bar, 1852, but never practiced; editor Miami Democrat, 1851; editor of Scott Battery for campaign of 1852; established Tiffin (O.) Tribune, 1853; editorial writer Cleveland Herald, 1862; editor Newark American, 1863-71; The Interior is a religious paper, but he is not a clergyman. Author: Campfire Musings; Clear Creek, etc. Address Chicago, Ill. Died 1901.

GRAY, William John, banker; b. Detroit, Mich., July 9, 1857; s. William and Mary (Stewart) G.; A.B., U. of Mich., 1877; studied law in office of R. P. Toms, Detroit; m. Hannah Van Vechten Hammond, June 2, 1887; children—Donald S., William J. Admitted to Mich. bar, 1879, and began practice at Detroit; mem. firm Gray & Gray, 1884-1912; elected v.p. First Nat. Bank (now First Wayne Nat. Bank), Detroit, 1912, pres. 1925-27, vice chmn. of bd., 1927—; dir. Detroit Br. Federal Reserve Bank of Chicago. Republican. Episcopalian. Home: Detroit, Mich. Deceased.

GRAY, William Rensselaer, educator; b. Aurora, Ill., Sept. 27, 1879; s. Frederick and Rella (Davis) G.; B.L., Dartmouth, 1904; Master Commercial Science, Amos Tuck Sch. (Dartmouth), 1905; C.P.A., New Hampshire, 1919; m. Lucia May Shattuck, Dec. 25, 1905. Clk. in U.S. Treasury, Washington, D.C., 1897-1900; with Dartmouth Coll., 1905—, instr. in accounting, 1905-08; asst. prof., 1908-14, sec. Amos Tuck Sch., 1911-16, prof. accounting, 1914—, acting dir. Amos Tuck Sch., 1917-19, dean, 1919—. Dir. Connecticut River Power Co. Dir. Ordnance Training Sch., Dartmouth, 1917-18; chief of div. business dept. Com. on Edn. and Spl. Training, War Dept., Sept. 1918-May 1919. Pres. trustees, Mary Hitchcock Memorial Hosp., Hanover, N.H., trustee Dartmouth Coll., Holderness Sch. for Boys, Plymouth, N.H., Protestant Episcopal Diocese of N.H. Home: Hanover, N.H. Died Mar. 31, 1937.

GRAYSON, Cary Travers, rear adm.; b. "Salubria," Culpeper County, Va., Oct. 11, 1878; s. John Cooke (M.D.) and Adelena (Pettus) G.; William and Mary Coll., 1895-98; Ph.G., U. of the South, 1902, M.D., 1902; M.D., Med. Coll. of Va.; grad. U.S. Naval Med. Sch., 1904; hon. LL.D., William and Mary College; m. Alice Gertrude Gordon, May 24, 1916; children—James Gordon, Cary Travers, Wm. Cabell. Interne, Columbia Hosp. for Women, Washington, 1902-03; commd. act. asst. surg. U.S.N., July 14, 1903; asst. surgeon, June 28, 1904; passed asst. surgeon, June 28, 1907; surgeon, Aug. 1916; med. dir. with rank of rear admiral, Aug. 29, 1916. Surgeon U.S. Naval Hosp., Washington, 1903-05, U.S.S. Maryland, 1905-07; cruise around the world, 1905-07; surgeon of the President's yacht, Mayflower, and attending and consulting physician, Naval Dispensary, Washington, during the Roosevelt and Taft administrations; physician to President Wilson. Mem. pub. health com. of Nat. Food Administration; med. mem. Council Nat. Defense; mem. staff Emergency Hosp.; formerly mem. staff Ear, Nose and Throat Hosp. and Providence Hosp.; chmn. Am. Nat. Red Cross, 1935—; chmn. Gorgas Memorial Inst. of Preventive Medicine and Tropical Research. Retired from Navy, Dec. 30, 1928. Dir. The Warwick Memorial Clinic; med. dir. Washington Gas Light Co. Decorated; Navy Cross (U.S.), Commander Order of Leopold (Belgium), Commander Legion of Honor (France). Dir. Nat. Capitol Horse Show (Washington). Episcopalian. Home: Washington, D.C. Died Feb. 15, 1938.

GRAYSON, Theodore J(ulius), prof. finance; b. Beverly, N.J., Mar. 4, 1880; s. Frederick William and Katherine (Julius) G.; Haverford (Pa.) Coll., 1897-99; LL.B., U. of Pa., 1902, B.S. in Economics, 1920; LL.D., Bucknell U., 1931; m. Grace Blakiston, Dec. 15, 1917 (divorced 1933); 1 dau., Louise Blakiston; m. 2d, Margaret Jacobs Whetstone, April 2, 1934. Admitted to Pa. bar, 1902; practiced at Philadelphia; instr. in finance, Wharton Sch. of Finance and Commerce, U. of Pa., 1914-20, asst. prof. finance, 1920-25, asso. prof., 1925-28, prof., 1928—, dir. evening and extension schs. of finance and accounting, 1918—. Sec. and treas. N.J. Pub. Utility Information Com.; treas. N.J. Utilities Assn. Rep. of U. of Pa. in Assn. of Urban Univs., Nat. Univ. Extension Assn.; pres. Nat. Univ. Extension Assn., 1932-33. Republican. Episcopalian (vestryman Ch. of St. Luke and Epiphany). Mason. Author: Law of Beneficial and Social Associations in Pennsylvania, 1904; Investment Trusts, 1928; Leaders and Periods of American Finance, 1932. Home: Philadelphia, Pa. Died Dec. 23, 1937.

GRAYSON, Thomas Wray, M.D.; b. Meadville, Pa., Nov. 22, 1871; s. Thomas Wray and Mary Elizabeth (Green) G.; A.B., Washington and Jefferson Coll., 1892, A.M., 1897; M.D. West Penn Med. Coll. (now Med. Dept. U. of Pittsburgh), 1897; m. Mary Elizabeth Bard, June 9, 1920. Interne, West Penn Hosp., 1898. First lieut. Medical R.C., 1917; in active service, Sept. 1, 1917, at Camp Greenleaf, Ga.; gastroenterologist, Base Hosp., Camp Shelby, Miss., Nov. 20, 1917; chief med. service, rank of maj., Base Hosp. No. 77, France, and comdg. officer, Camp Hosp. No. 108, to July 1919. Trustee P.E. Diocese of Pittsburgh. Progressive. Home: Pittsburgh, Pa. Died May 17, 1933.

GREATHOUSE, Charles A.; b. Mt. Vernon, Ind., July 17, 1869; s. Benjamin Franklin and Betheny (Welborn) G.; ed. Central Normal Coll. (Danville, Ind.); Ind. U., class 1893; m. Erma Ribyre, Nov. 4, 1903. State supt. pub. instrn., Ind., 3 terms; chmn. Dem. State Central Com., Ind., 1916-20; mem. Federal Bd. Vocational Edn. (representing agrl. interests), to March 1, 1919, resigned. Pres. and treas. Bookwalter-Ball-Greathouse Printing Co., Indianapolis. Mem. Dem. Nat. Com., 1923—, sec., 1924—; mem. Bd. Trustees Indiana State Teachers Coll. Mem. Phi Delta Theta. Episcopalian. Mason (32°), K.P. Clubs: University, Indiana Democratic, Highland Golf and Country, Woodstock Country. Home: 4326 Washington Boul. Office: Bookwalter-Ball-Greathouse Printing Co., Indianapolis, Ind. Died Nov. 5, 1931.

GREATHOUSE, Clarence R., journalist, diplomat; b. in Ky. about 1845; became a lawyer; settled in Calif.; entered journalism, becoming editor San Francisco Examiner; consul gen. Tokio, Japan, 1885-89; removed to Korea; became head Korean Postoffice Dept.; American counselor to Korean Minister of Foreign Affairs, 1893-98; during same period practically confidential adviser to the King. Dismissed from royal service on demand of Russian minister, 1898. Died 1899.

GREBLE, Edwin St. John, army officer; b. West Point, N.Y., June 24, 1859; s. John Trout and Sarah Bradley (French) G.; grad. U.S. Mil. Acad., 1881, Inf. and Cav. Sch., Ft. Leavenworth, Kan., 1884, Coast Arty. Sch., Ft. Monroe, Va., 1892; m. Gertrude, d. Gen. John S. Poland, June 24, 1885. Commd. 2d lt. 2d Arty., June 11, 1881; promoted through grades to brig. gen., Oct. 13, 1916; maj. gen. (temp.) World War. Served as adj. gen. 2d Div. of the Army Corps; asst. adj. gen. Dept. of Havana, under Gen. Ludlow; in charge guard to City of Havana, taking over pub. bldgs. and barracks during evacuation by the Spaniards, under Gen. Ludlow; organized Dept. of Charities while in Republic of Cuba, under Gen. Wood; supervisor sec. of interior in the 2d intervention, Cuba; mem. Gen. Staff, in charge field arty., U.S.A., 1910-14; comdg. 6th Field Arty., 1914-16; service on Mexican border—Naco, Douglas and El Paso—Sept. 13, 1914-Aug. 22, 1917; assigned as comdr. 36th Div., N.G.; Camp Bowie, Ft. Worth, Tex., Aug. 27, 1917; retired on account of disability incurred in active service, Oct. 1918. Home: Washington, D.C. Died Sept. 20, 1931.

GREELEY, Louis May, lawyer; b. Chicago, Ill., May 24, 1858; s. Samuel S. and Annie Morris (Larned) G.; A.B., Harvard, 1880; student Harvard Law School 2 years; LL.M., Northwestern Univ., 1910; m. Anna Lowell Dunbar, Oct. 3, 1895. Admitted to Ill. bar, 1884. Prof. law, Northwestern Law Sch. Democrat. Home: La Grange, Ill. Died June 17, 1939.

GREELY, Adolphus Washington, army officer; b. Newburyport, Mass., Mar. 27, 1844; s. John Balch and Frances (Cobb) G.; grad. Newburyport High Sch., 1860; m. Henrietta H. C. Nesmith, June 20, 1878; children—Antoinette, Adola, John Nesmith, Rose Ishbel, Adolphus W., Gertrude Gale. Served in Civil War, 1861-65, pvt. to capt., and bvt. maj. vols. (thrice wounded); apptd. 2d lt. 36th U.S. Inf., Mar. 7, 1867; 1st lt. 5th Cav., May 27, 1873; capt., June 11, 1886; brig. gen. chief signal officer U.S.A., Mar. 3, 1887; maj. gen., Feb. 10, 1906. First vol. pvt. soldier of Civil War to reach grade of brig. gen. U.S.A. Constructed 2,000 miles mil. telegraph in Tex., Dak. and Mont., 1876-79; in pursuance of recommendation of Hamburg Internat. Geog. Congress (1879) was placed, 1881, in command of U.S. expdn. to establish one of a chain of 13 circumpolar stations; his party of 25 reached further north (83°24') than any previous record; discovered new land N. of Greenland and crossed Grinnell Land to the Polar Sea; two relief expdns. failed to reach the party, which retreated S. to Cape Sabine, where, relief still failing, the party largely perished of starvation, only 7 survivors being found by 3d expdn. under Capt. Winfield S. Schley. During mil. operations abroad (1898-1902) there were built and operated under his direction 1,000 miles of telegraph in P.R., 3,800 miles in Cuba, 250 miles in China, and 13,500 miles of lines and cables in P.I.; installed system of 3,900 miles of telegraph lines, submarine cables and wireless in Alaska, 1900-04, the wireless section of 107 miles, from Nome to St. Michael, being the first successful long-distance wireless operated regularly as part of a commercial system. Mem. bd. to regulate wireless telegraphy in U.S., 1904; mem. bd. to report on coast defenses of U.S., 1905; U.S. del. Internat. Telegraph Conf., London, 1903, Internat. Wireless Telegraph Conf., Berlin, 1903. Comdg. Pacific Div. and in charge relief operations, San Francisco earthquake sufferers, Apr.-Aug. 1906; comdg. Northern Div. 1906, Dept. Columbia, 1907; retired by operation of law, 1908. Gold medalist, Royal, Am. and French geog. socs. Author: Isothermal Lines of the United States, 1881; Chronological List of Auroras, 1881; Diurnal Fluctuations of Barometric Pressure, 1891; Three Years of Arctic Service, 2 vols., 1885; Proceedings of Lady Franklin Bay Expedition, 1888; American Weather, 1890; American Explorers, 1894; Handbook of Arctic Discoveries, 1896; Rainfall of Western States and Territories, 1888; Climate of Oregon and Washington, 1889; Climate of Nebraska, 1890; Climatology of Arid Region, 1891; Climate of Texas, 1891; Public Documents First Fourteen Congresses of United States, 1900; Handbook of Polar Discoveries, 1909; Handbook of Alaska, 1925; True Tales of Arctic Heroism, 1912; Reminiscences of Travel and Adventure, 1927; Polar Regions in Twentieth Century, 1928. Rep. U.S.A. at coronation of George V of England, 1911. Died Oct. 20, 1935.

GREEN, Adolphus Williamson, lawyer; b. Boston, Mass., Jan. 14, 1843; s. John H. and Jane G.; grad. Boston Latin Sch., 1859; A.B., Harvard, 1863; m. Esther Walsh, July 3, 1881. Prin., high schools., Groton, Mass., 1863-64; 2d asst. librarian, 1864-67, librarian, 1867-69, Mercantile Library Assn., New York; studied law in offices of Evarts, Southmayd & Choate, New York, 1869-73; admitted to bar, 1873; went to Chicago; atty. Village of Hyde Park, Ill., 1882-84; later atty. of South Park Commrs.; mem. law firm of Goudy (William C.) & Green, 1884-94; later of Green, Willits & Robbins, and Green, Peters & Babst. Organized the Nat. Biscuit Co., 1898, and became its gen. counsel and mem. exec. com.; later elected chmn. bd. of dirs., and 1905 became pres. Home: Greenwich, Conn. Died Mar. 8, 1917.

GREEN, Andrew Haswell, lawyer; b. Green Hill, Worcester, Mass., Oct. 6, 1820; s. William E. G.; ed. in Mass.; studied law and practiced, New York; pres. bd. commrs. edn., 1856; pres. and exec. officer Central Park Bd., 1857-70; comptroller New York, 1871-76. Trustee and executor S. J. Tilden, William B. Ogden, and other large estates; originated, 1868, plan carried out in 1897, for creation of Greater New York and called "The Father of Greater New York"; also plan which resulted in consolidation of Astor, Lenox and Tilden libraries in New York Public Library; trustee same. Founder and pres. New York Zoöl. Soc.; pres. and commr. N.Y. State Reservation, Niagara Falls, 1883—, pres., 1888—; del. N.Y. State Constitutional Conv., 1894; spl. State commr. to locate bridge over North River, New York, to report on causes of decline of commerce of New York, to examine into tax legislation of New York, etc. Originator of plan and trustee Am. Mus. of Natural History; originator of plan and original trustee of the Met. Mus. of Art; dir. New York Juvenile Asylum, Soc. for Prevention of Cruelty to Children— trustee New York Homœ. Med. Coll. and Hosp.; dir. Isabella Heimath, etc. Home: New York, N.Y. Died 1903.

GREEN, Bernard Richardson, civil engr.; b. Malden, Mass., Dec. 28, 1843; s. Ezra and Elmina Minerva (Richardson) G.; S.B., Lawrence Scientific Sch. (Harvard), 1864; m. Julia E. Lincoln, Jan. 1, 1868. For 14 yrs. engaged with officers of U.S. corps of engrs. constructing permanent sea coast fortifications of Me., N.H., and Mass.; then in charge of erection of large pub. buildings in Washington, including the State, War and Navy building, Washington Monument, Army Med. Mus. and Library, U.S. Soldiers' Home buildings, Library of Congress, Washington Pub. Library and new Nat. Mus. Bldg.; also two of the principal hotels, etc.; supt. Congressional Library building and grounds. Address: Washington, D.C. Died Oct. 22, 1914.

GREEN, Berryman, clergyman, educator; b. Charlotte County, Va., 1864; s. Col. William E. and Jeanie Elliot (Boylan) G.; grad. P.E. Theol. Sem. in Va., 1890; D.D., Washington and Lee U., 1906; LL.D., William and Mary Coll., 1923; m. Nina Daniel Bouldin, 1891. Deacon, 1890, priest, 1891, P.E. Ch.; rector S. Farnham Parish, Va., 1891-93, St. James' Ch., Leesburg, 1893-96, Christ Ch., Alexandria, 1896-1902; prof. English Bible and homiletics, Theol. Sem. in Va., 1902—, also dean. Pres. Standing Com. Diocese of Va., 1903—. Address: Alexandria, Va. Deceased.

GREEN, Charles Henry, inventor, promoter; b. Dayton, O., Oct. 21, 1837; grad. Miami U., 1856; in produce commn. business, New York, 1863-70; organized, 1879, Hektograph Co., mfg. a device for reproducing drawings, writings, etc., pres., 1879—; also pres. Columbia Navigation Commercial Co., Washington City & Point Lookout (Md.) Ry. Co.; dir. other corps.; m. Lilla A. Wightman, 1872. Home: New York, N.Y. Died 1908.

GREEN, Charles Montraville, obstetrician, gynecologist; b. Medford, Mass., Dec. 18, 1850; s. George Bent and Melinda (Wetherbee) G.; A.B., Harvard, 1874, M.D., 1877; m. Helen Lincoln Ware, June 29, 1876; children—Charles Montraville (dec.), Robert Montraville. Asst. in obstetrics, 1883-86, instr., 1886-94, asst. prof., 1894-1904, asso. prof., 1904-07, prof. obstetrics, 1907-11, obstetrics and gynecology, 1911-15, prof. emeritus, 1915, sec. med. faculty, 1897-1907, acting dean, 1907-08, Harvard U. Sr. surgeon Boston City Hosp. Lt. col. M.N.G., retired. Home: Boston, Mass. Died Nov. 20, 1928.

GREEN, David Edward, lawyer; b. Renrock, O., Apr. 3, 1874; s. David Jacob and Mary (Fairchild) G.; prep. edn. Doan Acad., Granville, O.; B.S., Denison U., 1901, LL.D., 1937; LL.B., Western Reserve, 1904; m. Alice Dunham, July 31, 1909; children—Harriett, David Dunham, Isabel Alice, Helen Mary. Admitted to Ohio bar, 1904, and began practice at Cleveland; mem. firm Myers, Green & Keough, 1904-17, Griswold, Green, Palmer & Kapp, 1917—; gen. counsel Cleveland & Mahoning Valley Ry. Co.; special counsel to atty. gen. of Ohio, 1923-27; v.p. Equity Savings & Loan Co. Chmn. Legal Advisory Bd., Cleveland, World War. Mem. Bd. of Edn., Shaker Heights, O., 1927-35; pres. Federated Chs. of Cleveland, 1917-18; mem. Cleveland Metropolitan Housing Authority; mem. Community Fund Council, Cleveland. Chmn. bd. trustees Denison U.; pres. Shaker Heights Pub. Library Bd.; pres. Huntington Assn., Inc.; treas. Cleveland Welfare Fed.; trustee Bapt. Home of Northern Ohio, First Bapt. Ch. Republican. Baptist. Home: Cleveland O. Died July 30, 1940.

GREEN, David I., social economist; b. Independence, N.Y., Feb. 5, 1864; s. J. Chandler and Emily (Sherman) G.; A.B., Alfred U., 1885, A.M., 1886; Ph.D., Johns Hopkins, 1893; m. Mary Titsworth, Nov. 2, 1892. Taught in secondary schs., 1886-88; prof. Latin, Alfred U., 1888-90; instr. social science, Johns Hopkins, 1893-94; teacher in Hartford Sch. of Sociology, 1894-96; supt. Charity Organization Soc. of Hartford, 1894-1918; actg. prof. economics and sociology, Ia. State Teachers Coll., 1919; prof. economics and sociology, Kenyon Coll., 1919—. Home: West Hartford, Conn. Deceased.

GREEN, Edward Howland Robinson, capitalist; b. Langham, London, Eng. (while parents were touring Europe), Aug. 22, 1868; s. Edward H. and Hetty Howland (Robinson) G.; A.B., Fordham Coll., 1888; admitted to bar; m. Mabel E. Harlow, July 10, 1917. Began as section hand on an Eastern ry.; supt. and later mng. dir. O.&M. R.R.; pres. and gen. mgr. Tex. Midland R.R., 1893; dir. The Chase Nat. Bank (New York), Murray Co., Terrell Co.; trustee N.Y. Produce Exchange Safe Deposit & Storage Co. Chmn. Rep. State Com. of Tex., 3 terms; commr. and dir. St. Louis Expn., 1904. Home: South Dartmouth, Mass. Died June 8, 1936.

GREEN, Edward Melvin, clergyman; b. Darlington County, S.C., Sept. 10, 1838; s. James and Sarah Ann (James) G.; A.B., Oglethorpe U., Ga., 1859; grad. Columbia (S.C.) Theol. Sem., 1863; D.D., Southwestern Presbyn. U., Tenn., 1884; m. Sarah Emily Howe, June 24, 1863 (died 1890); m. 2d, Mrs. Fannie Wallace Anderson, Oct. 14, 1896. Ordained Presbyn. ministry, 1864; chaplain C.S.A., with Army of the Tenn., 1863-65; pastor Washington, Ga., 1866-71; editor Southern Presbyterian, 1872-73; pastor Washington, N.C., 1874-77, 1st Ch., Danville, Ky., 1877—. Moderator Gen. Assembly Presbyn. Ch. in U.S., 1898; mem. Pan Presbyn. Council, Washington, D.C., 1899. Trustee Columbia (S.C.) Theol. Sem., Central Univ., Ky., Ky. Theol. Sem. Democrat. Home: Danville, Ky. Deceased.

GREEN, Francis Mathews, comdr. U.S. Navy; b. Boston, Feb. 23, 1835; s. Mathews W. and Margaret A. (Gilchrist) G.; ed. English High School, Boston; m. Elizabeth S. Cushing, Sept. 1, 1870. Author: The Navigation of the Caribbean Sea, 1877; Telegraphic Determination of Longitudes, 1876, 1880, 1883; List of Geographical Positions, 1883. Died 1902.

GREEN, Fred Warren, gov., mfr.; b. Manistee, Mich., Oct. 20, 1872; s. Holdon Nathaniel and Adaline (Clark) G.; grad. high sch., Cadillac, Mich., 1890; B.S., Mich. State Normal Sch., Ypsilanti, Mich., 1893; LL.B., U. of Mich., 1898; m. Helen A. Kelly, June 18, 1901; 1 dau., Helen Nancy. Began practice of law at Ypsilanti, 1899; served as city atty., Ypsilanti; became identified with Ypsilanti Reed Furniture Co. and moved with it to Ionia, 1904, later chmn. bd.; v.p. Nat. Rattan & Willow Co., New York; dir. Lake Odessa (Mich.) Canning Co. Mgr. and dir. Ionia Free Fair Assn. Mem. Mich. N.G. 14 yrs., advancing to brig. gen.; served as 1st lt. Spanish-Am. War. Mayor of Ionia 12 terms; treas. Rep. State Central Com. of Mich., 10 yrs.; gov. of Mich., 1927-31. Nat. comdr. United Spanish War Vets., 1929-30. Mason. Home: Ionia, Mich. Died Nov. 30, 1936.

GREEN, Frederick Robin, physician; b. Cameron, Mo., July 17, 1870; s. Rev. John M. and Martha (McCreary) G.; A.B., Oberlin, 1894, A.M., 1898; M.D., Northwestern U., 1898; m. Helen Hutchinson, June 30, 1923. General practice, Chicago, 1898-1905; instr. anatomy, Northwestern U. Med. Sch., 1898-1904; asst. editor, Ill. State Med. Jour., 1904-05; asst. to gen. sec. A.M.A., 1905-10; sec. Council on Health and Pub. Instruction A.M.A., 1910-22. Editor of Health Magazine, May 1922-24; sec. of Medical and Dental Arts Club. First lt. Medical Reserve Corps, 1908-17, commd. capt., June 4, 1917; ordered to active duty Med. O.T.C., Ft. Riley, Kan., Aug. 11, 1917; instr. and asst. adj., Nov. 20, 1917; commd. maj., M.C. U.S.A., Feb. 3, 1918; adj. Med. O.T.C., Ft. Riley, May 1, 1918-July 17, 1918; personnel div. S.G.O., Washington, July 17, 1918-Dec. 15, 1918; hon. discharged, Dec. 15, 1918; lt. col. Med. O.R.C., Feb. 1, 1925. Home: Chicago, Ill. Died Apr. 26, 1929.

GREEN, Henry, asso. justice supreme court of Pa., 1879—; b. Warren County, N.J., Aug. 29, 1828; grad. Lafayette Coll., 1846 (A.M., 1849; LL.D., 1878). Studied law, 1846-49; admitted to bar, Sept. 1849; practiced law at Easton, Pa., until 1879. Mem. Constitutional Conv., 1873; mem. Nat. Rep. Conv. which nominated Fremont and Dayton, 1856. Republican. Home: Easton, Pa. Died 1900.

GREEN, Henry Woodhull, lawyer; b. Trenton, N.J., Apr. 30, 1868; s. Charles Ewing and Mary Livingston (Potter) G.; grad. Lawrenceville School, 1887; A.B., Princeton, 1891, A.M., 1894; LL.B., N.Y. Law Sch., 1894; m. Helen Wood Watts, Jan. 14, 1895. Sec.-treas. United Railroads of N.J.; v.p. Trenton Banking Co., 1910—. Dir. many corps.; trustee Princeton U., Princeton Theol. Sem. Home: Trenton, N.J. Died Nov. 24, 1939.

GREEN, Hetty Howland Robinson, financier; b. New Bedford, Mass., Nov. 21, 1835; d. Edward Mott Robinson, who died, leaving her large fortune, 1865; ed. Mrs. Lowell's Sch., Boston; m. Edward H. Green, 1867 (died Mar. 19, 1902); mother of Edward Howland Robinson G. Is said to be the richest woman in America, and probably the greatest woman financier in the world; interested in nearly every large corp. and enterprise of magnitude all over the world; personally manages her large property in stocks, bonds and real estate in Chicago, New York and elsewhere. Address: New York, N.Y. Died July 3, 1916.

GREEN, James, lawyer; b. Worcester, Mass., Mar. 2, 1841; s. James and Elizabeth (Swett) G.; A.B., Harvard, 1862, LL.B., 1864, A.M., 1865; traveled and studied in Europe and the East, 1872-74 and 1877-78; degree of French Civilization, Sorbonne, Paris, 1924; m. Mary A., d. of David Sewall and Harriet (Sawyer) Messinger, of Worcester, June 2, 1881 (died Mar. 22, 1925); children—Mary Sprague (Mrs. A. C. Higgins), Thomas Samuel. Admitted to N.Y. bar, 1865; in practice, Worcester, Mass., 1866-1920. Wrote "Causes of the War in South Africa from the American Lawyer's Standpoint," 1900 (reprinted by Impl. So. African Assn., London); also other pamphlets, including "Personal Recollections of D. H. Chamberlain, Once Governor of South Carolina," 1908. Unitarian. Home: Worcester, Mass. Died Apr. 21, 1926.

GREEN, James Gilchrist, naval officer; b. Jamaica Plain, Mass., June 27, 1841; s. Matthews W. and Margaret Augusta G.; ed. N.H. and Mass.; m. Cornelia F. Bond, Jan. 19, 1864. Entered U.S.N., volunteer service, as acting ensign, May 1861; transferred to regular navy at end of Civil war; commissioned lt. comdr. July 3, 1870; comdr., Mar. 1887; capt. Mar. 3, 1900; commandant Puget Sound Station, 1898-1900; retired May 11, 1901, as rear admiral, upon own request, after 40 yrs. service. Was commandant Havana, Cuba, Naval Station, 1900; comd. U.S.S. New Orleans, 1900-01. Died 1909.

GREEN, James Monroe, normal school prin.; b. Succasunna, N.J., Aug. 29, 1851; s. William Hampton and Alice (Hopkins) G.; ed. N.J. State Model and State Normal Schs., Trenton, N.J., class of 1870; A.M., Dickinson Coll., 1884, LL.D., 1905; Ph.B., Ill. Wesleyan U., 1884, A.M., 1887, Ph.D., 1890; m. Caroline E. Morris, Oct. 8, 1878. Prin. Long Branch schs., 1876-89; prin. N.J. State Normal and Model Schs., 1889-1917. Pres. State Teachers' Assn., 1881, State Sanitary Assn., 1886; chmn. State Teachers' Assn.'s Com. on Ednl. Progress; proposed, 1889, system of approving high schs. in N.J., which was adopted by the State Bd. Edn. Address: Trenton, N.J. Died Nov. 1, 1920.

GREEN, James Woods, lawyer; b. Cambridge, N.Y., Apr. 4, 1842; s. Robert and Margaret (Woods) G.; A.B., Williams Coll., 1866, A.M., 1890; m. May Stephens Banks, Dec. 7, 1875. Admitted to bar, 1869; began practice at Olathe, Kan., 1870; dean Law Sch. of U. of Kan., 1878—. County atty., Johnson County, Kan., 1875-77, Douglas County, Kan., 1878-80; Dem. candidate for justice Supreme Ct., 1884. Del. Universal Congress Lawyers and Jurists, St. Louis, 1904. Episcopalian. Home: Lawrence, Kan. Deceased.

GREEN, Jesse Cope, dentist; b. Birmingham, Pa., Dec. 13, 1817; s. William and Phebe (Hatton) G.; ed. neighborhood schs. of birthplace, and boarding schs., West Chester, Pa., and Wilmington, Del.; studied dentistry in West Chester, Pa., 1842-43; D.D.S., Pa. Coll. Dental Surgery, Phila., 1865; m. Alice W. Shields, Sept. 30, 1845 (died 1900). Taught sch., 1836-42; engaged in practice of dentistry in West Chester, Pa., 1843-1909, 66 yrs. continuous practice. Sch. dir., 1849-59, at times filling offices of pres. and treas.; pres. bd. health, 18 yrs.; formerly treas. Associated Health Authorities and Sanitarians of Pa. Volunteer observer for Smithsonian Instn. and Weather Bur., Washington, 1855—, and for Pa. State Weather Service from its organization. Mem. Pa. State Dental Examining Bd., 1876-98. Mem. Soc. of Friends. Address: West Chester, Pa. Died July 26, 1920.

GREEN, John, army officer; b. Germany, Nov. 20, 1825; s. Gottlieb and Mary G.; ed. pub. schs., Crawford County, O., 1832-42; m. Dec. 8, 1878, Mary Yeager. In army as sergt. and 1st sergt. Co. B. and sergt. maj. Mounted Rifles, 1846-48 and 1852-55; apptd. 2d lt. dragoons, June 18, 1855, 1st lt., Mar. 3, 1861, capt. 2d Cav., Aug. 13, 1861, maj. 1st Cav., June 9, 1868, lt. col. 2d Cav., July 3, 1885; retired for age, Nov. 20, 1889; col., Apr. 23, 1904, act of Congress; bvtd. maj., July 3, 1863, lt. col., Apr. 15, 1865, col., Feb. 27, 1890, brig. gen., Feb. 27, 1890; awarded Congressional Medal of Honor. Died 1908.

GREEN, John, physician; b. Worcester, Mass., Apr. 2, 1835; s. James and Elizabeth (Swett) G.; A.B., Harvard, 1855, S.B., 1856, A.M., 1859, M.D., 1866; admitted fellow Mass. Med. Soc. by exam., 1858; studied medicine at Cambridge and Boston, Mass., and in Europe, 1855-60, 1865-66; LL.D., Washington U., 1905, U. of Mo., 1906; m. Harriet Louisa Jones, Oct. 22, 1868. In med. service of Western Sanitary Commn., 1862, and acting asst. surgeon armies of the Tenn. and in Md., 1862-63; removed to St. Louis, 1866; prof. ophthalmology, St. Louis Med. Coll. (Washington U.), 1886—. Home: St. Louis, Mo. Died Dec. 8, 1913.

GREEN, John F(indley), lawyer; b. Clinton County, Mo., Feb. 14, 1864; s. Cyrus Estill and Wilmoth L. (Moberly) G.; grad. Westminster Coll., Fulton, Mo., 1884, St. Louis (Mo.) Law Sch., 1890; m. Eleanor Ibbotson, 1893. Admitted to Mo. bar, 1890; became law clk., office of Judson & Taussig, St. Louis, 1892; mem. Judson & Green, 1905-15, Judson, Green & Henry, 1915-29, Judson, Green, Henry & Remmers, 1929—. Democrat. Presbyn. Home: St. Louis, Mo. Died Aug. 24, 1932.

GREEN, John Orne, physician; b. Lowell, Mass., June 7, 1841; s. John Orne and Jane (McBurney) G.; A.B., Harvard, 1863, A.M., M.D., 1866; studied aural surgery in Berlin, Vienna and Würzburg; unmarried. Lecturer, 1869-70, 1871-75, instr. clin. otology, 1875-88, prof., 1888-1904, Harvard; aural surgeon, Boston City Hosp., Mass. Charitable Eye and Ear Infirmary, Mass. Gen. Hosp. Home: Boston, Mass. Died Jan. 5, 1922.

GREEN, John Pugh, ry. pres.; b. Phila., July 31, 1839; Central High Sch., Phila., class of 1855; admitted to bar; m. Jean Crissy Moore, Dec. 29, 1880. Served capt. in U.S.V., 1862-65. Entered ry. service, 1865; held various positions on different rys.; sec. to 1st v.p. Pa. R.R., 1869-74, asst. to pres., 1874-82, 4th v.p., 1882-88, 3d v.p., 1888-93, 2d v.p., 1893-97, 1st v.p., Feb. 10, 1897; retired July 31, 1909; pres. W.N.Y.&P. Ry. Co., Del. R.R. Co., D.,M.&V. R.R. Co., etc. Home: Rosemont, Pa. Died Mar. 9, 1924.

GREEN, Nathan, law prof.; b. Winchester, Tenn., Feb. 19, 1827; s. Nathan and Mary G.; A.B., Cumberland U., 1845, LL.B., 1849; LL.D., Centre Coll., Ky.; m. Betty McClain, Oct. 15, 1850; m. 2d, Mrs. Blanche Hunter Woodward, Oct. 14, 1902. Prof. law, Cumberland U., 1856—, chancellor, 1873—. Author: Tall Man of Winton; Sparks from a Back Log. Home: Lebanon, Tenn. Died Feb. 17, 1919.

GREEN, Rufus Lot, educator; b. Rush County, Ind., Mar. 3, 1862; s. Samuel and Elizabeth Anne (McKee) G.; student Ind. U., 1879-81, Cornell, 1881-83, Ind. U., 1883-85, B.S., 1885, A.M., 1888; Johns Hopkins, 1887-88; m. Emma Edwards, Aug. 11, 1886; children—Helen (Mrs. Robert W. Cross), Hazel, Thomas Edwards. Instr. mathematics, 1885-86, asso. prof. pure mathematics, 1886-90, prof., 1890-93, Ind. U.; asso. prof. mathematics, 1893-94, prof., 1894, exec. head dept. mathematics, 1925-27, Stanford (emeritus). Dir. Yosemite Park and Curry Co. Address: Stanford University, Calif. Died 1932.

GREEN, Samuel Abbott, physician, author; b. Groton, Mass., Mar. 16, 1830; s. Dr. Joshua and Eliza (Lawrence) G.; A.B., Harvard, 1851, A.M., M.D., 1854; LL.D., U. of Nashville, 1896; began practice, Boston, 1856; unmarried. Became surgeon, 2d Mass. Militia, May 1858; served in war as asst. surgeon 1st Mass. Vols., and surgeon 24th Mass. Vols., 1861-65; brevetted lt. col., 1864, for gallant and distinguished services in field. Supt. Boston Dispensary, 1865-72; city physician, 1871-81; mayor of Boston, 1882. One of bd. of experts apptd. by Congress to investigate yellow fever, 1878; overseer of Harvard Coll., 1869-80, 1882-1900; trustee Peabody Edn. Fund; many yrs. mem. Boston School Bd.; became librarian and v.p. Mass. Hist. Soc. Decorated Order Bust of Bolivar (Venezuela). Author: My Campaigns in America; A Journal Kept by Count William de Deux-Ponts, 1780-81, transl. from French MS., with introduction and notes, 1868; Account of Percival and Ellen Green, and of Some of Their Descendants, 1876; Epitaphs from the Old Burying Ground in Groton, Mass., 1878; The Early Records of Groton, 1662-1707 (edited), 1880; History of Medicine in Massachusetts, 1881; Inaugural Address as Mayor of Boston, 1882; Groton During the Indian Wars, 1883; The Boundary Lines of Old Groton, 1885; Groton Historical Series, 1887; also many others now out of print. Address: Boston and Groton, Mass. Died Dec. 5, 1919.

GREEN, Samuel Bowdlear, forester; b. Chelsea, Mass., Sept. 15, 1859; s. Thomas and Anna (Marden) G.; B.S., Mass. Agrl. Coll., 1879; spl. studies horticulture and forestry; m. Alice C. Hazelton, Sept. 15, 1887. Prof. horticulture, 1888-98, horticulture and forestry, 1898—, U. of Minn. Asso. editor Farm and Fireside, 1888—; studied forestry and horticulture in Germany, Denmark, Holland, Belgium, France and England, 1900, on leave of absence from U. of Minn. Pres. Minn. Hort. Soc., 1907; pres. bd. of administration Farmers' Institutes of Minn. Author: Amateur Fruit Growing (8 edits.), 1894; Vegetable Gardening (9 edits.), 1896; Forestry in Minnesota (2 edits.); Principles of American Forestry (2 edits.), 1898; Popular Fruit Growing (2 edits.), 1909. Address: St. Paul, Minn. Died 1910.

GREEN, Samuel Swett, student writer; b. Worcester, Mass., Feb. 20, 1837; s. James and Elizabeth (Swett) G.; A.B., Harvard, 1858, A.M., 1870, grad. Div. School, 1864; unmarried. Librarian, Jan. 15, 1871-Jan. 12, 1909, emeritus, Jan. 12, 1909, Worcester Free Pub. Library (trustee 1867-71). Apptd., 1890, by gov. of Mass. original mem. Free Pub. Library Commn.; reappointed, 1894, 1899, 1904. A founder and life fellow A.L.A. (v.p., 1887-89, 1892-93, pres., 1891, 1st pres. Council, 1896); mem. Am. Library Institute; a founder and 1st v.p. Mass. Library Club; hon. fellow Library Assn., United Kingdom; councillor Am. Antiq. Soc.; fellow Royal Hist. Soc. Del. A.L.A. to Internat. Congress Librarians, London, 1877 (mem. council); presided over World's Congress of Librarians, Chicago, 1893; v.p. Internat. Congress Librarians, London, 1897; delivered course of lectures on pub. libraries as popular ednl. instns. for several yrs., Library Sch., Columbia U.; trustee Leicester Acad. Author: Libraries and Schools, 1883; Library Aids, 1883; The Public Library Movement in the U.S., 1853-1893, 1913. Address: Worcester, Mass. Deceased.

GREEN, Thomas Edward, lecturer and author; b. Harrisville, Pa., Dec. 27, 1857; s. John M. and Martha (McCreary) G.; A.B., McKendree Coll., 1875, A.M., 1878; post-grad. studies, Princeton, 1877; Princeton Theol. Sem., 1879; S.T.D., Griswold, 1890; A.M. honoris causa, U. of Pittsburgh, 1915; Litt.D., St. John's Coll., Annapolis, 1931; LL.D., Coe Coll., 1932; m. Laura E. Johnson, Apr. 27, 1880; children—Eleanore (Mrs. R. W. Goodell), Gladys (Mrs. J. B. Terbell), Olga (dec.). Pastor Mt. Carmel, Ill., 1880, Sparta, Ill., 1881-83, Eighth Presbyn. Ch., Chicago, 1883-86. Deacon and priest, P.E. Ch., 1887; rector St. Andrew's Chicago, 1886-88, Grace Ch., Cedar Rapids, 1888-1903; lecturing, 1903—. Elected bishop of Ia., 1898, declined; chaplain Rep. Nat. Conv., 1884, Dem. Nat. convs., 1884, 92, 96; deputy to Gen. Conv. P.E. Ch., 1889, 92, 95, 98; chmn. deputation Canadian Synod, 1896; grand prelate, Knights Templar, 1897-98-99, 1901; chaplain 1st Regt. Ia. N.G., 1889-98; asso. editor Hampton's Mag., New York, 1910. Journeyed around the world, interest internat. peace, 1910-11; del.-at-large 4th Am. Peace Conf., 1913; internat. lecturer of Am. Peace Soc., 1913—; spl. lecturer Carnegie Endowment for Internat. Peace, 1915-16; extension lecturer, U. of Minn., 1915, U. of Kan., 1921; lecturer, Army Y.M.C.A., 1917; spl. lecturer Am. Red Cross, 1917; dir. nat. speakers' bur. same, 1918—; dir. speakers' bur. U.S. Treas. Dept., Victory Liberty Loan, 1919, European Relief Council, 1920. Gen. chaplain S.R., 1902, 05, 23, 26, and since 1929 (pres. D.C. soc. 1929—). Decorated Medal of French Red Cross, 1920; Medal of Honor by French Govt., 1921; Medal of Merit, Polish Red Cross, 1922; Medal of Honor, Chinese Red Cross, 1923; Chevalier of Legion of Honor (French), 1923; Chevalier Polonia Restituta (Poland), 1930. Mason (32°). Author: The Mantraps of the City, 1884; The Hill Called Calvary, 1898; In Praise of Valor, 1899-1900; The War Trust, 1914; The Burden of the Nations, 1914; The Forces That Failed, 1915; The Truth About Japan, 1915; War Facts and Peace, 1915; How Do You Do?, 1917; Eugenic Democracy, 1917; In This Thy Day, 1918; The Salt of the Earth, 1919; The Dream of the Ages, 1921; Guarding the Outposts, 1922; The Mason as a Citizen, 1926; The Man of Tomorrow, 1927. Deceased.

GREEN, Wharton Jackson, congressman; b. St. Marks, Fla., Feb. 28, 1831; s. Thomas Jefferson and Sarah Angelina (Wharton) G.; ed. Georgetown Coll. and U.S. Mil. Acad.; studied law U. of Va. and Cumberland U.; m. Esther Sargent Ellery, May 4, 1858; m. 2d, Mrs. Addie Burr Davis, Oct. 29, 1888. Lt. col. C.S.A.; twice wounded and taken prisoner. Del. Dem. Nat. convs., 1868, 76; candidate for presdl. elector, 1868; mem. 48th and 49th Congresses (1883-87); propr. Tokay Vineyard in Cumberland County, N.C. Author: Recollections and Reflections, 1907. Home: Fayetteville, N.C. Died 1910.

GREEN, William, printer, pub.; b. Brooklyn, N.Y., Apr. 1, 1861; s. Samuel Worcester and Cornelia (Wilcox) G.; A.B., Poly. Inst. Brooklyn, 1877; m. Bessie Beebe, Apr. 6, 1886. Began in composing room of father, 1877; entered business for self as printer and binder, 1886, inc., 1903, as William Green, of which was pres. and treas.; pres. New York Mfrs. Real Estate Co., Leslie-Judge Co. Pres. United Typothetae of America, 1919-20. Republican. Unitarian. Mason. Home: New Rochelle, N.Y. Died Feb. 24, 1925.

GREEN, William Elza, physician; b. Charlestown, Ind., Mar. 18, 1845; s. Richard E. and Frances J. (Davis) G.; ed. pub. schs. and Barnett Acad., Charlestown, Ind.; M.D., Eclectic Med. Inst., 1872; M.D., Pulte Med. Coll., Cincinnati, 1873; m. Adelaide E. Ward, Dec. 3, 1889. In homœ. med. practice, Little Rock, 1873—. Pres. Am. Inst. Homœopathy, 1905-06; pres. Southern Assn. Homœopathy. Home: Little Rock, Ark. Died Jan. 4, 1913.

GREEN, William Henry, clergyman, educator; b. Groveville, N.J., Jan. 27, 1825; grad. Lafayette Coll., Pa., 1840; Princeton Theol. Sem., 1848; D.D., Princeton, 1857; also U. of Edinburgh, 1884; LL.D., Rutgers Coll., 1873; m. Mary E. Colwell, June 24, 1852; m. 2d, Elizabeth Hayes, Apr. 28, 1858. Instr. in Hebrew, Princeton Theol. Sem., 1846-49; ordained by presbytery of New Brunswick, May 24, 1848; pastor Central Presbyn. Ch., Philadelphia, 1849-51; prof. Biblical and Oriental literature, Princeton Theol. Sem., 1851-59; prof. Oriental and Old Testament literature, 1859—. Moderator Presbyn. Gen. Assembly, 1891. Author: Hebrew Grammar; Elementary Hebrew Grammar; Hebrew Chrestomathy; The Pentateuch Vindicated from the Aspersions of Bishop Colenso; The Higher Criticism of the Pentateuch; The Unity of the Book of Genesis; The Argument of the Book of Job Unfolded; Moses and the Prophets; The Hebrew Feasts; General Introduction to the Old Testament. Home: Princeton, N.J. Died 1900.

GREENAWALT, Elmer Ellsworth, immigration commr.; b. Lancaster County, Pa., June 1, 1862; s. Jacob and Elizabeth (Kemrer) G.; ed. pub. schs.; m. Elizabeth Schaeffer, July 30, 1895. Worked as journeyman cigarmaker until 1886, then engaged in trades union orgn. work; editor Labor Leader, Lancaster, Pa., 23 yrs.; pres. Pa. Federation of Labor, 1902-12; represented organized labor at Harrisburg also before Congress 15 yrs.; Dem. candidate for congressman at large, Pa., 1912 (defeated); commr. of immigration, Port of Phila., 1914—. Mem. Cigar Makers' Internat. Union of America. Home: Philadelphia, Pa. Died Mar. 8, 1920.

GREENBAUM, Leo, dentist; b. Arva, Austria, Oct. 9, 1858; s. Philip and Marie (Goldfinger) G.; ed. Realschule, Vienna; D.D.S., Phila. Dental Coll., 1881; M.D., Medico-Chirurg. Coll., Phila., 1888; m. Nanna Newburgh, June 24, 1902. Came to America, 1871; demonstrator materia medica and chemistry, 1881-95, lecturer on materia medica, 1895-96, prof. materia medica, also prof. anæsthesia and anæsthetics, 1896-1905, asst. dean, 1905-06, dean, 1906-09, Phila. Dental Coll.; in practice in New York, 1909—. Author: Practice of Dentistry, 1912. Editor and pub. Stomatologist, 1897-1909. Home: New York, N.Y. Deceased.

GREENBAUM, Max, dentist; b. Austria, Feb. 28, 1868; s. Philip and Marie (Goldfinger) G.; brought to America, 1872; D.D.S., Phila. Dental Coll., 1890; m. Blanche Goldsmith, Nov. 28, 1893. Practiced, Phila., 1891—. Author: Practice of Dentistry, 1912. Home: Philadelphia, Pa. Died Sept. 1937.

GREENBAUM, Samuel, judge; b. London, Eng., Jan. 23, 1854; s. Louis and Rachel Deborah (Schlesinger) G.; came to New York, 1857; A.B., Coll. City of New York, 1872, A.M., 1875; LL.B., Columbia, 1875; m. Selina Ullman, Mar. 13, 1888; children—Lawrence Samuel, Edward Samuel, Grace Epstein, Isabel Stone. Teacher Grammar Sch. No. 59, New York, 1872-77; practiced law in New York, 1877-1902; justice Supreme Ct. of N.Y. for term 1902-16; reëlected term ending Dec. 31, 1929; designated asso. justice Appellate Div., 1920; resigned, 1923, resuming practice of law. Democrat. Pres. Aguilar Free Library Soc.; pres. Ednl. Alliance; trustee of New York Pub. Library, League for Polit. Edn., Jewish Welfare Bd., Jewish Theol. Sem. of America, Baron de Hirsch Fund, County Lawyers' Assn. Home: New York, N.Y. Died Aug. 26, 1930.

GREENDLINGER, Leo; b. Austria, Aug. 22, 1879; s. Nathaniel and Ruth (Glassman) G.; ed. Royal Seminarium, Austria; studied law in Austria 2 yrs.; came to U.S., 1900; B.C.S., New York U. Sch. of Commerce, 1907, M.C.S., 1908; C.P.A., U. State of N.Y., 1907; m. Rose Lichtenberg, June 14, 1903. Engaged in mfg., 1902-04; v.prin. Paine's Business Coll., New York, 1904-05; pres. South Brooklyn Business Coll., 1905-07; editor C.P.A. Question Dept. (first dept. of its kind), Jour. of Accountancy, 1907-11; asst. prof. accounting, New York U., 1907-15; practicing and cons. accountant, 1907-12; dir. and treas. Alexander Hamilton Inst., New York, 1912—, v.p., 1925—, gen. mgr., 1929—. Spl. lecturer on accounting, Case Sch. of Applied Science, 1915-16, U. of Wis., 1916-17. Republican. Author: Accountancy Problems with Solutions (2 vols.), 1909; (with R. H. Dennis) Graded Accounting Problems (3 vols.), 1910; Accounting Principles and Practice, 1910; Financial and Business Statements, 1917; Retail Financing (with Percy H. Johnson), 1927. Home: New York, N.Y. Died Oct. 11, 1935.

GREENE, Aella, author; b. Mass., 1838; s. Elijah S. and Ann Cartter G.; served twice in the Union army; engaged in journalistic work. Author: Rhymes of Yankee Land (poems), 1872, 1873, 1877; John Peters (novel), 1890; Culminations (novel), 1892; River, Bird and Star (poems), 1895-96. Home: Springfield, Mass. Died 1903.

GREENE, Benjamin Allen, clergyman; b. Harrisville, R.I., Nov. 6, 1845; s. Alvin and Maria (Arnold) G.; A.B., Brown U., 1872; B.D., Newton Theol. Instn., 1875; D.D., Brown, 1893; m. Nancy Wheeler Maine, May 12, 1891. Ordained Bapt. ministry, 1875; pastor Westboro, Mass., 1875-82, Lynn, 1882-97, Evanston, Ill., 1897-1909; professorial lecturer, Div. Sch. U. of Chicago, 1909—. Spl. lecturer Crozer Theol. Sem., 1895, Rochester Theol. Sem., 1896, U. of Chicago, 1903. Trustee Div. Sch. U. of Chicago. Republican. Author: Life of Stephen Greene, 1903. Address: Chicago, Ill. Died May 12, 1915.

GREENE, Charles Ezra, prof. civil engring., U. of Mich., 1872—; b. Cambridge, Mass., Feb. 12, 1842; s. James Diman and Sarah Adeline (Durell) G.; grad. Harvard, 1862, A.M., 1865; grad. Mass. Inst. Tech., B.S., 1868; hon. C.E., U. of Mich., 1884; m. Florence Emerson, 1872. Engaged in mfr. of rifles, 1862-63; clerk q.m. dept., Readville, Mass., 1864; q.m. 7th U.S. colored troops, 1865-66; engr. Bangor & Piscataquis R.R., 1868-70; U.S. asst. engr., 1870-71; city engr., Bangor, Me., 1871-72; consulting practice, 1872—. Asso. editor Engineering News, 1876-77. Author: Graphical Method of Analysis of Bridge Trusses, 1875; Trusses and Arches (3 vols.), 1876-79; Notes on Rankine's Civil Engineering, 1891; Structural Mechanics, 1897. Home: Ann Arbor, Mich. Died 1903.

GREENE, Charles Lyman, M.D.; b. Gray, Me., Sept. 21, 1862; s. Dr. William Warren and Elizabeth (Lawrence) G.; ed. Portland, Me., and began course at U. of Mich., class of 1885; M.D., U. of Minn., 1890; post-grad. work in hosps. of Harvard, Johns Hopkins, London, Paris, Merne, Heidelberg; m. Jessie Rice, Oct. 6, 1886. First asst. city physician, St. Paul, 1 yr.; prof. medicine, U. of Minn., and chief dept. medicine until 1915 (resigned); med. dir. Minn. Life Ins. Co., 1892-1904; chief of staff, St. Luke's Hosp.; attending physician, Miller Memorial Hosp.; consulting physician State Hosp. for Crippled Children. Was lt. col. M.C. U.S. Army; col. Med. Sect. O.R.C. Author: The Medical Examination for Life Insurance, and Its Associated Clinical Methods, 1900; Medical Diagnosis, 1907, 6th edit., 1925. Home: St. Paul, Minn. Died Jan. 19, 1929.

GREENE, Charles Samuel, librarian; b. Bridgeport, Conn., Dec. 6, 1856; s. Nathanael and Hannah Wells (Eldredge) G.; grad. E. Greenwich Acad., 1876; A.B., U. of Calif., 1886; m. Olivia Day, July 3, 1901. Asst. editor, 1887-90, mgr., 1891-94, asso. editor and acting editor, 1894-99, Overland Monthly; librarian Oakland Free Library, July 1, 1899-Dec. 31, 1926, emeritus. Pres. Alumni Association, U. of Calif., 1900-02, Library Assn. of Calif., 1901-02; councillor, A.L.A., 1909-14. Trustee Calif. State Library, 1904-17 (pres. bd. 1909-11). Wrote many poems, descriptive articles, reviews, editorials, etc., in Overland Monthly, 1883-99; poems in Californian, Argonaut, Lend a Hand, Our Continent, San Franciscan, etc. Home: Berkeley, Calif. Died May 7, 1930.

GREENE, Clay Meredith, playwright; b. San Francisco, Calif., Mar. 12, 1850; father, Irish, mother, American; ed. Santa Clara Coll., Calif., and U. of Calif.; did not grad.; Ph.D., Santa Clara Coll., 1901; m. Alice R. Wheeler, July 25, 1873. Shepherd, Lambs Club, 1890-98, and 1902-03-04; commodore Manhassett Bay Yacht Club, 1898-99; mem. Dramatic Authors' Soc., Actors' Order of Friendship. Republican. Author: Plays—M'Liss, Chispa, Sharps and Flats, The Golden Giant, "Last Days of Pompeii," An International Match; Forgiven; Sybil; The New South; Struck Oil; "Nazareth" (the American Passion Play); Paul of Tarsus; The Duchess; The Master Stroke; The Desert; It Is the Law; A House on the Sand; The Dazzler; The Seventh Moon (adaptation); Wia; Miss Go of Japan; also operas—Blue Beard; The Maid of Plymouth; The Little Trooper; The Conspirators; Napoleon; The Wandering Minstrel; and 50 other plays. Home: New York, N.Y. Died Sept. 5, 1933.

GREENE, Daniel Crosby, missionary; b. Roxbury, Mass., Feb. 11, 1843; s. Rev. David and Mary (Evarts) G.; A.B., Dartmouth, 1864, A.M., Rutgers Coll., 1879; LL.D., Dartmouth, 1909; m. Mary Jane Forbes, 1869; children—Evarts Boutell, Jerome Davis, Roger Sherman. Pvt. Co. B, 7th Squadron R.I. Cav., May-Sept. 1862; missionary A.B.C.F.M. in Japan, 1869—, at Kobe, 1870-74, Yokohama, 1874-80. Mem. "Yokohama" N.T. Translation Committee, 1873-80; prof. O.T. exegesis, Doshisha Kyoto, 1881-87, then resident of Tokyo. Pres. Asiatic Soc. of Japan, 1896 and 1901-02. Lecturer on Japan, Harvard, 1908-09. Author: Chinese New Testament, prepared for Japanese readers, 1878; Course of Study for Students of Japanese Language, 1903 (Tokyo). Mem. com. for revising Japanese N.T., 1910—; revised and brought up to date Ritter's History of Protestant Missions in Japan, 1898 (Tokyo). Editor of The Christian Movement in its relation to the New Life in Japan (now The Christian Movement in Japan), 1902-06, 1910-11. Address: Tokyo, Japan. Died Sept. 15, 1913.

GREENE, D(aniel) Crosby, laryngologist; b. Kobe, Japan, Jan. 29, 1873; s. Daniel Crosby and Mary J. (Forbes) G.; A.B., Harvard U., 1895; M.D., 1899; m. Marion Lockwood, Sept. 15, 1904; children—Marion, J. Evarts, D. Crosby, Roger S., Emily L. Laryngologist, Mass. General Hosp.; surgeon throat dept., Boston Children's Hosp.; instr. in laryngology, Harvard Med. Sch. Episcopalian. Home: Newton Center, Mass. Died Apr. 4, 1941.

GREENE, David Maxson, consulting engr.; b. Brunswick, N.Y., July 8, 1832; s. Joseph Langford and Susanna (Maxson) G.; grad. Rensselaer Polytechnic Inst. (C.E.), 1851; took private course, topog. engring., West Point, 1856; instr. Rensselaer Polytechnic Inst., 1851-52; asst. engr., enlargement Erie Canal, 1852-53; on railroads in Ohio and Ind., 1853-54; prof. geodesy and topog. drawing, Rensselaer Polytechnic Inst., 1855-61, dir. same, 1878-91; in corps of engrs., U.S.N., 1861-69; then in general practice; div. engr. and deputy State engr., New York, 1874-78; col. engrs., Nat. Guard, N.Y., 1872-93. Home: Troy, N.Y. Died 1905.

GREENE, Edward Lee, botanist; b. Hopkinton, R.I., Aug. 20, 1843; s. William M. and Abby (Crandall) G.; Ph.B., Albion (Wis.) Coll., 1866; LL.D., U. of Notre Dame, Ind., 1895; unmarried. Was Episcopal clergyman, 1871-85; then R.C. layman; prof. botany, U. of Calif., 1885-95, Catholic U. of America, 1895-1904; asso. in botany, Smithsonian Instn., 1904—. Pres. Internat. Congress of Botanists, Chicago Expn., 1893. Author: Manual of Botany for the region of San Francisco Bay, 1894; West American Oaks, 1887; Flora Franciscana, 1891; Plantæ Bakerianæ, 1901; Pittonia (5 vols.), 1887-1903; Leaflets of Botanical Observation (2 vols.), 1903-09; Landmarks of Botanical History, 1909. Address: Washington, D.C. Died Nov. 10, 1915.

GREENE, Francis Vinton, maj. gen. U.S. Vols.; b. Providence, R.I., June 27, 1850; s. Gen. George Sears and Martha (Dana) G.; apptd. from D.C., and grad. U.S. Mil. Acad., 1870; m. Belle Eugénie Chevallié, Feb. 25, 1879. Second lt. 4th Arty., June 15, 1870; transferred to engr. corps, June 10, 1872; 1st lt., Jan. 13, 1874; capt., Feb. 20, 1883. Served on Internat. Commn. for survey of northern boundary of U.S. as asst. astronomer and surveyor, 1872-76; on duty in War Dept.; mil. attaché U.S. Legation, St. Petersburg, 1877-79; was with Russian Army in Turkey, 1877-78; present at battles of Schipka, Plevna, Sophia, Philipopolis and minor engagements, receiving decorations of St. Vladimir and St. Anne and campaign medal from Emperor of Russia; afterward on U.S. engr. duties; engr. in charge of pub. works in Washington, 1879-85; prof. practical mil. engring., West Point, 1885; resigned, Dec. 31, 1886. Col. 71st N.Y. Inf., May 2, 1898; brig. gen. vols., May 27, 1898; maj. gen. vols., Aug. 13, 1898. Comd. 2d Div., 7th Army Corps, at Jacksonville, Fla., Savannah, Ga., and Havana, Cuba, Oct. to Dec. 1898; resigned Feb. 28, 1899. Chmn. com. on canals, N.Y., 1899. Del. Rep. Nat. Conv., Phila., 1900; pres. Rep. Co. Com., New York, July-Dec. 1900; police commr., Jan. 1, 1903-04. Pres. Niagara-Lockport & Ont. Power Co. Author: The Russian Army and Its Campaigns in Turkey (2 vols.), 1879; Army Life in Russia, 1881; The Mississippi Campaigns of the Civil War, 1882; Life of Nathanael Greene, Major General in the Army of the Revolution, 1893; The Revolutionary War and The Military Policy of the United States, 1911; The Present Military Situation in the United States, 1915; Our First Year in the Great War, 1918. Home: New York, N.Y. Died May 15, 1921.

GREENE, Frank Lester, senator; b. St. Albans, Vt., Feb. 10, 1870; s. Lester Bruce and Mary Elizabeth (Hoadley) G.; ed. pub. schs., Cleveland, and St. Albans, to 13; hon. M.A., Norwich U., 1908, LL.D., 1915; m. Jessie Emma Richardson, Feb. 20, 1895; children—Richard Lester, Dorothy, Stuart Hoadley. Began as errand boy in auditor's office Central Vt. Ry.; became stenographer, and chief clk. gen. freight dept.; reporter, 1891, editor, 1899-1912, St. Albans Daily Messenger; mem. commn. to prepare and propose amendments to state const.; chmn. Rep. State Conv., 1914; elected to 62d Congress July 30, 1912, for unexpired term of late David J. Foster; reëlected 63d to 67th Congresses (1913-23), 1st Vt. Dist.; elected to U.S. Senate 2 terms, 1923-35. Pvt. to capt., Vt. N.G., 1888-1900; a.-d.-c. staff of gov. of Vt.; raised and recruited Co. B, 1st Vt. Inf. Vols., Spanish-Am. War, and mustered into U.S. service as capt.; was adj. gen. 3d Brigade, 1st Div., 3d A.C. Regent Smithsonian Instn., Washington, 1917-23; trustee Vt. Soldiers' Home, Lyndon Inst. Mason. Home: St. Albans, Vt. Died Dec. 17, 1930.

GREENE, Frederick Stuart, civil engr.; b. Rappahannock County, Va., Apr. 14, 1870; s. Thomas Tileston and Elise Glenn Davis (Skinner) G.; C.E., Va. Mil. Inst., 1890; D.E., Syracuse U., 1929; m. Grace Emily Clapp, 1900; 1 son, Francis Thornton. Engr. on Central R.R. Ga., 1890-91; with cable rys., Washington, D.C., and New York, 1892-93; asst. engr., river and harbor work, U.S. Engrs., 1894-95; gen. supt. John Monks & Sons, dock builders, 1896-1900; with Am. Mfg. Co., 1900-05; v.p. Waterproofing Co. of N.Y. City, 1905-17; commr. of highways, State of N.Y., 1919-21; pres. Greene-Hule Co., engrs. and contractors, 1921-22; reapptd. commr. highways, 1923, and apptd. supt. pub. works, State of N.Y. Entered Plattsburg Mil. Camp, May 7, 1917; Camp Upton, Aug. 1917; comdr. Co. B, 302d Engrs., France, Apr. 14, 1918; batt. comdr. May 25, 1918, to close of war; participated in Oise, Aisne and Argonne offensives; colonel Engineers Auxiliary. Conspicuous Service Medal, State of N.Y. Democrat. Episcopalian. Author: The Blue Book of Rope Transmission, 1901. Editor: The Grim 13, 1917. Home: Rensselaerville, N.Y. Died Mar. 26, 1939.

GREENE, Gardiner, judge; b. Norwich, Conn., Aug. 31, 1851; s. Gardiner and Mary Ricketts (Adams) G.; grad. Norwich Free Acad., 1868; A.B., Yale, 1873; LL.B., Columbia, 1877; m. Louise Eustis Reynolds, Apr. 4, 1894. Practiced law, Utica, N.Y., 1877-78, Norwich, Conn., 1878-1910; judge Superior Court of Conn., 1910-21 (retired), now State referee. Mem. Conn. Ho. of Rep., 1891, 95; mem. commn. to revise Conn. statutes, revision of 1902. Pres. Dime Savings Bank, Norwich. Trustee Berkeley Div. Sch., Middletown, Conn., Norwich Free Acad. Episcopalian; sr. warden Christ Ch. parish, Norwich; lay del. Gen. Conv. P.E. Ch., 1907, 10, 13, 16, 19. Del. Am. Bankers' Conv., 1922. Republican. Home: Norwich, Conn. Died Feb. 10, 1925.

GREENE, George C., lawyer; b. Ballston Spa, N.Y., Jan. 16, 1833; s. William P. and Mary (Hough) G.; studied law; m. Emma Frances Green, May 11, 1857. Admitted to bar, 1857; mem. N.Y. State Court of Claims, 1870-73; practiced law, Lockport, N.Y., until 1881, when he removed to Buffalo and was local counsel for rys. in the Vanderbilt System until 1886; gen. counsel Lake Shore & Mich. Southern Ry. Co., 1886—. Home: Buffalo, N.Y. Died 1909.

GREENE, George Francis, clergyman; b. N. Greenbush, N.Y., June 5, 1858; s. George Washington and Jennie (Ewing) G.; A.B., Princeton, 1882, A.M., 1885, D.D., 1902; grad. Princeton Theol. Sem., 1885; m. Margaret L. Greene, Oct. 7, 1886; children—Margaret Cushing (dec.), Katharine Celia, Thomas Casey. Ordained Presbyn. ministry, 1885; pastor Cranford, N.J., 1885-1926. Dir. Princeton Theol. Sem., 1909—; pres. Bd. of Ministerial Pensions, etc., Presbyn. Ch. U.S.A. Author: The Many-Sided Paul, 1901; Christian Science and the Gospel of Jesus Christ, 1902. Home: Cranford, N.J. Died Nov. 19, 1926.

GREENE, George Sears, Jr., civil engr.; b. Lexington, Ky., Nov. 26, 1837; s. Gen. George Sears and Martha (Dana) G.; entered Harvard, 1856, but left before grad. to study civil engring. under father; m. Susan Moody, d. James Dana, Apr. 23, 1862 (died 1881). Asst. engr. on Croton Aqueduct, on various Cuban railroads and Lake Superior copper mines; conducted topog. surveys in 1868; introduced valuable improvements in instruments, some of which were adopted by U.S. Coast Survey. Became engr.-in-chief, dept. of docks, New York, 1875; consulting engr. in New York, 1898; advisory engr. on Barge Canal, N.Y., 1911-14. Home: South Orange, N.J. Died Dec. 23, 1922.

GREENE, George Wellington, lawyer; b. Hespeler, Ont., Nov. 26, 1866; s. Henry S. and Susan (Helmer) G.; ed. pub. schs.; LL.B., Boston U., 1889; m. Gertrude E. Nutting, 1889. Practiced law at Woonsocket, R.I. Sec. and dir. Woonsocket Napping Machinery Co. Mem. R.I. Ho. of Rep., 1890-92; mayor of Woonsocket, 1896 and 1899-1902; Dem. candidate for sec. of state, R.I., 1894, and for gov., 1899. Chmn. Dem. City Com. of Woonsocket, R.I.; mem. Dem. Nat. Com., 1900—, becoming mem. exec. com.; mem. R.I. State Com. 15 yrs. (chmn., 1898-1902); del. Dem. Nat. convs., 1896, 1900, 04, 08, 12, 16 (chmn. R.I. delegation 1900, 04). Home: Slatersville, R.I. Died Jan. 28, 1925.

GREENE, Henry Alexander, army officer; b. Matteawan, N.Y., Aug. 5, 1856; s. Edgar Gale and Margaret Dundee (Scott) G.; grad. U.S. Mil. Acad., 1879; m. Augusta B. Barlow, Dec. 21, 1881. Commd. 2d lt. 20th Inf., June 13, 1879; 1st lt., July 24, 1886; capt., Oct. 14, 1891; maj. 14th Inf., May 31, 1900; lt. col. 1st Inf., Aug. 8, 1903; col. 10th Inf., Oct. 20, 1906; brig. gen., Nov. 19, 1914; maj. gen., Aug. 5, 1917. Served in Tex.; in Mont. as lt. regtl. adj. and as organizer, and comdr. for nearly 3 yrs. of co. of Sioux Indians; comdr. of co. in Santiago Campaign, Cuba, and co. in field in Philippines, Jan. 1899-July 1900; a.-d.-c. to Maj. Gen. Otis, press censor, mem. Ct. of Claims, P.I.; mem. bd. to select 1st gen. staff of the army, 1903, and mem. and 1st sec. of staff; mem. War Coll. Bd., 1903-04; chief of staff, S.W. Div., Oklahoma City, Okla., 1904-05, Northern Div., St. Louis, 1905-07; comdr. 10th Inf. in Alaska, 1907-08, and at Ft. Benjamin Harrison, Ind., 1908-11; pres. Inf. Equipment Bd., Rock Island Arsenal, 1909-10; comd. regt. in Tex. and Panama Canal Zone to 1914; comd. Central Dept., Chicago, Apr.-Aug. 1914; comd. army service schs., Ft. Leavenworth, Kan., 1914-16; comdg. Eagle Pass dist., Mexican border, May-Aug. 1916, 12th Provisional Div., San Antonio, Aug. 1916-Mar. 1917, 2d Brigade, 3d Provisional Div., Douglas, Ariz., Mar.-May 1917, same div. and dist. of Ariz., May-Aug. 1917; comdg. 91st Inf. Div. and Camp Lewis, Am. Lake, Wash., Aug.-Nov. 1917; observation duty with British, French and A.E.F. in France and Belgium, Dec. 1917-Feb. 1918; comdg. 91st Div., Mar. 2-June 1918; comdg. Philippine Dept., Aug. 6, 1918, until retirement from active service, Nov. 29, 1918. Episcopalian. Mason. Home: Berkeley, Calif. Died Aug. 19, 1921.

GREENE, Henry Fay, lawyer; b. Newbern, N.C., May 30, 1859; s. Rev. Henry Fay and Alice Gray (Lawrence) G.; A.B., Princeton, 1880; LL.B., U. of Md., 1883; m. Susan Ryan Grady, Aug. 27, 1895. Lived in N.C. until 1865, Chicago until 1877, Baltimore, 1877-87, Duluth, Minn., 1887—. Admitted to bar, May 30, 1883; city atty., Duluth, 1893; U.S. civil service commr., 1903-09, resigned. Republican. Home: Duluth, Minn. Died Dec. 20, 1915.

GREENE, Herbert Wilber, musician; b. Holyoke, Mass., May 20, 1851; s. Myron E. and Amanda H. G.; ed. high sch., Holyoke; studied New York, London, Paris; m. Caia Aarup, May 20, 1902. Founder and dir. Met. Coll. of Music, 1886; dir. Brookfield Summer Sch. of Singing, 1900—; also pres. Associate School of Music, New York. Asso. editor Godey's Mag.; asso. editor Étude, Phila., 1895—, Boston Musician, 1907—; also of Musical Observer, N.Y. City. Lecturer on musical history of America, New York Bd. Edn., many yrs. Composer and lecturer on musical and hist. subjects. Author: The Singer's Ladder; The Standard Graded Course of Singing, 4 vols. Home: Brookfield Center, Conn. Died Sept. 25, 1924.

GREENE, Homer, author, lawyer; b. Lake Ariel, Pa., Jan. 10, 1853; s. Giles and Harriet L. (Schenck) G.; A.B., C.E., Union Coll., 1876, Litt.D., 1906; LL.B., Albany Law Sch., 1878; m. Matilda E. Gilbert, Sept. 1883 (died 1884); m. 2d, Catherine Gaines, June 30, 1886; children—Giles Pollard, Margaret Harriet. Began practice at Honesdale, Pa., 1879; mem. Greene & Male; dir., treas. Honesdale Cemetery Co.; dir. Honesdale Nat. Bank. Active in Pa. politics. Author: (poems) What My Lover Said; My Daughter Louise; The Banner of the Sea; St Peter, 1927; What My Lover Said (book of collected poems), 1931; (prose) The Blind Brother, 1887; Burnham Breaker, 1887; Coal and the Coal Mines, 1889, revised edit., 1928; The Riverpark Rebellion, 1892; A Tale of a Towpath, 1892; Whispering Tongues, 1902; Pickett's Gap, 1902; A Lincoln Conscript, 1909; Handicapped, the Story of a White-Haired Boy, 1915; The Unhallowed Harvest, 1917; The Flag, 1917; The Guardsman, 1919. Home: Honesdale, Pa. Died Nov. 26, 1940.

GREENE, Jacob L., pres. Conn. Mutual Life Ins. Co.; b. Waterford, Me., Aug. 9, 1837; ed. Freyburgh Acad., Me., and U. of Mich.; studied law; admitted to bar, 1859, and began practice in Lapeer County, Mich. Apptd. court comml., 1860; enlisted 7th Mich. inf., June 1861; captured and imprisoned at Libby, Macon and Charleston; paroled and exchanged, 1864, and joined staff of Gen. Custer with rank of maj., and was bvtd. lt. col.; mustered out Apr. 1866. Asst. sec. Berkshire Life Ins. Co., 1867-70; asst. sec., 1870-71, sec., 1871-78, and pres. Conn. Mutual Life Ins. Co., 1878—. Home: Hartford, Conn. Died 1905.

GREENE, James Leon, neurologist; b. Shelbyville, Ind., Nov. 1, 1861; s. John and Sarah (Victor) G.;

grad. high sch., Morgantown, Ind., 1880; M.D., U. of Vt., 1884; post-grad. work, U.S. and abroad; m. Julia King, Oct. 23, 1889; children—Margaret, John Ashbel. Served as asst. supt. Neb. hosps. for insane, at Norfolk and Lincoln until 1895; supt. Neb. Hosp. for Insane, 1901-06, Ill. Hosp. for Insane, Kankakee, Ill., 1906-09; state alienist, Ill., 1909-11; supt. Ark. State Hosp. for Nervous Diseases, Little Rock, 1911-14; settled in Hot Springs, Ark., 1914, specializing in neuro-psychiatry. Served as teacher med. jurisprudence, law dept. U. of Neb., and of diseases of mind and nervous system, U. of Ark. Republican. Methodist. Home: Hot Springs, Ark. Deceased.

GREENE, John Ernest, lawyer; b. Janesville, Wis., Jan. 10, 1858; s. William Maxon and Abby Maria (Crandall) G.; ed. common schs. of Wis. and Colo.; studied law in office M. W. Greene, Wells, Minn., 1878-82; m. Martha S. Polleys, May 9, 1882 (died 1898). Admitted Minn. bar, 1882; practiced at Wells, until 1885; removed to Fargo, N.D., and admitted to territorial bar, Jan. 1885; practiced there until 1903, at Minot, N.D., 1903—; became mem. bar U.S. Circuit Ct. of Appeals, 1899, U.S. Supreme Ct., 1912. Republican. Episcopalian. Mem. N.D. Commn. on Uniform State Laws. Home: Minot, N.D. Died 1921.

GREENE, John Priest, college pres.; b. Scotland County, Mo., 1849; s. Thomas W. and Nancy (Priest) G.; A.B., La Grange Coll., Mo., 1872; grad. Southern Bapt. Theol. Sem., 1879; studied U. of Leipzig; D.D., William Jewell, 1890; LL.D., Colgate, 1893, Wake Forest, 1894, Washington U., 1908; m. Lizzie Wikoff, 1888; children—John Wikoff, Dorothy. Licensed, 1870, ordained, 1872, Bapt. ministry; pastor East Ch., Louisville, Ky., 1879-82, Third Ch., St. Louis, 1882-92; pres. William Jewell Coll., 1892-1923, emeritus. Pres. Am. Bapt. Edn. Soc., 1897. Elected pres. of the Southern Bapt. Theol. Sem., Louisville, Ky., May 1899, but declined. Author: Commentary on Pastoral Epistles; The Happy Man; The Ideal Man; The Fundamental Virtues, 1928. Home: Santa Ana, Calif. Died Mar. 10, 1933.

GREENE, Myron Wesley; b. Monroe County, N.Y., Nov. 26, 1864; s. Ira Wesley and Hester A. (Ruliffson) G.; grad. Genesee Wesleyan Sem., 1887; student Syracuse U., 1887-88, Williams Coll., 1888-89; m. Nancy Laura Lancaster, Apr. 27, 1900; children—Lancaster Myron, Norvin Ruliffson, Zeta Priscilla (Mrs. M. Hubert Hilder), Nathan Ira, Myron Wesley II. With Bank of Honeoye Falls, N.Y., to 1892, Rochester Trust & Safe Deposit Co., 1892-99; founded business of investment banking and municipal bond financing and executor and trustee of estate, 1899—. Was in Europe, 1927 and 1929, in Alaska, above the Arctic Circle, 1928. Republican. Presbyn. One of organizers and charter mem. Investment Bankers' Assn. America. Grand Officer Zeta Psi, 1909-10, presiding at Internat. Conv., San Francisco, 1910. Mason. Author: Greene Family Genealogy, 1639-1891. Address: Rochester, N.Y. Died June 14, 1935.

GREENE, Oliver D., army officer; b. Cortland County, N.Y., Jan. 25, 1833; s. Geo. S. and Amelia Maxson G.; grad. West Point, July 1, 1854; m. Kate Rich, Oct. 1859. Commd. 2d lt., 1854; lt., 1861, 2d arty.; capt. arty., Aug. 3, 1861; maj., July 17, 1862; on staff lt. col., Feb. 27, 1887; retired as brig. gen. Jan. 25, 1897. Served in border troubles in Kan., 1857-58; in Civil war as asst. adj. gen. depts. Cumberland and Ohio, 1861-62; adj. gen. 6th corps, Army of the Potomac, 1862-63, dept. of Mo., 1863-64; took part in many battles; medal of honor for distinguished gallantry at Antietam; after war in various depts. as adj. gen.; last service as adj. gen., dept. Calif., 1890-97. Address: San Franicsco, Calif. Deceased.

GREENE, Richard Gleason, editor; b. East Haddam, Conn., June 29, 1829; s. Richard William and Charlotte (Gleason) G.; ed. Phila., Pa., 1835-45, Yale, 1849, but left because of father's death; hon. A.M., Yale, 1873; grad. Andover Theol. Sem., 1853; m. Augusta Ostrander, Oct. 1, 1856. Acting pastor Springfield, O., 1853-54, Eastern Ch., New York, 1854-56; ordained Congl. ministry, 1856; pastor Adrian, Mich., 1856-57, E. Cambridge, Mass., 1858-60, Brighton, Mass., 1860-62, Bedford Ch., Brooklyn, 1862-65, Valley Ch., Orange, N.J., 1865-66, North Ch., Springfield, Mass., 1866-74, Trinity Ch., East Orange, N.J., 1875-89; in editorial work, 1890—. Elected by the legislature of Mass. (1874) to preach the 243d in the line of annual election sermons before the governor and legislature, title, "Christianity a National Law." Editor: Library of Universal Knowledge (16 vols.); International Cyclopædia (16 vols.), 1st edit.; Columbian Cyclopædia (including a dictionary), 32 vols. Address: New York. Died July 7, 1914.

GREENE, Robert Holmes, surgeon; b. Brunswick, Me., Apr. 27, 1861; s. Benjamin and Susan T. (Holmes) G.; A.B., Bowdoin Coll., 1881, A.M., 1884; M.D., Harvard, 1886; m. Mabel A. V. Chubb, May 27, 1895 (died 1930). Consulting surgeon to City Hosp., New York, 1895-1923. Author: Healthy Exercise, 1899; Text Book on Surgery, 1917; Cancer, Its Nature, Causes, Diagnosis and Treatment, 1918. Address: New York, N.Y. Died 1933.

GREENE, Roger Sherman; b. Westborough, Mass., May 29, 1881; s. Daniel Crosby and Mary Jane (Forbes) G.; A.B., Harvard, 1901, A.M., 1902; m. Kate Brown, May 8, 1920. Vice and deputy consul-gen. at Rio de Janeiro, Brazil, 1903-04; vice-consul at Nagasaki, Japan, 1904-05; vice and deputy consul at Kobe, 1905; commercial agt. and later consul at Vladivostok, Siberia, 1905-07; consul at Dalny, Manchuria, 1907-09, at Harbin, China, 1909-11; consul-gen. at Hankow, China, 1911-14; resident dir. in China of China Med. Bd. of Rockefeller Foundation, 1914-21, dir., 1921-25, gen. dir., 1925-27; v.p. in Far East of Rockefeller Foundation, 1927-29; dir. China Med. Bd., Inc., 1929—; vice-dir. Peiping Union Med. Coll., 1929—. Address: Peiping, China. Died Feb. 17, 1930.

GREENE, Sarah Pratt, author; b. Simsbury, Conn., July 3, 1856; d. Dudley Bestor and Mary (Payne) McLean; acad. edn. at Mt. Holyoke, Mass.; m. Franklin Lynde Greene, July 27, 1887 (dec.); children—Dudley McLean (dec.), Lynde (dec.). Author: Cape Cod Folks, 1881; Some Other Folks, 1882; Towhead, 1883; Last Chance Junction, 1889; Leon Pontifex, 1890; Vesty of the Basins, 1892; Stuart and Bamboo, 1897; The Moral Imbeciles, 1898; Flood-Tide, 1901, Winslow Plain, 1902; Deacon Lysander, 1904; Power Lot, 1906. Address: Lexington, Mass. Died Dec. 29, 1935.

GREENE, S(tephen) Harold, cotton mfr.; b. Providence, R.I., Apr. 27, 1880; s. Stephen and Natalia (Schubarth) G.; Brown U., 1897-1900; studied Phila. Textile Sch.; m. Lillian May Eddy, June 4, 1902; 1 dau., Dorothy (Mrs. James A. Liddell). Began in cotton mfg. business, Boston, 1900; chmn. bd. Cosmos Imperial Mills, Ltd.; pres., treas. Mutual Boiler Ins. Co. of Boston; dir. Newton Trust Co., J. Spencer Turner Co. Trustee Newton Theol. Instn. Republican. Baptist. Home: Newton Center, Mass. Died Nov. 19, 1937.

GREENE, Thomas L., author, editor; b. Albany, N.Y.; ed. Albany Acad. V.p. The Audit Co. of New York. Author: Corporation Finance, 1897 P2. Home: New York, N.Y. Died 1904.

GREENE, Warwick; b. Washington, D.C., Dec. 18, 1879; s. Gen. Francis Vinton (U.S.V.) and Belle Eugenie (Checallié) G.; A.B., Harvard, 1901, LL.B., 1905; unmarried. Dir. Bur. Pub. Works, Manila, P.I., 1910-15; dir. War Relief Commn., Rockefeller Foundation, 1916. Maj. Air Service, A.E.F., 1917-18; lt. col., 1918-19; chief of mission to Finland, Esthonia, Latvia and Lithuania, 1919; pres. New England Oil Refining Co. Republican. Episcopalian. Home: New York, N.Y. Died Nov. 18, 1929.

GREENE, William Cornell, copper miner; b. New York, N.Y., 1851. Went west at 17; became govt. contractor in Colo. and Kan.; went to Ariz. and prospected around Prescott with varying success; farmed in San Pedro Valley; made success as rancher and cattleman; bought from the widow of Gov. Pesquiera of Sonora the La Cananea mines, 45 miles south of Ariz. line in Mexico; organized the Greene Consolidated Copper Co. Pres. and dir. Greene Consolidated Gold Co., Greene Gold Silver Mining Co., Greene Cattle Co., Turkey Track Cattle Cos. of Ariz., W.Va. and Sonora, Mex., Balvanera Mining Co., Belen Mining Co., Cananea Cattle Co., Cananea Realty Co., El Paso Southern R.R. Co., Guaynopita Copper Co., Internat. Ore Treating Co., Rey del Oro Mining Co., Rio Grande, Sierra Madre & Pacific R.R. Co., Santa Brigida Gold Co., Sierra Madre Land & Lumber Co.; v.p. Greene-Cananea Copper Co.; dir. Cananea Central Copper Co., Greene Land & Cattle Co. During Apaché troubles of early '80s organized and led several vol. forces against hostile Indians. Home: New York, N.Y. Died 1911.

GREENE, William Houston, chemist; b. Columbia, Pa., Dec. 30, 1853; s. Stephen and Martha (Mifflin) G.; A.M., Central High Sch., Phila.; M.D., Jefferson Medical College, Phila., 1873. Asst. prof. chemistry, Jefferson Med. Coll., 1870-77; demonstrator chemistry, same, 1875-77; pursued original research in lab. of Adolph Wurtz, Paris, and pvt. lab., Phila., 1877-79; demonstrator chemistry, U. of Pa., 1879-80; prof. chemistry, Central High Sch., 1880-92. Author: A Hand-book of Medical Chemistry, 1880; Lessons in Chemistry, 1884. Translator and editor Wurtz's Elements of Modern Chemistry, 1880, 84, 87. Am. editor Paul Berts' First Steps in Scientific Knowledge. Address: Philadelphia, Pa. Died Aug. 8, 1918.

GREENE, William L., congressman; b. on farm in Pike County, Ind., Oct. 3, 1849; ed. common schools and Ireland, Ind., Acad.; studied law; admitted to bar, 1876; practiced, Bloomington, Ind., 1876-83, at Kearney, Neb., 1883—; was a Democrat, but in 1890 aided in founding Populist party; candidate for U.S. senator, 1892, losing by 2 votes; judge 12th judicial dist., Neb., 1895-97; elected to Congress, 6th Neb. Dist., 1897; present term expires 1901. Populist. Home: Kearney, Neb. Died 1899.

GREENE, William Stedman, congressman; b. Tremont, Ill., Apr. 28, 1841; s. Chester W. and Abby (Stedman) G.; pub. sch. edn.; m. Mary E. White, Mar. 8, 1865. Engaged in real estate and ins. business, Fall River, 1866—. Mem. Common Council, 1876-79 (pres., 1877-79); mayor Fall River, 1880, 1881, 1886, 1895, 1896, 1897; postmaster, 1881-85 and 1898; gen. supt. prisons, Mass., 1888-93; elected 55th Congress, May 31, 1898, to fill unexpired term (1898-99) of John Simpkins, deceased; reëlected 56th to 63d Congresses (1899-1913), 13th Mass. Dist., and 64th to 68th Congresses (1915-25), 15th Dist. Republican. Home: Fall River, Mass. Died Sept. 22, 1924.

GREENEBAUM, Henry Everett, banker; b. Chicago, Ill., Sept. 1, 1854; s. Elias and Rosine (Straus) G.; grad. Central High Sch., Chicago, 1871; Bryant and Stratton Business Coll., 1871-72; m. Helen F. Leopold, Apr. 15, 1879; children—Carrie Nast, Walter Jerome, John. Began with First Nat. Bank, Chicago, 1872; with father's firm, Greenebaum & Foreman, 1873; with banks in N.Y. City, 1873-77; returned to Chicago, 1877, and entered the banking firm of Greenebaum Sons, Inc., 1911, as Greenebaum Sons Bank & Trust Co., later The Bank of America, later merged with Central Trust Co. of Ill.; v.p. Greenebaum Sons Investment Co. Republican. Mem. Sinai Temple. Address: Chicago, Ill. Died May 17, 1931.

GREENEBAUM, Moses Ernest, banker; b. Chicago, Ill., Mar. 17, 1858; s. Elias and Rosine (Straus) G.; ed. high sch.; m. Julia Friedman, Dec. 23, 1884. Began in father's banking business, and was admitted to firm, 1877; vice chmn. Central Trust Co. of Ill. until 1931; pres. Greenebaum Sons Investment Co.; dir. Central Republic Trust Co., Chicago Title and Trust Co.; dir. and treas. Travelers Aid Soc. Hon. dir. Michael Reese Hosp.; treas. Citizens Assn. of Chicago. Hon. pres. Chicago Sinai Congregation. Republican. Address: Chicago, Ill. Died June 22, 1934.

GREENEFIELD, Nathan R., lawyer, banker; b. nr. Freeport, Ill., Feb. 24, 1874; s. Fred and Ettie (Poppen) G.; LL.B., U. of Neb., 1897; m. Minnie B. Carr, Aug. 11, 1902. Admitted to Wyo. bar, 1897, and began practice at Rawlins; county atty., Carbon County, Wyo., 1904-10; pres. Rawlins Nat. Bank, 1923—; pres. Rawlins Development Co., Minnie Belle Oil Co., Lost Soldier Development Co.; treas. Hatfield Oil Co., Bush Lake Sheep, Dinner Lake Oil Co., Maggie B. Oil Co., Sunset Camps, Inc. Mayor of Rawlins, 1920-21; mem. State Bd. Law Examiners; mem. com. apptd. by Wyo. Supreme Ct. to revise statutes of Wyo. County exec., Carbon County, Boy Scouts America. Republican. Episcopalian. Mason. Home: Rawlins, Wyo. Died 1938.

GREENLAW, Edwin, univ. prof.; b. Flora, Ill., Apr. 6, 1874; s. Thomas Burton and Emma J. (Leverich) G.; A.B., Northwestern U., 1897, A.M., 1898, D.Litt., 1927; A.M., Harvard U., 1903, Ph.D., 1904; LL.D., U. of N.C., 1926; D.Litt., Northwestern U., 1927; m. Mary Elizabeth Durland, Sept. 1, 1898, children—Dorothy Durland, Margery Keith, Mary Edwin. Instr. English, Northwestern U., 1898-1902 and 1904-05; prof. English, Adelphia Coll., Brooklyn, N.Y., 1905-13; prof. English, 1913-18, Kenan prof. English, 1918-25, dean Grad. Sch., 1920-25, U. of N.C.; William Osler prof. of English lit. and dir. English Sem., Johns Hopkins U., 1925—. Author: Spenser and the Earl of Leicester, 1910; A Syllabus of English Literature, 1912; An Outline of the Literature of the English Renaissance, 1916; Builders of Democracy, 1918. Editor: Selections from Chaucer, 1907; Irving's Knickerbocker History of New York, 1909; Familiar Letters, English and American, 1915; National Ideals in British and American Literature, 1918; The Great Tradition (with J. H. Hanford), 1919; Literature and Life, Vols. I, II, 1922, III, 1923, IV, 1924. Also editor Studies in Philology (univ. quarterly), 1915-25; editor in chief Modern Lang. Notes, 1926-28; editor in chief A New Variorum Spenser. Home: Baltimore, Md. Died Sept. 10, 1931.

GREENLEAF, Charles Ravenscroft, brig. gen. U.S. Army; b. Carlisle, Pa., Jan. 1, 1838; s. Rev. Patrick Henry and Margaret (Johnson) G.; M.D., Ohio State Med. Coll., 1860; m. Georgie Franck de la Roche, Sept. 10, 1862. Asst. surgeon 5th Ohio Inf., Apr. 24-July 18, 1861 (1st surgeon commd. from Ohio for Civil War); asst. surgeon U.S. Army, Aug. 5, 1861; capt. asst. surgeon, July 28, 1866; maj. surgeon, June 26, 1876; lt. col. asst. med. purveyor, Feb. 24, 1891; col. asst. surgeon gen. U.S. Army, Oct. 10, 1896; retired, Jan. 1, 1902; brig. gen. retired, 1904. Built Mower Gen. Hosp., Chestnut Hill, Phila., 1862, where he was exec. officer; on staffs of Gens. McClellan, Lew Wallace, Hancock, George H. Wright, George H. Thomas; med. dir. after battle of Antietam; served with Army of Potomac through Peninsular, Antietam and Gettysburg campaigns; chief med. officer during Pittsburgh riots, 1876; Nez Perces and Sioux Indian campaigns, 1878-79; on staff Gen. Terry, 1882-83; exec. officer surgeon gen.'s office, 1887-93; author of present system for personal identification of soldiers in U.S.A.; organized hosp. corps, U.S.A.; originated and organized ambulance service, San Francisco; chief surgeon of army in the field during Spanish-Am. War, serving in Cuba and P.R., 1898; med. insp. of army, 1898-99; chief surgeon, div. of the Philippines, on staffs of Gens. Otis and MacArthur, 1900. Prof. pub. and mil. hygiene, U. of Calif. Del. Internat. Med. Congress, Rome, 1893. Author: Greenleaf's Manual for Medical Officers; Greenleaf's Epitome of the Examination of Recruits (present standard for the army). Died 1911.

GREENLEAF, Georgie H. Franck, founder and dir. of the "American Library," Manila, P.I.; b. Baltimore, Nov. 12, 1842; d. Baron George H. F. F. and Jane Belt de la Roche; grad. Georgetown (D.C.) Sem.; m. Charles Ravenscroft Greenleaf, Sept. 10, 1862. Started relief work on Pacific coast during Spanish-Am. War, in Berkeley, Calif., 1898. Author: My Life Among the Indians, 1885. Died Feb. 17, 1913.

GREENLEAF, James Leal, landscape architect; b. Kortright, N.Y., July 30, 1857; s. Thomas and Eleanor (Leal) G.; C.E., Sch. of Mines (Columbia), 1880; m. Bertha Potts, June 4, 1889 (died 1911); 1 son, Donald Leal. Spl. agt. 10th Census, reporting on water power of the Northwest, 1880-82; with engring. dept. of Columbia U., 1882-94, advancing to adj. prof.; pvt. practice, 1894—. Mem. Nat. Commn. Fine Arts. Republican. Presbyn. A.N.A. Home: New York, N.Y. Died Apr. 15, 1933.

GREENMAN, Milton J., anatomist; b. North East, Pa., June 14, 1866; s. J. B. G.; Ph.B., U. of Pa., 1889, M.D., 1892, Sc.D., 1919; Sc.D., U. of Pittsburgh, 1912; m. Frances A. Hancock, July 1, 1891. Instr. in biology, U. of Pa., 1889-92; lecturer on physiology, Biological Sch., U. of Pa., 1892-93; asst. dir., 1893-1905, dir., 1905—, Wistar Inst. of Anatomy. Trustee Marine Biol. Lab. (Woods Hole, Mass.), Vineland (N.J. Training Sch., Lab. of Biol. Survey of the Mt. Desert Region (Bar Harbor, Me.). Address: Philadelphia, Pa. Died April 8, 1937.

GREENOUGH, Chester Noyes, univ. prof.; b. Wakefield, Mass., June 29, 1874; s. William Smith and Elizabeth Macfarland (Noyes) G.; A.B., Harvard, 1898, A.M., 1899, Ph.D., 1904; m. Marietta McPherson, Aug. 10, 1907 (died 1925); m. 2d, Ruth Hornblower Atkins, June 13, 1931. Instr. in English, Harvard, 1899-1907; prof. English, U. of Ill., 1907-10; asst. prof. English, 1910-15, prof., 1915—, actg. dean of the coll., 1919-20, dean, 1921-27, Harvard. Spl. expert, U.S. Shipping Bd., 1918. Fellow Am. Academy Arts and Sciences. Author: A History of Literature in America (with Barrett Wendell), 1904; English Composition (with F. W. C. Hersey), 1917. Co-editor: Selection from the Writings of Joseph Addison, 1905; Specimens of Prose Composition (with others), 1907; Writing Well (with others), 1932. Home: Belmont, Mass. Died Feb. 26, 1938.

GREENOUGH, George Gordon, army officer; b. Washington, Dec. 8, 1844; s. John James and Mary Frances Ascough (Cushing) G.; ed. pvt. and pub. schs. to 1857, Paris, France, 1857-60, pvt. sch., Baltimore, 1860-61; grad. U.S. Mil. Acad., 1865; unmarried. Commd. 2d lt. and 1st lt. 12th Inf., June 23, 1865; transferred to 21st Infantry; Sept. 21, 1866; assigned to 4th Arty., Dec. 15, 1870; grad. Arty. Sch., 1882; capt., Dec. 1, 1883; maj. 7th Arty., Mar. 8, 1898; lt. col. Arty. Corps, July 1, 1901; col., Feb. 21, 1903; brig. gen. and retired, Dec. 8, 1908. Instr. asst. prof. and acting prof. of French, U.S. Mil. Acad., 1868-73; served in 3d Army Corps, 1863; in Modoc Indian campaign, 1873; Nev. expdn., 1875, and in Powder River expdn., 1876-77; mil. instr. U. of Calif., 1877-78; was one of the pioneers in range-finding work, 1882-98; sharp shooter for 5 yrs.; comd. arty. defenses of Washington, 1898; served in Cuba, 1898-99, and in P.I., 1900-02. Inventor of various devices for arty. operations. Died June 27, 1912.

GREENOUGH, James Bradstreet, A.B., prof. Latin, Harvard, 1874—; b. Me., 1833. Author: Special Vocabulary to Virgil; The Queen of Hearts; A Dramatic Fantasia; also (with Joseph H. Allen) a series of classical text-books. Address: Cambridge, Mass. Died 1901.

GREENOUGH, James Carruthers, educator; b. Wendell, Mass., Aug. 15, 1829; s. Thomas and Mary Johnstone (Carruthers) G.; A.B., Williams Coll., 1860, A.M., 1873; A.M., Brown U., 1876; LL.D., Berea Coll., Ky., 1899; m. Jeanie Ashley Bates, Nov. 27, 1860. Teacher in pub. schs., 1849-56; 1st asst. in State Normal Sch., Westfield, 1856-71; prin. R.I. Normal Sch., 1871-83; pres. Mass. Agrl. Coll., 1883-86; prin. State Normal Sch., Westfield, 1887-97. Visitor Wellesley and Williams Coll. for several yrs.; lecturer in teachers' insts. of Mass. and of other states. Author: Evolution of the Elementary Schools of Great Britain, 1903; History of Westfield (in History of Hampden Co.). Pres. trustees Westfield Acad.; pres. The Athenæum, Western Hampden County Hist. Soc. Address: Westfield, Mass. Died Dec. 2, 1924.

GREENOUGH, John, banker; b. Boston, Mass., Mar. 25, 1846; s. David Stoddard and Anna Augusta (Parkman) G.; A.B., Harvard, 1865, A.M., 1870; m. Carolina H. Storey, June 4, 1879. In mercantile business, New York, title of Wilder & Greenough, 1878-84, branch offices in Buenos Aires and Montevideo; member of Poor & Greenough, bankers (principally r.r. finance), 1884-98; devoted attention principally to philanthropies, 1898—. Republican. Episcopalian. Home: New York, N.Y. Died May 4, 1934.

GREENOUGH, Robert Battey, surgeon; b. Cambridge, Mass., Nov. 9, 1871; s. James Bradstreet and Mary (Ketchum) G.; A.B., Harvard, 1892, M.D., 1896; m. Amelia Mackay Goodwin, Oct. 16, 1900. House officer, Mass. Gen. Hosp., 1896, visiting surgeon, 1915-32, cons. surgeon, 1932—; asst. prof. surgery, Harvard Med. Sch., 1909-32; consulting surgeon Collis P. Huntington Memorial Hosp. Med. insp. (comdr.) U.S.N.R.F. Fellow Am. Acad. Arts and Sciences. Home: Brookline, Mass. Died Feb. 16, 1937.

GREENWAY, Charles Moore, newspaper pub.; b. London, Eng., Aug. 16, 1868; s. William Henry and Catherine Sarah (Moore) G.; brought to U.S., 1870; ed. high sch., London, Ont.; m. Jennie Manville, Oct. 22, 1896 (died 1911); children—Catherine Josephine (Mrs. John A. McDonald), Charles Moore; m. 2d, Elsa Mitchell Bucknum, Feb. 5, 1916. Cashier Grand Rapids Press, 1893, advancing to gen. mgr., 1910; in charge Saginaw Evening News, 1910-13, also in charge Flint Daily Journal, 1913-20; pres. Booth Newspapers, Inc., 1931—; editor and mgr. Grand Rapids Press, 1927-32. Trustee Cranbrook (Mich.) Inst. of Science, David Wolcot Memorial Art Sch., Grand Rapids, Blodgett Memorial Hosp., Grand Rapids, Grand Rapids Art Gallery. Republican. Mason. Home: Grand Rapids, Mich. Died Dec. 1, 1934.

GREENWAY, John Campbell, mining engr.; b. Huntsville, Ala., July 6, 1872; s. Gilbert Christian and Alice (White) G.; student U. of Va.; Ph.B., Yale U., 1895 (pres. of class); LL.D., U. of Ariz.; unmarried. Began as helper, Duquesne (Pa.) furnaces, Carnegie Steel Co., 1895; pvt. U.S. Volunteer Cavalry (Roosevelt's Rough Riders), Spanish-Am. War, 1898; commd. 2d lt. and promoted 1st lt. "for gallantry in action," at Battle of San Juan Hill; recommended to Congress by Col. Roosevelt for bvt. of capt. Asst. supt. mines of U.S. Steel Corp., Ishpeming, Mich., 1899-1906; gen. supt. Oliver Mining Co., Mesaba Range, Minn., 1906-10; gen. mgr. Calumet & Ariz. Mining Co.; gen. mgr. New Cornelia Copper Co., Tucson, Cornelia & Gila Bend Ry. (v.p.). Commd. maj. engrs. 1st and 26th divs., A.E.F., France; lt. col. 101st Inf., 26th Div.; in action on Cantigny, Chateau Thierry, St. Mihiel, Argonne and Meuse fronts; awarded D.S.C. (U.S.), Croix de Guerre with two Palms, Order Legion of Honor and Croix de l'Etoile Noire (France). Mem. bd. regents U. of Ariz.; chmn. defense com. Council of Defense of Ariz. Episcopalian. Address: Warren, Ariz. Died Jan. 19, 1926.

GREENWAY, Walter Burton, clergyman, educator; b. Broylesville, Tenn., Aug. 18, 1876; A.B., Washington (Tenn.) Coll., 1897; student Union Theol. Sem., N.Y. City, 1897-99; grad. study Columbia, 1899; grad. Princeton Theol. Sem., 1900; LL.D., Muskingum Coll., New Concord, O., 1931; D.D., Washington Coll.; m. Lillian Gilbert, June 28, 1905; children—Walter Samuel, William Lyndal, Dorothy Nancy. Ordained ministry Presbyn. Ch., 1900; pastor Elizabeth Av. Presbyn. Ch., 1900-05, Westminster Presbyn. Ch., Jersey City, N.J., 1905-11, Gaston Presbyn. Ch., Phila., Pa., 1911-19; gen. sec. dept. evangelism Presbyn. Gen. Assembly, 1919-22; pastor Bethany Temple Presbyn. Ch., Phila., 1922-28; pres. Beaver College for Women, 1928-39. Chaplain, Camps Mills, Gordon and McClellan, World War. Vice pres. Stony Brook Sch. for Boys: trustee Washington Coll., Berean Manual Training Sch., Pa. State S.S. Assn., Phila. S.S. Assn., Pa. Anti-Saloon League, Phila. Sabbath Sch. Assn. Republican. Mason. Author: Passion Week Sermons, 1926; Lenten Sermons, 1927; Sermons to Young People, 1927. Home: Stanhope, N.J. Died Dec. 21, 1940.

GREENWOOD, Grace, author. See Sara Jane Lippincott.

GREER, Benjamin Brinton; b. Chicago, Ill., Aug. 6, 1877; s. Robert and Katherine (Stewart) G.; ed. Dartmouth Coll., class 1901, and Armour Inst. Tech.; m. Augusta Jameson, 1910. V.p. in charge of operation, C.,M.&St.P. Ry., 1919; pres. N.Y. Air Brake Co., 1925—. Served as pvt. N.H. Inf., Spanish-Am. War. Republican. Died Feb. 28, 1932.

GREER, David Hummell, bishop; b. Wheeling, W.Va., Mar. 20, 1844; s. Jacob Rickard and Elizabeth (Yellott) G.; A.B., Washington Coll., Pa., 1862; studied theology at P.E. Sem., Gambier, O., 1863-66; D.D., Kenyon Coll., 1880, Brown U., 1890, U. of the South, 1901; LL.D., Washington and Jefferson College, 1902; S.T.D., Columbia U., 1904; D.D., Harvard U., 1915; m. Caroline A. Keith, 1869. Deacon, 1866, priest, 1868, P.E. Church; rector Clarksburg, W.Va., 1866-68, Covington, Ky., 1868-71, Grace Ch., Providence, R.I., 1871-88 St. Bartholomew's Ch. New York, 1888-1904; elected Sept., 1903, consecrated Jan. 26, 1904, bishop coadjutor, Diocese of New York, becoming bishop of New York, on death of Bishop Potter, July 21, 1908. Author: The Historic Christ, 1890; From Things to God, 1893; The Preacher and His Place, 1895; Visions, 1898. Address: New York, N.Y. Died May 19, 1919.

GREER, James Agustin, rear admiral U.S. Navy; retired Feb. 28, 1895; b. Cincinnati, O., Feb. 28, 1833; s. James and Caroline King G.; ed. private schools, Dayton, O.; m. Mary Randolph, d. Capt. T. T. Webb, U.S.N., Nov. 26, 1857. Entered navy as midshipman, Jan. 10, 1848; became lt., Sept. 16, 1855; lt. comdr., July 16, 1862; assisted in removal of Mason and Slidell from English steamer "Trent"; comd. iron-clad "Benton" and a div. of Admiral Porter's squadron at passage of Vicksburg batteries, April 16, 1863, and succeeding engagements; fought batteries of Grand Gulf for 5 hours, April 29, 1863; was with the Red River expdns., etc.; afterward promoted through various grades to rear admiral; comd. the "Tigress" in the "Polaris" search expdn., 1873, finding the wreck at Littleton Island, N. Greenland; comd. U.S. European naval Station, 1887-89. Chmn. of Lighthouse Bd., 1891-94. Became pres. Naval Examining and Retiring Bds., Dec. 1, 1894. Died 1904.

GREER, Lawrence, lawyer, ry. official; b. Providence, R.I., Oct. 25, 1872; s. Rt. Rev. David Hummell and Caroline A. (Keith) G.; A.B., Yale, 1893; LL.B. cum laude, N.Y. Law Sch., 1895; m. Georgiana Oakes, Oct. 19, 1896. Admitted to N.Y. bar, 1895, began practice in office of John F. Dillon, N.Y. City, 1895; mem. firm Pierce and Greer, 1902—. Pres. Western Md. Ry. Co., Apr. 3, 1918-Jan. 15, 1919, and Jan. 1-Feb. 29, 1920 (later chmn. bd.). Episcopalian. Home: New York, N.Y. Died Dec. 14, 1925.

GREGG, Alexander White, congressman; b. in Tex.; A.B., Kings College, Bristol, Tenn.; LL.B., U. of Va. Admitted to bar and practiced at Palestine, Tex. Mem. 58th to 65th Congresses (1903-19), 7th Tex. Dist. Democrat. Home: Palestine, Tex. Died Apr. 30, 1919.

GREGG, David, theologian; b. Pittsburgh, Pa., Mar. 25, 1845; s. David and Mary Margaret (Rafferty) G.; A.B., Jefferson Coll., Pa., 1865; D.D., New York U., 1888; LL.D., Livingston Coll., 1890, Washington and Jefferson Coll., 1902; m. S. Kate Etheridge, Mar. 2, 1871. Pastor New York, 1870-87, Third R.P. Ch., Boston, 1887-90, Park St. Congl. Ch. and Lafayette Av. Presbyn. Ch., Brooklyn, 1890-1904; pres. 1904-09, emeritus pres. and lecturer extraordinary, 1909—, Western Theol. Sem. Editor Our Banner, 1874-86. Author: Between the Testaments, 1907; The Master as a Preacher (translated into Greek and published in Athens, Greece), 1909; Pulpit Stars of the Nineteenth Century. Died Oct. 11, 1919.

GREGG, David McMurtrie, major gen., U.S.V.; b. Huntingdon, Pa., Apr. 10, 1833; s. Matthew D. and Ellen (McMurtrie) G.; grad. U.S. Mil. Acad., 1855; LL.D., Pa. Mil. Acad.; m. Ellen F. Sheaff, Oct. 6, 1862. Bvt. 2d lt. 2d Dragoons, July 1, 1855; 2d lt. 1st Dragoons, Sept. 4, 1855; 1st lt., Mar. 21, 1861; capt. 3d Cav., May 14, 1861, 6th Cav., Aug. 3, 1861; col. 8th Pa. Cav., Jan. 24, 1862; brig. gen. vols., Nov. 29, 1862; bvtd. maj. gen. vols., Aug. 1, 1864, "for highly meritorious and distinguished conduct"; comd. div. of cav. in Army of the Potomac; resigned from army, Feb. 3, 1865. U.S. consul at Prague, Bohemia, 1874; auditor gen. of Pa., 1891. Republican. Comdr. Pa. Commandery Loyal Legion, 1886—; comdr.-in-chief Mil. Order Loyal Legion U.S., 1903—. Author: Second Cavalry Division of the Army of the Potomac in the Gettysburg Campaign, 1907. Home: Reading, Pa. Died Aug. 7, 1916.

GREGG, James Bartlett, clergyman; b. Medford, Mass., Apr. 15, 1846; s. James Bartlett and Mary Bartlett (Bailey) G.; grad. Phillips Acad., Andover, Mass., 1862; A.B., Harvard, 1866; grad. Andover Theol. Sem., 1874; D.D., Colo. Coll., 1893; S.T.D., Harvard, 1906; m. Mary Needham, Dec. 3, 1874. Ordained Congl. ministry, Sept. 29, 1874; pastor Windsor Av. Ch., Hartford, Conn., 1874-82, First Ch., Colorado Springs, Colo., 1882-1909; acting pastor various chs. in Mass., 1909-19. Trustee Colo. Coll., 1855-1909; dir. Chicago Theol. Sem., 1894-1909. Chmn. Congl. Home Missionary Soc. Com. of Colo., several yrs.; pres. Rocky Mountain Harvard Club, 2 yrs. Home: Brookline, Mass. Died May 7, 1922.

GREGG, Willis Ray, meteorologist; b. Phoenix, N.Y., Jan. 4, 1880; s. Willis Perry and Jennie E. (Ray) G.; A.B., Cornell U., 1903; Sc.D., Norwich U., 1937; m. Mary Chamberlayne Wall, Oct. 15, 1914; 1 dau., Ruth Marguerite. With U.S. Weather Bur., 1904—; at Mt. Weather Obs., Va., 1907-14, Washington, D.C., 1915—; in charge Aerological Div. of Weather Bur., 1917-34; chief of U.S. Weather Bureau, 1934—; spl. meteorol. adviser trans-Atlantic flight for NC seaplanes (U.S.N.) at Trepassey, Newfoundland, May 1919, and for British dirigible R34, at Mineola, N.Y., July 1919, engaged in organizing weather service for commercial airways activities, 1926—. Mem. Nat. Advisory Com. for Aeronautics (chmn. exec. com. and of subcom. on meteorol. problems), Internat. Meteorol. Orgn., Internat. Meteorol. Com. (pres. comm. on projections of meteorol. maps), Daniel Guggenheim Com. on Aeronautical Meteorology, Interdepartmental Com. on Co-ordination of Meteorol. Service for Aeronautics, etc. Fellow Am. Meteorol. Soc. (treas. 1923-35). Mason (Past Master). Co-Author: Introductory Meteorology, 1918; Meteorology, 1931. Author: Aeronautical Meteorology, 1925, 2d edit., 1930; Aerological Survey of the United States (monograph), 1922 and 1926. Home: Takoma Park, Md. Died Sept. 14, 1938.

GREGORY, Carl C., clergyman; b. Birmingham, Ala., Nov. 27, 1888; s. Rev. John Bealle and Sue

Kathryn (Cain) G.; prep. edn. in prep. sch. of Birmingham-Southern U., Ph.B., Birmingham-Southern Coll., 1906, D.D., 1926; grad. theol. dept. Vanderbilt U., 1914 (winner of Founder's medal, 1913); m. Emma Farley Collins, Mar. 23, 1918; children—Carl C., John Collins, Vann Oliver. Ordained ministry M.E. Ch., S.; pastor St. John Ch., Birmingham, 1914-17; asso. pastor First Ch., South Birmingham, 1917-18; pastor Settle Memorial Ch., Owensboro, Ky., 1918-23, First Ch., Dallas, 1923-31 ($1,000,000 ch. bldg. erected), Travis Park Ch., San Antonio, 1931—; also chaplain Hella Temple Shrine, Dallas, 1931. Mem. World Alliance for Universal Peace, 1919-23. Democrat. Address: San Antonio, Tex. Died Apr. 9, 1933.

GREGORY, Caspar René, theologian; b. Phila., Pa., Nov. 6, 1846; s. Henry Duval and Mary (Jones) G.; A.B., U. of Pa., 1864, A.M., 1867; student Theol. Sem. R.P. Ch., Phila., 1865-67; Princeton Theol. Sem., 1867-73; Ph.D., U. of Leipzig, 1876 (S.T.D., 1893; LL.D., U. of Pa., 1894, Yale, 1901; D.D., U. of Glasgow, 1902); m. Lucy Watson Thayer, Sept. 29, 1886. Helped Dr. Charles Hodge publish his Systematic Theology, 1870-73; sub-editor Theologische Literaturzeitung, Leipzig, 1876-84; pastor Am. Chapel, Leipzig, 1878-79; Privatdocent, 1884-89, prof. theology, 1889—, U. of Leipzig. Hon. mem. Greek Philol. Syllogos, Constantinople, 1886; foreign hon. mem. Archæol. Inst. of America. Author: Canon and Text of the New Testament, 1907. Vol. in the German Army, 1914—. Died Apr. 9, 1917.

GREGORY, Charles Noble, internat. law; b. Otsego Co., N.Y., Aug. 27, 1851; s. Hon. Jared C. and Charlotte C. (Camp) G.; A.B., U. of Wis., 1871, LL.B., A.M., 1874, LL.D., 1901; unmarried. Practiced law at Madison, Wis., 1872-94, as mem. firms of Gregory & Pinney, Gregory & Gregory, and Gregory, Bird & Gregory, all of which represented C.,M.&St.P. Ry. there; retired from practice, 1894; asso. dean Coll. of Law, U. of Wis., 1894-1901; dean Coll. of Law, State U. of Ia., 1901-11; dean Dept. of Law, George Washington U., Sept. 1, 1911-14. Alderman, 1880-83, mem. bd. edn., 1883, Madison, Wis. Editor Tariff Reform Advocate, 1888; one of editors Am. Jour. of Internat. Law for 17 yrs. Episcopalian. Author: Life of Justice Miller, of the Supreme Court of United States; Abstracts of Cases Contained in Lloyds Reports of Prize Cases, vols. 1, 2, 3, 4 (pub. by State Dept.), 1919. Home: Washington, D.C. Died July 10, 1932.

GREGORY, Daniel Seelye, editor; b. Carmel, N.Y., Aug. 21, 1832; s. Horace and Betsy (Seelye) G.; grad. State Normal Coll., Albany, N.Y., 1850; A.B., Princeton, 1857; grad. Princeton Theol. Sem., 1860; (D.D., Princeton, 1873; LL.D., U. of Wooster, O., 1895); m. Jennie G. Brown, Nov. 5, 1860; m. 2d, Harriet Byram, Dec. 26, 1867. Instr. in rhetoric, Princeton, 1858-60; ordained Presbyn. ministry, 1861; pastor Galena, Ill., 1860-63, Troy, N.Y., 1863-66, New Haven, Conn., 1866-69, S. Salem, N.Y., 1869-71; prof. metaphysics, logic and English lit., U. of Wooster, 1871-78; pres. Lake Forest U., 1878-86; pastor Morgan, Minn., 1885-89; mng. editor Standard Dictionary, 1890-94; editor Homiletic Review, 1895-1904; gen. sec. Bible League of N. America, and mng. editor Bible Student and Teacher, 1904—. Author: Christian Ethics, 1875; Practical Logic, 1881. Home: East Orange, N.J. Died Apr. 14, 1915.

GREGORY, Eliot, artist, author; b. New York, N.Y., Oct. 13, 1854; studied at Yale; art edn., Rome and Paris, under Carolus-Duran. (Hon. mention Paris Salon.) Founder of the New Theatre, New York. Author (pen-name An Idler): Idler Papers; Worldly Ways and By-Ways; The Ways of Men, 1900. Chevalier de la Légion d'Honneur. Home: New York, N.Y. Died June 1, 1915.

GREGORY, Elisha Hall, M.D.; b. in Ky., Sept. 10, 1824; s. Charles and Sophia P. G.; ed. common schools, Booneville, Mo.; grad. med. dept., Univ. of St. Louis, 1849; prof. surgery, St. Louis Med. Coll. (med. dept. Washington Univ.); has been connected with same as teacher of surgery and anatomy, 1851—; pres. Am. Med. Assn., 1887. Home: St. Louis, Mo. Deceased.

GREGORY, John Henry, banker; b. Rochester, N.Y., Sept. 21, 1864; s. John and Alice (Redfern) G.; ed. pub. schs.; m. Helene La Barrere Valdes, Paris, France, Jan. 19, 1929. In banking business, at Rochester, June 1, 1881—; pres. Central Trust Co., 1915-33, chmn. bd., 1933—. Republican. Episcopalian. Mason. Home: Brighton, N.Y. Died Apr. 5, 1934.

GREGORY, John Herbert, engineer, educator; b. Cambridge, Mass., Aug. 7, 1874; s. John Porter and Mary Clerice (Stone) G.; New England ancestry; B.S. in C.E., Mass. Inst. Tech., 1895; m. Sarah Ann James, July 16, 1900; 1 son, Richard Sears. Engr. with Boston Metropolitan Sewerage Works, 1893-94, Boston Met. Water Works, 1895-97, Albany Water Filtration Works, 1897-1900, Phila. Water Filtration Works, 1900-02, Jersey City Water Supply Works, 1902-03, N.Y. Filtration Dept. Commn. on Additional Water Supply, 1903-04; engr. in charge Improved Water and Sewerage Works, Columbus, O., 1904-09;

resident engr. Passaic Valley Sewerage Project, Newark, N.J., 1909-10; engr. Met. Sewerage Commn., New York, 1910-11; mem. Rudolph Hering & John H. Gregory, cons. engrs., New York, 1911-17; practiced alone, 1917-19; settled at Baltimore as cons. engr., 1919; also prof. civil and sanitary engring., Johns Hopkins U., 1920—. Commd. capt. U.S.A., 1918. Mem. Engineers' Advisory Board, Reconstruction Finance Corp., 1932. Awarded Thomas Fitch Rowland prize, 1910, James Laurie prize, 1930, and Rudolph Hering medal, 1935, by Am. Soc. Civil Engineers. Episcopalian. Home: Baltimore, Md. Died Jan. 18, 1937.

GREGORY, Menas Sarkis, psychiatrist, neurologist; M.D., Albany Med. Coll., 1898. Interne, Craig Colony for Epileptics, Sonyea, N.Y.; dir. psychiatric division, Bellevue Hospital, 1904-34, consultant, 1936—; consultant in psychiatry N.Y. Neurol. Inst.; prof. psychiatry, N.Y. Post Graduate Med. Coll., 1914-16; prof. psychiatry, New York U. Coll. of Medicine, 1922-36, emeritus prof., 1936—. Maj. lt. col. U.S. Army Med. Corps. Fellow A.M.A. Home: New York, N.Y. Died Nov. 2, 1941.

GREGORY, Oliver Fuller, clergyman; b. Charleston, S.C., Mar. 7, 1844; s. Ferdinand Munson and Sarah Ann Brown (Fuller) G.; ed. Charleston (S.C.) Coll.; (D.D., Howard Coll., Birmingham, Ala., 1887); m. Kezia Ann Hobson, Mar. 6, 1866. Mem. Charleston Zouave Cadets; co. mustered into service one hour after State seceded, Dec. 20, 1860; on duty at Morris Island and Secessionville, Jan.-Apr. 1861; on Sullivan's Island during Battle of Ft. Sumter; mustered into Co. H, Hampton Legion, S.C.V., July 1861; wounded 4 times at 2d Battle of Manassas; wounded and captured at storming of Ft. Saunders, Knoxville, Tenn., and prisoner of war at Rock Island, Ill., Dec. 5, 1863-Mar. 7, 1865. Ordained Bapt. ministry, 1871; pastor, Mt. Pleasant, S.C., 1871-76, Kingstree, 1876, 1st Ch., Eufaula, Ala., 1877-79, 1st Ch., Tuscaloosa, 1879, Cheraw and Florence, S.C., 1880-82, 1st Ch., Charlotte, N.C., 1882-85, Valence St. Ch., New Orleans, La., 1885, 4th Ch., Baltimore, Md., 1885-1902, Adams St. Ch., Montgomery, Ala., 1902-05, 1st Ch., Staunton, Va., 1905-13; Gregory Memorial Ch., Baltimore, Apr. 1, 1913—. Corr. sec. exec. bd. Md. Baptists, 1887-1901; sec. Southern Baptist Conv., 1877-80, and 1883—; v.p. Md. Bapt. Mission Assn., 1915, 17 (sec. 1916); moderator Middle Dist. Assn. Md., 1915-17. Democrat. Mason. Home: Baltimore, Md. Died Jan. 12, 1919.

GREGORY, Stephen Strong, lawyer; b. Unadilla, N.Y., Nov. 16, 1849; s. J. C. and Charlotte C. G.; removed to Madison, Wis., 1858; A.B., U. of Wis., 1870, LL.B., 1871; m. Janet M. Tappan, Nov. 25, 1880. Practiced law at Madison, 1871-74, then in Chicago; partner of Judge A. H. Chetlain, 1874-79; then of Tenney & Flower, which later was succeeded by Flower, Remy & Gregory; mem. Gregory, Booth & Harlan, 1888-93; practiced alone and later the firm Gregory & McNab, Chicago, was formed. Was spl. counsel for city of Chicago before the Supreme Ct. of U.S. in the Lake Front case; with John P. Wilson defended and successfully maintained the constitutionality of the law creating the Sanitary Dist. of Chicago; defended the murder case of Prendergast and the conspiracy case against Eugene V. Debs. Was short time spl. counsel for Federal Trade Commn.; mem. Cook Co. Fuel Com. and war com. of Chicago Bar Assn., 1917—. Episcopalian. Democrat. Was election commr. of Chicago 2 yrs. Home: Chicago, Ill. Died Oct. 24, 1920.

GREGORY, Thomas T(ingey) C(raven), lawyer; b. Suisun, Calif., Oct. 4, 1878; s. John Munford and Evelyn Tingey (Craven) G.; A.B., Stanford U., 1899, studied law dept. same univ., 1900-01; m. Gertrude Martin, Apr. 15, 1903; children—John Munford, Gertrude Evelyn, Margaret Martin. Practiced at San Francisco, 1907—; dist. atty. Solano Co., Calif., 1903-07; dir. numerous companies. Trustee Stanford U. Capt. 144th F.A., with A.E.F. in France, World War; associated with Herbert Hoover in Europe as one of original members of Am. Relief Adminstrn.; dir. Central Europe A.R.A. and asst. to dir. of relief of Supreme Economic Council; Am. mem. Interallied Commn. Austro-Hungarian and Jugo-Slavian empires, feeding people and reinstating economic interchanges between Central and S.E. European countries. Republican. Episcopalian. Mason. Home: Stanford University, Calif. Died June 5, 1933.

GREGORY, Thomas Watt, attorney gen. U.S.; b. Crawfordsville, Miss., Nov. 6, 1861; s. Francis Robert and Mary Cornelia (Watt) G.; A.B., Southwestern Presbyn. U., Clarksville, Tenn., 1883; spl. student U. of Va., 1883-84; LL.B., U. of Tex., 1885; LL.D., Lincoln Memorial U., Southwestern Presbyterian U., Austin College; m. Julia Nalle, Feb. 22, 1893; children—Mrs. Jane Heyer, Thomas Watt, Joseph Nalle, Cornelia. Admitted to Tex. bar, 1885; practiced alone, 1885-1900; asst. city atty., Austin, Tex., 1891-94; declined appmt. as asst. atty. gen. of Texas, 1892, and dist. judge, 1896; firm of Gregory & Batts formed 1900; firm employed as spl. counsel State of Tex. to prosecute various corps. for violating anti-trust laws; mem. Gregory, Batts & Brooks, 1908-13; spl. asst. atty. gen. of U.S. in charge of investigation and

prosecution of N.Y.,N.H.&H. R.R. Co. for violation of Sherman Act, 1913; atty. gen. of the U.S., in cabinet of President Wilson, Aug. 29, 1914-Mar. 4, 1919; became mem. Gregory & Todd, Washington, D.C., June 1919. Mem. President Wilson's Second Industrial Conf., 1919-20; del. Dem. Nat. Convs., 1904, 12 (com. on credentials, 1904, v.p., 1912); regent U. of Tex., 1899-1907; trustee Austin Presbyn. Theol. Seminary. Democrat. Presbyn. Home: Houston, Tex. Died Feb. 26, 1933.

GREGORY, Warren, lawyer; b. Contra Costa Co., Calif., Sept. 30, 1864; s. Munson and Laura (Knox) G.; A.B., U. of Calif., 1887; LL.B., Hastings Coll. of Law, 1890; m. Sarah McLean Hardy, Apr. 20, 1896; children—Donald Munson, Elizabeth McLean, Jean Hardy, John Howard. Practiced at San Francisco, 1890—; sr. mem. Chickering & Gregory. Former mem. State Bd. of Bar Examiners, Calif.; mem. Dist. Bd. for Selective Service, World War; dir. Commn. for Relief in Belgium, 1916-17. Was regent U. of Calif. Decorated Chevalier Legion of Honor (French); Order of the Crown (Belgian). Unitarian. Home: Berkeley, Calif. Died Feb. 12, 1927.

GREGORY, Warren Fenno, publisher; b. Winchendon, Mass., July 12, 1863; s. George W. and Nancy (Miller) G.; A.B., Dartmouth Coll., 1888, A.M., 1895; m. Annie Laurie, Oct. 4, 1898 (died 1932); 1 daughter, Hope (Mrs. Courtney F. Bird). Educator and editor, 1888-98; mgr. Lee & Shepard, book publishers, 1898-1904; mgr. and treas. Lothrop, Lee & Shepard Co., 1904-34, retired. One of founders of Dartmouth Literary Monthly, Dartmouth College. Editor: (in Students' Series of English Classics) Oliver Goldsmith's Traveler and Deserted Village, 1894; John Dryden's Palamon and Arcite, 1896; Thomas Gray's Elegy in a Country Churchyard, 1909. Home: Newtonville, Mass. Died Mar. 29, 1936.

GREGORY, William, gov. R.I., elected April 4, 1900; b. Astoria, N.Y., Aug. 3, 1849; ed. Westerly, R.I.; pres. Wickford Nat. Bank and dir. Union Trust Co., Providence, R.I.; manufacturer; trustee R.I. Safe Deposit Co.; mem. and chmn. State bd. charities and corrections. Representative from North Kingstown to gen. assembly, R.I., 1888-92; senator, 1894-98; lt. gov., 1898-1900. Republican. Home: Providence, R.I. Died 1901.

GREGORY, William Voris, congressman; b. Graves Co., Ky., Oct. 21, 1877; s. William Jones and Azilee (Boyd) G.; A.B., West Ky. Coll., 1896; studied law Cumberland U.; m. Marie Elizabeth Myles, May 3, 1900; 1 dau., Elizabeth Myles (Mrs. Henry King Hill, Jr.). Formerly supt. schs., Mayfield; began practice at Mayfield, 1902; judge Graves Co. Court, 1913-19, resigned; U.S. atty., Western Dist. of Ky., 1919-22; resigned to resume law practice; mem. 70th to 74th Congresses (1927-37), 1st Ky. Dist. Dir. Odd Fellows Orphans' Home, Lexington, Ky. Democrat. Mason. Home: Mayfield, Ky. Died Oct. 10, 1936.

GREGORY, Willis George, prof. pharmacy; b. Theresa, N.Y., Apr. 19, 1857; s. Willis Lathrop and Frances (Beach) G.; M.D., U. of Buffalo, 1882; Ph.G., 1886; m. Gertrude A. Fargo, Apr. 15, 1885 (died 1915); children—Anna (dec.), Louise, Helen (Mrs. Harry F. Coward, dec.), Francis. In retail drug bus. with father, 1876-88; propr. drug store, 1888-1906; prof. pharmacy, U. of Buffalo, 1886—; dean Sch. of Pharmacy, 1890—. Was mem. New York State Bd. Pharmacy, 30 years. Trustee U. of Buffalo. Mem. U.S. Pharmacopœial Revision Com., 1890-1920. Republican. Baptist. Home: Buffalo, N.Y. Died Mar. 20, 1937.

GRENELL, Zelotes, clergyman; b. New York, N.Y., Feb. 25, 1841; s. Zelotes and Eliza (Burt) G.; U. of Rochester, 1859-60; A.B., Madison (now Colgate) U.; 1862, A.M., 1864; grad. Hamilton (N.Y.) Theol. Sem., 1864; (D.D., Colgate, 1882); m. Inez Augusta Budington, Oct. 14, 1868. Ordained Bapt. ministry, Oct. 24, 1864; pastor, Kingston, N.Y., 1864-73, Bay City, Mich., 1873-79, First Ch., Detroit, 1879-95, Chicago, 1895-98. Asso. editor Mich. Christian Herald, 1874-1900, Bapt. Teacher, 7 yrs. Trustee Kalamazoo (Mich.) Coll., 1874-90; pres. trustees, sem., Fenton, Mich., 1877; mem. bd. mgrs., Am. Bapt. Missionary Union. Author: The Sandals; The Young Christian and His Work, 1905; The Church Clerk, 1909. Home: La Grange, Ill. Died Apr. 29, 1918.

GRENFELL, Helen Loring, sociologist; b. Valparaiso, Chile; d. Charles and Mary Frances (Roby) Loring; descendant of John Howland, of the Mayflower; pub. schs., Colo.; State Normal Coll., Albany, N.Y.; M.A., U. of Denver, 1904; m. Edwin I. Grenfell, Apr. 6, 1889. Three times elected county supt. schs. Gilpin Co., Colo.; also 3 times elected state supt. pub. instrn., Colo., serving 1899-1905 (the first state official of Colo. to serve 3 consecutive terms); commr. State Penitentiary Reformatory and State Insane Asylum (mng. funds and controlling affairs penal instns.) by appmt. or gov., 1909-30; also director of Colorado Prison Assn. While state supt. pub. instrn. largely increased sch. revenues by new policy of leasing state lands, revised and annotated sch. laws, etc. Was mem. Am. Mission invited by British Govt., 1918, to speak on war issues and investigate war conditions in Gt. Britain and France. Conglist. Home: Denver, Colo. Died July 26, 1935.

GRENFELL, Sir Wilfred Thomason, supt. Internat. Grenfell Assn., surgeon, author; b. Mostyn House, Parkgate, nr. Chester, Eng., Feb. 28, 1865; s. Algernon Sydney and Jane Georgiana (Hutchinson) G.; ed. Marlborough Coll., Oxford U. and London Hosp.; hon. LL.D., Williams Coll., 1909; hon. M.A., Harvard, 1909; hon. M.D., Toronto U., 1911; L.H.D., U. of N.Y., 1928; LL.D., McGill U., Montreal, Can., 1928, Middlebury Coll., Vt., 1928, Princeton U., Bowdoin, St. Andrews, 1929, Berea Coll., Ky., 1930; D.S.C., U. of Louisville, 1933; m. Anne MacClanahan, 1909; (died 1938); children—Wilfred Thomason, Kinloch Pascoe, Rosamond Loveday. House surgeon London Hosp., 1890-91; entered med. service of Royal Nat. Mission to Fishermen, 1889; fitted out first hosp. ship for North Sea fisheries; cruised with fishermen, established houses and mission vessels for them; went to Labrador, 1892, and has built 5 hosps., 7 nursing stas., 2 orphanages, 2 large schools, coop. stores, and inaugurated industrial work and child welfare work; surgeon in charge hospital steamer, Strathcona II, of which is master, and cruises each year on coasts of northern Newfoundland and Labrador; owns and operates S.S. Maraval, S.S. Zavorah, M.V. Jessie Goldthwait, M.-V. George B. Cluett, and yawls in connection with hosps. F.R.C.S., L.R.C.P., London; fellow Am. Coll. Surgeons, 1915, Royal Coll. Surgeons, 1920; mem. Royal Instn. of Gt. Britain; awarded Murchison Bequest, Royal Geog. Soc., 1911; gold medal Nat. Acad. Social Sciences (U.S.), 1920; Livingston gold medal Royal Scottish Geog. Soc., 1930; lord rector St. Andrews U., 1929-31. Hon. fellow of Queen's Coll., Oxford, England, 1936. Decorated C.M.G. (Companion of St. Michael and St. George) by King Edward VII, 1907; K.C.M.G., by King George V, 1927; J.P., Colony of Newfoundland. Served as maj. Harvard Surg. Unit in France, World War. Episcopalian. Author: Harvest of the Sea; A Man's Faith, 1908; Labrador, 1909; Adrift on an Ice-Pan, 1909; Down to the Sea, 1910; What Life Means to Me, 1910; What the Church Means to Me, 1911; Down North on the Labrador, 1911; The Adventure of Life, 1912; Tales of the Labrador, 1916; Labrador Days, 1919; A Labrador Doctor (autobiography); Northern Neighbors, 1923; Yourself and Your Body, 1925; Labrador Looks at the Orient, 1928; Forty Years for Labrador, 1932; The Romance of Labrador, 1934. Died Oct. 9, 1940.

GRENIER, Arthur Sylvester, public utilities; b. Martinton, Ill., Apr. 21, 1872; s. Sylvester and Sophia (St. Pierre) G.; ed. pub. schs. and by pvt. studies; m. Mary Robinson, May 8, 1902; 1 son, Arthur Sylvester. With Electric Bond and Share Co. and associated cos. in N.Y., Tex., Kan., Neb. and other states, Apr. 1, 1912—; v.p. Electric Bond and Share Co., 1927—; chmn. bd. Tex. Electric Service Co.; v.p. and dir. American Power & Light Co., Tex. Power & Light Co., Houston Lighting & Power Co., Dallas Ry. & Terminal Co., Dallas Power & Light Co.; v.p. Electric Power & Light Corp. Republican. Conglist. Home: Montclair, N.J. Died Jan. 13, 1935.

GREVE, Charles Theodore, lawyer; b. Cincinnati, Jan. 3, 1863; s. Theodore L. A. and Clara Esther (Emrie) G.; A.B., Harvard, 1884; LL.B., Cincinnati Law Sch., 1885; m. Laura Belle, d. E. V. Cherry, Oct. 23, 1895; children—Theodore, Cherry. In practice of law at Cincinnati, May 1885—; asst. U.S. atty., 1894-98; referee in bankruptcy, 1898—; prof. of law, Cincinnati Law Sch. (U. of Cincinnati), 1904-17, Y.M.C.A. Law Sch., Cincinnati, 1919—, and Eclectic Med. Coll., 1920— (pres. trustees); sec. Sinking Fund trustees of Cincinnati, 1906. Lit. editor Cincinnati Tribune, 1894-97, Cincinnati Times-Star, 1898-1901. Dem. candidate for Congress, 2d Ohio Dist., 1892, for probate judge, Hamilton Co., O., 1902. Author: Centennial History of Cincinnati, 2 vols., 1904. Contbr. to encyclopædias Americana, International and Britannica; collaborated in Life of Alphonso Taft and Tafts of Today, 1919. Home: Vernonville, Cincinnati, O. Died Sept. 4, 1930.

GREVSTAD, Nicolay Andrew, newspaperman; b. Norway, June 2, 1851; s. Nils Carlson and Birgitte (Shetlein) G.; Candidatus Juris, Law Sch., U. of Norway, 1878; married; 1 dau., Dagny (Mrs. A. L. van Maarth). Came to U.S., 1883, naturalized citizen, 1890. In Dept. of Justice, Norway, 1878-80; editor Kristiania Dagbladet, 1880-83; editor Nordvesten (newspaper), St. Paul, Minn., until return to Norway, 1886-87; editorial writer, Minneapolis (Minn.) Tribune, 1887-90; editor and pub. Minneapolis Times, 1890-92; editor Chicago Skandinaven, 1892-1911; E.E. and M.P. to Paraguay and Uruguay, later Uruguay alone, 1911-15; asst. dir. Minn. Safety Commn., 1917-18; dir. information service of Rep. Nat. Com. for foreign lang. newspapers, 1919-25; rep. of Chicago financial syndicate, Montevideo, Uruguay, 1926-27; editor Chicago Skandinaven, 1930—. Decorated Knight Order of St. Olaf (Norway). Republican. Lutheran. Author of Report on the American Jury System, pub. as public document by Norwegian Storting, 1896. Home: Chicago, Ill. Died Feb. 20, 1940.

GREY, Zane, author; b. Zanesville, O., Jan. 31, 1875; s. Lewis M. and Alice Josephine (Zane) G.; Zanesville High Sch.; D.D.S., Univ. of Pa., 1896, also M.L.; m. Lina Elise Roth, Nov. 21, 1905; children—Romer Zane, Betty, Loren. Practiced in New York, 1898-1904; since followed lit. career. Author: Betty Zane, 1904; The Spirit of the Border, 1905; The Last Trail, 1907; The Last of the Plainsmen, 1908; The Short-Stop, 1909; The Heritage of the Desert, 1910; The Young Forester, 1910; The Young Pitcher, 1911; The Young Lion Hunter, 1911; Riders of the Purple Sage, 1912; Ken Ward in the Jungle, 1912; Desert Gold, 1913; The Light of Western Stars, 1914; The Lone Star Ranger, 1915; Rainbow Trail, 1915; The Border Legion, 1916; Wildfire, 1917; U.P. Trail, 1918; Desert of Wheat, 1919; Tales of Fishes, 1919; Man of the Forest, 1920; The Red-Headed Outfield, 1920; The Mysterious Rider, 1921; To the Last Man, 1922; The Day of the Beast, 1922; Tales of Lonely Trails, 1922; The Wanderer of the Wasteland, 1923; Tappan's Burro, 1923; The Call of the Canyon, 1924; Tales of Southern Rivers, 1924; The Thundering Herd, 1925; Roping Lions in the Grand Canyon, 1924; Tales of Fishing Virgin Seas, 1925; Tales of the Anglers' Eldorado, 1926; Under the Tonto Rim, 1926; Tales of Swordfish and Tuna, 1927; Forlorn River, 1927; Wild Horse Mesa, 1928; Tales of Fresh Water Fishing, 1928; Don, 1928; Fighting Caravans, 1929; The Shepherd of Guadaloupe, 1930; The Wolf Tracker, 1930; Sunset Pass, 1931; Zane Grey's Book of Camps and Trails, 1931; The Drift Fence, 1933; The Hash Knife Outfit, 1933; Code of the West, 1934; Thunder Mountain, 1935; The Trail Driver, 1936; The Lost Wagon Train, 1936; West of the Pecos, 1937; An American Angler in Australia, 1937. Home: Altadena, Calif. Died Oct. 23, 1939.

GRIBBEL, John, mfr.; b. Hudson City, N.J., Mar. 29, 1858; s. James and Anna (Simmons) G.; ed. Coll. City of N.Y.; hon. M.A., Wesleyan U., Middletown, Conn., Hahnemann Med. Coll. and Hosp., Phila.; LL.D., Temple U.; m. Elizabeth Bancker Wood, Jan. 8, 1880; children—Wakeman G., John B., Idella Louise, Elizabeth. With Importers and Traders Nat. Bank, 1876, Leather Mfrs. Nat. Bank, 1877; New York agent Harris, Griffin & Co., mfrs. gas meters, 1883-90; admitted to partnership John J. Griffin & Co., 1890, propr. of business under title John J. Griffin & Co., 1892-95, now Am. Meter Co. of which is pres.; pres. Tampa (Fla.) Gas Co.; dir. numerous companies. Trustee Wesleyan University (Conn.). Republican. Methodist. Home: Wyncote, Pa. Died Aug. 25, 1936.

GRIER, Alvan Ruckman, school pres.; b. Birmingham, Pa., Feb. 28, 1860; s. Dr. Lemuel G. and Sarah (Boileau) G.; ed. Mountain Sem., Birmingham, Princeton U., and U. of Pa.; A.M., Juniata Coll., 1927; Litt.D., Franklin and Marshall, 1928; m. Mary V. Campbell, Oct. 18, 1900. Business mgr. The Birmingham School for Girls, 1890-97, pres. and dir., 1907—; sec., treas., dir. Tyrone (Pa.) Electric R.R., 1897-99; pres. Home Electric Light Co., Tyrone, 1899-1902. Republican. Presbyn. Home: Birmingham, Pa. Died May 6, 1932.

GRIER, William, commodore U.S.N.; b. in Ireland, Oct. 5, 1816; s. William and Margaret (Hayes) G.; ed. at Baltimore; m. Margaret Watmough. Apptd. from Md., asst. surgeon U.S.N., Mar. 7, 1838; passed asst. surgeon and surgeon, Apr. 14, 1852; med. dir., Mar. 3, 1871; on board Cyane, 1838-41; storeship Erie, 1842-44; Shark, 1844-46; hospital, New York, 1848-49; Independence, 1849-52; Vincennes, as fleet surgeon, N. Pacific Surveying Expdn., 1853-56; spl. duty, 1857; Naval Acad., 1858-60; Macedonian, 1860-61; receiving ship at Baltimore, 1862; Naval hosps., Mound City, Ill., and Memphis, Tenn., 1862-65; spl. duty at Hartford, Conn., 1867; mem. Naval Examining Bd., 1868-69; spl. duty at Baltimore, 1869-71; mem. Examining and Retiring Bds., 1871-72; pres. Med. Examining Bd., 1872-76; surgeon gen. of the navy, and chief of Bur. of Medicine and Surgery, with the rank of commodore, 1877-78; retired, Oct. 5, 1876. Home: Washington, D.C. Died 1911.

GRIER, William Moffatt, pres. Erskine Coll., 1871—; b. York Co., S.C., Feb. 11, 1843; grad. Erskine, 1860 (D.D., LL.D.); m. Nannie McNorries, Oct. 25, 1864. Became minister in Associate Reformed Presbyn. church; is prof. mental and moral philosophy in the coll., and prof. pastoral theology and homiletics, Erskine Theol. Sem. Editor The Associate Reformed Presbyterian. Home: Due West, S.C. Died 1899.

GRIERSON, Benjamin Henry, brig. gen.; b. Pittsburgh, July 8, 1826; s. Robert and Mary (Shepard) G.; ed. Youngstown (O.) Acad.; m. Alice Kirk, Sept. 24, 1854 (died 1888); m. 2d, Mrs. Lillian Atwood King, July 28, 1897. Vol. a.d.c. to Gen. Prentiss, May 8, 1861; apptd. maj. 6th Ill. Cav., Oct. 24, 1861; col., Apr. 12, 1862; brig. gen. vols., June 3, 1863; maj. gen. vols., May 27, 1865; hon. mustered out of vol. service, Apr. 30, 1866; col. 10th U.S. Cav., July 28, 1866; brig. gen., Apr. 5, 1890. Bvtd.: maj. gen. vols., Feb. 10, 1865; brig. gen. U.S.A., Mar. 2, 1867, for gallant and meritorious services in raid through Miss. in 1863; maj. gen., Mar. 2, 1867, for same in raid through Miss. and Ala. in 1864. Home: Jacksonville, Ill. Died 1911.

GRIEST, William Walton, congressman; b. Christiana, Pa., Sept. 22, 1859; s. Ellwood and Rebecca (Walton) G.; grad. Millersville (Pa.) State Normal Sch., 1876; m. Elizabeth P. Smith, Oct. 17, 1888; children—Rebecca Walton, George Whittier. Pres. of electric rys. and lighting cos., and interested in other business enterprises. Editor Lancaster Inquirer, 1885-95. Chief clerk co. commr.'s office, Lancaster Co., Pa., 1887-99; sec. Commonwealth of Pa., 1899-1903; mem. 61st to 70th Congresses (1909-29), 10th Pa. Dist. Home: Lancaster, Pa. Died Dec. 5, 1929.

GRIFFIN, Anthony Jerome, congressman; b. N.Y. City, Apr. 1, 1866; s. James A. and Mary Ann (Zeluiff) G.; student Coll. City of New York, 1 yr.; B.S., Cooper Union, 1887; LL.B., from New York U., 1892; m. Katharine L. Byrne, Oct. 23, 1895. Practiced in New York, 1892—; founder, 1906, and editor Bronx Independent; mem. N.Y. Senate 2 terms, 1911-15; mem. State Constl. Conv., 1915; elected mem. 65th Congress, Mar. 5, 1918, to fill vacancy, 22d N.Y. Dist., for term ending 1919; reëlected 66th to 73d Congresses (1919-35). Democrat. Enlisted in 12th Regt., N.G. of New York, 1888; 2d lt., 1892; 1st lt. 69th Regt., 1895; organized Co. F, 69th Inf., N.G.N.Y., 1898, and served as capt. Spanish-Am. War. Author; Speeches and Addresses, 1917; Chaos (dramatic poem, published under nom de plume of "Altair"), 1919; War and Its Aftermath, 1922. Home: New York, N.. Died Jan. 13, 1935.

GRIFFIN, Appleton Prentiss Clark, librarian; b. Wilton, N.H.; s. Moses Porter and Charlotte Helen (Clark) G.; des. of prominent colonial Mass. families; removed in early childhood to Mass.; ed. pub. schs. and by pvt. tutors; m. Emily C. Osgood, Oct. 23, 1878; children—Mary Florence (dec.), George Appleton, Grace Gardner, Thomas Sergeant, Perry. Custodian of shelves, Boston Pub. Library, 1871-90; keeper of books, same, 1890-1904; preparing catalogue of books in Washington collection, Boston Athenæum, 1895-97; asst. librarian, 1897-1900, chief bibliographer, 1900-08, chief asst. librarian, Aug. 14, 1908—, Library of Congress (acting Librarian of Congress, Dec. 1918-Sept. 1919). Author: Discovery of the Mississippi (a bibliog. account), 1883; Index of Articles Upon American Local History in Collections in Boston Public Library, 1889; Index of Literature of American Local History in Collections Published 1890-95, 1896; Bibliography of American Historical Socities, 1905. Home: Washington, D.C. Died Apr. 16, 1926.

GRIFFIN, Daniel J., congressman; b. Brooklyn, Mar. 26, 1880; s. Daniel and Mary (Cleary) G.; St. Laurent Coll., Can.; A.B., St. Peter's Coll., Jersey City, N.J.; studied New York Law Sch.; m. Loretta McParland, Dec. 27, 1910. Admitted to N.Y. bar, 1902; was commr. of licenses, Borough of Brooklyn, later in charge administration and guardianship dept., Surrogate's Ct., County of Kings; mem. 63d and 64th Congresses (1913-17), 8th N.Y. Dist. Democrat. Catholic. Home: Brooklyn, N.Y. Died Dec. 11, 1926.

GRIFFIN, Edward Herrick, univ. dean; b. Williamstown, Mass., Nov. 18, 1843; s. Rev. Nathaniel Herrick and Hannah E. (Bulkley) G.; A.B., Williams, 1862, A.M., 1865; grad. Union Theol. Sem., 1867; D.D., Amherst, 1880; LL.D., Princeton, 1888, Williams, 1905; m. Rebekah Wheeler, May 22, 1872 (died 1906); children—Nathaniel Edward, John Wheeler. Prof. Latin, 1872-81, rhetoric, 1881-86, Mark Hopkins prof. intellectual and moral philosophy, 1886-89, Williams Coll.; prof. history of philosophy and dean coll. faculty, Johns Hopkins, 1889-1915; retired. Died Jan. 23, 1929.

GRIFFIN, Eugene, soldier, elec. engr.; b. Ellsworth, Me., Oct. 13, 1855; s. George K. and Harriet J. G.; grad. West Point, 1875; m. Allie Hancock, April 24, 1889. Served 2d lt., 1st lt. and capt. corps of engrs., 1875-89; resigned Oct. 5, 1889; col. 1st U.S. col. engrs., May 24, 1898; brig. gen. vols., Jan. 21, 1899. In regular army, served on various surveys until 1883; was asst. prof. civil and mil. engring. and the art of war, West Point, 1883-85; a.-d.-c. staff of Maj. Gen. Winfield Scott Hancock, 1885-86; chief engr. div. Atlantic and dept. of the East, 1885-86; asst. engr., commr. Dist. of Columbia, 1886-88; in volunteer service, organized 1st regt. U.S. vols., engrs., serving with it in Puerto Rico., 1898-99. Gen. mgr. ry. dept., and 2d v.p. Thomson-Houston Elec. Co., 1888-91; 1st v.p. Gen. Elec. Co., 1892—; pres. Thomson-Houston Internat. Elec. Co., 1893—; dir. British-Thomson-Houston Co. and of the Cie. Français pour l'Exploitation des Procédés Thomson-Houston, Paris, 1893—. Home: New York, N.. Died 1907.

GRIFFIN, Henry Lyman, clergyman; b. Williamstown, Mass., Dec. 1, 1848; s. Nathaniel Herrick and Hannah E. (Bulkley) G.; A.B., Williams, 1868, A.M., 1871 (D.D., 1905); studied univs. of Berlin, Leipzig and Marburg, German, and Oxford, Eng.; m. Lucy Frances Pickering, Sept. 18, 1884. Ordained Congl. ministry, 1873; pastor South Ch., New Britain, Conn., 1873-77, Hammond St. Ch., Bangor, Me., 1881-1904, Second Ch., Brewer, Me., Sept., 1907—. Lecturer on comparative religion and sec. trustees, Bangor Theol. Sem. Home: Bangor, Me. Died Sept. 27, 1917.

GRIFFIN, John, judge; b. Jersey City, N.J., June 26, 1858; ed. pub. schs.; studied law in office of Bedle, Muirheid & McGee. Admitted to N.J. bar as atty., 1881, counselor, 1884; practiced in Jersey City. Counsel to Bd. of Freeholders of Hudson County many yrs.; v. chancellor of N.J., Mar. 20, 1913—, term expires 1927. Democrat. Home: Jersey City, N.J. Died Jan. 26, 1927.

GRIFFIN, John Joseph, chemist; b. Corning, N.Y., June 24, 1859; s. Jeremiah and Mary G.; A.B., Ottawa (Can.) U., 1881, A.M., 1883; entered Ottawa Diocesan Sem., 1883. Ordained R.C. priest, May 1, 1885; instr. physics, Ottawa U., 1885-86; instr. chemistry, St. Thomas Aquinas Coll., Cambridgeport, Mass., 1886-87; prof. chemistry, Ottawa U., 1887-90; grad. student chemistry, physics and mathematics, Johns Hopkins, 1890-95, Ph.D., 1895, at same time conducting classes in chemistry, St. Joseph's Sem. and Notre Dame of Md.; prof. chemistry, 1895—, dean faculty philosophy, 1903-05, dean faculty science, 1908-11, Catholic U. of America. Home: Washington, D.C. Deceased.

GRIFFIN, Levi Thomas, lawyer, congressman; b. Clinton, N.Y., May 23, 1837; s. Charles Nathaniel and Margery (Thomas) G.; removed with parents to Rochester, Mich., 1848; ed. Rochester Acad. and grad. Univ. of Mich., 1857. Admitted to Mich. bar, 1858; practiced at Detroit until commd. 2d lt. Mich. cav., Dec. 18, 1862; promoted lt. adj. capt., and bvtd. maj. Mar. 13, 1865; returned to Detroit after war and practiced law; Fletcher prof. law, Univ. of Mich., 1886-97; candidate for justice Supreme Court, 1887, defeated; mem. Congress to fill vacancy, Aug. 17, 1893, to Mar. 4, 1895; defeated for re-election. Democrat. Home: Detroit, Mich. Deceased.

GRIFFIN, Martin Ignatius Joseph, editor; b. Phila., Oct. 23, 1842; s. Terrence and Elizabeth (Doyle) G.; ed. pvt. parochial and pub. schs., Phila., 1842-60; m. Mary A. E. MacMullen, Oct. 2, 1870. Editor and pub. Griffin's Journal, 1873, The Am. Catholic Hist. Researches, 1887. Founder Am. Catholic Hist. Soc., Phila.; historian Friendly Sons of St. Patrick, Philadelphia. Home: Philadelphia, Pa. Died 1911.

GRIFFIN, Michael, congressman, lawyer; b. in Ireland, Sept. 9, 1842; emigrated with parents to Canada, 1847; to Ohio, 1851; and to Wis., 1856; resided in Sauk Co. until 1868; then in Kilbourn City, Wis., until 1876, then at Eau Claire; m. Emma I. Daniels, Sept. 6, 1871. In Union army, Sept. 11, 1861, to July 16, 1865, pvt. and lt.; wounded at Atlanta, 1864. Mem. co. bd. of Columbia Co., Wis., 1874-75; mem. assembly, 1876; city atty., Eau Claire, 1878-81; State senator, 1880-81; dept. commander G.A.R., 1887-88; q.m. gen. State of Wis., with rank of brig. gen., 1889-90. Admitted to bar and began practice, 1868. Mem. Congress, 1894-99. Republican. Home: Eau Claire, Wis. Died 1901.

GRIFFIN, Nathaniel Edward, writer; b. Williamstown, Mass., Mar. 5, 1873; s. Edward Herrick and Rebekah (Wheeler) G.; A.B., Johns Hopkins Univ., 1894, Ph.D., 1899; m. Anne Waters McLean, June 5, 1917; children—Nathaniel Edward, Thomas McLean; m. 2d, Mary Anne Dye, Aug 2, 1938. Asst. prof. English, Princeton, 1905-19; edtiorial staff Webster's Dictionary, 1925-27; research under grant from Am. Council Learned Societies. Author: Dares and Dictys—An Introduction to the Study of Medieval Versions of Story of Troy; The Farther Shore (with Lawrence Hunt). Translator: (with A. B. Myrick) Boccaccio's Filostrato and author introd. to same. Home: Cambridge, Mass. Died Aug. 25, 1940.

GRIFFIN, Robert Stanislaus, naval officer; b. Fredericksburg, Va., Sept. 27, 1857; grad. U.S. Naval Acad., 1878; Sc.D., Columbia, 1915; D.Engring., Stevens Inst. Tech. Promoted asst. engr., June 20, 1880; passed asst. engr., Aug. 25, 1889; chief engr., Mar. 1, 1898; transferred to line as lt., Mar. 3, 1899; promoted through grades to rear adml., Aug. 29, 1916. Served on Mayflower, Spanish-Am. War, 1898, on Illinois, 1901-02, Chicago, 1902-03, Iowa, 1903-04; fleet engr. N. Atlantic Fleet, 1904-05; duty Bur. Steam Engring., Navy Dept., 1905-08; asst. to chief same, 1908-13; apptd. engr. in chief and chief Bur. Steam Engring., May 18, 1913, reappointed 1917; retired, Sept. 27, 1921. D.S.M. (U.S.); Comdr. Legion of Honor (France). Home: Washington, D.C. Died Feb. 21, 1933.

GRIFFIN, Simon Goddell, capitalist, soldier; b. Nelson, N.H., Aug. 9, 1824; s. Nathan and Sally (Wright) G.; reared on farm; became teacher; later mem. legislature; admitted to N.H. bar, 1860. Served in Union army from 1st battle of Bull Run to Appomattox, beginning as pvt. and becoming, Apr. 2, 1865, bvt. maj. gen. of vols.; mustered out, Aug. 24, 1865; participated in many heavy battles. After war settled in Keene; served 5 terms in N.H. legislature, 2 terms speaker; for 2 yrs. was comdr. Mass. Commandery Mil. Order Loyal Legion; has large interests in Texas lands and cattle. Home: Keene, N.H. Died 1902.

GRIFFIN, Solomon Bulkley, newspaper editor; b. Williamstown, Mass., Aug. 13, 1852; s. Rev. Nathaniel Herrick and Hannah E. (Bulkley) G.; brother of Edward Herrick and Henry L. G.; mem. class of 1872, Williams (A.M., 1880; L.H.D., 1907; LL.D., Amherst, 1919); m. Ida M. d. John H. Southworth, Springfield, Mass., Nov. 25, 1892. On staff, 1872-78, mng. editor, 1878-1919, Springfield Republican. Pres. Hampshire Paper Co.; v.p. Carew Mfg. Co., S. Hadley Falls, Mass. Alumni trustee Williams College, 1910-20, permanent member, 1920—. Author: People and Politics Observed by a Massachusetts Editor, 1923. Home: Springfield, Mass. Died Dec. 11, 1925.

GRIFFIN, Walter, artist; b. Portland, Me., Jan. 14, 1861; s. Edward Souther and Lydia (Libby) G.; ed. pub. schs., Portland; studied at Boston Mus. of Art, Art Students' League, New York, and Paris, France; pupil of R. Collin and Jean Paul Laurens; unmarried. Landscape painter; lived principally in France, 1887-1915, making occasional visits to U.S.; art instr. and dir. Sch. of Art Soc. of Hartford, Conn., 1898-1907. Medal of honor, San Francisco Expn., 1915; Jennie Sisson gold medal, Pa. Acad. Fine Arts. Represented in Memorial Art Gallery, Rochester, N.Y., Albright Art Gallery, Buffalo, Brooklyn Mus. of Art, Luxembourg Galley (Paris), Imperial Art Mus. in the Khoda bequest, Tokyo, Japan, and in many private collections. N.A.; mem. Nat. Inst. of Arts and Letters. Died May 18, 1935.

GRIFFIS, William Elliot, lecturer, author; b. Phila., Sept. 17, 1843; s. Capt. John Limeburner and Anna Maria (Hess) G.; served with 44th Pa. Regt. in Civil War, 1863; A.M., Rutgers, 1869; grad. Union Theol. Sem., 1877; D.D., Union Coll., 1884; L.H.D., Rutgers Coll., 1899; m. Katharine L. Stanton, June 17, 1879; children—Lillian Eyre, Stanton, (John) Elliot; m. 2d, Frances King, June 28, 1900. Went to Japan, 1870, to organize schools; supt. edn., province of Echizen, 1871; prof. physics, Imperial Univ., Tokio, 1872-74. Pastor First Reformed Ch., Schenectady, N.Y., 1877-86, Shawmut Congl. Ch., Boston, 1886-93, First Congl. Ch., Ithaca, N.Y., 1893-1903; in lit. work and on preaching tours, 1903—. Pres. DeWitt Hist. Soc. of Tompkins Co., N.Y.; mem. Nat. Inst. Arts and Letters. Has collected the money for and reared 17 hist. tablets, 2 in Schenectady, 5 in Ithaca, and 10 in The Netherlands. Mad 11th trip of study and investigation in Europe, 1925. Decorated by the Emperor of Japan, with the 4th Order of the Rising Sun, 1907, and 3d Order of the same, 1926; made 2d journey to Japan, Korea and Manchuria, 1926-27. Author: Brave Little Holland and What She Taught Us, 1894; Romance of Discovery, 1897; Romance of American Colonization, 1898; Romance of Conquest, 1899; The Pilgrims in Their Three Homes, 1898; The Pathfinders of the Revolution, 1900; A Maker of the New Orient, 1902; Mighty England—Our Old Home, 1902; Young People's History of Holland, 1903; China's Story in Myth, Legend, Art and Annals, 1910; Belgium, the Land of Art; A Modern Pioneer in Korea, 1912; Hepburn of Japan, Pioneer of Science and Religion, 1913; The House We Live In—Architect and Tenant, 1914; The Mikado—Institution and Person, 1915; Bonnie Scotland and What We Owe Her, 1916; Dutch Fairy Tales, 1918; Belgian Fairy Tales, 1919; Young People's History of the Pilgrims, 1920; Swiss Fairy Tales, 1920; Welsh Fairy Tales, 1921; Korean Fairy Tales, 1922; Japanese Fairy Tales, 1923; The Story of the Walloons, 1924; An American in the New Italy, 1925; The American Flag of Stripes and Stars, 1926. Editor: Sawyer's History of the Pilgrims and Puritans, 1922; Scheffer's History of the Free Churchmen in Holland, 1922. Home: Pulaski, N.Y. Died Feb. 5, 1928.

GRIFFITH, Benjamin Whitfield, banker; b. Hinds Co., nr. Jackson, Miss., Jan. 3, 1853; s. Richard and Sallie (Whitfield) G.; A.B., Miss. Coll., Clinton, 1872, A.M., 1874, LL.D., 1915; Eastman Business Coll., Poughkeepsie, N.Y., 1872; m. Cora Bertha Griffing, May 7, 1879; children—Richard, David C., B. Whitfield, Cora, Sallie, Walter H., Lucy. Prof. mathematics, Miss. Coll., 1872-74; admitted to bar, 1877; gave up practice and entered Capital State Bank, Jackson, Miss., as bookkeeper, 1878, made cashier, 1884; pres. 1st Nat. Bank, Vicksburg, 1893—; v.p. Savings & Trust Co. Alderman, Jackson, about 1890; elected mayor of Vicksburg on reform ticket, term 1905-09; treas. Warren Co., Miss., 1912-16. Pres. bd. Miss. Coll. Sound Money Democrat. Baptist. Pres. Miss. Bankers' Assn. (sec. 19 yrs.). Mason. Home: Vicksburg, Miss. Died Aug. 18, 1931.

GRIFFITH, Elmer Cummings, coll. prof.; b. Mt. Carroll, Ill., Oct. 16, 1869; s. Hugh J. and Lucy L. (Cummings) G.; A.B., Beloit Coll., Wis., 1895, A.M., 1898; student Oxford U. and U. of Berlin, 1899-1900; Ph.D., U. of Chicago, 1902; m. Martha McMillen, 1903. Prof. history and polit. science, 1902-05; dir. Summer Sch., 1903-05, Yankton (S.D.) Coll.; William Jewell Coll., 1905-18; actg. prof. hist., Brown U., 1918-19; actg. prof. history and head of dept., U. of Cincinnati, 1919-20; prof. economics and business adminstrn, Kalamazoo Coll., 1922—. Economic research investigation for Carnegie Instn., summers 1908, 09; in Europe, summer 1910; lecturer, Kansas City Sch. Social Service, 1914-18, summer session, U. of Mo., 1915, Brown U., 1919, U. of Cincinnati, 1920. Speaker 3d and 4th Liberty Loans. Baptist. Mason. Author: The Practice of Citizenship, 1914. Home: Kalamazoo, Mich. Died Feb. 21, 1928.

GRIFFITH, Frank Carlos, theatrical mgr.; b. Dixfield, Me., Dec. 30, 1851; s. Amos W. and Azubah F. (Stockbridge) G.; ed. Me. and Boston pub. schs.; m. Mary Catherine Lee, May 8, 1884. Acting mgr. Mrs. Langtry in U.S. and Great Britain, 1888, 1889, 1890; mgr. Margaret Mather, 1892; acting mgr. Minnie Maddern Fiske, 1893-1924. Dir. Poland Spring (Me.) Art Exhbn., 12 yrs.; organizer and librarian Poland Spring Library; editor-in-chief, The Hilltop, 12 yrs. A proprietor of the Boston Athenæum. Author: Maine's Hall of Fame; The Man from Maine; Mrs. Fiske, a biog. sketch. Publisher of the Mary Catherine Stories. Retired, 1930. Home: Middleboro, Mass. Died May 8, 1939.

GRIFFITH, George, educator; b. Trenton, N.Y., Sept. 11, 1853; s. Griffith D. and Catharine F. (Dopp) G.; grad. Hamilton Coll., A.B., 1877; Ph.D., in pedagogics, Ill. Wesleyan Univ., 1893; m. Mary C. Hill, Jan. 1880 (dec.); 2d, Elizabeth A. Stacy, July 1886. Teacher and supt. schs. from 1878; supt. schs., Utica, N.Y., 1892—. Pres. N.Y. State Council Supts. of Schs., 1901. Home: Utica, N.Y. Died 1903.

GRIFFITH, Griffith Jenkins, philanthropist; b. Glamorganshire, S. Wales, Jan. 4, 1850; s. Griffith M. and Margaret (Jenkins) G.; came to America, 1865; ed. pub. schs., Ashland and Danville, Pa., and Fowler Inst., New York; m. Miss M. A. C. Mesmer, Jan. 1886. Removed to Calif., 1873; business mgr. Herald Pub. Co., San Francisco, until 1878; mining corr. Alta Californian, San Francisco, during palmy days of Comstock Lode developments in Nev.; later engaged extensively in mining in Mexico. Purchased, 1882, Los Feliz Rancho of 4,074 acres nr. Los Angeles, and acquired extensive realty holdings in the city. Donated, 1896, without restriction, 3,016 acres of his ranch to City of Los Angeles for a pub. park; also presented, 1912, $100,000 for erection of an astronom. obs. on Mt. Hollywood, for free use of public for study and scientific research. Col. Calif. N.G., 1884-88. Republican. Mason. Home: Los Angeles, Calif. Died July 6, 1919.

GRIFFITH, Herbert Eugene, teacher chemistry; b. Titusville, Pa., Jan. 1, 1866; s. Micah H. and Amanda Merry (Studley) G.; B.S., Northwestern U., 1892; post-grad. work, Johns Hopkins, 1896-97; U. of Chicago Summer Sch., 1900; m. Caroline Porter Adams, Dec. 18, 1897. Teacher in pub. schs., Moline, Ill., 1885-87, high sch., 1887-89, 1892-94; teacher high sch., Oak Park, 1894-96; prof. chemistry, Knox Coll., Galesburg, Ill., 1897—, acting dean, 1914-15. Adviser to supt. pub. instrn. and Ill. State Exam. Bd. in the recognition of higher instns. of learning, 1916—. Presbyn. Home: Galesburg, Ill. Deceased.

GRIFFITH, Jefferson Davis, surgeon; b. Jackson, Miss., Feb. 12, 1850; s. Richard and Sallie (Whitfield) G.; ed. Summerville (Miss.) Inst.; M.D., Univ. Med. Coll. (New York U.), 1871; m. Sallie Coningo, Jan. 28, 1880. House surgeon, Bellevue Hosp., New York, 1873; prof. surgery, 1890-1905, dean, 1893-98, Kansas City Med. Coll.; prof. clin. surgery, U. of Kan., 1905—; prof. oral surgery, Kansas City Dental Coll., 1886—; prof. surgery, Kansas City Women's Med. Coll., 1890—; Surgeon-gen. of Mo., 1886-90; maj. surgeon vols., May 20, 1898; chief surgeon, 3d Div., 1st Army Corps; hon. disch., Dec. 2, 1898; retired chief surgeon N.G. Mo., with rank of colonel. Gold Democrat. Episcopalian. Home: Kansas City, Mo. Died Aug. 29, 1924.

GRIFFITH, J(ohn) P. Crozer, M.D.; b. Phila., Jan. 5, 1856; s. Benjamin and Elizabeth (Crozer) G.; A.B., U. of Pa., 1st in class, 1877, M.D., 1881, Ph.D. (1st prize for thesis), 1881; m. Julia E. Jenks, 1882. Instr. clinical medicine, U. of Pa., 1889-96; visiting physician St. Agnes Hosp., 1889, Howard Hosp., 1890; prof. clin. medicine, Phila. Polyclinic, 1891-1906; clin. prof. diseases of children, 1891-1913, prof. pediatrics, 1913—, U. of Pa.; visiting phys. Children's Hosp., 1891—; consulting phys. Women's Hosp., 1896—; consulting pediatrist Abington Memorial, Jewish, Misericordia and Babies Seashore hosps. Editor Proc. of Coll. of Phys. for several yrs. and of Internat. Clinics at its start. President board trustees Baptist Orphanage, Crozer Theological Seminary; chmn. bd. mgrs. Am. Bapt. Publ. Society. Author: The Care of the Baby, 1895; Diseases of Infants and Children, 2 vols., 1919; Diseases of Infants and Children, 1 vol., 1933, revised, 1936. Home: Philadelphia, Pa. Died July 28, 1941.

GRIFFITH, P. Merrill, consul; b. Bellbrook, O., 1872; Ph.B., U. of Chicago. Supt. schs.; admitted to bar; apptd. consul at Matamoros, Mexico, May 31, 1898; consul at Tampico, 1907-10, Pernambuco, Brazil, 1910-15, Santiago de Cuba, 1915-17; v.-consul, Neuvitas, 1917—. Died Dec. 1917.

GRIFFITH, William, editor, author; b. Memphis, Mo., Feb. 15, 1876; s. Samuel P. and Minerva (Downing) G.; pub. sch. edn.; m. Florence Vernon, June 25, 1909. On staffs of New York newspapers, 1901-06; mng. editor Hampton's Mag., 1906-09; editor, dir. and sec. Travel Mag., 1910; editor McCall's

Mag., 1911-12; editor, dir. and treas. National Sunday Mag., 1912-16; editor Current Opinion, 1917-25; editor William H. Wise & Co., 1925-29; editor Forum Press, Inc., 1929; editor The Authors Digest, 1931—. Pres. Poetry Soc. of America, 1929-31. Author: History of Kansas City and the Louisiana Purchase, 1899; Loves and Losses of Pierrot, 1916, revised and completed edit., 1924; Candles in the Sun, 1921; Selected Pierrot Lyrics, 1923. Editor: Life, Meaning, and Messages of Theodore Roosevelt, 1919; Great Painters and Their Famous Bible Pictures, 1925. Asso. editor, with Edwin Markham, of The Book of Poetry, 1926; The Book of Elbert Hubbard, 1934; Bermuda Troubadours, 1934. Editor American Scrap Book and European Scrap Book, 1928-29. Home: New York, N.Y. Died Apr. 1, 1936.

GRIFFITHS, Arthur Floyd, college pres.; b. Richville, N.Y., Sept. 16, 1878; s. Thomas Philip and Mary (Davies) G.; Ph.B., St. Lawrence U., 1897, A.M., 1899 (L.H.D., 1919); A.B., Harvard, 1899; m. Helen Alsy Clemence, June 26, 1901. Prin. Richville Union Sch., N.Y., 1897-98, Shepard Evening Sch., Cambridge, Mass., 1898-99; master St. George's Sch., Newport, R.I., 1899-1902; pres. Oahu Coll., Honolulu, H.T., 1902—. Conglist. Republican. Author of "The Chinese in Hawaii" in "China and the Far East" (Clark U. lectures). Contbg. editor Jour. of Internat. Relations (Clark U. Quar.). Died June 12, 1922.

GRIFFITHS, David, botanist; b. Aberystwith, Wales, Aug. 16, 1867; s. David and Rachel (Lewis) G.; B.S., Agrl. Coll., Brookings, S.D., 1892, M.S., 1893; Ph.D., Columbia, 1900; married; children—Elizabeth L., John D. Prin. or teacher in S.D. schs., 1889-98; prof. botany, U. of Ariz., 1900-01; asst. agrostologist, 1901-07, agriculturist, 1907-18, horticulturist, 1918—, U.S. Dept. Agriculture. Author: Torrey Bot. Club monograph on North Am. Sordariaceæ. Home: Takoma Park, D.C. Died Mar. 1935.

GRIFFITHS, Edwin Stephen, mfr.; b. Wales, Aug. 1872; s. Gwilym and Rachel (Davies) G.; ed. business coll. and corr. sch.; m. Margaret A. Rusk, 1902. In mfg. business, Cleveland, 1900—; pres. Bishop & Babcock Co., 1915-22; pres. Cleveland Machine & Mfg. Co., Buckeye Engine Co.; dir. Guardian Savings & Trust, etc. Republican. Baptist. Mason. Home: Cleveland, O. Died Jan. 20, 1930.

GRIFFITHS, John Lewis, consul-general; b. New York, Oct. 7, 1855; s. David and Elizabeth (Hughes) G.; A.B., State U. of Ia., 1874, LL.B., 1875; m. Caroline Henderson, June 5, 1889. Admitted to bar and engaged in practice at Indianapolis; dir. Security Trust Co. Mem. Ind. Ho. of Rep., 1887; reporter Ind. Supreme Ct., 1889-93; Am. consul at Liverpool, Eng., 1905-09; consul gen. at London, Aug. 1, 1909—. Mem. Indianapolis Bd. Trade. Conglist. Home: Indianapolis, Ind. Died May 17, 1914.

GRIGGS, Chauncey Wright, lumberman; b. Tolland, Conn., Dec. 31, 1832; ed. Monson Acad.; m. Martha Ann Gallup, Apr. 14, 1859. Took charge of a general store, St. Paul, Minn., 1856; served in Civil War, reaching rank of col.; afterward in banking and contracting in Minn. Alderman, St. Paul, 7 terms; mem. Minn. Ho. of Rep., 2 terms, Senate, 3 terms; removed to Tacoma, 1887; pres. The St. Paul & Tacoma Lumber Co., owning large mills and 80,000 acres of fir timber. Democratic caucus candidate for U.S. senator from Wash., 1889 and 1891. Home: Tacoma, Wash. Died 1910.

GRIGGS, Everett Gallup, lumberman; b. Chaska, Minn., Dec. 27, 1868; s. Col. Chauncey W. and Martha A. (Gallup) G.; B.A., Yale, 1890; m. Grace Isabel Wallace, July 6, 1895. With St. Paul & Tacoma Lumber Co., 1892—, pres., 1908-33, chairman of the board, 1933—. Pres. of the National Lumber Mfrs. Assn., 1911-13. Joined Wash. State N.G., 1890; capt., 1892; maj. coast arty. N.G. Wash., 1909-11; maj. U.S. Signal Corps, transferred to A.S.A.P., 1918-19. Home: Tacoma, Wash. Died Mar. 6, 1938.

GRIGGS, James M., congressman, lawyer; b. Lagrange, Ga., Mar. 29, 1861; grad. Peabody Normal Coll., Nashville, Tenn., 1881; m. Theodosia Stewart, July 14, 1886. Taught school and studied law; admitted to bar, 1883; practiced at Alapaha, Ga.; was for short time in newspaper business; removed to Dawson, Ga., 1885; solicitor-gen. (pros. atty.), Pataula jud. circuit, 1888-93; judge same circuit, 1893-96; mem. Congress, 1897-1909, 2d Ga. dist.; chmn. Dem. Congressional com., 1902. Home: Dawson, Ga. Died 1910.

GRIGGS, John William, attorney general; b. Newton, N.J., July 10, 1849; s. Daniel and Emeline (Johnson) G.; A.B., Lafayette Coll., 1868; (LL.D., Princeton Univ. and Rutgers Coll., 1896, Yale Univ., 1899); m. L. Elizabeth Price, Apr. 15, 1893. Admitted to bar, 1871, and since in practice at Paterson, N.J.; mem. N.J. Gen. Assembly, 1876-77, Senate, 1882-88 (pres., 1886); elected gov. of N.J., for term, 1896-99 (1st Rep. gov. in 30 yrs.); resigned Jan. 1898, to become atty. gen. of U.S. in Cabinet of President McKinley; resigned, 1901; mem. Permanent Court of Arbitration at The Hague, 1901-08. Now sr. mem. Griggs, Baldwin & Baldwin, New York. Home: Paterson, N.J. Died Nov. 28, 1927.

GRIGGS, Nathan Kirk, lawyer; b. Frankfort, Ind., Oct. 25, 1844; s. Lucien D. and Mary Townsend (Kirk) G.; common sch. edn.; taught sch. 4 yrs. in Clinton Co., Ind.; LL.B., Ind. U., 1867; m. Epsie E. Saunders, Dec. 21, 1869. Began law practice at Beatrice, Neb., 1867; removed to Lincoln, 1893; atty. for Northwestern div., C.,B.&Q. Ry., 1890—; dir. Columbia Oil Co. (Evanston, Wyo.), Cambria Fuel Co. (Cambria, Wyo.). Mem. Neb. Constl. Conv., 1871; Neb. Senate, 1872-76 (pres. 1875); U.S. consul at Chemnitz, Saxony, 1876-82; repeatedly chmn. Neb. Rep. State convs. Trustee Cotner U., Bethany, Neb. Mem. Disciples of Christ. Home: Lincoln, Neb. Died 1910.

GRIMES, George Simon, brig. gen., U.S.A.; b. in Eng., Feb. 15, 1846. Pvt. Co. G, 116th N.Y. Inf. and sergt. maj. 89th and 93d U.S. Colored Inf., Aug. 16, 1862-Mar. 29, 1865; 2d lt. 81st U.S.C.T., Mar. 30, 1865; 1st lt., Jan. 6, 1866; hon. mustered out of vol. service, Nov. 30, 1866; apptd. from N.Y., 2d lt. 39th Inf., Jan. 22, 1867; 1st lt., July 20, 1868; transferred to 25th Inf., Apr. 20, 1869; assigned to 2d Arty., Dec. 15, 1870; grad. Arty. Sch., 1886; capt., Nov. 20, 1887; maj., Mar. 31, 1899; lt. col. Arty. Corps, Aug. 22, 1901; col., July 19, 1903; brig. gen. and retired at own request, over 40 yrs.' service, Aug. 12, 1907. Died Aug. 9, 1920.

GRIMES, John, bishop; b. Co. Limerick, Ireland, Dec. 18, 1852; s. John and Bridget (Hammond) G.; ed. Nat. Sch. and Jesuits' Coll., Ireland, St. Hyacinth Coll., P.Q., Grand Sem., Montreal. Ordained R.C. ministry, 1882; St. Mary's Syracuse, 1882-87; pastor Whitesboro, N.Y., 1887-90, St. Mary's, Syracuse, 1890—; consecrated coadjutor bishop of Syracuse, N.Y., May 16, 1909, and bishop of Syracuse, Aug. 6, 1912. Died July 26, 1922.

GRIMES, J(ohn) Bryan; b. Raleigh, N.C., June 3, 1868; s. Gen. Bryan (C.S.A.) and Charlotte Emily (Bryan) G.; ed. high sch. and business coll.; U. of N.C., 1882-84; m. Elizabeth Forrest Laughinghouse, Feb. 3, 1904. Associated with brother in farming in several counties of N.C.; sec. of state, N.C., 6 terms, 1900-24. A.-d.-c. staff of Gov. Elias Carr, 1893-96, rank of col. Trustee U. of N.C. (exec. com.); mem. (ex officio) State Bd. Edn. Democrat. Episcopalian. Pres. N.C. Tobacco Growers' Assn.; mem. State Farmers' Alliance, N.C., State Farmers' Union, N.C. Agrl. Soc. (exec. com.). Mason. Author: Notes on Colonial North Carolina, 1700-1750, 1905; also editor and compiler North Carolina Wills and Inventories, etc. Mem. exec. com. N.C. Council of Defense. Pres. Scottish Soc. of America, 1918-19. Home: Raleigh, N.C. Died Jan. 1923.

GRIMKÉ, Archibald Henry, lawyer; b. Charleston, S.C., Aug. 17, 1849; s. Henry and Nancy (Weston) G.; brother of Francis James G.; A.B., Lincoln U., 1870, A.M., 1872; LL.B., Harvard, 1874; m. Sarah E. Stanley, Apr. 19, 1879. Editor the Hub, newspaper, Boston, 1883-85; spl. writer on Boston Herald and Boston Traveler, 1891-92; trustee Westborough Insane Hosp. and sec. of its bd., 1884-94; U.S. consul, Santo Domingo, 1894-98; pres. Am. Negro Acad., 1903-19 (emeritus). Trustee estate of Emmeline Cushing, Boston, for edn. of the colored race; treas. Com. of Twelve, for the advancement of the interests of the colored race. Author: Life of William Lloyd Garrison, 1891; Life of Charles Sumner, 1892. V.p. Nat. Assn. for Advancement of Colored People. Awarded the Spingarn medal for 1919. Home: Washington, D.C. Died Feb. 25, 1930.

GRIMM, Jacob Luther, United Brethren minister; b. Rohrersville, Washington Co., Md., Nov. 27, 1842; s. Rev. Joseph S. G.; ed. public schools and acad. Rohrersville, Md.; taught public schools from 1857-62, and took regular conference course in theology; entered U. B. ministry Jan. 1, 1866; m. Mary E. Harp, Feb. 10, 1870. Became U. B. itinerant minister, 1867; has been presiding elder, Oct. 1, 1897—. Pvt. 11th Md. vol. inf., U.S.A., during Civil War; chaplain dept. Md., G.A.R., 1896; elected chaplain-in-chief, G.A.R., at Nat. Encampment, Phila., Sept. 7, 1899. Republican. Editor Weekly Itinerant, 1887-89; supt. Eastern U. B. Book and Pub. House for 2 yrs.; corr. for Baltimore Daily American religious dept. 10 yrs. Member several gen. bds. of the Ch. of United Brethren in Christ; v.p. U. B. Orphanage and Home. Home: Harrisburg, Pa. Died 1905.

GRIMMELSMAN, Joseph, univ. pres.; b. Cincinnati, Mar. 17, 1853; s. Henry and Joanna (Reuter) G.; ed. St. Xavier Coll., Cincinnati, 1866-71; St. Stanislaus Sem., Florissant, Mo., 1871-74; Woodstock (Md.) Coll., 1874-77; Louvain, Belgium, 1881-86. Ordained priest R.C. Ch., 1884; prof. classics and mathematics, Detroit Coll., 1877-81; prof. philosophy, Woodstock Coll., 1887; prof. classics, and English, St. Stanislaus Sem., 1888; pres. Marquette Coll., Milwaukee, 1889-91, St. Louis U., 1891-98; provincial of Mo. Province, S.J., 1899-1905; pres. St. Stanislau Sem., 1905-08, St. Xavier Coll., 1908-11, Marquette U., 1911-15. Died Dec. 20, 1918.

GRINDALL, Charles Sylvester; b. Baltimore, Md., July 8, 1849; s. John Thomas and Eliza (Armstrong) G.; student St. Mary's Coll., Wilmington, Del., 1863, 64, Loyola Coll., Baltimore, 1865, 67 (M.A., 1896); D.D.S., Baltimore Coll. Dental Surgery, 1872; studied Sch. of Medicine, Univ. of Md.; m. Alverta Caughy, May 19, 1890. Practiced in Baltimore until 1902; trustee Estate of John T. Grindall, 1902—. Mem. bd. dirs. Soc. Cruelty and Immorality of Children of Md. Democrat. Home: Baltimore, Md. Died Feb. 14, 1920.

GRINNELL, Charles Edward, lawyer; b. Baltimore, May 7, 1841; s. Charles Andrews and Anna Almy (Cobb) G.; A.B., Harvard, 1862, A.M., 1865, grad. Div. Sch., 1865, LL.B., 1876; also studied div. at Yale, 1862-64, and U. of Göttinger, 1865-66; m. Elizabeth Tucker Washburn, July 11, 1865. Admitted to bar, 1876; a master in chancery, 1878-1913. Editor Am. Law Review, 1881-82 and 1907-09. Harvard Chapter. Author: A Study of the Poor Debtor Law of Massachusetts and Some Details of Its Practice, 1883; Points in Pleading and Practice Under the Massachusetts Practice Act, 1889; Subsequent Payments Under Resulting Trusts, 1887; Modern Murder Trials and Newspapers, 1901. Home: Boston, Mass. Died Feb. 2, 1916.

GRINNELL, Elizabeth, author, naturalist; b. Thorndyke, Me., May 9, 1851; d. Joseph H. and Martha E. (Hanson) Pratt; ed. Friends' Sch., Providence, R.I.; m. Dr. Fordyce Grinnell, 1874 (dec.), govt. phys. to plains Indians nr. Ft. Sill, I.T., and Sioux Indians, Dak.; children—Joseph, Fordyce, Elizabeth. Spent 10 yrs. with husband among Indians; studied birds with son, Joseph; her home at Pasadena, Calif., known as "the birds' retreat." Is interested in finding homes for orphan children. Author: How John and I Brought Up the Child, 1894; Our Feathered Friends (with Joseph Grinnell), 1898. Home: Sausalito, Calif. Died July 6, 1935.

GRINNELL, Frederick, mech. engr., inventor; b. New Bedford, Mass., Aug. 14, 1836; s. Lawrence and Rebecca S. G.; prep. edn. Friends' Acad., New Bedford; grad. Rensselaer Poly. Inst., Troy, 1855, as civ. and mech. engr.; m. Mary B. Page, Feb. 17, 1874. Was successively supt. Corliss Steam-engine Works, Providence; mgr. Jersey City Locomotive Works; supt. motive power Atlantic & Great Western R.R.; from 1869, pres., mgr. and mech. engr. Providence Steam and Gas Pipe Co. Introduced and has done much to perfect automatic fire exteinguisher and alarm, taking out about 40 patents in connection with it. Home: New Bedford, Mass. Died 1905.

GRINNELL, George Bird, editor, author, explorer; b. Brooklyn, Sept. 20, 1849; s. George Blake and Helen (Lansing) G.; A.B., Yale, 1870, Ph.D., 1880, Litt.D., 1921; m. Elizabeth Curtis Williams, Aug. 21, 1902. Six months in unmapped West, 1870; in business in New York, 1871-74; asst. in osteology, Peabody Mus., Yale, 1874-80; naturalist with Gen. Custer's expdn. to Black Hills, 1874, and with Col. William Ludlow's reconnaissance to Yellowstone Park, 1875; an editor Forest and Stream, 1876-1911; pres. Forest and Stream Pub. Co., 1880-1911, Bosworth Machine Co., 1887—, dir., 1886; member of Harriman Alaska Expedition, 1899. Member board of trustees, N.Y. Zoölogical Soc.; trustee and sec. Hispanic Society America. Commissioner to treat with Blackfoot and Ft. Belknap Indians, 1895. Awarded Roosevelt gold medal of honor, 1925. Mem. advisory bd. Federal Migratory Bird Law; student of N. Am. ethnology. Fellow of American Ornithologists Union; also member of National Parks Association (president). Author: Pawnee Hero Stories and Folk Tales, 1889; Blackfoot Lodge Tales, 1892; The Story of the Indian, 1895; Jack, the Young Ranchman, 1899; Jack Among the Indians, 1900; Jack in the Rockies, 1904; Jack, the Young Canoeman, 1906; Jack, the Young Trapper, 1907; Jack, the Young Explorer, 1908; Trails of the Pathfinders, 1911; The Indians of Today (to 1910), 1911; Jack, the Young Cowboy, 1913; Beyond the Old Frontier, 1913; Blackfeet Indian Stories, 1913; The Fighting Cheyennes, 1915; When Buffalo Ran, 1920; The Cheyenne Indians (2 vols.), 1923; Bent's Old Fort and Its Builders, 1923; By Cheyenne Campfires, 1926; Two Great Scouts, 1929. Also co-editor: American Big Game Hunting, 1893; Hunting in Many Lands, 1895; Trail and Campfire, 1897; Harper's Camping and Scouting, 1911. Editor: American Big Game in Its Haunts, 1904; Hunting at High Altitudes, 1913; Hunting and Conservation, 1925; Hunting Trails on Three Continents, 1933. Home: New York, N.Y. Died Apr. 11, 1938.

GRINNELL, Joseph, univ. prof., mus. dir.; b. Old Ft. Sill, Okla., Feb. 27, 1877; s. Fordyce and Elizabeth (Pratt) G.; A.B., Throop Poly. Inst., 1897; A.M., Stanford U., 1901, Ph.D., 1913; m. Hilda Wood, June 22, 1906; children—Willard Fordyce, Mary Elizabeth, Stuart Wood, Richard Austin. Asst. instr., Throop Poly. Inst., 1897-98; asst. in embryology, 1900, instr. ornithology, 1901-02, Hopkins Lab., Stanford U.; instr. High Sch., Palo Alto, 1901-03; instr., 1903-05, prof. biology, 1905-08, Throop Poly. Inst.; dir. Calif. Mus. Vertebrate Zoölogy, U.

of Calif., 1908—; asst. prof. zoölogy, 1913-17, asso. prof., 1917-20, prof., 1920—, U. of Calif. Editor The Condor. Fellow Am. Ornithologists' Union, Calif. Acad. Sciences, Am. Acad. Arts and Sciences. Home: Berkeley, Calif. Died May 29, 1939.

GRINNELL, Morton, physician, farmer; b. New York, Jan. 3, 1855; s. George B. and Helen Alvord (Lansing) G.; grad. A.B., Yale, 1875, Bellevue Hosp. Med. Coll., M.D., 1880; m. Jane Stanford Catherwood, Oct. 5, 1897. Practiced medicine in New York; house surgeon Bellevue Hosp., 1881, Munich and Göttingen, 1881-82; physician to Demilt and New York dispensaries; demonstrator of anatomy and asst. to chair of surgery, Bellevue Hosp. Med. Coll.; surgeon to out-door poor; surgeon to New York police dept., 1887-93; farmer, 1898—. Republican. Home: Milford, Conn. Died 1905.

GRINNELL, William Morton, lawyer; b. New York, Feb. 28, 1857; s. William F. and Mary (Morton) G.; ed. Anthon's and Mohegan Lake schs., Harvard Univ., Stuttgart (Germany), Univ. of France, grad. Bachelier-ès-lettres and Bachelier-en-droit; grad. Columbia Coll. Law Sch., LL.B., 1881; m. Elizabeth Lee Ernst, Dec. 8, 1898. Practiced law in Paris, France, as counsel to U.S. Legation, 1881-86; in New York, 1886-92; 3d asst. sec. of state of U.S., 1892-93; partner in banking house of Morton, Bliss & Co., 1893-1900, when firm became a trust co. under name of Morton Trust Co., resumed practice of law, acting as atty. for the co., the Mt. Morris Bank, etc., and still engaged in practice of law. Maj. U.S.V., in Spanish-Am. War, on staff Gen. Poland, 1st div., 2d army corps. Chevalier de la Légion d'Honneur, France, 1890. Dir. Illinois Central R.R. Co., Rio Grande & Sierra Madre R.R. Co., Loup Creek Coal Co., Mt. Morris Bank. Episcopalian. Republican. Home: New York, N.Y. Died 1906.

GRISCOM, Clement Acton, financier; b. Phila., Mar. 15, 1841; s. Dr. John D. and Margaret (Acton) G.; acad. edn.; m. Frances Canby Biddle, June 18, 1862; father of Clement Acton, Jr., and Lloyd Carpenter G. Became clerk, 1857, and partner, 1863, in business of Peter Wright & Sons, shipping mchts.; v.p. 1871-88, pres. 1888-1904. Internat. Navigation Co.; co. bought out the Inman Line, changing it to The Am. Line; also owns practically entire stock of Red Star Line, a Belgian corp., Internat. Navigation Co., Ltd., of Liverpool, Eng., and Empire Transportation Co., Seattle. In Sept. 1902, name of Internat. Navigation Co. was changed to Internat. Mercantile Marine Co. and capital increased to acquire fleets and businesses of the White Star Line, Atlantic Transport Line, Leland Line and Dominion Line; retired as pres. Internat. Mercantile Marine Co., Feb. 1904, and was elected chmn. of bd. Home: Haverford, Pa. Died Nov. 10, 1912.

GRISCOM, Clement Acton, financier; b. Philadelphia, June 20, 1868; s. Clement Acton and Frances Canby (Biddle) G.; bro. of Lloyd Carpenter G.; ed. Geneva, Switzerland, Frankfort-on-Main, Germany, and U. of Pa.; grad. (4th in class) Wharton Sch. of Political Economy, U. of Pa., 1887; m. Genevieve Sprigg, d. Gen. William Ludlow, U.S.A., of New York, Sept. 18, 1889. Supervisor Internat. Navigation Co., 1892, mgr., 1894—; gen. mgr. Internat. Mercantile Marine Co. until April 1904; pres. Griscom-Russell Co., Audiffren Refrigerating Machine Co. Mem. Chamber of Commerce, New York Produce Exchange. Home: New York, N.Y. Died Dec. 30, 1918.

GRISMER, Joseph Rhode, actor, manager; b. Albany, N.Y., Nov. 4, 1849; s. Valentine and Adelaide (Huba) G.; pub. sch., acad. and bus. coll. edn.; m. Phoebe Davies, June 7, 1882 (died 1912). Enlisted in 192d Regt. N.Y. Vols., Dec., 1864; hon. disch. as corporal, Sept. 15, 1865. First appearance on stage in Trimble Opera House, Albany, N.Y., 1871; continued as leading man and later as star until 1898; began playwriting, 1884, and as mgr., 1885; toured as joint star with wife for many yrs.; retired, 1910. Catholic. Vice-pres. Actors' Fund of America. Author (plays): The New South (with Clay M. Greene), 1892; Way Down East (re-wrote), 1898; The Manicure Girls (adapted from the French), 1899; The Gentleman from Mississippi. Home: Larchmont, N.Y. Died Mar. 3, 1922.

GRISWOLD, Augustus H., telegraph official; b. Milo, Ill., Sept. 29, 1879; s. Augustus Root and Mary (Swarthout) G.; B.S. in E.E., U. of Ill., 1901; m. Edna E. Holmes, Sept. 30, 1907; children—Janet Carter, Augustus Root. Engr. with Western Electric Co., Chicago, 1901-05; plant engr. Pacific Telephone & Telegraph Co., 1905-17; asst. chief engr. Internat. Western Electric Co., New York, 1920; asst. v.p. Am. Telephone & Telegraph Co., New York, 1921-24; v.p. Southern Calif. Telephone Co., 1924, Pacific Telephone & Telegraph Co., 1925-28; exec. v.p. Postal Telegraph and Cable Corp. and v.p. Internat. Telephone and Telegraph Corp., 1928-35; exec. v.p. Postal Telegraph and Cable Corp., 1935-38; v.p. Internat. Telephone and Telegraph Corp., 1938—. Commd. maj. Signal O.R.C., June 1917, and apptd. comdr. 411th Telegraph Battery, U.S. Army; went overseas, January 1918; apptd. dir. telephone and telegraph services, A.E.F., May 1918, in charge constrn., installation operation and maintenance of all signal corps lines of A.E.F. in Europe; lt. col., Sept. 1918; apptd. mem. Signal Corps Bd. of Adjustments, Nov. 1918, having disposition of all signal corps property in Europe; returned to U.S., Feb. 1919; hon. discharged, Mar. 4, 1919; returned to France as chmn. Am. Engring. Commn., to assist French in restoring communication in devastated areas. Cited by Gen. Pershing "for exceptionally meritorious service"; decorated Legion of Honor (French). Republican. Protestant. Home: New York, N.Y. Died Feb. 24, 1940.

GRISWOLD, Casimir Clayton, artist; b. Delaware, O., 1834; studied wood engraving in Cincinnati; removed to New York, 1850; received some instruction in painting from a brother, and in 1857 exhibited his first picture at Nat. Acad. Design. Splty. landscapes and coast scenes; lived in Rome, Italy, 1872-86. A.N.A., 1866, N.A., 1867; one of the original mems. of the Artists' Fund Soc., 1859. Home: Poughkeepsie, N.Y. Died June 7, 1918.

GRISWOLD, Edith Julia, patent lawyer; b. Windsor, Conn., Feb. 12, 1863; d. Thomas Newell and Cornelia Stanley (Babcock) Griswold; grad. Normal Coll., New York, 1883; pvt. studies in civ. and mech. engring., 1884-86, 2-yr. course in electricity, Normal Coll. and pvt. instrn. studied in patent law office and a few months in New York U. Law Sch.; unmarried. Taught geometry and algebra in pvt. sch., New York, winter 1885-86; opened an office as mech. draftsman, 1886; connected with patent law firm of Howson & Howson, first as draftsman and later as mng. clerk, 1887-97; admitted to N.Y. bar, June 28, 1898, to U.S. Circuit courts, July 1, 1901; practicing law and soliciting patents, 1898—; from 1901 chiefly occupied as expert in patent suits. Mem. Internat. Jury of Awards, Machinery Dept., St. Louis Expn., 1904. Home: Hastings-on-Hudson, N.Y. Deceased.

GRISWOLD, F(rank) Gray, merchant; b. N.Y. City, Dec. 21, 1854; s. George and Lydia (Alley) G.; grad. Handelschule, Dresden, Germany, 1875; studied later France and Germany; m. Josephine Houghteling, July 29, 1907. Agt. for P. Lorillard & Co., New York, 1879-93. Mem. bd. dirs. Met. Opera Co. Republican. Episcopalian. Author: Sport on Land and Water, 7 vols., 1913-23; Some Fish and Some Fishing, 1921; Fish Facts and Fancies, 1923; Race Horses and Racing, 1925; Horses and Hounds, 1927; Clipper Ships and Yachts, 1927; A Salmon River, 1928; International Polo Cup, 1929; French Wines and Havana Cigars, 1929; Old Madeiras, 1930; El Greco, 1930; Life of the Salmon (with R. D. Hunt), 1930; Memoirs of a Salmon, 1931; The Gourmet, 1933; Fra Filippo Luppi, 1934. Home: New York, N.Y. Died Mar. 30, 1937.

GRISWOLD, Glenn, congressman; b. New Haven, Mo., Jan. 20, 1890; s. Sylvanus C. (M.D.) and Annie Louise (Hasenfratz) G.; ed. pub. schs.; m. Edith Connally, Nov. 27, 1913. Admitted to bar of State of Indiana, 1917; began the practice of law at Peru, Ind.; served as city atty., Peru, 1921-25; pros. atty. Miami Co., Ind., 1925-26; elected to Congress, 1930; served as mem. 72d Congress (1931-33), 11th Ind. Dist., and 73d to 75th Congresses (1933-39), 5th Ind. Dist. Democrat. Home: Peru, Ind. Died December 5, 1940.

GRISWOLD, Hattie Tyng, author; b. Boston, Jan. 26, 1840; d. Rev. Dudley and Sarah (Haynes) Tyng; family removed to Wis., 1850; ed. by father; m. Eugene Sherwood Griswold, Feb. 18, 1863. Author: Apple Blossoms (poems), 1878; Home Life of Great Authors, 1887; Waiting on Destiny, 1889; Lucile and Her Friends, 1890; Fencing with Shadows, 1892; Personal Sketches of Recent Authors, 1899. Home: Columbus, Wis. Died 1909.

GRISWOLD, Latta, clergyman, author; b. Lancaster, O., Feb. 4, 1876; s. Samuel G. V. and Katharine (Latta) G.; B.A., Princeton, 1901, M.A., 1902; Princeton Theol. Sem., 1902-04; Gen. Theol. Sem., New York, 1905; unmarried. Deacon, 1905, priest, 1905. P.E. Ch.; asst. Trinity Ch., Newport, R.I., 1905-06; vicar St. Columba's Ch., Newport, 1906-15; master St. George's Sch., Newport, 1906-15; asst. Trinity Parish, New York, 1915-17; rector Trinity Ch., Lenox, Mass., 1917—. Author: Deering of Deal, 1912; Deering at Princeton, 1913; The Winds of Deal, 1914; Deal Woods, 1915; The Episcopal Church—Its Teaching and Worship, 1916; The Tides of Deal, 1921; Values of Catholic Faith, 1926; The Middle Way, 1928; The Teaching of the Prayer Book, 1929. Home: Lenox, Mass. Died Aug. 16, 1931.

GRISWOLD, Sheldon Munson, bishop; b. Delhi, N.Y., Jan. 8, 1861; s. Walter Hanford and Ann Elizabeth (Betts) G.; A.B., Union Coll., 1882, A.M., 1885; grad. Gen. Theol. Sem., 1885; D.D., Union, 1900, Gen. Theol. Sem., 1903; m. Kate Maxwell van der Bogert, Oct. 7, 1885. Deacon and priest P.E. Ch., 1885; rector Ilion, N.Y., 1885-88, Little Falls, N.Y., 1888-90, Hudson N.Y., 1890-1902; elected, Oct. 23, 1902, consecrated, Jan. 8, 1903, missionary bishop of Salina; suffragan bishop of Chicago, Jan. 8, 1917, bishop, Feb. 1930. Home: Evanston, Ill. Died Nov. 28, 1930.

GRISWOLD, Stephen Benham, librarian; b. Vernon, N.Y., July 14, 1835; s. Martin and Hannah (Smith) G.; acad. edn.; LL.B., Albany Law Sch., 1860; admitted to bar, 1860; m. Angeline E. Cornwell, Nov. 7, 1860. Librarian N.Y. State Law Library, 1868-1904; mem. faculty Albany Law Sch., 1899-1909. Home: Yonkers, N.Y. Died May 4, 1912.

GRISWOLD, William McCrillis, indexer and reviewer; b. Bangor, Me., Oct. 9, 1853; grad. Exeter Acad., 1871, Harvard, 1875; m. Anne D. Merrill, Sept. 14, 1882. Compiler of numerous indexes. Editor Passages from the Correspondence of R. W. Griswold. Home: Cambridge, Mass. Died 1899.

GROESBECK, Stephen Walley, army officer; b. Albany, N.Y., Nov. 26, 1840; s. Garrett E. and Elsie (Walley) G.; ed. commercial Sch., Albany, N.Y., and Mil. Sch., Phila.; m. Alice W. Thomas, Apr. 12, 1887. Enlisted 4th Ia. cav. vols., Oct. 28, 1861; mustered in as q.m. sergt., Jan. 1, 1862; apptd. 2d lt., Oct. 5, 1862; totally disabled by lodging of rifle ball in left foot, in battle Nov. 8, 1862; resigned Apr. 4, 1863; upon recovery accepted apptmt. as 2d lt., Vet. reserve corps, Sept. 16, 1864; served as such in South during reconstruction period; read law and later was admitted to bar. Apptd. 2d lt. 42d Inf., Jan. 15, 1867; transferred to 6th Inf., Apr. 22, 1869; adj. 6th Inf., 1875-80; acting judge advocate, Dept. of Mo., 1881-82; again adj. 6th Inf., 1883-86; acting judge advocate, Dept. Dakota, 1886-91; apptd. maj. judge advocate, Mar. 23, 1892; lt. col., Feb. 2, 1901; col., May 24, 1901; judge advocate 5th Army Corps during campaign against Santiago de Cuba, 1898, and of Div. of the Philippines, 1900-02. Apptd. brig. gen., U.S.A., Apr. 16, 1903; retired from active service, Apr. 17, 1903. Died 1904.

GROFF, George G., physician; b. Chester Valley, Pa., Apr. 5, 1851; s. John and Susan (Beaver) G.; M.D., L.I. Coll. Hosp., 1877; B.S., Pa. State Coll., 1897; (hon. LL.D., Judson Coll., N.C., 1887; Ph.D., Franklin and Marshall, 1898; Sc.D., Susquehanna U., 1902); m. Margaret Pusey Marshall, Apr. 14, 1880. Taught in pub. schs. 3 yrs., State Normal Sch. 2 yrs.; sch. dir. 8 yrs.; prof. anatomy, Bucknell U., 1879—. Mem. State Bd. Health, 1885-99, State Bd. Agr. 10 yrs., State Med. Council, 1 yr.; surgeon N.G. Pa. 3 yrs.; organized sanitary work at Johnstown after the flood of 1889. Maj. and brigade surgeon Spanish-Am. War, 1898-99. After war in P.R. as commr. Nat. Relief Commn.; dir. of vaccination (790,000 persons were vaccinated in 3 months); sec. and treas. Superior Bd. of Health. Insane Asylum, Leper Hosp.; pres. Insular Bd. Edn.; supt. pub. instrn.; acting commr. of edn.; mem. Exec. Council, P.R. Republican. Home: Lewisburg, Pa. Died 1910.

GROMER, Samuel David, univ. prof.; b. McFall, Mo., Sept. 8, 1865; s. Isaac and Mahala (Newby) G.; S.B., Pe.B., U. of Mo., 1889; studied U. of Chicago, 1896, Chautauqua Coll. Liberal Arts, 1897-98; A.M., Harvard, 1905; studied Columbia, 1905-06; LL.D., U. of Porto Rico, 1913; m. Mary Patton, June 1893 (died 1919); m. 2d, Helen Mueller, July 20, 1922; dau., Helen Jane Samuel. State inst. conductor, S.D., 1890-91; teacher of history, polit. science and economics, Stanberry (Mo.) Normal, 1891-96, 1897-1904; commr. of schs. Gentry Co., Mo., 1893-97; teacher of history, Coll. City of New York, 1906; teacher of history and economics, U. of Mo., 1906-07; treas. and mem. Exec. Council, Porto Rico, July 1, 1907-12; pres. P.R. Senate, Mar. 1910-12. Chmn. finance com.; mem. franchise com.; chmn. Insular Bd. of Agr. Mem. Mo. Rep. State Com., 1903-07 (exec. com., 1905-07); actg. pres. bd. trustees U. of P.R. Teacher rural economics, 1913-26, prof. agrl. economics, 1926—, U. of Mo.; studied in Oxford U., 1920; studied in U. of London. Author of Chapter 3, The Farmer and His Money, in Ency. of Farm Knowledge, 1918. Home: Columbia, Mo. Died Aug. 26, 1928.

GRONDAHL, Jens Kristian, newspaper editor; b. Eidsvold, Norway, Dec. 3, 1869; s. Lars and Inger Margrethe (Julsrud) G.; ed. in Norway, pub. schs. of Red Wing, Minn., and grad. Red Wing Sem.; attended U. of Minn.; m. Ottonie Gulbrandson, Jan. 11, 1911. Connected with Red Wing Daily Republican, 1892—; now editor same; pres., mgr. Red Wing Printing Co. Mem. Minn. Ho. of Rep., 1895-99. Successfully sponsored laws to abolish convict contract labor at Minn. State Prison; modernized bldgs. and care for chronic insane; revamped laws for juvenile reform schs. creating state agency and merit system, later copied by other states; refused free ry. passes resulting in state and nat. law prohibiting same. Republican. Pres. Minn. Rep. Editorial Assn. Has written numerous poems, sketches and songs, including "Fighting for Cuba," widely circulated during war with Spain. Active in promoting cost systems and better methods among printers and publishers. President Red Wing Commercial Club. Author: "The Madness of the Monarchs," a poem which has appeared in numerous publications; also anthem, "America, My Country," selected for nat. community singing, and adopted for schs. by edn. depts. of several states. Invented submarine detector, commended by Naval Consulting Bd. Selected del. to Press Congress of World, held at Honolulu, H.T., 1921, by Nat. Editorial Assn. Declined candidacy for gov. of Minn., 1924. Inventor of system for producing literature for blind and electrical devices for reading same; inventor of contrivance which converts any telephone into an automatic firealarm station; etc. Home: Red Wing, Minn. Died 1941.

GRONLUND, Laurence, author-correspondent; b. in Denmark, July 13, 1846; grad. U. of Copenhagen, 1865 (A.M.); lecturer on social topics; m. Dec. 24, 1895. Author: The Co-operative Commonwealth; Ca Ira, or Danton in the French Revolution; Our Destiny; Socialism and the Single Tax; The New Economy; etc. Died 1899.

GRONNA, Asle J., senator; b. Elkader, Ia., Dec. 10, 1853; reared on farm and ed. schs. of Huston Co., Minn., and Caledonia Acad.; removed to S.D., 1879; m. Bertha M. Ostby, Aug. 31, 1884. Extensively engaged in farming and banking. Mem. Territorial Legislature, 1889; pres. bd. trustees and bd. edn., Lakota, N.D., several terms; chmn. co. central com., Nelson Co., 1902-06; mem. 59th to 61st Congresses (1905-11), N.D. at-large; elected U.S. senator, Jan. 1911, for unexpired term (1911-15), of Martin N. Johnson, deceased; reëlected for term 1915-21. Republican. Regent U. of N.D. Home: Lakota, N.D. Died May 4, 1922.

GRONWALL, Thomas Hakon, cons. mathematician; b. Axberg, Sweden, Jan. 16, 1877; s. Carl T. G.; student U. of Upsala and U. of Stockholm, Ph.D., Upsala, 1898; C.E., U. of Berlin, 1902. Asst. in mathematics, U. of Stockholm, 1897; practiced civ. engring., 1902-13; instr. mathematics, Princeton, 1913-14, asst. prof., 1914-15; math. expert. Ordnance Dept., U.S.A., 1918-22; cons. mathematician, 1922—. Naturalized citizen of U.S., 1922. Editor Annals of Mathematics, 1913—. Died 1933.

GROSE, Howard Benjamin, clergyman; b. Millerton, N.Y., Sept. 5, 1851; s. Rev. Henry Laurenz and Emma Louisa (Seward) G.; prep. edn. old U. of Chicago; A.B., U. of Rochester, 1876, A.M., 1880; D.D., Brown Univ., Providence, R.I., 1907; m. Caroline Bristol, Aug. 13, 1877; children—Howard Bristol, Laurence Rich, Margaret Bristol. Ordained Bapt. ministry, 1883; pastor First Ch., Poughkeepsie, N.Y., 1883-87, First Ch., Pittsburgh, Pa., 1888-90; pres. State U. of S.D., 1890-92; recorder and asst. prof. history, U. of Chicago, 1892-96; asso. editor The Watchman, Boston, 1896-1900; editorial sec. Am. Baptist Home Mission Society, 1904-10, editor of Missions, 1910-33; retired as editor emeritus for life. Honorary vice-pres. for life, Internat. Society C.E., 1935; v.p. bd. trustees Federal Council Chs. of Christ in America, 1917-21; chief religious press section U.S. Food Administration, 1917. Author: Aliens or Americans?, 1906; The Incoming Millions, 1906; Advance in the Antilles, 1910; Never Man So Spake, 1924; George Edwin Horr, a Biography, 1928. Editor-in-chief, A Library of Knowledge, 1914. Died May 19, 1939.

GROSS, A(lbert) Haller, lawyer; b. Louisville, Ky., Mar. 18, 1844; s. Samuel D. (M.D., D.C.L., Oxon., LL.D., Cantab., Edin., Jefferson Med. Coll., Univ. of Pa.) and Louisa Ann Dulany (Weissell) studied U. of Va. 1 yr.; A.B., U. of Pa., 1864, A.M., 1867; m. Julia, d. John C. Bullitt, Mar. 9, 1896. Appointed U.S. attorney for New Mexico, 1869, but resigned because of ill health; declined position of deputy atty. gen. of Pa., 1871; apptd. U.S. consul at Athens, Greece, 1885, but declined; mem. Select Council, Phila., 1882-85; declined several nominations to city and co. offices, though taking active interest in municipal affairs. Democrat. Home: Langhorne, Pa. Died Oct. 28, 1918.

GROSS, Charles, prof. history, Harvard; b. Troy, N.Y., Feb. 10, 1857; s. Louis and Lottie (Wolf) G.; grad. Williams, 1878, A.M., 1882; Ph.D., Göttingen, 1883; (A.M., Harvard, 1901; LL.D., Williams, 1904); m. Annie Smith, July 15, 1889. In lit. work in England, 1884-88; instr. at Harvard, 1888—. Author: Bibliography of British Municipal History, 1897; Sources and Literature of English History, 1900. Translator: Lavisse's Political History of Europe, 1891; Kayserling's Christopher Columbus, 1893. Home: Cambridge, Mass. Died 1909.

GROSS, Charles Edward, lawyer; b. Hartford, Conn., Aug. 18, 1847; s. Mason and Cornelia (Barnard) G.; B.A., Yale, 1869, M.A., 1872; admitted to bar, 1872; m. Ellen C. Spencer, Oct. 5, 1875. Admitted to firm of Waldo, Hubbard & Hyde, 1877, succeeded by Hubbard, Hyde & Gross, Hyde, Gross & Hyde, Hyde & Shipman, and later firm of Gross, Gross & Hyde. Pres. Holyoke Water Power Co., 1898-1922; dir. and counsel Ætna Ins. Co., Phœnix Mut. Life Ins. Co., and First Reinsurance Co. (all of Hartford). Hon. mem. Conn. Medical Soc. Pres. Wadsworth Athenæum. Home: Hartford, Conn. Died Dec. 31, 1924.

GROSS, Christian (Canning), diplomatic service; b. Chicago, Ill., Oct. 9, 1895; s. Charles William and Natali (Watkins) G.; B.S., U. of Ill., 1916; studied law in Paris and Algeria; m. Virginia Randolph Harrison, Jan. 28, 1922; children—Peter Christian Channing, Barbara. Served as lt. inf., U.S.A., in France and Siberia, World War; hon. disch. as capt. (temp.), Aug. 1921. Apptd. 3d sec. Am. Embassy, Paris, Dec. 1923; chargé d'affaires of U.S. to Republic of Hayti, Oct. 1926—. Decorated D.S.C. (U.S.); Mil. Cross (British); Croix de Guerre (French). Episcopalian. Author: (under name of Fairfax Channing) Siberia's Untouched Treasure, 1923. Home: Washington, D.C. Died Mar. 26, 1933.

GROSS, Harold Judson; b. Providence, R.I., Apr. 15, 1866; s. John Mason and Elizabeth Harriet (Judson) G.; ed. high sch.; m. Mary Louise Colt, Jan. 17, 1907. Began in ins. and real estate business with bro. George L., 1888; now mem. G. L. & H. J. Gross; v.p. Union Trust Co., Maiden Lane Realty Co.; mem. bd. dirs. and exec. com. Industrial Trust Co. Aide on staff of Gov. Gregory, 1900; col. 1st Light Inf. Regt. 6 yrs.; police commr., Providence, 1904-10; lt. gov. R.I., 1920-22. Republican candidate for gov., 1922. Trustee Homeo. Hosp. of R.I. Episcopalian. Mason. Home: Providence, R.I. Died Apr. 3, 1927.

GROSS, Joseph Leonard, clergyman; b. Warren (now McDuffie) Co., Ga., June 22, 1862; s. William Munn and Sarah Anne Blanchard (Harrison) G.; A.B., U. of Ga., 1885, B.L., 1885; D.D., Baylor U., 1912; m. Ella Vann Turner, Feb. 11, 1892; children—Bayard Turner, Mary Frederica, Joseph Leonard, Luseale, William Victor, Sarah Lucy. Practiced law at Warrenton and Cedartown, Ga., to 1893; ordained Bapt. ministry, 1893; pastor Washington, Ga., 1893-99, 1st Ch., Griffin, 1899-1902, 1st Ch., Selma, Ala., 1902-05, Houston, Tex., 1905-17; enlistment sec. of Tex. Bapt. Gen. Conv., Dallas, Tex., 1917-21; pastor First Ch., Brownsville, Tex., 1921-22, Wornall Rd. Ch., Kansas City, Mo., 1922-23, Bales Av. Ch., 1923-25; field rep. Southern Bapt. Theol. Sem., 1925-26. Mem. bd. dirs. Tex. Bapt. Gen. Convention, Bapt. Edn. Bd. of Tex., Crittenton Home, Houston, Tex.; pres. bd. Star of Hope Mission, Bapt. Sanitarium and Hosp., Houston; v.p. Southern Bapt. Conv., 1915. Democrat. Home: Houston, Tex. Died Feb. 7, 1928.

GROSSCUP, Benjamin Sidney, lawyer; b. Ashland, O., Oct. 14, 1858; s. Benjamin and Susan (Bauermeister) G.; A.B., Wittenberg Coll., Springfield, O., 1879, hon. A.M.; m. Rebecca May Goucher, Jan. 15, 1884; children—Thaddeus Goucher, Benjamin Charles. Admitted to Ohio bar, 1884, and began practice at Ashland; practiced at Tacoma, Wash., 1890-1918, Seattle, 1918—; mem. Grosscup & Morrow, 1908—. Republican. Mason. Home: Seattle, Wash. Died Jan. 4, 1935.

GROSSCUP, Peter Stenger, judge; b. Ashland, O., Feb. 15, 1852; s. Benjamin and Susannah (Bowermaster) G.; A.B., Wittenberg Coll., 1872; LL.B., Boston Law Sch., 1874; m. Virginia Taylor. Admitted to bar, 1874; practiced law at Ashland, O., 1874-83 (city solicitor 6 yrs.); at Chicago, 1882-92; U.S. dist. judge, Northern Dist. of Ill., 1892-99; judge U.S. Circuit Ct. of Appeals, 7th Circuit, 1899-1905; presiding judge Mar. 1905-Oct. 23, 1911, resigned. Pres. John Crerar Library, Chicago, 1901—. Among his notable judicial acts are included his opinion (dissenting from the two circuit judges, but sustained by Circuit Ct. of Appeals) upon the application to close the World's Columbian Expn. on Sundays; also the injunction issued by him in conjunction with Judge Wm. A. Woods against Eugene V. Debs and other officers of the Am. Ry. Union, and subsequent proc. in that matter; the Standard Oil Case, etc. Home: Highland Park, Ill. Died Oct. 1, 1921.

GROSSMANN, Louis, rabbi; b. Vienna, Austria, Feb. 24, 1863; s. Rabbi Ignatz and Nettie (Rosenbaum) G.; ed. Vienna until 1874; B.A., U. of Cincinnati, 1884; grad. Hebrew Union Coll., rabbi, 1884; D.D., 1889, Dr. Hebrew Law, 1922; unmarried. Rabbi Temple Beth El, Detroit, 1884-98, Congregation B'nai Yeshurun, Cincinnati, 1898-1922, emeritus. Prof. ethics, theology and pedagogy, Hebrew Union Coll., 1898-1922; prof. emeritus, founder and prin. Teachers Coll. (training Jewish teachers), Cincinnati, 1909—; editorial writer The American Israelite. Pres. Jewish Religious Edn. Assn. Ohio, Rabbinical Assn. Ohio; pres. Central Conf. Am. Rabbis; founder and hon. pres. Western Assn. of Jewish Ministers, 1924. Lewissohn lecturer, 1918, on Jewish ethics. Author: Judaism and the Science of Religion, 1888; Maimonides, 1890; Responses, Psalms and Hymns, Detroit, 1895; The Jewish Pulpit, 1895; Biography of Isaac M. Wise, 1854-1900, in "Collected Writings of Isaac M. Wise," Cincinnati, 1900; Order of Service of Sabbath Schools, 1909; The Real Life, 1914; Glimpses into Life, New York, 1922; The Aims of Teaching in Jewish Schools; Work for Teachers in Jewish Schools; Order of Service for the Day of the New Year and the Day of Atonement, 1918; The Jewish Pulpit, 1919-21; Glimpses into Life, 1922. Died Sept. 21, 1926.

GROSSMANN, Rudolph, rabbi; b. Vienna, Austria, July 24, 1867; s. Rabbi Ignatz and Nettie (Rosenbaum) G.; B.L., McMicken U., Cincinnati, 1889; grad. Hebrew Union Coll., Cincinnati, 1889, D.D., 1894; m. Martha Keller, Jan. 11, 1892; children—Mrs. Justus Grun, Mrs. David Vorhaus, Mrs. Arthur Kitsheimer. Rabbi of Temple Rodeph Sholom, New York, 1897—. Grand chaplain of Masonic Order, N.Y.; pres. Jewish Religious Sch. Union, N.Y. Bd. of Jewish Ministers; v.p. N.Y. Assn. of Reform Rabbis; mem. Commn. of Jewish Religious Literature. Home: New York, N.Y. Died Sept. 22, 1927.

GROSVENOR, Charles Henry, congressman; b. Pomfret, Conn., Sept. 20, 1833; s. Maj. Peter and Ann (Chase) G.; went to Ohio, May 1838; attended country log schoolhouse; taught sch.; studied law; admitted to bar, 1857; engaged in practice; m. Samantha Stewart, 1858 (died); m. 2d, Louise H. Currier, 1865. Enlisted as pvt. 18th Ohio Inf., Aug. 1861; maj., Sept, 25, 1861; lt. col., June 9, 1863; col., Apr. 19, 1865; bvtd. col. and brig. gen. vols., Mar. 13, 1865, for gallant and meritorious services during the war; hon. mustered out, Oct. 9, 1865. Mem. Ohio Ho. of Rep., 1874-78 (speaker, 1876-78); presdl. elector, 1872, 1880; trustee Ohio Soldiers' and Sailors' Orphans' Home, Xenia, 1880-88 (pres. 1883-88); mem. 49th to 51st (1885-91) and 53d to 59th (1893-1907) Congresses, 11th Ohio Dist. Home: Athens, O. Died Oct. 30, 1917.

GROSVENOR, Edwin Augustus, educator, author; b. Newburyport, Mass., Aug. 30, 1845; s. Dr. Edwin Prescott and Harriet (Sanborne) G.; A.B., Amherst, 1867, A.M., 1871; grad. Andover Theol. Sem., 1872; LL.D., Wabash, 1903, Alfred, 1904, Marietta, 1910, Coll. of William and Mary, 1913; Litt.D., Amherst, 1914; m. Lillian H. Waters, Oct. 23, 1873; children—Gilbert, Hovey, Edwin Prescott, Asa Waters, Harriet Sanborne. Prof. of history, Robert Coll., Constantinople, Turkey, 1873-90; prof. European history, 1892-98, modern governments and their administration, 1898-1901, modern government and internat. law, Amherst, 1901-14. Prof. history, Smith Coll., 1892-94. Traveled in Europe and Asia; lecturer on hist. and diplomatic subjects. Author: The Hippodrome of Constantinople, 1889; Constantinople (2 vols.), 1895, 1900; The Permanence of the Greek Type, 1897; Contemporary History, 1899; The Races of Europe, 1919; etc. Editor Reference History of the World, in Webster's Internat. Dictionary, 1909. Home: Amherst, Mass. Died Sept. 15, 1936.

GROSVENOR, Edwin Prescott, lawyer; b. Constantinople, Turkey, Oct. 28, 1875; s. Edwin Augustus and Lillian Hovey (Waters) G.; twin brother of Gilbert Hovey G.; prep. dept. Robert Coll., Constantinople, 1884-90; Worcester Acad., 1891-93; A.B., magna cum laude, Amherst, 1897, A.M., 1900; LL.B., Columbia U. of Law Sch., 1904; m. Thelma Cudlipp, Oct. 26, 1918; children—Anne Somerville, Louise Taft. Master Latin and Greek languages, Chestnut Hill Acad., Phila., 1899-1900; admitted N.Y. bar, 1903; jr. counsel for U.S. Govt. in investigation and prosecution of Tobacco Trust, 1907-11; as spl. U.S. atty. won only criminal convictions secured against Ky. "night-riders," 1910; spl. counsel for U.S. in prosecuting window glass trust and enameled ware ("bath tub") trust, 1910-12; spl. asst. to atty. gen. at Washington, in a number of other cases relating to enforcement of anti-trust and interstate commerce laws, 1911-13; was spl. counsel for the U.S., in charge of suits brought under the anti-trust law against Internat. Harvester Co. ("harvester trust") and the Motion Picture Patents Co. and General Film Co. ("motion picture trust"), 1913-15; successfully defended Fur Dressers and Fur Dyers Assn., 1925, against govt. under Sherman Act, decision establishing for first time principle that members of a trade assn. may agree to refuse credit to delinquent customers. Mem. Cadwalader, Wickersham & Taft, New York, 1914—. Treas. Nat. Com. on Prisons and Prison Labor. Asso. mem. Legal Advisory Bd. of N.Y. City, under Selective Service Act, 1917-18. Commd. capt. U.S.A., Mil. Intelligence Div., Sept. 3, 1918; discharged Jan. 31, 1919. Homes: New York, N.Y., and Washington, Conn. Died Feb. 28, 1930.

GROSVENOR, Lemuel Conant, physician; b. Paxton, Mass., Mar. 22, 1833; s. Silas Newton and Mary (Conant) G.; ed. Williston Sem., Easthampton, Mass., High Sch., Worcester, Mass.; 7 yrs. master Mather School, Dorchester (the oldest free sch. in U.S.); M.D., Cleveland (O.) Homœ. Med. Coll., 1864; m. Ellen M. Prouty, Feb. 27, 1865 (died 1874); m. 2d, N. Josephine Basset, June 25, 1877. Practiced, Peoria, Ill., 1864-68, Galesburg, Ill., 1868-70, Chicago, 1870-1907, retired. Lecturer on anatomy and morbid anatomy, 1871-72, emeritus prof. obstetrics, 1899, Hahnemann Med. Coll.; prof. obstetrics, and sanitary science, Chicago Homœo. Coll., 1873-99. Home: Taunton, Mass. Died July 15, 1914.

GROSVENOR, William Mercer, clergyman; b. New London, Conn., June 22, 1863; s. Samuel Howe and Maria Stryker (Mercer) G.; A.B., Williams, 1885;

grad. Berkeley Div. Sch., Middletown, Conn., 1888; (D.D., New York U., Williams, 1905); unmarried. Deacon, 1888, priest, 1889, P.E. Ch.; asst. Grace Ch., Brooklyn, 1888-90; rector Trinity Ch., Lenox, Mass., 1890-95, Ch. of the Incarnation, New York, 1895-1911; dean Cathedral of St. John the Divine, 1911—. Deputy to Gen. Conv., P.E. Ch. Trustee Williams Coll., Barnard Coll., Gen. Theol. Sem., Berkeley Div. Sch., Cathedral of St. John the Divine, etc. Home: New York, N.Y. Died Dec. 9, 1916.

GROSZMANN, Maximilian Paul Eugen, educator; b. Brieg, Germany, June 29, 1855; s. Heinrich (M.D.) and Henriette (Bechler) G.; Gymnasium of St. Elizabeth, Breslau; Städtisches Gymnasium, Ohlau; U. of Greifswald, 1875-76; came to America, 1876; Pd.D., New York U., 1893; m. Clara Sickert, May 1875 (died 1900); m. 2d, Mary Scott Emmons, June 12, 1905. In Milwaukee, 1876-90; removed to New York, 1890; in charge of Workingmen's Sch. (now Ethical Culture Sch.), 1890-97; resigned on account of failure of health, and removed to farm in Va., where founded Groszmann Sch., for atypical children, 1900; removed to New York, 1901; located at Plainfield, N.J., 1904; founder, ednl. dir. and trustee Nat. Assn. for Study and Edn. of Exceptional Children; ednl. consultant and lecturer. Chmn. Com. on Pedagogical Research in Visual Education. Author: Education of Individual Children, 1912; The Exceptional Child, 1917. Was head of German dept., foreign press bur. of Com. on Pub. Information; lecturer Am. Friends of German Democracy and League to Enforce Peace. Home: Plainfield, N.J. Died Oct. 3, 1922.

GROTON, William Mansfield, theologian; b. Waldoboro, Me., Nov. 28, 1850; s. James Randall and Helen May (Richmond) G.; A.B., Harvard, 1873; grad. Phila. Div. Sch., 1876; (S.T.D., U. of Pa., 1903); m. Hannah Babcock, Jan. 21, 1883. Deacon, 1876, priest, 1877, P.E. Ch.; rector St. Anne's Ch., S. Lincoln, Mass., 1876-78, Trinity Ch., St. Stephen, N.B., Can., 1878-81, Christ Ch., Westerly, R.I., 1881-98; prof. systematic div., 1898—, dean, 1900—, Div. Sch. of P.E. Ch., Phila. Deputy to Gen. Conv., 1895, 98, and 1907—; mem. standing com. Diocese Pa., 1904-07; lecturer on Bohlen Foundation, Phila., 1912. Editor: Sunday School Teachers Manual, 1909 (2d edit. 1911). Home: Philadelphia, Pa. Died May 25, 1915.

GROUT, Edward Marshall, lawyer; b. New York, Oct. 27, 1861; s. Edward and Fanny (Marshall) G.; A.B., Colgate U., 1884 (LL.D., 1902); admitted to bar, 1885; m. Ida L. Loeschigk, June 4, 1889. Dem. candidate for mayor of Brooklyn, 1895; pres. Borough of Brooklyn, N.Y. City, 1897-1901; comptroller of New York, 2 terms, 1901-05; candidate for Dem. nomination for gov. N.Y., 1904; judge-advocate and maj. 2d Brigade, N.G.S.N.Y., 1894-1904; active in urging consolidation of New York and Brooklyn from 1893-98; conducted contests in courts against gratuitous gifts of st. ry. franchises in Brooklyn, 1892-95. Mem. Corp. Colgate U., 1895—. Home: Brooklyn, N.Y. Died Nov. 9, 1931.

GROUT, Josiah, governor; b. Compton, Que., Can. (of Am. parents), May 28, 1841; s. Josiah and Sophronia (Ayer) G.; ed. St. Johnsbury and Glover acads.; (LL.D., Univ. of Vt. and Norwich U., 1896); pvt. to capt. 1st Vt. Cav., 1861-63; maj. 26th N.Y. Cav., 1864-65; m. Harriet Hinman, Oct. 1868. Admitted to bar, 1865; practiced in Vt., 1865-75, in Ill., 1875-81; farmer, Newport, Vt., 1881-1917; in law practice at Newport, 1905-12. Mem. Vt. House of Representatives, 1872, 74, 84, 86, 88, 1904 (speaker, 1874, 86, 88), Senate, 1892; gov. of Vt., 1896-98; elected by the largest party vote of any governor of the state. Republican. Pres. trustees Derby (Vt.) Acad., 1880. V.p. Orleans Co. Memorial Hosp. Assn., Inc. Home: Newport, Vt. Died July 19, 1925.

GROUT, Lewis, clergyman, author; b. Newfane, Vt., Jan. 28, 1815; s. John and Azuba (Dunklee) G.; grad. Yale, 1842; studied theology Yale Divinity Sch., 1844-45; grad. Andover Theol. Sem., 1846; m. Lydia Bates, Oct. 8, 1846. Ordained on the day of his marriage, Congl. ministry, and sailed 2 days later as missionary to S. Africa, reaching Natal, Feb. 15, 1847; labored among the Zulus, 1847-62; made exhaustive study of Zulu and other African tongues; pastor Congl. Ch., Saxton's River, Vt., 1862-63, Feeding Hills, Mass., 1863-65; sec. and agt. for N.H. and Vt. of Am. Missionary Assn., 1865-84; spent a yr., 1884-85, collecting funds for Atlanta Univ.; pastor Sudbury, Vt., 1885-88; engaged in philol., hist. and other lit. pursuits, 1858—. Author: Translations of Psalms, Acts and Other Portions of the Bible into the Zulu Language, 1857; Zulu-Land, 1864. Home: W. Brattleboro, Vt. Died 1905.

GROUT, William Wallace, congressman, lawyer; b. Compton, Quebec, of Am. parents, May 24, 1836; s. Josiah and Sophronia (Ayer) G.; academic edn.; grad. Poughkeepsie Law School, 1857; LL.D., Norwich Univ., 1897; admitted to bar, 1857; engaged in practice; served as lt. col., 15th Vt. vols., in Union army, and brig. gen., Vt. militia, at time of St. Albans raid, 1864; State's atty., 1865-66; mem. Vt. Ho. of Reps., 1868, 1869, 1870 and 1874; was mem. and pres. pro tem. of Vt. senate, 1876; mem. Congress, 1881-83, and 1885-1901, 2d Vt. dist.; chmn. Com. on Dist. of Columbia in 51st Congress, and mem. Com. on Appropriations. Republican. Chmn. Com. on Expenditures of War Dept., 55th Congress. Home: Barton, Vt. Died 1902.

GROVER, La Fayette, senator; b. Bethel, Me., Nov. 29, 1823; s. Dr. John and Fanny (Leary) G.; ed. Gould's Acad., Me.; 2 yrs. at Bowdoin; (hon. A.M., Del. State Coll., 1854); m. Elizabeth, d. Thomas Carter, of Portland, Ore., Jan. 5, 1865. Admitted to Phila. bar, 1850; settled in practice at Salem, Ore., 1851; pros. atty., 2d Jud. Dist., and auditor pub. accounts, 1852; mem. Ore. Ho. of Rep., 1853-55, and (speaker) 1856 and 1886-87; served Indian wars, 1853 and 1855-56; U.S. commr. to audit Spoliation Claims of Indian wars, 1854-55, and Indian war expenses of 1855-56; mem. Ore. Constl. Conv., 1857; mem. 35th Congress (1857-59); chmn. Dem. State Central Com., 1866-70; gov. of Ore., 1870-77; U.S. senator, 1877-83. Home: Portland, Ore. Died 1911.

GROVER, Oliver Dennett, artist; b. Earlville, Ill., 1861; s. Alonzo Jackson and Octavia E. (Norton) G.; student U. of Chicago, 1877-79; studied painting Royal Acad., Munich, 1879-80, Duveneck Sch., Florence, Italy, 1880-84, Paris, 1884-86; m. Louise Rolshoven, 1887. Received first Yerkes prize for painting "Thy Will Be Done," Chicago, 1892; executed mural decorations Branford (Conn.) Memorial Library, 1897, Blackstone Memorial Library, Chicago, 1903. Has pictures in many pub. collections; silver and bronze medals, St. Louis Expn., 1904; Kahn prize, Chicago, 1913; Fine Arts Bldg. prize, 1906, 1914; silver medal, Panama P.I. Expn., San Francisco, 1915; gold medal, Art Inst. Chicago, 1918. A.N.A., 1913. Studio: Chicago, Ill. Died Feb. 14, 1927.

GROW, Galusha Aaron, congressman, lawyer; b. Ashford (now Eastford), Conn., Aug. 31, 1822; moved to Susquehanna Co., Pa., 1834; grad. Amherst, 1844; admitted to bar, 1847; mem. Congress, 1851-63 (first 6 yrs. as Free Soil Democrat; last 6 yrs. as Republican); speaker 37th Congress, July 4, 1861, to Mar. 3, 1863; pres. Internat. & Great Northern R.R., Tex., 1871-76; declined tender of mission to Russia, 1879; again mem. Congress (from Pa. at large) 1894-1903. Republican. Chmn. Com. on Edn., 54th, 55th, 56th and 57th Congresses. Home: Glenwood, Pa. Died 1907.

GROWOLL, Adolf, mng. editor The Publishers' Weekly; b. New York, 1850. Author: The Bookseller's Library and How to Use It, 1891; The Profession of Bookselling: Handbook of Practical Hints for the Apprentice and Bookseller (2 vols.), 1893, 1895; Publishers' and other Book Exhibits at the World's Columbian Exposition, 1893; American Book Clubs, Their Beginnings and History and a Bibliography of their Publications, 1897; Book-trade Bibliography in the United States in the XIXth Century, 1898; The Booksellers League—a History of Its Formation and Ten Years of Its Work, 1905. Died 1909.

GROZIER, Edwin Atkins, editor; b. San Francisco, Sept. 12, 1859; s. Joshua Freeman and Mary Louise (Given) G.; student Brown U., 1878-79; Ph.B., Boston U., 1881; m. Alice G. Goodell, Nov. 26, 1885. Reporter Boston Globe, Herald, 1881-83; pvt. sec. to gov. of Mass., 1884-85, to Joseph Pulitzer, of New York World, 1885-86; city editor World, 1887; editor Evening World, 1889, Sunday World, 1889-91; editor, publisher and chief propr. Boston Post, 1891—. Home: Cambridge, Mass. Died May 9, 1924.

GRUBB, Ignatius Cooper, judge; b. Grubbs Landing, Del., Apr. 12, 1841; s. Wellington and Caroline (Allmand) G.; has resided in Wilmington, Del., 1849—; classical edn.; LL.D., 1922; admitted to Del. bar, 1862; unmarried. Clerk Del. Ho. of Rep., 1867; deputy atty. gen., 1869; city solicitor, Wilmington, 1871; sec. of state, Del., 1875-79. Mem. Dem. Nat. Com., 1880-88; asso. justice Ct. of Appeals of Del., 1886-97; declined office of chief justice of Del., 1893; asso. judge-at-large, Supreme Ct. of Del., 1897-1909; retired, June 15, 1909. Pres. Hist. Soc. of Del., 1909—. Home: Wilmington, Del. Deceased.

GRUBB, William Irwin, judge; b. Cincinnati, Mar. 8, 1862; s. John and Sidney (Irwin) G.; A.B., Yale, 1883; m. Alice C. Vigo, June 18, 1906; children—Katharine, Archibald Irwin, William Irwin. Admitted to bar, 1884, practiced at Cincinnati and Birmingham, 1884-1909; U.S. Dist. judge, Northern Dist. of Ala., May 1909—. Mem. President Hoover's Law Enforcement Com. Democrat. Home: Birmingham, Ala. Died Oct. 27, 1935.

GRUENER, Gustav, univ. prof.; b. New Haven, Conn., Mar. 30, 1863; s. Leopold and Katharine (Kern) G.; A.B., Yale, 1884, Ph.D., 1896; Litt.D., Washington Coll., 1909; unmarried. Instructor German, Yale, 1885-87; studied abroad, 1887-89; tutor, German, 1889-92, asst. prof., 1892-97, prof. 1897—, Yale. Has edited school textbooks and contributed articles on German lit. to tech. jours. Home: New Haven, Conn. Died Dec. 5, 1928.

GRUHL, Edwin, pub. utilities; b. Milwaukee, Wis., Nov. 13, 1886; s. Fred J. and Emma (Shroeder) G.; A.B., U. of Wis., 1908; m. Helen E. Way, Mar. 26, 1924. Mem. staff joint engring. dept., Wis. State Railroad and Tax Commns., 1907-08; statistician in charge statis. and research depts., Wis. State R.R. Commn., 1909; spl. lecturer in economics, U. of Wis., 1911-12; asst. to v.p. The North American Co., 1912-14, asst. to pres., 1914-20, v.p., 1920, gen. mgr., mem. exec. com. and dir., 1921—; pres., v.p. or dir. many subsidiary and affiliated cos. Home: New York, N.Y. Died Jan. 21, 1933.

GRUNERT, Francis Eugene, clergyman; b. Salem, N.C., Jan. 31, 1859; s. Maximilian Eugene and Emma Theresa (Pfohl) G.; A.B., Moravian Coll., and Theol. Sem., Bethlehem, Pa., 1878, B.D., 1880; m. Gertrude Caroline Smyth, Aug. 26, 1884; children—James Ernest, Gertrude Frances (wife of Rev. George Fernando Weinland). Ordained deacon Moravian Ch., 1884, presbyter, 1888; pastor Grace Hill, Ia., 1884-87, West Salem, Ill., 1887-90, Castleton Corners, N.Y., 1890-1901, Lebanon, Pa., 1901-04, New Dorp, N.Y., 1904-16; principal and treas. Nazareth (Pa.) Hall Mil. Acad., 1916-18; pastor Brooklyn, N.Y., 1918—. Mem. of executive board Eastern District Northern Province Moravian Ch. in America, 1895-1917; sec. com. for preparation of new hymn book for Moravian Ch., 1914—; rep. of Moravian Ch. on Comity Com. of Greater N.Y. Fedn. of Churches, 1930—; pres. Moravian City Union of New York, 1919-33, v.p. 1933—. Trustee Moravian Sem. and Coll. for Women, Bethlehem, Pa. Republican. Home: New Dorp, N.Y. Deceased.

GRUNSKY, Carl Ewald, civil engr.; b. San Joaquin Co., Calif., Apr. 4, 1855; s. Carl Albert Leopold and Clotilde Josephine Frederica (Camerer) G.; grad. Realschule, Stuttgart, Germany, 1872-74; Polytechnikum, Stuttgart, 1874-77, grad., 1877, Dr. Ing., 1910; D.Eng., Rensselaer Poly. Inst., 1924; m. Mattie Kate Powers, Mar. 12, 1884 (died 1921); children—Carl Ewald, Kate Louise (Mrs. B. Grant Taylor), Eugene Lucius, Clotilde. First work as topographer with river surveying party of State Engring. Dept. of Calif., 1878; asst. and chief asst. state engr. of Calif., 1879-88; in pvt. practice, largely in irrigation work, sewerage and drainage, 1887-99, located at Sacramento and San Francisco; at work on river rectification and drainage problems as mem. Examining Commn. on Rivers and Harbors of Calif., 1889-90, and as cons. engr. to commr. of public works of Calif., 1893-94; mem. San Francisco Sewerage Commn., 1892-93; city engr., San Francisco, 1900-04; mem. Isthmian Canal Commn., 1904-05; cons. engr. U.S. Reclamation Service, 1905-07; in pvt. practice as cons. engr., New York and San Francisco, 1907-09; at San Francisco, 1910—; now sr. mem. C. E. Grunsky Co. and acting dir. Calif. Acad. of Sciences. Author: Valuation, Depreciation and the Rate-Base (with son), 1916; Topographic Stadia Surveying, 1917; Public Utility Rate Fixing, 1918; Ways to National Prosperity, 1929. Home: Berkeley, Calif. Died Jan. 9, 1934.

GRUPPE, Charles Paul, artist; b. Picton, Can., Sept. 3, 1860; s. Henry G.; studied art in Holland; m. Helen E. Mitchell, 1889; children—Paulo M., Karl H., Emil A., Virginia H. Represented in Library, Rouen, France, St. Louis Mus., Brooklyn Mus., Md. Inst., Baltimore, and in numerous pvt. galleries. Gold medals: Rouen, Exhbn. Paris et Province, Phila. Art Club, Phila. Art Soc.; 2 silver medals World's Fair, St. Louis, 1904; bronze medal, Knoxville, Tenn.; $500 landscape prize, Osborn Co., N.Y.; Tuthill prize, Art Inst. Chicago. Home: New York, N.Y. Died Sept. 30, 1940.

GUDE, Ove, diplomat; b. Jarlsberg, Norway, Sept. 11, 1853; s. Prof. Hans Frederik and Betsy (Anker) G.; ed. Nissen's Latin High School, Christiania, 1865-70; Candidatus Juris (LL.B.), Royal Frederiks U., Christiania, 1876; m. Lilly Ridley Egeberg, of Christiania, Sept. 11, 1879 (died 1900); 2d, Elna de Stiernholm, of Copenhagen, 1904. Apptd. attaché Swedish-Norwegian legation, Paris, 1877; sec. foreign office, Stockholm, 1879-84; 1st sec. Swedish-Norwegian Legation, Berlin, 1884-91; 1st sec. same, London, 1891-97; sent to China and Japan on spl. mission as minister plenipotentiary, 1897; E.E. and M.P., Madrid, Spain, 1897-1902, Copenhagen, 1902-05; gave in his demission at the separation of Sweden and Norway, 1905; E.E. and M.P. of Norway to U.S., Apr. 1, 1908—. Comdr. 1st class, Order of St. Olof, Great Cross of Order of Danebrog, of Isabella Catolica, The Conception, The Holy Treasure, The Double Dragon, The North Star; comdr. 2d class, Order of Albrecht; chevalier Order of the Red Eagle, The Crown, Charles the Third, Fahringer Lion; bearer of the Norwegian and Spanish Crowning medals. Died 1910.

GUDEMAN, Edward, chemist; b. N.Y. City, Jan. 25, 1865; s. Moritz T. and Clara (Alexander) G.; Ph.B., Columbia, 1887; post-grad. study Columbia and univs. of Berlin and Göttingen, Germany; Ph.D., Columbia, 1889; m. Clara E. Asher, Sept. 14, 1894; children—Richard M., Edward. Prof. chemistry and dyeing, Pa. Mus. and Sch. of Industrial Art, 1889;

instr. chemistry, Columbia, 1890-91; chemist and supt. for sugar, starch and glucose manufactories, 1891-1900; in Chicago, 1898—; pvt. practice as consulting chemist, chem. engr. and legal scientific expert, 1900—. Republican. Jewish religion. Home: Chicago, Ill. Died 1932.

GUDGER, Hezekiah A., judge; b. Marshall, N.C., May 27, 1850; s. Joseph Jackson and Sarah Emaline (Barnard) G.; ed. Leicester Acad. and Weaverville Coll., Buncombe Co., N.C., to 1870 (A.M.); grad. Bailey's Law Sch., Asheville, N.C., 1871; m. Jennie Hardy Smith, Aug. 10, 1875. Engaged in practice of law at Asheville, N.C., from 1871; elected to N.C. Legislature, 1872 and 1874; prin. N.C. Instn. for Edn. of the Deaf, Dumb and Blind, 1877-83; resigned to reënter practice of law, Jan. 1883. Elected to N.C. Senate, 1885; candidate for elector from N.C. at-large on McKinley ticket, 1896; Am. consul gen. to Panama, 1897-1905; justice Supreme Ct., Canal Zone, Panama, 1905-14, chief justice, 1909-14; resumed practice at Asheville. Mem. sch. bd. of Asheville several yrs. and trustee of U. of N.C. before going to Panama. Republican. Methodist. Mason. Home: Asheville, N.C. Died Sept. 22, 1917.

GUE, Benjamin F., journalist; b. Greene Co., N.Y., Dec. 25, 1828; s. John and Catherine (Gurney) G.; ed. pub. schs. and Canandaigua and Bloomfield acads., N.Y.; m. Elizabeth Parker, Nov. 12, 1855. One of founders Republican party; elected to Iowa legislature, 1858; served 4 yrs. in house, and also in senate; elected lt. gov. 1865; U.S. pension agt. for Iowa and Neb. 8 yrs.; editor of North West, Iowa Homestead, and State Journal newspapers 13 yrs. One of founders State Coll. of Agr.; one of founders Pioneer Law-makers' Assn. of Iowa. Home: Des Moines, Iowa. Died 1904.

GUENTHER, Francis Luther, brig. gen.; b. Buffalo, Feb. 22, 1838; s. Rev. Francis Henry and Katharine (Knouts) G.; apptd. from N.Y., and grad. U.S. Mil. Acad., 1859; unmarried. Bvtd. 2d lt. 1st Arty., July 1, 1859; 2d lt. 4th Arty., Nov. 2, 1859; 1st lt. 5th Arty., May 14, 1861; capt., July 2, 1863; maj. 2d Arty., June 26, 1882; lt. col. 5th Arty., July 1, 1891; col. 4th Arty., June 6, 1896; brig. gen. vols., May 4, 1898, to Oct. 31, 1898; brig. gen. U.S.A., Feb. 13, 1902. Bvtd.: capt., Apr. 7, 1862, for gallant and meritorious services at battle of Shiloh; maj., Dec. 31, 1862, for same at Stone River; lt. col. and col., Mar. 13, 1865, for same during the war. In Civil War served in W.Va. and in Army of the Ohio and Army of the Cumberland; took part in many battles, including Greenbrier, Virginia, Pittsburgh Landing, Shiloh, Corinth, Stone River, Tullahoma, Chattanooga, etc.; retired Feb. 22, 1902. Died Dec. 5, 1918.

GUENTHER, Richard, consul general; b. Potsdam, Prussia, Nov. 30, 1845. Came to U.S., 1866; broker drugs and chemicals, New York, 1866-67; settled in Oshkosh, Wis., 1867; engaged in business as pharmacist; mem. sch. bd. several terms; state treas. Wis., 1878-82; mem. 47th to 50th Congresses (1881-89); Am. consul gen. to City of Mexico, 1890-93; mem. State Bd. of Control, Wis., 1895-99 (pres. of bd., 1898-99); Am. consul gen. at Frankfort-on-the-Main, Germany, 1898-1910, at Cape Town, S. Africa, May 4, 1910—. Republican. Home: Oshkosh, Wis. Died Apr. 5, 1913.

GUERBER, Hélène Adeline, author; ed. abroad. Editor of French and German textbooks. Author: Myths of Greece and Rome; Myths of Northern Lands; Legends of the Middle Ages; Legends of the Rhine; Legends of Switzerland; Legends of the Virgin and Christ; Stories of the Wagner Operas; Stories of Famous Operas; Story of the Chosen People; Story of the Greeks; Story of the Romans; Story of the English; Story of the Thirteen Colonies; Story of the Great Republic; Empresses of France; Contes et Légendes (French reader); Märchen und Erzählungen (German reader); Yourself and Your House Wonderful; Stories of Popular Operas; Cupid and Psyche; How to Prepare for Europe; Prisoners of the Temple; Easy French Composition; Story of Old France; Story of Modern France; Stories of Shakespeare's Comedies; Stories of Shakespeare's Tragedies; Stories of Shakespeare's English History Plays; The Book of the Epic; Joan of Arc, French Composition, 1910; Marie Louise et el Duc de Reichstadt; Moni der Geisbub, German text; La Main Malheureuse, French text; Story of Our Civilization. Home: Upper Montclair, N.J. Died June 3, 1929.

GUERLAC, Othan Goepp, univ. prof.; b. of French Alsatian parentage, St. Louis, Oct. 4, 1870; s. Geoffroi and Amélie (Tafel) G.; raised and ed., France; served in French army; M.A., U. of Paris, 1893, LL.B., 1897; m. Helen Elizabeth Finch, Sept. 1, 1908; 1 son, Henry E. Asst. prof. French, 1904-19, prof., 1919—, Cornell U. Mobilized Aug. 1915, in 89th Territorial Regt., attaché French Foreign Office, Apr. 1917; mem. French High Commn. to U.S., Nov. 1917-Aug. 1919. Chevalier Legion of Honor, 1919. Corr. of Le Temps, of Paris, 10 yrs. Author: Les Citations Françaises, 1931. Translated into French (L'Autobiographie d'un Nègre) Up from Slavery by B. T. Washington, 1903. Editor: Selections from Standard French Authors, 1905; Le livre de mon Ami—by Anatole France, 1905 (with notes and introduction). Home: Ithaca, N.Y. Died Jan. 16, 1933.

GUERNSEY, Alice Margaret, editor; b. Rindge, N.H., Apr. 16, 1850; d. Rev. J. W. and Lucy Ann (Tucker) G.; grad. State Normal Sch., Salem, Mass., 1871; student Wellesley Coll., 1879-80; unmarried. Teacher, 1872-87; editor of The Young Crusader and of books and leaflets, Woman's Temperance Publ. Assn., 1887-94; asst. on The Silver Cross, 1895-1904; editor and bus. mgr. of gen. publs. for Woman's Home Missionary Soc. M.E. Ch. Author: Under Our Flag, 1903; Home Mission Readings, 1905. Died Sept. 1924.

GUERNSEY, Egbert, M.D., editor Med. Times, 1872—; b. Litchfield, Conn., 1823; grad. N.Y. Univ. (med. dept.), 1846; founder of Brooklyn Daily Times; pres. Metropolitan Hosp., etc. Author: Practice of Medicine. Home: New York, N.Y. Died 1903.

GUERNSEY, Frank Edward, congressman; b. Dover, Me., Oct. 15, 1866; s. Edward H. and Hannah M. (Thompson) G.; ed. Foxcroft Acad., Eastern Me. Conf. Sem., Me. Wesleyan Sem., Eastman Bus. Coll., Poughkeepsie, N.Y.; admitted to bar, 1890; m. Josephine F. Lyford, June 16, 1897. Treas. Piscataquis Co., Me., 1890-96; mem. Me. Ho. of Rep., 1897-99. Senate, 1903; del. Rep. Nat. Conv., Chicago, 1908; elec. to 60th Congress for unexpired term (1907-09) of Llewellyn Powers, deceased, and re-elected 61st to 64th Congresses (1909-17), 4th Me. Dist.; unanimously re-nominated for 65th Congress, declined to enter primaries for nomination to U.S. Senate; lost senatorial nomination by narrow margin. Pres. Piscataquis Savings Bank. Trustee U. of Maine. Home: Dover-Foxcroft, Me. Deceased.

GUERNSEY, Lucy Ellen, author; b. Pittsford, N.Y., Aug. 12, 1826; sister Clara F. Guernsey, author (dec.); ed. Rochester Female Sem.; began writing when quite young; first books published by Am. Sunday School Union; chosen as a deaconess by late Bishop Coxe of Western N.Y., but not publicly ordained on account of illness. Unmarried. Author: Irish Amy; Old Stanfield House; Through Unknown Ways; Winifred; The Stantoun-Corbet Chronicles (a series of historical tales); A Lent in Earnest; The Soldier of Christ; etc. (in all more than fifty titles). Home: Rochester, N.Y. Died 1899.

GUERNSEY, Nathaniel Taylor, lawyer; b. Davenport, Ia., Dec. 29, 1857; s. Jesse and Elizabeth (Eaton) G.; A.B., Yale, 1881, LL.B., 1883; m. Martha Godman Love, June 27, 1888. Admitted to Ia. bar, 1883; practiced at Des Moines, 1883-1912, latter part time mem. Guernsey, Parker & Miller; moved to New York; asso. counsel, 1912-14, gen. counsel, 1914-26, vice-pres., 1919-30, Am. Telephone & Telegraph Co.; asso. as counsel with Platt, Taylor & Walker, 1930—. Home: New York, N.Y. Died July 14, 1934.

GUERNSEY, Rocellus Sheridan, lawyer, author; b. Otsego Co., N.Y., Apr. 10, 1836; s. Richard and Orillia (De Les Dernier) G.; ed. dist. sch., Westford, N.Y., to 1852; learned printing business; studied law, 1853-59; m. Elizabeth Dunlop, Jan. 2, 1877. Admitted to bar, 1859, Supreme Ct. of U.S., 1863. Lit. editor N.Y. Law Register, 1873-84; editor Monthly Law Bulletin, 1878-83, Monthly Law Record, 1896, Journal of the Telegraph, 1881-83; collaborator The Sanitarian, Brooklyn, 1901-04. Trustee Am. Scenic and Historic Preservation Soc. (hon. mem.). Author: Taxation of Water, 1901; Utilitarian Principles of Taxation, 1902; Religious Liberty in Colonial New York, 1902; Introduction to the History of Treaty at Ghent, 1903; Taxation of Mortgages and Savings Banks, 1905; Tariff Reform and Taxation for Revenue, 1909. Retired, 1911. Home: New York, N.Y. Died Dec. 9, 1918.

GUERNSEY, Samuel James, anthropologist; b. Dover, Me., May 15, 1868; s. Edward H. and Hannah Morse (Thompson) G.; ed. Foxcroft Acad., Eastern Me. Conf. Sem., Me. Wesleyan Sem., and Cowles Art Sch., Boston; m. Drusilla E. Campbell, 1906; children—Isabel H., Edward E. Hemenway asst. in archæology, Peabody Mus., 1910-14, asst. curator archæology and ethnology, 1914-21, asst. dir., 1921-29, curator archæology, 1929—, instr. in anthropology, 1928-29. Explorations in northeastern Arizona and Utah, 1914-17, 1920-23, northeastern Arizona, 1931. Mem. Co. F, 2d Me. Regt., Spanish-Am. War. Republican. Methodist. Author: (with A. V. Kidder) Archæological Explorations in Northeastern Arizona, 1919; (with same) Basket-Maker Caves of Northeastern Arizona, 1921; Explorations in Northeastern Arizona, 1931. Home: Arlington, Mass. Died May 22, 1936.

GUERNSEY, Sarah Elizabeth; b. Salem, O., Sept. 13, 1860; d. Rev. Daniel Patrick and Ann Eliza (Baker) Mitchell; g.g.d. Rev. John Mitchell, Va., 1776; ed. State Normal Sch., Emporia, Kan.; m. George Thacher Guernsey (banker), Sept. 15, 1881. Began teaching at 16, and became prin. high sch., Independence, Kan., later pres. sch. bd.; a founder, now dir. Pub. Library, Independence. State regent D.A.R., 1908-17 and 1921-23; pres. gen. Nat. Soc. D.A.R., 1917-20; nat. pres. Daughters American Colonists. Republican. Methodist. Home: Independence, Kan. Died Feb. 28, 1939.

GUERRANT, Edward Owings, clergyman; b. Sharpsburg, Ky., Feb. 28, 1838; s. Dr. Henry Ellis and Mary Beaufort Howe (Owings) G.; A.B., Center Coll. (now Central U.), Danville, Ky., 1860; Jefferson Med. Coll., Phila., 1865-66; M.D., Bellevue Med. Coll., New York, 1867; grad. Union Theol. Sem., Va., 1876; (D.D., Austin Coll., Sherman, Tex.); m. Mary J. DeVault, May 12, 1863. Practiced medicine, Mt. Sterling, Ky., 1867-73; ordained Presbyn. ministry, 1876; pastor Salem, Ky., 1876-77, Mt. Sterling, 1877-79, 1st Ch., Louisville, 1880-83, Troy and Wilmore, 1885. Served in C.S.A., pvt. to capt. and asst. adj. gen. brigade of cav., Jan. 1862-Apr. 1865. Pres. Am. Inland Mission, 1897—, and editor The Soul Winner. Democrat. Mason. Home: Wilmore, Ky. Died Apr. 26, 1916.

GUERRY, William Alexander, bishop; b. Clarendon Co., S.C., July 7, 1861; s. Rev. Le Grand F. and Margaret Serena (Brailsford) G.; A.M., U. of the South, 1884, B.D., 1891; m. Anne McBee, Nov. 27, 1889. Deacon, 1889, priest, 1890, P.E. Ch.; rector Florence, Marion and Darlington, S.C., 1888-93; chaplain and prof. homiletics and pastoral theology, U. of the South, 1893-1907; consecrated coadjutor bishop of S.C., 1907; became bishop, 1908. Pres. Provincial Bd. of Social Service, Province IV, 1917-26. Home: Charleston, S.C. Died June 9, 1928.

GUERTIN, George Albert, bishop; b. Nashua, N.H., Feb. 17, 1869; s. George and Louise (Lefebvre) G.; ed. St. Charles-Borromeo Coll., Sherbrooke, P.Q.; St. Hyacinthe Coll., St. Hyacinthe, P.Q.; St. John's Sem., Brighton, Mass. Ordained R.C. priesthood, 1892; asst. St. Augustine's Ch., Manchester, N.H., 1892-96, Sacred Heart Ch., Lebanon, N.H., 1896-1900; pastor St. Anthony's Parish, E. Manchester, 1900-07; consecrated bishop of Manchester (N.H.), Mar. 19, 1907. Died Aug. 6, 1931.

GUFFEY, James McClurg, petroleum producer; b. Westmoreland Co., Pa., Jan. 19, 1839; ed. pub. schs. and a term in commercial sch.; railroad and express clerk in South; returned to Pa., 1872; since then in oil and gas production; probably the largest individual oil producer in U.S.; with large bituminous coal holdings; well known as a leader in Democratic politics. Died Mar. 20, 1930.

GUFFY, Bayless Leander Durant, jurist; b. Muhlenberg Co., Ky., Dec. 24, 1832; s. James and Malinda (Jameson) G.; reared on farm in Logan Co., Ky.; ed. in coll. at Glasgow, Ky.; m. Miss M. A. Monroe, May 28, 1857. Admitted to bar, 1856; began practice at Morgantown, 1857; asst. marshal to take census, Butler Co., 1860; police judge, Morgantown, 1860; co. judge, 1862, reëlected, 1866, 78, 82; presdl. elector, 1868; Greenback candidate for Congress, 1876; People's Party nominee for atty. gen. of Ky., 1891; returned to Rep. party, 1893; judge, 1894-1902, chief justice, 1902-03, Court of Appeals of Ky.; elected to Ky. legislature, 1903. Pres. John M. Carson Banking Co. Home: Morgantown, Ky. Died 1910.

GUGGENHEIM, Daniel, capitalist; b. 1856; s. Meyer and Barbara (Myers) G. Buyer for commercial house, in Switzerland, 1873-84; now mem. firm Guggenheim Brothers. Donor of $2,500,000 Daniel Guggenheim Fund for promotion of aviation, 1926. Home: Port Washington, L.I. Died Sept. 28, 1930.

GUGGENHEIM, Isaac, capitalist; b. Phila., June 7, 1854; s. Meyer and Barbara (Myers) G.; bro. Daniel, Simon and Solomon R. G.; grad. Phila. High Sch.; m. Carrie Sonneborn, Nov. 15, 1876. Dir. Mexican Union Ry., Am. Smelting & Refining Co., etc.; mem. Guggenheim Brothers. Home: New York, N.Y. Died Oct. 10, 1922.

GUGGENHEIM, Murry, capitalist; b. Philadelphia, Aug. 12, 1858; s. Meyer and Barbara (Myers) G.; pub. sch. edn.; m. Leonie Bernheim, Mar. 15, 1887. Assisted father and brothers in organizing firm of M. Guggenheim's Sons (later Guggenheim Brothers), 1881; firm merged smelting and refining branches of business, Jan. 1, 1901, with Am. Smelting & Refining Co. Home: New York, N.Y. Died Nov. 15, 1939.

GUGGENHEIM, Simon, senator; b. Phila., Dec. 30, 1867; s. Meyer and Barbara (Myers) G.; grad. pub. schs. of Phila., after which studied languages in Europe 2 yrs.; LL.D.; m. Olga H. Hirsh, Nov. 24, 1898; children—John Simon (dec.), George Denver. Went to Pueblo, Colo., 1888; mem. Guggenheim Bros., mining and smelting; pres. Am. Smelting & Refining Co., Jan. 21, 1919—. Elected U.S. senator from Colo. as a Republican, to succeed Thomas M. Patterson, Democrat, for term, 1907-13; declined to be a candidate for reëlection. Substantial contbr. to philanthropic and ednl. causes; established, jointly with wife, Feb. 1925, in memory of son, John Simon, who died in 1922, the John Simon Guggenheim Memorial Foundation for scholarships for advanced study abroad, without regard to sex, race, creed or color, making a preliminary gift of $3,000,000, later supplemented by an additional gift of $1,000,000 to include Latin-Am. scholarships. Home: New York, N.Y. Died Nov. 2, 1941.

GUGGENHEIM, William, industrialist, publicist, philanthropist; b. Phila., Nov. 6, 1868; s. Meyer and Barbara (Myers) G.; student in mining, metallurgy and chemistry, U. of Pa., 1885-89, A.B., 1899; m. Aimee L. Steinberg, Oct. 7, 1904; 1 son, William. Began with M. Guggenheim's Sons smelting works, Pueblo, Colo., 1889; mgr. Guggenheim mining and smelting interests, Mexico, 1890-1900. Decorated Commendatore dell' Ordine della Corona d'Italia, 1920. Fellow for life Metropolitan Mus. of Art. Author: William Guggenheim (under pseudonym Gatenby Williams), 1934. Home: New York, N.Y. Died June 28, 1941.

GUGGENHEIMER, Randolph, lawyer; b. Lynchburg, Va., July 20, 1848; studied Univ. of New York; clerked in woolen goods house in New York; later in law office; studied law; admitted to bar; head of Guggenheimer, Untermyer & Marshall; has been especially active in negotiating large transactions with English syndicates investing in Am. industries; has large real estate holdings; was mem. bd. of edn. of New York 3 terms; pres. council, 4 years. Home: New York, N.Y. Died 1907.

GUILBERT, Frank Warburton, good roads propagandist; b. Racine, Wis., Sept. 22, 1872; s. Albert Wright and Celia (Pease) G.; student civ. engring., U. of Wis., 1891-94; m. Marion Casseday, Oct. 5, 1899; children—David C., Marion C. Clk. on steamer Cyclone, on Miss. River, 1894; with S. C. Johnson & Son, Racine, Wis., 1895-98, Nat. Lead Co., St. Louis, 1898-1904; real estate business, Spokane, Wash., 1905-10; v.p. and sec. Spokane County Good Roads Assn., 1910—. Pres. Eastern Wash. Highway Assn.; manager Inland Automobile Assn. (trustee); pres. Wash. State Good Roads Assn. County Food Administrator World War, also mgr. 8 govt. war campaigns. A stone and bronze testimonial dedicated to him July 7, 1935, by State of Wash., in Mount Spokane State Park, in recognition of his public work, especially with reference to highway accomplishments. Home: Spokane, Wash. Died Oct. 22, 1940.

GUILD, Curtis, journalist; b. Boston, Jan. 13, 1827; s. Curtis and Charlotte L. (Hodges) G.; father of Curtis G., Jr.; ed. pub. schs.; m. Sarah Crocker Cobb, Sept. 22, 1858. Entered newspaper life on Boston Daily Journal; afterwards employed on Boston Daily Traveler, becoming one of proprietors of that paper under firm of Worthington, Flanders & Guild; left firm in 1858; founded, 1859, and edited, 1859-98, Boston Commercial Bulletin. Pres. Bostonian Soc. from foundation, until 1907, 25 yrs.; one of founders and pres. Home: Boston, Mass. Died 1911.

GUILD, Curtis, journalist, soldier; b. Boston, Feb. 2, 1860; son of Curtis and Sarah Crocker (Cobb) G.; A.B., summa cum laude, Harvard, 1881; (LL.D., Holy Cross Coll., 1906; Williams Coll., 1908; S.T.D., U. of Geneva, Switzerland, 1909); m. Charlotte H. Johnson, June 1, 1892. After graduation made tour of Europe; entered office Commercial Bulletin, Boston, founded by his father; served from bill collector to editor, and, 1902—, sole owner of the paper; pres. Anchor Linotype Printing Co. Pres. Rep. State Conv., 1895; del.-at-large from Mass. and a v.p. Rep. Nat. Conv., 1896. Active as volunteer public speaker on Rep. side, in N.E., Central West and Southern States. Brig. gen. state militia at outbreak of Spanish War; insp. gen. 7th Army Corps (Gen. Fitzhugh Lee), and later insp. gen. Dept. of Havana, until break-up of corps in Cuba; work praised by insp. gen. of army in report. Offered colonial commn. by President, declined; offered place 1st asst. postmaster gen., declined; offered chairmanship of Nat. Civil Service Commn., declined; Roosevelt's companion on stump tour of West, campaign of 1900; lt. gov. Mass., 1902-05, gov. Mass., 1906-09; received 75 votes for Vice-Presdl. nomination, Rep. Nat. Conv., 1908; spl. ambassador to Mexico, 1910; ambassador to Russia, July 21, 1911-13. Grand Officer Crown of Italy; Grand Cordon Order St. Alexander Nevski, Russia. Mem. Boston Chamber of Commerce. Home: Boston, Mass. Died Apr. 6, 1915.

GUILD, Reuben Aldridge, librarian emeritus, Brown Univ., 1893—; b. West Dedham, Mass., May 4, 1822; grad. Brown, 1847 (A.M.; also LL.D., Shurtleff Coll., Ill.); m. Jane Clifford, dau. Samuel Hunt (his wife desc. John Alden and Capt. Myles Standish, of the Mayflower), Dec. 17, 1849. Librarian Brown Univ., 46 years; resigned, 1893. Member city council, Providence, 7 years; school committee, 15 years. Author: Librarian's Manual; Early History of Brown University; Documentary History of Brown University. Home: Providence, R.I. Died 1899.

GUILER, Henry Anderson, lawyer; b. Belfast, Ireland, Aug. 14, 1877; s. James and Christina (Cheyne) G.; brought by parents to U.S., 1883; A.B., cum laude, Harvard, 1900, LL.B., 1904; m. Frances Merrill, Dec. 26, 1919. Admitted to Mass. bar, 1903, and practiced at Boston until 1909, at N.Y. City, 1909-23; in law dept. Erie R.R., 1909-10; with Breed, Abbott & Morgan, 1910-11; asst U.S. atty., spl. asst. to U.S. atty., N.Y. City, and spl. asst. to atty. gen. of U.S., 1911-22; spl. asst. to atty. gen., San Francisco, in charge anti-trust and interstate commerce cases, 1923-25; in gen. practice, San Francisco, 1925—. Republican. Methodist. Home: San Francisco, Calif. Died Nov. 21, 1938.

GUILFORD, Simeon Hayden, dentist; b. Lebanon, Pa., April 11, 1841; s. Simeon and Catharine E. (Doll) G.; A.B., Franklin and Marshall Coll., 1861, A.M., 1864 (Ph.D., 1887); DD.S., Pa. Coll. Dental Surgery, 1865; (hon. D.D.S., Phila. Dental Coll., 1884); m. Virginia S. Gleim, June 8, 1869. Served pvt. Co. E, 127th Pa. Vols., 1862-63; engaged in battles of Fredericksburg and Chancellorsville. Practiced dentistry, Lebanon, Pa., 1865-72, Phila., 1872—; prof. operative and prosthetic dentistry and orthodontia, 1881—, dean, 1895-1905 and 1908—, Phila. Dental Coll. Fellow Am. Acad. Dental Science. Author: Nitrous Oxide, Its Properties, Methods of Administration and Effects, 1887; Orthodontia, 1889, 1893, 1898, 1905. Home: Lansdowne, Pa. Died Jan. 18, 1919.

GUILLE, Andrew J., pianist; b. Bloomfield, Ia., May 16, 1862; s. Andrew J. and Susan L. (Wishard) G.; Southern Ia. Normal School, Bloomfield; unmarried. Dir. and teacher of piano, Kan. Wesleyan U., Salina, 1888-97; teacher music, German Acad., Enterprise, Kan., 1897-98; teacher, Emporia, Kansas, 1898-1904, Parsons, Kansas, 1904—. Composer: (books) Pastoral Scenes, 1900; Book of Polonaises, 1901; Sea Murmurs, 1904; Teaching Pieces for Piano, 1904; Six Laurel Leaves, 1904; 45 Melodic Studies, 1913. Home: Parsons, Kan. Deceased.

GUINEY, Louise Imogen, author; b. Boston, 1861; only child of Gen. Patrick Robert and Janet Margaret (Doylê) G.; grad. Elmhurst Acad., Providence, R.I.; studied afterward under pvt. tutors, and has lived over twelve yrs. abroad; unmarried. Author: The White Sail and Other Poems, 1887; Monsieur Henri—a Foot-Note to French History, 1892; A Little English Gallery, 1894; Patrins, 1897; A Roadside Harp, 1893; England and Yesterday, 1898; The Martyrs' Idyl and Shorter Poems, 1899; Happy Ending (poems), 1909; Hurrell Froude, 1904; Robert Emmet—His Rebellion and His Romance, 1904; The Blessed Edmund Campion, 1908. Died Nov. 2, 1920.

GUINEY, Patrick William, army officer; b. Fall River, Mass., Feb. 10, 1877; s. John and Johanna (Farrell) G.; ed. pub. schs., Fall River, 1884-95, U.S. Mil. Acad., 1895-99; m. Margaret Wells Buck, Feb. 24, 1906; 1 son, Patrick William. Commd. 2d lt. cav., U.S.A., 1899; advanced through grades to col., 1921; brig. gen., asst. to q.m. gen., U.S.A., 1933—. Served in China, Philippines, Mexican Border, World War. Awarded Silver Star Citation; Purple Heart with oak leaf cluster. Died Dec. 17, 1936.

GUION, Lewis, commr. Vicksburg Nat. Mil. Park; b. Parish of Lafourche, La., Aug. 28, 1838; s. George Seth and Caroline Lucretia (Winder) G.; g.s. Maj. Isaac G., U.S.A., also an officer Continental Army; St. James Coll.; A.B., U. of Miss., 1858; Law Dept. U. of Va., 1858-59; LL.B., Law Dept., U. of La., 1861; m. Mrs. Mary E. (Harris) Lanier, July 13, 1875. Admitted to La. bar, 1861; 1st lt. Co. A, 1st La. Inf., C.S.A., 1861; capt. Co. D, 26th La. Vols., 1863-65; acting asst. insp. gen. staffs of Gens. F. A. Shoup and Allen Thomas; paroled Aug. 1865. Resumed practiced after the war, also sugar planter; melter and refiner New Orleans Mint, 1893-98; mem. bd. commrs. Vicksburg Nat. Military Park, 1908—. Democrat. Episcopalian. Home: New Orleans, La. Died Jan. 12, 1920.

GUION, Walter, senator; practiced at Napoleonville, La.; served as judge District Court; atty. gen. of La., 1900-12; U.S. dist. atty., Eastern Dist. of La., 1912-17; apptd. U.S. senator, Apr. 21, 1918, for interim until election, Nov. 1918, to succeed Robert F. Broussard, deceased. Democrat. Home: New Orleans, La. Deceased.

GUITERAS, Gregario Maria, M.D.; b. Matanzas, Cuba, Mar. 12, 1863; s. Eusebio and Josefa (Gener) G.; A.B., LaSalle Coll., Philadelphia, 1880, A.M., 1881, hon. M.S., 1917; M.D., U. of Pa., 1885; m. Maria Hortensia Aranguren, Sept. 11, 1897; children—Nestor Ramon, Blanche Maria, John Raoul, Maria Hortense, Matilde Maria, George Gustavus, Mary Louise. Interne, Phila. Gen. Hosp. and U. of Pa. Hosp., 1885; in practice at Charleston, S.C., 1886-87; asst. surgeon, advancing through grades to sr. surgeon, U.S. Marine Hosp. Service (now U.S. Pub. Health Service), 1888-1927; retired, 1927, rank of lt. colonel. Served as quarantine officer, U.S. intervention in Cuba, 1899-1902; sanitation officer, 7th Naval Dist., World War. Del. to Pan-Am. Med. Congress, Havana, 1902, Guatemala, 1907, Santiago de Chili, 1911, Montevideo, Uruguay, 1920. Served in all yellow fever epidemics in U.S. and considered as authority on this disease. Home: Yeadon, Pa. Died July 5, 1934.

GUITERAS, Juan, physician; b. Matanzas, Cuba, Jan. 4, 1852; s. Eusebio and Josefa (Gener) G.; ed. at La Empresa, Matanzas; M.D., U. of Pa., 1873 (Ph.D.); m. Mrs. Dolores Guiteras, née Gener, of Matanzas, May 5, 1883. Resident and visiting phys. to Phila. Hosp., 1873-79; marine hosp. service, 1879-89; served as expert in yellow fever in all epidemics, 1881—; prof. medicine, Charleston Med. Sch., 1884-88; prof. pathology, U. of Pa., 1889-99; on staff Gen. Shafter as yellow fever expert in Santiago campaign, 1898; prof. gen. pathology and tropical diseases, U. of Havana, 1900-21; dir. of pub. health, Cuba, 1909-21, and pres. Nat. Bd. of Health; sec. Public Health and Charities, Cuba, 1921-22, resigned. Prominent in Cuban politics in this country. Editor La Revista de Medicina Tropical. Pres. 2d Nat. Med. Congress of Cuba; v.p. Assn. of Health Officers of N. America, Am. Public Health Assn.; mem. Yellow Fever Commn. of Internat. Health Bd. of the Rockefeller Foundation, 1916—. Discovered filaria Bancrofti in the U.S. and uncinaria in Cuba. Home: Benavides, Cuba. Died Oct. 28, 1925.

GULICK, Edward Leeds, clergyman; b. Honolulu, H.I., Mar. 21, 1862; s. Luther Halsey and Louisa (Lewis) G.; bro. Sidney Lewis and Luther Halsey G.; grad. St. Johnsbury Acad., Vt., 1879; A.B., Dartmouth, 1883, A.M., 1886; Union Theol. Sem., 1887; A.M., Harvard, 1893; m. Harriet Maria Farnsworth, Dec. 2, 1890. Teacher mathematics, Williston Sem., Mass., 1883-84; sub-master Lawrence (Mass.) High Sch., 1884-89; teacher evidences of Christianity, Dartmouth, 1889; ordained Congl. ministry; pastor Groton, Mass., 1889-92; head dept. of English, Lawrenceville Sch., N.J., 1893-1904; teacher English lit., Dartmouth Summer Sch., 1904; pastor W. Lebanon, N.H., 1906-10. Condr. (with wife) of the Aloha Camps for Girls, at Fairlee, Vt. Republican. Author (with Sidney Lewis Gulick): Outline Studies in the Growth of the Kingdom, 1910; editor of sch. edits. of Silas Marner and Macaulay's Essays on Milton. Home: Brookline, Mass. Died Apr. 27, 1931.

GULICK, John Thomas, missionary; b. Kauai, H.I., Mar. 13, 1832; s. Peter Johnson (Am. missionary) and Fanny Hinckley (Thomas) G.; was miner, Calif., 1849-50; A.B., Williams, 1859 (hon. A.M., 1889; Ph.D., Adelbert, 1889; Sc.D., Oberlin, 1905); studied in Union Theol. Sem., New York; m. Emily de la Cour, Sept. 3, 1864 (died 1875); m. 2d, Frances A. Stevens, May 31, 1880. Missionary to Pekin, China, 1864-65, Kalgan, China, 1865-75, missionary to Japan, 1875-99, for A.B.C.F.M. (Congl); at Oberlin, O., 1899-1905. Author: Evolution Racial and Habitudinal, 1905. Home: Honolulu, T.H. Died Apr. 16, 1923.

GULICK, John W., army officer; b. Goldsboro, N.C., Nov. 8, 1874; s. James Wharton and Susan Holland (Green) G.; grad. U.S. Arty. Sch., 1905, Army War Coll., 1925; m. Florence MacMullan, July 3, 1905. Served as 1st lt. U.S. Vols., 1898; commd. 1st lt., U.S.A., Sept. 17, 1901; promoted through grades to col., Aug. 19, 1925; maj. gen., Mar. 20, 1930. Instr., Coast Arty. Sch., 1905-11; on duty with Chilean Govt., 1911-15; dir. Coast Arty. Sch., 1915-17; chief of staff, 40th Div., 1917-18; chief of staff, Army Arty., First Army, A.E.F., 1918-19; on War Dept. General Staff, 1919-24; later chief of coast artillery. D.S.M. (U.S.); Legion of Honor (France). Died Aug. 18, 1939.

GULICK, Luther Halsey, educator, author; b. Honolulu, H.I., Dec. 4, 1865; s. Luther Halsey and Louisa (Lewis) G.; bro. of Frances Gulick Jewett and Sidney Lewis G.; student Oberlin Coll., 1880-82, 1883-86; student Sargent Normal Sch. of Physical Training, Harvard, 1885; M.D., Univ. Med. Coll. (New York U.), 1889; m. Charlotte Vetter, Aug. 30, 1887. Physical dir. Y.M.C.A., Jackson, Mich., 1886; supt. physical training dept., Y.M.C.A. Training Sch., Springfield, Mass., 1886-1903 (degree M.P.E., same, 1907); sec. physical training dept. Y.M.C.A. Internat. Com., 1887-1903; prin. Pratt Inst. High Sch., 1900-03; dir. physical training, pub. schs., New York, 1903-08. Editor Physical Education, 1891-96, Association Outlook, 1897-1900, Physical Education Review, 1901-03, Gulick Hygiene Series. Chmn. physical training lecture com. St. Louis Exposition, 1904; mem. Olympic Games Com., Athens, 1906, London, 1908; U.S. del. 2d Internat. Congress on Sch. Hygiene, London, 1907. Lecturer on hygiene, etc., New York U., 1906-09; consultant New York Hosp. for Deformities and Joint Diseases, 1907. Author: Physical Measurements and How They Are Used, 1889; Physical Education by Muscular Exercise, 1904; The Efficient Life, 1907; Mind and Work, 1908; The Healthful Art of Dancing, 1910; etc. Joint author: Medical Inspection of Schools, 1907. Dir. dept. of child hygiene, Russell Sage Foundation, 1907-13; pres. Camp Fire Girls, 1913. Home: South Casco, Me. Died Aug. 13, 1918.

GULICK, Thomas Lafon, clergyman, lecturer; b. Kauai, Hawaiian Islands, Apr. 10, 1839; s. Rev. Peter J. (Am. missionary) and Fanny (Thomas) G.; grad. Williams, 1865 (A.M.); grad. Andover Theol. Sem., 1868; m. Alice E. Walbridge, Nov. 25, 1872. Missionary of Am. Bd. in Spain and Cuba, 1873-84; pastor of Foreign Ch., on Maui, Hawaiian Islands, 1886-93. Has been shipwrecked 3 times; was shot at by 4 assassins in Spain; traveled from Africa to Spitzbergen, 1898; lectured and wrote for annexation of Hawaii; visited Turkey, Palestine, Egypt, Ceylon, India, China, Japan and the Hawaiian Islands, 1900-01; now supt. and chaplain of two sanitariums; brother John T. Gulick. Home: Devon, Pa. Died 1904.

GULLIVER, Julia Henrietta, college pres.; b. Norwich, Conn., July 30, 1856; d. John Putnam and Frances Woodbury (Curtis) Gulliver; A.B., Smith Coll., 1879, Ph.D., 1888; student Leipzig, Germany, 1892-93; LL.D., Smith Coll., 1910. Head dept. of philosophy and Bibl. lit., Rockford (Ill.) Sem., 1890-92; head dept. philosophy and Bibl. lit., 1893, pres. 1902-18, Rockford (Ill.) Coll.; pres. emeritus. Officier d'Académie, 1909. Author: Studies in Democracy. Home: Eustis, Fla. Died July 26, 1940.

GUMMERE, Francis Barton, college prof.; b. Burlington, N.J., Mar. 6, 1855; s. Samuel James (pres. Haverford Coll., 1862-74) and Elizabeth Hooton (Barton) G.; A.B., Haverford, 1872, A.M., 1875; A.B., Harvard, 1875; studed philology, Leipzig, Berlin, Strassburg, Freiburg; Ph.D., Freiburg, 1881; (Litt.D., Harvard, 1909); m. Amelia Smith Mott, Sept. 14, 1882. Teacher Friends' Sch., Providence, 1875-79; instr. English, Harvard, 1881-82; headmaster Swain Free Sch., New Bedford, Mass., 1882-87; prof. English, Haverford, 1887—. Fellow Am. Acad. Arts and Sciences. Author: The Anglo-Saxon Metaphor, 1881; Handbook of Poetics, 1885; Germanic Origins, 1892; Old English Ballads, 1894; The Beginnings of Poetry, 1901; The Popular Ballad, 1907; The Oldest English Epic, 1909; Democracy and Poetry, 1911. Home: Haverford, Pa. Died May 30, 1919.

GUMMERÉ, Samuel Réne, diplomat; b. Trenton, N.J., Feb. 19, 1853; s. Barker and Elizabeth (Stryker) G.; bro. of William S. G.; A.B., Princeton, 1870; unmarried. Admitted to bar, 1874, and practiced at Trenton. Sec. to U.S. minister at The Hague, 1881-84; U.S. consul-gen. to Morocco, 1898-1905; E.E. and M.P. to Morocco, 1905-09. Mem. commn. to represent U.S. at Algeciras conf., 1905. Republican. Presbyterian. Died May 28, 1920.

GUMMERE, William Stryker, judge; b. Trenton, N.J., June 24, 1852; s. Barker and Elizabeth (Stryker) G.; brother of Samuel Réne G.; A.B., Princeton U., 1870, A.M., 1873, LL.D., 1902. Admitted to bar and practiced at Newark and Trenton; was judge Circuit Ct. of Essex Co., N.J.; justice 1895-1901, chief justice, 1901—, Supreme Ct. of N.J. Republican. Home: Newark, N.J. Died Jan. 26, 1933.

GUNCKEL, John Elstner; b. Germantown, O., Aug. 14, 1846; s. William and Elisabeth (Elstner) G.; ed. pub. schs., and Oberlin Coll., winter mos. 2 seasons. In banking and ins. business with father, at Dayton, O., 1868-70; removed to Toledo, 1871; in real estate business, 1875-76; ticket and pass. agt., L.S.&M.S. Ry., 1876-1906; since at work among boys in the streets. Pres. (for life) Toledo and Nat. Newsboys' Assn., organized, 1892, on self-govt. principle; Toledo Assn. now has over 9,600 members and completely equipped bldg. which cost over $110,000. Republican. Conglist. Author: Boyville, 1907. Died Aug. 16, 1915.

GUNCKEL, Lewis B., lawyer; b. Germantown, O., Oct. 15, 1826; s. Col. Michael G.; grad. Farmers' Coll., 1848; Cincinnati Law Sch., 1851. Practiced law 50 yrs., Dayton, O.; retired, devoting himself to public charity and polit. reform. State senator, 1862-65; presidential elector, 1864, and canvassed State for Lincoln. Mgr. of Nat. Soldiers' Homes for 12 yrs.; spl. commr., 1871, to investigate frauds practiced upon Cherokee, Creek and Chickasaw Indians. Mem. Congress, 1873-75; candidate for re-election, 1874, but defeated; pres. Asso. Charities; pres. Ohio State Conf. Charities. Home: Dayton, O. Died 1903.

GUNDERSEN, Adolf, surgeon; b. Norway, Oct. 8, 1865; s. Martin and Olea (Melby) G.; B.A., M.D., Royal U. of Norway, 1890; m. Helga Isaksatre, of Solör, Norway, Sept. 16, 1894. Came to U.S., 1891, naturalized citizen, 1896. Practiced at LaCrosse, Wis., 1891—; surgeon LaCrosse, Lutheran and St. Francis hops.; mem. Bd. of Health, LaCrosse. Fellow Am. Coll. Surgeons, Scandinavian Surg. Soc.; hon. mem. Christiania Surg. Soc. Regent at large U. of Wis. Knight of 1st Class, Order of St. Olaf (Norway), 1926; made hon. mem. Med. Soc. of Norway, 1933. Home: LaCrosse, Wis. Died Sept. 15, 1938.

GUNDERSEN, Henrik, theologian; b. Tromsö, Norway, Jan. 31, 1857; s. Ole and Mette Bernthine (Olsen) G.; grad. Tromsö Acad., 1872, Bethel Theol. Sem., Stockholm, 1884. Christiania U. Candidatus Philosophiæ, 1888; (hon. D.B., Bapt. Union Theol. Sem., 1889; Th.D., Northern Baptist Theol. Sem., 1923); m. Hansine M. Hansen, of Trondhjem, Norway, June 28, 1888. Pastor Trondhjem, Norway, 1886-87; removed to U.S., 1888; prof. Greek and N.T. interpretation, Danish-Norwegian dept. Bapt. Union Theol. Sem., 1888-92; asst. prof. N.T. interpretation and bibl. lit., U. of Chicago, 1892-95;

dean and prof. systematic theology, N.T. interpretation and Bibl. lit., Danish-Norwegian Theol. Sem. (U. of Chicago), 1895-13; dean Norwegian Bapt. Div. House (U. of Chicago), 1913-21; dean Norwegian Bapt. Theol. Sem. (Northern Bapt. Theol. Sem.), 1921—. Died Nov. 4, 1925.

GUNDERSON, Carl, gov.; b. Clay Co., Dak. Ty., June 20, 1864; s. Hans and Isabel (Lee) G.; A.B., U. of S.D., 1890; student civ. engring., Cornell U., 1891; m. Gertrude Bertlesen, June 16, 1892. Mem. S.D. Senate 5 terms; U.S. Indian allotting agt., 1904-10; supervisor of allotting agts. 1 yr.; lt. gov. of S.D., 2 terms, 1921-24, gov., 1924-25. Republican. Mason. Home: Mitchell, S.D. Died Feb. 26, 1933.

GUNDRY, Richard Fitz Harris, physician; b. Dayton, O., Apr. 21, 1866; s. Richard and Mary Martha (Fitz Harris) G.; ed. at pvt. schs., Baltimore; M.D., Coll. Phys. and Surg., Baltimore 1888; m. Catherine A. Hines, Oct. 29, 1895. Asst. phys., Asylum for Insane, Dayton, O., July, 1888; transferred to Athens (O.) Asylum for Insane, 1889; established 1891, and has since conducted The Richard Gundry Home for the Treatment of Mental and Nervous Diseases, Catonsville, Md. Mem. bd. mgrs. Spring Grove State Hosp., Catonsville. Died Aug. 3, 1924.

GUNN, John Edward, bishop; b. Five Mile Town, Co. Tyrone, Ireland, Mar. 15, 1863; s. Edward and Mary (Grew) G.; ed. St. Mary's Coll., Dundalk, Ireland; Marist. Coll., Paignton, S. Devon, Eng.; Catholic U., Dublin; Gregorian U., Rome, Italy, J.C.B., D.D. Teacher moral theology, Catholic U., Washington, 1892-98; pastor, Atlanta, Ga., 1898-1911; consecrated bishop of Natchez, Miss., Aug. 29, 1911. Democrat. Died Feb. 19, 1924.

GUNNELL, Francis M., surgeon gen. U.S.N.; b. Washington, Nov. 27, 1827; s. James and Helen (Mackall) G.; A.B., Georgetown U., 1845, A.M., 1848; M.D., Columbian (now George Washington) U., 1846 (hon. A.M., 1852; LL.D., George Washington U., 1911); m. Harriet Patterson Chew. Apptd. from D.C., asst. surgeon, Mar. 22, 1849; passed asst. surgeon, Apr. 7, 1854; surgeon, Apr. 23, 1861; med. insp., Mar. 3, 1871; med. dir., Feb. 3, 1875; surgeon gen. U.S.N., 1884; retired with relative rank of commodore, Nov. 27, 1889; promoted to rank of rear admiral retired, June 1906. Served on various stas. and N. and S. Atlantic blockading squadrons, 1862; Naval Hosp., Washington, 1863-65, etc. Died June 10, 1922.

GUNNELL, George, clergyman; b. Pittsburgh, May 18, 1868; s. George and Sophia (Couling) G. B.A., Hobart Coll. 1891, M.A., 1894; B.A., Harvard, 1892; grad. Gen. Theol. Sem., 1895; m. Caroline Hogg Sibbett, Sept. 12, 1900. Deacon, 1895, priest, 1896, P.E. Ch.; minister in charge of Holy Innocents' Ch., Leechburg, Pa., 1895-96; asst., Calvary Ch., Pittsburgh, 1896-97; rector Ch. of the Epiphany, Bellevue, Pa., 1897-1903, St. Andrew's Ch., Phila., 1903-09, Trinity Ch., Toledo, O., 1909—. Clerical deputy Gen. Conv., New York, 1913. Republican. Home: Toledo, O. Died May 31, 1921.

GUNNISON, Almon, univ. pres.; b. Hallowell, Me., Mar. 2, 1844; s. Rev. Nathaniel and Ann Louisa (Foster) G.; bro. of Herbert Foster G.; student Tufts Coll., 1864; B.D., St. Lawrence U., 1868 (D.D.; LL.D., Union, 1902, Tufts, 1905); m. Ella I. Everest, July 8, 1868. Ordained Universalist ministry, 1868; pastor, Bath, Me., 1868-71, All Soul's Ch., Brooklyn, 20 yrs., First Ch., Worcester, Mass., 10 yrs.; pres. St. Lawrence U., Canton, N.Y., 1898-1914, pres. emeritus. Home: Brooklyn, N.Y. Died June 30, 1917.

GUNNISON, Frederic Everest, banker, lawyer; b. Canton, N.Y., May 28, 1869; s. Almon and Ella (Everest) G.; A.B., Columbia, 1890; A.M. and LL.B., New York U., 1892; m. Rose I. Fancher, Nov. 22, 1899. Admitted to N.Y. bar, 1892; v.p. Lawyers Title & Trust Co.; dir. Chase Securities Co., Stutz Motor Car Co.; trustee East Brooklyn Savings Instn., Sugar Planters Corp., Stromberg Carburetor Corp. Chmn. Kings Co. Fuel Commn., 1917. Republican. Universalist. Home: Brooklyn, N.Y. Died Jan. 11, 1922.

GUNNISON, Herbert Foster, newspaperman; b. Halifax, N.S., June 28, 1858; s. Rev. Nathaniel and Ann Louisa (Foster) G.; A.B., St. Lawrence U., 1880, A.M., 1882, LL.D., 1924; m. Alice May, Apr. 29, 1886 (died 1903); children—Raymond M., Mrs. Florence Brown, Foster; m. 2d, Mrs. Effie M. Baldwin, Jan. 20, 1923. Albany correspondent, 1884-86, v.p. and treas., 1921, publisher and dir., 1897—, pres., 1925-29, chmn. board of trustees, 1929—, Brooklyn Eagle; sec. and treas. Eagle Warehouse & Storage Co.; trustee Williamsburg Savings Bank; officer and dir. various corps. A founder, 3 yrs. treas., 2 yrs. sec., Am. Newspaper Pubs. Assn.; v.p. Associated Press, 1921, 1922; pres. New York City Publishers Assn., 1925. Trustee St. Lawrence U.; sec. and treas. Brooklyn Law Sch.; dir. Brooklyn Pub. Library several yrs.; dir. Brooklyn Bur. of Charities; a mgr. Brooklyn State Hosp. Editor Eagle Almanac, several yrs., from 1887. Trustee All Souls

Universalist Ch. Home: Brooklyn, N.Y. Died Nov. 24, 1932.

GUNNISON, Royal Arch, judge; b. Binghamton, N.Y., June 24, 1873; s. Christopher B. and Juliette (Turner) G.; LL.B., Cornell, 1896; m. Lena M. Cobb, Sept. 4, 1900. Admitted to N.Y. bar, 1897; U.S. referee in bankruptcy for Broome, Chenango and Delaware cos., 1898-1904; U.S. dist. judge, 1st Div., Dist. of Alaska, 1904-09; in practice at Juneau, 1909—; mem. Gunnison & Robertson. Non-resident lecturer on bankruptcy, Cornell Coll. of Law, 1901-08. Pres. Juneau Chamber Commerce, 1909-11; mem. 1st Alaska Bd. Commrs. on Uniform State Laws, 1912; reapptd. 1913, 17, and pres. bd. Federal food adminstr. for Alaska, Nov. 23, 1917—. Mason. Republican. Home: Juneau, Alaska. Died June 15, 1918.

GUNNISON, Walter Balfour, educator; b. Abington, Mass., May 2, 1852; s. Nathaniel and Ann (Foster) G.; A.B., St. Lawrence U., Canton, N.Y., 1875, Ph.D., 1876; m. Blanche Eaton, Jan. 18, 1876. Began teaching at St. Lawrence U., 1875; prin. Erasmus Hall High Sch., Brooklyn, 1885—. Trustee St. Lawrence U. Dir. Bank of Flatbush. Pres. N.Y. State Teachers' Assn., N.Y. Schoolmasters' Club. Author: First and Second Year of Latin, 1902, and Cicero, 1910. Home: Brooklyn, N.Y. Died Dec. 19, 1916.

GUNSAULUS, Edwin Norton, consul; b. Mt. Liberty, O., Dec. 13, 1859; s. Dr. Calvin and Eliza (Norton) G.; pub. and high sch. edn.; m. Harriet N. Mitchell, Mar. 28, 1888 (died May 8, 1901); children—Paul Mitchell, Edwin Norton, Eleanor, Frederick Knox (dec.); m. 2d, Maud Schooley, of Toronto, Ont., July 6, 1910; 1 dau., Elizabeth N. Became connected with newspaper at Mt. Gilead, O., 1884, later at Centerburg, where was mayor; owner and editor London (O.) Times, 1887-1900; Am. consul at Pernambuco, Brazil, 1900-01, Toronto, Can., 1901-05, Cork, Ireland, 1905-06, Rimouski, Can., 1906-08, Johannesburg, S. Africa, 1908-16; consul gen. Singapore, Straits Settlements, July 1916, at Halifax, Nova Scotia, 1920, Wellington, New Zealand, 1923; retired Dec. 13, 1924. Home: Chevy Chase, Md. Died June 11, 1930.

GUNSAULUS, Frank Wakeley, clergyman; b. Chesterville, O., Jan. 1, 1856; s. Joseph and Mary (Hawley) G.; A.B., Ohio Wesleyan U., 1875, A.M., 1887; (D.D., Beloit Coll., Wis. 1887); m. Anna Long, Sept. 20, 1875. Ordained Methodist ministry, 1875; preached 4 yrs.; entered Congl. ministry, 1879; pastor Eastwood Ch., Columbus, O., 1879-81, Newtonville, Mass., 1881-85, Memorial Ch., Baltimore, 1885-87, Plymouth Ch., Chicago, 1887-99, Central Ch., Chicago, 1899-1919; pres. Armour Inst. of Tech., 1893—. Lecturer Yale Theol. Sem., 1882; professorial lecturer, U. of Chicago. Author: Life of William Ewart Gladstone, 1898; The Man of Galilee, 1899; Paths to Power, 1905; Paths to the City of God, 1906; Higher Ministries of Recent English Poetry, 1907; The Minister and the Spiritual Life, 1911. Home: Chicago, Ill. Died Mar. 19, 1921.

GUNTER, Archibald Clavering, author, playwright, publisher; b. Liverpool, England, Oct. 25, 1847; ed. high school and univ.; studied, San Francisco, Calif., School of Mines; civil engr. Central Pacific R.R., 1868; chemist Calif. Assay Office, 1869-70; chemist Homanville Smelting Works, Utah, 1871; supt. McKay Mines, Utah, 1873-74; stockbroker, San Francisco, 1875-78; in New York, 1879—; m. Nov. 8, 1886, Esther Lisbeth Burns, niece George H. Story, curator Metropolitan Museum of Art, New York. Author: Mr. Barnes of New York; Miss Nobody of Nowhere; Miss Dividends; The Fighting Troubadour; Tangled Flags. His most successful plays are: Prince Karl; Two Nights in Rome; Fresh, The American; The Deacon's Daughter; Mr. Barnes of New York. Died 1907.

GUNTER, Julius Caldeen, governor; b. Fayetteville, Ark., Oct. 31, 1858; s. Thomas Montague and Marcella (Jackson) G.; student U. of Virginia, 1876-79; LL.D. from U. of Colorado in 1926; m. Bettie Brown, April 30, 1884. Admitted to Colorado bar, 1881, and practiced in Trinidad; mem. bar of U.S. Supreme Ct. and 10th Circuit Ct. of Appeals (1st to be admitted on court's motion); judge 3d Jud. Dist., Colo., 1889-95; judge Colo. Ct. of Appeals, 1901-05; justice Supreme Ct. of Colo., 1905-07; practiced at Denver, 1907-17; gov. of Colo., term 1917-19. Tendered appointment to Supreme Ct. of Colo., but declined. Pres. trustees Tillotson Acad., Trinidad, 1886-89, same, Clayton Coll., Denver, 1911-17; regent U. of Colo., 1913-15. Democrat. Episcopalian. Home: Denver, Colo. Died Oct. 26, 1940.

GUNTHER, Charles Frederick, mfr.; b. Wildberg, Wurtemberg, Germany, Mar. 6, 1837; s. John M. and Marie F. G.; came to U.S., 1842; pub. sch. edn.; m. Jennie Burnell, 1869. Cashier in bank; served in C.S.N. in Civil War. Manufacturing confectioner, 1868-1915. Served 2 terms Chicago Common Council; city treas., 1900-04. Extensive traveler. Owns one of finest collections of Washington and Lincoln relics in U.S.; also hist. manuscripts, etc. Pres. Coliseum. Mason. Democrat. Home: Chicago, Ill. Died Feb. 10, 1920.

GUNTHER, Franklin Mott, diplomatic service; b. N.Y. City, Feb. 28, 1885; s. Franklin L. and Louisa Dunmore (Mott) G.; A.B., Harvard, 1907; student École Libre des Sciences Politiques, Paris, France, 1907-08; m. Louisa Bronson Hunnewell, Apr. 27, 1918. Pvt. sec. to Am. ambassador to Japan, 1908-09; 3d sec. Am. Embassy at Paris, 1909-10; with Div. Latin-Am. Affairs, Washington, 1910-11; sec. Am. Legation, Managua, chargé d'affaires, 1911-12; Lisbon, sec. of Legation and chargé d'affaires, 1912; 2d sec. Embassy, Rio de Janeiro, 1912-14; sec. Legation, Christiania, Feb. 1914 (chargé d'affaires); sec. to Am. delegation to Internat. Conf., Spitzbergen, June 1914, and tech. del. to same conf.; 2d sec. Embassy, London, 1914-17, 1st sec. 1917-19; 1st sec. Legation, The Hague, and chargé d'affaires, 1919-20; counselor Am. Embassy, Rome, 1920-24 (chargé d'affaires); chief Div. of Mexican Affairs, Dept. of State, 1924-28; E.E. and M.P. to Egypt, 1928-30; apptd. E.E. and M.P. to Ecuador, 1930, but resigned Sept. 27, 1930; pres. Am. Inst. for Iranian Art and Archæology, 1930-37; financial and economic research, 1930-37; apptd. E.E. and M.P. to Rumania, July 31, 1937. Fellow Metropolitan Museum, New York, and Royal Society of Arts and Manufactures, London. Home: Washington, D.C. Died Dec. 22, 1941.

GUNTON, George, editor; b. Cambridgeshire, Eng., Sept. 8, 1847; s. Matthew and Ann (Middleton) G.; came to U.S., 1874, settling in Mass.; m. Mrs. Rebecca Douglas Lowe, Feb. 1904. Having made close study in Eng. and U.S. of industrial questions, became editorial writer on economic and kindred subjects until 1880; after that devoted himself entirely to scientific, economic and sociolog. work; in 1890 became pres. Inst. of Social Economics and editor Social Economist, which in 1896 was changed to Gunton's Magazine, of which became editor. Appointed, 1899, internat. examiner and dir. econ. and sociolog. work of Y.M.C.A. of N. America. Author: Wealth and Progress, 1887; Principles of Social Economics, 1891; Trusts and the Public, 1899; Outlines of Political Science, 1900; Outlines of Social Economics. Home: Hot Springs, Va. Died Sept. 11, 1919.

GURLER, Henry Benjamin, dairy farmer; b. Chesterfield, N.H., May 21, 1840; s. Benjamin and Harriet F. (Hopkins) G.; ed. country schs. and De Kalb (Ill.) High Sch.; m. Selenia Rolfe, Mar. 27, 1867; children—Mrs. Stella F. Lundberg, Mrs. May G. Ellwood; m. 2d, Cora A. Dodge, Oct. 5, 1904. Served in Civil War as corporal Co. K, 42d Ill. Inf. and 2d lt. Co. K, 132d Ill. Inf. In mercantile bus. in De Kalb, 1864-68; dairyman, 1868-82; propr. creamery, 1882—; pres. De Kalb Dairy Co. Instr. butter-making, Wis. Agrl. Coll., 1891; same, 2 terms in Vt. Agrl. Coll., and 3 terms in Pa. Agrl. Coll.; supplied certified milk to Chicago, 1895-1906, being pioneer in the business. Mem. De Kalb Common Council, 1896, Bd. Edn., 1886-92; supervisor, 1906. Republican. Christian Scientist. Author: American Dairying, 1894; The Farm Dairy. Home: De Kalb, Ill. Died Apr. 2, 1928.

GURLEY, William Fitzhugh, lawyer; b. Davenport, Ia., Apr. 30, 1861; s. William Henry Fitzhugh and Elizabeth Scott (Rittenhouse) G.; ed. common schs.; m. Elizabeth Buckey, June 12, 1890. Admitted to bar, 1886, and began practice at Omaha. Made speeches throughout the West in presidential campaign of 1896; chmn. Neb. delegation Rep. Nat. Conv., Phila., 1900. Delivered Grant oration, Galena, Ill., 1903; oration at dedication of Lewis and Clark Monument, Fort Calhoun, Neb., 1904; has spoken in leading cities of the country on legal, polit. and lit. subjects. Unitarian. Home: Omaha, Neb. Died Jan. 10, 1927.

GURLEY, William Wirt, lawyer; b. Mt. Gilead, O., Jan. 27, 1851; s. John J. and Anseville C. (Armentrout) G.; A.B., Ohio Wesleyan, 1870; read law in his father's office; m. Mary Eva, d. late Hon. Joseph Turney of Cleveland, O., Oct. 30, 1878. Supt. pub. schools, Seville, O., 1871-72; admitted to bar, 1873; practicing in Chicago since Sept. 1874; gen. counsel Chicago Rys. Co., Chicago Surface Lines, Baker Fentress & Co., Marquette Cement Co., and other corps. Home: Chicago, Ill. Died Mar. 11, 1923.

GUSHEE, Edward Manning, clergyman; b. Providence, R.I., Aug. 29, 1836; s. Dennis Stockbridge and Julia Lippitt (Hull) G.; A.M., Brown U., 1858; (D.D., U. of N.C., 1891). Deacon, 1861, priest, 1861, P.E. Ch.; chaplain 9th N.H. Regt., 1862-63; rector St. Thomas' Ch., Dover, N.H., 1861-64, St. Paul's, Wallingford, Conn., 1864-71, St. Peter's, Salem, Mass., 1871-76, St. Peter's, Cambridge, 1876-90, St. Philip's, Cambridge, 1890—. Author: The Dangers of Peace, 1898; The Church's Opportunity, 1903; Massacre of the Innocents, from 14 Years Old and Under, 1907. Home: Cambridge, Mass. Died Nov. 15, 1917.

GUSTAFSON, William, operatic basso; b. Arlington, Mass., Nov. 23, 1887; s. William and Wilhelmina (Olson) G.; student Columbia University; m. Mary Wells Capewell, July 11, 1921; children—Elizabeth, William. Made his first professional appearance at Boston, 1915; joined Metropolitan Opera Co., New York, 1920; principal rôles: Gurnemanz, in Parsifal; King Henry, in Lohengrin; King Mark, in Tristan and Isolde; etc.; created rôle of Maccus in world premier of The King's Henchman, Metropolitan Opera House, 1927. Second lt., 17th Inf., U.S.A., during World War; served at Camp Lee, Va., and Camp Meade, Md. Home: Windsor, Vt. Deceased.

GUSTAFSON, Zadel Barnes (Mrs.), author; b. Middletown, Conn., Mar. 9, 1841; d. Duane and Cynthia Sexton (Turner) Barnes; early edn. at home, later at St. Thomas' Hall Female Sem., Flushing, L.I., 1852, Wilbraham Acad., Mass., 1856; married. Began writing in local papers at 13; poems in The Home Journal at 15. Traveled and sojourned in Great Britain, Europe, India and Australia and contributed to periodicals published in those countries, in which she also lectured on drink and woman suffrage. Initiated and for short time edited National Philanthropist, London, 1884; accredited representative of and contbr. to Pall Mall Gazette in U.S., 1886; national del. and speaker before 1st Internat. Congress of Women, Washington, 1888. Was extensive contbr. to Harper's Monthly from 1870 to 1889 (20 years). Author: Biography of Genevieve Ward, 1881; (joint author with Mr. Gustafson), The Foundation of Death—A Study of the Drink Question (containing, in an appendix, the most extensive bibliography of the drink question ever published. Home: Huntington, L.I., N.Y. Died 1917.

GUTELIUS, Frederick Passmore, ry. official; b. Mifflinburg, Pa., Dec. 21, 1864; s. Jacob and Mary (Passmore) G.; desc. John Peter Gutelius, from France, M.D., Philadelphia, 1750; C.E., Lafayette Coll., 1887 (Sc.D., 1914); m. Anna Walker Eaton, Apr. 21, 1892. Began as engr. in charge constrn. sewer system, Englewood, N.J., 1887; asst. engr. Pa. Lines West of Pittsburgh, and asst. supervisor, 1888-92; hydraulic engring., Butte, Mont., 1892-94; county surveyor Silver Bow Co., Mont., 1894-95; took charge Trail Creek Tramway, B.C., 1895; later gen. supt. Columbia & Western R.R.; with Canadian Pacific Ry., 1898-1912, as div. supt. and various other positions, including gen. supt. Eastern Div., at Montreal, 1910-12; apptd. by Govt. as gen. mgr. Canadian Govt. Rys., 1912, also serving on Royal Commn. which was apptd. to investigate constrn. of Nat. Transcontinental Ry.; in active management Canadian Govt. Rys., 1913-17, making them pay $1,000,000 per yr. surplus, whereas never before had they paid operating expenses; made v.p. in charge operation and traffic D. & H. Co., June 1, 1917, now resident v.p.; federal mgr. same rd. during war period. V.p. Quebec, Montreal & Southern Ry. Co. Inventor smoke jack for railroad engine houses, and improved farm gate. Mason. Home: Westmount, P.Q. Died Sept. 12, 1935.

GUTH, William Westley, college pres.; b. Nashville, Tenn., Oct. 15, 1871; s. George and Susan Sophie (Le Grandlienard) G.; prep. edn. Acad. of U. of the Pacific; A.B., Stanford, 1895; student Hastings Coll. of Law; admitted to bar, 1895; practiced in San Francisco, 1895-98; S.T.B., Boston U., 1901; studied univs. of Halle and Berlin, Germany, 5 semesters; Ph.D., U. of Halle, 1904; m. Helen Louise Fischbeck, Mar. 10, 1896; 1 dau., Helen Louise. Ordained M.E. ministry, 1900; pastor West Chelmsford, Mass., 1900-01, Epworth Ch., Cambridge, Mass., 1904-08; pres. Coll. of Pacific, 1908-13; pres. Goucher Coll., Baltimore, Oct. 5, 1913—. Resigned from ministry, Apr. 1919. Has traveled extensively in Egypt, Palestine and Asia Minor and continent of Europe, and England. Author: The Assurance of Faith, 1911; Revelation and Its Record, 1912; Spiritual Values, 1912; The Teachers' Teacher, 1913. Home: Baltimore, Md. Died Apr. 19, 1929.

GUTHE, Karl Eugen, physicist; b. Hanover, Germany, Mar. 5, 1866; s. Otto and Anna (Hanstein) G.; ed. Gymnasium, Hanover, Hanover Tech. Sch., univs. of Marburg, Strassburg and Berlin; passed state exam., Marburg, 1889, Ph.D., 1892; m. Clara Belle Ware, 1892. Came to U.S., 1892; instr. physics, 1893-1900, asst. prof., 1900-03, U. of Mich.; asso. physicist, Bur. of Standards, 1903-05; prof. physics, State U. of Iowa, 1905-09; prof. physics, 1909—, dean of Grad. Dept., 1912—, U. of Mich. Mem. jury of awards (electricity) St. Louis Expn., 1904. Fellow A.A.A.S. (v.p. 1908). Author: Manual of Physical Measurements (with J. O. Reed), 1902, 07, 12; Laboratory Exercises with Primary and Storage Cells, 1903; Textbook of Physics (joint author), 1908, 1909; College Physics (with J. O. Reed), 1911; Definitions in Physics, 1913. Home: Ann Arbor, Mich. Died Sept. 10, 1915.

GUTHERZ, Carl, artist; b. Switzerland, 1844; s. Heinrich and Henrietta G.; came to U.S., 1851; modeled clay in his father's terra cotta art works at Cincinnati; commenced painting at Memphis, Tenn., 1866; studied in the Académie des Beaux Arts, Paris; also in Belgium and Italy; returned to Memphis, 1872; located in St. Louis, 1874-84; established art work in Washington Univ., now St. Louis School of Fine Arts; subsequently spent 12 yrs. in Paris; returned to U.S.; m. Kate Scruggs, 1879. Received medal and diploma Internat. Expn., Phila., 1876, and Paris, 1889; mem. Nat. Jury, Chicago World's Fair. His specialties are portraits and figure pieces, in oil and water-colors. Painted The Light of Incarnation; Evening of Sixth Day. Also mural paintings: The Spectrum of Light (in Library of Congress); Law and Justice (pictorial scheme in 14 parts), Fort Wayne Court House; and a pictorial development of the Unitarian Theology in People's Ch., St. Paul. Mem. advisory com. and Nat. Jury, St. Louis Expn., 1904. Home: Washington, D.C. Died 1907.

GUTHRIE, Anna Lorraine, editor; b. York, N.Y.; d. John and Alice H. (Crawford) G.; B.A., U. of Minn., 1892. Reference librarian U. of Minn., 1893-1904; editor Readers' Guide to Periodical Literature, 1902-14; Index to the Forum, 1902; Library Work, 1905-11; Eclectic Library Catalog, later Readers' Guide Abridged, 1907-10; Readers' Guide Supplement, 1913; Index to St. Nicholas, 1919. Compiler (study outlines): Municipal Civics, 1915; Early American Literature, 1916; Contemporary American Literature, 1917; American Art, 1917; Russian Literature, 1917. Christian Scientist. Home: Seattle, Wash. Died Jan. 2, 1936.

GUTHRIE, Charles Ellsworth, denominational sec.; b. Terra Alta, W.Va., May 26, 1867; s. George E. and Nancy Catherine (Dawson) G.; ed. normal sch. and under pvt. tutors; Johns Hopkins, 1894-98; D.D., Dickinson, 1911; m. Beulah Cowan, August 10, 1892 (died 1934); children—Freedom Cowan (dec.), Mrs. Eleanor Wallace, Philip Dawson, Carl Strawbridge; m. 2d, Gladys Mae Snyder, Oct. 5, 1936. Ordained to the ministry of M.E. church, 1890; pastor, Hancock, Md., 1887, Rawlings, Md., 1888, Walkersville, Md., 1889, Pikesville, Md., 1890-92, Baltimore, 1893-1907, Washington, D.C., 1908-10, Wilkes-Barre, Pa., 1911-15, Buffalo, N.Y., 1916-17; gen. sec. Epworth League, 1917-24; pastor University Ch., Syracuse, 1924-26; supt. Buffalo Dist. of M.E. Ch., 1927-33; pastor Baker Memorial Ch., East Aurora, N.Y., 1934-36, Coudersport, Pa., 1937-39; retired. Pres. Interdenom. Young People's Union; mem. council of benevolent bds. M.E. Ch.; mem. Gen. Conf. M.E. Ch., 1920, 24, 32; apptd. by bishops as rep. of M.E. Ch. to Sixth Ecumenical Meth. Conf., Atlanta, 1931; rep. of M.E. Ch. to Fed. Council of Chs. of Christ in America (com. on mercy and relief); mem. Council Internat. Friendship Through the Churches, 1927; trustee Genesee Wesleyan Sem., Blocher Homes (for aged), Williamsville, N.Y.; mem. bd. dirs. Methodist Home for Children (Williamsville, N.Y.). Mason. Republican. Home: East Aurora, N.Y. Died July 26, 1940.

GUTHRIE, George Wilkins, ambassador; b. Pittsburgh, Pa., Sept. 5, 1848; s. John B. G.; A.B., Western U. of Pa. (now U. of Pittsburgh), 1866, A.M., 1868; LL.B., Columbian (now George Washington) U., 1869; (LL.D., U. of Pittsburgh, 1905, Trinity Coll., 1907); m. Florence J., d. Thomas M. Howe, of Pittsburgh, Dec. 2, 1886. Admitted to bar, 1869, and since in practice at Pittsburgh. Mem. Pa. State Commn. which erected the Home for Feeble-Minded at Polk, Pa.; candidate for Citizens' Municipal League for mayor of Pittsburgh, in reform campaign, 1896; mem. com. Nat. Municipal League on Municipal Program (report published, 1900). Asso. counsel Tilden electors before Fla. Returning Bd., 1876; asst. sec. Dem. Nat. Conv., Chicago, 1884; Dem. candidate for lt. gov. Pa., 1902 (nominated unanimously by State Conv.). Mayor of Pittsburgh, 1906-09; ambassador extraordinary and plenipotentiary to Japan, 1913—. V.p. and trustee Dollar Savings Bank. Trustee U. of Pittsburgh; pres. St. Margaret's Memorial Hosp.; mem. bd. mgrs. Kingsley House Assn. Hon. mem. and mem. bd. govs. Pittsburgh Chamber of Commerce. Mason. Home: Pittsburgh, Pa. Died Mar. 8, 1917.

GUTHRIE, Joseph Edward, prof. zoölogy; b. York, N.Y., Sept. 24, 1871; s. James F. and Agnes (McCracken) G.; B.S., U. of Minn., 1900, M.S., 1901; m. Emma Florence Brooks, Dec. 28, 1904; children—Charles Francis, Jean Brooks. With Ia. State Coll. Agr. and Mechanic Arts, 1901—, consecutively asst. in zoölogy until 1904, asst. prof., 1904-14, asso. prof., 1914-17, prof., 1917—. Conglist. Author: The Collembola of Minnesota, 1903; The Snakes of Iowa, 1926. Home: Ames, Ia. Died Apr. 16, 1935.

GUTHRIE, Kenneth Sylvan, author; b. Dundee, Scotland, July 22, 1871; s. Dr. William Eugene and Frances Sylva Phiquepal (d'Arusmont) G.; A.B. and A.M., U. of the South, 1890; Ph.D., Tulane U., 1893; A.M., Harvard, 1894; M.D., Medico-Chirurg. Coll., Phila., 1903 (3 medals—surgery, practice, pediatrics); state diplomas, Pa. and N.J.; studied at Univs. of Marburg and Jena, 1910; also graduate of divinity; m. Mary Jane Cooper; children—Sylvia Camilla d'Arusmont, Kenneth Launfal Laureolus. Ordained deacon, 1892, ordained priest, 1897, P.E. Church; in charge at Natchitoches, La., 1892-93; rector of St. John's Ch., Hingham, Mass., 1893-94; asst. Ch. of Incarnation, Phila., 1894-99; vicar All Saints Ch., New York, 1915-25; St. Mark's Chapel, Nepera Park, N.Y., 1925—; teacher Boys' High Sch.,

New York, 1906, Washington Irving High Sch., 1907—. Prof. univ. extension, U. of the South, 1912, and Hunter Coll., N.Y., 1917; North Node lecturer, 1925, on Leaders and Message of Neoplatonism; has also lectured widely in the East and South. Mason. Author: Of Communion With God, 1895; The Philosophy of Plotinus, 1896; Plutarch's Genius of Socrates, 1904; The Spiritual Message of Literature, 1905; The Message of Philo Judæus, 1909; Once More Must the Methods of Modern Language Teaching Be Revised, 1912; also Of the Presence of God; Songs of the Presence; The Ladder of God, and Other Sermons; The Reuniting Pilgrimage; Perronik, the Simple-Hearted, 1915; Teachers' Problems Solved, 1917; Numenius Apamea, 1917, etc. Translator of numerous works. Home: Yonkers, N.Y. Died Apr. 1940.

GUTHRIE, Lewis Van Gilder, M.D.; b. Point Pleasant, W.Va., Jan. 8, 1868; s. Judge Francis Asbury and Clara Elizabeth (Van Gilder) G.; student Va. Poly. Inst., and Roanoke Coll., Salem, Va.; M.D., Coll. Phys. and Surg., Baltimore, 1889; m. Margaret L. English, June 1889; children—Kathleen Lewis (Mrs. Frank Witcher McCullough), F. Elizabeth (Mrs. Ben Williamson). Began practice at Point Pleasant, 1889; supt. 2d Hosp. for Insane, Spencer, W.Va., 1897-1901; supt. Huntington State Hosp. since 1901; cons. psychiatrist, U.S. War Risk Ins. for W.Va.; med. examiner Cabell Co. (W.Va.) Lunacy Commn.; v.p. First Nat. Bank, Huntington. Auditor Am. Psychiatric Assn.; chmn. State Commn. for Mental Hygiene. Republican. Mason. Died Sept. 20, 1930.

GUTHRIE, Walter James, lawyer; b. Apollo, Pa., Sept. 9, 1864; s. John Beatty and Mary Jane (Freetly) G.; grad. Blairsville (Pa.) Acad.; A.B., Allegheny Coll., 1884, A.M., 1889; m. Bella G. Giles, July 10, 1901; children—Douglas Giles (dec.), Laura Jean, Margaret Ruth (dec.), Walter J., Richard G. Admitted to Pa. bar, 1887, and began practice at Apollo; sec. and atty. for Pa., Gulf Oil Corp., Pittsburgh, 1907-20; sec. and asso. gen. counsel for same and subsidiary corps., 1920-38; v.p. Apollo Steel Co.; dir. Apollo Trust Co. Republican. Methodist. Mason. Home: Pittsburgh, Pa.; also Miami, Fla. Died Mar. 1940.

GUTHRIE, William Anderson, capitalist; b. nr. Dupont, Ind., May 13, 1851; s. Anderson Crawford and Ann (Wilson) G.; ed. College Hill Coll. (now defunct) and Moores Hill Coll. (now Evansville, Ind., Coll.); m. Sarah Lewis, Oct. 28, 1875; children—George Lewis, Lucy Anne (Mrs. Earl Willis Crecraft). V.p. Belt R.R. and Stock Yards Co., Fletcher Av. Saving & Loan Assn.; pres. Union Land & Timber Co., Fla. Orchards Co. Mem. State Senate, Ind., 1900-04; state chmn. Dept. of Conservation, Ind., 1917—; mem. Ind. Council Gt. Lakes-St. Lawrence Tidewater Assn. Republican. Baptist. Mason. Home: Dupont, Ind. Died Aug. 5, 1936.

GUTHRIE, William Buck, educator; b. Sand Spring, Ia., Sept. 8, 1869; s. Peter and Janann (Stewart) G.; B.S., Lenox Coll., Hopkinton, Ia., 1893; Ph.B., Ia. U., 1895; student U. of Chicago, 1897-98, U. of Berlin, 1900-02, U. of Paris, 1902-03, Ph.D., Columbia, 1907; m. Jennie Kelso Mar. 4, 1909; children—Jean Sophia, Mary Ellen. Tutor, Coll. of City of N.Y., 1903-09, instr., 1909-25, prof. of govt. and head dept. of govt. and sociology, 1925—; lecturer U. of the People, 1904-22; former lecturer on investments, N.Y. Univ.; former summer sch. lecturer, Colo. Teachers Coll., U. of Wyo.; supt. Riverside Settlement, 1903-07; lecturer Nat. Security League; radio lecturer, WNYC; organizer and chmn. Manhattan Community Council. Republican. Mem. Reformed Presbyn. Ch. Author: Socialism Before French Revolution, 1907; The American Government (with W. F. Barber), 1935; American Government (briefer edit. with C. P. Patterson), 1935. Reviser: Finer's Theory and Practice of Modern Government, 1935; Goodnow's Principles of Administrative Law in The United States, 1937. Home: Yonkers, N.Y. Died Nov. 6, 1940.

GUTHRIE, William Dameron, lawyer; b. San Francisco, Feb. 3, 1859; s. George Whitney and Emma (Gosson) G.; ed. France and Eng.; Columbia Law Sch., 1879-80; hon. A.M., Yale, 1904; LL.D., Fordham, 1916; Doctor honoris causa, U. of Paris, 1932; m. Ella Fuller, May 12, 1891; 1 dau., Ella G. (Mrs. Arthur W. Rossiter). Argued income tax, Calif. irrigation, Ill. inheritance tax, oleomargarine and Kansas City stock yards rate cases, also prohibition and Ore. sch. law cases in U.S. Supreme Court. Storrs lecturer at Yale, 1907-08; Ruggles prof. constl. law, Columbia U., 1909-22. Grand Officer of Legion of Honor (French); Comdr. Order of St. Gregory (by Pope Pius); Master Knight of Sovereign Order of Malta; Grand Cross of Order of St. Lazare of Jerusalem. Author: Lectures on the Fourteenth Amendment to the Constitution; Magna Carta and other Essays; The League of Nations and Miscellaneous Addresses; etc. Died Dec. 8, 1935.

GUY, Charles Lewis, judge; b. New York, N.Y., Jan. 6, 1856; s. Pierre A. and Sarah B. (Swift) G.; ed. Coll. City of New York, Columbia Law Sch.; m. Eliza M. Bowen, May 16, 1888. Admitted to bar, 1881; mem. N.Y. Senate, 13th and 20th N.Y. dists., 1894-99; asst. corp. counsel, New York, 1904-07; justice Supreme Ct. of N.Y., 1st dist., 1907—. Democrat. Home: New York, N.Y. Died July 21, 1930.

GUY, Harvey Hugo, lecturer; b. Osage City, Kan., Nov. 9, 1871; s. William Henry and Melissa (March) G.; student Garfield U. (now defunct), Wichita, Kan., 1888-90; B.D., Drake U., Des Moines, Ia., 1893, A.B., 1897, A.M., 1900; studied U. of Chicago, 1900-01; A.M., Yale, 1902, Ph.D., 1903; m. Martha Theoni Andrews, June 20, 1893; children—Bernard Andrews, Harriet Geraldine (Mrs. Henry Finke, Jr.). Missionary student and teacher, Japan, 1893-99; dean Sei Gakuin Theol. Sem., 1903-07; supt. Japanese missions in Calif., 1907-09; dean, Berkeley Bible Sem., 1909-12; prof. Ch. History, 1912-16, prof. history and philosophy of religion, 1916-19, Pacific Sch. of Religion. Lecturer history of the Far East, Coll. of Missions, Indianapolis, Ind., 1921-22. Dir. of research for Institute of Social and Religious Research in China and Japan, 1930-32. Republican. Lectured in Japan on Am.-Japanese relations, under Japanese-Am. Relations Com., of Tokyo, 1907-08. Home: Alameda, Calif. Died Jan. 30, 1936.

GUY, Seymour Joseph, artist; b. Greenwich, Eng., Jan. 16, 1824; studied art in London; from 1854 in New York; m. Anna M., d. late W. W. Barber, engraver U.S. Mint, Phila. Paints portraits and genre pictures, his later work being principally drawn from incidents in child life. A.N.A., 1861, N.A., 1865; mem. Am. Soc. Painters in Water Colors from its organization, 1866. Home: New York, N.Y. Died 1910.

GUY, William Evans, retired mining and civil engr.; b. Cincinnati, Dec. 22, 1844; s. Alexander (M.D.) and Susan Ann Livingston (Wade) G.; Miami U., Oxford, O., 1860-62, 1863; A.B., Princeton, 1865, A.M., 1868; U. of Heidelberg, Germany, 1865-66; Freiberg Sch. of Mines, 1866-69; Collége de France, Paris, 1869; LL.B., Cincinnati Law Sch., 1879; LL.D., Westminster Coll., Fulton, Mo., 1917; m. Katherine, d. of Dr. E. S. Lemoine, of St. Louis, Mar. 13, 1894; children—Katherine Lemoine (Mrs. Henry S. F. Cooper), William Edwin, David Wade, Evelyn Spotswood. Asst. supt., Stewart Silver Reduction Works, Georgetown, Colo., 1870-71; asst. geologist, Mo. State Geol. Survey, 1872; one of 3 founders, and v.p. St. Louis Bolt & Iron Co., 1872-81; also organized, and was pres. Tudor Iron Works, 1879-81; consolidated the two as Tudor Iron Works, of which was v.p., 1881-86; organized, built and was pres. of St. Louis & Eastern Ry., 1889-95; organized, and was pres. Madison Coal Co., 1889-99; organized, built and was pres. and gen. mgr. St. Louis, Peoria & Northern Ry., 1895-99, when it became part of the I.C. system; organized, built and was pres. and gen. mgr. St. Louis Valley Ry., 1901-03 (now part Mo.P. Ry.), also St. Louis & Gulf Ry., 1902-03 (now part Frisco system); retired. Pvt. and 1st sergt. 86th Ohio Inf., 1862. Nominated for pres. City Council, St. Louis, 1900; mem. exec. com. Civil Service Reform Assn. 20 yrs. Presbyn. Home: St. Louis; (summer) Cooperstown, N.Y. Died July 24, 1928.

GUYER, William Harris, clergyman, educator; b. Waterside, Pa., Sept. 2, 1870; s. Adam Bowers and Mary Ann (Mock) G.; A.B., Findlay (Ohio) Coll., 1906, A.M., 1909; D.D., Defiance (Ohio) Coll., 1914; m. Myrtle Emma Hartsock, Nov. 17, 1897; children—Carlos, James, Elizabeth, William, Dorothy, Tennyson. Teacher, pub. schs. and acads. several yrs.; ordained ministry Ch. of God, 1895; pastor Beaver County, Pa., 1898-1902, Barkeyville, 1902-08, Alverton, 1908-12, College Ch., Findlay, O., 1913—; prof. theology, Findlay Coll., 1912-14, pres., 1914—. Republican. Home: Findlay, O. Died July 22, 1926.

GWIN, Earl Stimson, banker; b. Carlisle, Ind., Sept. 7, 1875; s. Charles Polk and Isadora (Alsop) G.; pub. sch. edn.; m. Martha A. Cadwalader, Nov. 5, 1896. Began as messenger 2d Nat. Bank, New Albany, 1890, pres. Feb. 1908-June 1914; pres. Am. Southern Nat. Bank, June 1914-Feb. 1919, at which time consolidated with Nat. Bank of Ky. and Nat. Bank of Commerce, v.p. Nat. Bank of Ky. following consolidation; pres. Lincoln Bank & Trust Co., 1922—. Mem. Ky. State Council Defense; Ky. state chmn. Liberty Loan orgn. during the war. Dir. and treas. Ky. Chamber of Commerce; mem. Louisville Board of Trade. Democrat. Presbyn. Mason. Home: Louisville, Ky. Died Aug. 25, 1928.

GWYN, Herbert Britton, clergyman; b. Dundas, Ont., Can., May 5, 1873; s. Herbert Charles (K.C.) and Charlotte Elizabeth (Osler) G.; B.A., Trinity Coll., Toronto, 1893, M.A., 1896; completed theol. course, 1896; m. Katharine von Hof Maconochie, July 2, 1906 (died 1912); m. 2d, Virginia E. Percival, Aug. 6, 1914; 1 son, Herbert Campbell (dec.). Ordained Ch. of England in Can. ministry, 1896; curate All Saints' Ch., Toronto, 1896-99, St. Peter's Ch., Chicago, 1900-02; founder and first rector St. Simon's Ch., Chicago, 1902-12; editor-in-chief, The Churchman, 1913; priest in charge St. Edmund's Ch., Chicago, 1914-16; rector Ch. of Holy Comforter, Kenilworth, Ill., 1916-19; priest in charge of St. John's, Naperville, Ill., and of St. Catharine's, Brookfield, Ill., 1919-23; priest in charge, St. Lawrence's Ch., Libertyville, Ill., 1923-28; rector Holo Trinity Ch., Tiverton, R.I., 1928—. Corr. and contbr. The Living Church, 1915-28; editor The Diocese of Chicago, 1916-24. Chmn. Tiverton Chapter Red Cross, 1931—. Civilian chaplain at U.S. Base Hosp. No. 28, 1918-21. Republican. Home: Tiverton, R.I. Died Mar. 25, 1934.

GWYNNE, Walker, clergyman; b. Strabane, Ireland, June 7, 1845; s. Richard and Ann (Walker) G.; Strabane Acad.; B.D., Gen. Theol. Sem., New York, 1871; D.D., St. Stephen's Coll., N.Y., 1911; m. Helen Bowers Lee, Jan. 16, 1877; children—Helen Bowers, Walter Lee, Frederic Walker, Arthur, Edythe Stewart (Mrs. Reginald F. Pearson). Deacon, 1871, priest, 1872, P.E. Ch.; curate St. Paul's Ch., Albany, N.Y., 1871; priest in charge St. Paul's Free Chapel, Troy, N.Y., 1872-76; rector St. John's Ch., Cohoes, N.Y., 1876-84, St. Mark's Ch., Augustana, Maine, 1844-93, Calvary Church, Summit, N.J., 1893-1913, rector emeritus. Deputy Gen. Conv., 1889, 1892. Gen. sec. Sanctity of Marriage Assn.; hon. pres. Overlook Hosp. Corp. for Relief of Widows of Clergymen in N.J. Author: The Gospel in the Church, 1909; The Christian Year—Its Purpose and Its History, 1915; Primitive Worship and the Prayer Book, 1917; Divorce in America Under State and Church, 1925. Home: Summit, N.J. Died Feb. 19, 1931.

GYGER, Edgar Grant; b. Plattsmouth, Neb.; s. Godfrey Frederick and Sophie (Bauhof) G.; student high sch. and Burgess Acad., Plattsmouth, and high sch., Omaha, 1883-86; m. Caroline Mead Foss, Mar. 20, 1909. Began as clk., 1886; mem. staff John Wanamaker, New York, 1896-1900, Gyger of New York, Inc., 1900-04; sec., dir. Harperley Hall Co., 1913-30, pres., 1931-32, v.p., 1933-37, treas., 1937—; v.p., 1916-18, Lenox Corp., Interstate Transit Co., Motor Sales Co.—all of Greenwich, Conn.; v.p. and dir. Harperley Holding Corp., 1918—; treas. and dir. H. E. Lesan Advertising Agency, 1919-20; dir. 925 Park Avenue, Inc., 1922—, treas., 1930—; Christian Science practitioner, 1916—; first reader 8th Ch. of Christ, Scientist, New York, 1922-25, chmn. bd. trustees, 1935-38; Christian Science Com. on Publ., N.Y. State, 1926-27. Treas. and gen. mgr. Metals Fabricating Co., mfg. under U.S. Govt. supervision and contract ammunition for Ordnance Air Service, World War. Republican. Mason. Home: New York, N.Y. Died Apr. 30, 1941.

H

HAACKE, Henry, editor Cincinnati Volksfreund, 1872—; b. Hagenow, Mecklenburg, Germany, Oct. 22, 1832; s. William and Augusta (Paetow) H.; ed. common schools and Latin school, Hagenow, and grad. Med. Coll. of Ohio, 1869. Came to U.S., 1851; prof. German, Royal Coll. of Upper Canada; examiner dept. arts Univ. of Toronto; admitted to bar, Cincinnati, 1862; prof. German, Woodward High School; examiner teachers public schools, Cincinnati; trustee U. of Cincinnati; trustee Cincinnati Water Works; mem. bd. supervisors, Hamilton Co., O.; m. Katherine Tepker, Thiene, Hanover, Germany. Author: Poems (in German, original and transl. from Dutch and Russian), 1896. Died 1903.

HAAN, William George, army officer; b. Crown Point, Ind., Oct. 4, 1863; s. Nicholas and Anna M. H.; grad. U.S. Mil. Acad., 1889, Army War Coll., 1905; m. Margaret H. Haan, Aug. 16, 1905. Commd. 2d lt. 1st Arty., June 12, 1889; trans. to 5th Arty., Jan. 29, 1891; 1st lt., Aug. 29, 1896; capt. actg. q.m. vols., Oct. 17, 1898; hon. disch. from vols., Mar. 23, 1901; capt. Arty. Corps, U.S.A., Feb. 2, 1901; maj., Apr. 9, 1907; lt. col. Coast Arty. Corps, Dec. 6, 1911; col., July 1, 1916; brig. gen. N.A., Aug. 5, 1917. Served in Cuba and Philippines, 1898-1901; 3 times recommended for brevets "for conspicuous conduct in action"; served on Gen. Staff, 1903-06, 1912-14; was chief of staff Eastern Dept.; later mem. Panama Fortifications Bd. and Nat. Land Defense Bd.; apptd. comdr. 57th Field Arty. Brigade, Camp MacArthur, Tex., 1917, and of 32d Div., N.G., Jan. 1918 Died Oct. 26, 1924.

HAAS, George Christian Frederick, clergyman; b. Phila., May 5, 1854; s. John C. and Anna M. (Schur) H.; A.B., U. of Pa. (1st honor man), 1876, A.M., 1879; grad. Luth. Theol. Sem., Phila., 1880; D.D., Muhlenberg Coll., 1901; m. Anna S. Hansen, Apr. 25, 1882; children—George Christian Otto, Walter, Gertrude; m. 2d, Clara M. Holthusen, May 1, 1906. Ordained Luth. ministry, 1880; asst. pastor St. Mark's Luth. Ch., New York, 1880-82, sole pastor, 1882-1921; now prof. Wagner Memorial Lutheran Coll. Pres. N.Y. Ministerium (the Evang. Luth. Ministerium of N.Y. and adjacent states), 1893-96, 1899-1902, 1908-11, 1914-17; mem. or chmn. various important bds. and coms. of the Ministerium, and also of Gen. Council Evang. Luth. Ch. in America. Co-worker and editor of German S.S. Lesson Leaves, and of Bible Story for Sunday Schs. (English and German), 1889—, later editor same. Mem. gen. council Publication Bd. Died Sept. 29, 1927.

HAAS, Gustav, editor; b. Ludwigsburg, Wuerttemberg, Germany, July 14, 1861; s. Carl and Agnes (Binder) H.; ed. Gymnasium (Stuttgart), Royal Prussian Cadet Sch. (Berlin), War Sch. (Hanover); m. Ida Krueger, May 5, 1888; 1 son, Grant Carl. Became officer in German army, 1880; hon. disch. on application, 1883; came to U.S., 1883, naturalized citizen, 1890; draftsman constrn. dept. Pullman Palace Car Co., Pullman, Ill., writing also for German lang. newspapers; reporter Anzeiger, Cleveland, O., 1885; identified with Milwaukee Herold, 1886—, editor in chief, 1917—. Republican. Protestant. Author: A Book of Love (Ein Buch der Liebe), 1919. Home: Wauwatosa, Wis. Deceased.

HAAS, John A. W., college pres.; b. Phila., Aug. 31, 1862; s. John C. and Anna M. (Schur) H.; A.B., U. of Pa., 1884, A.M., 1887, B.D., 1887; student Lutheran Theol. Sem., Phila., 1887, U. of Leipzig, 1887-88; D.D., Thiel, 1902; LL.D., U. of Pa., 1914, Augustana Coll., 1917, Gettysburg Coll., 1922; m. Charlotte W. R. Boschen, Oct. 6, 1891. Ordained Luth. ministry; pastor Grace Ch., 1888-96, St. Paul's Ch., 1896-1904 (erected new ch., 1898), New York; pres. and prof. philosophy, Muhlenberg Coll., 1904—. University preacher at Harvard. Author: In the Light of Faith, 1922; Freedom and Christian Conduct, 1923; The Unity of Faith and Knowledge, 1926; The Truth of Faith, 1927; What Ought I to Believe?, 1929; The Christian Way of Liberty, 1930; Christianity and Its Contrasts, 1932. Home: Allentown, Pa. Died July 22, 1937.

HAASS, Julius Henry, banker; b. Detroit, Feb. 22, 1869; s. Charles W. F. and Marie (Clippert) H.; ed. pub. and pvt. schs.; m. Lillian Henkel, Nov. 21, 1898; 1 dau., Constance. Became connected with Home Savings Bank, Detroit, upon its orgn., 1889, cashier, 1894, pres. 1909 until consolidation with Wayne County Savings Bank, 1914, then pres. Wayne County & Home Savings Bank; became pres. Peoples Wayne County Bank, Detroit. Republican. Mem. Evangelical Ch. Home: Grosse Pointe Farms, Mich. Died Apr. 17, 1931.

HABBERTON, John, author; b. Brooklyn, N.Y., Feb. 24, 1842; s. J. J. and Esther E. (Peck) H.; lived in Ill., 1850-59; ed. in public schools there; learned printing trade in New York; m. Alice L. Hastings, Feb. 25, 1868. Served, private to lt., 1862-65, in New York vols. and U.S. colored inf.; employed in counting room, Harper & Bros., publishers; later in business for himself; literary editor Christian Union, 1874-77; on editorial staff New York Herald, 1876-93, and on Collier's Weekly, 1897-99. Author: Helen's Babies; Trif and Trixie; Poor Boys' Chances; Budge and Toddie, 1909. His only drama, Deacon Crankett, performed more than 500 times. Home: Westwood, N.J. Died Feb. 25, 1921.

HACKETT, Charles, operatic tenor; b. Worcester, Mass.; s. Charles A. and Bridget L. (Welch) H.; high sch. edn. m. Virginia Zucchi; children—Carla, Joan, Charles. Began singing in Glee Club of Worcester High Sch., then served as soloist in Arlington Street Ch., Boston; appeared in concert with Mme. Nordica, at Providence, R.I., at age of 19, and as tenor in Verdi's "Requiem Mass," with Gluck, Homer and Witherspoon, in Carnegie Hall, New York; studied voice in Florence, Italy; début in "Mignon," in Genoa, 1916, and was immediately engaged to sing at La Scala, making 14 appearances there; gave 68 performances in Buenos Aires; returned to Europe and later again visited South America. New York début with Metropolitan Opera Co., in "The Barber of Seville," 1919; joined Chicago Civic Opera Co., 1923; début in Romeo and Juliet; rejoined Metropolitan Opera Co. in Romeo and Juliet, 1933. Made Chevalier of the Crown of Italy by King Victor Emmanuel, 1931, for service to Italian art. Died Jan. 1, 1942.

HACKETT, Frank Warren, lawyer; b. Portsmouth, N.H., Apr. 11, 1841; s. William H. Y. and Olive (Pickering) H.; A.B., Harvard, 1861, A.M., 1864; studied law at Portsmouth, N.H.; Phila., with B. H. Brewster, afterward atty. gen. U.S., and at Harvard Law Sch.; m. Ida, youngest d. late Rear Admiral Thomas Tingey Craven, U.S.N., Apr. 1880; children—Chauncey, William Henry Young. Acting asst. p.m. U.S.N., 1862-64; was p.m. of U.S.S. Miami, N. Atlantic Squadron, on board at Plymouth, N.C., 1864, when Lt. Comdr. Charles W. Flusser was killed in engagement with Confederate ram Albemarle. Admitted to the bar, 1866; opened law office in Boston. Private sec. Caleb Cushing, sr. counsel Geneva Arbitration, 1872; in practice at Washington, 1873-1920; asst. sec. of the navy, Apr. 1900-Dec. 1901; resigned. Pres. N.H. Hist. Soc., 1912-13. Republican. Author: The Gavel and the Mace, 1900; Deck and Field, 1909; Reminiscences of the Geneva Tribunal of Arbitration (1872) of the Alabama Claims, 1911. Home: New Castle, N.H. Died Aug. 10, 1926.

HACKETT, Horatio Balch, architect; b. Philadelphia, May 8, 1880; s. Horatio Balch and Jane (Fraley) H.; grad. William Penn Charter Sch., Phila., 1899; grad. U.S. Mil. Acad., 1904; m. Winifred Marshall, Nov. 16, 1906. Served as 2d lt. U.S. Army, 1904-06 (resigned); architectural supt. D. H. Burnham & Co., Chicago, 1906-14; gen. supt. Embree Iron Co., Embreeville, Tenn., 1914-17; col. 124th F.A., 33d Div., U.S. Army, 1917-19; now col. F.A.O.R.C.; awarded D.S.M., Silver Star and Purple Heart decorations. With John Burnham & Co., stocks and bonds, Chicago, 1919-22; mem. Holabird & Root, architects, Chicago, 1922-34; apptd. gen. mgr. Federal Pub. Works Emergency Housing Corp., Feb. 1934, dir. housing PWA, June 1934, asst. adminstr. PWA, May 1935-Sept. 1937; mem. exec. com. Nat. Assn. Housing Officials, Dec. 1934; mem. President's Advisory Bd. on Allotments, May 1935; v.p. Chicago Venetian Blind Co. and Coath & Goss, Inc. (gen. contractors), Chicago, 1937; pres. and dir. Thompson-Starrett Co. (gen. contractors), New York, Mar. 1, 1938—. Mem. advisory bd. Football Rules Com. Mem. Bd. Local Improvements, Chicago, 1932-34. Mason. Home: New York, N.Y. Died Sept. 8, 1941.

HACKETT, James Keteltas, actor-mgr.; b. Am. parents sojourning in Can., at Wolfe Island, Ont., Sept. 6, 1869; s. James Henry (Am. actor) and Clara C. H.; B.A., Coll. City of New York, 1891; studied New York Law Sch.; m. Mary Mannering, May 2, 1897; 1 dau., Elise Mannering Keteltas; m. 2d, Beatrice Mary Beckley, of London, Dec. 17, 1911. Début in Palmer's Stock Co., Park Theatre, Phila., Mar. 1892; became leading man New York Lyceum at 24; first star to appear on screen for Famous Players on their foundation in "Prisoner of Zenda," 1912; produced many successful plays, either as mgr., actor or both. With Harrison Grey Fiske, Mrs. Fiske and Henrietta Crosman organized Independent Booking Agency, 1902, in opposition to trust; was pres. same. A noted production was Shakespeare's "Macbeth," prod. Criterion Theatre, New York, 1916; played in all-star cast of "Out There," for Am. Red Cross, 1918, netting for Red Cross $700,000 in 3 weeks (awarded Red Cross badge for exceptional service, 1919); appeared as Old Bill in "The Better 'Ole"; created rôle of Silas Lapham in "The Rise of Silas Lapham," Garrick Theatre, New York, 1919; took entire "Macbeth" production to London, 1920, and appeared as Macbeth at Aldwych Theatre, with a distinguished English company; accepted invitation of French Govt. to play "Macbeth" in Paris; received permission to invite English actors to participate, and for the first time in the history of the stage the dramatic art was represented by three nations in a state-subsidized theatre; the President of the U.S., through the Secretary of State and the U.S. ambassador, officially felicitated the player, and the Crown Prince of Japan and ambassadors of nearly every other nation in Paris were present at the performance; decorated by French Govt. with Cross of Legion of Honor; also appeared in Paris and London in "Othello," and at Stratford-on-Avon, as guest of honor, in same play, 1922; twice the guest of the King and Queen of England, at Buckingham Palace; represented Shakespeare and his works in Opera House, Paris, appearing as Shakespeare himself in the finale of the Tercentenary Celebration, in honor of Molière; decorated by the Authors and Composers of France in recognition of his "profound mastery of his great art." On return to New York, Jan. 1924, was tendered public reception at the City Hall and granted freedom of the city; also officially welcomed by the gov. of N.Y. at Albany, and nationally welcomed from Washington, D.C., by Sec. of State Charles E. Hughes. Chevalier Légion d'Honneur (France). Home: Clayton, N.Y. Died Nov. 8, 1926.

HACKETT, Karleton Spalding, musician; b. Brookline, Mass., Oct. 8, 1867; s. Francis Wilber and Isabelle Izette (Spalding) H.; ed. Boston and Roxbury Latin schs. and Harvard U., class of '91; studied at Florence, Italy, 1889-93, also at London and Munich; m. Gena Florence Castle, Mar. 9, 1896; 1 dau., Dorothy. Located at Chicago, 1893; head of vocal dept., Music School of Northwestern U., 1896-1911; became head of vocal dept., 1897, v.p., 1906, pres. 1932, Am. Conservatory of Music, Chicago. Formerly music critic and contbr. Chicago Evening Post, and The Chicagoan; asso. editor The Musician. Republican. Studio: Chicago, Ill. Died Oct. 7, 1935.

HACKETT, William Stormont, mayor, banker; b. Albany, N.Y., Dec. 7, 1868; s. John and Martha (Stormont) H.; ed. high sch.; unmarried. Discount clk. Albany City Nat. Bank, 1887-93; treas. and sec. City Savings Bank, Albany, 1893-1917, pres., 1917—; pres. City Safe Deposit Co., Central N.Y. Title Guaranty Co., Boulevard Garage Co. Admitted to N.Y. Bar, 1889; mayor of Albany, 1922-26. Democrat. Baptist. York and Scottish Rite Mason, Elk. Home: Albany, N.Y. Died Mar. 4, 1926.

HACKH, Ingo W(aldemar) D(agobert), prof. chemistry; b. Stuttgart, Germany, Mar. 25, 1890; s. Eugen and Frieda (Hack) H.; preparatory edn. Realgymnasium and Technische Hochschule, Stuttgart; student Drogisten Akademie, Braunschweig, Germany; A.B., U. of Calif., 1918; A.M. from the same university, 1933; m. Vera Eliot, Feb. 11, 1919. Came to U.S., 1912, naturalized citizen, 1921. Chemist, control lab., E. de Haen, Germany, 1908-10, Abbott Labs., Chicago, 1912-13, Research Lab. for Tuberculosis, Asheville, N.C., 1913-15; lecture and lab. asst., U. of Calif., 1916-18; prof. chemistry, Coll. Phys. and Surg., San Francisco, 1918—. Fellow A.A.A.S., Am. Inst. Chemists, Royal Soc. of Arts (London). Lutheran. Author: Chemical Reactions and Equations, 1922, 28; A Chemical Dictionary, 1929, 35; Structure Symbols of Organic Compounds, 1931. Home: San Francisco, Calif. Died Oct. 19, 1938.

HACKLEY, Charles H., lumberman; b. Michigan City, Ind., Jan. 3, 1837; moved in early boyhood to Southport (now Kenosha), Wis. When 15 yrs. old engaged in plank road building; worked passage on schooner to Muskegon, Mich., 1856; worked in mill as laborer and foreman; went to commercial school; became bookkeeper and, later, partner in mill firm; acquired large interests. Bought a square in Muskegon, removed the buildings, turned it into a park at a cost of $70,000 and in the center built a $20,000 soldiers' monument; gave the park to the city; also gave the city a $200,000 public library, a $60,000 high school and a $75,000 central school. Home: Muskegon, Mich. Died 1905.

HACKNEY, Walter S., banker; b. Aurora, Ill., 1860; s. Benjamin and Lydia (Wightman) H.; ed. Racine (Wis.) Coll.; m. Clara D. Child, Nov. 15, 1899. Credit mgr. Crane Co., Chicago, 10 yrs., until formation of Gen. Fire Extinguisher Co., 1892, by consolidation of various cos.; dir. and treas. same, 1893—; dir. Nat. Bank of Commerce, Providence, R.I., 1899-Oct. 1914 (resigned); dir. and mem. exec. com. R.I. Fire Ins. Co.; dir. Federal Reserve Bank, Boston, Oct. 1914—, and deputy federal reserve agt. and vice chmn. same. Republican. Episcopalian. Home: Providence, R.I. Died 1917.

HADDEN, Alexander, lawyer; b. Wheeling, Va. (now W.Va.), July 2, 1850; s. Alexander and Mary Eliza (Welch) H.; Shaw Acad., East Cleveland, O.; A.B., Oberlin Coll., 1873; m. Frances Hawthorne, July 17, 1883 (died 1914); m. 2d, Jessie E. Hutchins, Mar. 29, 1917 (died 1923). Began practice in Cleveland, 1875; partner Harvey D. Goulder, 1881, 82, prosecuting atty's. asst., 1882-85, pros. atty., 1886-90; probate judge, Cuyahoga Co., Feb. 2, 1905—; prof. criminal law, Western Reserve U. Law Sch., 1894—. Republican. Unitarian. Home: Euclid, O. Died April 1926.

HADDEN, Archibald; b. Wheeling, W.Va., Oct. 27, 1855; s. Alexander and Mary Eliza (Welch) H.; B.A., Oberlin, 1877; B.D., Yale, 1880; A.M., Olivet Coll., 1912, D.D., 1902; m. Sarah Bean, Feb. 23, 1881; children—Elizabeth M., Arthur A., Mrs. Helen G. Harkness and Mrs. Jean M. Reynolds (twins). Ordained ministry Congl. Ch., 1880; pastor Ortonville, Minn., 1880-84, Lyndale Ch., Minneapolis, 1884-91, First Ch., Muskegon, Mich., 1893-1921 (emeritus); field sec. Carleton Coll., Northfield, Minn., 1890-92. Dir. Muskegon Savings Bank. Pres. bd. trustees Hackley Hosp., Muskegon; dir. Muskegon Community Chest (chmn. 1922-25); pres. Boy Scout Council, 1927-28; trustee Chicago Theol. Sem., 1906-30. Chmn. Charter Revision Commn., Muskegon, 1919; mem. City Commn., Muskegon, 1920-28; mayor of Muskegon, 1923-24. Republican. Home: Muskegon, Mich. Died Aug. 3, 1937.

HADDEN, Crowell, banker; b. N.Y. City, Sept. 19, 1840; s. Crowell and Fanny (Ludlow) H.; student Poly. Inst. Brooklyn; m. Elizabeth H. Stevens, May 29, 1866. Pres. Long Island Bank until liquidation, 1896; pres. Brooklyn Savings Bank until Feb. 1, 1929; now chmn. bd. and trustee; dir. Bank of America, Bank of America Safe Deposit Co., N.Y. Investors, Brunswick Site Co. Treas. Brooklyn Acad. Music; trustee Children's Aid Soc., Brooklyn Savings Bank. Enlisted in 23rd Regt., N.G.N.Y., 1863, and served in Civil War. Presbyn. Home: Brooklyn, N.Y. Died Aug. 9, 1929.

HADDOCK, Frank Channing, author; b. Watertown, N.Y., Nov. 17, 1853; s. Rev. George C. and Cornelia B. (Herrick) H.; B.S. (class orator), Lawrence U., Appleton, Wis., 1876, M.S., 1879; Ph.D., Richmond Coll., O., 1901; admitted to Wis. bar, 1882; m. Mary Nash Conkey, Oct. 25, 1877. Lecturer on ethics and psychology. Author: The Power Book Library (direct methods in personal development), comprising Power of Will, Power for Success, The Will in Salesmanship, etc. Home: Auburndale Station, Boston. Died Feb. 9, 1915.

HADLEY, Arthur Twining, univ. pres.; b. New Haven, Conn., Apr. 23, 1856; s. Prof. James H. (of Yale) and Anne (Twining) H.; A.B., Yale (with highest honors), 1876; studied history and polit. science, Yale, 1876-77, U. of Berlin, 1878-79; LL.D., Yale, Harvard, Columbia, Johns Hopkins and others; Ph.D., Berlin; m. Helen Harrison, d. Gov. Luzon B. Morris, of Conn., June 30, 1891; children—Morris, Hamilton, Laura (Mrs. Nicholas Moseley). Tutor, 1879-83, lecturer on railroad administration, 1883-86, prof. polit. science, 1886-91, prof. polit. economy, 1891-99, pres., 1899-1921 (emeritus), Yale. Commr. labor statistics, Conn., 1885-87; asso. editor Railroad Gazette, New York, 1887-89; Roosevelt prof. at Berlin, 1907-08; lecturer, Oxford U., Eng., 1914. Author: Economics—An Account of the Relations Between Private Property and Public Welfare, 1896; The Education of the American Citizen, 1901; Freedom and Responsibility, 1903; Standards of Public Morality, 1907; Some Influences in Modern Philosophic Thought, 1913; Undercurrents in American Politics, 1915; The Moral Basis of Democracy, 1919; Economic Problems of Democracy, 1923; The Conflict between Liberty and Equality, 1925. Home: New Haven, Conn. Died Mar. 5, 1930.

HADLEY, Cassius Clay, lawyer; b. Avon, Ind., Aug. 9, 1863; s. Enos and Susan (Smith) H.; Butler Coll.; DePauw U., 1880-86; m. Frances S. Reed, Sept. 9, 1886. Admitted to Kan. bar, 1886; co.

atty., Scott Co., Kan., 1886-88; co. atty. Hendricks Co., Ind., 1890-96; pres. Town Bd., Danville, 1892-96; asst. atty. gen. of Ind., 1899-1907; judge Appellate Ct. of Ind., 1907-11; pres. and lecturer, Am. Central Law Sch., Indianapolis; lecturer Ind. State U. Dir. Commercial Club, Chamber of Commerce, Indianapolis, 1909— (pres. 1911). Trustee Ind. Reformatory, Jeffersonville. Republican. Methodist. Active worker in civic betterment. Home: Indianapolis, Ind. Died Nov. 24, 1913.

HADLEY, Everett Addison, chief engr. Mo. P. Ry.; b. Lowell, Mass., Nov. 19, 1879; s. Frank Milan and Susan Lillian (Eastman) H.; grad. high sch., Lowell, 1897; m. Lilla May Sturtevant, Feb. 5, 1902; children—Carleton Sturtevant, Raymond Everett (dec.). Engring. apprentice with Smith & Brooks, Lowell, 1897-1900; with engring. dept. B.&M. R.R., at Boston, 1900-10; engr. of design, with Mo. P. Ry., 1910-15; chief engr. same rd., 1915-18; engr. asst. to regional dir., U.S.R.R. Administration, at St. Louis, 1918-20; again chief engr. Mo. P. Ry., Mar. 1, 1920—. Republican. Conglist. Mason. Home: St. Louis, Mo. Died Nov. 11, 1932.

HADLEY, Henry Harrison, mission lecturer; b. Ohio; s. Col. William and Jane (Riddle) H.; ed. pub. schs.; volunteered, 1862, pvt. 90th O. vol. inf.; mustered out Apr. 27, 1866, as capt. and bvt. lt. col.; grad. Nat. Law Univ., Washington, 1875; m. Elizabeth Catherine Anderson, July 13, 1870. Mem. N.Y. bar and bar of D.C.; converted, 1886; went into rescue mission work, 1888; has since organized 60 Rescue Missions and several total abstinence socs., and raised $258,000 for their support; has addressed over 5,000 audiences on subject of total abstinence and rescue work. Dir. Nat. Christian Abstainers' Union; gen. Inter-State Blue Button Army of New York and Chicago. Mason. Died 1903.

HADLEY, Henry Harrison, clergyman; b. Brooklyn, N.Y., June 6, 1875; s. Henry Harrison and Elizabeth Catherine (Anderson) H.; grad. Pennington (N.J.) Sem., 1894; A.B., Princeton, 1898; B.D., Episcopal Theol. Sch., Cambridge, Mass., 1901; D.D., Syracuse U., 1917; m. Aurelia Moffatt Roe, June 1, 1904; children—Henry Harrison, Amy Roe. Deacon and priest P.E. Ch., 1901; curate St. Michael's Ch., N.Y. City., 1901-02; rector St. Paul's Ch., Richmond, Ind., 1902-06, St. Paul's Ch., Newark, N.J., 1906-16, St. Paul's Ch., Syracuse, N.Y., 1916—; dep. Gen. Conv. P.E. Ch. 5 times, 1913-31; examining chaplain Diocese of Newark; mem. standing com. Diocese of Central N.Y., 1932-33. Mem. and chaplain S.A.R., Sons of Vets. Republican. Home: Syracuse, N.Y. Deceased.

HADLEY, Henry K., composer; b. Somerville, Mass., 1871; studied under Stephen A. Emery and George W. Chadwick, Boston; studied violin and other branches in Vienna; Mus. Dir. Tufts Coll., 1925. Returned to U.S. from Europe, 1895, and was apptd. instr. in music in St. Paul's Sch., Garden City, L.I.; made kapellmeister of opera in Mainz, 1909, and prod. his one-act opera, Safie (text by Edward Oxenford) the same yr., in Germany; toured Europe, conducting principal orchestras; comdr. Seattle Symphony Orchestra, 1909-10, San Francisco Orchestra, 1911-15, later asso. condr. New York Philharmonic Orchestra; condr. Manhattan Symphony Orchestra, 1929—; also condr. Pa. Orchestra of Philadelphia, 1931—. Mem. Nat. Inst. Arts and Letters, Am. Acad. Arts and Letters. Has composed over 150 songs and piano pieces, 3 concert overtures, 4 symphonies, a festival march, trios, quartets, and other chamber music; 4 ballads for solo, chorus and orchestra; 2 comic operas, a cantata, "In Musical Praise," and several ballet suites; symphonic-fantasie, lyric drama—Merlin and Vivian, Japanese legend, "The Fate of Princess Kiyo" (women's voices and orchestra), and "Salome" (tone poem for grand orchestra), played by Boston Symphonic Orchestra, April 12 and 13, 1907; etc. Second symphony, "The Four Seasons," won Paderewski and New England Conservatory prizes, 1902. Composed operas "Azora" and "Bianca"; opera "Cleopatra's Night" (prod. Metropolitan Opera); composed work for 60th anniversary of Worcester Musical Festival, to Dr. Henry Van Dyck's text, "Music and Ode"; composed the work for double chorus, solos, children's voices and orchestra, "Resurgam," to Louise Ayres Garnett's text, for Cincinnati Festival, 1922; conducted this work in Queen's Hall, London, with London Choral Soc., 1924, and appeared as guest comdr. in Amsterdam and Stockholm, producing his tone poem, "Ocean," and his principal orchestras of U.S. in these three cities the same yr.; conducted Worcester Festival, 1924. Called to Buenos Aires to conduct a season of Symphony Concerts, 1927; to Tokyo, Japan, to appear as guest condr. Tokyo Symphony Orchestra, 1930; organizer, 1934, and condr. Berkshire Symphonic Festivals. Wrote music for Bohemian Club grove play "The Legend of Hani," 1933. Died Sept. 6, 1937.

HADLEY, Herbert Spencer, gov., educator; b. Olathe, Kan., Feb. 20, 1872; s. Maj. John Milton and Harriett (Beach) H.; A.B., U. of Kan., 1892; LL.B., 1st honors, Northwestern U., 1894; LL.D., Northwestern, 1909, U. of Mo., 1910, Mo. Valley Coll., 1911, Harvard, 1925; m. Agnes Lee, Oct. 8, 1901; children—John Milton, Henrietta, Herbert Spencer. Gen. practice, Kansas City, Mo., 1894-98; 1st asst. city counselor, in charge trial work for Kansas City, 1898-1901; pros. atty. Jackson Co., Mo., 1901-03; became widely known on account of successful prosecutions of legal offenders; defeated for re-election, 1902, atty. gen. of Mo., 1905-09; prosecuted cases successfully against the Standard Oil Co., the railroads, the Harvester Trust, the Ins. and Lumber Trust, the race-track gamblers of St. Louis, etc.; gov. of Mo., 1909-13; resumed practice at Kansas City; spl. counsel for rys. west of Chicago in federal valuation of rys., 1913-16; prof. law, U. of Colo., 1917-23; counsel State R.R. Commn. of Colo., 1919-21; chancellor Washington U., 1923—. Wrote: Standard Oil Trust; What the Railroads Owe the People; Rome and the World Today (award decoration Order of S.S. Maurizio e Lazzaro from Italian Govt. for this book). Home: St. Louis, Mo. Died Dec. 1, 1927.

HADLEY, Hiram, educator; b. nr. Wilmington, O., Mar. 17, 1833; s. John and Ann (Wildman) H.; ed. Friends' Boarding Sch. (now Earlham Coll.), Richmond, Ind., and Haverford Coll., Pa.; (hon. M.A., Earlham, 1886); m. Hannah Fulghum, Apr. 30, 1856 (dec.); 2d, Katharine E. Coffin, May 20, 1880. Began teaching at Grassy Run, O., 1850; taught at Carthage, Ind., 1854-56, Friends' Acad., Richmond, 1856-63; started Hadley's Normal Acad., Richmond, Ind., 1865; removed to Chicago; became head of Hadley Bros., booksellers; started Hadley's Classical Acad., Indianapolis, 1880; prin. of Friends' Academy, Bloomingdale, Ind., 1885-87; moved to N.M., 1887; assisted in organizing and was elected pres. Las Cruces Coll., N.M., 1888; pres. N.M. Coll. of Agr. and Mechanic Arts, 1889-94; pres. N.M. U., Albuquerque, 1894-97; prof. history and philosophy, N.M. Coll. of Agr. and Mechanic Arts, 1898-1905 (mem. bd. regents 1907-13); supt. pub. instrn., Ter. of N.M., 1905-07. Author: Hadley's Lessons in Language, 1871; Lee and Hadley's English Grammar (with Dr. Mary V. Lee), 1873. Home: Mesilla Park, N.M. Died Dec. 3, 1922.

HADLEY, Hiram Elwood, lawyer; b. Sylvania, Ind., Jan. 16, 1854; s. Jonathan and Martha (McCoy) H.; ed. Bloomingdale (Ind.) Acad. and Earlham Coll.; LL.B., Union Coll. of Law, Chicago, 1877; LL.D., Earlham Coll., 1908; m. Martha Musgrave, Jan. 16, 1879; children—Roy Overman, Clyde Musgrave, Earl Jonathan, Mrs. Inez Hadley Pierce, Mrs. Katharine Hadley Farris. Practiced law, Bloomington, Ill., 1877-81, Rockville, Ind., 1881-89; removed to Whatcom, Wash., 1889; city atty., 1891-92; superior judge, Whatcom Co., Wash., 1897-1901; associate justice, Mar. 1901-Jan. 1907, chief justice, Jan. 1907-Jan. 1909, Supreme Ct. of Wash.; declined reëlection; resumed practice, Jan. 1909; now mem. Hadley, Hay & Hadley, Seattle. Republican. Presbyn. Mason. Home: Seattle, Wash. Died Jan. 13. 1929.

HADLEY, John Vestal, judge; b. Hendricks Co., Ind., Oct. 31, 1842; s. Jonathan and Ara H.; ed. Northwestern Christian U., 1859-61; served in Union Army 3½ yrs.; twice wounded in battle; captured May 5, 1864; escaped from Columbia, S.C., to Knoxville, Tenn., Dec. 10, 1864; m. Mary J. Hill, Mar. 15, 1865. Studied in Ind. Law Sch., 1886; mem. Ind. Senate, 1869-72; circuit judge, 1888-99; justice Supreme Ct. of Ind., Jan. 2, 1899-1911. Republican. Home: Danville, Ind. Died Nov. 17, 1915.

HAESCHE, William Edwin, composer; b. New Haven, Conn., Apr. 11, 1867; s. Henry William and Rosina (Safney) H.; ed. New Haven schs.; Mus.B., Yale, 1897; studied violin with Bernhard Listemann and others, piano with Ernst Perabo and others, composition and theory with Dr. H. W. Parker and others; m. Nora Russell (soprano singer), 1890. One of the organizers of New Haven Symphony Orchestra; mem. faculty Dept. of Music, Yale U.: now in charge of the theoretical courses in music, Hollins College. Composer: For orchestra—A Forest Idylle, 1896; Fridthjol and Ingeborg, symphonic poem (prize composition), 1897; Springtime, overture, 1899; Symphony in A-flat, 1901; also Young Lovel's Bride, for women's chorus and orchestra, 1898; Sonata in E-minor, for violin and piano (prize composition); The Haunted Oak of Maunau, for full chorus and orchestra, 1902; The South, symphonic poem for orchestra; also Hungarian Dance, Souvenir de Wieniawski and other pieces for piano and violin, songs, anthems, symphonetta for orchestra in 4 movements; Red Godwin's Wooing, for Women's Chorus, soprano solo and orchestra or piano; etc. Home: Hollins, Va. Died Jan. 26, 1929.

HAGAN, Horace Henry, lawyer; b. St. Mary's, Kan., Oct. 13, 1891; s. Horace Henry and Eulalie Mary (Droege) H.; A.B., St. Mary's Coll., 1910, A.M., 1913; LL.B., Georgetown U., Washington, D.C., 1913; unmarried. Began practice at Oklahoma City, Okla., 1913; spl. asst. to atty. gen. of Okla., 1914; mem. West & Hagan, Oklahoma City, 1915-16; with legal dept. of Texas Co., Tulsa, Okla., 1917 and 1919; mem. Conner & Hagan, Tulsa, 1920-21; partner Hagan & Gavin, 1922—; spl. asst. to atty. gen. of U.S., 1934; prof. constitutional law, Tulsa and Law Sch. Apptd. by Senate of Okla. as one of three members of Soldiers Relief Commn. of Okla. and served, 1921-24. Served as corpl. C.A.C., U.S. Army, 1918. Mem. bd. dirs. Tulsa Y.M.C.A.; one of three founders of Georgetown Law Jour., 1913. Democrat. Author: Eight Great American Lawyers, 1923. Home: Tulsa, Okla. Died Nov. 3, 1936.

HAGAR, Edward McKim, pres. Universal Portland Cement Co. Home: Chicago, Ill. Died Jan. 18, 1918.

HAGAR, George Jotham, editor; b. Newark, N.J., Sept. 12, 1847; s. Jotham Meeker and Harriet Denman (Ross) H.; ed. pub. schs.; m. Emma L. Hubbard, Nov. 27, 1878. Mem. Auxiliary Relief Corps, U.S. Sanitary Commn., in Civil War; news editor Frank Leslie's Illustrated Newspaper, 1867-82; asso. editor Columbian Cyclopædia, 1888-93; one of revisers of Columbian, Johnson's, People's Americana, New Internat., New Standard, New Practical, Standard Am., Everybody's and Twentieth Century cyclops.; compiled What the World Believes, 1885 (republished under title Bibles and Reliefs of Mankind, 1895); the greater part of The History of the United States in Chronological Order, 1886; Our Great Continent (with B. J. Lossing), 1889, and Appendix to Encyclopædia Britannica, 1897-98; editor, cyclopædia section, Anglo-American Encyclopædia and Dictionary, 1900-02; reviser of Harper's Encyclopædia of United States History (10 vols.), 1910, 11, 15, asso. compiler Appleton's New Practical Encyclopædia (6 vols.), 1907; compiled chronology of the world in Standard Dictionary, 1912; revised Eggleston's History of the United States, 1913; edited the New Universities Dictionary, 1915; edited the Centennial edition of Crabb's English Synonyms, 1915; assembled documents in documentary edit. of President Wilson's History of the American People, 10 vols., 1917; edited the new World-Wide Cyclopedia, 1917; rev. Appleton's New Practical Cyclopedia for World War Activities, 1919. Home: Newark, N.J. Died July 25, 1921.

HAGEBOECK, Alfons Ludwig, surgeon; b. Davenport, Ia., Mar. 14, 1867; s. Gustav and Anna (Hitzeman) H.; M.D., State U. of Ia., 1889; studied surgery, Vienna, Paris and London, 1889-90; post-grad. work in surgery, Sorbonne, Paris, 1907-08; m. Ida Haller, 1892; children—Alfons E., William P. Practiced surgery at Davenport, 1890—; organizer, 1909, and chief surgeon clin. unit, which continues as Drs. Hageboeck, Stocks, Maxwell & Kornder; pres. Hageboeck Realty Co. Trustee for 6 yrs. of first Carnegie Library in Davenport; mem. Ia. Council of Defense, World War; organizer and pres. Municipal Art Gallery. Republican. Lutheran. Mason. Author: Romance and Reality in a Doctor's Life. Lecturer on art, State Univ. of Ia. Home: Davenport, Ia. Died July 28, 1938.

HAGERMAN, Frank, lawyer; b. Alexandria, Mo., Apr. 27, 1857; s. Benjamin F. and Ann Staunton (Cowgill) H.; ed. high sch., Keokuk, Ia.; m. Ella Comstock, Feb. 22, 1887; children—Abby Staunton (Mrs. Morrison Shofroth), B. Haywood Hagerman. Removed with parents to Keokuk, 1864; began practice in Keokuk, 1876; removed to Kansas City, Mo., 1887; mem. Pratt, McCrary, Ferry & Hagerman until death of Judge McCrary; then Pratt, Ferry & Hagerman; practiced alone, 1896-1922, retired. Democrat. Presbyn. Home: Kansas City, Mo. Deceased.

HAGERMAN, Herbert James, governor; b. Milwaukee, Dec. 15, 1871; s. James J. and Anna O. (Osborne) H.; B.L., Cornell U., 1894; unmarried. Practiced law, Colo., 1897-98; 2d sec. Am. Embassy in Russia, 1898-1901; territorial gov. of New Mexico, 1906-07. Pres. N.M. Taxpayers' Assn., 1915-33; chmn. Spl. Revenue Commn. of N.M., 1919-21; pres. Western States Taxpayers' Conf., 1926-27; apptd. federal commr. to Navajo Tribe of Indians, Jan. 3, 1923, in charge oil development and other tribal affairs of Navajo Nation; apptd. by sec. of interior, as his rep. on Pueblo Land Bd., to settle land rights of Pueblo Indians; spl. commr. to negotiate with Indians, 1923-32. Home: Santa Fe, N.M. Died Jan. 28, 1935.

HAGERMAN, James, lawyer; b. Clark Co., Mo., Nov. 26, 1848; s. Benjamin Franklin and Anne S. (Cogwill) H.; ed. pub. and pvt. schs. and Christian Brothers' Coll., St. Louis; m. Margaret M. Walker, Oct. 26, 1871. Admitted to Mo. bar, 1866 (before he was 18); practiced Keokuk, Ia., until 1884; gen. atty. A.,T.&S.F. Ry. Co., 1884-86; gen. solicitor M.,K.&T. Ry. System, 1887-1904, gen. counsel, Apr. 1904—. Democrat. Home: St. Louis, Mo. Deceased.

HAGERTY, Christian Dane, newspaperman; b. Bennington, Mich., July 24, 1876; s. Lorin D. and Eva (Galpin) H.; ed. public schools; m. Vina Halson Hankey, 1918. Reporter, Chicago Daily News, 1896-99; reporter and editor, Associated Press, 1899-1919. War corr. for Chicago Daily News, Spanish-Am. War, 1898; for Associated Press, Russo-Japanese War, 1904-06; disturbances, Venezuela, 1906-07, Nicaragua, 1910-10, Mexico, 1910-14; column conductor "CDH Broadcasting," Chicago Herald Examiner, 1925. Home: Chicago, Ill. Deceased.

HAGGARD, Alfred Martin, clergyman; b. nr. Cedar Rapids, Ia., Apr. 11, 1851; s. David M. and Mary Ann (Schmidt) H.; A.B., Oskaloosa (Ia.) Coll., 1879, A.M., 1889; studied divinity; minister Disciples of Christ; m. Florence Mary Johnson, Dec. 7, 1880; 1 son, Barton J. Prof. in Bryant & Stratton Business Coll., St. Paul, Minn., 1873-76; pres. Oskaloosa Coll., 1889-92; sec. Ia. Christian Conv., 1893-98; dean Bible Coll., 1899-1910, prof. Christian evidences, 1910-16, Drake U. In pulpit and pastoral work, 1876—, at Eddyville, Ia., DeSoto, Ia., Washington, Ill., Oskaloosa, Ia., Colfax, Ia. Prohibitionist. Sec. Ia. Christian Missionary Soc. 1917-22. Field worker Ia. Anti-Saloon League; sec. calendar com. Disciples of Christ Ch. Home: Des Moines, Ia. Died June 20, 1933.

HAGGARD, Sewell, editor; b. Lebanon, Tenn., Feb. 6, 1879; s. William Y. and Lucy (Sewell) H.; ed. under pvt. tutors; m. 1919, Flora Howard, d. Maj. A. L. Howard, D.S.O.V.C., British army, killed Boer War. Began as reporter Jackson (Miss.) News, 1896; later mng. editor Birmingham Age-Herald, Baltimore News; gen. work on New York Evening Sun, Times, and World; mng. editor McClure's Magazine, 1907-10; editor World Today and Hearst's Mag., 1911, 12, 15 and 18, Nash's Mag., London, 1913, Cosmopolitan Mag., 1914, Everybody's Mag., Apr. 1, 1921—; asso. editor Designer, and The Woman's Mag.; with Famous Players-Lasky Corp., 1925—; Editor The Shrine Magazine, 1926. Home: New York, N.Y. Died Jan. 3, 1928.

HAGGARD, William David, surgeon; b. Nashville, Tenn., Sept. 28, 1872; s. William David and Jane (Douglass) H.; M.D., U. of Tenn., 1893; D.C.L., U. of the South, 1931; m. Mary Laura Champe, Jan. 18, 1898 (died 1920); m. 2d, Lucile Holman, July 27, 1926. Practiced, 1893—; prof. gynecology and abdominal surgery, U. of Tenn., 1899-1912; prof. surgery and clin. surgery, Vanderbilt U. Med. Dept., 1913—; surgeon, president staff, St. Thomas Hosp.; visiting surgeon Vanderbilt U. Hosp. Served as major and lt. colonel Med. Corps, U.S.A.; surgeon Evacuation Hosp. No. 1, Toul, France, 1918-19, also consultant in surgery, Mesves Hosp. Center, France. Was chmn. med. sect. Council Nat. Defense, State of Tenn.; maj. and med. aide to gov. of Tenn.; mem. advisory bd. div. of surgery, Surgeon General's Office, Washington, D.C. Fellow Am. Coll. Surgeons (regent; pres. 1933), Am. Surg. Assn. Democrat. Episcopalian. Home: Nashville, Tenn. Died Jan. 28, 1940.

HAGGERTY, Melvin Everett, psychologist; b. Bunker Hill, Ind., Jan. 17, 1875; s. John Wright and Phoebe Ellen (Hann) H.; A.B., Ind. U., 1902, A.M., 1907; student U. of Chicago, 1904; A.M., Harvard, 1909, Ph.D., 1910; m. Laura Caroline Garretson, June 26, 1902; children—Helen Ruth, Margaret Elizabeth (Mrs. Norman Anderson), William James. Teacher in high schs. Indiana and Massachusetts, 1902-09; asst. in philosophy, Harvard, Radcliffe, 1909-10; asst. prof. and prof. psychology, Ind. U., 1910-15; prof. ednl. psychology, U. of Minn., 1915—; lecturer on ednl. psychology, Teachers Coll. (Columbia), 1917; dean Coll. of Education, U. of Minn., 1920. Maj. Sanitary Corps, U.S. Army, Jan. 1918-Mar. 1919; stationed in Surgeon, Gen.'s Office and identified with reëducation of disabled soldiers; lt. col. O.R.C. Dir. div. of tests and measurements, Va. Edn. Commn., 1919; same, North Carolina Sch. Survey, 1920; N.Y. State School Survey, 1921; chmn. U. of Minn. Com. on Edn. Research, 1924—. Mem. bd. of trustees College of St. Catherine. Democrat. Conglist. Mason. Home: Minnapolis, Minn. Died Oct. 6, 1937.

HAGGETT, Arthur Sewall, college dean; b. New Castle, Me., May 8. 1870; s. Ebenezer and Eleanor (Clark) H.; A.B., Bowdoin Coll., 1893, A.M., 1894; Ph.D., Johns Hopkins, 1897; studied U. of Berlin and Am. Sch. at Athens, 1897-98; m. Winnifred Sunderlin, Aug. 20, 1902. Instr. Greek Bangor (Me.) High Sch., 1898-99, Greek and Latin, Worcester (Mass.) Acad., 1899-1901; asst. prof. Greek and Latin, 1901-02, prof. Greek lang. and lit., 1902—, dean Coll. of Liberal Arts, 1911—, U. of Wash. Conglist. Home: Seattle, Wash. Died June 30, 1917.

HAGGIN, James B., capitalist; b. Harrodsburg, Ky., 1827; s. Ferah T. and Adaline S. (Ben Ali) H.; ed. for legal profession; m. a d. of Col. Lewis Sanders, of Natchez, Miss. (died 1894); 2d, Pearl Voorhies, Dec. 23, 1897. Practiced law for short time at St. Joseph, Mo., then at Natchez, Miss., until 1849, when went to Calif. and acquired fortune in mining enterprises; formed "silver trust," with other large mining capitalists, 1896; owns original interests of Marcus Daly in Anaconda Copper Co.; large owner of ranch property in Ky., and largest individual owner of horses in training, having large stock farms in Ky. Home: New York, N.Y. Died Sept. 12, 1914.

HAGGIN, Louis Terah, lawyer; b. Natchez, Miss., Nov. 1847; s. James B. and Eliza J. (Sanders) H.; A.B., Cambridge U., Eng., 1870; LL.B., Harvard, 1872; m. Blanche Butterworth, Feb. 12, 1873. Pres. Cerro de Baso Copper Corp.; dir. Am. Metal Co., Ltd. Home: New York, N.Y. Died Mar. 19, 1929.

HAGIN, Fred Eugene, missionary; b. Cambridge, Ill., June 3, 1869; s. Dan and Cordovia G. (Owens) H.; A.B., Eureka (Ill.) Coll., 1897, A.M.; studied Cotner U., Bethany, Neb.; passed state pharm. exam., Neb. 1887; m. Myrtle Edith Willett, Apr. 18, 1892; children—Edith G. (Mrs. Jack Francis), Dan W., Fanny Alice (Mrs. Mayer). Ordained ministry, Disciples of Christ Ch.; pastor in Ia., Ill., etc., for 22 yrs.; missionary to Japan, of United Christian Missionary Soc., of Indianapolis, 1900-22; opened work on Hachijo Island, founded East Tokyo Inst. ch. in 1919; pastor Figueroa Boul. Christian Ch., Los Angeles, 1924-29; exec. field sec. Calif. Christian Coll. (now Chapman Coll.), Los Angeles, 1929-31; field sec. United Christian Missionary Society of Indianapolis, 1931; pastor Vermont Sq. Christian Ch., Los Angeles, 1932-34; dir. of Bible institutes. Chairman S.S. Com. of Federated Missions of Japan 3 yrs.; traveled and lectured widely in Japan and U.S. Author: The Cross in Japan, 1914; His Appearing and His Kingdom, 1922. Home: Glendale, Calif. Died July 16, 1938.

HAGNER, Alexander Burton, judge; b. Washington, July 13, 1826; s. Peter and Frances (Randall) H. (first 3d auditor of the Treasury); A.B., Princeton, 1845, later A.M.; (LL.D., St. John's Coll., Md., 1879); m. Louisa Harrison, 1853. Admitted to Md. bar, 1848; practiced in Annapolis, Baltimore and elsewhere. Mem. Md. legislature, 1854 (chmn. Ways and Means Com.); elector on Bell and Everett ticket, 1860; Whig candidate, 1858, and Republican candidate, 1867, for Congress from Md. in Dem. dist.; asso. justice Supreme Ct. of D.C., 1879-June 1, 1903; retired. Home: Washington, D.C. Died June 30, 1915.

HAGNER, Francis Randall, genito-urinary surgeon; b. Washington, D.C., Feb. 19, 1873; s. Charles E. and Isabella (Davis) H.; M.D., George Washington U., 1894, hon. D.Sc., 1939; m. Elizabeth Allemong, June 1899. Practiced at Washington, D.C., 1896—; asst. resident in surgery, Johns Hopkins Hospital, Baltimore, 1895-96; prof. of genito-urinary surgery, George Washington U., 1905-39, emeritus. Fellow Am. Coll. Surgeons. Episcopalian. Home: Washington, D.C. Died July 7, 1940.

HAGUE, Arnold, geologist; b. Boston, Dec. 3, 1840; s. Rev. Dr. William and Mary Bowditch (Moriarty) H.; Ph.B., Sheffield Scientific Sch. (Yale), 1863; studied at univs. of Göttingen and Heidelberg and at Freiberg Sch. of Mines, 1863-66; (Sc.D., Columbia, 1901; LL.D., Aberdeen, 1906); m. Mary Bruce Howe, Nov. 14, 1893. Asst. geologist, U.S. Geol. Exploration, 40th parallel, and made investigations of mines and mining processes in Nevada, etc., 1867-77; govt. geologist, Guatemala, 1877-78; examining mines in northern China for the govt., 1878-79; geologist of U.S. Geol. Survey, 1879—. Mem. commn. apptd. by Nat. Acad. Sciences at request of U.S. Govt., 1896, to prepare plan of Nat. forest reserves; v.p. Internat. Geol. Congresses, Paris, 1900, Stockholm, 1910, Toronto, 1913. Author: Geology of the Yellowstone National Park (with others), 1899; Atlas of Yellowstone National Park (27 plates), 1904; The Origin of the Thermal Waters in the Yellowstone National Park, 1911. Died May 14, 1917.

HAGUE, James Duncan, cons. mining engr.; b. Boston, Feb. 24, 1836; s. Rev. Dr. William and Mary Bowditch (Moriarty) H.; ed. private schools; studied at Lawrence Scientific Sch., Harvard, 1854; Georgia Augusta Univ.; Göttingen, Germany, 1855; Royal School of Mines, Freiberg, Saxony, 1856-58; m. Mary Ward Foote, Apr. 1872 (died 1898). Exploring in South seas, 1859-61; brief service in U.S.N., 1862-63; mgr. copper mines at Lake Superior, participating in early development of Calumet mine, 1863-66; first asst. geologist, U.S. Geol. Survey, 40th parallel, 1867-70; cons. mining engr. in Calif., 1871-78; U.S. commr. to Paris Expn., 1878. Resident of New York, 1879; pres. and mgr. of mining companies. Home: New York, and Stockbridge, Mass. Died 1908.

HAHN, Adolf, musical dir.; b. Indianapolis, Ind., Jan. 13, 1875; s. Theodore and Wilhelmina (Roesch) H.; ed. pub. schs., Indianapolis and Cincinnati; grad. Cincinnati Coll. of Music, 1890, and first post-grad. student of same; awarded Ropes prize in composition; studied in Europe, mainly in London; m. Mary Davis, June 22, 1898. Orchestral and chorus conductor, Cincinnati, 1900—, also violin soloist; dir. Cincinnati Coll. of Music, 1923-31. Republican. Lutheran. Mason. Home: Cincinnati, O. Deceased.

HAHN, Benjamin Daviese, clergyman; b. Todd Twp., O., Aug. 21, 1856; s. David and Barbara Anna (Owen) H.; A.B., U. of Wooster, O., 1877; grad. Rochester Theol. Sem., 1882 (scholarship prize); D.D., Colby, 1899; m. Harriet Chapman Pendleton, Nov. 29, 1888; children—Barbara Mary, James Pendleton. Instr. in mathematics, Cook Acad. and acting pastor Bapt. Ch., Havana, N.Y., 1880-81; ordained Bapt. ministry, 1882; pastor Calvary Ch., Westerly, R.I., 1882-91, Sherman Av. Ch., Newark, N.J., 1891-93, State St. Ch., Springfield, Mass., 1893-1914, Pendleton St. Ch., Greenville, S.C., 1914-30, pastor emeritus. Invented rotary batten with fixed lay, slide batten with fixed lay for looms, also reed batten, 1928, and new picker action and automatic shuttle magazine, 1929. Home: Greenville, S.C. Died May 5, 1938.

HAHN, Conrad Velder, consulting engr.; b. Phila., Pa., May 9, 1890; s. John G. and Elizabeth (Velder) H.; B.S., U. of Pa., 1908, M.E., 1912; studied Temple U. (Phila.), D.Eng., Ph.D.; U. of San José (Costa Rica), Oxford U. (Eng.); married. Consulting practice, 1910—; mng. dir. The Hahn Co. (cons. engrs.); dir. and asso. engr. Internat. Development Co., Washington, D.C.; cons. mech. engr. Turbo Motor Co., East Radford, Va.; mem. N. T. Whitaker & Co., Washington, D.C.; mem. faculty, civ. engring. dept., Temple U., 1910-12, and of mech. engring. dept. U. of Pa., 1912-14; dir. mech. engring. dept. of evening schs., Drexel Inst., Phila., 1919—. 1st lt. and capt. Ordnance Dept., U.S.A., 1917-19; maj. Ordnance R.C.; spl. mention for tech. service, Am. Ordnance Base Depot, France, and Aberdeen Proving Ground, Scotland, World War. Mason. Republican. Baptist. Home: Aberdeen, Md. Died Dec. 3, 1933.

HAHN, George Philip, judge; b. Napoleon, O., June 26, 1879; s. Anton and Sophia (Yackee) H.; grad. high sch., Napoleon, 1899; art student Ohio State U., 1899-1902, LL.B., 1905; m. Stella Vocke, Nov. 14, 1906; children—Philip Vocke, Frances Elaine. Admitted to Ohio bar, 1905, and began practice at Toledo; judge, U.S. Dist. Court, Northern O. Dist., Dec. 27, 1928—. Republican. Lutheran. Elk. Home: Toledo, O. Died Feb. 12, 1937.

HAHN, J(oseph) Jerome, judge; b. Albany, N.Y., Aug. 20, 1868; s. Isaac and Rose (Stern) H.; LL.B., Boston U., 1889, LL.D., 1933; m. Katherine L. Marr, Mar. 16, 1911. Admitted to Mass. bar, 1889, R.I. bar, 1891, and began practice at Providence; asso. justice Superior Court, R.I., 1919-30; became asso. justice Supreme Court of R.I., 1930; pres. Washington Real Estate Co., Aetna Realty Co.; dir. Mortgage Guarantee & Title Co. Republican. Jewish religion. Mason. Home: Providence, R.I. Died Dec. 6, 1938.

HAID, Leo, bishop and abbot; b. Latrobe, Pa., July 15, 1849; joined Benedictine Order, 1869; (D.D.); ordained R.C. priest, 1872. Chaplain and prof. St. Vincent's Abbey, 1872-85; abbot Belmont Cathedral Abbey, July 1885—; blessed mitred abbot, Nov. 26, 1885; apptd., 1887, vicar apostolic of N.C., and titular bishop of Messene; consecrated July 1, 1888; designated abbot ordinary of Belmont Cathedral Abbey, June 13, 1910; mem. Roman Patriate and asst. at the Papal Throne, July 15, 1914. Home: Belmont, N.C. Died July 24, 1924.

HAIGHT, Albert, judge; b. Ellicottville, N.Y., Feb. 20, 1842; s. Henry and Sarah M. H.; ed. Springville (N.Y.) Acad.; admitted to bar, 1863. Held local offices; co. judge Erie Co., 1872; justice Supreme Ct., 8th Jud. Dist., 1876-94; justice for 5th dept., 1884-89; asso. judge 2d Div. Court of Appeals, 1889-94; asso. judge Court of Appeals of N.Y., Jan. 1, 1895-Dec. 31, 1912; (retired). Home: Buffalo, N.Y. Died Oct. 6, 1926.

HAIGHT, Charles Coolidge, architect, sculptor; b. New York, Mar. 17, 1841; s. Rev. Benjamin I. and Hetty (Coolidge) H.; A.B., Columbia, 1861, A.M., 1864; (hon. A.M., Yale, 1906); m. Euphemia Kneeland, Oct. 1870. Capt. U.S.V., 1862-64. Home: Garrison, N.Y. Died Feb. 8, 1917.

HAIGHT, Thomas Griffith, judge; b. Freehold, N.J., Aug. 4, 1879; s. John Tyler and Mary Louise (Drummond) H.; ed. Princeton U. and New York Law Sch.; hon. LL.D., Princeton; m. Annie M. Crater, Oct. 18, 1905; children—Nancy, Catharine, David. Admitted to N.J. bar, 1900; practiced with Queen & Tennant, Jersey City, 1901-05, then with George G. Tennant until latter's appmt. as judge of court of Common Pleas, Hudson County, May 1913; city atty., Jersey City, 1911-13; co. counsel, Hudson County, 1913-14; judge of U.S. Dist. Ct., Dist. of N.J., 1914-19; U.S. circuit judge, 3d Jud. Circuit and judge U.S. Circuit Ct. of Appeals, 1919-20, resigned; mem. Wall, Haight, Carey & Hartpence, Jersey City, N.J. Democrat. Episcopalian. Mem. 2d Troop N.G.N.J., 2 yrs. Signal Corps, 5 yrs. Mason. Home: Englewood, N.J. Died Jan. 26, 1942.

HAILE, Columbus, ry. official; b. Dallas Co., Ala., Sept. 8, 1860; s. Columbus and Louisa (McCaa) H.; ed. Staunton (Va.) Male Acad., Hampden-Sidney Coll. and U. of Va.; m. Temple Perry, Dec. 25, 1883; children—Columbus, Elise Perry. Began ry. service with Houston & Tex. Central Ry., as clerk, 1880; with Internat. & Great Northern R.R., 1881-85, Tex. Traffic Assn., 1885-89; asst. gen. freight agt. and gen. freight agt. M.,K.&T. Ry., 1889-95; mem. bd. of administration, Southwestern Traffic Assn., until 1896; freight traffic mgr., 1896-98, traffic mgr., 1898-1907, v.p. and traffic mgr., 1907-26, pres., 1926—, M.,K.&T. Ry. Co. Democrat. Episcopalian. Home: St. Louis, Mo. Died Nov. 14, 1931.

HAILEY, Orren Luico, clergyman; b. Fayette Co., Tenn., June 21, 1852; s. Luico Sanders and Elizabeth (Griffin) H.; McKenzie Coll., Tenn., 1 yr.; Henderson Masonic Inst., Tenn., 3 yrs.; A.B., Southwestern Bapt. U., Jackson, Tenn., 1878; grad. Southern Bapt. Theol. Sem., Louisville, Ky., 1884; (D.D., Miss.

Coll., 1895); m. Nora S. Graves, Oct. 14, 1885; children—Orrena Bearden (dec.), James Graves, Orren Luico, Robert William, George Norman, David Walter. Ordained Bapt. ministry, 1879; pastor various chs., Tenn. and Ky.; pastor Aberdeen, Miss., 1884-85; organizer, and pastor 2d Ch., Knoxville, Tenn., 1885-93; pastor Oxford, Miss., 1894-95, Ft. Smith, Ark., 1895-99, 1st Ch., Texarkana, 1900-06, Comanche, Tex., 1906-08, 1st Ch., Corsicana, 1908-14, Plainview, Tex., 1914-15; pres. Wayland Bapt. Coll., Plainview, Tex., 1915-17; pastor Ervay Street Ch., Dallas, Tex., 1917-19. Has served many yrs. as editor ch. papers, pub. as Nashville, St. Louis and Little Rock, and as officer ch. assns. and convs. Chmn. com. on order of business Southern Bapt. Conv., 1913-24; mem. joint commn. bet. Northern and Southern Bapt. convs., 1917-19; mem. and sec. commn. to establish theol. sem. for Negro Baptists at Nashville, and in charge, 1919—; acting pastor Eastland Bapt. Ch., Nashville, 1919-24. Chosen by Bapt. Conv., 1927, to write history of Tenn. Baptists, which was finished in 1929. Home: Nashville, Tenn. Died Feb. 10, 1934.

HAINER, Bayard Taylor, lawyer; b. Columbia, Mo., May 31, 1866; s. Ignace and Adelaide (Barthos) H.; moved to southern Ia. in childhood; B.S., Ia. State Coll., 1884; LL.B., U. of Mich., 1887; m. Florence Weatherby, Oct. 6, 1891; 1 son, Bayard T. Admitted to Mich. bar, 1887, Supreme Court U.S., 1897; practiced Larned, Kan., 1887-89; moved to Guthrie, Okla., Apr. 22, 1889 (1st settlement); city counsellor, Guthrie, 1893-98; judge U.S. Court for Okla. Ty., Feb. 16, 1898-Nov. 17, 1907; apptd. chief counsel for packers and stockyards adminstrn., Washington, D.C., 1921; chief counsel Federal Trade Commn., 1925-27. Republican. Episcopalian. Mason. Home: Oklahoma City, Okla. Died July 10, 1933.

HAINES, Henry Cargill, officer U.S.M.C.; b. Ft. Leavenworth, Kan., Nov. 19, 1859; s. Brig. Gen. T. J. (U.S.A.) and Anne Hays (Cargill) H.; grad. U.S. Naval Acad., 1881; m. Emma Burgers, Mar. 26, 1887; children—Thomas B., John Meade; m. 2d, Helen Rockwell, Mar. 28, 1898; children—Henry R., Barbara, Helen. Apptd. 2d lt. U.S.M.C., July 1, 1883; promoted through grades to brig. gen., Jan. 14, 1920; retired 1923. In charge office of asst. adj. and insp., San Francisco, Calif., 1903-05, Berkeley, Calif., 1906; duty Marine Corps Hdqrs., 1908-12; Pacific Inspection Dist., San Francisco, 1912-14; placed in charge asst. adj. and inspector's dept., San Francisco, Apr. 1, 1914. Republican. Episcopalian. Home: Berkeley, Calif. Died Aug. 8, 1926.

HAINES, John Allen, business executive; b. Chicago, Ill., Jan. 17, 1877; s. Charles John and Dora (Allen) H.; desc. Henry Adams, of Mass. and Ethan Allen, Vt.; prep. edn., Univ. School, Chicago and Belmont (Mass.) Sch.; B.S., Cornell, 1899; m. Edith, g.g.d. of Francis Scott Key, Oct. 22, 1902; 1 daughter (dec.). Pres. The Haines & Noyes Co., mfrs. of elec. devices, 1900-06; associated in Chicago with investment bankers, as western rep., partner, etc., 1906-17; a founder, 1917, v.p. Chicago Morris Plan Bank (now Personal Loan & Savings Bank), 1917-20; was organizer, 1922, inc., 1928, and chmn. bd., Haines, Spencer & Chancellor, financial advisers; dir. of Scott & Holladay, representatives of European distillers and vintners; business counselor. Founder, and pres. Chicago Municipal Christmas Assn., 1913-20; mem. finance com. Chicago Municipal Voters League, 1912-20. Enrolled as lt. (j.g.) U.S. Naval Training Sta., Great Lakes, Ill., Apr. 1917, and served as aide to comdt.; in naval aviation overseas, 1918, at Eastleigh, Eng., with field hdqrs. at Dunkirk, Belgium, as administrative and exec. aide to comdg. officer; returned to U.S. to serve as aide to Carter Glass, sec. of treasury, later exec. officer at Aviation Mechanics Sch., Great Lakes Sta. Inspector, rank lt. comdr. staff of rear adm. comdg. N.Y. Naval Militia; lt. comdr. U.S.N.R. Presbyn. Home: New York, N.Y. Deceased.

HAINES, John Michener, governor; b. Jasper County, Ia., Jan. 1, 1863; s. Isaac L. and Eliza (Bushong) H.; ed. Penn Coll., Oskaloosa, Ia., 3 yrs.; m. Mary Symons, May 20, 1883. In real estate and investment business, Boise, Ida., 1890—. Mayor of Boise, 1907-08; gov. of Ida., 1913-15. Republican. Quaker. Home: Boise, Ida. Died June 4, 1917.

HAINES, John Peter, humanitarian; b. New York, N.Y., Dec. 17, 1851; s. William Augustus and Emily S. H.; ed. by pvt. tutors and spl. course, Columbia; m. Mary, d. George Merritt, Irvington-on-Hudson, 1873 (died 1911). Prominently identified with humane and benevolent movements for many yrs.; pres. Am. Soc. for Prevention of Cruelty to Animals, 1889-1906 (resigned); during his administration the operations of the soc. were extended, new laws for protection of animals enacted, reforms in transportation of animals instituted, brutal and demoralizing "sports," pigeon shooting, rabbit coursing, suppressed, and many forms of cruelty checked or abolished. Life mem. Am. Soc. for Prevention Cruelty to Animals (was editor Our Animal Friends, official organ of the soc.). Owner of celebrated Cranmoor Farm, Toms River, N.J. Invented and patented the Haines' electric log, by means of which the speed of vessels is indicated and registered in any part of a vessel. Homes: Toms River, N.J., and N.Y. City. Died June 26, 1921.

HAINES, Walter Stanley, toxicologist; b. Chicago, Ill., Sept. 27, 1850; s. John C. and Emma A. (Adams) H.; Mass. Inst. Tech., 1869-71; M.D., Chicago Med. Coll. (Northwestern U.), 1873; (hon. A.M., Monmouth, 1881). Prof. chemistry, Chicago Med. Coll., 1872-76; student Paris and London, 1875-76; prof. chemistry and toxicology, 1876-85, chemistry, pharmacy and toxicology, 1885-1905, chemistry, materia medica and toxicology, 1905—, Rush Med. Coll. (U. of Chicago); professorial lecturer on toxicology, U. of Chicago, 1901—. Mem. Com. of Revision of U.S. Pharmacopœia, 1900-20; mem. Ill. State Food Standard Commn., 1909—. Author: A Text-Book of Legal Medicine and Toxicology, 1903, 04, 22; also chapters on alkaloidal poisons in Hamilton's System of Legal Medicine, 1894. Died Jan. 27, 1923.

HAINES, William T., governor; b. Levant, Me., Aug. 7, 1854; s. Thomas J. and Maria L. (Eddy) H.; A.B., U. of Me., 1876, LL.B., Albany (N.Y.) Law Sch., 1878; (LL.D., U. of Me., 1899); married. Began practice, Waterville, Me., 1879; county atty. Kennebec Co., Me., 1883-87; mem. State Senate, 1889-93, Me. Ho. of Rep., 1895; atty. gen. of Me., 1897-1901; mem. Exec. Council, Gov. John T. Hill, 1901-05; gov. of Me., 1913, 14. Republican. Mem. W. T. & F. E. Haines, logs, telegraph poles, etc.; dir. Ticonic Nat. Bank (Waterville); treas. Oakland Woolen Co. Unitarian. Mason. Home: Waterville, Me. Died June 4, 1919.

HAINS, Peter Conover, army officer; b. Phila., Pa., July 6, 1840; s. Reuben P. and Amanda M. H.; grad. U.S. Mil. Acad., 1861; m. Virginia P., d. Admiral Jenkins, U.S.N., Nov. 1864. Second and 1st lt. 2d Arty., June 24, 1861; transferred to topog. engrs., July 24, 1862, to engr. corps, Mar. 3, 1863; capt., July 18, 1863; maj., Sept. 22, 1870; lt. col., Sept. 16, 1886; col., Aug. 13, 1895; brig. gen. vols., May 27-Nov. 30, 1898; brig. gen. U.S.A., Apr. 21, 1903. Bvtd.: capt., May 27, 1862, "for gallant and meritorious services" in battle of Hanover C.H., Va.; maj., July 4, 1863, for same during siege of Vicksburg; lt. col., Mar. 13, 1865, for same during the war. Served as engr. of numerous works of harbor and river improvement; as engr. sec. Lighthouse Bd.; as engr. in charge Potomac Flats improvement, Washington; as engr. of numerous works of harbor defense; as mem. Bd. of Ordnance and Fortifications; as mem. Nicaragua Canal Commn., 1897-99, and as mem. of Isthmian Canal Commn., 1899-1903; retired from active service in army, July 6, 1904. Mem. Isthmian Canal Commn. (constructing commn.), 1905-07. Apptd. maj. gen. U.S.A., Nov. 1, 1916, under a special act of Congress; assigned to active duty, Sept. 18, 1917, as engr. Norfolk Harbor and River Dist.; div. engr. Eastern Div., May 28-Sept. 2, 1918, when returned to retired list. Died Nov. 7, 1921.

HALBERSTADT, Baird, engineer, geologist; b. Pottsville, Pa., Jan. 26, 1860; s. Andrew Howell (M.D.) and Augusta Mary (Baird) H.; U. of Pa.; Internat. Inst., Paris, France; m. Ida Ray Smith, Oct. 15, 1918; children—Lesley Richards, Anne Josephine. Aid, Geol. Survey of Pa., 1881-86; engr. and supt. Tazewell Coal & Iron Co., 1887; asst. to Dr. Charles A. Ashburner, coal expert, 1889; spl. agt. and expert, 11th U.S. Census, 1889-91; asst. geologist, Pa. Geol. Survey, 1891-93; spl. tech. corr. and representative mining jours., 1893-98; geol. expert for large coal cos. before important commns. and in local cts., 1902; consulting geologist, State Bd. Agr., 1909-19. Capt. Signal and Telegraph Corps, attached (but not mustered) Pa. N.G., 1893-95; 1st lt. and insp. 4th Regt. Inf., 1897; 1st lt. and regimental q.m. 4th Regt., 1898; 1st lt. and regimental q.m. Pa. Inf. U.S.V., Spanish-Am. War, 1898; capt. and regimental q.m. 4th Reg. Pa. N.G., 1899; maj. and a.d.c. on staff nat. comdr. Soc. P.R. Expdn. Mem. Advisory Commn. for Preservation of Pub. Records of Pa., 1918; chmn. Local (state) Armory Bd., 1916-22. Federal fuel adminstr. for Schuylkill Co., 1917-19; chmn. com. on materials and mem. com. on mil. of Com. Pub. Safety of Pa. Republican. Episcopalian. Home: Pottsville, Pa. Died Sept. 13, 1934.

HALBERT, Henry Sale, author; b. Pickens Co., Ala., Jan. 14, 1837; s. Percival Pickens and Jane (Owen) H.; A.M., Union U., Murfreesboro, Tenn., 1856; unmarried. Served in Tex. state troops, in campaigns against Kiowa and Comanche Indians, 1860-61; pvt. 6th Tex. Cav., C.S.A., through Civ. War. Taught in various schs. and colls., 1866-99; colonization agt. for removal of Miss. Choctaw Indians to west of Miss. River, 1900-03; from then engaged in lit., hist. and archæol. work at Montgomery, Ala. Baptist. Democrat. Author: Creek War of 1813-14, 1895; History of the Choctaw Indians, 1540-1900. Co-editor with Dr. John R. Swanton of Cyrus Byington's Choctaw Dictionary. Died May 9, 1916.

HALBERT, Homer Valmore, M.D.; b. Otsego, N.Y., Mar. 6, 1858; s. Morris and Anna Eliza (McFarland) H.; A.B., Williams, 1881; M.D., Hahnemann Med. Coll., Chicago, 1887; m. Abbie M. Sherman, June 2, 1892; children—Howard V., Frances (Mrs. Paul A. Frank). Adjunct lecturer in anatomy, prof. anatomy, 1888-90, prof. theory and practice of medicine, 1890-98, sr. prof. clin. medicine, 1898, Hahnemann Medical Coll. Author: Practice of Medicine. Home: Chicago, Ill. Died May 29, 1927.

HALDEMAN, Harry Marston, merchant; b. Oil City, Pa., Apr. 5, 1871; s. William and Sabra (Merridith) H.; grad. high sch., Oil City, 1889; m. Viola Flack, Dec. 31, 1894; children—Mrs. Josephine Fitger, Harry F., Dorothy E. With McElwaine-Richards Co., Indianapolis, 1899-1902; with Crane Co., Chicago, 1902-10; with Pacific Pipe & Supply Co., Los Angeles, Calif., 1910, pres. and gen. mgr., 1915—. Pres. Better Am. Federation of Calif.; v.p. Yosemite Nat. Park Co.; chmn. advisory council Salvation Army. Republican. Presbyn. Mason. Presented with gold watch by Los Angeles Realty Bd., 1920, as "the most useful citizen of Los Angeles." Home: Los Angeles, Calif. Died Mar. 10, 1930.

HALDEMAN, Isaac Massey, clergyman; b. Concordville, Pa., Feb. 13, 1845; s. Reuben Johnson and Rachel Ann (Massey) H.; ed. West Chester (Pa.) Acad.; (D.D., William Jewell Coll., Mo.); m. Edda Bell Quinby, Oct. 3, 1883. Ordained Bapt. ministry, 1870; pastor Brandywine, Pa., 1871-75, Wilmington, Del., 1875-84, First Bapt. Ch., New York, 1884—. Mem. emergency corps, 29th Pa. Regt., Civil War. Republican. Author: Second Coming of Christ (7th edit.); Christian Science in the Light of Holy Scriptures (9th edit.), 1909; The Signs of the Times, 1911; How to Study the Bible (9th edit.), 1912; Christ, Christianity and the Bible, 1912; Ten Sermons on the Second Coming, 1916; Why I Preach the Second Coming; Can the Dead Communicate with the Living? Home: New York, N.Y. Died Sept. 27, 1933.

HALDEMAN, Walter Newman, pub. Louisville Courier-Journal; b. Maysville, Ky., April 27, 1821; s. John and Elizabeth (Newman) H.; ed. Maysville Acad., until 16 yrs. old; settled in Louisville; clerk in commn. and grocery house until 1840; then clerk in office of Louisville Journal; conducted a magazine and book business, 1843-44; m. Elizabeth, d. William Metcalfe, of Cincinnati, Oct. 30, 1844. Bought Louisville Daily Dime, Feb. 12, 1844; changed name to The Courier. Office seized by Gen. Robert Anderson, Sept. 18, 1861; paper was circulated at Bowling Green, but was printed at Nashville; resumed at Louisville, Dec., 1865; bought the Journal, Nov. 8, 1868, calling the paper the Courier-Journal; pres. Louisville Courier-Journal Co.; also, from its origin, May 1, 1884, publisher of Louisville Times. Home: Louisville, Ky. Died 1902.

HALDEMAN, William Birch, editor, publisher; b. Louisville, Ky., July 27, 1846; s. of the late Walter Newman and Elizabeth (Metcalfe) Haldeman; A.B., from Kentucky Mil. Inst., 1869, A.M., 1871; m. Lizzie Robards Offutt, Nov. 30, 1876. Began newspaper work in Louisville, 1865; editor-in-chief Louisville Times, 1902-1918. Chairman exec. com. Louisville Courier-Journal Co. and Louisville Times Co., 1917-18. Presbyn. Mem. Co. G, 9th Ky. Inf., Orphan Brigade, C.S.A., and later midshipman C.S.N., in Civil War; paroled Washington, Ga., May 6, 1865. Col. 1st Inf. Ky. N.G., Apr. 1906-July 1909; adj. gen. of Ky., 1911-12; elected comdr. for life Orphan Brigade C.S.A., Sept. 8, 1915; maj. gen. comdg. Ky. Div., U.C.V., 1910-15; elected comdr. in chief U.C.V., Apr. 1923. Mem. Dem. Nat. Com., 1915-21. Pres. Ky. Press Assn., 1910—. Mem. bd. visitors Ky. Mil. Inst.; pres. Jefferson Davis Home Assn., 1919. Home: Louisville, Ky. Died Oct. 27, 1924.

HALDERMAN, John A., soldier, diplomatist; b. in Ky., April 15, 1838; s. Dr. John A. and Susan Henderson (Rogers) H.; academic edn. (LL.D., Highland Univ., Kan.). Private sec. to 1st gov. of Kan.; judge probate court; mayor of Leavenworth; mem. both houses Kan. legislature. Served in Union army in Civil war as maj. and as maj. gen.; named in General Orders and Official Report for "Conspicuous Gallantry" in action; was U.S. consul, Bangkok, Siam, 1880; later consul gen., and, 1882-85, minister resident in Siam. Received decorations from Kings of Siam and Cambodia and French govt. for services to civilization in Far East. Deceased.

HALE, Albert (Barlow), compiler; b. Jonesville, Mich., June 5, 1860; s. Edwin M. and Abba (George) H.; A.B., U. of Mich., 1882; M.D., Chicago Med. Coll., 1886; U. of Strassburg, 1886-87; m. Ida Viller, of London, Eng., Aug. 16, 1889. Asso. clin. prof. ophthalmology, Rush Med. Coll., Chicago, 1901-03; withdrew from active professional life, 1905, to travel in S. America; spl. compiler, Pan-Am. Union, Washington, 1908-14; commercial attaché, U.S. Department of Commerce to Argentina, Uruguay and Paraguay, Oct. 1914—. Asso. editor Ophthalmology, Anales de Oftalmologia, Mexico, Archivos de Oftalmologia, Spain. Home: Cherrydale, Va. Died Apr. 30, 1929.

HALE, Albert Cable, chemist; b. Adams, N.Y., Sept. 2, 1845; s. Abner Cable and Sally Ann (Barton) H.; A.B., U. of Rochester, 1869, A.M., 1872, E.M., 1881; Ph.D., U. of Heidelberg, 1880; m. Carrie Helen Angell, Dec. 23, 1889. Vice prin. high sch., Jersey City, N.J., 1873-77; commr. for ednl. exhibit of N.J. at U.S. Centennial Expn., 1876; pres. State Sch. of Mines, Colo., 1880-83; head teacher, physical science dept., Boys' High Sch., Brooklyn, 1883-1912; pres. dept. chemistry, Brooklyn Inst. of Arts and Sciences, 1890. Dir., 1887-1902, v.p., 1889, sec., 1889-1903, councilor, 1893-1909, Am. Chem. Soc.; councilor A.A.A.S., 1901, 1902; v.p. N.E. Assn. Chem. Teachers, 1901-02; examiner in chemistry, Coll. Entrance Bd., 1902-06; life mem. Chemists' Club, New York. Home: Brooklyn, N.Y. Died Apr. 24, 1921.

HALE, Anne Gardner, author; b. Newburyport, Mass.; d. Jacob and Mary Jane (Hoyt) H.; ed. pvt. schs. First published verse at 17 yrs.; has contbd. verse on nearly 400 different subjects to 21 different jours. and magazines. Originator and sec. Newburyport branch, Girls' Friendly Soc.; originator and for 10 yrs. mgr. Mary I. Woart scholarship, St. Augustine's Sch. for Colored Youth, Raleigh, N.C. Author: Uncle Mark's Amaranths, 1881; Folly's Bells (poem), 1897; Seedlings from My Wild Garden (poems), 1902; The Closed Balcony, 1907. Home: Newburyport, Mass. Died Nov. 1914.

HALE, Charles Reuben, P.E. bishop of Cairo, Ill., 1892—; coadjutor to Bishop of Springfield; b. Lewistown, Pa., 1837; grad. Univ. of Pa., 1858 (D.D., Hobart, 1876; LL.D., Griswold Coll., 1889); deacon, 1860; priest, 1861; asst. Christ Ch., Germantown, Pa., and All Saints, Lower Dublin, Pa., 1861-63; naval chaplain, 1863-70; rector St. John's, Auburn, N.Y., 1871-73; St. Mary the Virgin, Baltimore, 1875-76; asst. St. Paul's, Baltimore, 1877-85; dean of Davenport Cathedral, Ia., 1886-92. Home: Cairo, Ill. Died 1900.

HALE, Clarence, judge; b. Turner, Me., Apr. 15, 1848; s. James Sullivan and Betsey (Staples) H.; A.B., Bowdoin, 1869, later A.M. and LL.D.; m. Margaret Rollins, Mar. 11, 1880; children—Katharine (Mrs. Philip G. Clifford), Robert Hale. Admitted to bar, 1871, and practiced at Portland. City solicitor, 1879-82; mem. Me. Ho. of Rep., 1883-86; U.S. dist. judge, Dist. of Me., 1902. Republican. Conglist. Trustee overseers Bowdoin Coll. (pres.). Home: Portland, Me. Died Apr. 9, 1934.

HALE, Edward Everett, author, minister South Congl. (Unitarian) Ch., Boston, 1856—, chaplain U.S. Senate; b. Boston, Apr. 3, 1822; s. Nathan and Sarah Preston (Everett) H.; studied Boston Latin Sch.; grad. Harvard, 1839, S.T.D., 1879 (LL.D., Dartmouth, 1901, Williams, 1904); 2 yrs. usher Boston Latin Sch.; studied theology; licensed to preach; minister Ch. of the Unity, Worcester, Mass., 1846-56; m. Oct. 13, 1852, Emily Baldwin Perkins. Prominent promoter of "Chautauqua" circles and "Lend-a-Hand" clubs. Chmn. Mass. Commn. for Internat. Justice. Editor Lend-a-Hand Record. Author: (stories): The Man Without a Country; Ten Times One is Ten; Margaret Percival in America; In His Name; Mr. Tangier's Vacations; Mrs. Merriam's Scholars; His Level Best. Other works: Sketches in Christian History; Boy's Heroes; The Story of Massachusetts; A New England Boyhood; Memories of a Hundred Years, 1902; Ralph Waldo Emerson, 1902; We, the People, 1903; New England Ballads, 1903; Foundation of the Republic, 1906. Editor: Modern Achievement, 10 vols., 1905. Home: Roxbury, Mass. Died 1909.

HALE, Edward Everett, univ. prof.; b. at Boston, Mass., Feb. 18, 1863; s. Rev. Edward Everett and Emily Baldwin (Perkins) H.; A.B., Harvard U., 1883; Ph.D., Halle, 1892; Litt.D. from Union U., 1928; m. Rose Postlethwaite Perkins, June 15, 1893; children—Maurice Perkins, Nathan, Thomas Shaw. Instr. and asst. prof. English, Cornell, 1886-90; Harris fellow, Harvard, 1890-92; prof. English, U. of Ia., 1892-95, Union Coll., 1895—. Author: Constructive Rhetoric, 1896; Lowell, 1899; Dramatists of Today, 1905; Seward, 1910; Life and Letters of Edward Eeverett Hale, 1917. Home: Schenectady, N.Y. Died Aug. 19, 1932.

HALE, Edward Joseph, diplomatic service; b. "Haymount," near Fayetteville, N.C., Dec. 25, 1839; s. Edward J. and Sarah Jane (Walker) H.; A.B., U. of N.C., 1860 (LL.D., 1910); m. Maria Rhett Hill, Jan. 15, 1861; 2d Caroline Green Mallett, Dec. 5, 1905. A propr. and editor Fayetteville Observer, 1860-65; served pvt. to maj. and asst. adj. gen., of gen. staff, C.S.A., his last promotion being for "conspicuous gallantry and merit"; reëstablished Fayetteville Observer, 1882; Am. consul at Manchester, Eng., 1885-89; presented with an "illuminated address" by leading men of England, 1889; v.p. Internat. Congress on Internal Navigation, 1890; commr. Manchester Ship Canal in N. America, 1890-91; dir. a founder, Nat. Rivers and Harbors Congress, 1899-1913; E.E. and M.P. to Costa Rica, June 21, 1913-21; detained in the U.S. by exec. order on account of revolution in Costa Rica. Trustee U. of N.C. (exec. com.). Home: Fayetteville, N.C. Died Feb. 15, 1922.

HALE, Edwin Moses, M.D.; b. Newport, N.H., Feb. 2, 1829; ed. at Fredonia, O.; grad. Cleveland Homœopathic Med. Coll., 1859; practiced Jonesville, Mich., 1859-61; since then in Chicago; prof. materia medica and diseases of the heart, Hahnemann Med. Coll., Chicago, 18 years; prof. materia medica and therapeutics, Chicago Homœopathic Med. Coll. 5 years; mem. Am. Inst. of Homœopathy; Ill. State Med. Soc. Author: The Materia Medica and Therapeutics of New Remedies; Diseases of Women and

Sterility; The Practice of Medicine; etc. Home: Chicago, Ill. Died 1899.

HALE, Eugene, senator; b. Turner, Me., June 9, 1836; s. James Sullivan and Betsey (Staples) H.; bro. of Clarence H.; acad. edn.; (hon. A.M., Bowdoin, 1869; LL.D., Bates Coll., 1882, Colby, 1886, Bowdoin, 1896); m. Mary Douglas, d. Zachariah Chandler, of Michigan, Dec. 20, 1871, father of Chandler H. Admitted to bar, 1857; sr. mem. Hale & Hamlin. Co. atty. Hancock Co., 9 yrs.; mem. Ho. of Rep., 1867, 68, 80; mem. 41st to 45th Congresses (1869-79); U.S. senator for terms, 1881-87, 1887-93, 1893-99, 1899-1905, 1905-11. Now mem. Nat. Monetary Commn. Apptd. Postmaster Gen. by Pres. Grant, 1874, but declined; was tendered naval portfolio by Pres. Hayes, but declined. Home: Ellsworth, Me. Died Oct. 27, 1918.

HALE, Fletcher, congressman; b. Portland, Me., Jan. 22, 1883; s. Frederick Fletcher and Adelaide Louise (McLellan) H.; grad. English High Sch., Boston, 1900; B.S., Dartmouth, 1905; studied law, Harvard Law Sch. 6 mos. and in office of Batchellor & Mitchell, Littleton, N.H.; m. Alice Norma Armstrong, Mar. 29, 1913; children—Fletcher, Robert A. Admitted to N.H. bar, 1908; associated with Batchellor & Mitchell, Littleton, until 1912; practiced at Laconia, 1912—; city solicitor, Laconia, 1915; county solicitor, Belknap Co., 1915-20; mem. Bd. of Edn., Laconia, 1916-25, chmn., 1918-25; mem. N.H. Constl. Conv., 1918; mem. N.H. Tax Commn., 1920-25; mem. 69th to 71st Congresses (1927-31), 1st N.H. Dist. Republican. Episcopalian. Mason. Home: Laconia, N.H. Died Oct. 22, 1931.

HALE, Floyd Orlin, pres. Ill. Bell Telephone Co.; b. West Windsor, Vt., Apr. 13, 1882; s. Frank S. and Mary J. (Hale) H.; B.L., Dartmouth Coll., 1903; m. Gail Giddings Perkins, 1905 (died 1921); children—Elizabeth (Mrs. John H. Beardsley), Robert Locke. Associated with Bell System from 1903; with Central Dist. and Printing Telegraph Co., Pittsburgh, Pa., in various capacities, 1903-09; in engring. dept. Am. Telephone & Telegraph Co., New York, 1909-12; chief engr. Southwestern Bell Telephone System, St. Louis, 1912-16; gen. mgr. for properties in Mo. and Ark. for Southwestern Bell Telephone Co., St. Louis, 1916-21; chief engr. Ill. Bell Telephone Co. Chicago, 1921-22, vice pres. and gen. mgr., 1922-28, v.p. in charge of operations, 1928-30, pres., July 1, 1930—. Dir. Chicago Assn. of Commerce. Home: La Grange, Ill. Died Mar. 18, 1938.

HALE, Franklin Darius, consular service; b. Barnet, Vt., Mar. 7, 1854; s. Sprague Taylor and Nancy May (Moulton) H.; LL.B., U. of Mich., 1877; m. Addie L. Silsby, Nov. 2, 1881; m. 2d, Jennie A. Silsby, Nov. 26, 1907. Practiced, Lewiston, Me., and Lunenburg, Vt.; pros. atty. Essex Co., Vt., 1883-89; mem. Vt. Ho. of Rep. 3 terms, Senate, 1 term; state auditor, 1892-98; in service of U.S. Govt. as chmn. townsite bd. of trustees Oklahoma City, Okla., 1891; chief clk. to treas. of mil. govt. in Cuba, 1899-1900; consul at Coaticook, Can., 1902-08, Charlottetown, P.E.I., 1908-09, Trinidad, B.W.I., 1909-12, Huddersfield, Eng., Aug. 1912—. Republican. Conglist. Mason. Home: Lunenburg, Vt. Died Apr. 21, 1940.

HALE, Gardner, artist; b. Chicago, Ill., Feb. 1, 1894; s. William Gardner and Harriet Knowles (Swinburne) H.; grad. Univ. High Sch., Chicago, 1911; Harvard, 1911-14; pupil of Carlandi, Rome, Zanetti, Venice; studied Art Students' League, New York, Académie Julien, Paris, and under Maurice Denis; m. Marie Louise Gibson, Sept. 29, 1916 (divorced 1926); m. 2d, Dorothy A. Donovan, Dec. 18, 1929. Exhibited at Archtl. League, New York; Art Institute Chicago; "one man" exhbn., galleries of Marie Sterner (New York); Brooklyn Mus.; Soc. Independent Artists (New York). Mural work for residence of Edward Shearson, Palm Beach, Fla.; B. C. Work, Oyster Bay, N.Y.; Jay Carlisle, Islip, L.I.; T. M. Spelman and J. Walter Spalding, Florence, Italy; Ill. Merchants Trust Bldg., Chicago; residences of Mrs. Walter Lewisohn and Marquis Castel-Maurigi, Paris; church, Souvrain Moulin, France, for Comtesse d'Hinnisdal; frescoes in Château Fillerval, France, for Donald Harper; chapel for Mrs. Ellen Munroe, Ridgeway, Pau, France; Martin Saportas, New York, Mrs. Wm. Payne Thompson, London; Bishop Herbert Shipman, New York; Seton Porter, New York, etc. Episcopalian. A pioneer in revival of painting in "True Fresco." Home: New York, N.Y. Died Dec. 28, 1931.

HALE, George Ellery, astronomer; b. Chicago, Ill., June 29, 1868; s. William Ellery and Mary S. H.; S.B., Mass. Inst. Tech., 1890; studied Harvard College Obs., 1889-90, Univ. of Berlin, winter 1893-94; hon. Sc.D., U. of Pittsburgh, 1897, Yale, 1905, Victoria U., Manchester, 1907, Oxford, 1909, Cambridge, 1911, Chicago, 1916, Columbia, 1917, Harvard, 1921; LL.D., Beloit, 1904, U. of Calif., 1912, Princeton, 1917; Ph.D., Berlin, 1910; m. Evelina S. Conklin, June 5, 1890; children—Margaret, William Ellery. Dir. Kenwood Astrophys. Obs., 1890-96; asso. prof. astrophysics, 1892-97, prof., 1897-1905, organizer, and dir. Yerkes Obs., 1895-1905, U. of Chicago; organizer

and dir. Mount Wilson Obs. of Carnegie Instn. of Wash., 1904-23, hon. dir., 1923—. Trustee Calif. Inst. Technology (chmn. observatory council), Huntington Library and Art Gallery. Principal scientific researches have been made in solar stellar spectroscopy. Joint editor Astronomy and Astrophysics, 1892-95, Astrophysical Journal, 1895-1935. Janssen medal, Paris Acad. Sciences, 1894; Rumford medal, 1902; Draper medal, 1903; gold medal, Royal Astron. Soc., 1904; Bruce medal, Astron. Soc. of the Pacific, 1916; Janssen medal, Astron. Soc. of France, 1917; Galileo medal, Florence, 1920; Actonian prize, Royal Instn., 1921; Arthur Noble medal for civic service (Pasadena), 1927; Cresson and Franklin medals, Franklin Inst., 1926, 27; Holland Society medal, 1931; Copley medal, Royal Society, London, 1932; awarded Ives medal by Optical Soc. of America; Commander Order of Leopold II (Belgium); Commander Order of the Crown (Italy). Mem. com. on intellectual co-operation League of Nations, 1922. Author: The Study of Stellar Evolution; Ten Years' Work of a Mountain Observatory; The New Heavens; The Depths of the Universe; Beyond the Milky Way; Signals from the Stars. Died Feb. 21, 1938.

HALE, John Howard, nurseryman, pomologist; b. Glastonbury, Conn., Nov. 25, 1853; s. John A. and Henrietta (Moseley) H.; ed. pub. schs., Glastonbury; m. Addie R. Stancliff, Oct. 31, 1877. Pres. and gen. mgr. of The Hale Georgia Orchard Co., with orchards at Fort Valley, Ga.; "father" of commercial peach culture in N.E., with over 500 acres at Glastonbury and Seymour, Conn.; popularly known as America's "Peach King"; also extensive grower of apples; lecturer and writer on gen. hort. subjects. Master Conn. State Grange, 1887-91; trustee Conn. Agrl. Coll., 1886-96; mem. Conn. Gen. Assembly, 1893, 1894. Mem. Conn. Pub. Utilities Commn. Republican. Home: S. Glastonbury, Conn. Died Oct. 12, 1917.

HALE, Ledyard Park, lawyer; b. Canton, N.Y., May 17, 1854; s. Horace Winthrop and Betsy Russell (Lewis) H.; B.S., St. Lawrence U., 1876; LL.B., U. of Wis., 1878; LL.D., St. Lawrence, 1912; m. Georgettie Bacheller, May 21, 1879; children—Mrs. Irma Pfund, Horace Charles. Assistant dist. atty., St. Lawrence Co., 1882-88, dist. atty., 1894-99; apptd. co. judge by Gov. Odell, Oct. 1902; elected co. judge, Nov. 1903, for 6 yr. term (resigned 1908); mem. State Bd. Charities, 1907-08; counsel to Pub. Service Commn., 2d Dist., Apr. 1908-21, to Public Service Commn., 1921-23. Del. N.Y. Constl. Conv., 1915. Trustee St. Lawrence Univ., 1884— (pres. bd., 1919-24). Republican. Home: Canton, N.Y. Died 1926.

HALE, Louise Closser, actress, author; b. Chicago, Ill., Oct. 13, 1872; d. Joseph and Louise (Paddock) Closser; ed. pub. schs., Indianapolis; m. Walter Hale, Aug. 17, 1899. First appearance on stage, Detroit, 1895. Author: A Motor Car Divorce, 1906; The Actress, 1909; The Married Miss Worth, 1911; Her Soul and Her Body, 1912; We Discover New England, 1915; We Discover the Old Dominion, 1916; An American's London, 1920; Home Talent, 1926; The Canal Boat Fracas, 1926. Died July 26, 1933.

HALE, Lucretia Peabody, author; b. Boston, Mass., Sept. 2, 1820 (sister Edward Everett Hale). Author: The Peterkin Family; Peterkin Papers; The Last of the Peterkins; An Uncloseted Skeleton (with late E. L. Bynner); Stories for Children; The New Harry and Lucy (with Edward Everett Hale). Home: Brookline, Mass. Died 1900.

HALE, Matthew, lawyer; b. Albany, N.Y., May 30, 1882; s. Matthew and Mary (Lee) H.; A.B., Harvard, 1903 (Phi Beta Kappa), A.M., 1904; Harvard Law Sch., 1903-04, 1905-06; m. Anne Taggard Piper, Feb. 23, 1907. Began practice in offices of Dunbar, Brandeis & Nutter, 1907; opened pvt. office, 1908; asst. solicitor, B.&M. R.R., working on interstate commerce law, 1908-11; purchased Boston Journal, Mar. 1913; v.p. Liberty Shipbuilding Co., 1918; mgr. Liberty Shipbuilding Ship Yards, Brunswick, Ga., 1918; pres. S. Atlantic Maritime Corp., 1918-22, S. Atlantic Export Co., 1919-22. Alderman, Boston, 1909-10; Council, 1910-13; chmn. Prog. State Com., Mass., 1912; Mass. mem. Prog. Nat. Com., 1912. Apptd. mem. Wage Umpire Bd., July 1918. Unitarian. Mason. Home: Washington, D.C. Died Aug. 29, 1925.

HALE, Philip, music and drama critic; b. Norwich, Vt., Mar. 5, 1854; s. William Bainbridge and Harriet Amelia (Porter) H.; A.B., Yale, 1876; admitted to bar, Albany, N.Y., 1879; studied music in Berlin under Haupt and Bargiel, 1882-84; at Munich, Stuttgart, Germany, and in Paris under Guilmant, 1885-87; Mus.D., Dartmouth College, 1928; A.M. from Harvard U., 1933; m. Irene Baumgras, June 10, 1884. Was organist at Albany, N.Y., and Troy, N.Y.; organist of Dr. de Normandie's Ch., Boston, 1889-1905; on editorial staff and musical critic, Boston Post, 1890-91, Boston Journal, 1891-1903, Boston Herald, May 1903—. Editor Musical Record, Boston, 1897-1901, The Musical World, 1901-03; Boston Symphony Program Books, 1901—. Home: Boston, Mass. Died Nov. 30, 1934.

HALE, Philip Leslie, painter; b. Boston, Mass., May 21, 1865; s. Rev. Edward Everett and Emily Baldwin (Perkins) H.; ed. Roxbury Latin Sch.; studied Art Students' League, New York, Julian Acad., and École des Beaux Arts, Paris; m. Lilian C. Westcott, June 11, 1902. Hon. mention, Buffalo Expn., 1901; bronze medal, St. Louis Expn., 1904; gold medal, Internat. Expn., Buenos Aires, 1910; Norman Wait Harris silver medal, Chicago, 1914; Proctor portrait prize, N.A.D., 1916; 2d Lea prize, Pa. Acad. Fine Arts, 1916; popular prize, Phila., 1919; medal at Sesquicentennial, Phila. Mem. Internat. Art Jury, San Francisco Expn., 1915. Home: Dedham, Mass. Died Feb. 2, 1931.

HALE, Philip Thomas, clergyman; b. New Market, Ala., Aug. 18, 1857; s. Dr. Philip Perry and Caroline Susan (Gulledge) H.; A.B., with honors, Howard Coll., Ala., 1879; full grad. Southern Bapt. Theol. Sem., 1883, and post-grad. same; D.D., Howard, 1890; LL.D., Union U.; m. Lena Lyle Bolinger, Dec. 9, 1885; children—John Bolinger (dec.), Thomas Farris (dec.), Roy William, Philip Theodore, Davis Ward, Earl Douglas, Franklin Sevier. Ordained Bapt. ministry; pastor Danville, Ky., 1883-88, Birmingham, Ala., 1888-98, Roanoke, Va., 1898-1901, Owensboro, Ky., 1901-04; pres. Union U., Jackson, Tenn., 1904-06; corr. sec. Bapt. Edn. Soc. of Ky., 1906-09; lecturer, and financial sec., Southern Bapt. Theol. Sem., Sept. 10, 1909—. Mem. bd. State Missions of Ala.; v.p. Foreign Mission Bd., Southern Bapt. Conv. for Ala.; chaplain-gen. Sons of Confederate Vets. of Ala. Founder and the 1st pres. Southern Bapt. Ednl. Conf.; pres. Alumni Assn. Southern Bapt. Theol. Sem. Home: Louisville, Ky. Died Dec. 23, 1926.

HALE, Prentis Cobb, merchant, banker; b. South Haven, Mich., Dec. 12, 1858; s. Marshal and Prudence (Dyckman) H.; ed. high sch., San José, Calif.; m. Linda Hoag Bryan, Oct. 1, 1908; 1 son, Prentis Cobb; stepchildren—Hamilton Vose Bryan, lt. comdr., U.S.N., Florence Linda Bryan (Mrs. Edward Burke Corbet), Carleton Felton Bryan. Began as partner Hale Bros. & Co., Petaluma, Calif., 1879; consolidated with other brothers, 1881, as Hale Brothers & Co., inc. as Hale Brothers, Inc., 1892, pres. 1896-1926; pres. Hale Bros. Stores, Inc. (consolidation of all partnership interests), 1926-31, president bd. of dirs.; pres. Hale Real Estate Co.; v.p., dir. Hale Bros. Realty Co., Panama Realty Co. Decorated Cross of Chevalier of Crown of Italy. Republican. Mason. Mem. Ethical Culture Soc. Home: San Francisco, Calif. Died Nov. 21, 1936.

HALE, Susan, artist; b. Boston, Mass., Dec. 5, 1833; d. Nathan and Sarah Preston (Everett) H.; ed. pvt. sch.; unmarried. Taught school; artist in water colors; exhibited landscapes, Boston and New York. Author: Life and Letters of Thomas Gold Appleton; Family Flight series of travels, for young people (with her brother, Edward Everett Hale). Home: Roxbury, Mass. Died 1910.

HALE, Walter, illustrator; b. Chicago, Ill., Aug. 4, 1869; s. Robert W. and Virginia (Timberlake) H.; student Shattuck (Mil.) Sch., Faribault, Minn., 1884-85; Minneapolis Sch. of Fine Arts, 1888; studied later in New York and Paris; m. Louise Closser Hale, Aug. 17, 1899. Actor until 1913, keeping up art work in meantime; created parts in original productions of Augustus Thomas's "Oliver Goldsmith," "Arizona," "As a Man Thinks," etc.; played with Fanny Davenport, Sol Smith Russell, Julia Marlowe, William H. Crane, etc. Exhibited etchings, lithographs or illustrations, Royal Soc. of Painter-Etchers, London, 1894 (elected asso.), N.Y. Etching Club, 1894-96, St. Louis Expn., 1904, Salon of Société des Beaux Arts, Paris, 1911, San Francisco Expn., 1915, Musée des Invalides, Paris (war lithographs), 1916, Painters-Gravers of America, New York, 1917; etc. Served with 1st Regt. Minn. N.G., 1885-89; spl. corr. Century Mag., with armies of Northern France, June-Aug. 1915; spl. corr. for Harper's Mag. with French and British armies, Aug.-Oct. 1916. Author: The Ideal Motor Tour in France, 1914; By Motor to the Firing-Line, 1916. Illustrator: We Discover New England, 1915; On the Trail of Stevenson (by Clayton Hamilton), 1915; The Spirit of France (by Owen Johnson), 1915; We Discover the Old Dominion (by Louise Closser Hale), 1916; etc. Died Dec. 4, 1917.

HALE, William Barton, publisher; b. Adams Center, N.Y., Oct. 6, 1860; s. Abner C. and Sally Ann (Barton) H.; A.B., U. of Rochester, 1885 (Hull prize), A.M., 1888; m. Clara Louise Andrews, May 22, 1891. Admitted to bar, 1887; chmn. bd. Lawyers' Coöperative Pub. Co., Mechanics Savings Bank; pres. E. R. Andrews Printing Co.; dir. Genesee Valley Trust Co. Trustee U. of Rochester, 1906—, Colgate Rochester Div. Sch. Republican. Home: Rochester, N.Y. Died Dec. 27, 1938.

HALE, William Bayard, editor; b. Richmond, Ind., Apr. 6, 1869; s. William Hadley and Anna (Bunting) H.; ed. Boston and Harvard univs., and Episcopal Theol. Sem., Cambridge, Mass.; (S.T.D., Hobart Coll., 1896; LL.D., St. John's, Md., 1896); m. Olga, d. late Emil Unger, Oct. 5, 1909. For several yrs. P.E. clergyman, holding the rectorates of Our Saviour's, Middleborough, Mass. (founded the parish and built notable perpendicular ch.), and St. Mary's, Ardmore, Pa. Entered journalism, 1900, but retained clerical orders until 1909; mng. editor Cosmopolitan Mag., 1900; editor Current Literature, 1901; spl. corr. New York World, 1902; mng. editor Phila. Public Ledger, 1903-07; editor on staff New York Times and Paris corr. same, 1907-09; editor staff World's Work, 1909-13. Spl. agt. of President Wilson in Mexico, 1913-14. Has lived much abroad; student of internat. affairs; lectured at Oxford on U.S. Constitution and has advised several govts. on polit. questions. Decorated: Officer Order Leopold (Belgium); Knight Commander Imperial Order Rising Sun (Japan); Grand Cross Order Liberator (Venezuela), etc. Deputy gov. Soc. Colonial Wars; mem. bd. mngrs. Empire State Soc. S.A.R. Author: The Story of Style, 1920. Editor of President Wilson's book, The New Freedom, 1913. Died Apr. 1924.

HALE, William Benjamin, lawyer; b. St. Louis, Sept. 10, 1871; s. William Benjamin and Matilda (Nicholson) H.; LL.B., U. of Mo., cum laude, 1890; m. Anna B. De Forest, July 8, 1896. Admitted to bar, 1890. Author: Bailments and Carriers, 1895; Damages, 1896; Torts, 1896. Editor: Corpus Juris, 1914. Contributed numerous titles in Am. and English Encyclopædia of Law and in Encyclopædia of Pleading and Practice, 1896-1902. Home: Brooklyn, N.Y. Died Mar. 1924.

HALE, William Gardner, philologist; b. Savannah, Ga., Feb. 9, 1849; s. William Bradford and Elizabeth (Jewett) H.; A.B., Harvard, 1870, fellow, 1870-71; fellow and student univs. of Leipzig and Göttingen, 1876-77; (LL.D., Union U., 1895, Princeton, 1896, St. Andrew's, 1907, Aberdeen, 1907); m. Harriet Knowles Swinburne, June 13, 1883. Tutor in Latin, Harvard, 1874-76, 1877-80; prof. Latin lang. and lit., Cornell, 1880-92; prof. and head dept. Latin, U. of Chicago, 1892-1919, prof. emeritus. Asso. editor Classical Review, 1895-1907, Classical Quarterly, 1907—; hon. editor Am. Jour. Archæology, 1897-99; joint editor Cornell U. Studies in Classical Philology, 1887-92; mem. bd. of editors Classical Philology; chmn., 1894-99, and 1st dir., 1895-96, Am. Sch. Classical Studies, Rome. Author: The Art of Reading Latin, 1887; The Sequence of Tenses in Latin, 1887-88; Hale-Buck Latin Grammar (with Carl D. Buck), 1903; First Latin Book, 1907. Home: Stamford, Conn. Died June 24, 1928.

HALE, William Henry, lawyer; b. Albany, N.Y., Aug. 20, 1840; s. Silvester and Nancy Arzelia (Eames) H.; A.B., Yale, 1860, A.M., Ph.D., 1863; LL.B., Albany Law Sch., 1861; m. Louisa Gertrude Washington, Feb. 25, 1892. Admitted to bar, 1861; after some experience in business practiced at Albany, 1888, Brooklyn, 1888—; supt. pub. baths, Brooklyn, 1906—. Was for many years regular Am. corr. Nature, London, and was editor science dept. Bachelor of Arts Magazine. Mem. Com. on Tercentenary Celebration of Founding of New York City; del. 1st Internat. Conf. on Public and Sch. Baths, The Hague, 1912. Home: Brooklyn, N.Y. Died May 4, 1919.

HALE, William Thomas, author; b. Liberty, Tenn., Feb. 1, 1857; s. Charles Warren Lafayette and Malissa (Overall) H.; ed. Liberty, Tenn.; studied law in pvt. office, and practiced about 8 yrs. at Liberty and Lebanon; m. Lulu Lewis, Apr. 6, 1876; children—Charles Lewis, Herbert Lawrence, Hilda, Howell Lamar. Entered journalism in 1893; asso. editor Memphis Commercial-Appeal, 1895-96; asst. Sunday editor St. Louis Post-Dispatch, 1896; asso. editor Nashville American, 1897; editor in chief Knoxville Sentinel, portion of year 1898. Author: Great Southerners, Biographical and Critical Sketches, 1900; True Stories of Jamestown and Its Environs, 1907; Folklore of the Tennessee Hill People, 1911; A History of Tennessee and Tennesseans (8 vols.), 1913. Asso. editor and "colyum" man, Nashville Tennessean and American, 1917—. Home: Nashville, Tenn. Died July 12, 1926.

HALEY, George Franklin, judge; b. Saco, Me., Jan. 30, 1856; s. Henry U. and Martha P. (Borbthy) H.; common sch. edn.; m. Mariana Gains, Feb. 15, 1894 (died 1908); m. 2d, Ethel L. Bowie, Dec. 9, 1915. Admitted to Me. bar, 1882; asso. in practice at Biddeford, with B. F. Hamilton, as Hamilton & Haley, 1882-1900; practiced with brother Leroy H., 1904-11; apptd. justice Supreme Jud. Ct. of Me., Apr. 1911; term expiring Apr. 15, 1918. Democrat. Home: Saco, Me. Deceased.

HALEY, Jesse James, clergyman, editor; b. in Rockcastle Co., Ky., Mar. 18, 1851; s. John and Julia Anderson (Fish) H.; A.B., Ky. U., 1869, later A.M.; grad. Coll. of the Bible, Ky. U., 1872; 1 term at Northwestern Christian U. (now Butler Coll. of U. of Indianapolis); m. Elizabeth Clark, Apr. 13, 1874. Ordained Christian (Disciples of Christ) Ch. ministry, 1873; preached in Australia, 1874-85; edited the Australian Christian Watchman (organ Disciples of Christ in Southern Hemisphere), 1879-85; returned to U.S., 1885, preached at San Francisco, 1886; office editor, 1888, and 10 yrs. on editorial staff Christian Evangelist, St. Louis, and asst. editor Christian Quarterly Review. Went to England under auspices Foreign Christian Missionary Soc., 1890, and preached in Liverpool 5 yrs.; returned to U.S., Oct. 1894; pastor Christian Ch., Cynthiana, Ky., 9 yrs.; pastor 7th St. Christian Ch., Richmond, Va., 1904-08. Editor-in-chief of Christian Oracle, Chicago, 1898, and editor same paper under name of Christian Century up to 1908. Pres. Nat. Congress, Disciples of Christ, 1905. Author: Makers and Moulders of the Reformation, 1915; Debates that Made History, 1920. Home: Haines City, Fla. Died Apr. 8, 1924.

HALEY, Ora, stockman; b. East Corinth, Me., Dec. 4, 1845; s. Benjamin and Nancy Jane H.; ed. E. Corinth Acad.; m. Gussie Pfeiffer Jan. 8, 1872. Live stock grower and dealer in Wyo., 1871—; now one of the largest. Republican. Knight Templar, Mason. Home: Denver, Colo. Died Dec. 1919.

HALFHILL, James Wood, lawyer; b. Mercer, O., Mar. 1, 1861; s. Moses and Elanor Maria (Wood) H.; M.S., Ohio Northern U., 1884; LL.B., Cincinnati Law Sch., 1887 (pres. of class); m. Cora Agnes Miller, Sept. 23, 1896. Practiced at Lima, O., with Jacob C. Ridenour, 1887, until his death, July 5, 1908; mem. Halfhill, Quail & Kirk; atty. and dir. The Old Nat. Bank (Lima), 1st Nat. Bank (Ada), The Ridenour-Bayley Drug Co., Cincinnati Block Co., Ohio State Life Ins. Co., etc. City solicitor, Lima, 2 terms, 1890-94; mem. State Bd. of Law Examiners, 5 yrs.; mem. 4th Constl. Conv. of Ohio, 1911-12. Republican. Home: Lima, O. Died Apr. 15, 1923.

HALFORD, Albert James, journalist; b. Hamilton, O., Aug. 11, 1851; s. Elijah and Maria Ann (Walker) H.; bro. of Elijah Walker H.; common sch. edn.; (M. Dip., Columbian, now George Washington, U., 1900); m. Marie Dean, Jan. 24, 1877. Learned printer's trade in early youth; reported proceedings Ind. Legislature at 15; reporter Indianapolis News at 18; filled various positions in Indianapolis up to mng. editor until 1888; went to Washington, 1888, as mng. editor The Post, later connected with Associated Press and United Press; with New York Sun Bureau, 1897—. Compiler of the Congressional Directory, 1898—. Home: Washington, D.C. Died 1910.

HALFORD, Elijah Walker, lt. col.; b. Nottingham, Eng., Sept. 4, 1843; s. Elijah and Maria Ann (Walker) H.; ed. pub. schs., Hamilton, O., and at acad., Newtown, O., nr. Cincinnati; became printer, journalist, Indianapolis, Ind.; m. Mary Frances Armstrong, May 1, 1866 (dec.). Edited Indianapolis Journal; then was editorial founder Chicago Inter-Ocean, Mar. 1872, to Nov. 1893; returned to Indianapolis Journal and was again its editor until 1889; pvt. sec. to President Benjamin Harrison, Mar. 1889-Mar. 4, 1893; apptd. maj. p.-m. U.S.A., Jan. 10, 1893; disbursing officer Bering Sea Arbitration Commn., Paris, 1893; lt. col. deputy p.-m. gen., Sept. 13, 1906; retired by operation of law, Sept. 4, 1907. Mem. M.E. Ch.; v. chmn. exec. com. Interdenominational and chmn. Meth. Laymen's Missionary Movement, Internat. Com. Y.M.C.A. Home: Leonia, N.J. Died Feb. 27, 1938.

HALL, Alexander Wilford, editor, author; b. Bath, N.Y., Aug. 18, 1819; s. Samuel and Frances H.; became Christian evangelist and controversialist, especially known for his attacks on Universalism, and the theory of evolution; established The Microcosm, 1881 (Ph.D., Lebanon Valley Coll., Pa., 1882; LL.D., Fla. State U., 1885); fellow Victoria Inst., London; pres. Soc. for Philos. Research, 1893. Author: Universalism Against Itself; Problem of Human Life; Immortality of the Soul. Home: New York, N.Y. Died 1902.

HALL, Allen Garland, law school dean; b. Lafayette, Ky., July 12, 1862; s. Claudius Buchanan and Selina Jefferson (Garland) H.; ed. Central U. of Ky. and Vanderbilt U.; LL.B., Vanderbilt, 1885; (LL.D., Central U. of Ky., 1906); m. Lillie Carter Gunn, Feb. 26, 1885. Mem. 47th Gen. Assembly, Tenn., 1891 (speaker pro tem.). Prof. med. jurisprudence, U. of Nashville, 1893-95; prof. law, 1902, vice dean, 1906-10, dean, 1910—, Vanderbilt U. Law Sch. Moderator Gen. Assembly, Presbyn. Ch. U.S., 1906; mem. exec. com. State Anti-Saloon League; supt. Monteagle S.S. Assembly, 1907—. Ind. Democrat. Compiled and edited Tennessee Supreme Court Reports, vols. 83, 84, 1886. Home: Nashville, Tenn. Died Nov. 28, 1915.

HALL, Arnold Bennett, educator, political scientist; b. at Franklin, Ind., July 22, 1881; s. Columbus Horatio and Theodosia (Parks) H.; A.B., Franklin College, 1904; J.D., cum laude, U. of Chicago, 1907; post-grad. study, U. of Chicago, 1907-09; LL.D., Franklin Coll., 1924, U. of Calif., 1930, College of Puget Sound, 1932; m. Grace Stafford Carney, June 15, 1911; 1 dau., Grace Elizabeth. Scholarship, U. of Chicago Law Sch., 1904-07, U. of Chicago Grad. Sch., 1907-08, fellow in polit. science, 1908-09, asst. instr. polit. science and internat. law, 1907-09, U. of Chicago; lecturer Chicago Sch. of Civics and Philanthropy, 1908-09; instr. public law and politics, Northwestern U., 1909-10; instr. polit. science, 1910-11, asst. prof., 1911-14, asso. prof., 1914-21, prof. polit. sci. and asso. prof. law, 1921-26, U. of Wis.; pres. U. of Ore., 1926-32; dir. Inst. for Govt. Research, Brookings Instn., Washington, 1933—; mem. Wis. War History Commn., 1919-26; founder Nat. Conf. on Science of Politics, 1923, and became its chmn.; mem. Social Science Research Council, 1924-32; dir. Hanover Conf., 1926, 27; Am. del. to Inst. Pacific Relations, Honolulu, 1927, and exec. com. Am. br. of Inst., 1927—; mem. Ore. State Library Bd., 1926-32; chmn. Pacific Coast regional com.,

Social Science Research Council, 1929-32; pres. Social Sci. Research Conf. Pacific Coast, 1931-32. Admitted Ind. bar, 1907. Author: The Monroe Doctrine, 1919; Dynamic Americanism, 1920; Syllabus on The Past, Present and Future of the Monroe Doctrine, 1920; Popular Government, 1921. Republican. Baptist. Died June 1. 1936.

HALL, A(rthur) Cleveland, college prof.; b. New York, Oct. 25, 1865; s. Edward Smith and Marie Antoinette (Jarvis) H.; B.A., Trinity Coll., Conn., 1888, M.A., 1893; Johns Hopkins, 1892-94; Columbia, 1894-95, fellow in sociology, 1898-1900, 1902-03, Ph.D., 1901; m. Florence E. Clexton (B.A., Smith, 1902), June 18, 1907. In pub. and newspaper work, New York City and Mass., 1888-92; asst. supt. Bur. Charities and Corrections, Chicago Expn., 1893; in social settlement and boys' club work, New York, 1894-95, 1898-1900; headworker, Orange Valley (N.J.) Social Settlement, 1901-03; instr. economics and sociology, Kenyon Coll., Sept. 1904—. N.J. del. Nat. Prison Assn., 1903-04; Ohio del. Nat. Conf. Charities and Corrections, 1909; spl. agt. Bur. of Corps., 1908. Ind. Republican. Episcopalian. Author: Crime and Social Progress, 1902. Home: Gambier, O. Died 1910.

HALL, Arthur Crawshay Alliston, bishop; b. Binfield, Berkshire, Eng., Apr. 12, 1847; s. Maj. William Thomas and Louisa Astley (Alliston) H.; B.A., Christ Ch., Oxford, 1869, M.A., 1872; D.D., 1893; LL.D., U. of Vt., 1904; S.T.D., Columbia, 1916; unmarried. Took orders in Ch. of England; licensed preacher in Diocese of Oxford as mem. of Soc. of St. John the Evangelist (Cowley Fathers); asst. minister Ch. of the Advent, Boston, 1874; minister Mission Ch. St. John the Evangelist, Boston, 1882-91; consecrated bishop of Vt., Feb. 2, 1894. Author: Meditations on the Creed; The Example of the Passion; Christ's Temptation and Ours; Confirmation (Oxford Library of Practical Theology); Use of Holy Scripture in the Worship of the Church (Paddock Lectures); The Christian Doctrine of Prayer (Bohlen Lectures); Relations of Faith and Life (Bedell Lectures); The Forgiveness of Sins; Self Discipline; The Work of the Holy Spirit; The Sevenfold Unity of the Christian Church; The Example of Our Lord, Especially for His Ministers; Preaching and Pastoral Care; Reasonable Faith; Christian Unity; The Doctrine of the Church. Home: Burlington, Vt. Died Feb. 26, 1930.

HALL, Arthur Graham, college prof.; b. Memphis, Mich., Dec. 9, 1865; s. Clark Benedict and Agnes (Graham) H.; B.S., U. of Mich., 1887, student Grad. Sch., 1898-1900; Ph.D., U. of Leipzig, 1902; m. Octavia Rosaleen Stiling, Aug. 26, 1896. Teacher, 1887-91, prin., 1889-91, high sch., Laporte, Ind.; instr. mathematics, U. of Mich., 1891-93; teacher physics, Central High Sch., Grand Rapids, 1893-94; instr. mathematics, U. of Mich., 1894-1903; asst. prof. same, U. of Ill., 1903-05; prof. same, Miami U., Oxford, O., 1905-08; prof. mathematics and registrar, U. of Mich., Oct. 1908—. Episcopalian. Co-author: Plane and Spherical Trigonometry, 1910; Trigonometric and Logarithmic Tables, 1910. Died Jan. 10, 1925.

HALL, Asaph, prof. astronomy, Harvard, 1895—; b. Goshen, Conn., Oct. 15, 1829; ed. common school; worked at farming and carpentry; spl. studies at Norfolk Acad. and Univ. of Mich. (LL.D., Yale, Harvard; Ph.D., Hamilton). Taught school; became student and, 1857-62, asst. Harvard Coll. Observatory. Aide, 1862, prof. mathematics (relative rank of capt.), 1863, U.S. Naval Observatory. Has headed many govt. astron. expdns.; made numerous important discoveries, notably that of the two moons of Mars, which he named "Deimos" and "Phobos." Mem. from 1875, Nat. Acad. Sciences; foreign mem. Royal Astron. Soc.; m. Angeline Stickney. Home: Norfolk, Conn. Died 1907.

HALL, Asaph, Jr., astronomer; b. Cambridge, Mass., Oct. 6, 1859; s. Asaph and Angeline (Stickney) H.; A.B., Harvard, 1882; Ph.D., Yale, 1889; m. Mary Estella Cockrell, July 14, 1897. Asst., U.S. Naval Obs., Washington, D.C., 1882-85; asst. astronomer, Yale Obs., 1885-89, Naval Obs., 1889-92; prof. astronomy and dir. of the obs., U. of Mich., 1892-1905; asst. Naval Obs., 1905-08; prof. mathematics, U.S.N., rank of lt., 1908; now comdr. U.S.N., retired. Died Jan. 12, 1930.

HALL, Benjamin Mortimer, civil and mining engr.; b. Fairfield Co., S.C., Jan. 31, 1853; s. Dr. Nathaniel Barber and Nancy (Boulware) H.; moved to Ga., 1854; reared on father's plantation Webster Co., Ga., to age 16, when father moved to Floyd Co.; B.E., U. of Ga., 1876, C. and M.E., 1885, D.Sc., 1921; m. Kate Chamberlin, Jan. 5, 1881; children—Warren Esterly, Gertrude (Mrs. Brainard Clapp), Benjamin Mortimer. Prof. mathematics, N. Ga. Agrl. Coll., Dahlonega, 1876-80; engr. water supply investigations, construction and operation of Ga. gold mines, 1880-85; constrn. and operation, Southern Marble Co., Pickens Co., Ga., 1887-90; sr. mem. Hall Bros., civil and mining engrs., Atlanta, 1890-1903; consulting engr. U.S. Geol. Survey, 1896-1903; supervising engr. U.S. Reclamation Service for N.M., Tex., and Okla., 1904-07; constructed Hondo, Carlsbad and Leasburg projects; negotiated terms of Mexico-Rio Grande treaty, at El Paso, Tex.; made original plans Elephant Butte dam and Rio Grande project and supervised the settlement of all water rights disputes on Rio Grande; organized Puerto Rico Irrigation Service and was chief engr., Mar. 1908-July 1910; reconstructed and operated the plant of Amicalola Marble Co., Pickens Co., Ga., 1910-12; senior mem. B. M. Hall & Sons, cons. engrs., civil, mining and hydraulic, Atlanta; mem. Bd. Consulting Engrs., City of Atlanta. Mem. arbitration bds., Raleigh, N.C., Durham, N.C., New York and Washington, D.C.; was chmn. water power com., Nat. Conservation Congress. Democrat. Methodist. Home: Atlanta, Ga. Died Nov. 19, 1929.

HALL, Bolton, lawyer; b. Ireland, Aug. 5, 1854; s. Rev. John and Emily (Bolton) H.; brother of Thomas Cuming H.; ed. in Dublin until 1867, A.B., Princeton, 1875, A.M., 1878; LL.B., Columbia, 1888; m. Susie Hurlbut Scott, Feb. 6, 1884; 1 dau., Lois H. S. (Mrs. Gerard P. Herrick). Advocate of restoring the land to the people by taking rent of land instead of taxes. Univ. Extension lecturer. Founder "Free Acres" settlement in N.J. Treas. and founder Am. Longshoremen's Union, New York Tax Reform Assn. Author: Three Acres and Liberty, 1907, revised edit., 1917, 22; A Little Land and a Living, 1908; The Garden Yard (now out of print), 1909; What Tolstoy Taught, 1911; The New Thrift, 1916; The Living Bible—The Whole Bible in its Fewest Words, 1928. Home: New York, N.Y. Died Dec. 10, 1938.

HALL, C. Lester, physician; b. Saline Co., Mo., Mar. 10, 1845; s. Dr. Matthew W. and Agnes J. (Lester) H.; M.D., Jefferson Med. Coll., Phila., 1867; post-grad. studies, N.Y. Polyclinic, 1886; m. Katherine Sappington, June 16, 1869. Prof. diseases of women and pres. bd. dirs., Medico-Chirurg. Coll., Kansas City; prof. diseases of women, Kansas City Post-Grad. Med. Sch. and Hosp. Home: Kansas City, Mo. Died June 10, 1922.

HALL, Charles Badger, major gen. U.S.A.; b. at Portland, Me., Apr. 29, 1844; s. Charles Henry and Caroline (Page) H.; grad. Portland High Sch., 1862; widower. Commd. 2d lt. 25th Me. Vol. Inf., Sept. 29, 1862; 1st lt., Mar. 6, 1863; hon. mustered out, July 10, 1863; 1st lt. 30th Me. Vol. Inf., Jan. 1, 1864; hon. mustered out, Sept. 2, 1865; apptd. to U.S.A. from Me., 2d lt. 28th Inf., Jan. 22, 1867; promoted through grades to maj. gen., Mar. 28, 1908. Bvtd.: 1st lt., Mar. 2, 1867, "for gallant and meritorious services" battle of Sabine Cross Roads, La.; capt., Mar. 2, 1867, for same in battle of Pleasant Hill, La. Commandant Inf. and Cav. Sch., Signal Sch. and Army Staff Coll., Aug. 21, 1906-Apr. 29, 1908. Episcopalian. Mason. Died May 11, 1914.

HALL, Charles Cuthbert, pres. Union Theol. Sem., 1897—; b. New York, Sept. 3, 1852; s. William Cooper and Jane Agnes H.; grad. Williams, 1872; (D.D., Univ. of N.Y., 1890, Harvard, 1897, Yale, 1901; LL.D., Union Coll., 1905); 2 yrs.' course in theology at Union Theol. Sem., and a 3d yr. in London and Edinburgh; m. Jeanie Stewart Boyd, Aug. 2, 1877. Pastor Union Presbyn. Ch., Newburgh, N.Y., 1875-77, 1st Presbyn. Ch., Brooklyn, 1887-97. Barrows lecturer, Univ. of Chicago, to India and the Far East, 1902-03, and 1906-07; Cole lecturer, Vanderbilt Univ., 1905; Noble lecturer, Harvard, 1906. Author: Redeemed Life After Death, 1905; Universal Elements of the Christian Religion, 1905; Christ and the Human Race, 1906. Died 1908.

HALL, Charles Hershall, M.D.; b. Lexington, Ky., Apr. 5, 1833; ed. at Ind. Asbury Univ., 1848-53 (A.M., M.D.); m. Mary Waller, Aug. 10, 1857. Prof. theory and practice of medicine med. dept. Williamette Univ., Oct. 1871—; contract surgeon U.S. Indian Service, 1869-73; pres. Ore. State Med. Soc. Editor Ore. Med. Reporter, 1873-77. Home: Salem, Ore. Deceased.

HALL, Charles Martin, inventor; b. Thompson, O., Dec. 6, 1863; s. Rev. Heman B. and Sophronia (Brooks) H.; A.B., Oberlin, 1885, A.M., 1893 (LL.D., 1910); unmarried. Invented the electrolytic process for the mfr. of aluminum now universally used, Feb. 1886; commenced commercial manufacture of aluminum with Pittsburgh Reduction Co., 1888 (now Aluminum Co. of America), v.p. same, 1890—; U.S. court sustained the Hall patent and conceded priority of invention, 1893. Hall process has so reduced price of aluminum as to make it a common metal of commerce, whereas it was formerly as costly as silver and little used. Trustee Oberlin Coll. Awarded Perkin medal, for work in chemistry, Jan. 1911. Home: Niagara Falls, N.Y. Died Dec. 27, 1914.

HALL, Charles Mercer, clergyman; b. New York, Dec. 23, 1864; s. William Noble and Flora Margaret (McAlister) H.; student Gen. Theol. Sem., 1888-91; M.A., honoris causa, St. Stephen's Coll., Annandale, N.Y., 1903; m. Bertha, d. Alton Brooks Parker, 1898; children—Altar Parker, Mary Macalister. Missionary and rector, St. Barnabas Ch., Camden, N.J., 1891-93; curate Ch. of the Beloved Disciple, New York, 1893-94; curate St. John's Ch., and vicar Ch. of the Holy Cross, Kingston, N.Y., 1894; rector Ch. of the Holy Cross, Kingston, N.Y., 1895-1912, St. Mary's Ch., Asheville, N.C. 1914-25; examining chaplain to the Bishop of W.N.C., 1925; rector Trinity Parish, Bridgeport, Conn., Nov. 1925—. Chaplain 10th Regt. S, N.Y. N.G., 1925. Author: The Life of a Christian, 1907; The Little Valleys, 1913; Extra-Liturgical Use of The Blessed Sacrament, 1920. Died Nov. 28, 1929.

HALL, Christopher Webber, geologist; b. Wardsboro, Vt., Feb. 28, 1845; s. Lewis and Louisa (Wilder) H.; A.B., Middlebury Coll., 1871, A.M., 1874; m. Nellie A. Dunnell, July 26, 1875; 2d, Sophia L. Haight, Dec. 26, 1883. Prin. Glens Falls (N.Y.) Acad., 1871-72, high sch., Mankato, Minn., 1872-73; supt. schs., Owatonna, 1873-75; student U. of Leipzig, 1875-78; instr. geology, 1878-79, asst. prof., 1879-80, prof. geology, mineralogy and biology, 1880-90, geology and mineralogy, 1890—, dean Coll. Engring., Metallurgy and Mechanic Arts, 1892-97, U. of Minn. Asst. geologist, Minn. Geol. Survey, 1878-80, U.S. Geol. Survey, 1883—. Fellow A.A.A.S., Geol. Soc. America, Am. Geographers' Assn., Minn. Acad. Sciences (editor, 1888—, pres. 1900-01). Author: Syllabus of Physical Geography (with Prof. Kunze), 1897; Geography of Minnesota, 1903. Home: Minneapolis, Minn. Died 1911.

HALL, Daniel, lawyer; b. Barrington, N.H., Feb. 28, 1832; s. Gilman and Eliza (Tuttle) H.; A.B., Dartmouth, 1854; read law with Hon. D. M. Christie, Dover, N.H.; admitted to N.H. bar, 1860; m. Sophia Dodge, Jan. 25, 1877. Capt. and a.-d.-c. Union Army, 1862-64; served in army of Potomac, participating in its battles, 1862-63; provost marshal 1st N.H. dist., 1864, 1865; pres. N.H. Rep. State Conv., 1873; chmn. N.H. Rep. State Com., 1874-78; chmn. N.H. delegation Rep. Nat. Conv., 1876; maj. and judge-advocate, N.H. militia, 1875; law reporter, N.H. Supreme Ct., 1875-76; naval officer, Port of Boston, 1877-86. Dir. Strafford Nat. Bank; trustee Strafford Savings Bank. Trustee Berwick Acad., Dover Pub. Library, Wentworth Home for the Aged (chmn. bd.), Wentworth Hosp. (all of Dover); mgr. N.H. Soldiers' Home, Tilton, N.H., 1888-1907. Republican. Home: Dover, N.H. Died 1920.

HALL, Edward Hagaman, editor, writer, lecturer; b. Auburn, N.Y., Nov. 3, 1858; s. Benjamin Franklin (chief justice Colo., 1861-65) and Abbe Farnam (Hagaman) H.; grad. Auburn Acad. High Sch., 1877, with classical honor; Master of Letters, New York U., 1908; Dr. of Letters, Hobart Coll., 1909; Officier d'Académie, France, 1920; m. Irene Gilbert Gazzam, Feb. 7, 1893 (died 1929); 1 dau., Edwina Gazzam (Mrs. Samuel H. Knight). Editor Norwich (Conn.) Morning Bulletin, 1877-88, Waterbury (Conn.) Republican, 1888-89; corr. New York Tribune several years prior to 1890; later briefly connected with Tribune in New York City; publisher, printer and writer in New York, 1890-1900; writer and lecturer on Am. history, scenery and archæology, 1900—. Special agent New York Commerce Commn., 1898-99; trustee, assistant sec. and historian Hudson-Fulton Celebration Commn., 1906-11; trustee and sec. N.Y. Commercial Centenary Commn., 1912-14. Registrar Missionary Dist. of Wyoming (Episcopal); jr. warden St. Matthew's Cathedral Parish; mem. Cathedral Chapter. Author: Philipse Manor Hall, 1912; The Catskill Aqueduct, 1917 (official); Guide Book of Cathedral St. John the Divine, 1920; Guide Book of St. Matthew's Cathedral, 1931. Home: Laramie, Wyo. Deceased.

HALL, Edward Henry, clergyman; b. Cincinnati, Apr. 16, 1831; s. Edward B. and Harriet (Ware) H.; A.B., Harvard, 1851; grad. Harvard Div. Sch., 1855 (S.T.D., 1902). Ordained Unitarian ministry, 1859; chaplain Mass. vols. in Civil War; pastor Plymouth, Mass., 1859-67, Worcester, 1869-82, Cambridge, 1882-93. Fellow Am. Acad. Arts and Sciences. Author: Lessons on the Life of St. Paul, 1885; Paul the Apostle, 1906. Home: Cambridge, Mass. Died 1912.

HALL, Edward Kimball, public utilities; b. Granville, Ill., July 9, 1870; s. Charles Prentiss and Lucia Cotton (Kimball) H.; A.B., Dartmouth, 1892, A.M. from same, 1916 (Phi Beta Kappa); LL.B., Harvard, 1896; m. Sally Maynard Drew, July 1, 1902; children—Dorothy (Mrs. Lawrence G. Leavitt), Richard Drew (dec.), Edward Kimball. Admitted to Pa. bar, 1896, Mass. bar, 1898; began practice at Boston; moved to New York, 1917; v.p. Am. Telephone & Telegraph Co., 1919-30; resident lecturer Amos Tuck Sch. of Business Administration (Dartmouth), 1930—. Mem. Nat. Industrial Conf. Bd. Chmn. Inter-collegiate Football Rules Com. Republican. Episcopalian. Home: Hanover, N.H. Died Nov. 10, 1932.

HALL, Edwin Herbert, physicist; b. Gorham, Me., Nov. 7, 1855; s. Joshua E. and Lucy Ann (Hilborn) H.; A.B., Bowdoin, 1875, A.M., 1878; Ph.D., Johns Hopkins U., 1880; LL.D., Bowdoin, 1905; m. Caroline Eliza Bottum, August 31, 1882 (died 1921); 1 dau., Constance Huntington. Instructor physics, 1881-88, asst. prof., 1888-95, prof., 1895-1921, emeritus prof., 1921, Harvard. Awarded medal Am. Assn. of Physics Teachers, 1937. Fellow Am. Acad. Arts and Sciences; corr. mem. Brit. Assn. Adv. Science; fgn. mem. Société Hollandaise des Sciences. Author: A Text-book of Physics (with J. Y. Bergen), 1891, 3d edit., 1903; Lessons in Physics, 1900; The Teaching of Chemistry and Physics (with Alexander Smith), 1902; College Laboratory Manual of Physics, 1904; Elements of Physics, 1912. Home: Cambridge, Mass. Died Nov. 20, 1938.

HALL, Emery Stanford, architect; b. nr. Chatsworth, Ill., Nov. 25, 1869; s. Justin Smith and Sarah Mehitable (Stanford) H.; B.S. in architecture, Ill., 1895; m. Clara Louise Adams, June 1900; children—Halbert Hugo, Ruth Alden (Mrs. Arthur Larson), Josephine Sarah (Mrs. Armando Tejada U.), Eunice Stanford (Mrs. Stephen Diachun). Engaged in gen. archtl. practice in Chicago, 1897—. Principal works: Tabernacle Bapt. Ch. of Chicago; Harry Manaster & Bro. meat packing plant; Stearns Estate Apts., Chicago; 22d Street plant of Jackson Storage & Van Co.; 1st Baptist chs., Duluth, Minn., and Marietta, O.; Austin Congregational Ch.; Parish House of Riverside (Ill.) Presbyn. Ch.; George Williams Coll., Chicago and Lake Geneva, Wis.; plot plan of Conf. Point, Lake Geneva; invented steel asbestos theater curtain and rebuilt People's, Haymarket, Bijou, Alhambra, Great Northern and other Chicago theaters. Sec.-treas. Nat. Council Archtl. Registration Bds.; chmn. Ill. Archtl. Commn. for Examination of Architects. Fellow Am. Inst. Architects (Chicago Chapter), sec. 9 yrs., pres. 1935, 36. Editor Handbook for Architects and Builders, 1906—. Home: Chicago, Ill. Died Dec. 4, 1939.

HALL, Ernest, lawyer; b. London, Eng., Oct. 24, 1844; pub. sch. edn.; pvt. 71st N.Y. Vols., 1863; exec. clk. U.S.S. Mohican, 1864-65; LL.B., New York U., 1866 (LL.D., 1905). Mem. bd. of trustees Morrisiania, N.Y., 1869-72; corp. counsel, 1872-73; mem. Hall, Brown & Westcott, 1877-82; justice City (formerly Marine) Ct., New York, 1881-88; referee in bankruptcy, 1898-1902; justice of Supreme Ct., of N.Y., 1902. Republican. Home: New York, N.Y. Died June 13, 1920.

HALL, Florence Marion Howe, author; b. Boston, Aug. 25, 1845; d. Dr. Samuel Gridley and Julia (Ward) Howe; sister of Henry Marion Howe, Laura Elizabeth Richards and Maud Howe Elliott; ed. pvt. schs.; studied music with Otto Dresel, Boston; m. David Prescott Hall, Nov. 15, 1871 (died 1907). Has been prominent in club movement; 1st chmn. of correspondence for N.J. of Gen. Fedn. of Women's Clubs, later v.p., dir. and chmn. dept. edn. N.J. State Fedn. of Women's Clubs (v.p. 1911-13); hon. pres. N.J. Woman Suffrage Assn. (pres., 1893-1900); pres. Plainfield Alliance of Unitarian Women, 1893-1904; regent Continental Chapter, D.A.R., 1902-04, 1905-10 (elected hon. vice-regent 1914); leader Woman Suffrage Party, 12th Assembly Dist., Manhattan, 1914-16; pres. Newport Co. (R.I.) Women's Rep. Club. Lecturer. Author: The Correct Thing, 1888, 1902; Social Customs, 1911; Boys, Girls and Manners, 1913; The A B C of Correct Speech, 1916. Edited Julia Ward Howe and the Woman Suffrage Movement, 1913; Story of the Battle Hymn of the Republic; Good Form for All Occasions; Memories Grave and Gay, 1918. Home: High Bridge, N.J. Died Apr. 10, 1922.

HALL, Francis Joseph, theologian; b. Ashtabula, O., Dec. 24, 1857; s. Joseph B. and Juliet E. (Griswold) H.; A.B., Racine Coll., 1882, A.M., 1885; studied Gen. and Western Theol. seminaries; D.D., Kenyon Coll., 1898, Gen. Theol. Sem., 1910; m Prudence A. Griswold (cousin), Sept. 14, 1886; children—Leo Griswold, Mary Griswold, Margaret Griswold. Deacon, 1885, priest, 1886, P.E. Ch. Instr. and prof. dogmatic theology, Western Theol. Sem., 1886-1913; prof. dogmatic theology, Gen. Theol. Sem., 1913-28; in charge of Summer Chapel of St. John-by-the-Lake, Onekama, Mich., 1912—. Registrar of diocese of Chicago, 1894-1913; sec. diocesan standing com., 1898-1901; examining chaplain diocese of Chicago, 1901-06; apptd. on gen. convs. commn. on Swedish orders, 1901, and on World Conf., 1910; coöp. mem. of World Conf., Lausanne, 1927; theol. counsel for the ch. in trial of Dr. Crapsey, 1906. Author: Theological Outlines (3 vols.), 1892-95 (re-written 1905, 1915); Historical Position of the Episcopal Church, 1896; Dogmatic Theology, 1907-22; Recent Work of Anglican Theologians, 1912; The Bible and Modern Criticism, 1915; Moral Theology (with F. H. Hallock), 1923; Christianity and Modernism, 1924; Christian Reunion in Ecumenical Light, 1930. Home: Onekama, Mich. Died Mar. 12, 1932.

HALL, Frank Lucas, merchant; b. nr. Knightstown, Ind., May 18, 1856; s. Festus and Maria (Abernathy) H.; Ph.B., DePauw U., Ind., 1879, A.M., 1882; unmarried. Began in furniture merchandising business, Kansas City, 1879; pres. Abernathy Furniture Co., 1902—; dir. Duff and Repp Furniture Co., Fidelity Nat. Bank & Trust Co., Fidelity Savings Bank & Trust Co. Trustee DePauw U., Kansas City Art Inst. Republican. Methodist. Home: Kansas City, Mo. Died May 18, 1929.

HALL, Frank M., lawyer; b. Morgan Co., Ill., Jan. 27, 1852; s. James and Ellen (Hall) H.; ed. State Normal Sch., Peru, Neb., and U. of Neb.; m. Anna E. Reid, June 15, 1881. Admitted to Neb. bar, 1880, and since practiced at Lincoln; mem. Marquett, Deweese and Hall 15 yrs., later, Hall, Woods and Pound, and now Hall, Cline & Williams; specializes in corp. law. Pres. for many yrs. of Neb. Art Assn.; pres. Lincoln Sch. Bd. 6 yrs. Mem. Neb. State Bar Assn. (pres. 1917). Republican. Presbyn. Mason. Active in civic and polit. affairs; the moving spirit in erection of Lincoln statue on Capitol grounds at Lincoln; head of com. which erected the Temple Bldg. in connection with U. of Neb. Home: Lincoln, Neb. Died June 9, 1928.

HALL, Frank Oliver, clergyman; b. New Haven, Conn., Mar. 19, 1860; s. Oliver A. and Clara A. (Stanley) H.; B.D., Tufts Div. Sch., 1884; D.D., St. Lawrence U., 1900; S.T.D., Tufts, 1905; m. Vermeille A. Swan, Sept. 3, 1895; 1 dau., Dorothy; m. 2d, Mrs. Helen Chester Greanelle, 1919. Ordained Universalist ministry, 1884; pastor Ch. of the Divine Paternity, New York, 1902-10 (emeritus); emeritus prof. homiletics, Crane Theol. Sch., Tufts Coll. Chmn. Commn. on Public Welfare of Universalist Ch.; chmn. John Murray Lectureship of Universalist Gen. Conv.; trustee and chmn. exec. com. Church Peace Union. Author: Common People, 1901; Soul and Body, 1909; Divine Paternity Pulpit, 1919; (with Dorothy Hall) Handicapped (Life Story of Frederick A. Bisbee), 1925. Home: New York, N.Y. Died Oct. 18, 1941.

HALL, Frederic Aldin, univ. chancellor; b. Brunswick, Me., Nov. 20, 1854; s. James and Rebecca (Dixon) H.; A.B., Drury Coll., 1878, A.M., 1881 (Litt.D., 1901; L.H.D., Tufts, 1912; LL.D., Washington U., 1913, and U. of Missouri, 1917); studied U. of Göttinger, 1891-92; m. Mary Alice Linscott, June 16, 1881. Prin. Drury Acad., 1878-91; Goodell prof. of Greek, 1892-1901; dean, 1898-1901, Drury Coll.; dir. Summer Sch., Springfield, Mo., 1899-1901; Collier prof. Greek, 1901-17, acting dean of coll., 1906-07, dean of the coll., 1912-13, acting chancellor, Mar. 1913-Dec. 13, 1916, chancellor, Jan. 1, 1917-Sept. 20, 1923, emeritus, Washington U., Studied Am. Sch. Classical Studies, Athens, 1906-07. Trustee Drury Coll.; dir. and supt. St. Louis City Missionary Soc., 1909-10. Decorated Order of the Redeemer (Greek), 1918. Republican. Conglist. Author: Homeric Studies for Young Readers; Outline of the Odyssey. Home: St. Louis, Mo. Died Mar. 24, 1925.

HALL, Frederic Byron, judge; b. Saratoga Springs, N.Y., Feb. 20, 1843; s. Jonathan and Livonia (Hayward) H.; served in 17th Conn. Vols., 1862-63; disch. on account of sickness; A.B., Brown U., 1867, A.M., by spl. vote, 1890: (hon. A.M., Yale, 1890; LL.D., Brown, 1909); m. Jennie A. Lewis, Jan. 1, 1872. Admitted to bar, 1870; judge Court of Common Pleas, Fairfield Co., Conn., 1877-89; judge Superior Ct. of Conn., 1889-97; judge Supreme Court of Errors, 1897—, chief justice, 1909. Republican. Home: Bridgeport, Conn. Died Jan. 16, 1913.

HALL, George Eli, consul general: b. Nice, France, Mar. 17, 1863; s. Charles O. and Mary Abbie (Dale) H. (both Americans); ed. Galliard Coll. and Académie des Sciences, Lausanne, Switzerland, to 1878; U. of Leipzig, 1878-81, École des Beaux Arts, Paris, 1881-85; unmarried. Consul gen. of Turkey, 1891—; sec. gen. of the Ottoman Commission, St. Louis Expn., 1904. Knight Commander of following orders: Order of Christ, Order of Conception of Villa-ViCosa (Portugal); orders of Medjidié and of Osmanié (Turkey); order of Lion and Sun (Persia); Order of Nichan Iftikhar of Tunis. Deceased.

HALL, George Henry, artist; b. Boston, 1825; common sch. edn.; began study of art at 16; went to Europe, 1849, studied in Art Acad., Düsseldorf, and in Paris and Rome; settled in New York; unmarried. Has spent much time in Europe and one winter in Egypt making study of bazaar scenes in Cairo, from which he afterward painted pictures. Is a painter of figures—especially of Italian and Spanish peasants; also paints still life pictures. N.A., 1868. Home: New York. Died Feb. 17, 1913.

HALL, George Martin, geologist; b. Baltimore, Md., Sept. 13, 1891; s. George Arlow and Alice Josephine (Higgins) H.; A.B., Johns Hopkins, 1915, Ph.D., 1923; unmarried. Clerk and stenographer for city engr., Baltimore, 1910-11; inspector State Roads Commn. of Md., summers 1912-14; geol. aid Md. Geol. Survey, summer 1915; asst. geologist Md. Geol. Survey, part time, 1916-26, Roxana Petrol Corp., summer, 1917; asst. geologist U.S. Geol. Survey, part time, 1921-38, asso. geologist, part time, 1938—; instr. in geology, Johns Hopkins, 1923-26; asso. prof. of geology, U. of Tenn., 1926-29, prof. and head of dept. geology and geography, 1929—. Served as private Signal Corps, U.S. Army, 1918, 2d lt., 1918-20. Author: Ground Water in Yellowstone and Treasure Counties, Mont. (with Howard), 1929; Geology of Big Horn County, Mont. (with others), 1935; Ground Water in Southeastern Pa., 1934. Home: Knoxville, Tenn. Died Apr. 28, 1941.

HALL, George Washington, neurologist; b. Crawfordsville, Ind., June 18, 1869; s. Y. P. and Martha E. (Stillwell) H.; A.M., Wabash Coll., 1890; M.D., Rush Med. Coll., 1893; special post-grad. studies Nat. Hosp. for Paralyzed and Epileptics, London, Eng., and in Berlin, Germany, 1904; post-grad. work in Vienna and Munich, 1907; m. Nell Nicholson, June 5, 1894; children—Martha Nadine, Bertram Brower. Formerly prof. medicine, Rush Med. Coll.; sr. neurologist St. Luke's Hosp.; clin. prof. neurology, U. of Chicago (Rush Med. Coll.); formerly attending psychiatrist, Psychopathic Hosp. Fellow Inst. of Medicine (Chicago). Home: Chicago, Ill. Died Oct. 25, 1941.

HALL, G(ranville) Stanley, univ. president; b. Ashfield, Mass., Feb. 1, 1846; s. Granville Bascom and Abigail (Beals) H.; A.B., Williams, 1867, A.M., 1870; student Union Theol. Sem., 1867-68, Berlin and Bonn, 1868-71, Berlin and Heidelberg, 1871-72; Ph.D., Harvard, 1878; Leipzig, Berlin, London,, 1878-81; (LL.D., U. of Mich., 1888, Williams, 1889, Johns Hopkins, 1902); married. Prof. psychology Antioch Coll., 1872-76; instr. English, Harvard, 1876-77; lecturer, psychology, Harvard and Williams, 1880-81; prof. psychology, Johns Hopkins, 1881-88; pres. and prof. psychology Clark U., 1888-1920. Founder and editor Am. Jour. Psychology, 1887-1921; editor Pedagogical Sem., 1892—, Am. Jour. Religious Psychology and Edn., 1904-15, Jour. Applied Psychology, 1917—. Author: Adolescence (2 vols.), 1904; Youth—Its Education, 1907; Educational Problems (2 vols.), 1911; Founders of Modern Psychology, 1912; Jesus the Christ, in the Light of Psychology, 1917; Morale: The Supreme Standard of Life and Conduct, 1920; Recreations of a Psychologist, 1920; Senescence, 1922; Life and Confessions of a Psychologist, 1923. Home: Worcester, Mass. Died Apr. 24, 1924.

HALL, Grover Cleveland, editor; b. Haleburg, Ala., Jan. 11, 1888; s. William Rabun and Parmelia Ann (Davis) H.; ed. country schs.; m. Claudia McCurdy English, May 14, 1912; 1 son, Grover. Began as printer's devil Dothan (Ala.) Daily Siftings, 1905; editor Enterprise (Ala.) Ledger, 1907, Dothan Daily Siftings, 1908; mng. editor Selma Times, 1909; editorial writer Pensacola Journal, 1910; asso. editor Montgomery Advertiser, 1910-26, editor, 1926—. Apptd. Feb. 1933, judge Probate Court of Montgomery County. Pvt. Ala. N.G., 1906-08. Mem. personnel bd. State Merit System for Ala. Democrat. Winner Pulitzer prize of $500 for "the best editorial writing in 1928," for editorials in The Advertiser against gangism, flogging and racial and religious intolerance. Home: Montgomery, Ala. Died Jan. 9, 1941.

HALL, Harry Alvan, judge; b. Karthaus, Pa., Oct. 7, 1861; Benjamin McDowell and Susan (Geary) H.; A.B., Yale, 1879, LL.B., 1881; m. Currin McNairy, Jan. 10, 1886. Began practice at Ridgeway, Pa., 1881; mem. Pa. Senate, 1890-93; U.S. atty. Western Dist. of Pa., 1893-97; pres. judge 25th Jud. Dist. of Pa., 1907—. Capt. Co. H, 16th Pa. Inf., Spanish-Am. War; promoted to maj. "for gallantry" at battle of Coamo, P.R., Aug. 9, 1908, (apptd. by Gen. Miles to convey Spanish colors, captured in this action, to Washington, and present them to Pres. McKinley). Formerly gen. counsel in U.S. of Austro-Hungarian, and Italian govts. Officer's Cross of the Order of Francis Joseph (Austria), 1905. Fellow Am. Geog. Society. Episcopalian; sr. warden and judge of Ecclesiastical Ct., Diocese of Erie; mem. standing com. bd. trustees, and deputy to Gen. Conv., 1913. Home: Ridgway, Pa. Died Dec. 1, 1917.

HALL, Harry Hinckley, lawyer; b. Rock Island, Ill., Feb. 12, 1846; ed. Flushing (L.I.) Inst., and colls. at Halberstadt, Germany, and Tours, France; LL.B., Tulane U., 1869; m. Mary Fort-Adams, July 1870. Admitted to bar, New Orleans, 1869; counsel of New Orleans & North Eastern R.R. Co., Ala. & Vicksburg Ry. Co., Vicksburg, Shreveport & Pacific Ry. Co.; atty. for St. Charles Street R.R. Co., New Orleans; dean Law Sch. Tulane U. of La., New Orleans, 1889-1906. Died 1911.

HALL, Harry Melville, M.D.; b. Wheeling W.Va., Sept. 5, 1877; s. Andrew M. and Mary Jane (Godfrey) Hall; M.D., Western Res. Med. Coll., 1898; m. Jane Sutherland Wheat, May 20, 1909; 1 dau., Rebecca Wheat. Interne, St. Vincents Charity Hosp., Cleveland, O., 1898-99; began practice at Wheeling, 1900; mem. staff Ohio Valley Gen. Hosp. (pres. 1925-26) and Wheeling Hosp.; surgeon U.S. Steel Co. and Am. Sheet & Tin Plate Co., 1907-27; lecturer medicine, Nurses Training Sch., 1909-29, Med. Clinic Outdoor Dept., 1920-29; asso. editor W.Va. Med. Jour., 1921—. Examiner U.S. Pension Bd., 1922—. Examiner Selective Draft Bd. and Officers Res. Bd., World War. V.p. Alumni Assn. of Charity Hosp., 1929-30. Fellow Am. Coll. Physicians, A.M.A. Pres. Little Theatre, Wheeling, 1927-29. Republican. Presbyn. Home: Wheeling, W.Va. Died June 5, 1931.

HALL, Harvey Monroe, botany; b. Lee Co., Ill., Mar. 29, 1874; s. Reuben and Martha (Leist) H.; B.S., U. of Calif., 1901, M.S., 1902, Ph.D., 1906; m. Carlotta Case, Feb. 23, 1910; 1 dau., Martha.

Asst. in botany, U. of Calif., 1903, instr., 1903-08, asst. prof., 1908-16, asso. prof., 1916-19; also asst. botanist, Agrl. Expt. Sta., U. of Calif., 1902-19, and instr. in botany, mountain lab., U. of Colo., 1917; investigator in exptl. taxonomy, div. plant biology, Carnegie Instn. of Washington, D.C., 1919—. Fellow Am. Acad. Arts and Sciences, A.A.A.S., Bot. Soc. America, Calif. Acad. Science. Hon. curator Herbarium, U. of Calif.; acting prof. botany, Stanford U. Author: Botanical Survey of San Jacinto Mountain, 1902; Compositæ of Southern California, 1907; Yosemite Flora (with wife), 1912; Rubber Content of North American Plants (with F. L. Long), 1921; Phylogenetic Method in Taxonomy (with F. E. Clements), 1923, Haplopappus, 1928. Died 1932.

HALL, Henry, financial writer; b. Auburn, N.Y., Dec. 6, 1845; s. Benjamin Franklin (chief justice Colo., 1861-63) and Abbe Farnam (Hagaman) H.; bro. of Edward Hagaman and James P. Hall; ed. Auburn (N.Y.) Acad.; m. Sarah Virginia, d. L. Warren Houghton, of Bath, Me., Feb. 2, 1886. City editor, Auburn News, and Auburn Advertiser; an editor Norwich (Conn.) Daily Bulletin, 1873-75; in editorial dept., 1875-81, business mgr., 1882-1901, New York Tribune. Took census of shipbuilding industry for U.S. Census, 1881-82. Author: How Money Is Made in Security Investments. Home: Bronxville, N.Y. Died Feb. 6, 1920.

HALL, Henry, newspaper corr.; b. Edmondsley, Eng., Oct. 13, 1851; s. John and Mary Anne (Elstob) H.; came to America with parents in infancy; ed. common schs., Pa.; unmarried. Sch. teacher, 1875-78; editor and part propr., Mercer (Pa.) Dispatch, 1881-89; editorial writer Pittsburgh Commercial Gazette, 1884-85; legislative corr., Pittsburgh Dispatch, 1891; Washington corr. Pittsburgh Times, 1893-1906, Pittsburgh Chronicle-Telegraph, 1907—. Recorder of deeds, Mercer Co., Pa., 1879-82; mem. Pa. Ho. of Rep., from Mercer Co., 1887, 89, from Pittsburgh, 1901. Lt. col. and a.-d.-c. on staffs of Govs. D. H. Hastings and W. A. Stone, of Pa., 1895-1901. Republican. Episcopalian. Home: Washington, D.C. Died Oct. 22, 1934.

HALL, Henry Clay, lawyer; b. New York, Jan. 3, 1860; s. Henry Clay and Amanda Harwood (Ferry) H.; A.M., Amherst, 1881 (LL.D., 1914); LL.B., Columbia Law Sch., 1883; m. Mary Bacon Bartow, June 4, 1887 (died 1901); children—Bartow Harwood, Mrs. Ethel Hall Gilman, Mrs. Frances Hall Paige, Mrs. Elizabeth Hall Talcott; m. 2d, Alice Munsell Sweetser, Mar. 14, 1905; 1 dau., Janet Alling (Mrs. Oliver B. Lerch). Admitted to practice of law in State of New York, 1883; practiced in Paris, France, 1885-92, and counsel to U.S. Legation, 1888-92; removed to Colorado Springs, Colo., on account of health, 1892; mem. Interstate Commerce Commission, Washington, D.C., 1914-28 (chmn., 1917-18 and 1924). Democrat. Episcopalian. Mayor of Colorado Springs, 1905-07. President Colo. State Bar Assn., 1911-12; commr. for Colo. on Uniform State Laws, 1912. Home: Colorado Springs, Colo. Died Nov. 9, 1936.

HALL, Henry Harrington, fire underwriter; b. Boston, May 16, 1846; s. F. George and Mary Fikse (Harrington) H.; ed. Boston pub. schs. (hon. A.M., Middlebury Coll.); m. Aurelia Judd Twitchell, 1897. Began in fire ins. business in 1861 in Boston; later elected sec. Nat. Fire Ins. Co. of New York; served as pvt. 42d Mass. Vols.; later became U.S. mgr. Northern Assurance Co. of London; then organized Hall & Henshaw, fire underwriters, of New York, of which is still sr. mem. Pres. Underwriters' Salvage Co., Victoria Fire Ins. Co.; U.S. trustee Union Assurance Co. of London, Law, Union & Crown Ins. Co., London, and State Fire Ins. Co. of Liverpool. Pres. N.Y. Bd. Fire Underwriters, and of Nat. Bd. Fire Underwriters. Presbyn. Home: East Orange, N.J. Died 1906.

HALL, Herbert James, physician; b. Manchester, N.H., Mar. 12, 1870; s. Marshall Parker and Susan (James) H.; ed. pub. schs. of Manchester; M.D., Harvard, 1895; m. Eliza Pitman Goldthwait, Dec. 29, 1897. Practiced in Marblehead, 1897—; especially interested in developing manual work as a remedy in nervous disabilities; medical dir. Devereux Mansion (sanitarium), 1912—. Pres. Am. Occupational Therapy Assn., 1920, 21, and editor the Occupational Therapy and Rehabilitation Sect. The Modern Hospital. Author: The Untroubled Mind (essays), 1915; (with Mertice MacCrea Buck) The Work of Our Hands, 1915; (with same) Handicrafts for the Handicapped, 1916; War-Time Nerves, 1918; Moonrise, A Book of Poems, 1918. Home: Marblehead, Mass. Died Feb. 19, 1923.

HALL, Holworthy, author. See Harold Everett Porter.

HALL, James, artist; b. Boston, Mass., December 20, 1869; s. Joseph Henry and Alice (Ryder) H.; grad. Mass. Normal Art School, 1888-91, Art Students' League, New York, 1891-92, Paris, France, 1892-93; m. Grace Lydia Berney, June 22, 1898. Teacher drawing, N.H. Coll., Durham, 1893-95; supervisor drawing, Danvers (Mass.) pub. schs., 1894-96; asst. state supervisor, drawing, Mass., 1896; supervisor drawing Springfield (Mass.) pub. schs., 1896-1902, pub. schs., Newark, N.J., 1902-03; dir. art dept., Ethical Culture Sch., New York, 1903-11. Instr. Sch. of Edn., U. of Chicago, summer quarters, 1912-13. Illustrator and designer; exhibitor in various art exhibits, 1900—. Wrote: Chapters on Art in the Festival, in "Festivals and Plays" by Percival Chubb and his associates, 1912; etc. Home: North Scituate, Mass. Died Feb. 14, 1917.

HALL, James Alexander, prof. mech. engring.; b. Berlin, Vt., July 26, 1888; s. John Joseph and Agnes Brock (Hardie) H.; A.B., Brown U., 1908, Sc.B. in M.E., 1910; m. Leila Tucker, June 21, 1919; children—James Alexander, Flora, Margaret. Asst. and instr. in mech. engring., Brown U., 1910-14; with engring. dept. Link-Belt Co., Phila., 1914-15; with Brown U., 1915—, asst. prof., asso. prof. to 1925, prof. mech. engring., 1925; also cons. engr. Brown & Sharpe Mfg. Co., 1926—. Republican. Conglist. Co-author: (with D. T. Farnham, R. W. King and H. E. Howe) Profitable Science in Industry, 1925. Home: Providence, R.I. Died Oct. 29, 1936.

HALL, James Jabez, clergyman; b. London, Eng., Nov. 3, 1849; s. Samuel E. and Eliza (Coombs) H.; ed. Spurgeon's Coll., London; (D.D., Judson Coll., N.C., 1890); m. Angelina Bartlett, July 18, 1870. Ordained Bapt. ministry, 1871; pastor Auburn, Me., 1878-84, Minneapolis, 1884-87, Raleigh, N.C., 1889-93, Norfolk, Va., 1893-1904, Fafayetteville, N.C., 1904-12; pastor Harlem, Ga., 1918—. Pres. World Peace Assn., 1918-19. Naturalized Am. citizen, Feb. 1884. Chaplain Grand Lodge Odd Fellows of N.C., 1890-93. Home: Harlem, Ga. Died July 9, 1921.

HALL, James Parker, law school dean; b. Frewsburg, New York, 1871; s. of Edward L. and Charlotte (Parker) H.; A.B., Cornell, 1894; LL.B., Harvard, 1897; m. Evelyn H. Movius, 1900; children—Livingston, James Parker. Admitted to bar, 1897, and practiced at Buffalo, 1897-1900; lecturer on constl. law and real property, Buffalo Law Sch., 1898-1900; asso. prof. law, Leland Stanford Jr. U., 1900-02; prof. law, 1902—, dean Law School, 1904—, U. of Chicago. Maj., judge advocate U.S.A., 1918-19. Faculty rep. bd. trustees Cornell U., 1922-25; chmn. legal research com. Commonwealth Fund. Republican. Author: Constitutional Law, 1910; Cases on Constitutional Law, 1913. Editor: American Law and Procedure (12 vols.), 1910. Home: Chicago, Ill. Died Mar. 13, 1928.

HALL, James Whitney, M.D.; b. Alexandria, Ky., Aug. 27, 1869; s. James W. and Caroline (Horner) H.; student Central Acad., Georgetown (Ky.) Coll.; M.D., Ky. Sch. of Medicine, Louisville, 1891; m. Lucia Elizabeth Perry, Nov. 3, 1906; 1 son, James Whitney. Gen. practice, Bloomington, Ill., 1893-1900; in Chicago, 1900—, specializing in neuro-psychiatry and forensic medicine; served as med. counsel Ill. Central R.R. Co., C.,M.St.P.&Pacific, Pere Marquette and C.&E.I. rys.; chief of staff Goodheart Sanitarium; mem. Lunacy Commn., Cook Co. Court. Served as maj. Med. Corps, U.S.A., 1917-18; maj. Med. O.R.C. Mem. bd. govs. Thomas Jefferson Foundation; past nat. med. dir. Civil Legion. Democrat. Home: Chicago, Ill. Died Apr. 29, 1936.

HALL, Jennie, author; b. Grand Rapids, Mich., Jan. 7, 1875; d. Irving and Ella C. (Martin) H.; grad. high schs. of Topeka, Kan., and Englewood, Chicago; student U. of Chicago, 1895-7; unmarried. Teacher of history, Chicago Normal Sch., 1897-1902, Francis W. Parker Sch., Chicago, 1902-17, Lincoln Sch., N.Y. City, 1917-18, Francis W. Parker Sch., Chicago, 1918—. Author: Men of Old Greece, 1905; Story of Chicago, 1910; Our Ancestors in Europe, 1916; Weavers and Other Workers, 1917. Died June 12, 1921.

HALL, John Lesslie, college dean; b. Richmond, Va., Mar. 2, 1856; s. Jacob, Jr. and Emily G. (Moore) H.; ed. in Richmond, Va.; prep. schs., Randolph-Macon Coll.; Ph.D., Johns Hopkins U., 1892; (Litt.D., Wake Forest [N.C.] College; LL.D., from College of William and Mary, 1921); m. Margaret Fenwick Farland, Apr. 30, 1889; children—Channing Moore, John Lesslie, Joseph Farland, Emily Moore. Prof. English and history, 1888-1907, English lang. and lit., 1907—, and dean of faculty, William and Mary Coll. Author: Translation of Beowulf, 1892; Old English Idyls, 1899; Judith, Phœnix and other Anglo-Saxon Poems (trans.), 1902; English Usage, 1917. Joint editor of Half Hours in Southern History, 1907. Home: Williamsburg, Va. Died Feb. 23, 1928.

HALL, John Raymond; b. Elmira, N.Y., July 16, 1879; s. Francis Granger and Maria Almira (Angell) H.; A.B., Yale, 1902; m. Louise Hopkins Twichell, June 8, 1909; children—Joseph Twichell, Jesse Angell, Deborah Cushman, Anne Peyton. Bank clk. and pvt. sec., New York and Albany, 1902-07; mgr. bond dept., Crawford, Patton & Cannon, 1908-13, Hallgarten & Co., 1913-18; mem. Knauth, Nachod & Kuhn, 1920—; pres. John R. Hall Corp., 1927—; Pres. Nat. Personnel Service, World War. Republican. Presbyn. Mason. Homes: Washington, Conn., and New York, N.Y. Died July 29, 1936.

HALL, Josephine, actress; b. Greenwich, R.I.; début as Eulalie in Evangeline, 14th St. Theatre, New York; became a mem. of Eben Plympton's "Jack" co.; subsequently joined Frohman's co.; has played leading rôles in popular Am. dramas. Died Dec. 5, 1920.

HALL, Josiah Newhall, M.D.; b. North Chelsea, Mass., Oct. 11, 1859; s. Stephen A. and Evalina A. (Newhall) H.; B.S., Mass. Agrl. Coll., 1878; M.D., Harvard, 1882; m. Carrie G. Ayres, Apr. 12, 1885; children—Sigourney D., Oliver W. (dec.). House phys., Boston City Hosp., 1882-83; practiced medicine, Sterling, Colo., 1883-92, Denver, 1892-1937; prof. medicine, med. dept., U. of Colorado; physician to Denver City and Co., St. Joseph's, St. Anthony's hosps., and Mercy Sanitarium. Pres. State Bd. Med. Examiners, Colo., 1891; pres. Colo. State Bd. Health, 1903-04. Maj. and surgeon, Med. R.C., U.S.A., 1917; was chief of med. service, Base Hosp., Camp Logan, Tex., and later consultant in internal medicine to the 16 southwestern mil. hosps. during period of the war. Republican. Mayor Sterling, Colo., 1888-89. Author: Borderline Diseases, 2 vols., 1915. Home: Denver, Colo. Died Dec. 17, 1939.

HALL, Louis Phillips, prof. operative dentistry; b. Toledo, O., June 1, 1860; s. Israel and Olivia (Bigelow) H.; student lit. dept. U. of Mich., 1879-80; grad. in dentistry, same univ., 1889; m. Elizabeth Campbell, d. Judge S. T. Douglas, Feb. 14, 1885; children—Douglas, Louis Phillips, Richard Nelville (killed in France), Elizabeth Olivia (Mrs. J. R. Hayden). Began as asst. to prof. clin. and operative dentistry, U. of Mich., 1889; advanced through various positions to prof. operative and clin. dentistry, 1903; prof. operative dentistry, 1922—. Chmn. local br. Am. Red Cross, 1917-21. Republican. Episcopalian. Home: Ann Arbor, Mich. Died Dec. 19, 1941.

HALL, Luther Egbert, governor; b. Morehouse Parish, La., Aug. 30, 1869; s. Bolling C. and Antoinette (Newton) H.; A.B., Washington and Lee U., 1889; LL.B., Tulane U., 1892; m. Clara Wendel, Nov. 23, 1892. Began practice Bastrop, La., 1892; mem. La. State Senate, 1898-1900; judge 6th Dist. of La., 1900, reëlected 1904; elected judge Ct. of Appeals of La., 1906; elected asso. justice Sup. Ct. of La., 1910, for term beginning 1912; gov. of La., term 1912-16. Democrat. Mason. Home: New Orleans, La. Died Nov. 6, 1921.

HALL, Lyman, educator; b. Americus, Ga., Feb. 18, 1859; s. John E. and E. M. H.; prep. edn. Mercer Univ.; grad. West Point, 1881 (Washington and Lee Univ., LL.D., 1902); m. A. T. Jennings, Dec. 13, 1883. Commandant cadets and prof. mathematics Edgewood, Ga., 1881-83, 1868-88; asst. prof. mathematics S.C. Mil. Acad., Charleston, 1883-86; prof. mathematics, 1888-95, pres., 1895—, Ga. Sch. of Technology, Atlanta. Died 1905.

HALL, Lyman Beecher, chemist; b. New Bedford, Mass., Jan. 16, 1852; s. Isaac Dennis and Hannah (Norris) H.; A.B., Amherst, 1873; Ph.D., U. of Göttingen, 1875; fellow, Johns Hopkins, 1877-79; m. Carolyn Coffin Ladd, July 8, 1890. Instr. chemistry, Johns Hopkins, 1879-80; prof. chemistry, Haverford and Marion Wallace (Crowther) H.; S.B., Colo. (Pa.) Coll., 1880—. Died 1935.

HALL, Maurice Crowther, zoölogist; b. Golden, Colo., July 15, 1881; s. George Hemingway Birtby and Marion Wallace (Crowther) H.; S.B., Colo. Coll., Colorado Springs, 1905, hon. D.Sc., 1925; M.A., U. of Neb., 1906; Ph.D., George Washington U., 1915, D.V.M., 1916; m. Lola May Davis, June 18, 1906; children—Marion Millicent, Winifred Lois, Margaret Lola. Instr. botany and physiology, Cutler Acad., Colorado Springs, 1904-05; instr. biology and chemistry, Cañon City (Colo.) High Sch., 1906-07; jr. zoölogist, 1907-11, asst. zoölogist, 1911-16, U.S. Bur. Animal Industry; asst. zoölogist, U.S. Insecticide and Fungicide Bd., 1915-16; prof. zoölogy and parasitology, Coll. of Vet. Medicine, George Washington U., 1914-16; parasitologist, research lab. of Parke, Davis & Co., Detroit, 1916-18; 2d lt. and 1st lt. Vet. Corps, U.S.A., 1918-19; sr. zoölogist U.S. Bur. Animal Industry, 1919-36, chief of zoöl. div., 1925-36; asst. custodian Helminthol. Collection, U.S. Nat. Museum, 1925-31, custodian, 1931—. Pres. Permanent Internat. Commn. on Parasitology of Internat. Zoöl. Congress, 1930—; pres. Internat. Commn. on Control of Parasites of Internat. Veterinary Congress, 1934—. Mem. Nat. Research Council; prof. zoölogy and chief div. of zoölogy, Nat. Inst. of Health, U.S. Pub. Health Service, Apr. 1936—. Proposed the carbon tetrachlorid treatment, and, with Dr. J. E. Shillinger, the tetrachlorethylene treatment for hookworm disease. Home: Chevy Chase, D.C. Died 1938.

HALL, Newton Marshall, clergyman; b. Manchester, N.H., Jan. 10, 1865; s. Marshall Parker and Susan (James) H.; A.B., A.M., Dartmouth, 1888, D.D., 1908; grad. Andover Theol. Sem., 1891; m. Louise Buffum Varney, Aug. 20, 1891; 1 dau., Louise Marshall (Mrs. Carey Tharp). Ordained Congl. ministry, 1891; prof. English lang. and lit., Ia.

Coll., 1891-93; pastor *First Presbyn. Ch., Oneonta, N.Y., 1894-99*, North Congl. Ch., Springfield, Mass., 1899-1920, pastor emeritus, 1922—. College preacher Dartmouth, Amherst, Mt. Holyoke, and Mass. Agrl. Coll. Dir. Mass. Home Missionary Soc., 1916-19; pres. Nat. Congl. Summer Conf. Assn., 1916-19; vice moderator Mass. Congl. Conf., 1919. Mem.-at-large Springfield Bd. of Edn., 1912-21. Author: Stories of the Commonwealth of Israel, 3 vols., 1921. Coauthor: The Bible Story (5 vols.), 1906; The Early Days of Israel, 1906; Biblical Dramas, 1906; The Days of the Kings of Israel, 1907; The Book of Life (8 vols.), 1923. Commr. Chs. of Christ in America to Chs. of Europe, 1920-21. Home: Springfield, Mass. Died Jan. 25, 1926.

HALL, Pauline, actress, singer; b. Cincinnati, Feb. 26, 1860; m. G. B. McLellan. Début, Robinson Opera House, Cincinnati, as a dancer in ballet, 1875; later appeared with Alice Oates Opera Co.; played Lady Capulet, in "Romeo and Juliet." Hassan in "Blue Beard," etc.; toured with own company, 1892-96; appeared in "Erminie," "Dorcas," "Evangeline," "Puritania," "Orpheus and Eurydice," "Kitty Darlin," etc. Home: Yonkers, N.Y. Died Dec. 29, 1919.

HALL, Philip Louis, banker; b. White Co., Ind., Feb. 25, 1850; s. Edward and Eliza (McGrath) H.; M.D., Rush Med. Coll., Chicago, 1883; m. Catharine Barkley, 1873; 2d, Helena B. Link, Dec. 12, 1884. Practiced medicine at Millard and Mead, Neb., 1883-85; organized, and cashier, 1885-97, Bank of Mead; sec. Neb. State Banking Bd., 1897-1901; cashier Columbia Nat. Bank, Lincoln, Neb., 1901-07; organized, 1907, and from then pres., Central Nat. Bank, Lincoln; also pres. Bank of Mead, 1897—. Chmn. Dem. State Central Com., 1898-1904; member and v.-chmn. Dem. Nat. Com., 1908-12. Chmn. trustees State Sch. for Dependent Children. Regent U. of Neb. Home: Lincoln, Neb. Died Mar. 14, 1923.

HALL, Prescott Farnsworth, lawyer, author; b. Boston, Sept. 27, 1868; s. Samuel and Mary Elizabeth (Farnsworth) H.; A.B., Harvard, 1889, LL.B., 1892; m. Florence Gardiner, Sept. 24, 1895; 2d, Lucyle Irby, Oct. 17, 1908. In practice at Boston, 1892—. A founder, 1894, sec., 1896—, Immigration Restriction League; sec. for N.E. of Indianapolis Monetary Convention's Exec. Com., 1896; chmn. exec. com. Dem. Club of Mass., 1902-04. Republican. Author: Reference List of Wills Construed by the Supreme Court of Massachusetts, 1896; The Massachusetts Law of Landlord and Tenant, 1899, 1908; Examination of Land Titles, 1902; Massachusetts Business Corporations, 1903, 08, 17; Immigration and Its Effects on the United States, 1906, 1908. Vice-pres. Family Welfare Foundation. Home: Brookline, Mass. Died May 28, 1921.

HALL, Randall Cooke, theologian; b. Wallingford, Conn., Dec. 18, 1842; s. Francis C. and Elizabeth W. (Cooke) H.; A.B., Columbia, 1863, A.M., 1867; Gen. Theol. Sem., New York, 1866; (D.D., Racine Coll., 1881, Gen. Theol. Sem., 1885); m. Lizzie Eyland, July 23, 1878. Deacon, 1866, priest, 1870, P.E. Ch.; instr. Hebrew, 1869-71, prof. Hebrew and Greek, 1871-99, prof. emeritus, 1899, Gen. Theol. Sem.; chaplain House of the Holy Comforter, 1904—; curate Ch. of St. Mary the Virgin, New York, 1904—. Home: New York. Died July 27, 1921.

HALL, Reynold Thomas, naval officer; b. at Phila., Pa., Nov. 5, 1858; s. Edward Smyth and Katherine Piercy (Romney) H.; grad. Episcopal Acad., Phila., 1875; tech. course, Franklin Inst., Phila.; m. Anne Martin, Dec. 15, 1887. Apptd. asst. engr. U.S. Navy, Apr. 22, 1880; promoted through grades to rear adm., Dec. 12, 1914; retired, Nov. 5, 1922. Chief engr. U.S.S. Petrel, under Commodore Dewey in Battle of Manila Bay, May 1, 1898, and acting industrial mgr. of Cavite Navy Yard during Spanish-Am. War, 1898; squadron engr., Caribbean Squadron, 1903; fleet engr., European Sta., 1904; head of Dept. of Steam Engring., Navy Yard, New York, 1907, 1908. Advanced 3 numbers in rank "for eminent and conspicuous conduct in battle during Spanish-Am. War"; Dewey Medal. Mason. Home: Wynnewood, Pa. Died Feb. 10, 1934.

HALL, Richard Cartwright, merchant; b. Boston, Mass., Oct. 19, 1856; s. Henry Augustus and Susan Beddoes (Cartwright) H.; ed. high sch.; m. Grace Ellis, June 10, 1891; children—Richard Ellis, Dorothy, Grace. Began with Boston Belting Co., 1875; traveling salesman, Eastern Rubber Co., Boston, 1877-83; mgr. same, N.Y. City, 1883-85; mem. Elson, Hall & Co., Chicago, 1885-87; mem. Duck Brand Co., wholesale rubber and oil clothing, 1887—; western selling agt. U.S. Rubber Co. Mem. Chicago Assn. Commerce (pres. 1908). Trustee Boys' Homes, Lawrence Hall Homes, Chicago Sunday Evening Club. Republican. Episcopalian. Home: Evanston, Ill. Died Dec. 13, 1931.

HALL, Robert Henry, brig. gen.; b. Detroit, Nov. 15, 1837; s. Benjamin F. and Catherine F. (Mullitt) H.; grad. U.S. Mil. Acad., 1860; m. Georgianna K. Foote, Feb. 7, 1866. Bvt. 2d lt. 5th Inf., July 1, 1860; commd. 2d lt. 10th Inf., Jan. 23, 1861; 1st lt., June 1, 1861; capt., Aug. 31, 1863; maj. 22d Inf., May 21, 1883; lt. col. 6th Inf., Aug. 5, 1888; col. 4th Inf., May 18, 1893; brig. gen. vols., May 27, 1898; hon. disch. from vol. service, Apr. 15, 1899; brig. gen. vols., Apr. 15, 1899-Mar. 1, 1901; brig. gen. U.S.A., Feb. 5, 1901; retired by operation of law, Nov. 15, 1901. Bvtd. maj., Nov. 24, 1863, for battle of Lookout Mountain, Tenn.; lt. col., Aug. 19, 1864, for battle on Weldon R.R. in Va. After war served on frontier until 1871; U.S. Mil. Acad., 1871-88; comd. Ft. Sheridan, Ill., 1896-98; in P.I., 1899-1900. Mason. Died Dec. 29, 1914.

HALL, Robert Samuel, congressman; b. Williamsburg, Miss., Mar. 10, 1879; s. Evans and Effie (McDonald) H.; LL.B., Millsaps Coll., Jackson, Miss., 1900; m. Lenore Robinson, Apr. 10, 1901; children—Stanton A., Robert S., Edward Currie, Jack, George Calhoun, Effie Lenore, Lucile. Admitted to Miss. bar, 1900, and began practice at Hattiesburg. Mem. Miss. State Senate, 1906-08; county atty. Forrest Co., 1910-12; dist. atty. 12th Miss. Dist., 1912-18; judge Circuit Court, 12th Miss. Dist., 1918-29; mem. 71st and 72d Congresses (1929-33), 6th Miss. Dist.; now trial examiner Federal Trade Commn., Washington. Democrat. Presbyn. Mason. Home: Hattiesburg, Miss. Died June 10, 1941.

HALL, Thomas, teacher; b. Boston, 1869; s. Thomas and Mary (Putnam) H.; A.B., Harvard, 1893; unmarried. Instr. English, Harvard, 1894—. Editor Cambridge Literature Series. Boston, Mass. Died 1911.

HALL, Thomas, inventor; b. Phila., Feb. 4, 1834; ed. U. of Lewisburg, Pa. Devised mechanism for printing by touching keys, and in 1867 exhibited a keyed typewriter at Paris Expn.; later studied mechanics in Europe; invented and, 1881, placed on the market the Hall typewriter; has also invented several successful sewing machines, drill-grinding and other machinists' tools; now patent atty. Home: Brooklyn. Died 1911.

HALL, Thomas Bartlett, author; b. Springfield, Mass., July 26, 1824; s. Joseph Hall, Jr., and Maria Bartlett Hall; prep. edn. Boston Latin Sch.; grad. Harvard, 1843; admitted to bar, 1847; practiced Boston 10 yrs.; has been auditor of accounts; m. Miss Emily L. Dexter, May 29, 1851. Has lived in and near Boston 70 yrs. Deceased.

HALL, Thomas Cuming, historian; b. Armagh, Ireland, Sept. 25, 1858; s. Rev. John and Emily (Bolton) H.; brother of Bolton H.; A.B., Princeton, 1879, A.M., 1882; grad. Union Theol. Sem., 1882; studied univs. of Berlin and Göttingen, 1882-83; (D.D., Hamilton, 1894, U. of Marburg, 1921); m. Jenny L. E. Bartling, July 29, 1884 (dec.). Ordained Presbyn. ministry, 1883; pastor Omaha, 1883-86, First Ch. of Chicago, 1886-93, Fourth Church, Chicago, 1893-97; prof. Christian ethics, Union Theol. Sem., 1898-1917; prof. philos. faculty U. of Göttingen, 1921-31, emeritus. Work in aid of prisoners of war, traveling in Australia, Germany, Bulgaria, Servia, Turkey, neutral countries, 1915-19. Decorated Order of Crown, 3rd class, by Emperor of Germany. Author: John Hall, Pastor and Preacher—A Biography by His Son, 1901; Religious Background of American Culture, 1931. Died May 1936.

HALL, Thomas Winthrop, author; b. Ogdensburg, N.Y., Nov. 13, 1862; grad. U.S. Mil. Acad., 1887; adj. 1st U.S. vol. cav. (Rough Riders) during Spanish-American war; in all battles of the regiment. Dramatized The Bonnie Brier Bush. Author (verse): When Hearts Are Trumps; When Love Laughs; When Cupid Calls; When Love Is Lord; (prose): An Experimental Wooing; Tales by Tom Hall. Home: New York, N.Y. Died 1900.

HALL, Tomas Proctor, physician; b. Ontario, Can., Oct. 7, 1858; s. Robert Skirrow and Jane (Greenwood) H.; A.B., U. of Toronto, 1882; M.D., Nat. Med. U., Chicago, 1902; A.M., Ph.D., Ill. Wesleyan U., 1888; Ph.D., Clark U., 1893; m. Elizabeth Knight, July 16, 1885; 2d, Dr. Ruth M. McManus, Sept. 10, 1902. Fellow U. of Toronto, 1883-84, Clark U., 1891-94; prof. natural science, Tabor Coll., Ia., 1893-96; prof. physics, Kansas City U., 1897-1901. Home: Vancouver, B.C. Died 1931.

HALL, Walter Henry, choral conductor; b. London, Eng., Apr. 25, 1862; s. James and Mary (Neale) H.; studied 4 yrs. Royal Acad. Music, London; Mus.D., Wesleyan U., 1930; m. Celestia M. Younman, Apr. 7, 1885; children—Alice May, Alan, Cecil John. Came to America, 1883; organist and choirmaster, St. James' Ch., New York, 1896-1913; conductor, Brooklyn Oratoria Soc., 1893—; conductor, Musurgia, New York, 1901-07; lecturer on music, 1909—, dir. choral music, 1909-13, prof. ch. and choral music, 1913-20, now prof. emeritus and condr. Columbia Univ. Chorus, Columbia U. Author: Essentials of Choir Boy Training, 1907. Home: New York, N.Y. Died Dec. 11, 1935.

HALL, William Phillips; b. Stamford, Conn., Feb. 1, 1864; s. Thomas Shepard and Sarah Catherine (Phillips) H.; acad. edn.; m. Charlotte Sophia Hollister, Oct. 4, 1887; children—Mrs. Dorothy K. Peddle (dec.), Mrs. Mary P. Hirons, Mrs. Charlotte H. Stockton, Mrs. Margaret F. Moore, William Phillips, Charles Parker (dec.), Lyman Hollister (dec.), Melville Phillips, Theodore Dana, Thomas Shepard. Founder, many years pres. The Hall Signal Co.; introduced automatic block signals on many Am. rys. Pres. Am. Tract Soc.; originated, 1900, Twentieth Century Nat. Gospel Campaign. Lay evangelist; vice-pres. Am. Bible Soc.; pres. Bible League of N.A., General Conf. trustee Old John Street M.E. Ch. (N.Y. City); trustee Biblical Sem. in N.Y.; dir. N.Y. Christian Home for Intemperate Men; dir. Greenwich Library Assn. Republican. Mason. (K.T.). Wrote: Biblical Study of Union with God in Christ; The Name of God and Its Relationship to the Lord Jesus Christ; A Remarkable Biblical Discovery, or The Name of God According to the Scriptures. Home: Rowayton, Conn. Died Aug. 14, 1937.

HALL, William Preble, brig. gen.; b. Mo., June 11, 1848; apptd. from Mo., and grad., U.S. Mil. Acad., 1868. Second lt., 19th Inf., June 15, 1868, 5th Cav., July 14, 1869; 1st lt., July 1, 1876; capt., Mar. 8, 1867; maj. staff a.-a.-g., Nov. 6, 1893; lt. col. staff a.-a.-g., Sept. 11, 1897; col. a.-a.-g., Apr. 18, 1901; brig. gen. a.-a.-g., Apr. 23, 1904; brig. gen., adj. gen. U.S.A., Mar. 5, 1907, with rank from Apr. 23, 1904. Served principally on frontier duty until Spanish war; was in fight with Apaches at Whitestone Mountain, Ariz., July 13, 1873; Big Horn and Yellowstone Expdn., 1876, and in action at Indian Creek, Wyo., July 17, 1876, and combat of Slim Buttes, Dak., Sept. 9-10, 1876; attacked by Indians while in command of reconnoitering party near camp on White River, Colo., Oct. 29, 1879, and while going to rescue of brother officer was surrounded by about 35 warriors; awarded Congressional Medal of Honor for most distinguished gallantry on that occasion; adj. gen. dept. Puerto Rico, 1899-1900. Was mem. dept., div., army, and distinguished marksmen teams, 1879-92, and won medals upon all these teams, shooting, carbine and revolver. Retired June 11, 1912. Died Dec. 4, 1927.

HALLAM, Julia (Kirkland) Clark, author; b. Portage, Wis., Jan. 7, 1860; d. John T. and Louise (Holley) Clark; A.B., U. of Wis., 1881, A.M., 1884; A.M., U. of Chicago, 1910; m. Joseph W. Hallam, 1883; children—Marguerite Clark, Arthur Wood, Kirkland (dec.). Taught in high schs., Madison and LaCross, Wis., 2 yrs. Recording sec. Ia. Fedn. of Woman's Clubs, 1901-03; pres. Iowa Equal Suffrage Society, 1909-10; class speaker at U. of Wis. Alumni dinner, commencement, 1911; "mother's day" speaker at Hawarden, Ia., May 1912, and May 1913; state del. to Nat. Child Labor Conf., Jacksonville, Fla., Mar. 13-16, 1913; moved to Chicago, Sept. 1913; traveled in Japan and P.I., 1914-15; taught in provincial high sch., San Jose del Buena Vista, Antique, P.I., 1915; in charge Philosophy Library, U. of Chicago, 1919-21; lecturer to women's clubs and girls' schs., 1924—. Author: The Relation of the Sexes from a Scientific Standpoint; The Story of a European Tour, 1900; Studies in Child Development, 1913. Home: Chicago, Ill. Died Aug. 10, 1927.

HALLBERG, Carl Savantè Nicanor, pharmaceutical publicist; b. Helsingborg, Sweden, Oct. 13, 1856; s. Carl and Anna (Kohrtz) H.; ed. Latin sch., 1860-64; Gymnasium, Helsingborg, Sweden, 1864-69; came to U.S., July 4, 1869; grad. Phila. Coll. Pharmacy, 1876; (Harvey Med. Coll., M.D., honoris causa, 1903; Phar.D., Medico-Chirurg, Coll., Phila., 1909); m. Therese Bergstrom, Dec. 20, 1893. Prof. pharmacy Chicago Coll. Pharmacy (U. of Ill.), 1890—; prof. pharmacology, Ill. Med. Coll., 1894-96; organized, 1885, and from then dir. Nat. Inst. Pharmacy, a system of home-study in pharmaceutical sciences. Gold medal, Am. Pharm. Assn., Detroit, 1888; diploma, hon. mention, Chicago Expn., 1893. Mem. Nat. Com. Revision of the Nat. Formulary, 1886, 1895, 1906, Nat. Com. Revision of U.S. Pharmacopœia, 1890-1900, 1900-10. Editor Western Druggist, 1883-93; editor Bull. of Am. Pharm. Assn., 1906—. Home: Chicago, Ill. Died 1910.

HALLE, Edward Gustav, underwriter; b. Leipzig, Germany, Jan. 5, 1844; s. Heinrich and Henrietta F; ed. in Germany; came to U.S., 1866; m. E. Gutenberg, 1869. Became spl. agt. Germania Fire Ins. Co., of New York, 1873; later secured the state agency for Wis. and Minn. and from 1883 has been western mgr. for that co. at Chicago. Mem. Chicago Bd. of Edn., 1891-98 (pres., 1896-98); pres. of "German Day," Chicago Expn.; pres. advisory com. Rep. Nat. Com., 1896; McKinley elector, 1900. Col. on staff of Gov. Yates, 1900-04; decorated by German Emperor with Order of Crown II. Home: Chicago, Ill. Died July 25, 1917.

HALLECK, Reuben Post, author, lecturer; b. Rocky Point, L.I., Feb. 8, 1859; s. Rev. Luther Calvin and Fannie (Tuthill) H.; A.B., Yale, 1881, A.M., 189[illegible] LL.D., Ky. State U., 1912; m. Annie Ainslie, Oct. 29, 1896. Prin. Cherry Valley (N.Y.) Acad., 1881 [illegible] School, Louis[ville] instr., 1883-96, prin. Male High [illegible], 1896-1912. Dir. Louisville Bridge & Iron Works [illegible] as advisory editor Sch. Rev. Trustee Am. Prin[ting] House for the Blind, 1918—. Conglist. Auth[or]: Psychology and Psychic Culture,

1895; The Education of the Central Nervous System, 1896; History of English Literature, 1900; History of American Literature, 1911; New English Literature, 1913; Readings from Literature (with Miss Elizabeth G. Barbour), 1915; History of Our Country, 1923; Our Nation's Heritage (with Juliette Frantz), 1925; Founders of Our Nation (with same), 1929; Makers of Our Nation (with same), 1930; The Romance of American Literature, 1934; Our United States (with J. Frantz), 1935. Home: Louisville, Ky. Died Dec. 24, 1936.

HALLER, Frank Louis, business man; b. Davenport, Ia., Nov. 20, 1861; s. Frank and Mary (Hetzel) H.; B.A., State U. of Ia., 1883; m. Florence Lininger, Feb. 17, 1885. Began as shipping clk., Lininger Implement Co., 1885, pres., Dec. 15, 1906—; v.p. Bee Pub. Co.; dir. Omaha Corn Show, 1908-09; dir. Omaha Pub. Library 15 yrs., pres. 5 yrs.; chmn. bd. Neb. State Traveling Library Commn., 15 yrs.; regent U. of Neb., 1909-19 (pres. bd. 1918). Republican. Episcopalian. Mason. Home: Omaha, Neb. Died Sept. 1922.

HALLETT, Moses, judge; b. Galena, Ill., July 16, 1834; s. Moses and Eunice H.; acad. edn.; (LL.D., U. of Colo., 1893); studied law in Chicago; admitted to Ill. bar, 1858; m. Katharine Felt, Feb. 9, 1882. Removed to Colo., 1860; mem. Territorial Council, 1863-65; chief justice Supreme Ct. of Colo., 1866-76; U.S. Dist. judge, Dist. of Colo., 1877-1906. Republican. Prof. Am. constl. law and federal jurisprudence, U. of Colo., 1892—. Died Apr. 25, 1913.

HALLEY, James, banker; b. Sterling, Scotland, Jan. 7, 1854; brought to U.S., 1857; m. Lottie Smith, Sept. 20, 1878. Teller First Nat. Bank, Deadwood, Dak. (now S.D.), 1879; founder, 1884, and pres. First Nat. Bank of Rapid City; was mayor of Rapid City and mem. Rep. State Com. Died Feb. 27, 1920.

HALLIBURTON, Richard, author; b. Brownsville, Tenn., Jan. 9, 1900; s. Wesley and Nell (Nance) H.; grad. Lawrenceville (N.J.) Sch., 1917; A.B., Princeton U., 1921; unmarried. Mem. Princeton Naval Unit, 1918; climbed Matterhorn, 1921; Fujiyama in midwinter, 1923; Olympus, 1925; Popocatepetl, 1928; swam Hellespont in August 1925, Panama Canal, Atlantic to Pacific Aug. 1928, Sea of Galilee, Oct. 1931. Expedition to Western Tibet, 1922; Homeric expedition, 1925, tracing the travels of Ulysses from Ithaca back to Ithaca as recounted in the Odyssey. Mapped and traced on foot Cortez's Conquest of Mexico, and Balboa's march across Darien that led to the discovery of the Pacific, 1928; explorations in Yucatan, Peru, and Western Brazil, 1928; traveled over 50,000 miles around the world in own airplane "The Flying Carpet," 1931-32, London to Timbuctoo and back, route of First Crusade, Paris to Jerusalem, route of Alexander the Great; visited Mount Everest by air, Jan. 1932, also Borneo and Philippines; traveled in Russia, Arabia and Ethiopia, 1934-35, for newspaper syndicate; rode elephant from Lake Geneva, Switzerland, to Turin, Italy, over the Alps, via St. Bernard Pass, to retrace the elephant march of Hannibal in the 2d Punic War. Leading actor in moving picture, "India Speaks," 1933. Has adressed over 2,000 schs., colls., clubs, on travel and adventure. Democrat. Author: The Royal Road to Romance, 1925; The Glorious Adventure, 1927; New Worlds to Conquer, 1929; The Flying Carpet, 1932; Seven League Boots, 1935; Richard Halliburton's Book of Marvels—The Occident, 1937; Richard Halliburton's Book of Marvels—The Orient, 1937. Deceased.

HALLIDAY, Samuel Dumont, lawyer; b. Jan. 7, 1847; grad. Cornell Univ., 1870. Practiced law, Ithaca, N.Y., 1872—; dist. atty., 1874-75; mem. N.Y. Assembly, 1876-78; del. from N.Y., Dem. Nat. Conv., 1876, 1880. Trustee of Cornell Univ., 1874-84, and 1892—; dir. 1st Nat. Bank of Ithaca, and mem. Ithaca School Bd. Democrat. Home: Ithaca, N.Y., Died 1907.

HALLIGAN, John, naval officer; b. Boston, Mass., May 14, 1876; s. John and Margaret Elizabeth (McCarthy) H.; grad. U.S. Naval Acad., 1898; m. Katrina Hoskinson Loomis, Feb. 11, 1902; 1 dau., Katherine Porter (wife of Charles Adair, U.S.N.). Rear adm. U.S. Navy; served as naval cadet, U.S.S. Brooklyn, Spanish-Am. War; with U.S. Naval Forces, France, World War; engr.-in-chief, U.S.N., 1927-29; now comdr. aircraft, U.S. Scouting Force. Officer Legion of Honor (France); D.S.M. (U.S.). Catholic. Home: Annapolis, Md. Died Dec. 11, 1934.

HALLOCK, Charles, journalist, author, scientist; b. New York, 1834; s. Gerard and Eliza (Allen) H.; A.B., Amherst, 1854, A.M., 1871; m. Amelia J. Wardell, Sept. 10, 1855. Editor New Haven Register, 1855-56, New York Journal of Commerce, 1856-61, St. John (N.B.) Telegraph and Courier, 1863-65; broker at St. John and Halifax, 1865-66; founded financial editor Harper's Weekly, 1868; founded Nature's Realm, Forest and Stream, 1873; editor Stream, 1896-1890; editor Northwestern Field ... Park Assn., New 97. Was 1st sec. Blooming Grove ... Queens Co. Bank, York, 1870-72; dir. Flushing ... 1873; founded Internat. Assn. for Protection of Game, 1874; formulated uniform game laws, 1875; founder town of Hallock, Minn., 1880. Has done collecting and field work for Smithsonian Instn., 1860—. Author: Camp Life in Florida, 1876; Sportsman's Gazetteer, 1877; Vacation Rambles in Michigan, 1877; American Club List and Glossary, 1878; Dog Fanciers' Directory and Medical Guide, 1886; Our New Alaska, 1886; The Salmon Fisher, 1890; Hallock Ancestry, 1906; Peerless Alaska, 1908. Died Dec. 2, 1917.

HALLOCK, Frank Kirkwood, M.D.; b. Oyster Bay, L.I., Aug. 18, 1860; s. Winthrop Bailey (M.D.) and Mary Kirkwood (Kent) H.; A.B., Wesleyan U., 1882, A.M., 1885; M.D., Coll. Phys. and Surg. (Columbia), 1885; interne New York Hosp., 1885-87; student in Germany, 1887-89; m. Kate Camp Avery, May 7, 1890 (died 1930); children—Winthrop Avery (dec.), Abraham Avery, Mary (Mrs. S. W. Armstrong), Leonard Avery, Elizabeth (Mrs. J. G. Vermillion). Specialist in neurology, 1890—; med. dir. Cromwell Hall Health Sch., 1898—; established an instn. for the treatment of nervous invalidism on an educational basis, combining medical, physical, occupational and nature agencies with the psychological analysis and interpretation of the individual. Pres., now dir. Savings Bank (Cromwell); dir. Rand Avery Supply Co. (Boston), Industrial Securities Corp. (Middletown). Mem. bd. trustees Wesleyan U. (Middletown, Conn.); dir. Middlesex Hosp. (Middletown). Mason. Home: Cromwell, Conn. Died Apr. 29, 1937.

HALLOCK, Gerard, educator; b. Brooklyn, July 1, 1867; s. William Homes and Julia (Mack) H.; A.B., Rutgers, 1890, A.M., 1893; m. Mary Adele Page, June 30, 1903; children—Martha, Gerard, Harlan Page, Richards. Teacher St. Luke's Sch. (now), Wayne, Pa., 1890-92; instr. The Hill Sch., Pottstown, Pa., 1892-1906; headmaster, The Sedgwick Sch., Great Barrington, Mass., 1906-08; established, 1908, and from then prin. the Hallock School (a boys' sch.), Great Barrington, Mass. Deceased.

HALLOCK, Joseph Newton, editor; b. Franklinville, N.Y., 1834; s. Ezra and Lydia E. H.; A.B., Yale, 1857, A.M., 1860; grad. Yale Theol. Sem., 1860; (D.D., Ursinus Coll., Pa., 1896). Congl. minister several yrs. before entering lit. field; editor-in-chief and propr. The Christian Work, 1880—. Prizewinner in 1897 over 300 competitors from all parts U.S. for Brooklyn Eagle's essay on Sound Money. Received call, 1897, to presidency of Westminster Univ., Denver, but declined. Dir. in several large corps. Author: The Christian Life, 1890; Family Worship, 1892; First Principles of Temperance, 1892; Life of D. L. Moody, 1900. Home: Brooklyn, N.Y. Died Mar. 24, 1913.

HALLOCK, Robert Crawford, clergyman; b. Holliday's Cove, W.Va., Nov. 9, 1857; s. Homan Benjamin and Adelia Ann (Farnsworth) H.; one of family of 12 children—4 clergymen; A.B., Princeton, 1882; grad. Princeton Theol. Sem., 1885; Ph.D., New York U., 1888; D.D., Richmond (O.) Coll., 1900; m. Martha Austin Wells, Dec. 24, 1885; children—Allen Robert, Earl Kenneth, Constance M., Leland R., Marion Post, Hortense, Margaret Walton, Robert Farnsworth. Ordained Presbyn. ministry, 1885; pastor successively historic Old Tennent Ch., Monmouth Co., N.J., Southampton, L.I., Park Congl. Ch., Brooklyn, Stone Ch., Clinton, N.Y., until 1907; in Porto Rico 1 yr.; pastor Scottsville and Dundee, N.Y., later Presbyn. Ch., Havana, Cuba, until 1922, Valatie, N.Y., 1922-28. Twice del. Gen. Assembly Presbyn. Ch. U.S.A. Republican. Author: Dramatized Sermons, 1924. Co-author: Behind the Big Hill, 1930. Home: Valatie, N.Y. Died June 24, 1932.

HALLOCK, William, physicist; b. Milton, N.Y., Aug. 14, 1857; s. Isaac S. and Phœbe (Hull) H.; A.B., Columbia, 1879; Ph.D., U. of Würzburg, 1881 (hon. D.Phar., Nat. Coll. Pharmacy, Washington, 1892); m. Georgianna B., d. Charles Henri Ames, of Keesville, N.Y., Oct. 15, 1885. Asst. in physical lab., Würzburg, 1881-82; physicist, U.S. Geol. Survey, 1882-91; prof. physics, Corcoran Scientific Sch., Washington, 1884-86; prof. chemistry and toxicology, Nat. Coll. Pharmacy, 1889-92; asst. in charge, Astrophysical Obs., Smithsonian Instn., 1891-92; adj. prf., 1892-1902, prof. physics, 1902—, dean faculty of pure science, 1906-09, Columbia. Home: New York, N.Y. Died May 20, 1913.

HALLOWELL, John White; b. West Medford, Mass., Dec. 24, 1878; s. of late Col. Norwood Penrose and Sarah Wharton (Haydock) H.; A.B., Harvard, 1901; m. Marian H. Ladd, Oct. 10, 1905; children—William L., John W., Roger H., Eleanor, Phillips. Mem. Stone & Webster, 1901-17, partner, 1912-17; dir. Chicago, Wilmington & Franklin Coal Co.; asst. to Herbert Hoover, Fed. Food Administrator, May 1917-Mar. 1919; asst. to the Sec. of the Interior (Lane), Mar. 1919-20; mem. Commn. for Relief in Belgium, Ednl. Foundation, Inc. Overseer Harvard, 1914-20; mem. Harvard Fund Council, 1925—; trustee Middlesex Sch., Concord, Mass. Home: Milton, Mass. Died Jan. 5, 1927.

HALLOWELL, Richard Price, wool mcht.; b. Phila., Dec. 16, 1835; s. Morris L. and Hannah P. H.; ed. Haverford Coll.; m. Anna C., d. Edward M. and Maria (Mott) Davis, Phila., Oct. 26, 1859. Moved to Mass., 1859, and engaged in business in Boston; apptd. by Gov. Andrew of Mass. spl. agt. to recruit negro regts.; later v.p. New England Woman Suffrage Assn. and treas. Free Religious Assn. Home: West Medford, Mass. Died 1904.

HALLOWELL, Robert, artist; b. Denver, Colo., Mar. 12, 1886; s. Charles and Frances (Ferris) H.; prep. edn., Friends' Sch., Wilmington, Del., and Phillips Acad., Andover, Mass.; A.B., Harvard U., 1910; m. 2d, Aurelia Caloenesco (Rumanian painter); children—Robert Gilles (dec.), Carolyn Bayard. Was illustrator of juvenile book, 1908; pres. Harvard Lampoon, 1909-10; with Century Mag., doing occasional illustrations, 1910-14, American Mag., 1913-14; with Treasury Dept., Washington, D.C., 1917-18; one of founders, treas. and later pub., New Republic, 1914-25; v.p. Survey Associates, Inc., 1926-29. Painter in water color and oil, also etcher; self-taught. First public exhbn., Galerie Bernheim-Jeune, Paris, 1924. Other one-man shows same gallery, 1925; Druet, Paris, 1927; Montross Gallery, New York, 1924-27; jointly with wife, 1929; Rehn Gallery, N.Y. City, 1928; Ferargil, N.Y., 1929; Knoedlers, Chicago, 1930; McClees, Phila., 1933; Macbeth, N.Y., 1935; by invitation at Art Mus., Rochester and Baltimore, Corcoran Gallery, Washington. Rep. in permanent collections of Phillips Memorial Gallery, Washington; Cleveland Mus.; Brooklyn Mus.; Baltimore Mus.; Lewisohn collection, N.Y.; collection of late Arthur B. Davies; McBride collection, Cleveland; collection of Harvard U., etc. Asst. to dir., Federal Art Project, Washington, D.C., 1935-36, spl. adviser consumers div. on price study staff, reviewing the economics of contemporary Am. art, 1937. Quaker. Home: New Brighton, S.I., N.Y. Died Jan. 26, 1939.

HALPER, Benzion, editor, author; b. Lithuania, April 15, 1884; s. Abel Solomon and Miriam (Rosenbloom) H.; B.A., 1st class honors, U. of London, Eng., 1907, M.A., with mark of distinction, 1909; 1st holder of Gilchrist scholarship in Arabic; in Egypt, under auspices U. of London, 1910-11; Ph.D., Dropsie Coll., Phila., 1914; m. Lina Sacks, of London, Eng., June 2, 1908. Came to U.S., 1911, naturalized citizen, 1918. Custodian of manuscripts, Dropsie Coll., and asso. prof. Cognate Semitic langs.; editor Jewish Publn. Soc. America, 1916—. Author: Post-Biblical Hebrew Literature (2 vols.), 1921; Descriptive Catalogue of Genizah Fragments, 1922. Home: Philadelphia, Pa. Died Mar. 1924.

HALSEY, Abram Woodruff, clergyman; b. Elizabeth, N.J., Mar. 22, 1853; s. Maline W. and Henrietta P. H.; A.B., Princeton, 1879, A.M., 1822 (D.D., 1898); grad. Princeton Theol. Sem., 1882; m. Ella Gertrude Lithgow, Mar. 3, 1893. Ordained Presbyn. ministry, Oct. 10, 1882; pastor Spring St. Ch., New York, 1882-99; sec. Bd. Foreign Missions Presbyn. Ch. U.S.A., 1899—. Home: New York, N.Y. Died Apr. 20, 1921.

HALSEY, Francis Whiting, editor, author; b. Unadilla, N.Y., Oct. 15, 1851; s. Gaius Leonard (M.D.) and Juliet E. (Carrington) H.; bro. of Frederick Arthur H.; B.S., Cornell, 1873; m. Virginia Isabel Forbes, Dec. 18, 1883 (died 1899). On staff New York Tribune, 1875-80, New York Times, 1880-1902; edited New York Times Saturday Review from its first number, Oct. 15, 1896, until June 1902; lit. adviser D. Appleton & Co., 1902-05, Funk & Wagnalls Co., 1905—. Has lectured before N.Y. and N.J. hist. socs., students Columbia, Princeton and many other bodies. Trustee N.Y. State Hist. Assn., Am. Scenic Soc. Author: Two Months Abroad, 1878; The Old New York Frontier, 1901; Virginia Isabel Forbes (memoir of his wife), 1900; Our Literary Deluge, 1902; The Pioneers of Unadilla Village, 1902; hist. and biog. introduction to Mrs. Rowson's Charlotte Temple, 1905; hist. introduction and foot notes to Richard Smith's Tour of Four Great Rivers, 1906. Editor: The World's Famous Orations (asso. to William J. Bryan), 10 vols., 1906; The Best of the World's Classics (asso. to Henry Cabot Lodge), 10 vols., 1907; Great Epochs in American History Described by Famous Writers, 10 vols., 1912; Seeing Europe with Famous Authors, 10 vols., 1914. Wrote introduction and bibliographies for Pryde's "What Books to Read and How to Read," 1912. Home: New York, N.Y. Died Nov. 24, 1919.

HALSEY, Frederick Arthur, author; b. Unadilla, N.Y., July 12, 1856; s. Gaius Leonard (M.D.) and Juliet E. (Carrington) H.; B.M.E., Cornell, 1878; m. Stella D. Spencer, May 12, 1885; children—Olga S., Marion S. Engr. Rand Drill Co., 1880-90; engr. and gen. mgr. Canadian Rand Drill Co., 1890-94; asso. editor, 1894-1907, editor, Feb. 1, 1907-May 1, 1911, editor emeritus, the American Machinist. Inventor of the "premium plan" of paying for labor, now recognized factor in factory management, having been adopted by many mfrs. in Europe and America (gold medal Am. Soc. M.E. for this plan, 1923); active in opposition to the bill for the adoption of the metric system which was before the Ho. of Rep. 1902-06;

presented with a testimonial by mfrs. in recognition of these efforts, and since made commr. of Am. Inst. of Weights and Measures, organized by leading engrs. and mfrs. to oppose the metric system. Author: Slide Valve Gears, 1890; Slide Rule, 1899; Worm and Spiral Gearing, 1902; Metric Fallacy, 1904, rewritten edit., 1919; (with C. F. Smith) Design and Construction of Cams, 1906; Halsey's Handbook for Machine Designers and Draftsmen, 1913; Methods of Machine Shop Work, 1914; Metric System in Export Trade, 1917; Weights and Measures of Latin America, 1918. Home: New York, N.Y. Died Oct. 20, 1935.

HALSEY, John Julius, college prof.; b. Louisville, Ky., Nov. 23, 1848; s. LeRoy Jones and Caroline Augusta (Anderson) H.; B.A., (old) U. of Chicago, 1870; (LL.D., Centre Coll., 1898); m. Elizabeth Beadle Gardner, July 9, 1885. Instr. U. of Chicago, 1870-71; abstractor for Handy, Simmons & Co., 1872-74; fire ins. solicitor, 1874-78; prof. polit. science, 1878—, acting pres., 1896-97 and 1906-07, Lake Forest Co.; head prof. economics, Leland Stanford Jr. U., 1901-02. Alderman, 1893-96, pres. Library Bd., 1898-1901, pres. Bd. of Edn., 1903-07, dir. Law and Order League, 1905—, Lake Forest; pres. township high sch. bd., 1911-15. Republican. Presbyn. John J. Halsey, pub. sch., Lake Forest, Ill., dedicated Mar. 22, 1913. Joint author: The Halsey Family in America, 1895; A History of Lake County, Ill., 1911. Editor and contbr. of final chapter on "Reconstruction," Political History of Slavery, 1903. Dir. U.S. Navy League. Home: Lake Forest, Ill. Died May 29, 1919.

HALSEY, N. Wetmore, banker; b. Forreston, Ill., Dec. 25, 1856; s. Seton and Frances E. (Dean) H.; Beloit Coll.; grad. Union Coll. of Law, Chicago, 1882; m. Margaret C. Hitt, Oct. 20, 1885. In practice, Chicago, 1882-86; became asso. with N. W. Harris & Co., bankers and brokers, 1886, resident partner in New York, 1891-1901; organized, 1901, and from then sr. mem. N. W. Halsey & Co., municipal, railroad and pub. utility bonds, Chicago, Phila. and San Francisco; chmn. bd. dirs. Pacific Gas & Electric Co.; dir. and mem. exec. com. Electric Properties Co. Republican. Presbyn. Home: South Orange, N.J. Died 1911.

HALSEY, Rena Isabelle, writer; b. N.Y. City; d. Harlan Page and Henrietta Augusta H.; desc. of Rev. Francis Higginson, 1st Puritan clergyman at Salem, Mass.; ed. Nassau Inst., spl. courses Pratt Inst., Brooklyn, and New York U. Charter mem. Colonial Daughters of 17th Century (sec. 8 yrs.). Conglist. Author: Blue Robin, the Girl Pioneer, 1917; America's Daughter, 1918; The Liberty Girl, 1919 (last two books placed in Nat. War Museum, Paris, by request French Govt.); also of words One Hundred New Songs for the Kindergarten and Primary, 1905. Home: Brooklyn, N.Y. Died Oct. 24, 1932.

HALSEY, Richard T. Haines, broker; b. Elizabeth, N.J., May 28, 1865; s. William F. and Frances E. (Haines) H.; A.B., Princeton, 1886. Spl. partner Tefft, Halsey & Co., New York. Art critic and antiquarian; author on early Americana, and collector same. Mem. bd. dirs. Met. Mus. Art. Republican. Presbyn. Home: New York, N.Y. Died Feb. 7, 1942.

HALSTEAD, Albert Edward, surgeon; b. Ottawa, Ont., Apr. 21, 1868; s. William S. and Sara (Gibbons) H.; M.D., Northwestern U. Med. Sch., 1890; m. Mary S. Cochems, Feb. 1, 1893; children—Lucile Marie Byford, Dorothy Logan. Interne Cook Co. Hosp., 1890-91, then engaged in practice in Chicago; attending surgeon Cook Co. Hosp. for 20 yrs.; formerly prof. anatomy, Northwestern U. Med. Sch.; prof. surgery, Med. Dept. U. of Ill.; attending surg. Cook Co., St. Luke's hosps. Fellow Am. Surg. Assn., Chicago Surg. Soc. Lt. col. M.C.U.S.A., with A.E.F., 1917. Home: Chicago, Ill. Died Dec. 6, 1926.

HALSTEAD, Alexander Seaman, naval officer; b. Phila., Pa., Dec. 17, 1861; s. David and Janet (Gunn) H.; A.B., Central High Sch., Phila., 1879; grad. U.S. Naval Acad., 1883; grad. Naval War Coll., Newport, R.I., 1917; unmarried. Promoted asst. engr., July 1, 1885; passed asst. engr., Sept. 11, 1895; transferred to line as lt., Mar. 3, 1899; lt. comdr., Jan. 1, 1904; commander, July 1, 1908; capt., July 1, 1911; rear admiral (tem.), July 1, 1918; rear admiral (permanent), July 1, 1919. Served on Raleigh, Spanish-American War, participating in the Battle of Manila Bay, May 1, 1898, also capture of Corregidor Island, Manila Bay, capture of Grand Island, Subig Bay, and assault on Manila, Aug. 1898; on Chicago, 1904-06; insp. ordnance, San Francisco, Calif., 1906-09; comd. Vicksburg, 1909-10, Pensacola, 1910-11; comd. California, flagship of Pacific Fleet, 1912-13, participating in operations of U.S. forces in connection with revolution in Nicaragua; supervisor New York Harbor, 1915; comdr. Utah, 1915-16, Naval War Coll., Newport, R.I., 1916-17; apptd. sr. mem. Bd. for Appraisal for Mcht. and Pvt. Vessels, N.Y. City, Apr. 2, 1917. Comdr. dist. of Brest, France, Oct. 1918-Jan. 1919; comdr. U.S. naval forces in France, hdqrs., Brest, Jan. 30, 1919; returned to U.S., Oct. 1919; comdr. Navy Yard, Portsmouth, N.H., Dec. 1, 1919-20; comdt. 12th Naval Dist., San Francisco, Oct. 1920—. Holder Dewey medal, and Spanish-Am. War and Nicaragua campaign badges; awarded D.S.M., and Navy Cross; Comdr. Legion of Honor (French). Presbyn. Home: Philadelphia, Pa. Died Nov. 12, 1923.

HALSTEAD, Murat, journalist; b. Ross Twp., Butler Co., O., Sept. 2, 1829; s. Griffin and Clarissa (Willets) H.; reared on farm, attending school winters; attended select school 1 term; taught school 2 terms; grad. Farmers' Coll., nr. Cincinnati; m. Mary Banks, March 2, 1857. Began newspaper work on a literary weekly; joined staff of Cincinnati Commercial, March 8, 1853, bought interest, 1854, head of firm, 1865; later consolidated with Gazette as Commercial Gazette, of which he became editor-in-chief. Nominated, 1889, by Pres. Harrison as minister to Germany; rejected by Senate because of articles he had written about the purchase of senatorial seats. Later edited Brooklyn Standard-Union; during past few yrs. spl. corr. and mag. writer. Went to Philippine Islands during war with Spain. Author: Life of William McKinley; Life of Admiral Dewey. Home: Cincinnati, O. Died 1908.

HALSTEAD, William Riley, author; b. Vigo Co., Ind., Mar. 19, 1848; s. Reuben and Louisa (Brown) Halstead; B.S., Asbury (now DePauw) U., 1871, M.A., 1874, D.D., 1886; m. Candace Kennedy, 1873 (died 1873); m. 2d, Martha Taylor, 1875 (died 1902); children—William Leon, Eloise (dec.), Harry, Riley Courtlandt (dec.); m. 3d, Ella Briggs Pegg, Mar. 8, 1906. Ordained M.E. ministry, 1872; pastor Worthington, Ind., 1873, Spencer, 1875, Mitchell, 1876-80; pres. DePauw Coll., New Albany, Ind., 1880-81; pastor Indianapolis, 1882-84, Greencastle, 1884-87; presiding elder Indianapolis dist., 1887-90; pastor Bloomington, Ind., 1890-94; presiding elder Evansville dist., 1895-98; pastor St. Paul's Ch., Lincoln, Neb., 1898-99, Frankfort, Ind., 1899-1901; corr. sec. M.E. Deaconess Home and Hosp., 1901-03; retired, 1903. Author: The Tragedy of Labor, 1919; Some Social Aspects of Religion, 1919; Christ in the Universe, 1929. Home: Terre Haute, Ind. Died Dec. 19, 1931.

HALSTED, Abel Stevens, lawyer; b. New York, Aug. 20, 1870; s. Samuel Martin and Ida Russell (Stevens) H.; ed. common and high schs.; m. Eleanor Hall Halsted, May 27, 1897; children—Wyllys Stevens (dec.), Abel Stevens. Admitted to Calif. bar, 1893, and since practiced, Los Angeles; became connected with Los Angeles & Salt Lake R.R. Co., 1901, and successively gen. atty. for Calif., asst. gen. counsel and gen. solicitor same. Republican. Episcopalian. Home: Pasadena, Calif. Died July 21, 1932.

HALSTED, Byron David, botanist; b. Venice, N.Y., June 7, 1852; s. David and Mary (Mechem) H.; B.S., Mich. Agrl. Coll., 1871, M.S., 1874; Sc.D., Harvard, 1878; m. Susan E. Howe, Jan. 7, 1883. Mng. editor Am. Agriculturist, 1880-85; prof. botany, Ia. Agrl. Coll., 1885-89, Rutgers Coll., 1889—. Asso. editor Bull. of Torrey Bot. Club, 1890-93, Systematic Flora of N. America, 1905—. Silver medal, Mass. Hort. Soc., 1877. Home: New Brunswick, N.J. Died Aug. 28, 1919.

HALSTED, George Bruce, author; b. Newark, N.J., Nov. 25, 1853; s. Olive Spencer and Adela (Meeker) H.; A.B., Princeton, 1875; later A.M.; Ph.D., Johns Hopkins, 1879; m. Maggie Swearingen. Instructor in post-grad. mathematics, Princeton, 1878-81; prof. mathematics, U. of Tex., 1884-1903, St. John's Coll., Md., 1903, Kenyon Coll., Ohio, 1903-06, Colo. State Teachers Coll., 1906-12. Author: Elements of Geometry, 1885; Synthetic Projective Geometry, 1906; On the Foundation and Technic of Arithmetic, 1911. Died 1922.

HALSTED, William Stewart, surgeon; b. New York, Sept. 23, 1852; s. William Mills, Jr. and Mary Louisa (Haines) H.; A.B., Yale, 1874; M.D., Coll. Phys. and Surg. (Columbia), 1877; univs. of Vienna, Leipzig, Würzburg, 1878-80; (hon. F.R.C.S., Eng., 1900, Edinburgh, 1905; LL.D., Yale, 1904, Edinburgh, 1905; Sc.D., Columbia, 1904); m. Caroline Hampton, June 4, 1890. Attending phys., Charity Hosp., New York, 1881-83; attending surgeon, Bellevue and Presbyn. hosps., 1885-87; asso. surgeon, Roosevelt Hosp. and surgeon-in-chief, Out-Patient Dept., 1881-87; surgeon-in-chief Emigrant Hosp., New York, 1881-84, and Johns Hopkins Hosp., Baltimore, 1889—; prof. surgery, Johns Hopkins U., 1889—. Fellow Am. Surg. Assn., Am. Coll. Surgeons (hon.), Am. Soc. Exptl. Pathology. Home: Baltimore, Md. Died Sept. 7, 1922.

HAM, Guy Andrews, lawyer; b. Boston, Mass., July 8, 1878; s. Benjamin A. and Louise H. H.; A.B., Dartmouth, 1900; LL.B., Harvard, 1903; m. Anna E. Hellberg, Mar. 16, 1908. Began practice at Boston, 1902; pres. Citizens Nat. Bank, Canton (Mass.) Trust Co., Stoughton Trust Co.; dir. Eastern Casualty Ins. Co., Jamaica Plain Trust Co.; treas. Cedar Grove Cemetery; treas. and dir. New Eng. Equity Corp.; clk. and trustee Grove Hall Savings Bank. Second asst. U.S. atty., 1904-08; mem. Mass. Ho. of Rep., 1903-04; mem. Governor's Council, 1913. Republican. Mason. Home: Milton, Mass. Died May 23, 1926.

HAMAN, B(enjamin) Howard, lawyer; b. Kent Co., Md., June 26, 1857; s. James and Mary E. (Howard) H.; A.B., Baltimore City Coll., 1875; LL.B., U. of Md., 1878; m. Louise Cowgill, Sept. 19, 1882. Practiced, Baltimore, from 1878; engaged in corp. practice, 1898-1930; retired. Active worker in reform movements, notably the "new judge" movement in Md.; advocate at successive meetings of legislature, 1888— of "Haman Bill"; promoter of plan for nat. park surrounding Dist. of Columbia, proposed by Hon. James J. Bryce. Democrat. Episcopalian. Home: Baltimore, Md. Died Sept. 13, 1932.

HAMANN, Carl August, surgeon; b. Davenport, Ia., Jan. 26, 1868; s. Claus H. and Marie (Koenig) H.; M.D., U. of Pa., 1890; m. Ella F. Ampt, Oct. 31, 1900; children—Elizabeth Marie, Carl A. Practiced in Cleveland, 1893—; prof. anatomy, 1893-1912, prof. applied anatomy and clin. surgery, 1912—, Western Reserve U. Sch. of Medicine, also dean; visiting surgeon St. Vincent's Charity and Cleveland City hosps. Fellow Am. Coll. Surgeons, Am. Surg. Assn. Republican. Unitarian. Home: Cleveland, O. Died Jan. 12, 1930.

HAMANN, Carl Ferdinand, goldsmith; b. Hoboken, N.J., Nov. 14, 1857; s. John Adolf and Henriette (Engel) H.; certificate Cooper Inst., New York; studied art in Berlin, Munich, École des Beaux Arts, Paris; m. Else Jahr, of Guben, Germany, Sept. 18, 1892. Worked as a modeler in silverware, later as goldsmith and sculptor; teacher of goldsmithing and modeling, Pratt Inst., Brooklyn, 1904—. Represented by figure of Justice at Buffalo Expn., figure of Modern Art, St. Louis Museum; bronze tablet, Columbia Univ. Lutheran. Home: Brooklyn, N.Y. Deceased.

HAMBLETON, Thomas Edward, banker; b. New Windsor, Md., May 17, 1829; grad. St. Mary's Coll., Baltimore; m. Sept. 15, 1852, Arabella, d. Maj. Dixon Stansbury, U.S.A. Was formerly in mercantile business; sr. mem. Hambleton & Co., bankers, until Jan. 1, 1905; retired. Home: Lutherville, Md. Died 1906.

HAMBURGER, Walter Wile, M.D.; b. Chicago, Ill., Sept. 10, 1881; s. Max and Annette W. (Wile) H.; B.S., U. of Chicago, 1903, M.S., 1904; M.D., Rush Med. Coll. (now a dept. of U. of Chicago), 1906; m. Edna Levis, Dec. 27, 1911; children—Elizabeth, Peter. Practiced, Chicago, 1909—, specializing in internal medicine; interne Presbyn. Hosp., 1907-08, asst. attending phys., 1909-12; attending physician at the Cook County Hospital, 1913-23; clin. prof. medicine, U. of Chicago; emeritus attending physician Michael Reese Hospital. Served as maj. M.C., U.S.A., 1917-19. Mem. advisory bd. Am. Bd. of Internal Medicine, member advisory board Psychosomatic Medicine. Home: Chicago, Ill. Died June 27, 1941.

HAMBY, William Henry, writer; b. Wright Co., Mo., Mar. 18, 1875; s. John Washington and Martha Josephine (Craig) H.; ed. Drury Coll. and U. of Mo. (non-grad.); m. Edna Lodge Cornue, Oct. 6, 1898; 1 son, William C. Editor and owner of newspapers at Meadville, Mo., Boulder, Colo., and Marceline, Mo., 1895-1905. Author: Getting and Holding, 1910; The Way of Success, 1918; The Desert Fiddler, 1919; Ranch of the Thorn, 1923; The Seventh Hunch (London), 1925; The House of Truth (four-act comedy), 1924. Home: San Diego, Calif. Died Jan. 25, 1928.

HAMER, Francis Gregg, lawyer; b. nr. Fostoria, O., Feb. 20, 1843; s. Francis and Mary (Mahan) H.; ed. pub. schs. of Ohio, Ind., and Ill.; student law sch., Indianapolis; m. Rebecca A. McCord, Dec. 6, 1869. Admitted to bar, 1864; began practice at Lincoln, Neb., 1870; removed to Kearney, 1872; judge, 10th Jud. Dist. of Neb., 1883-92; justice Supreme Court of Neb., term 1912-19. Republican. Home: Lincoln, Neb. Died July 1918.

HAMERSCHLAG, Arthur Arton, educator, engr.; b. Neb., Nov. 22, 1867; s. William and Francesca H. (Brummel) H.; ed. pub. schs., Omaha and New York, and pvt. tutors; (Sc.D., Lehigh U., 1907, Western U. of Pa., 1907; LL.D., Trinity Coll., Conn., 1912, Allegheny Coll., Pa., 1915); m. Elizabeth Ann Tollast, Dec. 23, 1901. In engring. field work U.S., Cuba, Mex., 1888-92; supt. St. George's Evening Trade Sch., New York, 1892-1904; pres. Carnegie Inst. Tech., Pittsburgh, 1903-22; dir. industrial research, Office of Maj. Gen. George W. Goethals; pres. Research Corp. New York, 1923—. Consulting engr. New York Trade Sch., Boys' Prep. Trade Sch., New York, Highland Falls (N.Y.) Evening Trade Sch., etc., until 1904. During same period in independent practice as consulting elec. and mech. engr. for numerous corps. and industries; mem. Smoke and Dust Abatement League of Pittsburgh (pres.), Schenley Memorial Commn., Pittsburgh Chamber of Commerce; mem. Internat. Jury of Award of Dept. of Edn., Pamana P.I. Expn., 1915. Home: Pittsburgh, Pa. Died July 20, 1927.

HAMERSLEY, James Hooker; b. New York, Jan. 26, 1844; grad. Columbia, 1865 (A.M.); Columbia Law School, LL.B., 1867; m. Margaret Willing Chisolm, April 30, 1888. Practiced law; retired to manage family property; nominated for legislature, 1877, but withdrew in favor of William Waldorf Astor. Many yrs. dir. Knickerbocker Fire Ins. Co.; pres. Knickerbocker Bowling Club; pres. Babies' Hospital; exec. com. Y.M.C.A. (23d st. branch). Author: The Seven Voices, 1898. Home: New York, N.Y. Died 1901.

HAMERSLEY, William, judge; b. Hartford, Conn., Sept. 9, 1838; s. William James and Laura S. (Cooke) H.; grad. Trinity Coll., 1858, A.M., 1865 (LL.D., 1893); studied Harvard Law Sch., 1859; m. Cynthia, d. Henry Williams, of Painesville, O., Oct. 19, 1870; 2d, Jane, d. John Allen of Old Saybrook, Conn., Oct. 25, 1882. Admitted to bar, 1859; city atty. Hartford, 1865-68; state's atty., 1868-88; judge Superior Ct., 1893-94; asso. justice Supreme Ct. of Errors of Conn., 1894-1908; retired. Democrat. Home: Hartford, Conn. Died Sept. 17, 1920.

HAMILL, Charles Humphrey, lawyer; b. Chicago, Mar. 20, 1868; s. Charles D. and Susan Fannie (Walbridge) H.; A.B., Yale, 1890. Larned and Clark scholar, 1890-91; LL.B., Northwestern U. Law Sch., 1893; m. Kathleen McDonald Mather-Smith, May 25, 1910. Admitted to bar, 1893; mem. Hubbard (J. D.) & Hamill, Dec. 1897-June 1898, Deneen (Charles Samuel) & Hamill, 1898-1905, Rosenthal (Lessing), Hamill & Wormser, 1906-36; now counsel to Rosenthal, Hamill, Eldridge & King. Attorney for ins. dept. of Ill., 1905-09. Hon. pres. Orchestral Assn.; mem. bd. of mgrs. Presbyn. Hosp. Del. Ill. Constl. Conv., 1920; pres. 2d Ward Rep. Club, 1906-10. Home: Chicago, Ill. Died Aug. 10, 1941.

HAMILL, Ernest Alfred, banker; b. Bloomington, Ind., July 1, 1851; s. Robert C. (M.D.) and Eliza Jane (Davisson) H.; lived in Chicago from age of 10 mos.; ed. pub. and high schs.; m. Eliza Soulard Corwith, Dec. 29, 1880. Banker, July 16, 1889—; chmn. bd., Ill. Merchants Trust Co., Chicago; v.p. Elgin Nat. Watch Co., Ill. Trust Safety Deposit Co.; treas. Chicago Stock Exchange, Chicago Bd. of Trade, Art Inst. Chicago. V.p. trustees Rush Med. Coll.; trustee Presbyn. Hosp., Chicago Home for Incurables. Home: Chicago, and Lake Forest, Ill. Died Jan. 14, 1927.

HAMILL, Howard M., Sunday school fieldworker; b. Lowndesboro, Ala., Aug. 10, 1849; s. Edward Joseph and Ann Jane H.; A.B., E. Ala. Coll., Auburn, 1868 (A.M., 1900; D.D., Ill. Coll., 1900); m. Ada L. Tuman, July 7, 1885. Served C.S.A. under Gen. R. E. Lee, 1864-65; supt. city schs. in Mo. and Ill., 1872-85; pres. Mo. State Teachers' Assn., 1881; entered Meth. ministry, 1885; established in Ill., the first of the State S.S. normal depts., 1889; S.S. normal supt., Ill. State S.S. Assn., 1889-96; internat. S.S. field sec., 1896-1902; chmn. Ill. Conf. and S.S. com. at Gen. Conf., 1900; supt. training work, M.E. Ch., South, 1900—; chmn. com. on edn. Internat. S.S. Assn., 1902—. Chaplain-gen. U.C.V., 1913—. Author: Legion of Honor Normal Course of Study; The Sunday School Teacher; International Lesson History; The Bible and Its Books. Home: Nashville, Tenn. Died Jan. 22, 1915.

HAMILL, James A., congressman; b. Jersey City, N.J., Mar. 30, 1877; B.A., St. Peter's Coll., N.J., 1897; M.A., 1898, LL.D., 1912; LL.B., N.Y. Law Sch., 1899. Admitted to bar, 1900, and began practice at Jersey City; admitted to bar of U.S. Supreme Court, 1918, N.Y. bar, 1922. Mem. N.J. Assembly, 4 terms, 1902-06; mem. 60th to 62d Congresses (1907-13), 10th N.J. Dist. and 63d to 66th Congresses (1913-21), 12th Dist.; then 1st asst. corp. counsel of City of Jersey City, later corp. counsel. Chevalier of French Legion of Honor. Democrat. Home: Jersey City, N.J. Died Dec. 15, 1941.

HAMILTON, Albert Hine, micro-chem. investigator; b. Weedsport, N.Y., Dec. 10, 1859; s. James Theodore and Clarissa (Hine) H.; Ph.G., Coll. of Pharmacy of City of New York (now dept. Columbia U.), 1885; specialized later with expert tutors; m. Jessie Eccles, Feb. 1, 1888. Pharmacist, 1887-1911; formerly chemist, Auburn Bd. of Health; frequently called as expert chemist in legal proceedings, appearing in upwards of 300 homicide cases and hundreds of cases pertaining to forgery, arson, burglary, bomb assaults, etc. Discovered by test shots into human bodies, how to identify the "contact shot" in homicide cases; originated a system of examination of exhibits in circumstantial evidence cases whereby the exhibits reveal the truth, regardless of claims to the contrary; discovered by test shots, that the fine scratches on murder bullets which have been relied upon by forensic ballistics to identify a suspected firearm, are not made by the barrel interior but by the crimping of the cartridge shell and the hot escaping exploding powder. Republican. Presbyn. Mason. Home: Auburn, N.Y. Died July 1, 1938.

HAMILTON, Alexander, soldier; b. New York, Nov. 15, 1815; s. Col. John Church (a.d.c. to Gen. Harrison in War of 1812) and Maria Eliza (Van Den Heuvel) H.; grandson Alexander Hamilton (sec. treasury, 1789-95); ed. by pvt. tutors, attended lectures in Columbia Coll. at 14; spl. student U.S. Mil. Acad., 1838-40; m. Elizabeth Nicoll, 1842; m. 2d, Sarah E. Bodine, 1880. With Gen. Phil. Kearny, paying Winnebago Indians in West, 1840; afterward on duty in New York; returned to civil life, and in 1858 settled at Ramapo Valley (now Suffern), where, as lay reader, founded Christ Ch. (P.E.). When Ft. Sumpter was fired upon, reported for duty to Maj. Gen. Sandford; hurried troops to Washington from Apr. 16, 1861; reported to Lt. Gen. Scott, May 20, 1861; after that his a.d.c.; comd. div. guarding fords on Potomac River until Gen. Banks arrived at Harper's Ferry; sent to reconnoitre Fortress Monroe, Aug. 8; apptd. brig. gen. by President Lincoln, Aug. 12, 1861; later engaged in raising regts. in N.Y.; was in spl. service under President; took part in suppressing draft riots in New York. Took 6,000 men to Grant, in May 1864, etc., serving until end of war and becoming maj. gen. Episcopalian. Republican. Home: Tarrytown-on-Hudson, N.Y. Died 1907.

HAMILTON, Alexander, lawyer; b. Granville Co., N.C., Mar. 18, 1851; s. Robert Alston and Sarah (Alexander) H.; grad. Va. Mil. Inst., 1871; asst. prof., same, 1871-73; LL.B., Washington and Lee U., 1873; m. Helen Leslie McGill, Jan. 31, 1883. Admitted to Va. bar, 1873; 1st v.p., gen. counsel Atlantic Coast Line R.R. Co.; pres., gen. counsel Petersburg Savings & Ins. Co. Pres. bd. visitors Va. Central State Hosp. for Insane, 1882-85; mem. bd. visitors Va. Mil. Inst., 1891-1909 (pres. bd. about last 10 yrs. of service); mem. Va. Constl. Conv., 1901-02. Democrat. Episcopalian. Home: Petersburg, Va. Died Feb. 4, 1916.

HAMILTON, Allan McLane, physician; b. Brooklyn, Oct. 6, 1848; s. Philip (youngest son Alexander Hamilton) and Rebecca (McLane) H.; M.D., Coll. Phys. and Surg. (Columbia), 1870; m. May C. Tomlinson, Mar. 27, 1902. Specialist nervous diseases; testified for govt. as expert in trial of assassin Guiteau; prof. mental diseases, Cornell U. Med. Coll., 1900-03. Author: Medical Jurisprudence, 1883. Home: Great Barrington, Mass. Died Nov. 23, 1919.

HAMILTON, Alston, army officer; b. nr. Oxford, N.C., Oct. 20, 1871; s. Robert Alston and Martha Elizabeth (Venable) H.; prep. edn., University Sch., Petersburg, Va.; grad. U.S. Mil. Acad., 1894; grad. Army War Coll., Washington, 1914, again 1922; m. Nancy Thompson Creel, Oct. 20, 1896; children—John Creel, Alston (dau.). Commd. 2d lt. U.S.A., June 12, 1894; promoted through grades to brig. gen., Jan. 19, 1927. Served in Cuba, Spanish-Am. War (silver star citation for gallantry at El Caney), later in Philippines (silver star for gallantry at Calamba); instr. mathematics U.S. Mil. Acad., 1899-1903, in ballistics and seacoast engring., Ft. Monroe, Va., 1904-09; mem. and pres. Arty. Bd. for a number of yrs., later mem. Ordnance Bd., Sandy Hook Proving Ground; in comd. coast defenses Eastern N.Y., 1917; went to France as col. 58th Arty., C.A.C., May 1918; participated at St. Mihiel, Sept. 12-16, 1918; assigned as comdr. 35th Arty. Brigade, Oct. 1918; comdr. Panama Coast Arty. Dist., 1919-21; executive of 9th Coast Arty. Dist., hdqrs. Presidio, San Francisco, 1922-26; prof. mil. science and tactics, Mass. Inst. Tech., 1926-27; assigned as comdr. 2d Coast Arty. Dist., Jan. 1927, comdr. 11th Field Arty. Brigade, Schofield Barracks, Oahu, T.H., 1927-30; comdr. 1st Coast Arty. Dist., 1930-35; retired, Oct. 20, 1935. Presbyn. Died Dec. 18, 1937.

HAMILTON, Charles Elbert, clergyman; b. Delphi, N.Y., July 26, 1865; s. Rev. Burdette W. and Caroline (Leet) H.; A.B., Syracuse U., 1886, A.M., 1889, D.D., 1901; B.D., Drew Theol. Sem., 1889; m. Carrie May Cuykendall, July 14, 1886; 1 dau., Ruth (wife of Rev. Seth N. Genung). Entered M.E. ministry, 1882; pastor Eaton, N.Y., 1885-87, Leona, Pa., 1889, Cortland, N.Y., 1890-94, Geneva, N.Y., 1895, First Ch., Rochester, N.Y., 1896-1905, Trinity Ch., Albany, N.Y., 1905-08, University Av. Ch., Syracuse, 1908-15; pres. Cazenovia (N.Y.) Sem., 1915—. Pres. bd. trustees Central N.Y. Conf. M.E. Ch.; v.p. Ch. Ins. Assn., Rochester; mem. Bd. Edn. of M.E. Ch., 1924-28; mem. Univ. Senate M.E. Ch. Mason. Home: Cazenovia, N.Y. Died Aug. 5, 1933.

HAMILTON, Charles Sumner, surgeon; b. Columbus, O., Sept. 30, 1863; s. John Waterman and Rachel (Worden) H.; A.B., Princeton, 1884; M.D., Columbus Med. Coll., 1887; LL.D., Kenyon, 1917; m. Mrs. Elizabeth Loving Brown, 1909. Practiced at Columbus from 1887; prof. surgery, Ohio State U., 1921-27 (emeritus); surgeon Hawke's Hosp. of Mt. Carmel. Fellow Am. Coll. Surgeons. Republican. Episcopalian. Home: Columbus, O. Died June 1936.

HAMILTON, Clarence Grant, musician; b. Providence, R.I., June 9, 1865; s. John Alexander and Mary Elizabeth (Prentice) H.; A.B., Brown U., 1888, A.M., 1900; studied music with Edward Hoffman, H. C. Macdougall, Arthur Foote, G. W. Chadwick, Edward Dannreuther, Tobias Matthay; m. Ada Alice Anthony, Nov. 30, 1893; 1 son, Wallace Field. Teacher, Providence, 1888-89; teacher of music, Providence, 1889-1904, acting as organist at various chs.; asso. prof. music, 1904-17, prof., 1918-33, Wellesley Coll. Lecturer Boston U., 1917-19, 1923-25, 1930, Columbia U., summer 1926. Unitarian. Author: Outlines of Music History, 1908, 13, 24; Piano Teaching, 1910; Sound, and Its Relation to Music, 1911; Music Appreciation, 1920; Piano Music, 1925; Epochs in Musical Progress, 1925; Touch and Expression in Piano Playing, 1927; What Every Piano Pupil Should Know, 1928; Ornaments in Classical and Modern Music, 1929. Composer songs, piano pieces and anthems. Editor Music Students' Piano Course, 1918—. Departmental editor Étude, 1922—. Home: Wellesley Hills, Mass. Died Feb. 14, 1935.

HAMILTON, David Gilbert, capitalist; b. Chicago, Jan. 10, 1842; s. Polemus Draper and Cynthia (Holmes) H.; A.B., Asbury (now De Pauw) U., 1865, A.M., 1868; LL.B., Douglas U., Chicago, 1867; m. Mary Jane Kendall, Dec. 6, 1870. Was pres. Anglo-Am. Land & Claim Assn. in Tex., 1890; pres. Texas & Mexican Central R.R.; pres. Nat. Ry. of Ill. and its 7 subsidiary cos., St. Louis, 1889-99; pres. Chicago City Ry. Co., 1899-1905; dir. Union Mut. Life Ins. Co. of Me., Farmers' and Mechanics' Nat. Bank, Ft. Worth, Tex. Trustee U. of Chicago, De Pauw U. Mason. Home: Chicago, Ill. Died Feb. 16, 1915.

HAMILTON, Edward John, author; b. Belfast, Ireland, Nov. 29, 1834; s. William (D.D.) and Anna (Patterson) H.; A.B., Hanover (Ind.) Coll., 1853, later A.M.; grad. Princeton Theol. Sem., 1858; (S.T.D., Wabash Coll., 1877; D.D., Monmouth [Ill.] College, 1877; LL.D., Hanover [Ind.] College, 1917); m. Eliza Hume, Sept. 23, 1867. Ordained Presbyn. ministry, 1858; pastor Oyster Bay, L.I., 1858-61; evangelist Dromore, Ireland, 1862; chaplain 7th N.J. Vet. Inf., 1863-65; pastor Hamilton, O., 1866-68; prof. mental philosophy, Hanover Coll., 1868-79; acting prof. ethics, economics, politics and logic, Princeton, 1882-83; prof. philosophy, Hamilton Coll., 1883-91; definer and reviewer Standard Dictionary, 1891-94; prof. philosophy, Whitworth Coll., 1894-95; State U. of Wash., 1895-1900. Author of system of metaphysical philosophy, entitled "Perceptionalism." Author: A New Analysis in Fundamental Morals, 1870; The Human Mind, 1883; The Modalist, 1883; The Perceptionalist, or Mental Science, 1899; The Moral Law, or the Theory and Practice of Duty, 1902; Rational Orthodoxy, 1917. Home: Plainfield, N.J. Died Nov. 21, 1918.

HAMILTON, Edward La Rue, congressman; b. Niles, Mich., Dec. 9, 1857; s. Edward L. and Margaret (Jameson) H.; ed. in pub. schs.; m. Cora V. Eddy, Oct. 18, 1883. Admitted to bar, 1884, and since in practice at Niles, Mich. Mem. 55th and 66th Congresses (1897-21), 4th Mich. Dist. Republican. Home: Niles, Mich. Died Nov. 2, 1923.

HAMILTON, Finley, congressman; b. Vincent, Ky., June 19, 1886; s. William C. and Rachel H.; ed. Berea Coll. and spl. law course; m. Lily Bruner, Mar. 18, 1915; 1 dau., Laura Lee. Admitted to Ky. bar, 1915, and practiced since at London, Ky. Capt. Signal Corps, U.S.A., World War; participated in St. Mihiel and Argonne offensives; commended by Brig. Gen. U. G. Alexander for conduct under fire. Mem. 73d Congress (1933-35), Ky. at large. Democrat. Mason. Home: London, Ky. Died Jan. 10, 1940.

HAMILTON, Frank Hastings, ry. official; b. N.Y. City, Sept. 5, 1865; s. Frank Hastings and Julia Augusta (White) H.; B.S., U. of France, 1883; m. May Tappen, 1896; 1 son, Frank Hastings. Sec. to gen. agt. express dept. B.&O. R.R., at N.Y. City, 1885-87; clk. to 2d v.p. St.L.&S.F. Ry., N.Y. City, 1888-90; chief Lake R.R. Co., 1901, and successively gen. atty. for Calif., asst. gen. counsel and gen. solicitor same. Republican. Episcopalian. Home: Pasadena, Calif. Died Nov. 23, 1931.

HAMILTON, Franklin Elmer Ellsworth, bishop, educator; b. Pleasant Valley, O., Aug. 9, 1866; s. William Charles Patrick and Henrietta Maria (Dean) H.; bro. of John William Hamilton; A.B., Harvard U., 1887; S.T.B., Boston U., 1892, Ph.D., 1900; studied univs. of Berlin and Paris nearly 3 yrs.; m. Mary Mackie Pierce, Apr. 25, 1895. Prof. Greek and Latin, Chattanooga U., 1887, 1888; ordained M.E. ministry, 1892; organized and built ch., E. Boston, Mass., 1892-95; pastor Newtonville, Mass., 1895-1900, First Ch., Boston, 1900-08; chancellor and trustee American Univ., Washington, 1908-16; elected bishop M.E. Church, May 19, 1916. Made trip around the world to study missions and religions, 1905-06; has written on results of observations, and lectures widely before socs. and confs., prepared the handbook of bibliography used in the celebration in America of the 200th anniversary of the birth of John Wesley. Wrote: The Cup of Fire; Lodestar and Compass. Pres. Epworth League of N.E., 1902-04; v.p. Epworth League of the World. Republican. Home: Pittsburgh, Pa. Died May 4, 1918.

HAMILTON, Frederick William, clergyman, educator; b. Portland, Me., Mar. 30, 1860; s. Jonas and Angelina (Sawyer) H.; A.B., Tufts Coll., 1880, A.M., 1886; spl. course Tufts Div. Sch., 1890; D.D., Tufts, 1899; LL.D., St. Lawrence, 1906; m. Florence Quintard Mead, June 25, 1884; m. 2d, Emma Tuttle James, Mar. 4, 1912. Ry. clerk, 1880-89; entered Universalist ministry, 1889; pastor First Ch., Pawtucket, R.I., 1889-95, First Ch., Roxbury (Boston), 1895-1906; pres. Tufts Coll., Apr. 1, 1905-Dec. 31, 1913. Mem. Mass. State Bd. of Edn., 1909-20. Sec. Com. on Edn. United Typothetæ of America, 1913-27. Republican. Mason. Author: The Church and Secular Life, 1894. Home: Cambridge, Mass. Died May 22, 1940.

HAMILTON, George Anson, electrical engr.; b. Cleveland, O., Dec. 30, 1843; s. Daniel and Elizabeth A. (Beardsley) H.; ed. pub. schs.; m. Nellie F. Park, Dec. 15, 1880; children—Corinne F. (Mrs. R. H. Smith), Edith A. In telegraph and ry. signaling service, 1860-73; asst. to Prof. Moses G. Farmer, a pioneer elec. inventor of New England, 1873-75; asst. engr. and engr. Western Union Telegraph Co., at N.Y. City, 1875-89; engr., Western Electric Co., N.Y. City, 1889-1909 (retired). Fellow Am. Inst. Elec. Engrs. (treas., 1895-1930). Republican. Presbyterian. Home: Elizabeth, N.J. Died Jan. 10, 1935.

HAMILTON, George Hall, astronomer; b. of Am. parents, London, Eng., Jan. 31, 1884; s. John McLure and Clara Augusta (Raiguel) H.; brought to U.S. in infancy; M.A., Trinity Coll., Cambridge U., Eng., 1911; m. Elizabeth Langdon Williams, June 2, 1922. Prof. astronomy, Bellevue (Neb.) Coll., 1910-14; astronomer Lowell Obs., 1917-22; astronomer Jamaica br. Harvard Coll. Obs., 1922-24; working privately, 1924—. Fellow, Royal Astron. Soc. (Eng.). Republican. Episcopalian. Author: Mars at Its Nearest, 1925. Died Aug. 4, 1935.

HAMILTON, George Livingstone, univ. prof.; b. Boston, Mass., July 24, 1874; s. John and Ellen (Nicol) H.; A.B., Harvard, 1895, A.M., 1897; Columbia, 1899-1900, U. of Paris, 1901-02; Ph.D., Columbia, 1903; m. Anita Wheelwright Sargent, June 15, 1908; children—Anne S., G.L., Violet S. Instr. Romance langs., U. of Cincinnati, 1900-01; prof. same, Trinity Coll., Durham, N.C., 1902-03; instr. same, U. of Mich., 1903-11; asst. prof. Romance languages, 1911-16, prof., 1916—, Cornell U. Fellow Mediæval Acad. of America. Democrat. Author: The Indebtedness of Chaucer's Troilus and Creseyde to Guido delle Colonne's Historia Trojana, 1903. Home: Ithaca, N.Y. Died Sept. 25, 1940.

HAMILTON, Hamilton, painter; b. Eng., Apr. 1, 1847. Began as portrait painter at Buffalo, N.Y., 1872; specialty now landscapes. Represented in Buffalo Fine Arts Acad., etc., A.N.A., 1886, N.A., 1889; mem. Am. Water Color Soc. Home: Norwalk, Conn. Died Jan. 4, 1928.

HAMILTON, Hollister Adelbert, philologist; b. Savannah, N.Y., Jan. 14, 1870; s. Hollister and Mary Ann (Belcher) H.; A.B., U. of Rochester, 1892; student U. of Chicago; Ph.D., Johns Hopkins, 1899; m. Alice Wallbridge Dransfield, Apr. 25, 1905; children—Sarah Elizabeth, Dransfield, Mary Alice. Instr. Latin and Greek, U. of Rochester, 1894-96; lecturer in Greek, Bryn Mawr Coll., 1899-1900; prof. classical philology, 1900—, acting pres., 1918, v.p., 1918—, Elmira Coll. Pres. bd. of trustees Steele Memorial Library, Elmira, Fedn. for Social Service. Republican. Episcopalian. Author: The Negative Compounds in Greek (monograph), 1899. Home: Elmira, N.Y. Died May 23, 1939.

HAMILTON, James Edward, mfr.; b. Two Rivers, Wis., May 19, 1852; s. Henry Carter and Diantha (Smith) H.; ed. pub. schs., Two Rivers and Lockport, N.Y.; m. Etta Shove, Aug. 5, 1880; children—Grace Leigh (Mrs. John Steele Sweeney, dec.), George Spalding. Chmn. bd. Hamilton Mfg. Co., mfrs. printers' furniture, Two Rivers, The Aluminum Goods Mfg. Co., Manitowoc, Wis.; pres. Hotel Vista Corp., Pasadena, Calif. Alderman, Two Rivers, 1888; mayor of Two Rivers, 1893-95. Pres. Hamilton Foundation. Democrat. Conglist. Mason, Elk. Gave Community Recreation Bldg. to City of Two Rivers. Home: Two Rivers, Wis., and Pasadena, Calif. Died May 7, 1940.

HAMILTON, J(ames) Kent, lawyer; b. Milan, O., May 17, 1839; s. Thomas and Sarah O. (Standart) H.; A.B., Kenyon Coll., 1859, A.M., 1862 (LL.D., 1912); m. Ethel Beecher Allen, July 27, 1898. Asst. prof. English lit. and history, Kenyon Coll., 1860-61; pvt. to capt. 113th Regt., Ohio Vol. Inf., Civil War; participated in battles Middle Tenn., Chickamauga, Missionary Ridge, Atlanta Campaign, Sherman's March to Sea, etc. Admitted to bar, 1865; mem. Hamilton & Ford, 1870-88, Hamilton, Kirby & Conn, 1908—; dir. and atty. Ohio Savings Bank & Trust Co. (exec. com.), The B. A. Stevens Co. Pros. atty., Toledo, 1867; pros. atty., Lucas Co., O., 1867-71; city solicitor of Toledo, 1875-79; mayor of Toledo, 1887-91; mem. Bd. Sinking Fund Trustees, 12 yrs.; mem. Bd. of Edn., 7 yrs. (most of time pres.); judge advocate gen. of Ohio on staff of gov., 1896-1900; nominated for Congress, 1910; pres. of commn. to prepare new charter for Toledo, 1913-14. Republican. Episcopalian. Home: Toledo, O. Died Dec. 29, 1919.

HAMILTON, James McLellan, educator; b. Annapolis, Ill., Oct. 1, 1861; s. James and Mary (Burner) H.; B.S., Union Christian Coll., 1887, M.S., 1890; student, Harvard U., 1898; LL.D., Montana State U., 1830; m. Emma Shideler, June 6, 1888 (died 1909); m. 2d, Florence Ballinger, Aug. 21, 1918. Supt. city schs., Sumner, Ill., 1887-89, Missoula, Mont., 1889-1901; prof. history and economics, U. of Mont., Missoula, 1901-04; pres. Mont. State Coll. of Agr. and Mech. Arts, 1904-19; dean of men and prof. economics, same coll., 1919—. Mem. Mont. State Bd. Edn., 1893-1901. Republican. Unitarian. Mason. Traveled and studied agr. in Europe, 1912; studied agrl. economics at Cornell U., summer 1922, economics at U. of Calif., summer 1923, and terminal marketing at U. of Chicago, 1925. Wrote: Montana Civics (sect. of Hughes Civics), 1921. Home: Bozeman, Mont. Died Sept. 23, 1940.

HAMILTON, Jay Benson, clergyman; b. West Chester, O., Dec. 19, 1847; s. Rev. William C. Patrick and Henrietta Maria (Dean) H.; bro. of Bishop John W. and Bishop Franklin E. E. H.; B.S., A.B., Mt. Union Coll., Alliance, O. (D.D., 1892); m. Mary Florence Harvey, May 14, 1870. Ordained M.E. ministry, 1872; pastor Somerville, Mass., 1872-74, Manchester, N.H., 1875-77, Lewiston, Me., 1878-80, Providence, R.I., 1883-85; pres. Walden U., Nashville, Tenn., 1901-04; pastor 1st Ch., Williamsburgh, Brooklyn, 1917-18; retired from active ministry, Apr. 1919, closing 17 yrs. in pastorate of 5 chs. in Greater New York. Editor Bible Champion and gen. sec.-treas. of Bible League of N. America. Pioneer in movement to pension aged M.E. ministers. Republican. Mason. Died Jan. 1920.

HAMILTON, John, farmer; b. Juniata Co., Pa., Feb. 19, 1843; s. Hugh and Sarah Gettys (McDowell) H.; B.S., Pa. State Coll., 1871, M.A.S., 1872; m. Elizabeth McFarlane Thompson, Oct. 27, 1875. Was mem. Juniata cav. before Civil War; served in 1st Pa. Reserve Vol. Cav., 1861-64, pvt. to sergt. maj., in Army of Potomac. Prof. agr., 1871-80, business mgr. and treas., 1874-86, treas., 1874-1911, Pa. State Coll. Deputy sec. agr. of Pa., 1895-99, sec. agr. of Pa., 1899-1903; farmers' inst. specialist, U.S. Dept. of Agr., 1903-Jan. 1, 1914. Dir. Thompson Land & Coal Co. Presbyn. Republican. Mem. Union Veteran Legion. Author of ann. reports of Dept. of Agr. of Pa., 1899-1902. Address: State College, Pa. Died July 5, 1921.

HAMILTON, John Alan, lawyer; b. Toledo, O., Jan. 5, 1871; s. John A. and Harriet Hale (Rowland) H.; grad. Michigan Mil. Acad., Orchard Lake, Mich., 1888; Ph.B., Cornell U., 1892, LL.B., 1893, LL.M., 1894; m. Lorraine E. Melvin, June 2, 1896. Admitted to N.Y. bar, 1894, and began practice at Buffalo; apptd. mem. Inferior Criminal Courts Commn. (the Page Commn.), which reorganized the Magistrates' Courts of Greater New York, established the City Court of Buffalo, etc., 1909-10; apptd. a mem. Reconstruction Commn. of State of N.Y. and served as chmn. its com. on housing, 1919-20; asst. collector internal revenue, 28th Dist. of N.Y., 1921—. Lecturer on law of Insurance, U. of Buffalo, 1914-17. Mem. Legal Aid Bur. of Buffalo (counsel; pres.). Republican. Episcopalian. Home: Buffalo, N.Y. Died Oct. 5, 1930.

HAMILTON, John L., banker; b. Shipman, Ill., May 8, 1862; s. John L. and A. E. H.; ed. Watseka, Ill.; m. Mary A. Hall, Feb. 9, 1892. Went to Watseka, Ill., 1875, where was instrumental in organizing Citizens' Bank, and later became mem. Burwell, Hamilton & Morgan; now sr. mem. Hamilton & Cunningham, bankers, Hoopeston, Ill.; pres. Commercial Trust & Savings Bank, Danville, Ill. Mayor of Hoopeston, 1897-1901. Home: Hoopeston, Ill. Died Feb. 3, 1927.

HAMILTON, John Marshall, lawyer, gov.; b. Ridgewood, Ohio, May 28, 1847; s. Samuel and Nancy (McMorris) H.; went to Ill., 1854; brought up on farm nr. Wenoma; served in Civil war in 141st Ill., 1864-65; grad. Ohio Wesleyan U., 1866; taught in acad. at Henry, Ill., and later prof. languages Ill. Wesleyan; studied law; m. Helen W. Williams, 1870. Admitted to bar, 1870; practiced in Bloomington; mem. Ill. senate, 1876-80; lt. gov., 1880-82; gov., 1882-84, to fill remainder of term of Gov. Cullom, who was elected to U.S. Senate. Resumed law practice, 1885. Later removed to Chicago. Home: Chicago, Ill. Died 1905.

HAMILTON, John McLure, artist; b. Phila., Jan. 31, 1853; s. George (M.D.) and Caroline (Delaplaine) H.; studied at Pa. Acad. Fine Arts, Royal Acad., Antwerp, Jérôme Atelier, Beaux Arts, Paris; settled in London, 1878; married; 1 son, George Hall. Specialty, portraits and pastels; principal works: Gladstone (in Luxembourg Gallery); Gladstone at Hawarden, Richard Vaux, Cardinal Manning, George Meredith, and Henry Thonron, in Pa. Acad. Fine Arts.; Prof. Tyndall, Onslow Ford, Cosmo Monkhouse, and M. Ridley Corbet, in Nat. Portrait Gallery, London; Prof. Lewis Campbell, in University of St. Andrews; portraits of Gen. Booth, Dr. Archibald Geikie, Col. Edward M. House, Joseph Pennell, Charles M. Burns, Judge Alexander Simpson, etc. Hon. mention Paris Salon; gold medals, Buffalo, St. Louis, Pa. Acad., etc. Mem. advisory com. Panama-Pacific Expn., 1915; advisory council Art Assn. of Phila. Home: Kingston-on-Thames, Eng. Died Sept. 10, 1936.

HAMILTON, John Taylor, banker; b. Geneseo, Ill., Oct. 16, 1843; s. James Steel and Mary Elizabeth (Taylor) H.; acad. edn., Geneseo, Ill.; m. Sarah Ann Jones, of St. Andrews, Que., Can., Oct. 16, 1873. In mercantile business, Cedar Rapids, Ia., 1868—; pres. Hamilton Seed & Coal Co.; chmn. bd. Merchants Nat. Bank, and of Urbana Savings Bank; treas. St. Martin Land Co. Mayor of Cedar Rapids, 1878; co. supervisor, 1882-84; mem. Ia. Ho. of Rep., 1886-88 (speaker 1890); mem. 52d Congress (1891-93), 5th Ia. Dist.; mem. Bd. Control of State Instns., Ia., 1906-09; Dem. candidate for gov., 1914. Mason. Episcopalian. Home: Cedar Rapids, Ia. Deceased.

HAMILTON, John William, bishop; b. Weston, Va., Mar. 18, 1845; s. William Cooper Patrick and Henrietta Maria (Dean) H.; A.B., Mt. Union Coll., Ohio, 1865, LL.D., 1905, S.T.D., 1927; S.T.B., Boston U., 1871; A.M., Wesleyan U., Conn., 1877; D.D., Baker U., 1880; LL.D., U. of Southern Calif., 1905, De Pauw, 1905; L.H.D., American U.; m. Julia Elizabeth Battelle, Dec. 24, 1873 (died 1883); 1 son, Gordon Battelle; m. 2d, Emma Lydia Battelle, Dec. 18, 1888 (died 1915); 1 dau., Helene (Mrs. Geoffrey Wardle Stafford). Licensed to preach, M.E. Ch., 1865; deacon, 1868; elder, 1870; pastor Newport, O., 1866-68, Maplewood, Mass., 1868-70, Somerville, 1870-72, First Church, Boston, 1872-75, People's Church, Boston, 1875-84 (founder), Somerville, Mass., 1884-88, East Boston, 1888-92; corr. sec. Freedmen's Aid and Southern Edn. Soc., 1892-1900; bishop, May 1900—; chancellor American U., Washington, D.C., 1916-22, chancellor emeritus, 1922—. Chmn. commn. of Am. Methodists to create and present to Lincoln Coll., Oxford, memorial of John Wesley on 200th anniversary of his election as a fellow. Mason. Home: Washington, D.C. Deceased.

HAMILTON, Peter Joseph, author, lawyer; b. Mobile, Ala., Mar. 19, 1859; s. Peter and Anna Martha (Beers) H.; A.B., Princeton, 1879, A.M., 1882; mental science fellowship, and later attended U. of Leipzig; also law courses, univs. of Va. and Ala., 1881-82; LL.B., U. of Ala., 1882, LL.D., 1910, and Spring Hill Coll., 1911; m. Rachel Wheeler, d. Rev. Dr. J. R. Burgett, of Mobile, June 30, 1891; children—Peter Vernon (dec.), Anna Carlotta, Rachel Duke (wife of E. A. Can, U.S.A.). Practiced at Mobile; has been city atty. there; French consular agt., 1911-13; judge U.S. Dist. Ct., Dist. of P.R., 1913-21. Prof. constl. law, in Law Sch. of U. of P.R., 1921-25, also practicing law at San Juan. Pres. Iberville Hist. Soc. of Mobile. Author: International Public Law (with Hannis Taylor), 1901; Colonization of the South (Vol. 3, History of N. America), 1904; The Reconstruction Period (Vol. 16 in same series), 1906; Origin and Growth of the Common Law in England and America; Puerto Rico Federal Reports (Vols. 6 to 12). Home: San Juan, P.R. Died July 13, 1927.

HAMILTON, Samuel King, lawyer; b. Waterboro, Me., July 27, 1837; s. Benjamin Ricker and Sarah (Carle) H.; B.S and M.S., Chandler Scientific Sch., Dartmouth, 1859; m. Annie E. Davis, Feb. 13, 1867. Admitted to Me. bar, 1862; practiced at Alfred till 1867, Biddeford till 1872, Boston and Wakefield, Mass., 1872—; counsel in many important civ. and criminal causes; mem. Hamilton & Eaton. Mem. Me. Ho. of Rep., 1872; mem. Sch. Com., Wakefield, 13 yrs.; town counsel 20 yrs.; Bd. of Selectmen 4 yrs. (chmn.), etc. Mason. Author: The Hamiltons of Waterborough, their Ancestors and Descendants, 1912. Home: Wakefield, Mass. Died May 8, 1922.

HAMILTON, Schuyler, soldier; b. New York, July 25, 1822; s. John Church H.; g.s. Alexander H., the statesman; grad. U.S. Mil. Acad., 1841; served on frontier as lt., 1st inf.; was asst. instr. tactics, West Point; served with distinction through Mexican war, especially at battle of Monterey and at Mil Flores, where he overcame a number of Mexicans in hand-to-hand encounter, winning praise in official report of Gen. Scott; was a.d.c. to latter, 1849-54; retired from service, engaging in business in New York. Entered Union army as pvt., 1861, but soon after was on staff of Gen. B. F. Butler; later mil. sec. Gen. Scott, until latter retired, Oct. 31, 1861; promoted col. and asst. chief of staff to Gen. H. W. Halleck; brig. gen. vols., Nov. 12, 1861; took leading part in campaigns of armies of the Tenn. and Cumberland; for services at Island No. 10 and at battle of New Madrid, promoted maj. gen. vols., Sept. 17, 1862; comd. reserve at battle of Farmington, but Feb. 27, 1863, retired because of failing health. Was hydrographic engr., dept. of docks, New York, 1871-75. Died 1903.

HAMILTON, Stanislaus Murray, archivist; b. Washington, May 15, 1855; ed. Gonzaga Coll., Washington; Coll. Sainte Barbe, Paris, France; m. Katharine, d. Rev. Mark L. Olds, g.d. Nathan Sargent ("Oliver Oldschool"), Sept. 29, 1880. Associated from 1880 with the records of the Continental Congress and kindred hist. records in U.S. Dept. of State. Corr. mem. R.I. Hist. Soc.; mem. Va. Hist. Soc. Editor: The Writings of James Monroe (the 1st collected edit.); Letters to Washington, being the inauguration by The Soc. of the Colonial Dames of America of the printing of hitherto unpublished manuscripts. Attached to Diplomatic Bureau, July 1903—. Home: Brookland, D.C. Died 1909.

HAMILTON, Thomas Benton, ry. official; b. Columbus, O., Aug. 7, 1865; s. John Waterman (M.D.) and Rachel (Worden) H.; A.B., Princeton, 1888; m. Flora Brent, Jan. 26, 1897; children—Mrs. Winifred H. Bishop, John W., Mrs. Flora H. Cravens, Virginia R. With Pa. Co. or its subsidiaries, 1888—, beginning as rodman Jeffersonville, Madison & Indianapolis Ry., at Louisville, Ky.; asst. to engr. corps Pittsburgh div., P.,C.,C.&St.L. Ry., 1890-96; asst. engr. Pittsburgh div., P.,C.,C.&St.L. Ry., 1896-97; engr. maintenance of way, Toledo div. Pa. Co. until 1898; same, Cincinnati div., P.,C.,C.&St.L. Ry., 1898-1900; engr. m. of w. Cleveland and Pittsburgh div. Pa. Co., 1900-01; supt. Erie & Ashtabula div., 1901-03, Cleveland & Pittsburgh div., 1903-12; gen. supt. Central system Pa. Lines West of Pittsburgh, 1912-14; gen. mgr. Vandalia R.R., at St. Louis, 1914-17; resident v.p. Pa. Lines West of Pittsburgh, at St. Louis, 1917-18; gen. supt. St. Louis System, Pa. lines west of Pittsburgh, at Indianapolis, 1918-20; apptd. gen. mgr. Northwestern region Pa. System, at Chicago, Mar. 1920, regional v.p. and gen. mgr., Nov. 15, 1924, v.p. and gen. mgr. Western region, Chicago, June 1, 1925-29; v.p., Chicago, 1929-32, now retired. Home: Culver, Ind. Died Feb. 18, 1939.

HAMILTON, Thomas Jefferson, editor Augusta Chronicle; b. Grovetown, Ga., Nov. 20, 1885; s. William Winslow and Katherine Fleming (Mosley) H.; student Mercer U., Macon, Ga.; m. Daisye Ramsey, June 10, 1908; children—Thomas J., Alice Ramsey, Walton Winslow. Began as reporter Augusta Herald, 1906; city editor Augusta Chronicle, 1908-10; mng. editor Augusta Herald, 1910-17; editor Augusta Chronicle, 1919—; dir. Ga. & Fla. R.R. In charge Wm. G. McAdoo presdl. campaign in Ga., 1924. Pres. Savannah River Improvement Commn., 1931—; chmn. state advisory bd., Pub. Works Administration, 1933; postmaster, Augusta 1933—. Trustee Mercer U. Mem. Augusta Chamber Commerce (dir. 10 yrs.). Baptist. Mason. Decorated Chevalier Order of Polonia Restituta, for promoting friendly relations between Poland and U.S. Home: Augusta, Ga. Died Sept. 1, 1937.

HAMILTON, William Peter, editor; b. Great Britain, Jan. 20, 1867; m. Georgianna Tooker, June 20, 1901 (died 1916); m. 2d, Lilian Hart, May 19, 1917. Began newspaper work 1890; was on staff Pall Mall Gazette, under William T. Stead; traveled as corr. principal parts of world; served as lt. British auxiliary forces, Royal Engrs.; war corr. 1st Matabele War, S. Africa, 1893-94 (medal); came to America, 1899; editor Wall Street Journal, Jan. 1, 1908—. Catholic. Home: Brooklyn, N.Y. Died Dec. 9, 1929.

HAMILTON, William Reeve, army officer; b. Fond du Lac, Wis., June 13, 1855; s. Charles Smith (maj. gen. U.S.A.) and Sophia J. (Shepard) H.; student U. of Wis., 1871-72; apptd. from Wis., and grad. U.S. Mil. Acad., 1876; grad. Arty. Sch., 1894; (hon. M.S., Asbury, now De Pauw U., 1882); m. Jane H. Bond, June 21, 1902. Second lt. 5th Arty., June 15, 1876; promoted through grades to col. Coast Arty. Corps, Jan. 14, 1909; retired. Prof. mil. science and tactics, Asbury U., 1879-83; instr. N.G.S.N.Y., 1888-90; prof. mil. science and tactics, U. of Nev., 1894-97; served at Ft. Slocum, N.Y., Willetts Pt. Arty. Sub-post, and Tampa, Fla., in siege arty. train during Spanish-Am. War; comd. Ft. Schuyler, N.Y., 1899-1901, Ft. Terry, N.Y., 1901-03; stationed at Ft. Moultrie, S.C., 1903-05; on gen. recruiting duty, St. Louis, 1905-07. Statistician of mil. and naval tables, New York World Almanac, 1887—. Died Sept. 16, 1914.

HAMLEN, James C., lumber mfr.; b. Portland, Me., June 9, 1852; s. James H. and Anne C. P. Hamlen (née Patten) H.; ed. pub. and pvt. schs.; m. Caroline F. White, June 30, 1880; children—Joseph Rochemont, James Clarence, Robert Cushing. Head of J. H. Hamlen & Son (founded 1846), holders of timberlands in Me. and the Southern States, especially Ark., and largely engaged in exporting lumber and in shipbuilding. Dem. candidate for U.S. Senate, and Ho. of Rep., also for mayor of Portland; federal fuel adminstr. for Me., World War; commr. from Me. to Internat. Centennial Expn., Rio Janeiro, Brazil, 1923; mem. Nat. Advisory Commn., by apptmt. of President Coolidge, to Sesqui-centennial Internat. Expn., Phila., Pa., 1926-27. Home: Portland, Me. Died Nov. 7, 1936.

HAMLETT, Barksdale, state supt. schs.; b. Abilene, Va., Feb. 3, 1879; s. Coleman S. and Alice R. (Hale) H.; A.B., Hampden-Sidney Coll., Va., 1898; m. Daisy Crume, May 24, 1899. Asst. prin. Lynnland Acad., Hardin Co., K., 1898-99; asso. prin. East Lynn Acad., Buffalo, Ky., 1899-1902; prin. Corydon (Ky.) graded and high schs., 1902-04; prin. Henderson (Ky.) High Sch., 1904-05; supt. City Schs,. Hopkinsville, Ky., 1905-12; state supt. pub. instrn., Ky., Jan. 1, 1912—. Trustee State U. of Ky.; chmn. bd. trustees State Normal Schs. of Ky. Democrat. Baptist. Mason. Deceased.

HAMLIN, Alfred Dwight Foster, architect; b. Constantinople, Turkey, Sept. 5, 1855; s. Cyrus (D.D., LL.D., pres. Robert Coll., Constantinople) and Harriet Martha (Lovell) H.; ed. Constantinople, private schools and prep. classes, Robert Coll.; A.B., Amherst Coll., 1875, A.M., 1885; studied architecture, Mass. Inst. Tech., 1876-77; École des Beaux Arts, Paris, 1878-81; (L.H.D., St. John's College, 1912); m. Minnie F. Marston, June 4, 1885. Special asst., 1883, instr., 1887-89, asst. prof. architecture, 1889-91, adj. prof., 1891-1904, prof. history of architecture, 1904—, Columbia. Fellow A.I.A.; decorated Cross of Order of George I of Greece. Author: A History of Architecture, 1896; European and Japanese Gardens (in collaboration), 1902; History of Ornament, Ancient and Medieval, 1916; History of Ornament, Renaissance and Modern, 1923. Home: New York, N.Y. Died Mar. 21, 1926.

HAMLIN, Augustus Choate, surgeon; b. Columbia, Me., Aug. 28, 1829; s. Elijah Livermore and Eliza Bradley (Choate) H.; brother Hannibal H. (v.p. of U.S., 1861-65); grad. Bowdoin, 1851; Harvard, M.D., 1855; m. Helen A. Cutting, 1857. Raised co. at own expense, 1861; asst. surgeon 2d Me. inf., May 1861; brigade surgeon, April 1862; med. dir. 11th corps, 1862-63; apptd. Feb. 1863, lt. col. and med. insp., U.S.A. Served in Army of the Potomac, Army of Western Va., Army of the South, Seige of Fort Wagner, and Army of the Southwest on staff of Gen. George H. Thomas; mustered out, Nov. 1865; practiced medicine in Bangor; retired; made chevalier Order of St. Anne by late Czar of Russia, 1878; commr. of Me. Yorktown Centennial, 1881; surgeon gen. Me., 1882-86; twice mayor of Bangor; has been dept. comdr. Me. G.A.R. and chmn. Pension Com., Nat. G.A.R. Presented with Golden Loving Cup by 11th Army Corps Assn., New York, Nov. 17, 1904. Home: Bangor, Me. Died 1905.

HAMLIN, Charles, lawyer; b. Hampden, Me., Sept. 13, 1837; s. Hannibal (V.P. of U.S., 1861-65) and Sarah Jane (Emery) H.; A.B. Bowdoin, 1857, A.M., 1859; (LL.D., U. of Me., 1909); admitted to bar, 1858; m. Sarah P. Thompson, Nov. 28, 1860. Maj. 1st Me. Arty., Aug. 21, 1862; asst. adj. gen. U.S.V., 1863; bvtd. lt. col. and brig. gen. vols., Mar. 13, 1865, "for faithful and meritorious services" during the war; early in Civil War engaged in recruiting service; asst. adj. gen. of 2d div., 3d corps, Army of the Potomac; asst. insp. arty. U.S.A., 1864-65; took part in battles of Gettysburg, Kelly's Ford, Locust Grove, Mine Run, Harper's Ferry, etc.; hon. mustered out, Sept. 14, 1865. Resumed practice at Bangor, Me.; city solicitor, 1867-68; register in bankruptcy, 1867-78; U.S. commr., 1867-1909; reporter decisions Supreme Judicial Ct., 1885-1905; lecturer in Coll. of Law, U. of Me., 1899—; mem. Me. Ho. of Rep., 1883-85); Republican. Chmn. exec. com. Me. Gettysburg Commn.; trustee Penobscot Savings Bank, 1868—; pres. Eastern Me. Gen. Hosp., 1892. Author: Insolvent Laws of Maine, etc. Home: Bangor, Me. Died 1911.

HAMLIN, Charles Sumner, spl. counsel to Bd. of Governors of Fed. Reserve System; b. Boston, Aug. 30, 1861; A.B., Harvard Univ., 1883, A.M., 1886, LL.B. cum laude, 1886; LL.D., Washington and Lee U., 1895; LL.D., Columbia U. 1930; m. Huybertie Lansing Pruyn, June 4, 1898; 1 dau., Anna (dec.). In practice at Boston, 1886-93, and 1898-1913; asst. sec. of the treasury, U.S., 1893-97 and 1913-14; gov. Federal Reserve Bd., Washington, 1914-16, reapptd. mem. terms, 1916-26, 1926-36; special counsel to Board of Governors of Federal Reserve System, Feb. 4, 1936—; was apptd. chmn. Capital Issues Committee, Apr. 1918. Unanimously nominated for Congress, 1910, but declined; special commr. of U.S. to Japan, 1897; commr. at conv. between Russia, Japan and U.S., 1897; commr. at conv. between Great Britain and U.S. to determine fur-seal fishery controversy, 1897; mem. of bd. of Paris Expn. Commrs. from Mass., 1898; del. Dem. Nat. Conv., St. Louis, 1904; mem. exec. com. Indianapolis Monetary Conv., 1899; mem. U.S. Assay Commn. to examine Phila. Mint, 1903; U.S. Commn. on Limitation of Armaments, 1908; del. to fisheries conf. called by N.E. govs., 1908; Com. of 100, Boston Municipal Election, 1909; Com. of 25 to nominate mayor of Boston, 1909; Met. Water and Sewerage Bd. of Mass., 1913. Lecturer on U.S. Govt., Harvard, 1902, 03; mem. com. on govt. Harvard, 1906-15; trustee Mass. School for Feeble-Minded, 1905. Mem. Japanese Famine Relief Com., 1906 (decorated by Emperor for services, 1908). Trustee Carnegie Endowment Internat. Peace; mem. Nat. Grange many yrs. Acted as arbitrator between 1907-12, in many industrial disputes involving Boston Boiler Makers Union, Old Colony Street Ry. Co., Springfield Street Ry. Co., Boston Typog. Union, etc. Home: Mattapoisett, Mass.; and Washington, D.C. Died Apr. 24, 1938.

HAMLIN, Clarence Clark, lawyer; b. Manchester, Ia., Jan. 7, 1868; s. Henry F. and Harriet (Clark) H.; ed. pub. schs., Iowa; LL.B., State U. of Ia., 1890; m. Seddie Gunnell, Nov. 16, 1898; 1 dau., Elizabeth. Began practice at Rock Springs, Wyo., 1890; elected to Wyo. Senate, 1892 and 1894; mem. commn. to revise laws of Wyo., 1895; moved to Colorado Springs, Colo., 1896; elected dist. atty., 4th Jud. Dist., Colo., 1904; del. at large Rep. Nat. Conv., 1920; formerly mem. Rep. Nat. Com. for Colo.; pres. and editor Colorado Springs Evening Telegraph, and Colorado Springs Gazette. Apptd. by Gov. Gunter as mem. Colo. Council of Defense, 1917, and served during war. Home: Colorado Springs, Colo. Died Oct. 29, 1940.

HAMLIN, Cyrus, Congl. clergyman; b. Waterford, Me., Jan. 5, 1811; grad. Bowdoin Coll., 1834 (A.M., 1837; D.D.; also D.D., Cambridge; LL.D.; also LL.D., N.Y. Univ.); grad. Bangor Theol. Sem., 1837; missionary in Turkey, engaged in ednl. work for Am. Bd. Commrs. Foreign Missions, 1837-60. Founded Robert Coll., Constantinople; was its pres., 1860-77; prof. theology, Bangor Theol. Sem., 1877-80; pres. Middlebury College, 1880-85. Home: Lexington, Massachusetts. Died 1900.

HAMLIN, Elbert Bacon, judge; b. Troy, N.Y., Nov. 21, 1874; s. Rev. Teunis S. (D.D.) and Frances (Bacon) H.; grad. Westminster Sch., Simsbury, Conn., 1892; A.B., Yale, 1896; LL.B., New York Law Sch., 1898; m. Elizabeth Shields, Dec. 9, 1908; children—Eleanor Frances, Elbert Bacon. Admitted to bar State of N.Y., 1898, Supreme Court of U.S., 1903, Conn. bar, 1913; began practice at N.Y. City, 1898; mem. Hamlin and Conklin, 1906-16; moved 1910 to Litchfield County, Conn., where four generations resided; judge, Litchfield, County Court, Conn., 1925—, for term ending 1937. Formerly lecturer on commercial law, Y.M.C.A. Schs. of N.Y. City. Food adminstr., Litchfield, during World War. Mem. of board Westminster Sch. Republican. Presbyn. Home: Litchfield, Conn. Died Mar. 5, 1936.

HAMLIN, George John, singer, teacher; b. Elgin, Ill., Sept. 20, 1868; s. John Austin and Mary E. H.; acad. edn., Andover, Mass.; m. Harriet R. Eldredge, Dec. 27, 1892. Has appeared with prin. musical socs. and clubs in U.S. and Germany as tenor soloist; also leading tenor with Chicago Grand Opera Co., seasons 1911, 12, 13, 15. Died Jan. 10, 1923.

HAMLIN, Hannibal Emery, lawyer; b. Hampden, Me., Aug. 22, 1858; s. Hannibal (v.p. of U.S., 1861-65) and Ellen V. (Emery) H.; A.B., Colby Coll., 1879, LL.D., 1932; LL.B., Boston U., 1882, LL.D., 1935; LL.D., University of Me., 1934; unmarried. Admitted to bar, 1883, and practicing at Ellsworth; mem. Hale & Hamlin. Mem. Me. Ho. of Rep., 1893-95, Senate, 1899-1901 (pres. 1901); judge-advocate-gen. of Me., 1897-1904, on staffs Govs. Llewellyn Powers and John F. Hill; one of three commrs. on uniformity of legislation, 1895-1913; atty. gen. of Maine, 1905-08. Republican. Home: Ellsworth, Me. Died May 6, 1938.

HAMLIN, Simon Moulton, congressman; b. Standish (Richvill), Me., Aug. 10, 1866; s. Ebenezer C. and Abby M. (Hasty) H.; prep. edn. Gorham Normal Sch., 1888-90, Bridgton Acad., 1890-92; A.B., Bowdoin Coll., 1900; m. Luetta Higgins, 1894; children—Catherine, Zelma; m. 2d, Anne Wilson Hitchings, 1901 (died 1933); m. 3d, Mrs. Evelyn Field Ward, Dec. 15, 1934. Teacher pub. schs. and supt. schs., Me., 1890-1925; farmer and in real estate business; mayor of South Portland, Me., 1933; mem. 74th Congress, (1935-36), 1st Me. Dist. Democrat. Universalist. Mason. Home: Portland, Me. Died July 27, 1939.

HAMLIN, Teunis Slingerland, Presbyn. clergyman; b. Glenville, N.Y., May 31, 1847; s. Solomon Curtis and Christiana (Slingerland) H.; grad. Union Coll., 1867 (D.D., 1886). Pastor 13 yrs. at Troy, N.Y.; 2 yrs., Cincinnati; from 1886 at Washington, D.C.; m. Frances E. Bacon, Feb. 4, 1873. V.p. Memorial Assn. of D.C.; pres. bd. trustees Howard Univ.; trustee United Soc. of Christian Endeavor; visitor to Govt. Hosp. for Insane. Died 1907.

HAMLINE, John Henry, lawyer; b. Rotterdam, N.Y., March 23, 1856; s. Leonidas Price H., M.D., and g.s. Bishop L. L. H., M.E. Ch.; grad. Northwestern U., 1875; Columbia Coll. of Law, New York, 1877; began practice at Chicago; was several terms village atty. of Evanston until 1883, when he moved to Chicago; m. Josephine, d. Henry Meade, Norwich, N.Y., May 19, 1880. Alderman 3d ward, Chicago, 1887-89. Republican. Home: Chicago, Ill. Died 1904.

HAMM, Margherita Arlina (Mrs.), author, journalist; b. St. Stephens, N.B., Apr. 29, 1871; d. Rufus La Fayette and Almenia (Spencer) H.; ed. Convent of the Sacred Heart, Carleton, N.B.; Emerson Coll., Boston, New York Univ. Law Sch., Royal Coll., Hong-Kong; summer lecture course, Oxford, Eng.; m. John Robert McMahon, Aug. 1, 1902. Newspaper reporter and author from 1887; traveled in U.S., Hawaii and W. Indies in '90's for Sun, Herald and Mail, New York; later visited Japan, China, India, Egypt and Russia for same papers; made maps for Geog. Soc.; war corr. Chinese-Japanese War and Spanish-Am. War; also mil. nurse without salary; made hon. mem. of several regiments; decorated by Pres. Palma of Cuba; was commr. to England for Atlanta Expn. Protestant Episcopalian. Author: Famous Families of New York, 1903. Died 1907.

HAMM, William, capitalist; b. St. Paul, Minn., Sept. 26, 1858; s. Theodore and Louise (Buchholz) H.; student St. Johns U., Collegeville, Minn., 1870-72; m. Marie Scheffer, Oct. 27, 1892; children—William, Margaret Louise (Mrs. James E. Kelley), Theodor (Mrs. William H. Lang), Marie (Mrs. DeWalt Ankeny). Pres. and treas. Theo. Hamm Brewing Co., Hamm Realty Co., Inter-City Realty & Loan Co.; pres. Northwest Theatre Circuit, Inc. Mem. park bd., St. Paul, 10 yrs.; councilman (pres. of assembly), 2 yrs. Home: St. Paul, Minn. Died June 10, 1931.

HAMMER, John Schackelford, U.S. officer; b. Maysville, Ky., July 13, 1842; s. George and Panophy

H.; common school edn.; m. Belle Sanders, June 30, 1869 (died 1889); m. 2d, Ella C. Sloat, 1896. Served all grades private to col. 16th Ky. vol. inf., 1861-65; as 2d and 1st lt. 19th U.S. inf., 1866-73; deputy U.S. marshal, 3d div., U.S. Court, Ind. Ty., 1889-92; postmaster Ardmore, Ind. Ty., 1892-96; 1st mem. Nat. Rep. Com. from Ind. Ty., 1892-96; U.S. marshal, southern dist. Ind. Ty., 1897-1902; U.S. clerk, Ada, Ind. Ty., from Nov. 1, 1902. Dept. comdr. G.A.R. for Ind. Ty., 1901-02. Mem. mil. order Loyal Legion. Mason. Deceased.

HAMMER, William C., congressman; b. Asheboro, N.C., Mar. 24, 1865; student Western Md. Coll., Md. Univ.; m. Minnie Lee Hancock, Dec. 21, 1893. Admitted to N.C. bar, 1891, and began practice at Asheboro; served as mem. City Council, Asheboro, mayor of Asheboro, county supt. instrn.; solicitor Superior Court, 10th Jud. Dist., 12 yrs.; U.S. atty., Western Dist. of N.C., 1914-20; mem. 67th to 71st Congresses (1921-31), 7th N.C. Dist. Owner and editor Asheboro Courier. Democrat. Home: Asheboro, N.C. Died Sept. 26, 1930.

HAMMER, William Joseph, cons. engineer; b. Cressona, Pa., Feb. 26, 1858; s. William Alexander and Martha A. (Beck) H.; ed. pub. schs. and high schs., Newark, N.J.; m. Alice Maude White, Jan. 3, 1894; 1 dau., Mabel White (Mrs. Thomas Cleveland Assheton). Asst. to Edward Weston in Weston Malleable Nickel Co., Newark, N.J., 1878; became asst. in lab. of Thomas A. Edison, Menlo Park, N.J., Dec. 1879; chief engr. Edison Lamp Works, 1880-81; sent to Eng. by Mr. Edison in fall of 1881 and became chief engr. English Edison Co., and established in London 1st central sta. in world for incandescent elec. lighting; chief engr. German Edison Co. (now Allfemeine Elektricates Gesellschaft), 1883-84; had charge of interests of Mr. Edison and 8 Edison interests at Franklin Inst. Elec. Expn., 1884; represented Mr. Edison's interests Crystal Palace Elec. Expn., 1882, and Paris Expn., 1889; at close of latter expn. made balloon flight over France; chief insp. central stas., Edison Elec. Lab. Co., 1884-85; became confidential asst. of pres. of parent Edison Co., 1884, and incorporator and trustee Sprague Elec. R.R. & Motor Co.; installed the 8,000-light plant of Ponce de Leon Hotel at St. Augustine, Fla., 1887, and acted at cons. and contracting engr. in connection with the elaborate elec. effects at Cincinnati Expn., 1888; chief engr. and gen. mgr. Boston Edison Co., 1886-87; cons. practice as elec. engr., 1890—. Rep. of Am. Inst. E.E. at Hall of Fame ceremonies, 1901-07. Received 2 medals abroad for professional work, and John Scott Legacy medal and premium from Franklin Inst.; grand prize, St. Louis Expn., 1904, for hist. collection of incandescent elec. lamps; gold medal, St. Louis Expn., and Elliott Cresson gold medal, Franklin Inst., 1906; World War medal (U.S.), 1920; World War Medal, N.Y. State, 1920; Chevalier Legion of Honor (France), 1925. Past v.p. Am. Inst. Electrical Engrs. (life mem., fellow), N.Y. Elec. Soc. Aeronautical Soc.; pres. Edison Pioneers, 1920-21; pres. Franklin Exptl. Club; pres. Nat. Conf. on Standard Elec. Rules ten years; fellow Am. Physical Soc., A.A.A.S., Am. Inst. E.E., Am. Acoustical Soc.; chmn. Jamestown Expn. Aeronautical Congress, 1907; sec. and expert Aeronautics Com., Hudson Fulton Celebration, 1909. Served as maj., Gen. Staff, U.S.A., Inventions Sec. of War Plans Div., and later Operations Div., Army War College, Washington, D.C., after entrance of U.S. into World War; in charge elec. and aeronautical war inventions. Invented the radium luminous preparations used for watches, clocks, airplane and automobile instruments, etc.; brought 9 tubes of radium from Curie labs., 1902, and delivered 88 lectures on radium; first suggested and used radium for cancer and tumor treatment; inventor of motor-driven flashing electric sign. Republican. Episcopalian. Home: New York, N.Y. Died Mar. 24, 1934.

HAMMERLING, Louis Nicholas, editor; b. Honolulu, H.I., Mar. 23, 1874; s. August S. and Anna (Müller) H.; grad. U. of Lemberg, Austria, 1893; m. Sophie Jeane Von Brzezicka, of Lemberg, Austria, Feb. 25, 1915. Came to U.S., 1886; in Europe, 1889-93, returned to U.S., 1394; apptd. by Pres. Roosevelt as a mediator in anthracite coal strike, 1902; organizer, 1908, and since pres. Am. Assn. Foreign Lang. Newspapers, Inc. (represents 772 newspapers, pub. in 32 langs.), also editor American Leader. Del. Rep. Nat. Conv., 1908, 1912. Presented with gold medal by coal miners of Pa., 1902; medal by Naturalized Citizens' Com. of U.S., for efforts in defeating Burnett-Dillingham Immigration Bill before Congress, 1913; elected 1st hon. mem. Pub. Safety Commn. of Chicago and Cook Co., 1913. Republican. Catholic. Home: New York, N.Y. Died Apr. 27, 1935.

HAMMERSTEIN, Oscar, theater mgr.; b. Berlin, Germany, 1847; came to U.S., 1863. Invented and patented several labor saving devices; wrote 3 one-act comedies in German, 1868, prod. in New York; lessee and mgr. Stadt Theatre, New York, 1870; built Harlem Opera House, 1880; later Columbus Theatre, Manhattan Opera House, Olympia (later the New York) Theatre, Victoria Theatre, Belasco Theatre, and New Opera House. Pres. Hammerstein Opera Co. Home: N.Y. City. Died Aug. 1, 1919.

HAMMILL, Fred H., ry. exec.; b. Rockford, Ill.; s. John and Louisa (Pryor) H.; ed. high sch., Rockford; m. Jennie G. Lewis, June 6, 1894; 1 dau., Arline. Began as telegrapher, C.,M.&St.P. R.R., successively train dispatcher, supt., C.&N.W. Ry., gen. supt. U.P. Ry., gen. mgr. C.&N.W. Ry.; now exec. vice-pres. C.,R.I.&P. Ry. Mem. mgrs. com., Train Service Adjustment Bd. Mem. Ia. State Bd. of Defense, World War. Republican. Methodist. Mason. Home: Chicago, Ill. Died Aug. 30, 1931.

HAMMILL, John, gov.; b. Linden, Wis., Oct. 14, 1875; s. George and Mary (Brewer) H.; moved with family, in boyhood, to Hancock Co., Ia.; LL.B., State U. of Ia., 1897; m. Fannie B. Richards, June 7, 1899. Admitted to Ia. bar, June 9, 1897, and practiced at Britt; elected county atty., 1902, 04; mem. State Senate, 1908-12; lt. gov. of Ia., 1920, 22, gov., 3 terms, 1925-31. Republican. Mason. Home: Britt, Ia. Died Apr. 6, 1936.

HAMMITT, Jackson Lewis, banker; b. McKeesport, Pa., Aug. 8, 1862; s. John Kelly and Rebecca (Haney) H.; ed. pub. schs., McKeesport; m. Clara Covert Hodgkinson, Oct. 8, 1891; 1 son, Jackson Lewis. Gen. storekeeper, McKeesport, 1880-1906; dir. 1st Nat. Bank, McKeesport, 1904, vice-pres., 1913—, chmn. bd. 1921—. Mem. Bd. of Edn., McKeesport, 25 yrs. Republican. Baptist. Mason. Home: McKeesport, Pa. Died Oct. 7, 1937.

HAMMOND, Andrew B., lumberman; b. St. Leonards, N.B., Can., July 22, 1848; s. Andrew B. and Glorianna Harding (Coombes) H.; m. Florence Abbott, Feb. 22, 1879 (dec.); children—Edwina Clare (Mrs. Frank B. King), Florence (Mrs. Norman Whiteside), Leonard Coombes, Grace (Mrs. W. S. Burnett), Daisy Estelle. Went to Missoula, 1867, where organized Missoula Mercantile Co., First Nat. Bank, Big Blackfoot Mill Co.; built Bitter Root Valley and Philipburg rys.; went to Ore., 1895; built Astoria & Columbia River R.R.; in Calif., 1900—; pres. Hammond Lumber Co. Mason. Home: San Francisco, Calif. Died Jan. 15, 1934.

HAMMOND, Creed Cheshire, army officer; b. Eugene, Ore., Oct. 9, 1874; s. James Gilmore and Sarah Elizabeth (Cheshire) H.; ed. U. of Ore.; m. Mrs. Bertha Lois Titus, Apr. 6, 1917; stepson, Bruce Linville Titus. Mercantile business and realty broker, Eugene, 1900-11; chief dep. sheriff, Eugene, Oregon; dir. and assistant cashier Bank of Commerce, Eugene, 1911-17; dir. and cashier Portland (Oregon) National Bank, 1919-20. Served with U.S. Vols., Philippine Islands, Spanish-American War; colonel C.A.C., U.S.A., July 25, 1917-Apr. 19, 1919; on General Staff and in Militia Bureau, 1920-25; appointed major general and chief of Militia Bur. for 4 yrs. from June 29, 1925; insular auditor of Philippines, 1929-33. Republican. Episcopalian. Home: Portland, Ore. Died Apr. 2, 1940.

HAMMOND, Edward Payson, evangelist; b. Ellington, Conn., Sept. 1, 1831; s. Elijah and Esther (Griswold) H.; A.B., Williams Coll., 1858, later A.M.; student Union Theol. Sem., New York, 1858-59, Free Ch. Theol. Sem., Edinburgh, 1860-61; m. Eliza Plemer Overton, May 24, 1866. Ordained Presbyn. ministry, 1863; has devoted his life to evangelistic work in the U.S., Scotland and Eng. Author: Roger's Travels. Died 1910.

HAMMOND, Edwin Pollock, lawyer; b. Brookville, Ind., Nov. 26, 1835; s. Nathaniel and Hannah (Sering) H.; LL.B., Asbury (now De Pauw) U., Ind., 1857; (LL.D., Wabash Coll., Ind., 1892); admitted to bar, 1858, and began practice at Rensselaer, Ind.; m. Mary V. Spitler, Mar. 1, 1864. Served as 1st lt. Co. G, 9th Ind. Vol. Inf., Apr.-July 1861; capt. Co. A, 87th Ind. Inf. and maj. and lt. col. same regt., 1862-65. Resumed law practice, 1865; judge 30th circuit, Ind., 1873-83, 1890-92; asso. justice Supreme Ct. of Indiana, 1883-85; mem. Stuart, Hammond & Simms, Lafayette, Ind. Republican. Home: Lafayette, Ind. Deceased.

HAMMOND, Eleanor Prescott, author; b. Worcester, Mass., Apr. 26, 1866; d. Andrew Hill and Rhoda Maria (Barber) H.; U. of Leipzig, Germany, 1891; Oxford U., England, 1892-94, first class honors in English, 1894; fellow in English, U. of Chicago, 1895-98, Ph.D., 1898; unmarried. Docent in English, U. of Chicago, 1898-1904, resigned. Author: Chaucer: A Bibliographical Manual, 1908. Home: Chicago, Ill. Died Feb. 23, 1933.

HAMMOND, Eli Shelby, jurist; b. Brandon, Miss., Apr. 21, 1838; s. John Chesed Purnell and Priscilla Atalla (Shelby) H.; grad. Union Univ., Tenn., 1857; Lebanon Law Sch., 1858; served in C.S.A., 1861-65; m. Frances E. Davis, Jan. 13, 1864; m. 2d, Mrs. Margaret (Conly) Wilshire, July 17, 1895. Home: Memphis, Tenn. Died 1905.

HAMMOND, Harold, army officer; b. Rushville, Ill., Oct. 21, 1874; s. Jacob and Sarah Margaret (Lawler) H.; ed. Ill. Coll., Jacksonville, Ill., to 1892; grad. U.S. Mil. Acad., 1898; m. Mary Cragin Pierce, July 9, 1902. Commd. 2d lt. 9th U.S. Inf., Apr. 26, 1898; 1st lt., Mar. 2, 1899; capt. 19th Inf., Oct. 21, 1902; transferred to 23d Inf., July 3, 1903. Accompanied 1st expdn. to Cuba, June 1898; sailed for Manila, P.I., Mar. 1899; took part in China Relief Expdn. and relief of Peking siege, Aug. 1900; served in P.I., 1901-02; instr. drawing U.S. Mil. Acad., 1902-06; in charge Army and Navy Club, Jamestown Expn., 1907; detailed as p.m. U.S.A., Nov. 21, 1907. Author: Pinkey Perkins; Just a Boy, 1905; Further Fortunes of Pinkey Perkins, 1906. Died 1911.

HAMMOND, Jabez Dean, physician; b. Monroe Co., N.Y., July 29, 1860; s. Dr. Caleb Holton and Susan (Cutler) H.; ed. Geneseo State Normal Sch., Rochester Free Acad., U. of Rochester; med. studies New York, Boston, Ann Arbor and Chicago; M.D., Rush Med. Coll., 1884; supplementary courses at Paris and London; m. Margaret Maguire, 1898. In practice at Chicago, 1884—; attending physician to Auditorium and Congress hotels; physician to Victoria and Auditorium Annex hotels. Home: Winfield, Ill. Died Feb. 15, 1916.

HAMMOND, John Hays, mining engr.; b. San Francisco, Calif., Mar. 31, 1855; s. Richard Pindell and Sarah Elizabeth (Hays) H.; ed. pub. and pvt. schs.; Ph.B., Sheffield Scientific Sch. (Yale), 1876, A.M., Yale, 1898; mining course at Royal Sch. of Mines, Freiberg, Saxony; D.E., Stevens Inst., Tech., 1906; LL.D., St. John's Coll., 1907, Yale, 1925; Dr. Engring., U. of Pennsylvania, 1928; m. Natalie Harris, Jan. 1, 1881; children—Harris John Hays, Richard Pindell, Natalie Hays. Spl. expert U.S. Geol. Survey, 1880, examining Calif. gold fields; later in Mexico and afterward consulting engr. Union Iron Works, San Francisco, and to Central and Southern Pacific rys.; has examined properties in all parts of world; became consulting engr. for Barnato Bros., 1893, and later for Cecil Rhodes, of whom he became a strong supporter; consulting engr. Consolidated Gold Fields of S. Africa, British South Africa Co. and the Randfontein Estates Gold Mining Co. Was one of four leaders in reform movement in the Transvaal, 1895-96; after Jameson Raid (with which he was not in sympathy), was arrested and sentenced to death; sentence was afterward commuted to 15 yrs. imprisonment; and later was released on payment of fine of $125,000; went to London and became interested in many mining cos.; returned to U.S., 1900, and became associated with some of most important financial groups in this country, purchasing and promoting several of largest and most valuable mining properties in U.S. and Mexico; cons. engr. Guggenheim Exploration Co., 1903-07; has also been very active in various interests outside of mining, including hydro-electric enterprises, irrigation projects, etc. Has lectured at Columbia, Harvard, Yale and Johns Hopkins univs. Apptd. by Pres. Taft as spl. ambassador and rep. of the President to the coronation of King George V, 1911. Pres. Panama-Pacific Expn. Commn. to Europe, 1912; chmn. World Court Congress, 1914-15. Chmn. U.S. Coal Commn., 1922-23. Fellow A.A.A.S., Am. Acad. Arts and Sciences. Home: Gloucester, Mass. Died June 8, 1936.

HAMMOND, John Wilkes, judge; b. Rochester (now Mattapoisett), Mass., Dec. 16, 1837; s. John Wilkes and Maria Louisa (Southworth) H.; A.B., Tufts Coll., 1861 (LL.D., 1891, and Harvard, 1911); m. Clara E. Tweed, Aug. 15, 1866. Admitted to bar, 1866; in practice at Cambridge, Mass., 1866-86; mem. Mass. Ho. of Rep., 1872, 1873; city solicitor, 1873-86; justice Superior Ct. of Mass., 1886-98; justice Supreme Jud. Ct., Sept. 7, 1898-Dec. 1, 1914, resigned. Republican. Fellow Am. Acad. Arts and Sciences. Home: Cambridge, Mass. Died Mar. 26, 1921.

HAMMOND, John Winthrop, writer; b. Lynn, Mass., Feb. 19, 1887; s. Charles Adrian and Alice Cora (Oliver) H.; ed. high sch., Mt. Vernon, N.Y.; m. Jessie Louise Schofield, June 19, 1920 (died 1930); children—Jeannette Alice, Louise Estelle; m. 2d, Jennie Estelle Schofield, Feb. 6, 1932. Reporter Mt. Vernon Argus, 1903-11; reporter and dept. editor Evening Gazette, Worcester, 1911-17; publicity writer General Electric Co., Schenectady, 1920—. Student of electrical history, especially history of electrical inventions in United States; wrote first popular account of experiments of Charles P. Steinmetz with laboratory lightning, 1922. Y.M.C.A. service, Camp Devens, Mass., 1917-18; pvt. in personnel adjutant's office, Camp Upton, N.Y., 1918-19. Presbyn. Author: Charles Proteus Steinmetz—A Biography, 1924; A Magician of Science—The Boys' Life of Steinmetz, 1926. Home: Schenectady, N.Y. Died Dec. 27, 1934.

HAMMOND, Lily Hardy, author; b. of Southern parents, Newark, N.J., Sept. 24, 1859; d. Henry C. and Huldah E. (Daugé) Hardy; ed. in pvt. sch., Norfolk, Va., and at Packer Inst., Brooklyn; m. John Dennis Hammond, Sept. 10, 1879. Inaugurated the social service dept. of the women's work of the Southern Meth. Ch.; writer and speaker in advocacy of inter-racial justice and service. Mem. Inter-Racial Com. of State of Ga.; mem. Southern Commn. on Inter-Racial Coöperation. Author: In Black and White, 1914; In the Garden of Delight, 1916; In the Vanguard of a Race, 1922. Home: Islip, N.Y. Died Jan. 24, 1925.

HAMMOND, Matthew Brown, economist; b. South Bend, Ind., June 13, 1868; s. Seth and Sarah (Longley) H.; Ph.B., U. of Mich., 1891; M.L., U. of Wis., 1893; U. of Tübingen, 1893-94, U. of Berlin, 1894; Ph.D., Columbia, 1898; m. Sunie Butler Denham, July 2, 1902; children—Marjorie, Seth. Prin. Versailles (Mo.) Inst., 1891-92; acting asst. prof. economics, U. of Mo., 1896-97; instr. and asst. prof. economics, U. of Ill., 1897-1904; asst. prof. and asso. prof. economics, 1904-08, prof., 1908—, Ohio State U.; prof. economics U. of Chicago, summer, 1921, Columbia Univ., summer, 1922. Member of the Industrial Commn. of Ohio, 1913-15; mem. and sec. Ohio Coal Mining Commn., 1913; mem. Ohio Health and Old Age Ins. Com., 1917-19; labor adviser to U.S. Food Administration and mem. War Labor Policies Bd., 1918; tech. adviser, U.S. Anthracite Coal Commn., 1920. Conglist. Author: The Cotton Industry, 1897; Railway Rate Theories of Inter-State Commerce Commission, 1911; British Labor Conditions and Legislation During the War, 1919. Home: Columbus, O. Died Sept. 28, 1933.

HAMMOND, Monroe Percy; b. Columbia Co., Ark., Mar. 15, 1888; s. Joseph Alexander and Margaret (Sullivant) H.; A.B., Ouachita Coll., Arkadelphia, Ark., 1916; student U. of Chicago; A.M., Columbia, 1928; m. Estelle Afflerbach, July 6, 1914; children—Willard John, Joe Phil, Bennett Holloway. Served successively as teacher, principal high sch. and supt. schs., Hugo, Okla., 1916-22; pres. Northeastern State Teachers Coll., Tahlequah, Okla., 1923—. Democrat. Baptist. Mason. Died Mar. 11, 1935.

HAMMOND, Percy, dramatic critic; b. Cadiz, O., Mar. 7, 1873; s. Alexander and Charlotte (Hunter) H.; student Franklin (Ohio) Coll., 1892-96; m. Florence Carnahan, May 25, 1896. Reporter, corr., editorial writer and dramatic critic, Chicago Evening Post, 1898-1908; dramatic critic Chicago Tribune, 1908-21, also served as Paris corr.; now dramatic critic New York Herald Tribune. Author of "But—Is It Art." Home: East Hampton, L.I., N.Y. Died Apr. 25, 1936.

HAMMOND, Theodore Augustus, lawyer; b. Griffin, Ga., 1861; A.B., U. of Ga., 1880; m. Clifford Putnam, 1886. Mem. Am. and Ga. bar assns., Kappa Alpha. Home: Atlanta, Ga. Died Sept. 27, 1932.

HAMMOND, William Alexander, brig. gen. and surgeon gen. U.S.A.; b. Annapolis, Md., Aug. 28, 1828; grad. Univ. of City of New York, 1848; m. Helen Nisbet, 1849; m. 2d, Esther D. Chapin, 1886. Entered U.S. Army, 1849, as asst. surgeon with rank of 1st lt.; resigned, 1860, becoming prof. anatomy and physiology, Univ. of Md.; reëntered army on breaking out of Civil War, becoming surgeon gen., April 1862; tried by court-martial and dismissed from army, Aug. 1864; established practice in New York; special bill, 1878, authorized President to review court-martial proceeding, resulting in his honorable restoration to rank, and he was placed on the retired list. Is prof. diseases of the mind and nervous system in Baltimore and New York med. colleges. Home: Washington, D.C. Died 1900.

HAMMOND, Winfield Scott, congressman; b. Southboro, Mass., Nov. 17, 1863; s. John W. and Ellen (Panton) H.; A.B., Dartmouth Coll., 1884, A.M., 1889; unmarried. Prin. high sch., Mankato, Minn., Sept. 1884-June 1885; supt. schs., Madelia, Minn., 1885-90; admitted to bar, 1891, practicing at Madelia, Minn., 1891-95, at St. James, Minn., 1895—; Dem. candidate for Congress, 2d Minn. Dist., 1892; co. atty. Watonwan Co., 1895-96 and 1900-05; mem. state bd. dirs. normal schs. of Minn., 1898-1906; pres. bd. edn., St. James, Minn., 1898-1903; mem. 60th to 63d Congresses (1907-15), 2d Minn. Dist. Democrat. Home: St. James, Minn. Died Dec. 30, 1915.

HAMMONS, Earle Woolridge, motion picture producer; b. Winona, Miss., Dec. 2, 1882; s. Isaac Rollins and Sallie A. (Woolridge) H.; ed. pub. schs.; m. Violet Handy, Dec. 2, 1919. With Marshall, Spader & Co., 1903-07, Dean Alvord & Co., 1908-09; mgr. realty dept. U.S. & Mexican Trust Co., N.Y. City, 1910; organizer Jamaica Union Land Co., 1911, Jamaica Bay Building Co., 1911, Howard Estates Development Corp., 1912; pres. Ednl. Pictures, Inc., 1915—; pres. and gen. mgr. Ednl. Film Exchanges and subsidiaries; chmn. exec. com. World Wide Pictures, Inc. Maj. Signal Corps, U.S.R. Episcopalian. Home: Mamaroneck, N.Y. Deceased.

HAMP, Sidford Frederick, author; b. Liverpool, Eng., Mar. 10, 1855; s. Francis and Margaret (Sidford) H.; ed. Bedford Grammar Sch., Eng.; m. Josephine Cable, Nov. 11, 1899. Author: Treasure of Mushroom Rock, 1899; The Trail of the Badger, 1908; Coco Bolo (for children), 1910; Sheridan's Twins, 1917. Home: Colorado Springs, Colo. Died Sept. 3, 1919.

HAMPTON, Benjamin Bowles; b. Macomb, Ill., Mar. 19, 1875; s. David Hail and Mary (Bowles) H.; acad. edn.; m. Maria Somers Bartleson, Feb. 14, 1897 (died 1922); children—Catherine, David Bartleson, Helen Janet, Mary, Benjamin Randolph; m. 2d, Claire Adams, Sept. 1924. Newspaper editor and pub. in Ill. for several yrs.; moved to New York, 1900; editor Hampton's Mag., 1907-11; v.p. Am. Tobacco Co., 1911-16; author and producer of motion pictures, 1916-22, then engaged in writing. Mem. Authors' League America. Home: Pawling, N.Y., and New York, N.Y. Died Jan. 31, 1932.

HAMPTON, Wade, soldier, U.S. senator; b. Columbia, S.C., 1818; s. Col. Wade H., g.s. Gen. Wade H.; grad. Univ. of S.C.; studied law, but never practiced, devoting his attention to managing his plantations in S.C. and Miss. Was mem. S.C. legislature before war, and made notable speech against reopening of the slave trade; m. Margaret, d. Gen. Francis Preston; m. 2d, a d. of Senator George McDuffie of S.C. Enlisted at beginning of Civil war as pvt., but soon after raised command of inf., cav. and arty. known as Hampton's Legion, which distinguished itself at Bull Run, in Peninsula campaign, and many others, especially at Gettysburg; became maj. gen. Aug. 3, 1863; checked Sheridan at Trevilian's Station, 1864; was made comdr. Lee's cav., Aug. 1864, with rank of lt. gen.; later detached to command Gen. Joseph E. Johnston's cav.; several times wounded; cotton planter after war; gov. S.C., 1877-79; U.S. senator, 1879-91. Democrat, but advocate of the gold standard. Home: Columbia, S.C. Died 1902.

HANAN, John H., shoe mfr.; b. Ireland, July 28, 1849; s. James and Anne (Dalton) H.; ed. New York and Brooklyn schs. and pvt. tuition; m. Edith Evelyn Briggs Smith, Apr. 15, 1903. Sr. mem. Hanan & Son, New York, Hanan & Son, Ill.; pres. Hanan Shoe Co., Paris, Hanan Shoe Co., London; dir. Atlantic National Bank, United Shoe Machinery Co.; asso. dir. Title Guarantee Trust Co. Republican. Protestant. Mem. Chamber of Commerce, Bd. of Trade (New York). Home: New York, N.Y. Died Aug. 25, 1920.

HANAUER, Jerome J.; b. N.Y. City, July 30, 1875; s. M. G. and Henrietta (Rice) H.; student Coll. City of N.Y.; m. Carrie Hellman, Mar. 15, 1900; 1 dau., Alice Carrie (Mrs. Lewis L. Strauss). Formerly partner Kuhn, Loeb & Co., retired, Dec. 31, 1932; mem. board dirs. Westinghouse Electric and Mfg. Co., Westinghouse Electric Internat. Co., Westinghouse Acceptance Corp., Hudson and Manhattan R.R. Co., Ill. Central R.R. Co., Yazoo and Miss. Valley R.R. Co., etc. Pres. Loeb Memorial Home for Convalescents. Decorated Order of the Sacred Treasure (Japan). Mem. Chamber Commerce of New York. Home: New York, N.Y.; Greenburgh, N.Y. Died Sept. 3, 1938.

HANAW, Henry, lawyer; b. Jackson, Mich., Aug. 15, 1856; s. Joseph and Sarah (Isaacs) H.; LL.B., U. of Mich., 1878; m. Bettie Metzger, Jan. 20, 1886 (died 1913). Admitted to Mich. bar, 1879; practiced in Jackson, Mich., 1879-80, Mobile, Ala., 1881—; mem. Hanaw & Pillans. Democrat. Jewish religion. Home: Mobile, Ala. Died Feb. 1916.

HANCHETT, Benton, lawyer, banker; b. Oneida Co., N.Y., Apr. 6, 1835; s. Silas H. and Eliza (Dyer) H.; ed. Falley Sem., Fulton, N.Y., and Cazenovia (N.Y.) Sem.; grad. State and National Law Sch., Poughkeepsie, N.Y., 1858; LL.D., U. of Mich., 1896; m. Ann Broadwell, Nov. 18, 1861; m. 2d, Susan E. Kimberly, June 21, 1881. Practiced in Saginaw, 1865—; became chmn. bd. Bank of Saginaw, 1920; also chmn. Saginaw Clearing House. Home: Saginaw (West Side), Mich. Died June 24, 1931.

HANCHETT, Henry Granger, concert pianist; b. Syracuse, N.Y., Aug. 29, 1853; s. M. Waldo and Martha Anna (Huntington) H.; M.D., New York Homoe. Med. Coll., 1884; practiced several yrs.; retired to devote attention to lit. and music; m. Ophelia Murphey, June 22, 1886; m. 2d, Grace Mather, Feb. 22, 1898. Dir. piano dept., Martha Washington Coll., Va., 1876-78, Beethoven Conservatory, St. Louis, 1880-81; lecturer on music in New York "Free Lectures," 1889-1909, Brooklyn Inst. Arts and Sciences, 1895-1904; prof. musical analysis and history Met. Coll. of Music, New York, 1890-94; prof. theoretical music and dir. musical dept., Adelphi Coll., Brooklyn, 1900-04; dir. musical dept., Nat. Park Sem., Washington, 1907-10; dir. normal dept., Brenau Conservatory (Brenau Coll.), Gainesville, Ga., 1913-15; founder, 1917, and became director of the Orlando (Fla.) School of Musical Art. Director of music, chautauqua assemblies, Monteagle, Tenn., 1898-01, De Fumak Springs, Fla., 1899, Paterson (N.J.) Choral Union, 1886-88, Clifton (N.Y.) Choral Soc., 1889-90, etc. Inventor of the "sostenuto" or "tone sustaining" pedal. With Gerrit Smith organized Am. Guild of Organists, 1896. Author: Modern Domestic Medicine, 1887, 1891. Home: Orlando, Fla. Died Aug. 19, 1918.

HANCOCK, Albert Elmer, college prof.; b. Phila., Aug. 30, 1870; s. Clinton C. and Emily (Cummings) H.; B.S., Wesleyan U., 1891; A.M., Harvard, 1895, Ph.D., 1897; married. Lived in Germany, France, Spain and Italy, 1892-94; instr. English, French and Italian, Williams College, 1897-98; prof. of English, Haverford Coll., 1898-1915. Author: The French Revolution and the English Poets, 1899; Henry Bourland—The Passing to the Cavalier (novel), 1901; A Life of John Keats, 1908; Bronson of the Rabble (novel), 1909. Home: Atlantic City, N.J. Deceased.

HANCOCK, Elizabeth Hazlewood, author; b. "Ellerslie," nr. Charlottesville, Va., Sept. 10, 1871; d. Capt. Richard J. and Thomasia Overton (Harris) H.; ed. under tutelage; unmarried. Asst. editor Neale's Monthly, 1912—. Author: Betty Pembroke, 1907; The Betrayal (with Walter Neale), 1910. Editor: Autobiography of John E. Massey, 1909. Home: New York, N.Y. Died Apr. 1915.

HANCOCK, H(arrie) Irving, chemist, author; b. Waltham, Mass., Jan. 16, 1868; s. William Henry and Laura (Oakes) H.; ed. pub. schs. and spl. courses at colls. and tech. schs.; m. Nellie Stein, Dec. 21, 1887. Was with Boston Globe, 1885-90, New York Journal, etc.; war corr. in Cuba and Philippines; asst. editor Leslie's Weekly, 1900-01; edited revised edition Collier's Cyclopædia, 1901. Organized Ferguson-Hancock Laboratories, with Prof. George A. Ferguson, 1906. Author: Detective Johnson of New Orleans; His Evil Eye; Inspector Henderson; Life at West Point, 1902; Physical Training for Women by Japanese Methods, 1904; Jiu-jitsu Combat Tricks, 1904; The Physical Culture Life, 1905; Dave Darrin at Vera Cruz, 1914; Physical Training for Business Men, 1917; The Motor Boat Club Series, The High School Series, The Grammar School Series, The Annapolis Series, The West Point Series, The Boys of the Army Series, The Young Engineers Series, The Square Dollar Boys Series. Home: Blue Point, N.Y. Died Mar. 12, 1922.

HANCOCK, James Cole, ophthalmologist; b. Fulton, N.Y., Apr. 24, 1865; s. Chauncey B. and Lenna (Cole) H.; ed. Brooklyn Poly. Inst., 1884-85; M.D., Coll. Phys. and Surg. (Columbia), 1889; m. Florence Stevens Biddle, Aug. 18, 1905. Interne Chambers St. Bur. of N.Y. Hosp., 1889-90, New York Eye and Ear Infirmary, 1890-92; studied Berlin, Jan.-Apr. 1893; formerly ophthalmic surgeon and chief of clinic, Eastern Dist. Hospital; cons. ophthalmic surgeon Williamsburg Hosp.; ophthalmic surgeon, Howard Orphan Asylum, Jamaica Hosp., Hempstead Hosp.; asst. surgeon N.Y. Eye and Ear Infirmary, Brooklyn Eye and Ear Hosp.; now cons. ophthalmic surgeon, Coney Island Hosp.; visiting ophthalmic surgeon Brooklyn State Hosp., Creedmore State Hosp. Fellow Am. Coll. Surgeons. Episcopalian. Elk. Home: Brooklyn, and New York, N.Y. Died Nov. 28, 1933.

HANCOCK, Theodore E., lawyer; b. Fulton, N.Y., May 30, 1847; s. Freeman and Mary H.; A.B., Wesleyan U., Conn., 1871 (LL.D., 1897); LL.B., Columbia, 1873; A.M., Syracuse U., 1886; m. Martha B. Connelly, June 7, 1881. Admitted to bar, 1873, and engaged in practice at Syracuse; pros. attorney Onondaga Co., 1890-92; atty. gen. State of N.Y., 1894-99. Now sr. mem. Hancock, Spriggs & Hancock. Trustee Wesleyan U., 1907—. Home: Syracuse, N.Y. Died Nov. 19, 1916.

HAND, Alfred, judge; b. Honesdale, Pa., Mar. 26, 1835; s. Ezra and Catharine (Chapman) H.; A.B., Yale, 1857, A.M., 1866; m. Phebe A. Jessup, Sept. 11, 1861 (died 1872); m. 2d, Helen Sanderson, Nov. 26, 1873 (died 1907). Admitted to bar, 1859; practiced in Scranton; apptd. by gov., judge Court of Common Pleas, 1878; judge 45th Jud. Dist. of Pa., 1879-88; justice of the Supreme Ct. of Pa., to fill vacancy, 1888-89. Republican. Pres. Pa. Oral School for Deaf; pres. Public Library; pres. Third Nat. Bank 8 yrs. Home: Scranton, Pa. Died May 23, 1917.

HAND, John Pryor, judge; b. on farm in Henry Co., Ill., Nov. 10, 1850; s. Henry and Mary (Hanna) H.; ed. Rock River Sem., Mt. Morris, Ill., 1866-70; LL.B., State U. of Ia., 1875; m. Elizabeth Brayton, Oct. 26, 1871. Admitted to bar, 1875; co. judge Henry Co., Ill., 1885-90; asst. U.S. atty., Northern Dist., Ill., at Chicago, 1890-94; justice Supreme Ct. of Ill., 1900-July 15, 1913, resigned; chief justice, 1903-04, 1907-08. Republican. Home: Cambridge, Ill. Died May 22, 1923.

HAND, Richard Lockhart, lawyer; b. Elizabethtown, N.Y., Feb. 15, 1839; s. Augustus Cincinnatus and Marcia Seelye (Northrup) H.; sophomore yr., U. of Vt.; A.B., Union Coll., N.Y., 1858, A.M., 1865 (hon. chancellor and LL.D., 1887); m. Mary Elizabeth Noble, June 29, 1868. Admitted to bar, 1861, and since in practice at Elizabethtown; pres. Elizabethtown Water Co., Elizabethtown & Westport Plank Road Co.; sec., treas. Elizabethtown Cemetery Assn. Editor Elizabethtown Post, 1859-67. Was pres. of village and chmn. bd. edn.; commr. State Bd. Charities, N.Y., 1908—; commr. state prisons, apptd., 1907; commr. in charges against District Atty. Jerome, 1908; Dem. nominee for co. judge, 1878, 1890, for justice Supreme Ct., 1885, 1903. Home: Elizabethtown, N.Y. Died Oct. 7, 1914.

HANDLEY, William White, American consul; b. Washington, June 29, 1872; s. Joseph A. and Elizabeth (Langdon) H.; student Columbian (now George Washington) U.; m. Teresa, d. Dr. Ricardo Becerra, former Colombian minister to U.S., June 16, 1910. In shipping and trading business in Venezuela and Trinidad, 1898-1904, and commissions in Africa for U.S. Govt. in connection with the consular service; vice consul at Trinidad, W.I., Jan. 12-Aug. 17, 1904; consular agt. at Matanzas, Cuba, 1904-05; consul at Puerto Plata, Dominican Republic, June 5-Nov. 13, 1905, at Trinidad, Nov. 13, 1905-June 22, 1908; consul gen. at Boma, Belgian Congo, June 22, 1908-Dec. 14, 1910; consul at Naples, Dec. 14, 1910-13; consul gen. at Callao-Lima, Peru, 1913—. Republican. Home: Brooklyn, N.Y. Died Sept. 27, 1919.

HANDMAN, Max Sylvius, prof. economics; b. Roman, Rumania, Dec. 13, 1885; s. Melchior and Rosa (Saymon) H.; prep. edn., Gymasium, Roman; A.B., U. or Ore., 1907; Ph.D., U. of Chicago, 1917; grad. study, Collège de France, Columbia U., U. of Berlin; m. Della Doppelmayer, Sept. 3, 1914. Came to U.S., 1903, naturalized citizen, 1917. Docent in sociology, U. of Chicago, 1913; instr. in sociology, U. of Mo., 1913-16; prof. sociology, U. of Tex., 1917-26, prof. economics, 1926-31; visiting prof. sociology, U. of Minn., 1930-31; prof. economics, U. of Mich., 1931—. Special investigator for Library of Congress, 1918; mem. Com. on Pub. Information, 1918, and of staff U.S. Inquiry on Terms of Peace, 1918; dir. Red Cross Social Service Inst. for Tex., 1919; pres. Tex. Con. for Social Welfare, 1924; mem. Nat. Conf. Social Work (com. on immigration, 1926-32, on delinquents and correction, 1927, 28); mem. Social Science Research Council, 1931-34 (treas. 1933-34; chmn. com. on consumption and leisure; mem. com. on research fellowships, com. on study of population redistribution); spl. investigator Nat. Com. on Law Observance and Enforcement (Wickersham Commn.); mem. com. on Latin Am. studies. Decorated Order of Cultural Merit, Knight, first class (Rumania). Trustee Tex. Com. on Prisons and Prison Labor. Democrat. Home: Ann Arbor, Mich. Died Dec. 26, 1939.

HANDY, Henry Hunter Smith, civ. engr., mfr.; b. Phila. Pa., Nov. 30, 1856; s. Edward Smith and R. A. Virginia (Bryan) H.; spl. student in civ. engring., U. of Pa., 4 yrs.; m. Caroline Templeman Craighill, Jan. 6, 1886. Ry. work, principally with Norfolk & Western R.R., engring. and operating depts., advancing to div. supt. and supt. terminals, at Norfolk, Va., until 1899; entered employ Solvay Process Co., Syracuse, N.Y., 1901, later pres. Semet-Solvay Co. (and chmn. By Products Coke Corp.); dir. First Trust & Deposit Co., Syracuse. Assisted in establishing the first large industry in U.S. for production of aniline dyes, and in merger of Gen. Chemical, Solvay Process, Semet-Solvay Barrett, and Nat. Aniline and Chem. cos. into the Allied Chem. and Dye Corp.; retired from these industries in 1921. Republican. Episcopalian. Home: Syracuse, N.Y. Died Aug. 9, 1935.

HANDY, James A., bishop; b. Baltimore, Dec. 22, 1826; s. Ishmael and Nancy H.; his father was a slave and his mother a free woman; sch. edn. limited to 3 mos.; married. Early joined A.M.E. Ch.; began as sexton, and in 57 yrs. filled every position, including that of bishop; pastor chs. in Md., Va., S.C., New Orleans, La.; financial sec., 1888-92 (purchased dept. bldg., Washington, D.C., and turned it over to Gen. Conf. free of debt and $17,000 surplus); elected bishop, 1892, and acted as supt., successively, of 5th, 2d and 11th dists.; superannuated at age of 83, in 1908. Died 1911.

HANDY, Parker Douglas, banker, mfr.; b. Fairfield, Conn., Aug. 12, 1858; s. Parker and Cornelia (Sloane) H.; A.B., Princeton, 1879; m. Annie Kissam Warner, Dec. 12, 1887. In South Am. trade, 1879-87, representing Gogorza's Sons; became mem. of F. Handy & Harman, bankers and dealers in bullion and specie, 1887, elected pres. upon incorporation, May 1, 1905, and chmn. bd., April 1927, plants at Bridgeport, Conn., Providence, R.I., N.Y. City. Served in 7th Regt. N.G.N.Y., 5 yrs. Trustee Coll. City of New York, 1905-09; life trustee Princeton U., 1910. Mem. N.Y. Chamber of Commerce. Republican. Presbyn. Home: New York, N.Y. Died Nov. 12, 1929.

HANECY, Elbridge, judge; b. in Wis., Mar. 15, 1852; s. William and Mary (Wales) H.; studied at Coll. of Milwaukee; went to Chicago, 1869; admitted to bar, 1874; m. Sarah Barton, Mar. 1, 1876. Judge Circuit Ct. of Cook Co., Ill., 1893-1903, Superior Ct., 1903-04; was 3 times elected umpire of the bd. of arbitration for adjusting differences between the Brickmakers' and Stonemasons' Assn. and their employes. Rep. nominee for mayor of Chicago, 1901. Home: Chicago, Ill. Died Dec. 24, 1925.

HANEY, James Parton, art dir.; b. New York, Apr. 16, 1869; s. Jesse and Martha (Edwards) H.; B.S., Coll. City of New York, 1888; M.D., Coll. Phys. and Surg. (Columbia), 1892; studied Art Students' League, Artist Artisan Inst., N.Y. Sch. of Art; unmarried. Teacher of manual arts, New York pub. schs., 1888-91; practiced medicine, 1892-94; lecturer New York U. Sch. of Pedagogy, 1895-99, 1906-08; dir. of art and manual training in pub. schs., New York, boroughs of Manhattan and Bronx, 1896-1909; dir. of art, high sch., New York, 1909—; dir. art dept., New York U., Summer Sch., 1907—. Home: New York, N.Y. Died Mar. 3, 1923.

HANFORD, Ben; b. Cleveland, O., 1861; s. George Byington and Susan Elizabeth (Martin) H.; ed. under instrn. of stepmother; m. Alice M. Burnham. Learned printers' trade in office of Marshalltown (Ia.) Republican; removed to Chicago, 1879, and later to Phila. and New York; devoted 3 mos. each yr. for many yrs. as pub. speaker on socialistic platform; three times nominated as Socialist candidate for gov. of N.Y.; candidate of Socialist party for mayor of New York, 1901, and for V.P. of U.S., 1904 and 1908. Home: Brooklyn, N.Y. Died 1910.

HANFORD, Charles Barnum, actor and mgr.; b. Sutter Creek, Calif., May 5, 1859; s. Levi and Lucy (Barnum) H.; grad. Washington (D.C.) High Sch., 1881, followed by short time each in collegiate and law depts. Columbian U.; m. Mariella Twaddell Bear, June 30, 1885. Was in U.S. Pension Office, 1880-82; pvt. sec. Hon. H. F. Page, M.C., Calif., 1880-82. Began 1st season as actor at New London, Conn., Sept. 1882, with William Stafford, playing Shakespearean plays; with Thomas W. Keene, 1883-85, with Robson and Crane as Ægeon in "Comedy of Errors," 1885-86, with Edwin Booth, 1886-87, Booth and Barrett, 1887-89 (prin. success as Marc Antony to Booth's Brutus and Barrett's Cassius), Booth and Modjeska, 1889-90, Julia Marlowe, 1890-92; 1st starring tour, 1892-93, as Marc Antony in Julius Cæsar and in Ingomar; sub-star and mgr. with Thomas W. Keene, 1896-98, joint star with Louis James and Kathryn Kidder as James, Kidder & Hanford Co., 1899-1900, later starring with own co.; season 1910 and 11, engaged for Appius, in Maeterlinck's "Mary Magdalene," at the New Theatre, New York, with Miss Olga Nethersole; lecture tours with Captain Scott South Pole Expedition, motion pictures, 1913, 14, 15. Engaged for part of "King Duncan," by James K. Hackett, Criterion Theatre, New York, production of Macbeth, 1915-16; joint star with John E. Kellerd in Shakespearean plays, 1916-17. Enlisted June 19, 1917, as chief yeoman, U.S.N.R.F., and assigned to office of Naval Intelligence; detailed to duty with Thomas A. Edison, later as an editorial writer in hist. sect., Navy Dept. Mason. Died Oct. 16, 1926.

HANFORD, Cornelius Holgate, judge; b. Van Buren Co., Ia., Apr. 21, 1849; s. Edward and Abby J. (Holgate) H.; has lived on Pacific Coast since age of 4 yrs.; ed. common schs.; LL.D., Whitman Coll., 1904; m. Clara M. Baldwin, Nov. 15, 1875; children—Ada Levering, Mrs. Elaine Haynes, Edward Cornelius, William Brown. Admitted to bar, 1875, and engaged in practice at Seattle, Wash.; mem. Territorial Council, 1877; city atty., 1882, 84-85; asst. U.S. atty., Wash. Ty., 1881-86; last chief justice Supreme Court of Wash. Ty., 1889; U.S. dist. judge, Dist. of Wash., 1890-1905, and of Western Dist. of Wash., 1905-July 22, 1912; resigned and resumed practice of law. Republican. Home: Seattle, Wash. Deceased.

HANFORD, Franklin, rear adm. U.S.N.; b. Chili, N.Y., Nov. 8, 1844; s. William Haynes H., Jr., and Abbey (Pixley) H.; apptd. from N.Y., and grad. U.S. Naval Acad., 1866; m. Sara A. Crosby, Nov. 6, 1878 (died 1915); children—Mary Crosby (dec.), John Munn, Ruth Crosby. Promoted ensign Apr. 1868; master 1869; lt., 1870; lt. comdr., Oct. 1885; comdr., Sept, 1894; capt., Jan. 29, 1901; rear adm. Jan. 3, 1903. Served on various stas. and duties; circumnavigated the globe while attached to flagship Pensacola as navigator, 1881-84, taking observations for determination of the variations of the compass; protected Am. interests during revolutions in Ecuador and Nicaragua while comdg. U.S.S. Alert, 1895-97; comdt. U.S. Naval Sta., Cavite, P.I., 1900-02; retired after 40 yrs.' service, Jan. 3, 1903. Farming since retirement. Home: Scottsville, N.Y. Died Feb. 8, 1928.

HANGER, G. Wallace William, mem. U.S. Bd. of Mediation; b. Augusta Co., Va., Mar. 28, 1866; s. Henry Harrison and Cornelia (Glossbrenner) H.; A.B., Lebanon Valley College, Pa., 1884, A.M., 1886, Ph.D., 1897; m. Lucy Galt, Apr. 15, 1902; children—Wallace Galt, Harriet Turner, William Matthew Galt. Pres. Betheden (Miss.) Collegiate Inst., 1885-86; prof. Md. Coll. for Young Women, Lutherville, 1886-87; chief statistician and administrative asst., U.S. Bur. Labor, 1887-1913; mem. U.S. Bd. of Mediation and Conciliation, 1913-20; asst. dir. of labor, U.S. Railroad Administration, 1918-20; mem. U.S. Railroad Labor Bd., 1920-26; mem. U.S. Board of Mediation, 1926—. Mason. Home: Washington, D.C. Died Dec. 26, 1935.

HANGER, Harry Baylor, contractor; b. Staunton, Va., Nov. 1, 1864; s. George Alexander and Margaret (Trimble) H.; grad. Hoovers' Mil. Acad., Staunton, 1881; m. Elizabeth Arnold, 1893 (died 1921). Began at 17 with Mason & Hoge Co., contractors, Ky., later Mason & Hanger Co., of which has been pres., 1906—; also pres. Mason & Hanger-MacArthur Bros., Mason & Hanger Contracting Co., MacArthur-Hanger Co., State Bank & Trust Co., Richmond Ice Co., and various other ice cos. Has supervised construction on large scale in many parts of the country; built camp Zachary Taylor, Louisville, Ky., 1917, at cost approximately of $7,000,000; completed $20,000,000 contract in connection with Old Hickory Powder Plant, Nashville, Tenn.; $2,500,000 tunnel in mountains of Vt. for N.E. Power Co.; Port Newark Terminal, Newark, N.J.; 2½ mile subway, City of New York; extensive tunnel work to increase water supply of N.Y. City; 8 miles of Chicago Drainage Canal; etc. Coll. on staff of Gov. McCreary of Ky. Trustee Berea Coll., Ky. Democrat. Presbyn. Home: Richmond, Ky. Died Oct. 17, 1925.

HANIFAN, Lyda Judson; b. Elkins, W.Va., Feb. 12, 1879; s. John and Sara Susan (Taylor) H.; student W.Va. Wesleyan Coll.; A.B., W.Va. U., 1907; studied U. of Chicago, summer 1908; A.M., Harvard, 1909; grad. student, Harvard, 1919-20; m. Mary Pearl Agee, Mar. 26, 1913; 1 dau., Mary Elkin. Supt. schs., Belington, W.Va., 1904-05; principal Elkins (W.Va.) High Sch., 1905-08, Charleston High Sch., 1909-10; W.Va. agt. of Gen. Edn. Bd. attached to W.Va. State Dept. of Edn., 1910-19; supt. schs. Welch, W.Va., 1920-23; supt. schs. Paducah, Ky., 1923—. Teacher summer sessions, W.Va. U., 1913, 14, 15, 23, Concord State Coll., 1922, West Ky. State Coll., 1923, U. of Ky., 1925. Author: The Community Center, 1920. Republican. Presbyn. Institute lecturer. Home: Paducah, Ky. Died Dec. 12, 1932.

HANKS, Abbot Atherton, chem. engr.; b. San Francisco, Calif., 1869; s. Henry G. and Ellen F. (Barker) H.; student U. of Calif.; m. Vesta L. Jordan, 1900. Pres. Abbot A. Hanks, Inc., chemists, assayers, engineers, San Francisco. Served as member California National Gd. 13 yrs., retiring as major. Unitarian. Home: San Francisco, Calif. Deceased.

HANKS, Charles Stedman, author; b. Lowell, Mass., Apr. 10, 1856; s. Rev. Stedman Wright and Sarah Humphrey (Hale) H.; A.B., Harvard, 1879; LL.B., Boston Law Sch., 1882; m. Clarina Bartow Shumway, May 16, 1888. Author: Camp Kits and Camp Life, 1906. Home: Chestnut Hill, Mass. Died 1908.

HANKS, Henry G., chemist, geologist; b. Cleveland, O., 1826; went to Calif., 1852; established Pacific Chemical Works, 1866; has made important geol. and chem. investigations; mineral Hanksite named for him by its discoverer, W. E. Hidden; 6 yrs. State mineralogist of Calif.; Calif. commr. to Paris Expn., 1878, and supt. U.S. Mineral sect. at that expn. Fellow Am. Geol. Soc. (resigned, 1899); fellow Geol. Soc. of London. Home: San Francisco, Calif. Died 1907.

HANLEY, Stewart, lawyer; b. Detroit, Mich., Apr. 3, 1881; s. James and Mary (Dullea) H.; student U. of Mich., 1899-1901, LL.B., 1904; m. Violet E. Keenan, Feb. 14, 1912; children—Helen Hope, Elaine Elizabeth. Admitted to Mich. bar, 1904, and began practice at Detroit; asst. pros. atty. Wayne County, 1907-09; mem. firm Cullen, Casgrain & Hanley, 1909-13; judge Probate Court, Wayne Co., Mich., 1913-15; mem. Lightner, Oxtoby, Hanley & Crawford, 1915—. Mem. State Bd. Corrections and Charities, 1915-23. Democrat. K.C. Home: Bloomfield Hills, Mich. Died Sept. 25, 1931.

HANLY, J. Frank, governor; b. St. Joseph, Ill., Apr. 4, 1863; s. Elijah and Anna E. (Calton) H.; ed. common schs., Champaign Co., Ill.; m. Eva A. Simmer, Dec. 3, 1881. Taught in pub. schs., 1881-89; admitted to bar, 1889; practiced at Williamsport, 1889-96, Lafayette, Ind., 1896-1905; mem. Ind. Senate, 1890; mem. 54th Congress (1895-97); candidate for U.S. Senate, 1899; gov. of Ind., 1905-09. Prohibition nominee for Pres. of U.S., 1916. Now in practice at Indianapolis; also lecturer. Editor National Enquirer and Indianapolis Daily Commercial; pres. Flying Squadron Foundation and Enquirer Printing & Pub. Co. Home: Indianapolis, Ind. Died Aug. 1, 1920.

HANNA, Dan R., newspaper pub.; s. late Senator Marcus Alonzo and C. Augusta (Rhodes) H.; ed. Kenyon Coll., Gambier, O.; married 4 times, lastly Mrs. Molly Covington Warden, Nov. 2, 1916. Propr. Cleveland Leader and News, and interested in other enterprises. Endowed a sch. of journalism, 1913. Died Nov. 3, 1921.

HANNA, Hugh Henry, publicist; b. Lafayette, Ind., Sept. 19, 1848; s. Joseph S. and Hetty Ann H.; liberal edn. U.S. and Germany; (hon. M.A., Harvard, 1900; LL.D., Wabash Coll., 1900); m. Anna Hester Sharpe, d. of Thomas H. and Elizabeth C. Sharpe, of Indianapolis, Oct. 22, 1873. Began business in his father's bank at Lafayette; removed to Indianapolis, 1880; pres. Atlas Engine Works, 1880-1912. Became head of monetary movement that resulted in gold standard legislation; devoted 3 yrs. to the work, beginning with call issued by Bd. of Trade, Indianapolis, Nov. 1896, for a monetary conf.; organized the Monetary Commn. which developed plan of currency reform, part of which was included in legislation enacted by Congress, 1900. Hon. mem. New York Chamber of Commerce; awarded gold medal in recognition of his leadership for gold standard legislation; was apptd. chmn. of Commn. on Internat. Exchange, 1903. Served as vice-moderator Presbyn. Gen. Assembly and pres. Presbyn. Brotherhood of America; also several yrs. mem. Gen. Edn. Bd., Southern Edn. Bd., Hampton Inst. (Va.) and Tuskegee Inst. (Ala.). Home: Indianapolis, Ind. Died Oct. 31, 1920.

HANNA, James Robert; b. Geneseo, Ill., June 12, 1866; s. James Steel and Harriet Louise (Hunt) H.; B.S., Western Normal Coll., Shenandoah, Ia., 1890; A.B., Highland Park Coll. (now Des Moines U.), 1892, A.M., 1903, LL.D., 1916; m. Jessie Rosaline Pinney, Nov. 14, 1895; children—Robert Hamilton, Ruth, James Harmon (dec.). Ranching, farming and teacher rural schs. until 1888; teacher Highland Park Coll. until 1910; pres. Euclid Av. State Bank, Des Moines (now dir.); treas. Des Moines Morris Plan Co. Speaker throughout U.S. and writer for better city govt.; mem. citizens com. securing passage of the commission plan law by Ia. legislature and adoption of the plan by Des Moines; mayor of Des Moines, under commn. form, 1910-16; trustee Municipal Water Plant of Des Moines. Dir. Teachers Placement Div. of U.S. Bur. of Edn. (getting war-time teachers and placing men from service back into teaching positions), 1918-19. Active in prohibition movement. Prog. Republican. Unitarian. K. of P. Home: Des Moines, Ia. Died Feb. 24, 1931.

HANNA, Marcus Alonzo, U.S. senator from Ohio, 1897-1905; b. New Lisbon (now Lisbon), O., Sept. 24, 1837; s. Dr. Leonard and Samantha (Converse) H.; has lived in Cleveland, 1852—; ed. in common schs. and Western Reserve Coll.; LL.D., Kenyon Coll., 1900; m. C. Augusta, d. Daniel P. Rhodes, Sept. 27, 1864. Became employé and later partner in wholesale grocery house until 1867; now head M. A. Hanna & Co., coal; dir. Globe Ship Mfg. Co.; pres. Union Nat. Bank; pres. Cleveland City Railway Co.—all at Cleveland; pres. Chapin Mining Co., Lake Superior. Directed campaign which secured nomination and election and reëlection of William McKinley as President. Chmn. Nat. Rep. Com., 1896—. Home: Cleveland, O. Died 1904.

HANNA, Matthew Elting, diplomatic service; b. Gillespieville, O., Mar. 9, 1873; s. Robert and Eliza (Corken) H.; grad. U.S. Mil. Acad., 1897; honor grad. Inf. and Cav. Sch., 1906; honor grad. Staff Coll., 1907; m. Helen Richards, Nov. 12, 1902; children—Matthew Elting, Barbara; m. 2d, Gustava von der Tann née Baroness von Rheinbaben, Apr. 28, 1925. Second lt., 1st lt. and capt. cav., 1897-1913. Served on western frontier, 1897-98, in 2d Cav.; in Santiago Campaign, Spanish-Am. War; recommended for brevet for gallantry at Battle of San Juan Hill, July 1-3, 1898; a.d.c. to Maj. Gen. Leonard Wood, 1898-1902; mil. attaché, Hanava, 1902-04; with 3d Cav., 1904-05; instr. Staff Coll., 1907-10; special agt. of the United States in Panama, 1909; War Coll., 1910; capt. on Gen. Staff, U.S.A., 1910-12; spl. rep. of U.S. at German Imperial Maneuvers, 1911; resigned from army, 1913. In mfg. business, 1912-17; insp. gen. Mass. N.G., 1912-14; vol. asst., Am. Embassy, Mexico, Feb.-Aug. 1917; 3d 2d and 1st sec. Am. Embassy to Mexico, 1917-21, and chargé d'Affaires during portion of that period; chief Div. of Mexican Affairs, Dept. of State, 1921-24; 1st sec. Am. Embassy in Berlin, 1924-25; apptd. foreign service insp. for Latin America, Nov. 1925, for Europe, May 1927; apptd. counselor of Am. Embassy, Lima, Peru, Nov. 1927; sec. 6th Internat. Conf. of Am. States, at Havana, Jan. 16-Feb. 20, 1928; chargé d'affaires at Am. Legation, Managua, Nicaragua, May-Dec. 1929; apptd. E.E. and M.P. to Nicaragua, Dec. 16, 1929; apptd. E.E. and M.P. to Guatemala, Aug. 11, 1933. Developed pub. sch. system of Cuba, 1900-02. Decorated Service Medal, Santiago Campaign, Spanish-Am. War; Presidential Medal of Merit, Nicaragua, for services following earthquake at Managua, Mar. 31, 1931. Died Feb. 19, 1936.

HANNA, Philip C., consul gen.; b. Waterloo, Ia., June 27, 1857; s. George W. and Mary (Melrose) H.; the first white settlers in Black Hawk County (Ia.); built first house in county and were two of the four founders of Waterloo; mother was grand niece of Gen. Winfield Scott; ed. pub. schs.; m. Lulu May Cornick, 1891. In U.S. consular service since 1891; consul at La Guaira, Venezuela, 1891-94, at Trinidad, W.I., July 2-Aug. 30, 1897, at San Juan, P.R., Sept. 1, 1897-Apr. 21, 1898; apptd. consul-gen. at Monterey, Mex., Nov. 1, 1899 (now retired). Passed through 3 South American revolutions where became conspicuous by being backed, on several occasions, by U.S.N.; his efforts to protect Am. interests in Venezuela during time of Crespo revolution brought down upon him the enmity of the Venezuelan govt., and U.S. was asked to recall him; Secretary Blaine replied that he was satisfactory to U.S. and would remain until close of the revolution, and Admiral Walker, with White Squadron, was sent to back up this position, landing marines at port of Caracas until peace was restored. Following the Monterey and N. Mexico flood disaster of Aug. 1909, when more than 5,000 persons were drowned, in conjunction with Am. Red Cross and others assisted 90,000 needy persons, and kept open relief stores and free hosp. for 9 mos. Was thanked by President Taft, bd. dirs. of Am. Nat. Red Cross and was given the medal of merit for that yr.; also thanked by Mexican Red Cross, given a gold medal by the Mexican ladies, thanked by the govs. and legislature of two Mexican states and unanimously elected hon. mem. of Monterey Casino, being the only foreigner ever elected; member Monterey Foreign Club, and Club Campestre de Monterey. Following landing U.S. troops at Vera Cruz, 1914, was made prisoner of war by Huertistas and accused of sympathizing with revolutionists; was left in State House when Huerta troops evacuated Monterey; influential during the revolution in preserving friendly relations with Mexicans. Spl. official hdqrs. at Menger Hotel, San Antonio, Tex., 1916-19. Lecturer on Latin America and internat. subjects. Republican. Decorated Order of the Liberator (Venezuelan) and made hon. consul of Venezuela. Home: Waterloo, Ia. Died Feb. 17, 1929.

HANNA, Septimus James, lawyer; b. Spring Mills, Pa., July 29, 1844; s. Samuel Cook and Susanna (Miles) H.; ed. pub. schs. and acad.; m. Camilla Turley, 1869. Capt. Co. H, 138th Ill. Inf., last yr. of Civil War; admitted to Ill. bar. Located at Council Bluffs, Ia.; judge Co. Ct., 1867-69; city atty., 1869-71; practiced Chicago, 1872-79; removed to Leadville, Colo.; register U.S. land office, 1882-86; practiced law, 1886-90; editor Christian Science Journal, monthly, and Christian Science Sentinel, weekly, 1892-1902; first reader in "Mother Church," Boston, 1894-1902; apptd. mem. of Bd. Lectureship, First Church of Christ, Scientist, of Boston, July 1902; pres. Christian Science Bd. Edn., Boston. Home: Pasadena, Calif. Died July 23, 1921.

HANNA, William Brantly, pres. judge, orphan's court, Phila.; b. Phila., Pa., Nov. 23, 1835; grad. Central High School, Phila., 1853 (D.C.L., Bucknell Univ., 1885); studied law in his father's office and at Univ. of Pa.; admitted to bar, 1857; m. Mary V., d. Samuel M. Hopper, Phila., 1864. Asst. dist. atty. of Phila. several yrs.; mem. of Phila. city council, 1867-74; was mem. conv. which framed present constitution of Pa.; elected, 1874, one of the first 3 judges of newly created Orphans' Court of Phila.; became pres. judge, 1878; re-elected unanimously, 1884, 1894, 1904. Pres. trustees of Hahnemann Med. Coll. and Hosp.; trustee Bapt. Home; also Bucknell Univ.; v.p. W. Phila. Inst.; mgr. Home Missionary Soc. of Phila.; also Pa. Working Home for Blind Men. Home: Philadelphia, Pa. Died 1906.

HANNAFORD, Charles Edward, architect; b. Cincinnati, Apr. 7, 1860; s. Samuel and Phoebe (Statham) H.; ed. pub. schs. and Chickering Acad., Cincinnati; m. Agnes F. Moore, Apr. 25, 1889 (died 1931); children—Isabel, Samuel Northcotte, Charles Robert, Agnes, Roger Moore, William (dec.). Entered office of Samuel Hannaford, architect, 1878; mem. Samuel Hannaford & Sons, 1887—. In gen. practice, and as mem. of firm connected with a number of large undertakings, notably the City Hall, Cincinnati; the State Capitol, Columbus; the New Gen. Hosp. for Cincinnati; Postoffice Bldg., Cincinnati; bldg. for Cincinnati Times-Star. Republican. Methodist. Home: Cincinnati, O. Deceased.

HANNAFORD, Jule Murat, ry. official; b. Claremont, N.H., Nov. 19, 1850; s. Eli R. and Paulina (Jewett) H.; pub. sch. edn.; m. Miss C. L. Foster, 1882; 2 sons. Clk. gen. freight office, Vt. Central R.R., 1866-72; then with N.P. Ry., consecutively as chief clk., asst. gen. freight and pass. agt., gen. freight agt. Eastern div., asst. supt. freight traffic, traffic mgr., 3d v.p., 2d v.p., Apr. 1, 1902, and pres., Aug. 27, 1913; federal mgr. N.P. R.R., June 1918-Mar. 1920; elected pres., Dec. 1, 1920; resigned and was apptd. v.chmn. and elected dir. First National Bank; dir. N.P. Ry., State Savings Bank. Home: St. Paul, Minn. Died Sept. 24, 1934.

HANNAN, Frederick Watson, clergyman; b. Cochecton, N.Y., May 4, 1866; s. Michael and Catherine (Noonan) H.; grad. Hackettstown Collegiate Inst., 1886; A.B., Wesleyan U., Conn., 1890 (Phi Beta Kappa); B.D., Drew Theol. Sem., 1893; D.D., Wesleyan, 1907; m. Anna Louise Danes, Mar. 20, 1895. Began to preach at 16; ordained M.E. ministry, 1893; pastor Bayport, N.Y., 1893-94, 1st Ch., Meriden, Conn., 1894-98, 1st Ch., Waterbury, 1898-1901, Bushwick Av. Ch., Brooklyn, N.Y., 1901-09, New York Av. Ch., Brooklyn, 1909-13; prof. homiletics, Drew Theol. Sem. (now Drew U.), Sept. 1913—. Mem. Gen. Conf. Commn. on Courses of Study of M.E. Ch. Mason. Republican. Author: The Sunday School, an Evangelistic Opportunity; Evangelism for the New Age. Home: Madison, N.J. Died Feb. 11, 1929.

HANNIGAN, Francis James, librarian; b. Boston, Mass., Dec. 30, 1880; s. Thomas J. and Anne (Gill) H.; ed. pub. schs., Boston; m. Margaret M. Barry, June 7, 1911; children—Katharine Marie, Francis James. With Boston Pub. Library, 1894—; supervisor general reference depts. Boston Pub. Library; dir.-in-chief Federal Emergency Relief and Works Progress adminstrns. library projects, 1934-36. Editor: Up to Midnight, 1913. Compiler: Standard Index of Short Stories, 1900-14, 1915-33. Home: Dorchester, Mass. Died Oct. 14, 1940.

HANSBROUGH, Henry Clay, senator; b. Prairie du Rocher, Ill., Jan. 30, 1848; s. Eliab and Sarah (Hagen) H.; ed. common sch.; m. Josephine Orr (died 1895); m. 2d, Mary Berri Chapman, 1897. Removed to Calif., 1867; learned printing trade; published a daily paper at San José, Calif., 1869-70; with San Francisco Chronicle, 1870-79; published a paper at Baraboo, Wis., for 2 yrs.; removed to then Ty. of Dakota, 1882, engaging in journalism; was twice mayor of his city; mem. 51st Congress (1889-91); U.S. senator 3 terms, 1891-1909. Mem. Rep. Nat. Com., 1888-96. Home: Devils Lake, N.D. Died Nov. 16, 1933.

HANSCOM, Charles Ridgely, shipbuilder; b. Portsmouth, N.H., June 6, 1850; s. Pierpont and Eliza J. (Philbrick) H.; ed. largely under pvt. tutors; m. Eva L. Pettigrew, Feb. 1874 (died June, 1874); m. 2d, Adah L. Fernald, Jan. 8, 1879 (died June 1908). Asst. draftsman and draftsman navy yards, New York, Phila., Boston and Washington, 1873-80; draftsman and naval expert, U.S. Navy Dept., Washington, D.C., 1880-90; supt., 1890-96, gen. supt., 1896-1900, Bath (Me.) Iron Works, building govt. and mcht. vessels of all types; pres. Eastern Shipbuilding Co., New London, Conn., 1900-06 (retired); designed and built many steam yachts for private owners; also designed and built the large steamships, Minnesota and Dakota. Republican. Universalist. K.T. Home: New London, Conn. Died Oct. 31, 1918.

HANSCOM, Frank Edward; educator; b. West Poland, Me., Mar. 24, 1863; s. Edward H. and Emeline M. (McCann) H.; A.M., Bates Coll., 1899, Ed.D., 1931; A.M., Bowdoin Coll., 1907; m. Rose Ella Davis, Aug. 22, 1899; children—Kathryn (Mrs. Carroll P. Bailey), Robert Davis, Frank Edward, Margaret Emeline, Dorothy Jean. Supt. schs., Poland and Mechanic Falls, Me., 1886-92; prin. Oxford (Me.) High Sch., 1892-97, Gould Acad., Bethel, Me., 1897-1937, emeritus; propr. and mgr. Me. Teachers' Agency, 1892-1905; pres. Bethel Nat. Bank. Pres. Bethel Library Assn. Republican. Conglist. (deacon Bethel Congl. Ch.). Home: Bethel, Me. Died Apr. 11, 1940.

HANSCOM, John Forsyth, rear adm.; b. Eliot, Me., May 21, 1842. Served in vol. army, Sept. 10, 1862-July 17, 1863; apptd. from Mass., asst. naval constr. U.S.N., July 29, 1875; promoted naval constr., Oct. 10, 1888. On duty at navy yards, Boston and League Island, Pa., Bur. Constrn., Navy Dept. advisory bd., Chester, Pa., 1883-87, and New York, 1887-88; mem. Bd. Inspection and Survey, 1889-91, 1895-97; supt. constrn., Alabama and Maine, 1898-1903; sr. mem. bds. on hull changes for ships building on Atlantic Coast; retired with rank of rear admiral, May 4, 1904. Died Sept. 30, 1912.

HANSEL, Charles, cons. engr.; b. Peoria, Ill., July 31, 1859; s. John W. and Mary (Tillitson) H.; grad. high sch., Peoria, Ill.; studied civ. engring. under pvt. tutor; m. Frances Parker, 1887; children—Charles Francis, Anna Virginia Joy. Locating engr. D.&R.G. R.R. 4 yrs., and div. engr. in charge of building the first div. of D.&R.G. into New Mexico; chief engr. Wabash Ry., 1884-89; 1st cons. engr. Railroad and Warehouse Commn. of Ill., sent to Europe by state of Ill. to report on European railroads. Commd. to Europe, 1892, by dir. gen. Chicago Expn. to aid in getting exhibits of English equipment for railroads; apptd. by gov. of Mich. mem. Bd. of Review, 1901, to adjudicate problems in connection with valuation of railroads in that state; cons. engr. Indiana Harbor Ry., Ind., 1904-06, building 110 miles of double track; expert in charge valuation of railroads and canals of N.J., 1909; apptd., 1912, to make valuation Duluth, South Shore & Atlantic R.R.; made valuation of Reading System for Anthracite Rate Case, 1913; mem. Presidents' Conf. Engring. Com. of Railroads, 1913—; chmn. Valuation Com. of P.&R. Ry. Co., Central R.R. Co. of N.J., Phila. Rapid Transit Co., Internat. Ry. Co.; cons. valuation engr. Pa. System; etc.; head of Charles Hansel Cons. Specialists, practice in engring., law and economics in problems arising under Interstate Commerce Act and Federal Income Tax laws. Pres. Union County (N.J.) Park Commn. Author: Report on Revaluation Railroads and Canals of New Jersey, 1911. Home: Cranford, N.J. Died Dec. 24, 1936.

HANSEL, John Washington, clergyman; educator; b. Peoria, Ill., Mar. 6, 1853; s. John Washington and Mary Ann (Little) H.; ed. high sch., Peoria, and under private tutelage; (LL.D., Fargo [N.D.] Coll., 1917); m. Christina Mowat, Aug. 10, 1875. Connected with wholesale drug business, Peoria, 1870-82; gen. sec. Y.M.C.A., St. Joseph, Mo., 1882-87, Kansas City, Mo., 1887-90; gen. sec. Secretarial Inst. and Training Sch., Chicago and Lake Geneva, Ill., 1890-1900, and pres. same (now Y.M.C.A. Coll., Chicago), 1900-06; pres. Fargo (N.D.) Coll., 1913-18. Mem. A.B.C.F.M., Nat. Council Congl. Chs. of U.S., Congl. Conf. of N.D. Republican. Home: Richmond, Ind. Died Apr. 13, 1932.

HANSELL, Howard Forde, prof. ophthalmology; b. Phila., Pa., Oct. 25, 1855; s. Barnett and Rebecca (Wetherill) H.; A.B., Brown U., 1877, A.M., 1880; M.D., Jefferson Med. Coll., 1879; m. Emily Vogdes, Jan. 3, 1888; 1 son, Howard F. Practiced in Phila., 1881—; mem. faculty Jefferson Med. Coll., 1894—; prof. ophthalmology same coll. from 1904, emeritus; formerly prof. diseases of the eye, Phila. Polyclinic; ophthalmologist to Phila. Hosp. Baptist. Died Apr. 13, 1932.

HANSELMAN, Joseph Francis, priest; b. Brooklyn, Oct. 28, 1856; s. Henry and Margaret (Jacobs) H.; A.B., St. Francis Xavier Coll., New York, 1877; studied theology at Grand Sem., Montreal, 1877-78, philosophy, 1881-84, and theology, 1889-93, Woodstock Coll., Md.; became mem. of the Jesuit Order, 1878, priest in 1892. Taught Latin, Greek and English lit., St. Peter's Coll., Jersey City, 1884-88; surveying and philosophy, St. John's Coll., Fordham, N.Y., 1888-89; prefect of studies and discipline, 1893-97, prefect of discipline, 1898-1901, pres., 1901-06, Holy Cross Coll., Worcester, Mass.; provincial Md.-

N.Y. province of Jesuits, 1906-12; pres. Woodstock (Md.) Coll., 1912—. Died Jan. 16, 1923.

HANSON, Bert, lawyer; b. Sanford, Me., July 26, 1867; s. Benjamin Frank and Fannie (Thompson) H.; student Phillips Exeter Acad.; A.B., Yale U., 1890; LL.B., Cornell U., 1893; m. Helen Potter, July 16, 1919; 1 son, Potter. Admitted to N.Y. bar, 1894, and practiced in Syracuse; removed to N.Y. City, 1895; 3d dep. commr. of police, New York, under Gen. T. A. Bingham, 1907-09; asst. U.S. atty. gen., in charge of customs cases, 1914-21. Treas. Cornell Club of New York, 1904-14, v.p., 1914-17; pres. Municipal Art Soc., 1910-12; sec. Reform Club beginning 1904 and pres., 1923-28; trustee and sec. Nat. Acad. Assn. Democrat. Mason. Home: New York, N.Y. Died Dec. 13, 1938.

HANSON, Burton, lawyer; b. Rushford, Wis., Aug. 27, 1851; s. Cornelius and Catherine (Tremper) H.; ed. Whitewater (Wis.) Normal Sch.; m. Caro Lina McClure, June 3, 1896. Admitted to bar, 1876; solicitor Milwaukee, Lake Shore & Western Ry., 1879-83; asst. gen. solicitor, 1883-95, gen. solicitor, 1895-1910, gen. counsel, Jan. 1, 1911—, C.,M.&St.P. Ry. Home: Evanston, Ill. Died Aug. 5, 1922.

HANSON, George Charles, consular service; b. Bridgeport, Conn., Oct. 11, 1883; s. Charles and Josephine (Stegkemper) H.; C.E., Cornell U., 1908; unmarried. Apptd. student interpreter in China, 1909; dep. consul gen., later interpreter, at Shanghai, 1911; vice and dep. consul and interpreter, Chefoo, 1912-13, Dalny, 1913-14, Tientsin, 1914-15, Newchwang, Jan.-Mar. 1915; consul, Swatow, 1915-17, at Chungking, Mar. 20, 1917-July 10, 1918, Foochow, 1918-21, Harbin 1922-31, consul gen., 1931—. Fellow Am. Geog. Society. Presbyterian. Delegated by Secretary of State Stimson to report on conditions in Manchuria immediately following clash between Japanese and Chinese troops, 1931. Home: Bridgeport, Conn. Died Sept. 2, 1935.

HANSON, George M., asso. justice Supreme Jud. Court of Me. Democrat. Home: Calais, Me. Died Apr. 4, 1924.

HANSON, John Fletcher, ry. pres.; b. Monroe Co., Ga., Nov. 25, 1840; s. James B. and Permetea C. H.; country sch. edn.; m. Cora Alice Lee, Feb. 14, 1865. Was mem. U.S. Monetary Commn.; dir. Ga. Southern & Fla. R.R., 1894—; chmn. bd. dirs., 1900-03, pres., Dec. 7, 1903—, Central of Ga. Ry.; pres. Ocean Steamship Co., June 1902—. Home: Atlanta, Ga. Died 1910.

HANSON, Joseph Miles, social worker; b. Darlington, Wis., Mar. 24, 1868; s. Nelson and Jennie A. (Moody) H.; A.B., Grinnell (Ia.) Coll., 1893; m. Luetta M. Reece, Nov. 13, 1903. Asst. to pastor, Peoples Ch., St. Paul, Minn., 1893-94; apptd. supt. Men's Settlement Club, St. Paul, 1894; went to Kansas City, Mo., 1899, as gen. sec. Associated Charities, and established an industrial social settlement; called Franklin Inst. (now Swope Settlement); resigned, 1902, to give full time to settlement and gen. welfare movements; supt. self-help dept. Park Coll., Parkville, Mo., 1905-08; settled at Youngstown, O., 1908, and organized the charitable and welfare work of the city, title of gen. sec. Community-Service Society. Republican. Presbyn. Died Jan. 11, 1921.

HANSON, Martin H., impresario; b. Altona, Germany, July 11, 1864; ed. high sch., Altona, later univ. course; unmarried. First came to U.S., 1897; settled in N.Y. City, 1907; naturalized citizen of U.S., 1914. Introduced to Am. audiences Dr. Ludwig Wüllner, Leo Ornstein, Cecil Burleigh, Tilly Koenen, Max Pauer, Gottfried Galston, reintroduced Fegruccio Busoni, Ferenc Vecsey, etc. Originator and promoter of first concert tours of choirs from the Vatican, the first concert tour of chorus of 60 mixed voices from St. Olaf Coll., Northfield, Minn., Dayton (O.) Westminster Choir; mgr. Prague's Teachers Chorus tour of U.S., 1928-29. Pres. and concert dir. M. H. Hanson, Inc. Republican. Home: New York, N.Y. Died Apr. 29, 1931.

HANSON, Ole; b. Racine Co., Wis., Jan. 6, 1874; s. Thorsten and Goro (Tostofson) H.; ed. pub. schs., under priv. tutors, and grad. business coll.; studied law in the office of J. R. Dyer, Racine, Wis., 1890-94; LL.D., Lincoln Memorial Univ., Harrogate, Tenn.; m. Nellie Rose, May 12, 1895. Settled in Seattle, Wash., 1902, and engaged in real estate and investment business. Mem. Ho. of Rep., Wash., 1908, 09; sponsor of labor measures, mem. labor com., and leader in securing passage of anti-race track gambling act; defeated for U.S. Senate on state-wide issue of rural credit bank, of which he was advocate; elected mayor of Seattle, 1918, for term ending 1920. Gained nat. prominence by prompt and decisive measures in meeting and overcoming general strike at Seattle, Feb. 1919; after building 4,000-acre Spanish village called San Clemente, Calif., now developing 29 Palms, a desert community and health resort of Calif. Pres. All-Year Outdoor Ice Rinks, Inc. Has lectured widely in U.S. Mason. Author: Americanism vs. Bolshevism, 1920. Home: Los Angeles, Calif. Died July 6, 1940.

HANUS, Paul Henry, univ. prof.; b. Hermsdorf u.d. Kynast, Silesia, Prussia, Mar. 14, 1855; s. Gustaf and Ida (Aust) H.; came to U.S. in 1859 with widowed mother; B.S., U. of Mich., 1878; LL.D., U. of Colo., 1906, U. of Mich., 1925; m. Charlotte Hoskins, Aug. 10, 1881; 1 dau., Winifred (Mrs. Edward Clark Whiting). Was for 1 yr. in drug business in Denver; teacher, 1878—, except for 1 yr.; prof. pedagogy, Colo. State Normal Sch., Greeley, 1890-91; asst. prof. history and art of teaching, 1891-1901; prof., 1901-21, prof. emeritus, Harvard U. Chmn. Mass. State Commn. on Industrial Edn., 1906-09; mem. Mass. State Bd. of Edn., 1909-19; chmn. exec. bd., Boston Vocation Bur., 1909-17. In charge of ednl. aspects of an inquiry undertaken by a com. on sch. inquiry of Bd. of Estimate and Apportionment of N.Y. City, June 1, 1911-July 1, 1912; survey of Hampton Inst. (Va.) for Gen. Education Bd., 1917. Dir. sch. surveys in a number of cities, 1912—; counsellor on college problems; prin. founder Grad. Sch. of Edn., Harvard, 1920. On invitation of govt. of New Zealand, visited that country, 1914, with 13 others, also invited. Mem. editorial bd. School Review, Chicago, 1906-15; collaborator, Ednl. Adminstrn. and Supervision, Baltimore, 1915-17; lecturer Sch. of Edn., U. of Chicago, 1st term summer quarter, 1914, also summer sessions a number of state univs. Author: Geometry in the Grammar School, 1894; School Efficiency, 1913; School Administration and School Reports, 1920; Opportunity and Accomplishments in Secondary Education, 1926; Adventuring in Education, 1937. Home: Cambridge, Mass. Died Dec. 14, 1941.

HAPGOOD, Isabel Florence, author; b. Boston, Mass., Nov. 21, 1850; d. Asa and Lydia (Crossley) H.; ed. Miss Porter's Sch., Farmington, Conn., 1865-68. Author: (or compiler or translator) The Epic Songs of Russia, 1886; Russian Rambles, 1895; A Survey of Russian Literature, 1902; A Service Book of the Holy Orthodox Catholic (Greco-Russian) Church, 1906; (translations from Russian) Childhood, Boyhood, Youth, Sevastopol, Life, What Is to Be Done? (L. N. Tolstoy); Dead Souls, St. John's Eve and Other Tales (N. B. Gogol); Sonya, Kovalevsky, 1895; How Count Tolstoy Lives and Works (Sergeenko); Foma Gordyeeff, 1901; Orloff and His Wife (Maxim Gorky), 1901; The Novels and Stories of Ivan Turgenev (16 vols.), 1904; The Steel Flea (by N. S. Lyeskoff), 1916; (from Spanish) Faith; The Origin of Thought (Armando Palacio-Valdès); (from Italian) Cuore (A. De Amicis); (from French) Les Misérables, etc. (V. Hugo); Thoughts (Canon Joseph Roux); Recollections and Letters (Ernest Renan); The Evolution of France Under the Third Republic (Baron Pierre de Coubertin). Died June 26, 1928.

HAPGOOD, Marshall Jay; b. Peru, Vt., Jan. 13, 1850; s. Joseph Jackson and Hepsibah (Barnard) H.; ed. Williams Coll., and independent course at Harvard; m. Flora E. Huggins, June 1875. Began in gen. store business, Peru, 1875; entered lumber mfg. business, 1880, and now owns extensive tracts of timber land; entered hotel business, 1903, attaching an "outdoor fireplace," the only one of the kind known to exist. A leading propagandist of forestry in N.E.; attended, by spl. invitation, the 3 days' conference for the preservation of natural resources, called by President Roosevelt, at the White House, May 1908; lover of wild animals and earnest advocate of protection of deer, for which purpose he has an extensive park. Mem. Vt. Ho. Rep., 1880, 1904, 06, 12, 14, 16; known as "Vermont's Rugged Reformer"; advocate of unique plan to prevent undesirable legislation, by 3 mos. recess of legislature after all bills have passed successive readings, giving time for full discussion at home and in the press; candidate for gov., 1910, and was first one in history of the state to file sworn statement of expenses. Commissioner to devise a suitable memorial for the author of "The Green Mountain Boys," and Ira Allen. Has deeded Mt. Bromley, overlooking his native village, to the state upon condition that no trees shall ever be cut upon it and put the adjacent mountain range under perpetual protection of the state; owner of a "lodge" in the center of a 10,000-acre timber tract. Conglist. Home: Peru, Vt. Died June 1926.

HAPGOOD, Norman, editor, author; b. Chicago, Ill., Mar. 28, 1868; s. Charles H. and Fanny Louise (Powers) H.; A.B., Harvard, 1890, A.M., LL.B., 1893; m. Emilie Bigelow, June 17, 1896; m. 2d, Elizabeth K. Reynolds, Dec. 13, 1916. Dramatic critic New York Commercial Advertiser, and Bookman, 1897-1902; editor Collier's Weekly, 1903-12, Harper's Weekly, 1913-16, Hearst's Internat. Magazine, 1923-25. Author: Literary Statesmen, 1897; Daniel Webster, 1899; Abraham Lincoln, 1899; George Washington, 1901; The Stage in America, 1901; Industry and Progress, 1911; The Advancing Hour, 1920; Up from the City Streets (with Henry Moskowitz), 1927; Why Janet Should Read Shakespeare, 1929; The Changing Years, 1930. E.E. and M.P. from U.S. to Denmark, Feb.-Dec. 1919. Home: New York, N.Y. Died Apr. 29, 1937.

HARAHAN, James Theodore, ry. pres.; b. Lowell, Mass., Jan. 12, 1841; s. Thomas and Rose H.; m. Mary B. Kehoe, 1866; m. 2d, Mary Mallory, Apr. 19, 1899; father of William Johnson H. In employ Orange & Alexandria R.R., Alexandria, Va., 1864-65, Nashville & Decatur R.R., Nashville, Tenn., 1865-66, L.&N. R.R. at various points, 1866-70; in charge of Shelby R.R., 1870-72; roadmaster, Nashville & Decatur R.R., 1872-79; supt. Memphis line, L.&N. R.R., 1879-81, New Orleans div., same, 1881-85; gen. supt. L.&N. R.R., S. of Decatur, 1883-84, gen. mgr. entire line, same, 1884-85; gen. supt. Pittsburgh div., B.&O. R.R., Jan.-Apr. 1885; asst. gen. mgr. L.&N. R.R., Apr.-Oct. 1885, gen. mgr. same, 1885-88; afterward successively asst. gen. mgr. L.S.&M.S. Ry., gen. mgr. C.&O. Ry., gen. mgr. Louisville, New Orleans & Tex. Ry. until Nov. 1, 1890; 2d v.p. Nov. 1, 1890-Nov. 7, 1906, pres. Nov. 7, 1906—, Ill. Cent. R.R. Home: Chicago, Ill. Died 1912.

HARAHAN, William Johnson, ry. official; b. Nashville, Tenn., Dec. 22, 1867; s. James Theodore and Mary B. (Kehoe) H.; ed. St. John's Coll., New Orleans; m. Susan Smith, June 10, 1890; m. 2d, Elizabeth M. Smith, Mar. 23, 1935. Various positions on L.&N. R.R. at New Orleans, La., 1881-89; engr. of maintenance of way, Cincinnati div., C.&O. Ry., 1889-90; in charge of structures, B.&O.S.W. R.R., 1890-92; roadmaster and trainmaster, Pontiac div., I.C. R.R., 1892-95, asst. supt. and supt. Freeport div., 1895-96, supt. Louisville div., 1896-1901, chief engr. I.C. R.R., Chicago, May 1-Sept. 24, 1902; asst. gen. mgr., 1902-04, gen. mgr., June 1, 1904, 4th v.p., Feb. 20, 1905, I.C. R.R.; asst. to pres. Erie R.R., July 15, 1907-10; v.p. Erie R.R., Jan. 1, 1911-12; pres. Seaboard Air Line Ry., 1912-18; federal mgr. same rd., 1918-20; staff officer for Dir. Gen. of R.R.'s, Apr.-Dec. 1920; pres. C.&O. Ry., and Hocking Valley Ry., Dec. 1920-May 1929; sr. v.p. C.&O. Ry., Pere Marquette Ry. Co., May 1920-July 23, 1935; pres. C.&O. Ry., Pere Marquette Ry. Co., July 23, 1935—; pres. N.Y.C.&St.L. R.R. Co., July 30, 1935—. Home: Cleveland, O. Died Dec. 14, 1937.

HARALSON, Jonathan, judge; b. Lowndes Co., Ala., Oct. 18, 1830; s. William Browning and Temperance Martin (Dunklin) H.; A.B., U. of Ala., 1851, A.M., 1854; LL.B., U. of La.; (LL.D., Mercer U., 1892); m. Mattie Ellen Thompson, Apr. 9, 1859; 2d, Lida J. McFaddin, of Greensboro, Ala., May 20, 1869. Admitted to bar and practiced at Selma, Ala. Judge City Ct., Selma., 1876-92; judge Supreme Ct. of Ala., 1892-1910. Democrat. Pres. Ala. Bapt. State Conv., 1874-92; pres. Southern Bapt. Conv., 1888—; mem. exec. bd. Am. Bapt. Edn. Soc.; trustee Agrl. and Mech. Coll. of Ala., 1877—. Home: Selma, Ala. Died July 11, 1912.

HARBACH, Abram Alexander, army officer; b. Pa., Aug. 14, 1841. Sergt. Co. E, 1st Ia. Inf., May 7-Aug. 20, 1861; pvt. and corporal, Co. H, 11th U.S. Inf., Dec. 7, 1861-June 20, 1862; 2d lt. 11th Inf., June 11, 1862; 1st lt., July 2, 1863; transferred to 20th Inf., Sept. 21, 1866; capt., Jan. 22, 1867; maj. 18th Inf., Mar. 12, 1894; lt. col. 3d Inf., Aug. 8, 1897; served in Santiago campaign in Cuba, 1898, and P.I., 1900; col. 1st Inf., July 19, 1899; brig. gen. U.S.A., Mar. 16, 1902; retired, May 28, 1902, at his own request, after 40 yrs.' service. During Civil War was engaged in many battles, and bvtd. capt., July 2, 1863, "for gallant and meritorious services at Gettysburg." Home: Santa Barbara, Calif. Died Nov. 22, 1933.

HARBAUGH, Thomas Chalmers, author; b. Middletown, Md., Jan. 13, 1849; s. Morgan M. and Caroline R. H.; ed. common schs. Casstown, O.; unmarried. In lit. work, 1867—. Author: Loves of Gabrielle, 1913; Poisoned Pin, 1913; Borgia Shadow, 1913; Palace of Doom, 1913; Serpent and Dove, 1913; Kit Carson's Chum, 1913; The Leopard Woman, 1914; Washington's Boy Scouts, 1914; Ned Vinton's Quest, 1915; The Czar's Spy, 1915; Hearts and Swords, 1915; The Jewels of Jezebel, 1915, etc. Home: Troy, O. Died Oct. 28, 1924.

HARBEN, Will(iam) N(athaniel), author; b. Dalton, Ga., July 5, 1858; s. Nathaniel Parks and Myra (Richardson) H.; pvt. edn.; m. Maybelle Chandler, July 2, 1896. In business enterprises in South until 1888, then engaged in literature as profession; asst. editor Youth's Companion, 1891-93. Author: Abner Daniel, 1902; The Substitute, 1903; The Georgians, 1904; Gilbert Neal, 1908; The Desired Woman, 1913; The New Clarion, 1914; The Inner Law, 1915; Second Choice, 1916; The Triumph, 1917. Home: New York, N.Y. Died Aug. 7, 1919.

HARBER, Giles Bates, rear adm.; b. Youngstown, O., Sept. 24, 1849; s. Joseph and Ann Eliza (Darrow) H.; apptd. from Ohio, and grad U.S. Naval Acad., 1869; m. Jeannette Thurston Manning, Apr. 25, 1889. Promoted ensign July 12, 1870; master, July 12, 1871; lt., Sept. 19, 1874; lt. comdr., Sept. 4, 1896; comdr., Sept. 25, 1899; capt., Sept. 30, 1904; rear adm., Nov. 12, 1908. Served on Sabine and Franklin, European sta., 1869-71; Iroquois and Monocacy, China sta., 1872-75; Omaha, S. Pacific sta., 1875-78; Tennessee and Alarm, N. Atlantic sta., 1879-82; Saratoga and Tallapoosa, W.I. and S. Atlantic stas., 1885-88; Hassler (coast survey), in Alaska, 1892-95; aboard Texas, W.I., during Spanish-Am. War, 1898-99; New Orleans, China sta., 1903-05; comd. Independence, Mare Island Navy Yard, 1905-07; comd. 3d Squadron Pacific Fleet, 1907-10;

comdr.-in-chief Pacific Fleet, Feb. 19-Nov. 1, 1910; pres. Naval Examining and Retiring Bds., Dec. 1910-Oct. 1911; retired by operation of law, Sept. 24, 1911. Was in commd. of expdn. sent to search for survivors of the Jeannette Polar Expdn., 1882-84, and brought home bodies of DeLong and nine of his companions; naval attaché U.S. embassies, France and Russia, 1900-03. Promoted 5 numbers, Aug. 10, 1898, for "eminent and conspicuous conduct in battle." Died Dec. 30, 1925.

HARBERT, Elizabeth Morrisson Boynton, lecturer; b. Crawfordsville, Ind., Apr. 15, 1845; d. William and Abbey Upton (Sweetser) Boynton; grad. Terre Haute Female Coll., 1862; Ph.D., Ohio Wesleyan U.; m. William Soesby Harbert, Oct. 18, 1870. Editor "Woman's Kingdom," Chicago Inter Ocean, 8 yrs., The New Era, 1 yr. Asso. pres. World's Unity League; organized and 7 yrs. pres. Evanston Woman's Club; pres. Nat. Household Econ. Assn.; was for 12 yrs. pres. Ill. Equal Suffrage Assn.; v.p. Woman's Civic League of Pasadena; v.p. Southern Calif. Woman's Press Assn. Home: Pasadena, Calif. Died Jan. 19, 1925.

HARBISON, Robert Cleland, editor, pub.; b. Indianola, Ia., Sept. 10, 1866; s. William Porter and Amanda (Cleland) H.; A.B., Simpson Coll., Indianola, 1888, A.M., 1891; m. Nina Lezotte, Aug. 24, 1892; children—Rose (dec.), Robert Lezotte; m. 2d, Ida Miller Goodwin, Aug. 6, 1928. Newspaper business, Indianola, 1887; reporter in San Francisco, 1892-94; with San Bernardino (Calif.) Sun, 1894—, editor, 1896—; pres. Sun Co. Pres. San Bernardino chapter Am. Red. Cross, 1918-20, dir., 1920—; Rep. candidate for Congress, 11th Calif. Dist., 1916; mem. Calif. Water Resources Commn., 1931. Mason. Home: San Bernardino, Calif. Died Oct. 21, 1937.

HARBO, Elias Peter (adopted name), theologian; b. Fredrickshald, Norway, Feb. 6, 1856; s. Hans and Ellen Marie (Olson) Olson; B.A., Augsburg Sem., Minneapolis, 1886; grad. theol. course, same sem., 1889; m. Martha Marie Larson, Dec. 3, 1889; children—Elise M., Harold E., George M., Leif S., Alf F., Rolf T., Erling W., Anker B., Helen M. Ordained ministry Luth. Conf., 1889; pastor La Crosse, Wis., 1889-93, Duluth, Minn., 1893-1902, Minneapolis, 1902-09, prof. systematic theology, Augsburg Sem., 1909—; pres. Folkebladet Pub. Co. Pres. Luth. Free Ch.; pres. bd. of organization, Luth. Free Ch. and pres. Bd. of Home Missions, same. Prohibitionist. Home: Minneapolis, Minn. Died Apr. 10, 1927.

HARBOROUGH-SHERARD, Mrs. Robert (Irene Osgood), author; b. (de Belot) in Va.; descendant of French and Spanish ancestors; ed. pvtly.; m. Capt. Charles Pigott Harvey, high sheriff of North Hants, England, and lord of the manor in Lincolnshire, 1903 (died, 1904); granted name Irène Osgood by Royal Deed-Pole. Has lived principally in Paris and Eng. since she was a child; retains Am. citizenship. Maintained and managed 3 hosps. for wounded soldiers on her estate which she placed at the disposal of the Red Cross. Was specially mentioned by the war office for war work in England. Received in special private audience by Pope Benedict XV. Specially mentioned by French war office for war work. Author: Where Pharaoh Dreams, 1909, 1913; A Blood Moon, 1911; A Mother in Dreams (poems), 1913; The Indelicate Duellist, 1913; also short stories, verse, etc. Plays: Servitude; The Pale Witch Queen; Fatima Yasmeen; The Southern Widow; Une Aventure du Capitaine Lebrun, prod. Paris, Feb. 28, and Mar. 1913; The Menace, prod. 1914. Compiled: The Winged Anthology; The Garden Anthology. Home: Northampton, Eng. Died Dec. 12, 1922.

HARBOUR, Jefferson Lee, author; b. Oskaloosa, Ia., Mar. 31, 1857; s. R. R. and Mary C. (Roop) H.; ed. Oskaloosa; m. Alice E. Crowell, May 25, 1880; m. 2d, Mrs. Bertha Vella Borden, May 27, 1922. Asso. editor The Youth's Companion, 1884-1901. Author of more than 700 short stories published in The Youth's Companion, Harper's Bazar, St. Nicholas, The Outlook, and similar periodicals. Has lectured extensively on Blessed Be Humor, Wit and Humor of the Puritan, If I Were Twenty-one, Reminiscences of Famous Authors. Resided at Fall River, Mass. Died Feb. 25, 1931.

HARDAWAY, William Augustus, physician; b. Mobile, Ala., Jan. 8, 1850; s. William Augustus and Mary (del Barco) H.; ed. pvt. sch., St. Louis; spl. courses at Westminster Coll. and U. of Va.; M.D., Mo. Med. Coll., 1870; (hon. A.M., St. Louis U.; LL.D., Westminster Coll.); m. Lucy Nelson Page, Jan. 8, 1877. President Am. Dermatol. Assn., 1885. Author: Manual of Skin Diseases, 1890. Editor (with Dr. L. B. Bangs) of American Text-Book of Genito-Urinary Diseases, Syphilis and Diseases of the Skin, 1898; Handbook of Cutaneous Therapeutics (with Joseph Grindon), 1907. Home: St. Louis, Mo. Died Mar. 3, 1923.

HARDEN, William, librarian; b. Savannah, Ga., Nov. 11, 1844; s. Edward J. and Sophia H. (Maxwell) H.; ed. Savannah, Ga.; left school to enter mil. service of the state of Ga., 1861, and the C.S., 1862; served to end of war in 54th Ga. Inf. and in signal corps; admitted to bar, July 25, 1873; m. Mary E. Davenport, Dec. 11, 1879 (died 1921). Assistant librarian, 1866-69, librarian, Aug. 5, 1869—, Ga. Hist. Soc.; librarian Pub. Library of Savannah, 1903-16; editor Georgia Hist. Quarterly (Ga. Hist. Soc.), 1917-20. Mem. Ga. Ho. of Rep., 1900-05. Democrat. Organizer, and sec., 1891—, Georgia Society S.R.; past comdr. Georgia Div. U.C.V. Ruling elder in Presbyn. Ch., 1877—. Home: Savannah, Ga. Died Jan. 4, 1936.

HARDENBERGH, Henry Janeway, architect; b. New Brunswick, N.J., Feb. 6, 1847; s. John Pool and Frances Eliza (Eddy) H.; studied architecture under Detlef Lienau of New York, 1863-70; m. Emily Irene (Leeds) Keene, 1893 (died 1899). In active practice in New York, 1870—. Erected from his designs; Dakota Hotel, Waldorf-Astoria Hotel, Manhattan Hotel, Am. Fine Arts Soc. Bldg., Plaza Hotel, etc. A.N.A., 1910; mem. Nat. Inst. Arts and Letters, A.I.A. Home: Bernardsville, N.J. Died Mar. 18, 1918.

HARDIE, George Robert, college pres.; b. Gouverneur, N.Y., Sept. 10, 1869; s. James and Jessie (Telfer) H.; B.A., St. Lawrence U., Canton, N.Y., 1890, M.A., 1892; LL.D., Defiance (O.) Coll., 1931; student Harvard, 1891-92, U. of Chicago, 1895; m. Jessie Dell Stearns, July 2, 1901. Head of dept. Latin, St. Lawrence U., 1892-1917; mem. N.Y. State Dept. Edn., 1922-27; exec. head with title of dean, Long Island U., 1927-32; pres. Greenwich Coll., 1934—. Home: Greenwich, Conn. Died Dec. 4, 1935.

HARDIE, Robert Gordon, portrait, painter; b. Brattleboro, Vt., Mar. 29, 1854; only s. Maj. Robert Gordon and Frances (Hyde) H.; ed. in dist. and high school; studied drawing in schools of Cooper Inst., Acad. of Design and Art Students' League, New York; studied at École des Beaux Arts, Paris, pupil of M. Gérôme. Exhibited in Paris Salon, 1880, 1881, and several following yrs.; became pupil of Cabanel, 1882; had studio in Paris; exhibited at Nat. Acad. Design, 1888; exhibited portrait of his wife at World's Columbian Expn., 1893; m. 1884, d. U.S. Senator Shelby M. Cullom of Ill. (died, 1894); m. 2d, Oct. 26, 1899, Amy Sigourney, d. Dr. Robert Stone of New York. Capt., chief of staff, Albany Burgesses Corps (one of oldest mil. orgns. in U.S.). Died 1904.

HARDIN, Everitt C(hancy), banker; b. Monmouth, Ill., Nov. 2, 1869; s. Delevan S. and Mary E. (Parsons) H.; Monmouth (Ill.) Coll., 1883-85, Cornell Coll., Mt. Vernon, Ia., 1886; m. Caroline A. Baldwin, Jan. 18, 1893; children—Mrs. Clara Warfield, Dell B., Mrs. Mary Jane Brainard. In the banking business, July 15, 1886—; v.p., now pres. Second Nat. Bank, Monmouth. Mem. 43d and 44th Gen. Assemblies, Ill., 1903-07; mem. bd. Warren County Library; treas. Monmouth Park Bd. Republican. Mason. Home: Monmouth, Ill. Died Nov. 21, 1941.

HARDIN, George A., jurist; b. Winfield, N.Y., Aug. 17, 1832; s. Col. Joseph H.; grad. Union Coll. (LL.D., Hamilton); admitted to bar, 1854; elected State senator, 1861; m. 1868. Practiced at Little Falls until elected Supreme Court justice; apptd. by Gov. Cleveland, 1884; by. Gov. Hill, 1885, and by Gov. Morton, presiding justice 4th dept. for 1895-99. Pres. Nat. Herkimer Co. Bank of Little Falls, Jan. 1901—. Editor: History of Herkimer County, 1898. Home: Little Falls, N.Y. Died 1901.

HARDIN, Martin D., brig. gen.; b. Jacksonville, Ill., June 26, 1837; s. Gen. John J. H., of Ill. (killed at battle of Buena Vista, Mex.); grad. U.S. Mil. Acad., 1859; bvt. 2d lt. 3d U.S. Arty., July 1, 1859; Artillery School, Ft. Monroe, Va., 1859-60; on staff Col. R. E. Lee during John Brown raid at Harper's Ferry; crossed continent with Blake Expdn., May-Oct. 1860; stationed at Ft. Umpqua, Ore., Oct. 1860 to Oct. 1861; returned to east with Gen. Sumner's expdn., via Panama; served with U.S. arty., Army of Potomac, 1861-62; present at siege of Yorktown and 7 days' battles before Richmond, Va.; lt. col. 12th Pa. reserves, April 1, 1862; col., July 8, 1862; comd. regt. at Harrison's Landing; served in Pope's campaign; comd. 12th regt. Pa. reserves; present at Rappahannock Sta., battle of Groveton, Aug. 29, 1862 (slightly wounded); comd. 3d brigade Pa. reserves 2d Bull Run (severely wounded); comd. 12th Pa. reserves at Gettysburg and Falling Waters; 3d brigade same in Rapidan campaign, Sept.-Dec., 1863; comd. 2 regts. inf. and troop of cav. guarding O.&A. R.R., Dec. 1863; severely wounded by guerrillas, Dec. 14, 1863; comd. draft rendezvous Pittsburgh, to May 15, 1864; comd. 1st bridgade Pa. reserves Spottsylvania, North Anna, Bethesda Church. Brig. gen. U.S. vols., comdg. Hardin's div., defenses north of the Potomac, Washington, July 1864-Aug. 1865; present at attack of Early's forces on Washington; comd. dist. Raleigh, N.C., 1865-66; maj. 43d U.S. Inf., July 26, 1866; retired as brig. gen. U.S.A. on account of wounds, Dec. 15, 1870. Admitted to Ill. bar, Sept. 1870, and began practice at Chicago. Home: Lake Forest, Ill. Died Dec. 12, 1923.

HARDIN, Martin D., clergyman; b. Harrodsburg, Ky., June 5, 1873; s. Parker Watkins and Mary Elizabeth (Sallee) H.; A.B., Center Coll., Danville, Ky., 1893; student Danville Theol. Sem., 1 yr., also Free Ch. Div. Sch., Edinburgh, Scotland; grad. Auburn Theol. Sem., 1897; D.D., Davidson (N.C.) Coll., 1905; m. Julia Stevenson, June 2, 1896; children—Letitia Stevenson (dec.), Parker Calhoun, Adlai Stevenson, Martin D., Julia Stevenson. Ordained Presbyn. ministry, 1897; pastor Green Hill Ch., Phila., Pa., 1897-98, Andrew Ch., Minneapolis, Minn., 1899-1904, 2d Ch., Charlotte, N.C., 1904-08, 3d Ch., Chicago, 1908-17; capt. Am. Red Cross, 1917, and nat. speaker for same, 1917-18; pastor 1st Ch., Ithaca, N.Y., 1920—; preacher and lecturer in chs. of Scotland and England, 1927, through invitation of English com. of World Alliance for Internat. Friendship through the Chs.; Chautauqua lecturer on internat. understanding and peace 10 yrs. Democrat. Home: Ithaca, N.Y. Died Dec. 14, 1935.

HARDING, Alfred, bishop; b. Lisburn, Ireland, Aug. 15, 1852; s. Richard and Mary (Ferguson) H.; came to America, 1867; A.B., Trinity Coll., Conn., 1879; grad. Berkeley Div. Sch., Conn., 1882; (D.D., Trinity, 1902; LL.D., George Washington, 1909); m. Justine Butler Prindle, June 8, 1887. Deacon, 1882, priest, 1883, P.E. Ch.; asst., Trinity Ch., Geneva, N.Y., 1882-83; asst. rector St. Paul's Parish, Baltimore, 1883-87; rector St. Paul's Ch., Washington, 1887-1909; consecrated bishop of Washington (D.C.), Jan. 25, 1909. Pres. trustees Nat. Cathedral Sch. for Girls and Nat. Cathedral Sch. for Boys, and St. John's Orphanage; pres. Chapter of Cathedral of Saints Peter and Paul, Episcopal Eye, Ear and Throat Hosp., Episcopal Home for Children. Mem. War Commn. P.E. Ch., War-time Com. of One Hundred, Gen. Chaplain's Com. of Fed. Council of Chs. Died Apr. 30, 1923.

HARDING, Chester, army officer; b. Enterprise, Miss., Dec. 31, 1866; s. Horace and Eliza Procter (Gould) H.; B.E., U. of Ala., 1884; grad. U.S. Mil. Acad., 1889, U.S. Engr. Sch. of Application, Willetts Point, N.Y., 1892; m. Flora Krum, July 15, 1895. Commd. add. 2d lt. engrs., June 12, 1889; advanced through grades to lt. col., Feb. 27, 1913; brig. gen. and retired, Apr. 1, 1920. Served as asst. to engr. commr. of D.C., 1901-06; div. engr., Gatun Locks Div., Panama Canal, 1907-08; asst. div. engr., Atlantic Div., Panama Canal, 1908-13; engr. commr. of D.C., 1913-14; engr. of maintenance, Panama Canal, 1915-17; gov. Panama Canal, Jan. 1917-Mar. 1921. Unitarian. Home: Vineyard Haven, Mass. Died Nov. 11, 1936.

HARDING, George, lawyer; b. Phila., Oct. 26, 1827; grad. Univ. of Pa., 1846; studied law; admitted to bar, 1849; specialist in patent law; connected with the great telegraph patent case of Samuel F. B. Morse against O'Reilly; asso. with Abraham Lincoln and Edwin M. Stanton in the McCormick reaper case; and was in many great patent suits. Home: Philadelphia. Died 1902.

HARDING, George Franklin; b. Chicago, Aug. 16, 1868; s. George Franklin and Adelaide (Mathews) H.; student Harvard class, 1892; m. Ellen Osborn Davis, of Neenah, Wis., Sept. 29, 1896 (now deceased); children—Penelope (dec.), Mary; m. 2d, Katherine Fay (dec.). Pres. Chicago Real Estate Loan & Trust Co.; chmn. bd. Consumers Co. Alderman of 2d Ward, Chicago, 1903-13; elected state senator from 1st Dist., Ill., 1912; controller City of Chicago, 1919-23; treas. of Cook Co., 1926-30; Nat. Rep. committeeman of State of Ill., 1936. Pres. The George F. Harding Collection. Republican. Unitarian. Home: Chicago, Ill. Died Apr. 2, 1939.

HARDING, Henry, civil engr.; b. Hartland, Vt., Dec. 10, 1837; s. Dr. John H.; academic edn. with Job Atkins, mining engr., Richmond, Va., 1859-60; unmarried. One of pioneer civ. engrs. on surveys, construction, etc., U.P. Ry., 1865-70; employed at intervals, 1871-95, by U.S. engr. corps. on river and harbor improvements; engaged on fortifications, Ft. Adams, Newport, R.I., 1872-73; in private practice, 1895—. Home: Hartland (Four Corners), Vt. Died 1910.

HARDING, J. Horace, banker; b. Phila., July 31, 1863; s. William W. and Catherine (Hart) H.; m. Dorothea Barney, Apr. 30, 1898; children—Charles B., Mrs. L. Suffern Tailer, Laura, William Barclay. Began in banking business, 1883; sr. partner Charles D. Barney & Co. to Jan. 1, 1919, then spl. partner; chmn. bd. Am. Railway Express Co.; dir. numerous interests; trustee Am. Surety Co. Mem. 1st City Troop Cav., Phila., 8 yrs. Republican. Episcopalian. Home: New York, N.Y. Died Jan. 4, 1929.

HARDING, Russell, ry. official; b. Springfield, Mass., 1856; s. William H. and Mary E. H.; ed. pub. schs. of Portland, Me.; m. Miss Isabel Rowsey, 1887. Held various positions on different rys., 1870-97; gen. supt. Great Northern Ry., 1897-98; v.p. and gen. mgr. St. Louis Southwestern Ry., 1898-1900; pres. St. Louis Southwestern Ry. of Texas, 1898-1900; v.p. and gen. mgr. Mo. Pacific Ry., 1900-04; from Aug. 1, 1904, pres. Pere Marquette System, v.p. and gen. mgr. C.,H.&D. Ry. and v.p. Chicago, Cincinnati & Louisville R.R. Died 1908.

HARDING, Samuel Bannister, educator, writer; b. Indianapolis, July 29, 1866; s. George Canady and Julia Cora (Bannister) H.; A.B., Ind. U., 1890; A.M., Harvard, 1894, Ph.D., 1898; m. Caroline Hirst Brown, 1890; 1 son, Robert George; m. 2d, Margaret Snodgrass, 1918; children—John Snodgrass, Margaret, Mary Katharine. Asst. prof., asso. prof. and prof. history, Ind. U., 1895-1918; research and editorial war work with Com. on Pub. Information, Washington, Aug. 1917-Jan. 1919; editorial work, Chicago, 1919-21; acting prof. of English History, U. of Minn., 1921; prof. history, extension div., same, 1922-24, supervising all college subjects in extension, and prof. history, U. of Minn., 1924—; prof. history summer sessions, U. of Ore., 1922-24, summer session, State Teachers Coll., Colo., 1925. Author: The Contest Over the Ratification of the Federal Constitution in the State of Massachusetts (Harvard Hist. Studies series), 1896; Essentials in Medieval and Modern History, 1905; Ind. U., 1820-1904 (editor), 1905; Select Orations Illustrating American History, 1909; New Medieval and Modern History, 1913; Old World Background to American History, 1919. Mng. editor Compton's Pictured Ency. (for young people), 1919-21. Home: Minneapolis, Minn. Died Jan. 29, 1927.

HARDING, Warren G(amaliel), twenty-ninth President of the United States; b. Corsica, O., Nov. 2, 1865; s. George Tyron and Phebe Elizabeth (Dickerson) H.; student Ohio Central Coll. (now defunct), Iberia, 1879-82; m. Florence Kling, July 8, 1891. Engaged in newspaper business at Marion, 1884—; pres. Harding Pub. Co., pubs. Star (daily); mem. Ohio Senate, 1900-04; lt. gov. of Ohio, 1904-06; Rep. nominee for gov. of Ohio, 1910 (defeated); mem. U.S. Senate, from Ohio, term 1915-21, resigned, 1920. Nominated for President in Republican Nat. Conv., Chicago, 1920, and elected Nov. 4, 1920, for term, Mar. 4, 1921-Mar. 4, 1925, receiving 404 electoral votes, James M. Cox, the Democratic nominee, receiving 127 votes. Inaugurated Pres., Mar. 4, 1921. Mason. Baptist. Home: Marion, O. Died Aug. 2, 1923.

HARDING, William Lloyd, governor; b. Sibley, Ia., Oct. 3, 1877; s. O. B. and Emalyn (Moyer) H.; Morningside Coll., Ia., 1897-1901; LL.B., U. of S.D., 1905; m. Carrie M. Lamoreux, Jan. 7, 1907; 1 dau., Barbara Esther. Began practice 1905; mem. Ia. Ho. of Rep., 1907-13; lt. gov. of Ia., 1913-17; gov., terms 1917-19 and 1919-21; resumed practice, 1921. Lecturer. Republican. Methodist. Mason. Home: Des Moines, Ia. Died Dec. 17, 1934.

HARDING, William P. G(ould), banker; b. Greene Co., Ala., May 5, 1864; s. Horace and Eliza Procter (Gould) H.; A.B., U. of Ala., 1880, A.M., 1881 (youngest full grad. in its history); LL.D., U. of Ala., 1916, Harvard, 1922, Columbia, 1922; m. Amanda Moore, Oct. 22, 1895 (died 1910); children—Elizabeth (Mrs. Eugene V. R. Thayer), Alice (Mrs. Robert T. Pell). Began as clk. and bookkeeper pvt. bank of J. H. Fitts & Co., Tuscaloosa, Ala., 1882; bookkeeper to cashier, Berney Nat. Bank, Birmingham, 1886-96; v.p., 1896, pres., June 28, 1902-June 24, 1914, 1st Nat. Bank, Birmingham; mem. Federal Reserve Bd., Washington, D.C., 1914-22, and gov., Aug. 10, 1916; gov. Federal Reserve Bank of Boston, Jan. 1, 1923—; mng. dir. War Finance Corp., 1918-19. Pres. Ala. State Bankers Assn., 1908, Birmingham Chamber of Commerce, 1913. Episcopalian. Author: The Formative Period of the Federal Reserve System, 1925. Home: Boston, Mass. Died Apr. 7, 1930.

HARDMAN, Lamartine Griffin, gov., M.D.; b. Commerce, Ga., Apr. 14, 1856; s. William Benjamin Johnson and Susan Elizabeth (Colquitt) H.; M.D., U. of Ga., 1877; post-grad. study Bellevue Hosp., New York, N.Y. Polyclinic Hosp., U. of Pa., Guy's Hosp., London; hon. B S., U. of Ga., 1922; m. Emma Wiley Griffin, Mar. 26, 1907; children—Lamartine Griffin, Josephine Staten, Sue Colquitt, Emma Griffin. Began practice at Commerce, 1876; pres. Harmony Grove Cotton Mills, Northeastern Banking Co., Commerce Telephone Co., Hardman Drug Co.—all of Commerce; owner and operator Hurricane Shoals Light & Power Plant and Nora Mills; dir. 1st Nat. Bank, Commerce. Mem. Ga. Ho. of Rep., 1902-07, Ga. Senate, 1908-10; mem. state fuel administration for Ga., World War; elected gov. of Ga., 2 terms, 1927-31. Trustee Ga. State Coll. Agr. and Mechanic Arts, also of Expt. Sta., Griffin, Ga. Trustee Southern Bapt. Sem. (Louisville, Ky.), Shorter Coll. (Rome, Ga.). Democrat. Baptist. Home: Commerce, Ga. Died Feb. 18, 1937.

HARDY, Arthur Sherburne, diplomat; b. Andover, Mass., Aug. 13, 1847; s. Alpheus and Susan W. (Holmes) H.; apptd. from Mass., and grad. U.S. Mil. Acad., 1869; hon. A.M., Ia. Coll., 1872, Dartmouth, 1873; Ph.D., Amherst, 1873; m. Grace Aspinwall Bowen, Mar. 9, 1898. Second lt. 3d Arty., June 15, 1869-Nov. 12, 1870; prof. civ. engring., Ia. Coll., 1871-73; studied abroad École des Ponts et Chaussées, 1873-74; prof. civ. engring., 1874-78, mathematics, 1878-93, Dartmouth Coll.; editor Cosmopolitan Mag., 1893-95; U.S. minister resident and consul gen. Teheran, Persia, 1897-99; E.E. and M.P. of U.S. to Greece, Roumania and Servia, 1899-1901, to Switzerland, 1901-03, to Spain, 1903-05. Author: But Yet a Woman, 1883; Wind of Destiny, 1886; Passe Rose, 1889; Life and Letters of Joseph H. Neesima; His Daughter First, 1903; Helen, 1916; No. 13, Rue du Bon Diable, 1917; Things Remembered, 1923; (with Dorothy H. Richardson) A May and November Correspondence, 1928. Died Mar. 14, 1930.

HARDY, Ashley Kingsley, college prof.; b. Keene, N.H., Apr. 6, 1871; s. Silas and Josephine M. (Kingsley) H.; A.B., Dartmouth, 1894; U. of Berlin, 1894-95; Ph.D., U. of Leipzig, 1899; m. Adelaide B. Sanford, 1902. Instr. in German, 1897-1902, asst. prof. German and instr. in Old English, 1902-15, asso. prof., 1915-17, prof., 1917—, Dartmouth. Asso. editor Dartmouth Alumni Magazine, 1907-11. Mem. advisory council Simplified Spelling Bd. Editor: Wildenbruch's Das edle Blut, 1906. Compiler: (German portion) A Bibliography of Useful Books for the Library of Teachers in Secondary Schools, 1907. Home: Hanover, N.H. Died July 29, 1940.

HARDY, Caldwell, banker; b. Camden Co., N.C., May 13, 1852; s. Henry C. and Huldah E. H.; removed with parents to New York, 1859; ed. Poly. Inst. of Brooklyn; m. Lucy Hardy, Dec. 6, 1875. Entered broker's office Wall St., 1870, soon after removing to Norfolk, Va., and engaging in banking business; cashier on organization, 1885, pres., 1899-1916, Norfolk Nat. Bank; cashier, 1893, v.p., 1899, pres., 1901-1916, Norfolk Bank for Savings and Trusts; chmn. and federal reserve agt. Fed. Reserve Bank of Richmond, Apr. 1, 1916—. Home: Richmond, Va. Died Aug. 26, 1923.

HARDY, John Crumpton, college pres.; b. Newton Co., Miss., Dec. 24, 1864; s. John D. and Martha M. H.; A.B., Miss. Coll., 1889, A.M., 1891, LL.D., 1904; LL.B., Millsap's Law Sch., 1898; m. Kate, d. Albert Hall Whitfield, July 11, 1900; children—Dodie B. (dec.), Martha C., Katherine C., John Crumpton, Robert M. Supt. city schs., Jackson, Miss., 1890-1900; pres. Miss. Agrl. and Mech. Coll., 1900-12, Baylor Coll. for Women, Belton, Tex., 1912-37, emeritus. Candidate state supt. of edn., 1895; mem. State Bd. Examiners, 1897-1900; was pres. bd. trustees, State Blind Inst.; mem. State House Commn. to build a million-dollar State House, 1900. Pres. Law Enforcement League of Tex., 1922. Democrat. Home: Belton, Tex. Died Oct. 30, 1938.

HARDY, John Henry, judge; b. Hollis, N.H., Feb. 2, 1847; s. John and Hannah (Farley) H.; pvt. Co. E, 15th N.H. Inf. (enlisting at 15), Sept. 1862-Aug. 1863; A.B., Dartmouth, 1870; studied law with R.M. Morse, Jr., Boston; student Harvard U. Law Sch.; m. Anna J. Conant, Aug. 1871 (died 1902); m. 2d, Ada McNab, June 16, 1913. Admitted to Mass. bar, 1872; town counsel, Arlington, Mass., 1873-85; asso. justice Municipal Ct. of Boston, 1885-96; asso. justice Superior Ct. of Mass., Sept. 1896—. Mem. Mass. Ho. of Rep., from Arlington, 1883. Republican. Conglist. Mason. Home: Arlington, Mass. Died Oct. 10, 1917.

HARDY, Joseph Johnston, college prof.; b. New Castle, Eng., Oct. 4, 1844; s. James G. and Ann (Johnston) H.; brought to U.S., 1846; A.B., Lafayette Coll., Easton, Pa., 1870, A.M., 1873; (hon. Ph.D., Hamilton Coll.); m. Mary Montague, June 21, 1871. Prof. mathematics and astronomy, Lafayette Coll., 1891—. Author: Analytic Geometry; Infinitesimals and Limits. Home: Easton, Pa. Died May 2, 1915.

HARDY, Mary Earle, author; b. New Haven, Conn., July 22, 1846; d. George W. and Frances M. (Lay) Earle; A.B., Rockford (Ill.) Coll., 1867; m. Asa Strong Hardy, 1870; children—Asa Strong, Charles Willoughby, Sarah W. (dec.), Roy Earle (dec.), Mary Theoda, Alice Eldora (dec.), Faith Frances. Conglist. Author: Sea Stories for Wonder Eyes, 1904; Fairy Roads to Science Town, 1919; Hester's Easter Morning, 1923; The Girl of the Forest, 1927. Home: Grand Rapids, Mich. Died Sept. 29, 1928.

HARDY, Warren Follansbee, editor; b. Blue Hill, Me., Dec. 14, 1879; s. Daniel Warren and Lydia (Follansbee) H.; student Colby Coll., 2 yrs.; A.B., Amherst, 1900; m. Olive Milner, 1910; 1 son, Amherst Follansbee. Pres. Herald Printing & Stationery Co.; editor and dir. Decatur Newspapers, Inc. Chmn. Decatur City Plan Commn.; trustee Decatur Pub. Library; mem. bd. mgrs. James Millikin U. Conglist. Wrote: Pageant of Lake Decatur, 1923; Decatur Centennial Pageant, 1929. Home: Decatur, Ill. Died Dec. 20, 1933.

HARDY, William Edwin, merchant; b. Wyoming Co., N.Y., Aug. 5, 1863; s. Harvey Wesley and Charlotte Clement (Abbott) H.; grad. Rochester (N.Y.) Business Inst., 1883; student U. of Neb., 1883-85, hon. M.A., 1924; m. Gertrude H. Laws, Jan. 9, 1895. Mem. Hardy Furniture Co. (founded by father), 1885 until incorporation, 1907, pres., 1907—; pres. M. H. Tilton Furniture Co.; dir. Omaha Br. of Federal Reserve Bank of Kansas City. Member Board of Aldermen, Lincoln, Neb., 1908-10; chmn. Liberty Loan Drive, 1917; vice chmn. Neb. Capitol Commn., 1919—; chmn. Lincoln Community Chest, 1924. Chmn. Neb. Prison Reform Assn., 1891-97; chmn. Am. Red Cross, Lincoln Dist., 1917-22. Pres. Crete Chautauqua Assn., 1893-96. Mem. Lincoln Chamber of Commerce (past pres.). Republican. Mason. Home: Lincoln, Neb. Died Sept. 24, 1934.

HARE, George Andrew, M.D.; b. Mt. Pleasant, Ia., May 23, 1857; s. Jacob and Mary Ann (Corkhill) H.; M.D., U. of Mich., 1887; M.S., Ia. Wesleyan Univ., 1889; post grad. work, Harvard, 1887, Vienna, 1906; m. Jessie Blanche Daniells (M.D., U. of Mich.), Dec. 23, 1886; children—Herold Pittman, Gail Butler, Helen Mable, Mrs. Marion Alice Beem, Donald George C. Practiced in Fresno, Calif., 1891—, except three years in Washington, D.C.; former med. supt. Washington Sanitarium and asso. editor Life and Health. Del. Internat. Med. Congress, Lisbon, 1906; mem. Am. Acad. Medicine (pres. 1916-17), A.M.A. (house delegates, 1912-15), Calif. State Med. Soc. (v.p. 1895-1906, 1915-16, councilor 4th Dist. 1899-1904). Republican. Seventh Day Adventist. Home: Fresno, Calif. Died Apr. 4, 1936.

HARE, Hobart Amory, M.D.; b. Phila., Sept. 20, 1862; s. late Bishop William Hobart and Mary Amory (Howe) H.; g.s. Bishop Mark Antony de Wolfe Howe; B.S., U. of Pa., 1885, M.D., 1884; M.D., Jefferson Med. Coll., 1893; LL.D., U. of Pa., 1921; m. Rebecca Clifford Pemberton, May 8, 1884. Prof. children's diseases, U. of Pa., 1890; prof. therapeutics and diagnosis, Jefferson Med. Coll., 1891—. Editor Univ. Med. Mag., 1888-89, Med. News, 1890-91, Therapeutic Gazette, 1891-1927. Many prizes from univs. and med. socs., Am. and foreign, for med. essays. Fellow Coll. Physicians (Phila.), Assn. Am. Physicians. Author: Practical Therapeutics, 1890, 20th edit., 1927; Practical Diagnos, 1896, 9th edit., 1927. Editor: A System of Therapeutics, 4 vols., 1890, 1901, 11; Medical Compilations and Sequels of Typhoid and Other Fevers, 1901. Home: Philadelphia, Pa. Died June 15, 1931.

HARE, William Hobart, P.E. bishop; b. Princeton, N.J., May 17, 1838; s. Rev. George Emlen, D.D., LL.D., and Elizabeth Catharine (Hobart) H.; ed. P.E. Acad., Phila., and Univ. of Pa. (left at end of junior yr.); took up teaching in connection with studies preparatory to holy orders; (S.T.D., Columbia; D.D., Trinity, Hartford, and Kenyon Coll., O.); m. Mary Amory, d. Bishop M. A. DeW. Howe, 1861. Ordered deacon, 1859; ordained priest, 1862; asst. at St. Luke's, rector of St. Paul's, Chestnut Hill, and other Phila. chs. until 1870; sec. and gen. agt. of foreign com. of Domestic and Foreign Missionary Soc., 1870-73. Consecrated, 1873, bishop of Niobrara; diocese enlarged, 1883, made coterminous with newly created territory of S.Dak., and renamed, accordingly, S.Dak. Died 1909.

HARGIS, Thomas Frazier, lawyer; b. Breathitt Co., Ky., June 24, 1843; had little edn.; after serving 3 yrs. and 10 months in C.S.A., studied English grammar and then law; admitted to bar, 1866; chief justice Supreme Court, Ky., 1879-84; engaged in law practice, 1884—. Home: Louisville, Ky. Died 1903.

HARGITT, Charles Wesley, biologist; b. nr. Lawrenceburg, Ind., Mar. 28, 1852; s. Thomas and Mary Fisher (Lynas) H.; B.S., Moores Hill (Ind.) Coll., 1877; Ph.D., Ohio U., 1890; hon. Sc.D., Moores Hill Coll., 1908, Evansville Coll., 1920, Syracuse U., 1922; m. Susan E., d. Rev. Enoch G. Wood, of Moores Hill, Ind., July 26, 1877; children—Frank Wood, George Thomas, Charles Andrews. Prof. natural sciences, Moores Hill Coll., 1885-88; prof. biology and geology, Miami U., 1888-91; prof. ibology, 1891, prof. embryology, Coll. of Medicine, 1898-1912, curator Biol. Mus. and dir. Zoöl. Lab., 1893—, Syracuse U.; research prof. of zoölogy, same univ., 1921—. Asst. dir. Cold Spring Biol. Lab., 1891-93; trustee Marine Biol. Lab., 1900-21; studied and traveled in Europe, 1894, 1903, 1910-11, investigations Naples Biol. Sta. Chmn. local com. Nat. Research Council. Author: Outlines of General Biology, 1901. Home: Syracuse, N.Y. Died June 11, 1927.

HARGROVE, Robert Kennon, bishop M.E. Ch., South, 1882—; b. Pickens Co., Ala., Sept. 17, 1829; s. Daniel J. and Laodicea H.; grad. U. of Ala., 1852 A.M.; (D.D., Emory Coll., Ga.); m. Harriet C. Scott, Nov. 10, 1852; m. 2d, Ruth E. Scarritt, June 20, 1895. Prof. pure mathematics, Univ. of Ala., 1853-57, afterward in active pastoral work. Represented M.E. Ch., South, in Cape May commn., 1876, and in com. on federation, 1898; sec. Coll. of Bishops, 1884—; chmn. com. on applications for foreign mission field, and for transl. of theology for same; pres. bd. trustees, Vanderbilt Univ., 1889—; pres. bd. of management Epworth League, M.E. Ch., South, 1894-98; inaugurated Woman's Parsonage and Home Mission Soc. of M.E. Ch., South. Home: Nashville, Tenn. Died 1905.

HARISON, Beverly Drake, physician; b. Canton, N.Y., May 8, 1855; s. Minturn and Susan (Drake) H.; desc. Francis Harison, barrister (Oxford and Lincoln Inn), N.Y. City, 1708, Colonial Council, 1720-40; Bishops Coll. Sch., Lennoxville, Que.; Trinity Coll. Sch., Port Hope, Ont.; Univ. Trinity Coll.,

Toronto; M.B., U. of Toronto, 1882, M.D., 1901; hon. A.M., U. of Mich., 1910; m. Josephine, d. James Frederick Lister, K.C., justice Court Appeal, Toronto, Ont., Oct. 9, 1889. Practiced Sault Ste. Marie, Mich., 1888-1906, Detroit, 1906—. Organizer 1899, and sec. Mich. State Bd. of Registration in Medicine; organizer and sec. Am. Confederation Reciprocating State Med. Bds.; author of medical reciprocity, 1902; pres. State Hosp., Newberry, Mich. Fellow Am. Coll. Physicians. Capt. M.C., U.S.A., 1917-18. Republican. Episcopalian. Home: Detroit, Mich. Died Dec. 6, 1924.

HARK, J(oseph) Max(imilian), clergyman; b. Phila., June 4, 1849; s. Joseph and Maria Louisa (Bute) H.; grad. Moravian Coll. and Theol. Sem., 1870; (D.D., Franklin and Marshall, 1887); m. Milla T. Crosta, Oct. 7, 1873; children—Hugo Crosta, Mrs. Hilda Theresa Pilgrim, Anna Amelia. Formerly pastor Moravian churches in Lebanon, Phila. and Lancaster, Pa.; prin. Moravian Sem. and Coll. for Women, 1893-1909 (oldest girls' boarding sch. in America, founded, 1749); retired. One of founders of the Pennsylvania German Soc. and Pa. Chautauqua, of which was 1st chancellor. Home: Mt. Gretna, Pa. Died July 26, 1930.

HARKER, Catherine, educator; b. Portland, Ore.; d. James Bartlett and Sarah Ellen (Polk) H.; A.B., Vassar, 1889. Prin. Miss Harker's Sch., Palo Alto, Calif., Aug. 1902—. Episcopalian. Home: Palo Alto, Calif. Died Dec. 1938.

HARKER, Joseph Ralph, educator; b. in Co. of Durham, Eng., June 30, 1853; s. Ralph and Mary (Young) H.; A.B., Ill. Coll., 1888, A.M., 1891, and Ph.D., 1893; LL.D., Northwestern U., 1918; m. Susan Amass, Sept. 6, 1876 (died, 1880); 1 dau., Maude (Mrs. Albert C. Metcalf); m. 2d, Frances E. Wackerle, Dec. 26, 1882; children—Elizabeth (Mrs. Wallace C. Riddell), Jenne (Mrs. George R. Atherton), Ralph W., Louis (dec.), Albert Joseph (dec.), Frances Ruth (Mrs. Mark B. Hunt). Worked in coal mines in Co. of Durham, Eng., 1863-71; emigrated to Ill., and worked as coal miner at Du Quoin, Ill., till 1874, giving leisure time to study; began to teach pub. sch., Du Quoin, Ill., Mar. 1874; prin. schs., DeSoto, Ill., 1874-76; prin. grammar sch., Beardstown, Ill., 1876-77; supt. schs., Meredosia, 1877-81, Waverly, Ill., 1881-84; prin. Whipple Acad., Jacksonville, Ill., 1884-93 (during same period taking coll. course); prof. pedagogy, Ill. Coll., 1889-93; pres. Ill. Woman's Coll., Jacksonville, Ill., 1893-1925 (emeritus). Ordained M.E. ministry, 1891; del. Gen. Confs., 1904, 08, 16; mem. Bd. of Edn., and Council Bds. of Benevolence, M.E. Ch.; mem. Commn. of Life Service, M.E. Ch.; pres. Fedn. of Ill. Colleges, 1920-22. Republican. Home: Jacksonville, Ill. Died July 8, 1938.

HARKER, Oliver Albert, prof. law; b. Fountain City, Ind., Dec. 14, 1844; s. Miflin and Anna (Woods) H.; student Wheaton (Ill.) College, 1860-62; pvt. 67th Ill. Inf., 1863; A.B., McKendree College, Ill., 1866, A.M., 1869, LL.D., 1908, and Knox Coll., Galesburg, Ill., 1911; law sch., Ind. U., 1866-67; m. Siddie B. Bain, Mar. 3, 1870; children—George M., Oliver A., Mrs. Winifred Hewitt. Taught sch., Vienna, Ill., 1867-68, practiced law at Vienna, 1870-78; apptd. judge 1st Jud. Circuit, by Gov. S. M. Cullom, Aug. 1878, elected judge same circuit, 1879, 85, 91, 97; judge Appellate Court of Ill., 2d dist., 1891-97, 3d dist., 1897-1903; lecturer, 1897-1903, dean, 1903-16, Coll. Law, U. of Ill.; asso. legal counsel U. of Ill., also prof. law. Pres. Ill. State Bar Assn., 1895-96; pres. Ill. Soc. Am. Inst. Criminal Law and Criminology, 1910-11; Ill. Commr. to Nat. Conf. on Uniform State Laws, 1925-29, reappointed for 1929-33. Methodist. Republican. Author: Cases on Common Law Pleadings, 1924. Editor of Illinois Statutes Annotated (4 vols.), 1919. Home: Carbondale, Ill. Died Dec. 3, 1936.

HARKINS, Matthew, bishop; b. Boston, Nov. 17, 1845; grad. Boston Latin Sch., 1862; studied at Coll. of Holy Cross, Worcester, Mass., 1 yr.; studied theology at English Coll., Douay, and Sem. of St. Sulpice, Paris, 6 yrs. Ordained R.C. ministry, 1869; visited Rome; curate Ch. of Immaculate Conception, Salem, Mass.; rector St. Malachi's Ch., Arlington, Mass., 1876-84, St. James', Boston, 1884-87; consecrated bishop of Providence (R.I.), Apr. 14, 1887. Died May 25, 1921.

HARKNESS, Albert, prof. Greek, Brown, 1855—; b. Mendon, Mass., Oct. 6, 1822; s. Southwick and Phebe (Thayer) H.; grad. Brown, 1842 (LL.D., 1869; Ph.D., Bonn., 1854); teacher high school, 1843-53; senior master, 1845-53; student Univs. of Berlin, Bonn, Göttingen, 1853-55; m. Maria Aldrich Smith, May 28, 1849. A founder Am. Philol. Assn. (v.p., 1869-70, pres., 1875-76); one of organizers (mem. mng. com., 1880—) Am. School Classical Studies, Athens. Author: Cæsar's Gallic War with Notes, etc., 1870, 1886 (new edit. with C. H. Forbes, 1901); Select Orations of Cicero, with Notes, 1873, 1882; Easy Latin Method, 1890; Complete Latin Grammar, 1898; Short Latin Grammar, 1898; Cicero's Select Orations with Introduction, Notes and Dictionary (assisted by J. C. Kirtland, Jr.), 1905:—all A1. Home: Providence, R.I. Died 1907.

HARKNESS, Albert Granger, univ. prof.; b. Providence, R.I., Nov. 19, 1856; s. Prof. Albert and Maria Aldrich (Smith) H.; A.B., Brown U., 1879, A.M., 1882 (Litt.D., 1909); Berlin, Leipzig and Bonn, 1879-83; m. Katherine Beebee, Sept. 1884. Prof. Latin and German, Madison (now Colgate) U., 1883-89; asso. prof. Latin, 1889-93, prof. Roman lit. and history, 1893—, Brown U. Annual dir. Am. Sch. for Classical Studies in Rome, Italy, 1902-03. Home: Providence, R.I. Died Jan. 29, 1923.

HARKNESS, Charles William, lawyer; b. Monroeville, O., Dec. 17, 1860; s. Stephen V. and Anna M. H.; A.B., Yale, 1883; student, Columbia Law Sch.; m. Mary Warden, 1896. In law practice at New York, 1890—. Dir. Southern Pacific Co., C.,M.&St.P. Ry. Co., B.&O. R.R., Tilden Iron Mining Co. Home: New York, N.Y. Died May 1, 1916.

HARKNESS, Edward Stephen; b. Cleveland, O., Jan. 22, 1874; s. Stephen V. and Anna M. (Richardson) H.; A.B., Yale, 1897, M.A., 1925; LL.D., The University, St. Andrews, Scotland, 1926; LL.D., Columbia U., 1928; m. Mary Stillman, Nov. 15, 1904. Dir. Southern Pacific Co., N.Y. Central Lines. Trustee Met. Mus. of Art, Presbyn. Hosp. Presbyn. Home: New York, N.Y. Died Jan. 29, 1940.

HARKNESS, Harvey W., physician; grad. Berkshire Med. Coll., Pittsfield, Mass., 1847; pres. Calif. Acad. Sciences. Resides in San Francisco, Calif. Died 1901.

HARKNESS, William, astronomer, rear admiral U.S.N.; b. Ecclefechan, Scotland, Dec. 17, 1837; s. James and Jane Weild H.; studied Lafayette Coll., Pa., 1854-56, Rochester Univ., 1856-58, A.B., 1858, A.M., 1861, LL.D., 1874, Rochester (A.M., Lafayette, 1865); studied medicine, New York, M.D., 1862. Served as surgeon, U.S. army, at second battle of Bull Run; also during attack on Washington, July 1864. Apptd. from N.Y. as aide U.S. Naval Observatory, Aug. 1, 1862; commd. prof. mathematics, with relative rank of lt. comdr., Aug. 24, 1863; served at Naval Observatory until Oct. 4, 1865. Served on U.S. monitor Monadnock, 1865-66; attached to U.S. Hydrographic Office, 1867; discovered the coronal line K 1474, during total solar eclipse of Aug. 1869; mem., 1871, and from 1882 exec. officer U.S. Transit of Venus Commn.; had charge of transit of Venus parties in 1874 at Hobart, Tasmania, and in 1882 at Washington, D.C. In 1879, discovered the theory of the focal curve of achromatic telescopes, now universally adopted. Attached to U.S. Naval Observatory most of the time from Aug. 1862; designed most of its large instruments; astron. dir. Naval Observatory, 1894-99, and dir. U.S. Nautical Almanac, 1897-99. Attained relative rank of comdr., May 31, 1872, capt., April 17, 1878, rear admiral, Dec. 15, 1899; unmarried. Home: Jersey City, N.J. Died 1903.

HARLAN, Edgar Rubey, curator; b. Spartansburg, Ind., Feb. 28, 1869; s. Samuel Alexander and Marinda Ellen (Rubey) H.; Drake U., 2 yrs., LL.B., 1896, A.M., 1921; m. Minnie C. Duffield, June 9, 1897; children—John Edgar, George Duffield, Mary Adelaide, James Rubey, Ada Margaret. County atty. Van Buren Co., Ia., 1898-1901; mem. Work, Brown & Harlan, 1901-07; asst. and acting curator, Hist. Department of Ia., 1907-09, curator, 1909-37. Mem. bd. Ia. Soldiers' Roster Commn.; sec. Ia. Allison Memorial Commn., Grenville M. Dodge Memorial Commn.; chmn. Ia. Revolutionary Soldiers Graves Commn. A founder of Miss. Valley Hist. Assn., also of Ia. State Conservation Commn. Sec. Ia. State Conservation Assn., Ia. Forestry Conservation Assn., Ia. Plant Life Commn., Northern Miss. Valley Conservation Congress; founder and sec. Nat. Conv. on Parks; chmn. Revolutionary War Memorial Commn. Ia. Republican. Christian (Campbellite). Gave radio talks on early Iowa twice a week, 1927-32. Home: Des Moines, Ia. Died July 13, 1941.

HARLAN, George Cuvier, ophthalmologist; b. Phila., Jan. 28, 1835; s. Dr. Richard and Margaret (Simmons) H., ed. Del. Coll.; M.D., U. of Pa., 1858; held several hospital appointments before Civil War; med. officer on gun-boat Union in early part of war; later surgeon 11th Pa. Cav., 3 yrs. Ophthalmic surgeon Pa. Hosp.; consulting oculist Pa. Instn. for Blind and Pa. Instn. for Deaf and Dumb; surgeon to Wills' Eye Hosp.; formerly eye and ear surgeon to Children's Hosp., and prof. diseases of eye, Phila. Polyclinic. Home: Philadelphia. Died 1909.

HARLAN, James, lawyer, senator; b. Clarke Co., Ill., Aug. 26, 1820; s. Silas and Mary (Conley) H.; grad. Asbury (now De Pauw) Univ., Ind., 1845; m. Ann Eliza Peck. Prin. Iowa City Coll.; elected supt. public instruction, 1847; reëlected, 1848, but counted out by mems. of returning bd. Studied law; admitted to the bar; pres. Iowa Wesleyan U., 1853; prof. mental and moral sciences, 1853-55; elected U.S. senator, 1855; reëlected, 1861; resigned May 13, 1865, to take office of sec. of the Interior; apptd. by Pres. Lincoln. Elected to senate for 3d term, 1866, and resigned from Interior Dept., taking seat in senate March 4, 1867; presiding judge, court of commrs. of Alabama Claims, 1882-85. Home: Mt. Pleasant, Ia. Died 1899.

HARLAN, James Elliott, college pres.; b. Muskingum Co., O., June 25, 1845; s. Samuel and Sarah Ann (Elliott) H.; pvt. Co. D, 44th Ia. Inf., May-Oct. 1864; A.B., Cornell Coll., Ia., 1869, A.M., 1872; (LL.D., Upper Ia. U., 1904, Cornell Coll., 1904, Northwestern U., 1910); m. Harriet Janette McKinney, Dec. 29, 1869. Supt. pub. schs., Cedar Rapids, Ia., 1869-72; prin. ward sch., Sterling, Ill., 1872-73; alumni prof. mathematics and astronomy, 1873-1900, v.p. 1881-1908, chmn. exec. com., 1883—, financial sec., 1893-1914, pres., 1908-14, Cornell Coll., Ia. Mem. M.E. Ch. Republican. Home: Mt. Vernon, Ia. Died Dec. 13, 1933.

HARLAN, James S., lawyer; b. Evansville, Ind., Nov. 24, 1861; s. John Marshall and Malvina F. (Shanklin) H.; A.B., Princeton, 1883; studied law, at Chicago, 1884-88, in office of Melville W. Fuller (later chief justice Supreme Court of U.S.); m. Maud Noble, 1897. Admitted to bar, 1886; practiced at Chicago, firm Gregory, Booth & Harlan; atty. gen. Porto Rico, 1901-03; mem. U.S. Interstate Commerce Commn., Aug. 17, 1906-Dec. 31, 1918. Home: Washington, D.C. Died Sept. 20, 1927.

HARLAN, John Marshall, associate justice Supreme Court of U.S.; b. Boyle Co., Ky., June 1, 1833; s. Hon. James and Eliza D. H.; A.B., Centre Coll., Ky., 1850; studied law Transylvania U.; (LL.D., Bowdoin, 1883, Centre Coll., and Princeton, 1884, U. of Pa., 1900); m. Malvina F., d. John Shanklin, of Evansville, Ind., Dec. 23, 1856; father of Richard Davenport and James S. H. Practiced law at Frankfort, Ky.; co. judge, 1858; Whig candidate for Congress in Ashland dist., 1859; elector on Bell and Everett ticket, 1860; removed to Louisville in 1867 and practiced law there. Col. 10th Ky. regt. in Union Army, 1861-63; atty. gen. of Ky., 1863-67; returned to practice; Rep. nominee for gov., 1871 and 1875; his name was presented by Rep. Conv. of Ky. for v.p. of U.S. in 1872; mem. La. commn., 1877; commd., Nov. 29, 1877, took his seat, Dec. 10, 1877, as asso. justice Supreme Ct. of U.S.; one of Am. arbitrators on Bering Sea Tribunal which met in Paris, 1893; prof. constl. law, George Washington U., 1889—. Died 1911.

HARLAN, John Maynard, lawyer; b. Frankfort, Ky., Dec. 21, 1864; s. John Marshall and Malvina F. (Shanklin) H.; A.B., Princeton, 1884; U. of Berlin, 1885-86; LL.B., George Washington U., 1888; m. Elizabeth Palmer Flagg, Oct. 21, 1890; children—Elizabeth P. (Mrs. Roger A. Derby), John Marshall, Janet (Mrs. Walter Holcomb Stevenson), Edith. Alderman, Chicago, 1896-98; nominee for mayor of Chicago, 1897, 1905. Republican. Home: Chicago, Ill., and N.Y. City. Died Mar. 23, 1934.

HARLAN, Otis, actor; b. Zanesville, O.; m. Nellie Harvey, actress, Nov. 6, 1902; 1 dau., Marion Louise. Début 14th St. Theatre, New York, as Romantic Young Man, in "A Hole in the Ground," Sept. 12, 1887; toured with Frank Daniels, in "Little Puck," later played Major Yell, in "A Texas Steer"; scored success in "A Black Sheep," 1896; toured with Anna Held in "The Parisian Model," 1907; played Dupont in "Little Boy Blue," 1911; leading comedian, Folies Bergères Theatre, New York, 1912; motion pictures, 1920—, among them: "Abraham Lincoln"; "The Dixie Handicap"; "Lightnin'"; "What Happened to Jones"; "The Whole Town's Talking"; "The Cheerful Fraud"; "The Student Prince"; "The Shepherd of the Hills"; "Show Boat"; "Broadway"; King of Jazz"; "Port of Dreams"; "Man to Man"; "The Man I Killed"; "Prosperity"; "Dr. Bull"; "Hoopla." Home: Hollywood, Calif. Died Jan. 20, 1940.

HARLAN, Richard Davenport, educator; b. Evansville, Ind., Nov. 14, 1859; s. John Marshall and Malvina F. (Shanklin) H.; A.B., Princeton, 1881 (valedictorian), A.M., 1884; grad. Princeton Theol. Sem., 1885; D.D., Princeton, 1902; LL.D., Union U., 1904; m. Mrs. Augustus M. Swift, née Margaret M. Prouty, June 5, 1889. Ordained Presbyn. ministry, 1886; pastor First Ch., New York, 1886-90; spl. theol. studies U. of Berlin, 1890-91; pastor Third Ch., Rochester, N.Y., 1894-1901; pres. Lake Forest (Ill.) Coll., 1901-06; in charge of "The George Washington Univ. Movement," 1907-10, for the purpose of carrying out the spirit of Washington's last will and testament, by the development of a univ. for grad. work at the nat. capital. Home: Washington, D.C. Died Jan. 25, 1931.

HARLAND, Edward, banker; b. Norwich, Conn., June 24, 1832; s. Henry and Abby Leffingwell (Hyde) H.; A.B., Yale, 1853, A.M., 1856; admitted to bar at Norwich, 1855; unmarried. Capt. 3d Conn. Vols., Apr. 1861; col. 8th Conn. Inf., Oct. 5, 1861; brig. gen. vols., Nov. 29, 1862; resigned June 22, 1865. Mem. Conn. Ho. of Rep., 1869 and 1878; Senate, 1870, and was chosen its pres.; probate judge, 1862-76; mem. N.E. Soc. Republican. Home: Norwich, Conn. Died Mar. 9, 1915.

HARLAND, Henry, author; b. St. Petersburg, Russia, Mar. 1, 1861; ed. Coll. City of New York and Harvard; removed to London; was editor of

Yellow Book; married. Writes under pen-name "Sidney Luska." Author: Comedies and Errors, 1898; The Cardinal's Snuff Box, 1900; The Lady Paramount, 1902. Home: Norwich, Conn. Died 1905.

"HARLAND, Marion" (Mary Virginia Terhune), author; b. Amelia Co., Va., Dec. 21, 1830; d. Samuel Pierce and Judith A. (Smith) Hawes; ed. by tutors and governesses and at pvt. schs.; began to write for press at 14; m. Rev. Edward Payson Terhune, Sept. 2, 1856 (died 1907); mother of Christine Terhune Herrick, with whom she collaborated in National Cook Book and The Helping Hand, Virginia Terhune Vandewater, with whom collaborated in Everyday Etiquette, and Albert Payson Terhune, with whom she collaborated in Dr. Dale (a novel). V.p. Assn. Preservation of Va. Antiquities, Pocahontas Memorial Assn. (Conducted Babyhood 2 yrs., and later The Home-Maker; conducted depts. in Wide Awake and St. Nicholas; on staff Chicago Tribune). Author: Common Sense in the Household; The Cottage Kitchen; The Dinner Year-Book; National Cook Book; Some Colonial Homesteads; More Colonial Homesteads, 1899; When Grandmamma Was Fourteen, 1905; The Distractions of Martha, 1906; Marion Harland's Autobiography, 1911. Prepared Am. edition of Reader's Handbook; Everyday Etiquette; A Long Lane—A Chronicle of Old New Jersey; The Carringtons of High Hill, An Old Virginia Chronicle. Home: New York, N.Y. Died June 3, 1922.

HARLEY, Charles Richard, sculptor; b. Phila., Mar. 25, 1864; s. Charles Richard and Sarah Ann (McMullin) H.; ed. Phila. public schs., Spring Garden Inst., Pa. Acad. Fine Arts; in Paris at École Nationale des Arts Décoratifs, Académie Julian, École des Beaux Arts, and under Dampt and Aubé; also at New York under St. Gaudens and Martiny; also in Rome and Florence; m. Agnes Williams Palmer, Oct. 10, 1926. Medal, Buffalo Expn., 1901. Unitarian. Home: New Hope, Pa. Died Jan. 25, 1930.

HARLOW, William Page, physician; b. Dixon, Ill., Nov. 14, 1867; s. William Francis and Martha Samson (Besse) H.; M.D., U. of Mich., 1899; A.B. in geology, U. of Colo., 1907; post-grad. work, Johns Hopkins, Vienna, Berlin and Harvard, 1902-03; m. Jean Hoatson, Dec. 26, 1898. Engaged in copper mining in Mich., Mont. and Ariz., 1887-95; mine and ry. surgeon, Greenland, Mich., 1899-1902; prof. med. diagnosis, 1906-15, dean med. sch., 1907-15 and dean emeritus, 1916—, U. of Colorado. Republican. Fellow Fedn. of State Med. Bds. Mason. Capt., Med. R.C., May 21, 1918; maj., M.C., Aug. 7, 1918; chief med. service, Gen. Hosp. No. 8, Otisville, N.Y.; comdg. officer Gen. Hosp. No. 21, Denver, Aug. 27, 1918; lt. col., M.C., U.S.A., Apr. 28, 1919; hon. disch., June 19, 1919; lt. col., Med. Sect. O.R.C., Aug. 11, 1919; col. Med. O.R.C., Oct. 12, 1922. Home: Boulder, Colo. Died May 11, 1924.

HARMAN, Henry Elliott, author; b. Lexington, S.C., Mar. 18, 1866; s. Franklin James and Jane Rebecca (Meetze) H.; ed. Pa. Coll., Gettysburg, to middle of senior yr., A.B., 1909; Litt.D. from same coll., 1915; married. Established Southern Tobacco Journal, Winston-Salem, N.C., 1889, Cotton, and Cotton Oil Mag., Atlanta, 1899, Southern Engr., 1901, Concrete Age, 1903; purchased Southern Architect, 1904; owner and pub. Cotton Oil Magazine and Southern Architect. Pres. Southern Trade Press Assn. Methodist. Author (poems): Dreams of Yesterday, 1911; A Bar of Song, 1913; Idle Dreams of an Idle Day, 1917; Yuletide and You, 1920; Songs from Florida Shores, 1921 (complete edit. above named books, 1921); History of Famous Songs, 1925. Home: Atlanta, Ga. Deceased.

HARMAN, Pinckney Jones, business education; b. Franklin, W.Va., Oct. 5, 1879; s. Solon and Amanda (Nelson) H.; ed. pub. and normal schs., Strayer's Business Coll. (Baltimore) and Packard Commercial Sch. (New York); m. Pearle Jones, 1905 (died 1908); 1 dau., Margaret Amanda (Mrs. Rae Cohee); m. 2d, Isabel C. Zerega, Aug. 1910; children—Roland Nelson, Pinckney Jones, Isabel Miller. Teacher pub. schs. of W.Va., 1895-1901; teacher Strayer's Business Coll., 1903-04; asso. founder, 1904, prin. Strayer Coll., Washington, D.C., 1904-21, v.p. and dir., 1921—; v.p. and treas. Strayer Coll. of Accountancy. Dir. Columbia Nat. Bank of Washington, D.C. Mem. Washington Board of Trade. Republican. Mason. Home: Washington, D.C. Died May 24, 1938.

HARMATI, Sandor, conductor, composer; b. Budapest, Hungary, July 9, 1892; s. Morris and Sophia (Frohlich) H.; diploma of Prof. of Music, Royal Acad. of Music, Budapest, 1909; m. Ruth Sophia Tjader, June 28, 1919. Came to U.S., 1914, naturalized citizen, 1919. Violinist, chamber musician, Letz Quartet, 1917-20, Lenox Quartet, 1922-25; served as conductor Morristown (N.J.) Symphony Orchestra, Charleston (S.C.) Symphony Orchestra, Woman's Symphony Orchestra, New York, Omaha Symphony Orchestra, 1925-33; dir. Westchester County (N.Y.) Musical Festival. Am. del. to Internat. Soc. for Contemporary Music, Frankfort, Germany, 1927; appears yearly as guest conductor with European orchestras; guest conductor Chautauqua, N.Y., summers 1928, 29. Member Beethoven Assn. Lecturer and writer on music. Composer: Symphonic Poem (Pulitzer prize), 1922; string quartet, chamber music prize, Phila., 1924; incidental music for "Jeweled Tree," 1926; songs and music for violin, orchestra, etc. Died Apr. 4, 1936.

HARMER, Alfred C., congressman-capitalist; b. Germantown (now Philadelphia); ed. at public schools and Germantown Acad.; was in mercantile pursuits, now in railroad, mining and land enterprises. Member councils. Philadelphia, 1856-60; recorder of Philadelphia, 1860-63; from 1871 member Congress from 5th Pa. dist.; present term expiring 1901. Republican. Home: Philadelphia. Died 1900.

HARMON, Benjamin Smith, lawyer; b. Three Mile Bay, N.Y., Dec. 15, 1859; s. Gaius N. and Orpha I. (Smith) H.; A.B., Dartmouth, 1882; LL.B., cum laude, Columbia, 1885; m. Helen Lockwood Ketcham, June 3, 1897. In practice at New York, 1885—; mem. Strong, Harmon & Mathewson, 1891-98, Harmon & Mathewson, 1898-1909, Krauthoff (Louis C.), Harmon & Mathewson (Charles F.), 1909—. Gen. counsel or officer various ry. and mining cos. Home: New York, N.Y. Died Oct. 14, 1916.

HARMON, Frank Wilson, alienist; b. Cincinnati, O., May 18, 1851; s. Benjamin F. and Julia A. (Bronson) H.; student Denison U., Granville, O., 1869-72; M.D., Med. Coll. of Ohio (now Ohio Miami Med. Coll.), 1881; m. Cora Shaffer, Oct. 16, 1895; 1 dau., Frances Adele (Mrs. C. D. Dethlefsen). Interne, Cincinnati Hosp., 1880-81; asst. phys., 1881-90, supt., 1890-1918, Longview Hosp. for the Insane, Cincinnati. Home: San Diego, Calif. Died Dec. 8, 1931.

HARMON, Judson, governor; b. Newton, O., Feb. 3, 1846; s. Rev. B. F. and Julia (Bronson) H.; A.B., Denison U., 1866, LL.D., 1891; LL.B., Cincinnati Law Sch., 1869; m. a d. of Dr. William H. Scobey, of Hamilton, O., June 1870. Mayor Wyoming, O., 1875-76; judge Ct. of Common Pleas, 1876-77, Superior Ct., 1878-87; atty. gen. of U.S. in Cabinet of President Cleveland, June 8, 1895-Mar. 5, 1897; prof. of law, U. of Cincinnati, 1896—; receiver C.,H.&D., Pere Marquette, and Toledo Terminal rys., 1905-09; gov. of Ohio, 1909-11 and 1911-13. Democrat. Pres. Ohio Bar Assn., 1897-98. Home: Cincinnati, O. Died Feb. 22, 1927.

HARMON, William Elmer, real estate; b. Lebanon, O., Mar. 25, 1862; s. William R. and Mary (Wood) H.; ed. Nat. Normal U., Lebanon, O., Louisville Sch. of Medicine; m. Katharine Farnsworth Griffiths, Oct. 1, 1890; children—W. Burke, Helen G., Mrs. Henry Briggs. Originated, 1886, the first practical method of distributing real estate through small initial payments by giving a bond for a deed instead of a deed with mortgage, thus saving foreclosure costs in case of default in payment (this system widely copied); organized Wood, Harmon & Co., which at one time operated in the development of suburban property in 26 cities of U.S., later concentrating in N.Y.; founder Harmon Foundation (for charitable and humanitarian purposes); chmn. bd. Harmon Nat. Real Estate Corp.; pres. William E. Harmon & Co., Inc., United Cities Realty Co., Great New York Development Co., Brooklyn Development Co., and many other corps.; trustee Peoples Trust Co., Brooklyn. Trustee Poly. Inst. Brooklyn, Nat. Child Labor Commn., State Charities Aid Assn., N.Y., Civic Trust of Lebanon, O. Republican. Episcopalian. Home: New York, N.Y. Died July 15, 1928.

HARMONY, David Buttz, rear admiral U.S.N.; b. Easton, Pa., Sept. 3, 1832; s. William J. and Ebba (Herster) H.; apptd. from Pa., acting midshipman, 1847; passed midshipman, June 10, 1852; promoted through grades to rear admiral, Mar. 26, 1889. Served successively on the Brandywine, Ohio, Falmouth at Naval Acad., on the relief and receiving-ship Baltimore, Decatur and receiving-ship at New York; during the Civil War was exec. officer of the Iroquoisat; participated in bombardment and passage of Fts. Jackson and St. Philip, Chalmette batteries and at capture of New Orleans, at engagements at Vicksburg, and with Confederate ram Arkansas, 1861-62; on Nabant at engagements at Charleston, 1863; comd. Tahoma, and Sebago, W. Gulf Blockading Squadron, 1864-65; at the capture of Mobile, 1865; served at Navy Yard, New York, 1865-67; comd. Frolic, European Sta., 1867-69; Navy Yard, New York, 1869-72; comd. Portsmouth and Kearsarge, 1872-75; recruiting duty, New York, 1876; comd. Plymouth, Powhatan, Tennessee, and receiving-ship Colorado, 1878-83; spl. duty Navy Dept., 1883-84; chief Bur. of Yards and Docks, 1885-89; chmn. Lighthouse Bd., 1889-91; comdr.-in-chief Asiatic Sta., 1892-93; retired, June 26, 1893. Died Nov. 2, 1917.

HARNEY, George Edward, architect; b. Lynn, Mass., 1840; s. George Ballard and Mary Rand (Johnson) H.; ed. pvt. and pub. schs. and under pvt. tutors; studied architecture under Alonzo Lewis; m. Maria Renshaw, d. Col. Samuel Jaques, 1872 (died 1887). Established offices in Cold Spring and Newburgh, on Hudson River, N.Y., 1863, and designed many country places and residences; asso. with William I. Paulding in New York, 1873. Prin. works: St. Mary's Church, Cold Spring, N.Y.; Mercantile Library Bldg., New York; Lincoln Home and Hosp.; offices and ry. stas. for Del. & Hudson Co. Fellow Am. Inst. Architects, 1871 (mem. N.Y. Chapter). Home: New York, N.Y. Died Nov. 12, 1924.

HARPER, Carrie Anna, college prof.; b. Boston; d. Henry Mason and Caroline (Bennett) H.; ed. Girls' Latin Sch., 1890-92; Radcliffe, 1892-96; grad. student, Bryn Mawr, 1896-97, Radcliffe, 1897-98, A.B., Radcliffe, 1896, A.M., 1898; fellow in English, Bryn Mawr, 1898-99, Ph.D., 1910; unmarried. Teacher English, The Gilman Sch., Cambridge, Mass., 1899-1907; instr. English lit., Mt. Holyoke Coll., S. Hadley, Mass., 1907-11, asso. prof., 1911—. Wrote: Carados, in Modern Language Notes, 1898. Author: The Sources of the British Chronicle History in Spenser's Faerie Queene, 1910. Home: Sunderland, Mass. Died Dec. 13, 1918.

HARPER, Edward Thomson, theologian; b. Sabula, Ia., Sept. 28, 1857; s. Rev. Almer and Eunice (Thomson) H.; bro. of Robert Almer H.; A.B., Oberlin Coll., 1881; B.D., Chicago Theol. Sem., 1887; Ph.D., Leipzig, 1891; (D.D., Ia. Coll, 1902, Oberlin, 1908); m. Susan Amy Hosford, June 4, 1895. Prin. Port Byron Acad., 1882-84, and 1887-91; prof. Assyriology and comparative religion, 1892-1906, O.T. lit. and bibl. theology, 1906-11, Chicago Theol. Sem. Conglist. Home: Geneseo, Ill. Died Jan. 4, 1921.

HARPER, George Andrew, headmaster, author; b. Jamestown, O., Mar. 6, 1879; s. Andrew E. and Susan Jane (Spencer) H.; A.B., Cedarville (O.) Coll., 1901; A.B., U. of Chicago, 1908; student U. of Ariz., 1926-28; m. Mary Ellen Snyder, Aug. 22, 1906; children—Helen Elizabeth, Mary Alice. Began as supt. schs., Sugar Creek Twp., O., 1902; teacher New Trier High Sch., Winnetka, Ill., 1906-18, dean of boys, 1918-27; teacher and chmn. mathematics dept., Tucson (Ariz.) High Sch., 1927-30; headmaster Southern Ariz. Sch. for Boys, Tucson, 1930—, v.p., 1930—. Presbyterian. Co-author: (with Marquis J. Newell) Plane Geometry, 1914; Solid Geometry, 1915; A Year of Algebra, 1920; Second Course in Algebra, 1923; (with Marquis J. Newell and Gordon R. Mirick) Plane Geometry and Its Uses, 1929, rev. edit., 1935; Solid Geometry and Its Uses, 1929; (with Marquis J. Newell and Nathan Silberstein) Algebra and Its Uses, Books I and II, 1938. Home: Tucson, Ariz. Died July 7, 1939.

HARPER, Ida Husted, writer, lecturer; b. nr. Brookville, Ind.; d. John Arthur and Cassandra (Stoddard) Husted; grad. Muncie (Ind.) High Sch.; student Ind. U., 1 yr., Leland Stanford Jr. U., 2 yrs.; widow; 1 dau., Mrs. Winnifred Cooley. Prin. high sch., Peru, Ind., at 18; conducted dept., "A Woman's Opinions," in Terre Haute Saturday Evening Mail, for 12 yrs., and Woman's Dept., Firemen's Mag., same period; mng. editor Terre Haute Daily News, 1 yr.; editorial writer Indianapolis News for several yrs.; dept. editor N.Y. Sunday Sun, 5 yrs., Harper's Bazar, 4 yrs. Prepared Organized Work of Indiana Women, monograph for World's Columbian Expn., 1893; speaker and del. various meetings of Internat. Council of Women and Internat. Woman Suffrage Alliance, London, 1899, Berlin, 1904, Copenhagen, 1906, Amsterdam, Paris and Geneva, 1908, London, 1909, The Hague and Budapest, 1913, Rome, 1914. Mem. D.A.R. Unitarian. Author: Life and Work of Susan B. Anthony, 1898, 1908 (3 vols.); History of Woman Suffrage to Close of 19th Century (with Susan B. Anthony), 1902; same alone to 1921 (3 vols.); conducted own syndicate of metropolitan papers. Editorial chmn. Leslie Bur. of Suffrage Edn. Home: Washington, D.C. Died Mar. 14, 1931.

HARPER, Jacob Chandler, lawyer; b. Strickersville, Pa., Aug. 17, 1858; s. Samuel and Sarah F. (Phillips) H.; LL.B., Cincinnati (O.) Coll., 1879; LL.D., Pomona College, Calif., 1930; m. Alice E. Waggoner, Sept. 13, 1882; 1 dau., Ruth Holmes (Mrs. Alfred Oscar Anderson). Admitted to Ohio bar, 1879, U.S. Supreme Court, 1889; began practice at Cincinnati; moved to La Jolla, Calif., 1916; mem. State bar of Calif.; gen. counsel Scripps-McRae and Scripps newspapers and allied corps., 1899-1915. U.S. commr.; mem. Sch. Bd., Cincinnati, 6 yrs. Pres. bd. trustees Scripps Coll., Claremont, Calif., 1926—, La Jolla Library Assn., 1917-31; pres. bd. dirs. Scripps Memorial Hosp., Scripps Metabolic Clinic (both La Jolla), 1924—; trustee Claremont Coll., Bishops Sch. for Girls, La Jolla; mem. advisory bd. Scripps Instn. Oceanography). Presbyn. Author: Some Results in the Judicial Veto, 1930; Ellen Browning Scripps, 1936. Home: La Jolla, Calif. Died June 31, 1939.

HARPER, James Patterson, Jr., dentist; b. Fort Madison, Ia., Nov. 9, 1863; s. James Patterson and Elizabeth Bradford (Durfee) H.; ed. Indianapolis High Sch.; D.D.S., Chicago Coll. of Dental Surgery (Lake Forest U.), 1895; m. Elizabeth Pike, June 23,

1900; 1 son, James Durfee. Practiced in St. Louis, 1895—; prof. pathology and histology, Marion-Sims Dental Coll., 1895-1916; dean St. Louis U. Sch. of Dentistry, 1912—; mem. visiting staff St. Louis City Hosps., 1910—; mem. Bd. of Edn., St. Louis, 1911— (pres. 1915-16). Trustee Mo. Bot. Garden (Shaw's Garden). Democrat. Presbyn. Commd. 1st lt., D.R.C., U.S.A., Aug. 1917; maj., Mar. 1918; lt. col., Aug. 1919; col., Feb. 1923. Home: St. Louis, Mo. Died Feb. 13, 1934.

HARPER, John Erasmus, oculist, aurist; b. Cadiz, Ky., [illegible] 21, 1851; s. Robert W. and Harriet A. (Stimson) H.; M.D., Univ. Med. Coll. (New York U.), 1878; m. Elizabeth E. Walker, Feb. 13, 1893. Prof. ophthalmology and otology, Coll. Medicine of U. of Ill., Chicago, 1882-1914, emeritus. Editor Western Medical Reporter, 1881-91. Home: Chicago, Ill. Died Jan. 8, 1921.

HARPER, John Lyell, mechanical engr.; b. Harpersfield, N.Y., Sept. 21, 1873; s. Joseph F. and Quintilla Keturah (Hendry) H.; M.E., Cornell U., 1897; m. Linda E. Wheeler, Sept. 12, 1898. Electrician, Union Electric Co., Seattle, Wash., 1897-98; constrn. and operating engr. Twin City Rapid Transit Co., Minneapolis, 1898-99, St. Croix Power Co. (Apple River development), 1899-1901; asst. engr. Niagara Falls Hydraulic Power & Mfg. Co., 1902-03; chief engr., same, 1903-18, and Cliff Elec. Distributing Co., 1910-18; v.p. and chief eng. Niagara Falls Power Co. (merger of all power plants on Am. side of Niagara River, 1918—, also chief engr. Canadian Niagara Power Co., and Niagara Junction Ry. Co.; gen. cons. practice. Mem. Industrial Commn. and Grade Crossing Commn., Niagara Falls. Fellow Am. Inst. E.E. Republican. Presbyn. Home: Lewiston, N.Y. Died Nov. 28, 1924.

HARPER, Merritt Wesley, college prof.; b. Grove City, O., Oct. 24, 1877; s. James and Elizabeth Ann (Seeds) H.; B.S., Ohio State U., 1901; M.S., U. of Ill., 1902; m. Elizabeth May Tanton, July 29, 1909; children—James T., John T., George T. Asst. in agr., U. of Mo., and asst. in beef production, U. S. Dept. Agr., Columbia, Mo., 1902-05; instr. animal husbandry, 1905-06, prof., 1906—, Cornell U. Author: Manuel of Farm Animals, 1911, revised edit., 1924. Animal Husbandry for Schools, 1913, 24; Management and Breeding of Horses, 1913; Breeding Farm Animals, 1914; also agrl. reports. Home: Ithaca, N.Y. Died 1938.

HARPER, Paul Tompkins, M.D., prof. obstetrics; b. Schenevus, N.Y., Nov. 21, 1881; s. George Alexander nad Jeannette Morse (Tomkins) H.; Ph.B., Hamilton Coll., Clinton, N.Y., 1903, Sc.D., 1928; M.D., Columbia Coll. Phys. and Surg., 1907; m. Susan Ann Davis, Sept. 21, 1910; children—Sarah Ann, Richard Davis. Obstetric surgeon, Albany (N.Y). Hosp., 1912-27, asso. obstetrician, 1927—; attending obstetrician, Brady Maternity Home, Albany, 1915-24; clin. prof. obstetrics, Albany Med. Coll., 1915—; regional consultant in obstetrics, N.Y. State Dept. Health. Fellow Am. Coll. Surgeons, Am. Assn. Obstetricians, Gynecologists and Abdominal Surgeons, N.Y. Obstet. Soc. Republican. Presbyn. Mason. Author: Clinical Obstetrics, 1929. Home: Albany, N.Y. Died July 11, 1931.

HARPER, Robert Francis, Assyriologist; b. New Concord, O., Oct. 18, 1864; s. Samuel and Ellen Elizabeth (Rainey) H.; ed. Denison Coll., 1876-78, Muskingum Coll., 1879-80; A.B., (old) U. of Chicago, 1883; A.M., Ph.D., U. of Leipzig, 1886; (LL.D. from Muskingum Coll., Ohio, 1912); unmarried. Instr. Semitic langs., Yale, 1886-88, 1889-91; Assyriologist expdn. of Babylonian Exploration Fund, U. of Pa., 1888-89, British Mus., 1891-92; asso. prof. Semitic langs. and lits., 1892-1900, prof., 1900—, U. of Chicago. Editor Am. Jour. of Semitic Langs., 1907—; asso. ed. The Biblical World, and Am. Jour. of Theology. Director of expdn. to Babylonia of the Oriental Exploration Fund, 1903-06; curator Haskell Oriental Museum (Babylonian sect.), 1900—; dir. Am. Sch. for Oriental Study and Research in Palestine, 1908-09. Fellow Royal Geog. Soc., London. Author: Assyrian and Babylonian Letters belonging to the Kouyunjik Collections of the British Museum (13 parts published), 1892-1913; Babylonian and Assyrian Literature, 1901; The Code of Hammurabi, 1904. Editor: (with Francis Brown and George F. Moore) Old Testament and Semitic Studies in Memory of William Rainey Harper, 2 vols., 1908. Died Aug. 6, 1914.

HARPER, Robert N., banker; b. nr. Leesburg, Va., Jan. 31, 1861; s. Robert and Mary Armelia H.; Ph.G., Phila Coll., Pharmacy, 1885; m. Carolyn Roush, 1889. Organizer, 1903, and pres., 1903-08, Am. Nat. Bank, Washington, D.C.; sr. mem. Harper & Co. which was merged into Dist. Nat. Bank of which was organizer, pres. until 1930, chmn. bd., 1930-31, retired, 1931; dir. Potomac Electric Power Co., Peoples Nat. Bk. (Leesburg, Va.); organizer, pres. Farmers Banking & Trust Co., Leesburg, until it was merged with the Peoples Bank. Commr. of Pharmacy for Dist. of Columbia 6 yrs. Mem. staff of Gov. Montague, of Va., 4 yrs., title of col.; del. Dem. Nat. Conv., Kansas City, Mo., 1900, San Francisco, 1920; chmn. civic sect. at Pres. Wilson's inauguration, 1913; chmn. Inaugural Com., Pres. Wilson's inauguration, 1917; v. chmn. G.A.R. Reunion, Washington, 1914; chmn. Confederate Vets. Reunion, Washington, 1917; also chmn. at Home Coming of D.C. Soliders and chmn. Citizens' Com. at Gen. Pershing's reception. Pres. of Washington, D.C., Chamber of Commerce 4 terms, and for 25 yrs. mem. Washington, Bd. of Trade; pres. Washington and Leesburg Good Roads Assn., Washington, Drainsville and Great Falls Good Roads Assn.; v.p. Bankers Assn. of D.C.; v.p. Am. Bankers Assn. Presbyn. Mason. Pres. Washington Auditorium Corp. Home: Washington; (summer) near Leesburg, Va. Died Sept. 23, 1940.

HARPER, William Rainey, pres. Univ. of Chicago, 1891—; b. New Concord, O., July 26, 1856; s. Samuel and Ellen Elizabeth (Rainey) H.; grad. Muskingum Coll., 1870; (Ph.D., Yale, 1875; D.D., Colby, 1891; LL.D., Univ. of Neb., 1893, Yale, 1901, Johns Hopkins, 1902); m. 1875, Ellen, d. David Paul, New Concord, O. Prin. Masonic Coll., Macon, Tenn., 1875-76; tutor, 1876-79; prin. prep. dept. Denison U., Granville, O., 1879-80; prof. Hebrew, Bapt. Union Theol. Sem., Chicago, 1879-86; prof. Semitic langs., Yale, 1886-91, and prof. Bibl. lit., 1889-91; prin. Chautauqua Coll. Liberal Arts, 1885-91; head prof. Semitic langs. and lit. and pres., U. of Chicago, 1891—; mem. Chicago bd. of edn., 1896-98; dir. Haskell Oriental Mus. Author: Elements of Hebrew; Elements of Hebrew Syntax; Hebrew Vocabularies; Introductory New Testament Greek Method (with Revere F. Weidner); A Teacher's Manual for an Inductive Latin Primer (with I. B. Burgess), 1898; Elements of Latin (with I. B. Burgess), 1900; Constructive Studies in the Priestly Element in the Old Testament, 1902, 2d enlarged edit., 1905; Religion and the Higher Life, 1904; The Structure of the Text of the Book of Amos, 1904; The Structure of the Text of the Book of Hosea, 1905; The Trend of Higher Education, 1905; Amos and Hosea (Internat. Critical Commentary), 1905. Editor The Biblical World, The Am. Jour. of Theology, and the Am. Jour. of Semitic Languages and Literature. Home: Chicago, Ill. Died 1906.

HARPER, William St. John, painter; b. Rhinebeck, N.Y., Sept. 8, 1851; s. William R. and Mary J. (St. John) H.; ed. at Pittsfield, Mass., and Brooklyn; studied painting at Nat. Acad. Design, New York, and under Munkacsy and Bonnat, Paris; m. Mary Palmer Hedderwick, of London, Eng., 1886. In jewelry business in Brooklyn 5 yrs.; mgr. art dept., New York Daily Graphic, 1878; pres. Art Students' League, 1881-83; asso. mem. Nat. Acad. Design, 1892; instr. and mng. dir. Art Students' League, 1900-03; instr. drawing and painting, Cooper Union Art Sch., 1902-05; instr. same, art dept., Newark Tech. Sch., 1902-05, and Emma Willard Art Sch., Troy, N.Y., 1902-05; art critic Troy (N.Y.) Sch. Arts and Crafts, 1905-10; instr. Summer School of Painting, Northport, L.I., 1909-10. Received Clark prize, 1892, for painting "Autumn"; hon. memtion for painting "Winter's Veil," Buffalo Expn., 1901; other prominent paintings are: A Fairy Tale; An Opera Night; The Beach Patrol; A Legend of Spring; The Silent Snow; Mayflowers; Woodpinks; The Village Street; Easthampton, L.I.; An Old Long Island Homestead, Northport, N.Y.; A Long Lane, Larkfield, L.I.; etc. Home: Larkfield, L.I., N.Y. Died 1910.

HARPER, William Wade, surgeon; b. Richmond, Ala., Feb. 26, 1868; s. William Bolyn and Georgia (Wade) H.; A.B., U. of Ala., 1887, A.M., 1891; M.D., Tulane U., 1891; m. Rosa Frantz, Nov. 20, 1895. Practiced at Selma, 1891—, specializing as pediatrician; surgeon Ala. Bapt. Hosp., Southern Ry., Western Ry. of Ala.; dist. surgeon L.&N. R.R. Co.; dir. Selma Times Journal. Capt. Med. Corps, U.S.A., World War. Sch. trustee, Selma; pres. Y.M.C.A., Selma. Mem. Ala. State Bd. of Health. Fellow Am. Coll. Surgeons, Southeastern Surg. Congress. Democrat. Presbyn. Mason. Home: Selma, Ala. Died Jan. 14, 1941.

HARPSTER, Charles Melvin, surgeon; b. Carey, O., Sept. 13, 1873; s. David and Hannah (Holway) H.; M.D., Toledo Med. Coll., 1896; post-grad. work at Vienna, Berlin, Paris and London; registered Ohio State Bd. of Pharmacy; m. Luella A. Wilt, May 26, 1898; children—Helen, Hilda. Practiced at Toledo, 1898—; mem. Harpster, Brown & Vogelsang; cons. chief surgeon for Ohio for Henry L. Doherty & Co., and surgeon for many corps.; dir. dept. of surgery, St. Vincent's Hosp.; surgeon Hosp. Corps Ohio N.G. many yrs. Fellow Am. Coll. Surgeons, A.M.A. Republican. Episcopalian. Mason. Home: Toledo, O. Died Dec. 24, 1926.

HARPSTER, John Henry, missionary; b. Center Hall, Pa., Apr. 27, 1843; s. George and Frances H.; edn. interrupted by Civil War, in which he served, 1861-65, capt. and staff officer, 2 Corps, Army of Potomac; twice dangerously wounded in battle; after war student in instns. at Selinsgrove and Gettysburg, Pa.; (D.D., Wittenberg Coll., Springfield, O., 1893); m. Julia, d. Prof. Michael Jacobs, of Gettysburg, Pa., July 1882. Ordained Luth. ministry, 1871; missionary at Guntur, India, 1872-76; returned with impaired health; resided in Calif.; pastor Ellsworth and Hayes City, Kan., 1879-81, Trenton, N.J., 1882-84, Canton, O., 1884-93; reëntered foreign mission work, 1893; on furlough, 1902; returned to India as dir. of the Mission of the General Council, Dec. 1902. Home: Philadelphia, Pa. Died 1911.

HARRIES, George Herbert, major gen. (Aux.) U.S.A.; b. Haverfordwest, S. Wales, Sept. 19, 1860; s. John and Sarah (Davies) H.; ed. Haverfordwest Grammar Sch.; hon. A.M., Howard U., Washington, D.C., in recognition of lectures on Colonial history; LL.D., Ky. State U.; m. Elizabeth Langley, Apr. 23, 1884 (died May 29, 1925); children—Herbert Langley (lt. col. U.S.A.), Warren Godwin (1st lt. U.S.A., killed in France, 1918); m. 2d, Alice Loveland, Jan. 11, 1927. Printer, newspaper reporter and syndicate writer; mem. staff, later asso. editor Washington (D.C.) Evening Star; pres. Metropolitan R.R. Co., Washington, 1895-96; v.p. Washington Ry. & Electric Co. and of all cos. in that combination, 1900-11; on staff, 1911-12, v.p., Oct. 1912—, H. M. Byllesby & Co., Chicago. Vol. aide to Gen. Nelson A. Miles in Wounded Knee Campaign, S.D., 1890-91; active mem. Sioux Commn. which established boundary line between Pine Ridge and Rosebud Indian reservations and removed northern Cheyennes to old home on Lame Deer, Mont., 1891-92; brig. gen. comdg. militia (mil. and naval) of D.C., Nov. 30, 1897-May 8, 1915, by presdl. commn.; promoted maj. gen., May 18, 1915, and retired upon own request, May 26, 1915; col. 1st D.C. Inf., U.S.V., 1898, serving before Santiago de Cuba, during siege of that city and in Cuban Army of Occupation; mem. War Dept. Bd. on Promotion of Rifle Practice many yrs.; brig. gen. comdg. 1st Brig. Neb. N.G., June 25, 1917; brig. gen. U.S.A., Aug. 5, 1917-Sept. 30, 1919; comd. successively, 59th Depot Brig., 186th Inf. Brig. (13th Corps, 2d French Army), Base Sect. No. 5, A.E.F., 173d Inf. Brig.; chief U.S. Mil. Mission, Berlin, Germany, Dec. 3, 1918-Sept. 30, 1919, brig. gen. O.R.C., Dec. 28, 1920; maj. gen. (Aux.) Sept. 16, 1924. Awarded D.S.M. Army, and D.S.M. Navy; comdr. Légion d'Honneur (for constrn. and operation Port of Brest, etc.); also decorated by 8 other European govts. for mil. services. V.p. Bd. of Edn., Washington, D.C., 1895-1903; pres. Washington (D.C.) Bd. Trade, 1910-11. Nat. comdr. Order Indian Wars, U.S., 1912; comdr. in chief Mil. Order World War, 1920-25, declined reëlection; v.p. Soc. Army of Santiago de Cuba, 1924-25, pres. 1926-27. Fellow Am. Inst. E.E. Republican. Methodist. Home: Washington, D.C., and Bel Air, Los Angeles, Calif. Died Sept. 28, 1934.

HARRIGAN, Edward, actor, playwright; b. New York, 1845; married. Went on stage as variety performer and was asso. with Tony Hart as Harrigan & Hart until 1884 as actor and theatre mgr.; after 1884 conducted theatres in New York; built Theatre Comique (destroyed by fire) and later Garrick Theatre, 35th St. and Broadway, which he has leased. Author: (plays) Squatter Sovereignty; McSorley's Inflation; Editor's Troubles; and others, about 50 in all, latest being Under Cover for Season, 1903-04. Home: Brooklyn, N.Y. Died 1911.

HARRIMAN, Alice, author, publ.; b. Newport, Me., Mar. 12, 1861; d. James and Mary E. (Ladd) H.; high sch. edn.; widow. Writer for mags., 1896—; traveled for Northwest Mag., 1897-1902; established The Alice Harriman Co., pubs. of fine books, 1907, at Seattle, Wash.; moved to New York, 1910. Christian Scientist. Author: Stories of Montana (Pacific Coast Series), 1903; Songs o' the Sound, 1906; Songs of the Olympics, 1910; A Man of Two Countries, 1910; Bells and Their Overtones, 1918. Home: Hollywood, Calif. Died Dec. 24, 1925.

HARRIMAN, Edward Henry, capitalist; b. Hampstead, L.I., N.Y., Feb. 25, 1848; s. Rev. Orlando H.; common sch. edn.; became a broker's clerk in Wall St., at 14; later stock broker on own account; m. Mary Averell. Mem. N.Y. Stock Exchange, Aug. 13, 1870—; pres. and dir. Ore. R.R. & Navigation Co., Portland & Asiatic Steamship Co.; pres. and chmn. exec. com. U.P. R.R. Co.; chmn. exec. com. Wells-Fargo & Co.; mem. bd. mgrs. Del. & Hudson Co.; pres. and dir. Ore. Short Line R.R. Co., S.P. Co., Tex. & New Orleans R.R. Co., S. Pacific Coast Ry., Ore. & Calif. R.R. Co., Central Pacific Ry. Co., La. Western R.R. Co., Morgan's La. & Tex. R.R. & Steamship Co., Pacific Mail Steamship Co., Railroad Securities Co., S.P. Terminal Co.; dir. I.C. R.R. Co. from 1883 (v.p. 1887-90). Trustee Equitable Trust Co.; and dir. many other corps. Home: Tuxedo Park, N.Y. Died 1909.

HARRIMAN, Frederick William, clergyman; b. Crawfordsville, Ind., Nov. 22, 1852; s. Rev. Frederick Durbin and Mary Jones (Bostwick) H.; B.A., Trinity Coll., Conn., 1872, M.A., 1875, D.D., 1902; grad. Berkeley Div. Sch., Conn., 1876; m. Cora Elizabeth Jarvis, Oct. 19, 1882; children—Mary (Mrs. Paul L. Dole), Charles Jarvis, Lewis Gildersleeve. Ordained deacon 1876; priest 1877, P.E. Ch.; curate St. Andrew's Ch., Meriden, Conn., 1877-79; rector St. James, Winsted, Conn., 1879-80, Trinity Ch., Portland, Conn., 1880-86, Grace Ch., Windsor, Conn., 1886-1920, emeritus. Arch-deacon Hartford Co., 1893-96; sec. diocese of Conn., 1895-1912. Jr. fellow Trinity Coll., 1889-1910; trustee Berkeley Div. Sch.,

1915-22, Loomis Inst., 1917-21. Home: Buffalo, N.Y. Died Feb. 19, 1931.

HARRIMAN, Job, socialist; b. Clinton Co., Ind., Jan. 15, 1861; on farm till 18; attended Butler U., Irvington, Ind., 1884; entered the ministry, but his views changed so that he could not conscientiously remain in church; became a lawyer; brought up a Democrat; became dissatisfied with party; became interested in Socialism, 1890; Socialistic Labor party's candidate for gov. Calif., 1898; chosen state organizer Social Democracy, 1899; nominated for vice-presidency at Nat. Conv., Social Dem. party, at Indianapolis, 1900; socialist nominee for mayor of Los Angeles, 1911. Mem. Harriman & Ryckman. Home: Los Angeles, Calif. Died Oct. 26, 1925.

HARRIMAN, Karl Edwin, editor, author; b. Ann Arbor, Mich., Dec. 29, 1875; s. William Dexter and Harriett M. (Bliss) H.; student class of '96, U. of Mich., A.B., 1910, as of class of 1898; m. Edith M. Lee, 1899. Entered newspaper work on Detroit Journal, 1895; wrote daily editorial column, Detroit Free Press, 1898-99; in England for Free Press, 1899; editor The Pilgrim, 1905; later editor The Red Book, The Blue Book, and The Green Book (mags.), Chicago; mng. editor Ladies' Home Journal, 1912-19; editor Red Book and Blue Book mags., Chicago, 1919-27; v.p. J. H. Sears & Co., pubs., 1927—. Author: Ann Arbor Tales, 1902; Away from the Shore (serial in The Era), 1902; The Home Builders, 1903; Sadie, 1907. Home: Wyncote, Pa. Died Oct. 1, 1935.

HARRIMAN, Mary W.; b. New York City; d. W. J. Averell, of Ogdensburg, N.Y.; m. Edward Henry Harriman, capitalist and financier (died 1909); children—Mary (Mrs. C. C. Rumsey), Henry Neilson (dec.), Cornelia (Mrs. Robert Livingston Gerry), Carol Averell (Mrs. W. Plunkett Stewart), William Averell, Edward Roland Noel. Heir upon death of husband to estate appraised at about $100,000,000, of which is mgr. Actively interested in many charities. Home: Harriman, N.Y., and New York, N.Y. Died Nov. 7, 1932.

HARRIMAN, Oliver; b. N.Y. City, Nov. 29, 1862; s. Oliver and Laura (Low) H.; A.B., Princeton, 1883; m. Grace Carley, Jan. 28, 1891. Became mem. Harriman & Co., 1889, later consol. with Harriman & Keech; firm was mem. all prin. exchanges; retired 1938. Episcopalian. Home: New York, N.Y. Died Aug. 14, 1940.

HARRINGTON, Charles, educator, physician; b. Salem, Mass., July 29, 1856; s. George and Delphine Rose Eugenie H.; student Bowdoin Coll., 1873-74; grad. Harvard Coll., 1878, Harvard Med. Sch., 1881; studied univs. of Leipzig, Strassburg, Munich, 1881-83; m. M. Josephine Jones, Feb. 25, 1884. Began as asst. in chemistry, 1883, later instr., asst. prof., 1899-1906, prof. hygiene, 1906—, Harvard Med. Sch. Formerly chemist to State Bd. of Health of Mass. 9 yrs.; in charge of bureau of milk inspection, Boston Bd. Health, 1889-1904; sec. Mass. State Bd. of Health, Dec. 1904—. Author: Practical Hygiene, 1901, 02, 05. Home: Jamaica Plain, Boston. Died 1908.

HARRINGTON, Charles Kendall, missionary; b. Sydney, N.S., Can., Mar. 14, 1858; s. Clement Hubert and Sarah Ann (Reynolds) H.; B.A., Acadia Coll., 1879 (D.D., 1900); student Newton Theol. Instn., Mass., 1880-81; B.D., Morgan Park Theol. Sem., Chicago, 1884; post-grad work same, 1884-86; m. Jean L. Lovett, Sept. 9, 1886. Home missionary work in N.S. and N.B., 1879-82; sent to Japan as missionary Am. Bapt. Foreign Mission Soc., 1886; mem. teaching staff Japan Bapt. Theol. Sch.; mem. revising com. of Japanese New Testament, 1910-16; on furlough. Author: Five Old Friends, 1915; Captain Bickel of the Inland Sea, 1919. Home: Albany, N.Y. Died May 13, 1920.

HARRINGTON, Charles Medbury, grain mcht.; b. New Berlin, N.Y., July 11, 1855; s. Daniel and Elizabeth (Medbury) H.; ed. New Berlin Acad.; m. Grace Ross, Sept. 12, 1877. Telegraph operator and bookkeeper, Rochester, Minn., 1871-74; in employ wholesale house, Albany, N.Y., 1875-81; now pres. Van Dusen-Harrington Co., and identified with many large business enterprises. Pres. Minneapolis Chamber of Commerce. Republican. Episcopalian. Home: Wayzata, Minn. Deceased.

HARRINGTON, Francis Bishop, surgeon; b. Salem, Mass., Aug. 15, 1854; s. Samuel Bishop and Caroline Elizabeth (Hawes) H.; A.B., Tufts Coll., 1877; M.D., Harvard, 1881; m. Abbie Josephine Ruggles, Oct. 2, 1882. Began practice at Boston, 1882; surg. chief of service, Mass. Gen. Hosp., Boston; asst. in clin. surgery, 1889-94, lecturer, 1900—, Harvard; med. adviser to trustees of Peter Bent Brigham Hosp. Fellow Am. Surg. Assn. Died June 8, 1914.

HARRINGTON, Francis Clark, commr. of work projects, army officer; b. Bristol, Va., Sept. 10, 1887; s. William Clark and Victoria (Gauthier) H.; B.S., U.S. Mil. Acad., 1909; student Engr. Sch., U.S. Army, 1910-11, Gen. Staff Sch., 1927-28, Army War Coll., 1928-29, Ecole Superieure de Guerre, 1933-35; m. Eleanor Crozier Reyburn, June 30, 1915 (died 1938); children—William Stuart, Mary Eleanor. Commissioned 2d lt., Corps of Engrs., U.S. Army, 1909, and advanced through the grades to col., 1938; during World War was instr. in officer training camps, also with 603d Engrs. and comdg. 215th Engrs. and special duty Hdqrs., A.E.F.; has served as asst. prof. of mathematics at U.S. Mil. Acad., dir. Engr. Sch. of U.S. Army, dist. engr., Baltimore, asst. engr. of maintenance at Panama Canal and on War Dept. Gen. Staff; assigned asst. adminstr. Works Progress Administration, 1935, apptd. adminstr., Dec. 24, 1938, commissioner of work projects, July 1, 1939; dir. Panama R.R. Co. Home: Washington, D.C. Died Sept. 30, 1940.

HARRINGTON, Harry Franklin, prof. journalism; b. Logan, Ohio, July 25, 1882; s. Frank and Margaret (Walker) H.; student U. of Wooster, 1899-1901; B.A., Ohio State U., 1905; M.A., Columbia U., 1909; L.H.D., Oklahoma City U., 1931; m. Frieda Poston, July 15, 1913. Reportorial and editorial experience Ohio State Journal, Columbus and London (O.) Times until 1908; instr. in English, Ohio Wesleyan U., 1909-10; asst. prof. English, Ohio State U., 1910-14, also dir. courses in journalism; asst. prof. journalism, U. of Kan., 1914-15; asso. in journalism, 1915-18, asst. prof., 1918-21, U. of Ill.; dir. Medill School of Journalism, Northwestern Univ., 1921—. Dir. courses in journalism, U. of Calif., summer session, Southern div., 1918-19, U. of Wis., 1920, Sch. of Journalism, Columbia U., summer, 1921; editorial writer Christian Science Monitor, 1929—. Republican. Conglist. Author: Essentials in Journalism (with T. T. Frankenberg), 1912, 23; Typical Newspaper Stories, 1915; The Teaching of Journalism in a Natural Setting, 1919; Writing for Print, 1921, 29; Chats on Feature Writing, 1925; The Newspaper Club (with Evaline Harrington), 1927; Pathways to Print (with Lawrence Martin), 1931; The Copyreader's Workshop (with R. E. Wolseley), 1934. Editorial adviser to Harper & Bros. Home: Evanston, Ill. Died Sept. 2, 1935.

HARRINGTON, John T., mfr.; b. Rock Creek, O., May 22, 1873; s. Frederick and Hannah (Truesdale) H.; A.B., Oberlin, 1894; LL.B., U. of Mich., 1896; m. Grace Booth, Nov. 14, 1908; 1 dau., Florence Booth. Admitted to Ohio bar, 1896, and began practice at Jefferson; moved to Youngstown, 1900; mem. Arrel, McVey & Robinson, 1900-17, Harrington, De Ford, Huxley & Smith, 1917-25; pres. Trumbull Steel Co., Dec. 15, 1925—; pres. Pa.-Ohio Power & Light Co., Pa.-Ohio Electric Co.; v.p. and gen. counsel Republic Ry. & Light Co., Pa.-Ohio Edison Co. Republican. Presbyn. Home: Youngstown, O. Died Feb. 29, 1932.

HARRINGTON, Purnell Frederick, rear admiral U.S.N.; b. Dover, Del., June 6, 1844; s. Hon. Samuel M. and Mary (Lofland) H.; apptd. to U.S. Naval Acad., from Del., 1861; m. Mia N. Ruan, of St. Croix, D.W.I., Aug. 5, 1868; children—Helen Nelthrop, Ethel, Samuel Milby, Frederick Littell (dec.). Promoted ensign, Oct. 1, 1863; advanced through grades to rear adm., Mar. 21, 1903. Served on Ticonderoga, N. Atlantic Blockading Squadron, 1863; Monongahela, W. Gulf Blockading Squadron, 1864-65; participated in operations against defenses at mouth of Mobile Bay, and battle Mobile Bay, 1864; on bd. Monongahela, North Atlantic Squadron, 1865-68; at Naval Acad., 1868-70; California, 1870-73; Naval Acad., 1873-76; exec. officer Hartford, 1877-79; Naval Acad., 1880-83; comd. practice-ship Dale during the cruises of 1881 and 1882; comd. Juniata, 1883-85; Naval Acad., 1886-89; comd. practice-ship Constellation during cruises of 1888 and 1889; light-house insp. 4th dist., 1890-93; comd. Yorktown, 1893-94; pres. of Steel Bd., 1894-96; comd. Terror, 1896-97, Puritan, 1897-98; capt. of yard, Navy Yard, Portsmouth, 1898-1901, Navy Yard, New York, 1902-03; commandant, Navy Yard, Norfolk, 1903-06; retired, June 6, 1906; duty in connection with Jamestown Expn., 1906-07. Comdr.-in-chief, Loyal Legion, 1925-27. Home: Yonkers, N.Y. Died Sept. 20, 1937.

HARRINGTON, Thomas Francis, physician; b. Lowell, Mass., June 10, 1866; s. Thomas and Mary H.; M.D., Harvard, 1888; post-grad. work in Europe; m. Mary I. Dempsey, June 2, 1891. Practiced, Lowell, 1889-1907, since in Boston; visiting phys., St. John's Hosp., Lowell, 15 yrs.; cons. phys., same, 3 yrs.; U.S. pension examining surgeon 13 yrs.; chmn. Bd. Health, Lowell, 3 yrs.; dir. sch. hygiene, Boston pub. schs., 1907-15; med. deputy commr. labor, Mass., 1915—; instr. in sch. for health officers at Harvard and Mass. Inst. Tech.; phys.-in-chief St. Elizabeth's Hosp.; dir. St. Vincent's Orphan Asylum; examiner for Civ. Service Commn.; originator of "Health Day." Author: History of Harvard Medical School, 1636-1905, 3 vols. Capt., maj., lt. col., Mass. State Guard, 1917-18; chmn. Exemption Bd. Dist. 5, Mass., 1917-18. Home: Boston, Mass. Died Jan. 19, 1919.

HARRIS, Abram Winegardner, educator; b. Phila., Pa., Nov. 7, 1858; s. James Russell and Susanna (Reed) H.; A.B., Wesleyan U., Conn., 1880, A.M., 1883; Sc.D., Bowdoin, 1894; LL.D., U. of N.B., 1900, U. of Me., 1901, Wesleyan, 1904; m. Clara V. Bainbridge, Feb. 28, 1888 (died Feb. 3, 1908); 1 son, Abram Winegardner. Teacher mathematics, Dickinson Sem., Williamsport, Pa., 1880-81; tutor mathematics and registrar, 1881-84, instr. history, 1885-88, Wesleyan U., Conn.; asst. dir., 1888-91, and dir., 1891-93, Office of Expt. Stas., U.S. Dept. Agr.; pres. U. of Me., 1893-1901; headmaster and dir. Tome School, Md., 1901-06; pres. Northwestern U., 1906-16; corr. sec. Bd. of Edn. of M.E. Ch., 1916-24 and sec., 1924—. Prepared many scientific and administrative documents of U.S. Dept. Agr., etc. Chmn. exec. bd. Religious Edn. Assn., 1910-16; pres. Am. Social Hygiene Assn., 1915-17; ex-chmn. Vice Commn. of Chicago; v.p. Com. of 15 of Chicago, 1915-16; mem. Ednl. Assn. of the M.E. Ch.; trustee Drew University. Home: Manset, Me. Died Feb. 21, 1935.

HARRIS, Addison C., lawyer; b. Wayne Co., Ind., Oct. 1, 1840; s. Branson L. and Martha (Young) H.; student Northwestern U., 1860-63; m. India C. Crago, May 8, 1868. Admitted to bar, 1865, and engaged in practice at Indianapolis; mem. Ind. Senate, 1877-79; candidate for Congress, 1888; E.E. and M.P. of U.S. to Austria-Hungary, 1899-1901. Republican. Ex-officio pres. U. of Indianapolis, 1899-1904; trustee Purdue U.; pres. Ind. Law Sch., 1899—. Pres. Ind. Bar Assn., 1904-05. Home: Indianapolis, Ind. Died 1916.

HARRIS, Albert Hall, lawyer, ry. official; b. Rochester, N.Y., July 4, 1861; s. Edward and Emma L. (Hall) H.; A.B., U. of Rochester, 1881; m. Hebe Magee Beach, Dec. 13, 1887. Chmn. exec. com. and v.p. N.Y.C. R.R. Co., Cleveland, Cincinnati, Chicago & St. Louis Ry. Co., Mich. Central R.R. Co., Pittsburgh & Lake Erie R.R. Co.; v.p., Rutland R.R. Co., Cincinnati Northern R.R. Co., Canada Southern Ry. Co., Indiana Harbor Belt R.R. Co., Detroit River Tunnel Co., Peoria & Eastern Ry. Co. and other N.Y. Central Lines. Trustee, U. of Rochester. Home: New York, N.Y. Died Nov. 21, 1931.

HARRIS, Amanda Bartlett, author; b. Warner, N.H., Aug. 15, 1824; d. Harrison Gray and Mary (Bartlett) H.; acad. edn.; unmarried. Has been a writer since girlhood; has contributed to Christian Union, Congregationalist, Congregational Review, Appleton's Journal, St. Nicholas, Wide Awake, etc. Author: Pleasant Authors for Young Folks, 1884; Old School Days, 1886; American Authors for Young Folks, 1887; The Luck of Edenhall, 1888. Home: Warner, N.H. Died Jan. 13, 1917.

HARRIS, Andrew Lintner, governor; b. Butler Co., O., Nov. 17, 1835; s. Benjamin and Nancy (Lintner) H.; B.S., Miami U., 1860 (LL.D., 1906, Ohio Wesleyan, 1907). Second lt. 20th Ohio Inf., Apr. 17, 1861; capt., May 27, 1861; 2d lt. 75th Ohio Inf., Oct. 3, 1861; capt., Nov. 9, 1861; maj., Mar. 13, 1863; col., May 3, 1863; bvtd. brig. gen. vols., Mar. 13, 1865, for distinguished and gallant services; hon. mustered out, Jan. 17, 1865; m. Caroline Conger, Oct. 15, 1865. Admitted to bar 1865; probate judge, Preble Co., 1875-82; mem. Ohio Senate, 1865-67, Ho. of Rep., 1885-89; lt. gov. of Ohio, 1892-96; mem. U.S. Industrial Commn., 1898-1902; gov. of Ohio, 1906-09. Home: Eaton, O. Died Sept. 13, 1915.

HARRIS, Arthur M.; b. Madison, O., Dec. 2, 1865; s. Dwight J. and Elvira (Ingham) H.; ed. pub. schs., Ohio, and State Normal U., Normal, Ill.; LL.D., Denison U., O., 1936; m. Mary Alma Patrick, Apr. 25, 1889; children—Rae Myrtelle, Dwight J., Constance Ingham. Teacher, pub. schs., Lake Co., Ill., 1884-85; mem. N. W. Harris & Co., bankers, N.Y. City, 1907-12; v.p. and treas. Harris, Forbes & Co., 1912-20; retired; pres. Florida Bank, Winter Park. Pres. Northern Bapt. Conv., 1928-29; v.p., hon. treas. Ministers and Missionaries Benefit Bd., Northern Bapt. Conv. Treas. Y.M.C.A. for A.E.F., France, 1918. Mem. Chamber of Commerce (Winter Park, Fla.). Republican. Home: Winter Park, Fla. Died Mar. 27, 1941.

HARRIS, Benjamin Franklin, banker; b. Champaign Co., Ill., Sept. 30, 1868; s. Henry Hickman and Mary Melissa (Megrue) H.; student U. of Ill., 1889; LL.B., Columbia U., 1892; m. May Melish, Dec. 5, 1895. Pres. 1st Nat. Bank, Champaign, Ill. (bank owned by self and bro.); interested in farm lands and business enterprises. Progressive. Methodist. Chmn. Ill. Bankers' Assn. (cons. on agr. and vocational edn., pres. 1911-12); chmn. agr. commn. Am. Bankers' Assn. and pres. conf. of coms. on agrl. development and edn. of all state bankers' assns., and inaugurated movement among bankers to advance agrl. and rural development and state supervision of pvt. bks. Mem. com. on ocean transportation, Chamber Commerce U.S.A. Mason. Home: Champaign, Ill. Died Dec. 19, 1920.

HARRIS, Carlton Danner, clergyman, editor; b. Wardensville, W.Va., Nov. 26, 1864; s. Rev. David and Bernice Sophia (Danner) H.; A.B., Randolph-Macon Coll., 1888; D.D., St. John's Coll., Md., 1915; m. Katie Aileen Norris, Dec. 19, 1895 (died 1900); m. 2d, Katharine Elizabeth Matthaei, Apr. 27, 1904; children—Anna Bernice, Charles David, Carlton Matthaei, Katharine Danner. Ordained elder M.E. Ch., S., 1892; asso. pastor, Loudoun Circuit, Va., 1888-90; pastor Easton, Md., 1890-94, Calvary Ch., Baltimore, 1894-98, Mt. Crawford, Va., 1898-99, Easton, Md., 1899-1901, Martinsburg, W.Va., 1901-05, Emmanuel Ch., Baltimore, 1905-07, Central Ch., Baltimore, 1907-11; editor Baltimore Southern Methodist, 1911-

22; pastor, Alpheus W. Wilson Memorial Ch., Baltimore, 1921-27; editor Baltimore Southern Methodist, 1927—. Democrat. Mason. Home: Baltimore, Md. Died Sept. 28, 1928.

HARRIS, Charles K., music publisher, composer; b. Poughkeepsie, N.Y., May 1, 1865; s. Jacob and Rachel H.; ed. pub. schs., East Saginaw, Mich.; settled in Milwaukee; m. Cora Lehrberg, Nov. 15, 1893. Has written and composed many songs, including "After the Ball," 1892, and considerably over 100 later. Head of Charles K. Harris Pub. Co., established in Milwaukee, but now having hdqrs. in New York and many Am. and foreign branches. Author (plays): A Limb of the Tree; The Luckiest Man in the World; The Barker; The Heart of a Man. Treas. Music Publishers Protective Assn., Music Publishers Assn. of the U.S. Mason. Home: New York, N.Y. Died Dec. 22, 1930.

HARRIS, Cicero Richardson, bishop; b. Fayetteville, N.C., Aug. 25, 1844; s. Jacob and Charlotte H.; ed. pub. schs., Chillicothe and Delaware, O., grammar and high schs., Cleveland; (D.D., Howard U., Washington, 1891; A.M., Livingston Coll., N.C., 1902); m. Maria E. Guion, Dec. 17, 1879. Taught sch., Fayetteville, N.C., 1866-72; licensed as exhorter and as preacher, 1872; ordained deacon, Charlotte, N.C., Jan. 1873, as elder in Concord, N.C., Nov. 1874, and as bishop at Newbern, N.C., 1888, in A.M.E. Zion Ch. In Livingston Coll., Salisbury, N.C., 1882-88; gen. sec. A.M.E. Zion Ch., 1882; business mgr. Star of Zion, organ of the Ch., 1880-84. Prohibition Republican. Home: Salisbury, N.C. Died June 24, 1917.

HARRIS, Corra May (White), author; b. Farm Hill, Ga., Mar. 17, 1869; d. Tinsley Rucker and Mary Elizabeth (Matthews) White; educated at home; Litt.D., Oglethorpe U., 1921, U. of Ga., 1927; Lit.Hum., Rollins College, 1927; married Rev. Lundy Howard Harris, Feb. 8, 1887 (died 1910). Methodist. Began writing for the Independent, 1899; contbr. "Brasstown Valley Stories," to Am. Mag., 1905-09. Author: The Jessica Letters (with Paul Elmer More), 1904; A Circuit Rider's Wife, 1910; Eve's Second Husband, 1910; Recording Angel, 1912; In Search of a Husband, 1913; Co-Citizens, 1915; Making Her His Wife, 1918; Happily Married, 1920; My Son, 1921; Daughter of Adam, 1923; House of Helen, 1923; My Book and Heart, 1923; As a Woman Thinks, 1925; Flapper Anne, 1925; Happy Pilgrimage, 1927. Columnist in Atlanta Journal, 1931—. Home: Rydal, Ga. Died Feb. 9, 1935.

HARRIS, Elijah Paddock, chemist; b. Le Roy, N.Y., Apr. 3, 1832; s. Daniel and Mary (Paddock) H.; A.B., Amherst, 1855; Ph.D., U. of Göttingen, 1859; (LL.D., Victoria Coll., 1886); m. Ellen Park, July 26, 1860. Prof. chemistry, Victoria Coll., Can., 1859-66, Beloit (Wis.) Coll., 1866-68, Amherst, 1868-1907; retired under Carnegie Foundation, 1907. Congregationalist. Author: Qualitative Analysis, 1875 (10 edits.). Home: Warsaw, N.Y. Died Dec. 10, 1920.

HARRIS, Emerson Pitt, publisher, writer; b. Kennedy, N.Y., Dec. 30, 1853; s. Gilbert Dennison and Mary (Stratton) H.; ed. Jamestown (N.Y.) Union Sch. and Collegiate Inst., 1866-69, Fredonia (N.Y.) Normal Sch., 1878-80; m. Ella Florence Stevens, May 1, 1888 (died 1920); children—John F. (died at birth), Florence (Mrs. Robert Gay Hooke, dec.); m. 2d, Viola E. Rice, Oct. 14, 1922. Postmaster and country mcht., 1873-78; writer and rep. of engring. jours., 1880-84; owner and pub. engring. jours., 1884-89; pub. fruit grower publs., 1892-97; broker in publishing property, 1898-1920; organizer Harris-Dibble Co., specialists in pub. business, 1893; formerly pres. Am. Ry. Pub. Co.; retired. Founder of following publs.: Power, Electric Ry. Jour., Advertising and Selling, The Grape Belt. Republican. Unitarian; pres. Unity Ch., Montclair, N.J., 1900-10. Author: Coöperation, the Hope of the Consumer; The Community Newspaper. Home: Franklinville, N.Y. Died Feb. 17, 1937.

HARRIS, Frank, author; b. Galway, Ireland, 1854; s. Thomas (Brit. naval officer) and Mary (Vernon) H.; came to U.S., 1870; ed. univs. of Kan., Paris, Heidelberg, Strassburg, Göttingen, Berlin, Vienna and Athens (no degrees); m. Helen O'Hara, of Dublin, Ireland. Admitted to Kan. bar, 1875; later returned to Europe and became editor Evening News, and Fortnightly Rev., London, Eng., and secured control Saturday Review. Naturalized citizen of U.S. Author: Elder Conklin, 1892; The Bomb—A Story of the Chicago Anarchists of 1886, 1909; The Man Shakespeare, 1909; Montes (short stories), 1910; The Women of Shakespeare, 1911; Unpathed Waters, 1913; Contemporary Portraits, 1914; The Life and Confessions of Oscar Wilde (2 vols.), 1916; Contemporary Portraits, 2d series, 1919, 3d series, 1921, 4th series, 1923; Undream'd of Shores, 1925; My Life and Loves, vol. 1, 1923, vol. 2, 1925, vol. 3, 1927; Joan La Romee, 1926; Latest Contemporary Portraits, 1927. Died Aug. 26, 1931.

HARRIS, Garrard, editor, writer and foreign trade expert; b. Columbus, Ga., May 14, 1875; s. James Walton and Gertrude (Garrard) H.; attended U. of Ga., and N. Ga. Agrl. Coll.; LL.B., Billsaps Coll., Jackson, Miss., 1902; m. Mary Lou Sykes, Nov. 14, 1906; children—Frances Gertrude, Frank Sykes, Louise, Garrard. Reporter, city editor and editorial writer various Southern newspapers. Practiced law at Jackson, Miss., 1903-11; dist. atty. 7th Jud. dist.; mem. bar U.S. Supreme Court. Spl. agt. U.S. Dept. Commerce to Latin America, 1914-17; specialist, fgn. trade research and editor for Federal Bd. Vocational Edn., Washington, D.C., 1918-19; trade commr. U.S. Dept. Commerce, 1919-29; asso. editor Birmingham (Ala.) News, 1920—. Author: Joe the Book Farmer, 1914; Central America as an Export Field (U.S. Dept. Commerce), 1915; Trail of the Pearl, 1916; West Indies as an Export Field (U.S. Dept. Commerce), 1917; The Treasure of the Land, 1917; Redemption of the Disabled, 1919; Elements of Conservation, 1924. Home: Birmingham, Ala. Died Mar. 19, 1927.

HARRIS, George, educator; b. East Machias, Me., Apr. 1, 1844; s. George and Mary A. (Palmer) H.; A.B., Amherst, 1866; grad. Andover Theol. Sem., 1869; (D.D., Amherst, 1883, Harvard, 1899, Yale, 1901; LL.D., Dartmouth, 1899, Williams, 1908, Wesleyan, 1909); m. Jane A. Viall, Dec. 24, 1873. Ordained Congl. ministry, 1869; pastor High St. Ch., Auburn, Me., 1869-72, Central Ch., Providence, R.I., 1872-83; prof. Christian theol., Andover Theol. Sem., 1883-99; pres. Amherst College, 1899-1912, resigned. Author: Moral Evolution, 1896; Inequality and Progress, 1897; A Century's Change in Religion, 1914. Home: New York, N.Y. Died Mar. 1, 1922.

HARRIS, George B., ry. pres.; b. Brookline, Mass., 1848; s. George S. H. Went to Hannibal, Mo., 1864; began ry. services as office boy in office of treas. Hannibal & St. Joseph R.R.; clerk in land commr.'s office, 1871; later in service Atchison & Neb. R.R.; purchasing agent C.,B.&Q. R.R., 1882-83; asst. to gen. mgr. A.,T.&S.F. R.R., 1883-85; asst. to pres. Chicago, Burlington & Northern R.R. Co., 1885-90; then successively gen. mgr., v.p. and president same road; also 2d v.p. C.,B.&Q. R.R., 1890-1901; pres. C.,B.&Q. R.R., Feb. 21, 1901-Jan. 15, 1911; chmn. bd. dirs., Jan. 15, 1911—; chmn. bd. C.&S. Ry., Jan. 15, 1911—; also pres. Ft. Worth & Denver City Ry. Home: Chicago, Ill. Died June 10, 1918.

HARRIS, George William, librarian; b. Pictou, N.S., Dec. 18, 1849; s. John F. and Margaret (Johnson) H.; Ph.B., Cornell U., 1873; m. Annie Smith, of Campbellton, N.B., 1895. Asst. librarian, 1873-83, acting librarian, 1883-90, librarian, 1890-1915, librarian emeritus, Cornell U. Library. Mem. A.L.A. Editor of Library Bulletin of Cornell U.; Ten Year Book of Cornell U., 1888; Islandica, 1908-14. Home: Ithaca, N.Y. Died Oct. 11, 1917.

HARRIS, Hamilton, lawyer; b. Preble, N.Y., May 1, 1820; grad. Union Coll., 1841; admitted to N.Y. bar, 1845; practices at Albany; mem. N.Y. assembly, 1851; dist. atty. Albany Co., 1854-57; mem., 1862-70, chmn., 1864-70, Republican State committee; pres. bd. State capitol commrs., 1865-75; State senator, 1875-79; regent of the N.Y. State Univ. Home: Albany, N.Y. Died 1900.

HARRIS, Henry Burkhardt, theatrical mgr.; b. St. Louis, Mo., Dec. 1, 1866; s. William and Rachel (Freefield) H.; ed. pub. schs. St. Louis and Boston; m. Irene R. Wallach, Oct. 22, 1898. Connected with Howard Athenæum, Boston, several yrs.; became associated with Rich & Harris and undertook management of May Irwin, later mng. Pete Daily, Lily Langtry, Amelia Bingham in "The Climbers," and launched Robert Edeson as a star; became mgr. Hudson Theatre, 1903, Harris Theatre, 1906, Folies Bergere, 1911, and managed "The Lion and the Mouse," "The Traveling Salesman," "The Third Degree," etc.; had 18 cos. on tour season of 1910-11. Pres. Henry B. Harris Co. Dir. Theatre Mgrs. Assn. of Greater New York; treas. Actors' Fund of America; trustee Hebrew Infant Asylum of New York. Mason. Democrat. Home: New York, N.Y. Died Apr. 15, 1912.

HARRIS, Henry Tudor Brownell, rear admiral U.S.N.; b. Hartford, Conn., Mar. 10, 1845. Apptd. acting asst. p.m. in vol. navy, Nov. 1, 1864; hon. disch. Sept. 13, 1865; apptd. asst. p.m., from New York, Feb. 21, 1867; promoted passed asst. p.m., Feb. 17, 1869; p.m., Jan. 18, 1881; pay insp., Aug. 29, 1899; pay dir., June 13, 1902; paymaster gen. retired with the rank of senior rear admiral, Mar. 10, 1905. Served during the Civil War on the Napa, 1864-65; Nyack, 1867-69; Supply, 1871-72; Frolic, 1873-74; in charge of stores at Honolulu, 1875-77, at Rio de Janeiro, 1878-79; on various duties to 1897; receiving-ship Vermont, 1897-1900; fleet p.m., Asiatic Fleet, 1900-01, European Fleet, 1901-02; Navy Yard, League Island, 1902-03; paymaster gen. U.S.N., and chief of Bur. of Supplies and Accounts, with rank of rear admiral, 1903-06. Participated in N. China campaign and Philippine insurrection, 1900-01. Died July 12, 1920.

HARRIS, J(ames) Arthur, biologist, statistician; b. Plantsville, O., Sept. 29, 1880; s. Jordan Thomas and Ida Ellen (Lambert) H.; A.B., U. of Kan., 1901, A.M., 1902; Ph.D., Washington U., St. Louis, 1903; m. Emma Lay Apr. 20, 1910; children—James Arthur, Alanson Lay, Daniel Lambert, George Galton. Bot. asst., 1901-03, librarian, 1904-07, Mo. Bot. Garden, St. Louis; instr. botany, Washington U., 1903-07; bot. investigator, Sta. for Exptl. Evolution, Carnegie Instn., 1907-24; head dept. of botany, U. of Minn., 1924—. Studied U. of London, 1908, 09. Lecturer Grad. Sch. Agr., U. of Mo., 1914. An editor Bull. Torrey Bot. Club. Unitarian. Mem. Internat. Jury of Awards, St. Louis Expn., 1904. Author: Biometric Study of Basali Metabolism in Man (with F. G. Benedict). Collaborator Bur. Plant Industry, U.S. Dept. of Agr., 1918—. Awarded Weldon medal and Memorial prize by U. of Oxford, 1921. Home: St. Paul, Minn. Died Apr. 24, 1930.

HARRIS, James Coffee, educator; b. Magnolia, N.C., Apr. 28, 1858; s. Charles Hooks and Margaret Ann (Monk) H.; ed. pvt. schs., Ga.; hon. M.A., U. of Ga., 1886; m. Ellen Simmons, Dec. 2, 1879 (died 1895); children—George Simmons, Agnes Ellen, Mrs. Margaret Monk Blair; m. 2d, Kate Robeson, Feb. 5, 1897; 1 son, James Coffee. Began teaching at Cedartown, Ga., 1876; founder Boys' Prep. Sch., Marietta, Ga., 1885; supt. pub. schs., Cedartown, 1890-92, Rome, 1892-1916; supt. Ga. Sch. for the Deaf, 1916—. Democrat. Presbyn. Mason. Author: The Making of the Universe, 1920; The Making of Man, 1921; Astronomy for Children, 1921; Nature and God, 1929. Home: Cave Spring, Ga. Died June 23, 1940.

HARRIS, Joel Chandler, author; b. Eatonton, Ga., Dec. 8, 1848; ed. common schs. and Eatonton Acad.; served apprenticeship to printing trade, 1860; editorial writer on Southern newspapers; an editor of Atlanta Constitution 25 yrs., now retired; his first negro dialect stories were published in Atlanta Constitution; now editor Uncle Remus's Mag. Author: Uncle Remus—His Songs and His Sayings, 1880; Nights With Uncle Remus, 1883; Mingo and other Sketches in Black and White, 1884; Free Joe and Other Georgia Sketches, 1887; Uncle Remus and His Friends, 1892; On the Plantation, 1892; Little Mr. Thimblefinger, 1894; Mr. Rabbit at Home, 1895; Sister Jane, 1896; Daddy Jake, the Runaway; Balaam and His Master; The Story of Aaron, So-named, the Son of Ben Ali, 1896; Stories of Georgia; Aaron in the Wild Woods, 1897; Tales of the Home Folks; Georgia, From the Invasion of De Soto to Recent Times; Evening Tales; Stories of Home Folks; Chronicles of Aunt Minerva Ann, 1899; On the Wings of Occasion, 1900; The Making of a Statesman; Gabriel Tolliver; Wally Wanderoon; A Little Union Scout, The Tar Baby Story and other Rhymes of Uncle Remus, Told by Uncle Remus, 1905; Uncle Remus and Br'er Rabbit, 1907. Home: Atlanta, Ga. Died 1908.

HARRIS, J(ohn) Andrews, Jr., banker; s. John Andrews (S.T.D.) and Almy S. (Hale) H.; m. Georgiana French. Pres. Franklin Trust Co., Phila. Home: Philadelphia, Pa. Died Feb. 18, 1940.

HARRIS, John Howard, univ. pres.; b. Indiana, Pa., Apr. 24, 1847; s. Reese and Isabella (Coleman) H.; served 18 mos. in Union Army; A.B., Bucknell U., 1869; (Ph.D., Lafayette Coll., 1884; LL.D., Dickinson Coll., and Colgate U., 1891); m. Lucy Bailey, July 20, 1881. Founded, 1869, prin., 1869-89, Keystone Acad., Pa.; pres. Bucknell U., 1889-1919, prof. psychology same, 1889—. Home: Lewisburg, Pa. Died Apr. 4, 1925.

HARRIS, John Royall, clergyman, educator; b. nr. Murfreesboro, Tenn., Mar. 7, 1869; s. G. J. and Sarah Ann (Hill) H.; ed. Clark-Bledsoe Sch., Winchester, Tenn.; B.D., Cumberland U., Lebanon, Tenn., 1894; D.D., Waynesburg (Pa.) Coll., 1903, m. Emma Josephine Garber, July 6, 1909; children—Josephine Rea, Sarah Hill. Ordained Presbyn. ministry, 1894; pastor Lewisburg, Tenn., 1894-1903, Shady Av. Ch., Pittsburgh, Pa., 1903-17; supt. Dry Fedn. of Pa., 1917-19; was dir. industrial dept. Nat. Reform Assn., and founder of its southern hdqrs., at Nashville, Tenn., 1920; pres. Cumberland U., June 7, 1922—. Supt. Tenn. Anti-Saloon League, 1900-03. Served as pvt. and color sergt. Co. C, 3d Regt. Pa. R.M.; mem. Vet. Corps 18th Regt. (Duquesne Grays), Pa. N.G.; chaplain gen. S.C.V. Dept. of Gulf. Mem. Bd. of Temperance Presbyn. Ch., U.S.A.; trustee Waynesburg Coll. Mason. Home: Lebanon, Tenn. Died Sept. 12, 1926.

HARRIS, Joseph, telephone official; b. Chicago, Ill., June 19, 1854; s. Solomon and Hannah (Summerfield) H.; ed. high sch.; m. Grace Cole, May 15, 1877. A pioneer in development independent telephone service, and was the first to promote and carry to successful conclusion the automatic telephone as a commercial utility; organized the Automatic Electric Co., 1901, which co. has large automatic telephone installations all over the world; also an organizer of Chicago Tunnel Co. Hon. mem. Chicago Hist. Soc. (life). Died Oct. 30, 1936.

HARRIS, Joseph Hastings, clergyman, educator; b. nr. Plantsville, O., July 14, 1870; s. John Work and Martha Jane (Dille) H.; A.B., Otterbein Coll., Westerville, O., 1898, D.D., 1919; B.D. Bonebrake Theol. Sem., Dayton, O., 1903; worked way through coll. and sem.; m. Bertha Elizabeth Lambert, June 30, 1898; children—Paul Joseph, Robert Lambert (dec.), Daniel Alfred, Theodore Otterbein (dec.),

James Lowell, Richard Lambert. Ordained U.B. ministry, 1903; pastorates at Portsmouth, Hillsboro and Columbus, O.; served as supt. S.E. Ohio Conf. U.B. Ch.; pres. Bonebrake Theol. Sem., 1929-33; pastor, 1934—. Del. to Gen. Conf. 5 times; mem. Bd. of Adminstrn. U.B. Ch.; trustee Otterbein Coll., Bonebrake Theol. Sem. Republican. Woodman. Home: Columbus, O. Died Jan. 14, 1941.

HARRIS, Joseph Smith, ry. official; b. Chester, Co., Pa., Apr. 29, 1836; s. Stephen (M.D.) and Marianne (Smith) M.; A.B., Central High Sch., Phila., 1853, A.M., 1855; (Sc.D., Franklin and Marshall Coll., 1903); m. Delia Silliman Broadhead, June 20, 1865. Entered ry. service Apr. 1853 to Oct. 1854, rodman and topographer, N. Pa. R.R.; officer U.S. Coast Survey, 1854-64; detached in 1856 with Ky. Geol. Survey to trace and mark parallel of latitude in Ky.; asst. astronomer N.W. Boundary Survey, 1857-64; while in this service was also, Feb. to Sept. 1862, 1st officer and later comdr. U.S. steamer "Sachem," attached to Farragut's Miss. River Squadron; assisted in reduction of Forts Jackson and St. Philip on Miss. River below New Orleans. In private practice as civ. and mining engr., Pottsville, Pa., 1864-68, and at same time engr. Lehigh & Mahanoy R.R.; chief engr. Morris & Essex R.R., 1868-70; engr. Phila. & Reading Coal and Iron Co., 1870-77; supt. and engr. Lehigh Coal & Navigation Co., 1877-80; gen. mgr. Central R.R. of N.J., 1880-82; pres. Lehigh Coal & Navigation Co., 1882-93; also receiver and afterward v.p. Central R.R. of N.J., 1886-90; v.p. Phila. & Reading Coal & Iron Co., 1892; receiver and pres. Phila. & Reading R.R., 1893-96; pres. Reading Co., Phila. & Reading Ry. Co., and The Phila. & Reading Coal & Iron Co., 1896-1901; from 1901, mem. exec. com. of Reading Cos., Central R.R. of N.J., Lehigh & Wilkes-Barre Coal Co., Lehigh Coal & Navigation Co., and others, 1901—. Trustee U. of Pa., 1889—. Author: Record of the Harris Family, 1903; Record of the Smith Family, 1906; The Collateral Ancestry of Stephen Harris, M.D., and Marianne Smith, 1908. Home: Germantown, Philadelphia. Died 1910.

HARRIS, Leslie Huntington, electrical engr.; b. nr. Bradford, Pa., Oct. 23, 1883; s. Fernando C. and Clara (Ingoldsby) H.; B.S. in E.E., Purdue U., 1907; m. Alma Woods Kerr, Sept. 3, 1914. Elec. engr. with Westinghouse Electric & Mfg. Co., 1907-08; with U. of Pittsburgh, 1908—, prof. elec. engring., 1914—; cons. elec. engr. Pub. Service Commn. of Pa., 1913—. Commd. capt. Engr. R.C., U.S.A., Apr. 1917; called into service, Aug. 6, 1917; maj. Q.-M.C., Mar. 19, 1918; served as asst. constructing q.-m., Camp Stuart, Newport News, Va., and later as port utilities officer. Republican. Presbyn. Home: Pittsburgh, Pa. Died Feb. 21, 1920.

HARRIS, Louis Israel, formerly N.Y. City commr. of health; b. Austria, Jan. 27, 1882; s. Solomon and Edith (Bodenstein) H.; brought to U.S., 1884; student Coll. City of New York; M.D., Columbia U., 1905; D.P.H., New York U., 1917; m. Bertha Adler Harris, Oct. 12, 1913; children—Sophea Caroline, Carl Samuel. Began practice at New York, 1905; chief of div. industrial hygiene, Dept. of Health, N.Y. City, 1915-17; dir. bur. preventable diseases, same dept., 1917-26; commr. of health, N.Y. City, 1926-28; now consultant in pub. health. Democrat. Jewish religion. K.P. Radio broadcaster on health and med. topics; mem. editorial advisory bd. Life and Health (mag.). Home: New York, N.Y. Died Jan. 7, 1939.

HARRIS, Malcolm LaSalle, surgeon; b. Rock Island Co., Ill., June 27, 1862; s. Samuel G. and Frances (Greene) H.; ed. pub. schs. of Ia.; M.D., Rush Med. Coll., Chicago, 1882; m. Rose Breckenridge, Oct. 12, 1887; 1 dau., Florence. Practiced, Chicago, 1882—. Mem. Internat. Surg. Assn., Am. Surg. Assn., Am. Assn. Clinical Surgery, etc. Home: Chicago, Ill. Died Mar. 22, 1936.

HARRIS, Maurice Henry, rabbi; b. London, Eng., Nov. 9, 1859; s. Rev. Henry Lionel and Rachel (Lewis) H.; early edn. in London; A.B., Columbia, 1887, A.M., 1888, Ph.D., 1889; studied Emanuel Theol. Sem., New York; m. Kitty Green, of London, Aug. 14, 1888; children—Ruth Green, Mrs. Naomi Wolfson, Adriel. Rabbi Temple Israel, of City of New York, 1882—, full official, 1887. Past pres. New York Bd. of Jewish Ministers; founder and pres. Harlem Fedn. Settlement; pres. Eastern Council of Reform Rabbis. Author: People of Book—A Biblical History (3 vols.), 1895-97; Two Chautauqua Syllabi of Jewish History and Literature from the Kabbala to Mendelssohn, 1899. Wrote: Unitarianism and Judaism, North American Review, 1894; Are the Jews a Nation? Jewish Quarterly Review (London), 1890; A Thousand Years of Jewish History, 1904; Jews of the Middle Ages, 1907; Modern Jewish History, 1909; A Confirmation Manual, 1919. Home: New York, N.Y. Died June 23, 1930.

HARRIS, Merriman Colbert, bishop; b. Beallsville, O., July 9, 1846; s. Colbert and Elizabeth Catherine (Crupper) H.; A.B., Allegheny Coll., 1873, A.M., 1880 (D.D., 1887, LL.D., 1904); m. Flora Lydia Best, Oct. 23, 1873 (died 1909). Served 3 yrs. in 12th Ohio cav. in Civil War. Joined Pittsburgh Conf., M.E. Ch., 1869; in pastorate, 1869-73; apptd. to Japan, 1873; remained in Japan until 1886 and became mem. Japan Ann. Conf.; supt. Japanese Mission of M.E. Ch. in San Francisco, 1886-1904, establishing Japanese missions in Hawaii and on the Pacific Coast, and organizing them into a Pacific Japanese Mission; elected bishop of Japan and Korea, May, 1904; retired 1916, bishop emeritus. Decorated by Emperor of Japan, 1898 and 1905, third class Order Sacred Treasure, later 2d class same. Home: Aoyama, Tokyo, Japan. Died May 8, 1921.

HARRIS, Moses Henry, clergyman; b. Greene, Me., May 14, 1845; s. Capt. Andrew J. H.; A.B., St. Lawrence U., N.Y., 1870 (A.M., 1888, D.D., 1890); m. Zelia Ellis Willson, Sept. 6, 1871. Ordained Universalist ministry, Sept. 13, 1870; pastor Brattleboro, Vt., 1870-79; First Ch., Worcester, Mass., 1879-90, Ch. of the Redeemer, Chicago, 1890-95, All Souls' Ch., Worcester, Mass., 1895-1902; First Ch., Watertown, N.Y., Sept. 1, 1902—. Trustee St. Lawrence U., 1902—. Was dir. Universalist Pub. House, Boston, 9 yrs.; trustee Dean Acad., Franklin, Mass., 9 yrs.; mem. exec. bd. of Mass. Universalist State Conv., 9 yrs.; trustee Lombard Coll., Galesburg, Ill., 5 yrs. Republican. Home: Watertown, N.Y. Died 1911.

HARRIS, Nathaniel Edwin, governor; b. Jonesboro, Tenn., Jan. 21, 1846; s. Alexander Nelson and Edna (Haynes) H.; A.B., U. of Ga., 1870; LL.D., 1910; LL.D., Emory Coll., Ga., 1913; m. Fannie Burke, Jan. 12, 1873 (died 1898); children—Carrie E., Walter A., Nathaniel E. (dec.), Fannie B., John B., David W.; m. 2d, Hattie G. Jobe, July 6, 1899. Enlisted in C.S.A., Mar. 1, 1862, and served to close of Civil War, part of time on staff in Army of Northern Va.; began law practice, Sparta, Ga., 1872; removed to Macon, 1873. Corp. counsel Macon, 1874-82; mem. Ga. Ho. of Rep., 1882-86, Senate, 1894-96; Judge Superior Court, Macon Circuit, 1912; gov. of Ga., term 1915-17; pension commr. of Ga., by apptmt. of Gov. Walker, 1924-25. Founder, 1885, and from then chmn. trustees Ga. Sch. of Technology (acted as pres. while the pres. was absent in France); trustee U. of Ga., 1885—, Wesleyan Female Coll., 1882-1926; elected trustee Vanderbilt U. by Gen. Conf., 1910, but not seated. Dem. presdl. elector for state at large, and pres. Electoral Coll. for Ga., 1924. Mason. Author: Autobiography, 1925. Home: Macon, Ga. Died Sept. 21, 1929.

HARRIS, Norman Wait, banker; b. Berkshire Co., Mass., Aug. 15, 1846; s. Nathan Wait and C. Emeline (Wadsworth) H.; direct desc. of the 39th generation of Charlemagne, Frankish King and Roman Emperor, by his wife, Hildegarde, also descendant in the 26th generation of Countess Adelicia, the Fair Maid of Brabant, daughter of Godfrey I, who married Henry I, King of England, and whose second husband was William d'Albini, 2d earl of Sussex and Arundel; also desc. of the 7th generation of Thomas Harris of Eng. who settled in Mass. Bay Colony, 1630; ed. Westfield (Mass.) Acad., 1863; m. Jacyntha Vallandingham, Jan. 1, 1867 (died 1873); m. 2d, Clara Cochnower, 1875 (died 1876); m. 3d, Emma S. Gale, Apr. 1879. Aided in organizing, 1867, and sec., 1867-80, Union Cent. Life Ins. Co., Cincinnati; organized, 1882, banking house of N. W. Harris & Co., Chicago, New York and Boston; pres. Harris Trust & Savings Bank, Chicago, 1907-13; also of Harris, Forbes & Co., New York, and N. W. Harris & Co., Inc., Boston. Many years mem. Internat. Com. of Y.M.C.A. to which he has been a large financial contbr.; v.p. trustees Y.M.C.A., Chicago; pres. trustees Chicago Training School for Home and Foreign Missions (largest training school of its kind in the country to which he gave the land upon which its principal buildings are located and erected its chapel and one of its main buildings known as Harris Hall); founded the Deaconess Pension Fund, contributing thereto $100,000 and is pres. trustees thereof; trustee Northwestern U. Donated $250,000, in 1911, to Pub. Sch. Extension of Field Mus. of Natural History, Chicago; also, 1913, $250,000 to Northwestern U. to erect and maintain a building known as Harris Hall of Political Science and History. Home: Chicago, Ill. Died July 15, 1916.

HARRIS, Overton, banker, cattle breeder; b. Harris, Mo., July 3, 1856; s. Anderson Wood and Gabrilla (Neilson) H.; ed. State Normal School, Kirksville, Mo.; m. Mary Susan Jones, Jan. 16, 1876. Farmer since boyhood and now owns 3,000 acres in Sullivan Co., Mo.; formerly extensive cattle feeder; started breeding Hereford cattle about 1890; won most of prizes offered for cattle, with show herd at St. Louis Expn., 1904; herd now one of the foremost in U.S.; organizer, 1888, and pres. Harris Banking Co.; dir. various banks, Mo., Tex. and Mont. Trustee Harris (Mo.) Sch. Democrat. Mem. Christian (Disciples) Ch. Scottish and York Rite Mason. Home: Harris, Mo. Died Apr. 14, 1931.

HARRIS, Robert Orr, lawyer; b. Boston, Mass., Nov. 8, 1854; s. Hon. Benjamin Winslow and Julia A. (Orr) H.; A.B., Harvard, 1877; m. Josephine D. Gorton, Apr. 21, 1880; 5 children. Practiced at Boston and Brockton, Mass., 1879-1902; mem. Mass. Ho. of Rep., 1889; dist. atty., Southeastern dist. of Mass., 1892-1901; asso. judge Supreme Court of Mass., 1902-11; mem. 62d Congress (1911-13), 14th Mass. Dist.; U.S. dist. atty. for Mass. Republican. Home: Boston, Mass. Died June 13, 1926.

HARRIS, Rollin Arthur, mathematician; b. Randolph, N.Y., Apr. 18, 1863; s. Francis E. and Lydia Helen (Crandall) H.; bro. of Gilbert Dennison H.; Ph.B., Cornell U., 1885, fellow in mathematics, 1886-87, Ph.D., 1888; fellow Clark University, 1889-90; m. Emily J. Doty, June 13, 1890. On math. staff U.S. Coast and Geod. Survey, 1890—. Fellow A.A.A.S. Author of Manual of Tides, published in Coast Survey Reports for 1894, 97, 1900, 04, 07. Inventor of machines or instruments relating to tidal work. Died Jan. 20, 1918.

HARRIS, Sam H., theatrical mgr.; b. N.Y. City, 1872; self-educated; m. Mrs. Kathleen Brent Watson, Mar. 19, 1939. Thrown on own resources at 11; organized several holiday entertainments at 17; later managed various athletic enterprises; first success as theatrical mgr. was with "The Gay Morning Glories"; became partner of Sullivan, Harris & Woods, one of successes of this firm being the drama "The Fatal Wedding." Associated with George M. Cohan as Cohan & Harris, 1904-20; later produced independently "Welcome Stranger," "Little Old New York," "Six Cylinder Love," Irving Berlin's "Music Box Revues," "Rain," "Cradle Snatchers," "Cocoanuts," "Animal Crackers," "June Moon," "Once in a Lifetime," "Of Thee I Sing," "Dinner at Eight," "As Thousands Cheer," "First Lady," "Stage Door," "You Can't Take It With You," "I'd Rather Be Right," "Of Mice and Men," "The Fabulous Invalid," and other plays. Lessee and mgr. Music Box, New York. Home: New York, N.Y. Died July 3, 1941.

HARRIS, Samuel, prof. emeritus Yale Div. School; b. East Machias, Me., June 14, 1814; grad. Bowdoin, 1833; (D.D., Williams, 1854; LL.D., Bowdoin, 1871); m. Deborah R. Dickinson, 1839; m. 2d, Mrs. Mary S. Fitch, 1877. Prin. Limerick (Me.) Acad., 1833-34; Washington Acad., E. Machias, 1834-35 and 1838-41; student Andover Theol. Sem., 1835-38; pastor of Congl. chs., 1841-63; prof. systematic theology, Bangor (Me.) Theol. Sem., 1855-67; pres. Bowdoin Coll., 1867-71; prof. systematic theology, Divinity Sch., Yale, 1871-96; emeritus. Author: Zaccheus, a Prize Essay on the Scriptural Plan of Benevolence. Died 1899.

HARRIS, Samuel Henry, lawyer; b. Carrollton, Ark., Oct. 18, 1858; s. Samuel Yewell and Malinda (Curnutt) H.; ed. pub. schs.; studied law at home and in office Joseph G. Lowe, Washington, Kan.; m. Minnie Ernestine Carlock, Apr. 19, 1893; 1 son, Samuel Lowe. Admitted to Kan. bar, 1889, and began practice at Washington, Kan.; moved to Norman, Okla., 1891; gen. counsel Southwestern Bell Telephone System, St. Louis, Mo., 1912-16; same for state of Okla., 1916-27 (retired, age-limit); one of leaders in movement for admission of Okla. to statehood; chmn. Code Revision Com. of Okla., 1908-10, making revision of statute laws, adopted by state legislature, 1911. Mem. Okla. Game and Fish Commn., chmn., 1928-31. Home: Oklahoma City, Okla. Died Apr. 9, 1939.

HARRIS, Thomas LeGrand, prof. history; b. Hamilton Co., Ind., Apr. 8, 1863; s. Greene and Jane (Wilson) H.; A.B., Indiana U., 1892, A.M., 1895, Ph.D., 1922; A.M., Harvard, 1899; LL.D., Baker U., 1933; m. Adah Shafer, Aug. 14, 1913; 1 daughter, Mary Katharine (Mrs. Martin D. Phelan). Received teacher's license at age 15; taught in country and high schs. of Ind., instr. in history, Indiana U., 1905-12; prof. history and head of dept., Baker U., 1912-32 (emeritus); prof. history, Denver U., summers 1925, 27, 28. Democrat. Methodist. Wrote: The Trent Affair and Relations with England at the Beginning of the Civil War, 1896; Judge Ben B. Lindsay and His Work (in Greatest Living Americans), 1905; America and England in 1861, 1928. Home: Greencastle, Ind. Died Aug. 23, 1941.

HARRIS, Uriah Rose, rear admiral; b. Columbus, Ind., Sept. 14, 1849; s. John and Abigail (Rose) H.; grad. U.S. Naval Acad., 1869; m. Sophia Ann Simonton, Feb. 8, 1878. Midshipman, June 4, 1869; ensign, July 12, 1870; master, Jan. 1, 1872; lt., Feb. 11, 1875; lt. comdr., Feb. 25, 1897; comdr., Dec. 31, 1899; capt., Feb. 21, 1905; rear admiral, Jan. 7, 1909. Served on bd. Sabine, 1869-70; Ossipee, 1871-72; Frolic, 1873; Narragansett, 1874-75; coast survey schooner Earnest, 1876; navy yard, Mare Island, Calif., 1877; coast survey schooners Earnest and Yukon, 1877-78; Shenandoah, 1879-82; Naval Obs., 1882-84; navy yard, Mare Island, 1884-87, Ranger, 1887-90; Naval Acad., 1890-94; Ranger, 1895; Adams, 1896-97; navy yard, Boston, 1898; Chicago, 1899; light house duty, St. Louis, 1900-01; comdt. naval sta., Olongapo, P.I., 1902; Wilmington, 1903-04; navy yard, Boston, 1905-06; comdt. naval sta., Olongapo and Cavite, P.I., 1907-08; comdt. navy yard, Phila., May 27, 1909-Mar. 21, 1910; gov. Naval Home, Phila., to Sept. 14, 1911; retired, Sept. 14, 1911. Episcopalian. Home: Washington, D.C. Died June 20, 1930.

HARRIS, Wade Hampton, editor; b. Cabarrus Co., N.C., Jan. 1, 1858; s. Richard Sadler and Mary Annette (Hampton) H.; student Virginia Agrl. and Mech. Coll., Blacksburg, Va., 1874-75; LL.D., Davidson (N.C.) Coll., 1931; m. Cora Springs, Feb. 27, 1884. Began at 17 as editor Concord (N.C.) Sun (weekly); city editor Wilmington Sun, 1879-80, Charlotte Observer, 1882-88; founder, and editor, 1888-94, Charlotte News; returned to Observer, 1894; editor-in-chief same, 1912—. Alternate del. Dem. Nat. Conv., St. Louis, 1916; state rep. in formal notification of Pres. Wilson as nominee, Sept. 3, 1916. Presbyterian. Home: Charlotte, N.C. Died Sept. 14, 1935.

HARRIS, Walter Butler, civil engr., educator; b. Princeton, N.J., July 13, 1865; s. Rev. William and Christina Van Alen (Butler) H.; C.E., Princeton, 1886; m. Anne L. Yeomans, Nov. 22, 1892; children—Dorothy C., Walter Butler, George Yeomans (dec.), Helen Boyd. With Wilkes-Barre & Scranton Ry., 1886-87, Lehigh Coal & Navigation Co., 1887-88, Central R.R. of N.J., 1888-89; instr. civ. engring., 1889-95, asst. prof., 1895-99, prof. geodesy, 1899-1934, emeritus, Princeton University. Engr. and architect The Prospect Co.; designed and constructed a system of jetties for protection of N.J. coast at Asbury Park and other places. Former borough engr. and township engr.; pres. Bd. of Health, Princeton. Republican. Presbyn. (elder). Home: Princeton, N.J. Died Nov. 20, 1935.

HARRIS, Walter Edward, editor, pub.; b. Natural Bridge, Va., Apr. 27, 1868; s. John H. and Lumina J. Wallace (nee Luster) H.; LL.B., Washington and Lee U., 1893; m. Emma Power, Nov. 7, 1905. Began as reporter Roanoke (Va.) Herald, 1889; admitted to Va. bar, 1893, and began practice at Charleston; editor Charleston Gazette, 1893-95; successively with Washington (D.C.) Times, mng. editor Norfolk Virginian, with St. Louis (Mo.) Republic, St. Louis Globe-Democrat, political editor Richmond (Va.) Dispatch, Washington corr. Richmond Times-Dispatch to 1910; editor and pub. Petersburg (Va.) Index-Appeal, 1910, later merged with Petersburg Progress, as The Progress-Index, of which is editor and pub.; pres. Petersburg Newspaper Corp. Democrat. Home: Petersburg, Va. Died Nov. 9, 1939.

HARRIS, William Alexander, U.S. senator from Kan., 1897-1903; b. Loudoun Co., Va., Oct. 29, 1841; s. William A. and Frances (Murray) H.; grad. Columbian Coll., Washington, 1859; Va. Mil. Inst., 1861; in C.S.A. 3 yrs. as asst. adj. gen. and ordnance officer. Removed to Kan., 1865; civ. engr. in construction Kan. div. Union Pacific R.R., 3 yrs.; in 1868 became agt. for sale of Delaware Reservation and other lands; from 1876 farmer and breeder of pure-bred shorthorn cattle. Mem. Congress, 1893-95. Populist. Home: Linwood, Kan. Died 1909.

HARRIS, William Charles, author, editor; b. Baltimore, Md., May 30, 1830; s. James and Susan T. H.; public school and academic edn. Baltimore; widower. Served in Civil war, Apr. 30, 1861, to close; taken prisoner at Ball's Bluff, Oct. 30, 1861; was confined in Richmond 7 mos.; then released on parole, which ended with the war; was in comd. of Co. H, Gen. Baker's Calif. brigade. Democrat. Editor and pub. Afield and Afloat, 1876-80, and later of The American Angler and Nature's Realm; now editor angling dept., Outing Mag. Author and publisher: "The Fishes of North America," with colored lithographic plates, each 19x12; The Trouts of America; Game Fishes of the West; Game Fish of the Atlantic Coast; Sportsmen's Guide. Part author: Salmon and Trout, 1902. Died 1905.

HARRIS, William Fenwick, coll. prof.; b. Wolfville, N.S., Oct. 21, 1868; s. David Jewett and Rebecca (Elder) H.; arrived in U.S., 1876; A.B., Harvard, 1891, A.M., 1892; post-grad. work, Harvard, Berlin, Paris and Oxford, Eng.; m. Alice Mary Fogg, Sept. 19, 1894. Asst. prof. Greek, Harvard, 1898—. Instr. in Harvard R.O.T.C., with relative rank of lt., World War; mem. Com. Pub. Safety, chmn. Com. on Food Production and Conservation and mem. central com. Red Cross (Cambridge). Served with Francis Bacon in publn. of "Investigations at Assos," an account of the first excavation on Greek soil undertaken by the Archæol. Inst. America; with Herbert Weir Smyth and Charles Burton Gulick, as mem. com. Classical Dept., Harvard U., in bringing out "Agamemnon" of Æschylus, in the Stadium, 1906. Home: Cambridge, Mass. Died May 14, 1923.

HARRIS, W(illiam) Hall, lawyer; b. Baltimore, Md., Oct. 12, 1852; s. James Morrison and Sidney Calhoun (Hall) H.; ed. pvt. schs., Baltimore; admitted to bar, 1876; m. Alice Patterson, June 22, 1876; children—Mary Patterson (Mrs. Harris Sherburne), J(ames) Morrison, W(illiam) Hall, H(enry) Patterson. Sr. mem. Harris & Thompson, 1904-37; postmaster Baltimore, Feb. 1905-June 1913. Republican. Dir. Peabody Inst., Baltimore (v.p.). Presbyn. Home: Baltimore, Md. Died Apr. 29, 1938.

HARRIS, William Julius, senator; b. Cedartown, Ga., Feb. 3, 1868; s. Charles H. and Margaret Ann (Monk) H.; U. of Ga., 1890; m. Julia Knox, d. Gen. Joseph Wheeler, of Ala., July 27, 1905. Entered gen. ins., banking, Cedartown, 1890. Dir. U.S. Census, 1913-15; federal trade commr., 1915-18 (resigned). Chmn. Dem. State Com., Ga.; U.S. senator, Ga., terms 1919-25 and 1925-31. Home: Cedartown, Ga. Died Apr. 18, 1932.

HARRIS, William Laurel, mural painter; b. New York, N.Y., Feb. 18, 1870; s. Henry Earl and Julia (Gillingham) H.; ed. under pvt. tutors; studied Art Students' League, New York; Acad. Julien, Paris; École des Beaux Arts, Paris; traveled for several years, making studies of stained glass mosaics and mural painting, visiting prin. cities of Eng., France, Belgium, Holland, Germany, Italy, Egypt and Palestine; unmarried. Worked on decorations for Congressional Library, Washington, and asstd. Francis Lathrop in decorating St. Bartholomew's Ch., New York; began alone, 1898; best known and most important works are in Ch. of Paulist Fathers, New York. Mng. dir. Art Center Nat. Soc. Mural Painters (exec. com.), Municipal Art Soc. (pres. 1912), Fine Arts Fedn. (sec. 1918—); mem. Archtl. League (v.p. 1902-03). Dir. The Art Center, 1921-22. Home: New York, N.Y. Died July 3, 1924.

HARRIS, William Torrey, U.S. Commr. of Edn., 1889-July 1, 1906; b. N. Killingly, Conn., Sept. 10, 1835; s. William and Zilpah (Torrey) H.; 2½ yrs. in class of 1858, Yale—did not graduate (A.M., 1869, LL.D., 1895; Ph.D., Brown, 1893, U. of Jena, 1899; LL.D., U. State of Mo., 1870, U. of Pa., 1894, Princeton, 1896); m. Sarah T. Bugbee, Dec. 27, 1858. Teacher, prin., asst. supt., 1857-67; supt., 1867-80, St. Louis public schools; resigned because of failing health; settled at Concord, Mass., and became lecturer at School of Philosophy. At Paris Expn., 1878 was tendered the honorary title "Officier de l'Académie." Represented U.S. Bureau of Edn. at Internat. Congress of Educators, Brussels, 1880, and at Paris Expn., 1889 (received from French govt., 1889, title of "Officier de l'Instruction Publique"). Established, in St. Louis, 1867, Journal of Speculative Philosophy, and still conducts it; was chief editor of the Appleton School Readers; later edited Appleton's Ednl. series. Edited dept. of philosophy in Johnson's Cyclopædia, writing many important articles. Author: The Spiritual Sense of Dante's Divina Commedia, 1889, 1896; Psychologic Foundation of Education, 1898. Editor-in-chief Webster's Internat. Dictionary, 1900—. Home: Washington, D.C. Died 1909.

HARRIS, William Welton, publicist; b. Hudson, Mich., Feb. 10, 1866; s. Caleb H. and Eliza (Durling) H.; B.Ph., U. of Mich., 1889; m. Jessie Elizabeth Brown, Jan. 25, 1893; children—Jean, Janet, Ruth, Elizabeth (dec.). Began as reporter, Detroit News, 1890; with Chicago Inter Ocean and Chicago Tribune, 1891-95; New York World and New York Tribune, 1895, New York American, 1896-1901; telegraph editor and Sunday editor, New York Herald, 1901-05; mng. editor, New York Evening Telegram, 1905-08; night editor, New York Herald, 1908-14; mng. editor New York Sun, 1914-16; publicity counsel, 1916-24. Editor American Railroads, 1918-22; asso. editor Railroad Data, 1922-24; v.p. Fifth Av. Coach Co., 1924-27. Unitarian. Author: Daly's Billiard Book, 1914; How British Finance Met the Shock of War, 1918; Rapid Transit in New York City, 1923; Automotive Taxation, 1925; The Road to Farm Relief, 1931. Home: Yonkers, N.Y. Died Aug. 6, 1932.

HARRIS, Willis Overton, lawyer; b. Powhatan Co., Va., Feb. 5, 1847; s. Hilary and Phœbe Ann (Hobson) H.; grad. Va. Mil. Inst., 1866; LL.B., U. of Va., 1868; m. Caroline Throckmorton Adams, Nov. 22, 1877. In practice at Louisville, 1868—; dir. Citizens Nat. Bank, Louisville Pub. Warehouse Co., Guarantee Co. of N. America. Maj. Ky. State Guard, 1878; judge Circuit Ct. of Jefferson Co., Ky., 1887-89. Democrat (Gold). Episcopalian. Home: Louisville, Ky. Died 1911.

HARRISON, (Thomas) Alexander, artist; b. Phila., Pa., Jan. 17, 1853; ed. Pa. Acad. Fine Arts; École des Beaux Arts, Bastien-Lepage and Gérôme, Paris; unmarried. Hon. mention, Paris Salon, 1885; Temple silver medal, Pa. Acad. Fine Arts, 1887; first class gold medal, Paris Expn., 1889; medal (2d), Munich Salon, 1891; medal of honor, Brussels and Ghent, 1892; Gold medal of honor, Pa. Acad. Fine Arts, 1894. Chevalier of the Legion of Honor, 1889, Officier, 1901, and Officer of Public Instruction by French Govt. V.p. Jury Am. Art Sect. Internat. Expn., Paris, 1889; mem. Internat. Jury of Awards Expn. Universelle, Paris, 1900. Represented in Luxembourg Mus., Paris (2 pictures); Quimper Mus., France; Dresden Mus., Germany; Pa. Acad. Fine Arts; Corcoran Gallery, Washington, D.C.; Art Inst. Chicago, etc. A.N.A., 1898, N.A., 1902. Died Oct. 13, 1930.

HARRISON, Benjamin, pres. U.S.; b. North Bend, O., Aug. 20, 1833; prepared at Farmer's Coll., Cincinnati; grad. Miami Univ., 1852; served in Union army in Civil war, reaching bvt. rank of brig. gen.; was in law practice at Indianapolis before war; reporter supreme court Ind., 1860-62; reëlected while in field for term 1864-68; member Mississippi River Commn., 1879-81; U.S. senator, 1881-87; president of the United States, 1889-93; defeated for reëlection by Grover Cleveland, 1892. Republican. Distinguished as lawyer and constitutionalist; also prominent in Presbyn. ch. Author: This Country of Ours. Home: Indianapolis, Ind. Died 1901.

HARRISON, (Lovell) Birge, artist; b. Phila., Pa., Oct. 28, 1854; s. Apollos W. and Margaret (Belden) H.; pupil Cabanel in Paris; m. Eleanor Ritchie, 1882 (died 1895); m. 2d, Jenny Seaton Harrison, Nov. 28, 1896. Painted in Australia, South Seas, and Western U.S., 1889-93. Silver medal, Paris Salon, 1887; 2d medal, Paris Expn., 1889; unique medal, Chicago Expn., 1893; medal Buffalo Expn., 1901; 2d prize, Washington, 1903; silver medal, St. Louis Expn., 1904; gold medal, Phila., 1907; represented by oil paintings in public museums of Luxembourg, Paris, France, Marseilles, France, Phila., Chicago, St. Louis, Indianapolis, St. Paul, Detroit, Nashville, Lincoln, Neb., Oakland, Calif., Toledo, Washington, Memphis, Omaha, Atlanta, Madison, Wis. Hors Concours in Paris Salon; painter of Am. landscape; known most widely as a painter of snow and city streets. Dir. landscape sch. of Art Students' League, New York, N.A., 1910; mem. Nat. Inst. Arts and Letters; fellow Pa. Acad. Design. Author: Landscape Painting, 1909. Home: Woodstock, N.Y. Died May 11, 1929.

HARRISON, Charles Custis, educator; b. Phila., Pa., May 3, 1844; s. George Leib and Sarah Ann (Waples) H.; A.B., U. of Pa., 1862, A.M., 1865; (LL.D., Columbia, 1895, Princeton, 1896, Yale, 1901, U. of Pa., 1911); m. Ellen Nixon, d. Edward Waln, of Phila. and g.g.d. Robert Morris (died 1922). In business as a mfr., 1863-92. Trustee U. of Pa., 1876—, acting provost, 1894-95, provost, 1895-1911. Pres. University Museum. Home: St. Davids, Pa. Died Feb. 12, 1929.

HARRISON, Constance Cary, author; b. Fairfax Co., Va., Apr. 25, 1843; d. Archibald and Mominia (Fairfax) Cary; ed. by private governesses; lived in Richmond, Va., during Civil War, then went abroad with widowed mother to complete her studies in music and languages; m. Burton Harrison, lawyer, and thereafter resided in New York; mother of Fairfax and Francis Burton H. Author: Old Fashioned Fairy Books; Bar Harbor Days; The Anglomaniacs; Crow's Nest and Bellhaven Tales; A Daughter of the South; A Bachelor Maid; Externals of Modern New York; A Son of the Old Dominion; Good Americans; A Princess of the Hills, 1901; The Unwelcome Mrs. Hatch (play); Latter-Day Sweethearts, 1906; Transplanted Daughters, 1909; Recollections, Grave and Gay, 1911. Home: Washington, D.C. Died Nov. 21, 1920.

HARRISON, Edwin, mfr.; b. Washington, Ark., Jan. 29, 1836; s. James Harrison, 1st pres. of Iron Mountain Co.; grad. Harvard Univ., 1856, in dept. mechanics and engring., spl. student under Prof. Louis Agassiz, 1856-58, in geology and paleontology; m. Laura E. Sterne (late pres. Mo. State Fedn. of Women's Clubs), 1872. Asst. geologist Mo. Geol. Survey, in the field, 1859; Santa Fé merchant, 1860-62; head of pig iron mfg. firm of E. Harrison & Co., 1865-72; mem. bd. mgrs. Mo. Geol. Survey under three gubernatorial administrations, seventies; regular Democratic nominee for mayor St. Louis, 1896. Mem. bd. dirs. Washington U.; chmn. exec. com. St. Louis Provident Assn.; chmn. bd. mgrs. St. Louis Manual Training School; pres. St. Louis Smelting and Refining Co., Laclede Rolling Mills, Federal Lead Co., Iron Mountain Co., of Mo. Pres. St. Louis Acad. Science; trustee Mo. Bot. Garden. Home: St. Louis, Mo. Died 1905.

HARRISON, Elizabeth, kindergartner; b. Athens, Ky., Sept. 1, 1849; d. Isaac Webb and Elizabeth Thompson (Bullock) H.; grad. Froebel Kindergarten Training Sch., Chicago, 1880, St. Louis Kindergarten Training Sch., 1882, Kraus-Boelte Kindergarten Sch., New York, 1893; studied in Europe. A pioneer in kindergarten work in U.S.; pres. Nat. Kindergarten Coll., 1890-1920, emeritus. Mem. Internat. Kindergarten Union, N.E.A., Nat. Congress of Mothers, Nat. Child Labor Assn., etc. Author: Study of Child Nature, 1895, Two Children of the Foothills, 1899. Some Silent Teachers, 1903; Misunderstood Children, 1910; Offero, the Giant, 1912; Montessori and the Kindergarten, 1914; When Children Err, 1916; Legend of Christ-Child, with Musical Accompaniment, 1916; The Unseen Side of Child Life, 1922. Home: San Antonio, Tex. Died Oct. 31, 1927.

HARRISON, Fairfax, railway pres.; b. New York, Mar. 13, 1869; s. Burton and Constance (Cary) H.; A.B., Yale, 1890; A.M., Columbia, 1891; admitted to bar, New York, 1892. Practiced law at New York, 1892-96. Entered ry. service as solicitor Southern Ry. Co., 1896; asst. to pres. same rd., 1903-06, v.p., 1906-10; pres. Chicago, Indianapolis & Louisville Ry. Co., 1910-13; pres. Southern Ry. Co., 1913—. Home: Belvoir, Va. Died Feb. 2, 1938.

HARRISON, (William) Fred, lawyer; b. San Francisco, Calif., Dec. 26, 1874; s. William Frederick and Annie I. (Robinson) H.; ed. high sch. and business coll.; unmarried. Formerly court stenographer; mining in Alaska, 1898-1901; chief clk. in office of the crown prosecutor, Dawson, until 1911; began practice of law at Ruby, Alaska, 1911; U.S. dist. atty., Oct. 1921—. Republican. Protestant. Home: Nome, Alaska. Died July 13, 1929.

HARRISON, Gabriel, author; b. Phila., Mar. 25, 1825; removed to New York, 1831; became an actor;

also became known as a successful producer of pictures by Daguerre's process, 1841, taking several prizes; mem. of co. at Park Theatre, New York, 1845, supporting Charles Kean; later mgr. theatres in Troy, N.Y., and Brooklyn. Corr. Sec. Brooklyn Acad. of Design, 1867; an organizer of the Faust Club, Brooklyn, 1872; later teacher of elocution. Author: Life of John Howard Payne, 1873; also several plays, including dramatization of Hawthorne's Scarlet Letter (prod. 1878); Melanthia, tragedy (prod. by Matilda Heron), and others. Home: Brooklyn, N.Y. Died 1902.

HARRISON, George Moffett, judge; b. Staunton, Va., Feb. 14, 1847; s. Henry Harrison and Jane St. Clair (Cochran) H.; early edn. under father; served in C.S.A., 1864-65; studied law, U. of Va., 1869-70; m. Bettie Montgomery Kent, Sept. 23, 1874. Practiced at Staunton, 1870-94; mem. Harrison & Tucker few yrs.; justice Supreme Court of Appeals of Va., Jan. 1, 1895-Mar. 1, 1917, retired. Democrat. Episcopalian. Home: Staunton, Va. Died Nov. 22, 1923.

HARRISON, Hall, P.E. clergyman; b. Howard Co., Md., Nov. 11, 1837; grad. Coll. of St. James, Md.; (A.M., 1857; S.T.D., Trinity Coll., Hartford, 1889); m. Agnes Spottiswoode, dau. of Hon. Anthony Kennedy, 1875. Instructor Latin, Greek and English in Coll. of St. James, 1854-63; master St. Paul's School, Concord, N.H., 1865-79, then rector St. John's Ch., Howard Co., Md. Home: Ellicott City, Md. Died 1900.

HARRISON, Henry Sydnor, author; b. Sewanee, Tenn., Feb. 12, 1880; s. Caskie and Margaret Coleman (Sydnor) H.; Brooklyn Latin Sch. (founded by his father); B.A., Columbia, 1900, M.A., 1913; unmarried. With Am. Ambulance in France and Belgium, Mar.-June 1915; lt. U.S.N.R.F., 1917-19. Democrat. Episcopalian. Mem. Nat. Inst. Arts and Letters. Author: Queed, 1911; V. V.'s Eyes, 1913; Angela's Business, 1915; When I Come Back, 1919; Saint Teresa, 1922; Andrew Bride, of Paris, 1925. Home: New York, N.Y. Died July 14, 1930.

HARRISON, Ida Withers; b. Grand Gulf, Miss., May 9, 1851; d. William T. and Martha (Sharkey) Withers; grad. Patapsco (Md.) Inst., 1868; LL.D., Transylvania Coll., 1914; m. Albert M. Harrison, June 17, 1879 (dec.). Vice-pres. Christian Woman's Bd. of Missions, of Disciples of Christ; twice pres. Ky. Fedn. of Women's Clubs (now hon. pres. for life); 6 times pres. Woman's Club of Central Ky.; 1st woman to serve as mem. Bd. of Edn., Lexington, and now mem. bd.; chmn. Internat. Coöperation to Prevent War, of Ky. League of Women Voters, 1923—; etc. Author: History of the Christian Woman's Board of Missions, 1919; Memoirs of William Temple Withers, 1923; Gardens All the Year, 1927. Home: Lexington, Ky. Died Nov. 1927.

HARRISON, James Albert, philologist; b. Pass Christian, Miss., Aug. 21, 1848; s. J. P. and S. N. H.; reared in New Orleans; grad. U. of Pa., 1868; studied in Germany, 1871; (LL.D., Randolph-Macon, 1883, Washington and Lee, 1896, Tulane, 1904; L.H.D., Columbia, 1887); m. Miss L. S. Letcher. Prof. Latin and modern langs., Randolph-Macon Coll., 1871-76; prof. English and modern langs., Washington and Lee, 1876-95; prof. English and Romance langs., 1895, later prof. Teutonic langs., U. of Va. Lecturer on Anglo-Saxon Poetry, Johns Hopkins. Joint author: Anglo-Saxon Reader, 1899; Anglo-Saxon Dictionary; Easy French Lessons; Life of George Washington, 1906. Editor: Beowulf, 1883; Heine's Reisebilder; Library of Anglo-Saxon Poetry (5 vols.), 1883; Mme. de Sévigné's Letters, 1898; Cornielle's Nicomède, 1901; E. A. Poe's Complete Works (17 vols.), 1902. Home: Charlottesville, Va. Died 1911.

HARRISON, John Green, educator; b. Washington Co., Ga., Apr. 27, 1869; s. Green Berry and Rhoda Elephair (Mayo) H.; A.B., Mercer U., 1889, D.D., 1903; Th.M., Southern Bapt. Theol. Sem., 1899; grad. study of Chicago, 1901-12, U. of Berlin, 1905-06; m. Bessie Winn Gilmore, Dec. 28, 1893; m. 2d, Ruth Barrett, June 22, 1911; children—John Green, William Henry, Martha Elizabeth. Teacher and prin. high schs., Hiawassee, Ga., Cumming, Ga., Orangeburg, S.C., 1889-96; ordained ministry Bapt. Ch., 1896; pastor Tattnall Square Bapt. Ch., Macon, Ga., 1899-1905; prof. philosophy and edn., Mercer U., 1907-15; prin. Mercer U. Summer Sch., 1910, 15, 16, 17; sec. Ga. Bapt. Edn. Bd. (exec. sec. half-million debt paying campaign of Ga. Baptist 1918-19), 1915-19; prof. philosophy, Mercer U., 1919-29, dean of Sch. of Christianity, 1929—. Sr. partner of Harrison Farms. Mem. Ga. State Bd. Pub. Welfare, 1920-29, chmn., 1925-29; mem. Ga. State Bd. of Edn., 1929—. Supervisor Ga. Bapt. Secondary Edn., 1919-24. Democrat. Mason. Home: Macon, Ga. Died Jan. 28, 1934.

HARRISON, John Higgins, editor, pub.; b. Lebanon, Ind., Nov. 30, 1867; s. Thomas Henry and Minta (Higgins) H.; M.A., DePauw, 1891; unmarried. Newspaper reporter Chicago, 3 yrs.; publicity work, 3 yrs.; became connected, 1897, with Evening Commercial of Danville, Ill., merged with Danville News, 1903, and Danville Press, 1927, as Danville Commercial-News, of which is principal owner; pres. and treas. Commercial News Co.; pres. Home Theatre Co. Chairman Board of Commrs. of Ill. State Penitentiary, 1905-13; mem. Rep. State Central Com., Ill., 1914-16; mem. Ill. State Council of Defense, 1917-19; chmn. Ill. Rep. State Conv., 1918. Trustee DePauw U., Lakeview Hosp., Y.M.C.A., Danville. Methodist. Mason, Elk. Home: Danville, Ill. Died Mar. 2, 1930.

HARRISON, Jonathan Baxter, Unitarian clergyman; b. in Ohio, 1835; ordained to ministry, 1860. Author: Certain Dangerous Tendencies in American Life, H5; The Latest Studies on Indian Reservations. Home: Franklin Falls, N.H. Died 1907.

HARRISON, Leon, rabbi; b. Liverpool, Eng., Aug. 13, 1866; s. Gustave and Louisa (Nelson) H.; grad. into N.Y. City Coll., from pub. schs. at head of 920 candidates, ranking the entire city, 1880; thence went, 1882, to Columbia U., A.B., degree in first Honor Class, 1886; grad. Emanuel Theol. Sem., New York, as rabbi; post-grad. work in philosophy Columbia, 3 yrs.; unmarried. Ordained in Brooklyn by Rabbis Kohler and Gottheil, 1886; rabbi Temple Israel (Reformed Jewish), St. Louis, 1891—. At age of 21, delivered oration in Brooklyn before 3,000 people at funeral services of Henry Ward Beecher; delivered McKinley memorial address before 20,000 people in St. Louis Coliseum at invitation of municipality; also Thanksgiving oration at Festival Hall, St. Louis Expn., 1904, representing the Jewish community on that occasion; v.p. Anti-Tuberculosis Soc.; dir. Tenement-house Improvement Assn.; founder sisterhood of Personal Service, St. Louis (with 700 active members), with sections for kindergarten, day-nursery, evening classes, industrial sch., and for visiting sick and needy; founder Social Settlement League and Fresh Air Soc., with settlement at 9th and Carr Sts., St. Louis, Mo. Died Sept. 1, 1928.

HARRISON, Lynde, lawyer; b. New Haven, Conn., Dec. 15, 1837; s. James and Charlotte Nicoll (Lynde) H.; ed. pub. schs. and acad. at New Haven; grad. Yale Law Sch., 1860; m. Sarah Plant, May 2, 1867 (died 1879); m. 2d, Sept. 30, 1886, Harriet S. White. Established practice New Haven, 1863; clerk Conn. Ho. Reps. and Senate, 1862-64, senator 1865, 1866; judge city court, New Haven, 1871-74; mem. Ho. Reps., 1874-77 (speaker, 1877) and 1881-83; judge court common pleas, New Haven Co., 1877-81. Many yrs. on Rep. State Com. (chmn. 5 yrs.). Home: New Haven, Conn. Died 1906.

HARRISON, Orla Ellsworth, lawyer; b. Darke Co., O., Feb. 8, 1873; s. George Washington and Mary (Rupe) H.; B.S., Nat. Normal U., Lebanon, O., 1893; m. Virginia Eidson, Dec. 28, 1898. Admitted to Ohio bar, 1897, and began practice at Greenville; mem. Ohio Senate, 1902-06; del. Rep. Nat. Conv., 1904; spl. asst. to atty. gen. of Ohio, 1906-09, to atty. gen. of U.S., 1909-13; practiced at Columbus, O., 1913-21; moved to Washington, D.C., 1921; mem. Ellis, Harrison, Ferguson & Ellis. Mem. Christian Ch. Mason. Home: Washington, D.C. Died May 8, 1925.

HARRISON, Pat (Byron Patton), senator; b. Crystal Springs, Miss., Aug. 29, 1881; s. Robert and Myra Anna (Patton) H.; grad. high sch., Crystal Springs; attended La. State U., Baton Rouge; m. Mary Edwina McInnis, Jan. 19, 1905. Began law practice, Leakesville, Sept. 1902, later at Gulfport, Miss. Elected dist. atty., 2d Dist., Miss., 1905, 07; resigned, Sept. 1910; mem. 62d to 65th Congresses (1911-19), 6th Miss. Dist.; U.S. Senator, 4 terms, 1919-43; chmn. Senate Finance Com., 1933—. Democrat. Methodist. Home: Gulfport, Miss., and Washington, D.C. Died June 22, 1941.

HARRISON, Ralph Chandler, lawyer; b. Cornwall Bridge, Conn.; A.B., Wesleyan U., 1853, A.M., 1856; mem. Conn. Legislature, 1857; LL.B., Albany Law Sch., 1859. In practice at San Francisco, 1859-91 and from 1906; sr. mem. Harrison & Harrison. Mem. Bd. Freeholders to frame charter for San Francisco, 1880, pres. 2d bd., 1886; asso. justice Supreme Ct. of Calif., 1891-1903; mem. Supreme Ct. Commn., 1904; presiding justice Dist. Ct. of Appeal, 1st Dist., 1905-06. Republican. Life dir. Hastings Coll. of Law, 1886—; trustee San Francisco Law Library, 1884—, San Francisco Pub. Library, 1887—. Elected hon. life mem. Calif. Academy Sciences, 1874; pres. Geog. Soc. of the Pacific. Home: San Francisco, Calif. Died July 18, 1918.

HARRISON, Richard Almgill, lawyer; b. Thirsk, Yorkshire, Eng., Apr. 8, 1824; s. Robert and Mary (Almgill) H.; ed. pub. schs. and acad. at Springfield, O.; grad. Cincinnati Law Sch., 1846; m. Maria Louisa Warner, Dec. 21, 1847. Admitted to bar, Apr. 8, 1846; mem. lower house, 1858-59, senate 1860-61, Ohio legislature; mem. Congress, 1861-63; declined apptmt. to Supreme Court Commn. of Ohio, 1876, and to Supreme Court, 1887. Home: Columbus, O. Died 1904.

HARRISON, Richard B(erry), actor; b. London, Ont., Can., Sept. 28, 1864; s. Thomas and Isabella (Choteau) H.; ed. pub. schs., London, Ont., and Detroit (Mich.) Sch. of Dramatic Art; hon. M.A., Howard U., Washington, D.C., 1931; m. Gertrude Janet Washington, Dec. 11, 1895; children—Laurence Gilbert, Marian Ysobel. Began acting in Can., 1889; has toured U.S. and Can. as dramatic reader; teacher of dramatic art, N.C., many yrs.; conducts dramatic sch. in Agrl. and Tech. Sch. for Colored Race, Greensboro, N.C., 1921—; prin. role that of "God" in "The Green Pastures," in which play he has appeared over 1300 times, 640 in Mansfield Theatre, New York. Awarded Spingarn medal for "most outstanding achievement among colored people" for year 1930. Republican. Home: Chicago, Ill. Died Mar. 14, 1935.

HARRISON, Roland Rathbun, mng. editor Christian Science Monitor; b. Smithville, N.Y., June 10, 1878; s. Joseph Andrew and Florence Adela (Rathbun) H.; A.B., Cornell U., 1903; m. Hortense Long, Nov. 18, 1911; children—Joseph Graham, Frances Pauline. With Brooklyn (N.Y.) Standard-Union, 1903-06, New York Times, 1906-07; went to New York Herald, 1907, day city editor, 1919-20, night city editor, 1921-22; joined staff Christian Science Monitor, Boston, 1922, exec. editor, 1924-29; mem. editorial bd., 1927-39; mgr. Christian Science Publishing Society, 1929-39; administrative editor Christian Science Monitor, 1939—. Republican. Mason. Home: Newton Highlands, Mass. Died Jan. 16, 1940.

HARRISON, Russell Benjamin, lawyer; b. Oxford, O.; s. Benjamin Harrison (23d President U.S.) and Caroline (Scott) H.; g.s. William Henry Harrison (9th President U.S.); g.g.s. Benjamin Harrison, signer Declaration of Independence and mem. Continental Congress; ed. Pa. Mil. Acad., Chester, Pa.; M.E., M.S., Lafayette Coll.; m. Mary S. Saunders, Jan. 10, 1884; 1 son, William Henry. Engaged in newspaper work, New York, with "Judge," and Leslie's Weekly, later with Helena (Mont.) Daily Journal; supt. U.S. Assay Office, Helena, 1878-85; now in practice of law at Indianapolis; consul for Mexico for Ind. 25 yrs. Maj. insp. gen. vols., May 12, 1898; lt. col., Jan. 24, 1900; hon. disch., Dec. 1, 1900; served in Cuba and P.R., aided in establishing civil govt. in Porto Rico, 1900. Mem. Indiana Ho. of Rep., 1921-23 (chmn. judiciary com.); elected to Ind. Senate, 1924 and 1927 (chmn. judiciary com., 1925). Republican. Died Dec. 13, 1936.

HARRISON, Thomas Skelton, mfr.; b. Phila., Pa., Sept. 19, 1837; s. Michael Leib and Virginia Thomas Skelton (Johnston) H.; ed. Classical Acad. of John W. Faries, and at business coll.; m. Louise Harvey, Nov. 12, 1879. Acting p.m. U.S.N., 1861-Aug. 1864; mem. Harrison Bros. & Co. (founded by John Harrison, Phila., 1793), 1864-97; v.p. Harrison Bros. & Co., Inc., 1897-99, pres. 1899-1902. Apptd. by President McKinley, 1897, U.S. diplomatic agt. (minister) and consul gen. to Egypt. Prominent in polit. reform movement in Phila.; was mem. Com. of 100 and later Com. of 50, also Com. of 100 (1913). Trustee Pa. Mus. and Sch. Industrial Art. Episcopalian. Decorated twice by Khédive of Egypt, last time, with grand cordon Imperial Order of the Medjidia. Home: Philadelphia, Pa. Died May 3, 1919.

HARRISON, Thomas Walter, congressman; b. Leesburg, Va., Aug. 5, 1856; s. Matthew and Anne Harriette H.; M.A., and B.L., U. of Va.; m. Julia Knight, Mar. 8, 1882 (dec.); m. 2d, Nellie Cover, Winchester, July 3, 1903. Began practice at Winchester, Va., 1879; mem. Va. Senate 2 terms, 1888-95; judge Circuit Court, 17th Jud. Dist. of Va., 1895-1916; mem. State Constl. Conv., 1901; elected to 64th Congress, Nov. 1916, to fill vacancy, and at same time elected to 65th Congress (1917-19), 7th Va. Dist.; reëlected to 66th to 70th Congresses (1919-29), same dist.; in practice with son at Winchester, 1929—. Democrat. Home: Winchester, Va. Died May 9, 1935.

HARRISON, W(ilbur) Vernon, lyceum and Chautauqua mgr.; b. Grinnell, Ia., Oct. 22, 1879; s. Daniel B. and Elizabeth (Holland) H.; student Drake U., Des Moines, Ia., 1901-03; Ohio State U., 1905-06; m. Florence Lindenberg, Mar. 14, 1923. Began with Standard Lyceum Bur., Des Moines, 1901; became connected with Redpath Bur., Columbus, 1905; owner and mgr. Columbus office same, after 1908; organized Redpath Chautauqua circuit in Ohio, W.Va. and Ky., 1914; took over Redpath-Brockway Chautauqua in Pa., 1917, also Lincoln Chautauqua circuit in Ohio and adjoining states, 1920, Coit-Alber Seven-Day Chautauquas in Ohio, 1923, Swarthmore Five-Day Chautauquas in Ohio, 1927; now owner and mgr. Redpath Chautauquas in Ohio territory and Ohio mgr. Redpath Lyceum Bur., also dir. Redpath Lyceum Bur. (nat.). Mgr. Central Ohio Speakers' Bur. Liberty Loan Campaigns; tour of France under Am. Red Cross, 1918. Republican. Conglist. Mason. Home: Bexley, Columbus, O. Died May 14, 1929.

HARRISON, William Preston, art patron; b. Chicago, Ill., Apr. 12, 1869; s. Carter H. (5 times mayor of Chicago) and Sophinisba Grayson (Preston) H.; ed. Marquette Sch., Chicago, and Chicago U.; pvtly. tutored in Germany, France and Spain; m. Ada Marie Sandberg, July 3, 1915; 1 son, Carter. Entered real estate business, Chicago, 1889; editor and pub. Chicago Times, 1891-95; traveler and newspaper corr. for Times, Post, Inter-Ocean (all Chicago), 1895-1901; around the world, 1888-89, in Samoa, Fiji, Solomon Islands, New Hebrides (living with natives), 1894-96, in Europe and N. Africa, 1896-1901, and 1926, Mexico, Central America, West Indies, 1903, 07, 10, the Orient, 1919; continued real estate operations, 1901-15; art collector and patron, 1918—. Vice-president Board of Governors, Los Angeles Museum; vice-pres. Museum Association, Los Angeles Museum; director Friends of Huntington Library and Art Gallery; mem. board of trustees Associates of U. of Calif. in Los Angeles; founded Mr. and Mrs. William Preston Harrison Gallery Am. Art, Los Angeles, 1918, now part of Los Angeles Mus., consisting of 50 Am. oil paintings and 50 contemporary Am. water colors; founded Mr. and Mrs. William Preston Harrison Gallery of Modern French Art, Los Angeles, now part of Los Angeles Mus., 1926, consisting of 30 French oil paintings and 90 French water colors and drawings (all accepted by City of Los Angeles as vested rights in perpetuity). Episcopalian. Home: Los Angeles, Calif. Died June 28, 1940.

HARRISON, William Robert, supt. schs.; b. Florence, Ala., Jan. 16, 1869; s. Martin Luther and Edna (Smith) H.; student Florence (Ala.) Normal Sch., 1885-89; B.S., U. of Ala., 1899; m. Eva Trawick, Oct. 28, 1899; children—William Robert (dec.), Charles Trawick, Martin Leigh, Caroline. Teacher pub. schs., Opelika, Ala., 1890-97; supt. schs., Union Springs, 1900-12; teacher mathematics, Florence State Normal Sch., 1912-17; supt. schs., Florence, 1916-17, Montgomery, 1917—. Democrat. Mem. M.E. Ch. S. Rotarian. Home: Montgomery, Ala. Died 1937.

HARRITY, William Francis, lawyer; b. Wilmington, Del., Oct. 19, 1850; A.B., La Salle Coll., Phila., 1870, A.M., 1871; (LL.D., St. Joseph's Coll., Phila., 1902, Christian Brothers' College, St. Louis, 1904; Villanova College, 1911); m. Rose M. Devlin, 1883. Taught mathematics, Latin, etc., La Salle Coll., 1870-71; admitted Phila. bar, 1873; began practice in Phila. (firm Harrity, Thompson & Haig). Chmn. Dem. City Exec. Com., Phila., 1882; received 21 votes for V.P. of U.S., 1896); chmn. Dem. State Central Com., 1890; chmn. Dem. Nat. Com., 1892-96; postmaster of Phila., 1885-89; sec. state of Pa., 1891-95. Trustee Mut. Life Ins. Co. of New York; trustee La Salle Coll.; mem. Bd. Edn., Phila. Dir. numerous interests. Home: Overbrook, Pa. Died Apr. 17, 1912.

HARROD, Benjamin Morgan, civil engr.; b. New Orleans, La., Feb. 19, 1837; s. Charles and Mary (Morgan) H.; A.B., Harvard, 1856, A.M., 1859; (LL.D., Tulane, 1906); m. Eugenia Uhlhorn, Sept. 11, 1883. Pvt., lt. of arty., brigade and div. engr. and capt. engr. corps, C.S.A., in Civil War. Chief state engr. of La., 1877-80; mem. U.S. Miss. River Commn., 1879-1904; city engr. of New Orleans, 1888-92; chief engr. in charge of constructing drainage system, New Orleans, 1895-1902; mem. Panama Canal Commn., 1904-07. Home: New Orleans, La. Died Sept. 7, 1912.

HARROLD, Orville, tenor; b. Delaware Co., Ind.; s. John W. and Emily (Chalfant) H.; ed. pub. schs. and business course; m. Blanche Malli, Dec. 8, 1917. Began study of violin at 14, later singer in vaudeville, in New York; attracted favorable attention of Oscar Hammerstein who encouraged him to prepare for grand opera; student with Oscar Saenger; début Manhattan Opera House as Canio in "Pagliacci"; same in Phila., Baltimore, and made concert tour with Tetrazzini; served as leading tenor, London Opera House; toured U.S. with Century Opera Co.; with Met. Opera Co., 1919—. Home: Darien, Conn. Died Oct. 23, 1933.

HARSH, James Birney, banker, lawyer; b. Clinton Co., O., Sept. 8, 1845; s. Daniel and Nancy (McKay) H.; ed. Lombard Coll., Galesburg, Ill. (non-grad.); m. Anna E. Slater, July 1, 1869. Sergt. Co. K, 148th Ill. Vol. Inf., Civil War. Pres. J. B. Harsh & Co., bankers, Creston, Ia., 1870, Harsh & Perrin, 1875; pres. Creston Nat. Bank, 1880—, Creston Loan & Trust Co., 1880-05, Land Credit Bank, 1905—, Union Hardware Co. Founder, 1871, and editor Creston Daily and Weekly Gazette. Lawyer; mem. Harsh & Stafford, also Harsh & Higbee. Chmn. Rep. State Conv., Ia., 1888; mem. Iowa Senate, 8 yrs.; mayor Creston, 2 terms. Pres. Creston Dist. Fair, Blue Grass League of Southwest Ia., Blue Grass Palace. Pres. bd. trustees Lombard Coll. Universalist. Mason. Home: Creston, Ia. Died June 19, 1923.

HARSHBERGER, John William, botanist; b. Phila., Pa., Jan. 1, 1869; s. Dr. A. and Jennie (Waik) H.; A.B., Central High Sch., Phila., 1888; B.S., U. of Pa., 1892, Ph.D., 1893; spl. student Harvard, 1890; traveled and botanized in Europe, Brazil, Argentine, Chile, Mexico, Alaska, Ariz., Utah, Calif., Can., W.I., Southern Fla., Northwestern and Eastern states; m. Helen B. Cole, June 28, 1907 (died 1923); children—Jane Yard, Elyonta Cole. Instr. botany and zoölogy, 1892-1907, asst. prof. botany, 1907-11, prof., June 21, 1911—, U. of Pa. Formerly lecturer Soc. for Extension of Univ. Teaching; lectured in farmers' insts. in Pa., 1904-06; in charge nature study, Pocono Pines Assembly, summers 1903-08; in charge ecology, Marine Biol. Laboratory, Cold Spring Harbor, Long Island, 1913-21; in charge botany, Nantucket Maria Mitchell Assn., 1914-15. Author: Maize, a Botanical and Economic Study, 1893; The Botanists of Philadelphia, and Their Work, 1899. Bot. editor Worcester's New English Dictionary; Student's Herbarium for Descriptive and Geographic Purposes, 1901; A Phytogeographic Survey of North America, 1911, for the series of monographs, "Die Vegetation der Erde," The Vegetation of South Florida, 1914. The Vegetation of the New Jersey Pine Barrens, 1916; A Text-Book of Mycology and Plant Pathology, 1917; Colored Wall Map Vegetation of North America, 1919; Pastoral and Agricultural Botany, 1920. Bot. editor new Funk & Wagnall's College Dictionary. Home: Philadelphia, Pa. Died Apr. 27, 1929.

HARSHE, Robert Bartholow, artist; b. Salisbury, Mo., May 26, 1879; s. William and Emily (Robinson) H.; B.L., U. of Mo., 1899; M.T. Scholarship, Columbia; studied Art Inst. of Chicago, Art Students' League, N.Y., Colorossi Acad., Paris, Central Sch. of Arts and Crafts, London; Dr. Humane Letters, Northwestern U., 1926; Dr. of Fine Arts, U. of Nebraska, 1927; Dr. Humane Letters, Yale U., 1934; m. Marie Fuller Read, Aug. 15, 1907; 1 son, William R. Supervisor manual arts, Columbus, Ga., 1902-03; instr. fine arts, U. of Mo., 1905-06; asst. prof. graphic art, Leland Stanford Jr. U., 1908-13; dir. Oakland (Calif.) Pub. Mus., 1915-16; asst. dir. Dept. Fine Arts, Carnegie Inst., 1916-20; asso. dir. Art Inst. Chicago, 1920-21, dir., 1921—; dir. of A Century of Progress Expn. fine arts exhbn., Chicago, 1933, 34; advisory dir. dept. fine arts, Tex. Centennial Expn., 1936. Superintendent fine, applied and manual arts, Dept. of Edn., San Francisco Exposition, 1915, also asst. chief, Dept. Fine Arts and sec. Internat. Jury of Awards, same dept. Served as rep. abroad of San Francisco Expn., of Internat. Exhbn., Carnegie Inst., 1919; hon. adviser Roerich Mus., 1929. Mem. Am. com. of three to Internat. Congress of Art Edn., Paris; sec.-treas. Assn. Art Mus. Directors, 1917-22, pres., 1927-35. Represented in Luxembourg Museum (etchings), Los Angeles Museum, Brooklyn Museum. Chevalier Legion of Honor (France), 1925; Knight Royal Order North Star, 1929. Author: Reader's Guide to Modern Art, 1914; Prints and Their Makers, 1915. Member advisory council, Artistic Relations Sect., League of Nations, Internat. Inst. of Intellectual Coöperation, 1927; advisory com. L. C. Tiffany Foundation, 1931-34; exec. com. Olympic Games Internat. Field Athletic Competition, 1932, Internat. Assn. Museum Officials, Am. Hungarian Acad. Art (dir.). Died Jan. 11, 1938.

HARSHMAN, Walter Scott, prof. mathematics U.S.N.; b. N. Jackson, O., July 19, 1859; B.S., Western Reserve Sem., 1880; C.E., Ohio Normal U., 1883; studied Cornell U., 1888-89; M.S., Columbian (now George Washington) U., 1892, Ph.D., 1894; Johns Hopkins U., 1892-93; m. Frances M. Hodges, Dec. 9, 1890. Prof. mathematics Tri-State Normal Coll., 1884-85, Am. Normal Coll., 1885-88; asst. Am. Ephemeris, 1889-1900; prof. mathematics U.S.N., Aug. 1900-Jan. 1916 (retired with rank of comdr.). Dir. Nautical Almanac Office, 1901-07; prof. applied mathematics, Grad. Sch. of George Washington U., 1900-07. Assisted largely in work on astron. papers of the Am. Ephemeris, including Tables of Planets, Secular Variations; Orbit of Polyhymnia and Mass of Jupiter, etc. Deceased.

HARSON, M. Joseph; b. New York, July 1, 1856; s. John and Alice (O'Connell) H.; A.B., Brown U., 1884; m. Marianna F. Kelly (died 1903); children—Raymond Joseph, Henry Newman, Edwin Brownson (dec.); m. 2d, Elizabeth L. Rogers, 1915. In mercantile business in Providence, R.I., until 1904, then in real estate business, New York. Drew up Juvenile Court Law of R.I., 1897, and secured its enactment (first law of the kind in U.S.); authority and lecturer on land title registration, and largely instrumental in securing enactment of N.Y. Land Title Registration Law. At dinner at Brown U., Mar. 1894, delivered address on "The Catholic Aspect of Brown," which led to discussion resulting in amendment to the charter of the Univ., 1926, that permits 6 members of bd. of trustees to be elected without regard to religious affiliation. Was chmn. Brownson Memorial Nat. Com., and delivered dedicatory address at unveiling of the Brownson Monument, at Riverside Park, New York, Thanksgiving Day, 1910. Catholic. Proposed annual "Communion Day" of Catholic Young Men's Nat. Union, 1883, which was afterwards indulgenced by Pope Leo XIII; one of organizers Catholic Congress, Baltimore, 1889; the Columbus celebrations held under Catholic auspices throughout the country, Oct. 12, 1892, were due to his efforts; one of founders Am.-Irish Hist. Soc.; mem. U.S. Catholic Hist. Soc., Catholic Authors' Guild. Home: Brooklyn, N.Y. Died May 12, 1930.

HARSTROM, Carl Axel, educator; b. Westeros, Sweden, Dec. 20, 1863; s. Carl Gustaf and Emelia (Fosberg) H.; prep. edn., Peekskill (N.Y.) Mil. Acad. to 1880; A.B., Hobart Coll., 1886, A.M., 1889; Ph.D., Yale, 1899; m. Lee Selden Partridge, June 20, 1888; children—Frances, Carl Eric. Head master Peekskill Mil. Acad., 1886-87, Vieuland Prep. Sch., 1887-91, Norwalk Mil. Inst., 1891-93; founded, 1899, and from then prin. the Harstrom Sch., Norwalk, Conn. Elected mayor of the Consolidated Norwalks, Oct. 4, 1915. Republican. Episcopalian. Mason. Chmn. Draft Exemption Bd., Div. No. 14, of Conn. Home: Norwalk, Conn. Died Jan. 14, 1926.

HART, Archibald Chapman, congressman; b. Lennoxville, P.Q., Can., Feb. 27, 1873; s. Ruben M. and Caroline Isabel (Antrobus) H.; ed. pub. schs.; m. Lily L. Fenwick, June 4, 1901. Admitted to N.J. bar, 1896, and U.S. Supreme Court, 1910; mem. law firm of Hart & Vandewart; banker, publisher and real estate operator; prosecutor pleas, Bergen County, N.J., 1920-30; dir. Bogota National Bank and various mfg. and financial concerns. Mem. 62d, 63d and 64th Congresses (1911-17), 6th N.J. Dist. Democrat. Mem. 2d N.J. Vol. Inf. Spanish-Am. War, 1898; veteran 23d Regt. N.G.N.Y. and 2d N.J. Vol. Inf. Episcopalian. Mason. Home: Teaneck, N.J. Died July 24, 1935.

HART, Burdett, Congl. clergyman; b. New Britain, Conn., Nov. 16, 1821; s. Norman Hart; grad. Yale, 1842; studied divinity (D.D., Ripon Coll.); entered ministry, 1846; m. Rebecca Wheelock Fiske. Author: Biblical Epochs; Studies of the Model Life; Aspects of Heaven; Always Upward; The Crown Lost and Restored. Home: New Haven, Conn. Died 1906.

HART, Charles Edward, clergyman, univ. prof.; b. Freehold, N.J., Feb. 28, 1838; s. Walter Ward and Sarah (Bennett) H.; A.B., A.M., Princeton, 1858; grad. Princeton Theol. Sem., 1861; (D.D., Rutgers, 1880); m. Lucy Helena Carpender, June 19, 1884. Ordained Presbyn. ministry, 1863; pastor 40th St. (Murray Hill) Ch., New York C., 1863-66, N. Reformed Dutch Ch., Newark, N.J., 1866-80; prof. English philology and lit., 1880-97, prof. ethics, evidences of Christianity and English Bible, 1897-1906, emeritus, Rutgers Coll. Home: New Brunswick, N.J. Died Dec. 16, 1916.

HART, Charles Henry, author, art expert; b. Phila., Feb. 4, 1847; LL.B., U. of Pa., 1869; m. Armine Nixon, Nov. 16, 1869 (died 1897); m. 2d, Anita Beatriz Arabe, Dec. 7, 1912. Admitted to the Pennsylvania bar, Nov. 18, 1868; practiced until Feb. 17, 1894, when he met with severe railroad accident; since recovery devoted to literature; known as expert upon art and hist. portraiture. Dir. Pa. Acad. of Fine Arts, 1882-1902, resigned; chmn. com. on retrospective Am. art, Chicago Expn., 1893. Author: Portraits of Washington; Biography of Robert Morris; Turner the Dream Painter; Hints on Portraits and How to Catalogue Them; Abraham Lincoln's Place in History, 1900; Catalogue of Engraved Portraits of Washington, 1904; Portrait of Franklin Belonging to Royal Society London, 1908; Register of Portraits Painted by Thomas Sully, 1801-71, 1909; Historical, Descriptive and Critical Catalogue of Works of American Artists in Collection of Herbert L. Pratt, 1917. Selected and edited, with intro. and notes, 200 illustrations for Elson's History of United States, 5 vols., 1905; 100 portraits for The American Woman, by Ida M. Tarbell. Home: New York, N.Y. Died July 29, 1918.

HART, Edward, chemist; b. Doylestown, Pa., Nov. 18, 1854; s. George and Martha Longstreth (Watson) H.; B.S., Lafayette Coll., 1874, LL.D., 1924; Ph.D., Johns Hopkins, 1878. Asst. and tutor chemistry, 1874-76, adj. prof., 1876-82, prof., 1882-1924 (emeritus), Lafayette Coll., also dean Pardee Scientific Dept., 1909-24. Pres. Baker & Adamson Chem. Co., 1881-1913; propr. Chem. Pub. Co., 1892—. Has taken out 10 chem. patents (one awarded John Scott medal and premium by Franklin Inst., Phila.). Editor Jour. Analytical and Applied Chemistry, 1887-93, Jour. Am. Chem. Soc., 1893-1901. Pres. Easton City Improvement League, 1912—; chmn. City Planning Commn., 1913. Author: Text Book of Chemical Engineering, 1920; Our Farm in Cedar Valley, 1923; The Silica Gel Pseudomorph, 1924. Home: Easton, Pa. Died June 6, 1931.

HART, Ernest Eldred, banker; b. West Union, Ia., Dec. 9, 1859; s. Henry W. and Sarah H. H.; has lived in Council Bluffs, Ia., from 1868; grad. High Sch., Council Bluffs; A.B., Yale, 1881; m. Clara Bebbington, Oct. 16, 1889. In real estate business, 1881-84, investment banking, 1884—; pres. First Nat. Bank. Mem. Rep. Nat. Com., 1900—. Home: Council Bluffs, Ia. Died Feb. 1, 1913.

HART, Francis Russell, banker; b. New Bedford, Mass., Jan. 16, 1868; s. Thomas Mandell and Sarah Davis (Watson) H.; grad. Mass. Inst. Tech., 1889; hon. M.A., Tufts College (Mass.), 1935; m. Helen Bronson Hobbey, June 4, 1896; children—Mrs. Helen Nichols, Mrs. Gwendolyn Fargo, Francis R., Jr. Engaged as engr. in West Indies, 1889-91; gen. mgr., 1891-92, v.p. and gen. mgr., 1892-93, pres., 1893-1906, Cartagena-Magdalena Ry., Colombia, S.A.; v.p., 1896-1910, v.chmn. dirs., 1910-34, Old Colony Trust Co., Boston; pres. United Fruit Co., 1933—; dir. United Mail S.S. Co., Elders & Fyffes, Ltd., First Nat. Bank of Boston, Old Colony Trust Co., etc. Trustee Old Colony Trust Assos., Old Colony Investment Trust. Mem. Corp. of Mass. Inst. Tech. Vice-consul and consul, Colombia, 1908-19. Mem. Am. Acad. Arts and Sciences. Author: Admirals of the Caribbean, 1922; The Disaster of Darien, 1929; The Siege of Havana, 1931. Home: Boston, Mass. Died Jan. 18, 1938.

HART, George Overbury ("Pop"), artist; b. Cairo, Ill., May 10, 1868; s. Henry L. and Emma Elizabeth (Woods) H.; ed. pub. schs.; self-taught in art; unmarried. Water colorist; traveled and sketched in Iceland, Egypt, South Sea Islands, South America, Mexico and West Indies. Water colors, etchings or lithographs in permanent exhbn. in Met. Mus. of Art and Pub. Library, New York; Brooklyn Mus.; Smithsonian Instn., Washington; Art Inst. Chicago; Cleveland Mus.; Mus. National, Mexico City; British Mus.; etc. Awarded prize for 'landscape, "Santo Domingo," Brooklyn Mus. Exhbn., 1923-24; bronze medal for lithograph, "Springtime New Orleans." Sesquicentennial, Phila., 1926. Home: Coytesville, N.J. Died Sept. 9, 1933.

HART, Hastings Hornell, social worker; b. Brookfield, O., Dec. 14, 1851; s. Maj. Albert Gailord (M.D., surgeon of 41st O.V.I. in Civil War) and Mary Crosby (Hornell) H.; grad. Cleveland (O.) Inst., 1867; A.B. Oberlin Coll., 1875, A.M., 1885; B.D., Andover Theol. Sem., 1880; LL.D., Oberlin, 1898, Wilberforce U., 1915; m. Josephine M. Newton, Aug. 5, 1902; children—William Prosser (1st marriage), Laurence Hastings, Hornell, Helen, Frances Jeannette (all by 2d marriage), Elizabeth Haven and Albert Gailord (3d marriage). Clerk in U.S. Indian Service, Sisseton Agency, S.D., 1875-77; ordained Congl. ministry, 1880; pastor, Worthington, Minn., 1880-83; sec. Minn. State Bd. of Corrections and Charities, 1883-98; supt. Ill. Children's Home and Aid Soc., 1898-1908; dir. dept. child-helping, 1908-24, consultant in delinquency and penology, 1924—, Russell Sage Foundation, New York. Pres. Nat. Conf. of Charities and Correction, 1893, gen. sec. same, 1894-1901. Pres. Am. Prison Assn., 1921-22; Am. v.p. Internat. Prison Congress, 1925. Honorary member St. Paul Chamber of Commerce; mem. Loyal Legion, S.R. Awarded gold medal by Roosevelt Memorial Association "for the promotion of social justice," 1930. Round Table Studies for Trustees of Institutions. Also a Program for the State Council of Defense of W.Va., 1917; A Social Welfare Program for the State of Florida, 1918; The War Program of the State of South Carolina, 1918; Social Problems of Alabama, 1918; Social Progress of Mississippi, 1919; Report of Committee on Treatment of Persons Awaiting Court Action and Misdemeanant Prisoners, 1921; The Third Degree—Methods of Obtaining Confessions and Information from Persons Accused of Crime, 1921; The Restoration of the Criminal, 1922; Penology an Educational Problem, 1922; A Study of the Penitentiaries of Pennsylvania, 1923; Two Reports on Reorganization and Reconstruction of the New York City Prison System, 1925; United States Prisoners in County Jails, 1926; Report on the Penal and Reformatory System of Missouri, 1929; testimony before special com. of U.S. Ho. of Rep. on Federal Penal and Reformatory Institutions, 1929; Training Schools for Prison Officers, 1930. Home: White Plains, N.Y. Died May 9, 1932.

HART, H(enry) Martyn, clergyman; b. Otley, Yorkshire, Eng., Mar. 3, 1838; s. Joshua and Hannah H.; A.B., Trinity Coll., Dublin, 1861, A.M., 1864, B.D., D.D., 1889 (LL.D.); m. Eleanor Wilson, Kent, Eng., Apr. 19, 1865. Deacon, 1863, priest, 1864, P.E. Ch.; incumbent St. German's Ch., Blackheath, London, and head master of Montpelier House School, 1861-79; originator of the charity orgn. scheme, London, 1869; went to Denver, Colo., 1879; dean St. John's Cathedral, Denver, 1879—. Died Mar. 24, 1920.

HART, James MacDougall, artist; b. Kilmarnock, Scotland, May 10, 1828; s. James and Marion (Robertson) H.; came to U.S., 1830; sign and banner painter, Albany, N.Y., at 15; drifted into landscape work; studied at Düsseldorf, Germany, under Schirmer, 1850-53; painted and taught, Albany, 1853-57; located in New York, 1857; asso., 1858, academician, 1859, Nat. Acad. of Design; served in council many yrs. and as v.p., 3 yrs., Nat. Acad.; m. Marie Theresa Gorsuch, 1866. Is landscape and cattle painter. Prominent paintings: The Drove at the Ford (Corcoran Art Gallery, Washington); At the Brookside (Met. Museum of Art); In the Autumn Woods (Sayles Memorial Hall, Providence). Centennial medal, Phila.; gold medal, Mech. Inst., Boston; medal, Paris Expn., 1889. Home: Brooklyn, N.Y. Died 1901.

HART, James Morgan, philologist; b. Princeton, N.J., Nov. 2, 1839; s. John Seely and Amelia Caroline (Morford) H.; A.B., Princeton, 1860, A.M., 1863 (L.H.D., 1900); J.U.D., Göttingen, 1864; m. Clara Doherty, June 20, 1883. Asst. prof. modern langs., Cornell, 1868-72; prof. modern langs. and English lit., U. of Cincinnati, 1876-90; prof. English lang. and lit., Cornell, 1890-1907, emeritus. Author: German Universities, 1874; Syllabus of Anglo-Saxon Literature, 1887; Handbook of English Composition, 1895; Essentials of Prose Composition, 1902; Standard English Speech in Outline, 1907. Editor: Manual of Composition and Rhetoric, by John S. Hart (rev. edit.), 1897; German Classics, with notes, Hermann and Dorothea, 1875, Piccolomini, 1875, Goethe-Prose Selections, 1876, Faust—Part 1, 1878; De Quincey—The English Mail Coach, Joan of Arc, 1893. Translator: The Amazon, novel (from German of Franz

Dingelstedt), 1868; Cavé on Colour (from French), 1869. Home: Ithaca, N.Y. Died Apr. 18, 1916.

HART, Jerome Alfred, editor, author; b. San Francisco, Calif., Sept. 6, 1854; s. James and Sarah Marion (Burke) H.; ed. Calif. pub. schs.; m. Ann Clark, July 22, 1899. Asso. editor, 1880-91, editor, 1891-1907, San Francisco Argonaut, to which contributed letters of foreign travel (1887-1904), and translations from French, German, Spanish, etc. Mem. Calif. Acad. Sciences. Author: Sardou and the Sardou Plays, 1913; The Golconda Bonanza, 1923; In Our Second Century (from an Editor's Note Book), 1931. Editor: Argonaut Stories, 1906. Home: San Francisco, Calif. Died Jan. 3, 1937.

HART, Jesse Cleveland, judge; b. nr. Dardanelle, Ark., July 25, 1864; s. James E. and Sarah (Phila.) H.; A.B., U. of Ark., 1885; LL.B., Vanderbilt, 1890; m. Lillie Jacoway, Sept. 25, 1897; 1 dau., Ethel. Admitted to Ark. bar, 1888, and began practice at Dardanelle; apptd. chancellor 1st Chancery Dist. of Ark., 1893; asso. justice Supreme Court of Ark., 1907—; apptd. chief justice, Jan. 14, 1927. Democrat. Presbyterian. Home: Little Rock, Ark. Died Mar. 6, 1933.

HART, Lasher, physician; b. Taberg, N.Y., Jan. 11, 1879; s. Abram Eugene and Carrie (Lasher) H.; cadet U.S. Naval Acad., 1898-99; M.D., Syracuse U. Coll. of Medicine, 1903; m. Winona Elizabeth Dodge, Nov. 4, 1903. In employ State Custodial Asylum, Rome, N.Y., 1903-05; began study of diseases of the skin at N.Y. Skin and Cancer Hosp., 1905, and of urology at Post-Grad. Hosp., New York, continuing until 1907; studied in hosps. of London and Paris, 1907-08, U.S. Marine Hosp., until 1909; asso. with Dr. Granville MacGowan, 1909-12, alone, 1912—; practice limited to dermatology and urology. First lt. Medical Reserve Corps, U.S.A., 1914—; capt., M.C.U.S.A., with A.E.F. in France. Mason. Home: South Pasadena, Calif. Deceased.

HART, Louis Bret, judge; b. Medina, N.Y., Mar. 30, 1869; s. Edward and Hannah (Marcy) H.; ed. pub. schs., Lockport, N.Y. and Buffalo Law Sch.; m. Emelie Monteath Weed, Apr. 19, 1897. Sec. to Senator D. H. McMillan, 1887-88; stenographer to Grand Jury of Erie County, N.Y., 1891-95; clk. to Surrogate's Court of Erie Co., 1897-1905; surrogate of Erie Co., 1905—. Pres. bd. dirs. Grosvenor Library; v.p. Buffalo Musical Foundation. Republican. Protestant. Mason. Home: Buffalo, N.Y. Died July 17, 1939.

HART, Louis Folwell, governor; b. High Point, Mo., Jan. 4, 1862; s. Thomas J. and Harriett (Van Artsdalin) H.; ed. pub. schs.; m. Ella James, 1881. Admitted to bar, 1884, and practiced at California, Mo.; moved to Snohomish, Wash., 1889, to Republic, Wash., 1899; grand sec. Grand Lodge I.O.O.F., Wash., 1901-14. Elected lt. gov. of Wash., Nov. 1912, reëlected 1916, succeeded as gov. upon decease of Gov. Ernest Lister, June 14, 1919; term expired, Jan. 1921; reëlected 1921-25. Republican. Methodist. Mason. Home: Tacoma, Wash. Died Dec. 5, 1929.

HART, Marion Weddell, statistician; b. Rocky Mount, N.C., May 18, 1890; s. Richard Gatlin and Minnie Floy (Daughtridge) H.; grad. Tarboro (N.C.) Male Acad., 1907, Oak Ridge Inst., 1909, Eastman Business Coll., Poughkeepsie, N.Y., 1910; m. Carrie Sharp Shubrick, Sept. 16, 1912; children—Marion Weddell, Carrie Shubrick. Statistician with Atlantic Coast Line R.R. Co., 1910-18; with U.S. R.R. Labor Bd., 1918—, becoming chief statistician. Episcopalian. Mason. Home: Chicago, Ill. Died Mar. 28, 1938.

HART, Samuel, theologian; b. Saybrook, Conn., June 4, 1845; s. Henry and Mary Ann (Witter) H.; A.B., Trinity, 1866, A.M., 1869 (D.D., 1885, D.C.L., 1899; D.D., Yale U., 1902; LL.D., Wesleyan U., 1909); unmarried. Deacon, 1869, priest, 1870, P.E. Ch.; tutor, 1868-70; asst. prof. mathematics, 1870-73; prof. mathematics, 1873-83, Latin, 1883-99, Trinity Coll.; prof. doctrinal theology and prayer book, 1899—, vice-dean, 1899-1908, dean, 1908—, Berkeley Div. Sch. Registrar Diocese of Conn., 1874—; custodian of Standard Prayer Book, P.E. Ch. of U.S., 1886—; sec. House of Bishops, 1892—; historiographer and registrar of the church, 1898—. Trustee Wadsworth Athenæum, Watkinson Library, Russell Library (pres.), Ridgefield School (pres.), Trinity Coll., apptd. Paddock lecturer for 1915-16. Editor and author: Short Daily Prayers for Families, 1902; History of American Book of Common Prayer, 1910; Faith and the Faith (Bohlen lectures, 1914); Historical Sermons and Addresses. Home: Middletown, Conn. Died Feb. 25, 1917.

HART, Thomas Norton, mayor; b. N. Reading, Mass, Jan. 20, 1829; s. Daniel and Margaret (Norton) H.; country sch. edn.; removed to Boston, 1842; m. Elizabeth Snow, Apr. 30, 1850. Became partner in Philip A. Locke & Co.; subsequently founded Hart, Taylor & Co.; retired from mercantile business, 1879; pres. Mt. Vernon Nat. Bank, 1879-1903; identified with many socs. and eleemosynary instns. Mem. Boston Common Council, 1879-81, Bd. of Aldermen, 1882, 85, 86; mayor of Boston, 1889,

1890, 1900 and 1901; postmaster of Boston, 1891-93. Home: Boston, Mass. Died Oct. 4, 1927.

HART, William H., army officer; b. Winona, Minn., Mar. 20, 1864; s. John and Mary (Murphy) H.; grad. U.S. Mil. Acad., 1888; unmarried. Commd. 2d lt. 20th Inf., June 11, 1888; promoted through grades to col. Q.M.C., May 2, 1917; maj. gen., q.m. gen., Aug. 28, 1922. Q.m. 7th Cav., Ariz., 1896-98; adj. same, Cuba, 1899-1900; depot commissary, Manila, P.I., 1901-02; asst. com. gen., Washington, D.C., 1903-09; depot com., Honolulu, 1909-11, San Francisco, 1911-16, also supt. Army Trans. Service, 1913-16; base q.m., Base Sect. 1, St. Nazaire, France, 1918-19; depot q.m., New York, 1920-22; apptd. q.m. gen., Aug. 28, 1922. Initial Gen. Staff Corps Eligible List; awarded D.S.M. (U.S.); Officer Legion of Honor (French). Died Jan. 2, 1926.

HART, William Octave, lawyer; b. New Orleans, La., Aug. 19, 1857; s. Toby and Anna (Hussey) H.; ed. Clark's Sch. and Lusher's Acad., New Orleans; m. Evelyn Richards, Mar. 12, 1889 (died 1924). Mem. bd. dirs. Mut. Bldg. and Homestead Assn., Title and Mortgage Guarantee Co., Ltd. Lecturer on jurisprudence, La. Law Sch. (La. State U.), 1907; lecturer on La. statute law before Law Sch. of Tulane U., 1926. Commr. on uniform state laws from La., 1903—; treas. Nat. Conf. on Uniform State Laws, 1915—, mem. exec. com. from 1917, and v.p., 1903-07; mem. bd. to investigate Torrens system in La., 1904; mem. Conv. Internat. Jurists and Lawyers, St. Louis, Mo., 1904; mem. first State Tax Commn. of La.; mem. State Bar Examining Bd. 3 terms; mem. U.S. Sect. Inter-Am. High Commission. Mem. bd. govs. Washington Sulgrave Inst., and of Washington Lafayette Inst.; mem. exec. com. George Washington Bi-Centennial Celebration Com. Past comdt. and historian Camp Beauregard Sons Confederate Vets.; jr. mem. Army of Tenn. Confed. Vets. (recording sec. and mem. hist. com.); commissary gen. and chmn. finance com. United Confd. Vets.; mem. Bd. of Governors, Confed. Memorial Hall. Active in war work. Presbyn. Democrat. Wrote: Guide to New Orleans, 1904; compiled Laws of Louisiana, Am. Corp. Legal Manual, and Sharpe and Alleman's Legal Directory. Home: New Orleans, La. Died Oct. 19, 1929.

HARTE (Francis) Bret, author; b. Albany, N.Y., Aug. 25, 1839; went to mining regions of Calif.; later engaged in newspaper work; sec. branch U.S. mint, San Francisco, 1864-67; editor Overland Monthly; in New York, 1870-78; U.S. consul at Crefeld, Germany, 1878-80; at Glasgow, Scotland, 1880-85; since then resident in London. Author: The Heathen Chinee, 1869; Luck of Roaring Camp, 1870; Poems, 1870; Poems, 1871; East and West Poems, 1871; Mrs. Skagg's Husbands, 1872; Echoes of the Foothills, 1874; Tales of the Argonauts, 1875; Gabriel Conroy, and Two Men of Sandy Bar, 1876; Thankful Blossom, 1877; Story of a Mine, and Drift from Two Shores, 1878; The Twins of Table Mountain and Other Stories, 1879; Flip and Found at Blazing Star, 1882; In the Carquinez Woods, 1883; On the Frontier, 1884; By Shore and Sedge, and Maruja, 1885; Snowbound at Eagles, and The Queen of the Pirate Isle, 1886; A Millionaire of Rough and Ready, Devil's Ford, and The Crusade of the "Excelsior," 1887; A Phyllis of the Sierras, Drift from Redwood Camp, and The Argonauts of North Liberty, 1888; Cressy, and The Heritage of Dedlow Marsh, 1889; A Waif of the Plains; A Ward of the Golden Gate, 1890; A Sappho of Green Springs and Sally Dows, 1892; Susy, 1893; Three Partners, 1897; Tales of Trail and Town, 1898; Stories in Light and Shadow, 1898; A Ward of the Golden Gate, 1899; Mr. Jack Hamlin's Mediation, 1899; From Sandhill to Pine, 1900; Under the Redwoods, 1901. Died 1902.

HARTE, Richard Hickman, surgeon; b. Rock Island, Ill., Oct. 23, 1855; s. William H. and Mary A. (Betty) H.; M.D., U. of Pa., 1878; m. Maria H. Ames, 1888. Emeritus surgeon, Pa. Hosp.; cons. surgeon St. Mary's, St. Timothy's, Bryn Mawr and Abington hosps.; was adj. prof. surgery, U. of Pa. Was surgeon Am. Ambulance, Paris, 1916; col. in charge Gen. Hosp. 16, B.E.F. in France; now col., Med. R.C.U.S.A. Mentioned in despatches of Gen. Haig and awarded Brit. Order St. George and St. Michael; Companion Order of Leopold by King of Belgium, "for spl. service," rendered during the war; made a fellow of The Royal Coll. of Surgeons, Ireland, "for conspicuous service," to Brit. E.F.; medal for distinguished and meritorious services (U.S.). Dir. health and charities of Phila.; editor Transactions Am. Surg. Assn. 12 yrs. Fellow Am. Surg. Assn. (pres. 1910-11). Author: Hand Book of Local Therapeutics, 1893. Home: Philadelphia, Pa. Died Nov. 14, 1925.

HARTFORD, Fernando Wood, editor, pub.; b. Chateaugay, N.Y., Nov. 14, 1872; s. Mark and Eliza J. (Silver) H.; ed. pub. schs. and business coll.; m. Elizabeth Hill Downing, June 7, 1890; children—Beatrice Elizabeth (Mrs. Alexander Scarborough), Emma Helen (widow of W. A. Nelson), Justin Downing Hartford. Began as office boy with Manchester (N.H.) Union, 1885, later reporter for same paper and was made mgr. at Portsmouth, for Rockingham and Strafford counties; editor and pub. Portsmouth Herald, 1891—, and the New Hampshire Gazette (established Oct. 7, 1756); mem. N.H. Ho. of Rep., 1895; clk. of purchasing dept. Portsmouth Navy Yard 14 yrs.; mayor of Portsmouth 7 terms between 1921-32; served as chmn. Bd. of Instruction of Ports, 1921 to 1932; now pres. Portsmouth Theatre Corp.; dir. N.H. Nat. Bank; mem. N.E. R.R. Conf.; candidate for Congress, 1932; chmn. Rye Harbor Development Assn. Mem. staff of gov. of N.H., title of major. Republican. Conglist. Mason. Home: Portsmouth, N.H. Died July 22, 1938.

HARTLEY, Ellis Taylor, educator; b. Bellefontaine, O., June 7, 1848; s. Aaron and Eliza (Lyon) H.; B.A., Ohio Wesleyan U., 1870, M.A., 1873; studied in Europe, 1871; m. Luella Pierce, Aug. 2, 1881. Supt. schs., Galion, O., 1872-73, Fostoria, O., 1873-83, Lincoln, Neb., 1883-90; resigned to engage in fruit farming. In charge forestry exhibit, Chicago Expn., 1893. Mem. Hort. and Hist. socs., U. of Neb. Republican. Home: Lincoln, Neb. Died Oct. 7, 1914.

HARTLEY, Frank, surgeon; b. Washington, June 10, 1856; s. John F. and Mary D. (King) H.; A.B., Princeton, 1877, A.M., 1879; M.D., Coll. Phys. and Surg. (Columbia), 1880; student U. of Vienna, 1882-84; (LL.D., Princeton, 1909); m. Mrs. E. A. Parker, Aug. 1, 1899. Asst. surgeon Roosevelt Hosp., 1884-97; attending surgeon to Gen. Memorial and Bellevue hosps., 1890-98, N.Y. Hosp., 1895—; consulting surgeon Gen. Memorial Babies', French and Nyack hosps., White Plains, 1889—; instr. operative surgery and clin. lecturer surgery, 1888-1909, prof. clin. surgery, and instr. operative surgery, 1900—, Coll. Phys. and Surg. Has made numerous contributions to surgery; originator of intercranial method for the cure of trigeminal neuralgia (tic douloureux). Presbyterian. Democrat. Home: New York, N.Y. Died June 19, 1913.

HARTLEY, Isaac Smithson, Episcopal clergyman; b. New York, Sept. 27, 1830; grad. N.Y. Univ., 1852; Andover Theol. Sem., 1856 (D.D., Rutgers Coll., 1874); m. Isabella Aston White, Apr. 26, 1866. Author: Bedder Lectures on Modern Infidelity; Memorial of Robert Milham Hartley (his father, a philanthropist); Old Fort Schuyler in History; Sundays in the Adirondacks; The Twelve Gates. Member of the Evangelical Alliance, London, 1888, and Victoria Institute, London, 1895. Home: Great Barrington, Mass. Died 1899.

HARTLEY, Jonathan Scott, sculptor; b. Albany, N.Y., Sept. 23, 1845; s. Joseph and Margaret (Scott) H.; ed. Albany Acad.; m. a d. of George Inness, 1888. Sculptor Daguerre monument, Washington; Ericcson monument, New York; statue of Miles Morgan, Springfield, Mass.; statue of Alfred the Great, New Appellate Court Bldg., New York, 1900; statue of Thomas K. Beecher, Elmira, N.Y., 1901, and other public works. Pres. Art Students' League, New York, 1878-80. N.A., 1891. Home: New York, N.Y. Died Dec. 6, 1912.

HARTMAN, Charles S., lawyer; b. Monticello, Ind., Mar. 1, 1861; s. Sampson and Mary C. H.; ed. pub. schs.; m. Flora B. Imes, Dec. 2, 1884; children—Lois K., Flora (Mrs. Flora Salmon). Moved to Mont., 1882; admitted to bar, 1884; probate judge Gallatin Co., Mont., 1884-86; mem. Constl. Conv., Mont., 1888; mem. 53d to 55th Congresses, 1893-99; E.E. and M.P. to Ecuador, 1913-22; resumed practice of law; apptd. judge 12th Judicial Dist. Mont. Democrat. Home: Ft. Benton, Mont. Died Aug. 3, 1929.

HARTMAN, John Clark, editor, pub.; b. Waterloo, Ia., June 21, 1861; s. William Harrison and Dorinda Zidania (Clark) H.; ed. pub. schs.; m. Ida May Hummel, Nov. 8, 1886. With Waterloo Daily Courier, 1879—, editor and pub., 1895—; pres. W. H. Hartman Co., pubs. Republican. Mason. Home: Waterloo, Ia. Died Jan. 3, 1941.

HARTMAN, Lee Foster, editor; b. Ft. Wayne, Ind., Oct. 2, 1879; s. Lemuel R. and Eliza (Harter) H.; A.B., Wesleyan U., Conn., 1901, M.A., 1936; m. Estelle Douai Bosch, Apr. 28, 1906; children—Natalie Roberts (dec.), Elsa Allison, Alan Kerth; m. 2d, Adele Mingeaud, of Toronto, Canada, Feb. 16, 1926. With New York Journal, 1901-02; editorial dept., Asso. Sunday Magazines, 1903; lt. dept., Harper & Brothers, 1904-08; editorial staff, Harper's Magazine, 1908-18, asso. editor, 1918-31, editor, 1931—; v.p. Harper & Brothers, 1936—. Home: New York, N.Y. Died Sept. 23, 1941.

HARTMANN, F(rancis) M., prof. elec-engring.; b. Cochecton, N.Y., Aug. 31, 1870; s. Franz Eugen and Paulina (Hoenninger) H.; B.S., Cooper Union Night Sch., 1895, grad. course in chemistry, 1898, E.E., 1903; grad. study in mathematics, New York U., 1903. City surveyor, N.Y. City, 1891-94; computer, dept. pub. improvements, 1894-1901; instr. in physics and elec. engring., Cooper Union Night Sch. Engring., 1899, 1901-05, also same in Cooper Union Inst. Tech., 1901-05, asst. prof. physics and elec. engring., 1905-07, prof. 1907, prof. elec. and mech. engring., in charge dept., 1908-21, prof. elec. engring. and dean schs. of engring., 1921—; developed 5-year night course in elec. engring., Cooper Union. Fellow Am. Inst. E.E., A.A.A.S. Author: Elementary Mechanics, 1910; Heat and Thermodynamics, 1911; Biography of George W. Plympton, 1920; Alternating Currents and Transmission, 1923. Home: New York, N.Y. Died 1932.

HARTNESS, James, governor; b. Schenectady, N.Y., Sept. 3, 1861; s. John Williams and Ursilla (Jackson) H.; ed. Cleveland pub. schs.; M.E., Univ. of Vt., 1910; M.A., Yale, 1914; LL.D., U. of Vermont, 1921; m. Lena Sanford Pond, May 13, 1885; children—Anna (Mrs. William H. Beardsley), Helen (Mrs. Ralph E. Flanders). Successively, 1890—, supt., mgr., pres., Jones & Lamson Machine Co., Springfield, Vt.; inventor and patentee of over 100 patents including Hartness flat turret lathe, Hartness automatic die, Turret equatorial telescope, Hartness screw thread comparator, etc. Chmn. Com. of Pub. Safety, Vt., war period, also federal food administrator for Vt.; gov. of Vt., term 1921-23. Mem. commn. that represented U.S. Air Bd. at Inter-Allied Air Craft Standardization Conf., London and Paris; v. chmn. Congressional Screw Thread Standardization Commn. Chmn. State Bd. of Edn., Vt., 6 yrs. Fellow A.A.A.S., Royal Astron. Soc. Awarded John Scott medal by bd. of dirs. of City Trusts of Phila., 1921; Edward Longstreth Medal by Franklin Inst., Phila. Home: Springfield, Vt. Died Feb. 2, 1934.

HARTRANFT, Chester David, theologian; b. Frederick Tp., Pa., Oct. 15, 1839; s. Samuel and Salome (Stetler) H.; A.B., A.M., Phila. High Sch.; A.B., U. of Pa., 1861, later A.M.; New Brunswick Theol. Sem., 1864; (Mus. Doc. Rutgers; D.D., Williams); m. Annie Frances Berg, 1864; 2d, Ida T. Berg, Nov. 22, 1911. Capt. 18th Pa. Vols. in Civil War; ordained Dutch Reformed ministry; pastor, S. Bushwick, N.Y., 1864-66, New Brunswick, N.J., 1866-78; Waldo prof. ecclesiastical history, 1879-88, prof. Bibl. theology, 1892-97, prof. ecclesiastical dogmatics, 1897-1903, pres., 1888-1903, hon. pres., 1903—, Hartford Theol. Sem. Now editor Corpus Schwenckfeldianorum, in Germany. Pres. Conservatory of Music, New Brunswick, N.J.; conducted an oratorio soc., 10 yrs. Died Dec. 30, 1914.

HARTRIDGE, John Earle, lawyer; b. Madison, Fla., Nov. 16, 1849; s. Theodore and Susan (Livingston) H.; A.B., U. of Ga., 1873; m. Susan Fatio L'Engle. Practiced in Jacksonville, 1873—, city atty., Jacksonville, 1882; elected to Fla. Senate, 1894; has many times canvassed Fla. in Dem. campaigns; nominated, 1888, by Pres. Cleveland for judge U.S. Dist. Court, but nomination not confirmed. Episcopalian. Home: Jacksonville, Fla. Died Nov. 1929.

HARTSHORN, William Henry, college prof.; b. Lisbon, Me., June 17, 1863; s. Charles and Nancy (Hatch) H.; A.B., Bates Coll., 1886, A.M., 1889 (Litt.D., 1904); U. of Leipzig, 1890-91; m. Minnie Blake, Nov. 30, 1886. Supt. schs. and prin. High Sch., Laconia, N.H., 1886-89; instr. physics, 1889-90, prof., 1890-94, prof. English, 1894—, acting pres., 1919-20, Bates Coll. Chmn. State Library Commn.; pres. Me. Library Assn., 1910-12. Mason. Home: Lewiston, Me. Died Feb. 24, 1926.

HARTSHORN, William Newton, publisher; b. Greenville, N.H., Oct. 28, 1843; s. George and Mary A. (Putnam) H.; ed. pub. sch., Milford, N.H., and 1 yr. Appleton Acad., Mt. Vernon, N.H.; m. Ella S. Ford, Oct. 28, 1875. President The Priscilla Co., proprs. The Modern Priscilla. Chmn. exec. com. Internat. S.S. Assn., 1902-11, pres., 1911-14; v.p. World's S.S. Assn.; now devotes most of his time to state, nat. internat. and world S.S. work. Mem. Boston Bapt. Social Union (pres.), and various state and local denominational and charitable instns. Home: Cambridge, Mass. Died Sept. 1920.

HARTSHORNE, Charles, ry. official; b. Phila., Sept. 2, 1829; s. Dr. Joseph and Anna (Bonsall) H.; student Haverford Coll., 1843-45; grad. U. of Pa., 1847, A.M., 1850; m. Caroline C., d. Edward Yarnall of Phila., June 8, 1859. Entered ry. service, 1857; pres. Quakake R.R., 1857, Lehigh & Mahanoy R.R., 1862, until it merged with Lehigh Valley R.R.; v.p. Lehigh Valley R.R., 1868-99; formerly pres. Choctaw Coal & Ry. Co. and v.p. Phila., Reading & New England R.R. Trustee Lehigh Univ., Haverford, and Bryn Mawr Coll.; mem. bd. mgrs. of Pa. Hosp., Provident Life & Trust Society. Home: Merion Sta., Pa. Died 1908.

HARTSHORNE, Charles Hopkins, lawyer; b. Jersey City, N.J., Nov. 22, 1851; s. Samuel H. and Elizabeth Vincent (Holmes) H.; ed. home and Glenwood Acad., Delaware Water Gap, Pa.; m. Mariella Metcalf, Oct. 16, 1889 (died 1900); m. 2d, Sarah Murray Steuart, Oct. 20, 1909. Admitted to bar, 1872; mem. Hartshorne, Insley & Leake, 1900—. Chmn. State Bd. Bar Examiners, N.J., 1902—; lecturer in New York Law Sch., 1904—. Author: Courts and Procedure in England and New Jersey, 1905; Hartshorne's Practice Act, 1912. Home: Montclair, N.J. Died 1918.

HARTSUFF, Albert, army officer; b. New York, Feb. 4, 1837; M.D., Castleton Med. Coll., Vt. Apptd. from Mich., asst. surg. U.S.A., Aug. 5, 1861; capt. asst. surg., July 28, 1866; maj. surg., June 26, 1876; lt. col. dep. surgeon gen., Dec. 4, 1892; col. asst. surg. gen., Apr. 28, 1900; retired by operation of law, Feb. 4, 1901; advanced to rank of brig. gen. retired, by act of Apr. 23, 1904. Bvtd. capt. and maj., Mar. 13, 1865 for services during the war; lt. col., Nov. 26, 1866, for services during cholera epidemic in New Orleans. Died 1908.

HARTWELL, Alfred Stedman, lawyer; b. Dedham, Mass., June 11, 1836; s. Stedman and Rebecca Dana (Perry) H.; A.B., Harvard, 1858, LL.B., 1867; m. at Koloa, Kauai, H.I., Charlotte Elizabeth, d. Dr. James W. Smith, missionary physician, Jan. 10, 1872. Corporal 3d Mo. R.C., 1861; 1st lt. 44th Mass. vols., Sept. 12, 1862; capt. 54th Mass. Inf., Mar. 30, 1863; lt. col. 55th Mass. Inf., June 19, 1863; col., Dec. 1, 1863; bvtd. brig. gen. vols., Dec. 30, 1864, for gallantry at battle of Honey Hill, S.C.; mustered out Apr. 3, 1866. Mem. Mass. Legislature, 1867; 1st asso. justice of H.I., 1868-74; atty. gen. of H.I., 1874, 1877-78; spl. agt. Republic of Hawaii in Washington, 1899-1900; asso. justice Supreme Ct. of Hawaii, June 14, 1904, chief justice, Aug. 15, 1907-Feb. 2, 1911, resigned. Republican. Home: Honolulu, T.H. Died Aug. 30, 1912.

HARTWELL, Edward Mussey, statistician; b. Exeter, N.H., May 29, 1850; s. Shattuck and Catherine Stone (Mussey) H.; A.B., Amherst Coll., 1873, A.M., 1876; Ph.D., Johns Hopkins, 1881; M.D., Miami Med. Coll., Cincinnati, 1882; (LL.D., Amherst, 1898); m. Mary Lætitia Brown, July 25, 1889. Vice prin. high sch., Orange, N.J., 1873-74; teacher Boston Latin Sch., 1874-77; student medicine, Cincinnati, 1877-78; fellow Johns Hopkins, 1879-80; asso. physical training and dir. gymnasium, same, 1883-91; dir. physical training, pub. schs., Boston, 1891-97; sec. statis. dept., City of Boston, from its establishment, 1897. Chmn. Mass. State Commn. for the Blind, 1906-08. Spl. expert agt., U.S. Dept. Labor in Europe, 1888-89; has studied in Berlin, Vienna and Stockholm, and made spl. investigations in hygiene, edn. and statistics in Great Britain, Germany, Russia and Scandinavia. Translator from Swedish: Kleen's Handbok i Massage. Mem. Med. and Chirurg. Faculty of Md. Home: Jamaica Plain, Boston. Died Feb. 19, 1922.

HARTWELL, John Augustus, surgeon; b. Sussex, N.J., Sept. 27, 1869; s. Samuel S. and Clarinda (Stiles) H.; Ph.B., Yale, 1889, M.D., 1892; m. Mrs. Mary B. (Green) Fulton, Apr. 16, 1910. Practiced in New York from 1893; asso. prof. and clin. prof. surgery, Cornell U. Med. Coll., 1910—; consulting surgeon various hosps. Fellow Am. Coll. Surgeons. Republican. Commd. maj., M.C., U.S.A.; hon. discharged July 1, 1919. Retired. Home: New York, N.Y. Died Nov. 30, 1940.

HARTY, Jeremiah J., archbishop; b. St. Louis, Nov. 7, 1853; s. Andrew and Julia (Murphy) H.; ed. St. Louis U. and St. Vincent's Coll., Cape Girardeau, Mo.; also completed divinity studies in latter. Ordained R.C. priest Apr. 28, 1878; was asst. rector St. Lawrence O'Toole's Ch., later at St. Bridget's Ch., St. Louis, until Nov. 1888; organized parish of St. Leo's, St. Louis, and pastor same until apptd. Archibishop of Manila, P.I., June 6, 1903; consecrated, Aug. 15, 1903; transferred to the see of Omaha (Neb.), May 16, 1916. Died Oct. 29, 1927.

HARTZELL, Charles, lawyer; b. Canton, O., July 15, 1862; s. Josiah and Mary K. H.; ed. Canton, O., until 1878; studied law dept. Univ. of Mich., until 1881; m. Ida T. Jones, Dec. 13, 1893 (dec.); 1 son, Charles R. Admitted to bar, Ohio Supreme Court, 1883; lived in Colo., 1883-1901; practiced in Denver, 1886-1901, asso. with Senator T. M. Patterson and Gov. Charles S. Thomas. Mem. Colo. Senate, 1892-96; Rep. candidate for Congress, 1st Colo. Dist., 1898; chmn. Rep. Co. Com., 1900-01; sec. of Puerto Rico and pres. Exec. Council, 1902-04; now practicing law. Chmn. P.R. Chapter Am. Red Cross, 1918-19. Home: San Juan, P.R. Died Apr. 8, 1932.

HARTZELL, Joseph Crane, bishop; b. Moline, Ill., June 1, 1842; s. Michael Bash and Nancy (Worman) H.; A.B., Ill. Wesleyan U.; B.D., Garrett Bibl. Inst., 1868; A.M., D.D., LL.D.; m. Jennie Culver, Nov. 14, 1869. Ordained M.E. ministry, 1866; pastor, Pekin, Ill., 1869-70, St. Charles Ch., New Orleans, 1870-73; supt., ednl. and editorial work, New Orleans, 1873-82; asst. sec., 1882-87, sec., 1887-96, Freedmen's Aid and Ednl. Society, M.E. Ch.; missionary bishop of Africa, 1896-1916; retired on account age limit. Founded, 1875, Southwestern Christian Advocate; mem. sch. bd., New Orleans, several yrs. Del. Gen. Quadrennial Confs., 1876-96. Spl. envoy to U.S. and England in behalf of Republic of Liberia and succeeding in averting a crisis between that country and Germany. Mason. Knight Comdr. Order of Redemption of Africa (Liberia). Home: Cincinnati, O. Died Sept. 6, 1929.

HARTZELL, J(oseph) Culver, genealogist; b. New Orleans, Sept. 10, 1870; s. Joseph Crane and Jennie (Culver) H.; B.S., Chattanooga, 1892; M.S., Yale, 1899; M.D., Coll. Phys. and Surg., 1901; Ph.D., Munich, 1904; student, Harvard, 1896; Johns Hopkins, 1897-98; Pisa, 1903; Ohio-Miami Med. Coll., 1915; m. Helen Hitchcock Thresher, Aug. 31, 1893. Prof. of biology, Ill. Wesleyan U., 1899-1904; in Europe, 1903-04; prof. chemistry, U. of the Pacific, 1904-10; cons. engr. chemistry and metallurgy, 1910-13; Ill. Malleable Iron Co., 1913-14; research work, 1914-18; chief chemist, Cincinnati Milling Machine Co., 1918-19; cons. engr. to Dalton Adding Machine Co., 1920, to Victor Safe & Lock Div. of the Safe-Cabinet Co., and to the Hall's Safe Co., 1920-21; pres. and gen. mgr. Ohio Lesgas Co., 1921-25. Fellow Seismol. Soc. America, A.A.A.S.; charter mem. and chmn. exec. com. Cincinnati Chapter Am. Steel Treaters Society. Home: Blue Ash, O. Deceased.

HARTZLER, Henry Burns, bishop; b. Lower Windsor Tp., Pa., Mar. 23, 1840; s. Jacob and Magdalena (Colclazer) H.; ed. in common schs.; m. Sarah A. Zeller, Mar. 21, 1865. Licensed to preach M.E. Ch.; served at New Dover, N.J., 1866, Parsippany, N.J., 1867; ordained in Evangs. Assn.; served at Middleburg, Pa., 1869, Carlisle, Pa., 1870-73, Milton, Pa., 1874, York, Pa., 1875; in United Evang. Ch., 1892—. Instr. Bible, and chaplain, Mt. Hermon Sch., 1890-95; instr. Bible, Northfield Training Sch., 1890-95. Editor Evang. Messenger, Cleveland, O., 1879-87, The Evangelical, Harrisburg, Pa., 1888-90, 1895-1902 and from Oct. 1910; bishop United Evang. Ch., 1902-1910. Home: Harrisburg, Pa. Died Sept. 3, 1920.

HARVEY, Charles Henry, chmn. Tenn. Pub. Service Co.; b. Anamosa, Ia., Oct. 10, 1861; s. Edward Merton and Lucy Lucina (Clark) H.; Beloit Coll., 1881-83; A.B., U. of Mich., 1885; m. Ida Grace Locke, Apr. 19, 1892 (died 1899); children—Edith Clark, Mrs. Helen Whitney Arnold. In ry. service, 1885-95; became sec. Knoxville Electric Light & Power Co. and Knoxville Traction Co., 1895, and gen. mgr., 1902, the cos. consolidated, 1905, as Knoxville Ry. & Light Co. (now Tenn. Public Service Co.), of which was gen. mgr., 1902-25, pres., 1904-30, chmn. bd., 1930—; pres. Harvey Coal Corp.; dir. various corporations. Admitted to Tenn. bar, 1894, but never practiced. Served as colonel on staff of Gov. Ben W. Hooper. Republican. Episcopalian. Mason. Home: Knoxville, Tenn. Died Oct. 6, 1935.

HARVEY, Charles Mitchell, journalist; b. Boston, Oct. 15, 1848; s. John and Elizabeth (Flynn) H.; acad. edn.; m. Louise M. Lettré, Nov. 25, 1874 (died 1911). Was with newspapers in New York, St. Louis and Chicago; asso. editor and editorial writer on Globe-Democrat, St. Louis, 1886-1913, of which was leading polit. editorial writer; spl. corr. to many prominent newspapers, 1913—. Author: History of the Republican Party; Handbook of American Politics; History of Missouri. Home: St. Louis, Mo. Deceased.

HARVEY, Ford, restaurateur; b. Leavenworth, Kan., Mar. 7, 1866; s. Frederick Henry and Barbara Sarah (Mattes) H.; student Racine (Wis.) Coll., 1879-84; m. Josephine Lytle, dau. Gen. Blair, of Leavenworth, May 19, 1888 (died 1926); children—Katherine Medary, Frederick Henry. Left coll., 1884, because of failing health of father; made head of organization of restaurants, 1901, on Santa Fe R.R., which father had built up; pres. Fred Harvey, Inc., from incorporation, 1906; pres. Harvey Hotel & Restaurant Co., The Harvey Co., Santa Fe Transportation Co.; dir. First Nat. Bank, Sheffield Steel Corp. (Kansas City), Harris Trust & Savings Bank (Chicago), Leavenworth Nat. Bank. Home: Kansas City, Mo. Died Dec. 15, 1928.

HARVEY, Frederick Loviad, lawyer; b. Washington, May 6, 1856; s. Frederick Loviad (Sr.) and Helen Mary (Ford) H.; student Coll. City of New York; LL.B., Columbian (now George Washington) U., 1879, LL.M., 1880; m. Pamela Dean, d. Hon. W. S. Holman (congressman from Ind.), Apr. 8, 1889. Admitted to bar, 1879. Sec. to joint commn. for completion of Washington Nat. Monument, under act of Aug. 2, 1876, 1878-88; prin. examiner land claims and contests U.S. Gen. Land Office, 1888-96; law examiner U.S. Forest Service, 1906—. Asst. sec. and sec. Washington Nat. Monument Soc., 1874—, mem. 1894-1916. Author: History of the Washington Monument and of the Washington National Monument Society, 1902 (enlarged, illustrated and printed as a Senate document, 2d session, 57th Congress). Died Mar. 16, 1923.

HARVEY, George (Brinton McClellan), publicist, diplomat; b. Peacham, Vt., Feb. 16, 1864; s. Duncan and Margaret S. (Varnum) H.; ed. Peacham Acad.; LL.D., U. of Nev., U. of Vt., Middlebury Coll., Erskine Coll.; Litt.D., (Dartmouth); m. Alma A. Parker, Oct. 13, 1887; 1 dau., Dorothy (wife of M. H. Thompson, U.S.A.). Consecutively reporter Springfield Republican, Chicago News, and New York World, 1882-86; ins. commr. of N.J., 1890-91; mng. editor New York World, 1891-93; constructor and pres. various electric railroads, 1894-98; purchased, 1899, and editor 27 yrs., North American Review. Pres. Harper & Bros., 1900-15; formerly editor, pub. Harvey's Weekly; A.E. and P. to Great Britain, Apr. 1921-Dec. 1923. Col. and a.d.c. on staffs of Govs. Green and Abbett, of N.J., 1885-92; hon. col. and a.d.c. on staffs of Govs. Heyward and Ansel, of S.C. Trustee Stevens Inst. Tech. Home: Deal, N.J. Died Aug. 20, 1928.

HARVEY, George Cockburn, writer, editor; b. Thornby, Eng., 1858; s. George Cockburn and Mary (Barr) H.; ed. Cheltenham Coll. and Oxford U.; m. Josephine Palmer. Rancher in Ariz., later farmer and horse breaker in Eng.; contbg. editor University Ency., 1897; asso. editor New Standard Dictionary, 1898, 1912, and with Am. Book Co. until 1914; war work in Eng., 1914-19; returned to U.S., 1920; asso. editor College Standard Dictionary; editorial Staff The John C. Winston Co., 1923-27; mem. staff The Ency. Britannica, 1927—; corr. Empire Mail. Author: Famous Four-Footed Friends, 1916; also many short stories; (plays) Birds of a Feather, Hallucinations, Wanted—A Groom, Sally's Rival, The Dilemma, etc. Editor: Robin Hood, 1923; Black Beauty, 1927. Home: New York, N.Y. Died May 25, 1935.

HARVEY, Lawson Moreau, judge; b. Plainfield, Ind., Dec. 5, 1856; s. Thomas Burgess (M.D., LL.D.) and Delitha (Butler) H.; student Haverford Coll., Pa., 1877-78, Butler U., Ind., 1878-80; LL.B., Central Law Sch., Indianapolis, 1882; m. Kate Parrott, Oct. 18, 1882. Admitted to bar, 1882, and began practice at Indianapolis; judge Superior Court of Marion Co., Ind., 1894-98; sr. mem. Harvey, Pickens, Cox & Kahn, 1898-1907; asso. justice Supreme Court, of Ind., 1916—. Republican. Home: Indianapolis, Ind. Died June 25, 1920.

HARVEY, LeRoy, banker; b. Wilmington, Del., Apr. 28, 1873; s. Huxley and Mary Louise (Belt) H.; A.B., Harvard, 1894; m. Renée de Pelleport du Pont, Jan. 9, 1904; children—Alice Hounsfield, Mary Van Dyke, Edmund Huxley, Sophie Renée de Pelleport. In business, St. Petersburg, Russia, 1897-99; in lumber business, Phila., Pa., 1899-1914; pres. Farmers' Bank, Wilmington, 1925—. Mayor of Wilmington, 1921-23; mgr. and treas. Wilmington Pub. Library; mgr. Wilmington Savings Fund Soc. Home: Wilmington, Del. Deceased.

HARVEY, Lorenzo Dow, supt. of schs.; b. Deerfield, N.H., Nov. 23, 1848; s. John S. and Mary (Sanborn) H.; A.B., Milton (Wis.) Coll., 1872, A.M., 1876 (hon. Ph.D., 1885); m. Lettie Brown, Dec. 24, 1874. Became teacher, 1873; supt. schs., Sheboygan, Wis., 1875-85; inst. conductor and prof. polit. economy, State Normal Sch., Oshkosh, Wis., 1885-92; prin. State Normal Sch., Milwaukee, 1892-98; state supt. pub. instrn., Wis., 1899-1902; supt. Menomonie (Wis.) sch. system and Stout Training Schs., 1903-08; pres. Stout Inst., Menomonie, 1908—. Home: Menomonie, Wis. Died June 1, 1922.

HARVEY, Philip Francis, colonel U.S.A.; b. Thorneville, O., Dec. 12, 1844; s. Philip and Elizabeth Mary (Hodge) H.; ed. Bapt. U., Burlington, Ia., U. of Mich.; M.D., U. of Ia., 1864; M.D., Bellevue Hosp. Med. Coll. (New York U.), 1866; married. Apptd. from Iowa, asst. surgeon, U.S.A., Nov. 16, 1868; capt. asst. surgeon, Nov. 16, 1871; maj. surgeon, Feb. 9, 1890; lt. col. chief surgeon vols., July 8, 1898; resigned from vol. service, July 31, 1898; lt. col. deputy surgeon-gen., Feb. 2, 1901; col. asst. surgeon gen., Aug. 6, 1903. Served in med. dept. U.S.A. during Civil War, med. dept. U.S.A. during Sioux Indian wars, 1876, 1890-91, and during Spanish-Am. War and Philippine insurrection; prof. surgery, Nat. U., Washington, 1886-88; retired, Dec. 12, 1908. Unitarian. Republican. Home: Denver, Colo. Died July 7, 1922.

HARVEY, Roland Bridendall, diplomatic service; b. Baltimore Co., Md., Oct. 12, 1870; s. William Pinkney and Virginia (Jordan) H.; prep. edn., pvt. schs. in U.S. and tutors in Switzerland, France, Germany; B.A., Johns Hopkins, 1895; LL.B., U. of Md., 1896; unmarried. Admitted to Md. bar, 1896, N.Y. bar, 1897; practiced at New York, 1897-99; asst. state's atty., Baltimore, 1904-07, resigned; apptd. after examination, May 17, 1909, sec. Am. Legation and consul gen. to Roumania and Servia, and sec. of diplomatic agency in Bulgaria, Aug. 27, 1909; authorized to act as chargé d'affaires at Sofia, Mar. 24-July 1, 1910; sec. legation and consul gen. to Roumania, Servia and Bulgaria, June 24, 1910; apptd. sec. legation, Lima, Peru, Feb. 1, 1912, but did not serve; chargé d'affaires, May 22-Aug. 26, 1912, and Sept. 20, 1913-Feb. 6, 1914, sec. legation, Aug. 26-Sept. 20, 1913, at Santiago, Chile; 2d sec. embassy at Berlin, Feb. 21, 1914—. Democrat. Home: Baltimore, Md. Died Nov. 14, 1917.

HARVEY, William Edwin, soldier and lawyer; b. Kirkwood, Mo., Aug. 6, 1871; s. William Egbert and Martha Bates Beach H.; LL.B., Columbian, 1893, LL.M., 1894; m. Katherine E. Heydrick, Feb. 12, 1896. Practiced law in Washington, D.C., 1893-1919, as mem. King & King and asso. of its predecessors. Enlisted in D.C.N.G., 1890, and served through all grades; apptd. brig. gen. comdg. militia D.C., June 4, 1915; commd. brig. gen. N.A., Aug. 22, 1917, and assigned to command 75th Inf. Brigade, at Camp Shelby, Hattiesburg, Miss., trans. to command 1st Prov. Brig. Army Troops; hon. disch., May 9, 1918. Episcopalian. Home: Chevy Chase, D.C. Died Jan. 13, 1922.

HARVEY, William Hope ("Coin Harvey"); b. Buffalo, W.Va., Aug. 16, 1851; s. Col. Robert and Anna M. (Hope) H.; ed. Buffalo Academy and Marshall College, W.Va.; practiced law, 1871-84; m. Anna R. Halliday, 1876 (divorced 1929); m. 2d, Mrs. May Elliston Leake, April 21, 1929. With Paul's School of Statesmanship, 1924; builder of pyramid at Monte Ne, Ark. Chief executive officer World's Money Ednl. League. Author: Coin's Financial School, 1894; Coin's Financial School Up to Date, 1895; Coin on Money, Trusts and Imperialism, 1899; The Remedy, 1915; Common Sense, 1920; "The Book" (setting forth cause and remedy of present world conditions), 1930. Nominated as candidate of "Liberty Party" for pres. of U.S., Aug. 1931. Home: Monte Ne, Ark. Died Feb. 11, 1936.

HARVEY, William Lemuel, pres. Internat. Milling Co.; b. Pittsfield, Ill., July 13, 1871; s. Samuel Clemens and Julia (Chapman) H.; B.S., Mich. State Coll., 1893; m. Eleanora Holub, Aug. 26, 1899; children—Helen (wife of Dr. John A. T. Caine), Margaret, William Edward, Robert John, John Henry, Jane Louise. Sec. New Prague Flour Milling Co., 1896-1910; successively dir., sec. and treas. Internat. Milling Co., 1910-31, pres., 1931—; v.p. Robin Hood Mills Ltd. Republican. Home: Minneapolis, Minn. Died Mar. 13, 1938.

HARWOOD, Edwin, P.E. clergyman; b. Phila., Aug. 21, 1822; s. Lilburn and Sarah Ann H.; grad. Univ. of Pa.; studied theology, Andover and Gen. Theol. Sem., New York; ordained, 1844 (D.D., Trinity Coll., Hartford, 1862); m. Marion E. DeKay, Oct. 7, 1846. Successively rector Christ Ch., Oyster Bay; St. Paul's, E. Chester, N.Y.; St. James', New York; Ch. of the Incarnation, New York; prof. Berkeley Div. School; rector Trinity Ch., New Haven, 1859-95. Deputy to the Gen. Conv. P.E. Ch., 1877-1895. Home: New Haven, Conn. Died 1902.

HARWOOD, Frank James, mfr.; b. Crown Point, N.Y., Dec. 25, 1855; s. Allen Penfield and Ann (Penfield) H.; ed. Hudson River Inst. and Claverack (N.Y.) Coll.; m. Harriet Ann Harwood, Jan. 24, 1882; children—Ruth, Ann Penfield; m. 2d, Elizabeth P. Van Patten, Jan. 1, 1936. Moved to Ripon, Wis., 1874, to Appleton, 1876; entered woolen mfg. business, 1876, became gen. mgr. Appleton Woolen Mills, 1881, pres. and gen. mgr., 1910—; sec. Appleton Superior Knitting Works, from its orgn., 1899; dir. First National Bank, First Trust Co. Mem. Common Council, Appleton, 6 yrs.; mem. Sch. Bd., 9 yrs. Trustee Ripon Coll. Mem. exec. com. Nat. Council Congl. Chs., and elected moderator same, Oct. 20, 1925; supt. S.S. 40 yrs.; mem. Y.M.C.A. State Bd., 45 yrs.; pres. local Y.M.C.A. 16 yrs. Republican. Home: Appleton, Wis. Died Aug. 19, 1940.

HARWOOD, George Alexander, ry. official; b. Waltham, Mass., Aug. 29, 1875; s. Alexander Thorndyke and Emma Dean (Smith) H.; grad. English High Sch., Boston, 1892; B.S. in E.E. and C.E., Tufts Coll., 1898, M.S., 1901, D.Sc., 1913; m. Grace Isabelle Hawley, Sept. 19, 1900; children—Herbert H., Robert T. With N.Y.C. R.R., Apr. 1900—; apptd. chief engr. electric zone improvements, in charge constrn. Grand Central Terminal and improvements in connection with electrification to Peekskill and North White Plains, Nov. 1, 1906; engring. asst. to v.p. N.Y.C. Lines, July 1, 1916; engring. asst. to federal mgr., in charge of gen. engring. work on N.Y.C. R.R., June 10, 1918; corporate chief engr. N.Y.C. Lines and Rutland R.R. Co., 1918-20; asst. to pres. N.Y.C. Lines, 1920-24; v.p. same, in charge improvements and development, from Apr. 9, 1924. Trustee Tufts Coll.; pres. Bd. Edn. School Dist. No. 1, Scarsdale, N.Y. Republican. Conglist. Home: Scarsdale, N.Y. Died Nov. 4, 1926.

HARWOOD, William Sumner, writer; b. Charles City, Ia., Oct. 16, 1857; s. Sanford and Keziah (Dryer) H.; ed. pub. schs. and State Univ. of Ia.; m. Estelle L. Balch, June 17, 1885. Engaged in newspaper work in Chicago, Minneapolis, and St. Paul, 1883-97. Author: New Creations in Plant Life, an authoritative account of the life and work of Luther Burbank, 1905; The New Earth—A Recital of the Triumphs of Modern Agriculture in America, 1906. Home: Los Gatos, Calif. Died 1908.

HASBROUCK, Alfred, army officer; b. Poughkeepsie, N.Y., Nov. 1, 1858; s. Alfred and Margaret Anne (Manning) H.; grad. U.S. Mil. Acad., 1883, Army War Coll., 1913. Commd. 2d lt. 14th Inf., June 13, 1883; 1st lt. 13th Inf., Feb. 24, 1891; trans. to 14th Inf., July 20, 1891; capt. of inf., July 2, 1898; assigned to 14th Inf., Jan. 1, 1899; maj. 29th Inf., July 2, 1906; trans. to 14th Inf., Aug. 29, 1906; lt. col. 18th Inf., Nov. 27, 1911; col. of inf., Oct. 24, 1915; col. 20th Inf., Dec. 10, 1915. Prof. mil. science and tactics, Riverview Mil. Acad., Poughkeepsie, N.Y., 1895-98; went with regt. to Philippines, 1898; in China during Boxer troubles; again in Philippines, 1903-5 (in field against Pulajanes, Jan.-Mar. 1905) and 1908-10. Home: Poughkeepsie, N.Y. Died Aug. 19, 1920.

HASBROUCK, Henry Cornelius, brig. gen. U.S.A.; b. Newburgh, N.Y., Oct. 26, 1839; s. William Cornelius and Mary Elizabeth (Roe) H.; apptd. from N.Y., and grad. U.S. Mil. Acad., 1861; m. Laetitia Viele Warren, Oct. 26, 1882. Apptd. 2d lt. 4th Arty., May 6, 1861; 1st lt., May 14, 1861; capt., July 26, 1866; maj., Mar. 5, 1887; lt. col., Oct. 29, 1896; brig. gen. U.S.V., May 27, 1898; hon. discharged, June 12, 1899; col. 7th U.S. Arty., Feb. 13, 1899; brig. gen., Dec. 1, 1902. Bvtd.: capt., Oct. 25, 1862, "for gallant and meritorious services" in action at Blackwater Bridge, Va.; maj., Feb. 27, 1890, "for gallant services" in action against Indians at Sorass Lake, Cal., May 10, 1873. Commandant cadets U.S. Mil. Acad., 1882-88; mem. of bd. that prepared inf., cav. and arty. drill regulations for use in U.S.A.; comd. 2d Brigade, 2d Div., 7th Army Corps and Dept. of Pinar del Rio, Cuba, 1898-99; retired at own request, over 40 yrs.' service, Jan. 5, 1903. Home: Newburgh, N.Y. Died 1910.

HASCALL, Milo Smith, brig. gen. U.S. vols.; b. Le Roy, N.Y., Aug. 5, 1829; s. Amasa Hascall; went to Goshen, Ind., 1846; grad. West Point, 1852; served in garrison, 1852-53; resigned; practiced law in Ind.; pros. atty., 1856-58; clerk of court, 1859-61; served private to brig. gen. vols., 1861-64; at Stone River was the only gen. officer who held his ground and saved the day after the defeat and rout of Union army on the 1st day of the battle; took part in siege at Atlanta; resigned Commn. Oct. 27, 1864; after war banker at Goshen, Ind.; real estate operator, Chicago, 1890—. Home: Oak Park, Ill. Died 1904.

HASCALL, Wilbur (Fisk), composer; b. Shrewsbury, Mass., Dec. 15, 1854; s. Jefferson and Lavinia (Livermore) H.; ed. N.E. Conservatory of Music, Boston U. Coll. of Music and under pvt. tutors; m. Henrietta Hunt, Jan. 6, 1887. Connected with Fraternity Pub. Co., 1888—, now mgr. Author of many songs; among them are: The Survivor; We're A-Weary; The Galleon; Cavalier Song; Oh, that We Two Were Maying; The Night Has a Thousand Eyes (English); The Twinkle in Her Eye; To Hear the Wee Birds Sing (Irish); Behold My Love; The Lassie's Lament (Scotch). Home: Boston, Mass. Died Mar. 1, 1925.

HASE, William Frederick, army officer; b. Milwaukee, Wis., Aug. 31, 1874; s. Henry and Minnie (Bergeler) H.; LL.B., U. of Wis., 1897; grad. Coast Arty. Sch., 1902, advanced course, 1909, Sch. of the Line, 1920, Gen. Staff Sch., 1921, Army War Coll., 1922; m. Pearl Newman, June 6, 1906; children—Mary Elizabeth (wife of H. A. Brusher, U.S.A.), Hilda Houghton. Began as lawyer, 1897; commd. 2d lt. 6th Arty., July 9, 1898, advanced through grades to col., Feb. 1918; maj. gen., chief of coast arty., Mar. 1934—. Decorated D.S.M. (U.S.). Lutheran. Home: Washington, D.C. Died Jan. 20, 1935.

HASELTINE, George, lawyer; b. Bradford, Mass., Aug. 17, 1829; s. Col. Richard and Rebecca (Gage) H.; A.B., Dartmouth, 1854, A.M., 1857; LL.B., Albany Law Sch., 1856; (LL.D., U. of Chicago, 1872). Began practice of law at St. Louis, 1855; went to Eng. on law business, 1857; edited London American, 1860-62; engaged in patent practice, London, 1862-76, New York, 1876—. Gave evidence in 1871 before select com. of British Parliament on patents; was an organizer and active mem. of the Vienna Patent Congress, 1873; fellow British Soc. of Arts. Retired. Home: Hoboken, N.J. Died Sept. 9, 1915.

HASELTON, Seneca, judge; b. Westford, Vt., Feb. 26, 1848; s. Rev. Amos and Amelia (Frink) H.; A.B., U. of Vt., 1871, A.M., 1874; LL.B., U. of Mich., 1875; (LL.D., U. of Vt., 1909); unmarried. Instr. mathematics, U. of Mich., 1873-74; admitted to bar, 1875; mem. Vt. Ho. of Rep., 1886; mayor Burlington, 1891-94; U.S. minister to Venezuela, 1894-95; Dem. candidate for U.S. senator, 1900; judge Supreme Ct. of Vt., Apr. 3, 1902-Dec. 1, 1906; chief Superior judge, Dec. 1, 1906-Dec. 1, 1908; judge Supreme Ct., 1908-May 1, 1919. Democrat. Was for a time reporter of decisions of Supreme Ct., and edited Vols. 72, 73, Vt. Reports. Trustee Vt. State Library. Home: Burlington, Vt. Died July 21, 1921.

HASEMAN, Charles, prof. mathematics; b. Linton, Ind., Sept. 27, 1880; s. John Diederich and Elizabeth (Schultz) H.; A.B., Ind. U., 1903, A.M., 1906; Ph.D., U. of Göttingen, Germany, 1907; m. Lucile Bernice Ulery, May 28, 1917. Teacher of mathematics, pub. sch., Linton, Ind., 1898-1901; same, high sch., Elwood, Ind., 1904-05; student asst. in mathematics, Ind. U., 1905-06, instr., 1907-08, asst. prof., 1908-09; asso. prof. mathematics and mechanics, U. of Nev., 1909-10, prof. 1910—; dean of men, same university, 1929—. Dir. U. of Nev. Glee Club, 1910-27. Republican. Mason. Rotarian. Author of General Mathematical Analysis, Analytic Geometry, Differential Calculus, Integral Calculus, Applied Mechanics—all mimeographed textbooks. Home: Reno, Nev. Died July 9, 1931.

HASKELL, Charles Nathaniel, governor; b. Putnam Co., O., Mar. 13, 1860; s. George R. and Jane H.; ed. pub. schs.; m. Lucie Pomeroy, Oct. 11, 1881 (died 1888); m. 2d, Lillie E. Gallup, Sept. 1889. Admitted to bar, 1880, and began practice at Ottawa, O.; engaged in ry. building and other construction work, 1888; went to Muskogee I.T., 1901, and built various lines of ry. in Okla.; an organizer and chmn. bd. Middle States Oil Corp. Mem. Okla. Constl. Conv.; 1st gov. state of Okla., term 1907-11. Democrat. Died July 5, 1933.

HASKELL, Edward Howard, mfr.; b. Gloucester, Mass., Oct. 5, 1845; s. William H. and Mary (Smith) H.; ed. pub. schs., Gloucester; m. Hattie J. Smith, June 27, 1866. Signal officer in Civil War, 1861-64; taking part in Burnside's campaign in N.C.; campaigns, 1861-64, Army of Potomac, Va. and Tenn., and with Sherman in Ga. Paper and textile machinery mfr.; pres. Haskell-Dawes Machine Co., Am. Rotary Power Co.; dir. Great Northern Paper Co. Asst. adj. gen. staff of Gov. Long, 1880-83; mem. Mass. legislature, 1877; mem. exec. council of Mass., 1882-85. Home: Newton Center, Mass. Died Nov. 14, 1925.

HASKELL, Edwin Bradbury; b. Livermore, Me., Aug. 24, 1837; s. Moses Greenleaf and Rosilia Haines Haskell; ed. Kent's Hill Sem., Me.; m. Celia Hill, Aug. 29, 1861. Entered Portland (Me.) Advertiser office, 1854; went to Boston, 1856; became reporter on Boston Journal, 1857; changed to Boston Herald, Mar. 1860; purchased interest in Herald, Oct. 1865; editor Herald, 1862-87; owns interest in Minneapolis Journal. Mem. Met. Park Commn.; pres. trustees Newton (Mass.) Pub. Library, Newton Cemetery Corp. Home: Auburndale, Mass. Died 1907.

HASKELL, Eugene Elwin, civil engr.; b. Holland, N.Y., May 10, 1855; s. Addison Wells and Sarah (Colby) H.; ed. Forestville, N.Y., Acad.; B.C.E., Cornell, 1879, C.E., 1890; m. Lettie E. Wright, Feb. 4, 1880. With U.S. Lake Survey, Detroit, 1879; Sioux City & St. Paul R.R., 1880; Miss. River Commission, St. Louis, 1880-85; U.S. Coast and Geod. Survey, Washington, 1885-93; U.S. Lake Survey, Detroit, 1893-1906; dean Coll. Civil Engring., Cornell, 1906-21, emeritus; hon. chmn. Engring. Bd. of Review, Sanitary Dist. of Chicago, 1924-25. Mem. Am. Sect. Internat. Waterways Commn., 1906-15. Home: Hamburg, N.Y. Died Jan. 29, 1933.

HASKELL, Frederick Tudor, banker; b. Ogdensburg, N.Y.; s. Ralzamon and Annette C. (Ray) H.; married. Resident Chicago, 1867—; in banking business from young manhood; pres. Continental Ill. Safe Deposit Co.; dir. and v.p. Elgin Nat. Watch Co.; dir. Pittsburgh, Ft. Wayne & Chicago Ry. Co. Pres. bd. trustees Lawrence Hall; trustee James C. King Home for Old Men, Old Peoples Home, St. Luke's Hosp. Republican. Home: Chicago, Ill. Died Sept. 13, 1935.

HASKELL, Harriet Newell (Miss), educator; b. Waldoboro, Me., Jan. 14, 1835; d. Bela Bangs and Eliza (Sproul) H.; grad. Mt. Holyoke Coll., 1855 (Litt.D., 1904). Taught in pub. schs., Boston, Waldoboro, Me., and classical sem., Castleton, Vt., till 1867; prin. Monticello Female Sem., Godfrey, Ill., 1867—. Home: Godfrey, Ill. Died 1907.

HASKELL, Harry Leland, army officer; b. in Me., Sept. 24, 1840. Served as pvt. Co. A, and sergt. maj. 125th N.Y. Inf., Aug. 26, 1862-Mar. 16, 1863; 2d lt., Mar. 16, 1863; capt., Dec. 7, 1863; hon. mustered out, Sept. 22, 1864; commd. capt. 7th U.S. Vet. Inf., May 10, 1865; hon. mustered out, Apr. 27, 1866; apptd. from N.Y., 2d lt. 12th U.S. Inf., Aug. 30, 1867; 1st lt., June 30, 1877; capt., Jan. 2, 1888; maj., Mar. 2, 1899; transferred to 30th Inf., July 17, 1901; lt. col. 20th Inf., Sept. 27, 1901; transferred to 12th Inf., Oct. 15, 1901; col. 27th Inf., July 31, 1903; transferred to 3d Inf., Sept. 10, 1903; brig. gen., Jan. 20, 1904; retired at own request, over 30 yrs.' service, Jan. 21, 1904. Died 1908.

HASKELL, J(onathan) Amory, mfr.; b. N.Y. City, July 7, 1861; s. Samuel and Mary Frances (Amory) H.; ed. mil. inst., Briarcliff, N.Y.; m. Margaret Moore Riker, Dec. 9, 1891. With A. & L. Neilson, New York, 1879-83; became connected with Rochester & Pittsburgh Coal & Iron Co., New York, 1883, advancing to gen. mgr. and treas.; pres. Repauno Chemical Co., Wilmington, Del., 1892-1912; pres. Laflin & Rand Powder Co., 1895-1912; v.p., E. I. du Pont de Nemours & Co., General Motors Corp.; pres. Gen. Motors Export Co., Gen. Motors Acceptance Corp.; dir. Fidelity-Phenix Fire Ins. Co., Manhattan Eye, Ear and Throat Hosp. Homes: New York, and Red Bank, N.J. Died Sept. 9, 1923.

HASKELL, Thomas Hawes, asso. justice supreme judicial court Me., 1884—, present term expiring 1905; b. New Gloucester, Me., May 18, 1842; grad. Norway Liberal Inst., 1862 (A.M., Bowdoin); m. Elizabeth Parsons Whitman, 1867. In Union army, 1862-63; admitted to Me. bar, Feb. 1865; he began practice in Portland, 1866. Republican. Author: New Gloucester Centennial, 1874; Haskell's Reports (2 vols.). Home: Portland, Me. Died 1900.

HASKELL, William Edwin, newspaper publisher; b. Charlestown, Mass., June 18, 1862; s. Edwin Bradbury and Celia Anne (Hill) H.; A.B., Harvard, 1884; m. Helen Eggleston, Jan. 26, 1903. Started and ran for 3 yrs., Harvard Daily Herald, which became Harvard Crimson; became part owner and editor, Minneapolis Tribune, 1884; part owner Minneapolis Journal, 1885, sold Tribune, 1889; started (with J. T. Murphy) Superior (Wis.) Evening Telegram, 1889, and sold interest, 1890; bought Minneapolis Times, 1894; sold interest in Minneapolis Journal, 1900, and sold Times, 1902; business mgr. New York American and Journal, 1902-04; bought interest in Boston Herald, 1904, and was for a time editor and manager of same. Died May 2, 1933.

HASKIN, William Lawrence, brig. gen. U.S.A.; b. Houlton, Me., May 31, 1841; s. Gen. Joseph Abel and Rebecca E. (Sprague) H.; ed. Mexico Acad., Oswego Co., N.Y., 1852-57; C.E., Rensselaer Poly. Inst., 1861; m. Annie L. Davis, Apr. 26, 1865. Apptd. 2d lt. and 1st lt., 1st U.S. Arty., Aug. 5, 1861; promoted through grades to brig. gen., July 28, 1903. Bvtd. capt., July 8, 1863, "for gallant and meritorious services in capture of Port Hudson, La."; maj., Mar. 13, 1865, "for good conduct and gallant services during the war." After Civil War served in N.Y., S.C., Me., Calif., Ore., and Conn. Sent in command of regt. to Cuba, Dec. 1898, and in 1902 was designated to command U.S. troops still remaining there; retired at own request after 40 yrs.' service, July 29, 1903. Home: New London, Conn. Died Sept. 24, 1931.

HASKINS, Caryl Davis, electrical engr.; b. Waltham, Mass., May 22, 1867; s. John F. (mech. engr.) and Helen P. (Davis) H.; ed. in U.S. and Eng., including spl. work in London U.; E.E., U. of Vt.; m. Frances J. Parker, Nov. 1894. Elec. engr. with Ferranti, 1888, Gen. Electric Co., 1889, now mgr. lighting dept., Gen. Electric Co. Inventor autodirigible torpedo, 1896; volunteered for Spanish War and placed 2d in charge of submarine mining operations in Boston Dist., comdg. vol. electric corps, Boston battalion, 1898. Home: Schenectady, N.Y. Deceased.

HASKINS, Charles Homer, univ. prof.; b. Meadville, Pa., Dec. 21, 1870; s. George W. and Rachel A. (McClintock) H.; A.B., Johns Hopkins, 1887, Ph.D., 1890; hon. A.M., Harvard, 1908; Litt.D., U. of Wis., 1910, U. of Strassburg, 1919, Padua and Manchester, 1922, Harvard Univ., 1924, U. of Paris, 1926, U. of Louvain, 1927, U. of Caen, 1932; LL.D., Allegheny Coll., 1915; m. Clare Allen, July 11, 1912; children—George Lee, Charles Allen, Clare Elisabeth. Instr. in history, Johns Hopkins, 1889-90; instr. 1890-91, asst. prof. history, 1891-92, prof. European history, 1892-1902, U. of Wis.; lecturer on history, 1900, prof. history, 1902-12, Gurney prof. history and polit. science, 1912-28, Henry Charles Lea prof. of mediæval history, 1928-31, emeritus prof., 1931—, dean Graduate School of Arts and Sciences, 1908-24, Harvard. Chief of Division of Western Europe, Am. Commn. to Negotiate Peace, 1918-19; Am. mem. Commn. on Belgian and Danish Affairs and spl. com. on Alsace-Lorraine and the Saar Valley, Paris Peace Conf., 1919. Chmn. Am. Council of Learned Societies, 1920-26. Fellow Mediæval Acad. of America (pres. 1926-27). Officier Légion d'Honneur (France); Comdr. Order of Crown of Belgium. Fellow Am. Acad. Arts and Sciences. Author: The Normans in European History, 1915; Norman Institutions, 1918; Some Problems of the Peace Conference (with R. H. Lord), 1920; The Rise of Universities, 1923; Studies in the History of Mediæval Science, 1924; The Renaissance of the Twelfth Century, 1927; Studies in Mediæval Culture, 1929. Editor of the American Historical Series. Home: Cambridge, Mass. Died May 14, 1937.

HASKINS, Charles Waldo, public accountant; b. Brooklyn, N.Y., Jan. 11, 1852; s. Waldo Emerson H.; ed. public schools and Poly. Inst., Brooklyn; m. Henrietta Sherman, d. Albert H. Havemeyer, 1884. Expert under joint commn., 53d Congress, to revise methods of business exec. depts. of U.S., 1893-95; dean New York Univ. School of Commerce, Accounts and Finance, 1900—; examined accounts of Havana and Island of Cuba, for U.S. govt. at close of war; examined accounts of City of Chicago, 1901. Home: New York, N.Y. Died 1903.

HASKINS, Kittredge, congressman; b. Dover, Vt., Apr. 8, 1836; s. Asaph and Amelia (Ward) H.; ed. pub. schs.; admitted to bar, 1858; m. Esther M. Childs, July 1, 1860. Enlisted Co. I, 16th Vt. Vols., Aug. 1862; elected 1st lt.; resigned Mar. 23, 1863; clerk in office of asst. q.-m. vols. at Brattleboro, 1863-66; in law practice at Brattleboro, 1866—. Col. and a.-d.-c. on staff Gov. Washburn, 1869; mem. Rep. State Com., 1869-72; chmn. Rep. Congressional Com., 2d Dist., 1876-84; was state's atty., Windham Co.; U.S. atty., Dist. Vt., 1880-87; mem. Vt. Ho. of Rep., 1872-74, 1896-1900 (speaker, 1898-1900), Senate, 1892-94; mem. joint commn. which established boundary between Vt. and Mass., 1893; mem. 57th to 60th Congresses (1901-09), 2d Vt. Dist. Del. Gen. Conv., P.E. Ch., 4 terms. Now postmaster of Brattleboro. Mason. Home: Brattleboro, Vt. Died Aug. 7, 1916.

HASSAM, Childe, painter, etcher; b. Boston, Oct. 17, 1859; s. Frederick F. and Rose (Hathorne) H.; ed. Boston pub. schs.; art study in Boston and

Paris. Awards: Bronze medal, Paris Expn., 1889; gold medal, Munich, 1892; gold medal, Phila. Art Club, 1892; medal, Chicago Expn., 1893; prize, Cleveland Art Assn., 1893; Webb prize, Soc. Am. Artists, 1895; prize, Boston Art Club, 1896; medal, Carnegie Inst., Pittsburgh, 1898; Temple gold medal, Pa. Acad. Fine Arts, 1899; silver medal, Paris Expn., 1900; gold medal, Buffalo Expn., 1901; gold medal St. Louis Expn., 1904; Thomas B. Clark prize, Nat. Acad., 1905; gold medal, Carnegie Inst., Pittsburgh, 1905; Carnegie prize, Soc. Am. Artists, 1906; Walter Lippincott prize, Pa. Acad. Fine Arts, 1906; Jennie Sesnan gold medal, Pa. Acad. Fine Arts, 1910; Third W. A. Clark and Corcoran bronze medal, Corcoran Gallery, Washington, 1911; 1st W. A. Clark and gold medal, same, 1913; Hudnut prize, Am. Water Color Soc., 1919; water color prize, Phila., 1920; gold medal of honor, Pa. Acad. Fine Arts, 1920; gold medal Sesquicentennial Expn., 1926. Represented in permanent collections of Pa. Acad. Fine Arts; Carnegie Inst., Pittsburgh; Cincinnati Museum; Buffalo Fine Arts Acad.; Boston Art Club; R.I. Sch. of Design; Corcoran Gallery and Freer Collection, Washington, D.C.; Indianapolis Inst.; Smith Coll., Northampton, Mass.; Met. Mus. of Art, New York; Nat. Gallery, Walters Gallery, Baltimore; Portland (Ore.) Art Mus.; Art Inst. Chicago; Detroit Mus.; Worcester Mus.; City Art Mus., St. Louis; Mus. Fine Arts, Boston; Brooklyn Mus.; etc. N.A., 1906; mem. Ten Am. Painters, New York, Société Nationale des Beaux Arts, Paris, The Secession, Munich, Nat. Inst. Arts and Letters, Am. Acad. Arts and Letters, 1921. Home: New York, N.Y. Died Aug. 27, 1935.

HASSAM, John Tyler, lawyer; b. Boston, Sept. 20, 1841; s. John and Abby (Hilton) H.; grad. Harvard, 1863; A.M., 1866; 1st lt. 75th U.S. colored inf., Dec. 8, 1863, to Aug. 1, 1864, taking part in Red River expdn.; studied law; admitted to Suffolk bar, Dec. 13, 1867; gen. practice several yrs.; of late yrs. principally conveyancing; m. Nelly Alden, d. Dr. John Henry Batchelder, Feb. 14, 1878. Interested in hist., geneal. and antiquarian research; mem. New England Historic Geneal. Soc., etc.; apptd., 1884, by Superior Court, one of commn. to supervise ind'ces in the Registry of Deeds, Suffolk Co. Home: Boston, Mass. Died 1902.

HASSKARL, Joseph F., engineer; b. Hazleton, Pa., June 23, 1863; s. Rev. William R. (D.D.) and Elizabeth (Lang) H.; student Elmhurst (Ill.) Coll., 1880-83; m. M. Clara Baggy, June 17, 1913. Began as civ. and hydraulic engr., at Chicago, 1884; served as principal or chief engr., Phila. Dist., U.S. Engr. Dept.; dir. Dept. of Wharves, Docks and Ferries, Phila., 1909-12; commr. new water supply for Phila., 1920-24; chmn. Harbor and Navigation Com. of Philadelphia Chamber Commerce. Had charge various dredging enterprises, requiring removal of more than 50,000,000 cubic yds. of material from rivers and harbors; designed and built breakwater at entrance of Delaware Bay; first reinforced concrete pier (fireproof) in America. Republican. Lutheran. Mason. Home: Philadelphia, Pa. Died Mar. 5, 1926.

HASSLER, Ferdinand Augustus, author; b. nr. Norfolk, Va., Mar. 6, 1844; s. Charles W. (U.S.N.) and Anna J. (Nourse) H.; M.D., U. of Pa., 1866, Ph.D., 1875; m. Elizabeth Emily Hall, June 27, 1882. Page, U.S. Senate, 1856-62; prof. materia medica, Lincoln U., 1873; teacher W. Phila. Med. Inst., 1872. Author of numerous papers on scientific subjects and general literature, poems, children's stories, etc., 1866—; was principal writer of Medical Register and Directory of the United States, 1873. Invented and patented a word register for typewriters. Home: Santa Ana, Calif. Died Aug. 9, 1919.

HASSLER, Simon, musician, b. in Bavaria, July 25, 1832; came with parents to Philadelphia, 1842; studied music; made first public appearance as violinist in 1852; joined orchestra established by his father; later its leader; leader Walnut St. Theatre orchestra, 1865-72; then Chestnut St. Theatre; from 1882 leader Chestnut Street Opera House orchestra. Has conducted military band and orchestra summer concerts at Cape May; elected to direct Centennial orchestra, 1876, and has conducted many festivals; composed music for Shakespeare's plays, etc. Home: Philadelphia, Pa. Died 1901.

HASTINGS, Charles Douglas, automobile mfr.; b. Hillsdale, Mich., Aug. 25, 1858; s. Andrew M. and Mary A. (Weir) H.; ed. high sch., Detroit, Mich.; m. Mary Robinson, Apr. 3, 1883; children—Don T., Helen L. Began as traveling salesman, 18—; railroad accountant, 1890-94; wholesale business, 1894-1902; with Olds Motor Works, 1902-07; with Hupp Motor Car Co., Detroit, 1908-34, was chmn. bd. Mem. Detroit Bd. of Commerce, Automobile Chamber Commerce. Republican. Mason. Home: Detroit, Mich. Died Aug. 7, 1940.

HASTINGS, Charles Sheldon, physicist; Ph.B., Yale, 1870, Ph.D., 1873. Instr. physics, Yale, 1871-73; later asso. prof. physics, Johns Hopkins; prof. physics, Sheffield Scientific Sch. (Yale), 1884—. Mem. Nat. Acad. Sciences; fellow A.A.A.S. Author (with F. E. Beach) Text-Book on General Physics, 1899; Light—A Consideration of the More Familiar Phenomena of Optics, 1901. Home: New Haven, Conn. Died Feb. 1, 1932.

HASTINGS, Daniel Hartman, capitalist; b. Salona, Pa., Feb. 26, 1849; common school edn.; reared on farm; practiced law, 1875-88; largely interested in coal mines and banking; adj. gen. of Pa., 1887-91; had charge of the relief measures at Johnstown flood, 1889; delegate at large to Nat. Rep. Conv., 1888, and placed John Serman in nomination for President; chmn. Pa. delegation Nat. conv., 1896, placing M. S. Quay in nomination for President; gov. Pa., 1895-99. Home: Bellefont, Pa. Died 1903.

HASTINGS, Frank Seymour, banking; b. Mendham, N.J., May 31, 1853; s. Rev. Thomas S. and Fanny (de Groot) H.; ed. pvt. schs.; m. Caroline Fanning, Oct. 14, 1875. Began, 1869, in employ of Williams & Guion, shipping business; later with Fabbri & Chauncey; became asso. with various Edison cos., 1882 and later; became pres. and gen. mgr. Commercial Acetylene Supply Co.; pres. Transatlantic Trust Co. Pres. Ophthalmic Hosp., dir. MacDowell Memorial Assn. Skilled organist, and composer of songs. Decorated Order of St. Stanislaus, by Czar of Russia, 1908. Republican. Presbyn. Home: New York, N.Y. Died July 5, 1924.

HASTINGS, Frank Warren, author; b. Waterford, Vt., Dec. 31, 1856; s. Warren and Lydia (Richardson) H.; grad. St. Johnsbury (Vt.) Acad., 1875; m. Emilie E. Houghton, Aug. 14, 1878. Farmer. Republican. Author: Wed to a Lunatic, 1896, 1901; The Untamed Philosopher, 1906; With the Plugolians, 1906; Mariah and the Neighbors. Home: West Glover, Vt. Died Feb. 3, 1925.

HASTINGS, George Henry, lawyer; b. Coral, Ill., Aug. 26, 1848; s. Carlisle and Hannah (Granger) H.; pub. sch. edn.; m. Helen M. Richardson, Dec. 28, 1874 (dec.); 1 son, Robert Richardson. Admitted to bar, Lincoln, Neb., 1870; sr. mem. Hastings & McGintie, to 1896, Hastings & Hastings, 1896-99, Hastings & Ireland, 1904-17, Hastings & Hastings, Aug. 1, 1917—; also pres. Crete Loan & Savings Assn. County Judge, Saline Co., Neb., 1872-74; mem. Neb. Ho. of Rep., 1874-76; pros. atty. Saline Co., 1887-90; Rep. Presdl. elector, 1888; atty. gen., Neb., 1890-95; mayor rof Crete, 1900-01, city atty., 10 yrs. Episcopalian. Mason. Home: Crete, Neb. Died July 18, 1926.

HASTINGS, Samuel Dexter, merchant; b. Leicester, Mass., July 24, 1816; s. Simon and Elizabeth H.; ed. common sch. and 1 yr. in high sch., Boston; m. Margaretta Shubert, Aug. 1, 1837. Commission business, Phila., 1837-45; moved to Wis. where he was farmer, mcht., banker and real estate agt.; retired from active business over 25 yrs. ago. State treas., Wis., 1858-66; sec. State Bd. Charities and Reform, Wis., 1871-74; mem. Wis. legislature, 1849, 1857; head Order of Good Templars for the World, 1863-68, 1873; mem. exec. com. and treas. Nat. Prohibition Party, 1881-1902; for more than 60 yrs. interested in anti-slavery and temperance causes. Pres. Monona Lake Assembly, Madison, Wis. Home: Evanston, Ill., and Green Bay, Wis. Died 1903.

HASTINGS, Thomas, architect; b. New York, Mar. 11, 1860; s. Thomas Samuel and Fanny (de Groot) H.; grad. École des Beaux Arts Paris, France, 1884; LL.D., from Lafayette Coll., Easton, Pa. Partner with John M. Carrère, in firm Carrère & Hastings, 1885—. Firm architects of the Ponce de Leon and Alcazar hotels, St. Augustine, Fla., New York Pub. Library, Nat. Acad. Design, and many other notable buildings. N.A., 1907; mem. Am. Acad. Arts and Letters, Soc. Beaux Arts, Architects (pres.), Royal Inst. Brit. Architects, L'Institute de France. Royal medalist, 1922. Chevalier Legion of Honor (France). Home: Old Westbury, L.I. Died Oct. 22, 1929.

HASTINGS, Thomas Samuel, theologian; b. Utica, N.Y., Aug. 28, 1827; s. Thomas and Mary (Seymour) H.; A.B., Hamilton Coll., 1848; grad. Union Theol. Sem., 1851; (D.D., New York U., 1865; LL.D., Princeton, 1888; L.H.D., Hamilton, 1897); m. Fanny de Groot, July 1, 1852; father of Thomas H. Ordained Presbyn. ministry, 1852; pastor Mendham, N.J., 1852-56, West Ch., New York, 1856-82; prof. sacred rhetoric and pastoral theology, 1882-1904, prof. emeritus and lecturer pastoral theology, 1904—, pres. faculty, 1887-97, Union Theol. Sem., New York, N.Y. Died 1911.

HASTINGS, Wells Southworth, author; b. New Haven, Conn., June 24, 1878; s. Col. George Seymour and Harriet Mills (Southworth) H.; B.A., Yale, 1902; m. Elisabeth Putnam Stearns, June 28, 1902. Dir. Phoenix-Hermetic Co., Metallic Decorating Co. (New York), and Hampshire Paper Co. (S. Hadley Falls, Mass.). Progressive. Episcopalian. Author: The Professor's Mystery (with Brian Hooker), 1911; The Man in the Brown Derby, 1911. Home: Farmington, Conn. Died May 1923.

HASTINGS, William Granger, judge; b. Woodstock, Ill., Apr. 9, 1853; s. Carlisle and Hannah (Granger) H.; grad. U. of Chicago, 1876; LL.D., U. of Neb., 1925; m. Elizabeth Hackley, Oct. 20, 1880. Went to Neb., 1876; admitted to bar, 1877; mem. Neb. Senate, 1885-87; Dem. candidate for Congress, 1st Neb. Dist., 1888; pros. atty., Saline Co., 1889; dist. judge 7th Jud. Dist., 1891-1900; Supreme Court commr., 1901-04; Dem.-Populist candidate for judge Supreme Court, Neb., 1904; dean U. of Neb. Law Sch. (resigned, 1920); acting chancellor U. of Neb., 1918; judge 4th Jud. District, Omaha, reëlected, 1924, 28, 32, and candidate for reëlection in 1936. Member Commn. on Uniform State Laws. Author of the Development of Law as Illustrated by the Decisions Upon Police Power (Am. Philos. Soc. $2,000 prize essay). Translator, from the Russian of Korkunov's General Theory of Law. Home: Omaha, Neb. Died Jan. 9, 1937.

HASTINGS, William Wirt, congressman; b. of Cherokee parentage, Ind. Ty., Dec. 31, 1866; s. Yell and Louisa J. H.; grad. from Cherokee Male Sem., 1884; LL.B., Vanderbilt U., 1889; m. Lulu Starr, of Cherokee Nation, Dec. 9, 1896. Atty. gen. for Cherokee Nation, 1891-95, and has represented same in winding up of tribal affairs at Washington, D.C., 1890—; nat. atty. for Cherokee Tribe, 1907-14; mem. 64th to 66th Congresses (1915-21), and 68th to 73d Congresses (1923-35), 2d Okla. Dist. Home: Tahlequah, Okla. Died Apr. 8, 1938.

HASWELL, Charles Haynes, civil, marine and mech. engr.; b. New York, May 22, 1809 (English parentage); grad. Collegiate Inst. of Joseph Nelson; entered engine works of James P. Allaire; designed engines and boilers for U.S. steam frigate Fulton; was 1st chief engr. and engr. in chief U.S.N., 1836-51; designed and operated 1st steam launch; first to introduce zinc in marine boilers and in bottom of iron vessels to arrest oxidation of the plates; mem. navy bd. that designed 6 steam frigates; retired and began private practice; built merchant vessels; designed and constructed ballasted crib, Hart Island; was engr. health dept., Dept. Charities and Correction, trustee New York and Brooklyn bridge; from 1898 cons. engr. bd. public improvements New York, and engr. in charge extension and improvement Riker's Island, L.I. Sound; asst. engr. Bd. of Estimate and Appropriation. Mem. 1855-58, pres., 1858, New York Bd. Councilmen. Author: Mechanics' and Engineers' Book, 1842 (69th edit., 1903); Mechanics' Tables, 1854; Mensuration and Practical Geometry, 1856. Home: New York, N.Y. Died 1907.

HATCH, Edward Wingate, judge; b. Friendship, N.Y., Nov. 26, 1852; s. Capt. Jeremiah and Lacy Ann (Rigdon) H.; A.M., Williams Coll., 1901; (LL.D., Middlebury Coll., Vt., 1902, Alfred U., N.Y., 1907). Admitted to bar at Buffalo, 1876; dist. atty., Erie Co., 1881-86; judge Superior Ct., Buffalo, 1887-95; elected to Supreme Court of N.Y., 1895, for term expiring Dec. 31, 1909; assigned to Appellate Div., 2d Dept., Brooklyn, 1896-1900; transferred to Appellate Div., 1st Dept., New York, 1900; resigned, Sept. 30, 1905. Republican. Mem. Parker, Hatch & Sheehan, 1905-12; practiced with W. F. Sheehan, N.Y. City, 1912-15. Died June 1, 1924.

HATCH, Edwin Glentworth, engr.; b. Brooklyn, N.Y., Mar. 25, 1886; s. Edwin Austin (M.D.) and Emilie Jane (Pesinger) H.; M.E. Stevens Inst. of Tech., Hoboken, N.J., 1907; m. Amalia Riches, Apr. 5, 1920; 1 son, Edwin Pesinger. Held engineering position successively with Lackawanna Steel Co., Oakland Chem. Co., Safety Car Heating & Lighting Co., N.Y.C.&H.R. R.R. Co. until 1910; treas. and mgr. Clark Electric & Mfg. Co., 1910-15; cons. engr., Victoria Falls & Transvaal Power Co., serving the Rand Mines in S. Africa, 1915-24; pres. Edwin G. Hatch & Co., Inc., industrial engrs. and financial council specializing in corp. financing. Home: Brooklyn, N.Y. Died Jan. 24, 1933.

HATCH, Everard E., army officer; b. Montville, Me., July 18, 1859; s. Enos M. and Kate A. (Newham) H.; grad. U.S. Mil. Acad., 1884, Army War Coll., 1915; m. Mellie S. Rowe, Aug. 7, 1884; m. 2d, Annie K. Spring, Sept. 12, 1899. Second lt. 18th Inf., June 15, 1884; promoted through grades to brig. gen. N.A., Aug. 5, 1917. Duty U. of Me., 1888-91, Clinton Liberal Inst., Ft. Plain, N.Y., 1894-95; participated in assault and capture of Manila, P.I., Aug. 13, 1898; with regt. at capture of Iloilo, Feb. 11, 1899, and at engagement at Jaro, Feb. 12, 1899; again in Philippines, 1903-04 and 1907-09. Organized and trained 158th Inf. Brig., Aug. 1917-June 1918; comd. 154th Depot Brig., June-Nov. 1918, and in charge instrn. and training same, Nov. 1918-Mar. 1919, comd. same, Mar.-June 1919; with A.E.F., June-Aug. 1919; hon. disch. as brig. gen. N.A., May 24, 1918; comd. Fort Benjamin Harrison, Ind., Aug. 1919—. Episcopalian. Deceased.

HATCH, Francis March, lawyer; b. Portsmouth, N.H., June 7, 1852; s. Albert R. and Margaret Rooksby (Harris) H.; A.B., Bowdoin, 1873 (LL.D., 1917); m. Alicia Hawes, Oct. 31, 1888. Practiced law in Honolulu, 1878-1904; v.p. Provisional Govt. of Hawaii, Feb. 1893-July 1894; minister of foreign affairs, Republic of Hawaii, July 1894-Oct. 1895;

E.E. and M.P., Hawaii to Washington, Dec. 1895-July 1898; one of signers of the Hawaiian treaty of annexation; apptd. justice Supreme Court, Ty. of Hawaii, 1904; resigned account ill health, Jan. 31, 1905. Home: Honolulu, T.H. Died Mar. 19, 1923.

HATCH, Frederick Thomas, civil engr.; b. Haverhill, Mass., Nov. 21, 1855; s. Nathaniel and Catherine P. (Harbach) H.; ed. Phillips Acad., Andover, Mass.; m. Alice Gertrude Hill, Aug. 13, 1884; m. 2d, Mrs. Nola P. Underwood, May 9, 1916. Began with engr. corps Pittsburgh, Cincinnati & St. Louis Ry., 1880; became connected with Vandalia R.R. Co., 1894, as supt. Terre Haute & Logansport R.R.; chief engr. Vandalia Line, 1905-17; chief engr. maintenance of way, St. Louis System P.,C.,C.&St.L. R.R., consolidation of Vandalia with P.,C.,C.&St.L. R.R., Jan. 1, 1917, cons. engr. same. Republican. Conglist. Mason. Home: St. Louis, Mo. Died Mar. 9, 1920.

HATCH, Henry James, army officer; b. Charlotte, Mich., Apr. 28, 1869; s. Hiram F. and Sarah J. H.; B.S. in C.E., U. of Mich., 1891; grad. Arty. Sch., 1903; Army War Coll., 1925; m. Alice E. Hill, June 26, 1893; children—Walter A., Melton A. Cashier Farmers Nat. Bank, Arkansas City, 1891-97; commd. 2d lt. arty., U.S.A., July 9, 1898; promoted through grades to col., Feb. 6, 1918; brig. gen. N.A., June 26, 1918; col., C.A.C., July 1, 1920, brig. gen., Sept. 5, 1927. Chief of heavy arty. sect. of staff of chief of arty., A.E.F., 1918-19; comdr. Ry. Arty., 2d Army, Oct. and Nov. 1918; later comdr. coast defense of Los Angeles, Calif., later comdr. Harbor Defenses, Manila and Sobig Bay; now comdr. 2d Coast Artillery Dist. Decorated D.S.M. (U.S.); Officier Légion d'Honneur, France. Home: Washington, D.C. Died Dec. 31, 1931.

HATCH, John Porter, col. U.S.A., retired Jan. 9, 1886; b. Oswego, N.Y., Jan. 9, 1822, desc. in 7th generation from Thomas Hatch Freeman of Mass. Colony, 1635; mother was Hannah, d. Otis Reed, Salina, N.Y.; grad. West Point, 1845; served in Mexican war; bvtd. 1st lt. and later capt. for gallantry; capt., Oct. 13, 1860; brig. gen. vols., Sept. 28, 1861; took part in many battles; twice wounded; reached bvt. rank of brig. gen., U.S.A., and maj. gen. vols.; apptd. maj., 4th cav., at end of war; col., 3d cav., 1881-86; m. Adelaide, d. Christian J. Burckle, Oswego, N.Y., June 14, 1851. Home: New York, N.Y. Deceased.

HATCH, Samuel Grantham, ry. official; b. St. Louis, Mar. 22, 1865; s. George F. and Lavinia (Ford) H.; ed. pub. schs.; m. Mattie Sinclair, July 20, 1903; m. 2d, Anne Henry, Nov. 27, 1912. Began ry. service with C.,B.&Q. R.R., at Keokuk, Ia., 1882-85; afterward with the Cotton Belt Route at St. Louis, Louisville and Memphis, 1885-96; since 1896; with the I.C. R.R., as div. pass. agt. at Cincinnati, 1896-1900, asst. gen. pass. agt. at Chicago, Apr. 1, 1900-July 1, 1905, gen. pass. agt., July 1, 1905-Mar. 1, 1911, pass. traffic mgr., Mar. 1, 1911—. Home: Chicago, Ill. Died July 12, 1918.

HATCHER, John Bell, curator, dept. of vertebrate paleontology. Carnegie Museum, Pittsburgh, Pa., Feb. 1, 1900—; b. Cooperstown, Ill., Oct. 11, 1861; s. John and Margaret C. H.; grad. Yale Univ., 1884, spl. studies in natural history, more especially geology and vertebrate paleontology; m. Anna M. Peterson, Oct. 10, 1887. Asst. to Prof. O. C. Marsh on the U.S. Geol. Survey, July 1, 1884; asst. in geology, Yale Univ., 1890; curator of vertebrate paleontology and asst. in geology, Princeton U., 1893; conducted 3 scientific expdns. to Patagonia and Tierra del Fuego for Princeton, from 1896 to 1899. Author: Narrative of Princeton Expedition to Patagonia, 1903. Home: Pittsburgh, Pa. Died 1904.

HATCHER, William E., clergyman; b. Bedford Co., Va., July 25, 1834; s. Henry and Mary (Latham) H.; A.B. Richmond (Va.) Coll., 1858; (D.D., Richmond; LL.D., Denison; L.H.D., Colgate); m. Oranie Virginia Snead, 1864. Pres. bd. trustees Richmond Coll., 1893-1908, Woman's Coll. of Richmond, 1892-93, and now Fork Union (Va.) Mil. Acad.; pres. Bapt. Edn. Bd. of Va., 1875-1901, Bapt. Orphanage of Va., 1891—. Editor Religious Herald, Baltimore Baptist, Baptist Argus. Author: The Pastor and the Sunday School, 1902; John Jasper, 1908; Along the Trail of the Friendly Years, 1910. Home: Fork Union, Va. Died Aug. 24, 1912.

HATFIELD, Charles Folsom; b. Warren, O., May 2, 1862; s. Deming Niles and Adelia M. (Gay) H.; ed. high sch., Cleveland, O.; student organ under Prof. Frank Bassett, pres. Cleveland Conservatory of Music; m. Mary Williams, Oct. 1, 1885. With Standard Oil Co., Cleveland and New York, 1881-89, Waters-Pierce Oil Co. (S.O. Co. subdivision), St. Louis, 1889-1904; founder, and sec. Western Review (fraternal publn.), St. Louis and Chicago, 1904-22. Eastern rep. San Francisco Expn., 1913-15; sec. St. Louis Conv., Publicity and Tourist Bur., 1916—. Prominent many yrs. in fraternal orgns.; sec. and treas. Mo. Fraternal Congress 11 yrs. Prominent officially in Louisiana Pur. Expn. and sec. Nat. Fraternal Sanitarium for Tuberculosis. Mem. International Assn. Conv. Bureaus (ex-pres.), Nat. Assn.

Commercial Orgn. Secs. and over 100 nat., state civic and commercial orgns.; pres. for 20th yr. Am. Community Advertising Assn. and mem. nat. council Advertising Fedn. of America; sec. Am. Travel Development Assn.; ex-sec. Internat. Travel Federation. Mem. Chamber of Commerce of U.S. Mason. Church organist more than 25 yrs. Leader in effort to establish a U.S. travel commn. Home: St. Louis, Mo. Died June 1939.

HATFIELD, James Tobias, coal mine operator; b. Lincoln, Ill., Feb. 25, 1865; s. Henry and Amelia (Butts) H.; educated pub. and private schs.; m. Ellen Daisey Methven, Nov. 5, 1891; children—Eva Jane, Ruth Amelia (Mrs. Harry Lincoln Gordon), Louise, Virginia Thorpe, James Tobias, John Stanhope, Henry Reed, Helen Jean. Founder Hatfield Coal Co., Covington, Ky., 1892, and pres. until company merged with E. J. Hickey Transportation Co., Reliance Coal & Coke Co., Licking Valley Coal Digger Co., W.Va. Washed Coal Co., and Plymouth Coal & Mining Co., 1924, under title of the Hatfield-Reliance Coal Co., of which was v.p., and Julius Fleischmann, pres.; pres. same co. on decease of Mr. Fleischmann, 1925; now chmn. bd. Hatfield-Campbell's Creek Coal Co. (consolidation of Hatfield Reliance and Campbell Creek Coal Cos.); also officer or dir. various other corps. Pres. Hazard Coal Operators Exchange, 1925-26; Gt. Kanawha River Improvement Assn.; mem. exec. com. Ohio Valley Improvement Assn. Regarded as an authority on the bituminous coal industry. A founder and 1st pres. Covington Council Boy Scouts of America. Republican. Methodist. Mason. Home: Covington, Ky. Died July 20, 1938.

HATFIELD, Joshua Alexander, capitalist; b. Phila., June 11, 1863; s. Daniel Keyser and Margaret (Alexander) H.; ed. pvt. and pub. schs., and 2 yrs. Hill Sch., Pottstown, Pa.; m. Mary Ellen Byers, Nov. 8, 1888. With Pottstown Iron Co., office boy to gen. sales agent, 1880-96; with Pencoyd Iron Works, Phila., 1897, New York agent, same, 1898-1900; asst. to pres., 1900, pres. 1901, then pres. Am. Bridge Co. Mem. Met. Mus. of Art, Pa. Soc. Republican. Presbyn. Home: New York, N.Y. Died July 4, 1931.

HATFIELD, Marcus Patten, physician, author; s. Rev. R. M. and Elizabeth A. H.; grad. Wesleyan U. Conn., 1870. Chicago Med. Coll., 1872; student at Zurich and Univ. of Berlin; m. Hattie A., d. Bishop W L. Harris, 1876. Prof. Chicago Med. Coll., 1875-96; prof. pediatrics. Chicago Clinical Sch., 1898—. Pres. med. bd. Jackson Park Fresh Air Sanitarium; attending physician Children's Dept., Wesley Hosp.; cons. physician Chicago Orphan Asylum; clinical prof. pediatrics. Med. Dept. Univ. of Ill. Author: Compend of Diseases of Children, 1903; Acute Contagious Diseases of Children, 1902. Editor of the Chicago Clinic. Home: Chicago, Ill. Died 1909.

HATHAWAY, Arthur Stafford, college prof.; b. Keeler, Mich., Sept. 15, 1855; s. Aaron Stafford and Alizina B. (Robertson) H.; B.S., Cornell U., 1879; Johns Hopkins, 1880-85; m. Susan Hoxie, Dec. 22, 1878 (died Mar. 13, 1880); m. 2d, Ada J. Jackson, of Baltimore. Sept. 8, 1885. Instr. mathematics, 1885-90, asst. prof., 1890-91, Cornell U.; prof. mathematics, Rose Poly. Inst., 1891-1920; retired under pension, 1920. Reporter and editor Proc. U.S. Electric Conf., Phila., and Lord Kelvin's lectures on molecular dynamics. Baltimore, 1884. Trustee, treas. sch. bd. Terre Haute, 1910-14; pres. Terre Haute Chautauqua Assn., 1905-07. Progressive. Mem. Soc. of Friends. Home: Houston, Tex. Died Mar. 11, 1934.

HATHAWAY, Forrest Henry, brig. gen. U.S.A.; b. in Vt., Oct. 7, 1844. Enlisted as pvt. Co. G. 16th Vt. Inf., Sept. 4. 1862; hon. disch., Aug. 10, 1863; commd. capt. 107th U.S.C.T., June 30, 1864; bvtd. maj., July 25. 1866; hon. mustered out, Feb. 20, 1867; apptd. from Vt., 2d lt. 41st U.S. Inf., Mar. 7. 1867; transferred to 40th Inf., Nov. 27, 1867; assigned to 5th Inf., Dec. 17, 1869; 1st lt., Sept. 4, 1878; capt. asst. q.m., Feb. 13, 1882; maj. q.m., Sept. 12, 1894; lt. col. q.m. vols., Sept. 3, 1898-Mar. 2, 1899; lt. col. deputy q.m. gen., Aug. 12, 1900; col. asst. q.m. gen., Apr. 12, 1903; brig. gen., Jan. 20, 1904; retired at own request, after 40 yrs.' service, Jan. 21, 1904. Bvtd. 1st lt., Mar. 7, 1867, for battle of Fair Oaks, Va.; capt., Mar. 7. 1867, battle of Newmarket, Va. Died July 29, 1912.

HATHAWAY, George Henry, pres. Redpath Bur.; b. Sydney, Australia, May 19, 1843; s. Elisha and Phoebe B. (Williams) H.; came to U.S., 1854; grad. Boston Latin Sch., 1862; m. Georgiana Weber, June 11, 1891. Served as pvt. Co. E, 24th Mass. Vols., Civil War, 1862-65; entered dry goods commn. business as clk., 1865; 1st clk. Arlington Woolen Mills, Lawrence. Mass., 1867-68; joined Redpath Lyceum Bur., 1870; became propr. and mgr. same, 1875, pres. from incorporation, 1903. Republican. Episcopalian. Home: Brookline, Mass. Died Apr. 7, 1931.

HATTON, Charles Harold; b. Wichita, Kan., Apr. 23, 1880; s. Charles and Louisa (Davidson) H.;

student U. of Colo., 1900-02; A.B., Southwestern Coll., Winfield, Kan., 1905; grad. study, Sorbonne, Paris; m. Fode Stanley, Jan. 15, 1902. Began as ins. broker, Wichita, 1902; engaged in insurance and investment business, 1902-18; investment, loan and bond business, 1918—; pres. Interstate Public Utilities Corp., Republic Investment Co.; secretary Peoples Sand & Supply Co. In charge raising of war funds, Wichita, World War. Formerly civil service commr., Wichita; campaign mgr. Wichita Community Chest, 1930; v.p. Wichita Business Assn. Republican. Mem. Disciples of Christ Ch. Mason. Home: Wichita, Kan. Died Aug. 23, 1936.

HATTON, T. Chalkley, sanitary engr.; b. Avondale, Pa., Aug. 11, 1860; s. Chalkley and Hannah H.; ed. Maplewood Inst., Delaware Co., Pa.; hon. M.C.E., Pa. Mil. Coll.; m. Catharine E. Hinkson, 1888; 1 dau., Anna Elizabeth (Mrs. R. Horton Norris, Jr.). With engring. dept. S.P.,M.&M. Ry., 1878-82; hydraulic surveys, Dept. of Pub. Works, Dominion of Can., 1882-83; asst. engr. City of Wilmington, Del., 1883-89; chief engr. street and sewer dept., Wilmington, 1890-1900; cons. practice, water works, sanitation and street improvements, 1898-1914; chief engr. Sewerage Commn., City of Milwaukee, Wis., 1914-27; chief engr. Metropolitan Sewerage, County of Milwaukee, 1921-27; private practice as consulting engr. 1927—. Republican. Episcopalian. Home: Milwaukee, Wis. Deceased.

HATTSTAEDT, John James, teacher of piano; b. Monroe, Mich., Dec. 29, 1851; s. Rev. William and Mary (Schmid) H.; ed. Concordia Coll., Ft. Wayne, Ind.; musical edn. by pvt. instrn. in Boston and in Germany; m. Kate May Castle, Dec. 27, 1882; children—John Robert, Louise Annie (Mrs. Hugh Comer Winter). Began teaching piano, 1870, at Detroit; taught at St. Louis, 1872-73; teacher of piano, Chicago Musical Coll., 1875-86; founded Am. Conservatory of Music, Chicago, 1886, and became its pres., also a director. Lecturer on history of music, æsthetics, pedagogics, etc. Lutheran. Democrat. Home: Chicago, Ill. Died Nov. 30, 1931.

HAUBOLD, Herman A., author, surgeon; b. N.Y. City, Dec. 21, 1867; s. Arthur and Anna (Keppler) H.; M.D., Bellevue Hosp. Med. Coll. (New York U.), 1889; unmarried. Teacher of surgery, New York U. 1901—; now clin. professor; surgeon to Broad Street Hospital; consulting surgeon Nassau, Memorial, St. Mark's, Harlem and Broad Street hospitals. Capt. and asst. surgeon 8th N.Y. Inf., Spanish-Am. War. Catholic. Author: Preparation and After Treatment of Operative Cases, 1910; Surgery of the Brain, 1910; Principles and Practice of Surgery, 1921. Home: New York, N.Y. Died May 5, 1931.

HAUGAN, Henry Alexander, banker; b. Chicago, Ill., Aug. 14, 1878; s. Helge Alexander and Laura A. (Wardrum) H.; B.S., Dartmouth, 1903; m. Blanche Ernst, June 8, 1908; 1 son, Henry A. Messenger, 1903, in State Bank of Chicago (established by father, 1879, and inc. as state bank, 1891); successively clk., teller, asst. cashier, v.p., and pres., 1919—; dir. Fidelity & Deposit Co. of Md. Treas. U. of Ill. 1909-12, Chicago Assn. Commerce, 1922. Republican. Conglist. Home: Chicago, Ill. Died Dec. 1, 1928.

HAUGEN, Gilbert N., congressman; b. Rock Co., Wis., Apr. 21, 1859; common sch. edn.; at age of 14 entered business; at 18 purchased a farm in Worth Co., Ia., continuing his studies at Decorah, Ia., and finishing with a course at Janesville, Wis.; m. Bertha Elise Evensen, Oct. 25, 1885. One of organizers, and pres. Northwood Banking Co., 1890—, operating banks at Northwood and Kensett, Ia. Has held various local offices; co. treas. Worth Co., Ia., 1887-93; mem. Ia. Ho. of Rep. 2 terms; mem. 56th to 72d Congresses (1899-1933), 4th Ia. Dist.; chmn. Com. on Agr., and author of Haugen Packer Control and Stockyards Act. Republican. Home: Northwood, Ia. Died July 18, 1933.

HAUGEN, Nils Pederson; b. Norway, Mar. 9, 1849; s. Peder N. and Karen (Stensrud) H.; brought to U.S., 1854; Luther Coll., Decorah, Ia., 1868-71; LL.B., U. of Mich., 1874; m. Ingeborg A. Rasmussen, Mar. 1, 1875. Court reporter, 1874-81, also practice of law; mem. Wis. Ho. of Rep., 1879-80; Wis. State railroad commr., 1882-86; mem. 50th to 53d Congresses (1887-95), 8th and 10th Wis. dists.; practiced law at River Falls, Wis., 1895-1901; member State Tax Commn., 1901-21 (chmn. 1911-21); tax counsel to Bd. of Equalization, State of Mont. Republican. Mason, Elk. Was one of first advocates of income tax for State of Wis. and writer on that subject. Author: Pioneer and Political Reminiscenses, 1929. Home: Madison, Wis. Died Apr. 23, 1931.

HAUPT, Alexander James Derbyshire, clergyman; b. Greenfield, Mass., June 1, 1859; s. Gen. Herman and Ann Cecilia (Keller) H.; grad. Boys' Central High Sch., Phila., 1878 (distinguished rank and principal's certificate); A.B., U. of Pa., 1882; grad. Phila. Luth. Theol. Sem., 1884, D.D., Pa. Coll., 1907; m. Ida L. Boyer, June 10, 1885; children—Edith Anna (Mrs. H. A. Bossart), Margaret Cecilia (Mrs. O. V. Werner), A. James, John Boyer, George

Edward, Henry Harpster. Ordained Luth. ministry, 1884; assisted in organizing Memorial English Evang. Luth. Ch., St. Paul, Minn., 1883 (the first English Luth. mission in the city), and was its pastor, 1884-1907; supt. Luth. Inner Mission work, Pittsburgh, 1907-10; pastor Salem English Evang. Luth. Ch., Albert Lea, Minn., 1910-14; social service dir. League of Protestant Women, St. Paul, 1914-17, Church Fedn., 1917-21; exec. sec. Home Protective Assn. of St. Paul, 1921-23; sec. Luth. Colony of Mercy, 1919-22; spl. probation officer Juvenile Court, 1914-23; pastor St. Mark's Ch., Grand Forks, N.D., 1923-27; now pastor Zion Ch., Horicon, Wis. One of organizers, pres. 2 yrs., Synod of the Northwest; mem. Nat. and Minn. State confs. social work, Nat. Divorce Commn. of Minn., 1906, Luth. Brotherhood of America, Luth. Foundation of N.Dak. (v.p.) Minn. Inner Mission Soc., Inner Mission Soc. of N.Dak. (dir.). Scoutmaster, Boy Scouts America, 1925—. Mem. exec. bd. World's Purity Fedn., 1921—. Republican. Author: History of the Synod of the Northwest, 1901; The Golden Ladder, 1933. Home: Horicon, Wis. Died Sept. 29, 1934.

HAUPT, Charles Elvin, clergyman; b. Harrisburg, Pa., Oct. 6, 1852; s. Lewis Leeds and Louisa (Keeler) H.; A.B., U. of Pa., 1872; grad. Luth. Theol. Sem., Phila., 1875; (D.D., Franklin and Marshall Coll., 1900). Ordained Luth. ministry, 1875; asst. to Rev. Dr. E. Greenwald, pastor Holy Trinity Ch., Lancaster, Pa., 1875-80; pastor Grace Ch., Lancaster, Jan. 15, 1880. Organized Madam Cotta Coll. for Young Women (now Shippen Sch. for Girls); founder Lancaster Gen. Hosp.; organizer Emmanuel Luth. Ch. Home: Lancaster, Pa. Deceased.

HAUPT, Herman, engr.; b. Phila., Mar. 26, 1817; s. Jacob H.; grad. West Point, 1835; entered army but resigned, Oct. 1835; prof. civil engring., Pa. Coll., 1844-47; gen. supt. chief engr. and dir. Pa. R.R. and engr. Hoosac Tunnel, 1847-61; col., brig. gen. and chief of bureau, U.S. Mil. Rys., in Civil War; gen. mgr. Piedmont Air Line, 1875; later engr. Tide-Water Pipe Line Co. and gen. mgr. Northern Pacific R.R. Author: General Theory of Bridges, 1852; Military Bridges, 1863. Died 1905.

HAUPT, Lewis Muhlenberg, civil engr.; b. Gettysburg, Pa., Mar. 21, 1844; s. Gen. Herman and Ann Cecilia (Keller) H.; ed. Lawrence Scientific Sch. (Harvard); grad. U.S. Mil. Acad., 1867; hon. M.A., U. of Pa.; Sc.D., Muhlenberg; LL.D., Pa. Coll.; m. Isabella Christiana Cromwell, June 26, 1873 (died 1912); children—Eva Ruth (dec.), Elsie Catherine (dec.), Walter Cromwell (dec.), Bessie May, Eleanor (dec.), Florence Belle, Susan Gertrude, Edna Schaeffer, Lewis Herman. Second lt. engrs. U.S.A., June 17, 1867; engr. officer, survey of Great Lakes, till Feb. 1869; 5th mil. dist. Texas, 1869; resigned, Sept. 20, 1869; topog. engr. Fairmount Park, Phila., to 1872; prof. civ. engring., U. of Pa., 1872-92; practices his profession in Phila. In charge of hydrog. survey of Delaware River, 1873, Franklin Inst. Drawing Sch., 1874-79, triangulation of Eastern Pa., 1875-80. Member of Nicaragua Canal Commn., 1897-99, Isthmian Canal Commn., 1899-1902; pres. Colombia-Cauca Arbitration, 1897; chief engr. survey for ship canal across N.J., 1894; consulting engr. Lake Erie & Ohio River Ship Canal, etc.; prof. civil engring., Franklin Inst. Editor of Am. Engineering Register, 1885-86. Inventor of "Reaction Breakwater" for creating channels through ocean bars, 1887, successfully applied by the U.S. Premiums: Magellanic, by Am. Philos. Soc., 1887; Nat. Export Expn., 1899; Paris Expn., 1900; Elliott Cresson gold medal, Franklin Inst., 1901; also was awarded gold and silver medals, St. Louis Expn., 1904. Patented automatic devices for reclaiming eroded beaches by hooked jetties, 1911, since applied on the L.I. and N.J. coasts. Saved Barnegat Light, 1920, by two pile jetties, also beaches at Sea Isle City, Cape May Point, Surf City, Stone Harbor, Townsend's Inlet, Beach Haven, etc. Author: Physical Phenomena of Harbor Entrances (prize essay American Philos. Society), 1887; Canals and Their Economic Relation to Transportation, 1890; A Move for Better Roads, 1891; The Nation and the Waterways; The Miss. River Problems; Opening of Aransas Pass, Tex.; The New York Entrance. Home: Bala-Cynwyd, Pa. Died Mar. 10, 1937.

HAUPT, Paul, orientalist; b. Görlitz, Germany, Nov. 25, 1858; s. Karl Gottlieb and Elsie (Hülse) H.; grad. Gymnasium Augustum, Görlitz, 1876; Ph.D., U. of Leipzig, 1878; post-grad. studies univs. of Leipzig and Berlin and British Mus.; LL.D., Glasgow, 1902; m. Margaret Giede, June 9, 1884 (died 1884); m. 2d, Minnie Giede, Mar. 8, 1886; children—Walter C. (dec.), Erik G., H. Harold, Alida. Pvt. docent, 1880-83, prof. Assyriology, 1883-89, U. of Göttingen; Spence prof. Semitic langs. and dir. Oriental Sem., Johns Hopkins, 1883—. Hon. curator Oriental antiquities, 1888, hon. curator div. of historic archæology, 1898; asso. in historic archæology, 1905, U.S. Nat. Mus., Washington. Hon. asso. Soc. Oriental Research. Knight Royal Prussian Order Red Eagle, 1901. Am. mem. Internat. Com. on Oriental Congresses; 1st U.S. del. Internat. Congress Orientalists, Rome, 1899, Algiers, 1905, Copenhagen, 1908, Athens, 1912 (pres. Semitic sect. 1897, 99, 1912); 1st U.S. del. Internat. Congress History of Religions, Paris, 1900, Basel, 1904 (pres. Semitic sect.), Oxford, 1908; U.S. del. Internat. Congress Americanists, Stuttgart, 1904, Vienna, 1908. Mem. Soc. of Friends. Editor: The Polychrome Bible, 1898; New Critical Edition of Hebrew Text of the Old Testament, 1893. Co-editor: The Assyriological Library, 1881—; Johns Hopkins Contributions to Assyriology and Comparative Semitic Grammar, 1889—. Author: The Assyrian E-vowel, 1887; The Book of Ecclesiastes, 1905; The Book of Nahum, 1907; The Book of Esther, 1908; The Book of Micah, 1910. Home: Roland Park, Baltimore, Md. Died Dec. 15, 1926.

HAUSER, Samuel Thomas, governor; b. Falmouth, Ky., Jan. 10, 1833; s. Samuel Thomas and Mary Ann (Kennett) H.; ed. as civil engr.; m. Ellen Fanny Farrah, Oct. 4, 1871 (died 1906). Engr. on Mo. Py. Ry., 1854; prospector along upper waters Mo. and Columbia rivers, 1862; opened bank, with partner, at Virginia City, Mont., 1865; pres. First Nat. Bank, Helena, Mont., 1866—; built 1st smelter and 1st silver mill in Mont.; prominent mem. Vigilance Com. in pioneer days. Gov. of Mont., 1886-88. Democrat. Home: Helena, Mont. Died Nov. 10, 1914.

HAUSSLING, Jacob, mayor; b. Newark, N.J., Feb. 22, 1855; s. Henry and Josephine (Freund) H.; ed. parochial and pub. schs. and business coll.; m. Ellen Elligott, Jan. 11, 1874. Became sole owner, 1897, of mineral and soda water business established by father; pres. H. Haussling (Inc.), Haussling Soda Apparatus Mfg. Co. Sheriff Essex Co., N.J., 1891-93; was mem. N.J. Ho. of Rep.; mayor of Newark, 4 terms, 1906-14. Democrat. Roman Catholic. Home: Newark, N.J. Died Feb. 25, 1921.

HAVARD, Valery, surgeon U.S.A.; b. Compiègne, France, Feb. 18, 1846; grad. Inst. of Beauvais, France, 1865, Manhattan Coll., New York, 1869; M.D., Univ. Med. College, New York, 1869; m. Agnes J. Hewitt, Nov. 1885; children—Eugenie P., Aline, Valery. Asst. surgeon, Nov. 10, 1874; capt. asst. surgeon, Nov. 10, 1879; maj. surgeon, Feb. 27, 1891; lt. col. chief surgeon vols., Aug. 1-Nov. 5, 1898; lt. col. deputy surgeon gen., Oct. 24, 1901; col. asst. surgeon gen., Apr. 26, 1904. Chief surgeon 5th Corps under Gen. Shafter in Santiago de Cuba, 1898, and of Dept. of Cuba under Gen. Wood, 1900-01; mil. attaché to the Russian Army in Manchuria, Nov. 16, 1904-May 1, 1905; chief surgeon Dept. of the East, 1905-06; pres. Army Med. Sch. and in charge of Library and Museum Division, Med. Dept. U.S.A., 1906-10; retired by operation of law, Feb. 18, 1910. Recalled to active duty, Sept. 22, 1917, and ordered to Havana to reorganize med. dept. Cuban Army and Navy; relieved from Cuban service, May 1923. Author of Manual of Military Hygiene (pub. under authority and with approval of Surgeon Gen. U.S.A.). Home: Fairfield, Conn. Died Nov. 6, 1927.

HAVEMEYER, Henry Osborne, sugar refiner; b. New York, Oct. 18, 1847; s. Frederick Christian H.; ed. public and private schs.; m. Louisine Waldron Elder, 1883. Mem., 1869, and a few yrs. later mgr. Havemeyers & Elder, sugar refiners. Organized 1891, and became pres., Am. Sugar Refining Co. (capital now $75,000,000), uniting the large sugar interests of the U.S.; pres. and dir. Am. Coffee Co.; trustee Colonial Trust Co.; also officer or dir. in other corps. Presented public schoolhouse, costing $250,000, to Greenwich, Conn. Home: Greenwich, Conn. Died 1907.

HAVEMEYER, John Craig, sugar refiner; b. New York, May 31, 1833; s. William Frederick and Sarah Agnes (Craig) H.; bro. of William Frederick H.; ed. Anthon Grammar Sch., and New York U.; m. Alice Alide, d. Hon. John M. Francis, 1872. Clerk wholesale grocery, 1851-52; traveled in Europe, Syria and Egypt, 1852-53; clerk in sugar refinery, 1854-56; established sugar refinery, Brooklyn, 1856; partner Havemeyer Bros. & Co., 1871-80; sr. mem. J. C. Havemeyer & Bro. (retired); dir. in several railroads and other corps. Writer and speaker on polit., moral and religious topics. Home: Yonkers, N.Y. Died June 8, 1922.

HAVEMEYER, Theodore Augustus, corp. executive; b. N.Y. City; s. Theodore Augustus and Emily (deLoosey) Havemeyer; student Columbia; m. Katherine Aymar Sands. Dir. Brooklyn Eastern Dist. Terminal; dir. Brooklyn Elevator & Milling Co., Havemeyers & Elder, Inc., Scranton & Lehigh Coal Co. Pres. N.Y. Hort. Soc. Died July 30, 1936.

HAVEMEYER, William Frederick, banker; b. New York, Mar. 31, 1850; s. William F. and Sarah Agnes (Craig) H.; bro. of John Craig H.; ed. pvt. schs.; m. Josephine Harmon, Apr. 3, 1877. Pres. Nat. Bank of N. America; pres. Queens Co. Safe Deposit Co.; dir. N.Y. Mortgage & Security Co., Chelsea Realty Co., Colo. Eastern Ry. Co., Corn Exchange Bank, Title Ins. Co. of N.Y.; trustee N. River Savings Bank. Mem. Council of New York U.; founder Havemeyer Laboratory, New York U. Mem. Nat. Acad. of Design, etc. Home: New York, N.Y. Died Sept. 7, 1913.

HAVEN, Franklin, banker; s. Franklin H.; grad. Harvard, 1857; studied law, and was admitted to bar, 1861; served in Civil War as capt. and a.-d.-c. on staff of Maj. Gen. McDowell, Apr. 15, 1862; lt. col. 2d Calif. Cav., Jan. 11, 1865. U.S. asst. treas. at Boston, 1868-79; actuary N.E. Trust Co., 1879-84; succeeded his father as pres. Merchant's Nat. Bank, 1884; also pres. Boston Clearing House Assn.; v.p. Mass. Hosp. Life Ins. Co., N.E. Trust Co., etc.; treas. Mass. Gen. Hosp., 1884—. Home: Boston, Mass. Died 1908.

HAVEN, George Griswold, banker; pres. and dir. Metropolitan Opera and Real Estate Co., and Worcester, Nashua & Rochester R.R. Co.; v.p. Pittsburgh, Ft. Wayne & Chicago Ry. Co.; dir. Nat. Bank of Commerce, A.,T.&S.F. Ry. Co., Bank of America, N.Y. & Harlem R.R., Santa Fe Pacific R.R. Co., Fifth Av. Trust Co., Guaranty Trust Co. of N.Y., Morton Trust Co.; also many other corps. Home: New York, N.Y. Died 1908.

HAVEN, Joseph Emerson, consular service; b. Chicago, Ill., Jan. 19, 1885; s. Prof. Joseph (M.D.) and Fanny (Barnard) H.; ed. high sch.; studied medicine, U. of Lille, France; married. Consul at St. Christopher, W.I., 1904-07, Crefeld, Germany, 1907-08, Roubaix, France, 1908-14, Catania, Italy, 1914-16, Turin, Italy, 1916-20, Trieste, 1920-22, Florence, Mar. 30, 1923—. Spl. mission in Albania, Jan. 30-June 1, 1919; del. to Portorose Conf., 1921. Conglist. Mason. Home: Chicago, Ill. Died May 4, 1937.

HAVEN, William Ingraham, clergyman; b. Westfield, Mass., Jan. 30, 1856; s. Gilbert and Mary (Ingraham) H.; A.B., Wesleyan U., 1877, A.M. 1881, D.D., 1899, LL.D., 1921; student Drew Theol. Sem., 1878-79; S.T.B., Boston U., 1881; m. Minnie G. Speare, Apr. 25, 1894. Pres. Latin and Greek, Claflin U., 1877-78; ordained M.E. ministry, 1881; pastor Eggleston Sq., Boston, 1881-83, Newton Center, Mass., 1884-86, First Ch., Boston, 1887-91, Saratoga Street Ch., E. Boston, 1892-93, St. Mark's, Brookline, 1894-99; gen. sec. Am. Bible Society, Jan. 1, 1899—. Pres. Young People's Christian League, 1887; one of founders Epworth League (v.p., 1889-1909); pres. Epworth League in N.E., 1890; mem. Bd. of Foreign Missions M.E. Ch., 1899-1924; mem. Ecumenical Meth. Conf., 1901, 11; mem. various coms. Federal Council Chs. of Christ in America; trustee Boston U., Wesleyan U., Drew Theol. Seminary. Home: Summit, N.J. Died June 5, 1928.

HAVENS, Frank Colton, capitalist; b. Sag Harbor, N.Y., Nov. 21, 1848; s. Wickham Sayre and Sarah (Darling) H.; ed. pub. schs.; m. Sadie Bell, Nev. 1873 (dec.); m. 2d, Lila Rand, May 1892. Went to sea at 15; settled in San Francisco, Calif., 1865; clk., later teller for bank of Savings & Loan Soc.; mem. San Francisco Stock Exchange, 1880-84; organized successfully The Home Benefit Life Assn., Am. Investment Union, Mut. Investment Union, The Realty Syndicate, operating extensively in real estate and street rys., in Oakland, Calif., and vicinity; organizer, 1906, and pres. Peoples' Water Co., of Oakland; pres. Mahogany & Encalyptus Land Co. Home: Piedmont, Calif. Died Feb. 9, 1918.

HAVENS, James Smith, congressman; b. Weedsport, N.Y., May 28, 1859; s. Dexter E. and Lucy Bell (Smith) H.; A.B., Yale, 1884; m. Caroline Prindle Sammons, Jan. 16, 1894; children—Lucy Prindle (Mrs. Roland E. Parker), dec., Mary Eleanor, James Dexter, Nathaniel Foote. Admitted to bar, 1886, and began practice at Rochester; elected to 61st Congress, from 32d N.Y. Dist., Apr. 19, 1910, for unexpired term (1910-11), of James Breck Perkins, deceased. Resumed practice of law as mem. Havens & Havens; asst. treas., May 1918; v.p. in charge legal dept. and sec., Oct. 1919, Eastman Kodak Co. Democrat. Home: Rochester, N.Y. Died Feb. 27, 1927.

HAVENS, Paul Egbert, banker; b. Fulton Co., N.Y., May 4, 1839; s. Cevallos D. P. and Eleanor (Frey) H.; pub. sch. edn.; m. Matilda Moore, Dec. 18, 1860. Clerk U.S. Dist. Ct., Jefferson Co., Kan., 1858-64; mem. Kan. Ho. of Rep., 1862; admitted to bar, 1862; in ins. business, 1863-68; mem. Newman & Havens, pvt. bankers, 1868-74; in milling business, 1876-82; pres. Leavenworth Nat. Bank since orgn., 1883; pres. Leavenworth City & Ft. Leavenworth Water Co.; chmn. bd. Leavenworth Savings & Trust Co.; treas. Carr Coal Mining Co. Mem. syndicate which built Kan. Central (now Leavenworth, Kan. & Western) R.R. from Leavenworth to Miltonvale, Kan. (sec., treas. and dir., 1871-82); v.p. Leavenworth Light & Heating Co., 1889-98. Pres. City Council, Leavenworth, 1887. Republican. Unitarian. Mason. Home: Leavenworth, Kan. Died May 6, 1913.

HAVILAND, Clarence Floyd, psychiatrist; b. Spencertown, N.Y., Aug. 15, 1875; s. Norman H. and Henrietta B. (Newman) H.; grad. Fulton (N.Y.) High Sch., 1893; M.D., Syracuse U., 1896; m. Amy Amelia Miller, June 26, 1908. Med. interne, jr. phys., asst. phys. and 2d asst. phys. Manhattan State Hosp., Ward's Island, N.Y., 1897-1910; 1st asst. phys. Kings Park (L.I.) State Hosp., 1910-15; supt. Conn. State Hosp., Middletown, Conn., 1915-21; med. mem. and chmn. N.Y. State Hosp. Commn., 1921-26; supt. Manhattan State Hosp., Wards Island, New York, N.Y., 1926—; mem. N.Y. State Pension Commn. Formerly clin. asst. Dept. of Neurology and Psychiatry, Columbia U. and Cornell U.; clin. prof. psychiatry, Columbia, 1927—. Made survey of Pa. as to conditions attending care of insane, 1914; pres. Conn. Conf. Social Work; formerly mem. Conn. State Commn. on Psychopathic Hosps. Mem. advisory council Eugenics Com. of America; advisory council Milbank Memorial Fund; mental hygiene com. N.Y., State Charity Aid Assn. Asso. editor "The Modern Hospital." Home: New York, N.Y. Died Jan. 1, 1930.

HAWES, James William, lawyer; b. Chatham, Mass., July 9, 1844; s. James and Susannah (Taylor) H.; A.B., Harvard, 1866, A.M., 1869; studied Harvard Law Sch., 1867-68; admitted to bar, 1868; m. Amelia Appleton Prendergast, Oct. 14, 1873. Alderman, New York, 1881, 1882; leading organizer, 1887, of Rep. League of the U.S., and N.Y. State Rep. League; mem. of coms. that secured passage of reform measures relating to New York City; chmn. of various coms. of polit. clubs that secured the constl. conv. of 1894 and assisted in its work; drafted the naturalization law of 1895. Translator: The Letter from Brazil, 1886; The Guarany, a Brazilian Romance. Author: Legislative Reform, 1886; The New Constitution of Brazil, 1892; Edmond Hawes of Yarmouth, Mass., An Emigrant to America in 1635, His Ancestors, and Some of His Descendants, 1914. Retired from practice, 1910. Died Aug. 31, 1918.

HAWES, John Bromham II, M.D.; b. Montclair, N.J., July 11, 1877; s. George Elias and Adelaide Augusta (Dunning) H.; A.B., Harvard, 1900, M.D., 1903; m. Cornelia Lawrence Hyatt, June 1, 1909; 1 son, John Bromham, III. Practiced in Boston, 1904—, specializing in diseases of the chest and tuberculosis; formerly asst. visiting phys. and dir. of clinic for pulmonary diseases at Mass. Gen. Hospital; now dir. Rutland (Mass.) Cottage Sanatoria; consultant diseases of lungs, U.S. Vets.' Bur. Author: Early Pulmonary Tuberculosis, 1913; Consumption, 1915; Tuberculosis and the Community, 1921; Talks on Tuberculosis, 1931; (with Dr. M. J. Stone) Diagnosis and Treatment of Pulmonary Tuberculosis, 1936. Home: Brookline, Mass. Died July 20, 1938.

HAWGOOD, Harry, hydraulic engr.; b. Derbyshire, Eng., Apr. 28, 1853; s. William and Sarah A. (Pike) H.; ed. City of London Sch.; studied civ. and mech. engring. as student on municipal water works and in shipbuilding yard; m. Harriet E. McWain, 1887 (died 1927). Came to U.S., 1880, naturalized citizen, 1895. Asst. engr. maintenance and constrn. govt. rys., Cape of Good Hope, S. Africa, 1874-79; asst. engr. of constrn., C.&N.W. Ry., Madison, Wis., 1880-81; locating engr., Utah Northern Ry., 1881-83; resident engr. Ore. Ry. & Navigation System, 1884-85; in pvt. practice, Portland, Ore., 1885-88; resident engr., S.P. Ry., 1888-95; chief engr. of location and constrn., San Pedro, Los Angeles & Salt Lake R.R., 1900-04; cons. hydraulic engr., Los Angeles, 1895—. Republican. Episcopalian. Home: South Pasadena, Calif. Died Jan. 3, 1931.

HAWK, Wilbur C., newspaper pub.; b. Bakersville, O., Feb. 10, 1881; s. Layfette and Harriett (Pitt) H.; student U. of Kan., 1900-01; m. Mrs. Hallie Lucas, Mar. 16, 1929. Mgr. of clothing store, Atchison, Kan., 1901-11; dep. warden U.S. Penitentiary, Atlanta, 1911-14; in pub. business, 1914—; pres. Lindsay-Nunn Pub. Co., 1926—; co-owner of Globe and News (Amarillo), Globe (Atchison, Kan.), Journal (Falls City, Neb.), Democrat (Memphis, Tex.), Times (El Paso), Reporter-Telegram (Midland, Tex.), Avalanche-Journal (Lubbock, Tex.), Texan (Dalhart, Tex.), Texan (Shamrock, Tex.). Chmn. Rep. State Com. of Kan., 1922-24; chmn. Kan. delegation to Rep. Nat. Conv., Cleveland, 1924; pres. W. Texas Chamber of Commerce, 1932-33. Republican. Presbyn. Elk. Home: Amarillo, Tex. Died Feb. 12, 1936.

HAWKE, James Albert, rear admiral U.S.N.; b. Bristol, Pa., Jan. 31, 1841; s. William and Maria (Stackhouse) H.; M.D., U. of Pa., 1863; m. Mary Whilldin Halfmann, Jan. 29, 1868. Served as asst. surgeon 114th Pa. Vols. and surgeon 215th Pa. Vols. in Civil War; apptd. asst. surg. U.S.N., June 24, 1867; promoted passed asst. surgeon, Feb. 26, 1873; surgeon, May 1, 1879; med. insp., June 8, 1895; med. dir., Sept. 24, 1899; retired, Jan. 31, 1903, with rank of rear admiral for services during Civil War. In charge of Naval Hosp., Widows Island, June 2, 1890-Dec. 9, 1893, Naval Hosp., Mare Island, Calif., 1900-03. Home: Bristol, Pa. Died 1910.

HAWKES, Benjamin Carleton; b. Chicago, Ill., Oct. 8, 1875; s. Moses A. and Louise R. (Starrett) H.; ed. North Division High Sch. (Chicago), prep. dept. Northwestern U., and Chicago Coll. of Law; m. Mary A. Belknap, Oct. 5, 1898; 1 son, Belknap Carleton. Admitted to Ill. bar, 1896, and practiced at Chicago until 1906, mem. firm Varnahan, Slusser, Hawkes & Co.; pres. Standard Playing Card Co., 1898—; pres. U.S. Playing Card Co., 1929-30; pres. Caxton Printing Ink and Color Co., Great Northern Lumber Co. Mem. Art Inst. Chicago. Republican. Episcopalian. Mason. Home: Kenilworth, Ill. Died Dec. 16, 1931.

HAWKES, Forbes (Robert), surgeon; b. N.Y. City, 1865; s. W. Wright and Eliza (Forbes) H.; A.B., Yale, 1887; M.D., Coll. Phys. and Surg. (Columbia), 1891. Began practice at N.Y. City, 1891; consulting surgeon Nassau, St. Joseph's, Fifth Av., Flushing and Presbyn. hosps., Loomis Sanitarium, N.W. Dispensary. Fellow Am. Coll. Surgeons. Home: New York, N.Y. Died Aug. 24, 1940.

HAWKES, McDougall, lawyer; b. New York, July 29, 1862; s. W. Wright and Eliza (Forbes) H.; attended prep. schs. in Conn., Pa., Germany and France; E.M., Columbia, 1885, A.B., 1886, LL.B., 1887. Admitted to bar, 1887, and began practice at New York; authority on internat. matters; counsel for foreign investing interests in the United States. Active in Republican presdl. campaign, 1896; 1st v.p. N.Y. Rep. Co. Com., 1899; commr. of docks and ferries, New York, 1902-03, carrying out the Chelsea improvement; bridge and tunnel commr. State of N.Y., 1907-28. Founder and 1st pres. French Inst. in U.S., chartered by regents State of N.Y. as a pub. ednl. instn.; chmn. trustees French-Am. Chamber Commerce, Inc.; chmn. exec. com. Museum of French Art, New York; chmn. bd. Entente France-America, French Union; mem. exec. com. French-Am. Med., Chem. and Physics Soc.; trustee John Sanford Saltus Foundation, Am. Foundation for Safeguard of French Art. Comdr. Legion of Honor (French); Comdr. Order of Morocco, Order of Cambodia (French); Comdr. Order of Crown (Rumanian). Mem. N.Y. Chamber of Commerce. Homes: Palm Beach, Fla.; New York; and Paris, France. Died Mar. 22, 1929.

HAWKINS, Alvin, lawyer, gov.; b. Bath Co., Ky., Dec. 2, 1821; s. John M. and Polly G. H.; family removed, 1826, to Maury Co., and, 1828, to Carroll Co., Tenn.; did farm work and assisted his father in blacksmithing, but procured a good edn.; taught school; read law; admitted to bar, 1843; m. Justina M. Ott, 1847. Mem. general assembly, 1853; elector on Bell and Everett ticket, 1860; elected to Congress as a Unionist, 1862, but irregularities in election debarred him from seat. U.S. dist. atty., Western dist., Tenn., 1864-65; apptd. U.S. consul-gen. at Havana, 1868; soon thereafter resigned; judge Supreme Court Tenn., 1865-68, and 1869-70; gov. Tenn., 1881-83; defeated for ensuing term. Republican. Home: Huntingdon, Tenn. Died 1905.

HAWKINS, Chauncey Jeddie, author; b. at Vacaville, Calif., Sept. 3, 1876; s. Arculus and Margerette (Ellis) H.; A.B., U. of the Pacific, 1896; A.M., 1901; B.D., Yale, 1899; D.D., U. of the Pacific, 1908; m. Jessie Isabel Kemp, Apr. 8, 1902; children —Robert Boone, Philip Alba. Ordained Congl. ministry, 1898; asso. pastor Humphrey St. Ch., New Haven, Conn., 1897-1900; pastor Maple St. Ch., Danvers, Mass., 1900-02, First Ch., Spencer, Mass., 1902-05, Central Ch., Jamaica Plain, Mass., 1905-18, 1st Church, Lowell, Mass., 1918-21, Plymouth Ch., Seattle, Wash., 1921-27, First Church, San Francisco, California, 1927—. Author: The Mind of Whittier, 1904; Ned Brewster's Year in the Big Woods, 1912; Ned Brewster's Bear Hunt, 1913; Ned Brewster's Caribou Hunt, 1914; Life of Samuel B. Capen, 1914; The Little Red Doe, 1915; Do the Churches Dare? 1929. Home: Seattle, Wash. Died Aug. 9, 1930.

HAWKINS, George K., educator; b. Farmersville, N.Y., Dec. 16, 1862; s. Orson V. and Mary A. (Martin) H.; grad. State Normal Sch., Fredonia, N.Y., 1884; A.M., Union U., N.Y., 1894; D.Sc., St. Lawrence U., N.Y., 1905; m. Elizabeth Ringwood Garrity, July 12, 1893. Prin. Sherburne Union Sch. and Acad., N.Y., 1884-90; head dept. of mathematics, 1890-98, prin., 1898-1933, State Normal Sch., Plattsburg. Pres. Plattsburg Pub. Library. Home: Plattsburg, N.Y. Died Feb. 24, 1940.

HAWKINS, Hamilton Smith, brig. gen.; b. Ft. Moultrie, S.C., Nov. 13, 1834; s. Maj. Hamilton Smith (surgeon U.S.A.) and Ann Alicia (Chiffelle) H.; m. Annie Gray, Dec. 3, 1868. Apptd. from N.Y., and cadet U.S. Mil. Acad., July 1, 1852-Jan. 31, 1855; commd. 2d lt. 6th Inf., Apr. 26, 1861; 1st lt., May 14, 1861; capt., Sept. 20, 1863; maj. 10th Inf., Oct. 31, 1883; lt. col. 23d Inf., Feb. 17, 1889; col. 16th Inf., Aug. 13, 1894; brig. gen. vols., May 4, 1898; maj. gen., July 8, 1898; brig. gen., U.S.A., Sept. 28, 1898; hon. disch. from vol. service, Nov. 30, 1898. Bvtd. maj., Oct. 11, 1865 (declined). Commandant cadets, U.S. Mil. Acad., 1888-92; commandant Inf. and Cav. Sch., 1894-98; participated in battle of San Juan, 1898; retired at own request after 40 yrs.' service, Oct. 4, 1898. Gov. Soldiers' Home, Washington, Jan. 10, 1903—. Died 1910.

HAWKINS, John J., lawyer; b. in Saline Co., Mo., Jan. 4, 1855; s. George Scott and Frances M. (Gauldin) H.; ed. William Jewell Coll., and U. of Mo. (Phi Delta Theta Fraternity); left college, 1877; LL.D., William Jewell Coll., 1931; read law with Hon. Thomas Shackelford, Glasgow, Mo.; m Olive Birch, May 5, 1885 (dec.); 1 dau., Lila (dec., Mrs. R. J. Hutchins). Admitted to Mo. bar, 1878; moved to Ariz., 1883; judge Probate Court, Yavapai Co., Ariz., 1885-86; territorial auditor, 1887-89; mem. council 17th Ariz. Legislative Assembly; asso. justice Supreme Court of Ariz., 1893-97. Democrat. Chancellor missionary dist. Ariz.; lay del. general convs., P.E. Ch., San Francisco, 1901, Boston, 1904. Lectured on the law of mines, Okla. Coll. of Law, U. of Okla., 1915. Mason. Home: Los Angeles, Calif. Died May 1, 1935.

HAWKINS, John Parker, brig. gen. U.S.A.; b. Indianapolis, Sept. 29, 1830; s. John and Elizabeth (Waller) H.; student Wabash Coll., Ind., 2 yrs.; apptd. from Ind., and grad. U.S. Mil. Acad., 1852; m. Jane B. Craig, Oct. 10, 1867. Bvt. 2d lt. 6th Inf., July 1, 1852; apptd. 2d lt. 2d Inf., June 23, 1854; 1st lt., Oct. 12, 1857; capt. commissary subsistence, Aug. 3, 1861; lt. col. vols., Nov. 1, 1862-Apr. 13, 1863; brig. gen., Apr. 13, 1863; hon. mustered out, Feb. 1, 1866; maj. commissary subsistence, June 23, 1874; lt. col. asst. commissary gen., Sept. 3, 1889; col., Mar. 12, 1892; bri. gen. commissary gen. subsistence, Dec. 22, 1892; retired by operation of law, Sept. 29, 1894. Bvtd.; maj., Mar. 13, 1865, "for gallant and meritorious services during siege of Mobile;" lt. col. and col., Mar. 13, 1865, for same during the war; brig. gen. and maj. gen., Mar. 13, 1865, for same in the field during the war; maj. gen. vols., June 30, 1865, for same during the war. Home: Indianapolis, Ind. Died Feb. 7, 1914.

HAWKINS, Prince Albert, lawyer; b. Huntingdon, Tenn., Jan. 1, 1871; s. Chancellor A. G. and Ellen S. (Prince) H.; B.S., Edgewood (Tenn.) Normal Coll., 1888; student McTyeire (Tenn.) Inst., 1888-91, Southern Normal U., Huntingdon, Tenn., 1892; LL.B., Vanderbilt, 1894; m. Myrtle Ziemer, June 30, 1902; children—Robert Ziemer, Ellen-Prince, Carson, Elizabeth Ziemer, Prince Archer. Admitted to Tenn. bar, 1894, and began practice at Huntingdon; moved to Boulder, Colo., 1899, to Reno, Nev., 1910; mem. Cheney, Downer, Price & Hawkins, 1910-22, Price & Hawkins, 1922-29, Hawkins, Mayotte & Hawkins, 1929—. Dir. Y.M.C.A. (Reno), also of Congl.-Presbyn. Federated Ch. Commr. from Nevada on Uniform State Laws, 1928-31. Mason. Mem. Reno Chamber of Commerce. Home: Reno, Nev. Died Apr. 10, 1939.

HAWKINS, Rush Christopher; b. Pomfret, Vt., Sept. 14, 1831; s. Lorenzo Dow and Louisa Maria (Hutchinson) H.; ed. in common schs. (hon. A.M., Brown, 1874; LL.D., U. of Vt., 1900); m. Annmary, d. Nicholas Brown, of Providence, June 30, 1860. Col. 9th N.Y. Inf. ("Hawkins Zouaves"), May 4, 1861; bvtd. brig. gen. vols., Mar. 13, 1865, "for meritorious and valuable services during the war;" hon. mustered out, May 20, 1865. Mem. N.Y. Ho. of Rep., 1872; art commr. to Paris Expn., 1889. Officer Legion of Honor of France; book collector—especially of books relating to early history of printing and wood engraving. Has lately completed and opened to the public at Providence, R.I., the Annmary Brown Memorial, a building containing a collection of paintings by the early and later painters, a room of early printed books and another of family relics and manuscripts. Author: Titles of First Books from the Earliest Presses. Home: New York, N.Y. Died Oct. 25, 1920.

HAWKINS, William Edward, judge; b. Greenwood, La., Sept. 26, 1863; s. Rev. Samuel J. and Emeline M. (Burke) H.; U. of La. (now Tulane U.), 1881-82; B.S., Southwestern U., Georgetown, Tex., 1884; m. Ella Dickason, Nov. 11, 1886. Admitted to Tex. bar, 1887; practiced at Dallas, to 1905; 1st asst. atty. gen. of Tex., 1905-09; commr. of ins. and banking, Tex., 1910; asso. justice Supreme Court of Tex., 1913-21. Progressive Democrat. Mem. M.E. Ch., S. Home: Abilene, Tex. Died July 23, 1937.

HAWKS, Frank Monroe, aviator; b. Marshalltown, Ia., Mar. 28, 1897; s. Charles Monroe and Ida Mae (Woodruff) H.; grad. high sch., Long Beach, Calif., 1917; also grad. U.S. Sch., of Mil. Aeronautics; student U. of Calif., 2 years; m. Newell Lane, Aug. 16, 1918 (divorced); 1 dau., Dolly; m. 2d, Edith Bowie, Oct. 26, 1926. Began as aviator, Mar. 1916; entered U.S. Air Service, Apr. 1917, serving as instr. until Mar. 1919. Lt. comdr. U.S. Navy Reserve Air Force. Awarded Harmon trophy as outstanding aviator in U.S. for year 1930; French Aero Club decoration; Swiss Aero Club decoration; also Italian, Swedish, Norwegian, Danish and English decorations. Established transcontinental record of 12 hrs., 25 min., 3 seconds, west to east, Aug. 13, 1930, and east to west record of 14 hrs., 50 min., 43 seconds, Aug. 6, 1930, non-stop transcontinental record 13 hrs., 27 min., 15 seconds, June 2, 1933. Has established 214 city to city records in U.S., Europe, South America, Mexico and Cuba. Vice-pres. Quinn Aircar Co., Buffalo. Mem. advisory bd. Roosevelt Aviation Sch., Roosevelt Field, L.I., N.Y.; mem. advisory bd. Guggenheim Sch. of Aeronautics, New York Univ. Dir. Junior Birdmen of America. Author: Speed, 1931; Once to Every Pilot. Made hon. chief of Sioux Indian Tribe, Aug. 12, 1931. Home: Redding, Conn. Died Aug. 23, 1938.

HAWLEY, Alan Ramsay; b. Perth Amboy, N.J., July 29, 1869; s. Peter Radcliffe and Isabelle (Merritt) H.; ed. Trinity Sch.; unmarried. In stock brokerage until 1912 (retired). Mason. Winner of Nat. Championship Balloon Race from Indianapolis, 1910; also winner of Gordon Bennett Internat. Balloon Trophy, from St. Louis, Mo., 1910; holder Am. long-distance record for free balloons—1,172 miles. Permanent holder of Lahm Balloon Cup. Home: New York, N.Y. Died Feb. 16, 1938.

HAWLEY, Albert Henry, labor leader; b. Davenport, Ia., May 13, 1866; s. James F. and Ann E. (Hawley) H.; ed. pub. grammar schs., Port Henry, N.Y.; m. Mary T. Scully, Oct. 10, 1909. Hotel employe 13 to 19 yrs. of age; railroad fireman and engr., 1885-1901; insp. for Interstate Commerce Commission, 1901-09; gen. sec. and treas. Brotherhood of Locomotive Firemen and Engrs., Jan. 1, 1909—. Trustee Railroad Firemen's Home, Highland Park, Ill. Mason. Home: Rocky River, O. Died May 28, 1931.

HAWLEY, Bostwick, clergyman; b. Camillies, N.Y., Apr. 8, 1814; s. Isaac and Lucina (Bowen) H.; A.B., Wesleyan U., Conn., 1838 (D.D., 1863); m. Elizabeth R. Webber, Aug. 2, 1840. Prof. ancient langs. and lit., Cazenovia Sem., 1838-42; in active pastorates, 1842-75, when he retired. Has been trustee Wesleyan U.; pres. bd. of edn., Saratoga Springs, and pres. Troy Conf. Hist. Soc.; pres. Hawley Home for Children, 1889—. Author: Manual of Instruction for Baptized Children, 1865; Ministerial Education; Manual of Methodism, 1868; Prominent Doctrines and Usages of Methodist Episcopal Church; Lenten Season, 1882; Methodist Episcopacy Valid, 1892. Home: Saratoga Spring, N.Y. Died 1910.

HAWLEY, Edwin, ry. pres.; b. Chatham, N.Y., 1850. Connected with numerous rys., 1867—, in various capacities; sr. mem. firm Hawley & Davis; pres. Minneapolis & St. Louis R.R. Co., 1896—, Ia. Central Ry. Co., 1900—, Ia. Central & Western Ry.; also Des Moines & Ft. Dodge R.R. Co., Great Western Power Co., Western Power Co., v.p. U.S. Light & Heating Co.; dir. numerous railroad and other interests. Home: New York, N.Y. Died 1912.

HAWLEY, Fred Vermillia, clergyman; b. Bath, Mich., Nov. 2, 1862; s. Hanford H. and Mahala J. (Abel) H.; grad. Hillsdale Coll., 1891; studied in Theol. Sem., Hillsdale, Mich.; m. Mary Washburn, Aug. 3, 1891; children—Florence, Pearl. Ordained Bapt. ministry, 1891; was pastor Bapt. Ch., Brooklyn, Mich.; withdrew from Bapt. Ch., 1893, and organized People's Ch., Brooklyn, Mich.; pastor First Unitarian Ch., Jackson, Mich., 1897-1900, Ch. of the Messiah, Louisville, Ky., 1900-02; sec. Western Unitarian Conf., with supervision of Unitarian chs. in 14 states, 1902-04; pastor Unity Ch., Chicago, Mar. 1904—. Home: Chicago, Ill. Died Nov. 15, 1927.

HAWLEY, James H., governor; b. Dubuque, Ia., Jan. 17, 1847; s. Thomas and Annie (Carr) H.; ed. Dubuque High Sch.; m. Mary E. Bullock, July 4, 1875; children—Edgar T., Jess B., Mrs. Emma Atkinson, Mrs. Bessie Tucker, James H., Harry R. Went to Ida., 1862, and was one of earliest pioneers of territory; mined until 1871; admitted to bar, Feb. 14, 1871, and entered practice; sr. mem. Hawley & Hawley. Mem. Ida. Ho. of Rep., 1870-71, Senate, 1874-75; dist. atty., 2d dist., Ida., 1879-83; U.S. atty. for Ida., 1884-87; mayor of Boise, 1904-05; gov. for term, 1911-13; candidate for U.S. Senate, 1914. Democrat. Home: Boise, Ida. Died Aug. 3, 1929.

HAWLEY, John Blackstock, hydraulic engr.; b. Red Wing, Minn., May 27, 1866; s. Augustine Boyer (M.D.) and Harriet Bowman (Blackstock) H.; B.S., U. of Minn., 1887; M.S., Tex. Christian U., 1926, hon. D.Sc., 1938; m. Sue A. Terrell, Apr. 11, 1895; children—Judith Terrell, John Blackstock, Harriet Elizabeth, George Maxwell Blackstock. Engr., Water Bd., St. Paul, Minn., 1887-89; pvt. practice, Ft. Worth, 1890-97; city engr., Ft. Worth, 1897-1907; pres. Gen. Construction Co., 1909-17, also cons. engr.; pvt. practice, 1920-22; mem. Hawley & Sands, water supply and sanitary engrs., 1923, alone, 1923-27; mem. Hawley & Freese, 1927-29, Hawley, Freese & Nichols, 1930-38; consulting hydraulic and san. engr., 1938—. Major engrs., World War, comdg. 503d Engrs., A.E.F., in France, hdqrs. St. Nazaire; also engr. in charge water supply and sanitation, Base Sect. No. 1; hon. discharged Apr. 1919. Mem. Governor's Advisory Council Engrs. (Tex.), 1922-24; mem. Engineering Board of Review, Sanitary District of Chicago, 1924-25; mem. engr. advisory bd., 1924, asso. in biol. research, 1926-29, Texas Christian U., Fort Worth. Mason. Home: Ft. Worth, Tex. Died Jan. 9, 1941.

HAWLEY, John Mitchell, rear admiral U.S.N.; b. Northampton, Mass., July 28, 1846; grad. U.S. Naval Acad., 1868; m. Ella S. Moore, June 17, 1874. Promoted through all grades to capt., Mar. 15, 1904; rear admiral and retired, June 30, 1907. Has served at sea 22 yrs., 6 of which were in coast survey; during early career in navy was connected with 3 interoceanic surveys; exec. officer of U.S. ship Nipsic during Samoan hurricane, 1889, and received thanks of State of Mass. for services there; first officer to establish recruiting stations in West with view of bringing Western men into service; had charge of all recruiting stas. in West and Southwest during the war with Spain, enlisting about 1,900 men; comdr. Hartford, training ship for landsmen, 1899-1901; insp. 5th light house dist. at Baltimore, 1902-4; comd. flagship Brooklyn, Apr. 21, 1904; comdr.-in-chief S. Atlantic Squadron, Nov. 23, 1904-Jan. 12, 1905; comdg. Wabash, 1906-07. Presented with a jeweled sword by Ill. Naval Militia, 1898. Died Feb. 9, 1925.

HAWLEY, Joseph Boswell, U.S. senator, Conn., 1881-1905; b. Stewartsville, N.C., Oct. 31, 1826; grad. Hamilton Coll., N.Y., 1847 (LL.D., Hamilton, Yale and Trinity Colls.); admitted to bar, 1850, at Hartford, Conn.; practiced law 6 yrs.; became, 1857, editor Hartford Evening Press, which, in 1867, was consolidated with the Hartford Courant, of which he became editor. Enlisted in Union army as lt., Apr. 15, 1861; became brig. and bvt. maj. gen.; mustered out, Jan. 15, 1866. Del. to Free Soil Nat. Conv., 1852; gov. Conn., 1866; pres. Nat. Rep. Conv., 1868; presdl. elector, 1868; pres. U.S. Centennial Commn., 1873-76; mem. Congress, 1872-75 and 1879-81. Home: Hartford, Conn. Died 1905.

HAWLEY, Julius Sargent, retired banker; b. Troy, N.Y., June 1, 1844; s. James Simonds and Adeline Ann (Cook) H.; grad. high sch., Troy, 1861; m. Maria Lansing Drake, Sept. 7, 1869; children—Albert Drake (dec.), Louise (Mrs. Carroll Lewis Maxcy), Gertrude Morgan. Became connected with Nat. State Bank of Troy, as clk., 1861, cashier, 1887-1901, pres., 1901-26; became chmn. bd. and dir. Mfrs. Nat. Bank of Troy, 1927; retired. Republican. Presbyn. Home: Troy, N.Y. Died Jan. 2, 1935.

HAWLEY, Newton Fremont, banker; b. nr. Tipton, Ia., Nov. 28, 1859; s. Newton J. and Delia (Canfield) H.; A.B., Ia. (now Grinnell) Coll., 1879, A.M., 1882; m. Ellen M. Field, Sept. 5, 1884. Admitted to Minn. bar, 1884; asso. with W. J. Hahn, atty. gen. of Minn., 1892, as Hahn & Hawley, later Hahn, Belden & Hawley, and Belden, Hawley & Jamison; retired from practice of law, Jan. 1, 1906, to become trustee of Farmers & Mechanics Savings Bank of Minneapolis, later mng. exec. under title of treas.; v.p. Equitable Loan Co. Mem. Minneapolis Charter Commn., 1898, 1906; mem. Bd. of Edn., Minneapolis, 1899-1905; mem. Advisory Commn., same, 1915; mem. Minneapolis Water Commn., 1910; active in civic affairs. Trustee Grinnell Coll., Pillsbury Settlement Assn. (Minneapolis). Home: Minneapolis, Minn. Died July 16, 1918.

HAWLEY, Thomas Porter, U.S. dist. judge for dist. of Nev., Sept. 1890—; b. Ind., July 18, 1830; ed. in Versailles, Ind.; went to Calif., 1852; mined until 1855; in co. clerk's office, Nevada Co., Calif., 1855-57; admitted to practice law in Nevada Co., 1857, and in Supreme Court of Calif., 1859; dist. atty. Nevada Co., Calif., 1862-64; removed to White Pine Co., Nev., 1868; justice Supreme Court of Nev., 1872-90; m. Miss M. Eudora Murrell, Nov. 15, 1858 (died 1891). Home: Carson City, Nev. Died 1907.

HAWLEY, Willis Chatman, congressman; b. nr. Monroe, Ore., May 5, 1864; s. Sewel R. and Emma A. (Noble) H.; B.S., Willamette U., Salem, 1884, LL.B., and A.B., 1888, A.M., 1891, LL.D., 1909; m. Anna M. Geisendorfer, Aug. 19, 1885; 3 children. Prin. Umpqua Acad., Wilbur, Ore., 1884-86; pres. Ore. State Normal Sch., Drain, Ore., 1888-91; prof. mathematics, 1891-93, head prof. history, economics and constl. law, 1893-1906, pres., 1893-1902, v.p. and dean, 1902-05, Willamette U. Admitted to Ore. bar, 1894, also to U.S. Dist., Circuit and Supreme courts; mem. 60th to 72d Congresses (1907-1933), 1st Ore. Dist. (chmn. com. on ways and means); chmn. caucus of Republicans of the House, 69th to 72d Congresses; mem. Nat. Forest Reservation Commn.; mem. Joint Commn. of Senate and House on Celebration of 200th Anniversary of Birth of George Washington; chmn. Joint Com. of Senate and House on Internal Revenue Taxation. Head mgr. Pacific Jurisdiction, Woodmen of the World, 1896—, term ending 1936. Mason. Home: Salem, Ore. Died July 24, 1941.

HAWN, Henry Gaines; b. Richmond, Va., 1864; Washington and Lee U., 1884. Pres. The Hawn Sch. of the Speech Arts; dramatic instr. Cornell Univ. "Masque"; spl. lecturer Brooklyn Inst. Arts and Sciences; instr. elocution Brooklyn Poly. Inst., "The Castle," Tarrytown, N.Y., and Middlebury (Vt.) Coll.; dean Packard Theatre Inst. Lecturer for the Redpath Chautauqua System, Am. City Bureau. Author: Diction for Singers, 1911; Platform Pieces, 1917. Home: New York, N.Y. Deceased.

HAWORTH, Erasmus, geologist; b. on farm nr. Indianola, Ia., Apr. 17, 1855; s. Elwood and Matilda (Folger) H.; B.S., U. of Kan., 1881, M.S., 1884; Ph.D., Johns Hopkins, 1888; m. Ida E. Huntsman, Mar. 26, 1889; children—Henry Huntsman, Paul Eugene, Rose Elizabeth, Margaret Josephine. Teacher in coll., 1883—, except 1 yr., 1887-88; prof. geology and mineralogy, U. of Kan., 1892-1920; doing commercial expert work in geology. Organized Kan. State Geol. Survey, 1894, state geologist to 1915; has done much professional work for U.P. R.R. Co. in Wyo. and Kan., and for pvt. cos. in Mo., Kan., Ark., Oklahoma, etc.; connected with U.S. Geol. Survey for yrs.; recently has devoted much time to economic geology. Fellow and life mem. Geol. Soc. America; life mem. Kan. Acad. Science. Wrote vols. 1, 2, 3, 8, and Bulletin 1 on Well Waters of Kansas, 1895-1904, and parts volumes 5 and 9, Reports Kan. State Geol. Survey, and ann. reports Mineral Statistics of Kan., 1897-1904. Home: Ridgewood, N.J. Died Nov. 17, 1932.

HAWORTH, Joseph, actor; b. Providence, R.I., April 7, 1858; s. Benjamin and Martha H.; early removed to Cleveland, where he began stage career in John Ellsler's Stock Co.; supported Edwin Booth, as Laertes, Cassio, etc.; later with Lawrence Barrett; joined John McCullough as leading support in tragedies; later played prin. rôles in Hoodman Blind, The Bells and other dramas, and at the head of his own co. Home: New York, N.Y. Died 1903.

HAWORTH, Paul Leland, author; b. W. Newton, Ind., Aug. 28, 1876; s. John D. and Fanny (Hornor) H.; A.B., Ind. U., 1899, A.M., 1901; fellow in Am. history, Columbia, 1903-04, Ph.D., 1906; m. Martha B. Ackermann, Sept. 1, 1903; children—Leland J., Anna Ruth, Martha R. Prof. history and civics, Mich. Northern State Normal, 1901-02; tutor history, Teachers Coll., 1904-06; lecturer in history, Columbia, 1906, Bryn Mawr, 1910-11. Collaborator on "A History of the U.S. and Its People," of which he wrote the greater part of several vols. Made 1,000-mile canoe trip for Scribner's Mag., 1916, to a little known range of Canadian Rockies and discovered a new mountain, which he named Mt. Lloyd George, and a glacier that is probably the largest in the Rocky Mountain system; visited same region again 1919, and discovered two new lakes, many new mountains, and a waterfall 160 ft. high. Has large orchards near Indianapolis. Actg. prof. history, Ind. Univ., 1918-19; prof. history, Butler Coll., 1922—. Progressive nominee for Ind. legislature, 1912; mem. Ind. Ho. of Rep., 1921-22. Author: The Hayes-Tilden Disputed Presidential Election, 1906; Reconstruction and Union, 1912; George Washington—Farmer, 1915; On the Headwaters of Peace River, 1917; The United States in Our Own Times, 1865-1935; Trailmakers of the Northwest, 1921; Caverns of Sunset, 1930. Editor: The Problems of the Nations (4 vols.). Home: West Newton, Ind. Died Mar. 24, 1938.

HAWTHORNE, Charles Webster, artist; b. Me., Jan. 8, 1872; s. Joseph Jackson and Cornelia J. (Smith) H.; student Nat. Acad. Design, Art Students' League, New York, and under William M. Chase, Shinnecock, L.I.; m. Marion Campbell, 1903; 1 son, Joseph Campbell. Former teacher at Art Students' League; teacher New York Sch. of Art; owner and instr. Cape Cod Sch. of Art (summers), Provincetown, Mass. Represented in Metropolitan Mus. (New York); Corcoran Gallery (Washington); Syracuse Mus. of Fine Arts; R.I. Sch. of Design (Providence), Worcester Mus.; Buffalo Fine Arts Acad.; Art Inst. Chicago; Peabody Inst. (Baltimore); Hackley Gallery (Muskegon, Mich.); City Art Mus. (St. Louis); John Herron Art Inst., Indianapolis; Detroit Mus.; etc. Awards: Shaw prize, Salmagundi Club, 1903; 1st Hallgarten prize, Nat. Acad., 1904; 2d prize, Worcester Mus., 1904; hon. mention, Carnegie Inst., 1908; silver medal, Buenos Aires Expn., 1910; Clark prize, 1911, Isidor gold medal, 1913, Altman prize, 1914, Isidor gold medal, 1914, Nat. Acad.; silver medal San Francisco Expn., 1915; Temple medal, Pa. Acad., 1915; Harris prize and medal, Art Inst. Chicago, 1917; Lippincott prize Pa. Acad., Phila., 1922; Harris prize and silver medal, 1923; W. A. Clark prize and silver medal, Corcoran Gallery of Art, Washington, 1923; Carnegie prize, Acad. Design, 1924; 3d medal, Art week, Phila., 1925; medal of honor, Concord Art Assn., 1925; 3d prize, Internat. Exhbn., Carnegie Inst., 1925; Proctor prize, N.A.D., 1926; 1st W. A. Clark prize, Corcoran Gallery, 1926; gold medal, Sesquicentennial Expn., Phila., 1926; Richard S. Greenough memorial prize, Newport Art Assn., 1928; Mrs. Julius Rosenwald prize, Grand Central Art Galleries, New York, 1929; Boston Art Club medal, 1930. A.N.A., 1908, N.A., 1911; mem. Nat. Inst. Arts and Letters. Home: Provincetown, Mass., and New York, N.Y. Died Nov. 29, 1930.

HAWTHORNE, Julian, author; b. Boston, Mass., June 22, 1846; s. Nathaniel H., novelist; brother of Rose Hawthorne Lathrop; student, Lawrence Scientific Sch. (Harvard), and Dresden, but was not grad.; m. Mary Albertina Amelung, Nov. 15, 1870; father of Hildegarde H. Hydrographic engr. dept. of docks, New York, 1870-72; from then devoted to authorship and journalism; was corr. of New York Journal in Cuba and elsewhere, and spl. commr. of Cosmopolitan Magazine to India; lit. critic Phila. North American, 1901-03; spl. commr. New York American. Author: Nathaniel Hawthorne and His Wife; Prince Saroni's Wife; Golden Fleece; Archibald Malmaison, 1899; A Fool of Nature, 1899; One of Those Coincidences, and Other Stories, 1899; Hawthorne Reading; Hawthorne and His Circle, 1903. Home: Mt. Vernon, N.Y. Died July 14, 1934.

HAWTREY, Charles Henry, actor, manager; b. Eton, Eng., Sept. 21, 1858; s. Rev. John and Frances (Procter) H.; ed. Eton and Rugby schs.; Oxford U.; unmarried. First appearance, as Edward Langton, in "The Colonel," Prince of Wales Theatre, London, Oct. 1881; played Douglas Cattermole in "The Private Secretary," which he adapted from the German of Von Moser, at Cambridge, Nov. 1883; became mgr. Her Majesty's Theatre, 1885. First appearance in New York at the Garrick Theatre, Oct. 1901, in "A Message from Mars"; revived, at the Haymarket Theatre, "The Man from Blankley's," Mar. 1906; twice appeared "by command" at Windsor Castle, before King Edward. Home: London, Eng. Died July 30, 1923.

HAY, Eugene Gano, lawyer; b. Charlestown, Ind., Mar. 26, 1853; s. Andrew Jennings and Rebecca (Garrett) H.; pvt. sch. edn.; admitted to bar, 1877; m. Eleanora Farquhar, Nov. 4, 1891. Pros. atty. Jefferson and Switzerland cos., Ind., 1880-84; mem. Minn. legislature, 1889; U.S. dist atty., Dist. of Minn., 1890-94; U.S. gen. appraiser, 1903-23. Home: Summit, N.J. Died Feb. 21, 1933.

HAY, Henry Clinton, clergyman, editor; b. Portland, Me., Feb. 19, 1853; s. Henry Homer and Eleanor (Seavey) H.; A.B., Harvard, 1878; diploma New Ch. Theol. Sch., 1885; m. Sarah Alice Swazey, June 11, 1885; children—George Swazey (dec.), Donald Worcester (dec.), Clinton Allen (dec.). Ordained ministry Ch. of New Jerusalem, 1885; asst. minister, Fall River, Mass., 1885-87, Cincinnati, 1887-89; pastor Providence, R.I., 1889-96, Brockton, Mass., 1896-1902; became asso. editor New Church Review, 1897, mng. editor, 1909-17, advisory editor, 1917—; asso. pastor Boston Society, 1902-19, pastor, 1919-33, emeritus. Sec. Council of Ministers Gen. Conv., 1895-1915; sec. bd. of mgrs. New Ch. Theol. Sch., 1910-33. Pres. New Ch. Club of Boston, 1909-29; pres. New Ch. Sex-Edn. League, 1923-30. Author (with James Reed): Earthly Problems in Heavenly Light, 1905; Death and the Life Beyond, 1906; The Essential Needs of the Soul, 1907. Home: Bridgton, Me. Died Feb. 23, 1935.

HAY, James, judge; b. Milwood, Va., Jan. 9, 1856; s. William and Emily (Lewis) H.; ed. pvt. schs. in Md. and Va. and U. of Pa.; B.L., Washington and Lee U., 1877; m. Constance Tatum, Oct. 1, 1878; children—James, William; m. 2d, Frances B. Gordon, June 9, 1891; children—Ellen D., Frances B.; m. 3d, Eloise M. Cave, June 14, 1921. Admitted to bar, 1877; in practice at Madison, Va., 1879-1916; commonwealth's atty., 1883-96; mem. Va. Ho. of Dels., 1885-91, Senate, 1893; mem. Dem. State Com., 4 yrs.; mem. 55th to 64th Congresses (1897-1917), 7th Va. Dist.; resigned from 64th Congress upon appmt. as judge Court of Claims of U.S., July 15, 1916, resigned, Dec. 1, 1927. Home: Madison, Va. Died June 12, 1931.

HAY, James, Jr., writer; b. Harrisonburg, Va., Jan. 28, 1881; s. James and Constance (Tatum) H.; student U. of Va., 1899-1903; m. Maud Millicent Larrick, July 19, 1922. Reporter, Washington Post, 1903-04; Washington Times, 1904-09; contbr. fiction and spl. articles to mags., 1909—. Democrat. Author: The Unlighted House, 1921; The Bellamy Case, 1925; That Washington Affair, 1926; The Hidden Woman, 1928; The Wayside Inn for Birds, stories of bird life (with John L. Martin), 1929. Directed nation-wide mag. publicity campaign for U.S., George Washington Bicentennial Commn., 1931-32. Home: Washington, D.C. Died May 6, 1936.

HAY, John, sec. of state, U.S., 1898—; b. Salem, Ind., Oct. 8, 1838; s. Dr. Charles and Helen (Leonard) H.; common school edn., Warsaw, Ill., academic in Springfield, Ill.; grad. Brown, 1858 (A.M., LL.D.; also LL.D., Princeton, Yale, Harvard and Western Reserve univs.); m. Clara, d. late Amasa Stone, of Cleveland, Ohio, 1874. Admitted to Illinois bar; one of private secs. of President Lincoln; bvtd. col., U.S. vols., asst. adj. gen.; sec. of legation, Paris, Madrid, Vienna; chargé d'affaires, Vienna; 1st asst. sec. state, 1879-81; pres. Internat. Sanitary Conf., 1881; ambassador to England, 1897-98. Author: Castilian Days, 1871; Pike County Ballads, 1871; Translation of Castelar's Democracy in Europe, 1872 (serial); Abraham Lincoln, a History (with John G. Nicolay), 1890; Poems, 1890. Home: Washington, D.C. Died 1905.

HAY, Marion E., governor; b. Adams Co., Wis., Dec. 9, 1865; s. Edward Murry and Mary L. (Coming) H.; ed. dist. schs. and business coll.; m. Lizzie L. Muir, Jan. 16, 1887. Clk. in store, Minn., 1882-88; removed to Wash. Ty., 1888; in mercantile business, Davenport, Wash., 1888-89; moved to Wilbur, 1889, and to Spokane, 1908; pres. M. E. & E. T. Hay, Big Bend Land Co.; v.p. State Bank of Wilbur. Mayor of Wilbur, 2 terms; chmn. Rep. Co. Central Com., Lincoln Co., Wash., 1898-1902; elected lt. gov. of Wash., 1908, becoming gov., Mar. 29, 1909, on death of Gov. Cosgrove, for unexpired term, 1909-13. Home: Spokane, Wash. Died Nov. 21, 1933.

HAY, Mary Garrett, suffragist; b. Charlestown, Ind.; d. Andrew Jennings and Rebecca (Garrett) H.; ed. Western Coll. for Women, Oxford, O. Organizer Nat. Am. Woman Suffrage Assn. 10 yrs.; pres. N.Y. State Fedn. Women's Clubs, 1910-12; pres. N.Y. Equal Suffrage League, 1910-18; chmn. Woman Suffrage, 1912-18; chmn. Rep. Woman's Nat. Exec. Com., 1919-20; chmn. League of Women Voters of N.Y. City, 1918-23. Mem. D.A.R., Daughters of Ind. in N.Y. (pres.). Presbyterian. Died Aug. 29, 1928.

HAY, Oliver Perry, vertebrate paleontologist; b. Saluda, Ind., May 22, 1846; s. Robert and Margaret (Crawford) H.; A.B., Eureka (Ill.) Coll., 1870, A.M., 1873; Yale, 1876-77; Ph.D., Ind. U., 1884; m. Mary Emily Howsmon, of Eureka, Ill., June 30, 1870; children—William Perry, Mrs. Mary Minnick, Frances Steele, Robert Howsmon. Prof. natural sciences Eureka Coll., 1870-72, Oskaloosa (Ia.) Coll., 1874-76; prof. biology and geology, Butler Coll., Indianapolis, 1879-92; asst. curator zoölogy, Field Mus. Natural History, Chicago, 1895-97; asst. and asso. curator vertebrate paleontology, Am. Mus. Natural History, New York, 1901-07; engaged in pvt. investigations in vertebrate paleontology, 1907-11; research asso., 1912-17, and associate, 1917—, retired, Carnegie Institution of Washington, investigating history of Pleistocene vertebrata of N. America. Asst. Geol. Survey of Ark., 1884-88, of Ind., 1891-94, 1911-12, of Ia., 1911-13; asso. editor American Geologist, 1902-05. Author: Bibliography and Catalogue of the Fossil Vertebrata of North America, 1902; The Fossil Turtles of North America, 1908; Pleistocene Period in Indiana and its Vertebrates, 1912; Pleistocene Mammals of Iowa, 1914; Pleistocene and its Vertebrates, East Mississippi River, 1923; and of Middle Region of N.A., 1924; Pleistocene of Western Region, 1927; Second Bibliography and Catalogue of the Fossil Vertebrata of North America, Vol. I, 1929, Vol. II, 1930. Home: Washington, D.C. Died Nov. 2, 1930.

HAY, Stephen John, mayor; b. Griffin, Ga., Oct. 5, 1864; s. Stephen J. and Mary Eliza (Dobbs) H.; ed. pub. schs. and under pvt. tutelage; m. Mary N. Oxford, Mar. 15, 1903. Began as bookkeeper, 1885; removed to Dallas, Tex., 1887; pres. Dallas Trust & Savings Bank; v.p. Title & Guaranty Co., U.S. Bond & Mortgage Co. Mayor of Dallas, 1907-09, 1909-11. Democrat. Methodist. Home: Dallas, Tex. Died Feb. 29, 1916.

HAY, Thomas Abraham Horn; b. Easton, Pa., July 1, 1855; s. Jacob and Annie (Wilson) H.; B.A., Lafayette Coll., 1876, A.M., 1879; m. Helen Moore Ruger, Sept. 7, 1881. Partner, J. Hay & Sons, wholesale dry goods, Easton, 1876-96; mem. Hay Boot & Shoe Co., 1879-1912; chmn. Bangor & Portland Traction Co.; v.p. Doyle-DaCosta Mfg. Co.; exec. dir. Wahnetah Silk Co.; sec. Easton Bd. of Trade, 1915-23. Chmn. Com. Pub. Safety of Northampton Co., and mem. Com. Pub. Safety of Pa., 1917-19; was pres. Four Minute Men. Presbyn. Mason. Home: Easton, Pa. Died May 27, 1925.

HAYDEN, Austin Albert, M.D.; b. Shullsburg, Wis., Oct. 15, 1881; s. Albert (M.D.) and Emma C. (McNulty) H.; A.B., Creighton U., Omaha, Neb., 1900, A.M., 1903; B.S., U. of Chicago, 1902; M.D., Rush Med. Coll., 1904; grad. work St. Elizabeth's Hosp., 1906, New York Post-Grad. Med. Sch. and Hosp., 1908; m. Mary Forster Phillips, Apr. 28, 1915. Instr. in ophthalmology, New York Post-Grad. Med. Sch., 1906-08, Rush Med. Coll., 1908-16; chmn. dept. otolaryngology and ophthalmology, St. Joseph's Hosp. Fellow Am. Coll. Surgeons, A.M.A. (sec. bd. of trustees). Democrat. Home: Chicago, Ill. Died July 10, 1940.

HAYDEN, Charles, banker; b. Boston, July 9, 1870; s. Josiah W. and Emma A. (Tirrell) H.; desc. of Samuel H., Devonshire, Eng.; B.S., Mass. Inst. Tech. Sr. partner Hayden, Stone & Co. (founded 1892), bankers, New York and Boston; chmn. bd. Chicago, Rock Island & Pacific Railway; Internat. Nickel Co.; chmn. finance com. Kennecott Copper Corp., Utah Copper Co.; mem. exec. com. Am. Locomotive Co., Mack Trucks, Inc., Otis Elevator Co.; officer and dir. in many other corps. Mem. Corporation Mass. Inst. Tech. Mem. Mass. Militia 14 yrs. from pvt. to p.m. gen. of Mass. Home: New York, N.Y. Died Jan. 8, 1937.

HAYDEN, Charles H., artist; b. Plymouth, Mass., 1856; s. Edward Boyd and Anna (Goodspeed) H.; pupil of Museum of Fine Arts, Boston, Boulanger, Collin, and Lefebvre, Paris. Honorable mention, Expn. Universelle, Paris, 1889; Jordan prize, Boston, 1895; silver medal, Atlanta Expn., 1895; medal Paris Expn., 1900. Mem. St. Botolph Club, Boston. Home: Belmont, Mass. Died 1901.

HAYDEN, Charles Sidney, newspaper corr.; b. Holton, Kan., Sept. 22, 1880; s. Sidney and Mary (Walker) H.; student U. of Kan., 1899-1902; m. Alice Louise Boyer, Oct. 8, 1906; children—Dorothy Alice, Virginia Ann. Began as reporter Topeka Capital, 1902, continuing with Kansas City Journal, Chicago Tribune, Austin (Tex.) Tribune until 1911; staff writer San Antonio Express, later San Antonio Light, 1911-18; Washington corr. various newspapers, 1918—, now Nashville Banner, Chattanooga News. Exec. sec. Dem. Nat. Congressional Com. Democrat. Home: Falls Church, Va. Died Dec. 19, 1937.

HAYDEN, Edward Everett, naval officer; b. Boston, Apr. 14, 1858; s. William and Louise Annie (Dorr) H.; grad. U.S. Naval Acad., 1879; m. Kate Reynolds, Dec. 12, 1882; children—Reynolds, Herbert Bainbridge, William (dec.), Dorothy, Alfred Dorr, Mary Bainbridge. Promoted through grades to rear adm., retired, June 30, 1921. Asst. geologist, U.S. Geol. Survey, 1885; marine meteorologist, U.S. Hydrographic Office, and editor pilot chart, 1886-92; in charge Naval Obs., Mare Island, Calif., 1898, branch hydrographic office, Manila, 1899; in charge, dept. chronometers and time service, U.S. Naval Obs., Washington, 1902-10, comdt. U.S. Naval Sta., Key West, Fla., 1910-15; pres. Gen. Court Martial, Navy Yard, Norfolk, Va., 1916-21. Republican. Episcopalian. Died Nov. 17, 1932.

HAYDEN, Frank, banker; b. New Harmony, Ind., July 13, 1874; s. Henry and Mary E. (Saltzman) H.; student De Pauw U., Greencastle, Ind., 1893-95; A.B., Harvard, 1899; m. Jessie E. Matson, July 30, 1903. In wholesale implement business, Cincinnati, 1900-03; with financial dept. Union Central Life Ins. Co., Memphis, 1903-05; became pres. and mgr. Southern Abstract & Loan Co., 1906, and has been officer or dir. many other corps. Independent Democrat. Home: Memphis, Tenn. Died Jan. 31, 1936.

HAYDEN, Horace Edwin, clergyman; b. Catonville, Md., Feb. 18, 1837; s. Hon. Edwin Parsons and Elizabeth (Hause) H.; ed. St. Timothy's Mil. Coll., Md., and Kenyon Coll., Ohio (M.A., 1886); pvt. in Army Northern Va., C.S.A., 1861-65; grad. Va. Theol. Sem., 1867; m. Kate Elizabeth Byers, Nov. 30, 1868. Deacon, 1867, priest, 1868, P.E. Ch.; rector Christ Ch., Point Pleasant, W.Va., 1867-73, St. John's, West Brownsville, Pa., 1873-79; asst. minister St. Stephen's Ch., Wilkes-Barré, 1879-1916. An examining chaplain Diocese of Central Pa. and Bethlehem, 1885-1910. Corr. sec., librarian and editor Vols. IV-XIV Wyo. Hist. and Geol. Society. Mem. Free Library Com. of Pa.; mgr. Luzerne Co. Humane Assn., 1895-1914. Author: Virginia Genealogies, 1891; Massacre of Wyoming, 1895. Editor: Genealogical and Family History of the Wyoming and Lackawanna Valleys, Pa. (2 vols.), 1906. Compiler of the St. Johns Family History. Home: Wilkes-Barré, Pa. Died Aug. 22, 1917.

HAYDEN, John Louis, army officer; b. in Ill., Nov. 2, 1866; grad. U.S. Mil. Acad., 1888; grad. Arty. Sch., 1898. Commd. 2d lt. 1st Arty., June 11, 1888; 1st lt., Oct. 2, 1894; capt. Arty Corps, Feb. 10, 1901; maj., Jan. 25, 1907; lt. col. Coast Arty. Corps, Oct. 5, 1911; col., July 1, 1916; brig. gen. N.G., Aug. 5, 1917. Participated in campaign against Sioux Indians in S. Dak., 1890-91; in action at Wounded Knee, Dec. 29, 1890, and at White Clay Creek, Dec. 30, 1890; prof. mil. science and tactics, U. of Wash., 1892-96; apptd. comdr. 56th Field Arty. Brigade, Camp Wheeler, Macon, Ga., Sept. 1917. Died Feb. 22, 1936.

HAYDEN, Warren Sherman, investment banker; b. Danbury, Conn., Oct. 20, 1870; s. Warren Luce and Anna Flower (Sherman) H.; student Union Sch. and Washington and Jefferson Acad., Washington, Pa.; Ph.B., Hiram (O.) Coll., 1892; m. Blanche Rebecca Squire, 1893 (died 1903); 1 dau., Margaret (Mrs. Chester A. Thompson); m. 2d, Elizabeth Strong, 1906; children—Sherman Strong, Eleanor Warren. Admitted to Ohio bar, 1898 (never practiced); mgr. bond dept. Lamprecht Bros., Cleveland, 1892-1903; mem. Hayden, Miller & Co., 1903—; pres. Cleveland Union Terminals Co.; v.p. Malvern Land Co.; dir. N.Y. & Harlem R.R. Co., C.,C.,C.&St.L. Ry., M.C. R.R., N.Y.C. R.R., W.S. R.R., Zanesville & Western Ry., Western Reserve Investing Corp., Union Trust Co., White Motor Co., Strong, Carlisle & Hammond Co. Pres. Cleveland Metropolitan Park Bd.; trustee Western Reserve U., Adelbert Coll., Hiram Coll., University Hosp., Lakeside Hosp., Cleveland Mus. Natural History, Cleveland Community Fund. Mem. Cleveland Chamber of Commerce (pres. 1913-14). Republican. Protestant. Home: Cleveland Heights, Ohio. Died Mar. 14, 1933.

HAYDN, Hiram Collins, theologian; b. Pompey, N.Y., Dec. 11, 1831; s. David Ellsworth and Lucinda M. (Cooley) H.; A.B., Amherst, 1856; grad. Union Theol. Sem., 1859; (D.D., Wooster, 1875; LL.D., Amherst, and Marietta, 1888); m. Elizabeth Bill Coit, May 1, 1861; m. 2d, Sarah J. Merriman, Jan. 7, 1864. Ordained Congl. ministry, 1862; pastor First Ch., Meriden, Conn., 1862-66, First Ch., Painesville, O., 1866-71; asso. pastor, 1872-74, pastor, 1874-80 and 1884-1900, pastor emeritus, May 1903. First Presbyn. Ch., Cleveland; dist. sec. A.B.C.F.M., 1880-84; pres. Western Reserve U., 1887-90; prof. O.T. lit., Coll. for Women, Western Reserve. Author: Death and Beyond (sermons); American Heroes on Mission Fields; The Bible and Current Thought, 1891; Western Reserve University; From Hudson to Cleveland, 1878-1890, 1905. Home: Cleveland, O. Died July 31, 1913.

HAYES, Alfred, lawyer; b. Lewisburg, Pa., Oct. 15, 1873; s. Alfred and Mary Miles (Van Valzah) H.; Bucknell U., 1891-93; A.B., Princeton, 1895, A.M., 1898; LL.B., Columbia, 1898; m. Christine Grace Robertson, of Chicago, June 15, 1905; children—Chrintine MacEwan, Alfred, Miles Van Valzah. Practiced in New York, 1898-1907; tutor and lecturin law, Columbia, 1902-07; prof. law, Cornell, 1907-17. Pres. Hayes-Jackson Corp.; trustee Mutual Am. Securities Trust; dir. and mem. property com. N.Y. Transfer Co. Chevalier of Royal Order of the Savior (Greece), 1904. Del. Progressive Nat. Conv., 1912; Prog. candidate for justice of Supreme Court, 6th Dist., N.Y., 1912, Dem. and Prog. candidate, 1913—. Home: Greenwich, Conn. Died Oct. 19, 1936.

HAYES, Charles Harris, theologian; b. Newark, N.J., Sept. 1, 1868; s. Charles and Caroline Rosamund (Orton) H.; B.A., Columbia, 1890; fellow same, 1890-92, M.A., 1891; grad. Gen. Theol. Sem., 1894; fellowship Ch. Univ. Bd. of Bequests, 1894-96, B.D., 1897 (D.D., 1907); Berlin and Halle, 1894-95, Oxford, 1895-96; unmarried. Deacon, 1894, priest, 1896, P.E. Ch.; mem. staff St. Mark's Pro-Cathedral, Washington, 1896-1900; chaplain to bishop of Me., 1900-01; asso. prof. philosophy, Trinity Coll., Hartford, 1901-02; prof. Christian apologetics, Gen. Theol. Sem., 1902—. Democrat. Author: Bible Lessons on the Creed, 1906. Home: New York, N.Y. Died 1910.

HAYES, C(harles) Willard, geologist; b. Granville, O., Oct. 8, 1859; s. Charles C. and Ruth (Wolcott) H.; bro. of Ellen H.; A.B., Oberlin Coll., 1883; fellow chemistry and geology, Johns Hopkins, 1884-87, Ph.D., 1887; (LL.D., Oberlin, 1908); m. Rosa Paige, Mar. 22, 1894. Prin. Brecksville (O.) High Sch., 1883-84; apptd. asst. geologist, 1887, geologist, 1894, chief geologist, 1902-11, U.S. Geol. Survey; 1st v.p. and gen. mgr. Cia Mex. de Petrolea "El Aguila," S.A., Oct. 16, 1911—. Geologist to Nicaraguan Canal Commn., 1898-99. Home: Washington, D.C. Died Feb. 8, 1916.

HAYES, Daniel Webster, educator; b. Salem, Ia., Apr. 5, 1874; s. Lawrence M. and Mary Alice (Breach) H.; A.B., Neb. Wesleyan U., 1902; M.A., U. of Neb., 1912; m. Emma R. Parkyn, July 25, 1896; children—Doris W., Rachel R. (dec.), Jason M., Leonard U. Prin. High Sch., Alliance, Neb., 1902-06; supt. city schs., Alliance, 1906-10; pres. State Normal Sch., Peru, Neb., June 1, 1910-18. Mem. Neb. State Bd. Edn., 1908, 09; mem. N.E.A. (state rep. agrl. dept.); mem. Nat. Com. of Normal Sch. Presidents, to standardize normal sch. courses of study. Pres. Library Bd., Alliance, 1909-10; pres. Normal Sch. Sect. and state dir. for Neb. of N.E.A. Head of D. W. Hayes Land Co., Lincoln, Neb.; dir., treas. Western Good Roads Service Assn.; pres. Pathfinder. Dist. gov. Optimist Internat., 1925-29, v.p. 1929, dir. boys' work, 1929. Democrat. Methodist. Mason. Died July 4, 1938.

HAYES, Doremus Almy, theologian; b. Russelville, O., May 17, 1863; s. James Knox and Sarah Elizabeth (Wilkins) H.; A.B., Ohio Wesleyan U., 1884, A.M., 1887; Ph.D., S.T.B., Boston U., 1887; Jacob Sleeper fellow of Boston U., at Berlin and Leipzig, 1891-92; S.T.D., Boston U., 1901; LL.D., Missouri Wesleyan U., 1902; D.D., Garrett Bibl. Inst., 1933; Litt.D., College of the Pacific, 1933; m. Hester Ann Juvenal, July 28, 1887; 1 son, James Juvenal. Ordained M.E. ministry, 1887; pastor, San Leandro, Calif., 1887-88; prof. Greek lang. and lit., U. of the Pacific, 1888-91; pastor, Napa, Calif., 1892-95; prof. Bibl. theology, Iliff Sch. of Theology (U. of Denver), 1895-96; prof. English Bible, 1896-1901, N.T. interpretation, 1901-33, librarian Garrett Bibl. Inst. (Northwestern U.), 1906-26, prof. emeritus, 1933—. Author: The Synoptic Problem, 1912; The Most Beautiful Book Ever Written, 1913; The Gift of Tongues, 1913; Paul and His Epistles, 1915; John and His writings, 1917; The Synoptic Gospels and the Book of Acts, 1919; Great Characters of the New Testament, 1920; New Testament Epistles, 1921; Greek Culture and the Greek Testament, 1925; The Heights of Christian Love, 1926; The Heights of Christian Unity, 1927; The Heights of Christian Blessedness, 1928; The Heights of Christian Living, 1929; The Heights of Christian Devotion, 1930; The Resurrection Fact, 1932. Died 1936.

HAYES, Edward Cary, univ. prof.; b. Lewiston, Me., Feb. 10, 1868; s. Benjamin Francis (D.D.) and Arcy (Cary) H.; A.B., Bates Coll., Me., 1887; LL.D., 1927; studied Cobb Div. Sch., 1889-92, U. of Berlin, 1900-01; Ph.D., U. of Chicago, 1902; LL.D., Grinnell, 1920; m. Annie Lee Bean, Oct. 23, 1895; children—Edward Bean, Robert Cary, Harmon Phillips. Ordained ministry, 1893; pastor Augusta, Me., 1893-96; dean Keuka Coll., N.Y., 1897-99; prof. economics and sociology, Miami U., Ohio, 1902-07; prof. sociology and head of dept., U. of Ill., 1907—. Advisory editor Am. Jour. Sociology; coöperating editor Jour. Applied Sociology. Pres. Ill. State Conf. Charities and Correction, 1910-11; mem. Ill. Bd. Commrs. Pub. Welfare, 1917-18; sec. social psychol. sect. of World's Congress of Science, St. Louis Expn., 1904. Has taught in summer sessions, Harvard, Columbia, U. of Chicago, U. of Pa., U. of Colo. Conglist. Author: Introduction to the Study of Sociology, 1915; Sociology and Ethics, 1921. Home: Urbana, Ill. Died Aug. 7, 1928.

HAYES, Edward Mortimer, brig. gen.; b. in N.Y., Dec. 28, 1842. Enlisted in U.S.A., Aug. 28, 1855; served 2d Cav. in Tex., under Col. Lee and Capt. Kirby Smith, until Aug. 28, 1860; 1st lt. 10th Ohio Cav., Jan. 15, 1863; capt., Mar. 24, 1864; hon. mustered out, July 24, 1865; apptd. from N.J., 2d lt. 5th U.S. Cav., Feb. 23, 1866; promoted through grades to brig. gen., Jan. 15, 1903; retired, Jan. 26, 1903. Served on frontier in many Indian campaigns, in Cuba and P.I. Bvtd.; maj. vols., Mar. 13, 1865, "for gallant and meritorious services during campaign in Ga. and the Carolinas;" maj., Feb. 27, 1890, "for gallant services in action against Indians at Beaver Creek, Kan., Oct. 25, 26, 1868." Home: New York, N.Y. Died Aug. 15, 1912.

HAYES, Francis Little, clergyman; b. New Hampton, N.H., Jan. 5, 1858; s. Benjamin Francis (D.D.) and Arcy (Cary) H.; grad. Nichols Latin Sch., Lewiston, Me., 1876; pupil at Gymnasium of Frankischen Stiftungen, Halle, Germany; A.B., Bates Coll., Me., 1880, A.M., 1883; B.D., Cobb Div. Sch., Lewiston, Me., 1855; D.D., Bates, 1902, Washburn Coll., Kan., 1902; m. Cora Walker, June 26, 1884; children—Cary Walker, Doris Adelaide (dec.), Frank Little, Elinor Guthrie. Instr. Greek, 1880, prof. Greek lang. and lit., 1881-83, Hillsdale (Mich.) Coll.; gen. sec. Y.M.C.A., Lewiston, Me., 1884; ordained Free Bapt. ministry, 1885; pastor 1st Ch., Boston, 1885-90; elected pres. Hillsdale Coll., 1886 (declined); pastor 1st Church, Minneapolis, 1890-94; pastor Congl. Ch., Manitou, Colo., 1896-1902, 1st Congl. Ch., Topeka, Kan., 1902-11, California Av. Ch., Chicago, 1911-14; Western sec. Congl. Bd. of Ministerial Relief, and Annuity Fund for Congl. Ministers, 1914—. Pres. Evang. Alliance Boston and Vicinity, 1889-90, Western Free Bapt. Pub. Co., 1890-94, Western Assn. Free Bapts., 1890-94. Lecturer on homiletics, Bibl. Dept., Washburn Coll., 1909-10. Trustee Washburn Coll., 1902-11; dir. Chicago Theol. Sem., 1905-11; corporator A.B.C.F.M., 1906-11; chaplain Midwest div. Alden Kindred of America, 1912-21; regional dir. in the Midwest of the campaign for the Pilgrim Memorial Fund, 1917-20. Home: Oak Park, Ill. Died Apr. 3, 1926.

HAYES, Ellen, educator; b. at Granville, O., Sept. 23, 1851; d. Charles C. and Ruth (Wolcott) H.; sister of Charles Willard H.; A.B., Oberlin Coll., 1878; unmarried. Instr. and asso. prof., 1880-88, prof. mathematics, 1888-97, applied mathematics, 1897-1904, astronomy and applied mathematics, 1904-16, Wellesley Coll. Lecturer and writer on astron. and other scientific subjects. Candidate for sec. of state, Socialist party, Mass., 1912. Retired, 1916. Editor of The Relay. Foundation mem. History of Science Soc.; fellow A.A.A.S. Author: Wild Turkeys and Tallow Candles, 1910; How Do You Know? 1923; The Sycamore Trail, 1929. Deceased.

HAYES, Montrose W(hite), meterologist; b. Charlotte, N.C., Nov. 21, 1874; s. Junius W. and Lucie Connor (Morrow) H.; ed. pub. schs.; m. Marie C. Leuschen, Mar. 18, 1908; children—Idelia A., Montrose H. Observer, U.S. Weather Bur., 1892-1903; organizer nat. weather forecasting service, Argentina, 1904-06; in charge various offices of U.S. Weather Bur., 1907-09; in charge St. Louis (Mo.) office, 1910-29; chief of river and flood div., Weather Bur., Washington, D.C., 1930—. Home: Washington, D.C. Died Nov. 16, 1936.

HAYES, Patrick Joseph, cardinal; b. New York, N.Y., Nov. 20, 1867; s. Daniel and Mary (Gleason) H.; A.B., Manhattan Coll., New York, 1888, A.M., 1894; S.T.D., Catholic U. of America, 1894; D.D., Rome, 1904. Ordained R.C. priest, 1892; apptd. chancellor of New York, 1903; pres. Cathedral Coll., 1903-14; domestic prelate to the Pope, 1907; consecrated auxiliary bishop of New York, Oct. 28, 1914; rector St. Stephen's Ch., Oct. 1915; appt. Catholic chaplain bishop for U.S. Army and Navy, Nov. 24, 1917; apptd. archbishop New York, Mar. 10, 1919; created cardinal, Mar. 24, 1924. Decorated Officer Legion of Honor (France), 1919; Grand Cross of Devotion of Knights of Malta, 1927; Cardinal Protector of Am. Branch of Knights of Malta, 1928; Grand Official Order of St. Maurizio and St. Lazzaro, 1929; Grand Cross Order of St. Lazare de Jerusalem, 1929; Knight Grand Cross of Equestrian Order of the Holy Sepulchre, 1931; mem. of the Sacred Congregation "Pro Ecclesia Orientali," 1931; Knight Grand Officer Order of Can Marine, 1931; apptd. legate "a latere" to Eucharistic Congress, Cleveland, Aug. 20, 1935, by Pope Pius XI. Died Sept. 4, 1938.

HAYES, Philip Cornelius, congressman; b. Granby, Conn., Feb. 3, 1833; s. Gaylord and Mary (Goodrich) H.; A.B., Oberlin, 1860, A.M., 1863; grad. Oberlin Theol. Sem., 1863; m. Amelia E. Johnson, Jan. 25, 1865. Capt. 103d Ohio Inf., July 16, 1862; lt. col., Nov. 18, 1864; apptd. col. but not mustered in; bvtd. brig. gen. vols., Mar. 13, 1865, "for gallant and meritorious services during the war"; hon. mustered out, June 12, 1865. Actively engaged in journalism, 1866-95; mem. 45th and 46th Congresses (1877-81). Home: Joliet, Ill. Died July 13, 1916.

HAYES, Samuel Walter, judge; b. Huntsville, Ark., Sept. 17, 1875; s. John and Mollie (Cox) H.; ed. pub. schs. of Tex., and U. of Va. (non-grad.); m. Ida Poole, Oct. 8, 1899 (dec.); children—Kent Birch, Ruby Grace, Ida Lee; m. 2d, Mrs. Elizabeth Russell Crockett, July 28, 1925. Admitted to bar, 1899; practiced at Ryan, 1899-1902; mem. Welborne & Hayes, Chickasha, 1902-07; served as city atty. Ryan; mem. constl. conv. of Okla., 1906; justice Supreme Court of Okla., 1907-15 (chief justice, 1913-15); mem. Cottingham & Hayes, 1915-23; mem. Hayes, Richardson, Shartel, Gilliland & Jordan, 1923—. Democrat; chmn. Dem. State Central Com., Okla., 1930-31. Methodist. Home: Oklahoma City, Okla. Died Mar. 14, 1941.

HAYES, Stephen Quentin, electrical engr.; b. Washington, D.C., Dec. 17, 1873; s. Henry Gillespie and Maria Louisa (Hogan) H.; A.B., Georgetown U., 1892; E.E., Johns Hopkins, 1894; m. Helen Grace Buck, Nov. 6, 1901 (died 1931); children—Helen Grace (Mrs. R. J. Peterman), Jane Louise (Mrs. L. J. Hartman), Stephen Quentin, Charles Joseph, John Henry, Isabel Gillespie. With Westinghouse Electric & Mfg. Co., on students' course, 1894-95; draftsman, 1895-98, designing engr., 1898-1906, estimating and commercial engr., 1906-09, gen. and commercial engr., 1909-33. Temporarily with Westinghouse European cos. part 1917-18, with U.S. Govt. part 1919; in Australia and Japan, 1921-22; cons. engr. Japanese Imperial Govt. rys., 1922; in Colombia, Panama and Ecuador, 1928-31; cons. engr., Municipality of Quito, Ecuador, 1928; cons. engr., Quito Electric Light & Power Co., 1931. Lecturer U. of Pittsburgh and Carnegie Inst., 1933-36. Hon. Ecuadorean vice consul for Pittsburgh, 1931-35; sec. and treas. Consular Assn. of Pittsburgh, 1932-35. Fellow Am. Inst. E.E. Republican. Catholic. Author: Switching Equipment for Power Control. Asst. editor switchgear and control sect. Am. Elec. Engineers' Handbook, 1913-35; asst. editor E.M.F. (Electrical Year Book), 1920-26. Home: Pittsburgh, Pa. Died Apr. 4, 1936.

HAYES, Thomas Gordon, mayor Baltimore, Md., 1899-1903; b. Anne Arundel Co., Md., Jan. 5, 1844; s. Rev. Thomas C. and Juliana (Gordon) H.; grad. Va. Mil. Inst.; unmarried. Served Confederate soldier during Civil war; studied law; admitted to Md. bar, 1872; U.S. dist. atty. for Md. under Pres. Cleveland's 1st administration. Democrat. Home: Baltimore, Md. Died Aug. 27, 1915.

HAYES, Warren Howard, architect; b. Prattsburg, Steuben Co., N.Y., Aug. 22, 1847; grad. Cornell, 1871; m. Miss M. F. Beardsley, May 1881 (died 1882); m. 2d, Mrs. Lillie Cook Van Norman, Oct. 26, 1886. Practiced, Elmira, N.Y., 1874-81, Minneapolis, Minn., 1881—; originator of the "diagonal plan" of auditorium, which he has used in many churches; especially distinguished in the line of ecclesiastical architecture. Deceased.

HAYES, Webb Cook, mfr.; b. Cincinnati, O., Mar. 20, 1856; s. Rutherford Birchard (19th President of U.S.) and Lucy Ware (Webb) H.; student Cornell U., 1872-75; m. Mary Otis Miller, Sept. 30, 1912. Sec. to father, 1875-81; joint organizer, 1881-1901, and treas. Whipple Mfg., Nat. Carbon Co., Union Carbide Co. Served as maj. First Ohio Cav., later adj. gen., Spanish-Am. War, serving in Cuba and Porto Rico; wounded at crossing of San Juan River, Cuba; served as lt. col., U.S. Vols., Philippine Insurrection, Island of Mindanao; attached to staff Gen. Chaffee, China Relief Expdn., Boxer uprising, 1900; served on Mexican border, 1911, 13, 16; dispatch bearer between Am. ambassadors in Paris, London and Berlin, World War, 1916; served with Brit. and French brigades on Italian front, 1917-18; regional commr. A.E.F. in France and North Africa, 1918. Donated Spiegel Grove, 25-acre Hayes Homestead, to State of Ohio, building Hayes Memorial Library and Museum ($500,000 endowment), in memory of parents. Awarded Congressional Medal of Honor for "distinguished gallantry pushing through the enemy's lines alone on the night of Dec. 4th, 1899, from the beach to our beleaguered force at Vigan, P.I., and returning the following morning to report the condition of affairs to the Navy and get assistance." Decorated by Marshal Lyantey for the Sultan of Turkey, Aug. 15, 1918. Home: Fremont, O. Died July 26, 1934.

HAYFORD, John Fillmore, civil engr.; b. Rouse's Point, N.Y., May 19, 1868; s. Hiram and Mildred Alevia (Fillmore) H.; C.E., Cornell Univ., 1889; Sc.D. from George Washington Univ., 1918; m. Lucy Stone, Oct. 11, 1894. Apptd. computer U.S. Coast and Geod. Survey, June 1889; asst. astronomer to Internat. Boundary Commn. U.S. and Mexico, in charge of one of field parties, 1892-93; aid and later asst. U.S. Coast and Geod. Survey, 1894-95; instr. civ. engring., Cornell U., 1895-98; expert computer and geodesist, U.S. Coast and Geod. Survey, 1898-99, and inspr. of geodetic work and chief of computing div., 1900-09; dir. Coll. Engring., Northwestern U., Sept. 1, 1909—. Mem. Nat. Advisory Com. for Aeronatuics, 1915-23. Research asso. Carnegie Instn. of Washington, D.C. Author: Geodetic Astronomy, 1898. Home: Evanston, Ill. Died Mar. 10, 1925.

HAYLEY, John William, clergyman; b. Tuftonboro, N.H., June 8, 1834; s. John Smith and Mary Neal (Piper) H.; A.B., Dartmouth, 1860; grad. Andover Theol. Sem., 1864; D.D., Union Christian Coll., [illegible] 1900; m. Caroline S. Wadsworth, Nov. [illegible] (dec.); children—Evelyn C., Alice W.; Fer[illegible] Ordained Christian ministry, 1864; pasto[illegible]

Me., 1864-65; prof. Union Christian Coll., 1865; pastor Somerset, Mass., 1866-69, Duxbury, Mass., 1869-70, Tyngsboro, Mass., 1874-75, Hudson, N.H., 1876-78, Temple, N.H., 1880-82 and 1888-91, Lunenburg, Vt., 1891-92, Truro, Mass., 1892-95; in lit. work since 1895. Mem. Victoria Inst., London. Republican. Author: Alleged Discrepancies of the Bible, 1874; Some Aspects and Results of German Kultur, as Noted by an American Observer; Fancies and Follies of the Middle Ages. Translator (with 3 other clergymen) Book of Esther, 1885. Home: Center Tuftonboro, N.H. Died Oct. 3, 1927.

HAYMAKER, Jesse N., lawyer; b. Clark Co., Ind., Sept. 13, 1858; s. George W. and Foster (Henley) H.; student Hanover (Ind.) Coll. 1 yr.; LL.B., Ky. U., Louisville, 1855; m. Allie King, Nov. 30, 1881. City atty., Jeffersonville, Ind., 1885-87; co. atty., Clark Co., Ind., 1886; moved to Wichita, Kan., 1887; judge of probate, Sedgwick Co., Kan., 1897-1901; city solicitor, Wichita, 1917—. Pres. Gen. Conv. Disciples of Christ, 1916-17; dir. Phillips U., Enid, Okla.; dir. Wichita Y.M.C.A. Home: Wichita, Kan. Died Feb. 21, 1930.

HAYMAN, Al., theatrical manager; lessee Baldwin Theatre, San Francisco, 1883, and produced there many successful casts; purchased, 1889, play "Shenandoah," which prod. several seasons; leased Columbia Theatre, Chicago, 1889; was also mgr. Columbia Theatre, Brooklyn, and later Empire Theatre, New York; later with Charles Frohman and Nixon & Zimmerman owned or controlled theatres throughout the country. Pres. Actors' Fund of America. Died Feb. 10, 1917.

HAYNE, William Hamilton, author; b. Charleston, S.C., Mar. 11, 1856; s. Paul Hamilton H. (poet and author); ed. chiefly at home except few mos. at Porter Acad., Charleston, S.C.; unmarried. Family moved to Augusta, Ga., 1866. Wrote poem read at unveiling of bust of Sidney Lanier, the poet, at Public Library, Macon, Ga. Author: Sylvan Lyrics and Other Verses, 1892. Home: Augusta, Ga. Died Jan. 7, 1929.

HAYNER, Rutherford, editor; b. Clarendon, N.Y., Sept. 21, 1877; s. Nelson McChesney and Frances Adella (Frederick) H.; ed. high sch., Schaghticoke, N.Y.; m. Mabelle Beard, June 24, 1903; children—Dorothy (Mrs. Arthur R. Worrall), Warren Nelson. Printer, press photographer, reporter, editor, village weeklies and city dailies, 1893-1900; with Troy (N.Y.) Times, 1900—, city editor, 1917-26, editor, 1926-35; also program dir., announcer, station WHAZ, Rensselaer Poly. Inst. Republican. Unitarian. Author: History of Troy and Rensselaer County, 1924. Home: West Sand Lake, N.Y. Died Mar. 14, 1939.

HAYNES, Arthur Edwin, univ. prof.; b. Van Buren, N.Y., May 23, 1849; s. Horace and Adaline (Sweet) H.; B.S., Hillsdale Coll., 1875, M.S., 1877, M.Ph., 1879 (hon. Sc.D., 1896); several summers at U. of Mich., Harvard, Cornell; m. May Hewitt (coll. classmate), June 24, 1875. Instr., acting prof. and prof. mathematics and physics, Hillsdale Coll., 1875-90, Mich. Coll. Mines, 1890-93; asst. prof. mathematics, 1893-96, prof. in Coll. of Engring., 1896-1901, prof. of engring. mathematics, 1901-12, U. of Minn.; retired, on Carnegie allowance, May 6, 1912. Home: Minneapolis, Minn. Died Mar. 12, 1915.

HAYNES, David Oliphant, publisher; b. Detroit, Mich., Aug. 29, 1858; s. Levi Hasbrouck and Caroline (Oliphant) H.; high sch. edn.; m. Helen Dunham Williams, Oct. 15, 1885; children—Williams, Hasbrouck, David Oliphant, Helen D., Elise S. Pres. and gen. mgr. D. O. Haynes & Co., publishers, 1887—; established The Pharmaceutical Era, Detroit, 1887; removed to New York, 1894; established the New York Commercial as a daily business newspaper, 1898; planned and published Depew's One Hundred Years of American Commerce, 1896. Home: Garden City, L.I., N.Y. Died May 19, 1932.

HAYNES, Elwood, inventor; b. Portland, Ind., Oct. 14, 1857; s. Jacob March and Hilinda Sophia (Haines) H.; B.S., Worcester Poly. Inst., 1881; Johns Hopkins, 1884-85; m. Bertha Beatrice Lanterman, Oct. 21, 1887. Teacher sciences, Eastern Ind. Normal Sch., Portland, 1885-86; mgr. Portland Natural Gas & Oil Co., 1886-90; field supt. Ind. Natural Gas & Oil Co., 1890-1901; pres. Haynes Automobile Co., 1898—. Discovered tungsten chrome steel, 1881, alloy of chromium and nickel, 1897, alloy of cobalt and chromium, 1900; developed latter alloy for cutting instruments, 1910; designed and constructed a horseless carriage, 1893-94, which is the oldest American automobile in existence and is on exhibition at Smithsonian Instn.; first to introduce aluminum in automobile engine, 1895; invented and built rotary valve gas engine, 1903. Prohibitionist. Presbyn. Discovered alloys of cobalt, chromium, and tungsten, also alloys of cobalt, chromium and molybdenum, 1911-12, and pres. The Haynes Stellite Co., mfg. tool metals of same, 1912-20; discovered "stainless steel," 1911 (patented 1919). Trustee Western Coll., Oxford, O., Winona Assembly and Bible Conf., Winona Lake, Ind. Home: Kokomo, Ind. Died Apr. 13, 1925.

HAYNES, Emory James, clergyman; b. Cabot, Vt., Feb. 6, 1847; s. Zadoc S. and Marion W. (Bayley) H.; A.B., Wesleyan U., Conn., 1867, A.M., 1887 (D.D., 1874); m. Grace Forby, Apr. 28, 1874. Ordained M.E. ministry; pastor, Norwich, Conn., Fall River, Mass., Brooklyn, Boston and New York. Editorial staff New York Evening Mail. Author: Fairest of Three; Wedding in War-time; Dollars and Duty; Are These Things So?; None Such: A Farm House Cobweb. Home: Poughkeepsie, N.Y. Died Dec. 31, 1914.

HAYNES, Henry Williamson, archeologist; b. Bangor, Me., Sept. 20, 1831; s. Nathaniel and Caroline J. (Williamson) H.; A.B., Harvard, 1851, A.M., 1859; m. Helen Weld Blanchard, Aug. 1, 1867 (died 1902). Engaged in teaching; practiced law few yrs.; prof. Latin and later of Greek, U. of Vt., 1867-72; from 1873 devoted to archeology, making investigations and researches in Europe, Egypt and elsewhere. Received medal and diploma from Internat. Congress of Anthrop. Sciences, Paris, 1878. Fellow Am. Acad. Arts and Sciences. Home: Boston, Mass. Died 1912.

HAYNES, John Randolph, M.D.; b. Fairmount Springs, Pa., June 13, 1853; s. James Sydney (formerly of London, Eng.) and Elvira Mann (Koons) H.; moved to Phila. at age of 10; Ph.D., M.D., U. of Pa., 1874; began practice of medicine; m. Dora Fellows, Mar. 14, 1882. Removed to Los Angeles, practicing there from 1887; formerly asso. prof. gynecology, U. of Southern Calif. Mem. City Civ. Service Commn. of Los Angeles for 12 years and its pres. for 2 years; drafted and was instrumental in incorporating in the charter of city of Los Angeles, 1903, the initiative, referendum and recall amendments, the latter giving to majority of city's electors the power to discharge from office for incompetency or dishonesty any elected city official at any time. Los Angeles was not only the first city but the first political subdivision in the U.S. to incorporate this provision into its organic law. Pres. Direct Legislation League of Calif.; pres. League to Protect the Initiative of Calif.; mem. Los Angeles Pub. Service Commn., 1920-25; mem. Los Angeles Bd. of Water & Power Commrs. (successor to Public Service Commn.), 1925—; mem. Los Angeles Co. Probation Com., 1915-25. Nat. Child Labor Assn., 1915-25, Calif. State Bd. Charities and Corrections, 1912-23; state commr. to investigate mining accidents; v.p. Nat. Popular Govt. League. Mem. Los Angeles Co. Public Welfare Commn., 1915-26; mem. Calif. Tax Commn., 1927-29. Mem. Calif. State Council Defense, 1917; industrial adviser U.S. War Labor Bd., Div. No. 1, Southern Dist. of Calif., 1917-19; mem. Com. Efficiency and Economy (reorgn. state govt.), 1918; indsl. adviser U.S. Employment Service, 1919; mem. Met. Water Dist. Bd. (building aqueduct from Colo. River to Southern Calif.), 1928-30; mem. Calif. State Constl. Com., 1929-31, Calif. State Unemployment Com., 1930-31. Regent U. of Calif., 1923—; v.p. Good Hope Hosp. Assn. Home: Los Angeles, Calif. Died Oct. 1937.

HAYNES, Myron Wilbur, clergyman; b. Lunenburg, Mass., Jan. 1, 1855; s. Elnathan and Sarah (Wheeler) H.; A.B., Colgate U., 1879; D.D., Shurtleff Coll., Alton, Ill., 1890; LL.D., Shurtleff Coll., 1926; m. Florence G. Felt, June 20, 1879; children—Carey Dana, Mrs. Ethel Ada Arnold, Arthur Stanley. Ordained Bapt. ministry, 1879; pastor Frankfort, N.Y., 1879-82, Marblehead, Mass., 1882-84, Kalamazoo, Mich., 1884-88, Englewood Ch., Chicago, 1888-96, Belden Av. Ch., Chicago, 1896-1905, First Ch., Seattle, 1905-07, Delmar Av. Ch., St. Louis, 1907-08; engaged in endowment movement for Central U., Pella, Ia., 1908-11, for Franklin (Ind.) Coll., 1911-14, for McMinnville (Ore.) College, 1914-17, for Keuka Coll., Cook Acad., Shurtleff Coll., North Western Bible and Missionary Training Sch., McMinnville Coll., 1917—; endowment sec. Shurtleff Coll., 1919—; endowment and field sec. Keuka Coll., 1926—; field sec. Western Bapt. Theol. Sem., 1931—. Pres. trustees Shurtleff Coll., 1896-1902; pres. Central Bapt. Orphanage, 1895-1902, Ill. State Bapt. Conv., 1898-1902. Home: McMinnville, Ore. Deceased.

HAYNES, Nathaniel Smith, clergyman; b. Washington, Ky., Mar. 7, 1844; s. James and Amanda (Hampton) H.; grad. Eureka (Ill.) Coll., 1867 (A.M., 1868); post-grad. course, Ky. Univ.; m. Rose Frazier, Nov. 20, 1873. Pvt. 86th and 139th regts., Ill. Vol. Inf. in Civil War; prin. pub. schs., Kansas, Ill., 1867-68; pastor Christian (Disciples) Ch., Kansas, Ill., until 1873, Decatur, 1873-80; corr. sec. Ill. Christian Missionary Soc., 1880-86; pastor Peoria, Ill., 1886-92, Englewood, Chicago, 1892-98, Eureka, 1898-1902; First Church, Lincoln, Neb., 1902-06, and various other churches, 1906-15; retired 1916. Home: Gary, Ind. Died Jan. 12, 1925.

HAYNES, Roy Asa, commr. prohibition of U.S.; b. Hillsboro, O., Aug. 31, 1881; s. Charles Elliott and Mary (West) H.; Western Reserve U., 1903-04; m. Katherine Logan Mason, Sept. 9, 1903. Editor of Dispatch, Hillsboro, O., 1908—. Active worker in prohibition campaigns for many yrs.; federal prohibition commr., 1921-27; pres. Economy Fire Ins. Co., 1927-28; with Nat. Thrift Corp., 1928-29; investment banking, 1929-30; mng. distributor for Eastern territory, Air-Way Electric Appliance Corp., 1930-35, gen. sales mgr. and personnel dir., same co., 1936—. Twice del. Gen. Conf. M.E. Ch., heading lay delegation from West Ohio Conf. Republican. Methodist. Mason. Author: Prohibition Inside Out, 1923. Home: Hillsboro, O. Died Oct. 20, 1940.

HAYNIE, (James) Henry, author; b. Winchester, Ill., July 19, 1841; s. Ornsbe and Zerilda (Rucker) H.; ed. grammar and high sch., Winchester, Ill.; m. Mary Huguenin Bright, Dec. 19, 1893. Enlisted Apr. 15, 1861, in first inf. co. raised in Chicago; served in Gen. Swift's expdn. to Cairo, Ill., Apr. 17-May 6, 1861; mustered into Co. D, 19th Ill. Inf., June 17, 1861, for 3 yrs.; served in Army of the Cumberland; taken prisoner after being wounded at battle of Stone River, Dec. 31, 1862, and kept in Libby Prison several months in various battles and many engagements; mustered out July 9, 1864. After war reporter on Chicago newspaper; foreign editor New York Times, 1875-77; went to Paris, 1877, as spl. corr. Am. newspapers (principally Boston Herald, San Francisco Chronicle, and New Orleans Picayune); returned to U.S., 1895; traveling corr. Boston Herald in U.S. for some time; devoted entire time to lit. work, 1898—. Decorated Cross Legion d'Honneur, France, 1892, cross Chevalier Royal Order of the Saviour, Greece, 1895. Was pres. Assn. Foreign Press Corrs., Paris, several yrs. Was offered commn. as lt. col., Egyptian Army, 1876, by Khédive, but declined. Episcopalian. Independent Republican. Author: Paris, Past and Present, 2 vols., 1902; The Captains and the Kings, 1904. Home: Newton Centre, Mass. Died May 15, 1912.

HAYS, Calvin Cornwell, clergyman; b. Cumberland Co., Pa., May 21, 1861; s. Rev. Isaac N. (D.D.) and Rebecca H. (King) H.; A.B., Washington and Jefferson Coll., 1881, D.D. from same college, 1891; LL.D., Waynesburg Coll., 1928; student Western Theol. Sem., 1881-84; m. Lucy W. Alexander, Mar. 18, 1891. Ordained Presbyn. ministry, 1885; stated supply, Bethel Ch., Alleghany, Pa., 1883-84; pastor Bridgeport, O., 1885-90, First Ch., Johnstown, Pa., 1891-1925. Moderator Synod of Pa., 1909; moderator Gen. Assembly Presbyn. Ch. in U.S.A., 1922; synodical executive, Synod of Pa. Presbyn. Ch., 1925-29. Trustee Washington and Jefferson Coll., Lincoln U., Pa. Anti-Saloon League; trustee Western Theol. Sem. Home: Johnstown, Pa. Died Feb. 14, 1935.

HAYS, Charles Melville, ry. pres.; b. Rock Island, Ill., May 16, 1856; s. Samuel and Sarah Elisabeth (Morris) H.; ed. at St. Joseph, Mo., and Phila.; m. Clara J. Gregg, Oct. 13, 1881. Entered ry. service, Nov. 10, 1873, as clerk in passenger dept. Atlantic & Pacific R.R., St. Louis, later in auditor's and gen. supt.'s offices until 1877; sec. to gen. mgr. Mo. Pacific, 1877-84; sec. to gen. mgr., 1884-86, asst. gen. mgr., 1886-87, Wabash, St. Louis & Pacific; apptd., July 1887, gen. mgr. Wabash Western, and later of consolidated Wabash System; v.p. and gen. mgr., 1894; was dir. Chicago & Western Ill. R.R., Belt Ry. of Chicago, Detroit Union R.R. & Station Co., Hannibal Union Sta. Co., Keokuk Union Sta. Co., Kansas City Union Sta. Co., Terminal R.R. Assn. of St. Louis (chmn. exec. com.); represented Wabash R.R. in Western Traffic Assn., Central Traffic Assn. and on Joint Traffic Assn.; gen. mgr. Grand Trunk Ry. System, Jan. 1, 1896-Jan. 1, 1901; pres. S.P. Ry., Jan. 1, 1901, but retired latter part of 1901, becoming 2d v.p. and gen. mgr. Grand Trunk Ry. System; pres. Grand Trunk Ry. System, Jan. 1, 1910—. Is pres. Central Vt. Ry., Chicago, Detroit & Canada Grand Trunk Junction R.R., Grand Trunk Pacific Ry., Grand Trunk Western Ry., Detroit, Grand Haven & Milwaukee Ry., Canadian Express Co., St. Clair Tunnel Co., Internat. Bridge Co., Montreal Warehousing Co., Portland Elevator Co., N.E. Elevator Co. Died Apr. 15, 1912.

HAYS, Daniel Peixotto, lawyer; b. Pleasantville, N.Y., Mar. 28, 1854; s. David and Judith S. (Peixotto) H.; student Coll. City of New York, class 1873; LL.B., Columbia, 1875; m. Rachel Hershfield, Apr. 11, 1880. Practiced in New York, 1875—; sr. mem. Hays, Hershfield & Wolf, New York. Dir. Fleischmann Realty Co., Sickles Estate Improvement Co.; pres. Hays & Associates. Died Nov. 24, 1923.

HAYS, Edward D., congressman; b. Oak Ridge, Mo., Apr. 28, 1872; s. John W. and Mary J. (Horn) H.; grad. State Normal Sch., Cape Girardeau, Mo., 1893; m. Maggie Burford, Dec. 15, 1898; children—Dallas B., Cathryn M., Eddie Maxine (dec.), John Maxwell (dec.). Practiced at Jackson, Mo., 1896-1914; moved to Cape Girardeau, 1914; mayor of Jackson 2 terms, 1904-07; probate judge Cape Girardeau Co. 3 terms, 1907-18 inclusive; mem. 66th and 67th Congresses (1919-23), 14th Mo. Dist.; trial lawyer, Dept. of Justice in Court of Claims, 2½ yrs.; atty. for Interstate Commerce Commn. 8 yrs.; now in pvt. practice, general and departmental. Republican. Home: Cape Girardeau, Mo. Died July 25, 1941.

HAYS, Elmer D(ishman), lawyer; b. Barboursville, Ky., Sept. 13, 1891; s. Joseph Smith and Ella Belle (Helton) H.; B.S., Ky. Wesleyan Coll., Winchester, 1913; LL.B., U. of Ky., 1914; m. Isabelle Ruth Unkefer, Jan. 13, 1917; children—Elizabeth Helton, Elmer Dishman. Admitted to Ky. bar, 1914, gen. practice, 1914-16; with valuation dept. Interstate Commerce Commn., 1917-21, in charge N.Y. City office, 1921-24, traveling field instr., 1925, sr. and prin. valuation examiner, 1926-33; apptd. chief atty. license enforcement and revocation sect. of Agrl. Adjustment Administration, 1933. Pres. U. of Ky.

Alumni Assn. of Washington, D.C. Democrat. Presbyterian. Home: Chevy Chase, Md. Died Sept. 2, 1937.

HAYS, Frank W., clergyman, educator; b. Industry, Pa., Oct. 21, 1861; s. John and Ellen (Stevenson) H.; S.B., Grove City (Pa.) Coll., 1884, A.B., 1887, Ph.D., 1894; grad. Western Theol. Sem., Pa., 1890; D.D., Waynesburg, 1903; m. Harriet Gordon, June 25, 1890; children—Margaret (dec.), Frank Gordon (dec.), Ralph Lawrence, Quincy Gordon (dec.). Instr. and prof. mathematics, Grove City Coll., 1884-94; ordained Presbyn. ministry, 1890; pastor First Ch., North East, Pa., 1894-96; prof. history and polit. science, Grove City Coll., 1896-1911; pastor First Ch., New Bethlehem, Pa., 1911-18; prof. history, Coll. of Wooster, 1918—. Home: Wooster, O. Deceased.

HAYS, George Washington, governor; b. Ouachita County, nr. Camden, Ark., Sept. 23, 1863; s. Thomas and Parthena Jane H.; ed. dist. schs.; student Law Sch., Washington and Lee U., Lexington, Va.; m. Ida Virginia Yarbraugh, Feb. 26, 1895. Began practice, Camden, Ark., 1894; county and probate judge, Ouachita Co., 1900-04; judge 13th Jud. Circuit of Ark., 1906-13; gov. of Ark. for terms 1913-15, 1915-17. Democrat. Missionary Baptist. Mason. Home: Little Rock, Ark. Deceased.

HAYS, I(saac) Minis, physician; b. Philadelphia, July 26, 1847; s. Isaac (M.D.) and Sarah (Minis) H.; A.B., U. of Pa., 1866, M.D., 1868, A.M., 1869; m. Emma, d. George A. Wood, of Phila., Oct. 15, 1873. Editor Am. Jour. of Medical Sciences, 1869-90, The Medical News, 1869-89. Sec. gen. Internat. Med. Congress, Phila., 1876; fellow Am. Acad. Arts and Sciences. Editor: Am. edit. of Soelberg Wells on Diseases of the Eye, 1873; Calendar of the Franklin Papers, 1907. Author: Chronology of Benjamin Franklin, 1904, 2d edit., 1913. Home: Philadelphia, Pa. Died June 5, 1925.

HAYS, John, lawyer, mfr.; b. Carlisle, Pa., Feb. 2, 1837; s. John and Ellinor Blaine (Wheaton) Hays; A.B., Dickinson College, 1857 (LL.D., same, 1914); m. Jane Van Ness Smead, Aug. 8, 1865. In service Aug. 1862-May 1863, as 2d and 1st lt., 1st lt. and adj., 130th Regt. Pa. Vols.; acting asst. adj. gen. 2d Brigade, 3d Div., 2d Army Corps, and spl. inspecting officer; acting aid on staff of Gen. William Hays; selected to superintend burial of enemy's dead for front of ½ mile on "Bloody Lane"; participated in battles of Antietam, Fredericksburg and Chancellorsville; struck in clothing and person 7 times, and horse killed at Chancellorsville. Practiced, 1859-98; specialized in corp. law; established in U.S. Supreme Ct. liability of nat. banks for safe-keeping of special deposits held without compensation; mem. Henderson & Hays, 1863-74; pres. Carlisle Deposit Bank, 1874-93; editor and propr. Carlisle Herald, 1877-1909; pres. Carlisle Gas & Water Co., Frog Switch & Mfg. Co., etc. Trustee Metzger Coll., Carlisle. Presdl. elector, Pa., 1904. Presbyn. Home: Carlisle, Pa. Died Nov. 30, 1921.

HAYS, Margaret Gebbie, author; b. Philadelphia, Pa.; d. of George and Mary (Fitzgerald) Gebbie; sister of Grace Gebbie Drayton; ed. by governess, boarding sch. and Convent of Notre Dame, Phila.; m. Frank Allison Hays, Oct. 11, 1893. Began writing newspaper comics, Phila. Press, 1906. Author: The Turr'ble Tales of Kaptin Kiddo, 1910; Kiddie Land, 1910; Kaptin Kiddo and Puppo, 1911; Kiddie Rhymes, 1911; Kaptin Kiddo's 'Speriences, 1913. Home: Germantown, Pa. Died Sept. 13, 1925.

HAYS, William Jacob, painter; b. Catskill, N.Y., July 1, 1872; s. William J. (A.N.A.) and Helen (Dummer) H.; art. edn. Nat. Acad. Design, New York, Acad. Julian and Acad. Colorossi, Paris; m. Martha Stark, Feb. 13, 1903; 1 son, Hoffman R. Mem. 1st Ohio Vol. Cav., Spanish-Am. War, 1898. Has exhibited at Nat. Acad. Design, Pa. Acad. Fine Arts, Art Mus., Worcester, Mass., Portland, Ore., Internat. Exhbn., Venice. Shaw prize, Salmagundi Club, 1912. A.N.A., 1909; asso. Am. Fedn. of Arts. Home: Millbrook, N.Y. Died Sept. 30, 1934.

HAYS, William Shakespeare ("Will S. Hays"), ballad writer, composer; b. Louisville, Ky., July 19, 1837; academic edn.; became reporter on Louisville Democrat, 1857; later clerk and capt. of steamboats on Ohio and Mississippi rivers for 4 yrs.; now marine editor Louisville Courier-Journal and Times. Married. Wrote and composed Mollie Darling, Nora O'Neil, Shamus O'Brien, Write Me a Letter from Home, and over 300 other well-known songs. Author: Poems and Songs. Died 1907.

HAYT, Charles D., lawyer; b. Poughkeepsie, N.Y., May 20, 1850; s. Henry D. and Jane (Berry) H.; grad. Williston Sem., Easthampton, Mass., 1867; m. Julia Aline Palmer, Oct. 2, 1878, Practiced at Walsenburg, Colo., 1872-76, Garland City, 1876-77, Alamosa, 1878-83, Denver, 1889—. Dist. atty., 6th Jud. Dist., Colo., 1880-83; dist. judge, 1883-89; justice Supreme Court of Colo., 1889-98 (chief justice, 1892-98). Republican. Lecturer on taxation, U. of Colo., 1901-12. Mason, Elk. Home: Denver, Colo. Deceased.

HAYWARD, Benjamin Dover, educator; b. Pomeroy, O., Sept. 19, 1860; s. Benjamin and Sarah H.; ed. Carleton Coll., Syracuse, O., Nat. Normal U., Lebanon, O.; LL.B., U. of Neb., 1894; m. Mary E. Scanlin, Apr. 1, 1886. Teacher pub. schs., Ohio, 1880-88, Neb., 1888-92; co. supt. schs., Howard Co., Neb., 1890-92; practiced law in Neb., 1894-1903; supt. State Industrial Sch. for Boys, Neb., 1903-07; founded, Sept. 16, 1907, and from then supt., Neb. Mil. Acad. Republican. Presbyn. Home: Lincoln, Neb. Died Aug. 7, 1916.

HAYWARD, Edward Farwell, clergyman; b. Lowell, Mass., May 9, 1851; s. Asa Edward and Frances Caroline (French) H.; attended Tufts Coll. 2 yrs.; S.T.B., Harvard, 1874; m. Ellen Harriet Cross, Aug. 7, 1879. Ordained, Montreal, Can., Sept. 7, 1874; settled Fall River, Mass., 1877-82, Second Hawes Congl. (Unitarian) Soc., S. Boston, Mass., 1883-86, Chicopee, Mass., 1886-90, West Parish Unitarian Ch., Marlborough, Mass., 1890-1915, again at Chicopee, 1915—. Author: Ecce Spiritus, 1883; The Mothers, 1903; Life of Lyman Beecher, 1904. Home: Chicopee, Mass. Died Dec. 22, 1923.

HAYWARD, Florence, writer; b. St. Louis, 1865; d. George A. (col. C.S.A.) and Ellen (Erwin) H.; grad. Mary Inst. (coll. for women of Washington U.); unmarried. Has written extensively for Am. and English mags. Apptd., Nov. 1902, spl. commr. of St. Louis Expn. to Europe, only woman apptd. to this position; obtained for expn., from King Edward, loan of Queen Victoria's Jubilee presents for expn., and first Vatican exhibit ever sent to any expn. Elected Officier French Acad., 1904; pres. Mary Inst. Alumni Assn.; originator of Artists' Guild of St. Louis. Elected mem. Royal Soc. of Arts, and Meteorol. Soc. (London), 1913, in recognition of services rendered in 1904. Home: St. Louis, Mo. Deceased.

HAYWARD, Harry; b. Lewistown, N.Y., May 19, 1869; s. George Calvin and Frances (Baker) H.; B.S. in Agr., Cornell Univ., 1894; M.S., 1901; spl. courses in agr., U. of Minn., Hameln Dairy Sch., Germany, Reading (Eng.) Coll. and Harvard Med. Sch.; m. Lillian Woolson, Sept. 7, 1897; 1 dau., Mary Frances. Asst. in dairy husbandry, 1894-96, instr., 1896-98, asst. prof., 1898-1902, Pa. State Coll.; prof. animal and dairy husbandry, N.H. State Coll., 1902-03; asst. chief, dairy div., Bur. of Animal Industry, U.S. Dept. of Agr., 1903; organizer, and dir. Dept. of Agr., Mt. Hermon (Mass.) Boys' Sch., 1903-06; dir. Delaware Coll. Expt. Sta. and dean of dept. of agr., Delaware Coll., 1906-20; head Bur. Science and Agr., N. W. Ayer & Son, 1920—; dir. Dutton Investing Corp. Dir. Coll. of Agr., A.E.F. Univ., Beaune, France, 1919; twice decorated by French Govt. for services in education. Mem. Del. State Bd. Edn. Fellow Assn. Promotion Agrl. Science. Republican. Presbyn. Lecturer and writer on agr. Home: Devon, Pa. Died May 4, 1932.

HAYWARD, Harry Taft, mfr. woolen and cotton goods; b. Uxbridge, Mass., Sept. 18, 1868; s. William E. and Susan H. (Taft) H.; ed. pub. schs.; m. Edith C. Wires, Jan. 11, 1905; children—Mary Elizabeth, Harriet Taft. Purchased Charles J. McKenzie Woolen Mill, Franklin, Mass., 1892; organizer, treas. and pres. Forestdale (R.I.) Mfg. Co.; pres. Schuster Woolen Co. Home: Franklin, Mass. Died June 7, 1930.

HAYWARD, Joseph Warren, homeopathic physician; b. Easton, Mass., July 11, 1841; s. George Washington and Sylvia (Pratt) H.; ed. Easton, Mass., until 1858; grad. Bridgewater Normal Sch., 1859; studied medicine Harvard Med. Coll., Med. Sch. of Me. and Bellevue Med. Coll., New York Med. cadet, U.S.A. and asst. surgeon and bvt. maj., U.S.V., Mar. 1863-Nov. 1865. On staff Gen. E.O.C. Ord.; was at fall of Petersburg and surrender of Gen. Lee. Prof. fractures, dislocations and mil. surgery, Boston Univ. Sch. of Medicine, 1878—; a dir. and cons. surgeon, Morton Hosp., Taunton; operating surgeon, St. Botolph Hosp., Boston. Home: Taunton, Mass. Died 1905.

HAYWARD, Monroe Leland, lawyer, U.S. senator; b. Willsboro, N.Y., Dec. 22, 1840; grad. Ft. Edward (N.Y.) Coll. Inst., 1866; m. Jennie Pelton, Gold Spring, N.Y., June 14, 1870. Mem. Constl. Conv., 1875; judge dist. court, Neb. 1887; Republican candidate gov. Neb., 1898 (defeated); chmn. five State convs.; pres. Otoe Co. Nat. Bank. Served during Civil war in 5th N.Y. cav.; elected to U.S. Senate, term 1899-1905. Home: Nebraska City, Neb. Died 1899.

HAYWOOD, John Kerfoot, chemist; b. Raleigh, N.C., Dec. 19, 1873; s. Edward Graham and Margaret (Henry) H.; B.S., Cornell U., 1896; M.D., George Washington U., 1907; m. Margaret O'Brien Palmer, June 19, 1912; children—Walker H. (dec.), John H. Instr. in chemistry, Cornell U., 1897; became connected with Bur. of Chemistry, U.S. Dept. of Agr., 1897; chief of Miscellaneous Div., same bur., 1904-27, and chmn. Insecticide and Fungicide Bd., 1912-27; chief of office of insecticide, fungicide and caustic poison supervision in Food, Drug and Insecticide Administration, 1927—. In charge of enforcement of Federal Insecticide Act of 1910, also Federal Caustic Poison Act. Episcopalian. Specialist on insecticides, fungicides, disinfectants, caustic poisons. Home: Washington, D.C. Died Nov. 30, 1928.

HAYWOOD, Marshall De Lancey, librarian; b. Raleigh, N.C., Mar. 6, 1871; s. Dr. Richard B. and Julia Ogden (Hicks) H.; ed. Raleigh Male Acad., 1883-87; studied history, Johns Hopkins U., 1900-01; m. Mattie Hawkins Bailey, Oct. 16, 1926; 1 son. Sec. to atty. gen., N.C., 1889-96; asst. state librarian of N.C., 1901-02; librarian Agrl. and Mech. Coll. of N.C., 1902-03; asst. editor Biog. History of N.C., 1904—; historian U.S. War and Navy Depts., collecting N.C. Revolutionary records, 1914-15. Asst. librarian, N.C. Supreme Court, 1917-18; marshal and librarian same court, 1918—. Pres. S.R. in N.C., former historian Gen. Soc.; sec. N.C. Soc. of Cincinnati; historiographer P.E. Diocese of N.C. Author: Governor William Tryon and His Administration in the Province of North Carolina, 1765-71, 1903; Lives of the Bishops of North Carolina, 1910; Ballads of Courageous Carolinians, 1914. Owner pvt. library of N.C. hist. works. Home: Raleigh, N.C. Died Sept. 20, 1933.

HAZARD, Frederick Rowland, mfr.; b. Peace Dale, R.I., June 14, 1858; s. Rowland and Margaret Anna (Rood) H.; bro. of Caroline and Rowland Gibson H.; A.B., Brown U., 1881, A.M., 1884; studied chemistry in Europe, 1883-84; m. Dora Gannett Sedgwick, May 29, 1886. Identified with the Solvay Process Co., Syracuse, N.Y., 1884—, as asst. treas., 1884-87, treas., 1887-98, and pres., 1898—. Pres. Village of Solvay, N.Y., 1899-1909. Home: Solvay, N.Y. Died Feb. 27, 1917.

HAZARD, Lauriston Hartwell, cotton mcht.; b. Providence, R.I., Nov. 22, 1866; s. Jeffrey and Anna Lauriston (Hartwell) H.; prep. edn., Providence High Sch.; A.B., Brown U., 1889; m. Elizabeth Paine Sackett, June 19, 1907; children—Elizabeth, Marion. In cotton business, 1889-1932; elected treas. Hazard Cotton Co., Providence, 1893, pres., 1911-32; dir. Providence Washington Ins. Co., Anchore Ins. Co., Providence Nat. Bank; trustee Peoples Savings Bank. Pres. Butler Hosp.; mem. Providence Sch. Com., 1926—. Republican. Episcopalian. Home: Providence, R.I. Died Oct. 9, 1937.

HAZARD, Marshall Curtiss, editor; b. Tioga Co., Pa., June 28, 1839; s. Erastus W. and Mary F. H.; A.B., Knox Coll., 1861 (hon. Ph.D., 1894); m. Elizabeth W. Adams, June 28, 1862. Admitted to Ill. bar, 1864; asst. editor The Advance, Chicago, 1866-70; confidential agt. Jay Cooke & Co., bankers, 1871-72; editor Nat. Sunday School Teacher, 1874-82; asst. editor Sunday School Times, 1883-84; editor Congl. S.S. and Pub. Soc., 1885-1910, editor emeritus, 1910—. Author: Marriage Chimes, 1896; Outline Bible Studies, 1891; Concordance of the American Revised Version. Home: Dorchester Center, Mass. Died Feb. 14, 1929.

HAZARD, Rowland Gibson, mfr.; b. Phila., Pa., Jan. 22, 1855; s. Rowland and Margaret Anna (Rood) H.; bro. of Caroline H.; A.B., Brown U., 1876, A.M., 1879; m. Mary Pierrepont Bushnell, Nov. 16, 1880. Pres. Peace Dale Mfg. Co., 1898—; also chmn. bd. The Solvay Process Co., Semet-Solvay Co., By-Products Coke Corp.; pres. Narragansett Pier R.R. Co. Conglist.; mem. A.B.C.F.M. Independent Republican; presdl. elector, 1904; exec. com. Indianapolis Monetary Conv.; exec. com. R.I. State House Commn. (which built R.I. State House), 1890-94; mem. Providence Harbor Improvement Commn., 1900. Mem. exec. com., 1908, audit com., 1909—, N.Y. Life Ins. Co. Pres. Washington Co. Agrl. Soc. Fellow A.A.A.S.; fellow Brown U. Home: Peace Dale, R.I. Died Jan. 23, 1918.

HAZELTINE, Mayo Williamson, literary editor New York Sun, 1878—; b. Mass., 1841; grad. Harvard, 1865. Author: Chats About Books; British and American Education; The American Woman in Europe. Died 1909.

HAZELTON, George Cochrane, Jr., lawyer; b. Boscobel, Wis.; s. George Cochrane (M.C. from Wis.) and Ellen (Van Antwerp) H.; bro. of John Hampden H.; ed. Greylock Inst., Mass., and prep. dept. Columbian (now George Washington) U.; LL.B., Columbian, 1895, LL.M., 1896; m. Byrd C. Quin. To study the drama and dramatic writing practically, acted with the Booth-Barrett Co., season 1890-91, Modjeska Co., seasons 1891-92, 1892-93; practiced law at Washington, 1895-97, Phila., 1898-1900, New York, 1901—. Republican. Author: The National Capitol, Its Architecture, Art and History, 1897; Mistress Nell, A Merry Tale of a Merry Time, 1901; The Raven, 1909. Plays: Edgar Allan Poe (prod. Creston Clarke), 1895; Mistress Nell (prod. Henrietta Crosman), 1899; Captain Molly (prod. Mrs. Fiske), 1902; Yellow Jacket, a Chinese Play, etc., 1913; Mistress Nell, 1915. Home: New York, N.Y. Died June 24, 1921.

HAZEN, Allen, civil engr.; b. Hartford, Vt., Aug. 28, 1869; s. Charles D. and Abbie (Coleman) H.; ed. Hartford, Vt., and at Mass. Inst. Tech.; hon. Sc.D., N.H. and Dartmouth Colls.; m. Elizabeth McConw[illegible] Jan. 1, 1903. In charge of State Bd. of Health [illegible] Sta., Lawrence, Mass., 1888-93; in charge [illegible] posal, Chicago Expn., 1893; in private pr[illegible] ton, 1894-97, New York, 1897—; work mainly on city water supplies. Author: The Filtration of Public Water Supplies, 1895, 1900; Clean Water, 1907; Meter Rates for Water Works, 1917. Home: Dobbs Ferry, N.Y. Died July 26, 1930.

HAZEN, Azel Washburn, clergyman; b. Berlin, Vt., Apr. 10, 1841; s. Rev. Austin and Lucia (Washburn) H.; A.B., Dartmouth Coll., 1863, A.M., from same college, 1866; grad. Andover Theol. Sem., 1868; D.D., Dartmouth, 1888; m. Mary Butler Thompson, Sept. 1, 1869; children—Frances Elizabeth (dec.), Mary Washburn (dec.), Maynard Thompson. Ordained Congl. ministry, 1869; pastor of First Ch., Middletown, Conn., 1869-1916, emeritus. Home: Middletown, Conn. Died July 4, 1928.

HAZEN, Henry Allen, editor Congregational Year Book, 1883—; b. Hartford, Vt., Dec. 27, 1832; grad. Dartmouth, 1854; Andover Theol. Sem., 1857 (D.D., Marietta Coll., 1891); m. Charlotte Eloise Green, July 9, 1863; m. 2d, Martha Bethia Heath, Aug. 31, 1889. Ordained, 1858. Pastorates: Hardwick, Vt., 1858-59; Barton, 1860; Randolph, 1861-62; Plymouth, N.H., 1863-68; Lyme, 1868-70; Pittsfield, 1870-72; Billerica, Mass., 1874-79. Has resided in Auburndale, Mass., 1880—. Clerk secretary's dept. Am. Bd. For. Missions, 1880-83; sec. Nat. Council Congl. Chs.; asso. editor Congregational Quarterly, 1876-78; editor Triennial Minutes Nat. Council, 1833—; sec. N.H. General Assn., 1872-74; ditto in Mass., 1888—; sec. Andover Alumni Assn., 1880-90, editing its ann. Necrology, and Gen. Catalogue, 1880; asst. sec. First Internat. Congl. Council in London, 1891. Trustee: N.H. Missionary Soc., 1872-74; Kimball Union Acad., 1869-86; Howe School, Billerica, 1875-86. Dir. Am. Congl. Assn., 1890; corr. sec. N.E. Historic Geneal. Soc., 1892-93. Author: Historical Manual Congregational Church, Plymouth, N.H.; The Ministry and Churches of New Hampshire. Home: Auburndale, Mass. Died 1900.

HAZEN, Henry Allen, prof. meteorology, U.S. Weather Bureau, July 1, 1891—; b. Serur, India (where his father was missionary); grad. Dartmouth, 1871; 1 year in Thayer School of Civil Engring.; asst. in drawing, 1873-76, Sheffield Scientific Sch., Yale; private asst. to Prof. Elias Loomis in physics and meteorology, 1877-80. Joined U.S. Signal Service (now Weather Bur.), May 1, 1881. Devised sling psychrometer, 1884; established tables for reduction of barometric readings to sea-level; devised thermometer shelter, etc.; author numerous meteorol. papers; has made five balloon ascensions (one to 16,000 feet) for meteorol. research. Home: Washington, D.C. Died 1900.

HAZEN, John Vose, educator; b. Ralston, Mass., Nov. 22, 1850; s. Norman and Martha (Vose) H.; B.S., Dartmouth, 1875; C.E., Thayer Sch. Civ. Engring. (Dartmouth), 1876; m. Harriet A. Hurlbutt, July 20, 1881. Prof. civ. engring., Dartmouth, Aug. 1878—. Chmn. precinct commn. Village Precinct of Hanover; mem. Bd. of Edn. and auditor Town of Hanover. Republican. Conglist. Home: Hanover, N.H. Died Oct. 2, 1919.

HAZEN, Marshman Williams, lawyer; b. Beverly, Mass., July 20, 1845; s. Greenlief and Susan Perley (Towne) H.; A.B., Dartmouth, 1866, later A.M. Prin. Pinkerton Acad., 1866-69, high sch., West Cambridge (Arlington), Mass., 1869-73; mgr. Western house of Ginn & Co., publishers, 1873-77; mgr. New England br. D. Appleton & Co., pubs., 1873-78. Admitted to Mass. bar, 1882; has practiced in New York, 1885—; pres. of and dir. in various corps. Mason. Author: Observation, Thought and Expression (2 vols.); History of the United States (2 vols.); Government; A Course in Language; A Series of Readers. Died 1911.

HAZZARD, Charles, osteopath; b. Peoria, Ill., July 14, 1871; s. Joseph Frye and Louisa Adelaide (Phenix) H.; Ph.B., Northwestern U., 1895; D.O., Am. Sch. Osteopathy, Kirksville, Mo., 1898; m. Theodora Thoburn Craven, Apr. 20, 1897; children—Dorothea, Adelaide Jane (Mrs. William Webster Whitney), Margaret (dec.), Charles Theodore. Prof. histology and pathology, physical diagnosis, principles and practice of osteopathy, also chief of clinics, Am. Sch. of Osteopathy, 1897-1903; in pvt. practice, N.Y. City, 1903—. V.p. N.Y. State Bd. Med. Examiners, 1936—; treas. A. T. Still Research Inst., 1907-08; pres. Nat. Bd. Examiners for Osteopathic Physicians and Surgeons, 1934-37; pres. Stinson Lake (N.H.) Improvement Assn. Awarded Distinguished Service Certificate by Am. Osteopathic Assn., 1929. Republican. Methodist. Author: The Principles of Osteopathy, 1898; The Practice of Osteopathy, 1900. Home: Mt. Vernon, N.Y. Died Aug. 24, 1938.

HAZZARD, John Edward, actor, author; b. N.Y. City, Feb. 22, 1881; s. Edward John and Annie (Tillson) H.; ed. pub. schs., New York; unmarried. Professional début in "The Man from Mexico," 1901; later appeared in "The Two Orphans," "The Hurdy Gurdy Girl," "The Candy Shop," etc.; with Fritzie Scheff, in "The Duchess," 1911-12; with Lina Abarbanell, in "Miss Princess," 1912. Author: (verse) Poetry an' Rot, 1906; The Four Flusher, 1908; Verse and Worse, 1911; (with Winchell Smith) Turn to the Right (play), 1916. Home: New York, N.Y. Died Dec. 2, 1935.

HEAD, Franklin Harvey, mfr., banker; b. Paris, N.Y., Jan. 24, 1835; s. Harvey and Calista (Simmons) H.; A.B., Hamilton Coll., N.Y., 1856, A.M., 1859 (LL.D., 1896); m. Catherine P. Durkee, June 14, 1860 (died 1892). Practiced law, Kenosha, Wis., 1858-66; ranching in Utah about 4 yrs.; located at Chicago, 1872; pres. Bush Temple Conservatory, 1890—; v.p. Continental Casualty Co., Protection Mut. Fire Ins. Co., S. S. Hadley Co. Bank (Cedar Rapids, Neb.); dir. Toledo, Peoria & Western R.R., Street's Stable Car Line. Dir. Chicago Expn., 1893; mem. Jury Awards, Paris Expn., 1900. Chevalier Legion of Honor, France, 1901. Trustee Newberry Library; pres. Chicago Hist. Soc., Chicago Civic Federation, 1898-99. Author: Shakespeare's Insomnia and the Causes Thereof, 1896; A Notable Lawsuit, 1899; etc. Home: Chicago, Ill. Died June 28, 1914.

HEAD, Henry Oswald, lawyer; b. Sumner County, Tenn., Mar. 17, 1851; s. Dr. James Marshall and Barthenia P. (Branham) H.; ed. Greenwood and Rural acads., Sumner County, and by pvt. tutor; studied law Cumberland U., Lebanon, Tenn.; LL.D., Austin Coll., 1924; m. Sallie C. Wilson, Jan. 23, 1878; children—Henry Oswald, Hayden W. (dec.), Mary Orlena (Mrs. George D. Eader). Admitted to bar, 1871; judge 15th Jud. Dist. Tex., 1886-90, judge Court Civil Appeals, 1892-95 (resigned both offices before expiration of terms). Democrat. Home: Sherman, Tex. Died Apr. 1929.

HEAD, James Butler, lawyer; b. Greene County, Ala., Dec. 16, 1846; ed. common schools; private 16th C.S. cav., 1864-65; in agrl. pursuits until 1867; then in court and law offices at Eutaw, Ala.; clerk Circuit Court, Greene County, Ala., 1871-74; admitted to bar, Oct. 1874; practiced at Eutaw, 1874-88; at Birmingham, 1889; judge 10th jud. circuit, 1889-92; asso. justice Supreme Court, Ala., 1892-98; resumed practice, Nov. 1898; m. Virginia Leigh Pierce, July 9, 1874. Address: Birmingham, Ala. Died 1902.

HEAD, James Marshall, mayor; b. Sumner County, Tenn., July 25, 1855; s. Dr. James Marshall and Barthenia P. (Branham) H.; acad. edn., Gallatin, Tenn.; LL.B., Harvard, 1876; m. Minnie C. Cherry, June 30, 1885. In practice at Nashville, 1876-1903, Boston, 1904—. Mem. Tenn. Ho. of Rep., 1881-84; mayor of Nashville, 1899-1903; mem. Dem. Nat. Com., 1896-1904. V.p. and gen. counsel, Warren Brothers Co. Home: Brookline, Mass. Died Mar. 31, 1930.

HEAD, John Benedict, judge; b. Latrobe, Pa., Apr. 4, 1855; s. William S. and Sarah (Coulter) H.; A.B., Mt. Mary's Coll., Md., 1873, A.M., 1875, Litt.D., 1906; m. Naomi Jones, May 2, 1877. Admitted to bar, 1880; mem. firm Moorehead & Head, Greensburg, Pa., 1882-1906; judge Superior Ct. of Pa., 1906-16. Democrat. Roman Catholic. Address: Greensburg, Pa. Deceased.

HEAD, John Frazier, army officer; b. Boston, Jan. 9, 1821; s. George E. and Hannah (Catlin) H.; A.B., Yale, 1840, A.M., 1843; M.D., Harvard Med. Sch., 1843; m. Katharine Apthorp, Aug. 18, 1846. Entered U.S. Army, Aug. 6, 1846, as 1st lt., asst. surgeon; served in Mexican and Civil wars; retired for age with rank of col., Jan. 9, 1885; advanced in grade to brig. gen., retired Apr. 23, 1904. Address: Washington, D.C. Died 1908.

HEADDEN, William Parker, college prof.; b. nr. Red Bank, N.J., Sept. 21, 1850; s. John and Mehetable Trafford (Parker) H.; A.B., Dickinson, 1872, A.M., 1875; laboratory of R. Fresenius, Wiesbaden, 1873; A.M., Ph.D., U. of Giessen, 1874; D.Sc., U. of Colo., 1919; m. Mary Alice Ralston, Nov. 25, 1875; children—Helen Parker, William Ralston, Mary Alice, Margaret. Asst. to Prof. F. A. Genth, U. of Pa., 1874-76; prof. chemistry, Md. Agrl. Coll., 1880-84, U. of Denver, 1884-89, State Sch. of Mines, S.D., 1889-91, dean, same, 1892-93; prof. chemistry and geology, Colo. Agrl. Coll., and chemist to the Agrl. Expt. Sta., 1893—. Presbyn. Republican. Home: Fort Collins, Colo. Died Feb. 5, 1932.

HEADLEY, Phineas Camp, clergyman, author; b. Walton, N.Y., June 29, 1819; studied law; admitted to bar, 1847; studied theology; grad. Auburn (N.Y.) Theol. Sem.; held Presbyn. and Congl. pastorates; contributor to many newspapers and mags. Author: Women of the Bible; Biographies of the Empress Josephine, Kossuth, Lafayette, Mary Queen of Scots, Gen. Grant, Gen. O. M. Mitchell, Ericsson, Sheridan, Farragut and Sherman; Massachusetts in the Rebellion; Half-Hours in Bible Lands; Public Men of Today; etc. Home: Lexington, Mass. Died 1902.

HEALD, Daniel Addison, pres. Home Ins. Co.; b. Chester, Vt., 1818; worked on farm in youth; grad. Yale, 1841, LL.D., 1898; admitted to Vt. bar, 1843; took agency for several fire insurance companies in connection with his practice; operated gen. agency for Home Ins. Co., 1856-68; second v.p., 1868-83; v.p., 1883-88; pres., 1888—. Prominent in organizing Nat. Bd. Fire Underwriters, 1866; later pres. or chmn. exec. com. Home: Orange, N.J. Died 1900.

HEALD, William Henry, congressman; b. Wilmington, Del., Aug. 27, 1864; s. Charles H. and Mary E. (Talley) H.; B.S., Delaware Coll., Newark, 1883; LL.B., Columbian (now George Washington) U., 1888; unmarried. Examiner of nat. banks for Mont., Ida., Wash. and Ore., 1888-93; began practice of law, 1897; postmaster, Wilmington, 1902-06; mem. 61st and 62d Congresses (1909-13). Del. at-large. Republican. Home: Wilmington, Del. Died June 3, 1939.

HEALEY, Charles C., police official; b. N.Y. City, May 14, 1855; s. John J. and Mary (Sullivan) H.; ed. pub. schs., Chicago; m. Nellie J. O'Brien, Dec. 25, 1874. Entered police service in old Town of Lake, Chicago, 1890; in command of police and military force in railroad strike, 1903; organized the mounted squad, 1906, starting with 16 men; visited leading cities of Europe, 1910, on tour of street traffic investigation; organized the traffic div. of police, Chicago, 1914; gen. supt. of police, Chicago, 1915—. Mem. Street Traffic Com., Chicago Assn. of Commerce; mem. Pub. Safety Commn. Republican. Christian Scientist. Mason. Home: Chicago, Ill. Deceased.

HEALY, A(aron) Augustus, merchant; b. Brooklyn, June 26, 1850; s. Aaron and Elizabeth (Weston) H.; ed. Brooklyn Poly. Inst.; LL.D., Oberlin Coll., 1919; m. Elizabeth Bradley, Dec. 7, 1875; m. Mary Theodosia Curreir, Apr. 10, 1915. Formerly engaged as mfr. and dealer in leather, under firm name of A. Healy & Sons, New York; 1st v.p. Central Leather Co. until Feb. 1910, continues as dir. same. Collector internal revenue, Eastern Dist. N.Y., 1893-97. Independent Democrat. Pres. bd. trustees Brooklyn Inst. Arts and Sciences; mem. Art Commn. City of New York; dir. Brooklyn Acad. Music, Nassau Nat. Bank, Brooklyn. Home: Brooklyn, N.Y. Died Sept. 28, 1921.

HEALY, Daniel Joseph, physician; b. Toronto, Can., Mar. 26, 1873; s. William and Ellen (McCarthy) H.; student De LaSalle Coll., Toronto, 1886-89; M.D., C.M., McGill U., 1896; m. Louise Susette Bergmann (M.D.), June 26, 1902. Settled at Lexington, Ky., 1896; visiting physician, House of Mercy, 1896-99; pathologist Eastern Ky. Asylum for the Insane, 1897-99, Central Ind. Asylum for the Insane, 1899-1900; health officer City of Lexington, 1900-01; anatomist, office of Surgeon-Gen. U.S. Army, 1904-07; supt. Ky. Instn. for Feeble Minded Children, 1909-10; prof. bacteriology, 1910-19, prof. agrl. bacteriology, 1919—, U. of Ky., and research bacteriologist, Expt. Sta., 1910—. Mem. Vol. Med. Service Corps. Democrat. Home: Lexington, Ky. Died Nov. 24, 1935.

HEALY, Ezra Anthony, college dean; b. Smith's Falls, Ont., Can., Mar. 25, 1844; s. Almon and Lucy (Wood) H.; A.B., Victoria U., 1872, A.M., 1894, D.D., 1908; m. Mary Priscilla Edmunds, July 15, 1872. Entered Methodist ministry, 1867; pastor Stratford, Mitchell and Montreal, Can., 1867-78, North Dakota, 1878-86, cities of southern Calif., 1886-1907; dean Maclay Coll. of Theology, U. of Southern Calif., Oct. 1907-21; now prof. of systematic theology. Mem. bd. of trustees U. of Southern Calif.; former mem. bd. regents U. of N.D. Republican. Home: Los Angeles, Calif. Died Aug. 17, 1931.

HEALY, James Augustine, R.C. bishop of Portland, Me., 1875—; b. nr. Macon, Ga., 1830; went North in childhood; studied in Quaker schools in Long Island and N.J.; grad. Holy Cross Coll., Worcester, Mass., 1849; studied theology in Montreal and Paris; was ordained priest; missionary, and later diocesan chancellor, and bishop's sec., Boston; pastor St. James Ch., Boston, 1866-75. Address: Portland, Me. Died 1900.

HEALY, Patrick Joseph, clergyman, educator; b. Waterford, Ireland, July 26, 1871; s. Michael and Ellen (Keane) H.; S.T.B., Catholic U. of America, 1898, S.T.L., 1899, S.T.D., 1903. Ordained priest, R.C. Ch., 1897; instr. ch. history, 1903-05, asst. prof., 1905-07, asso. prof., 1907-10, prof., 1910—, Catholic U. of America, also dean Faculty of Theology. Author: The Valerian Persecution; Historical Christianity and the Social Question. Address: Washington, D.C. Died May 18, 1937.

HEALY, Robert Wallace, soldier; b. Chicago, Oct. 22, 1836; s. Robert and Ann (Wallace) H.; A.B., U. of Notre Dame, Ind., 1859, A.M., 1865, LL.D., 1908; took course Sloan's Commercial Coll., Chicago; entered mercantile life; del. Dem. State Conv., Springfield, Ill., 1860; m. Sarah J. Nolan, Oct. 1, 1862; m. 2d, Jeannette Cooke, Oct. 25, 1899. Enlisted 58th Ill. Inf., Sept. 25, 1861; capt., Dec. 25, 1861; maj., Oct. 20, 1864; lt. col., Apr. 10, 1865; col., Oct. 3, 1865. Bvtd. maj., Mar. 26, 1865, "for faithful and meritorious services during campaign against Mobile"; brig. gen. vols., Mar. 13, 1865, for same during the war; hon. mustered out, April 1, 1866. Served at Ft. Donaldson, Shiloh, Corinth, Iuka, Meridian, on Banks' Red River Expdn. at Ft. DeRussy, Pleasant Hill, Yellow Bayou, etc.; comdg. regt.; also in various engagements in A. J. Smith's campaign against Gen. Forest and Oxford, Miss.; transferred to Mo., serving under Rosecrans against Price; comdg. regt. in battle of Nashville and pursuit of Hood, Dec. 1864; apptd. insp. gen. 2d Div., 16th Army Corps, Mar. 1865; took part in the campaign against Mobile and battle of Blakely, Apr. 9, 1865; returned to command of regt., July 1865, and garrisoned Montgomery, Ala., after Lee's surrender. Cotton planter in Ala. after the war; purchasing agt. Erlanger Syndicate, operating Queen & Crescent system of railroads, until Jan. 1892, when he became pres. Ross-Meehan Foundry Co. U.S. marshal middle and southern judicial dists. of Ala., 1867-77; chmn. Ala. Rep. State Exec. Com., 1872-74; del. Rep. Nat. Conv., 1876; candidate for presdl. elector, 1876. Dir. Carnegie Library; mem. Loyal Legion, Soc. Army of Tenn. Home: Chattanooga, Tenn. Died Nov. 2, 1912.

HEAP, David Porter, army officer; b. at U.S. Legation, San Stefano, Turkey, Mar. 24, 1843; s. Gwynn Harris and Evelina Cora (Porter) H.; student Georgetown (D.C.) Coll.; apptd. from Pa., and grad. U.S. Mil. Acad., 1864; m. Elizabeth Brown Beale, Dec. 1, 1875 (died July 31, 1889); m. 2d, Josephine Bigelow Wright, Nov. 12, 1902. Apptd. 1st lt. engrs., June 13, 1864; promoted through grades to col., Apr. 13, 1903; brig. gen. retired, at own request after 40 yrs'. service, Feb. 16, 1905. Bvtd. capt., Apr. 2, 1865, "for gallant and meritorious services at Petersburg, Va." Engaged in river and harbor engring., fortifications, lighthouse engring.; later div. engr., Pacific Div.; pres. Calif. Debris Commn.; engr. officer on staff comdg. gen. Dept. of Calif.; mem. various bds. Mil. representative of U.S. at Paris Congress of Electricians, 1881; traveled in Europe, Asia and Africa. Author: Ancient and Modern Light-Houses, 1889; Electrical Appliances of the Present Day; Engineer Exhibit, Centennial Exhibition, 1882; History of the Application of Electricity to Lighting the Coasts of France, 1885; Report on the International Exhibition of Electricity at Paris, 1881, 1884, etc. Address: Pasadena, Calif. Died 1910.

HEARD, Arthur Marston, banker; b. Sandwich, N.H., Feb. 13, 1866; s. William Andrew and Emily Maria (Marston) H.; A.B., Amherst, 1888; m. Ora B. Farrar, June 12, 1895; children—Marston, Carlton Farrar. Clk. 1st Nat. Bank, Arkansas City, Kan., 1889-93; Nat. bank examiner, 1893-95; cashier Merchants, Nat. Bank, Manchester, N.H., 1896-1901; cashier Amoskeag Nat. Bank, 1902-05, pres., 1905—; pres. Manchester Gas Co., Amoskeag Trust Co., Amoskeag Investment Co.; dir. N.H. Fire Ins. Co. (finance com.), Granite State Fire Ins. Co.; trustee Amoskeag Savings Bank, Peoples Savings Bank. Treas. and trustee Currier Gallery of Art; trustee Cogswell Benevolent Trust, and Chandler Fund; trustee Alfred Quimby Fund, 1918-37. Mem. exec. com. N.H. Committee on Public Safety, 1917-19; dir. Federal Reserve Bank of Boston, 1914-18; mem. Federal Advisory Council, 1927-29. Mason. Home: Manchester, N.H. Died Nov. 27, 1938.

HEARD, Augustine, merchant, diplomat; b. Ipswich, Mass., Dec. 7, 1827; grad. Harvard, 1847; went immediately to China and engaged in mercantile pursuits; returned to U.S., 1857; m. Jane Leeps de Coninck, 1858. Resided many yrs. in Europe in supervision of large commercial interests in England, France and Russia in connection with China; was made officer of Order of Leopold of Belgium, 1871; apptd. Jan., 1890, minister resident and consul gen. of Korea, remaining until July 1893; resigned because of ill health. Address: Washington, D.C. Deceased.

HEARD, Dwight Bancroft; b. Boston, May 1, 1869; s. Leander B. and Lucy (Howard) H.; pub. sch. edn.; m. Maie B. Bartlett, Aug. 10, 1894; 1 son, Bartlett Bradford. With Hibbard, Spencer Bartlett & Co., wholesale hardware, Chicago, to 1894; located in Ariz. and engaged in investment and loan business and farming; pres. Dwight B. Heard Investment Co., Commonwealth Investment Co., Bartlett-Heard Land & Cattle Co., Monroe-Central Improvement Co., Security Improvement Co., San Carlos Hotel Co.; pres., publisher The Arizona Republican; pres. Palmcroft Development Co.; v.p. Arlington Improvement Co.; sec. Goldwater Improvement Co. Was chmn. Ariz. State Exec. Finance Com. of War Camp Community Service; chmn. com. of 30 which went to Washington, D.C., to fight point statehood with New Mexico; served as pres. Am. Nat. Live Stock Assn. (now exec. com.), Ariz. Cattle Growers Assn. (now exec. com.), etc.; Rep. candidate for gov. of Ariz., 1924; dir. Chamber Commerce of U.S., Ariz. Grain Growers' Assn., Roosevelt Hay Growers' Assn.; vice pres. St. Luke's Home; dir. Chamber Commerce of Phoenix; mem. exec. com. World Cotton Conf., Borderland Highway Assn.; trustee Am. Cotton Growers' Exchange; mem. exec. bd. Ariz. Pimocotton Growers, Roosevelt Council and of Boy Scouts of America. Chmn. Ariz. Council of Defense, World War. Episcopalian. Died March 14, 1929.

HEARD, Oscar Edwin, jurist; b. Freeport, Ill., June 26, 1856; s. William and Sarah Ann (Swanzey) H.; prep. edn. high sch., Freeport; student Northwestern U., 1874-76; m. Mary J. Peters, Dec. 25, 1879. Admitted to Ill. bar, 1879, and began practice at Freeport; state's atty. Stephenson County, Ill., 1884-1900; judge Circuit Court, 1903-24; judge Appellate Court, 2d Dist. of Ill., 1919-21, 3d Dist., 1921-24; justice Supreme Ct., Ill., term, 1924-33, chief justice, 1927-28, 1932-33; mem. law firm of Heard & Heard. Assigned to hold court in Chicago part of each yr. for over 20 yrs.; presided at the E. St. Louis Race Riot Cases, 1917. Mem. board of directors Freeport Pub. Library, 1896-1903; mem. Bd. of Edn., Freeport, 1897-1902. Republican. Presbyn. Mason. Home: Freeport, Ill. Died July 15, 1940.

HEARD, William H., bishop; b. Elbert County, Ga., June 25, 1850; s. George W. and Parthenia (Jones) H.; Atlanta (Ga.) U.; U. of S.C., Columbia; R.E. Div. Sch., W. Phila.; D.D., Allen U., S.C., 1891; m. Josephine D. Henderson, Jan. 22, 1882. Ordained A.M.E. ministry, 1879; elected bishop, 1904. Mem. S.C. Ho. of Rep., 1876; minister resident and consul gen. to Liberia, 1898-99. Trustee Wilberforce (O.) U., Payne Theol. Sem. Author: The Bright Side of African Life, 1900. Home: Philadelphia, Pa. Died Sept. 12, 1937.

HEARD, William Wright, gov.; b. Union Parish, La., Apr. 28, 1853; s. Stephen S. and Mary Ann (Wright) H.; ed. common schs. of the country and acad. at Farmerville, La.; m. Isabelle E. Manning, Dec. 3, 1878; children—William Wright (dec.), Alma Monroe (dec.), Eva Agusta, William Allan, Manning Wright, Louisiana Belle, Wilbur Wright. Clerk and deputy of court, 1876-92; elected to La. Ho. of Rep., 1884; Senate, 1888; auditor of pub. accounts on Anti-Lottery ticket, 1892-1900; gov. of La., 1900-04; v.p. State Nat. Bank of New Orleans, 1904; later sec. La. Securities Commn. Democrat. Baptist; moderator Comcord Bapt. Assn. for several yrs.; pres. Bapt. State Conv., 1 term, and v.p. Southern Bapt. Conv., 1 term. Was 2 terms vice-grand chancellor and 1 term grand chancellor K.P. of La. Home: New Orleans, La. Died June 1, 1926.

HEARN, Clint Calvin, army officer; b. Weston, Tex., Mar. 29, 1866; s. Levi A. and Margaret Adelaide (Routh) H.; grad. U.S. Mil. Academy, 1890, Artillery School, 1894, School of Submarine Defense, 1908, Army War College, 1912. General Staff College, 1920; m. Laura Wright Overaker, Dec. 2, 1897. Commd. add. 2d lt. 4th Arty., June 12, 1890; promoted through various grades to rank of colonel, May 15, 1917; brig. gen. N.A., Aug. 5, 1917-June 15, 1919; chief of staff Non-Divisional Group, Reserve Units, 3d Corps Area (reorganized reserves), Harrisburg, Pa., Apr. 10, 1922—. Died Feb. 11, 1928.

HEARN, David William, clergyman; b. Boston, Nov. 21, 1861; student Boston Coll., class of 1883; took 5 years' post-grad. courses in lit., science and philosophy; 4 yrs. in theol. courses; studies made at Woodstock Coll., Md., and in Europe; Roman Catholic priest; mem. Soc. of Jesus. Was prof. Georgetown U., v.p. Boston Coll.; v.p. Coll. of St. Francis Xavier, New York; pres. latter 1900-07; later prin. Loyola Sch. and rector Ch. of St. Ignatius Loyola, New York. Address New York, N.Y. Died Sept. 16, 1917.

HEARN, Lafcadio, author; b. in Ionian Islands, June 27, 1850; of Irish and Greek parentage; resided for yrs. in New Orleans; later in New York; for some time past in Japan. Author: Stray Leaves from Strange Literature; Some Chinese Ghosts; Chita; Two Years in the French West Indies; Youma; Glimpses of Unfamiliar Japan; Out of the East; Reveries and Studies in New Japan; Kokoro; Gleanings in Buddha-Fields; Exotics and Retrospectives, 1898; In Ghostly Japan, 1899; Shadowings, 1900; A Japanese Miscellany, 1901. Died 1904.

HEARST, Charles Ernest, farm bur. executive; b. Cedar Falls, Ia., Oct. 18, 1869; s. James and Maria Deborah (Dane) H.; student Ia. State Teachers Coll., Cedar Falls, 2 yrs.; m. Katharine Schell, Dec. 30, 1898; children—Helen Louise, James Schell, Robert Russell (dec.), Charles Joseph. Engaged in farming; pres. Black Hawk County Farm Bur., 1914-23; v.p. Ia. Farm Bur. Federation, 1921-23, pres., 1923—; v.p. Am. Farm Bur. Federation. Pres. Sch. Bd. of Cedar Falls Consolidated, 1919-23. Republican. Home: Cedar Falls, Ia. Died March 1936.

HEARST, Phoebe Apperson, philanthropist; b. Dec. 3, 1842; d. R. W. Apperson; taught sch. 1 yr.; m. George Hearst, June 15, 1862 (died 1891); mother of William Randolph H. Established and maintained kindergarten classes at San Francisco several yrs.; also classes and a training class for kindergarten teachers at Washington nearly 10 yrs. when about 90% of the pub. sch. teachers there were graduates of her classes; later conducted kindergarten classes at Lead, S.D., where her prin. mining interests were located. Gave $250,000 to build Nat. Cathedral School for Girls, Washington, D.C.; built, equipped and maintained several yrs. free library at Anaconda, Mont., finally presenting same to the municipality; has equipped and maintained for many yrs. a free library at Lead, S.D.; paid cost of a competition of best architects of Europe and America for plans for greater U. of Calif. and erected and equipped the mining bldg. as a memorial to her husband. Regent U. of Calif.; vice regent for Calif., Mt. Vernon Assn., etc.; hon. pres. Women's Bd. of Panama P.I. Expn., San Francisco, 1915. Address: Pleasanton, Calif. Died Apr. 13, 1919.

HEATH, Daniel Collamore, pres. D. C. Heath & Co.; b. Salem, Me., Oct. 26, 1843; s. Daniel and Mila Ann (Record) H.; A.B., 1868, A.M., 1873, Amherst; m. Mrs. Nelly Lloyd Knox, Jan. 1881. Was junior mem. Ginn & Heath until 1886, when he established, in Boston, house of D. C. Heath & Co., becoming pres. Home: Newtonville, Mass. Died 1908.

HEATH, Ferry Kimball, asst. sec. of Treasury; b. Grand Rapids, Mich., Oct. 23, 1876; s. Lewis Wadsworth and Jane Sophia (Worcester) H.; ed. U. of Mich.; unmarried. Asst. sec. of the Treasury, June 26, 1929-Apr. 17, 1933; became resident partner Harriman & Co., brokers, 1933, later Harriman & Keech. Pvt. U.S. Vol. Inf., Spanish-Am. War; maj., F.A., U.S.A., World War. Republican. Home: Grand Rapids, Mich. Died May 27, 1939.

HEATH, Frederic Carroll, physician; b. Gardiner, Me., Jan. 19, 1857; s. Alvan M. C. and Sarah Hinkley (Philbrook) H.; A.B., Amherst, 1878, A.M., 1886; M.D., Me. Med. Coll. (Bowdoin), 1884; m. Agnes Ralston Cochrane, June 19, 1895. Specialist in eye and ear practice; asst. surgeon U.S. Marine Hosp. Service, Detroit, 1887-90; clin. prof. diseases of the eye, Ind. Univ. Med. Coll., 1905—; eye and ear surgeon to Indianapolis City Hosp. and Dispensary. Home: Indianapolis, Ind. Died Oct. 16, 1918.

HEATH, Perry Sanford, pub. and editor; b. Muncie, Ind., Aug. 31, 1857; s. Rev. Jacob W. and Rhoda A. H.; ed. Muncie schs.; m. Ella Conway, Sept. 17, 1890. Established 1st daily paper Muncie, 1878, 1st paper Aberdeen (Dak. Pioneer), 1881; corr. at Washington, 1881-93; in charge lit. dept. Harrison nominating campaign, 1888, and renomination at Minneapolis, 1892. Identified framing constns. for div. of Dakota and govt. of proposed States of N. and S.D., 1884-86; declined appmt. by Pres. Harrison as provisional gov. of S.D. pending admission to statehood; declined nomination for Congress, 8th Ind. dist., 1890, with election by over 8,000 majority assured. Pres., gen. mgr. and editor Cincinnati Commercial-Gazette, 1894-96; gen. field manager in charge McKinley nomination and preliminary headquarters at St. Louis Conv., in charge publishing and printing, Rep. Nat. Com., 1896; 1st asst. postmaster-gen., 1897-1900; from unexpended balance of less than $30,000, for experimental purposes, made practical, developed, and established present system of rural free delivery of mail; thrice tendered resignation as 1st asst. postmaster-gen., to reënter private business, first in Feb. 1898, but each time was refused by President McKinley, until July 1900, when resignation accepted, upon election as sec. Rep. Nat. Com., which he held until 1904; arbitrated Govt's contention over telegraph rates, confirmed by U.S. Court and Congress; incorporator and dir. S.P.,L.A.&S.L. R.R., 1901-03; owner and pub. Salt Lake Tribune, 1901-05; established Salt Lake Telegram (evening), 1902. Author: A Hoosier in Russia (1887); also various treatises on nihilism, edn., resources and spl. phases of Russian life. Spent summer and autumn 1919 traveling in Japan, Philippines, China, Shantung, Manchuria, Mongolia and Korea (Chosen), studying their problems and critical political and financial situations. Address: Washington, D.C. Died Mar. 30, 1927.

HEATON, Augustus Goodyear, artist; b. Phila., Pa., Apr. 28, 1844; s. Augustus and Rosabella (Crean) H.; ed. in Phila.; was 1st U.S. student admitted to study at École des Beaux Arts, Paris (1863) under Cabanel; painted in Paris under Bonnat, 1878-80; m. Ada W. Griswold, Dec. 24, 1874; children- Augustus, John H., D. R. Perry. Gave Phila. Union League medals to Bright and Cobden in Manchester, 1863; prof. in Phila. Sch. of Design for Women, 1865-66; exhibited in Paris Salon, 1879, 80, and later years; painted "Washington at Fort Duquesne," Union League, Phila., 1881; The Recall of Columbus, bought by Congress for the Capitol, 1883, and engraved on 50-cent World's Fair stamp, 1893; painted portrait of Bishop Bowman for Cornell Coll., 1885; of Paul Tulane for Tulane U., 1892; painted The Promoters of the New Congressional Library, 1888. Author: The Heart of David—The Psalmist King, 1900; Coinage of the U.S. Branch Mints, 1893; Fancies and Thoughts in Verse, 1904. Privately issued "The Nutshell" (quarterly). Wrote "The Banner of Freedom" (Nat. anthem). Home: West Palm Beach, Fla. Deceased.

HEATON, John Langdon, newspaperman; b. Canton, N.Y., Jan. 29, 1860; s. Ira Willmarth and Lucinda (Langdon) H.; A.B., St. Lawrence, 1880, A.M., L.H.D.; m. Eliza Osborn Putnam, 1882. Entered journalism on Brooklyn Times, 1881; editorial writer later asso. editor New York World, 1899-1931. Author: The Story of Vermont, 1889; The Quilting Bee, 1896; The Story of a Page, 1913; Cobb of the World, 1924. Home: Brooklyn, N.Y. Died Feb. 21, 1935.

HEATON, Robert Douglas, congressman; b. Run, Pa., July 21, 1873; s. William H.

J. (Douglas) H.; prep. edn. Canandaigua Acad.; student U. of Pa., 1890-94; m. Louise Landefeld, June 2, 1897. Mem. 64th and 65th Congresses (1915-19), 12th Pa. Dist. Republican. Trustee State Hospital for Injured Miners, Fountain Springs, Pa. Home: Ashland, Pa. Died June 11, 1933.

HEATWOLE, Cornelius Jacob, college prof.; b. Dale Enterprise, Va., Oct. 20, 1868; s. David A. and Catharine (Driver) H.; grad. Peabody Coll. for Teachers, Nashville, Tenn., 1895; student U. of Va., 1897-98; apptd. Southern scholar to Teachers Coll. (Columbia), 1902, again 1907; B.S., Columbia, 1908, M.A., 1916; Litt.D., Hampden-Sydney College, Va., 1929; m. Sue Porter, Sept. 1, 1909; 1 dau., Margaret Porter. Began as teacher rural sch. Rockingham County, Va.; teacher French and history, West Central Acad., Mt. Clinton, Va., 1895-1901; prin. Oak Hill Acad., McGaheysville, Va., 1901-03; supt. schs., Morristown, Tenn., 1903-07; dean Dept. of Edn., State Coll. for Women, Tallahassee, Fla., 1908; prof. edn., State Teachers Coll., Harrisonburg, Va., 1909-17; prof. sociology and principles of edn., U. of Ga., 1917—; dir. Phelps Stokes Studies, same univ.; lecturer on edn., U. of Pittsburgh, 1920; lecturer on proposed internat. calendar, World Fed. Ednl. Assns., Geneva, Switzerland, July 1929. Editor Va. Jour. of Edn., 1922; exec. sec. Va. State Teachers' Assn., 1922. Presbyn. Author: History of Education in Virginia, 1916; History of the Heatwole Family, 1908. Home: Richmond, Va. Deceased.

HEATWOLE, Joel Prescott, congressman; b. Waterford, Ind., Aug. 22, 1856; s. Henry and Barbara (Kolb) H.; pub. sch. edn.; m. Mrs. G. L. Archibald, Dec. 4, 1890. Engaged in printing business, 1876—; went to Minn., 1882. Mem. 54th to 57th Congresses (1895-1903); declined renomination. Republican. Home: Northfield, Minn. Died 1910.

HEATWOLE, Lewis James, bishop; b. Dale Enterprise, Va., Dec. 4, 1852; s. David Abram and Catharine (Driver) H.; grad. Valley Normal Inst., Bridgewater, Va., 1872; student U. of Va., 1903; m. Mary Alice, d. Bishop Samuel Coffman, Nov. 11, 1875 (died 1926). Teacher 15 yrs.; ordained Mennonite ministry, 1887; pastor at Dale Enterprise, 1887-89; Garden City, Mo., 1890-93; bishop Middle Dist. of Va., 1892—. Officer or mem. various bds. of the ch. Author: Baptism—A Consecration, 1894; Moral Training in Public Schools, 1906; Key to the Almanac and the Sidereal Heavens, 1908; The Perpetual Calendar, 1911; Mennonite Hand-Book of Information, 1925; Best Graded Series of Readers; also astronomics for many almanacs. Home: Dale Enterprise, Va. Died Dec. 26, 1932.

HEBARD, Grace Raymond; b. Clinton, Ia., July 2, 1861; d. Rev. George Diah Alonzo and Margaret E. Dominick (Marven) H.; B.S., Ia. State U., 1882, M.A., 1885; Ph.D., Ill. Wesleyan U., 1893; unmarried. Draftsman, U.S. surveyor general's office and U.S. land office, Cheyenne, Wyo., 1882-91; librarian, 1891-1919, prof. polit. economy, 1906—, U. of Wyo. Admitted to Wyo. bar, 1898. Mem. of com. of 3 that drew up petition, 1889, asking Constl. Conv. of Wyo. to adopt woman suffrage clause. Trustee U. of Wyo., 1891-1904. Republican. Conglist. Regent D.A.R.; state historian Colonial Dames; mem. com. to mark Overland Trail, through Wyo.; mem. Wyo. Child Health Commn. Author: The History and Government of Wyoming, 1904; The Pathbreakers from River to Ocean, 1911; Sacajawea, Pilot for Lewis and Clark, 1907; The First Woman Jury, 1913; The Bozeman Trail (with E. A. Brininstool), 1921; Chief Washakie, 1929; Sacajawea, a Guide and Interpreter of the Lewis and Clark Expedition, 1933; The Pony Express and Telegraph Line in Wyoming, 1935; War Service of the University of Wyoming; Working the Oregon Trail; The Birth of Wyoming. Home: Laramie, Wyo. Died Oct. 11, 1936.

HEBDEN, John Calder, chemical engr.; b. Colgate, Wis., Dec. 22, 1862; s. John and Mary (Calder) H.; prep. edn., Mt. Pleasant Acad., Providence, R.I.; A.B., Brown U., 1885 (Phi Beta Kappa); post-grad. work, same univ., 1901-03; m. Lucie A. Mann, Nov. 2, 1898 (dec.); 1 dau., Ruth Dunham; m. 2d, Gertrude S. Beard, Oct. 8, 1919. Chemist and dyer Nat. & Providence Worsted Mills, and Silver Spring Bleachery, 1885-87; resident agt., technician and chemist, William J. Matheson & Co., and Cassela Color Co., 1887-1904; chemist and technician, A. Klipstein & Co., 1904-09; v.p. F. E. Atteaux & Co., 1909-10; v.p. and gen. mgr. Franklin Process Co., 1910-13, Federal Dyestuff & Chem. Corp., 1915-17; pres. and gen. mgr. Dyeing Processes Corp., v.p. Hebden Sugar Process Corp.; also practicing as consulting chemist and chem. engr. Republican. Baptist. Mason. Home: Brooklyn, N.Y. Died June 3, 1929.

HEBEL, John William, prof. English; b. Auburn, Ind., Apr. 1, 1891; s. John and Winifred (Richmond) H.; B.A., Indiana U., 1912; M.A., Cornell U., 1913, Ph.D., 1920; studied U. of Jena, 1911, U. of Paris, 1919; m. Mabel McGlynn, Sept. 9, 1922. Instr. in English, Cornell U., 1914-17 and 1919-21, asst. prof., 1921-29, prof., 1929—. Served in World War as capt. in 38th, 3d and 77th divs., A.E.F. Editor: A Concordance to the Poems of John Keats (with others), 1917; Drayton's Endimion and Phoebe, 1925; Poetry of the English Renaissance (with Hoyt H. Hudson), 1929; John Donne's Biathanatos, 1930; The Works of Michael Drayton, 1931. Home: Ithaca, N.Y. Died Feb. 7, 1934.

HECK, William Harry, prof. edn.; b. Raleigh, N.C., Nov. 1, 1879; s. Jonathan McGee and Mattie Anna (Callendine) H.; B.A., Wake Forest (N.C.) Coll., 1897, M.A., 1899; fellow Columbia U., 1900-02, Ph.D., 1914; m. Anna Seeley Tuttle, Sept. 9, 1911. Asst. sec., Gen. Edn. Bd., N.Y., 1902-05; prof. edn., U. of Va., 1905—. Author: Mental Discipline and Educational Values, 1909, 2d edit., 1911; Studies of Mental Fatigue in Relation to the Daily School Program, 1914; A Study of Home Study, 1915; A Study of School Recesses, 1917; International Source-Book on Home Study, 1918. Home: University, Va. Died Jan. 4, 1919.

HECKEL, Edward Balthasar, ophthalmologist; b. Pittsburgh, Pa., Jan. 30, 1865; s. John G. and Mary E. (Koch) H.; A.B., Allegheny Coll., 1887, A.M., 1889, Sc.D., 1930; M.D., Bellevue Hospital Medical Coll., New York, 1890; post-grad. work New York Polyclinic; m. Matilda Lautner, Nov. 21, 1894; children—Josephine L. (Mrs. J. V. Kimerer), Mary F. (Mrs. H. A. Sipe). Ophthalmologist, Allegheny Gen. Hosp., and for Pa. R.R., Carnegie Steel Co., and U.S. Pension Bur. Trustee Allegheny Coll.; trustee Am. Med. Assn., 1925-32, chmn. bd., 1925—, chmn. sect. on ophthalmology, 1929; mem. bd. mgrs. Allegheny Co. Industrial and Tr. Sch. for Boys. Pres. Pittsburgh Acad. Medicine, 1898, Pittsburgh Ophthal. Soc., 1912—; president Allegheny County Medical Society, 1905; president Med. Soc. State Pa., 1913-15; fellow Am. Coll. Surgeons. Home: Pittsburgh, Pa. Died Dec. 23, 1935.

HECKEL, George Baugh, editor; b. Chester County, Pa., Mar. 13, 1858; s. Edward Bowers (M.D.) and Harriet Rinehart (Baugh) H.; student Ursinus Coll., Collegeville, Pa., 1874-75, med. dept. U. of Pa., 1877-79; m. Ellen Theresa McCloskey, June 27, 1893; children—James Edward, George Baugh, Frank Price. Western corr. Lockwood Press of New York, at Chicago, 1881-83; ed. ry. publs.; lit. editor of Rand-McNally & Co., Chicago, 1884-87; spl. rep. L. J. McCloskey & Co., varnish mfrs., 1888-89; owner, editor and publisher The Paint Industry Magazine, formerly Drugs, Oils and Paints, 1890—. Sec.-treas. Paint Mfrs.' Assn. of U.S., 1905, Nat. Varnish Mfrs.' Assn., 1909; sec. Am. Paint and Varnish Mfrs.' Association, 1926-30; sec. emeritus Nat. Paint, Varnish and Lacquer Assn., Inc.; adv. manager The New Jersey Zinc Co., 1907-19, later consultant; organizer, 1921, and sec. Fed. Paint and Varnish Production Clubs; sec. Agricultural Insecticide and Fungicide Mfrs. Assn., 1924. Republican. Catholic. Joint Author: Jacob Valmont, Manager, 1885; A Paint Catechism, 5th edit., 1939; A Varnish Catechism, 1912-39; Materials of Paint Manufacture, 1925; The Paint Industry—Reminiscences and Comments, 1929; The New Paint, Varnish and Lacquer Catechism, 1936, 39. Translator: Nouma Roumestan (from the French of Daudet), 1886; Journal of Marie Bashkirtseff, 1886; The Dream (from the French of Zola), 1888; Fromont, Jr., and Risler, Sr. (from the French of Daudet), 1895. Home: Philadelphia, Pa. Died Jan. 19, 1941.

HECKER, Frank Joseph, capitalist; b. Freedom, Mich., July 9, 1846; s. Frank and Cynthia (Shield) H.; ed. in pub. schs.; pvt. and 1st sergt. Co. K, 41st Mo. Inf., Aug. 24, 1864-July 11, 1865; m. Anna M. Williamson, Dec. 8, 1868; children—Frank Clarence, Anna Cynthia (dec.), Louise May, Grace Clara, Christian Henry. Acting div. supt. U.P. Ry., 1869; gen. supt. Rondout & Oswego R.R., 1870-76, Eel River R.R., 1876-79; organized Peninsular Car Co., 1879, and remained with it and its successor, Mich. Peninsular Car Co., as pres., until 1900; dir. People's State Bank, Union Trust Co., Detroit Copper & Brass Rolling Mills, Detroit Lumber Co. Police commr., Detroit, 1880-90; col. q.m. vols., July 8, 1898-May 1, 1899; chief of div. of transportation of the army during Spanish-Am. War; mem. Isthmian Canal Commn., Mar.-Dec. 1904. Home: Detroit, Mich. Died June 26, 1927.

HECKERT, Charles Girven, college pres.; b. Northumberland, Pa., Mar. 22, 1863; s. Benjamin and Sarah Jane (Durst) H.; A.B., Wittenberg Coll., 1886, A.M., 1889; Wittenberg Theol. Sem., 1886-89; D.D., Carthage Coll., 1899; LL.D., Cedarville, 1919; m. Ada R. Royer, July 24, 1889. Ordained Luth. ministry, 1889; prin. Wittenberg Acad., 1891-93; prof. English and logic, 1893-1903, pres., 1903—, Wittenberg Coll. Pres. Miami (O.) Synod, 1892; mng. editor Lutheran World, 1900-03. Home: Springfield, O. Died Dec. 7, 1920.

HECKMAN, Wallace, lawyer; b. Morgan County, O., May 22, 1851; s. Philip and Sarah Ann (Farley) H.; M.S., Hillsdale (Mich.) Coll., 1874; m. Caroline Matilda Howe, Nov. 16, 1881; 1 dau., Jessie (Mrs. Marcus A. Herschel). Practiced, Chicago, 1875; sr. mem. Heckman, Elsdon & Shaw, 1885-1908; counsel and business mgr. U. of Chicago, 1903—; v.p. Chicago Rys. Co.; trustee Ida A. Richardson Estate; dir. Chicago Dock & Canal Co. Arbitrator of labor controversies, Union and Consolidated Traction cos., 1903, Met. Elevated R.R. Co., 1904, Elevated Roads, 1913; mem. operating bd. Chicago Surface Lines. Pres. Ill. Civ. Serv. Reform Assn.; mem. exec. com. Municipal Voters' League. Trustee Hillsdale Coll., Frances Shimer Acad., Mt. Carroll, Ill. Republican. Baptist. Home: Chicago, Ill. Died Mar. 6, 1927.

HECKSCHER, August, capitalist; b. Hamburg, Germany, Aug. 1848; s. John Gustav Maurice and Antoinette (Brautigam) H.; ed. high sch.; m. Anna Atkins, Oct. 13, 1881; children—G. Maurice, Antoinette (Viscountess Esher). With importing house of E. Nolting & Co., Hamburg, 3 yrs.; came to U.S., 1868, and engaged in coal business until 1884: an organizer of Lehigh Zinc & Iron Co., 1881, later consolidated with others into the New Jersey Zinc Co., of which was gen. mgr. until 1904, later dir.; pres. Anahama Realty Corp.; dir. Union Bag and Paper Corp., Empire Trust Co., Crucible Steel Co., etc. Chmn. Heckscher Foundation for Children. Home: New York, N.Y. Died Apr. 26, 1941.

HECKSCHER, Celeste Delongpre, composer; b. Phila., Pa., 1860; d. Robert Valantine and Julia Whitney (Pratt) Massey; m. Austin Stevens Heckscher, 1883 (dec.); children—Robert Valantine, Richard Maurice, Celeste (Mrs. Edward Troth), Anna Massey (Mrs. Richard Newbold). Episcopalian. Composer: (orchestral suite) Dances of the Pyrenees (performed by Phila. Orchestra, Theodore Thomas Orchestra, New York Symphony Orchestra, etc.); French Dance, Asiatic Dance; (violin suite) To the Forest; (opera) The Rose of Destiny; (piano pieces) Impromptu, Au Fond, Valse Bohême; book of seven songs; Romance for cello; etc. Home: New York, N.Y. Died Feb. 19, 1928.

HEDBLOM, Carl Arthur, surgeon; b. Dayton, Ia., Mar. 5, 1879; s. Peter and Maria S. (Johnson) H.; B.A., Colorado Coll., 1907; M.A., 1908, M.D., Harvard, 1911; Ph.D., Mayo Foundation, U. of Minn., 1920; m. Eleanor Pease, June 18, 1913; children—Carl Arthur, George Gordon, Richard Peter, Eleanor Jane. Interne Mass. Gen. Hosp., 1911-13; prof. surgery, Harvard Med. Sch. in China, 1913-16; fellow Mayo Foundation, 1917; surgeon Mayo Clinic, 1918-24; prof. surgery, U. of Wis. and chief of surg. dept., 1924-26; prof. surgery and head of dept., U. of Ill. Med. Sch., 1926—; surgeon in chief Research and Educational Hospital, U. of Ill.; senior surgeon St. Luke's Hospital. Republican. Conglist. Home: Chicago, Ill. Died June 6, 1934.

HEDGE, Charles Gorham, ry. official; b. Plymouth, Mass., May 15, 1852; s. Nathaniel L. and Sarah W. (Sylvester) H.; ed. Plymouth (Mass.) pub. schs.; m. Emma W. Bremner, 1877. Began ry. service, 1873; held various positions with different rys. and commercial cos., 1873-84; sec., treas. and purchasing agt. Mann Boudoir Car Co., 1885-89; asst. to 2d v.p. Pullman Palace Car Co., 1889-91; sec. and comptroller 1891-96, treas., 1891, v.p. and dir., 1896—, M.,K.&T. Ry. Co.; also v.p. and dir. M.,K.&T. Ry. Co. of Tex., M.,K.&T. Terminal Co. of Kansas City, Denison Union Passenger Depot Co., Boonville R.R. Bridge Co. Served 7th Regt. N.G.S.N.Y., 10 yrs. Republican. Unitarian. Mason. Home: Southampton, L.I., N.Y. Died Mar. 6, 1921.

HEDGES, Frank Hinckley, journalist; b. Springfield, Mo., Apr. 19, 1895; s. James Harrison and Edna Bertha (Houghton) H.; diploma, Western Mil. Acad., Alton, Ill., 1912; A.B., Drury Coll., Springfield, Mo., 1917; B.J., U. of Mo., 1919; unmarried. Successively news editor Miami (Okla.) Record-Herald, Corpus Christi (Tex.) Caller, and feature writer Washington (D.C.) Herald; staff of Japan Advertiser (Am. daily), Tokyo, Japan, in Peking and Tokyo; mng. editor same, in Tokyo, 1923-1927; was chief of the Far Eastern Bureau of the Christian Science Monitor, Tokyo, 1927-31; staff corr. The (London) Times, 1930-31; exec. sec. Press Congress of the World, 1934—; Far Eastern rep. of North Am. Newspaper Alliance; Japan corr. Washington Post, London Daily Telegraph, North-China Daily News; contributing editor The Japan Times and Mail, 1935—; contributor to American, English and Japanese magazines on Far Eastern topics. Served as 2d lieutenant 64th Pioneer Infantry, World War. Democrat. Conglist. Rotarian. Editor Trans. Asiatic Soc. of Japan, 1925-31. Author: The Kabuki Stage of Japan, 1929; What Do Americans Think of Japan? (bi-lingual), 1932; In Far Japan, 1935. Address: Springfield, Mo. Died Apr. 20, 1940.

HEDGES, Job Elmer, lawyer; b. Elizabeth, N.J., May 10, 1862; s. Job Clark and Elizabeth Wood (Elmer) H.; A.B., Princeton, 1884, A.M., 1887; LL.B., Columbia Law Sch., 1886; LL.D., St. Lawrence U. and U. of Pittsburgh, 1914, Muhlenberg Coll., 1922; married. Admitted to bar, 1886, and practiced in New York; sec. to Mayor Strong, 1895-97; city magistrate, 1897-98; dep. atty. gen. N.Y., resigned, 1902; mem. Hedges, Ely & Frankel. Commr. for U.S. of Internat. Fisheries Commn. Presbyn. Author: Common Sense in Politics, 1910. Address: New York, N.Y. Died Feb. 22, 1925.

HEDLESTON, Winn David, clergyman; b. Hale County, Ala., Apr. 25, 1862; s. W. D. and Martha Agnes (Fulton) H.; A.B., U. of Miss., 1883; D.D., Central U. of Ky.; m. Lillie Andrus, 1885. Prin.

Toccopola High Sch., 1883; acting prof. chemistry, U. of Miss., 1884; ordained to ministry, Southern Presbyn. Ch., 1885; pastor Pleasant Grove and Mackville Presbyn. chs., Washington County, Ky., 1886-88, Paint Lick Ch., Garrard Co., Ky., 1889-93, Presbyterian Ch., Oxford, Miss., 1893-1910; prof. ethics, U. of Miss., 1909—. Democrat. Author: Lamp Oil, 1898. Home: University, Miss. Deceased.

HEDRICK, Ira Grant, civil engr.; b. W. Salem, Ill., Apr. 6, 1868; s. Henderson and Mary Ann H.; C.E., U. of Ark., 1892; B.S., McGill U., Can., 1898, M.S., 1899, D.Sc., 1900; m. Louise Luther, Feb. 10, 1889. Established practice as civ. engr., Oct. 1892; has been identified with many large and important engrng. works; pres. Kansas City Viaduct & Terminal Ry. Co., 1907-09; later mem. firm of Hedrick & Cochrane. Address: Kansas City, Mo. Died Dec. 28, 1937.

HEEBNER, Charles, lawyer; b. Port Carbon, Pa., Feb. 6, 1859; s. Henry Reed and Elizabeth (Lewis) H.; A.B., Lafayette Coll., 1878, A.M., 1881; m. Alice Schuyler, Dec. 18, 1888; children—Charles Schuyler, Eleanor, Julia (dec.), Henry Reed, Alice. Admitted to Pa. bar, 1885; asst. gen. solicitor, Phila. & Reading R.R. Co., and its successor, Phila. & Reading Ry. Co., 1889-1910; gen. solicitor, Phila. & Reading Ry. Co., 1910—; also gen. solicitor Phila. & Reading Coal & Iron Co. and of Reading Co.; gen. counsel of these cos., 1918-29. Republican. Unitarian. Trustee Lafayette College. Home: Bryn Mawr, Pa. Died June 12, 1933.

HEERMANS, Forbes, author; b. Syracuse, N.Y., Oct. 25, 1856; s. Thomas Beekman and Annie (Forbes) H.; M.E., Cornell, 1878; unmarried. Engaged in journalism, 1880—. Author: Thirteen Stories of the Far West, 1887; Love by Induction, and Other Plays, 1889; The Silent Witness, drama, 1890; The Rancho of the Twelve Apostles, 1892; Between Two Foes, drama, 1899; The Investigators (novel); also The Vagabond, a play; Jess, of the Bar Z Ranch, a 4-act drama; Down the Santa Fe trail, 4-act drama; Twin Star (novel), 1907; Beacon Island (story), 1907; Buena Ventura (novel), 1911; Tales of West and East, 1922; The Greenwood Expedition. Home: Syracuse, N.Y. Died Sept. 18, 1928.

HEFFERN, Andrew Duff, theologian; b. Phila., Feb. 24, 1856; s. Andrew Duff and Elizabeth (Smith) H.; Amherst Coll., 1874-76; A.B., Harvard, 1878; U. of Berlin, 1879-80; grad. Episcopal Div. Sch., Phila., 1881; D.D., Western U. of Pa. (now U. of Pittsburgh), 1904; m. Louisa Fried Wagner, July 3, 1889. Deacon, 1881, priest, 1882, P.E. Ch.; rector, Hillsboro, O., 1881-82, Trinity Ch., Phila., 1882-87, Trinity, San Francisco, 1887-88, Ch. Good Shepherd, Pittsburgh, 1889-1900; prof. N.T. lit. and lang., Episcopal Divinity School, 1900—. Examining chaplain Diocese of Pa. Lecturer on the Bohlen Foundation, Phila., 1915. Home: Philadelphia, Pa. Died May 2, 1920.

HEFFRON, John Lorenzo, physician; b. New Woodstock, N.Y., Nov. 29, 1851; s. Dr. Lorenzo and Mary A. (Pettit) H.; A.B., Madison (now Colgate) U., 1873, A.M., 1876; student Coll. Phys. and Surg. (Columbia), 1879, 1880; M.D., Syracuse U., 1881; univs. Vienna and Heidelberg; D.Sc., Colgate, 1909; m. Marie A. Marcher, Aug. 13, 1881. Practiced at Syracuse; instr. in histology, 1882-85, prof. histology, 1885-87, materia medica and therapeutics, 1887-95, clin. medicine, 1895—, dean, Oct. 1907-22, dean emeritus, College of Medicine, Syracuse U.; visiting physician St. Joseph's Hosp., 1882-87; consulting physician Hosp. for Women and Children, 1888—; visiting physician, 1884-1907, physician-in-chief, 1907-15, consulting physician Hospital of the Good Shepherd. Alumnus trustee Syracuse U., 18 yrs.; dir. Syracuse Chamber of Commerce. Unitarian. Home: Syracuse, N.Y. Died Sept. 28, 1924.

HEFFRON, Patrick Richard, bishop; b. New York, June 1, 1860; s. Patrick and Margaret (O'Brien) H.; high sch., Mantorville, Minn.; business coll. and law sch., Rochester, Minn.; St. John's Coll., Minn., Master of Accounts, 1878; Grand Sem., Montreal, Can., 6 yrs., S.T.L., 1883; S.T.L., D.D., Minerva U., 1889; D.C.L., Appollinare U., Rome, 1889. Ordained R.C. priesthood, Dec. 22, 1884, after which he spent 2 yrs. on the European Continent, mostly in Rome; pastor Cathedral, St. Paul, 1886-96; vice rector, 1896-97, pres., 1897-1910, St. Paul Sem.; consecrated bishop of Winona, Minn., May 19, 1910; apptd. asst. at the throne by Benedict XV, 1920. Home: Winona, Minn. Died Nov. 23, 1927.

HEGEMAN, John Rogers, pres. Metropolitan Life Ins. Co.; b. Brooklyn, April 18, 1844; s. John G. and Charlotte Owen (Rogers) H.; ed. pub. and poly. schs., New York; m. Evelyn Lyon, Oct. 26, 1870. Became accountant for Manhattan Life Ins. Co., 1886; sec. Met. Life Ins. Co., June 1870, v.p., 1870, pres., 1891—. Dir. Metropolitan Bank, National Surety Co., Victor Chem. Co.; trustee Hamilton Trust Co., of Brooklyn, Union Dime Savings Bank. Home: Mamaroneck, N.Y. Died Apr. 6, 1919.

HEGER, Anthony, army officer; b. in Austria, Dec. 4, 1828. Apptd. from Pa. asst. surgeon, Aug. 29, 1856; capt. asst. surgeon, Aug. 29, 1861; maj. surgeon, Sept. 17, 1862; lt. col. surgeon, Jan. 24, 1886; col. surgeon, Jan. 2, 1891; retired by operation of law, Dec. 4, 1892; advanced to rank of brig. gen. retired, by act of Apr. 23, 1904. Bvtd. lt. col., Mar. 13, 1865, for services during the war. Died 1908.

HEHIR, Martin A., clergyman; b. County Clare, Ireland, Nov. 10, 1855; s. John and Mary (Clancy) H.; B.A., Blackrock Coll., Dublin, 1877; M.A., Catholic U., Dublin, 1880; studied theology at Chevilly, Paris, France; LL.D., Mt. St. Mary's, Md., 1909, Nat. U., Ireland, 1933; Litt.D., St. Vincent's Coll., Beatty, Pa., 1928. Joined Holy Ghost Fathers (C.S.Sp.), 1872; ordained priest R.C. Ch., at Paris, 1883; came to U.S., 1884; with Duquesne U. until 1899; pres. Holy Ghost Coll., 1899-1911, Duquesne U., 1911-30, Apostolic Coll., Cornwells Heights, Phila., 1930-32; rector St. Mary's Sem., Ferndale, Norwalk, Conn., 1932—. Mem. Diocesan Sch. Bd., examiner diocesan jr. clergy. Address: Norwalk, Conn. Deceased.

HEIDEL, William Arthur, univ. prof.; b. Burlington, Ia., Mar. 10, 1868; s. Rev. Charles and Mary Magdalen (Fengel) H.; A.B., Central Wesleyan Coll., 1888, A.M., 1891, LL.D., 1929; U. of Berlin, 1888-90; fellow in Greek, U. of Chicago, 1894-95, Ph.D., 1895; A.M., ad eundem, Wesleyan U., Conn., 1906; L.H.D., Ill. Wesleyan University, 1929; L.H.D., Trinity Coll., Hartford, Conn., 1939; m. Mary Elizabeth Mack, June 15, 1898; 1 son, Warren Clark. Acting prof. Latin, 1890-91, prof. Greek, 1891-94, Ill. Wesleyan U.; docent in ancient philosophy, U. of Chicago, 1895-96; prof. Latin, Ia. (now Grinnell) Coll., 1896-1905; prof. Greek, Wesleyan U., 1905-28, research prof. Greek, 1928-36, emeritus; research asso. Am. Council of Learned Societies and Carnegie Instn. of Washington, 1928—. Asso. editor of Classical Philology; mem. managing committee Am. Sch. Classical Studies at Athens. Author: On Certain Fragments of the Pre-Socratics, 1913; Anaximander's Book, the Earliest Known Geographical Treatise, 1921; Vergil's Messianic Expectations, 1924; The Day of Yahweh, 1929; The Heroic Age of Science, 1933; A Suggestion Concerning Plato's Atlantis, 1933; Hecataeus and the Egyptian Priests in Herodotus, Bk. II; The Frame of the Ancient Greek Maps, 1937; also other books now out of print. Home: Middletown, Conn. Died Jan. 15, 1941.

HEIL, William Franklin, bishop; b. Berlinsville, Pa., May 1, 1857; s. Nathan and Lydia (Meister) H.; ed. pub. schs., Berlinsville, Cedar Hill Sem. and Normal Sch., Pa.; m. Annie L. Reed, 1882. Ordained United Evang. ministry, 1880; pastor Lansdale, Pa., 1880-82, Bangor, Pa., 1882-85, Fredericksburg, Pa., 1885-87, Lebanon, Pa., 1887-90; presiding elder, 1890-95; pastor Reading, 1895-99, Allentown, 1899-1903; bishop, 1903-10; presiding elder Allentown Dist., East Pa. Conf., 1911-18; again bishop, 1918—. Home: Allentown, Pa. Died Nov. 6, 1930.

HEILMAN, Ralph Emerson, economist; b. Ida Grove, Ia., Apr. 15, 1886; s. Elwood C. (M.D.) and Nancy Jane (Blazer) H.; Ph.B., Morningside Coll., Sioux City, Ia., 1906; A.M., Northwestern U., 1907; Ph.D., Harvard, 1913; LL.D., Morningside Coll., 1920; m. Elsie May Weary, Sept. 8, 1909; children—Gwen, Mary Lou. Instr. in economics, Harvard, 1912-13; asst. prof. economics and chief Bur. of Social Welfare, U. of Ia., 1913-14; asst. prof. economics, U. of Ill., 1914-16; prof. economics and social science, 1916-19, dean Sch. of Commerce, Northwestern Univ., 1919—. Dist. representative of the Emergency Fleet Corp., and examiner Shipbuilding Labor Adjustment Bd., 1918-19; chmn. ways and means com. Chicago Assn. Commerce, 1929. Methodist. Author: (with others) Profit Sharing, 1918. Home: Evanston, Ill. Died Feb. 16, 1937.

HEILNER, Samuel; b. Phila., Pa., Sept. 30, 1855; s. Percival and Caroline (Can Camp) H.; Friends Central Sch.; LL.B., U. of Pa., 1877; m. Adelaide Breese Dunn, June 23, 1898; 1 son, Van Campen. Practiced law in Colo., 1877-82; returned to Phila. to asso. with father in mining and shipping coal, as Percy Heilner & Son; became mgr. of co. upon death of father, 1886, now owner and pres.; dir. N.Y.&N.E. R.R. Co., 1892-93; pres. Commonwealth Coal & Coke Co., 1903-22; v.p. Hastings Square Hotel Co. Apptd. mem. Ocean Boulevard Commn., 1908; represented N.J. at Am. Encampment G.A.R., 1910; apptd. mem. Waterways Commn. by Gov. Woodrow Wilson, 1912, also to rep. N.J. at Nat. Rivers and Harbors Congress, Washington, D.C., 1912; mem. Governors Conf., Richmond, Va., 1912, Madison, Wis., 1913; chmn. Red Cross, 1917, also mem. Liberty Loan Com. Chmn. bd. trustees Pub. Library, Spring Lake, also of Memorial Community House; v.p. bd. mgrs. Monmouth County Hosp.; mem. bd. mgrs. N.J. State Home for Girls, by apptmt. of Gov. Silzer, 1925—. Mem. Council Foreign Relations. Republican. Presbyn. Mason. Home: Spring Lake, N.J. Died May 29, 1938.

HEILPRIN, Angelo, naturalist; b. Sátoralja-Ujhely, Hungary, March 31, 1853; s. Michael and Henrietta H.; came to U.S., 1856; ed. in Europe, making spl. study of natural history. Successively prof. invertebrate paleontology and geology, 1880-1900, and exec. curator, 1883-92, Acad. Natural Sciences, Phila.; prof. geology, Wagner Free Inst., 1885-90; pres. for 7 yrs. Geog. Soc., Phila.; v.p. Am. Alpine Club, 1903. Leader Peary Relief Expdn., 1892. Exhibited paintings several exhbns. Author: The Animal Life of our Seashore, 1888 L5; The Bermuda Islands; A Contribution to the Physical History and Zoölogy of the Somers Archipelago, 1889 A7; Principles of Geology, 1890 O1; Peary Relief Expedition, 1893 O1; The Earth and Its Story, 1896 S6; Alaska and the Klondike, 1899 A2; Mont Pelée and the Tragedy of Martinique, 1903; Tower of Pelée, 1905 L5. Died 1907.

HEILPRIN, Louis, author; b. Miskolcz, Hungary, July 2, 1851; s. Michael and Henrietta H.; came to U.S., 1856; private edn. Unmarried. Author: Historical Reference Book, 1884. Brother of A. Heilprin. Home: New York, N.Y. Died 1912.

HEIMKE, William, diplomat; b. in France; educated in France and Germany, later pvt. and pub. schs., New York, at army posts, and at the U.S. Military Acad., class of 1875. General material, importing, and purchasing agt. Mex. Central Ry., 1881-82; gen. mgr. Chihuahua and Durango telephone cos., 1883-87; apptd. vice-consul at Chihuahua, Feb. 2, 1887, in charge of consulate from May 3, 1887; consul, Aug. 18, 1892; retired, Sept. 23, 1893; apptd. 2d sec. of legation at Mexico, May 3, 1897; chargé d'affaires at different times; sec. of legation at Bogotá, July 18, 1906; chargé d'affaires, de titre, Oct. 1, 1906-Oct. 16, 1907; E.E. and M.P. to Guatemala, 1908-09; E.E. and M.P., El Salvador, Aug. 5, 1909-May 1915; chief of Div. of Latin-Am. Affairs, Dept. of State, July 29, 1914; retired May 1915. Pres. Latin-Am. Coast and Car Lightning Co., 1915-Dec. 1917. During World War representative atty. for various Am., European, and Latin-Am. export and import houses before the different governmental bureaus in Washington, D.C.; E.E. and M.P. on spl. diplomatic mission to Peru, July-Aug. 1921, to attend the ceremonies in connection with the first Centenary of Peruvian Independence. Hon. v.p. Lincoln U. Endowment Assn.; life mem. Am. Red Cross, Acad. Internat. History (Paris); corr. mem. Geog. Soc. of Lima, Peru. Grand Officer Order of El Sol del Perú. Home: Leavenworth, Kan. Died July 14, 1931.

HEIN, Carl Christian, clergyman; b. Wiesbaden, Germany, Aug. 31, 1868; s. Julius and Ernstine (Buesgen) H.; came to U.S., 1884; A.B., Capital U., Columbus, O., 1885; grad. Theol. Sem., Joint Synod of Ohio, Columbus, 1888, D.D., 1922; m. Anna M. Froemke, Oct. 22, 1889; children—Hildegard Magdalene (dec.), Esther Hedwig (dec.), Reuben Froemke, Gerhard Carl (dec.), Carl Christian. Ordained Luth. ministry, 1888; pastor Marion, Wis., until 1891, Salem Ch., Detroit, 1891-1902; Trinity Ch., Columbus, 1902-25. Mem. publn. bd. Joint Synod of Ohio, 1902-25; pres. Western Dist. of Joint Synod, 1912-20; v.p. Nat. Luth. Council, 1927-32, pres., 1933—; pres. Evang. Luth. Joint Synod of Ohio and Other States, 1925; pres. Am. Lutheran Ch., Jan. 1, 1931—. Del. Luth. World Conv., Eisenach, Germany, 1923, Copenhagen, Denmark, 1929, Paris, France, 1935. Home: Columbus, O. Died April 30, 1937.

HEINEMAN, Walter Ben, lumber mfr.; b. Wausau, Wis., Mar. 15, 1879; s. Benjamin and Johanna (Ullman) H.; ed. pub. schs.; m. Elsie Deutsch, June 20, 1905; children—Marion, Marjorie L., Joan E., Ben W. Began with B. Heineman Lumber Co., founded by father, of which became pres., 1919; also pres. Cisco Lake Lumber Co.; treas. D. J. Murray Mfg. Co., Heineman-Johnson Lumber Co. Chmn. exec. com. Rep. State Central Com., Wis., 1913-22; vice treas. Rep. Nat. Com., 1928—; mem. Dist. Draft Bd., West Dist. of Wis., World War. Trustee D. L. Plummer Hosp. Mem. Nat. forestry com. of Chamber Commerce U.S. Home: Wausau, Wis. Died July 17, 1930.

HEINEMANN, E., artist; b. Brunswick, Germany, Feb. 19, 1848; s. J. August and Marie (Fricke) H.; pupil of A. Closs, and Brendeamour; studied drawing and painting Art Students' League, New York; m. Bertha Manzel, of Stuttgart, May 4, 1872. In art dept. Am. Book Co., June 1902—. Exhibited at Paris Expn., 1900; bronze medal Buffalo Expn., 1901. Engraved and published, The Land of Rip Van Winkle. Participated in Prussian-Franco War and received medal; gold and silver medals at athletic tournaments of N.Am. Turner Bund. Home: Fort Wadsworth, S.I., N.Y. Died May 11, 1912.

HEINMILLER, Louis Edward, educator; b. Utica, N.Y., Mar. 3, 1890; s. Louis and Louise (Holzwarth) H.; B.S., U. of Rochester, 1911; A.M., Columbia, 1918; Ph.D., New York U., 1926; m. Flora Shoemaker, Dec. 31, 1912. Prin. high sch., Freeville, N.Y., 1911-13, Cherry Valley, N.Y., 1913-15; head dept. mathematics high sch., Glen Ridge, N.J., 1915-20; prof. edn., State Teachers Coll., Slippery Rock, Pa., 1920-25; prof. and head dept. edn., State Teachers Coll., Kingsville, Tex., 1926-27; pres. Silliman Coll., Clinton, La., 1927-31; prin. and owner Loulie Compton Sem., Birmingham, Ala., 1931—. Republican. Presbyn. Mason. Author: A First Book ucation, 1925. Home: Birmingham, Ala. Died Feb. 25, 1939.

HEINRICH, Wilhelm, tenor soloist and teacher of singing; b. Rockford, Ill., Feb. 24, 1865; s. Christian and Wilhelmena (Hinze) H.; entire loss of sight from brain fever at age of 6 yrs.; grad. Ill. Sch. for the Blind, 1883; Berlitz Sch. of Langs., Boston; pvt. instrn. in vocalization under Charles R. Adams, Mrs. Henry M. Rogers, Boston; F. E. Bristol, New York; Herr Julius Stockhausen, Frankfort on the Main, Germany; Signor Sbriglia, Paris; William Shakespeare, London; unmarried. Began professional career at New Bedford Festival in Whiting's Tale of the Viking and Gounod's Redemption, 1896; later with Symphony Orchestra, Boston, at Old Music Hall, in the first production of Parsifal in America; later appeared in prin. cities of America and Europe, with Sembrich, Melba, Marchesi, Geraldine Farrar, Emma Eames, Claude Debussy, Anton Dvorak, Campanini, etc.; especially noted for his "Twentieth Century Song Recitals"; tenor soloist of quartette of S. Congl. (Unitarian) Ch., Boston, Apr. 1, 1900—. Home: Greenbush, Mass. Deceased.

HEINS, George Lewis, architect; b. Philadelphia, Pa., May 24, 1860; s. John and Anne Marie (Vaughn) H.; student Univ. of Pa., 1877-79; grad. Mass. Inst. Tech. (architecture), 1882; m. Aimee LaFarge, 1896. In architect's office, Minneapolis, 1882-83, St. Paul, 1883-84; joined his classmate, C. Grant LaFarge, and then removed to New York, 1884, both serving as archtl. assistants to John LaFarge, decorative artist. In 1886 formed partnership with C. G. LaFarge as Heins & LaFarge. Architect for P.E. Cathedral of St. John the Divine, New York, N.Y. Zoöl. Park. Consulting architects Rapid Transit Commn.; State architect of all N.Y. State Bldgs., 1898—. Home: Mohegan, N.Y. Died 1907.

HEINSHEIMER, Edward Lewis, philanthropist, banker; b. Cincinnati, Apr. 1, 1861; s. Lewis and Emma (Goodhart) H.; ed. Hughes High Sch., Cincinnati; m. Sallie Workum Freiberg, Nov. 16, 1886. Mem. P. J. Goodhart & Co., New York and Cincinnati, 1883-Jan. 1, 1916, when retired; charter mem. and pres. Cincinnati Stock Exchange. Identified with all the leading charity and eleemosynary instrns. of Cincinnati for more than 25 yrs.; pres. bd. govs. Hebrew Union Coll.; pres. Jewish Settlement; trustee Jacob H. Schiff Fund for Teachers' Inst. Republican. Jewish religion. Home: Cincinnati, O. Died Dec. 1917.

HEINTZELMAN, Stuart, army officer; b. N.Y. City, Nov. 19, 1876; s. C. S. (U.S. Army) and Emily (Bailey) H.; g.s. of S. P. Heintzelman (U.S. Army); grad. U.S. Mil. Acad., 1899; honor grad. Inf. and Cav. Sch., 1905; grad. Army Staff Coll., 1906, Army War Coll., 1920; hon. M.A., Princeton, 1917; m. Rubey Bowling, Mar. 14, 1910. Commd. 2d lt. cav., Feb. 15, 1899; promoted through grades to brig. gen., Dec. 29, 1922; major general, Dec. 1, 1931. Served in Nat. Army as lt. col., col. and brig. gen., World War. In Philippines, 1900-02, 1907-09; China Relief Expdn., 1900; instr. Army Service Schs., 1909-12, 1914-16; instr. Princeton Univ., 1916-17; arrived in France, July 1917; operation sect., G.H.Q., until Jan. 1918; chief of operation, 1st Corps, to June 1918; chief of staff, 4th Corps, to Sept. 1918; chief of staff, 2d Army, until demobolized, Apr. 1919; returned to U.S. July 1919; dir. Army War Coll., 1919; asst. chief of staff, 1921-24; comdt. Command and Gen. Staff Sch., Ft. Leavenworth, Kan., 1929-35. Holder of Philippine, China, Mexican border and Victory campaign badges; awarded D.S.M.; Croix de Guerre with Palm, and Comdr. Legion of Honor (France); Comdr. Order of Crown (Italy). Died July 6, 1935.

HEINZ, Henry John, mfr.; b. Pittsburgh, Pa., Oct. 11, 1844; s. Henry and Anna Margaretha (Schmidt) H.; ed. pub. schs. and Duff's Bus. Coll.; m. Sarah Sloan Young, Sept. 23, 1869 (died 1894). Began small business of packing food products at Sharpsburg, Pa., 1869; removed to Pittsburgh, 1872, where business was conducted by partnership of Heinz, Noble & Co.; firm name became F. & J. Heinz and in 1888, H. J. Heinz Co., which continued as a partnership until 1905, when business was organized as corp., of which he is pres.; besides main plant at Pittsburgh, co. has 16 branch factories (including 1 each in Can., Eng. and Spain), 98 salting houses, 45 branch houses, including 1 in London, and agencies in all parts of world; v.p. Western Pa. Expn. Soc.; dir. Union Nat. Bank, Western Ins. Co. Dir. Pittsburgh Chamber of Commerce; chmn. commn. to devise means to protect Pittsburgh from floods. Pres. Pa. State S.S. Assn.; chmn. exec. com. World's S.S. Assn. Presbyterian. Republican. Home: Pittsburgh, Pa. Died May 14, 1919.

HEINZ, Howard, mfr.; b. Pittsburgh, Pa., Aug. 27, 1877; s. Henry John and Sarah Sloan (Young) H.; prep. edn., Shady Side Acad., Pittsburgh; B.A., Yale, 1900; LL.D., Juniata College, Pa., 1926; m. Elizabeth Granger Rust, Oct. 3, 1906; children—Henry John, II, Rust. Began, 1900, in food product mfg. business estab. by father, 1869; became adv. mgr., 1905, sales mgr., 1907; pres. H. J. Heinz Co., 1919; dir. Pa. R.R. Co., Mellon National Bank of Pittsburgh; mem. bd. of govs. Yale Publishing Assn. Trustee Carnegie Endowment for Internat. Peace. Served during World War as mem. Nat. Council of Defense of Pa., also as follows: U.S. food adminstr. of Pa.; chmn. Food Supply Com. Nat. Council Defense, Pa.; zone chmn. U.S. Food Administration for Pa., Ohio, Va., W.Va., Md. and D.C.; mem. War Industries Bd. of Phila.; and mem. exec. com. Am. Relief Adminstration (European children's relief). Dir. gen. Am. Relief Adminstrn. for Southeastern Europe and Asia Minor, Jan.-June 1919. Pres. Heinz House, Pittsburgh; mem. bd. trustees U. of Pittsburgh, Carnegie Inst., West Pa. Hosp., W.Pa. Inst. for the Blind (Pittsburgh), Shady Side Acad. (Pittsburgh); pres. Pittsburgh Regional Planning Assn.; mem. Nat. Indsl. Conf. Bd., Inc., N.Y. City; trustee Commn. for Relief in Belgium, Ednl. Foundation, New York. Republican. Presbyterian. Home: Moorewood Heights, Pittsburgh, Pa. Died Feb. 9, 1941.

HEINZE, F. Augustus, mining engr.; b. Brooklyn, N.Y., Dec. 5, 1869; s. Otto and Lida M. (Lacey) H.; ed. Poly. Inst., Brooklyn; E.M., Columbia Sch. of Mines, 1889; studied in Germany; unmarried. Engaged in mining and smelting in Mont., 1889—; pres. United Copper Co.; dir. Montana Ore Purchasing Co. Active in Mont. politics as Democrat. Home: Butte, Mont. Died Nov. 4, 1914.

HEISCHMANN, John J., clergyman; b. Lyons, N.Y., Aug. 7, 1858; s. Charles Theodore and Marie A. (Nauen) H.; ed. Knapp's Inst., Baltimore, Md., and Collegiate Dept., Bloomfield (N.J.) Theol. Sem.; grad. Luth. Theol. Sem., Phila., 1879; D.D., Susquehanna U., 1891; m. Caroline M., née Ruoff, Aug. 7, 1879; children—Ruth A., Paul T. (dec.), Bruno J (dec.), Emma J., Marie W. Ordained ministry Evang. Luth. Ch., 1879; pastor St. Peter's Ch., Brooklyn, N.Y., Oct. 8, 1878, sr. pastor, Oct. 1914— (congregation grown from 225 to 2,000, and ch. property now valued at $238.000). Actively identified for more than 48 yrs. with interests of the ch.; many times del. to Pa. Ministerium and Gen. Council; pres. N.Y. Conf., 1899-1902; pres. Ministerium of N.Y. and adjacent States, 1902-05; del. to United Luth. Ch., 4 times; chmn. Luth. Liberty Loan Com. for Brooklyn and L.I., 3d and 4th loans, 1918. Vice-pres. German sect. Brooklyn Inst. Arts and Sciences, 1913; dir. Luth. Theol. Sem., Mt. Airy, Phila., 1891-95, 1918, 22; pres. Bedford Protestant Ministers' Assn., 1925. Entered on 50th yr. of pastorate, Oct. 8, 1927; dean of Protestant clergy of Brooklyn. Home: Brooklyn, N.Y. Died Mar. 1, 1929.

HEISEL, Thomas Bayard, judge; b. St. Georges, Del., Oct. 1, 1868; s. Joseph and Martha W. (Armstrong) H.; A.B., Delaware Coll., Newark, 1888; read law with late Chief Justice Charles B. Lore; m. Frances Clark, Nov. 26, 1896. Admitted to Del. bar, 1893; practiced in New Castle Co.; apptd., Sept. 1912, as mem. Code Commn. of Del. to fill vacancy caused by death of Chief Justice Lore; asso. justice Supreme Court of Del., Oct. 14, 1914—, for term expiring Oct. 13, 1926. Democrat. Presbyn. Home: Delaware City, Del. Died Dec. 26, 1921.

HEISKELL, Frederick Hugh, judge; b. Rogersville, Tenn., July 31, 1851; s. Joseph Brown and Sarah Ann (McKinney) H.; prep. edn., McMinn Acad., Rogersville, and pvt. schs.; student Washington and Lee U., 1870-72; m. Augusta Longstreet Lamar, May 5, 1880 (died 1926); children—Joseph Brown (dec.), Lucius Lamar (dec.), Virginia Longstreet (Mrs. William Forman Dunbar), Hugh McKinney, Augustus Longstreet, Mary Loretta, William Weatherford. Admitted to Tenn. bar, 1873, and began practice at Memphis; mem. Heiskell, Weatherford & Heiskell, later Heiskell & Heiskell until 1900; chancellor, Chancery Court, Shelby Co., Tenn., 1900-25; apptd. judge, Court of Appeals, Tenn., 1925, and elected to same office, 1926, for term 1926-34. Democrat. Presbyterian. Home: Memphis, Tenn. Died Sept. 9, 1933.

HEISKELL, Henry Lee, meteorologist; b. Washington, Oct. 17, 1850; s. Maj. Henry Lee (U.S.A.) and Elizabeth K. (Gouverneur) H.; g.g.s. President James Monroe; Rock Hill Coll., Ellicott City, Md.; U.S. Naval Acad., 1866-69 (resigned); spl. course in meteorology under Prof. Frank H. Bigelow and Prof. Cleveland Abbe; m. Emma L. Heiskell, Oct. 16, 1878 (died 1890); m. 2d, Henrietta Brent, Oct. 12, 1892. In mercantile business, St. Louis and Yazoo City, Miss., 1869-76; pvt. and sergt., U.S. Signal Corps, 1876, until that service was transferred to Agrl. Dept. as U.S. Weather Bur., 1888; clk., chief of div., marine meteorologist, and from Mar. 1, 1913, prof. meteorology, U.S. Weather Bur. Democrat. Catholic. Died Jan. 28, 1914.

HEISKELL, Samuel G., lawyer; b. Monroe Co., Tenn., Aug. 7, 1858; s. William and Julia Josephine (Gahagan) H.; A.B., U. of Tenn., 1877; m. Irene Kuhn, 1897. Practiced at Knoxville, Tenn., 1880—; mem. Bd. of Aldermen, 1882, city atty., 1884; mem. Tenn. Ho. of Rep., 1895 (chmn. judiciary com.); author of bill establishing Court of Chancery Appeals in Tenn. (now Court of Civ. Appeals); mayor of Knoxville, 5 terms (12 yrs.), last term expiring 1915; mem. Bd. of Edn. (pres. 1915-17); pres. State Asylum for the Insane. Chmn. Dem. State Com., Tenn.; Dem. presdl. elector, 1884. Trustee Hermitage Assn. (having charge of Andrew Jackson's old home), 1896— (pres. bd. 1916—). Protestant. Author: Andrew Jackson and Early Tennessee History, 3 vols., 1918. Died Sept. 17, 1923.

HEISLER, John Clement, M.D.; b. Jersey Shore, Pa., Feb. 27, 1862; s. Rev. Washington L. and Sarah Harriet (Kurtz) H.; ed. pub. schs., followed by pvt. tutoring in classical and modern langs., mathematics, lit., etc.; grad. Phila. Coll. Pharmacy, 1883; M.D., U. of Pa., 1887; m. Anna Mary, d. Rev. James D. Reardon; 1 dau., Laura Mary. Began med. practice, 1887; prosector to chair of anatomy, U. of Pa., 1888-97; and at intervals asst. demonstrator of anatomy and curator Wistar and Horner Museum, U. of Pa.; instr. in diseases of the chest, Phila. Polyclinic; prof. anatomy, Medico-Chirurg. Coll. of Phila., 1897-1916; prof. anatomy, U. of Pa., 1916-30, emeritus. Author: Embryology for Medical Students, 1899, 1901, 07; Practical Anatomy, 1912. Died Sept. 9, 1938.

HEISTAND, Henry Olcot Sheldon, army officer; b. on farm nr. Richmond, O., Apr. 30, 1856; s. Henry Olcot Sheldon and Lavina (Irwin) H.; grad. U.S. Mil. Acad., 1878; m. Mary J. Rippey, Sept. 19, 1878. Additional 2d lt. 11th Inf., June 14, 1878; 2d lt., June 28, 1878; 1st lt., June 1, 1886; capt., Mar. 19, 1891; maj. asst. adj. gen., Sept. 11, 1897; lt. col., Apr. 28, 1900; col. asst. adj. gen., July 22, 1902; col. adj. gen., Mar. 5, 1907. Apptd. govt. insp. and instr. Ohio N.G., May 19, 1892; confidential sec. to Maj. McKinley during presdl. campaign, 1896; a.d.c. to President McKinley, 1897-1900; U.S. mil. commr., Paris Expn., 1900; adj. gen. and chief of staff, China Relief Expn. for relief of Peking, 1900; adj. gen. Div. of the Philippines until Oct. 1902, Dept. of the East to Dec. 1909, Div. Philippines to Feb. 15, 1912; on duty in office of adj. gen. of the army, Feb. 1912-Dec. 1914; adj. gen. Central Dept., Chicago, Dec. 1914-Sept. 1917; adj. gen. Camp Grant, Rockford, Ill., and 86th Div., Sept. 1917-Apr. 3, 1918; dept. adjt. Central Dept., Chicago, Apr. 3, 1918-Apr. 30, 1919, Eastern Dept., Governors Island, N.Y., May 1, 1919—. Home: Richwood, O. Died Aug. 8, 1924.

HEITFELD, Henry, senator; b. St. Louis, Jan. 12, 1859; m. Anna M. Jacobs, Nov. 25, 1884 (dec.); children—Marie, Stephen Frederick, Louis George, Charles Anthony (dec.), Walter Bernard, Elaine Anna. Removed to Seneca, Kan., when 11 yrs. old; in 1882 emigrated to State of Wash.; located in Idaho, 1883; engaged in farming and stock-raising, 1883—. State senator, 1894-97; U.S. senator, 1897-1903. Populist Dem. candidate for gov., Idaho, 1904; mayor Lewiston, Ida., 1905-09. Register U.S. Land Office, Lewiston, Ida., 1914-22; engaged in fruit growing. Home: Lewiston, Ida. Died Oct. 21, 1938.

HELD, Anna, comedienne; b. Paris, Mar. 18, 1877; d. Maurice and Hélène Held; ed. in acad. at Rouen, France; m. Florenz Ziegfeld, Jr. (divorced 1915). Début as comedienne, Paris, 1890; since then in many rôles; began starring, 1896, in "A Parlor Match"; later appeared in "French Maid" and "Papa's Wife"; in "The Little Dutchess," at the New York Casino, 1903-04; "M'lle Napoleon," at the Knickerbocker Theatre, New York, 1905-06; in "The Parisian Model," at the Broadway Theatre, New York, 1907-08; in "Miss Innocence," at the New York Theatre, 1909-10. Appeared in vaudeville in America, 1916. Home: Paris, France. Died Aug. 12, 1918.

HELGESEN, Henry T., congressman; b. near Decorah, Ia., June 26, 1857; s. Thomas and Mary H.; ed. pub. schs., normal inst. and business coll., Decorah; m. Bessie H. Nelson, 1880. Removed to Milton, N.D., 1887; in hardware and lumber business until 1905, then engaged in farming. First commr. of agr. and labor, State of N.D., 1889-92; pres. Sch. Bd., Milton; mem. bd. regents State U. of N.D., 1898—; Rep. nominee for 61st Congress, 1908; elected 62d Congress (1911-13), N.D. at-large, to 63d and 64th Congresses (1913-17), 1st N.D. Dist. Home: Milton, N.D. Died Apr. 10, 1917.

HELLEMS, Fred Burton Renney, college dean; b. Welland, Ont., Sept. 1, 1872; s. Egerton Ryerson and Maria (Garner) H.; A.B., U. of Toronto, 1893, fellow, 1893-95; Am. Sch. Classical Studies at Rome, 1895-96; Ph.D., U. of Chicago, 1898; LL.D., Colo. Coll., 1913; m. Margaret Hortense Whiteley, Mar. 30, 1902. Dean, Coll. of Liberal Arts, U. of Colo., Sept. 1, 1899. Home: Boulder, Colo. Died Apr. 19, 1929.

HELLER, Edmund, naturalist; b. Freeport, Ill., May 21, 1875; s. Edward and Mary Ann (Schottle) H.; A.B., Stanford U., 1901. Stanford Zoölogy Expdn. to Galapagos Islands, 1898-99; asst. naturalist, U.S. Biol. Survey, Alaska, 1900; naturalist, Field Mus., Chicago, exploration in Calif., Mexico, Guatemala and E. Africa, 1901-07; curator of mammals in U. of Calif. Mus. of Natural History, 1907-08; naturalist, Smithsonian African Expdn. under direction of Col. Theodore Roosevelt, E. Africa, 1909-10, Rainey African Expdn., E. Africa, 1911-12; Peruvian Expdn., 1915, under auspices of Yale U. and Nat. Geog. Soc.; exploration in S.W. China on Tibetan and Burma borders for Am. Mus. Natural History, 1916-17; photographic staff of the Czecho-Slovak army, with Paul J. Rainey in Siberia, 1918; Cape to Cairo African Expdn. of Smithsonian Instn., 1919-

20; investigation big game animals, Yellowstone Nat. Park, 1921; expdn. across Peru and down Amazon to its mouth, 1922-23; expdn. Central Africa Mountains of Moon, Gorilla Volcanoes, 1924-26; served as asst. curator mammals, Field Museum, Chicago; dir. Milwaukee Zoöl. Gardens, 1928-35, Fleishhacker Zoo, San Francisco, 1935—. Joint author: (with Theodore Roosevelt) Life Histories of African Game Animals. Died July 18, 1939.

HELLER, Maximilian, rabbi; b. Prague, Bohemia, Jan. 31, 1860; s. Simon and Mathilde (Kassowitz) H.; grad. Neustaedter Staatsgymnasium, Prague, 1879; B.L., McMicken U., Cincinnati, O., 1882, M.L., 1884; rabbi, Hebrew Union Coll., Cincinnati, 1884; m. Ida Annie Marks, Mar. 6, 1889. Asso. rabbi, Zion Congregation, Chicago, 1884-86; rabbi Bethel Congregation, Houston, Tex., 1886; Sinai Temple, New Orleans, 1887-1927; prof. Hebrew and Hebrew lit., Tulane U., 1912—. Editor Jewish Ledger, New Orleans, La., 1896-97; leader writer Am. Israelite, Cincinnati, 1902-14; editor B'nai B'rith Magazine. Hon. v.p. Jewish Publ. Soc. America; mem. Central Conf. Am. Rabbis (pres. 1909-11). Home: New Orleans, La. Died Mar. 30, 1929.

HELLER, Otto, univ. prof.; b. Tietsch, Saxony, Germany, July 15, 1863; s. David and Emma (Feuerloescher) H.; Gymnasium Brüx, Dresden; univs. of Prague, Munich, Vienna and Berlin, 1881-83; came to America, 1883; Ph.D., U. of Chicago, 1900; Univ. of Berlin, 1900-01; hon. Litt.D. from Washington U.; m. Jean S. Blair, Feb. 5, 1922. Instr. in Greek, LaSalle Coll., Phila., 1887-90, modern langs., Mass. Inst. Tech., 1892; prof. German lang. and lit., Washington U., 1892-1936, prof. modern European lit., 1914-37, dean Grad. Sch., 1923-37, emeritus. Author: Studies in Modern German Literature, 1905; Henrik Ibsen, Plays and Problems, 1912; Prophets of Dissent, 1918; Faust and Faustus, 1931. Editor: Stifter's Das Heidedorf, 1890; C. F. Meyer's Gustav Adolf Page, 1894; Schuecking's Die drei Freier, 1896; Frenssen's Gravelotte, 1897; Baumbach's Der Schwiegersohn, 1908; Lessing's Minna von Barnhelm, 1909; Storm's In St. Juergen; Charles Nagel's Speeches and Writings; (with Th. Leon) Charles Sealsfield Bibliography and Handbook, 1939. Translator: Lessing's Minna von Barnhelm, 1909. Literary editor St. Louis Post-Dispatch, 1919-24. Died July 29, 1941.

HELLIER, Charles Edward, lawyer; b. Bangor, Me., July 8, 1864; s. Walter S. and Eunice (Bixby) H.; A.B., Yale, 1886; student U. of Berlin; LL.B., Boston U., 1890; completed legal studies in office of Robert M. Morse; m. Mary L. Harmon, July 8, 1886; children—Mary Louise, Walter Harmon, Edward Whittier, John. Admitted to Suffolk (Mass.) bar, 1889; mem. bar of Supreme Court of U.S.; in practice in Boston, 1890-1920, N.Y. City, 1920—. Served as member Citizens' Examining Com., Boston Public Library. Fellow Am. Geog. Soc. Conglist. Republican. Home: New York, N.Y. Died Apr. 29, 1940.

HELLMAN, Isaias William, banker; b. Bavaria, Germany, Oct. 3, 1842; ed. pub. schs. in Germany; came to U.S., 1859; m. Esther Newgass, Apr. 14, 1870. Began in banking at Los Angeles, 1868, at San Francisco, 1890; pres. Wells Fargo Nevada Nat. Bank, Union Trust Co. (San Francisco), Farmers & Merchants Nat. Bank (Los Angeles); dir. U.S. Nat. Bank (Portland, Ore.), S.P. Co. Regent U. of Calif. Republican. Jewish religion. Mason. Home: San Francisco, Calif. Died Apr. 9, 1920.

HELLMAN, Isaias William, Jr., banker; b. Los Angeles, Calif., Mar. 30, 1871; s. Isaias William and Esther (Newgass) H.; Ph.B., U. of Calif., 1892; m. Frances Jacobi, Sept. 7, 1898. In employ of Nevada Bank, San Francisco, 1892-94; mgr. Farmers & Merchants Bank, Los Angeles, 1894-95; cashier Union Trust Co., San Francisco, 1895-1900, v.p. and mgr., 1900-16, pres., 1916—. Also chmn. bd. Columbus Savings & Loan Soc.; v.p. Wells Fargo-Nev. Nat. Bank (San Francisco), Farmers and Merchants Nat. Bank (Los Angeles). V.p. Panama Pacific Internat. Expn. Republican. Jewish religion. Home: San Francisco, and San Leandro, Calif. Died May 10, 1920.

HELM, Harvey, congressman; b. Danville, Ky.; A.B., Central U. of Ky.; admitted to bar, 1890. Mem. Ky. Ho. of Rep., 1893-94; co. atty. Lincoln Co., Ky., 1897-1904; mem. 60th to 65th Congresses (1907-19), 8th Ky. Dist. Home: Stanford, Ky. Died Mar. 3, 1919.

HELM, James Meredith, naval officer; b. Grayville, Ill., Dec. 16, 1855; s. John Jacob and Mary Walden (Gray) H.; grad. U.S. Naval Acad., 1875; married. Promoted through grades to rear admiral, Sept. 1911. Served on various ships, on various stas. and in surveying expdns. in Alaska, coasts of Ore. and Wash.; comd. surveying steamers Patterson, McArthur, Gedney; comd. Gunboat Hornet during Spanish-Am. War, on blockade duty off Cuba; captured a Spanish steamer and 3 contraband schooners off Cape Cruz; advanced 5 numbers in grade "for eminent and conspicuous conduct in battle at Manzanillo, Cuba, June 30, 1898"; comd. Gunboat Frolic in Philippine waters, 1900-02; supt. lighthouse service, chief of coast guard and transportation and dir. navigation, civil govt., P.I., and comd. cruisers Baltimore and Galveston, Asiatic Squadron, 1902-06; naval sec. Lighthouse Bd., Washington, 1906-07; comd. Battleship Idaho, 1908-09, Receiving Ship Wabash, 1909-10; comdt. Naval Sta., New Orleans, 1910-11, Charleston, S.C., and supt. 6th naval dist., 1913-14; comdr. Atlantic Reserve Fleet, 1914-16; apptd. sr. mem. Commn. on Navy Yards and Naval Stations, 1916; apptd. comdt. 4th Naval Dist., Jan. 1918; apptd. sr. mem. Commn. on Navy Yards and Naval Stas., Sept. 16, 1919, and retired. Home: Washington, D.C. Died Oct. 28, 1927.

HELM, Joseph Church, judge; b. Chicago, Ill., June 30, 1848; s. Ruggles and Sarah A. (Bass) H.; grad. U. of Ia., 1870, LL.B., 1874 (LL.D., 1890); m. Marcia Stewart, Sept. 1881. Enlisted, 1861, 13th U.S. Inf., served through Civil War in that regt. and 6th Inf., Hancock's corps, armies of the Tennessee and Potomac; prisoner on Belle Isle; was in battles of Chickasaw Bayou, Champion Hills, Jackson, Vicksburg, Colliersville, etc. In charge pub. schs., Van Buren and Little Rock, Ark., 1870-73; admitted to bar, 1875; mem. Colo. Ho. of Rep., 1877, Senate, 1879; dist. judge, 1880; justice Supreme Ct. of Colo., 1882-92 and 1907-09 (chief justice, 1888). Republican candidate for gov. against David H. Waite, Populist. Home: Denver, Colo. Died May 13, 1915.

HELM, Thomas Kennedy, lawyer; b. Louisville, Ky., Nov. 18, 1874; s. James Pendleton and Pattie Anderson (Kennedy) H.; student Washington and Lee U., 1891-95, U. of Va., summer 1896; LL.B., U. of Louisville, 1897; m. Elizabeth Nelson, Nov. 14, 1900; children—Patty Anderson (Mrs. J. Carter Stewart), George Nelson, Katherine Tebbs (Mrs. Hubbard G. Buckner), Thomas Kennedy. Admitted to bar, State of Kentucky, 1897, and began practice at Louisville; atty. for various corps., now mem. Trabue, Doolan, Helm & Helm; chmn. exec. com. and gen. counsel Federal Chem. Co.; mem. exec. com. and general counsel Louisville Pub. Warehouse Co.; dir. and gen. counsel Indiana Cotton Mills. Chmn. Bd. Pub. Works, Louisville, 1907-08; chmn. Louisville chapter Am. Red Cross, 1918-26, chmn. disaster relief com. same, 1926—. Dir. Bd. of Trade, 1917-18. Episcopalian. Mason. Home: Louisville, Ky. Died May 19, 1939.

HELMER, B(essie) Bradwell, editor, pub., lawyer; b. Chicago, Ill., Oct. 20, 1858; d. Judge James B. and Myra (Colby) Bradwell; grad. Chicago High Sch., 1876; A.B., Northwestern U., 1880, A.M., 1883; LL.B., Union Coll. of Law, 1882; m. Frank Ambrose Helmer (lawyer), Dec. 23, 1885; 1 dau., Myra Bradwell (Mrs. James Stuart Pritchard). Admitted to Ill. bar, 1882; became asst. editor Chicago Legal News, 1894, chief editor same, 1907—, also pres. of the Chicago Legal News Co.; editor Hurd's Revised Statutes of Illinois, 1905—; also edited 9 vols. Appellate Court Reports of Ill. Sec. Soldiers' Home in Chicago, 1894—; v.-chmn. World's Congress Auxiliary (woman's com.) on Govt. Reform; chmn. for 12 yrs. of fellowship com. Assn. Collegiate Alumnæ, and now mem. council (pres. of assn. 2 yrs.). Republican. Deceased.

HELMER, Frank Ambrose, lawyer; b. nr. Cuba, N.Y., Apr. 8, 1854; s. Herman K. and Elizabeth (Keller) H.; A.B., U. of Chicago, 1878, A.M., 1881, LL.B., Union Coll. of Law, 1881; m. Bessie, d. late Judge James B. and Myra Bradwell, of Chicago, Dec. 23, 1885. Admitted to bar, 1881; began practice with Frank J. Smith, with whom was partner, 1882-89; firm changed to Smith, Helmer & Moulton, 1890, to Smith, Helmer, Moulton & Price, 1897, then Helmer, Moulton, Whitman & Holton. Asso. editor Chicago Legal News, 1908—. Republican. Home: Winnetka, Ill. Died Sept. 29, 1925.

HELMING, Oscar Clemens, prof. economics; b. Franklin, Wis., Jan. 17, 1867; s. Herman H. and Henriette (Schmiedel) H.; A.B., Butler Coll., 1888; B.D., Union Theol. Sem., 1894; studied U. of Berlin, 1889-90; m. Joanna S. Parker, Nov. 14, 1900; children—Ruth Parker (Mrs. Carl C. Mose), Vernon Parker, Oscar Clemens, James Herman. Ordained ministry Congl. Ch., 1894; pastor successively First Ch., Atchison, Kan., St. Paul's Ch., Nutley, N.J., University Ch., Chicago, until 1919; prof. economics, Carleton Coll., 1919—. Mem. Chicago Industrial Commn., World War; mem. Commn. for Replacement of Returning Soldiers, at close of war. Served as dir. Am. Religious Edn. Assn., 1909-18; mem. Congl. Social Service Commn., 1921—. Studied tech. and vocational ednl. systems in Germany, France and Eng., 1909; industrial, commercial and polit. conditions in Gt. Britain, France, Germany and the Near East, 1926. Trustee Chicago Theol. Sem., 1908-19. Progressive Republican. Home: Northfield, Minn. Died Apr. 10, 1935.

HELMLE, Frank J., architect; b. Marietta, O., Mar. 5, 1869; s. William and Maria (Peters) H.; ed. Pratt Inst., Brooklyn, N.Y., Cooper Union, New York; studied at Sch. of Fine Arts, Brooklyn Mus.; m. Louise Jamer, 1893 (died 1924); m. 2d, Florence Arnold, Dec. 8, 1925; children—Frank John, Edward Herbert. Began in architecture, 1890; mem. Helmle & Corbett, 1912-28; architect Bush Bldg., New York and London; 1 Fifth Av. Bldg., New York; Pa. Power & Light Bldg., Allentown, Pa.; George Washington Masonic Nat. Memorial, Alexandria, Va.; St. Gregory's R.C. Ch., Brooklyn; etc.; retired 1928. Universalist. Home: Sarasota, Fla. Died July 15, 1939.

HELMUTH, William Tod, physician; b. Phila., Oct. 30, 1833; grad. Yale, 1888 (LL.D.); grad. Homœ. Med. Coll., Phila., 1853; Hahnemann Coll., San Francisco, 1866; Regent's State N.Y. degree, 1877. Prof. surgery and dean Homœ. Med. Coll. and Hosp., New York; holds several hosp. apptmts.; ex-pres. Am. Inst. Homœopathy, N.Y. State Homœ. Med. Soc. and N.Y. County Homœ. Soc.; pres. Collins State Homœ. Hosp. Author: System of Surgery; Suprapubic Lithotomy; With the Pousse Café (postprandial verses). Died 1901.

HELMUTH, William Tod, M.D.; b. St. Louis, Feb. 24, 1862; s. William Tod (M.D.) and Fannie Ida (Pritchard) H.; ed. St. Paul's Sch., Concord, N.H.; Princeton U.; M.D., N.Y. Homœ. Med. Coll and Flower Hosp., 1887; m. Isabel Spaulding Lockman, Apr. 17, 1895. Practiced, New York, 1887—; prof. surgery, N.Y. Homœ. Med. Coll., 1900—; surgeon Flower Hosp.; cons. surgeon St. Mary's Hosp., Passaic, N.J., Jamaica (L.I.) Hosp., Homœ. Hosp., Essex Co., N.J., State (N.Y.) Hosp. for Crippled and Deformed Children, Middletown (N.Y.) State Hosp., Yonkers Hosp. Republican. Episcopalian. Fellow Am. Coll. Surgeons. Commd. maj., Med. R.C., June 1917. Home: New York, N.Y. Died June 15, 1932.

HELPER, Hinton Rowan, author, ry. projector; b. N.C., Dec. 27, 1829; m. Maria Rodriguez, Buenos Aires, 1863. Academic edn.; U.S. consul at Buenos Aires, 1862-66; devoted to promotion of his projected Three Americas Ry., to eventually run from Bering Strait to the Straits of Magellan. Author: Impending Crisis of the South (1857); The Three Americas Railway; Nojoque; The Negroes in Negroland; The Land of Gold; Oddments of Andean Diplomacy. Home: Washington, D.C. Died 1909.

HELPMAN, Dell A., fraternal insurance; b. Liberty Center, O., Mar. 3, 1867; s. Perry E. and Julia A. (Parrish) H.; ed. pub. schs. Elected sec. local lodge, Nat. Union Assurance Soc., 1898, dist. mgr., 1900, supt. of field, 1904, supreme v.p., 1916, sup. pres. N.U.A.S., 1918—. Republican. Methodist. Mason. Home: Toledo, O. Died Mar. 13, 1924.

HEMANS, Lawton Thomas, lawyer; b. Collamer, N.Y., Nov. 4, 1864; s. John A. and Frances Lavinia (Sherwood) H.; grad. Eaton Rapids (Mich.) High Sch., 1884; student U. of Mich. Law Dept., 1887-88; m. Minnie P. Hill, Dec. 31, 1889. Admitted to Mich. bar, 1888 and began practice at Mason; pres. and atty. Peninsular Life Ins. Co. of Detroit, Mich. Mayor of Mason, 1892 and 5 subsequent terms; mem. Mich. Ho. of Rep., 1901-03; mem. State Constl. Conv., 1907; candidate for gov. of Mich. on Dem. ticket, 1908, 1910; apptd. mem. Mich. R.R. Commn., Jan. 1911. Methodist. Author: History of Michigan, 1906; Life and Times of Stevens T. Mason, the Boy Governor of Michigan, 1912. Home: Mason, Mich. Died Nov. 16, 1916.

HEMBDT, Phil Harold, prof. English; b. Jeffersonville, N.Y., Mar. 27, 1875; s. Philip and Emma (Baum) H.; grad. Cortland (N.Y.) Normal Sch., 1896; A.B., New York U., 1901, A.M., 1905, Ph.D., 1916; studied Columbia 3 summers; m. Ruth Alida Phillips, Aug. 13, 1901; children—Florence Emma, Phillips Van Rensselaer, Ruth Alice. Prin. high sch., Mt. Kisco, N.Y., 1901-04; head dept. of English, State Normal Sch., Superior, Wis., 1905-11; head dept. English lang. and lit., Albion Coll., 1913—. Dean summer sch. of Bay View Univ. Lecturer and entertainer at Y.M.C.A. huts, World War. Trustee Wesleyan Foundation, Albion. Republican. Methodist. Co-author: An Analysis of English Prose Style, 1924. Home: Albion, Mich. Died Oct. 12, 1927.

HEMENWAY, Alfred, lawyer; b. Hopkinton, Mass., Aug. 17, 1839; s. Fisher and Elizabeth Jones (Fitch) H.; A.B., Yale, 1861, A.M., 1864; studied Harvard Law Sch.; m. Myra L. McLanathan, Oct. 14, 1871 (died 1896). Admitted to bar, Boston, 1863; apptd. by Gov. Wolcott, 1897, sole commr. to draft act embodying principles of Torrens System of Land Transfer; act drafted by him became law. Fellow Am. Acad. Arts and Sciences. Home: Boston, Mass. Died Oct. 25, 1927.

HEMENWAY, Augustus, trustee; b. Boston, Oct. 10, 1853; s. Augustus and Mary (Tileston) H.; A.B., Harvard, 1875; m. Harriet Lawrence, Dec. 28, 1881; children—Augustus, Mrs. Hope Richardson, Mrs. Charlotte Denny, Mrs. Hetty Richard, Lawrence, Mrs. Mary Callan. Trustee and mgr. estates, Boston, 1878—. Mem. Mass. Ho. of Rep., 1890, 1891; apptd. mem. Met. Park Commn., 1895. Built and presented to Harvard U., the Hemenway Gymnasium, 1878, and greatly enlarged it in 1895; also presented new high school bldg. and a library bldg. to the town of Canton, Mass. Formerly overseer Harvard. Home: Canton, Mass. Deceased.

HEMENWAY, Henry Bixby, sanitarian; b. Montpelier, Vt., Dec. 20, 1856; s. Francis Dana and S-

Louisa (Bixby) H.; A.B., Northwestern U., 1879, A.M., 1882; M.D., Chicago Med. Coll., 1881; m. Lilla Maggie Bradley, May 2, 1882 (died 1883); 1 dau., Ruth Lillian (Mrs. James H. Shaw); m. 2d, Victoria Stevenson Taylor, Oct. 13, 1885 (died 1910); children—Hazel (dec.), Margaret; m. 3d, Garnet Ruth Roe, July 11, 1919 (died 1922). Licensed to practice by state examination, Ill., 1880; practiced at Kalamazoo, Mich., 1881-90; health officer, Kalamazoo, 1884-85; sec. Bd. U.S. Examining Surgeons, Kalamazoo, 1887-90; instr. diseases of throat, Rush Med. Coll., Chicago, 1893-94; acting prof. pub. health, Coll. Phys. and Surg., Chicago, 1900; dist. health officer of Ill., 1918, now medical asst. registrar. Fellow Am. Pub. Health Assn., A.M.A., A.A.A.S. Republican. Episcopalian. Mason. Author: American Public Health Protection, 1916. Recognized as an authority on law of pub. health and administration. Home: Springfield, Ill. Died Jan. 1, 1931.

HEMENWAY, James Alexander, senator; b. Boonville, Ind., Mar. 8, 1860; s. William and Sarah (Clelland) H.; ed. common schs. Admitted to bar, 1885, and began practice at Boonville. Pros. atty., 2d Jud. Circuit, Ind., 1886-90; mem. Rep. State Com., 1890; elected 54th to 59th Congresses (1895-1907), 1st Ind. Dist.; resigned from 59th Congress, 1905, before taking seat; elected U.S. senator, Jan. 18, 1905, for unexpired term (1905-09) of Charles Warren Fairbanks, elected V.P. of U.S. Mem. Rep. Nat. Com. Home: Boonville, Ind. Died Feb. 11, 1923.

HEMING, Arthur (Henry Howard), artist, author; b. Paris, Ont., Can., Jan. 17, 1870; s. George Edward and Frances Ann (Morgan) H.; ed. pub. schs.; taught Hamilton (Can.) Art Sch., 1887-90; illustrator on Canadian publs. till 1899; studied at Art Students' League; under Frank Brangwyn, A.R.A., London, 1904. Unmarried. Illustrator of many books on animal and wild life. Student, by personal contact, of phases of life in Canadian wilderness. Represented by three pictures in Canadian Nat. Gallery; ten pictures in the Royal Ontario Museum; elected by artists of Can. to select for the Canadian Nat. Exhbn. the first collection of paintings by Am. artists ever exhibited in Canada. Episcopalian. Author: Spirit Lake, 1907; The Drama of the Forests, 1921. Home: Hamilton, Can. Died Oct. 30, 1940.

HEMINGWAY, Wilson Edwin, lawyer; b. Carroll Co., Miss., Jan. 4, 1854; s. William and Sarah Wesly (Jenkins) H.; ed. U. of Miss., 1868-70, U. of Ga., 1870-72, no degree; m. Mary Helen Girault, July 18, 1879. Admitted to bar, 1874; pros. atty., Washington Co., Mo., 1878-1881; city atty., Pine Bluff, Ark., 1885-89; judge Supreme Ct. of Ark., 1889-93; in Mar. 1893, resigned office of supreme judge, to which he had just been reëlected for term of 8 yrs., to enter practice of law at Little Rock, Ark., with U. M. and G. B. Rose; mem. Rose, Hemingway, Cantrell & Loughborough. Pres. Little Rock Ry. & Electric Co. Presbyn. Democrat. Home: Little Rock, Ark. Died Oct. 5, 1922.

HEMMETER, John Conrad, M.D.; b. Baltimore, Md., Apr. 25, 1864; s. John and Mathilde H.; grad. Royal Gymnasium, Wiesbaden, Germany; Baltimore City Coll., 1881; M.D., U. of Md., 1884; Ph.D., Johns Hopkins, 1890; LL.D., St. John's Coll., Annapolis, 1905; Sc.D., U. of Md., 1914; m. Helene Emilie Hilgenberg, Jan. 1893. Late prof. physiology and clin. prof. medicine, and regent med. dept., U. of Md., and dir. of Physiol. Lab.; practice limited to diseases of digestive organs. Now asso. editor Archives for Digestive Diseases, Berlin, Internationale Beitr. z. Physiol. u. Pathol. d. Verdauung u.d. Stoffwechsels, Berlin, and Archives of Clinical Medicine. Pres. Am. Sect. Internat. Assn. for History of Medicine; hon. pres. Am. Soc. Med. History. Mem. Med. R.C. U.S.A. Author: Master Minds in Medicine—a History of Evolution of Ideas in Medicine, 1927; and 150 different investigations in the physiol. history of medicine. Inventor of duodenal intubation; composer for orchestra, voice and piano. Home: Baltimore, Md. Died Feb. 25, 1931.

HEMPHILL, Alexander Julian, financier; b. Phila., Pa., Aug. 23, 1856; s. William Kerr and Sarah Jane (McCune) H.; B.A., Central High Sch., Phila., 1875 (65th class); m. Jeannette Cadmus, Apr. 29, 1880. Clk. Pa. R.R. Co., 1875-83; sec. Norfolk & Western Ry., until 1905; v.p., 1905-09, pres., 1909-15, chmn. bd., 1915—, Guaranty Trust Co., New York; dir. numerous corps. V.p. Friendly Aid Soc.; trustee Soc. for Employment and Relief of Poor Women. Mem. Chamber of Commerce (New York). Exec. com. Am. Com. for Armenian and Syrian Relief, Refugees Relief Fund; treas. Fatherless Children of France, Food for France Fund, Russian Orphans Fund, Inter-Racial Council, Nat. Security League. Homes: N.Y. City, and Spring Lake, N.J. Died Dec. 29, 1920.

HEMPHILL, Charles Robert, theologian; b. Chester, S.C., Apr. 18, 1852; s. James and Rachel E. (Brawley) H.; bro. of John James H.; grad. U. of S.C., 1869, and U. of Va., 1871; grad. Presbyn. Theol. Sem., Coumbia, S.C., 1874; fellow in Greek, Johns Hopkins, 1878-79; hon. A.M., 1878, D.D., 1884, Davidson Coll.; D.D., Central U., 1884; LL.D., Hanover Coll., 1895, Westminster Coll., 1898; m. Emma L. Muller, Sept. 1, 1875 (died 1920); children—Lucy B. (Mrs. E. W. Fay), James, Charles R. Ordained Presbyn. ministry; instr. Hebrew, Columbia Theol. Sem., 1874-78; prof. Greek and Latin, Southwestern Presbyn. U., 1879-82; prof. Bibl. lit., Columbia Sem., 1882-85; pastor 2d Presbyn. Ch., Louisville, 1885-99; prof., 1893—, pres., 1910-20, dean, 1920—, Louisville Presbyn. Theol. Sem. Moderator Gen. Assembly Presbyn. Ch. U.S., 1895; mem. Pan-Presbyn. Council, Glasgow, 1896, Internat. S.S. Lesson Com., 1902-14. Author of essay on Validity and Bearing of the Testimony of Christ and His Apostles to the Mosaic Authorship of the Pentateuch, in "Moses and His Recent Critics," 1899. Home: Louisville, Ky. Died Mar. 9, 1932.

HEMPHILL, James Calvin, journalist; b. Due West, S.C., May 18, 1850; s. Rev. William Ramsey and Hannah (Lind) H.; A.B., Erskine Coll., 1870, A.M., 1872, LL.D., 1909; m. Rebecca M., d. Rev. C. K. True, of Flushing, L.I., Nov. 19, 1878 (died 1923). Editor Abbeville (S.C.) Medium, 1871-80; reporter, exchange reader, spl. corr., 1880-81, chief Capitol (Columbia, S.C.) bur., 1881-82; city editor and acting mgr., 1886-88, mgr. and editor in chief, 1888-1910, Charleston (S.C.) News and Courier; editor Richmond (Va.) Times-Dispatch, 1910-11; editor Charlotte (N.C.) Observer, 1911; on editorial staff New York Times, 1912; was Washington corr. Phila. Public Ledger; editor Spartanburg (S.C.) Journal 5 yrs. Democrat. Actively identified with work of organizing mem. bd. dirs., and mgr. Dept. Publicity and Promotion of S.C. Inter-State and West Indian Expn., at Charleston, 1901-02. Bromley lecturer on journalism, Yale, 1909-10. First v.p. Associated Press, 1909. Home: Abbeville, S.C. Nov. 20, 1927.

HEMPHILL, John James, lawyer; b. Chester, S.C., Aug. 25, 1849; s. James and Rachel E. (Brawley) H.; bro. of Charles Robert H.; A.B., S.C. Coll., 1869; studied law with his father; admitted to bar, 1870; began practice Jan. 1, 1871; m. Elizabeth S. Henry, Dec. 23, 1891. Mem. S.C. legislature, 1876-82; mem. 48th to 52d Congresses (1882-92). Democrat; in practice Washington and S.C., 1893—. Author: Why the Solid South? Home: Washington, D.C. Died May 11, 1912.

HEMPHILL, Joseph Newton, rear admiral; b. Ripley, O., June 18, 1847; s. Samuel and Sarah (Campbell) H.; entered U.S. naval acad., Sept. 1862; cruised after Alabama, summer of 1863; grad. June 1866; m. Oro E. Stark, Dec. 1873 (died, Oct. 1886); m. 2d, Mrs. Dora A. Hancock, of Dubuque, Ia., Aug. 1893. Was on the Monongahela, wrecked in W. Indian earthquake Nov. 1867; promoted ensign, Mar. 12, 1868; master, Mar. 26, 1869; lt., Mar. 21, 1870; lt. comdr., Jan. 26, 1887; comdr., June 1895; capt., Mar. 3, 1901; rear admiral, Aug. 6, 1906. At Manila during Philippine outbreak and at Venezuela during the Andrade-Castro revolution; comdg. Kearsarge and chief of staff of North Atlantic Fleet, 1902-04; capt. New York Navy Yard, 1904-06; pres. Bd. of Inspection and Survey, 1906-07; comdg. Asiatic sta. and fleet, 1907-08; pres. Naval Examining and Retiring Boards, 1908-09; retired, June 18, 1909. Died July 8, 1931.

HEMPHILL, William Arnold, publisher and founder of Atlanta Constitution; b. Athens, Ga., May 5, 1842; s. W. S. H; early edn. Athens, Ga.; grad. Univ. of Ga., spl. studies in engring.; was in Civil War and wounded at Gettysburg; m. Mrs. E. B. Luckie, 1871 (died, 1900). Mayor of Atlanta, 1891. Home: Atlanta, Ga. Died 1902.

HEMPL, George ("Rudolph H. Rheinhardt"), philologist; b. Whitewater, Wis., June 6, 1859; s. Henry Theodore and Anna (Häntzsche) Hempel (both of German Slavic stock); A.B., U. of Mich., 1879; Ph.D., U. of Jena, 1889; (LL.D., Univ. of Wis., 1904, U. of Mich., 1915); m. Anna Belle Purmort, July 3, 1890. Prin. Saginaw (Mich.) High Sch., 1879-82, La Porte (Ind.) High Sch., 1882-84; instr. German, Johns Hopkins, 1884-86; studied Göttingen, Tübingen, Strassburg, Jena, and Berlin, 1886-89; asst. prof. English, 1889-93, jr. prof. English, 1893-97, U. of Mich.; prof. English, U. of Chicago, summer quarter, 1897; prof. English philology and general linguistics, 1897-1906, U. of Mich.; prof. Germanic philology, Stanford U., 1903—. Author: German Orthography and Phonology, 1897; English Nursery Rimes in German, 1898; Phonetic Text of Wilhelm Tell, 1900. Editorial critic of the English pronunciations in Pierce's French Dictionary, 1904. From 1908 devoted chiefly to the decipherment of prehistoric Mediterranean languages. Died Aug. 14, 1921.

HEMPSTEAD, Fay, poet; b. Little Rock, Ark., Nov. 24, 1847; s. Samuel Hutchinson and Elizabeth Rebecca (Beall) H.; St. John's Coll., Little Rock, 1859-61; acad. and law depts., U. of Va., 1866-68; m. Gertrude B. O'Neale, Sept. 13, 1871; children—Carrie (Mrs. Melville F. Riley), Lindsay Lee, Evlyn (Mrs. Thomas W. Newton), Robert O'Neale, Janet Laurie (Mrs. Charles R. Pierce), William Beall. Practiced law, Little Rock, 1868-74; register in bankruptcy, 1874-81; grand sec. Grand Lodge of Masons of Ark., 1881—. Grand recorder of Grand Council and Grand Commandery K.T. and of High Priesthood of Ark., 1899—; also sec. local lodge, chapter and council, Little Rock. Crowned Poet Laureate of Freemasonry, Chicago, 1908 (3d to hold this office). Democrat. Episcopalian. Author: Poems, 1878; School History of Arkansas, 1889; Pictorial History of Arkansas, 1890; Poems, 1898; Laureate Poems, 1908, complete edit., 1922; Historical Review of Arkansas, 1911. Sec. Ark. Soc. S.A.R., 1892—. Grand Master of Gen. Grand Council R. and S.M. of U.S., Sept. 27, 1921-Sept. 8, 1924. Home: Little Rock, Ark. Died April 24, 1934.

HENDEE, George Ellsworth, rear admiral; b. Roxbury, Mass., June 30, 1841; s. Charles J. and Adeline (Davis) H.; ed. pub. and pvt. schs.; m. Elsie S. Lewis, Apr. 21, 1870. Entered U.S.N. as paymaster's clerk, Oct. 10, 1861; promoted asst. p.m., Mar. 25, 1864; passed asst. p.m., July 26, 1866; p.m., Feb. 21, 1869; pay dir., Sept. 1, 1899; retired, June 30, 1902, with rank of rear admiral. Served in U.S.S. Brandywine, Pinola, Ossipee, Richmond, Saranac, Independence, and Philadelphia. Home: Brookline, Mass. Died Sept. 10, 1916.

HENDERSON, Charles, governor; b. Pike Co., Ala., Apr. 26, 1860; s. J. A. and Mildred (Hill) H.; ed. Howard Coll., Marion, Ala.; m. Laura Montgomery, Nov. 7, 1889. In business, at Troy, Ala., title of Chas. Henderson & Co.; pres. Troy Bank & Trust Co., Standard Telephone and Telegraph Co.; dir. First Farmers & Merchants Nat. Bank, Ala. Warehouse Co., Protective Life Ins. Co. Mayor of Troy, 1884-89, 1901-06; pres. Ala. R.R. Commn., 1906-15; gov. of Ala., 1915-19; mem. State Docks Commn. Democrat. Episcopalian. Mason. Home: Troy, Ala. Died Jan. 7, 1937.

HENDERSON, Charles English, ry. official; b. Jefferson Co., Va. (now W.Va.), Sept. 25, 1844; s. Richard and Elizabeth Ann Beall (English) H.; ed. pvt. sch., Jefferson Co., Va., 1850-59, Georgetown, D.C., 1859-61; M.D., U. of Pa., 1868; resident physician Bay View Hosp., Baltimore, 1869-70; m. Ida M. Lynn, Oct. 22, 1879. Entered ry. service Jan. 5, 1870, being clerk Ft. Scott Sta., Missouri River, Ft. Scott & Gulf R.R. to Apr. 1870, and clerk gen. freight and ticket office same, 1870-74; chief clerk to gen. supt. same road and to gen. supt. and receiver Leavenworth, Lawrence & Galveston R.R., 1874-79; prospecting routes and settling purchase accounts Springfield and Western Missouri R.R., 1879; gen. freight and ticket agt. Atchison & Nebraska R.R., 1879-80; auditor, cashier and paymaster, Apr. 1880, asst. gen. mgr., Oct. 1880, gen. mgr. and receiver, Oct. 1881 to Jan. 28, 1888, Ind., Bloomington & Western Ry.; gen. mgr. Ohio, Ind. & Western Ry., 1888-89; gen. mgr. Ohio Southern R.R., 1881-92; gen. mgr. Dayton & Ironton R.R., 1884-86; mgr. for purchaser Dayton & Toledo R.R., 1884-87; receiver Danville, Olney & Ohio River R.R., 1884-86; gen. mgr. Chicago & Ohio River R.R., 1886-88; gen. mgr. Phila. & Reading Coal & Iron Co., 1889-1903, 1st v.p., Oct. 1903-Apr. 1, 1906; 2d v.p. Phila. & Reading Ry. Co., Nov. 25, 1896-May 1, 1908. Home: Easton, Md. Died Apr. 8, 1919.

HENDERSON, C(harles) Hanford, head master; b. Phila., Dec. 30, 1861; s. J. Thomas and Mary E. (Hanford) H.; B.S., U. of Pa., 1882; Ph.D., Zürich, 1892; unmarried. Asst. to Dr. Persifor Frazer; lecturer Franklin Inst., 1883-85; on editorial staff Scientific American, 1885-86; science teacher, 1886-91, prin. N.E. Manual Training High Sch., Phila., 1892-96; asst. lit. editor Phila. Press 2 yrs.; lecturer on edn., Harvard, 1897-98; dir. Pratt Inst. High Sch., Brooklyn, 1898-1900; head master Marienfeld Summer Sch., Chesham, N.H., 1896-1912. Author: Elements of Physics, 1900; Education and the Larger Life, 1902; John Percyfield, 1903; Children of Good Fortune, 1905; The Lighted Lamp, 1908; Pay-Day, 1911; What Is It to Be Educated?, 1914. Died Jan. 9, 1941.

HENDERSON, Charles Richmond, sociologist; b. Covington, Ind., Dec. 17, 1848; s. Albert and Lorana (Richmond) H.; A.B. (old) U. of Chicago, 1870, A.M., 1873; B.D., Bapt. Union Theol. Sem., 1873 (D.D., 1885; Ph.D., Leipzig, 1901); m. Ella Levering, May 14, 1873. Ordained Bapt. ministry, 1873; pastor Terre Haute, Ind., 1873-82, Detroit, 1882-92; univ. chaplain, 1892—, asst. prof. sociology and univ. recorder, 1892-94, asso. prof., 1894-97, prof. sociology, 1897—, head dept. practical sociology, 1897—, head dept. practical sociology, 1904—, U. of Chicago. Asso. editor Am. Jour. Theology, Am. Jour. Sociology, 1895—, Journal Am. Inst. of Criminal Law and Criminology, 1911—. Pres. 26th Nat. Conf. Charities, 1898-99; pres. United Charities of Chicago, 1913; U.S. commr. Internat. Prison Commn., 1909; pres. Internat. Prison Congress, 1910; sec. Ill. Commn. Occupational Diseases, 1907. Author: Introduction to Study of Dependent, Defective and Delinquent Classes, 1893-1901; Development of Doctrine in the Epistles, 1894; The Social Spirit in America, 1896; Social Settlements, 1897; Social Elements, 1898. Died Mar. 29, 1915.

HENDERSON, David, journalist, theatrical mgr.; b. Edinburgh, Scotland, Apr. 26, 1853; s. William and Elizabeth (Bissett) H.; ed. at Edinburgh; began newspaper work in Scotland on the Courant, founded in Edinburgh by Daniel De Foe; came to America, 1871; m. Frances M. Raymonde, 1896. News editor The Scottish American, New York; later in publishing business; on staff of New York Herald, 1875; foreign corr. Chicago Tribune, 1878-79, and was with Gen. Grant on the European part of his tour of the world; dramatic critic Chicago Tribune, 1877-80; with Gen. John A. Logan and W. D. Eaton founded Chicago Herald, 1880-82; mng. editor Chicago Daily News, 1883. Built Chicago Opera House, 1884; produced "The Arabian Nights," 1887; "The Crystal Slipper," 1888-89; "Sinbad," 1890-91; "Bluebeard, Jr.," 1892-93; "Aladdin, Jr.," 1894; "Ali Baba," 1893-94; etc.; lessee Broadway Theatre, Denver, 1889-94, Great Northern and Schiller theatres, Chicago, 1897-98, Auditorium, Kansas City, 1895-96, Savoy, New York, 1901; built Duquesne Theatre, Pittsburgh, 1890. Died 1908.

HENDERSON, David Bremner, congressman; b. Old Deer, Scotland, March 14, 1840; brought to Ill., 1846, and to Ia., 1849; public schools and academic edn.; in Union army, Sept. 1861, as private; became 1st lt. 12th Ia. vols.; wounded at battle of Donelson; lost leg at battle of Corinth, because of which discharged; commr. bd. of enrollment, 3d dist. Ia., May 1863, to June 1864; resigned; re-entered army as col. 46th Ia. vols., 1864. Admitted to bar, 1865; m. Augusta A. Fox, March 4, 1866. Collector internal revenue, 3d dist. Ia., 1865-69; resigned; asst. U.S. atty., northern div., dist. of Ia., 1869-71; resigned; mem. Congress, 1883-1903; renominated 1902, but withdrew from ticket; 10 yrs. mem. Com. on Appropriations; chmn. Com. on Judiciary and mem. Com. on Rules, 54th and 55th Congresses; speaker 56th and 57th Congresses. Republican. Home: Dubuque, Ia. Died 1906.

HENDERSON, Ernest Flagg, author; b. New Brighton, S.I., N.Y., May 11, 1861; s. John Cleaves and Jane Louisa (Rapallo) H.; A.B., Trinity Coll., 1882, A.M., 1884; A.B., Harvard, 1883; Ph.D., U. of Berlin, 1890; L.H.D., Trinity, 1904; m. Berta von Bunsen, Berlin, Germany, Aug. 3, 1889; children—Hildegard Gertrude, Gerard Carl, George Bunsen, Edith May, Ernest Flagg, Frances de Bunsen. Author: History of Germany in the Middle Ages, 1894; History of Germany, 1902; Blücher (in Heroes of the Nation Series), 1911; Symbol and Satire in the French Revolution, 1912; Germany's Fighting Machine, 1914. Home: Dublin, N.H. Died Dec. 30, 1928.

HENDERSON, Ernest Norton, college prof.; b. La Salle Co., Ill., Dec. 17, 1869; s. Erastus Franklin and Julia (Norton) H.; Ph.B., U. of Calif., 1890, A.B., 1892, A.M., 1893; fellow in edn., Teachers Coll. (Columbia), 1901-02; Ph.D., Columbia, 1903; m. Margaret Rankin Wallace, Aug. 12, 1903; children—Adelaide Elizabeth, Margaret Norton, John Wallace. Teacher in secondary schs., San Mateo, Calif., 1890-92; fellow and asst. in philosophy, U. of Calif., 1892-95; prin. high sch., Woodland, Calif., 1895-97; instr. in psychology and edn., State Normal Sch., Chico, Calif., 1897-1901; asst. prof. edn. and psychology, 1902-03, prof., 1903-08, prof. edn. and philosophy, 1908-16, prof. philosophy and psychology, 1916—, Adelphi Coll. Instr. in edn., summer session U. of N.C., 1904, various summers Columbia, to 1917, Ohio State U., summer 1921-25; lecturer philosophy of edn., Teachers Coll. (Columbia), 1915. Unitarian. Author: Memory for Connected Trains of Thought, 1903; Text Book in the Principles of Education, 1910. Capt., Sanitary Corps U.S.A., 1918-19. Home: Brooklyn, N.Y. Died Mar. 4, 1938.

HENDERSON, Gerard C., lawyer; b. Williamstown, Mass., Aug. 13, 1891; s. Ernest Flagg and Bertha (von Bunsen) H.; A.B., Harvard, 1912, LL.B., 1916; m. Mary G. Taussig, Nov. 10, 1918; children—Edith Guild, Gerard Carl, Mary Merrick. Admitted to N.Y. bar, 1920; mem. Pitkin, Rosensohn & Henderson, 1920-23; gen. counsel War Finance Corp., Apr. 4, 1921-June 30, 1922; reapptd. to same position, 1923 and 1925, resigned. Author: The Position of Foreign Corporations in American Constitutional Law, 1917; The Federal Trade Commission, 1924. Home: New York, N.Y. Died Aug. 31, 1927.

HENDERSON, Howard Andrew Millet, clergyman; b. Paris, Ky., Aug. 15, 1836; s. Howard Millet and Jane Elizabeth (Moore) H.; LL.B., Gundry's Commercial and Law Sch., Cincinnati, 1856; A.B., Ohio Wesleyan U., 1858, A.M., 1876; (D.D., Ky. Mil. Inst., 1867; LL.D., Ky. Coll., 1870); m. Susan Watkins Vaughan, Feb. 5, 1861 (died 1903). Ordained M.E. ministry, 1856; pastor Newberne and Demopolis, Ala., 1857-61; capt. Col. Clay Cadets, Ky. State Guard, 1861; capt. Co. E, 28th Ala. Inf., C.S.A., 1861-62; asst. adj. gen., C.S.A., 1864; asst. commr. of exchange of prisoners of war, 1864-65; pastor Frankfort, Ky., 1866-70, Lexington, Ky., 1870-71; state supt. pub. instrn., Ky., 1871-79; pastor San Francisco, 1879-80, Hannibal, Mo., 1881-83, Jersey City, N.J., 1883-86, New York, 1886-88, Cincinnati, 1888-1903; pastor emeritus Park Av. Ch., Hartwell, O., 1903—. Prof. Ky. Mil. Inst., 1867-68; founder of system of colored schs., Ky., 1872. Chaplain Ohio N.G., 1892-98; chaplain 1st Inf., Ohio Vols., Spanish-Am. War, 1898; grand chaplain Ohio Commandery Spanish-Am. War Vets.; grand master I.O.O.F., Ky.; grand chaplain of Masons, Ky., 1867-79. Home: Hartwell, O. Died 1912.

HENDERSON, Isaac, author; b. Brooklyn, N.Y., Feb. 13, 1850; grad. Williams Coll., 1872 (D.C.L.); m. Marion Temple Brown, Feb. 13, 1880. Became connected with New York Evening Post, 1872; asst. publisher, 1875; publisher, 1876; mem. bd. of trustees had a stockholder; sold interest, 1880; has lived abroad from 1888; has a home in London and another in Rome. Author: The Prelate; Agatha Page, 1900; The Silent Battle; The Mummy and the Humming Bird. Died 1909.

HENDERSON, John Armstrong, clergyman, educator; b. Guernsey Co., O., July 9, 1853; s. John A. and Sarah (Stewart) H.; B.A., Monmouth (Ill.) Coll., 1877, M.A., 1880; grad. Xenia Theol. Sem., St. Louis, Mo., 1880; D.D., Grove City (Pa.) Coll., and Tarkio (Mo.) Coll., 1905; m. Flora E. McGaw, Feb. 5, 1880 (died 1925); children—Bessie McGaw (Mrs. Jacob M. Lashly), Arthur Waddle, Mabel McCoy. Ordained ministry U.P. Ch., 1880; pastor successively at Kenton, O., Omaha, Neb., Sparta, Ill., Erie and Pittsburgh, Pa., Dayton, O., Indianapolis, Ind., until 1925; promotional sec. and asst. to pres., Xenia Theol. Sem., 1925-30. Prohibition candidate for lt. gov. Ill., 1900, for gov. of Ohio, 1914, for Congress, 1916. Trustee Monmouth Coll., Westminster (Pa.) Coll., Xenia Theol. Sem. Home: St. Louis, Mo. Died Feb. 26, 1939.

HENDERSON, John Brooks, lawyer; b. Pittsylvania Co. Va., Nov. 16, 1826; s. James and Jane (Dawson) H.; acad. edn.; (LL.D., U. of Mo., 1882); m. Mary N. Foote, June 25, 1868; father of John Brooks H., Jr. In law practice, 1848—; mem. Mo. legislature, 1848, 1856-57; presdl. elector, 1856, 1860, mem. Mo. conv. to determine the question of secession, 1861-63; U.S. senator from Mo., Jan. 1862, to Mar. 4, 1869; spl. commr. to make peace with Indian tribes of West, 1867; Rep. candidate for gov. of Mo., 1872; spl. U.S. atty. for pros. "whisky ring" at St. Louis, 1875; pres. Rep. Nat. Conv., Chicago, 1884; mem. Pan-Am. Congress, 1889-90; elected by Congress, 1892 and 1898, a regent of the Smithsonian Instn. Author of the 13th Amendment to Constitution of U.S., abolishing slavery. Home: Washington, D.C. Died Apr. 12, 1913.

HENDERSON, John Brooks, lawyer; b. Louisiana, Mo., Feb. 18, 1870; s. John Brooks and Mary (Foote) H.; A.B., Harvard, 1891; LL.B., Columbian (now George Washington) U., 1893; m. Angelica Schuyler Crosby, Feb. 12, 1903. Pvt. sec. to Hon. John W. Foster while diplomatic adviser of Chinese govt., 1896-97; attached to Gen. Miles' suite in Europe on army inspection, 1897; Rep. nominee for 60th Congress, 1906, 8th Va. Dist. Author: American Diplomatic Questions, 1901; Cruise of the Tomas Barrera, 1916. Regent, Smithsonian Institute, 1910—. Home: Washington, D.C. Died Jan. 4, 1923.

HENDERSON, John Joseph, judge; b. Allegheny Co., Pa., Sept. 23, 1843; s. Rev. William C. and Eliza F. H.; A.B., Allegheny Coll., 1862, later A.M., LL.D.; unmarried. Served in U.S.V., 1862-65; admitted to bar, 1867; dist. atty., 1873-76; pres. judge 30th dist., Pa., 1888-98; apptd. judge Superior Ct. of Pa., Apr. 1903; elected to same position, 1903, 1913, and again in 1923 for term expiring 1933. Home: Meadville, Pa. Died Dec. 12, 1928.

HENDERSON, John Moreland, lawyer; b. Newville, O., Apr. 14, 1840; s. James Patterson and Ann Gilleland (Moreland) H.; A.M., Miami U., 1862; studied under Judge Darius Dirlam, Mansfield, O.; LL.B., Cleveland Law Sch., 1864; m. Anna Ramsey Cary, June 20, 1872; children—William Cary (dec.), Grace Moreland (Mrs. Charles Crothers Johnson), Anna (dec.), Rebecca (Mrs. Edward Scott Claflin), Janet (Mrs. Carl Fitch Adams), Florence, Ruth. Practiced with John G. Grannis, Cleveland, 1865-74, with Virgil P. Kline, 1875-82; mem. Henderson, Kline & Tolles, 1882-95; now Henderson, Quail, McGraw & Barclay. Pres. bd. trustees Case Sch. Aplied Science, 1899-1924; trustee McGregor Home. Home: East Cleveland, O. Died Aug. 24, 1934.

HENDERSON, John Steele, congressman; b. Salisbury, N.C., Jan. 6, 1846; s. Archibald and Mary Steele (Ferrand) H.; A.B., U. of N.C., 1865; (LL.D., Trinity Coll., N.C., 1890); m. Elizabeth Brownrigg Cain, Sept. 30, 1874. Left college and enlisted as pvt. Co. B, 10th Regt., N.C. State Troops, Nov. 1864; continued in army until surrender of Gen. Joseph E. Johnston, Apr. 26, 1865. Studied law in office of Judge Nathaniel Boyden, and in Judge Pearson's law sch., Richmond Hill, N.C.; licensed to practice in County Court, 1866, in Superior and Supreme courts, 1867; register of deeds, Rowan Co., N.C., 1866-68; mem. N.C. Ho. of Rep., 1876, Senate, 1878-1900, 1902; elected by gen. assembly as mem. code commn., N.C., and served 3 yrs. (code published, 1883); mem. 49th to 53d Congresses (1885-95), 7th N.C. Dist.; pres. People's Nat. Bank; chmn. Bd. Edn., Rowan Co.; mem. Bd. Edn., Salisbury, etc. Trustee U. of N.C. Democrat. Episcopalian. Home: Salisbury, N.C. Died Oct. 9, 1916.

HENDERSON, Junius, prof. natural history; b. Marshalltown, Ia., Apr. 30, 1865; s. Henry Clay and Ianthe (Fuller) H.; A.B., University of Colo., 1908; m. Nellie Bartlett, May 25, 1894 (died 1924); m. 2d, Bess R. Green, Sept. 10, 1929. Editor Puget Sound Mail, La Conner, Wash., 1887-92; admitted to Colo. bar, 1894, and practiced at Boulder until 1902; curator of museum, U. of Colo., 1903-33, prof. natural history, 1908-33, retired. Mem. Park and Planning Commn., Boulder, 1921-26. Republican. Methodist. Author: Geology in its Relation to Landscape, 1925; The Practical Value of Birds, 1927; (with Elberta L. Craig) Economic Mammalogy, 1932; Fossil Non-Marine Mollusca of North America, 1935. Home: Boulder, Colo. Died Nov. 4, 1937.

HENDERSON, Lawrence Joseph, biological chemist; b. Lynn, Mass., June 3, 1878; s. Joseph and Mary Reed (Bosworth) H.; A.B., Harvard, 1898, M.D., 1902, Sc.D., 1932; student U. of Strassburg, 1902-04; Sc.D., U. of Cambridge, Eng., 1934; Dr. Hon., U. of Grenoble, 1934; m. Edith Lawrence Thayer, 1910; 1 son, Lawrence Joseph. Lecturer biol. chemistry, 1904-05, instr., 1905-10, asst. prof., 1910-19, prof., 1919—, Harvard U. Exchange prof. Harvard to U. of Paris, 1921; Silliman lecturer, Yale, 1928; Leyden lecturer, U. of Berlin, 1928; Mills lecturer, U. of Calif., 1931. Sr. fellow and chmn. Soc. of Fellows (Harvard), 1933—. Decorated Legion of Honor (France). Fellow Am. Acad. Arts and Sciences. Author: The Fitness of the Environment, 1913; The Order of Nature, 1917; Blood, 1928; Pareto's Sociology, 1935. Home: Cambridge, Mass. Died Feb. 10, 1942.

HENDERSON, Robert Burns, pres. Pacific Portland Cement Co.; b. Indianapolis, Ind., Jan. 25, 1877; s. Alexander Campbell and Anna (Dunn) H.; student spl. course mining engring., U. of Calif., 1901-03; m. Louise McCormick, Nov. 30, 1911 (died 1919); 1 son, Alexander Scott; m. 2d, Jennie Crocker, Jan. 30, 1926; 1 son, Robert Easton. Treas. Pacific Portland Cement Co., 1910-13, gen. mgr., 1914-21, pres., 1921—; pres. Crocker Hotel Co., St. Francis Investment Co., The British Honduras Co.; v.p. Petroleum Rectifying Co., Crocker Estate Co.; dir. Occidental Ins. Co., Am. Trust Co. and affiliated cos. Vice-pres. Nat. Assn. of Mfrs.; dir. Golden Gate Internat. Expn. Republican. Episcopalian. Home: Burlingame, Calif. Died May 14, 1940.

HENDERSON, Robert Miller, lawyer; b. N. Middletown Twp., Pa., Mar. 12, 1827; s. William Miller and Elizabeth (Parker) H.; ed. pub. schs., Carlisle, Pa., Dickinson Coll., A.B., 1845 (A.M., LL.D.); m. Margaret Ann Webster, June 7, 1853. Admitted to bar, Aug. 25, 1847; mem. Pa. legislature, 1851-53; capt. Pa. Reserves (7th Pa.), 1861, 36th Pa. Vol. Inf., attached to 2d brigade McCall's Div., Army of Potomac; judge-advocate of div., 1861-June 1862; wounded at Charles City Cross Roads, June 30, 1862; promoted (on recommendation of Brig. Gen. Seymour) for "brilliant gallantry" to lt. col., July 4, 1862; severely wounded, Aug. 30, 1862, at 2d Bull Run; apptd. insp. gen. of div., June 2, 1863; provost-marshal, 15th Pa. dist., Apr. 18, 1863; hon. disch., November 10, 1865; bvtd. col. and brig. gen. U.S.V., for gallantry, Mar. 13, 1865. Apptd. Apr. 1874, and elected Nov. 1874, additional law judge, 12th jud. dist., Pa., and in Jan., 1882, became pres. judge of dist.; subsequently resigned and resumed practice. Original mem. and officer Pa. State Bar Assn.; 1st pres. Cumberland Co. Bar Assn.; pres. Carlisle Deposit Bank; pres. bd. trustees Metzgar Coll.; trustee Carlisle Indian Industrial Sch. Presbyterian. Republican. Home: Carlisle, Pa. Died 1906.

HENDERSON, Theodore Sommers, bishop; b. Milburn, N.J., May 14, 1868; s. William Henry and Louisa Elizabeth (Sommers) H.; Centenary Collegiate Inst., Hackettstown, N.J., 1885-88; A.B., Wesleyan U., Conn., 1892; B.D., Drew Theol. Sem., Madison, N.J., 1895; D.D., Allegheny Coll., Pa., 1909; LL.D., Lawrence Coll., 1912, Neb. Wesleyan, 1912, Conn. Wesleyan, 1921, Ohio Northern U., 1925; m. Dora Mooney, July 31, 1896. Ordained M.E. ministry, 1894; pastor Rockville Center, Conn., 1893-94; asso. pastor James Ch., Brooklyn, 1894-96; pastor Flushing, 1896-98, Simpson Ch., Brooklyn, 1898-1904, East Side Parish, New York, 1904, Stamford, Conn., 1905-06; gen. field sec. Gen. Conf. Commn. for Aggressive Evangelism, 1906-08; pastor Hanson Place Ch., Brooklyn, 1908-12; bishop M.E. Ch., May 21, 1912—. Trustee Ohio Wesleyan U., Ohio Northern U., White Cross Hosp. (Columbus, O.), Methodist Children's Home (Worthington, O.). Exec. sec. War Council M.E. Ch., 1917-18. Home: Cincinnati, O. Died Feb. 11, 1929.

HENDERSON, Thomas Jefferson, congressman; b. Brownsville, Tenn., Nov. 29, 1824; ed. Brownsville Male Acad., 1835-36; State U. of Ia., 1845-4

Henrietta Butler, May 29, 1849. Practiced law in Ill., 1852-75; clerk co. commrs. court Stark co., Ill., and co. court, same, 1847-52; mem. Ill. Ho. of Rep., 1854-56; Senate, 1856-60. Col. 112th Ill. Inf., Sept. 22, 1862; bvtd. brig. gen. vols., Nov. 30, 1864, "for gallant and meritorious services during the campaign in Ga. and Tenn." Presdl. elector, 1868; mem. 44th to 53d Congresses (1875-95). Republican. Was mem. bd. of mgrs. Nat. Home for Disabled Vol. Soldiers; mgr. Danville (Ill.) branch Nat. Home; now mem. Bd. Ordnance and Fortification, War Dept. Home: Princeton, Ill. Died 1911.

HENDERSON, Thomas Stalworth, lawyer; b. Washington, Tex., Jan. 12, 1859; s. Thomas Stalworth and Harriet (Red) H.; A.B., Waco (now Baylor) U., 1877; student St. Louis Law Sch., 1878-79; admitted to bar, 1879; m. Minnie Agnes Burns, Dec. 10, 1884; children—Thomas Stalworth, Eleanor (Mrs. P. B. Wells), Mary Lake, John Burns, Harriet Ada, Agnes Red. Co. atty. Milam Co., Tex., 1880-82; dist. atty., 20th Jud. Dist., Tex., 1882-86; mem. Tex. legislature, 1893; mem. bd. regents U. of Tex., 1895-1911 (chmn. 1900-11). Pres. Milam County Abstract Co.; v.p. Citizens Nat. Bank of Cameron; sr. mem. Henderson, Kidd & Henderson; also extensive cotton grower. Democrat. Mem. Council of Defense; chmn. County Legal Advisory Bd.; mem. of League to Enforce Peace. Home: Cameron, Tex. Died Feb. 1937.

HENDERSON, William James, author; b. Newark, N.J., Dec. 4, 1855; s. William and Ettie H.; A.B., Princeton, 1876, A.M., 1886, Litt.D., 1922; m. Julia Wall, May 9, 1904. On staff New York Times, 1883-1902; music critic New York Sun from 1902; asso. editor The Standard Dictionary, 1892-94. Mem. Nat. Inst. Arts and Letters, Am. Acad. of Arts and Letters. Author: The Story of Music, 1889; Afloat with the Flag, 1895; Elements of Navigation, 1895; What Is Good Music? 1898; How Music Developed, 1898; The Orchestra and Orchestral Music, 1899; Richard Wagner, His Life and His Dramas, 1901; Modern Musical Drift, 1904; The Art of the Singer, 1906; Early History of Singing, 1921. Home: New York, N.Y. Died June 5, 1937.

HENDERSON, William Olin, lawyer; b. Liberty Tp., O., Oct. 28, 1850; s. James Allen and Mary Josephine (Phifer) H.; A.B., Yale, 1874; m. Sarah Wilcox Ellis, Oct. 14, 1886. Admitted to Ohio bar, 1877; practiced, Columbus, O., successively as mem. Hamilton & Henderson, to 1882, Harrison, Olds & Henderson, 1889-1902, Henderson & Livesay, Henderson, Livesay & Burr, Henderson & Burr; solicitor 3d dist., P.,C.,C.&St.L. Ry. Co. Republican. Home: Columbus, O. Died Oct. 1934.

HENDREN, William Mayhew, lawyer; b. New Bern, N.C., Oct. 13, 1871; s. Linville Laurentine and Mary Elizabeth (Mayhew) H.; student U. of N.C.; m. Annie Rawley, Mar. 1899 (dec.); children—Mary Elizabeth (Mrs. Chas. W. Long), Carrie Shelton (Mrs. Alfred Z. Smith, Jr.). Admitted to North Carolina bar, 1894; mem. Manly, Hendren & Womble, 1894—; state senator, 1931-32; was commissioner uniform state laws, N.C. Democrat. Methodist. Home: Winston-Salem, N.C. Died July 19, 1939.

HENDRICK, Archer Wilmot, banker; b. Frankford, Ont., June 26, 1871; s. Wilmot Allen and Janet (Gunn) H.; B.A., U. of Toronto, 1897 (1st class honor in history and polit. science); post-grad. work, Queens U., Kinsgton, 1899-1901; grad. Ont. Normal Sch. and Ont. Normal Coll. (gold medalist); m. Blanche Estella Clark, Nov. 19, 1900. Modern lang. master, Picton Collegiate Inst., 1899-1902; chmn. Bd. of Examiners of Modern Langs. for Ont., 1902; prof. English, prin. prep. dept. and dean of men, Whitman Coll., Walla Walla, Wash., 1902-08, dean of faculty and sec. bd. trustees, 1908-12 (resigned); pres. U. of Nev., 1914-17; sec. Federal Land Bank of Berkeley, Calif., 1917-19; v.p. Calif. Joint Stock Land Bank of San Francisco, 1919-28, pres., 1928—; v.p. Bank of America Nat. Trust & Savings Assn., 1928—. Episcopalian. Mason. Home: Berkeley, Calif. Died Dec. 28, 1937.

HENDRICK, Ellwood, author, chemist; b. Albany, N.Y., Dec. 19, 1861; s. James and Anna (Wands) H.; student U. of Zürich, Switzerland; hon. Sc.D., Franklin and Marshall Coll., 1921; m. Josephine Pomeroy, Nov. 15, 1897; children—Grace V. Pomeroy (Mrs. George W. Patterson), James Pomeroy. Mgr. Albany Aniline & Chemical Works, 1881-84; engaged in fire ins. until 1900, then in stock brokerage in New York, until 1915. With indsl. research establishment of Arthur D. Little, Inc., Cambridge, Mass., 1917-22; cons. editor Chem. and Metall. Engring., 1918-23; now curator Chandler Chem. Mus. of Columbia U. Trustee, mem. exec. com. Research Corp. Author: Everyman's Chemistry, 1917; Opportunities in Chemistry, 1919; Percolator Papers, 1919; Life of Lewis Miller, 1925; Modern Views of Physical Science, 1925. Home: New York, N.Y. Died Oct. 29, 1930.

HENDRICK, Michael J., consular service; b. Penn Yan, N.Y., Dec. 23, 1847; s. Thomas and Catharine (Corcoran) H.; ed. Penn Yan Acad.; m. Genevieve Yates of Belleville, Ont., June 14, 1905. In mercantile business, Penn Yan, 1865-84; U.S. consul at Belleville, Ont., 1893-1908, Moncton, N.B., 1908-13, consul-gen. Christiania, Norway, 1913-15; consul Plauen, Saxony, Mar. 1915-Feb. 1917, then at Windsor, Ont., Can. Roman Catholic. Died Sept. 9, 1922.

HENDRICK, Peter Aloysius, judge; b. Penn Yan, N.Y., July 8, 1858; s. Thomas and Catherine (Corcoran) H.; A.B., Fordham U., 1878, A.M., 1881 (LL.D., 1908); m. Julia Sherwood, Apr. 27, 1881. Admitted to bar, 1880; practiced, Auburn, N.Y., 1880-86, New York, 1886-1906; corp. counsel, Auburn, 1881-83; justice Supreme Ct. of N.Y., 1907-20. Democrat. Home: New York, N.Y. Died Feb. 10, 1923.

HENDRICK, Thomas Augustine, R. C. bishop; b. Penn Yan, N.Y., Oct. 29, 1849; s. Thomas and Catherine (Corcoran) H.; A.B., Seton Hall Coll., S. Orange, N.J., 1870, A.M., 1872; grad. St. Joseph's Theol. Sem., Troy, N.Y., 1873; (LL.D., St. John's Coll., Fordham, N.Y., 1900, Seton Hall Coll., 1901). Ordained priest, 1873; asst. St. Mary's Ch., Rochester, N.Y., 1873-74, rector Holy Cross parish, Charlotte, N.Y., 1874-77, Union Springs, N.Y., 1877-91, St. Bridget's parish, Rochester, N.Y., 1895-1903; consecrated 1st Am. bishop of Cebu, P.I., at Rome, Aug. 23, 1903, took possession Mar. 6, 1904. Regent Univ. State of N.Y., 1900-03; v.p. N.Y. State and Nat. Assn. for Prevention of Cruelty, 1902; del. from nat. assn. to World's Conf., London, 1902. Died 1909.

HENDRICKS, Eldo Lewis, college pres.; b. Rossville, Ind., Oct. 2, 1866; s. Samuel and Henrietta (Stinehouse) H.; A.B., Franklin (Ind.) Coll., 1894, LL.D., 1916; A.M., Ind. U., 1899; studied Harvard, 1903, U. of Chicago, 1909-10, Columbia, 1923; m. Viola Murphy, 1910. County supt. schs., Johnson Co., Ind., 1894; supt. schs., Delphi, Ind., 1901-08; supervisor schs., Indianapolis, 1908-09; became pres. Central Mo. State Teachers' Coll., 1915, pres. emeritus. Mem. Fact Finding Commn. to India, 1930-31. Mason. Presbyn. Home: Warrensburg, Mo. Died Nov. 22, 1938.

HENDRICKSON, Charles Elvin, judge; b. New Egypt, N.J., Jan. 8, 1843; s. Jacob and Mary M. (Davis) H.; A.B., Princeton, 1863, A.M., 1866; m. Sarah Wood Noxon, Jan. 10, 1872. Admitted to bar, 1866; prosecutor of pleas, Burlington Co., 1870-90; mem. Legislative Assembly, N.J., 1868; spl. judge Ct. of Errors and Appeals, N.J., 1896-1901; justice Supreme Ct. N.J., 1901-08. Democrat. Home: Red Bank, N.J. Died July 27, 1919.

HENDRICKSON, William Woodbury, prof. mathematics, U.S.N.; b. Mt. Joy, Pa., June 21, 1844; s. James W. and Ellen (Woodbury) H.; grad. U.S. Naval Acad., 1863; m. Eleanor M. Burnham, Apr. 18, 1867. Apptd. acting midshipman from Ohio, 1860; ensign, 1863; served in Lancaster, Portsmouth and Plymouth; instr. mathematics, U.S. Naval Acad., 1870-73; resigned commn. as lt. comdr. to accept commn. as prof., Mar. 1873; head dept. mathematics, U.S. Naval Acad., 1873-90, and 1897-1907; in office Nautical Almanac, 1890-97; retired June 21, 1906, with rank of rear admiral. Home: Annapolis, Md. Died June 1, 1920.

HENDRIX, Eugene Russell, bishop; b. Fayette, Mo., May 17, 1847; s. Adam and Isabella (Murray) H.; A.B., Wesleyan U., Conn., 1867; grad. Union Theol. Sem., 1869; D.D., Emory Coll., 1878, Wesleyan, 1903; LL.D., U. of Mo. and U. of North Carolina, 1888, Washington and Lee U., 1892, and Wesleyan U., 1917; m. Annie E. Scarritt, June 20, 1872; children—Mrs. Evangeline Isabel Waring, Mrs. Mary Matilda Simpson, Nathan Scarritt, Mrs. Helen Chick Mohr. Ordained M.E. Ch., S. ministry, 1870; pastor Leavenworth, Kan., 1869-70, Macon, Mo., 1870-72, St. Joseph, Mo., 1872-76, Glasgow, Mo., 1877-88; pres. Central Coll., Mo., 1878-86; bishop M.E. Ch., S., 1886—. Pres. Federal Council of Schs. of Christ in Am., 1908-12. Made official visits to China, Japan, Korea, Mexico and Brazil; founded the mission of his church in Korea; fraternal messenger to British Wesleyan Conf., 1900; Cole lecturer at Vanderbilt U., 1903; Quillian lecturer at Vanderbilt U., 1903; Quillian lecturer at Emory Coll., 1903; Avera lecturer, Trinity Coll., 1916; Grover lecturer, Syracuse U., 1916. Owns John Wesley's manuscript jour., written in America, 1736-37. Author: Skilled Labor for the Master, 1900; The Religion of the Incarnation, 1903; The Personality of the Holy Spirit, 1904; Christ's Table Talk, 1908; If I Had Not Come, 1916. Home: Kansas City, Mo. Died Nov. 11, 1927.

HENDRIX, Joseph Clifford, banker; b. Fayette, Mo., May 25, 1853; academic edn. at Central Coll., Fayette, Mo.; 3 yrs. at Cornell; m. Mary Alice Rathbone, Oct. 28, 1875. Is pres. Nat. Bank of Commerce, New York; trustee Kings County Trust Co., Brooklyn (which he organized), Fifth Av. Trust Co., New York, and of Morton Trust Co., New York; postmaster, Brooklyn, 1886-90; pres. Brooklyn bd. of edn. 6 yrs.; trustee New York and Brooklyn Bridge 2 yrs.; mem. Congress, 1893-95; pres. Am. Bankers' Assn., elected Aug., 1897. Trustee Cornell; chmn. arbitration com., N.Y. Clearing House. Home: Brooklyn, N.Y. Died 1904.

HENDRIXSON, Walter Scott, chemist; b. Felicity, O., Jan. 11, 1859; s. Eber Adkins and Sarah (Hoover) H.; B.S., Union Christian Coll., Merom, Ind., 1881; A.M., Harvard, 1889, Ph.D., 1903; univs. of Berlin and Göttingen, 1894-95; m. Bessie Bradley, Apr. 18, 1906. Instr., 1882-85, prof. chemistry and physics, 1885-88, Antioch Coll., O.; asst. in chemistry, Harvard, 1889-90; prof. chemistry, Ia. (now Grinnell) Coll., 1890—. Prof. chemistry, State U. of Ia., summer, 1902; lecturer chemistry, U. of Ill., on leave, 1917; research fellow, Johns Hopkins U., 1920-21; connected with water resources branch U.S. Geol. Survey, 1905-09. Pres. Ia. Acad. of Science, 1899, Assn. of Ia. Colls., 1900; mem. council for Ia. of Am. Chem. Soc. Home: Grinnell, Ia. Deceased.

HENEY, Francis Joseph, lawyer; b. Lima, N.Y., Mar. 17, 1859; s. Richard and Julia (Schreiber) H.; resident San Francisco, 1864—; ed. pub. primary, grammar and night schs., 1866-75, U. of Calif., 1879-80, Hastings Law Sch., 1883-84; married. Admitted to bar, Sept. 1883; in cattle business in Ariz., 1885-89; conducted Indian trader store, Ft. Apache, Ariz., 1886-88; practiced law, Tucson, Ariz., 1889-95; took prominent part in litigation by which titles under Mexican land grants in Ariz. were settled, and in argument of three land-grant cases before Supreme Court of U.S.; was atty. gen., Ariz., 1893-94; removed to San Francisco, 1895, and confined cases to civil business until urged by Atty. Gen. Knox to undertake land fraud causes at Portland, Ore.; discovered conspiracy of U.S. Atty. John H. Hall to protect guilty politicians in consideration of reappointment; secured removal and indictment of Hall, and indictment of Senator Mitchell, George C. Brownell, and others; as dep. dist. atty., apptd. to prosecute offenders at San Francisco, brought about indictment and conviction of Mayor Eugene Schmitz and Abe Ruef, devoting 3 yrs., without compensation, to these and other cases; Progressive Party candidate for U.S. Senate, 1914; Dem. presdl. elector, 1916; spl. atty. for Federal Trade Commn., in charge of investigation of high cost of living, with special reference to the packing industry, July 1917-Apr. 1918. Dem. candidate for gov. of Calif., 1918, but prevented by decision of Supreme Court, on account of technicality, from having name appear on the ballot. Apptd. spl. counsel for U.S. Senate com. investigating Internal Revenue Bur., Apr. 1924; judge Superior Court of Calif., city and county of Los Angeles, 1931—. Home: Santa Monica, Calif. Died Oct. 31, 1937.

HENIUS, Max; b. Aalborg, Denmark, June 16, 1859; s. Isidor and Emilie H.; Ph.D., U. of Marburg, Germany, 1881; m. Johanne Louise Heiberg, Aalborg, June 4, 1883; children—Henry R., Emil Theodor, Gerda. Came to U.S., 1881; asso. with Dr. Robert Wahl as Wahl & Henius, analytical chemists; Chicago; established a brewing academy and analytical lab., 1886, now Wahl-Henius Inst., cons. and analyt. chemists, of which is pres. Sec.-gen. Second Internat. Brewers Congress, Chicago, 1911; pres. Jacob A. Riis League of Patriotic Service, 1916-18; mem. sub-com. on chemistry of fermentation, Nat. Research Council. Fellow Chem. Soc., London. Comdr. Order of Dannebrog, Denmark, 1911; the Merit Medal in Gold, 1925. Dir., v.p. and pres. Chicago Public Library, 1911-17, and 1925-30; pres. Am. Rebild Nat. Park Board (Denmark) of which was founder; formerly chmn., now mem., America-Denmark Com., Century of Progress Expn., Chicago, 1933; elected hon. citizen, Aalborg, 1929; founder Danish-Am. Archives, Aalborg, 1930, hon. pres., 1932; hon. mem. Am. and Danish Brewers' Assns., 1932. Joint author: American Handy Book of Brewing, 1902. Died Nov. 15, 1935.

HENKLE, Rae DeLancey, publisher; b. La Rue, O., Jan. 14, 1883; s. John D. and Jessie (Holliday) H.; ed. high sch. and law dept. George Washington U.; m. Pearl Wintermute, June 16, 1904; 1 dau., Henrietta DeLancey. Entered newspaper work, 1903; Sunday and dramatic editor, Cleveland Plain Dealer, 1905-07; polit. publicity work, 1908-10; asst. foreign editor, Sunday editor and fgn. editor, New York Herald, 1913-19; sec. and mng. editor Christian Herald, 1919-25; pres. Rae D. Henkle, Publisher; introduced modern Japanese fiction in U.S. through publication of "The Mother," by Yusuke Tsurumi, in 1932, the first contemporary Japanese novel to be translated. Chmn. exec. com. Am. Inst. of Christianity, 1926; gen. sec. Am. Com. for Famine Relief in China. Republican. Home: New York, N.Y. Died Nov. 28, 1935.

HENNEMAN, John Bell, educator, editor; b. Spartanburg, S.C., Jan. 2, 1864; s. John A. and Louisa H.; M.A., Univ. of Va., 1884; asst. prof. Wofford Coll., 1884-86; studied abroad, 1886-89; Ph.D., U. of Berlin, 1889; m. Marion, d. Hon. Robert T. Hubard, Sept. 7, 1897. Prof. English and history, Hampden-Sidney Coll., 1889-93; prof. English lang. and lit., U. of Tenn., 1893-1900; prof. English lang. and lit., 1900—, dean Coll. Arts and Sciences, 1907—, Univ. of the South. Editor Sewanee Review, 1900—; lecturer, U. of Chicago, 1899. Gen. editor Johnson Series of English Classics, 1900-

1903. Editor: (with W. P. Trent), The Complete works of Thackeray (30 vols.), including A Bibliography of Thackeray, 1904; Shakespeare's Twelfth Night, 1905; Thackeray's Henry Esmond, 1906; Kemper Bocock's The Antiphon to the Stars, 1907; Best American Tales (with W. P. Trent), 1907. Mem. exec. council Modern Lang. Assn. of America; mem. exec. com. Assn. of Colls. and Prep. Schs. of the Southern States. Home: Sewanee, Tenn. Died 1908.

HENNESSY, John, R. C. archbishop; b. Ireland, 1823; was a missionary priest in diocese of St. Louis; pastor New Madrid and Gravois, 1850-55; prof. dogmatic theology, 1855, and superior, 1857, R. C. Theol. Sem., Carondelet, Mo.; priest St. Joseph's Ch., St. Joseph, Mo., 1860-66; consecrated, 1866, bishop of Dubuque (Ia.), which was subsequently made an archdiocese, he becoming metropolitan. Died 1900.

HENNESSY, John Joseph, bishop; b. near Cloyne, Co. Cork, Ireland, July 19, 1847; s. Michael and Ellen (Cronin) H.; came to U.S. in childhood; grad. Christian Brothers' Coll., St. Louis, 1862; completed theol. course at Salesianum, Milwaukee; philos. course at Cape Girardeau Coll., Mo.; ordained priest (by Papal dispensation, being under canonical age), 1869. Missionary in 10 counties in Iron Mountain dist. of Mo., 1869-80; founded the Railroad Men's Benevolent Union, 1871; established, 1877, Ursuline Convent at Arcadia, Mo.; built chs. in Bismarck, Graniteville, Poplar Bluff, Doniphan and Gatewood, Mo.; procurator and v.p. bd. mgrs., St. Louis Protectory, 1878-86; editor St. Louis Youth's Magazine, 1880-86; rector St. John's, St. Louis, 1880-88; consecrated bishop of Wichita (Kan.), Nov. 30, 1888. Died July 13, 1920.

HENNESSY, William John, artist; b. Thomastown, Co. Kilkenny, Ireland, July 11, 1837; s. John and Catherine (Laffin) H.; came to New York with family, 1849; became student Nat. Acad. Design, 1856; m. Charlotte Mather, June 1870. N.A., 1863; mem. Soc. Oil Painters (London), Pastel Soc. (London); hon. mem. Am. Water Color Soc.; mem. Union Internationale des Beaux Arts and des Lettres, Paris. Died Dec. 26, 1917.

HENNEY, William Franklin, lawyer; b. Enfield, Conn., Nov. 2, 1852; s. John and Mene (Barclay) H.; A.B., Princeton, 1874, A.M., 1877; LL.D., Trinity Coll., Conn., 1906; unmarried. Admitted to Conn. bar, 1876, and practiced in Hartford; dir. and counsel, Hartford Electric Light Co., Southern N.E. Telephone Co.; mem. Common Council, Hartford, 1877; judge City Police Ct., 1883-89; corp. counsel, 1890-95; mayor of Hartford, 1904-08; mem. Bd. State Police Commrs., Conn., 1912-21; member Rep. Nat. Com. from Conn., 1913-16. Presbyn. Mason. Author: Songs of the Times, 1910. Home: Hartford, Conn. Died Feb. 7, 1928.

HENNING, Edward J., judge; b. Iron Ridge, Wis., Dec. 28, 1868; s. Gotlib and Henriette (Erdman) H.; B.L., U. of Wis., 1894; LL.B., Columbian (now George Washington) U., 1896, LL.M., 1897, LL.D., 1925; m. Eugenia Husting, Dec. 7, 1898; 1 dau., Beatrice (Mrs. George Shaw). In law practice at Milwaukee, 1897-1912; moved to San Diego, Calif., 1913. Campaign mgr. Am. Rep. Coll. League, 1896; asst. U.S. atty., Eastern Dist., Wis., 1901-10, U.S. atty., 1910-11; asst. sec. of labor, 1921-25; U.S. dist. judge, Southern Dist. of Calif., by apptmt. of President Coolidge, 1925-Dec. 31, 1929; industrial relations counsel "Big Five" Motion Picture Theatre Circuits, 1930-33; gen. counsel Internat. Order of Moose; in gen. practice Los Angeles, Washington and N.Y. City, 1932—. Member Harbor Commn. of San Diego. Headed American delegation to World Conf. on Emigration and Immigration, Rome, May 1924; mem. Am. delegation at conf. at El Paso, with Mexico to draft border treaty, May 1925. Republican. Methodist. Mason. Supreme Dictator Loyal Order Moose, 1915-16; trustee Mooseheart (Ill.). Home: Los Angeles, Calif. Died Sept. 6, 1935.

HENNISEE, Argalus Garey, brig. gen.; b. Trappe, Md., Jan. 16, 1839; s. Samuel and Ann (Garey) H.; ed. pub. sch. at Trappe, 1845-55; m. Ema Lone Rosette, Apr. 15, 1891. Entered Union Army as 1st lt. 1st Md. Inf., Sept. 30, 1861; capt., July 24, 1862; hon. mustered out, Feb. 11, 1865; apptd. from Md., 2d lt. 19th U.S. Inf., Jan. 22, 1867; 1st lt., May 14, 1868; assigned to 8th Cav., Jan. 1, 1871; capt., Mar. 16, 1881; maj. 2d Cav., May 31, 1898; lt. col. 11th Cav., Feb. 2, 1901; col. 5th Cav., Sept. 13, 1902; retired by operation of law, Jan. 16, 1903; advanced to rank of brig. gen. retired, by act of Apr. 23, 1904. Methodist. Republican. Home: Los Angeles, Calif. Died 1913.

HENNY, David Christian, hydraulic engr.; b. Arnhem, The Netherlands, Nov. 15, 1860; s. David and Berendina (Lorentz) H.; C.E., Poly. U., Delft, 1881; Dr. Engineering, Oregon State Coll., 1933; m. Julia A. H. Wetzel, 1893; children—George Christian, Frances Berendina, Arnold Lorentz. Railroad location, Holland, 1881-84; came to U.S., 1884, naturalized citizen, 1894; engaged in ry. waterworks and irrigation constrn., 1884-91; gen. mgr. Excelsior Redwood Pipe Co., San Francisco, 1892-1902, Redwood Mfrs. Co., 1902-05; supervising engr. U.S. Reclamation Bur. (Pacific Coast dist.), 1905-09; cons. engr. with U.S. Reclamation Service, 1909—, also pvt. practice, Portland, Ore., 1910—. Introduced wooden stave pipe on Pacific Coast, and built many pioneer lines; built first large factory in U.S. with individual motor drive, Pittsburgh, Calif., 1902; connected with constrn. and maintenance of many western irrigation projects and dams; cons. engr. various cities and states, irrigation dists. and power cos., also govts. of Puerto Rico and Cuba. Mem. Am. Concrete Inst. on Mass Concrete; mem. U.S. Reclamation Bd. on Hoover Dam. Home: Portland, Ore. Deceased.

HENRI, Robert, artist; b. Cincinnati, 1865; s. John and Theresa H.; lived in far west; ed. in schs. in New York, Cincinnati, Denver and elsewhere; student Pa. Acad. Fine Arts, Phila., 1886-88, in Académie Julian and École des Beaux Arts, Paris, 1888-91, and studied without instrn. for yrs. in France, Spain and Italy; m. Linda Craige, 1898 (died 1905); m. 2d, Marjorie Organ, 1908. Picture "La Neige," purchased from Salon, 1899, by French Govt. for Luxembourg Gallery; represented in permanent collections of Carnegie Inst., Pittsburgh, Art Inst. Chicago, New Orleans Art Assn., Dallas Art Assn., Pa. Acad. Fine Arts, Brooklyn Mus. Arts and Sciences, Art Inst., Kansas City, Met. Mus., New York, San Francisco Inst. Art, Minneapolis Mus., Buffalo Fine Arts Acad., Museum of Art and Archæology, Santa Fe, N.M., Detroit Mus. Art, Toledo Mus. Art, Milwaukee Art Inst., Telfair Acad. Arts and Scinces, Savannah, Ga., Corcoran Gallery, Washington, City Art Mus., St. Louis, Museum History, Art and Science, Los Angeles, Cincinnati Museum, and many others. Silver medal, Buffalo Expn., 1901; St. Louis Expn., 1904; gold medal, Phila. Art Club, 1909; Harris prize ($500), Art Inst. Chicago, 1905; silver medal, Internat. Expn., Buenos Aires, 1910; Carol H. Beck gold medal, Pa. Acad. Fine Arts; silver medal, Panama Pacific Expn., 1915; portrait prize, Wilmington Soc. Fine Arts, 1920. N.A., 1906; mem. Nat. Inst. Arts and Letters. Author: The Art Spirit, 1923. Home: New York, N.Y. Died July 12, 1929.

HENROTIN, Charles, banker; b. in Belgium, Apr. 15, 1843; s. Dr. Joseph F. and Adèle (Kinson) H.; ed. Poly. Sch., Tourney, Belgium; m. Ellen M. Martin, Sept. 2, 1869. Entered employ of Merchants' Loan & Trust Co., Chicago, 1861; cashier same (succeeding Lyman J. Gage), 1868-78; banker and broker from 1878; has served as broker in connection with many large corporate enterprises, including the sale for English cos. of the Am. Brewing & Malting Co., and the Union Stock Yards Co., and Am. rep. of large financial interests in London and on the European continent. Mem. New York Stock Exchange, Chicago Stock Exchange (prin. founder and pres. 3 terms), Chicago Bd. of Trade. Dir. World's Fair, Chicago, 1893. Resident consul for Belgium, 1876—, for Turkey, 1877—; became consul gen. for Turkey. Knight Order of Leopold (Belgium), 1889; later officer same order, and comdr. Ottoman Medjidie; comdr. of the Ismanieh; Knight of the Crown and Chevalier Legion of Honor (France); Civic Cross, 1st class, Belgium, 1911. Democrat. Home: Chicago, Ill. Died July 25, 1914.

HENROTIN, Ellen M. Martin; b. Portland, Me., July 1847; d. Edward Byam and Sarah Ellen (Norris) Martin; ed. in Europe; m. Charles Henrotin, Sept. 2, 1869 (died 1914). Vice-pres. of The Congress Auxiliary of World's Columbian Expn., 1893; pres. Gen. Fedn. of Women's Clubs, 1894-98. Decorated by the Sultan of Turkey with order of Chefakat in 1893, and made an Officier de l'Académie by French Republic, 1899; decorated by Leopold II, Chevalier de l'Ordre de Leopold, 1904. Home: South Berlin, N.Y. Died June 29, 1922.

HENROTIN, Fernand, physician; b. Brussels, Belgium, Sept. 28, 1847; s. Dr. J. F. Henrotin; grad. Rush Med. Coll., 1868; m. Emile B. Prussing, 1873. Prosector Rush Med. Coll., 2 yrs.; co-physician, Cook Co., 2 yrs.; was surgeon Chicago police dept., 15 yrs., fire dept., 21 yrs.; surgeon 1st brigade I. N. G., several yrs.; was surgeon and gynecologist Cook Co. Hosp. several yrs.; now connected with Alexian Brothers, Chicago Polyclinic, and St. Joseph's German hosps. Mem. Internat. Gynecol. and Obstet. Congress (sec.-gen.). Died 1906.

HENRY, Alexander, clergyman; b. Germantown, Pa., Dec. 29, 1850; s. Thomas Charlton and Mary Elizabeth (Jackson) H.; bro. Bayard H.; A.B., Princeton, 1870; grad. Princeton Theol. Sem., 1874; (D.D., Coe Coll., Ia., 1905, Temple U., Phila., 1907); m. Caroline R. Bayard, May 12, 1875. Ordained Presbyn. ministry, 1874; pastor Lycoming, Pa., 1875-87, Hermon Ch., Phila., 1887-1905; sec. Presbyn. Bd. of Publ. and Sabbath Sch. Work, Philadelphia, 1905-19. Home: Germantown, Phila., Pa. Died July 15, 1925.

HENRY, Alfred Judson, meteorologist; b. New Bethlehem, Pa., Sept. 1, 1858; s. John McConnell and Nancy (Reid) H.; ed. Reid Inst., Pa., 1871-73; studied telegraphy; student Columbian (now George Washington) U., 1885-86; spl. studies also, 1897-98; m. Jessie Holbrook Ide, July 25, 1883; 1 dau., Helen Hall (dec.). Signal Service of U.S.A., 1878; chief of the div. Meteorol. Records, 1895-1900; prof. meteorology, U.S. Weather Bureau, 1900-17, senior and principal meteorologist, Nov. 1917—; exec. officer Mount Weather Research Obs., May 1908-12. Editor Mo. Weather Review, 1921—. Home: Washington, D.C. Died Oct. 5, 1931.

HENRY, Bayard, lawyer; b. Phila., Jan. 15, 1857; s. Thomas Charlton and Mary Elizabeth (Jackson) H.; A.B., Princeton, 1876; m. Jane Irwin Robeson. In practice with George Wharton Pepper; pres., United New Jersey R.R. & Canal Co.; dir., Pa. R.R. Co., Ins. Co. of N. America, Tradesmen's Nat. Bank, Real Estate Trust Co., Lehigh Coal & Navigation Co., Alliance Ins. Co., Phila. & Trenton R.R., Lehigh & N.E. R.R., etc. Mem. Pa. Senate, 1898-1902; mem. Select Council of Phila., 1908-11. Trustee Princeton U. Republican. Presbyn. Mem. Cliosophic Soc. (Princeton U.). Home: Philadelphia, Pa. Died Sept. 17, 1926.

HENRY, Carl French, clergyman; b. Chagrin Falls, O., Oct. 7, 1867; s. Nelson Calvin and Mary Louisa (Chase) H.; B.S., Buchtel Coll. (now U. of Akron, O.), 1891; B.D., Tufts Div. Sch., 1894; A.M., Tufts, 1898; Bach. Religious Pedagogy, Hartford Sch. of Religious Edn., 1906; D.D., Lombard, 1924, Tufts, 1924; m. Rena M. Lathrop, Oct. 9, 1894; 1 dau., Helen. Ordained ministry Universalist Ch., 1893; pastor successively Cleveland, O., Bangor, Me., North Attleboro, Mass., until 1915, Pasadena, Calif., 1915—. Pres. Ohio Universalist Conv., Calif. Universalist Conv.; 2d v.p. Universalist Gen. Conv., 1927—. Trustee Buchtel Coll. Home: Pasadena, Calif. Jan. 23, 1929.

HENRY, Charles Lewis, capitalist; b. on farm in Hancock Co., Ind., July 1, 1849; s. George and Leah (Lewis) H.; ed. Asbury (now DePauw) U.; LL.B., Ind. U., 1872; m. Eva N. Smock, Sept. 2, 1873. Admitted to bar, 1872; practiced at Pendleton, Ind., 1872-75, later at Anderson and Indianapolis; owner Indianapolis Journal, 1903-04; now engaged in developing interurban lines; built lines of Union Traction Co. of Ind., etc.; pres. and gen. mgr. Indianapolis & Cincinnati Traction Co. Mem. Ind. Senate, 1881-83; mem. 54th and 55th Congresses (1895-99); declined renomination. Republican. Home: Indianapolis, Ind. Died May 2, 1927.

HENRY, Charles William, coll. pres.; b. Maryville, Tenn., Sept. 20, 1878; s. William Hutton and Martha Eleanor (Tedford) H.; A.B., Maryville Coll., 1901; student Commercial Coll., U. of Ky., 1901; grad. study, U. of Tenn., summers 1916, 17, 27; M.A., Columbia, 1928; LL.D., King Coll., Bristol, Tenn., 1932; m. Leola Clare Landon, Jan. 7, 1904; children—Martha Etta (wife of Dr. George W. Burchfield), Charles William (dec.), Irma Charles. Founder, 1904, owner until 1926, Maryville Poly. Sch.; asso. headmaster McCallie Sch., Chattanooga, Tenn., 1928-30; asso. pres. Sullins Coll., Bristol, Tenn., 1930-31; pres. King Coll., 1931—. Democrat. Elder in Presbyn. Ch., 25 yrs., teacher men's Bible class, 20 yrs. Home: Bristol, Tenn. Died Sept. 15, 1935.

HENRY, Claude Morrison, mem. Federal Bd. for Vocational Edn.; b. West Bend, Ia., Nov. 19, 1873; s. William Glenn and Nancy Matilda (Spangler) H.; grad. high sch., Emmetsburg, Ia., 1890; m. Lura Geneive Showen, Sept. 4, 1895; 1 dau., Claudia Maxica. In merchandising business, 1894-98; organizer, 1902, then cashier Redfield (S.D.) Nat. Bank; v.p. Hitchcock State Bank, Miranda State Bank. Served as 1st lt. inf., U.S. Vols., Spanish-Am. War. Chmn. S.D. Tax Commn., 1913-17; mem. S.D. Rural Credit Commn., 1917-25; mem. Federal Bd. for Vocational Edn., 1927—. Republican. Methodist. Mason. Address: Washington, D.C. Deceased.

HENRY, Edward Lamson, artist; b. Charleston, S.C., Jan. 12, 1841; art edn. in New York, Phila. and Paris; m. Frances Livingston Wells, June 1875. Paints genre pictures, interiors representative of early N.E. life and hist. pieces; painted the large picture of the 1st railroad train in America on the Mohawk & Hudson, now the New York Central (picture is now in Albany [N.Y.] Hist. Soc.). A.N.A., 1867, N.A., 1869. Hon. mention Paris Expn., 1889; medal, New Orleans, 1885, Chicago, 1893; bronze medal, Buffalo, 1901; silver medal, Charleston, 1902; bronze medal, St. Louis, 1904. Home: New York, N.Y. Died May 9, 1919.

HENRY, E(dward) Stevens, congressman; b. Gill, Mass., Feb. 10, 1836; s. Edward Fish and Elisa (Stevens) H.; removed when 12 with parents to Rockville, Conn.; ed. pub. schs.; m. Lucina E. Dewey, Feb. 11, 1860. Connected with various financial instns.; farmer and breeder of thoroughbred stock. Mem. Conn. Ho. of Rep., 1883, Senate, 1887-88; state treas., 1889-93; mayor of Rockville, 1894-95; mem. 54th to 62d Congresses (1895-1913), 1st Conn. Dist. Home: Rockville, Conn. Died Oct. 10, 1921.

HENRY, Guy Vernor, brig. gen. U.S.A.; b. Fort Smith, Indian Ty., Mar. 9, 1839; grad. West Point May 5, 1861; served through Civil war and wars as lt., capt., maj., lt. col. and brig. gen. Successive bvts. for gallantry in various battles; bvtd. brig. gen. for gallantry at Rose Bud, Mont., where he was shot through the face fighting Indians; received medal of honor from Congress for distinguished gallantry at Cold Harbor; later col. 10th cav.; bvt. brig. gen., commanding Fort Assinniboine, and May 1898, promoted brig. gen. vols.; brig. gen. U.S.A., Oct. 1898, and maj. gen. vols., Dec. 1898, serving in the war against Spain. Military gov. Puerto Rico, Dec. 1898, to May 1899—. Home: Washington, D.C. Died 1899.

HENRY, Horace Chapin, railroad contractor; b. Bennington, Vt., Oct. 6, 1844; s. Paul Mandell and Aurelia (Squier) H.; educated Norwich University, Vermont, 1861-62; Williams College, Massachusetts, 1864-65; Hobart College, N.Y., 1865-66; B.S. and C.E., Norwich, 1909, as of 1864; m. Susan Elizabeth Johnson, Dec. 1876; children—Langdon Chapin, Paul Mandell, Walter Horace (dec.), Florence Aurelia (dec.). Enlisted Co. A, 14th Vt. Vols., Aug. 27, 1862, and elected 1st sergt.; served defenses, Washington, fall of 1862 and following winter; regt. assigned to Vt. Brigade, 3d Div., 1st Army Corps; fought on Cemetery Ridge, at Gettysburg, Pa., July 2, 3 and 4, 1863; hon. mustered out July 30, 1863. Began in ry. contracting business at Minneapolis with R. B. Langdon, 1866; with associates built about 2,500 miles of ry. in the Northwest, principally for Minneapolis & St. Louis, Wis. Central, Duluth, South Shore & Atlantic, and Milwaukee, Lake Shore & Western rys., also 450 miles for the "Soo Line," etc. Moved to Seattle, Wash., 1890, and built the Belt Line and Palmer Cut Off for N.P. Ry., the Everett & Monte Cristo Rd. in Wash., the G.N. Ry. from Seattle, Bellingham and Everett to summit of the Cascade Range, also 700 miles of main line and branches (involving over $20,000,000 and at times employing 10,000 men) for C.,M.&St. P. extension to the Pacific Coast. Pres. Metropolitan Bank, Northern Life Ins. Co., Pacific Creosoting Co.; v.p. Metropolitan Bldg. Co.; dir. 1st Nat. Bank, Everett, etc. Pres. Anti-Tuberculosis League of King Co., Wash. Republican. Protestant. Mason. Decorated by President of France with B.S.M. medal and Cross of Legion of Honor, Apr. 1920, for assistance to fatherless children of France, having collected and sent money for support of 1,800 children. Built the Florence Henry Memorial Chapel, at Highlands, nr. Seattle; on account of land and money given, is located at Fairlands the Walter H. Henry Administration Bldg. of the Anti-Tuberculosis Sanitarium; erected art gallery and gave collection of 160 paintings to U. of Wash. Home: Seattle, Wash. Died June 1928.

HENRY, James Addison, Presbyn. clergyman; b. Cranbury, N.J., Oct. 28, 1835; s. Rev. Dr. Symmes C. Henry, 37 yrs. pastor 1st Presbyn. Ch., Cranbury, N.J.; grad. Coll. of N.J. (now Princeton U.), 1857; grad. Princeton Theol. Sem., 1860 (D.D., Central Coll., Ky.; D.D., Washington and Jefferson Coll., Pa.); pastor Princeton Presbyn. Ch., Phila., from June 1860, until the present time—over 44 yrs.; m. Mary S., d. Robert Steen, July 25, 1861 (died 1892). Trustee Princeton Univ.; dir. Princeton Theol. Sem.; trustee and dir. many benevolent instns.; pres. Pa. Industrial Home for Blind Women. Has visited Europe 15 times and represented the Presbyn. Ch. in several Pan-Presbyn. councils; moderator Gen. Assembly Presbyn. Ch. in U.S.A., Buffalo, May 1904. Republican. Home: Philadelphia, Pa. Died 1906.

HENRY, J(ohn) Norman, M.D.; b. Philadelphia, Pa., Sept. 12, 1873; s. Frederick Porteous and Josephine Bull (Nancrede) H.; prep. edn., Episcopal Acad., Phila., and St. Paul's Sch., Concord, N.H.; M.D., Univ. of Pa., 1895; m. Mary K. Gibson, Apr. 14, 1909; children—Mary Gibson, Josephine Nancrede, J. Norman, Howard G. Began practice at Phila., 1895; asst. visiting physician, later physician, Pa. Hosp., now cons. physician; mgr. Christ Ch. Hosp. Dir. Dept. of Public Health, Phila. Chief of med. dept., later comdg. officer, rank of maj., Base Hosp. 38, A.E.F., World War. Mem. Pa. State Sanitary Water Bd. Dir. Big Brother Assn.; pres. Gen. Alumni Soc. U. of Pa.; formerly trustee U. of Pa. Episcopalian. Home: Gladwyne, Pa. Died Oct. 4, 1938.

HENRY, Kate Kearney; b. Washington, D.C., Apr. 30, 1840; d. John A. (surgeon U.S.N.) and Mary M. (Forrest) Kearney; grad. Georgetown Female Sem., 1858; m. Capt. James H. Lake Henry, U.S.A., Apr. 7, 1859 (died 1881). Charter mem. D.A.R. and has served as v.p. gen., corr. sec. gen., and state regent; regent Mary Washington Chapter; del. to Continental Congress, D.A.R. (now mem. Continental Hall Com.); pres. D.C. Soc. U.S. Daughters of 1812; mem. Soc. Colonial Dames, Guadeloupe Club, Assn. for Preservation of Va. Antiquities. Episcopalian. Home: Washington, D.C. Deceased.

HENRY, Lemuel H., banker; b. Vernon, Ia., May 9, 1871; s. Thomas P. and Jennie M. (Bennett) H.; ed. high sch., Bonaparte, Ia.; unmarried. With Ottumwa (Ia.) Nat. Bank, 2 yrs.; office work, mercantile business, 9 yrs.; entered employ Ia. State Nat. Bank, Sioux City, Ia., 1902, cashier, 1906-15; elected v.p. First Nat. Bank, Sioux City, 1915, chmn. bd., 1924—. Republican. Mason. Home: Sioux City, Ia. Died Jan. 1929.

HENRY, Nelson Herrick, federal officer; b. Staten Island, N.Y., Apr. 27, 1855; s. Joshua J. and Maria C. H.; A.B., Coll. City of New York, 1877; M.D., Coll. Phys. and Surg. (Columbia), 1879; m. Mrs. Sarah B. Rodgers Sloan, Apr. 30, 1901. Practiced in New York; surgeon 12th Regt. N.G.S.N.Y., 1883; asst. surgeon gen. state of N.Y., 1893; chief surgeon, N.G.S.N.Y., 1898, reappointed, 1900; maj. Spanish-Am. War, 1898-99; mem. N.Y. Ho. of Rep., 1899-1901; adj. gen. N.Y., 1902-10; brevet maj. gen. N.G.S.N.Y., 1910; U.S. surveyor port of New York, 1910—. Republican. Episcopalian. Home: New York, N.Y. Died Mar. 15, 1933.

HENRY, O., author. See Sydney Porter.

HENRY, Philip Solomon; b. Adelaide, S. Australia, Mar. 17, 1863; s. Isaac S. and Rose (Marks) H.; ed. City of London Sch., U. of London and U. of Göttingen; m. Florine, d. Leonard Lewisohn, Apr. 10, 1900 (died 1903); children—Violet Rosalie, Leonore Gladys; m. 2d, Annie Hyatt-Woolfe, of London. Formerly in copper industry, now retired. Settled at Asheville, N.C.; citizen of U.S., 1907. Apptd. by gov. of N.C., spl. commr. to investigate municipal govts., conditions and pub. utilities in Eng. and Europe, 1914, as commr. to report on cotton conditions in Egypt, India and other countries, 1921, as unofficial observer to report on League of Nations, 1924, and as hon. commr. to Ibero-American Expn., 1929. Apptd. mem. League of Nations Internat. Inst. of Intellectual Coöperation, 1926; asso. mem. Académie Diplomatique Internationale, Paris. Pres. Asheville Art Assn. and Mus., Inc. Home: Asheville, N.C. Died Apr. 11, 1933.

HENRY, Robert Lee, congressman; b. Linden, Tex., May 12, 1864; went to Bowie Co. and resided there until Jan. 1895, when he removed to McLennan Co.; A.M., Southwestern U. of Tex., valedictorian, 1885; admitted to bar, 1886; LL.B., U. of Tex., 1887. Mayor of Texarkana, Tex., 1890; 1st office asst. to atty. gen. of Texas, 1891-93, asst. atty. gen., 1893-96; mem. 55th to 64th Congresses (1897-17), 7th, now 11th Tex. Dist. Democrat. Home: Waco, Tex. Died July 9, 1931.

HENRY, William Arnon, agriculturist; b. Norwalk, O., June 16, 1850; s. William and Martha Haines (Condict) H.; student Holbrook Normal Sch., Lebanon, O.; Ohio Wesleyan U., 1870-71; B.S. Agr., Cornell U., 1880; (D. Agr., U. of Ill., 1904; D.Sc., U. of Vt., 1904, Mich. Agrl. Coll., 1907); m. Clara Roxanna Taylor, Aug. 19, 1881. Prin. New Haven (Ind.) High Sch., 1871-73, Boulder (Colo.) High Sch., 1873-76; prof. botany and agr., U. of Wis., 1881, prof. agr., 1883; dir. Agrl. Expt. Sta., 1887, dean Coll. Agr., 1891-1907, emeritus prof. agr., 1907—. U. of Wis. Had charge from beginning of Agrl. Coll. and Expt. Sta. U. of Wis. Author: Feeds and Feeding, 1898 (17th edit., revised, with F. B. Morrison, 1917, and abridged edit., 1917). Home: San Diego, Calif. Died 1932.

HENRY, William Elmer, librarian; b. nr. Connersville, Ind., Nov. 7, 1857; s. of John and Elizabeth (Chapman) H.; grad. Ind. State Normal Sch., Terre Haute, Ind., 1885; A.B., Indiana U., 1891, A.M. from same, 1892; post-graduate work U. of Chicago, 1893-95, fellow in English, 1894-95; m. Margaret Atkinson Roberts, July 30, 1895 (died 1900); 1 dau., Elizabeth Gillette; m. 2d, Sylvia M. Allen, Mar. 26, 1903. Instr. English, Ind. U., 1891-93; prof. English, Franklin (Ind.) Coll., 1895-97; state librarian, Ind., 1897-1906; librarian U. of Wash., 1906-29, librarian emeritus, also dean emeritus of School of Library Science. Home: Seattle, Wash. Died Mar. 20, 1936.

HENRY, William Wirt, lawyer; b. Red Hill, Va., Feb. 14, 1831 (grandson of Patrick Henry, revolutionary orator); grad. Univ. of Va. (M.A., 1850); m. Lucy Gray, dau. Col. James P. and Elizabeth (Watkins) Marshall, Nov. 8, 1854. Admitted to bar, 1853; State's atty., Charlotte Co., several years; removed to Richmond; mem. legislature 4 sessions; pres. Va. Hist. Soc., before which he delivered a "Defense of Capt. John Smith's Narrative;" pres. Am. Hist. Assn.; a trustee of the Peabody Ednl. Fund; orator at the centennial of the laying of the corner-stone of the capitol at Washington. Home: Richmond, Va. Died 1900.

HENSEL, William Uhler, lawyer; b. Quarryville, Pa., Dec. 4, 1851; s. George W. and Anna M. (Uhler) H.; A.B., Franklin and Marshall Coll., 1870, A.M., 1873; (LL.D., Dickinson Coll., 1909, Washington and Lee, 1910; Litt.D., Franklin and Marshall, 1912); m. Emily C. Flinn, Oct. 13, 1874 (dec.). Admitted to bar, 1873; atty. gen., Pa., 1891-95. Chmn. Dem. State Com., Pa., 1882-87. Pres. Pa. State Bar Assn., 1898-89, Pa. Editorial Assn., 1881-83. Home: Lancaster, Pa. Died Feb. 26, 1915.

HENSHALL, James Alexander, govt. official; b. Baltimore, Feb. 29, 1836; s. Rev. James Gershom (M.D.) and Clarissa (Holt) H.; ed. Baltimore, New York and Cincinnati; grad. M.D., New York and Cincinnati; m. Hester Stansbury Ferguson, June 9, 1864. Practiced medicine until 1896; an accomplished angler, fishing in many Am. and foreign waters. Supt. U.S. Bur. of Fisheries Sta., at Bozeman, Mont., 1896-1909, at Tupelo, Miss., 1909-17. Was the first to propagate the grayling successfully; asst. chief fisheries dept., Chicago Expn., 1893. Received silver medal, Paris Expn., 1900; gold medal, St. Louis Expn., 1904, for literature on fish culture and fishing, etc. Pres. Am. Fisheries Soc.; sec. Cincinnati Soc. Natural History; pres. Mont. Soc. Natural Science. Author: Book of the Black Bass, 1881; More About the Black Bass, 1889; Bass, Pike, Perch and Others, 1903; Favorite Game Fish of Inland Waters, 1922; Autobiography, 1922. Home: Cincinnati, O. Died Apr. 4, 1925.

HENSHAW, Frederic Rich, dentist; b. Alexandria, Ind., Oct. 8, 1872; s. Seth B. and Mary Jane (Rich) H.; student Central Normal Coll., Danville, Ind., 1889-91; D.D.S., Ind. Dental Coll., Indianapolis, Ind., 1897; hon. D.Sc. from Wabash Coll., 1936; m. Mary Edith Strickler, Sept. 1, 1897; 1 son, Frederic Rich. Began practice at Middletown, Ind., 1895; removed to Indianapolis, 1909; dean Ind. Dental Coll., July 1914—; dean Ind. Univ. School of Dentistry, 1925—; mem. Ind. State Bd. of Health. Pres. Am. Assn. of Dental Schools, 1930-31. Fellow Am. Coll. Dentistry, N.Y. Acad. of Dentistry; member Am. Dental Assn., Ind. State Dental Assn. (sec. 1899-1901; pres. 1931), Indianapolis Dental Soc., Chicago Dental Assn., etc. Mem. Nat. Bd. Dental Examiners (v.p. 1907), Ind. State Bd. Dental Examiners (sec., 1903-14). Mem. Sch. Bd., Middletown, 9 yrs. Mason. Mem. Indiana State Council of Defense, 1917-18; spl. dental examiner for War Dept.; in active service as maj., Dental Corps, U.S.A.; disch. as lt. col.; col. Dental Officers' Reserve Corps, 1925. Home: Indianapolis, Ind. Died May 27, 1938.

HENSHAW, Frederick William, judge; A.B., U. of Calif., 1879. Asso. justice Supreme Court of Calif., 1894-1917; resigned Dec. 1917, to assist in war work. Home: San Francisco, Calif. Died June 8, 1929.

HENSHAW, Henry Wetherbee, naturalist; b. Cambridge, Mass., Mar. 3, 1850; s. William and Sarah (Holden) H.; ed. Cambridge pub. schs.; ed. as naturalist, chiefly by outdoor study; unmarried. Joined Wheeler Survey, 1872, as naturalist, and explored the West and made reports thereon until 1879, when began work with Bur. of Ethnology, with which was connected, chiefly in administrative capacity, until 1893, part of which time was editor American Anthropologist; administrative biologist, Biol. Survey, U.S. Dept. Agr., June 1, 1905—; Chief of Biol. Survey, June 1, 1910—. Was in H.I., 1894-1904, devoting much time to the study of biology. Author: Report on Ornithology of Nev., Utah., Calif., Colo., N.Mex., and Ariz., 1875; Birds of the Hawaiian Islands, 1902. Home: Washington, D.C. Died Aug. 1, 1930.

HENSLEY, Adelia Gates, educator; b. Springfield, Mass., Nov. 15, 1855; d. Benjamin Sanford and Eveline (Nelson) Gates; grad. Mt. Holyoke Sem. (now Coll.), 1877 (L.H.D., 1917); m. James Henry Hensley, Nov. 24, 1886. Teacher, Mt. Vernon Sem., Washington, 1884, asso. prin., 1899, prin., 1915—. Mem. Headmistresses' Assn., Fine Arts Soc. (Washington, D.C.), Am. Assn. Univ. Women, D.A.R. Home: Washington, D.C. Deceased.

HENSLEY, William Nicholas, Jr., army officer; b. Columbus, Neb., Oct. 18, 1881; s. William N. and Margaret Anna (McAllister) H.; grad. U.S. Mil. Acad., 1905, Mounted Service Sch. (Ft. Riley, Kan.), Sch. of the Line, 1922, Gen. Staff Sch., 1923, Army War College, 1926; G.S.C. eligible list; m. Matie Merle Manard, July 10, 1908; children—William Nicholas III, Gertrude Barbara. Commanding 2d lt. cav., June 13, 1905; promoted through grades to maj. regular army, July 1, 1920; organized div. of Philippine N.G., 1917; col. and chief q.m., Philippine N.G., 1917; col. Air Service, U.S.A., Aug. 24, 1918-June 30, 1920; comdr. army balloon sch., Pasadena, Calif., 1918-19; apptd. comdr. U.S.A. Air Service Sta., at Mitchel Field, L.I., July 17, 1923. First Am. to make non-stop flight, U.S. to Europe by air, as U.S. observer on return trip of R-34, from Eng., July 1919; made study of Zeppelin Airship Line in Germany, 1919, training as airship pilot; furnished War Dept. first detailed authentic information on the L-72, the giant dirigible built at Friedrichshafen for the bombing of N.Y. City, the dirigible being practically completed when armistice was signed. Free balloon pilot, kite balloon pilot, and observer, airship pilot, airplane pilot, and distinguished marksman. Episcopalian. Mason. Home: Ft. Sam Houston, Tex. Died Mar. 21, 1929.

HENSON, Poindexter Smith, clergyman; b. Fluvanna Co., Va., Dec. 7, 1831; s. John and Ann O. (London) H.; B.A., Richmond (Va.) Coll., 1848; B.A., M.A., U. of Va.; (D.D., Bucknell, 1867; LL.D., Richmond Coll.); m. Amoret C. Reese, Oct. 3, 1855; 2d, Mrs. Edith B. Boyden, July 2, 1901. Ordained Bapt. ministry, 1855; pastor Fluvanna, Va., 1883-89, Broad St. Ch., Phila., 1861-67, Memorial Ch., Phila., 1867-82, First Ch., Chicago, 1882-1901, Hanson Pl. Ch., Brooklyn, 1901-03, Tremont Temple, Boston, 1903-08. Editor Bapt. Teacher, 1867—. Home: Chicago, Ill. Died Apr. 24, 1914.

HEPBURN, A(lonzo) Barton, banker; b. Colton, N.Y., July 24, 1846; s. Zina Earl and Beulah (Gray) H.; A.B., Middlebury Coll., 1871 (LL.D., 1894; D.C.L., St. Lawrence, 1906; LL.D., Columbia Univ., 1911, Williams Coll., 1911, Univ. of Vt., 1915, and New York Univ., 1919); m. Hattie A. Fisher, Dec. 10, 1873; 2d, Emily L. Eaton, July 14, 1887. Instr. mathematics, St. Lawrence Acad.; prin. Ogdensburg Ednl. Inst.; practiced law at Colton, N.Y.; mem. N.Y. Assembly, 1875-80; supt. of Banking Dept. State of N.Y., 1880-83; U.S. bank examiner for N.Y., 1888-92; comptroller of the currency, 1892-93; pres. Third Nat. Bank, New York, 1893-97; v.p. Nat. City Bank, New York, 1897-99; pres. Chase National Bank, New York, 1899-1911, chmn. bd. dirs., 1911-17, chmn. advisory bd., 1918—; dir. numerous corporations. Trustee Middlebury Coll., Rockefeller Foundation, Columbia Univ., N.Y. Zoöl. Soc. Officer Legion of Honor, France, 1912. Mem. N.Y. Chamber Commerce (pres.), N.E. Soc. (pres.), St. Andrew Soc., The Pilgrims, Burns Soc., etc. Chmn. currency commn. of Am. Bankers' Assn. from its creation, 1906; pres. Acad. Polit. Science, N.Y. Clearing House, Nat. Currency Assn.; chmn. commn. to revise banking laws of N.Y. State, 1907, and of similar commn., 1913; mem. Fed. Advisory Council of Fed. Reserve Bd., 1918; gov.'s com. to study necessary legislation to protect public in security purchases, 1919; Internat. Trade Conf. (com. on finance and credits), 1919. Author: History of Coinage and Currency, 1903; Artificial Waterways and Commercial Development, 1909; A History of Currency in the United States, 1915. Homes: Ridgefield, Conn., and New York, N.Y. Died Jan. 25, 1922.

HEPBURN, Andrew Dousa, educator; b. Williamsport, Pa., Nov. 14, 1830; s. Samuel and Rebecca (Williamson) H.; A.B., Jefferson Coll., Pa., 1851; grad. U. of Va., 1854, Princeton Theol. Sem., 1857; (D.D., Hampden-Sidney, 1876; LL.D., U. of N.C., 1881); m. Henrietta McGuffey, July 10, 1857; father of Charles McGuffey H. Stated supply Harrisonburg, Va., 1857-58; ordained Presbyn. ministry, Oct. 22, 1858; pastor New Providence, Va., 1858-60; prof. logic, rhetoric and English lang. and lit., U. of N.C., 1860-67, same chairs Miami U., Oxford, O., 1868-73, pres., Miami U., 1871-73; prof. mental philosophy and English lit., 1874-85, pres., 1877-85, Davidson Coll., N.C.; prof. English lang. and lit., Miami U., 1885-1908, resigned. Died Feb. 14, 1921.

HEPBURN, Charles McGuffey, lawyer; b. Rockbridge Co., Va., Aug. 19, 1858; s. Andrew Dousa and Henrietta (McGuffey) H.; A.B., Davidson Coll., N.C. (valedictorian), 1878; LL.B., U. of Va., 1880; LL.D., Miami U., 1908; m. Julia Benedict, Oct. 10, 1891; children—Samuel Benedict, Henrietta, Janet Douglas (Mrs. Ralph W. Evans), Andrew Hopewell, Wm. McGuffey, Julia Cleveland (Mrs. Ben R. Ross), Charles Keith. Tutor, in charge prep. dept. Davidson Coll., 1880-81; admitted to Ohio bar, 1881; practiced at Cincinnati, 1881-1903; lecturer on code and on common law pleading, Cincinnati Law Sch., 1897-1903; apptd. prof. law, Ind. U., 1903, dean Law Sch., 1918-25, research prof. law, 1925—. Organized, 1909, Am. Inst. of Law, New York, for the purpose of establishing post-admission-to-the-bar courses of legal study. Presbyn. Democrat. Author: Cases on Torts, 1913. Home: Bloomington, Ind. Deceased.

HEPBURN, James Curtis, physician; b. Milton, Pa., Mar. 13, 1815; s. Samuel and Ann (Clay) H.; ed. Milton Acad., 1825-30; Princeton Coll., A.B., 1832, A.M., 1835; Univ. of Pa. Med. Dept., M.D., 1836; (LL.D., Lafayette, 1872, Princeton, 1905); m. Clara Marie Leete, Oct. 1840 (died 1906). Went to China as med. missionary, 1840; stationed in Singapore, 1841-43, in Amoy, China, 1843-46; returned to U.S., 1846; resided in New York, 1846-59; went to Japan, 1859; lived in Yokohama until 1892; returned to U.S., 1893; retired. Compiled first English dictionary of Japanese lang. (pub. 1867—went to 4 edits.), also English-Japanese Dictionary; wrote grammar of Japanese lang., 1867. Engaged, 1872, in transl. of Holy Bible into Japanese lang., which finished, 1888; pub. Japanese Dictionary of the Bible, 1891. Presbyn. Republican. Home: E. Orange, N.J. Died 1911.

HEPBURN, William Peters, congressman; b. Wellsville, O., Nov. 4, 1833; taken to Iowa Ty., Apr. 1841; ed. local schs. and in a printing office; (LL.D., Cornell Coll., Ia., 1904). Admitted to bar, 1854; pros. atty. Marshall Co., Ia., 1856-57; clerk Ia. Ho. of Rep., 1858; dist. atty. 11th Jud. Dist., 1858-61; capt., maj. and lt. col. 2d Ia. Cav., 1861-65; lived at Memphis, Tenn., 1865-67, Clarinda, Ia., 1867—; presdl. elector, 1876, at-large, 1888; mem. 47th to 49th Congresses, 1881-87; solicitor of the Treasury, 1888-93; mem. 53d to 60th Congresses (1893-1909), 8th Ia. Dist.; chmn. Rep. caucus 58th to 60th Congresses; chmn. Com. Interstate and Foreign Commerce, 59th and 60th Congresses. Home: Clarinda, Ia. Died Feb. 7, 1916.

HEPPENHEIMER, William Christian, chmn. bd. The Trust Co. of N.J.; b. N.Y. City, Mar. 27, 1860; s. Frederick and Christine (Hofer) H.; prep. edn., Hoboken (N.J.) Acad.; grad. Weinheim, Germany; LL.B., Columbia, 1880; grad. study Harvard, 1881-82; m. Blanche Miller, Apr. 30, 1890; children—Gladys (Lady Robert Vansittart), William C. Admitted to N.Y. bar, 1881, and began practice at N.Y. City, mem. Russ and Heppenheimer; admitted to N.J. bar, 1883; organizer and pres. People's Safe Deposit & Trust Co., Trust Co. of N.J., Bergen & Lafayette Trust Co., Carteret Trust; consol. same as The Trust Co. of N.J., 1913, now chmn. bd.; chmn. bd. Park Trust Co., Monitor Trust Co.; dir. and chmn. exec. com. Colonial Life Ins. Co. of America; dir. Empire Trust Co., Pub. Service Corp. of N.J. Mem. N.J. Gen. Assembly, 1887-91 (speaker 1890); comptroller of treasury, N.J., 1891-94; pres. bd. of finance, Jersey City, N.J., 1897, city treas., 1898-1901; mem. Port of New York Authority, 1928—; v.p. and commr. High Point Park. Mem. N.G.N.Y., 1879-86; a.d.c., rank of col., Gov. Green, 1887-89; brig. gen., serving as insp. gen., N.J.N.G.; chmn. dist. bd., N.J., World War. Former pres. and dir. N.J. State Chamber Commerce; chmn. bd. and dir. Jersey City Chamber Commerce. Democrat. Home: Jersey City, N.J. Died Sept. 16, 1933.

HEPWORTH, George Hughes, clergyman, author; b. Boston, Feb. 4, 1833; s. George and Charlotte H.; grad. Harvard Divinity School, 1855 (D.D.); m. Adaline A. Drury, April 25, 1860. Pastor Unitarian Ch., Nantucket, 1855-57; Ch. of the Unity, Boston, 1858-70; regimental chaplain, 1862-63; served on staff Gen. Banks in La.; pastor Ch. of the Messiah, New York, 1870-72; became a Trinitarian; pastor Ch. of the Disciples, 1872-79, and Belleville Av. Congl. Ch., Newark, 1882-85. From 1885 an editor on staff New York Herald and Telegram. Author: Hiram Golf's Religion; They Met in Heaven; The Life Beyond; Brown Studies; On Horseback Through Armenia; Rocks and Shoals; Starboard and Port; Whip, Hoe and Sword; The Farmer and the Lord. Died 1902.

HERBERMANN, Charles George, college prof.; b. near Münster, Westphalia, Prussia, Dec. 8, 1840; s. George and Elizabeth (Stipp) H.; came to U.S., 1851; A.B., Coll. St. Francis Xavier, New York, 1858, A.M., 1861, Ph.D., 1865 (LL.D., 1882; Litt.D., Holy Cross Coll., 1906, Catholic U., 1915; Knight of St. Gregory, 1909); m. Mary T. Dieter, July 6, 1873 (dec.); m. 2d, Elizabeth Scholb, 1880. Instr., 1858-69, prof. Latin lang. and lit., 1869-1915, emeritus prof., 1915, librarian, 1873—, Coll. City of N.Y. Editor-in-chief Catholic Ency., 1904—. Author: Business Life in Ancient Rome, 1879; also editions of Sallust's Jugurthine War and Bellum Catilinæ. Died Aug. 25, 1916.

HERBERT, Albert, cons. business engr.; b. Shrewsbury, Eng., Feb. 29, 1856; s. Thomas and Elizabeth (Norris) H.; ed. in Eng.; m. Jennie Wyatt, of Leamington, Eng., 1881; children—Harold (dec.), Major Wilwyn, Gladaid (dec., Mrs. Edward Neville Stent), Serval. Came to U.S., 1880; pres. Hub Gore Makers, mfrs. rubber elastic products, Boston, 1882-1900; pres., treas. Leolastic, Bayonne, Port of New York, 1903-13; dir. Everlastik Corp., rubber textile products, New York. Chmn. Carnegie Metric Com. of Nat. Assn. Mfrs., 1898, which reported unanimously for metric units; chmn. U.S. Am. Standardization Com., Internat. Chamber of Commerce, 1920 (Paris, London). Home: New York, N.Y. Deceased.

HERBERT, Hilary Abner, secretary of the navy; b. Laurensville, S.C., Mar. 12, 1834; s. Thomas E. and Dorothy Teague (Young) H.; family moved to Ala., 1846; student Univ. of Ala., 1853-54, Univ. of Va., 1854-56; (LL.D., Tulane Univ., and Univ. of Ala.); m. Ella B. Smith, Apr. 23, 1867. Admitted to bar, and practiced at Greenville, Ala., 1857-72; capt. to col. 8th Ala. Vols., C.S.A., 1861-64; moved to Montgomery, Ala., 1872; mem. 45th to 52d Congresses (1877-93); sec. of the navy in cabinet of President Cleveland, 1893-97. Democrat. In practice at Washington, 1897—; sr. mem. Herbert & Micou. Editor: Why the Solid South? or, Reconstruction and Its Results, 1890; The Abolition Crusade and Its Consequences, 1912. Grand marshal Confed. Vets. Reunion, Washington, June 1917. Home: Washington, D.C. Died Mar. 6, 1919.

HERBERT, James M., ry. pres.; b. Westmoreland Co., Pa., Jan. 15, 1863; s. John and Catherine (Dixon) H.; ed. Delmont (Pa.) Acad.; m. Emma M. Best, June 20, 1888. Telegraph operator, train dispatcher, chief train dispatcher and trainmaster, Wabash Ry., 1881-97; trainmaster and supt. Grand Trunk Ry. of Can., 1897-1901; supt. Mo. P. Ry., 1901-02; gen. supt. St.L.I.M.&S. Ry., 1902-03; mgr. S.P. Ry., 1903-04, D.&R.G. Ry., 1904-06; v.p. Colo. & Southern Ry.,1906-10; in other lines of business, 1910-14; pres. Colo., Wyo. & Eastern Ry., 1914-16, St.L.S.W. Ry., 1916—, also of subsidiary and affiliated cos. Republican. Episcopalian. Mason. Home: St. Louis, Mo. Died Aug. 5, 1923.

HERBERT, John F. J., federal prohibition administrator; b. Worcester, Mass. Formerly connected with newspapers in Mass.; served as prohibition administrator Baltimore-Washington dist., then Mont.-Ida. dist.; administrator dist. comprising Ill., Ind. and Wis., July 1930—. Served as comdr. 102d Field Arty., World War; overseas 19 mos. Deceased.

HERBERT, John Warne, lawyer; b. Marlboro, N.J., Aug. 3, 1853; s. John W. and Agnes D. (Wright) H.; B.S., Rutgers, 1872, M.S., 1875; LL.B., Columbia, 1876; also LL.D.; m. Olivia Antoinette Helme, Nov. 10, 1885; children—John Oliver (dec.), Gertrude A. (Mrs. Edward D. Dunn), John Warne III. Admitted to N.Y. and N.J. bars, 1876; practiced in Jersey City, 1876-89; counselor, 1879, special master in chancery, 1880; v.p. and treas. George W. Helme Co., 1889-1900; pres. Niagara, St. Catherine & Toronto R.R. Co. and Niagara, St. Catherine & Toronto Navigation Co., 1899-1905; v.p. Hudson Valley R.R. Co., 1900-06; became pres. Herbert Oil Co., Peoples Realty Co.; dir. numerous corps. Trustee Rutgers U., 1901—; mem. mng. com. N.J. State Agrl. Coll. Mayor of Helmetta, N.J., 1889-1902; chmn. N.J. State Highway Commn., 1916-19. Episcopalian; sr. warden St. Stephen's Ch., New York, and St. George's Ch., Helmetta. Homes: Helmetta, N.J., and New York, N.Y. Deceased.

HERBERT, Victor, conductor; b. Dublin, Ireland, Feb. 1, 1859; s. Edward and Fanny (Lover) H.; g.s. Samuel Lover, Irish novelist; began mus. edn. in Germany at 7, studying under leading masters; m. Therese Foerster, prima donna, Aug. 14, 1886. First position of prominence that of prin. violoncello player in Court Orchestra, Stuttgart; heard in concerts throughout Europe before coming to U.S. as solo violoncellist Metropolitan Orchestra, New York, 1886; since then has been connected with Theodore Thomas', Seidl's and other orchestral orgns. as soloist and conductor. Bandmaster 22d Regt. Band, New York, 1894; conductor Pittsburgh, Pa., Orchestra, 1898-1904. Victor Herbert's New York Orchestra, 1904—. Composer: "The Captive" (oratorio written for and performed at Worcester, Mass., Festival); "Prince Ananias"; "The Wizard of the Nile"; "The Serenade"; "Cyrano de Bergerac"; "The Ameer"; "The Viceroy"; "The Idol's Eye"; "The Fortune Teller"; "The Singing Girl"; "Babette"; "Babes in Toyland"; "It Happened in Nordland" (all comic operas); also several compositions for orchestra, songs and a concert for violoncello and orchestra. Mem. Nat. Inst. Arts and Letters. Wrote score for play "The Only Girl," prod. London, 1915. Home: New York, N.Y. Died May 26, 1924.

HERDMAN, William James, M.D.; b. Concord, O., Sept. 7, 1848; s. James H.; ed. Westminster Coll., Pa.; grad. Univ. of Mich. Ph.B., 1872; med. dept., 1875 (LL.D., U. of Nashville); m. Nancy Bradley Thomas, Sept. 16, 1873. Mem. faculty Univ. of Mich., 1875—; demonstrator of anatomy, 1875-89; prof. pathol. anatomy, 1880-82; prof. practical anatomy, 1882-90, then lecturer on med. jurisprudence in law dept. and prof. diseases of the mind and nervous system, U. of Mich. Home: Ann Arbor, Mich. Died 1906.

HEREFORD, William Richard, journalist, banker; b. St. Joseph, Mo., Feb. 2, 1871; s. Alfred P. and Elizabeth (Powell) H.; student Randolph-Macon Coll., Va., and Harvard Law Sch., 1892-93; m. Frances Reynolds, Dec. 26, 1899. Admitted to bar at Kansas City, 1893; began newspaper work on Kansas City Times, 1890; on editorial staff New York Recorder, 1895; sec. to Am. minister to Switzerland, 1895-97; on editorial staff New York Journal, 1897-1902, New York Herald, 1902-04; editor European edit. New York Herald, 1904-07; Paris corr. New York World, Nov., 1908-13. Made tour of S. America with Robert Bacon in interests of Carnegie Foundation of Internat. Peace, 1913; exec. sec. Am. Com. of Am. Ambulance Hosp., Paris, and Am. Ambulance Field Service, 1914-17; maj. and dep. commr. Am. Red Cross Commn. in Italy, Dec. 1917-Mar. 1919; dir. dept. publs. League of Red Cross Socs., hdqrs. Geneva, Switzerland, May 1919; now dir. fgn. information service, Bankers Trust Co., Paris. Awarded bronze medal, Conciliation Internationale, 1913; Chevalier Order of the Crown (Italy); silver medal of merit, Italian Red Cross; Am. Field Service medal. Author: The Demagog, 1909; When Fools Rush In, 1913. Home: Paris, France. Died Sept. 21, 1928.

HERFORD, Oliver, author; b. Dec. 1863; s. Dr. Brooke and Hannah (Hankinson) H.; ed. Lancaster Coll., Eng. and Antioch (O.) Coll.; art studies, Slade Sch., London, and Julian's, Paris; m. Margaret Regan, of London, May 26, 1904. Mem. Nat. Inst. Arts and Letters. Author: Rubaiyat of a Persian Kitten, 1904; The Fairy God-Mother-in-Law, 1905; The Astonishing Tale of a Pen and Ink Puppet, 1907; Peter Pan Alphabet, 1909; Cupid's Encyclopedia, 1910; Happy Days (with J. Cecil Clay), 1911; Kitten's Garden of Verses, 1911; The Mythological Zoo, 1914; Confessions of a Caricaturist, 1917; Cynic's Calendar, 1917; Excuse it Please, 1930; Sea Legs, 1931; The Deb's Dictionary, 1931. Also four plays The Devil, The Florist Shop, The Love Cure, Con & Co. Home: New York, N.Y. Died July 5 1935.

HERING, Carl, electrical engr.; b. Phila., Mar. 29, 1860; s. late Dr. Constantine and Therese (Buchheim) H.; B.S., U. of Pa., 1880, M.E., 1887, hon. D.Sc., 1912; post-grad. studies at Darmstadt, Germany, 1883-84; married; 1 dau., Mary Truesdell. Instr. several yrs., U. of Pa., and Polytechnikum, Darmstadt; practiced elec. engring. in Frankfort (Germany), 1884, and Phila. to date; splty. elec. furnaces, electrochemistry, physical research, and patent litigation. Del. and juror of wards at 12 expns.; U.S. juror, Paris expns., 1889, 1900; U.S. del. Internat. Elec. Congress, Paris, 1900; Am. delegate several internat. conferences. Decorated Légion d'Honneur, 1901; Officier de l'Instruction Publique, 1889, both by French Govt. Pres. Am. Inst. Elec. Engrs., 1900-01, Am. Electrochem. Soc., 1906-07, Engrs'. Club, Phila., 1904, Phys. Club of Phila., 1918; fellow Am. Institute Electrical Engineers, Physical Society, A.A.A.S. Formerly compiler of "Digest of Electrical Literature." Author: Conversion Tables, 1904; Tables of Electrochemical Equivalents, 1917, etc. Home: Philadelphia, Pa. Died May 10, 1926.

HERING, Daniel Webster, educator; b. Washington Co., Md., Mar. 23, 1850; s. Joshua and Susannah (Harman) H.; Ph.B., Sheffield Scientific Sch. (Yale), 1872, C.E., 1878; fellow Johns Hopkins, in engring., 1876-78; hon. Ph.D., Western Md. Coll., 1895; LL.D., U. of Pittsburgh, 1907, New York U., 1916; m. Mary Hollis Webster, Nov. 23, 1881; children—Doris Webster, Hollis Webster. Professor mathematics, Western Md. Coll., 1880-84; professor physics, Western Univ. of Pa., 1884-85; prof. physics and applied mechanics, 1885-1916, emeritus prof. physics, 1916, and dean grad. faculty, 1902-15, New York U. Fellow N.Y. Acad. Sciences (v.p.), A.A.A.S., Am. Physical Society, Am. Geog. Soc., etc. Author: Essentials of Physics, 2d edit., 1921; Physics the Science of the Forces of Nature; Foibles and Fallacies of Science, 1924; Electrical Units; The Lure of the Clock, 1932. Curator of James Arthur Collection of clocks and watches, New York Univ. Home: New York, N.Y. Died Mar. 24, 1938.

HERING, Hermann S., Christian Science lecturer; b. Phila., Pa., Aug. 24, 1864; s. Constantine (M.D.) and Therese (Buchheim) H.; B.Sc. and M.E., U. of Pa., 1886; spl. course in elec. engring., City and Guilds of London Inst., London, Eng., 1889; C.S.B., Mass. Metaphys. Coll., 1901; m. Marian White, June 9, 1887. Began with Phila. Manual Training Sch., 1886, prof. mechanics and elec. engring., 1889-91; asso. in elec. engring., Johns Hopkins, 1891-99; engaged in Christian Science work, 1897—; reader Christian Science Ch., Baltimore, Md., 5 yrs.; 1st reader in Mother Ch., Boston, 1902-05, and was made pres. of the ch. and mem. Bd. of Lectureship; reader of ch. at Concord, N.H., 1906-09; lecturer from 1905, in U.S., Can., and foreign countries. Republican. Home: Penacook, N.H. Died May 15, 1940.

HERING, Oswald Constantin, architect; b. Philadelphia, Jan. 12, 1874; s. Rudolph and Fanny Field (Gregory) H.; grad. Chauncy Hall Sch., Boston, Mass., 1890; student Mass. Inst. Tech., 1893-97, École des Beaux Arts, Paris, 1897-99; m. Adelaide Heriot Arms, June 17, 1933. Began practice in N.Y. City, 1900. Architect: Brentanos, N.Y. City, 1926; Lakewood Theatre, Skowhegan, Me., 1928; residences on Long Island and Westchester Co., N.Y., suburbs of Phila., Pa., and scattered through N.E., Middle Atlantic and Middle Western states, including "Trailsend," home of hon. James M. Cox. Vet. 7th Regt. N.G.N.Y. Independent Republican. Author: Concrete and Stucco Houses, 1912; Economy in Home Building, 1924; Designing and Building the Chapter House, 1931; Down the World, 1932. Editor Delta Kappa Epsilon Quarterly and Sons of The Revolution Quarterly. Home: New York, N.Y. Died Mar. 6, 1941.

HERING, Rudolph, hydraulic and sanitary engr.; b. Phila., Feb. 26, 1847; s. Dr. Constantine and Theresa (Buchheim) H.; grad. Dresden Poly. (Germany), 1867; asst. engr. Prospect Park, Brooklyn, 1868; asst. engr. Fairmount Park, Phila., 1869-71; astronomer Yellowstone Nat. Park, 1872; asst. city engr. Phila., 1873-80; from then in private practice. Investigation for new water supply of Phila., 1883-86; chief engr. Chicago Drainage and Water Supply Commn., 1886-88; cons. engr., dept. of public works, New York, 1889; m. Hermine, d. Prof. Dr. Buchheim, govt. councilor of Giessen, Germany, 1894. Consulting engr. for water supply and sewerage works, Phila., Baltimore, Washington, Buffalo, Cleveland, Atlanta, Montgomery, New Orleans, Los Angeles, Tacoma, Victoria, San Francisco, Honolulu, Columbus, O., and now for Dept. of Water Supply, Gas and Electricity, New York; etc. Home: Montclair, N.J. Died May 30, 1923.

HERMANCE, William Ellsworth, author; b. Cuba, N.Y., Apr. 17, 1862; s. Robert G. and Idah (Matthews) H.; ed. U. of Neb., 1877-79; m. Frances Ellen Paxson, Dec. 29, 1891. Cowboy, Kan. and Neb., 1879-84; warden insane dept. of almshouse, Pittsfield, Mass., 1885; trip in canoe, Yellowstone Park to Gulf of Mexico (4,500 miles), July 1885-Mar. 1886; settled in Norfolk Co., Va., 1889. Author: An Unorthodox Conception of Being, 1912; Common Sense Philosophy, 1924. Home: Indian River, Va. Died Sept. 27, 1927.

HERMANN, Binger, lawyer; b. Lonaconing, Md., Feb. 19, 1843; s. Dr. Henry and Elizabeth (Hopkins) H.; ed. in dist. schs. and at Independent Acad. (afterward Irving Coll.) near Baltimore; moved to Ore. with father, 1859; taught sch. in Canyonville, Ore. Admitted to Ore. bar, 1866; practiced at Roseburg; mem. Ore. Ho. of Rep., 1866, Senate, 1868-71; receiver U.S. land office Roseburg, 1871-73; mem. 49th Congress (1885-87) and 51st to 54th Congresses (1889-97); commr. Gen. Land Office, 1897-1903 (resigned); elected to 58th Congress, June 1, 1903, to fill vacancy; reëlected to 59th Congress (1905-07), 1st Ore. Dist. Republican. Judge advocate, with rank of col., Ore. militia, 1882-84. Mem. Nat. Com. to establish Univ. of U.S. Home: Roseburg, Ore. Died Apr. 16, 1926.

HERNANDEZ, José Conrado, judge; b. Aibonito, P.R., Feb. 19, 1849; s. Pedro José and Anna Maria (Santiago) H.; A.B., Jesuits' Coll., San Juan, P.R., 1865; LL.B., LL.M., U. of Salamanca, Spain, 1873; D.D., Salamanca Central Coll.; LL.D., U. of Puerto Rico, 1916; m. Angela Usera; children—José, Angela, Carmen, Dolores, Pedro A., Vicente, Maria Asuncion, Conchita, Ana Maria. After graduation, practiced as lawyer in Puerto Rico, 2 years; admitted to bar U.S. Supreme Court, 1917; entered Spanish judiciary as assisting prosecuting atty., 1877; held similiar position at Humacao, P.R., until Feb. 1880; judge of first instance of Aguadilla, P.R., 1880-83, of Mayaguez, P.R., 1883-84; asst. pros. atty., dist. of Catedral, San Juan, P.R., 1884-87; judge of first instance, dist. of Santiago de Cuba, 1888-89; judge in Criminal Ct. of Pinar del Rio, Cuba, 1889-90, Santa Clara, Cuba, 1890-91; transferred to P.I., as judge of Supreme Ct., Cebu, P.I., 1881-93; prosecuting atty., Vigan, Luzon Island, 1893-94; judge Supreme Ct., Manila, P.I., 1894-98; while in Philippines received spl. commn. from Manila Supreme Ct. to prosecute insular treas. and officials of Treasury Dept. for embezzlement of $1,500,000; later sent specially to Cebú to investigate charges against Gen. Junquera, then governor of that island, by order of Supreme Ct. of Spain; judge of Circuit Ct. (Audiencia Territorial), San Juan, P.R., Sept.-Oct. 1898; apptd. by Maj.-Gen. Brooke presiding judge Supreme Ct. of P.R., Oct. 1898, and asso. justice Supreme Ct. of P.R. by Gen. George W. Davis, Aug. 1899; upon establishment of civil govt. in P.R., became asso. justice Supreme Ct. until apptd. chief justice, Apr. 9, 1909; voluntarily resigned Dec. 7, 1921, after 10 yrs.' service. Catholic. Home: San Juan, P.R. Died June 20, 1932.

HERNE, James A., actor and playwright; b. Troy, N.Y., 1839; made his first appearance in a small traveling company, with which he remained a few weeks; in April, 1859, appeared at Adelphi Theatre, Troy, N.Y.; later in various companies; became a "star" and from 1878 has appeared in his own plays. Author (plays): Hearts of Oak; The Minute Men; Drifting Apart; Margaret Fleming; Shore Acres. Home: New York, N.Y. Died 1901.

HERO, Andrew, Jr., army officer; b. New Orleans, La., Dec. 13, 1868; s. Andrew and Otweana R. (Pugh) H.; Tulane U., New Orleans, 3 yrs., Columbia, 1 yr.; grad. U.S. Mil. Acad., 1891, Arty. Sch., 1896; m. Fanny Caroline, d. Capt. J. M. K. Davis, July 14, 1897; children—Jacklyn (wife of H. W. Brimmer, U.S. Army), Prentice, Elinor Kelso (Mrs. T. G. Murrell), Andrew. Commissioned 2d lt., 12th Infantry, June 12, 1891; promoted through grades to col., Coast Arty. Corps, May 15, 1917; brig. gen. N.A., Aug. 5, 1917. Special work in electricity, Arty. Sch., 1896-98; with 3d Div., 1st Army Corps, Chickamauga Park, 1898-99, Matanzas, Cuba, Jan.-May 1899; instr. in drawing, U.S. Mil. Acad., 1899-1902; editor Jour. U.S. Arty., 1902-07; asst. to chief Coast Arty., 1909-11; brigade adj., 1st Separate Brigade, Galveston, Tex., Mar.-June 1911; adj. S. Atlantic Coast Arty. Dist., Charleston, S.C., 1913-15; comd. 1st Federal Training Camp for Boys, Ft. Terry, N.Y., July 6-Aug. 10, 1916; comd. 154th F.A. Brig., 79th Div., Sept. 17, 1917-Dec. 9, 1918, and Feb. 1-May 25, 1919, Camp Meade, Md., training to July 14, 1918, Liverpool, Eng., July 31, 1918, firing schools, France, Aug. 8,-Nov. 19, 1918; with 153d F.A. Brig., Meuse-Argonne offensive, Nov. 1, 1918; on duty G.H.Q., A.E.F., Dec. 9, 1918-Jan. 31, 1919; army center of arty. studies, Treves, Germany, Feb. 16-Apr. 2, 1919; brigade joined div., Dec. 1918; left France, May 15, 1919; comd. 39th Arty. Brig. (C.A.C.), May 25, 1919-Oct. 4, 1921; staff, 2d C.A. Dist., Oct. 1921-Nov. 1922; Coast Defense, Manila and Subic Bays, Jan. 1923-Mar. 1925; comd. 4th C.A. Dist., June-Dec. 1925; chief C.A.C., rank of maj. gen., Mar. 1926-Mar. 1930; maj. gen. retired, May 1930. Republican. Episcopalian. Home: Washington, D.C. Died Feb. 7, 1942.

HEROD, William Pirtle, lawyer; b. Columbus, Ind., July 27, 1864; s. William Wirt and Susan Coons (Rogers) Herod; B.A., Yale, 1886; m. Mary Beaty Applegate, June 5, 1890 (died 1923); children—Bergen, Mary Beaty (Mrs. Nelson M. Graves), William Rogers. Admitted to Indiana bar, 1887, to bar of U.S. Supreme Court, 1905; mem. Herod & Herod, 1887-1904; now gen. counsel Grain Dealers Nat. Mutual Fire Ins. Co. U.S. commr. Dist. of Ind., 4 yrs.; mem. faculty and prof. med. jurisprudence, Central Coll. Phys. and Surg., Indianapolis, 4 yrs.; has served as spl. judge Superior Court, Marion Co., Ind. Trustee Boys Prep. Sch., Indianapolis; dir. James Whitcomb Riley Memorial Assn. Receiver Central Ind. Ry. Co., Lexington Motor Co. Vol. at War Coll., Washington, winter 1917, 1918, Mil. Intelligence Sect. Gen. Staff; mem. exec. com. War Camp Community Service; br. chmn. Mil. Training Camps Assn.; civilian aide to adj. gen. U.S.A., etc. Republican. Home: Indianapolis, Ind. Deceased.

HERR, Edwin Musser, electrical and mech. engr.; b. Lancaster, Pa., May 3, 1860; s. Theodore W. and Annie (Musser) H.; Ph.B., Sheffield Scientific Sch. (Yale), 1884; D.Sc., Franklin and Marshall Coll., Pa., 1911; A.M., Yale, 1915; m. Mary Forsyth, June 14, 1900. Engr. of tests, supt. telegraph and div. supt. C.,B.&Q. Ry., 1886-1900; div. master mechanic, C.,M.&St.P. Ry., 1891; gen. supt. Grant Locomotive Works, Chicago, 1892-93; gen. mgr. Gibbs Electric Co., Milwaukee, 1894; asst. supt. motive power C.& N.W. Ry., 1895; supt. motive power, N.P. Ry., 1896-98; gen. mgr., Westinghouse Air Brake Co., 1898-1905; 1st v.p., 1905-11, pres., Aug. 1911-May 1929, now vice-chmn. Westinghouse Electric & Mfg. Co. Republican. Home: New York, N.Y. Died Dec. 24, 1932.

HERR, Herbert Thacker, mech. engr.; b. Denver, Colo., Mar. 19, 1876; s. Theodore Witmer and Emma (Musser) H.; grad. East Denver High Sch., 1895; Ph.B., Yale, 1899; m. Irene Viancourt, Feb. 10, 1896; children—Herbert Thacker, Muriel Viancourt. Began with D.&R.G. R.R., 1899, later with C.G.W. Ry., and Norfolk & Western R.R.; apptd. gen. supt. D.&R.G. R.R., 1906; closely associated with George Westinghouse during the last 7 yrs. of his life, 1907-14; v.p., gen. mgr., Westinghouse Machine Co., 1908-15; v.p. Westinghouse Electric & Mfg. Co., 1915—; v.p. Westinghouse Gear & Dynamometer Co. Inventor locomotive air brake equipment (Westinghouse Air Brake Co.), improvements in turbines, oil and gas engines, remote control for marine steam turbines (in electrically propelled U.S. battleships), etc. Awarded Longstreth Medal by Franklin Inst., 1914; John Scott medal by Bd. of Dirs. of City Trusts, Phila., for sundry inventions, discoveries and improvements in mechanical apparatus, 1931. Republican. Episcopalian. Home: Philadelphia, Pa. Died Dec. 19, 1933.

HERR, Hiero Benjamin, mining engr.; b. Lancaster Co., Pa., Nov. 12, 1842; s. Benjamin G. and Mary Emma (Witmer) H.; grad. U.S. Mil. Acad., 1866; m. Martha A. Shenk, June 25, 1868. Second lt. and 1st lt., U.S. Arty.; resigned May 15, 1870; in charge mathematics, etc., Lehigh U., Bethlehem, Pa., 1870-74; supt. silver mines in Colo., 1874-78; in charge engring. parties in Miss., for U.S. Govt., 1879-82; made survey for location Miss. and Ill. Canal, 1882; in charge dept. civ. engring., U. of Calif., 1883-84; engring. business, Chicago, as Hiero B. Herr & Co., 1884-95; pres. Chicago Star Constrn. Co., 1895-1900; cons. mining engr., 1911—. Republican. Home: Carlisle, Pa. Died Sept. 3, 1920.

HERREID, Charles N., governor; b. Dane Co., Wis., Oct. 20, 1857; s. N. and Tena (Kytle) H.; ed. Galesville (Wis.) U.; LL.B., U. of Wis., 1882; m. Jeanette E. Slye, 1882; children—Mrs. Grace Lightner, Roscoe Conkling (dec.). Went to McPherson Co., S.D., 1883; state's atty., and judge Co. Ct.; lt. gov. of S.D., 1892-94, and 1894-96; never had a ruling questioned, or decision as presiding officer of Senate appealed from, during his 2 terms; chmn. Rep. State Central Com. and acting mem. Rep. Nat. Com., 1898-1900; gov. of S.D., 1900-02 and 1902-04. In law practice at Aberdeen, S.D., 1905-15; also dir. Western Mutual Life Ins. Co.; v.p. Dak. Central Telephone Co.; pres. Citizens Trust & Savings Bank. Federal food adminstr. for S.D. (exclusively), Oct. 1917-Nov. 1919; chmn. for S.D. of Mil. Training Camps Assn., and mem. state coms. of Red Cross and Belgian relief. Trustee U. of S.D., 1897, and mem. bd. regents of edn., S.D., 1898-1900. Past Grand Chancellor and Supreme Rep. K. of P. Mason. Presbyterian. Pres. S. Dak. Hist. Soc., 1923-24. Home: Aberdeen, S.D. Died July 6, 1928.

HERRESHOFF, James Brown, inventor; b. Bristol, R.I., Mar. 18, 1834; s. Charles Frederick and Julia Ann (Lewis) H.; student Brown U., 1853-56; m. Jane Brown, of Dromore, Ireland, 1875; children—James Brown, Charles Frederick, William Stuart, Jane Brown, Ann Frances. Supt. Rumford (R.I.) Chem. Works, 1858-63; mfr. fish oil, Prudence Island, R.I., 1863-69. Resided in Europe, much of time since 1869, giving attention to inventions, among the more important of which are: first naphtha driven motorcycle of internal combustion type in America (1870); coil boiler; fin-keel for sailing yachts; mercurial antifouling paint; sliding-seat for rowboats; thread-tension regulator for sewing machines; apparatus for measuring specific heat of gases; sounding apparatus, etc. Home: New York, N.Y. Died Dec. 5, 1930.

HERRESHOFF, John Brown, shipbuilder; b. Bristol, R.I., Apr. 24, 1841; s. Charles Frederick and Julia Ann (Lewis) H.; brother of Nathaniel Greene and J. B. Francis H.; ed. in schs. of Bristol; became totally blind at 15; m. Sarah Lucas Kilton, Oct. 6, 1870; m. 2d, Eugenia T. Tucker, Apr. 27, 1892. In 1863 began business of yacht-building in Bristol, firm being Herreshoff & Stone, 1863-66, John B. Herreshoff, 1866-79, Herreshoff Mfg. Co., 1879—, he being pres. Since 1868 the company has built steam as well as sailing yachts; also vessels for the U.S., English, French, Russian, Spanish and Peruvian govts. With brother, N. H., improved the "coil-boiler" invented by their brother, J. B. H. Address: Bristol, R.I. Died July 20, 1915.

HERRESHOFF, J(ohn) B(rown) Francis, chemist; b. Bristol, R.I., Feb. 7, 1850; s. Charles Frederick and Julia Ann (Lewis) H.; student Brown U., class of 1870, Ph.B., by spl. vote, 1905, hon. A.M., 1890, Sc.D., 1909; m. Grace Eugenia, d. John Dyer, of Providence, R.I., Feb. 9, 1876; m. 2d, at Phila., Emily Duval, d. Dr. Richard Henry Lee, Oct. 25, 1882; m. 3d, Carrie Ridley Enslow, d. Dr. James Lucas Ridley, of Hoboken, N.J., June 9, 1919 (died 1924); m. 4th, at Chattanooga, Tenn., Irma Grey, d. Dr. James Lucas Ridley, Apr. 14, 1925. Prof. analyt. chemistry, Brown U., 1869-72; supt. Laurel Hill Chem. Works, L.I., 1876; invented process for mfg. sulphuric acid; now v.p. and trustee Nichols Copper Co.; dir. Granby Consol. Mining, Smelting & Power Co.; hon. v.p. Gen. Chem. Co. Awarded Perkin medal (1st time awarded in America) for work in chem. and metall. industries. Home: New York, N.Y., and Atlanta, Ga. Died Jan. 30, 1932.

HERRESHOFF, Nathanael Greene, shipbuilder; b. Bristol, R.I., 1848; s. Charles Frederick and Julia Ann (Lewis) H.; ed. pub. schs., Bristol, R.I., and Mass. Inst. Tech., 1866-69; spl. tech. edn. in engring.; (Sc.M., Brown U., 1896); m. Clara A. DeWolf, Dec. 26, 1883 (died 1905); children—Agnes Muller, Algernon Sidney DeWolf, Nathanael G. (dec.), Alexander Griswold, Lewis Francis, Clarence DeWolf; m. 2d, Ann Roebuck, Oct. 7, 1915. Designer of many yachts and torpedo boats built by Herreshoff Mfg. Co., of which was supt., 1881-1915, pres., 1915-24 (retired). Home: Bristol, R.I. Died June 2, 1938.

HERRICK, Clarence Luther, supt. Socorro Gold Mining Co.; b. Minneapolis, Minn., June 21, 1858; s. Rev. Henry N. H.; grad. Univ. of Minn., 1880 (M.S., 1882; Ph.D., 1898); m. Alice Keith, June 21, 1883. Studied at Leipzig and Berlin; became, consecutively, instr. botany, U. of Minn. (served on geol. survey of Minn.); prof. natural history, Denison Univ.; prof. biology, U. of Cincinnati, Univ. of Chicago, Denison Univ.; pres. Univ. of N.Mex.; asso. editor Am. Geologist; editor Bulls. of Denison Univ.; editor-in-chief Jour. of Comparative Neurology. Author: Mammals of Minnesota; Entomostraca of Minnesota; Waverly Group of Ohio. Home: Magdalena, N.Mex. Died 1903.

HERRICK, D-Cady, lawyer; b. Esperance, N.Y., Apr. 12, 1846; s. Jonathan and Harriet H.; ed. Albany Classical Inst.; studied law with Lyman Tremain and Justice Rufus W. Peckham; LL.B., Albany Law Sch., 1868; admitted to bar, 1868; m. Orissa H. Salisbury. Dem. nominee for dist. atty., Albany Co., 1877; elected dist. atty., 1880, 1883; mem. Dem. State Com., 1885; corp. counsel, Albany, 1886-91; justice Supreme Ct. of N.Y., 1891-Dec. 31, 1905; served as asso. justice Appellate Div., 1894-1905; candidate for gov., N.Y., 1904. Democrat. Dir. Albany City Nat. Bank. Home: Albany, N.Y. Died Feb. 21, 1926.

HERRICK, Francis Hobart, biologist; b. Woodstock, Vt., Nov. 19, 1858; s. Rev. Marcellus Aurelius and Hannah Andrews (Putnam) H.; A.B., Dartmouth, 1881; Ph.D., Johns Hopkins, 1888; Sc.D., Western U. of Pa., 1897, Western Reserve U., 1936; m. Josephine Herkomer, Eng., June 24, 1897; children—Agnes Elizabeth (Mrs. Hans Platenius), Francis Herkomer. Instr. biology, 1888-91, prof., 1891-1929, prof. emeritus, 1929, Adelbert Coll., Western Reserve U. Fellow A.A.A.S., Am. Ornithologists' Union. Trustee Cleveland Mus. of Natural History, 1920—, v.p., 1928—. Author: Audubon the Naturalist, 2 vols., 1917, 1 vol. edit., 1938; The American Eagle on the Shores of Lake Erie, 1925, 27; The American Eagle—A Study in Natural and Civil History, 1934; Wild Birds at Home, 1935. Home: Cleveland Heights, O. Died Sept. 11, 1940.

HERRICK, George Frederick, missionary; b. Milton, Vt., Apr. 19, 1834; s. Russell and Maria (Tyler) H.; A.B., U. of Vt., 1856 (D.D., 1878); grad. Andover Theol. Sem., 1859; m. Helen M., d. C. S. Richards, LL.D., Aug. 16, 1861. Missionary A.B.C.F.M. (Congl.) in Turkey, 1859—; instr. Mission Theol. Sem., 1868-93; pres. Anatolia Coll., 1890-93; Bible translator and reviser into Turkish, 1873-78, 1883-85, and 1899-1903; joint supt. publ. work, 1893-1911, retired. Author of books in Turkish lang., published by Mission Press, Constantinople, including brief notes on most of the books of the Bible, 1866-1903; Christian and Mohammedan, 1912. Home: New York, N.Y. Died Oct. 28, 1926.

HERRICK, Harold; b. N.Y. City, Nov. 26, 1853; s. Jonathan K. and Elizabeth (Tiller) H.; ed. pvt. schs., N.Y. City; m. Annie T. Lawrence, Nov. 26, 1878. Began in ins. office of France, Hare & Lockwood, New York, 1872; became rep. of Mich., Mo. and Pa. cos. in New York, 1887, also gen. ins. business; v.p. Niagara Fire Ins. Co., 1894-96, pres., 1896-1917. Republican. Episcopalian. Home: Lawrence, L.I., N.Y. Died May 27, 1933.

HERRICK, Henry W., artist; b. Hopkinton, N.H., Aug. 23, 1824; s. Israel E. and Martha (Trow) H.; ed. Nashua, N.H., pub. schs. and Hancock Acad., Hancock, N.H.; m. Clara H. Parkinson, 1849. Was engraver in New York in 1844; teacher and mgr. New York Sch. of Design for Women, Cooper Inst., 1853-59; also designer and draftsman for book and periodical illustrations; has been designer and artist with Am. Bank Note Co. Home: Manchester, N.H. Died 1906.

HERRICK, Lott Russell, judge; b. Farmer City, Ill., Dec. 8, 1871; s. George W. and Dora C. (Knight) H.; B.L., U. of Ill., 1892; LL.B., U. of Mich., 1894; m. Harriet N. Swigart, Apr. 2, 1896; children—Mildred (Mrs. Ralph L. McClelland, dec.), Helen (Mrs. James G. Thomas). Admitted to Ill. bar, 1894; in practice, Farmer City, Ill., 1894-1933; co. judge De Witt County, Ill., 1902-04; justice Supreme Court of Ill., 1933—. Pres. bd. Moore Twp. High Sch. Democrat. Mason. Home: Farmer City, Ill. Died Sept. 18, 1937.

HERRICK, Lucius Carroll, M.D.; genealogist; b. Randolph, Vt., Sept. 2, 1840; s. Lorenzo Dow and Zilpha A. (Haskins) H.; grad. med. dept., Univ. of Vt.; m. Louise Taylor, Aug. 16, 1871. Private 8th Vt. inf., 1861-63; asst. surgeon 4th colored cav., Nov. 1863 to March 1866; practiced medicine, New York, 1866-68; Woodstock, O., 1868-82; then at Columbus, O. Author: Herrick Genealogy, 1885; sec. and librarian The "Old Northwest" Genealogical Soc. Editor The "Old Northwest" Genealogical Quarterly; also of The Year Book of the Ohio Soc. of the S.A.R. for 1898 and 1900. Home: Columbus, O. Died 1903.

HERRICK, Myron T., ambassador; b. Huntington, O., Oct. 9, 1854; s. Timothy R. and Mary L. H.; student Oberlin Coll. and Ohio Wesleyan U.; hon. A.M., Ohio Wesleyan, 1899; LL.D., Princeton, Harvard, Columbia, Western Reserve, 1915, Union, 1916, Yale, 1917; doctor, honoris causa, Univ. of Nancy, 1921; m. Carolyn M., d. of M. B. Parmley, of Dayton, O., June 30, 1880 (died as result of war work, Sept. 15, 1918); 1 son, Parmley. Admitted to bar, 1878; practiced at Cleveland, 1878-86; sec.-treas., 1886-94, later pres., chmn. bd. Soc. for Savings, Cleveland; chmn. bd. Union Carbide & Carbon Co.; dir. N.Y. Life Ins. Co. Mem. City Council, Cleveland, 1895-98; presdl. elector, Ohio-at-large, 1892; was mem. Rep. State Exec. Com. and mem. Rep. Nat. Com.; on staff Governor (later President) McKinley, with rank of col. Gov. of Ohio, 1903-06; ambassador to France, Feb. 15, 1912-Dec. 1914, again Apr. 1921—. Received Grand Cross of Legion of Honor, of France. Pres. Am. Bankers' Assn. and was 1st pres. savings bank sect. same. Trustee Carnegie Instn. of Washington. Chmn. Am. Com. for Devastated France. Organized Am. Relief Clearing House in Paris, and in the U.S.—the War Relief Clearing House—with which was associated during war; established the Am. Ambulance Hosp. at Neuilly, France; chmn. of War Camp Community Service; chmn. of Mayor's War Relief Com., Cleveland, Ohio. Home: Chagrin Falls, O. Died Mar. 31, 1929.

HERRICK, Parmely Webb, banker, realtor; b. Cleveland, O., Nov. 22, 1881; s. Myron Timothy and Caroline M. (Parmely) H.; student Harvard, 1900-04; m. Agnes Blackwell, June 6, 1906; children—Myron T. II (dec.), Parmely W. With Hayden-Clinton Bank, Columbus, O., and Citizens Savings & Trust Co., Cleveland, O., 1904-07; mgr. Herrick, Parmelee & Crawford, 1907-15; pres. The Herrick Co., 1915-30; pres. and dir. Cuyahoga Co., Sun Investing Co., Thomas Young Nurseries, Inc. (Del.). Served as maj., Q.M.C., liaison officer to dir. purchase, storage and traffic, and acting q.m. gen., also mem. U.S. Food Administration, World War. Treas. McKinley Nat. Memorial Assn. Decorated Chevalier Legion of Honor (France); Chevalier Order of Crown (Belgium). Republican. Episcopalian. Home: New York, N.Y. Died July 7, 1937.

HERRICK, Robert, author; b. Cambridge, Mass., Apr. 26, 1868; s. William Augustus and Harriet (Emery) H.; A.B., Harvard, 1890; m. Harriet Emery, June 9, 1894. Instructor in rhetoric, Mass. Inst. of Tech., 1890-93; instr. in rhetoric, 1893-95, asst. prof., 1895-1901, asso. prof., 1901-05, prof. English, 1905-23, U. of Chicago. Apptd. govt. secretary of Virgin Islands, Jan. 1935. Author: The Gospel of Freedom, 1898; Composition and Rhetoric (with Prof. L. T. Damon), 1899; The Web of Life, 1900; The Common Lot, 1904; The Memoirs of an American Citizen, 1905; The Master of the Inn, 1908; Together, 1908; One Woman's Life, 1913; Clark's Field, 1914; The World Decision, 1916; Homely Lilla, 1923; Waste, 1924; Wanderings, 1925; Chimes, 1926; Little Black Dog, 1931; The End of Desire, Sometime, 1933. Home: York Village, Me. Died Dec. 23, 1938.

HERRICK, Samuel Edward, Congl. clergyman; b. Southampton, N.Y., April 6, 1841; s. Austin and Mary Wells (Jagger) H.; grad. Amherst, 1859 (D.D., 1878); Princeton Theol. Sem., 1863; m. Sophia W. Foster, April 6, 1864. Minister of Mt. Vernon Ch., Boston, 1871—; mem. Mass. Hist. Soc. Author: Some Heretics of Yesterday, 1884. Home: Boston, Mass. Died 1904.

HERRICK, Sophia M'Ilvaine Bledsoe, author; b. Kenyon Coll., Mar. 26, 1837; d. Albert Taylor and Harriet (Coxe) Bledsoe; educated Miss Coxe's, Cincinnati, and Cooper Inst., Dayton, O.; m. James B. Herrick, 1860. Teacher and prin. of sch. in Baltimore, 1868-72; asso. editor and bus. mgr. Southern Review, Baltimore, 1875-78; on editorial staff Scribner's Magazine and its successor, The Century, 1878-1907. Author: The Earth in Past Ages; Wonders of Plant Life. Home: New York, N.Y. Died 1919.

HERRICK, Stephen Solon, M.D.; b. Randolph, Vt., Dec. 11, 1833; s. Lorenzo Dow and Zilpha Ann (Haskins) H.; grad. Dartmouth Coll., 1854; Univ. of La., M.D., 1861; m. Julia Cowand, 1867. Asst. surgeon C.S.A., 1862; asst. surgeon C.S.N., 1863-65; in health dept., New Orleans, insp. and sec., 1869-86; in health dept., San Francisco and State of Calif., 1888-90; prof. chemistry, New Orleans School of Medicine, 1869-70; prof. natural science, La. Agrl. and Mech. Coll., 1876-77; on editorial staff New Orleans Med. and Surg. Journal, 1866-84; practiced medicine New Orleans, 1865-87, then in San Francisco. Home: San Francisco, Calif. Died 1906.

HERRIN, William Franklin, lawyer; b. nr. Jacksonville, Ore., Aug. 7, 1854; s. John Stevenson and Nancy Katherine H.; B.S., Ore. State Agrl. Coll., Corvallis, 1873; LL.B., Cumberland U., Tenn., 1875; m. Annie S. Van Clief, Apr. 27, 1881. Practiced in San Francisco, chief counsel S.P. Co., July 1, 1893—, v.p. Mar. 1910—. Home: San Francisco, Calif. Died Feb. 28, 1927.

HERRING, Hubert Clinton, clergyman; b. Lowville, Wis., Oct. 30, 1859; s. Silas W. and Polly M. H.; student U. of Wis., 1878-79, U. of Chicago, 1879-80, McCormick Theol. Sem., 1884-86, Princeton Theol. Sem., 1886-87; m. Mary Woodbridge, Oct. 4, 1887. Ordained Presbyn. ministry, 1887; pastor Second Presbyn. Ch., Sioux City, Ia., 1887-90, First Presbyn. Ch., Winterset, Ia., 1890-94, Hyde Park Presbyn. Ch., Chicago, 1894-98, First Congl. Ch., Omaha, 1898-1907; gen. sec. Congl. Home Missionary Soc., Feb. 1, 1907-14; sec. Nat. Council Congl. Chs., 1914—. Home: New York, N.Y. Died Aug. 6, 1920.

HERRINGTON, Cass E., lawyer; b. nr. Pontiac, Mich., Dec. 23, 1856; s. Rev. Erastus C. and Sarepta (Warren) H.; Mich. Agrl. Coll. 3 yrs. to 1877; LL.B., U. of Mich., 1879; m. Isabella, d. Randolph Manning, chancellor and justice Sup. Ct. of Mich., Aug. 27, 1883. Practiced, Pontiac, Mich., 1879-89, then at Denver, Colo.; asso. in practice with brother, as C.E.&F. Herrington, 1889-99; with Colo. Fuel & Iron Co., 1901-19, as dir. exec. com., gen. atty. and gen. counsel. Mem. Mich. Ho. of Rep., 1887; mem. Bd. Pub. Works, Denver, 1897, 98. Mem. Colo. War Council, 1917-18. Pres. Denver Civic and Commercial Assn., 1916; pres. Colo. Development Fedn., 1917-19; dir. First Nat. Bank, Denver, Regional Adviser War Industries Bd., for Colo., Wyo., Utah and Northern N.M., 1918; dir. U.S. Chamber of Commerce, 1918. Presented medal, Denver Real Estate Exchange, for pub. services during the war. Apptd. spl. master, D.&R.G.W. R.R. receivership, Aug. 1922. Dir. Denver Art Museum, 1915—, pres., 1928-29. Officier Order of Knighthood of Crown of Italy, 1929. Home: Denver, Colo. Died Apr. 1934.

HERRMAN, Esther (Mrs.), patron and mem. A.A.A.S.; mem. Am. Acad. Polit. and Social Science, etc. Home: New York, N.Y. Died 1911.

HERRON, Clark Lincoln, educator; b. Gobles, Mich., Jan. 24, 1861; s. Harvey Thayer and Mary Elizabeth (Clark) H.; B.Ph., Hillsdale (Mich.) Coll., 1885, M.S., 1893; grad. study, U. of Minn., 1893-95, U. of Chicago, 1895-97; D.Sc., Bates Coll., Lewiston, Me., 1924; m. Bertha Harvey, Dec. 27, 1888 (died 1896); m. 2d, Martha Sisson, of Keokuk, Ia., Aug. 18, 1898 (died 1928). Teacher rural schs., Mich., 1885-87; prin. pub. schs., Hamilton, Mich., 1887-88; instr. Minneapolis (Minn.) Acad., 1888-93, prin., 1893-95; instr. Chicago Manual Training Sch., 1895-1901; asst. prin. Delaware Acad., Delhi, N.Y., 1901-02; prof. mathematics, Hillsdale Coll., 1902—, registrar, 1905-26, dean, 1926—, acting pres., 1932-33. Republican. Home: Hillsdale, Mich. Died Nov. 13, 1936.

HERRON, George Davis, lecturer, author; b. Montezuma, Ind., Jan. 21, 1862; s. William and Isabella (Davis) H.; ed. Ripon Coll., Wis., and 2 yrs. in Europe; (D.D., Tabor Coll., 1892); m. Carrie, d. E. D. Rand, of Burlington, Ia., May 25, 1901 (died 1914). Pastor Congl. Ch., Lake City, Minn.; later of First Congl. Ch., Burlington, Ia.; prof. applied Christianity, Ia. Coll., 1893-1900; resigned owing to opposition of trustees to his teachings. Became active in the Am. Socialist movement. Lecturer upon relations of Christianity to existing social conditions, but was not accepted as Christian in his views by the church and afterward dropped the Christian phraseology. Now living in Geneva; engaged in prolonged lit. work. Author: Defeat in the Victory, 1924. Died Oct. 10, 1925.

HERSCHEL, Clemens, hydraulic engr.; b. Mar. 23, 1842; **S.B.,** Lawrence Scientific Sch. (Harvard), 1860; m. Grace D. Hobart, May 12, 1869 (died 1898); children—Arthur Hobart, Winslow Hobart, Clementine (Mrs. Hobart Rawson); m. 2d, Jeannette B. Hunter, Mar. 5, 1910; 1 son, Clemens. Hydraulic engr., Holyoke (Mass.) Water Power Co., 1879-89; engr. and supt. E. Jersey Water Co., 1889-1900; r.r. commr. of Mass., 1881-83. Awarded Elliott Cresson gold medal of Franklin Inst., Phila., for his Venturi Water Meter. Author: Continuous Revolving Draw Bridges, 1875; 115 Experiments, 1897; Frontinus and the Water Supply of the City of Rome, 1899. Home: Glen Ridge, N.J. Died Mar. 3, 1930.

HERSCHELL, William, author; b. Spencer, Ind., Nov. 17, 1873; s. John Todd and Martha (Leitch) H.; ed. pub. schs.; hon. M.A., Wabash Coll., 1917, in recognition of war poetry; m. Josephine Pugh, June 3, 1908. Began, 1896, as writer for Princeton (Ind.) News; feature writer with Indianapolis News, 1902—. Republican. Mason, Elk. Author: Songs of the Streets and Byways, 1915; The Kid Has Gone to the Colors, 1917; The Smile Bringer, 1920; Howdy All, 1922; Meet the Folks, 1924; Hitch and Come In, 1928. Home: Indianapolis, Ind. Died Dec. 2, 1939.

HERSEY, George Dallas, surgeon; b. Foxboro, Mass., Aug. 12, 1847; s. David and Eliza Fitch (Mills) H.; A.B., Brown, 1869, A.M., 1872; M.D., Univ. Med. Coll. (New York U.), 1874. Surgeon out-patients' dept., 1878-88, visiting surgeon, 1888-1908, consultant, 1908-18, to Rhode Island Hosp. Editor Providence Medical Journal, 1899-1912. Fellow Am. Acad. Medicine, R.I. Med. Soc. (librarian, 1879-1912, sec., 1880-85, pres., 1899-1901). Home: Charleston, S.C. Died Sept. 28, 1919.

HERSEY, Heloise Edwina, lecturer; b. Oxford, Me., Feb. 22, 1855; d. Artemas Lendall (M.D.) and Heloise Helena (Keith) H.; A.B., Vassar Coll., 1876; hon. A.M., Bowdoin, 1921, Tufts, 1922; unmarried. Prof. English, Smith Coll., 1878-83; prin. Miss Hersey's Sch. for Girls, Boston, 1887-99; in lit. work and lecturer, 1899—; editorial writer on Youth's Companion, 1901-12. Editor: (with William J. Rolfe) Select Poems of Robert Browning, 1886; A Blot in the Scutcheon and Other Dramas by Robert Browning, 1887. Edited (with intro.) Christmas Eve and Easter Day, 1887. Lecturer on Shakespeare, the English Poets, novelists, and current lit. Home: Boston, Mass. Died Feb. 3, 1933.

HERSEY, Henry Johnson, lawyer; b. Sandwich, Mass., Feb. 18, 1863; s. Joseph Odell Bogart and Mary Knowles (Dyer) H.; A.B., Boston U., 1884; LL.B., cum laude, 1886; m. Annie Louise Budlong, June 15, 1886. In practice at Denver, 1886-1919; gen. counsel Denver, Lakewood & Golden R.R. Co., 1890-92; compiled charter and ordinances of City of Denver, 1898; represented State of Colo. in labor trouble cases, 1903-04, notably the Moyer habeas corpus case; was of leading counsel for Gov. Peabody in the gubernatorial contest before Colo. Legislature against Alva Adams, 1905; counsel for many large corps. Candidate for county judge, Arapahoe Co., 1895; deputy atty. gen. of Colo., 1903-04; judge advocate, judge advocate gen.'s dept., Colo. N.G., with rank of maj., Aug. 16, 1915-May 31, 1916, resigned; judge, Dist. Court, Denver, Jan. 1919-Jan. 1925 (presiding judge, 1919-20); resumed practice, 1925. Republican. Episcopalian. Lecturer and writer on U.S. Constitution and Our Form of Government. Home: Denver, Colo. Deceased.

HERSEY, Jacob Daniel Temple, capitalist; b. E. Bridgewater, Mass., Sept. 22, 1821; s. Jacob H.; ed. Wrentham Acad.; mfrd. thread and knitting cotton, 1837-40; mfd. straw goods, 1840-48; since then dealer in commercial paper, stocks and bonds; as pres. of Am. Straw Goods Assn., 1883, gave evidence which induced the ways and means com. of Congress to place raw straw-goods material on free list; mem. New York Chamber of Commerce, 1875—; m. Marcia E. Pennell. Home: New York, N.Y. Died 1902.

HERSEY, Mark Leslie, army officer; b. Stetson, Me., Dec. 1, 1863; s. George L. and Olive (Hodsdon) H.; A.B., Bates Coll., Me., 1884; grad. U.S. Mil. Acad., 1887; A.M., Bates Coll., 1902, LL.D., 1919; LL.D., U. of Me., 1921; m. Elizabeth Noyes, Sept. 16, 1887; children—Mark Leslie, Dorothy, Alice Elizabeth. Add. 2d lt. 19th Inf., June 12, 1887; promoted through grades to col. 58th Inf., July 27, 1917; brig. gen.; N.A., Aug. 28, 1917; maj. gen., Oct. 15, 1918; returned to grade of col. U.S.A., Aug. 31, 1919; brig. gen. (temp.), July 15, 1920-Mar. 4, 1921; reapptd. brig. gen., confirmed Mar. 5, 1921; maj. gen., Sept. 20, 1924; retired Nov. 2, 1924. Supt. supplies, City of Boston, Oct. 1925-26. Detached service at U. of Me., 1891-1895, with the Philippine Constabulary, 1905-14, chief of Mindanao Constabulary, 1909-14; assigned as comdr. 155th Inf. Brigade, Camp Dix, N.J., Aug. 29, 1917; comd. 155th Inf. Brigade in St. Mihiel offensive and defensive and at Bois des Loges in the Meuse-Argonne until Oct. 29, 1919, when assigned to command 4th Div.; comd. 4th Div. on march to the Rhine and throughout service with Army of Occupation; returned to U.S. with 4th Div., July 31, 1919. Decorated

D.S.M. (U.S.); officer Legion of Honor and Croix de Guerre with palm (France). Democrat. Episcopalian. Home: Washington, D.C. Died Jan. 22, 1934.

HERSHEY, Amos Shartle, univ. prof.; b. Hershey, Pa., July 11, 1867; s. Martin and Mary Ann (Shartle) H.; A.B., Harvard, 1892; Harvard Law Sch., 1891-92; Heidelberg, 1892-94, Ph.D., 1894; Paris, 1894-95; m. Lillian Wilcox, Sept. 6, 1892. Asst. prof. polit. science, 1895-1900; asso. prof. European history and politics, 1900-05, prof. polit. science and internat. law, 1905—, and head of (new) dept. polit. science, 1914—, Indiana U. Mem. staff Am. Commn. to Negotiate Peace, Paris, 1918-19; lecturer on government, Harvard, 1920. Kahn traveling fellow in Europe and Orient, 1913-14. Author: Modern Japan, 1919; (with Frank M. Anderson) Handbook for the Diplomatic History of Europe, Asia, and Africa, 1870-1914 (U.S. Govt. publ.), 1918; The Essentials of International Law and Organization, 1927. Home: Bloomington, Ind. Died June 12, 1933.

HERSHEY, Oscar H., mining geologist; b. Blue Rock, Pa., Mar. 27, 1874; s. Urias H. and Susan Ida (Hengst) H.; ed. high sch., Lebanon, Pa.; m. Mabel E. Zollers, Sept. 29, 1923. Began study of geology in the field, 1896; prospected in Calif. and Isthmus of Panama much of time until 1904; with U.S. Geol. Survey, Clear Creek Quadrangle, Colo., summer 1904; examining mines and prospects, 1904-08; mem. Burch, Caetani & Hershey, later Hershey & White; cons. geologist to Bunker Hill & Sullivan Mining and Concentrating Co. Fellow A.A.A.S. and Geol. Soc. of America. Republican. Home: Oakland, Calif. Died Dec. 11, 1939.

HERSHEY, Scott F., clergyman; b. Colburn, Ind., 1852; s. H. Y. and Elizabeth H.; grad. Heidelberg U., Ohio, 1875, Ph.D., 1881; LL.D., Mt. Hope Coll., 1899; m. Georgia E. Mayes, 1882. Ordained Ref. Ch. ministry, 1876; pastor Presbyn. Ch., Middletown, O., 1884-87, 6th Presbyn. Ch., Washington, 1887-94, First Presbyn. Ch., Boston, 1894-1905, Wooster, O., 1905-08, New Castle, Pa., 1908-13. Mem. World's Alliance of Reformed Chs.; 1880 (youngest mem. of Phila. Council); mem. Belfast, Ireland, Council, 1884, and Washington (D.C.) Council, 1899; elected, 1901, to fill the Twentieth Century Lectureship on Preaching. V.p. Universal Peace Union of the World; v.p. Am. Peace and Arbitration Soc. Specialist on the philosophy of health, and on Greek and Roman portraits of the first century. Teacher and lecturer on the Religious Drama. Home: Lake Helen, Fla. Died Jan. 10, 1931.

HERSHMAN, Oliver Sylvester, editor, publisher; b. Pittsburgh, Pa., July 2, 1859; s. Henry Logan (killed in Union Army, Civil War) and Lucy (Buhoup) H.; pub. sch. edn.; m. Belle C. Boyd, May 24, 1904. Entered business office Pittsburgh Evening Telegraph, 1873, becoming business mgr.; consolidated this paper with the Evening Chronicle, forming Chronicle Telegraph, 1884; pub. same until 1900, when he bought The Press, later acquiring Daily News, which he merged with The Press; pres. and treas. The Press Pub. Co. Republican. Apptd. a.d.c. on staff of Gov. Stuart of Pa., 1907, with rank of lt. col., and reapptd. by Govs. Tener and Brumbaugh. Mem. Pittsburgh Chamber Commerce. Home: Pittsburgh, Pa. Died July 9, 1930.

HERT, Alvin Tobias; b. Owensburg, Ind., Apr. 8, 1865; s. William and Isabel (Owen) H.; ed. pub. schs.; m. Sallie Aley, Nov. 20, 1893. Pres. Am. Creosoting Co., 1904—, operating 15 plants in U.S.; chmn. bd. Am. Tar Products Co.; dir. Nat. Bank of Ky. Mem. Rep. Nat. Com. from Ky., 1916-20, and of exec. com. same; western mgr. Rep. presdl. campaign, 1916. Episcopalian. Mason. Home: Jefferson Co., Ky. Died June 7, 1921.

HERTER, Christian Archibald, pathologist; b. Glenville, Conn., Sept. 3, 1865; s. Christian and Mary (Miles) H.; bro. of Albert H.; ed. Columbia Grammar Sch., New York; M.D., Coll. Phys. and Surg. (Columbia), 1885; m. Susan, d. David Dows, Dec. 9, 1886. Visiting phys. N.Y. City Hosp., 1894-1904; prof. pathol. chemistry, Univ. and Bellevue Hosp. Med. Coll. (New York U.), 1898-1903; prof. pharmacology and therapeutics, Coll. Phys. and Surg., New York, 1903—. Treas. Rockefeller Inst. for Med. Research; U.S. referee, Dept. of Agr. Fellow A.A.A.S., N.Y. Acad. Medicine. Died 1910.

HERTY, Charles Holmes, chemist; b. Milledgeville, Ga., Dec. 4, 1867; s. Bernard R. and Louisa T. H.; student Ga. Mil. and Agrl. Coll., 1880-84; Ph.B., U. of Ga., 1886; Ph.D., Johns Hopkins, 1890; at univs. of Berlin and Zürich, 1899, 1900; hon. Ch.D., U. of Pittsburgh, 1917; D.Sc., Colgate U., 1918, Oglethorpe U., 1934, U. of Fla., 1937; LL.D., U. of Ga., 1928, Univ. of N.C., 1933; m. Sophie Schaller, Dec. 23, 1895 (died 1929); children—Charles Holmes, Frank Bernard, Sophie Dorothea. Asst. chemist, Ga. State Expt. Sta., 1890-91; instr., 1891-94, adj. prof. chemistry, 1894-1902, U. of Ga.; collaborator, 1901-02, expert, 1902-04, Bur. of Forestry, U.S. Dept. of Agr.; with Chattanooga Pottery Co., 1904-05; prof. chemistry U. of N.C., 1905-16; editor Jour. Industrial and

Engring. Chemistry, 1917-21; pres. Synthetic Organic Chemical Mfrs.' Assn., 1921-26; advisor to The Chemical Foundation, Inc., 1926-28; became industrial consultant, N.Y. City, 1928; dir. div. pulp and paper research, Ga. State Dept. Forestry and Geol. Development, 1932-33; dir. Pulp and Paper Lab. of Industrial Com. of Savannah, Ga. Fellow A.A.A.S., Chemical Society (London). Home: Savannah, Ga. Died July 27, 1938.

HERTZ, Emanuel, lawyer; b. Austria (now Czechoslovakia), Sept. 2, 1870; s. Simon and Esther (Moskowitz) H.; came with parents to U.S., 1884; B.A., Coll. City New York, 1892; A.M., Columbia, 1894, LL.B., 1895; student Jewish Theol. Sem. 3 yrs.; LL.D., Lincoln Memorial U., 1925, L.H.D., 1928; Litt.D. from Knox Coll., Galesburg, Ill., 1935; m. Blanche Rosenthal, June 24, 1906; children—Edithe, Miriam, Lillian, Doris Judith, Hamilton Benjamin. In practice of law at N.Y. City, 1895—. Rep. candidate for Congress, 1926; Rep. presidential elector, N.Y., 1928. Sec. 8th Quinquennial Conv. B'nai B'rith; helped organize Jewish Community and erect 1st synagogue bldg. of Washington Heights. Contbr. 20,000 books to Lincoln Memorial U.; also instrumental in giving 20,000 books to Univ., in Jerusalem, 8000 books to Knox Coll., Galesburg, Ill. Extensive writer on Abraham Lincoln. Editor: Abraham Lincoln—The Tribute of the Synagogue, 1927; Abraham Lincoln—A New Portrait, 1931; The Hidden Lincoln, 1938; Lincoln Talks, 1939. Home: New York, N.Y. Died 1940.

HERTZBERG, Hans Rudolph Reinhart, newspaperman; b. San Antonio, Tex., July 1, 1871; s. Dr. Theodor Rudolph and Emilie (Grothaus) H.; ed. Lycée St. Louis, St. Etienne, France, agrl. and Mech. Coll. of Tex., San Antonio High School; LL.B., U. of Tex., 1892. Admitted to bar, 1892; practiced law and edited small newspaper, 1892-94; asst. city atty., San Antonio, 1897-99; edited a weekly, San Antonio, 1901, 2 weeklies, New Orleans, 1901-02; chief asso. editor New Orleans Harlequin, 1902-03-05, editorial and spl. writer on staff of Times-Democrat, 1903; spl. writer and dramatic critic on New York Journal, 1904; editorial writer, spl. writer, dramatic editor on New Orleans Item, Jan.-Nov. 1907; propr. and editor Hertzberg's Weekly, New Orleans, 1908-10; editorial writer and lit. editor Chicago Inter Ocean, May 1910-May 1914. Author: Lyrics of Love, 1906. Home: Chicago, Ill. Died Mar. 18, 1920.

HERVEY, Alpheus Baker, clergyman; b. Triangle, N.Y., Mar. 31, 1839; s. Joseph and Rhoda (Baker) H.; ed. Alfred and Oxford acads N.Y., pvt. schs. and St. Lawrence U.; grad. theol. dept. same, 1861; hon. A.M., Tufts Coll., 1880; A.M., 1878, Ph.D., 1885, LL.D., 1928, St. Lawrence; m. Sarah Eliza Andrew, 1863 (died 1884); m. 2d, Hanna Rion, June 1, 1921 (died 1924). Enlisted in Union Army for Civil War, but was not mustered in; from 1861 pastor of Universalist chs. at Malone, Afton and Troy, N.Y., Southbridge, Peabody and Taunton, Mass., and Bath, Me. Was pres. 1888-94, then trustee, St. Lawrence U.; retired, July 1, 1909. Democrat. Author: Sea Mosses, 1881; Beautiful Wild Flowers, 1881; Flowers of Field and Forest, 1882; (with Frank S. Collins) The Algæ of Bermuda, 1917. Translator: Guide to the Microscope in Botany (from German of Dr. Behrens), 1885; Manual of Microscopical Investigation in Botany (from German of Dr. Strasburger), 1886. Specialist in marine algæ. Home: Bath, Me. Died Mar. 10, 1931.

HERVEY, William Addison, prof. German; b. Rossville, S.I., N.Y., May 27, 1870; s. Edwin Addison (M.D.) and Grace Elinor (Moore) H.; A.B., 1893, post-grad., 1893-95, A.M., 1894, Columbia; studied U. of Leipzig, 1896; m. May Bogert, Mar. 10, 1896. University fellow, 1894-95, instr. German langs. and lits., 1896-1904, adj. asst. and asso. prof., 1904-15, prof. 1915—, Columbia, also registrar, 1908-13. Advisory foreign lang. expert, U.S. Dept. of Justice, Apr. 1917—. Democrat. Baptist. Author: Supplementary Exercises to Thomas's Practical German Grammar, 1901; (with Calvin Thomas) German Reader and Theme Book, 1901; Syllabus of Selected Bibliography of Lessing, Goethe, Schiller, 1918. Editor: Goethe's Hermann and Dorothea; Schiller's Kabala and Liebe, Maria Stuart, Jungfrau von Orleans; Fulda's Untervier Augen; etc. Home: New York, N.Y. Died Dec. 28, 1918.

HERZOG, Felix Benedict, patent atty.; b. New York, N.Y., Dec. 27, 1859; s. Philip and Henrietta (Benedict) H.; A.B., Columbia, 1881, LL.B., 1882, A.M., Ph.D., 1883. Published Railroad Transportation Question, 1883; engaged as elec. engr. and patent atty., 1883—. Inventor of electrical devices, including automatic switchboards, the teleseme, policecall and elevator signals, chem. annunciators, and various telephone devices. Received medals at Paris Expn., 1900, and Buffalo Expn., 1901; mem. jury of award (electricity), St. Louis Expn., 1904. Also artist-painter (pupil of Rondel and early mem. Art Students' League); reviews of his photographic compositions Century, Cosmopolitan, Current Literature, Camera Work, and other mags. Home: New York, N.Y. Died Apr. 21, 1912.

HERZOG, Maximilian Joseph, physician; b. Frankfort-on-the-Main, Germany, Sept. 17, 1858; s. Jesaias and Johanna (Maas) H.; studied biology, univs. of Giesen, Strassburg and Marburg, Germany, 1879-81; came to America, Jan. 1882; M.D., Med. Coll. of Ohio, Cincinnati, 1890; post-grad. studies, univs. of Munich, Würzburg, Berlin, etc., 1891-92; (LL.D., Loyola U., Chicago, 1913); m. Seraphine Ernau, Aug. 12, 1894. Laryngologist and otologist, German Hosp., Cincinnati, 1892-94; prof. pathology and bacteriology, Chicago Policlinic and Hosp., 1896-1903; pathologist, Govt. Labs., Manila, P.I., 1903-06; prof. pathology, Chicago Vet. Coll., 1906-16; chief dept. of pathology, Cook Co. (Ill.) Hosp., 1912—; dean and prof. pathology, Med. Dept., Loyola U., 1912—; supt. and dir. of labs. and research, Municipal Tuberculosis Sanitarium of Chicago, 1916—. Capt. Med. R.C., 1917. Home: Chicago, Ill. Died Aug. 10, 1918.

HESLIN, Thomas, bishop; b. Parish of Killoe, Co. Longford, Ireland, Apr. 1847; s. Patrick and Catherine (Hughes) H.; studied theology and philosophy under Lazarist fathers, Bouligny Sem., New Orleans; taught in St. Mary's Coll., Jefferson and Carrollton Parish School; ordained R.C. priest, 1869. Asst. priest, New Orleans Cathedral, St. Vincent de Paul's Ch., and St. Patrick's, and, 1874-89, pastor St. Michael's, New Orleans; consecrated bishop of Natchez (Miss.), June 18, 1889. Died 1911.

HESS, Alfred Fabian, M.D.; b. New York, N.Y., Oct. 19, 1875; s. Selmar and Josephine (Solomon) H.; A.B., Harvard, 1897; M.D., Coll. Phys. and Surg. (Columbia), 1901; post-grad. work in Prague, Vienna and Berlin; m. Sara Straus, Oct. 12, 1904; children—Eleanor Straus, Margaret Straus. Practiced in New York, 1901—; former prof. clin. pediatrics, Univ. and Bellevue Hosp. Med. Coll. Awarded John Scott medal, 1927, by Franklin Soc. for devising "a method of producing a vitamin factor in food by ultra-violet light." Home: New York, N.Y. Died Dec. 7, 1933.

HESS, Franklin, lawyer; b. Somonauk, Ill., Jan. 9, 1870; s. Paul E. and Mary A. (Graf) H.; B.A., Knox Coll., Ill., 1894, M.A., 1897; LL.B., Kent Coll. of Law, Chicago, 1897; m. Rilla Catherine Meeker, June 15, 1898; children—Rilla (dec.), Mrs. Mary Rachel Pett, Mrs. Ruth Cecil Barker. Began practice, Chicago, 1897; in charge legal dept. Warder, Bushnell & Glessner Co., until 1902; with Internat. Harvester Co. since it absorbed the Warder, Bushnell & Glessner Co., 1902, gen. atty., Dec. 12, 1920—. Trustee Knox Coll. Christian Scientist. Mason. Home: Chicago, Ill. Died Sept. 30, 1931.

HESS, Henry, mech. engr.; b. Darmstadt, Germany, 1863; s. George and Louise (Hess) H.; brought to America in infancy; ed. Heidenfeld's Inst., and under Dr. Douai, New York, and high sch., Germany; m. Caroline Annie Serle, of London, Eng., 1886. Served as designer with Pond Machine Tool Co., Watervliet Arsenal (U.S.A. heavy ordnance), Niles Tool Works Co., Bur. Constrn. and Repair, U.S. Navy; consulting engr. and mng. dir. German Niles Tool Works, Berlin; founder, and pres. Hess-Bright Mfg. Company, 1904-02, Hess Steel Co., Hess-Ives Co. Special lecturer, Columbia U. Home: Philadelphia, Pa. Died Mar. 22, 1922.

HESSBERG, Albert, lawyer; b. Albany, N.Y., Dec. 13, 1856; s. Simon and Hannah (Westheimer) H.; ed. Albany dist. and high schs.; m. Fredericka A. Cone, June 19, 1889. Admitted to bar, 1877; now mem. Rosendale (Simon Wolfe), Hessberg, Dugan & Haines; dir. Nat. Commercial Bank of Albany; trustee Albany City Savings Instn.; dir. City Safe Deposit & Storage Co. Asst. corp. counsel, Albany, 1883-86; elected recorder, City of Albany, 1888, 1896. Pres. Albany Jewish Home; gov. Albany Hosp.; trustee Albany City Dispensary, Schuyler Mansion. Home: Albany, N.Y. Died July 25, 1920.

HESSE, Bernard Conrad, chemist; b. East Saginaw, Mich., Oct. 3, 1869; Ph.C., U. of Mich., 1889, B.S., 1893; Ph.D., U. of Chicago, 1896. Asst. in chemistry, U. of Mich., 1890-93; research chemist at Ludwigshafen-on-Rhine, Germany, 1896-1906; consulting practice, New York, 1906—; consulting mem. General Chemical Co., N.Y. City. Died Apr. 1934.

HESSELBERG, Edouard, Gregory (D'Essenelli), pianist; b. Riga, Russia, May 3, 1870; s. Heinrich and Sahra (Davidoff) H.; classical gymnasium, Orel, Russia, 1878-87; grad., M.A., Philharmonique Conservatory of Music and Dramatic Art, Moscow (laureate and medal), 1892; later pvt. study under Rubinstein; came to America, 1892; naturalized, 1900; m. Lena, d. Gen. George T. Shackelford, of Mt. Sterling, Ky., 1898; children—Melvyn Edouard, Lamar (George). Dir. piano dept., Ithaca (N.Y.) Conservatory Music, 1895-96; dir. music, Coll. and Conservatory Music (U. of Denver), Acad. of Music, and Dick's Normal Coll., Denver, 1896-1900; dir. music, Wesleyan Coll. Conservatory, Macon, Ga., 1900-05; dir. music, Belmont Coll., Nashville, Tenn., 1905-12; sr. prof. and examiner in art of advanced pianoforte playing at Toronto Conservatory of Music, Hambourg Conservatory of Music, Loretto Abbey, Glen Mawr College, Westbourne Coll., all of Toronto, and Hamilton (Ont.) Conservatory of Music, London (Ont.) Conservatory of Music, 1912-17; dir. of staff, musical editor and critic, Met. Studies of Verse and Song; mem. faculty, Cosmopolitan Conservatory of Music and Dramatic Art, Chicago, 1917-21, Sherwood Music School, Chicago, 1921-24; on tour of Europe, introducing original compositions. Mason. Composer: New nat. hymn, "America, My Country," 1916 (poem by Lena Shackelford Hesselberg); (books) Juvenile Gems; A Russian Suite; Echoes from Fairyland; Russian Rhapsody; Slavic Fantasy; Hebraicana; also many songs and compositions for pianoforte, violin and orchestra; transcriptions for 2 pianos, 4 hands—Anthology of Modern Russian Composers; Chopin Études, op 10 and 25 (2 pianos, 4 hands). Deceased.

HESTER, St. Clair, clergyman; b. Oxford, N.C., Jan. 29, 1868; s. Capt. John Cason and Lucy Ann (Hamlet) H.; B.A., U. of N.C., 1888, M.A., 1890, D.D., 1908; grad. Gen. Theol. Sem., 1893; studied Keble Coll., Oxford U., Eng.; m. Sarah Conselyea Baker, June 17, 1896 (died 1901). Deacon, 1893, priest, 1894, P.E. Ch.; asst. Ch. of the Messiah, Brooklyn, 1893-95; rector St. George's Ch., Brooklyn, 1895-98, Ch. of the Messiah, 1898—. Archdeacon of N. Brooklyn, 1901-11; pres. standing com. Diocese of L.I.; mem. corp. Diocesan Missions; mem. bd. Ch. Charity Foundation (v.p.), Brooklyn Howard Colored Asylum. Trustee Gen. Theol. Sem., Estate of Diocese of L.I.; chancellor Cathedral of the Incarnation, Garden City, N.Y.; mem. bd. trustees Gen. Theol. Sem.; mem. bd. dirs. N.Y. Center of Dramatic League America. Democrat. Home: Brooklyn, N.Y. Died June 1933.

HESTER, William, publisher; b. Poughkeepsie, N.Y., Dec. 7, 1835; ed. Rhinebeck Acad., Poughkeepsie. Pres. Brooklyn Daily Eagle; dir. Eagle Warehouse & Storage Co. Died June 9, 1921.

HESTER, William Van Arden, pres. Brooklyn Daily Eagle; b. Brooklyn, N.Y., Dec. 1, 1858; s. William and Theodosia (Ward) H.; ed. Polytechnic Inst. Brooklyn; m. Ada Louisa Gibb, Apr. 28, 1896. Began in employ of Brooklyn Daily Eagle, 1881, pres., 1921—; dir. Eagle Warehouse & Storage Co., Corning Light & Power Co. Democrat. Mem. Dutch Ref. Ch. Home: Glen Cove, L.I. Died Dec. 14, 1924.

HESTON, John William, educator; b. Bellefonte, Pa., Feb. 1, 1854; s. Elisha B. and Katherine H.; A.B., Pa. State Coll., 1879, A.M., 1881; m. Mary Calder, Aug. 16, 1881. Prof. of pedagogy, Pa. State Coll., 1887-90; admitted to Pa. bar, 1890; prin. Seattle (Wash.) High Sch., 1890-92; pres. Wash. Sch. of Science and Agrl. Coll., 1892-93; practiced law, Seattle, 1894-96; pres. S.D. Agrl. Coll., 1896-1903; pres. State Normal Sch., Madison, S.D., 1905—. Mem. State Bd. of Edn., S.D. Republican. Baptist. Mason. Home: Madison, S.D. Died Feb. 1, 1920.

HETHERINGTON, John Edwin, apiculturist; b. Cherry Valley, N.Y., Jan. 7, 1840; s. James and Eliza (Judd) H.; grad. Cherry Valley Acad., 1858; m. Eva W. Booth, Nov. 20, 1879. Served in 1st regt. U.S. Sharpshooters, Nov. 23, 1861, to Sept. 20, 1864; made capt. at Gettysburg; four times wounded; discharged by reason of wounds. Apiculturist, 1856—; most extensive bee keeper in the world; inventor of numerous apiarian appliances, and recognized expert in all apiarian matters. Home: Cherry Valley, N.Y. Died 1903.

HETZLER, Howard George, ry. pres.; b. La Moille, Ill., Apr. 19, 1863; s. John and Harriet P. (Richardson) H.; B.S., C.E., U. of Mich., 1886; m. Frances E. Pickett, 1889 (died 1911); 2d, Ellen Harcourt Schonnthaler, 1914. In civil engring. dept., 1886-93, roadmaster at Chicago, 1893-99, supt. Chicago terminals, 1899-1903, supt. Chicago div., 1903-05, C.,B.&Q. R.R.; pres. Met. West Side Elevated Ry. Co., Chicago, Apr. 1905-Feb. 1910; elected pres. Chicago & Western Ind. R.R. Co., Feb. 7, 1910; gen. mgr. same under U.S.R.R. Administration, also of Belt Ry. of Chicago, again pres. same rys. after release from Govt. control. Republican. Conglist. Home: Hinsdale, Ill. Died Mar. 13, 1926.

HEWES, Fletcher Willis, author; b. LeRoy, N.Y., July 16, 1838; s. Ira, Jr., and Julia Ann (Scott) H.; ed. Clarkston (Mich.) Acad., State Normal Sch., Ypsilanti, Mich. served in Civil War in Union Army; mustered out as 1st lt. Co. D, 10th Mich. Inf., July 19, 1865; m. Alta J. Hemingway, Aug. 14, 1867. Pub. sch. teacher and supt., 1856-75, except during Civil War. Engaged in lit. work, 1880—; now engaged in writing the industrial, financial and commercial history of U.S. as a distinct part of a 10-vol. work entitled The United States, a History of Three Centuries, of which was projector. Baptist. Republican. Author: What Are the Facts—Protection and Reciprocity Illustrated, 1893; The United States, A History (with W.E. Chancellor), Vol. I, 1904, Vol. II, 1905. Home: E. Orange, N.J. Died 1910.

HEWES, M. Lewin, fire ins.; b. Baltimore, Md., June 14, 1861; s. James Ellicott and Gulielma (Warner) Hewes; student Friends Elementary and High Sch., Baltimore, 1867-73; Md. Agrl. Coll., 1874-75; m. Virginia Sumter Smith, Nov. 14, 1883; children—James Ellicott, Thomas, Phillip. Ins. clk., 1877-82; spl. agt. Royal Ins. Co., 1883-90; gen. agt. and adjuster Norwich Union Fire Office, 1890-97; sec. Howard Fire Ins. Co., Baltimore, 1897-99; sec. United Ins. Co., Baltimore, 1899-1901; agency supt. Scottish Union and Nat. Ins. Co., 1901-09; pres. Standard Fire Ins. Co., 1910-24, chmn. bd., 1924—. Democrat. Episcopalian. Home: Hartford, Conn. Died Feb. 16, 1940.

HEWETT, Edwin Crawford, educator; b. Sutton, Mass., Nov. 1, 1828; s. Timothy and Levina (Leonard) H.; grad. State Normal School, Bridgewater, Mass., 1852 (A.M., U. of Chicago; LL.D., Shurtleff Coll.); m. 1st, 1857 (wife died 1895); 2d, 1898. Taught in Bridgewater Normal, Grammar School, Worcester, Mass., and for 32 yrs. (pres., 1876-90) in Ill. State Normal. Treas. Nat. Ednl. Assn., 1886-90; became asso. editor School and Home Education. Author: Manual of Arithmetic, 1896; Rand-McNally Practical Arithmetic, 1896; Rand-McNally Primary Arithmetic, 1896. Home: Normal, Ill. Died 1905.

HEWETT, Waterman Thomas, univ. prof.; b. Miami, Mo., Jan. 10, 1846; s. Waterman Thomas and Sarah Woodman (Parsons) H.; A.B., Amherst, 1869, A.M., 1871; studied Univ. of Athens, and Heidelberg, 1869-70; at univs. of Leipzig, Berlin and Leiden, 1877-78, 1887-88; Ph.D., Cornell, 1879; m. Emma McChain, June 22, 1880 (died 1883); 2d, Katherine Mary Locke, of Paris, Dec. 18, 1889 (died 1910). Asst. prof. German, 1870-83, prof. German lang. and lit., 1883-1910, and head of the German dept., emeritus prof., 1910—, Cornell U. Lecturer at the Concord Sch. of Philosophy, 1885, at Goethe Sch., Milwaukee, 1886. Contributing editor Americana Germanica, 1896—; gen. editor Macmillan's German Classics, 1895—. Berlin corr. New York Nation, 1887-88. Del. of Cornell U. to Univ. of Bologna, 1907, and of Am. Philos. Soc. to univs. of Geneva and Leipzig, 1909. Author: German Reader; Cornell University, A History (4 vols.), 1905. Editor: Goethe's Hermann und Dorothea, 1891; Uhland's Poems, 1896; A German Reader, 1899; Bibliography of the Writings of Goldwin Smith. Resident in Europe, 1913—; in Oxford, Eng., 1914-17. Associated with Brit. Fgn. Office in presenting the Allied cause in America, etc., 1914-16. Died Sept. 13, 1921.

HEWINS, Caroline Maria, librarian; b. Roxbury, Mass., Oct. 10, 1846; d. Charles Amasa and Caroline Louisa (Chapin) H.; attended high schs. in Boston; received library training in Boston Athenæum; taught in private schs. several years; took a year's special course in Boston U.; hon. M.A., Trinity Coll., 1911; unmarried. Librarian, Hartford Library Assn., 1875-92, Hartford Pub. Library, 1892—. Sec. Conn. Pub. Library Commn., 1893—. Has done editorial work for Literary News, Library Journal, Babyhood, etc. Author: Books for the Young; Books for Boys and Girls; A Traveler's Letters to Boys and Girls, 1923. Died Nov. 4, 1926.

HEWITT, Abram Stevens, iron mfr., mayor of New York; b. Haverstraw, N.Y., July 31, 1822; s. John and Ann (Gurness) H.; grad. Columbia, 1842 (A.M., LL.D.); m. d. Peter Cooper, the philanthropist, 1855. Mem. Congress, 1874-87; mayor of New York, 1887-89; chmn. Nat. Dem. Com., 1876-77; sec. and organizer Cooper Union for the Adv. of Sciences and Art, New York; mem. Cooper & Hewitt, controlling Trenton Iron Co., N.J. Iron and Steel Co., and Peter Cooper's Glue Factory. Died 1903.

HEWITT, Charles Nathaniel, physician; b. Vergennes, Vt., June 3, 1835; s. Henry (M.D.) and Althea F. H.; A.B., Hobart, 1856, A.M., 1859 (LL.D., 1895); M.D., Albany Med. Coll., 1857; practiced at Geneva, N.Y., 1857-61; served in U.S.A., 1861-65, from asst. surgeon and surgeon, 50th N.Y. regt., to surgeon-in-chief engr. brigade, Army of Potomac; located at Red Wing, Minn., 1866; m. Helen Robinson Hawley, Apr. 22, 1869. Prof. pub. health, U. of Minn., 1873—; sec. and exec. officer Minn. State Bd. of Health, 1872-97; dir. Minn. Vaccine Sta., 1889—. Pres. Minn. State Med. Soc., 1881-82; pres. Am. Pub. Health Assn. Home: Red Wing, Minn. Died 1910.

HEWITT, Edwin Hawley, architect; b. Red Wing, Minn., Mar. 26, 1874; s. Charles Nathaniel and Helen (Robinson) H.; student Hobart Coll., Geneva, N.Y., 1 yr.; A.B., U. of Minn., 1896; student Mass. Inst. Tech., École des Beaux Arts, Paris, 1900-04; m. Caroline Christian, Apr. 18, 1900; children—Charles Christian, Helen (dec.), also (adopted) John Edwin, Mary, Elizabeth. Practiced alone in Minneapolis, Minn., 1904-11, with Edwin Hacker Brown, 1911-37; with Hewitt, Setter and Hamlin, 1937—; architect St. Mark's and Hennepin Avenue churches, McKnight and Metropolitan bldgs., C. S. Pillsbury's residence, Minneapolis Sch. Fine Arts, Northwestern Nat. Life Ins. Bldg., Y.W.C.A. Bldg., Northwestern Bell Telephone Building. President Minn. State Art Soc., 1915-20; pres. Minneapolis Housing Commn., 1932-33; chief archtl. supervisor Minn. Federal Housing Adminstrn., 1935-36; spl. architectural consultant Federal Housing Adminstrn., 1938; joint architect Summer Field Housing Development; trustee Minneapolis Inst. of Art. Fellow Am. Inst. Architects. Episcopalian. Home: Excelsior, Minn. Died Aug. 11, 1939.

HEWITT, Erskine, lawyer; b. New York, N.Y., Jan. 12, 1871; s. late Hon. Abram Stevens and Sarah Amelia (Cooper) H.; g.s. Peter Cooper; A.B., Princeton, 1891, A.M., 1893; LL.B., New York Law Sch., 1893; unmarried. Sec. and attaché spl. U.S. embassy to London, 1897. Pres. Ringwood Co. V.p. and trustee Winifred Masterson Burke Relief Foundation; trustee N.Y. Historical Soc. Capt. and asst. adj. gen. staff of Maj. Gen. James H. Wilson, Spanish-Am. War, 1898. Democrat. Episcopalian. Life mem. Am. Inst. Mining and Metall. Engrs. Home: Ringwood Manor, N.J. Died May 23, 1938.

HEWITT, Fayette, banker; b. Hardin Co., Ky., Oct. 15, 1831; s. Robert Hewitt and Eliza Chastain H.; ed. local schs. Teacher, 1850-59; supt. Dead Letter Office, Washington, 1859-61; served Confederate army, 1861-65, becoming brig. gen.; adj. gen. Trans-Mississippi Dept., 1861-62; transferred to Breckenridge's Div., 1863; was in battles of Pea Ridge, Elkhorn, Newtonia, Chicamauga and all battles during Atlanta campaign, and after that with troops opposing Sherman's March to the Sea; at time of final surrender was in S.C. with portion of Johnston's army. Practiced law, 1865-67; adj. gen. State of Ky., 1867-76; auditor Ky., 1879-97. Democrat. Unmarried. Pres. State Nat. Bank of Frankfort, Ky., Aug. 1890—. Home: Frankfort, Ky. Died 1909.

HEWITT, Henry, Jr., lumberman; b. Lancashire, Eng., Oct. 22, 1840; s. Henry and Mary (Proctor) H.; parents came to Racine, Wis., 1841; ed. 6 months in common sch., Kaukauna, Wis., Chicago Bus. Coll., 3 months, and 6 months at Lawrence U., Appleton, Wis.; m. Rocena L. Jones, 1870. Engaged in lumber, timber lands and banking business, beginning in 1858 at Menasha, Wis., where lived 20 yrs.; organized the Everett Land Co., the Everett Nat. and re-organized First Nat. Bank, and the Hewitt-Lombard Bank, the Everett Pulp and Paper Co. and other mills in Wis.; one of prin. organizers of St. Paul & Tacoma Lumber Co., was its treas. 15 yrs., now dir.; now largest individual owner of lumber and coal lands in State of Wash., owning two billion ft. of timber. Pres. and dir. Wilkeson Coal & Coke Co., Climax Coal Mining Co.; pres. of the Creek Coal Mine, Wilkinson, Wash.; v.p. and dir. Connellsville Coal & Coke Co.; pres. and large owner of Hewitt Investment Co., Hewitt Land Co., West Tacoma Iron Co. and New City Iron Industrials Co., and many other corps. Republican. Home: Tacoma, Wash. Died May 2, 1918.

HEWITT, John Haskell, college prof.; b. Preston, Conn., Aug. 8, 1835; s. Charles and Eunice (Witter) H.; A.B., Yale, 1859; grad. Yale Theol. Sem., 1863; post-grad. work, Yale, and librarian, Brothers in Unity Soc. Library and asst. in Yale Coll. Library, 1862-65; A.M., Yale, 1867, Williams Coll., 1888; (LL.D., Union Coll., N.Y., 1895); m. Mary Louisa Downing, Sept. 8, 1869. Prof. Latin lang. and lit., 1865-75, acting pres., 1872-75, Olivet Coll., Mich.; prof. Latin and Greek, 1875-77, Greek, 1877-81, acting pres., 1877-78, Lake Forest U.; studied and traveled in Europe, 1881-82, 1892-93; elected Garfield prof. ancient langs., 1882, acting pres., 1901-02, Lawrence prof. Greek lang. and lit., 1903-09, prof. emeritus, 1909—, Williams Coll. Republican. Home: Williamstown, Mass. Died Oct. 6, 1920.

HEWITT, Joseph William, prof. Greek; b. Leeds, Yorkshire, Eng., Aug. 23, 1875; s. Hosea and Martha Ann (Allen) H.; came to U.S., 1885, A.B., Bowdoin Coll., 1897, A.M., 1899; Litt.D., from same, 1927; A.M., Harvard U., 1900, Ph.D., 1902; m. Evelyn S. Clark, June 24, 1903; 1 dau., Dorothy. Assistant in Latin and in Greek, Bowdoin College, 1897-98; prin. Hanover (N.H.) High Sch., 1898-99; instr. Latin, 1902-03, master in Latin, 1903-05, Worcester (Mass.) Acad.; asso. prof. Latin and Greek, 1905-13, prof. classics, 1913-29, prof. Greek, 1929—, dean of freshmen, 1925—, Wesleyan U. Mem. exec. com. Am. Sch. Classical Studies at Athens. Odd Fellow. Methodist. Editor: (with M. W. Mather) Xenophon's Anabasis, I-IV, 1910. Home: Middletown, Conn. Died July 8, 1938.

HEWITT, Peter Cooper, scientist, inventor; b. New York, N.Y.; s. late Hon. Abram Stevens H. (congressman and mayor of New York) and Sarah Amelia (Cooper) H.; g.s. Peter Cooper, philanthropist; (hon. Sc.D., Columbia University, 1903, and Rutgers College, 1916); m. Lucy Work; m. 2d, Mrs. Maryon J. Bruguiere. Dir. N.Y. & Greenwood Lake Ry., Cooper, Hewitt & Co., Midvale Water Co., Hexagon Realty Co., Ringwood Co., Hewitt Realty Co., Lehigh & Oxford Mining Co. First v.p. Naval Consulting Board, 1915—. Trustee Cooper Union for Advancement of Science and Art, Hosp. House of Rest for Consumptives. Home: Ringwood Manor, N.J. Died Aug. 25, 1921.

HEWITT, William, mech. engr.; b. Trenton, N.J., Oct. 26, 1853; s. Charles and Anna (Conrad) H.; student Lehigh U., 1869-71; M.E., Stevens Inst. Tech., Hoboken, N.J., 1874; m. Josephine H. Walker, Dec. 11, 1878. Connected with Trenton Iron Co., 1874-1913, v.p., 1879-1903; estimating engr. and wire rope expert, tramway dept. Am. Steel & Wire Co., Trenton, 1903—. Inventor of machinery for mfr. of wire rope. Mem. Co. A, 7th Regt. N.J.N.G., 1874-82. Episcopalian. Home: Trenton, N.J. Died Aug. 3, 1922.

HEWLETT, A(lbion) Walter, physician; b. Petaluma, Calif., Nov. 27, 1874; s. Frederick and Cleora Melissa (Whitney) H.; B.S., U. of Calif., 1895; M.D., Johns Hopkins, 1900; studied in Germany, 1902-03; m. Louise Redington, June 12, 1907. House officer, New York Hosp., 1900-02; asst. instr. and asst. prof. medicine, Cooper Med. Coll., San Francisco, 1903-08; prof. internal medicine and dir. Clin. lab., U. of Mich., 1908-16; prof. medicine, Leland Stanford Jr. Univ., 1916—. Lt. comdr., M.C.U.S.N. R.F., 1917—. Republican. Episcopalian. Translator: Krehl's Clinical Pathology, 1905. Author: Functional Pathology of Internal Diseases, 1916-22. Died Nov. 10, 1925.

HEWLETT, James Monroe, architect; b. Lawrence, L.I., N.Y., Aug. 1, 1868; s. James Augustus and Mary Elizabeth (Sanderson) H.; Ph.B., Columbia, 1890; m. Anna Willets, Mar. 29, 1894; 9 children; m. 2d, Estelle Rodgers Wilbur, 1924. Practiced in New York, 1894—; mem. Lord & Hewlett. Prin. works: Brooklyn Masonic Temple, Brooklyn Hosp., Phila. War Memorial, St. John's Hosp., Brooklyn, N.Y., City Club, New York. Mural painter; decorative work in Bank of New York and Trust Co., Nat. Newark and Essex Bank, Willard Strait Memorial Theatre, Ithaca, N.Y., Bronx County Building, N.Y. City. Served as chmn. Committee for Erecting Carnegie Libraries in Borough of Brooklyn. Episcopalian. Fellow A.I.A. Elected Nat. Academician, 1931. Dir. Am. Acad. in Rome, 1932-35. Home: Lawrence, L.I., N.Y. Died Oct. 18, 1941.

HEWSON, Addinell, surgeon; b. Phila., Pa., Sept. 2, 1855; s. Addinell (M.D., 1828-89) and Rachel Macomb (Wetherill) H.; A.B., U. of Pa., 1876, A.M., 1879; M.D., Jefferson Med. Coll., 1879; m. Lucy Clabaugh, Sept. 4, 1883. Dispensary surg. St. Mary's Hosp., 1879-88; asst. surgeon, 1879-82, chief of surg. clinic, 1890-94, asst. ophthalmic clinic, 1882-84, Jefferson Med. Coll. Hosp.; asst. demonstrator of anatomy, 1879-86, prosecutor of anatomy, 1886-89, demonstrator of anatomy, 1889-1902, asst. prof. anatomy and demonstrator, 1902-06, Jefferson Med. Coll.; prof. anatomy, Phila. Polyclinic Coll. for Graduates in Medicine (now Post-Grad. Sch. of U. of Pa.), 1897-1928 (emeritus); sec. State Anat. Bd., 1899—; phys. to Phila. Orphan Soc., 1886-1900; surgeon to St. Timothy's (now Memorial) Hosp., Roxborough, 1894-1928 (emeritus); prof. anatomy and histology, Temple U., 1914—. Fellow Am. Coll. Surgeons. Editor Am. edit., "Holden's Dissector." Home: Bryn Mawr, Pa. Died Oct. 27, 1938.

HEXAMER, Charles John, civil engr.; b. Phila., Pa., May 9, 1862; s. Ernest and Marie (Klingel) H.; B.S., U. of Pa., 1882, A.M., 1884, Ph.D., 1886; (LL.D., Nat. U., 1899); m. Annie Josephine Haeuptner, Jan. 7, 1891. In practice, Phila., 1882-1917 (retired). Awarded Scott legacy medal and premium by Franklin Inst. for inventions. Republican. Lutheran. Author: Spontaneous Combustion, 1885; Fire Hazards in Textile Mills, Mill Architecture and Means for Extinguishing Fire, 1895; Finely Divided Organic Substances and Their Fire Hazard, 1896. Home: Atlantic City, N.J. Died Oct. 15, 1921.

HEYBURN, Weldon Brinton, senator; b. Delaware Co., Pa., May 23, 1852; acad. edn.; admitted to bar, 1876, and established practice. Removed to Shoshone Co., Ida., 1883, and entered practice there. Del. Rep. Nat. convs., 1888, 98, 1900; Rep. nominee for Congress, 1898; U.S. senator from Idaho for terms 1903-09, 1909-15. Home: Wallace, Ida. Died Oct. 17, 1912.

HEYDON, Henry Darling, capitalist; b. Coventry, R.I., Dec. 25, 1851; s. David and Remima Cordelia (Johnson) H.; ed. Mt. Pleasant Acad., Providence, R.I.; m. Charlotte Amanda Booth, Mar. 16, 1881. Began in mercantile business at Olneyville, R.I., 1871; formed partnership with Daniel W. Batchelder, 1874, and for over 30 yrs. operated gen. store at Crompton; now pres. Central Real Estate Co., Providence. Mem. R.I. Gen. Assembly, 1879-80, 1888-1902; mem. staff of Gov. Royal C. Taft of R.I., 1888-89, and of Gov. Herbert W. Ladd, 1889-92, rank of col.; served as chmn. State Armory Commn. and mem. Camp Ground Commn. for State Militia. Pres. bd. trustees R.I. Inst. for the Deaf; mem. bd. mgrs. Home for Aged Men and Aged Couples, Providence; mem. bd. dirs. Providence Lying-In Hosp. Republican. Episcopalian. Mason. Home: Providence, R.I. Died Jan. 8, 1925.

HEYDT, Herman A(ugust), lawyer; b. New York, N.Y., Dec. 5, 1868; s. Herman and Helene (Roemer) H.; A.B., Coll. of City of N.Y., 1933; LL.B., Columbia, 1894; Ph.B., St. Francis Xavier Coll., 1893; A.M., Fordham U., 1928, Ph.D., 1929, Litt.D., 1930; hon. LL.D., 1931; J.D., New York U., 1904, J.S.D., 1934; hon. D.C.L., Lincoln Memorial U., 1936; m. Margaret Sullivan, Nov. 15, 1906; 1 son, Herman August, Jr. Admitted to N.Y. bar, 1894, and began practice at New York; mem. H. A. & C. E. Heydt, 1900—; lecturer in law New York U., 1904; prof. of lit., Coll. of City of N.Y., 1933; has been yearly lecturer on lit., Fordham U.; voting trustee and dir. Frink Corp.; pres. Arbutus Realty Co.; pres. 510 Park Av. Corp. Mem. com. on Character and Fitness of the Appellate Div. of N.Y. Supreme Court for County of New York. Trustee Lincoln Memorial U., Harrogate, Tenn.; Stuyvesant Polyclinic in City of N.Y. Awarded 1st prize by Dickens Fellowship, City of N.Y. for essay on "The Pickwick Papers." Decorated by Government of Hungary with Order of the Cross and Star for his presentation of the Trianon Treaty at the Coll. of the City of New York and at Columbia U., 1936; Medallion of Honor by New York U. Republican. Presbyn. Mason. Home: New York, N.Y. Died Aug. 4, 1941.

HEYSHAM, Theodore, clergyman; b. Plymouth Twp., Pa., Jan. 14, 1864; s. Robert and Sarah Elizabeth (Hoopes) H.; Bucknell U., 1890-92; A.B., U. of Pa., 1894, Ph.D., 1898; Crozer Theol. Sem., 1894-97; m. Ella May Reese, Oct. 24, 1900; children—Anna Stewart (Mrs. Roy W. Schweiker), Theodore, Sara Reese. Ordained Bapt. ministry, 1897; pastor 1st Ch., Bridgeport, Pa., 1899-1904, Central Ch., Minneapolis, Minn., 1904-06; in San Francisco, at earthquake, 1906; rep. Calif. Bapt. Relief Com. on Atlantic seaboard, 1906-07; independent work for Christian unity, 1908-10; pastor 1st Ch., Bridgeport, 1911-14, Lower Providence Ch., Pa., 1914-23. Mem. Com. of Pub. Safety, World War. Republican. Mason. Organizer, dir. Hist. Pageant 100th Anniversary of Norristown, Pa., 1912. Author: The Birth of the Bible, 1923. Home: Norristown, Pa. Died Sept. 25, 1935.

HEYWARD, DuBose, author; b. Charleston, S.C., Aug. 31, 1885; s. Edwin W. and Jane (DuBose) H.; ed. pub. schs.; hon. Litt.D., U. of N.C., 1928, Coll. of Charleston, 1929; m. Dorothy Hartzell Kuhns, playwright, Sept. 22, 1923; 1 dau., Jenifer DuBose. Organizer Poetry Soc. S.C.; mem. Poetry Soc. America, MacDowell Colony. Democrat. Episcopalian. Author: (with Hervey Allen), Carolina Chansons, 1922; Skylines and Horizons, 1924; Porgy (novel), 1925; Angel (novel), 1926; Mamba's Daughters, 1929; Half Pint Flask, 1929; Jasbo Brown and Selected Poems, 1931; Peter Ashley (novel), 1932. "Porgy," dramatized in collaboration with Dorothy Heyward, and prod. by Theatre Guild, New York, 1927; "Brass Ankle," play, prod. 1931; "Porgy and Bess" (opera with George Gershwin, composer), prod. 1935; Lost Morning (novel), 1936; (with Dorothy Heyward) Mamba's Daughters, play prod. 1939; Star Spangled Virgin (novel), 1939. Home: Charleston, S.C. Died July 16, 1940.

HEYWOOD, Abbot Rodney, banker; b. Grafton, Mass., Sept. 16, 1855; s. Benjamin and Jane Abbie (Dennis) H.; Grafton High Sch.; read law in Salt Lake City; m. Mary Elizabeth Guthrie, Apr. 16, 1885. Practiced law in Ogden, Utah, 1879-1902; successively cashier, v.p., and pres. Commercial Nat. Bank, pres., 1906-13; sold controlling interest, 1913, and retired. City atty. of Ogden, 1889-91; mayor of Ogden, 1916-17; pres. Pub. Utility Commn., Utah. Republican. Conglist. Mason. Home: Ogden, Utah. Died Jan. 9, 1923.

HEYWOOD, Alba, oil producer and land development; b. Kingsville, O., Apr. 9, 1859; s. Chester Wright and Clarissa Beancia (Bannister) H.; ed. pub. sch., Cleveland, Geauga Sem., Chester, O., and at home; m. Genevieve Stoy, 1892; m. 2d, Frances Turner, July 19, 1906. Newsboy in Cleveland from 12 to 17; worked on farm after 20; became a canvassing agent; later an impersonator, traveling throughout U.S., 1885-1901. With brothers "struck oil," and developed oil fields at Beaumont, Tex., 1901-03; mem. Heywood Bros., who were first to discover oil in La., at Jennings, 1902; organized 1907, and was pres. San Benito (Tex.) Land & Water Co., which constructed an enormous system of gravity irrigation, drawing the water from the Rio Grande, and developed 55,000 acres, founding city of San Benito. Sr. mem. Heywood Bros. (Jennings, La.); pres. Jennings-Heywood Oil Syndicate; sec. Jennings Oil Co.; pres. San Benito Bank & Trust Co., etc. On staff Gov. N. C. Blanchard, of La., with rank of lt. col., 1904-08; Bryan Democrat. Elk. Sec. Cameron Co. Water Improvement Dist. No. 2. Home: San Benito, Tex. Died Nov. 15, 1921.

HEYWOOD, Albert Samuel, shoe mfr.; b. Worcester, Mass., May 31, 1867; s. Samuel R. and Harriet Butler (Milliken) H.; student Worcester (Mass.) Acad.; B.S., Mass. Inst. Tech., 1892; m. Laura Chester Foute, Sept. 28, 1899 (died May 5, 1913); children—Edward F. (dec.), Harriet B. (dec.), Dorothy, Anne N. (Mrs. Demeter Larisch), Elizabeth C. (dec.). Began as an engr., Gen. Electric Co., 1892; v.p. and treas. Heywood Boot and Shoe Co., 1900-13, pres., 1913—; vice-pres. Peoples Savings Bank; dir. State Mutual Life Assurance Co. Trustee Worcester Acad. Home: Worcester, Mass. Died May 31, 1938.

HEYWOOD, Charles, major general U.S. Marine Corps; b. Waterville, Me., Oct. 3, 1839; s. Lt. Charles (U.S.N.) and Antonia H.; m. Caroline Bacon, Oct. 25, 1866. Apptd. 2d lt. from N.Y., Apr. 5, 1858; promoted through grades to maj. gen., July 1, 1902.

Saw service in quelling quarantine riots, Staten Island, N.Y., Sept. 1858; then on spl. service taking captured Africans back to Africa; later at Greytown, Nicaragua, looking after the filibuster, Walker; served in U.S.S. Cumberland, Sept. 1860, until it was sunk, with flag flying, in battle with Merrimac, March 8, 1862; took part in battle of Hatteras Inlet, and capture Forts Clark and Hatteras, Aug. 1, 1861; was on Hartford, battle of Mobile Bay; also at capture Forts Gaines, Morgan, Powell, and capture ram Tennessee, and steamers Gaines and Morgan; bvtd. maj. and lt. col. "for distinguished gallantry in presence of the enemy." Had comd. battalion of marines at Baltimore, Phila. and Reading during labor riots, and was hon. mentioned by Maj. Gen. Hancock; organized and equipped, 1885, battalion to open transit and protect Am. lives and property at Panama. Comdt. U.S. Marine Corps, 1891-1903; retired Oct. 3, 1903. Died Feb. 26, 1915.

HEYWORTH, James Ormerod, contractor; b. Chicago, Ill., June 12, 1866; s. James O. and Julia F. (Dimon) H.; A.B., Yale, 1888; m. Martica G. Waterman, Jan. 15, 1902. Built (old) Coliseum, Chicago, 1894, and pres. 1894-96; mem. contracting firm Christie, Lowe & Heywoth, Chicago, 1897-1903, then alone. Among others has executed govt. contracts for jetties at Port Arthur, Tex., and Fernandino, Fla.; also for various rys.; recent yrs. specializing in hydro-electric plants. Mem. staff U.S. Shipping Bd., Washington, in charge of wood ship production, Nov. 1, 1917—. Home: Lake Forest, Ill. Died Mar. 15, 1928.

HIBBARD, Ellery Albee, lawyer; b. St. Johnsbury, Vt., July 31, 1826; s. Silas and Olive (Albee) H.; ed. there and at Derby (Vt.) Acad.; m. Mary H. Bell, Dec. 5, 1853. Admitted to bar, 1849; practiced Plymouth, N.H., 1849-53; removed to Laconia, N.H., 1853; clerk N.H. Ho. of Reps., 1852-54; mem. same, 1865-66; mem. Congress, 1871-73. Democrat. Judge Supreme Court, N.H., 1873-74; declined reapptmt.; resumed practice of law; mem. Constl. Conv., N.H., 1889. Home: Laconia, N.H. Died 1903.

HIBBARD, George, author; b. Buffalo, N.Y., Jan. 8, 1858; s. George B. and Abia T. (Hatch) H.; A.B., Harvard, 1880; unmarried. Admitted to bar, 1886; formerly devoted much time to painting; exhibited Nat. Acad. Design, 1887; illustrated own stories; asst. librarian Grosvenor Library, Buffalo. Author: Iduna, and Other Stories, 1891; The Governor, and Other Stories, 1892; Nowadays, and Other Stories, 1893; Eyes of Affection, 1906. Editor Grosvenor Library Bulletin; lecturer evening sessions, U. of Buffalo. Home: Buffalo, N.Y. Died July 3, 1928.

HIBBARD, George Albee, mayor; b. Boston, Mass., Oct. 27, 1864; s. Alonzo D. and Janette (Turner) H.; grad. Roxbury (Mass.) High Sch., 1880; m. M. Adelaide Ford, Oct. 27, 1886. Engaged in wholesale produce business with his father 8 yrs. and later in ins. business and mem. Weston K. Lewis & Co., commercial paper and bonds; treas. Hibbard & Mason Corp., tailors, 1900—. Mem. Mass. Ho. of Rep., 1894, 95; postmaster, Boston, 1900-08; mayor for term, 1908-10. Home: Boston, Mass. Deceased.

HIBBARD, H(erbert) Wade, mech. engr.; b. Maulmain, Burma, India, Sept. 10, 1863; s. Rev. Charles and Susan Ann (Robinson) H.; A.B., Brown U., 1886, A.M., 1899; M.E., Cornell, 1891; (1st Sibley prize man, 1890); m. Mary Coleman Davis, Aug. 20, 1896; children—Hope, Ruth (Mrs. Alfred S. Romer), Harlan Davis, Jeanne. With R.I. Locomotive Works, Providence, 1886-89; mech. dept., Pa. R.R., 1891-94; chief mech. engr., Lehigh Valley R.R., 1894-95; prof. machine design and locomotive engring., U. of Minn., 1895-98; prof. ry. mech. engring. and prin. Grad. Sch. Ry. Mech. Engring., Cornell U., 1898-1909; prof. mech. engring., U. of Mo., 1909—. Engring. work in Europe, 1892, 1900; engring. expert, N.Y. State Civ. Service Commn., 1904, 05, 08; smoke expert, 1908; cons. engr. on president's staff, Wabash Ry. War organizing work Council of Nat. Defense, Washington, May-Aug. 1917; U.S. dist. engr. in charge 18 Mo. counties, on power-plant fuel conservation, 1918-19. Presbyn. Member Internat. Jury Awards, San Francisco Expn., 1915. Home: Columbia, Mo. Died May 25, 1929.

HIBBEN, John Grier, pres. Princeton Univ.; b. Peoria, Ill., Apr. 19, 1861; s. Rev. Samuel and Elizabeth (Grier) H.; A.B., Princeton, 1882, A.M., 1885, Ph.D., 1893; studied Berlin U., 1882-83, Princeton Theol. Sem., 1883-86; m. Jenny Davidson, Nov. 8, 1887; 1 dau., Elizabeth Grier (wife of Prof. Robert M. Scoon). Minister Chambersburg, Pa., 1887-91; instr. logic, 1891-92, logic and psychology, 1892-94, asst. prof. of logic, 1894-97, prof., 1907-12, pres., Jan. 11, 1912—, Princeton U. Commander of Order of the Crown (Belgium); Grand Officer Order of St. Sava (Serbia). Author: The Problems of Philosophy, 1898; Hegel's Logic, 1902; Deductive Logic, 1905; The Philosophy of the Enlightenment, 1909; A Defense of Prejudice, and Other Essays, 1911; The Higher Patriotism, 1915. Home: Princeton, N.J. Died May 16, 1933.

HIBBEN, Paxton, journalist; b. Indianapolis, Ind., Dec. 5, 1880; s. Thomas Entrekin and Jeannie Merrill (Ketcham) H.; A.B., Princeton, 1903; A.M., Harvard, 1904; studied law, Harvard, 1 yr.; m. Cecile Craik, Oct. 17, 1916; 1 dau., Jean Constantine. Admitted to bar, 1906; 3rd sec. and 2d sec. Am. Embassy, Petrograd, Mexico City, 1905-08; sec. legation and chargé d'affaires, Bogota, Colombia, 1908-09, The Hague and Luxemburg, 1909-12, Santiago, Chile, 1912 (retired). War corr. Collier's Weekly, 1914-15; staff corr. Asso. Press, in Europe, 1915-17; war corr. Leslie's Weekly in Near East, and sec. Russian Commn. of Near East Relief, June-Dec. 1921. Commd. 1st lt. F.A., Nov. 27, 1917; capt., May 31, 1919; served at War Coll., Camp Grant, in France with 332d F.A., Finance Bur., S.O.S., at G.H.Q., in office Insp. Gen. A.E.F.; dischd., Aug. 21, 1919; capt. O.R.C., Feb. 7, 1920; recommd. Feb. 7, 1925. With mil. mission to Armenia, Aug.-Dec. 1919; staff corr. in Europe for Chicago Tribune, 1919-20; with Near East Relief, 1920-22; sec. Russian Red Cross Commn. in America, 1922; v. dir. for U.S. Nansen Relief Mission, 1923; sec. Am. Com. Relief Russian Children, Apr. 1922. Decorated Chevalier Order of St. Stanislas (Russian); Officer Order of the Redeemer (Greek), Order of the Sacred Treasure (Japan). Author: Constantine I and the Greek People, 1920; The Famine in Russia, 1922; Henry Ward Beecher—An American Portrait, 1927. Home: Irvington, Indianapolis, Ind. Died Dec. 5, 1928.

HIBBERD, James Farquhar, M.D.; b. nr. New Market, Md., Nov. 4, 1816; s. Joseph and Rachel (Wright) H.; grad. Coll. of Phys. and Surg., New York, 1849 (LL.D., Ind. Univ.); m. 1st, Nancy D. Higgins, March 30, 1842; 2d, Catherine Leeds, May 6, 1856; 3d, Elizabeth M. Laws, April 20, 1871. Practiced medicine in Ohio, 1840-48; on the ocean and in Calif., 1849-55; in Ind., 1856—; sec. bd. of health and health officer, Wayne Co., Ind., 1881—; prof. physiology and gen. pathology, Med. Coll. of Ohio, 1860-61. Mem. Ohio legislature, 1845-47; mayor Richmond, Ind., 1875-77. Home: Richmond, Ind. Died 1903.

HICHBORN, Philip, rear adm. U.S.N.; b. Charlestown, Mass., 1839; grad. Boston High Sch.; was 5 yrs. shipwright apprentice, Boston Navy Yards; took course of spl. instruction in ship construction, calculation and design, by direction of Navy Dept. Went from Boston to Calif., 1860; entered Mare Island Navy Yard, becoming master shipwright, 1862; entered navy, 1869, as asst. naval constructor, becoming, 1875, after competitive exam., full constructor; chief constructor, 1893-1901; retired, Mar. 4, 1901. Hon. mem. Instn. Naval Architects, Eng. Mason. Invented Franklin Life Buoy, Hichborn Balanced Turrets. Died 1910.

HICKENLOOPER, Andrew, engr., soldier; b. Hudson, O., Aug. 10, 1837; s. Andrew and Abigail H. (Cox) H.; removed to Cincinnati, 1844; ed. Woodward Coll.; practiced as civ. engr.; was chief engr., City of Cincinnati; entered army, 1861; capt. 5th O. battery; promoted to brig. gen., comdg. 3d brigade, 4th div., 17th army corps. For 5 yrs. U.S. marshal, Southern dist., O.; lt. gov. O., 1880-81; pres. Cincinnati Gas Light & Coke Co., 1872—. Author: Street Lighting, 1899; Fairy Tales, or Romance of an Arc Electric Lamp, 1901; Competition in the Manufacture and Delivery of Gas, 1881; Incandescent Electric Lights for Street Illumination, 1886. Home: Cincinnati, Ohio. Died 1904.

HICKENLOOPER, Smith, judge; b. Cincinnati, Feb. 13, 1880; s. Andrew and Maria L. (Smith) H.; B.A., U. of Cincinnati, 1901; LL.B., cum laude, Harvard, 1904; m. Anna Bailey Wright, Oct. 18, 1910; children—Smith, Gordon Wright, John Wright. Began practice at Cincinnati, 1904; was mem. Outcalt & Foraker, later Outcalt & Hickenlooper, until 1910, then Nelson & Hickenlooper, 1910-18; mem. Bd. of Edn., 1908-09; asst. pros. atty. Hamilton Co., 1916-18; judge Superior Court of Cincinnati, 1918-23; pvt. U.S.F.A. (unassigned), Camp Taylor, 1918; judge U.S. Dist. Court, Southern Dist. of Ohio, 1923-29; judge U.S. Circuit Court of Appeals, Jan. 8, 1929—. Dir. Columbia Life Ins. Co. Mem. bd. dirs. U. of Cincinnati, 1910-16. Republican. Protestant. Home: Cincinnati, O. Died Dec. 22, 1933.

HICKEY, James Burke, brig. gen.; b. in Md., May 8, 1848. Surgeon steward U.S.N., Apr. 4, 1864-May 15, 1865; grad. U.S. Mil. Acad., 1871; 2d lt. 8th Cav., June 12, 1871; 1st lt., Apr. 23, 1879; capt., Jan. 20, 1890; maj. a.-a.-g. vols., Sept. 5, 1899-Feb. 2, 1901; maj., 11th U.S. Cav., Feb. 2, 1901; transferred to 1st Cav., Nov. 29, 1904; lt. col., Nov. 30, 1904; mil. sec. U.S.A., Mar. 16, 1905; col. of cav., Nov. 15, 1908; brig. gen. retired, after 40 yrs.' service, Mar. 23, 1909. Home: New York, N.Y. Died Jan. 19, 1928.

HICKEY, Leo. J., lawyer; b. Brooklyn, N.Y.; s. Patrick Valentine and Agnes (Kavanagh) H.; A.B., St. Francis Coll., 1909; LL.B., Fordham U. Law Sch., 1912; unmarried. Admitted to N.Y. bar, 1913 and began practice at Brooklyn; now U.S. atty. Eastern Dist. of N.Y. Pres. of Boys Club Navy Yard Dist., Brooklyn. Democrat. Catholic. Home: Brooklyn, N.Y. Died Dec. 25, 1937.

HICKEY, Preston Manasseh, roentgenologist; b. Ypsilanti, Mich., Dec. 3, 1865; s. Rev. Manasseh and Sarah (Bush) H.; A.B., U. of Mich., 1888; M.D., Detroit Coll. Medicine, 1892; m. Grace Maley, Nov. 3, 1897. Practiced at Detroit, 1892-1922; prof. roentgenology, Detroit Coll. of Medicine, 1909-22; was roentgenologist Children's Harper and Receiving hosps.; lt. col. Med. Dept. U.S.A., consultant in roentgenology, A.E.F., in France, 1917-19; prof. roentgenology, U. of Mich., 1922—. Democrat. Methodist. Home: Ann Arbor, Mich. Died Oct. 30, 1930.

HICKEY, William Augustine, bishop; b. Worcester, Mass., May 13, 1869; s. William and Margaret (Troy) H.; Worcester Classical High Sch.; A.B., Holy Cross Coll., Mass., 1890; studied philosophy and theology, Sem. of St. Sulpice (Paris, France) and St. Joseph's Sem. (Brighton, Mass.). Ordained priest R.C. Ch., Christmas, 1893; asst. various chs. in Mass. until 1903; pastor St. Aloysius Ch., Gilbertville, Mass., 1903-17, St. John's Ch., Clinton, Mass., 1917-19; consecrated coadjustor bishop of Providence, R.I., Apr. 10, 1919, bishop of Providence, May 25, 1921. Pres. Providence Coll. Corp., LaSalle Acad., St. Xavier's Acad., R.I., Catholic Orphan Asylum, St. V. de Paul Infant Asylum, Visitor Printing Co. Translator: Life of Christ, 1906. Home: Providence, R.I. Oct. 4, 1933.

HICKLING, D(aniel) Percy, educator; b. Washington, D.C., Sept. 19, 1863; s. Daniel P. and Sarah A. (Russell) H.; ed. Columbian (now George Washington) U., M.D., Georgtown U. Medical School, 1884, M.A., 1925; spl. course in neurology and psychiatry, Fordham U., and further study in Paris, London, Chicago and Boston; LL.D., National U., 1927; D.Sc., Georgetown U., 1937; m. Harriet Frances Stone, Sept. 5, 1894; children—Daniel P., Mrs. John Dale Showell. Resident phys. Providence Hosp., 1884-85; visiting phys. in charge Washington Asylum Hosp., 1897-1914; cons. alienist St. Elizabeth's Hosp.; cons. neuropsychiatrist Providence Hosp.; psychiatrist in chief, Gallinger Municipal Hosp.; prof. med. jurisprudence, Nat. Univ. Law Sch.; formerly prof. clin. surgery, Georgetown U. Med. Sch.; now prof. psychiatry and neurology and head of dept. same; in charge dept. of neurology, Georgetown U. Hosp.; formerly attending specialist neuropsychiatric service, U.S. Vets'. Bur. Neuropsychiatrist Providence Hosp.; alienist for District of Columbia, 1914-33. Served as contract surgeon U.S. Army. Licensed by Am. Bd. of Psychiatry and Neurology, 1935. Episcopalian. Mason. Home: Washington, D.C. Deceased.

HICKMAN, Adam Clark, prof. law; b. Columbiana Co., Ohio, Apr. 30, 1837; s. Jeremiah and Mary (Martin) H.; Richmond Coll., Ohio, 1857-58; A.B., Allegheny Coll., Pa., 1862, A.M., 1865 (LL.D., 1902); LL.B., Ohio State and Union Law College, Cleveland, 1863; m. Ella B. Peck, Nov. 9, 1875. Practiced law, Akron, O., 1863-64, Owatonna, Minn., 1864-87, St. Paul, 1887-96; prof. law, U. of Minn., 1896-1912. Probate judge, Owatonna, 1869-72; mem. Minn. Senate, 1883-86; pres. Bd. Aldermen and acting mayor of St. Paul, 1892-93. Mason. Home: Minneapolis, Minn. Deceased.

HICKMAN, Eugene Christian, clergyman; b. Bath, S.D., Oct. 11, 1881; s. George William and Lydia (Wenz) H.; A.B., Hamline U., 1909, D.D., 1921; grad. Garrett Bibl. Inst., 1912, D.D., 1921; m. Nora D. von Berg, June 18, 1912; children—Mary Elizabeth, Jean Louise, William Hancher. Ordained M.E. ministry, 1910; successively pastor Albert Lea, Byron and Winona, Minn., until 1915; dir. publicity, Edn. Jubilee, M.E. Ch., 1915-16; nat. sec. Meth. Centenary, 1917-18; pastor Wilbur Ch., Portland, Ore., 1919-20; pres. Kimball Sch. of Theology, Salem, Ore., 1920-26; pastor Kenwood Ch., Milwaukee, Wis., 1926-29, Hamline Ch., St. Paul, Minn., 1929—. Supt. Winona Dist. M.E. Ch., 1933—. Republican. Home: St. Paul, Minn. Died June 25, 1937.

HICKOX, Ralph W., capitalist; b. Cleveland, O., 1850; A.B., Harvard, 1872. Engaged in mfg. until 1885, when retired from active business; 1st v.p. Hocking Valley Ry. Co.; dir. Toledo & Ohio Central Ry., Kanawha & Mich. Ry., N.Y., Chicago & St. Louis Ry.; officer and dir. other corps. Deceased.

HICKS, Frederick Cocks, congressman; b. Westbury, L.I., N.Y., Mar. 6, 1872; ed. Swarthmore Coll., and Harvard Law Sch., 1892-93; married. Trustee Roslyn Savings Bank; dir. Floral Park Bank, Glen Cove Ins. Co., Sea Coast Realty Co., Nassau County Trust Co., Mineola, N.Y. Defeated for 63d Congress, 1913; mem. 64th to 67th Congresses (1915-23), 1st N.Y. Dist. Republican. Friends' Ch. Home: Port Washington, L.I., N.Y. Died Dec. 14, 1925.

HICKS, John, newspaperman; b. Auburn, N.Y., Apr. 12, 1847; moved to Wisconsin in childhood; father was killed in Civil War; secured edn. by own efforts, at Lawrence U., Appleton, Wis. (LL.D., 1890). Began newspaper work at age of 20 on Oshkosh Northwestern, of which has for several yrs. been owner, and has spent life in the business. U.S. minister to Peru, 1889-93; made tour of Europe, 1895, and in 1899 spent several months in Egypt, Turkey, Italy and France. E.E. and M.P. of U.S.

to Chile, 1905-09. Author: The Man from Oshkosh, 1894; Something About Singlefoot, 1909. Home: Oshkosh, Wis. Died Dec. 20, 1917.

HICKS, Marshall, lawyer; b. Rusk, Tex., Aug. 26, 1865; s. Francis Marion and Anne Ellen (McDugald) H.; B.A., Southwestern Presbyn. U., Tenn., 1886; LL.B., U. of Tex., 1888; m. Lauraine Sedgwick Cooke, Dec. 30, 1891. Began practice at Mineola, Tex., Oct. 1888; mem. Hicks & Culberson (Robert U.), 1890-91; removed to San Antonio, 1895; mem. Lane & Hicks, 1895-97, Hicks & Hicks, 1897-1911, then Hicks, Hicks, Dickson & Bobbitt; atty. for Mexican Govt. during Huerta's administration. Dist. atty. 49th Jud. Dist. of Tex., Laredo, Tex., 1891-95; mayor San Antonio, 1899-1903; resigned to qualify as state senator 24th Senatorial District, 1903-07; mem. Dem. State Exec. Com., 1892-94; chmn. Dem. State Conv. Waco, 1900; presdl. elector at large for Texas, 1916; chmn. Tex. State Dem. Conv., San Antonio, 1922. Regent U. of Tex., term 1923-29. Chmn. Tex. State Dem. Conv., 1924. Presbyn. Home: San Antonio, Tex. Died July 18, 1930.

HICKSON, William James, psychopathologist; b. New York, Jan. 21, 1874; s. James Joseph and Mary Elizabeth (Heffernan) H.; A.B., Duquesne U., Pittsburgh, 1903; A.M., U. of Pittsburgh, 1906; M.D., Univ. of Pa., 1900; J.D. from Northwestern U., 1923; spent 2½ yrs. in Europe in research, normal and abnormal psychology, univs. and clinics of Berlin, Zürich, etc.; also post-grad. study 7 mos., 1921, 4 mos., 1927; m. Marie Katherine Kittner, July 2, 1902. Dir. Med. Research Dept. at The Training Sch., Vineland, N.J., 1912-15; psychopathologist, Psychopathic Lab. of the Municipal Court of Chicago, 1914-29. Acting chmn. Com. on Crime Prevention and Legislation, Eugenics Com. of U.S.A. First lt. Med. Corps Ill. N.G. Research work in Europe, 1929——. Died Oct. 4, 1935.

HIDDEN, William Earl, mineralogist; b. Providence, R.I., Feb. 16, 1853; s. James Edward and Abbie S. (Angel) H.; ed. pub. schs., Providence, New York and Washington; m. Josephine W. Morton, Oct. 30, 1883. Engaged as mineralogist, 1872——; discovered, 1880, mine producing emeralds and a transparent emerald-green gem, variety of spodumene (now known as hiddenite) in Alexander Co., N.C.; sent out by Edison, 1879, on a 5 months' search for platinum mines in Appalachian belt of N.C., S.C., Ga. and Ala.; discovered monazite (thought to be excessively rare) in commercial quantities in N.C., and this mineral now furnishes thoria for incandescent gas lights. Describer of iron meteorites known as the Lick Creek Iron (N.C.), the Chulafinnee (Ala.), Laurens Co. (S.C.), Elmo (Ark.), Maverick Co. (Tex.), and the thought-to-be "bielid" of Mazapil, Mex., in Am. Journal of Science. Co-discoverer and co-describer (with late Dr. James B. Mackintosh) of minerals hanksite, sulphohalite, yttrialite, thorogummite, nivenite; also (with late Samuel L. Penfield) of hamlinite; (with Dr. W. F. Hillebrand) of rowlandite and mackintoshite; (with Dr. J. H. Pratt) of the new gem rhodolite, and its associated minerals; discovered the 2d known locality for sperrylite (the only known ore of platinum) in Macon Co., N.C.; with Prof. John W. Judd of London discovered and described new mode of occurrence of ruby in Cowee Mountains of N.C.; discovered new mineral Yttrocrasite, a new yttrium-thorium-uranium titanate, from Burnet Co., Tex., an analysis by Prof. C. H. Warren, Am. Jour. Science, Dec. 1906. Solving the mineral. and geol. problems of Cobalt, Ont., 1906——. In Aug. 1911, traced the occurrence of the rich ore of thorium, auerlite, to its source in the Green River Zircon belt of Henderson Co., N.C., and found it in place there and mined several tons of zircons which were used in electric light glowers and in making "zircon-glas." Consulting mining geologist to Sunshine Copper Co. of Lavic, Calif., where is pursuing a mineral reconnaissance. Fellow Geol. Soc., London. Home: Ocean Grove, N.J. Died June 1918.

HIDER, Arthur, engineer; b. London, Eng., Feb. 29, 1844; s. James and Maria H.; ed. in London, Can., and Cleveland, O.; pvt. pupil, 1864-66, Peter Emslie, C.E. (dec.). Draftsman and asst. city engr., Louisville, Ky., 1866-74; prin. asst. city engr. Louisville, 1874-76; consulting engr., 1876-78; in charge surveys and physical exams. lower Mississippi, under U.S. Engrs. Corps, 1878-81; prin. engr. in local charge improvements on Mississippi River, 3d dist., under Mississippi River Commn., 1881——. Home: Grenville, Miss. Died July 28, 1916.

HIESTER, Anselm Vinet, college prof.; b. Annville, Pa., Nov. 27, 1866; s. Jonathan Ebling and Mary Catharine (Marshall) H.; B.S., Lebanon Valley Coll., Pa., 1887; B.A., Franklin and Marshall Coll., 1889; M.A., New York U., 1892; Union Theol. Sem., 1891-92; grad. Eastern Theol. Sem., Lancaster, Pa., 1894; fellow in sociology, Columbia, 1896-98; D.Sc., Ursinus, 1913; m. Mary Lincoln Morgan, Aug. 16, 1898; children—Ernest Morgan, Marian Anselma. Prof. mathematics, Palatinate College, Myerstown, Pa., 1889-91; instr., 1892-94, asst. prof. mathematics and German, 1894-96, prof. polit. and social science, 1898——, Franklin and Marshall Coll. Republican. Mem. Ref. Ch. Home: Lancaster, Pa. Died Nov. 18, 1927.

HIGBEE, Albert Enos, surgeon; b. Pike, N.Y., 1842; s. John Enos and Lucy (Patch) H.; M.D., Hahnemann Med. Coll., Chicago, 1871; m. Anna Maria Lynch, Sept. 26, 1872. Practiced, Red Wing, 1869-75, St. Paul, 1875-78, Minneapolis, 1878——; formerly mem. faculty U. of Minn. Coll. of Medicine and Surgery. Private Co. B, 12th Wis. Vols., 1862-65. Republican. Presbyn. Scottish Rite Mason. Home: Minneapolis, Minn. Died Apr. 3, 1924.

HIGBEE, Harry, judge; b. Pittsfield, Ill., Dec. 13, 1854; s. Chauncey L. and Julia M. (White) H.; A.B., Yale, 1875; student Sch. of Law, Columbia U., 1876; LL.B., Union Coll. of Law, Chicago, Ill., 1878; m. Maude Moreland. Admitted to bar, 1879; practiced at Pittsfield, Matthews, Wike & Higbee (except 1 yr., 1884, in Minneapolis). Pres. 1st Nat. Bank, Pittsfield. Mem. Ill. Senate, 1889-96; judge Circuit Ct. of Ill. 1897; justice Appellate Ct., 4th Dist., 1898——. Democrat. Home: Pittsfield, Ill. Died Jan. 29, 1929.

HIGBIE, Robert Winfield, banker; b. Springfield Gardens, N.Y., Mar. 5, 1863; s. Alexander and Sarah Frances (Davison) H.; A.B., New York U., 1882, A.M., 1887, LL.D., 1932; LL.D., Alfred U., 1928; m. Anna Augusta Pearsall, Sept. 12, 1888; children —Hamilton Alexander, Robert Winfield. With Hanover Nat. Bank, New York, 1882-85; Jamaica (L.I.) Lumber & Coal Co., 1885-88; mem. Carpenter & Higbie, Jamaica, 1888-93, Marsh & Higbie, New York, 1893-96; in business for self, 1896——; pres. Queensboro Development Corp., Higbie Corner; v.p. Forest Hill Estates, Jamaica Savings Bank. Pres. Nat. Wholesale Lumber Dealers' Assn., 1910-11; Chamber Commerce Borough of Queens, New York, 1913-15; chmn. for Borough of Queens, Roosevelt Memorial Com.; regent Univ. State of N.Y., 1925——; mem. Mayor's Com. on Plan and Survey, N.Y. City, also Mayor's Com. to Revise Teachers' Salaries; mem. commn. to investigate reforestation of N.Y. State; mem. N.Y. City Charter Revision Commn., 1934. An incorporator and dir. of World's Fair, N.Y., 1939. Dir. and trustee Y.M.C.A., Brooklyn and Queens. Republican presdl. elector, 1916. Conglist. Home: Kew Gardens, N.Y. Died June 20, 1936.

HIGGINS, Alice Louise, social worker; b. Boston, Mar. 28, 1870; d. Albert H. and Addie A. (Everson) H.; ed. pvt. schs., Boston; spl. training in Asso. Charities, Boston, 1898-1900; N.Y. Sch. of Philanthropy, summer of 1902; m. William H. Lothrop, May 1913. Dist. sec., 1900-02, gen. sec., 1902-13, Associated Charities, Boston; mem. exec. com. Mass. Child Labor Com.; mem. Mass. Civic League, Mass. Commn. to Investigate Employment Agencies, 1910-11; chmn. Am. Assn. for Organizing Charity, 1914—; dir. civilian relief for N.E. of Am. Red Cross, 1917-19. Unitarian. Home: Newtonville, Mass. Died Sept. 2, 1920.

HIGGINS, Alvin McCaslin, lawyer; b. Superior, Wis., Nov. 19, 1866; s. Rev. William Rayburn and Mary Elizabeth (Condon) H.; student Oberlin, 1884-88; m. Margaret Beatrice Keating, Apr. 12, 1899. Admitted to Ind. bar, 1888, and practiced at Terre Haute; 1st pres. Citizens Telephone Co., Terre Haute; a founder Terre Haute Commercial Club, and Ft. Harrison Savings Assn.; trustee Terre Haute Carriage & Buggy Co., 1896-1907. Pres. Rep. League of Clubs for Ind., campaign of 1896, reëlected, 1897; U.S. commr. for Western Ind., at Terre Haute, 1897-1908; pres. Bd. of Pub. Safety, Terre Haute, 1905. Enlisted in Vet. Corps Arty., N.G.N.Y., Mar. 1917; trans. to 9th Coast Arty., N.G.N.Y., Oct. 9, 1917; chmn. Washington Hgts. Legal Advisory Bd., N.Y. City, under Selective Service Act, World War. Author: Watch Your Step, 1915; We, the People—, 1920; Everything Lost but the Chains, 1920. Home: Croton-on-Hudson, N.Y. Died Apr. 6, 1938.

HIGGINS, A(ndrew) Foster, adjuster of averages; b. Macon, Ga., Jan. 24, 1831; s. Charles A. and Lucy R. (Crocker) H.; ed. U. of New York and Columbia; m. Sarah Hamilton Cornell, May 5, 1852; engaged in law practice at New York, 1847—; in firms of Jones & Johnson, Johnson & Higgins, and Higgins & Cox; atty., pres. U.S. Lloyds Marine Ins.; pres. Knickerbocker Trust Co., 1907-10; pres., dir. Mexican Northern Ry. Co., v.p. and dir. Compania Metalurgica Mexicana, Sombrerete Mining Co. Home: Greenwich, Conn. Died Nov. 28, 1916.

HIGGINS, Anthony, senator; b. Red Lion Hundred, Del., Oct. 1, 1840; s. Anthony Madison and Sarah Clark (Corbit) H.; bro. of John Clark H.; A.B., Yale, 1861; Harvard Law Sch., 1 yr.; (LL.D., Yale, 1891); unmarried. Admitted to bar, 1864, and practiced at Wilmington; chmn. Rep. State Com., 1868; U.S. atty. for Del., 1869-76; received vote of Rep. members Del. legislature for U.S. senator, 1881; Rep. candidate for Congress, 1884; U.S. senator, 1889-95. Counsel for Judge Charles Swayne in his impeachment trial before U.S. Senate, 1905. Home: Wilmington, Del. Died June 26, 1912.

HIGGINS, Edward, consul; b. Boston, Mass., May 30, 1856; s. James and Mary (Lucas) H.; ed. Cambridge (Latin) Sch., and Boston U. Sch. of Theology; m. Mary A. Willis. Joined N.E. Conf., M.E. Ch.; preacher and lecturer, 1881-1903. Consul at Berne, 1903-07, at Stuttgart, Apr. 29, 1907-July 1916, Bahia, Brazil, July 1916—. Died Nov. 17, 1919.

HIGGINS, Elmore Fitzpatrick, banker; b. Dallas, Tex., Oct. 21, 1882; s. Simeon Shy and Rosalie Virginia (Fitzpatrick) H.; ed. grammar sch., Montgomery, Ala.; m. Mary Shepherd Knowles, Nov. 12, 1912 (died 1924); children—Mary Knowles, Elmore Fitzpatrick, Roberta Shepherd; m. 2d, Catherine Prentice McMillan, Aug. 15, 1927; 1 daughter, Ann Prentice. Began as a boy in employ of Merchants & Planters Nat. Bank of Montgomery and after various mergers, resigned from First Nat. Bank to join Fourth Nat. Bank, 1912; asst. bank examiner, New Orleans Clearing House Assn., 1912-14; then nat. examiner in Ga., western Pa. and Chicago, Ill., advancing to chief nat. bank examiner 6th Federal Reserve Dist., at Atlanta; became connected in 1919 with Nat. Bank of Commerce, N.Y. City, as asst. cashier, later v.p.; v.p. Bank of America, New York, 1926, and when it was absorbed by the Nat. City Bank, was made v.p. of the latter; pres. Nat. Bank of Tulsa, Okla., 1932-33; v.p. Nat. City Bank of New York, 1933-38; pres. Royal Crown Bottling Corp. of Westchester, New Rochelle, N.Y., 1932—. Served as mem. Ala. N.G. Ind. Democrat. Home: Pelham Manor, N.Y. Died Mar. 27, 1941.

HIGGINS, Frank James, lawyer; b. New York, N.Y., March 18, 1869; s. William S. and Louise M. A. (Robb) H.; ed. pub. schs., Jersey City, N.J.; m. Naomie M. Millelot, Feb. 6, 1895; m. 2d, Ethel Jenkins, June 2, 1910; m. 3d, Lucy Adamy, Aug. 28, 1927. Reporter Jersey City News, and New York World, 1890-91; editor Town Talk, Jersey City, 1891-93; editor and propr. Jersey City Chronicle, 1893; under-sheriff, Hudson Co., N.J., 1893; clerk, N.J. Gen. Assembly, 1897; clerk, Criminal Ct. of Jersey City, 1898; admitted to N.J. bar, 1900; judge First Criminal Ct., 1904—. Pres. State Rep. League of N.J., 1894; treas. Nat. Rep. League of U.S., 1897—. Pres. Hudson Casualty Ins. Co. of N.J., 1921—. Home: Ridgewood, N.J. Died Mar. 14, 1937.

HIGGINS, Frank Wayland, gov.; b. Rushford, N.Y., Aug. 18, 1856; s. Orrin Trall and Lucia C. (Hapgood) H.; grad. Riverview Mil. Acad., Poughkeepsie, 1873; also took business course; m. Kate C. Noble, June 5, 1878. In mercantile business, Stanton, Mich., 1875-79; in Olean, N.Y., 1879. State senator, 50th dist. N.Y., 1894-1902; lt. gov. N.Y. for term, 1903-05; elected gov. N.Y., 1904, for term 1905-07. Republican. Trustee Western N.Y. Home for Friendless and Dependent Children, Chautauqua Assembly, etc. Home: Olean, N.Y. Died 1907.

HIGGINS, James Henry, governor; b. Lincoln, R.I., Jan. 22, 1876; s. Thomas F. and Elizabeth Ann (Mather) H.; A.B., Brown U., 1898; LL.B., Georgetown U., Washington, 1900; admitted to bar, 1900; m. Ellen F. Maguire, Nov. 17, 1908; children—James H., John T. Mem. R.I. Legislature, 1902; mayor Pawtucket, 1903-06; gov. of R.I., 1907-08, 1908-09. Democrat. Catholic. Home: Pawtucket, R.I. Died Sept. 16, 1927.

HIGGINS, John Wilfred, chmn. Chicago R.R. Presidents' Conf.; b. Newport, R.I., Oct. 12, 1864; s. Hugh and Mary (Fitzgerald) H.; ed. pub. schs.; m. Kate Eloise Evans, June 27, 1893; children— Eloise Winifred, Jeannette Lupton. Began, 1879, with Toledo, Peoria & Western Ry. and I.C. R.R. as joint messenger and U.S. transfer clk.; continued with I.C. R.R. in various positions, advancing to gen. supt. transportation, 1901; asst. supt. various divisions Grand Trunk Ry., in Can., 1903-04; with M.P. R.R. Co. and St. Louis, Iron Mountain & Southern R.R. (now M.P. System), 1904-15, serving as asst. gen. mgr. 6 yrs. and gen. mgr. 4½ yrs.; elected chmn. Gen. Mgrs. Assn. of Chicago, 1915, also exec. sec. Assn. Western Rys.; chmn. exec. com. Western Demurrage and Storage Bur., 1915-33; elected chmn. exec. com. and advisory com. Assn. Western Rys., 1920; chmn. exec. com. Western Assn. Ry. Execs., Feb. 1929-Dec. 1932; chmn. Chicago R.R. Presidents' Conf., Sept. 1930—. Chairman Conf. of Mgrs. handling negotiations before the President's Emergency Bd. under Ry. Labor Act in wage dispute, 1928. Home: Chicago, Ill. Died Mar. 1, 1936.

HIGGINS, Katharine Elizabeth Chapin, philanthropist; b. Manchester, N.H., Dec. 11, 1847; d. Aldus Manutius and Catherine Fisher (Sawin) Chapin; grad. Abbot Acad., Andover, Mass., 1868; m. Milton Prince Higgins, June 15, 1870 (died 1912). Teacher pub. schs., Manchester, 1869-70; regent Col. Timothy Bigelow Chapter D.A.R., 1908-10; Mass. state historian D.A.R., 1910-12; Mass. state pres. Congress of Mothers and Parent Teachers Assn., 1912-20; nat. pres. same, 1920-23; del. to Internat. Council of Women, Christiania, Norway, 1920. Prominent in war work and in securing relief for war vets. Republican. Conglist. Author: Richard Higgins and His Descendants, 1918. Home: Worcester, Mass. Died Jan. 9, 1925.

HIGGINS, Milton Prince, mfr.; b. Standish, Me., Dec. 7, 1842; s. Lewis and Susan (Whitney) H.; B.S., Dartmouth Coll., 1868; m. Katharine Elizabeth Chapin, June 15, 1870. Draftsman and engr. Washburn & Moen Mfg. Co., Worcester, Mass., 1868; supt. Washburn shops of Worcester Poly. Inst., 1869-96. Pres. Norton Emery Wheel Co., Worcester, 1885—, Plunger Elevator Co., 1896—, Norton Grinding Co.,

1900—, Worcester Pressed Steel Co., 1904—; dir. Mechanics Nat. Bank of Worcester. Expert in patent causes; consulting engr. in establishing shops at Miller Manual Labor Sch., Crozet, Albemarle Co., Va., 1880-82; cons. engr. and supt. of shops, Ga. Sch. of Tech., Atlanta, 1887-89. Mem. Mass. Commn. on Industrial Edn., 1908; pres. trustees Independent Industrial Schs., 1909—; trustee Worcester Poly. Inst.; mem. and dir. Worcester Bd. of Trade and Worcester Metal Trades Assn. Republican. Conglist. Home: Worcester, Mass. Died Mar. 8, 1912.

HIGGINS, Richard Thomas, lawyer; b. Washington, Conn., Sept. 24, 1865; s. Edward and Mary (Crowley) H.; ed. high sch., Woodbury, Conn., and St. Francis Coll., Brooklyn, N.Y.; studied law in office Huntington & Warner, Woodbury; LL.D., Fordham U., 1921; m. Margaret R. Bryan, Sept. 1, 1898; 1 son, Bryan Edward; m. 2d, Margaret B. Noonan, July 3, 1923. Admitted to Conn. bar, 1890, and began practice at Woodbury; moved to Winsted, 1891; dir. Winsted Savings Bank. Coroner, Litchfield Co., Conn., 1892-1910; corp. counsel, Town of Winchester, Conn., 1904-12; mem. Conn. Ho. of Rep. (minority floor leader), 1909; railroad commr., Conn., 1910-11; chmn. Pub. Utilities Commn., Conn., 1911—; chmn. Selective Draft Bd., Litchfield, 1917. Democrat. K.C. Home: West Hartford, Conn. Died Sept. 16, 1934.

HIGGINS, Robert Barnard, naval officer; b. Rockville, Md., Sept. 16, 1868; grad. U.S. Naval Acad., 1882. Promoted asst. engr., July 1, 1884; passed asst. engr., Jan. 15, 1895; transferred to the line as lt., Mar. 3, 1899; lt. comdr., Oct. 11, 1903; comdr., Jan. 30, 1908; capt., July 1, 1911. Served on Amphitrite, Spanish-Am. War, 1898, on Atlanta, 1904; fleet engr., S. Atlantic Squadron, 1904-05; duty at U.S. Naval Acad., 1905-07; fleet engr., Atlantic Fleet, 1907-08; at Navy Yard, N.Y. City, 1908-09; apptd. insp. engring. material, Conn. Dist., Sept. 1909. Died Jan. 6, 1928.

HIGGINS, William Edward, professor law; b. Rush Co., Ind., May 6, 1865; s. Silas Colfax and Hester Ann (Waller) H.; B.S., U. of Kan., 1888, LL.B., 1894; m. Ella Marie Anderson, Dec. 27, 1899. Practiced in Kansas City, Mo., 1894-1902; asst. prof. law, 1899-1902, asso. prof., 1902-04, prof. pleading and practice, 1904—, U. of Kan. On leave of absence, 1913-14, as commr. to investigate law courts of England and certain other European countries and report thereon to the Am. Judicature Soc. to promote the efficient administration of justice, Chicago; report to same, 1915; mem. spl. com. which revised Kan. code of civil procedure; chmn. spl. com. State Bar Assn. of Kan. on Criminal Law and Procedure and joint author of 9 spl. measures to improve criminal procedure; mem. bd. of edn., Lawrence, Kan., 1906-13. Republican. Methodist. Mem. Commn. on Uniform State Laws, 1913, 14; sec. Kan. State Soc. Criminal Law and Criminology, 1911-13. Mason. Home: Lawrence, Kan. Died May 13, 1920.

HIGGINSON, Ella, author; b. Council Grove, Kan.; d. Charles Reeves and Mary A. Rhoads; ed. Oregon City Sem. and pvt. sch.; m. Russell Carden Higginson (died 1909). Writer of short stories, novels, travel and verse; conducted literary dept. Seattle Sunday Times several yrs. Hon. life mem. Bellingham Library Bd. Republican. Author: Mariella, of Out-West (novel), 1904; The Voice of April-Land (poems), 1906; Alaska, The Great Country, 1908; The Takin' In of Old Mis' Lane (which won McClure's $500 prize for best short story); The Vanishing Race (poems), 1912; The Message of Anne Laura Sweet (winner $500 prize in Collier's), 1914. Home: Bellingham, Wash. Died Dec. 29, 1940.

HIGGINSON, Francis John, rear admiral U.S.N.; b. Boston, Mass., July 19, 1843; s. Stephen and Agnes Gordon (Cochrane) H.; apptd. from Mass., and grad. U.S. Naval Acad., 1861; m. Grace Glenwood Haldane, Jan. 5, 1878. Promoted lt., July 1, 1862; lt. comdr., July 25, 1866; comdr., June 10, 1876; capt., Sept. 27, 1891; commodore, Aug. 10, 1898; rear admiral, Mar. 3, 1899. Served on Colorado, W. Gulf Blockading Squadron, 1861-62; wounded in boat attack privateer Judith, Pensacola Harbor; participated in bombardments and passage of Fts. Jackson and St. Philip; engagements with Chalmette batteries, and capture of New Orleans; served Vixen, 1862, Powhatan, 1862-64, S. Atlantic Blockading Squadron; participated in bombardment of Ft. Sumter; exec. officer Housatonic when she was blown up by a torpedo off Charleston; Naval Acad., 1864-65; Hartford, Asiatic Squadron, 1865-68; Franklin, 1868-69; Richmond, 1869-71; Shenandoah, 1871-73; exec. officer Franklin, 1873-74, Dictator, 1874; comd. naval rendezvous, Boston, 1874-75; exec. officer receiving ship Ohio, 1875; Torpedo Sch., Newport, 1875; Bur. Ordnance, 1875-77; on various duties to 1894; capt. of yard, Navy Yard, Mare Island, 1894-95; comd. Monterey, Feb.-Sept. 1895; spl. duty, Navy Yard, New York, 1895-96; capt. of yard, Navy Yard, New York, 1896-97; comd. Massachusetts, 1897-98, during war with Spain; advanced 3 numbers in rank for eminent and conspicuous conduct in battle, during Spanish-Am. War; chmn. Lighthouse Bd., 1898-1901; comdr.-in-chief N. Atlantic Fleet, 1901-03; comdt. Navy Yard, Washington, 1903-05; retired, July 19, 1905. Home: Kingston, N.Y. Died Sept. 13, 1931.

HIGGINSON, Francis Lee, financier; b. Boston, Mass., Oct. 11, 1841; s. George and Mary C. (Lee) H.; A.B., Harvard, 1863. Entered 54th Mass. Inf. as 2d lt., Feb. 1863, becoming 1st lt. and capt. same; capt. 5th Mass. Cav., 1864; mustered out Nov. 1865; m. Miss Shattuck, April 11, 1898. Dir. Calumet & Hecla Consolidated Co., Merchants Nat. Bank, Mass. Hosp. Life Ins. Co., etc. Home: Boston, Mass. Died Aug. 19, 1925.

HIGGINSON, Henry Lee, banker; b. New York, Nov. 18, 1834; s. George and Mary C. H.; entered Harvard, 1851, but did not complete course (hon. A.M., Harvard U., 1882; LL.D., Yale U., 1901; LL.D., Williams Coll., 1912); m. Ida Agassiz, Dec. 5, 1863. Employe in counting-house of S. & E. Austin, Boston; then went to Vienna; studied music; served in U.S. Vols. in Civil War, becoming maj. and bvt. lt. col., 1st Mass. Cav.; severely wounded at Aldie, Va., June 1863. Mem. Lee Higginson & Co., bankers and brokers, 1868—; pres. New Boston Music Hall, Gauley Coal Land Co.; v.p. Provident Instn. for Savings, Smuggler Union Mining Co. Trustee Carnegie Instn. Washington, N.E. Conservatory of Music, Franklin Union; fellow Pres. and Fellows of Harvard, 1893—. Home: Boston, Mass. Died Nov. 15, 1919.

HIGGINSON, Mary P. Thacher, author; b. (Thacher) Machias, Me., Nov. 26, 1844; ed. pvt. schs., Portland, Me., and Springfield, Mass.; m. Thomas Wentworth Higginson, Feb. 6, 1879; children—Louisa Wentworth (dec.), Margaret Waldo. Author: Sea Shore and Prairie (sketches), 1876; Room for One More (story), 1879 (with her husband) Such as They Are (poems), 1894; Thomas Wentworth Higginson, the Story of His Life, 1914; Letters and Journals of Thomas Wentworth Higginson, 1921; The Playmate Hours (poems), 1904; Fugitives (poems), 1929. Home: Cambridge, Mass. Died Jan. 9, 1941.

HIGGINSON, Thomas Wentworth, author; b. Cambridge, Mass., Dec. 22, 1823; s. Stephen and Louisa (Storrow) H.; A.B., Harvard, 1841; grad. Harvard Div. Sch., 1847 (A.M., 1869, LL.D., 1898; LL.D., Western Reserve, 1896); in Civil War as capt., 51st Mass. Vol. Militia, later col. 1st S.C. (Union) Vols., afterward 33d U.S.C.T.; m. Mary P. Thacher, Feb. 6, 1879. Was a v.p. Liberal Congress of Religion; fellow Am. Acad. Arts and Sciences; corr. mem. Royal Soc. of Canada. Author: Outdoor Papers, 1863; Army Life in a Black Regiment, 1869; Young Folks' History of the U.S., 1875; Young Folks' Book of American Explorers, 1877; Short Studies of American Authors, 1879; The Monarch of Dreams, 1886; Women and Men, 1887; Cheerful Yesterdays, 1898; Tales of the Enchanted Islands of the Atlantic, 1898; Contemporaries, 1899; Collected Works (reprinted in 7 vols.), 1900; Henry W. Longfellow (in Am. Men of Letters Series), 1903; John G. Whittier (in English Men of Letters Series), 1903; A Reader's History of American Literature, 1903; Life of Stephen Higginson, Member Continental Congress, 1907; Carlyle's Laugh and Other Surprises, 1909. Home: Cambridge, Mass. Died May 9, 1911.

HIGHLAND, Virgil Lee, banker; b. Harrison Co., W.Va., Aug. 31, 1870; s. John Edgar and Lucy Earle (Patton) H.; student Scio (Ohio) Coll., 1898; Wesleyan U., Delaware, O., 1890; m. Gertrude E. Morgan, Dec. 31, 1902. Pres. Empire Nat. Bank (Clarksburg), West Chevy Chase Land Co., Union Co., Duncan Land Co., Clarksburg Pub. Co. (pubs. Clarksburg Daily Telegram and Clarksburg Exponent). Chmn. Rep. State Com., W.Va., 1912-16; mem. Rep. Nat. Com., 1916—; chmn. W.Va. Pub. Service Commn., 1913. Mason. Home: Clarksburg, W.Va. Died Aug. 9, 1930.

HIGHSMITH, Jacob Franklin, surgeon; b. on farm nr. Roseboro, N.C., Sept. 1, 1868; s. John James and Mary Ann (Fowler) H.; Wake Forest (N.C.) Coll., 1885-87; M.D., Jefferson Med. Coll., 1889; m. Mary Lou White, Nov. 14 1889; children—James Dacosta, Mrs. Mamie Wells, Mrs. Annie Campbell, Nita, Mrs. Louise Hardee, Jacob Franklin, William Cochran, Mrs. Rachel Caldwell. Practiced at Fayetteville until 1899; organizer, 1899, and pres. Highsmith Hosp. Co.; has devoted entire time from 1906 to hosp. surgery; now chief surgeon and med. dir. Highsmith Hosp.; surgeon to A.C.L. R.R., Norfolk Southern R.R.; extensively engaged in farming. Chmn. Med. Advisory Bd., U.S.A.; pres. N.C. State Med. Examining Bd., N.C. Med. Soc.; organizer and 1st pres. N.C. Hosp. Assn.; fellow Am. Coll. Surgeons. Democrat. Missionary Baptist. Mason. Home: Fayetteville, N.C. Died June 22, 1939.

HIGHTOWER, Emmett, clergyman; b. Cass Co., Tex., Mar. 31, 1866; s. Isaac Oslin and Rebecca Amanda (Dudley) H.; Southwestern U., Georgetown, Tex., 1883-89 (D.D., 1919); Vanderbilt U., 1890-91; m. Ruth Gertrude Dysart, Sept. 21, 1892; children—Ruth, Paul Alison, Mary (Mrs. W. P. Young), Emmennt Dysart, Frank Chapman. Ordained ministry M.E. Ch., S., 1887; pastor successively, Ft. Worth (Tex.) Circuit, Jacksboro, Vernon, Taylor, Mansfield, Colorado City, Dublin, Stephenville, Walnut Springs, Glen Rose, Sweetwater, Cisco, Gatesville, Belton, Morrow St. Ch., Waco; S.S. field sec. Central Tex. Conf., 1911-12; pastor 1st Ch., Weatherford, Tex., 1912-14; divisional field sec. S.S. Bd. M.E. Ch., S., 1914-18; supt. Bible class work, 1918-19; asso. editor S.S. lit. M.E. Ch., S., 1918—. Trustee Southwestern U., Weatherford Junior College. Home: Nashville, Tenn. Died Oct. 9, 1929.

HIGINBOTHAM, Harlow Niles, merchant; b. Joliet, Ill., Oct. 10, 1838; s. Henry D. and Rebecca H.; ed. Lombard U., Galesburg, Ill., and the Commercial Coll., Chicago; pvt. in Mercantile Battery of Chicago, Union Army, and chief clerk with chief q.-m., dept. of the Ohio, 1862-65; m. Rachel D. Davison, Dec. 7, 1865 (died 1909). Entered employ Field, Palmer & Leiter, dry goods, 1865; partner in that firm's successor, Field, Leiter & Co., 1868; and, 1881-1901, of the present firm of Marshall Field & Co.; now pres. Am. Luxfer Prism Co., Caxton Co. Pres. World's Columbian Expn. from 1892 until its close; pres. Field Mus. of Natural History, 1897-1909. The Chicago Home for Incurables, Municipal Sanitarium for Tuberculosis, etc. Home: Chicago, Ill. Died Apr. 18, 1919.

HIGLEY, Warren, lawyer; b. nr. Auburn, N.Y., July 1, 1833; s. Chester and Prudence (Miller) H.; A.B., Hamilton Coll., 1862, A.M., 1865; m. Mrs. Christina J. Haley, July 21, 1891. Prin. Cayuga Lake Acad., Aurora, N.Y., 1863-66, and 1868-70; prin. high sch. and supt. pub. schs., Auburn, N.Y., 1866-68; prin. high sch., Cleveland, O., 1870-71; supt. pub. schs., Dayton, O., 1871-73; admitted to bar, 1874; practiced at Cincinnati, 1874-84, at New York, 1884—. Judge City Ct., Cincinnati, 1881-83. Pres. Ohio State Forestry Assn., 1882-84, Am. Forestry Congress, 1885-86, Adirondack League, 1901-06; founder Assn. for Protection of the Adirondacks; trustee Hudson-Fulton Celebration Commn. Home: Larchmont, N.Y. and N.Y. City. Died 1911.

HILAND, James H., ry. official; b. in Vt., Sept. 27, 1848. Asst. traffic mgr. Chicago, St. Paul, Minneapolis & Omaha Ry., 1878-82; gen. traffic mgr., 1882-83, gen. freight agt., Oct. 1883-Dec. 1884, same rd.; arbitrator and referee, C.,St.L.&Mo. R. Pass. Assn., Dec. 15, 1884-July 1, 1885; gen. agt. Minneapolis Millers' Assn., July 1885-Sept. 1887, at Minneapolis; gen. agt., 1887-89, gen. frt. agt., 1889-1900, traffic mgr., 1900-03, 3d v.p., 1903-17, retired v.p., Dec. 15, 1917, C.,M.&St.P. Railway. Home: Chicago, Ill. Died May 20, 1929.

HILDEBURN, Charles Swift Riché, author, librarian; b. Phila., Aug. 14, 1855; ed. private schools; m. June 12, 1894, Sarah Elizabeth, d. Robert Winchester, Phila. Became librarian Phila. Athenæum, 1876. Author: The Issues of the Press in Pennsylvania, 1685-1784 (2 vols., 4to.); Sketches of Printers and Printing in Colonial New York; etc. Editor of Statutes at Large of Pa., vols. II. to VI. Home: Philadelphia, Pa. Died 1901.

HILDER, Howard, artist; b. London, Eng., Sept. 28, 1866; s. John and Julia (Sandys) H.; ed. Clifden House, Brentford, Middlesex, and U. Coll. Sch., London; practice of architecture, London, until 1900; studied art at Julian Académie in Paris under Bouguereau, Ferrier and other masters, 1900-03; paintings in The Hague, Holland, under Israels, Mesdag, de Bock; m. Carolien Enthoven, of London, 1891; 1 son, John Chapman. Came to U.S., 1905. Landscape and mural painter, formerly of Newport, R.I., and Charleston, S.C. Works: Scenery for Viking Pageant, Newport Art Assn., 1922; series of murals of life of Christ, St. Stephen's Ch., Coconut Grove, Fla.; murals, King Cole Hotel and Nautilus Hotel, Miami Beach, and Woman's Club, Miami; scenic paintings, auditorium Miami Sr. High Sch.; portrait of Admiral Albert Ross, Culver (Ind.) Mil. Acad.; scenery for opening of Bok-Annie Russell Presentation Theatre, Rollins Coll., Winter Park, Fla., 1932; Mabel Loomis Todd memorial painting, St. Stephens Episcopal Ch., Coconut Grove, 1933; Bok-Annie Russell Model Theatre scenery, 1933; portrait of Mrs. Moray Nairne Wootten (dau. Gen. R. E. Mead). Awarded Elliott silver medal for nude drawings, Nat. Acad. Design, 1906; hon. mention for "Florida Pines," Palm Beach Art Center Nat. Exhbn. Founder and 1st pres. Fla. Soc. Arts and Sciences. Homes: Coconut Grove, Fla., and Waban-Aki, Muscongus, Me. Died June 30, 1935.

HILDER, John Chapman, editor, writer; b. London, Eng., Aug. 11, 1892; s. George Howard and Carolien (Enthoven) H.; early education in France and England; came to U.S., 1905; student school of Architecture (Columbia), 1911; m. Eleanor B. Hotchkiss, June 12, 1915; 1 son, John Chapman; m. 2d, Vera de Wolfe, June 13, 1928. Lit. editor The Delineator, New York, 1913; asso. editor Vanity Fair, 1914-16; circulation mgr. Harper's Weekly, Jan.-May 1916; editor Motor Life, Bazar, 1917-18; editor same, 1918-20; mng. editor La France, 1920-21; mng. editor The Elks Magazine, Feb. 1922-Jan. 1930. Died May 21, 1936.

HILDRETH, David Merrill, civil engr.; b. Haverhill, N.H., Jan. 15, 1862; s. Sylvester Levi and Teressa (Nelson) H.; B.S., Dartmouth, 1887, M.S.,

1894; LL.M., Columbian (now George Washington) U. Law Sch., 1896; m. Cleora H. DeCoster, Jan. 1, 1889. Asst. on New Hampshire-Mass. boundary survey, 1887-88; topo. draftsman, Coast and Geodetic Survey, 1888-12; topographer Post Office Dept., Mar. 6, 1912-June 15, 1920; mem. U.S. Geographic Bd., Oct. 1912-Oct. 1920. Universalist. Mason. Home: Hanover, N.H. Died June 2, 1923.

HILDRETH, John Lewis, physician; b. N. Chelmsford, Mass., Nov. 29, 1838; s. John C. and Harriet Maria (Blanchard) H.; A.B., Dartmouth, 1879, as of 1864, M.D., 1867; (LL.D., Tufts, 1900); m. Achsah B. Colburn, Mar. 2, 1864. U.S. sanitary and relief agt. and insp. camps and hosps., 1864-65; prin. Peterborough (N.H.) Acad., 1865-67; in practice at Townsend, Mass., 1867-70, at Cambridge, Mass., 1870—; mem. sch. bd., 1875-89; surgeon 4th Battalion, Mass. N.G., 1875-76; med. dir. 1st Brigade, 1876-79; med. examiner Middlesex Co., 1877-82; organized Cambridge Dispensary, 1873 (clerk, 1873-79); phys. and surgeon Cambridge Hosp., 1886—; prof. clin. medicine, Tufts Med. School, 1894-1900, dean, 1897-1900, prof. emeritus, Tufts Med. Sch.; mem. Mass. State Bd. Lunacy and Charity, 1895-98. Trustee New Ipswich (N.H.) Library, New Ipswich Appleton Acad., Edward Hopkins Fund. Fellow Mass. Med. Society. Home: Winchester, Mass. Died Nov. 27, 1925.

HILDT, John Coffey, prof. history; b. Baltimore, Md., July 25, 1882; s. George Coffey and Margaret Catherine (Thomas) H.; A.B., Johns Hopkins, 1903, Ph.D., 1906; unmarried. Instr. in history, Smith Coll., 1906-12, asso. prof. history, 1912-18, prof., 1918-29, C. S. Parsons prof. history, 1929—; lecturer in history, Mt. Holyoke Coll., South Hadley, Mass., 1910-12. Served as capt., Mil. Intelligence Div., Gen. Staff, U.S.A., 1918-19; officer in charge mil. information, Am. Commn. to Negotiate Peace, Paris, 1919; maj. O.R.C. Awarded Henrico medallion, Johns Hopkins U., 1906. Author: Early Diplomatic Relations of the United States with Russia, 1906. Co-editor of Smith College Studies in History. Home: Northampton, Mass. Died Feb. 4, 1938.

HILGARD, Eugene Woldemar, prof. agr.; b. Zweibrücken, Rhenish Bavaria, Jan. 5, 1833; s. Theodore Erasmus and Margaretha (Pauli) H.; emigrated, 1836; ed. Belleville, Ill.; Ph.D., Univ. of Heidelberg, 1853 (re-conferred honoris causa, 1903); studied, also Zürich and Freiberg, Saxony; (LL.D., U. of Miss., 1882, Columbia and U. of Mich., 1887); m. J. Alexandrina Bello, of Madrid, Spain, 1860. State geologist of Miss., 1855-73; prof. chemistry, U. of Miss., 1866-73; prof. geology, zoölogy and botany, 1873-74, mineralogy, geology and zoölogy, 1874-75, U. of Mich.; prof. agr., 1874-1904, prof. emeritus, 1904—; U. of Calif.; dir. Calif. Agrl. Expt. Sta., 1888-1904. Spl. agt. cotton production reports 10th U.S. Census, 1879-83; in charge agr. div. Northern Transcontinental Survey, 1881-83. Specialist in direct investigation of soils in connection with their native vegetation; of the influence of climate upon the formation of soils, and of "alkali lands." Received Liebig medal for distinguished achievements in agrl. sciences from Acad. of Sciences, Munich; also gold medal, Paris Expn., 1900, as collaborator in agrl. science. Fellow Am. Acad. Arts and Sciences, A.A.A.S. Author: Soils of the Arid and Humid Regions, 1906; Agriculture for Schools of the Pacific Slope (with W. J. V. Osterhout), 1909. Author and editor: Cotton Culture in the U.S., 10th Census, 1880. Home: Berkeley, Calif. Died Jan. 8, 1916.

HILGARTNER, Henry Louis, M.D.; b. Baltimore, Md., July 10, 1868; s. Ludwig and Kunigunda (Dietz) H.; City Coll. of Baltimore, 1882-84; M.D., U. of Md., 1889; B.S., U. of Tex., 1896; studied Baltimore, New York and Vienna; m. Adela Belle Palm, Feb. 8, 1893; children—Mrs. Anna Belle Pendleton, Henry Louis. Interne Presbyn. Eye, Ear, Nose and Throat Charity Hosp., Baltimore, 1890-91; settled in Austin, 1891; oculist State Inst. for the Blind, Austin, 1893—; surgeon Tex. Eye, Ear, Nose and Throat Hosp. (later Austin Sanitarium), 1896-1912. Cons. eye, ear, nose and throat surgeon and examiner, U.S. Sch. Mil. Aeronautics, World War. Fellow Am. Acad. of Ophthalmology and Otolaryngology, Am. Coll. of Surgeons. Democrat. Episcopalian. Mason. Home: Austin, Tex. Died June 9, 1937.

HILL, Adams Sherman, univ. prof.; b. Boston, Jan. 30, 1833; s. Sherman Goldsmith and Joanna Catherine Elizabeth (Ballard) H.; A.B., Harvard, 1853, LL.B., 1855 (LL.D., 1903); m. Caroline Inches Dehon, Sept. 28, 1868. Law reporter, corr. and editor, New York, Washington and Chicago, 1856-68; asst. prof. rhetoric, 1872-76, Boylston prof. rhetoric and oratory, 1876-1904, emeritus prof., 1904, Harvard. Author: Principles of Rhetoric, 1878, 1895; Our English, 1889; Foundations of Rhetoric, 1892; Beginning of Rhetoric and Composition, 1903. Died 1910.

HILL, Agnes Leonard, author; b. Louisville, Ky.; d. Dr. Oliver Langdon and Agnes Howard (Sale) L.; grad. Henry Female Coll., New Castle, Ky.; m. Dr. S. E. Scanland, Oct. 29, 1868 (died 1871); m. 2d, Samuel Howe Hill, May 15, 1872 (divorced 1895). Began to write verse at 8 years of age; first verses published at 13; wrote stories for N.Y. Weekly at 16; began editorial work on daily Times in Chicago, and wrote editorials for all the principal dailies of Chicago. Edited at various times in Chicago, "Sorosis," "Home and Society," and "Elite News"; in Denver, "Western Society," and "Society"; "Daily Dispatch," Leadville, Colo.; "Chaffee Co. Times," at Buena Vista, Colo. Assistant pastor St. Paul's Ch. (Universalist), 1896; occupied, as temporary supply, various pulpits in Colo., Ill., and Conn. Went to Europe in summer of 1904 and became pastor of Congl. Ch. at Wollaston, England; winter of 1905, organized there children's soc. of over 100 children to refrain from use of tobacco and intoxicants before 21 yrs. of age. Author: The Divine Law of Divorce. Home: Denver, Colo. Died Jan. 1917.

HILL, Albert Hudgins, supt. schs.; b. Madison Co., Va., Feb. 3, 1866; s. J. Booton and Virginia (Byrd) H.; B.A., Richmond Coll., 1887; M.A. and diploma as supt. schs., Teachers Coll. (Columbia), 1914; m. Cora Bransford, Nov. 20, 1895; children—Katharine Byrd, Judith. Teacher night schs., Richmond, Va., 1896-1905; prin. elementary and high schs., Scottsville, Va.; connected with pub. schs., Richmond, 1889—, asst. supt., 1904, supt. schs., Richmond, 1919—; instr. in Summer Sch., U. of Va. and other summer schs. Mem. Pub. Library Bd., Richmond. Pres. Va. Supts.' Conf., 1921-22; mem State Bd. Edn., Va., 1923-27. Democrat. Baptist. Home: Richmond, Va. Died June 1933.

HILL, Arthur Edward, chemist; b. Newark, N.J., Mar. 20, 1880; s. Charles Edward and Caroline Greenwood (Hill) H.; B.S., New York U., 1901, M.S., 1903; Ph.D., U. of Freiburg, 1904; m. Grace L. Kent, Aug. 12, 1904; children—Douglas Greenwood, Dorothy Kent; m. 2d, Bess J. Talmadge, 1925. Fellow in chemistry, New York U., 1901-02; teacher, Newark High Sch., 1903-04; instr. chemistry, 1904-05, sec. Sch. Applied Science, 1906-19, asst. prof., 1906-08, asso. prof., 1908-12, prof. chemistry, and head dept., 1912—, New York U., acting dean, 1932, also acting dean College of Arts, 1935-36; prof. chemistry, N.J. Coll. Pharmacy, 1906-19; research chemist, Chem. Warfare Service, 1918-19; asso. editor Jour. of Am. Chem. Soc., 1923-33. Republican. Presbyn. Author: Laboratory Guide for Qualitative Analysis, 1910; chapter on Heterogeneous Equilibrium in Taylor's Treatise on Physical Chemistry, 1924. Died Mar. 16, 1939.

HILL, Arthur Turnbull, painter; b. N.Y. City, Apr. 26, 1868; s. George Waldo and Elizabeth (Turnbull) H.; ed. pvt. and pub. schs.; studied art under father (an artist) and George Inness, and at Brooklyn Inst., but mainly self-taught in art; m. Marion Estelle French, Dec. 6, 1898; 1 son, George Waldo II (dec.). Landscape, marine and portrait painter. First exhibited at Nat. Acad. Design, New York, 1895, later at principal art centres of U.S. and by invitation in western states circuit exhbns. Works on permanent exhbn. in Nat. Gallery, Washington, D.C.; Brooklyn Mus.; National Arts Club, New York. Marine camoufleur under U.S. Shipping Bd. Emergency Fleet Corp., 1918-19. Republican. Episcopalian. Wrote: Early Recollections of George Inness and George Waldo Hill (New Salmagundi Papers, Series 1922). Home: East Hampton, L.I., N.Y. Died Nov. 24, 1929.

HILL, Charles Edward, college prof.; b. Rochelle, Ill., Sept. 27, 1881; s. Peter and Engeborg (Hoversten) H.; A.B., U. of Mich., 1906, A.M., 1907; Ph.D., Harvard, 1916; m. Jane Blair, Sept. 1, 1911; children—Jane Engeborg, Annie Blair, Mary Richards, Caroline Esther (dec.). Teacher Am. history and govt., Kan. State Normal, Emporia, 1907-13; supervising prin. pub. schs., Pasadena, Calif., 1913-14; asst. prof. polit. science, 1916-18, prof., 1918—, dean of Columbian Coll., 1928-31, George Washington U. Spl. expert for U.S. Tariff Commn., 1917-18; reviser for Com. on Revision of Laws of (U.S.) House of Reps., 1920; lecturer Post Grad. Sch., U.S. Naval Acad., 1929, also, summers, Ill. Normal U., 1911, U. of So. Calif., 1930, and at Acad. of Internat. Law, The Hague, 1933. Republican. Presbyterian. Author: Leading American Treaties, 1922; The Danish Sound Dues, 1926; James Madison (in series on Secretaries of State), 1927; Le régime international des détroits maritimes, 1933. Home: Washington, D.C. Died May 10, 1936.

HILL, Crawford, capitalist; b. Providence, R.I., Mar. 29, 1862; s. Nathaniel Peter (U.S. senator) and Alice (Hale) H.; A.B., Brown U., 1885; m. Louise Bethel Sneed, Jan. 15, 1895. Pres. Denargo Land Co., Hill Land & Investment Co.; also director Mountain States Telephone & Telegraph Co., First Nat. Bank of Denver. Col. on staff of Gov. John L. Routt, 1891-92, and Gov. Albert W. McIntyre, 1895-96. Chairman Colo. delegation Rep. Nat. Conv., Chicago, 1908. Episcopalian. Home: Denver, Colo. Died Dec. 22, 1922.

HILL, Daniel Harvey, college pres.; b. Davidson, N.C., Jan. 15, 1859; s. Lt. Gen. Daniel Harvey (C.S.A.) and Isabella (Morrison) H.; A.B., Davidson (N.C.) Coll., 1880, A.M., 1885 (Litt.D., 1905; LL.D., U. of North Carolina, 1910); m. Pauline White, July 1885. Prof. English, Ga. Mil. and Agrl. Coll., 1880-89; prof. English, 1889-1907, v.p., 1905-08, pres., 1908-16, N.C. Coll. Agr. and Engineering, Raleigh; resigned to accede to request of State Confed. Vet. Assn. to write on the Ricks Foundation a history of N.C. in the Civil War. Exec. officer State Hist. Commn.; pres. State Teachers Assembly, 1910, State Forestry Conv., 1914, State Folk Lore Soc., 1920, State Lit. and Historic Soc., 1921; pres. S.R., 1923. Chmn. N.C. State Council Defense during World War. Democrat. Presbyn. Author: Agriculture for Beginners (joint author), 1903; Hill Readers (joint author), 1907; Young People's History of North Carolina, 1907; Corn Book (joint author), 1920. Home: Raleigh, N.C. Died July 31, 1924.

HILL, David Bennett, senator; b. Havana, N.Y., Aug. 29, 1843; s. Caleb and Eunice (Durfey) H.; ed. dist. schs. and Havana Acad. Admitted to bar, 1864; del. Dem. State convs., 1868-80 (chmn. 1877, 1881); mem. N.Y. Assembly, 1871-72; city atty., 1865, alderman, 1880 and 1881, mayor, 1882, Elmira, N.Y.; lt. gov. of N.Y., 1882-85, gov., 1885-91; U.S. senator, 1891-97; prominent candidate for presdl. nomination in Nat. Dem. Conv., 1892; candidate for gov., N.Y., 1894, defeated. Pres. N.Y. State Bar Assn., 1886-87. Home: Albany, N.Y. Died 1910.

HILL, David Jayne, diplomat, historian; b. Plainfield, N.J., June 10, 1850; s. Rev. Daniel T. and Lydia Ann (Thompson) H.; A.B., Bucknell U., Pa., 1874, A.M., 1877; univs. of Berlin and Paris; LL.D., Colgate, 1883, U. of Pa., 1902, Union, 1902, Bowdoin, 1925; Docteur es Lettres, U. of Geneva, Switzerland, 1906; D.C.L., Bucknell, 1924; m. Juliet Lewis Packer, June 3, 1886 (died 1923); children—Walter Liddell, Catharine Packer. Pres. Bucknell U., 1879-88; pres. U. of Rochester, 1888-96; resigned; spent nearly 3 yrs. in study of pub. law of Europe; prof. European diplomacy in Sch. of Comparative Jurisprudence and Diplomacy, Washington, D.C., 1899-1903; asst. sec of state, 1898-1903; E.E. and M.P. of U.S. to Switzerland, 1903-05, to the Netherlands, 1905-08; A.E. and M.P. to Germany, 1908-11. Del. 2d Peace Conf., The Hague, 1907. Author: Elements of Rhetoric, 1877; A History of Diplomacy in the International Development of Europe; World Organization as Affected by the Nature of the Modern State, 1911 (transl. into German and French); The People's Government, 1915; Americanism—What It Is, 1916; The Rebuilding of Europe, 1917 (2 latter transl. into French); Impressions of the Kaiser, 1918; Present Problems in Foreign Policy, 1919; American World Policies, 1920; The Problem of a World Court, 1927. Home: Washington, D.C. Died Mar. 2, 1932.

HILL, Eben Clayton, M.D., roentgenologist; b. Baltimore, Md., Oct. 9, 1882; s. Charles Ebenezer and Kate Watts (Clayton) H.; A.B., Johns Hopkins, 1903, M.D., 1907; matriculate research student, U. of Freiburg, Germany, 1904, 05; graduate of Army Medical School, 1909; m. Carolyn Sherwin Bailey, Oct. 14, 1936. Assistant in anatomy, Johns Hopkins U. Medical Sch., 1907-08; practiced, Baltimore, 1907-08, Poughkeepsie, N.Y., 1913-20; pathologist and radiologist, 1911-13, Roentgenologist, 1912-20, Vassar Hosp. and Dispensary. Instr. 1920-21, asso. in Roentgenol. anatomy, 1921-22, now lecturer roentgenology, Johns Hopkins. Roentgenologist U.S. Med. Advisory Bd., U.S.A., for N.Y., 1917-19. First lt. and capt., Med. Corps, U.S.A., 1908-13 (retired). Fellow A.A.A.S.; fellow and life mem. Am. Coll. Physicians, A.M.A. Republican. Episcopalian. Contbr. research X-ray technic for studying collateral circulation, sacroiliac injuries and effects of rays on cellular life. Proved the necessity in 1909, of massive doses of diphtheria antitoxin in laryngeal and other serious cases of dihptheria; proved the importance, 1910, of carriers in the spread of diphtheria, and the relative unimportance of disinfection and fumigation; showed, 1912, that salvarsan, even in frequent dosages, is not specific in action, and is not the complete curative drug as supposed; invented radiopaque injection method, etc. Completed in 1937 anatomical-surgical studies of sacro-iliac joint. Author of Cross Roads of the Mind, 1939. Died June 15, 1940.

HILL, Ebenezer J., congressman; b. Redding, Conn., Aug. 4, 1845; s. Rev. Moses and Charlotte Ilsely (McClellan) H.; student Yale, 2 yrs. (hon. A.M., 1892); m. Mary E. Mosman, June 15, 1868. Pres. Norwalk (Conn.) St. Ry. Co., and Norwalk Gaslight Co. several yrs.; now pres. Norwalk Mills Co. and Nat. Bank of Norwalk. Has held various local offices; mem. Conn. Senate, 1886-87; mem. Rep. State Central Com., 1 term; mem. 54th and 62d Congresses (1895-1913); and 64th Congress (1915-17), 4th Conn. Dist.; mem. Com. on Ways and Means 10 yrs. and of Banking and Currency Com. 8 yrs. Home: Norwalk, Conn. Died Sept. 27, 1917.

HILL, Edgar Preston, clergyman; b. Pontiac, Ill., July 27, 1861; s. Henry H. and Sarah E. H.; A.B., Williams Coll., 1884; grad. McCormick Theol. Sem., 1888; D.D., Beloit Coll., 1895; LL.D., Carroll Coll., Waukesha, Wis., 1913; D.D., Williams Coll., 1921; m. Hariette M. Rice, June 26, 1888. Ordained Presbyn. ministry, 1888; pastor Reunion Ch., Chicago, 1888-89, First Ch., Freeport, Ill., 1889-95, First Ch., Portland, Ore., 1895-1906; prof. homiletics and applied Christianity, McCormick Theol. Sem., Chicago, 1906-19. Supt., 1906-17, pres., 1917-19. Presbyn.

Ch. Extension Bd., Chicago; gen. sec. Gen. Bd. of Edn. of Presbyn. Ch. U.S.A., 1919-23; sec. Bd. of Christian Edn., 1925-26. Author: Calm Review of Christian Science, 1898; Christian Science in Its Second Stage, 1899. Home: Los Angeles, Calif. Died Nov. 26, 1938.

HILL, Edward Gurney, rose hybridizer; b. Rochdale, Lancashire, Eng., Sept. 11, 1847; s. Joseph and Mary Ann (Butterworth) H.; brought by parents to U.S., 1851; ed. pub. schs., western N.Y.; LL.D., Earlham Coll., Richmond, Ind., 1928; m. Eliza Lindley Stuart, Mar. 13, 1872; children—Flora Alice (Mrs. Frederic H. Lemon), Mary Stuart (Mrs. Earl H. Mann), Anna Woods (dec.), Joseph Herbert. With father and sister formed firm E. G. Hill & Co., florists, 1881; incorporated, 1900, and became pres. The E. G. Hill Co.; dir. 2d Nat. Bank of Richmond. Served as park commr., Richmond, many yrs.; former dir. Eastern Ind. Hosp. for Insane. Received over 50 medals, including gold medal, Paris, for rose production. Republican. Quaker. Rotarian. Home: Richmond, Ind. Died Nov. 27, 1933.

HILL, Edward Yates, clergyman; b. Rochester, Mo., Sept. 15, 1868; s. Rev. Isaac and Nancy Jane (Howard) H.; A.B., Baker U., Kan., 1891, D.D., 1905; grad. McCormick Theol. Sem., Chicago, 1894; A.M., Lake Forest (Ill.) U., 1895; m. Mary Moon, June 6, 1900; children—Helen, John Edward. Ordained Presbyn. ministry, 1894; minister Christ Chapel, Chicago, 1894-96; pastor 1st Ch., Warsaw, Ind., 1896-1900, 1st Ch., Logansport, Ind., 1900-04, 1st Ch., Phila. ("mother ch. of Presbyterianism in America"), 1904—. Am. exchange preacher to Great Britain in 1931. Trustee Gen. Assembly Presbyn. Ch. U.S.A., Presbytery of Phila., Tennent Coll. Dir. of Presbyn. Ministers' Fund for Life Ins.; mem. bd. of edn. Presbyn. Ch. U.S.A., 1907-18; dir. McCormick Theol. Sem., 1904-05; mem. Presbyn. Hist. Soc. (board mgrs.); vice-pres. Pa. Bible Soc.; Moderator of Synod of Pa., 1920-21. Home: Overbrook, Philadelphia, Pa. Died Aug. 26, 1941.

HILL, Emory, M.D.; b. Scottsville, Va., Sept. 8, 1883; s. James Christian and Mary (Emory) H.; A.B., Columbia U.; M.D., Med. Coll. of Va., 1907; grad. student U. of Chicago, 1914-16; m. Julia Duval Hawes, Apr. 18, 1911; children—Walker Hawes, James Christian. Practiced in Chicago, 1910-19; instr. ophthalmology, Rush Medical Coll., Chicago, 1914-19; practiced in Richmond, Va., 1919—; prof. ophthalmology, Med. Coll. of Va., 1929—. Fellow A.M.A.; Coll. of Physicians of Phila. Democrat. Home: Richmond, Va. Died Dec. 4, 1940.

HILL, Frank Alpine, sec. Mass. State Bd. of Edn., 1894—; b. Biddleford, Me., Oct. 12, 1841; s. Joseph S. and Nancy H.; grad. Bowdoin Coll., 1862 (Litt.D., 1894); m. Margaretta S. Brackett, 1865. Prin. Limington (Me.) Acad., 1862, Biddleford High Sch., 1862-63; studied law, 1863-64; prin. Milford (Mass.) High Sch., 1865-70; Chelsea (Mass.) High Sch., 1870-86; head master English High Sch., Cambridge, Mass., 1886-93, New Mechanic Arts High Sch., Boston, 1893-94. Home: Cambridge, Mass. Died 1903.

HILL, Frank Davis, consul general; b. in Minn., May 28, 1862; s. Charles (M.D.) and Jennie (Davis) H.; student U. of Minn., 1878-82, Columbian and Nat. Law schs., Washington, 1882-85; admitted to bar, 1884; unmarried. Consul at Asuncion, Paraguay, 1887-90, Montevideo, Uruguay, 1890-93, La Guayra, Venezuela, 1895-96, Santos, Brazil, 1896-99, Amsterdam, Netherlands, 1899-1907; consul gen. at St. Petersburg, 1907-08, Barcelona, Spain, 1908-10, Frankfort-on-Main, Germany, May 4, 1910—. Died May 23, 1912.

HILL, Fred Burnett, college prof.; b. Red Wing, Minn., May 15, 1876; s. Edwin Frederick and Grace Jeannette (Squires) H.; B.Litt., Carleton Coll., Minn., 1900; B.D., Hartford Theol. Sem., 1903; traveled around the world, 1905-06; post-grad. study Hartford Theol. Sem., 1906-07; m. Deborah Wilcox Sayles, June 14, 1905. Ordained Congl. ministry, 1903; prof. Bibl. lit., Carleton Coll., Sept. 1, 1907—. Mem. commn. on social service, Nat. Congl. Council; corporate mem. A.B.C.F.M.; pres. Northfield Hosp. Assn.; mem. Bd. of Edn., Northfield. Progressive Rep. Mason. Home: Northfield, Minn. Died Jan. 1919.

HILL, Frederick Trevor, lawyer, author; b. Brooklyn, N.Y., May 5, 1866; s. Edward and Mary H.; A.B., Yale U., 1887; LL.B., Columbia, 1889; hon. A.M., Yale, 1907; m. Mabel Wood, 1895; 1 son, Edward Trevor. Capt. Q.M.R.C., Feb. 1, 1917; attached to General Pershing's staff and sailed with him to France, May 1917; served in staff dept. A.E.F. to Feb. 1919; promoted to maj., Q.M.R.C., Dec. 1917; lt. col. U.S.A., Oct. 1918; recommissioned lt. col. R.C., July 1919; apptd. on General Staff U.S. Army initial elegibility list, Dec. 16, 1920. Chevalier Légion d'Honneur; cited by General Pershing for "exceptionally meritorious and conspicuous service," July 1919. Author: Miniatures of Balzac (with S. P. Griffin), 1893; Lincoln the Lawyer, 1906; On the Trail of Washington, 1909; On the Trail of Grant and Lee, 1911; Washington in Action, 1912; The Thirteenth Juror (novel), 1913; Tales Out of Court (short stories), 1920; High School Farces (plays), 1920. Home: Irvington-on-Hudson, N.Y. Died Mar. 17, 1930.

HILL, George Andrews, astronomer; b. Elizabeth, N.J., Apr. 11, 1858; s. late Rev. I. N. and Annie M. H.; ed. pvt. sch. and Columbia Coll.; married; children—George Cooper, Edgar Montgomery (dec.). An astronomer U.S. Naval Obs., 1893—. Spl. work has been in line of fundamental determination of star positions, determination of longitude by wireless, astronomical constants, and upon subject of variation of latitude. Died Aug. 29, 1927.

HILL, George Anthony, teacher; b. Sherborn, Mass., Aug. 25, 1842; s. James Nason and Jane (Whitney) H.; A.B., Harvard, 1865, A.M., 1870; unmarried. Tutor chemistry, 1865-71, asst. prof. physics, 1871-76, Harvard; lived in Germany, 1876-78; tutor and author from 1878. Author: Wentworth and Hill's Text Book of Physics, 1898; Wentworth and Hill's First Steps in Geometry, 1901; Essentials of Physics, 1912. Home: Cambridge, Mass. Died Aug. 17, 1916.

HILL, George Griswold, newspaper corr.; b. Montreal, Can., Apr. 24, 1868; s. George William and Frances Harriet (Griswold) H.; ed. pub. schs., Englewood (now Chicago) and St. Ignatius Coll., Chicago; m. Frances Mary Chaffee, May 3, 1893; children—George Chaffee (dec.), Marion Lancaster. Began newspaper work on the Farmer, St. Paul, Minn., 1886; mng. editor Am. Farmer, Chicago, 1890-97, of Product Trade Reporter, Chicago, 1895-97; Washington corr. Johnstown Democrat, Crawfordsville Journal and other papers, 1900-02; Washington Bur. New York Tribune, 1902-09, corr., 1909-14; asst. corr. London Times, Dec. 1, 1914. Was corr. New York Tribune at Russo-Japanese peace conf., 1905. Republican. Catholic. Home: Washington, D.C. Died Nov. 1935.

HILL, George William, astronomer; b. New York, Mar. 3, 1838; s. John William and Catherine (Smith) H.; A.B., Rutgers, 1859, A.M., 1862; (hon. Ph.D., Rutgers, 1872; Sc.D., U. of Cambridge, Eng., 1892; LL.D., Columbia, 1894, Princeton, 1896); unmarried. Became asst. in office of The Am. Ephemeris and Nautical Almanac, 1861; researches in connection with the lunar theory secured him gold medal of Royal Astron. Soc., London, 1887; awarded Damoiscan prize, Paris Acad. Sciences, 1898. Lecturer in celestial mechanics, Columbia U., 1898-1901. Asso. fellow Am. Acad. Arts and Sciences. Author: Collected Mathematical Works, vol. 1, 1905; etc. Home: West Nyack, N.Y. Died Apr. 16, 1914.

HILL, George William, editor; b. St. Peter's Port, Guernsey, Eng., Dec. 25, 1845; s. Dr. Ninian and Marion (Lancaster) H.; ed. in France at French Lycée and pvt. sch.; studied law at McGill Coll., Montreal, Can.; (Ph.D., Villanova Coll.); m. Frances Harriet Griswold, of Montreal, Mar. 30, 1867; father of George Griswold H. After leaving coll. was employed in Bank of Montreal, and later on staff of Montreal Herald; in service of Continental Ins. Co. of New York (located at Chicago), 1870-79. Established Farmers' Review, Chicago, 1879; removed to St. Paul, Minn., 1886, and managed and edited The Farmer until 1888; editor-in-chief U.S. Dept. Agr., 1899-1911; editor Year Book of Dept. of Agr., 1897-1911. Officier du Mérite Agricole. Cleveland Democrat. Catholic. Home: Washington, D.C. Died Mar. 30, 1914.

HILL, Gershom Hyde, alienist; b. Garnavillo, Ia., May 8, 1846; s. Rev. James Jeremiah and Sarah Elizabeth (Hyde) H.; pvt. Co. B, 46th Ia. Inf. in Civil War; A.B., Ia. (now Grinnell) Coll., 1871, hon. A.M., 1891; M.D., Rush Med. Coll., Chicago, 1874; m. Louisa Bliss Ford, Jan. 9, 1879; 1 dau., Julia Ford. Lectured on insanity, College of Medicine, State University of Iowa, 1890-1906; prof. mental diseases, Coll. of Medicine, Drake U., 1903-13; asst. phys., 1874-81, supt., 1881-1902, Independence (Ia.) Hosp. for Insane; supt. The Retreat (pvt. hosp.), 1905-24; on staff Ia. Methodist Congregational and Mercy hosps. Trustee Grinnell Coll.; pres. Ia. State Anti-Saloon League; exec. com. Associated Charities of Des Moines. Senior deacon Congl. Ch., Des Moines. Home: Des Moines, Ia. Died Nov. 23, 1925.

HILL, Henry Barker, chemist; b. Waltham, Mass., April 27, 1849; s. Thomas H. (pres. Harvard, 1862-68) and Anne Foster (Bellows) H.; grad. Harvard, 1869; studied chemistry, Univ. of Berlin, 1869-70; m. Ellen Grace Shepard, Sept. 2, 1871. Asst. in laboratory, 1870-74, asst. prof., 1874-84, and from 1884 prof. chemistry, Harvard; 1894, dir. chem. laboratory. Mem. Nat. Acad. Sciences, 1883—. Author: Notes on Qualitative Analysis; etc. Home: Cambridge, Mass. Died 1903.

HILL, Hiram Warner, judge; b. nr. Greenville, Ga., July 18, 1858; s. Alexander Franklin and Mary Jane (Warner) H.; ed. Emory Coll., Oxford, Georgia, and Harvard U. Law Sch.; m. Lena Harris, Sept. 24, 1884; children—Hiram Warner, Eliza (Mrs. C. E. Martin), Alexander Franklin, Mary Jane, Sarah Frances, Burwell Pope. Practiced law at Greenville; mayor of Greenville; served as chmn. Ga. R.R. Commn., and mem. Ga. Ho. of Rep.; asso. justice Supreme Court of Ga., 1911—. Democrat. Home: Atlanta, Ga. Died Jan. 13, 1934.

HILL, Howard Copeland, educator; b. St. Louis, Mo., Dec. 20, 1878; s. Rev. James Renwick (M.D.) and Margaret Agnes (Kirkpatrick) Hill; Eastern Indiana Normal, 1899-1901; A.B., Indiana Univ., 1906; A.M., U. of Wis., 1909; Ph.D., U. of Chicago, 1925; m. Hermione Ireland, Nov. 26, 1908; children—Betty Louise, Knox Calvin, Mary Lucile, Howard Copeland, Hermione Ireland (dec.), James Renwick. Instr. history, high sch., Brazil, 1907, Twp. High Sch., Highland Park, Ill., 1907-10, Oak Park (Ill.) High Sch., 1910-12, State Normal Sch., Milwaukee Wis., 1912-17; head dept. social science, U. of Chicago High Sch., 1917-35, Coll. of Arts and Sciences, 1935—, also asst. prof., 1924, U. of Chicago, lecturer summer sessions, U. of Chicago, 1918-30, Colo. State Teachers Coll., 1931, 32, 36, State Teachers Coll., Kansas City, Mo., 1933, U. of Hawaii, 1934, U. of Southern Calif., 1935, Teachers Coll., Columbia U., 1937, Grad. Sch. of Education, Harvard U., 1938. Presbyn. Author: Community Life and Civic Problems, 1922; Reading and Living (with R. L. Lyman), 2 vols., 1924, 3 vols., 1930; Literature and Living (same), 3 vols., 1925; Roosevelt and the Caribbean, 1927; Tests in Civic Information and Civic Attitudes, 1927; Community Civics, 1928; Vocational Civics, 1928; Readings in Community Life, 1930; Readings in Vocational Life, 1930; My Occupation (with D. H. Sellers), 1930; Our United States (with J. A. Woodburn), 1930; Tests in Community and Vocational Civics, 1931; Historic Background of Our United States (with J. A. Woodburn), 1932; United States History by Units (with R. B. Weaver), 1933; Early America (with J. A. Woodburn), 1934; Our Economic Society and Its Problems (with R. G. Tugwell), 1934; Life and Work of the Citizen, 1935. Co-author: American Literature, 1937; English Literature, 1937; World Literature, 1938; Contemporary Literature, 1938; Living Together in My Community, 1939. Home: Chicago, Ill. Died June 25, 1940.

HILL, James Ewing, lawyer; b. nr. Nashville, Tenn., Nov. 4, 1837; s. James Johnson and Elizabeth Lamb (Rogers) H.; ed. Gillett's Acad., Cold Springs, Tex.; m. Frances Eugenia Dunnam, Dec. 20, 1859. Served 1st lt. comdg. Co. G, 22d Tex. Regt., Walker's Div., C.S.A. Admitted to bar, 1871; mem. 17th and 18th Tex. legislatures (1881-84); served as spl. dist. judge; now mem. Hill & Hill. Chmn. com. Torrens Land System and author report and bill, approved by Judge Leonard A. Jones, of Boston. Chmn. com. Jurisprudence and Law Reform. Democrat. Home: Livingston, Texas. Died Oct. 13, 1916.

HILL, J(ames) Gilbert, banker, lawyer; b. Lowell, Mass., Nov. 24, 1872; s. Capt. J. Gilbert and Virginia G. (Bond) H.; A.B., Amherst, 1896; law study Harvard, 1896-98; m. Helen M. Frost, Oct. 16, 1909. Admitted to Mass. bar, 1899, and began practice at Lowell; trustee and atty., Mechanics Savings Bank of Lowell, 1902-13; trustee and atty., City Instn. for Savings, 1913-28, pres., 1928—; dir. Appleton Nat. Bank of Lowell, Lowell Morris Plan Co., etc. City solicitor, Lowell, 1905-09; mem. Rep. State Com., Mass., 1904-05. Treas. Lowell Day Nursery Assn., 1906-30. Republican. Episcopalian. Mason. Home: Lowell, Mass. Died Oct. 11, 1933.

HILL, James J(erome), ry. president; b. nr. Guelph, Ont., Sept. 16, 1838; s. James and Anne (Dunbar) H.; educated in Rockwood Academy; (LL.D., Yale U., 1910; LL.D. from Macalester Coll., in 1914); left his father's farm for business life in Minnesota; was in steamboat offices in St. Paul, 1856-65; m. Mary Theresa Mehegan, Aug. 19, 1867; father of James Norman and Louis Warren H. Agt. Northwestern Packet Co., 1865; later established gen. fuel and transportation business on his own account; head of Hill, Griggs & Co., same line, 1869-75; established, 1870, Red River Transportation Co., which was first to open communication between St. Paul and Winnipeg; organized, 1875, the Northwestern Fuel Co., and 3 yrs. later sold out his interest, in the meantime having organized a syndicate which secured control of the St. Paul & Pacific R.R., from Dutch owners of the securities; reorganized system as St. Paul, Minneapolis & Manitoba Ry. Co., and was its gen. mgr., 1879-81, v.p., 1881-82, pres., 1882-90; it became part Great Northern system, 1890; interested himself in building the Great Northern Ry., extending from Lake Superior to Puget Sound, with northern and southern branches, and a direct steamship connection with China and Japan, 1888-93; pres. entire G.N. system, 1889-1907; chmn. bd. dirs. same, Apr. 1, 1907-July 7, 1912. Chief promoter and now pres. Northern Securities Co. V.p. N.Y. Chamber of Commerce. Owner of one of finest collections of paintings of modern French school in the world. Contributed $500,000 toward erection and endowment of St. Paul Theol. Sem. Author: Highways of Progress, 1910. Home: St. Paul, Minn. Died May 29, 1916.

HILL, James Langdon, clergyman; b. Garnavillo, Ia., Mar. 14, 1848; s. Rev. James Jeremiah and Sarah Elizabeth (Hyde) H.; A.B., Grinnell (Iowa)

Coll., 1871; D.D., 1891; B.D., Andover Theol. Sem., 1875; m. Lucy B. Dunham, Mar. 28, 1878. Ordained Congl. ministry, 1875; pastor North Ch., Lynn, Mass., 1875-86, Mystic Ch., Medford, Mass., 1886-94; in lit. work and lecturing, 1894—. Asso. editor The Golden Rule, Boston, 1886-89. Was one of four clergymen in 1891 to make addresses and to plant societies of Christian Endeavor in Eng.; founded soc. at old Boston and has made addresses in Jamaica, Hawaii and Alaska. Lyceum lecturer on topics of social life, travel and reform. Trustee of United Soc. of Christian Endeavor from the beginning, and has given over 400 conv. and anniversary addresses before soc. of Endeavor; trustee Grinnell Coll. and mem. Grinnell Foundation. Republican. Author: The Immortal Seven, 1913; Yankees, 1923; Tiptops on Travel, 1925, and many others. Home: Salem, Mass. Died Mar. 5, 1931.

HILL, James Norman, ry. official; b. St. Paul, Minn., Feb. 13, 1870; s. James Jerome and Mary Theresa (Mahegan) H.; A.B., Yale, 1893; m. Marguerite Sawyer Fahnestock. Began ry. service as clk., 1893; v.p., 1905, later dir. N.P. Ry.; pres. United Securities Corp., St. Paul; trustee Great Northern Iron Ore Properties. Home: Wheatley Hills, L.I., N.Y. Died July 3, 1932.

HILL, Janet McKenzie, editor; b. Westfield, Mass., Dec. 1852; d. Alexander and Nancy (Lewis) McKenzie; grad. Mass State Normal Sch., 1871, Boston Cooking Sch., 1892; asst. teacher Stockbridge High Sch., 1871; m. Benjamin M. Hill, July 1873. Editor Boston Cooking School Magazine, June 1896—. Demonstrator of cookery, lecturer on domestic science. Author: Salads, Sandwiches and Chafing Dish Dainties, 1899; Practical Cooking and Serving, 1902; The Up-to-Date Waitress, 1906; Cooking for Two, 1909; The Book of Entrées, 1911; American Cook Book, 1914; Canning, Preserving and Jelly Making, 1915; Whys of Cooking, 1916. Home: Needham, Mass. Died Sept. 1933.

HILL, John Alexander, publisher; b. near Bennington, Vt., Feb. 22, 1858; s. George A. and Margaret H.; ed. pub. schs., Wis., up to 14 yrs. of age; from then to 20 in a printing office; self taught on tech. subjects; m. Emma B. Carlisle, 1882. Ran locomotive 8 yrs. Founded 1885, and edited, Pueblo, Colo., Daily Press. Contbr. to tech. press, 1880-88, when was selected to edit "Locomotive Engineering"; pres. and treas. Hill Pub. Co., pubs., Am. Machinist, Power, Engineering and Mining Journal, Coal Age, Engineering News; pres. McGraw-Hill Book Co., New York; chmn. Hill Pub. Co., Ltd., London; pres. Deutscher Hill Verlag A.G., Berlin. Author: Progressive Examinations for Locomotive Engineers and Firemen, 1889 (adapted by master mechanics of Am. rys., as standard form of examination for promotion). Home: East Orange, N.J. Died Jan. 24, 1916.

HILL, J(ohn) B(oynton) P(hilip) Clayton, lawyer; b. Annapolis, Md., May 2, 1879; s. Charles Ebenezer and Kate Watts (Clayton) H.; A.B., Johns Hopkins Univ., 1900; LL.B., Harvard Univ., 1903; m. Suzanne Howell, d. late John Howell and Mary Grafton (Rogers) Carroll, Oct. 28, 1913; children—Suzanne Carroll Clayton (Mrs. Phillips Huntington Clarke), Elise Bancroft Clayton, Catherine Coleman Clayton. Practiced at Boston, 1903-04, Baltimore and Washington, 1904-17; was mem. Hill, Randall & Leser (withdrew from firm, 1925, because of congl. duties); resumed practice, 1927, Howe, Hill & Bradley, later Hill, Ross & Hill, Baltimore, Washington and New York; U.S. atty. Dist. of Md., 1910-15; counsel for Baltimore and State of Md. in N.J.-N.Y. Lighterage, Boston, Baltimore and Phila. Differential cases, 1930-33; spl. counsel State of Md. in Albany Port Differential. Pres. Artesian Water Co.; Rep. nominee Congress, 4th Md. Dist., 1908; Rep. candidate for nomination for mayor of Baltimore, 1915; pvt. Battery A, Mass. V.M., 1904; 2d lt., 1st lt., capt. 4th Inf., Md. N.G.; mil. observer 11th German Army Corps maneuvers, Sept. 1911; maj., judge adv. gen., Md. N.G., 1910-17; judge adv. 15th Div. Mexican border service, Aug. 26-Dec. 15, 1916; active duty, Aug. 3, 1917; mem. staff, 29th Div., Aug. 25, 1917-Dec. 10, 1918, then judge adv. and asst. G-3, Gen. Staff, 8th Army Corps, A.E.F., until its dissolution; liaison officer 17th French Army Corps during offensive north of Verdun, Oct. 1918; promoted lt. col., Oct. 22, 1918. Served in defense of center sector, Haute Alsace, July 25-Sept. 23, and Meuse-Argonne offensive, north of Verdun, Oct. 8-30, 1918; hon. disch., May 9, 1919; col. R.C., comdg. 306th Cav. Member Am. Battle Monuments Commn.; military observer 1st and 2d cavalry brigades, Interbrigade Maneuvers, British Army, Salisbury Plains, Sept. 1933; apptd. mem. Md. Tercentenary Commn., 1934; apptd. brig. gen. the asst. adj. gen. State of Md., June 8, 1935. Decorated D.S.M. (U.S.); Legion of Honor (French); Croix de Guerre, with silver star, for "most distinguished services in the operations north of Verdun," Oct. 1918; La Solidaridad (Panama); Polonia Restituta (Poland); The Star of Abdon Calderon, 1st class (Ecuador). Mem. 67th Congress (1921-23), 3d Md. Dist.; reëlected to the 68th and 69th Congresses (1923-27), same dist.; not candidate for reëlection to House but candidate for Rep. senatorial nomination, 1926, 1934. Asst. in govt. Harvard, 1903; lecturer on Am. Government, Johns Hopkins, various periods to 1924, and at Harvard, 1924. Author: Hill and Padgett's Annotated Public Service Commission Law of Md., 1913; The Federal Executive, 1916; National Protection—Policy, Armament and Preparedness, 1916. Homes: Annapolis, Md.; and Army and Navy Club, Washington, D.C. Died May 23, 1941.

HILL, John Edward, civil engr.; b. N.Y. City, Nov. 9, 1864; s. Edward and Harriet (Smith) H.; B.S., Rutgers Coll., 1884, M.S., 1887, C.E., 1892 (D.Sc., 1905); M.C.E., Cornell, 1895; m. Jessie Louise Gould, Dec. 19, 1894; children—Berenice Gould, Audrey Chapman, Elsbeth, Jessica (Mrs. Eugene A. Bond). Instr. civ. engring., Cornell, 1890-94; instr., asso. prof. and prof. civ. engring., Brown, 1894—. Engaged in various branches civ. engring., 1884—. Fellow A.A.A.S. Home: Providence, R.I. Died Nov. 2, 1934.

HILL, John Fremont, governor; b. Eliot, Me., Oct. 29, 1855; s. William and Miriam (Leighton) H.; ed. Berwick (Me.) Acad.; M.D., Bowdoin, 1877; L.I. Coll. Hosp. Med. Sch., 1877; m. Lizzie G. Vickery, May 19, 1880 (died 1893); m. 2d, Mrs. Laura Colman Liggett, Apr. 25, 1897. Mem. Vickery & Hill, pubs. of periodical jours., Augusta, 1879—; pres. State Trust Co. Mem. Me. Ho. of Rep., 1888-92, Senate, 1892-96; mem. exec. council, 1898-99; gov. of Me., 1901-03, 1903-05. Home: Augusta, Me. Died Mar. 16, 1912.

HILL, John Wesley, clergyman; b. Kalida, O., May 8, 1863; s. John Wesley (D.D.) and Elizabeth (Hughes) H.; A.B., Ohio Northern U., 1887, later D.D.; Boston Theol. Sem., 1887-89; LL.D., Upper Ia. Univ., 1908; Litt.D., Lincoln Memorial U., 1918; m. Nora Holmes, June 1888; children—John Warren, Ruth Elizabeth, Charles Fowler; m. 2d, Sadie Harrison Schmidt, Nov. 1906. Ordained Methodist Episcopal ministry, 1889; pastor, Sprague, Wash., 1885-86, First Ch., Ogden, Utah, 1888-92, Helena, Mont., 1893-94, Fowler Memorial Ch. (founder), 1894-96, First Ch., Fostoria, O., 1897-99, Grace Ch., Harrisburg, Pa., 1899-1905, Jaynes Ch., Brooklyn, 1905-07, Met. Temple, New York, 1907-12; mem. N.Y. Conf. M.E. Ch.; chancellor Lincoln Memorial Univ., Cumberland Gap, Tenn., 1916-36. Civic, industrial and patriotic speaker; first appearance in Blaine campaign; took active part in McKinley campaign, 1896; chaplain Pa. Senate, 1900, Rep. Nat. Conv., Chicago, 1908, 12; platform and Chautauqua lecturer. Grand Chaplain Masons, State of N.Y.; supplied pulpit Marylebone Presbyn. Ch., London, summer of 1909; visited the Orient 1911, establishing the Asiatic Branch of Internat. Peace Forum (of which was pres.), in Japan and China; 1st gen. sec. World Court League in U.S., 1914. Trustee Lincoln Memorial U., Ohio Soc. of Washington, D.C.; dir. Archæol. Soc. of Washington, D.C. Author: Abraham Lincoln, Man of God, 1920; If Lincoln Were Here! 1926. Home: Washington, D.C. Died Oct. 12, 1936.

HILL, Joseph Adna, statistician; b. Stewartstown, N.H., May 5, 1860; s. Rev. Joseph B. and Harriet (Brown) H.; A.B., Harvard, 1885, A.M., 1887; Ph.D., Halle, Germany, 1892; unmarried. Lecturer, U. of Pa., 1893; instr. Harvard U., 1895; since 1898 engaged in statis. work on U.S. Census; apptd. chief statistician, 1909; appointed asst. dir. for 14th Census, 1921, 15th Census, 1929; apptd. chief statistician for statistical research, 1933; chmn. com. apptd. by secretaries of state, commerce and labor to determine immigration quotas. Author: The English Income Tax, 1899; Women in Gainful Occupations, 1929. Home: Washington, D.C. Died Dec. 12, 1938.

HILL, Joseph Henry, educator; b. Stockton, Pa., May 21, 1858; s. Joseph and Betsy (Moffatt) H.; grad. Kan. State Normal Sch., Emporia, 1876; A.B., Northwestern U., 1886, A.M., 1889; D.D., Baker U., 1906; LL.D., Kan. Agrl. Coll., 1909; m. Frances Meldrum, July 2, 1892; children—Alfred G., Ormond P., Mrs. Muriel Bardwell, Ruth Elizabeth, Joseph A. (dec.). Began teaching, 1876; prof. Latin, 1887-1906, v.p., 1901-06, Kan. State Normal Sch., Emporia; pres. Kan. State Normal Sch. (Emporia, Hays and Pittsburg), 1906-July 1913; prof. edn., Boston U., 1913-15; now ednl. lecturer; pastor Brown Road M.E. Ch., Kansas City, 1925—. Ordained M.E. ministry, 1886. Pres. Kan. State Teachers' Assn., 1901; v.p. N.E.A., 1907 (chmn. normal sch. dept., 1909). Republican. Home: Kansas City, Mo. Died Feb. 13, 1927.

HILL, J(oseph) Stacy, hotelman; b. Cincinnati, O., Mar. 19, 1862; s. Joseph Stacy and Anna (McKinnell) H.; educated in the public schools of Cincinnati; m. Carrie Tucker Webb, Oct. 15, 1884 (dec.); children—William Webb, Dorothy (Mrs. Douglas A. Warner). Engaged as cigar mfr. and jobber, 1884-1910; pres. The Hotel Gibson Co., 1910-27; pres. J. S. Hill Co. Pres. Cincinnati Expn. and Fall Festival, 1911; v.p. Dixie Highway, 1915-33 (made hon. mem. staff of Gov. Sampson of Ky.). Republican. Mason. Home: Cincinnati, O. Died Aug. 31, 1939.

HILL, Judson Sudborough, college pres.; b. Trenton, N.J., June 3, 1854; s. Hugh C. and Cornelia (Disbrow) H.; A.B., Madison (now Colgate) U., 1874, A.M., 1876; B.D., Central Tenn. Coll., 1893; D.D., Walden U., 1897; m. Laura E. Yard, Jan. 21, 1879; children—Anna E., Edward Y., Judson S., Howard L., Clara S., Carl K., Nabor Y., Warren K. Clk. New Jersey Senate, 1876; ordained M.E. ministry, 1879; pastor Chattanooga, Tenn., 1879-81; pres. Morristown Normal and Industrial Coll., 1881—; supervisor U.S. Census, 1900. Charter mem. and pres. Morristown (Tenn.) Chamber Commerce. Mem. Gen. M.E. Conf. 7 times. Nat. councillor U.S. Chamber Commerce. Mason. Home: Morristown, Tenn. Died Sept. 14, 1931.

HILL, Lamar, lawyer; b. Atlanta, Ga., May 27, 1885; s. Abner Welborn and Lucy Cobb (Erwin) H.; grad. Boys' High Sch., Atlanta, 1901; student U. of Ga., class of 1904; m. Adelaide Jaudon Singleton, Dec. 11, 1919; children—Adelaide Jaudon, Ellen Cobb. Admitted to Ga. bar, 1905, and began practice at Atlanta; removed to N.Y. City, 1919; counsel Continental Ins. Co. and its affiliated companies, 1922—, v.p. and general counsel of same companies, 1924—. Served as lt. col. adj. gen., A.E.F., World War; lt. col. adj. gen., O.R.C. Pres. Young Men's Dem. League of Ga., 1906-08; v.p. Citizen's Independent Democracy of New York, 1920-22. Episcopalian. Mason. Home: New York, N.Y. Died June 24, 1937.

HILL, Laurance Landreth, author; b. Denison, Tex., Nov. 9, 1887; s. John Corydon and Delia Amanda (Landreth) H.; A.B., Stanford, 1912; m. Ruth Alice Allum, Dec. 14, 1914; children—Ralph Laurance, Doris Ruth, Laurance Landreth. Sec. to David Starr Jordan, 1912; Calif. rep. of Allyn & Bacon, pubs., 1913-20; adv. mgr. Weinstock & Lubin, Sacramento, 1920-21; city editor Hollywood Citizen, 1921-22; publicity dir. Security-First Nat. Bank of Los Angeles, 1922—. Asst. publicity dir. at Chicago hdqrs. Prog. Nat. Com., presdl. campaign, 1912; publicity dir. Southern Calif. hdqrs. Woodrow Wilson Independent League, 1916, Hoover Campaign Com. Southern Calif., 1920; sec., dir. Hist. Soc. of Southern Calif. Democrat. Author: El Pueblo—Los Angeles Before the Railroads, 1928; La Reina-Los Angeles in Three Centuries, 1929. Dir. and chmn. publicity com. La Fiesta de Los Angeles Assn. Home: Hollywood, Calif. Died May 13, 1932.

HILL, Louis Clarence, engineer; b. Ann Arbor, Mich., Feb. 22, 1865; s. Alva Thomas and Frances (Bliss) H.; B.S. in Civ. Engring., U. of Mich., 1886; reëntered 1889, B.S. in elec. engring., 1890, hon. Master of Engring., 1911; m. Gertrude B. Rose, Aug. 26, 1890; children—Raymond Alva, Margaret. Asst. engr. Duluth, Red Wing & Southern R.R., 1887-88; asst. engr. U.S.A. (summer), 1887; div. engr. G.N. R.R., 1888-89, prof. hydraulic and elec. engring., Colo. Sch. of Mines, 1890-1903; engr. U.S. Geol. Survey, 1903-04, in charge Roosevelt Dam; supervising engr. U.S. Reclamation Service, in charge of all work in Ariz., Southern Calif., N.M., Texas and Utah, 1905-14. U.S. commr., div. of water of Rio Grande between U.S. and Mex., and for division of water of Colorado River; cons. engr. Boulder Canyon Dam, All American Canal, U.S. Reclamation Service, Los Angeles Co. Flood Control, Bouquet Canyon Dam, San Gabriel Dams Nos. 1 and 2, Bonneville Dam, El Capitan Dam, Long Valley Dam, Fort Peck Dam, Tygart Dam, Conchas Dam, Sardis Dam, and 10 dams of Muskingum Conservancy Dist. for War Dept.; cons. engr. Internat. Boundary Commission; mem. Quinton, Code, Hill, Leeds & Barnard, Los Angeles. Was cons. engr. for Camp Kearney. Mem. Jury Awards, Chicago Expn., 1893. Home: Hollywood, Calif. Died Nov. 5, 1938.

HILL, Lysander, patent lawyer; b. Union, Me., July 4, 1834; s. Isaac and Elizabeth M. (Hall) H.; A.B., Bowdoin, 1858, A.M., 1861; admitted to bar, 1860; capt. Co. I, 20th Me. Inf. in Civil War, 1862-63; m. Adelaide R. Cole, Feb. 2, 1864 (died 1897); m. 2d, Edith Healy, Nov. 26, 1904. Practiced at Alexandria, Va., and Washington, 1864-81; register in bankruptcy, 8th Jud. Dist., Va., 1867-68; judge Circuit Ct., 1869-70; chmn. Rep. State Com., Va., 1867-69; devoted to patent practice, Chicago, from 1881; retired. Home: Chicago, Ill. Died Oct. 30, 1914.

HILL, Marion, writer; b. Vicksburg, Miss., Feb. 20, 1870; d. Barton and Marian H.; grad. San Francisco Girls' High School; m. Charles R. Hill, Feb. 4, 1896. Wrote: June's Garden, serial in St. Nicholas, 1896-97; short stories and verse in most of current mags. Author: The Pettison Twins, 1906. Home: Paradise Valley, Pa. Died Jan. 2, 1918.

HILL, Nathaniel Peter, U.S. senator; b. Orange Co., N.Y., Feb. 18, 1832; grad. Brown Univ., 1857; prof. chemistry there, 1859-64; went to Colo., 1864, engaged in mining, organized, 1867, Colorado Smelting Co.; U.S. senator, 1879-85, from Colo.; mem. Internat. Monetary Commn., 1891. Home: Denver, Colo. Died 1900.

HILL, Owen Aloysius, clergyman; b. Washington, D.C., July 25, 1863; s. John Joseph and Bridget (Gorman) H.; A.B., Woodstock (Md.) Coll., 1885, A.M., 1887; Ph.D., Fordham, 1919. Mem. Soc. of Jesus (Jesuits); priest R.C. Ch.; teacher Boston Coll., 1888, Fordham, 1889-92, 1912-19, Holy Cross Coll., 1904-12; v.p. St. Peter's Coll., Jersey City, N.J., 1900-02, St. Joseph's Coll., Phila., 1902-04; preached in many chs. along Atlantic Coast from Boston to Washington, D.C.; teacher Georgetown U., 1921-23; lecturer, Law Sch. of Georgetown U., 1923-28. Home: Philadelphia, Pa. Deceased.

HILL, Percival Smith, merchant; b. Phila., Pa., Apr. 5, 1862; s. George W. and Sarah (White) H.; U. of Pa. 2 yrs., Harvard, 2 yrs.; m. Cassie Milnes, Apr. 3, 1882. Began as jobber in cotton and woolen goods; mem. Boyd, White & Co., carpet jobbers and retailers, 1882-94; was made mgr. sales dept. Blackwell Durham Tobacco Co., 1892; pres. Am. Tobacco Co., 1912—; chmn. bd. Am. Cigar Co., Havana Tobacco Co. Republican. Methodist. Home: New York, N.Y. Died Dec. 7, 1925.

HILL, Robert Potter, congressman; b. Ewing, Ill., Apr. 18, 1874; s. James B. and Rebecca A. (Spilman) H.; B.S., Ewing Coll., 1896; m. Lora Carder, Dec. 25, 1901. Admitted to Ill. bar, 1904; practiced, Marion, Ill.; police magistrate, Marion, 1903-04; city atty., 1907-09; mem. Ill. Ho. of Rep., 1910-12; mem. 63d Congress (1913-15), 25th Ill. Dist. Democrat. Baptist. Mason. Home: Marion, Ill. Died Oct. 29, 1937.

HILL, Robert Thomas, geologist; b. Nashville, Tenn., Aug. 11, 1858; B.S., Cornell, 1886; LL.D., Baylor, 1920; m. Justina Robinson, Dec. 28, 1887. Asst. paleontologist Smithsonian Instn., 1885; geologist U.S. Geol. Survey, 1885-1904; asso. geologist Ark. Geol. Survey, 1888-90; prof. geology, U. of Tex., 1890-91; geologist in charge U.S. investigation underground water and arid regions, 1891-92; cooperator with Prof. A. Agassiz in W. Indian and Central Am. explorations, 1895-1905; contract work, Geol. Survey of Southern Calif., U.S. Geol. Survey, 1911-17; lecturer various colleges and univs.; explored for first time great canons of the Rio Grande; spl. commr., Martinique eruptions for Nat. Geog. Soc.; etc.; cons. practice, 1918—. Fellow Am. Geol. Soc., A.A.A.S. Expert for State of Tex. in Okla.-Tex. boundary suit, U.S. Supreme Court, 1921. Home: Glendale, Calif. Died July 28, 1941.

HILL, Samuel, lawyer; b. Deep River, Randolph Co., N.C., May 13, 1857; s. Nathan Branson and Eliza Lenora (Mendenhall) H.; A.B., Haverford Coll., 1878; A.B., Harvard, 1879; LL.D., Penn Coll., Ia.; m. Mary, d. James Jerome Hill, Sept. 6, 1888; children—Mary Mendenhall, James Nathan. Admitted to bar, 1880; pres. Minneapolis Trust Co., 1888-1903, U.S. Trust Co., Seattle, Wash., many yrs. from 1908. Overseer Harvard Univ., 1900-06. Hon. consul-gen. of Belgium for Ida., Ore., and Wash. Hon. life pres. Wash. Good Roads Assn.; pres. Pacific Highway Assn., Everyday Highway Assn. (2,000 miles long, from Mexico to B.C.); hon. pres. B.C. Good Roads League; pres. Maryhill (Wash.) Mus. Fine Arts; v.p. Columbia River Highway Assn. A promoter of "Peace Portal" between U.S. and Canada, marking 100 yrs. of peace. Awarded spl. thanks by U.S. Senate and Canadian Govt.; Officer Legion of Honor (French), also medal of thanks; Comdr. Order of the Crown (Belgian); mem. Queen's Body Guard (Rumanian), also spl. medal of thanks; Order of the Sacred Treasure (Japanese). Builder and pres. Mary Hill Museum. Home: Maryhill, Wash. Died Feb. 26, 1931.

HILL, Theophilus Hunter, author; b. Raleigh, N.C., Oct. 31, 1836; s. William Geddy and Adelaide V. (Hunter) H.; academic edn.; m. Laura F. Phillips, Jan. 1861; m. 2d, Mary G. Yancey, Sept. 1879. Admitted to bar, but did not practice; edited (during war) The Spirit of the Age, at Raleigh, and later The Centenary, literary journal, at Florence, S.C.; State librarian N.C., 1871-72. Author: Hesper, and Other Poems (copyrighted by Confederate States), 1861; Poems, 1869; Passion Flower, and Other Poems, 1883. Home: Raleigh, N.C. Died 1901.

HILL, Thomas, artist; b. Birmingham, Eng., Sept. 11, 1829; direct desc. Sir Rowland Hill, founder of penny postage; family came to U.S., 1840, and settled in Taunton, Mass.; studied in Acad. Fine Arts, Phila., 1853-54; took 1st medal, Md. Inst., Baltimore, 1853; portrait painter in San Francisco, 1861-66; also did other figure work and received 1st prize, Art Union of San Francisco, 1865; studied under Paul Meyerheim, Paris, 1866; opened studio in Boston, 1867, but after a few yrs. returned to San Francisco; received prize medal for landscape painting Centennial Expn., 1876. Notable landscapes: Yosemite Valley; White Mountain Notch; Donner Lake; The Great Cañon of the Sierras; The Heart of the Sierras; The Driving of the Last Spike (connecting Union Pacific and Central Pacific railroads); The Grand Cañon of the Colorado; The Yellowstone Cañon; Muir Glacier; etc.; has received 31 medals. Died 1908.

HILL, Thomas Edie, author; b. Sandgate, Vt., Feb. 29, 1832; ed. in common schs. and Cambridge (N.Y.) Acad.; taught pub. and pvt. schs.; founded Herald, Aurora, Ill., 1866; made Aurora Silver Plate Factory a success in its early history; mayor, Aurora, 1876; shut off 600 cows from running at large in streets; established suburban purchasing agency, individuals going daily into metropolis buying for merchants and others; settled, 1885, at Glen Ellyn, Ill., which he named; made Spring Lake out of a swamp, supplying ice for that region; laid out the grounds, built several houses and set the groves of trees on estate now occupied by Chicago Salvation Army; formed an improvement assn. which made Lake Glen Ellyn; organized land syndicate, 1890, put 600 acres into market for sale, set aside 116 acres for a park; developed Glen Ellyn Springs; organized improvement assn. in Duluth, Minn., 1900. Author: Hill's Manual of Social and Business Forms; Hill's Album of Biography; Condensed Political History; Government Ownership of Banks; Ways of Cruelty; Modern Ornamental Grounds; Hill's Guide for Land Seekers; Hill's Reference Guide to Farm, Field and Garden. Home: Glen Ellyn, Ill. Died July 13, 1915.

HILL, Thomas Guthrie Franklin, Presbyn. clergyman; b. Pittsburgh, Pa., Oct. 15, 1865; grad. Washington and Jefferson Coll., 1887; Western Theol. Sem., Allegheny, Pa., 1890; post-graduate Univ. Edinburgh; m. Grace Livingston, New York, g.g.d. Philip Livingston, signer of Declaration of Independence. Pastorates: Presbyn. Ch., Parnassus, Pa., 1890-93; Wakefield Ch., Germantown, Philadelphia, 1893—. Author: Christian Endeavor Hour, Parts I, II, III (with Grace L. Hill). Home: Germantown, Phila., Pa. Died 1900.

HILL, Walker, banker; b. Richmond, Va., May 27, 1855; s. Lewis and Mary Elizabeth (Maury) H.; ed. at home and pvt. sch.; m. Jeanie Morrison Lockwood, Oct. 14, 1885. Messenger, 1871-72, asst. teller, 1872, teller, 1872-81, Planters Nat. Bank, Richmond, Va.; cashier City Bank, Richmond, 1881-88; cashier, 1888-94, pres., 1894-1905, Am. Exchange Nat. Bank, St. Louis, and pres. of its successor, the Mechanics-Am. Nat. Bank, 1905-19; exec. mgr. its successor, First Nat. Bank, St. Louis. V.p. Humane Soc. of Mo.; trustee David Ranken Jr. Sch. of Mech. Trades; trustee Barnard Board of Trustees. Cleveland Democrat. Episcopalian. Home: St. Louis, Mo. Died Oct. 6, 1922.

HILL, Walter Barnard, educator; lawyer; b. Talbotton, Ga., Sept. 9, 1851; s. Judge Barnard and Mary Clay (Birch) H.; grad. Univ. of Ga., 1870, law sch., 1871, A.M., 1871; (LL.D., Emory, Ga., 1899, Southwestern Presbyn. Univ., Tenn., 1899, S. C. Coll., 1905). Practiced law, Macon, Ga., 1871-99; chancellor Univ. of Ga., 1899—. Compiler Code of Ga., 1873, 1882; mem. Gen. Conf. M.E. Ch., S., 1886, 1894; mem. Western & Atlantic R.R. Commn., Ga.; trustee Vanderbilt Univ. Mem. Southern Bd. of Edn.; pres. Southern Ednl. Assn. Home: Athens, Ga. Died 1905.

HILL, Walter Henry, priest, educator, author; b. on farm 2 miles from Lebanon, Ky., Jan. 21, 1822; s. Clement and Mary (Hamilton) H.; grad. St. Mary's Coll., Ky., 1843; A.M., 1845; tutor St. Mary's Coll., 1840-46; attended lectures med. dept., St. Louis Univ., autumn, 1846; mem. Jesuit Soc. from 1847; taught different branches in colls.; completed study of theology; ordained priest, Aug. 24, 1861; pres. St. Xavier Coll., Cincinnati, 1865-69; socius of the provincial, St. Louis Univ., 1869-71; taught mental and moral philosophy, same, 1864-65, 1871-84; pastor Sacred Heart Ch., Chicago, 1884-96; returned to St. Louis Univ., giving up all active duties, Aug. 1896. Author: Ethics or Moral Philosophy, 1877; Historical Sketch of St. Louis University, 1879. Home: St. Louis. Died 1907.

HILL, William A., judge; b. Farmington, Ill., Nov. 4, 1864; s. Abner K. and Amanda (Martin) H.; collegiate edn.; m. Elizabeth Hunter, May 26, 1890. Admitted to bar, 1890; mayor of Ft. Morgan, Colo., 1892-93; county atty. Morgan Co., 1893-98; mem. Colo. Senate, 1899-1907; asso. justice Supreme Court of Colo., 1909-18, chief justice, 1918-19; resumed law practice. Chmn. Dem. State Central Com., Colo., 1920-22. Home: Denver, Colo. Died Mar. 10, 1932.

HILL, William Edwin, clergyman; b. Wilmington, N.C., June 20, 1880; s. William Edwin and Ella Kilchrist (Fillyaw) H.; A.B., Davidson (N.C.) Coll., 1900; B.D., Union Theol. Sem., 1905; D.D., Hampden-Sydney Coll., 1919; m. Zaida English, June 14, 1906; children—William Edwin, Thomas English, Sarah Dumond, Haywood Northrop, Zaida English (dec.), Dumond Peck. Ordained ministry Presbyn. Ch. in U.S., 1905; pastor successively Va. Hot Springs, Gadsden, Ala., Farmville, Va., West End Ch., Atlanta, Ga., First Ch., Fayetteville, N.C., until 1926, Second Ch., Richmond, Va., 1926-38, pastor emeritus. President board trustees General Assembly Training School; pres. bd. mgrs. Bible Society of Va.; mem. bd. dirs. Union Theol. Sem., Richmond div. William and Mary Coll., Collegiate Sch. for Girls (Richmond); mem. Com. of Publ. also Com. of Stewardship and Finance, Presbyn. Ch. in U.S.; moderator Synod of N.C., 1923. Mem. Council of Defense, 1917-18; chmn. Am. Red Cross, Cumberland Co., N.C., 1919-23. Democrat. Mason. Home: Richmond, Va. Died Apr. 23, 1940.

HILL, William Free, farmer, banker; b. Crawford Co., Pa., Mar. 4, 1867; s. Theodore Wallace and Rebecca (Free) H.; ed. Allegheny Coll., Pa.; m. Marie A. Hill, Nov. 4, 1897; children—Lina B. (Mrs. J. B. Holmes), Ned Wallace, Donald Mac, Gerald Bruce. Lecturer, Pa. State Grange, 4 yrs. and Master 10 yrs.; also lecturer at farmers' institutes; special representative Pa. Dept. Agr.; apptd. del. to Internat. Inst. Agr., Italy, 1904-08, and assisted in establishing the inst. permanently; studied system of farm credits in Europe and organized a dozen banks in Pa., serving on bd. dirs. of each several yrs.; del. by appmt. of govs. of Pa. to Farmers' Nat. Congress, Interstate Tax Congress, Interstate Road Congress, Charleston (S.C.) Expn., etc. Breeder thoroughbred white Plymouth Rock poultry. Trustee Pa. State Coll. Republican. Protestant. Mason. Home: Huntingdon, Pa. Died June 21, 1935.

HILL, William Henry, financier; b. Boston, July 14, 1838; s. William Henry and Abby F. (Remick) H.; grad. Roxbury High Sch., 1855; m. Sarah E., d. William B. May, of Boston, Jan. 8, 1862 (died 1904); m. 2d, Caroline Wright Rogers, 1906. Began business life as a clerk in pub. house, 1855-59; partner in firm as Chase, Nichols & Hill, 1859-61; bookseller and publisher on own account, 1861-69; from 1869, mem. Richardson, Hill & Co., bankers, and became spl. partner in that firm. Trustee several estates; pres. Renfrew Mfg. Co. (Adams, Mass.), Foster's Wharf Co. (Boston); dir. First Nat. Bank, Boston Ins. Co., Eastern Steamship Co., and many other cos. Mem. Boston Chamber of Commerce, Real Estate Exchange. Home: Brookline, Mass. Died Oct. 14, 1913.

HILL, William S., farmer, banker; b. Edgar Co., Ill., June 3, 1863; s. Joseph H. and Rebecca (Braden) H.; ed. high sch. and business coll.; m. Ida Kellogg, Sept. 3, 1890 (dec.); m. 2d, Inez Kelso, Sept. 24, 1914; children—Joseph L., William B., Emory K., Lawrence M., Robert D., Sherman R. Pres. Security Nat. Bank, Alexandria, S.D., 1914—; pres. Hill, Taylor Co., agrl. implements, Alexandria; propr. Hill's Riverview Ranch (home of one of the largest and best known herds of Red Polled Cattle in America). Mem. S.D. State Bd. Agr., 16 yrs., pres. 12 yrs.; mem. State Council of Defense, World War. Pres. Mitchell (S.D.) Bd. of Edn.; trustee Huron Coll.; appointed mem. U.S. Shipping Bd., terms 1924-33, resigned 1927. Republican. Conglist. Mason. Rotarian. Home: Mitchell, S.D. Died Sept. 3, 1940.

HILL, Wilson Shedric, lawyer; b. Choctaw County, Miss., Jan. 19, 1863; s. Samuel and Elizabeth (Witty) H.; student U. of Miss., 1882-84; LL.B., Cumberland U., Tenn., 1884; m. Mabel Laing Hill, Mar. 5, 1908. Admitted to Miss. bar, 1884, and began practice in Winona; mem. Miss. Ho. of Rep., 1888; dist. atty., 5th Jud. Dist. of Miss., 1892-1903; mem. 58th, 59th and 60th Congresses (1903-09), 4th Miss. Dist.; resumed practice in Greenwood, Miss.; U.S. atty. Northern Dist. of Miss., Feb. 2, 1914—; mem. Hill & Writy; dir. Bank of Winona. Democrat. Methodist. Mason. Home: Greenwood, Miss. Died Feb. 14, 1921.

HILLARD, Charles W., ry. official; b. England. Came to U.S., 1876; began as pvt. sec. to H. H. Porter, pres. Chicago, St. Paul & Minneapolis R.R.; asst. sec. same rd. until 1882; later v.p. and treas. Duluth & Iron Range Railroad; sec. and treas. Chicago & Ind. Coal Ry., 1885-87; v.p. and treas. C.&E.I. R.R., 1887-1902; comptroller St.L.&S.F. R.R., 1902-07; 4th v.p. C.,R.I.&P. Ry. (which acquired control of St.L.&S.F. R.R.), 1907-09; v.p. St.L.&S.F. R.R., 1907—, also v.p. C.&E.I. R.R., 1907-13. Died Mar. 8, 1921.

HILLARD, Mary Robbins, educator; b. Kensington, Conn.; d. Rev. Elias Brewster and Julia (Whittlesey) H.; ed. St. Margaret's Sch., Waterbury, Conn., and Abbot Acad., Andover, Mass.; hon. L.H.D. Teacher in Miss Porter's School, Farmington, Conn., 1885-91; prin. St. Margaret's Sch. for Girls, 1891-1909; founder, 1909, becoming prin. Westover Sch., Middlebury. Episcopalian. Home: Middlebury, Conn. Died Oct. 10, 1932.

HILLEBRAND, William Francis, chemist; b. Honolulu, H.I., Dec. 12, 1853; s. Dr. William and Anna (Post) H.; ed. there and at Oakland, Calif.; attended Cornell, 1870-72; studied 6 yrs. in Germany; Ph.D., U. of Heidelberg, 1875; studied at U. of Strassburg and Mining Acad., Freiberg, Saxony; m. Martha May Westcott, Sept. 6, 1881. Assayer, Leadville, Colo., 1879-80; chemist U.S. Geol. Survey, 1880-1908; chief chemist Bur. of Standards, Washington, June 1908—. Prof. gen. chemistry and physics, Nat. Coll. of Pharmacy, 1892-1910. Author: Some Principles and Methods of Rock Analysis (2 edits.), 1900, 1902; Methods of Silicate and Carbonate Analysis, 1907, 10, 19. Home: Washington, D.C. Died Feb. 7, 1925.

HILLEGAS, Howard Clemens, author; b. Pennsburg, Pa., Dec. 30, 1872; s. John Gery (M.D.) and Catharine A. (Ziegler) H.; A.B., Franklin and Marshall Coll., Pa., 1894; married. Staff New York

World, 1895-98; war corr. New York World in South Africa, 1899-1900; on staff New York Herald, 1906—. Author: Oom Paul's People, 1899; The Boers in War, 1900; With the Boer Forces, London, 1900. Home: New Brighton, S.I., N.Y. Died Jan. 29, 1918.

HILLER, Hiram Milliken, surgeon; b. Kahoka, Mo., Mar. 8, 1867; s. Col. Hiram M. and Sarah Fulton (Bell) H.; A.B., Parsons Coll., Ia. 1887; M.D., U. of Pa., 1891; short post-grad. courses, univs. of Berlin, Vienna and Paris. Began med. practice, 1891; spent most of the time, 1895-1902, in scientific exploration of Far East in interest of U. of Pa., visiting Japan, China, Malay States, Borneo and Sumatra; collections given to Mus. of Science and Art (U. of Pa.), and to Acad. Natural Science of Philadelphia; in practice at Chester, Pa., 1908—; surgeon B.&O. Ry., Sun Shipbuilding Co., Penn-Seaboard Steel Corp., etc. Writer on wild tribes of Borneo, Veddahs of Ceylon and other eastern peoples. Draft Exemption Bd. for Chester, Pa. Home: Swarthmore, Pa. Died Aug. 7, 1921.

HILLES, William Samuel, lawyer; b. Phila., Pa., May 5, 1865; s. John Smith and Sarah (Tatum) H.; ed. pub. schs.; A.B., Haverford Coll., 1885; m. Florence Bayard, Oct. 28, 1898. Admitted to Del. bar, 1888, and entered practice at Wilmington. Home: New Castle Hundred, Del. Died Jan. 26, 1928.

HILLIARD, John Northern, author; b. Palmyra, N.Y., Aug. 18, 1872; s. Allan D. and Augusta (Bortells) H.; mainly self-ed.; m. Ida Louise Harrison, 1898; children—Hamlin (dec.), Hilda Harrison, Helen Hope. Went West in early boyhood and lived on ranch; reporter on old Chicago Press, 1889, Chicago Herald, 1890-95; successively lit. editor, dramatic critic and editorial writer, The Post Express, Rochester, N.Y., 1895-1911 (resigned). Author: The Bear's Claws (with Grace S. Mason), 1913; Ysabel of the Blue Bird (with same), 1913; The Golden Hope (with same), 1916; also The Castaways (musical comedy), prod. Rochester, 1912; Tusitala, a Masque of Robert Louis Stevenson, prod. Forest Theater, Carmel-by-the-Sea, Calif., 1916; The Wings of Adventure (novel), 1927. Producer of The Yellow Jacket, 1921; Kismet, 1923. Died Mar. 14, 1935.

HILLIARD, Robert Cochran, actor; b. N.Y. City, May 28, 1857; m. Cora Bell, 1881; 1 son, Robert Bell, U.S.N.; m. 2d, Mrs. Nellie E. Whitehouse Murphy, 1896; m. 3d, Denver, Mrs. Olga Williams, Apr. 20, 1914. Entered dramatic profession in his own theatre, the Criterion, Brooklyn, as a star in "False Shame," Jan. 18, 1886; played in "Engaged" and "Led Astray," and later was identified with numerous leading parts, including the title rôle in "Mr. Barnes of New York," Richard Gray in "Adrift" (written by himself), and John Earl of Woodstock, in "Sporting Life," of which play he is half owner. Also starred with Paul Arthur in "The Nominee" and alone in "Lost 24 Hours," "The Mummy" and "The Sleepwalker;" created rôle of Dick Johnson, in "The Girl of the Golden West," 1905; played in "A Fool There Was," "The Argyle Case" and in "The Pride of Race" and "The Littlest Girl" (written by himself). Died June 7, 1927.

HILLIS, Newell Dwight, clergyman; b. Magnolia, Ia., Sept. 2, 1858; s. Samuel Ewing and Margaret (Hester) H.; A.B., Lake Forest Univ., 1884, later A.M.; grad. McCormick Theol. Sem., Chicago, 1887; D.D., Northwestern U., 1892; L.H.D., Western Reserve U.; m. Annie Louise Patrick, Apr. 14, 1887; children—Richard Dwight, Marjorie, Nathalie Louise (Mrs. Robert O. Kellogg). Ordained Presbyn. ministry, 1887; pastor First Ch., Peoria, Ill., 1886-89, Evanston, Ill., 1889-95, Central Ch. (independent), Chicago, 1895-99, Plymouth Congl. Ch., Brooklyn, Jan. 1899-Oct. 1924, now pastor emeritus. Pres. Plymouth Inst., 1914—. Author: The Investment of Influence; A Man's Value to Society; How the Inner Light Failed; Foretokens of Immortality; Great Books as Life Teachers; Influence of Christ in Modern Life; Quest of Happiness, 1902; Success Through Self-Help, 1903; Building a Working Faith, 1903; The Quest of John Chapman, 1904; The Fortune of the Republic, 1906; Contagion of Character, 1911; Anti-Slavery Epoch, 1911; Prophets of a New Era, 1912; All the Year Round, 1912; Battle of Principles, 1912; Misfortunes of a World Without Pain, 1912; Noble Thoughts, 1912; Studies of the Great War, 1915; Story of Phædrus, 1913; Message of David Swing, 1913; German Atrocities, 1918; The Blot on the Kaiser's 'Scutcheon, 1918; Rebuilding the Ruined Lands of Europe, 1919; The Better America Lectures, 1921. Compiler: Lectures of Henry Ward Beecher, 1913. Home: Brooklyn, N.Y. Died Feb. 25, 1929.

HILLIS, Mrs. Newell Dwight (Annie P.), author; b. Marengo, Ill., 1862; d. Richard Montgomery and Emma Hotchkiss (Page) Patrick; B.Ph., Lake Forest Coll., Ill.; m. Newell Dwight Hillis, Apr. 14, 1887. Conglist. Author: The American Woman and Her Home, 1911. Home: Brooklyn, N.Y. Died Nov. 1, 1930.

HILLQUIT, Morris, lawyer; b. Riga, Latvia, Aug. 1, 1869; s. Benjamin and Rebecca (Levene) H.; ed. Riga Gymnasium, 1881-86; emigrated with parents to U.S., 1886; LL.B., Univ. Law Sch., New York, 1893; m. Vera Levene, Dec. 31, 1893. Engaged in practice of law in New York, May 1, 1893. Mem. Socialist Party, 1888—; del. to nine national convs., 1899—; del. to Internat. Socialist Congress, Amsterdam, 1904, Stuttgart, 1907, Copenhagen, 1910, Hamburg, 1923, Marseilles, 1925, Brussels, 1928, Vienna, 1931; rep. on Internat. Socialist Bur., 1904—; chmn. Socialist Nat. Exec. Com.; Socialist candidate for mayor, N.Y., 1917. Author: History of Socialism in the United States, 1903; Socialism in Theory and Practice, 1909; Socialism Summed Up, 1912; Socialism—Promise or Menace (with John A. Ryan), 1914; From Marx to Lenin, 1921. Home: New York, N.Y. Died Oct. 7, 1933.

HILLS, Elijah Clarence, univ. prof.; b. Arlington, Ill., July 2, 1867; s. Elijah Justin and Mary Eleanor (Larkin) H.; grad. Bingham Sch., N.C.; A.B., Cornell, 1892, fellow in Romance langs., 1892-93; student U. of Paris, 1893-94; Ph.D., U. of Colo., 1906; Litt.D., Rollins Coll., 1906; m. Metta Vergil Strough, June 22, 1898; children—Elijah Justin, George Strough, Clarence Ballard, Ruth. Prof. modern langs. Rollins Coll., 1896-1901, Romance langs., Colo. Coll., 1902-18; librarian, The Hispanic Soc. of America, 1916-18; prof. Romance langs. and head of dept., Indiana U., 1918-22; prof. Spanish, U. of Calif., 1922-24; prof. Romance philology, same, 1924—; gen. editor Romance publications, D. C. Heath & Co., 1918—. Lecturer at Harvard, 1911-12; prof. at U. of California, summers, 1912, 14, 22, Univ. of Colo., summer 1916, U. of Wis., summer 1924, U. of Wash., summer 1928. Fellow Am. Acad. Arts and Sciences; mem. Hispanic Soc. America, Am. Assn. Univ. Profs. Knight Comdr. Royal Order of Queen Isabel (Spanish). Author: Bardos Cubanos, 1901; Spanish Grammar, 1904; Spanish Tales for Beginners, 1909; Spanish Short Stories, 1910; Modern Spanish Lyrics, 1913; First Spanish Course, 1917; The Odes of Bello, Olmedo and Heredia, 1919; ed. Fortuna and Zaragüeta, 1920; Cuentos y Leyendas, 1922; Portuguese Grammar, 1925; Contes Dramatiques, 1927; Spanish Grammar for Colleges, 1928; French Short Stories (anthology), 1929. Home: Berkeley, Calif. Died Apr. 21, 1932.

HILLS, Laurence, newspaperman; b. N.Y. City, July 29, 1879; s. Philip Knapp and Elinor (Babson) H.; grad. Staten Island Acad. and Latin Sch., 1896; m. Edith L. Willis, Oct. 4, 1899; children—Philip, Frances. Began as reporter New York Sun, 1897; polit. corr. reporting nat. convs., 1908-12, 16, and chief Washington corr. of the Sun, 1916-20; chief corr. of Sun, Paris Peace Conf., 1919, accompanying President Wilson to Eng., Italy and Belgium; reported opening and first four assemblies of League of Nations, at Geneva; interviewed Mussolini, 1922; chief Paris corr. New York Herald and New York Sun, 1920-24; editor-in-chief and gen. mgr. European Edition New York Herald Tribune; v.p. New York Herald Co. of Paris. Decorated Officier de l'Instruction Publique and Chevalier Legion d'Honneur (French). Republican. Episcopalian. Home: Paris, France. Died Mar. 28, 1941.

HILLS, Lewis Samuel, banker; b. S. Amherst, Mass., Mar. 8, 1836; s. Lewis and Rhoda (Thayer) H.; high school edn.; m. Theresa Burton, Oct. 17, 1866. Register U.S. Land Office, Council Bluffs, Ia., 1859-61; Receiver U.S. Land Office, Salt Lake City, Utah, 1868-69; bank cashier, 1869-91; pres. Deseret Nat. Bank, 1891-1911; retired. Home: Salt Lake City, Utah. Died July 21, 1915.

HILLS, Richard Charles, geologist; b. Ewhurst, Surrey, Eng., Feb. 5, 1848; s. Richard C. and Emily (Cooper) H.; ed. at Ewhurst and Shoreditch, London; m. Louise A. Bruce, Mar. 7, 1901. Came to U.S., July 1865; went to Calif., 1867, to Nev., 1869, and to Ida., 1870, to Colo., 1877; engaged for several yrs. in expert examinations of mines in the Western States and Territories and Mexico; geol. expert for the Colo. Fuel & Iron Co., 1883-1904; at intervals engaged on field work for U.S. Geol. Survey; now geol. expert for Victor-Am. Fuel Co. Hon. curator geology and mineralogy, Colo. Mus. Natural History. Fellow Geol. Soc. London, Geol. Soc. America. Home: Denver, Colo. Died Aug. 14, 1923.

HILLS, Victor Gardiner, mining engr.; b. Nunda, N.Y., Jan. 21, 1855; s. Milton Tyler and Mary Jane (Gardiner) H.; B.A., Highland (Kan.) Coll., 1877, M.A., 1880; spl. study in mining and assaying, Colo. Coll., 1879; m. M. Adaline Flick, Jan. 1, 1883. Began at Leadville, Colo., 1879; city engr., Pueblo, Colo., 1885, 86; co. surveyor, Pueblo Co., 1885-90; city engr., Cripple Creek, Colo., 1893; consulting engr., Portland Gold Mining Co., etc., at Cripple Creek; mgr. and consulting engr., Colo. Tungsten Corp., 1905-07; consulting engr. and mgr., Sheelite Mines, Ltd., N.S., 1910-12. Home: Denver, Colo. Died July 13, 1930.

HILLS, William Henry, editor; b. Somerville, Mass., June 6, 1859; s. John D. and Abby (Fosdick) H.; A.B., Harvard, 1880; m. Josephine Whitten, Oct. 2, 1882; children—Ruth Whitten (Mrs. Wm. E. Hartwell), Miriam Fosdick (dec.), Dorothy Thayer (dec.). When in coll. published Students' Songs; joined staff of the Boston Globe, 1881; founder, editor and publisher The Writer, 1887-1926; consulting editor, 1926—. Wrote humorous paragraphs and verse for Somerville Journal, of which he was several yrs. editor; New England corr. for Western papers, especially Chicago Daily News; exchange editor and editorial paragraph writer on Boston Globe. Home: Somerville, Mass. Died Nov. 7, 1930.

HILLYER, Virgil Mores, headmaster; b. Weymouth, Mass., Sept. 2, 1875; s. Virgil and Amey (Adlington) H.; A.B., Harvard, 1897; m. Reba Key Mitchell, 1902 (died 1906); m. 2d, Virginia Ann White, June 30, 1926. Headmaster, Calvert Sch., and "The New School," Baltimore, Md., 1899—. Appmt. officer U.S. Food Administration, Washington, 1917; capt., Mil. Intelligence Div., U.S.A., 1918. Episcopalian. Author: Child Training, 1915; A Child's History of the World, 1924; A Child's Geography of the World, 1929. Home: Baltimore, Md. Died Dec. 21, 1931.

HILPRECHT, Herman Volrath, educator; b. Hohenerxleben, Germany, July 28, 1859; s. Robert and Emilie (Wielepp) H.; grad. Herzogl. Gymnasium, Bernburg, Germany, 1880; studied, 1880-85, theology, philology and law, U. of Leipzig, Ph.D., 1883 (D.D., U. of Pa., 1894; LL.D., Princeton, 1896); "repetent" of O.T. theology, U. of Erlangen, Bavaria, 1885-86; m. Miss S. C. Haufe, 1886 (died 1902); m. 2d, Mrs. Sallie Crozer Robinson, d. Samuel Aldrich Crozer, Apr. 24, 1903. Curator Semitic sect. of mus., U. of Pa., 1887-1911, containing over fifty thousand original Babylonian antiquities, for the greater part presented by him; Clark research prof. Assyrian and prof. comparative Semitic philology, U. of Pa., 1886-1911. Assyriologist and from 1895 also scientific dir., U. of Pa. expdn. to Nippur, Babylonia (4 campaigns), and editor-in-chief of its publs., The Babylonian Expdn. of U. of Pa., 4 series; reorganized Babylonian sect., Imperial Ottoman Mus., Constantinople, 1893-1909; made frequent scientific explorations in Asia Minor and Syria, and trips to India, Ceylon, China, Japan and Korea, 1911-12. Leading authority in cuneiform research. Knight of first class, 1893, commander, 1898, Crown of Comthur of II class, 1909; Star of the Comthur I class, 1915; Albrecht der Baer (German decoration); comdr. Turkish Osmanië Order, 1895; comthur with star, same, 1897; comdr. Danish Order of Danebrog, 1898; German Order Frederika, 1901; Lucy Wharton Drexel Medal, 1902; Golden Liakat Medal, 1905. Author: Business Documents of Murashû Sons of Nippur, dated in the Reign of Artaxerxes I (with A. T. Clay); Mathematical Metrological and Chronological Texts from the Temple Library of Nippur, Part 1, 1906; Assyriaca, Eine Nachlese auf dem Gebiete der Assyriologie. Died Mar. 20, 1925.

HILTMAN, John Wolfe, publisher; b. Manchester, Eng., Feb. 27, 1862; s. John Thomas and Almira Virginia (Wolfe) H.; brought to U.S. in infancy; ed. pub. schs.; m. Rowena Large, 1884. Began as office boy American Express Co., Chicago, 1874, and advanced to agt.; gen. mgr. and treas. Edward Thompson Co., Northport, L.I., 1897-1912; v.p. and gen. mgr. D. Appleton & Co., publishers, 1912-19, pres., 1919-33; chmn. bd. D. Appleton-Century Co., 1933—. Capt. 1st Regt. Cav., Ill. N.G., 1881-84. Republican. Episcopalian. Home: Northport, L.I. Died Apr. 15, 1941.

HILTON, Alexander, ry. official; b. at Hamilton, Ont., June 19, 1865; s. Edward and Harriet (Hale) H.; ed. Hamilton pub. schs.; m. Grace Barr, May 10, 1886. Clerk G.W. Ry., Hamilton, Ont., Can., 1878-79; clerk at Chicago, Ill., 1879-84, city pass. and ticket agt., Kansas City, 1884-87, Pacific coast agt., San Francisco, 1887-88, gen. agt. pass. dept., Kansas City, 1888-1901, C.&A. R.R.; asst. gen. pass. agt., Kansas City, Fort Scott & Memphis Ry., Kansas City, 1901; gen. pass. agt. S.L.&S.F. R.R., 1901-13; pass. traffic mgr. S.L.&S.F. R.R., 1913-18; traffic mgr. Frisco Lines, 1918-20; v.p. in charge traffic, 1920—. Mason (32°). Home: St Louis, Mo. Died Dec. 25, 1922.

HIMES, John Andrew, college prof.; b. McAllisterville, Pa., June 3, 1848; s. Jacob and Margaret (Kenawell) H.; A.B., Pa. Coll., 1870, A.M., 1873; A.B., Yale, 1871; (Litt.D., Dickinson, 1898); m. Mary Jane Hay, June 30, 1874. Prof. English lit. and polit. science, Pa. Coll., 1873-1914; then engaged principally in literary work. Hon. mem. Sixth Corps Soc. of the Army of the Potomac. Author: A Study of Milton's Paradise Lost, 1878; Paradise Lost, with an introduction and notes on its structure and meaning, 1898; Miltonic Enigmas in the Minor Poems. Home: Gettysburg, Pa. Died Aug. 11, 1923.

HIMMEL, Joseph, univ. pres.; b. Annapolis, Md., Jan. 16, 1855; s. John and Mary (Himmelheber) H.; student St. John's Coll., Annapolis, 1869-70; grad. Woodstock (Md.) Coll., 1885. On teaching staff, Holy Cross Coll., Worcester, Mass., and Georgetown, D.C., 1877-82; dir. Jesuit Home Missions, 1890-98; superior Manresa Inst. (Jesuit summer sch.), 1899-1907; pres. Gonzaga Coll., D.C., 1907-08; pres. Georgetown (D.C.) U., 1908-12; dir.

Jesuit Home Missions and superior, Manresa Inst., Keyser Island, South Norwalk, Conn., 1912—. Rector St. Andrews-on-Hudson, 1918-21. Deceased.

HINCKLEY, Frederic Allen, clergyman; b. at Windsor, Vt., July 2, 1845; s. Rev. Frederic and Sarah A. (Hews) H.; ed. pub. schs., Lowell, Mass., 1856-64; m. Elizabeth S. Carter, Mar. 4, 1869; father of Allen Carter H. Ordained Unitarian ministry, 1878; took part in agitation for 10-hour factory law and for abolition of property qualification for voting in R.I.; was chmn. Woman's Suffrage Campaign Com. in R.I. for amendment to constitution giving women the right to vote; chmn. sch. com., Northampton, Mass., 1888-96, and introduced system of manual training there; minister Spring Garden Unitarian Ch., Phila., 1896-1910, Unitarian Ch., Wilmington, Del., 1913—. Author: Beckonings of the Spirit; Afterglow; The Deeper Meanings; Woodwork for Common Schools; What Unitarians Believe. Home: Wilmington, Del. Died Nov. 22, 1917.

HINCKLEY, Frederick Wheeler, lawyer; b. Princeton, Me., May 26, 1878; s. Adelbert E. and Sarah J. (McLaughlin) H.; ed. Eastern Me. Conf. Sem., Bucksport, Me.; Coburn Classical Inst., Waterville, Me.; m. Blanche Richards, Oct. 23, 1907. Admitted to Me. bar, 1901, and practiced at Calais 2 yrs., at Portland, 1903—; sr. mem. Hinckley & Hinckley, 1912-26, Hinckley, Hinckley & Shesong, 1926—; atty. in rate case vs. Cumberland County Power & Light Co., 1918, for gov. in state prison investigation, 1925; chief counsel for U.S. Senator Arthur R. Gould in handling his case before Com. on Privileges and Elections, U.S. Senate, in which an attempt was made to expel him from the Senate. Mayor of South Portland, 1919-20; mem. Me. Ho. of Rep., 1919-22, Senate, 1923-26, inclusive; mem. Legal Advisory Bd., World War. Mem. bd. trustees Juvenile Instns. of Me., 1914-19 (pres., 1913-16). Republican. Baptist. Mason. Designer, owner and builder Sylvan-Site, a $5,000,000 model community of 200 homes in South Portland Heights. Home: South Portland, Me. Died May 11, 1933.

HINCKLEY, George Lyman, librarian; b. Northampton, Mass., July 6, 1879; s. Henry Rose and Mary Wright (Barrett) H.; grad. Williston Sem., Easthampton, Mass., 1896; B.A., Yale, 1900, M.A., 1906; unmarried. Asst. in Forbes Library, Northampton, 1900-03; cataloguer Boston Pub. Library, 1903-13; in charge of the Allen A. Brown Dramatic Collection, 1910-13 (catalogued and classified it); worked on pvt. dramatic collection of Robert Gould Shaw, 1913-14; librarian Redwood Library, Newport, R.I., 1914-27. Republican. Congregationalist. Died Mar. 16, 1936.

HINCKLEY, Robert, portrait painter; b. Boston, Apr. 3, 1853; s. Samuel Lyman and Anne Cutler (Parker) H.; grad. École des Beaux Arts; studied painting, Paris, 17 yrs.; m. Eleanora O'Donnell, June 11, 1885. Founder of studio of Carolus Duran; teacher of portrait class, Corcoran Sch., Washington, several yrs. Best known work: Alexander at Persepolis; also about 350 portraits of eminent people in U.S. Author: Geyserland. Home: Rehoboth Beach, Del. Died June 1, 1941.

HINCKLEY, Thomas, diplomatic service; b. Washington, D.C., Aug. 4, 1888; s. Robert and Eleanora Columbus (O'Donnell) H.; student Stevens Inst. Tech., Hoboken, N.J.; unmarried. Engaged in elec. engring. and mining; sec. Am. Legation and consul gen. at San Salvador, 1912-14; 2d sec. Embassy, Vienna, Austria, 1914-15; sec. Embassy, Madrid, 1916—. Died Nov. 6, 1918.

HINCKS, Edward Young, theologian; b. Bucksport, Me., Aug. 13, 1844; s. John Winslow and Sarah Ann (Blodget) H.; A.B., Yale, 1866, A.M., 1883; student Union Theol. Sem., 1866-67; B.D., Andover Theol. Sem., 1870; (D.D., Yale, 1885); m. Elizabeth C., g.d. Commodore O. H. Perry, of Andover, Mass., Apr. 19, 1877; 1 dau., Annie Perry; m. 2d, Elizabeth T., d. Charles P. Clark, of Boston, July 20, 1887; children—Sarah, Carroll Clark, Elizabeth Mary, Caroline Tyler. Ordained Congl. ministry, 1870; pastor State St. Ch., Portland, Me., 1870-81; in Europe, 1881-82; prof. Bibl. theology, 1883-1900, systematic theology, 1900-08, Bibl. theology, 1908-19, Andover Theol. Sem., prof. emeritus, also emeritus Andover prof. Bibl. theology, Harvard. Joint author: Progressive Orthodoxy, 1886; Divinity of Christ, 1893. Home: Cambridge, Mass. Died Dec. 23, 1927.

HINDMAN, Albert Clare, U.S. attorney; b. Clarion, Pa., Nov. 28, 1884; s. Frank R. and Ella S (Craig) H.; grad. State Normal Sch., Clarion, 1901; student Ind. U.; LL.B., George Washington U., 1908; m. Blanche M. Hall. Began practice at Boise, Ida., 1910; v. chmn. Dem. State Central Com., 1916-18; asst. atty. gen. of Ida., 1917-18; mem. Nat. Congressional Com. from Ida., 1918-20; U.S. atty., Dist. of Canal Zone, April 1, 1919—. Elk. Home: Ancon, Canal Zone. Died Mar. 6, 1923.

HINDS, Asher Crosby, congressman; b. Benton, Me., Feb. 6, 1863; s. Albert Dwelly and Charlotte (Flagg) H grad Coburn Classical Inst., Waterville, Me., 1879; A.B., Colby Coll., 1883 (LL.D., 1905); m. Harriet Louise Estey, Sept. 3, 1891. Mem. editorial staff Portland (Me.) Daily Advertiser, 1884-85, Portland Press, 1885-1902; speaker's clerk, U.S. Ho. of Rep., 1889-91; clerk at speaker's table (parliamentary clerk) U.S. Ho. of Rep., 1895-1911; mem. 62d to 64th Congresses (1911-17), 1st Me. Dist. Republican. Trustee Colby Coll. Editor: Rules, Manual and Digest of House of Representatives; Parliamentary Precedents of the House of Representatives, 1899; Hinds' Precedents of the House of Representatives, 1908. Home: Portland, Me. Died May 1, 1919.

HINDS, Ernest, army officer; b. Ala., Aug. 18, 1864; grad. U.S. Mil. Acad., 1887; hon. grad. Arty. Sch., 1898; m. Mary Hatton Miller; children—Marjorie Hamilton (wife of Colonel Fred T. Cruse, F.A., U.S.A.), John Hamilton (Capt. F.A., U.S.A.). Commd. 2d lieut. 2d Arty., U.S. Army, June 12, 1887; promoted through grades to brig. gen., Mar. 5, 1921; maj. gen., Dec. 6, 1922. Comd. Light Battery F, 2d Arty., in campaign against Santiago de Cuba, 1898, and at various points in Cuba; comd. Battery L, 2d Arty., at Reina Battery, Havana, Aug.-Sept. 1899; maj. U.S. Vols. 49th Inf. in P.I., 1900-01; mem. Field Arty. Drill Regulations Bd., 1903-05; adj. gen. depts. of Colo. and Tex., 1907, Ft. Riley, Kan., 1907-09; asst. to adj. gen., Philippine Div., 1909-11; chief of staff, Philippine Dept., 1914-17; comdt. Saumur Arty. Sch., Dec. 1917-Jan. 1918; chief of arty., 1st A.C., Feb.-Mar. 1918, of 1st Army, Apr.-May 1918, of A.E.F., May 24, 1918-June 12, 1919; comdt. F.A. Sch. of Fire, Ft. Sill, Okla., Oct. 24, 1919-June 30, 1923; comdg. 2d Div., Ft. Sam Houston, Tex., July 3, 1923-Apr. 5, 1924; comdg. 8th Corps Area, Fort Sam Houston, Tex., April 6-Oct. 15, 1924, and Jan. 12, 1925-Jan. 3, 1928; retired Apr. 18, 1928. Atty., sec.-treas. and gen. mgr. United Services Automobile Assn., Jan. 1, 1928—. Awarded D.S.M. "for exceptionally meritorious and distinguished services" during World War; Comdr. Legion of Honor (French); Comdr. Order of Leopold (Belgian); Comdr. Order of Sts. Maurice and Lazarus (Italian). Died June 17, 1941.

HINDS, John Iredelle Dillard, educator; chemist; b. Guilford Co., N.C., Dec. 13, 1847; s. Rev. John and Rhoda (Webb) H.; A.B., A.M., C.E., Cumberland U., 1873; Ph.D., Lincoln U., 1879; grad. student U. of Berlin, 1880-81, Harvard, 1882; (LL.D., Cumberland, 1903); m. Mrs. Mary B. (Atkins) Lindsley, Nov. 21, 1880. Prof. science, Cumberland U., 1873-99; dean of coll. faculty, same, 1894-99; prof. chemistry, U. of Nashville, and Peabody Coll. for Teachers, 1899-1911; dean coll. faculty, same, 1907-11; prof. chemistry, Cumberland U., 1911-14; prof. science, Castle Heights' Sch., Lebanon, Tenn., 1914-17; chemist to Tenn. Geol. Survey, 1917—. Mason. Presbyn. Mem. Internat. S.S. Lesson Com., 1884-1902; supt. of platform Monteagle Assembly, 1891-96. Author: Qualitative Chemical Analysis from the Standpoint of Solubilities, Ionization and Mass Action, 1910. Home: Nashville, Tenn. Died Mar. 4, 1921.

HINDS, Warren Elmer, economic entomologist; b. Townsend, Mass., Sept. 20, 1876; s. Warren David and Mary Persis (Colby) H.; B.S., Mass. Agrl. Coll. (Boston U. Agrl. Dept.), 1899, Ph.D., 1902; m. Edith Goddard Gary, Mar. 4, 1903. Asst. in entomology, Mass. Expt. Sta., 1899; expert asst. U.S. Bur. Entomology, 1901, spl. field agent, 1902-07; prof. entomology, Ala. Poly. Inst., and entomologist, Ala. Expt. Sta., 1907-24; extension entomologist, Ala. Poly. Inst. Extension Service, 1914-24; entomologist La. Expt. Sta. and Extension Service, 1924-29; entomologist, La. Expt. Sta., 1929—; summer lecturer, U. of Md., 1901; in charge lab. work on Mexican boll weevil, 1902-07; studied cotton pest problems of Peru, S.A., 1926. Mem. City Council, Auburn, Ala., 1921-23; v.p. exec. com., La. State Schs. for Blind and Deaf, 1932—. Del. from Am. Assn. Econ. Entomologists to Centennial of French Entomol. Soc., and to 5th Internat. Congress of Entomology, Paris, 1932. Mason. Kiwanian (pres. Baton Rouge, La., Club, 1932). Author: The Boll Weevil, 1920. Died Jan. 11, 1936.

HINDS, William Alfred, author; b. Enfield, Mass., Feb. 2, 1833; s. Samuel and Lucy (Amsden) H.; Ph.B., Sheffield Scientific Sch. (Yale), 1870; unmarried. Stenographer, 1851-70; editor Oneida Circular, 1870-72; asso. editor The American Socialist, 1876-79; dir. Oneida Community, Limited, 26 yrs., pres., 1903—. Author: American Communities, 1878; revised and enlarged, 1902 and 1907. Home: Kenwood, Madison Co., N.Y. Died 1910.

HINE, Charles Daniel; b. Fair Haven, Vt., Feb. 26, 1845; s. Orlo Daniel and Ellen Caroline (Whittelsey) H.; grad. Phillips Acad., Andover, Mass., 1862; B.A., Yale, 1871; LL.B., Ia. State U., 1878; m. Mabel Elizabeth Moston, June 26, 1916. Supt. schs., Saginaw, Mich., 1871-74, Norwich, Conn., 1874-76; prin. high sch., Omaha, Neb., 1880-83; sec. (now commr.) Conn. State Bd. Edn., 1883-1920. Instr. grad. ednl. dept., Yale, 1915-19; chmn. Conn. Pub. Library Commn., 1893—. Republican. Episcopalian. Mason. Home: Winsted, Conn. Died Aug. 27, 1923.

HINE, Charles De Lano, organization expert; b. Vienna, Va., Mar. 15, 1867; s. Maj. Orrin Eugene (N.Y. Vol. Engrs., 1861-65) and Alma (De Lano) H., grad. U.S. Mil. Acad., 1891; LL.B., Cincinnati Law Sch., 1893, and admitted to bar same yr.; m. Helen Underwood, 1915. Commd. 2d lt. 6th Inf., June 12, 1891; served as instr. N.G. in D.C., Va. and N.C.; resigned from army, 1895, and entered ry. work as freight brakeman, later switchman, yardmaster, conductor, chief clk., trainmaster, right of way agt., asst. supt., gen. supt., gen. mgr. and v.p., and in various staff positions as expert adviser; originator unit system of orgn. for corps. installed on Harriman lines and other rys. Served as maj. U.S. Vols., in Santiago Campaign, Spanish-Am. War; in World War, 1917-19, as col. 69th N.Y. Inf. and in Motor Transport Corps; in action at Hoeville and St. Mihiel, France; col. O.R.C., Oct. 4, 1921. Republican. Author: Modern Organization, 1912. Homes: New York, N.Y., and Vienna, Va. Died Feb. 13, 1927.

HINE, Clint C., lawyer; b. Lafayette, Ind., Mar. 4, 1884; s. Frederick N. and Mary E. (Knauer) H.; ed. grade and high schs. and business coll.; LL.B., Ill. Coll. of Law, 1907; m. Florence Voelcker, Mar. 16, 1912; m. 2d, Kathryn Peetz, Sept. 30, 1922. Admitted to Ill. bar, 1907, and began practice at Chicago; with legal dept. C.,I.&L. Ry. Co., 1912—, successively gen. claim agt. until 1914, asst. gen. atty., 1914-16, gen. atty., 1916-20, gen. solicitor, 1920—; pres. Monon Coal Co.; dir. Monon Realty Co., Terminal & Warehouse Co. (Louisville, Ky.), Chicago & Indianapolis Coal Co. Atty. for U.S. R.R. Administration, World War. Republican. Episcopalian. Mason. Home: Glen Ellyn, Ill. Died Nov. 23, 1935.

HINE, Francis Lyman, banker; b. New Milford, Conn.; s. Dr. James and Catharine (Northrop) H.; ed. Oxford Acad., Oxford, N.Y.; m. Mrs. Mary Ide Low. Chmn. exec. com. First Nat. Bank of New York; v.p., dir. First Security Co. of City of N.Y.; dir. Nat. Biscuit Co., Fifth Av. Bank, Astor Safe Deposit Co., Lehigh Valley Coal Sales Co., Home Life Ins. Co., U.S. Rubber Co., etc.; trustee Brooklyn Trust Co., Am. Surety Co. Dir. Union Theol. Sem., 1903—; pres. N.Y. Clearing House Assn. Home: New York, N.Y. Died Oct. 9, 1927.

HINES, Edgar Alphonso, M.D., pediatrist; b. Wayne Co., N.C., Nov. 19, 1867; s. John Calhoun Caldwell and Nancy F. (Thompson) H.; prep. edn., Bingham Sch., N.C.; spl. student in chemistry, Clemson Coll.; M.D., Med. Coll. of S.C., 1891; post-grad. work, Johns Hopkins, Harvard, New York Post-Grad. Sch., New York Lying-In Hosp., Chicago Post-Grad. Sch., London (Eng.) Hosp.; m. Mary Woodbury Moore, July 25, 1894; children—Cornelia Ravenel, Nancy Thompson Brigman, Mary Moore (Mrs. L. E. Beard), Leola, Edgar Alphonso, Elizabeth (Mrs. W. E. Hall), John Elbridge. Began practice at Gillisonville, 1891; settled at Seneca, S.C., 1897; pioneer in child welfare work in the South; a founder Bur. Child Hygiene of State Bd. of Health, S.C.; one of inaugurators school med. inspection in the South. Vice chmn. S.C. State Bd. of Health, 1912—; session chmn. Internat. Congress Sch. Hygiene, Buffalo, N.Y., 1913; supt. Anderson Co. (S.C.) Hosp., 1915. Med. mem. Dist. Exemption Bd., West Dist. of S.C., World War; now maj. M.R.C., U.S.A. Democrat. Presbyn. Mason. Licentiate of Am. Bd. of Pediatrics. Home: Seneca, S.C. Died Nov. 27, 1940.

HINES, Edward, lumber mcht.; b. Buffalo, N.Y., July 31, 1863; s. Peter and Rose (McGarry) H.; removed to Chicago with parents, 1865; pub. sch. edn.; m. Loretta O'Dowd, June 12, 1895; children—Edward, Jr. (dec.), Ralph, Charles, Loretta. Began as clerk in grocery store at $10.00 per month; "tally boy" with the lumber firm of Fish & Bro., and later office boy with S. K. Martin & Co., advancing to bookkeeper and gen. office man, and later for 4 yrs. as traveling salesman; sec., treas. S. K. Martin Lumber Co., 1884-92; organized, 1892, and became pres. and gen. mgr., Edward Hines Lumber Co.; interested in numerous other business enterprises. Republican. Catholic. Home: Evanston, Ill. Died Dec. 1, 1931.

HINES, Edward Norris; b. St. Louis, Mo., Jan. 13, 1870; s. Henry and Eve (Ehret) H.; ed. pub. schs.; m. Clara Margaret Steers, June 8, 1898; children—Helen Margaret (Mrs. Ralph Thomas), Deming Lloyd (dec.). Started in printing business, 1889, as partner of William H. Speaker; business incorporated, 1907, as Speaker-Hines-Printing Co., treas., 1907-25, pres. and gen. mgr., 1925—. Rd. commr. of Wayne Co., Mich., 1906—. First mile of concrete road in the U.S. designed and built under his direction; originated white line device to separate traffic lanes, 1911; compiled and pub. 1st road tour book, 1893; sponsored adoption of county road law in Mich., 1893; organizer of Am. Road Builders Assn., 1903. Mem. Bd. of Co. Park Trustees, 1923—; mem. Macomb-Wayne Superhighway Commission, 1925—; mem. Oakland-Wayne Superhighway Commn., 1925—; mem. bd. of mgrs. Wayne Co. Airport. George S. Bartlett award for notable contributions to highway progress, 1935; B. F. Goodrich Co. plaque as originator center line safety stripe, 1936; Middle Rouge Parkway renamed Edward N. Hines Drive by County of Wayne, 1936. Christian Scientist. Mason. Home: Detroit, Mich. Died June 4, 1938.

HINES, Edward Warren, lawyer; b. Butler Co., Ky., Jan. 15, 1858; s. Warren Walker and Sarah (Carson) H.; student Bethel Coll., Russelville, Ky., 1869-70; Warren Coll., Bowling Green, Ky., 1873-75; studied law under Judge Thomas H. Hines, of Court of Appeals of Ky., 1879-81; Summer Law Sch. of U. of Va., 1882; (LL.D., Ky. State Univ., 1919); unmarried. Dep. clk., Warren Circuit Ct., Bowling Green, 1876-78, Ct. of Appeals of Ky., 1881; admitted to bar, 1881; practiced at Frankfort, Ky., 1881-1902, except 1 yr. in Washington, D.C.; official reporter Ct. of Appeals of Ky., 1887-96, and issued vols. 83-98 Ky. Repts.; gen. atty. and gen. solicitor, L.&N. R.R. Co., at Louisville, Ky., 1902-07; mem. McCord, Hines & Norman, 1908-11, Hines & Norman, 1911-14; asst. counsel and examiner-atty. Interstate Commerce Commn., 1914-17; chmn. Ky. State Council of Defense 1917-19; dean Law Sch. of U. of Louisville, 1919—. Trustee Emory Univ., Atlanta, Ga., 1919—. Editor Ky. Law Reporter (monthly), 1884-90. Democrat. Mem. M.E. Ch., S. Author: Abstracts of Cases Decided by Federal Courts, Relating to Limitations of 14th Amendment, upon Power of States to Regulate Rates, 1908. Home: Louisville, Ky. Deceased.

HINES, James Kollock, judge; b. Burke Co., Ga., Nov. 18, 1852; s. Joseph Henry and Susan Elizabeth (Harrison) H.; prep. edn., Oldfield and Bartow acads.; A.B., Emory Coll., Oxford, Ga., 1872; student law dept. Harvard U., 1 yr.; m. Belle Evans, Jan. 9, 1879 (died 1884); children—Mrs. Lucy Belle Livengood, Susan, Joseph Henry (dec.); m. 2d, Cora Lawson McBride, Dec. 28, 1885; children—Mrs. Elizabeth Hannah Jones, Mrs. Mary Gunsaulus, Daniel, Mrs. Lawson Carter. Admitted to Ga. bar, 1873, and began practice at Savannah; solicitor gen. Middle Jud. Circuit, Ga., 1877-81; mem. Ga. Ho. of Rep., 1884-85; judge Middle Jud. Circuit, 1887-91; atty. for R.R. Commn. of Ga., 1907-22; justice Supreme Court of Ga., 1922—. Democrat. Methodist. Home: Atlanta, Ga. Died May 19, 1932.

HINES, Linnæus Neal, educator; b. Carthage, Mo., Feb. 12, 1871; s. Hiram and Sarah Mary (Neal) H.; A.B., Ind. U., 1894, A.M., 1908; post-grad. work, Ind. U., Cornell U., Columbia and U. of Chicago; LL.D., Wabash Coll., 1929; m. Bertha Georgia Wiggs, Feb. 26, 1907; children—Neal Oldfield, Anne Emerson. Prin. grade sch., Noblesville, 1892-93; teacher and asst. to prin., Evansville, Ind., 1894-99; teacher mathematics, Shortridge High Sch., Indianapolis, 1900; supt. schs. Union City, Ind., 1901-06, Hartford City, Ind., 1906-08, Crawfordsville, Ind., 1908-19; state supt. pub. instr., Ind., terms, 1919-23, resigned Oct. 1, 1921; pres. Ind. State Normal Sch., Terre Haute, and Eastern Div., Ind. State Normal Sch., Muncie, 1921-24; pres. Ind. State Teachers Coll., Terre Haute, Dec. 1, 1924-Oct. 1, 1933; dir. of extension, placement and student activities, same coll., 1934. Asst. editor, 1914-16, editor and part owner, 1917-24, Educator-Journal, Indianapolis. Mem. Ind. State Bd. of Edn., 1919-33; Ind. State dir. Y.M.C.A. Republican. Methodist. Mason. Co-author: Educational Hygiene, 1913. Home: Terre Haute, Ind. Died July 14, 1936.

HINES, Walker Downer, lawyer; b. Russelville, Ky., Feb. 2, 1870; s. James M. and Mary Walker (Downer) H.; B.S., Ogden Coll., 1888; B.L., U. of Va., 1893; m. Alice Clymer Macfarlane, Oct. 24, 1900; 1 dau., Helen Macfarlane (Mrs. Paul Tison). Asst. atty., 1893-97, asst. chief atty., 1897-1901, 1st v.p., 1901-04, L.&N. R.R. Co.; mem. firm Humphrey, Hines & Humphrey, Louisville, Ky., 1904-06; gen. counsel A.,T.&S.F. Ry. Co., 1906-18, chmn. exec. com., 1908-16, and chmn. bd. of dirs., 1916-18; gen. law practice, New York, 1906-16; asst. dir. gen. of railways, Feb. 1918-19, dir. gen. of railroads, 1919-20, in Europe, June 1920-Oct. 1921, as arbitrator under Peace Treaties of questions of river shipping; law practice, New York, 1921—; mem. Hines, Rearick, Door, Travis & Marshall, 1927—; dir. C.,B.&Q. R.R. Co. Investigation and report on Rhine and Danube navigation for League of Nations, summer 1925. Commandeur de la Légion d'Honneur (France); Order of White Eagle, 1st Class, of Kingdom of Serbs, Croats and Slovenes; Cross of Grand Officer, Order of White Lion (Czecho-Slovakia). Author: War History of American Railroads. Home: New York, N.Y. Died Jan. 14, 1934.

HINGELEY, Joseph Beaumont, clergyman; b. Carmichaels, Pa., Jan. 26, 1856; s. Ezra and Anne (Warwick) H.; A.B., Amherst, 1877, A.M., 1885; Boston U. Sch. of Theology, 1877-78; (D.D., Hamline U., 1896); m. Emma Wert, Aug. 26, 1879. Prin. high sch., Montague, Mass., 1875, Provincetown, 1878-80; ordained M.E. ministry, 1883; pastor Bridgewater, Mass., 1881-82, New Bedford, Mass., 1883-84, Fergus Falls, Minn., 1884-86, Forest Heights, Minn., 1887; presiding elder Fergus Falls Dist., 1888-90; pastor Thirteenth Av. Ch., Minneapolis, 1891-92, Foss Ch., Minneapolis, 1893-96, Trinity Ch., Minneapolis, 1897-98; presiding elder Litchfield Dist., Minn., 1899-1905; corr. sec. Superannuated Fund Northern Minn. Conf., 1906-08; corr. sec. Bd. of Pensions and Relief, 1908-28; sec. Gen. Conf. of M.E. Ch., 1904, 08, 12, hon. secretary, 1916; del. to Gen. Conf., 1896-1928. Editor Northwestern Minn. Advocate, Fergus Falls, 1885-86, veteran preacher, Minneapolis and Chicago, 1907-20; editor Veteran Preacher; editor Minutes Northern Minn. Conf. M.E. Ch., 1896-98. Pres. Inter-denominational Secretaries' Conf. on Ministerial Pensions and Relief, 1916—; dir. survey dept. of Ministerial Support, Pensions and Relief of Inter-Ch. World Movement of America, 1919-20. Trustee Hamline U.; mem. Chicago Preachers' Meeting, Chicago Social Union, Northwestern Amherst Alumni Assn. Editor: Journal of General Conference M.E. Church, 1904, 08, 12; Discipline of the M.E. Church, 1908, 1912. Home: Evanston, Ill. Died July 25, 1929.

HINITT, Frederick William, clergyman; b. Kidderminster, Eng., Nov. 2, 1866; s. John and Selina H.; A.B., Westminster Coll., 1889, A.M., 1891; grad. McCormick Theol. Sem., Chicago, 1892; Ph.D., U. of Wooster, 1896, D.D., 1902; LL.D., Centre Coll. of Ky., 1915, Allegheny, 1915; m. Elfie H. Humphreys, June 29, 1892 (died 1918); children—Dorothy, Margaret (dec.), Frederick William (dec.), John Foster. Ordained Presbyn. ministry, 1892; pastor Warrensburg, Mo., 1892-95, Ottumwa, Ia., 1895-1900; pres. Parsons Coll., Fairfield, Ia., 1900-04, Centre Coll. of Ky., Danville, Ky., 1904-15, Washington and Jefferson Coll., 1915-18; pastor 1st Ch., Indiana, Pa., 1918—, Y.M.C.A. field sec. for army work, A.E.F., hdqrs. London, Eng., 1918-19, also dir. for United Kingdom of Army Ednl. Commn. Moderator, Synod of Ky., 1905; formerly mem. Gen. Assembly's coms. on ednl. policy and reorganization and consolidation of administrative agencies, also sec. of com.; mem. Gen. Council of Presbyn. Ch., 1923-24; dir. Western Theol. Sem., Pittsburgh, 1915—. Home: Indiana, Pa. Died Oct. 25, 1928.

HINKLE, Thornton Mills, lawyer; b. Cincinnati, Aug. 17, 1840; s. Philip and Frances (Quinn) H.; A.B., Yale, 1863, A.M., 1894; LL.B., Columbia, 1865; m. Helen F. Sage, Oct. 29, 1866; father of Frederick Wallis H. War corr. Cincinnati Gazette, 1864; admitted to bar, 1865, and began practice at Cincinnati; pres. and prof. med. jurisprudence, Pulte Med. Coll., 1886-96; v.p. and pres. trustees Cincinnati Sinking Fund, 1900-09; pres. trustees Cincinnati Pub. Library, 1891; v.p. Lane Theol. Sem., 1900—; trustee Cincinnati Law Sch. (U. of Cincinnati). Pres. Cincinnati Bar Assn., 1893-95; treas. Cincinnati Law Library Assn., 1878—. Home: Cincinnati, O. Died Sept. 17, 1920.

HINKLEY, John, lawyer; b. Baltimore, Mar. 1, 1864; s. Edward Otis and Anne M. (Keemlé) H.; A.B., Johns Hopkins, 1884; LL.B., U. of Md., 1886; unmarried. Sec. Am. Bar Assn., 1893-1909, mem. com. on professional ethics and grievances, 1923-34; dir. Baltimore National Bank; mem. Hinkley, Burger & Singley. Mem. Md. State Bd. Law Examiners, 1906-16. Capt. 5th Md. Inf. in Spanish War, May 14-Oct. 22, 1898; col. 5th Md. Inf., June 4, 1913-Feb. 28, 1917; Mexican border service, July 1, 1916-Feb. 24, 1917. One of Md. commrs. on Uniform State Laws, 1912—, mem. com. on uniform commercial acts, 1921—. Dir. Md. Sch. for the Blind. Home: Baltimore, Md. Died July 18, 1940.

HINMAN, Alice Hamlin; b. Constantinople, Turkey, Dec. 20, 1868; d. Cyrus and Mary (Tenney) Hamlin; A.B., Wellesley, 1893; Ph.D., Cornell U., 1896; m. Prof. Edgar L. Hinman, of U. of Neb., July 21, 1897. Teacher, Abbot Acad., Andover, Mass., 1889-92, 1893-94; prof. psychology, Mt. Holyoke Coll., 1897, 1898; has served as instr. and lecturer, U. of Neb., also lecturer teachers' insts.; lecturer in psychology, Univ.-Sch. of Nurses' Training, 1928-32; chmn. ednl. com. State Fedn. Women's Clubs, Neb., 2 terms, also chmn. civic com.; mem. Bd. of Edn., Lincoln, Neb., 1907-19 (pres.); state chmn. for internat. cooperation, League of Women Voters, 1928—. Pres. Missionary Fedn. of Neb., 1903-07. Conglist. Member Wellesley Council, 1912-16, Municipal Conservation Council, 1917; local chmn. Woman's Nat. League for Service, 1917-19. Mem. Congl. State Bd. of Dirs., 1920-23; chmn. University Y.W.C.A. Advisory Bd., 1921—, City Y.W.C.A., 1925. Home: Lincoln, Neb. Died Oct. 28, 1934.

HINMAN, George Warren, retired; b. Baraboo, Wis., Feb. 22, 1869; s. Horace Hannibal and Sarah Frances (Strong) H.; A.B., Oberlin, 1893; A.M., Harvard Div. Sch., 1898; research, Harvard, 1907-08; D.D., Pacific Sch. of Religion, 1918; m. Kate Rumsey Bailey, of Moreland, N.Y., Dec. 28, 1893. Prof. mathematics, Benzonia (Mich.) Coll., 1893-94; acting pres. Gates (Neb.) Coll., 1895-97; missionary A.B.C.F.M., Foochow, China, 1898-1909; gen. sec. United Soc. Christian Endeavor, China, 1902-05; dist. sec. Am. Missionary Assn. for Pacific Coast, 1909-26; editorial, survey and research work, 1926-31; asso. editor The Congregationalist and Herald of Gospel Liberty, 1930-31; hon. sec. Service Com. for Indians, 1930-34; hon. assistant to prin. Foochow (China) Coll., 1934—. Republican. Conglist. Author: Facing the Future in American Indian Missions (with Dr. Lewis Meriam), 1932; The American Indian and Christian Missions, 1933; Christian Activities Among American Indians, 1933. Died Oct. 13, 1940.

HINMAN, George Wheeler, publicist, editor; b. Mt. Morris, N.Y., Nov. 19, 1864; s. Wheeler and Lydia (Seymour) H.; B.A., Hamilton Coll.; studied Heidelberg, Berlin, Leipzig; M.A., Ph.D., Heidelberg; m. Maud M. Sturtevant, 1891; children—George W., Norman S., Sturtevant, Catherine S., Mrs. W. H. Coburn. Lecturer on foreign history and diplomacy; was on editorial staff New York Sun, 1888-97; editor in chief and pres. The Inter Ocean, Chicago, 1898-1913; pres. Marietta (O.) Coll., 1913-18. Home: Winnetka, Ill. Died Mar. 31, 1927.

HINMAN, Russell, editor; b. Cincinnati, Jan. 23, 1853; ed. Antioch Coll. Engaged as civ. engr. in surveying and constructing Cincinnati Southern Ry.; became, 1878, editor geog. textbook publs. of Van Antwerp, Bragg & Co., of Cincinnati; declined, 1890, appmt. as geographer, 11th U.S. Census, to accept charge of editorial office of Am. Book Co., New York. Author: Eclectic Elementary Geography; Eclectic Complete Geography; Eclectic Physical Geography. Joint author: Natural Elementary Geography; Natural Advanced Geography. Died Apr. 28, 1912.

HINMAN, Thomas Philip, prof. oral surgery, dentist; b. Stratford, Can., Mar. 4, 1870; s. George and Susannah (Birch) H.; brought by parents to U.S., 1871; D.D.S., Southern Med. Coll., 1891; Sc.D., U. of Ga., 1924; m. Florence Hand, June 7, 1899; 1 son, Thomas Philip. Began practice at Atlanta, Ga., 1891; prof. oral surgery, Atlanta-Southern Dental Coll., 1892—, dean, 1917—. Dir. First Nat. Bank, Atlanta Joint Stock Land Bank, Atlantic Steel Corp. Del. to Internat. Congress Dentists, London, 1914; mem. orgn. com. 7th Internat. Dental Congress, Phila., 1926; organizer Atlanta Midwinter Clinic, 1911. Fellow Am. Coll. Dentists (one of founders). Presbyn. Home: Atlanta, Ga. Died Mar. 19, 1931.

HINRICHS, Gustavus Detlef, chemist; b. Lunden, Holstein, Denmark, Dec. 2, 1836; s. Johan Detlef and Caroline C. E. (Andersen) H.; studied 8 yrs. in Poly. Sch. and U. of Copenhagen, Denmark; m. Auguste S. F. Springer, of Marne, Holstein, Apr. 1861 (died 1865); m. 2d, Anna C. M. Springer, July 1867; (died 1910); father of Carl Gustav H. Was 25 yrs. prof. physical science, State U. of Ia.; prof. chemistry, Coll. Pharmacy, St. Louis, 1889-1903; prof. chemistry, med. dept., St. Louis U., 1903-07. Originated graded courses in lab. work, mng. classes of several hundred students, about 1870; founded, 1875, and sustained, 1st state weather service in U.S.; has done practical scientific work for U.S. and state authorities; served as expert chemist before state and federal courts. Hon. and corr. mem. many scientific socs. in Austria, Eng., France, Germany and U.S. Author of 40 vols. and many scientific memoirs in German, Danish, English, French, main object of which is math. demonstration of Unity of Matter, by quantitatively determined physical, chem. and crystallographical properties of all chem. compounds known; many of his memoirs published in Trans. Acads. of Sciences of Vienna and Paris; also in Proc. Am. Philos. Soc., Philadelphia. Author: The Proximate Constituents of the Chemical Elements (32 plates), 1904; The Amana Meteorites (16 plates), 1905 (German edit., Berlin, 1906); La Matière est Une, Paris, 1906; Absolute Atomic Weights now confirmed; 60 articles in Comptes Rendus, Acad. Sciences, of Paris; from 1906, over 100 pp. in Moniteur Scientifique, Paris. Home: St. Louis, Mo. Died Feb. 14, 1923.

HINSCH, Charles Arthur, banker; b. Cincinnati, O., Oct. 22, 1865; s. William A. and Emily (Alcoke) H.; ed. pub. schs., Cincinnati; m. Myra Innes, Oct. 25, 1892; children—Charles A., Mary Innes. Began in employ of Exchange Nat. Bank of Cincinnati, 1881, later with Cincinnati Nat. Bank; dep. receiver of Fidelity Nat. Bank, 1887-89; became cashier Fifth Nat. Bank, 1889, pres., 1897, and pres. Fifth-Third Nat. Bank, since absorption of 3d Nat. Bank in 1908 (also absorbed Am. Nat. Bank, 1909, and S. Kuhn & Son's private bank, 1910, Market Nat. Bank, 1919); affiliated Fifth-Third Nat. Bank and Union Trust Co.; pres. Union Trust Co., 1919—; business of Security Safe Deposit & Trust Co., The Walnut Hills Savings Bank, and the Mohawk State Bank was consolidated with the Union Trust Co., 1919, and offices continued as branches, also Court House Savs. Bank, Winton Savs. Bank and First Nat. Bank of Madisonville, were acquired and banks continued as branches of Union Trust Co.; pres. Fifth-Third Union Trust Co. after merger of Fifth-Third Nat. Bank and Union Trust Co., Feb. 1927. Treas. Cincinnati Chamber of Commerce, 1897; pres. Cincinnati Clearing House, 1913; mem. U.S. Chamber of Commerce, Nat. Fgn. Trade Council. Home: Cincinnati, O. Died Dec. 18, 1928.

HINSDALE, Burke Aaron, prof. science and art of teaching, Univ. of Mich., 1888—; b. Wadsworth, O., Mar. 31, 1837; ed. public schools; m. Mary E. Turner, 1862. Taught in dist. school; later prin. of an acad.; pres. Hiram Coll., 1870-82; supt. Cleveland public schools, 1882-86; (A.M., Bethany Coll. and Williams Coll.; Ph.D., Ohio State Univ.; LL.D., Ohio Univ.). Author: Schools and Studies; President Garfield and Education; The Old Northwest; The American Government; How to Study and Teach History; Teaching the Language Arts; Jesus as a Teacher; Studies in Education; etc. Edited Pres. Garfield's works (2 vols.). Died 1900.

HINSDALE, John Wetmore, lawyer; b. Buffalo, N.Y., Feb. 4, 1843; s. Samuel Johnston and Elizabeth (Christopher) H.; acad. edn. at Fayetteville, N.C., and Yonkers, N.Y.; student, U. of N.C., 1858-61, Columbia Law Sch., 1865-66; m. Ellen, d. Maj. John Devereux, 1869. Served in C.S.A., 1861-65; adj. gen. of Gens. Pettigrew and Pender and Lt. Gen. T. H. Holmes; took part in many battles; comd. as col. 72d N.C. Regt. in battles of Kinston and Bentonville, N.C.; surrendered with Johnston's army at High Point, N.C. In practice at Raleigh, 1866—. Has been before Supreme Ct. of U.S. in important cases; retained by state in various tax suits. Was author of the Nonsuit Act and Equity Reference Act of N.C., as adopted by state legislature; also annotation of Winston's N.C. reports. Home: Raleigh, N.C. Died Sept. 15, 1921.

HINSON, Walter Benwell, clergyman; b. in Eng., 1862; s. Thomas C. and Mary L. (Benwell) H.; ed. Hulme Cliff Coll. and East London Coll., Eng.; M.A., Acadia U., N.S., 1890; D.D., Linfield Coll., Ore., 1910; D.D., Whitman Coll., Wash., 1911; m. Ethelwynne Wadsworth, Montreal, Can., 1898; children—Jean Dorothy, Kathleen Marie, Marjorie Austin, Lorraine, Walter Douglas. Came to America, 1883; ordained Bapt. ministry; pastorates at Montreal, Can., San Diego, Calif., The White Temple, Portland, Ore., and The East Side Baptist Church, Portland, 1909—. Trustee and lecturer, Linfield Coll. Republican. Author: Jesus the Carpenter; Bells and Echoes; The Real Lord's Prayer; A Grain of Wheat; The City of Tadmor; Dawn at Midnight; etc. Died Apr. 8, 1926.

HINTON, Edward Wilcox, prof. of law; b. Rocheport, Mo., Nov. 29, 1868; s. Judge John and Eliza (Wilcox) H.; student prep. dept. Christian College, Columbia, Mo., and U. of Mo.; LL.B., U. of Mo., 1890, LL.D., 1929; LL.B., Columbia, 1891; m. Mary Hood Turner, July 15, 1891. Began law practice at Columbia, June 1891; prof. pleading and practice, U. of Mo., 1903-13; prof. law, U. of Chicago, 1913—, also acting dean Law Sch., 1917-18, 1928-29, 1931. Democrat. Editor: Hinton's Cases on Code Pleading, 1906, 22, 32; Hinton's Cases on Trial Practice, 1915; Hinton's Cases on Evidence, 1919, 31; Cases on Equity Pleading, 1926. Co-editor: Cook and Hinton's Cases on Common Law Pleading, 1923. Home: Chicago, Ill. Died Jan. 2, 1936.

HIPPLE, Alpheus Hugh, dentist; b. St. Catharines, Ont., Can., Feb. 25, 1865; s. Jacob and Mary (Fry) H.; student Toronto Dental Coll., 1887-89; D.D.S., Toronto U., 1889; m. Emma J. Pritchard, of Brockville, Ont., Jan. 1, 1896; 1 dau., Dorothy Maud (Mrs. Donald W. Lyle). Came to U.S., 1892, naturalized citizen, 1899. Practiced at Omaha, Neb., 1892—; prof. oral surgery, Creighton Med. Coll., 1894-1905; dean and prof. operative dentistry, Creighton Dental Coll., 1908—. Mem. Omaha Water Bd., 1904-10. Maj. Dental O.R.C., U.S.A. Democrat. Methodist. Mason. Home: Omaha, Neb. Deceased.

HIPPLE, Frank K., lawyer; b. Phila., July 2, 1839; academic edn. Admitted to bar, 1863. Pres. Real Estate Trust Co. of Phila. from incorporation, Aug. 10, 1885; dir. Franklin Nat. Bank and other corps. Treas. trustees of Gen. Assembly, Presbyn. Ch.; treas. Sustentation Com. of Synod of Pa.; treas. Presbyn. Hosp., Phila.; Am. treas. Alliance of Reformed Chs. Holding the Presbyn. System. Home: Philadelphia, Pa. Died 1906.

HIRONS, Frederic C(harles), architect; b. Birmingham, Eng., Mar. 28, 1882; s. Charles Frederic and Esther (Rushton) H.; came with parents to U.S., 1892; grad. Boston Tech., 1903; student École des Beaux Arts, Paris, 1904-09; Rotch scholar, 1904; Paris prize fellow, 1906; hon. M.S., Catholic U. of America; m. Edna Bushnell Post, Aug. 24, 1910; children—Cornelia Post, Priscilla Bushnell (Mrs. D. C. Watson), Frederic Charles. Began practice as architect at N.Y. City, 1909. Principal works: George Rogers Clark Memorial, Ind.; Worcester (Mass.) War Memorial Auditorium; Rockland County Court House, New City, N.Y.; Beaux-Arts Inst. of Design Bldg., New York; Davidson Co. Courthouse, Nashville. A.N.A., 1931. Decorated Legion of Honor (France), 1926. Home: New York, N.Y. Died Jan. 23, 1942.

HIRSCH, Alcan, chem. engineer; b. Corpus Christi, Tex., Feb. 1, 1885; s. David and Olivia (Benedict) H.; A.B., U. of Tex., 1907; M.S., U. of Wis., 1908, Chem. Engr., 1909, Ph.D., 1911; m. Murilla Polakoff, Mar. 30, 1930; children—Alcene, (3 adopted daughters) Helene, Shirley and Audrey. Research asso. in chem. engring., Mass. Inst. Tech., 1909-10; established lab., New York, 1911; consultant to various indsl. corps., 1912-16; consultant to Japanese Govt. in chem. development, 1916-18; pres. Hirsch Labs., 1917—; formed Rector Chemical Co., 1917, consultant Bayer Co., 1918-20, and to various other cos., 1920-27; one of founders of Molybdenum Corp. of America, 1920, consultant, 1920—; part owner New Rochelle Research Labs., Inc., 1927—; chief consultant to Soviet Govt. in heavy chem. industry, 1931-33; chief consultant Giprokhim, U.S.S.R 1932; cons. engr., 1911—; formerly chem. dir. J. P. Devine Co. (Buffalo, N.Y.); consultant Treadwell Engring. Co. (New York); v.p. and chmn. bd. Hirestra Laboratories; started the pyrophoric alloy industry in U.S., 1915. Carnegie award of Iron and Steel Inst. of Gt. Britain, 1913. Mem. Am.-Russian Chamber of Commerce, Am.-Russian Inst. (dir.). Jewish religion. Author: Industrialized Russia, 1934. Home: New Rochelle, N.Y. Died Nov. 24, 1938.

HIRSCH, Emil Gustav, rabbi; b. Luxemburg, independent Grand-Duchy, May 22, 1851; s. Dr. Samuel and Louise (Mickolls) H.; acad. edn. in Germany; A.B., U. of Pa., 1872, A.M., 1875; student univs. of Berlin and Leipzig, 1872-76; alumnus of High Sch. for Jewish Science, Berlin, 1872-76; rabbi, 1877; (LL.D., Austin Coll., Ill., 1896; L.H.D., Western U. of Pa., 1900; D.D., Hebrew Union Coll., Cincinnati, 1901; D.C.L., Temple U., 1908); m. Matilda Einhorn, June 16, 1898. Minister of Har Sinai Congregation, Baltimore, 1877, Adath-Israel Congregation, Louisville, Ky., 1878, Sinai Congregation, Chicago, 1880—. Prof. rabbinical lit. and philosophy, U. of Chicago, 1892—; Trumbull lecturer Johns Hopkins, 1902. Editor Zeitgeist, Milwaukee, 1880-87, Reformer, New York, 1886, Reform Advocate, Chicago, 1894—, Bibl. Dept. Jewish Encyclopædia, 1903-06. Pres. bd. trustees Chicago Pub. Library, 1888-97; mem. Bd. of Commrs. of Pub. Charities of Ill., 1897, and 1906—; presdl. elector-at-large, 1896. Translator and editor of Dr. Einhorn's Ritual for Jewish Reform Congregations. Leader of radical liberal religions, Jewish movement. Died Jan. 7, 1923.

HIRSCH, Harold, lawyer; b. Atlanta, Ga., Oct. 19, 1881; s. Henry and Rosalie (Hutzler) H.; A.B., U. of Ga., 1901, LL.D.; LL.B., Columbia U., 1904; m. Marie Brown, Nov. 6, 1906; children—Ernestine, Harold. Began practice of law at Atlanta, Ga., 1904; counsel and dir. The Coca-Cola Co. and its subsidiaries; v.p., dir., general counsel Nat. Mfr. & Stores Corp. and The Lichens Co. (Atlanta); pres., dir. and counsel Scripto Mfg. Co. (Atlanta); dir., gen. counsel M. A. Ferst, Ltd. (Atlanta), Mutual Cotton Oil Co. (Ozark, Ala.). Farmers and Ginners Cotton Oil Co. (Birmingham); dir. and atty. Atlanta Title & Trust Co., Rich's, Inc.; dir. and mem. com. Trust Co. of Atlanta. Trustee War Memorial Fund of Ga. Mem. Hebrew Benevolent Congregation. Home: Atlanta, Ga. Died Sept. 25, 1939.

HIRSCHBERG, Michael Henry, judge; b. Newburgh, N.Y., Apr. 12, 1847; s. Henry M. and Fannie (Francks) H.; grad. Newburgh Free Acad., 1862; studied law in pvt. office; m. Lizzie McAlles, Mar. 16, 1878. Admitted to bar, 1868; spl. co. judge, Orange Co., 1875, dist. atty., 1889 (3 terms); del. Constl. Conv., 1894; justice Supreme Ct. of N.Y., 1896-1917; designated to Appellate Div. 2d Dept., at Brooklyn, by Gov. Roosevelt, 1900; apptd. presiding justice, by Gov. Odell, Jan. 1904; term expired Dec. 31, 1917; official referee, 1917—. Republican. Home: Newburgh, N.Y. Died Mar. 17, 1929.

HIRSCHFELDER, Joseph Oakland, physician; b. Oakland, Calif., Sept. 8, 1854; s. Aaron and Henrietta (Block) H.; student U. of Calif., 1869-71; M.D., U. of Leipzig, 1876; m. Clara Honigsberger, Nov. 28, 1878. Prof. materia medica, 1877-81, clin. medicine, 1881-82, Med. Coll. of the Pacific; prof. clin. medicine, Cooper Med. Coll., 1882—; prof. clin. medicine, 1909-12, prof. emeritus, 1912—, Leland Stanford Jr. U. Home: San Francisco, Calif. Died July 4, 1920.

HIRSH, Hugo, lawyer; b. in Germany, Dec. 22, 1848; s. Philip and Dorothea H.; ed. New York pub. schs.; m. Katie A. Burhans, May 24, 1872. Chmn. Kings Co. Rep. Exec. Com.; counsel for Assembly Cities Com. on Investigation of Charities Dept.; counsel for police dept.; counsel for sheriff and other officials; Rep. nominee for Supreme Ct. judge. Author: Hirsh on Juries, 1879; Hirsh's Tabulated Digest of the Divorce Laws of the United States, 1888, 1901. Home: Brooklyn, N.Y. Died May 1, 1933.

HIRSHFELD, Clarence Floyd, engineer; b. San Francisco, Calif., Jan. 30, 1881; s. Charles and Lotta (McCarthy) H.; B.S. in Elec. Engring., U. of Calif., 1902; M.M.E., Cornell U., 1905; Dr. Engring., Rensselaer Poly. Inst., 1932; m. Elizabeth Bishop Winslow, June 16, 1906; children—John Winslow, James Floyd. Successively instr., asst. prof. and prof. of mech. engring., Sibley Coll. (Cornell U.), 1903-14, also cons. practice, 1903-14; chief of research dept., Detroit Edison Co., 1913— (absent on leave 1918-19); cons. engr., 1919—; chief engineer Transit Research Corp. Major and lt. colonel Ordnance Dept., U.S.A., 1918-19. Mem. Am. Com. of World Power Conf.; mem. bd. nat. councillors, Purdue Research Foundation; mem. advisory council Yenching Univ. Mem. U.S. Bur. of Mines Advisory Bd., Ohio State Univ. Research Foundation. Republican. Episcopalian. Author: Engineering Thermodynamics, 1913; Farm Gas Engines (with T. C. Ulbricht), 1913; Steam Power (with same), 1913; Elements of Heat Power Engineering (with W. N. Barnard), 1915; Economic Operation of Steam-Turbo-electric Stations (with C. L. Karr), 1918; Elements of Heat Power Engineering (with W. N. Barnard and F. O. Ellenwood), 1933. Home: Detroit, Mich. Died Apr. 19, 1939.

HIRST, Barton Cooke, M.D.; b. Philadelphia, July 20, 1861; s. William Lucas and Lydia (Barton) H.; student U. of Pa., 1878-80, M.D., 1883; also studied at univs. of Heidelberg, Berlin, Munich and Vienna; m. Elizabeth Haskins Dupuy Graham, Apr. 22, 1890. Prof. obstetrics, U. of Pa., 1889-1927, emeritus. Hon. mem. Paris and Edinburgh Obstet. socs.; mem. Obstet. Soc. (pres.), Am. Gynecol. Soc. (pres.), Coll. of Physicians (pres. gynecol. sect.). Editor Am. System of Obstetrics. Author: A Text-book of Diseases of Women (2d edit.), 1905; A Text-book of Obstetrics (8th edit.); Atlas of Gynecology, 1919. Home: Philadelphia, Pa. Died Sept. 2, 1935.

HIRTH, Friedrich, univ. prof.; b. Gräfentonna, Germany, Apr. 16, 1845; s. Georg and Louise (Drevelle du Frênes) H.; grad. gymnasium in Gotha, 1865; univs. of Leipzig, Berlin and Greifswald, 1865-68, Ph.D., A.M., U. of Rostock, Germany, 1869; prof. by royal patent in Prussia, 1890; m. Hermine Schnare, 1871 (died 1917). Member Chinese customs service, 1870-97; attached to statis. dept., same, Shanghai, 1878-88; commr. customs in Tamsui (Formosa), Chinkiang, Ichang and Chungking, 1890-95; on leave in Munich, 1895-97; mem. Bavarian Acad., Munich, 1897-1902 and 1920—; prof. Chinese and head of Chinese dept., Columbia U., 1902-17, retired. Pres. China branch Royal Asiatic Soc., Shanghai, 1886-88. Comdr. Order of St. Stanislas. Foreign mem. Acad. Sciences, Petrograd and Budapest. Author: Notes on the Chinese Documentary Style, 2d edit., 1909; Scraps from a Collector's Note Book, 1905; History of China to the End of the Chóa Dynasty, 1908; (with W. W. Rockhill) Chau Jukua, Translated and Annotated, 1911. Home: Müchen, Germany. Died Jan. 9, 1927.

HISCOCK, Frank, senator; b. Pompey, N.Y., Sept. 6, 1834; s. Richard and Cynthia (Harris) H.; ed. Pompey Acad.; m. Cornelia King, Nov. 22, 1859. Admitted to bar, 1855; dist. atty. Onondaga Co., N.Y., 1860-63; mem. State Constl. Conv., 1867; mem. 45th to 49th Congresses (1877-87); U.S. senator, N.Y., 1887-93. Republican. Resumed practice as sr. mem. Hiscock, Doheny, Williams & Cowie; dir. State Bank of Syracuse, Syracuse Savings Bank, etc. Home: Syracuse, N.Y. Died June 18, 1914.

HISGEN, Thomas Louis, businessman; b. Petersburg, Ind., Nov. 26, 1858; s. William and Catherine Margaret (McNally) H.; common sch. end., Ind.; went to Albany, N.Y., at 17, and several yrs. salesman in a clothing store; m. Barbara A. Fox, 1900. Began mfr. of axle grease, 1889, with father and brothers, and in 1898, erected at Albany, N.Y., a complete, modern factory; refusing an offer to sell out to the Standard Oil Co., a fight was precipitated, resulting in the Hisgen Brothers going also into the kerosene oil business as competitors of the Standard Oil Co.; retired. Candidate Democratic and Independence League for state auditor of Mass., 1906; candidate of Independence League for gov. of Mass., 1907, and of Nat. Independence Party for pres. of U.S., 1908. Author of Anti-Discrimination-Unfair Trade Bill (first anti-monopoly bill passed in N.E.). Presbyn. Home: Springfield, Mass. Died Aug. 27, 1925.

HITCH, Robert Mark, lawyer; b. Morven, Ga., Feb. 14, 1872; s. Dr. Robert Marcus and Martha Serena (Fall) H.; A.B., Mercer U., 1892; LL.D., 1933; m. Virginia Eppes Walker, Nov. 21, 1900 (died 1935); children—Virginia Eppes (Mrs. Benjamin A. Oxnard, Jr.), Robert Mark; m. 2d, Mrs. Mildred Shelton Brooke, June 15, 1938; children—Shelton Brooke (stepson), William Stroud. Admitted to Ga. bar, 1892, and began practice at Quitman; moved to Savannah, Ga., 1893; mem. Alexander & Hitch, 1898-1904, Hitch & Denmark, 1904-21, Hitch, Denmark & Lovett, 1921—; v.p. and dir. Midland Properties Co.; asst. sec. Savannah & Atlanta Ry. Co. Served as pvt. and sergt. Spanish-Am. War. Mem. Ga. Ho. of Rep., 1900-01. Dem. presdl. elector, Ga., 1908. Mayor of Savannah, 1937-38. Chmn. exec. bd. Charity Hosp.; chmn. Armstrong Jr. Coll. Commn. Elder and trustee Ind. Presbyn. Ch., Savannah. Mason. Home: Savannah, Ga. Died Oct. 1940.

HITCHCOCK, Albert Spear, botanist; b. Owosso, Mich., Sept. 4, 1865; B.S., Iowa Agricultural College, 1884, M.S., 1886, D.S., 1920; m. Rania Belle

Dailey, Mar. 16, 1890; children—Horace Dailey, Frank Harold, Elizabeth Hortense, Helen Esther, Albert Edwin. Asst. in chemistry, State U. of Ia., 1886-89; asst. Mo. Bot. Garden, St. Louis, 1889-91; prof. botany, Kan. Agrl. Coll., 1892-1901; asst. agrostologist, 1901-05, systematic agrostologist, 1905-24, prin. botanist in charge systematic agrostology, 1924—, U.S. Dept. of Agr. Home: Washington, D.C. Died Dec. 16, 1935.

HITCHCOCK, Charles A., lawyer; b. Seneca Falls, N.Y., Feb. 8, 1859; s. Thomas Eugene and Mary Ann (Scrivener) H.; ed. high sch.; m. Florence E. Harp, July 25, 1883 (died 1884); children—Florence H., Hubbard; m. 2d, Alice B. Hanchett, Aug. 27, 1890; 1 son, Charles H. Admitted to N.Y. bar 1880; practiced in Madison Co., N.Y., 10 yrs.; settled at Syracuse, 1890; was mem. Hitchcock & Murphy; apptd. by gov., 1923, justice Supreme Court of N.Y., 6th Jud. Dist., for period ending Dec. 31, 1923; resumed practice. V.p. Salt Springs Nat. Bank, Syracuse, formerly mem. com. of 3d Jud. Dept. of N.Y. to examine applicants for admission to bar. Dem. candidate for presdl. elector, 1924. Home: Chittenango, N.Y. Deceased.

HITCHCOCK, Charles Henry, geologist; b. Amherst, Mass., Aug. 23, 1836; s. late Edward (pres. Amherst Coll.) and Orra (White) H.; brother of Edward H.; A.B., Amherst Coll., 1856, A.M., 1859; student Yale Div. Sch. and Andover Theol. Sem.; Royal Sch. Mines, London; (Ph.D., Lafayette, 1870; LL.D., Amherst, 1896); m. Martha Bliss, d. Prof. E. P. Barrows, June 19, 1862. Lecturer zoölogy, Amherst Coll., 1858-64; non-resident prof. geology and mineralogy, Lafayette Coll., 1866-70; prof. geology and mineralogy, Dartmouth, 1868-1908, emeritus prof., 1908—. Asst. state geologist, Vt., 1857-61; state geologist, Me., 1861-62, N.H., 1868-78; prof. geology, Va. Agrl. and Mech. Coll., 1880; prof. natural history, Williams Coll., 1881; lecturer geology, Mt. Holyoke Coll., 1870-96. Headed expdn. occupying Mt. Washington, N.H., in winter of 1870-71, the 1st high mountain observatory in the U.S.; best known as compiler of several geol. maps of U.S., and for researches in ichnology, geology of the crystalline schists, and glacial geology. Author: Elementary Geology (with Edward Hitchcock), 1861; Mt. Washington in Winter, 1871; Report on Geology of New Hampshire (3 vols.), 1873-78 (state publ.); Geological Map of the United States, 1881; Hawaii and Its Volcanoes, 1909. Home: Honolulu, T.H. Died Nov. 5, 1919.

HITCHCOCK, Edward, college prof.; b. Amherst, Mass., May 23, 1828; s. late Edward (pres. Amherst Coll.) and Orra (White) H.; bro. of Charles Henry H.; A.B., Amherst, 1849, A.M., 1852 (LL.D., 1899); M.D., Harvard, 1853. Taught chemistry and natural history, Williston Sem., 1853-61; prof. hygiene and physical edn., 1861—, acting pres., 1898-99, and dean of faculty, Amherst Coll. Mem. Mass. State Bd. of Health, Lunacy and Charity, 1879—. Trustee Mt. Holyoke Coll., 1869—, Williston Sem., 1884—. Author: Anatomy, Physiology and Anthropometry. Died 1911.

HITCHCOCK, Ethan Allen, sec. of interior U.S., 1898-1907; b. Mobile, Ala., Sept. 19, 1835; s. Judge Henry and Anne (Edwin) H.; attended private schools, Nashville, Tenn.; completing his course at a mil. acad. in New Haven, Conn., 1855; (LL.D., Univ. of Mo., 1902, Harvard, 1906, Washington Univ., St. Louis, 1907); settled in St. Louis and engaged in mercantile business until 1860, when he went to China to enter commission house of Olyphant & Co., of which firm he became a partner in 1866; retired from business, 1872, and spent 2 yrs. in Europe. Returned to U.S., 1874, and was engaged as pres. of several mfg., mining and ry. cos. until 1897. U.S. minister, 1897-98, and 1st ambassador, 1898-99, to Russia. Republican. Apptd. sec. of interior by President McKinley, Dec. 21, 1898, reapptd. Mar. 5, 1901, remained by request of Pres. Roosevelt, Sept. 14, 1901, and reapptd. by him, Mar. 6, 1905; resigned Mar. 4, 1907. Mem. bd. trustees Carnegie Instn., Washington. Home: St. Louis, Mo. Died 1909.

HITCHCOCK, Frank Harris, postmaster-gen.; b. Amherst, O., Oct. 5, 1869; s. Henry Chapman and Mary Laurette (Harris) H.; A.B., Harvard, 1891; LL.B., Columbian (now George Washington) U., 1894, LL.M., 1895; admitted to D.C. bar, 1894; Supreme Ct. of U.S., 1897; unmarried. Chief Div. Foreign Markets, Dept. Agr., 1897-1903; chief clerk Dept. Commerce and Labor, 1903-04; mem. Govt. Expn. Bd., 1903-04; mem. Keep Commn., 1905-06; 1st asst. postmaster-gen., 1905-08; postmaster-gen., in cabinet of President Taft, March 5, 1909-March 4, 1913; established postal savings banks and parcel post and started the first air mail service; resumed law practice, New York, 1913. Asst. sec. Rep. Nat. Com., 1904-08; mgr. Mr. Taft's campaign for presdl. nomination, 1908; chmn. Rep. Nat. Com., 1908-09, and managed presdl. campaign, 1908; managed campaign for nomination of Charles E. Hughes for President, 1916. Mem. Rep. Nat. Advisory Com., 1916; now mem. Rep. Nat. Committee. Col. O.R.C., Air Corps. Gov. for Ariz. of Nat. Aeronautic Assn.; mem. Am. Econ. Assn. Home: Tucson, Ariz. Died Aug. 5, 1935.

HITCHCOCK, Frederick Collamore, engr., contractor; b. Toledo, O., Sept. 19, 1864; s. Bailey Hall and Sarah Hatch (Collamore) H.; ed. high sch., Toledo, and preparatory sch., Ann Arbor, Mich.; studied engring. under father; unmarried. Engr. on constrn. of rys., 1883-92; gen. mgr. and partner George S. Good & Co., ry. contractors, Lock Haven, Pa., 1893-1905; v.p. and gen. mgr. Construction Co. of S. America, 1906-07; built Nat. Railways of Bolivia; v.p. and gen. mgr. MacArthur Bros. Co., New York and Chicago; engaged in bldg. rys., dams, docks, subways, tunnels, etc., including Ashokan Dam, N.Y., 1908-16; also as mgr. MacArthur, Perks & Co., built piers at Havana, Cuba; pres. Equipment Co. of America, 1908-16; in China as v.p. and gen. mgr. Siems, Carey & Co., holding contracts for 2,600 miles of railroads, and rehabilitation of Grand Canal, 1916-19; pres. Carey, Campbell & Co., highway contractors, 1919-22; v.p. W. F. Carey Co., building dam in Vt., 1921-22; pres. Hitchcock & Tinkler, Inc., 1923—; built Moffat Tunnel, Colo.; made reports on reclamation project in Greece, 1929; consultant of Soviet Govt. on 1,000,000 acre irrigation project, Turkestan, 1930; v.p. Ambursen Engineering Corp.; consultant. Republican. Unitarian. Home: New York, N.Y. Died June 28, 1937.

HITCHCOCK, Frederick Hills, publisher; b. Boston, July 4, 1867; s. Dr. Thomas Barnes and Sarah S. (Hills) H.; A.B., Amherst, 1891 (A.M., 1906); studied New York U. Law Sch., 1899; m. Ethel Olivia Hunter, June 9, 1896. Admitted to bar, 1899; mgr. mfg. dept. D. Appleton & Co., 1891-1900; founded, 1901, The Grafton Press; in pub. business, 1910—. Author: Bookbuilder's Handbook, 1899. Editor: The Building of a Book, 1906; The Grafton Historical Series, 1907; The Grafton Mag. of History and Genealogy, 1911. Home: New York, N.Y. Died July 10, 1928.

HITCHCOCK, George, artist; b. Providence, R.I., 1850; s. Charles and Olivia (Cowell) H.; B.A., Brown U., 1872; LL.B., Harvard, 1874; pupil of Boulanger and Lefebvre, Paris; m. Henrietta W. Richardson, 1881; m. 2d, in England, Cecil Jay. Represented in Dresden Gallery, Chicago Art Inst., Imperial Collection, Vienna, McCullouch Collection, London, Municipal Mus., Alkmaar, Holland, and R.I. Sch. of Design, Providence Art Mus., Telfair Gallery, Savannah, John Herron Art Inst., Indianapolis, St. Louis Mus. of Art, Minneapolis Art Inst., Allbright Gallery, Buffalo, Medals; Am. Art Assn., New York, 1887; gold medal, Paris, 1889; gold medal, Berlin, 1891; Chicago Expn., 1893; gold medals, Dresden, 1897, Vienna, 1898, Munich, 1899; exhibited Paris Expn., 1900. A.N.A.; officer Franz Joseph Order of Austria; Munich Secession, Vienna Acad. of Arts. Died Aug. 2, 1913.

HITCHCOCK, Gilbert Monell, senator; b. Omaha, Neb., Sept. 18, 1859; s. Phineas W. and Annie (Monell) H.; ed. Omaha and Baden-Baden, Germany; LL.B., U. of Mich., 1881; m. Jessie Crounse, Aug. 30, 1883 (died 1925); m. 2d, Martha Harris, June 1, 1927. Admitted to bar, 1881; in practice, Omaha, 1881-85; established Omaha Evening World, 1885; purchased Morning Herald, 1889, consolidating it with the World as the World-Herald, of which became publisher. Mem. 58th (1903-05), 60th and 61st Congresses (1907-11), 2d Neb. Dist.; U.S. senator, Nebraska, terms 1911-17, 1917-23. Democrat. Home: Omaha, Neb. Died Feb. 2, 1934.

HITCHCOCK, Henry, lawyer; b. Spring Hill, nr. Mobile, Ala., July 3, 1829; s. Henry H. (chief justice Ala.) and Anne (Erwin) H.; father died 1839; family moved to Nashville; grad. Univ. of Tenn., 1846, Yale, 1848 (LL.D., 1875); taught in Worcester (Mass.) High School; admitted to bar, St. Louis, Sept., 1851; m. Mary, d. George Collier, St. Louis, 1857. Asst. editor St. Louis Intelligencer, 1851-52; delegate, elected on Unconditional Union ticket, to conv., 1861, called by legislature to determine relations between Mo. and Union. Served maj. and judge advocate on staff Gen. Sherman on March to Sea, and S.C. and N.C. campaigns; bore dispatches to Washington announcing truce bet. Gens. Sherman and Joe Johnson, Apr. 1865. Resumed practice, 1866; dir., 1859, v.p. 1886, Washington Univ.; led in organizing (dean 1867-80) and successively prof. real property, equity, corporations, constl. law, St. Louis Law School. One of founders, 1877, pres., 1889-90, Am. Bar Assn.; v.p. bd. trustees Mo. Bot. Garden. Home: St. Louis, Mo. Died 1902.

HITCHCOCK, Henry Booth, foreign service officer; b. Canton Centre, Conn., Mar. 7, 1887; s. Edward Wilson and Evelyn McCurdy (Bentley) H.; B.A., Yale, 1909; m. Sarah Johnston, Mar. 30, 1919; children—James Johnston, Evelyn, Sarah. Student interpreter with Am. Embassy, Tokyo, Japan, 1912-14; assigned to Consulate General, Yokohama, 1914; promoted vice consul, 1915; in charge at Nagasaki, 1916-17; consul, 1918; consul at Taihoku, Formosa, 1919-22, Nagasaki, 1922-24; detailed temporarily at Consulate Gen., Tokyo, 1924-25; consul in charge at Kobe, May 1925; reassigned to Nagasaki, Nov. 1925. Republican. Protestant. Home: Ellenville, N.Y. Died Mar. 1, 1933.

HITCHCOCK, (James) Ripley (Wellman), author, editor, critic; b. Fitchburg, Mass., July 3, 1857; s. of late Dr. Alfred (distinguished physician, author and publicist) and Aurilla Phebe (Wellman) H.; A.B., Harvard, 1877; m. Martha Wolcott Hall, 1883 (died 1903); m. 2d, Helen Sanborn Sargent, Jan. 7, 1914. Went to N.Y., 1879, and engaged in lit. work; in summers of 1882 and 1883 made long journeys in the West, Mexico and Northwest as spl. corr. New York Tribune; art critic, Tribune, 1882-90; lit. adviser, D. Appleton & Co., 1890-1902; now literary adviser and mem. board of dirs. Harper & Brothers. Mem. Nat. Inst. Arts and Letters (v.p.). Author: An American Landscape Painter—George Inness; Etching in America; The Western Art Movement; Thomas De Quincey, a Study; The Louisiana Purchase and the Building of the West, 1904; The Lewis and Clark Expedition, 1905. Editor: The Life of an Artist, by Jules Breton; The Last Words of Thomas Carlyle; The Art of the World Illustrated in the Paintings, Statuary and Architecture of the Columbian Exposition, with an introduction and much other text; The Story of the West Series; Recollections, by Richard Henry Stoddard; The Trail-Makers, a Library of History and Exploration; Decisive Battles of America; Documentary edition of History of the American People by Woodrow Wilson. Home: New York, N.Y. Died May 4, 1918.

HITE, Bert Holmes, chemist; b. Morgantown, W.Va., Aug. 18, 1866; s. Isaac and Catherine (Hennen) H.; M.S., W.Va. U., 1890; student Johns Hopkins U., 1891-95; m. Evelyn Pratt, Nov. 2, 1898. Fellow in chemistry, Johns Hopkins, 1893-95; chemist W.Va. Agrl. Expt. Sta., 1895—, v.dir., 1902—; prof. organic chemistry, 1895-98, prof. agrl. chemistry, 1898—, W.Va. U.; chemist W.Va. Geol. Survey, 1898—; chemist W.Va. Dept. Agr.; consulting chemist U.S. Ordnance Dept., B.&O. R.R. Co. Republican. Episcopalian. Home: Morgantown, W.Va. Died Oct. 6, 1921.

HITT, Robert Roberts, congressman; b. Urbana, O., Jan. 16, 1834; moved to Ogle Co., Ill., 1837; ed. at Rock River Sem. and De Pauw Univ.; 1st U.S. sec. legation and chargé d'affaires ad interim, at Paris, 1874-81; Asst. Sec. of State, U.S., 1881; mem. Congress, 1881-1903, 9th Ill. dist., and 1903-07, 13th dist. Republican. Chmn. Com. on Foreign Affairs, 56th Congress. Apptd. July 1898, by President McKinley, one of commn. to establish govt. for Hawaii, on its annexation to U.S. Is a regent of Smithsonian Instn. Home: Mt. Morris, Ill. Died 1906.

HITT, R(obert) S(tockwell) Reynolds, diplomat; s. late Hon. Robert Roberts and Sally A. H.; A.B., Yale, 1898; LL.B., Harvard, 1901; m. Edith Romeyn Gray, Dec. 23, 1902; children—Edith Elizabeth (Madame Andor de Hertelendy), Robert Reynolds. Third sec. Am. Embassy at Paris, 1901-02; second secretary Am. Embassy at Berlin, 1902-05; sec. Am. Embassy at Rome, 1905-08, at Berlin, 1908-10; E.E. and M.P. to Panama, Dec. 1909-Sept. 1910, to Guatemala, Sept. 1910-Sept. 1913. Home: Washington, D.C. Died Apr. 16, 1938.

HITTELL, John Sherzer, author; b. Jonestown, Pa., Dec. 25, 1825; grad. Miami Univ., 1843; went to Calif., 1849; journalist in San Francisco 25 years. Author: History of San Francisco; The Resources of California; etc. Brother of Theodore Henry Hittell. Home: San Francisco, Calif. Died 1901.

HITZ, John, supt. Volta Bureau for increase and diffusion of knowledge relating to the deaf, from its formal organization, 1890; b. Sept. 14, 1828, Davos, Switzerland; s. John and Anna (Kohler) H.; resident U.S., 1831—; attended private schools; m. Jane C. Shanks, 1856. Trustee public schools; engaged for brief season in commercial and banking business; participated actively in various ednl. and philanthropic orgns.; apptd., 1864, consul gen. of Switzerland at Washington to succeed his father; served 17 yrs.; mem. foreign and domestic scientific and other socs. Edited Helen Keller Souvenirs and various other publs. relating to the deaf. Home: Washington, D.C. Died 1908.

HITZ, Ralph, hotel management; b. Vienna, Austria, Mar. 1, 1891; s. Josef and Leopoldine (Gans) H.; ed. Vienna grade and high schs.; m. Myrtle Dahl, Sept. 25, 1915; 1 son, Ralph. Came to U.S., 1906, naturalized, 1915. Began in hotel business, 1906; mgr. Fenway Hall Hotel, Cleveland, O., 1926-27, Hotel Gibson, Cincinnati, 1927-29; mng. dir. Hotel New Yorker, N.Y. City, 1929-31, pres., 1931—; pres. Nat. Hotel Management Co., Inc., 1932—; pres. Cincinnati Hotel Co., Van Cleve Hotel, Belmont Plaza Hotel; v.p. Book-Cadillac Properties, Inc.; dir. Dallas Hotel Co. Methodist. Mason. Home: Pittstown, N.J. Died Jan. 12, 1940.

HITZ, William, judge; b. Washington, D.C., Apr. 21, 1872; s. John and Jane C. (Shanks) H.; student Harvard, 1893-96; LL.B., Georgetown U. Law Sch., 1900; m. Esther Porter, June 28, 1902. Practiced in Washington, as mem. MacVeagh, McKenney, Flannery & Hitz until 1914; spl. atty., Dept. of Justice, 1914-16; justice Supreme Court of D.C., 1916-31; justice Court of Appeals, D.C., 1931—. Democrat. Home: Washington, D.C. Died July 3, 1935.

HIX, Charles H., ry. pres.; b. Nelson Co., Va., Apr. 5, 1862; ed. Norwood High Sch. In ry. service, 1880—, beginning as rodman Norfolk and Western

R.R.; with same rd. at Saltville, Va., as clk., asst. agt. and telegraph operator, 1881-84, agt. at Buford, 1884-86, relief agt., Roanoke, Va., 1886-88, train dispatcher, Roanoke, 1888-91, chief dispatcher, 1891-97, trainmaster and chief dispatcher, 1897-1900—all Norfolk and Western; with Seaboard Air Line Ry. as trainmaster 2d div., 1900-01, 1st div., June-Sept. 1901, supt. 1st div., 1901-05, gen. supt., 1905-09, gen. mgr., July-Dec. 1909, v.p. and gen. mgr., 1910-12; pres. and gen. mgr. Norfolk Southern Ry., 1912-14; in pvt. business, 1914-18; federal mgr. Hampton Roads Terminals, including Norfolk & Portsmouth Belt Line Ry., also Virginian Ry., during federal control; v.p., 1920-25, pres., 1925—, Virginian Ry. Died Dec. 23, 1933.

HIXSON, Fred Whitlo, coll. pres.; b. Dover Hill, Ind., Nov. 24, 1874; s. James (Rev.) and Nancy Elizabeth (Robinson) H.; A.B., DePauw U., 1899 (D.D., 1913; LL.D., Dickinson, 1918); m. Laura Edith Canady, Dec. 27, 1899. Ordained M.E. ministry, 1899; pastor Bloomington, Ind., 1900, Rockville, 1903-06, Grace Ch., South Bend, 1906-08, Centenary Ch., Terre Haute, 1908-09, 1st Ch., Crawfordsville, 1910-14; pres. U. of Chattanooga, Tenn., 1914-20; pres. Allegheny Coll., Meadville, Pa., 1920—. Sec. Univ. Senate of M.E. Ch.; mem. Gen. Conf. M.E. Ch., 1920 and 1924. Mason. Home: Meadville, Pa. Died Nov. 23, 1924.

HOADLEY, George Arthur, coll. prof.; b. Sheffield, Mass., Dec. 2, 1848; s. Henry H. and Jane (Callender) H.; ed. Ft. Edward (N.Y.) Collegiate Inst.; A.B., C.E., Union Coll., 1874, A.M., 1877, hon. Sc.D., 1907; m. Ida A. Burtch, July 5, 1876; children—Clarence Burtch, Arthur George, Russell Cowles, Mrs. Mildred Grace Ainsworth; m. 2d, Marie A. Kemp, June 27, 1895; 1 son, Anthony de Hothlegh; m. 3d, Fannie B. Kilgore, June 22, 1908; children—George Burnham, Florence Arnold, Alfred Damon, Henry Harold. Prin. Argyle (N.Y.) Acad., 1874-79, Ft. Edward Union Sch., 1879-83, Florence (Mass.) High Sch., 1883-87, Northampton (Mass.) High Sch., 1887-88; prof. physics, 1888-1914, v.p., 1894-1914, Swarthmore Coll.; actg. sec., 1917-18 and 1924-25, asst. in science and arts, 1919-23, sec. com. science and arts, Franklin Inst., 1925—. Author: Elements of Physics, 1908; Physical Laboratory Handbook, 1908; Teachers' Manual to Accompany the Elements of Physics, 1908; Essentials of Physics, 1913. Died May 18, 1936.

HOADLY, George, lawyer; b. New Haven, Conn., July 31, 1826; s. George and Mary Anne Woolsey (Scarborough) H.; removed to Cleveland, O., 1830; grad. Western Reserve Coll., 1844; studied Harvard Law School; admitted to bar, 1847; m. Mary B. Perry, Aug. 13, 1851. Partner of Salmon P. Chase, 1849-51; judge Superior Court, Cincinnati, 1851-53, 1859-66; practiced law in Cincinnati, 1866-87; mem. State Constl. Conv., 1873-74; was Republican until 1871, when became Democrat because of opposition to protective tariff; gov. Ohio, 1883-85; defeated for reelection by Joseph B. Foraker. Engaged in law practice in New York, 1887—. Mem. Hoadly, Lauterbach & Johnson. Home: New York, N.Y. Died 1902.

HOAG, David Doughty, pub. utilities; b. Sherman, Conn., Mar. 18, 1848; s. David D. and Eliza Oakley (Gardner) H.; student Yale, class of '73; m. Maria V. Kennedy, Oct. 1, 1872. Probate judge Ottawa Co., Kan., 1872-78; postmaster, Minneapolis, Kan., 1875-81; mem. Kan. Ho. of Rep., 1899, 1901. Promoter and sec. Solomon R.R. (branch of U.P. R.R.), in Kan., 1877-82; promoter, sec., v.p. and gen. mgr., Kansas City Elevated (St.) Ry. Co., in the two Kansas Cities, 1882-94; located and laid out addition to Kansas City, Kansas; established and laid out towns of Oakley, Colby, Sharon Springs and Winona, in western Kan., on line of U.P. R.R., 1886-89; consol. electric light and power cos. in southwest Mo., S.E. Kan. (1904-09), N.W. Okla., and Ark., also hydro-electric plant of Ozark Power & Water Co., all embraced in the Empire Dist. Electric Co., of which is v.p. (Empire Dist. Electric Co., a subsidary of Cities Service Co.). Republican. Presbyn. Mason. Home: Joplin, Mo. Died Dec. 4, 1933.

HOAG, Ernest Bryant, physician; b. Evanston, Ill., Mar 23, 1868; s. Thomas Clarkson and Louisa (Bryant) H.; B.S., Northwestern U., 1892, A.M., 1902, M.D., 1902; Leland Stanford U., 1892-94; U. of Wis., 1898; m. Sarah Blanchard Judd, 1896. Practiced at Pasadena, Calif., 1902-09; city bacteriologist, 1904-05; med. dir. Pasadena city schs., 1907-09; prof. biology, 1895-98, med. dir., 1907-09, Throop Poly. Inst.; med. dir. Berkeley schs., 1909-12. Republican. Episcopalian. Author: The Health Index of Children, 1910; Child Hygiene (joint author), 1912; Health of the Child in School, 1917. Co-author: Crime, Abnormal Minds and the Law, 1923. Contract surgeon U.S.A., S.A.T.C., U. of Calif., 1918; lecturer mental hygiene, U. of So. Calif.; spl. lecturer criminology, U. of Calif. Home: Pasadena, Calif. Died June 11, 1924.

HOAG, Junius Clarkson, obstetrician; b. Evanston, Ill., Feb. 6, 1858; s. Thomas C. and Maria L. (Bryant) H.; Ph.D., Northwestern U., 1878, Ph.M., 1880; M.D., Chicago Med. Coll., 1882; m. Adelaide Northup, Sept. 25, 1895. Practiced in Chicago from 1887; obstetrician to St. Luke's Hosp. Fellow Am. Coll. Surgeons, Brit. Gynecol. Soc., Chicago Gynecol. Soc. (pres.). Republican. Methodist. Home: Chicago, Ill. Died Oct. 25, 1930.

HOAR, George Frisbie, U.S. senator from Mass., 1877-1907; b. Concord, Mass., Aug. 29, 1826; s. Hon. Samuel and Sarah (Sherman) H.; grad. Harvard, 1846, and Dane Law Sch., Harvard (LL.D., William and Mary, Amherst, Yale, Harvard, Dartmouth); m. Mary Louisa Spurr; m. 2d, Ruth A. Miller. Settled at Worcester and practiced law; city atty., 1860; pres. trustees of city library; mem. Mass. Ho. of Reps., 1852; State senator, 1857; mem. Congress, 1869-77; one of mgrs. on behalf of House in Belknap impeachment trial, 1876; mem. electoral commn., 1876. Republican. Was regent Smithsonian Instn., 1880. Home: Worcester, Mass. Died 1904.

HOAR, Rockwood, lawyer; b. Worcester, Mass., Aug. 24, 1855; s. George Frisbie (U.S. senator, 1877-1904) and Louisa (Spurr) H.; ed. Worcester pub. schs. and Harvard Coll., A.B., 1876, LL.B., 1878, A.M., 1879; m. Christine, d. William E. Rice, June 1, 1893. Engaged in practice of law in Worcester, Mass., 1879—; asst. dist. atty., 1884-87, dist. atty., 1899-1905, middle dist. of Mass. Pvt. Co. C (Concord Co.), 5th Mass. Vol. Militia, 1875-78; a.d.c. on staff Gov. Oliver Ames, and judge adv. gen. on staff Gov. Roger Wolcott, 1887-90; mem. mil. advisory bd. in Mass. during Spanish-Am. War; pres. common council, Worcester, Mass.; mem. Congress, 3d Mass. dist., 1905-07. Republican. Unitarian. Trustee Clark Univ., Worcester Insane Hosp., and Worcester Insane Asylum. Home: Worcester, Mass. Died 1906

HOARD, William Dempster, governor; b. Stockbridge, N.Y., Oct. 10, 1836; common sch. edn.; removed to Wis., 1857; engaged in farming; m. Agnes Elizabeth Bragg, Feb. 9, 1860. Pvt. 4th Wis. Inf., and 1st N.Y. Arty., 1861-65; in nursery business, Columbus, Wis., 1865-70; publisher Jefferson County Union, Lake Mills, Wis., 1870-73; deputy U.S. marshal, 1870; justice of the peace, 1871; sergt.-at-arms, state senate, 1872; from 1873 in Ft. Atkinson; moved his paper there; pub. Hoard's Dairyman, organ of dairy interests; one of organizers Jefferson Co. Dairymen's Assn., 1871; also Wis. Dairymen's Assn. (of which he was sec. 3 yrs.), and Northwestern Dairymen's Assn., of which he became pres., 1878; pres. Farmers' Nat. Congress and Nat. Dairy Union; lecturer at farmers' institutes. Gov. of Wis., 1889-91. Republican. Pres. Wis. bd. of mgrs. St. Louis Expn.; pres. bd. of regents U. of Wis., 1907-11. Home: Ft. Atkinson, Wis. Died Nov. 22, 1918.

HOBAN, Michael John, bishop; b. Waterloo, N.J., June 6, 1853; s. Patrick and Brigid Agnes (Hennigan) H.; attended St. Francis Xavier Coll., N.Y., 1867-68, Holy Cross Coll., Worcester, Mass., 1868-71, St. Charles Sem., Phila., 1874-75, Am. Coll., Rome, Italy, 1875-80. Ordained priest by Cardinal Monaco La Valetta, May 22, 1880; consecrated by Cardinal Satolli, March 22, 1896, titular bishop of Alalis, and apptd. coadjustor bishop of Scranton, with right of succession; succeeded Bishop O'Hara (who died Feb. 3, 1899). Trustee State Hosp., Scranton Pub. Library, West Side Sanatorium, St. Patrick's Orphan Asylum, Assn. for the Blind, Mercy Hosp., Boys' Industrial Sch., St. Joseph's Infant Asylum, Pa. Oral Sch., etc. Mem. exec. com. Red Cross, also of Community Chest, Scranton; dir. Pub. Charities Assn. of Pa. Home: Scranton, Pa. Died Nov. 13, 1926.

HOBART, Alvah Sabin, clergyman; b. Whitby, Ont., Can., Mar. 7, 1847; s. Charles and Pathenia (Sabin) H.; A.B., Colgate U., 1873, A.M., 1875; grad. Hamilton Theol. Sem., 1875; (D.D., Denison U., 1886); m. Mary C. Bancroft, Sept. 30, 1874. Ordained Bapt. ministry, 1875; pastor, Morris, N.Y., 1874-79, Mt. Auburn, Cincinnati, 1879-85, First Ch., Toledo, O., 1885-88, Warburton Av. Ch., Yonkers, N.Y., 1888-1900; prof. English N.T., Crozer Theol. Sem., 1900-20; pastor Warburton Av. Ch., 1920-23, emeritus. Pres., 1886-87, Ohio Bapt. State Conv.; trustee Denison Univ., 1882-88, N.Y. Bapt. Edn. Soc., 1889-98, Am. Bapt. Edn. Soc., 1900-03; mem. bd. Am. Bapt. Home Missionary Soc., 1890—, rec. sec., 1890-1907, chmn. bd., 1897 and 1908-10; mem. exec. com. Baptist Congress, 1890-99; mem. Bapt. Social Union, New York, 1892-94, Philadelphia, 1900-04. Ind. Republican. Author: Our Silent Partner, 1908; Tillage of the Heart, 1909; Key to the New Testament, 1910; Seed-Thoughts for Right-Living, 1911; Religion for Men, 1912; Transplanted Truths from Ephesians, 1914; Transplanted Truths from Philippians, 1916; Pedagogy for Ministers, 1917; Transplanted Truths from Romans, 1919. Died May 7, 1930.

HOBART, Garret Augustus, Vice-president of the United States; b. Monmouth Co., N.J., June 3, 1844; grad. Rutgers Coll., 1863; taught school; studied law; admitted to bar, 1869; established practice at Paterson, N.J.; city counsel there, 1871; counsel for bd. of Chosen Freeholders, 1873; member legislature, 1873-78 (speaker, 1876); State senator, 1879-85; pres. N.J. senate, 1881. Long prominent in Republican politics; chmn. State committee of N.J., until elected Vice-president for term 1897-1901. Home: Paterson, N.J. Died 1899.

HOBART, George Vere, author, playwright; b. Cape Breton, N.S., Jan. 16, 1867; ed. in Nova Scotia; m. Sarah H. de Vries, July 14, 1897. Mng. editor Sunday Scimitar, Cumberland, Md., 1895; a yr. later went to Baltimore, 1st on Morning Herald, then sporting editor Baltimore News, later spl. humorous writer Baltimore American; originated the "Dinkelspiel" papers on Baltimore News, writing these articles for 16 yrs. Author of The John Henry Books (series of comic stories in 15 vols.), also 6 other books of comedy, and "Li'l Verses for Li'l Fellers" (children's poems). Co-author of drama, Wildfire, and of comedy, Our Mrs. McChesney, written for Ethel Barrymore; Buddies; Sonny. Most pronounced success is morality play entitled "Experience." Home: Ventnor, N.J. Died Jan. 31, 1926.

HOBART, Horace Reynolds, editor; b. Beloit, Wis., May 22, 1839; s. Horace and Charlotte (Field) H.; A.B., Beloit Coll., 1860, A.M., 1863; began as school principal in Ill., 1860-61; served pvt. and battalion q.m. 1st Wis. Cav., 1861-62; wounded in battle and mustered out; m. Emma M. Hastings, Dec. 3, 1872 (died 1914). Reporter Chicago Tribune, 1866-67; city editor Chicago Evening Post, 1867-70; western mgr. Am. Press Assn., 1870-74; mng. editor Chicago Evening Mail, 1870-73; editor and joint owner Jacksonville (Ill.) Daily Journal, 1874-75; editor Chicago Morning Courier, 1876; asso. editor and editor The Railway Age, and dir. and v.p., 1876-1907. Pres. (2 terms) Bd. Trustees Hyde Park, Ill., 1879-82. Republican. Conglist. Home: Evanston, Ill. Died Sept. 16, 1923.

HOBART, Marie Elizabeth Jefferys, author; b. Liège, Belgium, Feb. 16, 1860; d. C. P. B. and Elizabeth (Miller) Jefferys; came to America, July 1860; ed. at home by pvt. instrs.; m. Henry L. Hobart, Nov. 15, 1888; children—Margaret Jefferys (Mrs. George B. Myers), Rosamond (dec.), Charles Jefferys (dec.), Elizabeth Miller (dec.). Author: (plays) Lady Catechism and the Child, 1905; Little Pilgrims and the Book Beloved, 1906; The Vision of Saint Agnes' Eve, 1907; Athanasius, 1908; The Sunset Hour, 1911; The Great Trail, 1913; Conquering and to Conquer, 1917; Adeste Fideles, 1918; Advance the Line, 1920; Rebekah, 1920; The Angels of Magdalena, 1922. Home: Easthampton, L.I., N.Y. Died Sept. 19, 1928.

HOBBS, Charles Wood, army officer; b. Albany, N.Y., Feb. 2, 1842; s. George W. and Sarah (Boggs) H.; ed. pub. and pvt. schs., Albany (N.Y.) Classical Inst., Bryant and Stratton Business Coll.; m. Kate Beresford Potts, Nov. 25, 1874; children—Horace P., Mrs. Mary L. H. Pfeil, Charles W. Commd. 2d lt. 113th N.Y. Vol. Inf., Aug. 19, 1862; promoted to maj. in Civil War and entered regular army as 2d lt. 3d Arty., Sept. 21, 1867; promoted through grades to brig. gen., Apr. 12, 1905, and retired following day. Bvtd.: 1st lt., Sept. 21, 1867, "for gallant and meritorious services in battle of Spottsylvania, Va."; capt., Sept. 21, 1867, for same in battle of Cold Harbor, Va.; also breveted lt. col. N.Y. vols. Wounded in hand and leg at battle of Cold Harbor, June 3, 1864, with loss of part of left hand. Participated in campaigns in Spanish-Am. War and Philippine insurrection, July 1898-June 1900, wounded before Manila, July 31, 1898. Retired at own request after 40 yrs.' service, Apr. 13, 1905. Home: Washington, D.C. Died Dec. 21, 1929.

HOBBS, Edward H., lawyer; b. Ellenburgh, N.Y., June 5, 1835; s. Benjamin and Lucy Beaman H.; grad. Middlebury (Vt.) Coll. (LL.D.); m. Julia Ellen Buxton. Mem. Hobbs & Gifford; dir. Bedford Bank (Brooklyn), Mt. Vernon Suburban Land Co. Home: Brooklyn, N.Y. Died 1907.

HOBBS, Ichabod Goodwin, rear admiral U.S.N.; b. North Berwick, Me., Mar. 13, 1843; s. Wilson and Sarah Eliot (Goodwin) H.; bro. of John Edward H.; A.B., Dartmouth, 1864, A.M., 1865; m. Helen M. Hazard, June 29, 1882. Acting asst. p.m. U.S.N., 1864-65; asst. p.m., 1867-69; passed asst. p.m., 1869-78; p.m., 1879-98; pay insp., 1898-1902; pay dir., 1902-05; retired with rank of rear admiral, Mar. 13, 1905. Served on bd. U.S.S. Unadilla, 1864-65, Tallapoosa, 1867-71; Navy Dept., 1871-72; on bd. Tuscarora, 1872-75, Dispatch, 1876-78; Torpedo Sta., 1879-82; on bd. Juniata, 1882-85; Training Sta. and Torpedo Sta., Newport, 1886-89; on bd. Boston, 1890-93; Training Sta., Newport, 1894-96; on bd. Brooklyn, 1896-99, Kearsarge, 1900; navy pay office, Newport, R.I., 1900-05. Home: Newport, R.I. Died Dec. 2, 1918.

HOBBS, John Edward, farmer, mfr.; b. North Berwick, Me., Sept. 1, 1829; s. Wilson and Sarah Eliot (Goodwin) H.; bro. of Ichabod Goodwin H.; ed. pub. and pvt. schs., N. Berwick, Me., and 1 yr. pupil of his uncle, Rev. Daniel R. Goodwin, LL.D.; m. Elizabeth Tredick Kittredge, Sept. 21, 1859. Farmer from boyhood; from 1889 mfr. of attachable steel sleigh runners (his own patented invention), also mfr. of his patented double-ender spring sleigh. Mem., and from 1885 v.p. Am. Forestry Assn., and writer upon forestry. Author of the Maine forestry law, which has been a model for similar laws of many other States; was mem. of com. Am. Forestry Assn. which secured through ap plication to President Harrison, enactment of law by which more than 100,000,000 acres of pub. forest lands have already been withdrawn from sale and entry and made forest reserves. Episcopalian. Republican. Home: North Berwick, Me. Died Mar. 12, 1919.

HOBBS, Ralph Waller, clergyman; b. Mason City, Ill., Sept. 23, 1872; s. Charles A. and Loretta C. (Haight) H.; prep. edn., Kirkwood (Mo.) Mil. Acad. and Wayland Acad., Beaver Dam, Wis.; B.A., Shurtleff Coll., Alton, Ill., 1894, M.A., 1897; B.D., U. of Chicago Div. Sch., 1897; D.D., Fargo (N.Dak.) Coll., 1921, Shurtleff, 1923; m. Fannie Louise James, Oct. 12, 1898; children—Donald James (dec.), Elizabeth Loretta, Mary Eleanor. Ordained Bapt. ministry, 1897; pastor successively First Ch., Superior, Wis., First Ch., Boone, Ia., Rogers Park Ch. (Chicago), First Ch., Mankato, Minn., First Ch., Fargo, First Ch., Lansing, Mich., First Ch., Grand Island, Neb., 1929-36. Chmn. Safety League, Mankato, 1917-18; camp pastor, Camp Custer, 1918. Mem. Bd. Examiners, Kalamazoo Coll.; trustee Sioux Falls (S.D.) Coll.; mem. exec. com. bd. mgrs. Bapt. State Conv., Neb.; chmn. State Missions Dept.; pastor Neb. Bapt. Summer Assembly, 1929, 30, 31; mem. Neb. Bapt. Student Council, Grand Island Ministers Assn. (pres.); Bapt. mem. Neb. Interch. Council; mem. bd. dirs. Self-Help Corp.; mem. Denominational Day Com. of Northern Bapt. Conv., 1934-37; mem. Com. on Order of the Day, same, 1935. Fourth generation of Bapt. ministers. Home: Delavan, Wis. Died Nov. 24, 1936.

HOBBS, Roe Raymond, author; b. July 26, 1871; s. William Vincent and Ollie Theresa (Martin) H.; ed. pub. schs.; m. Emma May Kink, Mar. 30, 1903; children—Perry Gordon (dec.), Marjorie May, Garlan King. Supt. of telegraph, Louisville & Nashville R.R. Co., and Nashville, Chattanooga & St. Louis Ry. Mem. Am. Railroad Assn. Mason. Author: The Court of Pilate, 1906; Zaos, 1907; Gates of Flame, 1907. Home: Louisville, Ky. Died Mar. 21, 1933.

HOBEN, Allan, college pres.; b. Devon, N.B., Sept. 14, 1874; s. Thomas E. and Frances (Babbitt) H.; A.B., U. of New Brunswick, 1895, A.M., 1897; grad. Newton Theol. Instn., Mass., 1898; Ph.D., U. of Chicago, 1901; LL.D., University of New Brunswick, 1933; m. Jessie E. Lindsay, May 21, 1901; children—Lindsay, Frances Babbitt, Edmond Hume, John Burton, Elizabeth. Ordained Baptist ministry, 1899; pastor, Waupun, Wis., 1901-04; dir. Bapt. Students' Guild, U. of Mich., 1904-05; pastor First Bapt. Ch., Detroit, 1905-08; asso. prof. practical theology, U. of Chicago, 1908-19; prof. sociology, Carleton Coll., 1919-22; pres. Kalamazoo Coll., 1922—. Field sec. Juvenile Protective Assn., Chicago, 1910-13; pres. Hyde Park Center, 1915-17. Dir. Y.M.C.A., 5th Div. A.E.F., Apr.-Dec. 1918; pres. Mich. Council Religious Edn., 1923-25. Author: The Minister and the Boy, 1912; Church School of Citizenship, 1918. Home: Kalamazoo, Mich. Died Apr. 29, 1935.

HOBSON, Alfred Norman, judge; b. Allegheny City, Pa., Apr. 1, 1848; s. Joseph and Elizabeth (Baker) H.; student Upper Ia. U. and State U. of Ia. (non-grad.); m. Martha K. Ingham, Aug. 8, 1878. Admitted to Ia. bar, 1870, to Supreme Ct. of Ia., 1873, to U.S. courts, 1881; practiced in West Union as mem. Ainsworth & Hobson, 1875-93, Ainsworth, Hobson & Ainsworth, 18 mos. to close of 1894; mayor of West Union, Mar.-Sept. 1882 (resigned); judge Dist. Court, 13th Jud. Dist. of Ia., 6 terms of 4 yrs. each, 1894-18. Republican. Methodist. Mason. Home: West Union, Ia. Died Apr. 11, 1918.

HOBSON, Benjamin Lewis, theologian; b. Lexington, Mo., July 31, 1859; s. Benjamin Mosby and Martha G. (Barbour) H.; A.B., Central U. of Ky., 1877, A.M., 1880; studied Johns Hopkins; grad. Princeton Theol. Sem., 1885; U. of Berlin, 1888-90; (D.D., Central U. of Ky., 1894, LL.D., same, 1912); m. Katherine Prather Humphrey, Oct. 3, 1893. Ordained Presbyn. ministry, 1886; pastor, Springfield, Mo., 1886-87, Crescent Hill Ch., Louisville, Ky., 1891-93; prof. apologetics, McCormick Theol. Sem., 1893—. Home: Chicago, Ill. Died July 16, 1918.

HOBSON, Edward Henry, veteran gen. U.S.V.; b. Greensburg, Ky., July 11, 1825; ed. Greensburg and Danville common schools; enlisted, 1846, in 2d regt. Ky. vols. for Mexican war; apptd. 1st lt.; was in battle of Buena Vista, Feb. 22-23, 1847; mustered out, June, 1847; returned to Greensburg and resumed mercantile business; dir., 1853, pres., 1857-61, Branch Bank of Ky. Organized, 1861, and became col. 15th Ky. (Union) vols.; joined Gen. Buell's army in South, Feb., 1862; led regt. at battle of Shiloh; nominated by Pres. Lincoln as brig. gen.; before receiving commn. took part in siege of Corinth; was present at Perrysville; later at Mumfordsville, Ky., protected lines of communication and disciplined about 10,000 new troops; placed in command southern div. Ky. troops, ordered to Marrowbone, Ky., where he watched movements of Gen. John Morgan, and after slight engagement pursued him through Ky., Ind., and Ohio. Apptd. to command of Gen. Burnside's cav. corps, but owing to ill health, did not serve; engaged in repelling raids at Lexington, Ky.; mustered out, Sept. 1865. Actively engaged in business interests after the war. Pres. Southern div. Chesapeake & Ohio R.R. Co. Was v.p. Nat. Rep. Conv., 1880. Home: Greensburg, Ky. Died 1901.

HOBSON, John Peyton, judge; b. Powhatan Co., Va., Sept. 3, 1850; s. W. W. and Arabella (Bolling) H.; student Washington Coll., Va.; m. Mary E. Nourse, Feb. 25, 1885; children—Charles Nourse, John Peyton, Mrs. Mary Belle Carroll, Willis Ewing, Robert Pussey, Joseph. Taught at Lynnland Inst., Ky., 1870-72; practiced law Hardin Co., Ky., 1873-98; judge Ky. Court of Appeals, 1899-1915; resumed law practice; commr. of appeals, 1924—. Democrat. Home: Frankfort, Ky. Died June 3, 1934.

HOBSON, Richmond Pearson, rear adm.; b. Greensboro, Ala., Aug. 17, 1870; s. James Marcellus and Sarah Croom (Pearson) H.; educated in private school, 1878-82, Southern U., 1882-85; graduate U.S. Naval Acad., 1889; student École National Supérieur des Mines; grad. École d'Application du Génie Maritime, Paris, 1893; LL.D., Southern U., 1906; M.S., Washington and Jefferson Coll., 1898; m. Grizelda Houston Hull, May 25, 1905; children—Richmond P., Lucia Houston, George Hull. Midshipman cruise with White Squadron in Mediterranean and South Atlantic, 1889-90; duty Navy Department, 1894-95; on flagship New York, with North Atlantic Squadron, summer 1895; Navy Yard, New York, 1895-96; at Newport News in construction of battleships, 1896-97; organized and conducted post-grad. course for officers destined for construction corps, at U.S. Naval Acad., 1897-98; with N. Atlantic Squadron, taking post-grad. students, Mar. 1898; served as constructor with fleet; prin. work on stability and fire systems of vessels in action, on flagship New York in blockade duty, in bombardment of Mantanzas, in expdn. against San Juan de Puerto Rico.* Was commissioned collier Merrimac and with a crew of 7 volunteers sunk her in Santiago harbor; was held prisoner in Spanish fortress, June 3, to July 6, 1898. Insp. of Spanish wrecks; in charge of operations to save same; success with Teresa; on duty in far East, 1899-1900; directed reconstruction at Hong-Kong of 3 Spanish gunboats—Isla de Cuba, Isla de Luzon and Don Juan de Austria; in charge construction dept., Cavite, P.I.; spl. rep. Navy Dept., Buffalo Expn., 1901, Charleston Expn., 1901-02; superintending naval constrn., Crescent Shipyard, Elizabeth, N.J., May-June 1902; resigned from U.S.N. Feb. 6, 1903. Presdl. elector-at-large from Ala., 1904; mem. 60th to 63rd Congresses (1907-15), 6th Ala. Dist. Lecturer, speaker, writer, advocating Am. naval supremacy and Am. leadership in internat. movement for peace. Advocating nation-wide and world-wide prohibition; first to introduce in Congress and advocate prohibition amendment to Constitution for total prohibition; for long-time process of alcohol education for the nation to grow out of the drinking habit; organizer, 1921, and gen. sec. Am. Alcohol Edn. Assn.; organized, 1923, and pres. Internat. Narcotic Edn. Assn.; organized, 1926, World Conf. on Narcotic Education, of which is sec. gen. and chmn. bd. govs.; founder, pres. World Narcotic Defense Assn., 1927; founder, pres. Constl. Democracy Assn., 1935. Author Alcohol and the Human Race for Truth Inoculation of Society, 1919; Narcotic Peril, 1925; The Modern Pirates—Exterminate Them, 1931; Drug Addiction, a Malignant Racial Cancer, 1933. Awarded Congressional Medal of Honor, 1933, for sinking the Collier Merrimac, 1898; made rear adm. by act of Congress, 1934. Home: New York, N.Y. Died Mar. 16, 1937.

HOCH, August, psychiatrist; b. Basel, Switzerland, Apr. 20, 1868; s. Theodor and Valérie (Schneider) H.; came to America, 1887; pub. sch. and Gymnasium, Basel; M.D., U. of Md., 1890; Johns Hopkins U., 1889; Johns Hopkins Hosp., 1890-93; univs. of Strassburg, Leipzig and Heidelberg, 1893, 94; m. Emmy Münch, of Basel, July 1894. Asst. phys. McLean Hosp., Waverley, Mass., 1895-1905; instr. in neuropathology, Tuft's Med. Sch., Boston, 1902-05; 1st asst. phys. and spl. clinician, Bloomingdale Hosp., White Plains, N.Y., 1905-09; instr. in psychiatry, 1905-09, prof., 1909-17, Cornell U. Med. School, New York; dir. Psychiatric Inst. of N.Y. State Hosps. for the Insane, Ward's Island, N.Y., 1910-17. Editor Psychiatric Bulletin. Home: Montecito, Calif. Died Sept. 22, 1919.

HOCH, Edward Wallis, governor; b. Danville, Ky., Mar. 17, 1849; s. E. C. and Elizabeth (Stout) H.; ed. prep. dept. Central Coll., Danville, Ky.; m. Sarah Louisa Dickerson, May 23, 1876. Editor and propr., Marion (Kan.) Record, 1874—. Mem. Kan. Ho. of Rep., 1889, 93 (speaker pro tem., 1893); gov. of Kan., 1905-07 and 1907-09. Republican. Mem. State Bd. of Adminstrn., 1913-19. Methodist. Home: Marion, Kan. Died June 2, 1925.

HOCHWALT, Albert Frederick, author, pub.; b. Dayton, O., Dec. 24, 1869; s. George and Theresa (Lothammer) H.; grad. high sch., U. of Dayton, 1885; D.Litt., honoris causa, U. of Dayton, 1925; m. Adele M. Butz, Sept. 7, 1892; children—Albert G. (dec.), Cyril E., Norman C., Carroll A. Writer on field sports, nature, dogs, etc.; staff rep. The American Field, Chicago; head of A. F. Hochwalt Co., pubs. Author: The Modern Pointer, 1917, 23; The Modern Setter, 1919, 23, 35; Greymist (novel), 1925; Makers of Bird Dog History (Vol. 1), 1927; also serials, Field Trials and the Bird Dog, 1929; Side Lights of Field Trials, 1930-31; Random Notes (serial in American Field), 1932, 33, 34, 35, 36, 37. Home: Dayton, O. Died July 24, 1938.

HOCKENBEAMER, August Frederick, pub. utilities exec.; b. Logansport, Ind., Mar. 6, 1871; s. Frederick and Hulda H.; ed. pub. schs.; m. Ethel Fay Pryor, June 12, 1900; children—Embree Frederick, Ernest Pryor. In ry. service, Pa. Lines, B.&O. R.R., C.,R.I. &P. Ry., 1887-1903; with N. W. Halsey & Co., investment bankers, 1903-07; comptroller, later v.p. and treas. Pacific Gas & Electric Co., 1907-27, pres., 1927—; v.p. Bond & Share Co. Trustee Edison Electric Inst. Republican. Presbyn. Mason. Home: Berkeley, Calif. Died Nov. 11, 1935.

HODDER, Alfred, author; b. Celina, O., Sept. 18, 1866; s. Alfred James H.; ed. Cincinnati; did undergraduate work at home, 1880-86, under private tutor; read law in Senator Teller's office, 1886-89; admitted to bar, Denver, Colo., 1889; admitted to graduate school in Harvard, 1890-91; Morgan fellow, Harvard, 1891-92, studying philosophy, psychology and polit. economy (Ph.D., Harvard); m. Mary Gwinn, June 1904. Spent 2 yrs. in Europe; on return to U.S. became regular contbr. to New York Nation; received appointment Bryn Mawr Coll. to give courses in English drama and English literature; declined reappointment, 1898; from then devoted to writing. Author: The Powers that Prey (under pseudonym of "Francis Walton" and in collaboration with "Josiah Flynt"), 1900; The Specious Present, a metaphysical treatise, 1901; The New Americans, 1901; A Fight for the City, 1903. Collecting material for book on politics in dist. atty.'s office under W. T. Jerome, 1902—. Home: New York, N.Y. Died 1907.

HODDER, Frank Heywood, univ. prof.; b. Aurora, Ill., Nov. 6, 1860; s. John H. and Kate (Heywood) H.; Ph.M., U. of Mich., 1883; studied Göttingen and Freiburg (Baden), 1890-91; m. Anna Florence Moon, July 26, 1892; children—Frederika, Margaret (Mrs. D. D. Davis). Instr. and asst. prof. history and economics, Cornell U., 1885-90; prof. Am. history, 1891—, head of dept. history, 1908—, U. of Kan.; visiting prof., Cornell U., 1928-29. Lecturer summer sessions, universities of Chicago, Colo., Calif., Wash., Northwestern and Cornell. Author: Outline Historical Atlas of the United States, 1900. Editor Audubon's Western Journal and Pittman's Mississippi Settlements, 1905. Home: Lawrence, Kan. Died Dec. 27, 1935.

HODELL, Charles Wesley, coll. prof.; b. Lawrenceburg, Ind., Apr. 16, 1872; s. George and Mary E. (Shoemaker) H.; A.B., DePauw U., Ind., 1892; Ph.D., Cornell, 1894; m. Willa M. Ricketts, Apr. 5, 1899. Instr. English and history, Shady Side Acad., Pittsburgh, 1894-97; prof. English, Woman's (now Goucher) Coll., Baltimore, 1897-1912. Treas., dir. Finance & Guaranty Co., Baltimore. Author: Browning's Old Yellow Book, 1908; Browning's Poems, 1911; Browning's The Ring and the Book, 1911; The Old Yellow Book, 1911. Home: Roland Park, Md. Deceased.

HODGDON, Frank Wellington, civil engr., b. West Cambridge (now Arlington), Mass., Jan. 12, 1856; s. Richard Lord and Maria (Wellington) H.; B.S. in C.E., Mass. Inst. Tech., 1876; m. Grace M. Plumer, Oct. 1886. Engr., Harbor and Land Commrs. of Mass. until 1912; chief engr. Dirs. of Port of Boston, 1912-16; engr. Commn. on Waterways and Pub. Lands, Mass., 1916-20; chief engr. Mass. Dept. of Pub. Works, div. of waterways and pub. lands, 1920—. Republican. Unitarian. Home: Arlington, Mass. Died Jan. 25, 1923.

HODGE, Caspar Wistar, theologian; b. Princeton, N.J., Sept. 22, 1870; s. Caspar Wistar and Angelina (Post) H.; A.B., Princeton, 1892, Ph.D., 1894; D.D., Grove City (Pa.) College, 1935; studied univs. of Heidelberg and Berlin; m. Sarah Henry, Nov. 1897; 1 dau., Lucy Maxwell. Instr. philosophy, Princeton, 1896-97; asso. prof. ethics, Lafayette Coll., Pa., 1897-98; instr. systematic theology, 1901-07, asst. prof., 1907-15, prof. dogmatic theology, 1915-21, Charles Hodge prof. systematic theology, 1921—, Princeton Theol. Sem. Ordained Presbyn. ministry, 1901. Home: Princeton, N.J. Died Feb. 26, 1937.

HODGE, Edward B., corr. sec. Presbyn. bd. of edn.; b. Phila., Feb. 5, 1841; s. Hugh L., M.D., LL.D., prof. obstetrics, Univ. of Pa., and Margaret E. (Aspinwall) H.; grad. Univ. of Pa., 1859; grad. Princeton Theol. Sem., 1863; (D.D., Princeton, 1892); m. Alice Cogswell Van Rensselaer, May 7, 1868. Pastor Presbyn. Ch., Burlington, N.J., 1864-93; trustee and dir. Princeton Theol. Sem.; trustee Gen. Assembly Presbyn. Ch. in U.S.A.. Home: Philadelphia, Pa. Died 1906.

HODGE, Henry Wilson, civil engr.; b. Washington, Apr. 14, 1865; s. John Ledyard and Susan Savage (Wilson) H.; C.E., Rensselaer Poly. Inst., 1885; m. Sarah Cunningham Mills, Dec. 14, 1897. Asst. engr. Phoenix Bridge Co., Phila., 1885-91; chief engr. Union

Iron Works, New York, 1891-93; mem. Boller, Hodge & Baird, consulting engrs., 1899—; pres. The Porterfield Construction Co. Designed municipal bridge over Miss. River, at St. Louis, G.N. R.R. bridge, Duluth, Minn., C.,R.I.&P. bridge, Little Rock, Ark., all bridges for Choctaw, Okla. & Gulf R.R., Nat. R.R. Co. of Mex., and for Wabash-Pittsburgh Terminal Co., including the large cantilever bridges over Moongahela River and Ohio River, the former the largest R.R. bridge in U.S. Engr. for City of New York for Melrose Av. viaduct, 96th St. bridge; commr. for Blackwell's Island bridge and Manhattan Suspension bridge over East River; cons. engr. for Brooklyn Rapid Transit Co., N.Y. and N.J. Interstate Bridge and Tunnel Commn., and many other corps., etc. Apptd. pub. service commr., State of N.Y., Jan. 1916, resigned July 1917; commd. major Engr. R.C.U.S.A., and dir. of rys. in France, July 1917—. Presbyn. Republican. Home: New York, N.Y. Died Dec. 21, 1919.

HODGE, Hugh Lenox, clergyman; b. Mauch Chunk, Pa., May 25, 1864; s. Rev. John Aspinwall (D.D.) and Charlotte Gebhard (Morse) H.; B.A., Princeton, 1886, M.A., 1889; grad. Princeton Theol. Sem., 1889; D.D., Pittsburgh U., 1911; m. Annie Beith, of Glasgow, Scotland, Oct. 18, 1893; children—Gilbert Beith, Beatrice. Ordained Presbyn. ministry, 1890; pastor First Ch., Oxford, Pa., 1890-95, Central Ch., Erie, 1895-1908, First Ch., Sewickley, 1910-19, First Ch., Baltimore, Md., Feb. 1924—. Dir. religious edn., Ft. Myer, Va., 1917, and at Pontanasan and Brest, France, 1919, World War. Trustee First Presbyn. Ch. (Baltimore), Egenton Home for Girls. Democrat. Home: Baltimore, Md. Died Dec. 11, 1934.

HODGE, John Aspinwall, prof. Biblical instruction and church polity, Lincoln Univ., 1893—; s. Dr. Hugh Lenox and Margaret E. (Aspinwall) H.; b. Phila., 1831; grad. Univ. of Pa., 1851; Princeton Theol. Sem., 1856; (D.D., Princeton); m. Lottie G. Morse, 1857. Pastor 1st Presbyn. Ch., Mauch Chunk, Pa., 1856-65; 1st Presbyn. Ch., Hartford, Conn., 1866-92. Author: What Is Presbyterian Law?, 1882; Theology of the Shorter Catechism, 1888. Died 1901.

HODGE, Tobe, author. See Charles McIlvaine.

HODGE, Walter Roberts, mining engr.; b. Kirkwood, Mo., Apr. 1, 1884; s. Clarence Walcot and Mary (Roberts) H.; B.S. and E.M., Mich. Coll. of Mines, 1907; m. Olive C. Croze, June 29, 1908. Engr. and mill supt. for Carpenter, Brennon & Ryan, Salinas, Mex., 1907-10; exploration work in Shining Tree Dist., Ont., Can., 1911, 12; chief engr. mines dept., Tenn. Copper Co., Jan. 1913-20; private practice, 1920-21; inspector Minn. State Highway constrn., 1921-22; mining engr. Mariska Mine, 1922-23; supt. Delta Mine, 1923-24; mng. editor Skillings Mining Review, 1924—. Republican. Sigma Rho. Home: Duluth, Minn. Died Apr. 24, 1940.

HODGE, William, actor; b. Albion, N.Y., Nov. 1, 1874; s. Thomas and Mary (Anderson) H.; ed. pub. schs.; m. Helen Dale, actress, June 13, 1909. Began as property man in brother's theatrical co., Pa., and became joint mgr. New York Comedy Co.; first pronounced success was as the "Brazilian Heavy" in the musical comedy "The Reign of Error"; created rôle Freeman Whitmarsh in "Sag Harbor," 1899; later appeared in "The Sky Farm," "Peggy from Paris," "The Dream City," "The Man from Home," etc.; played "The Road to Happiness," season of 1913-14; in "Fixing Sister," season 1915-16; "A Cure for Curables," season 1917-18; "For All of Us," 1925-26. Died Jan. 30, 1932.

HODGES, Charles H(enry), mfr.; b. Fond du Lac, Wis., Oct. 26, 1859; s. Henry Clay and Julia (Bidwell) H.; prep. edn., Mich. Mil. Acad.; student U. of Mich., 1878-82; m. Eliza Wetmore, June 17, 1885 (died 1931); children—Wetmore, Charles H. Began as salesman, Detroit Radiator Co., 1882, successively asst. mgr. of factory and sec. until 1892; treas. Am. Radiator Co., 1892-1906, v.p. and mem. exec. com., 1892—; v.p. and dir. Am. Radiator & Standard Sanitary Corp.; chmn. bd. Detroit Lubricator Co.; dir. American Blower Co. Republican. Episcopalian. Home: Grosse Pointe, Mich. Died Aug. 7, 1937.

HODGES, Charles Libbens, brig. gen. U.S.A.; b. Providence, R.I., Mar. 13, 1847; ed. pub. and pvt. schs.; m. Anna L. Borden, Aug. 5, 1879. Served as pvt., corporal and sergt., cos. H, E. and G, and sergt. maj. 65th N.Y. Inf., Aug. 20, 1861-July 17, 1865; pvt., corp., sergt. and 1st sergt. Co. D, and sergt. maj. 18th U.S. Inf. and pvt. and corporal gen. service, Nov. 17, 1869-Feb. 13, 1875; commd. 2d lt. 25th Inf., Jan. 20, 1875; 1st lt., June 1, 1880; capt., Nov. 1, 1891; maj. 17th Inf., July 13, 1900; transferred to 23d Inf., Aug. 28, 1901; lt. col., Aug. 12, 1903; col. 24th Inf., Jan. 1, 1907; brig. gen. U.S.A., Apr. 30, 1907. Died 1911.

HODGES, George, theologian; b. Rome, N.Y., Oct. 6, 1856; s. George Frederick and Hannah (Ballard) H.; A.B., Hamilton, 1877, A.M., 1882; (D.D., Western U. of Pa., 1892, Brown U., 1914; D.C.L., Hobart Coll., 1902; LL.D., U. of Pittsburgh, 1911, Hamilton Coll., 1912). Deacon, 1881, priest, 1882, P.E. Ch.; asst., 1881-89, rector, 1889-94, Calvary Ch., Pittsburgh; dean Episcopal Theol. Sch., Cambridge, Mass., 1894—. Pres. South End House Assn. Author: The Episcopal Church, 1889; Christianity Between Sundays, 1892; The Heresy of Cain, 1894; In This Present World, 1896; Faith and Social Service, 1896; The Battles of Peace, 1897; The Path of Life, 1899; William Penn (Riverside Biog. Series), 1900; Fountains Abbey, 1904; The Human Nature of the Saints, 1904; When the King Came, 1904; The Cross and Passion, 1904; Three Hundred Years of the Episcopal Church in America, 1906; The Administration of an Institutional Church, 1906; The Happy Family, 1906; The Pursuit of Happiness, 1906; The Year of Grace, 1906; Holderness, 1907; The Apprenticeship of Washington, 1909; The Garden of Eden, 1909; The Training of Children in Religion, 1910; A Child's Guide to the Bible, 1911; Everyman's Religion, 1911; Saints and Heroes, 1911; Class Book of Old Testament History, 1914; The Early Church, 1914; Henry Codman Potter, Seventh Bishop of New York, 1915; Religion in a World at War, 1917. Died May 27, 1919.

HODGES, Harry Foote, army officer; b. Boston, Mass., Feb. 25, 1860; s. Edward Fuller and Anne Frances (Hammatt) H.; Boston Latin Sch. and Adams Acad., Quincy, Mass.; grad. U.S. Mil. Acad., 1881; m. Alma L'Hommedieu Raynolds, Dec. 8, 1887 (died 1926); children—Antoinette (dec.), Frances (widow of Col. A. H. Acher), Alma Louise (Mrs. G. L. Dickson), Duncan. Additional 2d lt., June 11, 1881; promoted through grades to maj. gen. N.A., Aug. 5, 1917; maj. gen. regular army, Dec. 21, 1921; retired Dec. 22, 1921. Lt. col. 1st U.S. Vol. engrs., June 10, 1898; col., Jan. 21, 1899; hon. mustered out, Jan. 25, 1899. Served with battalion of engrs. and on river and harbor duty, 1881-88; instr. and asst. prof. engring., U.S. Mil. Acad., 1888-92; river and harbor, and fortification duty, 1892-98; in field in P.R., 1898-99; river and harbor duty, 1899-1901; chief engr. Dept. of Cuba, 1901-02; in office of chief of engrs., U.S.A., 1902-07; gen. purchasing officer, asst. chief engr. and mem. Isthmian Canal Commn., 1907-14; in charge design of locks, dams and regulating works, Panama Canal; engr. of maintenance, Panama Canal, 1914-15; given thanks of Congress and advanced in rank Mar. 4, 1915; comdg. N. and Middle Atlantic Coast Arty. dists., 1915-17; comdg. 76th Div., U.S.A., Aug. 25, 1917-Jan. 1, 1919, at Camp Devens, Mass., and with A.E.F. in France; comdg. 20th Div., Camp Sevier, S.C., and Camp Travis, Tex., Jan. 1-July 1, 1919; comdg. N. Pacific and 3d Coast Arty. districts, July 1, 1919-Dec. 21, 1921. Awarded D.S.M. Episcopalian. Home: Lake Forest, Ill. Died Sept. 24, 1929.

HODGES, Henry Clay, brig. gen. U.S.A.; b. in Vt., Jan. 14, 1831. Grad. U.S. Mil. Acad., 1851; bvtd. 2d lt. 4th Inf., U.S.A., July 1, 1851, and promoted 2d lt., Aug. 1, 1852; promoted through grades to col. a.q.m. gen., Oct. 19, 1888; retired, Jan. 14, 1895; advanced to brig. gen. retired, Apr. 23, 1904. Bvtd. maj. and lt. col., Mar. 13, 1865, "for faithful and meritorious services during the war." Early service on frontier, and, 1853-54, on Pacific R.R. explorations; in Civ. War served in equipping troops and later as q.m. Center Grand Div., Army of the Potomac, chief q.m. Army of the Cumberland, on staff Maj. Gen. Rosecrans in Tenn. campaign; depot q.m. at Ft. Leavenworth, Kan., and at last part of war chief q.m. at Mobile, Ala., and New Orleans; after war in various duties as dept. q.m. and as a.q.m. gen. until retired. Died Nov. 3, 1917.

HODGES, John Sebastian Bach, clergyman; b. Bristol, Eng., 1830; s. Edward H. (Mus.Doc.); came to U.S., 1845; A.B., Columbia, 1850, A.M., 1853; grad. Gen. Theol. Sem., 1854; (S.T.D., Racine Coll., 1867). Deacon, 1854, priest, 1855, P.E. Ch.; asst. Trinity Ch., Pittsburgh, 1854-56; instr. Nashotah (Wis.) Sem., 1856-59; rector Ch. of the Holy Communion, Chicago, 1859-60, Grace Ch., Newark, N.J., 1860-70; rector, 1870-1906, rector emeritus, Jan. 1, 1906, St. Paul's Parish, Baltimore. Composer of many services, anthems, chants and hymn tunes. In 1868 compiled Book of Common Praise as a companion to the Book of Common Prayer. Died May 1, 1915.

HODGES, Nathaniel Dana Carlile, librarian; b. Salem, Mass., Apr. 19, 1852; s. John and Mary Osgood (Deland) H.; B.A., Harvard, 1874; U. of Heidelberg, 1874-75; m. Adele Louise Goepper, May 13, 1886. Pvt. tutor in mathematics and physics, Cambridge, Mass., 1876-77; asst. in physics, Harvard, 1877-81; asst. editor of Science, 1883-85, editor, 1885-94; asst. at Astor Library, New York, 1895-97, Harvard U. Library, 1897-1900; librarian Pub. Library of Cincinnati, Apr. 20, 1900-June 1924 (retired). Mem. Chicago Pub. Library Advisory Commn., 1909. For investigations in molecular physics, elected fellow Am. Acad. Arts and Sciences, 1879, A.A.A.S., 1882. Unitarian. Home: Cincinnati, O. Died Nov. 25, 1927.

HODGHEAD, Beverly Lacy, lawyer; b. nr. Lexington, Va., Mar. 21, 1865; s. Rev. Alexander Lewis and Mary (Moore) H.; ed. U. of Calif.; LL.B., Hastings Coll. of Law, San Francisco, 1891; m. Nelle M. Eckles, June 5, 1894; children—Evelyn Elizabeth, Beverly Eckles. Admitted to Calif. bar, 1891, and began practice at San Francisco; admitted to bar, Supreme Court of U.S., 1924. Mayor of Berkeley, Calif., 1909-11 (1st mayor under commn. form of charter); v.p. Bd. of Freeholders, Berkeley. Pres. John A. Roebling's Sons Co. of Calif., 1922-25. Pres. League of Calif. Municipalities, 1910-11. Chmn. com. of arrangements for meeting of Am. Bar Assn., San Francisco, Aug. 1922; presided at annual banquet of Commonwealth Club, given to Chief Justice Taft and Lord Shaw, 1922; rep. Calif. Bar Assn. at Am. Law Inst., Washington, 1924. Democrat. Presbyn. Home: Berkeley, Calif. Died Oct. 16, 1928.

HODGIN, Cyrus Wilburn, educator; b. nr. Farmland, Ind., Feb. 12, 1842; s. Tilnias and Rachel (Hinshaw) H.; grad. Ill. State Normal Univ., 1867; A.M., Earlham Coll., 1888; grad. student history and polit. science, Univ. of Chicago, 1892-93; m. Emily Caroline Chandler, Aug. 22, 1867. Prin. Richmond High Sch., 1868-69; prof. history, Ind. State Normal Sch., 1872-81; acting asso. pres. Ind. State Normal Sch., 1878-79; supt. city schs., Rushville, Ind., 1882-83; prin. Richmond Normal Sch., 1883-87; prof. history and polit. economy, Earlham Coll., Richmond, Ind., 1887—. Conductor Chautauqua Coll. of History, 1896-98. Extensive worker in co. teachers' institutes and assns.; lecturer on education, temperance, peace and arbitration; univ. extension lecturer. Died 1908.

HODGKIN, Henry Theodore, educator; b. Darlington, Eng., Apr. 21, 1877; s. Jonathan Backhouse and Mary Anna (Pease) H.; M.B., B.C. and M.A., with honors, Kings Coll., Cambridge, 1902; St. Thomas Hosp., London, 1899-1902; m. Elizabeth Joy Montgomery, Dec. 9, 1903; children—Herbert Montgomery, John Pease, Patrick Henry. Med. missionary in China, 1905-10; sec. Friends Foreign Mission Assn., London, 1910-20; sec. Nat. Christian Council of China, Shanghai, 1922-29; dir. Pendle Hill Grad. Sch., Wallingford, Pa., 1930—. Mem. bd. dirs. West China Union U. (Chengtu), Yenching U. (Peiping). Mem. Soc. of Friends. Author: Lay Religion, 1919; The Way of Jesus, 1924; Personality and Progress, 1929; Jesus Among Men, 1930; Living Issues in China, 1932. Home: Wallingford, Pa. Died Mar. 26, 1933.

HODGKINS, Howard Lincoln, univ. dean; b. Elgin, Ill., Jan. 23, 1862; s. David and Harriet (Shears) H.; A.B., A.M., Columbian (now George Washington) U., 1883, Ph.D., 1892; Sc.D., from the same univ., 1921; m. Marie E. Wilkinson, June 18, 1890; children—Howard W., George W. Tutor, Columbian Coll., 1883; dean Corcoran Scientific Sch. of Columbian U., 1897-1903; prof. mathematics, 1887-1903, physics, 1903-09, mathematics, 1909—, dean Coll. of Engring., 1900-02 and 1905-13, dean Dept. Arts and Sciences, 1913, pres. 1921-23, dean of the univ., 1923—, George Washington U. Computer, Nautical Almanac Office, U.S.N., 1882-92. Died Feb. 13, 1931.

HODGKINS, Louise Manning, author; b. Ipswich, Mass., Aug. 5, 1846; d. Daniel L. and Mary (Willett) H.; grad. Wilbraham (Mass.) Acad., 1870; A.M., Lawrence Coll., Wis., 1876; studied in Europe 4 different times, latest at Oxford U.; unmarried. Prof. English lit., Wellesley Coll., 1877-91; editor Woman's Missionary Friend, 1893-1905. In 1900 made tour of the world, visiting edni. instns. and Christian missions; traveled in Spain, Italy and Africa with four months on the Nile and in Cairo, Egypt, 1908-09. Diploma, Chicago Expn., 1893. Author: XIXth Century Authors, Great Britain and the United States. Edited Washington's Farewell Address, 1906. Home: Wilbraham, Mass. Died Nov. 29, 1935.

HODGKINS, William Candler, geodesist; b. Boston, Mass., Oct. 21, 1854; s. William E. and Ann M. (Bubier) H.; C.E., Lawrence Scientific Sch. (Harvard), 1877; m. Mary L. von Dodt, 1880. Aid and asst., 1871-1917, hydrographic and geodetic engr., July 1, 1917, U.S. Coast and Geod. Survey. Service has covered many parts of Atlantic, Gulf and Alaskan coasts, besides numerous spl. duties; relocated, 1892, circular boundary bet. Pa. and Del., originally surveyed for William Penn, 1701; took part in joint Am. and Canadian survey along Alaskan boundary, 1893; relocated part of boundary bet. Ia. and Mo., 1896; inspected survey of line bet. Greenville and Spartanburg cos., S.C., 1896; engr. for Md. in joint marking of water boundary bet. Md. and Va., 1897; in charge survey Puerto Rico and in command U.S.S. Blake, 1898-1900; chairman commn. apptd. by Supreme Ct. of U.S. to relocate boundary bet. Va. and Tenn., 1900-02; engr. in charge resurvey "Mason and Dixon's line" bet. Pa. and Md., 1900-03; cartographer to U.S. agency before Alaskan Boundary Tribunal, London, 1903; in command U.S.S. Patterson, on Alaska sta., 1905-08; in command U.S.S. Bache, Atlantic Coast and P.R., 1909-13; dir. coast surveys in P.I., 1914-Mar. 1916; insp. in charge of Boston Field Sta., June 25, 1919—. Author: An Historical Account of the Boundary Line Between Pennsylvania and Delaware, 1894. Deceased.

HODGMAN, Burns P., banker; b. Littleton, N.H., Dec. 30, 1875; s. Charles and Sarah Elizabeth (Taylor) H.; LL.B., cum laude, Boston U., 1898; m. Anne L. (Hackett), Jan. 16, 1901. Admitted to N.H. bar, 1898, and began practice at Littleton; clk. U.S. Circuit and Dist. courts, Dist. of N.H., 1900-23, also U.S. commr.; pres. First Nat. Bank, Concord,

Sept. 1, 1923—; treas. Union Trust Co.; pres. Rumford Printing Co.; dir. and treas. Eagle & Phenix Hotel Co.; chmn. advisory com. for N.H. of Reconstruction Finance Corp.; chmn. Stockholders Advisory Com. First Federal Rerserve Dist., 1935. Federal fuel adminstr., Concord Dist., World War; state fuel administration, N.H., 1923-24. Republican. Episcopalian. Home: Concord, N.H. Died Nov. 19, 1938.

HODGMAN, William Lansing, title ins.; b. Bath, N.Y., Sept. 28, 1854; s. Lansing D. and Abby (Cook) H.; A.B., Yale, 1876, U. of Berlin, 1877-78; LL.B., Albany Law Sch. (Union U.), 1881; m. Adelaide Knight, June 12, 1888. Practiced at Bath, N.Y., 1881-84, Buffalo, 1884-92, Providence, R.I., 1892-1902; in title ins. business, Providence, 1902—; pres. Title Guarantee Co. of R.I.; dir. R.I. Hosp. Trust Co., Providence Gas Co., Providence Journal Co., Providence Mut. Fire Ins. Co. Pres. Providence Lying-in Hosp. Republican. Episcopalian. Home: East Greenwich, R.I. Died Jan. 11, 1936.

HODGSDON, Daniel Bascome, officer U.S. Coast Guard; b. New York City, Feb. 4, 1836; s. George and Catharine (Evans) H.; ed. pub. and pvt. schs.; m. Georgia M. Smith, Oct. 26, 1869. Served in U.S. merchant marine, 1849-61; entered U.S. Revenue Service, Nov. 12, 1861, as 3d lt.; promoted 2d lt., July 14, 1863; first lieutenant July 11, 1864; captain, September 14, 1868; senior captain, April 16, 1908, by act of Congress "for a creditable record during the Civil War." During the Civil War on duty on lower Chesapeake Bay and its tributary waters; blockading duty in coöperation with the U.S.N. served in Alaskan waters at the time that Territory was transferred to the U.S. Govt., 1867; comd. revenue training schoolship S. P. Chase, 1887-91; spent about 25 yrs. on Atlantic coast stas., 10 on lakes and 3 on the Pacific; ordered, Nov. 1897, to comd. cutter McCulloch, which he took through Suez Canal, reaching Singapore, Apr. 8, 1898, reported to Commodore Dewey at Hongkong, Apr. 17, 1898, joined his squadron and took part in the battle of Manila Bay; later comd. cutter Fessenden; retired on full duty pay by joint resolution of Congress, May 3, 1900, "for efficient and meritorious service at battle of Manila Bay." Asst. insp. 10th and 11th Life Saving dists., 1902-05. Died Sept. 10, 1916.

HODGSON, Carey Vandervort, geodetic engr.; b. Wilmington, O., July 11, 1880; s. Lorenzo Dow and Clara Emma (Hyatt) H.; B.S., Wilmington Coll., 1902; B.S., Haverford Coll., 1903; m. Edith Hockett, Apr. 17, 1916; 1 son, William Hockett. With Coast and Geodetic Survey, 1904—, except when in mil. service; on geodetic work, 1911—; field observations for first order triangulation, astronomic latitudes and longitudes, 1911-20; asst. chief Div. of Geodesy, 1920—. Capt. and maj. Corps of Engrs., U.S.A., 1917-19; served overseas with 29th Div. Quaker. Mason. Author: Utah-Washington Arc of Primary Triangulation, 1922; Manual of First Order Triangulation, 1926; Manual of Third Order Triangulation and Traverse, 1928. Home: Washington, D.C. Died May 19, 1929.

HODGSON, Caspar Wistar, publisher, editor; b. Spiceland, Ind., Apr. 30, 1868; s. Lewis Nathan and Rebecca Martha (Parker) H.; ed. Richmond Normal Sch. (Ind.), Pasadena (Calif.) Acad., and State Normal Sch., Los Angeles, 1886-88; A.B. (in law), Stanford, 1896; m. Balm Mann, Nov. 5, 1900; children—Foresta (Mrs. Walter A. Wood III), Daphne and Kaspar Mann. Hoosier sch. master, 1885-87; prin. schs., Pasadena, Calif., 1888-93; rep. D. C. Heath & Co., pubs., in Pacific States and later mgr. their San Francisco office, 1888-1903; publicity mgr. New York office Silver, Burdett & Co., 1903-05; founder 1905, and pres. World Book Co., ednl. pub. house. Republican. Quaker. Editor of many textbooks; contbr. to mags., 1896—; cartographer map of Philippine Islands, 1908. Home: Usona, Mariposa, Calif. Died Feb. 17, 1938.

HODGSON, Laurence Curran, writer; b. Hastings, Minn., Nov. 6, 1874; s. William and Druscilla (Hutchinson) H.; ed. high sch., Hastings, and U. of Minn. (non-grad.); m. Elizabeth O. Schurch, June 21, 1900; children—William Frederick (dec.), Laurence Kirkwood. Editorial writer, dramatic critic and political reporter in Western cities, 1892—; contbg. editor Murray Co. (Minn.) Herald and Winnebago (Minn.) Times; columnist of the St. Paul Dispatch, 1930—; editorial writer, 1931—, St. Paul Pioneer Press. Sec. State Dept. of Education, Minn., 1898-1901; sec. to speaker of Minn. Ho. of Rep., 1905 and 1913; chief clk. State Census Bur., Minn., 1905-06; sec. to mayor of St. Paul, 1914-18; mayor of St. Paul, 1918-22, and 1926-30, also chmn. Ramsey County Bd. of Commrs. Dem. candidate for gov. of Minn., 1920; sec. City and County Bd. of Control, 1922-24; commr. of finance, St. Paul, 1924-26; v.p. for Minn. of Nat. Rivers and Harbors Congress, 1919; pres. Minn. Conf. of Mayors, 1919; an organizer America First Assn.; pres. League of Minn. Municipalities, 1921-23; v.p. Jefferson Highway Assn., 1927-28. Historian of Minn. Editorial Assn., 1915—; editor in chief "Minnesota Editor"; sec. Enterprise Newspaper Syndicate; life mem. Southern Minn. Editorial Assn.; sec. Minn. Territorial Pioneers, 1932—. Awarded medal "for distinguished service" by Cosmopolitan Internat. Club of St. Paul, 1933. Democrat. Methodist. Elk. Author: A Christmas Garland, 1909; Eastertide, 1914; Christmas Verses, 1916. Organizer St. Paul Santa Claus Club for Children, 1918. Home: St. Paul, Minn. Died Mar. 25, 1937.

HODGSON, Richard, sec. and treas., 1887—, Am. Branch Soc. of Psychical Research; b. Melbourne, Australia, in 1855; s. Richard and Margaret (Hyde) H.; grad. Melbourne Univ. (M.A., LL.D.); took law course at Melbourne; then grad. Univ. of Cambridge, England, in mental and moral sciences; spent 6 months at Univ. of Jena, Germany; unmarried. Lectured in North of England, 1882-83, univ. extension course; univ. lecturer at Cambridge, 1884-85, on Herbert Spencer's philosophy; active in investigations of Soc. for Psychical Research in England, 1882-87. Home: Boston, Mass. Died 1905.

HODSON, Clarence, lawyer, financier; b. Laurel, Del., Feb. 1868; s. Hon. Thomas Sherwood (LL.D.) and Alice (Mauck) H.; desc. Judge John Hodson, Md., 1664; ed. Crisfield (Md.) Acad. and under pvt. tutors; LL.D., Washington Coll., Chestertown, Md., 1922; m. Sara Marshall Payne, Sept. 1, 1893 (died 1898); children—Clarence, George, Leila (Mrs. James Neson Hynson); m. 2d, Lillian McKinley Brown, July 1901. Admitted to Md. bar, 1889, and practiced at Crisfield, later at Baltimore, Md.; formerly officer banks, trust cos. and fire ins. co.; chmn. bd. Clarence Hodson & Co., Inc., Am. Loan Co., Beneficial Loan Soc., Nat. Industrial Bankers, Inc., Collateral Bankers, Bankers Nat. Life Ins. Co. Mem. bd. Industrial Lenders Tech. Inst.; mem. bd. visitors and govs., Washington Coll. Col. on staff of gov. of Md., 1896. Presbyn. Mason. Home: East Orange, N.J. Died Jan. 13, 1928.

HOE, Robert, mfr., inventor; b. New York, 1839; s. Robert H. (the second); ed. pub. schs.; entered printing press factory of R. Hoe & Co., founded by his grandfather Robert. Has developed the printing press from the "Hoe cylinder" of the 1846 patent to the present double-sextuple Hoe, and also presses of greatly improved type for printing in colors; also mfr. of circular saws and saw-bits. Has large factories in New York and London. One of founders Met. Mus. of Art. Home: New York, N.Y. Died 1909.

HOEBER, Arthur, painter; b. New York, July 23, 1854; s. William Augustus and Ellen (Schenck) H.; ed. pub. schs. 35, New York; Art Students' League, under Beckwith; studied at École des Beaux Arts, Paris, under Gérome, 1881-86; m. Mary Gray Wildman. First exhibit at Salon, Sur la Grande Route, 1882; last exhibit Salon, Le Pain Quotidien, 1885; splty. landscapes. Writer and lecturer on art; art critic New York Times, 3 yrs.; asso. editor of Illustrated American, 1 yr.; art critic The Globe and Commercial Advertiser, New York. A.N.A. Author: Treasures of the Metropolitan Museum of Art; Painting in XIXth Century in France, Belgium, Spain and Italy. Internat. Art Assn., Chicago. Home: Nutley, N.J. Died Apr. 29, 1915.

HOEHLING, Adolph August, rear adm. U.S.N.; b. Phila., Mar. 5, 1839. Apptd. asst. surgeon U.S.N., Aug. 14, 1861; passed asst. surgeon, Apr. 24, 1865; surgeon, Oct. 2, 1867; med. insp., Jan. 31, 1885; med. dir., May 11, 1893; retired, June 14, 1895; advanced to rank of rear adm. retired, June 29, 1906. Served on various vessels and at various stas. during Civil War; in charge Naval Hosp., Washington, 1888-90; mem. various bds. Home: Washington, D.C. Died Apr. 25, 1920.

HOEING, Charles, univ. dean; b. Lexington, Ky., May 27, 1871; s. Joseph and Rebecca (Kastle) H.; A.B., U. of Ky., Lexington, 1890, A.M., 1892; Ph.D., Johns Hopkins, 1898; studied Am. Sch. Classical Studies in Rome (now Am. Acad. in Rome), 1896-97; m. Augusta Laney, June 20, 1905; 1 son, Frederick Walbridge. Instr. Latin, 1898-1905, asst. prof., 1905-14, prof., 1914-33, dean Coll. for Men, 1914-29, of grad. studies, 1928-33, U. of Rochester; retired, Sept. 1, 1933. Home: Rochester, N.Y. Died Mar. 9, 1938.

HOENSHEL, Eli J., teacher; b. in Westmoreland Co., Pa., Oct. 24, 1846; s. George and Mary (Smutz) H.; A.M., Ill. Wesleyan U., 1877; m. Abbie Moss, Mar. 27, 1872; 2d, Lola Sarchet, of Charleston, Ill., May 19, 1901. Engaged in teaching, 1865—. Author: English Grammar, 1895; Complete Grammar, 1897; Elementary Grammar, 1898; Advanced Grammar, 1899; Normal Note Reader, 1901; Essentials of Orthography and Orthoepy, 1903; Graded Note Reader, 1904. Home: Topeka, Kan. Deceased.

HOF, Samuel, army officer; b. Boscobel, Wis., Oct. 24, 1870; s. Philip Jacob and Elizabeth (Mayer) H.; grad. U.S. Mil. Acad., 1894, Army War Coll., 1921; M.B.A., Harvard, 1926; m. Alice Ingraham Mayo, May 1, 1900; 1 dau., Anne. Commd. 2d lt. U.S. Cav., June 12, 1894; promoted through grades to col., Aug. 5, 1917; asst. chief of ordnance, rank of brig. gen., 1927-30; apptd. chief of ordnance, rank of maj. gen., for period of 4 years, 1930; retired from active service, Oct. 31, 1934. Served at Fort Yellowstone, Wyoming, 1894-97; adj. and instr. law and history, U.S. Mil. Acad., 1897-98; at Tampa, Fla., and Montunk Point, Spanish-Am. War; comdg. officer Frankford (Pa.) Arsenal, World War; acting chmn. Ordnance Claims Bd. (settling $4,000,000,000 war contracts), 1919. Awarded D.S.M. (U.S.). Home: Washington, D.C. Died Mar. 11, 1937.

HOFF, Emanuel Buechley, Bibl. theology; b. Wooster, O., Dec. 21, 1860; s. John B. and Mary (Buechley) H.; student Mt. Morris (Ill.) Coll., 1883-86; student U. of Chicago, 1896-97, 1902-03; studied and traveled in Europe and the Orient, 1909; hon. M.A. from Manchester (Ind.) College, 1914; D.S.T., Bethany Bible School, Chicago, 1917; D.D. from McPherson (Kansas) College, 1927; m. Anna Gockley, 1889 (died 1891); 1 son, Ernest G.; m. 2d, Ida Wagner, 1894; 3 children. Ordained ministry Ch. of the Brethren, 1884; pastor Laporte, Ia., 1890, Des Moines, 1894, 95, Chicago, 1904; dean Bible dept. Manchester Coll., 1898, 99; with Bethany Bible Sch., 1905—; as prof. Bibl. evegesis and asso. pres. Mem. Chicago Theol. Faculty Union. Republican. Author: Training the Sunday School Teacher (2 vols.), 1913, 17; Studies in the Book of Acts, 1915: The Message of the Book of Revelation, 1919. Home: Maywood, Ill. Died Dec. 28, 1928.

HOFF, John Van Rensselaer, army officer; b. Mt. Morris, N.Y., Apr. 11, 1848; s. Bvt. Col. Alexander H. and Ann Eliza (Van Rensselaer) H.; A.B., Union U., N.Y., 1871, A.M., 1874; M.D., 1871; M.D., Coll. Phys. and Surg. (Columbia), 1874; U. of Vienna, 1886; (LL.D., Bucknell, 1907, Union, 1912); m. Lavinia, d. Gen. Hannibal Day, U.S.A., June 22, 1875. Apptd. from N.Y., 1st lt. asst. surgeon, Nov. 10, 1874; capt. asst. surgeon, Nov. 10, 1879; maj. surgeon, June 15, 1891; lt. col. chief surgeon vols., May 9, 1898; hon. disch. Nov. 5, 1898; lt. col. deputy surgeon gen., U.S.A., Jan. 1, 1902; col. asst. surgeon gen., Jan. 19, 1905. Organized the first detachment of the hosp. corps in U.S.A. at Ft. Reno, Ind. Ty., 1887, and the first co. of instrn. hosp. corps, at Ft. Riley, Kan., 1891; chief surgeon 3d corps, Spanish-Am. War, 1898, P.R., 1898-1900; organizer and pres. Superior Bd. of Health and Bd. of Charities, P.R.; in charge of hurricane relief work following disaster of Aug. 1899; chief surgeon China Relief Expdn., Aug. 1900; detailed as observer with Russian Army, 1905, Russo-Japanese War; chief surgeon Dept. of the Mo., 1906, P.I., 1907, Dept. of Lakes, 1909, Eastern Div., 1911; retired, 1912. Instr. ophthalmology, etc., U. of Cal., 1885; prof. Army Med. Sch., 1901-02; instr. in mil. hygiene, Gen. Service and Staff Coll., 1903-05; prof. mil. sanitation, U. of Neb., 1906. Acting editor The Military Surgeon. Pres. bd. dirs. The Lenthall Home; chmn. exec. com. Garfield Memorial Hosp.; vestryman Ch. of the Epiphany, Washington. Assigned to active duty July 10, 1916, in office of Surg. Gen. U.S.A. Home: Washington, D.C. Died Jan. 14, 1920.

HOFF, Nelville Soulé, dentist; b. Elizabeth, W.Va., July 20, 1854; s. Josiah Washington and Sarah (Hopkins) H.; D.D.S., Ohio Coll. Dental Surgery, Cincinnati, 1876; m. Addie L. Chickering, Oct. 24, 1884. Practiced at Cincinnati, 1876-88; became connected with U. of Mich., 1888, now prof. prosthetic dentistry, Coll. Dental Surgery. Conglist. Mason. Formerly editor Dental Register, Cincinnati. Home: Ann Arbor, Mich. Died Dec. 1926.

HOFF, Olaf, civil engr.; b. Smaalenene, Norway, Apr. 2, 1859; s. Martin C. and Gunhild (Smaadal) H.; grad. in engring., Poly. Inst., Christiania, 1879, and came to America same yr.; m. Josie Johnson, June 25, 1885. Engr. with Keystone Bridge Co., Pittsburgh, Pa., 1880; with Mexican Central Ry., 1881-83, Shiffler Bridge Works, Pittsburgh, 1883-85; cons. and contracting engr., Minneapolis, 1885-1901; in charge of bridges and bldgs., N.Y.C.&H.R. R.R., 1901-05; v.p. and chief engr. Butler Bros.-Hoff Co., gen. contractors, 1905-08; consulting engr., New York, 1908—; mem. Arthur McMullen & Hoff Co. Devised and executed method for tunneling Detroit River at Detroit, 1906-09, also the subway tunnel under Harlem River at N.Y. City, 1912-15, by constructing the tunnels from the water's surface; chief consultant to Cunard Steamship Co., Ltd., in connection with proposed steamship terminal in port of N.Y. Home: Montclair, N.J. Died Dec. 24, 1924.

HOFF, William Bainbridge, naval officer; b. Phila., Feb. 11, 1846; s. Rear Adm. Henry Kuhn and Louisa Alexina Wadsworth (Bainbridge) H.; prep. edn. Episcopal Acad., Phila.; entered U.S. Naval Acad., 1860; ordered into active service, Sept. 1863; m. Juliet A. Potts, Jan. 6, 1869. While midshipman he at one time comd. yacht America; promoted ensign Oct. 1, 1863; attached to steam frigate Niagara, 1864; served on E. Gulf Blockading Squadron, 1864-65; took part in expdn. to capture St. Marks, Fla., which terminated in battle of Natural Bridge. After war promoted master, May 10, 1866, lt., Feb. 21, 1867, lt. comdr., Mar. 12, 1868, comdr., Aug. 7, 1881, capt., May. 10, 1895; retired for physical disability, Mar. 13, 1897; served on various duties and stations; was naval commr. to London for World's Columbian Expn., 1892-93; originated system of tactics officially adopted in navy, 1890. Home: Washington, D.C. Died 1903.

HOFFECKER, John H., congressman from Del. for term 1899-1901. Republican. Home: Smyrna, Del. Died 1900.

HOFFMAN, Charles Frederick, real estate; b. Morristown, N.J., 1856; s. Charles Frederick and Eleanor Louisa (Vail) H.; A.B., Columbia, 1878; m. Zelia Krumbhaar Preston, Dec. 29, 1900. Began in real estate business, 1882; pres. Estate of Charles Frederick Hoffman, Inc.; v.p. Hoffman Brothers Realty Co., also Hoffman Brothers; trustee Greenwich Savings Bank, Commonwealth Ins. Co., U.S. Trust Co.; dir. Colonial Assurance Co. Trustee Cathedral of St. John the Divine (treas.), St. Luke's Home for Aged Women, New York P.E. Pub. School, All Angels' Church, and Columbia U., 1914—. Republican. Homes: Newport, R.I., and New York, N.Y. Died Aug. 28, 1919.

HOFFMAN, Christian Balzac, miller, banker; b. Azmoos, Switzerland, Nov. 30, 1851; s. Christian and Elsbeth (Lewis) H.; brought to America, 1854; ed. Central Wesleyan Coll., Mo., and pvt. study, specializing in economics; m. Catherine A. Hopkins, 1872; m. 2d, Anna Wares, July 21, 1910. Began in milling business with father, Feb. 3, 1873; inc., 1885, as The C. Hoffman & Son Milling Co.; became partner Kan. Flour Mills Co., 1910; founder and many yrs. pres. Dickinson Co. Bank; founded The Banking Trust Co. and The Peoples Nat. Bank, Kansas City, Kan.; retired from active business, 1910, and from then devoted attention to promotion of socialism and investigation of vice conditions on the Pacific Coast. Mem. Kan. Ho. of Rep., 1882-84; chmn. Rep. State Com. several terms; later active in organization of Socialist Party, becoming nat. lecturer same. Mem. and chmn. 7 yrs., Kan. State Agrl. Coll. Home: South Pasadena, Calif. Died July 18, 1915.

HOFFMAN, Edward George, lawyer; b. Springfield Twp., Ind., Oct. 1, 1878; s. George W. and Anna (Staebler) H.; A.B., Valparaiso (Ind.) Coll., 1900; LL.B., U. of Mich., 1903; m. Emily R. Hoffman, May 7, 1912; children—Anne Katharine, Edward George. Practiced in Ft. Wayne, Ind., 1903—; now mem. Hoffman, Shoaff & Hoffman; county atty., Allen Co., 1910-18; sec. and treas. Deister Machine Co.; was exec. v.p. and dir. of Tri-State Loan & Trust Co.; v.p., 1st and Tri-State Nat. Bank & Trust Co. Chmn. Dem. Co. Central Com., Allen Co., 1906; candidate for U.S. Senate, 1908; mem. Dem. Nat. Com., 1916-20; mem. com. in charge Dem. Nat. Conv., St. Louis, 1916; sec. Dem. Nat. Conv., San Francisco, 1920. Commr. Boy Scouts, Ft. Wayne. Presbyn. Mason. Home: Ft. Wayne, Ind. Died Feb. 10, 1931.

HOFFMAN, Eugene Augustus, dean of Gen. Theol. Sem., 1879—; b. New York, Mar. 31, 1829; grad. Rutgers Coll., 1847; Harvard, 1848; Gen. Theol. Sem., 1851; (D.D., Rutgers, 1864; Racine Coll., 1882; Gen. Theol. Sem., 1885; Columbia Coll., 1886; Univ. of Oxford, England, 1896; D.C.L., King's Coll., Windsor, N.S., 1890; LL.D., Univ. of the South, 1891; Trinity Univ., Toronto, 1893; Trinity Coll., Hartford, 1895); m. Mary Crooke, d. Peter Z. and Maria Elmendorf, New Brunswick, N.J., 1852. Ordained to P.E. ministry, 1851; in charge Grace Ch., Elizabeth Port, N.J., 1851-53; rector Christ Ch., Elizabeth, N.J., 1853-63; St. Mary's, Burlington, N.J., 1863-64; Grace Ch., Brooklyn Heights, 1864-69; Phila., 1869-79. Pres. N.Y. Hist. Soc. Home: New York, N.Y. Died 1902.

HOFFMAN, Frank Sargent, univ. prof.; b. Sheboygan Falls, Wis., Feb. 9, 1852; s. Wendel and Mary Currier (Sargent) H.; A.B., Amherst College, 1876, A.M., 1884, Ph.D., 1896; B.D., Yale Univ., 1880; Hooker Fellow, Yale, 1880-82; studied in Germany, 1882-83; (LL.D., Knox College, 1914); m. Jessie B. Lathrop, June 23, 1887 (died 1893); children—Emma Louise Booth, Grace May (dec.); m. 2d, Rebecca Russell Lowell, Apr. 25, 1900. Instr. philosophy, Wesleyan U., 1883-85; prof. philosophy, Union Univ., 1885—. Author: The Sphere of the State, 1894, 1898; The Sphere of Science, 1898; Psychology and Common Life, 1904, 1907; The Sphere of Religion, 1908. Home: Schenectady, N.Y. Deceased.

HOFFMAN, George Matthias, army engr.; b. Wilkes-Barre, Pa., June 15, 1870; s. Matthias and Margaretha (Schwab) H.; grad. U.S. Mil. Acad., 1896; grad. Army War Coll., 1921; m. Ruth Thompson, Dec. 5, 1901; children—George Matthias, Richard Thompson, Mary. Commd. 2d lt., May 18, 1896; promoted through grades to col. engrs., July 1, 1920. Served in Span.-Am. War and World War; served on Panama Canal and various river and harbor works; apptd. mem. Miss. River Commn., 1927. Awarded D.S.M. (U.S.). Died Nov. 1, 1936.

HOFFMAN, Herman S., bishop; b. nr. Salem, N.C., June 9, 1841; s. S. J. and Eliza (Holder) H.; ed. pvt. schs. in N.C., and at Moravian Theol. Sem., Bethlehem, Pa.; (D.D., Lawrence U., Wis., 1889); m. Eliza Looney, Phila., Apr. 16, 1872 (died 1898); m. 2d, Laura Goldsmith, Jan. 23, 1902. Ordained Moravian ministry, Mar. 15, 1864; founded 2d, 3d, 4th, 5th and Holy Trinity chs. of that denomination in Phila. up to Sept. 1, 1881; united with Ref. Episcopal Ch., Oct. 1881; pastor several parishes in Phila.; founded Christ Memorial Ch., 1885; made life trustee R.E. Theol. Sem.; built edifice of Ch. of Our Redeemer, Phila., 1893; consecrated bishop R.E. Ch., June 10, 1903. Made visitation of chs. in Canada, 1903, missionary visitation to stas. in India, 1903-04; has in spl. charge First Synod of Dominion of Canada; asst. bishop in charge of New York and Phila. Synod, 1905—. Home: Philadelphia, Pa. Died Nov. 23, 1912.

HOFFMAN, James David, practical mechanics; b. Auburn, Ind., Jan. 23, 1868; s. Daniel Zinn and Rachael Catharine (Goetschius) H.; B.M.E., Purdue, 1890, M.E., 1893; m. Kate Blanche Peterson, Aug. 7, 1890 (died 1902); m. 2d, Zoelah M. Burroughs, Aug. 3, 1913; 1 son, James David. Apprentice machinist with Auburn Foundry and Machine Co., 1883-86; draftsman and designer Buckeye Engine Co., Salem, O., summer 1890; became connected with Purdue U., 1890, successively instr. and asst. prof. in practical mechanics, asst. prof. machine design, asso. prof. and prof. engring. design until 1911; prof. mech. engring. and practical mechanics, U. of Neb., 1911-17; again with Purdue U. as prof. practical mechanics, 1917—, also head of dept., dir. practical mechanics lab. and dir. curriculum of industrial education. Presbyn. Author: Hand Book for Heating and Ventilating Engrs., 1910, 3d edit., 1920; (with C. H. Benjamin) Machine Design, 1913; Elements of Machine Design (with L. A. Scipio), 1928. Home: West Lafayette, Ind. Died Aug. 15, 1938.

HOFFMAN, Richard, musician; b. Manchester, Eng., May 24, 1831; removed to U.S., 1847; early became known as pianist; was with Julius Benedict in tour of Jenny Lind in U.S., 1850; long a teacher of piano; composer of many pieces for piano; also anthems, songs, etc. Hon. mem. Philharmonic Soc., New York, N.Y. Died 1909.

HOFFMAN, Richard Curzon, iron mcht.; b. Baltimore, July 13, 1839; s. Samuel and Elizabeth R. B. (Curzon) H.; ed. Chestnut Hill Sch. and McNally's Sch., Baltimore; m. Eliza Lawrence Dallam, Oct. 28, 1880. Served in C.S.A. Iron mcht. in Baltimore, 1866—; v.p., 1886-93, pres., 1893-99, Seaboard Air Line and Baltimore Steam Packet Co. Home: Baltimore, Md. Died Jan. 21, 1926.

HOFFMANN, Francis Arnold ("Hans Buschbauer"), agrl. editor; b. Herford, Westphalia, Prussia, June 5, 1822; s. Fred. William H., bookseller; ed. parochial school, 1827-34 and Royal Friedrichs Gymnasium, Herford, 1834-40; m. Cynthia Gilbert, Feb. 22, 1844. Emigrated to U.S., 1840; taught German school in Du Page Co., Ill., 1840-42; pastor of Lutheran congregations at Addison and Schaumberg, Ill., 1842-53; studied law; admitted to bar, 1854; established a law and real estate office, Chicago, 1854; subsequently engaged in banking; apptd. consul by King of Hanover, Grand Duke of Saxe-Weimar, etc.; elected lt. gov. of Illinois in 1860; for 4 yrs. commr. foreign land dept. Ill. Central R.R. Co.; retired on acount of ill health to farm in Rock River Valley, Jefferson Co., Wis.; is Republican, being one of founders of Rep. party. Decorated, The Knight's Cross of the Ducal Saxonian Ernstinian House Order. Was 1st editor of the Chicago "Illinois Staatszeitung," 1842; for nearly 20 yrs. past has been editor of "The Haus and Bauerfreund," weekly agrl. paper, Milwaukee, Wis.; also agrl. editor of "Chicago Warte" and "Buffalo Volksfreund." Home: Jefferson, Wis. Died 1903.

HOFFMANN, Ralph, museum dir.; b. Stockbridge, Mass., Nov. 30, 1870; s. Ferdinand and Caroline (Bullard) H.; grad. Williston Acad., Easthampton, Mass., 1886; A.B., Harvard, 1890; m. Gertrude Wesselhoeft, 1894; children—Eleanor, Walter Wesselhoeft, Gertrude (Mrs. Arthur Bliss). With Browne & Nichols Sch., Cambridge, Mass., 1891-1910; headmaster Country Day Sch., Kansas City, Mo., 1910-17, Country Day Sch., St. Louis, Mo., 1917-19, Santa Barbara (Calif.) Sch. for Boys, 1920-27; dir. Museum of Natural History, Santa Barbara, 1926—. Home: Santa Barbara, Calif. Died July 21, 1932.

HOFFSTOT, Frank N., mfr.; m. Annie Willard. Trustee New York Trust Co. Home: New York, N.Y. Died Dec. 25, 1938.

HOFMAN, Heinrich Oscar, metallurgist; b. Heidelberg, Germany, Aug. 13, 1852; s. Prof. Carl and Sophia (Proctor) H.; ed. U. of Heidelberg; E.M., Met.E., Sch. of Mines, Clausthal, 1877; Ph.D., Ohio U., 1889; m. Fanny E. Howell, Aug. 5, 1902. Came to U.S., 1881; practiced metallurgy, 1881-87; prof. metallurgy, Dak. Sch. of Mines, 1887-89, Mass. Inst. Tech., 1898—. Author: Metallurgy of Lead, 10th edit., 1918; Metallurgy of Iron and Steel, 2d edit., 1904; General Metallurgy, 3d edit., 1918; Metallurgy of Copper, 2d edit., 1917. Home: Jamaica Plain, Mass. Died May 28, 1924.

HOFMANN, Julius, clergyman; b. Friedberg, Hessen, Germany, Apr. 9, 1865; s. Peter and Marie (Engelter) H.; ed. Gymnasium and U. of Giessen, Germany; hon. Licentiate in Theology; studied Sem. of Friedberg, Johns Hopkins; (D.D., Franklin and Marshall, 1910); m. Adele L. Châtin, of Neuchâtel, Switzerland, July 26, 1890. Called to America, 1889; ordained Lutheran ministry, 1890; pastor Zion Ch., Baltimore. Home: Baltimore, Md. Died May 19, 1928.

HOGAN, Frank J., lawyer; b. Brooklyn, N.Y., Jan. 12, 1877; s. Maurice and Mary E. (McSweeney) H.; ed. pub. schools; LL.B., Georgetown U., 1902; m. Mary Cecil Adair, Feb. 14, 1899. Sec. to chief q.m. U.S.A., Cuba, 1898-99; to q.m. gen., Washington, 1899-1902; to comdg. gen. of The Army (temp.), 1904; practiced law at Washington, 1902. Lecturer on law of wills, evidence and partnership, Sch. of Law, Georgetown U. Advisory editor Georgetown Law Journal, 1912—. Mem. Prog. Nat. Com., 1912-16. Catholic. Home: Washington, D.C. Died May 29, 1923.

HOGAN, John Henry, banker; b. Dallas Center, Ia., June 6, 1882; s. William M. and Agnes H.; A.B., Drake U., Des Moines, Ia., 1906; m. Grace Power, June 4, 1918. Began active career with Marquardt Savings Bank, Des Moines, 1904; asst. cashier, dir. and v.p. Des Moines Nat. Bank, 1915-23, pres. 1923-26; v.p. Continental Ill. Bank & Trust Co., 1926—. Republican. K.C. Home: Chicago, Ill. Died Sept. 10, 1940.

HOGAN, John Joseph, bishop; b. Bruff, Co. Limerick, Ireland, May 10, 1829; came to St. Louis, 1848; entered Theol. Sem. Ordained R.C. priest, 1852; pastor at Old Mines and Potosi, Mo.; built, 1855, and was pastor of St. Michael's Ch., St. Louis; later missionary in charge of N.W. Mo. until consecrated bishop of St. Joseph, Mo., Sept. 13, 1868; transferred to new see of Kansas City, Mo., Sept. 10, 1880. Died Feb. 21, 1913.

HOGAN, Louise E. Shimer, author, editor—expert on dietetics and child study; b. Shimersville, Pa., Nov. 27, 1855; d. James O. and Elmira (Dubs) Shimer; grad. Allentown, Pa., Coll.; fitted for Vassar, but gave up studies because of ill health; m. John L. Hogan. During 1898 made personal study of Camp Alger, Camp Wikoff, and army and navy food question; gratuitously initiated army diet kitchen movement with coöperation of the President and Sec. of War; arranged, in 1899, for training classes in connection with army schools, where nurses and company cooks are taught to properly prepare and care for and select food. Pres. gen. and dir. Children's League and Internat. pres. jr. branches Sunshine Soc. Editor The Children's Library. Author: How to Feed Children, 1896; Study of a Child, 1898; Children's Diet in Home and School, 1902. Home: Washington, D.C. Died Jan. 10, 1929.

HOGAN, Michael J., congressman; b. N.Y. City, Apr. 22, 1871; ed. parochial schs. Forwarding and truck business; mem. Bd. of Aldermen, N.Y. City, 6 yrs.; mem. 67th Congress (1921-23), 7th N.Y. Dist. Republican. Home: Brooklyn, N.Y. Died May 7, 1940.

HOGATE, Enoch George, prof. law; b. Centreton, N.J., Sept. 16, 1849; s. Jonathan and Sarah Ann (Hanthorn) H.; prep. edn. Danville (Ind.) Acad.; A.B., Allegheny Coll., Pa., 1872, A.M., 1875 (LL.D., 1909); m. Anna C. Huston, Aug. 10, 1881. Admitted to Ind. bar, 1872, and practiced in Danville; mem. Ind. Senate, 1897-99; prof. Ind. U. Sch. of Law, 1903—, dean, 1906—; v.p. Bloomington Nat. Bank. Mem. Bloomington Chamber of Commerce. Trustee Ind. Village of Epileptics. Mem. Gen. Conf. M.E. Ch., 1884. Republican. Odd Fellow. Home: Bloomington, Ind. Died Sept. 8, 1924.

HOGE, Arthur Kenworthy, surgeon; b. Wheeling, W.Va., May 1, 1889; s. Kenworthy J. and Elizabeth (Rogers) H.; Ohio State U., 1909-12; M.D., Jefferson Med. Coll., Phila., 1914; post-grad. study, Polyclinic, Phila., U. of Rochester, Mass. Eye and Ear Infirmary, and U. of Vienna, Austria; m. Blanche Carlyle Cameron, Nov. 18, 1919; children—Arthur Kenworthy, Lawrence Allen. Resident phys., Pa. Hosp., 2 yrs., mem. staff 1 yr.; outpatient phys., Wills Eye Hosp., Phila., 1917; specialized as surgeon eye, ear, nose and throat, 1917—; oculist and otolaryngologist B.&O. R.R., Ohio Valley Gen. Hosp., Wheeling. Mem. Fawcett & Hoge. Certified by Am. Bd. Otolaryngology. Fellow Am. Coll. Surgeons. Republican. Presbyn. Home: Wheeling, W.Va. Died June 29, 1932.

HOGE, James Doster, banker; b. Zanesville, O., Sept. 21, 1871; s. James D. and Anna M. H.; ed. pub. schs. and business coll.; m. Ethel Hanna, Dec. 12, 1894. Mgr. and owner Seattle Post-Intelligencer, 1894-97; pres. First Nat. Bank, Seattle, 1898-1903; organized, 1903, and became pres., Union Savings & Trust Co. of Seattle; later chmn. bd. Union Nat. Bank which merged with the Dexter Horton Nat. Bank, of which is vice chmn.; dir. Pacific Alaska Steam Ship Co., Pacific Steamship Co., and Brown Mfg. Co. (Zanesville, O.), etc. Treas. Am. Bankers' Assn. Republican. Episcopalian. Home: Seattle, Wash. Died Nov. 25, 1929.

HOGE, John, mfr.; b. Zanesville, O., July 6, 1840; s. Israel and Betsey Ann (Doster) H.; common sch. edn.; unmarried. Began as partner of Schultz & Co., soap mfrs., about 1863, continuing until business was sold to the Procter & Gamble Co., 1903; pres. Brown Mfg. Co.; v.p. Guardian Trust & Safe Deposit Co.; dir. Homestead Bldg. & Savings Co., Am. Encaustic Tiling Co., etc.; v.p. First Nat. Bank, Peoples Savings Bank, Star Ice & Storage Co., Brown Manly Plow Co. (Malta, O.). Republican. Home: Zanesville, O. Died June 6, 1917.

HOGELAND, Albert Harrison, civil engr.; b. Southampton, Pa., Jan. 10, 1858; s. John and Keziah D. (Willard) H.; C.E., Lafayette Coll., Pa., 1877; m. Elizabeth T. Trego, Jan. 10, 1889; 1 dau., Anna Trego (wife of Dr. John de J. Pemberton). Rodman and leveler, St. Paul & Pacific R.R., Minn. and Dak., Apr.-Sept. 1879; leveler surveys for new ry. bet. Chicago and St. Paul, 1879-80; leveler, transitman and topographer, 1880-82, asst. engr., 1882-84, N.P. Ry.; asst. engr. St. Paul, Minneapolis & Manitoba, constrn. new lines in N.D., Apr.-Sept. 1884; asst. engr. constrn., Wis., N.P. Ry., 1884-85; with St. Paul, Minneapolis & Man. R.R. and its successor the G.N. Ry., July 1885—, as asst. engr. constrn. and maintenance lines in Minn., N.D., S.D., and Mont., 1885-90; engr. maintenance of way, Eastern dist., 1890-96; resident engr. Eastern dist., 1896-1902; asst. chief engr., 1902-03; chief engr., 1903-13, chmn. valuation committee, 1913-28, cons. engr., 1913-14, again chief engr., 1914-25, consulting engr., May 1, 1925—, G.N. Ry. Co. Presbyn. Home: St. Paul, Minn. Died May 14, 1930.

HOGG, James Stephen, lawyer; b. nr. Rusk, Tex., March 24, 1851; ed. common and high schools, Rusk; justice of the peace, Wood Co., Tex., 1873-75; co. atty., Wood Co., 1878-80; dist. atty., 7th jud. dist., Texas, 1880-84; atty. gen., Texas, 1886-90; gov. Texas, 1890-95; resumed practice of law. Democrat. Home: Austin, Tex. Died 1906.

HOGG, William Clifford, businessman; b. Quitman, Tex., Jan. 31, 1875; s. late Gov. James Stephen and Sarah (Stinson) H.; spl. course U. of Tex.; LL.B., same, 1897. Mem. Hogg Bros., Houston. Regent of U. of Tex., 1913-17. Democrat. Home: Houston, Tex. Died Sept. 12, 1930.

HOGG, William Stetson, commodore U.S.N.; b. Washington, D.C., Nov. 11, 1856; s. John Webb and Sarah Elizabeth (Dow) H.; grad. U.S. Naval Acad., 1876; m. Clara Whamm, d. Surgeon T. C. (U.S.N.) and Emma L. (Greene) Heyl, of Philadelphia. Promoted through the various grades to commodore, and retired, June 30, 1909. Served on board Vandalia during General Grant's tour of the world; on Miantonomah on blackading duty, Havana, during Spanish-Am. War, 1898; exec. officer Monocacy and present at bombardment of Taku forts in Boxer rebellion; comd. supply ship Glacier on trip around the world, 1908-09. Democrat. Episcopalian. Home: Washington, D.C. Died May 28, 1921.

HOGGATT, Wilford Bacon, governor; b. Paoli, Ind., Sept. 11, 1865; s. William M. and Isabelle (Bacon) H.; grad. U.S. Naval Acad., 1884; LL.B., Columbia, 1893; special student Columbia Sch. of Mines, 1898-99; m. Marie Hayden, Jan. 12, 1893 (died 1900). Naval officer, 1884-Aug. 1, 1898; mining engr., 1899—; pres. Keyes Products Co. Gov. of Alaska, 1906-09. Died Feb. 26, 1938.

HOGGSON, William John; b. New Haven, Conn., Nov. 19, 1861; s. Samuel James and Lucy (McLean) H.; ed. pub. schs.; m. Fanny D. Smith, Oct. 8, 1885; children—Bruce, Mrs. Harriet Roberts, Wallace, MacLean. Sec. Hoggson & Pettis Mfg. Co., New Haven, Conn., until 1890; partner of Hoggson Bros. until 1907 and pres. corp. until 1916; founder, and pres. Putnam Trust Co., 1914-16; pres. and gen. mgr. The Mario Co. (St. Augustine, Fla.); pres. W. J. Hoggson Corp., builders (New York), St. Augustine North Beach & Toll Bridge Co. Republican. Episcopalian. Mason. Home: Greenwich, Conn. Died May 13, 1933.

HOGUE, S. Fred, editor, publisher; b. Greene Co., Pa., Mar. 9, 1872; s. John H. and Irene (Penney) H.; A.B., Jefferson Coll., Pa., 1892; m. Ada Blech, 1903. Began as reporter Wheeling Register, 1893; became city editor Morning Sun, Los Angeles, Calif., 1896; city editor Herald, Los Angeles, 1904-06; spl. European corr. syndicate Am. newspapers, 1906-09; editor and pub. Evening Globe, San Francisco, 1909; pres. Evening Post Pub. Co. and editor Post, 1909—; dir. Panama-Pacific Internat. Expn. Co. Chmn. Taft Rep. State Com., 1912; represented Taft Republicans at contest over Calif. delegation to Chicago Conv., 1912. Presbyn. Home: San Francisco, Calif. Died June 27, 1941.

HOGUE, Walter Jenkins, clergyman; b. Short Creek, O., Nov. 16, 1878; s. Asa Hirst and Ruth Anna (Crew) H.; grad. Franklin Coll., New Athens, O., 1900, Pittsburgh (Pa.) Theol. Sem., 1903; grad. student New College, Edinburgh, Scotland, 1904, U. of Edinburgh, 1904; D.D., Westminster Coll., Fulton, Mo., 1919; m. Mary Gertrude Dickerson, Nov. 28, 1905; children—Arthur Reed, Walter Dickerson. Ordained ministry, Presbyn. Ch., 1904; pastor Swissvale, Pa., 1904-07, Unity, Pa., 1907-12, 2d Presbyn. Ch., Washington, Pa., 1912-20, 1st Ch., York, Pa., 1920—. Chaplain, U.S.A., July-Dec. 1918; capt.-chaplain, O.R.C. Trustee York Collegiate Institute, also of Wilson College and Newville Home. Moderator Presbyn. Synod of Pennsylvania. Pres. Pen-Mar Presbyn. Reunion. Republican. Mason. Home: York, Pa. Died Sept. 25, 1936.

HOGUE, Wilson Thomas, bishop; b. Lyndon, N.Y., Mar. 6, 1852; s. Thomas P. and Sarah Ann (Carpenter) Hogg (changed spelling to "Hogue"); ed. Ten Broeck Free Acad., Franklinville, N.Y., 1870-73; afterward completed 4 yrs. conf. course, Genesee Conf., Free Meth. Ch.; Ph.B., non-resident course, Ill. Wesleyan U., 1897, A.M., 1899, Ph.D., 1902; (LL.D., Greenville College, Ill., 1917); m. Emma Luella Jones, Dec. 29, 1874. Entered Free Meth. ministry, 1873; served as gen. supt. (bishop), 1893-94, and from 1903; pres. Greenville Coll., 1892-1904; editor The Free Methodist, 1894-1903, Earnest Christian, Oct. 1908-09. Author: Hymns That Are Immortal, 1906; The Class-Meeting as a Means of Grace, 1907. Editor and contbr. to A Symposium on Scriptural Holiness: The Believer's Personal Experience of Christ in the Process of Salvation, 1915; History of the Free Methodist Church of North America (2 vols.), 1915; The Holy Spirit—A Study, 1916. Home: Michigan City, Ind. Died Feb. 13, 1920.

HOHENTHAL, Emil Louis George, prohibition worker; b. N.Y. City, Oct. 15, 1864; s. Louis and Charlotte (Schomberg) H.; pub. sch. edn.; m. Eleanore Nipper, 1888 (died 1917); children—Emil Louis George, Louis Lester, Elmore Stewart; m. 2d, Almena E. Carpenter, 1922. Retired builder; prohibition worker, 1882—. Internat. sec. for Europe, and trustee Internat. Reform Fedn. of U.S., hdqrs. at Washington, D.C.; del. from Conn. to Internat. Anti-Alcohol Congress, Washington, D.C., 1920, and U.S. del., to similar congress at Lausanne, Switzerland, 1921, and attended similar congress at Copenhagen, Denmark, 1923; toured Europe 4 times 1922-27, to promote Prohibition orgns. for aggressive campaign. Chmn. Prohibition State Com. of Conn.; sec. Nat. Prohibition Com.; pres. Conn. Prohibition Trust, Inc.; pres. Prohibition Trust Assn. of New York; trustee Prohibition Foundation, Inc., of Ill.; commr. for Europe and mem. exec. com. World Prohibition Fedn.; mem. exec. com. Nat. Temperance Council; dir. and auditor Conn. Temperance Union; grand treas., trustee Sons of Temperance of Conn.; hon. mem. Women's Christian Temperance Union; past most worthy patriarch and trustee Nat. Div. Sons of Temperance of N.A.; etc. Pres. Manchester Chamber Commerce; former mem. Bd. of Selectmen, Manchester. Candidate on Prohibition ticket for U.S. Senator, for mem. Congress and for gov. of Conn. Conglist. Home: South Manchester, Conn. Died Dec. 8, 1928.

HOKE, Elmer Rhodes, coll. pres.; b. Ada, O., Sept. 16, 1892; s. Edward John and Mary Margaret (Rhodes) H.; B.A., Franklin & Marshall Coll., 1913, M.A., 1914; B.D., Theological Sem. of the Reformed Ch., Lancaster, Pa., 1917; M.A., Johns Hopkins, 1920, Ph.D., 1922; m. Mary Virginia Heller, Mar. 18, 1916; children—Elmer Rhodes, George Robert, Owen Heller, Richard Roy. Ordained ministry Ref. Ch. in U.S., 1917; pastor Trafford, Pa., 1917-18, Baltimore, 1918-20; prof. edn. and psychology, Hood Coll., Frederick, Md., 1920-22, Lebanon Valley Coll., Annville, Pa., 1922-24; pres. Catawba Coll., Salisbury, N.C., 1924—. Democrat. Mason. Author: The Measurement of Achievement in Shorthand, 1923. Home: Salisbury, N.C. Died Mar. 25, 1931.

HOKE, William Alexander, judge; b. Lincolnton, N.C., Oct. 25, 1851; s. Col. John Franklin and Catharine Wilson (Alexander) H.; early edn. under pvt. tuition, finishing in high sch. of Wetmore & Smith; finished law course at law sch. of Chief Justice Pearson, Richmond Hill, N.C.; licensed to practice, Oct. 25, 1872; m. Mary McBee, Dec. 16, 1897. Practiced law, Shelby and Lincolnton, N.C., until 1891; mem. N.C. Legislature, 1889; judge Superior Ct., 1891-1904; justice Supreme Ct. of N.C., 1904—. Democrat. Episcopalian. Home: Lincolnton, N.C. Died Sept. 13, 1925.

HOLABIRD, Samuel Beckley, brig. gen., U.S. Army, retired, 1890; b. Canaan, Conn., June 16, 1826; s. H. N. and A. M. (Beckley) H.; grad. West Point, 1849; 1st lt., May 1855; adj. at West Point, 1859-61; served in northern Va. and Md. campaigns with Army of Potomac, 1861-62; chief q.m. gen., Dept. of the Gulf, Dec. 1862 to July 1865; bvtd. brig. gen. for services in war. After war promoted regularly until July 1, 1883, became brig. gen. and q.m. gen. U.S. Army. Translator: Gen. Jomini's Treatise on Grand Military Operations of Frederick the Great, 1865 VI. Died 1907.

HOLABIRD, William, architect; b. Amenia Union, N.Y., Sept. 11, 1854; s. Gen. Samuel Becklay and Mary Theodosia (Grant) H.; grad. high sch., St. Paul, 1871; cadet U.S. Mil. Acad., 1873-75; m. Maria Ford Augur, Dec. 27, 1875. Studied in various architects' offices, 1875-80; in practice at Chicago, 1880—; head of firm Holabird & Roche. Home: Evanston, Ill. Died July 19, 1923.

HOLADAY, Ross Edgar, consul; b. Westboro, O., July 14, 1869; s. Samuel Andrew and Patience Louise (Pobst) H.; grad. Wilmington (Ohio) High Sch., 1890; m. Harriet Curl, June 24, 1902. Clk. in postoffice, Wilmington, 1890; teacher pub. schs., Ohio, 1891-94; prin. Academic Dept., Davis Mil. Sch., Winston-Salem, N.C., 1894-97; admitted to Ohio bar, 1898; practiced at Wilmington, 1898-1902; mem. Ohio Ho. of Rep., from Clinton County, 1899-1902 (resigned); U.S. consul at Santiago de Cuba, 1902-15, Manchester, Eng., 1915—. Republican. Mem. Soc. of Friends (Quakers). Mason. Home: Wilmington, O. Died Nov. 27, 1929.

HOLBROOK, Alfred, pres. Alfred Holbrook, Normal U.; b. Derby, Conn., 1816; ed. Groton (Mass.) Acad.; founded at Lebanon, O., a school for training of teachers which became the Nat. Normal U., becoming pres.; was chancellor Southern Normal U.; m. Melissa Pierson, 1843; m. 2d, Eason Thompson, Aug. 31, 1892. Author: The Normal, or Methods of Teaching; An English Grammar Conformed to Present Usage; School Management. Home: Lebanon, O. Died 1909.

HOLBROOK, Evans, prof. law; b. Onawa, Ia., Jan. 15, 1875; s. Bernard David and Mary Frances (Oliver) H.; student U. of Mich., 1893-95; A.B., Stanford, 1897; Northwestern U. Law Sch., 1897-98; LL.B., U. of Mich., 1900; m. Joanna Oliver, Oct. 2, 1902 (died 1905); children—Bernard David, Mrs. Joanna Oliver Denham; m. 2d, Elizabeth Brown, Dec. 26, 1908. Practiced at Chicago, 1900-05; with U. of Mich. Law Sch., 1905—, prof. law, 1910—, sec. same, 1917-22 (on leave as prof. law, U. of Calif., 1913-19. Episcopalian. Author: Cases on Judicial Opinions and Precedents, 1910; Cases on Bankruptcy (with Ralph W. Aigler), 1915; supplement, 1920, 2d edit., 1927. Home: Ann Arbor, Mich. Died June 6, 1932.

HOLBROOK, Florence, author, educator; b. Peru, Ill.; d. Edmund S. and Anne (Case) Holbrook; A.B., U. of Chicago, 1879, A.M., 1885; unmarried. Prin. Oakland High Sch., Chicago, 1886-89, Forestville Sch., Chicago, 1889-1924, Phillips Jr. High Sch., 1924—. Author: Elementary Geography, 1896; Round the Year in Myth and Song, 1897; The Hiawatha Primer, 1898; The Hawthorn Reader (No. 3), 1900; Dramatization of Hiawatha, 1902; The Book of Nature Myths, 1902; Northland Heroes, 1906; The Hiawatha Alphabet, 1910; Studies in Poetry, 1910; A Dramatic Reader, 1911; Cave, Lake and Mound Dwellers, 1911; The Holbrook Reader for Primary Grades, 1912; The Every Day Speller (co-author), 1917. Home: Chicago, Ill. Died 1932.

HOLBROOK, Frederick, gov.; b. Warehouse Point, Conn., Feb. 15, 1813; s. John and Sarah (Knowlton) H.; ed. village sch. and Berkshire Gymnasium, Pittsfield, Mass.; m. Harriet, d. Col. Joseph Goodhue, 1834. Elected at 18, capt. Floodwood Militia Co.; was partner in book store 2 yrs.; engaged in farming; mem. Vt. State senate, 1849-50; gov. Vt., 1861-63. Republican. Pres. Vt. State Agrl. Soc., 1850-56; mem. bd. trustees Vt. Asylum for Insane (now Brattleboro Retreat), 1852—. As war gov. floated $1,500,000 of bonds at a premium and equipped many regts. of troops. Address: Brattleboro, Vt. Died 1909.

HOLBROOK, Frederick, engineer, contractor; b. Lynn, Mass., July 20, 1861; s. Franklin F. and Anna E. (Nourse) H.; ed. pub. schs. and under pvt. tutors; m. Grace Cabot, Apr. 12, 1887. With engr. dept. U.P. R.R., 1880-88, N.Y.,N.H.&H. R.R., 1888-92; supt. for Dwight & Daly, contractors, Boston, 1902-04; an organizer Holbrook, Cabot & Rollins Corp., contractors, 1894, becoming v.p.; pres. Am. Internat. Shipbuilding Corp., 1918; pres. Grace Am. Internat. Corp.; v.p., Am. Internat. Corp. Large contractor for subway and aqueduct work for N.Y. City, also for extensive improvements for N.Y.,N.H.&H. R.R. Home: Brattleboro, Vt. Died Feb. 3, 1920.

HOLBROOK, John Swift, manufacturer; b. Boston, Mass., Mar. 4, 1875; s. Edward H. and Frances (Swift) H.; A.B., Harvard, 1896; m. Grace Morgan Sinclair, Apr. 11, 1908. Pres. Gorham Mfg. Co. (succeeding father), silversmiths, Providence, R.I. Home: Providence, R.I. Deceased.

HOLBROOK, Martin Luther, editor, author; b. Mantua, O., Feb. 3, 1831; ed. public schools and Ohio Agrl. Coll. (now Ohio U.); M.D., New York, 1864; asso. editor Ohio Farmer, Cleveland, 1859-61; edited Herald of Health (now Journal of Hygiene), 1864—; spent 1862-63 with Dio Lewis; grad. at his Normal School of Physical Culture; introduced his system into many schools, etc. Author: Hygiene of the Brain and Cure of Nervousness; Eating for Strength; Parturition Without Pain; Liver Complaint; Mental Dyspepsia and Headache; Chastity; Marriage and Parentage; Hygienic Treatment of Consumption; Stripiculture; etc. Home: New York, N.Y. Died 1902.

HOLBROOK, Richard Thayer, coll. prof.; b. Windsor Locks, Conn., Dec. 13, 1870; s. Dwight and Kalista (Thayer) H.; A.B., Yale, 1893; Ph.D., Columbia, 1902; student, U. of Paris, 1893-94, 1895-96, Italy, 1895, 1906, U. of Berlin, 1894-95, Spain, 1900; unmarried. Instr. Romance langs., Yale, 1896-1901, Columbia, 1902-06; head dept. of Italian and Old French philology, Bryn Mawr Coll., 1906-16; joined editorial staff D. C. Heath & Co., May 1917; enlisted in A.E.F. to work in Foyers du Soldat (France), June 1918; sr. prof. French, U. of Calif., June 1919—, also chmn. dept. of French, 1919-23. Chevalier Légion d'Honneur (France), 1920. Author: Boys and Men, 1900; Dante and the Animal Kingdom, 1902; The Farce of Master Pierre Pathelin (1st English transl.), 1905, 1914; Portraits of Dante—from Giotto to Raffael, 1911; Living French, 1917, 1921, 1923; Étude sur Pathelin, 1917; Maître Pierre Pathelin (small critical edition), Paris, 1924; Guillaume

Alecis et Pathelin, 1928. On editorial staff of New Internat. English Ency., 1903; edited stories by Balzac, 1912. Died July 31, 1934.

HOLBROOK, Willard Ames, army officer; b. Arkansaw, Wis., July 23, 1860; s. Willard F. and Mary (Ames) H.; grad. U.S. Mil. Acad., 1885; honor grad. Inf. and Cav. Sch., Ft. Leavenworth, Kan., 1891; grad. Army War Coll., Washington, 1912; m. Josephine Stanley, Oct. 6, 1909. Commd. 2d lt. 1st Cav., June 14, 1885; 1st lt. 7th Cav., Dec. 17, 1891; capt. a.a.g. vols., May 12, 1898; vacated, Apr. 11, 1899; capt. a.q.m., Apr. 1, 1899; maj. 38th U.S. Inf., Aug. 17, 1899; capt. 5th Cav., U.S. Army, Oct. 18, 1899; hon. discharged vols., June 30, 1901; maj. 8th Cav., Mar. 3, 1911; q.m., Dec. 10, 1911; assigned to 10th Cav., Apr. 12, 1912; lt. col. cav., Nov. 26, 1914; col., July 1, 1916; brig. gen. N.A., Aug. 5, 1917; maj. gen. N.A., Apr. 16, 1918; hon. discharged from N.A., Aug. 15, 1919. Aide to Gen. D. S. Stanley, 1891-92; tactical officer, U.S. Mil. Acad., 1892-96; in Cuba, Spanish-Am. War; participated in subduing Philippine insurrection, 1899-1901; civil gov. Province of Antique, Panay, 1901-02; on duty at Pa. Mil. Coll., 1905-09; dir. Army Staff Coll. and Sch. of the Line, Ft. Leavenworth, 1913-16; in comd. squadron of cav., after beginning of coal miners' strike, Trinidad, Colo., 1914; apptd. comdr. 165th Inf. Brigade, Camp Sherman, O., Aug. 25, 1917; comd. Southern Dept. and in charge of Mexican border, May 3-Sept. 26, 1918; comd. 9th Div., Camp Sheridan, Ala., Sept. 26, 1918, until demobilization of div., Feb. 1919; comd. Camp Grant demobilization center, Feb. 28-May 25, 1919; overseas service, May 1919; later chief of staff Southern Dept.; chief of cavalry, with rank of major gen., July 1, 1920; retired July 23, 1924. Died July 18, 1932.

HOLCOMB, Marcus Hensey, gov.; b. New Hartford, Conn., Nov. 28, 1844; s. Carlos and Adah L. (Bushnell) H.; ed. pub. and pvt. schs.; m. Sarah Carpenter Bennett, Nov. 15, 1872 (died 1901). Admitted to Conn. bar, 1871; practiced, Southington, 1872-93; mem. Holcomb & Pierce, Hartford, 1893-1910; judge Probate Court more than 30 yrs.; treas. Hartford County, 1893-1908; mem. Conn. Senate, 1893, Ho. of Rep., 1905 (speaker); mem. bd. State Police Commrs., 1903-10; atty. gen. of Conn., 1907-10; judge Superior Court, 1910-14; gov. of Conn. 3 terms, 1915-21. Republican. Pres. of Southington Savings Bank; dir. Southington Bank & Trust Co., Nat. Fire Ins. Co., Peck, Stow & Wilcox Co., Ætna Nut Co., Southington Hardware Co. Mason. Baptist. Home: Southington, Conn. Died Mar. 5, 1932.

HOLCOMB, Silas Alexander, gov.; b. Gibson County, Ind., Aug. 25, 1858; s. John C. and Lucinda Reavis (Skelton) H.; common sch. edn.; m. Alice Brinson, Apr. 13, 1882. Studied law in Neb.; admitted to bar, 1882; judge 12th Jud. Dist. of Neb., 1891-94; gov. of Neb., 1894-98. Populist; was elected by fusion of Populist and Democratic parties; justice Supreme Ct. of Neb., 1900-06. Mem. Bd. Commrs. of State Instns., 1913—. Home: Lincoln, Neb. Died Apr. 25, 1920.

HOLCOMBE, Armstead Richardson, newspaper man; b. Mobile, Ala., Nov. 10, 1876; s. Richard Spencer and Sallie (Taylor) H.; A.B., Centenary Coll., Jackson, La., 1897, LL.D., 1930; A.M., Vanderbilt U., 1899; m. Elizabeth Florence Bratney, Oct. 27, 1914. Teaching fellow in geology, Vanderbilt U., 1899-1900; instr. Vanderbilt U. Summer Sch., 1900; prin. Stanton (Tenn.) Training Sch., 1900-01; with Daily Picayune (now Times-Picayune), New Orleans, 1901-09, St. Louis Republic, 1909-11, Cleveland Leader, Mar.-Sept. 1911; city editor, 1914-15, mng. editor, 1915-18, St. Louis Times; cable editor New York Tribune, 1919-22, night editor, 1922-23; night editor New York Herald Tribune (consolidation of the New York Herald and the New York Tribune), 1923-26, mng. editor, 1926-31; editor and owner Eastern Shore Times, Berlin, Md. Decorated Chevalier Legion of Honor (France). Home: Berlin, Md. Died Apr. 22, 1936.

HOLCOMBE, Chester, author, diplomatist; b. Winfield, N.Y., Oct. 16, 1844; s. Chester and Lucy (Tompkins) H.; grad. Union Coll., 1861 (A.M.; L.H.D., 1910); m. Alice Reeves, Mar. 21, 1906. Interpreter and sec. U.S. legation, Peking, China, 1871-85; acting minister 1875-76, 1878-79, 1881-82; mem. commn. for negotiating new treaties with China, 1880; assisted in negotiating treaty with Corea, 1882; was offered decoration by Emperor of China; apptd. to U.S. legation, Colombia, 1884, but declined. In 1896, at request of Chinese authorities, prepared in detail, in Chinese and English, documents for govt. loan of $100,000,000; also developed in both languages, detailed plans for construction of about 3,000 miles of double-track ry., involving cost of about $240,000,000, a scheme for securing the necessary funds and the establishing of schools for instruction of Chinese in ry. construction and management. Lowell Inst. lecturer, Boston, Feb. 1902. Author: (in Chinese) Mental Arithmetic, 1873; Life of Christ, 1875; Translation of Declaration of Independence. In English: The Practical Effect of Confucianism Upon Chinese Nation, 1882; Travels in Western China, 1875; Catalogue and Hand-book of Antique Chinese Porcelains, 1890; The Real Chinaman, 1895; The Real Chinese Question, 1899. Address: Rochester, N.Y. Died Apr. 25, 1912.

HOLCOMBE, John Marshall, life underwriter; b. Hartford, Conn., June 8, 1848; s. James Huggins and Emily Merrill (Johnson) H.; A.B., Yale U., 1869, A.M., 1872; hon. A.M., 1900; LL.D., Trinity College, 1920; m. Emily Seymour Goodwin, Jan. 29, 1873. Actuary Conn. Insurance Dept., 1871-74; asst. sec. Phœnix Mutual Life Ins. Co., 1874-75, sec., 1875-89, v.p., 1889-1904, pres., 1904—; also pres. Mechanics Savings Bank; dir. Phœnix Nat. Bank, Phœnix Ins. Co., Peck, Stow & Wilcox, Nat. Surety Co.; trustee U.S. Security Trust Co.; pres. Hartford Meadows Development Co.; treas. Hartford Retreat. Former pres. Common Council and Bd. of Aldermen, Hartford; mem. City Plan Commn., Hartford. Republican. Conglist. Author: Lectures on Insurance (text book), 1908. Home: Hartford, Conn. Died Jan. 15, 1926.

HOLCOMBE, William Frederic, M.D.; b. Sterling, Mass., Apr. 2, 1827; s. Capt. Augustine and Lucy (Bush) H.; grad. Albany Med. Coll., 1849; studied in Europe; located in New York; lecturer on diseases of the eye, New York U. Med. Coll., 1861; prof. eye and ear diseases in New York Med. Coll., 1862, in New York Ophthalmic Coll. and Hosp., 1863, and New York Med. Coll. for Women, 1867. One of 9 founders of New York Geneal. and Biog. Soc. in 1869. Delivered centennial address of town of Sterling, Mass., 1881. Address: New York, N.Y. Died 1904.

HOLDEN, Albert James, organist, composer; b. Boston, Mass., Aug. 17, 1841; s. John and Lydia A. H.; studied entirely in New York. Organist over 47 yrs. at Ch. of the Divine Paternity (Universalist) and the Ch. of the Puritans. Has composed more than 300 anthems, hymns and other ch. music; has also written songs and part-songs, several ballads and choruses. Has edited and compiled numerous collections of music, both sacred and secular. One of founders Am. Guild of Organists. Mason. Home: Longmeadow, Mass. Died July 16, 1916.

HOLDEN, Edgar, physician; b. Hingham, Mass., Nov. 3, 1838; s. Asa Hall and Anna Louise (Seymour) S.; grad. Princeton, 1859, A.M., 1862, Ph.D., 1872; grad. Coll. Phys. and Surg., New York, 1861; m. Katherine Hedden, 1862 (died 1870); m. 2d, Helen Stewart Burgess, 1872. Before and after graduation, 1861, was interne Flatbush Hosp., entered U.S. Navy, 1861, as asst. surgeon; served on Minnesota, Passaic, Sassacus, etc., as surgeon; med. dir. James River Squadron, 1864; later commissioned surgeon, U.S. Army, and served in army hosp. for 1 yr. after war. Pres. med. bd., Mutual Benefit Life Ins. Co., 1870—. Republican. Presbyn. Author: Use of the Sphygmograph, 1872; Health and Mortality of Newark for 20 Years, 1880; The Waif from Minot's Ledge, 1888. Home: Newark, N.J. Died 1909.

HOLDEN, Edward Henry, newspaper editor; b. Boston, Mass., Feb. 10, 1858; s. John Henry and Elizabeth (Moakler) H.; ed. high sch., Tecumseh, Neb.; m. Alice Maud Lindsay, Oct. 16, 1891; children—Mabel Elizabeth (Mrs. Herbert Williams), John Edward, Mary Catherine (Mrs. Stanley Horine), Robert Roy. Reporter Stockton (Calif.) Independent, 1884; telegraph editor Butte (Mont.) Miner, 1891-1902, Salt Lake (Utah) Herald, 1902-11; telegraph editor Salt Lake Tribune, 1911-18, mng. ed., 1918-24, editor in chief, 1924-29. Deceased.

HOLDEN, Edward Singleton, astronomer; b. St. Louis, Nov. 5, 1846; s. Edward and Sarah Frances (Singleton) H.; B.S., Washington U., 1866, A.M., 1879; grad. U.S. Mil. Acad., 1870; LL.D., U. of Wis., 1886, Columbia, 1887; Sc. D., U. of the Pacific, 1896; Litt.D., Fordham U., 1910; m. Mary Chauvenet, May 8, 1871. Lt. engrs., U.S. Army, 1870-73; prof. mathematics, U.S.N., 1873-81; dir. Washburn Obs., Wis., 1881-85; pres. U. of Calif.; 1885-88; dir. Lick Obs., 1888-98; librarian U.S. Mil. Acad., 1901—. Mem. Nat. Acad. Sciences. Knight Order of the Danebrog (Denmark); Knight Comdr. Ernestine Order of Saxony; etc. Author: Bastian System of Fortification, 1872; Index Catalogue of Nebulæ, 1877; Life of Sir William Herschel, 1881; Writings of Sir William Herschel, 1881; Astronomy (with Simon Newcomb), 1887; Hand-book of the Lick Observatory, 1888; Briefer Astronomy (with Simon Newcomb), 1892; Mogul Emperors of Hindustan, 1895; Mountain Observatories, 1896; Memorials of W. C. and G. P. Bond, 1897; Pacific Coast Earthquakes, 1898; Earth and Sky, 1898; Our Country's Flag, 1898; Primer of Heraldry, 1898; Elementary Astronomy, 1899; Family of the Sun, 1899; Essays in Astronomy, 1900; Stories of the Great Astronomers; Real Things in Nature, 1903; The Sciences, 1903. Editor: Publications Washburn Observatory, 4 vols., 1881-85; Publications Lick Observatory, 3 vols., 1888-94; Centennial U.S. Military Academy, 1902 (2 vols.). Address: West Point, N.Y. Died Mar. 16, 1914.

HOLDEN, George Parker, surgeon, writer on angling; b. Yonkers, N.Y., Dec. 26, 1869; s. John George Parker and Maria Englehart (LeCount) H.; M.D., Homeo. Med. Coll. and Flower Hosp., New York, 1894; m. Anna Orrilla Wood, Aug. 29, 1900; children—Orrilla Anne W., Randall L., John P. W., Katharine M. Began practice, Yonkers, 1894; consulting surgeon Yonkers Gen. Hosp. Republican. Baptist. Author: Doughty-Holden Genito-Urinary Diseases, 1897; That Appendix Vermiformis and the Piscatorial Art (brochure), 1915; Streamcraft, An Angling Manual, 1919; The Idyl of the Split-Bamboo, 1920; Angling—Recollections and Practice, 1931. Home: Yonkers, N.Y. Died July 15, 1935.

HOLDEN, George Walter, M.D.; b. Barre, Mass., Sept. 17, 1866; s. James E. and Harriet A. (Wheelock) H.; Mt. Hermon Acad., Northfield, Mass.; M.D., U. of Vt., 1895; m. Elsie Greene, Dec. 31, 1896; children—Robert Greene, Lawrence Wheelock. Practiced in N. Brookfield, Mass., 1896-98, Denver, 1898—; supt. and med. dir. Agnes Memorial Sanatorium, 1904-32. Fellow Am. Coll. Phys.; chmn. Med. Advisory Bd., Denver; pres. Bd. Control Child Research Council; dir. Denver Community Chest. Mason. Republican. Capt. M.C., U.S. Army, World War; maj. M.C.O.R.C. Home: Denver, Colo. Died July 11, 1934.

HOLDEN, Hale, railway official; b. Kansas City, Mo., Aug. 11, 1869; A.B., Williams Coll., 1890; LL.D., 1925; student Harvard Law Sch. Practiced in Kansas City; general attorney C.,B.&Q. Ry. Co., 1907-10; asst. to pres., 1910-12, v.p., 1912-14, pres. same rd., also Colorado & Southern Lines, 1914-Dec. 31, 1928 (except 1918-20); chmn. exec. com. S.P. Co., 1929-32, chmn., 1932-39; dir. Am. Telephone and Telegraph Co., New York Life Ins. Co., Chemical Bank and Trust Co. Appointed member advisory bd. to U.S. dir. gen. of railroads, Dec. 1917, resigned Feb. 1918; regional dir. Central Western Region, R.R. Administration, June 1918-Feb. 15, 1920; chmn. exec. com. Assn. of Ry. Executives, Dec. 1922-Dec. 1924. Submitted to Interstate Commerce Commission, 1923, plan for consolidation of all western rys. into 4 systems—Burlington, U.P., Santa Fe, and S.P. Home: Niantic, Black Point, Conn.; and New York, N.Y. Died Sept. 23, 1940.

HOLDEN, Horace Moore, lawyer; b. Warren County, Ga., Mar. 5, 1866; s. William Frank H.; A.B., U. of Ga., 1885; m. Mary, d. Judge William Corry, June 1, 1893; children—Frank Alexander, Howard Lewis, Mrs. Mary Stephens Paul, Queen Elizabeth, Mrs. Anna Frances Johnston. Admitted to bar at 19, and practiced at Crawfordville, Ga.; Dem. nominee for legislature, 1894; mem. Dem. State Exec. Com., 1898; chmn. Dem. County Com., Taliaferro County; judge Superior Court of Ga., Northern Jud. Circuit, 1900-07; apptd. Oct. 12, 1907, elected, Oct. 1908, asso. justice Supreme Court of Ga. for term 1909-14; resigned, Oct. 30, 1911, and resumed law practice at Augusta, Athens, 1912-31, Atlanta, 1931—; dir. Southern Mut. Ins. Co. Home: Atlanta, Ga. Died Feb. 7, 1936.

HOLDEN, James, monetary reformer; b. Pontiac, Mich., Nov. 10, 1856; s. John D. and Harriet (Downer) H.; ed. pub. schs.; m. Beatrice Huggins, Sept. 1, 1880. Investment banker, Emporia, many yrs.; resident of Denver, Colo., 1902-14, N.Y. City, 1914—. Pres. Nat. Citizens' Alliance, 1890-95; editor and pub. The Independent League, Emporia, 1890-95, advocating a scientific certificate money system; the first to demonstrate that interest on a circulating medium is a wholly spurious and avoidable factor; the first to demonstrate that the currency deficit is exactly measured by the total amount of bank credit. Non-Conformist. Co-founder and editor "Money" (monthly mag.), New York, Jan. 1921. Address: New York, N.Y. Died June 13, 1925.

HOLDEN, John Burt, judge; b. Franklin County, Miss., Jan. 5, 1873; s. John E. and Laura (Curtis) H.; ed. Belton (Tex.) Male Acad.; studied law in office of Stockdale & Cassedy, and C. E. Williams, Summit, Miss.; m. Mary Cassedy, Oct. 17, 1894. Admitted to Miss. bar, 1894; practiced 20 yrs. at Summit and McComb City, Miss.; mayor of Summit, 1898-1910; pros. atty., Pike County, Miss., 1911-14; circuit judge 14th Dist., 1914-16; apptd. justice Supreme Court of Miss., Jan. 1916, and elected for term, 1917-24, reëlected, for term, 1924-33. Democrat. Mason. Home: Jackson, Miss. Died Jan. 7, 1928.

HOLDEN, Liberty Emery, newspaper publisher; b. Raymond, Me., June 20, 1833; s. Liberty and Sally Cox (Stearns) H.; student Waterville Coll., Me., 1854-56; A.B., U. of Mich., 1858, A.M., 1861; m. Delia Elizabeth Bulkley, Aug. 14, 1860. Prof. rhetoric and English literature, Kalamazoo Coll., 1858-59; supt. schs., Tiffin, O., 1861-62; admitted to bar, 1862; real estate business, Cleveland, 1862-72; removed to Utah, 1876; one of founders, and pres. 12 years., Salt Lake Acad.; editor Cleveland Plain Dealer, 1885—, and pres. Plain Dealer Pub. Co.; pres. Hollenden Hotel Co., Hub Transfer & Storage Co.; dir. First Nat. Bank, Cleveland Transfer & Carriage Co. First chmn. exec. com. Nat. Bimetallic League, 1884; under his direction data were collected and published which created a nat. interest in the free coinage of silver; del. from Ohio, Dem. Nat. convs., 1888, 96; mayor of Bratenahl Village, O.; commr. Chicago Expdn., 1893. Trustee Western Reserve U., Adelbert Coll., Cleveland Sch. of Art; mem.

bldg. com. Cleveland Mus. of Art. Home: Bratenahl, O. Died Aug. 26, 1913.

HOLDEN, Louis Edward, educator; b. Rome, N.Y., April 30, 1863; s. William Rufus and Ann Eliza (Davis) H.; A.B., Beloit Coll., 1888, A.M., 1891; grad. Princeton Theological Seminary, 1891; D.D., Beloit, 1899; LL.D., Lake Forest, 1900, Washington and Jefferson College, 1902, The College of Wooster (Ohio), 1937; m. Harriet Eliza Simmons, N.Y., September 29, 1890 (died 1917); m. 2d, Mary L. Murray, Apr. 20, 1918; children—Anne Elizabeth, Louis Edward. Ordained Presbyn. ministry, 1891; prof. oratory, Beloit Coll., 1891-99; pres. College of Wooster, Ohio, 1899-1915; associate secretary General Board of Education, Presbyterian Church of the U.S.A., 1917-20; president James Millikin University, Decatur, Illinois, 1920-23; vice president of Beloit (Wis.) College, 1923-33 (resigned). Mem. Phi Beta Kappa Fraternity. Home: Wooster, Ohio. Died April 12, 1942.

HOLDEN, Ward Andrews, oculist; b. Marietta, O., Feb. 15, 1866; s. William and Sarah Hyde (Andrews) H.; A.B., Marietta Coll., 1884, A.M., 1887; M.D., Med. Coll. of Ohio, Cincinnati, 1887; post-grad. work, univ. of Göttingen, Vienna and Marburg; unmarried. Practiced at N.Y. City, 1890—; formerly prof. clin. ophthalmology, Coll. Phys. and Surg. (Columbia U.); hon. surgeon at Knapp Memorial Eye Hosp. Republican. Author: An Outline of the Embryology of the Eye (Cartwright prize essay), 1893. Wrote sect. on The Pathology of the Eye, in Am. Textbook of Pathology, 1901. Address: New York, N.Y. Deceased.

HOLDER, Arthur Ernest, labor advocate; b. Pontypridd, Glamorganshire, Wales, Apr. 13, 1860; s. James and Caroline (Mathias) H.; ed. common schs. and Bapt. sch., Eng.; m. Sophia Elizabeth Bromfield, Nov. 4, 1881; children—James Arthur, Jack Walter, Sydney (dec.), Herbert Stanley. Came to U.S., 1878; machinist by trade; built and installed machinery in U.S. and various other countries; candidate for Ho. of Rep., in N.J., 1886, in Minn., 1894, in Iowa, 1897; dep. comm. Bur. of Labor, Ia., 3 terms, 1900-06; editor of the Machinists Journal, 1904-06; apptd. by President Wilson as labor representative on Federal Bd. for Vocational Edn., 1917-21; chief legislative division, People's Legislative Service, Washington, D.C., 1921-23; chief of research sec., conciliation service, U.S. Dept. of Labor, Washington, 1929-36; exec. sec. Conference Progressive Polit. Action, 1922-26. Rep. American Federation of Labor before Congress, 1906-17; pres. Ia. State Federation of Labor, 1900-04; mem. Council of Defense of D.C., 1917 (chmn. com. on labor). Made labor investigations for federal govt. in Europe, 1911; compiled much data for internat. trade union movement. Mason. Author: History of Railroad Strikes Since 1877 (series of articles), 1914. Home: Washington, D.C. Died Jan. 6, 1937.

HOLDER, Charles Frederick, author; b. Lynn, Mass., Aug. 5, 1851; s. Dr. Joseph Bassett and Emily A. (Gove) H.; ed. U.S. Naval Acad., class of 1869, but resigned before graduation, Friends' Sch., Providence, Allen's Sch., W. Newton, Mass., and pvt. tutors; m. Sarah Elizabeth Ufford, Nov. 8, 1879. Asst. Am. Museum Natural History, New York, 1871-75; pres. Pasadena Bd. Edn.; trustee Throop Coll. Tech. and elected to chair of zoölogy on its opening; now hon. curator of its mus. Author: Stories of Animal Life, 1900; The Adventures of Torqua, 1902; The Holders of Holderness, or Pioneer Quakers, 1902; Big Game Fishes of the United States, 1903; The Lower Animals, 1903; Crabs and Insects, 1903; Fishes and Reptiles, 1903; The Birds; The Mammals; Resources of Southern California; Animals of Forest Reserve (joint author); The Boy Anglers, 1904; Hand Book to Submarine Gardens, 1904; Life and Sport in the Open—in Southern California, 1905; Half Hours with the Lower Animals, 1905; The Log of a Sea Angler, 1906; Big Game at Sea, 1907; Fish Stories (with David S. Jordan, q.v.), 1908; The Recreations of a Sportsman, 1909; The Marooners, 1909; The Channel Islands, 1910; The Game Fishes of the Pacific Coast, 1910; Distinguished American Scientists, 1911; Game Fishes of the U.S., 1913; Game Fishes of the World (London), 1913; Marine Animals of the Pacific Coast, 1913; Quakers in England and America, 1913; The Ocean, 1914; Angling Adventures Around the World, 1914; Motoring in California. Fellow N.Y. Acad. Sciences. Gold medallist. Académie de Sport, France. Address: Pasadena, Calif. Died Oct. 11, 1915.

HOLDER, Francis Jerome, mathematician; b. Santa Fe, Fla., Aug. 11, 1876; s. Ivin and Priscilla (May) H.; B.S., Nat. Normal U., Lebanon, O., 1896; grad. Massey's Business Coll., Jacksonville, Fla., 1900; A.M., Yale, 1905, Ph.D., 1908; m. Isabella Leffingwell Pierson, June 17, 1908; children—Lois Rosalind, Mildred Louise, Curtis Raymond (dec.), Gladys May, Floyd Pierson. Prin. high sch., Alachua, Fla., 1896-1900; v.p. and mgr. King's Business Coll., Raleigh, N.C., 1901-03; prin. Sch. of Commerce, U. of Wyo., 1908-09; head dept. of mathematics, Colby Coll., Waterville, Me., 1909-11, Buchtel Coll., Akron, O., 1911-12, U. of Pittsburgh, 1912-18; established Sch. of Commerce, Mercer U., 1918, becoming dean and head dept. of mathematics. Democrat. Missionary Baptist. Home: Macon, Ga. Died Dec. 30, 1931.

HOLDERBY, William Matthew, clergyman lecturer; b. Chester, Ill., May 24, 1880; s. Andrew Jackson and Delphine Elizabeth (McCormack) H.; U. of Ill., 1901-04. Moody Bible Inst., Chicago, 1905; grad. Princeton Theol. Sem., 1908; m. Mary Minerva Neal, June 23, 1908; children—William Matthew (dec.), James Frederick, Alice Neal, Jane Elizabeth, Robert Andrew, Benjamin William (dec.). Ordained Presbyn. ministry, 1908; pastor First Ch., Northern Liberties, Phila., Pa., 1908-13, South Side Ch., Pittsburgh, 1913-14, Second Presbyterian Church, Dallas, Tex., 1916-17; evangelist and home missionary, 1915-18; gen. sec. Family Altar League, 1919-22; editor The Christian Home Mag. (formed by merging Daily Bible of World's Morning Watch and Family Altar Mag. of Family Altar League), 1922-23; asso. editor The Challenge (publ. of Nat. Federated Men's Bible Classes), 1933; became pres. and general dir. Christian Family Crusade, 1923 (movement to extend knowledge of family as organizing unit of home, church and nation as contrasted with the socialistic idea of the individual as the organizing unit of society; incorporated into Nat. Christian Family Defense League, 1933); conducted campaigns S.Dak., Mich., Ia., Tex., Calif., 1925-33. Pres. Prison Bible Soc., Nat. Religious Radio Service, Nat. Religious Poster Service, Nat. Pulpit and Forum Service, Religious News Service, Nat. Ch. Printers; dir. Nat. Anti-Cigarette League, Nat. Fed. Evangelistic Com. Master Chicago Boys' Club (organizing religious work dept.), 1905; mem. com. of 1,000 presenting appeal to Congress for submission of 18th Amendment for ratification. Civilian attaché Co. D, 4th Ill. Regt., Spanish-Am. War; civilian chaplain, Camp Logan, 33d Div., at Houston, Tex., 1918-19; Salvation Army war worker (hon. col.). Mem. Nat. Com. for Founding William Jennings Bryan Memorial U.; coöperator in work of White House Commn. on Child Welfare, 1929. Rep. campaign speaker for Rep. Nat. Com., 1924; active in campaign of Frank L. Smith for election to U.S. Senate, 1927. Chaplain of Senate, Ill. State Legislature, 1927; active in presdl. campaign, Tex., 1928; collaborator with Senator Sheppard in preparation of Senate Resolution 28, 72d Congress. Author: The Family Altar (series of articles), 1920. Chautauqua lecturer. Home: Springville, Calif. Died Dec. 5, 1933.

HOLDING, Archibald M., lawyer; b. West Chester, Pa., May 15, 1862; s. Eben B. and M. Phedora H.; prep. edn., Worrall's Acad., West Chester; law student U. of Pa., 1883-84; m. Florence K. Polk, Aug. 25, 1904; 1 dau., Lois E. In practice at West Chester, 1884—; mem. Holding & Harvey, 1920—; dir. First Nat. Bank of West Chester, Lukens Steel Co., Phila. & West Chester St. Ry. Co., Ardmore & Llanerck St. Ry. Co., Aronimink Transportation Co. Democrat. Episcopalian. Home: West Chester, Pa. Deceased.

HOLDOM, Jesse, judge; b. London, Eng., Aug. 23, 1851; s. William and Eliza H.; acad. edn. in London, until 1868, when he came to Chicago; m. Edith I. Foster, 1877; m. 2d, Mabel Brady (died Jan. 4, 1930). Studied in law office Judge Joshua C. Knickerbocker, 1870-72; admitted to bar, 1873; clk., Tenneys, Flower & Abercrombie, 1876-78; in firm of Knickerbocker & Holdom, 1878-88; alone, 1888-98; judge Superior Court of Cook County, Ill., 1898-1906; justice Appellate Court, 1st Dist., 1906-10; sr. mem. Holdom, Manierre & Pratt, Chicago, 1912-15; judge Circuit Court and justice of the Appellate Court of Ill., 1915-21; mem. law firm Holdom, Pratt & Zeiss, 1923-27; judge Superior Court of Cook County, 1928; justice Appellate Court, 1927-30. Republican. Was chmn. Legal Advisory Bd. of Exemption Bd. 13, Chicago; mem. Ill. State Council Defense. Pres. Endowment Fund, Episcopal Diocese Chicago. Home: Chicago, Ill. Died July 14, 1930.

HOLDREGE, George Ward, ry. official; b. New York, N.Y., Mar. 26, 1847; s. Henry and Mary (Russell) H.; A.B., Harvard, 1869; m. Emily Cabbot Atkinson, Feb. 12, 1872 (died Nov. 12, 1873); 1 son, Henry Atkinson; m. 2d, Frances Rogers Kimball, Apr. 23, 1878; children—Ward Kimball (dec.), Mary (Mrs. E. A. Holyoke), Susan (Mrs. R. R. Hollister), Leeta Arabel. Clk., 1869, to gen. mgr., Burlington & Mo. Ry., Plattsmouth, Neb.; gen. mgr., C.B.&Q. Ry. Co. lines west of Mo. River, 1886-1921. Republican. Home: Omaha, Neb. Died Sept. 14, 1926.

HOLLAND, Clifford Milburn, civil engr.; b. Somerset, Mass., Mar. 13, 1883; s. Edward John and Lydia Francis (Hood) H.; A.B., Harvard, 1905, S.B. in C.E., 1906; m. Anna Coolidge Davenport, Nov. 5, 1908. Asst. engr. East River tunnels, Rapid Transit Commn., New York, 1906-07; asst. engr. East River Tunnels and 4th Av. Subway, Pub. Service Commn., New York, 1907-15; div. engr. East River Tunnels, Public Service Commn., New York, 1915-19; chief engr. Hudson River Vehicular Tunnel, N.Y. State Bridge & Tunnel Commn. and N.J. Interstate Bridge & Tunnel Commn., 1919—. Home: Brooklyn, N.Y. Died Oct. 27, 1924.

HOLLAND, Edmund Milton, actor; b. New York, N.Y., Sept. 7, 1848; s. George and Catherine (De Luce) H.; m. Mary E., d. Benjamin F. Seward, Sept. 7, 1875. Identified with American stage for many years; connected at all times with prominent stock companies; has created numerous important rôles, among them Captain Redwood, the detective, in Jim the Penman; Col. Moberly, in Alabama; Col. Carter, in Col. Carter of Cartersville, etc. For 13 seasons at Wallack's Theatre, Lester Wallack, mgr., 1867-1880; following 10 seasons with A. M. Palmer; starring with his brother Joseph, in A Social Highwayman, 1896-97; later at the head of Charles Frohman's comedians; appeared as Eben Holden in Eben Holden, 1901-02; as Pope Pius X in Eternal City, 1902-03; as Captain Bedford, the Detective, in Raffles, with Kyrle Bellew, 1903-05; Measure of a Man, 1906-07; The Bishop with Otis Skinner, in The Duel; starred under management of James K. Hackett in The House of a Thousand Candles, 1907-08; "Gentle" in The Battle with Wilton Lackaye, 1908-09; starred with J. K. Hackett in Bishop's Candlesticks (vaudeville), 1909; "Mr. Baxter" in Foreign Exchange, 1909-10; mem. New Theatre Co., New York, 1911; with J. K. Hackett as "William Tetlow," in "A Grain of Dust," and "The Bishop's Candlesticks." Address: New York, N.Y. Died Nov. 24, 1913.

HOLLAND, Edward Everett, congressman; b. Nansemond County, Va., Feb. 26, 1861; s. Z. E. and Ann S. (Pretlow) H.; ed. Richmond Coll. and U. of Va.; LL.B., Richmond (Va.) Coll.; LL.D., Elon (N.C.) Coll.; m. S. Otelia Lee, Nov. 26, 1884 (died 1897); children—L. Pretlow, Mrs. E. F. Creekmore; m. 2d, Eunice M. Ensor, Sept. 29, 1920. Admitted to the bar, 1882, and practiced at Suffolk, Va.; pres. Farmers Bank of Nansemond, Suffolk, Va. Mayor of Suffolk, 1885-87; commonwealth atty., Nansemond Co., 1887-1908; mem. Va. Senate, 1908-11; mem. 62d to 66th Congresses (1911-21), 2d Va. Dist.; mem. Va. State Senate, 1930—. Chmn. Dem. County Exec. Com., 1883-85; mem. Dem. State Exec. Com.; del. San Francisco and New York Nat. Dem. convs. Trustee Elon (N.C.) Coll. Mason. Address: Suffolk, Va. Died Oct. 22, 1941.

HOLLAND, Frank P., editor, pub.; b. Galveston, Tex., Sept. 22, 1852; m. Pamelia D. Allen, Dec. 25, 1877; children—Frank P., Reginald V., Mrs. Gussie Jones, J. Porter, Marsh W. Connected with Texas Siftings, Austin, Tex., 14 mos.; established Texas Farm and Ranch, Dallas, Tex., 1882, also Holland's Magazine; mayor of Dallas, 1895-97 (declined 2d term); mem. bd. dirs. Agrl. and Mech. Coll. of Tex. Interested in promoting welfare of rural communities; originator of 1st social center conf. held in the Southwest, 1911; issued 1st call for Nat. Conf. on Marketing and Rural Credits, which met in Chicago, Ill., 1913; largely instrumental in founding nat. office of Marketing and Rural Organization, U.S. Dept. of Agr.; inaugurated "Cleanest Town Contest" movement in Tex. First pres. and hon. pres. for life Tex. Editorial Assn. Home: Dallas, Tex. Died Jan. 18, 1928.

HOLLAND, Frederic May, author; b. Boston, Mass., May 2, 1836; s. Rev. Frederick West and Harriet (Newcomb) H.; grad. Harvard, 1859; entered Unitarian ministry, 1862; resigned, 1874; m. Anna Maria Bicknell, Sept. 7, 1864. Author: The Reign of the Stoics, 1879; Sordello, a story from Robert Browning, 1881; Stories from Browning, 1882; Rise of Intellectual Liberty, 1885; Frederick Douglass, the Colored Orator, 1895; Liberty in the Nineteenth Century, 1899. Home: Concord, Mass. Died 1908.

HOLLAND, James Buchanan, judge; b. in Gwynedd Twp., Montgomery County, Pa., Nov. 14, 1857; s. James and Sarah H.; grad. Conshohocken (Pa.) pub. school, 1877; m. Lidie Sheard, November 14, 1882. Admitted to Pennsylvania bar, 1887; member firm of Holland & Dettra, 1887-98, Evans, Holland & Dettra, 1898-1904. Clk. county commrs., Montgomery County, 1882-87; solicitor for same, 1887-93; dist. atty., 1893-96; was naval officer, at Phila., 1898-1900; U.S. dist. atty. at Phila., 1900-04; U.S. dist. judge, Eastern Dist. of Pa., Apr. 19, 1904. Republican. Mason. Home: Conshohocken, Pa. Died Apr. 24, 1914.

HOLLAND, James William, dean; b. Nashville, Tenn., Apr. 24, 1849; s. Robert Chappell and Elizabeth Lewis (Turner) H.; A.B., U. of Louisville, 1865, A.M., 1868; M.D., Jefferson Med. Coll., 1868 (Sc.D., 1913; m. Mary B. Rupert, May 2, 1877; 1 son, Rupert Sargent. Prof. in med. dept. U. of Louisville, 1872-85; prof. med. chemistry and toxicology, 1885-12, dean faculty, 1887-1916, Jefferson Medical College. Editor Louisville Medical News, 1880. Author: Diet for the Sick, 1880; Common Poisons and the Urine, 1887; chapter on "Mineral Poisons" in Saunders' Text-book of Toxicology and Medical Jurisprudence; Text-book of Medical Chemistry and Toxicology, 1905. Address: Philadelphia, Pa. Died Feb. 10, 1922.

HOLLAND, Joseph Jefferson, actor; b. N.Y. City, Dec. 20, 1860; s. George and Catherine (DeLuce) H.; ed. pub. schs.; unmarried. First appeared on stage at age of 6 as footman with fairy coach, with Mrs. John Wood in "Cinderella," at Olympic Theatre, New York; later as the boy, with J. K. Stoddart, in "Grandfather Whitehead"; after serving as clk. various commercial houses, returned to stage permanently with George Rignold, Mar. 25, 1878, in Shakespeare's "Henry V"; played various rôles in New York, Phila., San Francisco; starred with brother, E. M. Holland, in "The Social Highwayman," under management of Richard Mansfield; starred alone in "The Mysterious Mr. Bugle"; retired 1904. Life mem. Actors' Fund. Episcopalian. Mason. Home: Falmouth, Mass. Died Sept. 25, 1926.

HOLLAND, Peter Olai; b. Skjold, Norway, July 28, 1878; s. Storker and Elizabeth (Langeland) H.; came to U.S., 1893; B.S., St. Olaf Coll., Northfield, Minn., 1904; LL.D., Luther College, Decorah, Iowa, 1934; student United Ch. Seminary, St. Paul, 1904; m. Amanda Nasby, Aug. 19, 1906. Instr. in chemistry and physics, St. Olaf Coll., 1904-06; prin. Scandinavia Acad. (now Central Wis. Coll.), 1906-07; returned to St. Olaf as instr. mathematics and asst. business mgr., 1907, business mgr. and treas., 1908-25, treas., 1925—; pres. Citizens State Bank (Enderlin, N.Dak.), Deering (N.D.) State Bank; v.p. Lutheran Brotherhood Ins. Co.; pres. Vergas (Minn.) State Bank; v.p. Bank of Elbow Lake, Citizens State Bank of Brandon, 1st State Bank of Kensington, Citizens State Bank of Barrett (all Minn.); chmn. Mineral Springs Tubercular Sanatorium Commn., 1935—; chmn. bd. Publications Norwegian Lutheran Church of America, 1937—; dir. finances St. Olaf Coll., 1930—. Mayor of Northfield, 1916-18; member Republican State Central Com., 1920-22; chmn. 3d Minn. Congressional Dist. Mem. Mineral Springs Tubercular Sanatorium Commn. Republican. Lutheran; mem. bd. trustees Norwegian Luth. Ch. of America, 1930—, chmn., 1933—. Home: Northfield, Minn. Died Nov. 15, 1939.

HOLLAND, Robert Afton, clergyman; b. Nashville, Tenn., June 1844; s. Robert Chappel and Elizabeth Lewis (Turner) H.; ed. Louisville Coll.; hon. (S.T.D., Racine Coll.; D.C.L., U. of the South); m. Theodosia Everett, 1864; m. 2d, Emma Carroll Sprague, 1901. Chaplain C.S.A., 1862-65; pastor Trinity M.E. Ch., Baltimore, 1866-70; editor Christian Advocate, 1870-72; took orders in P.E. ministry, 1872; rector St. George's, St. Louis, 1872-80, Trinity, Chicago, 1880-84, Trinity, New Orleans, 1884-86, St. George's, St. Louis, 1886—, emeritus. Author: The Philosophy of the Real Presence; Relations of Philosophy to Agnosticism and Religion; The Proof of Immortality; Midsummer Night's Dream, an Interpretation; What Is the Use of Going to Church?; Why Keep Lent?, 1900; Which Bible?; The Commonwealth of Man, 1905. Address: St. Louis, Mo. Died 1909.

HOLLAND, W(est) Bob, newspaperman; b. Goldsboro, N.C. Mar. 3, 1868; s. West and Sallie C. (Grice) H.; ed. pub. schs. of Cowley County, Kan.; m. Carl Emeline Boyle, Nov. 23, 1891. Began as country editor, later reporter in Chicago, Detroit, Kansas City, Denver and Phila.; joined staff of New York World, 1895; established Daily Record, Durham, N.C., 1898; with New York World and Hearst orgn., 1900-05, St. Louis Post-Dispatch, 1905-10, except 1907-08 as editor The Post, Havana, Cuba; newspaper and magazine work, New York, 1910-24; with Miami Herald, 1924—, editorial writer and condr. "Sidelights," 1925—; writer for many yrs. of jokes for Lire Puck, Truth, etc. Compiler of 25 Ghost Stories, 1902. Home: Miami, Fla. Died June 23, 1932.

HOLLAND, William J(acob), zoölogist, paleontologist; b. of Am. parents, Jamaica, W.I., Aug. 16, 1848; s. F. R. and Eliza Augusta (Wolle) H.; grad. Moravian Coll. and Theol. Sem., Bethlehem, Pa., 1867; A.B., Amherst, 1869, Phi Beta Kappa, A.M., 1872; grad. Princeton Theol. Sem., 1874; Ph.D., 1886, Sc.D., 1902, Washington and Jefferson; D.D., Amherst, 1888; LL.D., Dickinson, 1896, New York U., 1897, Bethany Coll., 1905, St. Andrew's, 1905; L.H.D., U. of Pittsburgh, 1928; m. Carrie T., d. John Moorhead, Jan. 23, 1879; children—Moorhead Benezet, Francis Raymond. Prin. high school, Amherst, Mass., 1860-70, Westboro, Mass., 1870-71; ordained Moravian ministry, 1872; pastor Phila., 1872-74, Bellefield Presbyn. Ch., Pittsburgh, 1874-91; chancellor of the Western U. of Pa. (now U. of Pittsburgh), 1891-1901; dir. Carnegie Inst., Pittsburgh, 1898-1922, dir. emeritus, 1922—. V.p. Carnegie Hero Fund Commn., 1904-22, pres., 1922—; mem. Carnegie Corp., 1922—. Naturalist U.S. Eclipse Expdn. to Japan, 1887, to West Africa, 1889. Ritter d. Kön. Preuss. Kronen-Ordens, III Kl.; Officier de la Légion d'Honneur, 1908; Offizier d. K.K. Franz Josefs Orden, 1909. Comdr. d. Corona d'Italia, 1910; Knight (II cl.) Order of St. Stanislas, Russia, 1911; Comdr. Ord. Civil Alfonzo XII, Spain, 1913; Comdr. Order of Crown of Belgium, 1919; was Belgian consul for Western Pa., 1918-22; authority upon zoölogy, paleontology and museum administration. Sr. trustee U. of Pittsburgh, Western Theol. Sem. Author: The Butterfly Book, 1898; The Moth Book, 1903; To the River Plate and Back, 1913; The Butterfly Guide, 1915. Editor "Annals" and "Memoirs" Carnegie Mus. Has traveled extensively in North and South America, Europe, Asia and Africa. Home: Pittsburgh, Pa. Died Dec. 13, 1932.

HOLLANDER, Jacob H., economist; b. Baltimore, July 23, 1871; s. Meyer and Rosa (Meyer) H.; A.B., Johns Hopkins U., 1891, Ph.D., 1894; LL.D., U. of Glasgow, 1938; m. Theresa G. Hutzler, Jan. 22, 1906 (died 1916); children—Rosamond Hutzler (Mrs. Siegfried Weisberger), David Hutzler, Bertha Hutzler. Asso. prof. finance until 1900, asso. prof. polit. economy, 1901-04, prof., 1904-25, Abram G. Hutzler prof. polit. economy, 1925—, Johns Hopkins. Was sec. Bimetallic Commn. abroad in 1897; chmn. of municipal lighting commn., City of Baltimore, 1900; was apptd. by Sec. of War, 1900, spl. commr. to revise the laws relating to taxation in P.R., and while engaged in this service was apptd. by President McKinley as treas. of P.R.; organized treasury dept. and devised and introduced present revenue system ("Hollander law") of island, resigning Aug. 1901, after system was in successful operation; U.S. spl. agent on taxation in Ind. Ty., 1904; was sent by President Roosevelt as spl. commr. to Santo Domingo, 1905, to investigate its public debt; confidential agent of Dept. of State with respect to Dominican affairs, 1906-07; financial adviser of the Dominican Republic, 1908-10, and largely instrumental in readjusting its public debt. Umpire in Md. and Upper Potomac coal field, 1918-20; impartial chmn. and mem. bd. referees, Cleveland Garment Industry, 1921-32; asso. editor Baltimore News, 1929-30; chmn. Tax Survey Commn. of Maryland, 1931-32. Author: The Cincinnati Southern Railway—A Study in Municipal Activity, 1894; The Financial History of Baltimore, 1899; edited Letters of David Ricardo to J. R. McCulloch; Letters of David Ricardo to Hutches Trower (with James Bonar); Studies in State Taxation—with particular reference to the Southern States, 1900; Reprint of Economic Tracts, 1903—; Report on Taxation in Indian Territory, 1904; Report on the Debt of San Domingo, 1906; David Ricardo, A Centenary Estimate, 1911; The Abolition of Poverty, 1914; War Borrowing, 1919; Economic Liberalism, 1925; Want and Plenty, 1932. Editor: Economic Essays in Honor of John Bates Clark, 1927; Ricardo's Notes on Malthus, 1928; Ricardo's Minor Papers on Currency, 1932. Home: Baltimore, Md. Died July 9, 1940.

HOLLEY, Francis, educator, traveler; b. Cook County, Ill., Nov. 21, 1863; s. David and Mary (Burch) H.; self-ed.; unmarried. Began at 13 as messenger in engr. corps on N.P. Ry. survey, later with Canadian Pacific Ry. engr. corps; became civ. engr.; admitted to bar in Minn. and Ill.; traveled 5 yrs. in Europe and 4 yrs. in the Orient, study and research; founder, 1913, and dir. Bur. Commercial Economics. Dir. gen. dept. of pub. welfare of Motion Picture Theatre Owners of America. Republican. Presbyn. Mason. Died Dec. 12, 1923.

HOLLEY, John Milton, banker; b. Lyons, N.Y., June 12, 1845; s. John Milton and Mary (Kirkland) H.; Hamilton Coll., Clinton, N.Y., class of 1866; m. Ann Orilla King, Oct. 12, 1869 (died 1904). Landsman, U.S. Navy, 1864-65; began banking as messenger, Portage, Wis., 1866; mem. firm Holley & Borresen, bankers, La Crosse, Wis., 1879-83, succeeded by State Bank of La Crosse, 1910, becoming pres.; dir. McMillan Co.; mem. Holley & Co., real estate. Republican. Conglist. Mgr. and sec. bd. mgrs. Nat. Home for Disabled Vol. Soldiers; sec. La Crosse Pub. Library; dir. Wis. State Y.M.C.A. Home: La Crosse, Wis. Died June 19, 1914.

HOLLEY, Marietta, author; b. Ellisburg, N.Y.; d. John M. and Mary (Taber) Holley; unmarried. Writer of poems, essays and stories. Author: My Opinions and Betsy Bobbett's, 1873; Samantha at the Centennial, 1877; My Wayward Pardner, 1880; The Mormon Wife (illus. poem), 1880; Miss Richard's Boy, 1883; Sweet Cicely, 1885; Poems, 1886; Samantha at Saratoga, 1887; Samantha Amongst the Brethren, 1890; Samantha Amongst the Colored Folks, 1892; Samantha at the World's Fair, 1893; Samantha in Europe, 1895; Around the World with Josiah Allen's Wife, 1899; Samantha at St. Louis Exposition, 1904; The Borrowed Automobile, 1906; Samantha on Children's Rights, 1909; Who Was to Blame? (booklet), 1910; Samantha at Coney Island and One Thousand More Islands, 1911; Samantha on Women's Rights, 1913; Josiah Allen on Women's Rights, 1914. Address: Pierrepont Manor, Jefferson County, N.Y. Died Mar. 1, 1926.

HOLLEY, William Welles, clergyman; b. Geneva, N.Y., Mar. 2, 1841; s. Alfred A. and Mary C. (Tillman) H.; Trinity Coll., Hartford, Conn., 1861; Yale Law Sch., 1862; St. Stephen's Coll., N.Y., 1863; Gen. Theol. Sem., New York, 1863; grad. Berkeley Div. Sch., Conn., 1865; D.D., U. of Miss., 1880; m. Katherine Ann Wyse, Nov. 13, 1866. Deacon, 1865, priest, 1866, P.E. Ch.; curate St. Paul's Ch., New Haven, Conn., 1865-66; rector Ch. of the Holy Comforter, Eltingville, S.I., N.Y., 1866-67, Christ Ch., Newton, N.J., 1868-70, Christ Ch., Hackensack, N.J., 1870-1910, emeritus. Deputy to Gen. Conv. P.E. Ch., 1898-1901; mem. Standing Com. Diocese of Newark, 1883-1912. Pres. Johnson Free Public Library, Hackensack, N.J.; trustee Christ Hosp., Jersey City, N.J., Clergymen's Retiring Fund Soc., Corp. for Relief of Clergymen's Widows and Orphans, Clergymen's Mut. Ins. League. Democrat. Home: Hackensack, N.J. Died Oct. 13, 1916.

HOLLICK, (Charles) Arthur, botanist, geologist; b. on Staten Island, N.Y., Feb. 6, 1857; s. Frederick and Eleanor Eliza (Bailey) H.; Ph.B. Columbia Sch. Mines, 1879; Ph.D., Columbian (now George Washington) U., 1897; m. Adeline Augusta Talkington, Sept. 19, 1881; children—Eleanor Adeline, Roger Frederick (dec.), Grace Eaton. Sanitary engr., later insp. and spl. insp. N.Y. City Health Dept., 1881-92; spl. insp. N.Y. State Bd. of Health, 1883-93; fellow, asst. tutor, Geol. Dept. Columbia, 1890-1900; curator dept. fossil botany, 1900-13, hon. curator, 1914-21, paleobotanist, 1921—, New York Bot. Garden. Sr. geologist U.S. Geol. Survey. Dir. Pub. Museum, Staten Island Inst. Arts and Sciences, 1914-June 30, 1919. Mem. Bd. of Health, New Brighton, N.Y., 1886-92; commr. and pres. Port Richmond, N.Y., boulevard commn., 1896; commr. and pres. Richmond Co. (N.Y.) park commn., 1897-1904; mem. Bd. of Edn., City of New York, 1907-10. Has written numerous works upon geology and botany. Article "Palæobotany," New Internat. Ency., 1903; "Palæobotany or Fossil Botany," Ency. Americana, 1904. Home: New York, N.Y. Died 1933.

HOLLIDAY, Carl, college prof., author; b. Hanging Rock, O., Mar. 2, 1879; s. George Hayes and Lucy (Sheppard) H.; B.S., U. of Tenn., 1901, M.A., 1903; post-grad. studies U. of Chicago and U. of Va.; Litt.D., Campbell Coll., 1915; D.C.L., Chicago Coll. of Law, 1920; Ph.D., Am. U., 1922; m. Winifred May Hocking, Aug. 20, 1901. Teacher pub. and pvt. schs. in N.C. and Tenn., 5 yrs.; prof. English, Ala. State Normal Coll., 1903-06; instr. English and lecturer on Southern lit., U. of Va., 1906-07; prof. English, Cox Coll., Atlanta, Ga., 1907-08, Southwestern Presbyn. U., 1908-10, Vanderbilt U., 1910-12; asso. editor Am. Library of Reference, Chicago, 1913; prof. English, dir. journalism dept., dir. bur. pub. information, U. of Mont., 1913-17; head of English dept. and dir. university extension dept., 1917-18, dean Coll. of Arts and Sciences, 1918-29, U. of Toledo; prof. English, Calif. State Coll., San Jose, 1929—, pastor San Jose Unitarian church, 1929-30. Field sec. Y.M.C.A., Jacksonville, Fla., during Spanish-Am. War; editorial dir. edn. dept. Y.M.C.A. in France, 1918. D.A.R. prize for treatise in Southern History, 1903; Colonial Dames prize for treatise on Colonial Virginia, 1906. Author: Grammar of Present-Day English, 1919; Woman's Life in Colonial Days, 1921; Business English, 1921; Drill Book in English Grammar, 1921; Old "Prof." Dickson and Other Poems, 1923; I Sat By the Gate Beautiful (novel), 1925; The Dawn of Literature, 1931; The Old Man of the Woods, 1932; Peeps through Colonial Windows, 1936; also others out of print. Asso. editor The Westerner, 1929-31; editor of A Year's Harvest, Vols. I and II, 1932-33. Address: San Jose, Calif. Died Aug. 16, 1936.

HOLLIDAY, John Hampden, financier; b. Indianapolis, May 31, 1846; s. Rev. William A. and Lucia S. (Cruft) H.; served in 137th Ind. Vols. in Civil War; A.B., Hanover Coll., 1864, A.M., 1867; LL.D., Wabash Coll., Indiana, 1916; m. Evaline M. Rieman, Nov. 4, 1875. Founded, 1869, editor, 1869-92, Indianapolis News; with William J. Richards, established Indianapolis Press, 1899, which was consolidated with the News, 1901; established, 1893, pres., 1893-99 and 1901-16, and chmn. bd., 1916—, Union Trust Co.; dir. numerous corps. Trustee Hanover College, Ind.; director McCormick Theol. Sem., Chicago; trustee Presbyn. Synod of Ind.; mem. Bd. State Charities; pres. Indianapolis Charity Orgn. Soc.; pres. Bd. Trade. Mason. Treas. Ind. and Indianapolis Red Cross; mem. Marion County Council of Defense. Home: Indianapolis, Ind. Died Oct. 20, 1921.

HOLLIDAY, William Helmus, merchant; b. Hamilton County, O., May 21, 1843; s. Eli and Annetta (Bogart) H.; later lived in Douglas County, Ill.; was in Rocky Mountains, nr. Denver, 1865-67; located Sept. 1867, in what is now Albany County, Wyo.; became lumber mfr., 1870; mcht., mfr. and builder, Laramie, Wyo., 1873—; pres. The W. H. Holliday Co.; m. Emily R. Coykendall, May 5, 1869 (died 1887); m. 2d, Sarah E. East, Feb. 20, 1897. Held several local offices; defeated as candidate, 1871, elected, 1873, to lower house Territorial legislature; elected to council (upper house of same), 1875, 77, 84 and 88, and defeated, on a tie vote, 1880; defeated for del. in Congress, 1882; del. to Washington, 1890, to assist in procuring statehood for Wyo.; state senator, 1892-94, 1908-16; defeated for gov., 1894; mem. Dem. Nat. Com., 1896-1900; mem. Wyo. Commn., St. Louis Expn., 1904; del. Dem. Nat. Conv., Denver, 1908. Address: Laramie, Wyo. Died Feb. 2, 1925.

HOLLINGWORTH, Leta S(tetter), prof. education; b. Chadron, Neb., May 25, 1886; d. John G. and Margaret (Danley) Stetter; B.A., U. of Neb., 1906; M.A., Columbia, 1913, Ph.D., 1916; m. Harry L. Hollingworth, Dec. 31, 1908. Teacher high sch., DeWitt, Neb., 1906-07, McCook, 1907-08; clin. psychologist Post-Grad. Hosp., N.Y. City, 1913-14, Bellevue Hosp., 1914-16; with Teachers Coll. (Columbia), 1916—, instr. ednl. psychology until 1919, asst. prof. edn., 1919-22, asso. prof., 1922-29, prof., 1929—. Author: Functional Periodicity, 1914; Psychology of Special Disability in Spelling (with C.

Amelia Winford), 1918; Psychology of Subnormal Children, 1920; Special Talents and Defects, 1923; Gifted Children, 1926; Psychology of the Adolescent, 1928. Co-author: The Problem of Mental Disorder, 1934. Asso. editor Jour. Genetic Psychology. Home: Montrose, N.Y. Died Nov. 27, 1939.

HOLLIS, Ira Nelson, engineer; b. Mooresville, Ind., Mar. 7, 1856; s. Ephraim Joseph and Mary (Kerns) H.; grad. U.S. Naval Acad., 1878; (hon. A.M., Harvard, 1899; L.H.D., Union Coll., 1899; Sc.D., U. of Pittsburgh, 1912); m. Caroline Lorman, Aug. 22, 1894; children—Janette Ralston, Oliver Nelson, Elinor Vernon, Carolyn. Commd. asst. engr., U.S.N., 1880; passed asst. engr., 1888; resigned from Navy, Oct. 1, 1893; prof. engring., Harvard, 1893-1913; pres. Worcester Poly. Inst., 1913-25. Fellow Am. Acad. Arts and Sciences. Author: War College Lectures on Naval Ships, 1892; History of the Frigate Constitution, 1900. Home: Worcester, Mass. Died Aug. 15, 1930.

HOLLIS, W(illiam) Stanley, consul gen.; b. Chelsea, Mass., Apr. 4, 1866; s. Capt. George Fearing (U.S.N.) and Eliza A. (Simmons) H.; ed. pub. schs. and pvtly. in Chelsea and Arlington, Mass.; U.S. Naval Acad., 1883-84, left on account injured eyes (gun accident); m. Lena Cogswell Hobbs, Mar. 9, 1898; 1 son, Theodore P.; m. 2d, Alice Davidson, May 18, 1918; 1 son, James G. Clerk Am. Consulate, Cape Town, 1889-91; consular agt. at Durban, 1891-92; consul at Mozambique, 1892-98; at Lourenco Marquez, S.E. Africa, 1898-1909 (in charge consulate at Pretoria, Dec. 1899-Feb. 1900), Dundee, Scotland, Oct. 1, 1909-Dec. 31, 1910; consul gen. Beirut, Syria, 1911-17. In charge, on entry of Turkey into war, of interests of France, Great Britain, Russia, Belgium, Italy, Roumania, Montenegro, Serbia and San Marino; also as Gerant, of consulates general, Netherland, Bulgaria, Denmark, Portugal, Argentina, and Spain, and charged with protection of interests Uruguay, Panama, Ecuador, and Cuba; head of Am. Red Cross, Beirut; distributed great quantity of relief amongst naturalized Americans, French, British, Italians, Russians, and Syrians, and assisted thousands of Christians and Jews to escape from that country to place of safety; July 1917, brought party of consular officers and other citizens out of Turkey. Temporarily detailed at Dept. of State, 1917; detailed to duty, London, Apr. 1918, and in charge of Consulate Gen., July-Nov. 1919, and during other periods; rep. in London of U.S. War Trade Bd.; mem. Allied Blockade Com.; mem. Interim Com. on Dyestuffs, and commercial adviser, ad interim, to Am. Embassy; trans. to Am. Consulate Gen., Lisbon, Portugal, and took charge 1920; attached to Dept. of State, Washington, 1928—. Home: Chevy Chase, Md. Died June 8, 1930.

HOLLISTER, Clay Harvey, banker; b. Grand Rapids, Mich., Oct. 7, 1863; s. Harvey James and Martha (Clay) H.; A.B., Amherst, 1886; m. Justina Hall Merrick, Dec. 19, 1888; children—Paul Merrick, Mrs. Martha Wadsworth, George Merrick (dec.), Clay H. Banking business at Grand Rapids, 1888—; pres. Old Kent bank; dir. Medusa Portland Cement Co., G. R. Store Equipment Corp., G. R. Industrial Foundation, Am. Seating Co. Chmn. Liberty Loan Com. for Kent County, Mich., World War. Mem. Bd. of Edn., Grand Rapids, 7 yrs. Republican. Conglist. Home: Grand Rapids, Mich. Died Feb. 18, 1940.

HOLLISTER, Granger A., capitalist; b. Rochester, N.Y., Dec. 7, 1854; s. Emmett H. and Sarah E. (Granger) H.; prepared for Princeton, but death of father prevented attendance at coll.; m. Elizabeth C. Watson, May 22, 1906. Associated with brother George C., 1873, as Hollister Bros. to carry on father's lumber business, later Hollister Lumber Co., Ltd., of which was pres.; active in orgn. and management of corps., especially local lighting and traction cos.; v.p. and mem. exec. com. Rochester Gas & Electric Corp., Rochester Sav. Bank; v.p., chmn. exec. com. Security Trust Co.; dir. New York Life Insurance Co., North East Electric Co. Dir. Rochester Chamber Commerce (pres.), Chamber of Commerce U.S.A.; pres. bd. of govs. Rochester Homœ. Hosp.; trustee Reynolds Library. Republican. Episcopalian. Home: Rochester, N.Y. Died Jan. 19, 1924.

HOLLISTER, Howard Clark, judge; b. Cincinnati, Sept. 11, 1856; s. George B. and Laura B. (Strait) H.; A.B., Yale, 1878; LL.B., Cincinnati Coll., 1880; m. Alice Keys, June 2, 1887. Admitted to bar, May 1880, and practiced at Cincinnati. Asst. pros. atty. Hamilton County, O., 1881-82; judge Ct. of Common Pleas, 1st Jud. Dist., O., 1893-1903; apptd. U.S. dist. judge, Southern Dist. of Ohio, Mar. 1910. Republican. Home: Cincinnati, O. Died Sept. 24, 1919.

HOLLISTER, John Hamilcar, physician; b. Riga, N.Y., Aug. 5, 1824; grad. Rochester Collegiate Inst., 1842; M.D., Berkshire Med. Coll., 1847; hon. A.M., Beloit Coll.; m. Jennette Windiate, Jan. 2, 1849. Practiced medicine in Chicago 52 yrs.; trustee and prof. Lind U., Chicago Med. Coll. (Med. Sch. of Northwestern U.), 1859-95, prof. emeritus; physician to Mercy Hosp., 1866-96, emeritus. Editor: North American Practitioner, 1893—. Home: Chicago, Ill. Died 1911.

HOLLISTER, Ned, zoölogist; b. Delavan, Wis., Nov. 26, 1876; s. Kinner Newcomb and Margaret Frances (Tilden) H.; ed. high sch., Delavan, and pvt. studies in zoölogy, 1896-1901; m. Mabel Pfrimmer, Apr. 15, 1908. Field work in vertebrate zoölogy, U.S. Biol. Survey, in Tex., N.M., Alaska, B.C., Wash., Ore., Calif., Utah, Nev., La. and Ariz., 1902-09; asst. curator of mammals, U.S. Nat. Mus., 1910-16; mem. Canadian Alpine Club expdn. to explore Mt. Robson region of B.C. and Alberta, 1911; mem. Smithsonian-Harvard expdn. to Altai Mountains, Siberia and Mongolia, 1912; supt. Nat. Zoöl. Park, Smithsonian Instn., Washington, 1916—. Author: The Birds of Wisconsin, 1903; A Systematic Synopsis of Muskrats, 1911; Mammals of the Philippine Islands, 1912; Mammals of Alpine Club Expedition to Mount Robson, 1913; Philippine Land Mammals in the U.S. National Museum, 1913; A Systematic Account of the Grasshopper Mice, 1914; A Systematic Account of the Prairie-dogs, 1916; East African Mammals in the U.S. National Museum, vol. 1, 1918, vol. 2, 1919. Home: Washington, D.C. Died Nov. 3, 1924.

HOLLISTER, Orlando Knapp, educator; b. North Montpelier, Vt., Jan. 12, 1865; s. Andrew Jackson and Elizabeth Ann (Knapp) H.; grad. Goddard Sem., 1884; A.B., Tufts Coll., 1889, A.M., 1890, Litt.D., 1905; m. Harriet Putnam Goodwin, June 27, 1891. Actively identified with Goddard Sem., Barre, Vt., 1890-1920, prin., 1897-1920, also trustee; pres. Westbrook Sem., Portland, Me., 1920-25. Has served as pres. Universalist State Conv., and trustee Anti-Saloon League of Vt. Mason. Republican. Home: North Montpelier, Vt. Deceased.

HOLLISTER, William Henry, Jr., lawyer; b. Coxsackie, N.Y., Oct. 11, 1847; s. William H. and Judith Ann (Lampman) H.; A.B., Williams Coll., 1870; m. Julia Frances Hillman, Oct. 16, 1878. Admitted to bar, 1874, and practiced at Troy, N.Y.; organized and dir. Troy Record Co. Sch. commr., Troy, 1878-81; pres. commn. to locate pub. market. Alumni trustee Williams Coll., 1901-06; (sec. of bd.); pres. Y.M.C.A. State Conv., Kingston, N.Y., 1900; commr. from Troy Presbytery to Gen. Assembly Presbyn. Ch., 1886, 1909, 1914; pres. Troy Vocal Soc.; trustee Troy Orphan Asylum. Republican. Home: Troy, N.Y. Died Feb. 25, 1925.

HOLLOMON, James Arthur, newspaperman; b. Winton, N.C., Nov. 24, 1873; s. Leonard and Temperance Ann (Evans) H.; B.A., Wake Forest (N.C.) Coll., 1890; m. Minnie Gertrude Kerner, Oct. 1, 1894; 1 son, James Arthur. With Atlanta Journal, 1895-1904, retiring as mng. editor; identified with banking and investments for a number of yrs.; mng. editor Jacksonville Times Union, 4 yrs.; Washington corr. Atlanta Constitution, 1917-21; asso. editor Atlanta Constitution, 1916—. Democrat. Baptist. Author of several books on econ. subjects. Home: Atlanta, Ga. Deceased.

HOLLOPETER, William Clarence, pediatrist; b. Muncy, Pa., 1858; s. Abram and Margaret (Crothers) H.; B.S., Bucknell U., 1874, A.M., 1878, LL.D., 1912; M.D., U. of Pa., 1877. Practiced in Phila., 1877—; prof. pediatrics, Medico Chirurg. Coll. of Pa., 1888—. Republican. Lutheran. Author: Hay Fever—Its Prevention and Cure, 1916, 22. Died Dec. 16, 1927.

HOLLOWAY, Edward Stratton, artist, author; b. Ashland, N.Y.; s. Rev. Charles Hoover and Rebecca (Stratton) H.; acad. edn. at private schs.; studied art at Pa. Acad. of Fine Arts, Philadelphia; m. Clara Augusta Githens. Splty. marines and landscapes; decorative designer—particularly of book covers and decorations; art director J. B. Lippincott Co., also mem. bd. dirs. Author: The Practical Book of Furnishing the Small House and Apartment; Practical Book of Learning Decoration and Furniture; American Furniture and Decoration—Colonial and Federal. Joint author: Practical Book of Interior Decoration. Home: Philadelphia, Pa. Died Nov. 3, 1939.

HOLLOWAY, Jacob James, banker; b. Bridgeport, O., Apr. 17, 1857; s. William Warfield and Martha Ann (Pryor) H.; ed. Western Reserve Coll., 1872-78; m. Mary Patterson Dubois, Nov. 14, 1883; children—William Warfield, Joseph Dubois, Eleanor Martha (Mrs. Hannibal Forbes Simpson). Pres. Bridgeport Nat. Bank; v.p. Superior Coal Co.; dir. Wheeling Steel Corp. (exec. com.), Hazel-Atlas Glass Co. (exec. com.), Fostoria Glass Co., and other corps. Republican. Episcopalian. Home: Wheeling, W.Va. Died Feb. 27, 1927.

HOLLOWAY, Thomas Beaver, M.D.; b. Danville, Pa., Mar. 24, 1872; s. William Kerling and Ruth Ann (Yeager) H.; B.S., Lafayette Coll., Easton, Pa., 1894, M.S., 1897, D.Sc., 1926; M.D., U. of Pa., 1897; m. Cordelia G. Woolley, June 4, 1902 (dec.); 1 son, Thomas Beaver, Jr.; m. 2d, Florence Jane Laird, Sept. 12, 1931. Prof. ophthalmology, Sch. of Medicine, and Grad. Sch. of Medicine, U. of Pa.; ophthalmic surgeon University Hosp.; consulting ophthalmologist neurol. dept. Phila. Gen. Hosp.; ophthalmologist to Pa. Instn. for Instrn. of Blind, Overbrook. Passed asst. surgeon U.S.N.R.F. Mem. Am. Ophthal. Soc. (sec. and treas. 1918-25; edited Trans. 1918-27; mem. council 1925-30; pres. 1932-33), A.M.A. (chmn. sect. on ophthalmology 1929-30), Pan-Am. Med. Assn. (pres. sect. on ophthalmology 1932). Republican. Author: (with G.E. de Schweinitz) Pulsating Exophthalmos, 1908. Home: Merion Station, Pa. Died Aug. 18, 1936.

HOLLOWAY, William Lawson, judge; b. Kirksville, Mo., Nov. 8, 1867; s. Silas N. and Charlotte A. H.; grad. Mo. State Normal, Kirksville, 1887; LL.B., U. of Mich., 1892; m. Lalia Holmes, Feb. 17, 1898. Admitted to bar, 1892; located in Mont.; elected county atty. Gallatin Co., Mont., 1894; dist. judge 9th Jud. Dist., Mont., 1900; asso. justice Supreme Court, Mont., 1902—. Republican. Address: Helena, Mont. Died Dec. 11, 1926.

HOLLS, George Frederick William, lawyer; b. Zelienople, Pa., July 1, 1857; s. Rev. Dr. George Charles and Johanna Louise (Burx) H.; grad. Columbia, 1878; D.C.L., U. of Leipzig, 1898; m. Feb. 20, 1889, Caroline M. Sayles, Pawtucket, R.I. Candidate for State senator, 1883; delegate at large constitutional conv., New York, 1894; chmn. com. on edn.; author amendments prohibiting public aid to sectarian schools, providing for civil service reform and separate State and municipal elections; commr. on government of cities of 3d class; mem. the Peace Conf., at The Hague from the U.S., 1899; mem. sub-com. on Arbitration of Conf.; author of article on "Special Mediation" in Treaty for the Peaceful Adjustment of International Differences; chmn. N.Y. State Commn. on Ednl. Unification, 1899; political orator in the English and German languages; extensive traveler in U.S. and abroad. Author: Franz Lieber (a sketch), 1884; Sancta Sophia and Troitza, 1888; Compulsory Voting, 1891; The Peace Conference at The Hague and Its Bearings on International Law and Policy, 1900. Home: Yonkers, N.Y. Died 1903.

HOLLY, James Theodore, bishop; b. Washington, Oct. 3, 1829; parents colored Roman Catholics; ed. Washington, New York, Buffalo and Detroit; D.D., Howard, 1874; LL.D., Liberial Coll., Monrovia, 1882. Asso. editor Voice of the Fugitive, Windsor, Can., 1851-53; pub. sch. prin., Buffalo, N.Y., 1854; deacon, 1855, priest, 1856, P.E. Ch.; rector St. Luke's, New Haven, Conn., 1856-61; missionary in Haiti, 1861-74; ordained missionary bishop of Haiti, 1874. Consul of Liberia at Port au Prince, Haiti, 1864-74, receiving commn. from Pres. Warner of Liberia and exequator from Pres. Geffrard of Haiti. Del. Lambeth Conf., England, 1878. Address: Port au Prince, Haiti. Died 1911.

HOLM, Frits Vilhelm (Duke of Kolachine); explorer, author; b. Charlottenlund, Denmark, July 23, 1881; s. Consul Gen. Frederik P. and Emma G. M. (Bording) H.; ed. pvt. and govt. Latin schs., 1887-95, and Danish Royal Navy, 1895-1900; D.C.L., Susquehanna U.; LL.D., Lincoln Memorial U., Litt.D., Thiel Coll.; m. Marguerite, Lady of Grace of Constantinian Order, dau. W. L. Green, pres. Am. Bank Note Co., Oct. 9, 1919. In journalism Far East, U.S.A., and Europe, 1901—; royal sworn interpreter, 1905-21; comd., 1907-08, the Holm-Nestorian Expdn. to Sian-fu, bringing out from far interior N.W. China a 2-ton replica of famous Nestorian Monument of A.D. 781, in Met. Museum of New York, 1908-16, now permanently in the Lateran, Rome, and of which has presented 9-foot casts to 14 countries. Commrs., B.S.A., 1913-16; chief of naval staff, F.A.C., 1914-17; mission to Vatican, 1916-17; Am. war-corr. in N. Europe, 1917-18; commr. abroad, Cuban Red Cross, 1918-19; bvt. lt. gen., R.M.A., 1919; E.E. of San Marino to President Harding's inauguration, 1921; hon. prof. under Mexican Govt., 1923; chamberlain to H.R.H. the Count of Caserta, 1923. Decorations: Grand Cross with Collar of Constantinian Order of St. George (const. prefix of Excellency); Grand Cross of Orders of Holy Sepulchre (Orthodox), of Danilo I, of St. Cyril and St. Methodius, and of Honor and Merit (Cuba); Knight Comdr. of Orders of the Redeemer, of St. Sylvester, of the Liberator; Coronation medal and Royal Red Cross (Spain); Cambodigan Medal of Merit in gold (France); 35 additional decorations conferred, 1902-25. Author: The Nestorian Monument, 1909; My Nestorian Adventure in China, 1923 (London), 1924; His Majesty's Secret Service (Memoirs of the Duke of Xensi), 1926; also numerous mag. articles and addresses. Address: Paris, France. Died Mar. 9, 1930.

HOLM, (Herman) Theodor, botanist; b. Copenhagen, Denmark, Feb. 3, 1854; s. Christian and Amalie H.; grad. U. of Copenhagen, 1880; Ph.D., Catholic U. of America, 1902; unmarried. Arrived in U.S., Apr. 12, 1888, naturalized citizen, 1893. Botanist and zoölogist, Danish North Pole Expdn., 1882-83; traveled in West Greenland as botanist and zoölogist for the Danish Govt., summers of 1884-86; explored the high alpine flora of Colo., 1896-99; was for about 8 yrs. bot. asst. Smithsonian Instn. and U.S. Dept. Agr. Home: Clinton, Md. Died 1932.

HOLM, Victor S(ophus Joachim), sculptor; b. Copenhagen, Denmark, Dec. 6, 1876; s. Wilhelm J. and Emma Emily (Buck) H.; came to America, 1890; pupil of Lorado Taft, Chicago; Art Inst. Chicago, 1894-98; student Art Students' League, New York; m. Elizabeth Baxter, 1900; m. 2d, Florence French, 1927. Instr. in sculpture and lecturer on history of art, St. Louis School of Fine Arts (Washington U.), 1909—. Prin. works: Mo. State Monument, at Vicksburg, Miss.; (in St. Louis) Halsey C. Ives Memorial, in City Art Museum, Barnes Memorial, Barnes Hosp., The Crucifixion and the Papal Trophy, St. Pious Ch., Washington Univ. War Memorial, Musicians' Memorial Fountain, Forest Park, Emile Zola Memorial, Dr. Beaumont Memorial, Gov. Thomas Carlin Monument, Carrollton, Ill., Luman Parker Monument, Rollo, Mo., Nelson Memorial Fountain, Leclair, Ill.; Aeronautic Gold Medal for Am. Soc. M.E.; statue of Washington, St. Louis Masonic Temple; Henry Shaw gold medal for horticulture; also numerous memorials, tablets, architectural decorations, etc. Mem. Municipal Art Commission of St. Louis (pres. 1917). Asso. field dir. Am. Red Cross, at various camps, 1918-19; active in war work. Mason. Address: St. Louis, Mo. Died Nov. 11, 1935.

HOLMAN, Alfred, editor; b. Yamhill County, Ore., July 6, 1857; s. Francis Dillard and Mary Catharine (McBride) H.; ed. pub. schs., Portland, Ore.; m. Caroline Durbrow, Jan. 28, 1891. Served as reporter and asst. editor, Portland Oregonian, 1877-88, editor Seattle Post Intelligencer, 1888-91, Pacific Rural Press, San Francisco, 1891-98; editor and pub. San Jose (Calif.) Mercury, 1898-1901, Sacramento Union, 1903-06, The Argonaut, San Francisco, 1907-24; Pacific States corr. New York Times. Mem. advisory bd. Pulitzer Sch. of Journalism, Columbia U., New York; mem. bd. trustees Carnegie Endowment for Peace. Republican. Home: San Francisco, Calif. Died Dec. 14, 1930.

HOLMAN, Frederick Van Voorhies, lawyer; b. Baker's Bay, Ore. Ty., Aug. 29, 1852; s. James Duval and Rachel Hixson (Summers) H.; Ph.B., U. of Calif., 1875; unmarried. Admitted to Ore. bar, 1879, and practiced at Portland; dir. and gen. counsel Portland Electric Power Co. Was member Charter Commission of Portland, 1902-03, 1908-09; regent U. of Ore., 1903-17; del.-at-large Dem. Nat. Conv., 1892, 1904, 12; Ore. mem. Dem. Nat. Com., 1904-08. Originated and caused to be adopted the name of "The Rose City" for Portland. Author: Dr. John McLoughlin, Father of Oregon, 1907. Home: Portland, Ore. Died July 6, 1927.

HOLMAN, Louis Arthur, writer, illustrator; b. Summerside, P.E.I., July 13, 1866; s. James Ludlow and Ada (Longmaid) H.; ed. pub. schs. and in art at Owen's Art Sch. (St. John, N.B.), Boston Night Art Sch., Cowles Art Sch.; also under C. H. Woodbury; m. Edna Lake Bourne, June 23, 1898; 1 son, Richard Bourne. With bookselling and pub. business in Canada and Boston, to 1889; art editor New England Mag., 1890-96; asst. art editor The Youth's Companion, 1896-1914. Republican. Baptist. Illustrator: Boston, the Place and the People, 1903; Boston Common, 1910. Contbr. pencil drawings and photographs to Scribner's, Century, Printing Art, etc. Authority on Keats, on prints and old maps. Author: Ten Scenes from the Life of Benjamin Franklin, 1916; Old Maps and Their Makers, 1925; The Graphic Processes, 1926. Editor of Within the Compass (monthly publ.). Address: Boston, Mass. Died Dec. 14, 1939.

HOLMAN, Minard Lafever, mech. engr.; b. Oxford County, Me., June 15, 1852; s. John Henry and Mary Ann (Richards) H.; A.B., Washington U., 1874, hon. A.M., 1905; m. Margaret H. Holland, Sept. 7, 1879. In supervising architect's office, U.S. Treasury Dept., 1874-76; with Flad & Smith, engrs., 1876-77; asst. engr., St. Louis Water Works, 1877-87; water commr., St. Louis, 1887-99; in gen. engrig. work, 1899-1900; gen. supt. Mo. Edison Electric Co., 1900-04; sr. mem. Holman & Laird, consulting engrs., St. Louis, 1904—. Home: St. Louis, Mo. Died Jan. 4, 1925.

HOLMBERG, Gustaf Fredrik, musician; b. Aug. 17, 1872; s. August and Eva (Sundstrom) H.; came to U.S., 1891; Mus.B., Bethany Coll., Lindsborg, Kan., 1899; post-grad. work at Bethany Coll. and in Chicago, 1899-1903; studied under masters at various times, 1903-14; m. Signy Hallberg, July 20, 1904; children—Linné Fredrik, Brunhild Louise. Instr. violin and harmony, Bethany Coll., 1898-1903; concert mastre, Bethany Symphony Orchestra, 1897-1903; instr. violin and theory of music, 1903-05, asst. prof. theory and condr. of music, 1905-08, prof. and dir. of music, 1908-10, dean Sch. of Fine Arts and prof. of music, 1910—, Okla. U.; condr. Okla. City Symphony Orchestra, 1921—. Lutheran. Mason. Author: Elementary Theory of Music for High Schools, 1920. Lecturer on music and art; state conductor Federated Clubs Chorus and Orchestra. Home: Norman, Okla. Died Jan. 1, 1936.

HOLME, John Francis, illustrator, printer; b. Corinth, W.Va., June 29, 1868; s. John Messenger and Eliza H.; ed. public schools, Keyser, W.Va.; m. Ida Van Dyke, May 10, 1893. Worked on country paper as printer till 1884; on civil engr. corps, 1884-85; reporter and artist, Wheeling (W.Va.) Register, 1885-87; Pittsburgh Press, 1887-89; artist Chicago Saturday Blade, 1889-92; Chicago Times through Columbian Expn. year, 1893; San Francisco Chronicle, 1893-94; Chicago Post, 1894-96; Chicago Chronicle, 1896-97; Chicago Daily News, 1897-98; started the School of Illustration, 1898, and Bandar Log Press incorporated New York, 1902, for printing limited editions hand-made books. Address: Chicago, Ill. Died 1904.

HOLMES, Bayard (Taylor), surgeon; b. N. Hero, Vt., July 29, 1852; s. Hector Adams and Olive A. (Williamson) H.; prep. edn. Carleton Coll., Minn.; B.S., Paw Paw Inst., 1874; M.D., Chicago Homœo. Coll., 1884; M.D., Northwestern U., 1888; m. Agnes Anna, d. Capt. James W. George, Aug. 14, 1878. Interne Cook County (Ill.) Hosp., 1885-86; began practice, 1886; for yrs. mem. surg. staff Cook County Hosp.; sec., 1891-95, sr. prof. surgery, med. dept., U. of Ill. (formerly Coll. Phys. and Surg.), 1892-1908. Organizer Chicago Med. Library Assn.; an organizer Nat. Christian Citizenship League. Socialist; candidate for mayor Chicago, 1895. Editor North American Practitioner, 1889-92. Author: Surgical Emergencies; Surgery of the Abdomen, 1905; The Friends of the Insane, 1911; Hieratic Egyptian Medicine, 1913; Adolescent Insanity, 1914. Editor Dementia Praecox Studies, 1915—. Home: Lakeside, Mich. Died Apr. 1, 1924.

HOLMES, Christian R., physician; b. Veile, Denmark, Oct. 18, 1857; s. C. R. and Karen (Mickelson) H.: ed. in Denmark, Germany and America; M.D., Miami Med. Coll., 1886; interne Cincinnati Hosp., 1885-86; m. Bettie Fleischmann, Oct. 26, 1892. Ophthalmologist and otologist Cincinnati Hosp., 1888-99; prof. otology, Miami Med. Coll., 1890-1904; prof. ophthalmology, Laura Memorial Med. Coll. and Presbyn. Hosp., 1892-1903; consulting ophthalmologist Cincinnati Hosp., 1908—; one of med. dirs. Cincinnati Gen. Hosp. and advisory commissioner new Cincinnati Gen. Hosp.; prof. otology, Coll. of Medicine (U. of Cincinnati), 1904—; dean Medical Dept. of U. of Cincinnati. Permanent chmn. New Hospital Commn., 1910—. Pres. Am. Acad. Ophthalmology and Oto-Laryngology, 1901-02; v.p. A.M.A., 1902-03, and chmn. sect. on Laryngology and Otology, 1904-05, chmn. sect. on Ophthalmology, 1905-06; pres. Am. Laryngol., Rhinol. and Otol. Soc., 1908-09. Commd. maj., Med. R.C., 1917; in charge ear, nose and throat dept. Base Hosp., Camp Sherman, O. Home: Cincinnati, O. Deceased.

HOLMES, Clarence Leroy, agrl. research; b. Lansing, Ia., Jan. 22, 1879; s. William Mason and Clarinda (Lees) H.; student Yankton (S.D.) Coll., 1899-1905; A.B., U. of Mich., 1907; Ph.D., U. of Wis., 1920; m. Frances Phillips, June 30, 1911; children—William Mason, Frances Phillips, Alice Arvilla (twins). Teacher, pub. schs., 1907-14; economist, U.S. Dept. Agr., Washington, D.C., 1917-19; asst. prof. agrl. economics, U. of Minn., 1919-21, Ia. State Coll., 1921-23, prof. and head of dept., 1923-29; prin. agrl. economist, in charge div. farm management and costs, Bur. of Agrl. Economics, U.S. Dept. Agr., Washington, D.C., 1929—. Conglist. Author: Economics of Farm Organization and Management, 1928. Home: Alexandria, Va. Died Dec. 16, 1938.

HOLMES, George Kirby, statistician; b. Great Barrington, Mass., May 10, 1856; s. Harvey and Mary J. (Kirby) H.; ed. com. and high schs., Great Barrington; studied law; m. Lilian C. Hunter, Apr. 27, 1898; children—Emma Biscoe (Mrs. Harold C. Taylor), Mary Kirby, George Kirby, John Hunter. Admitted to Mass. bar, 1877; spl. agt. in charge Div. of Farms, Homes and Mortgages, U.S. Census of 1890; agrl. statistician; mem. Crop Reporting Bd. of U.S. Dept. Agr., 1905-24, writer of interpretive comment concerning its reports to the press. Del. Gen. Assembly of Internat. Inst. of Agr., Rome. Fellow Am. Statis. Assn. Author: Farms and Homes; Real Estate Mortgages (both Census of 1890); numerous publs. of Dept. of Agr. Home: Washington, D.C. Died Feb. 1, 1927.

HOLMES, George Robert, newspaper corr.; b. Tippecanoe County, Ind., Jan. 28, 1895; s. George Fox and Rose Lincoln (Beaver) H.; grad. high sch., New Richmond, Ind., 1911; student U. of Wis., 1911-13; m. Mary Catherine Early, Apr. 23, 1921; children—Mary Catherine, Kathryn Early. Began as reporter Indianapolis Sun, 1914; with United Press, N.Y. City, 1914; reporter New York Evening Mail, 1915; with Internat. News Service, Washington, D.C., 1916—, chief of Washington Bur., 1920—. Commd. 2d lt. cav., U.S.A., 1917; served as asst. adj., 78th Div., A.E.F., and aerial observer, 258th Aero Squadron, World War. Received hon. mention in Pulitzer prize award for account of burial of Unknown Soldier, Arlington Cemetery. Chief polit. writer for Internat. News Service in all Presidential campaigns, 1916—; weekly news commentator on polit. events in Washington for Nat. Broadcasting Co. Home: Washington, D.C. Died Feb. 12, 1939.

HOLMES, Howard Carleton, civil engr.; b. Island of Nantucket, Mass., June 10, 1854; s. Cornelius and Maria (Folger) H.; removed with parents to San Francisco, Calif., 1860; ed. pub. schs.; tech. training in office of city engr., Oakland, Calif.; m. Josephine Bauer, 1883. Asst. engr. to State Bd. of Harbor Commrs. of Calif. until 1883; consulting engr., 1883—; built ferry terminal at Alameda, cable rys., Portland, Spokane, Seattle, San Francisco, also elec. rys. in various cities on Pacific Coast; chief engr. State Bd. Harbor Commrs. of Calif., 1892-1901; designed and built ferry terminus of the S.F., Oakland & San Jose R.R., pleasure pier at Long Beach, Calif.; designed yacht harbor and marine works, etc., for San Francisco Expn., also all ferry slips in Bay of San Francisco; completed largest graving dock in the world, at Hunter's Point, San Francisco Bay, for Bethlehem Steel Corp.; inventor of cylinder pier of San Francisco water front; chief engr. San Francisco Dry Dock Co., S.F.O.& S.J. R.R.; constructing engr., docks and wharfs Western Pacific Ry., A.,T.&S.F., and Calif. & N.W. rys.; consulting engr. Union Iron Works, etc. Republican. Unitarian. Home: San Francisco, Calif. Died Oct. 30, 1921.

HOLMES, John McClellan, clergyman; b. Livingston, N.Y., Jan. 22, 1834; s. Rev. Edwin and Sarah M. (McClellan) H.; son, Samuel Van Vranken; A.B., Williams, 1853, A.M., 1856, D.D., 1870; grad. New Brunswick Theol. Sem., 1857. Ordained Presbyn. ministry, 1857. Pastor in Brooklyn, 1857-65, Reformed Ch., Hudson, N.Y., 1865-77, State St. Ch., Albany, 1877-97. Pres. Gen. Synod, Reformed Ch., 1876; del. Pan-Presbyn. Council, Edinburgh, 1877, London, 1888; moderator N.Y. Presbyn. Synod, 1884. Trustee Auburn Theol. Sem., 1886-1900; dir. Union Theol. Sem., New York, 1888-1900. Address: Poughkeepsie, N.Y. Died 1911.

HOLMES, Joseph Austin, geologist; b. Laurens, S.C., Nov. 23, 1859; s. Z. L. and N. Catherine (Nickles) H.; B.S., Cornell U., 1881; D.Sc., U. of Pittsburgh; LL.D., U. of N.C.; m. Jeanie I. Sprunt, Oct. 20, 1887. Prof. geology and natural history, U. of N.C., 1881-91, lecturer on geology, 1891—; state geologist of N.C., 1891-1904; in charge U.S. Geol. Survey laboratories for testing fuels and structural materials, St. Louis, 1904-07, and Pittsburgh, 1908; chief technol. branch, U.S. Geol. Survey, in charge investigation of mine accidents, 1907-10; dir. Bur. of Mines, Dept. of the Interior, since its creation, July 1, 1910—. Chief dept. mines and metallurgy, St. Louis Expn., 1904; mem. Mining Legislation Commn. of Ill., Nat. Conservation Commission. Died July 12, 1915.

HOLMES, Ludvig, clergyman; b. in Sweden, Sept. 7, 1858; s. Carl and Joanna (Nystrom) H.; ed. Sweden, 1864-74; A.B., Upsala Coll., Kenilworth, N.J.; grad. Augustana Sem., Rock Island, Ill., 1886; A.M., 1891; L.H.D., Bethany Coll., Kan., 1897, Augustana, 1902; D.D., Wittenberg Coll., Ohio, 1900; m. Sophia Johnson, June 2, 1887. Ordained Luth. ministry, June 27, 1886; pres. Iowa Conf., Luth. Ch., 1899-1903; sec. Luth. Gen. Council of U.S. and Can., 1903—; pastor Immanuel Ch., Evanston, Ill. Hon. dir. Upsala Coll., N.J.; mem. bd. of Immigrant Mission of Augustana Synod. Only possessor in America of jubilee token in silver, 1897, and decoration Litteris et Artibus in gold, blue ribbon (highest award for literary merit), 1901—both conferred by King Oscar II, of Sweden and Norway; knighted by King of Sweden, Nov. 15, 1907, with insignia The Cross of The Order of Vasa, 1st class. Author: Dikter af Ludvig (poems), 1896; To Oscar II on his 25 Years Jubilee as King of Sweden and Norway, 1897; Outline for Final Examination of Catechumens, 1898; Nya Dikter af Ludvig (new poems by Ludvig), 1905. Address: Evanston, Ill. Died 1910.

HOLMES, Mary Caroline, author; b. Deposit, N.Y.; d. George W. and Mary M. (Rand) Holmes; ed. pvt. schs. Went as missionary to Syria, 1883; dir. relief work in Urfa, Turkey, 1919-22; during siege of French troops by Turks, 1920, served as intermediary between Turks and French and after massacre of French garrison continued for 2 yrs. in charge of foreign interests. Decorated Croix de Guerre, with Palm (French); Near East overseas medal; nat. speaker Near East Relief. Republican. Author: Who Follows in Their Train, 1917; The Knock on the Door, 1918; Bewteen the Lines in Asia Minor, 1923. Address: New York, N.Y. Died Mar. 3, 1927.

HOLMES, Mary Elisabeth, college prof.; b. Mystic, Conn., Dec. 28, 1870; d. Hiram Clift and Hannah Fish (Denison) Holmes; A.B., Wellesley Coll., 1892; U. of Chicago, 1895-97; Ph.D., U. of Pa., 1908. Teacher, Flushing, N.Y., Seminary, 1892-93, Alinda Prep. Sch., Pittsburgh, Pa., 1893-95, Walnut Lane Prep. Sch., Germantown, Pa., 1897-98; instr. chemistry, 1898-1904, asso. prof., 1904-17, Mt. Holyoke Coll.; prof. chemistry, Conn. Coll., New London, 1917—. Conglist. Address: New London, Conn. Died Mar. 12, 1927.

HOLMES, Mary Emilie; b. Chester, O., Apr. 10, 1850; d. Rev. Mead and Mary D. (Everette) Holmes;

grad. Rockford Sem., A.B., 1868, Conservatory of Music, 1870, U. of Mich., A.M., Ph.D., 1888; taught dept. natural science 8 yrs. Rockford Coll. Admitted fellow Geol. Soc. of America for "original scientific investigation and discovery," 1890. Pres. Presbyterial Missionary Soc., Freeport Presbytery; sec. for Freedmen, Synod of Ill., and Freedmen's sec. of the North West, under Gen. Assembly's Bd. of Missions; also editor and publisher of Freedmen's Bulletin, or Monthly News Letter. Founder and active supporter Mary Holmes Sem., West Point, Miss. Address: Rockford, Ill. Died 1906.

HOLMES, Mary Jane, author; b. Brookfield, Mass.; d. Preston and Fanny (Olds) Hawes; studied grammar at 6; taught school at 13; began writing at 15; m. Daniel Holmes. Extensive traveler in America and Europe. Author: Tempest and Sunshine, 1854; English Orphans, 1855; Homestead on Hillside, 1855; 'Lena Rivers, 1856; Meadow Brook, 1857; Dora Deane, 1858; Cousin Maude, 1860; Marian Grey, 1863; Edith Lyle, 1876; Daisy Thornton, 1878; Madeline, 1881; Queenie Hetherton, 1883; Bessie's Fortune, 1885; Marguerite, 1890; Dr. Hathern's Daughters, 1895; Paul Ralston, 1897; Darkness and Daylight, 1864; Hugh Worthington, 1865; Cameron Pride, 1867; Rose Mather, 1868; Ethelyn's Mistake, 1869; Millbank, 1871; Edna Browning, 1872; West Lawn, 1874; Mildred, 1877; Forrest House, 1879; Château d'Or, 1880; Christmas Stories, 1884; Gretchen, 1887; Mrs. Hallam's Companion, 1894; The Tracy's Diamonds, 1899; The Cromptons, 1902; The Merrivale Banks, 1903; Rena's Experiment, 1904; The Abandoned Farm, and Connie's Mistake, 1905. Address: Brockport, N.Y. Died 1907.

HOLMES, Nathaniel, jurist; b. Peterborough, N.H., Jan. 2, 1815; s. Samuel and Mary (Annan) H.; grad. Harvard, 1837, A.M., 1859; admitted to bar, 1839; established practice at St. Louis; circuit atty., 1846; judge Supreme Court, Mo., 1865-68; Royall prof. law, Harvard, 1868-72. Retired, 1883. Unmarried. Author: The Authorship of Shakespeare, 1866; Realistic Idealism in Philosophy Itself (2 vols.), 1888; Historical Address at Sesqui-Centennial Anniversary of Peterboro, N.H., 1890. Home: Cambridge, Mass. Died 1901.

HOLMES, Oliver Wendell, jurist; b. Boston, Mar. 8, 1841; s. Dr. Oliver Wendell H., poet and essayist (1809-94) and Amelia Lee (Jackson) H.; A.B., Harvard, 1861, LL.B., 1866, LL.D., 1895, Yale, 1886, U. of Berlin, 1910, Williams, 1912; D.C.L., Oxford, 1909; m. Fanny, d. Epes S. Dixwell, June 17, 1872 (died 1929). Served 3 yrs. with 20th Mass. Volunteers, lt. to lt. col.; wounded in breast at Ball's Bluff, Oct. 21, 1861, in neck at Antietam, Sept. 17, 1862, in foot at Marye's Hill, Fredericksburg, May 3, 1863; a.-d.-c. on staff Gen. H. G. Wright, Jan. 29, until mustered out July 17, 1864, with rank of capt. Admitted to Mass. bar, 1867; engaged in practice in Boston; instr. constl. law, Harvard Coll., 1870-71; editor Am. Law Review, 1870-73; mem. law firm of Shattuck, Holmes & Munroe, 1873-82; lecturer on common law, Lowell Inst., 1880; prof. law, Harvard Law Sch., 1882; asso. justice, 1882-99, chief justice, 1899-1902, Supreme Jud. Court of Mass.; asso. justice Supreme Court of U.S., Dec. 4, 1902-Jan. 12, 1932, resigned. Author: The Common Law (lectures at Lowell Inst.), 1881; Speeches, 1891, 1913; Collected Legal Papers, 1920. Editor: Kent's Commentaries (12th edit.), 1873. Home: Washington, D.C. Died Mar. 6, 1935.

HOLMES, Richard Sill, clergyman; b. Brooklyn, N.Y., July 6, 1842; s. Jacob, Jr. and Lucretia Frances (Harris) H.; A.B., Middlebury Coll., 1862, A.M., 1865, D.D., 1890, LL.D., 1900; grad. Auburn Theol. Sem., 1868; m. Fannie Pardee Olmsted, Oct. 14, 1869; m. 2d, Alida L. Dodge, Sept. 7, 1881. In business, Auburn, N.Y., 1866-70, 1878-84; teacher, 1870-78; registrar Chautauqua ednl. work, 1884-87; ordained Presbyn. ministry, 1887; pastor Warren, Pa., 1887-90, Shadyside Ch., Pittsburgh, 1890-1904; pres. The Holmes Press, Phila., 1904—; editor The Westminster, Phila., 1904-10, when consolidated with The Interior, of Chicago, under the name The Continent, New York, becoming corr. editor. Pres. N.Y. State Y.M.C.A., 1871; prof. langs., Latin Summer Sch., Chautauqua, N.Y., 1880. Author: The Maid of Honor, 1907; The Victor; The Outcome. Home: Philadelphia, Pa. Died Sept. 5, 1912.

HOLMES, Robert Shailor, author, educator, traveler; b. Unadilla, Mich., Feb. 8, 1870; s. William S. and Adelia E. (Howe) H.; ed. high sch. and business coll.; studied Met. Conservatory of Music, New York; Litt.D., U. of Ga., 1924; m. Katharine Alden Ayers, Oct. 4, 1893. Mem. firm W. S. Holmes & Son, music dealers, Lansing, 1890-1900; in realty business until 1910; retired for travel and study. Organizer, 1914, and pres. Fla. Forum and Assembly, Daytona Beach; pres. Florida Forum Assn. and Forum Speakers' Bur.; sec. Nat. Open Forum Council; founder Forum Lecture and Reading Courses for adults. Formerly v.p. Am. Bapt. Home Mission Soc. and trustee Winona Assembly. Mason. Rotarian. Author: Builders and Other Poems, 1925; Our Heritage and Other Poems, 1928. Has traveled widely in foreign countries. Home: Daytona Beach, Fla. Died **July 24, 1939.**

HOLMES, Samuel Van Vranken, clergyman; b. Brooklyn, Mar. 23, 1862; s. John McClellan and Frances (Van Vranken) H.; A.B., Williams, 1883, A.M., 1886; student U. of Berlin, 1884, 1886; grad. Princeton Theol. Sem., 1887; D.D., Williams, 1903; m. Helen Stanton, June 14, 1887; children—Marguerite, Richard Stanton. Ordained Presbyn. ministry, 1887; pastor First Ch., Richfield Springs, N.Y., 1887-92; asso. pastor First Ch., Washington, 1892-93; pastor Westminster Ch., Buffalo, 1893-1932, pastor emeritus, 1932—. Republican. Home: Buffalo, N.Y. Died May 9, 1935.

HOLMES, William Henry, art director; b. Harrison County, O., Dec. 1, 1846; s. Joseph and Mary (Heberling) H.; grad. McNeely Normal Coll., 1870, D.Sc., George Washington U., 1918; m. Kate Clifton Osgood, Oct. 1883 (died 1925); children—Osgood, William Heberling. Normal sch. teacher, 1871-72; asst., 1872-80, geologist, 1880-89, U.S. Geol. Survey; curator dept. aboriginal pottery, U.S. Nat. Museum, 1882-93; archæologist Bur. Am. Ethnology, in charge of explorations, 1889-98; curator anthropology, Field Mus. of Natural History, and prof. anthropic geology, U. of Chicago, 1894-97; head curator dept. anthropology, 1898-1902; curator prehistoric archæology, 1903, and Nat. Gallery of Art, 1907, U.S. Nat. Mus.; chief Bur. Am. Ethnology, Oct. 1902-09. Head curator, anthropology, U.S. Nat. Mus., 1910-20; curator, Nat. Gallery of Art, 1910-20; dir., 1920—. U.S. del. 1st Pan-Am. Scientific Congress, Santiago, Chile, 1908-09; chmn. organizing com. Internat. Congress of Americanists, 1915; chmn. section of anthropology, 2d Pan-American Congress, 1915. Chmn. mng. com. School of Am. Archæology; pres. Washington Acad. Sciences, 1917-18. Chmn. com. on anthropology of Nat. Research Council, 1917. Home: Washington, D.C. Died Apr. 20, 1933.

HOLSTEIN, Otto, geographer; b. Lexington, Ky., Jan. 14, 1883; s. Otto and Emilie Octavia (Gilman) H.; ed. pub. schs., Bourbon County, Ky., and S. Am. univs.; m. Ester San Martin, Aug. 20, 1911; children—Otto, Ester (dec.), Marion. With Panama R.R., 1908, Cerro de Pasco Ry., Peru, 1908-09; supt. of transportation and gen. supt. Central Ry. of Peru and supt. transportation, Guayaquil & Quito Ry., Ecuador, 1909-14; econ. survey in Brazil for Mercantile Bank of the Americas, 1920; with Northern Peru Mining & Smelting Co., 1922-27; sec. Am. Chamber Commerce of Mexico, 1927-31; prof. extraordinary of geography, Nat. U. of Mexico, 1927—. Served as lt. Philippines Constabulary, 1904-07; capt. Signal Corps, later F.A., U.S.A., later maj., F.A., 1915-19; spl. duty in Balkans, 1919-20; maj. Officers Res. Corps; grad. of Army War College, 1932; col. and aide de camp, staff of gov. of Ky. Fellow Royal Econ. Soc. (London), Royal Asiatic Soc., Royal Geog. Soc. (London), Royal Scottish Geog. Soc. (Edinburgh). Awarded Philippine Constabulary Service Medals, Mexican Border and World War Medals (U.S.), 4 war medals, Italy, 2 war medals, France; decorated Grand Officer Order of St. Stanislas, 2d Class, Order St. Anne, 2d Class, Order Vladimir, 4th Class (Russia); Comdr. Order Star of Rumania, with Swords; Comdr. Order of Prince Danilo I (Montenegro); Comdr. Order Polonia Restituta (Poland); Officer Order of St. Sava, 4th Class (Serbia); Officer Order Condor of the Andes (Bolivia); Order of Abdon Calderon, 2d Class (Ecuador); etc. Contbr. articles to 13th edit. Ency. Brit. Died Mar. 23, 1934.

HOLT, Adoniram Judson, clergyman; b. Somerset, Ky., Dec. 1, 1847; s. Aaron and Miriam (Buckner) H.; pvt. C.S.A., 1863-65; A.M., McKenzie Coll., Tex., 1866; Southern Bapt. Theol. Sem., 1874-76, 1881-83, grad. 1883; Ps.M., Atlanta Sch. of Psychology, 1899; D.D., Keachi Coll., La., 1887, Baylor U., Tex., 1888; m. Emma Dennis, June 16, 1875; children—Judson Toy, Mrs. Mittase Lockey, John Broadus, Verna, Carroll, Mrs. Carrie C. Wall. Ordained Bapt. ministry, 1868; 1st missionary to wild Indians of Ind. Ty. 4 yrs.; built 1st house of worship in what was later Okla. Ty.; pastor Webberville, Tex., 1870-74, missionary to Indians, 1878; pastor Denison, Tex., 1879-80, Portland Av. Ch., Louisville, Ky., 1880-82; supt. missions, Tex., 1882-89; visited Palestine, 1889-90; pastor Nacogdoches, Tex., 1890-92; sec. missions in Tenn., 1892-1902; pres. Tenn. Coll., 1905; pastor South Knoxville, 1905-09, Chickasha, Okla., 1909-10, Kissimmee, Fla., 1911-15, Arcadia, Fla., 6 yrs.; editor Florida Baptist Witness, 1916-17; later pastor 1st Ch., Punta Gorda, Fla. Pres. Tenn. Bapt. Pastors' Conf., 1905-09, Okla. Bapt. Conv., 1910-11, Fla. Bapt. Pastors' Conf., 1912—; trustee Southern Bapt. Theol. Sem. 10 yrs.; supt. Bapt. Orphanage, Tenn., 8 yrs. Author: Missionary Manual, 1884; Miriam Heth (5th edit.), 1889; Parthenia, 1890; Pastor's Record, 1923; Pioneering in the Southwest, 1923; The Seminole. Home: Arcadia, Fla. Died May 15, 1933.

HOLT, Arthur Erastus, denominational sec.; b. Longmont, Colo., Nov. 23, 1876; s. Asa Dutton and Fanny (Merrill) H.; A.B., Colorado Coll., 1898; Ph.D., U. of Chicago, 1904; studied McCormick Theol. Sem., 1903-04, Yale Theol. Sem., 1898-99; m. Grace Louise Bradshaw, Dec. 27, 1904; children—Frances Merrill, John Bradshaw, Florence Eugenie. Ordained Congl. ministry, 1904; pastor 1st Ch., Pueblo, Colo., 1904-09, 1st Ch., Manhattan, Kan., 1909-16, 1st Presbyn. Ch., Ft. Worth, Tex., 1916-19; apptd. social service sec. Congl. Ch., 1919; later prof. social ethics, Chicago Theol. Sem. and Divinity Sch. of U. of Chicago; also dir. research and survey of Chicago Congl. Union; nat. sec. of social edn. of Congl. Chs.; regional consultant for India, Burma and Ceylon, foreign work survey of Y.M.C.A. and Y.W.C.A., 1929-30; visiting prof. Sir Darabji Tata Sch. Social Service, Bombay, India, winter quarter 1936-37; lecturer Rauschenbusch Foundation, 1938. Author: The Bible as a Community Book, 1919; Social Work in the Church, 1922; Christian Fellowship and Modern Industry, 1923; Christian Ideals and Industry (with F. E. Johnson), 1923; The Fate of the Family, 1938; This Nation Under God, 1939. Home: Chicago, Ill. Died Jan. 13, 1942.

HOLT, Byron Webber, financial writer; b. Rutland, O., Dec. 12, 1857; s. Columbus Burse and Emira Jane (Nobles) H.; B.A., Cornell U., 1890; m. Elizabeth G. Kinsella, Nov. 25, 1891. Asst. sec., 1890-92, sec., 1892-1902, tariff com. of the Reform Club; editor lit. bur. Dem. Congressional Com., 1902-05; writing sec. for Gov. W. L. Douglas, of Mass., 1905; editor Moody's Magazine (financial), 1905-08; mgr. investment dept. Warren W. Erwin & Co., 1908-17; with Goodbody & Co., New York, 1917—. Testified before the Industrial Commn., 1901, as a tariff expert. Treasurer of Schalkenbach Foundation. Democrat. Agnostic. Author: Gold Supply and Prosperity, 1907. Home: Maplewood, N.J. Died Dec. **11, 1933.**

HOLT, Charles Sumner, lawyer; b. Chicago, Oct. 21, 1855; s. De Villo R. and Ellen M. (Hubbard) H.; A.B., Williams Coll., 1874; student Harvard Law Sch., 1878; m. Camilla McPherson, Oct. 9, 1889. In practice at Chicago, 1878—; sr. law firm of Holt, Cutting & Sidley. Independent Republican. Dir. McCormick Theol. Sem.; trustee Williams Coll., Chicago Orphan Asylum; pres. Presbyn. Brotherhood America. Home: Chicago, Ill. Died Dec. 13, 1918.

HOLT, Erastus Eugene, Sr., ophthalmologist, otologist; b. Peru, Me., June 1, 1849; s. Erastus and Lucinda (Packard) H.; ed. Hebron Acad. and Westbrook and Gorham Sems.; in mercantile life 5 yrs.; then in study and teaching; M.D., Bowdoin, 1874; M.D., Coll. Phys. and Surg. (Columbia), 1875; studied ophthalmology and otology in Europe, 1881; hon. A.M., Colby U., 1897; LL.D., U. of Me., 1904; m. Mary Brooks Dyer, Oct. 9, 1876. Demonstrator anatomy, Bowdoin, 1875-77; founded Me. Eye and Ear Infirmary, Portland, 1886, becoming exec. surgeon and supt. Secured passage of act in Me. legislature, 1891, for prevention of blindness. Founded Portland Med. Club, 1876, Me. Acad. Medicine and Science, 1894; one of founders, N.E. Ophthal. Soc. Commd. 1st lt. Med. R.C., 1917; assigned as med. aide to governor of Me. in formation and supervision of med. advisory bds.; also duty at Bur. War Risk Ins., Washington, D.C., for development and establishment of disability rating. Mason. Home: Portland, Me. Died Oct. 2, 1931.

HOLT, George Chandler, judge; b. Mexico, N.Y., Dec. 31, 1843; s. Hiram and Marian (Chandler) H.; A.B., Yale, 1866, LL.D., 1904; LL.B., Columbia, 1869; m. Mary Louisa Bowen, Oct. 12, 1871; 1 son, Hamilton H. Admitted to bar, 1869, and practiced at New York, 1869-98; referee in bankruptcy, 1898-1903; U.S. dist. judge, Southern Dist., of N.Y., Mar. 10, 1903-Jan. 1914, resigned. Independent. Lecturer federal jurisprudence, Columbia, 1890, on admiralty, Cornell, 1906, on patents, Columbia, 1912. Home: Woodstock, Conn. Died Jan. 26, 1931.

HOLT, George Hubbard, capitalist; b. Chicago, Ill., July 28, 1852; s. DeVillo R. and Ellen (Hubbard) H.; ed. Dearborn Sem. and Lake Forest Acad.; unmarried. Started in lumber business with father, 1869; pres. Holt Lumber Company, 1899—; pres. Home Lands, Inc., Holt Timber Co., Geo. H. Holt & Co. Owner of the Manhattan Bldg.; pres. Policy-Holders' Union; v.p. Columbian Nat. Life Ins. Co., of Boston. Republican. Presbyn. Homes: Lake Forest, Ill., and Chicago, Ill. Died Feb. 9, 1924.

HOLT, Guy, publisher; b. Boston, Jan. 18, 1892; s. Clarence Edwin and Adele (Durand) H.; ed. N.Y. pub. schs. and Columbia U.; married; 1 dau., Cicely Elizabeth; m. 2d, Margaret Van Vechten Saunders, Sept. 6, 1923; 1 dau., Margaret Van Vechten. With Doubleday, Page & Co., 1909-14; mng. editor Lippincott's Mag., 1914-15, McBride's Mag., 1915-16; in charge book editorial and sales depts., Robert McBride & Co., 1917-26; also sec. of co.; an organizer, 1926, sec. until 1930, The John Day Co.; dir. Whittlesey House. Editor: Jurgen and the Law, 1923; A Bibliography of the Writings of James Branch Cabell, 1924. Died Apr. 21, 1934.

HOLT, Henry, author, publisher; b. Baltimore, Jan. 3, 1840; s. Dan and Ann Eve (Siebold) H.; A.B., Yale, 1862; LL.B., Columbia, 1864; LL.D., U. of Vt., 1901; hon. Phi Beta Kappa, Johns Hopkins U., 1914; m. Mary Florence West, June 11, 1863 (died 1879); m. 2d, Florence Taber, Dec. 2, 1886. Began pub. business with G. P. Putnam, 1863; pres. Henry Holt & Co., 1873—. Trustee and councilor Am. Soc. Psych. Research. Mem. first exec. com. of Simplified Spelling Bd.; 1st chmn. New York U. Settlement Soc.; 1st chmn. University Club Library; trustee Geog. Soc. New York, 1891-1910; fellow A.A.A.S. Member Harvard Overseers Visiting Com. on philosophy and psychology, 1915—. Has lectured at Yale, Columbia, and at U. of Vt. Author: Calmire—Man and Nature, 1892; Talks on Civics, 1901; Sturmsee—Man and Man, 1905; On the Civic Relations, 1907; On the Cosmic Relations, 1914, 2d edit. The Cosmic Relations and Immortality, 1919; Garrulities of an Octogenarian Editor, 1923. Editor The Unpartizan (late the Unpopular) Review, 1914-21. Homes: New York, and Burlington, Vt. Died Feb. 13, 1926.

HOLT, Lawrence Shackleford, mfr.; b. Alamance County, nr. Burlington, N.C., May 17, 1851; s. Edwin M. and Emily (Farish) H.; ed. Dr. Alexander Wilson's Sch., Melville, N.C., Horner Mil. Sch., Oxford, Davidson Coll., 1 yr.; m. Margaret Locke Erwin, Apr. 2, 1872 (died 1918). Began in wholesale grocery business, Charlotte, 1869; an organizer, 1874, and for many years dir., Commercial Nat. Bank, Charlotte; received from father, 1873, one-fifth interest in Alamance and Carolina Cotton Mills and became actively identified with the business; built with brother, L. Banks, the Belmont Cotton Mills; organized and built the E. M. Holt Plaid Mills, Burlington, N.C., 1883; with others purchased the Altamahaw Cotton Mills, 1884 (now the Holt, Grant and Holt Cotton Mfg. Co.), the Lafayette (now the Aurora) Cotton Mills, and the Hiawatha (now the Gem) Cotton Mills; an incorporator and dir. Durham & Southern Ry. Co., and officer or member of many corps.; sr. mem. Lawrence S. Holt & Sons. Said to be the first mfr. in the South, voluntarily to shorten the hours of labor, which he did in 1886 and 1902. Home: Burlington, N.C. Died Jan. 15, 1937.

HOLT, L(uther) Emmett, physician; b. Webster, N.Y., Mar. 4, 1855; s. Horace and Sabrah (Curtice) H.; A.B., U. of Rochester, 1875, A.M., 1878; M.D., College of Physicians and Surgeons (Columbia U.), 1880; (LL.D., Rochester, 1902; Sc.D., Columbia U., 1904, Brown U., 1914); m. Linda Mairs, Apr. 26, 1886. Prof. diseases of children, N.Y. Polyclinic, 1890-1901; clin. prof. diseases of children, 1901—. Coll. Phys. and Surg.; physician in chief Babies Hosp. Mem. bd. dirs. and sec. Rockefeller Inst. Med. Research; trustee U. of Rochester, 1902—. Author: Care and Feeding of Children, 1894, 1902, 18; Diseases of Infancy and Childhood, 1896, 1902, 18. Address: New York, N.Y. Died Jan. 14, 1924.

HOLT, Roland, dramatic critic; b. New York City, Dec. 18, 1867; s. Henry and Mary Florence (West) H.; A.B., Yale U., 1890 (honor in English); m. Constance D'Arcy Mackay, Apr. 11, 1923. Dramatic critic of New Haven Palladium, at college; with Henry Holt & Co., pubs., 1890—, v.p., 1903-24. Visited theatres in Europe, 1896, 1901, 10, 24, 29, and has lectured in many cities on "The Power of the Playgoer," "The Great Little Theaters," "Play Hunting in England, France and Italy," etc. Dir. New York Drama League; for yrs. dir. of Oratorio Soc. of New York (treas. 1916-17), and of Century Opera Co. Democrat. Author: "A List of Music for Plays and Pageants" (1925). New York dramatic editor Cleveland Topics. Home: New York, N.Y. Died July 5, 1931.

HOLT, William Henry, lawyer; b. Bath County, Ky., Nov. 29, 1842; s. Gideon J. and Frances (Tyler) H.; ed. Twinsburg Inst., Ohio, Ft. Edward (N.Y.) Inst.; LL.B., New York Law U., Albany, 1862; LL.D., Ky. U., 1900; m. Sarah Roberts, Oct. 19, 1864. Practiced law, Mt. Sterling, Ky., 1863-84; judge Ky. Ct. of Appeals, Frankfort, 1884-93; chief justice of Ky., 1891-92; practiced law at Frankfort, 1893-1900; first U.S. dist. judge of P.R., 1900-04; practicing law, Louisville, Ky., 1904—. Past Grand Master Odd Fellows of Ky. Presbyn. Republican. Home: Pewee Valley, Ky. Died Mar. 6, 1919.

HOLT, William Sylvester, clergyman; b. Mt. Hawkins, Ill., Aug. 24, 1848; s. Wilson and Abigail Jerusha (Richmond) H.; A.B., Ripon (Wis.) Coll., 1870, M.A., 1873; McCormick Theol. Sem., Chicago, 1870-71; grad. Auburn (N.Y.) Theol. Seminary, 1873; D.D., Ripon Coll., 1892; LL.D., Albany Coll., 1915; m. Frances Adella Pratt, May 28, 1873; children—Abbie May (dec.), William Wilson Pratt, Laura, Edward Chester, Cleveland Byron, Margaret Richmond. Ordained Presbyn. ministry, 1873; sent as missionary to China, 1873; supt. Presbyn. Mission Press, Shanghai, 1876-85; missionary to the Chinese in Ore. and Wash., 1885-98; synodical missionary, Ore., 1898-1909; field sec. of Bd. of Home Missions, Pacific Coast dist., 1909-13; asso. sec. Bd. of Ministerial Relief and Sustentation, Phila., 1913-19; asso. gen. sec. New Era Movement of Presbyn. Ch. U.S.A., 1918-20; asso. sec. Bd. of Ministerial Relief and Sustenance, 1920—. Was moderator Presbytery and Synod of Ore.; corr. editor Pacific Presbyterian. Trustee Albany (Ore.) Coll.; dir. San Francisco Theol. Sem. (pres.). Republican. Mason. Home: Portland, Ore. Died Nov. 25, 1931.

HOLTON, Henry Dwight, surgeon; b. Rockingham, Vt., July 24, 1838; s. Elihu Dwight and Nancy (Grout) H.; ed. Saxton's River Sem.; M.D., Univ. Med. Coll. (New York U.), 1860; hon. A.M., U. of Vt., 1873; m. Ellen Jane Hoit, Nov. 19, 1862. Surgeon 12th Vt. Vols. in Civil War; prof. pathology and therapeutics, U. of Vt., 1873-86; med. examiner Vt. Asylum for Insane, 1873-78; mem. Vt. State Bd. of Health, 1896— (sec. and exec. officer, 1897—; consulting surgeon Mary Fletcher Hosp.; pres. Leland and Gray Sem., 1897—. Mem. Vt. Senate, 1884, Ho. of Rep., 1888; del.-at-large Rep. Nat. Conv., 1896; trustee U. of Vt., 1872-90; commr. Nat. Nicaragua Canal Conv., 1892, Chicago Expn., 1893. Pres. Conn. River Valley Med. Soc., 1869, Vt. State Med. Soc., 1873, Am. Congress Tuberculosis, 1901, Am. Pub. Health Assn., 1902 (treas. 9 yrs., many yrs. exec. com., hon. mem., 1915); pres. bd. trustees and chmn. exec. com. Pan-Am. Med Congress, 1893; pres. Vt. Soc. S.A.R., 1906; mem. Nat. Conf. Charities and Corrections, 1905; del. Internat. Med. Congress, 1875. Pres. Vt. Nat. Bank. Pres. trustees of Austine Instn. Author of Posological Tables (2 editions). Address: Brattleboro, Vt. Died Feb. 12, 1917.

HOLYOKE, Edward, clergyman; b. Galesburg, Ill., Oct. 7, 1858; s. Samuel Greenleaf and Amanda Lovisa (Hoag) H.; A.B., Knox Coll., 1881, D.D., 1931; A.M., Colgate, 1884, D.D., 1904; post-grad. work Brown U., 1890-93, D.D., 1918; m. Martha S. Douglass, July 16, 1885. Acting pastor, Bainbridge, N.Y., 1883-84; ordained Bapt. ministry, 1884; pastor 1st Ch., Pittsfield, Mass., 1884-87, Calvary Ch., Providence, 1887-1931, emeritus; pastor of First Church, Elmira, N.Y., 1932-34. Pres. R.I. Christian Endeavor Union, 1889-90, R.I. Bapt. Edn. Soc., 1895-97, R.I. Federation of Chs., 1910-12, R.I. Permanent Council; v.p. Bapt. State Conv.; pres. R.I. Anti-Saloon League. Lecturer at Colgate and Newton theol. sems. Home: Providence, R.I. Died Dec. 19, 1940.

HOMER, William J., prison warden; b. Elmira, N.Y., Feb. 1, 1869; s. William H. and Mary (Haight) H.; ed. Elmira Acad. and Warner's Business Coll., Elmira; m. Margaret J. Earl, June 18, 1890. Began in employ passenger dept. Erie R.R.; supt. Bradstreet Co., Elmira, 1900-07; mfr. boxes and shipping cases, 1907-11; warden, Great Meadow Prison, 1911—. Democrat. Conglist. Address: Comstock, N.Y. Died Oct. 5, 1919.

HOMER, Winslow, artist; b. Boston, Feb. 24, 1836; learned lithographing, 1854-56; engaged in drawing on block for wood engravers, and moved to New York; pupil night sch., Nat. Acad. Design, 1860-61; exhibited first pictures, 1863; studied at Paris, 1867. Splty. figure pieces, particularly negro studies; exhibited at Salon, 1867, 1877, and at other times; at Centennial Expn., Phila., 1876; frequently at Nat. Acad. A.N.A., 1864, N.A., 1865; mem. Am. Acad. Arts and Letters. Address: Scarboro, Me. Died 1910.

HONAN, James Henry, physician; b. Delphi, Ind., Nov. 6, 1859; s. James and Catharine (Dwyer) H.; Chicago Sch. of Tech.; U. of Chicago; M.D., Rush Med. Coll. (U. of Chicago), 1895; M.D., Royal Friedrich Wilhelm U., Berlin, 1897; post-grad. study London, Leipzig, Dresden; spl. work in cardio-vascular diseases in royal clinic, Berlin; certificate for scientific med. attainments conferred by Prussian Govt., 1909; m. Mary McMahon, April 20, 1896. Surgeon, Erie Ry., Ind. and Ill. to 1896; practiced in Berlin, Germany; until 1909, at Bad-Nauheim, Germany, and Augusta, Ga., 1909—; spl. lecturer on cardio-vascular diseases, U. of Ga., 1910—. Del. Internat. Md. Congress, Moscow, 1897; hon. pres. Anglo-Am. Med. Assn. in Berlin (pres.). Author: Carbonic Acid Baths in the Treatment of Chronic Heart Diseases, 1910; Chronic Heart Disease with Early Diagnostic Symptoms, 1911; Honan's Handbook to Medical Europe, 1912, 2d edit., 1913; What Heart Patients Should Know and Do, 1913; Clinical Observations of Carbonic Acid Brine Baths on the Circulation, 1913. Address: Bad-Nauheim, Germany; and Augusta, Ga. Died Nov. 11, 1917.

HONAN, William Francis, surgeon; b. Maysville, Ky.; s. Anthony and Anna Eliza (Bryan) H.; M.D., New York Homœ. Med. Coll. and Hosp., 1889; m. Annette Newdecker Dickey. Practiced in New York, 1889—; prof. clin. surgery N.Y. Homœ. Med. Coll. and Flower Hosp.; attending surgeon Met. Hosp. Dept. of Public Welfare; visiting surgeon Flower Hosp.; consulting surgeon 5th Av. Hosp., Carson C. Peck Memorial Hosp. Colonel M.R.C.; comdg. officer Gen. Hosp. 81. Catholic. Home: New York, N.Y. Died Oct. 7, 1935.

HONEY, Robertson, foreign service officer; b. Montevallo, Ala., Aug. 17, 1870; s. Samuel Robertson and Mary Jones Buffington Slaymaker (Edwards) H.; grad. U.S. Mil. Acad., 1893; LL.B., U. of Md., 1896; m. Mabel Elsworth Boggs, Nov. 16, 1904; children—Robertson, Marcus Elsworth. Served in U.S. Army, 1893-98 (resigned); maj. 13th Heavy Arty., N.Y., 1900-01; made unsuccessful efforts to reënter service, World War. Admitted to bar, Md., N.Y. and Supreme Court of U.S.; practiced in N.Y. City; asst. dist. atty., N.Y. County; apptd. U.S. Consul, Madrid, Spain, 1914, at Catania, Sicily, 1916-18, Bristol, Eng., 1918-24; foreign service officer, Bermuda, 1924-29, Nice, France, 1929-33, Calgary, Alberta, Can., 1933—. Episcopalian. Home: New York, N.Y. Died Aug. 30, 1941.

HONEY, Samuel Robertson, lawyer; b. Eng., 1842; s. William and Sarah Waynman (Robertson) H.; ed. in Eng.; taught sch. 2 yrs.; came to America, 1860; m. Mary Edwards; m. 2d, Frances H. Arkless, Feb. 21, 1906. Served pvt., corpl., sergt. and sergt. maj., 2d Batt., 15 U.S. Inf., Aug. 20, 1860-Aug. 13, 1862; 2d lt., Aug. 13, 1862; 1st lt. and adj., 1st Batt., 15th U.S. Inf., Feb. 17, 1863; capt. 33d Inf., Nov. 1, 1866; bvtd. capt., Sept. 1, 1864, "for gallant and meritorious services during Atlanta Campaign and at Battle of Jonesboro, Ga." (severely wounded); participated in Chickamauga, Missionary Ridge and Atlanta campaigns; acting asst. judge advocate gen. staffs of Generals Pope and Meade, 1867-68; hon. discharged at own request, Oct. 7, 1870. Read law with Judge W. P. Chilton, of Montgomery, Ala.; admitted to bar, 1869, to U.S. Supreme Court, 1887; retired from practice, Dec., 1905. Chief of staff to Gov. Van Zandt, 1877-79; lt. gov. of R.I., 1887-88; mayor of Newport, 1891-92; mem. Dem. Nat. Com., 1888-96; del. Dem. Nat. Convs., 1892, 1904; leader of Ho. of Rep., R.I., 1893-94. Mason. Home: Newport, R.I. Died Feb. 17, 1927.

HONEYCUTT, Francis Webster, army officer; b. San Francisco, Calif., May 26, 1883; s. John Thomas (capt. U.S.A.) and Jennie (Webster) H.; B.S., U.S. Mil. Acad., 1904; hon. grad. Command and Gen. Staff Sch., Ft. Leavenworth, Kan., 1923; grad. Army War Coll., Washington, D.C., 1929; m. Margaret Harmon, Aug. 28, 1910; children—John Thomas (U.S.A.), Margaret (wife of Donald P. Graul, U.S.A.), Jane. Commd. 2d lt., Arty. Corps, U.S. Army, June 15, 1904, and advanced through the grades to brig. gen., June 1, 1938; assigned to field arty., 1907; served as lt. col. and col., field arty., with A.E.F., 1917-19. Decorated Victory Campaign Medal. Mason. Presbyterian. Inter-collegiate fencing champion, 1903, 1904, capt. Am. Olympic Fencing Team, Antwerp, 1920; nat. foil champion, 1921; capt. Am. Fencing Team vs. British, in U.S., 1921, in England, 1923. Died Sept. 20, 1940.

HONLINE, Moses Alfred, religious educator; b. Hillsboro, O., May 19, 1873; s. Andrew and Ellen (Allen) H.; Otterbein U., Westerville, O., 1897-98, D.Litt., 1912; Ohio State U., 1898-1902; Columbia U., New York, 1912; Union Theol. Sem., 1912; m. DeForest Wenger, Aug. 10, 1907; 1 son, Robert Wenger. Ednl. sec. Ohio S.S. Assn., 1905-10; dir. religious edn., U.B. Ch., 1908-12; sec. religious edn. Internat. Y.M.C.A., 1911-14; prof. religious edn., Bonebrake Theol. Sem., Dayton, O., 1914-17; ednl. supt. Internat. S.S. Assn., 1917-20. Author: A Chart of Old Testament and Contemporaneous History, 1904; A Chart of Old Testament History, 1905; Man and His Ancestors, 1928; An Outline of New Testament History, 1929. Home: Pasadena, Calif. Died Mar. 14, 1932.

HOOD, Charles Crook, army officer; b. Somerset, O., Aug. 28, 1841; s. Thomas and Sarah H.; ed. pub. schs. of Somerset; m. Frances Skinner, Sept. 14, 1876. Pvt., corporal and sergt. Co. G, 31st Ohio Inf., Aug. 20, 1861-Feb. 3, 1864; 1st lt., Feb. 3, 1864; capt., Oct. 26, 1864, hon. mustered out of vol. service, July 20, 1865; capt. 41st U.S. Inf., July 28, 1866; transferred to 24th Inf., Nov. 11, 1869; maj. 7th Inf., July 4, 1892; lt. col., 19th Inf., Jan. 28, 1897; col. 16th Inf., May 5, 1899; brig. gen. U.S.A., Oct. 18, 1902; retired at own request, after 40 yrs.' service, Nov. 25, 1902. Wounded in skirmish with Roddy's Cav., Apr., 1863, and at battle of Chickamauga, Sept. 20, 1863. Served 4 yrs. in P.R. and P.I. Address: New York, N.Y. Died June 13, 1927.

HOOD, E(dmund) Lyman, theologian; b. Ravenna, O., Aug. 18, 1858; s. Edmund Bostwick and Mary (Lyman) H.; U. of Minn., 1877-80; B.D., Yale, 1885; grad. student in Europe, 1885-86; A.M., U. of Calif., 1896, fellow, 1897-98; Ph.D., New York U., 1899; m. Jessie Raymond, Jan. 28, 1886 (died 1922); children—Paul Kendall, Charis, Helen; m. 2d, Margaret Evans, Oct. 5, 1925. Supt. missions and schs. of Congl. Ch. in the Southwest, 1886-94; pres. and prof. ch. history, Atlanta (Ga.) Theol. Sem., 1905-19; pastor River Edge, N.J., 1919-24; prof. Honolulu Theol. Sem., 1924—, also prof. philosophy and ethics, U. of Hawaii. Mem. Internat. Council Congl. Chs., London, 1891, Boston, 1899, Edinboro, 1908. Mason. Author: Pedagogy in the Middle Ages, 1898; History of the National Council of the Congregational Churches, 1901; History of the Greek Russian Church in America, 1902; History of the New West Education Commission, 1905; Christ in the Church and in Literature, 1911. Died Aug. 14, 1931.

HOOD, Edwin Milton, newspaperman; b. Washington, D.C., Nov. 17, 1858; s. Henry Omen and Lura (Rymph) H.; ed. pub. schs., Washington; m. Sophie Ely, Oct. 4, 1883. With Associated Press, 1875—, beginning as office boy; has filled every position up to div. supt.; later dean corps of Washington correspondents. Home: Washington, D.C. Died Aug. 8, 1923.

HOOD, Horace, editor; b. Madisonville, Tenn., July 9, 1853; s. Alexander and Sallie (Frow) H.; ed. pub. schs. and under pvt. tutors; m. Susie Brame, May 27, 1875. Editor The Advance, Montgomery, 1873, Selma Daily Echo, 1874, Monroe Journal, 1875-85, Montgomery Daily Dispatch, 1885-87, Montgomery Journal, 1898—; mem. Ala. Ho. of Rep., 1898; apptd. sheriff Montgomery County, 1907, and elected to same office 1912. Democrat. Presbyterian. Home: Montgomery, Ala. Died 1925.

HOOD, James Walker, bishop; b. Kennett Tp., Chester County, Pa., May 30, 1831; s. Levi and Harriett (Walker) H.; went to school a few months only in New Castle Co., Del., and Chester Co., Pa., bet. yrs. 1841 and 1845; other gen. and theol. studies without a teacher; had tutor for Greek; (D.D., Lincoln U., Pa.; LL.D., Livingstone Coll., N.C.); m. Hannah L. Ralph, Sept. 1852; m. 2d, Sophia J. Nugent, May, 1858; m. 3d, Mrs. Keziah P. McKoy, June 6, 1877. Minister A.M.E. Zion Ch., 1858; sent from N.E. Conf., 1860, as missionary to Nova Scotia; missionary to freedmen within Union lines in N.C., 1863; mem. N.C. Const. Conv., 1868; asst. supt. pub. instrn. of N.C., 1868; ordained bishop, July 3, 1872; later senior bishop Am. M.E. Zion Ch. Author: The Negro in the Christian Pulpit, 1884; One Hundred Years of the Methodist Episcopal Zion Church, 1895; The Plan of the Apocalypse, 1900; Second Book of Sermons, 1908. Pres. trustees Livingstone Coll., Salisbury, N.C., 1879—. Address: Fayetteville, N.C. Died Oct. 30, 1918.

HOOD, John, naval officer; b. Florence, Ala., Dec. 3, 1859; s. John Murray and Mary Cornelia (Heslep) H.; grad. U.S. Naval Acad., 1879; m. Rosalie, d. Thomas Thompson Caswell, Jan. 28, 1890. Commd. midshipman, June 10, 1881; promoted through grades to rear admiral, Aug. 29, 1916. Wrecked with the Kearsarge, Feb. 2, 1894; blown up on Maine, Feb. 15, 1898; comd. Hawk during Spanish-Am. War, carried information of arrival of Spanish Squadron at Santiago to comdr. of Flying Squadron at Cienfuegos, and delivered orders for him to proceed to Santiago, May 23, 1898; made survey for Pacific Cable, 1899-1900, and prepared charts and data by which cable was laid; comd. Elcano in Chinese waters during Russo-Japanese War, 1903-05; comd. Tacoma, 1907-09, regulating Haitian and Central Am. revolutions and elections; comd. ships at Naval Acad., 1909-10; comd. Rhode Island, Atlantic Fleet, 1910-11; comd. Delaware, Atlantic Fleet, 1911-12, and won battle efficiency pennant; mem. Gen. Bd. of Navy, 1912-15; comd. Texas, Atlantic Fleet, 1915-16, won the battle efficiency pennant and gunnery trophy for the year, and awarded the "Red E" for excellence in engring. efficiency; comd. reserve force, U.S. Atlantic Fleet, Oct. 30, 1916-Apr. 6, 1917; ordered to command 4th Div., Atlantic Fleet, on mobilization of reserve for war, Apr. 6, 1917. Home: Florence, Ala. Died Feb. 11, 1919.

HOOD, Ozni Porter, mechanical engr.; b. Lowell, Mass., June 14, 1865; s. Harrison Porter and Vesta (Merrill) H.; Worcester Poly. Inst., 1882-83; B.S. in mech. engring., Rose Poly. Inst., 1885, M.S., 1895, M.E., 1898, Dr. Eng., 1933; m. Gertrude Benight, July 31, 1884; children—Ben Benight, Karl Kedzie, Harrison Porter. Began as pattern maker, 1885; supt. shops, 1886-89, supt. shops and prof. engring., 1889-98, Kan. State Agrl. Coll., Manhattan; prof. mech. and elec. engring., Mich. Coll. of Mines, 1898-1911; consulting engr. in mech. engring. relating to mines, 1900-11; chief mech. engr., U.S. Bur. Mines, 1911-26; chief of technologic br. U.S. Bur. of Mines, 1926—. Home: Washington, D.C. Died Apr. 22, 1937.

HOOD, Raymond Mathewson, architect; b. Pawtucket, R.I., Mar. 29, 1881; s. John Parmenter and Vella (Mathewson) H.; student Brown U., 1898-99; B.S., Mass. Inst. Tech., 1903; Architecte Diplomé par le Gouvernement Français, École, des Beaux Arts, Paris, France, 1911; hon. M.A., Brown U.; m. Elsie E. Schmidt, Oct. 25, 1920; children—Raymond, Trientje, Richard. Began practice in New York City, 1914. Mem. Am. Inst. Architects. Decorated Chevalier Order of Crown of Belgium. Home: Stamford, Conn. Died Aug. 14, 1934.

HOOD, William, civil engr.; b. Concord, N.H., Feb. 4, 1846; s. Joseph Edward and Maria (Savage) H.; B.S., Chandler Scientific Dept., Dartmouth, 1867; D.Sc., Dartmouth, 1923. With field engring. party, 1867-68; asst. engr., 1868-72, Central Pacific Ry.; asst. engr., 1872-75, chief asst. engr., 1875-83, S.P. R.R.; chief asst. engr., June-Oct. 10, 1883, chief engr., 1883-85, Central Pacific Ry.; chief engr. Southern Pacific Co. until May 3, 1921, retired. Home: San Francisco, Calif. Died Aug. 26, 1926.

HOOGEWERFF, John Adrian, naval officer; b. Howard County, Md., Nov. 27, 1860; s. Samuel Evans and Mary Elizabeth (Duval) H.; student Pa. Mil. Acad., 1875-76; grad. U.S. Naval Acad., 1881, Naval War Coll., 1913-14; m. Edwardine L. Hiester, Oct. 10, 1889. Ensign jr. grade, July 1, 1883; promoted through grades to capt., Mar. 4, 1911; temporary rear admiral, Aug. 31, 1917; permanent rear admiral, July 1, 1918. Landed with U.S. force at Alexandria, Egypt, after bombardment by British. 1882; at U.S. Naval Obs. with Prof. Asaph Hall, 1883-85; in charge Magnetic Obs., 1889-92; instr. electricity, etc., U.S. Naval Acad., 1895-98, 1901-04; served on Cincinnati, Spanish-Am. War, 1898; head Dept. Ordnance and Gunnery, U.S. Naval Acad., 1908-09; comd. Kansas, 1911-13; supt. U.S. Naval Obs., 1914-17; comd. Pennsylvania, Apr.-Sept. 1917; apptd. comdr. Mine Force, Atlantic Fleet, Sept. 1917; comdg. Battleship Div. One, Atlantic Fleet, Nov. 1917-Feb. 1919; supt. U.S. Naval Obs., Mar. 1919-June 1921; comdt. Navy Yard, Puget Sound, Wash., June 1921-Oct. 1924; retired Nov. 27, 1924. Medals for engagement at Matanzas, and for West Indian Campaign, Spanish-Am. War; Victory Medal and Navy Cross, World War. Episcopalian. Author: Magnetic Observations, 1891. Died Feb. 13, 1933.

HOOK, William Cather, judge; b. Waynesburg, Pa., Sept. 24, 1857; s. Enos and Elizabeth D. H.; LL.B., St. Louis Law School, 1878; m. Louise Dickson, Oct. 31, 1882. Practiced law, 1878-99; U.S. dist. judge, Dist. of Kan., 1899-1903; U.S. circuit judge, 8th Jud. Circuit, 1903. Chmn. Jud. Sect. of Am. Bar Assn., 1917, 18. Address: Leavenworth, Kan. Died Aug. 12, 1921.

HOOKER, Edward, comdr. U.S.N.; b. Farmington, Conn., Dec. 25, 1822; s. Edward and Elizabeth (Daggett) H.; ed. Farmington Acad.; m. Esther Ann Battey, May 11, 1851 (died 1896). Sailor and officer in merchant service, 1837-61; entered U.S. Navy, July 19, 1861; acting master on gunboat Louisiana; severely wounded, Oct. 5, 1861 (the 1st acting master wounded in the war); exec. officer of "Louisiana." Stationed at Washington, N.C., in unexpected absence of comdg. officer; comd. the ship in the fight of Sept. 5, 1862; promoted acting vol. lt. for gallantry in that action; comd. steamer Victoria, 1863, on Wilmington blockade, and captured brig. Minna and steamer Nicholai I; comd. boats on Rappahannock during advance of Gen. Grant and cleared the river of torpedoes; promoted, through various grades, to commdr. U.S.N., retiring 1884. Address: Brooklyn, N.Y. Died 1903.

HOOKER, Edward Beecher, M.D.; b. Hartford, Conn., Feb. 26, 1855; s. John and Isabella (Beecher) H.; student École de Médicine, Paris, France, 1874-75; M.D., Boston U., 1877; post-grad. work, New York, 1877-78; m. Martha Clarke Kilbourne, Sept. 18, 1879; children—Isabel Kilbourne (Mrs. Walter Gordon Merritt), Thomas (dec.), Joseph Kilbourne. In practice at Hartford, 1878—. Mem. Am. Inst. Homœopathy (pres. 1907). Mem. Hartford Vice Commn., 1912. Republican. Conglist. Home: Hartford, Conn. Died June 23, 1927.

HOOKER, Ellen Kelley, educator; b. Shoreham, Vt., May 23, 1833; d. George W. and Sibbel D. Kelley; grad. Troy Conf. Acad., Poultney, Vt., 1852; (A.E., Ingham U., 1882); m. Dr. Samuel L. Hooker, Jan. 26, 1854. Taught in Vt. and N.Y., 1848-55; pvt. sch., Black Earth, Wis., 1855-63; then asst. in work preparatory for U. of Wis.; later assisted her husband in supt.'s work in Dane County, Wis., until 1867; removed to N.Y.; taught in Le Roy Collegiate Inst. until 1876; prin. Ingham U., 1876-84; conducted Park Place Sch. for Young Ladies, Batavia, N.Y., 1884-88; prin. Sage Coll., Cornell, 1888-97; instr. English lit., Saginaw High Sch., 1899-1900; teacher psychology and administrative asst., Nat. Park Sem., Forest Glen, Md., 1901-06; tutor, Nat. Cathedral Sch., Washington, 1907-09; pvt. tutor, 1909-13. Charter mem. Coll. Women's Club, New York. Home: Le Roy, N.Y. Died Sept. 29, 1918.

HOOKER, Elon Huntington, civil engr.; b. Rochester, N.Y., Nov. 23, 1869; s. Horace B. and Susan (Huntington) H.; direct descendant of Thomas Hooker, founder, at Hartford, of the Colony of Connecticut, 1638; A.B., U. of Rochester, 1891, A.M., 1894; C.E., Cornell U., 1894, Ph.D., 1896 (European fellowship); post-grad. work Zürich (Switzerland) Polytechnicum, École des Ponts et Chaussées, Paris; m. Blanche Ferry, Jan. 25, 1901. Engring. work, 1888-98; mem. pvt. commn. inspecting Panama and Nicaragua Canal routes, 1898; deputy supt. pub. wks., N.Y., under Gov. Roosevelt, 1899-1900, under Gov. Odell, 1901; resigned, 1901, to engage in timber, mining and r.r. enterprises in the Southwest; organizer and pres. Hooker Electrochem. Co. (Niagara Falls and Tacoma). Pres. Mfg. Chemists' Assn. of the U.S., 1923, 24, 25; chmn., former pres. and dir. Research Corporation; mem. Nat. Industrial Conf. Bd. (exec. com.). Trustee U. of Rochester. Chmn. Am. Defense Soc.; treas. Progressive Nat. Com., 1912, also chmn. finance com., 1913; member Roosevelt Memorial Assn. (exec. com.). Baptist. Died May 10, 1938.

HOOKER, Forrestine Cooper, author; b. Phila., Pa., Mar. 8, 1867; d. Charles Lawrence (brig. gen. U.S.A.) and Flora (Green) Cooper (father organized Rough Riders, and named by Theodore Roosevelt, "Father of the Rough Riders"); grad. St. Joseph's Coll., Phila., 1884 (valedictorian); student Pierce Business Sch., Phila., 1910, 11; m. E. R. Hooker, May 4, 1886 (divorced 1907); children—Forrestine, Harry Edwin. Assisted in cattle work on Hooker ranches, 1886-1901; later assisted live stock insp., Willcox, Ariz., and in cattle commn. business until 1904; on editorial staff, Los Angeles Examiner, 1912-13; reorganized dept. and acted as sec. and mgr. court cases Los Angeles City and County Humane Soc. for Children; served as spl. preliminary investigator on failure to provide, under late Thomas Lee Woolwine until 1915, also active in polit. work. Assisted in promotion Soldiers' and Sailors' Welfare Bur., Los Angeles, World War. Republican. Protestant. Author: The Long Dim Trail, 1920, 21; Prince Jan, St. Bernard, 1922, 3d edit., 1929; Star—The Story of an Indian Pony, 1923, 3d edit., 1927; When Geronimo Rode, 1924, 3d edit., 1927; The Little House on the Desert, 1924, 29; Cricket—A Little Girl of the Old West, 1925; Just George, 1926; Civilizing Cricket, 1927; The Garden of the Lost Key, 1929. Home: Washington, D.C. Died Mar. 21, 1932.

HOOKER, Frank Arthur, judge; b. Hartford, Conn., Jan. 16, 1844; s. James Sedgwick and Camilla (Porter) H.; acad. edn.; LL.B., U. of Mich., 1865; m. Emma E. Carter, Aug. 5, 1868. Admitted to bar, 1865; practiced at Bryan, O., 1865-66, Charlotte, Mich., 1866-78; county supt. of schs., 1867-69; justice of the peace, 1869-72; pros. atty., 1872-76; judge 5th Jud. Circuit, Mich., 1878-93; justice Supreme Ct. of Mich., 1893-1914. Republican. Address: Lansing, Mich. Died 1911.

HOOKER, George Ellsworth, civic work; b. Peacham, Vt., Apr. 25, 1861; s. William Davenport and Esther H. (Bickford) H.; A.B., Amherst, 1883; LL.B., Columbia U. Law Sch., 1885; student Union Theol. Sem., New York, 1887-88; B.D., Yale Div. Sch., 1890; unmarried. Admitted to N.Y. bar, 1885, and practiced in N.Y. City till 1887; mem. "Yale Band" and pastor in State of Wash., under Am. Home Missionary Soc., 1890-93; traveled in Europe, 1894-95; investigated city conditions in U.S., 1896-97; sec. spl. street ry. com. of Chicago City Council, 1898; editorial writer, Chicago Tribune, 1899-1902, 1904-05; made many trips to Europe studying city problems; civic sec. City Club of Chicago, 1903-19; trade commr., Dept. of Commerce, investigating inland water transp., 1919-21; Am. labor press corr. 5th to 7th and 8th and 9th Assemblies of League of Nations, 1924, 25, 26, 28, 29, World Economic Conf., Geneva, 1927, and at 6th Pan-Am. Conf., Havana, Cuba, 1928. Mem. Chicago Plan Commn.; accompanied Chicago Ry. Terminals Commn. on European tour of investigation, summer 1914; apptd. by Gov. Dunne, 1915, chmn. Commn. to Investigate Ill. Pension Laws, and reapptd. by Gov. Lowden, 1917. Chmn. Local Exemption Bd., Div. 43, Chicago, 1917-19. Founder Inter-Am. (now World Policy) Council of Chicago, 1928. Conglist. Wrote: Report on Street Railway Franchises of Chicago, 1898; Through Routes for Chicago's Steam Railroads, 1914. Home: Chicago, Ill. Died Mar. 21, 1939.

HOOKER, Isabella Beecher, philanthropist; b. Litchfield, Conn., Feb. 22, 1822, d. Rev. Dr. Lyman Beecher; m. John Hooker, 1841. Made special study of the present right of women citizens of the U.S. to vote under the Constitution as interpreted by the Declaration of Independence; extempore public speaker; interested in various reform movements. Author: Womanhood: Its Sanctities and Fidelities. Home: Hartford, Conn. Died 1907.

HOOKER, John Daggett, mfr.; b. Hinsdale, N.H., May 10, 1838; s. Henry and Mary (Daggett) H.; ed. Hollister Acad. and Williams Coll.; m. Katharine Putnam, Aug. 26, 1869. Hardware mcht., San Francisco, 1861-76; mfr. steel pipe and established, 1885, J. D. Hooker Co., Los Angeles, of which was pres.; pres. Western Union Oil Co., 1900—; Baker Iron Works, 1895—. Invented riveting machine, 1888, patent enamel coating for water pipes, 1888. V.p. Acad. Sciences. Republican. Home: Los Angeles, Calif. Died 1911.

HOOKER, Thomas, banker; b. Macon, Ga., Sept. 3, 1849; s. Richard and Aurelia (Dwight) H.; A.B., Yale, 1869, A.M., 1872; m. Sarah A. Bowles, June 30, 1874 (died 1909). Entered banking business in New Haven, Conn., 1895; pres. New Haven Trust Co., 1902-09; v.p. 1st Nat. Bank, New Haven, 1902-09, pres. 1909-17, chmn. of the bd., 1917—; trustee Nat. Savings Bank. Pres. New Haven Dispensary; dir. New Haven Hosp. Republican. Conglist. Home: New Haven, Conn. Died Oct. 28, 1924.

HOOKER, Warren Brewster, judge; b. Perrysburg, N.Y., Nov. 24, 1856; s. John and Philena (Waterman) H.; ed. Forestville, N.Y.; m. Etta E. Abbey, Sept. 11, 1884. Admitted to bar, 1879; special surrogate Chautauqua County, 1878-1881; practiced at Tacoma, Wash., 1882-84; at Fredonia, N.Y., 1884-98; supervisor, 1889-1890; elected 52d to 56th Congresses (1891-98), 34th N.Y. Dist.; resigned, Nov. 10, 1898; apptd. Nov. 10, 1898, elected, Nov., 1899, for term 1900-13, justice Supreme Ct. of N.Y.; judge Appellate Div., 1902-08. Republican. Address: Fredonia, N.Y. Died Mar. 5, 1920.

HOON, Clarence Earl, clergyman, lecturer; b. West Middleton, Ind., Oct. 31, 1880; s. Francis Theodore and Hester Elizabeth (Quick) H.; desc. of Priscilla Alden, also William the Conqueror; attended Kokomo High Sch.; spl. student Northwestern U.; student Garrett Bible Inst., 1910; Litt.D., Lincoln Memorial U., 1928; D.D., Morningside Coll., 1928; m. Fannie

Ruth Waitman, Jan. 23, 1900; children—Bessie Evalynola, Paul Waitman. Ordained ministry M.E. Ch., 1897; pastor successively at Bayard, Clay City (Ill.), Greenstone Ch. (Chicago), Aurelia, Manson, First Ch., Sioux City (all of Ia.), Hyde Park Ch. of Cincinnati (built Hyde Park Temple), First Ch. of Seattle, Wash., 1929-32, Nardin Park Methodist Episcopal Church, Detroit, 1932—. Spl. lecturer for U.S. Treasury Dept. during World War; lecturer for Associated Advertising Clubs of the World. Mem. Portland Area Council; trustee Northwest Training Sch., Wesley Foundation, College of Puget Sound, Seattle Gen. Hosp., Ruth Home for Girls; mem. interdenominational com. Seattle Community Chest; dir. in ch. dept. of Associated Advertising Clubs of the World. Republican. Mason. Address: Detroit, Mich. Died Sept. 21, 1934.

HOOPER, Charles Edward, designer; b. at Medford, Mass., Apr. 28, 1867; s. Charles Otis and Deetta Maria (Hall) H.; pub. schs. Medford; spl. student Mass. Normal Art Sch., Boston; m. Mabel Emma Collins, Nov. 26, 1896. Draughtsman and designer in offices of Boston architects until 1894, when removed to New York and became designer of decorations for books; asst. art editor McClure's Mag., 1897-1900. Author: The Country House, 1906; Reclaiming the Old House, 1913. Home: Middle Haddam, Conn. Died May 16, 1920.

HOOPER, Franklin Henry, editor; b. Worcester, Mass., Jan. 28, 1862; s. William R. and Frances (Nelson) H.; A.B., magna cum laude, Harvard, 1883; m. Grace M. Sessions, Oct. 19, 1887; children—Catharine B., Leverett F. With Century Co., pubs., New York, 1883-96 (one of editors of Century Dictionary); lit. adviser and mgr. for James Clarke & Co., pubs., 1896-99; with Ency. Britannica (except during war period), 1899—, Am. editor 10th edit., 1902, mng. editor 11th edit., 1910, Am. editor 12th edit., 1922, 13th edit., 1926, 14th edit., 1928, and editor in chief, 1932-38, Ency. Britannica; also editor The World To-day, 1933-38; planned and edited These Eventful Years—The Twentieth Century in the Making (2 vols.), 1924; editor Britannica Junior—an Encyclopædia for Children (10 vols.), 1934. Mgr. New York office of British Ministry of Food, World War. Democrat. Episcopalian. Home: Montclair, N.J. Died Aug. 14, 1940.

HOOPER, Franklin William, institute dir.; b. Walpole, N.H., Feb. 11, 1851; s. William and Elvira (Pulsifer) H.; student Antioch Coll., O., 1867-71; A.B., Harvard, 1875, post-grad. in biology, 1875-1906, hon. A.M., 1897; LL.D., Middlebury, 1911, Antioch, 1912; m. Martha, d. Peter S. Holden, May 23, 1876. Prin. Keene (N.H.) High Sch., 1877-80; prof. natural science, Adelphi Coll., Brooklyn, 1880-89; dir. Brooklyn Inst. Arts and Sciences, 1889—. Organized Brooklyn Museum Arts and Sciences, Brooklyn Children's Museum and Brooklyn Botanic Garden. Lecturer on geology and biology; dir. Brooklyn Art Assn., 1890—; mem. Brooklyn Bd. Edn., 1892-99; dir. Brooklyn Pub. Library, 1895-1904; pres. Antioch College, Ohio, 1901-05, trustee, 1899—; trustee and sec. N.Y. State Sch. of Agr., L.I., 1912—; trustee Adelphi Coll., 1913—; sec. bd. mgrs. Biol. Lab., Cold Spring Harbor, L.I., 1890—. Editor year-books, the annual prospectus, and the Bulletin of Brooklyn Inst. of Arts and Sciences. Home: Brooklyn, N.Y. Aug. 1, 1914.

HOOPER, Jessie Annette Jack; b. Winneshiek County, Ia., Nov. 8, 1865; d. David and Mary Elizabeth (Nelings) Jack; ed. by governess; art study, Colnan Coll., Des Moines, Ia., and under D. F. Bigelow, Chicago, Ill.; m. Ben Hooper, May 30, 1888; 1 dau., Lorna (wife of Dr. Louis M. Warfield). Devoted time to philanthropic, civic and club work; former legislative and congressional chmn. Wis. Suffrage Assn.; mem. nat. bd., Nat. Am. Woman's Suffrage Assn.; chmn. internat. relations, Gen. Fed. Women's Clubs; recording sec. Conf. on Cause and Cure of War; mem. City Planning Commn., Oshkosh. Vice pres. Bemis-Hooper-Hays Co., wholesale grocers, at Oshkosh, Wis.; dir. Woman's Journal Corp. Dem. candidate for U.S. Senate, 1922. Active in securing ratification of suffrage amendment by Wis. legislature, 1919. Author of peace plan adjudged best of 400 presented before Conf. on Cause and Cure of War, 1927. Home: Oshkosh, Wis. Died May 8, 1935.

HOOPER, Joseph Lawrence, congressman; b. Cleveland, O., Dec. 22, 1877; s. Joseph R. and Florence R. (Merriam) H.; grad. high sch., Battle Creek, Mich., 1896; studied law in office of Williams & Lockton, Battle Creek; m. Leah L. Lucas, 1903 (died 1910); children—Marjorie F., Marion K.; m. 2d, Gertrude J. Clark, Sept. 15, 1923. Admitted to Mich. bar, 1899, and practiced at Battle Creek; pros. atty. Calhoun County, Mich., 1903-07; city atty. Battle Creek, 2 terms; elected mem. 69th Congress, 3d Mich. Dist., at spl. election, Aug. 18, 1925, to fill vacancy occasioned by death of Arthur B. Williams, for term expiring March 3, 1927; reëlected 70th to 72d Congresses (1927-33). Republican. Conglist. Mason, Elk. Home: Battle Creek, Mich. Died Feb. 22, 1934.

HOOPER, Osman Castle, college prof.; b. Alexandria, O., Apr. 10, 1858; s. Richard and Sarah Celestia (Castle) H.; A.B., Denison U., 1879 (L.H.D. 1918); m. Josephine Babbitt, May 20, 1880; 1 son, Richard Babbitt. Asso. editor Columbus Dispatch, 1880-86; editor and part owner Columbus News, 1886-93; editorial writer Columbus Dispatch, 1893-1917; literary editor same, 1917—; editor Ohio Newspaper, 1919-33. Prof. journalism, Ohio State U., 1918-32 (emeritus). Trustee Denison U. Author: The Joy of Things, 1910; The Shepherd Wind and Other Verses, 1916; History of Columbus, Ohio, 1919; History of the Ohio State University, 1910-25), 1925; Dodging a Sunbeam (verse), 1927; The Crisis and the Man (Samuel Medary), 1929; History of Ohio Journalism, 1933. Founder of Ohio Journalism Hall of Fame, 1928; elected only living member Ohio Journalism Hall of Fame, 1940. Home: Columbus, O. Died May 11, 1941.

HOOPER, Philo O., M.D., supt. Lunatic Asylum, 1885—; b. Little Rock, Ark., Oct. 11, 1833; s. Alanson and Maydalene H.; academic edn. at Nashville, Tenn.; M.D., Jefferson Med. Coll., Phila., 1856; m. Sept. 1860. Emeritus prof. med. dept. U. of Ark. was pres. Am. Med. Assn., State Med. Soc. and Am. Medico-Psychol. Assn. Address: Little Rock, Ark. Died 1902.

HOOPER, Shadrach K., ry. official; b. New Albany, Ind., May 30, 1841; s. D. M. and Annabelah H., ed. com. sch., New Albany, until 15 yrs. of age; m. Nancy A. Welch, May 17, 1865. At 15 began running on Ohio and Mississippi rivers; learned trade of steamboat blacksmith; enlisted in Union Army, June 1, 1861; served until Apr. 7, 1865, with armies under Grant and Sherman including March to the Sea; promoted from pvt. to corpl., q.-m.-sergt., 1st lt. and adj. and acting and bvtd. as maj. in 23d Ind. Inf. Entered ry. service Jan. 1, 1866, as clerk gen. pass. office, Louisville, New Albany & Chicago Ry.; agt. U.P. Ry., N. Platte, Neb., Mar. to Oct., 1867; chief clerk pass. dept., 1867-68, gen. pass. agt., 1868-73, Louisville, New Albany & Chicago; gen. pass. agt., Ft. Wayne, Jackson & Saginaw R.R., 1873-78; asst. gen. pass. agt., 1880-81, gen. pass. agt., 1881-84, Hannibal & St. Joseph R.R.; gen. pass. and ticket agt., Central Ia. R.R., 1884; gen. pass. and ticket agt., June 1, 1884-Oct. 1, 1910, asst. to gen. traffic mgr., Oct. 1, 1910—, D.&R.G. R.R. Co. Address: Denver, Colo. Deceased.

HOOPER, William Leslie, electrical engr.; b. Halifax, N.S., Aug. 2, 1855; s. Rev. William and Anne Jane (Whytal) H.; A.B., Tufts Coll., 1877, A.M., 1878, hon. Ph.D., 1898; m. Mary E. Heard, July 9, 1879. Instr. mathematics and sciences, 1878-80, prin., 1882, Bromfield Acad., Harvard, Mass.; asst. prof. physics, 1883-90, prof. elec. engring., 1890—, actg. pres., July 1, 1912-Nov. 15, 1914, Tufts Coll. Author: Electrical Problems, 1902. Address: Tufts College, Mass. Died Oct. 3, 1918.

HOOPER, William Thomas, clergyman; b. Bristol, Eng., Mar. 6, 1886; s. William and Maria (Norris) H.; A.B., Bishops U., Lennoxville, Quebec, Can., 1908; grad. Gen. Theol. Sem., 1913, B.D., 1914; grad. study Columbia; m. Florence Davenport Wight, June 17, 1914; children—William Thomas, Ellen Wells, Elizabeth Davenport. Instr. in chemistry, St. Paul's Sch., Concord, N.H., 1913-17; deacon, 1913, priest, 1914, P.E. Ch.; asst. rector St. John's Ch., Hartford, Conn., 1917-18, rector, 1918—. Canon of Aberdeen (Scotland) Cathedral, Aug. 1929. Mem. Bd. of Edn., West Hartford, 1923-25. Trustee Kingswood Sch., West Hartford; pres. Widows Homes, Hartford. Chmn. dept. religious Edn., Diocesan Council, 1922-28; mem. Diocesan Council, 1925. Exec. sec. Conf. of Masters and Headmasters in Ch. Schs. Republican. Mason. Home: West Hartford, Conn. Died Mar. 28, 1938.

HOOPES, Josiah, botanist, nurseryman; b. West Chester, Pa., Nov. 9, 1832; s. Pierce and Sarah (Andrews) H.; ed. public schools and Friends' Central High School, Phila.; m. Ellen A. Morgan, founder of the Maple Avenue Nurseries, in 1853, now Hoopes, Bro. & Thomas, Mar. 17, 1898. One of founders and pres. Hort. Soc. of Pa., 1869-79. Trustee West Chester State Normal School, 13 yrs. Author: Book of Evergreens, 1868. Address: West Chester, Pa. Died 1904.

HOOSE, James Harmon, college prof.; b. Cobleskill, N.Y., Jan. 24, 1835; s. Abram and Rosannah (Miller) H.; A.B., Genesee Coll. (now Syracuse U.), 1861, M.A., 1863; Ph.D., Syracuse U., 1873; LL.D., U. of Southern Calif.; m. Lemoyne Alida Hale, Nov. 29, 1861 (died 1871); m. 2d, Helen Kathleen Hubbard, July 31, 1872. Prin. Union Lit. Inst., Warnerville, N.Y., 1862; asso. teacher of English, Homer (N.Y.) Acad., 1862-63; teacher mathematics, Genesee Wesleyan Sem., Lima, N.Y., 1863-66; conductor teachers' insts., State of N.Y., 1866-68; teacher State Normal Sch., Brockport, N.Y., 1868-69; organized, 1869, prin., 1869-91, State Normal Sch., Cortland, N.Y., also temporary prin. State Normal Sch., Fredonia, N.Y., 1878, and supt. city schs., Binghamton, 1881-82; engaged in fruit-culture, Pasadena, Calif., 1891-95; prof. philosophy and edn., 1895-1909, prof. philosophy, 1895—, Coll. of Liberal Arts of U. of Southern Calif., and vice chmn. of the faculty; lecturer on logic, Law Coll. of same, 1908-09. Republican. Methodist. Home: Los Angeles, Calif. Died Aug. 31, 1915.

HOOTON, Mott, army officer; b. Phila., Apr. 16, 1838; s. Mott and Ann Eliza (Carpenter) H.; acad. edn., West Chester, Pa.; unmarried. First sergt. to capt. 1st Pa. Reserve Vols., June 4, 1861-June 13, 1864; apptd. from Pa., 2d lt. and 1st lt., 13th Inf., Feb. 23, 1866; transferred to 31st Inf., Sept. 21, 1866, to 22d Inf., May 15, 1869; capt., Aug. 5, 1872; maj., 25th Inf., May 1, 1896; lt. col., 5th Inf., Oct. 4, 1898; col. 28th Inf., Feb. 2, 1901; brig. gen., Apr. 15, 1902. Bvtd.; maj. vols., Mar. 13, 1865, "for gallant and meritorious services in Wilderness campaigns"; maj. U.S.A., Feb. 27, 1890, "for gallant services in action against Indians at Spring Creek, Mont., Oct. 15 and 16, 1876." Participated in campaigns of 7 days before Richmond, with Pope's army at Warrenton, Va., 2d battle of Bull Run (severely wounded), Gettysburg, Wilderness, etc.; after Civil War served in 13th U.S. Inf., 1866-67; 31st Inf., 1867-71; recruiting service, 1871-73; Yellowstone Expdn., 1873; New Orleans, 1874-75; Sioux campaigns, 1875-77; served in Mich., Texas, Colo., Mont., until Spanish-Am. War; served 9 mos. in Cuba; organized 28th Inf. and served in Philippines; retired by operation of law, Apr. 16, 1902. Has traveled extensively in Europe and the Far East. Home: West Chester, Pa. Died May 30, 1920.

HOOVER, Charles Franklin, M.D.; b. Miamisburg, O., Aug. 2, 1865; s. Abel and Clara Elizabeth (Hoff) H.; Ohio Wesleyan U., 1882-85; A.B., Harvard, 1887, M.D., 1892; univs. Vienna and Strassburg, 1890-94; m. Katherine Fraser, Aug. 9, 1900. Practiced in Cleveland, 1894—; teacher physical diagnosis and visiting physician, Cleveland City Hosp., 1894-1907; prof. medicine, Med. Coll. Western Reserve U., 1907—; visiting physician Lakeside Hosp. Commd. maj., Med. R.C., Apr. 15, 1917; served with Base Hosp., Unit No. 4, in France, May-Sept. 1917. Unitarian. Home: Cleveland, O. Died June 15, 1927.

HOOVER, Simon Robert, educator; b. Bedford County, Pa., Sept. 25, 1867; s. David S. and Mary Ellen (McCoy) H.; A.B., Baldwin-Wallace Coll., Berea, O., 1889; A.M. in Edn., Columbia, 1922; grad. study in accounting, Wharton Sch., U. of Pa.; m. Julia Egbert, Feb. 8, 1890; 1 dau., Haidee (Mrs. N. H. Allaman). Head of commercial dept., West High Sch., Cleveland, 1896-1909; asst. prin. West Commerce High Sch., Cleveland, 1909-29. Ordained ministry of Congregational Church. Author: The Science and Art of Salesmanship, 1916; Bookkeeping and Accounting Practice, 1920; A Son of the Nile, 1927. Address: Cleveland, O. Died June 28, 1936.

HOPE, John, univ. pres.; b. Augusta, Ga., June 2, 1868; s. James and Mary Frances (Butts) H.; grad. Worcester (Mass.) Acad., 1890; A.B., Brown U., 1894; U. of Chicago, summers 1897, 98; hon. A.M., Brown, 1907; LL.D., Howard U., Washington, 1920, Bucknell U., Lewisburg, Pa., 1923, McMaster U., Toronto, 1928, Bates Coll., 1932; m. Lugenia D. Burns, Dec. 29, 1897; children—Edward Swain, John. Has devoted entire time as teacher of colored youth; with Roger Williams U., Nashville, Tenn., 1894-98; became connected with Morehouse Coll. (then Atlanta Bapt. Coll.), 1898, pres., 1906-31, also prof. of ethics; pres. Atlanta (Ga.) U., 1929—. Y.M.C.A. war work among colored troops in France, July 1918-July 1919. Elected to Phi Beta Kappa, Brown U., 1919, "for achievements since graduation." Past pres. and dir., Commn. on Interracial Coöperation; pres. Assn. for Study of Negro Life and History, Ga. State Council for Work Among Negro Boys; dir. Atlanta Urban League, Nat. Urban League, Atlanta Sch. of Social Work, Encyclopedia of the Negro; del. to Citizens Conf. on the Crisis in Edn.; mem. Com. on Racialism of Bapt. World Alliance; mem. Gen. Bd., Nat. Council, Home Div. Com., Internat. Com., World's Com.—all of Y.M.C.A.; mem. Spingarn Medal Com.; dir. or trustee various instns. for colored people; active in amelioration of conditions among negroes in country places of the South. Republican. Baptist. Mason, Odd Fellow, K.P. Address: Atlanta, Ga. Died Feb. 22, 1936.

HOPEWELL, John, merchant, mfr.; b. Greenfield, Mass., 1845; s. John and Catherine (Maloney) H.; ed. dist. school to 14, night school, Springfield, 2 years, and business college; m. Sarah W. Blake, 1870. Became salesman for L. C. Chase & Co., 1868; L. C. & H. F. Chase sold out their interest, 1887, became sr. partner, 1890, and Frank Hopewell was admitted to firm; pres. Reading Rubber Mfg. Co., Electric Goods Mfg. Co.; dir. Sanford Mills. Mem. Mass. Ho. of Rep., 1890; del. Rep. Nat. Conv., St. Louis, 1896, and Nat. Bd. of Trade, Washington, 4 yrs. Universalist. Mason. Home: Newton, Mass. Died 1916.

HOPEWELL-SMITH, Arthur, author; b. Boston, Eng., May 20, 1865; s. Edward Smith-Smith and Mary Anne (Hopewell) Smith; grad. Royal Coll. Phys. and Surg., London, 1891, also dental surgery, 1887; Sc.D., U. of Pa., 1919; unmarried. Formerly mem. Faculty of Medicine, U. of London; extramural examiner in dental surgery at univs. of Birmingham, Leeds and Liverpool; came to U.S., 1914; prof. comparative odontology, dental histology and pathology, U. of Pa., 1914—; spl. lecturer on oral diseases, War Dept., World War. Author: Dental Microscopy, 1895; The Normal and Pathological Histology of the Mouth, 1903; An Introduction to Dental Anatomy and Physiology, Descriptive and Applied, 1913. Deceased.

HOPKINS, Abner Crump, clergyman; b. Powhatan County, Va., Oct. 24, 1835; s. Henry Laurens and Sarah Amelia (Crump) H.; A.B., Hampden-Sidney Coll., 1855, D.D., 1883; taught sch. 2 yrs.; grad. Union Theol. Sem., Va., 1860; m. Anne Pleasants Atkinson, May 16, 1861. Pastor Presbyn. ch., Martinsburg, Va., 1860-62; chaplain 2d Va. Inf., Stonewall brigade, C.S.A., 1862, 64; chaplain on staff Gen. John B. Gordon, 1864-65, at Appomattox, C. H., Va.; pastor Willis Ch., Va., 1865-66, Charlestown Presbyn. Ch., W.Va., 1866—. Chmn. many coms. of Gen. Assembly of Synod of Va. (moderator, 1881); mem. Gen. Assemblies Presbyn. Ch. in U.S., 1875, 81, 82, 98, 1903, 04, 06 (moderator, 1903, Lexington, Va.); mem. Pan-Presbyn. Council, Toronto, Can., 1892. Democrat. Address: Charlestown, W.Va. Died Dec. 4, 1911.

HOPKINS, Albert J., senator; b. DeKalb County, Ill., Aug. 15, 1846; A.B., Hillsdale (Mich.) College, 1870 (LL.D. same); m. Emma C. Etolp, 1873. Admitted to Illinois bar, 1871, and practiced at Aurora and Chicago; state's attorney, Kane County, Ill., 1872-76; mem. Rep. State Central Com., 1878-80; presdl. elector, 1884; mem. 49th to 57th Congresses (1885-1903), 8th Ill. Dist.; U.S. senator from Ill., 1903-09. Supported by Rep. congressional delegation of Ill. as candidate for Speaker, 56th Congress. Mem. law firm Hopkins & Hopkins, Chicago. Home: Aurora, Ill. Died Aug. 23, 1922.

HOPKINS, Alphonso Alva, author; b. Burlington Flats, N.Y., Mar. 27, 1843; s. Alvah and Mercy (Hale) H.; academic edn.; Ph.D., Am. Temperance U., Tenn., 1895; m. Adelia R. Allyn, 1867; m. 2d, Emma M. Santee, 1897. Editor Rural New Yorker, American Rural Home and American Reformer, 1867-85; was vice chancellor and prof. polit. economy, Am. Temperance U., 3 yrs. Lecturer on lit., temperance and econ. topics, 1868—. Prohibition candidate for gov. N.Y., 1882. Author: Geraldine (a novel in verse, first published anonymously), 1882; His Prison Bars, 1878; Sinner and Saint, 1880; Life of General Clinton B. Fisk, 1888; Wealth and Waste, 1896; Ballads of Brotherhood, 1900; Profit and Loss in Man, 1909; The Bugle of Right, 1913. Editor The National Advocate; on editorial staff Funk & Wagnalls Co. Address: Cliffside, N.J. Died Sept. 25, 1918.

HOPKINS, Archibald, lawyer; b. Williamstown, Mass., Feb. 1842; s. Mark and Mary (Hubbell) H.; A.B., Williams, 1862, A.M., 1865; capt., bvt. maj., lt. col. and col., 37th Mass. Vols., 1862-65; govt. officer under Reconstruction Acts, 1866; LL.B., Columbia, 1867; m. Charlotte Everett Wise, Nov. 14, 1878. Admitted to bar, 1867; practiced at N.Y. City, 1867-73; clerk U.S. Court of Claims, Washington, D.C., 1873-1914. Mem. bd. dirs. Garfield Hosp.; chmn. bd. Asso. Charities, bd. Washington Humane Soc.; mem. bd. visitors U.S. Mil. Acad.; del. Internat. Peace Conf.; trustee Legal Aid Soc.; v.p. trustees George Washington U. Mem. Com. of 100 for Beautification and Development of Washington Com. of 100 to Celebrate 100 Years Peace with Canada. Author: The Apostles' Creed, 1909. Address: Washington, D.C. Died June 18, 1926.

HOPKINS, Arthur John, prof. chemistry; b. Bridgewater, Mass., Sept. 20, 1864; s. Lewis Spring and Fanny Jane (Washburn) H.; A.B., Amherst (Mass.) Coll., 1885; Ph.D., Johns Hopkins, 1893 (fellowship); m. Margaret Sutton Briscoe, Apr. 16, 1895; 1 dau., Cornelia Dushane (Mrs. David Allen). Teacher Mass. pub. schs., 1885-88, Peekskill (N.Y.) Mil. Acad., 1888-90, Westminster Coll., New Wilmington, Pa., 1893-94; asst. prof. chemistry Amherst Coll., 1894-95, asso. prof., 1895-1907, prof., 1907-34 (emeritus). Awarded Eminent Service Medal, Amherst Coll. Democrat. Author: Alchemy, Child of Greek Philosophy, 1934. Home: Amherst, Mass. Died Nov. 10, 1939.

HOPKINS, Charlotte Everett (Mrs. Archibald Hopkins); b. Cambridge, Mass., June 7, 1851; d. Henry Augustus and Charlotte Brooks (Everett) Wise; ed. under pvt. teachers and in pvt. schs.; m. Archibald Hopkins, Nov. 14, 1878 (died 1926); children—Charlotte Wise (wife of Dr. Henry S. Patterson), Mary (Mrs. Crawford Blagden, dec.), Amos Lawrence, Archibald (dec.). President Home for Incurables, Washington, D.C.; mem. bd. U.S. Hosp. for the Insane; prominent in raising funds for erection of block of model homes for working people in Washington, D.C., under title of "The Ellen Wilson Memorial Homes." Mem. Nat. Red Cross; chmn. woman's div., D.C. sect. of Council Nat. Defense, 1917; chmn. D.C. Housing Com.; vice chmn. Camp Activities. Episcopalian. Home: Washington, D.C. Died Sept. 6, 1935.

HOPKINS, Cyril George, univ. prof.; b. nr. Chatfield, Minn., July 22, 1866; s. George Edwin and Caroline (Cudney) H.; B.S., S.D. Agrl. Coll., 1890; obtained S.D. state teacher's certificate, 1891; M.S., Cornell, 1894, Ph.D., 1898; studied agrl. chemistry at Göttingen, 1899-1900; m. Emma Matilda Stelter, May 11, 1893. Asst. in chemistry, Agrl. Coll. and Expt. Sta., Brookings, S.D., 1890-92, 1893-94; Cornell, 1892-93; acting prof. pharmacy, S.D. Agrl. Coll., 1893-94; chemist, 1894-1900, prof. agronomy and chief in agronomy and chemistry, 1900—, vice-dir., 1903—, U. of Ill. Agrl. Expt. Station. Invented Hopkins' condenser, Hopkins' distilling tube, 1898, and Hopkins' limestone tester, 1917. Author: Soil Fertility and Permanent Agriculture, 1910; The Story of the Soil, 1911; The Farm That Won't Wear Out, 1913. Also a number of bulls. on soil investigations and papers on chem. and agrl. subjects in various jours. Dir. agr., for Southern Settlement and Development Orgn., 1913-14. Address: Champaign, Ill. Died Oct. 6, 1919.

HOPKINS, Edna Boies, wood engraver; b. Hudson, Mich., Oct. 11, 1878; pupil of Art Acad., Cincinnati, and Arthur W. Dow; m. James R. Hopkins, Sept. 13, 1904. Awarded silver medal, San Francisco Expn., 1915. Works on permanent exhbn., Library of Congress, Washington, D.C.; Cincinnati Art Museum; Detroit Inst. Arts, Walker Art Gallery, Liverpool, Eng.; Nat. Museum, Stockholm; Kunst Gewerke Museum, Berlin; Bibliothèque d'Art et Archéologie, Paris. Home: Paris, France. Deceased.

HOPKINS, E(dward) Washburn, philologist; b. Northampton, Mass., Sept. 8, 1857; s. Lewis Spring and Frances (Washburn) H.; A.B., Columbia, 1878; A.M., Ph.D., U. of Leipzig, 1881; hon. A.M., Yale, 1895; LL.D., Columbia, 1902; hon. Ph.D., U. of Athens (Greece), 1912; m. Mary S. Clark, June 3, 1893; children—Mary Pauline, Clark, Francis Washburn, Edward Lewis, Howard, Allen Low. Tutor in Latin, Columbia, 1881-85; prof. Greek, Sanskrit and comparative philology, Bryn Mawr Coll., 1885-95; prof. Sanskrit lang. and lit. and comparative philology, Yale, 1895-1926 (emeritus). Mem. Am. Oriental Soc. (sec. 1896-1908; editor its jour., 1897-1907; twice pres.). Author: Caste in Ancient India, 1881; Manu's Lawbook, 1884; Religions of India, 1895; The Great Epic of India, 1901; India, Old and New, 1901; Epic Mythology, 1915; History of Religions, 1918; Origin and Evolution of Religion, 1923; Ethics of India, 1924; Legends of India, 1928. Home: New Haven, Conn. Died July 16, 1932.

HOPKINS, Edwin Butcher, petroleum geologist; b. Evans, W.Va., Oct. 25, 1882; s. Andrew Delmar and Delia (Butcher) H.; student W.Va. U., 1899-1901, George Washington U., 1903-04; m. Amy Longcope, June 20, 1913; children—Mrs. Ted Fitch, Mrs. Jack Munger, Louise, Madeleine, Edwin. With U.S. Geol. Survey, 1906-09; geologist Mexican Eagle Petroleum Co., 1909-13; mgr. Cuban Oil Co., 1913-14; mgr. Internat. Petroleum Co., 1914-16; cons. petroleum geologist, 1916—; pres. Delta Petroleum Co.; v.p. and gen. mgr. Am. Maracaibo Co.; v.p. Drilling and Exploration Co., Inc.; dir. Santa Fe Corp., Petroleum Finance Corp. Home: Dallas, Tex. Died July 5, 1940.

HOPKINS, Erasmus Guy, physician; b. Fredericksburg, Va., Apr. 9, 1877; s. Erasmus and Ida Gayle (Rowe) H.; student Fredericksburg (Va.) Coll., 1894-96; M.D., Univ. Coll. of Medicine, Richmond, Va., 1899; m. Pauline Dudley Gary, Dec. 27, 1905. Began practice at Richmond, 1899; city bacteriologist, 1906-07; pathologist St. Luke's Hosp., 1907—; asso. prof. pathology, 1913, prof. clin. pathology, 1917—, dir. clin. lab., 1913—, Med. Coll. of Va.; dir. laboratories, Retreat for the Sick and Stuart Circle Hosps., 1921—. Commd. capt. Med. Corps, U.S. Army, Aug. 23, 1917; maj., Feb. 17, 1919; ordered active duty, Sept. 28, 1917; chief of lab. service at Camp Doniphan, Okla., Base Hosp. 45, A.E.F., in France, and at Justice Hosp. Group, Toul, consecutively, Dec. 6, 1917-Jan. 31, 1919; hon. discharged, Apr. 25, 1919. Democrat. Home: Glen Allen, Va. Deceased.

HOPKINS, Evan Henry, lawyer; b. Johnstown, Pa., Nov. 4, 1864; s. David J. and Mary (Jeffreys) H.; A.B., Adelbert Coll., 1889; LL.B., Harvard, 1892; m. Frances P. M. Shain, Dec. 27, 1892; children—Percie Trowbridge (Mrs. A. M. Turner), Frances Shain, Margaret Elizabeth, Helen Jeffreys. Admitted to bar, 1891; practiced at Cleveland; mem. law firm of Herrick, Hopkins, Stockwell & Benesch, Cleveland. Mem. faculty and registrar, 1892-95, dean law dept., 1895-1910, Western Reserve U. Mem. and sec. Cleveland Pub. Library Bd., 1892-98; mem. Bd. Park Commrs., Cleveland, 1900-01. Presbyn. Republican. Home: Cleveland, O. Died June 28, 1938.

HOPKINS, Henry, educator, clergyman; b. Williamstown, Mass., Nov. 30, 1837; s. Mark H. and Mary H. H.; grad. Williams Coll., 1858 (A.M., D.D.; LL.D., Amherst and Marietta, 1902); studied theology 2 yrs. in Union Theol. Sem., New York; after that private pupil with his father; in ministry, 1861—; m. Alice Knight, 1866 (died 1869); m. 2d, Jeanette M. Southworth, 1876. Received, 1861, from Pres. Lincoln, personal commn. (before office was created by law) as U.S.A. hosp. chaplain, and served at Alexandria, Va., until 1864; chaplain in field, with 120th N.Y. vols., 1864-65; took ambulance corps, under flag of truce, on the battlefields of Chantilly and Bull Run; was at front through the campaigns and siege work of the Army of the Potomac, from the Rapidan to Appomattox; instrumental in securing legislation by Congress for nat. soldiers' cemeteries; pastor 2d Congl. Ch., Westfield, Mass., 1866-80; 1st Congl. Ch., Kansas City, Mo., 1880-1902; pres. Williams Coll., 1902-June 1908. Chaplain, 1887-99, 3d Regt. N.G. Mo., commander in chief Loyal Legion, 1899, Sons Revolution, State of Mo.; corporate mem. and v.p. A.B.C.F.M.; trustee Williams Coll., Mass., and Drury Coll., Mo.; nat. v.p. Am. Missionary Assn.; mem. Nat. Assn. Charities and Corrections. Several of his addresses on municipal and ednl. subjects, and sermons, have been published. Address: Williamstown, Mass. Died 1908.

HOPKINS, Herbert Müller, clergyman; b. Hannibal, Mo., Oct. 15, 1870; s. Rev. William C. and Cornelia (Stevens) H.; A.B., Columbia, 1893; A.M., Harvard, 1896, Ph.D., 1898; m. Pauline Bradford Mackie, Aug. 2, 1899. Instr. Latin, U. of Calif., 1898-1901; prof. Latin, Trinity Coll., Hartford, 1901-05; deacon, 1905, priest, 1906, P.E. Ch.; rector Ch. of the Holy Nativity, Bronx, New York, 1906—. Author: The Fighting Bishop, 1902; The Torch, 1903; the Mayor of Warwick, 1906; Priest and Pagan, 1908. Home: New York, N.Y. Died 1910.

HOPKINS, Isaac Stiles, clergyman; b. Augusta, Ga., June 20, 1841; s. Thomas and Rebecca (Lambuth) H.; A.B., Emory Coll., Ga., 1859, A.M., 1862, Ph.D., 1884; M.D., Med. Coll. of Ga., 1861; D.D., Central Coll., Mo., 1886; m. Emily Gibson, July 1, 1861; m. 2d, Mary Hinton, July 2, 1874. Prof., 1869-86, pres., 1883-87, Emory Coll. (with an interval at Southern U., Greensboro, Ala., 1875-77); organized, 1887, Ga. Sch. Tech. (branch of U. of Ga.) and was pres., 1888-96; ordained M.E. ministry, 1863; pastor, Atlanta, Ga., 1877-96, St. John's Ch., St. Louis, 1899-1902, Chattanooga, Tenn., 1902-03, Athens, Ga., 1903-06, La Grange, Ga., 1907-08. Lecturer before various ednl. assemblies. Address: Atlanta, Ga. Died Feb. 3, 1914.

HOPKINS, James Frederick, art educator; b. Newton, Mass., Feb. 26, 1868; s. Benjamin and Mary Malinda (Wood) H.; Newton High Sch.; grad. Mass. Normal Art Sch., 1889; spent many seasons abroad, study of schs., galleries and museums; m. Emma Augusta Asbrand, June 28, 1893. Instr., Pratt Inst., Brooklyn, 1889-96; dir. drawing, pub. schs., Boston, 1896-1906; dir. Schools of Art and Design, Md. Inst., Baltimore, 1906-12; dir. art edn. for Mass., 1912-20; dir. art efficiency surveys, 1920—. Active in organizing exhbns., reorganization of schs. and courses of study and in inst. work; del. 2d Internat. Congress for Promotion of Art Edn., Berne, 1904, 3d Congress, London, 1908; chmn. Am. representation, and U.S. del. 4th Congress, Dresden, 1912; etc. Mem. Jury of Art Edn., St. Louis Expn., 1904. Author: Outlines of Lessons in Drawing, 1897; Outlines of Art History, 1900. Spl. lecturer, Nat. War Council Y.M.C.A. in Northeastern, Eastern and Central depts., camps, cantonments, posts and naval bases, 1918. Address: Boston, Mass. Died Nov. 11, 1931.

HOPKINS, James Love, lawyer; b. St. Louis, Mo., July 20, 1868; s. Christian R. and Anna (Love) H.; LL.B., St. Louis Law Sch., 1894; m. Georgien Shields, Feb. 24, 1892; 1 dau., Anna Love (Mrs. Frank T. Hopkins). In practice at St. Louis, 1889—, except 1898-1902, when was located in San Francisco. Specialized in patent and trademark law. Spl. patent counsel for City of San Francisco, 1899-1900. Author: Hopkins on Unfair Trade, 1900; Hopkins on Trademarks, 1905 (4th edit. 1924); Hopkins' Judicial Code (3d edit., 1926); Hopkins on Patents, 1911; Hopkins' Federal Equity Rules, 1913 (6th edit. 1929); Hopkins' Federal Penal Code, 1927. Home: St. Louis, Mo. Died Aug. 30, 1931.

HOPKINS, Lindsey; b. nr. Reidsville, N.C., Apr. 22, 1879; s. Jonothan and Minerva (Jones) H.; ed. U. of N.C.; m. Leonora Balsley, 1906; children—Lindsey, Sarah. Formerly engaged in sales development of motor cars in the Southeast; settled in Atlanta, Ga., 1910. Principal residence Miami Beach, Fla.; also Lakemont, Ga., and Paces Ferry Road, Atlanta, Ga. Dir. Coca Cola Co., Am. Hide & Leather Co., Sperry Corp., North Am. Aviation, and many other corps. Died Aug. 17, 1937.

HOPKINS, Louis Bertram, college pres.; b. Hopkinton, N.H., Aug. 11, 1881; s. Adoniram Judson and Mary (Martin) H.; grad. Coburn Classical Inst., 1904; Dartmouth, 1904-06, M.A., 1925; LL.D., DePauw U., 1930, Marietta Coll., 1930; Litt.D., Hanover (Ind.) Coll., 1932; Sc.D., Rose Polytechnic Inst., 1933; m. Nora Lander, Oct. 2, 1907; children—Florence Martin, Margaret Lander. With Regal Shoe Co., 1907, Am. Optical Co., 1908, Gen. Electric Co., Pittsfield Works, 1909-11; treas. Pittsfield Spark Coil Co., 1912; asst. to mgr. in charge of personnel, labor relations, Gen. Electric Co., Pittsfield Works, 1914-16; dir. trade test div., Com. on Classification of Personnel, U.S. Army, 1917-18; asst. in personnel div. U.S. Dept. Labor, 1918; treas. The Scott Co., engrs. in industrial personnel, 1918; consultant in personnel and orgn. for industrial and commercial cos.; dir. of personnel, Northwestern U., 1922-26; pres. Wabash Coll., July 1926—. Mem. Apparel Industry Com., Wage and Hour Div., U.S. Dept. of Labor. Mem. of Commn. of Instns. of Higher Edn. of N. Central Assn. of Colls. and Secondary Schs. Home: Crawfordsville, Ind. Died Aug. 10, 1940.

HOPKINS, Nanette, educator; b. Sangersville, Va., Dec. 24, 1860; d. Benjamin Franklin and Frances Alexes (Fawcett) Hopkins; grad. Hollins (Va.) Inst. (now Coll.), 1880; Pd.D., Oglethorpe U., 1922; Litt.D., U. of Ga., 1930. Teacher Louisa (Va.) Home

Sch., 1884-87, Valley Sem., Waynesboro, Va., 1887-89; prin. Agnes Scott Inst., Decatur, Ga., 1889-97, lady prin., 1897-1906; dean Agnes Scott Coll., 1906—, mem. bd. trustees, 1927—. Democrat. Presbyn. Address: Decatur, Ga. Died Oct. 29, 1938.

HOPKINS, Robert Emmet, petroleum producer; b. Pompey, N.Y., Mar. 24, 1833; ed. in acad. there; taught school; entered lumber business at Brewerton, N.Y.; under-sheriff Onondaga County, 1861-62; capt. and maj. 149th N.Y. vols., 1862-64; resigned, July 1864, because of illness; in Libby prison 2 months in 1863; located in Titusville, Pa., in lumber and petroleum-producing business. One of organizers, 1878, The Tide Water Pipe Co., Limited, the 1st to lay a pipe for transportation of crude petroleum to the Atlantic seaboard. Home: Tarrytown, N.Y. Died 1901.

HOPKINS, Samuel Augustus, dentist; b. Jersey City, N.J., Sept. 12, 1858; s. Samuel A. and Helen (Carpenter) H.; ed. pub. schs. and Grinnell Coll., Ia.; M.D., Coll. Phys. and Surg. (Columbia), 1880; D.D.S., New York Coll. of Dentistry, 1882; m. Mrs. Harriet Woodworth Sherman, Jan. 10, 1898. Practiced dentistry, New York, 1882-84, then in Boston. Prof. theory and practice of dentistry, dental dept. Tufts Coll., until 1906. Author: Care of the Teeth, 1902. Home: Boston, Mass. Died Mar. 14, 1921.

HOPKINS, Samuel Miles, Presbyn. clergyman; b. Geneseo, N.Y., Aug. 8, 1813; grad. Amherst, 1932 (D.D., 1854); studied theology at Auburn Theol. Sem.; completed course at Princeton Theol. Sem., 1836; ordained, 1840; pastor Corning, Fredonia and Avon, N.Y., Presbyn. chs., 1840-47; in 1847 prof. ecclesias. history and ch. polity, Auburn Theol. Sem. (emeritus). Author: Manual of Church Polity; Liturgy and Book of Common Prayer. Home: Auburn, N.Y. Died 1901.

HOPKINS, Scott, banker; b. Waverly, N.Y., Feb. 2, 1860; s. John S. and Julia (Scott) H.; Highland U., Kan., 1876-77; B.A., U. of Kan., 1881, M.A., 1885; Columbia Law Sch., 1883-84; m. Cora E. Pierson, Nov. 25, 1885. Entered banking business at Horton, Kan., Nov. 1887; pres. First Nat. Bank, Horton; v.p. Prudential State Bank, Topeka; trust officer Prudential Trust Co. Pres. Kan. Bankers' Assn., 1901—. Regent U. of Kan. Republican. Presbyn. Home: Topeka, Kan. Died Dec. 2, 1917.

HOPKINS, Sherburne Gillette, lawyer; b. Washington, D.C., Oct. 5, 1868; s. Thomas S. and Caroline W. (Eastman) H.; student Columbia U., 1887-89; m. Hester I. Davis, Jan. 21, 1891. Admitted to bar, 1889, and since practiced in Washington, D.C.; associated with father as Hopkins & Hopkins; specializes in internat. matters and settlements with the Govt. Adviser to several Latin Am. govts.; adviser to provisional govt. of Mexico (Madero), 1911; constitutionalist govt. of Mexico, 1913-14; to provisional govt. of Mexico (de la Huerto), 1920. Lt. Naval Militia, D.C., 1898; lt. comdr., 1899, commanding U.S.S. Fern. Mason. Home: Washington, D.C. Died June 22, 1932.

HOPKINS, Thomas Snell, lawyer; b. Mt. Vernon, Me., Apr 22, 1845; s. Joseph and Hannah (Philbrick) H.; Wesleyan Sem., Kents Hill, Me.; served 3 yrs. during Civil War in 16th Regt., Me. Inf.; wounded at battle of Fredericksburg, Va., Dec. 13, 1862; law dept. Columbian (now George Washington) U., 1869; m. Carrie W. Eastman, Jan. 4, 1866. Admitted to bar, 1869; mem. bar Supreme Ct. U.S.; sr. mem. Hopkins & Hopkins; practice mostly confined to internat. law. Trustee George Washington U.; pres. bd. Soldiers' and Sailors' Temporary Home, Washington, D.C., 10 yrs. Gov. gen. Gen. Soc. Mayflower Descendants, 1912-15; past dept. comdr. G.A.R., Dept. of Potomac; judge advocate gen., G.A.R. Republican. Mason. Home: Washington, D.C. Died Apr. 17, 1925.

HOPKINS, William Hersey, college prof.; b. Greensborough, Md., Dec. 20, 1841; s. James and Elizabeth (Lyden) H.; A.B., with 1st honors, St. John's Coll., Md., 1859, A.M., 1867; (hon. Ph.D., Dickinson Coll., 1886); m. Eliza J. Brooke Brady, Sept. 29 1870. Tutor, 1859-61, asst. prof. Greek and Latin langs., 1867-80, prof. Greek and Latin langs., 1881-86, prof. German, 1871-86, pres., 1884-86, St. John's Coll.; organized, 1886, pres., 1886-90, prof. Latin, 1890-1915, emeritus prof. Latin, 1915, Woman's Coll. of Baltimore (now Goucher Coll.). Died Dec. 17, 1919.

HOPKINS, William John, author; b. New Bedford, Mass., June 10, 1863; s. John and Louisa Parsons (Stone) H.; ed. Friends' Acad., Harvard U., Mass. Inst. Tech.; m. Emma Laura Blauvelt, June 20, 1896; children—John Blauvelt, Lois Parsons. Author: Telephone Lines and Their Properties, 1893; The Telephone, 1898; The Sandman Series (4 vols.), 1902-08; The Clammer, 1906; Old Harbor, 1909; The Meddlings of Eve, 1910; The Indian Book, 1911; Concerning Sally, 1912; The Doers, 1914; The Clammer and the Submarine, 1917; She Blows! and Sparm at That, 1922; Tumbleberry and Chick. Home: Wellesley Hills, Mass. Died Nov. 24, 1926.

HOPKINSON, Ernest, lawyer, mfr.; b. Hyde Co., Chester, Eng., May 20. 1872; s. David and Mary (Penny) H.; ed. pub. schs.; m. B. B. Barnes, Feb. 16, 1899. Began practice at N.Y. City, 1895; v.p. in charge development dept., patent counsel and mem. exec. com. U.S. Rubber Co.; chmn. bd. Naugatuck Chem. Co., Rubber Regenerating Co.; vice pres. Hartford Rubber Works Co., Morgan & Wright; dir. numerous corps. Republican. Home: New York, N.Y. Died May 3, 1933.

HOPLEY, Elizabeth Sheppard; b. Granville, O., Dec. 11, 1870; d. Rev. Thomas J. and Margaret (Collins) Sheppard; grad. Chicago Kindergarten Training Sch., and studied under William L. Tomlins, Central Music Hall, Chicago, and Edmund Russell; taught in Chicago Mission kindergartens 2½ yrs.; in Shepardson College, Granville, 1891-93; m. James R. Hopley, Nov. 15, 1893. Pres. Ohio Fedn. Women's Clubs; only woman speaker at Centennial Celebration of 100th anniversary of admission of Ohio to the Union. Author of amendment to the constitution providing that women may hold membership in bds. of pub. instns. caring for women and as superintendents of same. Home: Bucyrus, O. Died Dec. 16, 1922.

HOPLEY, John Edward, editor; b. Elkton, Ky., Aug. 25, 1850; s. John Prat and Georgianna (Rochester) H.; removed with parents to Bucyrus, Ohio, 1856; ed. high sch. and under tutelage of father; unmarried. Admitted to Ohio bar, 1875; founded Evening Telegraph, Bucyrus, O., 1887; editor and owner Bucyrus Journal, and Evening Telegraph until May 1923, when sold both papers. Mem. Rep. State Central Com., 1894-96; consul to Southampton, Eng., 1898; consul to Montevideo, Uruguay, 1903-05; elector-at-large on Rep. ticket, 1912. Protestant. Wrote: History of Crawford Co., Ohio, 1912. Inherited his father's library handed down from ancestors for several hundred yrs.; also father's collection of autograph letters, including letters from every Republican president, beginning with Lincoln. State consul Lincoln Highway. Home: Bucyrus, O. Died July 10, 1927.

HOPPE, Herman Henry, neurologist; b. Cincinnati, O., Jan. 4, 1867; s. Dominick and Mary (Dusterberg) H.; A.B., St. Xavier's Coll., Cincinnati, 1886, A.M., 1890; M.D., Ohio-Miami Med. Coll. (U. of Cincinnati), 1889; post-grad. work in univs. of Strassburg and Berlin, specializing in nervous and mental diseases; m. Hermanie Richard, (died 1912); children—Rosemary Hermanie, Elizabeth Jaquelin; m. 2d, June 4, 1914, Mary Monica Mitchell, g.d. of Robert Mitchell, of Cincinnati. Practiced in Cincinnati, 1889—; prof. nervous diseases, U. of Cincinnati; dir. dept. of nervous and mental diseases, Cincinnati Gen. Hosp. Republican. Catholic. Home: Cincinnati, O. Died Oct. 20, 1929.

HOPPER, (William) DeWolf, comedian; b. N.Y. City, Mar. 30, 1858; s. John and Rosalie (DeWolf) H.; ed. J. H. Morse's Sch.; m. Ella Gardiner; m. 2d, Ida Mosher; 1 son, John Allan; m. 3d, Edna Wallace, Jan. 28, 1893; m. 4th, Nella Reardon Bergen, 1899; m. 5th, Ella Furry, May 24, 1913; (divorced from each); 1 son, Wm. DeWolf; m. 6th, Mrs. Lillian Glaser (singer), Oct. 20, 1925. Début in "Our Boys," 1879; later with Frohman's Madison Sq. Co. as Pittacus Green in "Hazel Kirke" and other rôles; studied vocal music and joined the McCaull Opera Co.; starred in comedy rôles at the head of own co.; later with Weber & Fields Co.; then starring at head of own co. and playing Mr. Pickwick; starring in revival of "Wang," "Happyland," "The Matinee Idol," and "Pinafore"; appeared as Reginald Bunthorne in "Patience," at Lyric Theatre, New York, 1912, later as Edward in "The Pirates of Penzance"; played as Ko-Ko, in "The Mikado," 1913, as the Lord Chancellor, in star revival of "Iolanthe," 1913; starred in "The Better 'Ole," 1918-19, in "Erminie," with Francis Wilson, 1921; head of own co. in revival of Gilbert & Sullivan operas, 1921-25; with Student Prince Co., 1925-26, 1927-28, White Lilacs Co., 1929; lecture and concert tour, 1930-31; spoke over radio 10 weeks, 1932; tour of Uncle Tom's Cabin, 1933. Author: (with W. W. Stout) Once a Clown Always a Clown, 1927. Home: New York, N.Y. Died Sept. 23, 1935.

HOPPIN, James Mason, univ. prof.; b. Providence, R.I., Jan. 17, 1820; s. Benjamin and Esther (Warner) H. g.s. Benjamin Hoppin, commd. officer of the Revolutionary Army; grad. Yale, 1840; at Harvard Law School, 1841-42; at Union Theol. Sem., N.Y., and Andover Sem., 1843-45; student of theology, Berlin Univ., Germany, 1847-49; (D.D., Knox, 1870; LL.D., Dartmouth, 1902); m. Mary D. Perkins, 1850. Ordained 1850; pastor Congl. Ch., Salem, Mass., 1850-59; prof. homiletics, 1861-79, history of art, 1879-99, Yale (emeritus); also pastor Coll. Ch., 1861-63. Author: Old England—Its Art, Scenery and People, 1867; Homiletics, 1881. Died 1906.

HOPPIN, Joseph Clark, archæologist; b. Providence, R.I., May 23, 1870; s. Courtland (M.D.) and Mary Frances (Clark) H.; A.B., Harvard, 1893; spl. studies in classical archæology, Athens, Berlin and Munich, 1893-98; Ph.D., Munich, 1896; m. Dorothy Woodville Rockhill, Nov. 26, 1901; 2d, Eleanor Dennistoun Wood, July 20, 1915. Took part in the excavations of the Argive Heræum., 1894, 1895; instr. Greek art, Wellesley Coll., 1898-99; asso. prof. classical art and archæology, Bryn Mawr Coll., 1899-1904; prof. Greek lang. and lit., Am. Sch. of Classical Studies, Athens, 1904-05. Took part in expdn. for excavating Cyrene, N. Africa, 1910-11; prof. classical archæology, Bryn Mawr, 1917-19. Fellow Am. Acad. Arts and Sciences, Royal Geog. Society. Author: Euthymides and His Fellows, 1916; Handbook of Attic Red-figured Vases, 1918; Handbook of Greek Black-figured Vases, 1923. Home: Pomfret, Conn. Died Jan. 31, 1925.

HOPPIN, William Warner, lawyer; b. Providence, R.I.; s. William Warner and Frances A. F. (Street) H.; A.M., Brown U., 1861; M.D., Coll. Phys. and Surg., New York, 1864; LL.B., Columbia, 1869; (Litt.D., Brown, 1911); m. Katharine Beekman. Served as pvt. and asst. surgeon U.S.V. during Civil War, 1861-65; admitted to bar, 1869, and began practice at New York. Was one of secretaries, Peace Conf., Washington, 1861; trustee Coll. Phys. and Surg., 1877-91; pres. Y.M.C.A.; trustee and v.p. Woman's Hosp.; gov. N.Y. Hosp. Home: New York. N.Y. Died Jan. 3, 1913.

HOPSON, George Bailey, college prof.; b. Naugatuck, Conn., Jan. 18, 1838; s. Rev. Oliver and Caroline (Allis) H.; A.B., Trinity Coll., 1857, A.M., 1860; (D.D., St. Stephen's, 1886, D.C.L., 1903); m. Mary Williamson Johnston, Mar. 29, 1864. Deacon, 1863, priest, 1864, P.E. Ch.; prof. Latin lang. and lit., 1863-1913, prof. emeritus, 1913, acting warden, 1898-99, 1903-04 and 1907-09, St. Stephen's Coll. Home: Annandale, N.Y. Died Aug. 1916.

HOPSON, William Fowler, artist; b. Watertown, Conn., Aug. 30, 1849; s. Orrin L. and Susan Caroline (Wilson) H.; pupil of L. Sanford, New Haven, and J. D. Felter and August Will, New York; m. Mary T. Allen, May 10, 1871; 1 son, Orrin L. (dec.); m. 2d, Ada M. Carter, June 27, 1899. Exhibited at Paris Expn., 1900, Buffalo Expn., 1901. Home: New Haven, Conn. Died Feb. 13, 1935.

HOPWOOD, Avery, playwright; b. Cleveland, O., May 28, 1884; s. James and Jule (Pendergast) H.; A.B., U. of Michigan, 1905. Went to New York as spl. corr. for Cleveland Leader, 1905, and almost immediately sold first play—"Clothes"—written in collaboration with Channing Pollock. Author: (plays) This Woman and This Man; Seven Days (in collaboration with Mary Roberts Rinehart); Judy Forgot; Nobody's Widow (prod. London, Eng., as "Roxana"); Fair and Warmer; Sadie Love; Our Little Wife; Double Exposure; The Gold Diggers; The Bat, and Spanish Love (both with Mary Roberts Rinehart); The Girl in the Limousine; Ladies' Night; The Demi-Virgin: Why Men Leave Home; Little Miss Bluebeard; The Alarm Clock; The Best People (in collaboration with David Gray); Naughty Cinderella; The Garden of Eden; etc. Plays have been prod. in U.S., Can., the principal countries of Europe, and in the Orient. Home: New York, N.Y. Died July 1, 1928.

HOPWOOD, Erie Clark, editor; b. North Eaton, O., Feb. 7, 1877; s. Henry Clay and Emily (Cook) H.; grad. Jefferson (O.) Ednl. Inst., 1897; B.Litt., Adelbert Coll. (Western Reserve U.), 1901; m. Ida R. Walter, July 20, 1903. Prin. high sch., Middletown, O., 1901-02; joined staff Cleveland Plain Dealer as police reporter, 1902; later asst. city editor, city editor, night editor, mng. editor, and editor, 1920—; dir. Plain Dealer Pub. Co. Mem. Cleveland Chamber of Commerce, Cleveland Council of Sociology. Mason. Home: Cleveland Heights, O. Died Mar. 18, 1928.

HORLICK, William, mfr.; b. Gloucestershire, Eng., Feb. 23, 1846; s. James and Priscilla (Griffiths) H.; ed. in Eng.; m. Arabella R. Horlick, Nov. 16, 1870; children—Alice Priscilla (dec.), Alexander James, William, Mrs. Mabelle Emma Sidley. Came to U.S., 1869, naturalized citizen, about 1887. Began mfg. food products in Chicago, 1873, business moved to Racine, Wis., 1876; originated malted milk and special process for producing malted milk, dry extract of malt, etc.; pres. and gen. mgr. Horlick's Malted Milk Corp., Horlick's Investment Co. Knight of St. Olav; first hon. mem. Order of St. George. Republican. Episcopalian. Home: Racine, Wis. Died Sept. 25, 1936.

HORLICK, William, Jr., mfr.; b. Chicago, Ill., Dec. 12, 1875; s. William and Arabella H.; ed. King's Coll., London, Eng., and Racine (Wis.) Coll.; unmarried. Chmn. bd. of dirs. and treas. Horlick's Malted Milk Corp., Racine, Wis. Treas. Racine Co. Council of Defense, World War. Pres. Racine Memorial Hall Commn. Hon. mem. G.A.R., Spanish War Vets., 32d Div. Republican. Episcopalian. Home: Racine, Wis. Died Apr. 1, 1940.

HORMELL, William Garfield, college prof.; b. Oakland, O., July 19. 1861; s. Milton John and Emeline (Hisey) H.; A.B., Ohio Wesleyan U., 1889, B.S., 1890, Ph.D., 1895; A.M., Harvard, 1892; m. Anne Johnston Buzzard, July 31, 1894; 1 dau., Elizabeth. Instr., Ohio Wesleyan U., 1889-91; asst. in physics, Harvard, 1892-93; prof. physics, 1894-1930, dean of men, 1909-26, acting dean of university, 1929-30, Ohio Wesleyan U. (emeritus). Republican. Methodist. Home: Delaware, O. Died June 1933.

HORN, Edward Traill, clergyman; b. Easton, Pa., June 10, 1850; s. Col. Melchior Hay and Matilda (Heller) H.; A.B., Pa. Coll., Gettysburg, 1869; grad. Theol. Sem. at Phila., 1872; (D.D., Roanoke, 1888, D.D., Newberry, 1888, LL.D., 1906); m. Harriet Chisolm, June 15, 1880. Ordained Luth. ministry, 1872; pastor Phila., 1872-96, Charleston, S.C., 1876-97, Trinity Ch., Reading, Pa., 1897-1911; prof. ethics and theory and practice of missions, Luth. Theol. Sem., Phila., 1911—. Pres. Luth. Ministerium Pa., 1909-11, Bd. of Foreign Missions of Gen. Council of the Evang. Luth. Ch. in N. America. Author: Outline of Liturgics, 1890. Home: Mt. Airy, Philadelphia. Died Mar. 4, 1915.

HORN, Frank Churchill, consulting engr.; b. Macomb, Ill., Jan. 8, 1861; s. Adam E. and Martha P. (Naylor) H.; ed. pub. and high schs. and under pvt. instruction; m. Margaret K. Ferguson, of Guelph, Ont., Can., June 24, 1888 (died 1899). Asst. engr., St.L.&S.F. R.R., in charge heavy mountain work and building bridges in western Ark., 1881-82; in gen. engring. practice and contr. water works sewerage systems, foundations, bldgs., rys., sts. and rds. until 1894; in charge constrn. of regulating work, Chicago Drainage Canal, Lockport, Ill., 1895; asst. chief engr. Denver Union Water Co., and built system of gravity filtration beds at Platte Canon, Colo., for purification of water supply for Denver, later built masonry dam for conserving water supply for Denver; constructing engr. U.S. Reclamation Service, 1905-08; apptd. spl. consulting engr., same, 1911. Invented pneumatic system for placing concrete in large units. Home: Boise, Ida. Died Feb. 16, 1919.

HORN, Henry John, ry. official; b. St. Paul, Minn., 1864; s. Henry J. and Francenia (Banning) H.; B.S. in C.E., Mass. Inst. Tech., 1888; m. Josephine M. Robinson, Feb. 15, 1898; children—Henry J., Francenia (Mrs. Ralph Shattuck Stevens). Asst. engr., Chicago, St. Paul & Kansas City Ry., 1888-89; entered service of Northern Pacific Railway, as draftsman, engineering dept., 1889, and continued as chief draftsman, middle dist., 1890-91, resident engr., 1891-93, supervisor bridges, Minn. div., 1893-97, supt. Mont. div., 1897-1902, asst. gen. supt. middle dist., 1902-03, gen. mgr. coal dept. Northwestern Improvement Co. (an auxiliary corp.), 1903-04, gen. mgr. N.P. Ry., 1904-07; in commercial business, 1907-10; asst. gen. mgr., C.,B.&Q. Ry., May-Dec. 1910; asst. to pres., N.Y.,N.H.&H. R.R., 1910-11; v.p., 1911-13; v.p. in charge of operation, 1912-13; railroad analysis, 1913—. Dep. commr. Am. Red Cross, 1917-18; Am. Commn. to Russia, also for a time vice-chmn. Am. Ry. Commn. to Russia. Home: Brookline, Mass. Died Dec. 29, 1940.

HORN, Paul Whitfield, college pres.; b. Booneville, Mo., Apr. 30, 1870; s. George Washington and Mattie (Myers) H.; A.M., Central Coll., Fayette, Mo., 1888; LL.D., Baylor U., 1917, Southwestern U., and Central Coll., 1917; m. Maud Keith, Aug. 28, 1890; 1 dau., Ruth. Teacher in rural schs., 1884-85; taught in Pryor Inst., Jasper, Tenn., 1889-92 (pres. 2 yrs.); prin. high sch., Sherman, Tex., 1895-97, supt. 7 yrs., 1897-1904; supt. schools, Houston, Tex., 1904-21; supt. Am. Sch., City of Mexico, 1921-22; pres. Southwestern U., Tex., 1922-23; pres. Tex. Tech. Coll., Lubbock, Tex., 1924—. Teacher summer sch., U. of Tex., 7 summers, summer sch., Tulane U., 1911, 21, Summer Sch. of South, Knoxville, 1913-16, Summer School, Peabody College, Nashville, 1914-15, Boston U., 1917, U. of Ore., 1920. Made school survey of Portland, Ore., 1917; mem. com. making survey of state schools of Ala., 1919; mem. Tex. Sch. Survey Commn., 1923. Democrat. Methodist. Author: New American Readers, 1919. Home: Lubbock, Tex. Died Apr. 13, 1932.

HORN, Tiemann Newell, army officer; b. Brooklyn, N.Y., Jan. 18, 1868; s. Daniel Tiemann and Frances (Capron) H.; grad. U.S. Mil. Acad., 1891, Arty. Sch., 1898, Sch. of Submarine Defense, 1903; honor grad. Army Sch. of the Line, 1911; grad. Army Staff Coll., 1912; m. Myra Rivers, Nov. 28, 1894. Commd. 2d lt. 3d Cav., June 12, 1891; trans. to 2d Arty., Dec. 15, 1891; 1st lt. 1st Arty., Oct. 7, 1898; promoted through grades to col. 9th F.A., July 1, 1917; brig. gen., Feb. 6, 1918. Dist. ordnance officer and arty. engr. Southern Arty. Dist. of N.Y., 1903-06; duty at Jamestown Expn., 1907; in Philippines, 1913-15, Hawaii, 1915-18; as brig. gen. comd. 7th F.A. Brigade, 7th Div., during war period. Mason. Episcopalian. Home: Plainfield, N.J. Died May 5, 1923.

HORN, William Melchior, clergyman; b. Charleston, S.C., Nov. 28, 1882; s. Edward Traill and Harriet (Chisolm) H.; student Charleston Coll., 1896-97; A.B., Muhlenberg Coll., Pa., 1900, D.D., 1925; A.M., Princeton, 1901; studied U. of Pa., 1901-02; grad. Luth. Theol. Sem., Phila., 1904; m. Marguerite E. Jacobs, June 30, 1908; children—Edward Traill III, Ruth Marguerite, William Melchior, Henry Eyster, John Chisolm, Robert Traill, Marguerite Eyster, James Gregg. Ordained ministry Luth. Ch., 1904; asst. pastor Ch. of the Advent, N.Y. City, 1904-07, pastor, 1907-17; resident pastor Cornell U., Ithaca, N.Y., 1917—. Founder Inner Mission Soc., N.Y.; pres. N.Y. Luth. Ministers' Assn., 1912-14; Evang. Luth. Synod of N.Y. and N.E., 1914-17; chmn. Bd. of Virgin Islands Missions, 1915-18; pres. Ministers Assn. Southern Tier, N.Y.; trustee Ithaca council, Boy Scouts America. Democrat. Died Sept. 21, 1932.

HORNADAY, James Parks, newspaperman; b. nr. Castleton, Ind., Nov. 7, 1863; s. Anson Deming and Sarah Hurid (Hanna) H.; ed. Central Normal Sch., Danville, Ind., and Central Acad., Plainfield, Ind.; m. Mary Gertrude Willis, June 6, 1893; children—Hilton P., Willis D. (dec.), James H., Fred E., Mary J. Teacher pub. schs., Hendricks Co., Ind., 1882-84; with Martinsville (Ind.) Republican, 1884-86, Indianapolis Journal, 1886-89; with Indianapolis News, 1889—, successively as state polit. writer, 1889-98, city editor, 1898-1901, Washington corr., 1901—. Christian Scientist. Home: Washington, D.C. Died Dec. 24, 1935.

HORNADAY, William Temple, zoölogist; b. Plainfield, Ind., Dec. 1, 1854; s. William and Martha (Varner) H.; ed. Ia. State Coll.; studied zoölogy and museology in U.S. and Europe; Sc.D., U. of Pittsburgh, 1906; A.M., Yale, 1917; Ph.M., Ia. State Coll., 1923; m. Josephine Chamberlain, Sept. 11, 1879; 1 dau., Helen Ross (Mrs. George T. Fielding). As collecting zoölogist visited Cuba, Fla., the W.I., S. America, India, Ceylon, the Malay Peninsula and Borneo, 1875-79; chief taxidermist U.S. Nat. Mus., 1882-90; in real estate business, Buffalo, N.Y., 1890-96; dir. New York Zoöl. Park, 1896-1926 (retired). Gold medalist Republic of France; British Royal Soc. for Protection of Birds, Royal Zoöl. Soc. of Antwerp; New York Zoöl. Soc.; Camp Fire Club of America; Inter-Nat. Congress for Study and Protection of Birds; silver medalist Société Nationale d'Acclimatation of France; holder of Cross of Crown of Belgium. Active in promoting game preserves and new laws for the protection of wild life generally; took initiative in creation of Mont. Nat. Bison Range, Wichita Nat. Bison Range, and Elk River Game Preserve (Mont.); the Bayne law to prohibit the sale of native game; and new tariff law to prohibit all importations of wild birds' plumage into U.S. for millinery purposes (1913); organized Permanent Wild Life Protection Fund, 1913-14. Author: Two Years in the Jungle, 1885; Taxidermy and Zoölogical Collecting, 1892; The American Natural History, 1904; Camp-Fires in the Canadian Rockies, 1906; Camp-Fires on Desert and Lava, 1908; Wild Life Conservation in Theory and Practice, 1914; Minds and Manners of Wild Animals, 1922; Tales from Nature's Wonderlands, 1924; A Wild-Animal Round-Up, 1925; Wild Animal Interviews, 1928; Thirty Years War for Wild Life, 1931. Home: Stamford, Conn. Died Mar. 6, 1937.

HORNBLOWER, Henry, broker; b. Lawrence, Mass., June 8, 1863; s. Edward Thomas and Martha Boyd (Whiting) H.; grad. Cotting High Sch., Arlington, Mass., 1878; m. Hattie Frances Wood, May 12, 1886; children—Ruth (Mrs. Chester N. Greenough), Helen (Mrs. Alfred R. Meyer), Ralph. Began as clerk in father's firm of Hornblower & Page, 1879; after death of Mr. Page, 1888, formed copartnership with John W. Weeks (Hornblower & Weeks), additions having been made to the firm, retired Jan. 1, 1936. Mem. gov. com. Boston Stock Exchange. Trustee N. Am. Civic League for Immigrants. Republican. Home: Boston, Mass. Died Apr. 11, 1941.

HORNBLOWER, Joseph Coerten, architect; b. Paterson, N.J., 1848; s. Rev. William H. (D.D.) and Matilda (Butler) H.; grad. Yale, Ph.B., 1869; Atelier J. L. Pascal, Paris, 1875-76; m. Caroline, d. Joseph P. Bradley, asso. justice of U.S. Supreme Court. Now mem. Hornblower & Marshal; architects of U.S. Custom House, Baltimore, U.S. Nat. Museum, etc. Fellow Am. Inst. Architects. Home: Washington, D.C. Died 1908.

HORNBLOWER, William Butler, lawyer; b. Paterson, N.J., May 13, 1851; s. Rev. William Henry and Matilda (Butler) H.; A.B., Princeton, 1871, A.M., 1874; LL.B., Columbia, 1875; (LL.D., Princeton, 1895). Mem. Hornblower, Miller & Potter, 1907-14; was a member of commn. apptd. by Gov. Hill, 1890, to propose amendments to the judiciary article of the N.Y. constn.; apptd., 1893, asso. justice Supreme Ct. of U.S., but was not confirmed by senate owing to opposition by N.Y. senators for polit. reasons; mem. Bd. Commrs. of Statutory Consolidation apptd. by Act. of N.Y. Legislature, 1904, which prepared Consolidated Laws passed by Legislature, 1909, consolidating and repealing all general laws of the state, 1777—; asso. justice Ct. of Appeals, N.Y., Feb. 1914—. Home: New York, N.Y. Died June 16, 1914.

HORNBROOK, Henry Hallam, lawyer; b. Evansville, Ind., Feb. 15, 1870; s. Sanders Richards and Lucy C. (Wheeler) H.; Ph.B., De Pauw U., 1892; student Law Sch., Harvard, 1893-94; m. Grace Smith, Nov. 25, 1896; 1 dau., Mrs. Margaret Winslow. Admitted to Ind. bar, 1892; began practice at Evansville; practiced at Indianapolis, 1894—. Republican. Methodist. Home: Indianapolis, Ind. Died Sept. 20, 1935.

HORNE, Frank Alexander, refrigeration executive; b. Brooklyn, N.Y., Feb. 25, 1869; s. Alexander and Ann Eliza (Nash) H.; grad. high sch., Brooklyn, 1887; S.C.D., Boston U., 1929; m. Daisalie S. Place, Feb. 21, 1913. Began in refrigeration business at N.Y. City, 1889; pres. Merchants Refrigeration Co., 1911—; dir. Cruikshank Co., East River Savings Bank. Chief of cold storage sect., U.S. Food Administration, 1917-19; chmn. U.S. Appraisal Commn., Washington market, 1921-22. Pres. and mgr. M.E. Hosp. of Brooklyn; v.p. and trustee Drew U. (Madison, N.J.). Home: Brooklyn, N.Y. Died Mar. 22, 1939.

HORNE, Perley Leonard, educator; b. Topeka, Kan., Dec. 30, 1866; s. John Blake and Mary White (Tay) H.; A.B., Harvard, 1892, A.M., 1894; m. Emma Sanderson, June 29, 1892. Master, Dummer Acad., South Byfield, Mass., 1896-1904; pres. The Kamebameha Schools, Honolulu, H.T., 1904-14. Owner and headmaster; The Norfolk School (country day sch.), Wellesley Hills, Mass., 1915-17; became prin. Pinkerton Academy, 1917. Mason. Home: Derry Village, N.H. Died Jan. 1, 1932.

HORNER, Henry, governor; b. Chicago, Ill., Nov. 30, 1878; s. Solomon A. and Dilah (Horner) H.; grad. pub. schs., Chicago and Chicago Manual Training Sch.; student U. of Chicago; LL.B., Chicago-Kent College of Law, 1898; LL.D., Lincoln Memorial U., 1929, Knox Coll., 1933, St. Viator's, 1934, Northwestern, 1935, Millikin U., 1936, Illinois Coll., 1937; Blackburn Coll., 1937; unmarried. Began practice in Chicago, 1899; mem. Whitney & Horner until 1905, Whitman & Horner until 1914; judge Probate Court of Cook Co., 1914-33; elected gov. of Ill. for term, 1933-37, reëlected for term, 1937-41. Mason. Democrat. Owner of a notable collection of Lincolniana. Home: Chicago, Ill. Died Oct. 6, 1940.

HORNER, John B., coll. prof.; b. near La Grange, Tex., Aug. 4, 1856; s. Rev. Elias Ruark and Mary Anne H.; B.S., Philomath (Ore.) Coll., 1877, M.S., 1881; A.B., Willamette U., Ore., 1885, A.M., 1887, Litt.D., 1929; grad. study, Harvard U., summer 1897; U. of Calif., summer 1907; L.H.D., Whitman Coll., 1930; m. Isabelle Skipton, Sept. 5, 1880. Successively prin. high sch., Buena Vista, Union, Brownsville, Roseburg and Albany, Ore., to 1890; prof. English lit., 1890-1900, prof. history, 1900—, Ore. Agrl. Coll. Editor Oregon Teachers' Journal, 1888-90; mem. Ore. State Bd. of Examiners, 1886-98; mem. Ore. Geog. Bd.; sec. State Teachers' Assn., 1882-98; sec.-treas. Ore. Authors' League, 1924-26; mem. Ore. Washington Bicentennial Commn. Presbyn. Author: Oregon—Her History, Her Great Men, Her Literature, 1919; A Short History of Oregon, 1923; Days and Deeds in the Oregon Country, 1928; Oregon History and Early Literature, 1931. Commended by Ore. Legislature for hist. research, 1919. Home: Corvallis, Ore. Died Sept. 1933.

HORNER, Junius Moore, bishop; b. Oxford, N.C., July 7, 1859; s. James Hunter and Sophronia (Moore) H.; A.B., Johns Hopkins, 1885; B.D., Gen. Theol. Sem., 1890; D.D., U. of the South, 1899; m. Eva Harker, Dec. 14, 1892; children—Eva, Katherine, Junius Moore. Deacon, 1890, priest, 1891, P.E. Ch.; prin. Oxford (N.C.) Sch. for Boys, 1890-98; consecrated first missionary bishop of Asheville (N.C.), Dec. 28, 1898, now Diocese of Western N.C. Died Apr. 5, 1933.

HORNICK, Charles W., newspaperman; b. Hoboken, N.J., Aug. 31, 1863; s. William and Marianne J. H.; ed. grammar schs., New York, high sch., Chicago, 2 yrs.; m. Juliet Bruner, June 28, 1885. Began newspaper work on staff of St. Paul Pioneer Press, 1888; mgr. St. Paul Pioneer Press, 1893-99, St. Paul Dispatch, 1899-1905, San Francisco Chronicle, 1905-06; editor-in-chief and pub. San Francisco Call, July 1, 1906—. Active in civic and polit. affairs in San Francisco. Republican; twice declined tendered nomination of mayor of St. Paul. Episcopalian. Dir. Am. Newspaper Pubs. Assn., 1900—; pres. San Francisco Newspaper Pubs. Assn., 1908; dir. Panama-Pacific Expn. Was one of original 100 mems. that organized 1st Inf. Ill. N.G.; retired with rank of capt. Mason. Home: San Francisco, Calif. Died Nov. 18, 1916.

HORNOR, Lynn Sedwick, congressman; b. Clarksburg, W.Va., Nov. 3, 1877; grad. high sch. Engaged in natural gas production; mem. 72d and 73d Congresses (1931-35), 3d W.Va. Dist. Democrat. Home: Clarksburg, W.Va. Died Sept. 23, 1933.

HORNSBY, John Allen, M.D.; b. St. Louis, Mo., Dec. 19, 1859; s. Doddridge Christopher and Elizabeth Matilda (Pim) H.; M.D., Washington U. Sch. of Medicine, 1882; m. Edith Primm, Sept. 18, 1883; children—Edith Marie, Hubert Primm. Interne St. Louis City Hosp., 1882-83; asst. supervising surg., M.P. Ry., 1883-84; coroner, St. Louis County, 1884-85; surgeon White Pass and Yukon Ry., Alaska, 1898-1900; spl. officer, Nome, Alaska, under U.S. Pub. Health Service, 1900-01; supt. Michael Reese Hosp., Chicago, 1907-14; supt. U. of Va. Hosp. and prof. Med. Sch. U. of Va. until 1931. Commd. 1st lt. M.R.C., U.S.A., 1911; maj. M.C., U.S.A., 1917; in active service throughout World War; promoted to lt. col., Apr. 1918; was chief of Hosp. Div., U.S.A., chief insp. of mil. hosps. and confidential adviser to Secretary of War Newton D. Baker. Author: (text book) The Modern Hospital; The Small Community Hospital; etc. Home: Washington, D.C. Died June 4, 1939.

HORR, George Edwin, theologian; b. Boston, Mass., Jan. 19, 1856; s. George Edwin and Matilda (Ellis) H.; A.B., Brown U., 1876, D.D., 1896; Union Theol. Sem., 1876-77; B.D., Newton Theol. Instn., 1879; LL.D., Colby, 1915; S.T.D., Harvard U.; m. Evelyn

Olmsted Sacchi, Mar. 16, 1886. Ordained Baptist ministry, 1879; pastor First Ch., Tarrytown, N.Y., 1879-84, First Ch., Charlestown, Mass., 1884-91; editor-in-chief The Watchman, 1891-1903; prof. ch. history, 1903—, pres., 1908—, Newton Theol. Instn. Fellow Brown U.; trustee Wellesley Coll., Worcester Acad., Shaw U. Author: The Baptist Heritage, 1923; The Christian Faith and Eternal Life, 1923. Dudleian lecturer, Harvard, 1913; Ingersoll lecturer, Harvard, 1923. Home: Newton Center, Mass. Died Jan. 22, 1927.

HORST, Emil Clemens, mcht., farmer; b. Tuttlingen, Germany, Mar. 18, 1867; s. Ernst Paul and Maria Barbara (Manz) H.; brought by parents to U.S., 1871; student Coll. City of N.Y., 1885-86, Cooper Union, N.Y. City, 1886-89; m. Daisy Brown, Feb. 14, 1893; children—Hazel (dec.), Helen (Mrs. Jose Moya del Pino), Beatrice (Mrs. Edouard Thys), E. Clemens. Employed, 1886-89, by Red Star Line, Knauth Nachod and Kuhne (foreign bankers in New York), A. S. Lascelles & Co. (exporters, New York) and Lilienthal Brothers (hop mchts., New York); in 1889 formed partnership with Paul and Louis Horst and Frank Jones under name of Horst Brothers, hop mchts., New York and San Francisco; organized, 1898, and pres. E. Clemens Horst Co., San Francisco. Engaged in growing hops and fruit; also canning and packing fruits and exporting barley. Inventor of the hop picking machine and natural air driers of hops. Mem. Grange, Farmers' Union. Home: San Francisco, Calif. Died May 24, 1940.

HORST, George Philip, clergyman; b. Detroit, Mich., Jan. 26, 1884; s. Peter William and Eliza Augusta (Jasper) H.; B.S., Alma (Mich.) Coll., 1908; M.A., Princeton, 1911; B.D., Princeton Theol. Sem., 1911; D.D., Washington Coll., Tenn., 1915; unmarried. Ordained ministry Presbyn. Ch., 1911; pastor Beacon Presbyn. Ch., Philadelphia, Pa., 1911-14, Second Presbyn. Ch., Portsmouth, O., 1914-21; dir. men's work, Presbyn. Ch., in U.S.A., 1921-31; pastor First Presbyn. Ch., Wichita Falls, Tex., 1931—. Served as chaplain, 1st lt., U.S.A., World War; now lt. col. Chaplain Res., U.S.A. Trustee Alma Coll. Mem. Gen. Council Presbyn. Ch. U.S.A. Republican. Mason. Home: Wichita Falls, Tex. Died Nov. 29, 1936.

HORSTMANN, Ignatius Frederick, R.C. bishop; b. Phila., Pa., Dec. 16, 1840; s. Frederick and Catharine (Weber) H.; grad. Central High Sch., Phila., 1857; studied at Jesuit Coll., and prep. sem., Glen Riddle, Pa.; grad. Am. College, Rome (D.D., 1866); ordained priest, June 10, 1865. Prof. St. Charles' Sem., Phila., 1865-77; pastor St. Mary's, Phila., 1877-85; chancellor archdiocese of Phila., 1885-92; consecrated bishop of Cleveland, Feb. 25, 1892. Asst. editor Am. Catholic Quarterly Review, 1889-92; edited Nampon's Catholic Doctrine as Defined in the Council of Trent. Died 1908.

HORTON, Albert Howell, lawyer; b. Orange Co., N.Y., March 13, 1837; s. Dr. Harvey A. and Mary B. H.; ed. Farmers Hall Acad., and 2 yrs., 1856-57, Univ. of Mich.; married; went to Kan., April 1860; has been city atty. of Atchison, Kan.; mem. legislature from Atchison Co., Kan., dist. judge 2d jud., Kan., U.S. atty. for dist. of Kan., and chief justice of Kan. from Jan. 1877 to May 1895; resigned to resume practice. Republican. Home: Topeka, Kan. Died 1902.

HORTON, Edward Augustus, clergyman; b. Springfield, Mass., Sept. 28, 1843; s. William Marshall and Ann (Leonard) H.; served in S. Atlantic Squadron during Civil War; student U. of Mich., 1865-66 (hon. A.M., 1880); grad. Meadville Theol. Sem., 1868; studied at Brunswick and Heidelberg, 1871; (D.D., Tufts Coll., 1919); m. Josephine Adelaide Rand, Dec. 1, 1875; 1 dau., Ruth (Mrs. B. Arthur Bensley). Pastor Leominster, Mass., 1868-75, Hingham, Mass., 1877-80, Second Ch., Copley Sq., Boston, 1880-92 (emeritus). President Unitarian S.S. Soc., and editor, Every Other Sunday, 1892-1910. Chaplain emeritus of Mass. Senate, Mass. Grand Lodge Freemasons, Ancient and Honorable Artillery Co., and of Kinsley Post G.A.R. Republican. Author: Noble Lives and Noble Deeds, 1893; Scenes in the Life of Jesus, 1895; Beginning of Christianity, 1896; Teaching of Jesus, 1896; The Story of Israel, 1896; Beacon Lights of Christian History (2 grades), 1897; Great Thoughts of Israel, 1896; Character Building, 1899; Foundation Truths in Religion, 1899; Great Passages from the Bible, 1901. Pres. Myles Standish Monument Assn., Boston Common Soc. Home: Boston, Mass. Died Apr. 15, 1931.

HORTON, Henry Hollis, governor; b. Princeton, Ala., Feb. 17, 1866; s. Henry Hollis and Anna Elizabeth (Moore) H.; prep. edn., Scott Acad., Scottsboro, Ala.; student Winchester (Tenn.) Coll., 1886-88, U. of the South, Tenn., 1891-92; m. Anna Adeline Wilhoite, Dec. 25, 1896; 1 son, John Wilhoite. Mem. Tenn. Ho. of Rep., 1907-09, Tenn. Senate, 1927 (speaker 1927); gov. of Tenn., 1927-33. Democrat. Baptist. Home: Nashville, Tenn. Died July 2, 1934.

HORTON, Katharine Loren Pratt; b. Buffalo, N.Y.; d. Pascal Paoli and Phebe (Loren) Pratt; ed. Buffalo Sem., Brooklyn Heights Sem.; m. John Miller Horton. Chmn. com. on ceremonies and entertainments Woman's Bd. of Pan-Am. Expn., Buffalo, 1901; commr. to Charleston (S.C.) Expn., 1901; mem. Woman's Bd. Lady Mgrs., St. Louis Expn., 1904; pres. Niagara Frontier Landmarks Assn. Regent of the Buffalo Chapter D.A.R.; founder and pres. Buffalo Fedn. Women's Clubs; pres. Nellie Custis Chapter, and v.p. Nat. Soc. Children of Am. Revolution; v.p. Order of Americans of Armorial Ancestry; trustee Nat. Soc. Daughters of Empire State. Three times del. to Internat. Peace and Arbitration Congress in Europe; pres. Woman's Bd. of Buffalo Celebration of 100 Years of Peace. V.p. Erie br. Am. Red Cross. Episcopalian. Home: Buffalo, N.Y. Deceased.

HORTON, McDavid, journalist; b. Greenville, S.C., Mar. 16, 1884; s. Eberle Roscoe and Laura (McDavid) H.; student Furman U., 1903-04, Mercer U., 1904; m. Sarah Flinn, July 18, 1907 (died 1930); 1 dau., Sarah Flinn (Mrs. Joseph Henry Moore). Became reporter Greenville (S.C.) News, 1900; editor The State, Columbia, Jan. 1938—. Served as capt., F.A., A.E.F.; major Res. Corps. Presbyn. Democrat. Home: Columbia, S.C. Died Oct. 1941.

HORTON, Oliver Harvey, lawyer; b. Cattaraugus Co., N.Y., Oct. 20, 1835; s. Rev. Harvey W. and Mary H. H.; ed. Rochester, N.Y., and Kingsville, O.; LL.B., Union Coll. of Law (now Law Sch. of Northwestern U.), 1863; (LL.D., Northwestern, 1889); m. Frances B. Gould, Dec. 27, 1857. Admitted to bar, 1863, and began practice at Chicago. Corp. counsel, 1887; judge of Circuit Ct., 1887-1903, serving in Appellate Ct., 1st Dist. of Ill., 1888-1903. Trustee Garrett Bibl. Inst., Northwestern U., Lewis Inst., and Wesley Hosp.; del. Gen. Conf. M.E. Ch., 1880, 1900, Ecumenical Conf., London, 1881; pres. Laymen's Assn., Rock River Conf. Home: Evanston, Ill. Died Feb. 6, 1915.

HORTON, Thomas Corwin, clergyman; b. Cincinnati, Aug. 3, 1848; s. Henry Victor and Sophia Matilda (Daugherty) H.; student Farmers' Coll., College Hill, O., 1 yr.; m. Anna Y. Kingsbury, May 15, 1872 (died 1920); children—Ruth Pierson (Mrs. C. L. Wells), Helen (Mrs. Paul E. Walker), Margaret (Mrs. V. V. Morgan), Jessie Blake (dec.); m. 2d, Harriet L. Ransom, Mar. 16, 1922. Trained in office work; partner in state agency Wheeler & Wilson Sewing Machines, Inc.; secretary Y.M.C.A. Indianapolis, 1876, later evangelist Presbyn. Ch.; regularly ordained to ministry, 1884; pastor St. Paul, Minn., 1 year; associate pastor with Rev. Dr. A. T. Pierson, Bethany Ch., Phila., 1885-89; sec. Y.M.C.A., St. Paul, 1890; pastor Independent Ch., St. Paul, 1894-1900, 1st Congl. Ch. (now Scofield Memorial Ch.), Dallas, Tex., 1900-03, and sec. Y.M.C.A., 1904-06; Bible Teacher Immanuel Presbyn. Ch., Los Angeles, 1906; organizer and pres. Internat. Fishermen's Club for Young Men; organized Bible Inst. of Los Angeles, 1907 (supt. emeritus); asso. pastor Ch. of the Open Door, 1915-24; editor in chief The King's Business, 1910-25. Republican. Author: Personal and Practical Christian Work, 1922; The Wonderful Names of Our Wonderful Lord, 1925; Outline Studies in Epistles of John and Jude, 1927; The Potency of Prayer, 1928; Forty Names of Satan, 1929. Editor Fishers of Men, 1930—. Home: Los Angeles, Calif. Died Feb. 27, 1932.

HORTON, William Edward, army officer; b. Washington, D.C., June 28, 1868; s. William Edward and Josephine Julia (Clarke) H.; grad. high sch., Washington, 1886; LL.B., Georgetown U., 1892, LL.M., 1893; unmarried. Commd. 1st lt. and adj. 1st D.C. Inf., U.S.A., May 11, 1898; advanced through grades to col., July 1, 1920; apptd. asst. to q.m.g., in charge constrn. service, rank of brig. gen. for 4 yrs. from Aug. 2, 1927; retired, 1929, and has practiced law since at Washington. Served in Spanish-American War, participating in charge of San Juan Hill; in campaigns against Aguinaldo, 1899, and Malvar, 1901-02, Philippine Islands; builder of Ft. William McKinley and Malate Bks., P.I.; in 2d intervention in Cuba, 1906-07; served as chief q.m., advance sect., and asst. to chief q.m., A.E.F., Tours, France, World War. Decorated D.S.M., Spanish Campaign Medal, silver star (citation for gallantry in action, Santiago, Cuba, July 1, 1898), Cuban Occupation Medal, Philippine Campaign Medal, silver star (citation for gallantry in action, Taboatin Bridge, P.I., Dec. 3, 1899), Cuban Pacification Medal, Victory Medal, World War (all U.S.); Officer Legion of Honor and Grand Cross Order Nichan El Anouar (France); Companion of Order St. Michael and St. George (Eng.); Comdr. Order Leopold II (Belgium); Comdr. Order of Crown of Italy; Officer Order of White Eagle (Serbia); Comdr. Order of Crown of Rumania; Grand Officer Order Prince Danilo I (Montenegro); Officer Mil. Medal La Solaridad (Panama); Grand Dignitary (Grand Cross) of Order of Crown of Charlemagne; Grand Official of Black Eagle Assn., also of Nat. Albanian Order of Skanderbeg. Comdr. Polonia Restituta (Poland); War Cross (Montenegro); Croix d' Honneur du Croix de Mérite (France); Star of Royal Acad. Hispano-Americana of Sciences and Arts (Spain). Hon. mem. Arts, Sciences, Lettres, Société d'Éducation and D'Encouragement de France; pres. and treas. Soc. of Am. Friends of Albania; mem. Baronial Order of Runnemede. Mason. Home: Washington, D.C. Died Sept. 13, 1935.

HORWITZ, Phineas Jonathan, med. dir. U.S.N.; b. Baltimore, March 3, 1822; ed. St. Mary Coll., Baltimore; grad. Univ. of Md., M.D., 1845; apptd. asst. surgeon, U.S.N.; Nov. 8, 1847; served in Mexican war, in charge of hosp. at Tampico; asst. surgeon gen., 1859-65; surgeon gen., 1865-69; med. insp., March 3, 1871; med. dir., Dec. 19, 1873, with relative rank of capt. While asst., 1859-65, and chief, 1865-69, of Bur. of Medicine and Surgery, had entire charge of tabulating casualties of war, indexing books of reference, etc.; had charge Naval Asylum, Phila., 1877-83; pres. examining bd., 1883-84; retired. Died 1904.

HOSKIER, Herman C., author; b. London, Eng., No. 12, 1864; s. Herman and Elizabeth Catherine (Byrne) H.; ed. Eton Coll., Eng., and in France and Germany; hon. A.M., Univ. of Michigan; Th.D., Amsterdam; m. Harriet A. Wood, May 23, 1888 (dec.); children—Cyril Herman (dec.), Walter Harald, Ronald Wood (dec.), Frank Roy Byrne. In banking and brokerage business, New York, as Hoskier, Wood & Co., then mem. L. von Hoffmann & Co. and F. S. Smithers & Co., until 1903; retired to devote attention to lit. occupations; endeavoring to solve the early interaction of the versions of the N.T. (Syriac, Coptic, Ethiopic and Latin), among each other and on the Greek, during the first four centuries of Christian era. Liberal Democrat. Episcopalian. In Europe 1914-19 during entire war; served in French Army, grade of lieutenant, with Am. Vol. Ambulance Sections VII and XI prior to U.S. entry into the war; decorated Croix de Guerre (two citations) and Legion of Honor; subsequently was rep. Am. Red Cross at French Gen. Hdqrs. Author: History of the Transmission of the Apocalypse (after examination of all existing MSS.), 1928. Editor: Collations of the Greek Codex Evan., 157-604, etc., 1890; The Golden Latin Gospels in the Library of J. Pierpont Morgan, 1910; Lost Commentary of Oecumenius (editio princeps), 1928; Bernard of Cluny's De contemptu mundi 1929; Immortality, 1925; In Tune With the Universe, 1931; The Back of Beyond, 1934. Died Sept. 8, 1938.

HOSKIN, Arthur Joseph, mining engr.; b. Shopiere, Wis., Jan. 4, 1869; s. Albert A. and Eliza M. (Taylor) H.; B.M.E., U. of Wis., 1890, M.E., 1905; m. Mary Margaret Allen, July 27, 1893; children—Elizabeth Louise (Mrs. A. S. Irvine), Margaret Jane. Began as mining engr., Idaho Springs, Colo., 1890; assayer, Omaha & Grant Smeltery, Denver, 1891-95; U.S. surveyor-gen.'s office, Denver, 1895; ore broker. Central City, 1896; mine engr., Cripple Creek, 1896-97; ore agencies, Florence, Leadville, Pueblo, Denver, 1897-99; U.S. sur.-gen.'s office, Denver, 1900-01; mine engr., Leadville, 1902; chief engr., Leyden Coal Co., Denver, 1903-06; asst. prof. and prof. mining, Colo. Sch. of Mines, Golden, 1905-11; editor, Mining and Metallurgical Jour., 1908; on Colo. Geol. Survey, 1910-11; western editor, Mines and Minerals, 1912-13; mgr., Square Deal G.M. Co., 1912-13; mine engr., consulting practice, 1913-16; mine engr., Leadville, 1916-17; editor The Mining American, Denver, 1917-18, oil-shale and consulting engr., 1918-21; research asst. prof. mining, 1921-23, research asso. prof. mining, 1923—, acting head of mining dept., 1923-24, U. of Ill. Research for Am. Ry. Assn. and asso. in geology and mineralogy, Purdue, 1926-29; editor Pit and Quarry, 1929—. Mason. Author: The Business of Mining, 1912. Home: Chicago, Ill. Died Mar. 13, 1935.

HOSKINS, Fermin Lincoln, bishop; b. Scio, Ore., June 8, 1865; s. James B. and Clarinda J. (Kenoyer) H.; prep. edn. Washington Sem., Huntsville, Wash.; student Philomath (Ore.) Coll., 1884-85; D.D., Central Coll., Huntington, Ind., 1905, M.A., 1910; m. Minnie A. Simonton, Dec. 18, 1892; children—Mrs. Beulah E. Luce, Mrs. Amelia M. Luce, Mrs. Gladys L. Calvert, Grace E. Formerly teacher in pub. schs., Ore., Wash. and Ida., and prin. Washington Sem.; ordained ministry U.B. Ch., 1895; became bishop U.B. Ch., 1905, emeritus, 1933. Pres. Central Coll., 1911 (resigned), Edwards Coll., Albion, Wash. (resigned). Prog. Republican. Home: Myrtle, Idaho. Died Feb. 18, 1935.

HOSKINS, Franklin Evans, missionary; b. Rockdale, Pa., Sept. 28, 1858; s. John Taylor and Jane (Brown) H.; A.B., Princeton, 1883, A.M., 1886; B.D., Union Theol. Sem., 1888; spl. studies, Yale; (D.D., New York U., 1903); m. Harriette Mollison Eddy, Aug. 22, 1888. Ordained Presbyn. ministry, 1888; prin. Prep. Dept., Syrian Protestant Coll., Beirut, 1883-86; touring missionary, with journeys of exploration in trans-Jordan country and Arabia, 1888-1900; editor Am. Mission Press, 1900—, issuing books and periodicals in Arabic lang., and extensive work in connection with various editions of Arabic bible. Pres. Theol. Faculty, 1911—; mem. exec. com. Lebanon Hosp. for Mental Diseases. Hon. life dir. Am. Bible Society. Hon. dir. British Relief in Palestine; commr. Syria and Palestine Relief, 1914-18. Died Nov. 12, 1920.

HOSKINS, John Deane Charles, brig. gen.; b. Potosi, Mo., Jan. 19, 1846; s. late Lt. Charles

(U.S.A.) and Jennie (Deane) H.; grad. U.S. Mil. Acad., 1868; m. Blanca Guiteras, of Matanzas, Cuba, Feb. 7, 1871. Second lt. 1st Inf., June 15, 1868; transferred to 3d Arty., May 13, 1869; grad. Arty. Sch., 1874; 1st lt. Dec. 20, 1875; capt. June 7, 1897; maj. Arty. Corps, July 1, 1901; lt. col., Mar. 22, 1905; col., June 22, 1906; brig. gen. U.S.A., Dec. 27, 1908, and retired at own request after 44 yrs.' service. Episcopalian. Mason. Died Mar. 1, 1937.

HOSKINS, J(ohn) Preston, univ. prof.; b. Rockdale, Pa., Jan. 16, 1867; s. John Taylor and Jane (Brown) H.; A.B., Princeton, 1891; fellow modern langs., Princeton, 1891-92; Ph.D., U. of Berlin, 1895; m. Mary Ella, d. John Barlow, June 28, 1900. Began teaching at Princeton, 1895, prof. Germanic langs. and lit., 1912—. Dir. propaganda div., Bur. of Investigation, U.S. Dept. Justice, N.Y. City and Washington, D.C., Sept. 1918-Sept. 1919; dir (foreign) radical publn. div., same bur., Washington, D.C., 1919-20. Democrat. Presbyn. A founder Modern Lang. Jour., 1917. Home: Princeton, N.J. Died July 15, 1935.

HOSKINS, Leander Miller, univ. prof.; b. in Wis., May 10, 1860; s. James H. and Araminta S. (Warren) H.; B.C.E., B.S., U. of Wis., 1883, M.S., 1885, C.E., 1887, Sc.D., 1918. Instr. engring., 1885-89, asst. prof. mechanics, 1889-91, prof. theoretical and applied mathematics, 1891-92, U. of Wis.; prof. applied mathematics, Stanford U., 1892—. Author: Graphic Statics, 1892; Theoretical Mechanics, 1900, 5th edit., 1915; Hydraulics, 1906, 3d edit., 1911. Home: Palo Alto, Calif. Died 1937.

HOSKINS, William, chemist; b. Covington, Ky., July 15, 1862; s. John and Mary Ann (Hoskins) H.; grad. Chicago High Sch., 1879, followed by chemical and other instrn.; m. Ada May Mariner, Dec. 8, 1885; children—Minna, Edna (Mrs. Fred Scheele), William, Florence (Mrs. Harvey Melcher). Joined Prof. G. A. Mariner in his analyt. chem. lab., 1880, and became partner, 1885, Mariner & Hoskins; sole propr., 1890—; pres. Mariner & Hoskins, Inc. Associate mem. Naval Consulting Bd., 1917, and mem. sub-com. in charge Chicago office; mem. advisory com. U.S. Bureau of Mines. Republican. Unitarian. Died May 19, 1934.

HOSKINS, William Horace, veterinarian; b. Rockdale, Pa., July 23, 1860; s. John T. and Jane B. H.; ed. pub. schs., Delaware Co., Pa.; grad. Am. Vet. Coll., New York, 1881; m. Annie E. Cheever, Mar. 19, 1885. Editor-in-chief Journal of Comparative Medicine and Veterinary Archives; prof. on veterinary jurisprudence, ethics and business methods, vet. dept. U. of Pa. until 1917; prof. jurisprudence and clin. medicine and dean, N.Y. State Vet. Coll. (New York U.), 1917—. Pres. and sec. Pa. State Bd. of Vet. Med. Examiners. Dem. candidate for mayor of Phila., 1899. Home: New York, N.Y. Died Aug. 10, 1921.

HOSMER, Frederick Lucian, clergyman; b. Framingham, Mass., Oct. 16, 1840; s. Charles and Susan (Carter) H.; A.B., Harvard, 1862; grad. Harvard Div. Sch., 1869; S.T.D., Buchtel, 1887; unmarried. Ordained Unitarian ministry, Northboro, Mass., 1869; settled in Quincy, Ill., 1872-77, Cleveland, O., 1878-92, in St. Louis, 1894-99; now resident Berkeley, Calif.; was minister Unitarian Ch. there. Lecturer on ch. hymnody, Harvard, 1908. Author: The Thought of God, in Hymns and Poems, 1st series, 1885, 2d series, 1894, 3d series, 1918 (with W. C. Gannett). Joint editor (with W. C. Gannett and J. V. Blake) Unity Hymns and Chorals, Chicago, 1880; (with W. C. Gannett), Unity Hymns and Chorals, rev. and enlarged, with Service Elements, 1911. Home: Berkeley, Calif. Died June 7, 1929.

HOSMER, George Stedman, judge; b. Detroit, May 13, 1855; s. John and Lucy Jane (Buttrick) H.; A.B., U. of Mich., 1875; (LL.D., 1910); studied law with Griffin & Dickinson, Detroit, and admitted to bar, 1878; m. Margaret S. Bagley, Oct. 30, 1889 (dec.); m. 2d, Mrs. Frances Bagley Brown. Mem. Griffin, Dickinson, Thurber & Hosmer, Detroit, to 1883, Dickinson, Thurber & Hosmer, 1883-88; judge circuit ct., 3d Jud. Circuit of Mich., Jan. 1, 1888. Democrat. Unitarian. Home: Detroit, Mich. Died Mar. 2, 1921.

HOSMER, Harriet Goodhue, sculptor; b. Watertown, Mass., Oct. 9, 1830; studied art in Boston under Stevenson, and anatomy under her father, a physician, supplemented by course at St. Louis Med. Coll.; studied with Gibson in Rome, 1852-53. Among her works are busts of Daphne and Medusa, Œnome, Zenobia in Chains, The Sleeping Faun, The Waking Faun, Beatrice Cenci, Puck, statue of Thomas H. Benton, at St. Louis; statue of Queen Isabella, statue of Queen of Naples; The Heroine of Gaeta; Triton and Mermaid Fountains for Louisa, Lady Ashburton, England; Siren Fountain for Lady Marian Alford, England. Died 1908.

HOSMER, James Kendall, author; b. Northfield, Mass., Jan. 29, 1834; s. Rev. Dr. George W. and Hanna P. (Kendall) H.; A.B., Harvard, 1855, A.M., 1867, grad. Div. Sch., 1859; hon. Ph.D., U. of Mo., 1877; LL.D., Washington U., 1897, Harvard, 1925; m. Eliza A. Cutler, Oct. 15, 1863; m. 2d, Jenny P. Garland, Nov. 27, 1878. Unitarian pastor Deerfield, Mass., 1860-66; served in Civil War as private (declining staff appmt.) in 52d Mass. Vols., 19th Army Corps; prof. rhetoric and English, Antioch Coll., 1866-72; prof. English and history, U. of Mo., 1872-74; prof. English and German lit., Washington U., 1874-92; librarian Minneapolis Pub. Library, 1892-1904; pres. A.L.A., 1902-03. Fellow Am. Acad. Arts and Sciences. Author: Life of Samuel Adams (Am. Statesmen Series), 1885; Life of Sir Henry Vane, 1888; Short History of Anglo-Saxon Freedom, 1890; History of the Civil War in America, Vols. XX and XXI ("Appeal to Arms" and "Outcome of the Civil War") of the "American Nation," 1907. Editor: Expedition Lewis and Clark, 1902; Journal of John Winthrop, 1908; The Last Leaf, 1912. Home: Minneapolis, Minn. Died May 11, 1927.

HOSMER, Samuel Monroe, univ. pres.; b. Tuscaloosa Co., Ala., July 22, 1846; s. Silas and Esther Ann (Cowley) H.; served 18 mos. in C.S.A. during Civil War; B.P. Southern U., 1874 (D.D., 1893); m. Fannie Parsons, Dec. 11, 1867. Joined the N. Ala. Conf., M.E. Ch., S., 1874; pastor Valley Head Circuit, 1875-77, Madison Circuit, 1878-79, Trinity Circuit, 1880, Florence Dist., 1881-84, Gadsden Dist., 1885-86, Huntsville Dist., 1887-89, Talladega Dist., 1890, Tuscaloosa Sta., 1891-92, Birmingham Dist., 1893, Talladega Dist., 1897-99; pres. Southern U., Greensboro, Ala., Feb. 1899-June 1910; presiding elder, Troy Dist., Ala. Conf., Feb. 1911-15; pastor Brundidge, Ala., 1915—. Mem. Gen. Conf., 5 times; mem. Gen. Bd. of Ch. Extension, 1890-1906, Bd. of Ins., M.E. Ch., S., 1902—. Home: Brundidge, Ala. Died Dec. 24, 1916.

HOSS, Elijah Embree, bishop; b. Washington Co., Tenn., Apr. 14, 1849; s. Henry and Anna M. (Sevier) H.; A.B., Emory and Henry Coll., Va., 1869 (D.D., 1885; LL.D., 1890; LL.D., Emory Coll., Ga., 1898, Ohio Wesleyan, 1906); m. Abbie Clark, Nov. 19, 1872. Ordained M.E. Ch., S., ministry, 1870; pastor Knoxville, Tenn., 1870-72, San Francisco, 1872-74, Asheville, N.C., 1875; pres. and prof. Martha Washington Coll., Abingdon, Va., 1876-81; v.p. and later pres. Emory and Henry Coll., 1881-85; prof. ecclesiastical history, Vanderbilt U., 1885-90; editor Nashville (Tenn.) Christian Advocate, 1890-1902; bishop M.E. Ch., S., May 1902—. Died Apr. 23, 1919.

HOSS, George Washington, educator; b. on farm, Brown Co., O., Nov. 6, 1824; s. Jacob and Jane H.; grad. Asbury (now DePauw) Univ., 1850, A.M., 1853; (LL.D., State Univ. of Ind.); m. Harriet J. Mitchell, Greencastle, Ind., Dec. 1850 (died June 1886); m. 2d, July 1888, May E. Engstrom. Head schs., 1850; prof. mathematics, 1852; pres., 1855-56, Ind. Female Coll., Indianapolis; prof. mathematics, N. W. Christian Univ., Indianapolis, 1856-64; State supt. pub. instruction, Ind., 1864-68; prof. English literature, Ind. State Univ., 1868-71; pres. Kan. State Normal Sch., Emporia, 1871-74; prof. English literature, Ind. State Univ., 1874-80. Editor and propr. Ind. Sch. Jour., 1863-71; editor and propr. Kan. Ednl. Jour., Topeka, 1880-85; prof. English lit. and oratory, prin. until 1903, Western Sch. of Elocution and Oratory, Wichita, Kan. Originally a Democrat; became a Republican on slavery issue; for several yrs. past Prohibitionist. Author: Memory Gems, 1883; First Steps in Public Speaking, 1903. Home: Wichita, Kan. Died 1906.

HOTCHKIN, Samuel Fitch, clergyman; b. Sauquoit, N.Y., Apr. 2, 1833; s. Rev. Dr. Beriah Bishop and Elizabeth Alice H.; A.B., Trinity Coll., 1856, A.M., 1859; grad. Gen. Theol. Sem., 1860; m. Sarah Sully, d. John Neagle, artist, of Phila., June 1, 1869 (died 1898); m. 2d, Helen Nicholson, d. Rev. Edmund Roberts, May 31, 1899. Deacon, 1860, priest, 1861, P.E. Ch.; asst., and later rector Ch. of Ascension, Claymont, Del., and Grace and Calvary chs., Brandywine Hundred, Del., 1860-76; rector, Trinity, Red Bank, N.J., and St. John's Chapel, Little Silver, N.J., 1876-77, St. Luke, the Beloved Physician, Phila., 1877-1909, rector emeritus, 1909, and registrar Diocese of Pa. (Phila.). Died Aug. 1, 1912.

HOTCHKISS, Chauncey Crafts, author; b. New York, Oct. 28, 1852; s. Hon. William B. and Rebecca B. H.; ed. at boarding schs. and old Sch. No. 35 on 13th St., New York; m. Kate N. Krugler, 1896. Was connected with various commercial ventures; writer, 1894—. Author: The Red Paper, 1912; The Spur of Danger, 1915; The Ivory Ball, 1919, and others. Home: Brooklyn, N.Y. Died Dec. 1920.

HOTCHKISS, George W., secretary; b. New Haven, Conn., Oct. 16, 1831; s. Elias and Almira (Woodward) H.; ed. Lancasterian School and Russell and French Acad., New Haven; m. Elizabeth St. John, Aug. 14, 1856. Went to Calif., 1849, via Cape Horn, reaching San Francisco after a voyage of 154 days; in lumber business at Pt. Dover, Can., 1852-60, and Bay City, Mich., 1861-77. With editorial dept. Saginaw Daily Courier, 1870, and was one of the originators of the Lumberman's Gazette (lumber jour.), and was editor Evening Tribune, Bay City, at intervals, 1871-76; asst. editor Northwestern Lumberman, Chicago, 1877-81; sec. Chicago Lumbermen's Exchange, 1881-87; pres. and editor Lumber Trade Journal, 1887-1905; editor Evanston (Ill.) Press, 1891; sec. Ill. Lumber Dealers' Assn. (emeritus). Mugwump (Dem.), opposing the Bryan policy. Alderman, 1865-69, and town supervisor, 1865-67, Bay City, Mich.; supervisor Evanston Township, Ill., 1896-1902. Presbyn. Mason Home: Evanston, Ill. Died Mar. 1, 1926.

HOTCHKISS, Henry DeWitt, judge; b. Albany, N.Y., July 2, 1856; s. Thomas Woodward and Emma (Burrell) H.; ed. under tutors and at pvt. schs.; m. Alice Strong. Admitted to N.Y. bar, 1878, and practiced at N.Y. City; mem. N.Y. Assembly, 1886; mem. N.Y. State Constl. Conv., 1894; justice Supreme Court N.Y., term Jan. 1, 1912-Dec. 31, 1925; designated to Appellate Div., Feb. 17, 1913. Democrat. Episcopalian. Home: New York, N.Y. Died Mar. 6, 1922.

HOTCHKISS, Horace Leslie; b. Auburn, N.Y., Mar. 27, 1842; s. Clark Beers and Caroline (Bennett) H.; ed. Auburn Acad.; m. Clara Taylor, June 26, 1867; m. 2d, Lucy May Johnson, Oct. 28, 1922. Was an organizer, and treas. Gold & Stock Telegraph Co., 1867; an organizer Am. Dist. Telegraph Co., 1871; assisted in developing the Exchange Telegraph Co., London, Eng., 1873; became mem. N.Y. Stock Exchange, 1874, and in brokerage and banking business until 1902; active in securing concession to build Nacaragua Canal, and was treas. Nicaragua Canal Constrn. Co., 1886-91. Served in the U.S. Navy, Civil War; participated in Battle of Mobile Bay; was treas. Grant Monument Assn. Republican. Christian Scientist. Organized Seniors' Golf Tournament, 1905; hon. pres. U.S. Seniors' Golf Assn.; hon. life mem. Canadian Seniors' Golf Assn. Home: New York, N.Y. Died May 10, 1929.

HOTCHKISS, Lucius Wales, surgeon; b. New Haven, Conn., Dec. 31, 1859; s. Wales and Frances Augusta (Collins) H.; A.B., Columbia, 1881; M.D., Coll. Phys. and Surg. (Columbia), 1884; m. Alice Hartley Greene, June 3, 1891; children—Henry G., Alice, Helen (dec.), Edna, Lucia. Began practice in New York, 1886; served as prof. clin. surgery, Coll. Phys. and Surg. (Columbia), and as consulting surgeon, Roosevelt, Bellevue, Knickerbocker, St. Joseph's, Yonkers and Greenwich hosps. Democrat. Episcopalian. Fellow Am. Surg. Assn. Home: Santa Barbara, Calif. Died Apr. 12, 1926.

HOTZ, Ferdinand Carl, physician, oculist; b. Wertheim, Baden, Germany, July 12, 1843; s. Gottfried and Rosa H.; ed. Lyceum there; studied medicine at Jena and Heidelberg (M.D., 1865), and afterward at Berlin, Vienna, Paris and London; surgeon South German army in war between Prussia and Austria, 1866; came to U.S., settling in Chicago, 1869; ophthalmic surgeon, Ill. Eye and Ear Infirmary, 1876—; prof. ophthalmology, Chicago Polyclinic, 1888—, and Rush Med. Coll., 1898—; dir. Chicago Public Library for many yrs. Died 1909.

HOTZ, Robert Schuttler, merchant; b. Chicago, Ill., Sept. 1, 1870; s. Christopher and Catharine (Schuttler) H.; Ph.B., Sheffield Scientific Sch. (Yale), 1891; m. Lila Frances Ross, Dec. 17, 1896. Entered service of Schuttler & Hotz, mfrs. of wagons, upon graduation from Yale; was in charge of their exhibit at World's Columbian Expn., 1893; became traveling salesman, 1894-96, traffic mgr., 1897, sec., 1902, and v.p., 1904; resigned Sept. 1, 1905; mem. Hotz & Rehm, real estate and investments, 1906-11. V.p. Citizens' Assn. of Chicago; commr. of Chicago Assn. Commerce to investigate the "Potentia" movement in Europe and spent a year, 1910, in visiting the capitals and principal cities in behalf of the assn. Republican. Home: Chicago, Ill. Died Aug. 25, 1918.

HOUCK, Louis, author; b. St. Clair Co., Ill., Apr. 1, 1840; s. Bartholomew and Anna (Senn) H.; ed. pub. schs.; m. Mary Hunter Giboney, Dec. 24, 1872. Admitted to Mo. bar, later engaged in farming. Pres. bd. regents Southeast Mo. Teachers' Coll., Cape Girardeau, Mo., 1884—. Built about 500 miles of railroad in southeast Missouri. Author: History of Missouri—Colonial and Territorial (3 vols.), 1908; The Spanish Regime in Missouri (2 vols.), 1909. Home: Cape Girardeau, Mo. Died Feb. 17, 1925.

HOUDINI, Harry, magician; b. Appleton, Wis., Apr. 6, 1874; s. Rev. Dr. Mayer Samuel and Cecelia (Steiner) Weiss, but name legally changed to Houdini; ed. pub. schs.; m. Wilhelmina Rahner, June 22, 1894. Began as trapeze performer, 1882; has made several tours of the world, performing before many rulers and notables. Inventor of a diving suit. Pres. Weehawken St. Corp., Film Developing Corp., Houdini Picture Corp. Awarded prize by Australian Aeronautic League, 1910, as being the first successful flier in Australia. Author: The Right Way to Do Wrong, 1906; Unmasking of Robert Houdini, 1908; Miracle Mongers, Paper Prestidigitation; Rope Ties and Escapes; A Magician Among the Spirits, 1924. Home: New York, N.Y. Died Oct. 31, 1926.

HOUGH, Alfred Lacey, soldier; b. Springfield Twp., N.J., Apr. 23, 1826; s. Jonathan and Jane Chapman (Lacey) H.; ed. local county sch., Juliustown, Burlington Co., N.J., and T. D. James Acad., Phila.; m. Mary Jane Merrill, Feb. 11, 1857 (dec). In mercantile business till Apr. 18, 1861, then in 17th Pa. vols. as pvt. and sergt. on upper Potomac until June 29, 1861, when discharged to accept apptmt. as capt. 19th U.S. Inf.; served as such with regt. and on staff of Maj. Gen. George H. Thomas in Army of Cumberland through the war; a.d.c. to Maj. Gen. Thomas, 1867, till his death, 1870; capt. 13th U.S. Inf., serving in Utah until 1874; maj. 22d U.S. Inf., serving in Northern Mich., Mont., in Pa. against rioters, in Colo., Ind. Ty. and Tex. until 1882; lt. col. 16th U.S. Inf., serving in Tex., in New York as supt. of recruiting service, again in Texas and in Utah till 1888; col. 9th U.S. Inf., serving in Ariz. till Apr. 23, 1890, when retired for age; brig. gen. retired, 1904. Bvtd. maj., 1863, lt. col., 1865, col., 1865. Episcopalian. Republican. Home: Princeton, N.J. Died 1908.

HOUGH, Charles Merrill, judge; b. Phila., Pa., May 18, 1858; s. Alfred Lacey and Mary (Merrill) H.; A.B., Dartmouth, 1879 (LL.D., 1908); studied law, admitted to bar, Phila., 1883; removed to New York, 1884; served N.Y. Naval Militia, 1892-98; m. Ethel Powers, Nov. 21, 1903. U.S. dist. judge, Southern Dist. of N.Y., 1906-16; U.S. circuit judge, Aug. 21, 1916—. Republican. Home: New York, N.Y. Died Apr. 23, 1927.

HOUGH, Emerson ("E. Hough"), author; b. Newton, Ia., June 28, 1857; s. Joseph Bond and Elizabeth H.; A.B., State U. of Ia., 1880; m. Charlotte A. Cheesebro, Oct. 26, 1897. Traveled over the wildest portions of the West; explored the Yellowstone Park, winter 1895, traveling on ski. The act of Congress protecting the Park buffalo was due to this trip. Author: The Story of the Cowboy, 1897; The Girl at the Half-way House, 1900; The Mississippi Bubble, 1902; The Way to the West, 1903; Heart's Desire, 1905; The Story of the Outlaw, 1906; The Way of a Man, 1907; Fifty-four Forty or Fight, 1909; The Young Alaskans, 1910; The Purchase Price, 1911; The Young Alaskans in the Rockies, 1913; Young Alaskans on the Trail, 1914; The Magnificent Adventure, 1915; The Man Next Door, 1916; The Broken Gate, 1917; Young Alaskans in the Far North, 1918; The Way Out, 1918; The Sagebrusher, 1919; The Web, 1919; North of '36, 1923. Died Apr. 30, 1923.

HOUGH, George Washington, prof. astronomy, Northwestern Univ., and dir. Dearborn Observatory, 1887—; b. Montgomery Co., N.Y. Oct. 24, 1836; s. William and Magdalene (Selmser) H.; grad. Union Coll., 1856 (A.M., LL.D.); m. Emma C., d. Jacob H. Shear, Albany, N.Y., 1870. Asst. astronomer, Cincinnati Observatory, 1859-60; astronomer and dir. Dudley Observatory, Albany, N.Y., 1860-74; dir. Dearborn Observatory and prof. astronomy Chicago Univ., 1879-87; discovered more than 600 new double stars and made a systematic study of the planet Jupiter; invented many instruments pertaining to astronomy, meteorology and physics. Died 1909.

HOUGH, Romeyn Beck, author; b. Albany, N.Y., Mar. 30, 1857; s. Franklin Benjamin and Mariah Ellen (Kilham) H.; B.A., Cornell, 1881; M. Anna Maria Galloway, Jan. 19, 1892. Invented a process of making and preparing sections of wood to be used (in lieu of pictures) for illustrating the various species in a publication on American woods; awarded gold medals or grand prizes on the above work at the internat. expns. of Paris, Chicago, Buffalo, St. Louis, Seattle and San Francisco; also spl. Elliott Cresson gold medal of Franklin Inst. (Phila.). Republican. Author: American Woods (14 vols. issued, one in course of preparation); Handbook of the Trees of the Northern States and Canada, 1907; Leaf Key to the Trees, 1910. Home: Lowville, N.Y. Died Sept. 2, 1924.

HOUGH, Theodore, univ. prof.; b. Front Royal, Va., June 19, 1865; s. Rev. Robert R. S. and Virginia (Baer) H.; A.B., Johns Hopkins, 1886, Ph.D., 1893; m. Ella Guy, d. Thomas Whitehead, of Richmond, Va., June 12, 1909. Instr. and asst. prof. biology, Mass. Inst. Tech., 1893-1903; instr. physiology and personal hygiene, Boston Normal Sch. of Gymnastics, 1893-1907; asso. prof. and prof. biology, Simmons Coll., Boston, 1903-07; prof. physiology, U. of Va., Sept. 1907—, and dean, Dept. of Medicine, 1916—. Co-author: The Human Mechanism, 1906. Died Nov. 30, 1924.

HOUGH, Walter, anthropologist; b. Morgantown, W.Va., Apr. 23, 1859; s. Lycurgus Stephen and Annie (Fairchild) H.; A.B., W.Va. U., 1883, A.M., 1884, Ph.D., 1894; m. Jennie Myrtle Zuck, Dec. 29, 1897; children—Ashbel Fairchild, Francis Zuck, Catherine Anne. Aid, 1886-94, asst. curator, div. ethnology, 1896-1910, curator of ethnology, 1910—, and head curator of anthropology, 1922—, U.S. Nat. Mus. Mem. U.S. Commission to Columbian Hist. Expn., Madrid, 1892-93; accompanied Dr. J. Walter Fewkes on archæol. expdns. to Ariz., 1896-97; extensive explorations in Southwest, 1901, 04, 05. Knight Order of Isabella, Spain, 1893. Home: Washington, D.C. Died Sept. 20, 1935.

HOUGH, Warwick, lawyer; b. Loudoun Co., Va., Jan. 26, 1836; s. George W. and Mary C. (Shawen) H.; moved to Mo., 1838; A.B., U. of Mo., 1854; A.M., 1857 (LL.D., 1881); m. Nina E. Massey, May 30, 1861. Shortly after graduation apptd. asst. state geologist, Mo.; studied law 1857-59; admitted to bar, 1859; sec. Mo. Senate, 1858-61; adj. gen. Mo., 1861; sec. of state of Mo. until Dec. 1863; resigned to enter C.S.A.; served on staff Lt. Gen. Polk, Gen. S. D. Lee, Lt. Gen. Taylor; surrendered in 1865; practiced law Memphis, Tenn., 1865-67, Kansas City, 1867-74; judge Supreme Ct. of Mo., 1874-84 (chief justice, 1882-84); judge St. Louis Circuit Ct., 1901-07; then engaged in practice of law. Home: St. Louis, Mo. Died Oct. 28, 1915.

HOUGH, Williston Samuel, college dean; b. Williston, Vt., Dec. 1, 1860; s. Jesse Winegar (D.D.) and Sarah (Holmes) H.; Mich. Agrl. Coll., 1879-81; Ph.B., Ph.M., U. of Mich., 1884; univs. of Heidelberg, Halle, Berlin, Paris and Oxford, 1884-88; m. Lotta, d. John Green Mills, of Washington, Aug. 8, 1901. Instr. philosophy, U. of Mich., 1888-89; asst. prof. philosophy, 1889-91, prof., 1891-94, U. of Minn.; research in history of philosophy, Oxford and Berlin, 1895-98; administrator, residing in New York, 1898-1901; study and lit. work abroad, 1901-04; prof. philosophy, 1905-07, prof. psychology and edn., in charge of div. of edn., 1907-09, dean Teachers Coll., June 1, 1909—, George Washington U. Republican. Translator: A Critique of Kant (from German of Kuno Fischer), 1888; The Problem of Human Life as Viewed by the Great Thinkers from Plato to the Present Time (from German of Rudolf Eucken, with W. R. Boyce Gibson), 1909. Editor: Erdmann's History of Philosophy (3 vols.), 1890, 3d edit., 1898. Died Sept. 18, 1912.

HOUGHTELING, James Lawrence, banker; b. Chicago, Nov., 29, 1855; s. William De Zeng and Marcia Elizabeth (Stockbridge) H.; Ph.B., Yale, 1876, A.M., 1901; m. Lucretia Ten-Broeck Peabody, Sept. 20, 1879. Mem. Peabody, Houghteling & Co., bankers, Jan. 1885—. Founded, 1883, pres., 1883-1900, Brotherhood of St. Andrew (P.E.), now the prin. young men's soc. in all branches of the Anglican communion; pres. 3 yrs., treas., 15 yrs., Y.M.C.A., Chicago. Home: Winnetka, Ill. Died 1910.

HOUGHTON, Alanson Bigelow, ambassador; b. Cambridge, Mass., Oct. 10, 1863; s. Amory, Jr., and Ellen Ann (Bigelow) H.; B.A., Harvard U., 1886, LL.D., 1927; post-grad. work at Göttingen, Berlin and Paris; m. Adelaide Wellington, June 25, 1890. Began in mfr. of glass at Corning, 1889; 2d vice-pres., 1903-10, pres. 1910-18, chmn. bd., 1918—, Corning Glass Works; dir. Met. Life Ins. Co., etc. Pres. Bd. of Edn., Corning; twice Rep. presdl. elector; mem. 66th and 67th Congresses (1919-23), 37th N.Y. Dist.; resigned to become A.E. and M.P. to Germany, Feb. 1922, resigned, Feb. 1925; apptd. A.E. and M.P. to Great Britain, Apr. 1925; resigned, 1929. Republican candidate for U.S. senator from New York, 1928. Trustee Brookings Instn.; chmn. Inst. for Advanced Study; treas. Carnegie Endowment for Internat. Peace. Home: Corning, N.Y., and Washington, D.C. Died Sept. 16, 1941.

HOUGHTON, Frederick Lowell, editor, lawyer; b. Brookline, Mass., Aug. 24, 1859; s. Charles and Edna Rebecca (Lowell) H.; LL.B., Boston U. Sch. of Law, 1884; m. Rosemarie MacCallum, June 20, 1896 (died 1899). Admitted to Suffolk bar, Boston, 1884, and practiced there until 1895; admitted to Vt. bar, 1896; in addition to law practice has given much attention to farming and breeding Holstein-Friesian cattle; sec. Holstein-Friesian Assn. America; editor Holstein-Friesian Register; trustee Vt. Savings Bank, Brattleboro; dir. Brattleboro Trust Co. Selectman and moderator, Putney, many yrs.; mem. Vt. Ho. of Rep., 1900-04. Trustee New England Agrl. Society. Republican. Episcopalian. Mason. Author: Holstein-Friesian Year Book, 1900-12; Holstein-Friesian Herd Book, 1894-1923. Home: Putney, Vt. Died Dec. 19, 1927.

HOUGHTON, George Clarke, clergyman; b. New York, N.Y., Dec. 17, 1852; s. Frederick E. and Anna E. (Dawson) H.; A.B., St. Stephen's Coll., N.Y., 1867, A.M., 1870, B.D., 1893 (D.D., 1895); grad. Gen. Theol. Sem., 1870; m. Mary Creemer Pirsson. Deacon, 1870, priest, 1871, P.E. Ch.; curate Trinity Parish, New York, 1870-78; rector Trinity Ch., Hoboken, N.J., 1879-97; also rector at same time of St. John's, West Hoboken, and Grace Ch., Weehawken, 1884-94; rector Ch. of the Transfiguration ("Little Church Around the Corner"), New York, and of Ch. of the Transfiguration, Pine Hill, N.Y., Nov. 20, 1897—. Supt. pub. instrn., N.J., 1885-97; pres. Manual Training Coll., N.J., 1887-95, chaplain N.G., N.J., 1879-92. Died Apr. 17, 1923.

HOUGHTON, Henry Clarke, physician; b. Roxbury, Mass., Jan. 22, 1837; s. Isaac Smith and Zebral Adams (Hill) H.; grad. Bridgewater Normal School, 1859; became instr. North Yarmouth (Me.) Acad.; grad. New York Univ., M.D., 1867; m. Mary Ella Pratt, Dec. 29, 1868. Resident physician Five Points House of Industry, 1867-69; prof. physiology New York Homœpathic Coll., 1868-70; prof. otology to present time; prof. physiology New York Coll. for Women, 1869-72; apptd. surgeon, 1868, New York Ophthalmic Hosp.; he later became dean; mem. and officer of many homœpathic med. socs.; specialist as oculist and aurist. Died 1901.

HOUGHTON, James Warren, judge; b. Corinth, N.Y., Sept. 1, 1856; s. Tilley and Charlotte (Dayton) H.; grad. Canandaigua (N.Y.) Acad., 1876; admitted to bar, Rochester, N.Y., 1879; m. Elizabeth M. Smith, Apr. 22, 1884. Practiced at Saratoga Springs; co. judge, Saratoga Co., 1888-99; apptd. Dec. 29, 1899, justice Supreme Ct. of N.Y., and elected 1900 for full term, expiring Dec. 31, 1914; served in Appellate Div., 3d Dept., 1903-05, 1st Dept., 1905-10, 3d Dept., 1910—. Republican. Home: Saratoga Springs, N.Y. Died Feb. 14, 1913.

HOUGHTON, John Henry, clergyman; b. Albany, N.Y., Mar. 29, 1848; s. Alfred and Julia Ann (Fenton) H.; A.B., St. Stephen's Coll., N.Y., 1869, A.M., 1876; grad. Gen. Theol. Sem., 1872; (S.T.D., St. Stephen's, 1910; LL.D., Denver U., 1914); m. Frances Amelia Hance, June 30, 1885 (died 1892). Deacon, 1872, priest, 1874, P.E. Ch.; rector St. Paul's, Salem, N.Y., 1874-92; established and conducted for 10 yrs. Rexleigh Sch. for boys; rector St. Mark's, Denver, 1892-1917, St. George's Ch., Englewood, Colo., 1917—. Canon St. John's Cathedral, 1895—; pres. Ministerial Alliance, Denver, 1903-06; mem. standing com. of Diocese, 1910—. Charter mem. Saturday and Sunday Hosp., 1902; trustee State Industrial Sch., 1905-07; chaplain Royal Arcanum, 1906-16; chaplain T.P.A., 1908; dir. Colo. Prisoners' Aid Soc., Apr. 1913—; mem. Charity Commn. of Denver; v.p. Anti-Saloon League. Died Dec. 8, 1917.

HOUGHTON, Louise Seymour, author; b. Piermont, N.Y., Nov. 22, 1838; d. Hon. H. C. and Mary (Sherrill) Seymour; ed. at home and Utica Female Sem.; m. E. R. Houghton, Dec. 30, 1856 (died 1878). Spent the yrs. 1872-75 abroad, and became active as volunteer in the McAll Mission in France; dir. Am. McAll Assn., and editor of its periodical. Charter mem. of first religious settlement in this country (1889), the King's Daughters Settlement, now Jacob A. Riis Neighborhood Settlement, New York. Asso. editor and editor The Evangelist, 1888-1902; asso. editor Christian Work and The Evangelist, 1902-04. Author: Faithful to the End, 1880; Life of David Livingstone, 1882; Telling Bible Stories, 1905; The Russian Grandmother's Wonder Tales, 1906; Our Debt to the Red Man, 1918; Handbook of French and Belgian Protestantism, 1919. Translator: Their Married Lives (from French), 1883; Little Hans and His Bible Leaf (from German), 1884; St. Francis of Assisi, 1894; Outre-Mer, 1896; Jesus Christ, 3 vols., 1898; Religions of Authority and the Religion of the Spirit, 1902; The Parting of the Ways, 1911; Byways of Paris, 1911; Letters and Despatches of Napoleon, 3 vols., 1913; The House, 1914; You No Longer Count, 1918; The People of Action, 1918 (all from French). Home: Philadelphia, Pa. Died Aug. 22, 1920.

HOUGHTON, William Addison, college prof.; b. Holliston, Mass., Mar. 10, 1852; s. Cyrus and Eliza Adaline (Sawin) H.; grad. Phillips Acad., 1869; A.B., Yale, 1873 (class orator), A.M., 1889; at U. of Berlin, 1882-83; m. Charlotte Johnson Morris, July 11, 1876. Prin. prep. dept. Olivet (Mich.) Coll., 1873-75; tutor Latin, Yale, 1876; prof. English lit., Imperial U., Tokio, Japan, 1877-82; asso. prof. English lit. and afterwards of Latin, New York U., 1884-92; Winkley prof. Latin lang. and lit., Bowdoin, 1892-1907. Mem. managing com. Am. Sch. Classical Studies, Rome, 1894—. Home: Brunswick, Me. Died Oct. 24, 1917.

HOUK, Eliza Phillips Thruston, author; b. Dayton, O., Oct. 23, 1833; d. Robert Alexander and Marianna Louise (Phillips) Thruston; grad. Cooper Female Sem., Dayton, 1849; m. George Washington Houk, of Dayton, mem. 52d and 53d Congresses (died 1894). Christian Scientist. Author: Puritan (poem), 1868; Diminution of Water on the Earth, 1873; The Lamarks, 1889; Louisa Varena, or Love's Recompense, 1905; Scientific Fire Fighting, 1908. Home: Dayton, O. Deceased.

HOURWICH, Isaac A., statistician, lawyer; b. Wilno, Russia, Apr. 26, 1860; s. Adolph and Rebecca (Sheveliovich) H.; grad. Classical Gymnasium, Minsk, 1877; St. Petersburg Acad. Med. and Surg.; U. of St. Petersburg; LL.M., Demidov Juridical Lyceum, Yaroslavl, 1887; Seligman fellow, Columbia, 1891-92, Ph.D., 1893; m. Helen Kushelevsky, of Minsk, Russia, 1881; m. 2d, Louise Joffe, 1893. Admitted to bar, Russia, 1887, Chicago, 1893, New York, 1896. Docent in statistics, U. of Chicago, 1893-95; translator, Bur. of the Mint, Washington, 1900-02; expert spl. agt. Bur. of the Census, 1902-06; statistician Pub. Service Commn., New York, 1908-09; expert spl. agt. on mining, Bur. of the Census, 1909-13. Lecturer on comparative commercial law, George Washington U., 1902-03. Author: Immigration and Labor, 1912, 2d edit., 1922; Mooted Questions of Socialism (in Yiddish), 1917. Editor Yiddish translation of "Capital," by Karl Marx, 1919. Died July 9, 1924.

HOUSE, Edward Howard, journalist, author; b. Boston, Mass., Sept. 5, 1836; self-educated; bank-note engraver, 1851-54; part propr. Boston Courier, 1854; editorial writer, war corr., musical and dramatic critic New York Tribune, 1858-69; on New York Times staff, 1869-70; wrote dramas (including Arrah-na-Pogue) in conjunction with Dion Boucicault, 1863-64. Has resided chiefly in Japan, 1870—; corr. Tribune, Herald, Times and World, New York, and Associated Press. Leading English teacher Univ. of Japan, 1871-72; established and conducted Tokio Times, 1877-80, has written extensively in support of Japan's internat. rights; declined Japanese govt. decoration, 1896; apptd., 1900, dir. Imperial Court Orchestra, Tokio. Prepared and conducted, 1900-01, the first orchestral concerts given in Japan. Unmarried. Author: The

Japanese Expedition to Formosa; Japanese Episodes. Died 1901.

HOUSE, Edward Mandell; b. Houston, Tex., July 26, 1858; s. Thomas William and Mary Elizabeth (Shearn) H.; Hopkins Grammar Sch., New Haven, Conn., 1877; Cornell U., 1878-79; m. Loulie Hunter, Aug. 4, 1881; children—Mrs. Mona Tucker, Mrs. Janet Auchincloss. Active in Dem. councils, state and national, but never a candidate for office. Personal representative of President Wilson to the European governments in 1914, 1915 and 1916; apptd. by the President, Sept. 1917, to gather and organize data to be used at the eventual peace conference; commd. as the special rep. of Govt. of U.S. at the Inter-Allied Conf. of Premiers and Foreign Ministers, held in Paris, Nov. 29, 1917, to effect a more complete coordination of the activities of the Entente co-belligerents for the prosecution of the war; designated by the President to represent the U.S. in the Supreme War Council at Versailles, Dec. 1, 1917; Oct. 17, 1918, designated by the President to act for the U.S. in the negotiation of the Armistice with the Central Powers; mem. Am. Commn. to Negotiate Peace, 1918-19; mem. Commn. charged by the Peace Congress to make the Covenant for the League of Nations; mem. Commn. of Mandates, London, 1919; elected mem. Internat. Diplomatic Acad., 1932. Joint editor, with Prof. Charles Seymour, of What Really Happened at Paris. Home: Austin, Tex. Died Mar. 28, 1938.

HOUSE, Elwin Lincoln, clergyman; b. Lebanon, N.H., Apr. 4, 1861; s. Captain Jerome B. and Nancy J. (Fowler) H.; A.B., Harvard, 1893, S.T.B., Boston U. Sch. of Theology, 1894; D.D., Furman, 1899; m. Sherlie D. Grow, May 10, 1883; children—Elmer Elwin, Arthur Everett. Ordained M.E. ministry, 1883; pastor, Boston, Mass., 1883-84, Henniker, N.H., 1884-86, Salem, 1886-88, Boston, 1888-90, Skowhegan, Me., 1890-91, Portland, 1892-93; entered Congl. ministry; pastor Attleboro, Mass., 1893-98, Providence, R.I., 1899-1902, Portland, Ore., 1902-07, Spokane, Wash., 1907-13; lecturer and writer on The Psychology of Religion, 1913—. Trustee Pacific Univ. (Forest Grove, Ore), Pacific Theol. Sem. (Berkeley, Calif.); moderator Pacific Coast Congress Congl. Chs., 1910-16; chaplain 5th Mass. Regt., U.S. Vols., Spanish-American War. Mason. Author: The Psychology of Orthodoxy, 1913; The Mind of God, 1917; The Drama of the Face, 1919; The Glory of Going On, 1920; How to Heal One's Self and Others, 1924; The Supreme Christ, 1927; The World's Greatest Things, 1929; Life's Masterpieces, 1930. Home: Hood River, Ore. Died Jan. 19, 1932.

HOUSE, Francis Edwin, ry. pres.; b. Houseville, N.Y., Nov. 15, 1855; s. Henry A. and Mary E. (Goff) H.; student Rensselaer Poly. Inst., 1873-77; m. Minnie McCracken, July 30, 1878. Began as mining engr. and assayer for Manhattan Silver Mining Co., Austin, Nev., 1877; entered engring. dept. C.,M.St.P. Ry., at Chicago, 1880; with engring. dept. L.S.&M.S. Ry., 1891; chief engr. Pittsburgh & Lake Erie R.R., 1894; chief engr. Pittsburgh, Bessemer & Lake Erie Ry., 1896, later gen. mgr.; pres. Duluth & Iron Range R.R., 1901—. Home: Duluth, Minn. Died Apr. 4, 1926.

HOUSE, Homer Clyde, prof. English; b. Manson, Ia., June 23, 1871; s. Rev. Albert V. and Mary (Sherman) H.; A.B., Doane Coll., Crete, Nebr., 1896; A.M., U. of Neb., 1898, Ph.D., 1909; m. Lilian Chase, 1901; children—Kingsley Albert, Hugh Osgood, Bolton Movius, Arthur Browning. Prof. English, Kingfisher (Okla.) Coll., 1898-1907, Neb. State Teachers' Coll., Peru, 1908-20; prof. and head dept. English lang. and lit., U. of Md., 1920—; mem. Adelphian Quartette. Author: A Theory of the Genetic Basis of Appeal in Literature, 1909; Sun-Dance (verse), 1935; (with S. E. Harman) Handbook of Correct English, 1926; Descriptive English Grammar, 1931; College Rhetoric, 1934. Home: College Park, Md. Died Aug. 28, 1939.

HOUSE, James Alford, inventor; b. New York, N.Y., April 6, 1838; ed. as architect, but became mech. engr. for the Wheeler & Wilson Sewing Machine Co. Inventor of buttonhole attachments and other sewing machine devices, and other useful articles. Home: Bridgeport, Conn. Died 1906.

HOUSE, Jay Elmer, writer; b. Plymouth, Ill., Apr. 3, 1870; s. Benjamin Franklin and Sarah Jane (Wier) H.; self-ed.; m. Julia Wikidal Wells, Oct. 17, 1911. Successively country printer, country editor, reporter, editor and, 1919—, columnist Phila. Pub. Ledger and New York Evening Post; newspaper columnist, 1901—. Mayor of Topeka, Kan., 1915-19. Republican. Home: Philadelphia, Pa. Died Jan. 5, 1936.

HOUSE, John Forde, lawyer; b. Williamson Co., Tenn., Jan. 9, 1827; s. John and Margaret S. H.; ed. Transylvania Univ., Lexington, Ky.; m. Julia Franklin Beech, Jan. 7, 1851. Admitted to bar, 1850; mem. Tenn. legislature, 1853; presdl. elector, 1860; mem. Confederate Congress, 1861-63; served C.S.A., 1863-65; mem. Tenn. constl. conv., 1870; mem. Congress, 1875-82. Democrat. Home: Clarksville, Tenn. Died 1904.

HOUSE, John Henry, missionary; b. Painesville, O., May 29, 1845; s. John and Jane Electa (Moseley) H.; A.B., Adelbert Coll. (Western Reserve U.), 1868; Union Theol. Sem., 1868-71; D.D., Adelbert Coll., 1886, LL.D., from same coll., 1920; m. Adeline Susan Beers, Sept. 17, 1872; children—John Henry, Florence Elisabeth, Grace Bigelow, Ethel Adeline, Ruth Eleanor, Charles Lucius, Gladys Edwards. Ordained Congl. ministry, 1871; missionary A.B.C.F.M., 1872—; in Eski Zaghra, Turkey, 1872-74; prof. and dir. Am. Coll. and Theol. Inst., Samokov, Bulgaria, 1874-91; editor Bulgarian paper Zornitza (Morning Star), Constantinople, 1891-92; evangelistic and ednl. work in Salonica (Thessalonica), Turkey (now Greece), 1894-1931. One of the incorporators, 1907, and pres., 1907-10, American Farm School, Salonica (pres. emeritus); succeeded by son, Charles L. Decorated Cross of Chevalier Order of the Savior (Greece). Home: Hastings-on-Hudson, N.Y. Died Apr. 19, 1936.

HOUSE, Ralph Emerson; b. Delhi, Ia., Dec. 31, 1873; s. Leroy Sunderland and Lydia Mary (Wolf) H.; Yankton (S.D.) Coll., 1894-95; B.L. and A.M., U. of Mo., 1900; studied Sorbonne, Paris, 1902-03, Madrid, Spain, 6 different periods; Ph.D., U. of Chicago, 1909; m. Clara Louise Keller, Mar. 26, 1911; 1 dau., Ruth DeMar. Prof. Latin and modern langs., Central State Normal Sch., Okla., 1900-04; prof. modern langs., U. of Utah, 1904-06; instr. and asst. prof. Romance langs., U. of Chicago, 1906-17; curator printed books, Library of the Hispanic Soc. America, New York, 1917-18; asso. prof. Romance langs., U. of Minn., 1918-21; prof. Spanish U. of Ia., 1921—. Author: The Essentials of Spanish Grammar (with E. K. Mapes), 1932. Editor: The Comedia Radiana of Augustin Ortiz, 1910; University of Iowa Studies in Spanish Language and Literature, 1928—. Joint Editor: Trois Contes de Theuriet, 1917; Le Voyage de M. Perrichon, 1923. Asso. editor Philol. Quarterly. Home: Iowa City, Ia. Died Apr. 4, 1940.

HOUSE, Robert Ernest, M.D.; b. Dallas, Tex., Aug. 3, 1875; s. John Ford and Marguerite Janie (Harper) H.; student U. of Tex., 1896-98; M.D., Tulane U., 1899; post-grad. work, New Orleans Polyclinic, Chicago, New York, etc.; m. Mary Alma Orr, Feb. 28, 1900; children—John Ford, Samuel David. House surgeon City Hosp., Dallas, 1897-98; practiced at Ferris, 1899—, specializing in obstetrics. Democrat. Presbyn. K.P. Originated the Florence-Rosser method in obstetrics; introduced the use of scopolamin to determine guilt or innocence of an individual charged with crime; also for the diagnosis and treatment of insanity by determining the cause of delusions. Home: Ferris, Tex. Died July 15, 1930.

HOUSER, Daniel M., newspaperman; b. Washington Co., Md., Dec. 23, 1834; s. Elias and Eliza H.; high sch. edn.; m. Marguerite J. Ingrem, Nov. 25, 1862 (died 1880); m. 2d, Agnes Barlow, Jan. 23, 1889 (died 1907). Began newspaper work, St. Louis Union, 1851, bookkeeper and gen. mgr., 1854-62, became propr., 1862; business and financial mgr., Missouri Democrat, 1862-72; founded St. Louis Globe, July 1872, which was consolidated with the Democrat, 1875, as the Globe-Democrat, of which became pres. and gen. mgr. Del.-at-large and chmn. Mo. delegation Rep. Nat. Conv., 1900. Presdl. elector-at-large, 1904. Home: St. Louis, Mo. Died Oct. 10, 1915.

HOUSTON, David Franklin, secretary of treasury and agriculture; b. Monroe, N.C., Feb. 17, 1866; s. William H. and Cornelia Anne (Stevens) H.; A.B., S.C. Coll., 1887; A.M., Harvard, 1892; LL.D., Tulane, 1903, U. of Wis., 1906, Yale, 1913, U. of Mo., 1914, Harvard, 1914, Rutgers, 1919, Brown, 1919, U. of N.C., 1922; m. Helen Beall, Dec. 11, 1895; children—Duval Beall (dec.), David Franklin, Elizabeth (dec.), Helen, Lawrence Reid. Tutor in ancient langs. and grad. student, S.C. Coll., 1887-88; supt. city schs., Spartanburg, S.C., 1888-91; grad. student, polit. science, Harvard, 1891-94; adj. prof., 1894-97, asso. prof., 1897-1900, prof. polit. science, 1900-02, and dean of faculty, 1899-1902, U. of Tex.; pres. Agrl. and Mech. Coll. of Tex., 1902-05; pres. U. of Tex., 1905-08; chancellor, Washington U., St. Louis, 1908-16; sec. of agr. in cabinet of President Wilson, 1913-20; sec. of treasury, Feb. 1920- Mar. 1921, also chmn. Federal Reserve and Farm Loan bds., Feb. 1920-Mar. 1921; mem. Council Nat. Defense, 1916-20; chmn. bd. Mut. Life Ins. Co., New York. Author: A Critical Study of Nullification in South Carolina, 1902; Eight Years with Wilson's Cabinet. Home: New York, N.Y. Died Sept. 2, 1940.

HOUSTON, Edwin James, electrical engr.; b. Alexandria, Va., July 9, 1847; s. John Mason and Mary (Larmour) H.; A.B., Central High Sch., Phila., 1864, later A.M.; (hon. Ph.D., Princeton). One of inventors of Thomson-Houston System of arc lighting; emeritus prof. physical geography and natural philosophy, Central High Sch.; emeritus prof. physics, Franklin Inst.; prof. physics, Medico-Chirurg. Coll.; elec. expert and consulting engr. Mem. U.S. Elec. Commn. and chief electrician, Internat. Elec. Exhbn., Phila., 1884. Author: Elements of Physical Geography (9 edits.), 1878, 1904; Dictionary of Electrical Word Terms and Phrases (4 edits.), 1894; The Boy Electrician, 1907; In Captivity in the Pacific, 1907; Wonder Book of Magnetism, 1908; Five Months on a Derelict, 1908; The Land of Drought, 1910; The Jaws of Death, 1910; The Yellow Magnet, 1911; Elements of Physics (with A. N. Seal), 1912. Home: Philadelphia, Pa. Died Mar. 1, 1914.

HOUSTON, Edwin Samuel, naval officer; b. Lancaster, Pa., May 13, 1845; s. William Houston and Mary Henderson H.; grad. U.S. Naval Acad., 1865. Promoted ensign Dec. 1, 1866, master, Mar. 12, 1868, lt., Mar. 29, 1869, lt. comdr., Mar. 1881, comdr., Sept. 27, 1891, capt., Mar. 3, 1899, rear admiral, Apr. 18, 1902, and retired, 1902, after 40 yrs. service on many duties and stas. Was capt. League Island Navy Yard, 1896-98; comd. U.S. Gunnery Training ship Amphitrite, 1899-1902. Home: Washington, D.C. Deceased.

HOUSTON, Frances C. (Mrs.), portrait painter; b. Hudson, Mich., 1851; d. Lafayette A. and Charlotte (Hand) Lyon; m. William Crowell Houston, 1874. Studied in Paris under Lefevre and Boulanger. Exhibited Paris Salon, 1889, London Acad., 1890; Boston, New York and Phila. yearly exhbns.; bronze medal Atlanta Expn. Home: Windsor, Vt. Died 1906.

HOUSTON, Francis A.; b. Keene, N.H., Dec. 16, 1858; s. Julius Augustine and Althea Louise (Temple) H.; A.B., Harvard, 1879, LL.B., 1882; m. Jennie Righter, Dec. 28, 1887. Admitted to Suffolk bar, 1882, and engaged in gen. practice; has been identified with N.E. Telephone & Telegraph Co., March 1885—; gen. mgr. same, 1904-13, v.p., 1910—; treas., May 1913-17. Mem. Boston Chamber Commerce, etc. Unitarian. Home: Concord, Mass. Died 1919.

HOUTS, Charles Alfred, lawyer; b. Warrensburg, Mo., Dec. 13, 1868; s. George William and Annie (Duffield) H.; A.M., DePauw, 1891; m. Eleanor Wright, Apr. 8, 1896. Admitted to Mo. bar, 1892, and began practice at Warrensburg; now at St. Louis; U.S. attorney Eastern Dist. of Mo., 1910-14. Mem. staff of Gov. Hadley with rank of col. Republican. Methodist. Mason. Home: Webster Groves, Mo. Died Aug. 19, 1932.

HOVEY, Alvah, prof. Biblical introductions and apologetics, Newton Theol. Instn., 1899—; b. Greene, N.Y., Mar. 5, 1820; s. Alfred and Abigail (Howard) H.; grad. Dartmouth Coll., 1844; Newton Theol. Instn., 1848 (D.D., Brown; LL.D., Denison Univ., Ohio, and Richmond Coll., Va.); m. Augusta Maria, 2d d. Marshall Spring Rice, Sept. 24, 1852. Ordained Bapt. minister. At Newton Theol. Instn., 1849—; Hebrew tutor, 1849-55; prof. ch. history, 1853-55; prof. theology and Christian ethics, 1855-99; pres., 1868-99. Editor American Commentary on the New Testament (writer of Commentaries on the Gospel of John and Epistle to the Galatians). Author: Manual of Christian Theology (5 edits.), 1861, 1900; The Scriptural Law of Divorce, 1866; Biblical Eschatology, 1888; Christian Teaching and Life, 1895. Trustee of Brown Univ., 1870-74, fellow same, 1874—; v.p. Wellesley Coll.; trustee New England Conservatory of Music; hon. mem. Bapt. Social Union, Boston, 1876—. Home: Newton Centre, Mass. Died 1903.

HOVEY, Edmund Otis, geologist; b. New Haven, Conn., Sept. 15, 1862; s. Horace Carter and Helen Lavinia (Blatchley) Hovey; A.B., Yale, 1884, Ph.D., 1889, U. of Heidelberg, 1890-91; m. Esther A. Lancraft, Sept. 13, 1888 (died 1914); m. 2d, Dell G. Rogers, Oct. 23, 1919. Prin. and supt. schs., Janesville, Minn., 1884-85, Elk River, Minn., 1885-86; asst. mineral. lab., Sheffield Scientific Sch., 1886-87; asst. prin., 1888-91, prin., 1891-92, high school, Waterbury, Conn.; supt. of Mo. mineral exhibit, Chicago Expn., 1892-93; asst. curator, 1894-1900, asso. curator, 1901-10, curator, 1910—, geol. dept., Am. Mus. Natural History. Asst. on U.S. Geol. Survey, 1890, 1901-06; in the Far Arctic of Greenland with the Crocker Land Expdn., winters of 1915-17. Fellow Geol. Soc. America (sec. 1907-22), N.Y. Acad. Sciences, Am. Geog. Soc. Compiled (with R. P. Whitfield) Catalogue of the Types and Figured Specimens of Geol. Dept., Am. Mus. Natural History. Home: Yonkers, N.Y. Died Sept. 27, 1924.

HOVEY, Horace Carter, clergyman; b. Rob Roy, Ind., Jan. 28, 1833; s. Prof. Edmund Otis and Mary (Carter) H.; A.B., Wabash Coll., 1853, A.M., 1856 (D.D., 1883); grad. Lane Theol. Sem., Cincinnati, 1857; m. Helen Lavinia Blatchley, Nov. 18, 1857; father of Edmund Otis Hovey. Ordained to Presbyn. ministry, 1858; home missionary, 1857-62; pastor, Florence, Mass., 1863-66, New Albany, Ind., 1866-69, Peoria, Ill., 1869-73, Kansas City, Mo., 1873-75, New Haven, Conn., 1876-83, Minneapolis, 1883-87, Bridgeport, Conn., 1887-93, Newburyport, Mass., 1893-1909; engaged in occasional preaching and lit. and scientific work, 1909—. Author: The Mammoth Cave of Kentucky, an Illustrated Manual (with R. E. Call), 1897; Hand Book of Mammoth Cave, 1909; revised and enlarged edit. of Hovey and Call's Mammoth Cave Manual, 1912; Bibliography of Mammoth Cave, Ky. (with R. E. Call), trans. into French by E. A. Martel, 1913. Editor: "The Hovey Book," of the descendants of Daniel Hovey of Ipswich, Mass., 1912. Home: Newburyport, Mass. Died July 27, 1914.

HOVEY, Richard, author-lecturer Columbia, 1898—; b. Normal, Ill., May 4, 1864; grad. Dartmouth, 1885; studied Gen. Theol. Sem., New York, 1 year; m. Mrs. Henriette Russell, 1893; a pupil of Delsarte and leader of the Delsarte movement in this country. For a time asst. Father Brown, Ch. of St. Mary the Virgin, New York. Subsequently journalist, actor and dramatist. Author: Launcelot and Guenevere, a poem in dramas, including The Quest of Merlin, The Marriage of Guenevere, The Birth of Galahad, Taliesin; Seaward, an elegy; Songs from Vagabondia, and More Songs from Vagabondia (with Bliss Carman); Along the Trail, a book of lyrics. Translator: The Plays of Maurice Maeterlinck. Home: Washington, D.C. Died 1900.

HOWARD, Ada Lydia, educator; b. Temple, N.H., 1829; d. William Hawkins and Lydia Adaline (Cowden) H.; ed. pvt. schs., Lowell, Mass., High Sch., and grad Mt. Holyoke Coll. (Litt.D., Mt. Holyoke, 1890); unmarried. Taught at Mt. Holyoke and later opened pvt. sch.; served, 1875-82, as first pres. Wellesley Co. and first woman pres. of a coll. in the world; resigned because of failing health; the Alumnae placed her life-sized portrait in Wellesley Art Gallery, 1890, and an honor scholarship, called the Ada L. Howard Scholarship, has been given to the college. Died 1907.

HOWARD, Albert Andrew, univ. prof.; b. Palmer, Mass., Oct. 6, 1858; s. Johnson P. and Lucy S. (Richmond) H.; A.B., Harvard, 1882, Ph.D., 1885; U. of Leipzig, 1882-83, 1885-86; m. Anna Hellrigl, of Meran, Tyrol, July 1, 1884. Prof. Latin, U. of Calif., 1888-90; tutor in Latin, 1890-93, asst. prof., 1893-1901, prof., 1901-08, Pope prof., 1908—, Harvard. Joint editor: Allen and Greenough's Shorter Latin Grammar, 1896; Allen Greenough's New Latin Grammar, 1903. Home: Cambridge, Mass. Died July 31, 1925.

HOWARD, Bronson, dramatist; b. Detroit, Mich., Oct. 7, 1842; s. Charles and Margaret Elizabeth (Vosburgh) H.; ed. Russell's Inst., New Haven, Conn.; m. Alice Wyndham, Oct. 28, 1880. Author of 17 comedies and other dramas. Principal plays, all produced originally in New York; Saratoga, 1870; Diamonds, 1872; The Banker's Daughter, 1878; Old Love Letters, 1878; Hurricanes, 1878; Wives (from Moliere), 1879; Young Mrs. Winthrop, 1882; One of Our Girls, 1885; Met by Chance, 1887; The Henrietta, 1887; Shenandoah, 1889; Aristocracy, 1892; Peter Stuyvesant (with Prof. Brander Matthews), 1899; etc. In London 3 of these are played under different titles —"Brighton" for "Saratoga"; "The Old Love and the New" for "The Banker's Daughter," and "Truth" for "Hurricanes." Others played in London have retained their original Am. names. In Berlin "Saratoga," adapted by Paul Lindau, was played under the title "Eine Erste und Enizige Liebe." Author: Kate —A Comedy, 1906; Norroy, Diplomatic Agent, 1907; Scars on the Southern Seas, 1907. Died 1908.

HOWARD, Burt Estes, univ. prof.; b. Clayton, N.Y., Feb. 23, 1862; s. Sebre C. and Josephine (Vincent) H.; A.B., Western Reserve U., 1883, A.M., 1886; grad. Lane Theol. Sem., Cincinnati, 1886, A.M., Harvard, 1900; Ph.D., Heidelberg, 1903; student, Berlin, 1903-04; m. Sarah C. Gates, July 31, 1890. Ordained Presbyn. ministry, 1886; pastor First Ch., Bay City, 1886-90, First Ch., Cleveland, O., 1890-92, First Ch., Los Angeles, Calif., 1892-97, Ch. of the Covenant (independent), Los Angeles, 1897-99; acting asso. prof. polit. science, Leland Stanford Jr. U., 1900-02; minister First Unitarian Ch., Los Angeles, 1905-08; prof. polit. science, Leland Stanford Jr. U., 1908—. Author: The German Empire, 1906; The Shepherd's Question, 1906. Died 1913.

HOWARD, Clara Eliza, library science; b. Bloomington, Ill., Oct. 24, 1879; d. Theodore Norman and Lilias (Capen) H.; B.L.S., U. of Ill., 1901; M.S., Columbia, 1928; grad. work, U. of Chicago and U. of Pittsburgh. Asst. in Carnegie Library, Pittsburgh, 1901-04; branch librarian same, 1904-13; sec. to Harrison W. Craver, librarian, Pittsburgh, 1913-16; teacher-librarian Schenley High Sch., Pittsburgh, 1916-27; dir. Library Sch., N.J. Coll. for Women, 1928-30; dean and prof. library science, Library Sch. of Emory U., 1930—; asso. prof., U. of Mich., summer 1922; prof., Columbia U. Sch. of Library Service, summer 1929, U. of Ore., summer 1930. Republican. Presbyn. Compiler: School Library Year Book No. 4 (pub. by A.L.A.), 1931. Home: Atlanta, Ga. Died Dec. 7, 1935.

HOWARD, Clarence Henry, steel mfr.; b. Centralia, Ill., Feb. 22, 1863; s. Blake C. and Sarah (Sawyer) H.; grad. highest honors, Manual Training Sch., Washington U., 1885; m. Minnie Morey, Feb. 22, 1894. Learned machinist's trade; foreman and gen. foreman M.P. shops, 1886; supt. Mo. Car & Foundry Co., 1886-88; asst. master mechanic, M.P. Ry., later mgr. Scarritt Car Seat Works, and asst. gen. mgr. St. Charles (Mo.) Car Co.; western mgr. and sec. Safety Car Heating & Lighting Co., 8 yrs.; v.p. and gen. mgr. Shickle, Harrison & Howard Iron Co., later v.p. Am. Steel Foundries; pres. Commonwealth Steel Co., 1904, until consolidation with Gen. Steel Castings Corp.; later dir. same. Pres. St. Louis Council Boy Scouts of America. Republican. Home: St. Louis, Mo. Died Dec. 6, 1931.

HOWARD, Fred Leslie, merchant; b. North Bridgewater, Mass., Feb. 2, 1849; s. Thomas Jefferson and Lavinia (Tilden) H.; common school edn.; m. Salome Torrey Barstow, Jan. 4, 1876. Began as bundle boy for C. A. Browning & Co., wholesale millinery and silk goods, and became v.p. C.A. Browning Co. Republican. Mason. Home: Boston, Mass. Deceased.

HOWARD, George Bronson, writer; b. "The Relay," Howard Co., Md., Jan. 7, 1884; s. William Warrington F. B. and Anne (Spese) H.; pvt. edn., Baltimore and London. In U.S. Govt. employ, 1898-1900, and for brief periods in employ Philippine Civil Govt. and in Imperial Chinese service at Canton, China. Corr. P.I. and war corr. London Daily Chronicle during earlier part of Russo-Japanese War; on staffs Baltimore American, Brooklyn Citizen, New York City News Assn., New York Herald, San Francisco Chronicle, Sunset Popular, Smart Set, Green Book mags., and dramatic citic New York Morning Telegraph and Smith's Mag. (1910-11); dir. Universal motion pictures, Hollywood, Calif., and with Fox and Lasky studios, 1914-17. Overseas service during World War; short period with American Intelligence, U.S.A., London Area, and with British Ambulance in France. Author: (books) Norroy, Diplomatic Agent, 1907; Scars on the Southern Seas, 1907; Meeresgold (in German only), 1909; An Enemy to Society, 1911; The Red Light of Mars, 1913; God's Man, 1915; Slaves of the Lamp, 1917; Birds of Prey, 1918; The Black Book, 1920. Also serially in The Century, Master François Villon of Paris; (plays) The Only Law (Hackett [Harris] Theatre, New York), 1909, revived as The Double Cross (Court Theatre, Chicago), 1913; Snobs (Hudson Theatre, New York), 1911; Springtime, a dramatization by Tarkington and Wilson (Liberty Theatre, New York), 1909; The Passing Show of 1912; Broadway to Paris (both Winter Garden, New York), with Harold Atteridge, 1912; A Night in Subterranea (Berkeley Lyceum, New York), 1914; The Red Light of Mars, N.Y., 1918; Easy Money (with Ethel Watts Mumford); and a play with David Belasco. Original photoplays include: The Spy; Come Through; Queen of the Sea; Sheltered Daughters; etc. Home: Huntington, L.I., N.Y. Died Nov. 20, 1922.

HOWARD, George Elliott, univ. prof.; b. Saratoga, N.Y., Oct. 1, 1849; s. Isaac and Margaret (Hardin) H.; A.B., U. of Neb., 1876, Ph.D., 1894; student history and Roman law, Munich and Paris, 1876-78; m. Alice May Frost, Jan. 1, 1880. Prof. history, U. of Neb., 1879-91; head, history dept., Leland Stanford Jr. U., 1891-1901; prof. history, Cornell U., summer, 1902; professorial lecturer in history, U. of Chicago, 1903-04; prof. institutional history, 1904-06, prof. polit. science and sociology, 1906—, U. of Neb. Author: Local Constitutional History of the United States, 1889; Preliminaries of the American Revolution, 1905. Home: Lincoln, Neb. Died June 9, 1928.

HOWARD, George H(enry), patent lawyer; b. Yorkshire, Eng., Oct. 5, 1844; s. William and Mabel Hornby (Thompson) H.; brought to U.S., 1856; ed. pvt. schools; studied Md. Inst. and Sch. of Design, Baltimore, 1858-63; matriculated Trinity Coll., Conn., 1868; read law in office of James Mason Campbell, Baltimore; m. Roberta Traill Brooke Macgill, Dec. 17, 1874. Practiced in U.S. Patent Office, title of G. H. & W. T. Howard, 1871-1920; individually in U.S. courts, 1876-1920; joint editor and pub. Am. Engineer, 1873-76; exclusive Washington corr. Western R.R. Assn. of Chicago, 1879-1920; appeared in 10 states and Supreme Court of U.S. from 1883, also extensive consultation work; discovered and took evidence, 1878-79, which destroyed patent monopoly on the hermetically sealed food process. A founder, 1888, and 1st pres. Monterey Library, Charmain, Pa. Republican. Roman Catholic. Trustee, dir. House of Good Shepherd, Washington. Died Jan. 15, 1925.

HOWARD, Harry Clay, clergyman; b. Monroe Co., Ala., Mar. 20, 1866; s. Alexander Travis and Mary Florence (Powell) H.; B.S., Southern U., Greensboro, Ala., 1889 (D.D., 1908); m. Lucia E. Smith, Apr. 30, 1891; children—Helen (Mrs. A. J. Phillips), Ruth (wife of Rev. J. A. Gray), Arthur Smith, Mildred, Marian. Ordained ministry M.E. Ch., S., 1891; pastor Avondale (Birmingham), Ala., 1893-97; presiding elder Florence Dist., 1897-1901; pastor 1st Ch., Anniston, 1902, Tuscaloosa, 1902-05, Huntsville, 1905-07; presiding elder, Jasper Dist., 1908, Talladega Dist., 1909; pastor Highlands's Ch., Birmingham, 1910, Talladega, 1911-13; presiding elder Tuscaloosa Dist., 1913, 14; prof. homiletics and pastoral theology, Candler Sch. of Theology (Emory U.), 1914—. Democrat. Author: Princes of the Christian Pulpit and Pastorate, First Series, 1927, Second Series, same, 1928; Prophetic and Personal Elements in Preaching. Died Dec. 28, 1930.

HOWARD, Henry, lawyer, mfr.; b. Cranston, R.I., Apr. 2, 1826; s. Jesse and Mary (King) H.; ed. Univ. Grammar Sch., Smithville Sem., Seekonk Sem. (A.M. Brown Univ., 1873); m. Catherine Greene, d. Gov. Elisha Harris, 1851. Practiced law until 1858; then mfr.; mem. State legislature, 1857-58; gov. R.I., 1873-74; declined renomination, 1875; presdl. elector, 1872; apptd. asst. comdr. to Paris Expn., 1878, to report on textiles. Pres. and dir. of several corporations. Home: Phenix, R.I. Died 1905.

HOWARD, Henry, clergyman; b. Melbourne, Australia, Jan. 21, 1859; s. Henry and Mary (Graham) H.; ed. Wesley Coll., Melbourne; Litt.D., Southwestern U., 1928; D.D., New York U., 1929; m. Sarah Jane Reynolds, Apr. 1885; children—Arthur E., Stanford, Egbert P., Winifred Jean. Minister of M.E. Ch., Australia, 40 years, London, Eng., 5 years; ordained ministry Presbyterian Church, 1926; pastor Fifth Av. Presbyterian Church, New York City, 1926—. Author: The Peril of Power, 1925; The Threshold, 1926; The Beauty of Strength, 1926; Fast Hold on Faith, 1927; When Wisdom Hides, 1929; The Shepherd Psalm, 1930; The Defeat of Fear, 1931. Home: New York, N.Y. Died June 29, 1933.

HOWARD, H(enry) Clay, diplomat; b. Mt. Sterling, Ky., Nov. 14, 1860; s. Henry Clay and Elizabeth Payne (Lewis) H.; ed. pvt. schs.; LL.B. (class pres.), Columbian (now George Washington) U., 1884, LL.M., 1885; m. Margaret Helm Clay, Jan. 27, 1897. Admitted to bar, 1885; practiced at Paris, Ky., 1887—. Co. judge Bourbon Co., Ky., 1894-98; referee in bankruptcy, 1898-1911; chmn. Rep. State Campaign Com., 1909, 1910; E.E. and M.P. to Peru, Mar. 4, 1911-Sept. 9, 1913; apptd. judge Circuit Court, 14th Jud. Dist. of Ky., to fill vacancy, Feb. 1923. Home: Paris, Ky. Died Jan. 9, 1928.

HOWARD, Herbert Burr, physician; b. Fitchburg, Mass., Mar. 24, 1855; s. Luther Grant and Sarah Burr (Damon) H.; A.B., Harvard, 1881, M.D., 1884; m. Margaret Emily Pagelsen, Oct. 1, 1886. In practice at Idaho Springs, Colo., 1885-87, Boston, 1897—; asst. phys., 1884-85, and 1887-91, supt. 1891-97, State Hosp., Tewksbury, Mass.; resident phys. Mass. Gen. Hosp., 1897-1908; supt. Peter Bent Brigham Hosp., Boston, 1908-19. Mem. Mass. State Bd. of Insanity, 1898— (chmn. 1908-13); trustee State Colony for Insane, 1901-16. Pres. Am. Hosp. Assn., 1909-10. Retired, May 1, 1919. Home: Reading, Mass. Died Mar. 8, 1923.

HOWARD, James E., engineer-physicist; b. Palmer, Mass., June 26, 1851; s. Sanford and Charlotte (Tupper) H.; ed. Nichols Acad., Dudley, Mass., Highland Mil. Acad., Worcester; hon. M.S., Dartmouth, 1910; m. Annie B. Potter, Aug. 23, 1882; 1 dau., Marion P. Engr. of tests, Watertown Arsenal, Mass., 1880-1910; engr. physicist, Bur. Standards, Washington, Mar. 1, 1910-Feb. 1914, Interstate Commerce Commn., 1914—. Home: Cohasset, Mass. Deceased.

HOWARD, James Quay, librarian; b. Newark, O.; s. George William and Elizabeth (Quigley) H.; ed. Ohio Wesleyan U., and Marietta Coll., A.M., 1859; admitted to bar, 1860; m. Florence A. Leach, 1876. U.S. consul, St. John, N.B., 1861-66; part owner and editor Ohio State Journal, 1867-71; chief U.S. appraiser, New York, 1879-83; head of Reference Library of Congress, 1897—. Editorial writer on 4 New York dailies and mag. contbr. Author: Lives of Presidents Lincoln (1860) and Hayes, 1876; History of the Louisiana Purchase, 1902. Died Nov. 15, 1912.

HOWARD, John Galen, architect; b. Chelmsford, Mass., May 8, 1864; s. Levi (M.D.) and Lydia J. (Hapgood) H.; grad. Boston Latin Sch., 1882; studied at Mass. Inst. Tech. 3 yrs., under H. H. Richardson, Shepley, Rutan & Coolidge, and McKim, Mead & White, 5 years at École des Beaux-Arts, Paris, 3 years (awarded medals in mathematics, archæology and design, and prize for his rapid advancement); m. Mary Robertson Bradbury, Aug. 1, 1893; children—Henry Temple, Robert Boardman, Charles Houghton, John Langley, Janette. Established practice in New York; architect of Hotel Renaissance, Hotel Essex and of several pub. buildings in the parks of New York; high sch., Newark, N.J.; Majestic Theatre, Boston; Pub. Library, Montclair, N.J., etc. Mem. bd. of architects of Pan-Am. Expn., Buffalo, 1901, and designed the Electric Tower there (awarded gold medal); supervising architect, 1901-25, and prof. architecture, 1901—, dir. Sch. of Architecture, 1913-27, U. of California. Designed there Hearst Memorial Mining Bldg., Greek Theatre, California Hall, Sather Gate, Boalt Hall, Doe Library, Agriculture Hall, Jane K. Sather Campanile, Wheeler Hall, Stephens Union, Gilman Hall, Hilgard Hall, Hesse Hall, LeConte Hall, Haviland Hall. Chmn. bd. of designers of Calif. Memorial Stadium. Mem. John Galen Howard & Associates, 1923—, architects of First Congl. Ch., Oakland, Calif., Le Conte School, San Francisco, and numerous pvt. houses. Advisory mem. of reconstruction com. of San Francisco after the earthquake and fire, 1906; one of the architects in chief Alaska-Yukon-Pacific Expn., 1909; mem. preliminary advisory com. Panama-Pacific Internat. Expn., 1911; mem. Bd. Consulting Architects, San Francisco, 1912-15; mem. Archtl. Advisory Com. on San Francisco War Memorial, 1923-27. Capt. Am. Red Cross, in France, 1918-19. Fellow A.I.A.; A.N.A., 1910; Nat. Inst. Arts and Letters; mem. advisory council to Com. on Sch. of Fine Arts of Am. Acad. in Rome, 1924—; U.S. del. 3d Pan Am. Congress of Architects, Buenos Aires, 1927; corr. mem. Montevideo Society Architects. Author: Brunelleschi (a poem); French Gardens; Pheidias, etc. Died July 18, 1931.

HOWARD, John Raymond, publisher; b. Brooklyn, May 25, 1837; s. John Tasker and Susan (Raymond) H.; A.B., U. of Rochester, 1857, A.M., 1860; instr. Poly. Inst. Brooklyn, 1858-59; traveled and studied in Europe, 1859-61; m. Susan R., d. George Merriam, Nov. 8, 1871; children—Frank Ward, George Merriam, Annie, Etta Spring (dec.), Rossiter, Tasker, John Raymond, Edward Ford (dec.), Carrington, James Merriam. Capt. and a.-d.-c. U.S. Vols., on staff of Gen. J. C. Fremont, Aug. 1861-Aug. 1863; court martial duty, 1863; div. judge advocate Gen. G. A. De Russy's heavy arty., to Feb. 1, 1865. Editorial writer, New York Times, Examiner and Chronicle, 1865-67; mem. pub. firms J. B. Ford & Co., 1867-77, Fords, Howard & Hulbert, 1877-1905. In Montclair, N.J., trustee Free Public Library, pres. bd. edn., bd. trustees First Congl. Ch., Outlook, Montclair and Tariff Reform clubs. Republican. Author: H. W. Beecher—A Study, 1888; Remembrance of Things Past (autobiography), 1925. Editor: Prose You Ought to Know; Best American Essays; Best American Orations; Best American Poems; Poems of Friendship; Daily Song—A Year-book of Spiritual Cheer; Changing Year; Poems of Heroism. Mng. editor of the World's Best Poetry, anthology of 10 vols. (with Bliss Carman, editor in chief). On editorial staff Webster's New Internat. Dictionary, 1908-09. Home: Sound Beach, Conn. Died Dec. 29, 1926.

HOWARD, Joseph, Jr., journalist; b. Brooklyn, June 3, 1833; ed. in Rensselaer Polytechnic Inst.; m. Anna Gregg, Oct. 22, 1856. From 1860 newspaper editor, corr. and spl. writer for New York Times, Tribune, Herald, Sun, World, Recorder, Boston Herald, Globe, Phila. Times, Press, San Francisco Chronicle, Chicago News, Tribune, Times-Herald, and other papers, over signature "Howard"; editor and propr. New York Star, 1868-76. Pres. New York Press Club, 1895-99, 1903, Internat. League of Press Clubs, 1897. Author: Life of H. W. Beecher; History of the Union League Club; History Makers of the 19th Century. Home: New York, N.Y. Died 1908.

HOWARD, Oliver Otis, army officer; b. Leeds, Me., Nov. 8, 1830; s. Rowland Bailey and Eliza (Otis) H.; attended dist. schs. and acads.; grad. Bowdoin Coll., 1850, A.M., 1853, West Point, 1854; (LL.D., Waterville Coll., 1865, Shurtleff Coll., 1865, Gettysburg Theol. Sem., 1866, and Bowdoin Coll.); m. Elizabeth Ann Waite, Feb. 14, 1855. Bvt. 2d lt. ordnance, July 1, 1854; apptd. 2d lt., Feb. 15, 1855; 1st lt., July 1, 1857; resigned, June 7, 1861; col. 3d Me. Inf. U.S.V., June 4, 1861; brig. gen., Sept. 3, 1861; maj. gen., Nov. 29, 1862; hon. mustered out of vol. service, Jan. 1, 1869; apptd. brig. gen. U.S.A., Dec. 21, 1864; maj. gen., Mar. 16, 1886; retired by operation of law, Nov. 8, 1894. Bvtd. maj. gen., Mar. 13, 1865, for gallant and meritorious services at battle of Ezra Church and during campaign against Atlanta; received thanks of Congress, Jan. 28, 1864, for Gettysburg; awarded medal of honor, Mar. 29, 1893, for distinguished bravery at battle of Fair Oaks, Va., June 1, 1862, where was twice severely wounded in right arm, necessitating its amputation. Served in Seminole campaign in Fla.; instr. and asst. prof. mathematics, West Point, 1857-61; comd. brigade at Bull Run, July 21, 1861; participated in many great battles; apptd. July 1864, comdr. Army and Dept. of Tenn. Was largely instrumental in establishing Howard Univ., Washington, which was named in his honor and was its pres., 1869-73, then trustee; commr. Freedmen's Bureau, 1865-74; peace commr. to Indians of Ariz. and N. Mex., 1872, in addition to bureau work; then dept. and div. comdr., successively, the Columbia (where comd. Nez Perces campaign, 1877, and Bannock War, 1878); supt. Mil. Acad., 1881-82; comd. depts. of the Platte, the Pacific and the Atlantic, 1882-88. Founder, 1895, and pres. bd. dirs. Lincoln Memorial Univ. (Coll., Normal and Industrial Sch.), Cumberland Gap, Tenn. Chevalier Legion of Honor, France, 1884. Author: Isabella of Castile; Fighting for Humanity; Henry in the War; Our Wild Indians; Autobiography, 2 vols. Home: Burlington, Vt. Died 1909.

HOWARD, Ralph Hills, ry. official; b. Zanesville, O., Aug. 15, 1870; s. Caleb Baxter and Violetta (McNeal) H.; ed. high sch. Zanesville and spl. study under Edmund Turner, C.E.; m. Sina Larzelere, May 20, 1897. Began as draftsman Cincinnati & Muskingum Valley Ry., Oct. 1889, and continued as asst. on engring. corps, chief clk. to engr. maintenance of way and asst. engr., till 1901; asst. on engr. corps P.,C.,C.&St.L. R.R., at Pittsburgh, Pa., 1901-02; asst. engr. St. Louis div., Vandalia R.R., 1902-05; prin. asst. engr., in charge constrn. and improvements, C.&E.I. R.R., Apr.-Oct. 1905; engr. maintenance of way, same rd., 1905-10; spl. engring. work for eastern capitalists, 1910-11; chief engr. Gt. Southern Lumber Co., Jan.-June 1911, also chief engr. N.O.&G.N. R.R.; gen. mgr. same ry., 1911-15; chief engr. maintenance of way, Wabash Ry. Co., at St. Louis, Mo., 1915-23, and chief engr. same rd., Oct. 1923—. Republican. Episcopalian. Mason. Home: St. Louis, Mo. Died Sept. 20, 1928.

HOWARD, Seth Edwin, adj. gen. (Calif.); b. Bouckville, N.Y., Aug. 17, 1884; s. Preston and Mary (Plunkett) H.; grad. Army War Coll., Washington, D.C., 1931; m. Mable Morris, Jan. 1, 1910; 1 son, Preston Seth.; m. 2d, Florence Stoddard Stockwell, Jan. 10, 1929. Began as a cabinetmaker, with Stirling Furniture Co., Grand Haven, Mich., 1900, continued in various capacities in furniture industry to 1931, except during World War; served as factory supt., traveling salesman and wholesale jobber; settled at Los Angeles, Calif., 1913. Served in Mich. N.G., 1901-03; student 2d O.T.C., Presidio, San Francisco, Aug.-Nov. 1917; commd. 1st lt. and assigned to 13th Inf., Camp Fremont; promoted capt. regtl. adj., Aug. 1, 1918; maj. inf., comdg. 2d Bn., 13th Inf., Camp Mills, N.Y., Nov. 1918-Apr. 2, 1919; upon return to Calif. was commd. capt. 160th Inf., later maj. and lt. col.; trans. to 185th Inf. as exec. officer in Southern Calif., June 1929; apptd. brig. gen. Calif. N.G., the adj. gen., Jan. 6, 1931. Republican. Mason. Home: Sacramento, Calif. Died June 26, 1935.

HOWARD, Sidney Coe, writer; b. Oakland, Calif., June 26, 1891; s. John Lawrence and Helen Louise (Coe) H.; A.B., U. of Calif., 1915; spl. dramatic work under George Pierce Baker in "47 Workshop," Harvard, 1915-16, A.M., 1935; hon. Litt.D., Washington and Jefferson Coll., 1935; m. Clare Jenness Eames, June 1, 1922 (dec.); 1 dau., Clare Jenness Eames; m. 2d, Leopoldine Blaine Damrosch, Jan. 10, 1931; children—Sidney Damrosch (daughter), 1 son, Walter Damrosch. Mem. editorial staff of Life, 1919, literary editor, 1922; spl. investigator and feature writer New Republic and Hearst's International Magazine, 1923. Served with Am. Ambulance on Western front and in the Balkans, earlier part of World War; capt. Aviation Service, after declaration of war by U.S. Mem. bd. dirs. Am. Civil Liberties Union; pres. Am. Dramatists Guild. Mem. Am. Acad. Arts and Letters, Nat. Inst. Arts and Letters. Author: The Labor Spy (with Robert Dunn), 1921; (plays) Swords, 1921; Bewitched (collaboration Edward Sheldon), 1924; Three Flights Up (fiction), 1924; They Knew What They Wanted (Pulitzer play prize), 1925; Lucky Sam McCarver, 1925; Ned McCobb's Daughter, 1926; The Silver Cord, 1926; Salvation (with Charles Mac Arthur), 1927; Yellowjack, 1928; Half-Gods, 1929; Alien Corn, 1931; Lute Song (with Will Irwin), 1931; The Late Christopher Bean, 1933; Dodsworth (with Sinclair Lewis), 1934; Gather Ye Rosebuds (with Robert Littell), 1934; Paths of Glory (with Humphrey Cobb), 1935; The Ghost of Yankee Doodle, 1937. Translator and adaptor: S.S. Tenacity, from the French of Charles Vildrac, 1922; Sancho Panza, from the Hungarian of Melchior Lengyel, 1923; Casanova, from the Spanish of Lorenzo de Azertis; Michel Auclair, from the French of Charles Vildrac, 1924; The Last Night of Don Juan, from the French of Edmond Rostand, 1925; Morals, from the German of Ludwig Thoma, 1925; Olympia, from the Hungarian of Ferenc Molnar, 1928; One, Two, Three, from the Hungarian of Ferenc Molnar; Marius, from the French of Marcel Pagnol, 1930; Ode to Liberty (from the French of Marcel Durand). Screen adaptations Bull Dog Drummond, Arrowsmith, Dodsworth, Gone With the Wind, etc. Homes: New York, N.Y., and Tyringham, Mass. Died Aug. 23, 1939.

HOWARD, Thomas Benton, rear admiral U.S.N.; b. Galena, Ill., Aug. 10, 1854; s. Bushrod Brush and Elizabeth (Mackay) H.; apptd. by President Grant, and grad. U.S. Naval Acad., 1873; m. Anne J. Claude, May 13, 1879. Promoted through the various grades to rear admiral, Nov. 14, 1910. Navigator, U.S.S. Concord, Manila Bay, May 1-Aug. 13, 1898; in Charleston and Monadnock during Philippine insurrection, Feb. 1890-May 1900; comd. caravel Pinta from Barcelona to Havana, 1892-93; comd. Chesapeake, 1901, Nevada, 1903-05, Olympia and Naval Acad. Squadron, 1907, Tennessee, 1907, Battleship Ohio, Admiral Sperry's fleet, on cruise around the world, 1908-09; mem. General Bd., 1909-10; comdg. 4th div. Atlantic Fleet, Oct. 1910-Jan. 1912, 3d div. Atlantic Fleet, Jan.-Apr. 1912; pres. Naval Examining and Retiring Bds., Apr. 1912-Dec. 1913; comdr.-in-chief Pacific Fleet, Feb. 1914-Sept. 1915, receiving rank of admiral the last 6 mos. of this service; pres. Naval Examining and Retiring Bds., Sept. 1915-Aug. 10, 1916, when retired by operation of law. Ordered on active duty as supt. U.S. Naval Obs., 1917-19. Was on duty at U.S. Naval Acad. at various times, as instr. in mathematics, applied mathematics and physics and chemistry; was twice head of dept. of ordnance and gunnery. Died Nov. 10, 1920.

HOWARD, Timothy Edward, judge; b. on farm nr. Ann Arbor, Mich., Jan. 27, 1837; s. Martin and Julia (Beahan) H.; U. of Mich., 1855-57; enlisted 12th Mich. Inf., Feb. 5, 1862; wounded at Shiloh, Apr. 6, 1862, and discharged; A.B., U. of Notre Dame, Ind., 1862, A.M., 1864 (LL.D., 1893); m. Julia A. Redmond, July 14, 1864. Instr. U. of Notre Dame, 1859-79; admitted to bar, 1883; mem. South Bend (Ind.) Common Council, 3 terms, 1878-84, councilman-at-large and pres. council, 1909; clerk Circuit Ct., 1879-83; city atty. and county atty., 1886-92; mem. Ind. Senate, 1886-92; justice Supreme Ct., Ind., 1893-99. Instr., law dept., Notre Dame U., 1908. Pres. Ind. Fee and Salary Commn., 1899; mem. commn. for revising and codifying laws of Ind., 1903; secured first park for South Bend, Howard Park. Mem. Tax Conf., Buffalo Expn., 1901. Awarded Lætare medal, U. of Notre Dame, 1898. Author: Excelsior; Uncle Edward's Stories; poems, essays. Home: South Bend, Ind. Died July 9, 1916.

HOWARD, Velma Swanston; b. in Sweden, Jan. 24, 1868; d. John and Caroline H. (Sundevall) Swanston; grad. Boston Sch. of Oratory, 1886, Am. Acad. Dramatic Art, 1888; m. Charles Howard. Fellow Am. Scandinavian Foundation. Translator: (from the Swedish of Selma Lagerlöf) The Wonderful Adventures of Nils, 1907; Christ Legends, 1908; The Girl from the Marshcroft, 1910; Further Adventures of Nils, 1911; Jerusalem, 1915; Emperor of Portugallia, 1916; The Holy City, 1918; Marbacka, 1924; Charlotte Lowenskold, 1927; also (from August Strindberg) Easter and Tales, 1912; Lucky Pehr, 1912. Home: New York, N.Y. Died Mar. 10, 1937.

HOWARD, Walter, on editorial staff New York Journal, 1895—; b. Floyd Co., Ga., July 18, 1870; grad. Ga. Mil. Acad., 1888; on staff Atlanta Jour. (Hon. Hoke Smith's paper), 1888-95, 3 yrs. as city editor; mem. exec. staff New York Jour., 1898—; was war corr. in Cuba and Puerto Rico during Spanish-Am. war; made city editor on return; now European editor. Unmarried. Home: Brooklyn, N.Y. Died 1902.

HOWARD, Walter Eugene, college dean; b. Tunbridge, Vt., May 29, 1849; s. William Bickford and Louisa (Cilley) H.; A.B., Middlebury Coll., 1871; admitted to bar in Wis., 1873, in Vt., 1878; matriculated in jurisprudence and economics, Oxford U., Eng., 1902-03; (LL.D., Ripon Coll., 1894); m. Maud A. Stevens, July 5, 1902. Taught sch. and studied law, 1871-81; practiced in Fairhaven, Vt., with interruptions, until 1888; prof. polit. science and history, 1888—, dean, 1909, Middlebury (Vt.) Coll. Prin. editor and compiler general catalogue Middlebury Coll., 1900; delivered centennial oration at celebration of 100th anniversary of founding of Middlebury Coll., 1900. Mem. Vt. Senate, 1882, Ho. of Rep., 1888; U.S. consul at Toronto, Can., 1883-85, at Cardiff, 1892-93; mem. State Bd. of Normal Sch. Commrs., 1894-1908 (pres. 1898-1908); mem. State Bd. of Edn., 1908— (v. chmn.). Died Apr. 12, 1912.

HOWARD, Wesley O., judge; b. Troy, N.Y., Sept. 11, 1863; s. Joel T. and Susannah M. (Sweet) H.; ed. common schs., and Lansingburgh (N.Y.) Acad.; m. Carrie A. Millis, Oct. 1, 1884. Admitted to bar, 1889, and practiced at Troy; atty. Bd. Supervisors, Troy, 1894-96; dist. atty., 1896-1902; justice Supreme Ct. N.Y., terms, Jan. 1, 1903-Dec. 31, 1930; apptd. to Appellate Div., Jan. 1, 1913. Republican. Home: Troy, N.Y. Died May 11, 1933.

HOWARD, William Lauriston, naval officer; b. Plainfield, Conn., Jan. 10, 1860; s. George F. and Mary (Phillips) H.; grad. U.S. Naval Acad., 1882; m. Louise G. Alden, Nov. 23, 1886; 1 dau., Helen. Ensign, July 1, 1884; promoted through grades and retired with rank of rear adm., Dec. 1919. For service record see Vol. 12 (1922-23). Home: Newport, R.I. Died Feb. 3, 1930.

HOWARD, William Lee, author; b. Hartford, Conn., Nov. 1, 1860; s. Mark and Angeline (Lee) H.; ed. by tutors in Eng. and France; at Williston Sem., Columbia, and Oxford U. (Eng.); left in sr. yr.; studied Coll. Phys. and Surg. (Columbia); M.D., U. of Vt., 1890; spl. courses in univs. of Bonn and Göttingen, École de Medicine, Paris, and U. of Edinburgh, 1883-89; m. Clara A. Oatman, 1885. Is a practical seaman and holds master's certificate; on whaling voyage 2 yrs.; in Iceland, 1880-81; practiced medicine in Baltimore, specialty—nervous diseases, 1890-1906, then engaged in lit. pursuits. Medalist, Royal Italian Soc. Psychology, 1913. Author: Plain Facts on Sex Hygiene, 1910; Confidential Chats with Boys; Confidential Chats with Girls; Start Your Child Right, 1910; Facts for the Married, 1914; Sex Problems in Worry and Work. Home: Westboro, Mass. Died Mar. 11, 1918.

HOWARD, William Marcellus, lawyer; b. Berwick, City, La., Dec. 6, 1857; Ph.B., U. of Ga., 1877; m. Augusta C. King, Jan. 3, 1883; children—Augusta K., William King, Henry Grady, Gussie Howard (dec.). Admitted to bar, 1880, and practiced at Lexington, Ga. Solicitor gen. Northern Jud. Circuit of Ga., 1884-96; mem. 55th to 61st Congresses (1897-1911), 8th Ga. Dist.; mem. the Tariff Bd., 1911-13. Democrat. Regent Smithsonian Instn.; trustee Carnegie Endowment for Internat. Peace, 1910-31. Mem. Callaway & Howard. Home: Augusta, Ga. Died July 5, 1932.

HOWARTH, Ellen Clementine, author; b. Cooperstown, N.Y., May 20, 1827; m. Joseph Howarth, 1846; contributor of verse to magazines, including 'Tis But a Little Faded Flower, and others which have been set to music. Author: The Wind-Harp and Other Poems; Poems (edited, with introduction, by Richard W. Gilder. Home: Trenton, N.J. Died 1899.

HOWAT, William Frederick, M.D.; b. P.E.I., Can., June 2, 1860; s. Alexander and Mary (Rogers) H.; ed. Prince of Wales Coll., 1888; M.D., U. of Pa., 1892; m. Alice A. Webb, of Charlottetown, P.E.I.,

Nov. 8, 1892 (died 1924); children—Mary Cuming (dec.), Colin Sholts, Frederick Malcolm, Grace Elizabeth (dec.). Began practice in Ind., 1892; mem. Sch. Bd., Hammond, Ind., 1903-10; pres. Pub. Library Bd., Hammond, 1903-18. Mem. various med. societies. Was capt., M.C., U.S.A., World War. Democrat. Mason. Home: Hammond, Ind. Died Aug. 27, 1929.

HOWBERT, Irving, banker; b. Columbus, Ind., Apr. 11, 1846; s. William and Martha (Marshall) H.; ed. high schs. of Ia. and Colo.; LL.D., Colorado Coll., 1911, D.Litt. from same. Cashier 1st Nat. Bank, Colorado Springs, 1878-80, pres., 1880-89, then v.p. many yrs. and now chmn. bd.; pres. Colo. Springs & Cripple Creek Dis. Ry., 1899-1905; etc. Mem. 3d Colo. Cav., 4 mos., 1864; county clk., El Paso Co., Colo., 1869-79; mem. State Senate, Colo., 1882-86; chmn. Rep. State Central Com., Colo., 1894, 95. Trustee Colo. Coll., 1880-1921. Mason. Author: Memories of a Lifetime in the Pike's Peak Region, 1925. Home: Colorado Springs, Colo. Died Dec. 21, 1934.

HOWE, Anna Belknap, club woman; b. Randolph, Vt., May 14, 1849; d. Lorenzo and Betsey L. (Austin) Belknap; ed. Northfield (Vt.) Acad.; m. Henry J. Howe, May 31, 1876. Active in library and woman's club work in Ia. many yrs.; mem. Ia. Library Commn., 1904—; v.p. Nat. League Library Commns., 1908-09; pres. Ia. Library Assn., 1903-04; trustee Marshalltown Pub. Library, 1892-1904; pres. Ia. Fedn. Women's Clubs, 1895-97, now hon. pres., also treas. S. and L. Com., 1913-25; mem. Ia. Memorial Monument Commn.; mem. Ia. Soc. Colonial Dames, D.A.R. Home: Marshalltown, Ia. Died Mar. 11, 1927.

HOWE, Archibald Murray, lawyer; b. Northampton, Mass., May 20, 1848; s. James Murray and Harriete Butler (Clarke) H.; A.B., Harvard, 1869, A.M., LL.B., 1871; m. Arria Sargent Dixwell, June 4, 1881. Admitted to bar, 1871; sec. to Henry L. Pierce, M.C., 1873-75; mem. Cambridge Common Council, 1875-77; one of Mass. Exec. Com. Independents, advocating Cleveland's election, 1884; civil service examiner, Cambridge, Mass.; mem. Mass. Gen. Court (legislature), 1891; independent in politics. Home: Cambridge, Mass. Died Jan. 6, 1916.

HOWE, Charles Sumner, college pres.; b. Nashua, N.H., Sept. 29, 1858; s. William R. and Susan D. (Woods) H.; B.S., Mass. Agrl. Coll. and Boston U., 1878; post-grad. course, mathematics and physics, Johns Hopkins; Ph.D., U. of Wooster, 1887; Sc.D., Armour Inst. Tech., Chicago, 1905, Mass. State Coll., 1931; LL.D., Mt. Union Coll., 1908, Oberlin, 1911; LL.D., Western Reserve, 1924; D. Engineering, Case Sch. of Applied Science; m. Abbie A. Waite, May 22, 1882 (died 1924); children—William Cordingley, Earle Waite, Francis Edward; m. 2d, Mrs. Ida E. Puffer, Sept. 20, 1929. Prin. Albuquerque (N.M.) Acad., 1879-81; prof. mathematics and astronomy, Buchtel Coll., 1883-89; prof. mathematics and astronomy, 1889-1902, acting pres., 1902-03, pres., 1903-29, Case School of Applied Science. Home: North Amherst, Mass. Died Apr. 18, 1939.

HOWE, Church, consul; b. Princeton, Mass., Dec. 13, 1839; s. Albert C. and Mary J. (Carr) H.; ed. pub. schs., Mass.; m. Augusta C. Bottomly, 1863. Pvt. and q.-m. sergt. Co. G, 6th Mass. Militia Inf., Apr. 15-July 23, 1861; apptd. 1st lt. and regimental q.-m., 15th Mass. Vols.; later commd. capt. and bvt. maj. U.S.V.; detached from regt. Nov., 1861, and assigned to duty as ordnance officer, staff Gen. Charles P. Stone; later sr. a.-d.-c. to Gen. John Sedgwick, serving through Peninsular and Md. campaigns (wounded at Antietam); later on staff Gen. Slocum; provost marshal Northern Md. and W.Va., with headqrs. at Harper's Ferry and later again a.-d.-c. Gen. Sedgwick; was in battles of Ball's Bluff, siege of Yorktown, Fair Oaks, Gaines' Hill, Peach Orchard, Savage Sta., Charles City Cross Road, Glendale, Malvern Hill, Flint Hill, Second Bull Run and Antietam. Apptd. first U.S. marshal Wyo. Ty., 1869; removed to Neb., 1871, and engaged in farming, banking and ry. bldg.; retired from business, 1895; Am. consul, Palermo, Italy, 1897-1900, at Sheffield, Eng., 1900-03; consul-gen. at Antwerp, Belgium, 1903-06, at Montreal, Can., 1906-07; consul at Manchester, Eng., Aug. 15, 1907-Oct. 1912; elected mayor of Auburn, Neb., Apr. 1913. Mem. Neb. Senate and Ho. of Rep. 24 yrs.; twice pres. Senate; mem. State Bd. Edn., 10 yrs.; mem. Rep. Nat. Com., 1884-88; sr. vice comdr., 1893, comdr., 1894, G.A.R., dept. of Neb. Home: Auburn, Neb. Died Oct. 7, 1915.

HOWE, Daniel Wait, lawyer; b. Patriot, Ind., Oct. 24, 1839; s. Daniel Haven and Lucy (Hicks) H.; desc. John Howe, 1st settler of Marlborough, Mass. (1657); A.B., Franklin (Ind.) Coll., 1857; LL.B., Albany Law Sch., 1867; m. Inez, d. Robert A. and Susan Hamilton, of Decatur Co., Ind., May 17, 1871. Pvt. 7th Ind. Vols. and capt. 79th Ind. Vols. in Civil War; was in battles of Carrick's Ford, Stone River, Chickamauga and Missionary Ridge, favorable mention in official reports, latter; discharged Nov. 10, 1864, because of wounds received in battle at Kenesaw Mountain, Ga. Began practice of law at Franklin, Ind., 1867, where held offices of city atty. and state pros. atty.; moved to Indianapolis, 1873; judge Superior Ct., 1876-90; resumed practice until retirement. Author: The Laws and Courts of the Northwest and Indiana Territories, 1895; A Descriptive Catalogue of the Official Publications of the Territory and State of Indiana from 1800 to 1890, 1895; Civil War Times, 1902; Political History of Secession, 1914. Joint editor Reprint of the Laws of Indiana Territory; The Executive Journal of Indiana Territory from 1800-16. Home: Indianapolis, Ind. Died Oct. 28, 1921.

HOWE, Edgar Watson, editor, author; b. Treaty, Ind., May 3, 1853; s. Henry and Elizabeth (Irwin) H.; common sch. edn.; has been in printing office since age of 12; Litt.D., Rollins Coll., 1926, Washburn Coll., 1927; m. Clara L. Frank, 1875; children—James Pomeroy, Eugene Alexander, Mateel (Mrs. Dwight Farnham). Published The Golden Globe, at Golden, Colo., at 19; editor and propr. The Atchison Daily Globe, 1877-1911; editor and pub. of E. W. Howe's monthly, Jan. 1, 1911—. Author: Daily Notes of a Trip Around the World, 2 vols.; Country Town Sayings; The Hundred Stories of a Country Town; Ventures in Common Sense; The Anthology of Another Town; Plain People, An Autobiography; When a Woman Enjoys Herself; The Indignations of E. W. Howe; About Nothing, by Nobody; In Defense of Men. Home: Atchison, Kan. Died Oct. 3, 1937.

HOWE, Ernest, geologist; b. N.Y. City, Sept. 28, 1875; s. Walter and Mary Bruce (Robins) H.; A.B., Yale, 1898; A.M., Harvard, 1899, Ph.D., 1901; m. Anne Wilson, June 7, 1905; children—Walter, Margaret Bruce. Asst. geologist U.S. Geol. Survey, 1900-08; geologist 1st Isthmian Canal Commn., 1906-07; cons. geologist, 1908—; chief of inspection labs., Air Service, aircraft production, 1918; mem. Conn. Gen. Assembly, 1921, State Senate, 1925; editor Am. Jour. Science, 1926—; pres. First Nat. Bank, Litchfield. Fellow Geol. Soc. America. Home: Litchfield, Conn. Died Dec. 18, 1932.

HOWE, Frederic Clemson, lawyer; b. Meadville, Pa., Nov. 21, 1867; s. A. J. and Jane (Clemson) H.; A.B., Allegheny Coll., Pa., 1889, A.M., 1890; Ph.D., Johns Hopkins, 1892; studied at Halle, Germany, U. of Md. Law Sch. and New York Law Sch.; m. Marie H. Jenney, June 1904. Admitted to bar, 1894, practiced, Cleveland, to 1909; dir. People's Inst., New York, 1911-14; commr. of immigration, Port of New York, 1914-19. Mem. City Council Cleveland, 1901-03; pres. Sinking Fund Commn., 1904-05; mem. Ohio Senate, 1906-09; spl. U.S. commr. to investigate municipal ownership in Great Britain, 1905. Chmn. Agrl. Adjustment Adminstrn. Consumers Council. Was prof. law, Cleveland Coll. of Law; lecturer on taxation, Western Reserve U., on municipal adminstrn. and politics, U. of Wis., 1906-09; consumers counsel Agrl. Adjustment Adminstrn., 1933-35; spl. adviser office of Sec. of Agr., 1935—. Author: The City, the Hope of Democracy, 1905; European Cities at Work; Why War? 1916; The High Cost of Living; The Only Possible Peace; The Land and the Soldier; Denmark—a Coöperative Commonwealth; Revolution and Democracy; The Confessions of a Reformer; Denmark—The Coöperative Way. Special economic adviser to the Philippine Commonwealth. Died Aug. 3, 1940.

HOWE, George, prof. Latin; b. Wilmington, N.C., Oct. 3, 1876; s. George and Annie Josephine (Wilson) H.; A.B., Princeton, 1897; A.M., Ph.D., U. of Halle, Germany, 1903; studied Oxford U., Eng., 1903, Am. Classical Sch. at Rome, 1912-13; m. Margaret S. Flinn, Oct. 27, 1903. Prof. Latin, U. of North Carolina, 1903—, and dean College of Arts, 1919-22. Mem. N. Carolina State Council of Defense, 1917-18. Democrat. Presbyn. Author: Latin Sight Reader, 1912; Latin for Pharmacists (with Beard), 1916; Handbook of Classical Mythology (with same), 1929. Asso. editor of Studies in Philology, and Classical Journal. Home: Chapel Hill, N.C. Died June 22, 1936.

HOWE, Henry Marion, metallurgist; b. Boston, Mar. 2, 1848; s. Dr. Samuel Gridley and Julia (Ward) H.; bro. of Florence Marion Howe Hall, Laura Elizabeth Richards and Maud Howe Elliott; A.B., Harvard, 1869, A.M., 1872; B.S., Mass. Inst. Tech., 1871; (LL.D., Harvard U. and Lafayette Coll., 1905; Sc.D., U. of Pittsburgh, 1915); m. Fannie Gay, Apr. 9, 1874. Now consulting metallurgist; prof. metallurgy, Columbia, 1897— (emeritus). V.p. Taylor-Wharton Iron & Steel Co. Bessemer medalist, Brit. Iron and Steel Inst., 1895; gold medalist, Verein zur Beförderung des Gewerbfleisses, 1895; Elliott Cresson gold medalist, Franklin Inst. Phila., 1895; gold medal, Société d'Encouragement pour l'Industrie Nationale, 1916; John Fritz gold medal, 1917. Pres. jury mines and mining, Chicago Expn., 1893; mem. jury, Paris expns., 1889, 1900. Chevalier Légion d'Honneur, France; Knight with star of 1st Order of St. Stanislas, Russia, 1906. Fellow Am. Acad. Arts and Sciences, N.Y. Acad. Sciences. Author: Metallurgical Laboratory Notes, 1902; Iron, Steel and Other Alloys, 1903; Metallography of Steel and Cast Iron, 1916. Hon. chmn. engring. div. Nat. Research Council; consulting metallurgist, U.S. Bur. of Standards. Home: Bedford Hills, N.Y. Died May 14, 1922.

HOWE, Henry Saltonstall, merchant; b. Haverhill, Mass., Aug. 12, 1848; s. Nathaniel S. and Sarah (Bradley) H.; A.B., Harvard, 1869, A.M., 1872; m. Katherine Dexter Wainwright, Oct. 20, 1874. Agent for various mills until 1887; mem. Lawrence & Co., dry goods commn., Boston, 1887-1927; also dir. Am. Telephone & Telegraph Co., Guarantee Co. of N. America, Nat. Shawmut Bank, Mass. Hospital Life Insurance Co., Merrimack Mfg. Co., Pacific Mills, Shawmut Corp.; trustee Provident Instn. for Savings. Trustee Peter Bent Brigham Hosp., St. Luke's Home for Convalescents, etc. Republican. Episcopalian. Home: Longwood, Mass. Died Mar. 2, 1931.

HOWE, Herbert Alonzo, astronomer; b. Brockport, N.Y., Nov. 22, 1858; s. Alonzo J. and Julia M. (Osgood) H.; A.B., U. of Chicago, 1875; A.M., U. of Cincinnati, 1877; Sc.D., Boston U., 1884; LL.D., U. of Denver, 1910, Colo. Coll., 1913; m. Fannie McClurg Shattuck, Dec. 23, 1884; children—Julian Osgood, Hubert Shattuck, Warren Francis, Ernest Joseph. Student and asst., Cincinnati Obs., 1875-80; prof. astronomy, U. of Denver, 1880—; dean Coll. Liberal Arts and dir. Chamberlin Obs., University Park, Denver, 1891—. Author: A Study of the Sky, 1896; Elements of Descriptive Astronomy, revised, 1909. Designed an impersonal micrometer for equatorial telescopes. Home: Denver, Colo. Died Nov. 2, 1926.

HOWE, Herbert Crombie, prof. English; b. Fulton, N.Y., Jan. 1, 1872; s. Henry Clay and Letitia Caroline (Crombie) H.; B.Litt., Cornell U., 1893, Sage scholar in philosophy, 1893-95, A.B., 1896; m. Georgia Van Wagenen Emeny, Sept. 14, 1892; children—Henry Van Wagenen, Lucy. Sec. to president of Cornell U., 1895-1901; with U. of Ore., 1901—, prof. English lit., 1902—, acting dean Coll. of Arts and Letters, 1936. Univ. of Ore. rep. Pacific Coast Intercollegiate Athletic Assn., 1915—, pres., 1925-26. Republican. Presbyn. Author: Rags and Tatters (verse), 1897. Home: Eugene, Ore. Died July 28, 1940.

HOWE, Herbert Marshall, capitalist; b. Roxbury, Mass., July 16, 1844; s. Mark Antony DeWolfe and Elizabeth (Marshall) H.; Rectory Sch., Hamden, Conn.; M.D., U. of Pa., 1865; m. Mary Wilson Fell, Nov. 28, 1871. Mem. Harrison, Havemeyer & Co. until 1874; for many yrs. past mem. A. Pardee & Co., coal miners and shippers; pres. Allentown Rolling Mills, Ogden Mine R.R. Co.; v.p. North Pa. R.R. Co. Trustee Pa. Acad. Fine Arts, Drexel Inst., Phila. Republican. Episcopalian. Home: Philadelphia, Pa. Died Oct. 1, 1916.

HOWE, James Blake, lawyer; b. Charleston, S.C., 1860; s. Rev. William Bell White and Catharine Gadsden (Edwards) H.; spl. student Coll. of Charleston; m. Rose Butler Ford, 1886; children—Catharine (Mrs. James Richard Goodfellow), Ellen (Mrs. John A. Goodfellow), William B. W., Rose (Mrs. Raymond H. Ensign), James Blake, Drayton F. Admitted to S.C. bar, 1881, and began practice at Charleston; moved to Seattle, Wash., 1889; gen. counsel Puget Sound Power & Light Co. and its subsidiaries, 1912—; mem. Howe & Graham, 1925—. Republican. Home: Seattle, Wash. Died Mar. 1930.

HOWE, J(oseph) Olin, journalist, writer; b. Norwich, Conn., Jan. 16, 1875; s. William Richards and Ethelyn (Brigham) H.; ed. pub. schs., Norwich, and Norwich Acad.; m. Mrs. Anna Elizabeth Lawlor, Jan. 12, 1902. Began with Norwich Bulletin, 1895, and long a prominent figure in N.E. journalism; legislative corr. various state papers, at Hartford, 6 sessions, between 1899 and 1913, also corr. N.Y. Tribune, 1907, and Springfield Republican, 1909, 11, 13; corr. United Press in Conn. legislature, 1907, 09, 11; spl. work with Asso. Press and rep. Am. Press Assn. at Hartford; conducted daily Connecticut edit. New York Tribune, 1907-08, and covered Southern N.E. in economic and political field for Boston Transcript and New York Evening Post, 1907-15; served as Washington corr. Conn. papers and New York corr. Boston Transcript. Pvt. sec. to Congressman George L. Lilley, of Conn., 1903-06; chief spl. agt. U.S. Census Bur., in charge Mfrs. Census, State of Conn., 1910; wrote popular feature on radio, syndicated by Phila. Pub. Ledger; on staff Success Mag., 1923-26. Home: Waterbury, Conn. Died Dec. 24, 1930.

HOWE, Julia Ward, author; b. New York, May 27, 1819; d. Samuel and Julia Rush (Cutler) Ward; private edn.; (LL.D., Tufts Coll., 1904; Litt.D., Brown U., 1909); m. the eminent philanthropist, Dr. Samuel Gridley Howe, 1843 (died 1876); mother of Henry Marion Howe, Florence Marion Howe Hall, Laura Elizabeth Richards and Maud Howe Elliott. With her husband conducted Boston Commonwealth (anti-slavery) prior to Civil War; after slavery question was settled became active in woman suffrage, prison reform, cause of peace, etc.; preacher, lecturer and writer. Her "Battle Hymn of the Republic" is widely known. Unitarian. Mem. Am. Acad. Arts and Letters. Author: Passion Flowers; Words for the Hour; A Trip to Cuba; The World's Own; From the Oak to the Olive; Later Lyrics; Sex and Education; Memoir of S. G. Howe; Life of Margaret Fuller; Modern Society; Is Polite Society Polite?

From Sunset Ridge; Reminiscences, 1899; Sketches of Representative Women of New England, 1905, etc. Home: Boston, Mass. Died 1910.

HOWE, Louis McHenry, sec. to the President; b. Indianapolis, Ind., Jan. 14, 1871; s. Edward Porter and Eliza Blake (Ray) H.; ed. Yates Saratoga Inst., Saratoga, N.Y.; m. Grace Hartley, May 6, 1899; children—Mary Howe (Mrs. Robert H. Baker), Hartley Edward. With New York Herald, 1888-1915; sec. to asst. sec. of navy Franklin D. Roosevelt, 1915-18, asst., 1918-20; personal sec. to Franklin D. Roosevelt, 1920—. Dir. Nat. Crime Commn.; mem. advisory council Boy Scout Foundation; mem. Legislative Correspondents Assn. Democrat. Episcopalian. Home: Fall River, Mass. Died Apr. 18, 1936.

HOWE, Lucien, ophthalmic surgeon; b. Standish, Me., Sept. 18, 1848; s. Marshall S. and Anna (Cleland) H.; A.B., Bowdoin, 1870, A.M., 1873; M.D., L.I. Coll. Hosp., Brooklyn, 1871; M.D., Bellevue Hosp. Med. Coll. (New York U.), 1872; (M.R.C.S., London, 1873); m. Elizabeth M. Howe, Aug. 16, 1893. Apptd. surgeon in charge Buffalo Eye and Ear Infirmary, 1876; prof. emeritus ophthalmology, U. of Buffalo, 1879; ophthal. surgeon, Buffalo Gen. Hosp., many years from 1885; dir. Howe Lab. of Ophthalmology, Harvard Univ. Fellow Royal Coll. Surgeons; v.p. Med. Soc. State of New York. Author: The Muscles of the Eye, 2 vols.; Universal Military Education; The Hereditary Eye Defects. Died Dec. 27, 1928.

HOWE, Marshall Avery, botanist; b. Newfane, Vt., June 6, 1867; s. Marshall Otis and Gertrude (Dexter) H.; Ph.B., U. of Vermont, 1890 (Sc.D., 1919); Ph.D., Columbia U., 1898; m. Edith Morton, d. of Rev. Edward N. Packard, D.D., June 8, 1909 (died 1928); children—Gertrude Dexter, Prentiss Mellen. Instr. cryptogamic botany, U. of Calif., 1891-96; curator herbarium, Columbia, 1899-1901, prof. botany, 1935—; asst. curator, New York Bot. Garden, 1901-06, curator, 1906-23, asst. dir., 1923-35, acting dir. in chief, 1929, dir., Oct. 1935—. Editor of Torreya, 1901-07; asso. editor, 1898-1907, editor, 1908-10, again asso. editor, 1911, Bull. of the Torrey Bot. Club. Mem. scientific expdns. to Newfoundland, the W.I., and Panama, 1901-15. Home: Pleasantville, N.Y. Died Dec. 24, 1936.

HOWE, Reginald Heber, clergyman; b. Roxbury, Mass., Apr. 9, 1846; s. Rt. Rev. M. A. DeWolfe and Elizabeth Smith (Marshall) H.; A.B., Brown U., 1866, A.M., 1869 (D.D., 1894); B.D., Phila. Div. Sch., 1869; m. Susan, d. Seth Adams, of Providence, R.I., June 22, 1868; father of Reginald Heber H., Jr. Deacon, 1869, priest, 1870, P.E. Ch.; asst. St. Luke's Ch., Phila., 1869, Grace Ch., Providence, 1869-71; rector Trinity Ch., Milford, Mass., 1871-72, Christ Ch., Quincy, Mass., 1872-77, Ch. of Our Saviour, Longwood, Mass., 1877-1921 (rector emeritus). Instructor Episcopal Theol. School, Cambridge, 1881; on Diocesan Bd. Missions, 1885-1918; v.p. and secretary of corp. of Ch. Home for Orphan and Destitute Children; pres. Dist. 15 Conf. of Asso. Charities; pres. Mass. Branch, Free Ch. Assn.; dir. Ch. Temperance Soc.; served as examining chaplain under Bishops Paddock, Brooks and Lawrence. Home: Brookline, Mass. Died June 6, 1924.

HOWE, Reginald Heber, naturalist; b. Quincy, Mass., Apr. 10, 1875; s. Reginald Heber and Susan (Adams) H.; ed. at home and at Noble's Sch., Boston; grad. spl. course Lawrence Scientific Sch. (Harvard), 1901; Docteur de l'Université, Sorbonne, Paris, 1912; S.M., Harvard, 1922; m. Marion Appleton Barker, Sept. 19, 1904; children—Susan Appleton, Richard Ollerton. Curator Thoreau Museum of Natural History; instr. natural sciences, Middlesex Sch., Concord, Mass., 1901-20; dir. of rowing and instr. Dept. Physical Edn., Harvard, 1919-23; research scholar, Bussey Instn., Harvard, 1921-23; headmaster, Belmont Hill Sch., Belmont, Mass., 1923—. Curator David Mason Little Memorial Mus. of Natural History. Writer serial "Contributions to North American Ornithology," containing Birds of Vermont, Index to Ornithologist and Oölogist, and The Birds of Florida (unfinished); Common and Conspicuous Lichens of New England in parts I-V, 1908; Education of the Modern Boy (co-author), etc. Died Jan. 28, 1932.

HOWE, Samuel Burnett, author, educator; b. Groton, N.Y., July 15, 1879; s. Samuel Burnett and Sarah Malvina (Crain) H.; B.A., Union Coll., Schenectady, N.Y., 1903, M.A., 1913; m. Harriet Augusta Strowbridge, 1901; children—Miriam S., Robert B., Constance S., John S. Principal of high sch., Saugerties, N.Y., 1903-04; head of dept. of history, Plainfield (N.J.) High Sch., 1904-14; head of dept. of social science, South Side High Sch., Newark, 1914-40; head of dept. of social sciences, N.J. State Summer Normal Sch., 1914-24; dept. of history, Extension and Summer Div. Hunter Coll., 1924-32; editor N.J. Jour. of Education, 1920-31. Was mem. of Commn. of N.E.A. on revision of courses on social science in secondary schs. and chmn. of com. that prepared syllabi in the social studies for schs. of N.J., 1924. Democrat. Episcopalian. Mason. Author: Essentials in Early European History, 1912; Essentials in Modern European History (with Daniel C. Knowlton), 1917; Actual Democracy (with Margaret K. Berry), 1923. Home: Mirocojo, Cranberry Lake, Sussex Co., N.J. Died Feb. 16, 1941.

HOWE, Thomas Carr; b. Charlestown, Ind., Aug. 5, 1867; s. Robert Long and Elizabeth Ellen (Carr) H.; Ph.B., Butler Coll., 1889, A.M., 1893, LL.D., 1922; U. of Berlin, 1890-92, Harvard, 1896-99; A.M., Harvard, 1897, Ph.D., 1899; m. Jennie Etta Armstrong, June 5, 1890; children—Mary Elizabeth (dec.), Charlotte Brandon, Thomas Carr, Addison Armstrong. Armstrong prof. Germanic langs., 1890-1910, dean, 1907-08, pres., 1908-20, Butler Coll.; pres. Armstrong Landon Hardware Co., Kokomo, Ind., and dir. in various corps. Mem. Ind. State Teachers Retirement Fund Bd.; v.p. Pension Fund, Disciples of Christ; pub. utilities trustee, City of Indianapolis. Mem. Indianapolis Chamber of Commerce. Home: Indianapolis, Ind. Died May 4, 1934.

HOWE, Walter, brig. gen.; b. in Ind., Dec. 31, 1846; s. James Montgomery Allison Higgins and Mary Frances (Graham) H.; grad. U.S. Mil. Acad., 1867; m. Elizabeth Dunn, Sept. 21, 1869. Second lt. 4th Arty., June 17, 1867; 1st lt., Sept. 1, 1872; grad. Arty. Sch., 1873; capt., July 1, 1891; col. 47th U.S. Inf. Vols., Aug. 17, 1899-July 2, 1901; maj. Arty. Corps, Feb. 2, 1901; lt. col., Dec. 20, 1902; col., May 20, 1904; brig. gen. U.S.A., Jan. 11, 1910. Participated in the Modoc war, 1873, and Powder River expdn., under General Crook, 1876; comd. provinces of Alboy and Sorsogon while on duty in the P.I.; retired, Dec. 31, 1910. Died Nov. 8, 1915.

HOWE, Willard B., banker; b. West Buxton, Me., Dec. 7, 1864; s. George Wilson and Ann (Bean) H.; A.B., Harvard, 1887; m. Annie Bean, Oct. 21, 1890; children—David W., George F., Edward G., Laurence P., Ruby Farwell, Mrs. Katharine Torrey, Mrs. Elizabeth Putney. Pres. Howard Nat. Bank, Burlington, Vt.; pres. City Trust Co.; trustee Burlington Savings Bank, 1912—; dir. O. C. Taylor & Co.; publisher, Burlington Free Press, 1895—. V.p. and sec. Mary Fletcher Hosp. Conglist. Mason. Home: Burlington, Vt. Died July 13, 1929.

HOWE, William Augustus, M.D.; b. Phelps, N.Y., Sept. 11, 1862; s. John Quincy and Nancy Amelia (Griffith) H.; B.S., Hobart Coll., 1885, LL.D. from same college, 1926; M.D., College of Phys. and Surgeons (Columbia U.), 1888; m. Elizabeth M. Partridge, May 17, 1892; children—Mrs. Margaret Partridge Drake, Mrs. Elizabeth Bellamy Rueckert, Mrs. Frances Griffith Wiltsie, John Quincy, Lee Selden MacLean. Gen. practice at Phelps, 1888-1909; coroner Ontario Co., 6 yrs.; health officer, village of Phelps, 10 yrs.; mem. bd., Phelps High Sch., 20 yrs.; former pres. U.S. Bd. Pension Examining Surgeons; dep. commr. of health, N.Y. State, 1910-14; state med. insp. of schs., Edn. Dept. N.Y., 1915-34. Awarded Ling Foundation medal, 1929. Republican. Presbyn. Editor-in-chief and business mgr. Sch. Physicians' Bull., 1930-37. Home: Phelps, N.Y. Died Sept. 11, 1940.

HOWE, William Henry, artist; b. Ravenna, O., 1846; s. Elisha B. and Celestia (Russell) H.; ed. in common schs. there; art edn. in Paris under Otto de Thoren and Vuillefroy; m. Julia May Clark, 1876. Especially noted as painter of cattle; gold and silver medals and other honors from various expns.; hon. mention Paris Salon, 1886; gold medal, 1888; New Orleans Expn., 1885; Expn. Universelle, Paris, 1889; Chicago Expn., 1893; London, Boston, New York, San Francisco, Atlanta, Officier d'Académie, 1896, and Cross of Légion d'Honneur, 1898 (France). Mem. jury, St. Louis Expn., 1904, A.N.A., 1894, N.A., 1897; mem. Nat. Inst. Arts and Letters. Represented in St. Louis Mus., Cleveland Mus., Nat. Gallery, Washington, D.C., Grand Rapids Art Museum, etc. Home: Bronxville, N.Y. Died Mar. 15, 1929.

HOWE, William Wirt, lawyer; b. Canandaigua, N.Y., 1833; s. Henry H.; served in Union Army to rank of maj., 1861-65. In law practice at New Orleans, 1865—; was judge of chief criminal ct. of New Orleans; later was asso. justice Supreme Ct. of La.; pres. Bd. Civ. Service Commrs., New Orleans, 1897-1900; U.S. atty. Eastern Dist. of La., 1900—. Trustee Carnegie Instn., Washington, D.C. Author: Municipal History of New Orleans; Studies in the Civil Law, 1896, 1905. Home: New Orleans, La. Died 1909.

HOWE, Wirt, lawyer; b. New Orleans, Nov. 15, 1875; s. William Wirt and Frances and Amelia (Gridley) H.; B.A., Tulane Univ., 1895; B.A., Harvard, 1896, LL.B., 1899; unmarried. Admitted to N.Y. bar, 1899; practiced in N.Y. City, successively with Seward, Guthrie & Steele, Delafield & Howe, Delafield, Howe & Burleigh, 1899-1919; mem. bd. of contract adjustment, Dept. of War, Washington, D.C., 1919-20; asst. counsel U.S. Shipping Bd. Bur., 1922-33; a principal atty. Tenn. Valley Authority, 1933—. Republican. Episcopalian. Mason. Asso. editor Harvard Law Review, 1898-99. Home: Gilbertsville, N.Y. Deceased.

HOWELL, Arthur Holmes, naturalist; b. Lake Grove, N.Y., May 3, 1872; s. Elbert Richard and Anne Judson (Holmes) H.; ed. pub. schs., Brooklyn, N.Y.; m. Grace Bowen Johnson, June 20, 1900; children—Ruth Alden (Mrs. E. E. Stansbury), Elizabeth Carolyn, Elbert Jerome. Biologist of the U.S. Biological Survey, Dept. of Agriculture, 1895—; in charge explorations in Tex. and N.M., 1903, Tex. and La., 1905-07, Ga. and Tenn., 1908, Mo., Ill. and Ky., 1909, Mont. and Ark., 1910, Ala., 1911-16, Fla., 1918-39, Ga., 1927-33, N.C., 1928-30. Fellow Am. Ornithol. Union. Conglist. Author: Birds of Arkansas, 1911; Biological Survey of Alabama, 1921; Birds of Alabama, 1924; Florida Bird Life, 1932. Home: Washington, D.C. Died July 10, 1940.

HOWELL, Benjamin Franklin, congressman; b. Cumberland Co., N.J., Jan. 27, 1844. Served 12th N.J. Vols., 1862-65; in business at S. Amboy, N.J., 1865-82; pres. People's Nat. Bank, New Brunswick, N.J., 1882—; v.p. First Nat. Bank, S. Amboy; dir. New Brunswick Savings Instn. Surrogate, Middlesex Co., N.J., 1882-92; mem. 54th to 61st Congresses (1895-1911), 3d N.J. Dist. Mem. U.S. Immigration Commn., 1907. Home: New Brunswick, N.J. Died Feb. 1, 1933.

HOWELL, Clark, editor; b. Barnwell Co., S.C., Sept. 21, 1863; s. late Evan P. and Julia A. (Erwin) H.; A.B., U. of Ga., 1883; m. Harriet Glascock Barrett, Apr. 9, 1887 (died 1898); m. 2d, Annie Comer, July 12, 1900 (died 1922); m. 3d, Margaret Cannon Carr. Connected with Atlanta Constitution, 1884—; succeeded Henry W. Grady as mng. editor, on latter's death, 1889, and succeeded his father as editor in chief on latter's retirement, 1897, also pres. of company. Mem. Ga. Ho. of Rep., 1886-91 (speaker, 1890-91); mem. Dem. Nat. Com., 1892-1924; mem. and pres. Ga. Senate, 1900-06. Dir. Associated Press since orgn., 1900; trustee U. of Ga., 1896-1927; apptd. mem. and chmn. Federal Aviation Commn., 1934; mem. U.S. Coal Commn., Nat. Transportation Commn. Home: Atlanta, Ga. Died Nov. 14, 1936.

HOWELL, Edwin Eugene, relief map and model maker; b. Genesee Co., N.Y., Mar. 12, 1845; s. John M. and Eunice (Elderkin) H.; ed. pub. schs.; spl. studies at U. of Rochester (hon. A.M., 1880); m. Anne Huntington Williams, artist, 1884. Geologist on the U.S. Geog. (Wheeler) Surveys west of the 100th meridian, 1872-73; also on U.S. (Powell) Survey of the Rocky Mountain region, 1874; made, 1875, relief map of Grand Cañon of the Colo., for Govt., exhibited at Phila., 1876; (the Island of San Domingo, which he modeled 5 yrs. earlier, was probably the first relief map and natural science systematic collections. Wrote: Report on the Geology of Portions of Utah, Nevada, Arizona and New Mexico in Explorations and Surveys West of the 100th Meridian, 1875; 56 of his relief maps and models were exhibited at St. Louis Expn., 1904. Home: Somerset, D.C. Died 1911.

HOWELL, Evan P., journalist, lawyer; b. Miltor Co., Ga., Dec. 10, 1839; s. Hon. Clark and Effie (Park) H.; ed. Ga. Mil. Inst. Marietta, Ga., and Lumpkin Law Sch., Athens, Ga.; m. Julia A. Erwin, June 5, 1861. Practiced law 1 yr. before the war and after up to 1876 in Atlanta, Ga.; then purchased half interest in the Atlanta Constitution and became pres. and editor-in-chief, retiring 1896. State senator, 1872-78; solicitor gen. of Atlanta circuit, and mem. State legislature later; mem. commn. to build new State capitol for Ga.; pres. Kimball House Co., and dir. in the two expns. in Atlanta; has been dir. in every new R.R. built into Atlanta following the war, now dir. Central R.R. of Ga. Apptd. by Pres. McKinley on com. to investigate conduct of war with Spain; mayor Atlanta, 1903, 1904. Apptd. consul to Manchester, England. Died 1905.

HOWELL, Francis Singleton, judge; b. Milton Co., Ga., July 17, 1863; s. Singleton Gideon and Agnes J. (Owsley) H.; student Emory Coll., Oxford, Ga., 1880-82; m. Clara A. Jones, Jan. 9, 1887; children—Mrs. Eunice Pollard, Guy R. (dec.), George L., Mrs. Francis L. McSweeney. Admitted to Neb. bar, 1884, and practiced at North Loup, Albion and Blair, Neb.; settled in Omaha, 1900; U.S. dist. atty., Dist. of Neb., 1910-15; mem. Smith, Schall, Howell & Sheehan, 1916-28; judge Supreme Court of Neb., Jan. 3, 1928-Jan. 3, 1929; mem. Howell, Tunison & Joyner, 1929—. Republican. Methodist. Mason. Elk. Home: Omaha, Neb. Died June 28, 1937.

HOWELL, James Edward, judge; b. Wantage, N.J., June 25, 1848; s. William Chauncey and Julia A. (Schofield) H.; LL.B., U. of Mich., 1870; m. Minnie L. Cummins, June 13, 1877. Practiced law in Newark, N.J., 1874-1907; mem. Coult & Howell, 31 yrs.; vice-chancellor of N.J., Apr. 9, 1907—. Trustee Newark Free Pub. Library, 1895-1914. Republican. Home: Newark, N.J. Died Sept. 26, 1916.

HOWELL, John Adams, rear admiral U.S.N.; b. Bath, N.Y., Mar. 16, 1840; s. William and Frances A. (Adams) H.; apptd. from N.Y., and grad. U.S. Naval Acad., 1858; m. Arabella E. Krausé, of St. Croix, W.I., May 1867. Passed midshipman, Jan. 19, 1861; promoted through grades to rear adm., Aug. 10, 1898. Served on Macedonian, Mediterranean Squadron, 1858-59; Pocahontas and Pawnee, 1860; store-ship supply, 1861; Montgomery, 1862; Ossipee,

W. Gulf Blockading Squadron, 1864-65; participated in battle of Mobile Bay, Aug. 5, 1864; served De Soto, spl. service, 1865-67; Naval Acad., 1867-71; coast survey, 1872-74; Naval Acad., 1875-79; comd. Adams, 1879-81; asst. Bur. of Ordnance, 1881; Navy Yard, Washington, 1882-84; mem. Advisory Bd., 1882-88; comd. Atlanta, 1888-90; pres. Steel Bd., 1891-94; comdt., Navy Yard, Washington, 1893-96, Navy Yard, League Island, 1896-98; comdr.-in-chief, European Squadron, Feb.-Apr. 1898; comd. Northern Patrol Squadron, Apr.-Oct. 1898; pres. Naval Examining and Retiring Bds., 1898-1902; retired, Mar. 16, 1902. Invented and patented a fly wheel torpedo, a disappearing gun carriage and an amphibious vehicle; originated the gyroscopic steering torpedoes, etc. Died Jan. 10, 1918.

HOWELL, John White, electrical engr; b. New Brunswick, N.J., Dec. 22, 1857; s. Martin A. and Abby Lucetta (Stout) H.; Coll. City of New York, 1874-76; Rutgers, 1876-78, Sc.D., 1925; Stevens Inst. Tech., 1878-81, hon. E.E., 1899, hon. Sc.D., 1932; m. Frederica Burckle Gilchrist, Apr. 23, 1895; children—Frederica B., John White, Jane Augusta, Cornelia Margaret, Robert G. With engring. dept., Edison Lamp Works, 1881-93; became chief engr. Lamp Works of Gen. Electric Co., 1893; retired 1931; mem. Research Council of Gen. Electric Co., Schenectady, 1900—. Mem. bd. mgrs. Howard Savings Instn. Trustee Newark Mus. Assn. Fellow Am. Inst. E.E. Awarded Edison medal by Am. Inst. E.E., 1924. Episcopalian. Home: Newark, N.J. Died July 28, 1937.

HOWELL, Joseph, congressman; b. Box Elder Co., Utah, Feb. 17, 1857; ed. common schs. and Utah U.; m. Mary Maughan, Oct. 24, 1878. Engaged in mercantile business at Wellsville, Utah. Formerly mayor of Wellsville; mem. Territorial Ho. of Rep., 3 terms, Utah Senate, 1 term; mem. 58th to 64th Congresses (1903-17), Utah at-large. Republican. Home: Logan, Utah. Died July 18, 1918.

HOWELL, J(oseph) Morton, diplomat; b. Uniopolis, Ohio, Mar. 17, 1863; s. Joseph Giles and Jane (Miller) H.; M.D., Starling Med. Coll., Columbus, O., 1885; M.A., Ohio Northern U., Ada, O., 1896; post-grad. work in U.S. and Europe; LL.D., Otterbein U., Westerville, O., 1922; m. Eva, d. Rev. Dr. Jonathan Mercer Flood, Apr. 10, 1884; children—Mrs. Lorena Turner; Frederick Morton. Began practice at Washington C.H., Ohio; settled at Dayton, O., 1896, specializing in surgery; pres. U.S. Bd. Med. Examiners for Nat. Military Home, Dayton, many yrs. Fellow A.M.A., Ohio State Med. Soc.; etc. Diplomatic agt. and consular gen. for Egypt, Oct. 7, 1921; apptd. E.E. and M.P. to Egypt, June 21, 1922; resigned July 6, 1927. Republican. Methodist. Mason. Homes: Danville, Calif.; Oakland, Calif. Died Dec. 27, 1937.

HOWELL, Mary Seymour, lecturer and philanthropist; b. Mt. Morris, N.Y., Aug. 29, 1850; d. Norman and Frances Hale (Metcalf) Seymour; classical edn.; m. George Rogers Howell, state librarian, Aug. 18, 1868 (died 1899). National lecturer for W.C.T.U.; prominent advocate of woman suffrage throughout U.S.; author of bills for women in N.Y. Legislature, and worked there for their successful passage; speaks before coms. in Congress. Campaigned with Susan B. Anthony through S.D., 1890, Kan., 1891, N.Y., 1893. Published, 1903, memoir to her husband and her son (who died in his jr. yr. at Harvard, Mar. 9, 1891). Home: Mt. Morris, N.Y. Died Feb. 18, 1913.

HOWELL, R(obert) Beecher, senator; b. Adrian, Mich., Jan. 21, 1864; s. Andrew (jurist and author) and Mary Adelia Beecher (Tower) H.; grad. U.S. Naval Acad., 1885; course in Detroit Sch. of Law, class of 1893; m. Alice Chase Cullingham, Sept. 12, 1905. Mem. R. Beecher Howell & Co., ins., loans, real estate, 1902-12. State engr. of Neb., 1895-96; city engr., Omaha, 1896-97; mem. Neb. State Senate, 1903-05; apptd. mem. Water Bd., Omaha, 1904, elected to same office, 1904-10; apptd. water commr. of Omaha, 1912. As state senator secured legislation resulting in pub. ownership of Omaha's water plant in 1912; undertook and continued in management of plant until 1923; secured legislation in 1913 creating Met. Utilities Dist., including Omaha and adjacent municipalities; add. legislation in 1917 established Omaha's municipal ice plants, also for acquisition of gas plant, acquired in 1920; dir. and gen. mgr. Met. Utilities Dist., 1913-23. Mem. Bd. of Visitors U.S. Naval Acad., 1896; served as lt. U.S.N., Spanish-Am. War, 1898; lt. U.S.N.R.F., 1917-21. Mem. Rep. Nat. Com., 1912-24 (exec. com. 1916-24); Rep. primary nominee for gov. of Neb., 1914; mem. U.S. Senate, 1923—, 2d term 1929-35. Chmn. Radio Service Commn. of U.S. Post Office and Agricultural Dept., 1921. Presbyn. Mason. Home: Omaha, Neb. Died. Mar. 11, 1933.

HOWELL, William Barbérie, U.S. general appraiser; b. Freehold, N.J., July 5, 1865; s. William H. and Josephine V. H.; grad. Spencerian Business Coll., Washington, D.C., 1882; LL.B., Columbian (now George Washington) U., 1889, LL.M., 1890; admitted to D.C. bar, 1891; m. Isabel S. Lauck, June 13, 1888; children—Kenneth Barbérie, Sidney Ierne. Apptd. to position in Treasury Dept., June 1882; passed the 1st competitive civ. service exam., Oct. 1883; apptd. to a $900 clerkship in Bur. of Internal Revenue, Jan. 1884; made. spl. employe in customs service, 1891; was pvt. sec. to Asst. Secs. Maynard, Tichenor, Spaulding and Hamlin; asst. sec. U.S. Treasury, 1897-99; U.S. gen. appraiser, Mar. 1899—. Home: Orange, N.J. Died Apr. 4, 1927.

HOWELLS, William Dean, author; b. Martins Ferry, O., Mar. 1, 1837; s. William Cooper and Mary (Dean) H.; bro. of Annie Howells Frechette; his father was a country editor and his edn. was largely gained in his father's and other Ohio newspaper offices in which he worked as compositor, corr. and editor; (hon. A.M., Harvard, 1867, Yale, 1881; Litt.D., Yale, 1901, Oxford, 1904, Columbia, 1906; LL.D., Adelbert Coll., 1904); m. Elinor G. Mead, Dec. 24, 1862. U.S. consul to Venice, 1861-65; studied Italian lang. and lit. there; editorial writer on New York Nation, 1865-66; asst. editor, 1866-71, editor, 1872-81, Atlantic Monthly; editorial contbr. Harper's Magazine, 1886-91; later editor Cosmopolitan Magazine for short time; now writer of "Editor's Easy Chair," Harper's. Pres. Am. Acad. Arts and Letters. Author: Poems of Two Friends (with John J. Piatt); Life of Abraham Lincoln; Venetian Life, new edit., 1907; Italian Journeys; Suburban Sketches; No Love Lost; Their Wedding Journey; A Chance Acquaintance; A Foregone Conclusion; Out of the Question; Life of Rutherford B. Hayes; A Counterfeit Presentment; The Lady of the Aroostook; The Undiscovered Country; A Fearful Responsibility, and Other Tales; Dr. Breen's Practice; A Modern Instance; A Woman's Reason; Three Villages; The Rise of Silas Lapham; Tuscan Cities; A Little Girl Among the Old Masters; The Minister's Charge; Indian Summer; Modern Italian Poets; April Hopes; Annie Kilburn; A Hazard of New Fortunes; The Sleeping Car, and Other Farces; The Mouse Trap, and Other Farces; The Shadow of a Dream; An Imperative Duty; A Boy's Town; The Albany Depot; Criticism and Fiction; The Quality of Mercy; The Letter of Introduction; A Little Swiss Sojourn; Christmas Every Day; The Unexpected Guests; The World of Chance; The Coast of Bohemia; A Traveler from Altruria; My Literary Passions; The Day of Their Wedding; A Parting and a Meeting; Impressions and Experiences; Stops of Various Quills (poems); The Landlord at Lion's Head; An Open-Eyed Conspiracy; Stories of Ohio; The Story of a Play; Ragged Lady; Their Silver Wedding Journey; Literary Friends and Acquaintance; A Pair of Patient Lovers; Heroines of Fiction; The Kentons, 1902; Literature and Life, 1902; The Flight of Pony Baker, 1902; Questionable Shapes, 1903; Miss Bellard's Inspiration, 1905; London Films, 1905; Certain Delightful English Towns, 1906; Between the Dark and the Daylight, 1907; Through the Eye of the Needle; Fennel and Rue; The Mother and the Father; Seven English Cities; New Leaf Mills, 1913; The Seen and Unseen at Stratford-on-Avon, 1914; Years of My Youth, 1915; The Leatherwood God, 1916. Gold medal, National Institute of Arts and Letters, "for distinguished work in fiction," 1915. Editor: Choice Autobiographies, with essays (8 vols.); Library of Universal Adventure. Home: New York, N.Y. Died May 10, 1919.

HOWER, Milton Otis, banker, mfr.; b. Doylestown, O., Nov. 25, 1859; s. John Henry and Susan (Youngker) H.; ed. Buchtel Coll., Akron, O.; m. Blanche Eugenia Bruot, Nov. 16, 1880. Formerly sec. The Hower Co., cereal millers; later dir. and dept. mgr. Am. Cereal Co.; pres. Akron Gear Co., Akron Wood Working Co., Sandusky Grille & Mfg. Co., etc.; v.p. and gen. mgr. Quaker Oats Co., Chicago; v.p. Central Savings & Trust Co. Progressive. Lutheran. Home: Akron, O. Died May 25, 1916.

HOWERTH, Ira Woods, college prof.; b. Brown Co., Ind., June 18, 1860; s. John and Elizabeth Amelia (Bright) H.; A.B., Northern Ind. Normal (now Valparaiso U.), 1885; admitted to Ill. bar, 1889; A.B., Harvard, 1893; A.M., U. of Chicago, 1894, Ph.D., 1898; m. Cora Olive Cissna, Aug. 16, 1881. Teacher and prin. schs. until 1891; instr. in sociology, U. of Chicago, 1896-1902, asst. prof. sociology, 1902-12; sec. Ill. Edn. Com., 1909-10, and wrote report; prof. edn. and dir. univ. extension, U. of Calif., 1912-18; prof. sociology and economics, Colo. State Teachers Coll., 1921—. Mem. Ednl. Corps, in Europe with A.E.F., 1919. Fellow A.A.A.S. Author: The Art of Education, 1912; The Theory of Education, 1926. Home: Greeley, Colo. Died July 1, 1938.

HOWERTON, James Robert, univ. prof.; b. Lafayette, Ky., Aug. 9, 1861; s. John Thomas and Anna (James) H.; M.A., Southwestern Univ., Tenn., 1882; grad. Columbia (S.C.) Theol. Sem., 1885; (D.D., Arkansas Coll., 1890; LL.D., Central U. of Kentucky, 1908); m. Mary N. Fullerton, Nov. 25, 1886. Ordained Presbyn. ministry, 1886; pastor Corpus Christi, 1886-87; prof. theology, Stillman Inst., Tuskaloosa, Ala., 1887-88; pastor Second Ch., Little Rock, Ark., 1888-95, First Ch., Norfolk, Va., 1895-96, First Ch., Charlotte, N.C., 1896-1906; prof. philosophy, Washington and Lee U., July 1, 1907—. Moderator Gen. Assembly Presbyn. Ch. in U.S. (Southern), Birmingham, Ala., 1907. Pres. Council of the Reformed Chs., 1910-12. Home: Lexington, Va. Deceased.

HOWES, Herbert Harold, college pres.; b. Dennis, Mass., May 10, 1881; s. Edwin Herbert and Chloe Crowell (Hall) H.; grad. Bridgewater (Mass.) Normal Sch., 1902; B.E., R.I. Coll. of Edn., 1925; Ed.M., Harvard, 1930; m. Cora Wheaton Luther, Aug. 16, 1905; children—Barbara Wheaton (Mrs. Charles Owen Nichols), Luther Hall, Harold Dudley. Elementary and jr. high sch. prin., Vt., Conn. and Mass., 1902-20; supt. pub. schs., Norwood, Mass., 1920-27, Medford, Mass., 1927-30; pres. State Teachers Coll., Hyannis, Mass., 1930—. Republican. Protestant. Mason. Rotarian. Home: Hyannis, Mass. Died Nov. 9, 1940.

HOWISON, George Holmes, univ. prof.; b. Montgomery Co., Md., Nov. 29, 1834; e.s. Robert and Eliza (Holmes) H.; A.B., Marietta Coll., 1852, M.A., 1855; grad. Lane Theol. Sem., Cincinnati, 1855; student U. of Berlin, 1881-82; (LL.D., Marietta Coll., 1883, Univ. of Michigan, 1909, U. of Calif., 1914); m. Lois Thompson Caswell, Nov. 25, 1863. Asst. prof. mathematics, 1864-66, Tileston prof. polit. economy, 1866-69, Washington U., St. Louis; prof. logic and philosophy of science, Mass. Inst. Tech., 1871-79; lecturer ethics, Harvard, 1879-80; lecturer philosophy, U. of Mich., 1883-84; Mills prof. philosophy, 1884-1909 (emeritus), U. of Calif. Fellow A.A.A.S. Author: Treatise on Analytic Geometry, 1869; The Conception of God (joint author), 1897; Limits of Evolution, and Other Essays in Philosophy, 1901, 2d edit., 1904; Philosophy—Its Fundamental Conceptions and Its Methods (in Vol. 1, Congress of Arts and Sciences, St. Louis Expn., 1904), 1905. Home: Berkeley, Calif. Deceased.

HOWISON, Henry Lycurgus, rear admiral U.S.N.; b. Washington, Oct. 10, 1837; s. Henry and Juliet Virginia (Jackson) H.; grad. U.S. Naval Acad., 1858; m. Hannah J. Middleton, Oct. 3, 1865. Warranted midshipman, June 11, 1858; passed midshipman, Jan. 19, 1861; promoted through grades to rear adm., Sept. 30, 1898. During Civil War was present at many important engagements, including skirmish with enemy's cav. while comdg. detachment of men and howitzer from U.S.S. Pocahontas, Clouds' Mills, Va., June-July 1861; battle of Port Royal, S.C.; engagements with rams off Charleston, 1862; engagements Forts Moultrie, Sumter and Wagner, 1863-64; battle of Mobile Bay, etc. After war in various branches of service; mem. 1st advisory bd., 1881; comd. Pacific Squadron, 1886; pres. Steel Inspection Bd., 1888-90; mem. Light House Bd., 1890-92; comdt. of Navy Yard, Mare Island, Calif., 1893-96; commissioned the battleship Oregon, as her first capt., July 15, 1896; comdt. Navy Yard, Boston, 1897-99; comdr.-in-chief South Atlantic Sta. until retired, Oct. 10, 1899. Home: Yonkers, N.Y. Died Dec. 31, 1914.

HOWISON, Robert Reid, Presbyn. clergyman, prof. Am. History, Coll. of Fredericksburg, Va., 1894—; b. Fredericksburg, Va., June 22, 1820; s. Samuel and Helen H.; ed. schools and acads. of Fredericksburg and private studies until 1840 (hon. LL.D., Hampden-Sidney Coll., Va.); studied law; admitted to bar June, 1841; practiced in Richmond 1 yr., then took full course Union Theol. Sem., Va., 1842-44; pastor Staunton, Va., Presbyn. Ch. 1 yr.; on account of health returned to law practice in Richmond; m. Mary Elizabeth, d. Rev. Dr. S. L. Graham of Union Theol. Sem., Nov. 24, 1847. Practiced law, Richmond, Va., 1846-70; injured in Capitol disaster, Richmond, Apr. 1870; after recovery reëntered ministry. Pastor or minister to Samuel Davis Ch., 3d Ch., Richmond City, Milden, Orange, Culpeper and Ashland. While in Richmond served as mem. city council; pres. Bd. of Lancastrian Schools; commr. of elections; sec. Joint Com. on Treatment of Prisoners of War. Author: History of Virginia, 2 vols., 1846, 1848; Fredericksburg Past and Present, 1880, 2d ed. 1898; Students' History of the United States, 1892. Died 1906.

HOWLAND, Alfred Cornelius, artist; b. Walpole, N.H., Feb. 12, 1838; s. Aaron P. and Huldah (Burke) H.; grad. Walpole Acad.; studied art in U.S.; also at Acad. of Düsseldorf, under Prof. Andreas Müller; in private studios under Prof. Flamm, and several yrs. under Emil Lambinet at Paris; m. Clara Ward, 1871. Asso., 1872, mem., 1882, Nat. Acad. of Design. Has exhibited in New York, Paris and Munich, and at World's Columbian Expn., Pan-Am. Expn., 1901, etc.; represented at Layton Art Gallery, Milwaukee, Yale Univ., etc. Homes: Williamstown, Mass., and Pasadena, Calif. Deceased.

HOWLAND, Charles P.; b. New York City, Sept. 15, 1869; s. Henry Elias and Louise (Miller) H.; A.B., Yale, 1891, A.M., 1894; LL.B., A.M., Harvard, 1894; m. Virginia C. Lazarus, Sept. 6, 1905. Admitted to N.Y. bar, 1894, and began practice with Guthrie, Morawetz & Steele, later with Anderson, Howland & Murray until 1900; successively mem. Howland & Murray, then Howland, Murray & Prentice, and Murray, Prentice & Howland, until 1921; mem. Rushmore, Bisbee & Stern, 1921-25; dir. Lawyers Mortgage Co., Mortgage Bond Co. of New York. Formerly civil service examiner and mem. Bd. of Aldermen, N.Y. City. Chmn. Greek Refugee Settlement Commn., 1925-26. Mem. Gen. Edn. Bd. and Rockefeller Foundation; trustee Johns Hopkins Univ. Home: New Haven, Conn. Died Nov. 12, 1932.

HOWLAND, Emily, humanitarian; b. Sherwood, N.Y., Nov. 20, 1827; d. Slocum and Hannah (Talcott) Howland; ed. pvt. and pub. schs.; Litt.D., Univ. State of N.Y., 1926; unmarried. Worked among negroes establishing schs. in Northumberland County, Va., after Civil War; maintained Sherwood Select Sch., 1882 until it was made a public sch., and renamed Emily Howland Sch., 1927; widely known as an advocate of women's rights, temperance, peace, and education. Dir. Aurora (N.Y.) Nat. Bank. Author: Early Friends in Cayuga County, 1880. Home: Sherwood, N.Y. Died June 29, 1929.

HOWLAND, Frederick Hoppin, newspaperman; b. New Bedford, Mass., Jan. 10, 1871; s. Richard Smith and Mary (Hoppin) H.; grad. Mass. Inst. Tech., 1893; m. Ellen Swan Dobbin, Apr. 10, 1901. Traveled abroad, 1889, 91; entered employ Providence Journal, 1893; Washington corr. same, 1894, New York corr., 1898-99. War corr. London Daily Mail, London Evening News and Providence Journal, with columns of General Hunter, Lord Methuen, and Gen. Broadwood in S. Africa, 1900, receiving Her Majesty's service medal; on return resumed post as Washington corr. Providence Journal; apptd. treas. and mgr. Providence Jour. Co., 1905; editor and part owner Providence Tribune, 1906-07; abroad and in Cuba, 1907-08; in charge of publ. dept., Boston Chamber of Commerce, and editor of Chamber of Commerce Journal, 1909-10; joined staff Phila. Press, 1910, asso. editor same, 1911-15. Home: Philadelphia, Pa. Died June 5, 1916.

HOWLAND, Gardiner Greene, gen. mgr. New York Herald; s. Gardiner Greene and Louisa (Meredith) H.; b. New York, 1834; m. Mary Grafton Dulany, 1856 (died 1897). Died 1903.

HOWLAND, Henry Elias, lawyer; b. Walpole N.H., June 30, 1835; s. Aaron P. and Huldah (Burke) H.; A.B., Yale, 1854, A.M., 1893; LL.B., Harvard, 1857; m. Louise Miller, Oct. 5, 1865. Admitted to bar, 1857, and since in practice at New York. Capt. 22d Regt. N.G.S.N.Y., 1862-63. Justice Marine Ct., 1873-74; Rep. candidate for judge Ct. of Common Pleas, 1884, for justice Supreme Ct., 1887; was alderman, 1875-76; pres. dept. of taxes, 1880; pres. Manhattan State Insane Hosp., 1895-1905, Home for Destitute Blind, 1898—. Fellow Yale Corp., 1892—. Home: New York, N.Y. Died Nov. 8, 1913.

HOWLAND, Henry Raymond, educator; b. Springfield, Mass., June 1, 1844; s. Job F. and Emily (Alvord) H.; A.B., Coll. City of New York, 1863; A.M., 1866; m. Rebecca Letchworth, 1866; children —Emily Alvord, Florence Letchworth. Pres. Thomas Indian Sch., Iroquois, N.Y., 1895-1913; pres. Buffalo Sem., 1910-23, emeritus. Dir. emeritus and corr. sec. Buffalo Soc. Natural Sciences; pres. Am. Assn. Museums; mem. Internat. Congress Americanists (v.p.). Republican. Episcopalian. Home: Buffalo, N.Y. Died Feb. 4, 1930.

HOWLAND, John, pediatrician; b. N.Y. City, Feb. 3, 1873; s. Henry Elias and Sarah Louise (Miller) H.; A.B., Yale, 1894; M.D., Univ. Med. Coll. (New York U.), 1897; m. Susan M. Sanford, Oct. 12, 1903. Began practice, N.Y. City, 1897; was phys. Willard Parker and Riverside and St. Vincent's hosps., pathologist Foundling Hosp., etc.; prof. pediatrics, Washington U., St. Louis, Mo., 1911-12; same, Johns Hopkins, and pediatrician in chief Johns Hopkins Hosp., 1912—. Home: Baltimore, Md. Died June 20, 1926.

HOWLAND, Louis, editor; b. Indianapolis, June 13, 1857; s. John D. and Desdemona (Harrison) H.; A.B., Yale, 1879; A.M., Wabash Coll., Ind., 1901, Litt.D., 1903; unmarried. Practiced law, 1879-88; editor The Freeman, an anti-Blane free trade weekly, 1884-87; in newspaper work and asso. editor The People's Cause, New York, 1888-92; editorial writer Indianapolis News, 1893-1911, editor, 1911—. Democrat. Episcopalian. Author: Day Unto Day; Stephen A. Douglas; The Mind of Jesus; Case and Comment, Autobiography of a Cathedral. Home: Indianapolis, Ind. Died Mar. 26, 1934.

HOWLAND, Silas Wilder, corp. official; b. Marion, Mass., May 15, 1879; s. Clark Phelps and Mary Bishop (Wilder) H.; A.B., Drury Coll., Springfield, Mo., 1898; A.B., Harvard, 1904, LL.B., 1907; m. Dorothy Gerrans, Mar. 16, 1912; children—Mary Wilder, Silas Wilder. Admitted to N.Y. bar, 1907, and began practice at N.Y. City with Byrne & Cutcheon; gen. atty. for receiver Southern Ind. Ry. Co., Chicago, Ill., 1909-11; gen. atty. The Texas Co., N.Y. City, 1911-13; mem. Buckner & Howland, 1913-14, Root, Clark, Buckner & Howland, 1914-25, Root, Clark, Buckner, Howland & Ballantine, 1925-30; partner Guggenheim Bros., 1930—. Republican. Conglist. Home: Rye, N.Y. Died Sept. 1, 1938.

HOWLAND, Thomas Smith, ry. official; b. North Dartmouth, Mass., Feb. 13, 1844; s. William and Louisa (Packhard) H.; B.S., Lawrence Scientific Sch. (Harvard), 1868; m. Eliza S. Harbach, Oct. 3, 1871. Engr. in service of the Burlington & Mo. River R.R., Mar. 1, 1868-76; sec. to v.p. C.,B.&Q. R.R., 1876-83; sec. same rd., 1883—, and 1902— also v.p. and treasurer. Home: Chicago, Ill. Died Aug. 8, 1921.

HOWLAND, William Bailey, publisher; b. Ashland, N.Y., June 10, 1849; s. Rev. Harrison O. and Hannah (Bailey) H.; ed. Williston Sem.; m. Ella May Jacobs, Apr. 3, 1873. Founder and pub. of Outing, 1882-85; editor and propr. Cambridge (Mass.) Tribune, 1885-90; pub. and treas. The Outlook, 1890-1913; pres. The Independent, N.Y. City, 1913—. Commr. State Reservation at Niagara; treas. Am. Civic Assn., Soc. for Italian Immigrants, Congl. Home Missionary Soc., 1893-1907; trustee Chautauqua Instn. Republican. Died Feb. 27, 1917.

HOWRY, Charles Bowen, judge; b. Oxford, Miss., May 14, 1844; s. Judge James M. and Narcissa (Bowen) H.; ed. U. of Miss. until war stopped course; LL.B., same univ., 1867, LL.D., 1896; m. Edmonia Beverley Carter, Jan. 14, 1869; children—Lucien Beverley, Willard Carter (dec.), Maude (dec.); m. 2d, Harriet Holt Harris, July 21, 1880; children—Hallie Harris (dec.), Charles Bowen, Elizabeth Butler, Mary Harris; m. 3d, Sallie Behethaland Bird (widow Buckingham Smith), July 25, 1900. Pvt. 2d and 1st lt. 29th Miss. Inf., C.S.A.; engaged in battle of Chickamauga and 8 other battles, also numerous skirmishes; severely wounded, Battle of Franklin. Practiced law at Oxford, Miss., 1867-74 and 1878-93; mem. Miss. Ho. of Rep., 1880-84; U.S. dist. atty., 1885-89; declined a mission to a S.Am. country offered by President Cleveland; trustee U. of Miss., 1882-94; asst. atty. gen. of U.S., 1893-97; mem. Dem. Nat. Com., 1891-96; asso. judge U.S. Court of Claims, 1897-1915; resigned and resumed cons. practice at Washington. Twice declined President Wilson's offer of appmt. to be chief justice U.S. Court of Claims. Canvassed, by request of Secretary of the Treasury, for subscriptions to Liberty Loan, without charge to Government. Elected by acclamation lt. gen. (supreme comdr.) Army of Northern Va., U.C.V. Home: Washington, D.C. Died July 20, 1928.

HOWSE, Hilary Ewing, mayor; b. Murfreesboro, Tenn., Jan. 25, 1866; s. L. H. and Mary (Blackman) H.; pub. sch. edn.; unmarried. Asso. judge County Court, 1st Dist., Tenn., 8 yrs.; elected mem. Tenn. State Senate, 1905, reëlected, 1909; mayor of Nashville, 1909—. Democrat. Methodist. Home: Nashville, Tenn. Deceased.

HOWZE, Robert Lee, army officer; b. Rusk Co., Tex., Aug. 22, 1864; s. James Augustus and Amanda Hamilton (Brown) H.; A.B., Hubbard Coll., Tex., 1883; grad. U.S. Mil. Acad., 1888; m. Anne Chifelle, d. late Hamilton S. Hawkins, Feb. 24, 1897; children—Harriot, Robert Lee, Hamilton Hawkins. Commd. 2d lt. 6th Cav., July 7, 1888; promoted through grades to brig. gen. vols., June 20, 1901; hon. disch. vols., June 30, 1901; maj. Puerto Rico provisional regt. of inf., Oct. 9, 1901-June 30, 1904; comdt. cadet, U.S. Mil. Acad., with rank of lt. col., 1905-09; lt. col. comdg. Puerto Rico Regt. and Mil. Dist. of P.R., Feb. 1909-Aug. 1912; maj. 4th Cav., Nov. 18, 1911; transferred to 11th Cav., Dec. 21, 1911; lt. cav., July 1, 1916; detailed to Gen. Staff, Sept. 1916; col. of cav., May 15, 1917; chief of staff 10th Provisional Div. and cav. div.; assigned chief of staff Northeastern Dept., June 1917; brig. gen. N.A., Dec. 1917, and assigned to command 2d Cav. Brig., Ft. Bliss, Mexican border duty; maj. gen. U.S.A., Aug. 8, 1918; comd. 38th Div. and overseas duty; served in Meuse-Argonne; comd. 3d (Marne) Div., marched to the Rhine and comd. that div. in Army of Occupation in Germany until Aug. 14, 1919; returned to U.S. in command of 3d Div. and assigned to Mexican border duty in command of the Dist. of El Paso, comdg. First Cav. Div.; maj. gen., regular army, Dec. 1922. Comd. detachment of 34th Vols. in rescue of Lt. Comdr. Gilmore, U.S.N., and 27 other Americans who had been prisoners of insurgents in Philippines 10 mos. or more; under Gen. Pershing performed distinguished service in Mexico while comdg. a selected squadron of 11th Cav. Awarded Congressional Medal of Honor, July 25, 1891, "for gallantry in repulsing attacks of Sioux Indians in S.D., Jan. 1, 1891." Awarded D.S.M. (U.S.), Croix de Guerre with palm, and Officer Legion of Honor (French). Home: Washington, D.C. Died Sept. 19, 1926.

HOXIE, Richard Leveridge, army officer; b. New York, Aug. 7, 1844; s. Joseph and Jacqueline (Barry) H.; ed. in N.Y., Pa., Italy, 1851-58; Ia. State U., 1858-61; grad. U.S. Mil. Acad., 1868; m. Vinnie Ream, May 28, 1878 (died Nov. 20, 1914); 1 son, Richard Ream; m. 2d, May Ruth Norcross, Apr. 30, 1917. Bugler, pvt., corporal Co. F., 1st Ia. Cav., June 13, 1861-June 9, 1864; cadet, West Point, 1864-68; 2d lt. Engr. Corps, June 15, 1868; 1st lt., Sept. 22, 1870; capt., June 15, 1882; maj., Mar. 31, 1895; lt. col., Apr. 23, 1904; col. June 9, 1907; brig. gen., Aug. 7, 1908 (retired). In engr. work in constrn. of defenses, improvements of rivers and harbors, the light house establishment, etc.; asst. on Western explorations under Lt. Wheeler, 1872-74; mem. bd. of pub. works, D.C., and engr., D.C. 1874-78, and asst. to engr. commn., D.C., 1878-83, etc. Home: Washington, D.C. Died Apr. 30, 1930.

HOXIE, Robert Franklin, economist; b. Edmeston, N.Y., Apr. 29, 1868; s. Solomon and Lucy Peet (Stickney) H.; Cornell U.; Ph.B., U. of Chicago, 1893, Ph.D., 1905; m. Lucy L. Bennett, Dec. 31, 1898. Acting prof. economics, Cornell Coll., Ia., 1897-98; instr. in economics, Washington U., 1898-1901; acting prof. economics, Washington and Lee U., 1901-02; instr. economics, Cornell U., 1903-06; instr. economics, 1906-08, asst. prof., 1908-12, asso. prof., 1912—, U. of Chicago. On leave of absence, 1914-15, and spl. investigator of scientific management and labor for U.S. Commn. on Industrial Relations. Asso. editor Jour. of Polit. Economy. Author: Scientific Management and Labor, 1915. Died June 22, 1916.

HOXIE, Solomon, agriculturist; b. Brookfield, N.Y., July 29, 1829; s. Nathan B. and Eliza (Langworthy) H.; ed. McGrawville Coll. and Madison (now Colgate) U.; m. Lucy P. Stickney, Sept. 22, 1859. Layman pastor Freewill Bapt. Ch., 8 yrs., Columbus, N.Y., 1868-76. One of first importers of Holstein Cattle in America; sec. Unadilla Valley Dutch Stock Breeders' Assn., 1876-85; sec. Dutch-Friesian Cattle Breeders' Assn. of America, 1878-85; originator of the earliest system for registering dairy cattle on the basis of product and supt. Advanced Registry of Holstein-Friesian Cattle Breeders' Assn., 1885-1904, emeritus, 1906—. Author: Holstein-Friesian Herd Book, 4 vols., 1880-85; Advanced Register Holstein-Friesian Cattle Breeders' Association, 14 vols., 1887-1903. Home: Edmeston, N.Y. Died Apr. 11, 1917.

HOXIE, Vinnie Ream, sculptor; b. Madison, Wis., Sept. 25, 1847; d. Robert Lee and Lavinia (McDonald) Ream; ed. Christian Coll., Mo.; studied art under Bonnât in Paris, and with Majoli, Rome, Italy; m. Richard Leveridge Hoxie, May 28, 1878. Received commn. from Congress to execute life-size statue of Abraham Lincoln; he sat for his bust at the White House, and his statue is now in rotunda of Capitol; later Congress commd. her to make the statue of Admiral Farragut which now stands in Farragut Sq., Washington; executed ideal statues of "Miriam," "The West," "Sappho," "The Spirit of the Carnival," "The Indian Girl"; also many busts in marble, including one of President Lincoln (for Cornell U.); has modeled from life portraits busts or medallions of Gen. George B. McClellan, Thaddeus Stevens, John Sherman, Ezra Cornell, Gen. J. C. Fremont, T. Buchanan Read, Elihu B. Washburn, Horace Greeley, Peter Cooper, and other prominent Americans; and of Cardinal Antonelli, Père Hyacinthe, Spurgeon, Franz Liszt, Gustave Doré, and Kaulbach; commd. by the state of Ia. to make statue of Gov. Samuel J. Kirkwood, and by Oklahoma to make statue of Sequoya, both to be placed in Nat. Capitol. Died Nov. 20, 1914.

HOXTON, William Winslow, banker; b. Jefferson Co., W.Va., May 20, 1871; s. Col. Llewellyn (C.S.A.) and Fanny (Robinson) H.; ed. Episcopal High School, Alexandria, Va.; m. Abbie Frances Haines, Sept. 20, 1897 (died May 12, 1902); children—Llewellyn Kennerly, Abbie Frances (Mrs. Clarence Johnston Robinson); m. 2d, Mabel Fraser Pearson, Sept. 10, 1904. Teacher, Trinity Hall, Louisville, Ky., 1890-91, Episcopal High School, Alexandria, 1891-94; newspaper and magazine writer, St. Louis, 1894-97; asst. mgr. St. Louis Clearing House Assn., 1897-1906, mgr., 1906-14; dep. gov. Federal Reserve Bank, St. Louis, 1914-19; gen. sec. Federal Reserve Bd., Washington, D.C., 1919-23; chmn. bd. and federal reserve agt. Federal Reserve Bank, Richmond, Va., 1923—. Episcopalian. Home: Richmond, Va. Died Dec. 20, 1935.

HOYLE, Eli DuBose, army officer; b. Canton, Ga., Jan. 19, 1851; s. George Summers and Margaret Amanda (Erwin) H.; grad. U.S. Mil. Acad., 1875; grad. U.S. Arty. Sch., 1880; m. Fanny DeRussy, d. late Bvt. Brig. Gen. R. E. DeRussy, U.S. Army, Dec. 11, 1878. Commd. 2d lt., 2d Arty., June 16, 1875; 1st lt., Oct. 28, 1883; maj. and chief ordnance officer, U.S. Vols., July 18, 1898; hon. disch., May 12, 1899; capt. 1st Arty., Sept. 18, 1898; maj. Arty. Corps, Aug. 10, 1903; lt. col. field arty., Jan. 25, 1907; col., Mar. 3, 1911; brig. gen., Sept. 24, 1913; retired (age limit), Jan. 19, 1915. Adj. U.S. Mil. Acad., 1882-85; adj. 2d Regt. Arty., 1885-89; served on staff Maj. Gen. James H. Wilson, in Puerto Rican Campaign, 1898; on staff Brig. Gen. Geo. M. Randall, 1898-99, and on staff of Major Gen. James H. Wilson as chief ordnance officer and provost marshal gen., Dept. of Matanzas, Cuba, until May 1899; asst. to insp. gen., Dept. of East, 1900-02; pres. bd. for preparation of drill regulations for rapid fire gun, 1903-06; pres. Field Arty. Bd., 1906-07; comd. recruit depot, Ft. Slocum, N.Y., 1907-08; comd. 6th Regt. Field Arty., 1908-11 and 1911-13; comdg. Central Dept. (Chicago), Mar.-June, 1913, Dist. of Luzon, P.I., 1913-14, Ft. William McKinley, Rizal, P.I., May-Dec. 1914. On active duty and comdg. Eastern Dept., hdqrs. Governors Island, N.Y., Aug.

25, 1917-Jan. 15, 1918. Medal Spanish-Am. War. Episcopalian. Died July 27, 1921.

HOYNE, Thomas Maclay, lawyer; b. Galena, Ill., July 17, 1843; s. Thomas and Lenora (Temple) H.; grad. Chicago High Sch.; studied law for 3 yrs. in offices of Hoyne, Miller & Lewis (of which father was sr. mem.), LL.B., old U. of Chicago Law Sch., 1866; m. Jeanie T., d. Moses B. Maclay, Jan. 25, 1871. Joined father's firm, 1867, changed to Horton & Hoyne, on death of father in 1883, so continuing until 1887, when Oliver H. Horton was elected to the bench, firm now Hoyne, O'Connor & Irwin; elected as additional circuit judge, 1903, but Supreme Court later declared act creating additional circuit judges invalid. Democrat. Home: Chicago, Ill. Died Sept. 28, 1941.

HOYNES, William, lawyer, university dean; b. nr. Callan, Co. Kilkenny, Ireland, Nov. 8, 1846; s. Patrick and Catherine (Kennedy) H.; came to America in early childhood; matriculated as student, U. of Notre Dame, Apr. 2, 1868, A.M., 1878, LL.D., 1888; LL.B., U. of Mich., 1872; unmarried. Learned printing trade with LaCrosse (Wis.) Republican. Enlisted June 9, 1862, Co. A, 20th Wis. Vol. Infantry; severely wounded at battle of Prairie Grove, Ark., Dec. 7, 1862; participated in capture of Van Buren on the Ark. River; participated in siege and capture of Vicksburg; discharged from service on account of wound, but reënlisted and joined Co. D, 2d Wis. Cav., participating in all actions and skirmishes with latter command; treated for wound in Adams St. Hosp., Memphis, in winter of 1865; returned with regt. from Austin, Tex., to Wis. at close of war; mustered out of U.S. service at Madison. Became editor New Brunswick (N.J.) Daily Times, 1873, and later associated with M. M. ("Brick") Pomeroy in editorial work at Chicago; editor Peoria (Ill.) Daily Transcript, 1881-82; practiced law at Chicago, 1882-83; admitted to Supreme Court of Mich., Apr. 10, 1872, U.S. Circuit Court, Apr. 11, 1872, Supreme Ct. of U.S., 1875, Supreme Ct. of Ill., 1877; prof. law and dean of law faculty, U. of Notre Dame, 1883-1918 (dean emeritus). Was organizer and commanded the University Light Guards, 1887. Rep. candidate for Congress, 1888; declined nomination for Congress, 1904; appointed U.S. commr. to treat with Turtle Mountain (N.D.) Indians, Oct. 4, 1890; apptd. three times to serve on state commns. Catholic. Apptd. Knight of St. Gregory, by Pope Pius X, 1912. Died Mar. 28, 1933.

HOYT, Allen Grey, banker; b. Aurora, Ill., Apr. 16, 1876; s. Willis and Jennie (Budlong) H.; Ph.B., U. of Chicago, 1899; LL.B., Georgetown U., 1902; m. Annette Taussig, Feb. 21, 1918; children—Allen Grey, Willis T. With Nat. City Bank of New York, 1902—, vice pres., 1928—; v.p. City Bank-Farmers Trust Co. Home: New York, N.Y. Died Nov. 4, 1941.

HOYT, Arthur Stephen, clergyman; b. Meridian, N.Y., June 3, 1851; s. Stephen Close and Betsey Ann (Barnes) H.; A.B., Hamilton Coll., 1872; grad. Auburn Theol. Sem., 1878; (D.D., Hamilton, 1891); m. M. Emma Hewson, Oct. 9, 1879. Tutor Robert Coll., Constantinople, Turkey, 1872-75; ordained Presbyn. ministry, 1878; pastor Oregon, Ill., 1879-86; prof. English lit. and pub. speaking, Hamilton Coll., 1886-91; prof. homiletics and sociology, Auburn Theol. Sem., 1891—. Author: The Work of Preaching, 1906; Public Worship for Non-liturgical Churches, 1911; The Vital Elements of Preaching, 1914; The Pulpit and American Life, 1921; The Spiritual Message of Modern English Poetry, 1923. Home: Auburn, N.Y. Died Mar. 1923.

HOYT, Charles Albert, mfr.; b. Burlington, Vt., July 27, 1839; s. Rev. William Henry and Anne (Deming) H.; grad. Univ. of Vt., 1857, A.M., 1861 (also A.M., Georgetown, D.C., Univ.); m. Julia Sherman, 1862. Entered business, 1858; one of pioneers in early development of hard rubber industry; more than 30 yrs. treas. Goodyear Hard Rubber Co. and India Rubber Comb Co., which owned Goodyear hard rubber patents; now dir. Am. Hard Rubber Co., New York, successor to those corporations. Mem. N.Y. Chamber of Commerce; a founder and dir. German Am. Ins. Co., New York. Retired. Mem. and treas. Soc. of the Cincinnati, N.Y. Home: Brooklyn, N.Y. Died 1903.

HOYT, Charles Hale, playwright and theatrical mgr.; b. Concord, N.H., July 26, 1860; ed. at Boston Latin School; 5 years editorial writer and dramatic and musical editor, Boston Post; engaged as playwright and later as mgr.; mem. Hoyt & Thomas, which later became Hoyt & McKee, lessees of the Garrick and Madison Square theatres, New York. Author: (of plays) A Bunch of Keys; A Rag Baby; A Tin Soldier; A Hole in the Ground; A Midnight Bell; A Brass Monkey; A Texas Steer; A Parlor Match; A Temperance Town; A Black Sheep; A Contented Woman; A Milk White Flag; A Trip to Chinatown; A Stranger in New York; A Day and a Night in New York; A Dog in the Manger; etc. Twice member N.H. legislature, and Democratic candidate for speaker. Home: Charlestown, N.H. Died 1900.

HOYT, Charles Oliver, college prof.; b. Middlesex, N.Y., July 12, 1856; s. William O. and Mary F. (Green) H.; A.B., Albion (Mich.) Coll., 1896; U. of Jena, 1901-03, Ph.D., 1903; m. Eva A. Green, Aug. 7, 1879; children—W. A., Mrs. Lucile Burnett. Began teaching in rural schs., Mich., at 16; prin. sch., Blissfield, Mich., 1877-81, supt. schs., Wyandotte, Mich., 1881-86, Grass Lake, 1886-89, Jackson, 1889-93, Lansing, 1893-96; dir. of Training Sch., 1896-98, prof. pedagogy, 1898-1900, prof. philosophy and edn., 1900-20, State Normal Coll., Ypsilanti, head dept. education. Republican. Methodist. Author: John D. Pierce (joint author), 1905; History of Modern Education, 1908. Home: Ypsilanti, Mich. Died Apr. 14, 1927.

HOYT, Colgate, banker; b. Cleveland, O., Mar. 2, 1849; s. James M. and Mary Ella H.; ed. Cleveland pub. schs., and Phillips Acad.; (hon. A.M., U. of Rochester, 1895); m. Lida Sherman, Oct. 16, 1873. Engaged in banking business. Govt. dir., 1882-84, company dir., 1884, U.P. Ry.; resigned when Charles F. Adams became pres.; later dir. Ore. & Transcontinental (v.p. 1889) and Ore. Ry. & Navigation Co., and of N.P. R.R.; was on exec. and financial coms. of latter, and v.p. Duluth & Manitoba R.R.; became interested in Wis. Central R.R., 1884, and one of its trustees; v.p. North Am. Co. until 1889; mem., 1889, of reorganized Com. of M.,K.&T. Ry. and soon after 1st v.p. M.,K.&T. Ry. of Tex.; later sr. partner in Stock Exchange house of Colgate Hoyt & Co.; also v.p. St. Joseph, South Bend & Southern R.R. Co.; dir., exec. com. U.S. Cast Iron Pipe & Foundry Co. Republican. Mem. Corp. of Brown U. Home: Oyster Bay, L.I. Died Jan. 30, 1922.

HOYT, David Webster, educator; b. Amesbury, Mass., Apr. 16, 1833; s. Enoch and Elizabeth (Williams) H.; student Brown U., class of 1855; (A.M., Middlebury, 1861, Brown, 1872; D.Sc., R.I. Coll., 1914); m. Mary E. Pierce, 1856; m. 2d, Martha J. Guild, 1868. Teacher, Putnam Free Sch., Newburyport, Mass., 1851-54, Union Sch., Beloit, Wis., 1854-55, high sch., Lexington, Mass., 1857-58; adj. prof. mathematics and mechanics, Poly. Coll. of Pa., 1858-59; prof. mathematics and natural sciences, New Hampton Instn., Fairfax, Vt., 1859-63; head of high sch., now English High School, Providence, R.I., 1864-1914; principal emeritus same. First secretary, 1871-79, pres., 1881-82, R.I. Bapt. Social Union; pres. R.I. Inst. of Instrn., 1875-76; commr. for Topog. Survey and Map of R.I., 1888-93; pres. Providence Franklin Soc., 1887-88, and chmn. of com. which prepared its report on the geology of R.I.; pres. Barnard Club, 1898-99. Baptist. Home: Providence, R.I. Died May 8, 1921.

HOYT, Edward C., leather merchant; b. New York, Nov. 1853; s. Oliver and Maria (Corse) H.; ed. Wilbraham, Mass.; m. C. Ida Bruggerhof, Nov. 1882. Chmn. bd. Central Leather Co.; dir. U.S. Leather Co., Union Tanning Co., Argentine Central Leather Co., Nat. Park Bank, N. R. Allen's Sons Co. Home: Stamford, Conn. Died Nov. 28, 1925.

HOYT, Franklin Chase, judge; b. Pelham, N.Y., Sept. 7, 1876; s. William Sprague and Janet Ralston (Chase) H.; g.s. Salmon P. Chase, chief justice of U.S.; grad. St. Paul's Sch., Concord, N.H., 1892; student Columbia, 1892-94, New York Law Sch., 1894-96; m. Maud Rives Borland, June 8, 1918; children—Constance Maud, Beatrix Chase. Began practice at N.Y. City, 1898; asst. corp. counsel, 1902-08; apptd. legal adviser to the mayor, 1905; justice Court of Spl. Sessions, City of New York, 1908-27; instrumental in organization of Children's Court of City of N.Y., of which was apptd. 1st presiding justice, 1915; urged N.Y. constl. amendment and creation of children's courts throughout state (adopted 1921); reorganized N.Y. City children's court, 1924, and again apptd. presiding justice, resigned, 1933, after 25 years' service, having handled over 75,000 cases. Federal Alcohol adminstr., 1935. President Big Brother Movement, 1911-25; pres. New York Conf. Charities and Corrections, 1919; hon. pres. N.Y. Council Boy Scouts America, 1918; chmn. Nat. Probation Assn., 1924-34; mem. N.Y. State Commn. to examine laws relating to child welfare. Republican. Episcopalian. Author: Quicksands of Youth, 1921. Winner of 1st prize of $25,000 in Hearst Temperance Contest, 1929. Home: Wappingers Falls, N.Y. Died Nov. 13, 1937.

HOYT, Henry Martyn, lawyer; b. Wilkes-Barre, Pa., Dec. 5, 1856; s. Gen. Henry Martyn (gov. of Pa., 1879-83, author, etc.) and Mary (Loveland) H.; A.B., Yale, 1878; LL.B., U. of Pa., 1881; m. Anne, d. Morton McMichael, Jan. 31, 1883. Admitted to bar, 1881; asst. cashier U.S. Nat. Bank, New York, 1883-86; treas. Investment Co. of Phila., 1886-90, pres., 1890-93; practiced law, Phila., 1893-97; asst. atty. gen. of U.S., 1897-1903; solicitor-gen. of U.S., 1903-09; counsellor for Dept. of State, 1909—. Republican. Home: Washington, D.C. Died 1910.

HOYT, James Humphrey, lawyer; b. Cleveland, O., Nov. 10, 1852; s. James M. and Mary Ella (Beebe) H.; bro. of Wayland Hoyt; A.B., Brown Univ., 1874; LL.B., Harvard, 1877; m. Jessie L. Taintor, 1885. Admitted to bar, 1877, and since in practice at Cleveland; sr. mem. Hoyt, Dustin, Kelley, McKeehan & Andrews; general counsel of Hocking Valley Railway; sec. Lake Superior & Ishpeming Ry., Munising, Marquette & South Eastern Ry. Home: Cleveland, O. Died Mar. 21, 1917.

HOYT, John Wesley, governor; b. near Worthington, O., Oct. 13, 1831; s. Joab and Judith (Hawley) H.; A.B., Ohio Wesleyan U., 1849, A.M., 1852; studied Cincinnati Law Sch. and Ohio Med. Coll.; M.D., Eclectic Med. Inst., 1853; (LL.D., U. of Mo., 1876); m. Elizabeth Orpha Sampson, 1854. Prof. chemistry and med. jurisprudence, Eclectic Med. Inst., 1853-57, Cincinnati Coll. Medicine, 1855-57; prof. chemistry, Antioch Coll., 1855-57. Took part in forming Rep. party and in most of its presdl. campaigns; publisher and editor agrl. jour., Madison, Wis., 1857-67; sec. and mgr. Wis. State Agrl. Soc., 1860-72; v.p. U.S. Agrl. Soc.; state commr. to London Expn., 1862; U.S. commr. to Paris Expn., 1867; reorganizer U. of Wis.; founder, 1870 (pres. 1870-77) Wis. Acad. Sciences, Arts and Letters; exec. and final chief commr. of U.S. to Vienna Expn., 1873 (pres. internat. jury edn. and science); Wis. state ry. commr., 1874-76; Wis. commr. water routes to seaboard; U.S. commr. to Centennial Expn. (pres. internat. jury edn. and science); gov. Wyo., 1878-83, making peace with the Indians; pres. Wyo. Development Co., 1882; pres. internat. jury edn. and science, New Orleans Expn., 1884-85; originated and was trustee Los Angeles & Santa Monica Ry., 1886; pres. U. of Wyo., 1887-90; founder and first pres. Wyo. Acad. Sciences, Arts and Letters, 1887-90; mem. Wyo. Constl. Conv., 1890; v.p. Pan-Republic Congress, 1891; chmn. Russian Famine Relief Com. of U.S.; located in Washington, D.C., 1891; spl. representative for foreign affairs, World's Columbian Commn., 1893; commr. plenipotentiary of Korea to Universal Postal Union, securing Korea's admission to Union, 1897; permanent chmn. Com. of 400 to Promote Nat. U. Received commander's cross, Imperial Order Francis Joseph; officier de l'Instruction Publique, France; gold medal from German Govt.; 2 medallion portraits of Emperor Napoleon III of France (from hand of Emperor himself); bronze plate from Japanese Government. Home: Chevy Chase, Washington, D.C. Died May 23, 1912.

HOYT, Lucius Warner, lawyer; b. Hartford, Mich., Dec. 31, 1860; s. Benjamin F. and Frances Elizabeth (Warner) H.; B.S., Mich. Agrl. Coll., 1882; LL.B., Columbia, 1889; (hon. A.M., U. of Denver, 1901, D.C.L., 1908); m. Catharine Connal Potter, Aug. 27, 1889. Admitted to bar, 1889; asso. prof., 1892-93, prof. law, 1893—, dean law dept., 1902—, Denver U. Presbyn. Republican. Home: Denver, Colo. Died 1910.

HOYT, Ralph Wilson, brig. gen. U.S.A.; b. Penn Yan, N.Y., Oct. 9, 1849; s. Benjamin L. and Celestia U. (Mariner) H.; grad. U.S. Mil. Acad., 1872; m. Mary C. Cravens, Jan. 17, 1878 (died 1910); m. 2d, Cora McK. Harbold. Commissioned 2d lt. 11th Inf., June 14, 1872; 1st lt., June 7, 1879; regtl. q.m., June 7, 1879-May 31, 1886; capt., Sept. 19, 1890; maj. 10th Inf., May 16, 1899; lt. col. 14th Inf., May 28, 1902; transferred to 10th Inf., Oct. 18, 1902; assigned to adj. gen. dept., Feb. 4, 1903; col. 25th Inf., Dec. 3, 1903; brig. gen. U.S.A., Mar. 18, 1910; retired by operation of law, Oct. 9, 1913. Home: Penn Yan, N.Y. Died Nov. 3, 1920.

HOYT, Richard Farnsworth, investments; b. Revere, Mass., July 3, 1888; s. Charles Chase and Emma Josephine (Farnsworth) H.; grad. Volkmann Sch., Boston, 1906; A.B., magna cum laude, Harvard, 1910; m. Katharine Stone, Sept. 5, 1911 (divorced 1931); children—Eleanor, Virginia, Constance; m. 2d, Martha Nicholson Doubleday, June 29, 1931; 1 child, Galen S. Began with Hayden, Stone & Co., investment bankers, 1910; with Wright-Martin Aircraft Corp., 1918; mem. Hayden, Stone & Co., 1919—; chmn. bd. Curtiss Wright Corp., Madison Square Garden Corp., Punta Alegre Sugar Corp., also officer or dir. many other corps. Vice chmn. com. on aeronautics, Chamber of Commerce of U.S.; mem. Aeronautical Chamber of Commerce of America; pres. bd. trustees Tabor Acad., Marion, Mass. Home: New York, N.Y. Died Mar. 7, 1935.

HOYT, Wayland, clergyman; b. Cleveland, O., Feb. 18, 1938; s. James M. and Mary Ella (Beebee) H.; bro. of James Humphrey H.; A.B., Brown U., 1860, A.M., 1863; graduate Rochester Theol. Sem., 1863; (D.D., U. of Rochester, 1877; LL.D., Ursinus Coll., 1901); m. Maud Fairfax Mansfield, 1864. Ordained Bapt. ministry, 1863; pastor Pittsfield, Mass., 1863-64, Ninth St. Ch., Cincinnati, 1864-67, Strong Pl. Ch., Brooklyn, 1867-73, 1876-82, Tabernacle Church, New York, 1873-74, Shawmut Av. Ch., Boston, 1874-76. Memorial Ch., Phila., 1882-89, First Ch., Minneapolis, 1889-95, Epiphany Ch., Phila., 1895—. Prof. religion and science and the art of public speech, Theol. Dept., Temple U. Author: Gleams from Paul's Prison, 1882; Along the Pilgrimage, 1884; Saturday Afternoon, 1890; For Shine and Shade, 1898; Home Ideals, 1904; The Teaching of Jesus Concerning His Own Person, 1907. Home: Philadelphia, Pa. Died 1910.

HOYT, Wilbur Franklin, teacher, author; b. Reedsville, O., Mar. 13, 1864; s. Noah Starr and Maria (Reed) H.; A.B., Ohio Wesleyan U., 1895, A.M., from same 1905; post-grad. work Harvard U. and Chautauqua Summer School; m. Love Smart, Aug. 26, 1895 (dec.); children—Esther Louise, Wilbur Reed (dec.), Philip Fenelon. Taught pub. schs., 1883-89; high sch. prin., Ohio, Mont. and Pa., 1888-98; prof. mathematics and science, Chamberlain Inst., Randolph, N.Y., 1898-1901; prof. science, 1901-10, acting pres., 1902-03, v.p., 1903-04, Kan. Wesleyan U.; head prof. phys. science, Neb. State Teachers Coll., Peru, 1910—. Mason. Methodist. Author: Laboratory Manual of General Chemistry; Manual of Qualitative Analysis, 1909; Manual Chemistry, 1913; Chemistry by Experimentation, 1917; Principles and Problems of Chemistry, 1927; Science and Life, 1927. Home: Peru, Neb. Died June 25, 1930.

HOYT, William Greeley, pres. Standard Gas Light Co.; b. Boston, Mass., Feb. 5, 1859; s. Benjamin Franklin and Annie Maria (Pike) H.; ed. pub. and pvt. schs.; m. Carrie J. Lathrop, June 22, 1896; 1 son, William Lathrop. Identified with gas lighting business, 1894—; pres. Standard Gas Light Co. of the City of N.Y., 1906—; pres. New Amsterdam Gas Co., East River Gas Light Co., New York Carbide & Acetylene Co. Republican. Episcopalian. Home: Garden City, N.Y. Died Nov. 26, 1935.

HUBARD, Robert Thruston, lawyer; b. Rosny, Va., March 9, 1839; s. Robert T. and Susan P. (Bolling) H.; A.B. (1st honor grad.), Hampden-Sidney Coll., 1859; studied law, U. of Va.; pvt. to 1st lt. and bvt. capt. Cumberland Co. Light Dragoons, which became Co. G, 3d Va. Cav. (Fitzhugh Lee's brigade, Stuart's div., Army Northern Va.) to close of war; twice wounded by musket ball; m. Sallie, d. Hon. John R. Edmund, of Va., Oct. 27, 1870. Mem. Va. House of Delegates, 1875-77; declined reëlection; joined Rep. party, 1880; in 1884 apptd. presdl. elector and nominated for Congress in the Richmond, Va., dist.; candidate for Congress, 1898, 1900, 10th Va. dist.; supervisor census, 1900, in same district. Home: Dillwyn, Va. Died 1921.

HUBBARD, Adolphus Skinner, secretary of Calif. Hist. Soc.; b. nr. Chicago, July 7, 1840; s. Theodore H. (Jr.) and Ann Ward (Ballou) H.; ed. pub. sch., Chicago; m. Sarah Isabelle Sylvester, Feb. 29, 1872. Formerly col. staff Territorial troops, N.M. Founder and pres. Calif. Soc. S.A.R.; pres. gen. Nat. Soc., same, 1890-91; mem. N.H. Soc. Colonial Wars; instituting mem. and treas. Mil. Order of Foreign Wars, Calif.; organizing mem. and v.p. Calif. Geneal. Soc.; hon. and corr. mem. various hist. socs. Home: San Francisco, Calif. Died Jan. 29, 1913.

HUBBARD, Alice, author; b. Wales, N.Y., June 7, 1861; d. Welcome and Melinda (Bush) Moore; grad. State Normal Sch., Buffalo, N.Y., 1882, Emerson Coll. of Oratory, Boston, 1892; m. Elbert Hubbard. Gen. supt. Roycroft Shops; mgr. Roycroft Inn; prin. Roycroft School of Life for Boys. Author: Woman's Work; Justinian and Theodora (with Elbert Hubbard), 1906; Life Lessons, 1909; The Basis of Marriage, 1911; The Apples of Discord, 1911; The Myth in Marriage, 1912. Home: East Aurora, N.Y. Died May 7, 1915.

HUBBARD, Elbert, author, lecturer; b. at Bloomington, Ill., June 19, 1859; s. Dr. Silas and Frances (Read) H.; common sch. edn.; (hon. M.A., Tufts College, 1899); m. Alice Moore. Editor of The Philistine; propr. The Roycroft Shop, devoted to making de luxe editions of the classics. Author: No Enemy but Himself; Little Journeys to Homes of Good Men and Great; Little Journeys to the Homes of American Authors; Little Journeys to the Homes of Famous Women; Little Journeys to the Homes of American Statesmen; Little Journeys to the Homes of Eminent Painters; Ali Baba of East Aurora; As It Seems to Me; A Message to Garcia; Time and Chance; The Legacy; Forbes of Harvard; One Day; A Tale of the Prairies; Little Journeys to Homes of Eminent Artists; Little Journeys to Homes of Eminent Orators; Little Journeys to Homes of Great Philosophers; Old John Burroughs: Contemplations; Consecrated Lives; The Man of Sorrows; Health and Wealth; Love, Life and Work; One Thousand and One Epigrams. Home: East Aurora, N.Y. Died May 7, 1915.

HUBBARD, Elbert Hamilton, congressman; b. Rushville, Ind., Aug. 19, 1849; s. Hon. Asahel Wheeler and Leah (Pugh) H.; B.A., Yale, 1872; m. Eleanor Heermance Cobb, June 6, 1882. Admitted to bar, 1874, and began practice at Sioux City, Ia. Mem. Ia. Ho. of Rep., 1882-83, Senate, 1900-04; mem. 59th to 62d Congresses (1905-13), 11th Ia. Dist. Republican. Home: Sioux City, Ia. Died June 4, 1912.

HUBBARD, Elijah Kent, financier; b. Chicago, Ill., Feb. 5, 1869; s. Elijah Kent and Anna Jones (Dyer) H.; preparatory edn., St. Paul's Sch., Concord, N.H.; B.S., Trinity Coll., Conn., 1892; M.A. from Wesleyan U., Conn., 1924; m. Helen Keep Otis, Jan. 15, 1901; children—Otis Livingston, Chauncey Keep, Helen Kent (Mrs. Hubbard Dodge), Mildred de Koven. Entered business in 1892 founded by uncle, Henry G. Hubbard, in 1834, as Russell Mfg. Co., mfrs. webbing, and elected treas., 1912, resigned, 1913; pres. Maxim Silencer Co., Hartford, Conn., 1913-16; pres. Mfrs. Assn. of Conn., 1918—; Dem. candidate for lt. gov. of Conn., 1903; nominated for state treas., 1910 (declined). Capt. 12 yrs. and p.m. 1st Co., Gov's Foot Guard. Mem. State Bd. of Finance, 10 yrs.; treas. Cheshire Reformatory, 12 yrs.; mem. Bd. of Parole of Conn. State Prison, also dir. Prison; dir. Middlesex Hosp.; gov.'s rep. New England R.R. Com. and chmn. Conn. Commn.; pres. Middletown Park Bd., Russell Library; v.p. Eastern States Expn.; trustee Wesleyan U. Chmn. and mem. exec. com. Nat. Industrial Conf. Bd.; mem. Tercentenary Commn., State of Conn. Mason. Home: Middletown, Conn. Died Aug. 7, 1941.

HUBBARD, Frank McKinney ("Kin Hubbard"), caricaturist; b. Bellefontaine, O.; s. Thomas and Sarah Jane (Miller) H.; pub. sch. edn.; m. Josephine Jackson, Oct. 1905. Employed almost continuously as caricaturist and paragrapher on Indianapolis News, 1891—. Author: Abe Martin's Sayings, syndicated widely, also pub. in book form annually. Home: Indianapolis, Ind. Died Dec. 26, 1930.

HUBBARD, Henry Wright, treasurer; b. Elgin, Ill., May 17, 1844; s. William G. and Charlotte (Wright) H.; B.S., U. of Mich., 1866, M.S., 1872; attended law school 1 yr.; pvt., 134th Ill. Vols., 1864; admitted to bar in Ill., 1868; practiced in Chicago and Denver, Colo., 1870. Prof. mathematics and asst. treas., Fisk U., Nashville, Tenn., 1871-73; entered New York office Am. Missionary Assn., 1873, asst. treas., 1876, treas., 1879—. Treas. Straight U., New Orleans, 1879—, Talladega Coll., Ala., 1885—, Tougaloo U., Miss., 1885—. Home: New York, N.Y. Died May 21, 1913.

HUBBARD, John, naval officer; b. S. Berwick, Me., May 19, 1849; s. John and Eleanor Augusta (Tucker) H.; grad. U.S. Naval Acad., 1870. Promoted ensign, 1871; master, 1873; lt., 1878; lt. comdr., 1898; comdr., 1901; capt., July 8, 1905; rear adm., 1909; retired May 19, 1911. In command U.S.S. Nashville and naval force on Isthmus of Panama during revolution of Nov. 1903, which resulted in independence of State of Panama; comd. U.S.S. Minnesota on cruise of the battleship fleet around the world; later on spl. duty Navy Dept. and mem. Gen. Bd.; comdr.-in-chief Asiatic Fleet, 1910. Home: Washington, D.C. Died May 28, 1932.

HUBBARD, Kin, author. See Frank McKinney Hubbard.

HUBBARD, Lucius Frederick, governor; b. Troy, N.Y., Jan. 26, 1836; s. Charles F. and Margaret (Van Valkenberg) H.; acad. edn., Granville, N.Y.; learned tinner's trade; went to Minn., 1857; m. Amelia Thomas, Apr. 17, 1868. Newspaper publisher at Red Wing, 1859-61; register of deeds, Goodhue Co., Minn., 1858-60; pvt. Co. A, 5th Minn. Inf., Dec. 19, 1861; capt., Feb. 4, 1862; lt. col., Mar. 24, 1862; col., Aug. 30, 1862; bvtd. brig. gen. vols., Dec. 16, 1864, "for gallant and distinguished services in actions before Nashville;" hon. mustered out, Sept. 6, 1865. In grain and milling business at Red Wing, 1866-84; built Midland R.R. in Minn., 1877-78; pres. Cannon Valley R.R., 1878-81; built, and operated Duluth, Red Wing & Southern R.R., 1888-1902. Mem. Minn. Senate, 1872-76; gov. of Minn., 1882-87. Brig. gen. vols., May 27-Oct. 31, 1898, in Spanish-Am. War; comd. 3d Div., 7th Army Corps. Mason. Home: St. Paul, Minn. Died Feb. 5, 1913.

HUBBARD, Lucius Lee, geologist; b. Cincinnati, Aug. 7, 1849; s. Lucius Virgilius and Annie Elizabeth (Lee) H.; A.B., Harvard, 1872; LL.B., Boston U., 1875; Ph.D., U. of Bonn, 1886; m. Frances Johnson Lambard, Sept. 29, 1875; children—Charlotte Armitage (Mrs. H. S. Goodell), Lucius Lambard (dec.), Frances Johnson (Mrs. R. J. Flaherty), Julia Lambard (Mrs. Platt Adams). Asst. Mich. Geol. Survey and instr. mineralogy, Mich. Coll. Mines, 1891-93; state geologist, 1893-99. Mem. bd. control Mich. Coll. of Mines, 1905-17; regent U. of Mich., 1911—. Author: Woods and Lakes of Maine, 1884; A Dutch Source for Robinson Crusoe—The Narrative of El-ho, "Sjouke Gabbes," 1921. Compiler: The University of Michigan—Its Origin, Growth, and Principles of Government, 1923. Home: Houghton, Mich. Died Aug. 3, 1933.

HUBBARD, Oliver Payson, univ. prof.; b. Pomfret, Conn., Mar. 1809; grad. Yale, 1828; (M.D., S. C. Med. Coll., 1837; LL.D., Hamilton, 1861). Prof., 1836-66; lecturer, 1866-71, chemistry, pharmacy, mineralogy and geology, afterward prof. chemistry and pharmacy, 1871-83 (emeritus), Dartmouth. Mem. N.H. legislature, 1863-64. Died 1900.

HUBBARD, Richard Bennet, gov. Texas; b. Walton Co., Ga., Nov. 1, 1836; s. Richard B. and Serena (Carter) H.; grad. Mercer Univ., 1852; grad. law dept. Harvard Univ. and Univ. of Va.; went to Texas, 1852; admitted to bar, practice at Tyler, Tex. Youngest delegate of 8 from Texas to Nat. Dem. Conv., Cincinnati, 1856; U.S. atty., western dist. Texas, 1857-59; resigned, 1859; mem. Texas legislature, 1859-62; resigned and raised 22d Tex. vol. inf. and was its col. in C.S.A. to end of war. Was disfranchised for some yrs. after war; when civil disabilities were removed entered politics; was pres. Dem. State Conv. and chmn. Dem. State Exec. Com.; lt.-gov., 1873-76; gov., 1876-79. E.E. and M.P. of U.S. to Japan, 1885-89. Home: Tyler, Tex. Deceased.

HUBBARD, S(amuel) Dana, dermatologist; b. Montgomery, Ala., Mar. 19, 1869; s. Samuel Dana and Mary C. (Taylor) H.; prep. edn., pvt. high sch., Montgomery; student U. of Ala., 1886; M.D., Bellevue Hosp. Med. Coll., N.Y. City, 1891; m. Armilla Monell, Oct. 23, 1895; children—Aileen (Mrs. Harry Chapin), Beryl. Interne, Bellevue Hosp., 1891-92; resident phys. Riverside Hosp., N.Y. City, 1892-95; began practice at N.Y. City, 1895; former dermatologist N.Y. City Children's Hosp. and attending dermatologist Letchworth Village. Maj. and surgeon, N.G.N.Y., 1891-98; maj. and surgeon, U.S. Vol. Inf., Spanish-Am. War. Presbyn. Author: Sex Facts, 1927; Diseases of Scalp and Hair, 1928. Home: Freeport, L.I., N.Y. Died July 12, 1937.

HUBBARD, Samuel Fairfield, settlement worker; b. Canaan, Me., Feb. 9, 1846; s. Samuel Fairfield and Mary (Ricker) H.; grad. Me. Wesleyan Sem., Kent's Hill, 1867; unmarried. Commercial traveler, 1870-79; in commn. business, 1880-92; supt. North End Union (social settlement), 1892-1917. Mem. Boston Sch. Com., 1896-98; v.p. Mass. Assn. Promoting Interests of Blind; trustee Boston Floating Hosp. Republican. Unitarian. Mason. Home: Boston, Mass. Died Mar. 3, 1928.

HUBBARD, Sara Anderson, author; b. East Berkshire, Vt., Sept. 7, 1832; d. David B. and Selena (Anderson) Blakely; ed. at Ladies' Sem., Newark, N.Y.; m. James M. Hubbard, 1853 (dec.). Engaged in journalism and teaching, 1869—. Author: Catchwords of Cheer, 1900, also Series No. 2 and No. 3, same; The Religion of Cheerfulness, 1906; The Duty of Being Beautiful; The Soul in a Flower. Home: Brooklyn, N.Y. Died July 31, 1918.

HUBBARD, Theodora Kimball, editor, author; b. Newton, Mass., Feb. 26, 1887; d. Edwin Fiske and Ellen Leora (Ripley) K.; grad. Girls' Latin Sch., Boston, 1904; S.B., Simmons Coll., 1908; M.S., 1917; m. Henry V. Hubbard, June 7, 1924. Librarian Sch. of Landscape Architecture, Harvard U., 1911-24, spl. adviser to same, 1924—; editor Research, Sch. of City Planning, Harvard, 1929—; asso. ed. Landscape Architecture (Boston); contbg. editor City Planning Quarterly (Boston). Consulting librarian and chief of reference library sect. U.S. Bur. Industrial Housing and Transportation, Washington, D.C., Apr. 1918-May 1919; expert on zoning information for Sec. Hoover's Advisory Com. on Zoning; mem. com. on research, President's Conference on Home Building and Home Ownership. Unitarian. Author: (with J. S. Pray) City Planning—a Comprehensive Analysis, 1913; (with H. V. Hubbard) Introduction to the Study of Landscape Design, 1917, 4th edit., 1929; Landscape Architecture Classification, 1920; Manual of Information on City Planning and Zoning, 1923, supplement to same (with K. McNamara), 1928; Our Cities Today and Tomorrow (with H. V. Hubbard), 1929; also Annual Survey of City and Regional Planning in the U.S. (pub. by City Planning Quarterly). Compiler: References on City Planning, 1915; Municipal Accomplishment in City Planning. Published City Plan Reports in the United States, 1920. Editor professional papers of Frederick Law Olmsted, Senior, Vol. I, 1922, Vol. II, 1928. Home: Milton, Mass. Died Nov. 7, 1935.

HUBBARD, Thomas Hamlin, lawyer; b. Hallowell, Me., Dec. 20, 1838; s. John and Sarah Hodge (Barrett) H.; A.B., Bowdoin, 1857, A.M., 1860 (LL.D., 1894); LL.B., Albany Law Sch., 1861; admitted to Me. bar, 1860, N.Y., 1861, Supreme Ct. of U.S., 1870; 1st lt. adj. 25th Me. Inf., Sept. 29, 1862; lt. col., 30th Me. Inf., Dec. 19, 1863; col., June 2, 1864; bvtd. brig. gen. vols., July 13, 1865, "for meritorious services"; resigned, July 23, 1865; m. Sibyl A. Fahnestock, Jan. 28, 1868. Mem. Butler, Stillman & Hubbard, New York, 1875-96; v.p. and dir. S.P. Co., 1896-1900; pres. Mexican Internat. R.R. Co., 1897-1901, Houston & Tex. Central R.R., 1894-1901; pres. Guatemala Central R.R. Co., 1901-12, Internat. Bank, 1905—; pres. and chmn. bd. Internat. Banking Corp., 1904—; pres. Pacific Improvement Co., 1903—; dir. Nat. Bank of Commerce; dir. and chmn. exec. com. Toledo, St. Louis & Western R.R. Co., Am. Light & Traction Co.; dir. and mem. exec. com. Wabash R.R. Co., Western Union Telegraph Co.; dir. and mem. finance com. Met. Life Ins. Co. Trustee Bowdoin Coll., Albany Law School. Died May 19, 1915.

HUBBARD, Walter Comstock, merchant; b. N.Y. City, June 25, 1851; s. Samuel Thomas and Mary (Hustace) H.; ed. Mt. Washington Collegiate Sch., N.Y. City; m. Helen Ingalls Valentine, 1872 (died 1918). Mem. Hubbard Bros. & Co., 1895—, became spl. partner; chmn. bd. Liverpool & London & Globe Ins. Co., Ltd., of Liverpool, Eng., also of subsidiary cos. and Globe Indemnity Co. of N.Y.; dir. Mechanics and Metals Nat. Bank. Home: New York, N.Y. Died Nov. 24, 1927.

HUBBARD, William H., banker; b. Renick, Mo., Sept. 1, 1860; s. S. W. and M. J. (Sears) H.; self-ed.; m. Alva R. Sears, June 14, 1881; children—

Mrs. Floy M. Beckett, M. Vilas, Catherine. Began as clk. in store at age of 14; entered business for self at 21; county assessor Randolph Co., Mo., 6 yrs.; then engaged in banking business; settled in San Diego, Calif., 1903, Pasadena, 1909; pres. Citizens Savings Bank from its orgn., 1912. Democrat. Methodist. Mason. Home: Pasadena, Calif. Deceased.

HUBBARD, William Henry, clergyman; b. Clark Co., Ky., Apr. 16, 1851; s. William Henry and Anna (Hinds) H.; A.B., Amherst, 1871; student Andover Theol. Sem., 1871-72; grad. Princeton Theol. Sem., 1874; (D.D., Berea Coll., Ky., 1905); m. Elizabeth Allen Skinner, Nov. 9, 1886. Ordained Presbyn. ministry, 1874; pastor Rutland, Mass., 1874-76, South Congl. Ch., Merrimac, Mass., 1876-83, Concord, N.H., 1883-85, Second Congl. Ch., Holyoke, Mass., 1885-86, First Presbyn. Ch., Auburn, N.Y., 1886-1911; mem. Exec. Commn. of Gen. Assembly Presbyn. Ch. U.S.A., 1908-11, exec. sec. same 1911—. Editor and publisher Assembly Herald of the Presbyn. Ch., 1894-98, Gospel Message, 1903-05. Sec. Gen. Assembly's com. on systematic beneficence, Presbyn. Ch. U.S.A., 1896-1909, when the com. was merged with the Exec. Commn. Commr. of charities, Auburn, 1906-07. Home: Auburn, N.Y. Died Jan. 31, 1913.

HUBBARD, William Pallister, congressman; b. Wheeling, W. Va., Dec. 24, 1843; s. Chester Dorman and Sarah (Pallister) H.; A.B., Wesleyan U., 1863, A.M., 1866; m. Anna Elizabeth Chamberlin, May 21, 1868. Lt. 3d W.Va. Cav., 1865; admitted to bar, 1865, and until 1903 in active practice in Wheeling. Clerk W.Va. Ho. of Delegates, 1865-70; mem. Ho. of Delegates, 1881-82; chmn. Commn. to Revise Tax Laws of State, 1901-03; mem. 60th and 61st Congresses (1907-11), 1st W.Va. Dist.; del. Rep. Nat. Conv., 1888, 1912. Home: Wheeling, W.Va. Died Dec. 5, 1921.

HUBBELL, Alvin Allace, ophthalmologist; b. Conewango, N.Y., May 1, 1846; s. Schuyler Phillip and Hepzibah (Farnsworth) H.; ed. Randolph (N.Y.) Academy (now Chamberlain Inst.); m. Evangeline Fancher, June 20, 1872. Practiced medicine and surgery at Leon, 1876-80, Buffalo, 1880-83; practiced ophthalmology at Buffalo, 1883—; prof. ophthalmology, Niagara U., 1883-98, U. of Buffalo, 1898—; ophthalmic surgeon, Sisters of Charity, Erie Co., and Charity Eye, Ear, Nose and Throat hosps. Author: Development of Ophthalmology in America, 1800-70, 1908. Home: Buffalo, N.Y. Died 1911.

HUBBELL, Burt G., telephone official; b. Cleveland, O., July 6, 1867; s. Henry S. and Mary (White) H.; ed. pub. schs., Cleveland, O.; m. Jessie Beach, Mar. 19, 1890. Mfr. telephone apparatus in Chicago, Ill., and Cleveland, 1896-1900; organized the Consolidated Telephone Co. of Delaware for purpose of financing telephone properties in N.Y., Pa. and O., 1900; financed many telephone cos., which were consolidated 1909, as the Federal Telephone & Telegraph Co., of which is pres.; pres. Consol. Telephone Co., Frontier Telephone Co., Inter Ocean Telephone & Telegraph Co., Century Telephone Constrn. Co., Gen. Drop Forge Co., Geneva (N.Y.) Telephone Co. Republican. Presbyn. Home: New York, N.Y. Died Jan. 24, 1925.

HUBBELL, Charles Bulkley, lawyer; b. Williamstown, Mass., July 20, 1853; s. Charles Lyman and Juliette E. (Bulkley) H.; B.A., Williams Coll., 1874, M.A., 1876; m. Emily Allen Chandler, June 5, 1879 (died 1934); children—Juliette E. (Mrs. Lewis Perry), Margaret H. (Mrs. Lewis Perry, dec.), Ruth Rossiter (Mrs. Robert Mason Derby). Was admitted to bar of State of New York, 1876, of State of Mass., 1915; mem. Common Council, Troy, N.Y., 1876; referee in adminstrn. of estates of incompetents in Co. of N.Y., 1896, 1900, 1907; mem. Bd. Edn., New York, 3 terms, elected pres., 1897, before consolidation, and after consolidation was 1st pres. Bd. Edn. Greater New York; chmn. Pub. Service Commn. N.Y., 1st Dist., 1918. Chmn. New Prison Commn. State of N.Y.; trustee Williams Coll., Hunter Coll., Coll. City New York, State Hosp. for Care of Crippled and Deformed Children, Mt. Holyoke Coll. Home: Williamstown, Mass. Died July 24, 1939.

HUBBELL, Frederick Marion; b. Huntington, Conn., Jan. 17, 1839; s. Francis Burritt and Augusta (Church) H.; ed. high sch., Birmingham, Conn., 3 yrs.; m. Frances Elizabeth Cooper, Mar. 19, 1863. Admitted to Ia. bar, 1858; mem. Cassidy & Polk, Des Moines, Ia., 1862-65, Polk & Hubbell, 1865-87; pres. F. M. Hubbell Son & Co., real estate, 1887—; chmn. bd. Equitable Life Ins. Co. of Ia., 1907—; dir. Des Moines Terminal Co. Pres. Home for the Aged, Des Moines, 1894—. Home: Des Moines, Ia. Died Nov. 11, 1930.

HUBBELL, Henry Wilson, brig. gen.; b. New York, Feb. 8, 1842; s. Henry Wilson and Jane Maria (Bostwick) H.; ed. Churchill's Mil. Sch., Sing Sing, N.Y., 1859, and pvt. tutors; m. Sarah, d. Col. John T. Sprague, U.S.A., Jan. 30, 1877. Pvt. Co. H, 7th N.Y. Militia, Apr. 17-June 3, 1861; 2d lt. 40th N.Y. Inf., Dec. 4, 1861; hon. mustered out, Oct. 4, 1863; apptd. from N.Y., 2d lt 1st U.S. Arty., June 18, 1867; grad. Arty. Sch. 1872, 1888; 1st lt., Nov. 17, 1873; capt., Aug. 9, 1889; col. 201st N.Y. Inf., July 11, 1898; hon. mustered out vol. service, Apr. 3, 1899; maj. 47th U.S. Inf., Aug. 17, 1899; hon. disch., Oct. 26, 1899; maj. 4th Arty., Aug. 10, 1900; lt. col. Arty. Corps., June 18, 1902; col., Aug. 10, 1903; brig. gen., and retired for disability in line of duty, May 20, 1905. Episcopalian. Died Dec. 15, 1917.

HUBBELL, Jay Abel, lawyer-congressman; (circuit judge for 12th judicial circuit, Mich.); b. Avon, Mich., Sept. 15, 1829; grad. Univ. of Mich., 1853; admitted to bar, 1855; practiced at Ontonagon, Mich., 1855-60; at Houghton, 1860-70; pros. atty., Houghton Co., 1861-65; State commr. to Centennial Expn., 1876; mem. Congress, 1873-83, from 9th Mich. dist.; after that State senator for several terms; largely interested in mines. Republican. Home: Houghton, Mich. Died 1900.

HUBBS, John Brewster, clergyman, educator; b. Elnora, N.Y., Nov. 23, 1856; s. Alexander and Mary (Dunsmore) H.; A.B., Union Coll., Schenectady, N.Y., 1877, D.D., 1922; B.D., Gen. Theol. Sem., 1880; D.C.L., Chicago Law Sch., 1897; m. Anna Frances Newton, Sept. 10, 1889; children—Horace Newton, Andrew Dunsmore. Deacon, 1880, priest, 1881, P.E. Ch.; rector St. Augustine's Ch., Ilion, N.Y., 1881-84, St. John's Ch., Johnstown, N.Y., 1888-91, Grace Ch., Grand Rapids, Mich., 1891-97, St. Peter's Ch., Geneva, N.Y., 1897-1913; built Grace Ch., and parish house and rectory at St. Peter's Ch.; chaplain Hobart Coll., 1913-29 (emeritus), became instructor in history and emeritus prof., 1929; lecturer on ethics, De Lancey Div. Sch., Buffalo; rector St. Paul's Ch., Delray Beach, Fla., 1929-38, built parish house for same, 1936. Dep. Gen. Conv. P.E. Ch., 1895, 1910. Republican. Mason. Home: Geneva, N.Y. Died May 26, 1938.

HUBER, G(ottheif) Carl, M.D.; b. Hoobly, India, Aug. 30, 1865; s. Rev. John and Barbara (Weber) H.; M.D., U. of Mich., 1887; post-grad. Berlin, 1891-92, Prague, 1895; m. Lucy A. Parker, Apr. 18, 1893. Asst. demonstrator anatomy, 1887-89, instr. histology, 1889-92, asst. prof., 1892-98, sec. med. and surg. faculty, 1897-1911, asst. prof. anatomy, 1898-99, dir. Histol. Lab., 1898—, jr. prof. anatomy, 1899-1903, prof. histology and embryology, dir. Histol. Lab., 1903—, prof. anatomy and dir. anatomic labs., 1914—, U. of Mich.; dean of the Graduate School, same, 1927. Prof. embryology, Wistar Inst. of Anatomy, Phila., 1911-12. Asso. editor Am. Jour. of Anatomy, 1901-20; mng. editor Anat. Record, 1909-20. Official reporter, sect. of anatomy, 17th Internat. Congress of Medicine, London; chmn. Med. Fellowship Bd., Nat. Research Council. Contract surgeon U.S.A. in charge of exptl. work on repair of severed peripheral nerves for Office of Surgeon Gen., 1918-19. Home: Ann Arbor, Mich. Died Dec. 26, 1934.

HUBER, Henry Allen, lt. governor; b. Pittsburgh, Pa., Nov. 7, 1869; s. Joseph and Anna Walburg (Schnitzer) H.; prep. edn., Albion (Wis.) Acad.; LL.B., U. of Wis., 1896; m. Minnie Pratt, Jan. 7, 1907. Admitted to Wis. bar, 1896, and began practice at Stoughton; city atty., Stoughton, 1897-1901; exec. clk. to Gov. R. M. La Follette, 1903-04; mem. Wis. Ho. of Rep., 1904-06, Wis. State Senate, 1912-24; lt. gov. of Wis., 1924—. Chmn. for Wis., La Follette presdl. campaign, 1924. Mem. Wis. State Hist. Soc. Progressive Republican. Lutheran. Author of Huber law for employment of prisoners for benefit of their families, also, with Prof. John R. Commons, of 1st bill in any Am. legislature for unemployment insurance. Home: Stoughton, Wis. Died Jan. 1933.

HUBER, John Bessner, physician; b. New York, N.Y., Mar. 14, 1864; s. John J. and Emily M. (Bessner) H.; A.B., Hamilton Coll., 1887, A.M., 1890; M.D., Bellevue Hosp. Med. Coll., 1889, Coll. Phys. and Surg., New York, 1890; M.D., Charity Hosp., Blackwell's Isl., 1891; m. Lucretia M. Harman Brown, June 9, 1903. Practiced in New York, 1892—; formerly professor in Fordham U. Med. Sch.; lecturer on tuberculosis, State Health Dept.; lecturer for New York Bd. of Edn. (evening free lecture courses); visiting physician, St. Joseph's Hosp. for Consumptives. Capt. and surgeon 112th Regt. N.Y. Vols., Spanish-Am. War. Author: Consumption and Civilization, 1906; A Doctor's Viewpoint, 1914; Why Die So Young?, 1920. Home: Pomfret, Conn. Died Feb. 16, 1924.

HUBERT, Philip Aklis, bishop; b. Antiqua, British W.I., Apr. 1, 1860; s. John and Cecelia (Thomas) H.; ed. Durham U., Eng., and Lady Mico Coll., St. John's, Antiqua; (LL.D., Prince's Coll., B.W.I., 1886, D.D., Livingstone Coll., N.C., 1893); m. Abigail Elizabeth Henry, Dec. 16, 1882 (died 1895). Ordained A.M.E. Zion Ch. ministry, 1888; consecrated bishop United Christian Ch., for N.Y., Mass. and Conn., May 3, 1909. Home: Brooklyn, N.Y. Deceased.

HUBERT, Philip Gengembre, author; b. Cincinnati, O., Jan. 9, 1852; s. Philip G. and Cornelia (Doisy) H.; ed. pvt. schs., Boston and College Chaptal, Paris; studied architecture; m. Anna Haight Holmes, June 1, 1878. Musical critic New York Evening Post, 1877-80, New York Herald, 1890-94; on editorial staff New York Herald, 1906-11. Author: Inventors, 1893; The Stage as a Career, 1900. Home: Bellport, N.Y. Died Jan. 3, 1925.

HUBNER, Charles William, librarian; b. Baltimore, Md., Jan. 16, 1835; s. John Adam and Margaret H.; ed. in common schs.; m. Mary Frances Whitney, Mar. 15, 1877. Lived in Germany several yrs.; served in C.S.A.; since war in Atlanta; asst. librarian Carnegie Library, Atlanta, 1899-1919. Author: The Wonder Stone (lyrical drama), 1883; War Poets of the South, 1896; Representative Southern Poets, 1906; Poems, 1906; A Sheaf of Sonnets, 1917; For Love of Burns (poems), 1919; Poems of Faith and Consolation, 1927. Home: Atlanta, Ga. Died Jan. 3, 1929.

HUCKEL, Oliver, clergyman; b. Phila., Pa., Jan. 11, 1864; s. William S. and Ruth A. H.; A.B., U. of Pa., 1887, A.M., 1890; S.T.B., Boston U., 1890; post-grad. work, Harvard, 1890-91; in theology and lit., U. of Berlin, 1894-95, and Oxford U., 1895-96; S.T.D., U. of Pa., 1907; grad. student comparative religions, Union Theol. Sem., 1916-17; m. Elizabeth F. Johnson, Jan. 7, 1902; children—Oliver Wentworth, Haldane Johnson. Ordained Congl. ministry, 1890; pastor Weymouth, Mass., 1890-94, Amherst, Mass., 1896-97, Associate Congl. Ch., Baltimore, 1897-1916, Greenwich, Conn., 1917-35; now engaged in literary work and lecturing. Member sch. bd., Braintree, Mass., 1890-94; one of coll. preachers, Amherst, 1898-99, and U. of Pa., U. of Va. and Cornell; George Dana Boardman lecturer Christian ethics, U. of Pa., 1906; Earle Foundation lecturer, Pacific Sch. of Religion, Berkeley, Calif., 1925. Corporate member A.B.C.F.M.; moderator Washington Conf. of Congl. Churches; mem. Nat. Council Commn. on New Polity for Congl. Chs. and speaker for same at Edinburgh, Des Moines, and Kansas City; pres. Conn. State Assn. Congl. Ministers, 1926-27. Author: Wagner's Parsifal, 1903; Wagner's Lohengrin, 1905; Wagner's Tannhäuser, 1906; Wagner's Rheingold, 1907; Wagner's Valkyrie, 1908; Wagner's Siegfried, 1910; Wagner's Götterdämmerung, 1911; Wagner's Meistersinger, 1912; Wagner's Tristan and Isolde, 1913; Through England with Tennyson, 1913; Wagner's Rienzi and Flying Dutchman, 1914; Richard Wagner; The Habit of Health, 1922; The Secret of the East, 1924; The Old Church Tells Her Story, 1930; The New Day, 1930; Book of Common Worship (with Bishop Thirkield), 1932. Home: New York, N.Y. Died Feb. 3, 1940.

HUDDLESTON, John Henry, physician; b. Boston, Mass., July 11, 1864; s. Charles H. and Susan H.; A.B., Harvard, 1886, A.M., 1891, M.D., 1891; m. Mabel Parker Clark, 1894. Has practiced in New York, 1892—; visiting phys. to Gouverneur and Willard Parker hosps. and Riverside Sanatorium; consulting phys. to United Hosp., Port Chester; capt. surgeon 7th Regt. N.G.N.Y., 1895-1907; Carpenter lecturer, N.Y. Acad. Medicine, 1902. Sec. Am. com. 14th Internat. Med. Congress, Madrid, 1903. Trustee N.Y. State Hosp. for Incipient Tuberculosis. Dir. Met. Life Ins. Co. Died Oct. 31, 1915.

HUDSON, Daniel E., clergyman, editor; b. Nahant, Mass.; ed. Holy Cross Coll., Worcester, Mass., U. of Notre Dame; LL.D. Joined Congregation of the Holy Cross (C.S.C.), 1870; ordained priest R.C. Ch., 1875; editor Ave Maria, 1875-1929. Pub. numerous Catholic books, some of which were edited by him. Address: Notre Dame, Indiana. Died Jan. 12, 1934.

HUDSON, Eric, artist; b. Boston, Mass.; m. Gertrude Dunton; children—Julie, Jacqueline. A.N.A., 1926. Home: Monhegan Island, Me. Died 1932.

HUDSON, James Fairchild, newspaperman; b. Oberlin, O., May 12, 1846; s. Prof. T. B. and Betsey (Branch) H.; served for short time in Civil War and was present at battle at Ft. Stevens, July 11 and 12, 1864; A.B., Oberlin Coll., 1867; m. Ina Burt, Oct. 27, 1885. Engaged in newspaper work on Toledo Blade; later on Youngstown (O.) Register; from 1874 in Pittsburgh on the Commercial-Gazette, and from 1883 as editorial writer and asso. editor of the Dispatch. Home: Ben Avon, Pa. Died May 1915.

HUDSON, John Elbridge, pres. Am. Bell Telephone Co.; b. Lynn, Mass., Aug. 3, 1839; grad. Harvard, valedictorian summa cum laude, 1862; tutor in Greek, Harvard, 1862-65; grad. Harvard Law School, 1865; general practice in Boston, 1865-80; gen. counsel, 1880-89, also v.p., 1887-89, then pres. Am. Bell Telephone Co.; m. Eunice W. Healey, Aug. 21, 1871. Home: Boston, Mass. Died 1900.

HUDSON, Joseph Kennedy, soldier, editor; b. Carrollton, O., May 4, 1840; s. John and Rebecca (Rohacker) H.; ed. Salem, O.; m. Mary W. Smith, Apr. 5, 1863. Served, pvt. to maj., in Mo., Ark., Indian Ty., La. and Tex., Civil war; farmer and stockraiser, 1865-73; regent State Agrl. Coll.; mem. Kan. legislature, 1871; editor Kansas Farmer, 1873; was independent candidate for Congress, 1874, and one of leading candidates for U.S. senator, 1874; founder, and for yrs. editor and propr., Topeka Daily Capital; editor Topeka Daily Herald, July 1901—; State printer, Kan., 1895-97; apptd. brig. gen. U.S. vols., May 27, 1898, for war with Spain. Home: Topeka, Kan. Died 1907.

HUDSON, Joseph Lowthian, merchant; b. New Castle-on-Tyne, Eng., Oct. 17, 1846; s. Richard and Elizabeth (Lowthian) H.; bro. of Richard H. Ed. pub. schs. of Eng. and Hamilton, Ont.; came to America, 1855; unmarried. In business with father at Ionia, Mich., 1866-77; removed to Detroit, 1877, and associated in clothing business with C. R. Mabley, 1877-81; with J. L. Hudson, 1881, J. L. Hudson & Co., Detroit, 1897—; chmn. bd. dirs. Hudson Motor Car Co. (Detroit); pres. J. L. Hudson Co. (Buffalo, N.Y., Cleveland, and Sandusky, O.), Thompson Hudson Co. (Toledo, O.); v.p. Am. Vapor Stove Co., Dime Savings Bank. Pres. Harper Hosp., McGregor Mission, Associated Charities, Municipal League, Florence Crittenton Home, Provident Loan Soc.; trustee Y.M.C.A., Central M.E. Ch. and Meth. Deaconess' Home; v.p. Soc. Prevention of Cruelty to Children; dir. Boys' Home, D'arcambal Assn.; treas. Fresh Air Soc.; mem. exec. com. Nat. Municipal League. Former Public Lighting Commr. and Water Commr.; now mem. Art Commn. of Detroit. Democrat. Died July 15, 1912.

HUDSON, Richard, univ. prof.; b. Gateshead, Eng., Sept. 17, 1845; s. Richard and Elizabeth (Lowthian) H.; brother of Joseph Lowthian H.; came to America with parents, 1855; A.B., U. of Mich., 1871, A.M., 1877; (LL.D., U. of Nashville, 1901); unmarried. Asst. prof. history, 1879-88, prof., 1888-1911, dean Dept. Lit., Science and the Arts, 1897-1907, U. of Mich. (Ann Arbor). Died Feb. 22, 1915.

HUDSON, Samuel Eddy, editor, pub.; b. Washington Village, Coventry, R.I., Mar. 12, 1870; s. Marinus Willett and Elizabeth (Austin) H.; ed. pub. and high schs., Woonsocket, R.I.; m. Harriet M. S. Buell, June 20, 1894; 1 son, Buell Wentworth. Clk. in stationery store, Woonsocket, 1886-89; Woonsocket corr. Providence Journal and Bulletin, 1889-1926; on staff of Woonsocket Reporter (absorbed 1908, by Woonsocket Call), 1892-95; pub. Woonsocket Call, 1895—, also editor, 1919—; treas. Evening Call Pub. Co., 1895—; v.p., asst. treas. and dir. Buell Realty Co.; mem. exec. com. Bd. of Mgrs. Woonsocket office of R.I. Hosp. Trust Co. Mem. spl. commn. to divide R.I. into 100 rep. dists., 1910; mem. Pub. Utilities Commn. of R.I., 1912-34. Pres., mem. bd. directors, Ballou Home for Aged. Republican. Baptist. Mason. Home: Woonsocket, R.I. Died June 17, 1941.

HUDSON, Thomson Jay, author, lecturer; b. Windham, O., Feb. 22, 1834; s. John and Ruth (Pulsifer) H.; ed. at acad. and by private tutor; (LL.D., St. John's Coll., Md.; Ph.D., Ewing Coll., Ill.); admitted to bar, 1857, at Cleveland, O.; practiced 3 yrs.; newspaper editor in Mich., 1860-76; prin. examiner U.S. Patent Office, 1886-93; m. Emma Little, May 28, 1861. Asso. editor Medico-Legal Jour. Author: The Law of Psychic Phenomena, 1893; A Scientific Demonstration of the Future Life, 1895; The Divine Pedigree of Man, 1899; The Law of Mental Medicine, 1903. Home: Detroit, Mich. Died 1903.

HUDSON, William Cadwalader, newspaperman; b. New Brunswick, N.J., Nov. 14, 1843; s. Rev. W. Cadwalader and Margaret (Wilde) H.; ed. pub. schs., Dutchess Co. Acad., Poughkeepsie, N.Y.; undergrad. Middleton U.; m. Mary E. Hogan, May 21, 1883. Began study of law, 1866, but abandoned it for journalism, 1867; working journalist in various capacities, editorial, etc., 1867-83; polit. corr. under pen-name of "Seacoal," 1878-83, varying this work with writing fiction; sec. Bd. R.R. Commrs., State of N.Y., 1883-94; on staff Brooklyn Eagle, 1901—. Independent Democrat. Author: The American Cavalier, 1894; also J. Percy Dunbar, Financier (serial in Brooklyn Eagle, 1905); Random Recollections of an Old Political Reporter, 1911. Plays (produced): Sealed Lips; Heroic Remedies; Man Among Men. Home: Brooklyn, N.Y. Died Oct. 16, 1915.

HUDSON, Woodward, lawyer; b. New York, Jan. 25, 1858; s. Frederic and Eliza (Woodward) H.; ed. pub. schs., Concord, Mass.; A.B., Harvard, 1879, LL.B., 1882; m. Bessie Van Mater Keyes, Aug. 31, 1880; children—Mary (dec.), Frederic (dec.), Marion. Mem. Parker, Thorp & Hudson, 1885-88; in office of Samuel Hoar, counsel N.Y.C.&H.R. R.R., lessee of B.&A. R.R., at Boston, as 1st asst. until latter's death, 1904, and in charge law dept. at Boston until 1916; v.p. and gen. counsel B.&M. R.R., Jan. 1916-June 1918, pres., June 1918-Dec. 1919; again v.p. and gen. counsel same rd., Dec. 19, 1919-Mar. 31, 1925 (resigned). Solicitor Middlesex Instn. for Savings, Concord, 1903-07. Home: Concord, Mass. Died Aug. 17, 1938.

HUDSPETH, C. B., congressman; b. Medina, Tex., May 12, 1877; s. Capt. H. S. and Elizabeth Anna H.; ed. 3 mos. in log cabin; studied law in office of Turney & Burgess, El Paso, Tex.; m. Marie Cliborne, 1903. Left home at age of 9; range rider in Western Tex., later peace officer, running down bandits; country editor; mem. Tex. Ho. of Rep., 1902-06, Senate, 1906-18 (elected pres. of Senate 4 times); admitted to Tex. bar, 1909, and began practice at El Paso; mem. Nealon, Hudspeth & McGill; mem. 66th to 71st Congresses (1919-31), 16th Tex. District. Democrat. Home: El Paso, Tex. Died Mar. 19, 1941.

HUDSPETH, Robert S., lawyer; served as prosecutor of pleas, Hudson Co., N.J.; judge Court of Common Pleas; mem. N.J. Assembly and Senate (was speaker in House, Dem. leader in Senate); mem. and chmn. Dem. State Com., N.J.; mem. Dem. Nat. Com. Home: Jersey City, N.J. Died Nov. 8, 1929.

HUEY, Samuel Baird, lawyer; b. Pittsburg, Pa., Jan. 7, 1843; grad. Princeton, 1863; Univ. of Pa. Law School, 1868; m. Mary Hunt Abrams, June 4, 1868. In U.S. navy, 1863-65, taking part in attacks on Ft. Fisher, Wilmington and Charleston; staff officer, capt., maj. and adj. gen., Philadelphia troop, Pa. Nat. Guard, 1866-78. Admitted to bar, Mar. 14, 1868; in independent practice, 1872—; counsel for several large corporations; pres. bd. of public education. Home: Philadelphia, Pa. Died 1901.

HUFF, George A., physical education; b. Champaign, Ill., June 11, 1872; s. George Alexander and Mary Marie (Martin) H.; B.S., U. of Ill., 1892; student Dartmouth Med. Coll., 1893-94; m. Kathrine Louise Naughton, Dec. 8, 1897; children—Mrs. Katherine Murphy, Mrs. Elizabeth Downs, George A. Director of physical training and athletics, U. of Illinois, Champaign, 1895-1924, dir. of physical welfare, 1925-32, dir. of Sch. of Physical Edn., 1932—. Director Summer School for Athletic Coaches, U. of Ill. (organized first sch. of this kind, 1914); dir. 4 yr. course in athletic coaching, U. of Ill. (organized first sch. of this kind, 1919). Fellow Am. Physical Edn. Assn., Soc. Dirs. Physical Edn. in Colleges. Died Oct. 1, 1936.

HUFF, George Franklin, congressman; b. Norristown, Pa., July 16, 1842; s. George and Caroline (Boyer) H.; ed. pub. schs., Middletown and Altoona, Pa.; m. Henrietta, d. Judge J. M. Burrell, Mar. 16, 1871. Cashier Ebensburg Bank, 1865-66; mem. Lloyd, Huff & Co., bankers, 1866-73; pres. Farmers' Nat. Bank, Greensburg, Pa., 1871-74; v.p. Fifth Nat. Bank, Pittsburgh, 1874-75; cashier Greensburg Banking Co., 1874-92; dir. First Nat. Bank, Greensburg, 1881—; treas. Southwestern Pa. R.R., 1871-74, and dir. same until road was merged into Pa. R.R.; pres. Keystone Coal & Coke Co. Mem. Pa. Senate, 1884-88; mem. 52d Congress (1891-93), 21st Pa. Dist., 54th Congress (1895-97), Pa.-at-large and 58th to 61st Congresses (1903-11), 22d Dist.; declined renomination. As chmn. Com. on Mines and Mining, 61st Congress, was largely instrumental in establishing the Bur. of Mines and Mining. Home: Greensburg, Pa., and Washington, D.C. Died Apr. 18, 1912.

HUFFCUT, Ernest Wilson, prof. law, 1893—, dean law faculty, 1903—, Cornell; b. Kent, Conn., Nov. 21, 1860; s. Ambrose and Luzina (Wilson) H.; grad. Cornell, 1884; Cornell Law Sch., 1888; unmarried. Instr. in English, Cornell Univ., 1885-88; in practice of law, Minneapolis, 1888-90; prof. law, Ind. Univ., 1890-92, Northwestern Univ., 1892-93. Author: American Cases on Contract (with E. H. Woodruff), 1894, 2d edit., 1900; Elements of Business Law, 1905. Editor American edition of Anson on Contract, 1895; Law of Agency, 1895, 2d edit., 1901; Cases on Agency, 1896; Law of Negotiable Instruments, 1898. Mem. bd. mgrs. Craig Colony, Lonyea, N.Y., 1900—. Home: Ithaca, N.Y. Died 1907.

HUFFMAN, Oscar Caperton, pres. Continental Can Co.; b. Augusta County, Va.; s. James and Mary E. (Hinton) H.; ed. Washington and Lee U.; m. Lucy Preston Beale, July 23, 1907; children—Lucinda Preston (Mrs. Ralph Christie Smith), Oscar Beale. Pvt. sec. Congressman Henry St. George Tucker, of Va., 1895-96; organizer, 1903, pres. until 1916, Virginia Can Co., Buchanan, Va.; organizer, 1908, pres. until 1928, U.S. Can Co., Cincinnati, O.; pres. Continental Can Co., N.Y. City, 1930-39, chmn. exec. com., 1939—. Mem. War Industries Bd., World War. Home: New Canaan, Conn. Died May 5, 1941.

HUG, George Willard, supt. schs.; b. Summerville, Ore., May 30, 1884; s. Rudolph and Mary (Nesser) H.; A.B., U. of Ore., 1907; student U. of Mich., summer 1930, U. of Calif., summers 1931-33; m. Gladys Mackenzie, July 5, 1910; children—George Wallace, Robert Mackenzie, Kathleen Ann. Prin. high sch. Eugene, Ore., 1907-15; supt. schs. McMinnville, 1915-20, Salem, 1920—. Instr. Ore. State Normal Sch., 5 summers, U. of Ore. Extension Center, 7 yrs. Republican. Presbyn. Mason. Home: Salem, Ore. Died May 17, 1937.

HUGER, Alfred, lawyer; b. Charleston, S.C., Oct. 10, 1876; s. Thomas Bee and Caroline Banks (Smith) H.; prep. edn. Porter Mil. Acad., Charleston; LL.B., Cornell U., 1903; pres. sr. Law Class, 1903; m. Margaret, d. Wilhelmus Mynderse, Apr. 17, 1906; children—Thomas Bee (dec.), Margaret, Wilhelmus Mynderse (dec.), Jeanne, Alfred. Chief passenger clk. S.C. Ry. Co., later asst. to div. passenger agt. Southern Ry. Co. until 1899; pvt. sec. in Europe, 1903-04, to Andrew D. White (first pres. Cornell U. and U.S. ambassador to Germany); in law office of Henry W. Sackett, New York, 1904, and with Butler, Notman & Mynderse, 1905-07; mem. Huger & Wilbur, Charleston, 1907, now Huger, Wilbur, Miller & Mouzon; first admiralty counsel U.S. Shipping Bd., June 1917-Apr. 1918. Former mem. Squadron A Cav., N.Y.N.G.; maj. Q.M.C., World War; assigned to 1st Sect. Gen. Staff, S. of S., Tours, France, chief of Div. of Staff representing Am. Shipping Control Com.; maj. O.R.C. Citation from Gen. Pershing; awarded Cross Legion of Honor (French); Order of Purple Heart (U.S.A.). Former member State Bd. Law Examiners of S.C.; trustee S.C. Med. Coll. 3 yrs.; dir. Internat. Chamber Commerce; pres. Charleston Chamber Commerce. Mason. Democrat. Episcopalian. Home: Charleston, S.C. Died May 18, 1936.

HUGER, William Harleston, physician; b. Charleston, S.C., May 20, 1826; grad. S.C. Coll., 1846, Med. Coll. State of S.C., 1849; attended lectures and hosps. in Paris and Dublin; diploma from Rotunda Hosp., Dublin, Ireland; surgeon C.S.A. during Civil war. Home: Charleston, S.C. Died 1906.

HUGGINS, Eli Lundy, brig. gen.; b. Schuyler Co., Ill., Aug. 1, 1842; s. Alexandre Gilliland and Lydia (Pettijohn) H. Pvt. and corporal Co. E, 2d Minn. Inf., July 5, 1861-July 14, 1864; pvt. Co. K, 1st Minn. Arty., Feb. 16-Feb. 28, 1865; 1st lt., Mar. 1-Sept. 27, 1865; apptd. from Minn., 2d lt. 2d U.S. Arty., Feb. 23, 1866; 1st lt., Dec. 24, 1866; trans. to cav., 1870; promoted through grades to brig. gen., Feb. 22, 1903; retired Feb. 23, 1903. Awarded Congressional Medal of Honor "for most distinguished gallantry" in action against Ogalalla Sioux Indians, Mont., Apr. 1, 1880; received surrender of Rain-in-the-Face, the slayer of Custer, and 800 other Sioux Indians, Oct. 1880. For other details of service see Vol. XI (1920-21). Author: Winona, a Dakota Legend, and Other Poems. Home: San Diego, Calif. Died Oct. 22, 1929.

HUGGINS, Raleigh Russell, gynecologist; b. Marietta, Ohio, Oct. 1, 1871; s. Jason and Margaret H.; student Marietta (Ohio) Coll., 1885-88; M.D., Miami (now Ohio-Miami) Med. Coll., Cincinnati, 1891; m. Catherine Thompson, Sept. 7, 1904. Practiced at Sharpsburg, 1892-1904, Pittsburgh, 1904—; prof. gynecology, Univ. of Pittsburgh, 1912—; gynecologist St. Francis Hosp.; medical director, Elizabeth Steel Magee Hosp. Home: Pittsburgh, Pa. Died Feb. 20, 1938.

HUGGINS, William Lloyd, judge; b. Highland Co., O., May 14, 1865; s. Milton Henderson and Elizabeth (DiBoll) H.; ed. State Normal Sch., of Emporia, Kan.; LL.D., Coll. of Emporia, Kan., 1922; m. Emma Elizabeth Spohr, May 31, 1898; children—William L., Mary Elizabeth (Mrs. H. L. Van Doren), Margaret Huntington (Mrs. John Philip Falter). Supt. schs., Lyon Co., Kan., 1893-97; admitted to bar, 1897, and practiced at Emporia; apptd. mem. Kan. Pub. Utility Commn., Jan. 1919, and author of bill known as the Kansas Industrial Law, creating the Court of Industrial Relations (law provides for adjudication of industrial controversies, discarding the theory of arbitration); apptd. presiding judge Kan. Court of Industrial Relations, term 1920-23; spl. atty. League for Industrial Rights, N.Y. City, 1923-26. Trustee Coll. of Emporia. Methodist. Mason. Author: Labor and Democracy, 1922. Home: Emporia, Kan. Died May 24, 1941.

HUGGINS, William Ogburn, lawyer, editor; b. Smith Co., Tex., July 8, 1878; s. Henry Clay and Susan Dolly (Ogburn) H.; ed. U. of Tex.; m. Ida Laura Parks, Feb. 12, 1908; children—Louise, William Ogburn. Admitted to Tex. bar, 1899, and began practice at Tyler; moved to Houston, Tex., 1910; mem. Huggins, Kayser & Liddell; v.p., counsel and editor Houston Chronicle, 1929—; v.p. Rice Hotel Co.; dir. Nat. Bank of Commerce. Home: Houston, Tex. Died Dec. 4, 1934.

HUGHES, Aaron Konkle, rear adm., U.S.A., retired, March 1884; b. Elmira, N.Y., March 31, 1822; apptd. acting midshipman, Oct. 30, 1838; promoted to passed midshipman, May 28, 1844; master, 1853; lt., Aug. 1853; lt. comdr., July 16, 1862; comdr., Nov. 16, 1862; capt., Feb. 10, 1869; commodore, Feb. 4, 1875; rear adm., July 2, 1882. Served in S. Atlantic and Gulf squadrons during Civil war. Home: Washington, D.C. Died 1906.

HUGHES, Charles Frederick, naval officer; b. Bath, Me., Oct. 14, 1866; s. John and Lucy Maria (Delano) H.; U.S. Naval Acad., 1884; m. Caroline Russell Clark, Jan. 31, 1898; 1 dau., Louisa Russell (wife of Otto Nimitz, U.S.A.). Promoted ensign, July 1, 1890; lt. jr. grade, Apr. 27, 1898; lt., Mar. 3, 1899; lt. comdr., July 1, 1905; comdr., Jan. 9, 1910; capt., July 10, 1914; rear adm., Oct. 10, 1918. Served on Monterey, Spanish-Am. War, 1898, and participated in Battle of Manila; duty Bur. of Equipment, Navy Dept., 1904-06; recorder Bd. of Inspection and Survey, Navy Dept., 1909-11; comd. Birmingham, 1911-12, Des Moines, 1912; was at Vera Cruz, Mexico, during Diaz revolution, 1912, and again when the city was captured, 1914; chief of staff, Atlantic Fleet, 1913-14; mem. Gen. Bd., Navy Dept., 1914-16; comd. New York, 1916-18; served with British Grand Fleet in the North Sea, Nov. 1917-Oct. 1918; comdt. Navy Yard, Phila., 1918-20; comdr. 2d Battleship Squadron, Atlantic Fleet, 1920-21, divs. 7 and 4, U.S. Battle Fleet, 1921-June 25, 1923; comdt. Naval War Coll., July 1, 1923-July 1, 1924; dir. fleet training, July 1, 1924-Oct. 10, 1925; later comdt. in chief U.S. battle fleet and chief of naval operations; retired, Nov. 1, 1930. Conglist. Died May 28, 1934.

HUGHES, Charles James, Jr., senator; b. Kingston, Mo., Feb. 16, 1853; s. Charles James and Serena C. (Pollard) H.; A.B., Richmond (Mo.) Coll., 1871; law student U. of Mo., 1872-73; m. Lucy S. Menefee, Sept. 1, 1874. In practice at Denver, 1879—;

Dem. candidate for presdl. elector, 1888 and 1904; presdl. elector, 1900; mem. Bd. Capitol Commrs., which built Colo. Capitol, 1889—; U.S. senator, 1909-15. Prof. mining law, Denver Law Sch., 1892—, Harvard Law Sch., 1903-06. Home: Denver, Colo. Died 1911.

HUGHES, Edward Smallwood, banker, mcht.; b. Raleigh, N.C., Jan. 16, 1863; s. Isaac Wayne and Annie M. H.; prep. edn., Bingham Sch., Mebane, N.C.; grad. Princeton U., 1882; m. Minerva Baker Rogers, Dec. 21, 1886; 1 dau., Elizabeth Graham. Began as merchant, Abilene, 1882, investment banker, 1900; pres. Ed. S. Hughes Co., Fellsmere Corp., Fellsmere Estates Corp.; chmn. bd. Roscoe, Snyder & Pacific Ry. Co. Democrat. Episcopalian. K.P. Home: Abilene, Tex., and New York, N.Y. Died Jan. 13, 1939.

HUGHES, Ellwood Clarke, lawyer; b. Columbia Co., Pa., Aug. 25, 1855; s. Ellwood and Elizabeth (Hill) H.; A.B., Carthage (Ill.) Coll., 1878; post-grad. Wittenberg Coll., Springfield, O., 1879; m. Emma De Hart, Dec. 30, 1880. Taught Latin and Greek in coll. 2 yrs.; practiced law in Ia., 1881-90, then in Seattle, Wash.; became asso. with Henry G. Struve, U.S. Senator John B. Allen and Maurice McMicken. Stuvre, Allen, Hughes & McMicken; now Hughes, McMicken, Ramsey & Rupp. Was elected pres. Carthage Coll., 1883, but declined; declined nomination for Congress, 1890; tendered office of U.S. dist. judge by President Taft, but declined. Republican. Home: Seattle, Wash. Died Nov. 26, 1918.

HUGHES, Fred C., church official; b. Bolivar, Mo., June 25, 1876; s. Lemon and Elizabeth (DePriest) H.; prep. edn., Pleasant Hope (Mo.) Acad.; student Cumberland U., Lebanon, Tenn., 1902-03; m. Amy I. Prock, July 20, 1898; children—James Harold, Marie, Glenn B., Helen, Kathryn, Robert. Ordained ministry Cumberland Presbyn. Ch., 1907; pastor successively Pleasant Hope, Springfield, and Odessa, Mo.; sec. and treas. Mo. Synodical Bd. of Missions, Cumberland Presbyn. Ch., 1908-27; pres. Bd. of Missions and Ch. erection, 1920—, field man of Mo. Mason. Home: Warrensburg, Mo. Deceased.

HUGHES, Hector James, civil engr.; b. Centralia, Pa., Oct. 23, 1871; s. James H. and Mary (Miller) H.; A.B., Harvard, 1894; S.B., Lawrence Scientific Sch. (Harvard), 1899; m. Elinor Lambert, Apr. 15, 1902; children—Katharine Porter, Elinor Lambert. In office of town engr., Brookline, Mass., 1894-98; asst. engr. maintenance, Chicago, 1899-1900, resident engr. in charge constrn. in Ia., 1900-02, C.,B.&Q. R.R.; designer, Am. Bridge Co., Pittsburgh, 1902; instr. civ. engring., 1902-03, asset. prof., 1903-13, asso. prof., 1913-14, prof., 1914—, Harvard; also prof. Mass. Inst. of Tech., 1914-18; dean Harvard U. Engring. Sch., 1920—. Fellow A.A.A.S., Am. Acad. Arts and Sciences. Unitarian. Author: (with A. T. Safford) A Treatise on Hydraulics, 1911; Roads and Toll Roads in America, 1913; Highway Engineering Education, 1914-27. Home: Cambridge, Mass. Died Mar. 1, 1930.

HUGHES, Herman Yeary, judge; b. Lee Co., Va., Jan. 8, 1863; s. Isaac T. and Louisa J. (Ciphers) H.; ed. Tazewell (Tenn.) Coll., to 1884; (LL.D., Lincoln Memorial U., Tenn.); m. Fannie C. Fulkerson, Sept. 3, 1907. Admitted to Tenn. bar, 1890; presdl. elector on Cleveland ticket, 1888; mayor of Tazewell 3 terms; co. judge Claiborne Co., Tenn., 1904-10; judge Ct. of Civil Appeals of Tenn., 1910-18; resumed practice at Tazewell. Democrat. Baptist. Home: Tazewell, Tenn. Died Feb. 25, 1921.

HUGHES, James Anthony, congressman; b. Ontario, Can., Feb. 27, 1861; s. James W. and Ellen (McNulty) H.; ed. Corunna, Can.; removed to Ashland, Ky., 1873, to Hunting, W.Va., 1890; m. Belle Vinson, Dec. 28, 1885; children—Mary Eloise, Tudelle. Engaged in lumber business, 1890—. Mem. Ky. Ho. of Rep., 1887-88; mem. W.Va. Senate, 1894-98; mem. 57th Congress (1901-03), 4th W.Va. Dist., and 58th to 63d Congresses (1903-15), 5th Dist., also 70th Congress (1927-29), same dist. Republican. Home: Huntington, W.Va. Died Mar. 2, 1930.

HUGHES, James Fredric, congressman; b. Green Bay, Wis., Aug. 7, 1883; s. James Vincent and Emma Louise (Leicht) H.; grad. high sch., Green Bay, 1901; m. Emma Lou Adams, Sept. 15, 1913; 1 son, James Adams. Western sales mgr. F. B. Stevens, Inc., foundry supplies, Detroit, Mich., 1905—. Mem. Bd. of Edn. and mem. Library Bd., DePere. Mem. 73d Congress (1933-35) 8th Wis. Dist. Catholic. Home: DePere, Wis. Died Aug. 9, 1940.

HUGHES, Levi Allen, banker; b. Minneapolis, Minn., Oct. 26, 1858; s. Levi and Amanda (Maxwell) H.; Ind. U., 1879; m. Christine Louise Proebstel, Oct. 31, 1903. Settled at Santa Fe, N.M., 1878; in banking business, 1903—; pres. First Nat. Bank, 1916—, also chairman of board, 1925. United States collector internal revenue, Santa Fe, 1892-94; special agent Court of Private Land Claims, 1898; treas. State of N.M., 1909. Trustee Sch. of Am. Research, Santa Fe. Republican. Presbyn. Home: Santa Fe, N.M. Died Apr. 8, 1934.

HUGHES, Louis C., governor; b. Philadelphia, May 15, 1844; ed. pub. schs., Allegheny Co., Pa.; partial acad. course, Meadville, Pa., 1866-68; served in Civil War in Co. A, 101st Pa. Vols., and Knapp's Pittsburgh battery; m. Josephine, d. John R. Brawley. Was a leader in labor reform movement in Pittsburgh after war; forwarded petition with 7,000 signatures asking for 8-hour day in Govt. work, to U.S. Senate; assisted in organizing and was a mem. of 1st lodge in U.S. of A.O.U.W. Studied law; began practice, Tucson, Ariz., 1871; dist. atty. 2 terms; probate judge 2 terms; atty. gen. Ariz.; U.S. Court commr. 4 yrs.; mem. and sec. bd. World's Fair Commrs. for Ariz., 1892-93; established, 1877, and published 30 yrs., the 1st daily journal in Ariz., the Tucson Star, as advocate of removal of Apaches from Ariz. (a policy adopted by govt. about 10 yrs. later); agitated for creation of federal ct. of private land claim, which returned to govt. over 12,000,000 acres in Ariz. claimed under Spanish and Mexican titles; gov. Ariz., 1893-96; chancellor U. of Ariz., 1898-1900. Engaged in practice of law. Home: Tucson, Ariz. Deceased.

HUGHES, Matt(hew) Simpson, bishop; b. Doddridge Co., Va. (now W.Va.), Feb. 2, 1863; s. Thomas Bayles (D.D.) and Louisa (Holt) H.; U. of W.Va. (non-grad.); (D.D., 1896, LL.D., 1909, Hamline); m. Harriet Frances Wheeler, Oct. 24, 1888. Ordained M.E. ministry, 1887; pastor Chestnut St. Ch., Portland, Me., 1890-95, Wesley Ch., Minneapolis, 1895-98, Independence Av. Ch., Kansas City, Mo., 1898-1908, 1st Ch., Pasadena, Calif., 1908-16; prof. practical theology, Maclay Coll. of Theology, U. of Southern Calif., 1908-11; elected bishop M.E. Ch., 1916. Chaplain 1st Minn. Regt., 1898. Mason. Author: The Logic of Prohibition, 1915. Home: Portland, Ore. Died Apr. 4, 1920.

HUGHES, Oliver John Davis, M.D., U.S. consul gen., Coburg, Germany, 1897-1904, and Sonneburg; b. Buenos Aires, S. America; s. John A. and Sophia Louise (Tidblom) H.; ed. at Harrow, England; grad., M.S., Univ. of London, England; M.D., L.I. Coll. Hosp., Brooklyn, 1875; m. Jennie Ward Toothe, Dec. 26, 1882; m. 2d, Baroness Charlotte von Petersdorff. Located in practice at New Rochelle, N.Y.; asst. surgeon, Franco-Prussian War, 1870-71; was on spl. service in Vera Cruz, City of Mexico, Japan and Cuba; served in Mexico as brigade surgeon with rank of lt. col.; was surgeon in U.S. Marine Service. Decorated by German, Bavarian, Saxon, Baden, French and Papal govts. and by Patriarch of Jerusalem. Knight Comdr. Royal Saxon Ernestine Order. K.T. Home: New Rochelle, N.Y. Deceased.

HUGHES, Percy Meredith, supt. schs.; b. Washington, D.C., Feb. 3, 1864; s. Carlton and Elizabeth Ann (Etchison) H.; grad. Emerson Inst., Washington, D.C., 1883; student Dickinson College, Pa., 1884; A.B., Johns Hopkins, 1886; LL.B., George Washington U., 1890, LL.M., 1891; D.Pd., Syracuse U., 1915; m. Annie Wilson Major, June 25, 1890. Began in pub. schs., Washington, D.C., 1886, and successively instr. and head of dept. Central High Sch. until 1897; prin. Central H.S., 1897-1902, dir. high schs., 1902-06, asst. supt. in charge of white schs., 1906-11, all of Washington, D.C.; supt. schs., Syracuse, N.Y., 1911—. Trustee Carnegie Pub. Library, Syracuse. Republican. Methodist. Mason. Author report on "The Gary (Ind.) Schools." Home: Syracuse, N.Y. Died Jan. 16, 1928.

HUGHES, Peter Davis, surgeon; b. Newport, Eng., Feb. 13, 1855; s. John R. and Elizabeth (Davis) H.; came to America, 1862; pub. sch. edn.; M.D., Ft. Wayne (Ind.) Coll. of Medicine, 1884; N.Y. Polyclinic, 1884-87; (hon. A.M., Taylor U., Ind., 1897); m. Katharine Stemen, May 10, 1885. Began practice at Brooklyn, 1884; removed to Kansas City, Kan.; sr. surgeon, chief of staff, Bethany Hosp., Kansas City, Kan., 1902—; prof. surgery, Coll. Phys. & Surg., Kansas City, Kan., 1894-1906; prof. clin. surgery, U. of Kan., 1906—. Pvt. Co. B, 17th Regt., Pa. N.G., 1874-77; inspr. dept. Animal Industry, U.S. Agrl. Dept., 1890-92. Trustee Coll. Phys. and Surg., Kansas City. Mason. Republican. Methodist. Died 1911.

HUGHES, Richard Cecil, college pres.; b. Springdale, O., Feb. 14, 1861; s. Rev. Thomas E. and Myra (Cross) H.; A.B., U. of Wooster, 1884, A.M., 1887 (D.D., 1900); Princeton Theol. Sem., 1884-85; grad. McCormick Theol. Sem., Chicago, 1887; m. Carrie Porter Wilson, May 13, 1886. Ordained Presbyn. ministry, 1887; pastor Sidney, Ia., 1887-91; prof. psychology, 1891-1901, pres. 1897-1901, Tabor Coll., Ia.; pres. and prof. psychology, Ripon Coll., 1901-09; asso. gen. sec. Gen. Board of Edn. of Presbyn. Ch. in U.S.A., 1909—. Home: Madison, Wis. Died Oct. 9, 1920.

HUGHES, Robert Morton, lawyer; b. Abingdon, Va., Sept. 10, 1855; s. Robert W. and Eliza M. (Johnston) H.; A.B., Coll. of William and Mary, 1873, LL.D., 1920; M.A., U. of Va., 1877; LL.D., from Washington and Lee U., 1926; m. Mattie L. Smith, Feb. 19, 1879; children—Robert Morton, Sydney Smith (dec.). Admitted to bar, 1877, and practiced at Norfolk (retired); pres. Va. Bd. of Law Examiners, 1910-23. Mem. Va. Commn. of 7 to Revise State Constitution, 1926-27; mem. Va. State Bd. of Edn., 1930-35, resigned. Republican. Episcopalian. Author: Hand Book of Admiralty Law, 1901, 20; Hand Book of Federal Jurisdiction and Procedure, 1904, 13; Law of Shipping, 1912. Home: Norfolk, Va. Died Jan. 15, 1940.

HUGHES, Robert Patterson, army officer; b. in Pa., Apr. 11, 1839; ed. Jefferson Coll., Pa. Enlisted as pvt. Co. E, 12th Pa. Inf., Apr. 25, 1861; hon. disch., Aug. 5, 1861; commd. 1st lt. 85th Pa. Inf., Oct. 11, 1861; capt., May 20, 1862; hon. mustered out, Dec. 6, 1864; lt. col. 199th Pa. Inf., Dec. 7, 1864; bvtd. col., Apr. 2, 1865; mustered out, June 28, 1865; apptd. from Pa. capt. 18th U.S. Inf., July 28, 1866; assigned to 3d Inf., July 5, 1870; maj. insp. gen., Feb. 19, 1885; lt. col., Mar. 11, 1885; col., Aug. 31, 1888; brig. gen. vols., June 3, 1898; hon. disch., Apr. 16, 1899; brig. gen. vols., Apr. 16, 1899; maj. gen. U.S.A., Apr. 1, 1902; retired Apr. 11, 1903. Bvtd. maj., Mar. 2, 1867, for assault on Ft. Gregg, Va. Provost marshal gen., Manila and suburbs, 1898; comd. 1st Mil. Dist., P.I., 1899, Dept. Visayan Islands, 1900. Died 1909.

HUGHES, Robert William, lawyer; b. Powhatan Co., Va., June 6, 1821; ed. Caldwell Inst., N.C., taught in high school, Hillsborough, N.C., 1840-42. Editor Richmond (Va.) Examiner, 1852-57; on staff of Washington Union, 1858-59; edited Richmond Examiner, 1861-65; Richmond Republic, 1865-66; later edited Richmond State Journal. While on State Journal fought and wounded, in duel, William E. Cameron, of Petersburg Index. U.S. atty. western dist. Va., 1871-73; Rep. candidate for gov. Va., 1873; U.S. judge Eastern dist. Va., 1874-98. Home: Norfolk, Va. Died 1901.

HUGHES, Royal Delaney, prof. music; b. Cuba, Ill., Sept. 13, 1884; s. Delaney Eckles and Arminda Claire (Powell) H.; grad. in voice, Monmouth (Ill.) Coll., 1907, A.B., 1910, A.M., 1918; studied with Klatte and Clark, at Berlin, 1914; John Knowles Paine traveling fellow, Harvard, 1924-25; and studied at Sorbonne and École Normale de Musique (Paris); Ph.D., Harvard, 1926; m. Adah J. Baily, June 15, 1910; 1 dau., Mary Katharine. Instr. in voice, Monmouth Coll., 1907-10, in voice and theory, 1910-12; dir. music, Ohio Northern U., 1912-16; dir. Conservatory of Music, Findlay (O.) Coll., 1916-22; dir. Summer Sch. of Music, Ohio State U., 1921-25; prof. music, same univ., 1925—, also chmn. dept. of music. Episcopalian. Home: Columbus, O. Died Nov. 7, 1938.

HUGHES, Simon P., gov.; b. Carthage, Tenn., Aug. 14, 1830; s. Simon P. and Mary H.; served, capt. and lt. col., C.S.A.; mem. Ark. legislature, 1866-67; delegate to constl. conv., 1874; atty. gen. Ark., 1875-77; gov., 1885-89; asso. justice Supreme Court, Ark., two terms; retired 1904; m. June 2, 1857. Democrat. Home: Little Rock, Ark. Died 1906.

HUGHES, Thomas Patrick, author, Orientalist; b. Ludlow, Eng., Mar. 26, 1838; s. Thomas and Elizabeth (Valentine) H.; student Ludlow Sch., Islington Coll.; fellow Punjab Oriental U., 1882; (B.D., 1876, by Archbp. Canterbury; D.D., 1886; LL.D., St. John's, Annapolis, 1897); m. Eliza Lloyd, Aug. 17, 1864; father of Percy H. Ordained clergyman in Ch. of Eng., by bishop of London, 1864; asst. St. Silas, Islington, London, 1865; missionary and chaplain, Peshawar, Afghanistan, 1865-85; govt. examiner in Oriental langs., 1875-85; asso. editor Civil and Military Gazette, Lahore; rector Lebanon Springs, N.Y., 1885-88; asst. All Souls' Ch., New York, 1888-89; rector Ch. of the Holy Sepulchre, New York, 1889-1902; asso. rector Ch. of the Epiphany, Brooklyn, 1902-03. Sec. Edgemere Assn., New York, 1904; on staff New York Churchman, 1890-96, Literary Digest, 1896-97; lit. editor N.Y. Commercial Advertiser, 1897; editor Sunday Reading, 1898, Long Island Gazette, 1906. Author: A Dictionary of Islam; Ruhainah, the Maid of Herat; Heroic Lives in Foreign Fields. Home: Kings Park, L.I., N.Y. Died Aug. 8, 1911.

HUGHES, Wilburn Patrick, lawyer; b. Yeager, Ky., May 1, 1892; s. James and Frankie (Tackitt) H.; B.Pd., Valparaiso (Ind.) U., 1913, LL.B., 1916; student officers' short course, U.S. Naval Acad., Annapolis, Md., 1918; m. Mollye Eversole, June 20, 1923. Teacher, rural schs., Ky. and W.Va., 1908-11; admitted to Calif. bar, 1916, and practiced at San Francisco, 1916-17; chief law clk. to atty. gen. of Ky., 1919-21; county atty. Pike Co., 1921-25; practiced at Clearwater, Fla., 1926; asst. U.S. dist. atty. Southern Fla. Dist., 1926-28; spl. asst. atty. gen. of U.S., Oct. 1928-Apr. 1929; acting U.S. dist. atty., Southern Fla. Dist., 1929, U.S. dist. atty., 1929-33; resumed practice of law. Served as ensign U.S.N., Overseas Transport Service, 1917-19. Republican. Mason. Home: Miami, Fla. Died Jan. 9, 1940.

HUGHES, William, U.S. senator; b. Ireland, Apr. 3, 1872; s. Thomas P. and Ellen H.; ed. common schs. and business course; m. Margaret Hughes, July 16, 1898. Served in 2d N.J. Vols. in Spanish-Am. War, 1898; admitted to bar, 1900, and began practice at Paterson. Mem. 58th Congress (1903-05) and 60th, 61st, 62d Congresses (1907-13), 6th N.J. Dist.; U.S. senator, N.J., 1913-19. Democrat. Home: Paterson, N.J. Died Jan. 30, 1918.

HUGHES, William F., clergyman; b. N.Y. City, Oct. 27, 1874; s. Edward and Jane Aldrich (Newton)

H.; A.B., Coll. of St. Francis Xavier, 1894; studied Urban Coll. of Propaganda, Rome, Italy; S.T.D., U. of St. Thomas, Rome, 1900; D.D., Sacred Congregation of Studies, Rome, 1909; LL.D., St. John's Coll., Brooklyn, 1923; S.T.D., Internat. U. of the Angelico, Rome, 1923. Ordained R.C. priest, 1898; prof. history, St. Joseph's Sem., Yonkers, N.Y., 1902-09, Catholic U. of America, 1909-10; sec. to Papal Legation, Washington, D.C., 1910-11; pres. Cathedral Coll., New York, 1911-17; pastor St. Gregory's Ch., New York, 1918—. Chaplain Camp Dix, N.J., 1916. Home: New York, N.Y. Died July 30, 1929.

HUGHES, William Joseph, lawyer; b. Upland, Pa., July 5, 1863; s. William John and Margaret (Kirkpatrick) H.; LL.B., Georgetown U., 1891, LL.M., 1892, LL.D., 1931; LL.D., Phila. Coll. Law, 1931; m. Josephine Elizabeth O'Sullivan, Oct. 17, 1894; children—William Joseph, Mary Margaret (Mrs. William J. Burlee), Josephine Alice (dec.). Admitted to Pa. bar, 1891; has held various positions with Dept. of Justice, Washington, D.C.; atty., Department of Justice, 1899-1933; retired July 31, 1933; in charge of questions of jurisdiction and procedure in federal courts, particularly in Supreme Court of U.S.; served as sec. com. of justices of Supreme Court of U.S. to revise rules of practice in courts of equity of U.S. Lecturer on federal practice and procedure, Georgetown U. Sch. of Law, 1914—. Catholic. Author: Hughes Federal Practice, Jurisdiction and Procedure (16 vols.), 1931. Home: Washington, D.C. Died Jan. 29, 1938.

HUGHITT, Marvin, ry. official; b. Genoa Twp., N.Y., Aug. 9, 1837; s. Amos and Miranda (Clark) H.; ed. Auburn, N.Y.; has lived in Ill., 1854—; m. Belle Barrett Hough, June 9, 1858. Was telegrapher and later in ry. service with C.&A. and I.C. rys.; with latter as div. supt. and gen. supt.; asst. gen. mgr. C.,M.&St.P. Ry., 1870-71; gen. mgr. Pullman Palace Car Co., 1871-72; gen. supt. C.&N.W. Ry., Mar. 1, 1872, gen. mgr. May 1, 1876, v.p. and gen. mgr., June 2, 1880, pres., June 2, 1887-Oct. 20, 1910, chmn. bd., Oct. 20, 1910-Apr. 9, 1918; dir. N.Y.C.&H.R. R.R., Ill. Merchants Trust Co., Chicago. Home: Lake Forest, Ill. Died Jan. 6, 1928.

HUHLEIN, Charles Frederick, mfr.; b. Louisville, Ky., Nov. 16, 1858; s. Erhart and Catherine (Scholler) H.; ed. high sch. Elected gen. mgr. B. F. Avery & Sons, mfrs. agrl. implements, 1889, pres., 1911-21, chmn. bd., 1921-31; dir. Citizens Union Nat. Bank, Louisville Title Mortgage Co., Title Ins. & Trust Co., Liberty Mutual Ins. Co. Member Kentucky N.G., 15 yrs., including 3 yrs. as capt. Battery A, Louisville Light Arty. Mem. Bd. of Water Works, Louisville, 1907-11; mem. bd. of judges, machinery sect.; San Francisco Expn., 1915, chmn. Bd. Pub. Safety, Louisville, 1921-25. Hon. mem. Nat. Implement and Vehicle Assn. (pres.). Pres. Hindman (Ky.) Settlement Sch., Isaac W. Bernheim Foundation, Forestry Assn. of Ky., South Eastern Economic Council. Republican. Presbyn. Home: Louisville, Ky. Died Sept. 11, 1938.

HUIDEKOPER, Arthur Clarke, farmer; capitalist; b. Meadville, Pa., June 15, 1845; s. Alfred and Catherine (Cullum) H.; Worcester (Mass.) Mil. Acad.; LL.B., Harvard Law Sch., 1867; m. Frances Reynolds, Sept. 21, 1869. Pres. U.S. & Steam Navigable Co., Conneaut Lake Expn. Co.; v.p. Bessemer (formerly Pittsburgh, Chenango & Lake Erie) R.R. Co.; dir. Meadville, Conneaut Lake & Linesville R.R. Co., Meadville Water Co., City Hosp.; trustee Meadville Theol. Sch., etc. Was capt. Co. A, 211th Regt. Pa. Vols. Unitarian. Home: Meadville, Pa. Died Nov. 30, 1928.

HUIDEKOPER, Frederic Louis, military writer; b. Meadville, Pa., Mar. 8, 1874; s. Frederic Wolters and Anna Virginia (Christie) H.; A.B., cum laude, Harvard, 1896; English lit. and law, Christ Ch., Oxford, 1896-98; Law Sch., Columbian (now George Washington) U., 1898-1900; admitted to bar, 1900; m. Helena K., d. late John Stuart and Helena F. (Ellis) Elliott, Sept. 14, 1916; children—Stuart Elliott, Frederic Fitz-James Christie; m. 2d, Anne Marie Amélie Debrinay de Montmort, dau. late Maj. A. A. G. Debrinay, June 7, 1933. Treas. The Disston Land Co., 1900-01; treas. United Land Co. of Fla., 1901-08, v.p., 1908-10; head of investment dept. W. B. Hibbs & Co., Washington, D.C., 1920-25. Has made extensive researches, 1897—, in archives of war offices at Paris, Vienna and St. Petersburg, being one of few Americans ever granted such permission, also given access to important pvt. archives; sec. Am. delegation to Internat. Opium Conf., The Hague, 1911-12. A founder Washington br. Nat. Cav. and Arty. Remount Assn. of U.S., 1912; founded, Apr. 3, 1912, and organized Army League of U.S.; sec. and dir. Nat. Remount Assn., 1913-14, v.p., 1914; one of founders of Nat. Security League, 1914, v.p., mem. army com. and pres. D.C. br., 1916-17. Commd. major, adjutant gen. sec., O.R.C., May 16, 1917, to rank from May 14, 1917; asst. to dept. adj., Southeastern Dept., Charleston, S.C., June 13-Aug. 23, 1917; div. adj. 33d Div. Ill. N.G., Aug. 28, 1917-Mar. 9, 1919; grad. Army Gen. Staff Coll., Langres, France, 1918; promoted lt. col. Sept. 25, 1918; served on British front and participated in Meuse-Argonne offensive; temporarily at-

tached to presdl. party, Am. peace Commn., Feb. 1919; hon. disch., Apr. 1, 1919. Cited, in G.O., 33d Div., "for gallantry in action against the enemy," and by Gen. Pershing "for exceptionally meritorious and conspicuous services as div. adj., 33d Division, France"; awarded D.S.M. (U.S.), 1921; Chevalier Legion of Honor, 1923, Médaille de Verdun (France), and silver star (U.S.), all for services in front of Verdun, Meuse-Argonne offensive. Wrote: Military Studies (Internat. Mil. Series), 1904; The Military Unpreparedness of the United States, with introd. by Maj. Gen. Leonard Wood, 1915; 33rd Division, A.E.F., 1919; The Thirty-third Division, in Vol. I of Ill. in the World War, 1921; The History of the 33rd Division, A.E.F. (3 vols. and portfolio of maps), officially published by State of Ill., 1921; Huidekoper, American Branch 1928; The American Ancestry of Frederic Louis Huidekoper and Reginald Shippen Huidekoper, of Washington, D.C., 1931. Episcopalian. Home: Washington, D.C. Died Mar. 7, 1940.

HUIDEKOPER, Frederic Wolters, ry. official; b. Meadville, Pa., Sept. 12, 1840; s. Edgar and Frances (Shippen) H.; grad. Harvard, 1862, A.M., 1871; m. Anna Virginia Christie, Jan. 22, 1867. Capt. 58th Pa. militia and participated in capture of Confederate raider, Gen. John H. Morgan; pres. Chicago & Eastern Ill. R.R., 1877-82; pres. Evansville & Terre Haute R.R., 1881-82; 1st v.p. Richmond & Danville R.R. and v.p. Richmond & West Point Terminal Ry. & Warehouse Co., and Va. Midland Ry., 1885-86; pres. Va. Midland Ry., 1886-87; pres. and receiver Pittsburgh, Shenango & Lake Erie R.R., 1889-91; pres. South Atlantic & Ohio R.R., 1890-92; receiver Richmond & Danville R.R., 1892-94; receiver Ga. Pacific Ry., Charlotte, Columbia & Augusta R.R., and Columbia & Greenville R.R., 1893-95; pres. Chicago, Peoria & St. Louis Ry., 1896-97; pres. The United Land Co. (of Fla.), 1901—(retired). Gov. Soc. Colonial Wars (of D.C.), 1901-02; pres. S.R. (D.C.), 1905-07. Home: Washington, D.C. Died 1908.

HUIDEKOPER, Henry Shippen, soldier; b. Meadville, Pa., July 17, 1839; s. Edgar and Frances (Shippen) H.; A.B., Harvard, 1862, A.M., 1872; m. Emma G. Evans, Oct. 26, 1864. Served in Civil War, July 1862-Mar. 1864; lt. col. comdg. 150th Pa. Regt., at Gettysburg, where he was twice wounded and lost right arm; received Congressional Medal of Honor "for gallantry in battle." After war was 15 yrs. brig. gen. and maj. gen. N.G. of Pa.; comd. 7th div. during railroad riots of 1877; postmaster of Phila., 1880-85. Overseer of Harvard, 1898-1910. Home: Philadelphia, Pa. Died Nov. 9, 1918.

HUIDEKOPER, Rush Shippen, physician; b. Meadville, Pa., May 3, 1854; s. Edgar and Frances (Shippen) H.; ed. Philips Acad., Exeter; grad. med. dept. Univ. of Pa., 1877; veterinarian, Nat. Veterinary School, Republic of France, Alfort, France, 1882, and following yr. in laboratories of Virchow, Koch, Chauveau and Pasteur; m. Anne P. Morris, 1877. Physician Phila. Dispensary; out-patient physician Children's Hosp.; asst. surgeon hosp., Univ. of Pa.; coroner's physician of Phila.; U.S. commr. gen., Agrl. Expn., Hamburg, Germany, 1883; dean veterinary dept. Univ. of Pa., and prof. internal pathology and contagious diseases, zoötechnics and hygiene, prof. comparative anatomy and veterinary surgery, New York Coll. Veterinary Surgery; maj. and a.d.c. Nat. Guard, Pa., 1874-78; maj. and brig. surgeon Nat. Guard Pa., 1878-91; acting asst. q.m. gen. Nat. Guard Pa., 1888 (Johnstown flood); late lt. col. and surgeon-in-chief, Nat. Guard Pa.; lt. col. and chief surgeon U.S. vols., 1898; chief surgeon 1st army corps and chief surgeon Puerto Rico; Pennsylvania Republican. Editor: Journal of Comparative Medicine and Veterinary Archives, Phila., 1889—. Died 1901.

HULBERT, Archer Butler, writer; b. Bennington, Vt., Jan. 26, 1873; s. Calvin Butler and Mary Elizabeth (Woodward) H.; B.A., Marietta Coll., 1895, hon. M.A., 1904, L.H.D., 1930; studied Western Reserve, Chicago, Wis., Columbia and Harvard univs., also in London and Paris; Litt.D., Middlebury (Vt.) College, 1929; m. Mary Elizabeth Stacy, Sept. 10, 1901; children—Marian Elizabeth, Katharine Wheelock; m. 2d, Dorothy Printup, June 16, 1923; 1 dau., Joan Woodward. Editor Korean Independent, Seoul, and Far East Am. newspapers, 1897-98; lit. work, 1898-1904; prof. Am. history, Marietta Coll., 1904-18; lecturer Am. history, Clark U., 1918-19; asso. prof., 1919-20, prof. history, Colo. Coll., 1920-25, prof. history and dir. Stewart Commn. on Western History, 1925—. Lecturer on economics of good roads for Office of Pub. Roads, U.S. Dept. Agr., 1905-14; lecturer, Univ. of Chicago, 1904 and 1923, Univ. Extension Soc. of Pittsburgh, Chautauqua Instn., 1909; instr. Columbia U., summer session, 1911; archivist Harvard Commn. on Western History, 1912-16; bd. editors Miss. Valley Hist. Review; lecturer War Work Council Y.M.C.A. of U.S., 1917-18. Author: Forty Niners (awarded Atlantic Monthly $5,000 prize), 1931. Bibliography of his writings (101 items) pub. by Vt. State Library, 1929. Home: Colorado Springs, Colo. Died Dec. 24, 1933.

HULBERT, Calvin Butler, clergyman; b. Sheldon, Vt., Oct. 18, 1827; s. Chauncey and Charlotte (Munsell) H.; A.B., Dartmouth 1853 (D.D., 1876); B.D.,

Andover Theol. Sem., 1859; m. Mary Elizabeth Woodward, Aug. 28, 1854; father of Henry Woodward, Homer Bebaleel and Archer Butler H. Teacher, Swanton, Vt., 1853-54, St. Albans, Vt., 1854-56; ordained and installed pastor Congl. Ch., New Haven, Vt., 1859-70, Bellevue Av. Congl. Ch., Newark, N.J. 1870-72, Congl. Ch., Bennington, Vt., 1872-75; pres. Middlebury Coll., 1875-80; supplied pulpits, Caledonia Co., Vt., 1880-90; pastor Presbyn. chs., Adams Mills and Rome, O., 1890-1904; retired to S. Dennis, Mass. Corporate mem. A.B.C.F.M., 1876-94. Died Feb. 12, 1917.

HULBERT, Edmund Daniel, banker; b. Pleasant Valley, Conn., Mar. 2, 1858; s. Henry R. and Emmeline (Stillman) H.; ed. pub. schs.; m. Emma Strayer, Aug. 8, 1897. Began with Hurlbut Nat. Bank, Winsted, Conn., as messenger, 1875; bookkeeper, later cashier, First Nat. Bank, Winona, Minn., 1877-95; 2d v.p. 1895-98, 1st v.p., dir., 1898-1916, pres., 1916—, Merchants Loan & Trust Co., Chicago; dir. Pullman Trust & Savings Bank, Marshall Field & Co., Roseland State Savings Bank, C.&N.W. Ry.; also pres. Ill. Trust & Savings Bank, 1919—, and pres. Corn Exchange Nat. Bank, Chicago. Democrat. Was treas. City of Winona, Minn., 3 terms; pres. Bd. of Edn., 2 terms. Died Mar. 30, 1923.

HULBERT, Eri Baker, head prof. church history and dean of the Divinity Sch., U. of Chicago; b. Chicago, Ill., July 16, 1841; grad. Union Coll., 1863 (A.M., 1866; Madison Univ., 1866; D.D., Union Theol. Sem., 1880; LL.D., Bucknell Univ., 1898); m. Ettie E. Spencer, 1869. Prof. church history, Baptist Union Theol. Sem., 1881-92; acting pres. same, 1884-85. On staff Am. Jour. Theology and Biblical World. Died 1907.

HULBERT, Henry Carlton, retired mcht.; b. Lee, Mass., Dec. 19, 1831; s. Amos Gear and Cynthia (Bassett) H.; of distinguished Puritan ancestry; ed. common schs. and Lee Acad.; m. Susan R. Cooley, Sept. 1854 (died 1882); m. 2d, Fannie Dwight Bigelow. Oct. 16, 1884. Entered dry goods business at 16 in firm of Plunkett & Hulbert, Pittsfield, Mass.; in New York clerking for White & Sheffield, paper dealers, 1851; admitted partner, 1856; organized H. C. & M. Hulbert, 1858; H. C. Hulbert & Co., 1872. Has large and varied financial interests; dir. and mem. finance com. The Pullman Co.; dir., mem. exec. com. Celluloid Co.; trustee, mem. exec. com. New York Life & Trust Co.; v.p., dir. Importers' & Traders' Nat. Bank; trustee Franklin Trust Co. (Brooklyn); v.p., trustee S. Brooklyn Savings Instn. Home: Brooklyn, N.Y. Died 1912.

HULBERT, Henry Woodward, clergyman; b. Sheldon, Vt., Jan. 26, 1858; s. Calvin Butler and Mary Elizabeth (Woodward) Hulbert; brother of Homer Bezaleel and Archer Butler H.; A.B., Middlebury Coll., 1879, A.M., 1882; grad. Union Theol. Sem., 1885; D.D., Middlebury and Marietta, 1900; m. Eliza Lyman Pinneo, Mar. 31, 1891 (died 1905); children—Winifred Elizabeth, Chauncey Pinneo (dec.), Woodward Dennis, Mrs. Kathryn Hall, Hilda Lyman, Ralph Wheelock (dec.); m. 2d, Annie Eliza McMaster, July 17, 1907. Investigated common schs. in Eng. for U.S. Bur. Edn., 1879-80; teacher Mechanicville (N.Y.) Acad., 1880-81; tutor Middlebury Coll., 1881-82; instr. Syrian Prot. Coll., Beirut, 1885-86; resident instr. ch. history, theol. Sem., Beirut, 1886-88; prof. history and polit. science, Marietta Coll., 1888-94; ordained Presbyn. ministry, 1889; prof. ch. history, Lane Theol. Sem., Cincinnati, 1894-97; pastor First Presbyn. Ch., Cleveland, 1897-1901; prof. ch. history, Bangor Theol. Sem., 1902-07; pastor High St. Congl. Ch., Portland, Me., 1907-11; pastor Groton (Conn.) Congl. Ch., 1914-30. Founder of "The Children of the Covenant." Investigator of Russian ecclesiastical affairs, 1906; ednl. dir. Y.M.C.A. war work, New London Dist., 1918. Sec. New London Fedn. of Chs. Author: The Church and Her Children. Home: Framingham, Mass. Died Oct. 31, 1937.

HULBERT, Milan Hulbert, real estate; b. Brooklyn, N.Y., July 24, 1867; s. William Augustus and Helen (Moore) H.; ed. Brooklyn Coll. and Poly. Inst.; m. Olive Evertsen Woodward, Oct. 1, 1891; children—Olive Woodward, Helen Mortimer, Ethel Plunkett, Milan Hulbert, Adèle Evertsen. Manufacturer until 1899; then engaged in real estate in Chicago, Illinois. Dir. Dept. of Mfrs. for U.S. Commn. to Paris Expn., 1900, and was mem. Internat. Jury of Award; chief Dept. of Mfrs., and mem. Superior Jury of St. Louis Expn., 1904. Officer Legion of Honor (France), officer Order of Civil Merit (Bulgaria), Royal Order of the Crown (Germany), Chevalier Order of Leopold (Belgium), Cavaliere of the Royal Order of Crown of Italy, Chevalier Order of Francis Joseph (Austria), Imperial Order of the Rising Sun (Japan), 1st Class of the Royal Order of Wasa (Sweden). Home: Chicago, Ill. Died July 14, 1931.

HULBERT, William Davenport, author; b. Mackinac Island, Mich., Oct. 12, 1868; s. Francis Robbins and Diantha Huldah (Gillett) H.; pvtly. educated; unmarried. Contributes to leading mags. Spent summer, 1911, in Alaska in interests of The Outlook, preparing a series of articles on the Alaskan situation. Author: Forest Neighbors, 1902. Home: Seattle, Wash. Died Nov. 2, 1913.

HULBURD, Charles Henry, capitalist; b. Stockholm, N.Y., May 28, 1850; s. Hiram and Amelia (Culver) H.; A.B., Oberlin Coll., 1871; LL.B., New York U., 1873; m. Anna R. Belknap, Feb. 3, 1880 (died 1906). Pres. Elgin Nat. Watch Co., 1898—; dir. Corn Exchange Nat. Bank, Union Special Machine Co., Hulburd, Warren & Chandler. Home: Chicago, Ill. Died Jan. 14, 1923.

HULBURT, David Willey, clergyman; b. Westfield, O., July 26, 1853; s. William and Sarah (Willey) H.; student Oberlin Coll., 2 yrs.; A.M., Denison Coll., Ohio, 1879, D.D., 1905; B.D., Bapt. Theol. Sem., Morgan Park, Ill., 1882; m. Ella J. Farrar, June 30, 1879; children—Arthur (dec.), Judson, Mary Ella, Willey (dec.), Clarence, Lillian Isabelle (Mrs. Maurice Carl Sjoblom). Preached first sermon, 1876; student pastor, 1880-83; ordained Bapt. ministry, 1883; successively pastor at Circleville (O.), South Ch., Milwaukee and Wauwatosa, Wis., until 1896; Wis. State supt. for Baptists, 1896-1921; exec. sec. City Missions in Wis., 1921-24; pastor at Woodlawn (suburb of Milwaukee), 1924-29; organizer and supt. Universal Sch. of Bibl. Education, Wauwatosa, Wis. Editor and publisher Wis. Baptist, 1898; hon. pres. Wis. Bapt. State Conv., 1925. Trustee Wayland Acad. 30 yrs. Home: Wauwatosa, Wis. Died Jan. 3, 1936.

HULING, Ray Greene, educator; b. Providence, R.I., Oct. 15, 1847; s. John G., Jr. and Huldah S. (Wilcox) H.; A.B., Brown U., 1869, A.M., 1872, Sc.D., 1894; post-grad. Harvard, 1893-98, A.M., 1897; m. Ellen C. Paine, July 10, 1879 (died 1896). Classical asst. Fall River High Sch., 1869-75; prin. Fitchburg (Mass.) High Sch., 1875-86, New Bedford (Mass.) High Sch., 1886-93; head master English High Sch., Cambridge, 1893-1908; consulting teacher, 1903-09; retired. Lecturer on organization and management of schs., Harvard, 1899; examiner, Boston U.; trustee Brown U., 1900—; one of founders and sec., 1887-1910, sec. emeritus, N.E. Assn. of Colls. and Prep. Schs.; mem. Madison Conf. on History, 1892, N.E. Conf. on History, 1895, and that at Columbia Coll., 1896; com. of N.E.A. on Coll. Entrance Requirements, 1899; chmn. com. on syllabus in civics, N.E. History Teachers' Assn.; pres. and now sec. Boston Bapt. Social Union; sec. Boston Bapt. City Mission Soc., 1895-1913; mem. exec. com. Am. Bapt. Foreign Mission Society. Editor: The School and College, 1892. Home: Cambridge, Mass. Died Sept. 4, 1915.

HULING, Sara Hawks; b. Bennington, Vt., Jan. 23, 1872; d. William Edward and Helen (Brown) Hawks; grad. Bradford (Mass.) Acad., 1890, Elderage Sch., New Haven, Conn., 1892; student Alliance Francaise, Paris, France, 1927; m. Edward Bentley Huling, Dec. 25, 1893; children—Katherine Brown (Mrs. Robert Franklin Hussey), Elizabeth Hinman, George Edward (dec.), Sara Frances. Adminstr. Estate of William E. Hawkes, 1911-14; v.p. and treas. Estate of William E. Hawkes, Inc., 1914—; trustee Helen Brown Hawks Gift, 1917-37. Treas. Bennington Chapter Am. Red Cross, 1915-25. Founder and regent gen. Order of the Three Crusades, 1096-1192, Inc.; organizing pres. Congress of Lineal Soc., Soc. Vt. Women in N.Y., Daughters of Founders and Patriots of America (Vt. Chapter), Daughters Am. Colonists (Vt. Soc.), U.S. Daughters of 1812 (Bennington Chapter), New England Women (Larchmont Colony), Nat. Defense Round Table and Study Class. Fellow Inst. of Am. Genealogy (a founder). Mem. or officer numerous patriotic societies. Has given over 500 addresses on national defense. Home: Larchmont, N.Y.; also Bennington, Vt. Died Oct. 11, 1940.

HULINGS, Garnet, naval officer; b. Oil City, Pa., Mar. 6, 1889; s. Gen. Willis James and Emma (Simpson) H.; grad. U.S. Naval Acad., 1912; m. Salena Shumard Carden, Aug. 14, 1913; children— Carol Carden, Isabel Simpson. Commd. midshipman, U.S. Navy, 1912, and advanced through grades to lt. commander; retired 1927; v.p. and gen. mgr. Continental Steamship Co., 1927—. Served on U.S.S. Texas, Occupation of Vera Cruz, 1914; comdr. Submarine C-4, Panama, 1914-17, comdr. Submarine AL-4, patrol of Irish coast, World War; naval attaché, Tokio, Japan, 1921-24; comdr. U.S.S. Billingsley, 1925-27. Awarded Navy Cross (U.S.). Home: Cockeysville, Md. Died Apr. 1932.

HULINGS, Willis James, congressman; b. Clarion Co., Pa., July 1, 1850; s. Marcus and Margaret H.; ed. as C.E.; admitted to bar, Pa., Ariz. and W.Va.; m. Emma Simpson, Apr. 28, 1874; engaged in mining and petroleum business, 1874—. Mem. Pa. Ho. of Rep., 1881-87, Senate, 1887-1911; mem. 63d Congress (1913-15), 28th Dist., Pa. (Progressive), and 66th Congress (1919-21). Republican. Served pvt. to brig. gen. Pa. N.G., 1876-1912; col. 16th Pa. Vol. Inf., Spanish-Am. War; promoted brig. gen. vols., "for meritorious conduct in action," Aug. 9, 1898; disch. from vols., Jan. 1, 1899; comd. 2d Brigade N.G.Pa., 1907-13. Was 1st comdr.-in-chief Nat. Assn. Spanish-Am. War Vets., 2 yrs. Home: Oil City, Pa. Deceased.

HULL, Charles Henry, prof. Am. history; b. Ithaca, N.Y., Sept. 29, 1864; s. Albert M. and Margaret (Visscher) H.; Ph.B., Cornell, 1886; student at Göttingen, Halle, Berlin, 1890-92, Ph.D., Halle, 1892; unmarried. Asst., Cornell U. Library, 1886-87; asst. librarian, 1887-90; instr. polit. science, Cornell U., 1892-93, asst. prof. polit. economy, 1892-1901, prof. Am. history, 1901-31, emeritus. Editor: The Economic Writings of Sir William Petty. Home: Ithaca, N.Y. Died July 15, 1936.

HULL, David Carlisle, univ. pres.; b. nr. McCool, Miss., Nov. 4, 1869; s. William Boley and Martha Elizabeth (Carlisle) H.; B.Sc., Miss. Agrl. and Mech. Coll., 1904, M.Sc., 1905; post-grad. work U. of Chicago; m. Madge Cooke Wilson, Mar. 27, 1908; children—William Wilson, David Carlisle (dec.), James Roger. Prin. high sch., Meridian, Miss., 1898-1902; head master prep. dept., Miss. A. and M. Coll., 1903-04; prof. industrial edn. and dean Sch. of Industrial Edn., same coll., 1904-10; pres. Millsaps Coll., Jackson, Miss., 1910-12; supt. city schs., Meridian, 1912-20; pres. Miss. A. and M. Coll., 1920-25; pres. Ky. Wesleyan Coll., Aug. 1, 1925—. Democrat. Mem. M.E. Ch. S. Home: Winchester, Ky. Deceased.

HULL, George Huntington, iron merchant, author; b. Dansville, N.Y., Nov. 22, 1840; s. Rev. Leverett and Sarah (Lord) H.; acad. edn.; m. Lucia Eugene Houston, Oct. 30, 1877. Partner Addy, Hull & Co., Cincinnati, 1868-71; head George H. Hull & Co., Louisville, 1871-90; pres. Hull Coal & Coke Co., Roanoke, Va., 1885-94, George H. Hull Freight Car Line, 1885-94; pres. Am. Pig Iron Storage Warrant Co., 1888—; retired from active business. Formerly regent Ohio Pub. Library, Cincinnati, and dir. Louisville Bd. of Trade; organizer and regent Charity Orgn. Soc. of Louisville. Republican, 1861-1900, since independent. Presbyn. Author: Industrial Depressions, 1911. Home: Tuxedo Park, N.Y. Died Mar. 12, 1921.

HULL, Harry Edward, commr. gen. of immigration; b. Belvidere, N.Y., Mar. 12, 1864; s. Henry D. and Isabel (Renwick) H.; educated grammar and high schools, Cedar Rapids, Ia.; m. Mary Louise Harris, June 3, 1891 (died 1917); 1 son, Harris B.; m. 2d, Ann Gittins, June 21, 1921. Engaged in grain business; pres. Williamsburg Telephone Co. Alderman, 1887-89, mayor, 1889-1901, postmaster, 1901-14, all of Williamsburg; mem. 64th to 68th Congresses (1915-25), 2d Ia. Dist.; commr. gen. of immigration, 1925-33. Pres. Williamsburg Fair Assn., 1900-15. Republican. Episcopalian. Mason. Home: Williamsburg, Ia. Died Jan. 15, 1938.

HULL, John Albert Tiffin, congressman; b. Sabina, O., May 1, 1841; parents removed to Iowa, 1849; acad. edn.; LL.B., Cincinnati Law Sch., 1862; lt. and capt. in Union army, July 1862-Oct. 1863; wounded at Black River and resigned; m. Miss Gregory, July 17, 1863. Engaged in farming, mfg. and banking at Des Moines, Ia. Sec. Ia. Senate, 1872, 73, 74, 76, 78; sec. of state, Ia., 1879-85; lt. gov., 1885-89; mem. 52d to 61st Congresses (1891-1911), 7th Ia. Dist. Republican; chmn. Com. Mil. Affaires, 55th to 61st Congresses. Chmn. exec. com. Rep. Congressional Com., 1898, 1900, 02, 04. Home: Washington, D.C. Died Sept. 26, 1928.

HULL, Morton Denison, congressman; b. Chicago, Jan. 13, 1867; s. Morton B. and Eudora (Denison) H.; A.B., Harvard, 1889, LL.B., 1892; m. Katharine Bingham, June 5, 1895 (died 1931); 1 son, Denison Bingham. Began practice at Chicago, 1893; formerly pres. Raymond Concrete Pile Co.; mem. Ill. Ho. of Rep., 1906-14, Senate, 1915-22; mem. Ill. Constl. Conv., 1920; mem. 68th to 72d Congresses (1923-33), 2d Ill. Dist. Republican. Unitarian. Home: Chicago, Ill. Died Aug. 20, 1937.

HULL, Roger Benton, lawyer; b. Greenfield, Mass., Feb. 18, 1885; s. Arthur Norton and Frances Roe (Benton) H.; A.B., Yale, 1907; LL.B., Harvard, 1911; married Miriam Marsh, Sept. 23, 1913; children—Beverly Marsh and Nancy Norton; m. 2d, Amelia Goodyear Crim, June 25, 1937. Admitted to New York bar, 1911; asst. atty. gen. of Puerto Rico, 1911-14; spl. counsel to the Insular Pub. Service Commn., 1912-14; spl. asst. to the atty. gen. of U.S., 1914-17; asso. Chadburne, Babbitt and Wallace, 1919-24; gen. atty. New York Rys. Corp., 1925-27; gen. counsel Nat. Assn. of Life Underwriters, 1927—. Served as maj. with A.E.F., U.S. Army, 1917-19. Awarded Thatcher prize, Demosthenes and De Forest medals (Yale), 1907. Republican. Conglist. Home: New York, N.Y. Died Jan. 23, 1942.

HULL, Theodore Young, M.D.; b. New York, N.Y., Aug. 24, 1860; s. Peter H. and Mary Jane (Lance) H.; B.Sc., Amity Coll., College Springs, Ia., 1884; studied law 2 yrs.; M.D., George Washington U., 1892; m. Maude Frances Hall, Jan. 19, 1888 (died 1916). U.S. Govt. service, Washington, D.C., several yrs.; practiced at Washington, D.C., also lecturer on psycholoy, Washington Coll. for Young Women, 5 yrs.; spent 1 yr. at Asheville, N.C., studying tuberculosis; settled at San Antonio, Tex., 1906, and has specialized in treatment of tuberculosis. Mem. San Antonio Bd. of Health, Bexar County Pub. Health Assn. (pres. 1926, 27). Republican. Methodist. Mason. Home: San Antonio, Tex. Died June 30, 1938.

HULL, William Isaac, college prof.; b. Baltimore, Nov. 19, 1868; s. Thomas Burling and Mary (Dixon) H.; A.B., Johns Hopkins, 1889, Ph.D., 1892; student Berlin, 1891, Leyden, 1907-08, Paris, 1914; m. Hannah Hallowell Clothier, Dec. 27, 1898; children—Mary Clothier, Elizabeth Powell. Associate prof. history and economics, 1892-94, Joseph Wharton prof. history and political economy, 1894-1904, prof. history and internat. relations, 1904—, Swarthmore Coll. Supt. summer charities, New York, 1896-97; examiner in history for Coll. Entrance Exam. Bd., 1900-05. Author: Maryland Independence and the Confederation, 1891; The Monroe Doctrine—National or International?, 1915; Preparedness the American vs. the Military Programme, 1916; The War-Method and the Peace-Method, 1929; India's Political Crisis, 1930; William Sewel of Amsterdam, 1934; William Penn and the Dutch Quaker Migration to Pennsylvania, 1935; Eight First Biographies of William Penn., 1936; William Penn—A Topical Biography, 1937. Trustee Church Peace Union. Home: Swarthmore, Pa. Died Nov. 14, 1939.

HULLEY, Lincoln, univ. pres.; b. Camden, N.J., May 3, 1865; s. George and Mary E. (Currie) H.; A.B., Bucknell U., 1888, A.M., 1891; A.B., Harvard, 1889; Ph.D., U. of Chicago, 1895; Litt.D., John B. Stetson U., 1906; LL.D., Denison U., 1907; J. D., Temple U., 1924; D.C.L., Bucknell, 1924; D.D., Mercer, 1925; L.H.D., Furman U.; Ed.D., Southern Coll., Lakeland, Fla.; m. Harriet E. Spratt, 1890 (dec.); m. 2d, Eloise Mayham, A.M., Sept. 19, 1893. Instr. science, 1889-92, prof. history, 1893-1904, Bucknell U.; pres. John B. Stetson U., 1904—. Pres. Fla. Bankers Assn. 1 term; mem. State Senate, Fla., 2 terms; trustee Bucknell U., Crozer Theol. Sem.; Lt. Col. on staff gov. of Fla. Home: De Land, Fla. Died Jan. 20, 1934.

HULME, Thomas Wilkins, ry. official; b. Mount Holly, N.J., Aug. 11, 1868; s. Joseph S. and Abigail (Wills) H.; B.S. and C.E., Univ. of Pa., 1889; m. Mary A. Oliphant, Oct. 30, 1900; children—Alice Oliphant (Mrs. Frank T. Lloyd, Jr.), Mary Wills (Mrs. Courtlandt K. Schenck), Thomas Read, Katherine (Mrs. Harold L. Yoh). Began in real estate dept. Lehigh Valley R.R. Co., 1890, asst. real estate agt., 1893-1904; with Penna. R.R. Co., June-Nov. 1904; asst. real estate agt. N.Y. Connecting R.R. Co., 1904-05; same, Penna. R.R. Co., 1905-13, real estate agt., 1913-18, gen. real estate agt., 1918-24, v.p. in charge real estate valuation and taxation, 1924—, also dir. of Pa. Railroad Co., 1932—; mgr. Western Saving Fund Society. Trustee U. of Pa., Bryn Mawr (Pa.) Hosp. Republican. Episcopalian. Home: Haverford, Pa. Died Sept. 23, 1939.

HULME, William Henry, univ. prof.; b. Cheatham Co., Tenn., Oct. 25, 1862; s. Fountain Eliot Pitts and Lucy Anderson (Phillips) H.; A.B., Vanderbilt U., 1890; studied univs. of Leipzig, Jena and Freiburg, 1891-94; Ph.D., Freiburg, 1894; m. Hedwig Haas, of Freiburg, July 10, 1897. Instructor German, 1894-96, asso. prof. English, Flora Stone Mather Coll., 1896-1900, prof. of English, 1900-33 (emeritus), Western Reserve U. Unitarian. Editor: Middle-English "Harrowing of Hell" and Gospel of Nicodemus, 1907; O. F. Emerson's Chaucer Essays and Studies, 1929. Editor: Early Lives of Milton, 1924. Translator: Antichrist and Adam (with S. F. Barrow), 1925. Home: Cleveland, O. Died Dec. 6, 1934.

HULSE, Hiram Richard, bishop; b. Middletown, N.Y., Sept. 15, 1868; s. Frederick Brewster and Selina (Richards) H.; B.D., Phila. Div. Sch., 1896, D.D., 1915; D.D., Hobart, 1915; m. Frances Seymour, May 20, 1903; children—Mary Frederick Seymour, Charity Brewster. Deacon and priest, 1896, P.E. Ch.; vicar Pro-Cathedral, New York, 1896-98; rector St. Mary's Ch., New York, 1899-1912; served as examining chaplain Diocese of New York and sec. Am. Ch. Missionary Soc., also archdeacon of New York; consecrated bishop of Cuba, Jan. 12, 1915. Home: Havana, Cuba. Died Apr. 10, 1938.

HULST, Nelson Powell, mining engr.; b. East Brooklyn, N.Y., Feb. 8, 1842; s. Garret and Nancy (Powell) H.; A.B., Yale, 1867, Ph.B., 1869, Ph.D., 1870; m. Florence Terry, May 12, 1875. Engr. and chemist, Milwaukee (Wis.) Iron Co., 1870-76; engr. and gen. supt. Menominee (Mich.) Mining Co., 1876-81; gen. supt. Pewabic Iron Co., 1886-96; gen. mgr. iron mining interests of Carnegie Steel Co. in Wis., Mich. and Minn., 1896-1901; v.p. various mining cos. of U.S. Steel Corp., 1901-04 (retired); chmn. bd. dirs. Milwaukee Gas Light Co. Trustee Milwaukee Assn. Commerce (chmn. pub. charities com.); dir. Asso. Charities of Milwaukee, Martha Washington Home, Free Employment Bur., Boys' Busy Life Club. Republican. Conglist. Home: Milwaukee, Wis. Died Jan. 11, 1923.

HULSWIT, Frank Theodore, pub. utilities; b. Grand Rapids, Mich., Sept. 10, 1875; s. Frank Michael and Johannah Ursula (Louis) H.; ed. high sch., Grand Rapids; m. Cornelia Maria Hoebeke, June 20, 1900; children—Charles Louis, Robert Marius. Pres. Child-Hulswit & Co., 1904-12, United Light & Power Co., 1910-26, Am. Commonwealths Power Corp., 1927—; pres. Jacksonville (Fla.) Gas Co., Bangor (Me.) Gas Light Co., St. Augustine (Fla.) Gas & Electric Light Co.; chmn. board and dir. Am. Community Power Co., Am. Gas & Power Co., Dominion Gas & Electric Co.; v.p. Minneapolis

Gas Light Co., Gen. Public Utilities Co. Mem. bd. dirs. Am. Gas Assn. Republican. Mem. Reformed Ch. Home: East Grand Rapids, Mich. Died Apr. 2, 1933.

HUME, Robert Allen, missionary; b. Bombay, India, Mar. 18, 1857; s. Rev. Robert Wilson and Hannah D. (Sackett) H.; A.B., Yale, 1868, A.M., 1871; Yale Div. Sch., 1869-71; grad. Andover Theol. Sem., 1873; D.D., Yale, 1895; m. Katie Fairbank, of Ahmednagar, India, Sept. 8, 1887; children—Ruth P., R. E., Mrs. Hannah H. Lee, W. M., W. F., Henry W., Mrs. Mary B. Maguire. Taught 1 yr. in Gen. Russell's Mil. Sch., New Haven, Conn., 1 yr. Edwards Sch., Stockbridge, Mass.; ordained Congl. ministry, 1874; missionary B.C.F.M., Admednagar, India, Aug. 12, 1874—. Presented by Queen Victoria, Jan. 1, 1901, with Kaiser-i-Hind gold medal for pub. service in India. Hyde lecturer on foreign missions, Andover Theol. Sem., 1904-05. Author: Missions from the Modern View; An Interpretation of India's Religious History Died June 24, 1929.

HUME, Thomas, univ. prof.; b. Portsmouth, Va.; s. Rev. Thomas H.; grad. Richmond Coll. and U. of Va. (A.M., D.D., Richmond; LL.D., Wake Forest Coll. and U. of N.C.). Chaplain C.S.A. in the field, afterward during siege of Petersburg, post chaplain there; prin. Petersburg, Va., Classical Inst., prin. Roanoke Female Coll., and pastor of Danville, Va., Baptist Ch.; prof. Latin and English, Norfolk, Va., Coll.; pastor Norfolk City; lecturer for 4 yrs. on lit. and English philology, Nat. Summer Sch., Glens Falls, N.Y.; prof. English lang. and lit., 1885-1902, English lit., 1902-07 (emeritus), U. of North Carolina. Author: Helps to the Study of Hamlet, 1880. Died July 15, 1912.

HUMPHREY, Alexander Pope, lawyer; b. Louisville, Ky., Jan. 26, 1848; s. Edward Porter (D.D.) and Martha Ann (Pope) H.; A.B., Centre Coll., Danville, Ky., 1866; B.L., U. of Va., 1868; m. Mary Moss Churchill, Apr. 3, 1879; children—Mrs. Edw. P. Mellon, Alexander Pope (killed in U.S. mil. service), Churchill, Mary Churchill. Admitted to bar, 1868, began practice at Louisville; mem. Humphrey, Crawford & Middleton; cons. counsel Southern Ry. Co.; v.p. Ky. & Ind. Terminal R.R. Co. Trustee for endowment fund of U. of Va. Presbyn. Democrat. Home: Glenview, Ky. Died Aug. 19, 1928.

HUMPHREY, Arthur Luther, mfr.; b. Buffalo, N.Y., June 12, 1860; s. Arthur K. and Hulda (Orcutt) H.; ed. high sch.; m. Jennie Field, Jan. 16, 1890; children—Arthur F., Frederick D. Farmer, later machinist's apprentice, advancing to supt. of motive power. Served with U.P., S.P., A.T.&S.F., Colo. Midland, Colo. Southern, and C.&A. rys.; apptd. western mgr. Westinghouse Air Brake Co., 1903; gen. mgr. same co. at Pittsburgh, 1905, v.p., 1910, pres., 1919, exec. dir., 1932, chmn. board dirs., 1933-36, chmn. exec. com., 1936—; chmn. exec. com. Union Switch and Signal Co.; director Chamber Commerce of Pittsburgh (pres.). Mem. Colorado Ho. of Rep. 2 terms, 1893-95 (speaker of House, 1895). Industrial expert Ordnance Dept., U.S.A., World War. Mem. President's Conf. on Unemployment, Sept. 1921. Trustee U. of Pittsburgh, St. Margaret Memorial Hosp. Republican. Episcopalian. Mason. Home: Edgewood, Pittsburgh, Pa. Died Nov. 1, 1939.

HUMPHREY, Charles Frederic, maj. gen.; b. New York, Sept. 2, 1844. Pvt. corporal, sergt. and 1st sergt. Co. E, 5th Arty., Mar. 17, 1863-June 28, 1866; commd. 2d lt. 5th Arty., May 8, 1866; transferred to 4th Arty., Oct. 23, 1866; 1st lt., May 21, 1868; grad. Arty. Sch., 1874; capt. asst. q.-m., June 23, 1879; maj. q.-m., Dec. 11, 1892; lt. col. deputy q.-m.-gen., Oct. 15, 1897; col. q.-m. vols., July 7-Sept. 20, 1898; brig. gen., Sept. 21, 1898; hon. disch. from vol. service, June 12, 1899; col. asst. q.-m.-gen., Oct. 26, 1901; brig. gen. q.-m.-gen. U.S.A., Apr. 12, 1903; maj. gen. and retired after over 44 yrs.' service, July 1, 1907. Served in following Indian campaigns: Nez Percé, 1877; Snake Bannock, 1878; Sioux, 1890-91; Shoshone-Snake, 1895. Bvtd. capt., Feb. 27, 1890, "for gallant service in action against Indians" at the Clearwater, Ida., July 11, 1877; awarded Congressional Medal of Honor, Mar. 22, 1897, "for most distinguished gallantry" in action at the Clearwater, Ida., July 11, 1877, when he voluntarily and successfully conducted, in the fact of a withering fire, a party which recovered possession of an abandoned howitzer and 2 Gatling guns lying between the lines and within a few yards of the Indians, while serving as 1st lt., 4th U.S. Arty. Was chief q.-m. Santiago de Cuba Expdn., 1898, Div. of Cuba, 1898-99, Chinese Relief Expdn., 1900-01, Philippines, 1901-03. Home: Washington, D.C. Died June 4, 1926.

HUMPHREY, Herman Loin, lawyer; b. Candor, N.Y., March 14, 1830; s. Lucius and Lydia (Chidsey) H.; ed. public schools and Cortland Acad.; studied law at Ithaca with Judge Francis M. Finch, author of "The Blue and the Grey"; m. Jane A. Cross 1855, (died 1880); m. 2d, Elvira Doty Door, Oct. 1881. Admitted to bar, 1854; moved to Hudson, Wis., 1855; was dist. atty and later judge St. Croix Co.; State senator, 1862; judge 8th jud. Dist. Wis., 1867-77; congressman, 1877-83; mem. Wis. legislature, 1887-88. Republican. Home: Hudson, Wis. Died 1902.

HUMPHREY, J. Otis, judge; b. Morgan Co., Ill., Dec. 30, 1850; s. William and Sarah (Stocker) H.; reared on farm; ed. Shurtleff Coll., Alton, Ill.; m. Mary E. Scott, Apr. 20, 1879. Taught sch. 2 yrs.; admitted to bar, 1880; legal clerk in office of railroad and warehouse commrs. of Ill., 1880-83; presdl. elector, 1884; U.S. dist. atty. Southern Dist. of Ill., 1897-1901; U.S. dist. judge Southern Dist. of Ill., 1901—. Home: Springfield, Ill. Died June 14, 1918.

HUMPHREY, Lewis Craig, editor; b. Louisville, Ky., Sept. 28, 1875; s. Edward Cornelius and Jessie (Barkley) H.; B.L., Centre Coll., Ky., 1896; m. Eleanor Belknap, Dec. 19, 1904. With Louisville Evening Post, 1896—, editor and v.p., 1917—. Mem. Jefferson Co. (Ky.) Election Bd., 1904-09. Democrat. Presbyn. Mason. Trustee Centre Coll., Ky. Home: Louisville, Ky. Deceased.

HUMPHREY, Lyman Underwood, governor; b. New Baltimore, O., July 25, 1844; at 17, enlisted in Co. I, 76th Ohio Inf.; served through war; was wounded; promoted orderly sergt. and 2d and 1st lt.; student Mt. Union Coll., Ohio; law student U. of Mich., 1866-67; m. Amanda Leonard, Dec. 25, 1872. In law practice at Independence, Kan., from 1871; sr. mem. Humphrey & Humphrey, farm loans. Mem. Kan. Ho. of Rep., 1876-77; lt. gov., 1877-84; mem. Kan. Senate, 1884-88; gov., 1889-93. Republican. Home: Independence, Kan. Died Sept. 12, 1915.

HUMPHREY, Marie E. Ives; b. New Haven, Conn.; d. Hon. Charles and Catherine M. (Osborn) Ives; desc. of John Howland, of the Mayflower; B.A., Vassar; m. Rev. William Brewster Humphrey, Sept. 14, 1905. Writer and lecturer on Am. Indians; devoting life to betterment of conditions of the Indians and promoting their music, arts, and native handicrafts; formerly interested in promotion of playgrounds, municipal improvements, etc. Organizer and pres. Am. Indian League, 1910—. Conglist. Home: New York, N.Y. Died Mar. 29, 1941.

HUMPHREY, Richard Lewis, engineer; b. Marblehead, Mass., Oct. 19, 1869; s. Richard Henry and Caroline (Curtis) H.; A.B., Central High Sch., Phila., 1888, A.M., 1893; C.E., U. of Pa., 1891; m. Anna Kay Thompson, Apr. 30, 1904. With Phila. Municipal Testing Lab., 1892-99; engr. and gen. mgr. Buckhorn Portland Cement Co., 1899-1903; consulting expert for Pa. R.R. Co. and for other large corps. Engr. in charge Collective Portland Cement Exhibit and Model Testing Lab. of Assn. Am. Portland Cement Mfrs. at St. Louis Expn., 1904; has served as cement and concrete expert U.S. Geol. Survey; was mem. War Industries Bd. Republican. Home: Westtown, Pa. Died Nov. 2, 1928.

HUMPHREY, Seth King, author; b. Faribault, Minn., Aug. 5, 1864; s. David W. and Adelaide W. (King) H.; grad. Faribault High Sch., 1881; course in Mass. Inst. Tech., 1895-97; unmarried. Engaged in flour milling, 1881-89; invented the Humphrey employes' elevator, 1886; engaged in western investments, 1889-1912. Author: The Indian Dispossessed, 1905; Mankind, 1917; The Racial Prospect, 1920; Loafing Through the Pacific, 1927; Loafing Through Africa, 1929; Following the Prairie Frontier, 1931. Home: Boston, Mass. Died May 24, 1932.

HUMPHREY, William E., federal trade commr.; b. nr. Alamo, Ind., Mar. 31, 1862; reared on farm; grad. Wabash Coll., Ind., 1887. Admitted to bar, 1887; in practice at Crawfordsville, Ind., 1887-93; moved to Seattle, Wash., 1893. Corp. counsel, Seattle, 1898-1902; mem. 58th, 59th and 60th Congresses (1903-09), Wash. at-large, and 61st to 64th Congresses (1909-17), 1st Dist.; resumed practice at Seattle and Washington, D.C.; chmn. Speaker's Bur., Rep. Nat. Com., 1922; apptd. mem. Federal Trade Commn., term 1925-31, reappointed, term 1931-37. Republican. Home: Seattle, Wash. Died Feb. 14, 1934.

HUMPHREYS, Albert Edmund, capitalist; b. Sissonville, W.Va., Jan. 11, 1860; s. Ira and Eleanor (Dawson) H.; ed. Marshall Coll., Huntington, W.Va.; granted teacher's certificate before he was 16; hon. D.M.E., Ohio Northern U.; m. Alice K. Boyd, 1887; children—Ira B., Albert E. Began at 17 in lumber business with father; went to Duluth, Minn., 1891, and was a pioneer in opening up the iron deposits of the Mesaba Range; founder of Virginia, Minn.; prospected widely for minerals and oil in Rocky Mountains and Southwest; organized the Merritt Oil & Gas Co. of Okla., 1914; asso. with F. Julius Fohs, geologist, in many enterprises; opened Big Muddy Pool in Wyo. and Mexia Field in Tex.; largely interested in coal deposits of W.Va.; pres. Humphreys Corp., Wyoming Investment Co., Ltd. Mem. Central Christian Ch., Denver; built Boyd Memorial Ch., Charleston, W.Va. Mason. Home: Denver, Colo. Died May 8, 1927.

HUMPHREYS, Alexander Crombie, coll. pres.; b. Edinburgh, Scotland, Mar. 30, 1851; s. Edward R. (M.D., LL.D.) and Margaret (McNutt) H.; ed. at his father's pvt. sch.; M.E., Stevens Inst. Tech., 1881; Sc.D., U. of Pa., 1903; LL.D., Columbia, 1903, New York U., 1906, Princeton, 1907, Brown, Rutgers, 1914; E.D., Rensselaer, 1918; m. Eva Guillaudeu, Apr. 30, 1872; children—Eva Margaret (Mrs. Henry S. Loud), Harold (dec.), Alexander Crombie (dec.). Began to work at 14; sec. and supt. Bayonne & Greenville Gas Light Co., 1872-81 (last 4 yrs. also a student at Stevens Inst. Tech.); chief engr. Pintsch Lighting Co., New York, 1881-85; gen. supt. and chief engr. United Gas Improvement Co., Phila., 1885-94; sr. mem. Humphreys & Glasgow, London and New York, 1892-1908; retired from that firm of London, 1908; reorganized Humphreys & Glasgow, of New York, as Humphreys & Miller, Inc., 1910; pres. Buffalo Gas Co.; dir., mem. finance com. Equitable Life Assurance Soc. Pres. Stevens Inst. Tech., Hoboken, N.J., Sept. 1902—, and pres. its bd. trustees, 1907—. Established a cadet corps in his professional work, students coming from coll. and getting in this corps a post-grad course in gas engring. Trustee and mem. exec. com. Carnegie Foundation for Advancement of Teaching. Author: Lecture Notes on Some of the Business Features of Engineering Practice, 1905. Home: Morristown, N.J. Died Aug. 14, 1927.

HUMPHREYS, Benjamin Grubb, congressman; b. Claiborne Co., Miss., Aug. 17, 1865; s. Gen. Benjamin G. (gov. of Miss., 1865-68) and Mildred Hickman (Maury) H.; student U. of Miss. to end of jr. yr.; m. Louise Yerger, Oct. 9, 1889. Admitted to bar, 1891, and began practice at Greenville. Supt. edn. Leflore Co., Miss., 1892-96; dist. atty., 4th Dist., 1895-1903; mem. 58th to 66th Congresses (1903-21), 3d Miss. District; del. at large Dem. Nat. Conv., San Francisco, 1920. First lt. 2d Miss. Inf. under Gen. Fitzhugh Lee during Spanish-Am. War, 1898. Home: Greenville, Miss. Died Oct. 16, 1923.

HUMPHREYS, David Carlisle, civil engr.; b. Chatham Hill, Va., Oct. 14, 1855; s. Dr. William Finley and Betsey (McFarland) H.; C.E., Washington and Lee U., 1878; m. Mary L., d. E. M. Sloan, Sept. 4, 1888. U.S. asst. engr. on improvement of Mo. River, 1879-85; adj. prof. applied mathematics, 1885-89, prof. civ. engring., 1889—, dean Sch. of Applied Science, 1904—, Washington and Lee U. Resident hydrographer, U.S. Geol. Survey, 1895-1908; sec. building commn. and supt. heating and power plant, Washington and Lee U.; mem. gov.'s Bd. of Mech. Survey of Va. Pres. bd. deacons Presbyn. Ch. Home: Lexington, Va. Died Jan. 10, 1921.

HUMPHREYS, Frank Landon, chaplain, author; b. Auburn, N.Y., June 16, 1858; s. Dr. Frederick and Frances M. (Sperry) H.; A.M., St. Stephen's Coll., 1883, Mus. Doc., 1888; S.T.D., Hobart Coll., 1894; LL.D., U. of Maryland, 1915; m. Jean Todd, Apr. 29, 1886; children—Landon, Malcolm, George, David. Deacon, 1879, priest, 1883, P.E. Ch.; asst. Ch. of Heavenly Rest, New York, 1879-81; rector Short Hills, N.J., 1883-85; precentor in charge Cathedral of Incarnation, Garden City, 1885-90; canon Cathedral St. John the Divine, New York, 1900-06. Acting chaplain U.S. Mil. Acad., 1897; gen. sec. Ch. Univ. Bd. of Regents, 1894-1900; sec. Parochial Fund, Diocese of New York, 1898. Chaplain Soc. of the Nazarene; gen. chaplain Soc. of the Cincinati, 1896—; chaplain Naval Order of U.S., Soc. of 1812, 1895—. Naval Reserves (U.S.S. Portsmouth); staff chaplain Naval Reserve, rank comdr., World War, —, also was comdr. in the line, N.J. Naval Militia, Spanish-Am. War; chaplain N.Y. Soc. S.R. 27 yrs.; chaplain for spl. service, U.S. Naval Res.; historian Soc. Colonial Wars 15 yrs.; pres. Soc. of Cincinnati in N.J. 10 yrs. Officer Legion of Honor (France), 1921; medal Reconnaissance (France); Officer French Acad., decorated with palms; Knight Comdr. Order St. George, 1929; Comdr. of Order of St. Lazare (Italy); Commander of Our Lady of Bethlehem. Mayor of City of Boynton, Fla. Author: What We Owe to France, 1915; Life and Times of David Humphreys, 1917; Ce Que Nous Devoir a la France, 1922; France and America (are our present negotiations worthy of American traditions?), 1926. Home: New Canaan, Conn., and Boynton, Fla. Died July 18, 1937.

HUMPHREYS, Lester Warren, lawyer; b. Brookville, Pa., May 20, 1883; s. Thomas Norris and Margaret (Yost) H.; student Oregon Agricultural Coll., Corvallis; LL.B., U. of Oregon, 1908; special course U. of Paris, France, 1919; m. Evangeline Bard, Jan. 29, 1921; children—Lester Warren, Richard Howard, Marian Margaret. Began law practice at Portland, 1909; member Chamberlain, Thomas, Kraemer & Humphreys, 1915-19; U.S. atty. for Ore., 1919-23; mem. Simon, Gearin, Humphreys & Freed, 1925—. Chairman Soldiers & Sailors Commn. of Ore. Mem. 17th U.S. Inf., in Philippines, 1900-03; entered O.T.C., May 12, 1917; commd. capt., Aug. 15, 1917, and assigned to 91st Div., A.E.F.; served in France, 1918-19; maj. 364th Inf., Oct. 17, 1918; awarded Croix de Guerre (Belgian). Democrat. Home: Portland, Ore. Died May 14, 1929.

HUMPHREYS, Marie Champney (Mrs.), arist; b. Deerfield, Mass., 1876; d. James Wells and Elizabeth (Williams) Champney; pupil Mlle. Noeme Schmitt, Paris, and Virginia Reynolds, Chicago Art Inst.; m. John Sanford Humphreys, Nov. 22, 1899. Has exhibited in Europe, America and Paris Expn., 1900; mem. Woman's Art Club. Home: New York, N.Y. Died 1906.

HUMPHREYS, Mary Gay, author; b. Ripley, O.; d. William Smith and Henrietta (Wright) H.; unmarried. Has traveled extensively in the Orient; was in the Philippines at outbreak of insurgent war and volunteered as nurse and served 8 months in hosp.; from Philippines continued journey around the world, 1899. Author: Catherine Schuyler, 1897; Jack Racer, 1901; Racer of Illinois, 1902. Editor: The Boys Catlin, 1909; The Boy's Story of Zebulon M. Pike, 1911; Missionary Explorers Among the North American Indians, 1914. Home: New York, N.Y. Died Oct. 10, 1915.

HUMPHREYS, Milton Wylie, university prof.; b. Greenbrier Co., Va. (now W.Va.), Sept. 15, 1844; s. Dr. Andrew Cavet and Mary McQuain (Hefner) H.; gunner C.S.A., 1862-65; A.M., Washington and Lee U., 1869; Ph.D., U. of Leipzig, 1874; LL.D., Vanderbilt and Washington and Lee univs.; m. Louise, d. Dr. Landon C. Garland, chancellor Vanderbilt U., 1877; children—Louise Garland, Annie Fulton, Mary Meredith, Jeannette Rose. Asso. prof. Latin and Greek, 1867-70, adj. prof. ancient langs., 1870-75, Washington and Lee (on leave of absence, 1872-74, in Europe); prof. Greek, Vanderbilt U., 1875-83; prof. Latin and Greek, U. of Tex., 1883-87; prof. Greek, U. of Va., 1887-1912; retired Sept. 15, 1912. Am. chief editor of Revue des Revues, appended to Revue de Philologie, Paris, 1878-88. In artillery service invented indirect fire and discovered "terrestrial shift." Editor: (with notes) The Clouds, of Aristophanes, 1885; The Antigone, of Sophocles, 1891; Demosthenes, On The Crown, 1913. Home: University, Va. Deceased.

HUMPHREYS, Solon, merchant; b. Canton, Conn., Oct. 27, 1821; ed. public schools and St. John's Coll., Annapolis, Md.; m. Ellen, dau. Edward Walsh, St. Louis, Mo., 1857. Clerk for Wm. Harrison, 1838-39; clerk E. D. Morgan & Co., New York, 1839-44. Founded, 1844, and was senior member until 1853, Humphreys & Thatcher, St. Louis. Partner in E. D. Morgan & Co. from 1854, then in sugar and tea trade, later in banking and other business. Home: Bergen Point, N.J. Died 1900.

HUMPHREYS, Willard, prof. of German, Princeton, 1894—; b. New York, N.Y., 1867; s. A. Willard and Mary (Cunningham) H.; grad. Columbia, 1888 (A.M., 1889; Ph.D., 1890; M.D., N.Y. Univ., 1890); m. Mary Prince, 1898. Studied Columbia Law School; School of Political Science, and N.Y. Univ. Med. School. Admitted to N.Y. bar, 1892. Sec. New York Medico-Legal Soc.; editor Columbia Law Times; asso. editor Medico-Legal Journal. Instr. Latin, Princeton, 1892-94. Editor: Selections from Quintus Curtius, 1896; Schiller's Jungfrau von Orleans, 1899. Home: Princeton, N.J. Died 1902.

HUMPHREYS, William Yerger, congressman; b. Greenville, Miss., Sept. 9, 1890; s. Benjamin Grubb and Louise (Yerger) H.; ed. pub. schs. of Miss. and pvt. schs., Washington, D.C.; studied law George Washington U., 1911-14 (no degree); m. Clara Mai Nulsen, June 1, 1911; children—Wm. Yerger, Louise, Clara Mai. Began practice of law at Greenville, 1914; mem. Humphreys & Anderson; mem. 68th Congress (1923-25), 3d Miss. Dist. Served as 1st lt. C.W.S., World War. Democrat. Episcopalian. Home: Greenville, Miss. Died Feb. 26, 1933.

HUMPHRIES, John Edmund, lawyer; b. Calhoun, Ill., Mar. 17, 1852; s. Francis McFarland and Maria (Ridgway) H.; ed. common and high schs., Ill. and Ind. and Ind. U.; m. Estelle M. Freshman, Mar. 11, 1888. Practiced law at Rockville, Ind., 1872-78, Crawfordsville, 1878-89, Seattle, Wash., June 1889—. Rep. candidate for justice Supreme Ct. of Wash. under direct primary law, 1908; candidate for U.S. senator under direct primary statute, 1910; judge Superior Ct., King Co., Wash., 1912—. Presbyn. Mason. Home: Seattle, Wash. Died May 29, 1915.

HUMSTONE, Walter Coutant, telegraph service; b. Esopus, N.Y., June 1, 1849; s. John Reddrop and Juliette (Coutant) H.; ed. pub. schs.; m. Mary I. Millard, Sept. 11, 1872. Telegraph operator, 1862-70; supt. Atlantic & Pacific Telegraph Co., 1871-81; spl. agt. Western Union Telegraph Co., 1881, 82; supt. W.U. Tel. Co., at N.Y., 1882-1902 (retired); dir. Met. Life Ins. Co., West Penn Steel Co., Gamewell Fire Alarm Telegraph Co., U.S. Title Guaranty Co.; mem. exec. com. Telegraph & Telephone Life Ins. Assn. Pres. bd. Central Congl. Soc.; v.p. Brooklyn Soc. Prevention Cruelty to Children; pres. Industrial Home for Blind. Republican. Mem. Chamber Commerce. Mason. Home: Brooklyn, N.Y. Died Mar. 12, 1925.

HUN, Henry, neurologist; b. Albany, N.Y., Mar. 21, 1854; s. Thomas and Lydia Louisa (Reynolds) H.; Ph.B., Sheffield Scientific Sch. (Yale), 1874; M.D., Harvard, 1879; (hon. M.A., Yale, 1914); m. Lydia Marcia Hand, Apr. 28, 1892. Asst. in physics, Sheffield Scientific Sch., 1873-75; prof. nervous diseases, Albany Med. Coll. (Union U.), 1885-1914; cons. physician to Albany, Anthony Brady Memorial hospitals and Albany Hosp. for Incurables; attending physician to Child's Hospital, Albany. Pres. trustee Albany Acad.; trustee Dudley Obs., gov. Albany Hosp. Chmn. Med. Advisory Bd. No. 27, N.Y. State, World War. Home: Albany, N.Y. Died Mar. 1924.

HUNDLEY, Henry Rhodes, educator; b. Louisa Co., Va., Aug. 10, 1867; s. Rev. John W. and Virginia (Quarles) H.; B.A., Richmond Coll., 1888; M.A., Denison U., 1910; Crozer Theol. Sem., 1895; D.Sc., Bucknell U., 1900; m. Mabel Parker Lewis, 1896; children—Henry Rhodes (dec.), John Walker, Bernard Lewis, William Thomas, Marion Lee. Teacher Johnston Inst., S.C., 1888-89; prin. high sch., Batesburg, S.C., 1889-92; master modern langs., Peddie Inst., Hightstown, N.J., 1895-1900; v.-prin., 1898-1900; prin., 1900—, Doane Academy, Granville, O.; also prof. English and German, Denison U., 1927—. Trustee Ohio Bapt. Edn. Soc., 1900—, sec., 1901—. Mason. Home: Granville, O. Died Jan. 26, 1934.

HUNDLEY, Oscar R., judge; b. Limestone Co., Ala., Oct. 30, 1855; s. Orville M. and Mary E. H.; LL.B., Vanderbilt U., 1877; (LL.D., Marietta Coll., 1907); m. Bossie O'Brien, June 24, 1897. Admitted to bar, 1878, and practiced at Huntsville, Ala., 1878-1907; div. counsel Nashville, Chattanooga & St. Louis Ry., 1884-1907. Mem. Ala. Ho. of Rep., 1886-90, Senate, 1890-98; city atty., Huntsville, 1886-90; nat. commr. Chicago Expn., 1893 (mem. com. on judiciary and sec. bur. of awards); Rep. nominee for Congress, 8th Ala. Dist., 1896, defeated by Gen. Joseph Wheeler; apptd. Apr. 9, 1907, U.S. dist. judge, Northern Dist. of Ala.; retired May 1909. "Four Minute Man," speaking in Ala. and other states, 1917-18. Home: Birmingham, Ala. Died Dec. 22, 1921.

HUNEKER, James Gibbons, critic, author; b. Phila., Pa., Jan. 31, 1860; s. John and Mary H.; g.s. James Gibbons (Irish poet), and of John H., organist; grad. Roth's Mil. Acad., Phila., 1873; studied law and conveyancing at Law Acad., Phila., 5 yrs.; studied piano with Georges Mathias, Paris. Associated for 10 yrs. with Rafael Joseffy as teacher of piano at Nat. Conservatory, New York; music and dramatic critic New York Recorder, 1891-95, Morning Advertiser, 1895-97; formerly music and dramatic, and art editor New York Sun. Author: Mezzotints in Modern Music, 1899; Chopin—The Man and His Music, 1900; Melomaniacs, 1902; Overtones, 1904; Iconoclasts—A Book of Dramatists, 1905; Visionaries, 1905; Egoists—A Book of Supermen, 1909; Promenades of an Impressionist, 1910; Franz Liszt, 1911; The Pathos of Distance, 1913; Ivory Apes and Peacocks, 1915; New Cosmopolis, 1915; Unicorns, 1917; Philharmonic Society, 1918; Charles Baudelaire, 1919; Steeplejack, 1919; Mary Garden, 1920. Home: New York, N.Y. Died Feb. 9, 1921.

HUNGERFORD, Frank Louis, lawyer; b. Torrington, Conn., Nov. 6, 1843; s. John and Charlotte A. H.; m. Sarah Churchill, Dec. 21, 1869; ed. Univ. of Vt. (A.B.), and Harvard Law Sch. Republican. Mem. firm of Hungerford, Hyde, Joslyn & Gilman. Home: New Britain, Conn. Died 1909.

HUNKER, John Jacob, rear admiral U.S.N.; b. Pittsburgh, Pa., June 12, 1844; s. Andrew and Margaret (Donaldson) H.; ed. Toledo High Sch. to 1861; grad. U.S. Naval Acad., 1866; m. Mary Monroe, Dec. 22, 1875. Served as pvt., Co. H, 1st Ohio Arty., for 7 months, 1861-62, in Civil War; midshipman, Naval Acad., 1862-66; ensign, Apr. 1868; master, Mar. 26, 1869; lt., Mar. 21, 1870; lt. comdr., Oct. 1855; comdr., Sept. 1894; capt., Dec. 11, 1900; rear admiral, June 6, 1906. Organized and comd. transport fleet and convoys assembled at Tampa, Fla., June 1898, to carry Shafter's army to Santiago, Cuba, during Spanish-Am. War; comdr. expdn. capturing Nipe Bay, Cuba, July 21, 1898, in Spanish-Am. War; advanced 3 numbers "for eminent and conspicuous conduct in battle"; retired, June 12, 1906. Home: Put-in-Bay, Ohio. Died Dec. 16, 1916.

HUNNEWELL, James Frothingham, merchant, author; b. Charlestown, Mass., July 3, 1832; s. James and Susan (Lamson) H.; ed. pvt. schs.; m. Sarah M. Farnsworth, Apr. 3, 1872. Holds offices and membership in many hist. and business orgns.; pres. Bostonian Soc., Club of Odd Volumes. Author: The Lands of Scott, 1871; The Historical Monuments of France, 1884. Editor: Relation of Virginia, by Henry Spelman, 1609, 1872; Early American Poetry (5 vols.), 1894-99. Home: Charlestown and Boston, Mass. Died 1910.

HUNNEWELL, Walter, trustee; b. Boston, Mass., Jan. 28, 1844; s. H. H. and Isabella P. H.; grad. Harvard, 1865; m. Jane A. Peele, May 15, 1873. Trustee Commonwealth Av. Land Trust, Provident Instn. for Savings, Summer St. Firemen's Fund, Boston Lying-in Hosp.; dir. Webster and Atlas Nat. Bank, Calumet & Hecla Mining Co.; v.p. St. Mary's Mineral Land Co. Dir. Peter Bent Brigham Hosp.; treas. bd. trustees Boston Y.M.C.U. Home: Wellesley, Mass. Died Sept. 30, 1921.

HUNSAKER, Walter Jerome, newspaper pub.; b. Keokuk, Ia., Sept. 19, 1857; s. George T. and Emeline (Coddington) H.; ed. pvt. and high schs. and Carthage (Ill.) Coll.; m. Alma Lyle Clarke, Oct. 21, 1885; 1 son, Jerome Clarke. Newspaper work at Carthage, 1872; publisher Creston Republic, Daily Gazette, 1879-85; editorial writer Minneapolis Journal, 1885; night editor, 1885-87, mng. editor, 1888-92, Detroit Tribune; mng. editor Detroit Evening Journal, 1892-1902; editor and owner Saginaw Daily Courier-Herald, 1902-19; mem. Booth Newspapers, Inc. Pres. Mich. Fish Commn., 1912-21. Home: Saginaw, Mich. Died Sept. 28, 1939.

HUNT, Andrew Murray, consulting engr.; b. Sioux City, Ia., Aug. 12, 1859; s. Andrew Murray and Marion (Kent) H.; grad. U.S. Naval Acad., 1879; unmarried. Engr. officer on several vessels of U.S. Navy; was instr. mech. engring., Orchard Lake Mil. Acad., Mich., 1 yr.; mem. Naval Steel Inspn. Bd., having charge of chem. work of inspn. and started the chem. lab. at Mare Island Navy Yard; chief engr. of U.S. Fish Commn. steamer Albatross, 1893, and detailed as chief of the Dept. Mech. Arts, Mid-winter Fair, San Francisco; resigned from Navy, July 1894, and engaged as consulting engr. in San Francisco. Built 4 steamers in Alaska, 1897-98, for service on Yukon River; resumed practice, San Francisco, 1899; was consulting engr. for Claus Spreckels in erection of plant of Independent Elec. Light and Power Co., of which became gen. mgr., also gen. mgr. Independent Gas and Power Co.; consulting engr. many important constructions on Pacific Coast; removed to New York, 1915; pres. Peyton Hunt Co., Inc., consulting engrs., N.Y. City, 1915—. Mem. Naval Consulting Bd., Sept. 4, 1915—; mem. ship protection gen. com. of U.S. Shipping Bd., 1917. Died Dec. 8, 1930.

HUNT, Arthur Prince, clergyman, educator; b. Springfield, Mass., Aug. 5, 1874; s. George and Eleonora (Prince) H.; B.A., Amherst, 1897, M.A., 1900; grad. Gen. Theol. Sem., 1900, B.D., 1901; studied U. of Oxford, Eng., 1903; m. Una Atherton Clarke, June 18, 1908. Deacon, 1900, priest, 1901, P.E. Ch.; canon All Saints Cathedral, Albany, N.Y., 1901-03; instr. Christian ethics, 1904-08, prof., 1908—. Gen. Theol. Sem. Compiler: Stories of the Life of Jesus Christ in the Words of the Bible, 1901, 2d Series, 1902. Home: New York, N.Y. Died July 1925.

HUNT, Benjamin Weeks; b. Chappaqua, West Chester Co., N.Y., May 18, 1847; s. Benjamin Weeks and Mary (Quinby) H.; ed. Mt. Kisco Acad., N.Y.; D.Sc., U. of Ga., 1922; m. Louise Prudden, May 18, 1876. Began in banking business at Eatonton, 1891; former pres. Middle Ga. Bank. Known as animal and plant breeder; original investigations in diseases of animals; created a cross-bred fig; an organized Ga. Pasteur Inst.; curator Eatonton Pub. Library. Mem. Soc. of Friends. Mason. Home: Eatonton, Ga. Deceased.

HUNT, Carleton, lawyer; b. New Orleans, Jan. 1, 1836; s. Thomas (M.D., founder Med. Coll. of La., pres. U. of La.) and Aglaé H. (d. of Justice Henry Carleton); A.B., Harvard, 1856, A.M., 1859; LL.B., U. of La., 1858 (LL.D., 1880); m. Louise Elizabeth Georgine Cammack, Dec. 24, 1860. Mem. Bd. of Administrators, 1866-69, prof. admiralty and internat. law, 1869-78, prof. civil law, 1878-82, and dean 9 yrs., U. of La. (now Tulane U.); mem. 48th Congress (1883-85); corp. counsel city of New Orleans, 1888-92. One of organizers Am. Bar Assn. (chmn. coms. on organization, legal edn. and admission to bar). Declined appmt. as justice of Supreme Court of La., 1879. Home: New Orleans, La. Died Aug. 14, 1921.

HUNT, Caroline Louisa, home economist; b. Chicago, Ill., Aug. 23, 1865; d. Homer Conkey and Ann (Gleed) H.; A.B., Northwestern U., 1888; grad. work in chemistry, same, 1892-93, and at U. of Chicago, 1893-94. Dietary studies in Chicago, for U.S. Dept. of Agr., 1894-96; teacher of home economics, Lewis Inst., Chicago, 1896-1901; prof. home economics, U. of Wis., 1903-08; scientific asst., nutrition investigations, U.S. Dept. Agr., 1909-15; scientific asst., Office of Home Economics, 1915-23; specialist Bur. of Home Economics, Washington, 1923—. Author: Home Problems, 1908; Life of Ellen H. Richards, 1912. Died 1927.

HUNT, Charles Wallace, engineer; b. Candor, N.Y., Oct. 13, 1841; s. William Walter and Elizabeth Bush (Sackett) H.; m. Frances Martha Bush, 1868; 2d, Katharine Humphrey, 1889; spl. agt. War Dept., 1864, to care for freedmen coming into the Union lines. V.p. Richmond County Savings Bank; engaged in engring. and mfg. Pres. Am. Soc. Mech. Engrs., 1898, United Engring Soc., 1909; mem. N.Y. Chamber of Commerce. Home: Stapleton, N.Y. Died 1911.

HUNT, Charles Warren, civil engr.; b. New York, May 19, 1858; s. Charles Havens and Anna de Peyster (Livingston) H.; B.S. and C.E., 1876, LL.D., 1909, New York U.; m. Mary Osgood, d. George S. Riggs, of Baltimore, Sept. 8, 1883. Asst. sec., 1892-95, sec., 1895-1920 (emeritus), Am. Soc. Civil Engineers. Died July 23, 1932.

HUNT, Emory William, educator; b. East Clarence, N.Y., Feb. 2, 1862; s. Rev. Harrison P. and Caroline (Holmes) H.; A.B., U. of Rochester, 1884; grad. Crozer Theol. Sem., 1887; D.D., Denison, 1901; LL.D., U. of Rochester, 1902; D.C.L., Hillsdale (Mich.) Coll., 1927; m. Elizabeth Olney, Aug. 24, 1892. Ordained Bapt. ministry, 1887; pastor Ashland Av. Ch., Toledo, 1887-1900, Clarendon St. Ch., Boston, 1900-02; pres. Denison U., Granville, O., Jan. 1902-June 1913; gen. sec. Am. Bapt. Foreign Mission Soc., Boston, June 1913-15; pastor First Ch., Newton Center, Mass., 1915-19; pres. Bucknell

U., Lewisburg, Pa., June 1919-31 (pres. emeritus). Pres. Northern Bapt. Conv., 1910-12. Home: Lewisburg, Pa. Died May 20, 1938.

HUNT, Frank W., gov. of Idaho; b. Newport, Ky., Dec. 16, 1861; s. Thomas B. and Eugenia A. H.; m. Ruth Maynard, Nov. 10, 1896. Elected gov. Idaho, Jan. 7, 1901, for term expiring Jan. 5, 1903. Died 1906.

HUNT, Gaillard, author; b. New Orleans, Sept. 8, 1862; s. William H. (sec. of the navy) and Elizabeth Augusta (Ridgely) H.; bro., of William Henry H.; ed. Hopkins Grammar Sch., New Haven, and Emerson Inst., Washington; (Litt.D., Washington and Lee U., 1912; LL.D., U. of S.C., 1912, William and Mary, 1913); m. Mary, d. Maj. Henry Goodfellow, U.S. Army, Oct. 24, 1901. Representative of State Dept. to Chicago Expn., 1893; chief Bur. of Citizenship, Dept. of State, 1900-09; chief Div. of Manuscripts, Library of Congress, 1909-17; special officer of the Dept. of State to prepare history of the World War, 1918-20; editor for Department of State, 1921—. Member Naturalization Commn. apptd. by the President, 1905; mem. Citizenship Bd., 1906; adviser to Dept. State in citizenship matters, 1915, 17. Was lecturer on Nationality, Grad. Sch. of Polit. Sciences, George Washington U., and on materials for history, Johns Hopkins, 1913. Author: The Department of State of the United States, 1892, 2d edit., Life of James Madison, 1902; John C. Calhoun (Am. Crisis Biographies), 1907; Dis-union Sentiment in Congress in 1794, 1905; Life in America One Hundred Years Ago, 1914. Editor: The Writings of James Madison (8 vols.); The First Forty Years of Washington Society, 1906; The Journals of the Continental Congress in Succession to Worthington C. Ford, 1909; James Madison's Journal of Debates in the Constitutional Convention, 1917. Died Mar. 20, 1924.

HUNT, George Edwin, dentist; b. Indianapolis, Apr. 29, 1864; s. Phineas George Canning and Hannah Mary (Phipps) H.; student Asbury Coll. (now Pe Pauw U.), 1880-82, U. of Mich., 1882-83; D.D.S., Ind. Dental Coll., 1890; M.D., Med. Coll. of Indiana, 1892; m. Maria Foster Buchanan, June 23, 1908. Engaged in ry. engring. in Fla., 1883-88; practiced dentistry in Indianapolis, 1890-96; dean, sec. and treas., Ind. Dental Coll., Indianapolis, 1896—. Editor and publisher Indiana Dental Journal, 1898-1900; editor Desmos, official mag. Delta Sigma Delta Fraternity, Nov., 1900—; editor, Oral Hygiene, 1911. Mason. Home: Indianapolis, Ind. Deceased.

HUNT, George Wylie Paul, governor; b. Huntsville, Mo., Nov. 1, 1859; s. George Washington and Sarah Elizabeth (Yates) H.; ed. pub. and pvt. schs. about 8 yrs.; m. Duett Ellison, Feb. 24, 1904. Ranchman on Salt River, Ariz., 1890-1900; became connected with Old Dominion Commercial Co., Globe, Ariz., 1890, sec., 1896—, pres., 1900—. Elected mem. Ariz. legislature, 1892, reëlected, 1894; elected to Upper House, 1896, 98, 1904, 06, 08 (pres. of council 1905, 09); pres. Constl. Conv., 1910; elected 1st gov. State of Ariz., Dec. 12, 1911; reëlected for terms 1914-19. Apptd. U.S. commr. of conciliation, 1917, to negotiate settlement of miners' strike in Arizona. Exponent of prison reform; pres. Anti-Capital Punishment League; apptd. Envoy Extraordinary and M.P. to Siam, Mar. 1920; resigned Oct. 1, 1921; again gov. of Ariz. terms, 1923-28 and 1931-33; elected chmn. Ariz. Colo. River Commn., 1927 and 1931. Home: Phoenix, Ariz. Died Dec. 24, 1934.

HUNT, Harry Hampton, elec. engr.; b. Melrose, Mass., Nov. 18, 1868; s. Harry and May Imogen (Covel) H.; S.B. in E.E., Mass. Inst. Tech., 1889; m. Louisa Cleaves Sargent, June 8, 1897; 1 dau., Helen. With Stone & Webster, Mar. 26, 1900—, admitted as member firm Jan. 1, 1920; v.p., May 26, 1920; chairman bd. Stone & Webster Service Corp.; dir. Stone & Webster Engring. Co., Stone & Webster Realty Corp., Tarrant County Traction Co., etc. Mem. Boston Chamber Commerce. Home: Melrose, Mass. Died Nov. 30, 1937.

HUNT, Henry Warren, real estate; b. Dorchester, Mass., Dec. 23, 1844; s. Charles and Louisa Minot (Wilson) H.; common sch. edn.; studied Boston Nautical Sch., 1861; vol. U.S.N. and Army, 1862; in charge Mass. marine exhibit, Centennial Expn., Phila., 1876; apptd. to Russian Navy, and decorated by Czar with order of St. Stanislaus, 1876; confidential marine agt. of Russia in America, 1878-81. Interested colossal real estate operations in Mass. water fronts, 1890—. Mem. Boston Dock Commn. Home: Dorchester, Mass. Died Jan. 16, 1915.

HUNT, Isaac Hamilton, lawyer; b. Fernandina, Fla., May 3, 1868; s. Walter Herbert and Susan (McCaughrin) H.; ed. Newberry Male Acad., Newberry Coll., S.C. Coll. (now U. of S.C.), Eastmans Bus. Coll., Poughkeepsie, N.Y.; m. Unity Elizabeth Gibson, June 27, 1906. Admitted to S.C. bar, 1894, and began practice at Newberry; dir. and atty. Oakland Cotton Mills, Mollohon Mfg. Co. (both divisions of Kendall Co.). Mem. legal advisory bd., Selective Draft, and govt. rep., Newberry Co., World War. Has acted as spl. asso. justice, Supreme Court; S.C., and spl. referee and commr., U.S. Dist. Court, Western Dist., S.C.; same, S.C. Circuit Court; mem. S.C. Ho. of Rep., 1925-26. Trustee Newberry County Hosp., Furman U. Vice pres. Bapt. State Conv., S.C., 1923, pres. gen. bd., 1925; mem. advisory council Yenching U., Peiping, China. Democrat. Mason. Home: Newberry, S.C. Died July 16, 1935.

HUNT, James Ramsay, M.D.; b. Phila., Pa., 1874; s. William R. and Eva (Ramsay) H.; M.D., U. of Pa., 1893, hon. Sc.D., 1931; studied Vienna, Berlin and Paris; m. Alice St. John Nolan, Sept. 26, 1908; children—James Ramsay, Alice St. John. Asso. prof. nervous diseases, Columbia, 1910-15; clin. prof. nervous diseases, Columbia, 1924; prof. clin. neurology, 1931—; director neuropsychiatric division, New York Neurol. Institute; cons. neurologist Psychiatric Inst., the Babies', N.Y. Eye and Ear and Lenox Hill hosps., and Letchworth Village for Mental Defectives; formerly cons. psychiatrist to Lying-In Hosp., New York Hospital and Randall's Island institutions. Consulting neuropathologist to Craig Colony for epileptics. Lt. Col. Medical Corps, U.S.A., World War; consultant in neuropsychiatry with A.E.F. Home: New York, N.Y. Died July 22, 1937.

HUNT, James Winford, clergyman, educator; b. Kaw Agency, Ind. Ty., July 9, 1875; s. William (Govt. physician) and Elizabeth (Pruitt) H.; grad. Central Plains Acad., Estacado, Tex., 1893; D.D., Central College, Fayette, Mo., 1927; LL.D., Asbury College, Wilmore, Ky., 1931; m. Mary Anthony, 1906; children—Anthony, Elizabeth, Julian, Margaret, David Glenn. Circuit rider, 1903-06; ordained ministry M.E. Ch., S., 1906; pastor successively Dumas, Channing Dalhart, Snyder, St. Paul's Ch., Abilene, Tex., until 1916; pres. Stamford (Tex.) Coll., 1916-18; again pastor St. Paul's Ch., 1918-21; founder, and pres. McMurry Coll., Abilene, 1921—. Mason. Democrat. Home: Abilene, Tex. Died Mar. 12, 1934.

HUNT, Leigh S. J.; s. Franklyn Leigh and Martha Long Leigh Hunt; m. Jessie Noble. Engaged in ednl. work and became pres. State Agrl. Coll. of Ia., at Ames, Ia., continuing until 1885; entered business career at Seattle, Wash., 1886, as owner and editor Seattle Post-Intelligencer; later organized the Oriental Consolidated Mines, Korea, and developed properties on an extensive scale; introduced cotton growing in the Anglo-Egyptian Soudan. Republican. Home: Las Vegas, Nev. Died Oct. 5, 1933.

HUNT, Mary Hannah, temperance reformer; b. S. Canaan, Conn., July 4, 1830; d. Ephraim and Nancy Hanchett; grad. Patapsco Inst., nr. Baltimore, Md.; teacher chemistry and physiology, same; m. Leander B. Hunt, 1852. Was attracted, 1874 and 1875, by some chem. experiments made by her son to scientific study of the nature and effects of alcoholic drinks and other narcotics; proposed compulsory instruction on that subject, in connection with physiology and hygiene, for all pupils in all public schools; drafted the laws for compulsory scientific temperance edn. now on statute books of Congress, all States of U.S. and some provinces of Canada, Chile and other countries; personally conducted campaigns which secured enactment of these laws, appearing as their advocate before Congress and the legislatures of State and Canadian provinces. Attended as del. from U.S. and was 1st v.p. Internat. Anti-alcoholic Congress, Brussels, under auspices of King of Belgium, 1897, and at Bremen, Apr. 1903; supt. for dept. Scientific Temperance Instruction for World's and Nat. W.C.T.U. from organization of dept., in 1880; life dir. Nat. Ednl. Assn. Edits and publishes School Physiology Journal, monthly. Was summoned to personal audience by German Empress to explain Am. system of temperance edn.; dir. Bureau Scientific Temperance Investigation. Died 1906.

HUNT, Ralph Hudson, M.D.; b. Camden, Me., Dec. 9, 1869; s. Abel and Evelina (Knight) H.; A.B., Bowdoin, 1891, A.M., 1893; M.D., Med. Sch. of Me. (Bowdoin), 1894; m. May Williams, June 6, 1903; 1 dau., May Hayward. Began practice, Portland, Me., 1894; removed to East Orange, N.J., 1899; attending phys., Orange Memorial Hosp., and phys.-in-chief to tuberculosis dispensary of same; mem. East Orange Bd. of Health, 1907—; pres. Essex Co. Mosquito Extermination Commn. Hosp. steward, Essex Troop, 1st Troop, N.G.N.J., 1905-09; commd. capt., Med. R.C., May 15, 1917; Med. O.T.C., Camp Greenleaf, Ft. Oglethorpe, Ga., Aug. 2, 1917; maj., M.C., U.S.A., Jan. 15, 1918; lt. col., May 2, 1919; regtl. surgeon 22d Cav. to Nov. 20, 1917, 80th F.A. to June 20, 1919; overseas service, Aug. 22, 1918-June 20, 1919; pres. med. bd., Camp Merritt, N.J., to Sept. 12, 1919. Unitarian. Fellow Am. Coll. Phys. Mason. Home: East Orange, N.J. Died July 9, 1928.

HUNT, Richard Howland, architect; b. Paris, France, Mar. 14, 1862; s. Richard Morris and Catharine C. H.; ed. Mass. Inst. Tech. and École des Beaux Arts, Paris; m. Pearl, d. Francis D. Carley; children—Richard Carley, Frank Carley, Jonathan; m. 2d, Margaret Livingston Watrous, d. S. Otis Livingston, 1891. From small sketch left by his father (a distinguished architect) completed new wing for Met. Mus. of Art; was architect Quintard Hall and Hoffman Hall, U. of the South; Kissan Hall, Vanderbilt U.; pvt. residences of Wm. K. and George W. Vanderbilt, Mrs. O. H. P. Belmont; etc. Fellow A.I.A. Home: New York, N.Y. Died July 12, 1931.

HUNT, Robert Woolston, metall. engineer; b. Fallsington, Pa., Dec. 9, 1838; s. Robert A. (M.D.) and Martha L. (Woolston) H.; ed. in Covington, Ky.; studied analyt. chemistry, Phila., 1859-60; (Dr. Engring., Rensselaer Poly. Inst., 1916); m. Eleanor Clark, Dec. 5, 1866. Worked in rolling mill at Pottsville, Pa.; chemist Cambria Iron Co., 1860-61; supt. steel works, Wyandotte, Mich., 1865-66, Cambria Iron Co., 1866-73, John A. Griswold & Co., Troy, N.Y., 1873-75, Troy Steel & Iron Co., 1875-88; head of Robert W. Hunt & Co., cons. engrs., iron insps., etc., 1888—. Served pvt. and sergt. Pa. Vols. and capt. in command Camp Curtin, Harrisburg, Pa., 1861-65. Trustee Rensselaer Poly. Institute. Awarded John Fritz Medal, 1912. Republican. Protestant. Home: Chicago, Ill. Died July 11, 1923.

HUNT, Samuel Furman, jurist; b. Springdale, O., Oct. 22, 1844; s. John Randolph (M.D.) and Amanda (Baird) H.; grad. Miami Univ., 1864, Cincinnati Law School, 1867 (LL.D., 1890, L.H.D., Univ. of Cincinnati; A.M., 1867, LL.D., 1893, L.H.D., 1896, Miami Univ.); unmarried. Admitted to bar, 1867; mem. Ohio State senate, 1870-71 (pres. pro tem); introduced bill organizing Univ. of Cincinnati; candidate for lt. gov., 1871; mem. Ohio Constl. Conv., 1873; judge advocate gen. of Ohio, 1878-79; chmn. Univ. Bd. of Cincinnati, 1878-90; judge Superior Court of Cincinnati, 1890-98. Home: Glendale, O. Died 1907.

HUNT, Sumner P., architect; b. Brooklyn, N.Y., May 8, 1865; s. Stephen P. and Harriet (Conklin) H.; ed. pvt. schs.; studied architecture in office of Clarence B. Cutler, of Troy, N.Y., and N.Y. City; m. Mary Hancock Chapman, Jan. 21, 1892; 1 dau., Louise. Settled in Los Angeles, Calif., 1889; was member Hunt & Burns until 1930; in practice alone, 1930—; architect of the South West Museum, Los Angeles Country Club Wilshire Country Club, Automobile Club, Ebell Club, Los Angeles Tennis Club, Roosevelt and Alhambra high schs., Robert Louis Stevenson Junior High Sch., Academic Hall, Scripps Coll., Claremont, Calif., Bancroft Jr. High Sch., new bldgs. Virgil Jr. High Sch., new Louis Pasteur Jr. High Sch.; also many residences, etc., in Los Angeles. Fellow Am. Inst. Architects. Home: Los Angeles, Calif. Died Nov. 19, 1938.

HUNT, Theodore Whitefield, university prof.; b. Metuchen, N.J., Feb. 19, 1844; s. Holloway W. and Henrietta (Mundy) H.; A.B., Princeton, 1865; Union Theol. Sem., 1866-68; grad. Princeton Theol. Sem., 1869; hon. Ph.D., Lafayette, 1880; Litt.D., Rutgers, 1890; tutor English, Princeton, 1868-71; studied U. of Berlin, 1871-72; m. Sarah Cooper Reeve, June 29, 1882. Ordained Presbyn. ministry, 1878; adj. prof. rhetoric and English lang., 1873-81, professor English language and literature, 1881-1918 (emeritus), Princeton U. Author: Ethical Teachings in Old English Literature, 1894; Literature—Its Principles and Problems, 1906; Timely Topics, 1921. Home: Princeton, N.J. Died Apr. 12, 1930.

HUNT, Thomas Forsyth, agriculturist; b. Ridott, Ill., Jan. 1, 1862; s. Thomas Marshall and Mary A. (Kirk) H.; B.Sc., U. of Ill., 1884, D.Agr., 1904; D.Sc., Mich. Agrl. Coll., 1907; m. Juniata G. Campbell, Aug. 22, 1888; children—Theodore Morrow, Marion Juliet. Asst. to Ill. State entomologist, 1885-86; asst. in agr., U. of Ill., 1886-88; asst. agriculturist, Ill. Agrl. Expt. Sta., 1888-91; prof. agr., Pa. State Coll., 1891-92; prof. agr., 1892-1903, dean Coll. Agr. and Domestic Science, 1896-1903, Ohio State U.; registrar Grad. Sch., held at Ohio State U., 1902; prof. agronomy, Cornell U., 1903-07; dean Sch. of Agr. and dir. Pa. Agrl. Expt. Sta. of Pa. State Coll., 1907-12; dean Coll. of Agr., 1912-23, prof. agr., 1912—, U. of Calif., dir. Agrl. Expt. Sta. same 1912-19. Author: The Cereals in America, 1904; How to Choose a Farm, 1906; The Forage and Fiber Crops in America, 1907; The Young Farmer, 1913; Soil and Crops (with Charles W. Burkett), 1913; Farm Animals (with Charles W. Burkett), 1914. Home: Berkeley, Calif. Died Apr. 26, 1927.

HUNT, William Southworth, newspaper editor and pub.; b. Newark, N.J., Jan. 17, 1879; s. William Tallmadge and Lucy Bardine (Southworth) H.; grad. St. George's Hall, Summit, N.J., 1896; A.B., Yale, 1901, A.M., 1903; m. Lorentha Storms Lum, Sept. 9, 1903; 1 dau., Alice Southworth (Mrs. Charles Edward Burton, Jr.). Reporter N.Y. Herald, 1901-03, Newark Sunday Call, 1903-19; editor Newark Star-Eagle, 1919-24; mng. editor Newark Sunday Call, 1924-32; pres. Newark Call Printing and Pub. Co., 1932—. Mem. bd. mgrs. Howard Savings Inst.; mem. exec. com. Newark Pubs. Assn. N.J. labor statistician, 1904; pres. South Orange Village, 1919-23; commr. N.J. State budget, 1924-25; pres. bd. trustees N.J. Training Sch. for Women, 1926-31. Progressive Republican. Episcopalian. Mason. Author: Frank Forester, 1927. Home: South Orange, N.J. Died Jan. 26, 1940.

HUNTER, Adison I., banking; b. Freetown, Ind., July 29, 1860; s. Cyrus R. and Margaret A.; student Depauw U., 1879-82; m. Alice C. Bailey, Feb. 6, 1889; 1 dau., Alice M. Chmn. bd. First Nat. Bank, Grand Forks; pres. First Nat. Bank (Munich N.D.),

First State Bank (Gilby, N.D.), Red River Valley Brick Corp.; v.p. Arvilla (N.D.) State Bank, Grand Forks St. Ry. Co. Trustee Jamestown Coll. Republican. Presbyn. Home: Grand Forks, N.D. Deceased.

HUNTER, Alexander Stuart, college prof.; b. Bavington, Pa.; s. Joseph and Margaret (Stewart) H.; A.B., Washington and Jefferson, 1880, A.M., 1883, LL.D., 1902; grad. Western Theol. Sem., 1885; Ph.D., U. of Wooster, 1888; m. Laetitia Hunter, Dec. 31, 1885; children—Laetitia, Alexander Hays, Joseph Fisher. Licensed by Presbytery of Washington, Pa., 1885; pastor-elect Brownsville, Pa., 1886; prof. physics and astronomy, 1887-90, ethics and English lit., 1890-95, Hanover Coll.; prof. ethics and English lit., Western U. of Pa. (now U. of Pittsburgh), 1895—. Pres. Pittsburgh Bd. of trade 2 terms; pres. bd. of trustees Presbyn. Hosp.; mem. Chamber Commerce. Presbyn. Author: Ethics—Theoretical and Practical, 1900. Home: Pittsburgh, Pa. Died July 31, 1926.

HUNTER, Alfred M., army officer; b. in Ill., Jan. 21, 1864; s. Nelson F. and Elizabeth (Williamson) H.; grad. U.S. Mil. Acad., 1887, grad. Arty. Sch., 1896, Army War Coll., 1909; m. Elizabeth Martin, Oct. 19, 1904. Commd. 2d lt. 5th Cav., June 12, 1887; trans. to 4th Arty., Apr. 3, 1888; 1st lt. 1st Arty., Mar. 22, 1894; promoted through grades to col. Coast Arty. Corps, Aug. 25, 1915. With siege train 5th Army Corps, campaign against Santiago, Cuba, 1898; comd. Ft. Mott, N.J., 1899-1901; observer for Bd. of Ordnance and Fortification, at Sandy Hook, N.J., and Ft. Riley, Kan., 1901-02; comdr. Ft. Fremont, S.C., 1903-04, Ft. Rodman, Mass., 1906-07, Ft. Constitution, N.H., and Arty. Dist. of Portsmouth, 1907-08, Army War Coll., 1908-09, Ft. Mott, N.J., 1909-10; duty hdqrs. Dept. of the Gulf and hdqrs. Eastern Dept., 1910-14; Ft. Winfield Scott, Calif., 1914-16; comdg. coast defense of Oahu, Honolulu, 1916-17; comd. S. Pacific Coast Arty. Dist., San Francisco, Sept. 1917-Jan. 1919. Died May 12, 1929.

HUNTER, George King, army officer; b. Lancaster, O., Apr. 6, 1855; s. Henry B. and Josephine L. (King) H.; grad. U.S. Mil. Acad., 1877; m. Mary E. Hinman, Dec. 17, 1878. Commd. additional 2d lt., 4th Cav., June 15, 1877; promoted through grades to brig. gen. N.A., Aug. 5, 1917. Participated in numerous Indian campaigns; wounded at Battle of San Juan Hill, Cuba, July 1, 1898; actively engaged in subduing Philippine Insurrection, 1899-1903; assigned to duty Camp Funston, Kan., 1917; retired, Feb. 1, 1918; comd. Jefferson Barracks, Mo., Feb. 22, 1918-July 28, 1919. Mem. Loyal Legion, Soc. Foreign Wars, Mil. Order Carabao, S.A.R. Episcopalian. Home: Cleveland, O. Died Feb. 2, 1940.

HUNTER, George Leland, author; b. Bellingham, Mass., May 8, 1867; grad. Phillips Exeter Acad., N.H., 1885; A.B., Harvard, 1889; m. Esther Kennedy Boardman, Mar. 24, 1913. Writer, lecturer on tapestries and other decorative subjects; decorative art editor, new edit. New Internat. Ency., 1914. Author: Tapestries, Their Origin, History and Renaissance, 1912; Home Furnishing, 1913; Inside the House that Jack Built, 1914; Italian Furniture and Interiors, 1917; Decorative Textiles, 1918; Decorative Furniture, 1923; Practical Book of Tapestries, 1925; Tapestries of Clarence H. Mackay, 1925. Home: Redding, Conn., and New York, N.Y. Died Oct. 30, 1927.

HUNTER, Hubert Samuel, newspaper editor; b. Shelby County, Ill., Aug. 12, 1886; s. Robert and Sophronia Jane (Longenbaugh) H.; A.B., Stanford U., 1908; m. Willa Frances Hickman, Sept. 18, 1909; children—Hubert Shipley, Allen Martin, Charles Benton Hickman, Phyllis Ann. Reporter and managing editor Ariz. Democrat, Phoenix, 1909; reporter, news editor, editorial writer Tucson (Ariz.) Citizen, 1910-13; asst. news editor and editorial writer El Paso (Tex.) Herald, 1913-19; Asso. Press Bureau mgr. for Ariz. and N.M., 1919-21; asst. to editor El Paso Herald, 1921-29; editor El Paso Herald and Times, 1929-31, editor El Paso Times, 1931—; dir. El Paso Times, Inc. Lt. col. on staff Gov. of Tex. Republican. Home: El Paso, Tex. Deceased.

HUNTER, James Boyd, clergyman, editor; b. Irvine, Ayrshire, Scotland, Apr. 5, 1863; s. Peter Carmichael and Mary Masson (Boyd) H.; came with parents to U.S., 1867; A.B., Princeton, 1889, A.M., 1892; grad. Union Theol. Sem., 1892; D.D., Central College, Pella, Iowa, 1930; m. Harriet Condit Leake, Oct. 4, 1892; children—James Boyd, Paul Rutherfurd. Ordained ministry Presbyn. Ch., U.S.A., 1892, Ref. Ch. in America, 1898; pastor N.Y. City, 1892-1908, Jersey City, 1909-23; lit. editor The Church Economist, 1896-99; editor The Christian Intelligencer, 1920—. Republican. Mason. Home: River Edge, N.J. Died Mar. 18, 1933.

HUNTER, John Lathrop, lawyer; b. Gardiner, Me., March 13, 1834; s. John Patten and Mary Averill (Stone) H.; grad. Bowdoin Coll., Me., 1855; studied law; admitted to bar, Me., 1859; Conn., 1871; has practiced law in Willimantic, Conn., 1871—; state's atty., Windham Co., 1894—; m. Mary Lyon Cheesebrough, Nov. 1882. Home: Willimantic, Conn. Died 1903.

HUNTER, Paull Stuart, physician; b. Morgantown, W.Va., Mar. 29, 1877; s. Rev. Stephen A. (LL.D.) and Sarah Moreland H.; B.A., U. of W.Va., 1899; M.D., U. of Colo., 1904; m. Cora May Allen, May 6, 1908. Practiced, Denver, 1904; mem. Colo. State Bd. of Health, 1908-15, sec. and exec. officer, 1911-15. Interpreter to chief surgeon U.S.A. in China relief expdn., 1900, and corr. Pittsburgh Press during the expdn.; platform lecturer on China, 1900—. Democrat. Presbyn. Sec.-treas. Colo. Assn. Health Officers, 1914—. Discovered and made public a new process of bone shadow photography and skiagraphy without X rays, 1919. Home: Denver, Colo. Died Oct. 20, 1923.

HUNTER, Rudolph Melville, consulting engr.; b. N.Y. City, June 20, 1856; s. Robert (M.D.) and Sarah (Barton) H.; M.E., Polytechnic Coll. State of Pa., 1878; m. Emilie M. Phillips, Aug. 1879. Began in Cincinnati, O., making distillery plans for U.S. Govt., 1871; gen. engineering and patents, Ironton, Ohio, blast furnaces and steel works, 1874-75, Chicago, 1875-76, Phila., 1877; developed spl. process for mfg. gas at Coney Island, N.Y., 1878; organizer Atlantic & Pacific Electric Mfg. Co., 1879; developed and patented transformer system of electric power and lighting, 1879-86; developed complete electric railway systems, 1881-89; placed before Brit. Parliament elec. ry. plan for proposed tunnel, Dover to Calais, May 1883; developed submarine vessel, 1879-81, and pub. pamphlet on torpedo boats, 1882; sold telephone patents to Am. Bell Telephone Co., 1882; tests, smokeless powder for French Govt., 1883-84; demonstrated submarine inventions before members of Congress, 1885; sold electric transformer system inventions to Westinghouse Electric Co., 1886; organized Hunter Electric Co., 1886-87; organized Elec. Car Co. of America, 1887; sold many patents to Thomson-Houston Electric Co. and retained as elec. engr. and patent counsel by said co., 1889, and continued by General Electric Co. for 22 yrs.; later licenses, covering about 300 patents, granted to General Electric Co. and to Westinghouse Elec. & Mfg. Co.; designed and built first moving picture projector in the world, 1894; organized Gen. Electric Automobile Co., 1898, Tractor Truck Automobile Co., 1899, etc.; inventor of many devices now in use by various corps.; pres. Electric Car Co. of America, U.S. Assay & Bullion Co., The Mirabile Corp., Hunter Pressed Steel Co.; dir. Herr Automatic Press Co., etc. Expert of Victor Talking Machine Co. with spl. reference to acoustics. Original research, 1902—, include breaking down and reconstruction of atomic matter; "growth" of cells, and discovering of nature's processes in multiplying atoms; causes for different members of the elements in various stars and sun from those of the earth; physical properties of atomic structure; has discovered and commercialized transmutation of the elements, duplicating nature's processes in creating the precious metals; cause of gravitation; etc. Republican. Episcopalian. Home: Philadelphia, Pa. Died Mar. 20, 1935.

HUNTER, Stephen Alexander, clergyman; b. Christiana, Pa., Mar. 23, 1851; s. Rev. William and Ann Eliza (Heard) H.; B.A., Washington and Jefferson Coll., 1874; grad. Western Theol. Sem., 1876; M.D., Jefferson Med. Coll., Phila., 1878; (LL.D., W.Va. U., 1892; Ph.D., Western U. of Pa., 1895); m. Sarah H. Moreland, June 3, 1875. Ordained Presbyn. ministry, 1877; missionary in China, 1879-91; pastor W. Bridgewater, Pa., 1892-94, S. Side Presbyn. Ch., Pittsburgh, 1894-1904, Sheraden Church, Pittsburgh, 1904-12, Arlington Heights, Pittsburgh, 1914-20. Author: A Manual of Therapeutics and Pharmacy (in Chinese), with an introduction by H. E. Li Hung Chang, Prime Minister of China, 1890; An Analysis of the Book of Hebrews (in Chinese), 1890; Studies in the Book of Revelation (a Bible sch. manual), 1921. Home: Pittsburgh, Pa. Died Feb. 20, 1923.

HUNTER, Walter David, entomologist; b. Lincoln, Neb., Dec. 14, 1875; s. Joseph H. and Mary Abbey (Crooker) H.; A.B., U. of Neb., 1895, A.M., 1897; (LL.D., Tulane U. of La., 1916); m. Mary P., d. of Dr. E. H. Smith, of Victoria, Tex., Mar. 1906. Asst. entomologist, U. of Neb., 1895-1900, Ia. Agrl. Expt. Sta., 1901; asst. entomologist in charge of boll weevil investigation, Bur. of Entomology, U.S. Dept. Agr., 1902-05; in charge southern field crop insect investigations and mem. Federal Hort. Bd., in charge field work against pink boll worm of cotton, 1908. Died Oct. 13, 1925.

HUNTER, William Armstrong, clergyman; b. Peterboro, Ont., Can., Mar. 23, 1855; s. William and Anne (Armstrong) H.; B.A., Toronto U., 1877, M.A., 1879; Ph.D., Illinois W. Univ., 1896; (D.D., U. of Denver, 1902); m. Lizzie Chambers, d. Capt. Chambers, of Woodstock, Ont., Oct. 12, 1881 (died 1894); m. 2d, Sara B. Holden, d. J. C. Holden, of Montreal, Can., Jan. 3, 1901. Ordained Presbyn. ministry, 1880; pastor Parkdale Ch., Toronto, 1880-88, Erskine Ch., Toronto, 1888-89, First Av. Ch., Denver, Colo., 1899-1909, Calvary Ch., Riverside, Calif., 1909—. Moderator Presbytery of Toronto, 1892, Synod of Colo. and Wyo., 1906, Synod of Calif. and Nev., 1912. Home: Riverside, Calif. Died Feb. 21, 1920.

HUNTER, William Forrest, lawyer; b. Woodsfield, O., May 26, 1839; s. William Forrest and Mary (Kinkeade) H.; ed. pub. schs., Woodsfield; studied law under late Justice John W. Okey (Supreme Court, Ohio) and at law sch., U. of Mich.; m. Elizabeth Fitz Randolph, Jan. 1, 1867. Admitted to Ohio bar, 1861; served in Union army; adj. 62d O.V.I., capt. 97th O.V.I.; served on staffs Gens. Wagner and Woods, in Army of the Cumberland; shot in mouth in charge on Missionary Ridge. Resumed practice after war; counsel for ry. cos. Republican. Dean Coll. of Law, Ohio State Univ., 1892—. Home: Columbus, O. Died 1904.

HUNTING, George Coolidge, bishop; b. Milwaukee, Wis., Oct. 22, 1871; s. George Coolidge and Mary Ann (Ladd) H.; Va. Theol. Sem., 1894 (D.D., 1914); m. Mary Grace Pullman, Oct. 15, 1894. Deacon, 1894, priest, 1897, P.E. Ch.; in charge St. Paul's Ch., Virginia City, Nev., 1894-98; gen. missionary Nev. and Utah, 1898-99; rector St. Paul's Ch., Evanston, Wyo., 1899-1902; supt. and chaplain St. Mark's Hosp., Salt Lake City, 1902-07; missionary, Ely, Nev., 1907-12; sec. 8th Missionary Province, P.E. Ch., 1912-15; consecrated bishop of Nev., Dec. 16, 1914. Sec. of Convocation, 1899-1912; examining chaplain, 1899-1912. Editor The Nevada Churchman, 1909-11. Mason. Home: Reno, Nev. Died Feb. 6, 1924.

HUNTINGTON, Adoniram Judson, emeritus prof. Greek, Columbian Univ.; b. Braintree, Vt., 1818; s. Rev. Elijah Huntington; ed. Braintree, Vt., Randolph, Vt., 1833-36; grad. Columbian Coll., Washington; A.B., 1843; A.M., 1846; (D.D., Brown Univ., 1868); m. Bettie G. Christian, 1844. Taught in Columbian Coll. and Univ., at 3 different periods, beginning 1843 and ending 1900, in all 47 yrs.; tutor Latin and Greek, 1843-46; prof. Latin and Greek, 1846-49, 1852-59, 1866-82; prof. Greek, 1882-1900; dean Columbian Coll., 1897-1900; prof. mental and moral philosophy, Corcoran School, 1884. Bapt. preacher and pastor, 1849-52, 1859-65. Deceased.

HUNTINGTON, Charles Pratt, architect; b. Logansport, Ind., Nov. 22, 1871; s. Capt. Edward Stanton (U.S.A.) and Julia A. (Pratt) H.; A.B., Harvard, 1893; studied École des Beaux Arts, Paris, 6 yrs., Certificat d'Études, 1901; m. Maude Mary Bagly, of England, May 5, 1894; m. 2d, Eleanor Moretti, Sept. 11, 1913. Practiced in New York, 1903—; architect of buildings of Hispanic Soc. of America, Am. Geog. Soc., Am. Numismatic Soc. (all of New York), also Ch. of Our Lady of Hope, etc. Republican. Home: New York, N.Y. Died Oct. 15, 1919.

HUNTINGTON, Clarence William, ry. consultant; b. Newark, N.J., May 31, 1857; m. Edith Chapin, May 23, 1883; children—William Chapin, Mrs. Helen Berryhill, John Chadwick. Began as freight brakeman, C.R.I.&P. Ry., 1876; asst. supt. and supt. Des Moines Northern & Western Ry.; gen. supt. Ia. Central Ry., 1894-1902; gen. supt. Central R.R. of N.J., 1902-14; v.p. and gen. mgr. Minneapolis and St. Louis R.R., 1914-17; pres. Virginian Ry., 1917-25. Pres. Bd. of Mgrs. New Jersey State Prison. Home: Elizabeth, N.J. Died July 12, 1927.

HUNTINGTON, Collis Potter, pres. Southern Pacific R.R. Co.; b. Harwinton, Conn., Oct. 22, 1821; went to Calif., 1848; became hardware merchant in Sacramento. With Leland Stanford, Charles Crocker and Mark Hopkins, built the Central Pacific and Southern Pacific railroads; later he built Chesapeake and Ohio and other railroads, making a continuous system from San Francisco to Newport News, Va. Died 1900.

HUNTINGTON, Daniel, artist; b. New York, Oct. 14, 1816; s. Benjamin H.; ed. Hamilton Coll.; m. Sophia Richards, 1842; studied art, 1835, with Samuel F. B. Morse, then pres. Nat. Acad. Design; painted that yr. "The Bar-Room Politician" and "A Toper Asleep." Subsequently painted several landscapes, but later portraits and figure pieces, with a number of hist. canvases; portraits of Abraham Lincoln, Martin Van Buren, Albert Gallatin; Gens. Grant, Sherman, Sheridan and Admiral Dupont and others of the Civil war; full length portraits of Mrs. Hayes and Mrs. Harrison (at White House); also Louis Agassiz, John Sherman, William Cullen Bryant, etc. Also figure pieces "Mercy's Dream," "Sacred Lesson," "Philosophy and Christian Art," "Mrs. Washington's Reception," "The Good Samaritan," "Righteousness and Peace," "The Atlantic Cable Projectors," and upwards of 40 portraits in collection of New York Chamber of Commerce. Asso., 1839, academician, 1840—, pres. 1862-69 and 1877-91, Nat. Acad. Design; one of founders Century Assn., Met. Mus. of Art (v.p. several yrs.); life mem. Am. Geog. Soc., N.Y. Hist Society. Died 1906.

HUNTINGTON, David Lynde, pres. Washington Water Power Co.; b. New London, Conn., Oct. 18, 1870; s. David Low and Gertrude Elizabeth (Shoemaker) H.; Ph.B., Yale, 1891; hon. M.S., Wash. State Coll., 1916; m. Helen Longacre, Dec. 8, 1896. With Thomson-Houston Electric Co., 1891-92; asst. engr. Gen. Electric Co., Phila., 1892-94; with Washington Water Power Co., Spokane, Wash., 1894—, pres., 1910—; dir. Washington Water Power Co. Fellow Am. Inst. E.E. Republican. Home: Spokane, Wash. Died Sept. 27, 1929.

HUNTINGTON, DeWitt Clinton, univ. prof.; b. Townsend, Vt., Apr. 27, 1830; s. Ebenezer and Lydia (Peck) H.; alumnus of Syracuse U., N.Y. (D.D.,

Genesee Coll., 1868; D.D., Syracuse U., 1874, LL.D., 1900, L.H.D., 1906); m. Mary E. Moore, May 24, 1853 (died 1866); m. 2d, Frances H. Davis, Oct. 27, 1868. Entered M.E. ministry, May 1853; pastor Rochester, N.Y., 1861-71; presiding elder, 1871-73; pastor Syracuse, 1873-76, Rochester, 1876-79; presiding elder, 1879-82; pastor Bradford, Pa., 1882-85, 1889-91, Olean, N.Y., 1885-89, Lincoln, Neb., 1891-96; presiding elder, 1896-98; chancellor, 1898-1908, prof. English Bible, June 1908—, Neb. Wesleyan U. Died 1912.

HUNTINGTON, Emily, educator, writer; b. Lebanon, Conn., Jan. 3, 1841; d. Dan and Emily (Wilson) H.; moved to Norwich, Conn., in infancy; ed. Wheaton Sem., Norton, Mass.; unmarried. Went to New York, 1872; took charge of Wilson Industrial Sch. for Girls, first of kind in this country; lived there 20 yrs.; started 1st boys' club, 1st kitchen garden, and 1st small centers for teaching children cookery in U.S. Author: Child's Kitchen Garden Primer, 1884; Introductory Cooking Lessons; Cooking Garden; Little Housekeeper, 1873; How to Teach Kitchen Garden, 1903. Died 1909.

HUNTINGTON, Frank, writer, editor; b. Rochester, N.Y., July 14, 1848; s. Elon and Annjeannette (Cole) H.; A.B., U. of Rochester, 1868; studied Coll. of Law (Columbia), univs. of Berlin and Munich; unmarried. Recorded polit. mil. and commercial history of all foreign countries except Japan and Korea, in Appleton's Ann. Cyclo., 1874-1902; on staff Johnson's Cyclo., 1873-74, Appleton's Cyclo. Am. Biography, 1886-88, Standard Dictionary, 1891-93; in service U.S. Govt., 1902—, editing, translating and making bibliog. researches; worked on Dictionary of Am. Indians, assisted in Bureau Ethnology; with Dept. of Agr., 1907—. Home: Washington, D.C. Died Feb. 27, 1928.

HUNTINGTON, Frederic Dan, first P.E. bishop of Central N.Y.; consecrated April 8, 1869; b. Hadley, Mass., May 28, 1819; s. Rev. Dan H.; grad. Amherst Coll., 1839 (S.T.D., Amherst and Columbia; LL.D., Amherst; L.H.D., Syracuse Univ.); grad. Harvard Divinity School; m. Hannah Dane Sargent, 1843. Ordained pastor South Congl. Ch., Boston (Unitarian), but in 1860 withdrew from that denomination and was ordered deacon in P.E. Ch.; ordained priest, 1861. Prof. and preacher Harvard Coll., 1855-60; later lecturer Episcopal Theol. Sem., Cambridge, Mass., and Gen. Theol. Sem., New York; rector Emmanuel Ch., Boston, 1861-69. Was consecutively editor The Christian Register, The Monthly Religious Magazine, The Church Monthly. Author: Helps to a Holy Lent; New Helps to a Holy Lent; Sermons for the People; The Fitness of Christianity to Man; Unconscious Tuition; etc. Died 1904.

HUNTINGTON, George, educator; b. Brooklyn, Conn., Nov. 5, 1835; s. Rev. Thomas (M.D.) and Paulina (Clark) H.; A.B., Brown U., 1863; Andover Theol. Sem., 1864-65; (hon. A.M., Beloit, 1879; Litt.D., Carleton, 1911); m. Caroline A. Mason, June 30, 1863 (died 1912); m. 2d, Margaret J. Evans, L.H.D., Nov. 7, 1914. Ordained to the Congregational ministry, 1863; pastor Central Village, Conn., 1863-64, Providence, R.I., 1865-70, Oak Park, Ill., 1870-79; professor of rhetoric and logic, 1879-1900, rhetoric and Bibl. lit., 1900-04, asso. prof. Bibl. lit., and librarian, 1904-06, Carleton Coll.; retired on Carnegie Foundation, 1906. Editor The Scholar, juvenile mag., and The Sunday School Teacher, Chicago, 1874-76. Author: Charms of the Old Book, 1909. Six of these books first published serially in The Advance, Chicago. Died Jan. 2, 1916.

HUNTINGTON, George Sumner, surgeon; b. Hartford, Conn., Mar. 21, 1861; s. Hezekiah and Katherine Brinley (Sumner) H.; A.B., Trinity Coll., Hartford, 1881, A.M., 1884; M.D., Coll. Phys. and Surg. (Columbia), 1884, Sc.D., 1904; m. Annie McNair Elderkin, June 18, 1885. Interne Roosevelt Hosp., 1884-86; asst. demonstrator of anatomy, 1886-88, demonstrator and lecturer 1888-89, prof. anatomy, May 1899—, Columbia; asst. attending surgeon, Roosevelt Hosp., 1887, Bellevue Hosp., 1887; chief surg. clinic Vanderbilt Clinic, 1888. Am. editor, Journal of Anatomy and Physiology, 1899—. Home: New York, N.Y. Died Jan. 5, 1927.

HUNTINGTON, Harwood, clergyman, author; b. New Haven, Conn., Dec. 1, 1861; s. John Taylor (D.D.) and Elisabeth Tracy (Williams) H.; A.B., cum honore in chemistry, Trinity Coll., Conn., 1884; studied in Europe, 3 yrs.; Ph.D., Columbia, 1894; m. Grace Goodhue, Feb. 22, 1908. Admitted to bar, 1895, and practiced at New York; deacon, 1906, priest, 1907, P.E. Ch.; missionary in China and Korea, 1908; rector Hot Springs, Va., 1913-17 (retired) volunteer chaplain Army camps in southern Fla. Republican. Author: Chemical Jurisprudence, 1900; Year Book for Chemists, 1900; "Cui Bono?" 1912, 3d edit., 1914. Died at his home, Los Angeles, Calif., Jan. 1923.

HUNTINGTON, Henry Alonzo, soldier; b. Chicago, Mar. 23, 1840; s. Alonzo and Patience Lorain (Dyer) H.; ed. Phillips Acad., Andover, Mass.; m. Frances S. Tucker. Began study of law in father's office at 19; raised a troop of cav. and was commd. 2d lt. 9th Ill. Cav., Oct. 9-Nov. 6, 1861; 2d lt. 4th U.S. Arty., Oct. 24, 1861; 1st lt., May 3, 1863; apptd. a.-d.-c. to Maj. Gen. Hallock, July 12, 1865; resigned Nov. 19, 1869. Bvtd. 1st lt., Apr. 7, 1862, for gallant and meritorious services at battle of Stone River, Tenn.; maj., Mar. 13, 1865, for same during the war. One of founders Chicago Civ. Service Reform League and for 2 yrs. v.p. Nat. Reform League. Mem. Am. Art Assn. (life), L'Association pour l'Encouragement des Etudes Grecques en France (both of Paris). Died 1907.

HUNTINGTON, Henry Edwards, ry. official; b. Oneonta, N.Y., Feb. 27, 1850; s. Solon and Harriet (Saunders) H.; ed. pub. and pvt. schs.; m. 1873, Mary E. Prentice; m. 2d, Mrs. Arabella D. Huntington, July 16, 1913. Began business life in hardware business in Oneonta, later in New York; lumberman at St. Albans, W.Va., 1874-80; supt. constrn. Chesapeake, Ohio & Southwestern Ry., 1880-84; supt., 1884, receiver, 1885, v.p. and gen. mgr., 1886-90, Ky. Central Ry.; v.p. and gen. mgr. Elizabeth, Lexington & Big Sandy, and Ohio Valley rys., 1890-92; 1st asst. to pres., 1892-1900, 2d v.p., Mar.-June 1900, later 1st v.p., S.P. Co.; pres. S.P. rys. of Ariz. and N.M., Carson & Colo. Ry., Market St. Cable Ry., San Francisco. Now chmn. bd. Newport News (Va.) Shipbuilding & Dry Dock Co., Safety Insulated Wire & Cable Co. (New York); pres. Huntington Land & Imp. Co. (Calif), Huntington-Redondo Co. (Calif.), Los Angeles Ry. Land Co., Los Angeles Ry. Corp., Oak Knoll Co.; v.p. San Gabriel Valley Water Co. Mem. New York, Los Angeles and Newport News chambers of commerce, Los Angeles Realty Bd. Life mem. Am. Mus. Natural History, Am. Asiatic Assn., Am. Defense Soc., Am. Red Cross, Am. Forestry Assn., Bibliog. Soc. America, Bibliog. Soc. London. Owns one of the finest pvt. collections of English lit. and Americana in the world, including the original mss. of Benjamin Franklin's autobiography, the first collection of Washington mss., largest pvt. collection of Lincoln letters and mss., etc. Home: San Marino, Calif. Died May 23, 1927.

HUNTINGTON, James Otis Sargent, clergyman; b. Boston, Mass., July 23, 1854; s. Frederick Dan and Hannah Dane (Sargent) H.; B.A., Harvard, 1875; student St. Andrew's Divinity Sch., 1876-79; D.D., Nashotah (Wis.) House, 1924. Deacon, 1878, priest, 1880, P.E. Ch.; asst. Calvary Mission, Syracuse, N.Y., 1875-81, Holy Ch. Mission, New York, 1881-89; joined order of the Holy Cross, West Park, N.Y., 1884; superior same various periods and 1921—. Died June 29, 1935.

HUNTINGTON, Margaret Evans, educator; b. Utica, N.Y., Jan. 9, 1842; d. Daniel M. and Sarah (James) Evans (Welsh ancestry); A.B., Lawrence U., 1869, A.M., 1872, preceptress, 1870-74; studied Paris and Berlin, 1878-79; Berlin, Heidelberg and Oxford, 1892-93; (L.H.D., Lawrence, 1898); m. Rev. George Huntington, L.H.D., Nov. 7, 1914. Prof. English lit. and dean women's dept., Carleton Coll., 1874-1908. Chmn. Minn. State Pub. Library Commission Pres. Minn. Congl. Woman's Bd. Missions, 1879-1914; 1st woman corporate mem. A.B.C.F.M.; pres. Minn. Federation Women's Clubs, 1895-99; chmn. ednl. com., 1896-1900 and 1902-04, 2d v.p., 1900-02, hon. v.p., 1908—, General Fedn. Women's Clubs; chairman Minn. State Pub. Library Assn., 1900—. Home: Northfield, Minn. Died Mar. 17, 1926.

HUNTINGTON, Oliver Whipple, teacher; b. Marietta, O., June 9, 1858; s. James Freman and Ellen (Whipple) H.; A B., Harvard, 1881, A.M., 1882; Ph.D., 1883; studied at The Sorbonne, Paris, and traveled over Europe, Egypt and the East; m. Ellen Balch, Aug. 30, 1886. Asst. and instr. mineralogy and chemistry, Harvard, 1882-94; studied schs. in Europe 1 yr.; founded, 1896, Cloyne House Sch., Newport, R.I. Publisher the Cloyne Magazine, 1897—. Fellow Am. Acad. Arts and Sciences; pres. Newport Natural History Soc.; v.p. N.E. Fedn. of Harvard Clubs. Loaned the Cloyne House Sch. to Navy Dept. for duration of war; worked for the Navy Dept. during war. Retired. Home: Newport, R.I. Died Aug. 22, 1924.

HUNTINGTON, Theodore Sollace, banker; b. Columbus, O., Sept. 2, 1873; s. Pelatiah Webster and Frances (Sollace) H.; grad. Lawrenceville (N.J.) Sch., 1891; A.B., Princeton, 1895; m. Grace Livingston Lee, Jan. 29, 1902 (died 1908); 1 son, Theodore Lee; m. 2d, Mary E. Bugh, Aug. 4, 1914. Began with P. W. Huntington & Co., bankers, Columbus, 1895; treas. Beaumont & Chauncey Coal Co., 1897-99; mem. P. W. Huntington & Co., 1899-1905; cashier, Huntington Nat. Bank, 1905-13, v.p., 1913-28, pres., 1928-32, chmn. bd., 1932—; pres. Greenlawn Cemetery Assn. Republican. Home: Columbus, O. Died Jan. 1937.

HUNTINGTON, Thomas Waterman, surgeon; b. Rockford, Ill., Jan. 16, 1849; s. Charles A. and Lucretia A. (Waterman) H.; A.B., U. of Vt., 1871, LL.D., 1913; M.D., Harvard, 1876; m. Harriet O. Pearson, Nov. 1882; children—Thomas Waterman, Emily H. Surgeon Southern Pacific Hosp., 1882-99; prof. surgery, 1899-1912 (emeritus), U. of Calif.; chief surgeon, Western Pacific R.R. Co., Aug. 1910—. Fellow Am. Surg. Assn. (v.p. 1906-07). Mem. Am. Red Cross Commn. to Italy, 1917. Home: San Francisco, Calif. Died Apr. 19, 1929.

HUNTINGTON, Tuley Francis, author and printer; b. near Barrington, Ill., Sept. 23, 1770; s. Seth Phinney and Angeline (Kelsey) H.; A.B., Cornell Coll. (Ia.) 1892, Litt.D., 1912, A.M., Harvard, 1894; m. Ada McKee, Sept. 21, 1892; children—Frances, Katharine (Mrs. David Coit Elliott), Hartley (dec.), Evelyn Hope (Mrs. Theodore Kesler Sterling), Virginia. Instr. in English, Lake Forest (Ill.) U., 1894-96; head of dept. of English, S. Side High Sch., Milwaukee, Wis., 1896-99; instr. English, Stanford U., 1899-1900; owner apricot ranch, Los Altos, Calif., 1900-16; mfrs. agt., 1905—; author, creator, and printer of fine books, 1928—. Author: Elements of English Composition, 1903; Elementary English Compositioun, 1907; The Acre of the Earth Turner, 1929; (prose poems) Iron Rain and Green, 1929; Jacqueline of Very Near, 1931; The Lagday Letter, 1932—. Home: Palo Alto, Calif. Died May 4, 1938.

HUNTINGTON, Warner Dare, mfg. chemist; b. Sandusky, O., Apr. 19, 1874; s. Henry Clay and Josephine Holden (Warner) H.; grad. Sandusky High Sch.; student Oberlin Coll. 3 yrs.; m. Ola Craige Gibbins, June 4, 1902; children—Josephine Warner (Mrs. Robt. P. Bradford), William Henry; m. 2d, Edna Alice Gery Thomas, May 13, 1933. In business with father until 1898; served in Spanish-Am. War, 1898; sales mgr. Jarecki Chem. Co., 1899-1903, Buffalo Fertilizer Co., 1903-09; mgr. Internat. Agrl. Corp., 1909-15; v.p. Davidson Chem. Co., fertilizer and chemicals, 1915—; dir. fertilizer sales, Am. Cyanamid Co., N.Y. City, 1932—; v.p. Silica Gel Corp., Southern Phosphate Co.—both of Baltimore; treas. Va. Barrel Co. Chmn. acid com. War Industries Board, 1917-18. Chmn. soil improvement com. Nat. Fertilizer Assn., 1915-29; v.p. Nat. Fertilizer Assn., 1916-18, pres., 1918-20. Presbyn. Died Nov. 26, 1938.

HUNTINGTON, William Edwards, university pres.; b. Hillsboro, Ill., July 30, 1844; s. William Pitkin and Lucy (Edwards) H.; pvt. 40th and 1st lt. 49th Wis. Inf., 1864-65; A.B., U. of Wis., 1870, A.M., 1874; B.D., Boston U., 1873, Ph.D., 1882; S.T.D., Syracuse, and Wesleyan, 1903; LL.D., U. of Wis., 1904, Tufts, 1905, Boston U., 1923; m. Ella M. Speare, May 10, 1881. Ordained M.E. ministry, 1868; pastor Nahant, Mass., 1870-71, Roslindale, 1872-75, Newton, 1875-76, Cambridge, 1877-79, Boston, 1880-82; dean Coll. Liberal Arts, 1882-1904, pres., 1904-11, dean Grad. Dept., 1911-17 (pres. emeritus), Boston U. Home: Newton Centre, Mass. Died Dec. 6, 1930.

HUNTINGTON, William Reed, P.E. clergyman; b. Lowell, Mass., Sept. 20, 1838; grad. Harvard, 1859 (D.D., Columbia, Princeton, Harvard, Yale; D.C.L., Univ. of South; L.H.D., Hobart; LL.D., Union); m. Theresa, d. late Dr. Edward Reynolds, Boston, and niece Wendell Phillips, 1863. Deacon, 1861; priest, 1862; curate Emmanuel Ch., Boston, 1861-62; rector All Saints Ch., Worcester, Mass., 1862-83; rector Grace Ch., New York, 1883—. Author: The Spiritual House, 1895; Sonnets and a Dream, 1899; A Good Shepherd and other Sermons, 1907. Died 1909.

HUNTLEY, Charles R., corp. official; b. West Winfield, N.Y., Oct. 12, 1853; s. Russell and Clorinda (Talbot) H.; ed. pub. schs.; m. Ida Richardson Huntley, June 1878. Identified with elec. engring. from 1888; chmn. bd. Buffalo, Niagara & Eastern Power Corp.; pres. Buffalo Gen. Electric Co.; v.p. George Urban Milling Co., Peoples Bank; dir. Niagara Falls Power Co., Niagara, Lockport & Ontario Power Co., etc. Mem. bd. dirs. Pan-Am. Expn., Buffalo, 1901; commr. State of N.Y. to Lewis and Clark Expn., Portland, Ore., 1905; mem. Buffalo Park Commn. 3 yrs. Republican. Episcopalian. Home: Lancaster, N.Y. Died Sept. 17, 1926.

HUNTLEY, Elias DeWitt, M.E. clergyman; b. Elmira, N.Y., April 19, 1840; grad. Genesee Coll., 1866 (D.D., E. Tenn. Wesleyan Univ., 1879, Grant Memorial Univ., 1886; LL.D., Univ. of Ia., 1879); entered M.E. ministry, 1866; prof. ancient langs., Genesee Wesleyan Sem. 6 months; presiding elder Madison, Wis., dist.; pres. Lawrence Univ., Appleton, Wis., 1879-83; resigned to become pastor Metropolitan Ch., Washington; transferred to Baltimore conf., 1883; pastor successively of Madison Av. M.E. Ch., Baltimore, 1st Ch., Annapolis, Md., 1st Ch., Baltimore, Trinity Ch., Washington; made superannuated, Apr. 1903; chaplain U.S. senate, 1883-86; del. to Ecumenical Methodist Conf., London, Eng., 1881. Home: Washington Grove, Md. Died 1909.

HUNTLEY, Florence, author; b. Alliance, Ohio; d. Rev. Henry and Charlotte (Trego) Chance; m. Stanley Huntley (author) (died 1885). Entered journalism, 1886, corr. St. Paul Pioneer Press and Minneapolis Tribune; followed by editorial work and humorous paragraphing on latter and Washington Post; editor Iowa City Republican, 1901-02; now engaged on Harmonic Series, a system of science and philosophy intended to connect the demonstrated and recorded knowledge of ancient spiritual schools with the discovered and published facts of modern physical school of science. Author: Harmonics of Evolution, 1899; The Gay Gnani of Gingelee, 1908. Editor:

The Great Psychological Crime, 1903; The Destructive Principle of Nature in Individual Life, 1903; The Great Work, the Constructive Principle of Individual Life, 1907; Who Answers Prayer, 1908. Home: Oak Park, Ill. Died Feb. 1, 1912.

HUNTON, Eppa, lawyer; b. Faruquier Co., Va., Sept. 22, 1822; chiefly self-taught; studied and practiced law; m. Lucy C. Weir. Commonwealth atty. Prince William Co., 1849-62; mem. Va. conv., 1861; col. 8th Va. Inf., 1861-63; brig. gen., 1863-65, C.S.A.; prisoner of war at Ft. Warren, April 6 to July 1865. Mem. Congress, 1873-81; U.S. senator from Va. for unexpired term, 1892-95. Democrat. Home: Richmond, Va. Died 1908.

HUNTON, Eppa, Jr., railroad exec.; b. Brentsville, Va., Apr. 14, 1855; s. Eppa and Lucy Caroline (Weir) H.; LL.B., U. of Va., 1877; m. Erva Winston Payne, Nov. 18, 1884 (dec.); m. 2d, Virginia S. Payne, Apr. 24, 1901; children—Mary Winter Payne (dec.), Eppa IV. Admitted to Va. bar, 1877, and began practice with father at Warrenton; moved to Richmond, Va., 1901; mem. Munford, Hunton, Williams & Anderson, 1901-20; gen. counsel Richmond, Fredricksburg & Potomac R.R. Co., 1914-20, pres., 1920—; pres. Richmond Terminal Ry. Co.; dir. 1st & Merchants Nat. Bank, Dominion Securities Corp. (both of Richmond), etc. Mem. Va. Ho. of Delegates, 1893-94; mem. constl. conv., Va. (chmn. con. on cts. of justice), 1901; counsel for dir. gen. of railroads, during federal control. Pres. bd. visitors, Med. Coll. Va.; mem. alumni bd. trustees, U. of Va. Endowment Fund. Democrat. Episcopalian. Home: Richmond, Va. Died Mar. 5, 1932.

HUNTON, William Lee, clergyman, editor; b. Morrisburgh, Ont., Can., Feb. 16, 1864; s. Rev. John H. and Lavinia (Baker) H.; A.B., Thiel College, Greenville, Pa., 1886; A.M. from same, 1889, Ph.D., 1899, D.D., 1920; grad. Phila. Theol. Sem., 1889; m. Emma M. Hoppe, July 3, 1894; children—William Hoppe, Marion Hoppe Porch. Ordained Luth. ministry, 1889; pastor, Amanda, O., 1889-91, Rochester, N.Y., 1891-94, Buffalo, 1894-98, Wilkes-Barre, Pa., 1898-1901, Chicago, 1901-06; instr. Chicago Theol. Sem., 1902-06; supt. Chicago Synod Missions, 1902-06; asso. editor Luth. Graded S.S. Lessons, 1901—, Luth. Lesson Commentary (annual), 1901—, The Lutheran, 1907-20, Teacher Training Magazine, 1914-21, The Parish School, 1921—; editor Lutheran Young Folks (illustrated weekly), 1908—; mgr. Gen. Council Pub. House, Phila., 1917-19; literature mgr. United Luth. Pub. House, 1919—. Religious writer for secular press; sec. press com. United Luth. Ch., 1919—; mem. com. on common hymnal for English Lutherans; sec. Parish and Ch. Sch. Bd., United Luth. Ch., 1920—. Dir. Mt. Airy Summer Sch., 1914-26. Author: Favorite Hymns, 1917; I Believe, 1922; Facts of Our Faith, 1925. Co-editor Parish School Hymnal, 1926; Children's Hymnal and Service Book, 1929. Home: Philadelphia, Pa. Died Oct. 12, 1930.

HUNTOON, Benjamin Bussey, educator; b. Milton, Mass., Jan. 30, 1836; s. Benjamin and Susan Mehetabel (Pettingill) H.; A.B., Harvard, 1856, A.M., 1859; m. Sara Josephine Huntoon, Aug. 14, 1860. Taught in pvt. family and pvt. sch. in Ky., 1856-71; supt. Ky. Inst. for Edn. of the Blind, Sept. 10, 1871-Aug. 1913; also supt. Am. Printing House for the Blind, 1871-1913. Home: Louisville, Ky. Died Aug. 9, 1919.

HUNTSMAN, Owen Benjamin, ry. official; b. Conyngham, Pa., Sept. 23, 1871; s. Benjamin T. and Martha Grove (Brown) H.; grad. State Normal Sch., West Chester, Pa., 1892; A.B., Harvard, 1897, A.M., 1898; fellow in philosophy, Columbia U., 1898-99; m. Elizabeth Marie Van Buskirk, Sept. 18, 1902. Teacher pub. schs., Stroudsburg, Pa., 1887-89; instr. St. George's Hall, Summit, N.J., 1892-93, acting head master, 1895; instr. Wilson-Vail Sch., New York, 1899-1900; ednl. work, 1900-07; v.p. Tex. and Pacific Ry. Co., 1907-15, 1921-31; dir. same 1913-15 and 1921-24; dir., mem. exec. com. Western Pacific Ry. Co., 1915; v.p., 1908-15, dir., 1914-15, v.p. and asst. sec. and asst. treas., Mar. 1915-June 1917, Mo.P. Ry. Co. and St. Louis, Iron Mountain & Southern Ry. Co., and of the newly organized Mo.P. R.R. Co., June 1917—; asst. sec. New Orleans, Tex. & Mexico Ry. Co., 1925, asst. treas., 1929—; asst. sec. and asst. treas. Internat.-Gt. Northern R.R. Co., Mar. 1929—, v.p., Oct. 1929—; v.p., asst. sec. and asst. treas. Mo.-Ill. R.R. Co., June 1929; dir. N.Y. County Nat. Bank, 1918-21; retired July 1931. Republican. Quaker. Home: New York, N.Y. Died May 10, 1935.

HURD, Albert Arthur, lawyer; b. Lafayette, Ill., Sept. 27, 1849; s. Theodore F. and Catherine M. (Driscoll) H.; student Northwestern U. and State U. of Ia. Law Sch.; m. Theo. E. Oosley, Dec. 22, 1885. Admitted to bar, 1870; in gen. practice until 1875; asst. atty., 1875-81, solicitor for Kan., 1881-1905, spl. counsel, July 1, 1905—, A.,T.&S.F. Ry. Home: Topeka, Kan. Died Dec. 20, 1915.

HURD, Arthur William, physician; b. Galesburg, Ill., Dec. 26, 1858; s. Henry Stirling and Eleanor Eunice (Hammond) H.; A.B., Knox Coll., 1880, A.M., 1883; M.D., Coll. Phys. and Surg. (Columbia), 1883; m. Mary L. Wheeler, June 20, 1895. Asst. phys., 1885-94, supt., 1894-1918, Buffalo State Hosp.; instr. and prof. insanity, U. of Buffalo, 1892-94. Pres. Knox Coll. Alumni Club of Southern Calif., 1919—. Home: Hollywood, Calif. Died Nov. 19, 1924.

HURD, Charles Edwin, journalist, author; b. Croydon, N.H., June 15, 1833; s. Henry and Abigail (Gibson) H.; pub. sch. and pvt. edn.; m. Frances Margey Tooker, Dec. 30, 1866. Began newspaper work, 1850; contbr. to Boston and New York publs., 1852-55; asso. editor Yarmouth (N.S.) Semi-Weekly Tribune, 1855-57; successively edited Chelsea (Mass.) Herald, Lynn (Mass.) Reporter, Boston Sunday Leader, Erie (Pa.) Dispatch and Providence (R.I.) Daily Herald; on staff Boston Journal, 1870-72; associate editor Boston Globe, 1872-74; assistant clerk Ho. of Reps., few months in 1874; lit. editor Boston Transcript, 1874-1901. Author: New England Library of Genealogy and Personal History, 1901; History of the United States (4 vols.), 1906. Home: Yonkers, N.Y. Died 1910.

HURD, Edward Melville, banker, mcht.; b. Brantford, Ont., Can., Feb. 18, 1873; s. James Christie and Mariana (Lockwood) H.; brought to U.S. at age of 2; ed. pub. schs., Burlington; m. Zora Finek, July 17, 1897; 1 dau., Mrs. John L. Bland. Clk. Denver (Colo.) Nat. Bank, 1890-1902; mgr. chain of banks in Ariz. for Gila Valley Bank & Trust Co., 1902-12; v.p. First Nat. Bank, El Paso, Tex., 1913-14; in wholesale grocery and dry goods business, 1914—; pres. The H. Lesinsky Co., El Paso, until acquired all interests in same and reorganized as E. M. Hurd, wholesale grocer; dir. El Paso Br. of Federal Reserve Bank of Dallas. Home: El Paso, Tex. Died Feb. 25, 1933.

HURD, Edward Payson, registrar and prof. pathology and dermatology Coll. Phys. and Surg., Boston; grad. McGill Univ., Montreal, A.M. and M.D., 1865. Home: Newburyport, Mass. Died 1899.

HURD, Edward Payson, corp. officer; b. Medway, Mass., June 28, 1841; s. Julius Curtis and Rebecca Ann (Robinson) H.; ed. Phillips Acad., Andover, Mass.; m. Almira Gardner Pope (died 1869), Feb. 25, 1869; 2d, Sarah Louise Pope, both daughters of James Pope, of Dorchester, Mass., Oct. 16, 1872. Enlisted in Co. K, 16th Conn. Vols., and served in Civil War 3 yrs.; prisoner of war at Andersonville and other Southern prisons 8 mos. After war began under father, later with Samuel Slater & Sons, mfrs., Webster, Mass.; with Stevenson Bros. & Co., importers and commn. mchts., New York and Boston, George F. Hall, Boston, and successively with Continental Nat. Bank, Boston, McKay Sewing Machine Assn., McKay Metallic Assn., Gordon McKay Trustee, McKay & Thompson Consolidated Lasting Machine Assn., and McKay & Copeland Lasting Machine Co., all of Boston. A promoter of United Shoe Machinery Co. and identified with same from Feb. 1899; v.p., asst. treas. and mem. exec. and finance coms. United Shoe Machinery Co. of N.J., United Shoe Machinery Corp. of N.J., United Shoe Machinery Co. of Me., of Mexico, and S. America. Republican. Unitarian. Home: Newtonville, Mass. Died Feb. 23, 1927.

HURD, Eugene, surgeon; b. Ft. Atkinson, Wis., July 7, 1881; s. Samuel Curtis and Emily Ann (Wilds) H.; M.D., West Coast Coll. Medicine and Surgery, San Francisco, 1905; m. Baroness Nella von Hochstetter, Aug. 20, 1913; 1 son, John Gavin. Began practice at Seattle, Washington, 1906; mem. of Washington House of Representatives, 1913. Apptd. capt. Russian Army, Oct. 14, 1914; lt. col., Feb. 2, 1915; col. Sept. 1, 1915; capt. Med. Corps, U.S. Army, Aug. 26, 1917; hon. disch., July 22, 1918. Served as med. officer at the front with the Russian Army, in numerous engagements; surgeon to Root Commn. from Petrograd, Russia, to Washington, D.C., 1917; with Am. Army in France, Dec. 1917-July 1918. Corr. on Russian front for Chicago Tribune. Decorated Order of St. Stanislaus; Order of St. Anna, 3d and 2d degrees with crossed swords; Order of St. Vladimir, 3d degree; Order St. George, 3d degree; Order St. Nicolis, 2d degree. Mason. Republican. Episcopalian. Home: Auburn, Calif. Died May 19, 1941.

HURD, George Arthur, chmn. bd. Mortgage-Bond & Title Corp.; b. N.Y. City, Aug. 20, 1869; s. Melancthon Montgomery and Clara Armstrong (Hatch) H.; prep. edn., St. Paul's Sch., Concord, N.H.; A.B., Yale, 1890; LL.B., Harvard, 1893; m. Emily Lea Gazzam, Mar. 18, 1898; children—Arthur Melancthon, Katharine, Charles Gazzam, Clarissa. Resident agt. U.S. Mortgage and Trust Co., at Seattle, Wash., 1895-1903; asst. sec. same, 1903-05; v.p. Mortgage-Bond Co. of New York, 1905-10, later pres.; now chmn. bd. directors Mortgage-Bond & Title Corp. Republican. Home: New York, N.Y. Died Nov. 1929.

HURD, Harvey Bostwick, lawyer; b. Huntington, Conn., Feb. 14, 1828; s. Alanson and Elizabeth H.; ed. common schools; m. Cornelia Hilliard (died 1857), 1853; 2d, Sarah W. Collins (died 1890), 1860; 3d, Susannah M. Van Wyck (died 1896), 1892. At printer's trade, Bridgeport, Conn., 1842-44; Jubilee Coll., Peoria Co., Ill., 1844-45 (LL.D., Northwestern Univ.); came to Chicago, Jan. 7, 1846; studied law; admitted to bar, March 8, 1848; prof. in Chicago Law School (now dept. Northwestern U.), 1862-1902. First pres. village of Evanston; sec. Nat. Kansan Com., which conducted Kansas war on part of the North (1856-58). Official reviser of gen. statutes of Ill.; edited State edit. of same, 1874; has since edited 17 edits.; originator of the great Chicago drainage canal scheme; author Torrens Act of Ill. for registration of land titles; also of Juvenile Court Act of Ill., Apr. 22, 1899 (now also enacted in Pa. and other States) and producing revolution in treatment of juvenile dependents and offenders. Pres. Evanston Hist. Society. Home: Evanston, Ill. Died 1906.

HURD, Henry Mills, M.D.; b. Union City, Mich., May 3, 1843; s. Theodore C. and Eleanor Eunice (Hammond) H.; A.B., U. of Mich., 1863, M.D., 1866, A.M., 1870, LL.D., 1895; m. Mary Doolittle, Sept. 16, 1874 (died Mar. 14, 1913). Supt. of the Eastern Mich. Asylum at Pontiac, 1878-89; prof. psychiatry, 1889-1906 (emeritus), Johns Hopkins; supt. Johns Hopkins Hosp., 1889-1911. Editor Johns Hopkins Hosp. Bull. and Johns Hopkins Hosp. Reports, 1890-1911; one of editors Am. Journal of Insanity, 1897-1920, editor emeritus; editor Modern Hospital, 1913-20. Mem. Md. State Lunacy Commn. Sec. bd. of trustees Johns Hopkins Hosp., 1911—. Author: Hints to Hospital Visitors (with Dr. John S. Billings), 1895; also editor (with same) Hospitals, Dispensaries and Nursing, 1893; (also editor) Institutional Care of the Insane in the United States and Canada (4 vols.), 1916, 17. Home: Baltimore, Md. Died July 19, 1927.

HURD, Louis Guthrie, lawyer; b. Morgan Co., O., Jan. 8, 1847; s. Uri Keeler and Sylvia Augusta (Guthrie) H.; LL.B., Law Sch. of Cincinnati Coll., 1870; m. Lymna O. Maxfield, Mar. 25, 1872. Practiced in Dubuque, Ia., 1871—; sr. mem. Hurd, Lenehan, Smith & O'Connor. Mem. Bd. of Edn., Dubuque, 1895-1901 (pres. 1900-01). Trustee Public Library; pres. Dubuque Humane Soc. Republican. Home: Dubuque, Ia. Deceased.

HURD, Richard Melancthon; b. N.Y. City, June 14, 1865; s. M. M. and Clara A. (Hatch) H.; A.B., Yale, 1888; m. Lucy Gazzam, Sept. 22, 1898. Became pres. Lawyers Mortgage Co., New York, 1903, now chmn. bd. Republican. Episcopalian. Author: Principles of City Land Values. Home: Locust, N.J. Died June 6, 1941.

HURD, William Daniel, educator; b. De Witt, Mich., Dec. 19, 1875; s. Edgar and Elizabeth Anna (Appleton) H.; B.S., Mich. Agrl. Coll., 1899 (M.Agr., 1908); m. Sarah B. Cooper, Dec. 31, 1902. Taught in Lansing High Sch., 1899-1901; nursery insp., U. of Ill., summer, 1900; prof. horticulture Sch. of Practical Agr. and Horticulture, Briarcliff Manor, N.Y., 1901-03; organized extension work for R.I. State Coll., summer, 1903; prof. agr. U. of Me., 1903-06, dean, Coll. of Agr., 1906-09; dir. of extension service, Mass. Agrl. Coll., 1909-19; western mgr. soil improvement com. Nat. Fertilizer Assn., Chicago, 1919-20; dir. same, 1920; special asst. (temp.) to Sec. of Agr., Washington, 1917. Republican. Episcopalian. Home: Chevy Chase, Md. Died Aug. 22, 1924.

HURLBUT, Byron Satterlee, univ. prof.; b. Shelburne, Vt., Feb. 10, 1865; s. Hiram Fuller and Roxcy Jane (Satterley) H.; A.B., Harvard, 1887, A.M., 1888; student Harvard Grad. Sch., 1887-90; m. Eda Adams Woolson, July 12, 1904; children—James Woolson (dec.), David Huntington (dec.), Robert Satterlee. Instr., 1890-1901, asst. prof., 1901-06, dean, 1902-16, prof. English, 1906—, Harvard. Home: Cambridge, Mass. Died Dec. 19, 1929.

HURLBUT, Edwin Wilcox, judge; b. Linneus, Mo., May 12, 1854; s. Hiram E. and Teresa A. (Booker) H.; removed to Colo., 1862; cadet U.S. Mil. Acad., 1875-77, at time excitement over gold discoveries; resigned to go to Black Hills, Dak. Ty.; studied law in office of Teller & Orahood, Denver; m. Elizabeth G. Arnold, Feb. 1, 1883. Admitted to Colo. bar, 1883, and began practice at Central City, Colo.; lived in Creede, Colo., 1½ yrs., Cripple Creek, 2 yrs.; law partner of H. M. Orahood, Denver, 1905-11; pres. Gilpin Lumber Co. Capt. militia co., Gilpin Co., Colo., 3 yrs.; capt. vols., Spanish-Am. War; served in P.R., Tampa, Fla., and Huntsville, Ala., to close of war; later apptd. by President McKinley maj. and p.m., but declined. Dist. atty., 1st Jud. Dist., Colo., 1887-89; mem. Colo. Ho. of Rep., from Gilpin Co., 1889, from El Paso Co., 1897 (speaker of House); 1st mayor of Creede, Colo., 1902; asso. judge Colo. Ct. of Appeals, Aug. 1911, until court expired by operation of law, LaFollette Republican. Home: Denver, Colo. Died Feb. 6, 1925.

HURLBUT, Jesse Lyman, clergyman; b. New York, Feb. 15, 1843; s. Samuel and Evelina H.; A.B., Wesleyan, Conn., 1864, A.M., 1867; D.D., Syracuse, 1883; S.T.O., Wesleyan, 1923; m. Mary M. Chase, March 5, 1867 (died 1913); children—Charles Chase, Mary Evelyn (Mrs. H. B. Hurlbut), Bertha Grace (wife of Rev. George P. Dougherty). Ordained to the M.E. ministry, 1865; pastor Newark, N.J., 1865-67, Montclair, 1867-69, Paterson, 1869-72, Staten Island, 1872-74, Plainfield, N.J., 1874-77, Hoboken, 1877-79; agt. S.S. Union, M.E. Ch., 1879-84; asst. editor S.S. Lit., 1884-88; editor S.S. Lit. and sec. S.S. Union and Tract Soc., 1888-1900; pastor Morristown, N.J., 1901-04, S. Orange, 1904-05, Bloomfield, 1906-09; dist. supt. Newark Dist., Mar. 1909-Mar. 1914. Counselor Chautauqua Lit. and Scientific Circle. Author: Outline Normal Lessons, 1884; Hurlbut's Story of the Bible, 1901; Sunday Half Hours with the Great Preachers, 1905; Handy Bible Encyclopedia, 1906; Teacher Training Lessons, 1908; Organizing and Building Up the Sunday School, 1909; Traveling in the Holy Land Through the Stereoscope, 1913; Hurlbut's Story of Jesus, 1915; Story of the Christian Church, 1918; The Story of Chautauqua, 1921. Home: Montclair, N.J. Died Aug. 2, 1930.

HURLEY, Edward Nash, mfr., financier; b. Galesburg, Ill., July 31, 1864; s. Jeremiah and Ellen (Nash) H.; pub. sch. edn.; LL.D., U. of Notre Dame; D.C.L., Knox Coll., Galesburg, Ill.; m. Julia Keeley, Sept. 30, 1891 (died Oct. 18, 1900); children—Edward Nash, Raymond J.; m. 2d, Florence Agnes, d. John H. Amberg, of Chicago, July 24, 1905; children—Helen Mary, John R. Traveling salesman, later mgr. U.S. Metallic Packing Co., Phila., 1888-96; originated and developed pneumatic tool industry in U.S. and Europe; organizer, and pres. and treas. Standard Pneumatic Tool Co., Chicago, 1896-1902; sold out interests in that co. and Internat. Pneumatic Tool Co. of Eng., and engaged in farming and stock raising at country home, Wheaton, Ill., 1902-08; pres. Hurley Machine Co., Chicago, 1908-15; pres. 1st Nat. Bank, Wheaton, 1909-19. Apptd., Nov. 1913, by sec. of commerce, as U.S. trade commr. to Latin-Am. Republics; v. chmn., later chmn., Federal Trade Commn. until Feb. 1917 (resigned); mem. War Council, Am. Red Cross; chmn. U.S. Shipping Bd. and pres. Emergency Fleet Corp., July 24, 1917-July 31, 1919 (resigned); mem. World War Funding Commn., 1924—; mem. President Hoover's Advisory Shipping Commn.; mem. Chicago Council on Foreign Relations. Now chmn. bd. Hurley Machine Co., mfrs. electrical home labor saving devices. Dir. Chamber of Commerce of U.S.; mem. Internat. Chamber Commerce. A receiver of Middle West Utilities Co., 1932. Dir. Nat. Foreign Trade Council; pres. Am. Mfrs. Export Assn; trustee U. of Notre Dame, Chicago Century of Progress Expn., 1933. Awarded D.S.M. by Gen. Pershing, 1916, "for exceptionally meritorious and distinguished services in connection with the shipment of troops and supplies"; Comdr. Legion of Honor (French); Order Ta Sho Cha Ho (Chinese); Grand Officer Crown of Italy; Knight of St. John of Malta; Laetare medal, U. of Notre Dame. Author: The Awakening of Business, 1916; The New Merchant Marine, 1920; The Bridge to France, 1927. Homes: Wheaton, Ill., and Chicago. Died Nov. 14, 1933.

HURLEY, James E., ry. mgr.; b. at Wapello, Ia., June 1, 1860; ed. Wapello High Sch., and Bloomfield (Ia.) State Normal Sch., winters, 1873-75. In service of A.,T.&S.F. Ry., 1880—; held various minor positions, 1880-88; trainmaster eastern div. at Topeka, Kan., 1888-91; asst. supt. Mo. div., Sept.-Oct. 1891; Chicago div., 1891-94; supt. N.M. div., June-Oct. 1894; supt. N.M. and Rio Grande divs., 1894-1901; acting gen. supt. lines west of Albuquerque, Jan.-Oct. 1901; gen. supt. western grand div., 1901-02; gen. supt. eastern grand div. at Topeka, 1902-05; gen. mgr. A.,T.&S.F. System, May 1, 1905—. Home: Topeka, Kan. Died 1910.

HURLEY, James Franklin, editor, pub.; b. Concord, N.C., Sept. 20, 1870; s. Alexander Franklin and Jane (King) H.; prep. edn. Kings Mountain (N.C.) Inst. and Davis Mil. Sch.; student Davidson (N.C.) Coll.; m. Jeanette Erwin, Aug. 6, 1895; 1 son, James Franklin. Founder Concord Tribune, 1910; editor and pub. Salisbury (N.C.) Post, 1912—; president Post Pub. Co., Citizens Bldg. & Loan Assn.; dir. Wachovia Bank & Trust Co. Chmn. Bd. of Edn., Rowan County, N.C. Democrat. Presbyn. Mason, K.P. Home: Salisbury, N.C. Died Mar. 5, 1936.

HURLL, Estelle May, author; b. New Bedford, Mass., July 25, 1863; d. Charles W. and Sarah S. Hurll; grad. Wellesley Coll., 1882; (A.M., 1892); m. John C. Hurll, June 29, 1908. Teacher of ethics, Wellesley Coll., 1884-91. Author: Child Life in Art, 1895; The Madonna in Art, 1897; Life of Our Lord in Art, 1898; also (in Riverside Art Series), Rembrandt, 1899; Michelangelo, 1900; Millet, 1900; Reynolds, 1900; Murillo, 1900; Greek Sculpture, 1901; Titian, 1901; Landseer, 1901; Correggio, 1902; Tuscan Sculpture, 1902; Van Dyck, 1902; The Bible Beautiful, 1905; Portraits and Portrait Painting, 1907; How to Show Pictures to Children, 1914; Home Book of Great Paintings, 1914. Editor: Mrs. Jameson's Art Works. Home: Watertown, Mass. Died May 8, 1924.

HURRELL, Alfred, ins. official; b. Fort Erie, Ont., Can., Feb. 12, 1874; s. Alfred Brooking and Helen (Foster) H.; LL.B., Buffalo Law Sch. (U. of Buffalo), 1902; m. Harriet Gertrude Mason, Oct. 15, 1903; children—Ruth Louise (Mrs. Ruth H. Crawford), Helen (Mrs. Helen McHorney). Came to U.S., 1891, naturalized, 1898. Admitted to New York bar, 1902, and began practice, Buffalo, N.Y., 1904; asst. dist. atty. Erie Co., N.Y., 1909; counsel, N.Y. State Ins. Dept., 1909-11; atty. Assn. Life Ins. Pres., 1911-15; v.p. and gen. counsel Prudential Ins. Co. America, 1925—; dir. Prudential Ins. Co. of America. Was mem. borough council and later mayor of Glen Ridge; mem. Edison Park Commn. Republican. Unitarian. Mason. Home: Glen Ridge, N.J. Died June 23, 1938.

HURST, John, bishop; b. Port-au-Prince, Haiti, May 10, 1863; s. Thomas and Sylvanie (Gordon) H.; ed. Lycée National de Port-au-Prince; B.D., Wilberforce (Ohio) U., 1886; LL.D., Morris Brown U., 1917; m. Kathrine Bertha Thompson, Oct. 29, 1890. Ordained ministry A.M.E. Ch., 1886; pastor St. Paul's Ch., Port-au-Prince, 1886-87; supt. A.M.E. missions, Haiti, 1888-89; 1st sec. Haitian Legation at Washington, D.C., by appmt. of Pres. Hyppolite, 1889-93; joined Baltimore Conf., A.M.E. Ch., 1893; pastor Crowdensville Circuit, 1893-94, Waters Ch., Baltimore, 1894-98, Bethel Ch., Baltimore, 1898-1903, Waters Ch. again, 1903-08; financial sec. A.M.E. Ch., 1908-12; bishop, May 1912—. Chancellor of Edward Waters Coll., Jacksonville, Fla.; mem. bd. dirs. Payne Theol. Sem., Wilberforce, O.; trustee Wilberforce U., Howard U. Del. to Ecumenical Conf., London, 1921; Conf. on Faith and Order, Lausanne, Switzerland, 1927. Dir. Nat. Assn. Advancement Colored People. Mason. Home: Baltimore, Md. Died May 6, 1930.

HURST, John Fletcher, M.E. bishop, 1880—; b. Dorchester Co., Md., Aug. 17, 1834; grad. Dickinson, 1854 (D.D., LL.D., Asbury); studied theology at univs. of Halle and Heidelberg, Germany; entered Methodist ministry, 1858, in Newark conf.; instr. Methodist Mission Inst., Bremen, Germany, 1866-68; Frankfort-on-the-Main, 1868-71; traveled, 1869-71; prof. hist. theology, 1871-80; pres., 1873-80, Drew Theol. Sem., Madison, N.J. Chancellor American U., Washington. Author: Outlines of Bible History, 1873; Outlines of Church History, 1874; Short History of the Christian Church, 1893; History of the Christian Church (2 vols.), 1897. Died 1903.

HURTH, Peter Joseph, titular archbishop; b. Nittel-on-Moselle, Germany, Mar. 30, 1857; s. Peter John and Susanna (Wolf) H.; came to America, 1874; ed. in Germany and at U. of Notre Dame, Ind. Ordained priest R.C. Ch., 1880; rector St. Joseph's Coll., Cincinnati, 1881-84, St. Edward's Coll., Austin, Tex., 1885-94; apptd. bishop of Dacca, India, 1894; left India on account of ill health, 1910; became bishop of Nueva Segovia, P.I., Dec. 30, 1912, resigned, Nov. 5, 1926; titular archbishop of Bostra, Nov. 12, 1926; named asst. to Papal Throne, Jan. 17, 1926. Died Aug. 1, 1935.

HURTY, John N., physician; b. Lebanon, O., Feb. 21, 1852; s. Josiah and Ann H.; M.D., Med. Coll. of Ind., Indianapolis, 1881; m. Ethel Johnstone, Oct. 25, 1877. In practice at Indianapolis, 1881—; prof. hygiene and sanitary science, med. dept. Ind. U.; sec. Ind. State Bd. Health; state health commr. of Ind., 1896—; supt. hygiene exhibit, St. Louis Expn., 1904. Author: Health with Life. Home: Indianapolis, Ind. Died Mar. 27, 1925.

HUSBAND, Joseph, author; b. Rochester, N.Y., July 25, 1885; s. Thomas and Ella (Wright) H.; grad. St. Mark's Sch., Southboro, Mass., 1904; A.B., Harvard, 1908; m. Eleanor Brown. Entered as seaman, 2d U.S. N.R.F., Jan. 7, 1918; commd. ensign, May 24, 1918; served on Noma, Benham and Christabel, in French waters, until Jan. 1, 1919. Republican. Author: A Year in a Coal Mine, 1911; America at Work, 1915; The Story of a Pullman Car, 1917; A Year in the Navy, 1919; On the Coast of France, 1919; Americans by Adoption, 1920; High Hurdles, 1923; Citadel, 1925. Died Sept. 21, 1938.

HUSBAND, Richard Wellington, educator; b. Milton, Ont., Can., Nov. 27, 1869; s. Richard and Eleanor Lowry (Teeple) H.; A.B., Leland Stanford Jr. U., 1895, A.M., 1896; A.B., U. of Toronto, 1896; studied U. of Calif., U. of Leipzig; m. Helene Borgman (Vassar Coll.), June 20, 1901. Instr. in Latin, Mills Coll., Calif., 1898-99; same, Stanford Univ., 1899-1900; instr., asst. prof. and prof. classical langs., 1900-19, asso. dean, 1919-23, dir. personnel research, 1923—, Dartmouth Coll. Sec. N.H. Com. on Pub. Safety, 1917-21; office mgr. Dist. Bd. for State of N.H., 1917; historian N.H. Com. on Pub. Safety and state war historian to compile mil. records of N.H. in the war against Germany, 1917-20. Republican. Episcopalian. Author: The Prosecution of Jesus, 1916. Home: Hanover, N.H. Died Apr. 9, 1924.

HUSIK, Isaac, univ. prof.; b. Vaseutinez, Government of Poltava, Russia, Feb. 10, 1876; s. Wolf and Hannah Pia H.; came to America, 1888; A.B., Univ. of Pennsylvania, 1897, A.M., 1899, Ph.D., 1903, LL.B., 1919; m. Rose Gorfine, July 1926. Instr. Hebrew, Gratz Coll., Phila., 1898-1916; lecturer in philosophy, 1911-16, asst. prof., 1916-22, prof., 1922—, Pa. U. Lecturer philosophy, Columbia Summer Sch., 1914, Yeshiva Coll., New York, 1928-31, Hebrew Union Coll., summer 1929. Editor Jewish Publ. Soc., 1924—. Trustee Gratz Coll., Hebrew Edn. Soc., Phila. Author: Judah Messer Leon's Commentary on the Vetus Logica, 1906; Matter and Form in Aristotle, 1912; A History of Mediæval Jewish Philosophy, 1916, 2d edit., 1930. Translator: Van Ihering Law as a Means to an End, Vol. 1, 1913; Stammler—The Theory of Justice, 1925. Contributor to philos. and other jours. Translator and editor: Albo's Ikkarim (5 vols.), 1929. Editor dept. philosophy in new edit. Standard Jewish Encyclopædia to 1933. Home: Festerville, Pa. Died Mar. 22, 1939.

HUSSEY, Charles Lincoln, rear admiral; b. Rochester, N.H., Aug. 18, 1870; s. George D. and Mary J. (Foss) H.; grad. U.S. Naval Acad., 1892; Naval War Coll., 1920; m. Mrs. Harriet Brownson Tooker, Dec. 21, 1908; 1 dau., Faith. Ensign U.S.N., July 1, 1894; promoted through grades to capt., July 1, 1917; rear admiral, June 4, 1926. Served on Oregon, Spanish-Am. War, 1898; comd. expdn. to Abyssinia, 1903; duty Bur. of Navigation, Navy Dept., 1906-08; navigator New Hampshire, 1908-10; exec. officer, Georgia, 1912-13; duty Gen. Bd., Navy Dept., 1914-17, and mem. commn. on Navy Yards and Naval Stas., 1916-17; comdr. Birmingham, World War, 1917-19; comd. Idaho, 1920-21; naval attaché to American Embassy, London, 1922-24; comd. train, Scouting Fleet, 1925-27; retired Oct. 1, 1927. Awarded Navy Cross (U.S.); decorated Companion Order St. Michael and St. George; Star of Ethiopia. Conf. leader Williamstown Inst. Politics, 1929. Presbyn. Author: (with Sir Norman Angell and Carl Russell Fish) The United States and Great Britain, 1931. Home: Litchfield, Conn. Died Dec. 4, 1934.

HUSSEY, William Joseph, astronomer; b. at Mendon, O., Aug. 10, 1862; s. John Milton and Mary Catherine (Severns) Hussey; B.S., Univ. of Michigan, 1889; Sc.D., Brown U., 1912; m. Ethel Fountain, June 27, 1895; children—Roland Fountain, Allis Fountain; m. 2d, Mary McNeal Reed, Sept. 1, 1917. Instr. in mathematics, U. of Mich., 1889-91; acting dir. Detroit Obs., 1891-92; asst. prof. astronomy, 1892-93, asso. prof., 1893-94, prof., 1894-96, Leland Stanford Jr. U.; astronomer in Lick Obs., 1896-1905; prof. astronomy and dir. obs., U. of Mich., 1905—; also prof. astronomia y geodesia, U. of La Plata, Argentina and dir. Observatorio Nacional de La Plata, La Plata, Argentina, Sept. 1, 1911-17. Expert on observatory sites in Southern Calif., Ariz. and Australia, to com. on observatories of Carnegie Instn., 1903; in charge of Lick Obs. eclipse expdn. to Egypt, 1905, of La Plata eclipse expedition to Brazil, 1912; discoverer of 1,650 double stars; awarded Lalande prize of French Acad., 1906, for double star discoveries and investigations. Foreign asso. Royal Astron. Soc.; hon. mem. Sociedad Astronomica de Mexico. Author: Logarithmic and Other Mathematical Tables, 1891, 1895; Mathematical Theories of Planetary Motions, 1892; Micrometrical Observations of the Double Stars Discovered at Pulkowa (Vol. V, Lick Observatory publ.), 1901. Home: Ann Arbor, Mich. Died Oct. 28, 1926.

HUSTED, James Delno; b. Clarksfield, O., Sept. 26, 1857; s. Obadiah J. and Mary W. (Hurlbutt) H.; common sch. edn.; m. Jennie Thorpe, Sept. 26, 1881 (died 1913); 1 son, Elbert E. Investment business; actively interested in corps. dealing in land and livestock (Denver, Colo.); identified with public and religious organizations. Col. in U.S. Army Res. Republican. Deceased.

HUSTED, James William, congressman; b. Peekskill, N.Y., Mar. 16, 1870; s. James William and Helen M. (Southard) H.; A.B., Yale, 1892, LL.B., New York Law Sch., 1894; m. Louise Wetmore Spaulding, June 12, 1895 (died 1914); m. 2d, Bertha Frances (Herrick) Lloyd, Sept. 21, 1915. Admitted to N.Y. bar, 1894, and practiced in Peekskill; pres. N.E. Pin Co.; pres. Peekskill Nat. Bank. Mem. N.Y. Assembly, 1895, 96, 97; pres. Village of Peekskill, 1903, 1904; mem. 64th to 67th Congresses (1915-23), 25th N.Y. Dist. Republican. Episcopalian. Home: Peekskill, N.Y. Died Jan. 2, 1925.

HUSTING, Paul Oscar, senator; b. Fond du Lac, Wis., Apr. 25, 1866; s. Jean Pierre and Mary Magdelena (Juneau) H.; g.s. Solomon Juneau, first white settler and founder of Milwaukee, Wis.; student U. of Wis. Coll. of Law, 1895; unmarried. Admitted to Wis. bar, 1895, and practiced in Mayville; pres. E. Swartz Printing Co.; dist. atty., Dodge Co., Wis., 1902-06; mem. Wis. Senate, 1906, 1910; elected mem. U.S. Senate for term, 1915-21, at 1st direct election of senator by people in Wis. Author of Wis. waterpower law; active in securing passage of income tax, workmen's compensation, and 2-cent railroad fare laws in Wis., also initiated investigation leading to enactment of Corrupt Practices Act. Democrat. Home: Mayville, Wis. Died Oct. 21, 1917.

HUSTON, Abraham Francis, mfr.; b. Coatesville, Pa., July 7, 1852; s. Charles and Isabella Pennock (Lukens) H.; A.B., Haverford Coll., 1872; m. Alice Calley, Jan. 17, 1889 (died 1906); m. 2d, Alfie Frances Sly, Oct. 24, 1907. Began with Lukens Iron Works, 1872, now chmn. bd. successor, Lukens Steel Co.; also v.p. Nat. Bank of Chester Valley, Coatesville; pres. Coatesville Trust Co.; dir. Commercial Trust Co. of Phila. (now Bank of North America & Trust Co.), Pa. Sugar Co. Mem. bd. dirs. Haverford Coll., Bryn Mawr Coll. Republican. Soc. of Friends (Quaker). Home: Coatesville, Pa. Died Jan. 12, 1930.

HUSTON, Charles Andrews, prof. of law; b. Stratford, Ont., Can., May 5, 1876; s. James and Harriet (Andrews) H.; U. of Manitoba, 1899-1900; A.B., U. of Chicago, 1902, fellow in polit. economy, 1902-03, J.D., 1906; S.J.D., Harvard, 1913; m. Margaret Davidson, June 9, 1909. Asst. in English, 1903-04, asso., 1904-06, U. of Chicago; instr. law, 1906-07, asst. prof., 1907-09, asso. prof., 1909-11, prof., 1911—, and dean of Law School, 1916—, Leland Stanford Jr. University. Methodist. Democrat. Author: The Enforcement of Decrees in Equity, 1915. With War Trade Bd. and Provost Marshal Gen's. Dept., Washington, 1917-18. Died July 19, 1922.

HUSTON, Joseph Waldo, lawyer; b. Painesville, O., Apr. 10, 1833; ed. public schools, Willoughby, O.; m. Lucia Wilder, July 5, 1855; m. 2d, Frances Collister, Dec. 28, 1864. Went to Kalamazoo, Mich., Oct. 1845; studied law; clerk U.S. Treasury Dept., 1855-57; admitted to Mich. bar, 1857; lt. 3d Mich. cav., 1861-62; maj. 4th Mich. cav., 1862-63; U.S. atty. for Idaho, 1869-78; asso. justice Supreme Court, Idaho, 1890-1900. Republican. Home: Boise City, Ida. Died 1905.

HUSTON, Thad, judge Superior Court of Pierce Co., Wash., 1901-09; b. Washington Co., Ind., Apr. 15, 1846; s. William A. H.; ed. at Macomb, Ill.; served in Union army in Civil war, 1864, in Co. C, 137th Ill. Vol. Inf., as 1st sergt.; severely wounded in action at Memphis, Tenn., Aug. 21, 1864; m. Rose L. Kenrich, June 20, 1900. Admitted to bar, Mar. 1868, at Macomb, Ill. Republican. Home: Tacoma, Wash. Deceased.

HUTCHENS, Frank Townsend, artist; b. Canandaigua, N.Y.; s. Hiram L. and Mary A. H.; ed. Canandaigua Acad., student art, Art Students' League, N.Y., Acad. Colorossi, and Acad. Julian, Paris, France; m. Mabel Reynolds, Nov. 1, 1900. Exhibited Royal Acad. (London), Paris Salon, Amsterdam Internat. Expn., Nat. Acad. Design (New York), Pa. Acad. Fine Arts, Art Inst. Chicago, Corcoran Gallery (Washington, D.C.); Allied Artists of America; New York Water Color Club; Am. Water Color Soc.; Salmagundi Club; etc. Awarded silver medal, Paris. Works on permanent exhbn. in Toledo, Mus., John Herron Art Inst., West Point Mus., in Capitol at Albany, N.Y., Erie Mus., Contemporary Exhbn., Baltimore, Md., Milwaukee (Wis.) Art Inst., Syracuse (N.Y.) Mus. Fine Arts, High Mus. Art, Atlanta, Ga., Delgado Mus. Art, New Orleans, La., Memorial Gallery, Rochester, N.Y.; 24 portraits in oil of past presidents of Florida Senate, in the Senate Chambers of The Capitol in Tallahassee; portraits of Gov. Doyle E. Carlton and Gov. David Sholtz in Governors Chambers of The Capitol, in Tallahassee; portrait U.S. Senator Duncan U. Fletcher, owned by city of Jacksonville, Fla. Mason. Homes: Norwalk, Conn., and Taos, N.M. Died Feb. 6, 1937.

HUTCHEON, Robert James, clergyman, educator; b. Campbellford, Ont., Can., Oct. 22, 1869; s. James and Jemima (Minte) H.; A.M., Queen's U., Kingston, Ont., 1892; A.M., Harvard, 1906; m. Margaret Allen, of Kingston, Oct. 20, 1897; 1 son, Allen Grant. Ordained Presbyn. ministry, 1896; pastor St. Andrew's Ch., Almonte, Ont., 1896-1902, Unitarian Ch., Ottawa, Ont., 1902-05, Toronto, 1906-13; prof. philosophy and psychology of religion, Meadville Theol. Sch., 1913—. Author: The Causes of Germany's Moral Downfall, 1919; Star Island Lectures, 1928; Frankness in Religion, 1929; Humanism in Religion Examined, 1931. Home: Chicago, Ill. Died Dec. 18, 1940.

HUTCHESON, John Bell, judge; b. Jonesboro, Ga., Nov. 20, 1860; s. Leander Caruth and Julia Ann (Sims) H.; grad. Jonesboro High Sch.; student U. of Ga., 1882-84; m. Rebecca Shepard, June 30, 1903. Began practice of law, Jonesboro, 1886; editor Jonesboro News, 1885-88; admitted to Ga. bar, 1886 and practiced in Jonesboro; mayor of Jonesboro, 1892, 1917; mem. Ga. Ho. of Rep., 1915-16; judge of Superior Court, Stone Mountain Circuit, 1919-34; asso. justice Supreme Court of Ga., 1934-38. Mem. Bd. of Selective Service, Northern Dist. of Ga., World War. Mem. bd. dirs. Ga. State Coll. for Women, 1913-32. Democrat. Methodist. Mason. Home: Jonesboro, Ga. Died May 21, 1939.

HUTCHINGS, Frank Day, judge; b. on farm, N.Y., Oct. 24, 1859; s. Samuel D. and Betsy R. (Ashley) H.; A.B., U. of Kan., 1883, LL.B., 1886; m. Mabel Wemple, niece of late Senator Edmund G. Ross, of Kan., Nov. 24, 1892; children—W. F., Mrs. Kate Colt. Began practice in St. Paul, Kansas, 1886; removed to Kansas City, Kan., 1888; apptd. city atty., 1898, elected same yr., for full term; apptd. judge Circuit Ct. of Wyandotte Co., 1908; held office until law creating ct. was declared unconstitutional by Supreme Court; elected judge Div. No. 2 Dist Ct. of Wyandotte Co., created to take place of Circuit Ct., Nov. 1910, reëlected 4 times. Republican. Conglist. Mason. Home: Kansas City, Kan. Died Dec. 29, 1929.

HUTCHINS, Charles Henry, mfr.; b. East Douglas, Mass., Jan. 13, 1847; s. Charles and Harriet (Hunt) H.; ed. pub. and high schs., Douglas; m. Eliza E. Knowles, Sept. 2, 1874 (died 1898); m. 2d, Laura N. Nicolle, June 1, 1918. Began in axe works of which his father was supt.; engaged in dry goods business, Worcester, 1867-74; entered mfr. of tapes and webbing, 1874; became connected with the Knowles Loom Works, 1884, later pres. and treas.; pres., 1897-1917, chmn. bd. dirs. and mem. exec. com., 1917—, Crompton & Knowles Loom Works; president U.S. Envelope Co., 1898—; v.p. Peoples Savings Bank; dir. Worcester Trust Co. Trustee Home for Aged Women, Home for Aged Men (Worcester); pres. Hosp. Cottages for Children. Republican. Conglist. Homes: Shrewsbury and Worcester, Mass. Died Nov. 15, 1922.

HUTCHINS, Charles Pelton; b. Brooklyn, Sept. 10, 1872; s. Alexander (M.D.) and Mary F. (Pelton) H.; Williams Coll. and Columbia U. (non-grad.); M.D., L.I. Coll. Hosp., 1897; m. Margaret E. Snowden, May 5, 1897. Practice of medicine, 1897-1902; prof. physical training and physiology, Dickinson Coll., 1902-04; prof. physical training, U. of Wis., 1906-10, Indiana U., 1910—. Episcopalian. Home: Bloomington, Ind. Died Dec. 28, 1938.

HUTCHINS, Charles Thomas, rear admiral U.S.N.; b. Kingston, Pa., Feb. 5, 1844; s. Richard and Emily (Little) H.; grad. U.S. Naval Acad., 1866; m. Marion Clementine Borup, Nov. 17, 1876. Ensign, 1868; master, 1869; lt., 1870; lt. comdr., 1887; comdr., 1896; capt., 1901; rear admiral and retired, June 30, 1905. Served on sailing-ship Relief on voyage to France with supplies for starving French, 1871; served as navigator of Wyoming, with Comdr. Cushing, when he went to Santiago de Cuba to retake Virginius; was watch officer and navigator, flagship Lancaster, European Sta., at bombardment of Alexandria, Egypt, and in command of fleet landing party on shore for 5 days; personally thanked by Kings of Sweden and Norway; at Kronstadt, Russia, coronation of the Czar, 1884; comd. several vessels, 1893-1900; comdg. U.S.S. Buffalo, spl. service, carrying recruits to China and training landsmen, 1900-02; naval sec. Lighthouse Bd., 1902-04; comdg. new U.S. battleship Maine, 1904-05. Episcopalian. Home: Washington, D.C. Died Aug. 9, 1920.

HUTCHINS, Edward Webster, lawyer; A.B., Harvard, 1872; LL.B., Harvard, 1875. Mem. Hutchins & Wheeler; dir. 2d Nat. Bank, Boston Safe Deposit & Trust Co., Cambridge Gas Light Co., etc. Pres. Social Law Library. Home: Boston, Mass. Died June 23, 1929.

HUTCHINS, Harry Burns, university pres.; b. Lisbon, N.H., Apr. 8, 1847; s. Carleton Brown and Nancy W. (Merrill) H.; Ph.B., U. of Mich., 1871; LL.D., U. of Wis., 1897, Wesleyan, 1916, Notre Dame, 1917, U. of Calif., 1918, U. of Mich., 1920; m. Mary L. Crocker, Dec. 26, 1872. Instr. and asst. prof. history and rhetoric, 1872-76, Jay prof. law, 1884-87, U. of Mich.; prof. law, Cornell, 1887-94; prof. law, and dean Dept. of Law, 1895-1910, acting pres., 1897-98, and Oct. 1, 1909-June 29, 1910, pres., June 1910-20 (pres. emeritus), U. of Michigan. Mem. of advisory bd. Mich. Law Review. American member Internat. Commn. provided for in the treaty between U.S. and Uruguay for the advancement of peace. Revised and annotated 5 vols. Mich. Supreme Court Reports, under appmt. Supreme Court, 1882-83; edited Am. edition Williams on Real Property; consulting editor Am. and English Encyclo. of Law and Procedure; author biography of the late Thomas M. Cooley in "Great American Lawyers." Home: Ann Arbor, Mich. Died Jan. 25, 1930.

HUTCHINS, James Calhoun, lawyer; b. Chicago, Dec. 15, 1857; s. James Cass and Martha C. (Phillips) H.; LL.B., Northwestern U. Law Sch. (Union Coll. of Law), Chicago, 1879; m. Agnes Potter, Sept. 3, 1884. Has practiced in Chicago, 1880—; dir. and vice-pres. Ill. Trust & Savings Bank. Home: Chicago, Ill. Died Feb. 28, 1921.

HUTCHINS, John Corbin, banker; b. Wolcott, Vt., Feb. 3, 1864; s. Lewis S. and Marcia M. (Aiken) H.; grad. Hardwick (Vt.) Acad., 1885; m. Saidee H. Mayo, Oct. 24, 1889; children—Ralph Mayo, Ruth Ward (dec.), Paul Aiken. Registered druggist, 1886; now drug, furniture and real estate business; extensive owner timber lands. Selectman 30 yrs.; mem. N.H. Gen. Court, 1899; mem. N.H. Senate, 1913, 14; Dem. candidate for gov. of N.H., 1914, 16. Dollar a year man, World War; chmn. Liberty Loan drives; county chmn. Near East Relief, etc. Baptist. Mason. Home: N. Stratford, N.H. Died Mar. 21, 1938.

HUTCHINS, Stilson, capitalist; b. Whitefield, N.H., Nov. 14, 1838; s. Stilson and Clara (Eaton) H.; ed. Hopkinton, N.H., and Dana Prep. Sch., Harvard U. Removed to Iowa, 1855, and later founded Dubuque Herald; founded St. Louis Times, 1866; founded The Washington Post, Dec. 6, 1877, sold it Jan. 1, 1889; exploited the Mergenthaler Linotype and was one of the prin. founders of the company. Home: Washington, D.C. Died Apr. 22, 1912.

HUTCHINSON, Cary Talcott, engineer; b. St. Louis, Mo., Mar. 4, 1866; s. Robert Randolph and Mary (Mitchell) H.; Ph.B., Washington U., 1886; fellow in physics, Johns Hopkins, 1888-89, Ph.D., 1889. With the Sprague Electric Ry. Co. and Edison Gen. Electric Co., 1889-90; mem. of Sprague, Duncan & Hutchinson, consulting elec. engrs., 1891-92, then alone. Chief engr., McCall Ferry Power Co., bldg. large hydro-electric plant on Susquehanna River; consulting engr. G.N. Ry., in charge of electrification of Cascade Tunnel, state of Wash. Sec. Engring. Foundation, and Nat. Research Council. Mem. Electrification Commn., Ill. Central R.R. Co., 1921; in charge Ry. Div., Superpower Report, 1921; cons. engr. with Sanderson & Porter, 1922-32; in private practice, N.Y. City, 1932—. Died Jan. 18, 1939.

HUTCHINSON, Charles Lawrence, banker; b. Lynn, Mass., Mar. 7, 1854; s. Benjamin P. and Sarah (Ingalls) H.; has lived in Chicago from 1856; grad. Chicago High School, 1873; hon. A.M., Tufts College, 1901, and Harvard U., 1915; degree of LL.D. from Tufts College, 1919; m. Frances, d. Herbert M. Kinsley, 1881. Became grain merchant and later banker; v.p. Corn Exchange National Bank (formerly pres.); dir. Northern Trust Co. Has been pres. Chicago Bd. of Trade; was dir. and chmn. fine arts com., World's Columbian Expn.; pres. Art Inst. of Chicago from its orgn.; pres. Chicago Orphan Asylum; pres. gen. convs. Universalist Ch., 4 terms; v.p. Egypt Exploration Fund; trustee, 1890—, and treas. U. of Chicago; treas. Rush Med. Coll., McCormick Memorial Inst. for Infectious Diseases, and Sanitary Dist. of Chicago; v.p. South Park Commn., Chicago; trustee Hull House, Old People's Home, Carnegie Instn. of Washington. Hon. mem. Am. Inst. of Architects. Home: Chicago, Ill. Died Oct. 7, 1924.

HUTCHINSON, Elijah Cubberley, congressman; b. Windsor, N.J., Aug. 7, 1855; s. Spafford W. and Mary E. (Cubberley) H.; ed. pub. schs. and business coll.; m. 2d, Mrs. Ella C. Stults Reese, June 12, 1922. Sec. and treas. Trenton Bone Fertilizer Co.; dir. Broad St. Bank (Trenton). Member New Jersey Ho. of Assembly, 1896, 1897, Senate, 1899-1904 (pres. 1903); state road commd. of N.J., 1905-08; mem. 64th to 67th Congresses (1915-23), 4th N.J. Dist. Republican. Presbyn. Mason. Home: Trenton, N.J. Died June 25, 1932.

HUTCHINSON, Frederick Lane; b. Elizabeth, N.J., Apr. 2, 1866; s. John and Elizabeth (Pring) H.; M.E. in Electrical Engring., Cornell U., 1893; m. Grace Lawrence Duryee, June 27, 1921. With Westinghouse Elec. & Mfg. Co., Newark, N.J., New York and Pittsburgh, 1893-1901; mgr. publication dept. C. W. Hunt Co., New York, 1901; mgr. electric sales dept., Nat. Electric Co., Milwaukee, 1902-03 with Am. Inst. Elec. Engrs., 1904—, became nat. sec. and exec. manager. Home: Glen Ridge, N.J. Died Feb. 26, 1932.

HUTCHINSON, John, surgeon; b. Hebron, Conn., Feb. 28, 1860; s. John Calvin and Maryette (Keeney) H.; ed. prep. sch. and under pvt. tutors; M.D., New York Homœ. Med. Coll. and Flower Hosp., 1898; m. Adaline Gillette Eldridge. Practiced in N.Y. City, 1898—; specialist in treatment chronic diseases; formerly active in hosps. and in post-graduate institutions. Founder of Council for Homœopathy. Pres. International Hahnemannian Assn.; mem. Am. Press Humorists. Republican. Episcopalian. Opposed to vivisection, vaccination and compulsory inoculations. Died May 2, 1941.

HUTCHINSON, John Irwin, mathematician; b. Bangor, Me., Apr. 12, 1867; s. Rev. Henry H. and Bessie Jane (Frank) H.; A.B., Bates Coll., Lewiston, Me., 1889; Clark Univ., Worcester, Mass., 1890-92, U. of Chicago, 1892-94, Ph.D., 1896; m. Genevra Barrett, June 17, 1896. Instr. math., 1894-1903, asst. prof., 1903-10, prof., 1910—, Cornell U. Republican. Conglist. Author: Differential and Integral Calculus (with Prof. Virgil Snyder), 1902; Elementary Treatise on the Calculus (with same), 1912. Home: Ithaca, N.Y. Died Dec. 1, 1935.

HUTCHINSON, John Wallace, vocalist, song composer; b. Milford, N.H., 1821; s. Jesse and Mary (Leavitt) H.; ed. pub. schs., Milford, N.H.; m. Fanny B. Patch, 1843 (died 1888). His parents and their 13 children formed, under name of The Hutchinson Family, a well-known quartet of vocalists, composed of John, Judson, Asa and Abby, in the '40s sang all over North and West. They were abolitionists, temperance advocates and favored woman suffrage, and sang in behalf of these reforms; took part in Rep. campaigns of 1856 and 1860. The quartet visited Army of Potomac and were expelled, but were readmitted by personal order of President Lincoln, and were afterwards singers and active nurses in hosp. camps. Sang in British Isles, 1845-46; visited and were entertained at White House by President John Tyler; visited President Lincoln by spl. request and sang in Green Room, White House, 1862; Mr. Hutchinson has given 11,670 concerts; sang 62 yrs.; founded Am. Temperance Union, 1866; conducted a farm in Mass.; founded Hutchinson, Kan., and Hutchinson, Minn.; gave site of 10 acres at Hutchinson for Ansgar College. Author: The Granite Songster, 1848; Story of the Hutchinsons, 1896. Home: Lynn, Mass. Died 1908.

HUTCHINSON, Joseph Baldwin, ry. official; b. Bristol, Pa., Mar. 20, 1844; s. Joseph B. and Selina Knapp H.; grad. Polytechnic Coll. of Pa., 1861; followed by a yr. in Delamater Iron Works, New York, and received certificate as 3d asst. engr.; employed on steamer, 1862-63; employed on various rys., 1863-79; served as vol. in Gettysburg campaign, 1863; supt. Lewistown div., Pa. Ry., 1879-81, Frederick div., 1881-84, Altoona div., 1884-90, Western Pa. div., 1890-91; supt. Md. div. Phila., Wilmington & Baltimore, Baltimore & Potomac, Washington Southern, 1891-93; gen. supt. transportation Pa. Ry. east of Pittsburgh, and Erie Ry. at Phila., 1893-97; gen. mgr., 1897-1903, asst. to 2d v.p., 1903-09, asst. to 1st v.p., 1909-11, asst. to 5th v.p., Mar. 3, 1911-May 8, 1912, and asst. to v.p., May 8, 1912—, Pa. R.R. Co. Home: Philadelphia, Pa. Died Feb. 12, 1934.

HUTCHINSON, Norman, consul-general; b. San Francisco, Aug. 10, 1875; s. Henry Loring and Josephine (Rees) H.; ed. Belmont (Calif.) Sch., "Bellerive," Vevey, Switzerland, Cornell U., École libre Sciences Politiques, Paris, Merton Coll., Oxford, Eng.; LL.B., Cornell U., 1897; m. Juanita Davies, of Santiago, Chile, Aug. 27, 1902. Apptd. sec. Am. Legation at Santiago, Chile, Jan. 8, 1902, at Caracas, Mar. 24, 1904, Stockholm, June 28, 1906; apptd. sec. legation and consul-gen. to Rumania and Servia, and sec. diplomatic agency, Bulgaria, July 24, 1907; retired from diplomatic service, Sept. 26, 1909; residing in Paris. Vol. orderly at Am. Ambulance at Neuilly, France, Jan. 1, 1915—. Died Dec. 21, 1924.

HUTCHINSON, S(ydney) Pemberton, capitalist; b. Phila., Pa., Apr. 27, 1861; s. Pemberton Sydney and Agnes (Wharton) H.; student St. Paul's Sch., Concord, N.H., 1873-79; student U. of Pa., 1879-81; m. Amy Lewis, Apr. 13, 1887; children—Sophie Lewis (Mrs. Henry S. Drinker, Jr.), Agnes Wharton (Mrs. George W. Martin), Aimee (Mrs. Joseph T. Thayer), S(ydney) Pemberton. Began as rodman engr. corps, Pa. R.R., 1881; with same rd. as asst. engr., supervisor, div. engr., div. supt., and asst. gen. agt. at N.Y. City until 1901; became connected with Phelps, Dodge & Co., in its railroad enterprises, May 1901; supt. B.&O. R.R., at Pittsburgh, Pa., 1902; asst. gen. supt. and gen. supt. M.C. R.R., 1902-05; resigned, Nov. 15, 1905; mem. Cramp, Mitchell & Shober, bankers, Phila., 1906-10; pres. Westmoreland Coal Co., June 1910—; trustee Penn Mut. Life Insurance Co.; mem. bd. mgrs. Phila. Savings Fund Soc.; mem. Tidewater Coal Exchange during World War. Mem. European Commn. of Nat. Industrial Conf. Bd., 1919; mem. employers' group of President Wilson's Industrial Conf., Washington, D.C., 1919. Mem. Phila. Bd. of Trade (exec. council), Phila. Bourse (dir.). Republican. Episcopalian. Home: Merion, Pa. Died Feb. 16, 1929.

HUTCHINSON, Woods, M.D.; b. Selby, Yorkshire, Eng., Jan. 3, 1862; s. Charles and Elizabeth (Woods) H.; came with parents to U.S., 1874; A.B., Penn Coll., Oskaloosa, Ia., 1880, A.M., 1883; M.D., U. of Mich., 1884; m. Cornelia M. Williams, May 15, 1893; 1 son, Alexander Williams. Began practice, 1884; prof. anatomy, State U. of Ia., 1891-96; prof. comparative pathology, U. of Buffalo, 1896-1900; state health officer of Ore., 1903-05; clin. prof. medicine, New York Polyclinic, 1907-09. Lecturer on comparative pathology, London Med. Graduates' Coll., Eng., 1899-1900; lecturer on biology, extension dept., U. of London, 1899-1900. Fellow Am. Acad. Medicine (pres. 1915-16), A.M.A. Author: Preventable Diseases, 1909; Conquest of Consumption, 1910; The Child's Day, 1912; Common Diseases, 1913; Civilization and Health, 1914; Community Hygiene, 1915; The Doctor in War, 1918; Exercise and Health, 1918; Building Strong Bodies, 1924; New Handbook of Health, 1926. Home: Brookline, Mass. Died Apr. 26, 1930.

HUTCHISON, Benjamin Franklin, naval officer; b. St. Louis, Mo., Feb. 12, 1868; s. Walter Raleigh and Sarah (Murphy) H.; grad. U.S. Naval Acad., 1889; m. Helen Seymour Weaver, Apr. 20, 1907. Promoted ensign U.S. Navy, June 1891; lt., 1899; lt. comdr., 1896; comdr., 1910; capt., Aug. 6, 1915. Midshipman on U.S.S. Boston, until 1891; served on Yorktown, Mohican, Petral, Detroit and again on Mohican until 1898; service ashore on training stas., San Francisco and Norfolk, Va., U.S. Naval Acad., Naval War Coll., Navy Yard (New York), Hydrographic Office, Washington; administrator tanker floating equipment, New York and comdt. Navy Yard, Norfolk, Va.; comdr. Kansas, 1917, Mississippi, 1918. Episcopalian. Home: Utica, N.Y. Died Sept. 16, 1927.

HUTCHISON, Martin Bell, banker; b. Altoona, Pa., Jan. 5, 1860; s. Joseph and Mary M. (Scott) H.; student Lafayette Coll., Easton, Pa., 1880-82; m. Inez V. Jordan, Apr. 25, 1888. Settled in Ottumwa; became connected with Ottumwa Nat. Bank, 1882, cashier, 1885-92; cashier, First Nat. Bank, Ottumwa, 1893-1904; organizer, 1903, and pres., M. B. Hutchison Lumber Co.; v.p. Union Trust & Savings Bank; dir. First Nat. Bank, Ottumwa Automobile Co.; elected dir. Federal Reserve Bank, Chicago, Class B, Group 2, July 1914. Pres. Bd. of Edn., Ottumwa. Republican. Presbyn. Home: Ottumwa, Ia. Died Aug. 6, 1918.

HUTCHISON, Robert Alden, clergyman; b. Claysville, Pa., Feb. 8, 1862; s. James and Mary (Robinson) H.; student Westminster Coll., New Wilmington, Pa.; A.B., Monmouth (Ill.) Coll., 1888, A.M., 1891; grad. Xenia (O.) Theol. Sem., 1891; D.D., Grove City, Muskingum and Monmouth colleges, 1907; LL.D., Cedarville (O.) Coll., 1927, Monmouth (Ill.) Coll., 1927; m. Mary Orr, Oct. 19, 1892 (died 1896); 1 son, James Renwick; m. 2d, Jean Stirling, Dec. 16, 1909; children—Robert Alden, Russell Stirling, Margaret Jean, Mary Joan. Ordained ministry U.P. Ch., of North America, 1891; pastor 1st Ch., Altoona, Pa., 1891-1907; elected pres. Muskingum (O.) Coll., 1904, but declined; gen. sec. and mem. Bd. of Home Missions U.P. Ch., 1907—; opened many schs. and chs. in mountains of Ark., Ky. and Tenn.; elected moderator Gen. Assembly U.P. Ch., 1926; moderator Synod of Pittsburgh, 1901. An organizer Keystone Party, 1910, and member state com., vice chmn. and chmn. Allegheny County Com. of Keystone Party; mem. bd. trustees Am. Anti-Saloon League, also of State Bd. of Pa. Anti-Saloon League; chmn. of 75th Anniversary Com. of United Presbyn. Ch.; one of fifteen Dry delegates selected in Pa. as candidate to the 18th Amendment Convention. Republican. Author: Memory Talks on Spiritual Power, 1899; Save America, 1920; also Holy Spirit—Word Outline, 1924. Home: Pittsburgh, Pa. Died Dec. 11, 1937.

HUTSON, Charles Woodward, author, artist; b. McPhersonville, S.C., Sept. 23, 1840; s. William Ferguson and Sophronia (Palmer) H.; A.B., S.C. Coll., 1860; LL.D., U. of S.C., 1911; m. Mary Jane Lockett, July 5, 1871; children—Ethel, William F., Henry L., A. Cary, Sophie P., Mary L., Miles B., Albert L. Served in Hampton Legion and Beaufort Arty., C.S.A., 1861-65. Prof. Greek, La. State U., 1869-73; prof. modern languages, Univ. of Miss., 1881-89; professor Agricultural and Mechanical College, Tex., 1893-1908; began as painter, 1905; exhibited Art Assn. of New Orleans, 1911—; Soc. Independent Artists, New York, 1917; Southern States Art League, 1923—; Arts and Crafts Club of New Orleans, 1921— (awarded Blanche Benjamin prize for best Southern landscape, 1925). Author: Out of a Besieged City, 1887. Editor: Fantastics and Other Fancies (by Lafcadio Hearn), 1914; Creole Sketches (by same), 1924; Editorials (by same), 1926. Home: New Orleans, La. Died May 27, 1936.

HUTTIG, Charles Henry, banker, mfr.; b. Muscatine, Ia., Feb. 14, 1861; s. Frederick and Sophia (Schnell) H.; ed. pub. schs., Muscatine; m. Annie E. Musser, Apr. 13, 1902. Began as clerk in bank at Muscatine; moved to St. Louis and established as mfr. of sash, doors and blinds; still pres. Huttig Sash & Door Co.; pres. Third Nat. Bank, 1897—. Mem. Sch. Board, St. Louis, 1891-95. Methodist. Democrat. Was 6th v.p. St. Louis Expn. Home: St. Louis, Mo. Died July 12, 1913.

HUTTON, Edward Hyatt, surgeon; b. West Troy, N.Y., Nov. 5, 1872; s. Alfred J. (D.D.) and Harriet (Hyatt) H.; student U. of Rochester, 1890; A.B., Williams, 1894; M.D., Coll. Phys. and Surg. (Columbia), 1900; m. Alice Kathryn Simpson, Oct. 1, 1902; children—Ruth, Alice Kathryn. Practiced at Corning, N.Y., 1901—; surgeon Corning Hosp., 1902-33; expert to N.Y. Dept. of Health, 1906-15; surgeon to N.Y.C. R.R.; formerly mem. bd. mgrs. Pleasant Valley Sanitarium, Bath, N.Y. Capt. U.S.A., 1918; now maj. M.R.C. Chmn. Steuben County Alcoholic Beverage Control Board. Fellow Am. Coll. Surgeons, 1921; pres. Steuben Co. Med. Soc., 1926. Home: Corning, N.Y. Died May 7, 1934.

HUTTON, Frederick Remsen, mech. engr.; b. New York, May 28, 1853; s. Mancius Smedes and Gertrude (Holmes) H.; brother of Mancius Holmes H.; A.B., Columbia, 1873, A.M., E.M., C.E., 1876, Ph.D., 1881 (Sc.D., 1904; Sc.D., Rutgers, 1913); m. Grace Lefferts May 28, 1878. Asst. civ. and mech. engring., 1876-77, instr. mech. engring., 1877-82, adj. prof., 1882-91, prof., 1891-1907, prof. emeritus, 1907, dean faculty applied science, 1899-1905, Columbia. Consulting engr. Dept. Water, Gas and Electricity, City of New York, and of Automobile Club of America, 1911-12. Trustee Collegiate Sch., New York, 1885—. Asso. editor Engineering Mag., 1892, Johnson's Encyclopædia, 1893, Century Dictionary, 1904, New Internat. Encyclopædia, 1913. Fellow Am. Acad. Arts and Sciences. Author: Mechanical Engineering of Power Plants, 1897; Heat and Heat Engines, 1899; Machine Tools (U.S. Census, 1880); The Gas Engine, 1904. Died May 14, 1918.

HUTTON, James Buchanan, clergyman; b. Indian Run, Va., Mar. 19, 1866; s. Arthur Dixon (M.D.) and Sarah E. B. (Ryburn) H.; A.B., Emory and Henry Coll., 1885, D.D., 1911; studied law, U. of Va., summer 1887; B.D., Union Theol. Sem., Va., 1891; D.D., Southwestern Presbyn. U., Clarksville, Tenn., 1903; m. Irene Rosalind Gwin, May 8, 1895; children—Arthur Dixon, Martha Gwin, Mary Ryburn, Samuel Gwin, James Buchanan, Irene Rosalind, Charlton Dobyns. Teacher and prin. schs., 1885-87; home mission work, summers, 1890, 91; licensed to preach, 1891; pastor Lexington and Durant chs., Miss., 1892; ordained ministry Presbyn Ch., U.S., 1892, and continued as pastor same chs.; pastor First Ch., Jackson, Miss., 1896—; established missions in Jackson, growing into Central, Power Memorial and Fondren chs. Moderator Synod of Miss., 1913; chmn. Synod's exec. com. of edn., 1913-27; chmn. home missions, Synod of Miss. and of Central Miss. Presbytery; mem. judicial com. of Gen. Assembly Presbyn. Ch. in U.S., 1925-1933; mem. Gen. Assembly's com. on union of chs.; leader in establishing Belhaven Coll.; mem. bd. dirs. Southwestern Coll., Memphis, Tenn.; trustee Columbia Theol. Sem., Decatur, Ga., 1924—; trustee Y.M.C.A. (Jackson). Democrat. Home: Jackson, Miss. Died Sept. 22, 1940.

HUTTON, James Morgan, investment banker; b. Cincinnati, O., Feb. 21, 1870; s. William Edward and Cornelia Pendleton (Morgan) H.; ed. pub. schs., Cincinnati; m. Sarah Peters Johnston, Jan. 4, 1899; children—James Morgan, Elizabeth J., William Edward II. Began with W. E. Hutton & Co., investment bankers, Cincinnati, 1889, became sr. mem. on retirement of father (the firm is member of New York, Cincinnati, Philadelphia, Baltimore and Detroit stock exchanges, Chicago Stock Exchange, Chicago Bd. of Trade, New York Cotton Exchange, New York Curb Exchange); dir. U.S. Shoe Corp., Aluminum Industries, Inc., Cincinnati Street Railway Co., Am. Thermos Bottle Company, Am. Rolling Mill Co. (chmn. finance com.), Hatfield Co., Campbell-Creek Coal Co., Champion Paper & Fibre Co., Interchemical Corp., Richardson Co., Morristown Securities Corp., Printing Machinery Co., Multi-Colortype Co., Duplex Paper Bag Co. Pres. Cincinnati Stock Exchange, Cincinnati Chamber Commerce; trustee Cincinnati Childrens Home; dir. Cincinnati Fine Arts Society, Ohio Chamber of Commerce. Republican. Episcopalian. Home: Cincinnati, O. Died Mar. 1, 1940.

HUTTON, Laurence, author, essayist, journalist, lecturer; b. New York, Aug. 8, 1843; s. John and Eliza Ann H.; ed. private schools (A.M., Yale, 1892; Princeton, 1897); m. Eleanor Varnum Mitchell, Apr. 7, 1885. Literary editor Harper's Mag., 1886-98; univ. lecturer on English literature, Princeton. Author: Literary Landmarks of Venice; Literary Landmarks of Florence; Literary Landmarks of Rome: Literary Landmarks of Jerusalem; Boy I Knew; Literary Landmarks of Oxford. Home: Princeton, N.J. Died 1904.

HUTTON, Levi W., philanthropist; b. Fairfield, Ia., Oct. 22, 1860; s. Levi and Nancy (Hutton) H.; left an orphan at age of 6 and brought up by uncle; ed. dist. sch.; m. Mary Arkwright, 1887 (died 1915). Went to Portland, Ore., 1879; locomotive fireman, later engr. N.P. Ry., trans to Coeur d'Alene mining dist., Ida., and was one of original owners Hercules Mine, one of the largest lead-silver producing mines of the country; built Hutton Bldg., Spokane, 1907; purchased Fernwell Bldg., 1914; built Liberty Theatre; operated Regal shoe store 10 yrs.; dir. Old Nat. Bank, Union Trust Co. Founder, 1917, The Hutton Settlement, a home for orphans, fully endowed, comprising 300 acres of land near Spokane, with modern bldgs., on cottage plan, now housing 80 children. Trustee Community Welfare Federation. Mem. Brotherhood of Locomotive Engrs. Mason. Home: Spokane, Wash. Died Nov. 3, 1928.

HUTTON, Mancius Holmes, clergyman; b. New York, Oct. 13, 1837; s. Mancius Smedes and Gertrude (Holmes) H.; bro. of Frederick Remsen H.; A.B., New York U., 1857; Union Theol. Sem., 1857-59; grad. New Brunswick Theol. Sem., 1860; (D.D., Rutgers, 1879); m. Mary Eleanor Clark, Oct. 8, 1879. Ordained Ref. Ch. in America ministry, 1864; pastor Mt. Vernon, N.Y., 1864-79, Second Ch., New Brunswick, N.J., 1879-1908 (emeritus). Pres. Gen. Synod, 1886; pres. Bd. Foreign Missions, 1896—; mem. deputation to visit missions in Arabia, India, China and Japan, 1905. Home: New Brunswick, N.J. Died 1909.

HUTTON, Norman, clergyman; b. Baltimore, Md., June 20, 1876; s. Richard Graham and Frances (Allan) H.; Hobart Coll., Geneva, N.Y., 1903, S.T.D.,

1918; grad. Gen. Theol. Sem., 1905; m. Anne Butler, June 20, 1905; children—Norman, Nancy Butler, Eduard Butler. Deacon, 1904, priest, 1905, P.E. Ch.; priest in charge Ch. of Nativity, Mineola, L.I., 1905-07; successively rector Trinity Ch., Roslyn, L.I., St. Chrysostom's Ch., Chicago (rector honorarius) rector St. Andrews Ch., Wellesley, Mass. Trustee Hobart College. Home: Wellesley, Mass. Died Sept. 25, 1935.

HUYCK, Edmund Niles, mfr.; b. Rensselaerville, N.Y., May 17, 1866; s. Francis Conkling and Emily Harriet (Niles) H.; grad. Albany Acad., 1884; A.B., Williams, 1888; m. Jessie Van Antwerp, Dec. 9, 1891. Entered father's business, mfg. woolen felts for paper mfrs., 1888; title of firm changed, 1894, to F. C. Huyck & Sons, of which is pres.; pres. Kenwood Mills, Ltd., Arnprior, Ont., Can.; trustee Albany Savings Bank; dir. Nat. Commercial Bank & Trust Co.; mem. War Industries Bd. (felt sect., in charge dept. woven felts), 1918; advisory com. State Fund for Compensation Ins.; mem. Albany Chamber Commerce (pres. 1918). Pres. bd. trustees Albany Med. Coll. (Union U.); pres. bd. govs. Union U.; trustee Union Coll., Bennington Coll.; mem. bd. govs. Albany Hosp. Presbyn. Home: Albany, N.Y. Died July 15, 1930.

HYATT, Alpheus, curator Boston Soc. of Natural History and asst. Museum Comparative Zoölogy, Cambridge, Mass.; b. Washington, April 5, 1838; academic edn. at Yale; grad. Lawrence Scientific School, Harvard, S.B., 1862 (LL.D., Brown, 1898); m. Andella Beebe, Jan. 7, 1867. Served in Civil War, becoming capt.; has been officer in the Essex Inst. and Peabody Acad., Salem, Mass.; also prof. zoölogy and paleontology Mass. Inst. Technology; mem. Nat. Acad. Sciences; foreign mem. Geol. Soc. London, Am. Acad. Arts and Sciences; etc. Author: Observations on Fresh Water Polyzoa; Genesis of Planobis at Steinheim; Genesis of the Arietidæ Phylogeny of an Acquired Characteristic. Home: Boston, Mass. Died 1902.

HYATT, Charles Eliot, college pres.; b. Wilmington, Del., Nov. 27, 1851; s. Theodore and Matilda Eliot (Rice) H.; C.E., Pa. Mil. Coll., 1872; (LL.D., 1913); brevetted brig. gen. N.G.P., June 1923; m. Kezia West Dyer, July 6, 1880; children—Mrs. A. M. Burt, Mabel Lee, Frank Kelso, Leslie Starr. Teacher from 1872, pres. Pennsylvania Military Coll., 1888—. Home: Chester, Pa. Died Apr. 9, 1930.

HYATT, Edward, state supt. schs.; b. Huntington, Pa., Mar. 8, 1858; s. Thomas Jefferson and Mary (Atkinson) H.; B.S., Ohio State U., 1881; m. Margaret Gill, Jan. 26, 1881. State supt. pub. instrn., Calif., Jan. 1, 1907—. Republican. Presbyn. Home: Sacramento, Calif. Died Dec. 1919.

HYATT, John Wesley, inventor; b. Starkey, N.Y., Nov. 28, 1837; s. John Wesley and Anne (Gleason) H.; common sch. edn. and 1 yr. at Eddytown Sem.; m. Anna E. Taft, July 21, 1869. Removed to Ill. at 16 and became a printer; subsequently gave whole attention to inventing; first patent, 1861, a knife-sharpener; new method of making dominoes and checkers, 1869; discovered method of dissolving pyroxylin under pressure and with his late brother I. Smith H., invented "celluloid"; established mfg. at Newark, N.J.; began mfg. of sch. slates, 1875; invented Hyatt billiard ball, both material and machinery; invented water purifying system, 1881, now in use in 1,000 places in the U.S.; about 1892 invented Hyatt Roller Bearing and organized Hyatt Roller Bearing Co., Harrison, N.J.; invented, 1900, lockstitch sewing machine, with 50 needles, for sewing belting; has also invented machine for squeezing juice from sugar cane, obtaining 8 per cent more sugar than former machines, and at less cost; has recently patented new method of solidifying Am. hard woods, from which bowling balls, golf heads, mallets, etc., are being made. Awarded Perkin medal of Soc. Chem. Industry, 1914. Home: Short Hills, N.J. Died May 10, 1920.

HYDE, Albert Alexander, mfr.; b. Lee, Mass., Mar. 2, 1848; s. Alexander and Cornelia (Hull) H.; ed. boarding sch. and high sch.; m. Ida E. Todd, Jan. 1875; children—Albert Todd, Edward Knowlton, Alexander, Mrs. Mary Lewis, Charles Hewett, Mrs. Ruth Purviance, Paul Hull, George Alvan, Mrs. Martha Barclay. Began as clk. in bank of Clark & Co., Leavenworth, Kan., 1865; organized for same, Wichita Savings Bank, 1872, later cashier Farmers & Merchants Bank, Wichita; in loan business, and mem. Hyde & Humble Stationery Co.; organized, 1888, the Yucca Co., later the Mentholatum Co., of which became pres. Trustee Fairmount Coll., Wichita; mem. Internat. Com. Y.M.C.A. Republican. Presbyn. Home: Wichita, Kan. Died Jan. 10, 1935.

HYDE, Ammi Bradford, college prof.; b. Oxford, N.Y., Mar. 13, 1824; s. Asabel J. and Mary O. (Hinckley) H.; A.B., Wesleyan U., Conn., 1846, A.M., 1848; (D.D., Genesee, 1867, Syracuse, 1874; Litt.D., U. of Denver); m. Mira Smith, July 20, 1850. Prof. langs., Cazenovia (N.Y.) Sem., 1846-'62; ordained M.E. ministry, 1850; pastor Rushville, N.Y., 1862-64; prof. Greek, English and Hebrew, Allegheny Coll., 1864-84; formerly prof. langs. and librarian, prof. philology, 1909—, U. of Denver. Editor Rocky Mountain Christian Advocate, 1887-90; pastor University Park, Colo., 1897-98. Author: Essays, 1884; Story of Methodism, 1890. Contbr. to Methodist Review 58 yrs. Died Mar. 23, 1921.

HYDE, Charles Leavitt, banker; b. on farm, Pike Co., Ill., June 23, 1860; s. James Franklin and Harriett L. (Blake) Hyde; educated in country school; m. Katherine Robinson, July 28, 1886. Commercial traveler, hardware trade, 1882-86; merchant, Lima, O., 1886-87; moved to Pierre, S.D., 1888; engaged in real estate, banking and cattle raising; pres. Am. Exchange Bank, 1st Nat. Life Ins. Co., Onida Nat. Bank. Trustee Yankton Coll., Pierre Congl. Ch. for 20 yrs. Lt. gov. of S.Dak. Kiwanis. Park in Pierre named in his honor Hyde Park. Home: Pierre, S.D. Died Sept. 10, 1938.

HYDE, Edward Warden, shipbuilder; b. Bath, Maine, August 9, 1868; s. Thomas W. and Annie (Hayden) Hyde; ed. at Phillips Exeter (N.H.) Acad. and Mass. Inst. Tech.; m. Alice Mayo Morse, Dec. 4, 1902. Began as storekeeper, Bath Iron Works, Ltd., 1892, and was pres., 1898-1903; pres. First Nat. Bank 6 yrs.; incorporator and 1st v.p. Bath Trust Co.; treas. Hyde Windlass Co., 1897-1901. Mayor City of Bath, 1902-04, inclusive; mem. Rep. City Com. 6 yrs. (chmn. 2 yrs.); mem. Me. Ho. of Rep., 1908-09. Episcopalian. Home: Bath, Me. Deceased.

HYDE, Edward Wyllys, mathematician; b. Saginaw, Mich., Oct. 17, 1843; s. Rev. Harvey and Julia Dwight (Taylor) H.; lt. 33d U.S.C.T. in Civil War; B.C.E., Cornell, 1872, C.E., 1874; m. Sarah J., d. James Rowe, Sept. 11, 1878. Instr. civ. engring., Cornell, 1871-73; prof. mathematics, Pa. Mil. Acad., 1873-74; asst. prof., 1875-78, prof. mathematics, 1878—, dean 1892-93 and 1898-1900, chmn. of faculty, 1894-95, U. of Cincinnati. Treas. and actuary Columbia Life Ins. Co., 1903—. Author: Skew Arches, 1875; Directional Calculus, 1890; A Portion of Higher Mathematics, 1896. Died Nov. 4, 1930.

HYDE, Edwin Francis, banker; b. New York, June 23, 1842; s. Edwin and Elizabeth A. (Mead) H.; A.B., New York Free Acad. (now Coll. City of New York), 1861; LL.B., Columbia Law Sch., 1863; m. Marie E. Brown, Nov. 18, 1868. Served in Civ. War as mem. 22d N.Y. Regt., at Harper's Ferry, Va., 1862; practiced law, 1863-86; v.p. Central Trust Co., 1886-1919. Trustee Princeton Theol. Sem. (treas. 1898-1924); treas. New York Sabbath Committee. President Am. Bible Society. Member Reformed Dutch Church. Republican. Fellow Philharmonic Society of London, Royal Geog. Soc.; pres. Philharmonic Soc. of New York, 1888-1901. Home: New York, N.Y. Died Mar. 30, 1933.

HYDE, George Merriam, editorial writer The Commercial Advertiser and reviewer of books and plays; b. Middlebury, Vt., Feb. 26, 1865 (son of late Prof. James T. Hyde of Chicago Theol. Sem.); studied in Chicago public schools; grad. Amherst, 1888 (A.M., 1892); post-graduate and theol. studies Yale; traveled and studied in Europe, 1891-92; taught English literature Minneapolis High School, 1892-96; m. Violet McDougall Buel, dau. late Col. D. H. Buel, U.S.A., Jan. 11, 1899. Author of numerous essays and sketches in The Bookman, The Book-Buyer and in newspapers. Home: New York, N.Y. Died 1899.

HYDE, Helen, artist; b. Lima, N.Y.; d. William Bierlie and Marietta (Butler) H.; grad. Wellesley Sch., Phila.; studied art under Emil Carlsen, San Francisco Art Inst.; Frank Skarbina, Berlin; Raphael Collin, Paris; Kano Tomonobu, Tokyo; unmarried. Best known by etchings in color and woodcuts of women and children; first success, etchings in color of Chinese children, of Chinatown, San Francisco; spent 14 yrs. in Japan making etchings, woodcuts and water colors of Japanese children and women; also made series of woodcuts, Mexican subjects. Entire series in Congressional Library, Washington; also some in New York Pub. Library, Art Mus., San Francisco. Episcopalian. Home: Chicago, Ill. Died May 14, 1919.

HYDE, James Nevins, physician; b. Norwich, Conn., June 21, 1840; s. Edward Goodrich and Hannah Huntington (Thomas) H.; A.B., Yale, 1861, A.M., 1865; M.D., U. of Pa., 1869; (hon. M.D., Rush Med. Coll., Chicago, 1879); asst. and passed asst. surgeon U.S.N., 1863-69; m. Alice Louise Griswold, July 31, 1872. Lecturer on skin diseases, Rush Med. Coll., 1873-76; prof. dermatology, Northwestern U., 1876-88; prof. skin and genito-urinary diseases, Rush Med. Coll., 1879—. Professorial lecturer on dermatology, U. of Chicago, 1902—; sec. council administration and of faculty, Rush Med. College. Mem. Internat. Congresses of Dermatology, 1889-1907 (sec. for America, 5th congress); corr. mem. French, Italian, Berlin and Vienna Dermatol. socs.; pres. Am. Dermatol. Assn., 1881, 1896. Author: Early Medical Chicago; Diseases of the Skin, 8th edit., 1909. Home: Chicago, Ill. Died 1910.

HYDE, Jesse Earl, geologist; b. Rushville, O., May 2, 1884; s. Eber and Flora Belle (Johnson) H.; B.A., Ohio State U., 1906; M.A. Columbia, 1907; post-grad. work Columbia and Harvard; m. Edna M. McCleery, Aug. 1, 1911; children—William McCleery, Eber Johnson. Asst. in physiography, Harvard, 1908, in paleontology, Columbia, 1909-11; asst. prof. geology, Queen's U., Can., 1911-15; asso. prof. geology, Western Reserve U., 1915-21, prof., 1921—. Asst. geologist, Geol. Survey of Ohio, many summers; paleontologist Geol. Survey of Can., 1912-14; consulting practice, 1919—; curator of geology, Cleveland Mus. Natural History, 1922—. Fellow Geol. Soc. America, Ohio Acad. Science, A.A.A.S. Protestant. Author: Geology of Camp Sherman Quadrangle (Geol. Survey of Ohio), 1921. Home: Cleveland Heights, Celveland, O. Died July 3, 1936.

HYDE, Joel Wilbur, M.D.; b. Westbrook, Conn., Mar. 20, 1839; s. Rev. William Albert and Martha (Sackett) H.; grad. Yale, 1861; Yale Med. School; m. Mary E. Richardson, 1861. Staff officer and later surgeon Conn. vols., 1861-65; brigade surgeon Nat. Guard, N.Y., 1872-79; Loyal Legion, New England Soc., Hamilton Club; also has practiced in Brooklyn from 1865; has held important positions in Long Island and St. Mary's hosps.; mem. Am. Assn. of Obstetricians and Gynaecologists, and many med. socs. Home: Brooklyn, N.Y. Died 1907.

HYDE, John, statistician, geographer; b. Stalybridge, Eng., Dec. 16, 1848; s. Abel and Emily (Adshead) H.; ed. Stamford Acad., and Owens Coll. (now U. of Manchester); m. Emily Watson, of Leamington, Eng., 1874; children—Edith Emily, Elizabeth Adshead, Edward Alderson, John Lawrence, Mrs. (Mary) Winifred Lee. Began as clk. country bank; made researches into econ. effects of preventable disease; traveled in U.S. and Can., 1882-83; asso. editor Prairie Farmer, 1884-85, Bankers' Monthly, 1885-86; investigations of econ. conditions in U.S. and Can., 1886-90; spl. agent 11th U.S. Census, in charge agr., 1890-94; editor Nat. Geog. Mag., 1895-1901; chief Bur. of Statistics, Dept. of Agr., 1897-1905; mem. U.S. Geog. Bd., 1899-1905; cotton expert U.S. Commn. to Paris Expn., 1900 (grand prize for Am. cottons); mem. Jury of Awards, Trans-Miss. Expn., Omaha, 1898, St. Louis Expn., 1904. Studied Far Eastern problems in China and Japan, 1906-10; contrib. editor Japan Mail, 1908-09; Washington corr. N. China Daily News and Herald, 1911-24. Presented library of 4,000 vols. of statis. ("Hyde Library") to Tokyo Statis. Soc., 1913; presented collection N. Am. Indian ethnologica to Harris Mus., Preston, Eng., 1914. Home: Washington, D.C. Died Jan. 18, 1929.

HYDE, John McEwen, brig. gen. U.S.A.; b. New York, Nov. 1, 1841; s. Joseph and Catherine Maria (McEwen) H.; m. Katharine Hubbard, Oct. 21, 1885. Pvt. Co. A, 71st Regt., N.G.S.N.Y., June 16, 1861; disch., July 30, 1861; 2d lt. 38th N.Y. Inf., Jan. 11, 1862; promoted through grades to lt. col. deputy q.m. gen., Apr. 12, 1903; brig. gen., July 9, 1904. Bvtd. lt. col. vols., Mar. 13, 1865, "for gallant and meritorious services in battle of Cold Harbor, Va."; col. vols., Mar. 13, 1865, for same in front of Petersburg, Va. Wounded in battle of Bull Run; was in siege of Yorktown and at 2d Bull Run, where was again wounded, and at Fredericksburg; served at Chancellorsville in Miles' Div., 2d Corps, Army of Potomac, in action of Morton's Ford, battles of the Wilderness, Po River, Spottsylvania C.H., North Anna, Tolopotomoy Creek, Cold Harbor, Petersburg. Surveying expdn. N.P. R.R., 1872; served in Wyo., Ariz., Nev., Ida. and Calif., 1874-83; on recruiting service, New York, 1883-85; took part in Bannock campaign, 1878, in Chimehueva troubles in Ariz., 1880, and Cibicu troubles, 1881; adj. 8th Inf., 1886; capt. and asst. q.-m., 1889; at Davids Island, New York Harbor, 1889-92; Jefferson Barracks, Mo., 1892-93; Vancouver Barracks, Wash., 1893-96; at Boston, 1896-99, adding to q.-m. work that of purchasing commissary during Spanish War; ordered to Manila, Oct. 1899; sent to Nagasaki, Japan, where established depot; was depot q.-m. when expeditionary force went to Peking; chief q.-m. Dept. of Visays, at Iloilo, Panay, Sept., 1901-September 1902; assigned to Portland, Oregon, Jan. 1903; chief q.-m. Dept. of Calif., May 1903; chief of q.-m. Dept. of Dakota, at St. Paul, Aug. 1903; retired at own request after 40 yrs.' service, July 10, 1904. Episcopalian. Died Oct. 25, 1916.

HYDE, John Sedgwick, shipbuilder; b. Bath, Me., Mar. 25, 1867; s. Thomas Worcester and Annie (Hayden) H.; ed. Mass. Inst. of Tech. and in Europe; (hon. A.M., Bowdoin, 1912); m. Ernestine Shannon, June 4, 1898. Apprentice, draftsman, p.-m., auditor, asst. suptg. engr., supt., v.p. and gen. mgr., and since Jan. 1, 1905, pres. and gen. mgr., Bath Iron Works, Ltd.; dir. First Nat. Bank. Mem. bd. of overseers, Bowdoin Coll. Mem. Me. Ho. of Rep., 1899-03, Me. Senate, 1903-05; mayor of Bath, 1909-11. Republican. Episcopalian. Home: Bath, Me. Died Mar. 17, 1917.

HYDE, Mary Caroline, author; b. Plainfield, Vt.; d. Col. Breed Noyes H., of Hyde Park, Vt.; privately educated; unmarried. Author: Guy and Gladys; Goostie; Under the Stable Floor; Yan and Nochie of Tappan Sea; also serials Hollyberry and Mistletoe (St. Nicholas); The Pink Diamond; Karoama, an

Egyptian mummy story; Grit. Home: Pottsville, Pa. Died 1904.

HYDE, Mary Kendall, writer; b. Boston, Mass.; d. George Swan and Mary Freeman (Kendall) Bryant; ed. pub. schs., Boston, and Tilden Academy, N.H.; C.L.S.C. diploma awarded for 4 yrs. course; spl. courses, Boston U.; m. Elliott J. Hyde (died 1917). Began as spl. writer for New York papers; extensive contbr. to religious publs., 1905—; editor children's page of New York Christian Advocate, 1907-12; in charge publicity work for Woman's Nat. Foreign Missionary Jubilee, 1911; religious editor New York Press, 1912-16. Dir. of publicity Evangelistic Com. of N.Y. City, 1906-16. Methodist. Author: Girls' Book of the Red Cross, 1919; Children, Meet the Birds, 1929. Home: Cambridge, Mass. Died Aug. 1940.

HYDE, William DeWitt, college pres.; b. Winchendon, Mass., Sept. 23, 1858; s. Joel and Eliza (DeWitt) H.; A.B., Harvard, 1879; grad. Andover Theol. Sem., 1882; (S.T.D., Harvard, 1886; D.D., Bowdoin, 1886; LL.D., Syracuse, 1897); m. Prudence M. Phillips, Nov. 6, 1883. Ordained Congl. ministry, 1883; pastor Paterson, N.J., 1883-85; pres. and prof. mental and moral philosophy, Bowdoin Coll., 1885—. Author: Practical Ethics, 1892; School Speaker and Reader, 1900; Jesus' Way, 1902; The New Ethics, 1903; The College Man and the College Woman, 1906; Self-Measurement, 1908; The Teacher's Philosophy In and Out of School, 1910; The Five Great Philosophies of Life, 1911. Fellow Am. Acad. Arts and Sciences. Home: Brunswick, Me. Died June 29, 1917.

HYDE, William Waldo, lawyer; b. Tolland, Conn., Mar. 25, 1854; s. Alvan Pinney and Frances Elizabeth (Waldo) H.; A.B., Yale, 1876 (Phi Beta Kappa); studied law under his father and at Boston U. Law Sch.; admitted to bar, 1878, and began practice at Hartford; m. Helen Eliza Watson, Dec. 1, 1877. Supt. of schs., Hartford, 6 yrs.; mayor of Hartford, 1892-94; pres. Bd. of St. Commrs., 1890-92. Democrat. Conglist. Home: Hartford, Conn. Died Oct. 30, 1915.

HYDRICK, Daniel Edward, judge; b. Orangeburg, S.C., Aug. 6, 1860; s. Jacob H. and Margaret (Hildebrand) H.; student Wofford Coll., S.C., 1877-80 (medal for highest proficiency in gen. scholarship); A.B., Vanderbilt U., Tenn., 1882; m. Rosa, d. Maj. John A. Lee, Oct. 24, 1882. Prin. Darlington (S.C.) Male Acad., 1882-85; admitted to bar, 1886; mem. Carlisle & Hydrick, Spartanburg, 1887-94, Hydrick & Wilson, 1895-1900, Hydrick & Sawyer, Union, S.C., 1894-1905; co. atty., Spartanburg Co., 1895-1900; mem. S.C. Ho. of Rep., 1897-99, Senate, 1900-05 (resigned); judge Circuit Ct. of S.C., 7th Jud. Circuit, 1905-09 (resigned); justice Supreme Ct., 1909—. Democrat. Home: Spartanburg, S.C. Died Jan. 15, 1921.

HYER, Robert Stewart, univ. pres.; b. Oxford, Ga., Oct. 18, 1860; s. William L. and Laura H.; A.B., Emory Coll., 1881, A.M., 1883; LL.D., Central Coll., 1901, Baylor U., 1907; m. Maggie Hudgins, Feb. 24, 1888. Prof. physics, 1882-1911, pres., 1897-1911, Southwestern U.; first pres. and head dept. physics, Southern Meth. U., Dallas, Tex., 1911-19, now emeritus. Del. Ecumenical Conf., London, 1902, Toronto, 1912; mem. Commn. on Federation, 1906-18, Gen. Conf. Commn. on Edn., 1900-18. Home: Dallas, Tex. Died May 29, 1929.

HYLAN, John F., mayor; b. on farm, Hunter, N.Y., Apr. 20, 1868; s. Thomas H. H.; ed. pub. schs.; LL.B., New York Law Sch., 1897; m. Marian O'Hara; 1 dau., Mrs. Virginia Sinnott. Admitted to bar, 1897, and began practice in Brooklyn; candidate for municipal judge, 1905; city magistrate, 1906-14; apptd. 1914, elected, 1915, judge County Court; mayor of N.Y. City, 2 terms, 1918-25; now justice Children's Court of City of New York. Democrat. Catholic. Home: Forest Hills, N.Y. Died Jan. 12, 1936.

HYNDMAN, James Gilmore, physician; b. Cincinnati, Sept. 12, 1853; s. William Graves and Barbara (Gilmore) H.; ed. high schs., Cincinnati; grad. Med. Coll. of Ohio, 1874; m. Mary E., d. Samuel M. Mitchell, of Martinsville, Ind., June 20, 1883. Was 2 yrs. interne Cincinnati Hosp.; practices Cincinnati; editor Cincinnati Clinic, and asso. editor Cincinnati Lancet-Clinic several yrs.; sec. faculty, 1883—, and prof. diseases of the throat, Med. Coll. of Ohio. Home: Cincinnati, O. Died 1904.

HYNES, William J., lawyer; b. Kilkee, Co. Clare, Ireland, Mar. 31, 1842; s. Thomas and Catherine (O'Shea) H.; father died in 1847, and mother brought family to U.S. in 1853, settling in Springfield, Mass.; ed. common schs.; Columbian U. Law Sch., Washington, 1868-70; m. Jennie W., d. Judge George B. Way, of Ohio, Sept. 1871. Admitted to bar, 1870, and practiced at Little Rock, Ark.; elected to 43d Congress from Ark. at-large on Greeley ticket, 1872; reëlected by popular vote, 1874, but "counted out"; in practice at Chicago, 1875—. Home: Chicago, Ill. Died Apr. 21, 1915.

HYNICKA, Rudolph Kelker, theatre enterprises; b. Myerstown, Pa., July 6, 1859; s. Luther Reily and Elizabeth (Moyer) H.; ed. pub. schs.; m. Laura Elizabeth Campbell, 1894 (died 1912); m. 2d, Dorothy Dresselhouse, 1918. Reporter on Cincinnati daily newspapers, 1881-86; clk. Police Court, Cincinnati, O.; treas. Hamilton Co., O., 1 term; chmn. Hamilton Co. Rep. Com., 1900—; mem. Rep. Central and Controlling Com. Cincinnati, 40 yrs.; mem. Rep. Nat. Com. from Ohio, 1916—. Identified with theatre enterprises from 1906; treas., dir. Columbia Amusement Co., owning or operating about 40 theatres in U.S. and Can., including Columbia Bldg., and Theatre Co. (New York), Baltimore Theatre Co., Empire Theatre Co. (Baltimore), Washington Theatre Co., Washington Capitol Theatre Co., Cincinnati Theatre Co., Chicago Gayety Theatre Co., Kansas City Theatre Co., Buffalo Theatre Co., Toronto Theatre Co., etc. Mem. Ref. Dutch Ch. Elk. Home: Cincinnati, O. Died Feb. 22, 1927.

HYPES, Benjamin Murray, physician; b. Lebanon, Ill., July 31, 1846; s. Benjamin and Caroline (Murray) H.; A.B., McKendree Coll., 1866, A.M., 1869; M.D., St. Louis Med. Coll. (now Washington U. Med. Dept.), 1872; unmarried. Interne St. Louis City Hosp., 1872-74; practiced, St. Louis, 1874—; prof. obstetrics, St. Louis U., 1890—. Pres. St. Louis Dental Coll., 1906-13. Republican. Methodist. Home: St. Louis, Mo. Deceased.

HYPES, Oran Faville, merchant; b. Xenia, O., Dec. 18, 1862; s. Samuel Henry and Hannah (Van Brocklin) H.; grad. Xenia High Sch., 1879; m. Jessie Beatrice Johnson, Sept. 10, 1889. In mercantile business, Springfield, 1883—; mem. Ohio Ho. of Rep., two terms, 1901-05, Senate, 2 terms, 1905-13. Republican. Methodist. Trustee Clark Co. Children's Home 14 yrs.; dir. Ohio State Y.M.C.A, Springfield Y.M.C.A. Lay del. from Cincinnati Conf. to Gen. Conf. M.E. Ch., Baltimore, 1908, Minneapolis, 1912. Mason. Home: Springfield, O. Died Mar. 9, 1915.

HYSLOP, James Hervey, psychologist; b. Xenia, O., Aug. 18, 1854; s. Robert H.; A.B., U. of Wooster, 1877; U. of Leipzig, 1882-84; Ph.D., Johns Hopkins, 1887; (LL.D., Wooster, 1902); m. Mary Fry Hall, Oct. 1, 1891. Instr. philosophy, Lake Forest U., Ill., 1880-82 and 1884-85, Smith Coll., 1885-86, Bucknell U., Pa., 1888-89; tutor philosophy, ethics and psychology, 1889-91; instr. ethics, 1891-95, prof. logic and ethics, 1895-1902, Columbia; organizer, and sec. Am. Inst. for Scientific Research, 1903—. Editor Proceedings and Journal Am. Society for Psychical Research. Author: Logic and Argument, 1899; Psychic Research and Survival, 1913; Life After Death, 1918; Contact with the Other World, 1919. Home: New York, N.Y. Died June 17, 1920.

HYVERNAT, (Eugene-Xavier-Louis) Henry, orientalist; b. St. Julien-en-Jarrêt, Loire, France, June 30, 1858; s. Claude and Léonide (Meyrieux) H.; ed. Petit Séminaire de St. Jean, Lyons, France, 1867-76. Bachelier-es-Lettres, U. of France, Lyons, 1876; studied divinity, Séminaire de St. Sulpice, Issy, 1877-79; same, Paris, 1879-82; D.D., Pontifical U. of Rome, 1882; Doctor of Letters, honoris causa, U. of Mich., 1919. Chaplain St. Louis of the French, Rome, 1882-85; prof. interpreter of Oriental langs. for Propaganda, Rome, 1885-89; prof. Assyriology and Egyptology, Roman Sem., 1885-88; scientific mission in Armenia for French government, 1888-89; Andrews prof. Biblical Archæology, 1889—; curator Museum Oriental Antiquities, 1889-95; head dept. Semitic and Egyptian langs and lits., 1895—; founded and organized the Museum of Oriental Antiquities, 1889 at Catholic Univ. of America; organized dept. Semitic and Egyptian langs. and lits., and head dept., 1895—; curator General Museum, 1896-1917; one of founders, in Paris (1902), of the Corpus Scriptorum Christianorum Orientalium, and one of its editors to 1930; instrumental (1910) in the late J. P. Morgan securing for his library the newly discovered Hamouli Coptic manuscripts and entrusting them to Catholic U. of America; in 1896 was instrumental in transference of ownership of Corpus Scripti Orient. to Catholic U. of America, and the Université Catholique de Louvain (Belgium). In 1931 established and endowed at Catholic U. of America a Foundation for Research in Christian Oriental Literature. Fellow Am. Acad. Arts and Sciences. Author: Les Actes des Martyrs de l'Egypte, vol. I, Paris, 1886; Album de Paléographie Copte, Paris, 1888; Du Caucase au Golfe Persique (with Paul Muller-Simonis), Washington, 1892; A Check List of Coptic Manuscripts in the Pierpont Morgan Library, New York, 1919; Bybliothecæ Pierpont Morgan Codices Coptici photographice expressi, Rome, 1922 (56 Tomes and Index). Mem. Institut Français de Washington. Chevalier de la Légion d'Honneur, 1926, Officier, 1938. Protonotary Apostolic by Pope Pius XI, 1938. Died May 29, 1941.

HYZER, Edward M., lawyer; b. Janesville, Wis., Dec. 10, 1854; ed. pub. schs. and pvt. tutors; twice married; m. 2d, Mary L. Cantillon, 1902. Admitted to bar, 1879; practiced at Janesville, 1879-98, Milwaukee, 1898-1909; counsel in Wis. for C.&N.W. Ry. Co. several yrs. until became gen. counsel at Chicago, Apr. 1, 1909. Was also mem. Cary, Upham & Black, Milwaukee, 6 yrs. Home: Chicago, Ill. Died Jan. 1925.

I

IDDINGS, Joseph Paxson, geologist; b. Baltimore, Md., Jan. 21, 1857; s. William Penn and Almira (Gillet) I.; Ph.B., in engring. course, Sheffield Scientific Sch. (Yale), 1877, grad. student in chemistry and mineralogy, 1877-78; asst. in mech. drawing and surveying same, 1877-78; grad. student geology and assaying, Columbia Sch. of Mines, 1878-79; in microscopic petrography, Heidelberg, 1879-80; Sc.D., Yale, 1907. Asst. geologist, 1880-88, geologist, 1888-92, and again, 1895—, U.S. Geol. Survey; asso. prof. petrology, 1892-95, prof. 1895-1908, U. of Chicago. Silliman lecturer at Yale U. for 1914; hon. asso. in petrology, U.S. Nat. Museum, 1917—. Joint Author: Geology of the Yellowstone National Park, 1899; Quantitative Classification of Igneous Rocks, 1903. Translated and abridged H. Rosenbusch's Microscopical Physiography of the Rock-Making Minerals, 1898. Author: Rock Minerals, 1906; Igneous Rocks, 1909, Vol. II, 1913; The Problem of Volcanism, 1914. Address: Washington, D.C. Died Sept. 8, 1920.

IDDINGS, Lewis Morris, diplomatist; b. Warren, O., Apr. 23, 1850; s. Lewis J. and Jane (Chesney) I.; Ph.B., U. of Mich., 1872; LL.B., cum laude, Columbia, 1881; admitted to N.Y. and Colo. bars, but never practiced; m. Louise A. Belden, Oct. 29, 1885. On staff New York Tribune, 1876-89, Evening Post, 1889-91; 2d sec. of embassy, Rome, Aug. 3, 1897, 1st sec., Jan. 14, 1898, being chargé d'affaires each summer, 1897-1905; diplomatic agt. and consul gen. at Cairo, 1905-10. Rep. of Am. Red Cross in Italy during early part of the war as dir. American War Relief Clearing House in Rome, Commendatore di SS. Maurizio e Lazare (Italian). Republican. Episcopalian. Home: New York, N.Y. Died Dec. 27, 1921.

IDE, Alba M., pres. George P. Ide & Co., mfrs. shirts and collars; v.p. Mfrs. Nat. Bank, Troy, N.Y.; dir. B.&M. R.R., Troy Gas Co., Securities Properties Co., etc. Home: Troy, N.Y. Died May 14, 1933.

IDE, Fannie Ogden ("Ruth Ogden"), author; b. Brooklyn, N.Y., Dec. 27, 1853; d. Jonathan and Abigail (Murphey) Ogden; ed. Brooklyn private schools; m. Charles W. Ide, Dec. 1875 (dec.). Writer of juvenile stories. Author: His Little Royal Highness, 1897; A Loyal Little Red-Coat, 1889; A Little Queen of Hearts, 1892; Courage, 1894; Little Homespun, 1896; Tattine, 1900; Loyal Hearts and True, 1900; Friendship—The Good and Perfect Gift, 1904; Little Pierre and Big Peter, 1915. Home: Brooklyn, N.Y. Died July 2, 1927.

IDE, George Edward, life underwriter; b. Brooklyn, N.Y., May 10, 1860; s. Henry and Lydia (Smith) I.; student Poly. Inst., Brooklyn; B.A., Yale, 1881 (M.A., 1906); m. Carrie W. Hester, Oct. 21, 1885. With firm Dominick & Dickerman, bankers, 1881-90; sec., 1890-92, v.p., 1892-94, pres. and dir., 1894—, Home Life Ins. Co.; dir. Fidelity and Casualty Co., Brooklyn City R.R.; trustee Title Guarantee & Trust Co. Episcopalian. Republican. Home: New York, N.Y. Died July 9, 1919.

IDE, George Elmore, naval officer; b. Zanesville, O., Dec. 6, 1845; s. Dr. William E. and Angelina (Sullivan) I.; grad. U.S. Naval Acad., 1865; m. Alexandra Louise Bruen, July 28, 1889. Served on various ships, including Juniata in Greenland after Polaris survivors, 1873; brought home Virginius filibusters from Santiago, 1873; comd. U.S.S. Justin, off Santiago, in Spanish-Am. War, 1898; took U.S.S. Yosemite to Guam, 1899, and surveyed harbor; comd. U.S.S. New Orleans in Manila, 1900, thence capt. navy yard, Mare Island, Calif., until retired as rear admiral U.S. Navy, Sept. 26, 1901, after 40 yrs.' service. Address: New York, N.Y. Died Feb. 12, 1917.

IDE, Henry Clay, diplomatist; b. Barnet, Vt., Sept. 18, 1844; s. Jacob and Lodoska (Knights) I.; A.B., Dartmouth, 1866; LL.D., 1900, Tufts, 1903; m. Mary M. Melcher, Oct. 26, 1871 (died 1892). State's atty., 1876-78; mem. Vt. Senate, 1882-85; pres. Rep. State Conv., 1884; del. Rep. Nat. Conv., 1888; U.S. commr. to Samoa, 1891; chief justice of Samoa, under joint appmt., Eng., Germany and U.S., 1893-97; mem. Taft Commn. to establish civil govt. in P.I., Apr. 1900; sec. finance and justice for P.I., Sept. 1, 1901, vice gov., 1904-05, acting gov., 1905-06, gov. gen., 1906; receiver of Knickerbocker Trust Co., New York, 1907-08; E.E. and M.P. to Spain, 1909-13. Dir. several banks and mfg. corps. Author: Code of Procedure in Civil Actions and Special Proceedings in the Philippine Islands, 1901; The Land Registration Act, 1903; The Internal Revenue Law of 1904 of the Philippine Islands. Address: St. Johnsbury, Vt. Died June 13, 1921.

IDLEMAN, Finis Schuyler, clergyman; b. Vandalia, Ill., Sept. 12, 1875; s. Winfield Scott and Barbara (Switzer) I.; A.B., Eureka (Ill.) Coll., 1900; grad. study U. of Chicago, 1901-02; D.D., Drake U., 1914; m. Etta May Johnson, Dec. 25, 1900; children—Margaret May (Mrs. Gordon W. Stearns), Harold A., Holland B., Miriam J. (Mrs. Eugene Knapp), H. Kingsley. Ordained ministry

Christian (Disciples) Ch., 1901; pastor First Christian Ch., Paris, Ill., 1904-06, Central Christian Church, Des Moines, Iowa, 1906-15, Central Ch. of Disciples, N.Y. City, 1915—; asst. editor Christian Union Quarterly. Administrative officer Federal Council of Chs. of America; mem. exec. com. World Alliance for Friendship, Am. Tract Soc. Home: New York, N.Y. Died Mar. 22, 1941.

IDLEMAN, Silas Ellsworth, clergyman; b. Mansfield, O., Dec. 29, 1863; s. Amos H. and Sarah (Hippard) I.; A.B., Ohio Wesleyan U., 1889, A.M., 1899, D.D., 1908; Boston U., 1891; B.D., Drew Theol. Sem., Madison, N.J., 1898; m. Maude E., d. Dr. J. E. Kendall, Aug. 27, 1889; children—Pearl Kendall (wife of Rev. R. T. Lowman), Lowell. Entered M.E. ministry, 1889; pastor, Chesterville, O., 1889-91, Utica, O., 1903-07, Huntington, W.Va., 1898, Iberia, O., 1899-1900, Galion, O., 1900-04; presiding elder Mansfield (O.) Dist., 1904-08, dist. supt., 1908-10; pres. Clark U., South Atlanta, Ga., 1910-12; pres. Gammon Theol. Sem., South Atlanta, 1910-14; pastor First Ch., Bradford, Pa., 1914-16; dist. supt. Olean (N.Y.) Dist. Genesee Conf. M.E. Ch., 1916-18; regional religious dir. Y.M.C.A., St. Nazaire, France, 1918-19; pastor Grace Ch., Rochester, N.Y., 1919-20, Snyder Memorial Ch., Jacksonville, Fla., 1920-23; dist. supt. Miami Dist. St. Johns River Conf., 1923-26; pastor First M.E. Ch., South Miami, 1926—. Mem. Emergency Com. Near East Relief, also mem. Nat. Com. of same. Mason. Home: Miami, Fla. Died Sept. 20, 1931.

IGLEHART, Ferdinand Cowle, clergyman; b. Warrick County, Ind., Dec. 8, 1845; s. Asa and Ann (Cowle) I.; A.B., DePauw U., 1867, A.M., 1869, D.D., 1892; m. Nannie Dorsey Stewart, Oct. 14, 1869. Ordained M.E. ministry, 1870; pastor at Sullivan, New Harmony, New Albany, Salem, Greencastle and Evansville, Ind., 1870-82, First Ch., Bloomington, Ill., 1882-83, Delaware Av. Ch., Buffalo, N.Y., 1884-86, Central Ch., Newark, N.J., 1886-90, Park Av. Ch., New York, 1891-95, Simpson Ch., Brooklyn, 1896-97, Trinity Ch., Newburgh, N.Y., 1898-1901, Asbury Ch., Tarrytown, N.Y., 1902, St. Paul's Ch., Peekskill, N.Y., 1903-05; dist. supt. New York Anti-Saloon League, 1906-15. Republican. Author: The Speaking Oak, 1903; King Alcohol Dethroned, 1917; Theodore Roosevelt, the Man As I Knew Him, 1919. Editorial staff Christian Herald. Home: Dobbs Ferry, N.Y. Died July 21, 1922.

IGLESIAS, Santiago, territorial delegate; b. Coruña, Spain, Feb. 22, 1872; s. Manuel and Josefa (Pantin) I.; ed. pub. schs., Coruña; m. Justa B. Iglesias, 1902; children—Santiago, Josefina (Señora José Antonio Laborde), Libertad (Señora Robert L. Moore), America (Señora Frank W. Thatcher, Jr.), Fraternidad, Igualdad (Señora Bolivar Pagán), Justicia, Laura, Luz, Manuel, Eddie. Founded, 1898, Free Fed. of Workingmen, P.R.; organizer A.F. and L., P.R. and Cuba; sec. Pan Am. Fed. of Labor, 1925—; senator P.R. Legislature, 1917-32; territorial del. from P.R., 73d, 74th and 75th U.S. Congresses; editor Porvenir Social, 1898-1900, Union Obrera, 1903-06, Justicia, 1914-25. Home: Santurce, P.R. Died Dec. 5, 1939.

IHLSENG, Axel Olaf, mining engr.; b. N.Y. City, Feb. 20, 1855; s. Lars and Anna M. (Anderson) I.; B.S., Coll. City of New York, 1874; E.M. and C.E., Sch. of Mines, Columbia, 1877; m. Susan M. Reston, Apr. 18, 1887; 1 dau., Ulga Kathryn (Mrs. Thomas Richard Nunan). Chemist, Havemeyer Sugar Refining Co., 1877-82; mgr. Mountain Queen Mining Co. and other mines, Silverton, Colo., and metallurgist, Martha Rose Smelter, Silverton, and La Plata Smelter, Leadville, Colo., 1882-89; operator of zinc mines (owner of Orinogo Circle, Pleasant Valley and other mines), Joplin (Mo.) dist., 1889-1908; cons. engr., 1908—; co-owner and cons. engr. Keystone (S.D.) Consol. Mines; engaged in examination of strip coal mines, 1920-26. Democrat. Episcopalian. Home: New York, N.Y. Died Dec. 9, 1934.

IHMSEN, Maximilian Frederick, newspaperman; b. Pittsburgh, Mar. 14, 1868; s. Frederick Lorenz and Josephine (Darr) I.; ed. pub. schs., Stuttgart, Germany, Allegheny (Pa.) pub. schs., grad. high sch., 1886, Pittsburgh Catholic Coll.; m. Angeline Arado, Mar. 17, 1894. Clerk in Pittsburgh post-office, 1887; reporter Pittsburgh Leader, 1888, Pittsburgh Post, 1889; was first newspaperman to reach the dam above South Fork, Pa., which dam, by bursting, caused Johnstown flood; Washington corr. Pittsburgh Post, 1890; attached to Washington bur., New York Herald, 1891; polit. reporter same, 1893; Albany corr. New York Journal, 1895; city editor, 1896-98, and 1901-02, Washington corr., 1898-1900, and later polit. editor New York American; later pub. of the Los Angeles Examiner. Active in the movement to nominate William Randolph Hearst as presdl. candidate, 1904. Sec. Nat. Assn. Dem. Clubs, 1900-04; mem. exec. com. Nat. Dem. Congressional Com., 1902; organized Municipal Ownership League of New York, 1905; mgr. W. R. Hearst's mayoralty campaign, New York, 1905; organized Independence League and chmn. Independence League N.Y. state com. during governorship campaign, 1906; fusion nominee for sheriff N.Y. County, 1907. Home: Los Angeles, Calif. Died May 4, 1921.

ILES, Orlando Buff, pres. Internat. Machine Tool Co.; b. Brown County, O., May 31, 1869; s. Thomas and Elizabeth Mary (Ewing) I.; grad. DePauw U., 1894; m. Esther D. Jordan, Oct. 25, 1899; children—Elizabeth Ewing (Mrs. Sidney Alden), Arthur Jordan. Admitted to Ind. bar, 1897, and became asso. in law office of Judge Henry Clay Allen; police prosecutor, Indianapolis, 1897-98; reading clerk in Ind. House of Rep., 1897-99; dep. atty. gen. of Ind., 1899; formed partnership with Arthur Jordan and in wholesale produce business, 1899-1903; mgr. Capitol Gas Engine Co., later internat. Machine Tool Co., 1903-06, pres., 1923-39. Baptist. Mason. Home: Ft. Lauderdale, Fla. Died Apr. 7, 1941.

ILIFF, Thomas Corwin, clergyman; b. McLuney, O., Oct. 26, 1845; s. Wesley and Harriet (Teal) I.; A.B., Ohio U., 1870; D.D., Ohio U., DePauw U., 1887; m. Mary A. Robinson, Mar. 22, 1871. Served pvt. U.S. vols., 1862-65. Entered M.E. ministry, 1870; missionary in Rocky Mountains, 1870-1901; supt. Utah Mission, at Salt Lake City, 1875-1901; asst. sec. Bd. Home Missions and Ch. Extension M.E. Ch., 1901-09; ch. extension sec., Colo. Conf., and gen. dedicator of chs. throughout the nation, 1909—. Traveled in Europe, Egypt and Holy Land, 1880-81. Mem. G.A.R. (chaplain-in-chief, 1895). Address: Denver, Colo. Died Feb. 22, 1918.

ILLINGTON, Margaret, actress; b. (Maude Light) Bloomington, Ill., July 23, 1881; d. I. H. and Mary Ellen Light; ed. Ill. Wesleyan U. and studied at Chicago Musical Coll.; m. Daniel Frohman, Nov. 22, 1903; m. 2d, Edward J. Bowes, Nov. 14, 1909. Début in "The Pride of Jennico," at Criterion Theatre, New York, 1900; played in Daniel Frohman's stock co., Lyceum Theatre, New York, 1902-03; created leading rôle in "The Japanese Nightingale," 1903; "The Two Orphans," 1904; "Mrs. Leffingwell's Boots," 1905; "The Lion and the Mouse," London, Eng., 1906; "His House in Order," Empire Theatre, New York, 1906; "The Thief," Lyceum Theatre, New York, 1907; star in "Kindling," 1911-12, "Within the Law," 1913-14; "The Lie," 1915-16; "Our Little Wife," 1916-17; co-star with John Drew in "The Gay Lord Quex," 1917-18. Home: Ossining-on-Hudson, N.Y. Died Mar. 11, 1934.

ILLOWAY, Henry, M.D.; b. Kolin, Bohemia, Nov. 29, 1848; s. Rev. Bernard and Katherine (Schiff) I.; M.D., Miami Med. Coll., Cincinnati, O., 1869. Resident phys., Cincinnati Hosp., 1869-70; was prof. of diseases of children, Cincinnati Coll. Medicine and Surgery, and visiting physician, Jewish Hosp., Cincinnati; removed to New York. Author: Constipation in Adults and Children; Summer Diarrhœas of Infants. Collaborator on American Text Book of the Diseases of Children. Died Jan. 15, 1932.

ILSLEY, James Keeler, banker; b. Milwaukee, Wis., Apr. 14, 1854; s. Charles Ferdinand and Sarah (Keeler) I.; A.B., U. of Mich., 1876; student law dept. Harvard 1 yr.; m. Mary Stevens, Feb. 24, 1892. Began with Marshall & Ilsley, pvt. bankers, 1877; firm incorp., 1888, as Marshall & Ilsley Bank, of which was cashier, v.p. and pres.; retired, 1915; trustee Estate of Daniel Wells, Jr. Episcopalian. Home: Milwaukee, Wis. Died Apr. 30, 1924.

IMLAY, Lorin Everett, elec. engr.; b. Guernsey County, O., Nov. 2, 1864; s. Thomas Johnson and Lavina Catherine (Conner) I.; B.C.E., Cornell Coll., Ia., 1888, C.E., 1892; post-grad. work, U. of Calif., 1892; m. Helen Maria Smith, Dec. 2, 1889; children—Helen Louise (dec.), Robert; m. 2d, Marie H. Rose, June 16, 1919; 1 son, Alexander Rose. In civ. engring. work Calif. and H.I., 1888-91; with San Antonio Light & Power Co., Pomona, Calif., 1891-94; engr. of constrn. Westinghouse Electric & Mfg. Co., Pittsburgh, 1894-1902; supt. Niagara Falls Power Co. and Canadian Niagara Power Co., 1902-19; became operating engr. Niagara Falls Power Co., 1920; engr. superpower survey, U.S. Geol. Survey, 1920-21; statis. engr., Buffalo, Niagara & Eastern Power Corp., 1926; dir. statistics Niagara-Hudson Power Corp., 1930; retired, 1938. Republican. Unitarian. Author: Mechanical Characteristics of Transmission Lines. Home: Niagara Falls, N.Y. Died June 9, 1941.

INCE, Thomas Harper, motion pictures; b. Newport, R.I., Nov. 16, 1880; s. John E. (comedian) and Emma B. I.; ed. pub. schs.; m. Elinor Priscilla Kershaw, Oct. 19, 1907. Began career with Charles Frohman, New York, as an actor in "Poet and Puppets," appeared in "Shore Acres," "The Ninety-nine"; starred in "For Love's Sweet Sake"; apptd. dir. gen. New York Motion Picture Corp., 1909; v.p. Triangle Film Corp., 1915-17; pres. Thomas H. Ince Studios, Inc. Notable productions: "The Battle of Gettysburg," "The Wrath of the Gods," "The Cup of Life," "The Coward," "Civilization," "Peggy," "The Narrow Trail," "Wolves of the Rail," "The Aryan," "Hell's Hinges," "Hail the Woman," "Her Reputation," "The Hottentot," "Anna Christie." Episcopalian. Studio: Culver City, Calif. Died Nov. 19, 1924.

INCH, Richard, naval officer; b. Washington, June 29, 1843; s. Philip and Mary (O'Neil) I.; ed. East Washington Sem. and Washington Sem. Apptd. 3d asst. engr. U.S. Navy, Sept. 8, 1863; promoted 2d asst. engr., Oct. 15, 1865; passed asst. engr., Sept. 28, 1874; chief engr., Aug. 3, 1892; comdr., Mar. 3, 1899; capt., Nov. 12, 1902; retired as rear admiral, June 29, 1905. Served on Lancaster and Powhatan, 1863-67; Navy Yard, New York, 1867-68; Nyack, 1868-70; Triana, 1871-72; Richmond, 1872-73; Tallapoosa, 1873; Gettysburg, 1873-74; Navy Yard, Washington, 1875-77; Wyoming, 1877-81; Passaic, 1881; spl. duty Exec. Mansion, Washington, 1881; Passaic, 1881-82; Pinta, 1883; Yantic, 1884-86; Navy Yard, Washington, 1887-90; Lancaster 1891-92; Marion, 1892-94; Navy Yard, Mare Island, 1895-97; Concord, 1897; Boston, 1898; Charleston, 1898-99; naval sta., Cavite, P.I., 1899; insp. machinery, Newport News, 1900-05; advanced 3 numbers on the comdrs. list, Feb. 11, 1901, "for eminent and conspicuous conduct in battle." Address: Washington, D.C. Died 1911.

INGALLS, Charles Russell, judge; b. Greenwich, N.Y., Sept. 14, 1819; read law with his father, Judge Charles F. I.; admitted to bar, 1844; practiced with his father until 1860; in Troy, N.Y., 1860-63; justice Supreme Ct., 1863, until retired by age limitation, Jan. 1, 1890, part of time serving on bench Court of Appeals, and, after 1877, becoming mem. gen. term of Supreme Ct. for 1st dept., comprising the City of New York. Address: Troy, N.Y. Died 1908.

INGALLS, George Hoadly, ry. official; b. Boston, Mass., July 28, 1872; s. Melville Ezra and Abbie (Stimson) I.; A.B., Harvard, 1893; m. Katherine Davis Hinkle, Nov. 12, 1898; children—Katherine Elizabeth (Mrs. Katherine Ingalls), George Howard, Melville Ezra, Louise (dec.). Began as clk. in office of gen. mgr. C.&O. Ry., 1893, and successively clk., gen. supt.'s office, Western Div., 1895-96, clk. in office of pres., 1896, asst. to pres., 1896-1900, same rd.; asst. gen. frt. agt. C.,C.,C.&St.L. Ry., at Cincinnati, 1901-02; gen. frt. agt. same rd., Cincinnati Northern, and Dayton & Union rys., 1902-06; frt. traffic mgr., 1906-17, traffic mgr., Aug. 1917-July 1918, N.Y.C. Lines West of Buffalo, traffic asst. to regional dir. U.S. R.R. Administration, July 1918-Nov. 1919; v.p. in charge of traffic, York Central Lines, 1919—. Democrat. Episcopalian. Home: New York, N.Y. Died June 14, 1931.

INGALLS, James Monroe, army officer, author; b. Sutton, Vt., Jan. 25, 1837; s. James and Mary (Cass) I.; prep. edn. Evansville (Wis.) Sem., 1859-63; grad. Artillery Sch., Ft. Monroe, Va., 1872; m. Eliza H. Niles, July 29, 1860; children—Arthur Niles, Hilda Eliza; m. 2d, Harriet Elizabeth Thurston, July 17, 1877; 1 dau., Fanny Thurston. Pvt. and corporal Co. A, 1st Battalion, 16th Inf., and commissary sergt. and q.-m. sergt. 16th Inf., Jan. 2, 1864-May 21, 1865; commd. 2d lt. and 1st lt., May 3, 1865; transferred to 2d Inf., Apr. 17, 1869, to 1st Arty., Jan. 1, 1871; capt., July 1, 1880; maj., June 1, 1897; transferred to 5th Arty., Oct. 28, 1899; lt. col. 3d Arty., Oct. 5, 1900; retired, Jan. 25, 1901; advanced to rank of col.; retired, by act of Apr. 23, 1904. Participated in Atlanta campaign and was engaged in reconstruction duty in South until Jan. 1, 1871. Founded Dept. of Ballistics at U.S. Arty. Sch., Ft. Monroe, 1882; was prin. instr. until school suspended operations, Apr. 1898, at outbreak of war with Spain. Author: Exterior Ballistics, 1883, 85, 86; Ballistic Machines, 1885; Handbook of Problems in Exterior Ballistics, 1890, 1901; Interior Ballistics, 1894, 1911; Ballistic Tables, 1891, 1900; Ballistics for the Instruction of Artillery Gunners, 1893. Wrote: Articles Gunnery Gunpowder, Johnson's Universal Cyclopædia, 1894; article Ballistics in New Internat. Ency., 2d edit., 1915. Home: Providence, R.I. Died May 1, 1927.

INGALLS, John James, U.S. senator; b. Middleton, Mass., Dec. 29, 1833; grad. Williams Coll., 1855 (LL.D., 1884); studied law; admitted to bar, 1857; removed to Atchison, Kan., 1858; mem. Wyandotte conv., 1859; sec. Territorial council, 1860, and of State senate, 1861; State senator, 1862; same year unsuccessful candidate for lt. gov.; U.S. senator from Kan., 1873-91; (pres. pro tempore, U.S. Senate, 1887-91). Republican. Lecturer and journalist, 1891—. Home: Atchison, Kan. Died 1900.

INGALLS, Melville Ezra, railroad pres.; b. Harrison, Me., Sept. 6, 1842; reared on farm; ed. Bridgton Acad. and studied Bowdoin Coll.; LL.B., Harvard, 1863; hon. A.M., Bowdoin, 1902, also Wabash College. Practiced first at Gray, Me., but soon removed to Boston; mem. Mass. Senate, 1867. President, 1870, receiver, 1871, the Indianapolis, Cincinnati & Lafayette R.R., and from bankrupt condition, with aid of reorganizations in 1873 and 1880, put its successor, the Cincinnati, Indianapolis, St. Louis & Chicago, upon a sound footing, consolidating it with other roads into the C.,C.,C.&St.L. R.R., of which he was chmn.—comprising the "Big Four" system; resigned 1912; pres. C.&O. Ry. Co., 1888-1900. Dem. candidate for mayor of Cincinnati

1903; pres. Nat. Civic Federation, 1905. Home: Washington, D.C. Died July 11, 1914.

INGALS, E(phraim) Fletcher, physician; b. Lee Centre, Ill., Sept. 29, 1848; s. Charles Francis and Sarah (Hawkins) I.; ed. Rock River Sem., Mt. Morris, Ill.; M.D., Rush Med. Coll., Chicago, 1871; A.M. (old), U. of Chicago, 1879; visited hosps. and med. schs., London and Paris, 1873; m. Lucy S., d. Dr. Ephraim Ingals, Sept. 5, 1876. Interne of Cook County (Ill.) Hosp., 1871; asst. prof. materia medica, 1871-73, lecturer diseases of chest and physical diagnosis, 1874-83, prof. laryngology, 1883-90, laryngology and practice of medicine, 1890-93, laryngology and diseases of chest, 1893-98, registrar, 1891-98, prof. diseases of chest, throat and nose, and comptroller, 1898—, Rush Med. Coll.; prof. diseases of throat and chest, Northwestern Woman's Medical Sch., 1879-98; prof. laryngology and rhinology, Chicago, Polyclinic, 1890—; professorial lecturer on medicine, U. of Chicago, 1901—. Chmn. sect. laryngology, Pan-Am. Med. Congress, 1893. Author: Diseases of the Chest, Throat and Nose, 4th edit., 1900. Commd. capt., Med. R.C., 1917. Home: Chicago, Ill. Died Apr. 29, 1918.

INGALSBE, Grenville Mellen, lawyer; b. S. Hartford, N.Y., July 26, 1846; s. Milo and Laura Cook (Chapin) I.; student Union Coll., class of '68; left to become prin. Argyle (N.Y.) Acad., 1867-70, but received A.B. (in course), Union Coll., 1870, A.M., 1873, hon. L.H.D., 1917; LL.B., Harvard U., 1872; m. Franc E. Groesbeck, Sept. 20, 1876. Admitted to bar, 1874; pres. Sandy Hill Nat. Bank of Hudson Falls; sec., dir. Imperial Wall Paper Co., Imperial Color Works, Inc., Little River Lumber Co.; v.p., dir. C. C. Allen Realty Co., Inc.; dir. Sandy Hill Realty Co., Plattsburgh Wall Paper Co., Underwood Paper Mills. Was member 1885-88 (chmn. 1887-88), bd. supervisors; surrogate (judge Probate Ct.), 1895-1901, Wash. Co., N.Y. Del. Universal Congress Lawyers and Jurists, St. Louis, 1904. Mem. Am. Bar Assn. (mem. local council for N.Y., 1895-1905), N.Y. State Bar Assn. (exec. com., 1892—, 3 yrs. chmn.). Trustee Glens Falls Acad. Unitarian. Address: Hudson Falls, N.Y. Died Apr. 21, 1918.

INGERSOLL, Charles Edward, lawyer; b. Phila., June 17, 1860; s. Edward and Anna Chester (Warren) I.; A.B., U. of Pa., 1882; admitted to bar, 1884; m. Henrietta A. Sturgis, Dec. 23, 1886; children—Anna Warren, Harry (dec.), R. Sturgis, C. Jared, Susan B. (Mrs. Orville H. Bullitt), John H. W. Practiced with Franklin B. Gowen, 1885-89; was organizer and pres. Choctaw Northern R.R.; pres. and builder Midland Valley R.R.; pres. Kansas, Oklahoma and Gulf Railroad, North Pa. Railroad; dir. Central-Penn Nat. Bank, Pa. R.R., Midland Valley R.R., Phila. & Western Ry., Girard Trust Co., Phila. Elec. Co. U.S. Appaiser Port of Phila., 1893-96; del. Dem. Nat. Conv., 1896; Dem. nominee for Congress, 7th Pa. Dist., 1902. Home: Philadelphia, Pa. Died June 6, 1932.

INGERSOLL, Edward Payson, clergyman; b. Lee, Mass., May 6, 1834; s. William and Samantha (Bassett) I.; prep. edn. Oberlin, O.; grad. Williams Coll., 1855 (A.M., D.D.); grad. in law, Ohio State, and Union Law colls., Cleveland, 1859; grad. Andover Theol. Sem., 1863; m. Julia A. de Forest, Sept. 11, 1860; m. 2d, Helen E. Abbott, Oct. 25, 1866. Ordained Congl. ministry, 1863; pastor Sandusky, O., 1863-67, Indianapolis, 1867-70, Middle Reformed (Dutch) Ch., Brooklyn, 1870-82, Puritan Congl. Ch., Brooklyn, 1882-91, Park Congl. Ch., St. Paul, 1891-97; Immanuel Congl. Ch., Brooklyn, 1897-1902; sec. Am. Bible Soc., 1902—. Republican. Home: Brooklyn, N.Y. Died 1907.

INGERSOLL, George Pratt, diplomat; b. New Haven, Conn., Apr. 24, 1861; s. Colin Macrae (M.C., 1848-52) and Julia Harriet (Pratt) I.; grad. of Hopkins Grammar Sch., New Haven, 1879; B.A., Trinity Coll., Conn., 1883, M.A., 1885; LL.B., Yale, 1885; m. Alice, d. Rev. Orlando Witherspoon, Nov. 3, 1891; children—Colin Montaigue, Gertrude Victoria. Practiced law Stamford, Conn., and N.Y. City, 1885-1917 and 1918—; U.S. commr. for Conn., 1889; mem. Conn. State Bd. of Health, 1893-99; Dem. nominee for Congress, Conn. at large, 1910; E.E. and M.P. to Siam, 1917-18; also acting minister to Siam for Switzerland, 1917-18. Trustee Conn. Sch. for Boys, 1914-17, Berkeley Div. Sch., 1916—, Christ Ch. Cathedral, Conn., 1918—, French-Am. Chamber of Commerce, 1918—; pres. Stanford Hist. Soc., 1923; del. Internat. Peace Conf., Washington, 1910. Episcopalian. Publications: The Measure of Success; Our Connecticut Heritage; Diplomatic Life in Siam. Home: Stamford, Conn. Died Feb. 23, 1927.

INGERSOLL, Henry Hulbert, lawyer; b. Oberlin, O., Jan. 20, 1844; s. William and Samantha (Bassett) I.; student Oberlin Coll., 1857-61; pvt. 7th Ohio Vol. Inf., in W.Va. campaign, 1861; grad. Yale, 1863, A.M., 1866; LL.D., Washington Coll., Tenn., 1889; studied law in office Probasco & Ramsey, Cincinnati; m. Emily G. Rogers, 1864. Admitted to bar, 1865; asst. atty. gen. 1st Circuit, Tenn., 1866-67; Tilden elector 1st Dist., Tenn., 1876; judge Supreme Ct., Commn. of Tenn., 1879-80; spl. judge Supreme Ct., 1884-85; dean law faculty, U. of Tenn., 1891-1914. Sec. Dem. Nat. Conv., St. Louis, 1888. Pres. Tenn. State Bar Assn., 1887-88; v.p. Am. Bar Assn., 1907-13. Trustee Emory and Henry Coll., 1885-93, U. of the South, 1898-1908. Grand Master Freemasons of Tenn., 1888. Deputy to Gen. Conv. P.E. Church, 1898-1912. Editor: Barton's Suit in Equity, 1886. Author: University of Tennessee Law Syllabi, 1900; Ingersoll on Public Corporations, 1904. Contbd. Municipal Corporations, in "CYC," 1907; Towns, in "CYC," 1911; Equity, in Library of Am. Sch. of Correspondence, 1912; Municipal Corporations, in Standard Ency. of Law and Procedure, 1913. Address: Knoxville, Tenn. Died Mar. 12, 1915.

INGERSOLL, Raymond Vail, lawyer; b. Corning, N.Y., Apr. 3, 1875; s. Andrew Jackson and Ellen (Vail) I.; A.B., Amherst Coll., 1897; LL.B., New York Law Sch., 1900; m. Marion Crary, Sept. 29, 1908; children—Jerry, Asho, Raymond, Marion. Practiced law at Brooklyn, 1902-09, New York, 1909—. Elected city magistrate, 1901, serving 6 months. Chmn. exec. com. and campaign mgr. Com. of 100, New York City campaign of 1909; park commr. of Brooklyn, 1914-17. Vol. with "Foyer du Soldat," on French Army front, 1918; mem. Paris com. of League to Enforce Peace, at Peace Conf. Sec. City Club of New York, 1919-24. Mgr. Gov. Alfred E. Smith's campaign, 1924; arbitrator in New York cloak and suit industries, 1924-31; chmn. of first New York Minimum Wage Board, 1933; elected pres. Brooklyn Borough on Fusion, ticket, 1933, re-elected, 1937; mem. state commn. which revised tenement and housing laws, 1928-29; apptd. by President Roosevelt, 1934, as one of commn. of three who settled textile strike. Independent Democrat. Home: Brooklyn, N.Y. Died Feb. 24, 1940.

INGERSOLL, Robert Green, lawyer; b. Dresden, N.Y., Aug. 11, 1833; childhood in Wis., and, after 1843, in Ill.; studied law; practiced at Shawneetown, Ill., 1855-57; removed to Peoria, Ill., 1860. Defeated as Democratic candidate for Congress, 1860; col. 11th Ill. cav., 1862; joined Republican party, 1864; apptd atty. gen., Ill., 1866; attained nat. fame as orator in a nominating speech in favor of James G. Blaine at Nat. Rep. Conv., 1876; refused post of minister to Germany, 1877; defended Star Route defendants, securing their acquittal, 1883. Practised law; lectured and wrote against Christian religion. Author: The Gods; Ghosts; Some Mistakes of Moses; Complete Lectures; Prose Poems; etc. Address: New York, N.Y. Died 1899.

INGERSOLL, Robert Hawley, watch mfr.; b. Delta, Mich., Dec. 26, 1859; s. Orville Boudinot and Mary Elizabeth (Beers) I.; ed. pub. schs.; m. Edith Maria Bannister, June 20, 1904. Settled in N.Y. City, 1879; mfr. rubber stamps, 1880, later in mail order business; conceived idea and commenced manufacture of the "dollar watch," 1892, over 70,000,000 being sold by 1919; pres. and gen. mgr. Robert H. Ingersoll & Bro.; pres. New Era Mfg. Co. Republican. Conglist. Home: New York, N.Y. Died Sept. 4, 1928.

INGERSOLL, Royal Rodney, rear admiral U.S.N.; b. Niles, Mich., Dec. 4, 1847; s. Harmon W. and Rebecca A. (Deniston) I.; grad. U.S. Naval Acad., 1868; m. Cynthia Eason, Aug. 26, 1873; 1 son, Royal Eason. Has served as naval officer in all parts of the world; commd. capt., Mar. 21, 1903; rear admiral, July 11, 1908. Comd. U.S.S. Supply during Spanish-Am. War; comdg. Maryland, 1905; chief of staff Atlantic Fleet, voyage from Hampton Roads to the Pacific; mem. Gen. Bd. of the Navy; retired, Dec. 4, 1909. Pres. spl. bd. on naval ordnance, July 9, 1917-Jan. 2, 1919. Presbyterian. Author: Text-book of Ordnance and Gunnery, 1887; Exterior Ballistics, 1891; Elastic Strength of Guns, 1891. Home: LaPorte, Ind. Died Apr. 21, 1931.

INGHAM, William Armstrong, lawyer; b. Bucks County, Pa., May 25, 1827; s. Samuel D. and Deborah Kay (Hall) I.; C.E., B.N.S., Rensselaer Poly. Inst., 1846; grad. Princeton, 1849; m. Catherine Keppele Hall, June 30, 1857 (dec.). Admitted to Phila. bar, 1855; pres. Union Improvement Co., Highland Coal Co., and several other corps. Home: Philadelphia, Pa. Died Sept. 23, 1913.

INGLE, Edward, writer; b. Baltimore, May 17, 1861; s. William Pechin and Eliza (Crummer) I.; A.B., Johns Hopkins U., 1882; m. Mary Friend Mayo, Apr. 28, 1892. Author: Southern Sidelights; The Negro in the District of Columbia; Local Institutions of Virginia; Parish Institutions of Maryland; Capt. Richard Ingle, the Maryland Pirate and Rebel; In the Maze; Realism of Southern Dreams of Material Progress. Active in newspaper work over 30 yrs. Home: Baltimore, Md. Died Jan. 6, 1924.

INGLE, James Addison, bishop, missionary; b. Frederick, Md., Mar. 11, 1867; s. Rev. Osborne (D.D.) and Mary Mills (Addison) I.; ed. Frederick Acad. to 1882, Episcopal High Sch., Alexandria, Va., 1882-84; grad. U. of Va., M.A., 1888; studied divinity, Va. Theol. Sem., Alexandria; m. Charlotte Thomson Rhett, Aug. 2, 1894. Taught in Pantops Acad., Charlottesville, Va., 1886-87; went as missionary to China, Nov. 1891; consecrated in Hankow 1st P.E. bishop of Hankow, Feb. 24, 1902. Has published some books in Chinese. Address: Hankow, China. Died 1903.

INGLIS, Alexander James, college prof.; b. Middletown, Conn., Nov. 24, 1879; s. William Grey and Susan (Byers) I.; B.A., Wesleyan U., Conn., 1902; M.A., Columbia, 1909, Ph.D., 1911; m. Antoinette Clark, Dec. 20, 1911. Teacher secondary schs. in Pa., N.Y. City and Calif., 1902-12; prof. edn. and dir. summer sch. and extension courses, Rutgers Coll., 1912-14; asst. prof. edn., 1914-19, prof. edn., 1919—, Harvard U. Mem. orgn. com. on edn. and spl. training war plans div. of Gen. Staff, 1918; dir. edn. survey of State of Va. for Legislature Commn., 1919; mem. survey staff for ednl. instns., states Wash., Ind. and S.D. Author: First Book in Latin (Inglis and Prettyman), 1906; Exercise Book in Latin Composition, 1908; High School Course in Latin Composition (Baker and Inglis), 1909; Rise of the High School in Massachusetts, 1911; Principles of Secondary Education, 1918; Virginia Public Schools, 1919; Intelligence Quotient Values, 1921. Editor of series of text books on Theory and Practice of Education. Home: Cambridge, Mass. Died Apr. 1924.

INGRAHAM, Darius Holbrook, lawyer; b. Camden, Me., Oct. 14, 1837; s. Samuel P. and Mary (Adams) I.; ed. in Me. and U.S. Naval Acad.; m. Ella, d. William Moulton, June 1868. Admitted to Me. bar, 1859; represented Portland in Legislature, 1879; U.S. consul, Cadiz, Spain, 1885-89; sent to Morocco by State Dept., to investigate Tangier consulate, receiving thanks of dept.; mayor of Portland, Me., 1892-93; Dem. candidate for Congress, 1892; consul gen. Halifax, N.S., 1893-97; Dem. candidate for mayor of Portland, 1898, 1902 and 1903. Address: Portland, Me. Died July 11, 1923.

INGRAHAM, Frances Adelaide Leverich (Mrs. D. Phoenix Ingraham); b. Brooklyn, N.Y.; d. Richard Berrien and Margaret M. (Schoonmaker) Leverich; ed. in private schs., Brooklyn; m. D. Phœnix Ingraham. Pres. N.Y. State Chapter Daughters of Founders and Patriots of America; pres. gen. Daughters of Revolution; directress-gen. Daughters of Holland Dames, Ancient and Honorable Families of New Netherland; mem. Huguenot Soc., Order of the Constitution, Nat. Soc. Colonial Dames in State of N.Y. Home: New Canaan, Conn. Died Sept. 7, 1934.

INGRAHAM, George Landon, judge; b. New York, Aug. 1, 1847; s. Daniel Phœnix and Mary (Landon) I.; LL.B., Columbia, 1869, LL.D., 1904; admitted to bar, 1869; m. Georgina Lent, Dec. 4, 1873. Judge Superior Court, City of New York, 1883-91; became justice Supreme Court of N.Y., May 1891; judge appellate div. Supreme Court, Jan. 1, 1896-Dec. 1915 (resigned). Address: New York, N.Y. Died Jan. 24, 1931.

INGRAHAM, Henry Cruise Murphy, lawyer; b. Amenia, N.Y., May 2, 1838; s. George and Mary (Michelle) I.; B.A., Wesleyan U., Conn., 1864, M.A., 1867, LL.D., 1903; m. Winifred Andrews, Sept. 3, 1873. Admitted to bar, 1865; practiced at Brooklyn; counsel to commrs. of Williamsburg Bridge, 1894-98; chmn. com. for admission to bar, in 2d Dept., N.Y., 1899-1902; dir. Glen Cove (N.Y.) Bank, Toluca (Mex.) Light & Power Co. Trustee Wesleyan U., 1897— (pres. bd. 1903—), Pekin U. (China), Bd. of Edn. M.E. Ch.; mgr. Am. Bible Soc.; mem. exec. com. Federal Council of Chs. of Christ in America. Mem. Brooklyn Bar Assn. (dir. 1889—, pres. 1899-1903). Republican. Home: Brooklyn, N.Y. Died Feb. 15, 1911.

INGRAHAM, John Phillips Thurston, P.E. clergyman; b. Hallowell, Me., Aug. 29, 1817; s. James Milk and Elizabeth (Thurston) I.; grad. high school, Portland, Me.; grad. Theol. Sem., Waukesha County, Wis. (S.T.D., Racine Coll., 1875); m. Cornelia Fanning Root, Sept. 14, 1848. Ordained, 1847; rector St. James' Ch., Milwaukee, 1852-62; chaplain in Army Hosp., in Tenn., 1862-64; rector Christ Ch., Indianapolis, 1864-67; St. John's Ch., St. Louis, 1867-81; rector Grace Ch., St. Louis, 1881-1902, emeritus. Author: Why We Believe the Bible, 1885; Mother's Talks with Her Little Folks, 1880. Address: St. Louis, Mo. Died 1906.

INGRAHAM, Prentiss, soldier, author; b. Adams County, Miss., Dec. 22, 1843; s. Rev. Prof. J. H. I. and Mary (Brooks) I.; ed. private tutor, St. Timothy's Mil. Acad., Md., and Jefferson Coll., Miss.; studied medicine, Mobile Med. Coll., but left to enter C.S.A., Apr. 1861; m. Rosa Langley, 1875. Served in light arty., Withers' Miss. Regt.; wounded and captured at Ft. Hudson; also served on staff as lt. and in Ross' brigade, Texas cav., commdr. of scouts; wounded at battle of Franklin; served after Civil war in Mexico under Juarez; also in Austria, in war with Prussia; in Crete and in Africa; extensive traveler in Eastern lands; served afloat and ashore in Cuban ten years' war for independence, with ranks of capt. of navy and col. of cav.; was tried as filibuster and condemned to death by Spaniards; escaped. Entered upon literary career in London, England, 1870; later in New York. Democrat. Author: Zuleikah: A Story of Crete, 1887; Darkie Dan, 1888; In Golden Fetters, 1888; Cadet Carey, of West Point, 1890; Red Rovers on Blue Waters, 1890;

In Satan's Coil, 1890; An American Monte Cristo, 1891; The Vagabond, 1891; Wandering Jew of the Sea, 1891; Given for Gold, 1893; Trailing with Buffalo Bill; Land of Legendary Lore, 1899; Girl Rough Rider, 1903; Satan's Slave, 1903; and over 600 novels. Home: Chicago, Ill. Died 1904.

INGRAM, Eleanor Marie, author; b. New York, Nov. 26, 1886; d. John Wharton and Anna Augusta (Shields) Ingram. Ed. under pvt. tutelage; unmarried. Author: The Game and the Candle, 1910 (also issued as "John Allard," 1911); The Flying Mercury, 1911; Stanton Wins, 1911; From the Car Behind, 1912; The Unafraid, 1913; A Man's Hearth, 1915; Twice American, 1917. Home: New York, N.Y. Died Mar. 22, 1921.

INGRAM, Frederick Fremont, mfg. pharmacist; b. Irving, Mich., May 9, 1856; s. Orrin Lorenzo and Lydia (Benson) I.; student Olivet (Mich.) Coll.; m. Laura A. Mayo, June 15, 1889; 1 son, Frederick F. In retail drug business, at Ypsilanti, Mich.; traveled for pharmaceutical house several yrs.; became partner Milburn & Williamson, mfg. pharmacists, Detroit, 1885, succeeded, 1890, by Frederick F. Ingram & Co., Inc., 1909, as Frederick F. Ingram Co., of which was pres.; founder and pres. The Frederick F. Ingram Foundation, Ingram Institute of Social Science. Elected charter commr. at large, for Detroit, 1913; mem. Detroit Pub. Lighting Commn., 1899-1905 (twice pres.); mem. Mich. Constl. Conv. and Detroit Charter Commn.; president of Civic Forum Institute. Home: Detroit, Mich.; and San Diego, Calif. Died Sept. 29, 1932.

INMAN, Edward Hamilton, cotton mcht.; b. Atlanta, Ga., Aug. 29, 1881; s. Hugh Theodore and Margaret Josephine (Van Dyke) I.; A.B., Princeton, 1903; m. Emily MacDougald, June 19, 1901; children—Hugh Theodore, Edward H. Mem. Inman, Smith & Co., 1900-03, Inman, Akers & Inman, 1903-18, Inman & Howard, 1918-21; pres. Kimball, House Co.; v.p. Atlanta Woolen Mills; dir. Trust Co. of Georgia, Atlanta Lowry Nat. Bank, Atlantic Ice & Coal Co. Mem. Com. on Cotton Distribution of War Industries Bd., 1918; regional adviser, Region No. 12, same bd. Mem. Atlanta City Council, 1915-16 and 1924-25. Presbyn. Home: Atlanta, Ga. Deceased.

INMAN, Henry, writer; b. New York, N.Y., July 30, 1837; s. Henry Inman; ed. Brooklyn pub. schs. and Athenian Acad. (1846); m. Miss E. C. Dyer, Oct. 22, 1862. Author: The Old Santa Fé Trail; The Ranch on the Oxhide; Great Salt Lake Trail (with W. F. Cody); Tales of the Trail; Pioneer from Kentucky; The Delahoyles; etc. Address: Topeka, Kan. Died 1899.

INNES, Frederick Neil, musician; b. London, Eng., Oct. 29, 1858; s. William and Sara Julia (Delaney) I.; m. Frances Boyden, Apr. 6, 1903. Came to America, 1879, as soloist of Gilmore's Band; established the Innes Band in N.Y. City, 1899. Home: Chicago, Ill. Died Dec. 31, 1927.

INNES, Katherine, art director; b. N.Y. City; d. John R. and Jeanne D. (Macfarlane) Innes; ed. Hunter Coll., New York. Asst. sec. Nat. Arts Club 9 yrs.; sec. Painting Com., MacDowell Club, and mgr. of group exhbns. of the club for several years; dir. Montclair (N.J.) Art Museum, 1916—. Conglist. Address: Montclair, N.J. Died June 1, 1929.

INNESS, George, Jr., painter; b. Paris, France, Jan. 5, 1854; s. George I. Was a pupil of his father in Rome, 1870-74; studied 1 yr. in Paris, 1875; m. Julia G. Roswell-Smith; children—Elizabeth (Mrs. Howard Greenley), Juliet (Mrs. Harry B. Cox). Lived in Boston and New York, where he occupied studio with his father, 1878; resided with family, Montclair, N.J., after 1880, but had studio in Paris, 1895-99; exhibited annually at Paris Salon; hon. mention Paris Salon, 1896, and gold medal, 1900. Officier Académie des Beaux Arts, Paris, 1902; A.N.A., 1895, N.A., 1899. Art signature always "Inness, Jr." Author: Art, Life and Letters of George Inness, 1917. Home: Tarpon Springs, Fla. Died July 27, 1926.

INNIS, William Reynolds, mfr.; b. Poughkeepsie, N.Y., Jan. 7, 1859; s. Aaron and Katherine (Reynolds) I.; B.A., Yale, 1880; m. Dora L., d. Peter E. Studebaker, Feb. 21, 1884 (died 1909); m. 2d, Edith Donaldson Clark, Oct. 28, 1911. Dir. New York Life Ins. Co.; trustee Union Dime Savings Bank of New York. Home: New York, N.Y. Died Oct. 1920.

INSULL, Frederick William, pub. utility exec.; b. London, Eng., July 5, 1875; s. Henry and Helen (Pasfield) I.; ed. pub. schs.; m. Margaret Parkinson, Apr. 24, 1905; children—Margaret, Rosemary. Came to U.S., 1901, naturalized citizen, 1912. Began as trolley wagon driver, Winnipeg Electric St. Ry. Co., 1891; sec.-treas. North Shore Electric Co., Chicago, Ill., 1901-09; auditor, H. M. Byllesby Co., 1909-12; pres. Pub. Service Co. of Okla., 1913—; pres. Southwestern Light & Power Co., 1928—. Pres. Community Chest Fund, 1928-31. Presbyn. Mason. Home: Tulsa, Okla. Died Jan. 14, 1939.

INSULL, Samuel, pub. utility executive; b. London, Eng., Nov. 11, 1859; s. Samuel and Emma (Short) I.; ed. pvt. schs. in London, Reading and Oxford, Eng.; Sc.D., Union Coll., Schenectady, N.Y., 1917; LL.D., Northwestern U., 1926, Notre Dame, 1926, Queens U., Kingston, Can., 1930; m. Margaret A. Bird, May 23, 1899; 1 son, Samuel Jr. Came to U.S., Feb. 1881, becoming pvt. sec. to Thomas A. Edison, of whose business affairs had full charge for many yrs.; represented Mr. Edison in organization and management of The Electric Tube Co., Edison Machine Works, and Edison Lamp Co.; built and operated, for Mr. Edison, Edison Machine Works, at Schenectady, N.Y., as gen. mgr., and in 1889, when the various Edison mfg. concerns, with the Edison Electric Light Co., were consolidated into Edison Gen. Electric Co., was made 2d v.p. in charge of mfg. and selling depts. of the co., and when it was consolidated, 1892, with Thomson-Houston Co., as the Gen. Electric Co., became 2d v.p. of latter (resigned, June 1892); pres. Chicago Edison Co. and Commonwealth Electric Co., 1892-1907, and of the Commonwealth Edison Co. (consolidation), 1907-30, chmn. bd., 1930-32; officer and dir. many other pub. utility companies until retired, 1932. Chmn. Ill. State Council of Defense, May 3, 1917-19. Decorated Chevalier Legion of Honor (France), 1930. Home: Chicago, Ill. Died July 16, 1938.

IRBY, John Laurens Manning, U.S. senator; b. Laurens, S.C., Sept. 10, 1854; ed. Princeton and U. of Va.; admitted to bar and practiced law, 1876-79; planter near Laurens, 1879—; mem. S.C. legislature, 1886-90 (speaker, 1890); chairman State Dem. Com., 1890; U.S. senator, 1891-97. Home: Laurens, S.C. Died 1900.

IRBY, John St. John; b. Vernon Hill, Va., Aug. 9, 1867; s. Meade Adams and Amanda Tanner (James) I.; student Richmond (Va.) Coll., 1887-89; m. Harriet Ryland, Oct. 12, 1901. Began on Richmond Times, 1889, and became mng. editor of Times and Evening Leader; reporter Evening Times, later Evening Post, Denver, Colo., 1899-1903; propr. Cripple Creek (Colo.) Times, 1903-04; pvt. sec. to Mayor Robert W. Speer of Denver, 1904-12; mem. Colo. Senate, 1909-13; sec. of commn. apptd. by President Wilson, 1915, to investigate diplomatic relations of J. M. Sullivan, U.S. minister to Santo Domingo; pvt. sec. to U.S. Senator James D. Phelan of Calif., 1915-17; U.S. surveyor of customs, Port of San Francisco, 1917-21. Democrat. Episcopalian. Home: San Francisco, Calif. Died 1924.

IRELAND, Clifford, congressman; b. Washburn, Ill., Feb. 14, 1878; s. Frank N. and Fidelia A. (Bangs) I.; prep. edn. Cheltenham Mil. Acad., Ogontz, Pa.; Knox Coll., Galesburg, Ill., 1897-98; U. of Wis., 1899-1901, LL.B., Ill. Coll. of Law, 1908, M.L., 1909, D.C.L., 1911; m. Louise Savage, Sept. 16, 1903; children—Clifford, Eloise. Cashier Washburn (Ill.) Bank, 1901-07; admitted to Ill. bar, 1909, and began practice in Peoria; gen. counsel State T.&S. Bank, 1910-13; pres. Western Live Stock Ins. Co. Mem. 65th to 67th Congresses (1917-23), 16th Ill. Dist.; dir. Dept. of Trade and Commerce, State of Ill., 1923-26. Republican. Methodist. Pres. Nat. Assn. Live Stock Ins. Companies. Served as pvt. Battery B, I.N.G., Spanish-Am. War, 1898. Mason. Home: Peoria, Ill. Died May 24, 1930.

IRELAND, John, archbishop; b. Ireland, Sept. 11, 1838; came to U.S. in boyhood; ed. Cathedral School, St. Paul; studied theology in France; (LL.D., Yale, 1901). Ordained R.C. priest, Dec. 21, 1861; chaplain 5th Minn. Regt. in Civil War; rector cathedral, St. Paul; consecrated bishop of Maronea and coadjutor to Bishop Thomas L. Grace, Dec. 21, 1875; succeeded to the see of St. Paul, July 31, 1884; named archbishop, May 15, 1888. Author: The Church and Modern Society, etc. Home: St. Paul, Minn. Died Sept. 25, 1918.

IRELAND, Oscar Brown, actuary; b. New York, N.Y., Oct. 28, 1840; s. George, Jr., and Anna Mary (Brown) I.; ed. pvt. and pub. schs., and in Free Acad. (now Coll. City of New York), class of 1859 (A.M., Coll. City of New York); m. Jeannie Gordon, Dec. 11, 1877. Clerk in New York, 1859-63; 2d lt. Signal Corps, U.S.A., 1863-65; again clerk, New York, 1865-67; in commercial work in U.S. of Colombia, S.A., 1867-69; in office of D. P. Fackler, consulting actuary, New York, 1870-72; actuary Mass. Mutual Life Ins. Co., 1872—, 2d v.p., 1909—. Unitarian. Republican. Mem. Springfield Sch. Com., 1898-1903. Address: Springfield, Mass. Deceased.

IRELAND, Robert Livingston, corp. official; b. Stratford, Conn., Aug. 20, 1867; s. John Busteed and Adelia Duane (Pell) I.; A.B., Yale, 1890; m. Kate Benedict Hanna, May 2, 1894; children—Robert Livingston, Elizabeth; m. 2d, Mary E. Wood, Apr. 1, 1920. Began as sec. and treas. Hackney Bicycle Co., Cleveland, O., 1892; elected v.p. and gen. mgr. Shipowners' Dry Dock Co., 1898, also v.p. Globe Iron Works; v.p. Am. Shipbuilding Co., 1899-1904; partner M. A. Hanna & Co., 1904-17. Republican. Home: New York, N.Y. Died Feb. 17, 1928.

IRELAND, William (Addison), cartoonist; b. Chillicothe, O., Jan. 8, 1880; s. William Welch and Elizabeth (Pearson) I.; pub. sch. edn.; m. Florence Sayre, June 27, 1906; children—Ruth Winters, Elizabeth Pearson. Began as cartoonist with Chillicothe Daily News, 1897; with Chillicothe News-Advertiser, 1899, Columbus Evening Dispatch, 1899—. Episcopalian. Mason. Home: Columbus, O. Died May 29, 1935.

IRISH, John Powell, customs officer; b. Iowa City, Ia., Jan. 1, 1843; s. Frederick Macy and Elizabeth (Robinson) I.; ed. Iowa City; became teacher and grammar school master, and began journalistic career, 1864, on State Press, Iowa City; m. Annie Fletcher, 1875. Mem. Ia. Legislature, 1868-72; edited Oakland (Calif.) Times, and Alta California, San Francisco, 1882-91; apptd. naval officer of customs, San Francisco, 1894. Candidate for Congress in Iowa, 1868 and 1872—in latter yr. beaten by James Wilson, later Sec. of Agr.; Dem. candidate for gov. Ia., 1877; candidate for Congress in Calif., 1890, against Joseph McKenna. Took part in Monetary Conf., 1897; mem. exec. com. which framed the gold standard and other related financial legislation. Gold Democrat. Has made spl. study of means for making blind adults self-supporting. Pres. Calif. Blind Home Directory, 25 yrs. Advocate of Japanese who are legally domiciled in U.S., and organized Am. Com. of Justice to resist their persecution. Home: Oakland, Calif. Died Oct. 6, 1923.

IRONQUILL, author. See Eugene Ware.

IRONS, James Anderson, army officer; b. Phila., Pa., Feb. 21, 1857; s. James R. and Sarah M. (Anderson) I.; grad. Central High Sch., Phila., 1875, U.S. Mil. Acad., 1879, Inf. and Cav. Sch., 1885; m. Florence Farrell, June 7, 1888. Commd. 2d lt. 20th Inf., June 13, 1879; 1st lt., May 14, 1887; capt., Aug. 25, 1893; maj. engr. vols., June 13, 1898; hon. discharged vols., Feb. 16, 1899; maj. U.S.A., Feb. 2, 1901; insp. gen., Feb. 28, 1901; assigned 16th Inf., Mar. 1, 1905; lt. col. 14th Inf., Apr. 9, 1905; col. 20th Inf., June 26, 1909; brig. gen. N.A., Aug. 5, 1917. Served in campaign against Santiago, Cuba, 1898, engaging in actions at El Caney, San Juan and siege of Santiago; with regt. to Philippines, 1899; in action at Guadaloupe, Pasig, Cainta, Mar. 1899; insp. gen. Dept. of Colo., 1901-03; mem. Gen. Staff Corps, 1903-05; mil. attaché Am. Embassy, Tokyo, Japan, 1907-10, 1914-17; mil. observer at Tsingtao, China, during Japan-German campaign, 1914; with Japanese mission to U.S., Aug. 13-Oct. 12, 1917; apptd. comdr. 166th Depot Brigade, Camp Lewis, American Lake, Wash., Sept. 1917; comdr. 5th Inf. Brigade, Camp Greene, N.C., Dec. 23, 1917. Died July 20, 1921.

IRVINE, Alexander Fitzgerald; b. Antrim, Ireland, Jan. 19, 1863; s. James and Anna (Gilmore) I.; student Oxford U., Eng., 1887-88, Yale U., 1900-04; m. Maude Hazen, June 2, 1897. In British Army in Egypt, 1883-84; awarded Queen's medal and Khedive's bronze star. Ordained Congl. ministry, 1894; pastor successively Omaha (Neb.), Avoca (Ia.), Cleveland (O.), New Haven (Conn.) to 1906; colleague of Dr. Percy Stickney Grant, Ch. of the Ascension, New York, 1907-10; organized first ch. forums in U.S.; became an actor, 1913, and appeared in own playlet, "The Rector of St. Jude's"; chief morale raiser in British Army in France, 1916-18; received personal thanks of King George. Author: The Master and the Chisel, 1904; From the Bottom Up, 1909; The Magyar, 1910; My Lady of the Chimney Corner, 1913; God and Tommy Atkins, 1916; A Life of Christ, 1917; Souls of Poor Folk, 1919; A Yankee with the Soldiers of the King, 1920; The Man From World's End, 1922; Children of Ishmael, 1927; A Fighting Parson, 1929. Address: Santa Barbara, Calif. Died Mar. 15, 1941.

IRVINE, Alonzo Blair, lawyer; b. Salt Lake City, Utah, Feb. 14, 1875; s. William and Jane (Yeates) I.; student Brigham Young Coll., Logan, Utah, 1890-92, U. of Utah, 1890-91; LL.B., U. of Mich., 1902; m. Rosannah Cannon, June 29, 1898; children—Wendell Cannon, Bruce Lincoln, Marian. Began as a teacher, 1893; admitted to Utah bar, 1902, and practiced at Salt Lake City; v.p. and gen. counsel Bamberger Electric R.R. Co.; dir. and gen. counsel Inter-Mountain Electric Co.; pres. Irvine-Cannon Co.; v.p. Abraham Irrigation Co.; dir. Cannon Investment Co.; mem. Utah State Senate, 1924-32, pres., 1926-30; asst. county atty., Salt Lake County, 1902-03; reporter of decisions Utah State Supreme Ct., 1906-12, chmn. Judicial Council, Utah, 1932-34, 1936-37. Judge advocate gen. Utah Nat. Guard, 1906-10. Republican. Mem. Ch. of Latter Day Saints. Home: Salt Lake City, Utah. Died July 12, 1940.

IRVINE, Benjamin Franklin, newspaper editor; b. nr. Scio, Ore.; s. Jesse Baird and Salina Emeline (Humphreys) I.; B.S., A.M., LL.D., Willamette U., Salem, Ore.; LL.D., Ore. State Coll., 1927; m. Gertrude Avery; children—Edna, Ward Avery. Editor and owner Corvallis (Ore.) Times, 1892-1908; editorial writer Oregon Daily Journal, 1908-19, editor, 1919-37. Mem. Ore. State Americanization Board. Former member State Board of Higher Education (resigned 1937). Democrat. Home: Portland, Ore. Died May 1, 1940.

IRVINE, Frank, lawyer; b. Sharon, Pa., Sept. 15, 1858; s. John Mitcheltree and Mary (Winter) I.; B.S., Cornell, 1880; LL.B., Nat. U., Washington, 1883; m. Clara Christy, Nov. 16, 1887; children—Lida (Mrs. C. J. Pope), Winifred (Mrs. C. S. Woolford), Marjorie (dec.). Admitted to bar, Mar. 23, 1883; asst. U.S. atty., D.C., 1883-84; removed to Omaha, Neb., 1884; judge 4th Dist. Neb., 1891-93; Supreme Ct. commr., 1893-99; prof. pleading and practice, 1901-14, dean faculty of law, 1907-14, Cornell U. Coll. of Law; pub. service commr., 2d Dist. N.Y., 1914-21; Dem. candidate for Congress, 37th N.Y. Dist., spl. election, 1922. Home: Ithaca, N.Y. Died June 23, 1931.

IRVINE, Julia Josephine, educator; b. Salem, O., Nov. 9, 1848; d. Owen and Mary Frame (Myers) Thomas; prep. edn. Antioch Coll., Ohio; A.B., Cornell, 1875, A.M., 1876; (Litt.D., Brown, 1895); m. Charles James Irvine, 1875 (died 1886). Prof. Greek, Wellesley Coll., 1890-99, pres., 1895-99. Died Mar. 14, 1930.

IRVINE, Robert Tate, lawyer; b. Danville, Ky., July 11, 1862; s. Abram Walter and Sophia (Tate) I.; Danville Mil. Acad.; A.B., Central U., (now Centre Coll., Danville, Ky.), 1884, LL.D., 1919; LL.B., Law Dept., U. of Va., 1889; m. Roberta Nölting, June 11, 1907. Adj. prof. English, Central U. of Ky., 1883-85; prin. select sch., Winchester, Ky., 1885-87; prof. prep. dept., Central U. of Ky., 1887-88; in practice at Big Stone Gap, Va., 1890—; represents chiefly railroad and mining corps., land and industrial cos. Pres. Intermont Coal & Iron Co., Big Stone Gap Bldg. & Investment Co.; dir. Log Mountain Coal Co. Mem. Va. Ho. of Dels., 1893, 94; mem. Dem. State Exec. Com., 1898—; Dem. presdl. elector, 1900; del.-at-large Dem. Nat. Conv., Baltimore, 1912. Mem. bd. of visitors, U. of Va., 1895-1904, 1908-20, and rector, 1918-20. Presbyn. Home: Big Stone Gap, Va. Mar. 28, 1929.

IRVINE, William, lumberman; b. Mt. Carroll, Ill., Oct. 28, 1851; s. John and Amanda M. (Fitch) I.; ed. pub. schs. and sem., Mt. Carroll; m. Adelaide M. Beardsley, Oct. 8, 1873. Sec. Chippewa Lumber & Boom Co. (successor to Union Lumbering Co.), 1881-85; mgr. same, 1885—, and dir., 1896—; pres. Am. Immigration Co., Lumbermen's Nat. Bank, Chippewa Falls; dir. Wis. Central R.R. Co.; sec. and dir. Northern Lumber Co., Cloquet, Minn.; trustee Northwestern Mut. Life Ins. Co. Republican. Mason. Home: Chippewa Falls, Wis. Died Dec. 26, 1927.

IRVINE, William Burriss, banker; b. Smithfield, O., June 7, 1866; s. George Fleming and Rachael (Burriss) I.; ed. pub. schs. and Linsly Inst., Wheeling, W.Va.; m. Eva A. Drake, Feb. 25, 1886; 1 son, Russell Drake. Asst. cashier, Nat. Exchange Bank, Wheeling, 1898-1901; cashier Bank of Wheeling, 1901-07; v.p. and mgr. Nat. Bank of W.Va., 1907-26, pres., 1926—; also pres. Farmers Nat. Bank, Claysville, Pa. Mem. W.Va. Bankers Assn. (sec., 1907, 08, pres. 1909, 10). Republican. Methodist. Mason. Home: Elm Grove, W.Va. Died Feb. 1, 1940.

IRVINE, William Mann, head master; b. Bedford, Pa., Oct. 13, 1865; s. Henry F. and Emma E. (Mann) I.; Phillips Acad., Exeter, N.H., 1881-84; A.B., Princeton, 1888, Ph.D., 1891; Reformed Ch. Sem., Lancaster, Pa., 1889-92; LL.D., Franklin and Marshall Coll., Pa., 1910, Fafayette Coll., 1916; m. Camille Hart, June 26, 1894. Prof. social science, Franklin and Marshall Coll., 1892-93; head master Mercersburg (Pa.) Acad., 1893—. Mem. Board of Fish Commrs. of Pa., 1924—. Democrat. Home: Mercersburg, Pa. Died June 11, 1928.

IRVINE, Wilson Henry, landscape painter; b. Byron, Ill., Feb. 28, 1869; s. Edwin Alexander and Mina (Underwood) I.; grad. High Sch., Rockford, Ill., 1888; student Art Inst. of Chicago; m. Lydia C. Weyher, Apr. 8, 1891. Represented in Art Inst. Chicago, collection of Friends of Am. Art, Municipal Art League, Union League Club, Chicago, and many pvt. collections. Awarded Martin B. Cahn prize, 1912, and Clyde M. Carr prize, 1915, Art Inst. Chicago; silver medal, San Francisco Expn., 1915, Chicago Soc. Artists, 1916; Charles Noël Flagg prize, Conn. Acad. Fine Arts, 1928. Winner William Eaton prize, $500, 1921; Mr. and Mrs. Wm. O. Goodman prize, Old Lyme Art Assn., 1934. A.N.A., 1926. Home: Old Lyme, Conn. Died Aug. 21, 1936.

IRVING, George Henry, Jr. (George Irving), actor; b. New York, Oct. 5, 1874; s. George Henry and Caroline Matilda (Roberts) I.; ed. Coll. City of New York; grad. Am. Acad. Dramatic Arts, New York, 1897; m. Mary Katharine Gilman, Apr. 9, 1906. Made first appearance in Garrick Theatre, New York, in "Secret Service," 1896; played with Maude Adams in "The Little Minister," "Quality Street," "L'Aiglon"; with Francis Wilson in "The Mountain Climber" and "When Knights Were Bold"; performed as "Jimmy" in "Alias Jimmy Valentine"; etc. Progressive. Episcopalian. Home: Bayside, L.I., N.Y. Died May 29, 1914.

IRVING, Sir Henry Brodribb, actor; b. Keinton, nr. Glastonbury, Eng., Feb. 6, 1838; s. Samuel Brodribb; assumed name of "Irving" by royal license, 1887. Ed. in pvt. sch. in London; (D.Litt., Dublin; Litt.D., Cambridge; LL.D., Glasgow); on stage in provinces, 1856; appeared in London, 1859, but returned to provinces until 1866, when he reappeared in London; played in several London theatres; at the Lyceum, 1871—, lessee and mgr., 1878-99; has made many tours through Great Britain and U.S.; was knighted, 1895. Author: The Drama, 1893; addresses, etc. Address: London, Eng. Died 1905.

IRVING, John Duer, mining geologist; b. Madison, Wis., Aug. 18, 1874; s. Roland Duer and Abby Louise (McCulloh) I.; A.B., Columbia University, 1896, A.M., 1898, Ph.D., 1899; hon. A.M., Yale U., 1907); unmarried. Geologic aid, 1899-1900, asst. geologist, 1900-06, geologist, 1906-07, U.S. Geol. Survey; acting prof. mining and geology, U. of Wyo., 1902-03 (while on leave of absence); apptd. asst. prof. geology, 1903, prof. geology, 1906, Lehigh U.; prof. economic geology, Sheffield Scientific Sch. (Yale), 1907—. Geologist for Alaska Syndicate (N. Guggenheim Sons and J. P. Morgan & Co.) summer of 1907. Editor of the journal, Economic Geology. Wrote Economic Resources of the Northern Black Hills, etc. Capt. engr., O.R.C., in active service. Home: New Haven, Conn. Died July 27, 1918.

IRVING, John Treat, author; b. New York, Dec. 2, 1812; grad. Columbia, 1929; studied law; admitted to bar. Author: Indian Sketches, 1835 and 1888; Hawk Chief; The Attorney; Harry Harson; The Van Gelder Papers. Home: New York, N.Y. Died 1906.

IRVING, Minna (Mrs. Harry Michener), writer; b. Tarrytown, N.Y.; d. William R. and Marian Odell; ed. under pvt. tutors; studied music with Ferdinand de Angelis, Rome, Italy; m. Hasbrouck Delamater (divorced); m. 2d, Harry Michener, Aug. 10, 1911. Episcopalian. Author: Songs of a Haunted Heart; Marriage of the Future; A Cunning Culprit. Contbr. verse to mags. and New York Herald, also sketches and stories, chiefly of the sea. Presented with gold medal, 1899, by survivors of the Maine, in appreciation of her writings on that battleship's destruction. Selected by French authorities, Nov. 1923, to write memorial verse for bronze tablet to Lt. Quentin Roosevelt, at Chamery, France. Home: Tarrytown, N.Y. Died July 23, 1940.

IRWIN, Agnes, coll. dean; b. Washington, Dec. 30, 1841; d. William W. and Sophia A. (Bache) I.; ed. pvt. schs.; (hon. degree from Western U. of Pa.; Litt.D., U. of Pa., 1898; LL.D., St. Andrew's 1906); unmarried. First taught in sch. of Mrs. Hoffman, New York, later conducted pvt. sch. in Phila.; dean Radcliffe Coll., 1894-1909. Commr. Paris Expn. from Mass., 1900; commr. on the adult blind for Mass. Address: Philadelphia, Pa. Died Dec. 5, 1914.

IRWIN, Bernard John Dowling, brig. gen. U.S.A.; b. in Ireland, June 24, 1830; s. James and Sabina Maria (Dowling) I.; ed. by pvt. tutors, classical and modern langs., U. of New York, 1848-49, Castleton (Vt.) Med. Coll., 1850; M.D., New York Med. Coll., 1852; m. Antoinette Elizabeth Stahl, June 20, 1864 (died 1912). Pvt. 7th Regt., N.G.S.N.Y., 1848-51; house surgeon and house physician, N.Y. State Emigrant Hosp., 1853-55. First lt. asst. surgeon, U.S.A., Aug. 28, 1856; capt. asst. surgeon, Aug. 28, 1861; maj. surgeon, Sept. 16, 1862; lt. col. asst. med. purveyor, Sept. 16, 1885; col. asst. surgeon gen., Aug. 28, 1890; bvtd. lt. col. and col. "for meritorious services during war"; retired, June 28, 1894; advanced to rank of brig. gen., retired, by act of Apr. 23, 1904. Served in N.M. and Ariz., 1855-61; comd. detachments from cos. C and H, 7th U.S. Inf., in engagement with Chiricahua Indians, near Apache Pass, Ariz., Feb. 13-14, 1861, and awarded Congressional Medal of Honor for "distinguished gallantry in action" on that occasion. Active service as med. insp. Army of the Ohio, and Army of the Cumberland, 1862; med. dir. Army of Ky. and Army of Southwest, 1862-63; supt. U.S.A. Gen. Hosps., Memphis, Tenn., 1863-65; chief med. officer, U.S. Mil. Acad., 1873-78; med. dir. Dept. of Ariz., 1882-85, Dept. Columbia, 1890-91, Dept. Mo., 1891-94; in charge medical purveying dept., U.S.A., New York, 1885-86, San Francisco, 1886-90. Mem. Pub. Health Congress Auxiliary, Chicago Expn., 1893; v.p. Pan-Am. Med. Congress, 1893; pres. Army Med. Bd. of Examiners, 1892; v.p. and hon. mem. Assn. Mil. Surgeons, U.S., 1891; del. of U.S.A. at 11th Internat. Med. Congress, Rome, 1894; v.p. Am. White Cross First Aid Soc., 1904-06. Home: Chicago, Ill. Died Dec. 15, 1917.

IRWIN, Charles Walter, educator; b. Mt. Vernon, O., Nov. 4, 1868; s. George Alexander and Hannah Antoinette (Johnson) I.; grad. Mt. Vernon High Sch., 1887; B.A., Battle Creek (Mich.) Coll., 1891; M.A., U. of Neb., 1898; studied U. of Calif.; m. Minnie Velara Hennig, Aug. 14, 1895 (died 1927); m. 2d, Mrs. Minnie B. Edwards, July 31, 1930. Prof. Greek and Latin langs., Union College, College View, Neb., 1891-98; prin. Graysville (Tenn.) Acad., 1898-1901; prin. and business mgr. Avondale Sch., Cooranbong, New South Wales, Australia, 1901-09; pres. Pacific Union Coll., 1909-21, also business mgr., 1909-18, and mem. bd. dirs. Advocate of correlation of lit. work and manual labor; student required to work 2½ hours per day; all the bldgs. at Pacific Union Coll. erected by students under direction of teachers. Studied endl. conditions in Europe 6 mos., 1921; sec. dept. of edn., General Conf. Seventh Day Adventists; mem. bd. dirs. Washington Missionary Coll., Review and Herald Pub. Assn. (Takoma Park, D.C.), and Oakwood Jr. Coll. (Huntsville, Ala.); chmn. Assn. Seventh Day Adventist Colleges and Secondary Schs. Home: Washington, D.C. Died July 31, 1934.

IRWIN, Edward M., congressman; b. Crawford County, Mo., Apr. 14, 1869; student U. of Mo.; M.D., Mo. Med. Coll., St. Louis, 1892; m. Emelia Flack; 1 dau., Agnes (Mrs. A. Weaver). Began practice, St. Clair County, Ill., 1892; coroner St. Clair County, 1904-08; chmn. Rep. County Central Com. 24 yrs.; mem. 69th to 71st Congresses (1925-31), 22d Ill. Dist. Republican. Home: Belleville, Ill. Died Jan. 30, 1933.

IRWIN, George Le Roy, army officer; b. Fort Wayne, Mich., Aug. 26, 1868; s. Brig. Gen. Bernard John Dowling and Antoinette Elizabeth (Stahl) I.; grad. U.S. Mil. Acad., 1889, Coast Arty. Sch., 1894, Army War Coll., 1910; m. Maria Elizabeth Barker, Apr. 30, 1892. Commd. additional 2d lt. 5th Arty., June 12, 1889; 2d lt. 3d Arty., Feb. 11, 1890; 1st lt. 5th Arty., Sept. 23, 1897; capt. a.q.m. vols., July 13, 1899; hon. discharged vols., Mar. 21, 1901; capt. Arty. Corps, U.S Army, Feb. 28, 1901; promoted through grades to major gen., Mar. 1928. Served in Philippines, 1899-1901, Cuba, 1906-09, later in Panama, C.Z.; comdr. 161st F.A. Brigade, Camp Grant, Ill., 1917; sailed for France in command 41st Inf. Div., Dec. 12, 1917; comd. 66th, 2d, and 57th F.A. brigades, and (Nov. 1918-Feb. 1919) the Saumur Arty. Sch.; served on Verdun front, Alsace front, in Marne-Aisne offensive and in the Oise-Aisne and Meuse-Argonne offensives; returned to U.S., May 1919. Comdr. Field Arty. Sch., Ft. Sill, Okla., 1923—. Officer Legion of Honor (France). Episcopalian. Died Feb. 19, 1931.

IRWIN, John, rear admiral U.S. Navy, retired Apr. 15, 1894; b. Pa., Apr. 15, 1832; apptd. to navy, Sept. 4, 1847; passed midshipman, June 10, 1853; master 1855; lt., Sept. 6, 1855; lt. comdr., July 16, 1862; comdr., July 25, 1866; capt., May 15, 1875; commodore, Mar. 1886; rear admiral, May 19, 1891. Served on frigate "Wabash" in Civil war; participated in capture of forts at Hatteras Inlet and of Forts Walker and Beauregard; also in battle of Port Royal and capture of Fort Pulaski, 1862. Died 1901.

IRWIN, John Nichol, E.E.&M.P. of U.S. to Portugal, 1899-1902; b. Ohio, 1847; attended Keokuk, Ia., public schools and Miami Univ., O.; private in 45th Iowa vol. inf., 1864; grad. Dartmouth, 1867; m. Mary L. Rankin, 1870; apptd. gov. Idaho by Pres. Arthur, 1883; gov. Ariz., by Pres. Harrison, 1890. Republican. Home: Keokuk, Ia. Died 1905.

IRWIN, John Scull, educator; b. Pittsburg, Apr. 4, 1825; s. Dr. John S. and Mary I.; grad. Western U. of Pa., 1842; U. of Pa., M.D., 1847; LL.D., U. of Ind., 1875; m. Martha C. Mahon, Sept. 30, 1847. Practiced medicine until 1852; went to Fort Wayne, Ind., and became connected with banking, and was several yrs. cashier Merchants Nat. Bank there. School trustee, Ft. Wayne, 1865-75; supt. of schools, 1875-96; retired, 1896, and moved to Lafayette. Home: Lafayette, Ind. Died 1901.

IRWIN, May, actress; b. Whitby, Ont., 1862; d. Robert E. and Jane (Draper) Campbell; m. Frederick W. Keller, 1878 (died 1886); m. 2d, Kurt Eisfeldt, May 26, 1907. Début Adelphi Theatre, Buffalo, Feb. 1876; mem. of Tony Pastor's co. (with her sister Flora), 1877-83; Augustin Daly's co., 1883-87; later with Charles Frohman, in "Junior Partner," "His Wedding Day," "Poets and Puppets," "A Straight Tip," with James T. Powers; "A Country Sport," with Peter F. Dailey; subsequently starring in "The Widow Jones," "The Swell Miss Fitzwell," "Courted into Court," "Kate Kip-Buyer," "Sister Mary," "Belle of Bridgeport," "Madge Smith, Attorney," "Mrs. Black Is Back," "Mrs. Wilson—Andrews," "Mrs. Peckham's Carouse," "Getting a Polish," "She Knows Better Now," "Widow by Proxy," "No. 33 Washington Square," "On the Hiring Line," "The Water's Fine." Home: Clayton, N.Y. Died Oct. 22, 1938.

IRWIN, Noble Edward, naval officer; b. Greenfield, O., Sept. 29, 1869; s. Henry Wilson and Lavina Ann (Rogers) I; grad. U.S. Naval Acad., 1891; m. Elma Natalie Norris, Sept. 26, 1896; 1 dau., Phyllis Natalie. Ensign, July 1, 1893; promoted through grades to rear adm., Dec. 1924. Served aboard U.S.S. Newark at Rio de Janeiro during Brazilian Revolution, 1893-94; wounded while serving on U.S.S. Baltimore at Battle of Manila Bay, May 1, 1898; participated in Philippine Campaign; in comd. at Tientsin, China, during Boxer trouble; as comdr. destroyer Barry, accompanied first flotilla to Philippines; comdr. U.S.S. New Orleans, West Coast of Mexico, 1913-15, and in charge during Turtle Bay incident; first dir. naval aviation, May 1917-May 1919, also arranged for trans-Atlantic flight; comdr. U.S.S. Oklahoma, 1919-21; comdt. Naval Yard, Portsmouth, N.H., 1921-22; comdt. 15th Naval Dist., Canal Zone, 1923-25; comdg. Destroyer Squad., Scouting Fleet, 1925-27; chief of naval mission, Brazil, 1927-30; comdt., 15th Naval Dist., Canal Zone, 1931-33, retired. Medals: Battle of Manila Bay, Spanish-American War, Philippine Campaign, Chinese Campaign, Mexican Campaign, World War; Navy Cross; Officer Legion of Honor (French). Died Aug. 10, 1937.

IRWIN, Richard William, judge; b. Northampton, Mass., Feb. 18, 1857; s. William and Mary (Blake) I.; LL.B, Boston U., 1885; m. Florence E. Bangs, Nov. 16, 1892. Practiced law at Northampton; mem. Common Council, 1888, 89 (pres. 1889); city solicitor, 1890-94; mem. Mass. Ho. of Rep., 1894-95, Senate, 1896-98; mem. Gov.'s Council, 1903-04; dist. atty., Northwestern Dist., Mass., 1905-11 (resigned); justice Superior Ct., Mass., Oct. 7, 1911—. V.p. Northampton Co-operative Bank; trustee Monotuck Savings Bank. Served as 1st lt. and capt. Co. I, 2d Regt. Inf., M.V.M., 1887-92 (resigned). Republican. Mason. Home: Northampton, Mass. Died Mar. 9, 1932.

IRWIN, W(illiam) Francis, clergyman; b. Waveland, Ind., Mar. 12, 1866; s. Robert (D.D.) and Kate (Matthews) I.; A.B., Hanover Coll., Ind., 1887, A.M., 1891; B.D., McCormick Theol. Sem., 1891; D.D., Hanover, 1904; LL.D., Centre Coll., Ky., 1917. Ordained Presbyn. ministry, 1891; pastor Cote Brilliante Ch., St. Louis, 1891-93, Westminster Ch., Bay City, Mich., 1893-96, Fifth Ch., Chicago, 1896-1900, Second Ch., Springfield, Ill., 1900-06, Fourth Av. Ch., Louisville, Ky., 1906-16, Irvington-on-Hudson, N.Y., 1916. Trustee Central U. of Ky., Hanover (Ind.) Coll., Presbyn. Theol. Sem. of Ky.; commr. Gen. Assemblies Presbyn. Ch., Los Angeles and Atlantic City; chmn. synod's exec. com. of Ky.; mem. Permanent Jud. Commn. Presbyn. Ch., 1912-15; mem. Bd. Home Missions, New York, 1913—; chmn. spl. com. on prison reform, 1913-15; mem. exec. commn. of Alliance of Reformed Chs., Aberdeen, Scotland, 1913—; mem. Board of Christian Edn., 1923. War relief work, France and Germany, 1918-19. Home: Irvington-on-Hudson, N.Y. Died Apr. 22, 1932.

ISAACS, Abram Samuel, univ. prof.; b. New York, Aug. 30, 1851; s. Samuel M. and Jane (Symmons) I.; A.B., New York U., 1871, A.M., 1873 and Ph.D., 1878; U. of Breslau, 1874-77; m. Lily Lee Harby, Apr. 23, 1890. Prof. Hebrew, 1886-94, German, 1887-95, German lit., post-grad. dept., 1895-1906, prof. Semitic langs., 1906—, New York U. Editor of The Jewish Messenger, 1878-1903; rabbi Barnert Memorial Temple, Paterson, N.J., 1896-1905. Interested in ednl. and benevolent work; lecturer on lit. and ednl. topics. Author: Moses Chaim Luzzatto, 1878; Stories from the Rabbis, 1894; Step by Step, 1910; What Is Judaism?, 1912; The Young Champion, 1913; Under Sabbath Lamp, 1919. Editor Jewish dept. Encyclopedia Americana, 1907, and Semetic Dept., 1919. Wrote lit. vol. in Young People's Foundation Library, 1911. Home: Paterson, N.J. Died Dec. 22, 1920.

ISAACS, Charles Applewhite, mathematician; b. Brownstown, Ind., Apr. 9, 1881; s. William MacKenzie and Martha Adeline (Robertson) I.; B.A., U. of Ind., 1905; M.A., Columbia, 1908; m. Harriett May McRae, Dec. 21, 1910; children—Catherine Mabel, Doris May, Harriett Marea. Instr. mathematics and civ. engring., State Coll. of Wash., 1905-07; asst. in mathematics, Columbia, 1907-09; prof. mathematics, 1909—, State Coll. of Wash. Served as asst. ednl. dir. S.A.T.C. in states of Wash., Ore., Ida., and Mont., Oct. 1-Dec. 31, 1918. Democrat. Mem. Christian (Disciples) Ch. Mason, K.P. Home: Pullman, Wash. Died Aug. 12, 1937.

ISAACS, Myer Samuel, lawyer; b. New York, May 8, 1841; s. Rev. Samuel M. and Jane (Symmons) I.; grad. New York U., 1859 (A.M., LL.M.); m. Maria Solomon, Feb. 10, 1869; admitted to bar, 1862; one of the founders of the Jewish Messenger, 1857; pres. Baron de Hirsch Fund and of Woodbine Land and Improvement Co.; founder and officer of ednl. and benevolent organizations; justice marine court, 1880; Republican and citizens' candidate for Supreme Court, State of N.Y., 1895; trustee Columbia Bank, Lawyers' Mortgage Co., Borough Homes Co. Home: New York, N.Y. Died 1904.

ISAACS, Nathan, prof. law; b. Cincinnati, O., July 10, 1886; s. Abraham and Rachel (Friedman) I., A.B., U. of Cincinnati, 1907, A.M., 1908, Ph.D., 1910; LL.B., Cincinnati Law Sch., 1910; S.J.D., Harvard U., 1920; m. Ella Davis, Mar. 21, 1912; 1 dau., Carol. Admitted to Ohio bar, 1910, and began practice at Cincinnati; instr. in law, prof. and asst. dean, Cincinnati Law Sch., 1912-18; Thayer teaching fellow, Harvard Law Sch., 1919-20, prof. law, U. of Pittsburgh, 1920-23; prof. business law, Columbia, summers 1921-23, 1925-26; lecturer business law, Harvard, 1923-24, prof. business law, 1924—; special lecturer, Army Industrial Coll., 1932-35; Cutler lecturer on constitutional law, U. of Rochester, 1934; lecturer, Yale Law Sch., 1937-39; dir. Gimbel Bros., Inc. Served as capt. M.I. Div., U.S. Army, 1918-19. Trustee Hebrew Teachers Coll., Associated Jewish Philanthropies. Jewish religion. Author: The Law in Business Problems, 1921, revised, 1934; Course in Business Law, 1922; Study as a Mode of Worship, 1925. Contbr. chapters to Ways to Peace, 1924, Selected Essays on the Law of Torts, 1924, The Legacy of Israel, 1927, Ballantine's Problems in Law, 1927, Ency. Britannica, 1930, Ency. Social Sciences, 1931-35. Editor The National Law Library (with Roscoe Pound), 1939; University Business Book Series. Asst. editor Internat. Standard Bible Ency., 1915. Home: Cambridge, Mass. Died Dec. 18, 1941.

ISAACSON, Charles David, writer, lecturer; b. 1891; s. Mark N. and Kate (Arons) I.; ed. pub. and high schs.; m. Emolyn Gloria Silverman, 1915; 1 son, Charles David. Studied violin with father; concertized; various lines of business and advertising with George Batten Co., Æolian Co.; pres. Joseph Ellner Co., 1914-15, A. M. Sweyd Co., 1916-19; with Goldwyn Distributing Corp., 1919; editor dept. "Our Family Music," New York Globe, 1916-21, Evening Mail, 1921-23; served as asso. mgr. Gallo. San Carlo Grand Opera, Chicago Opera Co.; conducted 4,000 free concerts in New York; was dir. WRNY (radio) Roosevelt Hotel, New York; was gen. mgr. WGL (radio), New York; music critic, N.Y. Morning Telegraph, 1927-30, later dir. Speech Center, New York. Author: Face to Face with Great Musicians, Vol. I, 1918, Vol. II, 1922; Simple Story of Music, 1927; Jews, Money and Such, 1932; also Stories from the Hindu; New Democratic Philosophy. Narrator WOR opera hours. Died Feb. 15, 1936.

ISELIN, Adrian, banker; s. Adrian and Eleanora (O'Donnell) I.; m. Louise Caylus, Apr. 4, 1872 (died 1909); m. 2d, Mrs. Sara Gracie King Bronson, 1914 (died 1931). Engaged in banking, 1868—; mem. A. Iselin & Co. Dir. many corps. Home: New York, N.Y. Died Jan. 29, 1935.

ISELIN, Charles Oliver, banker, yachtsman; s. Adrian and Eleanora (O'Donnell) I.; LL.B., Columbia, 1874; m. 1st, d. of Thomas Garner; m. 2d, Hope, d. Col. William Goddard. Owner of the yachts, Vigilant, Defender and Reliance (cup defenders); also mug owner the yacht Columbia. Home: Glen Head, L.I., N.Y. Died Jan. 11, 1932.

ISELIN, Columbus O'Donnell, financier; s. Adrian and Eleanora (O'Donnell) I.; m. Edith C. Jones; children—Lewis, O'Donnell, Adrienne M. Pres. Codi Corp., New Rochelle Homestead Co.; v.p. Interlaken and Helvetia Realty Cos., Neptune Realty Co., Two Lakes Corp.; treas. Allegheny & Western Ry. Co.; dir. Adrian Furnace Co., Manhattan Storage Safe Deposit Co., Clearfield & Mahoning Ry. Co., Mahoning Valley Ry., Queens Ins. Co. of America, Reynoldsville & Falls Creek R.R., Allegheny & Western Ry. Co., 150 William St. Corp.; trustee Bank of N.Y. & Trust Co., Manhattan Storage & Warehouse Co. Home: New York, N.Y. Died Nov. 10, 1933.

ISHAM, Frederic Stewart author; b. Detroit, Mich., Mar. 29, 1866; s. Charles S. and Lucy B. (Mott) I.; grad. high sch., Detroit; studied 2 yrs. Royal Acad. Music, London, and 2 yrs. Munich; m. Helen M. Frue, Apr. 15, 1895. On editorial staff Detroit Free Press and other newspapers 10 yrs. Author: The Strollers, 1902; Under the Rose, 1903; Black Friday, 1904; The Lady of the Mount, 1908; Half a Chance, 1909; The Social Buccaneer, 1910; The Treasure (novelette), 1910; A Man and His Money, 1912; Aladdin from Broadway, 1913; Nothing But the Truth, 1915 (dramatized and presented at Longacre Theatre, N.Y., 1916-17, by William Collier; 18 mos. at Savoy Theatre, London, 1918-19; 4 mos., Paris, 1918); This Way Out, 1917; Three Live Ghosts, 1918; The Daisy Pushers (comedy-drama, with Max Marcin), 1919; The Nut-Cracker (play), 1919; Blue Is True (play), 1919. Address: Detroit, Mich. Died 1922.

ISHAM, Samuel, artist; b. New York, N.Y., May 12, 1855; s. William B. and Julia (Burhans) I.; A.B., Yale, 1875, B.F.A., 1901; art edn. at Paris in Atelier Julien; unmarried. Has exhibited at both Paris salons and in most of the larger Am. exhibitions; mem. jury Buffalo Expn., 1901; 2d medal, St. Louis Expn., 1904. Dir. Am. Fine Arts Soc.; N.A., 1906; mem. Nat. Inst. Arts and Letters. Author: A History of American Painting, 1905. Address: New York, N.Y. Died June 12, 1914.

ISHERWOOD, Benjamin Franklin, commodore U.S. Navy; b. June 6, 1822. Entered U.S. Navy, May 23, 1844, as 1st asst. engr.; promoted chief engr., Oct. 31, 1848; was engr.-in-chief U.S. Navy, 1861-69; afterward at Mare Island Navy Yard, Calif., and on spl. duties; retired by operation of law, June 6, 1884, with relative rank of commodore. Address: New York, N.Y. Died June 19, 1915.

ISOM, Mary Frances, librarian; b. Nashville, Tenn., Feb. 27, 1865; d. John Franklin (M.D.) and Frances A. (Walter) I.: student Wellesley, 1883-84; student library science, Pratt Inst. Library Sch., Brooklyn, 1899-1901; unmarried. Librarian, Library Assn. of Portland, 1901—. Hosp. rep. of A.L.A. in France, 1918-19. Pres. Pacific Northwestern Library Assn., 1911; life mem. A.L.A. (2d v.p. 1912); mem. Nat. Advisory Bd. of Special Libraries; ex-officio mem. Ore. Free Library Commn.; pres. Professional Woman's League of Portland, 1912-13. Home: Portland, Ore. Died Apr. 15, 1920.

ISRAEL, Edward L., rabbi; b. Cincinnati, O., Aug. 30, 1896; s. Charles and Emma (Linz) I.; A.B., U. of Cincinnati, 1917; studied Harvard, summers 1916, 17; Rabbi, Hebrew Union Coll., Cincinnati, 1919; LL.D., Washington Coll., 1938; m. Amelia Dryer, Nov. 23, 1919; children—Charles Edward, Edward L. Acting chaplain Jewish Welfare Bd., Chaumont and Brest, France, 1919; rabbi B'rith Sholom Congregation, Springfield, Ill., 1919-20, Washington Av. Temple, Evansville, Ind., 1920-23. Har Sinai Congregation, Baltimore, 1923—. Mem. White House Conf. on Children in Democracy, 1939; 1st v.p. Synagogue Council of America; mem. Commn. on Social Justice of Central Conf. Am. Rabbis, 1926—, chmn., 1927-33; pres. Baltimore Branch Am. Jewish Congress, 1934—; mem. exec. com. World Jewish Congress; mem. Regional Nat. Labor Bd., 1934-35; summer lecturer, U. of N.C., 1927-29, U. of Va., 1931. Mem. Nat. exec. com. and chmn. administrative com. Seaboard Region. Zionist Orgn. America; mem. nat. exec. bd., Nat. Pub. Housing Conf. and Nat. Housing Com., Nat. Religion and Labor Foundation; mem. nat. com. Nat. Conf. Jews and Christians, League for Industrial Democracy, Am. Assn. for Social Security, Am. Civil Liberties Union, bd. trustees Christian Social Justice Fund, B'nai B'rith Hillel Foundation, Municipal Commn. on Employment Stabilization of Baltimore City (chmn.); chmn. Arbitration Men's Clothing Industry, Baltimore, 1935—; chmn. Social Justice Commn., Synagogue Council of America, 1936—. Mason. Author: (with others) The Western Maryland Railway Strike, 1927; The Centralia Tragedy (in collaboration) 1930; The Message of Israel, 1934. Editor Bull. of Commn. on Social Justice of Central Conf. Am. Rabbis, 1927-33; contbg. editor The World Tomorrow, 1929-33, The Reconstructionist. Columnist and special feature writer magazines and newspapers. Lecturer Jewish Chautauqua and various univs. and forums. Home: Baltimore, Md. Died Oct. 19, 1941.

ISRAEL, Rogers, bishop; b. Baltimore, Md., Sept. 14, 1854; s. Thomas Beale and Elizabeth Rogers (Hiss) I.; A.B., Dickinson Coll., Pa., 1881, A.M., 1884; D.D., Dickinson, 1900, Allegheny College, 1915; m. Sara Frances, d. Judge James H. Graham, Sept. 22, 1882. Deacon, 1885, priest, 1886, P.E. Church; rector Christ Ch., Meadville, Pa., 1885-92, St. Luke's, Scranton, Pa., 1892-1911; consecrated bishop, Diocese of Erie, Pa., Feb. 24, 1911. Deputy 5 Gen. Convs.; examining chaplain Diocese of Bethlehem, 10 yrs. Chaplain, Base Hosp. No. 20, U. of Pa. in France, July 1917-Feb. 1919. Address: Erie, Pa. Died Jan. 11, 1921.

ITTNER, William Butts, architect; b. St. Louis, Mo., Sept. 4, 1864; s. Anthony and Mary Isabella I.; grad. Manual Training Sch. of Washington U., 1884; grad. spl. student in architecture, Cornell U., 1887; LL.D., U. of Mo., 1930; m. Littie Crane Allan, June 6, 1888; m. 2d, Marie Anderson, Oct. 1, 1923. Commr. of sch. bldgs. for Bd. of Edn. of St. Louis, June 22, 1897-1910; architect for the Bd. of Edn. and in gen. practice of architecture, 1910—. Has designed sch. bldgs. in most of states, including Central High Sch. (Washington, D.C.), Emerson, Froebel and Horace Mann schs. (Gary, Ind.), Central Tech. High Sch. (Columbus, O.), 3 bldg. group (Greenfield, O.); designed many Masonic bldgs., among them St. Louis Scottish Rite Cathedral; architect for St. Louis Unit of Shriners' Hosp. for Crippled Children, Central Inst. for the Deaf, Pharmacal Coll., Continental Life Ins. Bldg. (all St. Louis); Pottsville (Pa.) High School (cost $1,000,000); also sch. buildings in suburban cities near St. Louis; Mo. State Prison, Lincoln Univ. (Jefferson City). Fellow A.I.A., and pres. chapter same, 1893-95. Home: St. Louis, Mo. Died Jan. 26, 1936.

IVERSON, Samuel Gilbert, lawyer; b. Rushford, Minn., Apr. 21, 1859; s. John and Gunhild (Gunderson) I.; prep. edn. Shattuck Mil. Acad., Faribault, Minn.; LL.B., U. of Minn. Law Sch., 1893; m. Calista Bentley, Apr. 24, 1900 (died 1912). Began as clk. in store at Rushford; postmaster Rushford, 1881-86; mem. Minn. Ho. of Rep., 1887; accountant, state auditor's office, 1887-91; deputy state treas., Minn., 1891-95; deputy state auditor, 1895-1902, state auditor 3 terms, 1902-14; candidate for gov., 1916. As state auditor was in charge of 3,000,000 acres school and other trust fund lands, with timber and ore valued at $200,000,000; conducted many successful claims in Interior Dept. and secured decree of Supreme Court of Minn. that iron ore under public lakes and rivers in the state belongs to the people and not to shore owners. Commd. 1st lt. Adj. Gen.'s Dept., N.A., Aug. 15, 1917; served 8 mos. in France with A.E.F. Republican. Episcopalian. Mason. Home: St. Paul, Minn. Died Mar. 27, 1928.

IVES, Brayton, banker; b. Farmington, Conn., 1840; A.B., Yale, 1861. First lt. adj. 5th Conn. Inf., July 23, 1861; capt., Sept. 25, 1861; capt. asst. adj. vols., Apr. 28, 1862; resigned, Aug. 5, 1863; maj. 1st Conn. Cav., May 31, 1864; lt. col., Nov. 1, 1864; col., Jan. 17, 1865; bvtd. brig. gen. vols., Mar. 13, 1865, "for gallantry at battles of Reams Sta., Deep Bottom, Five Forks and Sailors Creek"; hon. mustered out, Aug. 2, 1865. Stock broker in Wall St., New York, 1867-89; pres. Standard Milling Co., Hecker-Jones-Jewell Milling Co., Kanona & Prattsburgh Ry. Co., Metcalf Land Co., Northwestern Consolidated Milling Co., Barney Estate Co.; dir. Metropolitan Trust Co., Am. Round Bail Press Co., Atlantic Safe Deposit Co. Pres. New York Stock Exchange, 1878-79. Died Oct. 22, 1914.

IVES, Frederic Eugene, inventor; b. Litchfield, Conn., Feb. 17, 1856; s. Hubert Leverit and Ellen A. (Beach) I.; ed. pub. schs., Litchfield, Norfolk, Newtown, Conn.; m. Mary Elizabeth Olmstead, June 15,

1879 (died 1904); 1 son, Herbert Eugene; m. 2d, Mrs. Margaret Campbell Cutting, Nov. 15, 1913 (died 1928). In charge of photography laboratory, Cornell U., 1874-78; realized first practically successful process of orthochromatic photography, and invented 1st practically successful process of half-tone photo-engraving, 1878; invented the half-tone photo-engraving process now universally employed, 1886; (inscribed gold testimonial Internat. Photo-Engravers' Assn., 1911; gold medals United Typothetae of America, Printing House Craftsman, Poor Richard Club, 1926); experiments in color photography on the so-called trichromatic principle commenced in 1878, culminating in the three-color printing process in typographic press, now an important industry, and in "Kromskop," "Tripak," "Hicrom" and "1931 Polychrome" processes; and a successful process for moving pictures in natural colors; 70 U.S. patents granted. Awarded Cresson gold medal, Franklin Inst., Philadelphia; spl. gold medal, Photo. Society of Philadelphia, and Progress medal, Royal Photo. Society for work in color photography; Science medal, Royal Photo. Society, London, and Scott Legacy medal, Franklin Inst., for The Parallax Stereogram; Rumford medal, Am. Acad. Arts and Sciences, for inventions in color photography and photo-engraving; and 14 other medals by scientific socs. for various inventions and discoveries. Author: The Autobiography of an Amateur Inventor, 1928. Home: Philadelphia, Pa. Died May 27, 1937.

IVES, George Burnham, editor and translator; b. Salem, Mass., Oct. 18, 1856; s. Stephen Bradshaw and Mary Eliza (Burnham) I.; A.B., Harvard, 1876; m. May Manley Creamer, Apr. 10, 1879 (died 1919). Lit. work, 1893—, largely, at first, translating from the French, especially Balzac, Daudet and George Sand; editorial proofreader for Riverside Press, 1903-17; asst. to editor Atlantic Monthly, 1917-23; editorial proofreader for Harvard U. Press, 1923-29. Editor: Florio's Montaigne (folio), 1903-04. Compiler: Bibliography of Oliver Wendell Holmes, 1907. Translator: Bernard's Life of Geofrey Tory, 1909; Tory's Champ Fleury (1529), 1927; The Essays of Montaigne (4 vols.), 1925; Weygand's Turenne, 1929. Wrote: Text, Type and Style—a Compendium of Atlantic (Monthly) Usage, 1921. Home: Salem, Mass. Died Aug. 21, 1930.

IVES, Halsey Cooley, art director; b. Montour Falls, N.Y., Oct. 27, 1846; s. Hiram DuBoise and Teresa (McDowell) I.; ed. tech. schs. of S. Kensington, London, and various art schs.; student of Piatowski; LL.D., Washington U., 1905; m. Margaret A. Lackland, Feb. 21, 1887. Dir. St. Louis Sch. of Fine Arts (art dept. Washington U.), 1874-1909; dir. City Art Mus., St. Louis, 1909—. Has several times represented U.S. Govt. as commr. abroad; was chief Art Dept., Chicago Expn., 1893, St. Louis Expn., 1904; mem. St. Louis Art Commn. Lay mem. Nat. Sculpture Soc.; hon. mem. Am. Inst. Architects. Decorations: Knight of the Danebrog by Christian IX, 1894; Knight, Order of Vasa, Sweden, 1895; Knight Comdr., Order Saint Alexander, Bulgaria, 1904; Knight Comdr., Order Double Dragon, China, 1904; Chevalier, Order Leopold, Belgium, 1905; Knight, Order Saint Maurice and Leazar, Italy, 1905; Knight, Order Christ, Portugal, 1905; Knight, Order Iron Cross of Francis Joseph, Austria, 1905; Knight, Order of Rising Sun, Japan, 1906; Officer Pub. Instrn., France, with insignia of the Palms of the Acad., 1908; spl. medal from bd. of directors, Chicago Expn.; medal and diploma from French Govt.; grand prize for ednl. services, St. Louis Expn., 1904; silver medal for landscape "Waste Lands," Portland Expn. Home: Redcroft, Mo. Died 1911.

IVES, Joel Stone, clergyman; b. Colebrook, Conn., Dec. 5, 1847; s. Rev. Alfred E. and Harriet Platt (Stone) I.; A.B., Amherst, 1870, A.M., 1873; B.D., Yale Div. Sch., 1874; m. Emma Sarah Butler, July 15, 1874. Ordained Congl. Ministry, 1874; pastor East Hampton, Conn., 1874-83, Stratford, 1883-99; director Missionary Society of Conn., 1894-99, and trustee Fund for Ministers; sec. same socs., 1899-1914, treas., 1909-14; treas. Nat. Council Congl. Chs. of U.S., 1908-15. Moderator Conn. State Assn. Conglists, 1893. Republican. Author of Quarto Millennial of the Stratford Congregational Church, 1889. Home: Meriden, Conn. Died Jan. 21, 1924.

IVES, Joseph Moss, lawyer; b. Danbury, Conn., Feb. 5, 1876; s. George Edward and Mary (Parmelee) I.; LL.B., Yale Law Sch., 1899; LL.D., Loyola Coll., Baltimore, 1934; m. Minnie L. Goodman, Dec. 4, 1900; children—Richard Goodman, Lyman Brewster, Moss White, Walter Bigelow, Chester Brown, Sarane Wilcox. Admitted to Conn. bar, 1899; corp. counsel City of Danbury, 1901-13, pros. atty., 1907-10; mem. Conn. Gen. Assembly, 1905; judge City Ct. of Danbury, 1918-26; judge of 1st Dist. Traffic Ct. in Conn., 1929, 1933; mem. firm Ives & Sherwood; dir. Danbury Nat. Bank, Savings Bank of Danbury. V.P. and trustee Danbury Pub. Library; trustee Brewster Home for Aged, Am. Legion Home; mem. Child Welfare Commn., 1919-21; sec. Nat. Conf. on Uniform State Laws, 1899-1904. Judge advocate gen. on Gov.'s staff, 1907-11, 1921-23; judge advocate, Conn. Nat. G., 1914-16; mem. mil. Emergency Bd. and adj. gen. Conn. State Guard, World War; maj. U.S. Res.; with War Dept., Gen. Staff, Washington, in work of reorganization of N.G. and U.S. Res., 1920-21. Republican. Conglist. (deacon 1st Ch.). Mason. Author: The Ark and the Dove, 1936. Lecturer. Home: Danbury, Conn. Died Apr. 8, 1939.

IVES, Percy, portrait painter; b. Detroit, Mich., June 5, 1864; s. Lewis Thomas and Margaret Wright (Leggett) I.; ed. high sch., Detroit; studied Pa. Acad. Fine Arts 4 yrs., Paris, France, 6 yrs.; m. Elsie Caron, June 16, 1890 (died 1915). Exhibited Paris, New York, Boston, Phila., Cincinnati, Chicago, etc. Most important works: President Grover Cleveland; Brittany Fisherman (World's Columbian Exposition); Mrs. Ives (Am. Painters' Exhbn., Detroit); Gen. Alger (U.S. War Dept.); quarter-centennial portrait (1921) of Prof. R. M. Wenley, U. of Mich.; Treaty of Saginaw (Cass High Sch., Detroit). Hon. mention, Buffalo Exposition, 1901; mem. Jury of Admission, Art Dept., St. Louis Expn., 1904. Mem. Detroit Museum of Art (incorporator, trustee and treas.), Soc. Western Artists, Fine Arts Soc. (Detroit), Archæol. Inst. America (treas. Detroit br.). Republican. Unitarian. Address: Detroit, Mich. Died Feb. 14, 1928.

IVES, Ralph Burkett, corp. official; b. Hartford, Conn., Jan. 27, 1873; s. John S. and Annie (Chapin) I.; ed. pub. schs., Hartford; m. Edith King, Nov. 3, 1897; children—Mrs. Nettie K. Miner, Louis K. Began with Aetna Ins. Co., Hartford, 1905, spl. agent, New England, 1907-12, asst. sec., 1912-15, with Western dept., Chicago, Ill., 1915-19, v.p., 1919-23, pres., 1923—; pres. World Fire & Marine Ins. Co., Piedmont Fire Ins. Co., Century Indemnity Co. Republican. Conglist. Home: Hartford, Conn. Died Jan. 2, 1934.

IVEY, Thomas Neal, clergyman, editor; b. Marion, S.C., May 22, 1860; s. George Washington and Selina (Neal) I.; A.B., Trinity Coll., N.C., 1880, A.M., 1882 (D.D., 1896); m. Lenora Ann Dowd, Aug. 8, 1883. Prin. Shelby (N.C.) High Sch., 1880-83; prin. Oak Inst., Mooresville, N.C., 1883-88; entered M.E. Ch., S., ministry, 1888; pastor, Lenoir Station, N.C., 1888, Roxboro, N.C., 1888-92, Wilson, N.C., 1892-96; editor N.C. Christian Advocate, 1896-98, Raleigh (N.C.) Christian Advocate, 1898-1910; editor Christian Advocate, Nashville (gen. organ M.E. Ch., S.), 1910—. Del. Ecumenical Conf., Toronto, 1911; v.p. for Southern Methodism of Federal Council of Chs. of Christ in America. Mem. Ecumenical Commission for 1921. Trustee Trinity Coll., N.C., Meth. Orphanage, Raleigh, N.C. Mem. Nat. Editorial Assn. Democrat. Mason (Grand Chaplain Grand Lodge N.C., 2 yrs.). Editor: Southern Methodist Handbook (ann. yearbook, M.E. Ch., S.), 1896—. Author: Bildad Akers—His Book. Mem. Commn. on Unification of Methodism. Died May 15, 1923.

IVINS, Anthony W., ch. official; b. Toms River, N.J.; s. Israel and Anna (Lowrie) I.; ed. pub. schs.; m. Elizabeth Ashby Snow, Nov. 9, 1878; children—Antoine Ridgway, Anna Lowrie, Florence S., Leah, Heber Grant, Stanley, Fulvia. Farmer, rancher and breeder of horses and cattle, also engaged in banking and merchandising. Counseller Ch. of Jesus Christ of Latter Day Saints. Served as town marshal, dep. sheriff, mayor, pros. atty., county assessor and collector; mem. Utah Ho. of Rep. and mem. Utah Constl. Conv. Democrat. Rotarian. Home: Salt Lake City, Utah. Died Sept. 23, 1934.

IVINS, William Mills, lawyer; b. Monmouth County, N.J., Apr. 22, 1851; s. Augustus and Sarah (Mills) I.; ed. Adelphi Acad., Brooklyn; LL.B., Columbia, 1873; admitted to bar, 1873; m. Emma L. Yard, Feb. 3, 1879. Mem. law firm of Ivins, Wolff & Hoguet; mem. bd. of edn., 1882-85; chamberlain, New York, 1885-89; judge advocate gen. State of N.Y., 1886-88. Rep. candidate for mayor New York, 1905; spl. counsel to Pub. Service Commn., 1st Dist., 1906-07; chmn. New York Charter Commn., 1907-09. Home: New York, N.Y. Died July 23, 1915.

IVISON, David Brinkerhoff, publisher; b. Auburn, N.Y., June 28, 1835; s. Henry and Sarah B. I.; m. Emeline M. Crane, Oct. 17, 1860. Employe, 1857, and later partner, house of Ivison, Blakeman & Taylor, school-book publishers, founded by father. Of this firm he became head, and when it, in 1890, united with other firms in The American Book Co., became pres. of latter. Elder in Presbyn. Ch. Home: Rutherford, N.J. Died 1903.

J

JACCHIA, Agide, musical dir.; b. Lugo, Italy, Jan. 5, 1875; s. Leone and Volunnia (Camerini) J.; grad. Rossini Conservatory, Pesaro, Italy, 1898, with diplomas in composition and conducting; studied under Maseagni; m. Ester Ferrabini (operatic soprano), Mar. 5, 1911; 1 dau., Elsa. Came to U.S., 1902, as asst. condr. Mascagni Opera Co.; naturalized citizen, 1922; toured U.S. and Central America with Milano Opera Co., 1907-09; gen. mus. dir. Montreal Opera Co., 1910-14; mus. dir. Century Opera Co., New York, 1914; condr. Boston Symphony "Pops," 1917-26; also condr. Cecilia Soc. of Boston, 1920-24, Fitchburg (Mass.) Choral Soc., 1923-25; dir. Boston Conservatory of Music, 1920—. Composer of cantatas, arrangements, songs. Home: Boston, Mass. Died Nov. 29, 1932.

JACK, George Whitfield, judge; b. Natchitoches, La., Nov. 1, 1875; s. William Houston and Mary Catherine (Whitfield) J.; grad. La. State Normal Sch., 1893; LL.B., Tulane U. Law Dept., 1898; m. Roberta Pegues, May 9, 1900. Admitted to La. bar, 1898, and began practice in Shreveport. City atty., Shreveport, 1910-13; U.S. atty., Western Dist. of La., 1913-17; U.S. dist. judge, Western Dist. La., 1917—. Democrat. Home: Shreveport, La. Died Mar. 15, 1924.

JACKMAN, Wilbur Samuel, educator, author; b. Mechanicstown, O., Jan. 12, 1855; s. Barnard C. and Ruth L. J.; grad. Pa. Normal School, California, Pa., 1877; studied Allegheny Coll., 1880-82; grad. Harvard Coll., 1884; m. Ellen Amelia Reis, Dec. 23, 1884. Traveled in England, Holland, France and Germany studying edn., 1899-1900. Prof. teaching of natural science, 1901—, dean Coll. of Edn., U. of Chicago, 1901-04; prin. Univ. Elementary Sch., 1904—. Editor Elementary Sch. Teacher. Author: Nature Study for the Common Schools, 1891; Number Work in Nature Study, 1893; Field Work in Nature Study, 1894; Nature Study and Related Subjects, 1898; Nature Study for the Grammar Grades, 1898; Nature Study Record, 1895. Home: Chicago, Ill. Died 1907.

JACKSON, A(braham) V(alentine) Williams, univ. prof.; b. New York, Feb. 9, 1862; s. David Sherwood and Elizabeth (Williams) J.; A.B., Columbia, 1883, A.M., 1884, L.H.D., 1885, Ph.D., 1886, LL.D., 1904; U. of Halle, 1887-89; m. Dora Elizabeth Ritter, June 25, 1889 (died, 1909); m. 2d, Kate Brigham, Feb. 28, 1911. Asst. in English and instr. Zend, 1886-89, instr. Anglo-Saxon and Indo-Iranian langs., 1889-91, adj. prof. English lang. and lit., 1891-95, prof. Indo-Iranian langs., 1895-1935, prof. emeritus in residence, 1935—, Columbia U. Pub. lecturer; traveled for research in India, 1901, 1911, Persia and Central Asia, 1903, 07, 10, receiving spl. attention from Parsi community, India; revisited India and Persia, 1918, as mem. Am. Persian Relief Commn. (decorated by the Shah and received hon. degree from Dár'ul-Funún University, Teheran, 1918); again, in 1926, made a journey of research in India, Afghanistan, Baluchistan and Eastern Persia. Trustee Yonkers Bd. Edn., 1898-1909; trustee Yonkers Pub. Library, 1893-1926; trustee Am. Sch. Oriental Research, 1921—; pres. Omar Khayyam Soc. of America, 1927-29. Mem. Am. Oriental Soc. (pres., 1915-16 and 1929-30, dir. many years). Episcopalian. Author: A Hymn of Zoroaster, Yasma XXXI, 1888; An Avestan Grammar, in comparison with Sanskrit, 1892; An Avestan Reader, 1893; Zoroaster, the Prophet of Ancient Iran, 1899; Die iranische Religion, 1900-01 (Strassburg); Persia, Past and Present, 1906; From Constantinople to the Home of Omar Khayyam, 1911; Descriptive Catalogue of the Persian MSS. in the Metropolitan Museum of Art, New York (with A. Yohannan), 1914; Early Persian Poetry, 1920. Joint translator: Priyadarsika, a Sanskrit Drama, 1923, Zoroastrian Studies, 1928; Researches in Manichaeism, 1932. Editor: A History of India (9 vols.), 1906-07; Columbia Univ. Indo-Iranian Series (13 vols.), 1901—. Home: New York, N.Y. Died Aug. 8, 1937.

JACKSON, Abraham Willard, author; b. Portland, Me., Apr. 7, 1843; s. Robert and Ruth Shaw (Lucas) J.; pvt. 8th Me. Vols. and 2d lt., 1st lt. and capt. 33d U.S.C.T. in Civil War; incurred deafness in service; A.B., Colby Coll., 1869, A.M., 1898, D.D., 1901; S.T.B., Harvard, 1872; m. Caroline B. Bigelow, July 8, 1872. Unitarian pastor Peterboro, N.H., 1872-80, Santa Barbara, Calif., 1880-88; acting prof. philosophy, Meadville Theol. Sch., 1894-95. Author: The Immanent God, 1889; James Martineau, a Biography and Study, 1900; Deafness and Cheerfulness, 1902. Home: Melrose, Mass. Died 1911.

JACKSON, Albert Atlee, banker; b. Stamford, Conn., May 28, 1867; s. Charles McClintock and Emily Boude (Haldeman) J.; ed. Episcopal Acad., Phila., and U. of Pa.; m. Lucy, d. John S. Runnells, Nov. 20, 1901. Began as clk. with Pa. R.R., 1884; became connected with Girard Trust Co. as clerk, 1889, pres., 1928-38, chmn. of bd., 1938—; dir. Western Savings Fund Soc., Buffalo & Susquehanna R.R. Corp., Penn Mutual Life Ins. Co., Keystone Watch Case Corp., Westmoreland Coal Co. Republican. Episcopalian. Home: Philadelphia, Pa. Died July 30, 1939.

JACKSON, Albert Mathews, educator; b. W. Middlesex, Pa., Nov. 12, 1860; s. William A. and Adelaide (Mathews) J.; student Westminster Coll., Pa., 3 yrs.; A.B., Princeton, 1884; m. Jennie B. Simons, July 16, 1865. Teacher mathematics, Blair Acad., Blairstown, N.J., 1884-86; teacher mathematics and prin. Wyman Inst., 1886-92; name of inst. changed, 1892, to Western Mil. Acad. of which was pres., supt. and prin. owner. Holds bvt. rank of col. in Ill. N.G. Address: Upper Alton, Ill. Died Mar. 28, 1919.

JACKSON, Charles Cabot, broker; b. Boston, Sept. 22, 1843; s. Charles Jr., and Susan (Cabot) J.; A.B., Harvard, 1863; Harvard Law Sch., 1863-64; m. Frances Elizabeth Appleton, June 7, 1876; children—Charles, Robert, Appleton, Susan (Mrs. R. B. Williams), George S. (deceased), Frances Appleton (deceased). Mem. firm Richardson & Jackson, wool brokers, Boston, 1868-70; with Lee, Higginson & Co., bankers, 1870-75; sr. mem. Jackson & Curtis, 1879-1916; retired. Pres. Boston Stock Exchange, 1903-05; treas. Rep. City Com., 1883; mem. corp. Mass. Inst. Tech., 1887-1912; treas. Greater Boston Council Boy Scouts of America, 1911-14, and pres., 1915-18; treas. Girls' Trade Edn. League, 1910—. Sec. of Class of 1863, Harvard. Wrote: Has Gold Appreciated? 1894; Six Industrial Crises. Home: Boston, Mass. Died Oct. 24, 1926.

JACKSON, Charles Loring, chemist; b. Boston, Apr. 4, 1847; s. Patrick Tracy and Susan Mary (Loring) J.; A.B., Harvard, 1867, A.M., 1870; studied Heidelberg and Berlin, 1873-75; unmarried. Asst. in chemistry, 1868-71, asst. prof., 1871-81, prof., 1881-99, Erving prof. chemistry, 1899-1911, prof. emeritus, 1911—, Harvard. Author: Gold Point and Other Strange Stories, 1926. Address: Boston, Mass. Died 1935.

JACKSON, Charles Samuel, newspaper pub.; b. Jackson's Creek, Va., Sept. 15, 1860; s. James Henry and Anna (Boss) J.; ed. pvt. and pub. schs., Va., and Bryant & Stratton's Business Coll., Baltimore; m. Maria Foster Clopton, Mar. 9, 1886. Bought East Oregonian, Pendleton, and made it semi-weekly, 1881, daily, 1888; published till 1903; bought Oregon Journal, 1902; publisher and chief owner Journal Pub. Co. Home: Portland, Ore. Deceased.

JACKSON, Charles Warren, physician; b. N.Y. City, Oct. 29, 1864; s. Ebenezer Conover and Mary Frances (Sillcocks) J.; ed. pub. and pvt. schs.; M.D., New York U., 1887; interne Bellevue Hosp., 1887-89; m. Alma de Forrest Curtiss, Oct. 18, 1892. Practiced, New York, 1889-1902, Watertown, Conn., 1902—; owner "On the Hill," Health Resort. First lt. and asst. surg. 1st Signal Corps, N.G.N.Y., 6 yrs.; health officer, Watertown; chmn. Watertown Fire Dist. Republican. Conglist. Mason. Home: Watertown, Conn. Deceased.

JACKSON, Clifford Linden, lawyer; b. Dayton, O., Nov. 25, 1857; s. George and Ann Amelia J.; reared in La. and Mo.; ed. country schs. of Pettis County, Mo.; studied law in office; m. Kate Pugh Williams, Apr. 17, 1895. Deputy circuit clerk, Pettis County, Mo., 1880-81; dist. atty. 2d Jud. Dist., N.M., 1887-88; U.S. dist. atty. for Ind. Ty., 1893-94; U.S. dist. atty., Northern Dist. Ind. Ty., 1895-97; gen. atty., M.,K.&T. Ry. Co. for Ind. Ty., 1889-1907; gen. atty. for Okla. of M.,K.&T. Ry. Co., 1907—. Pres. Ind. Ty. Bar Assn., 1902-03, Muskogee Bar Assn., 1905, 10, 12, 17, Okla.-Ind. Ty. Bar Assn., 1906, Okla. State Bar Assn., 1907; v.p. Am. Bar Assn., 1909-10; pres. Muskogee Commercial Club, 1907-08, Oklahoma State Poultry Federation, 1914. Mem. Legal Advisory Bd., 1917-19. Democrat. Address: Muskogee, Okla. Died Apr. 14, 1921.

JACKSON, Daniel Dana, prof. chem. engring.; b. Gloucester, Mass., Aug. 1, 1870; s. Daniel and Lucy Agnes (Langsford) J.; B.S., Mass. Inst. Tech., 1893; student Harvard Graduate School, 1896-97; M.S., New York U., 1908; hon. Sc.D., U. of Pittsburgh, 1924; m. Ella Howard Phillips, Nov. 26, 1902; children—Daniel Dana, Elizabeth Purdy. Began as chemist, Boston (Mass.) Water Works, 1893; biologist, Mass. State Bd. of Health and lecturer Mass. Inst. Tech., 1895-97; chief chemist Brooklyn Water Supply Dept., 1897-1904; dir. labs. New York dept. water supply, gas and electricity, 1904-12; lecturer on sanitary engring. and bateriology, Columbia, 1911-13, asst. prof. chem. engring., 1913-17, asso. prof., 1917-18, prof. and exec. officer, dept. chem. engring., 1918—; v.p. Leavitt-Jackson Engring. Co., 1912-20; tech. mgr. Permitut Co., 1912-17; dir. Chem. Treatment Co. Mem. advisory com. on training camps, office of sec. of war, dean Sch. of Mil. Photography, U.S. Signal Corps, prof. Sch. of Explosives, Ordnance Dept., World War. Mem. advisory com., New York Health Dept. Consultant for cities and companies on water and drainage, factory processes. Home: New York, N.Y. Died Sept. 1, 1941.

JACKSON, Dorothy Branch; b. Brooklyn, N.Y., Dec. 6, 1881; d. Oliver E. and Sarah M. (Chase) Branch; ed. high sch., Manchester, N.H., and Bradford (Mass.) Acad.; m. Robert Jackson, Oct. 14, 1909; children—Sarah Branch, Hope. Mem. Dem. Nat. Com., 1919—. Trustee Laconia State Sch.; mem. Sch. Bd., Concord. Christian Scientist. Home: Concord, N.H. Died May 31, 1933.

JACKSON, Edward Payson, master in Boston Latin School, 1887-1905; b. Erzeroum, Turkey, March 15, 1840; s. Rev. William C. J. (Congl. missionary) and Mary A. (Sawyer) J.; ed. Amherst Coll. (A.M., 1870); m. Helen Maria Smith, Mar. 23, 1865 (died 1876); m. 2d, Mrs. Mary Elizabeth Clarke, June 24, 1904. Lt. 5th Mass. regt., also served in 45th Mass. in Civil war. Author: Mathematical Geography; A Demigod (novel), 1886; The Earth in Space, 1887; Character Building, 1892. Joint Author: Conduct as Fine Art, 1892. Address: New Dorchester, Mass. Died 1905.

JACKSON, Elihu Emory, gov.; b. Wicomico Co., Md., Nov. 3, 1837; s. Hugh and Sallie M. J.; reared on farm; ed. at country school; m. Nannie R. Rider, 1869. Conducted country store at Delmar, Md., 1859-63; moved to Salisbury, 1863, and engaged in lumber business, later opening branches at Baltimore and Washington. Mem. legislature, 1882-83; State senator, 1884-88; gov. Md., 1888-92; again elected to State senate, 1895. Democrat. Home: Salisbury, Md. Died 1907.

JACKSON, Frank Dar, gov.; b. Arcade, N.Y., Jan. 26, 1854; s. Hiram W. and Marion (Jenks) J.; removed to Ia. in boyhood; ed. pub. sch., Jesup, Ia., and Ia. State Agrl. Coll.; LL.B., State U. of Ia., 1874. Sec. Ia. Senate, 1882-84; sec. of state, Ia., 1884-89; gov. of Ia., 1894-96. Pres. Royal Union Life Ins. Co. Home: Des Moines, Ia. Died Nov. 16, 1938.

JACKSON, Fred Schuyler, lawyer; b. Stanton, Kan., Apr. 19, 1868; s. Martin V. and Eliza B. (Cure) J.; LL.B., U. of Kan., 1892; m. Inez S. Wood, Oct. 30, 1895; 1 son, Schuyler Wood. Admitted to Kan. bar, 1891, and began practice, Eureka, Kan.; county atty., Greenwood County, Kan., 1893-97; atty. gen. of Kan., 1907-11; mem. Congress (1911-13), 4th Kan. Dist.; atty. Kan. Pub. Service Com., 1915-25. Republican. Conglist. Mason, Elk. Home: Topeka, Kan. Died Nov. 21, 1931.

JACKSON, Frederick John Foakes, theologian; b. Ipswich, Eng., Aug. 10, 1855; s. Stephen and Catharine (Cobbold) J.; B.A., Trinity Coll. (Cambridge U.), 1879, M.A., 1882, B.D., 1903, D.D., 1905; D.Theol., Strasbourg, France; hon. D.Litt., U. of South, 1935; m. Anna Maria Everett, Oct. 1895 (died 1931); m. 2d, Clara Fawcett, widow of Arthur Jackson Tomlinson, 1932. Fellow, Jesus Coll., Cambridge, 1886—, dean and asst. tutor, 1895-1916; Briggs grad. prof. Christian instns., Union Theol. Sem., 1916-34. Lowell lecturer at Boston, 1916. Lecturer at Jewish Inst., New York, 1924, Gen. Theol. Sem., New York, 1925-26. Episcopalian. Past Grand Chaplain Grand Lodge of Eng., A.F. and A.M. Author: History of the Christian Church, 1891, 7th edit., 1921; Christian Difficulties, 1903; Biblical History of the Hebrews, 1903, 4th edit., 1921; St. Luke and a Modern Writer, 1916; English Society, 1750-1850 (Lowell Lectures), 1916; Introduction to Church History (590-1314), 1921; Anglican Church Principles, 1924; Studies in the Life of the Early Church, 1924; Life of St. Paul, 1926, 2d edit. Life and Letters series, 1933; Rise of Gentile Christianity, 1927; Peter, Prince of Apostles, 1927; Josephus and the Jews, 1930; The Church in England, 1931; Eusebius Pamphili, 1933; The Church in the Middle Ages, 1934; History of Church Historians, 1939. Editor: Parting of the Roads, 1911; Faith and the War, 1916; Beginnings of Christianity (with K. Lake), Vol. I, 1919, Vol. II, 1922, Vol. III, 1926, Vols. IV and V, 1932. Home: Englewood, N.J. Died Dec. 1, 1941.

JACKSON, George, educator; b. Cincinnati, O., Mar. 22, 1878; s. Dudley Elmer and Sarah (George) J.; grad. high sch., Cincinnati; grad. Cincinnati Tech. Sch., 1894; B.S., U. of Cincinnati, 1898; m. Blanche Rowe Randolph, Sept. 4, 1906; children—William Randolph, Sarah George. Began teaching at the Asheville Sch., 1900, headmaster, 1924—. Republican. Episcopalian. Home: Asheville School, N.C. Deceased.

JACKSON, George Anson, Congl. clergyman, librarian, Gen. Theol. Library of Boston, 1897—; s. Jerome B. and Lydia Ann (Ward) J.; b. North Adams, Mass., March 17, 1846; grad. Yale, Ph. B., 1868, M.A. hon. 1887; Andover Theol. Sem., 1871; m. Belle Donald, Nov. 21, 1871. Ordained and engaged in pastorates Congl. chs. at Leavenworth, Kan., Southbridge and Swampscott, Mass., 1872-97. Author: The Apostolic Fathers, 1879; Fathers of the Third Century, 1881; Post-Nicene Greek Fathers, 1883; Post-Nicene Latin Fathers, 1883; The Son of a Prophet (historical novel), 1894; The Ladye Susan (poem), 1904; New-Creed Catechisms. Home: Swampscott, Mass. Died 1907.

JACKSON, George Edwards, educator; b. Newton, Mass., Nov. 5, 1828; s. Ephraim and Beulah (Murdock) J.; A.B., Yale, 1852, A.M., 1855; LL.D., Washington U., 1905; m. Maria E. Fisher, June 15, 1861 (died 1884). Taught at Alexandria, Va., 1852-57, in La Grange Female Coll., Tenn., 1859, in New Haven (Conn.) High Sch., 1860-61; prof. Latin, 1866-1902, prof. emeritus, 1902, Washington U. Dir. Am. Sch at Rome. Conglist. Home: St. Louis, Mo. Died 1910.

JACKSON, George Somerville; b. Baltimore, Md., June 30, 1867; s. John James and Esther (Gill) J.; B.L., U. of Md.; m. Anne Triplett Harrison, Apr. 15, 1898. Clk., Gill & Fisher, grain exporters, Baltimore, 1881-98, mem. firm, 1898-1917; v.p. U.S. Grain Corp., 1917-20; v.p. Barnes-Jackson Co., grain exporters, 1921-23; pres. Western Md. Dairy Corp., 1925-29, chmn. bd., 1929—; dir. and mem. exec. com. Mercantile Trust Co.; dir. Fidelity & Deposit Co. of Md., Md. Life Ins. Co., Fidelity & Guarantee Fire Co., Savings Bank of Baltimore, Industrial Corp. of Baltimore. U.S. rep. Allied Food Commn., London, 1918; mem. Royal British and Allied Wheat Commn., 1918; mem. U.S. Food Commn. for Relief of Central and Eastern Europe, 1921; dir. relief, Russian Food Shortage, 1922; mem. Hoover Commn. for Examination into U.S. Shipping Bd. and Shipping, 1930. Pres. N. Am. Grain Exporters Assn., 1912, Baltimore Chamber Commerce, 1914. Democrat. Episcopalian. Home: Garrison, Md. Died June 20, 1935.

JACKSON, George Thomas, dermatologist; b. New York, N.Y., Dec. 19, 1852; s. George T. and Letitia Jane Aiken (Macauley) J.; ed. pub. and pvt. schs. and Coll. City of New York; student, Berlin, Vienna, Strassburg, 2 yrs.; M.D., Coll. Phys. and Surg. (Columbia), 1878; m. Caroline G. Weidemeyer, Oct. 3, 1878. General practice until 1884; specialist in dermatology, 1884—; prof. dermatology, Woman's Med Coll. of New York Infirmary, 1890-99, U. of Vt., 1895-1900; instr. dermatology, 1890-1908, prof., 1908-13, Columbia; consulting physician in skin diseases to the Presbyterian Hospital, New York, until 1913 and later to the New York Infirmary for Women and Children. Author: Diseases of Hair and Scalp, 1894, 1912; The Ready Reference Handbook of Dermatology, 1896-1913. Home: New York, N.Y. Died Jan. 3, 1916.

JACKSON, George Washington, engineer; b. Chicago, July 21, 1861; ed. pub. schs. of Chicago and at Oxford, Eng.; m. Rose Tracy Casey, 1883 (died 1913); m. 2d, Pearl Monroe, Dec. 1914. Engaged in engring. and contracting, 1893—; contractor for the Strickler tunnel through Pike's Peak; for 14-foot subway at Reading, Pa.; pneumatic tube system for the Associated Press; Wentworth Av. drainage system, Chicago, and about 90 per cent of the entire underground system for Chicago Telephone Co., Postal-Telegraph Cable Co., and Western Union Telegraph Co.; also systems at Columbus, O., Indianapolis, Ind., Muscatine, Ia., Phila., etc.; engr. and contractor for the entire system of tunnels in Chicago for the Ill. Telephone Constrn. Co.; consulting engr. for the local transportation com. of Chicago in its study of the traction problem, and hydraulic engr. for the high pressure water commn. of the city; constructed sect. 3 of Southwest Land Tunnel for City of Chicago, as well as sect. of Yonkers (N.Y.) Pressure Tunnel, 21 feet in diameter through granite, 2½ miles long, contract price, $2,000,000; was pres. George W. Jackson, Inc. Mason, Elk. Home: Chicago, Ill. Died Feb. 5, 1922.

JACKSON, Henry, army officer; b. in Eng., May 31, 1837. Pvt. and corporal Co. A, 14th Ill. Cav., and sergt. maj. 5th U.S.C.T., Dec. 28, 1863-May 13, 1865; commd. 2d lt., 5th U.S. Cav., May 14, 1865; 1st lt., Dec. 28, 1865; hon. mustered out, Mar. 16, 1866; apptd. from Ill., 2d lt. 7th U.S. Cav., July 28, 1866; 1st lt., July 31, 1867; capt., June 25, 1876; maj. 3d Cav., Aug. 27, 1896; lt. col. 5th Cav., Jan. 23, 1900; col. 3d Cav., Apr. 29, 1901; retired by operation of law, May 31, 1901; advanced to rank of brig. gen. retired, by act of Apr. 23, 1904. Deceased.

JACKSON, Henry Ezekiel, clergyman; b. Chester County, Pa., Feb. 21, 1869; s. Oliver Cloud and Margaret (Hamilton) J.; York (Pa.) Collegiate Inst., 1889-90; A.B., Lafayette Coll., 1893, A.M., 1896; A.M., Princeton, 1896; grad. Princeton Theol. Sem., 1896; m. Mary Viola Laughead, Dec. 14, 1897; children—Robert Davis, Ruth Lee. Ordained Presbyn. ministry, 1896; founder and pastor Presbyn. Ch., Swarthmore, Pa., 1896-1907; pastor Christian Union Congl. Ch., Upper Montclair, N.J., 1907-15; spl. lecturer to the students of China, under appmt. of a com. of Princeton U., 1915; spl. agt. in community orgn., U.S. Bur. of Edn., Washington, D.C., 1916-20; pres. Nat. Community Bd., Washington, D.C. Apptd. mem. advisory com. on Federal Pub. Schs., Oct. 1918; pres. Social Engring. Inst., New York. Democrat. Author: Benjamin West, His Life and Work, 1900; Great Pictures as Moral Teachers, 1910; The Message of the Modern Minister, 1908; The Meaning of the Cross, 1911; The Legend of the Christmas Rose, 1914; The New Chivalry, 1915; A Community Center, What It Is and How to Organize It, 1918; The League of Nations, 1919; A Community Church, 1919; What America Means to Me, 1920; Robinson Crusoe, Social Engineer, 1922; The Thomas Jefferson Bible, 1923. Home: Ridgefield, Conn. Died Apr. 20, 1939.

JACKSON, Henry Melville, coadjutor P.E. bishop of Ala., consecrated 1891; b. Leesburg, Va., July 28, 1849; ed. Va. Mil. Inst.; grad. Va. Theol. Sem., 1873 (D.D., Randolph-Macon, 1885; U. of the South, 1891). Ordered deacon, 1873, priest, 1874; pastor in Montgomery County, Va., and at Christ Ch., Greenville, S.C.; rector Grace Ch., Richmond, Va., 1876-91. For years editor The Southern Pulpit, afterward The Pulpit Treasury. Home: Anniston, Ala. Died 1900.

JACKSON, Henry S.; b. Memphis, Tenn., Aug. 31, 1860; s. Howell E. and Sophia Harrison (Molloy) J.; Vanderbilt U., 1878-81; m. Eula Maddox, Dec. 12,

1889; children—Eula (Mrs. E. H. Alsop), Howell E. Head of H. S. Jackson & Co., iron, steel and pig iron, Nashville, Tenn., until 1893; gen. agt. Southern Ry. Co., at Atlanta, Ga., 1893-98; ins. business from 1898; retired. Collector U.S. internal revenue, Ga., 1908-12; was state pres. Taft Club, Ga.; Ga. mem. Rep. Nat. Com., 1912-20. Methodist. Home: New York, N.Y. Deceased.

JACKSON, Herbert Worth, banker; b. Asheboro, N.C., Feb. 15, 1865; s. Samuel Spencer and Elvira E. (Worth) J.; prep. edn. Bingham Mil. Sch., Mebane, N.C.; A.B., U. of N.C., 1886; m. Annie H. Philips, Oct. 22, 1890; children—Evelyn H., Herbert W., Samuel S. Began in banking business with The Commercial & Farmers Bank, Raleigh, N.C., 1891; pres. Va. Trust Co., 1909—; chmn. bd. Aberdeen & Rockfish R.R.; dir. Va. Electric & Power Co., Johnson Pub. Co., Tredegar Co. Chmn. Liberty Loan Com., Richmond, World War. Trustee Sheltering Arms Free Hosp., Hampden-Sydney Coll. Democrat. Presbyn. Home: Richmond, Va. Died Dec. 30, 1936.

JACKSON, Holmes Condict, physiologist; b. New York, Feb. 18, 1875; s. William Holmes and Jane Eliza (Freeman) J.; Ph.B., Sheffield Scientific Sch. (Yale), 1896, post-grad. work same, 1896-99, Ph.D., 1899; Germany, 1899-1900; m. Mary Abby Read, Dec. 18, 1901; children—Kathleen C., Audrey R., Enid F. Instr., Sept. 1901, asst. prof. physiol. chemistry, 1902-05, Univ. and Bellevue Hosp. Med. Coll., New York; adj. prof. physiol. chemistry and experimental physiology and dir. of these laboratories, Albany Med. Coll., 1905-09; prof. physiology, Univ. and Bellevue Hosp. Med. Coll., 1909—; asst. dean, 1925—; dean New York U. Dental Coll., 1925—. Sec.-treas. Soc. Exptl. Biology and Medicine, 1912-23, pres., 1923—. Food administrator for E. Orange, 1917. Presbyn. Democrat. Author: Manual of Physiological Chemistry, 1902; Laboratory Exercises in Physiology, 1917. Home: East Orange, N.J. Died Oct. 25, 1927.

JACKSON, Jabez North, surgeon; b. Labaddie, Mo., Oct. 6, 1868; s. John Wesley (M.D.) and Jennie Clark (North) J.; A.B., Central Coll., Fayette, Mo., 1889, A.M., 1890; M.D., Univ. Med. Coll., Kansas City, 1891; D.Sc., Park Coll., 1926; LL.D., University of Mo., 1927; post-grad. work, New York Polyclinic, 1891; m. Virlea Wayland, Oct. 12, 1899; children—Virginia, Margaret. Demonstrator anatomy, 1891-95, prof., 1895-98; prof. surg. anatomy and adj. prof. surgery, 1898-1900, prof. principles and practice of surgery and clin. surgery, 1900-11, Univ. Med. Coll., also trustee, 1891-1911, and pres.; surgeon Kansas City Gen. Hosp., Research Hospital, Trinity Hosp.; dir. of health, Kansas City, Mo., 1923—. Asst. surg. and surg. 3d Regt., Mo. N.G., 1893-98; maj. and brigade surgeon U.S. Vols. in charge hospital, Spanish-Am. War, July-Nov. 1898. Democrat. Mem. Christian (Disciples) Ch. Mason. Home: Kansas City, Mo. Died Mar. 8, 1935.

JACKSON, James Frederick, lawyer; b. Taunton, Mass., Nov. 13, 1851; s. Elisha T. and Caroline (Forbes) J.; A.B., Harvard, 1873; LL.B., Boston U., 1875; m. Caroline S. Thurston, June 15, 1882; 1 dau., Edith (Mrs. Theodore R. Godwin). Began practice in Fall River, 1875; later was mem. firm Jackson, Slade & Borden; in practice at Boston, 1907—. City solicitor, Fall River, 1881-89, mayor of Fall River, 1890-91; chmn. Mass. R.R. Commn., 1899-1907; chmn. bd. pub. trustees Boston Elevated Ry., 1919-25 (resigned). Served with 1st Inf. Mass. N.G., advancing to lt. col. (resigned 1891). Republican. Conglist. Home: Winchester, Mass. Died Apr. 25, 1937.

JACKSON, James F(rederick); b. Wabasha, Minn., Aug. 16, 1861; s. William Sharpless and Mary Augusta (Pendleton) J.; B.S., Carleton Coll., Minn., 1883, L.H.D., 1921; m. Linda Carrie Pomroy, June 4, 1885. In lumber business, St. Paul, Minn., 1886-90; sec. St. Paul Associated Charities, 1892-98, Minn. Bd. of Corrections and Charities, 1898-1901; asst. sec. New York Charity Orgn. Soc., 1901-02; mgr. Minneapolis Associated Charities, 1902-04; exec. sec. of Cleveland Associated Charities, 1904-10 and 1911—. Gen. sec. Cleveland Pub. Charities and Corrections, 1910, 11; formerly dir. Div. of Family Welfare and Social Work, Sch. of Applied Social Sciences, Western Reserve Univ.; dir. Dept. of Social Administration, Sch. of Applied Social Sciences, same univ., 1925—; founder, trustee and asst. dir. Welfare Federation, Cleveland; gen. sec. Cleveland A.C.; active in work of Am. Red Cross and soldiers' relief, etc.; 1st v.p. Nat. Conf. Social Work; pres. Cleveland chapter Am. Assn. Social Workers; pres. Ohio State Conf. Charities and Correction, 1913. Chmn. U.S. Exemption Board, Dist. 7, 1917. Republican. Conglist. Writer and speaker on social and economic subjects. Home: Cleveland, O. Died Jan. 4, 1927.

JACKSON, John Brinckerhoff, diplomat; b. Newark, N.J., Aug. 19, 1862; s. F. Wolcott and Nannie (Nye) J.; grad. U.S. Naval Acad., 1883; A.M., Princeton, 1896; after 2 yrs.' cruise in European waters (part of time jr. aide to comdr.-in-chief European Squadron), passed final exam. in 1885; commd. ensign U.S. Navy, July 1, 1885. Attended course at Torpedo Sta., Newport, R.I., and was stationed at Ordnance Proving Grounds, Annapolis; resigned from Navy June 30, 1886; m. Florence A. Baird, Apr. 26, 1886. Admitted N.Y. bar, 1889; apptd. 2d sec. U.S. Legation, Berlin, Dec. 30, 1890; sec. of embassy, Nov. 15, 1894; frequently served as chargé d'affaires at Berlin; was mem. spl. missions at 25th anniversary of the accession of King Albert of Saxony, and of accession of Queen Wilhelmina of the Netherlands, 1898; offered and accepted mission to Chili but apptd. E.E. and M.P., U.S. to Greece, Roumania and Servia, Oct. 13, 1902, and diplomatic agt. in Bulgaria, June 5, 1903; represented U.S. at coronation King Peter of Servia, Sept. 21, 1904; apptd. E.E. and M.P. to Greece and Montenegro and diplomatic agt. in Bulgaria, Mar. 6, 1905; apptd. E.E. and M.P. to Persia, June 18, 1907, to Cuba, Dec. 1909, to Roumania, Servia and Bulgaria, Aug. 1911; resigned, 1913. Vol. asst. at Am. Embassy, Berlin, from Sept. 1914; spl. agt. of Dept. of State to report on German prisoners of war in Eng., Jan.-Feb. 1914; later at Embassy, Berlin, until Feb. 1917, in charge British sect.; visited camps of British, Servian and Roumanian prisoners of war. Declined position as counsellor to Siamese Foreign Office, Oct. 1914. Del. to International Maritime Law Conf., Hamburg, 1902, Internat. Archæol. Congress, Athens, 1905; Am. rep. at Olympic games, Athens, 1906; spl. rep. of the President with rank of ambassador, at Sofia, Feb. 1912, for the coming of age of the Crown Prince (Boris) of Bulgaria. Died Dec. 20, 1920.

JACKSON, John Henry, physician; b. Lee, Me., Mar. 26, 1838; s. John and Sarah (Cunningham) J.; grad. Colby Coll., 1860, Bowdoin Coll. Med. School, 1868; m. Clara Wentworth, Jan. 29, 1862. Taught school, Me., Wis. and Ill., 1860-65; now registrar and for past 13 yrs. prof. theory and practice of medicine, and nervous diseases, Boston Coll. Phys. & Surg.; consulting physician to Union Hosp., Fall River, Mass. Home: Fall River, Mass. Died 1908.

JACKSON, John Jay, U.S. judge, dist. of W.Va., 1861-1905; b. Parkersburg, Va., Aug. 4, 1824; s. Gen. John Jay J.; grad. Princeton, 1845; studied law; admitted to bar, 1847; m. Carrie C. Glime, July 8, 1847. When Wirt Co. was organized, 1848, was apptd. its 1st pros. atty.; apptd. pros. atty., Ritchie County, Va., 1849; elected, 1851, reëlected succeeding term; mem. Va. legislature; elector on Whig ticket, 1852 and 1856, and on Bell and Everett ticket, 1860, for presidential elector; apptd., 1861, to present position, dist. being originally that of Va. (changed later to W.Va.). Address: Parkersburg, W.Va. Died 1907.

JACKSON, Joseph Cooke, lawyer, brig. gen.; b. Newark, N.J., Aug. 5, 1835; s. Hon. John P. and Elizabeth (Huntington Wolcott) J.; A.B., Yale, 1857, A.M., 1860; LL.B., New York U., 1859; LL.B., Harvard, 1860. Admitted to N.Y. bar, 1860, and began practice at New York. Del. Rep. Nat. Conv., Chicago, 1861. Volunteered on fall of Ft. Sumter and was ordered to staff of Gen. Robert Anderson, U.S.A.; commd. 2d lt. 1st N.J. Vols., and assigned to staff Gen. Philip Kearny; promoted to div. staff of Maj. Gen. Franklin, Oct. 11, 1861; commd. capt. and a.d.c. vols., Aug. 20, 1862, "for gallantry during Seven Days' Battles before Richmond," and assigned to Sixth Corps staff as a.d.c. to Gen. Franklin; commd. lt. col. 26th N.J. Inf., Dec. 2, 1862; served in nearly 30 engagements of war as a.d.c. on staffs of Generals Anderson, Kearny, Franklin, Meade and Wool, U.S.A., in campaigns of McDowell, McClellan, Pope, Burnside and Meade; bvtd. col. vols., Mar. 13, 1865, "for gallant and meritorious conduct at battle of Fredericksburg, Va.," Sept. 13, 1862; a.d.c. to Gen. Wool, U.S.A., quelling July riots, 1863; bvtd. brig. gen. vols., Mar. 13, 1865, "for faithful and meritorious services in the field"; resigned, Jan. 5, 1863. While holding present commn. of brig. gen. U.S.V. was also commd. a.d.c. to Gov. Marcus L. Ward, N.J., in Reconstruction period. During war was apptd. by Secretary Stanton special War Dept. commr. U.S. Naval Credits, and established 1,900 naval enlistments, which were credited to quota of troops from N.J., and thereby rendered a draft unnecessary and saved nearly $1,000,000 to the state. Admitted to U.S. Supreme Court, 1864; del. Ship Canal Conv., Chicago, 1864; resumed general law practice, New York, near close of war and for nearly 30 yrs. was atty. and counsel for railways, banks, express and other corps.; m. Katharine Perkins, d. Hon. Calvin and Catherine (Seymour) Day, Oct. 12, 1864. Apptd. by President Grant, asst. atty., Southern Dist. N.Y., 1870; was counsel for Soc. of Polit. Reform which created first Com. of 70; counsel for removal police commrs.; also N.Y. Bar Assn. and N.Y. Supreme Ct. in their proceedings to purify N.Y. bar; active in Law Inst. and com. of bar assn.; retired from office engagements, 1890. Organizer by request of N.Y. Rep. Club and grand marshal of citizen night parade of over 60,000 Republican voters assembled from different states, in New York City, 1889; campaign and convention speaker and liberal contbr. to Rep. measures. Was an original founder of the earliest Am. coll. local alumni assn. (Yale); its treas., v.p., and mem. exec. com. many years; trustee and v.p. De Milt Dispensary 15 yrs. Home: New York, N.Y. Died May 22, 1913.

JACKSON, Mary Anna; b. Mecklenburg County, N.C.; d. Robert Hall (D.D.) and Mary (Graham) Morrison; ed. Salem (N.C.) Acad and Coll., finishing in 1849; m. Thomas Jonathan Jackson ("Stonewall"), the famous Southern general (died from wounds received in battle, May 10, 1863), July 16, 1857. Pres. Stonewall Jackson Chapter, United Daughters of the Confederacy. Presbyn. Author: Memoirs of "Stonewall" Jackson. Home: Charlotte, N.C. Died Mar. 24, 1915.

JACKSON, Percy (Van de Linde), lawyer, ins. exec.; b. Belleville, N.J., May 21, 1863; s. Wm. and Elizabeth Brinckerhoff (McNulty) J.; student Coll. of Geneva, Switzerland, U. of Heidelberg, Germany; Ph.B., Yale, 1885; LL.B., Columbia, 1887; m. Alice Hooker Day, Nov. 9, 1909 (died 1926); m. 2d, Mrs. Edna Morse Walker, July 20, 1932. Admitted to N.Y. bar, 1887, and began practice at N.Y. City; mem. exec. com. Firemen's Ins. Co. of Newark, N.J., Mechanics Fire Ins. Co. of Philadelphia, Nat. Ben Franklin Fire Ins. Co. of Pittsburgh, and many other ins. cos.; dir. Worthington Pump & Machinery Corp. Pres. Manhattan council, also mem. exec. com. Greater New York Foundation; mem. at large and chmn. of Indian division of Interracial Com. of Boy Scouts America. Pres. Culley & Martin Co. of N.Mex. (cattle and sheep). Dir. and mem. exec. com. Am. Sch. of Research (br. Archeol. Inst. America); pres. Class of 1885 (S.) Yale. Home: New York, N.Y. Died Apr. 4, 1941.

JACKSON, Reginald Henry, surgeon; b. De Pere, Wis., Jan. 17, 1876; s. James Albert and Josephine Syndonia (Hobbins) J.; student U. of Wis., 1892-95; M.D., Coll. Phys. and Surg., Columbia, 1899; m. Elizabeth Breese Stevens, June 4, 1908; 1 son, Reginald Henry. House surgeon, Presbyn. Hosp., N.Y. City, 1900-02; began practice at Madison, 1902; organizer, 1912, and chief of staff, Jackson Clinic; chief of staff, Methodist Hosp., 1922—; prof. clin. surgery, U. of Wis. Med. Sch., 1926—; 1st v.p. Capitol City Bank; dir. 1st Nat. Bank. Mem. Draft Bd., Madison, Med. Res. Corps, 1918. Republican. Episcopalian. Home: Madison, Wis. Died Sept. 7, 1939.

JACKSON, Richard Arbuthnot, lawyer; b. Richmond, Ind., Sept. 5, 1858; s. Richard and Anna M. (Knott) J.; ed. Earlham Coll. to 1875; LL.B., U. of Va., 1879; m. Anna V. Scott, Sept. 19, 1882. Admitted to bar, Jan. 1880; pros. atty. Wayne County, Ind., 1886-90; gen. practice to 1902; gen. solicitor and 1st v.p. C.,R.I.&P. Ry. Co., 1904-09; pres. Rock Island Co., Apr. 1909-Jan. 1910; v.p. and gen. counsel G.N. Ry. Co., St. Paul, 1910-16. Home: Ridgefield, Conn. Died Apr. 29, 1934.

JACKSON, Roscoe Bradbury, mfr.; b. Ionia, Mich., Jan. 30, 1879; s. Andrew Jarus and Agnes Frances (Bradbury) J.; B.S. and M.E., U. of Mich., 1902; m. Louise A. Webber, Sept. 12, 1907; children—Eleanor Webber, Richard Webber. Asst. supt. Olds Motor Works, Lansing, Mich., 1904; asst. to gen. mgr. same co., and factory mgr., 1906-07; gen. mgr. E. R. Thomas Motor Co., Buffalo, N.Y., 1908; organizer Hudson Motor Co., Detroit, 1909, pres., 1923—. Republican. Presbyn. Home: Detroit, Mich. Died Mar. 19, 1929.

JACKSON, Russell, lawyer; b. De Pere, Wis., May 10, 1874; s. Dr. James Albert and Syndonia Josephine (Hobbins) J.; prep. edn., Miss Richmond's Pvt. Sch. and Wis. Acad., Madison, Wis.; LL.B., U. of Wis., 1899; m. Lucile Durley, Aug. 14, 1909; children—Russell, Jonathan Durley. Admitted to Wis. bar, 1899, and began practice at Madison; mem. firm Gilbert & Jackson, 1899-1907, Gilbert, Jackson & Ela, 1907-13; gen. counsel for Uihlein interests, 1913-29; associated with Lines, Spooner & Quarles, 1929—; pres. Wis. Shares Corp.; v.p. Bankers Farm Mortgage Co.; dir. Oval-Wood-Dish Co., Marblehead Lime Co., Leader Card Works, Terre Haute Malleable Mfg. Co., Columbus Food Corp. Dep. atty. gen., Wis., 1907-13. Republican. Home: Milwaukee, Wis. Died Aug. 7, 1937.

JACKSON, Samuel Macauley, editor; b. New York, N.Y., June 19, 1851; s. George T. and Letitia Jane Aiken (Macauley) J.; A.B., Coll. City New York, 1870, A.M., 1876; studied Princeton Theol. Sem., 1870-71; grad. Union Theol. Sem., 1873; studied abroad, 1873-75; LL.D., Washington and Lee U., 1892; D.D., New York U., 1893; unmarried. Ordained Presbyn. ministry, 1876; pastor Norwood, N.J., 1876-80; prof. ch. history, New York U., 1895-1912. Mem. Prison Assn. (rec. sec.), Charity Organization Soc. (v.p.); pres. bd. trustees Canton Christian Coll., China; sec. Am. Soc. Ch. History, 1888-1912, pres., 1912. Asst. editor Schaff's Bible Dictionary, Phila., 1880; asso. editor Schaff-Herzog Encyclopædia of Religious Knowledge, 1884; also (for religious literature) Johnson's Universal Cyclopædia, 8 vols., 1893-95, and new edition same, called The Universal Cyclopædia, 12 vols., 1900; dept. religion New International Encyclopædia, 18 vols., 1902-04. Joint Editor: Cyclopædia of Living Divine, 1887. Editor: Concise Dictionary of Religious Knowledge, 1891; Heroes of the Reformation (9 vols.), 1898-1906; Hand-books for Practical Workers in Church and Philanthropy, 9 vols., 1899-1904; Papers and Proceedings Huguenot Soc. of America (Tercentenary of the Edict of Nantes, 1899, and vols. in 1902 and 1904); church terms in Standard Dictionary, 1895; same in New International Dictionary, 1900. Editor-in-chief New Schaff-Herzog Encyclopædia of Religious

Knowledge, 12 vols., 1907-11; Zwingli Selections, 1901; The Latin Works and the Correspondence of Huldreich Zwingli, Together with Selections of His German Works, in English Translation, Vol. I, 1912. Author: Huldreich Zwingli (Heroes of Reformation Series), 1901, 1903; The Source of Jerusalem the Golden, and other pieces attributed to Bernard of Cluny, 1910. Home: New York, N.Y. Died Aug. 2, 1912.

JACKSON, Sheldon, U.S. gen. agt. of edn. in Alaska, 1885—; b. Minaville, N.Y., May 18, 1834; s. Samuel Clinton and Delia (Sheldon) J.; grad. Union, 1855, LL.D., 1897; grad. Princeton Theol. Sem., 1858; D.D., Hanover, 1874; LL.D., Union U., N.Y., and Richmond, O., Coll., 1897; ordained Presbyn. minister, May 5, 1858; m. Mary Voorhees, May 18, 1858. Colporteur Presbyn. Bd. Publication, 1856; agt. Am. Systematic Beneficence Soc., 1857; missionary to Chostaw Indians, 1858; to Western Wis. and Southern Minn., 1859-69; agt. U.S. Christian Commn. Army Cumberland, 1863; pastor La Crescent, Minn., 1859-64, Rochester, Minn., 1864-69; prin. Rochester Female Inst., 1864-69; supt. Presbyn. missions Western Ia., Neb. and Rocky Mountain territories, 1869-70; same, Wyo., Colo., N.Mex., Ariz., Utah and Mont., 1870-82, and of Alaska, 1877—. Assisted in organizing Presbyn. synods of St. Paul, 1860, Colo., 1871 (stated clerk, 1872-81), Wash., 1890; Presbyteries of Chippewa, 1859 (a reorganization), Southern Minn., 1865, Colo., 1870, Wyo., 1871, Mont., 1872, Utah, 1874, Alaska, 1884; stated clerk Presbyteries of Chippewa, 1863-64, Southern Minn., 1865-69, Alaska, 1884; spl. agt. of Presbyn. Bd. Home Missions to Ida., Eastern Ore. and Eastern Wash., 1877. Prin. founder Woman's Bd. Home Missions, Presbyn. Ch., 1870-79. Spl. agt. govt. to gather and bring to Indian Schs. at Carlisle and Hampton children of Pueblo, Pima, Papago and Apache tribes of N.Mex. and Ariz.; first ordained missionary to begin religious work in Alaska, 1877; mem. spl. govt. commn. to investigate condition of natives of S.E. Alaska, 1879; spl. agt. of U.S. Govt. to report on agrl. possibilities of Yukon Valley. Editor Rocky Mountain Presbyterian, Denver, 1872-82, Presbyn. Home Missionary, New York, 1882-84, North Star, Sitka, 1887-94; organized the Alaskan Soc. Natural History and Ethnology, Sitka, 1887; established first canoe mail service in Alaska, 1883; secured from Congress, dist. organization for Alaska, 1884; introduced pub. sch. system into Alaska, 1885; introduced domestic reindeer into Alaska, 1891; organized 1st reindeer mail service in Alaska, 1898-99; spl. agt. U.S. Govt. to procure colony of Laplanders for Alaska, 1898; gave valuable real estate to found a Christian coll., Utah, 1896; collected from Rocky Mountain region valuable ethnol. collection and donated to Princeton U.; commr. to represent Alaska at Internat. Expn., City of Mexico, 1896; commr. to Gen. Assembly, Presbyn. Ch., 1860, 65, 67, 70, 75, 80, 97 (moderator), and 1898; mem. 7th Gen. Council Alliance Reformed Chs. throughout the world holding Presbyn. system, 1899. Awarded two diplomas, two medals, World's Columbian Expn., 1893; diploma Pan-Am. Expn., Buffalo, 1901. Author: Education in Alaska, 1872; Hand-Book on Alaska; Alaska and Missions on the North Pacific Coast, 1880; Education in Alaska, spl. report to U.S. Senate, 1881; also annual reports from 1886 on Education in Alaska; and annual reports from 1891, on Introduction of Domestic Reindeer Into Alaska; etc. Mem. editorial advisory council World's Best Orations (11 vols.), 1899; World's Best Essays (10 vols.), 1900. Home: Washington, D.C. Died 1909.

JACKSON, Thomas Herbert, brig. gen.; b. Westmeath, Ont., Can., Jan. 18, 1874; s. Noah Willard and Pauline (Adams) J.; brought to U.S., 1880; grad. U.S. Mil. Acad., 1899, Engr. Sch. of Application, Washington Bks., D.C., 1902; m. Maude Edgar Jurich, Aug. 24, 1912. Commd. add. 2d lt., Corps Engrs., U.S. Army, Feb. 15, 1899; advanced through grades to col., May 11, 1921; brig. gen., June 10, 1928. Served in Philippines, 1903-05; served as engr. dist. officer, San Francisco, Calif., 1907-11, Dallas, Tex., 1911-14, Wheeling, W.Va., 1914-17; engr. supply officer, France, 1917; sect. engr., Advance Sect., 1918; chief engr., Am. Forces in France, July-Nov. 1919; div. engr., San Francisco, 1926-28, St. Louis, Mo., 1928, Norfolk, Va., 1932-34, San Francisco, 1934—; pres. Miss. River Commn., 1928-32. Decorated D.S.M. (U.S.); Officer Legion of Honor (France); Comdr. Order of Leopold II (Belgium). Author of flood control plan for Sacramento River, 1907-10. Home: San Francisco, Calif. Died 1937.

JACKSON, William, civil engr.; b. Brighton, Mass., Mar. 13, 1848; s. Samuel and Mary (Field) J.; ed. pub. schs. and Mass. Inst. Tech. (non-grad.); m. Mary Stuart MacCorry, Apr. 27, 1886. Rodman, in Boston city engrs. office, 1868; city engr. of Boston, 1885—. Home: Boston, Mass. Died 1910.

JACKSON, William Benjamin, engineer; b. Kennett Square, Pa., June 23, 1870; s. Prof. Josiah and Mary Detweiler (Price) J.; B.S. in Mech. Engring., Pa. State Coll., 1890, M.E., 1895; m. Isabel Morrison West, Sept. 3, 1903; children—Isabel Morrison, Josiah Kennett, Mary Price, John West. In banking business, Colorado Springs, Colo., 1890-93; in charge Pa. mining exhibit, Chicago Expn., 1893; with United Electric Light & Power Co., New York, then asst. to chief engr. Stanley Electric Mfg. Co., Pittsfield, Mass., 1894-95, and engr. for the Northwest, at Chicago, for same, 1895-96; mgr. Lowell Water & Light Co., and Peninsular Light, Power & Heat Co., Grand Rapids, Mich., 1896-97; chief engr. and gen. supt. N.Y.&S.I. Electric Co., and consulting engr. S.I. Electric Ry. Co., 1897-99; chief engr. and gen. supt. Colo. Electric Power Co., Cripple Creek, Colo., 1899-1901; spl. engr. Stanley Electric Mfg. Co., including services in Eng., Germany, Austria, Hungary and Switzerland, 1901-02; mem. engring. firm of D. C. & Wm. B. Jackson, 1902-18; rate engr. and consultant New York Edison Co. and N.Y. Edison Co., Inc., 1919—. Major U.S. Army, officer in charge of utilities and constructing quartermaster, Camp Merritt, N.J., during 1918; lt. col. Engr. R.C.U.S.A. Fellow Am. Inst. E.E. (mgr. 1912-15; v.p. 1918). Home: Scarsdale, N.Y. Died Jan. 20, 1937.

JACKSON, William Hicks, soldier, stock man; b. Paris, Tenn., Oct. 7, 1836; served in C.S.A., 1861-65, becoming brig. gen.; stock-raiser; partner of Richard Croker in the Belle Meade stock farm in Tenn. Home: Nashville, Tenn. Died 1903.

JACKSON, William Humphreys, congressman; b. on farm near Salisbury, Md., Oct. 13, 1839; s. Hugh and Sarah McB. J.; ed. common schs.; m. Arabella Humphreys, 1864. Cattle dealer, 1864-67; lumber dealer, 1867-89, under firm name of E. E. Jackson & Co., later Jackson Bros. Co. Mem. 57th and 58th Congresses (1901-05), and 60th Congress (1907-09), 1st Md. Dist. Mem. Rep. Nat. Com., 1908-12. Address: Salisbury, Md. Died Apr. 3, 1915.

JACKSON, William J., railway official; b. Toronto, Ont., 1859; s. John and Jane J.; ed. pub. schs., Toronto; m. Eliza J. Preston, 1884. Began in the G.T. Ry. shops at Toronto as machinist's helper, 1877; in May 1878, became freight clk. same rd., at Toronto, and in Jan. 1882, chief claim clerk at Chicago for C.&G.T. Ry.; gen. freight foreman, 1885-90, and asst. agt., 1890-91, same rd., at Chicago; in service of C.&E.I. R.R., 1891—; asst. local freight agt. to 1893, local agt. to 1899, at Chicago; asst. gen. supt. until 1903; gen. supt. to 1906; gen. mgr. to 1909; v.p. and gen. mgr. same to 1913, receiver, to 1918, and pres. to 1918; federal mgr. C.&E.I.,C., T.H.&S.E., and E.&I. rys., 1918-20; reapptd. receiver, C.&E.I. R.R., 1920, and pres. after reorganization, Jan. 1, 1922, chmn. exec. com., 1925—. Mason. Home: Chicago, Ill. Died Apr. 4, 1932.

JACKSON, William Purnell, senator; b. Salisbury, Md., Jan. 11, 1868; s. William Humphreys and Arabella (Humphreys) J.; ed. Wilmington Conf. Acad., Dover, Del.; m. Sallie McCoombs, 1890 (died 1899); m. 2d, Katherine Shelmerdine, 1900. Entered lumber mfg. business, 1887, as partner E. E. Jackson & Co., firm dissolved, 1889; then formed partnership with father, and in 1893, assisted in organizing Jackson Bros. Co., becoming pres. Mem. Rep. Nat. Com. from Md., 1908-32; apptd. U.S. senator, Nov. 29, 1912, to fill vacancy caused by death of Isador Rayner, and served until Jan. 27, 1914; treas. State of Md., 1918-20. Methodist. Mason. Home: Salisbury, Md. Died Mar. 7, 1939.

JACKSON, William Trayton, mayor; b. Toledo, O., May 8, 1876; s. Joseph and Rebecca (Moon) J.; ed. pub. schs. and Steadman Bus. Coll., Toledo; m. Maude Atkins, Sept. 28, 1907 (died 1915); 1 dau., Nan Betty; m. 2d, Cora Kuhns, Jan. 25, 1919. Began as stenographer, Snell Bicycle Works, Toledo, 1895; corr. clk., Nat. Cash Register Co., Dayton, O., 1899-1900; purchasing agt., Consol. Mfg. Co., 1901-04; mem. firm Joseph Jackson & Sons, gen. contractors, Toledo, 1904—, pres., 1910—; pres. Toledo Citizens System Co., 1927—. Service dir., Toledo, 1922-27; mayor of Toledo, 1928-32; rep. presdl. elector from Ohio, 1928. V.p. Ohio State Conf. on City Planning, Ohio League of Municipalities; dir. Nat. Conf. on City Planning; mem. Toledo Mus. Art, Mchts. and Mfrs. Assn., Associated Gen. Contractors America, Northwestern Ohio Hist. Soc., Izaak Walton League, Toledo Chamber Commerce. Republican. Methodist. Mason, Elks. Home: Toledo, O. Died Oct. 3, 1933.

JACOB, Richard Taylor, soldier; b. Oldham County, Ky., Mar. 13, 1825; s. John Jeremiah and Lucy Donald (Robertson) J.; joined emigrant party leaving Missouri River, May 11, 1846, for Calif.; chosen 2d in command of Republican Fork of Blue at Ft. Laramie; reached Calif. Sept. 9, 1846, with 8 of his party; found Californians in rebellion; raised company, becoming its capt. and joined Frémont, serving under him until surrender of the Mexican army to Col. Frémont, 40 miles from Los Angeles. Returned to Ky., raised a vol. co. for Mexican war, which was not accepted; went to Washington as witness in Frémont courtmartial; m. 1st, Sarah, 3d d. Senator Thomas H. Benton, Jan. 17, 1848 (died 1863); m. 2d, Laura, d. Dr. Wilson, June 6, 1865 (died 1895). Lived on farm in Mo., 1848-54; returned to Ky.; Breckenridge elector, 1860; representative from Oldham County in Ky. legislature, 1857-61; drafted com. report in favor of remaining loyal to Union, which was adopted. Raised, 1862, and was col. 9th Ky. vols.; served in Ky., driving Scott's brigade and the Secession govt. out of Frankfort; lt. gov. Ky., 1863-67; supported McClellan, 1864; opposed enlistment of Negro troops in Ky.; was arrested by Gen. Burbridge and escorted across enemy's lines; appealed to President Lincoln, who directed his return to his home. Park Commr. Louisville, 1895-99. Home: Louisville, Ky. Died 1903.

JACOBI, Abraham, physician; b. Hartum, Westphalia, May 6, 1830; studied univs. of Greifswald, Göttingen; M.D., Bonn, 1851; LL.D., U. of Mich., 1898, Columbia, 1900, Yale, 1905, Harvard, 1906, Jefferson, 1913; m. Dr. Mary C. Putnam, 1873 (died 1906). Identified with German revolutionary movement; in detention, Berlin and Cologne, 1851-53, for "high treason"; settled in practice in New York, 1853; prof. diseases of children, New York Med. Coll., 1860-64, U. of New York, 1865-70; prof. diseases of children, 1870-1902, prof. emeritus, 1902, Coll. Phys. and Surg. (Columbia). Has held many important hosp. appmts. Co-editor American Journal of Obstetrics and Diseases of Women and Children, 1868-71. Pres. New York Pathol. Soc., 1866, New York Obstet. Soc., 1868, N.Y. Co. Med. Soc., 1870-72, N.Y. State Med. Soc., 1882, N.Y. Acad. Medicine, 1885-89, Am. Pediatric Soc., 1891, 1906, Assn. Am. Physicians, 1896, Am. Climatol. Soc., 1896, A.M.A., 1912-13. Author: Dentition and Its Derangements, 1862; The Raising and Education of Abandoned Children in Europe, 1870; Infant Diet, 1872, 1875; Diphtheria, 1876; Treatise on Diphtheria, 1880; Pathology of the Thymus Gland, 1889; Therapeutics of Infancy and Childhood, 1896, 1898, 1903; Intestinal Diseases; Collectanea Jacobi, 8 vols., 1909. Address: New York, N.Y. Died July 10, 1919.

JACOBI, Mary Putnam, physician; b. London, Eng., Aug. 31, 1842; d. George P. Putnam; studied Phila. Woman's Med. Coll.; grad. New York Coll. of Pharmacy; 1st woman admitted to École de Medicine, Paris, France, grad. 1871; m. Abraham Jacobi (M.D.), 1873. First woman to become mem. N.Y. Acad. of Medicine, and to be sent as delegate to the State Med. Assn. Twelve yrs. dispensary physician, Mt. Sinai Hosp.; was prof. Woman's Med. Coll. of New York Infirmary for 10 yrs., and later during 3 yrs., of New York Post-Graduate Med. School. Won Boylston prize, Harvard, with an essay: "The Question of Rest for Women During Menstruation." Author: The Value of Life; Cold Pack and Massage in Anæmia, Hysteria, Brain Tumor, and Other Essays; Studies in Primary Education; Common Sense Applied to Woman Suffrage. Address: New York, N.Y. Died 1906.

JACOBS, Benjamin Franklin, chmn. exec. com. Internat. Sunday School Assn.; b. Paterson, N.J., Sept. 18, 1834; s. Charles P. and Eliza (Pelton) J.; liberal edn.; moved to Chicago, 1854; in produce commn. business until burned out in fire of 1871; in real estate business, 1871—; m. Frances M. Eddy. Was supt. of the First Bapt. Mission Sunday School, 1856, and First Bapt. Sunday School, 1864; sec. Northwestern branch U.S. Christian Commission during Civil war, 1861-65; founder Waifs' Mission, Chicago. Organized, with others, Immanuel Bapt. Ch., Chicago, 1881; supt. of its Sunday School, 1881—; has been pres. Y.M.C.A., and pres. World's Sunday School Conv. Was originator and suggester of the Internat. Sunday School Lessons, now used by all evangelical denominations; and mem. Internat. Lesson Com., 1872—. Home: Chicago, Ill. Died 1902.

JACOBS, Charles M., civil engr.; b. Hull, Eng., June 8, 1850; married June 1, 1876. First practiced in Eng.; consulting engr. Phila. & Reading Ry. Co., N.Y.&N.E. Ry. Co., L.I. R.R. Co.; chief engr. East River Gas Tunnel; designed tunnel plans for Pa. R.R., connecting Pa. and L.I. rys.; chief engr. N.Y.&N.J. R.R. Co.; in charge of North Tunnel; chief engr. Hudson Cos., etc. Designed complete system of ry. tunnels under Manhattan Island and vicinity, requiring outlay of $50,000,000, 1890; consulting engr. for constrn. of tunnel under River Seine, France, at Paris. Pres. Jacobs & Davies, Inc. Died Sept. 7, 1919.

JACOBS, Charles Michael, clergyman, educator; b. Gettysburg, Pa., Dec. 5, 1875; s. Henry Eyster and Laura H. (Downing) J.; A.B., U. of Pa., 1895; grad. Luth. Theol. Sem., Mt. Airy, Phila., 1899; studied U. of Pa. and U. of Leipzig; D.D., Muhlenberg Coll., 1913, LL.D., 1929; L.H.D., Augustana Coll., 1929; m. Abigail Shearer, Oct. 5, 1905; children—Margaret Abigail, Hilda Elinor, Charles Shearer. Ordained Luth. ministry, 1899; pastor St. Peter's Ch., North Wales, Pa., 1899-1904, Christ Ch., Allentown, Pa., 1904-13; prof. ch. history and dir. Grad. Sch., Luth. Theol. Sem., 1913—, pres. 1927—. V.p. Nat. Luth. Commn., 1917-22; mem. Nat. Luth. Council, 1918—; chmn. Am. Com. for Luth. World Conv., 1920-23. Co-editor: Luther's Work in English Volumes I and II, 1915, Volumes III and IV, 1930, Volume V, 1931, Volume VI, 1932; (with Preserved Smith) Luther's Correspondence, Volume II, 1916. Author: The Way—A Little Book of Christian Truth, 1922; The Story of the Church—An Outline of Its History, 1925; Helps on the Road (addresses), 1933; An Outline of Christian Doctrine (trans., from German of W. Elert), 1926. Mem. bd. editors Am. Ency. of Christianity, 1923-26, Luth. Ch.

Quarterly, 1827; contbr. to Outlines of Christianity, Ency. Britannica, etc. Address: Philadelphia, Pa. Died Mar. 30, 1938.

JACOBS, Henry Barton, M.D.; b. S. Scituate, Mass., June 2, 1858; s. Barton Richmond and Frances Almira (Ford) J.; A.B., Harvard, 1883, M.D., 1887; asst. in botany Harvard, 1884-85; interne Mass. Gen. Hosp., 1887-88; m. Mary Frick Garrett, Apr. 2, 1902. Practiced at Boston, 1888-90; asso. in medicine, Johns Hopkins, 1896-1904. Pres. Hosp. for Consumptives of Md.; mem. original bd. mgrs. Md. State Tuberculosis Sanatorium. Trustee, mem. executive com. Johns Hopkins Hosp., Peabody Inst. of Baltimore, Harriet Lane Home for Invalid Children, Ch. Home and Infirmary, Md. Inst., Children's Hosp. Sch.; pres. and dir. Redwood Library, Newport, R.I. Mem. exec. com. Family Welfare Assn. of Baltimore. Fellow A.A.A.S.; original sec., dir. Nat. Tuberculosis Assn. Vestryman, Grace and St. Peter's Chs., Baltimore, Md., and Trinity Church, Newport, R.I.; pres. Churchmen's Club; trustee and treas. Md. Cathedral; mem. exec. council, Diocese of Maryland. Associate editor Annals of Medical History. Homes: Newport, R.I., Baltimore, Md. Died Dec. 18, 1939.

JACOBS, Henry Eyster, theologian; b. Gettysburg, Pa., Nov. 10, 1844; s. Michael J. (D.D.) and Julianna M. (Eyster) J.; A.B., Pa. Coll., 1862, A.M., 1865; grad. Lutheran Theol. Sem., Gettysburg, 1865, D.D., 1877; LL.D., Thiel Coll., Greenville, Pa., 1892; S.T.D., Muhlenberg Coll., Pa., 1907; m. Laura H. Downing, July 3, 1872; children—Eugenia Anna (dec.), Charles Michael, Henry Downing, Laura Winifred (Mrs. Luther R. Shearer), Marguerite Eyster (wife of Rev. William M. Horn). Tutor Pa. Coll., 1864-67; home missionary, Pittsburgh, 1867-68; prin. Thiel Hall, Water Cure, Beaver County, Pa., 1868-70; prof. Latin and history, 1870-80, ancient langs., 1880-81, Greek, 1881-83, Pa. Coll.; prof. systematic theology, 1883—, dean of faculty, 1894-1920, pres., 1920-27, Lutheran Theol. Sem. Pres. Bd. of Foreign Missions, Gen. Council Lutheran Ch., 1902-07; pres. Gen. Conf. of Lutherans, 1899, 1902, 04; mem. Common Service Com. Luth. Ch., 1885—; chmn. Commn. of Adjudication of United Luth. Ch. in America, 1919—. Pres. Am. Soc. Ch. History, 1907-08, Pa. German Soc., 1910-11; v.p. Pa. Bible Soc., 1893-95, pres., 1926—. Sr. Luth. Ministerium of Pa., 1927—. A corporator Presbyn. Ministers' Fund for Life Ins., 1912. Asso. editor Johnson's Cyclopædia, 1893-95; editor Luth. Ch. Rev., 1882-96; Luth. Commentary, 1895-98, Lutheran Cyclopædia, 1899. Author: The Lutheran Movement in England, 1891; History of Lutheran Church in America, 1893; Elements of Religion, 1894; Commentary on Romans, 1896; Commentary on I Corinthians, 1897; Life of Martin Luther, 1898; The German Emigration to America, 1709-40, 1899; Summary of Christian Doctrine, 1905; Lincoln's Gettysburg World Message, 1920. Contbr. to Hasting's Encyclopædia of Religion and Ethics, 1916, 19; Internat. Standard Bible Encyclopedia, 1915. Translator of various theol. works from German, and contbr. to theol. periodicals. Home: Philadelphia, Pa. Died July 7, 1932.

JACOBS, J(ames) Arthur, contractor; b. Boston, Mass., Oct. 15, 1848; s. David H. and Elizabeth (Ayers) J.; ed. pub. schs., Boston; hon. A.M., Tufts Coll., 1905; m. Anna E. Dupee, Dec. 4, 1872. Pres. and treas. David H. Jacobs & Son, Inc.; trustee Franklin Savings Bank. Trustee Tufts Coll.; trustee charity fund Mass. Charitable Assn. Republican. Universalist. Home: Roxbury, Mass. Died Oct. 16, 1923.

JACOBS, Joseph, author, editor; b. Sydney, New South Wales, Aug. 29, 1854; ed. Sydney Grammar Sch., St. John's Coll., Cambridge, Eng. (senior moralist, 1876); Litt.D., U. of Pa., 1906. Came to U.S., 1900, to take part in editing of Funk & Wagnalls' Jewish Encyclopædia. Visited Spain for hist. purposes, 1888, U.S. on lecturing tour, 1896. Corr. mem. Royal Acad. of History, Madrid, and Brooklyn Inst. Was for some time editor of Folk-Lore; sec. Russo-Jewish com.; pres. Jewish Hist. Soc.; one of the leading contbrs. to Athenæum; leading authority in Eng. on Fairy Tales, of which he has published a great many collections, and on the Migration of Fables. Editor of the Jewish Year-Book, 1896-99, Lit. Year-Book, 1898-99, Am. Hebrew, 1906. Prof. English lit. and rhetoric, Jewish Theol. Sem. of America, 1906-13. Author: English Fairy Tales, 1890; Studies in Jewish Statistics, 1890; Celtic Fairy Tales, 1890; Indian Fairy Tales, 1892; Tennyson, and In Memoriam, 1892; Jews of Angevin, England, 1893; More English Fairy Tales, 1893; More Celtic Fairy Tales, 1894; Studies in Biblical Archæology, 1894; Statistics of Jewish Population in London, etc., 1894; Æsop's Fables, 1894; Literary Studies, 1895; Reynard the Fox, 1895; As Others Saw Him (Jewish Life of Christ), 1895; Sources of the History of the Jews in Spain, 1895; Jewish Ideals, 1896; Wonder Voyages, 1896; Story of Geographical Discovery, 1898. Edited: North's Fables of Bidpai, 1887; Caxton's Æsop, 1889; Painter's Palace of Pleasure, 1891; Howell's Familiar Letters, 1892; Day's Daphnis and Chloe, 1890. Home: Yonkers, N.Y. Died Jan. 30, 1916.

JACOBS, Joshua W., soldier; b. in Ky., June 24, 1843. Entered mil. service as pvt. Co. K, and sergt. maj. 4th Ky. Vol. Inf., Nov. 10, 1861-Sept. 25, 1862; commd. 1st lt. 4th Ky. Vol. Inf., Sept. 25, 1862; capt., Sept. 1, 1863; maj. 6th Ky. Vols., July 1, 1865; hon. mustered out of vol. service, Aug. 17, 1865. Apptd. 2d lt. 18th U.S. Inf., June 28, 1866; transferred to 36th Inf., Sept. 21, 1866; capt. and a.-q.-m., Mar. 8, 1882; maj. q.m., Dec. 31, 1894; lt. col. deputy q.-m. gen., Nov. 1, 1900; col. a.-q.-m. gen., 1903; brig. gen., 1904, and retired after 40 yrs. service. Deceased.

JACOBS, Pattie Ruffner (Mrs. Solon Harold Jacobs); d. Lewis, Jr., and Virginia Louise (West) Ruffner; grad. Ward Sem., Nashville, Tenn.; grad. Birmingham Training Sch. for Teachers; studied under pvt. tutors in N.Y. City 2 yrs.; m. Solon Harold Jacobs, Feb. 8, 1898; children—Madeleine Ruffner, Virginia West. Past auditor Nat. Am. Woman Suffrage Assn.; chmn. Liberty Loan Com. of Ala., 1st four loans, and then made mem. Nat. Woman's Liberty Loan Com.; pres. Ala. Equal Suffrage Assn., 1911-20; 1st woman asso. mem. Dem. Nat. Com. for Ala., also Exec. Com. Dem. Nat. Com.; 2d v.p. Nat. League of Women Voters. Chief of women's sect. Consumers Advisory Bd. of NRA, Washington. Presbyterian. Home: Birmingham, Ala. Died Dec. 22, 1935.

JACOBS, Walter Ballou, college prof.; b. Providence, R.I., May 5, 1861; s. James Carroll and Mary Velina (Lamson) J.; A.B., Brown U., 1882, A.M., 1885; Union Theol. Sem., 1882-83; m. Josephine Jones Chace, June 27, 1888. Instr., 1893-95, asso. prof., 1895-1901, prof. of edn., 1901-31, dir. univ. extension, 1915-31, dir. Sch. of Edn., 1923-27, Brown U.; sec. N.E. Assn. of Colls. and Secondary Schs., 1909-30; mem. dept. of superintendence, N.E.A. Conglist. Home: Providence, R.I. Died July 23, 1932.

JACOBSEN, Bernhard Martin, congressman; b. Klixbuel, Schleswig, Germany, Mar. 26, 1862; s. Boh and Magdelena (Tadsen) J.; came to U.S. at 14; ed. pub. schs.; m. Lena Trager, May 28, 1885; children—Marvin, William, Mrs. C. L. Callendar, Mrs. P. W. Svenksen, Mrs. J. M. Hammond. Worked in lumber yard, brick yard and dry goods store; entered mercantile business on own account at Clinton, Ia., 1886; postmaster of Clinton, 1914-23; mem. 72d and 74th Congresses (1931-37), 2d Ia. Dist. Democrat. Lutheran. Mason, Odd Fellow, Elk, Eagle. Home: Clinton, Ia. Died June 20, 1936.

JACOBSOHN, Simon Eberhard, musician; b. Mitau, Kurland, Russia, 1839; studied music from childhood at home and later with Weller at Riga, where he became known as violin soloist; studied at Leipzig Conservatory; was soloist Gewandhous Concerts, Leipzig; toured in Europe; became concertmeister in Bremen; concertmeister with Theodore Thomas' Orchestra in U.S., 1872-78; established Jacobson Violin School, Cincinnati, which, in 1886, became the violin dept., Chicago Musical Coll., of which was asso. dir. Home: Chicago, Ill. Died 1902.

JACOBSON, Fritz, clergyman; b. in Sweden, Mar 17, 1863; s. Joseph and Maria (Kruse) J.; was brought to America, 1869; A.B., Augustana Coll., Rock Island, Ill., 1885; Yale, 1886-89, Ph.D., 1889; B.D., Augustana Theol. Sem., 1890; m. Othelia Holland, June 29, 1887. Ordained Luth. ministry, 1890; pastor, New Haven, Conn., 1890-92, Swedish Lutheran Bethlehem Ch., Brooklyn, 1892—. Pres. N.Y. Conf. Augustana Synod, 1909—; v.p. Bd. of Edn. Gen. Council; trustee Bd. of Foreign Missions of Gen. Council; pres. Augustana Home for Aged, Brooklyn, N.Y.; mem. Council of Augustana Synod; pres. Bd. Home Missions of the N.Y. Conf. Decorated by King of Sweden with Order of North Star, 1910. Editor Lutheran Monthly. Home: Brooklyn, N.Y. Deceased.

JACOBUS, Melancthon Williams, educator; b. Allegheny City, Pa., Dec. 15, 1855; s. Melancthon Williams (D.D., LL.D.) and Sarah (Hayes) J.; A.B., Princeton, 1877; grad. Princeton Theol. Sem., 1881; studied Göttingen, Berlin, 1881-84; D.D., Lafayette, 1892, Yale, 1910; m. Clara M. Cooley, Jan. 8, 1896; children—Maritje Kip, Clarissa Cooley, Melancthon Williams. Ordained Presbyn. ministry, 1884; pastor, Oxford, Pa., 1884-91; prof. N. T. Exegesis and criticism, 1891-1928, acting pres., 1902-03, dean faculty, 1903-27, Hartford Theol. Sem., emeritus. Stone lecturer, Princeton Theol. Sem., 1897-98; acting pastor, Center Congregational Church, Hartford, Conn., 1899-1900; lecturer on New Testament, Mt. Holyoke Coll., 1901, 1903-04. Trustee Lincoln U., 1887-1904, Princeton, 1890—, Wadsworth Atheneum; trustee Kingswood Country Day Sch., (v.p. 1921, pres. 1922-23, hon. pres. 1934—), Watkinson Library of Reference (pres. 1924-25); mem. bd. of dirs. Hartford Hosp. Author: A Problem in New Testament Criticism (Stone lectures), 1900. Contributing editor-in-charge N. T. dept. New International Encyclopædia, 1902-04, 2d edit., 1914-15; chmn. editorial bd. Standard Bible Dictionary, 1909, now in 3d edit.; editor Zahn's N. T. Introduction (English transl.), 1909, 2d edit., 1917; Commentary on Gospel of Mark (The Bible for Home and School Series), 1915. Home: Hartford, Conn. Died Oct. 31, 1937.

JACOBY, George W., neurologist; b. St. Louis, Mo., Sept. 1856; s. Samuel and Rosalie J.; M.D., Bellevue Hosp. Med. Coll. (New York U.), 1877; M.D., U. of Berlin, 1878; m. Miss Deborah Kaufmann, Mar. 1884. Attending physicians German Dispensary, New York, 1882-1902; lecturer on nervous diseases, 1887-89, clin. prof. nervous diseases, 1890-95, prof. nervous and mental diseases, 1895-1900, Women's Med. Coll. of New York Infirmary; consulting neurologist, Lenox Hill and Beth Israel hosps., Craig Colony for Epileptics, etc. Republican. Author: Electrotherapy, 2 vols. (with others), 1901; Suggestion and Psychotherapy, 1912; Child Training as an Exact Science, 1914; The Unsound Mind and the Law, 1918; Electricity in Medicine (with J. Ralph Jacoby), 1919; Physician, Pastor and Patient, 1936. Address: New York, N.Y. Died Sept. 11, 1940.

JACOBY, Harold, astronomer; b. New York, Mar. 4, 1865; s. Max and Eve M. (Jackson) J.; A.B., Columbia, 1885, Ph.D., 1895; m. Annie Maclear, Dec. 28, 1890; children—Maclear, Eve (Mrs. Edward Terhune Van de Water). Asst. and instr. geodesy and practical astronomy, Columbia, 1888-92, instr. astronomy, 1892-94, adj. prof., 1894-1904, prof., 1904-30, acting dir. Obs., 1903-06, dir., 1906-30. Asst. astronomer U.S. eclipse expdn. to W. Africa in U.S.S. Pensacola, 1889-90. Civilian instr. navigation Submarine Officers' Material Sch., Pelham Bay Naval Training Sta., 1918. Author: Practical Talks by an Astronomer, 1891; Astronomy, a Popular Handbook, 1913; Navigation, 1917. Home: Westport, Conn. Died 1932.

JACOBY, William Lawall, pres. Kellogg Switchboard and Supply Co.; b. Bethlehem, Pa., Dec. 12, 1873; s. Cyrus and Mary (Weierbach) J.; prep. edn., Ulrichs Prep. Sch.; M.E., Lehigh U., 1892; m. Laura F. Warren, Nov. 1903; children—Charles Warren, Mary, Laura Farson, William Lawall, Sarah F. (dec.). Began in employ R. D. Wood & Co., Camden, N.J., 1892; with Latrobe Steel & Coupler Co., 1893-1908, advancing to pres.; organizer, and pres. Inter-Ocean Steel Co. (notable for improvements in methods of mfg. steel tires for locomotives and cars), 1908-11; engr. for Daniel C. Reid, 1911-12; pres. Am. Dist. Telegraph Co., 1912-18; v.p. A. G. Becker & Co., 1918-27; pres. Kellogg Switchboard & Supply Co., 1927—. Republican. Episcopalian. Home: Chicago, Ill. Died Jan. 11, 1930.

JACQUES, William White, physicist; b. Haverhill, Mass., Aug. 30, 1855; s. John Thurston and Lucy (Withington) J.; S.B., Mass. Inst. Tech., 1876; A.M., Ph.D., Johns Hopkins, 1879; studied Berlin, Leipzig, Vienna, Göttingen, 1877; m. Kate Shakespeare Haman, Nov. 10, 1880; children—Helen Louise (Mrs. John Lawrence Miller), Margaret Howard (Baroness Margaret de Brueggen). Fellow Johns Hopkins, 1876-80: lecturer on elec. engring., Mass. Inst. of Technology, 1887-90; expert for Am. Bell Telephone Co., 1880-97; originator of many of the salient inventions and engring. devices that have made long-distance telephony practicable; expert for numerous elec. and chem. industries in Eng., France and America, 1897-1914, and originator of many processes and mechanisms therein used; expert for anti-submarine div. of British Admiralty during war; originator of device by which submarines were detected and located; engaged in scientific investigations. Home: Boston, Mass. Died June 23, 1932.

JADWIN, Edgar, army officer; b. Honesdale, Pa., Aug. 7, 1865; s. Hon. C. C. and Charlotte E. (Wood) J.; student Lafayette Coll., Easton, Pa., 1884-86; grad. head of class, U.S. Mil. Acad., 1890; grad. Engr. Sch. of Application, 1893; hon. Dr. Engring., Lafayette, 1925; m. Jean Laubach, Oct. 6, 1891; children—Charlotte (Mrs. Thomas G. Hearn), Cornelius C. (U.S. Cav.). Apptd. add. 2d lt. engrs., June 12, 1890; promoted through grades to lt. col., Oct. 12, 1913; col. N.A., July 6, 1917; brig. gen. (temp.), Dec. 17, 1917-Oct. 31, 1919; col. engrs., Sept. 10, 1919; apptd. asst. to chief of engrs. with rank of brig. gen., 1924, chief of engrs. with rank of major gen., 1926; retired Aug. 7, 1929. In charge improvements, Ellis Island, 1890-91; duty, Office Chief of Engineers, Washington, D.C., 1897-98, Panama Canal, 1907-11, Office Chief of Engrs., Washington, D.C., 1911-16; dist. engr. in various engring. dists.; organized and comd. 15th U.S. Engrs. (Ry.), the first Am. regt. to pass under arms through England, 1917; dir. light rys. and roads, A.E.F., in France, later dir. constrn. and forestry, in charge gen. construction program, working 160,000 men in dredging, building railroads, barracks, hosps., warehouses, roads, lumbering, etc.; mem. Am. Mission to Poland, 1919; observer in Ukraine, 1919; engr. 8th Corps Area, San Antonio, Tex., 1920-22; div. engr. Southeast Div., Charleston, S.C., 1922-24. Served as sr. mem. Am. sect. Joint Engring. Bd. St. Lawrence Waterway Project and as sr. mem. Bd. of Engrs. for Rivers and Harbors; was mem. tech. advisory com. of Federal Oil Conservation Bd., and mem. Am. delegation to Internat. Conf. on Oil Pollution of Navigable Rivers; served as chmn. Nat. Capital Park and Planning Commn.; supervised, 1927, plan which was adopted by congress for control of floods in Mississippi Valley, etc.; appointed 1929, chmn. Interocean Canal Bd. Presbyn. Awarded D.S.M. (U.S.); Companion Order of the Bath (British); Comdr. Legion of Honor (French). Home: Honesdale, Pa. Died Mar. 2, 1931.

JAECKEL, Theodore, foreign service officer; b. N.Y. City, Dec. 29, 1882; s. Hugo Ernest Francis and Elizabeth (Bernius) J.; B.A., Williams, 1904; studied Harvard 1 yr.; LL.B., New York Law Sch., 1908; m. Violet Ridgway, Nov. 21, 1914; children—Theodore Ridgway, John J. Ridgway, Hugo Francis; m. 2d, Barbara Ross, Sept. 1935. Practiced law at N.Y. City, 1909-12; Am. consul at Stavanger, Norway, 1914-15, Stettin, Germany, 1915-17; chief of Visa Office, Dept. of State, Washington, 1917-19; consul at Bordeaux, France, 1919-23; consul gen. at Hamburg, Germany, 1923-24, at Warsaw, 1924, at Milan, Italy, 1927-28, at Halifax, Canada, 1928-29, at Rome, Italy, 1930-33, at Victoria, B.C., 1934—. U.S. commr. to Volta Centennial Exhbn., Como, Italy, 1927; Am. del. plenipotentiary at 3d Internat. Conf. on Private Aerial Law, Rome, 1933. Died Dec. 26, 1935.

JAEGERS, Albert, sculptor; b. Elberfeld, Germany, Mar. 28, 1868; s. Albert and Elizabeth (Loser) J.; ed. in pub. schs. in Germany and U.S.; m. Matilda Holdt, July 8, 1890. Sculptor, 1890—; won various competitions by decision of Nat. Sculpture Society; executed statuary for Buffalo and St. Louis expns., for Fine Arts Bldg., St. Louis, new Custom House, New York; also pvt. monuments, busts and tablets in marble and bronze; commd. by U.S. Govt. to erect the Baron von Steuben Statue for Washington; executed the Germantown monument. Home: Suffern, N.Y. Died July 22, 1925.

JAFFA, Myer Edward, chemist; b. Sydney, Australia, Oct. 6, 1857; s. H. S. and Rebecca S. J.; Ph B., U. of Calif., 1877, M.S., 1896; m. Adele R. Solomons, Mar. 21, 1895; children—Edward Moss, Aileen Raby, Robert Leon (dec.). Asst. chemist, 10th U.S. Census, 1879-80; asst. agrl. dept., U. of Calif., 1880-81; asst. chemist, Northern Transcontinental Survey, 1881-83; 1st asst. and chemist, dept. of viticulture, 1883-89, 1st asst. chemist in charge lab. of agrl. chemistry, 1889-93, instr. agr., 1893-96, asst. prof. agr. in charge lab. of agrl. chemistry, 1896, asst. prof. nutrition, 1906, asso. prof., 1907, prof. nutrition, 1908-25, emeritus, U. of Calif.; chief Bur. Food and Drugs, Calif. State Bd. of Health, 1925—; dir. State Food and Drug Lab., 1908-15. Spl. agt. and food expert, U.S. Dept. Agr., 1900; consulting nutrition expert, Calif. State Bd. Health, 1915—. Jewish religion. Home: Berkeley, Calif. Died June 28, 1931.

JAGEMANN, Hans Carl Günther von, philologist; b. Grottkau, Germany, Aug. 2, 1859; s. Hans C. W. and Juliane (Ingermann) von J.; ed. Gymnasium at Naumburg and univs. of Leipzig and Tübingen; came to U.S., 1881; Ph.D., Johns Hopkins, 1884; m. Frances A. Whitman, 1884. Prof. modern langs., Earlham Coll., 1884-86; prof. Germanic langs., Ind. U., 1886-89; prof. Germanic philology, Harvard, 1889—. Author of articles on Germanic and Romance langs. and of textbooks for the study of German. Address: Cambridge, Mass. Died Jan. 22, 1926.

JAGGAR, Thomas Augustus, bishop; b. New York, June 2, 1839; s. Walter and Julia (Niles) J.; ed. in city schs. and by pvt. tutors; was bank clerk; prepared for ministry; D.D., U. of Pa., 1874; m. Anna Louisa, d. Hon. John W. Lawrence, Apr. 22, 1862; 1 son, Thomas Augustus, Jr. Deacon, 1860, priest, 1863, P.E. Ch.; rector Bergen Point, N.J., 1861-63, Anthon Memorial Ch., New York, 1863-68, St. John's, Yonkers, N.Y., 1868-70 (founded St. John's Riverside Hosp.); rector Holy Trinity Ch., Phila., 1870-75; consecrated bishop of Southern Ohio, 1875. Retired from charge of diocese, Oct. 1905, but retained seat and vote in House of Bishops; morning preacher St. Paul's Ch., Boston, until 1908; bishop in charge of Am. chs. in Europe, 1908—. Author: Bohlen Lectures for 1900 and various essays, printed sermons and addresses. Died Dec. 13, 1912.

JAGGARD, Edwin Ames, judge; b. Altoona, Pa., June 21, 1859; s. Clement and Annie Jane (Wright) J.; A.B., Dickinson Coll., 1879, A.M., 1882; LL.B., U. of Pa., 1882, LL.D., 1906; m. Anna, d. Gen. John T. Averill, Dec. 17, 1890. Admitted to bar, 1882; lecturer med. jurisprudence, St. Paul Med. Coll., 1888; mem. law faculty, U. of Minn., 1892—; judge Dist. Court, 2d Dist., Minn., 1898-1904; asso. justice Supreme Court, Minn., 1905—. Republican. Author: Jaggard on Torts (2 vols.), 1893; Jaggard on Taxation in Minnesota and North and South Dakota, 1901; Jaggard on Taxation in Iowa, 1902; also hist. Anomalies in the Law of Libel and Slander, N.E.A., 1903. Home: St. Paul, Minn. Died 1911.

JAMES, Arthur Curtiss, capitalist; b. New York, June 1, 1867; s. D. Willis and Ellen S. (Curtiss) J.; A.B. and A.M., Amherst, 1889; m. Harriet Eddy Parsons. Pres. Curtiss Southwestern Corp., Curtiss Southwestern Co.; dir. Phelps Dodge Corp. and subsidiaries, C.,B.&Q. Ry. Co., C.&S. Ry. Co., G.N. Ry. Co.; trustee U.S. Trust Co. Trustee Amherst Coll., Hampton Normal and Industrial Inst., Met. Mus. Art; mem. bd. of dirs. Union Theological Sem. Home: New York, N.Y. Died June 4, 1941.

JAMES, Bushrod Washington, oculist; b. Phila., Aug. 25, 1836; s. David James (M.D.) and Amanda (Worthington) J.; grad. Central High School, Phila., 1855 (A.M.); Pa. Homœ. Med. Coll., 1857 (M.D.); Am. U., Harriman, Tenn., 1897 (LL.D.); unmarried. Pres. Am. Inst. of Homœopathy, 1883; pres. Pa. Homœ. Med. Soc., 1873; pres. Hahnemann Club, Phila., several yrs.; pres. Children's Homœ. Hosp., 1890-96; hon. v.p. Homœ. Med. Congress, 1896, London, England; pres. Food-Fish Protective Assn. of Pa.; pres. Masonic Veterans' Assn.; trustee Am. U., Harriman, Tenn. Author: American Climates and Resorts, 1889; Alaskana, containing the legends of Alaska, 1892; Echoes of Battle, 1895; Dawn of a New Era in America, 1894; Alaska: Its Neglected Past and its Brilliant Future, 1897, revised, and 2d edit., 1901. Address: Philadelphia, Pa. Died 1903.

JAMES, Charles, prof. chemistry; b. Earls Barton, nr. Northampton, Eng., Apr. 27, 1880; s. William and Mary Diana (Shatford) J.; grad. inst. of Chemistry, London, 1904, fellow, 1907; hon. D.Sc., U. of N.H., 1928; m. Marion Elizabeth Templeton, 1915. Formerly chemist New Cransley Iron & Steel Co., Kettering, Eng.; came to U.S. 1906, naturalized citizen, 1920; asst. prof. inorganic chemistry, New Hampshire Coll., 1906-12, prof., 1912—. Awarded Ramsay silver medal, 1901; Nicholas medal, 1911. Episcopalian. Mason. Home: Durham, N.H. Died Dec. 10, 1928.

JAMES, Charles Fenton, clergyman, educator; b. Loudoun County, Va., Nov. 13, 1844; s. Robert and Winnifred (Simpson) J.; grad. Richmond Coll., 1870 (D.D., 1886); Southern Bapt. Theol. Sem., 1873; m. Mary Alice Chamblin, Oct. 28, 1873. Mem. cav. co. during John Brown's raid, 1859; enlisted 8th Va. regt. Pickett's div. C.S.A., 1861; became lt., 1863, capt., 1864. Ordained Bapt. ministry, 1873; pastor Buchanan, Va., 1873-82, Culpepper, Va., 1882-89; prin. Alleghany Inst., Danville, Va., 1892—. Author: Documentary History of the Struggle for Religious Freedom in Virginia, 1900. Home: Danville, Va. Died 1902.

JAMES, Charles P., asso. justice supreme court of D.C.; b. Cincinnati, May 11, 1818; admitted to Ohio bar; prof. law school, Cincinnati Coll., 1850-56; afterward judge superior court, Cincinnati; removed to Washington, 1864; 4 years prof. law, Georgetown U.; mem. commn. to revise the statutes of U.S.; apptd. to district bench, 1879. Home: Washington, D.C. Died 1899.

JAMES, D(aniel) Willis, philanthropist; b. Liverpool, Eng., Apr. 15, 1832; s. Daniel J., leading mcht. New York and Liverpool, more than 50 yrs.; m. Ellen S. Curtiss. Metal importer and mfr.; v.p. and trustee U.S. Trust Co.; dir. Ansonia Brass & Copper Co., Ansonia Clock Co., Commercial Mining Co., Copper Queen Consolidated Mining Co., Northern Pacific Ry. Co., and United Globe Mines. Trustee Amherst Coll. Home: New York, N.Y.; and Madison, N.J. Died 1907.

JAMES, Darwin Rush, mcht.; b. Williamsburg, Mass., May 14, 1834; ed. there until age 13; then 4 yrs. at Mt. Pleasant Boarding Sch., Amherst, Mass.; m. Mary E. Fairchild, Jan. 14, 1858. Importer of indigo and spices from the East Indies, 1857—; has visited the Philippines, East Indian Islands and Oriental countries generally. Was park commr. in Brooklyn, 6 yrs.; mem. Congress, 1883-87; leader of the minority which defeated Bland free-coinage bill, 1886; mem. and chmn. U.S. Bd. of Indian Commrs., 1889—; pres. N.Y. Bd. of Trade and Transportation, 6 yrs.; dir. various financial, ednl. and religious organizations. Home: Brooklyn, N.Y. Died 1908.

JAMES, Darwin Rush; b. Brooklyn, Jan. 10, 1873; s. Darwin Rush and Mary E. (Fairchild) J.; grad. Adelphi Acad., 1891; A.B., Princeton, 1895; m. Alice B. Fonda, Dec. 23, 1896. Pres. East River Savings Bank, Fairchild Realty Co.; dir. Aldar Realty Co., Savings Banks Trust Co., Institutional Securities Corp., Brooklyn Public Library. Pres. Brooklyn Bur. of Charities. Republican. Presbyn. Home: Brooklyn, N.Y. Died Aug. 7, 1937.

JAMES, D(avid) Bushrod, gynecologist; b. Franklin, Pa., July 14, 1874; s. William H. and Sarah E. (Le Vake) J.; M.D., Hahnemann Med. Coll. and Hosp., Phila., 1896; m. M. Mae A. Evans, June 3, 1902; children—David B., Mary Alice, William H. Practiced in Phila., 1896—; asst. in pathol. histology, 1898, demonstrator gynecology, pathology and microscopy, 1899, asso. prof. gynecology, 1905, prof., 1910—, also head of dept., Hahnemann Med. Coll. and Hosp.; gynecologist in charge Hahnemann Dispensary; consulting gynecologist, State Hosp. for Insane (Rittersville, Pa.), Homeo. Med. and Surg. Hosp. (Reading, Pa.). Republican. Methodist. Home: Philadelphia, Pa. Died Jan. 19, 1933.

JAMES, Edmund Janes, univ. pres.; b. Jacksonville, Ill., May 21, 1855; s. Rev. Colin Dew and Amanda Keziah (Casad) J.; ed. Ill. State Normal Sch., and Northwestern and Harvard univs.; A.M., Ph.D., U. of Halle, 1877; LL.D., Cornell Coll., Ia., 1902, Wesleyan, 1903, Queen's Coll., 1903, Harvard, 1909, Northwestern, 1914, University of Mich., 1914; m. Anna Margaret Lange, Aug. 22, 1879. Prin. High Sch., Evanston, Ill., 1878-79; prin. Model High Sch., Normal, Ill., 1879-82; prof. pub. finance and administration, Wharton Sch. of Finance and Economy, U. of Pa., 1883-95; prof. polit. and social science, U. of Pa., 1884-95; prof. pub. administration and dir. extension div. U. of Chicago, 1896-1901; pres. Northwestern U., 1902-04; pres. U. of Ill., 1904-20, emeritus. Editor publs., U. of Pa., Political Economy and Public Law Series, 1886-95. Mem. bd. trustees Ill. State Hist. Library, 1897-1907; National Municipal League, 1896—; pres. Ill. State Highway Commission, 1904-09; sec. Illinois State Geol. Commn., 1906—; mem. Bd. Nat. Resources and Conservation; pres. Am. Econ. Assn.; founder, and pres. Am. Acad. Polit. and Social Science, 1889-1901 (editor of its "Annals," 1890-95; asso. editor, 1895-98); pres. Am. Soc. for Extension of Univ. Teaching, 1891-95, Internat. Arbitration Soc., Chicago, 1903, Ill. Assn. for Prevention of Tuberculosis, 1905; fellow Royal Statis. Soc. Dublin. Author: Relation of the Modern Municipality to the Gas Supply, 1886; The Legal Tender Decisions, 1887; The Canal and the Railway, 1890; Federal Constitution of Germany, 1890; Federal Constitution of Switzerland, 1890; Education of Business Men in Europe, 1899; Charters of City of Chicago, 1900; Growth of Great Cities in Area and Population, 1900; Government of a Typical German City—Halle, 1900; The Land Grant Act of 1862, 1910; A National Economic Program, 1916; Military Training in Our Land Grant Colleges, 1916; A Naval Program, 1916. Home: Urbana, Ill. Died June 17, 1925.

JAMES, Francis Bacon, lawyer; b. Cincinnati, June 10, 1864; s. Francis Bacon and Elizabeth (Faris) J.; LL.B., with first honors, Cincinnati Law Sch., 1886; m. Miriam Loud. Admitted to bar, 1886; counsel for shippers in general advance of rate cases, 1910-11, and other cases of interstate commerce; commerce counsel various short line railroads. Instr. law Dept., U. of Cincinnati, 1895-1912; formerly dean of faculty, Cincinnati College of Commerce, Finance and Accounts. Del. Universal Congress Lawyers and Jurists, St. Louis Expn., 1904; del. 2d Pan-Am. Scientific Congress, 1916; pres. Ohio State Com. Uniform State Laws; life fellow of Royal Economic Soc., London. Former pres. Union Bd. of High Schs. of Cincinnati. Republican. Author: Ohio Law of Opinion Evidence, 1889; Advertising and Other Addresses, 1907; The New Jurisprudence (U.S. Senate doc.), 1915; Introduction to Clark on Interstate Commerce, 1919; Am. Nat. Economic Series, 1921. Compiler of Collection of Cases on Construction of Statutes, 1897. Home: Cincinnati, O. Deceased.

JAMES, Frank Lowber, physician, editor; b. Mobile, Ala., Aug. 27, 1841; s. Thomas Simmons and Laura (Spaulding) J.; ed. Mobile, Ala., 1847-57; Carlsruhe (Baden), Munich (Bavaria), Paris, France; grad. Munich, ad eundem, St. Louis, Mo.; spl. studies medicine, and chemistry under Baron von Liebig; unmarried. Democrat. Author: Elementary Microscopical Technology; editor The National Druggist for past 21 yrs. Wrote notable monograph on The Microscope in the Investigation of Scorches and Burns on Textile Fabrics, Proc. Am. Micros. Soc., 1891. Home: St. Louis, Mo. Died 1907.

JAMES, George Francis, educator; b. Normal, Ill., Aug. 18, 1867; s. Rev. Colin Dew and Amanda Keziah (Casad) J.; student Northwestern U., 1882-85; A.B., U. of Mich., 1886, A.M., 1887; studied history of edn. and sch. systems in France, Germany and Italy, 3 yrs.; Ph.D., U. of Halle, 1894; m. Pauline Ten Eyck Sholes, Aug. 10, 1899; children—Alice Felicia, Bertha Ten Eyck (Mrs. Daniel C. Rich), Margaret Pauline (Mrs. Wade H. Coleman, Jr.), George Francis, Barbara Sholes. Sec. Univ. Extension Soc., Phila., 1891-93; sec. Chicago Ednl. Commn., 1898-99; prof. pedagogy, State Normal Sch., Los Angeles, Calif., 1899-1902; prof. edn., 1902-05; dean Coll. of Edn., 1905-15, U. of Minn.; dean in edn., U. of Nev. and dir. State Normal Sch., Reno, Nev., 1915-18; ednl. dir. western dept., Nat. War Work Council of Y.M.C.A., 1918-19; asst. dir. Army Ednl. Corps of A.E.F., 1919; ednl. sec. Mil. Training Camps Assn., 1919-23; nat. exec. sec., same, 1923—. Author: Hand Book of University Extension, 1892. Editor Procs. of First Nat. Conf. on University Extension, 1892. Sec. Report of Chicago Educational Commission, 1899; Unveiling of Logan Monument, 1899; The Schools of a Democracy, 1918. Editor Nat. Series of Reports on Citizens' Military Training Camps, 1922—. Address: Chicago, Ill. Died Aug. 29, 1932.

JAMES, George Oscar, mathematician; b. Bowers Hill, Va., Aug. 1, 1873; s. George W. and Augusta C. (Walker) J.; A.B., Johns Hopkins, 1895, scholar, 1895-96, 1897-98, fellow, 1898-99, Ph.D., 1899; unmarried. Instr. in physics, U. of Utah, 1896-97;

examiner U.S. Civil Service Commn., 1900-01; instr. mathematics and astronomy, Lehigh U., 1902-03; instr. mathematics and astronomy, 1903-08, asst. prof. astronomy and mathematics, 1908-13, asso. prof. astronomy and mechanics and dean of coll., 1914-17, Thayer prof. applied mathematics and dean, 1918—, Washington U. Author: Elements of Rational Mechanics, 1905. Address: St. Louis, Mo. Died Nov. 24, 1931.

JAMES, George Roosa, merchant, mfr.; b. Memphis, Tenn., Sept. 12, 1866; s. Henry and Caroline (Roosa) J.; ed. pub. schs.; m. Elizabeth Carpenter, Jan. 12, 1888. Sec. James & Graham Wagon Co., Memphis, 1886, pres., 1889; pres. State Nat. Bank of Memphis, 1910, and served as v.p. of its successor, the Central State Nat. Bank, after consolidation with Central Bank & Trust Co., 1912; pres. William R. Moore Dry Goods Co., 1915; mem. Federal Reserve Board, until Jan. 1936. Mem. Memphis City Council, 1892-93; chief of cotton and cotton linter sect. of War Industries Bd., Mar.-Dec. 1918; mem. industrial bd. of Dept. of Commerce, Feb.-May 1919; mem. Industrial Conf., Oct. 6-21, 1919. Trustee Peabody Coll. for Teachers, Nashville, Tenn. Democrat. Episcopalian. Mason. Home: Washington, D.C. Died Mar. 9, 1937.

JAMES, George Wharton, explorer, ethnologist; b. Gainsborough, Lincolnshire, Eng., Sept. 27, 1858; s. John and Ann (Wharton) J.; m. Emma George Farnsworth, Nov. 12, 1895. Devoted yrs. to geog., geol., ethnol., and archæol. researches in Calif., Nev., Utah, Colo., Ariz., and N.M., especially in the regions of the Grand Canyon of the Colo. River, the Colo. Desert in Southern Calif. and among the Wallapai, Navaho, Apache, Havasupai, Zuni, Hopi, Acoma, and other Pueblo Indians, and the various tribes of Calif. Lecturer on these subjects with stereopticon views taken by himself; mem. several Indian tribes. Asso. editor The Craftsman, 1904-05; editor Out West, 1912-14; lit. editor of Oakland (Calif.) Tribune, 1919; editor California Indian Herald. Author: In and Around the Grand Canyon, 1900; Indian Basketry, 1900; Practical Basket Making; In and Out of the Old Missions, 1905; Indian Blankets and Their Makers, 1914; California, Romantic and Beautiful, 1914; The Lake of the Sky, Lake Tahoe, 1915; Living the Radiant Life, 1915; Our American Wonderlands, 1915; Quit Your Worrying, 1916; Arizona, the Wonderland, 1916; Rose H. Thorpe and the Story of the Curfew, 1916; House Blessing and Guest Book, 1918; New Mexico, the Land of the Delight Makers, 1919; Utah, the Land of Blossoming Valleys, 1921; also many other books now out of print. Home: Pasadena, Calif. Died Nov. 8, 1923.

JAMES, Henry, author; b. New York, Apr. 15, 1843; s. Rev. Henry and Mary R. (Walsh) J.; ed. in France and Switzerland, and Harvard Law School; L.H.D., Harvard U., 1911. Began as contributor to periodicals, 1866. Author: Watch and Ward, 1871; A Passionate Pilgrim, 1875; Roderick Hudson, 1875; Transatlantic Sketches, 1875; The American, 1877; French Poets and Novelists, 1878; The Europeans, 1878; Daisy Miller, 1878; An International Episode, 1879; Life of Hawthorne, 1879; A Bundle of Letters, 1879; Confidence, 1879; Diary of a Man of Fifty, 1880; Washington Square, 1880; The Portrait of a Lady, 1881; Siege of London, 1883; Portraits of Places, 1884; Tales of Three Cities, 1884; A Little Tour in France, 1884; Author of Beltraffio, 1885; The Bostonians, 1886; Princess Casamassima, 1886; Partial Portraits, 1888; The Aspern Papers, 1888; The Reverberator, 1888; A London Life, 1889; The Tragic Muse, 1890; Terminations, 1896; The Spoils of Poynton, 1897; What Maisie Knew, 1897; In the Cage, 1898; The Two Magics, 1898; The Awkward Age, 1899; The Soft Side, 1900; A Little Tour in France, 1900; The Sacred Fount, 1901; The Wings of the Dove, 1902; The Better Sort, 1903; Question of Our Speech, The Lesson of Balzac (2 lectures), 1905; American Scene, 1906; Italian Hours, 1909; Julia Bride, 1909; also Novels and Tales, 24 vols., 1909; Finer Grain, 1910; The Outcry, 1911; Small Boys and Others, 1913. Address: Rye, Sussex, Eng. Died Feb. 28, 1916.

JAMES, Louis, actor; b. Tremont, Ill., 1842; s. Benjamin F. and Almira H. J.; joined McAuley's Stock Co., Louisville, Ky., 1864; later to Mrs. John Drew's Arch St. Theatre, Phila., 1865-70; Augustin Daly's, 5th Av., New York, 1871; McGuire's, San Francisco; later to Ford's, in Baltimore; then to Boston Theatre; leading man with Lawrence Barrett, 5 yrs.; starred, 1886-89; with Joseph Jefferson, 1891-92; starred with Frederick Warde, 1892-95; star with Wagenhals & Kemper, 1895—, in The Two Orphans and She Stoops to Conquer, 1904-05; starring in Virginius, Merchant of Venice and Merry Wives of Windsor, 1905—; m. Lillian Scanlan, 1871 (died 1876); m. 2d, Aphie Hendricks, Dec. 24, 1892. Home: Monmouth Beach, N.J. Died 1910.

JAMES, Mary E. (Fairchild); b. Stockbridge, Mass., July 21, 1834; d. Daniel and Octavia (Briggs) Fairchild; grad. Maplewood Inst., Pittsfield, Mass.; m. Darwin R. James, Jan. 14, 1858 (died 1908). For 40 yrs. devoted to social, philanthropic and religious work; in Washington, 1885, with others, secured opening of night schs. for colored people, also organized and was pres. soc. for helping the newsboys; v.p. 1881-86, pres., 1886—, Woman's Bd. of Home Missions of Presbyn. Ch. (representing over half million Presbyn. women); also pres. other religious and benevolent organizations. Led uprising of women which prevented Brigham H. Roberts (of Utah) from taking seat in 56th Congress; platform speaker and writer on reforms. Address: Brooklyn, N.Y. Died 1912.

JAMES, Ollie M., U.S. senator; b. Crittenden County, Ky., July 27, 1871; s. L. H. and Elizabeth J. J.; acad. edn.; page Ky. Legislature, 1887; studied law under his father; m. Ruth Thomas, Dec. 2, 1903. Admitted to Ky. bar, 1891, was one of attys. for late Gov. Goebel in his contest for gov. of Ky.; del. Dem. Nat. Conv., 1896, del.-at-large, 1904 and 1908 (chmn. Ky. delegation in each; seconded nomination of W. J. Bryan for President, 1908); chmn. Ky. State Dem. Conv., 1900; mem. 58th to 62d Congresses (1903-13), 1st Ky. Dist.; elected U.S. senator, Jan. 10, 1912, for term 1913-19. Chmn. Dem. Nat. Conv., 1912. Home: Marion, Ky. Died Aug. 28, 1919.

JAMES, Thomas Lemuel, Postmaster Gen.; b. Utica, N.Y., Mar. 29, 1831; s. William and Jane Maria (Price) J.; ed. common schs.; A.M., Hamilton Coll., 1863; LL.D., Madison U., 1883, St. John's Coll., 1884, St. Francis Xavier Coll., 1886; m. Flora MacDonnell, May 10, 1911. Learned the printing trade; published paper at Hamilton, N.Y., 1851-61; collector canal tolls there, 1854-55. Insp. customs, New York, 1861-64; weigher, 1864-70; deputy collector customs, 1870-73; postmaster of New York, 1873-81; Postmaster Gen. in cabinet of President Garfield, Mar. 5, 1881-Jan. 4, 1882. Chmn. bd. of dirs. Lincoln Nat. Bank, New York, 1882—; pres. Lincoln Safe Deposit Co.; dir. Met. Life Ins. Co. Mayor of Tenafly, N.J., 1896. Home: New York, N.Y. Died Sept. 11, 1916.

JAMES, Walter Belknap, M.D.; b. Baltimore, May 11, 1858; s. Henry and Amelia (Cate) J.; B.A., Yale, 1879; M.D., Coll. Phys. and Surg. (Columbia), 1883; LL.D., Columbia, 1904; M.A., Yale, 1906; LL.D., Harvard, 1922; m. Helen G. Jennings, 1894. Practicing in New York, 1883—; clin. lecturer medicine, 1889-97, instr. gen. diagnosis, 1897-1900, med. diagnosis, 1900-01, lecturer practice of medicine, 1901-02, prof., 1902-04, Bard prof., 1904-09, prof. clin. medicine, 1909—, mem. Univ. Council, 1903—, Columbia U. Visiting physician, Presbyn. Hosp., 1904-09; consulting physician, Bellevue Hosp., Hosp. for Ruptured and Crippled. Trustee Columbia U. Address: New York, N.Y. Died Apr. 6, 1927.

JAMES, William, psychologist; b. New York, Jan. 11, 1842; s. Rev. Henry J. and Mary R. (Walsh) J.; student Lawrence Scientific Sch. (Harvard), 1861-63; M.D., Harvard, 1869; Ph.D., and Litt.D., Padua, 1893; LL.D., Princeton, 1896, Edinburgh, 1902, Harvard 1903; D.Sc., Oxford, 1908; Litt.D., Durham, 1908; D.Sc., Geneva, 1909; m. Alice H. Gibbens, 1878. Instr. physiology, 1872-76, anatomy, 1873-76, asst. prof. physiology, 1876-80, philosophy, 1880-85, prof. same, 1885-89, prof. psychology, 1889-97, philosophy, 1897-1907, emeritus prof. 1907, Harvard. Gifford lecturer on natural religion, U. of Edinburgh, 1899-1901; Hibbert lecturer on philosophy, Oxford, 1908. Author: Principles of Psychology (2 vols.), 1890; Psychology—Briefer Course, 1892; The Will to Believe, and Other Essays in Popular Philosophy, 1897; Talks to Teachers on Psychology and to Students on Life's Ideals, 1898; Human Immortality—Two Supposed Objections to the Doctrine, 1899; The Varieties of Religious Experiences, 1902; Pragmatism—A New Name for Some Old Ways of Thinking, 1907; A Pluralistic Universe, 1908; The Meaning of Truth, 1909. Address: Cambridge, Mass. Died 1910.

JAMES, William Hartford, gov.; b. Marion County, O., Oct. 16, 1831; s. Isaac Even and Betsy (Bates) J.; ed. pub. schs., Marion, O.; m. Louisa Epler, Feb. 12, 1857. Admitted to Ia. bar, 1855. Apptd. register land office at Dakota, Neb., 1864, later becoming sec. of state of Neb.; gov. of Neb., 1871-73; apptd., 1887, register land office, Colfax, Wash., removing to that state Oct. 1887. Republican. Home: Colfax, Wash. Died Feb. 1, 1920.

JAMES, William John, librarian; b. Cincinnati, Sept. 7, 1860; s. Thomas and Alice Pearson (Williams) J.; Poly. Inst. Brooklyn, 1876-79; B.A., Wesleyan U., 1883, M.A., 1886; L.H.D., Dickinson College, 1920; studied univs. of Leipzig and Berlin and traveled in Europe, 1883-87; m. Saidee Brakeley Walters, July 16, 1890. Tutor in mathematics, 1887-90, instr., 1890-95, librarian, 1891-1929, Wesleyan U., also asst. treas. Democrat. Methodist. Address: Middletown, Conn. Died Jan. 5, 1941.

JAMES, William Knowles; b. nr. Georgetown, Del., Aug. 20, 1852; s. Urias Thomas and Eliza Jane (Knowles) J.; Central Coll., Fayette, Mo.; A.B., Yale, 1878; m. Mary Tootle, Oct. 31, 1883; children—Ellen Tootle, Thomas Tootle (dec.). Admitted to Mo. bar, 1880, and practiced at St. Joseph; judge Circuit Court, St. Joseph, 1898-1902; mem. Mo. Ho. of Rep., 1917-18; active in securing passage of Casey-James Prison Reform Bill, and industrial training of Negroes in Mo. Retired to Hillcrest Farm, Andrew County, 1913; elected pres. Internat. Farm Congress, 1921, reelected 1923, 25; a leader in organizing the Farm Bur. in county, state and nation; elected chmn. Mo. dirs. Mo. River Navigation Assn., 1925. Pres. Bartlett Agrl. and Industrial Sch. (for Negroes), Dalton, Mo.; trustee Y.M.C.A., St. Joseph. Democrat. Presbyn. Mason, Odd Fellow. Home: St. Joseph, Mo. Died Nov. 11, 1927.

JAMES, William P., judge; b. Buffalo, N.Y., Jan. 10, 1870; s. David and Jane (Parry) James; m. Ella V. Haas, 1896. Began practice of law at Los Angeles; judge Superior Court of Los Angeles County, 1905-10; judge Calif. Court of Appeals, 1910-23; U.S. dist. judge, Southern Dist .of Calif., 1923—. Republican. Presbyn. Mason. Died July 29, 1940.

JAMESON, Henry, physician; b. Indianapolis, Ind., Sept. 9, 1848; s. Alexander and Lydia C. (Thompson) J.; B.S., Northwestern Christian U. (now Butler Coll.), Indianapolis, 1869, LL.D., 1906; M.D., Bellevue Hosp. Med. Coll. (New York U.), 1871; m. Gertrude Carey, Nov. 25, 1875. Practiced in Indianapolis; mem. staffs of all hosps. in Indianapolis; surgeon gen. Ind. N.G. under Gov. W. T. Durbin, 1901-05; chmn. Bd. of Park Commissioners, Indianapolis, 1906-15; pres. Indianapolis Street Ry. Co., 1914—. Republican. Mem. Christian (Disciples) Ch. Mason. Home: Indianapolis, Ind. Died Feb. 13, 1924.

JAMESON, John Franklin, historian; b. nr. Boston, Sept. 19, 1859; s. John and Mariette (Thompson) J.; A.B., Amherst, 1879, LL.D., 1898; fellow Johns Hopkins, 1881, Ph.D., 1882, LL.D., 1902; LL.D., U. of Mich., 1923; Litt.D., Brown, 1914, Princeton, 1922; m. Sara E. Elwell, Apr. 13, 1893. Asst. and asso. in history, Johns Hopkins, 1882-88; prof. history, Brown U., 1888-1901; prof. and head dept. history, U. of Chicago, 1901-05; dir. dept. hist. research, Carnegie Instn., Washington, 1905-28; chief div. of manuscripts, Library of Congress, 1928—. Mng. editor Am. Hist. Review, 1895-1901 and 1905-28; chmn. Hist. Manuscripts Commn., 1895-99 and 1905-08. Pres. Am. Hist. Assn., 1906-07. Author: Willem Usselinx, Founder of the Dutch and Swedish West India Companies, 1887; History of Historical Writing in America, 1891; Dictionary of United States History, 1894; The American Revolution Considered as a Social Movement, 1926; etc. Editor: Correspondence of John C. Calhoun, 1900; Original Narratives of Early American History, 1906-17; Privateering and Piracy, 1923. Chmn. com. of management of Dictionary of Am. Biography. Died Sept. 28, 1937.

JAMIESON, Charles Clark, army officer, cons. engr.; b. Glover, Vt., Nov. 3, 1866; s. Williams S. and Isabella A. (MacDowell) J.; grad. U.S. Mil. Acad., 1892; m. Frances Floyd, June 12, 1894; children—Floyd M., Eleanor; m. 2d, Anne Uezzell, July 12, 1930. Commd. 2d lt. 15th Inf., June 11, 1892; 1st lt. ordnance, Apr. 9, 1895; capt., Feb. 7, 1901; maj., June 25, 1906; retired on account of disability in line of duty, Oct. 12, 1910; recalled to active service Apr. 13, 1919; col. N.A., Jan. 11, 1918; brig. gen. (temp.), Oct. 1, 1918; discharged as brig. gen., at his own request, Jan. 3, 1919; resumed business as v.p. firm George W. Goethals & Co., Inc., New York; consulting industrial engineer; pres. Asfalterra Co., Jacksonville, Fla., Duty Ft. Sheridan, Ill., 1892-95, Sandy Hook Proving Ground, 1897-1900; instr. U.S. Mil. Acad., 1900-03; duty Rock Island Arsenal, 1903-05, Watervliet Arsenal, N.Y., 1905-10; duty Washington, D.C., World War, as asst. to chief of production div., chief of production division, and spl. asst. to chief of ordnance until appmt., Dec. 1918, as dir. of sales of property acquired by War Dept. after Apr. 6, 1917. Presbyn. Address: Ocala, Fla. Died Aug. 21, 1935.

JAMIESON, Edmund Scudder, educator; b. Lawrenceville, N.J., Oct. 3, 1886; s. Alexander Fridge and Mary (Scudder) J.; grad. Lawrenceville Sch., 1903; A.B., Princeton, 1907; post grad. work, Columbia, 1923, U. of Mich., 1929, 34; studied law pvtly.; m. Ruth Amelia Mason, Dec. 22, 1919 (died 1935); m. 2d, Marian Ruth Frank, May 22, 1937; 1 dau., Prudence King. Admitted to N.J. bar, 1910, and practiced in Trenton, 1910-13; atty. Lawrence Township, 1911-13; teacher Adirondack-Fla. Sch., Onchiota, N.Y., 1913; housemaster Chestnut Hill (Pa.) Acad., 1913-23; headmaster Howe (Ind.) Sch., 1923—. Served as lt. N.J. N.G., 1911-13; in U.S. Army, 1918. Democrat. Episcopalian. Mason. Author: School Songs. Address: Howe, Ind. Died Apr 2, 1941.

JAMISON, Joseph Warren, lawyer; b. Bolivar, Mo., Jan. 23, 1868; s. Harrison H. and Sarah R. (Montgomery) J.; ed. pub. schs. and acad.; studied law pvtly.; m. Anna L. McCracken; children—Wylla (Mrs. Wylla Viley), William C., Lorena (Mrs. Lorena Christophel), Ruth (Mrs. Howard McCord). Admitted to Mo. bar, 1891; practiced in Versailles,

1891-93, Boonville, 1893-1903, St. Louis, 1903—; register U. S. Land Office, Boonville, 1893-97, by apptmt. Pres. Cleveland; city counselor, Boonville, 1898-1900; gen. practice, St. Louis, 1903-13; mem. St. Louis Bd. Election Commrs., 1909-13; gen. atty. (State of Mo.) M.K.&T. Ry., 1913-23; gen. counsel Southwestern Bell Telephone Co., 1923-33; gen. counsel for trustees St.L.-S.F. Ry., 1934—. Democrat. Home: St. Louis, Mo. Died July 15, 1940.

JAMISON, Monroe Franklin, bishop; b. Rome, Ga., Nov. 27, 1849; s. George Shorter and Olivia (Shorter) J.; never attended sch.; m. M. A. Flournoy, Feb. 24, 1874. Bishop, Colored M.E. Ch., 1910—. Address: Leigh, Tex. Died May 19, 1918.

JAMISON, William Arbuckle, merchant; b. Sept. 18, 1863; s. Robert and Catherine (Arbuckle) J.; ed. Western U. of Pa.; m. Inez Mermier, Dec. 1902. Directing partner Arbuckle Bros., coffee importers and sugar refiners; dir. Chase Nat. Bank, U.S. Mortgage & Trust Co., U.S. Safe Deposit Co., Wabash Ry. Co., etc.; pres. Jay Street Connecting Railroad. Mem. Internat. Sugar Com., 1917. Home: New York, N.Y. Died June 27, 1928.

JANAUSHEK, Francesca, actress; b. Prague, Bohemia, 1830; became prominent as an actress in her own country and Germany; came to U.S., 1867, and played Medea and other rôles in German; studied English and later made a success in tragic rôles in that tongue, including Deborah, Bianca, Mary Stuart, Queen Elizabeth, Lady Macbeth, Meg Merrilies and others. Home: Brooklyn, N.Y. Died 1904.

JANES, George Milton, economist; b. Utica, N.Y., Apr. 18, 1869; s. Joseph and Jane (Isaacs) J.; grad. Bangor Sem., 1899; B.Litt., Dartmouth, 1901; A.B., Middlebury Coll., 1903; A.M., Harvard, 1910; Ph.D., Johns Hopkins, 1913; m. Mary Alice Helme, Nov. 21, 1904; children—Bernon Helme, Robert Brown, Milton. Instr. polit. and social science, U. of Wash., 1913-17; asst. prof. economics and polit. science, U. of N.D., 1917-19; prof. economics, Washington and Jefferson Coll., 1919-25; prof. economics and sociology, and head of dept., Kenyon Coll., 1925-34, emeritus. Author: The Pilgrim Spirit and Other Essays, 1904; The Control of Strikes in American Trade Unions, 1916; American Trade Unionism, 1922; Who Should Have Wealth, and Other Papers, 1925; Man and Society, 1927; Seven Social Thinkers, 1934. Asso. editor New Century Book of Facts. Home: Oberlin, O. Died Dec. 24, 1936.

JANES, Lewis George, dir. Cambridge Confs. and Monsalvat School of Comparative Religion, 1896—; b. Providence, R.I., Feb. 19, 1844; s. Alphonso Richards and Sophia (Taft) J.; grad. Providence High School (A.M., Brown); m. Gertrude Pool, June 2, 1869 (died 1875); 2d, Helen Hall Rawson, June 17, 1882. Pres. Brooklyn Ethical Assn., 1885-96; instr. in history, Adelphi Acad., Brooklyn, 1894-95; lecturer on sociology and civics, School of Political Science, Brooklyn, 1893-96; pres. Free Religious Assn. of America, 1899—. Author: A Study of Primitive Christianity, 1887; Evolution of Morals, 1889; Scope and Principles of the Evolution Philosophy, 1890; Life as a Fine Art, 1891; The Problem of City Government, 1892; War and Progress, 1893; Cosmic Evolution as Related to Ethics, 1895; Samuell Gorton, First Settler of Warwick, R.I., 1896; Social Ideals and Social Progress, 1899; Health and a Day, 1901. Home: Cambridge, Mass. Died 1901.

JANEWAY, Edward Gamaliel, physician; b. in N.J., Aug. 31, 1841; A.B., Rutgers, 1860, A.M., 1863; acting med. cadet U.S. Army Hospital, Newark, N.J., 1862-63; M.D., Coll. Phys. and Surg. (Columbia), 1864, LL.D., 1904. Curator, 1868-72, prof. pathology and practical anatomy, 1872-79; diseases of the mind and nervous system, 1881-86, medicine, 1886-92, Bellevue Hosp. Med. Coll.; prof. medicine, 1898—, dean, 1898-1905, Univ. and Bellevue Hosp. Med. Coll. Has held many hosp. appmts.; health commr. New York, 1875-82. Address: New York, N.Y. Died 1911.

JANEWAY, Theodore Caldwell, physician; b. New York, Nov. 2, 1872; s. Edward Gamaliel and Frances Strong (Rogers) J.; Ph.B., Yale, 1892; M.D., Coll. Phys. and Surg. (Columbia), 1895; hon. A.M., Yale, 1912; Sc.D., Washington U., 1915; m. Eleanor C. Alderson, Sept. 27, 1898. Instr., then lecturer on med. diagnosis, New York U., 1898-1906; asso. in medicine, 1907-09; prof. practice of medicine, 1909-14, Coll. Phys. and Surg. (Columbia); prof. medicine Johns Hopkins U. and physician-in-chief Johns Hopkins Hosp., Baltimore, 1914—. Sec. Russell Sage Inst. Pathology, New York, 1907—; mem. editorial bd. Archives of Internal Medicine, 1908—; mem. bd. scientific dirs. Rockefeller Inst. for Med. Research, 1911—. Author: The Clinical Study of Blood-Pressure, 1904. Home: Baltimore, Md. Died Dec. 27, 1917.

JANNEY, O(liver) Edward, M.D.; b. Washington, Mar. 8, 1856; s. Henry and Hannah Russell (Scholfield) J.; State Normal Sch., Millersville, Pa., 4 yrs.; M.D., U. of Md., 1881; M.D., Hahnemann Med. Coll., Phila., 1882; m. Anne B. Webb, Oct. 22, 1885; children—Eleanor (Mrs. W. R. Johns), William W. (dec.), Rebecca S. (Mrs. H. G. Timbres). Practiced in Baltimore, 1882. Minister, Soc. of Friends (Quakers), 1895; chmn. Friends' Gen. Conf., 1900-20. Actg. asst. surgeon U.S. Pub. Health Service. Author: The Medical Advisor, 1910; The White Slave Traffic in America, 1911; The Gateway to the Kingdom, 1912; The Making of a Man, 1914; Quakerism, 1917. Address: Baltimore, Md. Died Nov. 17, 1930.

JANNEY, Thomas B., merchant, banker; b. Shanesville, O., Oct. 5, 1838; s. Phineas M. and Frances (Smith) J.; ed. acad., Henry, Ill.; m. Mary Wheaton. Clk. in gen. store until 1862; at Nashville, Tenn., 1862-66; entered hardware business, with brothers, in Minneapolis, 1866, firm becoming Janney, Brooks & Eastman, 1875, Janney, Semple & Co., 1884, inc., 1898, as Janney, Semple, Hill & Co., becoming pres.; pres. Farmers & Mechanics Savings Bank; dir. Northwestern Nat. Bank. Democrat. Presbyn. Home: Minneapolis, Minn. Died Feb. 5, 1924.

JANSEN, Marie, actress; b. (Johnson) Boston; début Park Theatre, Boston; stage name of "Jansen," Sept. 13, 1881; soon took leading rôles in Olivette, Iolanthe, The Beggar Student, etc.; played one season, Criterion Theatre, London, with Francis Wilson's Co. several seasons; afterward in various operas and comedies at head of her own co. until 1901; retired for 2 seasons; played title rôle Iolanthe, Standard Theatre, New York; created rôle of "Featherbrain" in play of same name, with Sir Charles Wyndham, Criterion Theatre, London, an adaptation from the French "Tête de Linotte." Address: Winthrop, Mass. Died Mar. 20, 1914.

JANSSEN, John, bishop; b. Keppeln in Rhine-Prussia, Mar. 3, 1835; after classical studies entered theol. sem. of Diocese of Münster. At solicitation of Bishop Juncker, of Alton, Ill., came to U.S., 1858; completed his theol. studies. Ordained R.C. priest, Nov. 19, 1858; in missionary work, Springfield, Ill.; later at Alton, where became sec. to Bishop Juncker until latter's death, 1868; vicar-gen. Diocese of Alton, 1870-77 and 1879-86; pastor St. Boniface, Quincy, Ill., 1877-79; administrator of Diocese of Alton, 1886-88; consecrated bishop of Belleville, Apr. 25, 1888. Address: Belleville, Ill. Died July 2, 1913.

JANVIER, Caesar A(ugustus) Rodney, college prin.; b. Abington, Pa., Jan. 5, 1861; s. Levi and Mary Rodney (Parvin) J.; A.B., Princeton, 1880, A.M., 1883; grad. Princeton Theol. Sem., 1884; D.D., Ursinus Coll., 1911; m. Susan Duryee Rankin, May 15, 1884; children—Rodney Parvin (dec.), Ernest Paxton. Ordained Presbyn. ministry, 1884; pastor Trenton, N.J., 1884-87; missionary in India, 1887-1901; pastor Hollond Memorial Ch., Phila., 1901-13; prin. Ewing Christian Coll., Allahabad, India, Sept. 1913—. Awarded Kaisar-i-Hind Medal by govt., 1925. Mem. exec. council Allahabad U. Republican. Author: Sketch of Presbyterian Missions in India, 1903. Address: Allahabad, Ind. Died Nov. 3, 1928.

JANVIER, Catharine Ann, painter, author; b. Phila.; d. Henry Sandwith and Susannah (Shober) Drinker; early life passed in China; studied in the Pa. Acad. Fine Arts, and Art Students' League, New York; m. Thomas Allibone Janvier, Sept. 26, 1878 (died 1913). Pictures: Geoffrey Rudel and the Countess of Tripoli; The Princess Badroulbadour; The Guitar Player (prize picture Pa. Academy); Daniel at Prayer; The Violinist, etc. Author: Ceramics for Students, 1880; London Mews, 1904. Translator: (from the Provencal of Félix Gras) The Reds of the Midi, 1896; The Terror, 1898; The White Terror, 1900. Died July 17, 1923.

JANVIER, Charles; b. New Orleans, La., Sept. 8, 1857; s. Charles A. and Zelime Coiron J.; ed. Coll. of Immaculate Conception, New Orleans; m. Josephine Celeste Bush, Oct. 3, 1883 (died 1899); 7 children. Was pres. Sun Ins. Co. of New Orleans; gen. agt. for La. and Miss., Sun Isn. Office of Eng. and Palatine Ins. Co., Ltd., of London; was pres. Canal-La. Bank & Trust Co.; postmaster of New Orleans, 1916-24. Took part in White League movement, 1874, as mem. of Roman Rifles; elected to lead Citizens' League movement in New Orleans, 1896, which resulted in defeat regular Dem. municipal ticket, and installation of a reform administration; mem. and vice chmn. Dem. State Central Com., 1900-06 (chmn. 1906-08); mem. La. Senate, session 1904, resigned, Sept. 1904; chmn. Yellow Fever Fund Com., 1905. Mem. and 2d v.p. Bd. of Administrators Tulane Ednl. Fund. First Grand Knight of 1st council Knights of Columbus instituted in La.; Past Grand Knight Marquette Council, No. 1437, K. of C. Home: New Orleans, La. Died Jan. 21, 1927.

JANVIER, Margaret Thomson ("Margaret Vandegrift"), author; b. New Orleans, 1844; d. Francis de Haes and Emma (Newbold) Janvier. Writer of juvenile stories and verses. Author: Under the Dog-Star; Clover Beach; Little Helpers; The Dead Doll and Other Verses; The Queen's Body-Guard; Doris and Theodora; Rose Raymond's Wards; Ways and Means; Holidays at Home; The Absent-Minded Fairy; Little Bell and Other Stories; Umbrellas to Mend (novel), 1905. Address: Philadelphia, Pa. Died Feb. 1913.

JANVIER, Thomas Allibone, author; b. Phila., July 16, 1849; s. Francis de Haes and Emma (Newbold) J.; common sch. edn.; m. Catharine Ann Drinker, Sept. 26, 1878. Editorial work on Philadelphia Press, Bulletin and Times, 1870-81; in Colo., N.M., and Mex. during major portion of the yrs. 1881-87; in Provence, 1894-97; in Eng., 1897-1900. Author: Color Studies, 1885; The Mexican Guide, 1887 et seq.; the Aztec Treasure House, 1890; Stories of Old New Spain, 1891; The Uncle of an Angel and Other Stories, 1891; An Embassy to Provence, 1893; In Old New York, 1894; In the Sargasso Sea, 1898; The Passing of Thomas and Other Stories, 1900; In Great Waters, 1901; The Christmas Kalends of Provence, 1902; The Dutch Founding of New York, 1903; Santa Fé's Partner, 1907; Henry Hudson—His Aims and his Achievements, 1909; Legends of the City of Mexico, 1910; From the South of France, 1912. Died June 18, 1913.

JANVRIN, Joseph Edward, gynecologist; b. Exeter, N.H., Jan. 13, 1839; s. Joseph Adams and Lydia Ann (Colcord) J.; ed. Phillips Exeter Acad.; asst. surgeon 15th N.H. Vols., in Civil War; M.D., Coll. Phys. and Surg. (Columbia), 1864; m. Laura L. LaWall, Sept. 1, 1881. Asst. surgeon Woman's Hosp., State of N.Y., 1872-82; gynecologist, N.Y. Skin and Cancer Hosp., 1883—, also consulting surgeon same. One of founders Internat. Congress Gynecology and Obstetrics, 1893; pres. Am. Gynecol. Soc., 1902-03, N.Y. Obstet. Soc., 1890, 1891, New York County Med. Assn., 1896-97. Address: New York, N.Y. Died Dec. 21, 1911.

JAQUES, Alfred, lawyer; b. Geneseo Tp., Henry County, Ill., Feb. 9, 1857; s. William Cowpen and Elizabeth Anne (Beers) J.; ed. pub. and pvt. schs.; studied law in office of Judge George E. Wait, Geneseo, Ill.; m. Mary Josephine Shaw, Apr. 15, 1885; children—Robert, Lawrence, Wilfrid, Randal. Admitted to Minn. bar, 1883, and practiced in Duluth; spl. judge Municipal Court, Duluth, 1887-89; Dem. candidate for judge, 11th Judicial Dist., Minn., 1896 (defeated); for Congress, 8th Minn. Dist., 1910 (defeated); del. to Dem. Nat. Conv., Baltimore, 1912, and seconded nomination of Woodrow Wilson for pres. of U.S., for State of Minn.; U.S. atty., Dist. of Minn., 1914-22; Dem. candidate for gov. of Minn., 1926. Pres. The New Duluth Co. Unitarian. Home: Duluth, Minn. Died July 2, 1937.

JAQUES, Herbert, architect; b. Framingham, Mass., Jan. 23, 1857; s. Francis and Caroline Louisa (Merriam) J.; grad. Boston Latin Sch., 1873; in Europe, 1874; spl. course, Mass. Inst. Tech., 1875-76; m. Harriet Sayles Francis, Apr. 26, 1883. In office of Messrs. Snell & Gregerson, Boston, 1876-79; office of H. H. Richardson, 1879-83; mem. firm of Andrews & Jaques, 1883-90, Andrews, Jaques & Rantoul, 1890—. Fellow A.I.A. Home: Chestnut Hill, Mass. Died Dec. 21, 1916.

JAQUES, Willard W(ight), mfr.; b. Chicago, Ill., Feb. 7, 1875; s. Frank F. and Abbie L. (Everett) J.; ed. Chicago Manual Training Sch., high sch., Kansas City, Mo., and Univ. Med. Sch., Kansas City; m. Mabel Kohlsaat, 1902; children—Mabel Alice, Willard Kohlsaat. Began with F. F. Jaques & Co., mfrs. K. C. baking powder, Kansas City, Jan. 1901, was sec. 1901-03, and has been pres., 1903—, Jaques Mfg. Co., main office and factory in Chicago. Republican. Home: Chicago, Ill. Died Aug. 20, 1940.

JAQUES, William Henry, engineer and naval architect; b. Phila., Dec. 24, 1848; ed. pub. schs., Newark, N.J.; grad. U.S. Naval Acad., 1867; remained in service until 1887; resigned 1887, to inaugurate mfr. of heavy ordnance and armor at works of Bethlehem Iron Co. Has served as asst. in U.S. Coast and Geod. Survey; mem. and sec. gun foundry bd., sec. senate com. on ordnance and war ships. Introduced into U.S. the fluid compression and hydraulic forging of heavy masses of steel and invented reforging process; was mem. international jury on marine transportation and war material, Chicago Expn., 1893. Organized, and comd. N.J. Naval Reserve, 1895-98. Pres. Hampton (N.H.) Water Works Co. Civil War service medal; mem. Loyal Legion U.S.; decorated Naval Order of the United States, Order of the Rising Sun, Japan. Republican. Mem. bd. visitors U.S. Naval Acad., 1905. Author: The Establishment of Steel Gun Factories in the United States, 1884. Address: Little Boar's Head, N.H. Died Nov. 23, 1916.

JARRETT, Edwin Seton, civil engr.; b. Brooklyn, N.Y., Mar. 7, 1862; s. James M. and Sarah Olivia (Heather) J.; C.E., Rensselaer Poly. Inst., 1889; m. Cora Hardy, June 26, 1906; children—Edwin Seton, William Armistead, Olivia Heather. Began, 1889, as engr. with firm of Sooysmith & Co., foundation specialists, New York, continuing until 1900, consulting practice, 1900-02; an organizer, and v.p. The Foundation Co., 1902-14; pres. Jarrett-Chambers Co., 1914-28; cons. engr., 1928-37; exec. v.p., actg. pres. Rensselaer Poly. Inst., 1935-37, retired; trustee Rensselaer Poly. Inst., 1937—; has been connected with design and building of many notable structures throughout U.S., including bridges, docks, retaining walls, dams, etc. Unitarian. Home: Princeton, N.J. Died Dec. 26, 1938.

JARRETT, William Paul, territorial del.; b. Honolulu, T.H., Aug. 22, 1877; ed. St. Louis Coll., Honolulu. Dep. sheriff and sheriff City and County of Honolulu 8 yrs.; high sheriff Ty. of Hawaii and warden Oahu Prison, 1914-22; del. 68th to 70th Congresses (1923-29), Hawaii. Democrat. Home: Honolulu, T.H. Deceased.

JARVIE, James Newbegin, capitalist; b. Manchester, Eng.; s. William and Isabella (Newbegin) J.; ed. Adelphi Acad., Brooklyn; m. Helen Vanderveer Newton, Aug. 28, 1909. Dir. Cuba Cane Sugar Corp., Southern Pacific Co., Manhattan Fire & Marine Ins. Co., and many other cos.; trustee Central Union Trust Co., London Assurance Corp. Home: Montclair, N.J. Died June 21, 1929.

JARVIS, Samuel M., banker; b. McDonough County, Ill., Jan. 31, 1853; s. James and Permelia J.; m. Priscilla Wear, 1873. Admitted to bar, 1876, and began practice, but soon became interested in banking and finance; one of organizers and first pres. N. Am. Trust Co.; opened branch at Santiago de Cuba immediately after Am. occupation, 1898; rendered important assistance to U.S. Govt.; offered post of fiscal agt. of U.S. in Cuba by President McKinley, but at his request appmt. was given to the trust co. instead; became v.p. Nat. Bank of Cuba, fiscal agt. and depositary of Republic of Cuba; dir. numerous corps. Home: New York, N.Y. Died Dec. 27, 1913.

JARVIS, Thomas Jordan, senator; b. Jarvisburg, N.C., Jan. 18, 1836; s. Rev. B. H. and Elizabeth J.; grad. Randolph-Macon Coll., 1860; served in C.S.A., 1861-64, pvt. to capt.; right arm shattered by bullet and compelled to leave service; m. Mary Woodson, Dec. 23, 1874. Mem. State Constl. convs., 1865 and 1875; admitted to bar, 1868, and began practice; presdl. elector, 1868, 1872; mem. Legislature, 1868-69 and 1870-71 (speaker last term); lt. gov., 1877; became gov. on election of Gov. Vance to U.S. Senate, 1879; elected gov. for term, 1881-85; U.S. minister to Brazil, 1885-89; elected to fill Senator Vance's term on latter's death, 1894, serving until 1895; del.-at-large to Dem. Nat. Conv., 1896. Address: Greenville, N.C. Died 1915.

JASTROW, Marcus, clergyman; b. Rogasen, Posen, Prussia, June 5, 1829; s. Abraham and Yetta J.; pub. sch. edn., Rogasen, and under pvt. teachers of Bible, Talmud and languages; later in gymnasium of Posen, and 1852-55, at U. of Berlin; grad. U. of Halle; Litt.D., U. of Pa.; m. Bertha Wolfsohn, May 16, 1857. Jewish clergyman in Warsaw, 1857-63, Worms, 1864-66, Philadelphia, 1866—. Author: Kazania (Polish), 1862; Die Lage der Juden in Polen (anonymous), 1858; Die Vorläufer der Polnischen Revolution (anonymous), 1864; Abodath J'srael (prayer book) English edition, 1873; Dictionary of the Targumim and the Talmud Babli and Yerushalmi (16 parts), 1886-1902. Home: Philadelphia, Pa. Died 1903.

JASTROW, Morris, Jr., univ. prof.; b. in Europe, Aug. 13, 1861; s. Rev. Marcus and Bertha (Wolfsohn) J.; A.B., U. of Pa., 1881; Ph.D., U. of Leipzig, 1884; also studied in Germany and France; (LL.D., 1914); m. Helen Bachman, Feb. 28, 1893. Prof. Semitic langs., U. of Pa. Recognized authority on Semitic religions, langs. and lits. Author: Religion of the Babylonians and Assyrians, 1898; two grammatical treatises of "Abu Zakariyya Hayyug," 1897; A Fragment of the Babylonian Dibbarra Epic, 1891; The Study of Religion, 1902; Die Religion Babyloniens und Assyriens, 1902-12 (3 vols.); Aspects of Religious Belief and Practice in Babylonia and Assyria, 1911; Hebrew and Babylonian Traditions, 1914; Babylonian-Assyrian Birth Omens and their Cultural Significance, 1914; The Civilization of Babylonia and Assyria, 1915; The War and the Bagdad Railway, 1917; The War and the Coming Peace, 1918; The Gentle Cynic, 1919; Zionism and the Future of Palestine, 1919. Editor: (with memoir) Selected Essays of James Darmesteter (translated by Helen Bachman Jastrow), 1895; series Handbooks on the History of Religion; Semitic dept., International Encyclopedia. Home: Philadelphia, Pa. Died June 22, 1921.

JAUREGUI, Guillermo Patterson y, ambassador; b. Havana, Cuba, May 20, 1868; s. Jacobo Patterson y Dolarea and Rita Maria y (Lamar) J.; LL.D., U. of Havana Law Sch.; m. Maria Bausa y Ruiz de Apodaca, Feb. 10, 1892 (dec.); children—Guillermo, Margarita (wife of Valentin Riva); m. 2d, Zoe Sofiano y Wainwright, Apr. 7, 1903 (dec.); children —Enrique, Zoe, Olga. Entered Cuban diplomatic service, 1902; consul at Liverpool, Eng., 1902-06; consul gen. in Great Britain, 1906-08; first sec. Cuban Legation, Spain, 1908-09; consul gen. in Germany, 1908-09; asst. sec. of State, Cuba, 1911-25; became E.E. and M.P. to Great Britain, 1925; ambassador of Cuba to U.S., Washington, D.C., 1934—. Died July 27, 1937.

JAY, John Clarkson; b. N.Y. City, Jan. 20, 1880; s. John Clarkson and Harriette Arnold (Vinton) J.; B.A., Williams Coll., 1901; m. Marguerite Soléliac, Apr. 20, 1903 (died 1937); children—Sarah Livingston (Mrs. Arthur M. R. Hughes), Marguerite Montgomery (wife of Rev. W. D. F. Hughes, she died 1934), Alice (Mrs. Vivian Wilshire Harcourt), John Clarkson. Began as apprentice, Pennsylvania Steel Co., 1901, v.p., 1912-15; chmn. bd. Maxwell Motor Car Co., 1915-16; chmn. bd. Republic Truck Co., 1916-19; pres. Pierce-Arrow Motor Car Co., 1920-21; partner J. W. Seligman & Co., bankers, N.Y. City, 1921-34; chmn. exec. com. Globe & Rutgers Fire Ins. Co., and affiliated cos., 1935-39; pres. 5th Av. Bank of New York, 5th Av. Bank Safe Deposit Vaults, Inc.; trustee Franklin Savings Bank. Republican. Episcopalian. Home: New York, N.Y. Died Jan. 22, 1941.

JAY, Lawrence Merton, banker; b. Sturgis, Mich., Apr. 15, 1878; s. Marion J. and Sarah (Blue) J.; A.B., U. of Chicago, 1899; m. Elizabeth Williams, Aug. 8, 1906; children—Muriel Millicent, Halford Howard, Rutledge Lawrence. Asst. statistician of Philippine Islands, 1901, deputy treas., 1902-03; European rep. of Nat. City Bank of New York, 1909-15; pres. Internat. Bank, N.Y. City, 1915; v.p. and treas. Internat. Banking Corp., 1915-26; retired, 1926. Republican. Episcopalian. Home: West Palm Beach, Fla. Died May 11, 1934.

JAY, Milton, surgeon; b. Dayton, O., May 10, 1833; s. Isaac and Rhoda J.; grad. Eclectic Med. Inst., Cincinnati, 1859, Rush Med. Coll., Chicago, 1895; m. Miss Webster, Apr. 17, 1861. Chief surgeon Chicago and Eastern Ill. R.R. Home: Chicago, Ill. Died 1905.

JAY, Peter Augustus, diplomat; b. Newport, R.I., Aug. 23, 1877; s. Augustus and Emily Astor (Kane) J.; student Eton Coll., Eng.; A.B., Harvard, 1900; m. Susan Alexander McCook, Mar. 16, 1909; children—Emily Kane, Susan Mary. Third sec. Am. Embassy at Paris, Oct. 1902-June 1903; 2d sec. Legation, June-Sept. 1903, sec. Sept. 1903-June 1906, sec. Embassy, June 1906-June 1907, at Constantinople; sec. Embassy at Tokyo, 1907-09; diplomatic agt. and consul-gen. at Cairo, Egypt, Dec. 1909-Dec. 1913; appointed sec. Am. Embassy at Rome, Italy, Dec. 1913, and counselor same; minister to Salvador, 1920, to Roumania, 1921-25; ambassador to Argentina, 1925-27, resigned; apptd. Am. mem. Permanent Internat. Commn. established under Treaty of Sept. 15, 1914, between U.S. and Spain, 1928. Episcopalian. Home: Washington, D.C. Died Oct. 18, 1933.

JAY, William, lawyer; b. New York, Feb. 12, 1841; s. John and Eleanor (Field) J.; A.B., Columbia, 1859, A.M., 1863, LL.B., 1867; m. Lucy Oelrichs, June 12, 1878. Served as capt., gen. staff, U.S.V. in Civil War; bvtd. maj., Aug. 1, 1864, "for faithful and meritorious service in the field," and lt. col. vols., Apr. 9, 1865, "for gallant and meritorious services during operations resulting in fall of Richmond and surrender of Gen. Lee"; resigned, Mar. 29, 1865. Practiced in New York, 1869—; mem. firm of Jay & Chandler; pres. New York Herald Co., Valley Farms Co.; dir. Commercial Cable Co., Manhattan Storage & Warehouse Co., New York Mortgage & Security Co. Atty. Trinity Corp. and sr. warden and clerk, Trinity Ch. Home: Bedford House, nr. Katonah, N.Y. Died Mar. 28, 1915.

JAYCOX, Walter Husted, judge; b. Wassaic, N.Y., Sept. 3, 1863; s. Lorin R. and Hannah A. (Darling) J.; common sch. edn.; admitted to bar, 1889; m. Inez Leaming, Dec. 3, 1890. Dist. atty., 1893-99, county judge, 1902-06, Suffolk County, N.Y.; justice Supreme Ct. of N.Y., 2d Dist., 1906-34. Republican. Home: Patchogue, N.Y. Died Feb. 3, 1927.

JAYNE, Caroline Furness, author; b. Wallingford, Pa., July 3, 1873; d. Horace Howard and Helen Kate (Rogers) Furness, ed. Agnes Irwin's Sch., Phila.; m. Dr. Horace Jayne, Oct. 10, 1894. Author: String Figures: A Study of Cats-Cradle in Many Lands, 1906. Home: Philadelphia, Pa. Died 1909.

JAYNE, Henry LaBarre, lawyer; b. Phila., Nov. 3, 1857; s. David and Hannah (Fort) Jayne; A.B., U. of Pa., 1879; studied law in offices of George W. Biddle; admitted to Phila. bar, 1881, Supreme Ct. of U.S., 1896; studied polit. economy and civ. law, Leipzig, 1882-83; m. Elizabeth Matthews, May 23, 1893. In 1884 formed a partnership with Arthur Biddle, merging, in 1891, into firm of Biddle & Ward, Phila. and New York; later Biddle, Paul & Jayne. Has devoted much time to politics as a reformer; pres. Am. Soc. for Extension of Univ. Teaching; treas. Am. Philos. Soc.; dir. Pa. Inst. for the Deaf and Dumb, Edwin Forrest Home for Actors and Actresses, Presser Home for Retired Music Teachers. Home: Philadelphia, Pa. Died May 10, 1920.

JAYNE, Horace, univ. dean; b. Phila., Mar. 5, 1859; s. David and Hannah (Fort) J.; A.B., U. of Pa., 1879, M.D., 1882; studied biology, U. of Leipzig and at Jena, 1882-83, Johns Hopkins, 1883-84; hon. Ph.D., Franklin and Marshall Coll., 1893; m. Caroline Furness, Oct. 10, 1894 (died 1909). Asst. instr. biology, 1883-84, prof. vertebrate morphology, 1884-94, prof. zoölogy and dir., 1894-1905, Wistar Inst. of Anatomy; sec. biol. faculty, 1884-89, dean coll. faculty, 1889-94, U. of Pa. Author: Mammalian Anatomy; Revision of the Dermestidæ of North America; Abnormities Observed in North American Coleoptera; etc. Address: Wallingford, Pa. Died July 8, 1913.

JAYNE, Joseph Lee, naval officer; b. Brandon, Miss., May 30, 1863; s. William McAfee and Julia Hamilton (Kennon) J.; grad. U.S. Naval Acad., 1882; studied Johns Hopkins, 1885-88 (certificate in applied electricity for which awarded B. Engring. degree, 1927); courses Torpedo Station and Naval War Coll.; m. Elizabeth Tilton Eastman, Dec. 5, 1894; children—John Kennon, Anna Morwell. Ensign, July 1, 1884; promoted, through grades to rear adm., Oct. 15, 1917; retired May 1921. Comd. Torpedo boat Rodgers during Spanish-Am. War, blockade duty, Cuban coast; comd. various vessels, including armored cruisers Colorado and New York; has served as mem. Naval and Inter-Departmental Wireless Telegraph bds. and sec. Gen. Bd. of Navy; supt. Naval Obs., Oct. 16, 1911-14; comd. U.S.S. New Jersey and U.S.S. Mississippi, 1914-17; comd. Naval Air Sta., Pensacola, Fla., Apr.-Oct. 29, 1917; comd. Mississippi to Jan. 31, 1918; comd. div. 3, Battleship Force 1, Atlantic Fleet, Feb. 1-Sept. 13, 1918; comdt. 12th Naval Dist., 1918-20; comdr. Train Pacific Fleet, 1920-21. Methodist. Home: Newton, Miss. Died Nov. 24, 1928.

JAYNE, Walter Addison, surgeon; b. Orange, N.J., Dec. 4, 1853; s. Alfred Addison and Eleanor (Fordyce) J.; M.D., Coll. Phys. & Surg. (Columbia), 1875; unmarried. Began practice, New York; removed to Colo., 1883; prof. gynecol. and abdominal surgery, med. dept. U. of Colo., 1895-97, 1910-17; prof., trustee former Denver and Gross Coll. of Medicine, 1897-1910. Commd. maj., Med. R.C., 1917, lt. col. M.C., 1918. Author: The Healing Gods of Ancient Civilizations. Home: Denver, Colo. Died Aug. 29, 1929.

JAYNES, Allan Brown; b. Delaware, O., Dec. 4, 1879; s. Willis Clark and Adelaide (Brown) J.; B.Ph., Ohio State U., 1900; m. Kathryn Moore Feighan, May 11, 1904. Sec. Tucson Chamber of Commerce, 1902-05; pub. Tucson Post, 1902-06; clk. U.S. Dist. Court, 1st Dist., Ty. of Ariz., 1906-12; admitted to bar, 1912; Clk. U.S. Dist. Court, State of Ariz., 1912-13; mem. Rep. Nat. Com., 1916-20. Pub. Tucson Citizen. Home: Tucson, Ariz. Died Nov. 7, 1920.

JEFFERIS, William W., banker; b. West Chester, Pa., Jan. 12, 1820; s. Horatio Townsend and Hannah (Paul) J.; common sch. edn., West Chester; m. Anna E. Elmore, Dec. 14, 1898. Entered Bank of Chester County (Pa.) Dec. 1843, as receiving teller; cashier same Sept. 1857, to June 1883, when he resigned. Always a student of mineralogy; sold collection of over 12,000 fine specimens to Carnegie Mus., Pittsburgh. Emeritus prof. mineralogy, State Normal Sch., W. Chester, Pa., 1878—. Address: New York, N.Y. Died 1906.

JEFFERS, Eliakim Tupper, college pres.; b. in Novia Scotia, Apr. 6, 1841; s. James Dickey and Mary A. B. (Tupper) J.; A.B., Jefferson Coll., 1862; grad. Princeton Theol. Sem., 1865; studied U.P. Theol. Sem., Allegheny, Pa., 1 yr.; D.D., 1872, LL.D., 1902, Washington and Jefferson Coll.; LL.D., Westminster Coll. (Pa.) 1911; m. Esther Graham Hodgens, May 14, 1867. Ordained United Presbyn. ministry, Sept. 25, 1865; pastor U.P. Ch., Oxford, 1865-72; pres. Westminster Coll., Pa., 1872-83; prof. theology, Lincoln U., 1883-90; pastor First Presbyn. Ch., Oil City, 1900-03; pres. York Collegiate Inst., 1893—. Moderator U.P. Assembly, 1880; pres. Pa. State Teachers' Assn., 1895; mem. Victoria Inst., London. Author: Shortest Road to Cæsar, 1896. Address: York, Pa. Died Nov. 18, 1915.

JEFFERS, LeRoy, librarian, author, lecturer; b. Ipswich, Mass., Aug. 1878; s. Charles P. and Elizabeth B. (Stalker) J.; m. R. E. Miller, 1918. Mgr. for the Booklovers Libraries, 1901-04; mgr. Book Order Office, New York Pub. Library, for its system of 52 branches, 1905—; also in main reading room for evening service, 1906-14; visited European libraries, 1908. Mem. New York Library Club. Published various bibliographies through the A.L.A. and the New York Pub. Library. Lecturer on The Natural Wonders of U.S., Canada and Mexico; on mountaineering in N. America, etc. Organizer, 1916, and sec. Associated Mountaineering Clubs of N. America, comprising 65 clubs and socs. active in creation, development and protection of nat. parks and forests; mem. Council on Nat. Parks, Forest and Wild Life; gen. council Nat. Conf. on Outdoor Recreation; librarian Am. Alpine Club; fellow Royal Geog. Soc., London. Editor F. S. Van Eps, Your Right to be Happy, 1922, and other works. Author: The Call of the Mountains, 1922. Home: New York, N.Y. Died July 25, 1926.

JEFFERS, William Hamilton, theologian; b. Cadiz, O., May 1, 1838; s. Joseph and Barbara (Moore) J.; A.B., Geneva Coll., Beaver Falls, Pa.,

1855; studied Xenia Theol. Sem., completing course, 1859; D.D., Western Reserve, 1873; LL.D., U. of Wooster, 1882; m. Maria L. Robinson, July 1, 1868; m. 2d, Anna R. Tuttle, Apr. 12, 1885. Ordained Presbyn. ministry, 1862; pastor U.P. chs., Northwood and Bellefontaine, O., 1862-65; prof. Latin and Hebrew, Westminster Coll., Pa., 1865-69; studied in Egypt, Syria and Greece, 1869-70; prof. Greek lang. and lit. U. of Wooster, 1870-75; pastor Euclid Av. Ch., Cleveland, 1875-77; prof. hist. theology, Western Theol. Sem., 1877-1903, prof. emeritus and lecturer on ecclesiastical history, 1903—. Home: Pasadena, Calif. Died Dec. 20, 1914.

JEFFERSON, Charles Edward, clergyman; b. Cambridge, O., Aug. 29, 1860; s. Dr. Milton and Ella (Sarchett) J.; B.S., Ohio Wesleyan, 1882, A.B., 1886; supt. pub. schs., Worthington, O., 1882-84; S.T.B., Boston U., 1887; D.D., Oberlin Coll., 1898, Union Coll., 1898, Yale, 1903; LL.D., Ohio Wesleyan U., 1905, Miami U., 1923; D.D., U. of Vt., 1921; m. Belle Patterson, Aug. 10, 1887; children—Charles Frederic, Ralph Waldo (dec.). Ordained Congl. ministry, 1887; pastor Central Ch., Chelsea, Mass., 1887-98, Broadway Tabernacle, New York, 1898—. Fellow Yale Corp., 1902-24. Author: Quiet Hints to Growing Preachers in My Study, 1891; Quiet Talks with Earnest People in My Study, 1898; Things Fundamental, 1903; The Minister as Prophet, 1905; The Character of Jesus, 1908; The Building of the Church, 1910; Why We May Believe in Life After Death, 1911; The Minister as Shepherd, 1912; Forefathers' Day Sermons, 1917; Old Truths and New Facts, 1918; Quiet Talks with the Family; Under Twenty, 1922; The Friendship Indispensable, 1923; The Character of Paul, 1923; Five Present-day Controversies, 1924; Cardinal Ideas of Isaiah, 1925; Cardinal Ideas of Jeremiah, 1928; Christianizing a Nation, 1929; Other Nature Sermons, 1931; Like a Trumpet, 1934; also other books now out of print. Home: New York, N.Y. Died Sept. 12, 1937.

JEFFERSON, John Percival, mfr.; b. New Castle County, Del., Mar. 11, 1852; s. John and Sarah (Ware) J.; grad. U.S. Mil. Acad., 1875; assigned 2d lt. 5th Arty.; grad. U.S. Artillery School, 1878; m. Alice M. Wetmore, June 6, 1877; m. 2d, Mary C. Trunkey, Dec. 16, 1915. Garrison duty, Atlantic Coast, 1875-79; head of mil. dept. (by assignment War Dept.), Brooks' Sch., Cleveland, 1879-80; resigned 1881. Became mem. firm Struthers, Wells & Co., 1881, mng. partner, 1886-1902; pres. Struthers-Wells Co., mfrs. of gas and steam engines, boilers, etc., 1902—; was identified with one of first orgns. for transporting natural gas, 1882; investor in timber, 1884—; v.p. Redondo Development Co., also lumber and timber cos. in Ore., N.M., N.C., Wash. and Pa. Republican. Presbyn. Home: Warren, Pa.; and Santa Barbara, Calif. Died Sept. 2, 1934.

JEFFERSON, Joseph, actor; b. Phila., Feb. 20, 1829; s. Joseph J.; ed. at home (M.A., Yale, M.A., Harvard); m. Margaret Lockyer, 1848 (dec.); m. 2d, Sarah Warren, 1867. First appearance on stage as the child in "Pizarro." In 1843, after his father's death, joined party of strolling players who played through Tex., and followed U.S. army into Mex. Played in minor theatres and later in better companies and became known as a good stock actor. First became prominent as Asa Trenchard in "Our American Cousin," beginning Oct. 18, 1858, at Laura Keene's Theatre, New York, and continuing 150 consecutive nights. Later notable parts have been Newman Noggs in "Nicholas Nickleby;" Caleb Plummer in "Cricket on the Hearth," Dr. Pangloss in "The Heir at Law," Bob Acres in "The Rivals," Dr. Ollapod in the "Poor Gentleman," and especially Rip Van Winkle, which he has played in every important city in the United States. Has played in England and Australia. Painter; several of his paintings have attracted much attention. Author: Autobiography of Joseph Jefferson; Reply to Ignatius Donnelly on the Shakespeare-Bacon Argument. Home: Buzzard's Bay, Mass. Died 1905.

JEFFERSON, Joseph, actor; b. New York, July 6, 1869; s. Joseph and Sarah A. (Warren) J.; ed. Columbia Grammar Sch., Challier Inst., New York, English Grammar Sch., London, Upson Sem., Conn.; m. Blanche Bender, June 13, 1891. First appearance on stage, Denver, 1885, with his father as supernumerary, in "Rip Van Winkle"; played Sir Lucius O'Trigger, in "The Rivals," Jim Farren, in "Shadows of a Great City," Chambers, in "Pudd'n Head Wilson," Beverly Clay, in "Playing the Game"; played in vaudeville in "In 1999," by Wm. C. de Mille, 1912-13; in "Poor Old Jim," by Wm. C. de Mille, 1913-14. Mason. Home: Buzzards Bay, Mass. Died May 1, 1919.

JEFFERSON, Samuel Mitchell, univ. prof.; b. Kent County, Del., July 28, 1849; s. John Warren and Elizabeth (Lynch) J.; A.B., Ind U., 1874; traveled in Europe, summers, 1882, 1885; A.M., Bethany Coll., W.Va., 1891, LL.D., 1896; grad. student philosophy, Columbia, 1903; m. Julia M. Barclay, 1888; m. 2d, Annie M. Waterman, 1891. Ordained to ministry Disciples of Christ, 1869; prof. N.T. Greek and Bibl. lit., Bethany Coll., 1893-96; dean Berkeley Bible Sem., 1896-1900; prof. philosophy, Transylvania U., 1900—. Public speaker, lecturer. Home: Lexington, Ky. Died Feb. 20, 1914.

JEFFERY, Edward Turner, ry. official; b. Liverpool, Eng., Apr. 6, 1843; s. William S. and Jane (McMillan) J.; came to U.S., 1850; m. Virginia Osborne Clarke, 1877. Entered service of I.C. R.R. Co., 1856, became its gen. supt., 1877-85, gen. mgr., 1885-89; resigned. Commr. to Paris Expn., 1889, on behalf of the Exec. Com. of the citizens of Chicago, for the purpose of studying and reporting upon the expn.; chmn. grounds and bldgs. com., Chicago Expn., until Sept. 1891. Pres. 1891-1912 (gen. mgr., 1891-1900), and later chmn. bd. dirs. D.&R.G. R.R. Co.; receiver, 1893-95, later pres., Rio Grande Southern R.R. Co.; dir. First Nat. Bank of Chicago, First Trust & Savings Bank of Chicago, Nat. Safety Deposit Co. of Chicago, Manhattan Ry. Co., Pleasant Valley Coal Co., Rio Grande Junction Ry. Co., trustee Equitable Trust Co. of N.Y. Home: Chicago, Ill. Died Sept. 24, 1927.

JEFFERY, Elmore Berry, banker; b. Harford County, Md., Sept. 9, 1870; s. William Grafton and Elizabeth (Heith) J.; ed. high sch., Bel Air, Md.; m. Nellie Waters French, June 6, 1908; children—Eleanor Miller, Janet Bartram. Pres. Equitable Trust Co., 1921; pres. Md. Title Guarantee Co.; v.p. New Amsterdam Casualty Co.; dir. Mid-Continent Petroleum Co. Finance commr., Baltimore. Pres. bd. trustees Goucher Coll.; dir. Baltimore Y.M.C.A., Baltimore Assn. Commerce. Methodist. Home: Baltimore, Md. Died Apr. 1929.

JEFFERY, Robert Emmett; b. Mt. Olive, Ark., Jan. 30, 1875; ed. pub. schs. Admitted to Ark. bar, 1899; mem. Ark. Ho. of Rep., 1900; pros. atty. 3d Jud. Dist. of Ark., 1906-10; judge Circuit Court, same dist., 1910-15; E.E. and M.P. to Uruguay, 1915—. Died May 19, 1935.

JEFFRIES, Benjamin Joy, ophthalmic surgeon; b. Boston, Mass., Mar. 26, 1833; s. Dr. John and Ann Geyer (Amory) J.; A.B., Harvard, 1854, A.M., 1857, M.D., 1857; U. of Vienna, 1858-59; m. Marian Shimmin, Jan. 4, 1872. Specialist in diseases of the eye and skin, 1859—; spl. investigations in color-blindness. Ophthal. surgeon Mass. Charitable Eye and Ear Infirmary, 1866-1902; lecturer Harvard, 1869-71; consulting surgeon State Hosp., Tewksbury, Mass.; consulting ophthalmologist N.E. Hosp. for Women. Author: The Eye in Health and Disease, 1872; Color Blindness: Its Dangers and Its Detection, 1879. Address: Boston, Mass. Died Nov. 21, 1915.

JEFFRIES, Louis Eugene, lawyer; b. Uniontown, Ala., Feb. 14, 1868; s. John Miller and Emily Epps (Norris) J.; U. of Ala., 1884, 85; law dept. U. of Va., 1886-87; m. Virginia Caperton Hardie, June 24, 1891; children—Josephine (wife of Alfred A. Cunningham, U.S.M.C.), Virginia (Mrs. George G. Munce), Louis Eugene, Alexander Hardie. Admitted to Ala. bar, 1888, and practiced at Selma; later mem. firm Pettus & Jeffries; apptd. gen. atty. Southern Ry. Co., at Washington, D.C., 1912, gen. counsel, 1916, v.p. and gen. counsel, 1918—; also v.p. and gen. counsel C.,N.O.&T.P. Ry., Ala. Great Southern R.R., N.O. & Northeastern R.R., M.&O. R.R., Ga. Southern & Fla. Ry., Riggs Nat. Bank, Washington, etc. Democrat. Presbyn. Mason. Home: Washington, D.C. Died Jan. 6, 1932.

JEFFRIES, Millard Dudley, clergyman; b. Culpeper County, Va., Nov. 18, 1855; s. Thomas and Mary Mildred J.; ed. Bleak Hill Sem., Culpeper County, and Culpeper Male Acad.; M.D., U. of Va., 1875; B.D., Southern Bapt. Theol. Sem., 1881; m. Anna B. Newcomer, Nov. 30, 1881. Ordained Bapt. ministry, 1881; pastor successively Montgomery County, Va., Chapel Hill, N.C., East Ch., Louisville, and Broadway Ch., Knoxville, to 1903; pres. Carson and Newman Coll., 1903-11; pastor Edgefield, later Southside Ch., Spartanburg, S.C., until 1918, Bapt. Memorial Hosp., Memphis, Tenn., 1918—. Wrote brochures "Sanctification as Taught in the Scriptures," "Adventism or Millenarianism, Pre— and Post—"; also Questions on the Bible for Little Folks, and Primary Catechism on the Bible. Address: Memphis, Tenn. Died Dec. 24, 1936.

JEFFRIS, Malcolm George, lawyer; b. Janesville, Wis., Aug. 18, 1862; s. David and Grace (Mouat) J.; ed. by self-study after 12 yrs. of age; studied law in law offices; m. Nancy Roys, Jan. 22, 1885; children—Malcolm R., Helen (Mrs. Pierpont J. E. Wood), Rufus R. Admitted to bar, Aug. 18, 1883, and practiced at Janesville; also mfr. and banker, and connected with electric light and power cos., water works, lumber in Fla., La., Wash., and British Columbia. Prominent in fraternal ins. organizations; pres. Nat. Fraternal Conf.; pres. Nat. Union. Home: Janesville, Wis. Died Dec. 26, 1933.

JELKS, William Dorsey, governor; b. Russell County, Ala., Nov. 7, 1855; s. J. W. D. and Jane Goodrum (Frazer) J.; A.M., Mercer U., 1876; LL.D., U. of Ala., 1923, Mercer, 1924; m. Alice Keitt Shorter, June 7, 1883. Editor at Eufaula, Ala., for 20 yrs.; pres. Protective Life Ins. Co., Birmingham, Ala., 1907—. Was mem. Alabama Senate (pres., 1900); became gov. of Ala., on death of Gov. Samford, June 11, 1901; elected gov., term 1903-07; mem. Dem. Nat. Com., 1912-16. Home: Birmingham, Ala. Died Dec. 13, 1931.

JEMISON, Robert, Sr., banker, mcht.; b. Tuscaloosa, Ala., Sept. 12, 1853; s. William Henry and Elizabeth Ann (Patrick) J.; LL.B., U. of Ala., 1874, LL.D., 1906; m. Eugenia R. Sorsby, Oct. 25, 1876; 1 son, Robert. Began as merchant, Tuscaloosa, Ala., 1870; removed to Birmingham, 1884, and became mng. officer st. ry., gas and lighting cos., retiring after 21 yrs., in 1907; pres. Central Mortgage & Trust Co.; v.p. Allen & Jemison Co., Tuscaloosa Ice & Light Co.; dir., exec. com. 1st Nat. Bank, Birmingham Ry., Light & Power Co. Trustee Y.M.C.A., Bishop Wilmer Ch. Home for Orphans. Episcopalian. Home: Birmingham, Ala. Died Sept. 16, 1927.

JENKINS, Arthur, publisher; b. Buffalo, N.Y., July 23, 1851; ed. common schools, Milwaukee, Wis., to 1865; became a printer and worked at various places in Wis., Ill., Ohio and Pa.; m. Emma Hogan, June 11, 1874. Settled in Syracuse, 1871; established Syracuse Herald, Jan. 15, 1877; June 3, 1878, the Syracuse Herald Co. was organized, he becoming its pres. Pres. Syracuse & Suburban R.R. Co. Home: Syracuse, N.Y. Died 1903.

JENKINS, Charles Francis, physicist, inventor; b. nr. Dayton, O., Aug. 22, 1867; s. Amasa Milton and Mary Ann (Thomas) J.; prep. edn., high sch., Fountain City, Ind., and Spiceland (Ind.) Acad.; student Earlham Coll.; spl. lectures, Johns Hopkins; Sc.D., Earlham Coll., Richmond, Ind., 1928; m. Grace Love, Jan. 30, 1902. Inventor of projecting machine for motion picture theatres, spiral-wound paraffin paper box; granted 400 patents, foreign and domestic, on inventions in radio-photography, television, radio-movies; pres., Jenkins Laboratories; research v.p. Jenkins Television Corp.; dir. Park Savings Bank, Federal-Am. Bank & Trust Co. Medalist, Franklin Inst. and City of Philadelphia. Quaker. Author: Picture Ribbons, 1896; Animated Pictures, 1898; Motion Picture Handbook, 1908; Vision by Radio, Radio Photographs, 1925; Visual Radio and Television, 1928. Home: Washington, D.C. Died June 6, 1934.

JENKINS, Daniel Edwards, theologian; b. Flintshire, N. Wales, Dec. 13, 1866; s. John M. and Jennie E. J.; came with parents to U.S.; U. of Wooster, 1882-85; went to Australia; grad. Melbourne U., 1889, A.M., 1890; student Ormond Div. Hall, Melbourne, 1889, Princeton Theol. Sem., 1890; Ph.D., Washington and Jefferson Coll., 1898; D.D., U. of Pittsburgh, 1906; m. Annie Finley, June 15, 1892; children—Finley Dubois, Lucille Edwards (dec.), John Laurie, Annie B., William Robert, Daniel Edwards. Ordained Presbyterian ministry, 1891; pastor, New London, Pa., 1891-96; pres. and Armstrong prof. mental and moral sciences, Parsons Coll., Fairfield, Ia., 1896-1900; prof. didactic and polemic theology, Presbyn. Theol. Sem., Omaha, Neb., 1900—; also pres. U. of Omaha, 1909—. Stone lecturer at Princeton Theol. Sem., 1905-06. Mem. Nat. Council of Nat. Econ. League; pres. Neb. Assn. for Charities and Correction, 1911-12; del. Congress of Am. Prison Assn., Omaha, 1911; mem. spl. vice commn. apptd. by gov. of Neb., 1915. Address: Omaha, Neb. Died Nov. 24, 1927.

JENKINS, E(dmund), Fellows; b. Weedsport, N.Y., July 28, 1844; s. John Stillwell and Minerva Porter (Fellows) J.; ed. Mt. Vernon Boarding Sch. (prep. to Hamilton Coll.), but did not enter coll., owing to father's death; served pvt. to 1st lt. in Civ. War, Apr. 19, 1861-June 8, 1865; m. Adelaide M. Montgomery, July 11, 1889. Sec. and supt. New York Soc. for Prevention of Cruelty to Children from its organization, Dec. 28, 1874-Dec. 1909, resigned. Aided in organizing socs. for prevention of cruelty to children in Eng., Scotland, Ireland, Germany, France, Austria, Hungary, Switzerland, Italy, etc. Address: New York, N.Y. Died May 16, 1923.

JENKINS, Edward Hopkins, chemist; b. Falmouth, Mass., May 31, 1850; s. John and Chloe (Thompson) J.; A.B., Yale, 1872, spl. studies in chemistry, 1872-75; U. of Leipzig, 1875-76; Ph.D., Yale, 1879; m. Elizabeth Elliot Foote, June 18, 1885. Chemist, 1877-1900, vice dir., 1882-1900, dir., 1900-23, treas., 1901-23, Conn. Agrl. Expt. Station. Chmn. State Sewage Commn., 1897-1903. Author of Connecticut Agriculture in History of Connecticut. Home: New Haven, Conn. Died Nov. 7, 1931.

JENKINS, Frederick Warren; b. Bradford, Mass., Jan. 22, 1878; s. Benjamin Albert and Sarah Kate (Poor) J.; A.B., Dartmouth, 1900; m. Mabel Lant Chamberlain, Oct. 22, 1907. Reference librarian, Dartmouth Coll., 1900-05; dir. library dept. Charles Scribner's Sons, 1905-11; librarian Russell Sage Foundation, 1911-27, and dir. publs. 1917-27; organized a library on social problems and inaugurated a series of social bibliographies. Organized ednl. work at Naval Air Sta., Pensacola, Fla., 1918, and later served as editor Statistical News of War Industries Bd. Republican. Episcopalian. Collaborated with E. M. Rushmore in preparation of Social Workers Guide to Serial Publs., 1921. Home: Mt. Vernon, N.Y. Died Apr. 12, 1940.

JENKINS, George Franklin, physician; b. Clark County, Mo., July 15, 1842; s. Robert and Elizabeth (Rambo) J.; M.D., Mo. Med. Coll., St. Louis, 1867; hon. A.M., Parsons Coll., Ia., 1884. In practice at Keokuk, Ia., 1867—; prof. diseases of children, 1879-82, principles and practices of medicine and clin. medicine, 1882-90, pres. of faculty, 1885-90, Coll. Phys. and Surg., Keokuk; one of organizers, Keokuk Coll., 1890, pres. annd prof. principles and practice of medicine, and clin. medicine and physical diagnosis, 1890—; chief med. staff St. Joseph's Hosp. Address: Keokuk, Ia. Died Sept. 4, 1914.

JENKINS, Hermon Dutilh, clergyman; b. Columbus, O., Jan. 14, 1842; s. Rev. Warren and Marion (Dutilh) J.; A.B., Hamilton Coll., 1864; B.D., Union Theol. Sem., New York, 1867; D.D., Beloit, 1881; m. Harriet Newell Burrill, Oct. 29, 1868; 1 son, Paul Burrill J. Ordained Presbyn. ministry, 1868; pastor Central Ch., Joliet, Ill., 1868-73, 1st Ch., Freeport, Ill., 1873-89, 1st Ch., Sioux City, Ia., 1889-95, 2d Ch., Kansas City, Mo., 1895-1900, Riverside, Ill., 1900-13; editor Great Lakes Presbyn., Chicago, 1913—. Served in 35th Pa. Vol. Militia during Gettysburg campaign, summer of 1863. Republican. Author (by apptmt. Gen. Assembly Presbyn. Ch. U.S.A.); Presbyterianism, 1893. Editorial writer, The Interior, 1892-1910, The Great Lakes, 1913-15, The Advance, 1916—. Home: Evanston, Ill. Died Oct. 31, 1918.

JENKINS, Howard Malcolm, editor Friends' Intelligencer, 1885—; b. Gwynedd, Pa., March 30, 1842; s. Algernon S. and Anna Maria (Thomas) J.; ed. at public and select schools, and Friends' Boarding School, Gwynedd, Pa.; m. Mary Anna Atkinson, Mar. 16, 1865. Editor Norristown (Pa.) Republican, 1862-64; Norristown Herald and Republican, 1864-66; Wilmington, Del., Daily Commercial, 1866-77; and The American, Phila., 1881-91; formerly Republican, now Independent. Author: Historical Collections Relating to Gwynedd, 1884, 1897; vol. 1, Memorial History of Philadelphia, 1895; The Family of William Penn, 1899; Genealogical Sketch of the Descendants of Samuel Spencer, 1900. Home: Gwynedd, Pa. Died 1902.

JENKINS, James Graham, judge; b. Saratoga Springs, N.Y., 1834; s. Edgar and Mary E. (Walworth) J.; received liberal edn. in N.Y.; LL.D., U. of Wis., 1893, Wabash Coll., Ind., 1897; m. Mary, d. Hon. Andrew G. Miller, 1st U.S. dist. judge for the Dist. of Wis., Feb. 16, 1870. Admitted to N.Y. bar, 1855; removed, 1857, to Milwaukee, practicing there until 1888; city atty. Milwaukee, 4 yrs.; defeated on Dem. ticket for gov. of Wis., 1879; received Dem. vote in Legislature for U.S. senator, 1881; declined appmt. as asso. justice Supreme Ct. of D.C., 1885; U.S. dist. judge, Dist. of Wis., 1888-93; U.S. circuit judge 7th Circuit, 1893-1905; presiding judge U.S. Circuit Ct. of Appeals, 7th Circuit, 1901-05, retired 1905; several yrs. dean Coll. of Law, Marquette U., Milwaukee. One of his noteworthy official acts was his injunction, issued in Dec. 1893, forbidding employes of N.P. Ry. (then under management of receivers apptd. by the ct.) from combining or conspiring together, or with others, to strike against a reduction of their wages; this injunction, somewhat modified in form, was sustained by the Circuit Ct. of Appeals, but the dissatisfied labor leaders took steps looking to the impeachment of Judge Jenkins, of which, however, nothing ever came. Address: Milwaukee, Wis. Died Aug. 6, 1921.

JENKINS, John J., congressman; b. Weymouth, Eng., Aug. 20, 1843; settled in Baraboo, Wis., June 1852; common sch. edn. Served during Civil War in Co. A, 6th Wis. Vols.; admitted to bar, and practiced at Baraboo and Chippewa Falls, Wis. Was clerk Circuit Ct., Baraboo; city atty., Chippewa Falls; mem. Wis. Assembly; county judge; U.S. dist. atty., Wyo. Ty., 1876-80; mem. 54th to 60th Congresses (1895-1909). Republican. Address: Chippewa Falls, Wis. Died 1911.

JENKINS, MacGregor, author; b. Amherst, Mass., Apr. 14, 1869; s. Johnathan Leavitt and Sarah Maria (Eaton) J.; grad. Williams Coll., 1890, L.H.D., 1927; m. Alice Boorum Duncan, June 2, 1904; children—Julia Duncan, Sarah Eaton. With Houghton, Mifflin Co., publishers, Boston, Mass., 1890-1908; one of organizers, 1908, treas. and pub. until 1928, The Atlantic Monthly Co. Congregationalist. Author: The Reading Public, 1914; Literature With a Large L, 1919; Bucolic Beatitudes, 1925; Puttering Around, 1927; Shriner Watson, The Autobiography of a Boy, 1929; The Last Cruise of the Panther, 1929; Emily Dickinson, Friend and Neighbor, 1930; Emily (a novel), 1930; Sons of Ephraim, The Spirit of Williams College, 1934; Emily Dickinson, 1939. Home: Williamstown, Mass. Died Mar. 6, 1940.

JENKINS, Michael, banker. Pres. Safe Deposit & Trust Co.; chmn. bd. Merchants & Miners Transportation Co.; one of chief owners of Atlantic Coast Line R.R.; trustee and treas. Catholic U. of America; treas. trustees Peabody Inst., Baltimore; m. Mary Isabel Jenkins, Oct. 2, 1866 (died Mar. 5, 1911). Together with Andrew Carnegie donated site and bldg. for Md. Inst. to cost about $1,000,000. Knighted by Pope Pius X. Home: Baltimore, Md. Died Sept. 7, 1915.

JENKINS, Oliver Peebles, college prof.; b. Bantam, O., Nov. 3, 1850; s. George P. (D.D.) and Caroline M. (Hitch) J.; A.B., Moores Hill Coll., 1869, A.M., 1872, LL.D., 1916; M.S., Ind. U., 1886, Ph.D., 1889; supt. schs., prin. high sch., etc., Ind., Wis., Calif., 1870-76; grad. student Northwestern U., 2 yrs.; grad. student Johns Hopkins, 1882-83; m. Lizzie R. Hester, 1878; children—Mrs. Alice M. Weymouth, Hubert Oliver, Olaf Pitt. Prof. natural science Moores Hill Coll., 1876-82, Ind. State Normal Sch., 1883-86; prof. biology, DePauw U., 1886-91; prof. physiology and histology, Leland Stanford U., 1891-1916, emeritus. Dir. (with C. H. Gilbert) Stanford Marine Lab., 1892-1916. Author of Indiana State Series of text-books on physiology. Home: Stanford University, Calif. Died Jan. 9, 1935.

JENKINS, Paul Burrill, clergyman, writer; b. Joliet, Ill., Aug. 25, 1872; s. Hermon Dutilh and Harriet Newell (Burrill) J.; A.B., Princeton U., 1894, A.M., 1907; grad. Princeton Theol. Sem., 1897; D.D., Carroll Coll., Wis., 1907; m. Gertrude M. Halbert, Nov. 23, 1897; 1 son, Halbert Dutilh. Ordained Presbyn. ministry, 1897; asst., Vermilye Chapel, New York, 1897; pastor, Linwood Ch., Kansas City, Mo., 1897-1907, Immanuel Ch., Milwaukee, 1907-23. Mem. standing com. V. and S. Gen. Assembly Presbyn. Ch. U.S.A., 1912-23; del. World's Presbyn. Council, Edinburgh, 1913; mem. Presbyn. Nat. Service Com. and Social Service Commn. Gen. Assembly Presbyn. Ch. U.S.A., 1917. Sergt. Co. L, 9th Training Regt., Plattsburg, N.Y., Aug. 1916; chaplain U.S. Base Hosp. 22 and 2d U.S. Arty. Aerial Observn. Sch., A.E.F., 1917-18; attached U.S. Evac. Hosp. 41, St. Mihiel campaign; chaplain (capt.) Hdqrs., 101 Div., O.R.C., U.S.A., 1924-34; chaplain Northwestern Mil. and Naval Acad., Lake Geneva, Wis., 1933—. Historian of Geneva Lake Centennial, 1931; mem. outdoors advisory staff, Milwaukee Journal. Author: The Battle of Westport, 1906; The Book of Lake Geneva, 1922; History and Indian Remains of Lake Geneva, Wis., 1930. Co-author: Church Advertising, 1917. Contbr. on travel and nature subjects. Asst. editor Outdoor Recreation, 1915-27; editor catalog Nunnemacher Firearms Collection, Milwaukee Pub. Museum (3,000 specimens), 1927, advisor on arms, same, 1927—. Adopted into Wis. Pottawatomi Indian tribe, 1927. Lecturer, "Book-Talks," Lake Geneva, Wis., Pinehurst and Southern Pines, N.C., and Milwaukee, 1924—. Home: Williams Bay, Wis. Died Aug. 4, 1936.

JENKINS, Robert Edwin, lawyer; b. Clark County, Mo., Feb. 6, 1846; s. Robert and Elizabeth (Rambo) J.; ed. at St. Francisville, Mo., and at Ill. Coll.; grad. Union Coll. of Law, Chicago, 1867; m. Marcia Raymond, Chicago, Sept. 2, 1869. Admitted to Ill. bar, 1867; was assignee in bankruptcy under law of 1867 in over 1,200 cases; has been pres. Law Inst., and several yrs. treas. Chicago Bar Assn.; was chmn. of commn. which drew present jury commission law, and secured its passage through legislature; was mem. "reform" bd. of Cook County Commrs., 1888, and chmn. of its finance com.; for many yrs. v.p. Citizens Assn.; v.p. Chicago City Missionary Soc.; supt. for 10 yrs. of Sunday Sch. of Union Park Congl. Ch., and for 8 yrs. of that of South Congl. Ch., Chicago. Home: Chicago, Ill. Died 1907.

JENKINS, Stephen, author; b. Mt. Vernon, N.Y., June 25, 1857; s. William Leavitt and Janet Gunn (Raeburn) J.; grad. U.S. Naval Acad., 1876; spl. courses, New York U. and Columbia; m. Eva Florence Gowen, Sept. 6, 1880. Served in U.S. Navy, 1876-80, resigned; teacher, 1889—; lecturer, 1894—. Served as lt. and exec. officer collier Abarenda during Spanish-Am. War. Democrat. Episcopalian. Author: A Princess and Another, 1907; The Greatest Street in the World, 1911; Story of the Bronx, 1912; Old Boston Post Road, 1913. Home: Mt. Vernon, N.Y. Died Oct. 10, 1913.

JENKINS, Thomas Atkinson, univ. prof.; b. Wilmington, Del., May 24, 1868; s. Howard M. and Mary Anna (Atkinson) J.; A.B., Swarthmore Coll., 1887; Ph.B., U. of Pa., 1888; Ph.D., Johns Hopkins U., 1894; Litt.D., Swarthmore Coll., 1924; m. Marian Magill, June 19, 1894; children—Beatrice M. (dec.), Edward Magill, Francis Arthur, Wilmer Atkinson. Instr. and adj. prof. Romance langs., Vanderbilt U., 1895-1900; prof. French, Swarthmore, 1900-01; with U. of Chicago, 1901-33, prof. history of French lang., 1911-33, emeritus. Mem. editorial bd. Modern Philology. Home: Chicago, Ill. Died Mar. 23, 1935.

JENKINS, William Dunbar, civil engr.; b. Adams County, Miss.; ed. mil. schs., France and Belgium; studied civ. engring., Lexington, Va., 1870-72, engaged in practice. Has done some important bridge work, including Randolph bridge over Mo. River at Kansas City, Mo., etc.; work on Miss. levees; chief engr. of railroads in South and Southwest; chief engr. Aransas Pass harbor and jetty works, Tex.; maj. vol. engrs., and chief engr. officer, 1st Div. 2d Army Corps, 1898-99; chief engr. Chattanooga Station Co. Address: Chattanooga, Tenn. Died Mar. 12, 1914.

JENKINS, William M., governor; b. Alliance, O., Apr. 25, 1856; s. William and Lydia (Miller) J.; attended Mt. Union Coll., Alliance, O., 1875-77; m. Delphina White, Dec. 31, 1878. Taught sch., Stark County, O., 1876-78; removed Shelby County, Ia., 1880; admitted to bar, 1883; removed to Arkansas City, Kan., 1884; del. Rep. Nat. Conv., 1888; apptd. spl. allotting agt. by President Harrison; allotted Siletz Indians in Ore. and Pawnees in Okla.; removed to Okla., 1893; sec. Okla. Ty., 1897-1901; gov. May to Nov. 1901; in law practice at Sapulpa, Okla., 1908-11, Guthrie, 1911—. Address: Guthrie, Okla. Died Oct. 19, 1941.

JENKINSON, Isaac, lawyer, editor; b. Piqua, O., Apr. 29, 1825; s. John and Isabel (Knox) J.; pvt. edn.; m. Narcissa Lewis, Feb. 15, 1854. Admitted to bar, 1850; practiced at Ft. Wayne, Ind., until 1863; editor Ft. Wayne Gazette, 1863-69, Richmond Palladium, 1875-96. Rep. presdl. elector, Ind., 1860; del. Nat. Rep. Conv., 1864; U.S. consul at Glasgow, 1869-74; postmaster Richmond, Ind., 1889-93; trustee, 1872—, pres. bd., 1890—, Ind. U., Bloomington. Home: Richmond, Ind. Died 1911.

JENKINSON, Richard C., mfr.; b. Newark, N.J., Apr. 14, 1853; s. George Bestell and Jane (Stringer) J.; ed. pub. and pvt. schs., Newark, and study in Europe; m. Emily Pendleton Coe, Dec. 21, 1876 (died 1922); children—Louise (Mrs. Thos. J. Skillman), Charlotte (Mrs. Harry O. May), Margaret (Mrs. Charles Blake Carrington). Founder, 1876, and pres. R. C. Jenkinson & Co., mfrs. metal goods; mem. advisory bd. Ironbound Trust Co., Newark. Rep. candidate for mayor of Newark, 1900; v.p. Pan-Am. Expn., Buffalo, 1901. Chmn. first N.J. Commn. for the Blind; pres. Newark Chamber of Commerce, 1898-1900; mem. N.Y. and N.J. Harbor Commn., 1912; v.p. N.J. Bd. of Commerce and Navigation, N.J. Sch. for Girls (Vineland); mem. exec. com. Newark Museum; mem. advisory bd. Coll. of Pharmacy, Newark; pres. Newark Free Pub. Library. Trustee N.J. Inst. of Arts and Sciences. Presbyn. Home: Newark, N.J. Died Aug. 1930.

JENKS, Almet Francis, judge; b. Brooklyn, May 21, 1853; s. Grenville Tudor and Persis Sophia (Smith) J.; A.B., Yale, 1875; LL.B., Columbia, 1877; (LL.D., Colgate, 1906); m. Lena Barré, Apr. 29, 1891. Admitted to bar, 1877; asst. dist. atty., Kings County, 1884-86; corp. counsel, Brooklyn, 1886-93; judge advocate gen., N.Y., 1891-95; mem. Constl. Conv., 1895; asst. corp. counsel, Greater New York, in charge of Brooklyn office, 1898; justice Supreme Ct. of N.Y., 1898—; apptd. to Appellate Div., 1900, reapptd., 1905, presiding justice, 1911-12; reappointed Justice Supreme Ct. of N.Y. for term expiring Dec. 31, 1926. Democrat. Home: New York, N.Y. Died Sept. 18, 1924.

JENKS, Arthur Whipple, clergyman; b. Concord, N.H., Aug. 9, 1863; s. George Edwin and Eliza J. (Grover) J.; B.A., Dartmouth, 1884, M.A., 1887, D.D., 1911; B.D., Gen. Theol. Sem., 1896; unmarried. Deacon, 1892, priest, 1893, P.E. Ch.; rector St. Luke's Ch., Woodsville, N.H., 1892-95; prof. ecclesiastical history, Nashotah House, Wis., 1895-1901, Trinity Coll., Toronto, Can., 1901-10, Gen. Theol. Sem., 1910—. Author: Beatitudes of the Psalter, 1914; Use and Abuse of Church History, and other lectures, 1915; Moments Rich in Blessing, 1916; History of the American Church interpreted for English Readers. Also articles in New Internat. Ency., and Am. and English theol. periodicals. Editor: A Handbook of the American Episcopal Church. Asso. editor Anglican Theological Review, Chicago. Address: New York, N.Y. Died Apr. 18, 1922.

JENKS, Edward Watrous, physician; b. Victor, N.Y., Mar. 31, 1833; s. Nathan and Jane (Bushnell) J.; ed. La Grange Collegiate Instn.; M.D., Castleton, Vt., 1855, and Bellevue Hosp. Med. Coll., New York, 1864; LL.D., Albion Coll.; m. Sarah R. Joy. Asst. surgeon in mil. hosps., Detroit, 1864-65; one of founders (pres. 1868-69) Detroit Med. Coll.; prof. surg. diseases of women, Bowdoin Coll., Me., 1871-75, Chicago Med. Coll., 1879; commr. Mich. State bd. of corrections and charities. Author of many well-known med. works. One of founders Am. Gynecol. Soc. Home: Detroit, Mich. Died 1903.

JENKS, Edwin Hart, clergyman; b. Janesville, Wis., Mar. 24, 1862; s. Ira C. and Harriet (Hart) J.; A.B., Hamilton Coll., 1886, A.M., 1890; grad. Auburn Theol. Sem., 1888; D.D., Coe Coll., Ia., 1902; m. Jessie E. Keys, Oct. 1, 1883; children—Chester Keys, Eloise (Mrs. Benjamin A. Funk), Edwin Hart, Florence Alice (Mrs. Harold J. Pratt). Ordained Presbyterian ministry, 1888; home missionary Lakeport, Calif., 1888-91; pastor Red Bluff, Calif., 1891-96; colleague pastor First Ch., San Francisco, 1896-99; pastor Second Ch., Los Angeles, Calif., 1899-1900, First Ch., Omaha, Neb., 1900—. Pres. bd. trustees Bellevue Coll.; dir. Presbyn. Theol. Sem. of Omaha. Moderator Synod of Neb., 1921-22; dir. bds. of Church Erection and Nat. Missions, Presbyn. Ch. U.S.A. Home: Omaha, Neb. Died Dec. 16, 1927.

JENKS, George Augustus, lawyer; b. Punxsutawney, Pa., Mar. 26, 1836; grad. Jefferson College, Pa., 1858; m. Mary A. Mabon, Jan. 3, 1860. Mem. Congress, 1875-77; nominated for judge Supreme Court, Pa., 1880; U.S. asst. sec. of interior, 1885-86; solicitor gen. of the U.S., 1886-89; Dem. nominee for gov., 1898; nominee for U.S. senator by Dem. mems. Pa. legislature, 1899. Address: Brookville, Pa. Died 1908.

JENKS, George Charles, newspaper man; b. London, Eng., Apr. 13, 1850; s. George Stilwell and Eliza (Miller) J.; ed. in Eng.; came to America, 1872; m. Sarah Jane Lambert, Nov. 21, 1878 (died 1895); m. 2d, Elizabeth J. Aylward, May 4, 1897 (died 1897); m. 3d, Kate Baird, July 24, 1899. Began as newspaper writer, Pittsburgh, 1882; editorial writer Pittsburgh Press, 6 yrs.; went to New York, 1895; dramatic critic a number of yrs.; N.Y. corr. Dispatch and Gazette-Times (Pittsburgh). Republican. Methodist. Mason. Author: Official History of the Johnstown Flood, 1890; The Climax, 1910; The Deserters, 1911; Stop Thief, 1913; also plays, motion pictures. Lectures on "Story Writing as a Business"; etc. Contbr. Cyclopedia of Am. Biography. Home: Auburn, N.Y. Died Sept. 13, 1929.

JENKS, James Lawrence, lawyer; b. Smithfield, R.I., Apr. 15, 1858; s. John A. and Martha (Connor) J.; Ph.B., Brown U., 1884; m. May Bromley, 1890; 1 son, James Lawrence. Practiced at Pawtucket, 1837—; dir. Pawtucket Mut. Fire Ins. Co., Adams Sutliffe Co., Pawtucket br. Industrial Trust Co., Lonsdale Bakery Co. Sec., trustee Memorial Hosp.; sec. Pawtucket Business Men's Association, 1889—. Mem. R.I. House of Rep., 1892, 93, Senate, 1907. Republican. Baptist. Home: Pawtucket, R.I. Died Nov. 19, 1940.

JENKS, Jeremiah Whipple, political economist; b. St. Clair, Mich., Sept. 2, 1856; s. Benjamin Lane and Amanda (Messer) J.; A.B., U. of Mich., 1878, A.M., 1879, LL.D., 1903; Ph.D., U. of Halle, 1885; m. Georgia Bixler, Aug. 28, 1884; children—Margaret Bixler (Mrs. Stanley Doty Brown), Benjamin Lane, Ernest Ellsworth. Admitted to Mich. bar, 1881; taught Greek, Latin and German, Mt. Morris Coll., 1879-80 and 1881-83; prof. polit. science and English lit., Knox Coll., 1886-89; prof. polit. economy and social science, Ind. U., 1889-91; prof. polit. economy and politics, Cornell, 1891-1912; prof. govt. and dir. div. of pub. affairs, 1912-17, research prof. govt. and pub. adminstrn., 1917—, dir. div. of Oriental Commerce and Politics, New York U. Expert agent of U.S. Industrial Commn. on investigation of trusts and industrial combinations in U.S. and Europe, 1899-1901, and consulting expert of U.S. Dept. of Labor on same subject; spl. commr. War Dept., to investigate questions of currency, labor, internal taxation and police in the Orient, 1901-02; spl. expert on currency reform of Govt. of Mexico, 1903; mem. U.S. Commn. on Internat. Exchange in spl. charge of reform of currency in China, 1903-04; mem. U.S. Immigration Commn., 1907-10; mem. High Commn. of Nicaragua, 1918—; also dir. Pacific Railways of Nicaragua and National Bank of Nicaragua. Pres. and chmn. bd. Alexander Hamilton Inst.; founder, director Far Eastern Bur., 1913-21. Pres. Am. Econ. Assn., 1906-07; mem. advisory commn. Council Nat. Defense, Washington, 1917; formerly mem. exec. com. of com. of 15 on ednl. preparation for foreign service (under Bur. Edn.); pres. and chmn. bd. Nat. Council on Religion in Higher Edn.; chmn. dept. on current economics and mem. exec. council, Nat. Civic Federation; hon. v.p. Nat. Monetary Assn.; dir. and v.p. China Soc. America; mem. exec. bd. and com. on edn. Boy Scouts of America. Author: Henry C. Carey als Nationalökonom, Jena, 1885; The Trust Problem, 1900 (enlarged edit. with Pres. Walter E. Clark, of U. of Nev., 1917); Vol. XVIII Report-Industrial Commission Industrial Combinations in Europe, 1901; Report on Certain Economic Questions in the English and Dutch Colonies in the Orient, 1902; Citizenship and the Schools, 1906; Great Fortunes, The Winning, The Using, 1906; The Political and Social Significance of the Life and Teachings of Jesus, 1906; Life Questions of High School Boys, 1908; Principles of Politics, 1909; Governmental Action for Social Welfare, 1910; The Immigration Problem (with W. J. Lauck), 1913, 6th edit., revised by Rufus D. Smith, 1925; The Making of a Nation; The Testing of a Nation's Ideals (with Prof. Chas. F. Kent), 1915; Personal Problems of Boys Who Work, 1913; Business and the Government, 1917; Jesus' Principles of Living (with C. F. Kent), 1920; Great American Issues (with John Hays Hammond), 1921; We and Our Government (with R. D. Smith), 1922; Science of Business (vol. 1, Modern Merchandising Course), 1927. Part author and editor: Trusts and Industrial Combinations (Reports U.S. Industrial Commn.), Vol. I, 1900, Vol. XIII, 1901; Reports of Commission on International Exchange, 1903-04. Compiler of Statutes and Digested Decisions of Federal, State and Territorial Law Relating to Trusts and Industrial Combinations, Vol. II, 1900. Address: New York, N.Y. Died Aug. 24, 1929.

JENKS, John Edward, editor; b. St. John, N.B., Dec. 15, 1866; s. John Moore and Caroline Elizabeth (Fernald) J.; ed. Boston pub. schs.; unmarried. In editorial work, 1885—; editor Army and Navy Register, 1898—; pres. U.S. Govt. Advertiser, 1890—; also sec. Nat. Capital Press; v.p. U.S. Ordnance Co. Unitarian. Home: Washington, D.C. Died Nov. 8, 1932.

JENKS, Phœbe A. Pickering, portrait painter; b. Portsmouth, N.H., July 28, 1847; d. Denis and Fidelia (Barton) Hoyt; High School edn.; m. **Lewis E. Jenks.** Has exhibited numerous ideal paintings, and has been especially successful with portraits of women and children. Home: Boston, Mass. Died 1907.

JENKS, Tudor, author; b. Brooklyn, N.Y., May 7, 1857; s. Grenville Tudor and Persis Sophia (Smith) J.; grad. Polytechnic Inst., Brooklyn, 1874; A.B., Yale, 1878; LL.B., Columbia, 1880; m. Mary Donnison Ford, Oct. 5, 1882. Studied art in Paris winter of 1880-81; practiced law, New York, 1881-87; on staff of St. Nicholas Mag., 1887-1902; clerk with Appellate Div., Borough Hall, Brooklyn, N.Y.; mem. law firm Jenks & Britton, Bronxville. Author of many juvenile books. Address: Bronxville, N.Y. Died Feb. 11, 1922.

JENNE, James Nathaniel, M.D., educator; b. Berkshire, Vt., Dec. 21, 1859; s. John Gilbert and Charlotte (Woodworth) J.; M.D., U. of Vt., 1881, M.S., 1924; grad. study N.Y. Post-Grad. Sch. and Hosp. (6 weeks annually), 1890-95, École de Médecin, Paris, 1896; m. Abbie Cushman, Sept. 19, 1883. Began practice of medicine and surgery in Ga., 1881; surg. dir. Central Vt. R.R., 1891-1901; adjunct prof. materia medica, U. of Vt., 1891-93, prof., 1894-99, prof. therapeutics and clin. medicine, 1900-31, dean of Coll. of Medicine and mem. of univ. council, 1926—; dir. U. of Vt. Coll. of Medicine Dispensary; cons. physician Mary Fletcher Hosp.; cons. surgeon Bishop De Goesbriand Hosp., Burlington, Vt., Fanny Allen Hosp., Winooski, Vt. Mem. bd. trustees U. of Vt. Surgeon gen. Vt. N.G.; maj.-chief-surgeon U.S.A., Spanish-Am. War. Republican. Home: Burlington, Vt. Died Sept. 9, 1937.

JENNEY, Charles Francis, judge; b. Middleborough, Mass., Sept. 16, 1860; s. Charles Edwin and Elvira Frances (Clark) J.; grad. Brockton (Mass.) High Sch., 1878; LL.B., Boston U., 1883; m. Mary E. Bruce, Oct. 12, 1886. Practiced Hyde Park, Mass., and Boston, 1882-89, Boston, 1889—; served as atty. for Town of Hyde Park, County of Norfolk, etc.; mem. Mass. Ho. of Rep., 1886, Senate, 1907, 08 (chmn. com. of judiciary. 1908); asso. justice Superior Ct., Mass., 1909-19; asso. justice Supreme Jud. Court, Mass., 1919—. Lecturer on Mass. practice, Boston U. Law Sch., 1886-1909; trustee Hyde Park Pub. Library, 1886-1910. Conglist. Author of The Fortunate Island of Monhegan, 1922. Home: Hyde Park, Mass. Died Nov. 29, 1923.

JENNEY, William Le Baron, architect; b. Fairhaven, Mass., Sept. 25, 1832; ed. Phillips Acad., Andover, Harvard Scientific School; grad. École Centrale des Arts et Manufactures, Paris, 1856; studied art and architecture in Paris studios, 1858-59; was capt., U.S. Army, assigned to engr. duty; on staff Gen. U. S. Grant, Cairo to Corinth; on staff Gen. W. T. Sherman, Corinth, until 1866; bvtd. maj., 1864; located in Chicago as architect, 1868; landscape engr. for West Chicago Parks, 1870-71; invented, 1883, and first used in Home Ins. Bldg., 1884, the skeleton construction now generally used for tall bldgs., in honor of which the Bessemer Steam Ship Co., named one of its vessels the W. L. B. Jenney; architect of Union League Club, Siegel & Cooper Bldg., Y.M.C.A. Bldg., New York Life Bldg.; The Fair, and the Horticultural Bldg. at World's Columbian Expn., etc., in Chicago. Address: Chicago, Ill. Died 1907.

JENNINGS, Andrew Jackson, lawyer; b. Fall River, Mass., Aug. 2, 1849; s. Andrew M. and Olive B. (Chace) J.; A.B., Brown U., 1872; LL.B., Boston U., 1876; m. Marion G. Saunders, Dec. 25, 1879. Admitted to bar, 1876; sr. mem. Jennings, Morton & Brayton; trustee Union Savings Bank; dir. Mchts. Mfg. Co., Samoset Co. Mem. Fall River Sch. Com., 1875-78, Mass. Ho. of Rep., 1878-79, Senate, 1882; dist. atty., 1894-98. Pres. Fall River Bar Assn., Y.M.C.A.; trustee Brown U. Republican. Baptist. Home: Fall River, Mass. Died Oct. 19, 1923.

JENNINGS, Charles Godwin, M.D.; b. Leroy, N.Y., Feb. 4, 1857; s. Thomas A. and Matilda (Godwin) J.; grad. Mynderse Acad., Seneca Falls, N.Y., 1875; M.D., Detroit Medical College, 1879; M.A., U. of Mich., 1931; M.S., Detroit City College; m. Helen Louise Felch, Mar. 6, 1884. Practicing physician, Detroit, 1880; prof. medicine (chief of dept.), Detroit Coll. of Medicine and Surgery, 1897-1917; physician to Harper Hosp. (chmn. med. bd., 1913-20). Capt. M.C. U.S.A., 1917. Home: Detroit, Mich. Died Jan. 9, 1936.

JENNINGS, Edward Henry, oil producer, banker; b. Brady's Bend, Pa., Aug. 10, 1852; s. Richard and Katharine (Evans) J.; ed. pub. schs.; m. Mary J. Colwell, 1879 (died 1896). Associated with father in production of petroleum in Western Pa., 1872-91; became mem. E. H. Jennings & Bros., Pittsburgh, 1891; later pres. Columbia Nat. Bank and dir. Germania Savings Bank; trustee Dollar Savings Bank. Home: Pittsburgh, Pa. Died Nov. 17, 1923.

JENNINGS, Elzy Dee, educator; b. McMinnville, Tenn., Mar. 11, 1880; s. Walker R. and Nancy (Wiseman) J.; A.B., Randolph Coll., Lancaster, Tex., 1900; B.A., M.A., U. of Tex., 1913, Ph.D., 1924; LL.D., Emory U., 1931; m. Ora Dickie Long, May 6, 1902; 1 dau., Lova Zell. Teacher pub. schs., Tex., 1900-04; co-prin. Huckabay (Tex.) Acad., 1904-08; admitted to Tex. bar, 1906; pres. John Tarleton Coll., Stephenville, Tex., 1909-11; dean Tex. Woman's Coll., Ft. Worth, Tex., 1915-22, v.p., 1918-22; dean Coll. Arts and Sciences, Southern Meth. U., 1922—. Mem. bd. mgrs., Tex. Anti-Saloon League. Democrat. Mem. M.E. Ch., S. Mason, Odd Fellow, K.P. Wrote: A Survey of the Austin City Schools, 1925. Home: Dallas, Tex. Died Apr. 28, 1938.

JENNINGS, Frederic Beach, lawyer; b. Bennington Center, Vt., Aug. 6, 1853; s. Isaac and Sophia (Day) J.; A.B., Williams Coll., 1872, A.M., 1875; LL.B., Harvard, 1874; LL.B., New York U. Law School, 1875; LL.D., Middlebury (Vt.) Coll., 1917; m. Laura Hall Park, July 27, 1880. Admitted to bar, 1875; mem. firm Stetson, Jennings & Russell. Dir. and gen. counsel Hudson & Manhattan R.R. Co.; dir. First Nat. Bank, N. Bennington, Vt., Chicago & Erie R.R. Co., Am. Trading Co., Internat. Paper Co., N.Y. Trust Co., etc.; gen. counsel Erie R.R. Co., Internat. Paper Co., The Associated Press, Am. Trading Co., Continental Paper Bag Co., and other corps. Trustee Williams Coll., Barnard Coll. Republican. Home: New York, N.Y. Died May 26, 1920.

JENNINGS, Hennen, mining engr.; b. Hawesville, Ky., May 6, 1854; s. James R. and Katharine Sharpe (Hennen) J.; C.E., Lawrence Scientific School (Harvard), 1877; hon. M.A., Harvard U., 1918; m. Mary L. Coleman, Oct. 7, 1886. Identified with mining in Calif., 1877-87, in Venezuela, 1887-89; consulting engr. to H. Eckstein & Co., Johannesburg, and to many Transvaal gold mining cos., 1889-98; consulting engr. Wernher, Beit & Co., London, 1898-1905, Convey Placer Mining Co., Mont., U.S. Bur. of Mines. Mem. tech. edn. commrs. in Transvaal, 1902-04; pres. London Inst. Mining and Metallurgy, 1903-04. Home: Washington, D.C. Died Mar. 5, 1920.

JENNINGS, Henry Burritt, cotton mgr.; b. Charleston, S.C., Aug. 1, 1883; s. Henry Burritt and Martha Glen (Reeves) J.; B.S., Clemson (S.C.) Coll., 1902; m. Josephine Sibley, Jan. 8, 1913; children—Josephine Sibley, Henry B., J. L. Sibley, Erwin R. Engaged in cotton mfg, 1902—; v.p. and gen. mgr. Union-Buffalo Mills Co., Union Mfg. and Power Co.; v.p. Buffalo-Union Carolina R.R.; dir. Fairmont Mfg. Co., Nicholson Bank & Trust Co. Dir. Wallace Thomson Hosp., Union, S.C. Rotarian. Home: Union, S.C. Died July 10, 1927.

JENNINGS, Henry C., publishing agent; b. Fremont, Ill., Dec. 21, 1850; s. George R. and Clementine S. (Trumbull) J.; ed. Northwestern U. and pvtly.; hon. A.M., Chaddock Coll., 1883; D.D., Hamline, 1894; LL.D., Upper Ia. U., 1905, Hamline, 1921; m. Helen A. Culver, Dec. 24, 1871. Mem. Minn. Conf., M.E. Ch., 1871; ordained, 1873; pastor in Minn. at Caledonia, La Crescent, Chatfield, Waseca, Spring Valley, Faribalt, Red Wing, Grace and Oxford chs. in St. Paul, and presiding elder Marshall Dist.; sr. pub. agt. (Jennings & Graham) Western Meth. Book Concern, Cincinnati, 1896-1913; gen. publishing agt. Meth. Book Concern, New York, Cincinnati and Chicago, 1913-20; retired with title agent emeritus. Mem. Gen. Conf. M.E. Ch., 1892, 96, 1900, 04, 08, 12, 16; mem. bd. of control of Epworth League first 7 yrs. of its history. Home: Portland, Ore. Died Nov. 9, 1927.

JENNINGS, John Joseph, editor; b. St. Louis, Mo., Mar. 1, 1853; s. Michael and Mary (O'Meara) J.; grad. Christian Brothers Coll., St. Louis, A.B., 1873, A.M., 1875; m. Emma M. Hall, Mar. 8, 1904. Began newspaper work, 1875; dramatic editor Globe-Democrat, St. Louis, 1878-86, New York World, 1887; mng. editor Post-Dispatch, St. Louis, 1888-89; on editorial staff New York World, 1890-91; on editorial staff New York Evening World, 1892—. Exposed the Ignatius Donnelly Bacon-Shakespeare cipher; author of many humorous sketches and poems, including "Irish Widow" series of dialect sketches in New York Mercury, 1880-95; has also rewritten plays. Author: Theatrical and Circus Life, 1882; Widow Magoogin, 1900. Home: New York, N.Y. Died 1909.

JENNINGS, Martin Luther, clergyman; b. Ohio, July 10, 1847; s. Abraham M. and Louisa (Foreman) J.; A.B., Adrian (Mich.) Coll., 1871, A.M., 1874, D.D., 1890, LL.D., 1906; post-grad. student, Yale, 1874-75; m. Lettie A. Heberling, May 18, 1893. Ordained M.P. ministry, 1871; pastor Zanesville, O., 1871-72; instr., 1872-74, prof. Latin and Greek, 1875-80, Adrian Coll.; pastor Wellsville, O., 1882-83, Cambridge, O., 1883-87; agent, Adrian Coll., 1888-89; pastor Coschocton, O., 1889-90; pres. Muskingum Conf., 1890-93; pastor 1st M.P. Ch., Des Moines, Ia., 1893-94; prof. Greek, Adrian Coll., 1894-96; editor Meth. Recorder, Pittsburgh, 1896—. Del. to Ecumenical Conf. of Methodism, London, 1901, Toronto, Can., 1911; v.p. for M.P. Ch. of Federal Council of Chs. in America; mem. Joint Commn. on Union of Congl., U.B. and M.P. Chs., 1906-08; mem. Joint Commn. on Union of Am. Methodism, 1908—. Address: Pittsburgh, Pa. Died Aug. 30, 1913.

JENNINGS, Oliver Gould; A.B., Yale, 1887; LL.B., Columbia, 1889. **Dir. Bethlehem Steel Corp., McKesson & Robbins, Inc., U.S. Industrial Alcohol**

Co., Nat. Fuel Gas Co. and other cos. A founder of the Stable Money Assn. Home: Fairfield, Conn. Died Oct. 13, 1936.

JENNINGS, Richard William; b. Brighton, Sussex County Eng., Aug. 11, 1866; s. Richard and Jane (March) J.; ed. pvt. schs.; m. Gertrude Johnson, June 21, 1892. Came to U.S., 1886, naturalized citizen, 1892. Reporter Providence Jour., 1889-92; sec. to Governor Brown, 1892-95, State Census Bd., 1895-1900, State Returning Bd., 1900-18; gen. treas. of R.I., 1918-22 and 1925-26; state law revision commr., 1927—; sec. Criminal Law Revision Commn., 1927—. Mem. R.I. Ho. of Rep., 1910, 12, 1914-18 (leader of House most of time); chmn. Criminal Law Revision Com., 1910, Constl. Revision Com., 1912. Dir. William H. Hall Free Pub. Library. Republican. Unitarian. Mason. Home: Cranston, R.I. Died June 14, 1928.

JENNINGS, Sidney Johnston, mining engr.; b. Hawesville, Ky., Aug. 13, 1863; s. James Rody and Katherine Sharp (Hennen) J.; early edn. Tours, France, and in Germany; C.E., Lawrence Scientific Sch. (Harvard), 1885; post-grad. course, U. of Calif.; m. Amy Florence (Horne) Valpy, Aug. 18, 1893; children—John Morris, Amy Sidney, Mary Agnes, Philip Hennen. Surveyor, New Alameda Quicksilver Mining Co., Calif., 1885-87, Anaconda Copper Co., Butte, Mont., 1887-89; mgr. Willow Copper Co., S. Africa, 1889-90; asst. gen. mgr. De Beers Consol. Mines, Kimberley, 1891-93; mgr. Crown Deep Mine, Ltd., Johannesburg, 1893-96; mgr. Crown Mines and consulting engr. H. Eckstein & Co., 1896-1907; v.p. U.S. Smelting, Refining & Mining Co., 1908—; dir. Cia de Real del Monte y Pachuca; pres. Hanover Bessemer Iron & Copper Co. Was chmn. works com. of Town Council, Johannesburg, after occupation of the city by the British, providing the city with electric trolley lines, adequate water supply and underground sewers. Pres. American Mining Congress, 1922-23. Democrat. Episcopalian. Home: New York, N.Y. Died Nov. 17, 1928.

JENNINGS, T(homas) Albert, business man; b. Jennings, Fla., Jan. 8, 1865; s. George S. and Mary Elizabeth (Stewart) J.; common schs. of Fla. and at Emory Coll., Ga.; m. Annie Beall Wood, June 18, 1899. Pres. Jennings Naval Stores Co. (Pensacola), Bank of Jennings; organized Globe Naval Stores Co., 1913; dir. Gulf, Fla. & Ala. Ry. Co., etc. Chmn. Bd Pub. Works, Pensacola, 1909-10; mem. Fla. Ho. of Rep., 1911 (speaker). Mem. and sec. Dem. State Exec. Com., 1892-94; del. Dem. Nat. Conv., St. Louis, 1888, Chicago, 1892; presdl. elector, 1904; Fla. mem. Dem. Nat. Com., 1908-12. Methodist. Mason, K.P., Elk. Address: Pensacola, Fla. Died Aug. 16, 1917.

JENNINGS, Walter, capitalist; b. San Francisco, Calif., Sept. 14, 1858; s. Oliver Burr and Esther Judson (Goodsell) J.; B.A., Yale, 1880; LL.B., Columbia, 1882; m. Jean Pollock Brown, Nov. 11, 1891. With Pratt Mfg. Co., New York, 1882-86, Oil City, Pa., 1886-88; dir. Standard Oil Co. of N.J., 1903—; sec. 1908-11; was also pres. Nat. Fuel Gas Co., 1908-19; trustee New York Trust Co. Chmn. New York Co. A.R.C., 1918-19. Mem. bd. govs. New York Hosp. Home: Coldspring Harbor, L.I. Died Jan. 9, 1933.

JENNINGS, W(illiam) Beatty, clergyman; b. Bennettsville, S.C., Sept. 26, 1859; s. Jonathan Beatty and Sally Ann H. (McCully) J.; A.B., Davidson Coll., N.C., 1880; A.M., Princeton, 1882; grad. Princeton Theol. Sem., 1883; D.D., Centre Coll., Ky., 1896; m. Mattie J. C. Huff, Sept. 12, 1893; children—Arnold Huff, Judith, Martha Haraden. Ordained Persbyn. ministry, 1883; pastor First Ch., Rock Hill, S.C., 1883-87, First Ch., Macon, Ga., 1887-95, Central Ch., Louisville, Ky., 1895-98, First Ch., Detroit, 1898-1906, First Ch., Germantown, Pa., 1906—. Mem. Presbyn. Gen. Assembly, 6 times; mem. Gen. Assembly's Com. which drafted plan for jud. commissions; mem. com. which issued Book of Common Worship; mem. Bd. of Home Missions Presbyn Ch., U.S.A. Trustee Princeton Theol. Sem. Author: Social Teachings of Jesus Christ, 1915; (brochure), The Bible and Social Living, 1916. Address: Philadelphia, Pa. Died Sept. 7, 1935.

JENNINGS, William Sherman, governor; b. Centralia, Ill., Mar. 24, 1863; s. Josephus W. and Amanda J.; ed. Marion County, Ill., 1869-79, Southern Ill. Normal U., Carbondale, 1879-83, Union Coll. of Law, Chicago, 1884-85; m. May Mann, May 12, 1891. Admitted to Fla. bar, 1886, U.S. courts, 1892; apptd. circuit ct. commr., May 1887; apptd. county judge Hernando County, Fla., May 1888; elected county judge, 1888; mem. Fla. Ho. of Rep., 1893-95 (speaker 1895); alderman 9 yrs., pres. council 8 yrs., city of Brooksville; presdl. elector, 1896; messenger to deliver Fla. vote in Washington; elected chmn. Dem. State Conv., 1898; gov. of Fla., 1901-05. Democrat. First v.p. and gen. counsel Fla. Bank & Trust Co., 1905—; gen. counsel Internat. Improvement Fund of State of Fla., 1905—; gen. counsel Bd. Drainage Commrs. of Fla.; v.p. and gen. counsel Fla. State Drainage Land Co.; chmn. ways and means com. Naval Stores Assn. of Fla.; pres. Leesburg State Bank, Depositors Trust Co.; dir. Barnes & Jessup Co., naval stores factors. Author of Fla. Drainage Law and plan of draining the Everglades. Mem. advisory bd. of federal drainage and reclamation commn.; chmn. com. apptd. by Sec. of Interior Lane to prepare amendments to drainage bill; spl. counsel in drafting and settling contract for comprehensive investigation and survey of Everglades of Fla. by commn. of expert engrs.; gen. counsel for Everglades Sugar & Land Co.; pres. Jennings Artesian Farm Land Co.; counsel Furst-Clark Construction Co., everglades contractors, Bowers Southern Dredging Co. Chmn. Fla. Tax Commn., 1911-12. Address: Jacksonville, Fla. Died Feb. 28, 1920.

JENT, John William, educator; b. Franklin, Ky., Mar. 19, 1877; s. William Thomas and Nancy Wilson (Jackson) J.; diploma, Pierce City Bapt. Acad., 1901; Th.B., Southern Bapt. Theol. Sem., 1907; Th.M., Baylor U., 1908, B.L., 1910; A.B., Yale, 1911, A.M., 1914; Th.D., Southwestern Bapt. Theol. Sem., 1912, A.M., with professional diploma as Rural Community Worker, Columbia U., 1922; LL.D., Okla. Bapt. U., 1926; m. Jessie Annie Pollard, Aug. 30, 1904; children—William Pollard, John Thomas. Teacher rural sch., Chautauqua County, Kan., 1897-99; student and commercial prin. Pierce City Bapt. Coll., 1899-1901; pastor Bapt. chs. during coll. days; student registrar S.W. Bapt. Theol. Sem., 1909-13; registrar and prof. social sciences, Okla. Bapt. U., 1914-17, prof. sociology, 1916-26, bursar, 1918, acting dean, 1921, dean, 1922-26; prof. rural ch. and dean Theol. Sem. of Mercer U., 1926-28; pres. Southwest Bapt. Coll., Bolivar, Mo., 1928-30; prof. edn. and sociology, Union U., 1930-32, acting dean, 1931; prof. psychology, philosophy, and rural edn., Okla. Bapt. U., 1932-36, prof. philosophy, 1936—, v.p., 1932, dean of faculties, 1933-36, v.p. and dir. Personnel Department, 1936-39, prof. and dir., 1939—. Lecturer Southwestern Baptist Theol. Seminary, 1924 (trustee 1924-26), Southern Bapt. Theol. Sem., 1934, 37 (trustee), Bapt. Bible Inst., New Orleans, 1935, U. of Fla., 1937. Mem. Edn. Bd. Southern Baptist Conv., 1925-26; v.p. S.W. Philos. Conf., 1938; chairman Rural Church Com. of Ga. Bapt. Conv., 1925-26. Former officer Mo. N.G.; college adj. Okla. Bapt. U., World War. Democrat. Mason (K.T.). Author: The Primacy of Personality in Pedagogy, 1914; The Challenge of the Country Church, 1924; Rural Church Development, 1928; Chapter I, Introduction to Religious Education, 1932; Rural Church Problems, 1935; After Fifty-Eight Years (autobiography), 1935; Sermons and Addresses, 1935; The Philosophy of a Christian Philosopher, 1935; Editor O.B.U. Faculty Symposium, Why Christian Education, 1935. Address: Shawnee, Okla. Died May 29, 1941.

JEPSON, Samuel L., physician; b. nr. St. Clairsville, O., April 7, 1842; s. John and Hannah (Hunt) J.; A.B., Washington Coll., Pa., 1862, A.M., Washington and Jefferson, 1865; M.D., Med. Coll. of Ohio, Cincinnati, 1868; Sc.D., Western U. of Pa. (now U. of Pittsburgh), 1907; m. H. Isabella Scott, Sept. 14, 1871. Resident physician Cincinnati Hosp., 1868-69; health officer, Wheeling, W.Va., 1873-79, 1895-1901; studied in Edinburgh, London, Vienna, 1877-78; acting asst. surgeon, U.S. Marine Hosp. Service, 1884-89; sec. U.S. Bd. Examining Surgeons for Pensions, 1889-93, and mem. bd., 1907-15; attending physician City Hosp., 1890-1913; consulting physician to same, 1913-15 (now called Ohio Valley Gen. Hosp.); med. examiner for a number of ins. cos. Editor West Virginia Medical Journal, 1906-16; author many med. papers. Mem. Wheeling City Council, 1881-84; mem. bd. edn., 1881-92, 1897-98, and 1913-16 (pres. 1891-92); state commr. of health, 1913-20. Trustee of Washington and Jefferson Coll., 1904—. Home: Wheeling, W.Va. Died May 2, 1922.

JERMAIN, Louis Francis, M.D.; b. Manitowoc County, Wis., Oct. 10, 1867; s. George and Laura (Simon) J.; student Oshkosh (Wis.) Normal Sch.; M.D., Northwestern U., 1894; studied U. of Berlin and U. of Vienna, 1910; m. Rose Barth, June 26, 1894; children—Teresa (Mrs. Raymond F. Jaekels), William Michael, Angeline Marie (Mrs. Cyril Boemer). Practiced at Milwaukee, 1894—; dean Marquette U. Sch. of Medicine, 1913-26. Dir. and mem. bd. trustees Marquette U., 1913—. Catholic. Decorated Knight of St. Gregory by Pope Pius XI, 1927. Home: Milwaukee, Wis. Died July 24, 1935.

JEROME, Harry, economist; b. Bloomington, Ill., Mar. 7, 1886; s. Moses and Sarah Amanda (Brakey) J.; A.B., U. of Omaha, 1912; M.A., U. of Wis., 1915, Ph.D., 1918; m. Gladys Walker Solomon, Aug. 12, 1913; adopted children—Richard Francis, Margaret Lois. Instr. history and economics, U. of Omaha, 1912-14; asst. in economics, U. of Wis., 1914-15; instr., 1915-19, asst. prof., 1920-23, asso. prof., 1925-26, prof., 1926—, chmn. dept., 1931-36; dist. assessor of incomes, Wis. Tax Commn., 1919-20; dir. productivity survey Nat. Research Project, 1936-37. Dir. Nat. Bur. of Econ. Research. Presbyterian. Author: Statistical Method, 1924; Migration and Business Cycles, 1926; Mechanization in Industry, 1934. Home: Madison, Wis. Died Sept. 11, 1938.

JEROME, William Travers, lawyer; b. New York, N.Y., Apr. 18, 1859; s. Lawrence R. and Katherine (Hall) J.; ed. Williston Sem. and Amherst Coll., hon. A.M., 1892; LL.B., Columbia, 1884; m. Lavinia Howe, May 9, 1888. Admitted to bar, 1884; asst. dist. atty. N.Y. Co., 1888-90; justice of spl. sessions, 1895-1902; dist. atty. New York County, 1901-09; mem. law firm Jerome & Rand. Democrat. Address: New York, N.Y. Died Feb. 13, 1934.

JESSEN, Karl Detlev, college prof.; b. Winnemark, Schleswig-Holstein, Germany, July 13, 1872; s. Peter and Maria Katharina Dorothea (Petersen) J.; ed. real gymnasium, Itzehoe, Gymnasium, Glückstadt, Germany; A.B., U. of Chicago, 1896; studied univs. of Kiel and Berlin; Ph.D., Berlin, 1901; emigrated to U.S., Dec. 1892; m. 2d, Myra Stephanie Richards, Sept. 15, 1915. Instr. and lecturer German lit. and æsthetics, Harvard, 1901-04; prof. German lit., Bryn Mawr Coll., 1904—. Lutheran. Author: Heinses Stellung zur bildenden Kunst, 1902. Editor: Wackenroder's Herbensergiessungen, 1904. Address: Bryn Mawr, Pa. Died Sept. 24, 1919.

JESSUP, Henry Harris, missionary; b. Montrose, Pa., Apr. 19, 1832; s. William (LL.D.) and Amanda (Harris) J.; A.B., Yale, 1851, A.M., 1854; grad. Union Theol. Sem., 1855; D.D., Princeton, 1865; m. Caroline Bush, Oct. 1857; m. 2d, Harriet Elizabeth Dodge, Oct. 1868; m. 3d, Theodosia Davenport Lockwood, Aug. 1884; 1 son, Henry Wynans J. Ordained Presbyn. ministry, 1855; missionary in Tripoli and Syria, 1856-60, at Beirut, 1860—. Missionary-editor Arabic journal, "El-Neshrah"; prof. theology and homiletics, Moderator Gen. Assembly in Saratoga, 1879. Author: The Women of the Arabs, 1874; Syrian Home Life, 1874; Mohammedan Missionary Problem, 1879; The Greek Church and Protestant Missions, 1885; Kamil, Moslem Convert, 1893; Autobiography and History of the Syria Mission, 1909. Address: Beirut, Syria. Died 1910.

JESSUP, Henry Wynans, lawyer; b. Beirut, Syria, Jan. 20, 1864; s. Henry Harris and Caroline (Bush) J.; came to America, 1878; A.B., Princeton, 1886, A.M., 1889; LL.B., New York U. Law Sch., 1888, LL.M., 1892, J.D., 1917; LL.D., Hamilton Coll., 1928; m. Mary Hay, dau. of James M. Stotesbury, Oct. 15, 1889; children—Henry Herbert, Theodore Carrington, John Butler, Philip Caryl, Richard Stotesbury. Prof. law, New York U. Law Sch., to 1893. Mem. 1st Permanent Jud. Commn. Gen. Assembly Presbyn. Ch. U.S.A.; mem. com. on union of Presbyn. and Cumberland Presbyn. chs. Mem. Draft Bd., world war; dir. Am. Defense Soc. Sec. Princeton Class of '86. Republican. Author: Law and Practice in Surrogates' Courts, 1899, 9th edit., 1930; Centennial History Fifth Avenue Presbyterian Church, New York City, 1908; (booklet) Faith and Everyday Life, 1917; (booklet) Songs for Uncle Sam's Soldiers, 1917; Professional Ideals of the Lawyer, 1925; Bill of Rights, Its Destruction, 1927; Law for Wives and Daughters, 1927. Home: New York, N.Y. Died Dec. 9, 1934.

JESSUP, Samuel, missionary; b. Montrose, Pa., Dec. 21, 1833; s. William (LL.D.) and Amanda (Harris) J.; studied at Yale, 1856-58, M.A., 1863; grad. Union Theol. Sem., 1861; D.D., Princeton, 1890; m. Miss A. E. Jay, 1862 (died 1895). Ordained Presbyn. ministry, 1861; chaplain U.S. Army, 6th Pa. reserve corps, 1861-62; missionary in Syria, 1862—. Editor Arabic Weekly, 1883-89; mgr. Arabic Publishing House, Beirut, 1883-96; prin. Gerard Inst., Sidon, Syria, 1903-07. Acting sec. Presbyn. Bd. Foreign Missions, N.Y., 1880-90, while on furlough. Home: Montrose, Pa. Deceased.

JESUP, Henry Griswold, clergyman, educator; b. Westport, Conn., Jan. 23, 1826; s. William Henry and Mary Hannah (Riley) J.; grad. Yale, 1847, A.M., 1850; Union Theol. Sem., New York, 1853; unmarried. Pastor Congl. Ch., Stanwich, Conn., 1854-62; prof. botany Dartmouth Coll., 1877-99. Author: Edward Jesup and His Descendants, 1887; Flora and Fauna Within Thirty Miles of Hanover, N.H., 1891. Home: Hanover, N.H. Died 1903.

JESUP, Morris Ketchum, banker; b. Westport, Conn., June 21, 1830; s. Charles and Abby Sherwood (DeWitt) J.; hon. A.M., Yale, Williams, Columbia; LL.D., Princeton, 1902. Clerk for mfg. firm, New York, until 1852; active banker, 1852-84, New York; m. Maria Van Antwerp, d. Rev. Thomas DeWitt, Apr. 26, 1854. Pres. New York City Mission and Tract Soc., 1881-1903, for which he built the DeWitt Memorial Ch., in Rivington St., in memory of his father-in-law; pres. Five Points House of Industry, 1872—; one of founders (pres., 1872) Y.M.C.A., of New York; pres. Chamber of Commerce of New York, Am. Sunday Sch. Union, Peary Arctic Club, Sailors' Snug Harbor, Audubon Soc. State of N.Y.; trustee Union Theol. Sem., to which he presented the building called Jesup Hall; pres. Am. Mus. Natural History, 1881—, to which he gave a $100,000 collection of native woods and marble busts of ten most prominent scientists; trustee Brick Presbyn. Ch., Syrian Protestant Coll. (Beirut), John F. Slater Fund (treas.), Peabody Edn. Fund, Gen. Edn. Bd., Hosp. Sat. and Sunday Assn., Soc. for Relief of Half-Orphan and Destitute Children; v.p. Am. Soc. for Prevention of Cruelty to Animals, 1885-1901; dir. N.Y. Instn. for Instrn. of Deaf and Dumb. Trustee Atlantic Mut. Ins. Co.; dir. Western Union Telegraph Co., Met. Trust Co. Address: New York, N.Y. Died 1908.

JEWELL, Frederick Swartz, clergyman, educator; b. Eliot Mission Sta., Chictaw Nation, Miss., Jan. 23, 1821; s. Moses and Elmina (Conger) J.; ed. Groton and Munro acads., N.Y., prepared for sophomore class Yale; health failed; grad. Auburn Theol. Sem.; hon. A.M., Amherst Coll.; Ph.D., Lafayette Coll.; S.T.D., Nashotah Sem., Wis.; m. Julia Adelaide Chapin, Jan. 27, 1855. Pastor at different periods from 1847; Presbyn. until 1875; ordained priest, 1875, P.E. Ch., Presbyn. chs., Cincinnati and Greenbush, Congl. ch., Morrisville, N.Y.; rector (P.E. chs.): St. James, Winsted, Conn., St. Mark's, Evanston, Ill., St. Paul's, Watertown, and St. John's, Portage, Wis., and chancellor All Saints' Cathedral, Milwaukee. Asst. and prin. various acads. in N.Y.; prof. English lang. and lit., State Normal Sch., Albany, N.Y., 14 yrs.; several yrs. State teachers' inst. conductor and lecturer, N.Y.; 4 yrs. asst. prof. ethics and evidences, Racine Coll., Wis.; later prof. history and philosophy, Grafton Hall, Fond du Lac, Wis. Mem. Guild of All Souls; Confraternity of the Blessed Sacrament. Author: School Government, 01; Grammatical Diagrams; Christion Science Examined. Address: Fond du Lac, Wis. Died 1903.

JEWELL, John Franklin, consul; b. nr. Galena, Ill., May 11, 1874; s. Edwin and Ann (Reed) J., LL.B., U. of Mich., 1896; m. Mrs. Jeannette Sherwood Seers, June 2, 1923. Practiced law at Galena, 1896-1902; Am. consul at Martinique, French W.I., 1902-06, at St. Michaels, Azores, Portugal, 1906-08, at Melbourne, Australia, 1908-11, at Vladivostok, Siberia, 1911-14. at Chefoo, China, 1914-16, at Lourenço Marques, Portuguese East Africa, Aug. 3, 1916-June 17, 1918, at Batavia, Java, 1918-21; Birmingham, Eng., 1922—. Has traveled extensively in N. America, W.I., Australasia, Northern Asia, Europe, the Far East and Africa. Home: Galena, Ill. Died Oct. 23, 1927.

JEWELL, Theodore Frelinghuysen, rear admiral; b. Georgetown, D.C., Aug. 5, 1844; s. Thomas and Eleanor (Spencer) J.; grad. U.S. Naval Acad., 1864; m. Elizabeth Lindsay, d. Rear Admiral C. H. Poor, U.S.N., June 15, 1871. Acting midshipman, Nov. 28, 1861; comd. naval battery of field howitzers in defense of Washington, June and July 1863; commd. ensign, Nov. 1, 1866; promoted through grades to rear adm., Mar. 15, 1904; retired, Nov. 22, 1904. Served on all foreign stas.; comd. Naval Torpedo Sta., 1890-93; supt. naval gun factory, 1893-96; comd. U.S. protected cruiser Minneapolis through war with Spain, on scouting service in W.I.; also comd. armored cruiser Brooklyn serving in the P.I.; mem. Naval Examining Bd.; comdr.-in-chief, European Squadron, 1904. Author numerous pamphlets and articles on professional subjects. Companion Mil. Order Loyal Legion. Home: Washington, D.C. Died July 26, 1932.

JEWETT, Charles, physician; b. Bath, Me., Sept. 27, 1839; s. George and Sarah (Hale) J.; A.B., Bowdoin, 1864, A.M., 1867 (Sc.D., 1894); M.D., Coll. Phys. and Surg. (Columbia), 1871; m. Abbie E. Flagg, 1868 (dec.). Has practiced medicine at Brooklyn; prof. obstetrics, 1880-1900, gynecology and obstetrics, 1900—, and gynecol. surgeon, L.I. Coll. Hosp.; consulting obstetrician Kings Co. Hosp., 1893—; consulting gynecologist Bushwick, Swedish and German hosps.; consulting surgeon St. Christopher's Hospital; trustee Brooklyn Eye and Ear Hosp., 1887—. Was first in America to perform symphyseotomy. Pres. Medical Soc. County of Kings, 1878-80, Brooklyn Gynecol. Soc., 1893, New York Obstet. Soc., 1894. Author: Essentials of Obstetrics; Manual of Child-Bed Nursing. Editor Practice of Obstetrics, by Am. authors. Address: Brooklyn, N.Y. Died 1910.

JEWETT, Edward Hurtt, clergyman, theologian; b. Nottingham, Eng., 1830; s. William and Elizabeth J.; grad. Hobart Coll., 1855, A.M., 1856, LL.D., 1891; grad. Gen. Theol. Sem., New York, 1856, D.D., 1890; S.T.D., Racine Coll., 1875; m. Sophia Seymour Miller, Dec. 30, 1863. Ordained deacon, 1856, priest, 1857, P.E. Ch. Pastorates: Boonsville, N.Y.; Forrestport, N.Y., and Dayton, O.; Norwich, Conn.; many yrs. prof. pastoral theology, Gen. Theol. Sem. Author: Communion Wine, 1856; Diabolology (Bishop Paddock Lectures, 1889), 1890; The Two Wine Theory Discussed. Address: Redlands, Calif. Died 1907.

JEWETT, George Anson, mcht.; b. Red Rock, Ia., Sept. 9, 1847; s. George Enoch and Patty Maria (Matthews) J.; Ph.B., Central Coll., Pella, Ia., 1864, A.M., 1922; grad. Bryant and Stratton's Commercial Coll., Chicago, 1865; LL.D., Drake Univ., 1892; m. Annie Henry, Oct. 28, 1868 (died 1933); children—Bonnie Ella (wife of Dr. Hugh Gilmer Welpton), Margaret (Mrs. David Lewis Jewett). Became bookkeeper, later gen. mgr. agrl. implement house, Des Moines, 1865-73; organizer, sec. and gen. mgr. Des Moines Scale Co.; entered lumber business, 1873, and became mgr. H. F. Getchell & Sons; organizer lumber firm of Ewing, Jewett & Chandler, 1879, later Ewing & Jewett, and, 1906—, Jewett Lumber Co., of which is pres. and gen. mgr.; pres. Jewett Realty Co.; organized, 1888, and 20 yrs. pres. and gen. mgr. Jewett Typewriter Co.; pub. Christian Worker, 1887—. A founder, 1881, and sec. and trustee Drake U. Founder and pres. Jewett Family in America, Inc. Republican. Mem. Ch. of Christ (Disciples); ch. clk., 1866—, and ch. treas, 1879—. Author: Hunting an Ancestor, 1914; Year Book, Jewett Family of America, 1914; also 138 Generations from Adam (series in Christian Worker), 1929. Home: Des Moines, Ia. Died July 15, 1934.

JEWETT, George Franklin, educator; b. Pepperell, Mass., Mar. 19, 1859; s. Charles Franklin and Georgiana Shipley (Loring) J.; grad. Bridgewater (Mass.) State Normal Sch., 1879; A.B., Harvard, 1886, A.M., 1911; studied in Europe, 1890; m. Abbie Burgess Fay, June 20, 1882. Teacher in Cambridge (Mass.) Latin Sch., 1887-88; prin. Marlboro (Mass.) High Sch., 1888-89, Rutgers Grammar Sch., New Brunswick, N.J., 1889-90, Rayen-High Sch., Youngstown, O., 1891-1901; asst. prin. Lasell Sem., 1901-02; founder, 1902, and prin. Mt. Ida Sch. for Girls, Newton, Mass. Congregationalist. Home: Newton, Mass. Died Apr. 1925.

JEWETT, Harry Mulford, corp. official; b. at Elmira, N.Y., Aug. 14, 1870; s. Arthur Le Roy and Gertrude (Osborne) J.; C.E., U. of Notre Dame, Ind., 1890; m. Mary Visscher Wendell, Feb. 19, 1900; children—Eleanor Osborne, Edward Huntting. Began as civil engr. on Chicago Drainage Canal, later with Mich. Central R.R. as asst. engr., at Detroit; entered coal mining business with W. P. Rend Coal Co., Chicago, and began for self in same business, 1903, at Detroit; an organizer firm of Jewett, Bigelow & Brooks, miners and wholesale coal dealers; pres. Colonial Laundry Co. (Detroit). Mem. Appalachian Engineers' Soc. Mem. Mich Naval Reserve, on board U.S.S. Yosemite, Spanish-Am. War. Republican. Mason. Home: Detroit, Mich. Died June 15. 1933.

JEWETT, Harvey C., merchant, mfr.; b. Newark, O., Aug. 5, 1863; s. David Doud and Sarah Shapley (Niles) J.; ed. high sch., Newark; m. Kate P. Kennedy, Feb. 18, 1886. Established first wholesale grocery in S.D., 1883; established wholesale grocery in Sioux Falls, 1889, wholesale drug co., 1903, investment co., 1913, and assisted in establishing biscuit cos., 1902, 10; pres. Aberdeen Nat. Bank, Jewett Bros., Jewett Drug Co. and Jewett Investment Co. (all of Aberdeen, S.D.); dir. Northwestern Bell Telephone Co. Mem. Industrial Loan Committee, 9th Federal District, Minneapolis, Minn. Elected first chairman Brown County (South Dakota) Chapter American Red Cross. also active mem. state bd.; formerly chmn. Bd. of Edn., Aberdeen. Republican. Episcopalian. Mason, Elk. Home: Aberdeen, S.D. Died June 22, 1937.

JEWETT, John Howard, author; b. Hadley, Mass., Jan. 19, 1843; s. Edwin and Elizabeth (Jones) J.; grad. Hopkins Acad., Hadley, 1861; entered army, Apr. 26, 1861, Co. C, 10th Mass. Inf.; resigned, Aug. 1864, with rank of lt. and brigade a.-q.-m. and ordnance officer; m. Sarah Hart Phelps, Oct. 1, 1867. Editor and business mgr. Holyoke (Mass.) Transcript, 1867-73; business mgr., 1873-96, pub. 1896-99, Worcester Gazette; editor "The Profession" mag., New York, 1901-02; mng. editor the Craftsman mag., 1905-06; in spl. lit. work, 1906—. Has written popular verse over own name and nom de plume "Hannah Warner." Author: The Bunny Stories, 1890; More Bunny Stories, 1900; The Easter Story, 1901; Christmas Stocking Stories (5 vols.), 1905-07; Little Mother Stories (10 vols.), 1906; Grandmother Goose Stories (4 vols.), 1907; Friends of the Hunted, 1909; also juvenile stories, army songs, poems, etc. Died Sept. 18, 1925.

JEWETT, Rutger Bleecker, editor, pub.; b. Dayton, O., Nov. 24, 1867; s. Rt. Rev. Edward Hurt and Sophia Seymour Bleecker Miller J.; A.B., Hobart Coll., N.Y., 1890, Litt.D., 1927; traveled and studied in Europe; unmarried. Prof. Greek and Latin, N.Y. Mil. Acad., 1890-92; prin. high sch., Passaic, N.J., 1892-95; prof. classics, Berkeley Sch., N.Y., 1895-99; partner and editor J. F. Taylor & Co., pubs., 1899-1904; v.p., mng. dir. John Lane Co., 1904-11; v.p. and editor in chief, D. Appleton Co., 1911-33; editor D. Appleton-Century Co. Mem. Co. K, 7th Regt. Nat. Guard N.Y., 1895-1901. Mem. Paderewski Relief Orgn. for Poland, 1915-21. Home: New York, N.Y. Died Jan. 25, 1935.

JEWETT, Sarah Orne, author; b. S. Berwick, Me., Sept. 3, 1849; d. late Dr. Theodore H. and Caroline F. (Perry) J.; ed. Berwick Acad.; Litt.D., Bowdoin Coll. Author: Deephaven, 1877; Play Days, 1878; Old Friends and New, 1879; Country By-Ways, 1881; The Mate of the Daylight and Friends Ashore, 1883; A Country Doctor, 1884; A Marsh Island, 1885; A White Heron, and Other Stories, 1886; The King of Folly Island, and Other People, 1888; Betty Leicester—A Story for Girls, 1889; Strangers and Wayfarers, 1890; The Country of the Pointed Firs, 1896; Betty Leicester's English Christmas, 1897; The Queen's Twin, 1899; The Tory Lover, 1901. Address: South Berwick, Me. and Boston, Mass. Died 1909.

JEWETT, Sophie (Miss), educator, author; b. Moravia, N.Y., June 3, 1861; d. Charles Carroll (M.D.) and Ellen Ransom (Burroughs) J.; ed. pvt. sch., Buffalo, N.Y. Instr., 1889-97, asso. prof., 1897—, English literature, Wellesley Coll. Author: The Pilgrim and Other Poems, 1896; also God's Troubadour (serial in The Churchman, Jan. to April), 1903. Editor: (with intro. and notes) The Holy Grail (Tennyson), 1901. Pseud. "Ellen Burroughs." Home: Buffalo, N.Y. Died 1909.

JEWETT, Stephen Shannon, lawyer; b. Gilford, N.H., Sept. 18, 1858; s. John Glines and Caroline E. (Shannon) J.; ed. Gilford Acad., Laconia, N.H.; hon. A.M., Dartmouth, 1913; m. Annie L. Bray, June 30, 1880; 1 son, Theo. S. Admitted to N.H. bar, 1880; dir. Laconia Nat. Bank, Laconia Bldg. & Loan Asn.; v.p. City Savings Bank. Clk. Superior Ct., Belknap County, N.H., 1884; clk. N.H. Ho. of Rep., 1891-93; mem. N.H. Ho. of Rep., 1895, 97 (speaker 1895); mem. N.H. Senate, 1899—; mem. N.H. Constl. Conv., 1902; mem. Exec. Council, N.H., 1907-08; city solicitor, Laconia, 1893-1900, and 1903-13. Del. Rep. Nat. Conv., St. Louis, 1896. Naval officer, port of Boston, 1922-23; resigned, 1923, to resume practice of law; mem. firm Jewett & Jewett. Chmn. trustees N.H. State Prison, 1919; mem. N.H. Commn. on Uniform State Laws. Conglist. Pres. N.H. Bar Assn., pres. 1916-17. Mason. Home: Laconia, N.H. Died Oct. 24, 1932.

JOB, Herbert Keightley, lecturer, author; b. Boston, Nov. 29, 1864; s. Daniel Ward and Susan Grey (Adams) J.; A.B., Harvard, 1888; grad. Hartford Theol. Sem., 1891; m. Elsie Ann Curtiss, Sept. 10, 1891; children—George Curtiss, Muriel Marion. Congl. pastor, N. Middleboro, Mass., 1891-98, Kent, Conn., 1898-1908; state ornithologist of Conn. and mem. faculty Conn. Agrl. Coll., 1908-14; econ. ornithologist in charge dept. applied ornithology, 1914-24; dir. Summer Sch. and Ornithol. Expt. Sta., 1918—, of Nat. Assn. Audubon Socs., Amston, Conn.; field agent for S.C. of Nat. Assn. of Audubon Socs. and state dir. of nature and conservation education, South Carolina, 1926-30. Has made frequent scientific expeditions to wilder parts of Northwestern states, Canada and South; nature photographer, securing large series of photographs and motion pictures of wild birds from life. Author: Among the Water Fowl, 1902 ; Wild Wings (introduction by President Roosevelt), 1905; The Sport of Bird Study, 1908; How to Study Birds, 1910; Blue Goose Chase, 1911; The Propagation of Wild Birds, 1915. Home: West Haven, Conn. Died June 17, 1933.

JOCELYN, Stephen Perry, army officer; b. Brownington, Vt., Mar. 1, 1843; s. William and Abigail Nims (Wilder) J.; ed. Brownington Acad. to 1855 People's Acad., Morrisville, Vt., 1856-57, Barton (Vt.) Acad., 1858-62; m. Mary Chamberlain Edgell, Feb. 2, 1886. Enlisted in 6th Vt. Vols., Aug. 22, 1863, serving to July 6, 1864; 1st lt. 115th U.S. Vols., Aug. 1, 1864-Feb. 10, 1866; entered regular army as lt. 6th Inf., Feb. 23, 1866; capt. 21st Inf., May 19, 1874; maj. 19th Inf., June 27, 1897; lt. col. 25th Inf., Mar. 31, 1899; col. 14th Inf., Feb. 28, 1901; brig. gen., June 16, 1906. Bvtd. maj., Feb. 27, 1890, "for conspicuous gallantry in action against Indians at the Clearwater, Ida., July 11, 12, 1877." During Civil War served in Army of the Ohio and Army of the James, being present at the fall of Richmond; served on Rio Grande border of Tex., 1865-66; in numerous Indian campaigns west of the Miss. River, 1867-91; participated in Spanish-Am. War and in P.I., 1898-1901; comd. forces in Samar, 1903, and Dept. of the Visayas, 1904; mem. Gen. Staff U.S. Army and chief of staff Pacific Div., 1904-06; comd. Dept. of the Columbia, 1906-07. Episcopalian. Home: Burlington, Vt. Died Mar. 8, 1920.

JOHANN, Carl, college pres.; b. Chaux-de-Fonds, Switzerland, Mar. 2, 1849; s. Albert Johann and Helene Mathilda (Russ) J.; ed. Chaux-de-Fonds; Coll. of Lausanne, and U. of Aarau, Switzerland; Coll. of France, Paris; hon. A.M., Eureka (Ill.) Coll., 1879, LL.D., 1887; m. Georgina Callender, Oct. 8, 1879. Came to U.S., 1869; pvt. tutor, Collinsville, Conn., 1870; pub. sch. teacher in Ill., 1872-76; prof. modern langs., 1876-98, pres., 1887-98, Eureka Coll.; supt. pub. schs., Eureka, 1898-1902; pres. Christian U., Canton, Mo., 1902-15, emeritus. Candidate for supt. public instrn., Ill., 1892. Prohibitionist. Mem. Christian Church. Mason. Address: Canton, Mo. Died Feb. 26, 1930.

JOHANNES, Francis, bishop; b. Mittelstren, Bavaria, Feb. 17, 1874; s. Urban and Anna M. (Zwierlein) J.; came with parents to U.S., 1882; ed. St. Benedict's Coll., Atchison, Kan., 1888-92, St. Francis Sem., Milwaukee, 1892-96. Ordained priest R.C. Ch., 1897; asst. pastor Immaculate Conception Ch., St. Joseph, Mo., 1897-1918, pastor, 1918-28; coadjustor bishop of Leavenworth, 1928-29, bishop of Leavenworth, Apr. 20, 1929. Home: Kansas City, Kan. Died March 13, 1937.

JOHN, John Price Durbin, educator; b. Brookville, Ind., Nov. 25, 1843; s. Robert and Martha (Wiles) J.; ed. Brookville Coll. until 16 yrs. old; A.M., McKendree Coll., Ill., 1867; (D.D., DePauw

U., 1895); m. Orra Poundstone, June 24, 1869. Taught in pub. schs., Franklin County, Ind., 1860-63; prof. mathematics, 1863-72, pres., 1869-72, Brookville (Ind.) Coll.; prof. mathematics, 1872-76; pres., and prof. philosophy, 1876-82, Moores Hill (Ind.) Coll.; prof. mathematics, 1882-95, pres., 1889-95, DePauw U.; platform lecturer, 1895—. Mem. Ind. Conference M.E. Church, 1867—. Author: Did Man Make God, or Did God Make Man?, 1899; Signs of God in the World, 1907; The Worth of a Man, 1907. Address: Greencastle, Ind. Died Aug. 7, 1916.

JOHNES, Edward Rodolph, lawyer; b. Whitesboro, Sept. 8, 1852; s. William Pierson and Anna Louisa (Gold) J.; grad. Yale (class poet), 1873; Columbia Coll. Law School, 1876; admitted to bar, 1876; partner Henry C. Wilcox 14 yrs.; later of Governor Hoffman, until latter's death; later of Robert G. Ingersoll and Hon. Thomas Fitch. Represented Venezuela in boundary dispute (received Venezuelan decoration of cross and star of Order of Bolivar); counsel in Nicaragua and Costa Rica boundary case; for Consolidated Stock Exchange in their litigation with New York Stock Exchange and Western Union Telegraph Co.; in Canon Bernard case against the King of Belgium; in Crouse will case; etc. Held options and brought about Am. Malting Co. (capital, $30,000,000), controlling 75 per cent of maltsters in U.S.; m. Winifred Wallace Tinker, Apr. 26, 1892. Author: The Monroe Doctrine as Applied to Venezuela Boundary Question; English and American Bankruptcy and Insolvency Laws; Briefs by a Barrister (verse); History of Southampton, L.I.; Circumstantial Evidence of a Future State. Home: New York, N.Y. Died 1903.

JOHNS, Charles A., judge; b. Jackson County, Mo., June 25, 1857; s. James McClellan and Elizabeth Ann (Darby) J.; A.M., Willamette U., 1878; m. Elizabeth Busch, Oct. 7, 1921; children—Barbara Elizabeth, Marguerite. Admitted to Ore. bar, 1881, and began practice at Dallas; county judge, Polk County, Ore., 1883-85; asso. justice Supreme Court of Ore., 1918-21; asso. justice Supreme Court of P.I., 1921—. Mayor of Baker, Ore., 4 terms; mem. Sch. Bd., Baker, 21 yrs.; mem. State Sch. Book Commn., Ore., 3 terms. Republican. Mason, Elk. Home: Portland, Ore. Died Jan. 12, 1932.

JOHNS, Clayton, pianist; b. New Castle, Del., Nov. 24, 1857; s. James McCalmont and Eliza (Hopkins) J.; ed. pub. and pvt. schs. there and Rugby Acad., Wilmington, Del.; spl. student, Harvard, 1879-81; studied music at Berlin until 1884; unmarried. In Boston as musician, composer and teacher, 1884—; has been abroad much of time, particularly in London, where his compositions were frequently performed. Compositions include about 100 songs, various pieces for piano, piano and violin, short choral works, several movements for string orchestra and music for a 14th Century Mystery Play (voices and instruments), etc. Author: Songs of Sleep, 1892; English Songs, 1894; Wonder Songs, 1895; Album of Songs, 1896; German Songs, 1898; French Songs, 1899; Essentials of Pianoforte Playing, 1909; The Reminiscences of A Musician, 1929; etc. Editor From Bach to Chopin, 1906. Address: Boston, Mass. Died Mar. 5, 1932.

JOHNS, George Sibley, editor; b. St. Charles, Mo., Dec. 27, 1857; s. John J. and Jane A. (Durfee) J.; A.B., Princeton, 1880; studied law; m. Minnie McDearmon, Nov. 17, 1884. Founded St. Charles Journal, 1882; joined St. Louis Post-Dispatch, 1883, successively dramatic critic, city editor, mng. editor and editor in charge, editor editorial page, asso. editor. Dir. Municipal Theatre; patron Little Theatre of St. Louis. Home: Sappington, Mo. Died July 16, 1941.

JOHNSEN, Erik Kristian, theologian; b. Stavanger, Norway, Sept. 20, 1863; s. Erik and Else Kristine (Finkelsen) J.; B.Ph., Royal U., 1883, B.D., 1887; D.D., Augustana Coll. and Theol. Sem., Ill., 1920; m. Helene Johnsen, Apr. 27, 1915. Came to U.S., 1892, naturalized citizen, 1914. Prof. theology, Luther Theol. Sem., St. Paul, Minn., 1892—. Chmn. com. on books considered for publication, Augsburg Pub. House, Minneapolis. Author: Folke Kalender (yearly), 1901—; Vor Herres Jesu Kristi Lidelses historie, 1909; Lykke-Livet, 1911; I Kirke, 1913; Paulus, 1917; Paa Reisegjennem England, Norge Danmark, 1918; Paul of Tarsus—I, Paul, a character sketch, II. Paul's Epistles, 1919. Address: St. Paul, Minn. Died Jan. 21, 1923.

JOHNSON, Alba Boardman; b. Pittsburgh, Pa., Feb. 8, 1858; s. Samuel Adams and Alma Sarah (Kemp) J.; A.B., Central High Sch., Philadelphia, 1876; LL.D., Ursinus Coll., Pa., 1909; LL.D., U. of Vt., 1928; m. Elizabeth Thomas Reeves, Apr. 30, 1883 (died 1908); m. 2d, Leah Goff, June 23, 1910. Entered Baldwin Locomotive Works (then owned by firm of Burnham, Parry, Williams & Co.), as jr. clerk, May 14, 1877; with Edge Moor Iron Works, Wilmington, Del., 1878-79, when returned to Baldwin Locomotive Works; admitted to partnership in successor firm Burnham, Williams & Co., 1896, and upon incorporation, July 1, 1909, became v.p. and treas. and pres., 1911; resigned 1919; dir. Federal Res. Bank (Phila.), N.Y. Life Ins. Co. Past pres. Am. Mfrs.' Export Assn.; past pres. and dir. Phila. Art Alliance; v.p. Y.M.C.A. of Phila. Past pres. Presbyn. Social Union, 1906-07; pres. Jefferson Med. Coll. and Hosp. Pres. Pa. State Chamber Commerce; v.p. Phila. Chamber Commerce. V.p. Art Jury of City of Phila. Republican. Home: Rosemont, Pa. Died Jan. 8, 1935.

JOHNSON, Alex Carlton, railway official; b. Crawford County, Pa., May 20, 1861; s. Abraham Carlton and Clara Maria (Sigler) J.; ed. Meadville (Pa.) Coll., 1880-82; LL.D., Dakota Wesleyan U., 1929; LL.B., Kent Coll. of Law; m. Ida R. DeVore, Jan. 4, 1881. Began with C.&N.W. Ry., 1892, spl. agt., 1894-99; gen. agt. for S.D., 1899-1900; gen. agt. at Winona, Minn., 1900-10; pass. traffic mgr., 1910-16; gen. traffic mgr., 1916, v.p., 1920-29; pres. Alex Johnson Hotel Co., Rapid City, S.D., North Western Warehouse Co.; also spl. rep. C.&N.W. Ry. Chmn. Western Freight Traffic Com., U.S.R.R. Adminstrn., 1918-20, v.p., 1921; chmn. Western Exec. Traffic Officers, 1921-29. Republican. Conglist. Mason. Home: Monrovia, Calif.; and Rapid City, S.D. Died Mar. 18, 1938.

JOHNSON, Alexander, humanitarian; b. Ashton-under-Lynn, Lancashire, Eng., Jan. 2, 1847; s. John and Amelia (Hill) J.; ed. pvt. schs., Mechanics' Inst., and Owens Coll. (now Victoria U.), Manchester, Eng.; m. Eliza Ann Johnston, June 6, 1872 (died 1911). Came to America, 1869; in clothing business until 1884; gen. sec. Asso. Charities, Cincinnati, 1884-86, Charity Orgn. Soc. of Chicago, 1886-89; sec. Ind. State Bd. of Charities, 1889-93; supt. Ind. Sch. for Feeble Minded Youth, 1893-1903; gen. sec. Nat. Conf. Charities and Correction, 1904-13; dir. extension dept., Training Sch. at Vineland, N.J., 1913-15; field sec. of Nat. Com. on Provision for the Feeble Minded, Phila., 1915-18; asst. field dir., Camp Greene, N.C., later supervisor of home service, Southern div., Atlanta, Am. Red Cross, 1918-19; dir. Alexander Milne Home-Sch. for (feeble minded) Girls, Frellsen, La., 1919-20; staff rep. Southern Div. Am. Red Cross, 1921—. Asso. dir. New York Sch. of Philanthropy, 1904-06. Democrat. Unitarian. Grand Master I.O.O.F., Ind., 1904-05. Author: Guide to the Study of Charities and Correction, 1906; The Almshouse, 1910. Home: Atlanta, Ga. Died May 17, 1941.

JOHNSON, Alfred Sidney, editor; b. L'Orignal, Ont., Dec. 15, 1860; s. Eden P. and Sarah Jane (Marston) J.; grad. Govt. Sch. of Mil. Instn., Toronto, 1882, and gazetted 1st lt. 18th Battalion vol. militia, Feb. 16, 1882; A.B., U. of Toronto (gold medalist), 1883, A.M., 1885; Ph.D., Illinois Wesleyan U., 1888; Oph.D., McCormick Med. Coll., Chicago, 1915; Opt.D., Los Angeles Med. Sch. of Ophthalmology and Optometry, 1916; m. Emma Alexandria, d. John Clarke, Sept. 1884 (died 1920). Fellow Univ. Coll., Toronto, 1883-86; examiner U. of Toronto, 1885-87; sub-examiner, ednl. dept., Prov. of Ontario, 1883-86; instr. psychology and logic, Cornell, 1886-87; prin. Denmark (Ia.) Acad., 1887-90; editor Current History, 1890-1901; mng. editor Technical World, 1904-07; editor in charge cyclo. dept. Radford Architectural Co., Chicago, and asso. editor Am. Carpenter and Builder, 1909-15; asso. editor, 1909-10, editor, 1911-15, of Cement World; editorial staff Rand McNally & Co., 1920—. As official press representative, accompanied Canadian Govt. eclipse expdn. to Labrador, 1905; on staff of Columbian Cyclopedia and United Editors' Encyclopedia; editor textbook dept., Am. Sch. Correspondence, 1903-09. Author: The Materials and Manufacture of Concrete, 1909; New Light on the Origin and Early History of Portland Cement, 1910; Steel Square Manual for Builders, 1920. Mason. Cruise to Northern Labrador, Hudson Strait, and Ungava Bay, 1923, investigating feasibility of Hudson Bay route to Europe. Died May 24, 1925.

JOHNSON, Allen, historian, editor; b. Lowell, Mass., Jan. 29, 1870; s. Moses Allen and Elmira (Shattuck) J.; A.B., Amherst Coll., 1892, A.M., 1895, also L.H.D.; U. of Leipzig, 1895-97, École des Sciences Politiques, Paris, 1897; Ph.D., Columbia U., 1899; Litt.D., 1929; m. Helen K. Ross, June 20, 1900 (died 1921); 1 son, Allen Sheppard. Instr. in history, Lawrenceville (N.J.) Sch., 1892-94; prof. history, Ia. (now Grinnell) Coll., Grinnell, Ia., 1898-1905; prof. history and polit. science, Bowdoin Coll., 1905-10; Larned prof. Am. history, Yale, 1910-26; editor Dictionary of American Biography, 1926—. Author: The Intendant Under Louis XIV, 1899; Stephen A. Douglas, 1908; Report on the Archives of Maine, 1910; Readings in American Constitutional History, 1912; Union and Democracy, 1915; Jefferson and His Colleagues, 1921; The Historian and Historical Evidence, 1926; Readings in Recent American Constitutional History (with W. A. Robinson), 1927. Editor of Chronicles of America, 1918-21. Address: Washington, D.C. Died Jan. 18, 1931.

JOHNSON, Andrew Gustavus, editor and pub.; b. Ljungby, Sweden, Dec. 25, 1857; s. Jonas and Anna (Anderson) J.; came to America, 1873; Northwestern U., 1875-78; grad. Swedish Theol. Sem., Evanston, Ill., 1878; m. Selma C. Johnson, 1889. Ordained M.E. ministry, 1878; pastor 1st Ch., Minneapolis, 1878-81, New York, 1881-85, St. Paul, 1885-90, Galesburg, Ill., 1891-92; apptd. financial agt., Bethany Home, Ravenswood, Chicago, 1893; mgr. and treas. Swedish M.E. Book Concern, Chicago, 1893-1901; pastor Moline, Ill., 1901-04, St. Paul, 1905; editor and pub. Svenska Folkets Tidning and the Royal Peoples Magazine, 1908—. Mem. Minn. Ho. of Rep., 1907-08. Home: Minneapolis, Minn. Died Jan. 10, 1924.

JOHNSON, Arthur Newhall, civil engr.; b. Lynn, Mass., Nov. 11, 1870; s. David Newhall and Amanda Malvina (Richardson) J.; S.B. in civ. engring., Lawrence Scientific Sch. (Harvard), 1894; hon. Dr. Engring., U. of Md., 1924; m. May Louise Ash, Sept. 12, 1900. Instr. descriptive geometry, Harvard, 1895-96; asst. engr. Calumet and Hecla Mine, Calumet, Mich., 1896-97; asst. engr. Mass. Highway Commn., 1897-98; state highway engr. of Md., 1898-1905; chief engr. U.S. Office of Pub. Roads, Washington, 1905; state highway engr. of Ill., 1906-14; with Bur. Municipal Research of New York, 1914-16; consulting highway engr., Portland Cement Assn., Chicago, 1916-20; dean Coll. of Engring., U. of Md., 1920-36, emeritus. Chmn. Highway Research Bd., Nat. Research Council, 1923-26; del. to Pan Am. Road Congress, Buenos Aires, 1925. Received Bartlett award for outstanding contribution to highway progress, 1933. Home: Baltimore, Md. Died July 10, 1940.

JOHNSON, Ashley Sidney, college pres.; b. Knox County, Tenn., June 22, 1857; s. Jeremiah Crockett and Barbara Jane (Johnson) J.; student U. of Tenn. short time; hon. A.M., Hiram (O.) Coll., 1889; LL.D., Christian (now Culver-Stockton) U., Canton, Mo., 1897; m. Emma Elizabeth Strawn, Dec. 31, 1884. Founder, 1893, and pres. Johnson Bible Coll. (training of young men for the ministry), Kimberlin Heights, Tenn. Democrat. Mem. Ch. of Christ. Author: The Great Controversy; The Tennessee Evangelist; Letters to a Young Methodist Preacher; Out of Darkness Into Light; The Life of Trust; Moses or Christ—Which?, Ten Lessons in How to Read, Understand and Remember the Bible; Bible Readings and Sermon Outlines in Our Plea; The Self-Interpreting New Testament; The Resurrection and the Future Life; The Condensed Biblical Cyclopedia; The Holy Spirit and the Human Mind; The C.B.C. Lesson Book; Johnson Speeches—A Debate. Home: Kimberlin Heights, Tenn. Died Jan. 13, 1925.

JOHNSON, Benjamin Franklin, publisher; b. Fauquier County, Va., Apr. 3, 1856; s. Richard Nutt and Ann Miller (Wheatley) J.; ed. pub. and pvt. schs.; m. Lucie Davis, Oct. 2, 1877 (died 1891); m. 2d, Blanche T. Wynne, July 19, 1892. Began publishing sch. books in Richmond, Va., 1876; organizer, 1900, pres., 1900-07, and still largest stockholder, B. F. Johnson Pub. Co., Richmond; organizer, 1908, and pres., B. F. Johnson, Inc., Washington, D.C.; dir. Equity Savings Bank, Washington. Baptist. Author: Johnson's Physical Culture, 1898; Johnson's Readers, 1902; Tripartite Education, 1904; Brighter Side of Washington, 1918; Army and Navy Portrait Gallery and Historical Register, 1918. Home: Washington, D.C. Died June 11, 1921.

JOHNSON, Benjamin Newhall, lawyer; b. Lynn, Mass., June 19, 1856; s. Rufus Augustus and Ellen Maria (Newhall) J.; prep. edn., Chauncy Hall Sch., Boston, and Phillips Exeter Acad., Exeter, N.H.; A.B., cum laude, highest honors in philosophy, Harvard, 1878; law study Boston U. and offices Ives, Lincoln & Huntress, Boston; hon. A.M., Tufts Coll., 1929; m. Ida Moore Oliver, June 15, 1881 (died May 27, 1894); children—Romilly, Marian (Mrs. Samuel Buchanan Charles); m. 2d, Virginia Vernon Newhall (died July 5, 1926); children—Virginia, Benjamin Newhall, Richard Vernon. Admitted to Mass. bar, 1880, and practiced at Boston; mem. firm Ives, Johnson & Ives, 1882-84, Johnson, Clapp & Underwood, 1889-1924, Johnson, Clapp, Ives & Knight, 1919—; pres. Carver Cotton Gin Co.; v.p. Essex Trust Co. of Lynn, Lynn Instn. for Savings, Lynn Gas & Electric Co.; dir. Atlantic Nat. Bank of Boston, Boston Woven Hose & Rubber Co. Chmn. Metropolitan Improvements Commn., Mass., 1907; mem. Sch. Bd., Lynn, 6 yrs.; chmn. exec. com. Tercentenary Celebration, Lynn, 1929. Four-minute man and mem. Com. on Pub. Information, World War. Was active trustee Yorktown Sesquicentennial Assn. Republican. Universalist. Donor of museum to Lynn Hist. Soc., 1929. Home: Lynn, Mass. Died Feb. 19, 1932.

JOHNSON, Bolling Arthur, editor, pub.; b. Fayette County, O., Aug. 5, 1862; s. Cyrus F. and Clarinda Tivus (Adams) J.; student Monmouth (Ill.) Coll., 1885; m. Rose, d. Maj. Thomas J. Shumate, Aug. 30, 1905. One of founders of Huffman & Johnson, pubs., Lexington, Ky., 1884; with business dept. Chicago Mail, 1886-87; market editor The Timberman, Chicago, 1887-89; staff rep. Lumber Trade Journal, Chicago, 1889-94; part owner and business mgr. Lumber Trade Journal, New Orleans, 1894-95; staff rep. The Timberman, Chicago, 1896-99, American Lumberman, Chicago, 1899-1900; pres. Am. Lecture Assn., Chicago, 1900-02; gen. staff rep. American Lumberman, 1902-11; pres. Lumber Review Co. and editor and pub. Lumber World Review, Chicago, 1911—. Home: Chicago, Ill. Died Dec. 19, 1925.

JOHNSON, Bradley Tyler, lawyer; b. Frederick, Md., Sept. 29, 1829; s. Charles Worthington and

Eleanor Murdock (Tyler) J.; grad. Princeton, 1849 (A.M., 1851); studied law at Harvard, 1850-51; practiced in Frederick; State's atty., Frederick County, 1851; Dem. candidate for comptroller of treasury, Md., 1857; chmn. Dem. State Com., Md., 1859; del. to Charleston conv., 1860; voted for State's Rights platform; withdrew from adjourned conv., Baltimore; supported Breckinridge and Lane ticket. Served as capt. to brig. gen. in Confederate army through Civil war. Practiced law, Richmond, Va., 1865-79, Baltimore, 1879-90. Mem. Nat. Dem. Conv., 1872; mem. Va. State senate, 1875-79; pres. Electoral Coll. of Md., 1884. Author: Chase's Decisions; The Foundation of Maryland; Memoir of Joseph E. Johnston; Life of General Washington ("Great Commanders" series), 1886; The Confederate History of Maryland; etc. Address: Amelia C.H., Va. Died 1903.

JOHNSON, Burt W., sculptor; b. Flint, O., Apr. 25, 1890; s. Harvey William and May (Burt) J.; ed. Pomona Prep. Sch. and Coll., Claremont, Calif.; studied art under Louis St. Gaudens and under James E. Fraser, Sr., George Bridgeman and Robert I. Aitken, Sr., Art Students' League; m. Ottilie Marie Schmucker, Aug. 19, 1916; children— Lillian (dec.), Harvey William, Cynthia Mae. Exhibited at Am. Acad. Design and Architectural League, New York; Pa. Acad. Fine Arts; Albright Galleries, Buffalo, N.Y.; Columbus Gallery of Fine Arts; etc. Principal works: Pomona Valley war memorial statue and Spanish music fountain, Pomona Coll.; Woodside memorial statue, N.Y. City; E. N. Dimick memorial statue, West Palm Beach, Fla.; Children's World War memorial fountain, Huntington Park, Calif.; sculpture on Memorial Shaft, College Park, Atlanta, Ga.; etc. Republican. Conglist. Lecturer on civic sculpture and history of Am. sculpture. Home: Claremont, Calif., and Cornish, N.H. Died Mar. 27, 1927.

JOHNSON, Byron Bancroft ("Ban" Johnson), baseball promoter; b. Cincinnati, O., Jan. 6, 1865; s. Alexander Byron and Eunice C. (Fox) J.; A.B., Marietta (O.) Coll., 1897; m. Sarah Jane Laymon, 1894. Pres. Am. League of Professional Baseball Clubs, 1900-27, also treas. and sec. Presbyn. Home: Chicago, Ill. Died Mar. 28, 1931.

JOHNSON, Charles Eugene, prof. zoölogy; b. Oslo, Norway, Apr. 24, 1880; s. Capt. Christen and Ottomine Marie (Anderson) J.; brought to U.S., 1882, naturalized, 1886; A.B., U. of Minn., 1906, A.M., 1907, Ph.D., 1912; post-grad. work, U. of Wis., 1910, Harvard Med. Sch., 1911; m. Jane A. Wood, Dec. 20, 1914; children—Lucia Marie, Jane Louise. Began as instr. gen. zoölogy and histology, Hamline U., St. Paul, 1907; asst. and instr. in gen. zoölogy and comparative anatomy, U. of Minn., 1907-19; asst. prof. and asso. prof. zoölogy, U. of Kan., 1919-23; prof. zoölogy, N.Y. State Coll. of Forestry, 1923—, head dept. forest zoölogy and dir. Roosevelt Wild Life Sta., 1926—. Republican. Home: Syracuse, N.Y. Died June 6, 1936.

JOHNSON, Charles Fletcher, judge; b. Winslow, Me., Feb. 14, 1859; s. William F. and Ruth S. Johnson; A.B., Bowdoin, 1879, LL.D., 1911; m. Abbie W. Britton, Dec. 21, 1881; children—William F. (dec.), Emma L. (wife of Henry W. Abbott, M.D.). Prin. high sch., Machias, Me., 5 yrs., 1881-86; admitted to Me. bar, 1886, and began practice at Waterville. Was mayor of Waterville; Dem. candidate for gov. of Me., 1892, 94; mem. Me. Ho. of Rep., 1905, 07; del. Dem. nat. convs., 1904, 12, 16; U.S. senator from Me. for term 1911-17; U.S. circuit judge, 1st Circuit, 1917—. Mason (Grand Master Grand Lodge of Me., 1906-07). Home: Waterville, Me. Died Feb. 15, 1930.

JOHNSON, Charles Frederick, author; b. New York, N.Y., May 8, 1836; s. Charles F. and Sarah Dwight (Woolsey) J.; A.B., Yale, 1855, A.M., 1885, Litt.D., 1898; LL.D., Trinity, 1909; m. Elizabeth J. McAlpine, Jan. 4, 1872 (died 1882); m. 2d, Ellen Wadsworth Terry, Dec. 27, 1883 (died 1896). Studied law but did not practice, asst. prof. mathematics, U.S. Naval Acad., 1865-70; prof. English lit., Trinity Coll., Conn., 1883-1907; emeritus prof. under Carnegie Foundation, 1909. Author: English Words (text-book), 1897; Three Englishmen and Three Americans, 1890; Elements of Literary Criticism, 1898; What Can I Do for Brady?, and Other Verses, 1897; Outline History of English and American Literature, 1900; Forms of English Poetry, 1904; Shakespeare and His Critics, 1909. Engaged in newspaper work, 1909—. Address: Hartford, Conn. Died Jan. 9, 1931.

JOHNSON, Charles Nelson, dentist; b. Brock Twp., Ont., Can., Mar. 16, 1860; s. Winthrop and Laura (Moore) J.; ed. Port Perry high schs.; L.D.S., Royal Coll. Dental Surgeons, Toronto, 1881, M.D.S., 1921; D.D.S., Chicago Coll. Dental Surgery, 1885; hon. A.M., Lake Forest U., 1897; LL.D., Loyola U., 1924, U. of Toronto, 1932; m. Fannie Patterson, Mar. 7, 1883; children—Mignon, Nelyon. Practicing dentistry in Chicago, 1885—; students' dean, and prof. operative dentistry, Chicago Coll. Dental Surgery, 1891—. Editor Dental Review, 1902-19; editor Jour. of the American Dental Assn., 1925—. Author: The Hermit of the Nonquon, 1893; Filling Teeth, 1900; Poems of the Farm and Other Poems, 1901; Success in Practice, 1903; Operative Dentistry, 1908; The Hand Clasp, 1919. Home: Chicago, Ill Died July 17, 1938.

JOHNSON, Charles Philip, lawyer; b. Lebanon, Ill., Jan. 18, 1836; s. Henry and Elvira (Fouke) J.; ed. McKendree College, 1855, later awarded degrees M.A., LL.B., same coll.; m. Estelle Parker, June 1861; m. 2d, Louise Stevens, Mar. 1881; m. 3d, Anne, d. Doctor Maurice and Clementine (Bernays) André, of St. Louis, November 18, 1898. Was editor of Independent Spartan, Sparta, Ill., at age of 17; city atty., St. Louis, 1859, 1860; mem. Mo. Ho. of Rep., 1862, 63, 65, and 1881; circuit atty. of St. Louis City and County, 1866-72, lt. gov. of Mo., 1872-74; lecturer on law, Washington U., for number of yrs. Specializes in criminal law. Democrat. Home: St. Louis, Mo. Died May 21, 1920.

JOHNSON, Charles Willison, zoölogist; b. Morris Plains, N.J., Oct. 26, 1863; s. Albert Fletcher and Sarah Elizabeth (Willison) J.; ed. pub. and pvt. schs., Morristown, N.J.; m. Carrie W. Ford, Jan. 14, 1897 (died 1931). Moved to St. Augustine, Fla., 1880, continuing studies in natural history, and making large collection of insects, mollusca and fossils. Curator Museum of Wagner Free Inst. of Science, Phila., 1888-1903; curator Boston Soc. Natural History, 1903—. Especially interested in study of mollusca and diptera, and contbr. to biol. jours. of papers relating to these splties.; asso. editor and mgr. The Nautilus, 1890—. Fellow Am. Acad. Arts and Sciences, Entomol. Soc. America (pres. 1924), A.A.A.S. Home: Brookline, Mass. Died 1932.

JOHNSON, Clarke Howard, judge; b. Foster, R.I., Nov. 18, 1851; s. Elisha and Matilda (Howard) J.; A.B., Brown U, 1877, LL.D., 1914; LL.D., R.I. State Coll. of Agr., 1919; m. Ida S. Harrington, Dec. 21, 1889. Admitted to bar, 1879; practiced law in Providence. Mem. R.I. Ho. of Rep., 1879-80, and 1899-1903; clerk of R.I. Ho. of Rep., 1881-86; justice District Ct., 8th Jud. Dist. R.I., 1886-1903; asso. justice Supreme Ct. of R.I., 1903-17 (chief justice, Jan. 27, 1913-Mar. 7, 1917). Republican. Home: Foster, R.I. Died Sept. 14, 1930.

JOHNSON, Clifton, author, illustrator; b. Hadley, Mass., Jan. 25, 1865; s. Chester L. and Jenette (Reynolds) J.; ed. common schs. there, 1870-80; m. Anna McQueston, 1896; children—Margaret, Arthur, Roger, Oliver (dec.), Irving, Catherine. Republican. Unitarian. Author: The New England Country, 1892; The Country School, 1907; The Farmer's Boy, 1907; What They Say in New England, 1896; Among English Hedgerows, 1899; Along French Byways, 1900; The Isle of the Shamrock, 1901; New England and Its Neighbors, 1902; The Land of Heather, 1903; Old-Time Schools and School-Books, 1904; American Highways and Byways, 7 vols., 1904-15; The Picturesque Hudson, 1909; The Picturesque St. Lawrence, 1910; Battleground Adventures in the Civil War, 1915; New England, 1917; Highways and Byways of Florida, 1918; What to See in America, 1919; John Burroughs' Talks, 1922; The Rise of An American Inventor, 1924; The Parson's Devil, 1926; Historic Hampshire in the Connecticut Valley, 1932. Has edited or illustrated about 50 juveniles, school books and other works. Home: Hadley, Mass. Died Jan. 22, 1940.

JOHNSON, Cone, lawyer; b. Dawsonville, Ga., June 11, 1860; s. Samuel Calaway and Emily (Swilling) J.; student Emory Coll., Oxford, Ga., 1878, Peabody Normal Coll., Nashville, Tenn., 1878-80; A.B., U. of Nashville, 1889; m. Sophie Elizabeth Robertson, May 8, 1889 (died 1926); m. 2d, Ethel Frances Hilton, Aug. 2, 1928. Began practice in Tyler, Tex., 1884; in partnership with T. O. Woldert, 1886-91, with H. C. Johnson, 1891-1901; sr. mem. Johnson & Edwards, 1901-25. Mem. Tex. Ho. of Rep., 1886-88, Senate, 1888-92; candidate for gov. of Tex., 1908; del.-at-large Dem. Nat. convs., 1912, 20, solicitor Dept. of State, Washington, 1914-17. Mem. Smith County Highway Commn., 1918-21, Tex. State Highway Commn., 1927—. Methodist. Mason. Home: Tyler, Tex. Died Mar. 17, 1933.

JOHNSON, David, artist; b. New York, N.Y., May 1827; s. David and Eliza (Daymon) J.; ed. common schools; except for a few lessons from Jasper F. Cropsey, is self-taught in art; m. Marie Louise West, Jan. 20, 1869. His landscapes, all American subjects, are in many of the best public and private collections. Received medals at Centennial Expn., 1876, Boston, etc. Elected asso., 1861, academician, 1862—, Nat. Acad. of Design. One of the founders of Artists' Fund Soc. Home: Walden, N.Y. Died 1908.

JOHNSON, David Bancroft, college pres.; b. La Grange, Tenn., Jan. 10, 1856; s. David Bancroft and Margaret E. J.; A.B., U. of Tenn., 1877, A.M., 1880; LL.D., S.C. Coll., 1905; LL.D., Presbyterian Coll., Clinton, S.C., 1924; m. Mai R. Smith, Aug. 6, 1902. Asst. prof. mathematics, U. of Tenn., 1879-80; prin. graded schs., Abbeville, S.C., 1880-82; supt. and organizer city schs., Columbia, S.C., 1883-95; organized, 1886, Winthrop College, the S.C. College for Women, pres. 1896—. Established, and pres. 1885-94, Columbia (S.C.) Y.M.C.A.; chmn. state executive com. Y.M.C.A., 1886—; organized S.C. Assn. of School Supts., 1890, Rural Sch. Improvement Assn., of S.C., 1902; mem. S.C. State Com. to Revise School Laws, 1910-11, State Bd. of Edn. of S.C., 1891-94, Conservation Soc. of S.C., 1924. Pres. State Teachers' Assn., 1884-88; v.p. 1906-07, pres. dept. rural and agrl. edn., 1909, pres. normal sch. dept., 1911, mem. nat. com. on normal sch. statistics, 1911, pres., 1915-16—all of N.E.A.; pres. Southern Ednl. Assn., 1910. Pres. S.C. State S.S. Assn.; mem. Internat. Com. Y.M.C.A. Assns. Elector Hall of Fame, 1919—. First Distinguished Service Medal award by Am. Legion of S.C., 1927. Home: Rock Hill, S.C. Died Dec. 26, 1928.

JOHNSON, Duncan Starr, botanist; b. Cromwell, Conn., July 21, 1867; s. Edward Tracy and Lucy Emma (Starr) J.; B.S., Wesleyan U., Conn., 1892, D.Sc., 1932; student, Yale, 1887; Ph.D., Johns Hopkins, 1897; U. of Munich, 1901; m. Mary E. G. Lentz, June 22, 1904; children—George Duncan, David Starr. Asst. in botany, 1898-99, asso., 1899-1901, asso. prof., 1901-06, prof., 1906—, dir. bot. garden, 1913—, Johns Hopkins U. In charge of botany, 1896-1900, cryptogamic botany, 1902-11, Cold Spring Harbor, L.I., N.Y.; botanical exploration and investigation, Jamaica, B.W.I., 6 times to 1932; investigator, Carnegie Institution, Washington, D.C., 1912, 15; in charge of inspection for disease of grain fields of Atlantic States for Bureau of Plant Industry, May-Aug. 1918; v.p. Mt. Desert Biol. Lab., 1921—; lecturer Mt. Lake Biol. Sta., U. of Va., summer 1935. Dir. 6th Bot. Expdn. of Johns Hopkins U. to West Indian tropics, and Guatemala, June-Aug. 1932, and of 7th Expdn. of Bot. Dept., Johns Hopkins, to Jamaica and Central America, summer 1936. Mgr. L.I. Biol. Assn., 1923-24. Mem. Nat. Research Council, 1927-1933, chmn. division biology and agr., 1931-32. Fellow A.A.A.S. (v.p. sect. G, 1912); mem. Bot. Soc. America (sec. 1907-09). Author: The Relation of Plants to Tide Levels (with H. H. York), 1915; The Fruit of Opuntia fulgida and Proliferation in Fruits of the Cactaceæ, 1918 (monograph); Littoral Vegetation on Mt. Desert Island (with A. F. Skutch), 1928. Home: Roland Park, Md. Died Feb. 16, 1937.

JOHNSON, Eastman, artist; b. Lovell, Me., 1824; s. Philip C. J. (many yrs. Sec. of State of Me.); ed. public schools, Augusta, Me.; studied 2 yrs. in Royal Acad., Düsseldorf. Mem. Nat. Acad. of Design, 1860—, and Soc. of Am. Artists. Among many notable genre pictures are "The Kentucky Home," "Husking Bee," "The Stage Coach," "Pension Agent," "Prisoner of State," and portraits "Two Men," Presidents Arthur, Cleveland and Harrison, W. H. Vanderbilt, Commodore Vanderbilt, Secretary Folger, Daniel Webster, John Quincy Adams, Wm. B. Astor, John D. Rockefeller, W. D. Sloane, Mrs. Alexander Hamilton, Mrs. Dolly Madison (from life), Mrs. August Belmont, Mrs. Hamilton Fish, Mr. and Mrs. I. A. Burden, Mrs. W. T. Blodgett; Coll. Presidents McCosh, Noah Porter, Barnard and Andrew White; Charles O'Conor, Wheeler H. Peckham, Longfellow, Hawthorne, Emerson, Bishop Potter, Morris K. Jesup, etc. Exhibited and received medals at Paris, London, Phila. Centennial, World's Columbian, Buffalo and Charleston Expns. Represented in the Metropolitan Mus. of Art and Lenox Galleries, New York; Corcoran Gallery, White House and Treasury Bldg., Washington; Capitol at Albany; Knickerbocker, Century and Union League Clubs, Chamber of Commerce, Board of Trade, etc., New York. Address: New York, N.Y. Died 1906.

JOHNSON, Eben Samuel, bishop; b. Warwickshire, Eng., Feb. 8, 1866; s. William and Catherine (Sidwell) J.; teachers' training course, Eng.; engaged in newspaper work in London; came to U.S., 1889; A.B., A.M., Morningside Coll., Ia.; studied Oxford U., Eng.; D.D., Syracuse; m. Sarah Tilsley. Ordained M.E. ministry, 1889; pastor in Ia. for many yrs., also dist. supt.; elected missionary bishop of Africa, 1916, bishop, 1920. Del. and Journal sec. Gen. Conf. M.E. Ch., 1904, 08, 12, 16; secretary and publisher minutes Northwest Ia. Conf. 13 yrs.; chmn. Conf. Bd. Examiners 10 yrs.; pres. Northwest Ia. Conf. Bd. of Edn. 8 yrs.; was trustee Morningside Coll. Chaplain Ia. N.G. 18 yrs.; chaplain 52d Ia. Vols., Spanish-Am. War, 1898; on Mexican border with 2d Ia. Regt., 1916. Extensive missionary travels in Africa, including journey across the wilds of Angola and Belgian Congo, 800 miles of which was accomplished on foot, 1919; traveled by motor car through southern and northern Rhodesia, Belgian Congo and Angola and back to Cape Town, over 8,000 miles, 1927, and more extensive journeys in succeeding years. Mason (Past Grand Prelate, Grand Commandery K.T. of Ia.). Address: New York, N.Y. Died Dec. 9, 1939.

JOHNSON, Edward Bryant, stockman, banker; b. nr. Ft. Arbuckle, Ind. Ty., Oct. 1, 1863; s. Montford Thomas and Mary Elizabeth (Campbell) J.; student Chickasaw Male Acad., Tishomingo, Okla., 1877-78, Cane Hill (Ark.) Coll., 1879-80, Poly. Inst. of Brooklyn (N.Y.), 1881-83; m. Mollie Elizabeth Graham, Feb. 17, 1887; children—Veta (Mrs. L. C. Giles), Ina Johnson (Mrs. Phil C. Kidd), Neil Robert, Montford Tilford, Graham Belton, Froma Adelaide (Mrs. Roy S. Johnson), Arline (Mrs. LeRoy Le Flore), Edward Bryant. Engaged in stock raising many years; formerly pres. First Nat. Bank, Norman, Okla. Democrat. Mem. Disciples of Christ Ch. Mason, Odd Fellow, Elk, Woodman of the World. Mem. Chickasaw Tribe of Indians and del. from same to Washington, D.C., as treaty commr. Home: Norman, Okla. Died Dec. 25, 1935.

JOHNSON, Edward Payson, clergyman; b. Peru, Ind., Jan. 26, 1850; s. Rev. Asa and Julia Warner (Sadd) J.; A.B., Wabash Coll., 1871, A.M., 1875; grad. Auburn (N.Y.) Theol. Sem., 1875; D.D., Rutgers, 1896; m. Clara Brownell, Jan. 23, 1878. Ordained Presbyn. ministry, 1875; pastor Presbyn. chs., Sandy Hill, N.Y., 1875-79, Marshall, Mich., 1879-86, Woodlawn Park, Chicago, 1886-91; pastor First Ref. Ch., Albany, 1891-1906; prof. sacred and ecclesiastical history, Theol. Sem. of Ref. Ch. in America, 1906—. Address: New Brunswick, N.J. Died May 31, 1924.

JOHNSON, Edwin S., senator; b. Owen County, Ind., Feb. 26, 1857; s. Allison C. and Emily J. (Brenton) J.; ed. pub. schs., Osceola, Ia. Began in clothing business with father, in S.Dak., 1884, and engaged in banking business at Grandview and Armour; admitted to bar, 1891; state's atty. Douglas County, S.D., 1893; served as mem. Senate, S.D., and as mem. Dem. Nat. Com.; mem. U.S. Senate, 1915-21. Home: Yankton, S.D. Died July 19, 1933.

JOHNSON, Effie, author. See Euphemia Johnson Richmond.

JOHNSON, Elias Finley, judge; b. Van Wert, O., June 24, 1861; s. Abel J.; B.S., Nat. U., Lebanon, O.; LL.B., U. of Mich., 1890, LL.M., 1891; m. Clara A. Smith, Sept. 6, 1883; children—Mrs. A. D. Gibbs, David Cecil (dec.). Mem. Ohio Ho. of Rep., 1883-87; asst. and instr. law, 1890-94, asst. prof., 1894-95, prof. law, 1895-1901, U. of Mich.; judge Supreme Court of P.I., 1901—; mem. Mich. State Bd. Edn., 1897-1901; mem. Bd. of Regents U. of Philippines. Republican. Author: Johnson on Bills and Notes. Editor: 2d edit. Norton on Bills and Notes; 3d edit. Bliss on Code Pleading. Address: Manila, P.I. Died July 31, 1933.

JOHNSON, Elias Henry, prof. systematic theology, Crozer Theol. Sem., 1882—; b. Troy, N.Y.; Oct. 15, 1841; s. Elias and Laura Gale J.; grad. U. of Rochester, 1862; Rochester Theol. Sem., 1871; (A.M., 1871, D.D., 1878, U. of Rochester; A.M., Brown U., 1877; LL.D., Bucknell U., 1898); m. Mary A. Lyon, Feb. 14, 1867. Acting asst. paymaster U.S.N., 1864-66; entered Bapt. ministry, 1866; visited Europe, Egypt, Sinai and Palestine, 1871-73. Pastorates in LeSueur, Minn., 1866-68; Ballston, N.Y., 1873-75; Providence, R.I., 1875-83. Author: Outline of Systematic Theology, 1892, 3d edit., 1895; Uses and Abuses of Ordinances, 1890; Review of Ethical Monism, 1896; Religious Use of Imagination, 1900; The Highest Life, 1901; The Holy Spirit Then and Now, 1904. Editor: Songs of Praise for Sunday Schools, 1882; asst. editor of Baptist Hymnal, 1883; editor Our Sunday School Songs, 1885, 2d edit., 1901; Ezekiel Gilman Robinson, 1896; Sursum Corda, a hymnal, 1898. Home: Upland, Pa. Died 1906.

JOHNSON, Evan Malbone, army officer; b. Brooklyn, Sept. 26, 1861; s. Capt. Evan M. (U.S.V.) and Amy (Grant) J.; ed. Alexander Mil. Inst., White Plains, N.Y.; Poly. Inst., Brooklyn; M.S., Mt. Union Coll., 1904, LL.D., 1918; M.M.S., Pa. Mil. Coll., 1914; grad. Inf. and Cav. Sch., Ft. Leavenworth, Kan., 1889; grad. Army War Coll., Washington, 1911; m. Bessie Seaman, Feb. 12, 1896. Enlisted as pvt. Co. F, 10th Inf., June 12, 1882; 2d lt., Aug. 15, 1885; 1st lt. 23d Inf., June 28, 1892; trans. to 17th Inf., Aug. 12, 1892, to 19th Inf., Dec. 15, 1892; capt., Mar. 2, 1899; maj. 29th U.S. Vol. Inf., July 5, 1899; hon. discharged vols., May 10, 1901; trans. to 8th Inf., Apr. 9, 1904; maj. 6th Inf., July 3, 1908; lt. col. 19th Inf., July 20, 1914; trans. to 29th Inf., Jan. 5, 1915; col., July 1, 1916; brig. gen. N.A., Aug. 5, 1917. Campaign against Apache Indians, 1885-86, against Geronimo, in Ariz. and N.M.; prof. mil. science and tactics, Mt. Union Coll., 1891-94; Puerto Rican Expdn., Spanish-Am. War, 1898; Philippine Insurrection, 1899-1901, operations Island of Leyte, 1907; insp.-instr., organizing militia of N.J., 1911-12; with Div. Mil. Affairs, Office Chief of Staff, Washington, 1912-14; expdn. to Vera Cruz, Mex., Apr. 1914; assigned as comdr. 154th Inf. Brigade, Camp Upton, L.I., N.Y., Aug. 25, 1917; comd. 77th Div., Dec. 1, 1918-May 10, 1919, and Aug. 18-28, 1919; transferred to command 158th Brig., Oct. 28, 1919; comd. 79th Div., Jan. 17-Apr. 1, 1919; mil. attaché to Am. Embassy, Rome, Italy, Sept. 15, 1919—. Sec. Inf. Assn. and editor Inf. Jour., 1912-14. Medalist Mil. Service Instn., 1906. Died Oct. 13, 1923.

JOHNSON, Francis Howe, author; b. Boston, Jan. 15, 1835; s. Samuel and Charlotte A. (Howe) J.; A.B., Harvard, 1856; grad. Andover Theol. Sem., 1860; m. Mary A. Dove, 1867; m. 2d, Mary Beach, 1894. Ordained Congl. ministry, 1861; pastor Hamilton, Mass., 1861-64; resided in Andover, Mass., 1864—. Author: What Is Reality? an Inquiry as to the Reasonableness of Natural Religion and the Naturalness of Revealed Religion, 1891; God in Evolution, 1911. Died Oct. 27, 1920.

JOHNSON, Frank Fisk, public utility exec.; b. Shawano, Wis., Nov. 15, 1862; s. Albert and Elizabeth S. (Fisk) J.; prep. edn., high school, Denver; student Mass. Inst. Tech.; m. Marie L. Gieson, Apr. 17, 1888; children—Albert Dorman, Clara Louise (Mrs. Pasco B. Carter), Ellsworth Egbert. Asst. cashier Bank of Murray, Idaho, 1887-90; with Bank of North Ida., 1890-96; organizer and pres. First Nat. Bank, Wallace, Ida., 1892-1910; began with Boise City Nat. Bank, 1910, successively cashier, pres., became chmn. bd., 1926; chmn. bd. Ida. Power Co.; dir. Nev. Power Co., Salmon River Power & Light Co. Treas. Shoshone County, Ida., 1891, 92. First chmn. Ida. Liberty Loan Com.; treas. Am. Red Cross, Ida., before and during World War. Republican. Mason, Elk. Home: Boise, Ida. Died Jan. 4, 1937.

JOHNSON, Frank Pearson, banker; b. Lexington, Miss., Aug. 9, 1872; s. Herbert Pearson and Lucy Chase (Fultz) J.; B.S., Agrl. and Mech. Coll. of Miss., 1890; m. Aida Allen, Mar. 28, 1894; children—Mrs. Ethelyn J. Hightower (dec.), Hugh Allen (dec.). Owner, editor weekly newspaper, Kosciusko, 1890-95; settled in Oklahoma City, Okla., 1895; published daily newspaper, taught sch., engaged in mortgage and title business; established Oklahoma City Savings Bank, 1901, pres. 1901-03; bank merged, 1903, with Am. Nat. Bank, of which was cashier until 1906, pres., 1906-27; pres. Am.-First Nat. Bank (consolidation of First Nat. and Am. Nat. banks), 1927-30; pres. First Nat. Bank & Trust Co. (consolidated Am.-First Nat. and Security Nat. banks), 1930—; also pres. Am.-First Trust Co., Hightower Building Co., Union Mortgage Co.; dir. Oklahoma City Building & Loan Assn., Oklahoma Savings & Loan Assn. Served as mil. cadet, 1886-90, advancing to capt. Democrat. Presbyn. Elk. Home: Oklahoma City, Okla. Deceased.

JOHNSON, Frank Seward, physician; b. Chicago, Apr. 18, 1856; s. Homer Allen and Margaret (Seward) J.; A.M., Northwestern U., 1878; M.D., Chicago Med. Coll., 1881; m. Elizabeth Burbank, d. Edward Everett Ayer, Sept. 3, 1900. Emeritus dean and prof. medicine and clin. medicine, Med. Dept., Northwestern U.; consulting physician to Michael Reese and Mercy hosps., Chicago; 1st lt. Med. Reserve Corps U.S.A. Died Apr. 23, 1922.

JOHNSON, Frank Tenney, artist; b. on ranch nr. Big Grove, Pottawattamie Co., Ia., June 26, 1874; s. Abner Morse and Cordelia Rebecca (Tenney) J.; ed. high sch., Oconomowoc, Wis., Art Students' League, N.Y. City, and New York Sch. of Art; m. Vinnie Reeve Francis, Dec. 31, 1896. Painter of Western life; dir. Biltmore Salon, Los Angeles, Calif. Awarded $1,000 Shaw purchase prize, Salmagundi Club, N.Y. City, 1923; $1,250 Edgar B. Davis purchase prize, San Antonio, Tex., 1929; silver medal, Allied Artists America, 1929; silver medal, Painters of the West, Los Angeles, 1930. Rep. in Nat. Gallery, Washington, D.C., Dallas (Tex.) Art Assn., Fort Worth (Tex.) Mus. Art, Phoenix (Ariz.) Municipal Art Gallery, Nat. Arts Club, N.Y. City, Amherst Coll., Royal Palace, Copenhagen, Denmark, Dunedin Mus. (New Zealand), Cathay Circle Theater (Los Angeles); A.N.A., 1929, N.A., 1937. Republican. Methodist. Mason. Address: Alhambra, Calif. Died Jan. 1, 1939.

JOHNSON, Franklin, theologian; b. Franklin, O., Nov. 2, 1836; s. Rev. Hezekiah and Eliza Shepherd (Harris) J.; grad. Colgate Theol. Sem., 1861; studied German univs. and traveled in Egypt and Holy Land, 1868-69; D.D., U. of Jena, 1869; LL.D., Ottawa U., Kan., 1898; m. Mary Alma Barton, Sept. 28, 1863 (died 1882); m. 2d, Persis Isabel Swett, June 29, 1886. Ordained Bapt. ministry, 1862; pastor Bay City, Mich., 1861-63, Lambertville, N.J., 1864-66, Passaic, N.J., 1866-72, Newark, N.J., 1872-74, Cambridge, Mass., 1874-88, Athens, Greece, 1888-89; pres. Ottawa U., 1890-92; asst. prof. ch. history and homiletics, 1892-94, asso. prof., 1894-95, prof., 1895-1908, prof. emeritus, 1908, U. of Chicago. Coeditor The Watchman, 1876. Author: The Dies Iræ, 1880; The Stabat Mater Dolorosa and The Stabat Mater Speciosa, 1886; The Gospel According to Matthew, with notes, 1873; Moses and Israel, 1874; Heroes and Judges from the Law-Givers to the King, 1875; True Womanhood—Hints on the Formation of Womanly Character, 1884; A Romance in Song—Heine's Lyrical Interlude, 1884; The New Psychic Studies in Their Relation to Christian Thought, 1886; The Quotations of the New Testament from the Old Considered in the Light of General Literature, 1896; The Home Missionaries, 1899; Have We the Likeness of Christ? The Christian's Relation to Evolution, 1904. Contbr. to encys. and revs. and transls. of Latin and Anabaptist hymns. Investigations in Japan, China and India, 1913-14. Was mem. Rep. Nat. Conv., Chicago, 1860, which nominated Lincoln. Home: Chicago, Ill. Died Oct. 7, 1916.

JOHNSON, Fred Page, ry. official; b. N.Y. City, Jan. 27, 1874; s. Barton McKay and Susan Martha (Cook) J.; ed. pub. schs., St. Louis, Mo.; m. Minnie Jean Smith, June 2, 1897; children—Alice Dell (Mrs. Eustice Waggoner), George Fred. Began as messenger boy with accounting dept., Mo.P. Ry., 1889, clk., 1889-1910, chief accountant, 1910-12, auditor of disbursements, 1912-13, asst. gen. auditor, 1913-18, federal auditor, 1918-20, gen. auditor, 1920-26; v.p., in charge finance and accounts, 1926—; pres. Kan.-Mo. Elevator Co.; v.p. Boonville, St. Louis & Southern Ry. Co., Mo.P. R.R. Corp. in Neb., Mo. Improvement Co., and many other rys.; sec. and treas. Southern Ill. & Mo. Bridge Co., Chester & Mount Vernon R.R. Co., Doniphan, Kensett & Searcy Ry.; gen. auditor Mo. P. Transportation Co. Republican. Presbyn. Odd Fellow. Home: St. Louis Mo. Died Nov. 11, 1938.

JOHNSON, Frederick Green, newspaper pub.; b. Wilkes-Barre, Pa., Oct. 22, 1890; s. Frederick Charles (M.D.) and Georgia (Post) J.; prep. edn., Harry Hillman Acad. (now Wilkes-Barre Acad.); A.B., Cornell U., 1913; studied Columbia U. Sch. of Journalism, 1913-14; m. Kathleen MacBeth Cable, Apr. 9, 1914 (died 1916); 1 dau., Kathleen Cable; m. 2d. Thelma Rhea Neiger, June 25, 1921; children—Eleanor Lindsey, Marjory Holt, Marilyn, Frederick G., Gail; m. 3d, Lillian Yow Weller. With U.S. Marine Corps, Res., in U.S. and overseas, Dec. 1917-Apr. 1919. Pub. of Wilkes-Barre Record. Ind. Republican. Episcopalian. Mason. Home: Wilkes-Barre, Pa. Died Oct. 21, 1941.

JOHNSON, George Ellsworth, educator; b. Springfield, Vt., June 21, 1862; s. Rawson Taft and Adaline (Allbee) J.; A.B., Dartmouth, 1887, A.M., 1890; Hartford Theol. Sem., 1892-93; scholar and fellow, Clark U., 1893-95, A.M., 1895; m. Alice Williams, July 14, 1897. Teacher, Peshtigo, Wis., 1881-83; prin. Colebrook (N.H.) Acad., 1887-88, Springfield (Vt.) High Sch., 1888-92; supt. schs., Andover, Mass., 1895-1901; teacher, Cleveland, O., 1901-03; supt. schs. Tewksbury (Mass.) Dist., 1903-05, Hyde Park, Mass., 1905-07; supt. Pittsburgh Playground Assn., 1907-13; was also prof. play, Sch. of Edn., U. of Pittsburgh; head of dept. play and recreation, New York School of Philanthropy, 1913-15; asst. prof. div. education, 1915-20, asso. prof., 1920—, Grad. Sch. of Edn., Harvard U. Lecturer Teachers College, Columbia University, 1914-15. Author: Elementary Rational Speller, 1903; Contagious Diseases of Children, 1906; Education by Plays and Games, 1907; What to Do at Recess, 1910; Education Through Recreation, 1916. Home: Cambridge, Mass. Died Aug. 26, 1931.

JOHNSON, George K., life underwriter; b. Bucks County, Pa., Dec. 11, 1848; s. George K. and Elizabeth R. (Shotwell) J.; grad. Friends' Central Sch., Phila.; m. Sarah K. Cooper, Oct. 1, 1873. Partner Belknap, Johnson & Powell, New York and Phila., 1880; retired from mercantile bus., 1897; mem. bd. of trustees Penn Mut. Life Ins. Co., 1889, elected v.p. and in charge of underwriting branch, 1897, pres., 1906-1922; dir. Pa. Co. for Insurance, Fourth St. Nat. Bank, Cincinnati, Indianapolis & Western R.R. Co., N.E. Power Co. Treasurer Jeanes Hosp. Home: Philadelphia, Pa. Died 1923.

JOHNSON, Hale, lawyer, prohibition advocate; b. Montgomery County, Ind., Aug. 21, 1847; s. John B. and Sarah A. (Davisson) J.; academic edn.; m. Mary E. Loofbourrow, Feb. 19, 1871. Admitted to bar, 1875; has practiced at Newton, Ill., 1877—; joined Prohibition party, 1882; has been that party's candidate for Congress, gov. and (1896) for Vice-President; active in state and national campaigns, and in amendment campaigns in Mich. and Ohio; now mem. Nat. Prohibition Com. Home: Newton, Ill. Died 1902.

JOHNSON, Harry McCrindell, genito-urinary surgeon; b. St. Francesville, La., Jan. 14, 1867; s. Charles James (M.D.) and Louisa Bulter (McCrindell) J.; grad. Episcopal High Sch., Alexandria, Va., 1886; M.D., Tulane U., 1890; m. Constance Walker, July 16, 1913; children—Harry McCrindell, Margaret Read (Mrs. Creston Alexander King), Stewart Courtney, James Walker, Charles James. Instr., Trinity Hall High Sch., Louisville, Ky., 1886; began practice at St. Louis, Mo., 1891; clin. prof. genito-urinary surgery, Washington U., 1903-14, asso. in surgery, 1910-14; chief genito-urinary surgeon, Mulanphy Hosp., 1903-14, Washington Univ. Hosp., 1911-14; consultant, Skin and Cancer Hosp., 1911-14, St. Louis Eye, Ear, Nose and Throat Infirmary and St. Johns Hosp., 1912-14; moved to San Antonio, Tex., 1916. Mem. Med. Advisory Bd., San Antonio, 1917-18. Episcopalian. Asso. editor Interstate Med. Jour., 1903. Home: San Antonio, Tex. Died Sept. 26, 1930.

JOHNSON, Hayden, lawyer, educator; b. Washington, D.C., Feb. 28, 1874; s. Robert M. and Katherine (Minitree) J.; grad. Washington High Sch., 1893; LL.B., Georgetown Law Sch., 1895, LL.M., 1896; LL.D., National U., 1925; m. Jeannette Blanchard Gatewood, 1910. Practiced law in Washington, D.C., 1896—; chancellor Nat. U., 1931—; also trustee of the univ. and dean Nat. U. Law Sch. Pres. Board of Edn., Washington, D.C. Home: Washington, D.C. Died May 4, 1936.

JOHNSON, Helen Kendrick, author; b. Hamilton, N.Y., Jan. 4, 1844; d. Asahel C. and Anne (Hopkins) Kendrick; ed. at The Oread, Worcester, Mass.; m. Rossiter Johnson, May 20, 1869. Edited American Woman's Journal, 1893-94. Originated "The Meridian," a woman's club, that meets at noonday, founded 1886. Active mem. of the Assn. Opposed to the Extension of Suffrage to Women and author of some of its publs.; founder and pres. the Guidon Club. Editor: The Nutshell Series, 1883; Poems and

Songs for Young People, 1884; and other collections. Author: The Roddy Books, 3 vols., 1874-76; Our Familiar Songs, 1881; Raleigh Westgate, 1889; Woman and the Republic, 1897. Address: New York, N.Y. Died Jan. 3, 1917.

JOHNSON, Henry, college prof.; b. Gardiner, Me., June 25, 1855; s. Richard Elliot and Louisa Abbie (Reed) J.; A.B., Bowdoin Coll., 1874; student univs. of Göttingen, Leipzig, and Berlin; Ph.D., Berlin, 1884; has studied and traveled about 5 yrs. in Europe at various periods, 1875—; Litt.D., Bowdoin Coll., 1914; m. Frances M. Robinson, July 26, 1881. Prof. modern languages, 1877, librarian, 1880-83, Bowdoin Coll., and curator Bowdoin Art Collection, Walker Art Building, 1894—. Editor: Schiller's Ballads, 1888; Midsummer Night's Dream, 1888. Author: Where Beauty Is, and Other Poems, 1898; The Seer, and Other Poems, 1910. Translator: Les Trophées, José-Maria de Heredia, The Sonnets, 1910; La Comedia di Dante Alighieri, 1892-1914. Address: Brunswick, Me. Died Feb. 7, 1918.

JOHNSON, Henry Clark, lawyer, educator; b. Homer, N.Y., June 11, 1851; s. Eardley N. and Elizabeth Matilda (Hay) J.; grad. Cortland (N.Y.) Acad., 1867, Cornell U., 1873; law dept., Hamilton Coll., 1875; A.M. Hobart, 1877; m. Kate Loder Webb. Student of Roman Law, Yale Coll., 2 yrs.; prof. Latin lang. and lit., Lehigh U., 1881-88; pres. Central High Sch., Phila., and prof. constl. and internat. law in same, 1888-94. Pres. Nat. Corporation Agency, Internat. Steel Car Co., Atlas Ball Co., and Met. Correspondence Coll.; counsel for several corps. Editor: First Three Books of Homer's Iliad, 1886; The Satires of Aulus Persius Flaccus, 1885; The Bucolics and Georgics of Vergil, 1885; The Agricola and Germania of Tacitus, 1885; The Æneid of Vergil, Book I, 1893; Cicero de Amicitia, 1894; The Satires of Juvenal, 12; also contbr. to Johnson's Encyclopedia. Address: New York, N.Y. Died 1904.

JOHNSON, Henry Herbert, dentistry; b. Elko, Ga., Nov. 11, 1861; s. Needham Thomas and Sarah (Holmes) J.; D.D.S., Baltimore (Md.) Coll. Dental Surgery, 1886; m. Wilhelmina Wheeler, Feb. 9, 1897; children—Henry Herbert, Polhill Wheeler. Began practice at Hawkinsville, Ga., 1886; prof. of prosthetic dentistry and metallurgy, Southern Dental Coll., Atlanta, Ga., 1897-1918 (retired); dir. Ga. Kaolin Co., Commercial Bank of Macon. Mem. Ga. State Bd. Dental Examiners, 1893-97, 1918-30. Editor Southern Dental Jour., 1890-1900. Democrat. Baptist. Mason. Author: Biographies of Ex-Presidents of Georgia Dental Society, 1907; Care and Preservation of the Teeth, 1909. Home: Crescent, Ga. Died May 23, 1937.

JOHNSON, Henry Lincoln, lawyer; b. Augusta, Ga., July 27, 1870; s. Peter and Martha Ann (Brown) J.; A.B., Atlanta U., 1888; LL.B., U. of Mich., 1892; LL.D., Morris Brown Coll., Atlanta, 1920; m. Georgia Douglas, Sept. 28, 1903. Practiced at Jackson, later Atlanta, Ga.; recorder of deeds, Dist. of Columbia, 1912-16; del. at large to Rep. Nat. Conv. 4 times between 1896-1924; mem. from Ga. of Rep. Nat. Com., 1920-24. Formerly mem. Ga. State Troops (colored). Baptist. Mason, Odd Fellow, K.P., Elk. Author: The Negro Under Wilson, 1912. Home: Washington, D.C. Died Sept. 10, 1925.

JOHNSON, Henry Lowry Emilius, physician; b. Washington, D.C., Nov. 11, 1858; s. Henry L. and Emily E. J.; M.D., Columbian (now George Washington) U., 1882; m. Eugenie Reel Taylor, June 19, 1901. Prof. surg. gynecology, Columbian, 1889-1906; prof. gynecology, Washington Post-Grad. Sch. Medicine, 1897—; consulting gynecologist Providence Hosp., Woman's Clinic, and U.S. Govt. Hosp. for the Insane. Represented U.S. Dept. of State at Internat. Congress of Hygiene, Berlin, 1907, Internat. Sanitary Conf. of Am. Republics, Mexico City, 1907, Internat. Med. Congress, Budapest, 1909; v.p. 1st, 2d, 3d, 4th, 7th Pan-Am. Med. Congresses; v.p. 1st, 2d, and 3d Internat. Sanitary convs. of Am. Republics; mem. exec. com. Internat. Am. Congress of Medicine and Hygiene, Buenos Aires, 1910; member nat. com. Internat. Hygiene Exhbn., Dresden, Germany, 1911; pres. internat. exec. commn. Pan-Am. Med. Congress, 1915; mem. bd. dir. Columbia Hosp. and Lying-in Asylum, 1915—. Trustee A.M.A., 1898-1909, v.p. 1910-11; mem. and founder Am. Assn. Aeronautical Engrs. Patentee of safety aeroplane, 1912; ship and aeroplane compass and inclinometer, 1912. Address: Washington, D.C. Died Dec. 1915.

JOHNSON, Herbert Fisk, mfr.; b. Kenosha, Wis., May 27, 1868; s. Samuel Curtiss and Caroline (Fisk) J.; ed. pub. schs.; m. Helen Converse, July 14, 1894; children—Herbert Fisk, Henrietta Converse. Partner and gen. mgr. S. C. Johnson & Son; dir. Wis. Electric Co., Wright Rubber Products Co., Twin Disc Clutch Co., Am. Trades & Savings Bank (all of Racine), Metro-Nite Products Co. (Milwaukee); trustee Northwestern Mut. Life Ins. Co. Head of Am. Red Cross Chapter, Racine, World War; pres. Racine Community Welfare Fund. Republican. Presbyn. Home: Racine, Wis. Died Feb. 14, 1928.

JOHNSON, Herbert Morris, gen. dir. Chicago Grand Opera Co.; b. Lockport, Ill., July 31, 1876; s. Morris P. and Emma (Parks) J.; grad. high sch., Lockport, 1891; m. Laura Elizabeth Alexander, Mar. 20, 1901. Formerly auditor Internat. Harvester Co.; became connected with Chicago Grand Opera Co., 1913, became mgr., 1916, later Chicago Civic Opera Co. of which was v.p.; gen. dir. Chicago Grand Opera Co. Republican. Protestant. Address: Chicago Ill. Died Mar. 16, 1937.

JOHNSON, Herrick, clergyman, educator; b. Kaughnewaga, N.Y., Sept. 22, 1832; s. John J. and Lydia (French) J.; grad. Hamilton Coll., N.Y., 1857, Auburn (N.Y.) Theol. Sem., 1860; D.D., Western Reserve, 1867; LL.D., U. of Wooster, 1882; D.C.L., Omaha U., 1890; m. Catharine Spencer Hardenbergh, Sept. 6, 1860 (died 1907). Ordained Presbyn. ministry, 1860; pastor Troy, N.Y., 1860-62, Third Ch., Pittsburgh, 1862-67, First Ch., Phila., 1868-74; prof. homiletics and pastoral theology, Auburn Theol. Sem., 1874-80; pastor Fourth Ch., Chicago, 1880-83; prof. homiletics, McCormick Theol. Sem., Chicago, 1880-1905. Moderator Presbyn. Gen. Assembly, 1882; pres. Presbyn. Bd. of Edn. and Bd. of College Aid. Author: Christianity's Challenge, 1881; Revivals, Their Place and Power, 1882; Plain Talks About the Theatre, 1883; Presbyterian Book of Forms, 1889; From Love to Praise, 1903; The Ideal Ministry, 1908. Address: St. Louis, Mo. Died Nov. 20, 1913.

JOHNSON, Jackson, shoe mfr.; b. La Grange College, Ala., Nov. 2, 1859; s. James Lee and Helen (Rand) J.; ed. common schs.; m. Minnie Alva Wooten, Dec. 30, 1880; children—Helen (Mrs. Lee I. Niedringhaus), Andrew W., Florence (Mrs. Bradford Shinkle), Ada (Mrs. J. Russell Forgan). In mercantile business, Mississippi, until 1892; removed to Memphis, Tennessee, and joined in organizing Johnson, Carruthers & Rand Co., of which was pres. 5 yrs.; sold out and settled in St. Louis; an organizer Roberts, Johnson & Rand Shoe Co., of which was pres.; chmn. of bd. Internat. Shoe Co., 1915—; dir. First Nat. Bank. Democrat. Presbyn. Trustee Washington U. Home: St. Louis, Mo. Died Jan. 23, 1929.

JOHNSON, James Gibson, clergyman; b. Providence, R.I., June 25, 1839; s. Lorenzo D. and Mary (Burges) J.; grad. Union Coll., 1863; Princeton Theol. Sem., 1866; D.D., Middlebury Coll.; m. Mary A. Rankin, June 30, 1870. Ordained to Congl. ministry, Dec. 27, 1866; was pastor New England Ch., Chicago, 1891-97; corporate mem. Am. Bd. Commrs. Foreign Missions; sent by Am. Bd. to Japan, 1895; visited Europe several times; once through Palestine and Egypt. Address: Farmington, Conn. Died 1905.

JOHNSON, James Granville, judge; b. Springfield, O., Dec. 3, 1857; s. James and Catherine (Eby) J.; A.B., Wittenberg Col., Springfield, 1878; m. Blanche Obenshane, Dec. 4, 1888. Admitted to bar, Oct. 1880, and practiced at Springfield. Mayor, 1895-98; became judge Supreme Court of Ohio, 1911. Democrat. Trustee Springfield Pub. Library. Mason, Elk. Home: Springfield, O. Died Oct. 24, 1936.

JOHNSON, James Weldon, author; b. Jacksonville, Fla., June 17, 1871; s. James and Helen Louise (Dillette) J.; A.B., Atlanta U., 1894, A.M., 1904; Columbia 3 years; Litt.D., Talladega College, Alabama, 1917, Howard Univ., 1923; m. Grace Nail, Feb. 3, 1910. Prin. colored high sch., Jacksonville, several yrs.; admitted to Fla. bar, 1897, and practiced at Jacksonville; removed to N.Y. City, 1901, to collaborate with bro., J. Rosamond Johnson, in writing for light opera stage; apptd. U.S. consul to Puerto Cabello, Venezuela, 1906; consul at Corinto, Nicaragua, 1909-12; serving during revolution which overthrew Zelaya, and through abortive revolution against Diaz; sec. Nat. Assn. for Advancement of Colored People, 1916-30; prof. creative literature, Fisk U., 1930—, visiting prof. same, New York U., 1934—. Dir. Am. Fund for Pub. Service. Trustee Atlanta U. Awarded Spingarn medal, 1925. Author: (novel) The Autobiography of an Ex-Colored Man, 1912, republished, 1927; Fifty Years and Other Poems, 1917; Self-Determining Haiti, 1920; The Book of American Negro Poetry, 1921; The Book of American Negro Spirituals, 1925; Second Book of Spirituals, 1926; God's Trombones (poems), 1927; Black Manhattan, 1930; St. Peter Relates an Incident of the Resurrection Day, 1930; Along This Way (an autobiography), 1933; Negro Americans, What Now?, 1934; also wrote words of a number of songs. Contributor to Ency. Britannica. Wrote English version of libretto to the grand opera, "Goyescas," prod. Met. Opera House, New York, 1915. Address: Nashville, Tenn. Died June 26, 1933.

JOHNSON, Jeremiah Augustus, lawyer; b. Boston, Mass., June 3, 1836; s. Lorenzo Dow and Mary (Burgess) J.; m. Sarah M. Barclay, 1857; m. 2d, Fanny V. Matthews, 1887. Admitted to bar, Washington, 1867, to Supreme Ct. of U.S. and New York courts, 1870. U.S. consul, Beirut, Syria, 1858-67, consul gen., 1867-70; resigned to practice law in New York; counsel for many rys. and other corps. Discovered famous Hamath stones (in Syria) with Hittite inscriptions, and wrote account, 1870; was mem. Com. of Seventy, New York, and pres. Confederated Council of Good Govt. Home: S. Orange, N.J. Died Feb. 28, 1914.

JOHNSON, John, P.E. clergyman; b. Charleston, S.C., Dec. 25, 1829; s. Joseph J. (M.D.) and Catharine (Bonneau) J.; ed. U. of Va.; D.D., U. of the South; LL.D., Charleston Coll.; m. Floride Cantey, Dec. 1865. Civil engr. on surveys, construction and operation of railways, 1847-57; then went to U. of Va.; served lt., capt. and maj. of engrs., Confederate army, 1861-65, in the Carolinas and Ga. Was 15 months engr. in charge of Fort Sumter during the heavy and prolonged bombardments; twice wounded there; present at battles of Averysboro and Bentonville, N.C. Ordained to P.E. ministry, 1866; in charge Grace Ch., Camden, S.C., 5 yrs.; rector St. Philip's Ch., Charleston, 1871—; repeatedly deputy to Gen. Conv., P.E. Ch. Author: The Defense of Charleston Harbor, 1863-65, 1890. Home: Charleston, S.C. Died 1907.

JOHNSON, John A., journalist, gov.; b. St. Peter, Minn., July 28, 1861; s. G. and Caroline (Haden) J.; ed. pub. schs., St. Peter; LL.D., U. of Pa., 1907; m. Elinore Preston, June 1, 1894. Care of family devolving upon him at 12, went to work in drug store in St. Peter; later obtained interest in St. Peter Herald of which became editor. Served 7 years in Minn. Nat. Guard, becoming capt. Was State senator from St. Peter dist.; elected gov. Minn., 1904, reëlected 1906. Democrat. Presbyn. Home: St. Peter, Minn. Died 1909.

JOHNSON, John Albert, bishop; b. Oakville, Ont., Can., Oct. 29, 1857; s. John Garrison and Mary (Mackay) J.; m. Minnie S. Goosley, Jan. 16, 1881. Ordained A.M.E. ministry, 1875; elected bishop, 1904. Address: Philadelphia, Pa. Died Nov. 22, 1928.

JOHNSON, John B., lawyer; b. Live Oak, Fla., Oct. 15, 1868; s. Archibald and Martha Elizabeth (Bachlotte) J.; ed. common schs.; m. Mary Wagner, Oct. 14, 1903 (died 1923); children—Wagner B., John Paul. Admitted to Fla. bar, 1893, and began practice at Live Oak; mayor Live Oak 5 terms; mem. Fla. State Senate, 1907-23 (pres. 1917); atty. gen. of Fla., 1925-27; judge Circuit Court. Served as sergt. Co. L, 1st Fla. Vols., Spanish-Am. War. Democrat. Methodist. Mason. Home: Tallahassee, Fla. Deceased.

JOHNSON, John Butler, dean Coll. of Mechanics and Engring., U. of Wis.; b. Marlboro, O., June 11, 1850; s. Jesse J.; grad. U. of Mich., C.E., 1878; m. Phoebe E. Henby, Nov. 12, 1879. Served as civil engr. U.S. lake and Miss. river surveys; prof. civil engring., Washington U., St. Louis, 1883-98; conducted a large testing laboratory in St. Louis, in which all the U.S. timber tests were made; superintended the index dept., Journal of Assn. of Engring. Socs., and published 2 vols. of Index Notes to Engring. Literature; has contributed largely to engring. literature; prof. civil engring., Washington U., St. Louis, 1883; later to U. of Wis. Author: Theory and Practice of Surveying, 1886; Modern Framed Structures, 1893; Engineering Contracts and Specifications, 1895; Materials of Construction. Address: Madison, Wis. Died 1902.

JOHNSON, John Edward, clergyman, banker; b. Omaha, Neb., Feb. 7, 1864; s. Harrison and Minerva (Hambright) J.; A.B., Cornell Coll., Mt. Vernon, Ia., 1892, D.D., 1913; S.T.B., Boston U. Sch. of Theology, 1895; studied Harvard, 1896; research work, Sch. of Theology, same univ., 1920-21; m. Martha Cadwallader, July 2, 1895; children—Harold Edward, Paul Emanuel, Margaret Eleanor. Ordained ministry M.E. Ch., 1895; pastor Pearl St. Ch., Brockton, Mass., 1892-97, Niantic, Conn., 1897-1900, First Ch., Waterloo, Ia., 1900-03, Sumner, 1904-05, St. Paul's Ch., Waterloo, 1907-13; asst. pastor First Ch., Waterloo, 1913-15; city missionary, Waterloo, 1915-20; asst. prof. practical theology, Boston U., Sch. of Theology, 1920-21. Sec.-treas. Waterloo Gasoline Engine Co., 1908-18, gen. mgr., 1918-19; pres. Ia. Life Ins. Co., 1921-22; pres. Waterloo Savings Bank, 1922-30, chmn. bd. dirs., 1931—; dir., sec.-treas. Hawkeye Building Corp. Trustee Cornell College, 1913-26 (pres. board 1917-26). Republican. Home: Waterloo, Ia. Died Oct. 29, 1938.

JOHNSON, John Gilmore, lawyer; b. Brooklyn, Feb. 22, 1852; s. Samuel G. and Matilda J.; ed. pub. schs.; family moved to Ill., 1865; m. Lura Will, 1876. Moved to Kan., 1878; gen. atty. Modern Woodmen of America. Mem. for Kan. of Dem. Nat. Com., 1896-1904; mem. exec. and campaign com. of Nat. Com., 1896-1904; one of the active mgrs. Mr. Bryan's campaign, 1896; in May 1899, placed in charge of Dem. Nat. Com. during absence of Chmn. Jones in Europe; chmn. Nat. Exec. Com. during Mr. Bryan's second campaign, 1900; sec. nat. advisory com., campaigns, 1904, 08, 12. Pres. Nat. Fraternal Congress, 1897. Home: Peabody, Kan. Died June 1921.

JOHNSON, John Graver, lawyer; b. Germantown, Phila., Pa., 1841; grad. Central High Sch., Phila., 1858; studied law in offices of Benjamin & Murray Rush, and Power, Wallace & Judson, Phila. Practiced in Phila., 1863—; has represented many of the prin. corps. of the country in state and federal courts; defended Sugar Trust, the Am. Tobacco Co., the Standard Oil Co., the Northern Securities Merger, etc., before U.S. Supreme Court; declined appmt. to bench of U.S. Supreme Court, tendered by Presidents Garfield and Cleveland, and the atty. generalship of U.S., under Pres. McKinley. Art expert, and owns one of most valuable collections of pictures in the U.S. Died Apr. 14, 1917.

JOHNSON, John Lipscomb, coll. pres.; b. Spottsylvania County, Va., Aug. 10, 1869; s. John Lipscomb and Julia Anna (Toy) J.; B.S., U. of Miss., 1887; post-grad. work U. of Ga., 1894; M.A., Miss. Coll., 1900; studied Berlin and Paris, 1907; m. Sue Bell Moody, June 29, 1898; children—Cecil Slaton, Mary Rachel, Julia Toy, Jacqueline Van Raden, Sue Bell. Asst. in mathematics, U. of Miss., 1887-88; prin. high sch., Maxeys, Ga., 1889-95; supt. city schs., Jackson, 1896-99; v.p. Hillman Coll., Clinton, Miss., 1899-1905, pres., 1905-06; prof. modern langs., Mississippi Coll., 1906-12; pres. Mississippi Woman's Coll., 1912—. Trustee Southwestern Bapt. Theol. Sem., Ft. Worth, Tex.; mem. bd. visitors U. of Ga. Democrat. Pres. Miss. State Bapt. Conv., 1915-17, v.p. Southern Bapt. Conv., 1918-19; pres. Miss. Bapt. S.S. Conv., 1920-22. Mason, K.P. Home: Hattiesburg, Miss. Died Feb. 1, 1932.

JOHNSON, J(ohn) Lovell, mfr.; b. Worcester, Mass., June 26, 1876; s. Iver and Mary Elizabeth (Spiers) J.; ed. Fitchburg High School, Worcester Poly. Inst.; m. Margaret M. Dwyer; 1 dau., Mary Margaret. Began, 1896, with the Iver Johnson cos.; later pres. Iver Johnson's Arms & Cycle Works of Fitchburg, Iver Johnson's Arms & Cycle Works (Can.) Ltd. (Montreal), Iver Johnson Sporting Goods Co. of Boston, Worcester and Fitchburg; dir. Merchants' Nat. Bank of Boston, Boston Casualty Co. (mem. finance com.); vice-pres. and trustee Fitchburg Savings Bank (chmn. bd. of investment); dir. and mem. exec. com. Fitchburg Mut. Fire Ins. Co.; dir. Fitchburg Co-operative Bank (chmn. finance com.); mem. advisory com. Worcester County Trust Co. of Fitchburg. Alderman of Fitchburg, 1901-03 (pres. bd., 1902-03); state senator, 3d Worcester Senatorial Dist., 1907-08; councilor 7th Dist., 1909-10. Treas., Rep. State Com., Mass.; del. Rep. Nat. Conv., Chicago, 1910. Episcopalian. Mason, Elk. Home: Fitchburg, Mass. Deceased.

JOHNSON, John Samuel Adolphus, educator; b. Cismont, Va., Aug. 10, 1878; s. William Whitfield and Willie Catherine Morris (Anderson) J.; B.S., Va. Poly. Inst., 1898, M.E., 1899; studied summers, Cornell and Lehigh univs.; m. Margaret Adger Smyth, June 27, 1905; children—Sarah Smyth, James Edger Smyth, Katharine Morris, Anne Ransom. With Va. Poly. Inst., 1898—, successively, instr. until 1900, prof. mil. sci. and tactics and asso. prof. mech. engring., 1900-06, prof. exptl. engring., 1906-14, prof. applied mechanics and exptl. engring., 1914—, also dir. Engring. Expt. Sta., 1921—. Democrat. Episcopalian. Mason. Home: Blacksburg, Va. Died Oct. 21, 1931.

JOHNSON, John William, theologian; b. Willington, County Durham, Eng., Jan. 31, 1872; s. Joseph and Jane Ellen (Galley) J.; Shurtleff Coll., Upper Alton, Ill., 1899-1900, U. of Chicago, summer 1903, Harvard, 1904-05; grad. Rochester Theol. Sem., 1906, B.D., 1910; Ph.B., Rochester, 1909; grad. work philosophy, U. of Calif., 1914-18; D.D., Pacific Sch. of Religion, 1922; Lic. Theol., honoris causa, U. of Göttingen, 1925; m. Sarah Brown Johnson, Aug. 12, 1902; children—Josephine Ella, Constance Howard, John William Stewart, Faith Seville. Pastor's asst. in England, 1893-96; ordained Bapt. ministry, 1901; pastor Le Roy, N.Y., 1906-09, Wenatchee, Wash., 1909-11, Emanuel Ch., Spokane, 1911-13; prof. systematic theology, Berkeley (Calif.) Bapt. Div. Sch., 1913—. Traveled in Eng. and Scotland, 1911, Eng., 1920; sabbatic yr. spent in research at Heidelberg and Göttingen. Chmn. publicity com. Men and Religion Forward Movement for Spokane and Inland Empire, 1911-12; pres. East Wash. State Bapt. Pastors' Conf., 1911. Republican. Supply pastor various chs. Author: Die Bestimmung des Wesens der christlichen Religion bei Troeltsch und Wobbermin; Reviews. Naturalized citizen, 1904. Home: Berkeley, Calif. Died June 6, 1933.

JOHNSON, Joseph French, univ. dean; b. Hardwick, Mass., Aug. 24, 1853; s. Gardner Nye and Eliza (French) J.; early life in Aurora, Ill.; A.B., Harvard, 1878; studied polit. economy and history in Germany, 1 yr.; Dr. Commercial Science, Union Coll., 1909; LL.D., Hobart Coll., 1915; m. Caroline T. Stolp, Aug. 4, 1884. Was engaged on Springfield Republican, and later as financial editor Chicago Tribune; established Spokane, Wash., Spokesman, 1890; sold it 1893; prof. in Wharton Sch. of Commerce, U. of Pa., 1893-1901; lecturer upon finance, Columbian U., 1899-1903; prof. polit. economy, 1901—, dean Sch. of Commerce, Accounts and Finance, 1903—, New York U. Author: Money and Currency, 1905; Syllabus of Money and Banking, 1899; Report on the Canadian Banking System, for the Nat. Monetary Commission; Business and the Man, 1916; We and Our Work, 1922; Organized Business Knowledge, 1923. Editor Journal of Accountancy. Editor Modern Business series. Mem. Commn. on New Sources of Revenue for New York City, 1912; mem. Commn. to Revise Banking Laws of State of N.Y., 1913. Home: New York, N.Y. Died Jan. 22, 1925.

JOHNSON, Joseph Horsfall, bishop; b. Schenectady, N.Y., June 7, 1847; s. Stephen Hotchkiss and Eleanor (Horsfall) J.; A.B., Williams, 1870; grad. Gen. Theol. Sem., 1873; D.D., Nasbotah, Wis., 1895; S.T.D., Gen. Theol. Sem., 1908; m. Isabel Greene, d. Isaac Davis, June 14, 1881; 1 son, Reginald Davis. Deacon, 1873, priest, 1874, P.E. Ch.; in charge Holy Trinity Ch., Highland, N.Y., 1873-79; rector Trinity Ch., Bristol, R.I., 1879-81, St. Peter's, Westchester, N.Y., 1881-86, Christ Ch., Detroit, 1886-96; consecrated bishop of Los Angeles, 1896. Address: Los Angeles, Calif. Died May 16, 1928.

JOHNSON, Joseph Taber, physician; b. Lowell, Mass., June 30, 1845; s. Lorenzo Dow and Mary (Burgess) J.; M.D., Georgetown (D.C.) Med. Coll., 1865; M.D., Bellevue Hosp. Med. Coll., 1867; hon. A.M., Columbian (now George Washington) U., 1869; Ph.D., Georgetown U., 1904, LL.D., 1914. Began practice, Washington, 1867; took degree in obstetric operations, Vienna, 1870; prof. obstetrics and diseases of women and children, Howard U., 1868-72; acting asst. surgeon U.S.A., assigned to duty Freedmen's Hosp., D.C.; lecturer, 1874, prof. obstetrics and pres. faculty, 1876-1915, emeritus, 1915—, medical dept., Georgetown U. Consulting surgeon to six hosps. Pres. Am. Gynecol. Soc., 1898-99, Southern Surg. and Gynecol. Assn., 1898-99; fellow Brit. Gynecol. Soc., Am. Col. Surgeons (gov.). Wrote part Dennis' American System of Surgery. Lectured to soldiers during the war; mem. Vol. Med. Service Corps. Home: Cherrydale, Va. Died Mar. 12, 1921.

JOHNSON, Joseph Travis, U.S. judge; b. Brewerton, S.C., Feb. 28, 1858; s. Benjamin and Mary J.; A.B., Erskine Coll., 1879, LL.D., 1917; m. Sarah Anderson, July 30, 1890. Admitted to bar, 1883, and practiced at Spartanburg, S.C. Mem. 57th to 63d Congresses (1901-15), 4th S.C. Dist., and re-elected to 64th Congress (1915-17), but resigned Apr. 19, 1915, to become U.S. dist. judge for Western Dist. S.C. Democrat. Address: Greenville, S.C. Died May 8, 1919.

JOHNSON, Julia Macfarlane (Mrs. Richard W. Johnson), educator; b. Salem, Pa., Mar. 1, 1862; grad. Mt. Holyoke Sem. (now Coll.), 1885; U. of Pa., 1887-88; U. of Cincinnati, 1889-90; M.A., U. of Minn.; U. of Oxford, Eng., 1923-24; m. General Richard W. Johnson, U.S.A., 1894 (died 1897); 1 son, John Macfarlane. Teacher Coates College, Terre Haute, Ind., before marriage; head of dept. English, 1897—, also dean of women, 1897-1917, Macalester Coll., St. Paul, Minn. Active in patriotic and religious work; lecturer before clubs, city missions, etc. Presbyn. Home: St. Paul, Minn. Died July 4, 1935.

JOHNSON, Livingston, clergyman, editor; b. Spring Hill, N.C., Nov. 7, 1857; s. Duncan and Catharine (Livingston) J.; student Wake Forest (N.C.) Coll., 1877-78, D.D., 1913; student Southern Bapt. Theol. Sem., 1887-88; m. Mary Frances Memory, Oct. 18, 1882; children—Wingate Memory, Foy Elizabeth, Duncan Monroe (dec.), Frances Livingston, Mary Lynch. Ordained Bapt. ministry, 1888; pastor Rockingham, N.C., 1888-95, Lumberton, Jan.-Oct. 1895, 1st Ch., Greensboro, 1895-1900; corr. sec. Bapt. State Com., N.C., 1900-15; pastor 1st ch. Rocky Mount, North Carolina, 1916-17; editor Biblical Recorder, 1917—. Mem. bd. dirs. Wake Forest Coll., Meredith Coll.; trustee Southern Bapt. Theol. Sem. Mem. exec. com. Southern Bapt. Conv. (v.p. 1918). Democrat. Author: History of the Baptist State Convention of North Carolina, 1908; Christian Statesmanship, 1913. Home: Raleigh, N.C. Died Feb. 8, 1931.

JOHNSON, Lorenzo M., gen. mgr. Mexican Internat. R.R. Co. and related cos., 1883—; b. New York; grad. Yale, 1874, B.A. and C.E.; m. Helen Wolcott, d. Gen. Hart L. Stewart, Apr. 28, 1878. Served on Keokuk & Des Moines R.R., engr. chief engr., asst. to gen. supt. and gen. supt., 1874-77; gen. mgr., 1877-80; dir. and v.p., 1881-83, Cairo & St. Louis R.R.; asst. to pres. Pullman Palace Car Co., 1881-83. Is gen. mgr. Mexican Internat. R.R. and of large coal mining and cattle-raising interests in Mexico. Mgr. railroad and fuel dept. Am. Smelting & Refining Co. in Mexico, 1903—; gen. mgr. Mexican Union Ry., El Carmen Ry., Aguascalientes Ry., Viladeña Ry. Address: Mexico City, Mexico. Died 1904.

JOHNSON, Lucius E., ry. pres.; b. Aurora, Ill., Apr. 13, 1846; s. J. Spencer and Eliza (Brown) J.; pub. sch. edn., Aurora; m. Ella Parker, Apr. 10, 1869. Entered ry. service, 1866, as fireman, C.,B.& Q. R.R.; remained in locomotive dept. that road until 1886, holding various positions, including master mechanic at Aurora, Ill.; supt. St. Louis div., 1886-88, Chicago div., 1888-90, same road; supt. Mont. Central Ry., 1890-93; supt. Mich. div. L.S. & M.S. Ry., 1893-97; gen. supt., 1897-99, v.p. and gen. mgr., 1899-1903, pres. and gen. mgr., Oct. 1, 1903, pres., 1904-18, chmn. bd., Jan. 1-June 1, 1918, and again pres., 1918—, Norfolk & Western Ry. Address: Roanoke, Va. Died Feb. 9, 1921.

JOHNSON, Lucius Henry (Lute H.), newspaperman; b. Mt. Vernon, Ill., Feb. 9, 1863; s. James D. and Martha (Boswell) J.; self-ed.; special student Harvard, 1919-21; unmarried. Widely known for many yrs. as mining editor and corr., mining camps of Colo. Sunday editor and editorial writer, Denver Republican, then spl. writer Denver Post. Author: (periodical publs. and plays) A Spare Million, 1911, Magnolia Plantation (drama), and other dramatic compositions; By Law's Decree; Nada; Coming Home; also Colorado, Bright Land, Little Coon Lullaby and Mary Carey (songs). Address: Denver, Colo. Deceased.

JOHNSON, Luther Appeles, prof. English, 1889—, chmn. faculty, 1896—, Trinity U., Texas; b. Tishomingo County, Miss., May 5, 1858; grad. Trinity U., 1886; A.M., U. of Chicago; Ph.D., Bethel Coll. Before going to Texas studied at Cumberland U. (Tenn.) and Southern Ill. Normal U., while completing his collegiate studies; mem. faculty of Trinity U. Author: Inductive Studies in Shakespeare; Foundation Principles of Literature; The Work and Place of Denominational Colleges and Universities. Home: Tehuacana, Tex. Died 1900.

JOHNSON, Magnus, congressman; Varmland, Sweden, Sept. 19, 1871; s. Johannes Janson; ed. common and high schs. for short time; m. Harriet Dorman, 1897. Came to U.S., 1891, naturalized citizen, 1899. Farmer; mem. Minn. Ho. of Rep., 1915, 17, Senate, 1919, 21; candidate for gov. of Minn. on Farmer-Labor ticket, 1922; elected to U.S. Senate, July 16, 1923, to fill vacancy caused by death of Senator Knute Nelson; term ending Mar. 3, 1925; elected to 73d Congress (1933-35), on Farmer-Labor ticket, at large, Minn. Connected with many coöp. orgns. in Minn.; pres. State Union of Am. Soc. of Equity; v.p. Equity Coöp. Exchange. Lutheran. Home: Kimball, Minn. Died Sept. 13, 1936.

JOHNSON, Marietta Louise (Mrs. John Franklin Johnson), educator; b. St. Paul, Minn.; d. Clarence D. and Rhoda Matilda (Morton) Pierce; grad. State Normal Sch., St. Cloud, Minn., 1885; m. John Franklin Johnson, June 6, 1897 (died 1919); children—Clifford Ernest, Franklin Pierce (dec.). Teacher St. Paul Teachers' Training Sch., 1890-92, State Teachers Coll., Moorhead, Minn., 1893-95, State Teachers Coll., Mankato, Minn., 1896-99; founder, 1907, and prin. Sch. of Organic Edn., Fairhope, Ala., beginning in cottage with 6 children; admits children of the vicinity without charge; all grades represented from kindergarten to coll., also 2-yr. course for teachers in training. In charge of special winter school for teachers, parents, social workers and children, at Fairhope, Ala., 1920—. Advocate of educational program "eliminating grades, marks and promotions as tending to develop self-consciousness and insincerity, every effort being made to respect the order of the development of the nervous system, the integrity of the intellect, and the sincerity and fearlessness of the emotional life." Home: Fairhope, Ala. Died Dec. 23, 1938.

JOHNSON, Martin (Elmer), moving picture explorer; b. Rockford, Ill., Oct. 9, 1884; s. John Alfred and Lucinda (Constant) J.; ed. pub. schs., Independence, Kan.; m. Osa Helen Leighty, May 15, 1910. Traveled around the world 6 times; in South Sea Islands 12 yrs., Australia 1 yr., Borneo 2 yrs., Africa 5 yrs., wife sharing every expdn.; the only member of Jack London's "Snark" voyage to complete the trip (1917); helped build the Snark and was last to leave her; began, 1924, to make 5-yr. film record of vanishing wild life of Africa for Am. Mus. Natural History, under title of Martin Johnson African Expdn. Corp.; returned to Africa, Nov. 1929, to study pygmy life in Belgian Congo. Author: Through the South Seas with Jack London, 1912; Cannibal Land, 1917; Camera Trails in Africa, 1924; Safari—A Saga of the African Blue, 1928; Lion—African Adventure with the King of Beasts, 1929. Died Jan. 13, 1937.

JOHNSON, Martin Nelson, lawyer; b. Wis., 1850; s. Nelson and Anna (Selheim) J.; removed to Iowa same year; grad. Iowa State U., 1873; taught 2 yrs. in Calif. Mil. Acad., Oakland; studied law; admitted to bar, 1876; served a term in each branch of Iowa legislature; was a Hayes elector in that State; removed to Dakota, 1882, and took up Govt. land, residing there until death. Elected dist. atty., 1886 and 1888; mem. Constitutional Conv., N.D., 1889. Mem. Congress, 1891-99. Republican. Engaged in farming. Home: Petersburg, N.D. Died 1909.

JOHNSON, Merle DeVore, illustrator; b. Oregon City, Ore., Nov. 24, 1874; s. William Carey and Josephine (DeVore) J.; A.B., Leland Stanford Jr. U., 1897; m. Margaret Keough, Sept. 7, 1905; children—Helen Carey, Marion Josephine. Mgr. art dept. New York Evening Journal, 1910-13; cartoonist, "News in Rime" dept. of Puck, 1914-17. Created Boy Scout series in N.Y. Press, 1915; illustrated many books. Author: Bibliography of Mark Twain, 1910; Bibliographic Check-List James Branch Cabell, 1921. Compiler of Howard Pyle's Book of Pirates, 1921; Howard Pyle's Book of the American Spirit, 1923; American First Editions, 1929; High Spots of American Literature, 1929; You Know These Lines, 1934. Home: New York, N.Y. Died Sept. 1, 1935.

JOHNSON, Mortimer Lawrence, rear admiral U.S.N.; b. Nahant, Mass., June 1, 1842. Apptd. from Mass. and grad. U.S. Naval Acad., 1862; promoted ensign, Sept. 16, 1862; lt., Feb. 22, 1864; lt. comdr., July 25, 1866; comdr., Apr. 26, 1878; capt., May 9, 1893; rear admiral, Jan. 29, 1901. Served on Mississippi, 1861; Susquehanna, 1861; Sabine and Wabash, 1862-63; S. Atlantic Blockading Squadron, and was in all engagements under Admiral Du Pont and Dahlgren, 1863-64; served on Colorado, 1864-65, participated in both attacks on Ft. Fisher; comd. Estrella, W. Gulf Blockading Squadron, 1865; Dacotah, 1866-88; Kenosha and Plymouth, 1869-70; Navy Yard, Portsmouth, 1870-71; Worcester, 1871; Wyoming, 1872-73; exec. officer receiving-ship Sabine, 1873-74, Powhatan, 1874-75; served on receiving ship Wabash, 1875-78; Navy Yard, Portsmouth, 1878-79; comd. Ashelot, 1879-81; spl. duty, 1882-83; Navy Yard, Boston, 1884-87; comd. Monocacy, 1889-91; Naval War Coll., 1892; Navy Yard, Portsmouth, 1893; comd. receiving ship Franklin, 1894-95; comd. Cincinnati, 1895-97, San Francisco, 1897; comd. Miantonomoh during Spanish War, 1898; Navy Yard, Boston, 1898-1901; commandant, Naval Sta., Port Royal, 1901; commandant, Navy Yard, Boston, 1901-04; retired, June 1, 1904. Address: Portsmouth, N.H. Died Feb. 14, 1913.

JOHNSON, Oliver Francis, ry. official; b. Hopkinton, Mass.; s. Edward Andrew and Ellen (Lyden) J.; ed. pub. schs.; m. Anna Traphagen, Feb. 19, 1921. Began in employ Lehigh Valley R.R. Co., at Boston, Mass., Apr. 1, 1902; has continued with same co. through various positions, freight traffic mgr., 1927—. Capt. Air Service, U.S. Army, World War. Home: New York, N.Y. Deceased.

JOHNSON, Otis Coe, chemist; b. Kishwaukee, Ill., Sept. 11, 1839; s. William H. and Alma (Otis) J.; A.B., Oberlin, 1868, A.M., 1877; grad. Sch. of Pharmacy, U. of Mich., 1871; m. Katharine Crane, July 18, 1878. Instr., 1873-80, asst. prof., 1880-89, prof. qualitative chem. analysis, 1889-1911, emeritus prof. qualitative analysis, 1911—, U. of Mich. Author: Prescott's and Johnson's Qualitative Chemical Analysis (with A. B. Prescott), 1888, 1901. Wrote: Chemical Theory of Negative Bonds and Rule for Balancing Equations, Chemical News, 1880 (later incorporated in books of other authors). Home: Ann Arbor, Mich. Died June 6, 1912.

JOHNSON, Philander Chase, editor; b. Wheeling, W.Va., Feb. 6, 1866; s. Sylvanus E. and Martha A. (Mann) J.; ed. in Cincinnati; m. Louise Covert, Oct. 21, 1890 (dec.); m. 2d, Mrs. Mary A. Hagman, d. of late Brig. Gen. Daniel W. Adams, C.S.A., Apr. 8, 1908. Conducted humorous and lit. depts. in Merchant Traveler, Chicago and Washington (D.C.) Critic, also Capital, column "Postscripts" in Post; later editorial contbr. to Washington Star; has written for that paper daily contbns. of miscellaneous verse and dialogue, under caption, "Shooting Stars," also reviews of theater, 1915—. Mason. Author: Sayings of Uncle Eben, 1897; Now-a-Day Poems, 1900; Senator Sorghum's Primer of Politics, 1906. Song verse of the war ballad, "Somewhere in France Is the Lily," 1917. Home: Rockville, Md. Died May 18, 1939.

JOHNSON, Richard Harvey, lawyer; b. Silver City, Ida., July 19, 1870; s. Richard Zina and Kathrina (Brög) J.; grad. Boise (Ida.) High Sch., 1886; student 2 yrs. Concordia Coll., Zürich, Switzerland, and traveled and studied a yr. in Germany; 1 yr. in acad. dept. Yale, LL.B., 1892; m. Catherine M. Ashdown, Dec. 29, 1889; 1 dau., Kathrina Cecilia (Mrs. C. H. Nixon). Mem. bar Supreme Ct. of U.S.; with father in law firm of Johnson & Johnson, 1892, until father's death, 1912; later mem. firm Johnson & Nixon. Democrat. Mem. Idaho Ho. of Rep., 1896-98; temporary and permanent chmn., Dem. State Conv. of Ida., Aug. 1904. Home: Boise, Ida. Died July 14, 1929.

JOHNSON, Richard Zina, lawyer; b. Akron, O., May 21, 1837; s. Harvey Hull and Calista F. (Munger) J.; ed. pub. and pvt. schs., Ohio and N.Y.; LL.B., Yale, 1859; LL.D., U. of Ida., 1894; m. Kathrina Brög, 1868. Admitted to bar in Minn., 1858; later moved to Calif. and Nev., and to Ida., 1864; sr. mem. law firm of Johnson & Johnson. Mem. Territorial Council, Ida., 1880-82; atty. gen. of Ida., 2 terms, 1887-91; one of commrs. who completed Revised Statutes, 1887; author of bill creating Boisé Independent Sch. Dist., 1881, and mem. Bd. of Edn., 1881-96 (chmn.); mem. bd. of regents, U. of Ida., 1889-94. Democrat. Pres. Ida. State Bar Assn., 1898-1902. Has made frequent and extended visits to Europe, and has villa on Lake Constance, at Wasserburg, Bavaria. Address: Boisé, Ida. Died Sept. 10, 1913.

JOHNSON, Robert Underwood, editor, author; b. Washington, Jan. 12, 1853; s. Nimrod H. and Catherine C. (Underwood) J.; B.S., Earlham Coll., Ind., 1871, hon. Ph.D., 1889; hon. A.M., Yale, 1891; hon. L.H.D., N.Y. U., 1911; m. Katharine McMahon, Aug. 31, 1876 (died 1924); children—Owen McMahon, Agnes McMahon (Mrs. Frank H. Holden). On staff Century Mag., 1873, asso. editor, 1881-1909, editor, Nov. 1909-May 31, 1913, succeeding Richard Watson Gilder. Had charge with Clarence Clough Buel of editing of "Century War Series" and subsequent 4 vols., extending it to "Battles and Leaders of the Civil War," 1887-88; induced Gen. Grant to write his Memoirs, half of which appeared in the "Century War Series"; originated and, with John Muir, set on foot the movement resulting in creation Yosemite Nat. Park. Sec. Am. Copyright League, 1888—; for services in cause of internat. copyright received hon. A.M. degree from Yale, 1891, and decorations of Chevalier Legion of Honor, France, 1891, and Cavaliere of the Crown of Italy, 1895; took leading part in securing abolition of manufacturing condition in copyright of books in foreign langs., 1908-09. Originator of Memorial to Keats and Shelley in Rome and sec. Am. Com.; first proposed by formal letters of Aug. and Sept. 1906, to President Roosevelt, Conf. of Govs. to conserve forests of Eastern States, out of which grew White House confs. on conservation. Chmn. Nat. Com. for Preservation of Yosemite Nat. Park, 1913; active in opposing bill to give San Francisco the Hetch Hetchy valley for a reservoir, and in movement for repeal of the exemption of Am. coast wise shipping in Panama Canal Act. Mem. Nat. Inst. Arts and Letters (sec. 1903-09); preliminary sec. Am. Acad. Arts and Letters during its organization, later sec. and mem.; hon. v.p. Sierra Club, Calif.; mem. Nat. Citizens Com. on 3d Hague Conf.; mem. Independence Hall conf. to found League to Enforce Peace. Originator and chmn. "Am. Poets Ambulances in Italy," 1917, which presented 112 ambulances to Italian Army within 4 mos.; pres. N.Y. com. Italian War Relief Fund of America, 1918-19. Dir. Hall of Fame (N.Y. Univ.), 1919—. Ambassador to Italy, Feb. 1920-July 1921; rep. U.S. as an observer at San Reno Conference of the Supreme Council, Apr. 1920. Comdr. Order Crown of Italy, 1919; Officier de l'Odre de Léopold II (Belgian), 1919; Comdr. Order of St. Sava (Serbian), 1920; Grand Cordon Order of SS. Maurice and Lazarus (Italian), conferred by King Victor Emanuel III, 1921, "as a mark of personal esteem and in recognition of work for good relations between Italy and United States"; Grand Officier Légion d'Honneur (France), 1922; Grand Cordon, with star, Order Polonia Restituta. Author: The Winter House, and Other Poems, 1891; Songs of Liberty, and Other Poems, 1897; Poems (collected), 1902, enlarged, 1908; Saint Gaudens, An Ode (3d edit. of poems), 1910, 4th edit., 1913; Poems of War and Peace, 1916, 2d edit., 1917; Italian Rhapsody and Other Poems of Italy, 1917; Collected Poems, 1919, 23; Poems of the Longer Flight, 1928; Remembered Yesterdays (Memoirs), 1923, 5th printing, 1929; The Pact of Honor and Other Poems, 1929; Poems of the Lighter Touch, 1930; Poems of Fifty Years (definitive edition of his verse), 1931; Aftermath (poetry), 1933; Heroes, Children and Fun (poetry), 1934; Your Hall of Fame (prose), 1935. Home: New York, N.Y. Died Oct. 14, 1937.

JOHNSON, Robert Wilkinson, surgeon; b. Rockland, Md., Sept. 8, 1854; s. William Fell and Ann Mifiin (Barker) J.; grad. St. Paul's Sch., Concord, N.H., 1873; A.B., Princeton, 1876; M.D., U. of Pa., 1879; European hosps.; post-grad., Johns Hopkins; m. Julia Watts Hall Brock, Oct. 1, 1879; 5 children. In surg. practice at Baltimore, 1879—; asst. surgeon, U.S. Marine Hosp., Baltimore, 1883-86; prof. surgery, 1892-1909, emeritus prof., 1909—, Baltimore Med. Coll. Surgeon, Md. Steel Co., Church Home; brigade surgeon, 1st Brigade, Md. N.G., 1888-97. Republican. Episcopalian. Address: Baltimore, Md. Died Nov. 14, 1930.

JOHNSON, Rossiter, author, editor; b. Rochester, N.Y., Jan. 27, 1840; s. Reuben and Almira (Alexander) J.; A.B., U. of Rochester, 1863, A.M., 1875, hon. Ph. D., 1888, LL.D., 1893; m. Helen Kendrick, May 20, 1869 (died 1917); children—Laurence Kendrick (dec.), Florence Kendrick, Evelyn (dec.), Mildred (dec.); m. 2d, Mary Agnes Keyes, May 24, 1924. Asso. editor Rochester Democrat, 1864-68; editor Concord (N.H.) Statesman, 1869-72; asso. editor American Cyclopædia, 1873-77, Standard Dictionary, 1892-94; editor Annual Cyclopedia, 1883-1902; mng. editor Cyclo. of Am. Biography, 1886-89. Editor Authorized History of the Columbian Expn., 1898; editor-in-chief The World's Great Books (40 vols. of masterpieces), 1898-1901; editor-in-chief Universal Cyclopedia, 1900-04; originator and editor of Little Classics (18 vols.), 1875-80; Famous Fugitive Poems, 1878; Play-day Poems, 1879; Fifty Perfect Poems (with Charles A. Dana), 1882; The Great Events, by Famous Historians (20 vols.), 1905; The Literature of Italy (with Dora Knowlton Ranous), 16 volumes, 1907; The Author's Digest (20 vols.), 1908; hist. vol. in Young Folks' Ednl. series, 1911; Fortier's History of Louisiana, 1904; also wrote the Whispering Galley in Overland Monthly, 1898-99. Asso. editor The Lincoln Library, 1924. Lectures frequently on American hist. subjects. Pres. New York Assn. Phi Beta Kappa, 1897-98, Univ. Extension Soc., 1898—, Soc. of the Genesee, 1899, Quill Club, 1899, Delta Upsilon Club, 1901; sec. Authors' Club 6 yrs. (chmn. 2 yrs., treas. 1904-17); mem. Rochester Hist. Soc., contbr. to its publs. Author: Phaeton Rogers—a Novel of Boy Life, 1881; A History of the French War, Ending in the Conquest of Canada, 1882; A History of the War Between the United States and Great Britain, 1812-15, 1882; Idler and Poet (poems), 1883; A History of the War of Secession, 1888; The End of a Rainbow, an American Story, 1892; Campfire and Battlefield, 1894; The Turning-Points of the Civil War, 1894; Three Decades (poems), 1895; Chapter on Gettysburg, added to Creasy's Decisive Battles, 1898; A Short History of the War Between the United States and Spain, 1899; The Hero of Manila, 1899; Morning Lights and Evening Shadows (poems), 1902, 18; The Alphabet of Rhetoric, 1903; The Blank Cartridge Ballot, 1904; The Story of the Constitution of the United States, 1906; The Clash of Nations, 1914; Captain John Smith, 1915; A Simple Record of a Noble Life, 1916; The Fight for the Republic, 1916; Biography of Helen Kendrick Johnson, 1917; The Grandest Playground in the World, 1918. Originator and editor of Liber Scriptorium, 2 issues, 1893, 1921. Home: New York, N.Y. Died Oct. 3, 1931.

JOHNSON, Royal Cleaves, congressman, lawyer; b. Cherokee, Ia., Oct. 3, 1882; s. Eli and Philena (Everett) J.; studied Yankton Acad.; LL.B., U. of S.D., 1906; m. Florence Thode, Oct. 5, 1907; children—Everett Royal, Harlan Thode (U.S.N.). Admitted to S.D. bar, 1906, D.C. bar, 1933; practiced in Highmore, S.D.; deputy state's attorney, Hyde County, 1906-09, state's atty., 1909-10; removed to Aberdeen, 1912; atty. gen. S.D., 1911-15; mem. 64th to 72d Congresses (1915-33), 2d S.D. Dist. Apptd. mem. Mt. Rushmore Nat. Memorial Com., 1929. Republican. Enlisted as pvt. in U.S. regular army, Jan. 5, 1918; sergt. Co. K, 313th Inf., Apr. 23, 1918; 2d lt., June 1, 1918; assigned Co. D, 313th Inf.; overseas, July 6, 1918; 1st lt., Sept. 3, 1918; wounded Montfaucon, Sept. 27, 1918; discharged, Dec. 20, 1918. Awarded D.S.C., and Purple Heart (U.S.), French Croix de Guerre. Conglist. Mason. Died Aug. 2, 1939.

JOHNSON, Samuel William, prof. emeritus agrl. chemistry, 1896—, Sheffield Scientific School, Yale; b. Kingsboro, N.Y., July 3, 1830; s. Abner A. and Annah W. (Gilbert) J.; studied at Yale (now Sheffield) Scientific School and univs. of Leipzig and Munich. Prof. analytical and agrl. chemistry, 1856-74; prof. theoretical and agrl. chemistry, 1874-95, Sheffield Scientific Sch. Dir. Conn. Agrl. Expt. Sta., 1877-1899. Pres. Am. Chem. Soc., 1878; chmn. sub-section of chemistry, A.A.A.S., 1875; mem. Nat. Acad. Sciences. Author: Essays on Peat Muck and Commercial Manures, 1859; Peat and Its Uses as Fertilizer and Fuel, 1866; How Crops Grow, 1868, 1890; How Crops Feed, 1870. Home: New Haven, Conn. Died 1909.

JOHNSON, Stanley H., ry. official; b. Bunker Hill, Ill., Feb. 22, 1872; s. Benjamin and Amelia E. J.; ed. high school, St. Louis; m. Jane C. Daniels, Apr. 9, 1893. Began as stenographer Southern Interstate Assn., St. Louis, 1888; with Southwestern Freight Bur., St. Louis, 1894-1902; with C.,R.I.&P. Ry., 1902—, as chief clk. to 3d v.p., 1902-04, asst. gen. freight agt. at Little Rock, Ark., 1904-06, Chicago, 1906-09, asst. freight mgr., 1909-15, freight traffic mgr., 1915-20, v.p. and freight traffic mgr., 1920—. Home: Chicago, Ill. Died Feb. 16, 1926.

JOHNSON, Sylvanus Elihu, journalist; b. Island Creek Tp., O., Jan. 19, 1841; ed. country schs., Richmond (O.) Coll. and McNeely Sch., Harrison Co., O.; m. Martha A. Mann, Mar. 30, 1865 (died 1899); m. 2d, Bertha B. Bowersmith, Apr. 29, 1903. Learned printers' trade; was city editor Ohio Statesman and later city editor, mng. editor and editorial writer Ohio State Journal; with Cincinnati Enquirer, 1879—, as state corr., mng. editor, Washington corr. and editorial writer, except 1 yr. when he was on staff New York World; in addition to Enquirer work was editorially connected with New York Journal, 1895. Has participated in Ohio and Nat. Dem. politics; sat in Dem. Nat. Com., 1900, 1904. Home: Washington, D.C. Died 1908.

JOHNSON, Thomas, artist; b. London, Eng.; pupil of F. Williams. Medal World's Columbian Expn., 1893. Exhibited at Paris Expn., 1900. Deceased.

JOHNSON, Thomas Cary, theologian; b. Fishbok Hill, Va., July 19, 1859; s. Thomas and Minerva (Hinchman) J.; A.B., Hampden-Sidney Coll., 1882, D.D., 1891, LL.D., 1899; diplomas in schs. of Latin, Greek and mathematics, U. of Va., 1883-84; grad. Union Theol. Sem. in Va., 1887; spl. student, Yale, 1887-88; m. Ella Faulkner Bocock, Dec. 26, 1894; children—Thos. Cary, Elinor Holmes, Anne Faulkner. Prof. Old and N.T. exegesis, Austin (Tex.) Theol. Sch., 1888-90; ordained Presbyn. ministry, 1890; pastor elect Third Ch., Louisville, Ky., 1890-91; prof. English Bible and pastoral theology, 1891-92, eccles. history and polity, 1892-1913, systematic theology, 1913-30, emeritus, Union Theol. Sem., Richmond. Mem. Advisory Bd. for Preservation of Va. Antiquities. Author: History of the Southern Presbyterian Church, 1894; Brief Sketch of the United Synod of the Presbyterian Church in the United States of America, 1897; John Calvin and the Geneva Reformation—A Sketch, 1900; The Life and Letters of Robert Lewis Dabney, 1903; The Life and Letters of Benjamin Morgan Palmer, 1906; Virginia Presbyterianism and Religious Liberty, 1907; Introduction to Christian Missions, 1909; Baptism in the Apostolic Age, 1912; Some Modern Isms, 1919; God's Answer to Evolution, 1924; edited collected writings of Rev. Prof. Thomas E. Peck, D.D., LL.D., 1895-97. Home: Richmond, Va. Died Feb. 15, 1936.

JOHNSON, Thomas Humrickhouse, civil engr.; b. Coshocton, O., Jan. 12, 1841; s. William Kerr and Elizabeth (Humrickhouse) J.; A.B., Jefferson (now Washington and Jefferson) Coll., Pa., 1861, A.M., 1866 (Sc.D., 1911); m. Martha E. Patterson, Oct. 28, 1868. Rodman on constrn. of Steubenville bridge, 1863, Marietta & Cincinnati R.R., 1864-65; asst. engr. Pana, Springfield & N.W. R.R., 1866-67, P.,C.C.&St.L. Ry., 1867-72; engr. Union Depot Co., Columbus, O., 1873-75; civil engr. and architect, Columbus, 1875-78; engr. for contractors, Ind. State House, 1878-83; prin. asst. engr., 1883-96, chief engr. Pa. Lines West of Pittsburgh, 1901—. Republican. Presbyterian. Home: Pittsburgh, Pa. Died Apr. 16, 1914.

JOHNSON, Thomas Joseph Allan, pres. Johnson Marble Co.; b. Boston, Mass., Sept. 20, 1876; s. William Andrew and Mary Elizabeth Allan (Buckley) J.; grad. Roxbury High Sch., 1894; unmarried. Owner and mgr. pvt. bank, foreign quarter of Boston, 1900-06; pres., treas. and mgr. Johnson Marble Co., importers and mfrs., 1906—. Mem. bd. dirs. Boston Port Authority. Decorated Cavaliere by King of Italy. Asst. treas. Nat. Rep. Com. Catholic. Home: Boston, Mass. Died Jan. 15, 1934.

JOHNSON, Thomas Moore, platonist; b. Osceola, Mo., Mar. 30, 1851; s. Waldo Porter and Emily (Moore) J.; A.B., U. of Notre Dame, Ind., 1871, A.M., 1874; m. Alice Barr, 1881. Began practice, Osceola, 1872; pros. atty., St. Clair County, Mo., 1874-76 and 1898-1900; retired to devote entire time to study and dissemination of philosophy of Plato. Mayor of Osceola 13 yrs.; mem. Osceola Sch. Bd. 30 yrs. Democrat. Author: Plato and His Philosophy, 1906. Translator: Iamblichus' Exhortation to the Study of Philosophy, 1907; Opuscula Platonica, 1908; Proclus' Metaphysical Elements, 1909. Home: Osceola, Mo. Died Mar. 3, 1919.

JOHNSON, Tom Loftin, mayor; b. Georgetown, Ky., July 18, 1854; s. Albert L. and Helen (Loftin) J.; went to Ind. in boyhood; ed. there; clerk in street ry. office, Louisville, Ky., 1869-75; invented several street ry. devices; bought a street ry. in Indianapolis; later acquired large street ry. interests in Cleveland, Detroit and Brooklyn; also iron mfr. in Cleveland; retired from business. Mem. Congress, 1891-95. Democrat; prominent advocate of the "single-tax" theories of late Henry George. Mayor of Cleveland, 4 terms, 1901-10. Address: Cleveland, O. Died 1911.

JOHNSON, Virginia Wales, author; b. Brooklyn, Dec. 28, 1849; d. M. Augustus and Sarah (Benson) Johnson; ed. at home; unmarried. Made her home in Europe, 1875—. Author: Kettle Club Series, 1870; Travels of an American Owl, 1870; Joseph, the Jew, 1873; A Sack of Gold, 1874; The Catskill Fairies, 1875; The Calderwood Secret, 1875; Miss Nancy's Pilgrimage, 1877; A Foreign Marriage, 1880; The Neptune Vase, 1881; An English Daisy Miller, 1882; The Fainalls of Tipton; Tulip Place, 1886; The House of the Musician, 1887; America's Godfather; Genoa the Superb; The Lily of the Arno; The World's Shrine, 1902; Lake Como; Two Old Cats. Died Jan. 16, 1916.

JOHNSON, Wallace Clyde, civil engr.; b. Granville, Mass., May 21, 1859; s. James W. and Frances A. (Whitney) J.; ed. public and high schools to 1880; Williams Coll., 1880-82; grad. Worcester Polytechnic Inst., 1884; m. Eloise Gertrude Murlless, May 31, 1893. Asst. engr. Holyoke Water Power Co., 1884; chief engr. The Niagara Falls Hydraulic Power & Mfg. Co., 1886-1900; consulting engr., 1900—; also chief engr. Shawinigen Water & Power Co., Montreal; engr. mem. River Improvement Commission, State of N.Y. Home: Niagara Falls, N.Y. Died 1906.

JOHNSON, William Allen, clergyman, theologian; b. Hyde Park, N.Y., Aug. 4, 1833; s. Rev. Dr. Samuel Roosevelt and Elizabeth (Johnston) J.; ed. Columbia Grammar Sch., New York, Columbia Coll., A.B., 1853, A.M., 1856, Gen. Theol. Sem., New York, 1857; m. Henrietta A. Chamberlin, June 12, 1860. Ordained deacon, 1857, priest 1858, in Prot. Episcopal Ch.; rector St. Peter's Ch., Bainbridge, N.Y., and Christ Ch., Guilford, N.Y., 1857-62; missionary in copper mine region of Lake Superior, Mich., 1862-64; rector St. Mary's Ch., Burlington, N.J., 1864-70, St. John's Ch., Salisbury, Conn., 1871-83; prof. homiletics and evidences of religion, 1883-86, prof. ecclesiastical history, 1887-1900, Berkeley Divinity Sch., Middletown, Conn.; prof. emeritus, 1900—. Democrat. Author 3 pamphlets on Church Doctrine of Confession, Annihilation, and Confirmation. Address: Littleton, Colo. Died 1909.

JOHNSON, William Christie, past commander-in-chief G.A.R.; b. Clermont County, O., Mar. 19, 1843; s. John Sutton and Susan (Sheldon) J.; attended Ohio Wesleyan U., 1860-61; m. Lide Littelle, May 10, 1866. Pvt. 89th Ohio Inf., 1862, participating in campaigns of Western Va., Tullahoma to Chattanooga, Sherman's March to Sea, Sherman's march through "the Carolinas," battle of Bentonville, N.C.; 2d lt. 42d U.S.C.T.; mustered out of service Jan. 1866. Senior vice comdr.-in-chief G.A.R., Sept. 1898, acting comdr.-in-chief same, Feb. 5, 1899, to Sept. 6, 1899; elected comdr.-in-chief, Sept. 6, 1899; presided at Nat. Encampment, Sept. 6 and 7, 1899, Phila., retiring Sept. 7, 1899. In drug business, Union City, Ind., 1866-73; cashier People's Bank, Portland, Ind., 1873-78; in hardware business, Cincinnati, 1881-99; mem. Bd. of Public Service, Cincinnati, 1900-06 (pres. 1904-06); asst. postmaster of Cincinnati, 1906-15. Home: Cincinnati, O. Died Apr. 1917.

JOHNSON, William Hannibal, editorial writer; b. Monroe County, O., Mar. 26, 1860; s. Enoch Dye and Charlotte (Dibble) J.; A.B., Denison U., 1885, L.H.D., 1920; post-grad. work Johns Hopkins, 1 yr.; m. Augusta Gieze, June 19, 1890; children—Arthur Lowell, Alfred Janney. Prof. Latin, Denison U., Granville, O., 1894-1919; asso. editor The Review, New York, 1919-20; chief editorial writer Columbus Evening Dispatch, 1920—. Home: Columbus, O. Died Jan. 4, 1934.

JOHNSON, William Henry, author; b. Beaufort, S.C., Mar. 29, 1845; s. Benjamin J. and Caroline A. Richardson J.; ed. Beaufort, S.C., till 1858; academic edn., Dresden, Germany; studied Theol. Sem. of Va., Alexandria, Va.; served in C.S.A. as an officer in the regt. which garrisoned Fort Sumter; m. Sarah Ursula Edmondston, 1867. Ordained in Episcopal Ch., 1872; in 1886 retired from Episcopal ministry to enter the Unitarian. Author: The King's Henchman, 1898; King or Knave, Which Wins?, 1899; The World's Discoverers, 1900; Pioneer Spaniards in North America, 1903. Also wrote Immortality: Its Place in the Thought of To-day, Arena, May 1898. Home: Cambridge, Mass. Died 1907.

JOHNSON, William Howard, originator of—Tiny Town; b. City Point, Va., Oct. 9, 1866; s. William Seylatheal and Norah (Onstot) J.; ed. Mich. Mil. Acad., 1881-83, Georgetown U. Law Coll., 1885-86 (LL.B., 1886); m. Sarah Elizabeth Wood, Feb. 23, 1887; children—William Wood, Eugene Francis, James Cedric, Elizabeth (Mrs. Russel Jules Tuche). Admitted to Mo. bar, Nov. 20, 1885; practiced in Springfield, Mo., 1885—, Forsyth, Taney Co., Mo., 1893-1902; city atty., Springfield, 1887-88; specialized in land law and became asso. with St.L.&S.F. R.R. and Mo.P. Ry. in land promotion; founded Hollister, Taney Co., Mo. (featured for unique architecture). Served on Mo. State Rep. Com. 4 yrs. Republican. Originated and supervised "Tiny Town," Springfield, Mo., first Lilliputian city built and officered by children, 1919, 1925. Home: Springfield, Mo. Died Apr. 2, 1940.

JOHNSON, William Mindred, lawyer; b. Newton, N.J., Dec. 2, 1847; s. Whitfield S. (sec. of state of N.J., 1861-65) and Ellen (Green) J.; A.B., Princeton, 1867, A.M., 1870, LL.D., 1919; m. Maria E. White, Oct. 22, 1872; children—Walter Whitfield (dec.), George White, William Kempton. Admitted to bar, 1870, and practiced at Hackensack, N.J. Mem. N.J. Senate, 1895-1900 (pres. 1900); acting gov. of N.J., May and June 1900, during absence of Gov. Voorhees in Europe; 1st asst. postmaster-gen., 1900-02. Del. Rep. Nat. convs., 1888, 1904; chmn. N.J. Rep. State Conv., 1900, 1904. Donor of Pub. Library to Hackensack, 1901, and of Nurses' Home to Hackensack Hosp., 1917. Pres. N.J. State Bar Assn., 1911-12; trustee N.J. Hist. Soc. Dir. Mut. Benefit Life Ins. Co., N.J. Home: Hackensack, N.J. Died Sept. 10, 1928.

JOHNSON, William Samuel, author; b. Ellicottville, N.Y., Dec. 1, 1859; s. Samuel William and Frances Ann (Sanderson) J.; LL.B., cum laude, Columbia, 1884; m. Carrie Gately Beers, June 19, 1894 (died 1925). Admitted to bar, 1885; clerk, U.S. atty.'s office, 1886-87; practiced at New York, 1887-1905; resided at Paris, France, 1905-10. Author: Glamourie, 1911; Nothing Else Matters, 1913; Prayer for Peace (poem in Forum, Dec. 1914), used by Theodore Roosevelt as the introduction to his book America and the World War, 1915; Prayer for Peace and Other Poems, 1915; Buttadeus, 1916. Address: New York, N.Y. Died Mar. 2, 1937.

JOHNSON, William Woolsey, mathematician; b. Owego, N.Y., June 23, 1841; s. Charles Frederick and Sarah Dwight (Woolsey) J.; A.B., Yale U., 1862, A.M., 1868; LL.D., St. John's Coll., Md., 1915; m. Susannah Leverett Batcheller, Aug. 12, 1869 (died 1916). In U.S. Nautical Almanac Office, Cambridge, Mass., 1862-64; asst. prof. mathematics, U.S. Naval Acad., at Newport, R.I., and Annapolis, 1864-70; prof. mathematics, Kenyon Coll., Ohio, 1870-72, St. John's Coll., Md., 1872-81, U.S. Naval Acad., 1881—; prof. mathematics in the Navy, 1913—. Author: Differential Calculus (Rice and Johnson), 1879; An Elementary Treatise on the Integral Calculus, 1881; Curve Tracing in Cartesian Co-ordinates, 1884; The Theory of Errors and Method of Least Squares, 1890; Treatise on Differential Equations, 1889; Theoretical Mechanics, 1901; Treatise on Differential Calculus, 1904; Differential Equations (math. monographs), 1906; Treatise on Integral Calculus, 1907; an Elementary Treatise on the Differential Calculus, 1908. Home: Baltimore, Md. Died May 14, 1927.

JOHNSON, Willis Fletcher, editor; b. New York, Oct. 7, 1857; s. William and Alathea (Coles) J.; A.B., New York U., 1879; hon. A.M., 1891, L.H.D., 1901, Dickinson; L.H.M., New York U., 1895; m. Sue Rockhill. Prin. pub. sch., Tuckerton, 1876-77; on editorial staff, 1880-87, day editor, 1887-94, editorial writer, 1894—, literary editor, 1917-20, of the New York Tribune; contbg. editor of North American Review, 1914—. Lecturer, 1882—, at a number of schools and colleges; mem. council New York U., 1898—; hon. prof., history of Am. foreign relations, New York U., 1913—; instr. Columbia U., 1923. Pres. N.J. State Civil Service Commn., Apr. 1908-12. Republican. Editor of History of New York University, 1903. Author: A Century of Expansion, 1903; Four Centuries of the Panama Canal, 1906; Col. Henry Ludington, a Memoir, 1907; America's Foreign Relations, 2 vols., 1916; America and the Great War for Humanity and Freedom, 1917; History of Cuba, 5 vols., 1920; Life of Warren G. Harding, 1922; Political and Governmental History of the State of New York, 2 vols., 1923; George Harvey—A Passionate Patriot, 1929; Jilted (trans. from René Bazin), 1929. Home: Summit, N.J. Died Mar. 28, 1931.

JOHNSON, Willis Grant, editor; b. New Albany, O., July 4, 1866; s. William H. and Mary (Humphrey) J.; ed. Ohio State U., 1884-87, Cornell U., 1888-92; post-grad. student in science, instr. and asst. registrar Leland Stanford Jr. U., 1892-94, A.B., 1892, A.M., 1894; m. Fannie Phillips, Apr. 19, 1892. Was instr. U. of Ill. and engaged in spl. agrl. investigations for Ill. State Lab. of Natural History, 1894-96; State entomologist of Md.; organized and was chief of State Hort. Dept. of Md.; prof. entomology and invertebrate zoölogy, Md. Agrl. Coll. and entomologist Md. Expt. Sta., 1896-1901. Editor for Orange Judd Co., N.Y., 1901—. Episcopalian. Republican. Author: The San José Scale, 1898; Fumigation Methods, 1902; The Peace Crop, 1906; The Poultry Book, 3 vols., 1903-04-05. Address: New York, N.Y. Died 1908.

JOHNSTON, Adelia Antoinette Field, educator; b. Lafayette, O., Feb. 5, 1837; d. Leonard and Margaret (Gridley) Field; A.B., Oberlin, 1856; hon. A.M., 1878, Hillsdale Coll., 1873; LL.D., Western Reserve, 1906; studied history 2 yrs. in Germany; m. James M. Johnston, 1859. Began teaching when 14 yrs. old; dean women's dept., 1870-1900, prof. mediæval history, 1894-1907, prof. emeritus, 1907, and mem. prudential com., Oberlin Coll. Address: Oberlin, O. Died 1910.

JOHNSTON, Annie Fellows, author; b. Evansville, Ind., 1863; d. Rev. Albion and Mary (Erskine) Fellows; ed. pub. schs., Evansville, and State U., Ia., 1881-82; m. William L. Johnston, 1888 (died 1892). Author: Big Brother, 1893; The Little Colonel, 1895; Joel—A Boy of Galilee, 1895; In League with Israel, 1896; Ole Mammy's Torment, 1897; Songs Ysame, poems (with her sister, Mrs. Albion Fellows Bacon), 1897; The Gate of the Giant Scissors, 1898; Two Little Knights of Kentucky, 1899; The Little Colonel's House Party, 1900; The Little Colonel's Holidays, 1901; The Little Colonel's Hero, 1902; Cicely, 1902; Asa Holmes, or At the Crossroads, 1902; Flip's Islands of Providence, 1903; Little Colonel at Boarding School, 1903; Little Colonel in Arizona, 1904; The Quilt that Jack Built, 1904; Little Colonel's Christmas Vacation, 1905; In the Desert of Waiting, 1905; Three Weavers, 1905; Mildred's Inheritance, 1906; Maid of Honor, 1906; The Little Colonel's Knight Comes Riding, 1907; Mary Ware, 1908; Legend of the Bleeding Heart, 1908; Keeping Tryst, 1908; Rescue of the Princess Winsome, 1908; The Jester's Sword, 1909; Little Colonel Good Times Book, 1909; Mary Ware in Texas, 1910; Travellers Five, 1911; Mary Ware's Promised Land, 1912; Miss Santa Claus of the Pullman, 1913; Georgina of the Rainbows, 1916; Georgina's Service Stars, 1918; Story of the Red Cross, 1918; The Road of the Loving Heart, 1922; The Land of the Little Colonel, 1929. Home: Pewee Valley, Ky. Died Oct. 5, 1931.

JOHNSTON, Charles, author; b. Ballykilbeg, County Down, Ireland, Feb. 17, 1867; s. William J. (M.P. for Belfast, Ireland) and Georgina Barbara, d. Sir John Hay, Bart., of Park, Scotland; ed. in Derby, Eng., and Dublin U.; entered on course for India civil service, 1886; passed final exam. for Bengal civil service, Aug. 1888, reaching India in Nov., visiting Bombay, Madras, Calcutta and Allahabad; invalided 2 yrs. later; traveled on Continent, Holland, Belgium, Germany, Russia, Austria and France; came to U.S., Oct. 1896; citizen of U.S., 1903. Captain, Military Intelligence Division U.S. Army, 1918-19. Spl. lecturer in polit. science, U. of Wis., 1908. Translator: From the Upanishads, Archaic Sanskrit, 1896; Bhagavad Gita, 1908; What Is Art? (from the Russian of Count L. N. Tolstoi), 1898; Julian, the Apostate (from the Russian of Mereshkovski), 1899; The System of Vedanta (from the German of Prof. Paul Deussen); Yoga Sutras of Patanjali. Author: The Memory of Past Births, 1900; Kela Baj, 1900; Ireland, Historic and Picturesque; The Parables of the Kingdom, 1909; Why the World Laughs, 1912. Home: New York, N.Y. Died Oct. 1, 1931.

JOHNSTON, Charles Hughes, univ. prof.; b. nr. Chapel Hill, N.C., Dec. 21, 1877; s. Charles Wilson and Agnes Watkins (Hughes) J.; A.B., U. of N.C., 1898; post-grad. Harvard, Ph.D., 1905; m. Nell Converse Bomar, June 21, 1906. Teacher and vice prin. Bingham School, Mebane, N.C., 1898-1902; registrar, Harvard Summer Sch., 1903-05; prof. psychology and v.p. State Normal Sch., East Stroudsburg, Pa., 1905-06; substitute for prof. philosophy, Dartmouth, 1906-07; asst. prof. edn., 1907-09, jr. prof., 1909-10, U. of Mich.; dean Sch. of Edn., U. of Kan., 1910-13; prof. secondary edn., U. of Ill., 1913—. Prof. secondary edn., summer session, Columbia, 1913. Progressive Democrat. Presbyn. Author: Syllabus in Philosophy of Education, 1908; School of Education of University of Kansas, 1910. Editor and Part Author: High School Education, 1912; The Modern High School, 1914. Mng. editor Educational Administration and Supervision. Home: Urbana, Ill. Died Sept. 4, 1917.

JOHNSTON, Charles Worth, cotton mfr.; b. Cabarrus County, N.C., Oct. 14, 1861; s. Samuel and Mary (Smith) J.; student Davidson (N.C.) Coll., 1879-80; m. Jennie Stough, Feb. 22, 1882 (died 1921); children—Flora J. (Mrs. E. J. Braswell), Rosa (Mrs. R. W. Stokes), Richard Horace; m. 2d, Jeannett Elliott Newcombe, Apr. 12, 1926 (died 1930). Began as a merchant, 1884; then in cotton mfg. business; chmn. bd. Highland Park Mfg. Co.; pres. Anchor Mills Co., Cornelius Cotton Mills, Brown Manufacturing Co., Union Mills Co., Worth Spinning Co., Park Yarn Mills Co., Eastern Mfg. Co., Johnston Mfg. Co., Monroe Mills Co., Spinners Processing Co. Democrat. Presbyn. Home: Charlotte, N.C. Died July 4, 1941.

JOHNSTON, Christopher, univ. prof.; b. Baltimore, Dec. 8, 1856; s. Christopher (M.D.) and Sarah Lucretia Clay (Smith) J.; B.Litt., U. of Va., 1876, B.A., 1878, M.A., 1879; M.D., U. of Md., 1880; spl. student Johns Hopkins, 1888, prin. subject, Assyriology, fellow in Semitics, 1889-91, Ph.D., 1894; LL.D., U. of Md., 1911; m. Madeline Tasker Tilghman, June 2, 1897. Practiced medicine, 1880-88, devoting much time to study of ancient and modern langs.; instr. Semitics, 1891-94, asso., 1894-99, asso. prof. Oriental history and archæology, 1899-1908, prof., 1908—, Johns Hopkins. Del. from Med. and Chirurg. Faculty of Md. to Internat. Med. Congress at Copenhagen, Denmark, 1884. Author: Epistolary Literature of the Assyrians and Babylonians, 1896. Editor: Ancient Empires of the East, 1906. Contbr. on Egyptology to New International Encyclopedia. Address: Baltimore, Md. Died June 26, 1914.

JOHNSTON, Clarence Howard, architect; b. Okaman, Minn., Aug. 26, 1859; s. Alexander and Mary Louise (Buckhout) J.; ed. pub. and high sch., St. Paul, Minn.; studied architecture in office A. M. Radcliff, St. Paul, 3 yrs.; spl. course, Mass. Inst. Tech.; made architectural tour through Europe and Asia Minor, 1881; m. Mary L. Thurston, Oct. 1, 1885; children—Cyrus Thurston (dec.), Clarence Howard, Helen, Harrison Requa, Mary Louise. Employed in office E. P. Bassford, St. Paul, 1 yr.; with Herter Bros., N.Y. City, 2 yrs.; practiced in St. Paul, 1882—. Prin. bldgs.: Minn. State Prison, Stillwater; U. of Minn. bldgs.; Minn. Hist. Soc. Bldg., Central High Sch. Bldg., Gordon & Ferguson and Golden Rule store bldgs., Minn. Club Bldg., all of St. Paul. Fellow Am. Inst. Architects, Minn. Chapter A.I.A. (a founder); a founder Architectural League of New York. Republican. Conglist. Home: St. Paul, Minn. Died Dec. 29, 1936.

JOHNSTON, Elizabeth Bryant (Miss), author; b. Mason County, Ky.; mem. Columbia Hist. Soc., The Literary Soc. Washington, D.A.R. Author: George Washington Day by Day; Original Portraits of George Washington; Visitors' Guide to Mount Vernon; The Days That Are No More, 1901; Christmas in Kentucky, 1862, 1892. Contbr. to series in Home Mag. giving in 22 papers history of the various depts. of the govt. at Washington. Lecturer and dialect reader. Address: Washington, D.C. Died 1907.

JOHNSTON, George Ben, surgeon; b. Tazewell, Va., July 25, 1853; s. John Warfield and Nicketti (Floyd) J.; student U. of Va., 1870-75; M.D., Univ. Med. Coll. (New York U.), 1876; LL.D., St. Francis Xavier Coll., 1897; m. Helen Rutherfoord, 1892. Prof. surgery, Med. Coll. of Va.; surgeon Memorial Hosp., Richmond, to Johnston-Willis Sanatorium, and to Abingdon (Va.) Hosp. Fellow Internat. Surg. Soc., American Surg. Assn. (pres. 1904-05). Address: Richmond, Va. Died Dec. 20, 1916.

JOHNSTON, George Doherty, soldier; b. Hillsboro, N.C., May 30, 1832; s. George Mulhollan and Mary Eliza (Bond) J.; early edn. at Marion, Ala.; A.B., Howard Coll., Ala., 1849, later A.M.; LL.B., Lebanon (Tenn.) Law Sch.; LL.D., U. of Ala.; m. Euphradia Poellnitz, 1854; m. 2d, Maria Barnett, 1865; m. 3d, Stella Searcy, 1876. Entered C.S.A. as 2d lt. 4th Ala. Regt., Apr. 15, 1861; maj. 25th Ala., Jan. 27, 1862; lt. col., Apr. 6, 1862; col., Sept. 9, 1863; brig. gen. C.S.A., July 24, 1864, serving to close of war; wounded at Murfreesboro and at Atlanta. Commandant of cadets, U. of Ala., 1871-73; supt. S.C. Mil. Acad., 1885-90; U.S. civil service commr., 1892-93; mem. Ala. Senate, 1900-06. Democrat. Presbyterian. Lectured on Memories of the Old South, The Confederate War, Jefferson Davis and Women of the Confederacy. Address: Tuscaloosa, Ala. Died 1910.

JOHNSTON, Gordon, army officer; b. Charlotte, N.C., May 25, 1874; s. Gen. Robert Daniel (C.S.A.) and Elizabeth Johnston (Evans) J.; A.B., Princeton, 1896; hon. grad. Inf. and Cav. Sch., 1903; grad. Gen. Staff Coll. A.E.F., June 1918; m. Anna Julia, d. Dr. Robert W. Johnson, May 25, 1904. Sergt. Co. M, 2d Miss. Inf. and pvt. Troop M, 1st U.S. Vol. Cav. (Rough Riders), June 8-Sept. 15, 1898, Spanish-Am. War; commd. 2d lt. 43d U.S. Inf., Aug. 17, 1899; 2d lt. cav., Aug. 5, 1901; maj. N.A., Aug. 21, 1917; lt. col., June 1918; col., Oct. 1918; promoted through various grades in regular army to lt. col., July 1, 1920. Served Philippine Insurrection, Cuban occupation, on Mexican border, and with A.E.F., in France; chief of staff, 82d Div., Oct. 1918; later acting chief of staff, 7th Army Corps, chief of staff, 7th Regular Div., and asst. chief of staff, 2d Army; selected by Maj. Gen. Wood as mem. Wood-Forbes Mission to P.I., and as asst. to gov. gen., 1921. Decorated Congressional Medal of Honor for "extraordinary gallantry in action at Bud Dajo, Sulu, P.I.," Mar. 1906; D.S.M. (U.S.); Officer Legion of Honor (France). Presbyn. Died Mar. 8, 1934.

JOHNSTON, Harold Whetstone, univ. prof.; b. Rushville, Ill., Mar. 18, 1859; s. DeWitt Clinton and Margretta Hay (Bower) J.; A.B., Ill. Coll., Jacksonville, 1879, A.M., 1882, Ph.D., 1891; L.H.D., Kenyon Coll.; LL.D., Ill. Coll., Jacksonville, 1909, Indiana U., 1911; m. Eugenia Hinrichsen, Mar. 25, 1882. Instr. and prof. Latin, Ill. Coll., 1880-95; prof. Latin, Ind. U., 1895—. Editor-in-chief of The Inter-Collegiate Latin Series; editor Cicero's Orations and Letters (selections), 1891; Cæsar's Commentaries on the Gallic War, 1906. Author: Latin Manuscripts, 1897; Metrical Licenses of Vergil, 1897; The Private Life of the Romans, 1903. Address: Bloomington, Ind. Died 1912.

JOHNSTON, Henry Phelps, univ. prof.; b. 1842; A.B., Yale, 1862. Prof. history, Coll. City of New York. Author: Battle of Harlem Heights; The Campaign of 1776 Around New York; The Yorktown Campaign; Yale and Her Honor Roll in the American Revolution; Observations on Judge Jones; Loyalist History of the Revolution; The Storming of Stony Point on the Hudson, July 15, 1779; Nathan Hale, 1901; Memoir of Col. Benjamin Tallmadge, Vol. I, collections Soc. S.R. of Md., 1905. Home: New York, N.Y. Died Mar. 2, 1923.

JOHNSTON, Howard Agnew, clergyman; b. Greene County, O., June 29, 1860; s. David Steele and Eliza Elmira (Bogle) J.; A.B., U. of Cincinnati, 1882 (Phi Beta Kappa); B.D., Lane Theol. Sem., 1885; Ph.D., U. of Wooster, 1889; D.D., Parsons Coll., Ia., 1894; LL.D., Carroll Coll., 1930; m. Mary Este Hubbard, Oct. 21, 1885 (died 1909); 1 dau., Mary Montfort; m. 2d, Mrs. Ida C. Lamson, Mar. 15, 1917 (died 1929); m. 3d, Grace A. Young, Oct. 28, 1930. Ordained Presbyterian ministry, 1885; pastor Seventh Church, Cincinnati, 1884-90, Central Ch., Des Moines, Ia., 1890-93, Forty-first St. Ch., Chicago, 1893-99, Madison Av. Ch., New York, 1899-1905; spl. representative Presbyn. Ch. to its missions in Asia, 1905-07; pastor First Ch., Colorado Springs, 1908-10, First Ch., Stamford, Conn., 1910-17; conf. and institutional work, Chicago, 1917-20; pres. Chicago Ch. Federation, 1920-23; pastor Immanuel Presbyn. Ch., Milwaukee, 1923—. Author: Moses and the Pentateuch, 1891; Studies in God's Methods of Training Workers, 1900; Bible Criticism and the Average Man, 1902; Studies for Personal Workers, 1903; Scientific Faith, 1904; The Beatitudes of Christ, 1905; The Famine and the Bread, 1908; Victorious Manhood, 1909; Enlisting for Christ and the Church, 1919; Scientific Christian Thinking, 1922; The Son of Nicodemus, 1925; We Can Surely Believe; A Christian Answer to Current Atheism, 1928. Home: Milwaukee, Wis. Died Apr. 15, 1936.

JOHNSTON, Hugh, clergyman; b. County of Elgin, Ont., Can., Jan. 5, 1840; s. John and Mary Ann (Teetzel) J.; A.B., Victoria U., valedictorian, 1865, A.M., 1869, B.D., 1874, D.D., 1889; m. Eliza Holland, June 18, 1867. Ordained Methodist ministry, 1865; pastor Centenary Ch., Hamilton, 1873-76, St. James', Montreal, 1878-82, Carleton St., Trinity, Queen St. and Metropolitan chs., Toronto, 1882-93, Metropolitan Memorial M.E. Ch., Washington (attended by Pres. McKinley), 1893-98, First Ch., Baltimore, Md., 1898-1904, asso. pastor, 1904—. Acting chaplain of the U.S. Senate, 1897. Author: Toward the Sunrise (sketches of travel in Europe and Holy Land); Beyond Death (work on Eschatology), 1903; Travel Films, 1913; also biographies of William Morley Punshon and Senator John Macdonald and of collections of sermons and addresses. Home: Baltimore, Md. Died Sept. 24, 1922.

JOHNSTON, James Steptoe, bishop; b. Church Hill, Miss., June 9, 1843; s. James Steptoe and Louisa C. B. J.; attended Oakland Coll., and U. of Va., 1860-61; D.D., U. of the South, 1888; pvt. Hood's div. and 2d lt. Stuart's cav., C.S.A., 1861-65; m. Mary M. Green, Aug. 24, 1865. Admitted to bar, 1868; studied for ministry; deacon, 1869, priest, 1871, P.E. Ch.; rector Port Gibson, Miss., 1870-76, Mt. Sterling, Ky., 1876-80, Trinity Ch., Mobile, Ala., 1880-88; consecrated bishop of Western Tex., Jan. 6, 1888. Retired, May 1914. Address: San Antonio, Tex. Died Nov. 4, 1924.

JOHNSTON, John, banker; b. Aberdeenshire, Scotland, June 8, 1836; s. George and Margaret (Mitchell) J.; grad. U. of Aberdeen, 1855; hon. A.M., U. of Aberdeen, U. of Wis; m. Sept. 1, 1881, Ethelinda Thorsen, Sept. 1, 1881. Banker, 1856—; pres. Marine Nat. Bank, Milwaukee. Represented Milwaukee at opening of Bd. of Trade, Chicago, and Chamber of Commerce, Cincinnati, and at several meetings of Nat. Bd. of Trade; was 2 yrs. pres. Chamber of Commerce, Milwaukee, and mem. exec. com. Am. Bankers' Assn.; is mem. exec. com. Northwestern Mutual Life Ins. Co. Carried off championship rifle shooting at 800, 900 and 1,000 yards at the Wapinschaw, Aberdeen, Scotland, 1879; also several prizes shooting at Wimbledon, London; was 2 yrs. pres. Grand Nat. Curling Club of America. Was 10 yrs. mem. and part time pres. bd. regents, U. of Wis.; 12 yrs. pres. State Hist. Soc., Wis.; pres. bd. trustees Milwaukee-Downer Coll. for Young Women. Presented the city of Milwaukee with a valuable central site for the City Emergency Hosp. Gold Democrat. Wrote articles on Milwaukee in Ency. Brittannica and Universal Ency.; also other articles in cyclopedias. Home: Milwaukee, Wis. Died 1904.

JOHNSTON, John Alexander, army officer; b. Allegheny, Pa., Feb. 22, 1858; s. Alexander and Sarah R. J.; grad. U.S. Mil. Acad., 1879; honor grad. Inf. and Cav. Sch., Ft. Leavenworth, Kan., 1883; m. Henrietta V. Vandergrift, 1888. Commd. 2d lt., June 13, 1879; 1st lt., Jan. 20, 1886; capt., Jan. 3, 1895; maj. a.a.g., May 19, 1898; lt. col. a.a.g., Feb. 21, 1901; brig. gen., Jan. 7, 1903; resigned Jan. 15, 1903. Frontier service in Tex., 1879-82, 1885-87, in S.D., 1891-93, and 1895-97; instr. art of war and engring., Inf. and Cav. Sch., 1883-85; instr. history, law and tactics, U.S. Mil. Acad., 1887-91; in charge mounted instrn., Cav. Depot, Jefferson Barracks, Mo., 1893-95. Duty in office of adj. gen. in charge of orgn. and muster in and out of all vol. forces raised during Spanish-Am. War, 1898, and the vols. raised for the Philippines 1898-1901; in charges reorgn. of gen. recruiting service U.S.A., incident to army increase; prepared reports upon German Army maneuvers, 1902; was commr., Dist. Govt., D.C.; apptd. comdr. Northeastern Dept., U.S. Army, Boston, 1917. Address: Washington, D.C. Died Jan. 5, 1940.

JOHNSTON, John T(homas) M(orris), banker; b. Ashland, Mo., Mar. 17, 1856; s. John T. M. and Minerva (Waters) J.; grad. Ashland High Sch., 1872, Jones Commercial Coll., St. Louis, 1873; Southern Bapt. Theol. Sem., Louisville, Ky., 1885-87; (D.D., Southwest Coll., 1890); m. Florence Brooks, Oct. 15, 1879. Ordained Bapt. ministry, 1887; pastor 1st Ch., Jefferson City, Mo., 1887-97; chaplain Mo. State Senate, 1887-97, Mo. State Prison, 1895-97; pastor Delmar Av. Ch., St. Louis, 1897-1907; prof. biography and history, William Jewell Coll., Liberty, Mo., 1907, 08; an organizer, 1910, and pres., 1910-14, Nat. Reserve Bank, Kansas City. Trustee William Jewell Coll., Stephens Bapt. Coll. Del. at large Dem. National Conv., St. Louis, 1916. Mason, K. of P. Author: A Man with a Purpose, 1895 (3 edits.); The Question of the Hour, 1897; Moral Heroes; World Patriots (3 edits.). Home: Washington, D.C. Died Nov. 9, 1930.

JOHNSTON, Joseph Forney, senator; b. Lincoln County, N.C., 1843; s. Dr. William and Nancy (Forney) J.; was attending high sch. when war broke out; served in C.S.A., 1861-65, pvt. to capt.; 4 times wounded. Practiced law at Selma, Ala., 1866-84; lived at Birmingham, 1884—; pres. Ala. Nat. Bank, 1884-94; was 1st pres. Sloss Iron and Steel Co. Gov. of Alabama, 2 terms, 1896-1900; unanimously elected U.S. senator, Aug. 1, 1907, for unexpired term (1907-09) of Edmund W. Pettus, deceased, and for term 1909-15. Democrat. Address: Birmingham, Ala. Died Aug. 8, 1913.

JOHNSTON, J(osiah) Stoddard, editor; b. New Orleans, Feb. 10, 1833; s. John Harris and Eliza (Davidson) J.; orphaned at 5; reared by maternal relatives in Ky.; A.B., Yale, 1853; LL.B., Louisville U., 1854; m. Eliza W., d. George W. (afterward gov.) Johnson, June 13, 1854. Cotton planter in Ark., 1855-59; farmer in Scott County, Ky., 1859-62; on staffs Gens. Bragg, Buckner and Breckinridge, C.S.A., 1862-65; practiced law at Helena, Ark., 1866-67; editor Frankfort (Ky.) Yeoman, 1867-86; asso. editor Louisville Courier-Journal, 1903-08; consulting geologist, 1908—. Adj. gen. of Ky.,

1871; sec. of state, 1875-79; candidate for Dem. nomination for gov., 1875; sec. or chmn. Dem. State Com. (the latter most of the time), 1868-88; del. Dem. Nat. convs., 1884, 1888. Pres. Ky. Press Assn., 1870-86, Yale Alumni Assn. of Ky., 1890-1902; v.p. Filson Club, 1893—. Author: Memorial History of Louisville (2 vols.), First Explorations of Kentucky, 1898; Confederate History of Kentucky, 1898. Address: Louisville, Ky. Died Oct. 4, 1913.

JOHNSTON, Julia Harriette, writer; b. Salineville, O., Jan. 21, 1849; d. Rev. Robert and Jane Grey (Waters) J.; grad. Peoria (Ill.) High Sch., 1867; unmarried. Writer for The Presbyn. and Reformed Presbyn., and other publs. Also David C. Cook Pub. Co., Chicago; lesson writer, particularly in primary dept.; has written about 500 hymns and gospel songs for composers. Pres. Presbyterial Missionary Soc. of Peoria Presbytery, 1899. Author: The School of the Master (poems), 1880; Life of Adoniram Judson, 1887; Bright Threads, 1897; Indian and Spanish Neighbors, 1906; Who Was It? Stories, 1911; Fifty Missionary Heroes Every Boy and Girl Should Know, 1913. Also booklets, Marginal Readings, Benedictions of the Bible. Address: Peoria, Ill. Died Mar. 6, 1919.

JOHNSTON, Lawrence Albert, clergyman; b. Sugar Grove, Pa., Aug. 12, 1855; s. Frederick and Charlotte J.; A.B., Augustana Coll., Rock Island, Ill., 1879, D.D., 1901; grad. Augustana Theol. Sem., 1881; m. Anna S. Lindgren, Oct. 18, 1881. Ordained Luth. ministry, 1881; pastor Des Moines, Ia., 1881-86, Rockford, Ill., 1886-94, St. Paul, Minn., 1894-1904, Moline, Ill., 1904-11, St. Paul, 1911—. Asso. editor Bethania, Des Moines, Ia., 1883-85, also Ungdorsnvannen, Rock Island; several yrs.; editor Young Peoples Messenger, Moline, Ill., 1904-11. Dir. Augustana Book Concern, Rock Island, 1890-93; Augustana College, 1893—; Augustana Adolphus Coll., Minn., 1895-98, 1902-04; Augustana Hosp., Chicago, 6 yrs., Bethesda Hosp., St. Paul, Emanuel Hosp., Omaha, for various terms; City Library, Moline, 3 yrs. Has served as pres. or v.p. various confs., Ia., Ill. and Minn.; pres. Evang. Luth. Augustana Synod, 1911—; Swedish sec. gen. council Lutheran Ch. of America, 1905-11, etc. Republican. Author: Be Thou Faithful, 1902; "Minnesshrift," 1910. Home: St. Paul, Minn. Died June 10, 1918.

JOHNSTON, Lucy Browne (Mrs. William Agnew Johnston), club woman; b. Camden, O., Apr. 7, 1846; d. Robert Henning and Margaret (Wright) Browne; student Western Female Sem. (now Western Coll. for Women), 1865-66, LL.D., 1921; grad. Chautauqua course; m. William Agnew Johnston, Nov. 25, 1875; children—John Jacob, Margaret Agnes. Mem. Ottawa County (Kan.) Teachers' Exam. Bd. 3 yrs.; mem. Minneapolis (Kan.) Sch. Bd., 1887-90; pres. Kan. Federation Women's Clubs, 1901-03; mem. bd. dirs. Gen. Federation Women's Clubs, 1906-10; pres. Kansas Equal Suffrage Association, 1911-13; pres. Kansas Day Club, 1914; mem. Kan. Traveling Library Commn., 1899—. Elected chmn., later hon. chmn., Woman's Com., Kan. Div. of Council National Defense, 1918-19; chmn. 1st dist. Kan. div. Woman's Liberty Loan Com. Mem. bd. dirs. Kan. State Hist. Soc., 1917—. Republican. Presbyn. Home: Topeka, Kan. Died Feb. 17, 1937.

JOHNSTON, Marbury, naval officer; b. Albany, Ga., Dec. 2, 1860; s. Thomas Henry and Laura Camilla (Hill) J.; grad. U.S. Naval Acad., 1878; unmarried. Promoted ensign, July 1, 1884; promoted through grades to capt., June 14, 1911; temporarily apptd. rear admiral, Aug. 31, 1917; rear admiral (permanent), Nov. 28, 1918; retired Dec. 2, 1924. Served on New Orleans and Cassius, Spanish-Am. War, 1898; comd. 2d Torpedo Flotilla, 1903-05, Navy Yard, N.Y. City, 1906-07, Albatross, 1907-08, Galveston, 1908-09, Navy Yard, Puget Sound, 1909-10; capt. of yard, Navy Yard, Portsmouth, N.H., 1910-11; comd. Georgia, 1911-13; at Naval War Coll., Newport, R.I., 1913-14; comd. Naval Sta., New Orleans, 1915-17; comd. Squadron Four, Patrol Force, 1917; apptd. comdr. Div. Three and Four, Cruiser Force, 1917. Home: Cuthbert, Ga. Died Mar. 15, 1934.

JOHNSTON, Mary, author; b. Buchanan, Va., Nov. 21, 1870; d. John William and Elizabeth (Alexander) J.; ed. at home; unmarried. Author: Prisoners of Hope, 1898; To Have and to Hold, 1900; Audrey, 1902; Sir Mortimer, 1904; The Goddess of Reason, 1907; Lewis Rand, 1908; The Long Roll, 1911; Cease Firing, 1912; Hagar, 1913; The Witch, 1914; The Fortunes of Garin, 1915; The Wanderers, 1917; Pioneers of the Old South, 1918; Foes, 1918; Michael Forth, 1919; Sweet Rocket, 1920; Silver Cross, 1921; 1492, 1922; Croatan, 1923; The Slave Ship, 1924; The Great Valley, 1926; The Exile, 1927; Hunting Shirt, 1931; Miss Delicia Allen, 1932. Home: Warm Springs, Va. Died May 9, 1936.

JOHNSTON, Rienzi Melville, editor; b. Sandersville, Ga., Sept. 9, 1850; s. Freeman W. and Mary J. J.; ed. common schs., Bainbridge, Ga.; served 2 yrs. in C.S.A.; m. Mary E. Parsons, 1875. In newspaper work in Ga. in early manhood; moved to Texas, 1878; long pres., editor and one of the largest stockholders the Daily Post. Declined nomination for lt. gov. of Tex., 1898; apptd. U.S. senator, Jan. 4, 1913, to succeed Joseph W. Bailey, resigned, and served until successor was elected by legislature, Jan. 29, 1913; Tex. mem. Dem. Nat. Com., 1900-12; later mem. Tex. Senate. First v.p. Associated Press, 2 yrs. Address: Houston, Tex. Died Feb. 28, 1926.

JOHNSTON, Robert Matteson, univ. prof.; b. Paris, France, Apr. 11, 1867; s. William Edward and Bertha (Matteson) J.; ed. in U.S., France, Eng., Germany; M.A., Cambridge U., 1889; of the Inner Temple, barrister-at-law; m. Emily Dawson, 1895. Lecturer in history, Harvard and Mt. Holyoke colls., 1904; prof. history, Bryn Mawr Coll., 1907-08; asst. prof. history, Harvard, 1908—. Author: The Roman Theocracy and the Republic, 1846-49, 1901; Napoleon, a short biography, 1904; The Napoleonic Empire in Southern Italy and the Rise of the Secret Societies, 1904; The Memoirs of Malakoff, 1907; American Soldiers, 1907; The French Revolution, 1909; The Corsican, 1910; The Holy Christian Church, 1912; Mémoire de Marie Caroline, reine de Naples, 1912; Bull Run, 1913; Arms and the Race, 1915. Editor of The Military Historian and Economist. Address: Cambridge, Mass. Died Jan. 28, 1920.

JOHNSTON, Rowland L., congressman; b. Louisiana, Mo., Apr. 23, 1872; educated pub. schs. Admitted to Mo. bar, 1894; mem. Mo. Ho. of Rep. 3 terms from St. Louis County, also served 3 terms as pros. atty. same county; asst. circuit atty., City of St. Louis, 5 yrs.; del. Rep. Nat. Conv., Chicago, 1908; mem. 71st Congress (1929-31), 16th Mo. Dist. Mem. Mo. N.G. 5 yrs.; recruiting duty, Spanish-Am. War. Republican. Episcopalian. Mason. Home: Rolla, Mo. Died Sept. 22, 1939.

JOHNSTON, Rufus Perry, clergyman; b. New Cambria, Mo., June 9, 1861; student, Lincoln U., Ill.; A.M., William Jewell College, Mo., 1888, D.D., 1895; Th.M., Southern Bapt. Theol. Sem., 1891. Ordained Bapt. ministry, Clifton Hill, Mo., Aug. 29, 1886; pastor, Roanoke and Lathrop, Mo., 1887-88, Athens, and David's Fork, Ky., First Ch., St. Joseph, Mo., Third Ch., St. Louis, Fifth Av. Ch., New York. Home: New York, N.Y. Died Aug. 24, 1924.

JOHNSTON, Stewart, steel mfr.; b. Pittsburgh, Pa., Sept. 17, 1865; s. William G. and Sarah M. (Stewart) J.; C.E., Rensselaer Poly. Inst., 1887; m. Eleanor Dudley Hogg, 1891; 1 dau., Caroline (Mrs. S. A. Hartwell, Jr.). Pres. Pittsburgh Steel Foundry Co., 1899—, chmn. bd., 1925—. Trustee Rensselaer Poly. Inst. Republican. Presbyn. Home: Pittsburgh, Pa. Died Dec. 29, 1933.

JOHNSTON, Thomas Alexander, educator; b. Cooper County, Mo., Nov. 13, 1848; s. John Benoni Thaxton and Margaret (Harris) J.; grad. Kemper Sch., Boonville, Mo., 1869; A.B., U. of Mo., 1872, A.M., 1875; LL.D., Mo. Valley Coll. and Westminster Coll., 1923, U. of Mo., 1924, Kenyon Coll., 1927; m. Caroline Frances Rea, June 27, 1877; children—Bertha, Rea Alexander, Harris Cecil, Alice Ewing. Asso. prin. (with its founder, Frederick T. Kemper, of Va.), of Kemper Mil. Sch., 1872-81, supt. and owner, 1881-1909, pres. and supt., 1909-28, pres., 1928—. Dir. and chmn. bd. Kemper State Bank; pres. of several corps. Presbyn. (elder). Home: Boonville, Mo. Died Feb. 5, 1934.

JOHNSTON, Thomas William, editor; b. Youngstown, O., Dec. 1, 1862; s. Thomas William and Sarah Ellen (Johnston) J.; ed. pub. schs.; m. Maud St. Aubert Leavens, Mar. 15, 1897. Mng. editor, 1887-1904, asso. chief editor, 1904-13, Kansas City Star. Home: Kansas City, Mo. Died May 18, 1917.

JOHNSTON, William (Andrew), author; b. Pittsburgh, Pa., Jan. 26, 1871; s. Prof. William Andrew and Agnes (Parry) J.; A.B., Western U. of Pa., 1891; Litt.D., U. of Pittsburgh, 1919; m. Hattie Belle McCollum, Apr. 12, 1910. Pub. Wilkinsburg (Pa.) Independent, 1893-94; reporter New York Journal and New York Press, 1894-96; editorial staff N.Y. Herald, 1897-1900, N.Y. World, 1900-27; v.p. Celotex Co., 1927—. Founder grammar sch. field days in N.Y. pub. schs.; chmn. Parker Independent League, 1904. Proposed Fulton Aerial Flight, for which $10,000 prize was offered in Hudson-Fulton celebration, 1909; managed New York's "safe and sane" Fourth of July celebrations, 1910-12; trustee N.Y. Tercentenary Commission. Author: History Up to Date, 1898; The Innocent Murderers, 1910; The Yellow Letter, 1911; Limpy, 1916; The House of Whispers, 1917; The Apartment Next Door, 1919; The Mystery in the Ritsmore, 1920; The Flying Hoof, 1921; The Tragedy at the Beach Club, 1922; The Fun of Being a Fat Man, 1923; The Waddington Cipher, 1923; Webster's Bridge (with H. T. Webster), 1924; These Women, 1925; The Affair in Duplex Mine B, 1927; An Accidental Accomplice, 1928. Editor: World's Best Stories, 1925, 26, 27. Contbr. to mags. Home: Chicago, Ill. Died Feb. 16, 1929.

JOHNSTON, William Agnew, judge; b. Oxford, Ont., July 24, 1848; s. Mathew and Jane (Agnew) J.; ed. common schs.; LL.D., Washburn Coll., 1900, Baker U., 1901; m. Lucy Holsington, 1871 (died 1871); m. 2d, Lucy Browne, 1875; children—John J., Mrs. Margaret J. Brandenburg. Practiced law in Kan., 1872-84; mem. Kan. Ho. of Rep., 1875, Senate, 1876-80; asst. U.S. atty. for Kan., 1879; atty. gen. of Kan., 1880-82, 1882-84; mem. Supreme Court of Kan., continuously, 1884-1935, reëlected 9 times, last time, 1930, chief justice, 1903-35. Home: Topeka, Kan. Died Jan. 21, 1937.

JOHNSTON, William Atkinson, mech. engr.; b. South Boston, Mass., Aug. 31, 1868; s. Archibald and Mary (Watt) J.; B.S., Mass. Inst. Tech., 1892; m. Eleanor Chant, June 12, 1895 (died 1920); 1 dau., Ruth Stevens; m. 2d, Edith Crane Lanphere, Aug. 8, 1922. Prof. theoretical and applied mechanics, 1912-33, Mass. Inst. Tech., prof. emeritus, 1933—. Republican. Baptist. Co-Author: (with C. E. Fuller) Applied Mechanics, Vol. I, Statics and Kinetics, 1913; Applied Mechanics, Vol. II, Strength of Materials, 1919. Home: Belmont, Mass. Died Aug. 6, 1937.

JOHNSTON, W(illiam) Dawson, librarian; b. Essex Center, Vt., June 11, 1871; s. Rev. James Arthur and Janette (Cass) J.; A.B., Brown U., 1893; student U. of Chicago, 1893-94; A.M., Harvard, 1897-98; Litt.D., Rutgers Coll., 1911; m. Jean McVicker Browne, July 12, 1895. Instr. history, U. of Mich., 1894-97, Brown U., 1899-1900; asst., Library of Congress, 1900-07; lecturer bibliography, Simmons Coll., 1905-07; librarian, Bur. of Edn., Washington, 1907-09, Columbia U., 1909-14, St. Paul Pub. Library, 1914-21, Am. Library in Paris, 1921-25; European rep. Library of Congress, 1926—. Author: History of the Library of Congress (Vol. I), 1904. Address: Washington, D.C. Died Nov. 18, 1928.

JOHNSTON, W(illiam) Dawson, librarian; b. Es- Cincinnati, Oct. 19, 1861; s. William Hartshorne and Mary (Neele) J.; student Washington U., 1876-79, LL.B., 1897; honor grad. Inf. and Cav. Sch., Ft. Leavenworth, Kan., 1887; Army War Coll., Washington, D.C., 1907-08; grad. Gen. Staff Coll., 1920; m. Lucille Barat Wilkinson, June 27, 1888 (died 1917); m. 2d, Isabelle Gros, Mar. 17, 1923. Pvt., corpl. and sergt., Lafayette Guard, St. Louis, 1878-81; 1st lt. Prescott Rifles, Co. B, Ariz. Territorial Militia, 1881-82; commd. 2d lt. 16th Inf., U.S.A., Oct. 10, 1883; promoted through grades of vol. service to maj. 46th U.S. Inf. Vols., Aug. 17, 1899; hon. mustered out vols., May 31, 1901; maj., Philippine Scouts, Apr. 1904-Oct. 6, 1906; col., June 12, 1916; brig. gen. N.A., Aug. 5, 1917; maj. gen., Aug. 8, 1918-July 31, 1919; brig. gen., U.S.A., Apr. 30, 1921; maj. gen., Nov. 3, 1924. Gov. Province of Isabela, 1901-02; comd. 1st Bn., Philippine Scouts, campaign against Pulajanes, 1905-07; mem. Gen. Staff Corps, Army War Coll., 1914-17; organized, and comd. 180th Inf. (Texas) Brig., Aug. 25, 1917-Aug. 27, 1918; served with Texas Brig., 90th Division, 1st Army Corps, in Toul sector, Aug. 1918; maj. gen. U.S.A. and assigned to the 91st Div., Aug. 1918; comd. 91st Div. in St. Mihiel offensive, Sept. 12-13, Meuse-Argonne, Sept. 26-Oct. 15, and with the French Army in Belgium in the Group of Armies of Flanders, under command King of Belgians, during the Ypres-Lys campaign in Belgium, Oct. 19-Nov. 11, 1918. Served at Camp Lewis, Wash., during demobilization of 91st Div., Gen. Staff Coll., Aug. 1919-July 1920; with Am. Forces in Germany from Aug. 18, 1920; chief of Staff A.F. in G., Aug. 25, 1920-May 11, 1921; comdg. 1st Brig., July 1, 1921-Apr. 6, 1922; gen. liaison officer French Army of the Rhine, Apr. 1922-Jan. 1923; sr. mil. adviser Am. Delegation Commn. of Jurists, studying rules of war at The Hague, Dec. 1, 1922-Mar. 1923; comdg. 4th C.A. Dist., Ft. McPherson, Ga., July 15, 1923-Nov. 15, 1924; comdg. 3d Div., Dec. 3, 1924-Oct. 19, 1925; retired, Oct. 19, 1925. Awarded silver star citation, Philippine Insurrection, 1900; D.S.C. "for extraordinary heroism in action" during Meuse-Argonne; D.S.M. "for distinguished services in command of 91st Div. in Meuse-Argonne and in Belgium"; Victory medal (three major offensives, one defensive sector); Comdr. Legion of Honor, Croix de Guerre with palm; Comdr. Order of Leopold I of Belgium. Died Feb. 19, 1933.

JOHNSTON, William Hugh, labor leader; b. Nova Scotia, Can., Dec. 30, 1874; s. Adam and Jane (Murray) J.; ed. grammar sch.; m. Harriet L. Lunn, Nov. 1, 1907. Brought to U.S., 1885; apprentice machinist trade, Rhode Island Locomotive Works, and worked at all branches of the trade; joined Internat. Assn. Machinists, 1895; elected pres. of New England Dist. of that orgn., 1905; elected business rep., Providence, 1907; elected pres. Dist. 44, embracing all machinists in navy yards and arsenals and other govt. depts., 1909; pres. Internat. Assn. Machinists, 1912—. Mem. Nat. War Labor Bd., by apptmt. of President Wilson, 1917-19; sent by the President on mission to Great Britain and France, 1918. Conglist. Mason. Odd Fellow. Home: Washington, D.C. Died Mar. 26, 1937.

JOHNSTON, William Milton, lawyer; b. Milledgeville, Ill., Feb. 5, 1867; s. Joseph and Harriet (Meyers) J.; student normal sch., Holton, Kan.; A.B., U. of Neb., 1894; m. Mabel Sleeper, July 27,

1898; children—Paul F. (dec.), Margaret, Harriet. Admitted to Mont. bar, 1895; sr. mem. firm Johnston & Johnston, Billings, Mont., 1895-1901; practiced alone, 1901-13; mem. Johnston & Coleman, 1913-20, Johnston, Coleman & Johnston, 1920-29, Johnston, Coleman & Jameson, 1929—; dir. Mont. Coal & Iron Co. County attorney Yellowstone County, 1897-1901; city atty., Billings, 1901-03; mem. Mont. Ho. of Rep., 1905-07; mayor of Billings, 1917-19; mem. State Bd. of Edn. Mem. and pres. bd. trustees pub. schs., Billings; mem. of Board of Park Commrs. of Billings; trustee Poly. Inst., Billings. Chmn. of finance com., War Chest, World War; mem. Legal Advisory Bd.; four-minute speaker; chmn. Near East Relief, 1920; pres. Billings Community Chest; chmn. relief campaigns in 1931, 32 and 33. Mason. Home: Billings, Mont. Died Jan. 21, 1938.

JOHNSTON, William Pollock, educator; b. Harrison County, O., Jan. 26, 1839; s. Samuel P. and Eleanor (Thomson) J.; A.B., Jefferson Coll., Pa., 1858, later A.M.; studied Reformed Presbyn. Theol. Sem.; D.D., Grove City Coll., 1891; LL.D., Washington and Jefferson Coll., 1902; m. Clara Dawson Anderson, June 16, 1874. Ordained R.P. ministry, 1864; pastor Baltimore, 1864-73, Washington, Ia., 1873-81; prin. Washington (Ia.) Acad., 1879-81; prof. Latin and English lit., 1881-90, prof. philosophy and English lit., and pres., 1890-1907, pres. emeritus, 1908, Geneva Coll., Pa.; prin. Mercer (Pa.) Acad., 1908. Moderator R.P. Synod, 1898. Address: Beaver Falls, Pa. Died Feb. 1920.

JOHNSTON, William Preston, pres. Tulane U., 1883—; b. Louisville, Ky., Jan. 5, 1831; grad. Yale, 1852; LL.D., Washington and Lee; m. Rosa E. Duncan, 1853; m. 2d, Margaret H. Avery, 1888. Was col. and aide-de-camp on staff of Jefferson Davis, pres. of the Confederacy, 1862-65; prof. history and literature, Washington and Lee U., 1867-77; pres. La. State U. and Agrl. and Mech. Coll., Baton Rouge, La., 1880-83. Author: Life of General Albert Sidney Johnston; The Prototype of Hamlet; The Johnstons of Salisbury; also the poems "My Garden Walk," "Pictures of the Patriarchs" and "Seekers After God." Address: New Orleans, La. Died 1899.

JOHNSTON, William Waring, physician; b. Washington, Dec. 28, 1843; s. Dr. William P. Johnston; prof. in med. dept., Columbian; ed. private schools and Coll. of St. James, Md.; grad. med. dept. U. of Pa., 1865; studied U. of Edinburgh, 1866-67, and in Paris; m. Virginia Stoughton, 1897. Resident physician, Charity Hosp., Blackwell's Island, and in Bellevue Hosp., 1865-66; prof. theory and practice of medicine, 1871—, and later apptd. prof. clinical medicine, med. dept., Columbian U. Mem. and pres. Med. Soc., D.C., and Obstet. and Gynecol. Soc., Washington; mem. Bd. Visitors Govt. Hosp. for Insane, Washington. Contributed articles on diseases of intestines to following: System of Practical Medicine (Pepper), 1885; American Text-Book of Applied Therapeutics (Wilson), 1896; American System of Practical Medicine (Loomis & Thompson), 1898; System of Practical Therapeutics (Hare), 1897. Address: Washington, D.C. Died 1902.

JOHNSTON, Wirt, M.D.; b. Raymond, Miss., Aug. 31, 1846; grad. Jefferson Med. Coll., Philadelphia, 1868; recording sec. Miss. State Med. Assn., 1876-78; sec. Miss. State bd. of health, 1877—. Address: Jackson, Miss. Died 1900.

JOHNSTONE, Edward Robert, editor; b. Utica, N.Y., Apr. 30, 1849; s. Mervin E. and Julia (Waters) J.; student Princeton, 1866, Dickinson Coll., 1866-70; m. Mary Griswold; 1 dau., Julia Waters; m. 2d, Ida Louise Abell, Jan. 27, 1887. With various papers from 1870; in campaigns against Chief Joseph, 1877, Sitting Bull, 1880-81; city editor St. Paul Pioneer Press, 1882-92; corr. in Riel rebellion, 1885; city and county assessor, St. Paul, Minn., 1892-95; with Associated Press, 1897-98, in New York; in charge fleet of dispatch boats, Spanish-Am. War, Feb. to Aug. 1898, at Key West, in Havana and Santiago blockades, and in Puerto Rico. Editor Minneapolis Times, 1898-1903; mng. editor New York Commercial Advertiser, 1903-04; editor-in-chief Cleveland Leader, 1904-06; in charge of cargoes of flour-famine relief in China, 1907; nat. registrar Am. Red Cross, 1908-09. Special writer. Address: New York, N.Y. Deceased.

JOHNSTONE, William Jackson, clergyman; b. Daviess County, Ind., Aug. 7, 1867; s. Brison Blair and Lydia (Overton) J.; grad. normal sch., Bloomfield, Ind., 1884; student DePauw U., Greencastle, Ind.; Ind. U., Bloomington; Johns Hopkins U.; D.D., Ursinus Coll., 1913; LL.D., Jamestown Coll., 1916; A.B., Johns Hopkins U., 1935 (as of 1892); m. Jeanette C. Walls, Nov. 21, 1888; children—Mrs. Florence Lucile Hauser, Mrs. Ruth Allyne Hillman. Teacher country schs., 1883-85; prin. high sch. and normal sch., Odon, Ind., 1885-86; licensed U.B. ministry, 1887; pastor, Odon, 1887-88; prin. normal dept., Otterbein U., Westerville, O., 1888-90; pastor Salem U.B. Ch., Baltimore, 1891-93; lecture platform, 1893-95; ordained Presbyn. ministry, 1895; pastor Cloquet, Minn., 1895-97, Luverne, Minn., 1897-99; field sec. Macalester Coll., St. Paul, 1899-1902; pastor 5th Ch., Minneapolis, 1905-10; field rep. eastern dist., Bd. of Ministerial Relief and Sustentation, Phila., 1910-14, campaign rep., 1914-17; asso. sec. Presbyn. Bd. of Temperance and Moral Welfare, 1917-22; lecturer for Nat. Reform Assn., 1923-24; minister Knox Presbyterian Ch., St. Paul, 1924-31. Dir. Dry Chicago Federation, 1917-19. President International Magna Charta Day Assn., 1921-27. Author: Abraham Lincoln, the Christian, 1913; George Washington, the Christian, 1919; Manual of Moral Welfare, 1920; Prohibition Addresses, 1921; How Lincoln Prayed, 1931; How Washington Prayed, 1932; Robert E. Lee, the Christian, 1933. Home: St. Paul, Minn. Died Apr. 18, 1939.

JOHONNOTT, Edwin Sheldon, physicist; b. Richmond, Ill., Nov. 9, 1868; s. Edwin Sheldon and Frances L. (Brown) J.; B.S., Rose Poly. Inst., Terre Haute, Ind., 1893, M.S., 1897; Johns Hopkins, 1895-96, U. of Chicago, 1896-99; Ph.D., 1898; m. Mabel M. Stevens, Aug. 22, 1900. Prof. mathematics, physics and astronomy, Drury Coll., 1894-95; asst. in lab., U. of Chicago, 1898-99; asso. prof. physics, 1899-1909, prof., 1909—, Rose Poly. Inst. Home: Terre Haute, Ind. Died Jan. 2, 1925.

JOLINE, Adrian Hoffman, lawyer; b. Sing Sing, N.Y., June 30, 1850; s. Charles O. and Mary (Hoffman) J.; A.B., Princeton, 1870, A.M., 1873, LL.D., 1904; LL.B., Columbia, 1872; m. Mary E., d. Francis Larkin, July 12, 1876. Admitted to bar, 1872; sr. mem. firm Joline, Larkin & Rathbone, 1905—; pres. M.,K.&T. Ry. Co. and M.,K.&T. Ry. Co. of Tex., 1906-09; dir. Albany & Susquehanna R.R. Co., Am. & Foreign Marine Ins. Co., Nat. Surety Co., United Traction & Electric Co., Chatham-Phenix Nat. Bank; receiver Met. St. Ry. Co., New York, 1907—. Author: Meditations of an Autograph Collector, 1902; Diversions of a Book Lover, 1903; At the Library Table, 1909; Edgehill Essays, 1910. Homes: Bernardsville, N.J.; New York, N.Y. Died Oct. 15, 1912.

JONAS, August Frederick, surgeon; b. Arlington, Wis., June 12, 1858; s. August Otto and Fredericka (Gundlach) J.; ed. pub. schs., Madison, Wis.; M.D., Bennett Med. Coll., Chicago, 1877; Ludwig Maximilian U., Munich, 1884; post-grad. work, Vienna, Berlin, Paris; LL.D., U. of Neb., 1928; m. Jessica Stebbins, Nov. 16, 1907; children—August F., Mary Elizabeth, Carl Stebbins. Began practice of medicine, 1877; became prof. surgery, med. dept., U. of Neb., 1892, emeritus; later surgeon to Neb. Methodist and Douglas County hosps.; formerly chief surgeon U.P. R.R., div. surgeon C.&N.W. Ry., asst. surgeon C.,St.P.,M.&O. R.R.; retired from practice, 1928. Capt. Med. Corps and governor's aide, World War. Home: Omaha, Neb. Died Nov. 13, 1934.

JONAS, Benjamin Franklin, senator; b. Williamstown, Ky., July 19, 1834; s. Abraham and Louisa (Block) J.; ed. in Ill. and La.; LL.B., U. of La., 1855; m. Josephine Block, Feb. 9, 1859. Pvt. and acting adj. of arty., Hood's corps, Army of the Tenn., 1861-65. Mem. La. Ho. of Rep., 1865, 1876, 1877, Senate, 1872; chmn. La. delegation Dem. Nat. Conv., 1868; city atty., New Orleans, 1874-78; mem. Dem. Nat. Com., 1876-88; U.S. senator from La., 1879-85; collector port of New Orleans, 1885-89; mem. law firm Farrar, Jonas, Goldborough & Goldberg. Home: New Orleans, La. Deceased.

JONES, Adam Leroy, prof. philosophy; b. Dunlap, Ill., July 2, 1873; s. Josiah and Sarah Jane (Yates) J.; A.B., Williams, 1895; univ. scholar, Columbia, 1896, fellow, 1897, Ph.D., 1898, Litt.D., 1929; m. Lily Sylvester Murray, May 24, 1909; children—Murray Leroy, Alfred Welwood, Wallace Sylvester. Asst. tutor in philosophy, Columbia, 1898-1905; preceptor, Princeton, 1905-09; adj. prof. philosophy, Columbia, 1909, asst. prof., 1910, asso. prof., 1911—, also dir. univ. admissions, 1909—. Mem. N.Y. State Examination Bd. Trustee Collegiate Sch., N.Y. City. Chmn. commn. on instns. of higher edn., Assn. Colls. and Secondary Schs. of Middle States and Md., 1918—; chmn. com. on classification of univs. and colls., Assn. American Univs., 1922—. Conglist. Author: Early American Philosophers, 1898; Logic, Inductive and Deductive, 1909. Active in standardization of univs. and colls. Home: Montclair, N.J. Died Mar. 2, 1934.

JONES, Alfred, engraver, artist; b. Liverpool, England, April 7, 1819; came to New York, 1834; m. Louisa Major, May 1841. Served apprenticeship to bank-note engraving; first became prominent by engraving a plate, "The Proposal," for Graham's Magazine, followed by others for that and Godey's Magazine. Later made many artistic plates for art publishers until 1848; almost exclusively in bank-note engraving, 1848—; among others engraved the 2-cent, 30-cent, $4 and $5 postage stamps in the "Columbian" series for Am. Bank Note Co.; became v.p. British-Am. Bank Note Co., 1867. Became asso., 1841, academician, 1851, Nat. Acad. of Design, and was long its sec. and treas. Among his later works are two portraits of Thomas Carlyle, for the Grolier Club, New York, and a large portrait of George Washington. Address: Yonkers, N.Y. Died 1900.

JONES, Alfred Miles, pres. Bethesda Springs Co., Waukesha, Wis.; b. New Durham, N.H., 1837; s. Alfred S. and Rebecca (Miles) J.; ed. Rutland, Vt., and Rockford, Ill.; ran away from home at 14, traveling through West 3 yrs.; m. Emeline A. Wright, Oct. 1857; m. 2d, Blanche P. Smart, July 7, 1908. Was coroner Jo Daviess County, Ill.; mem. Ill. Ho. of Rep., 1872; pres. Ill. State Penitentiary Commn.; U.S. marshal, Northern Dist. Ill., 12 yrs.; mem. Ill. Rep. State Central Com., 1878-94; mem. Wis. Senate, 1898. Address: Waukesha, Wis. Died 1910.

JONES, Amanda Theodosia, author; b. E. Bloomfield, N.Y., Oct. 19, 1835; d. Henry and Mary Alma (Mott) J.; grad. normal classes Aurora Acad., and High Sch., Buffalo; unmmarried. Wrote for Methodist Ladies' Repository, 1853-62, Frank Leslie's Illustrated, 1861-65; lit. editor The Western Rural, 1869-70, The Bright Side, 1870-71. Author: Ulah and Other Poems (2 edits.), 1861; Atlantis and Other Poems, 1866; A Prairie Idyl, 1882; Flowers and a Weed (booklet), 1899; Rubaiyat of Solomon and Other Poems, 1905; Poems, 1854-1906, 1906; A Mother of Pioneers, 1908; A Psychic Autobiography, 1910 (republished in London). Inventor: Vacuum preserving processes for canning without cooking, canning with cooking and desiccation of fruits, meats, etc., without use of preservatives; appliances, retorts, etc., for carrying on vacuum processes; the Jones Direct Feed Safety Oil-Burning System; the Jones Protection Valve (all patented); also improvements upon protection valve and additions thereto, comprising a series of valves applicable to oil, air, vacuum, steam, gas, etc. Address: Junction City, Kan. Deceased.

JONES, Andrieus Aristieus, senator; b. nr. Union City, Tenn., May 16, 1862; s. Rev. James H. W. and Hester A. A. (May) J.; Bethel Coll., McKenzie, Tenn.; B.S., Valparaiso (Ind.) U., 1884, A.B., 1885; law course of study, Valparaiso U.; m. Natalia Stoneroad, Aug. 7, 1902. Taught school, Tenn., 2 yrs.; prin. pub. schs., Las Vegas, 1885-87; admitted to N.M. bar, 1888, bar of Supreme Ct. U.S., 1894. Mayor, Las Vegas, 1893-94; spl. U.S. dist. atty., 1894-98; del. Dem. Nat. Conv., Chicago, 1896; chmn. N.M. Dem. Com., 1906-08; chmn. Dem. State Com. during 1st state campaign, 1911; received vote of Dem. members 1st state legislature of N.M. for U.S. senator; mem. Dem. Nat. Com., 1908-22; first asst. sec. of the Interior, 1913-16; elected U.S. senator for terms, 1917-23 and 1923-29. Mason. Home: East Las Vegas, N.M. Died Dec. 20, 1927.

JONES, Arthur Gray, theologian; b. Memphis, Tenn., Dec. 19, 1868; s. William Henry and Sarah Adelaid (Means) J.; B.A., Arkansas Coll., Batesville, Ark., 1888, M.A., 1892; grad. Union Theol. Sem., Richmond, Va., 1890; D.D., Arkansas Coll., 1903, Daniel Baker Coll., Brownwood, Tex., 1903; LL.D., Arkansas Coll., 1922, Austin Coll., Sherman, Tex., 1923; m. Irene Jeanette Long, Jan. 1891 (died 1894); 1 son, Arthur Long (dec.); m. 2d, Anne McDugald Hicks, Dec. 1897. Ordained ministry Presbyn. Ch. in U.S., 1890; pastor Batesville, 1890-95; prof. Hebrew, Arkansas Coll., 1890-92; pastor First Ch., San Antonio, 1895-1921; prof. systematic and pastoral theology, Austin Theol. Sem., 1921—, also prof. homiletics, 1921-25. Mem. Gen. Assembly's Com. on Revision of Ch. Law, 1921-26; del. to Council Ref. Chs. of World Holding Presbyn. System, 1916, 20; commr. to Gen. Assembly 5 times to 1921. Pres. bd. trustees Austin Theol. Sem., 1907-21; a founder, 1906, Westminster Presbyn. Encampment, Kerrville, Tex. Democrat. Author: Thornton R. Sampson (biog. sk.), 1917. Home: Austin, Tex. Died May 1, 1929.

JONES, Augustine, teacher; b. St. China, Me., Oct. 16, 1835; s. Richard M. and Eunice (Jones) J.; A.B., Bowdoin, 1860, A.M., 1863; LL.B., Harvard, 1867; law student of Gov. John A. Andrew, of Mass.; m. Caroline Alice Osborne, Oct. 10, 1867. Admitted to bar, 1867, and practiced at Boston, 1867-79; prin. Friends' (now Moses Brown) Sch., Providence, R.I., 1879-1904. Was selected by Poet Whittier, 1874, to represent Society of Friends in a series of discourses on the Universal Ch., in Boston. Pres. Park Assn. of Providence and one of first promoters of its met. park system; twice pres. Annual Conv. of Rep. party of R.I. Author: Life of Thomas Dudley, Second Governor of Massachusetts, 1899; Sketch of Joseph Dudley, Ninth Governor of Massachusetts. Home: Newton Highlands, Mass. Died Sept. 10, 1925.

JONES, Benjamin Franklin, mfr.; b. Washington County, Pa., Aug. 8, 1824; ed. New Brighton, Pa.; clerk in a transportation enterprise, Pittsburgh, 1843-45; joined his employer, Samuel M. Kier, in purchasing, 1845, an iron furnace and forges in Westmoreland Co. Established, 1852, The American Iron Works (now Jones & Laughlins) and became head of same; pres. Am. Iron and Steel Assn., 1884—; chmn. Rep. Nat. Com., 1884; candidate for U.S. senator before State legislature, 1899. Address: Pittsburgh, Pa. Died 1903.

JONES, Benjamin Franklin, Jr., steel mfr.; b. Pittsburgh, Pa., Apr. 21, 1868; s. Benjamin Franklin and Mary (McMasters) J.; A.B., Princeton, 1891; m. Sue D. Dalzell, Nov. 16, 1892; children—Benjamin Franklin, Adelaide Dalzell Burgwin. Began with Jones & Laughlin, Ltd., 1891, mgr., 1891, treas.,

1899, pres., 1900; pres. Jones & Laughlin Steel Co., 1902-23, chmn. bd., 1923—; dir. Nat. Union Fire Ins. Co., Union Trust Co. of Pittsburgh. Trustee Allegheny Gen. Hosp., Mercy Hosp. Republican. Chmn. Electoral Coll. of Pa., 1908. Presbyn. Home: Pittsburgh, Pa. Died Jan. 1, 1928.

JONES, Benjamin Franklin, lawyer; b. N.Y. City, Jan. 1, 1870; s. Rev. John and Elizabeth (Holland) J.; grad. high sch.; LL.B., New York U., 1895, LL.M., 1896; m. Mabel Stevens, May 1917; children—Benjamin F., Mabel Elizabeth. Admitted to N.Y. bar, 1897, N.J., 1899; mem. N.J. Assembly, 1899-1901 (speaker of House, 1900-01); judge Dist. Court, 1906-11; pres. Essex County Tax Bd., 1917-20; county counsel Essex Co., 1911-14; Govt. appeal agt. during World War. Republican. Methodist. Mason. Home: Maplewood, N.J. Deceased.

JONES, Breckinridge, lawyer, banker; b. Boyle County, Ky., Oct. 2, 1856; s. Daniel W. and Rebecca Robertson (Dunlap) J.; A.B., Centre Coll., Danville, Ky., 1875; studied law, 1876-78; student St. Louis Law Sch., 1878-79; U. of Va. summer sch., 1879; m. Frances Reid, Oct. 21, 1885 (died 1904); children—Reid, Breckinridge, Frances Reid (Mrs. Kent S. Clow), Daniel W., Mary D. (Mrs. Harrison Hoblitzelle); m. 2d, Sarah Brant Colwell, Sept. 21, 1910. Practiced, St. Louis, 1879-90; officer, 1890—, Miss. Valley Trust Co., of which was chmn. bd.; mem. advisory council Federal Reserve Bd.; mem. Mo. Ho. of Rep., 1882-84. V.p. Mo. Hist. Soc. 20 yrs. Democrat. Mem. Christian (Disciples) Church. Home: St. Louis, Mo. Died Nov. 21, 1928.

JONES, Burr W., judge; b. Evansville, Wis., Mar. 9, 1846; s. William and Sarah M. Jones; A.B., U. of Wis., 1870, LL.B., 1871, A.M., 1874 (LL.D., 1916); m. Olive L. Hoyt, Dec. 1873 (died 1906); 1 dau., Marion Burr (Mrs. Walter M. Smith); m. 2d, Katharine I. MacDonald, 1908. Admitted to bar, 1871; in practice at Madison, Wis., until Sept. 1920; dist. atty., Dane County, Wis., 1872-76; mem. 48th Congress (1883-85); prof. law, U. of Wis., 1885-1915; asso. justice Supreme Court of Wis., 1921-26. Chmn. Dem. State Conv., 1892; del. Dem. Nat. (gold standard) Convention, Indianapolis, 1896; chmn. Wis. State Tax Commn., 1897-98. Pres. Wis. State Bar Assn., 1908; chmn. Dane County Legal Advisory Board in World War; curator Wis. State Hist. Soc. Author: Law of Evidence in Civil Cases, 1896, 2d edit., 1908, enlarged and pub. in 5 vols., 1913, in 6 vols., 1926. Address: Madison, Wis. Died Jan. 7, 1935.

JONES, Burton Rensselaer, bishop; b. York, N.Y., Dec. 3, 1845; s. James and Eleanor S. J.; ed. Geneseo (N.Y.) Acad.; m. Helen M. Hart, July 16, 1895; children—Nellie Edith, Ella Mabel, Ruth Elizabeth. Entered Free Meth. ministry, 1867; dist. elder, Mich. and Ohio confs., 14 yrs.; prof. Spring Arbor (Mich.) Sem., 1886-88; editor Free Methodist, Chicago, 1890-94; bishop, 1894; retired 1919. Home: Pasadena, Calif. Died Apr. 20, 1933.

JONES, Charles Davies, corp. exec.; b. Cincinnati, Apr. 3, 1871; s. Frank Johnston and Frances Dering (Fosdick) J.; A.B., Yale, 1893; LL.B., Cincinnati Law Sch., 1895; m. Grace E. Hinchman, Jan. 19, 1904; children—Frank J. II, Ford H., Grace D. Admitted to Ohio bar, 1895, and practiced at Cincinnati until 1908; sec. and treas. Little Miami R.R. Co., 1908-27, pres., 1927—; pres. Cincinnati Gas & Electric Co., 1915-28, chmn. bd., 1928—; also dir. many corps. Republican. Episcopalian. Home: Cincinnati, O. Died Oct. 24, 1935.

JONES, C(harles) Edward, educator; b. Richland, N.Y., Feb. 23, 1867; s. Charles and Vytie M. (Brown) J.; Pd.B., N.Y. State Coll. for Teachers, Albany, N.Y., 1904, Pd.M., 1905; B.S., New York U., 1907, M.A., 1908, Ph.D., 1911; m. Clara Walker, Aug. 5, 1915; children—Helen Elizabeth (Mrs. Wm. W. Gibson), Ruth Eliza, Louis Clark. Teacher Richland, N.Y., 1884-86, Alhambra, Calif., 1886-95; sch. commr. Oswego County, N.Y., 1896-1901; examiner State Edn. Dept., N.Y., 1901-09; prin. Teachers Training Sch., Albany, N.Y., 1909-12; supt. schs., Albany, 1912-32; writer and lecturer. Mem. exec. bd. Ft. Orange Council Boy Scouts America; dir. Albany Inst. Mason. Author: Sources of Interest in High School English, 1912. Address: Albany, N.Y. Died Jan. 10, 1941.

JONES, Charles Fremont, U.S. attorney; b. nr. Brookville, Ind., May 12, 1856; s. John and Maria (Colescot) J.; ed. Brookville Coll.; studied law in law office and U. of Va.; m. Mary Rose, Oct. 23, 1879 (died 1909); children—2 died in infancy. Admitted to Ind. bar, 1879, and practiced at Brookville until 1901; atty. for U.S. before Spanish Treaty Claims Commn. during its life, 1901-10; organized work of Commn. in Spain, 1904, and in Cuba, 1905, visiting both countries; admitted to bar of Supreme Court of U.S., 1905, and practiced before that court; atty. Court of Claims Div., U.S. Dept. of Justice, 1910—, spl. asst. to atty. gen., 1921. Mem. Rep. State Central Com. Ind., 1886-90; Rep. elector at large, Ind., 1896; del. to Rep. Nat. Conv., 1900. Officer Grenfeld Assn. Methodist. Mason, Odd Fellow, K.P. Home: Washington, D.C. Died Feb. 16, 1931.

JONES, C(harles) Hampson, physician; b. Baltimore, Dec. 11, 1858; s. Isaac Soloman and Mary Ann (Hampson) J.; Johns Hopkins, 1877-79; U. of Edinburgh, Scotland, 1879-83, M.B. and C.M., 1883; M.D., Coll. Phys. & Surg., Baltimore, 1889; m. Emma M. White, June 26, 1902. Practiced, Baltimore, 1883—; prof. physiology, Women's Med. Coll.; prof. pub. health and preventive medicine, Coll. Phys. and Surg. Insp. of health, Baltimore, 1896-98; commr. of health, 1898-1900; asst. commr. of health, 1900—. Republican. Episcopalian. Mason. Address: Baltimore, Md. Died Apr. 11, 1932.

JONES, Charles Henry, journalist; b. Talbotton, Ga., Mar. 7, 1848; s. George Washington and Susan Elinor J.; entered C.S.A. at 15, serving under Gen. Joe Johnston in campaign ending in fall of Atlanta; transferred to naval dept., and was in Ga. Reserves when war closed; m. Eliza Cowperthwaite, 1871 (died 1888); m. 2d, Mrs. L. E. Parsons, 1890. Lived in New York, 1865-81; edited Eclectic Magazine, Appleton's Journal, etc., and contributed to leading periodicals; established Florida Daily Times, Jacksonville, 1881, consolidating it with the Union, 1882, as the Times-Union; removed to St. Louis as editor Missouri Republican (later St. Louis Republic), 1888, mng. it until 1893; editor New York World, 1893-95; leased and edited St. Louis Post-Dispatch, 1895-97. Mem. World's Columbian Commission, and originated the idea of the La. Purchase Expn. of 1904, St. Louis. Prominent in Democratic party; wrote Chicago Platform of 1896 and Kansas City Platform of 1900. Pres. Nat. Editorial Assn., 1885; one of leaders in organizing Am. Newspaper Publishers' Assn. Home: Paris, France. Died Jan. 27, 1913.

JONES, Charles Sumner, physician; b. Middlesex, N.Y., July 27, 1858; s. Joshua and Ursula Betsey (Case) J.; B.S., Cornell U., 1884; M.D., U. of Buffalo, 1888; studied in Vienna, Paris and London; m. Emma Pratt, Dec. 26, 1893 (dec.); 1 son, Pascal Pratt. Practiced at Buffalo, 1889—; mem. Council of U. of Buffalo, also chmn. Administration Bd., emeritus prof. pediatrics, dean, 1918—, Sch. of Medicine, U. of Buffalo; physician in chief Buffalo Orphan Asylum; consulting phys. Children's Hosp., Buffalo. Presbyn. Home: Buffalo, N.Y. Died Nov. 16, 1927.

JONES, Chester Lloyd, commercial expert; b. Hillside, Wis., Mar. 6, 1881; s. Enos Lloyd and Eleanor B. (Lloyd) J.; B.L., U. of Wis., 1902; U. of Pa., 1902-03, U. of Berlin, 1904, U. of Madrid, 1905; Ph.D., U. of Pa., 1906; m. Caroline Franck Schock, June 30, 1909; children—Caroline, Eleanor Christine, Mary, Chester. Instr. polit. science, U. of Pa., 1906-10; prof. polit. science, U. of Wis., July 1910-20. Asst. editor Annals of Am. Acad. Polit. and Social Science, 1906-10. Mem. ednl. commn. of Pan-Am. Assn. for Internat. Conciliation, to visit univs. of S. America, 1914; mem. E. L. Doheny Research Foundation, 1917; dir. Bur. Fgn. Agents of War Trade Bd., Washington, 1918-19; commercial attaché, Am. Embassy, Madrid, Spain, 1919-20, Am. Legation, Havana, Cuba, 1921-22, Am. Embassy, Paris, France, 1922-27; adviser Pan Am. Conf., Havana, 1928; spl. rep. U.S. Dept. Commerce, Mexico, 1928; dir. School of Commerce, U. of Wis., 1929-35, prof. econs., 1929—; dir. Am. Corporation of Foreign Bondholders. Author: The Consular Service of the United States, 1906; The Economic History of the Anthracite-Tidewater Canals, 1908; Statute Law Making, 1912; Caribbean Interests of the United States, 1916; Mexico and Its Reconstruction, 1921; Handbook of Switzerland, 1925; The United States and the Caribbean (with others), 1929; Caribbean Backgrounds and Prospects, 1931; Costa Rica, 1935; The Caribbean since 1900, 1935; Guatemala, 1940. Compiler: Readings on Parties and Elections in the United States, 1912. Address: Madison, Wis. Died Jan. 13, 1941.

JONES, Clement Ross, engineer; b. Knottsville, W.Va., Apr. 19, 1871; s. Uriah and Pernissa Jane (Ford) J.; B.S., C.E., W.Va. U., 1894, M.E., 1897; Worcester Poly. Inst., summer 1896; Stevens Inst. Tech., summer 1897; M.M.E., Cornell, 1900; m. Elizabeth Charles Gambrill, July 22, 1915; 1 son, Ross Gambrill. Mem. engring. firm Jones & Jenkins, 1894-98; asst. in mech. engring., 1895-97, instr., 1897-99, asst. prof., 1899-1901, prof. and head dept., 1901-11, dean Coll. Engring. and prof. steam and exptl. engring., W.Va. U., 1911-32, dean emeritus and prof. power engring., 1932—. Sec. engring. sect. Land Grant Coll. Assn., 1921-24, mem. com. on engring. expt. sta., 1924-27; chmn. engineering sect. of same assn., 1928-29. Editor Experiment Station Record, 1921-24. Chmn. fuel com., 1917-18. Grad. as No. 1, and 1st lt. adj. W.Va. Corps of Cadets, 1894; 1st lt. W.Va. N.G., 1894; capt. 1896. Republican. Methodist. Mason. Home: Morgantown, W.Va. Died Aug. 16, 1939.

JONES, Daniel Fiske, surgeon; b. Minneapolis, Minn., June 2, 1868; s. George Edward and Emma Maria (Hall) J.; A.B., Harvard, 1892, M.D., 1896; m. Mary Haughton Richardson, May 1, 1898. House officer, Mass. Gen. Hosp., 1896-97; cons. surgeon Mass. Gen. Hosp.; hon. cons. surgeon N.E. Deaconess and Palmer Memorial hosps. Surgeon-in-chief Harvard Surg. Unit, with British Forces in France, Sept.-Dec. 15, 1916, rank of lt. col. (temp.); commissioned maj. M.C., U.S.A., July 1918; lt. col. Med. Corps, U.S.A., May 1919; served in France; hon. discharged, May 21, 1919. Regent Am. College of Surgeons, 1921-24; overseer Harvard U., 1932—. Republican. Episcopalian. Home: Boston, Mass. Died Sept. 11, 1937.

JONES, Daniel Webster, governor; b. Bowie County, Republic of Tex., Dec. 15, 1839; s. Dr. Isaac N. J.; ed. in acad., Washington, Ark.; m. Margaret P. Hadly, Feb. 9, 1864. Entered C.S.A., 1861; became col. 20th Ark. Inf., Dec., 1862; was comdg. a brigade of inf. at close of war. Admitted to bar, 1865; elected pros. atty., 1874; presdl. elector, 1876, 1880; elected atty. gen., Ark., 1884, 1886; mem. legislature, 1891, 1915; gov. of Ark., 2 terms, 1897-1901; resumed practice on expiration of 2d term. Home: Little Rock, Ark. Died Dec. 25, 1918.

JONES, David Percy; b. Minneapolis, Minn., July 6, 1860; s. Judge Edwin S., and Harriet (James) J.; A.B., U. of Minn., 1883; m. Alice Gale, May 13, 1891; children—David Gale, Anna (Mrs. E. S. Mariette), Helen Holmes (Mrs. P. S. Duff). Began in real estate and banking business established by father, 1900, as David P. Jones & Co., of which is pres.; pres. Jones Davis Agency, v.p. Hennepin Co. Savings Bank. Pres. Bd. of Aldermen, Minneapolis, 1898-1902; mayor of Minneapolis, 1905-07. Pres. bd. trustees Carleton Coll., Northfield, Minn.; corporate mem. A.B.C.F.M. (v.p.); pres. Social Settlement Assn. Republican. Home: Minneapolis, Minn. Died Aug. 3, 1927.

JONES, Edgar Laroy, dentist; b. Dexter, Me., Mar. 15, 1853; s. Samuel Straw and Dianna (Lane) J.; ed. com. schs., Dexter, and 1 yr. dental dept., U. of Me.; m. Adele Curtis, Oct. 20, 1875. Practiced, Waterville, Me., 1879—. Mayor of Waterville, 1891, 92, 1906; chmn. Dem. State Central Com., 1904—; mem. Dem. Nat. Com., 1908-16; trustee Pub. Library. Address: Waterville, Me. Died July 24, 1915.

JONES, Edmund Adams, univ. prof.; b. Rockville, Mass., Feb. 11, 1842; s. Elisha A. and Rhoda (Ellis) J.; served in 42d Mass. Vols. in Civil War; A.B., Amherst, 1865, A.M., 1871; hon. Ph.D., Ohio U., 1903; m. Flora Richards, Dec. 23, 1873 (dec.); children—Flora Ellis (dec.), Walter Elisha. Teacher, 1865-67, asso. prin., 1867-68, prin., 1868-69, Lake Forest (Ill.) Acad.; supt. schs., Massillon, O., 1869-73, Marietta, O., 1873-75, Massillon, O., 1875-1904; state commr. of common schs. of Ohio, 1904-09; prof. history and economics, 1909-10, prof. Am. history and Bible, 1910-15, prof. Bible and edn., 1915-20; prof. English Bible, 1920-23, emeritus, Otterbein U. Sec. Massillon Board of Trade, 14 yrs.; treas. McClymond's Pub. Library, 1898-1904; sec. trustees Charity Rotch Sch., 20 yrs.; trustee U. of Wooster, 6 yrs.; mem. State Bd. Examiners, Ohio, 8 yrs.; bd. control Ohio Teachers' Reading Circle, 1883-1905; mem. Nat. Council of Edn., 1909-15. Past comdr. Hart Post G.A.R.; patriotic instr. dept. of Ohio, 1908-09; pres. Stark Co. Soldiers' Relief Commn., 14 yrs. Presbyn. Republican. Author: Ohio Supplement Morton's Geography; Ohio State School Reports, 5 vols., 1904-09. Home: Westerville, O. Died Dec. 23, 1926.

JONES, Edward Campbell, gas engr.; b. South Boston, Mass., Feb. 8, 1861; s. Edward and Hannah Frances (Campbell) J.; ed. Lowell (Mass.) Inst., and Hawes Sch. of Art; m. Mary Stratton Jones, Nov. 22, 1883 (died 1922); children—Edward Stratton, Leon Barrett, Dwight Williams; m. 2d, Florence C. Harris, May 19, 1926. Began in the employ of South Boston Gas Light Co., 1876, and became asst. supt. and clerk of corp.; with Boston Gas Light Co. as supt. North End Sta., and asst. engr., 1889-90; asst. engr., later chief engr., San Francisco Gas Light Co., 1891-1902; chief engr. Calif. Central Gas & Electric Co., 1902-04; chief engr. gas dept. Calif. Gas & Electric Corp., 1904-06; chief engr. gas dept. Pacific Gas & Electric Co., 1906-20; later cons. gas engr. Had charge of restoration of gas in San Francisco after earthquake, 1906; lecturer in gas engring., U. of Calif., 1913; advisory gas engr., U.S. Bur. Standards. Del. Am. Gas Assn. to U.S. Chamber of Commerce. Awarded medal of honor and gold medal, San Francisco Expn., 1915; gold medal, Pacific Coast Gas Assn. Republican. Conglist. Mason. Author of numerous professional papers relating to heating and gas. Inventor of Jones Oil Gas Process and Jones Jet Photometer. Home: Palo Alto, Calif. Died July 22, 1933.

JONES, Edward Franc, scale mfr.; b. Utica, N.Y., June 3, 1828; s. Lorenzo Baldwin and Sophronia (Chapman) J.; ed. schs. and acad., Leicester, Mass.; m. Sarah Antoinette Tarbell, May 1850; m. 2d, Susan Annie Brown, May 1863. Col. 6th Regt. Mass. Vol. Militia—first regt. in Civil War; attacked in Baltimore and reached Washington Apr. 19, 1861; met on arrival by President Lincoln. Col. 26th Mass. Inf., Oct. 18, 1861; bvtd. brig. gen. vols., Mar. 13, 1865, "for meritorious services during the war." Mem.

Mass. Legislature, 1865; has held several municipal offices in Binghamton; lt. gov. of N.Y., 1886-91. Democrat. Conducted Jones Scale Works at Binghamton, N.Y., under corporate name "Jones of Binghamton," 1865—; originator of phrases "He pays the freight," and "Do it now." For past several yrs. has been totally blind. Mason. Author of "Origin of the Flag," "Richard Baxter," "Uncle Jerry." Address: Binghamton, N.Y. Died Aug. 14, 1913.

JONES, Edward Groves, surgeon; b. Chattooga County, Ga., Jan. 14, 1874; s. John A. and Margaret (Kendrick) J.; A.B., Emory Coll., Ga., 1895; M.D., Atlanta Coll. Phys. and Surg., 1900; post-grad. studies Johns Hopkins Hosp.; m. Lillian Taylor, Nov. 1906. Prof. surgery, Emory U. Sch. of Medicine; surgeon to Grady, Ga. Bapt., and Wesley Memorial hosps. Author: Notes on Obstetrics and Gynecology, 1900; Outlines of Physiology, 1901. Fellow Am. Coll. Surgeons. Home: Atlanta, Ga. Died Oct. 6, 1921.

JONES, Edwin Frank, lawyer; b. Manchester, N.H., Apr. 19, 1859; s. Edwin R. and Mary A. (Farnham) J.; A.B., Dartmouth, 1880; studied law in office on Hon. David Cross, Manchester; admitted to bar, 1883; m. Nora F. Kennard, Dec. 21, 1887. Mem. firm of Copeland & Jones, Manchester, 1883-86; practiced alone, 1886-1902, as mem. Burnham, Brown, Jones & Warren, 1902-12, Jones, Warren, Wilson & Manning, 1912—. Asst. clk. and clk. N.H. Ho. of Rep., sessions 1881, 83, 85; city solicitor, Manchester, 1887-98; treas. Hillsborough Co., 1887-95; pres. Rep. State Conv., 1900; mem. N.H. Constl. Conv., 1902; del.-at-large Rep. Nat. Conv., 1908; pres. N.H. Constl. Conv., 1912. Trustee of Cemeteries, Manchester, 21 yrs., of City Library 12 yrs.; trustee N.H. State Library. Unitarian. Mason (Grand Master of Grand Lodge of Masons, N.H., 1910-11). Mem. Manchester Com. on Pub. Safety and Defense, 1917. Address: Manchester, N.H. Died Oct. 6, 1918.

JONES, E(rnest) Lester, hydrographic and geodetic engr.; b. E. Orange, N.J., Apr. 14, 1876; s. Charles Hopkins and Ada (Lester) J.; mem. class of 1898, Princeton, A.M., 1919; m. Virginia Brent Fox, Sept. 28, 1897; children—Mrs. Elizabeth Brent Barker, Cecil Lester. Business, research and secretarial work 10 yrs.; U.S. dep. commr. fisheries, 1913-15; apptd. supt. U.S. Coast and Geod. Survey, Apr. 1915, title changed to dir., 1919, and commd. dir., 1920. Commr. Internat. Boundary bet. U.S. and Can. (Alaska and Can.); mem. first Aerial Coastal Patrol Commn.; mem. Federal Bd. Surveys and Maps, Federal Personnel Bd. Served pvt. to maj., D.C. Militia; commd. lt. col. Signal Corps U.S.A., World War, later col. Div. Mil. Aeronautics; served with A.E.F. in France and Italy. An organizer and incorporator Am. Legion; organizer, 1st comdt. 1st American Legion Post (Pioneer Post) and 1st Am. Legion Dept. Diploma of Honor, Aerial League America; decorated Officer Order S.S. Maurizio e Lazzaro, by King of Italy, and Fatigue de Guerre (Italy); Officer Legion of Honor (France); Verdun medal. Cited for D.S.M. Author: Alaska Investigations, 1914; Hypsometry, 1915; Elements of Chart Making, 1915; Neglected Waters of the Pacific, 1916; Safeguard the Gateways of Alaska, 1917; Aerial Surveying, 1919; Earthquake Investigation in United States, 1925; Tide and Current Investigations of the U.S.C. and G.S., 1926—all Govt. publs.; Surveying from the Air, 1922; The Evolution of the Nautical Chart, 1924; Science and the Earthquake Perils, 1926. Called first meeting, Feb. 5, 1919, and first caucus World War Vets., at Washington, D.C., Mar. 7, 1919; wrote first draft Preamble and Constn. of Am. Legion, and presented same, St. Louis Conv., May 1919. Home: Rixeyville, Va. Died Apr. 9, 1929.

JONES, Fernando, title examiner; b. Chautauqua County, N.Y., May 26, 1820; s. William and Anna (Gregory) J.; moved to Buffalo, 1824; ed. public sch., Buffalo, and an acad., New York; removed to Chicago, 1835; m. Jane Grahame, 1853. On coming to Chicago was clerk in his father's hardware store; learned the Pottawatomie tongue; was employed in the Land Office, Chicago, 1836; went into abstract business (with partners) and compiled abstracts of all titles in Cook County, which became of enormous value when the records of the county were destroyed; business was consolidated with that of the two other abstract firms and finally merged in Chicago Title & Trust Co. Alderman, 1859-60; South Town supervisor during war; helped establish Camp Douglas. Was trustee Orphan Asylum, State Asylum for Insane, Jacksonville, Ill., and the old Chicago U. Address: Chicago, Ill. Died 1911.

JONES, Francis Coates, painter; b. Baltimore, July 25, 1857; s. Hugh B. and Laura E. J.; in France, 1876-82; studied at École des Beaux Arts under Yvon, Lehmann, Boulanger and Lefebvre; unmarried. Studio in New York, 1882—; splty. figure painting. Clark prize, Nat. Acad. Design, 1885; silver medal, Buffalo Expn., 1901, St. Louis Expn., 1904. N.A., 1894; mem. Nat. Inst. Arts and Letters. Address: New York, N.Y. Died May 27, 1932.

JONES, Frank, capitalist; b. Barrington, N.H., Sept. 15, 1832; went to school winters, worked on father's farm summers; clerk at 17 in brother's hardware store, later partner; became owner of ale brewery, Portsmouth, N.H., 1857; later bought one in Boston; 4 yrs. pres. Boston & Me. R.R. Mayor Portsmouth, 1865-66; mem. Congress, 1875-79; Dem. candidate for gov., N.H., 1880. Address Portsmouth, N.H. Died 1902.

JONES, Frank Johnston, lawyer; b. Cincinnati, Apr. 22, 1838; s. John Davies and Elizabeth (Johnston) J.; B.A., Yale, 1859, hon. M.A., 1906; LL.B., Cincinnati Law Sch., 1866; m. Frances Dering Fosdick, May 30, 1866. Enlisted pvt. Co. A, 6th Ohio Inf., Apr. 1861; 2d lt. 13th Ohio Inf., May 1861, later 1st lt. and adj., and afterward capt. same regt.; bvtd. maj. vols., Mar. 13, 1865, "for gallant and meritorious services during the war." Practicing law at Cincinnati, 1866—; pres. Little Miami R.R. Co., 1890—, Cincinnati Equitable Ins. Co.; dir. Cleveland & Pittsburgh R.R. Co., Dayton & Mich. R.R. Co., Cincinnati St. Ry. Co., Columbia Life Ins. Co., Cincinnati, First Nat. Bank, Cincinnati. Republican. Episcopalian. Trustee Cincinnati Orphan Asylum; dir. Spring Grove Cemetery Assn. Home: Cincinnati, O. Died June 7, 1927.

JONES, Franklin D., lawyer, author; b. Webster, Neb., Oct. 5, 1887; s. Daniel and Fannie Louise (Roberts) J.; A.B., U. of Ia., 1910; LL.B., George Washington U., 1915; m. Aura Belle Fike, 1916; children—Lawrence Fike, Dorothy Fike. Acting sec. and asst. sec. Federal Trade Commn., 1916; atty. same commn. and mem. Bd of Review, 1917-19; mem. law firm Davies, Jones & Beebe. Decorated Silver Cross of Order of Redeemer (Greece), 1926. Democrat. Author: Trade Association Activities and the Law; Historical Development of the Law of Business Competition. Home: Washington, D.C. Died Apr. 19, 1929.

JONES, F(rederick) Robertson, insurance; b. Wicomico County, Md., Jan. 4, 1872; s. John Bayley and Anne A. (Follin) J.; A.B., Western Maryland Coll., 1892, A.M., 1895; Ph.D., Johns Hopkins, 1896; m. Eleanor Dwight Cook, June 20, 1905; children—Eleanor Robertson (Mrs. Eric Paepcke), Katharine Robertson (Mrs. Hamilton Southworth). Acting prof. history and economics, Western Md. Coll., 1896-97; acting instr. economics, Johns Hopkins, 1897; instr. and asst. prof. history and sociology, Union U., 1897-1902; asso. in economics and politics, Bryn Mawr, 1902-06; asst. supt., Charity Orgn. Soc., Hartford Conn., 1894-95; spl. rep. of U.S. Bur. of Edn. in Eng., 1897; in employ Fidelity and Casualty Co. of New York, June 12, 1906-13, asst. sec., Feb. 1910-13; sec.-treas. Workmen's Compensation Publicity Bur., 1913-29. Gen. mgr. Assn. of Casualty and Surety Execs., 1929-36; hon. sec. bur. of Personal Accident and Health Underwriters. Apptd., 1918, mem. advisory bd. U.S. Bureau of War Risk Ins. (mil. and naval div.). Author: The History of Taxation in Connecticut, 1896; Colonization of the Middle States and Maryland, 1904; History of the United States since the Civil War, 1905; Digest of Workmen's Compensation Laws of the United States and Territories, 1913-37; Taxation of Insurance Companies for Revenue, 1915; Essential Factors of a Good Workmen's Compensation Law, 1915; Case against State Managed Insurance under Workmen's Compensation Laws, 1916; History and Proceedings of the World's Insurance Congress (San Francisco, 1915), 1917; Dangerous Tendencies in Workmen's Compensation Laws, 1926; Workmen's Compensation Laws of the United States and Territories (editor). Home: New York, N.Y. Died Dec. 27, 1941.

JONES, Gardner Maynard, librarian; b. Charlestown, Mass., June 27, 1850; s. Nahum and Lucy (Blake) J.; grad. Dorchester, Mass., High Sch., 1866; attended Sch. of Library Economy, Columbia Coll., 1888; m. Kate Emery Sanborn, June 30, 1897. In book-stores in Boston, Mass., 1867-87; librarian Salem Pub. Library, 1889-1931. Mem. A.L.A. (treas. 1897-1906, member council, 1907-12), Mass. Library Club (sec. 1890-91, pres., 1893-94), Appalachian Mountain Club (treas. 1885-87, pres. 1908). Author: List of Subject Headings for Use in Dictionary Catalogs, 1895, 2d edit., 1898. Home: Salem, Mass. Died May 19, 1941.

JONES, George H., Standard Oil Official; b. Carthage, N.Y., Sept. 22, 1872; s. Charles and Mary M. (Barlett) J.; ed. pub. schs. (West Carthage), Chaffee's Phonographic Inst. (Oswego, N.Y.), and under pvt. tutors; m. Blanche K. Fry, June 8, 1892; children—Mrs. Ruth E. Koechling, Mrs. Mildred M. Berran. Began as stenographer with Nat. Transit Co., Oil City, Pa., 1890; sec. to v.p. South Penn Oil Co., Pittsburgh, Pa., 1897-99, to v.p. Nat. Transit Co., New York, 1899-1907; became connected with legal dept. special, Standard Oil Co. (N.J.), 1907, and has continued with same co. successively as chief accountant, comptroller of subsidiaries, dir., 1917, treas., 1919, v.p. and treas., 1920 and chmn. bd., 1925—. Republican. Methodist. Home: Pelham, N.Y. Died Nov. 22, 1928.

JONES, George Heber, missionary; b. Mohawk, N.Y., Aug. 14, 1867; s. Charles Edward and Susan Jane (Cosser) J.; ed. pub. schs., Utica, N.Y.; A.B. (non-resident course), Am. U., Harriman, Tenn., 1892, D.D., Ill. Wesleyan U., 1906; m. Margaret Josephine Bengel, missionary, May 10, 1893. Apptd. missionary to Korea by M.E. Ch., 1887; in ednl. work, Seoul, Korea, 1888-91; prin. Pai Chai English Sch., Seoul, 1892-93; presiding elder Chemulpo Dist., 1893-1903; supt. Korea Mission M.E. Ch., 1897-99; in America, 1903-07, served as a sec. Bd. of Missions M.E. Ch., and as lecturer on missions at Morningside Coll., Sioux City, Ia.; returned to Korea, 1907; pres. Bible Inst. of Korea, the Union Theol. Sch. of M.E. Ch. and M.E. Ch., S., 1907-11. Del. from Korea to Gen. Conf. M.E. Ch., Baltimore, 1908; spl. lecturer on missions, Boston U. Sch. Theology, 1915-18; exec. sec. Korean Quarter Centennial Movement of M.E. Ch., Sept. 1, 1910-12; ministerial reserve del. from Korea to Gen. Conf., 1912; editorial sec. Bd. of Foreign Missions, M.E. Ch., 1913—. Author: Korea, Country and People, 1907; An English Korean Dictionary of Scientific and Technical Terms, 1910. Editor Korean Repository, 1895-98; contbr. various scientific and secular periodicals in Japan, China and Korea. Contributing editor, Journal of Race Development, Clark U., Worcester, Mass. Made extensive investigations in history, lang., lit. and religious beliefs of the Koreans. Home: Leonia, N.J. Died May 10, 1919.

JONES, George Herbert, corp. official; b. Brixton, Eng., Jan. 25, 1856; s. Charles J. and Caroline (Wilson) J.; ed. pvt. schs., Eng., and on continent of Europe; m. Myrtilla Colbert, Aug. 15, 1876; children—Harold (dec.), Ruth Caroline. Came to Chicago, 1871; began as clk. for Hall, Kimbark & Co., iron merchants; an organizer, 1893, Inland Steel Co., became pres. serving until 1921; pres. Hillside Fluorspar Mines, Pershing Quicksilver Co., Mid-West Forging Co. Republican. Home: Chicago, Ill. Died July 6, 1941.

JONES, George Salley, lawyer; b. Rockdale County, Ga., Sept. 12, 1871; s. George Salley and Martha Ruth (Carr) J.; prep. edn., Mrs. Birch's Pvt. Sch. and Alexander Free Sch., Macon, Ga.; LL.B., Mercer U., Macon, 1893; m. Roberta Elizabeth Hardeman, 1890 (died 1912); children—George Salley, Isaac Hardeman, Charles Baxter, Bascom Sidney, Giles Paul, Elizabeth Hardeman (Mrs. Homer B. Williamson), Robert Bruce, Roberta (Mrs. Alfred S. Gardiner), Richard Lord; m. 2d, Alice Horton, 1925. Admitted to Ga. bar, 1893, and began practice at Macon; mem. Jones, Johnston, Russell & Sparks; v.p. Guaranty Trust Co. of New York, 1920-21; chmn. bd. Fourth Nat. Bank, Macon, 1921-22; chmn. bd. Continental Trust Co., 1921-22, 1927-30; v.p. Cornell-Young Co., Isaac Hardeman Estate, Inc.; dir. The Dannenberg Co., First Nat. Bank & Trust Co. in Macon, Standard Realty Company. Vice-pres. Y.M.C.A., Ga. Republican. Methodist. Home: Macon, Ga. Died Apr. 1, 1938.

JONES, George Washington, lawyer; b. Hardin County, Ky., Oct. 25, 1865; s. Samuel Harris and Fanny Evans (Smith) J.; student Sonora (Ky.) Collegiate Inst. (completed course in 1884 and afterwards an instr. and asst. prin. at the instn.); grad. Bryant & Stratton Business Coll., Louisville, Ky., 1885; m. Ruth Norton, Dec. 21, 1892; children—Roger Alston, Ruth Norton (dec.). Admitted to Ala. bar, 1892, and began practice at Montgomery; formerly v.p. South & North Ala. R.R. Co.; dist. atty. for Ala. of L.&N. R.R. Co., 1905—; dir. Woodstock & Blocton Ry. Co. Chmn. Council Nat. Defense, pres. volunteer Mil. Training Class, and mem. exec. com. Am. Red Cross (all of Montgomery), World War. Mem. Bd. of Edn., Montgomery, 15 yrs.; lt. col., staff of gov. of Ala.; chmn. Dem. Exec. Com., Montgomery County, 18 yrs.; former mem. Dem. State Exec. Com., Ala. Episcopalian. Mason, Elk. Home: Montgomery, Ala. Died Nov. 3, 1930.

JONES, George William, mathematician; b. E. Corinth, Me., Oct. 14, 1837; s. George William and Cordelia (Allen) J.; A.B., Yale, 1859, A.M., 1862; m. Caroline Tuttle Barber, Aug. 11, 1862. Teacher mathematics, Russell's Mil. Sch., New Haven, 1859-62, Del. Lit. Inst., Franklin, N.Y., 1862-68; prof. mathematics, Ia. State Coll., 1868-74; asst. prof., asso. prof., and prof. mathematics, Cornell, 1877-1907. Author: Treatise on Algebra (joint author), 1882; Treatise on Trigonometry (joint author), 1881; Logarithmic Tables, 1889; Drill-book in Algebra, 1892; Drill-book in Trigonometry, 1896; Five-place Logarithms, 1896; Four-place Logarithms, 1896; Some Proofs in Elementary Geometry, 1904. Address: Ithaca, N.Y. Died 1911.

JONES, Guernsey, coll. prof.; b. Foreston, Ia., Aug. 4, 1868; s. John A. (Rev.) and Ann (Davies) J.; Ph.B., U. of Calif., 1891; studied univs. of Munich and Heidelberg, 1892-96; Ph.D., Heidelberg, 1896; unmarried. Mem. U. of Neb. faculty, 1897—, becoming prof. English history. Author: Cromwell and Charles X of Sweden, 1897. Co-Editor: Copley-Pelham Letters, 1914. Home: Lincoln, Neb. Died May 5, 1929.

JONES, Harry Clary, chemist; b. New London, Md., Nov. 11, 1865; s. William and Joanna C. J.; A.B., Johns Hopkins, 1889, fellow, 1891-92, Ph.D., 1892; univs. of Leipzig, Amsterdam and Stockholm, 1892-94; m. Harriet Brooks, May 22, 1902. Instr. physical chemistry, 1895-98, asso., 1898-1900, asso. prof., 1900-04, prof., 1904—, Johns Hopkins. Asso. editor Journal de Chimie Physique, Journal of Franklin Inst., and Zeitschrift für physikalische Chemie. Langstreth medalist, Franklin Inst., 1913. Author: Freezing Point, Boiling Point, and Conductivity Methods, 1897; The Modern Theory of Solutions (Harper's Scientific Series), 1898. Translator: Biltz's Practical Methods for Determining Molecular Weights, 1899; The Theory of Electrolytic Dissociation, 1900; Outlines of Electrochemistry, 1902; Elements of Physical Chemistry, 1902 (translated into Russian, 1911, and Italian, 1912); Principles of Inorganic Chemistry, 1903; Elements of Inorganic Chemistry, 1903; The Electrical Nature of Matter and Radioactivity, 1906; Hydrates in Aqueous Solutions, 1907; Conductivity and Viscosity in Mixed Solvents, 1907; The Absorption Spectra of Solutions, 1909; Introduction to Physical Chemistry, 1910; The Absorption Spectra of Solutions, 1910, 11; Electrical Conductivity of Salts and Organic Acids, 1912; A New Era in Chemistry, 1913; Absorption Spectra Studied by Radiomicrometer, 1913; Freezing Points, Conductivities and Viscosities of Solutions of Salts in Mixed Solvents, 1913; The Absorption Spectra of Solutions; The Conductivities, Dissociations and Viscosities of Solutions of Electrolites in Aqueous, Nonaqueous and Mixed Solvents, 1915; Conductivities and Viscosities in Pure and in Mixed Solvents; Radiometric Measurements of the Formation Constants of Indicators, 1915. Address: Baltimore, Md. Died Mar. 19, 1916.

JONES, Harry Stuart Vedder, prof. English; b. Charleston, S.C., Aug. 8, 1878; s. Daniel Henry and Roberta Stuart (Hare) J.; A.B., Coll. of Charleston, 1899; A.B., Harvard, 1901, A.M., 1904, Ph.D., 1906; m. Margaret Murdoch Walker, June 12, 1907; children—Anne Prioleau, Margaret Walker, Robert Hare. Prof. English, Mount Union Coll., Alliance, O., 1901-02; acting asst. prof. English, U. of Mo., 1902-03; asst. in English, Harvard, 1904-05; instr. in English, U. of Ill., 1906-07, asso. in English, 1907-12, asst. prof. English, 1912-20, asso. prof., 1920-30, prof., 1930—; temporary apptmts. at U. of Texas, Northwestern U., U. of Mich., U. of N.C., and New York U. Asso. editor Jour. English and Germanic Philology, 1911-27, mng. editor, 1927—. Participating mem. Conf. on Science, Philosophy and Religion, Columbia U., 1941. Democrat. Author: Words and Sentences, 1919; Spenser's Defense of Lord Grey, 1919; A Spenser Handbook, 1930. Home: Champaign, Ill. Died Jan. 10, 1942.

JONES, Harry Wild, architect; b. Schoolcraft, Mich., June 9, 1859; s. Howard Malcolm and Mary White (Smith) J.; Brown U., class of 1882, A.B., 1903; studied Mass. Inst. Tech.; m. Bertha J. Tucker, Sept. 6, 1883; children—Malcolm, Mary White, Arthur L. Practiced, Minneapolis, 1884—; prof. architecture, U. of Minn., 1891-93; lecturer on ch. architecture, U. of Chicago, 1908—. Architect and supt. of many bldgs. of all classes in Minn. and other states, notably Cream of Wheat Bldg., Minneapolis, Butler Bros. Warehouse, etc.; specializes in ch. architecture. Mem. Bd. of Park Commrs., Minneapolis, 1892-1904. Dist. vocational officer, Federal Bd. Vocational Edn., for Minn., N. and S.D. and Mont., Oct. 1918-Aug. 1919. Dir. Minneapolis Y.M.C.A., 3 yrs. Republican. Baptist. Mem. A.I.A. Author: Churches, 1912. Home: Minneapolis, Minn. Died Sept. 25, 1935.

JONES, Heber, physician; b. Philip County, Ark., Sept. 11, 1848; s. John T. and Sarah C. (McEwen) J.; ed. Nottingham (Tenn.) Acad.; M.D., U. of Va., 1869; m. Valerie Wooten, Dec. 23, 1873. In med. practice at Memphis, 1871—. Pres. Tenn. State Bd. Health, 10 yrs., Bd. Health, Memphis, 8 yrs., State Bd. Med. Examiners, 10 yrs.; surgeon Tenn. N.G. with rank of col. Presented with silver service by citizens of Memphis, 1898, and with check for $10,000 for services against yellow fever epidemic, 1905. Address: Memphis, Tenn. Deceased.

JONES, Henry Craig, law school dean; b. Central City, Ia., June 18, 1879; s. John Barnard and Jennie Louise (Craig) J.; A.B., Cornell Coll., Ia., 1900, LL.D., 1922; A.B., Harvard, 1903, LL.B., 1906, S.J.D., 1921; m. Louise Russell Livermore, June 9, 1908 (died 1919); m. 2d, Caroline Louise Critchett, June 18, 1921. Practiced with Rubens, Fischer & Mosser, Chicago, 1906-11; asst. prof. law, George Washington U., 1911-14; dean College of Law, W.Va. U., 1914-21; dean Coll. of Law, U. of Ill., 1921-22; dean Coll. of Law, U. of Ia., 1922—. Mem. W.Va. Bd. Law Examiners, 1914-21, and commrs. on Uniform Laws, W.Va., 1919-21. Mem. Am. Bar Assn. (council for W.Va., 1917-18, gen. council, 1918-19), W.Va. Bar Assn. (council 1916-21, pres. 1918-19); sec.-treas. Assn. Am. Law Schs., 1919-22, pres., 1923. Republican. Methodist. Compiler: Illinois Cases on Suretyship, 1912; asso. editor of Barnes' Federal Code, 1919. Home: Iowa City, Ia. Died Oct. 25, 1929.

JONES, Herschell V., editor; b. Jefferson, N.Y., Aug. 30, 1861; s. William S. and Helen E. (Merchant) J.; ed. common schs. and Delaware Lit. Inst., Franklin, N.Y.; m. Lydia A. Wilcox, Sept. 30, 1885. Owned Jefferson (N.Y.) Courier, 1879, at 18 yrs. of age; removed to Minneapolis, Minn., 1885; began as reporter on Minneapolis Journal and continued through various positions for 17 yrs.; established newspaper market service in Northwest late in the '80's and as commercial editor was the 1st to make estimate of wheat yields in all the states by personal inspection of grain in fields, covering 30,000 miles in a yr. in travel and gaining internat. reputation in the work; established The Commercial West (weekly), 1901-08; publisher The Journal and pres. Journal Printing Co., 1908—. Republican. Protestant. Collector of very rare books. Home: Minneapolis, Minn. Died May 24, 1928.

JONES, Hilary Pollard, naval officer; b. Va., Nov. 14, 1863; m. Virginia Lippincott, Oct. 2, 1917. Grad. U.S. Naval Acad., 1884; ensign, July 1, 1886; promoted through grades to rear admiral, Dec. 24, 1917; vice admiral, July 1, 1919; adm., July 1, 1921. Served on Dorothea, Spanish-Am. War, 1898; comd. Scorpion, 1904-06, Navy Yard, Washington, 1906-09; exec. officer on Idaho, 1909; at Naval Sta., Cavite, P.I., 1909-10, Navy Yard, Washington, D.C., 1910-11; commanded Birmingham, 1911, Tennessee, 1911, Rhode Island, 1911-12; comd. Navy Yard and supt. Naval Gun Factory, Washington, D.C., 1913-14; comd. Florida, 1914-16; at Naval War Coll., 1916-17; comd. Squadron One, Patrol Force, Atlantic Fleet, Apr.-July 1917; apptd. comdr. Div. One, Cruiser Force raider guard, Atlantic Fleet, July 17, 1917; comdr. Newport News div. cruiser and transport force, Apr. 1918-Jan. 1919; dir. naval overseas transportation, Jan.-July 1919; vice admiral comdg. 2d Battleship Squadron Atlantic Fleet, July 1919-21; adm., comdr. in chief Atlantic Fleet, 1921-22; comdr. in chief U.S. Fleet, Dec. 1922-Aug. 1923; apptd. to Gen. Bd., Aug. 1923. E.E. and M.P. on special mission to Brazil, 1922; naval adviser on Am. delegation to Preparatory Commn. for Limitation of Armaments, Geneva, 1926-27; del. to Conf. for Limitation of Naval Armaments, Geneva, 1927; retired from active service, Nov. 14, 1927; commd. admiral on retired list, Oct. 15, 1930. Home: Doswell, Va. Died Jan. 1, 1938.

JONES, Horace Conrad, mfr., banker; b. Conshohocken, Pa., June 16, 1857; s. Ellwood and Rachel (Conrad) J.; ed. U. of Pa. 1 yr., class of 1877; m. Linda Loch, Feb. 5, 1889; 1 son, Spencer L. Pres. The H. C. Jones Co.; chmn. bd. First Nat. Bank of Conshohocken; dir. Norristown-Penn Trust Co., Lee Tire & Rubber Co., Buck Hill Falls Co., Schuylkill Valley Lines, Norristown, Pa. Trustee Carson Coll. for Orphan Girls; pres. Visiting Nurse Assn. of Conshohocken. Mem. Soc. of Friends. Home: Conshohocken, Pa. Died Aug. 29, 1940.

JONES, H(ugh) Bolton, landscape painter; b. Baltimore, Oct. 20, 1848; s. Hugh B. and Laura Eliza J.; studied in France. Splty. landscapes; 3d class medal, Paris Expn., 1889; medal, Chicago Expn., 1893; bronze medal, Paris Expn., 1900; Webb prize, Soc. Am. Artists, 1902; gold medal, St. Louis Expn., 1904; silver medal, Panama Pacific Expn., San Francisco, 1915. Works on exhbn.: "Spring," "Autumn," Met. Museum, New York; "Springtime," Corcoran Gallery, Washington; "Sheep Pasture," Pa. Acad. Fine Arts, Phila.; Landscape, Brooklyn Inst. Museum. N.A., 1883; mem. Nat. Inst. Arts and Letters. Address: New York, N.Y. Died Sept. 24, 1927.

JONES, Isaac Thomas, jurist; b. West River, Md., Dec. 2, 1838; s. Edward and Maria F. (Croxall) J.; grad. Lafayette Coll., 1857; studied law in Baltimore; admitted to bar, 1861; began practice at Ellicott City, Md.; m. Mary, d. Richard Gambrill, June 3, 1869. Mem. Md. legislature, 1868; elected judge circuit court 5th jud. circuit twice for 15 yrs. each, and 2 yrs. after second election was elected chief judge of the circuit, and ex-officio judge Court of Appeals of Md. Democrat. Address: Ellicott City, Md. Died 1907.

JONES, J. Catron, prof. politics; b. Barbourville, Ky., Mar. 26, 1889; s. Nathan B. and Elizabeth (Hibbard) J.; grad. Eastern Ky. State Normal Sch., Richmond, Ky., 1909; A.B., Transylvania Coll., Lexington, Ky., 1911; grad. study, Columbia, 1913-16, A.M., 1914; studied U. of London, 1919, Robert Brookings Grad. Sch., Washington, D.C., 1923-24, Ph.D. from latter, 1925; m. Lois Elizabeth Sauters, 1921; 1 son, William Catron. Teacher and supt. schs., Hazard, Ky., 1911-13; part-time social worker, N.Y. City, 1913-17; asst. prof. polit. science, U. of Ky., 1920-23, asso. prof., 1923-25, prof., 1925—, head of dept., 1926—; dir. Bur. Govt. Research, U. of Ky., 1930—; on leave of absence serving as business analyst Agrl. Adjustment Administration, Washington. Served with machine gun bn., U.S.A., 1917-19. Democrat. Author: Digest of Kentucky Election Laws, 1922; Direct Primaries, 1923; (with Dr. A. Vandenbosch) Readings in Citizenship, 1929. Editor: Comments on Kentucky Constitution, 1931. Compiler of Ky. Directory and Blue Book. Home: Green Acres, Lexington, Ky. Died Dec. 1934.

JONES, J. Claude, geologist; b. Merrimac, Wis., July 2, 1877; s. John Dorence and Alberta Rosella (Van Sice) J.; A.B., U. of Ill., 1902; Ph.D., U. of Chicago, 1923; m. Belle McCurdy, June 23, 1904; children—Alberta Rosella, Ellen May (dec.), Claude Dorence, Dorothy Ellen. Instr. geology, U. of Ill., 1904-06; field asst., Ill. State Geol. Survey, 1906-09; research asst., U. of Chicago, 1906-09; prof. geology, U. of Nev., 1909—, dean of men, 1931—; also in practice as consulting geologist. In charge Nevada mining exhibit San Francisco Expn., 1915; geologist Nev. State Mining Lab.; has served as mem. Nev. Cement Commn. Universalist. K.P. Home: Reno, Nev. Died 1932.

JONES, J. Levering, lawyer; b. Phila., July 26, 1851; s. John Sidney and Catharine Elizabeth (Riter) J.; LL.B., U. of Pa., 1875; LL.D., U. of Ky., 1910; m. Elisabeth Mercer MacLean, Oct. 26, 1887. Dir. Ft. Wayne & Northern Ind. Traction Co., Real Estate Trust Co., Alliance Ins. Co.; in practice in Phila., 1875—. Trustee U. of Pa., Chestnut Hill Acad., Ridgefield Sch., Thomas W. Evans Mus. and Inst. Society. Republican. Editor: Binney's Reports (Pa.) with Notes; Finlason's edition of Reeve's History of the English Law, 1879; Chronicle of the Union League of Philadelphia, 1902. Was asso. editor of Legal Gazette. Interested in ednl. matters. Delivered many addresses on legal and other subjects. Address: Philadelphia, Pa. Deceased.

JONES, James Emlyn; b. Youngstown, O., Jan. 9, 1875; s. Thomas B. and Mary A. (Davis) J.; ed. pub. schs. and Columbian U. Law Sch. (non-grad.); m. Marguerite B. Zimmerman, May 1, 1906; children—Ruth E., James E., Lambert E. With Dept. of Agr., in various capacities, 1893-1921; was rep. of the dept. on U.S. Supply Com. 5 yrs., as chmn. subcom. on furniture and fuel; secured establishment of govt. coal yard at Washington; asst. prohibition commr., 1921-25, dir. of prohibition, 1925-27; dep. federal commr. of prohibition, 1927-28; dir. of finance, City of Youngstown, 1928-32; a senior administrative officer, Agrl. Adjustment Administration U.S. Dept. Agr., 1933—. Home: Washington, D.C. Died Dec. 30, 1938.

JONES, James Kimbrough, U.S. senator from Ark., 1885-1903; b. Marshall County, Miss., Sept. 29, 1839; classical edn.; private in C.S.A. through Civil war; lived on his plantation until 1873; then entered on practice of law; mem. State senate, 1873-79; pres. same, 1877-79; mem. Congress, 1881-87. Chmn. Dem. Nat. Com., 1896—, and conducted campaigns, 1896, 1900; del. Nat. Dem. Conv., 1896 and 1900. Home: Washington, Ark. Died 1908.

JONES, James Marion, Jr., pres. Commn. of City of Birmingham; b. Eufaula, Ala., Sept. 18, 1884; s. James Monroe and Emma Louise (Davis) J.; grad. Eastman Business Coll., Poughkeepsie, N.Y., 1905; m. Cynthia Byram, Sept. 17, 1907; children—William Marion, Mildred Louise (Mrs. David Daniels), James Byram, Mary Elizabeth, Joe Chester. City clk. and tax collector, East Lake, Ala., 1908-10; tax collector Birmingham, Ala., 1910-17, city comptroller, 1917, resigned, 1921; in warehouse business, Birmingham, 1921-25; pres. Commn. of City of Birmingham, 1925—; mem. Park and Recreation Bd. Democrat. Methodist. Mason, Elk. Home: Birmingham, Ala. Died Feb. 7, 1940.

JONES, James Sumner, soldier, mcht.; b. Wheeling, W.Va., Apr. 23, 1881; s. Henry and Anna (Stone) J.; grad. Linsly Inst., Wheeling, 1896; student Washington and Jefferson Coll., 1897-99, hon. D.Sc., 1938; grad. U.S. Mil. Acad., 1903; m. Marguerite Westinghouse Sands, Oct. 4, 1905; children—Wilbur Stone, Pearson Sands. Commd. 2d lt. Cav., U.S.A., 1903; 1st lt., 1911; resigned Oct. 1913; maj., lt. col. and col. Adj. Gen.'s Dept., U.S.A., staff of Gen. Pershing, June 1917-July 1919; brig. gen. Adj. Gen.'s R.C., 1923—. With Stone & Thomas, Inc., dept. store, Wheeling, 1913—, except 1917-19, later pres. and gen. mgr.; pres. Security Trust Co.; dir. M. Marsh & Son, Inc., Ohio Valley Drug Co., Clarksburg Drug Co., Stone & Thomas, Inc., Hazel Atlas Glass Co., U.S. Stamping Co., Sterling Products, Inc., Wheeling & Belmont Bridge Co., Wheeling Tile Co. Member Wheeling (W.Va.) Park Com. Awarded D.S.M. (U.S.); Legion of Honor (French); Order of The Crown (Italian). Republican. Episcopalian. Mason. Home: Wheeling, W.Va. Died Aug. 17, 1940.

JONES, Jenkin Lloyd, minister; b. Cardiganshire, South Wales, Nov. 14, 1843; s. Richard Lloyd and Mary (Thomas) J.; parents moved to Wis. when an infant; worked on farm until 1862; pvt. 6th Wis. Battery, 3 yrs. in Civil War; grad. Meadville (Pa.) Theol. Sem., 1870; LL.D., U. of Wis., 1909; m. Susan C. Barber, June 1870 (died 1911); m. 2d, Mrs. Edith Lackersteen, 1915. Pastor of All Souls Ch., Janesville, Wis., 1871-80; sec. Western Unitarian Conf., 1875-84; organized, and was 1st sec. Western Unitarian S.S. Soc., 1874-80; with others established Unity, a weekly paper, 1878, now organ of the Congress of Religion and of the Free Religious Assn. of America, editor, 1879—; organized, 1882, and pastor of All Souls Ch., Chicago; dir. Abraham Lincoln Centre, Chicago, 1905—. Sec. World's Parliament of Religions, 1892-93; instrumental in organizing the Congress of Religion, 1894 (gen. sec. till 1905); 1st pres. Ill. State Conf. of Charities, 1895-97; lecturer in English, U. of Chicago, 1893—; pres. Tower Hill Summer Sch. of Lit. and Religion; founder and 1st pres. Chicago Browning Soc. Author: The Faith That Makes Faithful (with William C. Gannett), 1886; Practical Piety, 1890; Word of the Spirit, 1897; Jess: Bits of Wayside Gospel, 1899; A Search for an Infidel; Bits of Wayside Gospel (2d series), 1901; Nuggets from a Welsh Mine, 1902; Reinforcement of

Faith, 1905; Conscience Calls, 1906; Love and Loyalty (sermons), 1907; What Does Christmas Really Mean? (with John T. McCutcheon); On the Firing Line in the Battle for Sobriety, 1910; An Artillery Man's Diary, 1862-65; Love for Battle-torn Peoples, 1917. Mem. bd. of dirs. Church Peace Union, founded by Andrew Carnegie. Address: Chicago, Ill. Died Sept. 12, 1918.

JONES, Jerome, merchant; b. Athol, Mass., Oct. 13, 1837; s. Theodore and Marcia (Estabrook) J.; ed. pub. sch., Athol, Mass.; m. Elizabeth R. Wait, Feb. 11, 1864; m. 2d, Mrs. Maria E. Dutton, Feb. 16, 1881. Pres. Jones, McDuffee & Stratton Co.; 1st v.p. Home Savings Bank; dir. Boston Safe Deposit & Trust Co.; trustee Mt. Auburn Cemetery. Chmn. maritime com. Chamber of Commerce. Unitarian. Mason. Home: Brookline, Mass. Died Dec. 1916.

JONES, John Carleton, univ. pres.; b. Sharpsburg, Ky., July 30, 1856; s. Daniel Ralls and Margaret (Comingo) J.; A.B., Westminster Coll., Fulton, Mo., 1879, A.M., 1882, Ph.D., 1891; Johns Hopkins, 1882-83, U. of Leipzig, 1895-96, U. of Munich, 1903-04; LL.D., U. of Mo., 1908; LL.D., Washington U., 1923; m. Clara Field Thompson, July 7, 1886; children—Lloyd Edmonstone, Katherine Edmonstone, Marjorie Comingo. Prof. Latin, Westminster Coll., 1880-82; asst. prof. Latin and Greek, 1883-87, asso. prof. Latin, 1888-91, prof. Latin, 1891—, dean of Coll. of Arts and Sciences, 1900—, acting pres., 1905-06, v.p., 1918—, acting pres., 1921-22, pres., 1922-23, pres. emeritus, U. of Mo.; dir. Memorial Union and Stadium Campaign, U. of Mo., 1923—. Mem. mng. com. Am. Sch. Classical Studies in Rome. Presbyterian. Home: Columbia, Mo. Died Apr. 22, 1930.

JONES, John Edward, consul gen.; b. Washington, Feb. 21, 1868; s. John William and Kate Jessie (Williams) J.; ed. Georgetown U., Nat. Law Sch., and Columbian (now George Washington) U.; M.D., Columbian, 1897; m. Hilda Virginia Tyssowski, June 1902. Asst. sec. Rep. Nat. Com., 1900 campaign; del. Dep. Nat. Conv., 1900; on staff Washington Evening Star, 16 yrs. Consul (consul gen., Jan.-June 1906) at Dalny, Manchuria, 1905-06; consul at Winnipeg, 1907-08, consul gen., 1908-13; consul gen. at Genoa, Italy, 1913-15, Lyon, 1915—. Episcopalian. Died May 20, 1918.

JONES, John Percival, senator; b. Herefordshire, Eng., Jan. 27, 1829; s. Thomas and Mary (Pugh) J.; came with parents to U.S. in infancy; ed. pub. schs., Cleveland, O.; m. Mrs. Cornelia (Conger) Greathouse, Calif., Jan. 1861. In early part of Calif. excitement went to that State and engaged in mining; mem. Calif. Senate, 1863-67; went to Nev., 1867; engaged in development of mines there, 1867—. U.S. senator 5 terms, 1873-1903, separated himself from Republican party when money question became leading issue between the parties; reaffiliated with his old party when that question ceased to be polit. issue. Address: Santa Monica, Calif. Died Nov. 27, 1912.

JONES, John Sills, lawyer; b. Champaign County, O., Feb. 12, 1836; grad. Ohio Wesleyan, 1855; admitted to bar, 1857; pros. atty. Delaware County, 1860-61; served in Union army 1861-65, pvt. to col., 174th Ohio regt., and bvt. brig. gen. vols.; mayor Delaware, O., 1866; pros. atty. Delaware County, 1866-71; presidential elector, 1872; congressman, 1877-79; mem. Ohio legislature, 1879-84. Republican. Address: Delaware, O. Died 1903.

JONES, J(ohn) Sparhawk, clergyman; b. Phila., June 5, 1841; A.B., U. of Pa., 1862; grad. Princeton Theol. Sem., 1867; D.D., Princeton, 1880, U. of Pa., 1901. Asst. pastor First Ch., Baltimore, 1867-71; ordained Presbyn. ministry, 1871; pastor Brown Memorial Ch., Baltimore, 1871-84, Calvary Ch., Phila., 1893—. Address: Philadelphia, Pa. Died Aug. 10, 1910.

JONES, J(ohn) William, clergyman, lecturer; b. Louisa, Va., Sept. 25, 1836; s. Col. Francis William and Ann Pendleton J.; grad. U. of Va., 1859; Southern Bapt. Theol. Sem., 1860; D.D., Washington and Lee, 1874; m. Judith Page Helm, Dec. 20, 1860. Was under appmt. as missionary to China when war broke out; served pvt. soldier, 1861-62, chaplain, 1862-63, in 13th Va. inf., C.S.A.; missionary chaplain A. P. Hill's corps, Nov. 1863, to close of war; active worker in great revivals in which over 15,000 of Lee's veterans professed conversion, personally baptizing 410 soldiers. Pastor Lexington, Va., 1865-71, and one of chaplains Washington Coll.; successively agent Southern Bapt. Theol. Sem., supt. Va. Bapt. Sunday School and Colportage Work, asst. sec. Home Mission Bd., Southern Bapt. Conv., chaplain U. of Va., pastor of several chs. Has been for some yrs. chaplain gen. United Confederate Veterans; sec. and supt. Confederate Memorial Assn.; lecturer on Lee, Jackson, etc. Was sec. Southern Hist. Soc., 1876-87, and edited 14 vols. Southern Hist. Papers. Author: Personal Reminiscences, Anecdotes and Letters of R. E. Lee, 1874; Army of Northern Virginia Memorial Volume; Christ in the Camp; School History of the United States; Life and Letters of R. E. Lee, 1906, N3; Jefferson Davis Memorial Volume; High School and College History of the United States. Address: Richmond, Va. Died 1909.

JONES, Joseph Russell; b. Conneaut, O., Feb. 17, 1823; ed. in local school; was clerk in store there; became clerk and later partner in store, Galena, Ill., retiring 1856; sec. and treas., 1846-61, The Galena and Minnesota Packet Co.; mem. Ill. legislature, 1860; U.S. marshal at Chicago, 1861-69; U.S. minister to Belgium, 1869-75; collector port of Chicago, 1875-76. Organized, 1863, and was for yrs. pres. Chicago West Division Ry. Co. Home: Chicago, Ill. Died 1909.

JONES, Joshua H., bishop; b. Pine Plains, S.C., June 15, 1856; s. Joseph and Sylvia J.; B.A., Claflin U., S.C., 1885; student Howard U., Washington, D.C.; B.D., Wilberforce (Ohio) U., 1887, D.D., 1893; m. Elizabeth Martin, 1875; m. 2d, Augusta E. Clark, Nov. 1888. Local preacher A.M.E. Ch. at 18; pastor in S.C., Wheeling, W.Va., Wilberforce, O., Lynn, Mass., Providence, R.I., and Columbus, O.; presiding elder Columbus dist., 1894-99; pastor Zanesville, O., 1899; pres. Wilberforce U., 1900-08; bishop A.M.E. Ch., 1912—. Home: Wilberforce, O. Died Nov. 24, 1932.

JONES, Lake, judge; b. Vicksburg, Miss., Feb. 10, 1867; s. The. Allan and Alice (Lake) J.; grad. State Normal Sch., Florence, Ala., 1883; LL.B., Northwestern, 1909; m. Cecille Moragné, Jan. 14, 1892. Formerly ry. postal clk. and post office insp.; admitted to Fla. bar, at age of 42, in 1909, and began practice at Jacksonville; dist. counsel for U.S. Shipping Bd. Emergency Fleet Corp., 1921-24, for dist. covering states of Fla., Ga., Ala., Miss., La. and Tex.; apptd. U.S. dist. judge, Southern Dist. of Fla., 1924. Republican. Episcopalian. Elk. Address: Jacksonville, Fla. Deceased.

JONES, Leonard Augustus, chief judge of Land Court, Mass., 1898—, law author; b. Templeton, Mass., Jan. 13, 1832; s. Augustus Appleton and Mary (Partridge) J.; grad. Harvard, 1855, Harvard Law School, 1858; m. Josephine, d. Col. A. Lee. Admitted to bar, Boston, 1858. Commr. for Mass. for promotion of uniform legislation in U.S., 1891-1902. Asso. editor, 1884-1904, editor, 1904-07, Am. Law Rev.; Am. editor English Ruling Cases (after vol. 18), 1899-1901; editor Memoirs of the Judiciary and Bar of New England for the 19th Century, 1900-01. Author: Law of Mortgages of Real Property, 2 vols., 6 edits., 1878-1904; Law of Corporate Bonds and Mortgages, 1879-90, 3 edits., 1907; Law of Mortgages of Personal Property, 5 edits., 1881-94, 1907; Law of Pledges, 2 edits., 1883, 1901; Law of Liens, 2 vols., 1888, 1894; Forms in Conveyancing, 5 edits., 1886, 1894, 1899; Law of Real Property, as Applied Between Vendor and Purchaser in Modern Conveyancing, 1896; Law of Easements, 1898; Law of Landlord and Tenant, 1906; An Index to Legal Periodical Literature, 1st vol., 1888, 2d, 1899 (Boston Book Co.). Home: Boston, Mass. Died 1909.

JONES, Lewis Henry, college pres.; b. Noblesville, Ind., July 3, 1844; s. William and Huldah (Swain) J.; ed. Spiceland Acad., Ind.; grad. Oswego Normal School, 1868, 70; hon. A.M., DePauw, 1888, Wabash, 1889; D.Pd., Miami, 1911; m. Sarah Ellen Good, Mar. 21, 1872 (died 1901). Teacher, Ind. State Normal Sch., 1871-74; instr. Indianapolis High Sch., 1875; prin., Indianapolis Normal Sch., 1876-84; supt., Indianapolis schs., 1884-94; supt. pub. schs., Cleveland, O., 1894-1902; pres. of Mich. State Normal Coll., Sept. 1902-12; lecturer on edn., 1912—. Mem. Nat. Council Edn.; pres. dept. superintendence N.E.A., 1896. Author: The Jones Readers, 1903; Education as Growth, 1911. Address: Ypsilanti, Mich. Died Aug. 11, 1917.

JONES, Lewis Henry, mfr.; b. Detroit, Mich., May 3, 1856; s. Edward D. and Mary (Griffith) J.; ed. pub. schs., and at Detroit Business U.; m. Ida Sales, Feb. 8, 1883; children—Charles B. (dec.), Janet Lewis (Mrs. Frank E. Caulk), Marion A. (Mrs. Robert Lockhart Wilbur). In employ of Second Nat. Bank, 1873-77, Peninsular Car Works, 1879-81; became identified with the Detroit Copper and Brass Rolling Mills, 1882, pres., 1907; chmn. bd. Grace Harbor Lumber Co.; dir. First Nat. Bank, First Nat. Co., Mich. Sugar Co. Republican. Presbyn. Home: Grosse Pointe Farms, Mich. Died Nov. 1, 1932.

JONES, Livingston French, missionary; b. Tuckerton, N.J., June 1, 1865; s. Hazelton and Mary A. (O'Brien) J.; studied arts, sciences and langs. under Rev. Joseph H. Bradley, D.D.; grad. Princeton Theol. Sem., 1891; m. Nellie A. Shinn, Sept. 16, 1891. Ordained Presbyn. ministry, 1891; pastor Delanco, N.J., 1891-92; missionary in Alaska, 1892-1914 (baptized 700 natives and built 2 chs., a schoolhouse and a council hall). Odd Fellow, Moose, Mason. Author: A Study of the Thlingets of Alaska; Indian Vengeance. Has lectured widely upon Alaska. Home: Fresno, Calif. Died Aug. 27, 1928.

JONES, Mabel Cronise (Mrs. Thomas MacDowell Jones), author; b. Tiffin, O., June 18, 1860; d. Charles and Martha Maria (Lyttle) Cronise; grad. Toledo High Sch., 1878; student Lake Erie Coll., Painesville, O., 1878-82; m. Thomas MacDowell Jones, June 4, 1890 (died 1917). Began in newspaper editorial work at Toledo, O., 1886, and has written extensively for newspapers and mags., also editor Children's page, Phila. and Pittsburgh newspapers; legislative corr. at Harrisburg, 1891. Mem. Pa. Bd., Chicago Expn., 1892-93; pres. Central Pa. Woman Suffrage Assn., 1911—; regent U.S. Daughters of 1812 for 15 yrs. Presbyn. Author: Gettysburg, 1902; Six of Them, 1902; Dolly's College Experiences, 1909; Achsah, 1911; In Days of Old, 1912; Rome's Fool, 1915. Developed system of edn. by which daughter, Dorothea, read newspapers at 3, entered Dickinson Coll. at 13, grad. A.B., U. of Mich., at 17, A.M., at 18. Home: Harrisburg, Pa. Deceased.

JONES, Marcus Eugene, botanist, geologist; b. Jefferson, O., Apr. 25, 1852; s. Publius Virgilius and Lavinia (Burton) J.; A.B., Ia. (now Grinnell) Coll., 1875, A.M., 1878; m. Anna E. Richardson, Feb. 18, 1880; children—Mabel Anna, Howard Marcus, Mildred Lavinia. Tutor, Ia. Coll., 1876-77; prin. Lemars (Iowa) Acad., 1877; prof. natural science, Colorado Coll., 1879; same at Salt Lake City, 1880-81; prin. Jones High Sch., Salt Lake City, 1884-86; spl. expert, U.S. Treasury Dept., 1889; geologist Rio Grande Western R.R., 1890-93; spl. field agt., U.S. Dept. Agr., 1894-95; botanist, geologist and mining expert. Pres. Utah Acad. Sciences. Hon. curator of botany, Pomona Coll. Author: Excursion Botanique, 1879; Ferns of the West, 1883; Salt Lake City, 1889; Some Phases of Mining in Utah; Utah supplement to Tarr and McMurry's Geography, 1902; Contbns. to Western Botany (18 parts), 1879-1934. Exploring in Mexico, 1924—. Home: Claremont, Calif. Died June 3, 1934.

JONES, Matt Bushnell, lawyer; b. Waitsfield, Vt., May 15, 1871; s. Walter A. and Elvira (Bushnell) J.; A.B., Dartmouth, 1894; LL.B., Harvard Law Sch., 1897; Litt.D., Brown U., 1936; m. Grace A. Smith, Sept. 12, 1899; children—Walter Leland, Catharine Bushnell, Matt Bushnell. Began practice, Boston, 1897; mem. firm of Powers, Hall & Jones, 1898-1904; counsel N.E. Telephone & Telegraph Co., 1904-17, 1st v.p., dir. and gen. counsel, 1917-19, pres. 1919-34, chmn. of board, 1934-36, retired; dir. First National Bank of Boston, 1923-36. Mem. Bd. of Aldermen, Newton, 1907-11 (pres. 1910-11). Republican. Author: History of Waitsfield, Vt., 1909; Vermont in the Making, 1939. Home: Newton Center, Mass. Died July 1, 1940.

JONES, Nelson Edwards, physician; b. Liberty Twp., Ross County, O., Sept. 20, 1821; s. Henry and Rachel (Corkin) J.; ed. at home and at an acad. at Chillicothe, O.; entered coll. at Augusta, Ky.; grad. Cleveland Med. Coll., 1846; m. Virginia Smith, June 9, 1846. Practiced at Circleville, O., 1852—. Commd. May 4, 1864, surgeon Bd. of Enrollment, 12th dist. of Ohio, serving to end of war. Served 31 yrs. as examining surgeon for pensions. Author: The Squirrel Hunters of Ohio: or Glimpses of Pioneer Life, 1896. Home: Circleville, O. Died 1901.

JONES, Norman L., judge; b. Patterson, Ill., Sept. 19, 1870; s. John and Minerva (Patterson) J.; m. Almeda Pegram, June 28, 1906; 1 son, Norman P. Admitted to Ill. bar, 1896, and began practice at Carrollton; was mem. Ill. House of Rep.; served as city atty. Carrollton, states atty. Greene County, judge of Circuit Court and later judge Court of Appeals, 2d Dist. of Ill.; justice Supreme Court of Ill., 1931—, chief justice, 1934-35. Dem. nominee for gov. of Ill., 1924. Home: Carrollton, Ill. Died Nov. 15, 1940.

JONES, Philip Lovering, editor; b. Devonshire, Eng., Sept. 19 1838; came to U.S., 1850; A.B., U. of Rochester, 1865; grad. Rochester Theol. Sem., 1868; D.D., U. of Rochester, 1894; m. Mary Kerbaugh, July 11, 1888. Ordained Bapt. ministry, 1868; pastor Dunkirk, N.Y., 1868-70, S. Broad St. Ch., Phila., 1870-89 (organized ch. and built new bldg. at cost of $60,000). Asso book editor, 1889-94, Am. Bapt. Publication Soc., Phila., book editor, 1894—. Author: Divine Fatherhood; A Restatement of Baptist Principles; Script and Print; Henry Drummond, A Study. Home: Narberth, Pa. Died Aug. 26, 1913.

JONES, Philip Mills, medical editor; b. Brooklyn, N.Y., Jan. 17, 1870; s. Lysander Mills and Pauline (Both-Hendriksen) J.; Poly. Inst. of Brooklyn to 1886; New York U., 1886-87; M.D., L.I. Coll. Hosp., 1891; m. Helen Louise Spalding, Dec. 30, 1915. Practiced medicine at Brooklyn, 1891-1900; archæol. work for U. of Calif., 1900-02; organized Med. Soc. State of Calif., 1902, and editor Calif. State Jour. of Medicine. Mem. Nat. Com. of 100 on Pub. Health. Home: San Francisco, Calif. Died Nov. 27, 1916.

JONES, Richard, university prof.; b. Berlin, Wis., July 18, 1855; s. Rev. John A. and Ann (Davis) J.; student univs. of Oxford, Munich and Heidelberg, Ph.D., Heidelberg, 1893; m. Carrie Holmes, d. late Hon. J. B. Grinnell, Dec. 28, 1881. Prof. literature, Vanderbilt U., Nashville, 1899-1910, Tufts Coll., Mass., Sept. 1910-15. Author: The Growth of the Idylls of the King, 1895; The Arthurian Legends, Kuno Fischer (in Warner's Library of the World's Best Literature), 1896; College Entrance English, 1897 (U. of State of N.Y.). Editor: The Tragedy of Macbeth, 1899; The Merchant of Venice, 1903; History of English Literature, 1905. Contbr. to Educational Review, articles on Oxford degrees (transl. into German and Russian mags.), and various articles to other American and English publs.; articles on Carlyle, Ruskin, and Wordsworth in the Macmillan Co. Cyclo. of Edn. Trustee of Grinnell College for 30 yrs. Address: Cambridge, Mass. Died Oct. 21, 1923.

JONES, Richard Channing, lawyer; b. Brunswick Co., Va., April 12, 1841; s. Rev. John Cargill and Mary (Walker) J.; grad. Univ. of Ala., 1859 (A.M., LL.D.); m. Stella H., d. Maj. Frank Boykin, Camden, Ala., Oct. 19, 1864. Removed to Camden, Ala., 1844; admitted to bar, 1861; served in C.S.A. 4 yrs., as line and staff officer; in law practice at Camden, Ala., since war, State senator, 1882-83, 1884-85; pres. Univ. of Ala., and prof. internat. and constitut. law, 1890-97; pres. Ala. State Bar Assn., 1896. Del. Ala. Constitutional Conv., 1901; apptd. by Gov. Wm. J. Samford mem. State Commn. to confer with like commn. on part of Fla., looking to annexation of territory of West Fla. to Ala. Address: Camden, Ala. Died 1903.

JONES, Richard Mott, head master; b. South China, Me., June 29, 1843; s. Eli and Sibyl (Jones) J.; A.B., Haverford Coll., 1867 (hon. A.M., 1879, LL.D., 1891; LL.D., U. of Pa., 1902); after graduation spent 18 months as tutor in Ireland, followed by 18 months' study on the Continent of Europe; m. Annie Virginia Costello, of S. China, June 5, 1873. Head master Oak Grove Sem., Me., 1870-74; head master William Penn Charter Sch., Phila., Feb. 2, 1875—, reorganizing the sch. Mem. Soc. of Friends (Quakers). Home: "The Gladstone," Philadelphia, Pa. Died Aug. 1, 1917.

JONES, Richard Saxe, lawyer; b. Chatfield, Minn., Feb. 22, 1861; s. Richard Asbury (chief justice Wash. Ty.) and Sarah Jane (McClelland) J.; grad. Rochester (Minn.) High Sch., 1877; U. of Minn., 1878-81; m. Helen Maud Tayler (dec.); children—Richard Saxe (dec.), Richard Seelye; m. 2d, Margaret Tillotson Barr, Aug. 2, 1898; children—Marjorie, Stephen Barr. In practice at Seattle, Wash., 1892—, specializing in admiralty law; counsel of Pacific Steamship Co., Columbia Salmon Co., Ferro Concrete Co., etc. Democrat. Episcopalian. Trustee Trans-Miss. Commercial Congress (v.p.), etc. Mason; Past Exalted Ruler B.P.O.E.; Past Chancellor Comdr. K.P. Home: Seattle, Wash. Died Nov. 3, 1926.

JONES, Richard Uriah, chemist; b. Ottawa, Minn., Jan. 25, 1877; s. William R. and Mary (Hughes) J.; B.A., Macalester Coll., St. Paul, Minn., 1901, hon. D.Sc., 1926; student U. of Minn., 1901-02, U. of Chicago, summers 1908, 09; M.A., U. of Wis., 1916; m. Mary Helen Smith, Aug. 18, 1909; children—Richard Herbert, Donald Caldwell, George William. Prof. physics and chemistry, 1903, prof. chemistry, 1907—, dean of coll., 1917-36, Macalester Coll. Presbyn. Specialized in researches in organic chemistry, particularly sugars, starches and volatile oils. Author: The Scientific Eye of Faith. Home: St. Paul, Minn. Died July 9, 1941.

JONES, Richard Watson, educator; b. Greensville County, Va., May 16, 1837; s. Mordecai and Martha Randolph (Grigg) J.; A.B., Randolph-Macon Coll., 1857; A.M., U. of Va., 1861; LL.D., U. of Miss., 1881; in C.S.A., 1861-65; m. Bettie S. Spratley, Jan. 6, 1864. Prof. mathematics, Randolph-Macon Coll., Va., 1866-68; pres. Petersburg (Va.) Female Coll., 1868-71, Martha Washington Coll., Va., 1871-76; prof. chemistry, U. of Miss., 1876-85; pres. Miss. State Instn. for Girls, 1885-88, Emory and Henry Coll., 1888-90; prof. chemistry, U. of Miss., 1890—. Lit. editor Rural Messenger, Petersburg, Va., 1870, of Petersburg Courier, 1868-71; one of asso. editors People's Encyclopædia, 1881-82. Wrote pamphlets on Cotton Army Worm, 1880, and Cotton Boll Worm, 1880; also various reports as coll. pres., papers before scientific and ednl. bodies, pub. lectures, addresses, etc. Del. Meth. Ecumenical Conf., London, 1881, to six gen. confs., M.E. Ch., South, etc. Trustee State Dept. Archives and History; dir. Miss. Orphans' Home. Address: University, Miss. Deceased.

JONES, Robert Ellis, clergyman; b. New York, Mar. 18, 1858; s. Eleazer and Anna (Parry) J.; A.B., Williams Coll., 1879, D.D., 1897; student Va. Theol. Sem., 1879-80, Berlin and Heidelberg, 1894-95; topographer U.S. Geol. Survey, 1880-82; m. Lattie Tilden Gill, Dec. 4, 1900. Deacon, 1882, priest, 1884, P.E. Ch.; rector, St. John's Williamstown, Mass., 1882-84, St. Luke's, Kalamazoo, Mich., 1884-89, Trinity, Columbus, O., 1889-94; sr. curate Grace Ch., New York, 1894-97; pres. Hobart Coll., Geneva, N.Y., 1897-1902; canon Cathedral of St. John the Divine, New York, 1905—. Home: New York, N.Y. Died July 19, 1929.

JONES, Robinson Godfrey, educator; b. Kansas City, Mo., Dec. 14, 1871; s. John Godfrey and Rovilla (Robinson) J.; grad. Ohio Central Normal Sch., 1890; A.B., Ohio Northern, 1894, D.Ped., 1921; A.B., A.M., Columbia, and Teachers Coll., 1912; m. Minnie Linn Gish, July 26, 1899; 1 son, Robert Stanley. Supt. schools Gibson City, Ill., 1895-1900, Lexington, 1900-02, Harvard, 1902-07, Kewanee, 1907-13, Rockford, 1913-17; dep. supt. Cleveland (O.) pub. schs., 1917-18, actg. supt., 1918-19, supt., 1919-33; asst. supt. sr. high schools, Cleveland, 1933-36, dir. of guidance, 1936—. Mem. dept. of superintendence N.E.A. (pres. 1921); pres. Ohio State Teachers Assn., 1923-24; mem. exec. com., N.E.A., Cleveland Conf. for Ednl. Coöperation; mem. advisory board Progressive Edn. Assn.; mem. Nat. Adv. Council on Radio in Education; mem. advisory board, Western Reserve Acad. (Hudson, O.), Nat. Com. on Visiting Teachers. Republican. Presbyterian. Mason. Author: Rockford Survey; also various elementary text books. Editor "The Crippled Child," magazine. Awarded Butler medal (Columbia U.) for public school administration, 1933. Home: Cleveland, O. Died Aug. 18, 1938.

JONES, Samuel J., physician; b. Bainbridge, Pa., Mar. 22, 1836; s. Robert H. J. (M.D.) and Sarah Morret (Ekel) J.; grad. Dickinson Coll., Pa., 1857, A.M., 1860; LL.D., 1884; grad. med. dept., U. of Pa., 1860. Asst. surgeon U.S.N., Dec. 1860; served in Civil war in Atlantic blockading squadron, later at Phila., 1863, promoted surgeon; assigned to duty at Chicago as examiner of candidates for med. corps, U.S.N.; later in West Gulf blockading squadron and surgeon New Orleans Naval Hosp. to close of war; afterward on various duties until resigning from navy in 1868; in Chicago, 1868—. Prof. ophthalmology and otology Northwestern U. Med. School, 1870-97; surgeon to eye and ear dept., St. Luke's Hosp., 1869—, Mercy Hosp. and South Side Dispensary, 1870-80. Editor Chicago Med. Jour. and Examiner, 1887-92. Home: Chicago, Ill. Died 1901.

JONES, Samuel Milton, mayor; b. nr. Beddgelert, N. Wales, Aug. 3, 1846; s. Hugh Samuel and Margaret (Williams) J.; came to U.S. with parents when 3 yrs. old; was compelled by poverty to engage in labor as a child, and in 1864 went to Titusville, Pa., worked in the oil-fields; later oil producer in Pa., W.Va. and Ohio; invented improved oil-well appliance and established in Toledo the Acme Sucker Rod Factory, in which he has introduced various reforms in labor conditions; elected mayor of Toledo, 1897, as Republican; re-elected, 1899, 1901 and 1903, as independent; non-partisan candidate by petition for gov. Ohio, 1900; noted for advocacy of municipal ownership, direct legislation, the 8-hour day, and of the doctrine that the people should nominate their own candidates for all offices by free petition without the intervention of caucuses, primaries, delegates or parties. Author: The New Right, 1899; Letters of Love and Labor, 1900. Home: Toledo, O. Died 1904.

JONES, Samuel Porter ("Sam Jones"), clergyman; b. Chambers County, Ala., Oct. 16, 1847; removed to Cartersville, Ga., 1859; studied under private tutors and at boarding schools; admitted to Ga. bar, 1869; began professional life under bright prospects of success but broke down in health from nervous dyspepsia, began to drink and soon ended his professional career as a lawyer. Professed religion, 1872, became a clergyman of M.E. Ch., South, same yr.; pastor various charges, North Ga. Conf., 8 yrs.; then agt. of North Ga. Orphanage, 12 yrs.; devoted great deal of time to evangelistic work over the country, evangelistic work and the lecture platform for the past 6 or 8 yrs.; has held revival meetings in almost all cities of U.S., and in summer months on platform of various chautauquas. Author: Sermons and Sayings; Music Hall Sermons; Quit Your Meanness; St. Louis Series; Sam Jones' Own Book; Thunderbolts. Address: Cartersville, Ga. Died 1906.

JONES, Sebastian Chatham, educator; b. Geneseo, N.Y., Oct. 4, 1863; s. John P. (D.D.) and Minerva A. (Chatham) J.; student Centre Coll., Ky., 1883-84, Cornell U., 1885-87; M.S., Norwich, 1916; m. Mary A. Hale, Sept. 28, 1892. Headmaster Cayuga Lake Mil. Acad., 1887-89; div. engr. L.&N. R.R., 1889-94; supt. N.Y. Mil. Acad., Cornwall-on-Hudson, N.Y., 1894-1922; supt. Calif. Mil. Acad, 1922—. Republican. Presbyn. Home: Palo Alto, Calif. Died Aug. 9, 1929.

JONES, Stephen Alfred, educator; b. China, Me., Mar. 21, 1848; s. Alfred H. and Mary R. (Jones) J.; A.B., Dartmouth, 1872, A.M., 1875, Ph.D., pro meritis, 1885; m. Louise M. Coffin, Nov. 29, 1877. Teacher Spiceland Acad., 1872-74; prof. Greek and Latin, Pa. Coll., 1874-82; student U. of Münster, Germany, 1882-83, U. of Bonn., 1883-85; investigating Greek and Latin texts, 1885-87; prin. Colorado Springs (Colo.) High Sch., 1887-89; pres. Nev. State U., 1889-94; dir. Agrl. Expt. Sta., Nev., 1888-94; prof. pedagogy, State Normal Sch., San José, Calif., 1895—. Has made numerous addresses before teachers' insts. and assns. Address: San José, Calif. Died Dec. 10, 1915.

JONES, Thomas Alfred, judge; b. Oak Hill, O., Mar. 4, 1859; s. Eben and Ann (Williams) J.; B.A., Ohio U., Athens, 1881, later M.A. and LL.D.; m. Grace U. Hoyt, June 30, 1886. Mem. Tripp & Jones, Jackson, O., 1883-85, Tripp, Jones & Phillips, 1888-92. Mayor of Jackson, 1885-87; judge Circuit Court, 4th Jud. Circuit, 1901-13; judge Court of Appeals, 4th Ohio Dist., 1913-15; justice Supreme Court of Ohio, 4 terms, 1915-39. Republican. Presbyn. Mason. Home: Columbus, O. Died Aug. 31, 1937.

JONES, Thomas Davies; b. Iowa County, Wis., Aug. 13, 1851; s. John and Phoebe (Davies) J.; A.B., Princeton, 1876, A.M., 1879; unmarried. Admitted to Ill. bar, 1879; mem. Swift, Campbell & Jones, Chicago, several yrs.; retired from practice, 1900; pres. Mineral Point Zinc Co.; dir. Internat. Harvester Co., New Jersey Zinc Co. Nominated by Pres. Wilson as mem. Federal Reserve Bd., 1914, but was not confirmed by Senate and name wtihdrawn. Mem. War Trade Board, 1917—. Dir. John Crerar Library, Chicago; trustee Princeton U., 1906-12. Democrat. Presbyterian. Mem. group representing the public in Nat. Industrial Conf., Washington, Oct. 6-23, 1919. Home: Chicago, Ill. Died Sept. 27, 1930.

JONES, Thomas Goode, judge; b. Macon, Ga., Nov. 26, 1844; s. Samuel G. and Martha Ward (Goode) J.; grad. Va. Mil. Inst., 1862; m. Gena C. Bird, Dec. 20, 1866. Served C.S.A. of Northern Va., as staff officer under Gen. John B. Gordon, attaining rank of maj.; was several times wounded; carried a flag of truce, sent out by Gordon, to Sheridan's lines to Appomattox C.H., Apr. 9, 1865. Esstablished law practice, Montgomery; reporter decisions Supreme Ct. of Ala., 1870-80; alderman, 1875-84; mem. Ala. Legislature, 1884-88 (speaker, 1886-88); gov. of Ala., 1890-94; U.S. dist. judge, Middle and Northern dists. of Ala., 1901—. Del. Ala. Constl. Conv., 1901. Democrat. Col. 2d Regt. Ala. state troops, 1880-90; chmn. relief com. yellow fever epidemic, 1897; pres. Ala. State Bar Assn., 1901. Compiled 18 vols. of Alabama Supreme Court Reports; author of Code of Ethics Ala. State Bar Assn. and also of state laws regulating employment of military in enforcement of law and suppression of riots. Address: Montgomery, Ala. Died Apr. 28, 1914.

JONES, T(homas) Sambola, lawyer; b. Jackson, La., Oct. 5, 1859; s. Thomas Spec and Eliza Perkins (Perry) J.; B.A. and M.A., Centenary Coll., Jackson, La., 1878; LL.B., Tulane U., 1880; LL.D., Centenary Coll., Shreveport, La., 1920; m. Deborah, d. Chief Justice Spencer, 1885 (dec.); 1 dau., Eliza Perry (dec.). m. 2d, Julia, d. Chief Justice R. E. de Buron, June 11, 1919. Supt. schs., Baton Rouge, 1882; editor State Journal, 1886-1901; owner and editor La. Educator, 1888-92; col. on staffs several govs. of La.; was pvt. sec. to Gov. M. J. Foster; judge Inferior Criminal Court, Baton Rouge, 10 yrs.; commr. to St. Louis Expn., 1904, and commr. at large to San Francisco Expn., 1913-15; mem. La. Ho. of Rep., 2 terms 1912-20, and term, 1924-28 (vice-chmn. judiciary com. 12 yrs., also vice-chmn. joint judiciary com. of House and Senate for 12 yrs.); M.P. and E.E. to Honduras July 1918-June 1, 1920 (resigned); received spl. approval of sec. of state "for general conduct of affairs as U.S. minister in Central America." Chmn. and mgr. State Council of Defense, La., World War. One of founders of La. Chautauqua. Democrat. Home: Baton Rouge, La. Died May 15, 1933.

JONES, Thomas Samuel, Jr., author; b. Boonville, N.Y., Nov. 6, 1882; s. Thomas Samuel and Mary (Clarke) J.; A.B., Cornell U., 1904; unmarried. On dramatic staff The New York Times, 1904-07; with Reuter Cable Service, New York, 1907; asso. editor The Pathfinder, 1911—. Author (poems): The Path o' Dreams, 1904; From Quiet Valleys, 1907; Interludes, 1908; Ave atque Vale (in memoriam Arthur Upson), 1909; From the Heart of the Hills (with Clinton Scollard), 1909; The Voice in the Silence, 1911 (4th edit., with a Foreword by James Lane Allen, 1917), 6th edit., 1924; The Rose Jar, 7th edit., 1924; Sonnets of the Cross, 1922; Sonnets of the Saints, 1925; Six Sonnets, 1926. Home: New York, N.Y. Died Oct. 16, 1932.

JONES, Virginia Smith; b. New London, Conn., Sept. 9, 1827; d. Anson and Amy C. (Beckwith) Smith; m. Dr. Nelson E. Jones, June 9, 1846 (died Dec. 15, 1901). Author: Illustration of the Nests and Eggs of Birds of Ohio (with 68 hand-colored plates, 15¼x17¼ inches; only 90 copies produced). Address: Circleville, O. Died 1906.

JONES, Walter, physiol. chemist; b. Baltimore, Apr. 28, 1865; s. Levin and Zeanette J. (Bohen) J.; A.B., Johns Hopkins, 1888, Ph.D., 1891; m. Grace C. Clarke, Sept. 1, 1891; 1 dau., Marion E. (Mrs. Gilbert A. Jarman). Prof. chemistry, Wittenberg Coll., Springfield, O., 1891-92; prof. analyt. chemistry, Purdue U., 1892-95; asst., asso. prof., 1895-1908, and prof. of physiol. chemistry, 1908-27, prof. emeritus, 1927, Johns Hopkins. Author: Nucleic Acids, 1921. Home: Baltimore, Md. Died Feb. 28, 1935.

JONES, W(alter) A(delard) Fleming, lands; b. Birmingham, Eng., Nov. 30, 1871; s. Walter Robert and Mary Matilda (Greening) J.; came to America, 1891; m. Catherine Olive McBride, June 6, 1905. Interested in land and mining, New York, 1898-1900, in Mo., 1900-01, in N.M., 1901—; pres. Lost River Irrigation Co.; pres. N.M. Incorporators Trust Co.; pres., treas. Cutter (N.M.) Land & Improvement Co. Del. Rep. Territorial Convs., 1904, 1908; mem. exec. com. N.M. Territorial Central Com., 1909—; U.S. commr., 3d Jud. Dist., N.M., 1906—; del to Washington in interest of statehood for N.M., 1907; regent N.M. Sch. Mines, 1906—; capt. N.M. N.G., 1910; a.d.c. on staff of Governor Mills with rank of col., 1910; mem. gen. com. N.M. Statehood League; sec. and treas. Conservation Commn. N.M., 1909-12. Del. Nat. Irrigation Congress, Boisé, 1906, Spokane, 1909, Am. Mining Congresses, 1907, 14, Legislative and Good Roads Conv., Buffalo, 1908, Nat. Conservation Congress, Seattle, 1909 (mem. exec. com.), Lakes to Gulf Deep Waterways Conv., and Southern Conservation Congress, New Orleans, 1909, Rivers and Harbors Congress, Washington, 1909 (v.p.), Conf. of Govs. of Western States, 1914; mem. council Nat. Conf. on Highways and Roads of Nat. Highways Assn., 1914. Mason, Elk. Address: Las Cruces, N.M. Died Nov. 1917.

JONES, Walter Clyde, lawyer; b. Pilot Grove, Ia., Dec. 27, 1870; s. Jonathan and Sarah (Buffington) J.; M.E., Ia. State Coll., 1891; LL.B., Chicago Coll. of Law (Lake Forest U.), 1895; m. Emma Boyd, 1896; children—Walter Clyde, Helen Gwendolyn, Clarence B. Admitted to Ill. bar, 1895, in gen. and patent practice, Chicago; mem. law firm of Jones, Addington, Ames & Seibold, Chicago and New York; v.p., dir. Benjamin Electric Mfg. Co. Mem. Ill. Senate, 5th Dist., 1906-14 (author Ill. Direct Primary Law, Women's Ten-Hour Law and reform rules for legislature insuring majority control); candidate for gov. of Ill., Prog. Rep. ticket, 1912; mem. War Industries Bd., 1918. Joint author and editor (with K. H. Addington): Jones and Addington's Annotated Statutes of Illinois; Cyclopedia of Illinois Law; Appellate Court Reports of Illinois. Home: Evanston, Ill. Died Mar. 28, 1928.

JONES, Washington, mech. engr.; b. Phila., Feb. 22, 1822; s. Thomas J. and Eliza (Ransted) J.; common sch. edn. until 1938; apprenticed Southwark Foundry, 1838-44; studied under pvt. instrs., 1849-56. Chief draughtsman Penn Works, marine engines; then until 1861 supt. Port Richmond Iron Works; asst. supt. Southwark Foundry, 1861-66; gen. supt. and constructing engr. Port Richmond Iron Works, 1866-91; dir. Am. Dredging Co. Address: Philadelphia, Pa. Deceased.

JONES, Wesley Livsey, senator; b. nr. Bethany, Ill., Oct. 9, 1863; s. Wesley and Phoebe McKay J.; A.B., Southern Ill. Coll., 1886; m. Minda Nelson, Oct. 13, 1886; children—Harry B., Mrs. Hazel E. Coffin. Admitted to bar, 1886; moved to Ty. of Washington just before its admission as state, 1889, and located at N. Yakima; began law practice, 1890; moved to Seattle, 1917. Took part as speaker in Blaine campaign, 1884, and Harrison campaign, 1888, in Ill., and in every campaign in Wash., 1888—; mem. 56th to 60th Congresses (1899-1909), Wash. at large; U.S. senator from Wash., 4 terms, 1909-33. Republican. Home: Seattle, Wash. Died Nov. 19, 1932.

JONES, Wharton Stewart, supt. schs.; b. Nashville, Tenn., Sept. 14, 1849; s. Sandy Elrod and Catherine (Stewart) J.; A.B., 1st honors, Ky. U. (now Transylvania Coll.), 1873, later M.A.; m. Mattie Boyd, Dec. 20, 1888; children—Boyd Jones (dec.), Mrs. Mary Wharton Ramsey, Mrs. Martha Wharton Jones. Pres. Bourbon Female Coll., Paris, Ky., 1875-81; prin. Memphis Mil. Inst., 1881-1902; asst. supt. schs., Memphis, 1902-13; prof. mathematics, W. Tenn. State Normal Sch., 1914-18; supt. schs., Memphis, 1918—. Mem. State Bd. Edn., 7 yrs. Chmn. State Bd. Preliminary Examiners of Grad. Physicians; membership sec. Chamber of Commerce. Mem. N.E.A. (v.p.), Tenn. State Teachers' Assn. (pres. 1890). Democrat. Mem. Christian (Disciples) Ch. Mason. Author: Elements of Arithmetic, 1904; Practical Arithmetic, 1909. Home: Memphis, Tenn. Died Oct. 28, 1936.

JONES, Wiley Emmet, lawyer; b. Springfield, Ill., Oct. 19, 1856; s. Joshua Walden and Polly Ann (Wills) J.; ed. pub. schs.; studied law in office of Gen. John M. Palmer, Springfield; unmarried. Admitted to Ill. bar, 1886, and practiced in Springfield; mem. Ill. Ho. of Rep., 1887, 1889; removed to Tacoma, Wash., 1889; founder, 1889, and 1st city atty. of Anacortes, Wash.; removed to Ariz., 1892; dist. atty. Graham County, Ariz., 8 yrs.; asst. U.S. atty., Dist. of Ariz., Mar.-Dec. 1914; apptd. atty. gen. Ariz., Dec. 5, 1914, to fill unexpired term ending Dec. 31, 1914; elected 3 terms, 1914-20. Del. Democratic Nat. Conv., 1896; presdl. elector, 1912. First lt., 1st Ariz. Regt., Spanish-Am. War, 1898. Home: Phoenix, Ariz. Deceased.

JONES, Will Owen, editor; b. Berlin, Wis., Oct. 6, 1862; s. Rev. John A. and Anne (Davies) J.; A.B., U. of Neb., 1886; m. Edith P. Doolittle, Sept. 18, 1889; 1 dau., Mariel Theresa. City editor, 1886-89, asso. editor, 1889-92, mng. editor, 1892—, Neb. State Jour.; dir. Lincoln Jt.-Stock Land Bk. Instr. journalism, U. of Neb., 1893-98. Del. at organization of La. Purchase Expn., 1899; apptd. by Pres. Roosevelt, mem. bd. of visitors to U.S. Naval Acad., 1907. Republican. Conglist. Mason. Author of By Land and Sea, a series of foreign travel interpretations. Home: Lincoln, Neb. Died Jan. 29, 1928.

JONES, William Albert, brigadier gen. U.S. Army; b. St. Charles, Mo., June 26, 1841; s. Stillman and Ann J (Perkins) J.; grad. U.S. Mil. Acad., 1864; m. Louisa V. Test, Nov. 25, 1873. Commd. 1st lt. engrs., June 13, 1864; capt., Mar. 7, 1867; maj., June 30, 1882; lt. col., Oct. 2, 1895; col., Apr. 21, 1903; brig. gen. and retired by operation of law, June 26, 1905. Asst. prof. civil and mil. engring., law and ethics, and instr. practical mil. engring., and comdg. Co. A Battalion of Engrs., also treas., U.S. Mil. Acad., 1864-66; served in 6th Corps, Army of the Potomac, Civil War; comd. U.S. Army exploring expdn. in northwestern Wyo. and Yellowstone Park, 1873; discovered Two Ocean Pass, Togwotee Pass and Shoshone Mountains; served on constrn. of fortifications, harbors and lighthouses on Atlantic coast and Great Lakes, on improvement of rivers in northwest, Yellowstone Park, etc.; mem. commn. to investigate salmon fisheries of Columbia River; div. engr. of the Chesapeake, etc.; consulting engr. location and construction rys., mining and treating ores, bldg. dams and water works in various localities; consulting engr. state of Calif., Golden Gate Park, San Francisco; consulting engr. Commonwealth of Mass., Marine Park, Charles River Dam. Owner and manager 2,000 acres oyster plantation on eastern shore of Va. Protestant. Author: Report of Exploration of Northwestern Wyoming and Yellowstone Park, 1874; The Salmon Fisheries of the Columbia River. Home: Ft. Monroe, Va. Died Nov. 10, 1914.

JONES, William Alexander, M.D.; b. St. Peter, Minn., May 24, 1859; s. Henry and Virginia (Christian) J.; high sch., St. Peter; M.D., U. Med. Coll. (New York U.), 1881; m. Annie R. Johnson, Oct. 2, 1886. Asst. physician, St. Peter State Hosp. for Insane, 1879-83; practiced, Minneapolis, 1883—; instr. nervous diseases, Coll. Hosp., 1889-95; prof. mental and nervous diseases, U. of Minn., 1900-19. Editor Journal-Lancet, representing med. prof. of Minn., N.D., S.D. and Mont.; official jour. of N.D. and S.D. State med. assns. Pres. Minn. State Bd. Health, 1905-17. Trustee State Hospital for Insane, 1890-94. Democrat. Presbyn. Home: Minneapolis, Minn. Died Jan. 15, 1931.

JONES, William Alfred, author; b. New York, June 26, 1817; grad. Columbia, 1836; studied law, but never practised; librarian Columbia Coll., 1851-65; critic and essayist. Author: The Analyst; Essays upon Authors and Books; Characters and Criticisms; Literary Studies (2 vols.); Memorial of Hon. David S. Jones (his father); The Library of Columbia College; The First Century of Columbia College; Long Island. Home: Norwich, Conn. Died 1900.

JONES, William Ambrose, bishop; b. Cambridge, N.Y., July 21, 1865; s. Thomas and Mary (Hurly) J.; Cambridge High Sch.; A.B., Villanova (Pa.) Coll., 1887, and completed scholasticate of Augustinian Order of same instn. Ordained priest R.C. Ch., 1890; asst. priest Ch. of St. Augustine, Phila., 1890-95; master of novices, Augustinian Scholasticate, and prof. English and mathematics, 1895-99, Villanova Coll.; placed in charge first English speaking Catholic Ch. in Cuba at beginning of mil. occupation of the island by U.S., Jan. 1899; pres. Coll. of St. Augustine, Havana, 1902-07, and pastor Ch. of Santo Cristo, Havana, 1904-07; consecrated bishop of P.R., Feb. 24, 1907 (oldest diocese of R.C. Ch. in America, dating from Feb. 1511). Address: San Juan, P.R. Died Feb. 17, 1921.

JONES, William Atkinson, congressman; b. Warsaw, Va., Mar. 21, 1849; s. Thomas and Anne S. (Trowbridge) J.; in winter, 1864-65, entered Va. Mil. Inst., and remained until evacuation of Richmond, serving with cadets in the defense of that city; B.L., U. of Va., 1870; m. Claude D. Motley, Jan. 23, 1889. Admitted to bar, 1870, and practiced at Warsaw. Del.-at-large Dem. Nat. convs., 1880, 1896, 1900; mem. 52d to 64th Congresses (1891-1917), 1st Va. Dist. Address: Warsaw, Va. Died Apr. 17. 1918.

JONES, William Carey, college prof.; b. Washington, D.C., Oct. 15, 1854; s. William Carey and Eliza (Benton) J.; A.B., U. of Calif., 1875, A.M., 1879; m. Alice H. Whitcomb, 1880 (died 1882); m. 2d, Ada M. Butterfield, 1893. Admitted to bar, 1879; instr. Latin, 1877, U.S. history, 1882, asst. prof. U.S. history, 1887, asso. prof., 1889, prof. jurisprudence, 1894—, dir. Sch of Jurisprudence, 1912—, dean grad. div., 1918-1920, U. of Calif.; also chmn. Administrative Bd. of univ., 1919. Pres. Bd. of Edn., Berkeley, Calif., 1884-90; mem. City Council, 1894-96; pres. Bd. of Free-Woodrow Wilson Foundation, 1921. Author: Illustrated History of University of California, holders, Berkeley, 1894, 1908. Mem. Nat. Com. 1895, 2d edit., 1900. Editor: Jones' Blackstone's Commentaries on the Laws of England (2 vols.), 1915. Home: Berkeley, Calif. Died Oct. 2, 1923.

JONES, William Carey, lawyer; b. Remsen, N.Y., Apr. 5, 1855; student U. of Wis.; admitted to Minn. bar, 1876; in active practice, 1876—. Several times city atty.; dist. atty., 12th Dist., Wash., 1886-89; atty. gen. of Wash., 1889-97; mem. 55th Congress (1897-99). Free Silver Republican. Address: Spokane, Wash. Died June 14, 1927.

JONES, William James, Jr., chemist; b. Watseka, Ill., Dec. 9, 1870; s. William James and Sallie Davenport (Jones) J.; B.S., Purdue U., 1891, M.S., 1892, A.C., 1899; m. Nelle Parker, Dec. 25, 1894. Asst. in chemistry, Purdue U., 1891-92; asst. state chemist of Ind., 1892-1901, chief deputy state chemist, 1901-07, state chemist, 1907—; spl. observer U.S. Weather Bur., 1894—; asso. chemist, Purdue Expt. Sta., 1903-07; prof. agrl. chemistry, Purdue U., 1907—. Collaborating chemist, U.S. Dept. of Agr. Mason, Odd Fellow. Address: Lafayette, Ind. Died Aug. 31, 1917.

JONES, William Otterbein, clergyman, educator; b. Va., Aug. 22, 1874; s. Henry and Catherine (Hulvey) J.; A.B., Shenandoah Coll., Dayton, Va., 1895; A.B., Lebanon Valley Coll., Annville, Pa., 1899; B.D., Bonebrake Theol Sem., Dayton, O., 1902; A.M., D.D., York (Neb.) Coll., 1910; m. Olive Tilzey, Aug. 19, 1908; children—Virginia Gertrude, William Otterbein, Dorothy Mabel. Ordained ministry U.B. in Christ, 1895; pastor in Va., Pa., Ohio and Neb. until 1916; conf. supt. in Neb. and S.Dak. 7 yrs.; pres. York Coll., 1922-24; mem. Gen. Bd. of Administration U.B. Ch., 1921-27; chancellor Kansas City U., 1925-31; pastor Winfield Ch., 1931-33; elected supt. Topeka Dist., Kan. Conf., U.S. Ch., 1933; mem. Gen. Conf. 7 consecutive terms (28 yrs.). Home: Lawrence, Kan. Died July 30, 1938.

JORDAN, Arthur, industrialist; b. Madison, Ind., Sept. 1, 1855; s. Gilmore and Harriet Isabel (McLaughlin) J.; ed. high sch., Indianapolis; m. Rose Burke, Dec. 15, 1875; 1 son, Robert Gilmore (dec.). Established Arthur Jordan Co., 1877, wholesale dealer and shipper of poultry, eggs and butter, operated until 1903 with many branches; founder, 1892, and owner of The Keyless Lock Co., sr. partner same; founded, 1894, and owner until 1920, City Ice & Coal Co., Indianapolis; pres. and principal owner of Meridian Life Ins. Co. of Indiana, 1898-1916; organizer, 1904, and v.p. until 1923, The Cloverdale Co., Boston, chain of retail grocery stores; organizer, 1907, owner until 1920, Internat. Machine Tool Co., Indianapolis; owner Printing Arts Co., Indianapolis, 1910-20; organizer, 1914, and pres. Arthur Jordan Piano Co., Washington, D.C.; pres. Postal Life Insurance Company of New York and Postal Nat. Life Ins. Co. of America, 1931—; v.p. Homer L. Kitt Co., Washington, D.C.; Internat. Printing Co., Indianapolis; dir. Clairemont Sterilized Egg Co., Am. Coll. Bur. and Fisk Teachers Agency, Chicago; established, 1928, The Arthur Jordan Conservatory of Music, combining the Metropolitan Sch. of Music and the Indiana Coll. of Music and Fine Arts, at Indianapolis. Trustee Indianapolis Y.M.C.A.; dir. Butler U. Mem. bd. of corporators Crown Hill Cemetery, Indianapolis. Republican. Baptist. Donor of Arthur Jordan Memorial Hall, Butler U., also of Y.M.C.A. buildings at Rangoon, Burma, and Tsinau Fu, China; founded Arthur Jordan Foundation, 1928, endowed with $2,000,000, chmn. bd. trustees. Address: Indianapolis, Ind.; also New York, N.Y. Died Sept. 5, 1934.

JORDAN, Chester Bradley, governor; b. Colebrook, N.H., Oct. 15, 1839; s. Johnson and Minerva (Buel) J.; ed. Colebrook schs.; grad. Kimball Union Acad., Plainfield, N.H., 1866; A.M., Dartmouth, 1882, LL.D., 1901, M.Sc., N.H. Coll. of Agr. and Mech. Arts, 1901; m. Ida R. Nutter, July 19, 1879. Clerk Supreme Ct., 1868-74; admitted to bar, 1875; speaker N.H. Ho. of Rep., 1881; pres. N.H. Senate, 1897; gov. of N.H., 1901-03. Republican. Mason. Address: Lancaster, N.H. Died Aug. 24, 1914.

JORDAN, Conrad N., banker; b. New York, N.Y., April 20, 1830; ed. private schools; learned printing trade and was compositor until 1852; clerk Hanover Bank, New York, 1852-64; cashier 3d Nat. Bank, 1864-80; treas. New York, Ontario & Western R.R., 1884; asst. U.S. treas., New York, 1885-87 and 1893—; and v.p. Western Nat. Bank, New York, 1887-93. Address: New York, N.Y. Died 1903.

JORDAN, David Starr, educator, author, naturalist; b. Gainesville, N.Y., Jan. 19, 1851; s. Hiram and Huldah Lake (Hawley) J.; M.S., Cornell, 1872; M.D., Ind. Med. Coll., 1875; Ph.D., Butler U., 1878; LL.D., Cornell, 1886, Johns Hopkins, 1902, Ill. College, 1903, Ind. U., 1909, U. of Calif., 1913, Western Reserve U., 1915; m. Susan Bowen, Mar. 10, 1875 (died 1885); m. 2d, Jessie L. Knight, Aug. 10, 1887; children—Edith, Harold, Thora (dec.), Knight, Barbara (dec.), Eric (dec.). Instr. botany, Cornell, 1871-72; prof. natural history Lombard U., 1872-83; prin. Appleton (Wis.) Collegiate Inst., 1873-74; teacher Indianapolis High Sch., 1874-75; prof. biology, Butler U., 1875-79; prof. zoölogy, 1879-85, pres., 1885-91, Ind. U.; pres. Stanford, 1891-1913, chancellor, 1913-16, emeritus. Coöperating asst. to U.S. Fish Commn., 1877-91, 1894-1909; also U.S. commr. in charge of fur seal and salmon investigations; internat. commr. of fisheries, 1908-10. Chief dir. World Peace Foundation, 1910-14; pres. World's Peace Congress, 1915; v.p. Am. Peace Soc. Pres. A.A.A.S., 1909-10, N.E.A., 1915. Author: Manual of Vertebrate Animals of Northern United States, 1876-1929; Science Sketches, 1887; Fishes of North and Middle America, 4 vols. (with B. W. Evermann), 1896; Care and Culture of Men, 1896; The Innumerable Company, 1896; To Barbara (verse), 1897; Footnotes to Evolution, 1898; The Story of Matka, 1898; Book of Knight and Barbara (stories), 1899; Imperial Democracy, 1899; The Strength of Being Clean, 1900; Standeth God Within the Shadow, 1900; Animal Life (with V. L. Kellogg), 1900; The Philosophy of Hope, 1902; The Blood of the Nation, 1902; Animal Forms (with others), 1903; Voice of the Scholar, 1903; Food and Game Fishes of North America (with B. W. Evermann), 1905; A Guide to the Study of Fishes, 1905; The Call of the Twentieth Century, 1905; The Human Harvest, 1907; Evolution and Animal Life (with V. L. Kellogg), 1907; Fishes, 1907; Life's Enthusiasms, 1907; College and the Man, 1907; The Higher Sacrifice, 1908; Fish Stories (with C. F. Holder), 1908; The Religion of a Sensible American, 1909; The Stability of Truth, 1909; The Fate of Iciodorum, 1909; Unseen Empire, 1912; War's Aftermath (with Harvey E. Jordan), 1912; Eric's Book of Beasts (children), 1913; War and Waste, 1914; World Peace and the College Man, 1914; War and the Breed, 1915; Ways to Lasting Peace, 1915; Alsace-Lorraine, a Study in Conquest, 1915; The Genera of Fishes, 1918-20, 4 parts; Democracy and World Relations, 1918; Fossil Fishes of Southern California, 1919-26, 9 parts; The Days of a Man, 1922; Autobiography (2 vols.); Classification of Fishes, 1922; (with K. D. Cather) High Lights of Geography, North America, 1925, Europe, 1925; The Higher Foolishness, 1927; Your Family Tree (with S. L. Kimball), 1929; The Trend of the American University, 1929. Home: Stanford University, Calif. Died Sept. 19, 1931

JORDAN, Eben Dyer, merchant; b. Boston, Mass., Nov. 7, 1857; s. Eben Dyer and Julia M. (Clark) J.; student Harvard (course unfinished on account of ill health); m. May Sheppard, Nov. 22, 1883. Became mem. firm of Jordan, Marsh Co., 1880, later becoming pres.; pres. N.E. Conservatory of Music, Boston Opera Co.; dir. Met. Opera Co.; hon. dir. Royal Opera, London; dir. Boston Dry Goods Co., Globe Newspaper Co.; trustee Avon Street Trust. Home: Boston, Mass. Died Aug. 1, 1916.

JORDAN, Edwin Oakes, bacteriologist; b. Thomaston, Me., July 28, 1866; s. J. L. and E. D. (Bugbee) J.; S.B., Mass. Inst. Tech., 1888; Ph.D., Clark U., 1892; student Pasteur Inst., Paris, 1896; hon. Sc.D., U. of Cincinnati, 1920; m. Elsie Fay Pratt, June 16, 1893; children—Henry Donaldson, Edwin Pratt, Lucia Elisabeth. Chief asst. biologist Mass. State Bd. of Health, 1888-90; lecturer on biology, Mass. Inst. Tech., 1889-90; fellow in morphology Clark U., 1890-92; asso. in anatomy, 1892-93, instr., 1893-95, asst. prof. bacteriology, 1895-1900, asso. prof., 1900-07, prof., 1907-33, and chmn. dept. hygiene and bacteriology, 1914-33, emeritus, 1933—, U. of Chicago. Chief of serum div. and trustee McCormick Memorial Inst. for Infectious Diseases, Chicago, Ill. Editor of Journal of Preventive Medicine; joint editor (with L. Hektoen and W. H. Taliaferro) Jour. Infectious Diseases. Mem. Internat. Health Bd. of Rockefeller Foundation, Feb. 1920-27; mem. bd. scientific dirs., Internat. Health Div. of Rockefeller Foundation, 1930-33; mem. Med. Fellowship Bd. of Nat. Research Council. Author: General Bacteriology, 1908; Food Poisoning, 1917, 2d edit., 1931; A Pioneer in Public Health—W. T. Sedgwick (with G. C. Whipple and C. E. A. Winslow), 1924; Epidemic Influenza, 1927; (with I. S. Falk) The Newer Knowledge of Bacteriology and Immunology, 1928. Home: Homewood, Ill. Died Sept. 2, 1936.

JORDAN, Francis, Jr., importer of chemicals; b. Phila., Pa., Aug. 28, 1843; s. Francis and Emily (Woolf) J.; grad. Nazareth Hall (Moravian Coll.), Pa.; m. Mary A. Harding, Dec. 7, 1875. V.p. Numismatic and Antiquarian Soc., Phila. Author: The Remains of an Aboriginal Town of Rehoboth, Del.; Aboriginal Village Sites of the Middle Atlantic States; Life of William Henry of Lancaster. Home: Philadelphia, Pa. Died 1911.

JORDAN, Frank Craig, astronomer; b. Cordova, Ill., Sept. 24, 1865; s. John Henry and Louisiana (Craig) J.; B.Ph., Marietta Coll., 1889, M.A., 1892; Ph.D., U. of Chicago, 1914; Sc.D., Marietta (Ohio) Coll., 1929; m. Cora A. Ross, June 22, 1893; 1 son, Frank Warren (dec.); m. 2d, Mrs. Harriet C. Roy, Nov. 25, 1909; 1 son, John William. Instr. astronomy and mathematics, Marietta Coll., 1889-1900, high sch., Portland, Ore., 1900-02, at Colorado Springs, Colo., 1902-05; fellow Yerkes Obs., Williams Bay, Wis., 1905-08; with Allegheny Obs., 1908—; asst. prof. astronomy U. of Pittsburgh, 1910-19, prof., 1919—; asst. dir. Allegheny Obs., 1920-30, dir., 1930—. Democrat. Presbyterian. Has specialized in photometry; determined and published light curves of many short period variable stars. Home: Pittsburgh, Pa. Died Feb. 15, 1941.

JORDAN, Frederick Freas; b. Jefferson County, Pa.; s. William Alexander and Sarah Loretta (Freas) J.; B.S., U. of Pittsburgh, 1919; studied at Ia. State Coll. Agr. and Mech. Arts, 1919; A.M., U. of Chicago, 1921, grad. study, 1922; m. Olivette May Gourley, Sept. 9, 1920; children—Mary Jane, Frederick Freas. Began as reporter The Punxsutawney Spirit, 1913; sec. U. of Pittsburgh Employment Bur., 1915-18; instr. in economics, U. of Pittsburgh, 1918-19, Ia. State Coll. Agr. and Mech. Arts, 1919; asst. in political economy, U. of Chicago, 1920-22; also prof. political economy, De Paul U., 1920-22; asso. prof. marketing, U. of Cincinnati, also consulting practice, 1922-24; economist Emery Candle Co. (now Emery Industries Inc.), Cincinnati, 1924; v.p. and gen. mgr., 1925-31; pres. Jordan, Kelleher & Co., New York, 1932—; v.p. Ralph H. Jones Co., Cincinnati, 1932—; dir. The Ruppert Co., Snow King Baking Powder Co., Walter F. Haehnle Advertising Co. Trustee and mem. steering com., Am. Wildlife Inst.; originator and dir. of Wildlife Restoration Week, General Wildlife Federation. War relief work, Russia, 1916-17. Republican. Methodist. Mason. Home: Wilton, Conn. Died Oct. 1938.

JORDAN, G(eorge) Gunby, mfr.; b. Sparta, Ga., June 19, 1846; s. Sylvester Franklin and Rachel (Gunby) J.; ed. grammar and high schs., Sparta; m. Lizzie Curtis, Feb. 1881 (died 1882); 1 son, Ralph Curtis. Began as clk. with wholesale mercantile firm, Columbus, Ga., 1866; elected treas. and credit man, Eagle & Phenix Mfg. Co., woolen and cotton mfg., 1867, and continued later as treas., until 1887; cashier Eagle & Phenix Savings Bank, 1875-86; elected pres. Ga. Midland Construction Co., 1886; was gen. mgr. Ga. Midland & Gulf Ry., also organizer Columbus Southern R.R.; organizer, 1888, pres. 3d Nat. Bank til Jan. 1921; organizer, 1889, pres. till Jan. 1921, Columbus Bank & Trust Co.; pres. Eagle & Phenix Mills, 1898-1916, Bibb Mfg. Co., Macon, 1909-13, The Jordan Co.; chmn. bd. Columbus Electric & Power Co.; dir. Perkins Hosiery Mills, Southern Mut. Ins. Co., Gen. Fire Extinguisher Co. (Providence and N.Y.). Enlisted in Confederate Army 1863 and served until Apr. 26, 1865; mem. staff of Gov. Alexander H. Stephens, 1882; mem. Western Atlantic Commn., 1918; railroad commr. of Ga., 1894, 1901; pres. Ga. Immigration Assn., 1904; mem. Commn. for Industrial Peace, 1907; chmn. Western and Atlantic Commn., 1913; v.-chmn. Western & Atlantic Leasing Commn., 1915; commr. Roads and Revenues, Muscogee County. Pres. Bd. of Edn., Columbus, 1905. Democrat. Unitarian. Home: Green Island Ranch, Muskogee County, Ga. Died May 9, 1930.

JORDAN, James Henry, judge; b. Woodstock, Va., Dec. 21, 1842; s. Charles B. and Elizabeth R. J.; removed to Ind., 1853; lived on farm until 1861. Served in 45th Ind. Vols., 3d Ind. Cav. through Civil War, participating in all important battles of Army of the Potomac; twice wounded in battle; B.S., Ind. U., 1868, LL.B., 1871; LL.D., Wabash Coll., 1907; m. Emma R. Johnson, Jan. 13, 1886. Admitted to bar, 1869; pros. atty., 1872; mem. Rep. State Central Com., 1880-86 (chmn. 1882); judge Supreme Ct. of Ind., 3 terms, 1895-1913. Trustee Ind. U., 1891-95; mem. Nat. Arbitration and Peace Congress, 1907. Home: Martinsville, Ind. Died Apr. 5, 1912.

JORDAN, Jules (Julius), conductor; b. Willimantic, Conn., Nov. 10, 1850; s. Lyman and Susan (Beckwith) J.; ed. pub. schs. there; Mus.Doc., Brown U., 1895; unmarried. First known musically as tenor singer (created part of Faust at first performance in America, of Berlioz's "La Damnation de Faust," 1880), afterward as a conductor and finally as a composer. Among his compositions are the romantic opera "Rip Van Winkle" (produced in Providence, May 1897); musical setting of Whittier's "Barbara Frietchie"; grand opera in 3 acts, Nisida; miniature operas, Leapyear Furlough, 1 act, Thistledown, 1 act, The Rivals, 1 act; also many songs and much ch. music. Address: Providence, R.I. Died Mar. 5, 1927.

JORDAN, Kate, author. See Mrs. Kate Jordan Vermilye.

JORDAN, Lyman Granville, college prof.; b. Otisfield, Me., Mar. 12, 1845; s. David and Thankful (Clark) J.; A.B., Bates Coll., 1870, A.M., 1873, Ph.D., 1895; in Europe, 1889-90; m. Hattie True Knowlton, Dec. 25, 1871. Prin. Nichols' Latin Sch., Lewiston, Me., 1870-74, Lewiston High Sch., 1874-89; prof. chemistry and biology, 1890-1902, prof. of chemistry, 1902—, Bates Coll.; from 1894-1912 served as acting pres. of the coll. intermittently. On leave of absence for travel and study in Europe, 1908-09. Pres. Sch. Bd., Lewiston, 12 yrs. Mem. Internat. Chem. Congresses, London, 1909, New York, 1912. Republican. Free Baptist. Author of system of qualitative analysis, and of organic chemistry. Address: Lewiston, Me. Died Feb. 27, 1921.

JORDAN, Mary Augusta, coll. prof.; b. Ironton, O., July 5, 1855; d. Edward and Augusta W. (Ricker) Jordan; A.B., Vassar, 1876, A.M., 1878; L.H.D., Smith, 1910; Pd.D., Syracuse, 1921. Librarian, 1877-80, teacher English, 1880-84, Vassar; prof. emeritus English and Old English, Smith Coll., 1921—. Editor: Vicar of Wakefield; Burke on Conciliation; Milton's Minor Poems; Correct Writing and Speaking; Ten Essays of Ralph Waldo Emerson. Home: New Haven, Conn. Died Apr. 14, 1941.

JORDAN, Thomas Walden, univ. dean; b. Newbern, Va., Dec. 2, 1848; s. Col. William Jasper and Lucretia (Howe) J.; A.B., Emory and Henry Coll., 1869, A.M., 1872, LL.D., 1897; grad. U. of Va., 1871; m. Kate H. Longley, 1874. Prof. Latin and history, Ky. Wesleyan Coll., 1872-78; joint prin. Science Hill Female Coll., Shelbyville, Ky., 1879-81; prof. Latin and Greek, 1882-86, pres., 1886-89, Emory and Henry Coll.; dean of coll. and prof. Latin lang. and lit., U. of Tenn., 1889-1907; retired. Died Apr. 13, 1919.

JORDAN, Whitman Howard, agrl. scientist; b. Raymond, Me., Oct. 27, 1851; s. James and Sarah (Symonds) J.; B.S., U. of Me., 1875; M.S., Cornell, 1878; D.Sc., U. of Me., 1896; LL.D., Mich. Agrl. Coll., 1907, Hobart, 1911; m. Emma L. Wilson, Mar. 3, 1880. Asst., Conn. Agrl. Expt. Sta., 1878-79; instr. U. of Me., 1879-80; prof. agrl. chemistry, Pa. State Coll., 1881-85; dir. Me. Agrl. Expt. Sta., 1885-96; dir. N.Y. Agrl. Expt. Sta., 1896-1921. Author: The Feeding of Animals, 1901; Principles of Human Nutrition, 1912. Home: Orono, Me. Died May 8, 1931.

JORDAN, William Frederick, author; b. Compton, Quebec, Can., Sept. 27, 1867; s. William E. and Persis (Smith) J.; Coaticook Acad., Quebec; A.B., Elon Coll., N.C., 1921; m. Ethel M. Merrill, Jan. 1903; children—May Olive (wife of T. C. Pendersen, U.S.A.), Tenneva M., Mercedes P., George W., David C. Began teaching, 1884; missionary to India, with Salvation Army, 1886-92; in business, 1892-1904; teacher, Union Missionary Training Inst., Brooklyn, N.Y., 1904-08; with Am. Bible Soc., 1908—, in West Indies, Mexico, Central and S. America, then agency sec. Upper Andes Agency. Minister Christian Ch. Naturalized citizen of U.S., 1917. Author: Crusading in the West Indies, 1922; Glimpses of Indian America, 1923. Central American Indians and the Bible, 1925. Address: Cristobal, C.Z. Deceased.

JORDAN, William George, author; b. N.Y. City, Mar. 6, 1864; s Henry and Mary (Moat) J.; ed. Coll. City of New York; m. Nell Mitchell, May 6, 1922. Began literary career as editor of Book Chat, 1884; later editor Current Literature, from which retired to lecture on his system of education called "Mental Training by Analysis, Law and Analogy." Mng. editor of Ladies' Home Journal, 1897; editor Saturday Evening Post, Phila., 1898-99; editor and v.p. Continental Pub. Co., 1899-1905; editor The Search-Light, 1905-06. In 1907 he proposed the organization of the govs. of the country as a House of Governors to work for uniform legislation between the states; this led to the call by President Roosevelt of a conv. of govs. at Washington, May 1908, at which the govs. apptd. a com. to arrange for a permanent organization; the first meeting of the House of Governors held, 1910. Author: Mental Training a Remedy for Education, 1896; The Kingship of Self-Control, 1899; The Majesty of Calmness, 1900; The Power of Truth, 1902; The House of Governors, 1907; The Crown of Individuality, 1909; The Power of Purpose, 1910; Little Problems of Married Life, 1910; The Wood-Carver, 1915; What Every American Should Know About the League of Nations, 1919; One Hundred Years of Fire Insurance (with Henry R. Call), 1919; The Trusteeship of Life, 1921. Home: New York, N.Y. Died Apr. 20, 1928.

JORDEN, Edward Fletcher, clergyman; b. Prince Edward Island, Can., 1858; s. Edward James and Rehumah (Sensebaugh) J.; grad. McMaster Coll., Toronto, 1884; Ph.B., Ill. Wesleyan U., 1888, Ph.D., 1890; B.D., U. of Chicago Div. Sch., 1887; D.D., Neb. Wesleyan, 1900; m. Jemima Laurie, June 11, 1890; children—Mary Eloise, Edward Laurie. Ordained Bapt. ministry, 1885; pastor First Ch., Muscatine, Ia., 1890-92, Grand Island, Neb., 1892-1902, Fremont, 1902-04 (6 mos. leave of absence, during which served as chaplain 3d Neb. Vols., Spanish-Am. War; pres. Sioux Falls (S.D.) Coll., 1904-14; pastor 1st Ch., Shenandoah, Ia., 1914-16; pres. Grand Island (Neb.) Coll., 1916-19, later v.p. Home: Grand Island, Neb. Died Sept. 26, 1927.

JOSEPH, Don Rosco, physiologist; b. Chatsworth, Ill., Nov. 24, 1881; s. George and Electa (Combs) J.; B.S., U. of Chicago, 1904; M.S., St. Louis U., 1906, M.D., 1907; m. Lura I. Licklider, 1905; children—Don Roscoe, Evelyn. Fellow, Rockefeller Inst., 1907-08, asst., 1908-10, asso., 1910-12; asso. prof. physiology, Bryn Mawr Coll., 1912-13; prof. physiology and dir. dept., St. Louis U. Sch. of Medicine, 1913—, vice dean, 1919—. Capt. Med. R.C., 1918; maj. Med. Corps U.S.A., 1918-19. Home: Clayton, Mo. Died July 9, 1928.

JOSHI, Samuel Lucas, educator; b. Buldana, India, Oct. 11, 1874; s. Rev. Lucas M. and Karunabai J.; A.B., U. of Madras, India, 1896; law student U. of Bombay, 1897-99; A.M., Columbia U., 1905; student Union Theol. Sem., New York, N.Y., 1904-06; Litt.D., Colo. Coll., 1932; m. Ramabai Banawalkar, Sept. 1901; children—Sunder, Anandibai (Mrs. Prabhakarrao Madgaokar), Manoramabai (Mrs. Chitale). Came to U.S. with his family, 1902, returned to India, 1909, again in U.S., 1921—. Began career as prin. Am. Presbyn. High Sch., Punjab, 1900; lecturer on India on staff of N.Y. Bd. Edn. Pub. Lectures, 1904-09; represented India at Internat. Peace Conf., New York, N.Y., 1907, at Congress of Religious Liberals, Boston, 1908; prof. English lit., State Coll., Baroda, India (div. U. of Bombay), 1909; appointed Carnegie Exchange prof. from India for one year, 1922 (first native of India to rep. univs. of India in N. America); prof. comparative religion, U. of Colo., 1923-26, with Colo. Coll., 1926; prof. comparative religion and Indian philosophy, Dartmouth Coll., 1926-36; then prof. comparative culture, Carleton College, under the dept. of internat. relations. Delivered many lectures at various Am. colls. and univs. as interpreter ancient and modern culture of India; Earl Foundation lectures at Pacific Sch. of Religion, Berkeley, Calif.; Ropes Foundation lectures at U. of Cincinnati; Francis Bergen

Memorial Foundation at Yale; McBride Foundation lecture at Western Reserve U., Cleveland. Episcopalian. Mason. Visited India, China and Japan, during 1935, to study current problems of the Orient. Address: Northfield, Minn. Deceased.

JOSLIN, Cedric Freeman, civil engr.; b. Staten Island, N.Y., Apr. 12, 1889; s. William Carey and Elizabeth Florine (Freeman) J.; B.S. in C.E., Brown U., 1913; m. Elizabeth O'Neill, Mar. 8, 1919. Engr. with F. L. Dillon Constrn. Co., 1914-15; erection foreman, Aberthaw Constrn. Co., Boston, 1915-17; chief of physics dept., U. of Puerto Rico, 1917-19, prof. civ. engring., 1921—. Student Officers' T.C., San Juan, 1918; coörganizer and capt. Mayaguez Home Guard, World War; served as chief Sanitary engr. Mil. Govt. of Santo Domingo, Dec. 1919-June 1921. Mason. Episcopalian. Address: Mayaguez, P.R. Died Sept. 10, 1922.

JOSLIN, Falcon, lawyer; b. Belleview, Tenn., Sept. 27, 1866; s. John M. and Margery (Allison) J.; LL.B., Vanderbilt U., 1890; m. Lora Price, May 10, 1900. Practiced law in Seattle, 1890-1907; was counsel for Seattle Street Ry. System and other important enterprises; west to the Klondike in 1907; surveyed and began constrn., 1907, of Tanana Valley R.R., the first ry. in interior of Alaska; organized and built the Dawson Electric Light & Power Co., Yukon Telephone Co.; opened Coal Creek Co. Mines; organizer and pres. Bering River Coal Co., Chilkat Oil Co.; dir. Arctic Constrn. Co. Served as mem. Wash. N.G., retiring as lt. col. Democrat. Mason, K.P. Home: Seattle, Wash. Died Jan. 12, 1928.

JOSLIN, Harold Vincent, civil engr.; b. Belleville, N.Y., June 22, 1883; s. William Cary and Elizabeth Florine (Freeman) J.; A.B., Brown, 1904 (Phi Beta Kappa); m. Annie Devereux Hinsdale, Dec. 2, 1908; children—Harold V. (dec.), Nell Devereux, John Devereux, William, Elliott Hinsdale. Surveyor for White Mountain Lumber Co., N.H., 1904, engr. with Norfolk Southern Ry., N.C. and Va., 1905-10, Norfolk City Water Dept., 1910-11, Yadkin River Power Co., N.C., 1911-13, Phoenix Constrn. Co., Utah and Idaho, 1913-14, Carolina Power & Light Co., N.C., 1914-18, U.S. Housing Corp., Washington, D.C., 1918-19; engr., contractor, Wilson (N.C.) Housing Corp., 1919-20; asst. to chmn. and purchasing agt. N.C. State Highway Commn., 1921-23; asst. engr. in charge constrn. and surveys, Carolina Power & Light Co., 1923, later engr. Episcopalian. Mason. Home: Raleigh, N.C. Died Nov. 3, 1928.

JOSLIN, William Cary, educator; b. Thompson, Conn., Nov. 17, 1852; s. William and Harriet (Shumway) J.; grad. Williston Sem., Easthampton, Mass., 1872; A.B., Brown U., 1876, A.M., 1897; L.H.D., Tufts Coll., 1899; m. Elizabeth Florine Freeman, Aug. 3, 1882. Editor, Times, Webster, Mass., 1876-77; prin., acad., Watertown, Conn., 1878-79; teacher, Cottage Hill Sch., Poughkeepsie, N.Y., 1879-80; vice-prin., Staten Island Acad., Stapleton, N.Y., 1884-95; prin., acad., Oxford, N.Y., 1895-97; Clinton Liberal Inst., Ft. Plain, N.Y., 1897-1900; master Payson Hall, Williston Sem., 1900-01; prin., high sch., Scranton, Pa., 1901-03, New Brunswick, N.J., 1903-04; v.prin. Peddie Inst., Hightstown, N.J., 1904-05; pres. Westbrook Sem., Portland, Me., 1905-07; Latin master, Bethlehem (Pa.) Sch., 1907-09; supt. schs., Media, Pa., 1910-20; Latin master Yeates Sch., Lancaster, Pa., 1920—. Mem. advisory bd., N.Y. Regents, 1898-1900; pres. Tri-county Council, Montgomery, Fulton and Herkimer counties, N.Y., 1899-1900. Address: Lancaster, Pa. Died Dec. 30, 1923.

JOSSELYN, Freeman Marshall, author; b. Boston, July 30, 1866; s. Freeman Marshall and Elizabeth (Rowe) J.; B.A., Boston U., 1898; Docteur de l'Université de Paris, 1900; Maître de Phonétique, de l'Institut Catholique de Paris, 1900; unmarried. Prof. Romance langs., Boston U., 1900-08; later lived in Europe. Author: Étude sur la phonétique italienne, 1900; Revision of Monsanto and Languellier's Spanish Grammar, 1904; Études de phonétique espagnole, 1907; Flamini's Study of the Divine Comedy (transl.), 1910; also various modern lang. text-books in collaboration, and articles on phonetics. Address: Munich, Bavaria. Deceased.

JOUETT, James Edward, rear admiral U.S. Navy, retired, 1890; b. Lexington, Ky., Feb. 27, 1828; s. Matthew Harris J. (artist) and Margaret H. (Mamer) J.; m. Galena Stockett, 1852. Entered U.S.N. as midshipman, 1841; fought in Mex. war; grad. U.S. Naval Acad., 1847; served in Paraguay expdn. and in Berriby war, 1845; promoted to passed midshipman; became master and lt., 1855. For services on expdn. into Galveston harbor, 1861, when he destroyed Confederate war vessel "Royal Yacht," he was given command of U.S.S. "Montgomery." Promoted to lt. comdr., July 16, 1862; took prominent part in entrance to Mobile bay under Farragut, Aug. 1864; promoted in course to rear admiral and comd. North Atlantic squadron. In 1885, when rebels closed the transit across the Isthmus of Panama, he opened the transit and restored peace, for which he was thanked by pres. of the United States of Colombia. Home: Orlando, Fla. Died 1902.

JOUIN, Louis, R.C. clergyman; b. Berlin, Prussia, June 14, 1818; originally Protestant; became Roman Catholic, 1840; entered Society of Jesus, 1841; prepared for priesthood in Roman Coll.; was prof. mathematics Coll. of Reggio, in Lombardy, until forced to leave Italy by revolution of 1848. In U.S., 1848—, as prof. mental philosophy in Jesuit colleges, which chair he long held at Fordham. Author: Elementa Philosophiæ Moralis; Compendium Logicæ et Metaphisicæ; Evidences of Religion. Address: Fordham, N.Y. Died 1899.

JOURDAN, James H., dir. bd. Brooklyn Union Gas Co.; mem. advisory com. Nat. City Bank of New York (Peoples Trust br.); trustee and mem. exec. com. Brooklyn Trust Co.; etc. Home: New York, N.Y. Died Nov. 25, 1938.

JOURNET, Marcel, operatic bass; b. Grasse, France, July 1870; s. Jule and Virginie (Delphin) J.; ed. Lycée de Nice; m. Paule Brunet, 1895. Début at Brussels, Belgium, 1891, and appeared in prin. opera houses of Europe and America; first sang in Covent Garden, London, 1897; mem. Metropolitan Opera Co., New York, 8 seasons; appeared in Grand Opera House, Paris, 6 seasons; with Chicago Opera Co., seasons, 1914-15, 1915-16; prin. rôles: Marco, in "Monna Vanna"; Toreador, in "Carmen"; Wolfram in "Tannhauser"; etc. Officier l'Instruction Publique, France. Home: Paris, France. Died Sept. 6, 1933.

JOWETT, John Henry, clergyman; b. Halifax, Eng., Aug. 25, 1864; s. Josiah and Hannah J.; M.A., U. of Edinburgh, 1887; Oxford U., Eng., 1887-90; m. Lizzie Ann, d. Francis Winpenny, 1891. Ordained Congl. ministry, 1890; pastor St. James Ch., Newcastle-on-Tyne, Eng., 1890-95, Carr's Lane Ch., Birmingham, Eng., 1895-1911, Fifth Ave. Presbyn. Ch., New York, 1911-18, Westminster Chapel, London, Eng., Apr. 1918—. Author: Apostolic Optimism; From Strength to Strength; Meditations for Quiet Moments; Brooks by the Traveller's Way; Thirsting for the Springs; The Passion for Souls; Silver Lining; The High Calling; Our Blessed Dead; School of Calvary; The Transfigured Church; The Pastor, His Life and Work; Things That Matter Most; My Daily Meditation. Address: London, Eng. Died Dec. 19, 1923.

JOY, Henry Bourne, automobile mfr.; b. Detroit, Nov. 23, 1864; s. James Frederick and Mary (Bourne) J.; grad. Phillips Acad., Andover, Mass., 1883; Sheffield Scientific Sch. (Yale), jr. yr., 1886; m. Helen Hall Newberry, Oct. 11, 1892. Began as office boy, Peninsular Car Co., and became clk., p.m. and asst. treas.; in mining business in Utah, 1887-89; asst. treas., dir. Fort St. Union Depot Co., Detroit, from 1889; pres. Detroit Union Depot Co., 1896-1907; receiver C.&G.T. Ry. Co., 1900-03; dir. Federal Res. Bank of Chicago, 1913-14; pres., mgr. and dir. Packard Motor Car Co., 1901-18; former pres. Detroit Union Railroad Depot & Station Co.; former treas. and sec. Fort Street Union Depot Co. Pres. Lincoln Highway Assn.; v.p. Navy League of U.S.; dir. Chamber Commerce, U.S.A., Am. Protective Tariff League, Am. Fair Trade League; dir. Detroit Bd. of Commerce, 1914-15, v.p., 1915-16 and 1922-23. Republican. Presbyn. Mem. State Naval Militia, Mich., 9 yrs.; served in U.S. Navy during Spanish-Am. War as chief boatswain's mate U.S.S. Yosemite; capt. and lt. col. U.S.A., World War. Home: Grosse Pointe Farms, Mich. Died Nov. 6, 1936.

JOYCE, Isaac W., M.E. bishop; b. Hamilton County, O., Oct. 11, 1836; s. James W. and Mary Ann J.; removed to Tippecanoe, Ind., 1851; grad. Hartsville, 1858; joined N.W. Ind. Conf., M.E. Ch., 1859; m. Miss C. W. Bosserman, 1861. Was pastor and presiding elder; transferred to Cincinnati Conf., 1880; pastor St. Paul's and later of Trinity Ch., Cincinnati, until elected bishop, 1888. Mem. Gen. Conf., 1880 and 1888; 5 yrs. pres. U.S. Grant Univ. Spent 2 yrs. in the Orient, presiding over the conf. and inspecting work various missions Methodist Ch., returning in 1898; went S. America on 2 yrs. tour of supervision of ch. work. Address: Minneapolis, Minn. Died 1905.

JOYCE, John Alexander, author; b. Shraugh, Ireland, July 4, 1840; s. Michael and Catherine (Gibbons) J.; reared in Ky.; grad. Highland Lit. Inst., Mt. Sterling, Ky., 1859; studied law; served in Union Army as pvt., 24th Ky., Sept. 1861; 2d lt., Mar. 1862; adj., Sept. 1862; discharged for wounds, Nov. 4, 1864. After war practiced law. Author: A Checkered Life, 1883; Peculiar Poems, 1885; Zig-Zag, 1888; Jewels of Memory, 1896; Complete Poems, 1899; Oliver Goldsmith, 1901; Edgar Allan Poe, 1901; Brickbats and Bouquets, 1902; Beautiful Washington; Personal Recollections of Shakespeare; Bullets of Truth; Robert Burns; Life of Lincoln. Address: Washington, D.C. Died Jan. 18, 1915.

JOYCE, William Henry; b. San Antonio, Tex., Mar. 11, 1868; s. William J. and Laura (Mitchell) J.; grad. Coronal Inst., San Marcos, Tex., 1886, Alamo Business Coll., 1887; m. Josephine Haskins, 1897; children—Thomas H., W. H., Robert P., Mary, Frances. Ranching, railroading, and banking in Tex., until 1895; sec. Globe Grain & Milling Co., Los Angeles, Calif., until 1910; real estate, banking and mgr. San Fernando Mission Land Co., Calif., 1910-17; pres. Federal Land Bank, Berkeley, Calif., 1917-20; mem. Federal Farm Land Bd., Mar. 15, 1921-June 1922. Pres. Assn. of Pacific Coast Joint Stock Land Banks; pres. Sperry Flour Co., 1924—; estate and corp. mgr. and liquidator, 1927—. Episcopalian. Home: San Marino, Calif. Died Sept. 30, 1941.

JOYNES, Edward Southey, coll. prof.; b. Accomack County, Va., Mar. 2, 1834; s. Thomas R. and Anne Bell (Satchell) J.; M.A., U. of Va., 1853; LL.D., Delaware Coll., 1875, William and Mary Coll., 1878; m. Eliza W. Vest, Dec. 14, 1859. Prof. langs., William and Mary Coll., 1858-66, Washington and Lee U., 1866-75, Vanderbilt U., 1875-78, U. of Tenn., 1878-82; prof. modern langs., U. of S.C., 1882-1908, prof. emeritus, 1908. Author and Editor: Joynes-Meissner German Grammar, 1887; Minimum French Grammar, 1892; also other text-books in French and German. Address: Columbia, S.C. Died June 18, 1917.

JUCH, Emma Antonia Joanna (Mrs. Emma Juch Wellman), operatic singer; b. Vienna, Austria, July 4, 1865; d. Justin (musician) and Augusta (Hahn) Juch; parents returned to U.S. when she was 2 yrs. old, making their home in New York; grad. normal sch., 1879; m. Francis Lewis Wellman, June 25, 1894 (divorced July 1911). Studied 3 yrs. with Murio-Celli; début in concert, Chickering Hall; operatic début in Her Majesty's Grand Italian Opera, London, June 1883, as Felina in Mignon, and later sang during 3 seasons under Col. Mapleson in soprano rôles; sang alternate nights with Nilsson as Elsa in Lohengrin under management of Theodore Thomas in U.S.; prima donna Am. Opera Co. 3 seasons; sang in festivals, orchestral symphonic concerts and in Emma Juch English Grand Opera Co. Address: New York, N.Y. Died Mar. 6, 1939.

JUDAH, Noble Brandon, lawyer; b. Vincennes, Ind., Sept. 7, 1851; s. Samuel and Harriet (Brandon) J.; student Vincennes U., and Ind. State U.; Ph.B., Brown U., 1872; studied law in office Hitchcock & Dupee, Chicago, and in law dept., U. of Mich.; widower. Admitted to bar, 1874; partner, 1875, in firm of Hitchcock & Dupee, and after Mr. Hitchcock's death, in firm Dupee & Judah, later Dupee, Judah, Willard & Wolf, and then sr. mem. Judah, Willard, Wolf & Reichmann. V.p. South Side Elevated R.R. Co. Home: Chicago, Ill. Died Dec. 10, 1918.

JUDAH, Noble Brandon, lawyer; b. Chicago, Ill., Apr. 23, 1884; s. Noble Brandon and Kate (Hutchinson) J.; grad. Chicago Manual Training Sch., 1900; A.B., Brown U., 1904, LL.D., 1929; law study, Northwestern U., 1907; m. Dorothy Patterson, May 12, 1917 (divorced, 1933); twin daughters—Katharine Patterson, Ann Patterson (adopted). Admitted to Ill. bar, 1907, and began practice at Chicago with Judah, Willard, Wolf & Reichmann; mem. Judah, Reichmann, Trumbull, Cox & Stern; dir. Chicago Title & Trust Co. Mem. 1st Ill. F.A., I.N.G., 1915-17, lt., later capt., in service on Mexican border, 1916; served as capt., maj. and lt. col., F.A., U.S.A., and as asst. chief of staff 42d Div., World War; took part in Champagne offensive, 2d Battle of the Marne, St. Mihiel offensive and Meuse-Argonne offensive; col., F.A., O.R.C. Mem. Ill. Ho. of Rep., 1911-12; ambassador to Cuba, 1927-29. Trustee Brown U. Decorated D.S.M. (U.S.); Croix de Guerre with Palm and Legion of Honor (France). Republican. Home: Chicago, Ill. Died Feb. 26, 1938.

JUDD, Edward Starr, surgeon; b. Rochester, Minn., July 11, 1878; s. Edward F. and Emma J. J.; M.D., U. of Minn., 1902; m. Helen Berkman, Sept. 7, 1908; 5 children. Prof. surgery, Post-Grad. Med. Sch., U. of Minn. (Mayo Clinic), 1918—; surgeon St. Mary's Hosp., Rochester, Minn. Fellow A.M.A. (pres. 1932), Am. Coll. Surgeons. Episcopalian. Home: Rochester, N.Y. Died Nov. 30, 1935.

JUDKINS, Charles Otis, clergyman; b. Bristol, N.H., Oct. 2, 1868; s. George Janvrin and Myra Smith (Dolloff) J.; A.B., Wesleyan U., Conn., 1895; studied Boston U. and Boston U. Theol. Sch. 1 yr.; m. Eva Austin, Mar. 30, 1898; children—Ruth Elizabeth (Mrs. Richard J. Johnson), Eleanor Austin, Margaret Nelson (Mrs. William Mason Duncan, Jr.), Barbara, Winthrop. Ordained M.E. ministry, 1896; pastor Windsor, Vt., 1896-98, Montpelier, 1898-1901, Glens Falls, N.Y., 1901—. Trustee Wesleyan U., 1910-17. Republican. Has lectured widely in defense of the modern critical constructive view of the Bible. Home: Glens Falls, N.Y. Died Jan. 23, 1934.

JUDSON, Adoniram Brown, surgeon; b. Maulmain, Burma, Apr. 7, 1837; s. Adoniram and Sarah Hall (Boardman) J.; A.M., Brown U., 1859; Harvard Med. Sch. (recitations), 1860; M.D., Jefferson Med. Coll., Phila., 1865; M.D., Coll. Phys. and Surg. (Columbia), ad eundem, 1868; m. Anna Margaret Haughwout, Nov. 19, 1868. Asst. surgeon, U.S.N., July 1, 1861; surgeon, Dec. 26, 1866; resigned, May 11, 1868; then engaged in practice of medicine in New York, 1868—; specialist in orthopædic surgery. Insp. New York City Bd. of Health, 1869-77; pension examining surgeon, 1877-84, 1901-14; med. examiner N.Y. State Civ. Service Commn., 1901-09; orthopædic surgeon to out-patient dept., New York Hosp., 1878-1908. Pres. Am. Orthopædic Assn., 1891. Author: The Influence of Growth on Congenital and Acquired Deformities, 1905. Address: New York, N.Y. Died Sept. 20, 1916.

JUDSON, Edward, clergyman; b. Maulmain, Burma, Dec. 27, 1844; s. Adoniram and Sarah Hall (Boardman) J.; came to U.S., 1850; A.B., Brown U., 1865, A.M., 1868; D.D., Colgate, 1881. Prin. Leland and Gray Sem., Townshend, Vt., 1865-67; prof. Latin and modern langs., Madison (now Colgate) U., 1867-74; traveled abroad, 1874-75; ordained Bapt. ministry, 1875; pastor Orange, N.J., 1875-81; Berean Ch., New York, which later changed to Memorial Bapt. Ch. of which he became pastor. Lecturer on theology, U. of Chicago, 1904-06, on Bapt. principles and polity. Union Theol. Sem., 1906-08; became prof. pastoral theology, Colgate U. Fellow Brown U.; trustee Vassar Coll. Author: Life of Adoniram Judson, 1899; The Institutional Chuch. Address: New York, N.Y. Died Oct. 23, 1914.

JUDSON, Frederick Newton, lawyer; b. St. Mary's, Ga., Oct. 7, 1845; s. Dr. Frederick Joseph and Catherine (Chappelle) J.; A.B., Yale, 1866 (valedictorian, Woolsey and Bristed scholar), A.M., 1869; LL.B., St. Louis Law Sch., 1871; LL.D., U. Mo., 1906, Yale, 1907; m. Jennie W. Eakin, Feb. 8, 1872 (died 1914). Admitted to bar, 1871; pvt. sec. Gov. B. Gratz Brown, 1871-73; pres. bd. edn., St. Louis, 1880-82, 1887-89; spl. counsel of U.S. in matter of A.T.&S.F. R.R. and Colo. Fuel & Iron Co. rebates, 1905; also in injunction by U.S. against increased rates by Western railroads, 1910; chmn. State Taxation Commn. of Mo., 1906. Nat. Democrat. Lecturer Washington U., St. Louis. Chmn. Nat. Conf. on Taxation, Buffalo, 1901; mem. of commn. for investigation of power of Congress in regulation of security issues of railroads, 1910; mem. bd. arbitration to settle differences between railroads and locomotive engrs. of East, 1912. Storrs lecturer, Yale Law Sch., 1913. Pres. Mo. Bar Assn., 1908-09. Mem. Freeholders' Charter Commn. of St. Louis, 1913, Mo. Code Commn., 1914; state chmn. Mo. Branch League to Enforce Peace; chmn. Exemption Bd. 17th Ward, St. Louis, 1917. Author: Law and Practice of Taxation in Missouri, 1900; The Taxing Power, State and Federal, in the United States, 1902, 2d edit. 1917; The Law of Interstate Commerce, 1905, 3d edit. 1916. Home: St. Louis, Mo. Died Oct. 18, 1919.

JUDSON, Harry Pratt, educator; b. Jamestown, N.Y., Dec. 20, 1849; s. Rev. Lyman P. and Abigail C. (Pratt) J.; A.B., Williams, 1870, A.M., 1883, LL.D., 1893; LL.D., Queen's U., Can., 1903, State U. of Ia., 1907, Washington U., 1907, Western Reserve U., 1909, Harvard U., 1909, U. of Mich., 1911, Northwestern U., 1916, and Dalhousie U., 1919; m. Rebecca A. Gilbert, Jan. 14, 1879; children—Mrs. Alice Cleveland Laing, Edith Pratt (dec.). Teacher and prin. high sch., Troy, N.Y., 1870-85; prof. history, U. of Minn., 1885-92; prof. polit. science and head dean of the colls., 1892-94, prof. and head dept. polit. science and dean faculties arts, lit. and science, 1894-1907, acting pres., 1906-07, pres. Feb. 20, 1907-Feb. 20, 1923, U. of Chicago, pres. emeritus. Co-editor Am. Hist. Rev., 1895-1902. Author: History of Troy Citizens' Corps, 1884; Cæsar's Army, 1885; Cæsar's Commentaries (co-editor), 1885; Europe in the Nineteenth Century, 1894, 1898, revised, 1901; The Growth of the American Nation, 1895, 1900; The Higher Education as a Training for Business, 1896; The Mississippi Valley (in Shaler's United States of America), 1894; The Young American, 1895; The Government of Illinois, 1900; The Essentials of a Written Constitution (Decennial Publications, U. of Chicago, Vol. IV); Our Federal Republic, 1925. Mem. Gen. Edn. Bd., 1906—; mem. Rockefeller Foundation, 1913-24; chmn. China Med. Commn., 1914. Chmn. Dist. Bd. No. 1, for Northern Dist. of Ill. (Appeal Bd. in the first draft), 1917. Dir. Am. Relief Commn., in Persia, 1918. Home: Chicago, Ill. Died Mar. 4, 1927.

JUDSON, William Lees, artist; b. Manchester, Eng,. Apr. 1, 1842; s. John Randle and Ann (Smithurst) J.; came to America, 1852; ed. pub. schs., Brooklyn, N.Y., and London, Ont.; studied art under John B. Irving, New York, and Boulanger and Lefebvre, Paris; m. Maria Bedford, May 17, 1869 (died 1885); children—Maude Alethe, Frank Besinerk, Walter Horace, Bertha May, Paul Richard, Lionel, Meria Pearl. Enlisted in Ill. State Militia, about May 1861, and served to close of Civil War, in detached service in commissary dept. (field), after first yr. Farmed in Ont., 1865-67; followed profession in New York, Toronto and London, Can., until 1890, Chicago, 1890-93, in Calif., 1893—; prof. of drawing and painting, U. of Southern Calif., 1896-1901; founded, 1901, and dean, Coll. of Fine Arts. Pres. Arroyo Guild of Craftsmen, Southern Calif. Hist. Soc. Calif. Painters Club. Mason. Independent Republican. Methodist. Home: Los Angeles, Calif. Died Nov. 1928.

JUDSON, William Pierson, cons. engr.; b. Oswego, N.Y., May 20, 1849; s. John W. and Emily (Pierson) J.; ed. Oswego schs. and pvt. tuition; m. Mrs. Anna L. T. McWhorter, Oct. 9, 1888. U.S. asst. engr. on forts, rivers, and harbors, 1870-99; commr. Varick power canal, Oswego, 1876-1922; dep. state engr. N.Y., May 1899-1905; pres. Broadalbin (N.Y.) Electric Light & Power Co., 1905—; pres. Broadalbin Supply & Constrn. Co., Inc., 1919—; dir. Broadalbin Knitting Co., Broadalbin Bank; consulting engr., 1905—. Mason. Republican. Episcopalian. Author: City Roads and Pavements, 1894, 1902, 1906, 1909; Road Preservation and Dust Prevention, 1908; From the West and Northwest to the Sea by the Way of the Niagara Ship Canal, 1890; Lake Ontario to the Hudson River through the Oswego-Oneida-Mohawk Valley from Oswego to Troy, 1896; History of various projects for reaching the Great Lakes from Tide-water, 1768-1901, 1901; also many reports on harbors to engring. jours. Home: Broadalbin, N.Y. Died Feb. 12, 1925.

JUDSON, William Voorhees, col. Corps Engrs. U.S.A.; b. Indianapolis, Ind., Feb. 16, 1865; s. Charles E. and Abby (Voorhees) J.; ed. Harvard, 1882-84, M.A., 1911; grad. U.S. Mil. Acad., 1888, U.S. Engr. Sch. of Application, 1891; m. Alice Carneal Clay, Apr. 21, 1891. Additional 2d lt. Engr. Corps, June 11, 1888; 2d lt., July 23, 1888; 1st lt., May 18, 1893; capt., July 5, 1898; maj., Mar. 2, 1906; lt. col., Mar. 2, 1912; col., May 15, 1917; brig. gen. N.A., 1917-19. Recorder board of engineers U.S.A.; mem. U.S. bd. of engrs. for rivers and harbors; harbor improvements at Galveston, etc.; river improvements, Miss. River, etc.; instr. mil. engring., U.S. Engr. Sch.; asst. to chief of engrs.; mil. attaché with Russian Army during Russo-Japanese War; in charge of harbor improvements and light house constrn. on Lake Michigan; engr. commr. of D.C.; on duty with Panama Canal Commn.; in charge of river and harbor improvements, Chicago and vicinity. With Root mission to Russia, 1917; detached therefrom and remained in Russia as mil. attaché and chief of Am. Mil. Mission to Russia until spring 1918. Comd. 38th Div., Camp Shelby, Miss., until Aug. 1918; thereafter until after Armistice comd. Port of Embarkation, New York; div. engr., Northwestern Div. Awarded D.S.M. Address: Chicago, Ill. Died Mar. 29, 1923.

JUERGENS, Alfred, artist; b. Chicago, Aug. 5, 1866; s. Louis and Wilhelmina (Prosch) J.; studied at Royal Acad., Munich, under Prof. N. Gysis and Prof. W. Dietz, 1884-89; unmarried. Awards: silver medal, Royal Acad., Munich, and at Madrid; San Francisco Expn., 1915; Cahn prize, 1915, Hearst prize, 1918, Art Inst. Chicago, business men's art club prize, Art Institute Chicago, 1923. Exhibited in principal exhbns. of Europe and America; specialty, garden, genre and landscapes. Home: Oak Park, Ill. Died Apr. 18, 1934.

JUETTNER, Otto, physician; b. Nimptsch, nr. Breslau, Germany, Feb. 3, 1865; s. Amandus and Augusta (Haenel) J.; prep. edn. St. Mathias Gymnasium, Breslau, and Grandducal Lyceum, Carlsruhe, Germany; came to America, 1881; A.B., St. Xavier Coll., Cincinnati, 1885, Sc.M., 1891; M.D., Med. Coll. of Ohio, Cincinnati, 1888; practiced at Cincinnati; m. Estelle Regina Bode, 1913. Attending phys. Seton Hosp.; dir. Cincinnati Post-Grad. Sch. of Physiol. Therapeutics, 1903—; prof. clin. medicine and Physical therapeutics, Cincinnati Polyclinic and Post-Grad. School, 1909—. Permanent sec. Western Assn. for Preservation of Med. Records; fellow Am. Acad. Medicine, Am. Electro-therapeutic Assn., Am. Physio-therapeutic Assn., A.A.A.S., Royal Soc. Medicine (Eng.), Royal Micros. Soc. (Eng.), Royal Anthropologic Inst. of Great Britain and Ireland. Author: Modern Physio-therapy, 1906; Songs of the University of Cincinnati, 1908; Physical Therapeutic Methods, 1909; Daniel Drake and His Followers, 1909; A Narrative of Medicine in Ohio, 1912; Life of John L. Richmond, 1913; Life of Alexander Dunlap, 1913; Treatise on the Practice of Medicine Based on the Physical Therapeutic Methods, 1915. Apptd. 1st lt. Med. Reserve Corps U.S.A., 1915, capt., 1917. Home: Cincinnati, O. Died Aug. 23, 1922.

JUHRING, John Christopher, merchant; b. N.Y. City; s. John C. and Lena (Stucke) J.; ed. Mt. Washington Inst., New York; m. Frances Bryant Fisher, Oct. 19, 1901; 1 son, John C. Chmn. bd. Francis H. Leggett & Co. for many years; v.p. and trustee Citizens Savings Bank. Home: New York City and Ferry, N.Y. Died Mar. 10, 1932.

JUILLIARD, Augustus D., capitalist; b. Canton, O.; m. Helen Cossitt. Sr. mem. firm A. D. Juilliard & Co.; dir. A.,T.&S.F. R.R., Realty Associates, N. British & Mercantile Ins. Co., Guaranty Trust Co. of New York; trustee Central Trust Co., Title Guarantee & Trust Co., New York Life Ins. & Trust Co., Mut. Life Ins. Co. of New York; dir. Guaranty Safe Deposit Co., Bank of America, Mercantile Ins. Co. of America; pres. Metropolitan Opera & Real Estate Co. Trustee Am. Mus. Natural History; gov. New York Hosp. Juilliard Foundation created by his will. Home: New York, N.Y. Died Apr. 25, 1919.

JUILLIARD, Frederic A., merchant, philanthropist; chmn. bd. A. D. Juilliard & Co., Inc.; dir. Chem. Bank & Trust Co., Metropolitan Opera Co., Metropolitan Opera & Real Estate Co., Juilliard Foundation (fund of 20 million dollars left by uncle A. D. Juilliard to improve musical condition in U.S.). Home: New York, N.Y. Died June 29, 1937.

JULIAN, George Washington, lawyer, congressman; b. Centreville, Ind., May 5, 1817; attended dist. schools; taught 3 years; studied law; admitted to bar, 1840. Elected to Congress, 1849, as Free Soiler; championed homestead policy and opposed the compromise measures; again in Congress, 1861-71; was mem. com. on conduct of the war, and reconstruction com.; joined Liberal Republican movement, 1872; later acted with Democrats. Surveyor-gen. N.Mex., 1885-89. Author: Speeches on Political Questions (1872); Later Speeches (1889); Political Recollections; Life of Joshua R. Giddings. Address: Irvington, Ind. Died 1899.

JULIAN, Isaac Hoover, journalist; b. nr. Centreville, Ind., June 19, 1823; s. Isaac and Rebecca (Hoover) J.; chiefly self-ed.; m. Virginia M. Spillard, 1859 (died 1873); m. 2d, Mrs. Isabel McCoy Harvey, 1893. Lived some yrs. in Ia., returned to Ind., admitted to Ind. bar, 1851; early contbr. to periodicals; was prominent in anti-slavery and temperance reforms; edited The True Republican, Centreville, Ind., and later Richmond, Ind., 1858-72; removed to San Marcos, Tex., 1873; edited there Free Press 17 yrs., later the People's Era until June 1900. Author: Sketches of the Early History of the Whitewater Valley, 1857; Late-Gathered Leaves in Verse and Prose; Outline History of the Julian and Hoover Families. Address: San Marcos, Tex. Deceased.

JULIEN, Alexis Anastay, geologist; b. New York, N.Y., Feb. 13, 1840; s. Pierre Denis and Magdalen (Cantine) J.; A.B., Union Coll., 1859, A.M., 1864; hon. Ph.D., New York U., 1881; m. Annie Walker, d. P. I. Nevius, June 1, 1882. Resident chemist, guano island of Sombrero, 1860-64; studied geology and natural history there; collected birds and land shells and made meteorol. observations on the island for Smithsonian Instn.; asst. analytical chemistry, 1865-85, instr. microscopy, microbiology, 1885-97, curator geology, 1897-1909, Sch. of Mines, Columbia. Connected with Mich. Geol. Survey, 1872, N.C. Geol. Survey, 1875-78; reported on bldg. stones of New York City, 10th U.S. Census. Address: South Harwich, Mass. Died May 7, 1919.

JUMP, Herbert Atchinson, clergyman; b. Albany, N.Y., July 21, 1875; s. Joseph Burnett and Cynthia (Atchinson) J.; A.B., Amherst, 1896; B.D., Yale Div. Sch., 1899; m. May Ellis Brock, Apr. 20, 1908; children—Ellis Burnett, Laurence Atchinson, Cynthia. Ordained Congl. ministry, 1900; pastor Hamilton (N.Y.) Ch., 1899-1903, First Parish Ch., Brunswick, Me., 1903-09, South Ch., New Britain, Conn., 1909-11, First Ch., Oakland, Calif., 1911-13, First Ch., Redlands, Calif., 1913-16, First Ch., Manchester, N.H., 1917-22, First Ch., Ann Arbor, Mich., 1922-27, Union Congl. Ch., Boston, 1927—. Dir. Boston Friendship Tours, 1928—. Mason, Odd Fellow. Author: The Yosemite, a Spiritual Interpretation, 1916; Evolution and Restatement of Faith, 1924. Home: Brookline, Mass. Died Aug. 12, 1934.

JUNKERMAN, Gustavus S., dentist; b. Cinicinnati, O., Feb. 14, 1859; s. Gustavus F. and Elwine (Kuchenbuch) J.; D.D.S., Ohio Dental Coll., 1881; M.D., Med. Coll. U. of Cincinnati, 1884; A.M., Ohio U., 1905; m. Pearl Hall, June 3, 1890. Organized, 1893, and dean 1893—, Cincinnati Coll. of Dental Surgery, Dental Dept., Ohio U. Mason. Address: Cincinnati, O. Died May 22, 1931.

JUNKERSFELD, Peter, engineer; b. Champaign County, Ill., Oct. 17, 1869; s. Peter J. and Josephine (Schmitz) J.; B.S., U. of Ill., 1895, E.E., 1907; m. Anna Boyle, June 19, 1901; children—Florence Rita, Josephine. In charge engring. dept. Chicago Edison Co. and its successor, Commonwealth Edison Co., 1895-1909, asst. to v.p. same, 1909-17; engring. mgr. Stone & Webster, Boston, 1919-22; mem. firm McClellan & Junkersfeld, Inc., engrs. Commd. maj. engrs., U.S.R., Feb. 23, 1917; called to active service June 7, 1917, as supervising officer cantonment and other war constrn., hdqrs., Washington, D.C.; lt. col. Feb. 1918; col., Mar. 1918; hon. discharged, Mar. 4, 1919. Awarded D.S.M., Aug. 1919. Pres. Assn. Edison Illuminating Cos., 1916-17. Home: Scarsdale, N.Y. Died Mar. 18, 1930.

JUNKIN, Francis Thomas Anderson, lawyer; b. Falling Spring, Va., Feb. 3, 1864; s. William Finney (D.D.) and Anna Aylett (Anderson) J.; A.B., Kenyon, 1884, A.M., 1890; LL.B., Columbia, 1887; LL.D., Kenyon, 1913, Washington and Lee, 1913; m. Mrs. Emily Sprague (Hutchinson) Crane, Apr. 30, 1913. Admitted to N.Y. bar, 1887; practiced, N.Y. City, 1887-98; gen. atty. A.,T.&S.F. Ry. System, 1898-1915 (retired). Identified with reorganization of many large ry. systems, 1893-97, notably the N.P. Ry., Erie Ry., Central Ry. of Ga., Ore. Ry. & Nav. Co., U.P. Ry., Chicago & N.P. Ry., etc. Lt. col. U.S.A. and mem. Bd. Contract Adjustment P.S. and T. Div., Gen. Staff, 1919—. Trustee Kenyon Coll., Western Theol. Sem. Democrat. Vestryman and sr. warden Trinity P.E. Ch., Chicago. Address: New York, N.Y. Died May 6, 1928.

JUSSERAND, Jean Adrien Antoine Jules, ambassador; b. Lyons, France, Feb. 18, 1855; m. Elise

Richards, Oct. 15, 1895. In the diplomatic service of France; minister to Denmark, 1898-1902; ambassador to U.S., 1902—. Grand Cross Legion of Honor; LL.D., Chicago, McGill, Columbia, Harvard, New York, Temple, Princeton, State of New York, St. John (Md.), Yale, George Washington (D.C.), Washington (St. Louis). Pres. Am. Hist. Assn., 1921; gold medal, Pa. Soc. Author: English Wayfaring Life; English Novel in the Time of Shakespeare; Piers Plowman, 1894; Les sports et jeux d'exercise dans l'ancienne France; A Literary History of the English People; Ronsard, 1913; With Americans of Past and Present Days, 1916; also (essays) A French Ambassador at the Court of Charles II, Shakespeare in France. Address: Washington, D.C. Died July 18, 1932.

JUST, Ernest Everett, prof. zoölogy; b. Charleston, S.C., Aug. 14, 1883; s. Charles Frazier and Mary (Mathews) J.; grad. Kimball Union Acad., Meriden, N.H., 1903; A.B., Dartmouth, 1907; Ph.D., U. of Chicago, 1916; m. Ethel Highwarden, June 26, 1912. With Howard U., Washington, 1907—, prof. zoölogy, 1912—. Author: (with others) General Cytology, 1924; The Biology of the Cell Surface, 1939; Basic Methods for Experiments on Eggs of Marine Animals, 1939. Contbr. papers on physiology of development, including results of research on fertilization, artificial parthenogenesis, cell division. Asso. editor Physiol. Zoölogy (Chicago) and The Biol. Bull. (Woods Hole, Mass.), Jour. Morphology. Home: Washington, D.C. Died Oct. 27, 1941.

JUSTICE, Edwin Judson, lawyer; b. Rutherfordton, N.C., June 30, 1867; s. Michael Hoke and Margaret L. (Smith) J.; B.S., Wake Forest (N.C.) Coll., 1887; m. Louisa Cutlar, Oct. 8, 1896. Began practice at Rutherfordton, N.C., 1888; mem. Justice & Broadhurst, Greensboro, N.C.; mem. N.C. Ho. of Rep., 1899, 1907, 13 (speaker of House, 1907), N.C. Senate, 1903. Spl. asst. to atty. gen. of U.S. in suits of U.S. Govt. against S.P. Co. to set aside patents, covering $500,-000,000 worth of oil lands; also in charge of litigation involving $60,000,000 worth of unpatented oil lands. Democrat. Episcopalian. Home: Greensboro, N.C. Died July 25, 1917.

JUUL, Niels, congressman; b. in Denmark; s. Niels and Anna (Kergaard) J.; came to Chicago, 1880; grad. Chicago Coll. of Law (Lake Forest U.), 1898. Admitted to Ill. bar, 1899; elected mem. Ill. Senate, 1898, and served 16 yrs.; asst. atty. Sanitary Dist. of Chicago, 1907-11; was mem. and sec. Ill. Wage Commn.; mem. 65th and 66th Congresses (1917-21), 7th Ill. Dist.; sr. mem. law firm Juul & Juul. Republican. Mason. Home: Chicago, Ill. Died Dec. 5, 1929.

K

KAELIN, Charles Salis, artist; b. Cincinnati, Dec. 19, 1858; s. Maurus and Augusta K.; pupil of Cincinnati Art Sch., Art Students' League of New York, and Cincinnati Mus. Assn. Exhibited at Paris Expn., 1900; silver medal, Panama Expn., San Francisco, 1915. Home: Rockport, Mass. Died Mar. 28, 1929.

KAEMMERLING, Gustav, naval officer; b. Cincinnati, O., May 15, 1858; grad. U.S. Naval Acad., 1881. Promoted asst. engr., July 1, 1883; passed asst. engr., Aug. 10, 1893; transferred to the line as lt., Mar. 3, 1899; promoted through grades to rear adm., July 1, 1919. Served on Olympia, Spanish-Am. War, 1898; insp. engring. material, Mass. Dist., 1905-08; duty Bur. Steam Engring., Navy Dept., 1908-09; insp. engring. material, Chester Dist., 1909-12; with Bur. Steam Engring., 1912-15; assigned as insp. machinery, Camden, N.J., Jan. 5, 1915; sr. insp. for Navy Dept., at New York Shipbuilding Corp., Camden, N.J., during the war; sr. insp. of Engring. Dept. at Cramp's Shipyard, Phila., 1920-22; retired, May 15, 1922. Died Aug. 30, 1934.

KAHLENBERG, Louis, chemist; b. Two Rivers, Wis., Jan. 27, 1870; s. Albert and Bertha (Albrecht) K.; B.S., U. of Wis., 1892, fellow chemistry, 1892-93, M.Sc., 1893; Ph.D., summa cum laude, U. of Leipzig, 1895; m. Lillian Belle Heald (B.L., U. of Wis., 1893), July 21, 1896; children—Hester (Mrs. Jas. R. Davidson), Herman Heald, Eilhard (dec.). Instr., 1895-97, asst. prof. physical chemistry, 1897-1900, prof., 1900-07, prof. chemistry, 1907—, chmn. chem. dept. and dir. course in chemistry, 1908-19, U. of Wis. Fellow A.A.A.S. (v.p. Sect. C, 1907-08). Engaged in study of the celluloses, the keratins, separation of crystalloids by dialysis, potentiometric titrations, gas electrodes, and nature of metallic state, activation of gases by metals; exptl. studies of elemental carbon and phosphorus; with Dr. Edward H. Ochsner, boric acid treatment of blood poisoning, also use of colloidal gold in cases of malignancy, and the introduction of the use of dichloracetic acid in med. practice. Author: Outlines of Chemistry, 1909, 15; Qualitative Chemical Analysis (with J. H. Walton), 1911; Chemistry and Its Relations to Daily Life (with E. B. Hart), 1914. Inventor of Equisetene, new skin suture material. Home: Madison, Wis. Died Mar. 18, 1941.

KAHLER, Frederick August, clergyman; b. Erie, Pa., Sept. 21, 1850; s. Henry Christian and Anna M. (Ottesen) K.; A.B., McGill U., Montreal, Can., 1869; grad. Luth. Theol. Sem., Phila., 1874; D.D., Thiel Coll.; LL.D., Muhlenberg Coll., 1925; m. Margaret Torbert MacNair, Aug. 6, 1879. Ordained Luth. ministry, 1874; pastor Germantown, Pa., 1874-84, Holy Trinity Ch., Buffalo, 1884—. Trustee Lutheran Theol. Sem., Phila.; a leader in founding Luth. Synod of N.Y. and N.E. (pres., now mem. exec. bd.); a founder, 1895, Luth. Ch. Home, Buffalo, and its v.p.; a founder Luth. Ch. Rev., and led in establishing 7 chs. Home: Buffalo, N.Y. Died Jan. 24, 1931.

KAHLER, John Henry, business executive; b. Zurich, Can., Dec. 10, 1863; s. Henry and Amelia (Allworth) K.; brought to U.S. at age of 3; ed. pub. schs., Mich. and Minn.; m. Mabel Van Campen, 1901; 1 dau., Mary Genevieve. Created the plan and successful operation of hotel, hosp. and convalescent hosp. as a unit, in collaboration with Mayo Clinic; pres. and gen. mgr. The Kahler Corp.; chmn. bd. First Nat. Bank, Rochester. Dir. of Am. Red Cross, Olmsted Co., Minn., World War. Republican. Mason. Home: Rochester, Minn. Died Jan. 18, 1931.

KAHN, Julius, congressman; b. Kuppenheim, Grand Duchy of Baden, Feb. 28, 1861; s. Herman and Jeanette (Weil) K.; went to Calif., 1866; ed. pub. schs., San Francisco; m. Florence Prag, Mar. 19, 1899. After leaving school entered theatrical profession, playing with Edwin Booth, Joseph Jefferson, Tomasso Salvini, Clara Morris, etc.; returned to San Francisco, 1890, and studied law. Elected Calif. Legislature, 1892; sec. finance com., Calif. Midwinter Internat. Exhbn.; admitted to bar, 1894; mem. 56th and 57th Congresses (1899-1903) and 59th to 67th Congresses (1905-23), 4th Calif. Dist. Republican. Led and won the campaign in 61st Congress to hold the Panama-Pacific Internat. Ex
n. at San Francisco; leader in securing passage of the Selective Draft Act in extra session of 65th Congress; chmn. Com. Mil. Affairs, 66th and 67th Congresses. Home: San Francisco, Calif. Died Dec. 18, 1924.

KAHN, Lazard, stove mfr.; b. Ingwiller, Alsace, Nov. 22, 1850; s. David and Caroline (Meis) K.; ed. common sch. of native village and superior sch., Bouxwiller, Alsace; came to U.S., 1866; m. Coralie Berthelot Lemann, May 17, 1881; children—Milton David, Bertrand Berthelot, Lucian Lemann, Mrs. Marie Berthelot Heyn, Jerome Lemann. Was in business in Indianapolis, Ind., and Marshall, Ill., 1866, Nashville, Tenn., 1867-72, Selma, Ala., 1870-75; became partner in 1873 of Martin Henderson & Co., stove foundry, established 1845, at Hanging Rock, O.; in 1881 with brother, Felix, purchased entire business, continuing afterwards under name of F. & L. Kahn & Bros. and in 1884 erected extensive plant at and removed business to Hamilton, O.; incorporated The Estate Stove Co., 1906, becoming its v.p. Is also v.p. The Lemann Co., engaged in sugar planting in Ascencion Parish, La. Invented and patented numerous improvements in stoves. Participated during reconstruction period and since in numerous notable polit. contests; presdl. elector, 1888; mem. sewerage bd., Hamilton; juror Paris Expn., 1889, 1900. Chevalier Légion d'Honneur, France, 1901. Mem. Nat. Assn. Stove Mfrs. (pres. 1895-97), Stove Founders' Nat. Defense Assn. and coöperated in initiating continuing annual conferences with labor unions for settlement of wage scale; mem. Cincinnati and Hamilton (O.) chambers of commerce. Councillor Nat. Chamber Commerce; del. Internat. Congress Chambers of Commerce, Paris, 1914, London, Eng., 1921; and of other nat. socs. Mason. Home: Cincinnati, O. Died Mar. 7, 1928.

KAHN, Otto Hermann, banker; b. Mannheim, Germany, Feb. 21, 1867; s. Bernhard and Emma (Eberstadt) K.; father came to America, 1848, having taken part in unsuccessful German revolution of that year; became naturalized Am. citizen, returning to Germany 10 yrs. later; ed. coll. in Germany; LL.D., U. of Mich., George Washington U., and Lincoln Memorial U.; m. Addie, d. Abraham Wolff, 1896; children—Mrs. John C. O. Marriott, Margaret Dorothy (Mrs. John Barry Ryan, Jr.), Gilbert Wolff, Roger Wolff. Learned banking in Germany, and afterward was 5 years in London branch, Deutsche Bank; came to U.S., Aug. 1893; with banking house of Speyer & Co., 1893-95; traveled in Europe, 1895-96; mem. Kuhn, Loeb & Co., Jan. 1897—; dir. Los Angeles & Salt Lake Railroad Company. Pres. and chmn. bd. Met. Opera Co. of New York until Oct. 26, 1931, now dir. same; v.p. Philharmonic Symphony Orchestra Society; trustee Rutgers Coll.; mem. trustees com. Carnegie Inst. Tech.; mem. visiting com. for dept. of art and archæology of Princeton U.; former chmn. com. on finance and currency, Chamber of Commerce State of N.Y.; dir. Am. Federation of Arts; treas. Am. Shakespeare Foundation; mem. Mayor's Com. on Plan and Survey. Dir. Italy America Society; v.p. English-Speaking Union. Comdr. Legion of Honor (France), 1918; Knight Order of Charles II (Spain); Grand Officer Order of the Crown (Italy); Comdr. Order of the Crown of Belgium; Officer Order of SS. Maurizio e Lazzaro (Italy); Order of the Rising Sun (Japan). Home: New York, and Cold Spring Harbor, L.I. Died Mar. 29, 1934.

KAIN, John Joseph, R.C. archbishop; b. Martinsburg, W.Va., May 31, 1841; grad. prep. sem. of St. Charles; completed course in theology and philosophy at St. Mary's Coll., Baltimore; ordained priest, July 2, 1866; located at Harper's Ferry, Va., several yrs.; consecrated bishop of Wheeling, May 23, 1875; there until he became coadjutor archbishop of St. Louis (Mo.), 1893; succeeded late Archbishop Kenrick in 1896. Died 1903.

KALANIANAOLE, J(onah) Kuhio, delegate to Congress; b. Koloa, Island of Kauai, Hawaii, Mar. 26, 1871; s. D. Kahalepouli and Princess Kekaulike, cousin to late King Kalakaua and Queen Liliuokalani, monarchs of the then Kingdom of Hawaii, and nephew of Queen Kapiolani, consort of Kalakaua; created Prince, by royal proclamation, 1884; ed. in Honolulu, the U.S., and Eng.; m. Elizabeth Kahanu, d. of a chief of the island of Maui, Oct. 8, 1896. Was employed in office of minister of the interior, and in the custom house under the monarchy. Delegate 58th to 66th Congresses (1903-21), from H.T. Republican. Home: Honolulu, H.T. Died Jan. 7, 1921.

KALDENBERG, Frederick Robert, sculptor; b. New York, June 7, 1855; s. F. W. and Henrietta (Schlesinger) K.; ed. pub. schs., N.Y.; self taught in art; unmarried. Took up carving in meerschaum at 10 yrs. of age, and at 14 commenced ivory carving, being 1st native Am. to do this work. Some of productions are in possession of Russian Emperor, King of Belgium and Presidents of Venezuela and Mexico, and in the relics of Gen. U. S. Grant, the gallery of George W. Vanderbilt, Smithsonian Instn., palace of Li Hung Chang, etc. Home: New York, N.Y. Died Oct. 8, 1923.

KALER, James Otis ("James Otis"), author: b. Winterport, Me., Mar. 19, 1848; m. Amy L. Scammon, Mar. 1, 1898. Began at 17 to work on Boston Journal; continued newspaper work until 1880, when he wrote Toby Tyler; from then has been engaged in writing books for juveniles. Author: Raising the Pearl; Tim and Tip; Jenny Wren's Boarding House; Teddy and Carrots; Across the Delaware; The Castaways; The Graganza Diamond; When Israel Putnam Served the King; The Charming Sally; Little Joe; The Wreck of the Circus; Minute Boys of the Mohawk Valley, 1905; When Washington Served the King, 1905; Aboard the Hylow on Sable Island Bank, 1907; Minute Boys of South Carolina, 1907; The Wreck of the Ocean Queen, 1907; Afloat in Freedom's Cause, 1908; Cruise of the Phœbe, 1908; Minute Boys of Long Island, 1908; Two Stowaways Aboard the Ellen Maria, 1908. Home: Portland, Me. Died Dec. 11, 1912.

KALES, Albert Martin, lawyer; b. Chicago, Mar. 11, 1875; s. Francis Henry and Ellen P. (Davis) K.; A.B., Harvard, 1896, LL.B., 1899; m. Anna M. Bradley, Nov. 22, 1899. Admitted to Ill. bar, Oct. 1899; mem. Fisher, Boyden, Kales & Bell; asst. prof. law of property, 1902-10, prof. law, 1910-16, Northwestern U. Law Sch.; prof. law, Harvard U., 1916-17. Republican. Episcopalian. Author: Future Interests in Illinois, 1905; Case Book on the Law of Persons, 1911; Case Book on Contracts and Combinations in Restraint of Trade, 1916; Unpopular Government in the United States, 1914; Case Book on Future Interests, 1917; Summary of the Law of Contracts and Combinations in Restraint of Trade, 1917; Estates and Future Interests, 1920. Home: Winnetka, Ill. Died July 26, 1922.

KALISCH, Samuel, judge; b. Cleveland, O., Apr. 18, 1851; s. Isidor (D.D.) and Charlotte (Bankman) K.; ed. pub. schs. and under tutelage of father; LL.B., Columbia U. Sch. of Law, 1870; m. Caroline E. Baldwin, Apr. 26, 1877. Admitted to N.J. bar, 1870, and practiced in Newark. City atty., Newark, 1875; apptd. justice Supreme Ct. of N.J. by Gov. Woodrow Wilson, for term 1911-18; reapptd. for term 1918-25, and by Gov. George S. Silzer, for term 1925-32. Jewish religion. Democrat. Mason. Home: Newark, N.J. Died Apr. 29, 1930.

KALMAN, Charles Oscar, investment banker; b. N.Y. City, May 9, 1872; s. Arnold and Sarah W. K.; student Phillips Exeter Acad., 1889-90; Ph.B., Sheffield Scientific Sch. (Yale), 1893; m. Margaret Rugg, 1900; 1 dau., Margaret (Mrs. Mark DeF. Orton); m. 2d, Alexandra Robertson, Jan. 8, 1917; 1 son, Arnold. Began as bank clk., 1893; treas. and later gen. auditor, C.G.W. Ry., 1894-1908; entered investment banking business, 1908; pres. Kalman & Co., 1929—; chmn. bd. Schuneman's, Inc.; pres. Jackson St. Corp., Watertown & Sioux Falls R.R.; dir. numerous corporations; trustee Gt. Northern Iron Properties. Home: St. Paul, Minn. Died Aug. 9, 1935.

KALMAN, Paul Jerome, steel co. exec.; b. New York, N.Y., Apr. 1, 1879; s. Arnold and Sarah (Greeve) K.; ed. pub. schs., St. Paul, Worcester (Mass.) Acad.; m. Roxana W. Smith, Nov. 20, 1903 (died 1911); 1 dau., Elizabeth Livingstone; m. 2d, Leeslie B. Bradshaw, October 11, 1915. In employ C.G.W. Ry., 1897-1901; formed Paul J. Kalman Co., 1901, name changed to Kalman Steel Co., 1922, and sold to Bethlehem Steel Co., 1931; organized Twin City Motor Car Co., 1911, Kalman Floor Co., 1916, Hudson Motor Co. of Ill., 1919 (liquidated 1930); reorganized Bliss & Laughlin, Inc., chmn. bd., 1920—; reorganized Globe Steel Tubes Co., 1922, chmn. bd., 1924—; organized Kal Products, Inc., pres., 1932—; dir. 1st Nat. Bank and affiliates, St. Paul, 1st Bank Stock Corp., Minneapolis, North West Airways, Inc. Vice pres. Miller Hosp. (St. Paul). Episcopalian. Home: White Bear, Minn. Died Aug. 8, 1935.

KAMENSKY, Theodore, sculptor; b. St. Petersburg, Russia, 1836; s. Gen. Theodore and Adelaida (Wolfe) K.; ed. pvt. sch.; student Acad. Fine Arts, St. Petersburg, 1850-60; received 3 silver medals, 1857, gold medal, 1858, great gold medal, 1860, and pension for 6 yrs. to continue study abroad; received medal, London Internat. Exhbn., and later, a medal at Vienna; m. Catherine Esimontoffsky, of Province of Tchernigoff, Russia, 1869; 2d, Emily Meyer, of Switzerland. Went to Italy, 1864; settled in Florence, 1865; engaged as sculptor there until 1871; mem. Acad. Fine Arts, St. Petersburg, 1863; settled in Kan. as farmer, 1872; since 1882 in Fla., as orange grower. Became a naturalized citizen of the U.S. Won competition for crowning statue and two bas reliefs for capitol, Topeka, Kan., 1889; made bust for Memorial Hall, Normal Coll., New York; employed on decorations Chicago Expn., 1893, and was commr. Fine Arts Dept. of Russia at World's Fair; exhibited in Anthrop. Dept. same, collection from shell mounds of Fla., and after the fair sent it to Moscow and was made hon. mem. Geog. and Anthrop. Soc., Russia. Notable statues: "The Little Sculptor," "The Widow and Child" (both in Acad. Fine Arts, St. Petersburg); "The First Step" (in Nat. Museum, St. Petersburg), etc.; last work, sketch-model representing "The Evolution of Peace." Home: Clearwater, Fla. Died Aug. 26, 1913.

KAMMERER, Frederic, surgeon; b. N.Y. City, Feb. 4, 1856; s. Joseph (M.D.) and Léonie (von Weisseneck) K.; M.D., U. of Freiburg, 1880; m. Ida Knapp, Mar. 23, 1907. Returned to U.S. from Europe, 1886, and since practiced in N.Y. City; prof. clin. surgery, Cornell U. Med. Sch., New York, 1898-1909, Coll. Phys. and Surg. (Columbia), 1909—; attending surgeon, Lenox Hill Hosp.; consulting surgeon, St. Francis Hosp. Fellow Am. Coll. Surgeons. Home: New York, N.Y. Died 1928.

KAMMEYER, Julius Ernest, prof. economics; b. Washington, Franklin Co., Mo., Aug. 31, 1867; s. William and Wilhelmina (Voss) K.; A.B., Central Wesleyan Coll., Mo., 1886, A.M., 1889; studied U. of Chicago; LL.D., Kansas City U., 1912; m. Josephine Weber, Oct. 25, 1888; children—Marie (Mrs. R. B. Easson, Emma (Mrs. D. R. Hull), Wilma (Mrs. G. E. Thompson), Herbert L., Lillian (Mrs. C. M. Holmes). Principal of Schools, Spanish Lake, Mo., 1886-87, Wyandotte Co., Kan., 1889-93; instr. history and civics, later v. prin., Kansas City, Kan., High Sch., 1893-1903; prof. oratory, 1903-04, prof. economics, 1904—, Kansas State College; visiting lecturer on economics, New York U., 1928-29; lecturer on banking fundamentals, Am. Inst. Banking, 1930-31. Fellow Royal Econ. Soc. (England). Mason. Home: Manhattan, Kan. Died Jan. 11, 1936.

KANAVEL, Allen Buckner, surgeon; b. Sedgwick, Kan., Sept. 2, 1874; s. George W. and Mary A. (Paugh) K.; Ph.B., Northwestern U., 1896, M.D., cum laude, 1899, hon. D.S., 1924; grad. study in medicine, Vienna, Austria, 1899; m. Olive Rosencranz, Oct. 1907; children—Patricia, David, Richard. Interne, Cook County Hospital, 1900-01; instr. clinical surgery, 1901, asst. prof. surgery, 1908-17, asso. prof., 1917-19, prof. surgery, 1919—, Northwestern U. Med. Sch.; attending surgeon Wesley and Passavant hosps. Commd. maj. in the Med. R.C., 1917; col. M.C. U.S.A., 1918. Fellow Am. Surg. Assn., Am. Coll. Surgeons (regent, pres., 1931-32), Western Surg. Assn., Soc. Clinical Surgery. Author: Infections of the Hand. Editor of Surgery, Gynecology and Obstetrics. Home: Chicago, Ill. Died May 27, 1938.

KANE, Elisha Kent, prohibition advocate; b. Germantown, Phila., Pa., Nov. 25, 1856; s. Thomas Leiper and Elizabeth Dennistoun (Wood) K.; prep. edn., Rugby Acad. (Wilmington, Del.) and Germantown and Barker's acads., Germantown; C.E., Princeton, 1878; m. Zella E. Hays, June 21, 1892; children—Harriet Griselda (Mrs. Howard N. Butler), Evan O'Neill, Elisha Kent, Florence Mabel, Virginia. Began, 1879, as civ. engr. with the Big Level & Bradford R.R. (now part of B.&O. R.R.), and continued with Mount Jewett, Kinzua & Riterville R.R., and subsidiaries until r.r. and subsidiaries were made part of B.&O. R.R. Co.; engaged in mfr. of lumber, 1890-1912; pres. and mgr. Kushequa Brick Co., mfrs. oxblood vitrified brick; pres. and lessee Kushequa Keramic Co., mfrs. oxblood vitrified floor tiles. Active from 1890 in councils of Prohibition Party, state and national. Mem. bd. dirs. Kane Summit Hosp. Assn. Elder Presbyn. Ch., Kane, Pa. Home: Kushequa, Pa. Died Feb. 18, 1935.

KANE, James Johnson, chaplain U.S.N.; b. Ottawa, Ont., Oct. 18, 1837; s. Capt. Clement (Royal Navy) and Barbara (Price) K.; student Chambale Coll. 1 yr. and Montreal Coll. 1 yr.; Stonyhurst Coll., Eng., 1847-51; studied medicine in Toronto (A.M.). On account of ill health went to sea, 1853, and became comdr. of coastwise vessel; entered U.S.N. as vol. officer, 1861; comd. a dispatch gunboat, under Admiral Farragut, 1862, who promoted him for spl. services; served under Admiral Porter, 1864-65; participated in both battles of Ft. Fisher; at close of war declined appmt. in regular navy, and resigned to enter U. of Lewisburgh (now Bucknell), Pa., grad. theol. dept. same, 1867; student Harvard Law Sch., 1869-70; chaplain U.S.N., 1868; served in various vessels and stas.; retired with rank of capt., 1896; rear admiral retired, Dec. 1906, for services during Civil War. Was chaplain pro tem. of U.S. Senate at various times. Mason. Died Mar. 10, 1921.

KANE, Matthew John, judge; b. in Niagara Co., N.Y., Nov. 28, 1863; s. Anthony and Mary (Dunn) K.; ed. pub. schs.; LL.B., Georgetown U., 1887 (LL.D., 1917); m. Kathleen Reagan, June 9, 1909. Practiced law at Wichita, Kan., 1888-89, at Kingfisher, Okla., Apr. 22, 1889, on opening of Okla. to settlement; mem. Okla. Constl. Conv., 1907; elected justice Supreme Ct. of Okla., Sept. 1907 (chief justice, 1909-12); reëlected 2 terms 1917-29. Del. Universal Congress Lawyers and Jurists, St. Louis, 1904. Elector Hall of Fame, N.Y. Univ., spl. law lecturer, Okla. Univ. Democrat. Catholic. Home: Oklahoma City, Okla. Died Jan. 2, 1924.

KANE, William Patterson, pres. Wabash Coll., Sept. 1899—; b. Scroggsfield, O., April 13, 1847; grad. Monmouth Coll., 1871 (D.D.); Newburgh Theol. Sem., 1873; m. Jeannette Thompson, Oct. 12, 1881. Pastor Presbyn. chs. in Argyle, N.Y.; Lafayette, Ind., and Bloomington, Ill. Home: Crawfordsville, Ind. Died 1906.

KAPLAN, Bernard Michael, rabbi; b. Linkovo, Lithuania, July 15, 1874; s. Michael Sheftel and Feigel (Mayor) K.; father of Blanche Lilian Kaplan, pianist; came to America in childhood; B.A., Columbia, 1897, M.A., 1899; grad. Jewish Theol. Sem. America, 1897; m. Lena Hanales, Dec. 23, 1895 (died 1916); children—Blanche Lillian (Mrs. M. D. Mosessohn), Naomi Miriam (Mrs. Louis R. Raphal), Daniel Boaz, Amos Montefiore; m. 2d, Ray L. Steinman, July 18, 1918. Rabbi McGill Coll. Av. Synagogue, Montreal, Can., 1898-1902; apptd. hon. Jewish Chaplain of the Dominion by the minister of justice; rabbi, Sacramento, Calif., 1902-05, Bush St. Temple, San Francisco, 1905-15; editor Emanu El (Jewish weekly), 1906-15; grand sec. Dist. 1, I.O.B.B., 1915-20; rabbi Temple Emanuel, Kingston, N.Y., 1920-23, Temple Israel, Waterbury, Conn., 1923-26. Mem. I.O.B.B. Founder and gen. dir. Camp Kinaani for Boys and Camp Pinecrest for Girls, Naples, Me. Capt. (chaplain), O.R.C., U.S.A. Pres. Waterbury sector of U.S. Officers' Reserve Corps., 1925. Mason. Home: New York, N.Y. Died Nov. 22, 1941.

KARCH, Charles Adam, congressman; b. nr. Mascoutah, Ill., Mar. 17, 1875; s. Charles and Mary (Heberer) K.; student Ill. State Normal, Normal, Ill., 1892-93, Wesleyan Law Coll., Bloomington, Ill., 1896-98; m. Hulda Bischof, June 27, 1905; 1 dau., Marguerite Marie. Admitted to Ill. bar, 1898, and began practice at Belleville, 1903; settled in East St. Louis, 1914; mem. Karch, Hendricks & Moran; mem. Ill. Ho. of Rep., 1904-06 and 1910-14 (floor leader 1912-14); Dem. candidate for Congress, 1908; U.S. atty., Eastern Dist. of Ill., 1914-18; a leader in impeachment of Federal Judge George W. English, 1924-25; mem. 72d Congress (1931-33), 22d Ill. Dist. Mem. Evang. Protestant Ch. Home: East St. Louis, Ill. Died Nov. 6, 1932.

KARGER, Gustav J., newspaperman; b. Berlin, Germany, July 12, 1866; s. Samuel and Therese (Rosenthal) K.; brought to U.S., 1873; ed. high schs., Cleveland and Columbus, O.; studied law; m. Rachel Levison, Oct. 25, 1892. Reporter, Cincinnati Freie Presse, later Volksfreund, 1884-90; reporter and city editor, Cincinnati Commercial-Gazette, 1890-95; city editor and actg. mng. editor, Cincinnati Post, 1895-99; Washington corr. same, Scripps McRae papers and Scripps-McRae Press Assn., 1889-1906; Washington corr. Cincinnati Times-Star, 1906—. Chmn. standing com. of corrs. Member Rep. State Central Committee, Ohio, in charge Congressional Press Galleries, 1917-21, 1893; personal press rep. of Hon. W. H. Taft in campaign of 1908; dir. bur. of orgn. Rep. Nat. Com., campaign of 1912. Jewish religion. Mason. Home: Washington, D.C. Died Nov. 16, 1924.

KARNES, Joseph V. C., lawyer; b. Boone Co., Mo., Feb. 11, 1841; A.B., U. of Mo., 1862, A.M., 1865 (LL.D., 1903). Admitted to bar, 1865; mem. Karnes, New, Hall & Krauthoff. Republican. Hon. mem. Commercial Club. Home: Kansas City, Mo. Died 1911.

KARSTEN, Gustaf E., educator; b. Petershagenfeld, West Prussia, Germany, May 22, 1859; studied, Leipzig, Königsberg, Heidelberg, Tübingen univs. (Ph.D., Freiburg, 1883); m. Eleanor S. Daggett, Mar. 24, 1891. Was docent Germanic and Romance philology Univ. Geneva, Switzerland; prof. Germanic languages, Univ. of Ind., 1886-1906; head dept. modern languages and prof. German, Univ. of Ill., 1906—. Chmn. sect. Germanic languages, Internat. Congress of Arts and Science, St. Louis Expn., 1904; chmn. of central div. Modern Lang. Assn. of America, 1907. Editor-in-chief and pub. Jour. of English and Germanic Philology, 1896—. Died 1908.

KÄSEBIER, Gertrude, photographer; b. Des Moines, Ia., May 18, 1852; d. John and Muncy Stanton; studied art at Pratt Inst., Brooklyn, and Paris, France, and tech. features of photography in Germany; m. Eduard Käsebier, of Wiesbaden, Germany, May 18, 1874; children—Fredrick William, Mrs. Gertrude Elizabeth O'Malley, Mrs. Hermine Mathilde Turner. Has exhibited all over Europe; in S. America, and U.S.; has received numerous awards. Home: New York, N.Y. Deceased.

KASSABIAN, Mihran Krikor, physician; b. Cesaria, Asia Minor, Turkey, Aug. 25, 1868; ed. Argeus (Am. missionary) High Sch., Cesaria, taught there, 1887-90; came to America, 1894; M.D., Medico-Chirurg. Coll., Phila., 1898; married. Enlisted 1898, in hosp. med. corps U.S.A.; instr. electro-therapeutics and skiagrapher, Medico-Chirurg. Coll. and Hosp., 1899-1902; dir. Röntgen Ray Lab. and lecturer on the Röntgen ray, Phila. Gen. Hosp., 1903—. Del. to Internat. Congress, Physio-therapy and Internat. Congress, Radiology and Ionization, Liege, Belgium, 1905, to Am. Congress for Tuberculosis, 1902. V.p. Am. Electro-Therapeutic Assn. Republican. Conglist. Author: Electro-Therapeutics and Röntgen Rays with Chapters on Radium and Phototherapy, 1907. Home: Philadelphia, Pa. Died 1910.

KASSON, John Adam, diplomat; b. Charlotte, Vt., Jan. 11, 1822, of Scotch-Irish ancestry; A.B., U. of Vt., 1842 (LL.D.); admitted to Mass. bar, 1845; removed to Iowa and engaged in practice of law, 1857; unmarried. Del. to Free Soil Conv., Buffalo, 1848, Rep. Nat. Conv., Chicago, 1860; 1st asst. postmaster gen., 1861-62; commr. to Internat. Postal Congress, Paris, 1863; mem. 38th and 39th Congresses (1863-67); mem. 12th, 13th and 14th Ia. Gen. Assemblies (1868-72); mem. 43d and 44th Congresses (1873-77); U.S. minister to Austria, 1877-81; mem. 47th and 48th Congresses (1881-84); U.S. minister to Germany, 1884-85; commr. to Congo Internat. Conf., 1885; spl. envoy to Samoan Internat. Conf., 1893; U.S. spl. commr. plenipotentiary to negotiate reciprocity treaties, 1897-1901; mem. Am.-Canadian Joint High Commn., 1898. Author: Evolution of the U.S. Constitution and History of the Monroe Doctrine, 1904. Died 1910.

KAST, Ludwig, M.D.; b. Vienna, Austria, Mar. 2, 1877; s. Surgeon-Gen. T. and Antonia (Windisch) K.; M.D., German U. of Prague, 1903; Sc.D. honoris causa, Syracuse U., 1934; studied in Vienna, Munich, Berlin, Paris and London. Came to U.S., 1906; research work at Rockefeller Inst. 1 yr.; prof. clin. medicine, New York Post-Grad. Med. Sch., 1910-26, also trustee same; consulting phys. N.Y. Post-Grad. Hosp., Columbia U. Pres. Josiah Macy, Jr. Foundation. Lt. Colonel Medical Reserve Corps, U.S. Army. Decorated Officer of the Order of the Crown (Belgium); Officer of the Palmes Academique (France). Home: New York, N.Y. Died Aug. 14, 1941.

KASTER, John P., surgeon; b. Burlington, Ia., Oct. 7, 1857; s. William and Lydia (Penny) K.; M.D., Rush Med. Coll., Chicago, 1881; m. Ide Miller of Sperry, Ia., Apr. 1882. Practiced at Burlington, Ia., 1881-87, Albuquerque, N.M., 1887-97, Topeka, Kan., 1897—; chief surgeon A.,T.&S.F. Ry., 1897; prof. railroad and clin. medicine, Kan. Med. Coll., Topeka, 1900-13. Republican. Home: Topeka, Kan. Died Dec. 13, 1938.

KASTLE, Joseph Hoeing, chemist; b. Lexington, Ky., Jan. 25, 1864; s. Daniel and Thane (Vallandingham) K.; B.S., State Coll. of Ky., 1884, M.S., 1886; post-grad. studies Johns Hopkins, 1884-88, Ph.D., 1888; m. B. Callie Warner, June 18, 1895. Prof. chemistry, State Coll. of Ky., 1888-1905; chief div. chem. hygienic lab., U.S. Pub. Health and Marine Hosp. Service, 1905-09; prof. chemistry, U. of Va., 1909-11; research prof. chemistry, Ky. Agrl. Expt. Sta., State U. of Ky., July 1, 1911-12; dir. Ky. Agrl. Expt. Sta. and dean Coll. of Agr., State U., Lexington, 1912—. Author: The Chemistry of Metals, 1900; The Chemistry of Milk; Oxidases. Home: Lexington, Ky. Died Sept. 24, 1916.

KATO, Frederick, mfr. artistic metal and bronze work; b. New York, June 12, 1866; s. George Phillip and Cathrine K.; ed. public schools and private acad.; lectured, 1892-93, on botany and physiology, N.J. Coll. of Pharmacy; active in local scientific societies. Home: Jersey City, N.J. Died 1909.

KATTE, Edwin Britton, electrical engr.; b. St. Louis, Oct. 16, 1871; s. Walter and Elizabeth Pendleton (Britton) K.; M.E., Cornell, 1893, M.M.E., 1894; m. Elva King, Jan. 26, 1907; children—Elizabeth, Edwin Britton. Apprentice and engring. student, H. R. Worthington shops, Brooklyn, 1894-96; asst. engr. Park Av. Improvement Commn., 1896-98; successively, 1898—, draftsman, asst. engr., mech. engr., elec. engr., and 1906—, chief engr. of electric traction N.Y. Central R.R., in charge of design, constrn. and operation of electric traction systems; consulting elec. engr. Cleveland Union Terminals Co. Democrat. Episcopalian. Home: Irvington, N.Y. Died July 19, 1928.

KATTE, Walter, civil engr.; b. London, Eng., Nov. 14, 1830; s. Edwin and Isabella (James) K.; ed. King's Coll. Sch.; pupil in civil engr's. office, 1846-49. Came to U.S., May 1849; m. Elizabeth Pendleton Britton, Nov. 22, 1870. Entered ry. service, 1850; resident engr. state canals, Pa., 1857-58; afterward engr. of several rys.; in U.S. mil. engring. service, 1861-62; with Keystone Bridge Co., Pittsburgh, as engr., sec. and gen. Western agt., 1865-75; superintended erection St. Louis steel arch bridge; chief engr. New York Elevated R.R., 1877-80, New York, West Shore & Buffalo R.R., 1880-86, N.Y.C.&H.R., New York & Harlem, and West Shore railroads, 1886-99; retired. Home: New York, N.Y. Died Mar. 4, 1917.

KATZ, Frank J(ames), geologist; b. N.Y. City, Jan. 27, 1883; s. Edward Marc and Alice (Neustadt) K.; B.A., U. of Wis., 1905; fellow in geology, U. of Chicago, 1906-07; m. Martha Valiant Wills, Nov. 1, 1913. Pvt. geol. work, 1904-07; mem. U.S. Geol. Survey, 1907-25; successively jr. geologist, asst. geologist, asso. geologist, to 1918, geologist, 1918-24, geologist in charge Div. of Mineral Resources, 1924-25; engr. in charge Div. of Mineral Resources and Statistics, U.S. Bur. of Mines, July 1, 1925—. Expert spl. agt. for mines and quarries, U.S. Census, 1919-22; specialist on mineral abrasives and feldspar resources. Author: Mines and Quarries, 1922. Home: Washington, D.C. Died Aug. 1930.

KÄTZ, Mark Jacob, lawyer; b. New York, Mar. 7, 1863; s. Jacob H. and Ester (Schaumberg) K.; ed. pub. schs. and Cooper Inst., New York; m. Ettie Barasch, Feb. 22, 1888. Studied law in office of Oscar S. Straus; admitted to bar, 1888; del. Tercentenary of modern shorthand, London, 1887; instr. in Evening High Sch., New York, 1890-1911; legislative representative in Washington, 1906, Nat. Liberal Immigration League, of which has been sec., 1905—; sec. and dir. Baltimore & Southern R.R. Co. Republican. Home: New York, N.Y. Died Nov. 10, 1927.

KATZENBACH, Edward Lawrence, lawyer; b. Trenton, N.J., Oct. 21, 1878; s. Frank Snowden and Augusta (Mushbach) K.; A.B., Princeton, 1900, A.M., 1901; student Harvard Law Sch., 1903-05; A.M., Harvard U., 1906; LL.D., Rutgers, 1925, Lafayette, 1928; m. Marie Hilson, Nov. 7, 1911; children—Edward Lawrence, Nicholas de Belleville. Fellow and instr. polit. economy, Princeton, 1900-03; lecturer in politics, Princeton, 1929—. Admitted to N.J. bar as atty., 1905, counsellor, 1908, to U.S. Supreme Court, 1920; atty. gen. of N.J., 1924-29; chancellor Diocese of N.J., 1928—; counsel for Trenton Banking Co., Trenton Trust Co., E. I. duPont de Nemours & Co., Reading Co., etc. Mem. N.J. State Bd. of Control of Instns. and Agencies, 1922-24. Trustee Trenton Free Pub. Library, 1910—, Rutgers University, 1924—, Gen. Theol. Seminary, 1931—; pres. Trenton Y.M.C.A. Democrat. Warden of Trinity Cathedral, Trenton. Home: Trenton, N.J. Died Dec. 18, 1934.

KATZENBACH, Frank S., Jr., judge; b. Trenton, N.J., Nov. 5, 1868; s. Frank S. and Augusta M. (Mushbach) K.; A.B., Princeton, 1889; LL.B., Columbia, 1891; m. Natalie McNeal Grubb, d. Andrew H. McNeal, of Burlington, N.J., Nov. 10, 1904. Admitted to N.J. bar, 1891, and began practice at Trenton; councilman at large, Trenton, 1898-1900; mayor Trenton, 1902-05; Dem. candidate for gov. of N.J., 1907; apptd. asso. justice Supreme Court of New Jersey, June 1, 1920. Dir. Trenton Banking Co. Pres. bd. trustees, Trenton Sch. Industrial Arts. Episcopalian. Home: Trenton, N.J. Died Mar. 13, 1929.

KATZER, Frederic Xavier, R.C. archbishop of Milwaukee, 1891—; b. Ebensee, Austria, Feb. 7, 1844; ed. at schools at Gmünden, Austria, 1850-57; academic edn. at Linz, Austria, 1857-64; grad. in theology at St. Francis, Wis., 1866; then prof. of philosophy and theology there until 1875. Sec. to bishop of Green Bay, Wis., and rector of the Cathedral; then vicar gen. In 1886 consecrated bishop of Green Bay (Wis.). Died 1903.

KAUFFMAN, Calvin Henry, botanist, mycologist; b. Lebanon, Pa., Mar. 10, 1869; s. John Henry and Mary Ann (Light) K.; A.B., Harvard, 1896; student U. of Wis., 1900-01, Cornell U., 1902-04; Ph.D., U. of Mich., 1906; m. Elizabeth Catharine Wolf, Sept. 3, 1895. Teacher secondary schs. of Pa., Ind., and Ill. until 1900; asst. in botany, Cornell U., 1902-04; instr. botany, 1904-08, asst. prof., 1908-17, U. of Mich.; pathol. insp. (leave of absence from univ.), Federal Hort. Bd., U.S. Dept. Agr., 1917-19; asso. prof. botany and dir. Univ. Herbarium, 1920-23, prof. and dir., 1923—. Presbyn. Author: Agaricaceæ of Michigan (2 vols.), 1918. Home: Ann Arbor, Mich. Died June 14, 1931.

KAUFFMANN, Rudolph, journalist; b. Zanesville, O., Oct. 5, 1853; s. Samuel Hay and Sarah (Fracker) K.; A.B., Amherst Coll., 1875; m. Jessie Kennedy, 1882 (dec.). Mng. editor and part owner, Washington Evening Star; pres. Columbia Planograph Co.; dir. Nat. Metropolitan Bank, Washington. Mem. bd. trustees, Nat. Geog. Soc.; trustee Corcoran Art Gallery. Home: Washington, D.C. Died Sept. 19, 1927.

KAUFFMANN, Samuel Hay, pres. Washington (D.C.) Evening Star Co.; b. Wayne Co., O.; s. Rudolph and Jane (Hay) K.; common school edn.; married. Learned printing business early in life and has been almost continuously connected with journalism since, in Ohio and D.C.; for more than 30 yrs. one of proprs. Washington Evening Star. Extensive traveler in all parts of world; patron of art and literature; pres. bd. trustees Corcoran Gallery Art. Died 1906.

KAUL, John Lanzel, lumber mfr.; b. St. Marys, Pa., Oct. 9, 1866; s. Andrew and Walburga (Lanzel) K.; ed. Rock Hill Coll., Baltimore, Md., and Eastman's Business Coll., Poughkeepsie, N.Y.; m. Virginia Roy Head, June 18, 1901. Began in lumber business at Hollins, Ala., 1890; pres. and treas. Kaul Lumber Co.; pres. Kaul Land & Lumber Company; dir. First Nat. Bank, Elmwood Cemetery Corp., Tutwiler Hotel Co. Mem. Am. Commn. to Study Rural Credits in Europe, 1913; dir. Southern Pine Emergency Bureau, member Southern War Service Committee of War Industries Bd., during World War; chmn. Birmingham and Jefferson Co. (Ala.) Victory Liberty Loan Com.; pres. Birmingham Chapter Am. Red Cross. Mem. Birmingham Chamber Commerce, Ala. State Forestry Commn. Democrat. Home: Birmingham, Ala. Died Sept. 8, 1931.

KAUTZ, Albert, rear admiral U.S.N., retired Jan. 29, 1901; b. Georgetown, O., Jan. 29, 1839; s. George and Dortha (Lewing) K.; entered navy, acting midshipman, Sept. 25, 1854; grad. Naval Acad., and apptd. midshipman, June 11, 1858; promoted passed midshipman, Jan. 19, 1861; master, Feb. 23, 1861; lt., April 21, 1861; prisoner of war in N.C. and Richmond, Va., June-Oct. 1861; served as Farragut's flag lt. on board Hartford at capture of New Orleans, April 1862; personally hauled down the "Lone Star" flag from the city hall (which Mayor Munroe refused to strike), and hoisted "Stars and Stripes" on custom-house; served on Hartford during engagements with the Vicksburg batteries, June and July, 1862; afterwards on various stations and duties; promoted lt. comdr., 1865, comdr., 1872, capt., 1885, commodore, 1897, rear admiral, Oct. 1898; placed in command of Pacific sta.—flagship Philadelphia; was in command at Apia, Samoa, March and April 1899, during the troubles of the native chiefs, and was commended for his conduct on that occasion. Died 1907.

KAUTZ, John Arthur, editor, pub.; b. Wabash Co., Ind., Sept. 26, 1860; s. Henry and Eliza (Baker) K.; A.B., Butler Coll., Indianapolis, 1885, A.M., 1886. Editor and pub. Kokomo Tribune, 1887—. Home: Kokomo, Ind. Died May 18, 1938.

KAVANAGH, Leslie J., clergyman; b. Litherland, Eng., Sept. 25, 1866; s. John Thomas and Annie (Leslie) K.; ed. St. Joseph's Coll., Louvain, Belgium; St. Francis Xavier, Liverpool, Eng.; Marist Coll., Brookland, D.C.; Marist Sem., Belley, France; LL.D., Duquesne U., Pittsburgh, Pa., 1926. Ordained priest R.C. Ch., 1903; prof. rhetoric, Jefferson Coll., Convent, La., 1897-99, 1901-03; apptd. pastor Our Lady of Lourdes Ch., 1905; apptd. mil. vicar gen. of Cath. chaplains, U.S. Army and Navy Gulf Vicariate, 1918; domestic prelate, 1919. Compiler of Crown Hymnal (children's edition and organist's edition), 1912. Home: New Orleans, La. Died July 1934.

KAVANAGH, Marcus A., judge; b. Des Moines, Ia., Sept. 3, 1859; s. Marcus and Mary (Hughes) K.; grad. Niagara U., 1876; LL.B., State U. of Ia., 1878; LL.D., Univ. of Notre Dame, Niagara Univ., Loyola Univ.; m. Mrs. Herminie Templeton, d. Maj. George McGibney, of Longford, Ireland, Aug. 19, 1905 (died 1933); m. 2d, Jeanne Velma Latour, Nov. 8, 1934. Admitted to Ia. bar, 1878; elected city atty. of Des Moines, 1880; reëlected 1882; elected dist. judge of the 9th Jud. Dist. of Ia., 1885, but resigned in 1889; moved to Chicago, 1889, becoming a partner with John Gibbons, under firm name of Gibbons & Kavanagh, later Gibbons, Kavanagh & O'Donnell, and after the election of Judge Gibbons to the bench, title changed to Kavanagh & O'Donnell and so continued until 1888; judge Superior Court of Cook Co., 1898-1935. Was maj. and lt. col. 3d Inf. Ia. N.G.; elected lt. col. 7th Regt., I.N.G., 1894, col., 1896; served in Spanish-Am. War as col. 7th Ill. Vol. Inf. Republican. Known generally for work in law reform; apptd., 1923, with Charles S. Whitman of New York and Wade H. Ellis, of Washington, to make study of European legal procedure and report upon same. Author: The Criminal and His Allies, 1928; You Be the Judge. Home: Ocean Grove, N.J. Died Dec. 31, 1937.

KAVANAUGH, William Harrison, engr.; b. Williamsport, Pa., Aug. 19, 1873; s. Daniel and Emma (Ramsey) K.; M.E., Lehigh U., 1894; m. Julia Sara Vogt, Feb. 20, 1896; children—Emma Cosette (wife of William Harry Regelman, M.D.), William Ramsey. Prin. Miners and Mechanics Inst., Freeland, Pa., 1894-95; mercantile business, Williamsport, 1895-97; instr. mech. engring., U. of Ill., 1897-98; draftsman and chief draftsman Pa. R.R., 1898-1901; instr. mech. engring. and asst. prof. exptl. engring., U. of Minn., 1901-07, prof. exptl. engring., 1907-16; prof. exptl. engring., U. of Pa., 1916—, also cons. practice and servicing as engring. expert in many cases of patent and other litigation. Mem. Exam. Bd. Civil Service Commn., Minneapolis, 1913-16. Mem. Internat. Jury of Awards, Panama-Pacific Expn., San Francisco, 1915, and Sesquicentennial Expn., Phila., 1926; mem. commn., Chicago, to report on "mushroom" system of concrete constrn., 1913; designed Exptl. Engring. Lab., U. of Minn. Progressive Republican. Mason. Home: Philadelphia, Pa. Died May 6, 1939.

KAVANAUGH, William Kerr, businessman; b. nr. Sweet Springs, Mo., July 13, 1860; s. Richard Parsons and Sarah (Talbot) K.; ed. pub. sch. and Westminster Coll., Fulton, Mo., until 16; m. Edna Lee Boggs, Aug. 21, 1890; children—J. Boggs, Mrs. Evan C. H. Alban; m. 2d, Mrs. Cora Shupp Mulliken, Apr. 15, 1920. In coal business, St. Louis, 1905—; pres. Southern Coal, Coke & Mining Co. Pres. Lakes-to-Gulf Deep Waterway Assn., 1906—; chmn. Mo. Waterways Commn., 1909—; mem. Bd. of Nat. Rivers and Harbors Congress, Washington, D.C.; mem. Nat. Bd. Steam Navigation, New York; vice pres. Miss. Valley Assn.; Mo. state v.p. Great Lakes-St. Lawrence Tidewater Assn.; mem. Municipal Nurses Bd. of St. Louis; mem. St. Louis Chamber of Commerce (chmn. river com.). Independent Democrat. Methodist Episcopal. Home: St. Louis, Mo. Died Sept. 26, 1932.

KAVANAUGH, Williams Marmaduke, banker; b. Greene Co., Ala., Mar. 3, 1866; s. Hubbard Hinde and Anna Maria (Kimbrough) K.; grad. Ky. Mil. Inst., 1885; m. Ida Floyd, Oct. 9, 1889. Began as reporter on Arkansas Gazette, 1886, and became editor and mgr.; sheriff and collector, Pulaski Co., Ark., 1896-1900; co. and probate judge, 1900-04; mem. U.S. Senate from Ark., Jan. 29-Mar. 4, 1913, to fill unexpired term of Jeff Davis, deceased; mem. Dem. Nat. Com. from Ark., 1912-16. Pres. Southern Trust Co., 1905—, Little Rock Ry. & Electric Co., Natural Gas Supply Co., Consumers' Coal Co., Southern Assn. Base Ball Clubs, etc. Dir Lakes to the Gulf Deep Waterways Assn. Methodist. Mason. Home: Little Rock, Ark. Died Feb. 21, 1915.

KAY, Edgar Boyd, civil engr.; b. Warriors Mark, Pa., Jan. 15, 1860; s. Dr. Isaac Franklin and Catharine (Bell) K.; acad. edn., Bellwood and Birmingham, Pa., 1872-77; C.E., Rensselaer Poly. Inst., 1883; m. Florence Edna Means, Sept. 26, 1900. Instr. civ. engring., Rensselaer Poly. Inst., 1883-85, Union Coll., Schenectady, N.Y., 1896-97, Cornell U., 1897-1903; prof. engring., 1903-07, civ. engring. and dean Coll. Engring., 1907-12, U. of Ala. Consulting engr. Ala. R.R. Commn., 1903-15; chief engr. State Convict Bur. Ala. and for several steam and hydroelectric power cos., and cities; has designed and built many water works, sewer and lighting systems, steam and electric rys.; pres. Mt. Union (Pa.) Water Co., Dillsburg (Pa.) Water Co.; consulting engr. City of Mobile, water works dept., 1912; chief engr. City of Winchester water works and hydro-electric plant. Inventor of U.S. Govt. incinerators; also municipal incinerator plants for Niagara Falls, Wellsville, Tonawanda, Valley Stream, N.Y.; Highlands, Long Branch, Hackensack, N.J.; Munhall, McKees Rocks, Homestead, Woodland, Easton, Wilson, Pa.; Steubenville, Martins Ferry, Mingo Junction, Ohio; La Grange, Ill.; Portsmouth, Va Chief of hydraulic and sanitary div., Office Quartermaster Gen. U.S.A., 1918-27; consulting engr. Democrat. Episcopalian. Mem. Bd. of Trade and Chamber Commerce, Washington, D.C. Mason. Home: Washington, D.C. Died Apr. 20, 1931.

KAY, Gertrude Alice, illustrator, author; b. Alliance, O.; d. Charles Y. and Gertrude Emily (Cantine) K.; Phila. Sch. of Design for Women, 4 yrs., 1903-07; studied with Howard Pyle. Began work, illustrating for mags.; illustrated her own books. Author: When the Sand-Man Comes; The Book of Seven Wishes; The Jolly Old Shadow Man; Helping the Weatherman; Adventures in Our Street; The Friends of Jimmy; Us Kids and the Circus; Adventures in Geography; Peter, Patter & Pixie. Home: Alliance, O. Died Dec. 18, 1939.

KAY, William Edward, lawyer; b. Atlanta, Ga., Nov. 15, 1859; s. William and Margaret (Burke) K.; grad. high sch., Atlanta; student Pio Nono Coll., Macon, Ga., 1875-76; m. Emma Lucas, Feb. 2, 1882; children—Marie Lucile (dec.), William A., Vivien (Mrs. R. C. Muncaster, dec.), Raymond (dec.), Olivia (Mrs. J. W. Pope, Jr.), Ramona (Mrs. E. A. Inglis). Admitted to Ga. bar, 1878, and began practice at Atlanta; in gen. practice at Brunswick, Ga., 1879-1905; moved to Jacksonville, Fla., 1905; mem. Kay, Adams, Ragland & Kurz, 1928-35, Kay, Ragland & Kurz, June 1, 1935—. General Solicitor for Georgia, Florida, and Alabama, 1906—; v.p. Jacksonville Realty & Mortgage Co. Catholic. Elk. Home: Jacksonville, Fla. Died Feb. 28, 1939.

KAYE, James Hamilton Barcroft, educator; b. Farnworth, Eng., Mar. 12, 1862; s. Rev. John Barcroft and Jane Dagleish (Duckworth) K.; came to U.S., 1883; A.B., U. of Mich., 1892, A.M., 1912; A.M., Albion (Mich.) Coll., 1902; m. Ina L. Tracey, Aug. 22, 1893. Teacher pub. schs., Custer, Chase and Ludington, Mich.; supt. schs., Reed City, Mich.,

1892-96, Cadillac, 1896-1904; pres. of Northern State Teachers College, Marquette, 1904-23, pres. emeritus and prof. philosophy and edn., 1923—. Lecturer teachers' institutes. Republican. Presbyn. Mason. Rotarian; gov. 15th dist., 1920-21. Home: Marquette, Mich. Died July 1932.

KAYE, John William, clergyman; b. Huddersfield, Yorkshire, Eng., Jan. 9, 1846; s. Thomas and Lucy (Cully) K.; came to Phila., 1852; student U. of Pa., 1870-72; A.B., Princeton, 1874, A.M., 1877; B.D., Divinity Sch., P.E. Ch., Phila., 1876. Served in Pa. militia on emergency call, June and July 1863; pvt. 3d Pa. Vols., 1864-65, becoming 2d lt., June 1865. Deacon, 1876, priest, 1877, P.E. Ch.; rector St. Timothy, Phila., 1883-88, All Saints', Norristown, Pa., 1890-94; asst. rector St. David's, 1894-1900. Author: Luray Cave, 1882; Flight, Capture and Imprisonment of Jefferson Davis, 1883; Night Ascent of Vesuvius, 1887; The Royal Tomb at Charlottenburg, 1888. Deceased.

KEALING, Joseph B., lawyer; b. Indianapolis, Ind., June 25, 1859; s. Peter and Phoebe (Bloomer) K.; A.B., Butler U., 1879; LL.B., Indianapolis Law Sch., 1881; m. Lenora E. Franken, Mar. 19, 1899. Practiced at Indianapolis, 1881—; asst. pros. atty. Marion Co., 1883-85; U.S. dist. atty. for Ind., 1891-99; corp. counsel, Indianapolis, 1900-04; mem. Kealing & Hugg; mem. Rep. Nat. Com. Mason. Home: Indianapolis, Ind. Died Dec. 7, 1927.

KEAN, Hamilton Fish, senator; b. Ursino, Union Twp., N.J., Feb. 27, 1862; s. John and Lucy (Halsted) K.; grad. St. Paul's Sch., Concord, N.H.; m. Katharine Taylor Winthrop, Jan. 12, 1888; children—John, Robert Winthrop. Dealer in securities and farmer; sr. mem. of Kean, Taylor & Co., investments; chmn. bd. Hackensack Water Co., Weehawken, N.J.; dir. numerous corps. Mem. Rep. State Com., 1905-19, Rep. Nat. Com., 1919-28; mem. U.S. Senate, term 1929-35. Episcopalian. Home: Union County, N.J. Died Dec. 27, 1941.

KEAN, John, senator; b. Ursino, N.J., Dec. 4, 1852; s. John and Lucy K.; student Yale, class of '76 (hon. A.M., 1890); LL.B., Columbia, 1875. Admitted to N.J. bar, 1877, but never practiced; treas., dir. Pacific Coast Co.; dir. Securities Co.; trustee Atlas Ins. Co., Ltd., of London. Mem. 48th (1883-85) and 50th (1887-89) Congresses; chmn. Rep. State Com., 1891-92; candidate for gov., 1892; mem. com. to revise judiciary system of N.J.; U.S. senator, 1899-1905, 1905-11. Home: Ursino, nr. Elizabeth, N.J. Died Nov. 4, 1914.

KEANE, James John, archbishop; b. Joliet, Ill., Aug. 26, 1857; s. John and Margaret (O'Connor) K.; ed. St. John's U., Minn., and Grand Sem., Montreal. Ordained R.C. priest, Dec. 1882; asst., St. Mary's Ch., and pastor St. Joseph's Ch., St. Paul, 1882-85; prof. and bursar, 1886-88, pres., 1888-92, St. Thomas' Sem., St. Paul; pastor Ch. Immaculate Conception, Minneapolis, 1892-1902; consecrated 3d bishop Diocese of Cheyenne, Wyo., Oct. 28, 1902; transferred to archbishopric of Dubuque (Ia.), Aug. 11, 1911. Died Aug. 2, 1929.

KEANE, John Joseph, archibishop; b. Ballyshannon, Ireland, Sept. 12, 1839; s. Hugh and Fannie K.; came to U.S., 1846; A.B., St. Mary's Sem., Baltimore, 1864, A.M., 1865, S.T.B., 1866; (D.D., Laval, 1889, Manhattan Coll., 1892; LL.D., Harvard, 1893). Ordained R.C. priest 1866; asst. pastor St. Patrick's Ch., Washington, 1866-78; consecrated bishop of Richmond, Va., Aug. 25, 1878; transferred to Titular See of Jasso, Aug. 12, 1888; rector Catholic U. of America, 1886-97; elevated to archiepiscopal dignity with title of archbishop of Damascus, Jan. 9, 1897; transferred to See of Dubuque (Ia.), July 24, 1900. Author: Onward and Upward, 1902. Died June 22, 1918.

KEARFUL, Francis Joseph, lawyer; b. St. Joseph, Mo., June 28, 1871; s. of Charles and Phoebe (Van Dyke) K.; LL.B., Yale, 1896, LL.M., 1897. Began practice in Oklahoma City, Okla., 1893; asst. atty. gen. in charge of Pub. Lands Div., Dept. of Justice, Washington, Mar. 19, 1917-July 15, 1919; counsel for Senate sub-com. investigating Mexican affairs, Sept. 1, 1919-May 1, 1920; counsel for Pantepec Petroleum Co., Tampico. Democrat. Home: Brookline, Mass. Deceased.

KEARNEY, Edward Francis, ry. official; b. Logansport, Ind., Mar. 27, 1865; s. James and Margaret (Kane) K.; ed. pub. schs., Logansport; m. Emma Hoover, Oct. 1883. Began as telegraph operator Pa. Lines, 1882, and continued 20 yrs., advancing to trainmaster, at Indianapolis; supt. Terminal R.R. Assn. and St. Louis Merchants' Bridge Terminal Ry., 1903-04; supervisor of mails, C.,R.I.& P.Ry., Feb.-Apr. 1904; gen. supt. transportation, St.L.&S.F. R.R., 1905-08; supt. and gen. supt. transportation, Mo.P., and St.L.,I.M.&S. rys., 1908-13; 1st v.p. T.&P. Ry., 1913-15; pres. Wabash R.R., 1915—. Home: New Orleans, La. Died Mar. 10, 1919.

KEARNEY, Edward James, mfr. machinery tools; b. Mitchell Co., Ia., Apr. 7, 1868; s. James Hamilton and Emeline (Smith) K.; B.M.E., Ia. State Coll., 1893; m. Ella Berdine Morton, Dec. 31, 1895; children—Katherine Morton (Mrs. W. Carpenter, Jr.), Alice Morton. Began as mech. engr., C.,M.& St.P. Ry., 1893; with Kempsmith Machine Tool Co., Milwaukee, Wis., 1894-98; became partner Kearney & Treckler, 1898; later mem. Kearney & Treckler Co.; now sec. Kearney & Treckler Corp.; sec. and treas. Investment Corp. Dir. sales 4th and 5th Liberty Loan Drives, 7th Federal Dist., World War. Formerly mem. Wis. State Vocational Sch. Bd. Trustee Milwaukee Downer Coll. Conglist. Home: Milwaukee, Wis. Died Jan. 12, 1934.

KEARNS, Charles Cyrus, congressman; b. Tonica, Ill., Feb. 10, 1869; s. Barton and Amanda (Salisbury) K.; ed. pub. schs., coll. 2 yrs., and grad. Cincinnati Law Sch.; m. Philena Penn. Admitted to Ohio bar, 1894, and practiced in Batavia; mem. 64th to 71st Congresses (1915-31), 6th Ohio Dist. Republican. Was mng. editor Las Vegas (N.M.) Daily Record, 1900-01, Daily Record, Hot Springs, Ark., 1901-02. Mason. Presbyterian. Home: Amelia, O. Died Dec. 7, 1931.

KEARNS, Thomas, senator; b. nr. Woodstock, Ontario, Can., Apr. 11, 1862; s. Thomas and Margaret (Meagher) K.; ed. pub. schs., Holt Co., Neb.; worked on farm 4 yrs.; began freighting and hauling goods to camps in Black Hills; went to Utah, 1883; employed in mines; later became one of the owners of Mayflower and Silver King mines; m. Jennie Judge, Sept. 15, 1890. Mem. City Council, 1895; Constl. Conv., 1895. U.S. senator, 1901-05. Home: Salt Lake City, Utah. Died Oct. 18, 1918.

KEASBEY, Edward Quinton, lawyer; b. Salem, N.J., July 27, 1849; s. Anthony Q. and Elizabeth (Miller) K.; (mother a d. of U.S. Senator Jacob W. Miller); A.B., Princeton, 1869, A.M., 1872; LL.B., Harvard, 1871; m. Eliza G. Darcy, Oct. 22, 1885. Now mem. Edward Q. & George M. Keasbey; counsel for B.&O. R.R. Co. in New Jersey. Was U.S. commr. for N.J., 1873-1900; now Supreme Court commr. and spl. master in chancery. Mem. N.J. Assembly, 1884-85. Del. Universal Congress Lawyers and Jurists, St. Louis, 1904. Trustee Howard Savings Instn., Hosp. of St. Barnabas, Episcopal Fund. Republican. Episcopalian. Author: Courts of New Jersey, 1903; Courts and Lawyers of New Jersey, 1912. Home: Newark, N.J. Deceased.

KEASBEY, George Macculloch, lawyer; b. Salem, N.J., Oct. 25, 1850; s. Anthony Q. and Elizabeth (Miller) K.; B.S., Sheffield Scientific Sch. (Yale), 1871; m. Annie W. Lewis, Jan. 14, 1885. With Yale Paleontol. Expdn., under Prof. O. C. Marsh, 1871; with U.S. Geol. Survey, 1873; admitted to N.J. bar, 1875. In practice of law many years in Newark, N.J.; retired. Asst. U.S. atty. for Dist. of N.J., 1880-87. Republican. Episcopalian. Home: East Orange, N.J. Died July 31, 1924.

KEATING, Cecil A., mfr.; b. Halifax, N.S., Mar. 20, 1850; s. W. H. and Eliza W. K.; ed. pub. schs., Halifax. Began mfr. agrl. implements in Chicago, 1870; married; 1 dau., Mrs. Smith H. Latta. Created and was pres. many yrs. of Keating Implement & Machine Co., and Tex. Disc Plow Co.; since 1891 has been pres. Trinity River Navigation Co., organized for purpose of securing govt. aid to convert into a canal the Trinity River, 500 miles, from Dallas to Gulf of Mexico, which measure was successful in Congress, 1902, and for which Congress has since appropriated over $1,000,000. Retired from active business. Home: Dallas, Tex. Died Jan. 2, 1931.

KEATING, Frank Webster, psychiatrist; b. Centerville, Md., Feb. 20, 1870; s. Thomas James and Sarah Frances (Webster) K.; M.D., U. of Md., 1896; unmarried. Sec. and supt., Md. Asylum and Training Sch. for Feeble Minded, 1896—; lecturer on psychiatry, U. of Md. Trustee St. James Sch. for Boys. Democrat. Episcopalian. Home: Owings Mills, Md. Died Feb. 18, 1934.

KEATOR, Frederic William, bishop; b. Honesdale, Pa., Oct. 22, 1855; s. Jerman S. and Mary (Baldwin) K.; B.A., Yale, 1880, LL.B., 1882; grad. Western Theol. Sem., Chicago, 1891 (S.T.D., 1902; D.D., Yale, 1905; LL.D., Coll. of Puget Sound, Wash., 1920); m. Emma Victoria Lyon, Oct. 30, 1894. Practiced law, Chicago, 1882-90, then studied for ministry; ordained 1891; rector Ch. of the Atonement, Chicago, 1891-96, Grace Ch., Freeport, Ill., 1896-99, St. John's, Dubuque, Ia., 1899-1902; consecrated bishop of Olympia, Jan. 8, 1902. Pres. Pub. Library Bd., Tacoma, 1907-10, 1912—; overseer Whitman Coll., Walla Walla, Wash.; pres. trustees Annie Wright Sem., Tacoma. Mason. Hon. Chaplain Coast Arty. Corps N.G. Wash. Trustee Shriners' Hosp. for Crippled Children. Home: Tacoma, Wash. Died Jan. 31, 1924.

KEDNEY, John Steinfort, theologian; b. in Essex Co., N.J., Feb. 12, 1819; s. Henry S. and Maria R. (Algood) K.; A.B., Union Coll., 1838, later A.M.; grad. Gen. Theol. Sem., 1844; (hon. A.M., Trinity, 1856; S.T.D., Racine, and Hobart, 1872); m. Elizabeth T. Cooke; 2d, Sarah Ingham. Deacon, 1841, priest, 1843, P.E. Ch.; missionary in N.C., 1842-45; rector Salem, N.J., 1847-52, Saratoga Springs, N.Y., 1852-59, Society Hill, S.C., 1859-65, Potsdam, N.Y., 1865-70, Camden, S.C., 1870-71; prof. divinity, Seabury Div. Sch., 1871-1908; retired. Author: Christian Doctrine Harmonized, 1888; Mens Christi, 1890; Problems in Ethics, 1899. Home: Salem, N.J. Died 1911.

KEDZIE, Frank Stewart, educator; b. Vermontville, Mich., May 12, 1857; s. Robert C. and Harriet E. (Fairchild) K.; B.S., Mich. State Agrl. Coll., 1877, M.S., 1882, Sc.D., 1912; m. Kate Marvin, Dec. 30, 1885. Instr. chemistry, 1880-87, asst. prof., 1887-91, adj. prof., 1891-1902, prof., 1902—, and pres., 1916-21, dean div. applied science, 1921-27, coll. historian, 1927-32, Mich. State Agrl. Coll., retired. Home: Lansing, Mich. Died Jan. 5, 1935.

KEDZIE, Robert Clark, prof. chemistry, Mich. Agrl. Coll., 1863; b. Delhi, N.Y., Jan. 23, 1823; s. William K.; grad. Oberlin, 1847 (A.M., 1864); M.D., Univ. of Mich., 1850; Sc.D., Mich. Agrl. Coll., 1898 (LL.D., Univ. of Mich.); m. Harriet Eliza Fairchild, 1850. Has resided in Mich., 1826—, except when at Oberlin. Mem. Mich. legis., 1867; mem., 1873-81, and pres., 1877-81, Mich. State Bd. of Health; has been pres. Mich. State Med. Soc.; Am. Public Health Assn.; and Sanitary Council of the Mississippi Valley; v.p. Am. Med. Assn., A.A. A.S.; fellow Am. Acad. of Medicine; pres. Assn. of Agrl. Colls., 1898. Died 1902.

KEDZIE, William Roscoe, clergyman; b. Oberlin, O., May 10, 1879; s. William Knowlton and Ella M. (Gale) K.; B.S., Mich. State Coll., 1899; B.D., Oberlin (O.) Sch. of Theology, 1902; D.D., Olivet (Mich.) Coll., 1922; m. Ida Barton; children—Kathryn (Mrs. Albert J. Isbell), Faith (Mrs. Frederic B. Dutton), William Roscoe, Hope (dec.); m. 2d, Elsie C. Dean, May 10, 1938. Ordained ministry Congregational Ch., 1902; pastor Vicksburg, Mich., 1902-06; Pontiac, Mich., 1906-12, Glen Ellyn, Ill., 1912-15, St. Johns, Mich., 1915-18, First Congl. Ch., Cleveland, O., 1918-29; sec. of ednl. instns., Congl. Edn. Soc., 1929-35; sec. Cleveland Congl. Union, 1929; pres. Council of Ch. Bds. of Edn., 1934. Republican. Home: Eaton Rapids, Mich. Died Sept. 26, 1940.

KEEBLE, John Bell, lawyer; b. Murfreesboro, Tenn., May 13, 1868; s. Edwin Augustus and Sallie Dickinson (Bell) K.; prep. edn. East Nashville Acad.; Vanderbilt U., 1885-88, LL.B., 1888; LL.D., Southwestern Presbyn. U., 1919; m. Emmie Frazer, Jan. 6, 1897; children—Cornelia, John Bell, Sydney Frazer, Edwin A., David Maney, Emmie. Began practice as mem. Barthell & Keeble, Nashville, 1889; now mem. Keeble & Seay; dist. atty. Louisville & Nashville R.R. Co. City atty., Nashville, 1895-97; presdl. elector (Palmer and Buckner), 1896; prof. law, 1900—, dean Law Sch. and prof. constl. law, Jan. 1916—, Vanderbilt U. Pres. Monteagle S.S. Assembly, 1907-17 and 1918-21. Democrat. Baptist. Home: Nashville, Tenn. Died Oct. 10, 1929.

KEEDY, Charles Cochran, lawyer; b. Baltimore, Md., Feb. 28, 1891; s. Martin Luther and Ella (Cameron) K.; A.B., Roanoke (Va.) Coll., 1912; LL.B., Harvard, 1915; m. Anastasia H. Coady, June 3, 1927; children—Robert Beresford, Jane. Practiced at Hagerstown, as mem. Keedy & Lane, 1915-18; atty. U.S. Fuel Administration, Washington, D.C., 1917-18; capt. J.A.G.D., U.S. Army, 1918-19; spl. dep. atty. gen. State of Del., 1926-28; mem. Keedy & Duane, Wilmington, Del., 1931—; atty. and dir. Industrial Trust Co.; atty. The Corp. Trust Co., N.Y. City. Republican. Episcopalian. Editor: Delaware Corporation Law and Equity Practice, 1931, 2d edit., 1934. Home: Wilmington, Del. Died May 15, 1934.

KEEFE, Daniel J., labor leader; b. South Chicago, Sept. 1855. Began work in shingle mill at 8 yrs. of age; later became lumber handler and longshoreman. Pres. Lumber Unloaders' Assn., 1882; pres. Internat. Longshoremen, Marine and Transport Workers' Assn., 1893—, with exception of 2 yrs.; an original mem. exec. com. Nat. Civic Fedn., 6th v.p. A. F. of L.; mem. Industrial Peace Commn., Washington, 1906; commr. gen. of immigration of U.S., Dec. 1, 1908-May 31, 1913. Died Jan. 2, 1929.

KEEFE, John William, surgeon; b. Worcester, Mass., Apr. 25, 1863; s. Denis and Alice (McGrath) K.; student U. of Mich. Dept. of Medicine and Surgery, 1882-83; M.D., Univ. Med. Coll. (New York U.), 1884; LL.D., Manhattan College, N.Y. City, 1909, Providence (R.I.) College, 1932; m. Statia Sherman Maher, Apr. 24, 1895; children—Alice Sherman, Helen Constance, Gertrude Sherman, Mary Ruth. Interne Bellevue Hosp., N.Y. City, 1884-86; practiced in Providence, R.I., 1886—; surgeon in chief to The John W. Keefe Surgery. Maj. Med. R.C. Fellow Am. Coll. Surgeons, N.E. Surg. Soc. (pres. 1924-25), Am. Assn. Obstetricians, Gynecologists and Abdominal Surgeons (pres. 1916-17). Home: Providence, R.I. Died Aug. 3, 1935.

KEELER, Charles (Augustus), author; b. Milwaukee, Wis., Oct. 7, 1871; s. James and Harriet Newell (Green) K.; ed. pub. and pvt. schs., Milwaukee and New York, and Berkeley (Calif.) High Sch.; spl. course U. of Calif.; m. Louise Mapes Bunnell, Oct. 14, 1893 (died 1907); children—Merodine, Leonarde, Eloise Keeler; m. 2d, Ormeida Curtis

Harrison, June 26, 1921. Voyage around Cape Horn, Feb.-June 1893, with Harriman expdn. to Alaska, 1899; voyage to South Seas—Tahiti, New Zealand, Australia, Samoa, Hawaiian Islands—1900-01; formerly dir. museum of Calif. Acad. Sciences. Mem. Philos. Union, Berkeley, Calif. Founder of the Cosmic Society, 1925, and managing director of same. Author: San Francisco and Thereabout, 1902; San Francisco Through Earthquake and Fire, 1906; The Victory (poems), 1916; Sequoia Sonnets, 1919; An Epitome of Cosmic Religion, 1925. Around the World tour recital of original poems, Japan, China, India and Europe, 1912-13. Home: Berkeley, Calif. Died July 31, 1937.

KEELER, Fred Lockwood, educator; b. Sharon Tp., Washtenaw Co., Mich., July 4, 1872; s. Mathew E. and Annie (Lockwood) K.; B.S., U. of Mich., 1893; post-grad. work, same, 1893-94; student summer sessions, U. of Chicago; m. Bertina B. Bliss, Nov. 29, 1894. Prin. high sch., Houghton, Mich., 1894-95; head dept. science, Central Mich. Normal Sch., Mt. Pleasant, 1895-1908; department supt. pub. instrn., Mich., 1908-13; apptd. supt. pub. instrn. to fill vacancy, by Gov. Ferris, Nov. 1913, and elected for terms 1915-19. V.p. Isabella County State Bank, Mt. Pleasant, Mich. Republican. Presbyn. Mason. Home: Lansing, Mich. Died Apr. 4, 1919.

KEELER, Harriet Louise, teacher; b. at S. Kortright, N.Y., 1846; d. Burr and Elizabeth (Barlow) K.; A.B., Oberlin, 1870 (hon. A.M., 1900; LL.D., Western Reserve U., 1913); supt. primary instrn. in pub. schs. of Cleveland, 1871-79; teacher in Central High Sch., Cleveland, 1879-1909; supt. pub. schs., Jan. 1912-Sept. 1912. Author: Wild Flowers of Early Spring, 1894; Our Native Trees, 1900; Our Northern Shrubs, 1903; High School English (Keeler and Adams), 1906; Our Garden Flowers, 1910; The Life of Adelia A. Field Johnston, 1912; Ethical Readings from the Bible (Keeler and Wild), 1915; Our Early Wild Flowers, 1916; Wayside Flowers of Summer, 1917. Home: Cleveland, O. Died 1921.

KEELER, James Edward, astronomer; b. La Salle, Ill., Sept. 10, 1857; ed. public schools; grad. Johns Hopkins, 1881 (Sc.D., Univ. of Calif.). Was with Mt. Whitney (Calif.) expedition for study of solar physics, 1881. Studied in Heidelberg and Berlin; asst. astronomer, 1886-88, astronomer, 1888-89, Lick Observatory; dir. Allegheny Observatory, 1889-98; dir. Lick Observatory, June 1898—. Foreign asso. Royal Astronomical Soc., etc.; m. Cora S. Matthews, June 16, 1891. Home: Mt. Hamilton, Calif. Died 1900.

KEELER, John Everett, judge; b. Stamford, Conn., Feb. 26, 1856; s. Samuel Smith and Mary Jane (June) K.; B.A., Yale, 1877; read law in office of Calvin G. Child, of Stamford; m. Alice Horne, Oct. 14, 1885; children—Ralph, Margery. Admitted to Conn. bar, 1879, and began practice in Stamford; judge of Borough Court, 1883-87; mem. Hart & Keeler, 1887-1906, Keeler & Durey, 1913-18; judge Superior Court of Conn., 1918-22; asso. justice Supreme Court of Conn., 1922—. Trustee Ferguson Library, Stamford Hosp. Republican. Episcopalian. Home: Stamford, Conn. Died May 28, 1927.

KEELEY, James, vice pres. of The Pullman Co.; b. London, Eng., Oct. 14, 1867; common school edn.; m. Gertrude E. Small, June 5, 1895. Was reporter, night city editor, city editor, Chicago Tribune for several yrs. prior to 1898; mng. editor and gen. mgr. Chicago Tribune until 1914; editor Chicago Herald, 1914-18; asst. to pres., later vice pres. The Pullman Company. Died June 7, 1934.

KEELEY, Leslie E., M.D.; pres. The Leslie E. Keeley Co.; grad. Rush Med. Coll., Chicago, 1864; founder of the Keeley Institute, Dwight, Ill., system for the treatment and cure of inebriety and the use of narcotic drugs, commonly known as the "Keeley Cure." Died 1900.

KEEN, Gregory Bernard, curator; b. Phila., Mar. 3, 1844; s. Joseph Swift and Lucy Ann (Hutton) K.; A.B., U. of Pa., 1861, A.M., 1864; grad. P.E. Div. Sch., Phila., 1866; LL.D., Gustavus Adolphus Coll., 1907; m. Stella Maria Stokes (née Watson), June 29, 1885; children—John Francis Gregory, Joseph Bernard. P.E. clergyman, 1866-68; became a Catholic, 1868; prof. mathematics, Theol. Sem. of St. Charles Borromeo, 1871-72. Corr. sec., 1880-98, librarian, 1898-1903, curator, 1903—, Hist. Soc. of Pa.; librarian U. of Pa., 1887-97. Del. Columbian Catholic Congress, 1893; vice-pres. Colonial Soc. of Pa.; historian of Pa. Soc. Colonial Wars; pres. Swedish Colonial Society. Author: The Descendants of Jöran Kyn of New Sweden, 1913. Home: Bryn Mawr, Pa. Died Apr. 30, 1930.

KEEN, William Williams, surgeon; b. Phila., Jan. 19, 1837; s. William W. and Susan (Budd) K.; A.M., Brown U., 1859; M.D., Jefferson Med. Coll., Phila., 1862, Sc.D., 1912; LL.D., Brown, 1891, Northwestern, and Toronto, 1903, Edinburgh U., 1905, Yale, 1906, St. Andrews U., 1911, and U. of Pa., 1919; Ph.D., U. of Upsala, 1907; Sc.D., Harvard, 1920; Dr., honoris causa, U. of Paris, 1923; asst. surgeon 5th Mass. Regt., 1861; acting asst. surgeon U.S.A., 1862-64; studied in Europe, 1864-66; m. Emma Corinna Borden, 1867 (died 1886); children—Corinne (Mrs. Walter J. Freeman), Florence, Dora (Mrs. Geo. W. Handy), Margaret (Mrs. Howard Butcher, Jr.). In practice at Phila., 1866—; conducted Phila. Sch. of Anatomy, 1866-75; lecturer pathol. anatomy, Jefferson Med. Coll., 1866-75; prof. artistic anatomy, Pa. Acad. Fine Arts, 1876-89; prof. surgery, Woman's Med. Coll., 1884-89; prof. surgery, 1889-1907, prof. emeritus, 1907, Jefferson Med. Coll. 1st lt. med. R.C. U.S.A., Dec. 28, 1909; maj., Apr. 16, 1917; hon. disch., Mar. 18, 1918. Mem. Nat. Research Council during World War. Trustee and fellow Brown U., 1873—. Pres. Am. Surg. Assn., 1899, A.M.A., 1900, Coll. Physicians, Philadelphia, 1900-01, Internat. Congress of Surgery, Paris, 1920, Congress Am. Physicians and Surgeons, 1903, Am. Philos. Soc., 1907-17; hon. fellow Royal College of Surgeons of England, Edinburgh, Italian Surgical Soc., Royal College of Surgeons in Ireland, American Coll. Surgeons; asso. fellow Am. Acad. Arts and Sciences; hon. fellow Boston Surg. Soc. (awarded Bigelow gold medal); awarded Colver-Rosenberger medal of honor, Brown U.; gold medal by Pennsylvania Soc. of New York. Officer Order of the Crown of Belgium, 1920; Officier Légion d'Honneur, France, 1923. Author: Surgical Complications and Sequels of Typhoid Fever, 1898; Animal Experimentation and Medical Progress, 1914; Treatment of War Wounds, 1917; Surgical Operations on President Cleveland, 1917. Editor: Heath's Practical Anatomy, 1870; Diagrams of the Nerves of the Human Body, by W. H. Flower, 1872; American Health Primers, 1879-80; Holden's Medical and Surgical Landmarks, 1881; Gray's Anatomy, 1887; American Text-Book of Surgery, 1892, 1903; I Believe in God and in Evolution, 1922; Everlasting Life, 1924; Keen's System of Surgery, 8 vols., 1906-21. Home: Philadelphia, Pa. Died June 7, 1932.

KEENA, James Trafton, lawyer, banker; b. Ogdensburg, N.Y., Nov. 19, 1850; s. John C. and Margaret (Trafton) K.; ed. Christian Brothers Coll., Buffalo, N.Y., and spl. course U. of Mich.; m. Henrietta M. Boyle, May 1874 (died 1904); m. 2d, Mabel Smith, May 1909. Admitted to Mich. bar, 1874, and began practice with firm of Atkinson & Atkinson; formed Trowbridge & Keena, later Keena & Lightner, now Keena, Lightner, Oxtoby & Hanley; retired from practice 1914, upon being elected v.p. Peoples State Bank; elected pres. same bank, 1916, chmn. bd., 1919; dir. and mem. exec. com. Standard Accident Ins. Co.; dir. Standard Loan & Investment Co., Union Trust Co. Served in U.S. Navy 3 yrs. Home: Detroit, Mich. Died Jan. 8, 1924.

KEENAN, Frank, actor; b. Dubuque, Ia., Apr. 8, 1858; s. Owen and Frances (Kelly) K.; ed. Boston Coll.; m. Katherine Agnes Long, of St. John, N.B.; children—Mrs. Frances Sloan, Mrs. Hilda Wynn. First appeared on stage in Boston, 1880; mem. Boston Museum Stock Co., later in New York for many yrs., and touring in U.S.; played in "The Capitol," "The Christian," "The Girl of the Golden West," as Cassius, in "Julius Cæsar," as Rip Van Winkle, as leading character in "John Ferguson"; starred in "Hearts of Oak," "McKenna's Flirtation," "A Texas Steer," "A Poor Relative," "The Heights," "The Pawn," "The Warrens of Virginia," etc.; directed original productions of "The Christian," "The King's Musketeers," "Such a Little Queen," and many others. Home: Hollywood, Calif. Died Feb. 24, 1929.

KEENAN, Thomas Johnston, journalist, real estate; b. Pittsburgh, Pa., Nov. 22, 1859; s. Thomas Johnston and Sophie Latimer (Gaskell) K.; ed. Western U. of Pa. (now U. of Pittsburgh). Founded, 1884, and editor and publisher, 1884-1901, Pittsburgh Press. Noted as an organizer and executive; interested in numerous charities. Organized, 1891, Internat. League Press Clubs; founder and 1st pres. Publishers' Press Assn. (now the United Press). Chmn. com., 1910-11, which secured a new charter for the city of Pittsburgh from the legislature. Raised $40,000 by popular subscription and built the Pittsburgh Newsboys' Home; erected by same means a monument to Stephen C. Foster, Pittsburgh. Home: Pittsburgh, Pa. Died Oct. 31, 1927.

KEENE, Amor Frederick, mining engr.; b. Minneapolis, Minn., Dec. 18, 1879; s. Albin and Maria (Jeschka) Kuehn; ed. pub. and high schs., Minneapolis; E.M., U. of Minn., 1904; m. Muriel Leslie Carmody, Jan. 2, 1915; 1 son, Frederick Arthur. Gen. mining engring., U.S. Peru, Chile and Mexico, 1904-09; consulting practice, New York, 1909-11, London, 1911-18, New York and London, 1919—; v.p. Mego Corp.; dir. Internat. Marble Corp. Mem. Am. Relief Com., London, 1914; mem. Col. House Com., Sept. 1918-Feb. 1919, on World's mineral resources. Spl. commendation from Pres. Wilson and Ambassador Walter Hines Page for work done for Am. Relief Commrs. in London. Republican. Lutheran. Home: Douglaston, N.Y. Died Sept. 25, 1940.

KEENE, Carter Brewster, lawyer; b. Freedom, Me., July 3, 1868; s. Orris Hewitt and Abbie Susan (Carter) K.; Me. Wesleyan Sem., Kents Hill; LL.B., Columbian (now George Washington) U., 1895, LL.M., 1896. Post office insp., 1901-10; insp. in charge Washington div., 1910-Feb. 16, 1913; chief post office insp., Feb. 17-June 30, 1913; dir. Postal Savings System, July 1, 1913-21. Democrat. Trustee Me. Wesleyan Sem. Mem. bar U.S. Supreme Ct. Mason. Home: Chevy Chase, Md. Died Apr. 2, 1938.

KEENE, Edward Spencer, college prof.; b. Rock Island, Ill., Oct. 8, 1864; s. Philip H. and Margaret K. (Baxter) K.; B.S., U. of Ill., 1890 (M.E., 1912); m. Myrtle Pearman, Sept. 1893; children—Margaret Elizabeth, Dorothy Ann, Rebecca Reed, Philip Edward, Virginia Frances. Instr. mech. engring., U. of Ill., 1890-92; prof. mech. engring., 1892-1900, dean engring. and physics, 1900-18, dean Sch. of Mechanic Arts, 1918—, acting pres., 1921, N.Dak. Agrl. College. Mason. Author: Mechanics of the Household, 1918. Home: Fargo, N.Dak. Died Aug. 1928.

KEENE, Floyd Elwood, gynecologist; b. Kewanee, Ill., Oct. 9, 1881; s. John Elam and Lalla Rooke (Robinson) K.; grad. high sch., Peoria, Ill., 1899; M.D., U. of Pa., 1904; m. Martha Bussiere, of Chatel Guyon, France, Jan. 27, 1919; children—Martha Jeannette, John Clark. Began practice at Phila., Pa., 1906; instr., later asso. in gynecology, U. of Pa., 1908-27, William Goodell prof. gynecology, 1927—; gynecologist University Hosp.; consulting gynecologist Chestnut Hill, Bryn Mawr and Abington Memorial hospitals. Served as major Medical Corps, U.S. Army, Base Hosp. No. 20, 1917-19. Fellow Am. Gynecol. Society (pres. 1932), Am. Coll. Surgeons, Phila. Coll. Physicians, Phila. Acad. Surgery. Republican. Conglist. Home: Wynnewood, Pa. Died Nov. 15, 1938.

KEENE, James Robert, stockbroker, etc.; b. London, Eng., 1838; went with family to Calif., 1852; became miner in Calif. and Nev., later speculator in mining stocks, San Francisco; accumulated $6,000,000 during "bonanza" period of the 70's; was pres. San Francisco Stock Exchange; since 1877 an operator on Wall St., New York. Pres. U.S. Graphotype Co.; v.p. Westchester Racing Assn. Home: Cedarhurst, L.I., N.Y. Died Jan. 3, 1913.

KEENER, John Christian, M.E. Ch., So., bishop, 1870—; b. Baltimore, Feb. 7, 1819; grad. Wesleyan, Conn., 1835 (D.D., 1854; LL.D., 1880); in business, Baltimore, 1835-41; entered Methodist ministry, 1841; preached in Ala., 1841-48; New Orleans, pastor and presiding elder, 1848-61; supt. chaplains C.S.A., west of Miss. river, 1861-64; presiding elder, New Orleans, and editor New Orleans Christian Advocate, 1865-70; founded a mission in Mexico, 1873. Author: The Post Oak Circuit; Studies of Bible Truths, 1899; The Garden of Eden and the Flood, 1900, etc. Home: New Orleans, La. Deceased.

KEENER, Walter Ney, newspaper editor; b. Lincoln Co., N.C., Aug. 2, 1880; s. Elijah Washington and Rhoda Caroline (Loftin) K.; A.B., Wake Forest (N.C.) Coll., 1902, LL.B., 1903; m. Mamie E. Dunn, Feb. 2, 1904 (died 1918); children—Walter Ney, John Washington, Edward Bruce; m. 2d, Ruth Duhling, Jan. 7, 1922. Editor Lincoln County News, Lincolnton, N.C., 1904-07; city editor Raleigh Times, 1909-11; mng. editor Durham Sun, 1912-13; city editor Charlotte Chronicle, 1913-14; mng. editor High Point Enterprise, 1914-16; editor Wilmington Dispatch, 1917-18, Durham Morning Herald, 1918-29; editor in chief latter and Durham Evening Sun, 1929—. Mem. N.C. Ho. of Rep., 1907-08. Mem. exec. com. N.C. State Sch. for Blind and Deaf. Democrat. Presbyn. Mason. Home: Durham, N.C. Died Nov. 25, 1932.

KEENER, William Albert, lawyer; b. Augusta, Ga., Mar. 10, 1856; s. Henry and Isabella K.; A.B., Emory Coll., Ga., 1874; LL.B., Harvard, 1877; (LL.D., Western U. of Pa., 1895); m. Frances McLeod Smith, July 16, 1878. Admitted to N.Y. bar, 1879; justice Supreme Ct. of N.Y.; asst. prof. law, 1883-88, Story prof., 1888-90, Harvard; prof. law, 1890-92, Kent prof. law, 1892-1902, dean Law Sch., 1891-1901, Columbia. Author: Treatise on Quasi-Contracts. Editor: Cases on Contracts; Cases on Equity Jurisdiction; Cases on Quasi-Contracts; Cases on Corporations. Died Apr. 18, 1913.

KEEP, Albert, ry. official; b. Homer, N.Y., Apr. 30, 1826; s. Chauncey and Prudence (Wolcott) K.; ed. Cortland Acad., Homer, N.Y.; m. Harriet S. Gunn, Sept. 3, 1861. Dir., 1873— (pres. 1873-87, chmn. bd. dirs., 1887-1901), C.&N.W. Ry. Co., retired from chmnship, 1901; dir. Lake Shore & Mich. So. Ry. Co., 1865-83. Dir. Crerar Library; trustee Chicago Home for Incurables; trustee Merchants' Loan & Trust Co. Home: Chicago, Ill. Died 1907.

KEEP, Charles Hallam, banker; b. Lockport, N.Y., Feb. 26, 1861; s. Charles and Caroline (Crockett) K.; A.B., Harvard, 1882, LL.B., 1885; m. Margaret Turner Williams, May 17, 1894; children—Eleanor, Mrs. Martha G. Shipley. Practiced law at Buffalo, 1885-1903; asst. sec. of the treasury, 1903-07; supt. banks, N.Y. State Banking Dept., Jan.-June 1907; mem. N.Y. Pub. Service Commn., 1907-08; pres. Knickerbocker Trust Co., New York, 1908-12; chmn. bd. Columbia Trust Co., 1912-23. Republican. Home: New York, N.Y. Died Aug. 30, 1941.

KEEP, Chauncey, capitalist; b. Whitewater, Wis., Aug. 20, 1853; s. Henry and Phebe (McCluer) K.; ed. pub. schs., Chicago; m. Mary H. Blair, Jan. 19, 1888; children—Margaret (Mrs. James C. Hutchins), Henry Blair (killed in action in France), Katharine Frances (Mrs. Robert A. Gardner). Identified with numerous large interests; v.p. Ill. Merchants Trust Co. (Chicago); trustee U.S. Trust Co. (New York); trustee estate of Marshall Field. Republican. Episcopalian. Home: Chicago, Ill. Died Aug. 12, 1929.

KEEP, Robert Porter, educator; b. Farmington, Conn., Apr. 26, 1844; s. Rev. John R. and Rebecca (Porter) K.; grad. Yale, 1865 (Ph.D., 1869). U.S. consul, Piræus, Athens, Greece, 1869-71; teacher of Greek, Williston Sem., Easthampton, Mass., 1876-85; prin. Norwich Free Acad., 1885-1903. Author: Homeric Dictionary; Stories from Herodotus and Book Seventh of the History; Essential Uses of the Moods in Greek and Latin; Books I-VI of the Iliad, with Notes and Vocabulary; Greek Lessons; etc. Home: Farmington, Conn. Died 1904.

KEEP, William John, mfr.; b. Oberlin, O., June 3, 1842; s. Rev. Theodore John and Mary A. (Thomson) K.; student Oberlin, 1858-64; C.E., Union Coll., 1865; m. Frances Sarah, d. Dr. William Gates and Hannah (Stewart) Henderson, of Oberlin, May 22, 1866. Was corporal "Squirrel Hunters," 1862; stove manufacturer, 1865—; now of Mich. Stove Co.; also mfr. of testing machines. In 1885, discovered the relation between the shrinkage and the chemical composition of cast iron, which is named "Mechanical Analysis." Author: Cast Iron, 1902. Home: Detroit, Mich. Died Sept. 30, 1918.

KEESE, William Linn, author, business mgr.; b. New York, Feb. 25, 1835; s. late John and Elizabeth K.; ed. private schools; pursued a mercantile career; m. Helen K. Thorne, Oct. 4, 1864. Author: John Keese, Wit and Litterateur, 1883; William E. Burton, Actor, Author and Manager, 1885; William E. Burton, Sketch of Career Other than that of Actor, 1891; A Group of Comedians, 1901; The Siamese Twins and Other Poems, 1902. Home: Brooklyn, N.Y. Died 1904.

KEFFER, Charles Albert, horticulturist; b. Des Moines, Ia., June 11, 1861; s. S. B. and Rebecca (Kagey) K.; ed. Des Moines High Sch.; student Ia. Agrl. Coll., 1881-83; unmarried. Prof. horticulture and forestry, S.D. Agrl. Coll., 1887-91, U. of Agrl., 1891-95; asst. chief forestry div., U.S. Dept. Mo., 1895-99; prof. agr. and horticulture, N.M. Agr. Coll., 1899; prof. horticulture, 1900-14, dir. div. of extension Coll. of Agr., U. of Tenn., 1914—. Died Dec. 31, 1935.

KEIFER, J(oseph) Warren, lawyer, soldier; b. Clark County, O., Jan. 30, 1836; s. Joseph and Mary (Smith) K.; ed. Antioch Coll.; m. Eliza Stout, Mar. 22, 1860 (died 1899); children—Joseph Warren, William White, Horace Charles (dec.), Margarette Eliza (dec.). In law practice at Springfield, O., 1858; pres. Lagonda Nat. Bank, 1873-1927. Maj. 3d Ohio Inf., Apr. 27, 1861; lt. col., Feb. 12, 1862; col. 110th Ohio Inf., Sept. 30, 1862; bvtd.: brig. gen. vols., Oct. 19, 1864, "for gallant and meritorious services in battles of Opequan, Fisher's Hill and Middletown, Va."; maj. gen. vols., Apr. 9, 1865, for same, during campaign ending with surrender of Gen. Lee; wounded 4 times; hon. mustered out, June 27, 1865; apptd. lt. col., 26th U.S. Inf., Nov. 30, 1866, but declined; maj. gen. vols., June 9, 1898-May 12, 1899, Spanish-Am. War. Mem. Ohio Senate, 1868-69; mem. 45th to 48th (speaker 47th, 1881-83) Congresses (1877-85), and 59th to 61st Congresses (1905-11), 7th Ohio Dist. Trustee Ohio Soldiers' and Sailors' Orphans' Home, 1870-78, 1903-04, Antioch Coll., 1873—. Nat. mem. Perry's Victory Centennial Commn., 1911—; life member Interparliamentary Peace Conf. of the World, Paris, 1912. Author: Slavery and Four Years of War, 1900. Home: Springfield, O. Died April 22, 1932.

KEILEY, Benjamin J., bishop; b. Petersburg, Va., Oct. 13, 1847; studied Am. Coll., Rome, Italy. Ordained R.C. priest, Dec. 31, 1873; pastor New Castle and Wilmington, Del., 1873-86, Atlanta, Ga., 1886-96, Savannah, Ga., 1896-1900; consecrated bishop of Savannah, June 3, 1900; resigned the See of Savannah, Feb. 1923, on account of loss of sight; apptd. titular bishop of Scilium, 1923. Home: Atlanta, Ga. Died June 17, 1925.

KEILLER, William, M.D.; b. Midlothian, Scotland, July 4, 1861; s. Mathewson and Hannah (Napier) K.; ed. in Scotland at Perth Acad., 1868-69, 1870-77, Montrose Acad., 1869-70, U. of Edinburgh, 1877-81 (academic), med. dept. same and Royal Coll. of Surgeons, Edinburgh, 1885-88, licentiate of Royal Coll. of Phys. and Surg., Edinburgh, 1888, fellow by exam., 1891, Royal Coll. Surg., Edinburgh; licentiate Faculty Phys. and Surg., Glasgow; m. Eliza Henrietta McLaughlin, Mar. 6, 1883 (Died 1894); children—Mabel Mathewson, Eric William (dec.), Violet Hannah, William Henry (dec.); m. 2d, Jane Julia McLaughlin, June 27, 1895; children—Thomas Mitchell, Eliza Margaret. Lecturer anatomy, Sch. of Medicine, Edinburgh, 1889-91; prof. anatomy, U. of Tex., Oct. 1891—, also dean medical br. of Univ., 1923—. Author: Nerve Tracts of the Brain and Cord and Applied Neurology, 1927. Joint author: Text-book on Anatomy by American Authors, 1899. Home: Galveston, Tex. Died Feb. 22, 1931.

KEISTER, Abraham L., congressman; b. Fayette Co., Pa., Sept. 10, 1852; B.S., Otterbein U., 1874; law student, 1876-78. Practiced law at Columbus, O., for a short time; mfr. of coke, Fayette Co., Pa., 1882—. Mem. 63d and 64th Congresses (1913-17), 22d Pa. Dist. Republican. Home: Scottdale, Pa. Died May 28, 1917.

KEITH, Arthur Monroe, lawyer; b. Roxbury, Mass., July 9, 1852; s. James Monroe and Adeline Wetherbee (Clapp) K.; A.B., Harvard, 1874; LL.B., Boston U., 1876; m. Helen K. Benchley, June 12, 1884. Admitted to Boston bar, June 1876; practiced Boston 2 yrs.; in Minneapolis, Nov. 1878—; now sr. mem. Keith, Kingman, Cross & Wallace; v.p. Minn. Loan & Trust Co. Home: Minneapolis, Minn. Died 1918.

KEITH, Benjamin Franklin, theatre mgr.; b. Hillsboro Bridge, N.H.; ed. N.H. dist. schs. Prop. of a circus until 1885; became part owner of the Gaiety Theatre, Boston, and began the continuous performance theatre, 1885; with F. F. Proctor formed the Keith & Proctor Amusement Co., 1906, operating many theaters throughout the U.S. Pres. United Booking Office of America. Home: Brookline, Mass. Died Mar. 26, 1914.

KEITH, Charles Penrose, author; b. Phila., Mar. 15, 1854; s. Washington and Anne M. (Penrose) K.; B.S., U. of Pa., 1873, Litt.D., 1919; admitted to bar, 1877; m. Elizabeth Harvey Wister, Dec. 18, 1883. Clerk in Title Ins. Co., 10 yrs.; chief clerk U.S. Appraiser's Office, 1889-93. Author: The Provincial Councillors of Pennsylvania, Between 1733 and 1776, and Their Descendants, 1883; The Ancestry of Benjamin Harrison, and Notes on Families Related, 1893; Chronicles of Pennsylvania from the English Revolution to the Peace of Aix-la-Chapelle (1688-1748), 1917. Home: Philadelphia, Pa. Died Apr. 23, 1939.

KEITH, David, capitalist; b. Mabou, Cape Breton Island, N.S., May 27, 1847; s. John and Margaret (Ness) K.; ed. pub. schs.; m. Mary Ferguson. Ran away to sea in boyhood; landed in Calif., 1867, and later employed in constrn. of S.P. R.R., nr. Reno, Nev.; engaged in mining on Comstock Lode for a number of yrs.; went to Park City, Utah, 1883, and became foreman, later supt. of Ontario Mine No. 3; asso. with Thomas Kearns and others in leasing mining claims, and developed the celebrated Silver King Mine; now pres. Silver King Coalition Mines Co., 1st Nat. Bank, Park City. Extensive owner of real estate in Salt Lake City, and of timber lands. Home: Salt Lake City, Utah. Died Apr. 1918.

KEITH, Dora Wheeler, artist; b. Jamaica, L.I., Mar. 12, 1857; ed. in U.S., Germany and Paris; pupil of William Chase, New York. Won Prang prizes 2 consecutive yrs.; studied 2 yrs. in Paris, designed in stained glass, and other decorative work, book illustrations, etc.; m. Boudinot Keith (dec.); children—Elisha Boudinot (dec.), Lois Pickering (wife of C. V. Simpson, U.S.A.). Specialty is portraits; has painted Samuel L. Clemens, Frank Stockton, Mrs. Burnett, Charles Dudley Warner, Col. John Hay, William Dean Howells, etc. A.N.A., 1906. Home: New York, N.Y. Died Dec. 27, 1940.

KEITH, Elbridge G., bank pres.; b. Barre, Vt., July 16, 1840; s. Martin K.; ed. Barre and Newbury sems., Vt.; m. Harriet S. Hall. Mem. Keith Bros., 1865; mem. bd. edn., Chicago, 1877-84; pres. Union League Club, 1883; pres. Commercial Club, 1892; pres. Metropolitan Nat. Bank from 1884 to 1902, Clearing House, 1888; pres. Bankers' Club, 1890; pres. Chicago Title & Trust Co., 1902. Republican. Home: Chicago, Ill. Died 1905.

KEITH, George Eldon, mfr.; b. Brockton, Mass., Feb. 8, 1850; s. Franklin and Betsey (Bailey) K.; ed. Brockton High Sch.; m. Anna G. Reed, Oct. 23, 1877; m. 2d, Elizabeth W. Archibald, 1908. Worked in shoe factory of father, 1863-74; mfr. of shoes, 1874—(employing 5,000 persons); pres. Brockton Nat. Bank; dir. Old Colony Trust Co. (Boston), United Shoe Machinery Co. Republican. Conglist. Home: Brockton, Mass. Died Dec. 9, 1920.

KEITH, James, judge; b. Fauquier Co., Va., Sept. 1839; s. Isham and Juliet (Chilton) K.; ed. schs. of Fauquier Co. and U. of Va.; m. Miss Morson, Feb. 1887. Practiced at Warrenton, Va., until becoming judge, 1870; pres. Supreme Ct. of Appeals of Va., 1895-1916. Home: Richmond, Va. Died Jan. 2, 1918.

KEITH, John Alexander Hull, state supt. schs.; b. Homer, Ill., Nov. 28, 1869; s. Harvey Hamilton and Juliet Carter (Hull) K.; grad. Ill. State Normal U., 1894; A.B., Harvard, 1899, A.M., 1900; Pd.D., Miami U., 1919; Ed.D., Temple U., 1928; LL.D., Grove City Coll., 1929; m. Rebecca A. Foley, June 7, 1900; children—Mary Lee, John A. H. Teacher co. and village schs., 1889-92, Model Sch., Ill. State Normal U., 1894-96; prof. pedagogy and asst. in psychology, Northern Ill. State Normal Sch., 1899-1906; head of training dept., Ill. State Normal U., 1906-07; pres. State Normal Sch., Oshkosh, Wis., Nov. 1, 1907-Sept. 1, 1917; prin. Normal Sch., Indiana, Pa., 1917-27; supt. pub. instrn., Pa., Jan. 24, 1927—. Author: Elementary Education, Its Processes and Problems, 1905. Joint author: The Nation and The Schools, 1919; An Introduction to Teaching, 1923. Died Feb. 22, 1931.

KEITH, Minor Cooper, capitalist; b. Brooklyn, N.Y., Jan. 19, 1848; s. Minor Hubbell and Emily (Meiggs) K.; ed. pvt. schs.; m. Cristina, d. José Maria Castro, pres. Republic of Costa Rica, Oct. 31, 1883. In lumber business until 1870; in cattle business, Tex., 2 yrs.; became identified with ry. construction in Costa Rica, 1872, and later with pub. improvements there; organized United Fruit Co., 1899; v.p. Premier Gold Mining Co.; pres. Atlanta & St. Andrews Bay Ry. Co., St. Andrews Bay Lumber Co., Guatemala Central R.R. Co., Internat. Ry. of Central America; dir. Empire Trust Co. Fellow Royal Geog. Soc. Trustee Museum of Am. Indian, Heye Foundation. Republican. Episcopalian. Died June 14, 1929.

KEITH, Nathaniel Shepard, electro-metallurgist; b. Boston, July 14, 1838; s. Bethuel (M.D.) and Elizabeth P. K.; ed. Dover, N.H., and New York; tech. edn. in mining and elec. engring.; ed. as physician but never practiced. Mining and metallurgical engr. in Colorado, 1860-69; then elec. and electro-metall. engr.; inventor, with many patents in these lines; scientific editor Electrical World, 1884-85. Mfr. elec. appliances, as applied to mining and metallurgy, San Francisco, 1884-93; expert in same line in England till 1897. Organizer and 1st sec. Am. Inst. E.E., 1884. Author: Magnetic and Dynamo-Electric Machines, 1884. Sec.-treas. Am. Venture & Mines Corp. and officer other cos. Home: Philadelphia, Pa. Died Jan. 28, 1925.

KEITH, William, artist; b. Aberdeenshire, Scotland, 1839; s. William and Elizabeth (Bruce) K.; ed. in Scotland; studied portrait painting in Munich; came to New York, 1851, and was engaged as engraver until 1859; removed to Calif., 1859 and worked first as an engraver and later as landscape painter. Home: Berkeley, Calif. Died 1911.

KELCEY, Herbert, actor; b. London, Eng., Oct. 10, 1856; ed. pvtly. First appearance in "Flirtation," at Brighton, Eng., 1880; later played leading parts in Drury Lane Theatre and Royalty Theatre; came to U.S., 1882, with Lester Wallack, in "Taken from Life"; leading man in Frohman's Lyceum Co., and other cos.; later starred with Effie Shannon with their own company. Died July 10, 1917.

KELHAM, George William, architect; b. Manchester, Mass., May 15, 1871; s. Daniel, Jr., and Mary I. (Brown) K.; studied architecture at Harvard, Paris and Rome; m. Katharine Taft Bruce, Apr. 23, 1902; 1 son, Bruce. Practiced in N.Y. City, 1898-1906. San Francisco, 1906—; chief Dept. of Architecture, Panama P.I. Expn., 1912-15; supervising architect U. of Calif. Trustee San Francisco Pub. Library; chmn. Archtl. Commn., San Francisco Bay Expn. Served as mem. Co. K, 7th Regt. N.G. N.Y. Home: San Francisco, Calif. Died Dec. 7, 1936.

KELLAR, Harry, public entertainer; b. Erie, Pa., July 11, 1849; s. Francis P. and Elizabeth (Anthony) K.; grad. Painesville (O.) High Sch., 1866; m. Eva Medley, of Melbourne, Australia, Nov. 1, 1887 (dec.). When a young man was asst. to the "Fakir of Ava," the magician; joined Davenport Brothers, spirit mediums, as business mgr., 1867; with Fay toured S. America and Mexico as Fay & Kellar, 1871-73; with Ling Look and Yamadura, under name of Kellar, Ling Look & Yamadura, royal illusionists, played through S. America, Africa, Australia, India, China, Philippine Islands and Japan (Ling Look and Yamadura died in China, 1877); then with J. H. Cunard, as Kellar & Cunard; traveled 5 yrs. through India, Burmah, Siam, Java, Persia, Asia Minor, Egypt and Mediterranean ports; performed in leading Am. cities, 1884—. Died Mar. 10, 1922.

KELLEHER, Daniel, banker; b. Middleboro, Mass., Feb. 5, 1864; s. Daniel and Mary K.; A.B., Harvard, 1885; m. Elise C., d. Gen. Gilbert S. Meem, Apr. 26, 1894; children—Hugh Garland Meem, Campbell. Lived in Syracuse, N.Y., 1885-90; settled in Seattle, Wash., 1890, and engaged in practice of law; has devoted entire attention to banking, 1910—; chmn. bd. Seattle Nat. Bank; pres. Bank for Savings; v.p. Yukon Investment Co. Served as state dir. War Savings for Wash. and Alaska, World War. Democrat. Owner of "Dunmore-Mt. Airy," an estate of 2,400 acres in the Shenandoah Valley, Va., regarded as one of the finest estates in the U.S. Home: Seattle, Wash. Died Feb. 20, 1929.

KELLER, Arthur Ignatius, artist, illustrator; b. New York, July 4, 1867; s. Adam and Matilda (Spohr) K.; pupil Nat. Acad. Design, Prof. Wilmarth, New York, and Prof. Loeffts, Munich; m. Myra A. C. Hayes, June 20, 1894; m. 2d, Edith Livingston Mason, June 3, 1908. Awarded 1st class medal, Nat. Acad.; 1st Hallgarten composition prize; gold medal, Phila. Art Club; silver medal, Paris Expn., 1900; Evans water color prize, 1902; gold and silver medals, St. Louis Expn., 1904; gold medal, Panama P.I. Expn., San Francisco, 1915. Among his best works are: At Mass (bought by Munich Acad.), Lead Kindly Light, The Sisters, The Finishing Touches. Books illustrated: The First American, George Washington; Jerome—A Poor Man; Autobiography of a Quack; The Virginian; Bret Harte's Stories; The Law of the Land; The Clansman; The Legend of Sleepy Hollow, Irving; etc. Home: Riverdale-on-Hudson, N.Y. Died Dec. 2, 1924.

KELLER, Benjamin Franklin, judge; b. Boalsburg, Pa., Apr. 21, 1857; s. Henry and Margaret (Schneck) K.; B.S., Pa. State Coll., 1876, M.S., 1879; LL.B., Columbian (now George Washington) U., 1882 (LL.D., 1903); m. Mercy J. Baldy, Oct. 25, 1887. Admitted to bar, 1882; practiced at Bramwell, W.Va., 1891-1901; U.S. dist. judge, Southern Dist. of W.Va., 1901—. Republican. Home: Charleston, W.Va. Died Aug. 8, 1921.

KELLER, Harry Frederick, chemist, educator; b. Philadelphia, Dec. 15, 1861; s. William C. C. and Augusta Maria (Cramer) K.; B.S., U. of Pa., 1881; Ph. Nat. D., Strassburg, 1888; studied in chem. labs., of Prof. Fresenius, Wiesbaden, and U. of Strassburg; (Sc.D., U. of Pennsylvania, 1915); m. Henrietta M. Hexamer, 1892. Assayer and chemist various iron and metall. works, 1881—; asst. chemistry, 1883-86, instr. organic chemistry, 1888-90, U. of Pa.; prof. chemistry, Mich. Coll. Mines, 1890-92; prof. chemistry, 1892-1915, head dept. science, 1908-15, Central High Sch., Phila.; prin. Germantown (Pa.) High School, 1915—. Author: Experiments in General Chemistry (with E. F. Smith), 1892. Editor: Greene's Lessons in Chemistry, 1900; Am. edit. Wurtz's Modern Chemistry, 1902. Asst. dir. of allied bodies, Dept. of Pub. Safety of Pa., 1917. Home: Philadelphia, Pa. Died Feb. 5, 1924.

KELLER, John William, newspaperman; b. Bourbon Co., Ky., July 5, 1856; s. John Cantrill and Mary E. (Simpson) K.; ed. Yale until 1879; widower. Reporter, dramatic critic, editorial writer and mng. editor on Truth, Dramatic News, Times, World, Press, Recorder and Journal, New York, from 1879; pres. and commr. of Pub. Charities of New York, 1898-1902. Del. Dem. Nat. Conv., Kansas City, 1900, and was named in caucus as candidate of State of N.Y. for vice-presidential nomination. Pres. Dem. Club of New York, 1899-1900; mem. exec. com. Tammany Hall, 1898-1903; sachem of Tammany Soc., 1899-1903; chmn. speakers bur. of Tammany Hall, 1914, 15. Was pres. New York Press Club 2 terms. Wrote: Journalism as a Career, Forum, 1894; Pauperism and Municipal Charity, Arena, 1900; Charities, Ency. Americana, 1904. Home: New York, N.Y. Died 1919.

KELLER, Lewis Henry, clergyman, educator; b. Upper Sandusky, O., Feb. 24, 1858; s. Levi Washington and Margaret (Shriver) K.; ed. Valparaiso (Ind.) U., 1879-80; Adrian (Mich.) Coll., 1881-85; B.D., Yale Div. Sch., 1889; D.D., Ripon (Wis.) Coll., 1909; study U. of Chicago, summer 1910; m. Nettie Cutter Hardy, Apr. 17, 1890; children—Eleanor Hardy (wife of Homer M. Carter, M.D.), Fanny Margaret. Ordained ministry Congl. Ch., 1886; pastor successively Edgerton, Wis., Lyndale Ch., Minneapolis, Pilgrim Ch., Milwaukee, Fond du Lac, Wis., until 1912; gen. supt. Wis. Congl. Conf., 1912-18; supt. Congl. Extension Bds. of Southeast, 1918-25; pres. Atlanta Theol. Seminary, 1925-29. Moderator Wis. Congl. Conf., 1903; editor Wis. Congl. Ch. Life 6 yrs., Southern Conglist., 8 yrs.; as mem. exec. com. Nat. Anti-Saloon League assisted in adoption of 18th Amendment. Trustee Piedmont Coll., Thornsby (Ala.) Acad., Rural Life Acad., Star, N.C. Republican. Home: Penney Farms, Fla. Died Aug. 5, 1938.

KELLER, Oscar Edward, congressman; b. Helensville, Wis., July 30, 1878; ed. high sch. and course in dairying and agr., U. of Wis.; m. Alice Seebeck, 1911. Moved to Minn., 1901; mem. Assembly, City of St. Paul, 2 terms; elected commr. pub. utilities, St. Paul, 1916, 18; lost Rep. nomination for Congress but ran as independent candidate and elected 66th to 69th Congresses (1919-27), 4th Minn. Dist. Home: St. Paul, Minn. Died Nov. 22, 1927.

KELLER, Walter, organist, composer; b. Chicago, Ill., Feb. 23, 1873; s. Rev. William and Anna B. (Walther) K.; musical edn., Am. Conservatory of Music, Chicago, 1891-94, Royal Conservatory of Music, Leipzig, Germany, 1894-96, and under Frederic Grant Gleason; honorary Mus. Doc., De Paul Univ., 1916; m. Anna Marie Talbot, June 20, 1900; children—Robert Stewart, Charlotte Victoria, Richard Talbot, Margaret Anne; m. 2d, Helen Morris Barnes, Aug. 26, 1938. Instructor in piano, Northwestern U. School of Music, 1898-1904; organist St. Vincent's Church, Chicago, 1903-18; instr. in organ and theory, Sherwood Music Sch., 1906—, dir., 1911—; dean music dept., DePaul U., 1912-20; played organ concerts from Mass. to Calif., including Jamestown Expn. and Mormon Tabernacle, Salt Lake City; organist Fifth Ch. of Christ, Scientist, 1922-38. Fellow Am. Guild Organists (dean Ill. chapter, 1914-16). Republican. Mason. Composer of Synchronous Prelude and Fugue in F, also ch. music, works for orchestra, chorus, organ, piano, voice. Home: Chicago, Ill. Died July 8, 1940.

KELLER, William Simpson, civil engr.; b. Tuscumbia, Ala., Feb. 20, 1874; s. Arthur Henley and Sally (Simpson) K.; State Normal Coll., Florence, Ala., 2½ yrs.; B.C.E., U. of Ala., 1893; m. Aileen Moore, May 18, 1904 (died 1912); m. 2d, Annie Searcy, Dec. 1913. Practiced at Tuscumbia, 1893-1900; asst. engr. Shiloh Nat. Mil. Park, 1900-05; asst. engr., Apr.-Oct. 1905, engr., 1905-07, Madison Co. (Tenn.) Good Roads Commn.; supt. road construction, Office of Pub. Roads, U.S. Dept. Agr., 1907-10; co. engr., Dallas Co., Ala., 1910-11; state highway engr. of Ala., May 1, 1911—. Democrat. Presbyn. Home: Montgomery, Ala. Died Sept. 9, 1925.

KELLERMAN, Karl Frederic, bacteriologist; b. of American parents, Göttingen, Germany, Dec. 9, 1879; s. William Ashbrook and Stella V. (Dennis) K.; student Ohio State U.; S.B., Cornell, 1900; D.Sc., Kans. Agrl. Coll., 1923; m. Gertrude Hast, Aug. 17, 1905; 1 son, Karl Frederic. Asst. in botany, Cornell, 1900-01; asst. physiologist Bur. of Plant Industry, U.S. Dept. Agr., 1901-04; physiologist in charge lab. plant physiology, 1905-06; physiologist in charge soil bacteriology and water purification investigations, 1906-14; asst. chief of bur., 1914-17; asso. chief of bureau, 1917-33; chief Div. of Plant Disease Eradication and Control, Bureau of Entomology, 1933—. Organized the Journal of Agricultural Research, 1913, and was chmn. editorial com., 1913-24; mem. Federal Hort. Bd., 1914-24; organized, 1915, and thereafter directed the coöperative campaign of the Gulf States and Bur. of Plant Industry to eradicate citrus canker, one of the most contagious of all known diseases of citrus trees. Designated by President Wilson, 1917, as mem. Nat. Research Council, serving as sec. agrl. com., 1918—, as mem. Div. of Biology and Agr. and Div. of Federal Relations. Republican. Clubs: Cosmos, Columbia Country, Federal. Home: Washington, D.C. Died Aug. 30, 1934.

KELLERMAN, William Ashbrook, prof. botany, Ohio State Univ., 1891—; b. Ashville, O., May 1, 1850; s. D. K. and Ivy K.; grad. Cornell, 1874 (Ph.D., Univ. of Zürich, 1881); m. Stella Dennis, July 25, 1876. Taught natural science in Wis. State Normal School 5 yrs.; prof. botany and zoölogy, Kan. State Agrl. Coll., 8 yrs.; State botanist of Kan. and botanist Kan. Expt. Sta. 4 yrs.; founder and editor Journal of Mycology and Mycol. Bulletin. Author: Flora of Kansas; Elementary Botany; Phyto-Theca; Spring Flora of Ohio; etc. Home: Columbus, O. Died 1908.

KELLEY, Albert Wesley, univ. prof.; b. Attica, O., Jan. 8, 1853; s. Benjamin and Sarah (Rhodes) K.; A.B., Union U., 1876, later A.M.; student Yale, 1884; Ph.D., Otterbein U., 1892; M.D., Chicago Physio-Med. Coll., 1896; m. Harriet E. McCulloch, July 27, 1877. Prof. science, Fostoria (O.) Coll., 1879-86; prof. science and medicine, Battle Creek (Mich.) Coll., 1886-98, Union Coll., Neb., 1898-1902; dean and prof. natural science, Adrian (Mich.) Coll., 1902-06; prof. biology and dir. Steinheim Lab., Alfred (N.Y.) U., 1906-08; prof. chemistry, Milton (Wis.) Coll., Sept. 8, 1908—. Teacher and lecturer Chicago Physio-Med. Coll., 1893-98; lecturer pathology and gen. biology, Coll. of Medicine and Surgery, 1904-06. Died Apr. 18, 1916.

KELLEY, Alfred Kendall, lawyer; b. Cleveland, O., Sept. 22, 1891; s. Hermon Alfred and Florence (Kendall) K.; A.B., Yale, 1914; LL.B., Harvard, 1917; m. Elizabeth Vinson, Apr. 21, 1925; children—Alfred Kendall, Florence Katherine, Robert Ernest Vinson. Admitted to Ohio bar, 1917; associated with Hoyt, Dustin, Kelley, McKeehan & Andrews, 1917-19; associated with Kelley, David & Cottrell, 1919-29; mem. Morley, Stickle & Kelley, 1936—. Served at Camp Sherman, Ohio, 1918. Pres., treas. and trustee the Horace Kelley Art Foundation. Republican. Home: Shaker Heights, O. Died Apr. 8, 1941.

KELLEY, David Campbell, clergyman M.E. Ch., South; b. Leeville, Tenn., Dec. 25, 1833; s. John Kelley and Margaret L. (Campbell) Kelley; grad. Cumberland Univ., 1851 (A.M.; D.D., 1868); Univ. of Nashville, M.D., 1853 (LL.D., 1896); missionary to China, 1853; col. cav. with Gen. N. B. Forrest in C. S. army; m. Mary Owen Campbell, 1870; m. 2d, 1892, Mrs. May Elliott Knight. Has been pastor of leading chs., Nashville, Tenn.; also sec. and treas. Bd. of Missions, M. E. Ch., South; candidate for gov. of Tenn. on Prohibition ticket, 1890; projector of the schemes from which came Vanderbilt Univ. and the Nashville Coll. for Young Ladies; presiding elder Nashville dist., Tenn., 1898—; 7 times elected to gen. conf. Lieut. gen. commanding Forrest's Veteran Cav. Corps, U.C.V., 1900—; pres. Humane Soc. Tenn.; trustee Vanderbilt Univ., 1872-85; missionary sec. Tenn. Conf. M. E. Ch., South, 1904-07. Home: Lebanon, Tenn. Died 1909.

KELLEY, Eugene Robert, sanitarian; b. Bancroft, Me., Nov. 5, 1882; s. George Washington and Clara Blanch (Hinch) K.; A.B., Bowdoin, 1902; M.D., Johns Hopkins, 1906; m. Grace Elizabeth Boutelle, June 9, 1909. Asst. commr. of health, State of Wash., 1909-11, commr. of health, 1911-15; dir. Div. of Communicable Diseases, Mass. State Dept. of Health, 1915-18; commr. of pub. health, State of Mass., 1918—. Sec. Conf. of State and Provincial Health Authorities of North America, 1916-19, pres., 1921-22; pres. Mass. Conf. on Social Work, 1923-24. Conglist. Mason. Home: Dorchester, Mass. Died Sept. 27, 1925.

KELLEY, Florence; b. Philadelphia, Sept. 12, 1859; d. William D. K. (congressman from Pa.) and Caroline (Bonsall) Kelley; B.Litt., Cornell, 1882; LL.B., Northwestern U., 1894; children—Nicholas, John Bartram. Served as chief inspector of factories for Illinois, 1893-97; American editor Archiv für Soziale Gesetzgebung, Berlin, 1897-98; gen. sec. Nat. Consumers' League, 1899—. Sec. U.S. Bd. of Control of Labor Standards for Army Clothing, 1917-18. Translated Friedrich Engels' Condition of the Working Class in England. Resident at Hull House, Chicago, 1891-99, Henry Street Settlement, N.Y. City, 1899-1924. Edited Edmond Kelly's Twentieth Century Socialism, 1910. Compiled: The Supreme Court and Minimum Wage Legislation; Comment of the Legal Profession on the District of Columbia Minimum Wage Case, 1925. Address: New York, N.Y. Died Feb. 17, 1932.

KELLEY, Francis Alphonsus, clergyman; b. Cohoes, N.Y., Apr. 19, 1888; s. John Francis and Mary Annette (Mulvihill) K.; ed. St. Michael's Coll., Toronto, Ont., Can., Toronto U.; philosophy and theology, St. Bernard's Sem., Rochester, N.Y. Ordained priest R.C. Church, 1912; asst. pastor St. Joseph's Church, Albany, St. Vincent de Paul's, Albany, St. Mary's, Troy; now pastor church of the Sacred Heart, Cairo, New York. Commd. chaplain 10th Inf., N.G.N.Y., May 16, 1916; served on Mexican border; called out with same regt., Feb. 4, 1917; trans. to 104th Machine Gun Batt., 27th Div., U.S.A., Dec. 19, 1917; sailed for France Apr. 18, 1918; trans. to Hdqrs. 27th Div., July 13, 1918; returned to U.S., Feb. 27, 1919; hon. disch., Apr. 1, 1919. Decorated D.S.C. (U.S.); Mil. Cross (British); cited in gen. orders by Gen. Rawlinson, comdr. 4th Brit. Army, Sept. 20, 1918; cited in gen. orders, U.S.A., "for gallantry on field of battle," Sept. 29 and Oct. 17, 1918. First nat. chaplain, 1919, Am. Legion. Now mem. Com. of Relief of Disabled Vets., N.Y. City. Mem. K. of C., Elks. Toured Pacific Coast, May 1919, in interest of Victory Loan. Home: Cairo, N.Y. Died Oct. 15, 1931.

KELLEY, Hermon Alfred, lawyer; b. Kelley's Island, O., May 15, 1859; s. Alfred Stow and Hannah (Farr) K.; Joshua Stow, great uncle, was with Moses Cleveland party, which founded Cleveland, 1796; great uncle Alfred Kelley, 1st mayor Cleveland, 1814; B.S., Buchtel Coll., 1879, A.B., 1880, A.M., 1884, LL.D., 1907, Harvard University Law School, 1880-82; studied at Göttingen U., Germany (Roman law and German literature); m. Florence Alice Kendall, Sept. 3, 1889. Member Stearns & Kelley, Cleveland, 1884-90; first assistant corp. counsel of Cleveland, 1890-91; mem. Hoyt, Dustin & Kelley, 1891, later Hoyt, Dustin, Kelley, McKeehan & Andrews; now Kelley, David & Cottrell; dir., gen. counsel, dir. Pittsburgh Steamship Co.; sec., gen. counsel Am. Shipbuilding Co., Great Lakes Towing Co.; pres., gen. counsel Atchison & E. Bridge Co.; chmn. bd. Morris Plan Bank of Cleveland. Pres. and treas. The Horace Kelley Art Foundation; sec., trustee Cleveland Mus. of Art (exec. com. and bldg. com.). Republican. Unitarian. Homes: Euclid Heights; Cleveland, O. Died Feb. 2, 1925.

KELLEY, Howard G., civil engr.; b. Phila., Jan. 12, 1858; s. Edwin A. and Mary B. (Peterson) K.; grad. Poly. Coll. Pa.; m. Cora J. Lingo, Jan. 11, 1899. Entered ry. service, 1881, being asst. engr. on location, bridge constrn. and harbor work and div. engr. in charge design and field constrn. of 250 miles of the original constrn. in Wash., Ida. and Mont. on west. and Pac. divs. of N.P. Ry. until 1884; supt. mines in Mont., 1884-87; resident engr. and supt. bridges and bldgs., St. Louis Southwestern Ry. System, 1887-90; chief engr. same, 1890-98; chief engr. Minneapolis & St. Louis R.R. Co., including Ia. Central Ry. and leased and operated lines, 1898-1907; also cons. engr. St. Louis S.W. Ry., Mar. 1, 1898-May 1899; chief engr., July 4, 1907-Oct. 1, 1910, v.p. in charge operation, constrn. and maintenance, Oct. 1, 1910-Aug. 31, 1917, pres., Sept. 1, 1917—, Grand Trunk Ry. System; also pres. Grand Trunk Pacific Ry. and chmn. bd. Central Vt. Ry., Sept. 1, 1917—. Received decoration Order of St. John of Jerusalem in England, June 1913. Home: Montreal, Can. Died May 15, 1928.

KELLEY, James Douglas Jerrold, commander U.S.N., author; b. New York, Dec. 25, 1847; ed. pvt. and pub. schs. and Seton Hall Coll., N.J.; apptd. to navy by Pres. Lincoln; entered Oct. 5, 1864; grad. U.S. Naval Acad., 1868; m. Isabel de P. Morrell. Ensign, 1869; master, 1870; lt., 1872; lt. comdr., 1893; comdr., 1899. Served on many duties and stations; prize essayist and gold medalist U.S. Naval Inst., 1881; mem. and chmn. Bd. Auxiliary Vessels,

1898; insp. merchant vessels at New York; senior aid to comdt., Navy Yard, New York; in command of Resolute, West Indies, and again insp. merchant vessels; retired, Apr. 1, 1901. Co-author: Modern Ships of War; The Barbary Corsairs; The Army and Navy. Home: New York. Died Apr. 30, 1922.

KELLEY, Jay George, mining engr.; b. Worcester, Mass., July 4, 1838; ed. common schools, Boston; m. Lida Elliott, 1870. Ran away from home, 1850, and as a stowaway on "Witch of the Wave" went to Calif.; pony express rider, 1860; capt. Co. C, Nev. Inf., during Civil War; member U.S. Assay Commn., 1883; admitted to bar Deadwood, S.D., 1877, but has never practiced. Author: The Boy Mineral Collectors. Home: Denver, Colo. Died 1899.

KELLEY, John William, lawyer; b. Portsmouth, N.H., Dec. 3, 1865; s. John and Ellen (Nagel) K.; grad. Dartmouth Coll., 1888; admitted to bar, 1893; m. Romaine G. Sherwood, Jan. 8, 1897. Practiced at Portsmouth, 1893—; mem. Kelley, Harding & Hatch. Mem. Bd. of Edn., Portsmouth, 3 yrs., Water Bd., 3 yrs.; city solicitor, 2 yrs., and co. solicitor Rockingham Co., 1901-06. Republican. Catholic. Home: Portsmouth, N.H. Died Sept. 20, 1913.

KELLEY, Patrick Henry, congressman; b. Cass Co., Mich., Oct. 7, 1867; LL.B., U. of Mich., 1900. Began practice, Lansing, Mich., 1900; mem. Mich. State Bd. of Edn., 1901-05; state supt. pub. instrn., 1905-07; lt. gov., Mich., 1907-11; mem. 63d Congress (1913-15), Mich. at-large; reëlected to 64th to 67th Congresses (1915-23), 6th Dist. Republican. Home: Lansing, Mich. Died Sept. 11, 1925.

KELLEY, Robert Weeks; b. N.Y. City, Mar. 2, 1853; s. James E. and Roxanna (Drew) K.; A.B., Yale, 1874. Began as sec. Phila. Oil Co., 1876, and later served as officer many cos.; pres. Echo Farm Co., Litchfield, Conn., 1881-88, and was pres. Kanawha & Ohio R.R. Co., Kanawha & Mich. R.R. Co., The Warren-Burnham Co., Va. Portland Cement Co., Vulcan Portland Cement Co., Holly Sugar Co., etc.; now pres. William Holland Wilmer Foundation; chmn. bd. Am. Ice Co. Mem. Navy League of U.S. Republican. Home: New York, N.Y. Died Aug. 4, 1928.

KELLEY, Samuel Walter, M.D., surgeon; b. Adamsville, O., Sept. 15, 1855; s. Walter and Selina Catherine (Kaemmerer) K.; M.D., Western Reserve U., Cleveland, 1884; also studied in hosps. of London; m. Amelia Kemmerlein, July 2, 1884; children—Walter Paul (dec.), Katherine Mildred. Chief dept. of diseases of children, Polyclinic, Western Reserve U., 1886-93; prof. diseases of children, Cleveland Coll. Phys. and Surg. (Ohio Wesleyan U.), 1893-1910; surgeon to the children St. Luke's Hospital, sr. staff; secretary med. staff Cleveland City Hosp., 1891-99, pres., 1899-1902; pediatrist City Hosp., 1893-1910. Entered service as civilian surgeon, Spanish-Am. War; recommended for "efficiency in the field under most trying circumstances"; commd. brigade surgeon of vols. with rank of maj., Aug. 17, 1898. Editor: Cleveland Medical Gazette, 1885-1901. Pres. Ohio State Pediatric Soc., 1896, 97; chmn. sect. on diseases of children A.M.A., 1900-01; pres. Assn. Am. Teachers of Diseases of Children, 1907-08; fellow Am. College of Surgeons; mem. governing com. Gorgas Memorial Institute. Republican. Author: About Children, 1897; In the Year 1800, 1904; Surgical Diseases of Children, 1909, 2d edit., 1914; The Witchery o' the Moon and Other Poems, 1919; Lo Studente, 1925. Home: Cleveland, O. Died Apr. 20, 1929.

KELLEY, William Vallandigham, mfr.; b. Gratis, O., Feb. 13, 1861; s. William J. and Susan E. (Taylor) K.; ed. high sch. and commercial coll.; m. Lilian Phelps, Nov. 14, 1894; children—William V., Russell P., Phelps, Gordon P. Began as clerk and bookkeeper in hardware store, Springfield, O., 1883; sales agent Springfield Malleable Iron Co., 1885-88, Charles Scott Spring Co., Phila., 1888-97; organized Simplex Ry. Appliance Co., 1897, of which was pres. and treas.; stock of this co. sold to Am. Steel Foundries, Jan. 1905; was president American Steel Foundries from 1905 to 1912; chmn. bd. Miehle Printing Press & Mfg. Co. Republican. Home: Chicago, and Lake Forest, Ill. Died Jan. 21, 1932.

KELLICOTT, William Erskine, prof. biology; b. Buffalo, N.Y., Apr. 5, 1878; s. David Simmons and Valeria Erskine (Stowell) K.; Ph.B., Ohio State U., 1898; Ph.D., Columbia, 1904; m. Mary Hicks, Sept. 11, 1901. Asst., tutor, and instr. zoölogy, Barnard Coll. (Columbia), 1901-06; prof. biology, Goucher Coll., Baltimore, 1906—. In charge embryological instruction, Marine Biol. Lab., Woods Hole, Mass., 1908—. Fellow, Kahn Foundation for the Foreign Travel of American Teachers, 1912-13. Author: Social Direction of Human Evolution, 1911; Text-Book of General Embryology, 1913; Outlines of Chordate Development, 1913. Asst. statistician, U.S. Food Administration, Washington, 1917—. Home: Roland Park, Baltimore. Died Jan. 29, 1919.

KELLNER, Elisabeth Willard Brooks, author; b. Williamsport, Pa.; d. William Waldo and Sarah A. (Maynard) Willard; m. Rev. Arthur Brooks (dec.); 2d, Prof. Max Kellner, June 28, 1905. Author: (as Elisabeth Willard Brooks) As the World Goes By, 1905. Home: Cambridge, Mass. Died Apr. 16, 1916.

KELLNER, Max, theologian, orientalist; b. Detroit, May 21, 1861; s. Prof. Charles Frederick and Teresa (Mary) K.; A.B., Hobart Coll., 1881, A.M., 1884, D.D., 1895; A.B., Harvard, 1885, A.M., 1886; B.D., Cambridge Theol. Sch., 1885, D.D., 1922; m. Elisabeth (Willard) Brooks, June 28, 1905 (died 1916); 1 son, Waldo. Instr. Hebrew, 1887-91, asst. prof. Old Testament languages, 1891-98, prof., 1898-1907, prof. lit. and interpretation of the O.T., 1907-22, Cambridge Theol. School, prof. emeritus. Episcopalian. Author: An Outline Study on the History of the Hebrews, 1901; An Outline Study on the Old Testament Literature and Religion, 1902; Magic—Its Origin and Survivals, 1934. Home: Cambridge, Mass. Died Aug. 5, 1935.

KELLOGG, Amos Markham, editor; b. Utica, N.Y., June 5, 1832; s. Henry and Serena (Beach) K.; grad. Albany State Normal Sch., 1851; (A.M., Hamilton Coll., 1857); m. Lavinia Livingston Steele, July 7, 1857. Instr. Palmyra (N.Y.) Union Sch., 1851, State Normal Sch., Albany, 1852-56; prin. N.J. Prep. Normal Sch., 1856-57; conducted Teachers' Inst., Mich., 1858-60; prin. Union Sch., Monroe, Mich., 1861-63, Bergen Inst., 1866-75. Editor of The School Journal, 1874-1904; was also editor Teachers' Institute, Educational Foundations, Primary School, Our Times, Teachers' Magazine. Author: How to Teach the Writing of Compositions; How to Manage Busy Work, 1897; How to Teach Clay Modeling, 1894; How to Teach Botany, 1897; How to Teach Fractions, 1900; How to Teach to Read, 1900; How to Make School Charts, 1901; Best Primary Songs, 1893; Elementary Psychology, 1894; Nature Study, 1900. Home: New Rochelle, N.Y. Died Oct. 3, 1914.

KELLOGG, Arthur Piper, editor; b. Kalamazoo, Mich., Mar. 18, 1878; s. Frank Israel and Mary Foster (Underwood) K.; grad. Kalamazoo High School, 1897, New York Sch. of Philanthropy, 1903; m. Augusta Louise Coleman, June 24, 1902; m. 2d, Florence Loeb, Aug. 10, 1925. Reporter, city editor, Daily Telegraph, Kalamazoo, 1898-1902; press rep., Mich. Legislature, 1900; joined staff of The Survey (then called Charities), 1903, and has held various positions, chiefly that of mng. editor, 1908-19, business mgr., 1919-25, mng. editor, 1925—, also treas. Survey Associates, Inc., which pub. The Survey (monthly) and Survey Graphic (monthly). Democrat. Home: New York, N.Y. Died July 20, 1934.

KELLOGG, Charles Collins, postmaster; b. Plymouth, Mich., Dec. 25, 1858; s. Jason and Caroline Elizabeth K.; grad. high sch., Detroit; student U. of Mich., 1878-82; m. Emma Elizabeth Borchardt, July 8, 1885; 1 dau., Annabel (Mrs. Don W. Van Winkle). Teacher, pub. schs., 1882-84; dep. county clk., Wayne Co., Mich., 1884-96; asst. postmaster, Detroit, later supt. of mails until 1925, postmaster, 1925—. Republican. Mason. Home: Detroit, Mich. Died May 15, 1933.

KELLOGG, Clara Louise, prima donna; b. Sumterville, S.C., 1842; removed to New York, 1856, and received mus. edn. there; m. Carl Strakosch, 1887. Début Acad. Music, New York, 1861, as Gilda in Rigoletto; London début, Her Majesty's Theatre, 1867. Toured U.S., 1868-82; reappeared in London, May 1872; sang in Italian opera for several yrs. and organized her own English opera co. Appeared principally in concerts the later years; retired. Died May 13, 1916.

KELLOGG, Daniel Fiske; b. Chittenango, N.Y., Mar. 19, 1865; s. Charles and Ann Elizabeth (Moody) K.; A.B., Amherst, 1886; m. Maud Isabel Forbes, Sept. 2, 1891. Joined staff of New York Sun, 1886; city editor and editorial writer, same, 1891-1902, financial editor, 1902-13; associated with J. P. Morgan & Co., 1913—. Republican. Episcopalian. Home: New York, N.Y. Died Oct. 28, 1920.

KELLOGG, Edgar Romeyn, brig. gen.; b. New York, Mar. 25, 1842; s. Moses Curtis (M.D.) and Elizabeth (Swartwout) K.; pub. sch. edn.; m. Mary E. Wickham, Feb. 13, 1866. Served as sergt. Co. A, and sergt. maj. 24th Ohio Inf., Apr. 22-July 23, 1861; commd. 2d lt. 24th Ohio Inf., July 23, 1861; resigned, Oct. 28, 1861; pvt. Co. B, and sergt. maj. 1st battalion, 16th U.S. Inf., Nov. 29, 1861-Aug. 1, 1862; apptd. from N.Y. 2d lt. 16th Inf., Apr. 7, 1862; 1st lt., May 3, 1862; capt., Feb. 16, 1865; transferred to 25th Inf., Sept. 21, 1866, to 18th Inf., Apr. 26, 1869; maj., Dec. 26, 1888; lt. col. 10th Inf., Sept. 16, 1892; col. 6th Inf., June 30, 1898; brig. gen. vols., Oct. 1, 1898; hon. disch. from vol. service, Feb. 24, 1899; brig. gen. U.S.A., Dec. 5, 1899; retired at own request, over 30 yrs.' service, Dec. 16, 1899. Bvtd.: capt., Dec. 31, 1862, for battle of Murfreesboro, Tenn.; maj., Sept. 1, 1864, for Atlanta campaign and battle of Jonesboro, Ga. Home: Toledo, O. Died Oct. 7, 1914.

KELLOGG, Frank Billings, diplomat, sec. of state; b. Potsdam, N.Y., Dec. 22, 1856; s. Asa F. and Abigail (Billings) K.; went to Minn. with parents, 1865; common sch. edn.; admitted to bar 1877; LL.D., McGill U., Montreal, 1913, U. of Pa., 1926, New York U., 1927, George Washington Univ., 1927, Carleton Coll., 1928, St. Lawrence U., 1929, Harvard Univ., 1929, Brown Univ., 1930, Univ. of Minn. and Princeton Univ., 1931, Occidental U., 1931, Hamline U., 1931; D.C.L., Trinity College (Conn.) and Oxford Univ., 1929; m. Clara M. Cook, 1896. City atty., Rochester, Minn., 3 yrs.; co. atty., Olmsted Co., 5 yrs.; removed to St. Paul, 1887, forming partnership with late Senator Cushman Kellogg Davis and Cordenio A. Severance as Davis, Kellogg & Severance; was spl. counsel for U.S. in case against the paper and Standard Oil trusts; spl. counsel for Interstate Commerce Commn. in investigation of Harriman railroads, and for U.S. in action to dissolve U.P.-S.P. merger; U.S. senator from Minn., term 1917-23; mem. Davis, Kellogg, Severance & Morgan, 1923; apptd. A.E. and P. to Great Britain, 1924; sec. of state in Cabinet of President Coolidge, Mar. 4, 1925-Mar. 4, 1929; mem. Kellogg, Morgan, Chase, Carter & Headley, 1929—; judge of Permanent Court of Internat. Justice, 1930-35. Government del. Universal Congress Lawyers and Jurists, St. Louis, 1904; mem. Rep. Nat. Com. for Minn., 1904-12; del. 5th Internat. Conf. of Am. States, Santiago, Chile, 1923. Awarded Nobel peace prize for 1929; Order of Olive Branch of Argentina, 1930; Grand Cross French Legion of Honor, 1929; Hon. Bencher of the Middle Temple, 1929. Home: St. Paul, Minn. Died Dec. 21, 1937.

KELLOGG, Frederic Rogers, lawyer; b. Middlebury, Vt., May 6, 1867; s. Brainerd and Julia (Cutter) K.; B.S., Poly. Inst. Brooklyn, 1885; LL.B., Columbia, 1888; LL.D., Middlebury, 1919; m. Cornelia Van Wyck Halsey, June 24, 1903; children—Mary Darcy, Frederic Brainerd, Edmund Halsey, Cornelia Rogers. Practiced at New York, 1888—; member firm of Kellogg, Emery and Inness-Brown. Republican. Episcopalian. Home: Morristown, N.J. Died Aug. 18, 1935.

KELLOGG, Frederick William, newspaper publisher; b. Norwalk, Ohio, Dec. 7, 1866; s. Theron Hotchkiss and Frances (Penfield) K.; ed. pub. schs.; m. Florence Scripps, May 8, 1890. Advertising mgr. Detroit News, 1887-94, Scripps-McRae League, 1895-99; pub. Omaha Daily News, 1899; associated with L. V. Ashbaugh and B. D. Butler and established Omaha Daily News, St. Paul Daily News, 1900, Minneapolis Daily News, 1902, San Francisco Call, 1913; sold San Francisco Call, 1919; part owner and gen. mgr. Los Angeles (Calif.) Evening Express, 1919-25 (sold to Los Angeles Evening Herald 1931); founded Pasadena Evening Post, 1919; pres. and principal stockholder Kellogg Newspapers, Inc., including Pasadena Evening Post, Monrovia Evening Post, Hollywood News, San Fernando Valley News, Glendale Daily Press, Burbank Daily Press, Eagle Rock Daily Press, Sawtelle Tribune, Santa Monica Evening Outlook, Venice Evening Vanguard, Redondo Daily Breeze, Hermosa Daily Breeze, San Pedro Daily News, Alhambra Post-Advocate, and Culver City Star-News, all sold to Ira C. Copley, of Aurora, Ill., 1928; retired. Episcopalian. Mason. Home: Altadena, Calif. Died Sept. 5, 1940.

KELLOGG, James C., consul; b. Woodville, Mass., 1859; ed. U. of South, Sewanee, Tenn.; univs. of Germany, France and Austria, 8 yrs.; M.D., Vanderbilt U., Nashville, Tenn. Practiced medicine at New Orleans; consul at Settin, Germany, 1890-93, Barranquilla, Colombia, 1905, Colon, Panama, May 27, 1905—. Home: Colon, Panama. Died Nov. 18, 1916.

KELLOGG, James Lawrence, biologist; b. Kewanee, Ill., Sept. 15, 1866; s. Hosmer L. and Emily (Platt) K.; B.S., Olivet (Mich.) Coll., 1888; Ph.D., Johns Hopkins, 1892; hon. A.M., Williams, 1900; m. Ida M. Archambeault, June 16, 1892; children—Emilie (Mrs. E. A. Carrier), Louise, Helena (Mrs. W. E. Wright), Margaret (Mrs. J. R. Nelson). Prof. biology, Olivet Coll., 1892-99; asst. prof. biology, 1899-1903, prof., 1903-34 (emeritus), Williams College. Specialized in anatomy and habits of Lamellibranchiate mollusks. Author: (brochure) Oyster Culture Experiments for State of Louisiana, 1904; Shell-Fish Industries, 1910. Home: Williamstown, Mass. Died July 8, 1938.

KELLOGG, John Morris, judge; b. Taylor, N.Y., Aug. 28, 1851; s. Stephen and Nancy (Dillenbeck) K.; ed. Cincinnatus Acad., Cazenovia Sem. and Cornell U.; LL.B., Albany Law Sch., 1873; m. Henrietta Guest Mathews. Admitted to bar, 1873; has been recorder City of Ogdensburg, co. judge St. Lawrence Co.; judge Ct. of Claims State of N.Y., 1899-1902; apptd. justice Supreme Ct., Oct. 16, 1902; elected same, 1903, for term 1904-17; designated asso. justice Appellate Div., 3d Dept., Nov. 1905, and as presiding justice thereof, Nov. 1915; reëlected justice Supreme Ct., for term Jan. 1, 1918-Jan. 1, 1922; redesignated presiding justice Jan. 1, 1918. Republican. Home: Ogdensburg, N.Y. Died Jan. 16, 1925.

KELLOGG, John Prescott, judge; b. Waterbury, Conn., Mar. 31, 1860; s. Stephen Wright and Lucia Hosmer (Andrews) K.; B.A., Yale, 1882; LL.B., Yale Law Sch., 1884; m. Clara Mason, June 1, 1892. Admitted to Conn. bar, 1884; jr. mem. Kellogg, Burpee & Kellogg, 1884-93, Kellogg & Kellogg, 1893-1904, alone 1904-17. President Bd. of Councilmen, Waterbury, 1887-91; atty. City Ct. of Waterbury, 1891-93; town atty. Town of Waterbury, 1891-95; pros. atty. Dist. Ct. of Waterbury, 1893-97; corp. counsel City of Waterbury, 1896-1909 and July 1, 1911-Jan. 1, 1912; state's atty., Waterbury, 1897-1917; judge Superior Court of Conn., Mar. 1917—. Chmn. Rep. Town Com., Waterbury, 1895-1906, Rep. State Central Com., 1898-1900. Agt. Bronson Library, Waterbury; trustee St. Margaret's Sch. Episcopalian. Home: Waterbury, Conn. Died Jan. 16, 1925.

KELLOGG, Joseph Augustus, lawyer; b. Wilmington, Del., May 13, 1865; s. Rev. Charles Dor and Mary Jane (Baucus) K.; grad. Island Grove Sch., Ft. Edward, N.Y., 1880; LL.B., cum laude, Columbia, 1885; m. Emma Ada Cronkhite, Nov. 29, 1893; children—Mrs. Emma Ada Kramer, Baucus Cronkhite, Joseph Augustus, Preston Paris. Began practice at Hudson Falls, 1886; settled in Glens Falls, 1894; justice Supreme Court of N.Y., 1911; 1st dep. atty. gen. of N.Y., 1912, 13, 14; counsel to gov. of N.Y., Jan.-Apr. 1919; pub. service commr. 2d Dist. of N.Y., 1919-21; mem. Conway, Kellogg & O'Brien, New York, May 1921—. Elected chmn. Dem. State Com., N.Y., 1918. Presbyn. Home: Glens Falls, N.Y. Died Sept. 8, 1929.

KELLOGG, Luther Laflin, lawyer; b. Malden, N.Y., July 1, 1849; s. Nathan and Helen M. K.; A.B., Rutgers, 1870, A.M., 1873; LL.B., Columbia, 1872; (LL.D., Rutgers, 1901); admitted to bar, 1872; m. Eliza S., d. Gen. John B. McIntosh, U.S.A., 1874. Now sr. mem. Kellogg & Rose; makes a specialty of municipal law. The unconstitutionality of the following labor laws: Prevailing Rate of Wages Law, Cut Stone Law, Eight Hour Law, law relating to contracts with state and municipalities, have recently been declared by the Court of Appeals of the State of N.Y. in their separate decisions upon his arguments. Dir. Colonial Assurance Co. Home: New York, N.Y. Died Dec. 6, 1918.

KELLOGG, Martin, prof. (emeritus) Latin, Univ. of Calif.; b. Vernon, Conn., Mar. 15, 1828; s. Allyn and Eliza (White) K.; grad. Yale, 1850; (A.M., 1853, LL.D., 1893); m. Louise Wells Brockway, Sept. 3, 1863. Prof. Latin and mathematics, Coll. of Calif., 1860-69; prof. Latin and Greek, Univ. of Calif., 1869-76; prof. Latin language and literature, Univ. of Calif., 1876-93; pres. Univ. of Calif., 1893-99; resigned and apptd. prof. emeritus Latin, 1899; took trip around the world, 1899-1900; resumed teaching Sept. 1900. Editor: Ars Oratoria, Selections from Cicero and Quintilian, 1872; The Brutus of Cicero, 1889. Died 1903.

KELLOGG, Oliver Dimon, college prof.; b. Linwood, Pa., July 10, 1878; s. Rev. Day Otis and Sarah Cornelia (Hall) K.; A.B., Princeton, 1899, A.M., 1900, fellow, 1899-1902; U. of Berlin, 1901; Ph.D., U. of Göttingen, 1902; m. Edith Taylor, 1911; 1 dau., Margaret Philbrick. Instr. mathematics, Princeton, 1902-05; asst. prof. mathematics, 1905-10, prof., 1910-20, U. of Mo. Mathematician, U.S. Naval Exptl. Sta., New London, Conn., June 1918-June 1919; lecturer on mathematics, 1919-20, asso. prof., 1920-27, prof., 1927—, Harvard. Fellow Am. Acad. Arts and Sciences, A.A.A.S. Mem. editorial com. Zentralblatt für Mathematik und ihre Grenzgebiete. Home: Cambridge, Mass. Died Aug. 27, 1932.

KELLOGG, Spencer, mfr.; b. West Galway, N.Y., June 16, 1851; s. Lauren and Elizabeth (Miller) K.; grad. Gloversville (N.Y.) Sem.; studied under pvt. tutors; m. Jane Morris, Apr. 10, 1875. Entered linseed oil business, Amsterdam, N.Y., 1872; pvt. banker, Des Moines, Ia., 1878; mfr. linseed oil, Buffalo, 1879—; now largest individual mfr. linseed oil in U.S., with mills in Buffalo, Minneapolis, Superior, Wis., and N.Y. City; also identified with grain elevator business, mfr. brooms and brushes, and white lead, paints, varnishes, etc.; pres. N.Y. State Steel Co., Buffalo, 1905-07. Founder, 1911, and trustee Lincoln Memorial Hall, Hodgenville, Ky. Charter mem. Nat. Marine League. Republican. Presbyn. Author: From Boyhood to Manhood, 1914; A Capitalist's View of Socialism, 1916. Home: Buffalo, N.Y. Died Nov. 14, 1922.

KELLOGG, Stephen Wright, jurist, congressman; b. Shelburne, Mass., Apr. 5, 1822; s. Jacob Poole and Lucy (Wright) K.; grad. Yale, 1846; m. Miss Lucia Wasmer Andrews, Sept. 10, 1851. Admitted to Conn. bar, June, 1848; practiced at Waterbury; judge New Haven Co. court, 1854; judge probate court, 1854-60; congressman, 1869-75; candidate for congress, 1874 and 1876; presdl. elector at large, 1900. Home: Waterbury, Conn. Died 1904.

KELLOGG, Thomas Moore, architect; b. Washington, June 24, 1862; s. George Ward and Maria Elizabeth (Douglas) K.; Baltimore City Coll., 1 yr.; in office of Chas. L. Carson, architect, 4 yrs.; Mass. Inst. Tech., 1883-84; in office of McKim, Mead & White, architects, New York, 1884-91; m. Antoinette Reed Gardner, Nov. 24, 1885 (died 1932); children—Sara Lawrence, Margaret Harper, Arthur Cottrel, Eleanor May. Mem. Rankin & Kellogg, 1891-1903, Rankin, Kellogg & Crane, 1903-26, again Rankin & Kellogg, 1926—. Republican. Fellow A.I.A. Home: Chestnut Hill, Philadelphia, Pa. Died July 8, 1935.

KELLOGG, Vernon Lyman, zoölogist; b. Emporia, Kan., Dec. 1, 1867; s. Lyman Beecher and Abigail (Homer) K.; A.B., U. of Kan., 1889, M.S., 1892; Cornell, 1891; U. Leipzig, 1893, 97; U. of Paris, 1904; LL.D., U. of Calif., 1919, Brown, 1920; Sc.D., Oberlin, 1922; m. Charlotte Hoffman, Apr. 27, 1908; 1 dau., Charlotte Jean. Asst. and asso. prof. entomology, U. of Kan., 1890-94; prof. entomology and lecturer bionomics, Stanford U., 1894-1920. Mem. Nat. Acad. of Science and various other American and European scientific societies. Officer Legion of Honor (France); Comdr. Order of Crown (Belgium); Comdr. Order of Leopold I (Belgium); Comdr. Order of Polonia Restituta (Poland); gold medal (Poland). Dir., in Brussels, of Am. Com. for Relief in Belgium, 1915-16; asst. to U.S. Food administrator, 1917-19; chief of mission to Poland, special investigator in Russia, and other service in Europe with Am. Relief Administrator, 1918-21; permanent sec. Nat. Research Council, Washington, 1919-31, and chmn. div. of endl. relations, 1919-29, sec. emeritus, 1932. Trustee Rockefeller Foundation (1922-33), Brookings Institution, Gallaudet Coll. (1925-32) and other organizations. Author: Am. Insects, 1904; Animal Studies (with D. S. Jordan and H. Heath), 1905; Evolution and Animal Life (with D. S. Jordan), 1907; Insect Stories, 1908; Scientific Aspects of Luther Burbank's Work (with D. S. Jordan), 1909; Economic Zoölogy and Entomology (with R. W. Doane), 1915; Losses of Life in Modern Wars and Race Deterioration (with G. Bodart), 1916; Headquarters Nights, 1917; The Food Problem (with A.R. Taylor), 1917; Fighting Starvation in Belgium, 1918; Germany in the War and After, 1919; Herbert Hoover—The Man and His Work, 1920; Nuova, the New Bee, 1921; Human Life as the Biologist Sees It, 1922; Mind and Heredity, 1923; Evolution, 1924; Reading with a Purpose—Biology, 1925. Died Aug. 8, 1937.

KELLOGG, William Pitt, senator; b. Orwell, Vt., Dec. 8, 1830; s. Rev. Sherman K.; ed. Norwich Mil. Inst.; removed to Ill.; m. Mary E. Wills, June 6, 1865. Admitted to Ill. bar, 1852; practiced at Canton, Ill., 1852-61; Lincoln elector for Ill., 1860 (only elector for that yr. now living); apptd., 1861, chief justice Neb. Ty.; raised and became col. 7th Ill. Cav., summer of 1861 (granted leave of absence from jud. duties by Mr. Lincoln); after 2 yrs'. service resigned from army because of ill health; resigned chief justiceship, 1865; collector port of New Orleans, 1865-68 (last civil commn., dated Apr. 13, 1865, signed by President Lincoln before he was assassinated); U.S. senator, 1868-72 and 1877-83; gov. La., 1873-77; mem. Congress, 1883-85; one of the 306 dels. who voted for Gen. Grant Divides his time between La. and Washington; has large interests in Washington. Mem. D.C. Commandery Loyal Legion. Died Aug. 10, 1918.

KELLY, Aloysius Oliver Joseph, physician; b. Philadelphia, June 13, 1870; s. Joseph V. (M.D.) and Emma Jane (Ferguson) K.; A.B., La Salle Coll., Phila., 1888, A.M., 1891; M.D., U. of Pa., 1891; post-grad. London, Dublin, Vienna, 1892-94, and again (Vienna), 1897; m. Elizabeth Morrison McKnight, Oct. 30, 1897. Engaged in med. practice in Phila., 1894—; asst. prof. medicine, U. of Pa.; asst. phys. to Univ. Hosp.; prof. theory and practice of medicine, U. of Vt.; prof. pathology, Woman's Med. Coll. of Pa.; pathologist to German Hosp. of Phila.; phys. to St. Agnes Hosp. Editor Am. Jour. Medical Sciences. Fellow Coll. of Physicians of Phila., Am. Acad. Medicine. Author: The Practice of Medicine, 1910. Died 1911.

KELLY, Dennis Francis, mcht.; b. Chicago, Ill., Aug. 23, 1868; s. John and Mary (Murphy) K.; ed. St. Mary's Sch., Chicago; LL.D., De Paul University, 1923; LL.D., U. of Notre Dame, 1930; m. Irene E. Sullivan, Jan. 4, 1894; 1 dau., Eileen Glassbrook (Mrs. Charles P. Vogel). Started as a boy with Mandel Brothers, dept. store, Chicago, 1879, supt. of store, 1888-1901, gen. mgr., 1901-23; v.p. and gen. mgr. The Fair, 1923-24, pres. and gen. mgr., 1925-38, dir.; dir. Kresge Dept. Stores, Inc. Incorporator and trustee Century of Progress Expn., Chicago, 1933-34. President Catholic Charities of Chicago from organization, 1918. Commissioned by Gov. Lowden, lt. col. Ill. Res. Militia. Knight Order of St. Gregory, 1920, Knight Comdr., 1925; Knight of Malta, by Pope Pius XI, 1931. Home: Lake Forest, Ill. Died July 23, 1938.

KELLY, Edward A., clergyman; b. Brooklyn, N.Y., June 15, 1853; s. Charles and Mary (Donlin) K.; student Ignatius Coll., Chicago, 1869-71; St. Charles Coll., Ellicott City, Mo., 1872-76, St. Mary's Sem., Baltimore, 1876. Ordained priest R.C. Ch., 1880; asst. St. Bridget's Ch., Chicago, 1880-81, All Saints Ch., 1881-85; founder, and pastor St. Cecilia Ch., 1885-1909; pastor St. Anne's Ch., 1909—. Chaplain 7th Regt., Ill. N.G., 1893-1918. Democrat. Home: Chicago, Ill. Died Aug. 24, 1925.

KELLY, Florence Finch, author; b. Girard, Ill., Mar. 27, 1858; d. James G. and Mary Ann (Purdum) Finch; A.B., U. of Kan., 1881, A.M., 1884; m. Allen Kelly, 1884 (died 1916); children—Morton Finch (dec.), Sherwin Finch. Has been engaged on various newspapers in Chicago, Boston, Troy, N.Y., Lowell and Fall River, Mass., New York, San Francisco, Los Angeles. In 1905 visited Australia and New Zealand to study social and economic legislation and its results. Author: With Hoops of Steel, 1900; The Delafield Affair, 1909; Fate of Felix Brand, 1913; What America Did, 1919; The Dixons, 1921; Flowing Stream, the Story of Fifty-Six Years in Newspaper Life, 1938. On staff New York Times Review of Books, 1906—. Home: New York, N.Y. Died Dec. 17, 1939.

KELLY, George Henderson, editor, pub.; b. Poplar Bluff, Mo., Feb. 5, 1854; s. John Garland and Rebecca (Cash) K.; ed. pub. schs.; m. Alice Valera Beatty, Mar. 4, 1875 (died 1924); children—William Beatty, Jennie Valine (Mrs. Charles L. Rawlins). Began with Poplar Bluff (Mo.) Citizen, 1869; moved to Ariz., 1887; editor, pub. Arizona Bulletin, weekly, 1890-1903, Douglas Daily International, 1903-25. Active worker in Dem. Party; apptd. state historian, Ariz., Jan. 1, 1923. Presbyn. Mason. Author: Legislative History of Arizona Territory, 1926. Home: Phoenix, Ariz. Died Nov. 10, 1929.

KELLY, Guy Edward, lawyer; b. Rochester, Minn., May 23, 1876; s. Jeremiah Elmer and Alice Louise (Fleming) K.; S.Dak. State Coll., Brookings, 1899-1901; LL.B., George Washington U., 1905; m. Margaret Mary McNamee, June 22, 1903; children—Jean Mary, Margaret, Guy Edward. Pvt. sec. to U.S. Senator Alfred B. Kittredge, 1902-05; began practice at Brookings, 1905; moved to Tacoma, Wash., 1906. Mem. Wash. House of Rep., 1915 (speaker, 1917); Wash. mem. Rep. Nat. Com., 1920-24. Sergt. Co. H, 1st S.D. Volunteer Inf., Philippines, 13 mos., 1898-99. Mason. Home: Tacoma, Wash. Died July 28, 1940.

KELLY, Harry Eugene, lawyer; b. Des Moines, Ia., Dec. 27, 1870; s. Michael Joseph and Margery A. (Lytle) K.; Ph.B., State U. of Ia., 1892, M.A., 1897; post-grad. work, U. of Chicago, 1895; studied law, U. of Denver, 1899-1900; admitted to Colo. bar, 1900; m. Jessie L. Speer, Jan. 1893 (died 1899); m. 2d, Edna McElravy Smalley, Aug. 1903; 2 sons: William M., Will Abbott. Editor Daily Herald, Litchfield, Ill., 1892-94; prin. Litchfield High Sch., 1894-95; supt. schs., Sullivan, Ill., 1895-96; instr. English lit., State U. of Ia., 1896-99. Began practice, Denver, Colo., 1900; ten yrs. counsel in West for Western Union Telegraph Co.; mem. Kelly & Haines, 1907-14. Mem. Colo. Ho. of Rep., 1906-08 (secured passage of pure food bill and bill establishing state r.r. commn.); asst. U.S. dist. atty., 1909-12; U.S. dist. atty., 1912-14; atty. at Washington, D.C., of Interstate Commerce Commn., 1914-16; regional counsel U.S. Railroad Administration, at Chicago, 1920-21; now mem. Kelly, Pratt & Zeis. In practice at Chicago, 1916—. Served as Colo. commr. on Uniform State Laws. Mem. Gov. Lowden's Chicago Commn. on Race Relations, 1919; pres. State U. of Ia. Alumni Assn., 1922-23. Mem. Chicago Assn. Commerce (exec. com. and chmn. Ways and Means com., 1926-27); Com. of 15 (bd. dirs.). Trustee Union League Foundation for Boys' Clubs. Republican. Unitarian. Mem. Electoral College for Ill., 1929. Author: Literary Style of Edmund Burke, 1897; Third Degree Inquisition, 1909; Regulation of Physicians by Law, 1924. Home: Evanston, Ill. Died Jan. 14, 1936.

KELLY, Harry McCormick, biologist; b. Harrisburg, Pa., May 27, 1867; s. George Correy and Susan Hauer (Bradley) K.; A.B., Bucknell U., Lewisburg, Pa., 1888, A.M., 1891; A.B., Harvard, 1891, A.M., 1893; LL.D., John B. Stetson U., DeLand, Fla., 1911; m. Caroline May Vanderslice, Dec. 27, 1894; 1 dau., Caroline. Prof. mathematics, Central Pa. Coll., 1888-90; asst. in zoölogy, Harvard, 1891-93; instr. biology, Northwestern U., 1893-94; prof. biology, Cornell Coll., Mt. Vernon, Ia., 1894—. Library trustee Mt. Vernon, 1903-23. Republican. Methodist. Died Apr. 10, 1936.

KELLY, J. Redding, portrait painter; b. New York, N.Y.; s. Maurice and Mary (Redding) K.; ed. N.Y. City Coll., Cooper Union and Nat. Acad. of Design; unmarried. Mem. faculty Coll. of City of N.Y., 1905-30, tutor in art, 1905-08, instr., 1908-18, asst. prof., 1918-21, asso. prof., 1921-30; prof. art and drafting Brooklyn Coll., 1930—, head of dept., 1931—, Portrait painter, 1905—; his portrait of Abraham Lincoln reproduced in Ency. Britannica; other portraits at Columbia U., Barnard Coll., Coll. of City of N.Y., Brooklyn Coll., 71st Regt. Armory; also exhibited at Nat. Acad. of Design, Pa. Acad. Awarded Silver Suydam medal of Nat. Acad. of Design, 1895; Canon prize for figure painting from same, 1897. Catholic. Home: New York, N.Y. Died Dec. 9, 1939.

KELLY, James Edward, sculptor; b. New York, N.Y., July 30, 1855; s. Patrick Paul and Julia Finly (Golden) K.; ed. pub. schs.; studied art, Nat. Acad. Design; studied wood engraving, 1871; m. Helen McKay, Feb. 27, 1922. In Harper's art dept., 1874; illustrator for Scribner's, St. Nicholas, etc., until 1881; since then exclusively sculptor. His first piece of sculpture was Sheridan's Ride, 1878; 40 gens., including Grant, Sherman, Sheridan and Hancock, gave him sittings for a series of bronzes. Prominent works: relief of Edison, from life, with first phonograph, 1879; Monmouth Battle Monument, including Molly Pitcher, 1885; Paul Revere, 1882; 6th New York Cav., Gettysburg, 1890; Call to Arms, Troy, N.Y., 1891; Long Island—Panel; Gen. John Bulford at Gettysburg,

1895; Battle of Harlem Heights Memorial, Columbia Coll., 1897; equestrian figures Gen. Sherman, Col. Roosevelt at San Juan Hill; busts from life of Admiral Dewey, Admiral Sampson, Lt. Hobson, Admiral C. E. Clark, and President Roosevelt as col. of the "Rough Riders," panels from life of Dewey's captains, Sampson's captains, and Gens. Joseph Wheeler, Leonard Wood, J. H. Wilson and equestrian statue of Gen. Fitz John Porter at Portsmouth, N.H.; Washington at Valley Forge, Sub-Treasury Bldg., New York; McKinley memorial at Wilmington, Del.; Defenders' monument, New Haven, 1909; "Wilson at Selma"; Count Rochambeau at Southington, Conn.; Father Hecker, founder and the superior gen. of the Paulist order; memorial to Gen. Thomas W. Sweeney; memorial to Gen. O. O. Howard, for Howard U., Washington; war memorial to soldiers and sailors, Kingston, N.Y., 1919; equestrian bronze of George Hope Ryder, M.D., 1922; Caesar Rodney equestrian monument, Wilmington, Del., 1923; bronze reliefs of Rodney Declaring for Independence, 1924, Rodney's Arrival at Independence Hall, 1925; bronze group of Leather Stocking and the Last of the Mohicans, 1926; bust of Thomas A. Edison, 1927; bronze, Destruction of Bridge at Princeton (1777), 1928; bronze of Isaac Sears Striking First Blow for Liberty (1770), 1931. Home: New York, N.Y. Died May 25, 1933.

KELLY, James Kerr, lawyer, U.S. senator; b. Centre County, Pa., Feb. 16, 1819; grad. Coll. of N.J. (Princeton), 1839, A.M., 1842; m. Mary Buchanan Millar, Nov. 26, 1863. Admitted to Pa. bar, 1842; deputy atty. gen. for Mifflin Co., Pa., 1847-49; went to Calif., 1849, to Portland, Ore. Ty., 1851; one of com. of 3 apptd. 1852 to draw up set of laws for Ty.; lieut. col. 1st regt. Ore. mounted vols., and served against Yakima Indians, 1855-56; mem. Territorial Council, 1853-57; one of framers of Ore. constitution, 1857; mem. State Senate, 1860-64; U.S. Senator from Ore., 1871-77. Democrat. Chief justice Supreme Court Ore., 1879-81. Died 1903.

KELLY, John C., editor, publisher; b. Cortland, N.Y., Feb. 26, 1852; s. Thomas C. and Mary G. (Kelly) K.; ed. pub. schs. and commercial coll.; m. Martha A. Hill, May 1, 1878. Part owner and editor Des Moines Leader, 1877-80; owner and editor Sioux City Tribune, 1880—; pres. The Tribune Co., Sioux City Printing Co. Collector of internal revenue, Northern Dist. of Ia., 1894-98. Home: Sioux City, Iowa. Died Oct. 27, 1920.

KELLY, John Forrest, electrical engr.; b. Carrick-on-Suir, Ireland, Mar. 28, 1859; s. Jeremiah and Kate (Forrest) K.; B.S. in physics and chemistry, Stevens Inst. Tech., 1878, Ph.D., 1881; m. Helen Tischer, 1892. Chemist in lab. of Thomas A. Edison, 1879; electrician New York factory Western Elec. Co., 1879-82, asst. electrician U.S. Elect. Lighting Co., 1882; with Parker Electric Lighting Co., 1882-84; with U.S. Electric Lighting Co., 1884-86; electrician Newark shops of Westinghouse Elec. Co. until Jan. 1892; with Stanley Lab. Co., 1892-95; consulting engr. for Stanley Electric Mfg. Co., Pittsfield, and Stanley Instrument Co., Great Barrington, Mass., until 1905; founded Teleelectric Co., 1905, pres. until 1910; introduced Cooke-Kelly food drying process which preserves primal freshness. Has received over 90 U.S. patents for utilization of electricity, covering apparatus for generating transmitting, distributing and measuring; first to produce stable iron for electromagnetic purposes; pioneer in long distance, high tension transmission work. Fellow Am. Inst. Elec. Engineers. Received John Scott medal of Franklin Inst., Phila., 1909, for electric piano-players. Home: Pittsfield, Mass. Died Oct. 15, 1922.

KELLY, John H., newspaper pub.; b. Sioux City, Ia., June 18, 1885; s. John Charles and Martha (Hill) K.; prep. edn., Mercersburg (Pa.) Acad.; Litt.B., Princeton Univ.; m. Edna M. Hanford, July 3, 1912; children—Constance M., Marjorie A., Janice H., Doris Hanford. Editor and pub. Sioux City Tribune. Served as maj. inf., U.S.A., World War; lt. col., Specialist Res., U.S.A. Mason. Home: Sioux City, Ia. Died Mar. 2, 1933.

KELLY, Joseph Luther, judge; b. Smyth Co., Va., Mar. 4, 1867; s. Judge John A. and Martha (Peck) K.; A.B., Emory and Henry Coll., Va., 1886; B.L., Univ. of Va., 1889; LL.D., Washington and Lee U., 1923; m. Mary Eloise Hull, July 29, 1896. Practiced in Big Stone Gap, Va., with R. A. Ayers, atty. gen. of Va., 1889-95; mem. Bullitt & Kelly (J. F. Bullitt), 1895-1909; judge Corp. Ct., Bristol, 1909-14; judge Supreme Ct. of Appeals, Va., term 1915-27, pres. ct., 1920—. Trustee Emory and Henry Coll. Democrat. Methodist. Home: Bristol, Va. Died Apr. 14, 1925.

KELLY, Lon Hamman, lawyer; b. Sutton, W.Va., Jan. 28, 1871; s. John McH. and Alzira Virginia (Hamman) K.; LL.B., Washington and Lee U., 1893; m. Bertha Gorrell, Mar. 3, 1897 (died 1904); children—Robert G., Mrs. Janet Savage; m. 2d, Nellie Kiddy, June 19, 1907; 1 dau., Virginia Elizabeth. Admitted to W.Va. bar, 1893; mem. Brown, Jackson & Knight. Mayor of Sutton, 1896; pros. atty. Braxton Co., W.Va., 1897-1900; asst. U.S. atty. Southern Dist. of W Va., 1916-17, and U.S. atty., Oct. 1917-22; nominated by Dem. Party for Judge Supreme Ct. of Appeals of W.Va., 1924. Pres. W.Va. State Bar Assn., 1933-34; gov. Rotary Internat., 24th Dist., 1935-36. Presbyn. Mason. Home: Charleston, W.Va. Died Dec. 23, 1938.

KELLY, M(elville) Clyde, congressman; b. Bloomfield, Ohio, Aug. 4, 1883; s. William M. and Mary C. (Clark) K.; educated Muskingum Coll., New Concord, O.; hon. A.M., same coll., 1916; m. Vida Ruth Clementson, 1917; children—Ruth, Mary, Hilda Fletcher, Vida Clyde. City editor, Daily News, Braddock, Pa., 1901-03; founded Braddock Leader, 1903; purchased Daily News, 1905, Evening Herald, 1907; published Daily News-Herald, 1907—. Mem. Pa. Ho. of Rep., 1910-13; mem. 63d Congress and 65th to 72d Congresses (1913-15 and 1917-32), 33d Pa. Dist., and 73d Congress (1932-35), 31st Pa. Dist. Republican. United Presby. Pres. Pa. Soc. D.C., Gen. Council United Presbyn. Ch. of N. America, Belvedere Gen. Hosp. (Pittsburgh). Author: Machine Made Legislation, 1911; The Community Capitol, 1921; U.S. Postal Policy, 1931. Home: Pittsburgh, Pa. Deceased.

KELLY, Robert Morrow, lawyer; b. Paris, Ky., Sept. 22, 1836; s. Thomas and Cordelia (Morrow) K.; ed. pvt. schs.; taught sch. several yrs.; admitted to bar, 1860; capt. to col. 4th Ky. Inf., U.S.V., 1861-65; m. Harriet Holley Warfield, June 27, 1867. Resumed law practice at Paris, Ky.; collector internal revenue, 7th Ky. Dist., 1866-70; with brief intermission, had charge of Louisville Daily Commercial, 1870-97; U.S. pension agt., 1873-86. Republican. Home: Louisville, Ky. Died Dec. 27, 1913.

KELLY, William, mining engr.; b. New York, N.Y., Apr. 17, 1854; s. Robert and Arietta A. (Hutton) K.; B.A., Yale, 1874; E.M., Columbia, 1877; D.Eng., Rensselaer Polytech. Inst., 1924; D.Sc., Mich. Coll. Mining and Technology, 1930; m. Annie Ashcom, June 24, 1886; 1 son, William Ashcom (dec.). Asst. supt. Chem. Copper Co., Phoenixville, Pa., 1876, 79, 80; chemist Himrod Furnace Co., Youngstown, O., 7 mos., 1878; supt. Kemble Coal & Iron Co., Riddlesburg, Pa., 1881-85, Glamorgan Iron Co., Lewistown, Pa., 1885, Kemble Iron Co., 1886-89; gen. supt., gen. mgr. Penn Iron Mining Co., Vulcan, Mich., 1889-1923; gen. mgr. Republic (Mich.) Iron Co., 1902-14; treas. Penn Store Co., 1902-23; v.p. Commercial Bank, Iron Mountain, Mich. Pres. Bd. Examiners Bituminous Mine Inspectors of Pa., 1885-89; chmn. Bd. County Road Commrs., Dickinson Co., Mich., 1904—; mem. Pub. Domain Commn. Mich., 1909-21, chmn., 1917-21; pres. Bd. Edn., Norway Twp., Mich. several yrs.; mem. 1897-1929, chmn., 1904-29, bd. control Mich. Coll. Mines. Mem. State Highway Advisory Bd., Mich., 1919-30. Fellow A.A.A.S., Nat. Inst. Social Sciences; hon. mem. Instn. Mining Engrs. (London). Home: Iron Mountain, Mich. Died Oct. 1, 1937.

KELLY, William Joseph, judge; b. Brooklyn, N.Y., Apr. 13, 1860; s. William and Mary (Holden) K.; educated pvt. and pub. schs., Brooklyn; LL.D., Manhattan Coll., 1919; m. Elizabeth A. Scott, 1883 (died 1906). Admitted to bar, 1881, and engaged in gen. practice of law in New York and Brooklyn; justice Supreme Ct. of N.Y. for terms 1903-17, 1918-31; temporarily assigned to Appellate Div., 2d Dept., by Gov. Whitman, Jan. 1, 1918; apptd. justice Appellate Div. for term, 1921-26, by Gov. Miller, Apr. 16, 1921; apptd. presiding justice, by Gov. Smith, Jan. 1, 1923. Democrat. Home: Brooklyn, N.Y. Died Oct. 11, 1927.

KELMAN, John, clergyman; b. Dundonald, Ayrshire, Scotland, June 20, 1864; s. Rev. John and Margaret Harper (Urquhart) K.; ed. Royal High Sch., Univ., and New Coll., Edinburgh, and Ormond Coll., Melbourne, Australia (one session); M.A., Edinburgh, 1884 (D.D., 1907; D.D., Yale, 1917, Princeton, 1921; Litt.D., Lafayette, 1920); m. Ellin Runcorn Bell, of Edinburgh, May 18, 1892. Asst. to Rev. George Adam Smith, of Queen's Cross United Free Ch., 1890-91; ordained Presbyn. ministry, 1891; pastor Peterculter United Free Ch., Aberdeenshire, 1891-97, New North United Free Ch., 1897-1907, St. George's United Free Ch., Edinburgh, 1907-19, Fifth Av. Presbyn. Ch., New York, Nov. 1919—. Served as chaplain in British Territorial Army 6 yrs. Decorated Officer Order of the British Empire for services with Army in France and Flanders. Mem. bd. dirs. Lafayette U., Union Theol. Sem. Author: The Holy Land, 1901; The Faith of Robert Louis Stevenson, 1903; The Courts of the Temple; Honor Towards God; The War and Preaching, 1919; Some Aspects of International Christianity, 1920; Foundations of Faith, 1921; Prophets of Yesterday and Their Message for Today, 1923. Home: New York, N.Y Died May 3, 1929.

KELSEY, Charles Boyd, physician; b. Farmington, Conn., Nov. 19, 1850; s. Rev. Charles and Eliza (Boyd) K.; A.B., Free Acad. (now Coll. City of New York), 1870; M.D., Coll. Phys. and Surg. (Columbia), 1873; m. Carolyn Terry, Apr. 1876. House surgeon St. Luke's Hosp., 1873-76; asst. demonstrator anatomy, Coll. Phys. and Surg., 1874-79; prof. diseases of the rectum, U. of Vt., 1889-90; same chair (and dir.), N.Y. Post-Grad. Sch. and Hosp., 1890—. Home: New York, N.Y. Died Aug. 4, 1917.

KELSEY, Charles Edward, publisher; b. Evans Mills, N.Y., June 7, 1862; s. Erastus S. and Elizabeth (Sill) K.; A.B., Amherst, 1884, hon. A.M., 1924; m. Carrie M. Pratt, May 24, 1894; children—Robert P., Marion (Mrs. John H. Underhill). Connected with The Youth's Companion, 1889—; formerly sec.; pres. Perry Mason & Co., publishers Youth's Companion, 1912—. Pres. Newton Hosp.; trustee Atlanta (Ga.) U. Republican. Conglist. Home: Boston, Mass. Died Nov. 25, 1931.

KELSEY, Clarence Hill, banker; b. Bridgeport, Conn., Dec. 23, 1856; s. Courtland and Sarah (Hoyt) K.; A.B., Yale, 1878, A.M., 1880; LL.B., Hamilton Law Sch., 1880; m. Elizabeth B. Tomlinson, Dec. 1, 1885. Admitted to bar, 1880; practiced in New York, 1880-83; office mgr., 1883, later sec., v.p., pres. and from 1923 chmn. bd., Title Guarantee & Trust Co.; also chmn. bd. Bond & Mortgage Guarantee Co.; dir. Corn Exchange Bank, Home Ins. Co., U.S. Life Ins. Co., Westchester Title & Trust Co. Presbyn. Republican. Home: West Orange, N.J. Died May 1, 1930.

KELSEY, Francis Willey, univ. prof.; b. Ogden, N.Y., May 23, 1858; s. Henry and Olive Cornelia (Trowbridge) K.; A.B., U. of Rochester, 1880, Ph.D., 1886, LL.D., 1910; studied in Europe, 1883, 1884-85; m. Isabelle Badger, Dec. 22, 1885; children—Ruth Cornelia (Mrs. Frederick Carl Diel), Charlotte Badger (Mrs. Frank T. Hubley), Easton Trowbridge. Instr. classics, 1880-82, prof. Latin, 1882-89, Lake Forest U.; prof. Latin lang. and lit., U. of Mich., 1889—; dir. U. of Mich. Expdns. to Near East, 1919, 24, 25, 26. Editor: Am. edit. Cicero's Cato Major De Senectute and Lælius De Amicitia (with introduction and notes by James S. Reid), 1883; T. Lucreti Cari De Rerum Natura (with introduction and notes to Books 1, 3 and 5), 1884, 6th edit., 1906; Cæsar's Gallic War (with introduction, notes and vocabulary), 1886-1917; Selections from Ovid, 1891-1906; Select Orations and Letters of Cicero, 1892-1911; Xenophon's Anabasis (with Andreas C. Zenos), 1889-98; Latin and Greek in American Education, 1911, 26; Handbooks of Archæology and Antiquities (with Prof. Percy Gardner, of U. of Oxford), 1896—; University of Michigan Studies, Humanistic Series (with Prof. H. A. Sanders), 1904—. Translator: Pompeii—Its Life and Art, by August Mau, 1889-1904. Died May 14, 1927.

KELSEY, Frederick Wallace, nurseryman; b. Ogden, N.Y., Apr. 25, 1850; s. Henry and Olive Cornelia (Trowbridge) K.; ed. pub. schs., Ogden, and Chili (N.Y.) Acad.; m. Ella Abigail Butts, Jan. 1874; children—Frederick Trowbridge, Ronald Butts; m. 2d, Vergelia Adelia Butts, June 1914. In nursery business, 1878—; now exec. pres. F. W. Kelsey Nursery Co., nursery stock and tree seeds; founder of The Kelsey Trust. Chmn. Tariff Com. on Nursery Products, retained through two tariffs; author of N.Y. law for inspection of fruit trees and nursery stock; chmn. com. that prepared street tree planting law of N.J., 1893 (since adopted in main features by several states); originator of Essex County (N.J.) Park Commn. (first county park system); known as "father of the Essex County Parks"; chmn. of com., 1905, that framed the original limited utility franchise law of N.J.; chmn. stockholders' com., 1915, that selected bd. dirs. of New York Title & Mortgage Co.; long active in betterment of local, state and nat. affairs. Author: The First County Park System, 1905. Home: South Orange, N.J. Died Oct. 20, 1935.

KELSEY, Henry Hopkins, clergyman; b. Evans Mills, N.Y., Apr. 9, 1853; s. Erastus Spencer and Elizabeth (Sill) K.; A.B., Amherst, 1876, A.M., 1879; grad. Hartford Theol. Sem., 1879; D.D., Marietta, 1911; m. Alice Watson Miller, Nov. 22, 1892. Instr. and asst. librarian, Hartford Theol. Sem., 1879-82; asst. pastor Shawmut Ch., Boston, 1882-83; ordained Congl. ministry, 1884; pastor 2d Ch., Winsted, Conn., 1884-88, 4th Ch., Hartford, Conn., 1888-1910, 1st Ch., Marietta, O., 1910-15; sec. A.B.C.F.M. for coast dist., 1915-25, emeritus. Chaplain 1st Regt., Conn. Vols., Spanish-Am. War, May 14-Oct. 31, 1898; chaplain 1st Regt. Conn. N.G., 1900-08. Trustee Pacific Sch. of Religion. Republican. Home: Berkeley, Calif. Deceased.

KELSEY, Joseph A., fire insurance; b. St. Mary's, O. Began ins. business at Denver, Colo., 1880; spl. agt. New York Underwriters Agency, 1881; spl. agt. Ins. Co. of North America and Pa. Fire Ins. Co. in Ia., later in Ind., 1881-90; asst. mgr. Western dept. Royal Ins. Co., Chicago, 1890-97; mgr. Aachen & Munich Ins. Co., 1897-1918; gen. agt. Tokio Marine & Fire Ins. Co., 1918—; pres. Standard Ins. Co. of N.Y., 1922—. Home: Montclair, N.J. Died Sept. 13, 1938.

KELSEY, Rayner Wickersham, prof. history; b. Western Springs, Ill., Jan. 29, 1879; s. Asa and Sarah (Atwater) K.; Ph.B., Earlham Coll., Richmond, Ind., 1900; M.L., Ph.D., U. of Calif., 1909; m. Naomi Harrison Binford, Feb. 23, 1901; 1 son, Rayner Wilfred. Prof. history, Pacific Coll., Newberg, Ore., 1900-04; prof. history, Whittier (Calif.) Coll., 1904-06; fellow U. of Calif., 1906-09; instr. in Am. history, Haverford (Pa.) Coll., 1909-11, asso. prof., 1912-19, prof., 1920—. Author: U.S. Consulate in California, 1910; Friends and the Indians, 1917; Centennial History of Moses Brown School, 1919; The Tariff, 1929; Farm Relief, 1929; Prohibition, 1929; Political Parties, 1930; Internationalism, 1930. Editor Cazenove

Jour., 1922, and Bull. of Friends' Hist. Assn., 1922-32. Home: Haverford, Pa. Died Oct. 29, 1934.

KEMBLE, Edward Windsor, writer, illustrator; b. Sacramento, Calif., Jan. 18, 1861; s. Edward Cleveland (founder and pub. Alta Californian) and Cecilia (Windsor) K.; ed. pub. schs., New York; m. Sara Briggs; children—Edward Brewster, Beth Elsie, Schuyler, Gail. From 1881 has been connected with various mags. and weekly periodicals as illustrator and cartoonist; for Collier's, 1903-07, Harper's Weekly, 1907-12; splty. negro characters. Illustrator: Uncle Tom's Cabin, Huckleberry Finn, Pudd'nhead Wilson, Colonel Carter of Cartersville, etc. Author: Blackberries; Kemble's Coons; Rosemary; Virginia Creeper; Billy-Goat and Other Comicalities, 1898; Comical Coons, 1898; A Coon Alphabet, 1898; Coon Calendar, 1899; Kemble's Sketch Book, 1899; Coontown's 400, 1900; A Pickaninny Calendar, 1900. Died Sept. 19, 1933.

KEMEYS, Edward, sculptor; b. Savannah, Ga., Jan. 31, 1843; s. William and Abby Brenton (Greene) K.; ed. in New York until 1860; served in Civil war, capt. arty., Union army, until 1866; m. Laura Swing. After war farmed in Illinois for a short time; later mem. of corps of civ. engrs., Central Park, New York. Became a sculptor, 1870; went abroad, 1877; exhibited in London and in the Paris Salon. His specialty is N. Am. Indians and animal figures, particularly of wild beasts; pioneer animal sculptor of U.S. Home: Washington, D.C. Died 1907.

KEMP, Agnes, physician, reformer; b. (Nininger) Harrisburg, Pa., Nov. 4, 1823; ed. Harrisburg Sem.; grad. Woman's Med. Coll., Phila., 1879; m. Col. William Saunders; 2d, 1860, Joseph Kemp, lawyer. Was 1st woman mem. of Med. Soc. of Dauphin Co., Pa.; practiced medicine 6 yrs.; then traveled abroad nearly 4 yrs. Prominent in W.C.T.U.; active in woman suffrage, social purity and other reform movements; also active in anti-slavery work. Home: Swarthmore, Pa. Died 1908.

KEMP, Bolivar Edwards, congressman; b. Amite, La., Dec. 28, 1871; s. William Breed and Elizabeth (Neson) K.; student La. State U.; LL.B., Tulane, 1897; m. Lallie Conner, Apr. 21, 1903; children—Bolivar Edwards, Eleanor Ogden. Admitted to La. bar, 1898, and began practice at Amite; associated with father as mem. Kemp & Kemp, later Kemp & Spiller, now Kemp & Buck; mem. 69th to 72d Congresses (1925-33), 6th La. Dist. Mem. bd. supervisors La. State U. Democrat. Episcopalian. Home: Amite, La. Died June 19, 1933.

KEMP, James Furman, geologist; b. New York, N.Y., 1859; s. James Alexander and Caroline (Furman) K.; A.B., Amherst, 1881, hon. Sc.D., 1906; E.M., Columbia, 1884; LL.D., McGill, 1913; m. Kate Taylor, Sept. 5, 1889; children—James Taylor, Philip Kittredge, Katherine Furman. Instr. and asst. prof. geology, Cornell U., 1886-91; adj. prof. geology, 1891-92, prof., 1892—, Columbia. Mgr. and scientific dir. New York Bot. Gardens, 1898—; formerly geologist U.S. and N.Y. Geol. Surveys. Hon. mem. and res. Am. Inst. Mining and Metall. Engrs., Mining and Metall. Soc. America (gold medalist). Author of textbooks and many scientific papers. Home: Great Neck, N.Y. Died Nov. 17, 1926.

KEMP, Theodore, lecturer; b. near Rising Sun, Ind., Apr. 16, 1868; s. George C. and Minerva Dora (Stone) K.; A.B., DePauw U., Ind., 1893; Garrett Bibl. Inst., Evanston, Ill., 1885-87; sch. of theology (formerly at DePauw U.), 1891-93; D.D., Ill. Wesleyan, 1907, LL.D., 1911; m. Flora B. Truitt, Nov. 28, 1893. Ordained M.E. ministry, 1895; pastor, Allerton, Ill., 1893-96, Petersburg, 1896-1900, Grace Ch., Jacksonville, 1900-02, Charleston, 1902-05, Grace Ch., Bloomington, 1905-08; teacher English Bible and ethics, 1906-07, pres., 1908-22, Ill. Wesleyan U.; asso. sec. Commn. Internat. Justice and Goodwill of Federal Council of Chs., 1923-24; pastor Hollywood M.E. Ch., South, Los Angeles, 1924-26. Mason. Republican. Home: Los Angeles, Calif. Died May 20, 1937.

KEMP, W(illiam) Thomas, lawyer; b. Talbot Co., Md., Apr. 16, 1877; s. J. H. Caulk and Hester Ann (Hopkins) K.; B.A., St. John's Coll., Md., 1897; M.A., in Polit. Science, Columbia, 1899, LL.B., 1900; m. Elsie C. Melvin, June 4, 1904. Began practice at Baltimore, 1900, in association with the late George Whitelock; became mem. Keech, Deming, Kemp & Carman; asst. sec. Am. Bar Assn., 1910-19, sec., 1920—. Chmn. State Conservation Commn. of Md., 1916-20; pres. Eastern Shore Soc., 1919; pres. Roland Park Civic League, 1921. Mem. bd. govs. St. John's Coll. Democrat. Episcopalian. Mason. Revised Conservation Laws of Md., 1916, 18. Edited annual reports of Am. Bar Assn., 1910-23. Home: Roland Park, Baltimore, Md. Died Feb. 7, 1925.

KEMPER, General William Harrison, M.D.; b. Rush Co., Ind., Dec. 16, 1839; s. Arthur Smith and Patience (Bryant) K.; ed. common schs.; pvt. 7th Ind. Vols., 3 months, 1861; hosp. steward 17th Ind. Vols., 1861-63; asst. surgeon, 1863-64; attended med. lectures, U. of Mich., 1864-65; M.D., L.I. Coll. Hosp., 1865; post-grad. course New York Polyclinic, 1886; m. Harriet Kemper, Aug. 15, 1865; children—Mrs. Georgette Moodey Smith, Arthur Thomson, William Winter. In practice at Muncie, Ind., 1865; was asst. to chair of obstetrics and diseases of women, Central Coll. Phys. and Surg. Indianapolis, 1875-76; mem. and sec. bd. trustees Med. Coll. of Ind., Indianapolis, 1890—; coroner Delaware Co., Ind., 1870-75; U.S. examining surgeon for pensions, 1872-93. Author: The World's Anatomists, 1905; Medical History of the State of Indiana, 1911. Home: Muncie, Ind. Died Sept. 26, 1927.

KEMPER, William Thornton, banker; b. Davies Co., Mo., Nov. 3, 1866; s. of James Madison and Sarah Ann (Paxton) K.; ed. high school; m. Lottie Crosby, June 10, 1890. Began as clk. in shoe store, later traveling salesman; in commercial business, Valley Falls, Kan., and became bank cashier there; settled in Kansas City, Mo., 1893, an organizer Commerce Trust Co., 1906; sold interest to Southwest Nat. Bank of Commerce, Jan. 1, 1917, and after 5 mos. was invited back as chmn. bd. of both Nat. Bank of Commerce and Commerce Trust Co.; now chmn. bd. Commerce Trust Company; pres. Kemper Mill & Elevator Co., Kemper Investment Co., Kemper Mercantile Co. Operates 7 large farms. Mem. State Council Defense, Mo., also Jackson Co. Council Defense; mem. exec. com. 3 Liberty Loan campaigns; dir. Tenth Federal Res. Dist. Advisory Council. Mem. K.C. Bd. of Trade (pres.), K.C. Chamber of Commerce (dir., treas. 6 yrs.). Trustee William Woods Coll. (Fulton, Mo.), Nettleton Home for Aged Women; v.p., trustee Thomas M. Spofford Home for Dependent Children; mem. exec. com. Red Cross; mem. bd. govs. Liberty Memorial Assn. Del. 3 Dem. Nat. Convs.; formerly mem. Dem. State Central Com.; mem. Dem. Nat. Com. until Feb. 1936. Mason. Mem. Industrial Advisory Bd. of NRA, 1933—. Home: Kansas City, Mo. Died Jan. 19, 1938.

KEMPFF, Louis, rear admiral U.S.N.; b. nr. Belleville, Ill., Oct. 11, 1841; s. Friedrich and Henrietta K.; apptd. to U.S. Naval Acad., from Ill., 1857; m. Cornelia R. Selby, July 16, 1873. Promoted lt., Aug. 1, 1862; lt. comdr., July 25, 1866; comdr., Mar. 9, 1876; capt., May 19, 1891; rear admiral, Mar. 3, 1899. Served on Vandalia, Atlantic Blockading Squadron, 1861; captured, and took to New York, schooner Henry Middleton, of Charleston; participated in battle of Port Royal, S.C., Nov. 7, 1861; served on Wabash, Atlantic Blockading Squadron, 1861-62; capture of Fernandina, Fla., St. Mary's, Ga., Jacksonville, Fla., and St. Augustine, Fla.; Susquehanna, West Gulf Blockading Squadron, part of 1862, and 1863; bombardment of Sewell's Point, Va., May 1862, and reoccupation of Norfolk, May 10, 1862; Sonoma, June and July, 1863; Connecticut, 1863-64; Suwanee, Pacific Squadron, 1865-67; training-ship Portsmouth, 1867-68; receiving-ship Independence, 1868-70; exec. officer Mohican, on eclipse expdn. to Siberia, 1869; Pacific Squadron, 1870-73, as exec. officer Mohican, 1871-72, Saranac, 1872, California, 1872-73; Naval Rendezvous, San Francisco, 1873-74; light house insp., 13th dist., 1874-76; sr. aid to commandant, Navy Yard, Mare Island, 1877-78; equipment officer, Navy Yard, Mare Island, 1878-80; comd. Naval Rendezvous, San Francisco, 1880-81; comd. Alert, 1881-82; ordnance officer, Navy Yard, Mare Island, Calif., 1883-85; comd. Adams, 1885-88; Navy Yard, Mare Island, 1888-90; mem. Bd. of Inspection, San Francisco, 1890-93; comd. Monterey, 1893-95; Naval War Coll., 1895; mem. Naval Examining and Retiring Bds., 1895-96; comd. receiving-ship Independence, 1896-99; comdt., Navy Yard, Mare Island, 1899-1900; squadron comdr., Asiatic Fleet, 1900-02; declined to join foreign admirals in firing on Taku forts, 1900, but after U.S.S. Monocacy was struck by a shot from the Chinese forts, joined in with forces at hand for protection of life and property of Americans; comdt. Pacific Naval Dist., 1902-03; retired, Oct. 11, 1903; special duty, 1904-05. Home: San Francisco, Calif. Died July 29, 1920.

KEMPSTER, Walter, physician; b. London, Eng., May 25, 1841; s. Christopher and Charlotte (Treble) K.; infancy in Syracuse, N.Y.; acad. edn.; M.D., L.I. Med. Coll., 1864; m. J. L. J. Poessel, June 28, 1913. Served in Civil War, May-Nov. 1861, in 12th N.Y. Inf.; then in 10th N.Y. Cav. to Nov. 1863; 1st lt., June 9, 1863; actg. asst. surgeon U.S.A., June 1864-July 1865; asst. supt. N.Y. State Asylum for Idiots, 1866-67; asst. phys. N.Y. Hosp. for Insane, Utica, 1867-73; supt. Northern Hosp. for Insane, Wis., 1873-84; asst. editor Am. Jour. of Insanity, 1874-84; commr. of health, Milwaukee, 1894-98; prof. mental diseases in Wis. Coll. Phys. and Surg. First phys. in U.S. to make systematic microscopic exam. of brains of insane, and first to photograph through microscope the actual disease (1867); has filled important spl. med. commns. for U.S. Govt. Author: Hospital Gangrene in Army Hospitals, 1866; Entero-Colitis in United States Army, 1866. Home: Milwaukee, Wis. Died Aug. 22, 1918.

KENDAL, William Hunter, actor, mgr.; b. London, Eng., Dec. 16, 1843; real name Grimston; ed. private school and by tutor; m. Margaret Brunton Robertson (see "Mrs. Kendal"), Aug. 7, 1869; began career on stage (under theatrical name of Mr. Kendal) at Glasgow, 1862, supporting various stars there until 1866; 1st London appearance, Oct. 31, 1866, at Haymarket Theatre in A Dangerous Friend; after that played leading rôles in modern dramas at Haymarket, Prince of Wales' and Court theatres; lessee and mgr. with John Hare of St. James' Theatre, 1879-88; professionally toured U.S. and Canada (with Mrs. Kendal), 1889-95. Died Nov. 6, 1917.

KENDALL, Calvin Noyes, commr. of education; b. Augusta, N.Y., Feb. 9, 1858; s. Leonard J. and Sarah M. K.; A.B., Hamilton Coll., 1882; (hon. A.M., Yale U., 1900, U. of Mich., 1909; Litt.D., Hamilton Coll., 1911, Rutgers, 1912; LL.D., New York U., 1913); m. Alla P. Field, June 30, 1891. Taught pvt. schs. in West 3 yrs.; prin. Jackson High Sch., 1885-86; supt. schs., Jackson, 1886-90, Saginaw, Mich., 1890-92; in business 3 yrs.; supt. schs., New Haven, Conn., 1895-1900; supt. schs., Indianapolis, and mem. Ind. State Bd. Edn., 1900-11; commr. of edn., State of N.J., July, 1911—. Has lectured in summer schs. of Columbia, Calif., Chicago, Ind., and Yale univs. President Conn. Council of Edn., 1897-98, Conn. State Teachers' Assn., 1899-1900, Southern Ind. Teachers' Assn., 1904-05, Ind. State Teachers' Assn., 1910-11, N.J. Council Edn., 1914-15. Apptd. mem. advisory com. on federal tubercular schs., Oct. 1, 1918. Mem. Order of Double Dragon (Chinese), 1904. Joint editor: (with late Reuben G. Thwaites) History of the United States for Elementary Schools; (with George A. Mirick) Teaching the Fundamental Subjects; (with Florence A. Stryker) How to Teach History in the Elementary Schools; (with George A. Mirick) How to Teach the Special Subjects. Home: Princeton, N.J. Died Sept. 2, 1921.

KENDALL, Edward Hale, architect; b. July 31, 1842; ed. Boston Latin School and Paris, France. Pres. New York Chapter of Am. Inst. of Architects, 1887-91; pres. Am. Inst. Architects, 1892-93; mem. Architectural League, Century Assn., etc. Home: New York, N.Y. Died 1901.

KENDALL, Ezra Fremont, comedian, author; b. Allegany Co., N.Y., Feb. 15, 1861; s. Ezra W. and Eliza R. (Pratt) K., (father, lt. 64th N.Y. Vols., killed at battle of Fair Oaks); ed. pub. schs.; learned printer's trade; went to New York at 17, worked at trade and as reporter (was youngest mem. New York Press Club); m. Jannette Dunn, 1887. In theatrical life from 1881; first success in "Wanted, a Partner," later in "We, Us & Co.," "A Pair of Kids," "The Substitute." In vaudeville, 1896-1902, in monologues; began starring in "The Vinegar Buyer," Sept. 22, 1902. Author: Spots of Wit and Humor, 1901; Good Gravy, 1902 H12; Tell It to Me. Plays: We, Us & Co.; A Pair of Kids; The Substitute; One of the Old Stock; Just Landed. Home: Mt. Vernon, N.Y. Died 1910.

KENDALL, John Chester, agriculturist; b. Harrisville, N.H., Mar. 13, 1877; s. Gilman and Lucy Ann (Felch) K.; B.S., N.H. Coll., Durham, 1902; post-grad., Ohio State U., 1902; m. Marjorie Louise Foster, Oct. 2, 1912. Instr. dairying, winter of 1902, later instr. and asst. prof. in charge of dairying, 1902-07, N.C. Coll. of Agr. and Mechanic Arts, West Raleigh; state dairy commr. of Kan., at Manhattan, Kan., 1907-08; prof. dairy husbandry, Kan. State Agrl. Coll., Manhattan, 1908-10; dir. N.H. Agrl. Expt. Sta., Sept. 15, 1910-39, and dir. extension service, 1911-38. Republican. Unitarian. Mason. Home: Dunham, N.H. Died Mar. 16, 1941.

KENDALL, Margaret, artist; b. Staten Island, N.Y., Nov. 29, 1871; d. late Albert and Elizabeth (Weston) Stickney; pupil of J. Alden Weir, Julius Rolshoven and Sergeant Kendall; m. (William) Sergeant Kendall, Feb. 17, 1896; children—Elisabeth, Beatrice, Alison. Exhibited Pa. Acad. Fine Arts, 1898-1902, Soc. Am. Artists, 1898-1902, Minneapolis, 1900, Paris Expn., 1900, Soc. Miniature Painters, 1901-04, Boston Expn., Buffalo Expn., 1901; bronze medal, St. Louis Expn., 1904. Home: Hot Springs, Va. Died Apr. 27, 1933.

KENDALL, Nathan E., governor; b. Greenville, Ia., Mar. 17, 1868; dist. sch. edn.; m. Belle Wooden, Apr. 20, 1896. Began practice of law at Albia, Ia., 1887; city atty. 1 term; co. atty. Monroe Co., Ia., 1893-97; mem. Ia. Ho. of Rep., 1899-1909 (speaker last term); mem. 61st and 62d Congresses (1909-13), 6th Iowa Dist. gov. of Ia., 1921-25. Republican. Home: Des Moines, Ia. Died Nov. 1936.

KENDALL, Samuel Austin, congressman; b. Somerset Co., Pa., Nov. 1, 1859; s. John C. and Elizabeth (Kendall) K.; student Mt. Union Coll., Alliance, O., 1879-80; m. Edith Wiley, 1883; children—Grace Maeona (wife of Rev. H. B. Angus), Samuel Austin, John Wiley, Grant Van Nest (dec.). In lumber business, 1890—. Mem. Pa. Ho. of Rep., 1899-1903; mem. 66th to 72d Congresses (1919-33), 24th Pa. Dist. Republican. Lutheran. Mason. Home: Meyersdale, Pa. Died Jan. 8, 1933.

KENDALL, (William) Sergeant, painter, sculptor; b. Spuyten Duyvil (now part of N.Y. City), Jan. 20, 1869; s. Benjamin Franklin and Elizabeth Anne (Sergeant) K.; pupil of Thomas Eakins, 1883, Art Students League, New York, 1886, Academie Julien, Paris, 1888, École des Beaux Arts, 1890, Luc Olivier Merson, Paris, 1891; hon. M.A., Yale, 1913; m. Margaret Weston Stickney, Feb. 17, 1896; children—Elizabeth (Mrs. Pierson Underwood), Beatrice, Alison

(Mrs. Edward L. Parker); m. 2d, Christine Herter, Aug. 2, 1922. Hon. mention Paris Salon, 1891; awarded medal, Chicago Expn., 1893; Lippincott prize, Pa. Acad. Fine Arts, 1894; hon. mention, Tenn. Expn., 1897, Omaha Expn., 1898; 2d prize, Worcester Art Mus., 1900; bronze medal and prize, Carnegie Inst., 1900; medal, Paris Expn., 1900; silver medal for painting, bronze medal for drawing, and hon. mention for sculpture, Buffalo Expn., 1901; Shaw prize, Soc. Am. Artists, 1901; 2d prize, Worcester Art Mus., 1902; Shaw Fund purchase prize, Soc. Am. Artists, 1903; gold medal, St. Louis Expn., 1904; Isidor gold medal, N.A.D., 1908; Harris prize, Art Inst. Chicago, 1908; Potter Palmer gold medal and $1000 prize, Art Inst. Chicago, 1910; gold medal for painting and silver medal for sculpture, Panama Pacific Expn., 1915; Edward B. Butler prize, Art Inst. Chicago, 1918; gold medal, Miss. Art Assn., 1926; Isidor gold medal, N.A.D., 1927, with Ranger Fund Purchase; Chauncey Woodworth prize, Palm Beach Art Center Expn., 1934. Represented in Met. Mus. of Art, Pa. Acad. Fine Arts, Albright Art Gallery (Buffalo), Peabody Inst. (Baltimore), Nat. Gallery and Corcoran Gallery (Washington, D.C.) R.I. Sch. of Design, Coll. of Physicians and Surgeons (New York), Johns Hopkins U., Williams Coll., Yale Univ., U.S. War Coll. (Newport, R.I.), Detroit Mus. of Art, St. Paul's Sch. (Concord, N.H.), and numerous pvt. collections. Exhibited in France, Italy, Germany, U.S. and S. America. Nat. Academician; mem. Nat. Inst. Arts and Letters, Art Assn. of Newport (pres. 1911-13). Dean Sch. of Fine Arts, Yale, 1913-22. Home: Hot Springs, Va. Died Feb. 16, 1938.

KENDALL, William Converse, naturalist; b. Freeport, Me., Apr. 4, 1861; s. William Pote and Frances Ann (Carver) K.; A.B., Bowdoin College, Brunswick, Maine, 1885, A.M., 1890, Sc.D., 1935; M.D., Georgetown Univ., 1896; m. Ida W. Aschenbach, Apr. 3, 1893; 1 dau., Minerva Converse (Mrs. Harrison Warner). Taught sch. in Minn., 1885-87; prin. Patten (Me.) Acad., 1887-89; naturalist with U.S. Commn. of Fish and Fisheries, 1889-1921; ichthyologist, Roosevelt Wild Life Forest Expt. Sta., 1921-23; ichthyologist, U.S. Bur. Fisheries, 1923-32. Has written papers and reports on fishes and other natural history subjects in bulls. and reports U.S. Fish Commn.; proc. of the U.S. Nat. Mus. and publications of Boston Soc. Natural History, Portland Soc. Natural History and Mus. of Comparative Zoölogy. Member MacMillan Arctic Expdn., summer, 1929. Mason. Home: Freeport, Me. Died Jan. 28, 1939.

KENDALL, William Mitchell, architect; b. Jamaica Plain, Mass., Feb. 13, 1856; s. Joshua and Phoebe (Mitchell) K.; A.B., Harvard, 1876; studied architecture for 2 yrs. at Mass. Inst. Tech. and for several yrs. in Italy and France; L.H.D., Bowdoin, 1923; A.M., Wesleyan U., 1930; m. Grace Eliot Endicott, July 14, 1897 (died 1919). Mem. McKim, Mead & White, New York. Among bldgs. designed by the firm are the new Post Office and the Municipal Office Bldg., New York; the Journalism and Avery Library bldgs., and dwelling of the president, at Columbia U.; houses for Percy R. Pyne and Geraldyn Redmond, New York, and house for Thos. Newbold, New York; Butler Art Gallery, Youngstown, Ohio, the McKinley memorial, Niles, O.; bldg. for Acad. of Arts and Letters, New York; Plymouth Rock Portico, Plymouth, Mass.; restoration St. John's Ch., Washington; bldg. for Am. Acad. in Rome; Tenn. War Memorial, Nashville; Arlington Memorial Bridge; bldg. for Harvard Sch. of Business; John W. Weeks Memorial Bridge, Cambridge, Mass.; Casa Italiana, New York; Chapel, U. of Vt.; Rochester Savings Bank; Savoy Plaza Hotel, New York; additional wings to Met. Mus. of Art, New York; Olin Memorial Library, Wesleyan Univ.; City Hall, Burlington, Vt.; War Memorial, Newport, R.I.; Ira Allen Chapel, Burlington, Vt.; gymnasium and other buildings for Adelphi College. National Academician; fellow Am. Inst. Architects; trustee Am. Acad. in Rome, mem. Nat. Acad. Arts and Letters. Apptd., 1916, mem. Nat. Commn. of Fine Arts; mem. commn. for beautification permanent Am. mil. cemeteries, France and England, 1921. Awarded gold medal, N.Y. Chapter Am. Inst. Architects, 1929. Home: New York, N.Y. Died Aug. 8, 1941.

KENDRICK, Eliza Hall, coll. prof.; b. Nashua, N.H., Mar. 14, 1863; d. Benjamin F. and Clara (Dodge) K.; B.A., Wellesley, 1885; Ph.D., Boston U., 1895; studied Radcliffe, 1895-96, Berlin, 1908-09. Instr., 1894-95, 1900-06, asso. prof. Bibl. history, 1906-08, prof., 1909—, Wellesley. Mem. Soc. Bibl. Lit. and Exegesis. Conglist. Home: Wellesley, Mass. Died Apr. 11, 1940.

KENDRICK, Georgia (Avery), educator; b. Rochester, N.Y., July 1848; d. Solon C. and Susan (Cook) Avery; edn. chiefly pvt.; m. Rev. James Ryland Kendrick, Apr. 30, 1880 (died 1889). Principal Vassar Coll., 1891-1913, (emeritus). Presbyn. Home: Poughkeepsie, N.Y. Died 1922.

KENDRICK, John Benjamin, senator; b. Cherokee Co., Tex., Sept. 6, 1857; s. John Harvey and Anna (Maye) K.; ed. pub. schs.; m. Eula Wulfjen, Jan. 20, 1891; children—Rosa-Maye, Manville. Cattleman in Northern Wyo. and Southern Mont., 1885—, and owner one of largest range ranches in the West. Mem. Wyo. Senate, 1910-14; elected governor of Wyo. for term 1915-19; nominated for U.S. senator at primaries, 1916, although name did not appear on ballots and was written in by voters; elected senator 3 terms, 1917-35; resigned as gov., Feb. 1917. Democrat. Mason. Home: Sheridan, Wyo. Died Nov. 3, 1933.

KENDRICK, John Mills, bishop; b. Gambier, O.; A.B., Marietta Coll., 1856 (D.D., 1880, Kenyon, 1888); admitted to N.Y. bar, 1858; 1st lt. adj. 33d Ohio Inf., Aug. 3, 1861; capt. asst. adj. vols., Feb. 19, 1862; resigned, Sept. 30, 1862. Deacon, 1864, priest, 1865, P.E. Ch.; missionary, Put-in-Bay, O., 1865-67; rector, St. Andrew's, Ft. Scott, Kan., 1867-69, St. Paul's, Leavenworth, Kan., 1869-75, Ch. of the Good Shepherd, Columbus, O., 1875-78; gen. missionary, Diocese of Southern Ohio, 1878-89; consecrated bishop of Ariz. and N.M., Jan. 18, 1889. Home: El Paso, Tex. Died Dec. 16, 1911.

KENDRICK, John William, ry. official; b. Worcester, Mass., Oct. 14, 1853; s. John Abbot and Mary Elizabeth (Crosby) K.; grad. Worcester Poly. Inst., 1873; m. Elizabeth Foster Dolliver, Jan. 14, 1880. Entered ry. service with N.P. Ry., beginning, 1879, as levelman on constrn. party, in Yellowstone Valley; continuing as mem. and head of constrn. forces on various divs. until 1883; chief engr. St. Paul & Northern Pacific, 1883-88; chief engr., 1888-93, gen. mgr., 1893-98, 2d v.p., 1898-1901, N.P. R.R. and leased lines; 3d v.p., in charge of operation, 1901-05, 2d v.p., 1905-09, v.p. in charge operation, Oct. 1, 1909-May 1911, A.T.&S.F. System; cons. railway expert, 1911—; now chmn. bd. Internat. Great Northern R.R. Co. Home: Chicago, Ill. Died Feb. 16, 1924.

KENISTON, James Mortimer, alienist; b. Newburyport, Mass., Oct. 30, 1848; s. James Robinson and Sarah Norris (Pearson) K.; Amherst, 1864-66; M.D., Harvard, 1871; m. Charlotte Elizabeth Littlefield, Jan. 1, 1872. Interne, Butler Hosp., Providence, R.I., 1870-71; practiced at Cambridge, Mass., 1871-82; mem. staff Conn. Hosp. for Insane, Middletown, 1882-1904; supt. Hartford (Conn.) Hosp., 1904-06; mem. staff Conn. Hosp. for Insane, 1906—. Mason. Democrat. Conglist. Author: Paranoia (3d edit.), 1915; The Kingdom of the Mind, 1916. Home: Portland, Me. Died July 13, 1927.

KENLON, John; b. Dundalk, Ireland, Dec. 26, 1859; s. James and June (Smyth) K.; ed. pub. schs. and by pvt. study; m. Kathryn Fitz Gerald, of Co. Limerick, Ireland, Dec. 25, 1887. Began as farm boy; went to sea at 14 and served apprenticeship in China trade, rising to master mariner and chief engr.; joined New York Fire Dept., Apr. 2, 1887; served through all grades, advancing through competitive examinations; chief of dept., Aug. 1, 1911—. Awarded dept. medal "for saving life at great personal risk," 1911; commended 5 times "for meritorious conduct at great personal risk." Democrat. Catholic. Author: Fires and Fire Fighters, 1913. Home: New York, N.Y. Died May 30, 1940.

KENLY, John Reese, ry. pres.; b. Baltimore, Md., Jan. 21, 1847; ed. pub. schs. Began in employ Pittsburgh & Connellsville R.R., July 1868, and served as resident engr. construction until 1871; same position with Union R.R. tunnel, Baltimore, 1871-73; engr. and roadmaster same rd., 1873-76, engr. and supt., 1876-82; supt. Richmond & Petersburg R.R., 1882-85; with Atlantic Coast Line, 1885—, successively as supt. transportation until 1889, asst. gen. mgr., 1889-91, gen. mgr., 1891-1902, 4th v.p. and gen. mgr., 1902-05, 4th v.p., Apr.-Nov. 1905, 3d v.p., 1905-13, pres., Dec. 8, 1913—. Home: Wilmington, N.C. Died Mar. 1, 1928.

KENLY, Ritchie Graham, civil engr.; b. Ritchie Mines, W.Va., Mar. 13, 1866; s. William L. and Elizabeth Marion (Hook) K.; Baltimore City Coll., 1879-84; m. Grace I. Erdman, Oct. 16, 1888 (dec.); children—Ritchie Graham (dec.), Guy, Grace Marion (Mrs. John A. Buck), Allen Jackson, Katherine Erdman (deceased, wife of Dr. Paul G. Bovard), Grace Isabella (Mrs. Edgar R. Bjorklund), Edith Lilian (Mrs. C. Hume Ritchie); m. 2d, Mrs. Augusta Davidson Kenly, Oct. 1, 1932. Held minor railway positions, 1885-91; supervisor Radford division, 1891-93, asst. engineer, 1893-97, asst. trainmaster Radford and Pulaski divs., 1897-98, N.&W. Ry.; asst. to chief engr. W.Va. Central & Pittsburgh Ry., 1898-99; draftsman and constrn. engr. Phila. & Erie R.R. and Northern Central Ry. (Pa. R.R.), 1899-1900; supervisor Lehigh div., L.V. Ry., June 1900; div. engr. Lehigh & N.J. divs., same rd., 1900-04; trainmaster same divs., Easton, Pa., 1904-07; gen. supt. Lehigh & N.E. Ry., 1907-08; engr. maintenance of way, L.V. R.R., 1908-09; chief engr., 1909-17, gen. mgr., May 17, 1917, asst. to pres. and chief engr., Mar. 1920, later chief engr., Minneapolis & St. Louis R.R., retired 1939. Mason. Conglist. Home: Minneapolis, Minn. Died Nov. 15, 1939.

KENLY, William Lacy, army officer; b. in Md., Feb. 18, 1864; grad. U.S. Mil. Acad., 1889, Arty Sch., 1894. Commd. 2d lt. 4th Arty., June 12, 1889; promoted through grades to brig. gen. N.A., Aug. 5, 1917. In Cuba with 5th Army Corps, 1898; in action at El Caney, July 1, and at Santiago, July 10 and 11, 1898; served successively under Gens. Lawton, Wheaton and MacArthur in Philippine Islands, 1899-1902; Battle Zapote Bridge, June 13, 1899; again in Philippine Islands, 1906-07; in charge recruiting, N.Y. City, 1907-12; duty on Mexican border, 1914-15. Student Aviation Sch., San Diego, Calif., Nov. 12, 1916-May 21, 1917; took 7th F.A. overseas, landed St. Nazaire, France, Aug. 11, 1917; brig. gen. N.A., Aug. 5, 1917; chief of Air Service A.E.F., Aug. 24-Nov. 27, 1917; comdg. 2d F.A., Brigade to Jan. 4, 1918; returned to U.S., Mar. 11, 1918; dir. Mil. Aeronautics, Apr. 26, 1918—; maj. gen. U.S.A., Apr. 29, 1918; retired from active service, Oct. 31, 1919. Comdr. Legion of Honor (France), 1919; Companion Order of the Bath (Eng.), 1919; Grand Officer Crown of Italy, 1920. First pres. Army Air Service Assn., 1918. V.p. Marland Oil Co. of Mexico. Home: Ponca City, Okla. Died Jan. 20, 1928.

KENNAN, George, author, lecturer; b. Norwalk, O., Feb. 16, 1845; s. John and Mary Ann (Morse) K.; ed. in grammar and high schs.; (Litt.D., Williams College, Mass., 1910 and U. of Rochester, 1916); m. Emeline Rathbone Weld, Sept. 25, 1879. Became telegraph operator, later mgr. Western Union office, Cincinnati, 1863-64; went to N.E. Siberia as explorer and telegraphic engr., 1865; supt. constrn. middle div. Russo-Am. Telegraph Line, 1866-68; explored Eastern Caucasus, 1870-71; night mgr. Associated Press, Washington, 1877-85; investigated Russian exile system in Siberia, 1885-86; lecturer in U.S. and Great Britain. In May 1898 went to Cuba on the steamship State of Texas, with Am. Nat. Red Cross Soc., and as spl. commr. for The Outlook; went to Martinique for The Outlook to study volcano Mont Pelée, May 1902; went to Japan, Mar. 1904, to report Russo-Japanese War for The Outlook; on staff McClure's Mag., 1907, The Outlook, 1909; v.p. Medina Tribune Pub. Corp., 1923—. Gold war medal (Japan), 1906; Order of the Sacred Treasure (Japan), 1908. Author: The Chicago & Alton Case, 1916; Misrepresentation in Railroad Affairs, 1916; E. H. Harriman's Far Eastern Plans, 1917; E. H. Harriman—A Biography, 2 vols., 1922. Home: Medina, N.Y. Died May 10, 1923.

KENNARD, Frederic Hedge, landscape architect; b. Brookline, Mass., Nov. 19, 1865; s. Martin Parry and Caroline Augusta (Smith) K.; A.B., Harvard, 1888; post-grad. work, Bussey Inst. and Lawrence Scientific Sch., 1 yr.; m. Sarah Harrison Eisenbrey, May 27, 1896; children—Margaret Alice, Frederic Hedge, Harrison Eisenbrey, Robert Martin Parry, John Harold. Began as landscape architect at Boston, 1896; retired, 1916. Asso. in ornithology, Mus. of Comparative Zoölogy, Harvard; asso. curator of birds, Boston Soc. Natural History. Unitarian. Home: Newton Center, Mass. Died Feb. 24, 1937.

KENNARD, Samuel M., merchant; b. Lexington, Ky., Jan. 1842; s. John and Catherine (Fishburne) K.; ed. Lexington pub. schs.; m. Annie R. Maude, 1867. Joined Landis' Battery, C.S.A., attached to Cockrell's Brigade, 1861; saw active service in Miss., especially around Vicksburg in 1863, and command was surrendered to Grant when that place fell; remained prisoner of war until exchanged and became a lt. in Landis' and Guiboir's batteries; comd. a section of the battery at battle of Franklin, Tenn., Oct. 30, 1864, under Gen. J.E. B. Stuart; during last 6 months of war was a.-d.-c. to Gen. N. B. Forrest. Returned to St. Louis after war and became partner with father, 1865, in J. Kennard & Sons, now J. Kennard & Sons Carpets Co. of which became president. One of original organizers of St. Louis Expn., pres. St. Louis Expn. Assn. 8 yrs.; pres. first meeting of Autumnal Festivities Assn. (Veiled Prophet), 1891. Democrat. Methodist (Southern). Home: St. Louis, Mo. Deceased.

KENNEDY, Chase Wilmot, army officer; b. Portsmouth, O., Jan. 4, 1859; s. Milton and Josephine Barclay (Hutchinson) K.; grad. U.S. Mil. Acad., 1883, Army War Coll., 1914; m. Elizabeth Lord Jewett, Nov. 13, 1889. Commd. 2d lt. 3d Inf., June 13, 1883; promoted through grades to brig. gen., May 15, 1917; maj. gen. (temp.), World War; promoted maj. gen., retired, June 21, 1930. Served in Cuba, Philippines, Alaska, France and Panama; comdg. 78th and 85th Divs. to Mar. 31, 1919; comdg. Panama Canal Dept., Apr. 28, 1919-May 23, 1921; comdg. 9th Coast Arty. Dist. and 9th Training Center, Nov. 1, 1921-Nov. 30, 1922; retired, Nov. 30, 1922. Awarded badges Indian Wars, Spanish-Am. War, Philippine Insurrection, Cuban Occupation and war with Germany. Home: Washington, D.C. Died Nov. 23, 1936.

KENNEDY, Crammond, lawyer; b. North Berwick, Scotland, Dec. 29, 1842; s. Alexander James and Mary (Blair) K.; ed. there and in Edinburgh; came to New York, 1856; attended night school; delivered religious addresses, 1857-60, to large audiences, and was widely known as "the boy preacher"; studied, Madison U., 1861-63; chaplain 79th N.Y. Regt. ("Highlanders"), 1863-64; bvtd. maj. for services in E. Tenn. and the Wilderness, by gov. of N.Y.; m. Agnes Gorman, July 9, 1867. Lectured in Eng. and Scotland on the Civil War, 1864-65; connected with Freedmen's Commn., 1865-67; editor and propr. Church Union, 1869; joined Henry Ward Beecher in establishing Christian Union, 1869; became its mng.

editor, 1870; LL.B., Columbia, 1878; practiced in New York and now in Washington, chiefly in internat. cases; of counsel in Mora case against Spain and Alsop & Co. against Chile, decided in favor of claimants by King George V. Home: Washington, D.C. Deceased.

KENNEDY, Daniel Joseph, clergyman, educator; b. Knox Co., Eastern Tenn., Jan. 12, 1862; s. Daniel Bernard and Ellen (Boland) K.; St. Joseph's Convent, Somerset, O., 1876-81 (S.T.M., 1898); Dominican Coll., Louvain, Belgium, 1881-85; S.T.Lr., Louvain, 1885. Joined Dominican Fathers (O.P.), 1876; ordained ministry R.C. Ch., 1884; prof. philosophy and theology, Dominican House of Studies, Somerset, 1885-90; prof. philosophy, U. of Freiberg, Switzerland, 1890-91; prof. theology, Dominican House of Studies, 1892-1905, and regent of studies, 1896-1905; regent of studies, Dominican House of Studies, Washington, D.C., 1905-19; lecturer on sacramental theology, 1906-09, prof., 1909-20, prof. dogmatic theology, 1920-23, Catholic U. of America. Mem. commn. of 3 by apptmt. of Gov. Herrick of Ohio, for erection of equestrian statute of Gen. Philip H. Sheridan in his home town, Somerset, O. Author: The Summa Theologica of Saint Thomas, 1915; Saint Thomas and Medieval Philosophy, 1919. Deceased.

KENNEDY, David Scott, editor; b. Phila., July 16, 1856; s. Joseph H. and Jane (Sloan) K.; B.S., U. of Wis., 1883; grad. McCormick Theol. Sem. Chicago, 1886; D.D., Western U. of Pa., 1896; m. Frances P. Shulze, July 30, 1888; children—Joseph E. (dec.), Francis S., David G., Edgar S., Margaret J. Ordained Presbyn. ministry, 1886; pastor Ft. Wayne, Ind., 1886-88, 1st Church, Allegheny, Pa., 1888-1911; editor The Presbyterian, 1911-July 16, 1927, at which time retired from all public activities. Dir. Western Theol. Sem.; trustee Presbytery of Pittsburgh; mem. Bd. of Freedmen, Pittsburgh; pres. Presbyn. Hosp., Pittsburgh. Mem. Nat. Service Commn. Presbyn. Church, U.S.A. Dir. Lincoln University. Republican. Home: Wayne, Pa. Died Aug. 27, 1938.

KENNEDY, Elijah Robinson, author; b. Hartford, Conn., May 6, 1844; s. Leonard and Parthenia (Robinson) K.; ed. high sch., Milwaukee; Milwaukee U. (now defunct); m. Lucy Grace Pratt, Dec. 2, 1874; children—Sidney R., Susan Pratt Marion, Frank W. Tully, Leonard. Elected 2d lt. Co. E, 5th Calif. Inf., Apr. 1861; declined to be mustered into federal service, and resigned. For many yrs. in ins. business in New York, now pres. Weed & Kennedy, Inc. Was chmn. com. that drew up standard fire ins. policy of New York; twice pres. New York Bd. Fire Underwriters. Park commr. Brooklyn, 2 terms; trustee Brooklyn Inst. Arts and Sciences. Republican. Conglist. Author: Life of General John B. Woodward; The Contest for California in 1861, 1912; The Real Daniel Webster, 1923. Home: Brooklyn, N.Y. Died Apr. 25, 1926.

KENNEDY, Emma Baker, philanthropist; b. N.Y. City; hon. degree L.H.M., Univ. of New York, 1929; d. Cornelius Baker, of Elizabeth, N.J.; m. Oct. 14, 1858, John Stewart Kennedy, philanthropist and financier, of New York (died 1909). Founded the Hartford Sch. of Missions, and the Hartford Sch. of Religious Pedagogy, with an endowment of $250,000, later increased; also has helped largely Berea (Ky.) Coll., Robert Coll. (Constantinople, Turkey), Internat. Coll. (Smyrna, Turkey), Northfield (Mass.) Sem., Canton Christian Coll., China; built institutional ch. and theol. sem. for the Waldensians, in Rome, Italy. Presbyn. Home: New York, N.Y. Died July 23, 1930.

KENNEDY, Francis Williard, prof. social science; b. Pittsburgh, Pa., Apr. 3, 1874; s. James and Elizabeth (Williard) K.; student Ohio Normal U. (now Ohio Northern U.); A.B., Heidelberg U., Tiffin, O., 1898, A.M., 1900; student Theol. Sem. Ref. Ch., Lancaster, Pa., 1899-1900; grad. Heidelberg Theol. Sem., 1903, B.D., U. of Chicago, 1904; hon. Litt.D., Ursinus Coll., Pa., 1920; m. Mayme Bisco Troxell, Aug. 16, 1905; children—Anna Matilda, Lorene Elizabeth. Prof. Latin and English Bible, Heidelberg Coll., 1900-10; prof. social science, same, 1910—, dean Dept. of Liberal Arts, 1920—. Pres. City Council, Tiffin, most of time, 1916-33, mayor, 1933-36. Mem. Selective Service Bd., World War. Trustee Eden Theol. Sem., Webster Groves, Mo. Home: Tiffin, Ohio. Died Nov. 22, 1938.

KENNEDY, F(rank) Lowell, educator; b. Cambridge, Mass., Oct. 7, 1870; s. Frank Artemas and Charlotte Grosvenor (Lowell) K.; A.B., Harvard, 1892, S.B., in mech. engring., 1898; m. Grace Lowell Forbes, Nov. 29, 1899; children—Lowell Francis, Forbes (dec.), Charlotte, Sargent. Instr. in drawing, 1899-1903; asst. prof. drawing and machine design, 1904-13, asso. prof. engring, drawing, 1914-31, now emeritus, Harvard. Died Apr. 14, 1937.

KENNEDY, Howard Samuel, mfr.; b. Troy, N.Y., July 11, 1858; s. Peter H. and Elizabeth M. (Van Volkenburgh) K.; ed. in pub. schs. and Troy Business Coll.; m. Josephine A. Sharp, Dec. 17, 1874 (died 1920); children—Howard W. (dec.), Richard Oakley, Josephine W. (Mrs. Fred R. Bull). Entered employ Cluett, Peabody & Co. as office boy, 1872, mem. firm, 1898-1905, v.p., 1905-17, pres., 1918-20; chmn. bd. National City Bank, Troy, N.Y., 1928—. Pres. bd. trustees Troy Conf. Academy, Green Mountain Jr. College (Poultney, Vt.). Republican. Methodist. Mason. Home: Troy, N.Y. Died Jan. 20, 1938.

KENNEDY, James, editor; b. Aberlemno, Forfarshire, Scotland, Nov. 3, 1850; s. David and Jessie (MacKintosh) K.; ed. high sch., Dundee, Scotland, and evening high school, New York City. Served apprentice machinist's trade in Scotland; served in 42d Highlanders (Dundee Vols.), 1867-68. Came to America, 1868; m. Isabella Low, 1873 (died 1910). With New York Elevated R.R., 1879-1902; chief cashier Water Dept., New York, 1902-03; asso. editor Railway and Locomotive Engring., 1905-10, mng. editor, 1910—, and pres. Angus Sinclair Co., pubs. Pres. Harlem Rep. Club, 1902-06, 1908-12; Rep. and Independent Dem. candidate for Bd. of Aldermen, 1901, Assembly, 1908, Senate, 1909. First lt. 79th Highlanders, N.Y., 1875-76. Mem. St. Andrew's Soc. State of N.Y., Burns Soc. City of N.Y. (pres. 1915-16). Presbyn. Mason. Editor: The Complete Scottish and American Poems of James Kennedy, 1921. Home: New York, N.Y. Died Aug. 14, 1922.

KENNEDY, James Henry, editor; b. Farmington, O., Jan. 17, 1849; s. James C. and Sally Ann (Curry) K.; ed. Western Reserve Sem., Ohio; m. Mary G. Pierce. Formerly city and news editor, Cleveland Leader, and mng. editor Cleveland Herald; editor Magazine of Western History, 1889-1902; editor Hardware Dealers' Magazine; one of owners of Cleveland Voice. New York corr. Cleveland Plain Dealer, 10 yrs. Mem. Pub. Library Bd., Cleveland, 7 yrs.; trustee Washington Heights br. N.Y. City Library 3 yrs.; mem. Bd. of Assessors, N.Y. City, 4 yrs. Mem. Ohio Soc. N.Y. (historian), Montclair (N.J.) Civic Assn. (pres.). Republican. Editor of The American Nation (3 vols.), 1888. Home: Altadena, Calif. Died Jan. 22, 1934.

KENNEDY, James Madison, med. officer U.S.A.; b. Abbeville Co., S.C., Dec. 4, 1865; s. Archibald Boggs and Mary (McCaslan) K.; student Erskine Coll., Due West, S.C.; A.B., S.C. Coll., Columbia, S.C., 1884; M.D., Med. Coll. and Coll. Phys. and Surg., U. of Maryland, 1892; LL.D., Univ. of S.C., 1928; m. Mary Edith Baldwin, Apr. 16, 1898; children—Laurence Baldwin, Katharine (Mrs. William B. Kean), Archibald Boggs. Apptd. asst. surgeon U.S.A., May 12, 1893; advanced through grades to col., May 15, 1917; apptd. brig. gen., asst. to surgeon gen., U.S.A., Mar. 3, 1927. Comdr. ambulance train, Port Tampa, Fla., and Santiago, Cuba, Spanish-Am. War; dist. surgeon and comdg. officer base hosp., Calamba, Luzon, P.I., 1900, in office chief surgeon, Div. of Philippines, 1900-02; assigned U.S.A. Gen. Hosp., Presidio, San Francisco, Calif., 1902-10, comdg. hosp. during San Francisco earthquake and fire, 1906; surgeon and comdg. officer Dept. Hosp., Ft. Shafter, T.H., 1910-12, operating and attending surgeon, 1912; surgeon and sr. recruiting officer Jefferson Barracks, 1913-16; gen. sanitary insp. Ariz. sect., Mexican border, July 1916-May 1917; comdg. officer Base Hosp., Ft. Bliss, Tex., May-July 1917; surgeon, Port of Embarkation, Hoboken, N.J., 1917-19; comdg. officer Letterman Gen. Hosp., San Francisco, 1919-22; surgeon, Philippine Dept., Manila, P.I., 1922-24; comdg. officer Letterman Gen. Hosp., 1924-26; comdg. general, Army Med. Center, Washington, D.C., 1926; retired, Dec. 4, 1929. Fellow Am. College Surgeons. Presbyn. Awarded D.S.M., Navy Cross; Spanish-Am. War, Philippine Insurrection, Cuban Occupation and Victory Campaign medals; War Dept. citation—all of U.S. Died Oct. 15, 1930.

KENNEDY, John Stewart, banker; b. Scotland, Jan. 4, 1830; s. John K.; ed. in Glasgow, Scotland, 1836-43; m. Emma Baker, Oct. 14, 1858. Came to New York, June 1850; returned to Scotland, Aug. 1852; came to New York again, 1856, and settled there; banker, 1857-85. V.p. and dir. Northern Securities Co.; trustee Central Trust Co., Provident Loan Soc. of New York, Title Guarantee & Trust Co., U.S. Trust Co., Hudson Trust Co. of N.J.; dir. many rail road cos.; pres. Spence Sch. Co., Central Syndicate Bldg. Co. Trustee Columbia Coll., Met. Mus. Art (v.p.); pres. Presbyn. Hosp., United Charities; pres. bd. trustees Robert Coll., and Am. Bible House (Constantinople); v.p. Soc. for Ruptured and Crippled, N.Y. Oratorio Soc.; v.p. and trustee N.Y. Pub. Library, Astor, Lenox and Tilden Foundations. Home: New York, N.Y. Died 1909.

KENNEDY, Joseph, educator; b. Oshawa, Minn., July 14, 1858; s. Patrick and Elizabeth (Meaney) K.; B.S., U. of Minn., 1886, M.A., 1902; LL.D., U. of N.D., 1918; m. Elizabeth M. Davis, June 20, 1889; children—James P., Laurence E. (dec.). Prin. pub. schs., Hillsboro, N.D., 1886-88; co. supt. schs., Traill Co., N.D., 1888-92; asst. prof. edn., 1892-93, prof. edn., 1893-96, prof. philosophy and edn., 1900—, dean Sch. of Edn., 1901-28, Univ. of N. Dakota, dean emeritus and prof. philosophy and education. Pres. N. Dak. Ednl. Assn., 1895-96. Institute and summer school conductor and lecturer. Mem. Sch. Law Compilation Commn. apptd. by gov. of N.D., 1909-11; mem. State Bd. Examiners for Certification of Teachers, 1911-13; mem. Park Commn. Grand Forks Dist., 1907-24. Author: Rural Life and the Rural School, 1915; Fundamentals in Methods, 1915. Editor School of Education Record, 1915-28. Home: Grand Forks, N.D. Died Apr. 1, 1937.

KENNEDY, Julian, mechanical engr., inventor; b. Poland, O., Mar. 15, 1852; s. Thomas Walker and Margaret (Trusdale) K.; ed. Poland Union Sem.; Ph.B., Sheffield Scientific Sch. (Yale), 1875, A.M., 1900; D.Eng., Stevens Inst. of Tech., 1909; m. Jennie Eliza, d. Joseph Brenneman; children—Lucy Bell (Mrs. J. O. Miller), Joseph Walker, Julian, Hugh Truesdale (dec.), Eliza Jane (Mrs. R. T. Smith), Thomas Walker (dec.). Before going to Yale he had been draftsman, under his father, in the construction of the Struthers Iron Co., where he was employed three years; was supt. blast furnaces, 1876-85, at Briar Hill Iron Co.'s works, Struthers Iron Co.'s works, Morse Bridge Works, Edgar Thomson Steel Works and at the Lucy furnaces; gen. supt. for Carnegie, Phipps & Co., at Homestead, 1885-88; chief engr. Latrobe Steel Works, 1888; gen. consulting and contracting engr., 1890—; has been connected with nearly every important steel plant in U.S. and Europe. Home: Pittsburgh, Pa. Died May 28, 1932.

KENNEDY, Moorhead Cowell, ry. official; b. Chambersburg, Pa., Mar. 10, 1862; s. Thomas Benton and Ariana Stuart (Riddle) K.; grad. scientific dept. Andover (Mass.) Acad., 1880; John C. Green's Sch. of Science; C.E., Princeton, 1884; m. Margaret Coyle, June 25, 1891; children—Thomas B. II (dec.), James Coyle, Mrs. Margaret Riddle Clark, Moorhead Cowell. Cattle ranching on Powder River, Wyo., 1884-87; mem. Kennedy & Kennedy, pvt. bankers, Junction City, Kan., 1887-89; became asst. to pres. Cumberland Valley R.R., 1889; v.p. same rd., 1892, v.p. and gen. supt. 1903, pres. 1913-19; resident v.p. Cumberland Valley Dist., 1919-20, v.p., 1920-32, Pa. R.R. Co. Dir. First Nat. Bank of Phila., N.&W. Ry. Co. Commd. col. N.A., 1917; dept. dir. gen. of transportation A.E.F. in France and Eng.; returned to U.S., Dec. 30, 1918, demobilized Jan. 7, 1919. Awarded D.S.M. (U.S.); Officer Legion of Honor (France). Trustee Wilson Coll., Chambersburg, Pa.; v.p. Pa. Soc. of N.Y. Presbyn. Home: Chambersburg, Pa. Died Nov. 3, 1936.

KENNEDY, Paca, clergyman, educator; b. Charles Town, W.Va., Aug. 2, 1878; s. Edmund Pendleton and Julia Chew (Paca) K.; B.A., Roanoke Coll., Salem, Va., 1899, M.A., 1902; grad. Theol. Sem. in Va., 1902, B.D., 1904, D.D., 1910; student Oxford Univ., Eng., 1902-04; m. Erin Paine, Aug. 16, 1906; 1 son, William Paca. Deacon, 1902, priest, 1904, P.E. Ch.; served in mission field in W.Va., 1904-08; prof. N.T. Greek, Theol. Sem., Alexandria, Va., 1908. Democrat. Died Sept. 10, 1931.

KENNEDY, Robert Patterson, lawyer; b. Bellefontaine, O., Jan. 23, 1840; s. William G. and Mary E. (Patterson) K.; student Yale, and Geneva Coll., class of 1861; m. Maria L. Gardner, Dec. 29, 1862; m. 2d, Mrs. Emma (Cowgill) Mendenhall, Sept. 4, 1894. Second lt. 23d Ohio Inf., June 11, 1861; capt. asst. adj. vols., Oct. 7, 1862; maj., Nov. 16, 1864; resigned, Apr. 8, 1865; col. 196th Ohio Inf., Apr. 14, 1865; bvtd. lt. col. vols., Mar. 13, 1865, "for gallant and meritorious services during campaign in W.Va. and in Shenandoah Valley"; bvtd. brig. gen. vols., Mar. 13, 1865, "for distinguished gallantry during the war"; hon. mustered out, Sept. 11, 1865. Admitted to bar, 1866, and practiced at Bellefontaine, O.; U.S. internal revenue collector, 1878-83; lt. gov. of Ohio, 1885-87; mem. 50th and 51st Congresses (1887-91); mem. U.S. Insular Commn., to investigate conditions and formulate a code of laws for Cuba and P.R., 1899-1900. Republican. Died May 6, 1918.

KENNEDY, Samuel Macaw, utility engr.; b. Toronto, Can., June 20, 1863; s. Warring and Jane (Macaw) K.; ed. Model Sch. Collegiate Inst., Upper Can. Coll., Toronto, and under pvt. tutors; m. Mattie, d. of late J. C. Wallace, of Alhambra, Calif., Oct. 1, 1902. Entered business of father, Samson, Kennedy & Co., wholesale importers, Toronto, 1882; resigned, 1894, on account of ill health, and settled in Calif.; apptd. asst. to pres. United Electric Power & Gas Co., Los Angeles, 1900, and has been closely identified with development of light and power utilities in Calif.; served as v.p. Southern Calif. Edison Co., Santa Barbara & Suburban Ry., Pacific Gasoline Co., and as dir. Alhambra Savings and Commercial Bank; owing to accident retired from active business, 1927. Republican. Episcopalian. Mason. Author: Winning the Public, 2 edits. Home: Alhambra, Calif. Died July 1929.

KENNEDY, Sara Beaumont, author; b. Somerville, Tenn.; d. Dr. Robert H. and Nora (Devereux) Cannon; grad. St. Mary's P.E. Sch., Raleigh, N.C.; m. Walker Kennedy, Jan. 10, 1888 (died 1909). In journalistic work on Memphis papers. Author: Jocelyn Cheshire, 1901; The Wooing of Judith, 1902; Told in a Little Boy's Pocket, 1908; Cicely, A Tale of The Georgia March, 1911; One Wish (poems), 1915; Poems, 1919. Home: Memphis, Tenn. Died Mar. 12, 1921.

KENNEDY, Thomas F., bishop; b. Conshohocken, Pa., Mar. 23, 1858; s. Patrick and Maria (Burns) K.; ed. at St. Matthew's Sch., Conshohocken, Tremont Acad., Norristown, Pa., and Theol. Sem. of St. Charles Borromeo, and Am. Coll. in Rome, 1882-88 (D.D.). Ordained to R.C. priesthood, July 25, 1887; rector N. Am. Coll. at Rome, June 15, 1901. Named domestic prelate by His Holiness Leo XIII, Dec. 16, 1901; named prothonotary apostolic by Pius X, Mar. 15, 1904; apptd. titular bishop of Adrianapolis, Nov. 30, 1907; promoted titular archbishop of Seleucia in Isauria, June 17, 1915. Home: Rome, Italy. Died Aug. 28, 1917.

KENNEDY, Walker, journalist, editor, Commercial-Appeal, 1896—; b. Louisville, Ky., June 8, 1857; s. James and Kate E. K.; ed. Louisville public schools; m. Sara Beaumont Cannon, Jan. 10, 1888. In journalism, 1878—; Louisville Courier-Journal, 1878-81; Memphis Appeal, 1881; 1 yr. chief editorial writer Nashville American. Author: In the Dwellings of Silence, 1893; Javan ben Seir, 1898; The Secret of the Wet Woods, 1899. Home: Memphis, Tenn. Died 1909.

KENNEDY, William, congressman; b. Naugatuck, Conn., Dec. 19, 1854; s. John and Mary K.; pub. sch. edn.; m. Mary H. Clerkin, Nov. 1882. Began practice of law, 1879; atty. for town of Naugatuck, Conn., 1893; mem. Conn. State Senate, 2 terms, 1900-04; del. Dem. Nat. Conv., Chicago, 1896, Kansas City, Mo., 1900, Denver, 1908, Baltimore, 1912; mem. 63d Congress (1913-15), 5th Dist., Conn. Home: Naugatuck, Conn. Died June 19, 1918.

KENNEDY, William Sloane, author; b. Brecksville, nr. Cleveland, O., Sept. 26, 1850; s. Rev. William Sloane and Sarah Eliza (Woodruff) K.; A.B., Yale, 1875; studied 2 yrs. at Harvard; m. Adeline E. Lincoln, 1883; 1 son, Mortimer Lincoln (dec.). Has been on staff Boston Transcript. Author: John G. Whittier, the Poet of Freedom, 1892; The Real John Burroughs, 1924; The Fight of a Book for the World, 1926; Poems of the Weird and the Mystical, 1926; An Autolycus Pack or What You Will, 1926; Italy in Chains—A Nation Under the Microscope, 1926. Editor: Walt Whitman's Diary in Canada, 1904. Translator: Camille Flammarion's Mysterious Psychic Forces, 1907; Cesare Lombroso's After Death—What?, 1909. Years 1907-20 given entirely to Italian lang. and lit.; spent summer 1914 and years, 1924-25 and 1926-27, in Italy and Eng. Home: West Yarmouth, Mass. Died Aug. 3, 1929.

KENNELLY, Arthur Edwin, electrical engr.; b. Bombay, East India, Dec. 17, 1861; s. Capt. David Joseph and Cathrine (Heycock) K.; ed. pvt. schs., France and England, Univ. Coll. Sch., London; hon. Sc.D., U. of Pittsburgh, 1895; hon. A.M., Harvard, 1906; hon. Sc.D., U. of Toulouse, France, 1922; hon. Dr.Engring., University of Darmstadt, 1936; m. Julia Grice, July 22, 1903; 1 son, Reginald Grice. Telegraph operator in Eng., 1876; asst. electrician in Malta, 1878; chief electrician of a cable repairing steamer, 1881; senior ship's electrician Eastern Tel. Cable Co., 1886; prin. elec. asst. to Thomas A. Edison, 1887-94; asso. with Edwin J. Houston in firm Houston & Kennelly, consulting elec. engrs., Phila., 1894-1901; prof. elec. engring., Harvard, 1902-30, now prof. emeritus same and Mass. Inst. Tech. prof. elec. engring., 1913-24, dir. elec. engring. research, and chmn. faculty, 1917-18, Mass. Inst. Tech. Exchange prof. to French univs. in applied science, 1921-22; research asso. Carnegie Instn., 1924-30. Engr. in charge laying Vera Cruz-Frontera-Campeche cables for Mexican Govt., 1902. Mem. Nat. Research Council. Pres. Am. Inst. E.E., 1898-1900, Soc. Promotion Metric System of Weights and Measures, 1904, Illuminating Engring. Soc., 1911, Inst. of Radio Engrs., 1916; a vice pres. Am. Acad. Arts and Sciences; chmn. Rumford Com. 1924; hon. pres. U.S. Nat. Com. of Internat. Elec. Commn. (chmn. adv. com. on elec. and magnetic magnitudes and units, 1930—). Elected juror at expns. of Phila., 1898, Buffalo, 1901, St. Louis, 1904. Author: The Application of Hyperbolic Functions to Electrical Engineering Problems, 1911; Artificial Electric Lines, 1917; Electrical Vibration Instruments, 1923; Vestiges of Premetric Weights and Measures Persisting in Metric-System Europe, 1926-27; Electric Lines and Nets, 1928. Recipient of the Institution and Fahie premiums from the British Institute E.E., Howard Potts gold medal and Edward Longstreth silver medal Franklin Institute for electrical research; gold medal, Inst. Radio Engrs., 1932; Edison gold medal, Am. Inst. Elec. Engrs., 1933. Civilian liaison officer, U.S.A. Signal Corps, 1918, A.E.F. Third Order Mejidieh, Egypt, 1885; Chevalier Légion d'Honneur, France, 1922; Mascart medal, 1936. Hon. mem. Tau Beta Pi. First visiting elec. engring. lecturer, Iwadare Foundation, Japanese univs., 1931. Home: Cambridge, Mass. Died June 18, 1939.

KENNERLY, John Hanger, educator; b. Hermitage, Va., May 2, 1856; s. Samuel and Frances Cathren (Hanger) K.; prep. edn. New Hope (Va.) Acad.; D.D.S., Mo. Dental Coll. (now Washington U. Dental Sch.), 1883; M.D., Marion Sims Med. Coll., 1897; m. Alice Virginia Starke, July 23, 1890. Began practice at St. Louis, 1888; prof. prosthetic dentistry and sec. faculty of dental dept., Marion Sims Coll. of Medicine, 1894-1900; same to faculty of Mo. Dental Coll., 1900-01; prof. clin. dentistry and dean dental dept., Washington Univ., 1901-22. Democrat. Methodist. Mason. Home: Petersburg, Fla. Died Jan. 22, 1926.

KENNESON, Taddeus Davis, prof. law; b. Tewksbury, Mass., May 23, 1859; s. Zebulon Davis and Lucy (Shedd) K.; A.B., Harvard, 1880, A.M., 1883, LL.B., 1883; (hon. LL.M., New York Univ., 1898, J.D., 1903); married. Admitted to N.Y. bar, 1884, later to bar U.S. Sup. Ct.; practiced, various firms, until 1910, when retired on account of ill health; prof. law, Met. Law Sch., 1892-95, New York U., 1895—. Republican. Presbyn. Author: Cases on Trusts, 1911. Died May 28, 1924.

KENNEY, Edward A., congressman; b. Clinton, Mass., Aug. 11, 1884; s. Thomas H. and Elizabeth Gertrude (Moriarty) K.; A.B., Williams, 1906; LL.B., New York U., 1908; m. Elizabeth Jane Linkletter, July 10, 1910. In practice of law, N.Y. City, 1908—, also in Jersey City, 1917—; judge of City Court, 1919-23, and atty. for Bd. of Edn., Cliffside Park, 1921-23; mem. 73d and 74th Congresses (1933-37), 9th N.J. Dist. Mem. legal advisory bd., Bergen Co., N.J., 1917-18. Democrat. Elk. Home: Cliffside Park, N.J. Died Jan. 27, 1938.

KENNEY, Richard Rolland, senator; b. Sussex Co., Del., Sept. 9, 1856; s. Samuel and Hettie (Short) K.; grad. Laurel Acad., Del.; student Hobart Coll.; m. Harriet Calley Pennewill, Dec. 1881; 2d. M. Walker, of Dover, Del., Mar. 4, 1908. Admitted to bar, 1881, and began practice in Dover. State librarian, 1879-83; adj. gen. of Del., 1887-91; mem. Dem. Nat. Com., 1896-1908; U.S. senator, for an unexpired term, Jan. 1897-Mar. 3, 1901. Died Aug. 14, 1931.

KENNEY, William Francis, editor; b. Woburn, Mass.; s. Peter and Katherine Hannan (Ryan) K.; A.B. and A.M., Boston Coll., 1910; m. Margaret T. Guinan, June 2, 1886; children—Mary Loretto, Inez Marguerite, William Peter (dec.), Catherine Madeline, Francis Russell (dec.), Heloise Guinan, Helen Hannan. Day editor in charge Boston Evening Globe, 1888-1918; spl. corr. at The Hague Peace Conf., 1910; at the Consistory, Rome, Italy, 1911, etc.; spl. writer on Fla. development, 1922—; Fla. corr. Wall Street Journal. Mem. School Bd., Woburn, Mass., 12 yrs. (pres. 1 yr.); trustee Boston Pub. Library, 1908-21 (v.p. bd. 1912-17, pres. 1917-20); trustee Boston Mus. Fine Arts, 1917-20; del. and v.p. Internat. Congress of Librarians, Brussels, Belgium, 1910; pres. Boston War Library Council 1917. Decorated Knight Comdr. Order of St. Sava (Serbia) 1920. Died Aug. 9 1940.

KENNEY, William P., ry. official; b. Watertown, Wis., Jan. 10, 1870; ed. high sch., Minneapolis, Minn. Began as telegraph operator with C.G.W. Ry., 1888; clk. and stenographer to gen. agt., same rd., at Minneapolis, 1890-92; contracting agt., same rd., 1892-99; contracting agt., Emporia Line, Jan.-Sept. 1899; chief clk., gen. freight office, St. Paul & Duluth R.R., 1899-1900, N.P. Ry., 1900-02; chief clk. gen. freight office 1902-03, asst. gen. freight agt., 1903-05, asst. to 4th v.p., 1905-08, asst. traffic mgr., 1908-11, gen. traffic mgr., 1911-12, v.p. in charge of traffic, 1912-18, federal mgr. until Mar. 1, 1919, later v.p. and dir. traffic, G.N. Ry. Co., pres., Jan. 1, 1932—. Home: St. Paul, Minn. Died Jan. 24, 1939.

KENNON, Lyman Walter Vere, army officer; b. Providence, R.I., Sept. 2, 1858; s. Charles Henry Vere and Adelaide (Hall) K.; Grad. U.S. Mil. Acad., 1881, Army War Coll., 1910; m. Anne Beecher Rice, Apr. 3, 1883. Commd. add. 2d lt. 1st Inf., June 11, 1881; promoted through grades to brig. gen. N.A., Aug. 5, 1917. Served in Indian Wars, in Cuba during Spanish-Am. War, Cuban occupation and Philippines; explorations and surveys in Central America for Intercontinental Ry.; constructed the Benguet Road to Baguio, the summer capital of Philippines, for which was complimented by Pres. Roosevelt. Apptd. comdr. 86th div., N.A., Camp Grant, Rockford, Ill., Nov. 1917. Author: Manual of Guard Duty, 1891. Died Sept. 9, 1918.

KENNY, Albert Sewall, rear adm. U.S.N.; b. Van Buren Co., Ia., Jan. 19, 1841; s. Sewall and Mary (Strong) K.; A.B., U. of Vt., 1861; m. Ellen Barnes, Oct. 27, 1874. Commd. asst. p.m. U.S.N., Mar. 19, 1862; p.m., Mar. 9, 1865; pay insp., July 31, 1884; pay dir., Sept. 26, 1897; p.m. gen., May 5, 1889; with rank of rear adm., Dec. 13, 1899. Served in S. Atlantic blockading squadron, 1862-63; N. Atlantic blockading squadron, 1864-65; present at both attacks on Ft. Fisher. After Civil War, service on west coast of Africa, San Francisco, in cruising ships, at Naval Acad. and at New York Navy Yard; retired, Jan. 19, 1903; relieved from duty as p.m. gen., July 1, 1903; treasurer Isthmian Canal Commn., May 1904-May 1905. Died May 17, 1930.

KENNY, William John, bishop; b. Delhi, N.Y., Oct. 9, 1853; s. John and Ann (McDonough) K.; A.B., St. Bonaventure's Coll., Allegany, N.Y. Ordained priest, St. Augustine, Fla., Jan. 15, 1879; pastor Jacksonville, Fla., 1879-81, Palatka, Fla., 1881-84, Jacksonville, 1884-1902; vicar gen., 1889-1901, administrator, 1901-02; consecrated 3d bishop of St. Augustine, May 18, 1902. Died Oct. 23, 1913.

KENT, Alexander, Independent clergyman; b. Truro, N.S., Nov. 27, 1837; s. James and Sara (Archibald) K.; ed. Truro, 1843-54; began preaching in Universalist Ch., in Iowa; studied Lombard Univ., Ill., part of 2 yrs.; student 2½ yrs. Canton, N.Y., Theol. School, St. Lawrence Univ.; left, 1865, and settled over Universalist Ch., Halifax, N.S., until 1867; pastor Universalist Ch., Portland, Me., 1867-69; State missionary in Minn., part of 1869; in Baltimore, 1869-77; part of time out of health and out of ministry; in Washington, D.C., 1877; pastor Universalist Ch. there 12 yrs.; built ch.; for over 10 yrs. past, pastor of undenominational People's Ch.; liberal, independent, progressive; m. Carrie E. Gove, Jan. 24, 1878. Died 1908.

KENT, Charles Artemas, lawyer; b. Hopkinton, N.Y., Oct. 11, 1835; s. Artemas and Sarah (Weed) K.; A.B., U. of Vt., 1856; student Andover Theol. Sem., 1857-59; (LL.D., U. of Mich., 1899, U. of Vt., 1904); m. Frances King, Apr. 30, 1874. Admitted to Mich. bar, 1860, and began practice at Detroit. Prof. law, U. of Mich., 1868-86; mem. Mich. Tax Commn., 1882; v.p. Mich. Mut. Life Ins. Co.; dir. Citizens' Savings Bank; trustee Harper's Hosp. Republican. Congregationalist. Home: Detroit, Mich. Died May 7, 1917.

KENT, Charles Foster, univ. prof.; b. Palmyra, N.Y., Aug. 13, 1867; s. William Hotchkiss and Helen Maria (Foster) K.; A.B., Yale, 1889, fellow, 1889-91, Ph.D., 1891; U. of Berlin, 1891-92; m. Elizabeth Middleton Sherrill, July 9, 1895. Instr., U. of Chicago, 1893-95; asso. prof. Bibl. lit. and history, 1895-98, prof., 1898-1901, Brown U.; Woolsey prof. Bibl. lit., Yale, 1901—; dir. Nat. Council Sch. of Religion, 1922—. Author: A History of the Hebrew People, the United Kingdom, 1896; A History of the Hebrew People, the Divided Kingdom, 1897; A History of the Jewish People—the Babylonian, Persian and Greek Periods, 1899; The Messages of Israel's Lawgivers, 1902; Narratives of the Beginnings of Hebrew History (Student's O.T.), 1904; Origin and Permanent Value of the Old Testament, 1906; Israel's Laws and Legal Precedents, 1907; The Heroes and Crises of Early Hebrew History, 1908; The Founders and Rulers of United Israel, 1908; The Kings and Prophets of Israel and Judah, 1909; The Makers and Teachers of Judaism, 1911; The Great Teachers of Judaism and Christianity, 1911; Biblical Geography and History, 1912; Life and Teachings of Jesus in the Light of the Oldest Records, 1913; Songs, Hymns and Prayers of the Old Testament, 1914; The Testing of a Nation's Ideals (with J. W. Jenks), 1915; The Social Teachings of the Prophets and Jesus, 1917; The Shorter Bible, the N.T., 1919; A History of the Hebrew Commonwealth (with A. E. Bailey), 1919; Jesus' Principles of Living (with J. W. Jenks), 1920; The Shorter Bible, the Old Testament, 1921. Editor: The Historical Series for Bible Students; The Messages of the Bible; Student's Old Testament; Religious Education Manuals for School and Home. Pres. Assn. Bibl. Instrs. in Am. Colleges and Secondary Schools. Home: Mt. Carmel, Conn. Died May 2, 1925.

KENT, Charles William, univ. prof.; b. Louisa Court House, Va., Sept. 27, 1860; s. Robert Meredith and Sarah Garland (Hunter) K.; M.A., U. of Virginia, 1882; student Göttingen, Berlin, Leipzig, 1884-87, Ph.D., 1887; (LL.D., U. of Alabama, 1906; Litt.D., Colgate Univ., 1914); m. Eleanor A., d. Prof. Francis H. Smith, June 4, 1895. Joint founder and head master Univ. Sch., Charleston, S.C., 1882-84; licentiate in German and French, U. of Va., 1887-88; prof. English and modern langs., U. of Tenn., 1888-93; prof. English lit., rhetoric and belles lettres, Linden Kent Memorial Sch. of English Literature, U. of Va., 1893—. Pub. lecturer on Am. and English lit., Southern poets, etc., 1888—; chmn. state exec. committee of Y.M.C.A. Editor: Cynewulf's Elene, 1888; Idyls of the Lawn, 1899; Selected Poems from Burns, 1901; Tennyson's Princess, 1901; Poe Memorial Volume, 1901; Poe's Poems (Vol. VII, Virginia Edition), 1902; Poe's Poems in Pocket Classics, 1904; The Book of the Poe Centenary, 1909; Library of Southern Literature, 15 vols., 1909-10; Southern Poems, 1912; Judge Lucas's Poems, 1912. Progressive Democrat. Mem. Christian Church. Died Oct. 5, 1917.

KENT, Edward, judge; b. Lynn, Mass., Aug. 8, 1862; s. Edward (gov. Me., 1838-40—mentioned in famous political song "Have You Heard the News from Maine" of campaign of 1840) and Abby (Rockwood) K.; A.B., Harvard, 1883; LL.B., Columbia Law School, New York, 1887; (LL.D., U. of Ariz., 1915); m. Edith Chadwick, Sept. 14, 1893. Admitted to N.Y. bar, 1887; mem. firm Butler, Stillman & Hubbard, New York, 1893-96; removed to Denver, 1897; Rep. candidate for mem. Colo. Ho. of Rep., 1900; asst. U.S. dist. atty., Colo., 1901-02; chief justice Supreme Ct. of Ariz., 1902-12; mem. Chalmers, Kent & Stahl. Home: Phoenix, Ariz. Died July 30 1916.

KENT, Henry Oakes, banker; b. Lancaster, N.H., Feb. 7, 1834; s. Richard Peabody and Emily Mann (Oakes) K.; B.S., Norwich U., 1854, later M.A., and LL.D.; m. Berenice A. Kent, Jan. 11, 1859. Commr. to adjust N.H. and Me. boundary, 1858; a.-a.-g. State of N.H., 1861; col. 17th N.H. Vols., 1862; postmaster, U.S. Senate, 1863; aide to Pres. Lincoln at Gettysburg, Nov. 1863; has been identified with banking from 1868; newspaper editor and pub. 12 yrs.; pres. Lancaster Trust Co. 40 yrs.; sec. and mng. dir. Lancaster Savings Bank; treas. Lancaster Paper Mill. Naval officer port of Boston, 1885; invited by Sec. Lamont to become asst. sec. of war, 1892 (declined); was mem. N.H. Ho. of Rep. and Senate; was temporary chmn. State Constl. Conv.; thrice Dem. nominee for Congress and twice for gov. of N.H.; chmn. State Forestry Commn. Sr. trustee Norwich U., 1862—, and pres. Associate Alumni 20 yrs. Episcopalian (sr. warden St. Paul's Ch.). Mason. Home: Lancaster, N.H. Died Mar. 21, 1909.

KENT, Jacob Ford, brig. gen.; b. Phila., Sept. 14, 1835; s. Rodolphus and Sarah (Deily) K.; ed. at Samuel Crawford's Sch., Phila. and Mt. Pleasant Mil. Acad., Sing Sing, N.Y.; grad. U.S. Mil. Acad., 1861; m. Mary M. Eaton, June 3, 1885. Commd. 2d lt. 3d Inf., May 6, 1861; promoted through grades to brig. gen. vols., May 4, 1898; maj. gen. vols., July 8, 1898; brig. gen. U.S.A., Oct. 4, 1898; retired at own request, after 40 yrs.' service, Oct. 15, 1898; hon. disch. from vol. service, Nov. 30, 1898. Bvtd.: maj., May 3, 1863, "for gallant and meritorious services in battle of Marye's Heights, Va."; lt. col., May 12, 1864, for same in battle of Spottsylvania, Va.; col. vols., Oct. 19, 1864, "for faithful and meritorious services during campaign before Richmond, Va." Home: Troy, N.Y. Died Dec. 22, 1918.

KENT, James Tyler, physician; b. Woodhull, N.Y., Mar. 31, 1849; s. Stephen and Caroline (Tyler) K.; Ph.B., Madison (now Colgate) U., 1868; M.D., Eclectic Med. Inst. Cincinnati, 1871; M.D., Homœ. Med. Coll. of Mo., 1879; m. Clara Louise Tobey, July 2, 1896. Practiced at St. Louis, 1873-88, Phila., 1888-1900; prof. materia medica, Homœ. Med. Coll., St. Louis, 1881-88; prof. materia medica and dean Post-Grad. Sch. of Homœopathy, Phila., 1890-99; prof. materia medica, Hahnemann Med. Coll. and Hosp., 1903-09, Hering Med. Coll. and Hosp., 1909—. Author: Repertory of the Homœopathic Materia Medica, 1877; Homœopathic Philosophy, 1900; Lectures on Homœopathic Materia Medica, 1905. Home: Evanston, Ill. Died June 5, 1916.

KENT, Russell, newspaper corr.; b. Story Co., Ia., July 5, 1885; s. Weston William and Edith (Pierce) K.; ed. pub. and pvt. schs., St. Louis, Houston and Chattanooga; m. Oneata White, Oct. 1, 1907. Began as reporter on Chattanooga Times, 1905, continuing with various Southern and New York newspapers; mng. editor New Orleans Times-Picayune, 1911-14, Memphis News-Scimitar, 1915-17, Knoxville Journal and Tribune, 1918-22; Washington corr., 1922—, then corr. Birmingham News and Age-Herald, Memphis Commercial Appeal and Evening Appeal, Chattanooga Times, Montgomery Advertiser, Mobile Register and Press. Independent Democrat. Died Oct. 30, 1940.

KENT, Walter Henry, chemist; b. Levant, N.Y., March 29, 1851; s. Ara W. and Lucy A. (Neate) K.; grad. Cornell, B.S., 1876 (M.S., 1880; Ph.D., Göttingen, Germany, 1884). Instr. chemistry Cornell, 1877-81; prof. chemistry Drake Univ., Des Moines, Ia., 1881-82; student at Göttingen, 1883-84; chemist Brooklyn Health Dept., through a civil service exam., 1885-94; chemist New York Navy Yard, 1895-99; asst. prof. Brooklyn Coll. of Pharmacy, 1900-02; m. Ann Elizabeth Hall, June 30, 1904. Home: Brooklyn, N.Y. Died 1907.

KENT, William, engineer; b. Philadelphia, Mar. 5, 1851; s. James and Janet (Scott) K.; A.B., Central High Sch., Phila., 1868, A.M., 1873; M.E., Stevens Inst. Tech., 1876; (Sc.D., Syracuse U., 1905); m. Marion Weild Smith, Feb. 25, 1879. Editor of Am. Manufacturer and Iron World, Pittsburgh, 1877-79; held positions as mech. engr. and supt. in iron and steel works, steam boiler business and Torsion balance scale factory, 1879-90; consulting engr. (office practice), 1890—; asso. editor Engineering News, 1895-1903; dean L. C. Smith Coll. Applied Science, Syracuse U., 1903-08; editor Industrial Engineering, 1910-14. Lecturer steam engring., Newark Tech. Sch., 1888-95; has also lectured at Purdue, Brooklyn Inst., Franklin Inst. (Phila.), Worcester Poly. Inst., W.Va. U., U. of Ill., Cornell, Stevens Inst., etc. Mem. N.J. State Commn. on Pollution of Streams, 1898-99. Has taken out over 20 patents on weighing machinery, water-tube boilers, smokeless furnaces, etc. Author: The Strength of Materials, 1879; The Mechanical Engineer's Pocket Book, 1895, 9th edition, 1915; Investigating an Industry, 1915; Bookkeeping and Cost Accounting for Factories, 1918. Home: Montclair, N.J. Died Sept. 18, 1918.

KENT, William, congressman; b. Chicago, Mar. 29, 1864; s. Albert Emmett and Adaline Elizabeth (Dutton) K.; parents removed to Marin Co., Calif., 1871; A.B., Yale, 1887, hon. A.M., 1908; m. Elizabeth Thacher, Feb. 26, 1890; children—Albert Emmett, Thomas Thacher, Elizabeth Sherman, William, Adaline Dutton, Sherman, Roger. Located in Chicago, 1887; owner of real estate in Chicago and interested in lands and live stock in several states; mem. Kent & Burke, cattle feeders, Genoa, Neb. Mem. Chicago City Council, 1895-97; pres. Municipal Voters' League, 1899-1900 (exec. com. 1897-1904); was mem. Ill. Civ. Service Assn., Civ. Service Reform League. Returned to Marin Co., Calif., 1907; mem. 62d Congress (1911-13), 2d Calif. Dist.; reëlected to 63d and 64th Congresses as Independent from new 1st Dist., Calif.; mem. U.S. Tariff Commn., Apr. 1917—. Home: Kentfield, Calif. Died Mar. 13, 1928.

KENYON, Alfred Monroe, mathematician; b. Medina, O., Dec. 10, 1869; s. Charles Champlin and Lucy Elizabeth (Gouldin) K.; A.B., Hiram (O.) Coll., 1894; grad. student Western Reserve U., and Case Sch. Applied Science, Cleveland, O., 1896-97; A.M., Harvard, 1898; m. Grace Greenwood Finch, Sept. 1, 1897. Instr. mathematics, 1898, asso. prof., 1900, prof., 1905—, head of dept., 1908—, Purdue U., also registrar, 1900-08. Fellow Ind. Acad. Science. Progressive Rep. Presbyn. Author: (with Louis Ingold) Plane and Spherical Trigonometry, 1913; (with William V. Lovitt) Mathematics for Students of Agriculture and General Science, 1917; (with Louis Ingold) Elements of Plane Trigonometry, 1919. Home: Lafayette, Ind. Died July 27, 1921.

KENYON, Alpheus Burdick, college dean; b. Hopkinton, R.I., Aug. 2, 1850; s. Edwin Orsando and Cordelia (Burdick) K.; B.Sc., Alfred (N.Y.) U., 1874, M.Sc., 1877, D.Sc., 1905; Cornell, 1887-88; m. Mary Veola Babcock, Aug. 30, 1873; children—Grace (dec.), Dora, Agnes. Prof. mathematics, 1874-1920, pres. stockholders, 1896—, dean, 1908-20, Alfred U.; retired on Carnegie Foundation, 1920. Pres. Alfred Mut. Loan Assn., 1884-96, 1918 (sec. 1896-1910). Pres. Village of Alfred, 1887-88; trustee, 1906-08; pres. bd. edn., 1896-1902; treas. Alfred Rural Cemetery, 1916—; treas. Village of Alfred, 1924—. Dir. Seventh-day Bapt. Edn. Soc., 1888—(treas. 1888-1910); pres. Seventh-day Bapt. Gen. Conf., 1914. Trustee Alfred Univ., 1920—. Home: Alfred, N.Y. Died Sept. 15, 1931.

KENYON, James Benjamin, poet; b. Frankfort, N.Y., Apr. 26, 1858; s. Delos M. and Nancy M. (Piper) K.; grad. Hungerford Collegiate Inst., 1875; (hon. Litt.D., Syracuse U., 1892); m. Margaret J. Taylor, Jan. 2, 1878. Studied theology and entered M.E. ministry, 1878; retired 1906; mem. editorial staff Standard Dictionary, 1910-12; editor revision of Appleton's Cyclo. of Am. Biography, 1912-13; editor White's Nat. Cyclo. of Am. Biog., 1913—. Modern Am. Poetry Series, 1917—. Author: Retribution, 1903. Home: New York, N.Y. Died May 11, 1924.

KENYON, William Houston, lawyer; b. Hartford, Conn., Jan. 5, 1856; s. Robert and Jean Borland (Houston) K.; A.B., Coll. City of New York, 1876, A.M., 1883; LL.B., Columbia, 1879; m. Minnie Wellington Stanwood, Apr. 1887 (died 1905); children—Dorothy, Theodore Stanwood, W. Houston, Jr.; m. 2d, Lestra Kinney, June 1909. Admitted to N.Y. bar, 1880, and since practiced in N.Y. City; mem. Browne, Witter & Kenyon, 1883-86, Witter & Kenyon, 1886-99, Kenyon & Kenyon, 1899—; specializes in patent law. Served as chmn., in 1897, Com. of 53, in revolt against Republican city machine, out of which revolt came the first N.Y. State Primary Law. Author: Design Patent Law, 1887. Home: New York, N.Y. Died Sept. 5, 1933.

KENYON, William Squire, judge; b. Elyria, Ohio, June 10, 1869; s. Fergus L. and Hattie A. (Squire) K.; ed. Ia. (now Grinnell) Coll., and law school of State U. of Ia.; m. Mary Duncombe, May 11, 1893. In law practice at Ft. Dodge; pros. atty., Webster Co., Ia., 5 yrs.; dist. judge, 11th Jud. Dist., 2 yrs.; asst. to the attorney general U.S., Mar. 1910-Apr. 1911; elected U.S. senator, Apr. 12, 1911, for an unexpired term ending Mar. 3, 1913; reëlected for terms 1913-25, resigned; judge U.S. Circuit Court, 8th Dist., by apptmt. of President Harding, 1922—; apptd. mem. Law Enforcement Commn., 1929. Republican. Home: Ft. Dodge, Ia. Died Sept. 9, 1933.

KEOGH, Martin Jerome, judge; b. in Ireland, 1855; s. John and Margaret K.; ed. pub. schs.; LL.B., New York U., 1875; LL.D., Manhattan Coll., 1903, New York U., 1906; m. Katharine Temple Emmet, 1894; children—Richard E., Grenville Temple, John, Mrs. Katharine Semple, Hugh, Mrs. Margaret Phelan Gotte, Terence Jerome, Mary, Brigid Temple; also 2 children by first marriage—Alexander (dec.), Martin J. Admitted to bar, 1875, and practiced at New York, 1875-95; presdl. elector, 1886; justice Supreme Court of N.Y., for the terms 1896-1909, 1910-22. Democrat. Home: New Rochelle, N.Y. Died Oct. 24, 1928.

KEPHART, Cyrus Jeffries, bishop; b. Clearfield Co., Pa., Feb. 23, 1852; s. Rev. Henry and Sarah (Goss) K.; A.B., Western Coll., Ia., 1874, A.M., 1877; grad. Union Bibl. Sem., Dayton, O., 1878; D.D., Lebanon Valley Coll., Pa., 1895; LL.D., Otterbein U., 1915, Kansas City U., 1916; m. Sallie S. Perry, Dec. 4, 1873 (died 1928). Ordained ministry of United Brethren Ch., 1879; pres. Avalon (Mo.) College, 1878-85; prof. mathematics, Western Coll., Ia., 1885-87; pastor Des Moines, Ia., 1887-89; pres. Lebanon Valley Coll., 1889-90; pastor Lebanon, Pa., 1890-94; gen. sec. Pa. State Sabbath Sch. Assn., 1894-97; again pres. Avalon Coll., 1897-99; pastor Summit Park Ch., Des Moines, 1899-1903, Lisbon, Ia., 1903-05; pres. Western (later Leander Clark) Coll., Toledo, Ia., 1905-08; pastor First U.B. Ch., Dayton, O., 1908-13; bishop, May 14, 1913, emeritus; head Bible dept. Kansas City U. Author: Christianity and the Social Weal, 1914. Home: Shelby, Neb. Died July 22, 1932.

KEPHART, Ezekial Boring, U.B. bishop, May 12, 1881—; b. Decatur Tp., Clearfield Co., Pa., Nov. 6, 1834; s. Rev. Henry and Sarah (Goss) K.; reared on farm; later cut and floated lumber on Susquehanna River; afterward pilot on that river; earned money with which to go to college; m. Susan J. Trefts, Nov. 4, 1860. Attended Dickinson Sem., Pa., and Mt. Pleasant Coll., Pa.; grad. Otterbein Univ., 1865 (A.M., D.D., same; LL.D., Lebanon Valley Coll.). Entered ministry, 1857; lived 23 yrs. in Iowa; pres. Western Coll., Ia., 1868-81; State senator, Ia., 1872-76; traveled extensively in Africa, Egypt, Palestine and in Europe. Author: Apologetics, or a Treatise on Christian Evidences, 1901. Home: Annville, Pa. Died 1906.

KEPHART, Horace, author; b. East Salem, Pa., Sept. 8, 1862; s. Isaiah L. and Mary (Sowers) K.; A.B., Lebanon Valley Coll., Annville, Pa., 1879, A.M., 1882; post-grad. work Cornell U., Boston U., Yale; m. Laura White Mack, Apr. 12, 1887; children—Cornelia Ferris, Margaret, Leonard Wheeler, Lucy, George Stebbins, Barbara. Asst. Cornell U. Library, 1880-84; in Europe, 1884-86; asst. Yale U. Library, 1886-90; librarian St. Louis Mercantile Library, 1890-1903. Pres. State Lit. and Hist. Assn. of N.C., 1929-30. Democrat. Author: Our Southern Highlanders, 1913; Camping and Woodcraft, 1916; Sporting Firearms, 1918; The Camper's Manual, 1923. Home: Bryson City, N.C. Died Apr. 2, 1931.

KEPHART, Isaiah Lafayette, clergyman, editor The Religious Telescope, 1889—; b. Decatur Tp., Clearfield Co., Pa., Dec. 10, 1832; s. Rev. Henry and Sarah (Goss) K.; reared on farm; ed. country schools and various sems. (A.M., Otterbein Univ.; D.D., Western Coll.); licensed to preach, 1859, by Allegheny Conf. U.B. Ch.; ordained, 1863; m. Mary E. Sowers, 1861. Was in pastoral work, 1859-63; chaplain 21st Pa. cav. vols., 1863-65; resumed preaching until 1867; prin. public schools, Jefferson, Ia., 1867-69; supt. schools, Greene Co., Ia., 1869-71; prof. natural science, Western Coll., Ia., 1871-76; actuarry U.B. Aid Soc. of Pa., 1876-83; prof. mental and moral science, San Joaquin Valley Coll., Woodbridge, Calif., 1883-85; pres. Westfield, Ill., Coll., 1885-89. Home: Dayton, O. Died 1908.

KEPLER, Charles Ober, surgeon; b. Burbank, O., Aug. 20, 1868; s. William and Anna (Ober) K.; A.B., Baldwin U., Berea, O., 1887, A.M., 1890; M.D., Harvard, 1899; grad. St. Elizabeth's Hosp., Boston, 1900; U. of Vienna, 1906; m. Effie Alene Sweet, June 27, 1900; children—Aura Elizabeth, Helen, Edith Katharine. Practiced at Boston, Jan. 1, 1900—; specialist in gynecology and abdominal surgery; examining surgeon Boston Consolidated Gas Co. Commd. capt., Med. O.R.C., 1917, and in active service, Camp Devens, Mass. Home: Brookline, Mass. Died Nov. 1, 1934.

KEPPEL, Frederick, importer of art; b. Tullow, Ireland, Mar. 22, 1845; s. John and Ellen (Hadden) K.; prep. edn. Eng. and Ireland; student Wesley Coll., Dublin; m. Fannie M. Vickery, of Cork, Ireland, 1875. Sr. mem. Frederick Keppel & Co., dealers in and importers of pictures. Lecturer on art subjects before Yale, Columbia and Johns Hopkins, Met. Mus. of Art, Grolier Club, etc. Home: New York, N.Y. Died 1912.

KERBY, William Joseph, clergyman, educator; b. Lawler, Ia., Feb. 20, 1870; s. Daniel and Ellen (Rochford) K.; grad. St. Joseph's Coll., Dubuque, 1889; theol. course, St. Francis Sem., Milwaukee. Ordained R.C. priest at Dubuque, Ia., 1892; S.T.B., Catholic U. of America, 1893, S.T.L., 1894; student social sciences, univs. of Berlin and Bonn, Germany, and Louvain, Belgium, 1895-97; Doctor of Social and Polit. Sciences, U. of Louvain, 1897. Prof. St. Joseph's Coll., Dubuque, Ia., 1895-96; asso. prof. sociology, 1897-1906, prof., 1906—, dean of the faculty of philosophy, 1917-19. Catholic U. Sec. Nat. Conf. of Catholic Charities, 1910-20; mem. D.C. Board of Charities, 1920-26. Author: Le Socialisme aux États-Unis, 1897; The Social Mission of Charity, 1921; Prophets of the Better Hope, 1922. Editor The Ecclesiastical Review, 1927. Died July 28, 1936.

KERENS, Richard C., ambassador; b. Killberry, Co. Meath, Ireland, 1842; s. Thomas and Elizabeth (Gugerty) K.; came to U.S. in infancy; ed. pub. schs. Jackson Co., Ia.; served in the Union Army, Civil War, 1861-65; m. Frances Jane Jones, June 2, 1867 (died 1914). Lived in Arkansas after war; became contractor for the Southern Overland Mail, controlling many frontier routes, residing at San

Diego, Calif.; removed to St. Louis, 1876; identified with constrn. of Cotton Belt System, W.Va. Central & Pittsburgh Ry. System, St. Louis & N.Ark. R.R., San Pedro, Los Angeles & Salt Lake Ry. System, Coal and Coke R.R. of W.Va.; also interested in the A.,T.&St.F. System. Mem. Rep. Nat. Exec. Com., 1884-1900; mem. Rep. Nat. Com., 1892—; commr.-at-large from Mo., Chicago Expn., 1893; mem. U.S. Inter-Continental Ry. Commn., 1892-1900; received Rep. votes in Mo. Legislature for U.S. senator 3 times; ambassador extraordinary and plenipotentiary to Austria-Hungary, Dec. 21, 1909-13. Recipient of Lætare Medal from U. of Notre Dame, 1904. Home: St. Louis, Mo. Died Sept. 4, 1916.

KERFOOT, John Barrett, writer; b. Chicago, Nov. 18, 1865; s. Samuel H. and Annie W. (Lawrence) K.; early edn. in Europe, 1873-76; Shattuck Sch., Faribault, Minn., 1879-82; grad. Columbia Grammar Sch., New York, 1883; A.B., Columbia U., 1887; m. Annie Haight Hunter, 1920. Literary editor of Life, 1900-18; asso. editor Camera Work, New York, 1905—. Author: Broadway, 1911; How to Read, 1916; American Pewter, 1923. Home: Freehold, N.J. Died Apr. 17, 1927.

KERFOOT, Samuel Fletcher, educator; b. Ontario, Can., Feb. 11, 1865; s. Samuel and Eliza Jane (Neeland) K.; A.B., Hamline U., Minn., 1889, A.M., 1892; B.D., Drew Theol. Sem., N.J., 1892; D.D., Hamline, 1904, Northwestern, 1916; LL.D., Dickinson, 1917; m. Margaret Share, Dec. 28, 1892; children—Paul S., Harold Lemont, Kenneth Share, Margaret, William Neeland. Ordained M.E. ministry, 1892; pastor Minneapolis and Winona, Minn., 1892-1905; sec. Conf. Claimants Endowment Fund of Minn. Conf. M.E. Ch., 1906; dist. supt. Mankato Dist., 1907, 1908; pres. Dak. Wesleyan U., 1908-12; pres. Hamline U., June 1912-27. Home: St. Paul, Minn. Died Aug. 27, 1930.

KERKER, Gustave Adolph, composer; b. Herford, Germany, Feb. 28, 1857; s. Gustave Adolph and Elizabeth K. (both parents musicians); m. Mattie Belle Rivenburg, June 1, 1908. Began to conduct German opera at 16; conductor at New York Casino, 1889—. Invited to Berlin, Germany, to compose the comic opera The Upper 10,000, prod. Metropole Theatre, Apr. 1909; invited to Vienna to compose the comic opera "Schneeglöckchen," which was produced at Vienna, Oct. 14, 1910. Composer (comic operas): "The Pearl of Pekin"; "The Belle of New York"; "The Billionaire"; "Tourists"; "Lady Slavey"; and 20 others. Died June 29, 1923.

KERN, Frederick John, editor, pub.; b. nr. Millstadt, Ill., Sept. 2, 1864; s. Henry L. and Catherine (Engler) K.; ed. Ill. State Normal U., Normal, Ill.; m. Alma E. Eidmann, July 23, 1893. Entered newspaper business at Belleville, Ill., 1891; owner and pub. News-Democrat. Chief enrolling clk. Ill. Senate, 1892; mem. 57th Congress, 1901-03; mayor Belleville 5 terms, 1902-12; pres. State Bd. of Administration, 1913-19. Home: Belleville, Ill. Died Nov. 9, 1931.

KERN, John Adam, theologian; b. Frederick Co., Va., Apr. 23, 1846; s. Nimrod and Eliza (Bentley) K.; student U. of Va., 1868-70; D.D., Washington and Lee, 1888; m. Virginia Eskridge, Jan. 25, 1875. Ordained M.E. Ch., S., ministry, 1867; pastor at Baltimore, Washington, Alexandria, Va., and other places; prof. moral philosophy, 1886-99, v.p., 1893-97, pres., 1897-99, Randolph-Macon Coll.; prof. practical theology, Vanderbilt U., 1899-1914; prof. Christian Instns., Randolph-Macon Coll., 1914-22. Author: The Ministry to the Congregation, 1897; The Way of the Preacher, 1902; A Study of Christianity as Organized, 1910; Vision and Power, 1915. Died Mar. 24, 1926.

KERN, John Worth, senator; b. Alto, Ind., Dec. 20, 1849; s. Dr. Jacob H. and Nancy (Ligget) K.; prep. edn. at Kokomo (Ind.) High Sch.; LL.B., U. of Mich., 1869; m. Annie Hazzard, Nov. 10, 1870 (died 1884); m. 2d, Araminta Cooper, Dec. 23, 1885. Admitted to bar, 1869; practiced at Kokomo, 1869-85, Indianapolis, 1885—. Candidate for mem. Ind. Ho. of Rep., 1870; city atty., Kokomo, 6 terms, 1871-84; reporter Supreme Ct., 1885-89, and edited and pub. Vols. 100-116 Ind. Reports; mem. Ind. Senate, 1893-97; spl. asst. U.S. dist. atty., 1893-94; city solicitor, Indianapolis, 1897-1901; candidate for gov., 1900, 1904; received vote of party for U.S. senator, 1905; Dem. nominee for Vice-Pres. of U.S., 1908; U.S. senator, term 1911-17. Chmn. Dem. conf. and majority floor leader, U.S. Senate, 1914-15. Died Aug. 17, 1917.

KERN, Josiah Quincy, lawyer; b. on farm nr. Alliance, O., Oct. 27, 1838; s. Jacob and Christina (Riseley) K.; A.B., Mt. Union Coll., 1861, A.M., 1864, Ph.D., 1884; LL.B., Nat. U. Law Sch., Washington, D.C., 1882, LL.M., 1883; m. Edith Kingman, Feb. 20, 1903. Clerk, law clerk and digest clerk, U.S. Treasury, Washington, D.C., 1865—. Republican. Author: Digest of Decisions of the Second Comptroller of the Treasury, Vol. III, 1884-93, Vol. IV, 1893-94. Died Nov. 28, 1913.

KERNEY, James, editor, publisher; b. Trenton, N.J., Apr. 29, 1873; s. Thomas Francis and Maria (O'Farrell) K.; ed. parochial schs.; hon. M.A., Lafayette Coll., 1925; m. Sarah Mullen, Oct. 4, 1897; children—Mrs. Mary Kuser, Thomas Lincoln, Mrs. Katharine Welling, James, John Edward, Margaret. Began as reporter, 1895; editor Trenton Times, 1903, editor, publisher, 1924; treas. Trenton Times Corp.; State civil service commr., 1908-11. At suggestion of President Wilson, went to France, Feb. 1918, to direct distribution to European countries of all official information regarding Am. war activities, remaining overseas until shortly before signing of armistice; mem. commn. to Haiti, with rank of ambassador; judge of N.J. Court of Errors and Appeals. Trustee Prudential Ins. Co. of America. Decorated Legion of Honor (France). Catholic. Author: The Political Education of Woodrow Wilson. Home: Trenton, N.J. Died Apr. 8, 1934.

KERR, Abram Tucker, anatomist; b. Buffalo, N.Y., Jan. 7, 1873; s. Abram and Rebecca (Marshall) K.; B.S., Cornell, 1895; M.D., U. of Buffalo, 1897; grad. student Göttingen, 1899, Johns Hopkins Med. Sch., 1899-1900, U. of Freiburg, 1909; m. Agnes Rogers Sherman, July 10, 1895; children—Bruce Duncan, Cynthia Jean. Student asst. in histology and pathology, 1894-97, acting and adj. prof. anatomy, 1898-1900, U. of Buffalo; asst. prof. anatomy, 1900-04, prof. anatomy and sec., 1904—, acting prof. hygiene, 1920-22, acting prof. and dir. hygiene, 1935-37, Cornell U. Med. Coll., Ithaca. Ind. Democrat. Mason. Episcopalian. Home: Ithaca, N.Y. Died Aug. 15, 1938.

KERR, Alexander, univ. prof.; b. Aberdeenshire, Scotland, Aug. 15, 1828; s. George and Helen L. K.; A.B., Beloit Coll., 1855, A.M., 1858 (Litt.D., 1912); m. Katharine F. Brown, Jan. 1, 1857 (died 1890). Teaching, 1856—; prof. Greek lang. and lit., 1871-1907 (emeritus), U. of Wisconsin. Spent six summers in travel and study in Great Britain, France, Germany, Italy, Greece, etc. Pres. Wis. Teachers' Assn. Author and editor: The Republic of Plato (translation into English), Books I-X, with introduction to I-V, 1901-13; Atlantis Found, and other verse, 1917. Home: Madison, Wis. Died Sept. 25, 1919.

KERR, Alexander Thomas Warwick, glass mfr.; b. San Francisco, Sept. 7, 1888; s. Alexander H. and A. (Alison) K.; prep. edn., Portland (Ore.) Acad.; student Harvard, 1907-10. Began in manufacture of glass at Portland, Ore., 1903; removed to Okla.; pres. Kerr Glass Mfg. Corp.; pres. Alexander H. Kerr & Co., Inc.; mem. Kerr, Hubbard & Kelly. Republican. Presbyn. Home: Tulsa, Okla. Died May 14, 1931.

KERR, Alvah Milton, editor, author; b. Athens, O., July 22, 1858; s. Joseph and Rebecca (Sanders) K.; ed. pub. schs., Monroe, Wis.; married. Telegraph operator and train dispatcher, C.,R.I.&P. R.R., 1876-88; editor and writer, 1888—. Was consecutively editor of Up-to-Date, asso. editor Belford's Magazine, editor Iroquois Magazine, and also editor The Chicago Ledger. Author: Heroes of Wire and Rail, 1903; Two Young Inventors, 1904; The Diamond Key, 1907. Died Sept. 26, 1924.

KERR, David Ramsey, college pres.; b. nr. Cadiz, O., Mar. 2, 1850; s. James and Julia Ann (Carrick) K.; A.B., Franklin Coll., New Athens, O., 1874, A.M., 1877; Ph.D., Bellevue Coll., Neb., 1889; D.D., U. of Omaha, and Franklin Coll., Ohio, 1891; LL.D., Westminster Coll., Mo., 1912; m. Martha S. Hill, June 12, 1879; children—Willis Holmes, James Fred (dec.), Mrs. Mary Sherrard Page, David Rhea, Mrs. Julia Carrick McCarty, Robert Hill. Ordained Presbyterian ministry, 1876; pastor Atlantic, Pa., 1876-78, Jamestown, Pa., 1876-82, Mercer, Pa., 1882-87, Omaha, Neb., 1887-89; pres. U. of Omaha, 1891-1904, Bellevue Coll., 1889-1904, Westminster Coll., Fulton, Mo., 1904-11; prof. history and polit. science, Coll. of Emporia, Kan., 1911-12; asso. pres. Beechwood Sch. for Women, Jenkinton, Pa., 1912-16; again pres. Bellevue Coll., 1916-18 (emeritus). Honorably retired minister, 1920. Home: Topeka, Kan. Died Dec. 29, 1929.

KERR, Duncan J(ohn), ry. pres.; b. Glasgow, Scotland, Dec. 3, 1883; s. Alexander and Barbara Balfour (Sleigh) K.; B.S., C.E., U. of Glasgow, 1904; m. Elizabeth Muir Hendrie, May 6, 1911; children—William S., Alexander D., John D., Douglas H., Elsie M. Came to U.S., 1904, naturalized, 1919. Rodman Pa. R.R., 1904-08; constrn. work Chicago, Milwaukee & Puget Sound R.R., 1908-10, Ore. Trunk Line & Spokane, Portland & Seattle Ry., 1910-13; engr. Great Northern Ry., St. Paul, Minn., 1913, asst. to v.p. of operations to 1936; also pres. Cottonwood Coal Co. and Somers Lumber Co. (subsidiaries of Great Northern Ry.) for 10 years; asst. to pres. Lehigh Valley R.R., 1936, pres., 1937—. Served as chief engr. and asst. to exec. v.p. U.S. R.R. Adminstrn. during World War. Home: Sayre, Pa. Died Oct. 8, 1940.

KERR, Frank Marion, pub. utility management; b. Gilman, Ill., Mar. 22, 1869; s. Joseph Lee and Candas Ellen (Roberts) K.; ed. high sch., Gilman; m. Kate M. Ottis, Jan. 12, 1893. Went to Butte, 1890, to install electric light plant for the Northwest Thomson-Houston Co., St. Paul, Minn., and remained there; advanced through various positions to gen. supt. Silver Bow Electric Light Co., Butte Gen. Electric Co., Butte Electric Light Co., Butte Electric & Power Co., Madison River Power Co., Great Falls Power Co., Thompson Falls Power Co., Rocky Mountain Power Co., all of which were merged with The Mont. Power Co., of which was pres. and gen. mgr. until Jan. 1940, hon. pres. and dir.; pres. Glacier Production Co.; v.p. Great Falls Townsite Co. Republican. Home: Butte, Mont. Died May 17, 1941.

KERR, Henry Hampton, elec. engr.; b. St. Peter, Minn., Apr. 12, 1864; s. Aaron Hervey and Elizabeth (Craig) K.; ed. high sch.; m. Jessie C. Smith, June 17, 1894; children—Henry H., Malcolm C. With Westinghouse, Church, Kerr & Co., 1886-1920, advanced to v.p.; company taken over, 1920, by the Dwight P. Robinson Co., Inc., of which was v.p.; company absorbed with others, 1928, now United Engineers & Constructors, of which is v.p. Republican. Episcopalian. Home: Evanston, Ill. Died July 1932.

KERR, James, surgeon; b. Portstewart, Co. Derry, Ireland, Dec. 14, 1848; s. Abraham John and Isabella (Gilliland) K.; grad. Royal U., Dublin, Ireland, 1870; M.D., M.Ch., Queen's Coll., Belfast, 1870; m. Laurie J. Bell, of Dublin, Ireland, July 26, 1876. Surgeon Royal Canadian Mail Service, 1871-73; surgeon to H. M. Transport No. XII, Gold Coast Expdn., 1873-74; chief surgeon Canadian Pacific Ry., 1882-88; surgeon Canadian Militia, Riel Rebellion, 1885; pres. and prof. surgery, Manitoba Med. Coll., 1883-88; prof. surgery, Georgetown Med. Coll., Washington, 1891-94. Died 1911.

KERR, James Bremer, lawyer; b. Beloit, Wis., Sept. 28, 1867; s. Alexander and Katharine Fuller (Brown) K.; A.B., U. of Wis., 1889, fellow in Latin, 1889-90, M.A., 1890; LL.B., U. of Wis., 1892; m. Mabel Bushnell, Sept. 6, 1893; children—Katharine Hope (Mrs. Matthew C. Riddle), Elizabeth Bushnell (Mrs. John L. Day, Jr.). Began practice at Madison, 1892; gen. land attorney, 1896-1902, asst. general counsel, 1902-07, Northern Pacific Ry., St. Paul; mem. firm Carey & Kerr, Portland, Ore., 1907—; gen. counsel Spokane, Portland & Seattle Ry. Co. Member commn. to draft workmen's compensation act, passed by Ore. Legislature, 1913. Republican. Home: Portland, Ore. Died Mar. 26, 1930.

KERR, John Brown, army officer; b. nr. Lexington, Ky., Mar. 12, 1847; s. John and Rachel (Fry) K.; grad. U.S. Mil. Acad., 1870; m. Eva Paddock, June 7, 1894. Apptd. 2d lt., 6th U.S. Cav., June 15, 1870; promoted through grades to brig. gen. U.S.A., Apr. 13, 1908; retired, May 20, 1909. Engaged in mil. duty on frontier in Tex., Ind. Ty., Kan., Ariz. and N.M., 1870-88, and active in movements against and engagements with Indians; hon. mentioned in gen. orders, June 25, 1888, "for meritorious conduct in defeating attempt made by Navajo Indians to rescue from custody Indian prisoners, between Fts. Wingate and Gallup, N.M."; engaged in campaign against Sioux Indians, under Gen. Miles, 1890-97; awarded medal of honor "for distinguished bravery while comdg. his troop against Sioux on White River, S.D., Jan. 1, 1891"; comd. 2d squadron, 6th Cav., in Spanish-Am. War, and in campaign against Santiago de Cuba, and wounded in assault on San Juan Ridge, July 1, 1898; mil. attaché to Germany, 1900-02; asst. adj. gen., July 15, 1902; chief of staff, Philippines Div., 1903-04, Atlantic Div., 1904-06. Won many medals for marksmanship; won Army gold medal in Army Competition, 1890. Died Feb. 27, 1928.

KERR, John Brown, ry. official; b. Newburgh, N.Y., Feb. 1, 1851; s. George W. and Margaret (Brown) K.; grad. Trinity Sch., N.Y. City, 1866; studied law in office of E. A. Brewster, Newburgh; m. Elizabeth R. Case, Nov. 16, 1881. Admitted to N.Y. bar, 1872, and began practice at Newburgh; apptd. atty. N.Y., Ontario Western Ry., 1881; dir. same rd., 1883, v.p. and gen. counsel, 1892; pres., 1913-29. Home: Wainscott, N.Y. Died June 25, 1939.

KERR, John Henry, clergyman; b. Monongahela City, Pa., Apr. 7, 1858; s. John and Anne Bakewell (Campbell) K.; A.B., Princeton, 1878, A.M., 1888; grad. Western Theol. Sem., Pittsburgh, Pa., 1881; D.D., U. of Pittsburgh, 1896; m. Margaretta Campbell, Sept. 21, 1882 (died 1926); children—William Campbell, Benjamin Warfield, Marcia. Ordained Presbyn. ministry, 1882; pastor successively at Oconto, Wis., Normal, Ill., Central Ch., Rock Island, Ill., Trinity Ch., San Francisco, until 1902; prof. N.T. lang. and lit., San Francisco Theol. Sem., 1895-1902; publishing sec. Am. Tract Soc., 1902-08; pastor Arlington Av. Ch., Brooklyn, N.Y., 1909-28; prof. N.T. Exegesis, Bloomfield (N.J.) Theol. Sem., 1931-32. Moderator Synod of N.Y., 1925. Republican. Author: Harmony of the Gospels, 1903. Home: Berkeley, Calif. Died June 3, 1936.

KERR, John Steele, nurseryman; b. nr. Columbia, Tenn., Jan. 15, 1847; s. Green Williamson and Mariah (Henderson) K.; removed to Tex., 1859; ed.

high schs. and acads., Tex., to 1866; m. Amelia Rutherford Murray, later of Bonham, Tex., Nov. 18, 1874. Pvt. Roberts' Co., Chambers' Battalion, Tex. Reserve Corps, 1864-65; farmer nr. McKinney, Tex., 1865-84; began in horticulture, 1870, nursery business, with brother, A. W. Kerr, 1874; moved to Sherman, Tex., 1884; founder, and pres. Commercial Nursery & Orchard Co., to 1906; now 1st v.p. Tex. Nursery Co.; also pres. and mgr. John S. Kerr Nursery Co. Democrat. Mem. Presbyn. Ch., S. Home: Sherman, Tex. Died Oct. 4, 1925.

KERR, Mark Brickell, mining engr.; b. St. Michaels, Md., June 28, 1860; s. John Bozman and Lucy Hamilton (Stevens) K.; ed. pub. schs. of Washington, and spl. edn. as civil engr. under pvt. instruction; m. Kate Shepard, June 5, 1889. Made ascent of Mt. Shasta, 1886; geographer of expdn. sent out in 1890 by U.S. Geol. Survey and Nat. Geog. Soc. Home: Berkeley, Calif. Died Mar. 15, 1917.

KERR, Robert Floyd, editor; b. Sugar Grove, Ind., Apr. 12, 1850; s. Andrew Jackson and Nancy (Sayers) K.; A.B., DePauw U., 1877, A.M., 1880; post-grad. in economics, U. of Chicago, 1892-93; unmarried. Taught sch., Kentland, Ind., 1877-78; taught English and mathematics in a provincial sch., Hirosaki, Japan, 1879-80; prin. Blair (Neb.) High Sch., 1884; prin. prep. dept., 1885-86, prep. dept., 1885-86, prof. history and economics, 1887-92, librarian and instr. in civics, 1899-1904, S.D. Agrl. Coll.; pvt. sec. to Gov. Elrod, of S.D., 1905-06; editor Minnesota and Dakota Farmer, Brookings, S.D., Mar. 1, 1909—; sec. Brookings Bldg. & Loan Assn. Supt. schs., Newton Co., Ind., 1878, Brookings Co., S.D., 1895-98; mem. S.D. Ho. of Rep., 1911, 13. Methodist. Mason. Republican. Home: Brookings, S.D. Died Oct. 17, 1921.

KERR, Robert Pollok, clergyman; b. Greensboro, Ala., July 19, 1850; s. John Poole and Sarah (Howard) K.; grad. William Jewel Coll., Liberty, Mo., 1871; (D.D., Washington and Lee, 1887); m. Nellie T. Webb, Sept. 17, 1873. Ordained Presbyn. ministry, 1874; pastor Lexington, Mo., 1874-77, Thomasville, Ga., 1878-82, Independent Ch., Savannah, Ga., 1882-86, First Ch., Richmond, Va., 1886-1906, Northminster Ch., Baltimore, 1906-17. Dir. Princeton Theol. Sem. Author: History of Presbyterianism, 1884. Compiler: Hymns of the Ages, 1901. Home: Baltimore, Md. Died Mar. 25, 1923.

KERR, Walter Craig, mechanical engr.; b. St. Peter, Minn., Nov. 8, 1858; s. Aaron H. and Elizabeth (Craig) K.; common sch. edn. there; B.M.E., Cornell, 1879; m. Lucy Lyon, Dec. 27, 1883. Asst. prof. Cornell, 1880-83; since then mech. engr. in the Westinghouse interests; pres. Westinghouse, Church, Kerr & Co., 1902—. Trustee Cornell, 1890—. Home: Dongan Hills, S.I., N.Y. Died 1910.

KERRIGAN, Frank Henry, judge; b. Contra Costa Co., Calif., Sept. 17, 1868; s. Henry Patrick and Elizabeth (Donlin) K.; ed. pub. schs.; m. Jessie McNab, Nov. 30, 1905; children—Stewart, Jane. Admitted to Calif. bar, 1889; justice of the peace, San Francisco, 1894-1900; judge Superior Court, 1900-06; asso. justice Dist. Court of Appeals, 1906-22; justice Supreme Court of Calif., 1923-24; judge U.S. Dist. Court, Northern Dist. of Calif., Feb. 10, 1924—. Republican. Mason. Home: San Francisco, Calif. Died Feb. 9, 1935.

KERWIN, Hugh Leo, dir. U.S. Conciliation Service, Dept. of Labor; b. Blossburg, Pa., Feb. 18, 1873; s. Hugh and Annie (Bennett) K.; ed. high sch. and business coll.; m. Angie Dickinson, June 10, 1896; children—Hugh A., Myra F., Frank W. County auditor, Tioga Co., Pa., 1902-06; sec. to Hon. William B. Wilson, chmn. Com. on Labor of Ho. of Rep., Washington, 1911-13, and continued as his sec. after he became sec. of labor, 1913-17; asst. to sec. of labor, 1917-18; sec., 1st Federal, State and Municipal Employment Conf., San Francisco, 1915; mem. Fuel Production Com. of Council Nat. Defense, 1917; dir. U.S. Labor Adjustment Service (war emergency, which included Conciliation Service), 1918-19; mem. Federal Mediation Board, Oil Industry, Calif., 1919, and Packing House Com. same year; dir. U.S. Conciliation Service, Dept. of Labor, 1917—, also dir. U.S. Housing Corp. Mem. Assn. of Govt. Labor Officials of U.S. and Canada. Home: Wellsboro, Pa. Died June 10, 1937.

KERWIN, James Charles, judge; b. Menasha, Wis., May 4, 1850; s. Michael and Mary (Buckley) K.; ed. Menasha High Sch.; LL.B., U. of Wis., 1875; m. Helen E. Lawson, 1877. Admitted to bar, 1875; practiced at Neenah and Milwaukee; city atty., Neenah, 12 yrs.; regent U. of Wis., 1901-04; asso. justice Supreme Ct. of Wis., Jan. 1905—. Republican. Home: Neenah, Wis. Died Jan. 29, 1921.

KESLER, Martin Luther, clergyman; b. Iredell Co., N.C., Aug. 25, 1858; s. Charles Washington and Elizabeth Keziah (Lazenby) K.; A.B., Wake Forest (N.C.) Coll., 1888, D.D., 1916; Th.M., Southern Bapt. Theol. Sem., 1891; m. Ethel Browne, Sept. 14, 1892; children—John Malcolm, James Courtney, Martin Luther. Ordained ministry Southern Bapt. Ch., 1890; pastor Laurinburg, N.C., 1891-93, Red Springs, 1893-96, Rocky Mount, 1897-1900, Scotland Neck, 1900-03, Morgantown, 1903-05; supt. Thomasville Bapt. Orphanage, 1905—; inaugurated system of mothers' aid, 1921. Trustee Wake Forest Coll., Meredith Coll., N.C. State Sch. for the Blind, State Bd. of Charities and Pub. Welfare. Democrat. Home: Thomasville, N.C. Died Aug. 19, 1932.

KESSLER, George Edward, landscape architect; b. Frankenhausen, Germany, July 16, 1862; s. Edward Carl and Clotilde K.; came to America with parents, 1865; ed. in pub. schs., by pvt. tutors, and spl. instrn. in civ. engring., forestry and botany, in Europe; m. Ida Grant Field, May 14, 1900. Engaged as landscape architect at Kansas City, 1882—, and St. Louis, 1903—. Landscape architect, Park Dept., Kansas City, 1892—. Planned grounds La. Purchase Expn., St. Louis, 1904; designer of park systems and improvements for Kansas City, Memphis, Cincinnati, Denver, Dallas, Syracuse, Houston, Salt Lake, Indianapolis and many other cities; planned layout for cantonment, Camp Travis, San Antonio, Tex.; town planner for Rock Island dist. under U.S. Housing Corp. Mem. exec. bd. Nat. City Planning Inst.; mem. Chamber of Commerce, St. Louis. Home: St. Louis, Mo. Died Mar. 19, 1923.

KESSLER, Harry Clay, bvt. brig. gen. U.S.V.; b. Phila., Mar. 18, 1844; s. John K., Jr.; ed. Phila. until 1861; m. Josephine A. Dilworth, Nov. 1876. Entered Union army, 1861, as 2d lt. 104th regt. Pa. vols.; promoted 1st lt., Jan. 1863; served in Army of Potomac; disch., Sept. 1863; went to Mont., Jan. 1875; engaged in mining; identified with Nat. Guard from organization; comdg. col. 1st Mont. Inf., U.S.V., Apr. 1898; served in the Philippines; bvtd. brig. gen. U.S.V., Mar. 1899; disch., Oct. 1899. Jr. vice comdr.-in-chief, G.A.R., 1903-04. Home: Butte, Mont. Died 1907.

KESTER, Paul, dramatist, author; b. Delaware, O., Nov. 2, 1870; s. Franklin Cooley and Harriett (Watkins) K.; ed. pvt. schs. and under pvt. tutors; unmarried. Author: His Own Country; Tales of the Real Gypsy; Diana Dauntless; also numerous poems. Plays: The Countess Roudine (with Minnie Maddern Fiske), prod. by Mme. Modjeska; Zamar, prod. by Alexander Salvini; The Student of Salamanca, prod. by A. Salvini; What Dreams May Come, prod. by Mme. Janauschek; Guy Mannering (new version), prod. by Madame Janauschek; The Cousin of the King (with Vaughan Kester), prod. by Walker Whiteside; Eugene Aram, prod. by Walker Whiteside; Sweet Nell of Old Drury, prod. in England by Julia Neilson and Fred Terry, in America by Mlle. Rhea and later by Ada Rehan, in Australia by Nellie Stewart, in Orient by Matheson Lang, revived in New York, 1923; When Knighthood Was in Flower, prod. in America by Julia Marlowe, in London by Julia Marlowe and E. H. Sothern, in Australia by Nellie Stewart; Mademoiselle Mars, prod. by Mrs. Langtry; Rachel Vour, prod. in England by Maud May; The Cavalier (with George Middleton), prod. by Julia Marlowe; Queen Fiametta (with Mildred Aldrich, from the French of Catule Mendes), prod. by Julia Marlowe; Dorothy Vernon, prod. in America by Bertha Galland, in Eng. by Julia Neilson and Fred Terry; Friend Hannah, prod. by Annie Russell, revived under title of The Love of a King, by Albert Brown; Don Quixote, prod. by E. H. Sothern; The Bill Toppers, prod. by Marie Tempest; The Lady in the Case, prod. by Annie Russell; Beverly's Balance, prod. by Margaret Anglin; The Woman of Bronze (adapted from the French of Kistermaeckers and Dellard), produced by Margaret Anglin; Lady Dedlock (founded on Bleak House by Charles Dickens), prod. by Margaret Anglin, 1923; Tom Sawyer (dramatization of Mark Twain's story), prod., 1931. Also Conservative Democracy. Home: Hague, Westmoreland Co., Va. Died June 20, 1933.

KESTER, Vaughan, writer; b. New Brunswick, N.J., Sept. 12, 1869; s. Franklin Cooley and Harriett (Watkins) K.; bro. of Paul K.; ed. common schs., Mt. Vernon, O., and under tutor at Cleveland; m. Jessie B. Jennings, Aug. 31, 1898. Held position on staff of Cosmopolitan Magazine and the International, Literary and News Syndicates, Irvington-on-Hudson, N.Y. Has done miscellaneous literary work, short stories published by the various mags., songs and two plays. Author: The Manager of the B and A, 1901; The Fortunes of the Landrays, 1905; John o' Jamestown, 1907; The Just and the Unjust, 1912. Home: Gunston, Va. Died 1911.

KETCHAM, Daniel Warren, army officer; b. nr. Burns City, Ind., May 1, 1867; s. Seth L. and Almira (Benham) K.; grad. U.S. Mil. Acad., 1890, Arty. Sch., 1894, Sch. of Submarine Defense, 1904; m. Edith Varnum Smith, Oct. 9, 1897. Commd. add. 2d lt. 2d Arty., June 12, 1890; promoted through grades to col., Coast Arty Corps, May 15, 1917; brig. gen. (temp.), Oct. 1, 1918; returned to grade of col., May 15, 1919; retired from active service May 24, 1919, on own application, after more than 32 yrs.' service. Duty at Ft. Warren, Mass., 1895-97, Boston, 1899; at Honolulu, 1899-1901, Ft. Hamilton, N.Y., 1902-03, Ft. Totten, N.Y., 1903-04, Presidio, San Francisco, 1904-09; in Philippines, 1909-11; at Forts Strong and Warren, Mass., 1911-12; on Gen. Staff, Washington, D.C., 1912-14; at Ft. DuPont, Del., 1915, Ft. Monroe, Va., as pres. Arty. Bd., 1916-17; mem. Ordnance Bd., 1917; on Gen. Staff, Washington, D.C., 1917-18; arrived in France, June 17, 1918; grad. Gen. Staff Coll., Langres, Sept. 1918; comdr. 34th Brigade, C.A.C., Sept. 1918-Feb. 1, 1919; comdr. Camp Taylor, Ky., Mar.-May 1919. Died July 19, 1935.

KETCHAM, John Clark, congressman; b. Toledo, O., Jan. 1, 1873; s. John Clark and Mary L. (Davis) K.; grad. high sch., Hastings, Mich., 1892; hon. LL.D. conferred by Albion College in 1929; hon. D.Agr., Michigan State College, 1932; m. Cora E. Rowlader, June 30, 1897 (died 1923); children—Mildred Clare (Mrs. Robert E. Houston), John Clark, Ruth Madeline (Mrs. E. C. Sackrider); m. 2d, Ada Belle Shelton, Mar. 29, 1924; 1 dau., Mary Shelton. Teacher, high schs., 1892-99; county commr. schs., Barry Co., Mich., 1899-1907; postmaster, Hastings, 1907-13; master Mich. State Grange, 1912-20; lecturer Nat. Grange, 1917-21. Mem. 67th to 72d Congresses (1921-23), 4th Mich. Dist. Pres. Nat. Bank of Hastings, 1933-37. Commr. of ins., State of Mich., 1935-36. Agr. counsel Mich. Chain Stores, 1938—. Member I.O.O.F. Republican. Mem. Gen. Conf. M.E. Ch., 1916, 20. Mason. Home: Hastings, Mich. Died Dec. 4, 1941.

KETCHAM, John Henry, congressman, farmer; b. Dover, N.Y., Dec. 21, 1832; academic edn.; engaged in farming. Town supervisor, 1854-55; mem. N.Y. assembly, 1856-57; State senator, 1860-61; served, col. 150th N.Y. vols., 1861-65; promoted brig. gen. and bvtd. maj. gen.; commr. of D.C., 1874-77; mem. Congress, 1865-73, 1877-93, and 1897-1903, 18th N.Y. dist., and 1903-07, 21st dist. Republican. Home: Dover Plains, N.Y. Died 1906.

KETCHAM, Rosemary, prof. of design; b. Springfield, O., d. Charles Wesley and Mary Dyer (Parkison) K.; Litt.B., Ohio Wesleyan U.; post grad. work Columbia, 1905-06, Harvard, 1908, Westminster Tech. Inst., London, Eng., 1914-15; pupil of Frank Brangwyn, London, 1909. Asso. prof. of design, Syracuse (N.Y.) U., 1908-12, prof., 1912-20; prof. of design, head of department, University of Kansas, 1920; exhibited landscape paintings in London, 1915, Syracuse, 1916; hand bookbinding in Syracuse, N.Y. City, Kansas City, Mo., and San Francisco, 1922 and 1928. Mem. regional com. Am. Coll. Soc. of Print Collectors; regional advisor Federated Council on Art Edn. Methodist. Home: Lawrence, Kan. Died July 19, 1940.

KETCHAM, William Alexander, lawyer; b. Indianapolis, Ind., Jan. 2, 1846; s. John Lewis and Jane (Merrill) K.; prep. edn. Halle, Germany, and Gymnasium, Stuttgart, 1859-61; student Wabash Coll., Crawfordsville, Ind., 1861-63; A.B., Dartmouth Coll., 1867; (LL.D., Wabash Coll., 1894, also Dartmouth Coll., 1917); m. Flora McDonald, June 25, 1873. Enlisted as pvt. Co. A, 13th Ind. Vols., Feb. 24, 1864; 2d lt. Co. E, Dec. 16, 1864; capt. Co. I, May 1, 1865; hon. mustered out Sept. 5, 1865. Admitted to Ind. bar, 1868, and began practice at Indianapolis; firm Ketcham, McTiernan & Higgins. Co. atty. Marion Co., 1884-86; atty. gen., Ind., 2 terms, 1894-98; mem. Bd. Control Ind. Soldiers' and Sailors' Monument. Mem. George H. Thomas Post G.A.R.; 1907-08. Republican. Presbyn. Home: Indianapolis, Ind. Died Dec. 27, 1921.

KETCHAM, William Ezra, M.E. minister, editor Preacher's Magazine; b. New York, Feb. 19, 1837; s. Ezra and Jerusha K.; ed. City Inst., New York, and Amenia Sem. (D.D., Univ. of Omaha, 1894); m. Selina Bowers, March 18, 1858. Mem. N.Y. Conf. M.E. Ch., 1858, and has filled various pastorates; solicited large amounts for chs. Author: Funeral Sermons and Outlines. Home: Yonkers, N.Y. Died 1903.

KETCHAM, William Henry, missionary; b. Sumner, Ia., June 1, 1868; s. Alonzo and Josephine (Shanafelt) K.; A.B., St. Charles Coll., Grand Coteau, La.; studied divinity, Theol. Cem., Mt. St. Mary's of the West, Cincinnati, O. (LL.D., from Fordham U., June 1915). Ordained R.C. priest in Pro-Cathedral, Guthrie, Okla., Mar. 13, 1892; apptd. missionary to Creek and Cherokee Indians, with residence at Muskogee, I.T., 1891; apptd. missionary to full-blood Choctaw Indians, with residence at Antlers, I.T., 1897; dir. Bur. Catholic Indian Missions, Washington, D.C., 1901—; mem. Bd. of Indian Commrs., Dec. 3, 1912—. Made Domestic Prelate, Apr. 5, 1919. Died Nov. 14, 1921.

KETCHUM, Alexander Phœnix, lawyer; b. New Haven, Conn., May 11, 1839; s. Edgar and Elizabeth (Phœnix) K.; grad. with honors, Coll. City of New York, 1858 (M.A.); tutor there, 1858-59; grad. Albany Law School, 1860, and admitted to bar; m. Clara McFarland Dwight, June 10, 1870 (dec.). Served in Civil War in Dept. of South, and as staff officer of Gen. Rufus Saxton, mil. gov. of S.C.; transferred to staff of Maj. Gen. O. O. Howard, 1865; served as A.A.A.G., in Charleston and Washington; resigned from army Sept. 1867, with rank of bvt. col.; apptd., 1869, assessor Internal Revenue,

9th dist., N.Y.; later collector same; gen. appraiser and chief appraiser Port of New York, 1874-85; from then engaged in practice of law, N.Y. City. One of founders, and 1st pres. Mt. Morris Bank; 2 yrs. pres. Presbyn. Union, New York; prominent in Y.M.C.A.; was for 4 yrs. mem. bd. education. Republican. Deceased.

KETCHUM, Edgar, lawyer; b. New York, July 15, 1840; s. Edgar and Elizabeth K.; grad. Coll. City of New York, 1860 (A.M., 1863); Law School Columbia Coll., 1862; m. Angelica Schuyler Anderson, Oct. 1869. Was mem. 7th N.Y. regt.; afterward entered U.S.A. as 2d lt. signal corps; received 2 bvts. for gallant and meritorious conduct at capture of Ft. Fisher, N.C., and for such service during the war; hon. discharge, 1865; later three yrs. engr. with rank of maj. in N.Y. Nat. Guard. Republican. Home: New York, N.Y. Died 1905.

KETCHUM, John Buckhout, editor; b. New York, July 11, 1837; s. David C. and Ann (Requa) K.; ed. pub. sch.; 1845-51, and 1 yr. at New York U.; m. Rachelle A. Terhune, Nov. 14, 1858. Writer on New York Leader, 1857; on Rockland County Journal, 1879; mem. U.S. Sanitary Commn., 1862; mem. staff Gov. Reuben E. Fenton of N.Y., 1865, with rank of major; over 50 yrs. corresponding sec. U.S. Soldiers' Christian Aid Assn., of New York; has made two voyages to Europe for purpose of observing moral condition of European soldiers. Editor United States Soldier. Republican. Home: Brooklyn, N.Y. Died Dec. 8, 1914.

KETCHUM, Milo Smith, civil engr., educator; b. Burns, Ill., Jan. 26, 1872; s. Smith and Martha Ann (Clement) K.; grad. Elmwood (Ill.) High Sch., 1889; B.S., U. of Ill., 1895, C.E., 1900; Sc.D., Colo. Sch. Mines, 1926, U. of Colo., 1927; m. Mary Esther Beatty, Sept. 17, 1903; children—Martha Esther (Mrs. N. C. Debevoise), Elizabeth Jane, Milo Smith, Jr. Instructor in civil engineering, U. of Illinois, 1895-97; bridge and structural engr. Gillette-Herzog Mfg. Co., 1897-99; asst. prof. civ. engring., U. of Ill., 1899-1903; contracting mgr. Am. Bridge Co., Kansas City, 1903-04; prof. civ. engring., 1904-19, dean Coll. of Engring., 1905-19, U. of Colo. prof. civil engring. and dir. dept., U. of Pa., Sept. 1919-Sept. 1922; dean of Coll. of Engring. and dir. Engring. Expt. Sta., U. of Ill., Sept. 1922—. Asst. dir. U.S. Govt. explosives plants, in charge of contsrn. of smokeless powder plant at Nitro, W.Va., Feb. 1918-19. Mem. Crocker and Ketchum, consulting engrs., Denver, Colo., 1909-10. Registered structural engr. state of Ill. Author: Surveying Manual (with Prof. W. D. Pence), 1900, 5th edit., 1931; Design of Steel Mill Buildings, and The Calculation of Stresses in Framed Structures, 1903, 4th edit., 1921; Design of Walls, Bins and Grain Elevators, 1907, 3d edit., 1918; Design of Highway Bridges of Steel, Timber and Concrete, 1908, 2d edit., 1920; Design of Mine Structures, 1912; Structural Engineers' Handbook, 1914, 3d edit., 1924. Presbyn. Home: Urbana, Ill. Died Dec. 19, 1934.

KETLER, Isaac Conrad, college pres.; b. Northumberland, Pa., Jan. 21, 1853; s. Adam and Mary (Kyle) K.; A.B., Nat. Normal Coll., Lebanon, O.; A.M., Allegheny Coll., 1882; Ph.D., U. of Wooster, 1884; Western Theol. Sem., Pa., 1885-88; (D.D., U. of Wooster, 1893; LL.D., Washington and Jefferson Coll., 1902); m. Matilda Gilson, Dec. 24, 1878. Ordained Presbyn. ministry, 1888; organized pvt. sch. at Pine Grove (now Grove City, Pa.), 1876, acad., 1879, Grove City Coll., 1884, of which became president. Author: The Tragedy of Paotingfu, 1901. Home: Grove City, Pa. Died July 2, 1913.

KETTIG, William Henry, merchant; b. Louisville, Ky., Aug. 6, 1863; s. Ernest and Josephine (William) K.; ed. grade and high schs., Louisville; m. Laura E. Moody, Dec. 29, 1890; children—William Henry, Mildred (Mrs. J. Reese Murray), Dorothy. Organizer, 1886, Milner & Kettig Co., Birmingham, pres. and mgr. 20 years until co. was absorbed by the Crane Co. of Chicago; mgr. Crane Co., Birmingham, 15 yrs.; chmn. and federal reserve agent Federal Reserve Bank of Atlanta, 23 yrs. Col. on staff of Gov. Braxton B. Comer, 1907-11. Chmn. Liberty Loan Com. and Capital Issues Com., Birmingham, World War. Mem. Chamber Commerce, Birmingham (pres.). Democrat. Presbyn. Mason. Home: Birmingham, Ala. Died July 1939.

KETTLE, Edgar Ulf, kiln drying expert; b. Birmingham, Eng., March 22, 1868. Came to U.S., 1912, naturalized citizen, 1921. Designer of many lumber-drying installations in U.S. and Canada. V.p. Grand Rapids Veneer Works. Author: Practical Kiln Drying, 1922. Home: Grand Rapids, Mich. Died Feb. 17, 1933.

KETTNER, William, congressman; b. Ann Arbor, Mich., Nov. 20, 1864; s. John Kettner and L. Fredericka (Lang) K.; pub. sch. edn.; m. Marion Morgan, Aug. 24, 1905. Lived in St. Paul, Minn., to 1884; miner, Calif., later with newspapers; engaged in gen. ins. business, 1892—. Mem. 63rd to 66th Congresses (1913-21), 11th Calif. Dist. Democrat. Mem. Disciples of Christ. Mason. Home: San Diego, Calif. Died Nov. 11, 1930.

KEY, David McKendree, jurist; b. Green Co., Tenn., Jan. 27, 1824; grad. Hiwassee Coll., Tenn., 1850 (A.M., LL.D., also LL.D., Univ. of Tenn.); practised law in Tenn.; lt. col. in Confederate army during Civil War; member Constl. Convention, Tenn., 1870; chancellor, 3d Chancery dist., Tenn., 1870-75; U.S. senator from Tenn., 1875-77; U.S. postmaster general, 1877-80; U.S. dist. judge, 1880-95; resigned latter year; m. Elizabeth J. Lenoir, July 1, 1857. Home: Chattanooga, Tenn. Died 1900.

KEY, James Lee, lawyer; b. De Kalb Co., Ga., July 27, 1867; s. Thomas Terrell and Rhoda (Carroll) K.; A.B., Emory Univ., Atlanta, Ga., 1888; m. Ela Tillman, June 20, 1906. Admitted to Ga. bar, 1889, and began practice at Atlanta; mem. City Council 2 yrs., Bd. of Aldermen 3 yrs., Bd. of Edn., 12 yrs.; mayor of Atlanta, term ending 1936. Democrat. Mem. M.E. Ch., S. Mason. Home: Atlanta, Ga. Died May 28, 1939.

KEY, Joseph Staunton, bishop; b. La Grange, Ga., July 18, 1829; s. Rev. Caleb W. and Elizabeth (Hames) K.; A.B., Emory Coll., Ga., 1848, later A.M.; (D.D., U. of Ga., 1868); m. Lucy Kidd, Apr. 5, 1894. Entered M.E. Ch., S. ministry, 1848; in active pastorates in Ga., until 1886; bishop M.E. Ch. S., May 1886—. Removed to Tex., 1889. Home: Sherman, Texas. Died Apr. 6, 1920.

KEY, William Mercer, judge; b. Oglethorpe Co., Ga., Oct. 20, 1850; s. Jasper Newton and Mary (Howard) K.; mainly self ed.; m. Izora Scott, 1876. Admitted to Tex. bar, 1875; practiced Georgetown, Tex.; co. Judge, Williamson Co., Tex., 1885-88; dist. judge, 1888-92; elected asso. justice Ct. of Civil Appeals, 3d Dist. of Tex., 1892, chief justice same court, Feb. 1910—. Democrat. Mason. Home: Austin, Tex. Died Dec. 13, 1923.

KEYES, Charles Henry, educator; b. Banfield, Wis., Sept. 6, 1858; s. Henry and Joan K.; grad. St. John's Coll., 1878; spl. law courses 2 yrs.; admitted to bar, 1880; m. Helen E. Brown, 1881. Prin. River Falls (Wis.) High Sch., 1880-82; prof. Fourth State Normal Sch., River Falls, 1882-84; city supt. schs., Janesville, Wis., 1884-89; conducted teachers' insts. for the state in the summers, 1882-89; mem. bd. visitors, U. of Wis., 1886-88; supt. schs., Riverside, Calif., 1889-91; pres. Throop Poly. Inst., 1891-96; resigned to take graduate course in pedagogy and philosophy, U. of Calif., 1896-97; studied Clark U., Worcester, Mass., 1897-99; prin. High Sch., Holyoke, Mass., 1898-99; supervisor schs., So. Dist., Hartford, Conn., 1899-1910; grad. student, Columbia U., 1910, 1911; received doctor's diploma in edn., Teachers Coll., Ph.D., Columbia; exec. sec. New York Com. on Safety, 1911; lecturer on vocational education and sch. administration in summer terms Colo. Teachers' Coll. and Missouri Normal Coll., 1910, 11, 12. President Skidmore College, July 1, 1912—. Pres. Southern California Teachers' Assn., 1893-96; elected pres. Pasadena Bd. of Trade, 5 times; conductor of teachers' insts. in U.S. and Canada. Home: Saratoga Springs, N.Y. Died Jan. 17, 1925.

KEYES, Edward Lawrence, surgeon; b. Charleston, S.C., Aug. 28, 1843; s. Erasmus D. (maj. gen. U.S.A.) and Caroline M. K.; A.B., Yale, 1863, A.M., 1866; M.D., Univ. Med. Coll. (New York U.), 1866; studied in France; (LL.D., Coll. St. Francis Xavier, 1897); m. Sarah M. Loughborough; father of Edward Loughborough K. Prof. dermatology, Woman's Med. Coll., 1870; asst. demonstrator anatomy, 1869-70, instr. surgery, 1870, lecturer dermatology, 1871, adj. prof. surgery, 1875, prof. dermatology, syphilology and genito-urinary surgery, and adj. prof. operative surgery to 1890, Bellevue Hosp. Med. Coll.; surgeon, St. Elizabeth's Hospital. Home: New York, N.Y. Died Jan. 24, 1924.

KEYES, Henry Wilder, senator; b. Newbury, Vt., May 23, 1863; s. Henry and Emma Frances (Pierce) K.; A.B., Harvard, 1887; (B.S., LL.D., N.H. Coll.; A.M., Dartmouth); m. Frances Parkinson Wheeler, June 8, 1904; children—Henry W., John P., Francis. Has engaged extensively in farming for many yrs.; pres. Woodsville (N.H.) Nat. Bank. Mem. N.H. Ho. of Rep., 1891-95, 1915-17, Senate, 1903-05; chmn. State Excise Commn., 1915-17; gov. of N.H., 1917-19; U.S. senator 3 terms, 1919-37. Republican. Trustee N.H. Coll. Episcopalian. Mason. Home: North Haverhill, N.H. Died June 19, 1938.

KEYES, Homer Eaton, editor; b. Brooklyn, N.Y., Dec. 21, 1875; s. Emerson Willard and Rowena (Saxe) K.; studied art, Pratt Inst., Brooklyn, 1 year; B.L., Dartmouth, 1900; studied and traveled in Europe, 1903-05; M.A., Princeton, 1912; m. Caroline Gardner Abbott, Apr. 2, 1903; 1 dau., Katharine. Instructor English, 1900-03, asst. prof. modern art, 1906-13, business dir., 1913-21, Dartmouth. Asso. editor Dartmouth Alumni Magazine, 1907-11, managing editor, 1911-20; editor "Antiques," 1921—. Congregationalist. Editor: Dana's Two Years Before the Mast, 1908. Home: New York, N.Y. Died Oct. 8, 1938.

KEYES, Rollin Arthur, merchant; b. Somerville, Mass., Dec. 14, 1854; s. Rollin Webb and Abigail A. (Chandler) K.; ed. pub. schs. and 1 yr. Chicago Acad.; m. Katharine D. Officer, Oct. 4, 1876. Began

as clk. with E. H. Sargent & Co., retail druggists, Chicago, Ill., 1871; entered service of Franklin Mac-Veagh & Co., wholesale grocers, 1872, as clk.; admitted to the firm, 1880, and pres. from its incorp., 1909. Dir. First State Pawners' Soc. Republican. Episcopalian. Home: Evanston, Ill. Died Apr. 3, 1925.

KEYES, Thomas Bassett, physician; b. Oneonta, N.Y., Oct. 22, 1874; s. Melville (atty.) and Elizabeth (Bassett) K.; M.D., Albany Medical Coll., 1895; m. Elsie Holden. Chmn. first organization com. Am. Congress of Tuberculosis (held under auspices Medico-Legal Soc. of N.Y.); a v.p. Internat. Congress of Tuberculosis, St. Louis Expn., 1904; chmn. com. on relation of insanity to tuberculosis, and 2d v.p. Am. Internat. Congress on Tuberculosis, New York, 1906; editor The Tubercle, 1897-1902; hon. collaborator editorial staff Pacific Med. Jour., 1907-17. Mason. Author: The Cure of Consumption with Subcutaneous Injections of Oil, 1904; The Renewal of Life, 1909. Home: Butternut, Wis. Died Oct. 2, 1938.

KEYES, Victor Ernest, atty. gen. of Colo.; b. Oneonta, N.Y., Jan. 16, 1879; s. Melville and Elizabeth (Bassett) K.; Ped B., State Teachers' Coll. of Colo., Greeley, 1901; Ph.B., Colo. Coll., Colorado Springs, 1905, later M.A.; J.D., U. of Chicago, 1907; m. Dora Ladd, June 22, 1909; children—Charles M., Ernest V., Elizabeth Jane. Began practice at Greeley, Colo., 1908; dep. dist. atty., Weld Co., 1908-14; atty. gen. Colo. 2 terms, 1918-22; now in law practice. Republican. Presbyn. Home: Greeley, Colo. Died June 14, 1927.

KEYES, Winfield Scott, mining engr.; b. Brooklyn, N.Y., Nov. 17, 1839; s. Erasmus D. K. (maj. gen. U.S.A.); grad. Yale, 1860; studied 3 yrs. at School of Mines, Freiberg, Saxony; widower. Supt. of mines; joint inventor Keyes & Arent's automatic tap for molten metals; mem. bd. of judges, Centennial Expn., Phila., 1876; hon. commr. to Paris Expn., 1878; leading expert in many mining suits. Pres. trustees Calif. State Mining Bureau, 16 yrs.; mem. exec. com. Calif. Miners' Assn. Owns vineyards in Napa Co., Calif.; received gold medal for exhibit of wines, Paris Expn., 1900, grand prize, St. Louis Expn., 1904. V.p. Humboldt Bank, San Francisco; gen. mgr. Pan-Am. Development Co., operating mines in State of Sinaloa, Mex. Died 1906.

KEYSER, Charles Shearer, lawyer; b. Phila., June 18, 1825; s. Joseph and Susan (Shearer) K.; grad. U. of Pa., 1845, A.M.; studied law (LL.D. conferred by Archbishop Wood); m. Sophronia McKay Norris (dec.). Was prominently identified with the establishment of Fairmount Park and the preservation of Independence Hall; in legal practice, 1848. Author: Fairmount Park, 1871-75; Penn's Treaty, 1882; The Keyser Family, 1889; Independence Hall, 1895; The Liberty Bell, 1901. Residence: Philadelphia, Pa. Deceased.

KEYSER, Ephraim, sculptor; b. Baltimore, Oct. 6, 1850; s. Moses and Bertha (Preiss) K.; ed. pub. schs. and City Coll., Baltimore, Royal Actd. Fine Arts, Munich, and Berlin; unmarried. Executed statue of Maj. Gen. Baron de Kalb for U.S. Government, 1887; designed tomb of President Chester A. Arthur and modeled figure on same erected at Rural Cemetery, Albany, N.Y.; silver medal for a bronze statue, "The Page," at Munich; M. Beer scholarship to Rome for "Psyche," now in possession of Cincinnati Art Mus. Executed busts of Sidney Lanier, Henry Harland, Cardinal Gibbons and Dr. Daniel C. Gilman. Formerly instr. Rinehart Sch. for Sculpture, Baltimore. Home: Baltimore, Md. Died Jan. 26, 1937.

KEYSER, Leander Sylvester, clergyman; b. Tuscarawas Co., O., Mar. 13, 1856; s. David A. and Barbara A. (Biddle) K.; grad. Wittenberg Div. Sch., 1883; A.M., Ohio Northern U., 1886; A.M., Wittenberg Coll., 1893, D.D., 1900; m. Mary C. Foltz, Nov. 18, 1879; children—Ort Albert, Dorner Luther, Tedrow Sylvester. Ordained Lutheran ministry, 1879; pastor La Grange, Ind., 1879-81, Elkhart, 1883-89, Springfield, O., 1889-95; mng. editor Lutheran Evangelist, 1895-97; pastor Midland College Ch., Atchison, Kan., 1897-1903, Dover, Ohio, 1903-11; prof. systematic theology, Hamma Divinity Sch. (Wittenberg Coll.), Springfield, O., 1911-32; prof. emeritus, 1932—. Author: The Only Way Out, 1888, revised edit., 1906; Our Bird Comrades, 1907; The Rational Test, 1908; A System of Christian Ethics, 1913; A System of Natural Theism, 2d edit., 1922; A System of General Ethics, 4th edit., 1934; In the Redeemer's Footsteps, 2 vols., 1919; In the Apostles' Footsteps, 2 vols., 1920; Contending for the Faith, 1921; A System of Christian Evidence, 1922, 6th edit., 1935; Man's First Disobedience, 1924; The Doctrines of Modernism, 1925; The Problem of Origins, 1926; The Conflict of Fundamentalism and Modernism, 1926; A Manual of Christian Ethics, 1926; A Handbook of Christian Psychology, 1928; The Philosophy of Christianity, 1928; A Reasonable Faith, 1933. Contbr. to mags. Home: Springfield, O. Died Oct. 18, 1937.

KEYSER, R. Brent, mfr.; b. Baltimore, Aug. 5, 1859; s. William and Mary (Brent) K.; ed. pvt.

schs., Baltimore, 1866-72, Ury, Pa., 1872-75, St. Paul's, Concord, N.H., 1875-78; m. Ellen Carr McHenry, June 14, 1888. With Keyser Brothers & Co., iron and steel mchts., 1878-83; with Baltimore Copper Smelting & Rolling Co., 1883-1910, treas., 1885, pres., 1905-10; treas. Old Dominion Copper Co., Globe, Ariz., 1887-95; dir. B.&O. R.R. Co., Merchants & Miners Transportation Co.; mem. exec. com. Mercantile Trust & Deposit Co. Pres. bd. trustees Johns Hopkins U., 1903—; trustee St. Paul's Sch., Concord, N.H. Vestryman Emmanuel P.E. Ch. Chmn. Baltimore Chapter Am. Red Cross, 1917-19. Home: Baltimore, Md. Died Mar. 1, 1927.

KEYWORTH, Maurice Reed, school supt.; b. Shabbona, Mich., Jan. 29, 1884; s. William and Eliza Ann (Lovejoy) K.; B.A., Mich. State Normal Coll., 1918; M.A., U. of Mich., 1923, Ph.D., 1930; m. Ora G. Moore, Aug. 28, 1907. Supt. schs., Lake City, Mich., 1909-14, Gaylord, Mich., 1914-18, East Jordan, Mich., 1918-21, Hastings, Mich., 1921-23, Hamtramck, Mich., 1923—; gave courses in city sch. adminstrn., U. of Mich., summers 1927, 28, Detroit City Coll., summer 1931. Republican. Mason. Author: Legal Aspects for the Records of Proceedings of Boards of Education, 1931. Editor: Hamtramck Public School Code, 1927. Home: Detroit, Mich. Died June 22, 1935.

KIBBEY, Joseph H., governor; b. Centreville, Ind., Mar. 4, 1853; s. John F. and Caroline E. K.; ed. Earlham Coll., Richmond, Ind.; m. Nora Burbank, 1877. Admitted to Ind. bar, 1875; removed to Ariz., 1888, and engaged in practice; asso. justice Supreme Ct., 1889-93; mem. Territorial Council, 1902-04; atty. gen., 1904-05; gov. of Ariz., 1905-09. Republican. Home: Phoenix, Ariz. Died June 14, 1924.

KIDDER, Benjamin Harrison, naval officer; b. Edgartown, Mass., Jan. 23, 1836. Apptd. asst. surgeon U.S.N., Sept. 30, 1861; passed asst. surgeon, June 28, 1865; surgeon, Mar. 2, 1868; med. insp., Jan. 30, 1887; med. dir., Aug. 21, 1893; retired Jan. 23, 1898; advanced to rank of rear admiral retired, June 29, 1906, for services during Civil War. Home: Malden, Mass. Died 1909.

KIDDER, Daniel Selvey, journalist, consul; b. Newark, N.J., Feb. 13, 1848; s. Daniel Parrish (D.D., LL.D.) and Harriette (Smith) K.; ed. Northwestern Univ.; m. Marie Huse Wilder, Apr. 1893. Engaged in newspaper work, 1870-1900; mayor of Clearwater, Fla., 1899; consul to Algiers, Algeria, 1900-05; consul-gen. to Hankau, China, 1905—. Republican. Died 1907.

KIDDER, Fred Thomas, physician; b. Woodstock, Vt., Oct. 14, 1858; s. Rev. Moses and Laura W. (Hazen) K.; A.B., U. of Vt., 1880, M.D., 1883; m. Ellen S. Warren, Oct. 11, 1893. Mem. Vt. State Bd. of Health, 1906— (pres. 1918—); mem. Vt. Ho. of Rep., 1906, Senate, 1908-10; pres. Woodstock Hotel Co., Woodstock Electric Co. Chmn. Windsor Co. Y.M.C.A. Com., 1906—; trustee U. of Vt., 1908—. Republican. Mem. Disciples of Christ. Home: Woodstock, Vt. Died May 10, 1925.

KIDDER, Kathryn, actress; b. Newark, N.J.; d. Col. H. M. Kidder; lived at Evanston, nr. Chicago, from childhood; studied dramatic art, New York, London and Paris; m. Louis Kaufman Anspacher, Oct. 1905. Début as Lucy Fairweather in Mayo's "The Streets of New York," Chicago, 1885; then played the lead in Mayo's "Davy Crockett"; created Countess Wanda in "Nordeck"; later the original Rachel McCreery in "Held by the Enemy" and Dearest in "Little Lord Fauntleroy"; then played leading rôles in various cos. producing French romantic dramas and Shakespearean tragedies; beginning 1894, has continuously starred in "Mme. Sans Gêne," old English comedies, "Lady Teazle," "Lydia Languish," "The Country Girl," and Shakespearean tragedies, playing Helena, Ophelia, Lady Macbeth, Desdemona, Portia, and Rosalind. Created: Elizabeth in "Embarrassment of Riches," 1906; Leanora in "A Woman of Impulse," 1909; Elinor, in "The Glass House," 1911; Katherine in "The Washerwoman Duchess," 1912; Madame Cecile, 1917; Nora Cathleen, in Synge's "Shadow of the Glen," 1917; Ruth Prescott in "All the King's Horses," 1919. Home: Ossining, N.Y. Died Sept. 7, 1939.

KIDDER, Nathaniel Thayer; b. Boston, Oct. 29, 1860; s. Henry Purkitt and Caroline W. (Archbald) K.; B.A. in Agrl. Science, Harvard, 1882; unmarried. Trustee Mass. Gen. Hosp., Milton Pub. Library, Mass. Hort. Soc. Unitarian. Home: Milton, Mass. Died July 13, 1938.

KIDDER, Wellington Parker, engr., inventor; b. Norridgewock, Me., Feb. 19, 1853; s. Wellington and Annie (Winslow) K.; ed. dist. school and Eaton Prep. School; m. Emma Louise Hinckley, Sept. 4, 1878. Patented, 1868, when but 15 yrs. old, improvement in rotary steam engines; studied applied mechanics and drawing, Boston; invented web adjustable press, 1874, which received diploma Mass. Charitable Mechanics Inst., 1878; Kidder press now in large use, especially for printing consecutive numbering of railroad and other tickets from continuous roll; invented many other improvements in presses, typewriters, automobile appliances, etc. Consulting engr. Rochester Industries, Inc., mfrs. of his later improvements in writing machines, 1923—. Home: Rochester, N.Y. Died Oct. 2, 1924.

KIECKHEFER, Ferdinand A. W., mfr.; b. Milwaukee, Feb. 10, 1852; s. Carl and Justine K.; ed. St. John's Luth. Sch. and Spencerian Business Coll., Milwaukee; m. Minnie Kuetemeyer, May 13, 1875. Began business life as clerk and cashier in hardware house for 5 yrs.; started on his own account with a little hardware and tinware shop, 1872; with brother as F. Kieckhefer & Bro., 1880, as mfrs. of tinware; business in 1899 was merged in Nat. Enameling & Stamping Co., of which became pres. Republican. Home: New York, N.Y. Died Mar. 26, 1919.

KIEFER, Andrew R., congressman; b. Marienborn, nr. Mainz, on the Rhine, Germany; ed. there; came to U.S., 1849; to St. Paul, 1855; organized on Lincoln's first call, 1861, and comd. Co. G, 2d Minn. vol. inf.; took part in several battles; apptd. provost marshal, 1863; commissioned col. 32d regt., State militia, 1864; served in State legislature; elected clerk dist. courts, 1878; mem. Congress, 1893-97; mayor of St. Paul, Jan. 1, 1899, to Jan. 1, 1901. Republican. Retired to country villa, "Marienborn," Lake Gervais, nr. St. Paul, Minn. Died 1904.

KIEFER, Daniel, political reformer; b. Cincinnati, Jan. 29, 1856; s. Charles and Sera (Bohm) K.; pub. sch. edn.; m. Rosa Danziger, May 1, 1888. In wholesale clothing mfg. business, Cincinnati, 1877-1901, Chicago, 1901-02; since retired from active business. An organizer of a semi-charitable concern to loan money on chattel mortgage at less than market rates, of which was sec. 1898-1901; devoted to polit. and econ. reforms, 1901—; advocate of views of Henry George; prominent in reorganization of Dem. party in Hamilton Co., O., and election of Dem. ticket, 1905; chmn. Fels Fund Commn. to supervise expenditure of $50,000 per annum in interest of single tax propaganda until Jan. 1, 1917; chmn. Nat. Single Tax League, Jan. 1, 1917—. Was one of signers of call for nat. Conf. on Democracy and Terms of Peace at Madison Square Garden, New York, May 30 and 31, 1917, which resulted in the creation of the Peoples Council. Home: Philadelphia, Pa. Died Aug. 18, 1923.

KIEFER, Emil, newspaper editor; b. Baden, Germany, Sept. 22, 1872; educated in schools of Germany; m. Freda Schmidt, Sept. 25, 1901; children—Gertrude Marie, Joseph, Frederick George, Louise. Came to U.S., 1889, naturalized, 1921. Editor in chief "Phila. Gazette-Democrat," 1908—. Home: Philadelphia, Pa. Died Sept. 5, 1941.

KIEFER, Guy Lincoln, M.D.; b. Detroit, Mich., Apr. 25, 1867; s. Hermann and Franciska (Kehle) K.; A.B., U. of Mich., 1887, A.M. and M.D., 1891, hon. D.P.H., 1911; m. Josephine Fannie Henion, May 2, 1893. Began practice, 1893; county phys., Wayne Co., 1895-96; city phys., Detroit, 1897-98; U.S. pension examiner, 1898-1901; health officer, Detroit, 1901-13 (resigned). Chief of staff Herman Kiefer Hosp. (municipal, contagious); consulting phys. on contagious diseases at Harper and Children's Free; consulting physician on internal medicine Woman's Hosp.; prof. preventive medicine and contagious diseases, and head dept. preventive medicine and public health, Detroit Coll. of Medicine; health commr. State of Mich., 1927—; med. dir. Mich. State Telephone Co. Fellow Am. Coll. Physicians. Republican. Died May 9, 1930.

KIEFER, Hermann, physician; b. Sulzburg, Baden, Germany, Nov. 19, 1825; s. Conrad and Friedericke (Schweyckert) K.; ed. lyceums, Freiburg and Carlsruhe, 1839-44; studied medicine, univs. of Freiburg, Heidelberg, Prague and Vienna, 1844-49; grad. Carlsruhe, May 1849; (hon. M.D. and prof. emeritus, U. of Mich., 1902); m. Francisca Kehle, of Bonndorf, Baden, July 21, 1850. Took active part in revolutions of 1848 and 1849; had to leave country, July 1849; came to U.S., settled as phys., Oct. 1849, at Detroit. Mem. bd. of edn., 1855-56; presdl. elector, 1872; commr. of Pub. Library, 1882; U.S. consul Stettin, Germany, 1883-85; regent U. of Mich., 1889-1901. Home: Detroit, Mich. Died Oct. 13, 1911.

KIEFFER, George Linn, church statistician; b. nr. Millersburg, Pa., Nov. 25, 1883; s. Solomon Winfield and Abbie Ophelia (Romberger) K.; student spring terms, Millersville (Pa.) State Normal Sch., 1902-05; A.B., Gettysburg Coll., 1909; grad. Luth. Theol. Sem., Gettysburg, 1912; B.D., Union Theol. Sem., 1914; A.M., Columbia, 1915; D.D., Hartwick Sem., 1928; Litt.D., Newberry (S.C.) Coll., 1928; m. Maude Gertrude Hostetter, Nov. 25, 1916. Teacher pub. schs. of Pa., 1901-05; engaged in Chautauqua management, and lecture work on Battle of Gettysburg, 1909-16; licensed in ministry Luth. Ch., 1911, ordained, 1916; pastor Rosedale, L.I., 1916-26, serving without salary, 1919-26; statistician and reference librarian Nat. Luth. Council, 1919—; statis. sec. United Luth. Ch., 1921-32. Asst. sec. N.Y. City Com. for 400th Anniversary of Reformation, 1916-17; financial sec. Nat. Luth. Commn. for Soldiers' and Sailors' Welfare, 1917-22; same, Nat. Luth. Council, 1919-23; asso. editor Luth. Year Book, 1919; same, United Luth. Year Book and Luth. World Almanac, 1921—; sec. New York Luth. Ministers' Assn., 1924—, Southern Conf. N.Y. Synod, 1925-26; pres. L.I. Conf. United New York Synod, 1929-32; now gen. ch. statistician, preparing Annual Census of Chs. of U.S. for The Christian Herald. Chmn. awards com. Alumni Assn. of Grad. Schs. of Columbia U., 1933—. Trustee The Hartwick Sem., 1926—, Hartwick Coll., 1928-32, Hartwick Acad., 1930-32. Home: Long Beach, also Rosedale, L.I., N.Y. Died Apr. 25, 1937.

KIEFFER, Henry Martyn, clergyman; b. Mifflinburg, Pa., Oct. 5, 1845; s. Rev. Ephraim and Eleanor (Spangler) K.; enlisted as drummer boy 150th Pa. Vols. at 16; served 3 yrs.; A.B., Franklin and Marshall Coll., 1870, with the highest grade ever made in the history of the coll.; grad. Theol. Sem. of Reformed Ch., Lancaster, Pa., 1873; D.D., Ursinus Coll., 1887; m. Mary E. Miley, Sept. 2, 1873; children—Evelyn (dec.), Edna Jeanne (dec.), Henry Mylin. Pastor Reformed Ch., Norristown, Pa., 1873-84, Easton, Pa., 1884-1903; received into P.E. Ch., Jan. 1903. Author: The Recollections of a Drummer Boy, 1883. Joint Editor: The Reformed Church Hymnal, 1890; The First Settlers of the Forks of the Delaware, 1905; It Is to Laugh, 1907; The Funny-Bone, 1910; Short Stories of the Hymns, 1912; Laugh Again, 1913; More Laughs, 1923. Home: Atlantic City, N.J. Deceased.

KIEFFER, Joseph Spangler, clergyman; b. Mifflinburg, Pa., Feb. 3, 1842; s. Rev. Ephraim and Eleanor (Spangler) K.; brother Henry Martyn K.; A.B., Franklin and Marshall Coll., 1860; grad. Theol. Sem. Ref. Ch. in U.S., Lancaster, Pa., 1866; (D.D., Franklin and Marshall, 1884, LL.D., 1910; LL.D., Heidelberg U., Ohio, 1911); m. Mary M. Clark, Nov. 11, 1869. Ordained Ref. Ch. ministry, 1866; pastor Huntingdon, Pa., 1866-88, Hagerstown, Md., Jan. 1868—. Asso. editor Reformed Church Messenger, 1884—. Pres. Gen. Synod, Ref. Ch.; mem. bd. visitors Theol. Sem. Ref. Ch. Mem. bd. regents Mercersburg Acad.; pres. Washington Co. (Md.) Free Library. Republican. Died May 16, 1919.

KIERAN, James Michael, coll. pres.; b. N.Y. City, Aug. 23, 1863; s. Michael and Catherine (Lynch) K.; A.B., Coll. City New York, 1882; A.M., St. Francis Xavier Coll., New York, 1887; grad. study, Columbia, New York U.; LL.D., Fordham, 1905, Holy Cross, 1929; m. Kate Donohue, July 16, 1890; children—Helen Margaret (Mrs. Paul Reilly), John Francis, Catherine (Mrs. Joseph Vincent Hogue, Marie (Mrs. James King Duffy), Leo Augustine, James Michael, Laurence Donohue. Teacher and prin. day and evening schs., N.Y. City, 1883-1904; prof. philosophy and edn., organizer of dept., Hunter Coll., N.Y. City, 1904-27, dean of coll., 1927-28, acting pres., 1928-29, pres., 1929-33 (emeritus). Trustee Hunter Coll., Acad. of Pub. Edn., N.Y. City. Democrat. Catholic. Home: New York, N.Y. Died Apr. 1936.

KIERNAN, James George, neurologist; b. New York, June 18, 1852; s. Francis and Mary (Aiken) K.; student Coll. City of New York, 1868-71; M.D., Univ. Med. Coll. (New York U.), 1874; m. Jane Ann Trumper, Feb. 10, 1881 (died 1903); m. 2d, Grace Cole, Dec. 11, 1917. Assistant physician Ward's Island (now New York State Insane) Hosp., 1874-78, and as officer N.Y. Neurol. Soc. was active in reforms brought about by that soc. in Am. psychiatry and neurology; asst. prof. nervous and mental diseases, Northwestern U., Ill., 1881-82; insp. Nat. Bd. Health, 1882; supt. Cook Co. Insane Hosp., Chicago, 1885-89, and forced investigation of co. charities, 1885, which led to the "boodle" trials and convictions of 1887; prof forensic psychiatry, Kent Coll. of Law, Chicago, 1890-1902; prof. mental and nervous diseases, Milwaukee Med. Coll., 1894-97; prof. neurology, Chicago, Post-Grad. Sch., 1903-04; prof. med. jurisprudence, Dearborn Med. Coll., Chicago, 1904; prof. nervous diseases, Illinois Medical Coll., 1906-08; prof. mental and nervous diseases, Chicago Medical School. Was expert for the defense in Guiteau trial, 1881, Mooney trial, 1884, and in many other criminal and civil cases involving medicolegal issues. Democrat. Home: Chicago, Ill. Died July 1, 1923.

KIERSTED, Andrew Jackson, rear admiral; b. New Point Comfort, Va., Dec. 25, 1832; s. Luke and Catharine Sophia (Myer) K.; ed. schs. of Va. and Me.; m. Isabella Stuart Henderson, Jan. 25, 1866. Apptd. asst. engr. U.S.N., June 26, 1856; promoted 1st asst. engr., Aug. 2, 1859; chief engr., Nov. 12, 1861; retired, Dec. 25, 1904; advanced to rank of rear admiral in recognition of services during Civil War, June 29, 1906. Served on spl. duty during Civil War; mem. Naval Examining Bd., Mar. 18-Aug. 28, 1873, and Apr. 18-Nov. 9, 1878, pres. same, Feb. 4-July 27, 1875; fleet engr. N. Atlantic Squadron, Sept. 19, 1881-Aug. 7, 1882, Pacific Sta., June 19, 1888-Apr. 15, 1889. Home: Philadelphia, Pa. Died 1910.

KIERSTED, Wynkoop, hydraulic engr.; b. Mongaup Valley, N.Y., Feb. 9, 1857; s. Wynkoop and Jane A. (Swan) K.; ed. at home to age of 20; C.E., Rensselaer Poly. Inst., 1880; m. Medora R. Smith; children—Martha (dec.), Jeanette, Wynkoop, Louise.

Chief engr., 1892, in design and construction of new water supply of Galveston, Tex.; chief engr. Kansas City (Mo.) water works, Kansas City (Kan.) water works, and several pvt. water cos. Valued Los Angeles water works, 1898, Dubuque, Ia., water works, 1899, Oakland, Calif., water works, 1900; arbitrator at Eau Claire and Beloit, Wis., 1901, in valuation of water works property. Designed water supply systems for various cities and has been otherwise associated with over 50 water works in different parts of the country; supervising engr. for water works and sewerage of the U.S. Cantonment, Camp Funston, Fort Riley, Kan.; div. engr. U.S. Housing Corp.; mem. engring. bd. of review, sanitary problems of Chicago, Ill.; bd. of advisory engrs., new water works of Kansas City, Mo.; chief engr. Amarillo (Tex.) sewage disposal works and new water supply works; designed and supervised constrn. of new water supply works, Fort Collins, Colo., Abilene, Tex., Providence, Ky.; retired. Home: Liberty, Mo. Died Nov. 7, 1934.

KIESEL, Fred J., merchant. Crossed plains to Salt Lake City, 1863; employed in commercial houses until 1873, when founded The Fred J. Kiesel Co., wholesale mchts., Ogden, Utah, of which became head. Elected mayor of Ogden, 1889; commr. to Chicago Expn., 1893; mem. Utah Constl. Conv., 1895; mem. Utah State Senate, 1898-1900. Chmn. exec. com. Nat. Irrigation Congress, 1903. Pres. Security Nat. Bank. Home: Ogden, Utah. Died Apr. 22, 1919.

KIESS, Edgar Raymond, congressman; b. Warrensville, Pa., Aug. 26, 1875; s. Samuel S. and Annie (Winner) K.; grad. Lycoming Co. (Pa.) Normal Sch., 1892; m. Roemer Clarke, June 4, 1919; children—Anne Winner, Mary Jane. Pres. The Eagles Mere Co. (owners of Forest Inn and Eagles Mere Park); pres. Eagles Mere Land Co., Raymond Hotel Co., Eagles Mere Hotel Co., The Edgar R. Kiess Co. Mem. Pa. Ho. of Rep., 1904-10; mem. 63d to 71st Congresses (1913-31), 16th Pa. Dist. Republican. Trustee Pa. State Coll. Presbyn. Mason. Home: Williamsport, Pa. Died July 20, 1930.

KIEST, Edwin John, newspaper pub.; b. Cook Co., Ill., Sept. 24, 1861; s. John Christian and Ann Barbara (Sharkey) K.; ed. pub. schs., Chicago, Joliet and Elgin, Ill.; m. Elizabeth Patterson Lyon, Oct. 20, 1893 (died 1917). Newsboy, Chicago, 1871-73; learned printer's trade; compositor Chicago Times and other newspapers, 1876-89; with Western Newspaper Union, Omaha, Neb., 1889-96; owner and pub. Dallas (Tex.) Daily Times-Herald, 1896—. Dir. Agrl. and Mech. Coll. of Tex., Scottish Rite Crippled Children Hosp. Democrat. Protestant. Mason. Home: Dallas, Tex. Died Aug. 11, 1941.

KILBOURN, Judson Giles, surgeon; b. Plainfield, N.Y., Jan. 11, 1860; s. Francis Smith and Agnes (Smith) K.; prep. edn., West Winfield and Sauquoit acads.; M.D., Univ. Med. Coll., New York U., 1884; m. Nella E. Armstrong, Oct. 30, 1889. Practiced, Utica, N.Y., 1884—; surgeon St. Luke's Hosp., 1906—; surgeon N.Y.C.&H.R. R.R. and D.L.&W. Ry.; cons. surgeon St. Elizabeth's Hosp., Saranac Lake Hosp. Republican. Protestant. Mason. Home: Utica, N.Y. Died Feb. 1915.

KILBOURNE, Charles Evans, army officer; b. Columbus, O., Jan. 17, 1844; s. Lincoln and Jane (Evans) K.; grad. West Point, 1866; under instruction Arty. Sch., Ft. Monroe, Va., 1869-70 (honor grad., 1870); m. Ada J. Coolidge, Apr. 13, 1868. Apptd. 2d lt. 2d arty., June 18, 1866; 1st lt., Dec. 3, 1868; capt. signal corps, Dec. 20, 1896; maj. in pay dept., Nov. 6, 1893. Served in signal corps, 1871-84 and 1890-93; prof. mil. science and tactics, Ohio State Univ., 1887-90. In Philippines, 1898-99; auditor public accounts, P.I., Oct. 1898; treas. Philippine Archipelago and Island of Guam, Oct. 11, 1898, to Nov. 22, 1899. Died 1903.

KILBOURNE, James, mfr.; b. Columbus, O., Oct. 9, 1842; s. Lincoln K., g.s. Col. James K., Ohio pioneer; A.B., Kenyon Coll., 1862, A.M., 1864 (LL.D., 1910); LL.B., Harvard, 1868; enlisted as pvt. 84th Ohio Vols. in Civil War; 2d lt., 1st lt. and capt. 95th Ohio Vols. to end of war; on staffs Gen. J. M. Tuttle, comdg. 3d Div., 15th Army Corps, and Gen. John McArthur, comdg. 1st Div., 16th Army Corps, Army of the Tenn.; bvtd. maj., lt. col. and col. vols., "for gallant and meritorious services during the war"; m. Anna B., d. Gen. George B. Wright, Oct. 3, 1869. Admitted to bar and practiced at Columbus; founder and pres. the Kilbourne & Jacobs Mfg. Co.; dir. Columbus, Hocking Valley & Toledo Ry. Co., Columbus, Cincinnati & Midland R.R. Co., Hayden-Clinton Nat. Bank, First Nat. Bank. Dem. nominee for gov. of Ohio, 1901. Pres. Ohio Centennial Commn., 1898; pres. trustees Columbus Pub. Library, 10 yrs.; organized Columbus Children's Hosp., and pres. 5 yrs.; mem. bd. mgrs. Associated Charities; mem. Columbus Bd. Trade (dir. 1887-91, pres., 1891). Home: Columbus, O. Deceased.

KILBURN, Charles Lawrence, soldier; b. Lawrenceville, Tioga Co., Pa., Aug. 9, 1819; grad. U.S. Mil. Acad., 1842; apptd. lt. artillery, served through Mexican war, including battles of Monterey and Buena

Vista; promoted capt. and commissary of subsistence; maj., May 11, 1861; lt. col. and asst. commissary-gen., Feb. 9, 1863; col., June 29, 1864; bvt. brig. gen. at close of war; after war chief commissary Dept. of Atlantic and later of Dept. of Pacific, until retired, May 20, 1882. Home: Germantown, Pa. Died 1899.

KILBY, Quincy, writer; b. Eastport, Me., Feb. 9, 1854; s. William Henry and Lydia Frances (Sherman) K.; grad. Roxbury High Sch., Boston, 1870; studied architecture, Mass. Inst. Tech., 1873-74; m. Mrs. Fanny A. Spink, Feb. 8, 1885; children—Mrs. Barbara Phillips (dec.) Barbara Phillips (grandchild, adopted). Entered theatrical business, 1876, becoming associated with the Boston Theatre traveling cos., 1879; treas. Boston Theatre, 1886-1901; afterward business mgr. Bijou Theatre, Boston, Hanlon's "Superba," and Bertha Kalich. Co-author (with Eugene Tompkins); History of the Boston Theatre, 1854-1901, 08. Author of "Superba," "Fantasma," and vaudeville sketches. Home: Brookline, Mass. Died May 3, 1931.

KILDAHL, John Nathan, college pres.; b. Beitstaden, Norway, Jan. 4, 1857; s. Johan and Nicolina (Buvarp) K.; A.B., Luther Coll., Decorah, Ia., 1879; grad. in divinity, Lutheran Sem., Madison, Wis., 1882; m. Bertha Soine, July 11, 1882. Ordained Luth. ministry, 1882; pastor Wang and Urland Luth. chs., Goodhue Co., Minn., 1882-89; Bethlehem Luth. Ch., Chicago, 1889-99; pres. St. Olaf Coll., Northfield, Minn., 1889-1914; prof. systematic theology, Luther Theological Sem., St. Paul, Minn., Sept. 1, 1914—. Died Sept. 25, 1920.

KILDARE, Owen Frawley, journalist, author; b. New York, June 11, 1864; s. Owen Frawley and Regine (Fernault) K.; ed. in evening classes of pub. schs., Cooper Union lectures, pvt. instrn., Y.M.C.A. courses after 30. In 1871 was a newsboy of the gang of which Timothy D. Sullivan, congressman, of New York, was leader; was pugilist, professional athlete, soldier of fortune, filibuster, manager of sporting and theatrical ventures, 1880-94; dock laborer, freight handler and truck driver from 1884; became practical reformer of the slum district, 1900; contbr. for Herald, Press, Telegraph, World, etc., 1901; asso. editor Pearson's Mag. In Brazilian Revolution shipped from Key West as capt. of marines in Republican Brazilian Navy; served as sergt. Légion des Étrangers, Algiers, in 1901 gen. of Army of Liberation, Venezuela, in unsuccessful revolution against President Castro; sentenced to be shot. Now pres. Kildare Publishing Co. Mem. Reformed Ch. Author: My Mamie Rose (autobiography), 1903 (London edit. under name of Up from the Slums). Plays: The Tipster; An Intermezzo; A Raid on Policy; The Czar of the Precinct; dramatization of My Mamie Rose. Home: New York, N.Y. Died 1911.

KILEY, Michael H., judge; b. Horicon, Warren Co., Aug. 28, 1861; s. William and Mary (Cronin) K.; grad. Cazenovia (N.Y.) Sem., 1883; studied law with D. W. Cameron, Cazenovia; m. Chloe Celia Sterling, Nov. 27, 1887. Admitted to N.Y. bar, 1886, and practiced at Cazenovia; dist. atty. Madison Co., N.Y., 1896-1905; county judge and surrogate, same co., 1905-12; justice Supreme Ct. of N.Y. 6th Dist., term 1912-26; apptd. to appellate div. 3d Judicial Dept., term 1920-25. Dir. Cazenovia Nat. Bank. Republican. Catholic. Home: Cazenovia, N.Y. Died May 19, 1923.

KILGO, John Carlisle, bishop; b. Laurens, S.C., July 22, 1861; s. James T. and Catherine (Mason) K.; ed. various schs.; A.M., Wofford Coll., 1892; (D.D., Wofford, and Randolph-Macon colls., 1895; LL.D., Tulane, 1910); m. Fannie Turner, Dec. 20, 1882. Ordained M.E. Ch., S. ministry, 1882; agent, Wofford Coll., Spartanburg, S.C. 1889-94, prof. philosophy, 1890-94; pres. Trinity Coll., Durham, N.C., 1894-1910; then pres. emeritus until 1917 (resigned); elected bishop M.E. Ch., S., May 1910. Del. Gen. Conf. 5 times; del. Ecumenical Meth. Conf. London, 1901; fraternal del. from M.E. Ch., S. to M.E. Ch., 1904; del. to Meth. Ecumenical Conf., Toronto, Can., 1911. Home: Charlotte, N.C. Died Aug. 11, 1922.

KILIANI, Otto George Theobald, surgeon; b. Munich, Bavaria, Sept. 5, 1863; s. Hermann (Supreme Ct. judge) and Caroline (Faulstich) K.; grad. gymnasium, Augsburg, 1881; med. edn., U. of Munich, 1886, Halle, 1888; M.D., U. of Leipzig, 1888; m. Lilian Bayard Taylor, Aug. 12, 1887. Surgeon 3d Royal Bavarian Arty. Regt., Munich, 1890; came to U.S., 1891, and began practice at New York; surgeon to consulate-gen. of German Empire, at New York, 1900—; surgeon German Hosp.; prof. clin. surgery, Columbia. Knight, Order of the Crown (Prussian); knight, Order of St. Michael (Bavarian). Catholic. Home: New York, N.Y. Died June 1, 1928.

KILLEBREW, Joseph Buckner; b. Montgomery Co., Tenn., May 29, 1831; s. Bryan Whitfield and Elizabeth Smith (Ligon) K.; grad. Univ. of N.C. (A.M., Ph.D.); spl. law and scientific studies; m. Mary Catherine Wimberly, Dec. 3, 1857. Commr. agr. and mines, Tenn., 1871-81; agt. Peabody Fund, Tenn., 1871-73; acting supt. public instruction, 1871-73; editor "Rural Sun"; spl. expert for 10th Census,

1880, on tobacco for U.S.; one of editors of Standard Dictionary; pres. Industrial League and promoter of several large industrial establishments. Author: Tobacco Leaf, 1898. Special agent Bur. of Road Inquiries, Dept. of Agriculture. Home: Nashville, Tenn. Died 1906.

KILLIKELLY, Sarah Hutchins, author; b. Vincennes, Ind., Jan. 1, 1840; d. B. B. K. (D.D., P.E. clergyman) and Mary (Meech) K.; grad. Eden Hall Sem., Pa.; grad. as pianist and organist under Prof. Karl Merz; unmarried. Foundation Fellow Soc. of Science, Letters and Art, London; received from that soc. gold crown prize for papers on the Victorian era, 1897. Author: "Curious Questions" in History, Literature, Art (3 vols.), 1900; The History of Pittsburgh, 1907. Home: Pittsburgh, Pa. Died May 14, 1912.

KILLITS, John Milton, judge; b. Lithopolis, O., Oct. 7, 1858; s. Andrew W. and Clarissa (Crumley) K.; A.B., Williams Coll., 1880, A.M., 1887, LL.D., 1914; LL.B., Columbian (now George Washington) U., 1885, LL.M., 1886; m. Alice N. Steuart, June 21, 1887. Editor and pub. Red Oak (Ia.) Express, 1881-83; editor publs. of Signal Bureau and sec. to chief signal officer, 1884-87; admitted to bar, 1887; practiced at Bryan, O., 1888-1904; pros. atty. Williams Co., O., 1893-99; judge Ct. Common Pleas, 3d Ohio Dist., 1905-10; U.S. dist. judge, Northern Dist. Ohio, June 24, 1910—. Republican. Mem. Charter Commrs., City of Toledo, 1914, 28. Mason. Home: Toledo, O. Died Sept. 13, 1938.

KILMER, Aline (Murray), author; b. Norfolk, Va., Aug. 1, 1888; d. Kenton C. and Ada (Foster) Murray; ed. Rutgers Prep. School, New Brunswick, N.J., and Vail-Deane School, Elizabeth, N.J.; m. Joyce Kilmer, poet, June 9, 1908 (died 1918). Vice-pres. Catholic Poetry Society of America. Author: (poems) Candles That Burn, 1919; Vigils, 1921; Hunting a Hair Shirt and Other Essays, 1923; The Poor King's Daughter, 1925; Emmy, Nicky and Greg, 1927; A Buttonwood Summer, 1929; Selected Poems, 1929. Lecturer on poetry and kindred subjects, 1919-26. Home: Stillwater, N.J. Died Oct. 1, 1941.

KILMER, Frederick Barnett, chemist; b. Chapinville, Conn., Dec. 11, 1851; s. Charles and Mary Ann (Langdon) K.; ed. Wyoming Sem., Kingston, Pa.; grad. New York Coll. Pharmacy, with spl. courses in chemistry, etc., at New York Coll., Columbia, and Rutgers; also spl. course under Hoffman; Pharm.M., Phila. Coll. Pharmacy and Science, 1920; m. Annie E. Kilbourn, Dec. 25, 1871 (dec.); 4 children (all dec.). Dir. scientific dept., Johnson & Johnson, chemists, New Brunswick, 1889—. Pres. Bd. Health, 1901-14; dean Nurses' Training Sch. of St. Peter's Hosp., New Brunswick. Warden Christ Episcopal Ch. Author: First Aid Manual, 1925. Editor Red Cross Notes, Messenger. Home: Brunswick, N.J. Died Dec. 28, 1934.

KILMER, Joyce, author; b. New Brunswick, N.J., Dec. 6, 1886; s. Frederick Barnett and Annie Ellene (Kilburn) K.; Rutgers Coll., 1904-06; A.B., Columbia, 1908; m. Aline Murray, June 9, 1908. Instr. Latin, Morristown (N.J.) High Sch., 1908-09; editorial asst., Standard Dictionary, 1909-12; lit. editor The Churchman, 1912-13; member staff New York Times Sunday Mag. and New York Times Review of Books, 1913—. Democrat. Catholic. Author: Summer of Love, 1911; Trees and Other Poems, 1915; Main Street and Other Poems, 1917; Literature in the Making, 1917. Editor: Verses, by Hilaire Belloc, 1916; Dreams and Images, an Anthology of Catholic Poets, 1917. Pvt. 165th Inf. N.A. (69th N.Y.), 1917—. Home: Larchmont, N.Y. Died Aug. 1, 1918.

KILNER, Walter Glenn, army officer; b. Shelby, N.Y., July 8, 1888; s. Charles Windsor and Mary Elizabeth K.; B.S., U.S. Mil. Acad., 1912; m. 2d, I. M. Givenwilson, Oct. 10, 1924. Commd. 2d lt. Inf., June 12, 1912; transferred to Aviation sect. Signal Corps, 1915, and advanced through the grades to brig. gen., Air Corps, 1938; served with 1st Aero Squadron on Punitive Expdn. into Mexico, 1916; comdr. Aviation School, Mineola, L.I., N.Y., Mar.-Oct. 1917; with A.E.F. in France, Oct. 1917-Jan. 1919, as organizer and comdr. U.S. Aviation Center at Issoudun, and in charge of training of flying personnel for the front; exec. officer Army Air Service, 1924-25. Mem. Nat. Advisory Com. for Aeronautics. Decorated D.S.M., 1919; Companion Order of St. Michael and St. George (British); Officer Legion of Honor (French). Author: Cantonment Manual, 1917. Died Aug. 30, 1940.

KILPATRICK, James Hines, clergyman; b. Burke Co., Ga., Oct. 18, 1833; s. James Hall Tanner and Harriet Eliza (Jones) K.; grad. Mercer Univ. (then at Penfield, Ga.), 1853, D.D., 1880; m. Cornelia Hall, May 9, 1856; 2d, Edna P. Heard, Dec. 20, 1870. Ordained to ministry of regular Bapt. ch., Dec. 30, 1854, and from then pastor White Plains (Ga.) Bapt. Ch. Trustee Mercer Univ. (now at Macon, Ga.), Southern Bapt. Theol. Sem., Louisville, Ky.; pres. Bapt. Conv. of Ga.; moderator Ga. Bapt. Assn. Died 1908.

KILPATRICK, Thomas, dry goods mcht.; b. Scotland, Aug. 20, 1841; ed. there; came to U.S. and engaged in mercantile business; m. Harriet N. Burnham, Apr. 21, 1873. Head of Thomas Kilpatrick & Co., dry goods, Omaha; dir. Society for Savings, Cleveland, O. Park commr., Omaha, Neb., 5 yrs.; dir. Transmississippi Expn. at Omaha, 1898. Home: Omaha, Neb. Died Jan. 14, 1916.

KIMBALL, Alfred Redington; b. Orange, N.J., Sept. 29, 1848; s. Horace (M.D.) and Mary Davenport (Fisher) K.; Coll. City of New York; m. Caroline F. Hildreth, Feb. 4, 1874. With L. T. Hoyt, mem. N.Y. Stock Exchange, 1867-71; then with A.B. Baylis & Co., now Baylis & Co., mem. firm, 1884-1919. Mem. bd. edn., W. Orange, N.J., 1894-1904; trustee N.Y. Law Sch., Mt. Holyoke Coll., Skidmore Coll., Saratoga Springs, N.Y.; treas. N.Y. Skin and Cancer Hosp. Presbyterian. Treas. Church of the Covenant, New York; treas. Federal Council Chs. of Christ in America, 1908-24. Home: West Orange, N.J. Died Dec. 8, 1929.

KIMBALL, Alfred Sanders, lawyer; b. Waterford, Me., Dec. 20, 1842; s. Sanders and Jemima (Burnell) K.; grad. Bridgton Academy, Me., 1862; m. Florence A. Houghton, Apr. 29, 1866. Admitted to Me. bar, 1865; began practice at Waterford; removed to Norway, Me., 1882; mem. Kimball & Son, 1888—; pres. Norway Savings Bank. Mem. Me. Ho. of Rep., 1874-78; state's atty., 1880-82; appraiser U.S. customs, Portland, Me., 1894-98; mem. Governor's Council, 1911, 1912. Democrat. Universalist. Mason, Odd Fellow. Home: Norway, Me. Died Apr. 12, 1915.

KIMBALL, Alonzo, artist; b. Green Bay, Wis., Aug. 14, 1874; s. Alonzo Weston and Myra (Mahan) K.; studied under Jules Lefebvre, Gustave Courtois, and James McNeill Whistler in Paris, 1894-1900; m. Madeline Williams, Apr. 26, 1902. Exhibited portrait, Paris Salon, 1899; book and mag. illustrator and portrait painter. Home: New York, N.Y. Died Aug. 27, 1923.

KIMBALL, Amos Samuel, army officer; b. Lawrence, N.Y., July 14, 1840; s. James and Sophia (Taft) K.; grad. State Normal Sch., Albany, N.Y., 1859; m. Hattie F. Crary, 1861. Commissioned Nov. 1861, 1st lt. 98th N.Y. vol. inf.; served in Army of Potomac to Nov. 1862, including McClellan's peninsular campaign; afterward in Carolinas with Hunter and Heckman; acting q.-m. Roanoke Island, N.C.; capt. and a. q. m. vols. Apr. 7, 1864, in charge water transportation Ft. Monroe; later q. m. at Newbern, N.C., during yellow fever epidemic, where he became ill with the disease; ordered to New York, Apr., 1865; bvtd. capt., maj., lt. col. and col. by State and apptd. maj. vols. by bvt. and asst. q. m. U.S.A. Served under Sheridan in Indian campaign, 1868-69; field q. m. with Gen. Miles in Ariz. campaign against Geronimo, etc.; assigned to charge of gen. depot, New York, 1897, and during Spanish war, 1898, distributed over $8,000,000 in 4 months; promoted col. Nov. 13, 1898, and brig. gen. U.S.A., Oct. 1902; retired. Died 1909.

KIMBALL, Arthur Lalanne, physicist; b. Succasunna Plains, N.J., Oct. 16, 1856; s. Horace and Mary D. (Fisher) K.; A.B., Princeton, 1881, fellow in science, 1881-82; Ph.D., Johns Hopkins, 1884; m. Lucilla P. Scribner, 1884; m. 2d, Julia S. Scribner, June, 1913. Asso. in physics, 1884-88, asso. prof., 1888-91, Johns Hopkins; prof. physics, Amherst, 1891—. Author: The Physical Properties of Gases, 1890; College Physics, 1911. Home: Amherst, Mass. Died Oct. 22, 1922.

KIMBALL, Arthur Reed, editor; b. New York, Feb. 1, 1855; s. J. Merrill and Elizabeth (Chapin) K.; A.B., Yale, 1877; studied law at Yale, and at Chicago; admitted to Ill. bar, 1879; m. Mary E. Chase, May 15, 1895. City editor Iowa State Register, Des Moines, 9 mos., 1880; asso. editor (and later business mgr.) Waterbury American, 1881-1922, sold interest and retired, 1922; officer and dir. in a number of brass corps. and 3 banks. Has lectured on journalism, at Yale. Active in work of stamping out tuberculosis; mem. Conn. Tuberculosis Commission, and chmn. exec. com. Gaylord Farm Sanatorium; pres. State Assn. Conn. Charity Orgns.; pres. trustees Long Lane Farm (state industrial sch. for girls), Middletown. Died Jan. 27, 1933.

KIMBALL, Charles Dean, governor; b. Providence, R.I., Sept. 13, 1859; s. Emery S. and Mary C. (Briggs) K.; grad. Providence High Sch.; hon. A.M., R.I. State College, 1926; m. Gertrude C. Greenalgh, Nov. 24, 1885 (died 1929); 1 dau., Marion Dean (Mrs. Walter S. Ball). Engaged in mercantile business, Providence. Mem. R.I. Ho. of Rep., 1894-99; lt.-gov. of R.I., 1900, 01; governor, 1902-03; Republican presdl. elector, 1916. Pres. South Kingston Town Council; federal commr. of jurors. Chmn. Draft Bd. Div. No. 1, R.I., June 17, 1917-Mar. 31, 1918. Deputy Fair Price Commr. R.I., 1919; pres. bd. mgrs. R.I. Coll., 1903-13. Col. 1st Light Inf. Vet. Assn.; mem. Providence Chamber of Commerce. Republican. Mason. Home: Wakefield, R.I. Died Dec. 8, 1930.

KIMBALL, Clarence Oliver, clergyman; b. Golconda, Ill., Aug. 23, 1868; s. George Washington and Sarah (Thompson) K.; A.B., Austin Coll., Ill., 1895; A.M., McKendree Coll., Ill., 1896, Ph.D., 1897; D.D., Willamette U., 1908; m. Josephine Dear, Oct. 11, 1890; children—Mary Jo, Dorothy, Clarence O.; m. 2d, May Agee Miller, Nov. 28, 1922; children—Elizabeth A. and Jessica May (stepdaughters), Patricia May. Admitted to Ill. bar, 1889; ordained M.E. ministry, 1894; pastor in Ill. until 1902, La Junta, Colo., 1902-04, Trinidad, 1904-06, Spokane, Wash., 1906-10, Walla Walla, 1910-12, Manhattan, Kan., 1912-14, St. Joseph, Mo., 1914-16, Glendora, Calif., 1916-20, Porterville, Calif., 1920-22, Highland Park, Los Angeles, 1922-25, First Ch., San Pedro, Calif., 1925, First Ch., Burbank, Calif., 1926-28, Vermont Square Ch., Los Angeles, 1928-30, First Ch., Ontario, Calif., 1930-33, First Ch., Escondido, 1933—. Republican. Mason. Home: Escondido, Calif. Died Oct. 6, 1934.

KIMBALL, Curtis Nathaniel, mfr. musical merchandise; b. Wayne Tp., Mitchell Co., Ia., Jan. 4, 1862; s. David W. and Sarah (Moore) K.; ed. pvt. schs. and business coll.; m. Fannie C. B. Hadley, Nov. 3, 1894; children—William Wallace, David W., Mary H. (Mrs. Harold F. Van Steenderen), Elizabeth M. With W. W. Kimball Co., mfrs. pianos and pipe organs, 1879—, treas., 1893-98, v.p., 1898-1905, pres., 1905—. Home: Highland Park, Ill. Died July 30, 1936.

KIMBALL, David Pulsifer, lawyer; b. Boston, Sept. 30, 1833; s. David and Augusta (Blanchard) K.; A.B., Harvard, 1856; admitted to bar, 1858; m. Clara M. Bertram, Sept. 30, 1858. Practiced law at Boston many yrs. from 1858; retired; pres. Nashua & Lowell Ry. Co.; dir. C.&N.W. Ry., C.,St.P.,M.& O. Ry. Co. Republican. Unitarian. Home: Boston, Mass. Died Aug. 7, 1923.

KIMBALL, Edward Partridge, organist, teacher; b. Salt Lake City, Utah, June 12, 1882; s. Albert Heber and Harriet (Partridge) K.; studied piano with Alberto Jonas, Berlin, and New York, organ with Walter Fischer, Berlin, and R. Huntington Woodman, New York, theory with Wilhelm Klatte, Berlin; m. Hazel Young Beatie, Aug. 1, 1905; children—Marion Young, Edward Beatie, Willard Young. Dir. Music Brigham Young U., 1898-99, Latter Day Saints U., 1908-09; asst. organist Tabernacle, 1905-25, sr. organist, 1925—; prof. organ and lecturer on music history, McCune Sch. of Music, Salt Lake City. Formerly sergeant Utah N.G.; chmn. Com. on Music of War Camp Community Service; state dir. Liberty Choruses and Community Singing for Utah. Mormon (vice chmn. Gen. Music Com. and chmn. Com. on Sunday School Music, Latter Day Saints Church). Home: Salt Lake City, Utah. Died Mar. 15, 1937.

KIMBALL, George Albert, civil engr.; b. Littleton, Mass., May 14, 1850; s. William and Mary (Lawrence) K.; ed. Appleton Acad., New Ipswich, N.H.; studied engring. City engr. Somerville, 1876-86; mem. Somerville bd. of health, 1879-86; mem. Mystic water bd.; mem. Met. Sewerage Commn., 1896-1901; chief engr. elevated and subway construction, Boston Elevated Ry. Co. Home: Arlington, Mass. Died Dec. 3, 1912.

KIMBALL, G(eorge) Cook, steel mfr.; b. Newtonville, Mass., Oct. 13, 1879; s. Edwin, Nelson and Emma (Cook) K.; B.S., Harvard, 1900; m. Elizabeth W. Leeds, Nov. 19, 1902; children—Marjorie Stuart, Richard, Edwin Nelson. Engr. Am. Tin Plate Co., Pittsburgh, Pa., 1901-05; chief engr. Am. Sheet & Tin Plate Co., 1905-31, v.p., 1931-32; v.p. in charge operation and dir. Ill. Steel Co., 1932-35, pres., 1935—; exec. v.p. and dir. Carnegie-Ill. Steel Corp., 1935-39; exec. vice-pres. and dir. U.S. Steel Corporation of Delaware. Dir. Chicago Assn. of Commerce. Vice chairman Pittsburgh Chapter Am. Red Cross, World War. Pres. Associated Harvard Clubs, 1919; v.p. Harvard Alumni Assn., 1920. Republican. Episcopalian. Home: Chicago, Ill. Died Jan. 13, 1942.

KIMBALL, George Henry, consulting engr.; b. Newburyport, Mass., Dec. 8, 1849; s. Lafayette and Mary (Grover) K.; student Mass. Inst. Tech.; m. Emma A. Carpenter, Feb. 25, 1874. Supt. bridges and bldgs. Pittsburgh, Cincinnati & St. Louis Ry., 1876-79; supt. Columbus & Sunday Creek Valley Rd., 1879-80; engr. maintenance of way, Little Miami Rd., 1880-81; chief engr. southern extension, Toledo, Cincinnati & St. Louis Ry., 1881-82; supt. N.Y.,C.& St.L. Rd., 1882-89; chief engr. L.S.&M.S. Ry., 1889-91; in gen. practice as consulting engr., 1891-98; supt. and chief engr., Columbus, Sandusky & Hocking Rd., 1898-99; chief engr. Pere Marquette R.R., 1899-1902, Central Electric Constrn. Co., New York, 1902-03; engaged in designing a system of freight terminals for trunk lines at Buffalo, N.Y., 1903-04; chief engr. C.&A. R.R., 1904-06; in gen. practice, 1906—. City commr., Pontiac, Mich., 1920-23, mayor, 1923-24. Mason. Home: Pontiac, Mich. Deceased.

KIMBALL, George Selwyn, author; b. Hampden, Me., June 20, 1846; s. Robert S. and Mary A. (Cram) K.; ed. Hampden (Me.) Acad.; m. Flora Humphrey, June 1, 1869. Served in Co. F, 26th and Co. I, 14th Me. Vol. Inf. in Civil War. Mem. G.A.R. Republican. Unitarian. Author: Piney Home, 1904; Jay Gould Harmon, 1905; The Lackawannas on Moosehead, 1907. Home: Bangor, Me. Died 1909.

KIMBALL, Gustavus Sylvester, educator; b. Yale, Mich., Nov. 27, 1860; s. Sylvester and Sara Ann (Beardsley) K.; ed. Valparaiso (Ind.) U., 1879; Spencerian Business Coll., Cleveland, O., 1881-82; Ohio Wesleyan U., 1882-88; m. Marie Esther Guy, Dec. 25, 1879 (died 1910); children—Guy W., LeRoy E., Ralph T., Keith K.; m. 2d, Laura E. Adams, July 15, 1912 (died 1921); m. 3d, Mrs. Pearlina D. Lamb, Jan. 11, 1922. Was teacher in pub. schs., Mich., 1876-82; prin. business dept. Ohio Wesleyan U., 1882-88; prin. Detroit Business U., 1891-97; prin., business dept. Albion (Mich.) Coll., 1897-1906; prin. of banking dept., Rider Coll., Trenton, N.J., 1906-10; prin. Yale Business Coll., New Haven, Conn., 1910-12; pres. Kimball Sch., New York, 1912—; pres. Isaac Pitman Short Hand Writers' Assn. of America, 1913-14, dean, 1914-15. Mason. Author: Kimball's Business Speller, 1905; Kimball's Business English, 1908; Kimball's New Business English, 1928. Home: New York, N.Y. Died Apr. 22, 1937.

KIMBALL, Harriet McEwen, poet; b. Portsmouth, N.H., Nov. 1834; ed. there; unmarried. Specially known as a religious poet, although she has also written much secular verse; chief founder of the Portsmouth Cottage Hosp. Author: Hymns; Swallow Flights; Blessed Company of All Faithful People; Poems (complete edit., 1889; new revised edition, 1911). Home: Portsmouth, N.H. Died Sept. 3, 1917.

KIMBALL, Henry Dox, college dean; b. Raymertown, N.Y., Aug. 11, 1841; s. Rev. Isaac and Jeanie (McBain) K.; ed. Collegiate Inst., Charlottesville, N.Y., Methodist Gen. Bibl. Inst., Concord, N.H. (now Sch. of Theology, Boston U.); (D.D., Allegheny Coll., 1890; LL.D., Neb. Wesleyan U., 1907, Dalles Coll., Ore., 1907); m. Charlotte A. Baker, 1865; m. 2d, Mrs. Luella D. Eastman, June 1, 1903. Ordained M.E. ministry, 1864; pastor Schaghticoke, 1864-65, State St. Ch., Troy, 1874-77, Grace Ch., Albany, 1879-82, County St. Ch., New Bedford, Mass., 1882-85, St. Paul's Ch., Fall River, 1885-87, Chicago, 1887-97, Spokane, Wash., 1902-06; founder, 1906, and prof. systematic theology, and dean, Kimball Coll. of Theology (Willamette U.). Mem. Univ. Senate of M.E. Ch., 1908-12. Republican. Home: Salem, Ore. Died May 31, 1915.

KIMBALL, James Putnam, geologist; b. Salem, Mass., Apr. 26, 1836; s. James and Maria Grace (Putnam) K.; ed. Lawrence Scientific Sch. (Harvard), univs. of Berlin and Göttingen and Freiberg Sch. of Mining; m. Mary Elizabeth Farley, July 20, 1874 (now deceased). Geologist Wis. and Ill. State geol. surveys; prof. chemistry and economic geology, N.Y. Agrl. Coll., Ovid, 1861-62; capt. and asst. adj. gen. vols., 1862-63; on gen. staffs of McClellan, Burnside, Hooker and Meade; provost marshal, general's div.; bvtd. maj., Mar. 23, 1865, "for gallant and meritorious services." Resumed mining practice, New York, 1864-74; hon. prof. geology, Lehigh U., 1874-85; apptd. dir. of the Mint, 1885-88. Home: Cody, Wyo. Died Oct. 23, 1913.

KIMBALL, John C., clergyman; b. Ipswich, Mass., May 23, 1832; s. John and Rebecca (Gould) K.; A.B., Amherst, 1854; prof. langs., Marshall U., Tex., 1854-55; grad. Harvard Div. Sch., 1859; m. Emily O. Richardson, Feb. 1, 1860 (died 1902). Ordained Unitarian ministry, 1860; pastor Beverly, Mass., 1860-62; chaplain 8th Mass. Vols., 1862-63; pastor Beverly, 1863-70; agt. Am. Unitarian Assn. on Pacific Coast, 1871-73; pastor Newport, R.I., 1873-78, Hartford, Conn., 1878-88; lecturer and preacher, 1888-1900; pastor Sharon, Mass., 1899-1904, Greenfield, Mass., 1905—. Author: The Ethics of Evolution, 1902; The Humanitarian Side of Religion, 1904; A New Answer to an Old Question, 1908; Romance of Evolution, 1913. Home: Greenfield, Mass. Died 1910.

KIMBALL, John White, soldier; b. Fitchburg, Mass., Feb. 27, 1828; s. Alpheus and Harriet (Stone) K.; ed. Fitchburg Acad.; m. Almira Melissa Lesure, July 15, 1851. Entered army, capt. Co. B, 15th Mass. Vols., June 28, 1861; maj., Aug. 1, 1861, lt. col., Apr. 29, 1862, col., 53d Mass. Vols., Nov. 12, 1862; bvtd. brig. gen. vols., Mar. 13, 1865, "for gallant and distinguished services during the war." Mem. Mass. Legislature, 1864, 65, 1872, 1888, 89, 1890, 91; auditor Commonwealth of Mass., 1892-1900; custodian Bur. of Engraving and Printing, Treasury Dept., Washington, 1877-78; postmaster, Fitchburg, 1879-87. Trustee and auditor Fitchburg Savings Bank many yrs. Republican. Mason. Home: Fitchburg, Mass. Died 1910.

KIMBALL, Kate Fisher, secretary; b. Orange, N.J., Feb. 22, 1860; d. Horace and Mary D. K.; grad. Plainfield (N.J.) High Sch., 1877; unmarried. Exec. sec. Chautauqua Lit. and Scientific Circle, 1878—. Edited "The Round Table," in The Chautauquan, 1899-1909. Author: An English Cathedral Journey, 1913. Home: New York, N.Y. Died Jan. 17, 1917.

KIMBALL, Sumner Increase, gen. supt. U.S. Life Saving Service; b. Lebanon, Me., Sept. 2, 1834; s. Increase Sumner and Miriam White (Bodwell) K.; A.B., Bowdoin, 1855 (hon. Sc.D., 1891); m. Ellen Frothingham Fenno, Oct. 12, 1858. Admitted to bar,

1858; mem. legislature, 1859; clerk and chief clerk 2d auditor's office, U.S. Treasury Dept., 1862-71; chief Revenue Marine Service and Life-Saving Service, 1871-78; gen. supt. U.S. Life-Saving Service and chief officer of the bureau, 1878-1916. By act of Congress approved Jan. 28, 1915, organizing the Coast Guard, by combining the Life-Saving Service and the Revenue Cutter Service, was retired 1916, at the age of 81, on three-quarters pay—a distinction rarely, if ever, before accorded a public official outside the Army and Navy and the judiciary; pres. bd. on life-saving appliances, 1915—. Has been actg. chief clk., actg. comptroller and actg. solicitor of the Treasury; mem. Bd. Civil Service Examiners for the Treasury Dept., 1872. U.S. del. Internat. Marine Conf., 1889. Author: Organization and Methods of the United States Life-Saving Service, 1889; Joshua James—Life-saver, 1909. Home: Washington, D.C. Died June 21, 1923.

KIMBALL, Thomas Rogers, architect; b. Linwood, O., Apr. 19, 1862; s. Thomas Lord and Mary Porter (Rogers) K.; student U. of Neb., 1877-78, Mass. Inst. Tech., 1884-87, Cowles Art Sch., Boston, 1883-86; studied drawing and painting under Ross Turner, Theodore Langerfeldt and Emil Carlson, of Boston, and Henri Harpignies and A. Vignal, Paris, France; m. Annie L. McPhail, Sept. 25, 1889. Began practice at Boston, 1889; mem. Walker, Kimball & Best, Boston and Omaha, 1891, Walker & Kimball, 1891-99; practiced alone, 1899-1903, and as Walker & Kimball for St. Louis Expn., 1903-04, then alone, 1904-27; mem. Kimball, Steele & Sandham, Walker & Kimball, architects C.,B.&Q. Station, Omaha, and architects-in-chief Trans-Miss. and Internat. Expn., 1897-98, also members Archtl. Bd. Louisiana Purchase Expn. and architects of its Electric Bldg.; architect, alone, for Battle Mountain Sanatorium, Hot Springs, S.Dak., for U.S. Treasury Dept.; St. Cecelia's Cathedral, and Hotel Fontenelle, Omaha; professional adviser Neb. Capitol Commn., Kansas City Liberty Memorial and Indiana War Memorial bds. Mem. exec. council Fontenelle Forest Assn.; mem. Commn. of Fine Arts (U.S.), 1909. Pres. Thomas L. Kimball Co., Sheridan Land Co. Mem. Omaha Chamber Commerce, Omaha Civic League (pres.). Fellow Am. Inst. Architects (pres. 1918-20); hon. mem. Ill. State Soc. of Architects. With Henry D. Bates, at Boston, 1888, founded and pub. Technology Architectural Rev.; with Bates and Guild founded and pub. The Brochure series of architectural illustrations, Boston, 1890. Home: Omaha, Neb. Died Sept. 7, 1934.

KIMBALL, William Coggin; b. Boxford, Mass., Feb. 11, 1847; s. Jefferson and Mary (Griffin) K.; ed. common schs. and Putnam Acad., Newburyport, Mass.; m. Blanche Read, June 4, 1873. Began with Palmer & Bachelder, Boston, 1862; removed to New York, 1868; with Wilcox Silver Plate Co. and H. F. Barrows Co. until 1888; entered silk business with Strange & Bro., later the William Strange Co. (now real estate); v.p., sec. The William Strange Co., Paterson, N.J.; dir., treas. Am. Clay Products Co., New York; treas. Hawthorne Apartment Assn., New York. Active in securing passage of bill for Public Library Commn. of N.J., 1899, and apptd. by Gov. Voorhees, chmn. of bd., in which position continues; trustee Carnegie Endowment Fund of A.L.A., 1908—; pres. Passaic Pub. Library. Presbyn. Home: Passaic, N.J. Died Jan. 17, 1914.

KIMBALL, William Wallace, mfr.; b. Oxford Co., Me., 1828; s. David K.; common school edn.; later clerk in Boston until 1857; became dealer in pianos and organs, Chicago, 1857; began as mfr. reed organs, 1881; added pianos, 1887, and pipe organs soon after; now pres. W. W. Kimball Co., which has one of the largest outputs in the world of pianos and organs. Home: Chicago, Ill. Died 1904.

KIMBALL, William Wirt, rear admiral; b. Paris, Me., Jan. 9, 1848; s. Brig. Gen. William King and Frances Freeland (Rawson) K.; grad. U.S. Naval Acad., 1869; m. Esther Smith Spencer, July 18, 1882. Ensign, 1870; promoted through grades to rear admiral, Dec. 17, 1908. Served on N. and S. Atlantic, European, Asiatic, and Pacific stas.; mem. of the first class of officers at the Torpedo Sta., 1870; assisted in capture of Am. steamers in the Orinoco, 1872; torpedo officer of the first two torpedo craft of the navy, 1874; engaged in development of magazine and machine guns in the early 80's; designed, constructed, and operated the first armed cars used by U.S. forces and assisted in occupation of Isthmus of Panama, 1885; reported to Congress progress of work on Panama Canal, 1886; exec. officer Detroit in the affair of Enchadas in Rio harbor, 1894; engaged in development of submarine boats in early 90's (John P. Holland, inventor of the Holland boats, wrote of him, "Submarining owes more to him than to any other living man."); organized first torpedo boat flotilla of U.S.N., and comd. Atlantic Torpedo Boat Flotilla in war with Spain; comd. Cæsar, Glacier, Supply, Vixen, Concord, Wheeling, Abarenda, Alert and New Jersey; on bds. of Construction, Examination and Retirement, 1907-09; selected for command of Nicaraguan expeditionary squadron, Dec. 1, 1909; retired by operation of law, Jan. 9, 1910, but retained in active command afloat until withdrawal of squadron from Nicaraguan waters, Apr. 1910; relieved from active duty, June 1, 1910; recalled to active duty during the World War as pres. bd. for the examination of officers, and officer in charge of hist. sect., Office of Operations, Navy Dept. Sr. officer present at and awarded medal for 2d action at Matanzas bar for Santiago; medal for Spanish-Am. War. Home: Paris, Me. Died Jan. 26, 1930.

KIMBERLY, Lewis Ashfield, rear admiral U.S.N.; b. Troy, N.Y., Apr. 2, 1830; apptd. to navy from Ill., Dec. 8, 1846, acting midshipman; grad. U.S. Naval Acad., passed-midshipman, June 8, 1852; master, Sept. 15, and lt., Sept. 16, 1856; comdr., July 16, 1862; comdr., July 25, 1866; capt., Oct. 3, 1874; commodore, Nov. 27, 1884; rear admiral, Sept. 4, 1887; retired Apr. 2, 1892. Served on frigate Potomac, 1861-62; then exec. officer on the Hartford, Admiral Farragut's flagship, participating in actions of Port Hudson, Grand Gulf, Warrington, Mobile Bay, etc. Was in expdn. to Korea and comd. the force which landed and captured the forts. Was comdr.-in-chief of Pacific station; was in the great hurricane of Mar. 15 and 16, 1889, at Apia, Samoa; was commended by the sec. of the navy for his conduct of affairs there. Home: West Newton, Mass. Died 1902.

KIMBLE, John Haines, executive sec.; b. Nottingham, Pa., Oct. 26, 1860; s. Anson Bennett and Mary Hannah (Kirk) K.; pub. sch. edn., Oxford (Pa.) Sem. and Eastman Business Coll., Poughkeepsie, N.Y.; m. Mary Jane Tome, Jan. 31, 1883; children—Chester Tome, Anna May. Clerk in mercantile house, 1878-82; teller Cecil Nat. Bank, Port Deposit, 1883-1909; sec. Jacob Tome Inst., Port Deposit, Md., 1900-16, treas., 1916-37; pres. Mutual Fire Ins. Co. of Cecil Co. Mem. Md. Ho. of Dels., 1900, special session, 1901. Democrat. Mem. bd. dirs. Md. Penitentiary, 1908-16. Assistant secretary, 1905-11, sec., 1911-13, legislative agt., 1914—, pres., 1918-19, Farmers' Nat. Congress. Methodist. Mason. Home: Port Deposit, Md. Died Aug. 15, 1938.

KIMBROUGH, Bradley Thomas, lawyer; b. in Jefferson Co., Tenn., Nov. 30, 1846; s. Duke W. and Eliza (Cooke) K.; ed. Mulberry Acad., Tenn., Georgetown (Ky.) Coll., Cumberland Univ. (law dept.), Lebanon, Tenn., LL.B. Served in Co. A, 59th Tenn. Vols., C.S.A., Nov. 1863-May 11, 1865; engaged in law practice at Ripley, Miss., 1870; co. atty., Benton Co., Miss., several yrs. in '70s; mem. Miss. legislature, 1872-73; chancellor 2d Miss. dist., 1884-88, and 3d dist., 1889-97; then resumed law practice at Oxford, in firm of Kimbrough & Kimbrough. Pres. Oxford Oil Mill Co., Merchants' and Farmers' Bank of Oxford. Mason. Baptist. Democrat. Home: Oxford, Miss. Deceased.

KIMMEL, Gustav Bernard, clergyman, educator; b. Dayton, O., Apr. 22, 1874; s. Christian and Sara (Ecki) K.; B.A., Northwestern Coll., Naperville, Ill., 1897; B.D., Evang. Theol. Sem., Naperville, 1900, D.D., 1914; M.A., U. of Chicago, 1925; m. Esther C. Breyfogel, May 19, 1904; children—Charles Breyfogel, William Breyfogel, Dorothy. Formerly membership and social sec. Y.M.C.A., Dayton, O.; ordained ministry Evang. Ch., 1900; pastor Indianapolis, Ind., 1900-08, Dayton, O., 1908-13; prof. practical theology, Evang. Theol. Sem., Sept. 1913—, and pres., 1919—. Republican. Home: Naperville, Ill. Died July 14, 1939.

KINCAID, Charles Euston, journalist; b. Danville, Ky., May 18, 1855; s. Capt. William Garnett (served Mexican war) and Elizabeth Frances (Banford) K.; grad. Centre Coll. (now Central Univ.), 1878. Edited Anderson News; was elected judge with jurisdiction for city of Lawrenceburg, Ky., and Anderson Co.; legislative corr. Louisville Courier-Journal at Frankfort, Ky.; mem. 1st State R.R. Commn. of Ky.; was sec. State Central Dem. Com., Ky.; pvt. sec. to Gov. Proctor Knott and Senator John Stuart Williams of Ky.; commr. of Ky. to bring remains of Joel T. Hart, the sculptor, from Florence, Italy, to Frankfort, Ky., for burial; consular agt. of U.S. in St. Helen's dist., Lancashire, Eng., 1885-89; in Internal Revenue dept., 1893-95. In journalism has been city and news editor, Louisville Courier-Journal; Washington corr. New York and San Francisco papers; from 1895 on regular staff, Cincinnati Enquirer. Unmarried. Home: Cincinnati, O. Died 1906.

KINCAID, William A., lawyer; b. Pilot Grove, Tex., Aug. 30, 1859; ed. pub. schs.; m. Elizabeth Padgett, Sept. 20, 1879. Admitted to Tex. bar, 1879; mem. Tex. Ho. of Rep., 1889; apptd., Apr. 1901, by Pres. McKinley as one of judges of Court of First Instance, Manila, P.I.; now in practice at Manila; mem. Kincaid, Perkins & Kincaid. Chmn. 1st Insular Dem. Conv., 1904. Author: Codigo Civil Anotado, 2 vol. annotated edit. in Spanish of the Philippine Civil Code. Died Jan. 5, 1922.

KINDEL, George John, congressman; b. Cincinnati, Mar. 2, 1855; s. Gabriel and Anna (Herkommer) K.; ed. St. Augustine Sch. and pub. night schs.; m. Minnie A. Danner, May 1, 1883. Learned upholsterer's trade with Robert Mitchell Furniture Co.; removed to Denver, 1877; pres. Kindel Bedding & Renovating Co. Mem. Bd. of Supervisors City and County of Denver, 1910-14. Recognized as an authority on railroad and express rates; has instituted many suits before Interstate Commerce Commn. against railroad cos. for discrimination against Denver, beginning 1892; won 1st suit filed before Interstate Commerce Commn. against express cos. for excessive charges, 1908; prominent advocate of parcels post; mem. 63d Congress (1913-15), 1st Colo. Dist. Democrat. Author of "Kindel's ABC on Freight Rates." Home: Denver, Colo. Died Feb. 28, 1930.

KINDLE, Edward Martin, paleontologist, geologist; b. near Franklin, Ind., Mar. 10, 1869; s. Martin V. and Tabitha Ann K.; A.B., Ind. U., 1893, LL.D., 1939; M.S., Cornell, 1896; Ph.D., Yale, 1899; m. Margaret Ferris, Dec. 31, 1901; children—Winona Helen, Leroy Ferris, Cecil Haldane, Edward Darwin, Virginia Tomlinson, Margaret Crane, Madeleine Barton, Katharine, Charlotte. Instr. geology, Ind. U., 1894-95; mem. Cornell expdn. to Greenland, 1896; asst. geologist, Ind. Geol. Survey, 1898-1900; asst. geologist, 1900-08, paleontologist, 1908-10, geologist, 1911, U.S. Geol. Survey; paleontologist in charge of paleontology, Geol. Survey of Can., 1912-38. Spl. lecturer in geology, U. of London, Eng., 1928. Fellow Geol. Soc. America, Am. Geog. Soc., Royal Soc. of Can. Home: Ottawa, Can. Died Aug. 29, 1940.

KINDLEBERGER, David, medical dir. U.S.N.; b. Smithville, O., Sept. 2, 1834; s. T. J. (M.D.) and Katherine (Newcomer) K.; A.B., Wittenberg Coll., Springfield, O., 1857; m. Olivia M. Bishop, Mar. 10, 1906. Entered U.S. Naval service, 1859; advanced through various grades to med. dir. with rank of capt.; retired, Sept. 2, 1896, on account of age limit; advanced to rank of rear adm. retired, June 29, 1906. Served on African coast on U.S.S. San Jacinto, 1859-61; participated in all the battles of Admiral Farragut's squadron in Civil War except Vicksburg; fleet surgeon Asiatic Squadron, 1877-80, S. Pacific Squadron, 1882; comd. U.S. Naval Hosp., Phila., 1892-96. In command naval hosp., Guam, 1914. Died Mar. 25, 1921.

KINDRED, John Joseph, physician; b. Southampton County, Va., July 15, 1864; s. John J. and Caroline A. (Drewry) K.; ed. Suffolk (Va.) Mil. Acad., Randolph-Macon Coll., and U. of Va.; M.D., Medical Dept., Univ. of Louisville, 1889; hon. grad. dept. mental diseases, U. of Edinburgh; LL.B., John B. Stetson U.; m. Ella W. Cramer (A.B., LL.B.), July 10, 1902; one son, John C. (M.D.). Began med. practice at New York, 1889; conducted a sanitarium, Stamford, Conn., 1896-97; established, 1897, and since owner, River Crest Sanitarium, Astoria, L.I., for mental and nervous diseases, Belle Mead (N.J.) Sanatorium and Farm for Mental and Nervous Diseases; consultant mental diseases; prof. med. jurisprudence, John B. Stetson U., DeLand, Fla.; also largely interested in real estate, building of homes and agr.; mem. 62d, and 67th to 70th Congresses (1911-13 and 1921-29), 2d N.Y. Dist. Democrat. Home: Astoria, L.I., N.Y. Died Oct. 23, 1937.

KINEALY, John Henry, engineer; b. Hannibal, Mo., Mar. 18, 1864; s. Michael and Sarah (Briscoe) K.; M.E., Washington U., 1884; m. Grace Sampson Strong, June 26, 1890; children—Mrs. Winifred Bryan, Mrs. Grace Pierson, Mrs. Virginia Jackson, Mrs. Sarah Wentworth, J. Henry. Instr. Washington U., 1886-87; asso. prof. Agrl. and Mech. Coll. of Tex., 1887-89; prof. N.C. Coll. of Agr. and Mech. Arts, 1889-92; prof. mech. engring., Washington U., 1892-1902; consulting engr., Boston, 1902-04; mech. engr., St. Louis, 1904—. Patent expert; inventor of devices used in heating and ventilation. Active in Progressive Party, 1912, mayor of Ferguson, St. Louis Co., Mo., 1913-23, chmn. local exemption board, 1917-19; pres. League of Municipalities of St. Louis Co., 1918-23. Author: Steam Engines and Boilers, 1895, 4th edit., 1903; Mechanical Draft, 1906. Home: Ferguson, Mo. Died May 6, 1928.

KING, Albert Freeman Africanus, physician; b. in England, Jan. 18, 1841; s. Dr. Edward and Louisa (Freeman) K.; M.D., Columbian (now George Washington) U., 1861; M.D., U. of Pa., 1865; (hon. A.M., U. of Vt., 1883, LL.D., 1904); m. Ellen A. Dexter, Oct. 17, 1894. Acting asst. surgeon U.S.A., 1864; prof. obstetrics, 1871-1913, dean Medical Sch., 1879-94, Columbian U.; prof. obstetrics, U. of Vt., 1871-1913; obstetrician George Washington U. Hospital. Author: A Manual of Obstetrics, 1st edit., 1882, 11th edit., 1910; Mosquitoes and Malaria, 1883. Died Dec. 13, 1914.

KING, Alexander Campbell, judge; b. Charleston, S.C., Dec. 7, 1856; s. J. Gadsden and Caroline Clifford (Postell) K.; D.C.L., U. of the South, 1916; m. Alice May Fowler, July 13, 1881; children—Edward, Alexander C. Admitted to bar, 1875; asso. gen. counsel Atlanta & West Point R.R., 1887-93; gen. counsel East & West R.R. of Ala., 1887-89; asst. gen. counsel Richmond & Danville R.R., and Richmond & West Point Terminal Co., 1890-92; gen. counsel Chattanooga, Rome & Columbus R.R., 1894-1901; counsel Seaboard Air Line Ry. Solicitor gen. of U.S., 1918-20; U.S. circuit judge, 5th Circuit, 1920-25; resigned to become mem. King, Spalding, MacDougald & Sibley. Counselor Am. Red Cross, 1918-20. Mem. bd. State Bar Examiners, 1913-18 (chmn.); apptd. by U.S. Circuit Ct. Appeals, 5th Circuit, mem. com. to report on revision of rules in equity in U.S. Ct., 1912. Home: Atlanta, Ga. Died July 25, 1926.

KING, Alfred Rufus, jurist; b. Kewanee, Ill., Feb. 12, 1857; s. Rufus D. and Rebecca J. (Whitney) K.; Hedding Coll. and Chaddock Coll., Ill.; Union Coll. of Law, Chicago, 1881-82; (LL.D., U. of Denver, 1910); m. Annie R. Caldwell, Dec. 24, 1884. Practiced, Gunnison and Delta, Colo., 1882-1911; mayor of Delta, 1885; co. judge, Delta Co., 1883-90; atty. for D.&R.G. R.R., 1902-11; asso. justice, Ct. of Appeals, Colo., term Oct. 1911-Oct. 1, 1915. Col. and a.-d.-c., staff of gov. of Colo., 1907. Trustee U. of Denver. Republican. Methodist. Mason. Home: Delta, Colo. Died May 13, 1916.

KING, Arno Warren, judge; b. Aug. 2, 1855; student Colby Coll., Me., 1879-80; LL.B., Boston U. Law Sch., 1883; (LL.D., Colby, 1908). Admitted to bar, 1883, and practiced at Ellsworth, Me., until 1907; now asso. justice Supreme Ct. of Me. Republican. Pres. Ellsworth Loan & Bldg. Assn.; trustee Union Trust Co., Colby Coll. K.T. Home: Ellsworth, Me. Died July 21, 1918.

KING, (William Benjamin) Basil, author; b. Charlottetown, Can., Feb. 26, 1859; s. William and Mary Anne Lucretia K.; ed. St. Peter's Sch., Charlottetown, and King's Coll., Windsor, Can.; m. Esther Manton Foote, June 28, 1893. Episcopalian. Author: The Side of the Angels, 1916; The Lifted Veil, 1917; The High Heart, 1917; The City of Comrades, 1919; The Abolishing of Death, 1919; The Thread of Flame, 1920; The Empty Sack, 1921; The Conquest of Fear, 1921; The Dust Flower, 1922; The Discovery of God, 1923; The Happy Isles, 1923; The High Forfeit, 1925; Faith and Success, 1925; The Spreading Dawn, 1927. Home: Cambridge, Mass. Died June 22, 1928.

KING, Charles, soldier, author; b. Albany, N.Y., Oct. 12, 1844; s. Rufus and Susan McKown (Eliot) K.; grad. U.S. Mil. Acad., 1866; m. Adelaide Lavander, d. Capt. Yorke, of Carroll Parish, La., Nov. 20, 1872; children—Adelaide Patton (dec.), Carolyn Merritt, Elinor Yorke, Rufus. Second lt. 1st Arty., June 18, 1866; 1st lt., May 15, 1870; transferred to 5th Cav., Dec. 31, 1870; regimental adj., 1876-78; capt., May 1, 1879; retired for wounds, June 14, 1879. Insp. and instr. Wis. Nat. Guard, 1882-89; col. comdg. regt., 1890; adj. gen., 1895; brig. gen. vols., May 27, 1898-Aug. 2, 1899; served in P.I. under Gen. Lawton. Supt. Mich. Mil. Acad., 1901. Author: Famous and Decisive Battles; Between the Lines; The Colonel's Daughter, 1883; Marion's Faith, 1885; Captain Blake, 1892; The General's Double, 1897; The Iron Brigade, 1902; A Conquering Corps Badge, 1902; Medal of Honor, 1905; and others. Home: Milwaukee, Wis. Died Mar. 18, 1933.

KING, Charles Francis, school prin.; b. Wilton, N.H., Jan. 30, 1843; s. Sanford and Susan (Burnham) K.; A.B., Dartmouth Coll., 1867; m. Elizabeth Boardman, Aug. 1, 1867; 2d, Gratia Cobb, July 6, 1897. Began teaching, 1864; prin. Dearborn Grammar Sch., Boston, 1887-1913. Has lectured on methods of teaching geography before teachers' institutes, assns., etc., in various cities; founder and mgr. Nat. Sch. of Methods, Saratoga and Glens Falls, N.Y. Conglist. Republican. Author: Methods and Aids in Geography, 1888; Picturesque Geographical Readers for Home and School, 1889; New England Supplement of Geography, 1909. Retired, Aug. 1913. Home: Boston, Mass. Died May 22, 1924.

KING, Clarence, geologist; b. Newport, R.I., Jan. 6, 1842; grad. Sheffield Scientific School, Yale, 1862; crossed continent on horseback and joined Calif. geol. survey, 1863, working with it until 1866; made palæontol. discoveries which furnished the evidence upon which the accepted age of gold-bearing rocks was determined. Originated the plan and comd. the expdn. for geol. survey of 40th parallel, under auspices of army engr. dept., 1867-72; exposed Arizona "diamond-fields" fraud, 1872; suggested and organized U.S. Geol. Survey, of which he was dir., 1878-81; then in spl. investigations. Author: Systematic Geology (Vol. I, Professional Papers of Engr. Dept., U.S.A.); Mountaineering in Sierra Nevada, etc. Died 1901.

KING, Clyde Lyndon, author; b. Burlington, Kan., May 1, 1879; s. Peter and Sarah (Talliaferro) K.; grad. Kan. State Normal Sch., Emporia, 1904; A.B., U. of Mich., 1907, A.M., 1908; Harrison fellow, University of Pa., 1910-11, Ph.D., 1911; Sc.D., Temple U., Phila., 1933, m. Irene B. Marschall, June 29, 1931. Acting prof. economics and sociology, U. of Colo., 1908-10; instr. polit. science, 1911-14, asst. prof., 1914-20, prof., 1920—, U. of Pa. Chmn. Pa. Unemployment Com., 1930-31; sec. of revenue of Pa., Jan. 1931-Oct. 1932; chmn. Pub. Service Commn. of Pa., Oct. 1932-May 1933. Member Christian (Disciples) Church. Chmn. gov.'s Tri-state Milk Commn. (Pa., Md., Del.), 1916-18; milk commr. for Eastern States for U.S. Food Administration, 1918-19; milk price arbitrator of Pa., 1919; sec. of State and budget officer, Pa., 1923-27; sec. of Revenue, Pa., 1931-32; chairman of Public Service Commission, Pa., 1932-33. Member Agrl. Conf., called by President Harding, 1921, of Unemployment Conf., 1922; chmn. Citizens Com. apptd. by gov. of Pa. to investigate State finances, 1922; chief of the dairy section, Agricultural Adjustment Administration, Washington, D.C., 1933. Author: History of the Government of Denver, 1911; Regulation of Municipal Utilities, 1913; Trolley Freight and Philadelphia Markets, 1913; Lower Living Costs in Cities, 1915; The Price of Milk, 1920; Community Civics, 1926; Public Finance, 1935. Home: West Chester, Pa. Died June 21, 1937.

KING, Cora Smith, physiotherapist; b. Rockford, Ill., Sept. 7, 1867; d. Col. Eliphaz and Sara Emma (Barnes) Smith; grad. Nat. Sch. of Elocution and Oratory, Phila., 1886; Sc.B., U. of N.D., 1889; M.D., Boston U. Sch. of Medicine, 1892; m. Judson King, Feb. 14, 1912 (divorced 1925); 1 dau., Sylvia More (adopted). Practiced in Grand Forks, N.D., 1892-96, Minneapolis, Minn., 1896-1906, Seattle, Wash., 1906-12, Washington, D.C., 1912-24, Pasadena, Calif., 1924-27, Hollywood, Calif., 1927—; dir. Physiotherapy dept. Hollywood Hosp., 1927—. Active worker and speaker for woman suffrage from 1887; chmn. congl. com. National Council of Women Voters. Unitarian. Acting sec. com. of women physicians of Council Nat. Defense, organizing med. women of U.S. for war service; pres. Nat. Soc. Physical Therapeutics, 1917; 2d v.p. Am. Inst. Homœpathy, 1919; sec. Pacific Physiotherapy Assn., 1925-28, pres., 1935-36. Author: A Course in Physiotherapy, 1933. Home: Hollywood, Calif. Died Nov. 1939.

KING, Dougall Macdougall, physician; b. Berlin, Ont., Nov. 11, 1878; s. John and Isabell Grace (Mackenzie) K.; prep. edn. Harbord Collegiate Inst., Toronto; M.B., Toronto U., 1902; m. May Wookey, of Toronto, Oct. 18, 1911. In gen. practice, Ottawa, Can., 1905-13; removed to Denver, Colo., 1913; practice confined to treatment of diseases of the chest. Veteran S. African War. Presbyn. Author: The Battle with Tuberculosis and How to Win It, 1917. Home: Denver, Colo. Died Mar. 18, 1922.

KING, Edmund Burritt, lawyer; b. Montville, O., July 4, 1850; s. Cyrus and Harriet (Bennett) K.; ed. Oberlin Acad., 2 yrs., Baldwin U., 1 yr.; admitted to Ohio bar, 1873; m. Emma Hackett, Feb. 26, 1874. Pros. atty., Medina Co., O., 1874-75; presdl. elector, 1888-89; judge 6th Jud. Circuit, Ohio, 1894-99; sr. mem. King & Ramsey, 1899-1931; mem. King, Flynn & Frohman, 1931—. Second lt., capt. and maj. 16th Inf. Ohio N.G., 1880-96. Mem. 4th Constl. Conv. of Ohio, 1912. Mason. Republican. Home: Sandusky, Ohio. Died Dec. 30, 1934.

KING, Edward, banker; b. Highwood, Weehawken, N.J., 1833; s. James Gore and Sarah Rogers (Gracie) K.; grad. Harvard; m. Isabella Ramsay Cochrane (died); m. 2d, Elizabeth Fisher, Phila. Pres. and trustee Union Trust Co., 1873—; trustee Northern Assurance Co. of London. Mem. N.Y. Stock Exchange (pres.); treas. bd. trustees, N.Y. Pub. Library, Astor, Lenox and Tilden Foundation; gov. N.Y. Hosp. Home: New York, N.Y. Died 1908.

KING, Edward J., congressman; b. Springfield, Mass., July 1, 1867; s. John A. and Alice L. (Houghton) K.; B.S., Knox Coll., Galesburg, Ill., 1891; m. May B. Roberts, Jan. 1, 1895 (died 1925). Admitted to Ill. bar, 1893, and practiced in Galesburg; city atty., Galesburg 1893-94; mem. Ill. Ho. of Rep., 1907-14; mem. 64th to 70th Congresses (1915-29), 15th Ill. Dist. Republican. Home: Galesburg, Ill. Died Feb. 17, 1929.

KING, Edward Leonard, army officer; b. Bridgewater, Mass., Dec. 5, 1873; s. Francis Dane and Mary Ann (Malloy) K.; grad. U.S. Mil. Acad., 1896; distinguished grad. Army Sch. of the Line, 1913; grad. Army Staff Coll., 1914; Army War Coll., 1917-22; m. Nancy Vose Sumner, Jan. 18, 1898; 1 dau., Nancy Sumner (Mrs. Chas. Lee Andrews). Commd. 2d lt. 9th Cav., Dec. 22, 1896; promoted through grades to brig. gen., Dec. 4, 1922; promoted to major general, U.S.A., Oct. 1, 1931. Participated in Spanish-Am. War, and Philippine Insurrection; a.d.c. to Gen. H. W. Lawton; chief of staff 28th Div., and comdr. 65th Inf. Brigade, A.E.F., World War; comdr. Cav. Sch., Ft. Riley, Kan., July 1, 1923-June 30, 1925; comdt. Gen. Service Schs., Ft. Leavenworth, Kan., 1925-29; asst. chief of staff, War Dept. Gen. Staff, 1929-32; commander Fourth Corps Area, Feb. 1932—. Decorated D.S.C. and D.S.M. (U.S.); Officer Legion of Honor and Croix de Guerre with palm (French). Conglist. Mason. Died Dec. 27, 1933.

KING, Edward S(kinner), astronomer; b. Liverpool, N.Y., May 31, 1861; s. Nathaniel and Cornelia C. (Skinner) K.; A.B. from Hamilton College, 1887, A.M., 1890, and Sc.D. from the same college, 1927; m. Kate Irene Colson, July 23, 1890; children—Harold Skinner, Margaret Wight, Everett Tryon (dec.). Connected from 1887, with Harvard Coll. Obs. (except 3 yrs. absent on account of ill health); observer in charge Harvard Sta. on Mt. Wilson, Calif., 1889; asst. prof. astronomy, 1913-26, Phillips prof., Harvard, 1926—. Obtained first photog. observation of the occultation of a star, also first photograph of spectrum of the aurora; perfected method of obtaining circular photographic images of the stars without visual guiding of the telescope; devised method of transforming prismatic to normal spectra, both photographically and mechanically; determined photographic magnitudes of bright stars and planets, from images photographed out of focus; made photographic measures of the light of the moon, also of the sun; has maintained systematic tests of photographic plates, 1896—; also determined photovisual magnitudes of stars, and derived color indices of planets; etc. Fellow Am. Acad. Arts and Sciences, A.A.A.S. Republican. Conglist. Home: Cambridge, Mass. Died Sept. 10, 1931.

KING, Francis Scott, artist; b. Auburn, Me., Mar. 24, 1850; s. William and Marian K.; pupil of John W. Orr and August Will, New York; unmarried. Designer and engraver on copper; designed and engraved the now famous "Ex Libris" of the printer's devil; designed the "Sylvester" bronze tablet for Johns Hopkins U., and seal for The Rockefeller Inst. for Med. Research, New York; designed and engraved copper plates for The Boston Port Bills, published by Grolier Club, New York; designed and engraved on copper numerous important plates for the Society of Iconophiles, New York. Medals, Paris Expn., 1889, Chicago Expn., 1893; exhibited Paris Expn., 1900; silver medal, Buffalo Expn., 1901. Home: Newark, N.J. Deceased.

KING, Franklin Hiram, agrl. scientist; b. Whitewater, Wis., June 8, 1848; s. Edmund and Deborah L. K.; grad. State Normal Sch., Whitewater, 1872; m. Carrie H. Baker, 1880. On Wis. Geol. Survey, 1873-76; took spl. course at Cornell, 1876-78; prof. natural sciences, River Falls State Normal Sch., 1878-88; prof. agrl. physics, U of Wis., 1888-1901; chief Div. of Soil Management, U.S. Bur. of Soils, 1901-04. Author: The Soil, 1895; Principles of Agricultural Irrigation and Farm Drainage, 1899; Physics of Agriculture, 1900; Ventilation for Dwellings, Rural Schools and Stables, 1908. Home: Madison, Wis. Died 1911.

KING, Frederick Allen, editor; b. Thompsonville, Conn., Feb. 20, 1865; s. E. Wolcott and Cecilia (Pease) K.; A.B., Wesleyan U., Conn., 1891, A.M., 1893. Asst. librarian, Wesleyan U., 1891-92; teacher, Franklin Sch. (Phila.), Peekskill (N.Y.) Mil. Acad., De Lancey Sch. Smith Coll., until 1898; lit. and editorial work, New York; lit. editor Literary Digest, 1909-33. Died Oct. 31, 1939.

KING, George Anderson, lawyer; b. Minneapolis, Minn., Feb. 10, 1855; s. Charles and Eleanor Frances (Anderson) K.; Gonzaga Coll., Washington, 1864-68; A.B., Columbian Coll. (now George Washington U.), 1870, LL.B., 1871, LL.M., 1872; LL.D., Nat. U. Law Sch., 1902; m. Ada Edmonston, June 14, 1881 (died 1933); children—Archibald, Francis Anderson (dec.), Marion Edmonston (wife of Comdr. Robert M. Hinckley, U.S.N.), Charles Wadsworth (dec.), George Anderson, Elizabeth (wife of Capt. Lawrence M. Jones, U.S.A.). Clerk in law office, Washington, 1872-76; admitted to D.C. bar, 1876, and entered practice at Washington; mem. King & King, specializing in matters affecting U.S. Govt.; dir. and mem. trust com. Washington Loan & Trust Co. Republican. Episcopalian; mem. Conv. of Diocese of Washington. Home: Washington, D.C. Died July 19, 1938.

KING, Grace Elizabeth, author; b. New Orleans, La., 1852; d. William Woodson and Sarah Ann (Miller) K.; ed. at New Orleans; unmarried. Author: New Orleans, the Place and the People; Jean Baptiste Lemoine, Founder of New Orleans; Balcony Stories; History of Louisiana, Stories from History of Louisiana; Pleasant Ways of St. Médard, 1916; Creole Families of New Orleans, 1921; Madame Girard, an Old French Teacher of New Orleans, 1922; La Dame de Sainte Hermine, 1924. Home: New Orleans, La. Died Jan. 12, 1932.

KING, Hamilton, diplomat; b. St. Johns, Newfoundland, June 4, 1852; s. William and Maria (Squires) K.; A.B., Olivet (Mich.) Coll., 1878, A.M., 1881 (LL.D., 1910); studied at Chicago Theol. Sem., 1878-79, U. of Leipzig, 1883-84, Am. Sch. at Athens, Greece, 1884; m. Cora Lee Seward (of the old N.Y. Seward family), 1884. Prin. prep. dept. Olivet Coll., 1879-98; lecturer, preacher and polit. speaker; minister resident and consul gen. to Siam, 1898-1903, E.E. and M.P., Apr. 27, 1903—. Spl. rep. of President Taft at the cremation of the late King of Siam, Mar. 16, 1911; same, with the rank of ambassador extraordinary and plenipotentiary at the coronation of King Vajiravudh of Siam, Dec. 2, 1911. Home: Olivet, Mich. Died Sept. 1, 1912.

KING, Harry Andrews, college pres.; b. Kansas City, Mo., Oct. 27, 1867; s. David Clark and Sarah Louise (Andrews) K.; A.B., Baker U., Kan., 1897, D.D., 1910; S.T.B., Boston U., 1904; m. Susie Amarette Newgent, Sept. 1, 1891; children—Marie Sophia, Susie Newgent, Martha (dec.), Sarah Elizabeth. Ordained M.E. ministry, 1897; pastor Belton, Mo., 1897-98, Kansas City, Mo., 1898-1900, Egleston Sq. Ch., Boston, 1901-04, Kents Hill, Me., 1904-05, Oakley Ch., Kansas City, 1905-07; ednl. sec. Baker U., 1907-09; pres. Moores Hill (Ind.) Coll., 1909-15; pres. Clark U., S. Atlanta, Ga., 1915-22; dist. supt. Indianapolis Dist., M.E. Ch., 1922—. Died Aug. 7, 1927.

KING, Henry, editor; b. Salem, O., May 11, 1842; s. Selah W. and Eliza (Aleshire) K.; common sch. edn.; m. Maria Louise Lane, Nov. 17, 1861 (dec.).

Served in Union Army 4 yrs., during Civil War; editor newspapers at Quincy, Ill., and Topeka, Kan.; on staff, 1883—, mng. editor, 1897—, St. Louis Globe-Democrat. Home: St. Louis, Mo. Died Mar. 16, 1915.

KING, Henry Churchill, educator; b. Hillsdale, Mich., Sept. 18, 1858; s. Henry Jarvis and Sarah (Lee) K.; A.B., Oberlin Coll., 1879; B.D., Oberlin Theol. Sem., 1882; A.M., Harvard, 1883, Berlin, 1893-94; D.D., Oberlin, 1897, Western Reserve, 1901, Yale, 1904, Chicago, Harvard, 1916; LL.D., U. of Ill., 1908, Miami U., 1909; S.T.D., Columbia, 1909; L.H.D., Colgate, 1916; m. Julia M. Coates, July 7, 1882; children—Harold Lee, Philip Coates, Donald Storrs, Edgar Weld. Tutor Latin and mathematics, Oberlin Acad., 1879-82; asso. prof. mathematics, 1884-90, philosophy, 1890-91, prof. philosophy, 1891-97, theology, 1897-1925, dean, 1901-02, pres., Nov. 19, 1902-Aug. 31, 1927 (emeritus), Oberlin Coll.; Haverford Coll. Library lecturer, 1906; Taylor lecturer, Yale, 1907; Noble lecturer, Harvard, 1909; lectured in India, China, Japan, 1909-10; Earl lecturer, Pacific Theol. Sem., 1910; lecturer on religious life, Columbia, 1913; Cole lecturer, Vanderbilt U., 1920; Gates lecturer, Grinnell Coll., 1921; Deems lecturer, New York U., 1922. Trustee Carnegie Foundation Advancement of Teaching. Chmn. commn. on missions Nat. Council Congl. Chs., 1913-19; moderator Nat. Council Congl. Chs., 1919-21; chmn. Congl. Foundation for Edn., 1921-27. Dir. religious work dept. Y.M.C.A., for France, Oct. 1918-Apr. 1919; with Charles R. Crane forming Am. sect. of the Peace Conf. Inter-Allied Commn. on Mandates in Turkey, Apr.-Sept. 1919. Chevalier Legion of Honor (France), 1929. Author: Rational Living, 1905; The Laws of Friendship, Human and Divine, 1909; The Ethics of Jesus, 1910; Religion as Life, 1913; It's All in the Day's Work, 1916; Fundamental Questions, 1917; The Way to Life, 1918; For a New America in a New World, 1919; A New Mind for the New Age, 1920; Seeing Life Whole, 1923. Home: Oberlin, O. Died Feb. 27, 1934.

KING, Henry Melville, clergyman; b. Oxford, Me., Sept. 3, 1838; s. Samuel Hall and Eliza (Shaw) K.; A.B., Bowdoin, 1859, A.M., 1862; grad. Newton Theol. Instn., 1862; (D.D., Colby, 1877; S.T.D., Bowdoin, 1899); m. Susan Ellen Fogg, Sept. 2, 1862; father of Lida Shaw K. Ordained Bapt. ministry, Aug. 28, 1862; instr. Hebrew lang., Newton Theol. Instn., 1862-63; pastor Dudley St. Ch., Boston, 1863-82, Emanuel Ch., Albany, 1882-91, First Ch., Providence, 1891-1906, emeritus, 1906. Chmn. bd. mgrs., 1884-87, and mem. exec. com., 1874-82, 1894-1901, 1906-09, Am. Bapt. Missionary Union; pres. R.I. Bapt. State Conv., 1891-95, Northern Bapt. Edn. Soc., 1875-82. Trustee Newton Theol. Instn., Vassar Coll., Hamilton Theol. Sem., Rochester Theol. Sem., Worcester Acad., Hartshorn Memorial Coll., and Brown U. Author: Our Gospels, 1895; Summer Visit of Three Rhode Islanders to Massachusetts Bay, 1896; The Baptism of Roger Williams, 1897; Religious Liberty, 1903; John Myles and the Founding of the First Baptist Church in Massachusetts, 1905; Sir Henry Vane, Jr., 1909. Died June 16, 1919.

KING, Horatio Collins, lawyer; b. Portland, Me., Dec. 22, 1837; s. Horatio (Postmaster Gen., 1861) and Anne (Collins) K.; reared in Washington; A.B., Dickinson Coll., 1858, A.M., 1863; (LL.D., Allegheny Coll., 1897); admitted to bar, 1861; m. Emma C. Stebbins, Oct. 1862 (died 1864); m. 2d, Esther A. Howard, June 14, 1866. Capt. and a.q.m. vols., Aug. 19, 1862; maj. q.m., Feb. 20-May 19, 1865; bvtd.: maj. vols., Mar. 13, 1865, "for meritorious services during the war," and lt. vol. and col. vols., May 19, 1865, "for faithful and meritorious services"; Congressional Medal of Honor "for distinguished bravery nr. Dinwiddie C.H., Va., Mar. 29, 1865." Practiced law, 1865-71, and 1877—; asso. editor New York Star, 1871-73; publisher Christian Union and Christian At Work, 1873-77. Maj. 13th Regt. N.G.S.N.Y., 1877; judge advocate 11th Brigade, 1880; judge advocate gen. of N.Y., 1883; mem. Brooklyn Bd. Edn., 1883-94; trustee N.Y. State Soldiers' and Sailors' Home, 1894-1900; trustee Dickinson Coll., 1896—; chmn. Fredericksburg Nat. Park Assn., 1898. Dem. nominee for sec. of state, N.Y., 1895; Progressive Republican, 1900—; mem. state commn. on law's delays; mem. N.Y. State Monument Commn. Author: History of Dickinson College, 1896; Sketch of Army of Potomac, 1896; Songs of Dickinson, 1901; Souvenir of Poems and Compositions, 1908. Mason, Elk. Home: Brooklyn, N.Y. Died Nov. 15, 1918.

KING, James A., late minister of the interior, Republic of Hawaii. Residence: Honolulu, H.I. Died 1899.

KING, James Joseph, M.D.; b. Columbia, Tenn., Mar. 9, 1882; s. Meredith David and Katharine Lavinia Jane (Smith) K.; A.B., U. of Tenn., 1904; M.D., U. of Louisville, 1907; m. Virginia P. Lawrence; 1 son, John Pernet. Resident physician, Children's Hosp., Phila., 1907-08; practiced in Freeland, Pa., 1908-11; house surgeon, St. Bartholomew's Clinic, 1911-12; practice limited to treatment of ear, nose and throat, 1913—; attending laryngologist, Hospital for the Ruptured and Crippled; consultant to French Hospital in diseases of the ear, nose and throat, etc. Author: Diseases of Ear, Nose and Throat from the Practitioners' Viewpoint, 1916; Local Anaesthesia in Oto-Laryngology, 1926. Has devised surg. instruments for use in throat. Capt. M.C., attached to air med. service, during the war. Died Nov. 29, 1935.

KING, James Marcus, M.E. clergyman; b. Girard, Pa., 1839; grad. Wesleyan Univ.; was prof. natural science, Collegiate Inst., Ft. Edward, N.Y., 6 yrs.; joined Troy Conf., 1868; pastor 5th Av. Ch., Troy, N.Y., 3 yrs., 1st Ch., Saratoga Springs, N.Y., 3 yrs.; transferred to New York Conf., 1873; since then successively pastor St. Johns, Washington Square, St. James, 18th St., Park Av., St. Andrew's and Union M.E. chs., New York; gen. sec. Nat. League for Protection of Am. Instns.; corr. sec. Bd. Ch. Extension, M.E. Ch., May 1899—. Died 1907.

KING, John A., banker; b. DeWitt Twp., N.Y., 1834; s. William M. and Hannah (Hadley) K.; reared on farm; married. Entered employment of grocery firm of Syracuse at 15; later served messenger to teller Mechanics' Bank of Syracuse; in business in Toledo, O., 1859-61; bookkeeper and later treas. S. M. Nickerson & Co., distillers, 1861-67; wholesale drug business, 1867-88; bought controlling interest in McAvoy Brewing Co., 1888, selling property to English syndicate, 1889; pres. Ft. Dearborn Nat. Bank, 1889-1903; trustee Chicago Sanitary Dist., 1889-91. Democrat. Home: Chicago, Ill. Died Sept. 12, 1916.

KING, John Jefferson, lawyer; b. Franklin Parish, La., July 26, 1863; s. John and Virginia (Ship) K.; ed. pub. schs. of Tex.; m. Caroline Wyse, Mar. 18, 1894; children—Mable, John R. Admitted to Tex. bar 1886 and began practice at Texarkana; county atty., Bowie Co., Tex., 1886-90; mem. Tex. Ho. of Rep., 1890-92; judge County Court, Bowie Co., 1892-96; senior mem. King & Wheeler; 1st v.p. and dir. Texarkana & Fort Smith Ry. Co., Port Arthur Canal & Dock Co. Mem. bd. dirs. Chamber Commerce, United Charities and Community Chest, Texarkana. Democrat. Presbyn. Mason. Home: Texarkana, Tex. Died Feb. 6, 1940.

KING, John Rigdon; b. Hagerstown, Md., June 24, 1844; s. Samuel L. and Eliza (Lane) K.; ed. pvt. and pub. schs., Washington Co., Md.; m. Annie Maria Snyder, May 28, 1874. Enlisted at 17 in Co. H, 6th Md. Vol. Inf., served through Civil War, in 3d and 6th Army Corps, Army of the Potomac; prisoner of war in Salisbury, N.C., and Libby Prison, 6 months; wounded 3 times. Assisted in forming 1st G.A.R. post in Md.; held every office including dept. comdr.; elected sr. vice-comdr.-in-chief, G.A.R., 1904, and became comdr.-in-chief, 1905. In Baltimore Custom House 30 yrs.; U.S. pension agt., Washington, till 1913. Pres. Grand Army Club of Md., Md. Union Soldiers and Sailors Monument Commn. Republican. Presbyn. Home: Baltimore, Md. Died Mar. 3, 1934.

KING, Joseph Elijah, educator; b. Laurens, N.Y., Nov. 30, 1823; s. Rev. Elijah and Catherine (Olmstead) K.; A.B., Wesleyan U., Conn., 1847; (D.D., Union Coll., 1863; Ph.D., from Regents of U. of N.Y., 1865); m. Melissa Bayley, July 20, 1850; m. 2d, Josephine M. Batcheller, Dec. 28, 1889. Began teaching in pub. schs. at 17; ordained M.E. ministry, 1848; prin. Newbury (Vt.) Sem., 1847-53, Ft. Plain (N.Y.) Sem., 1853-54; pres. Ft. Edward (N.Y.) Collegiate Inst., 1854—. Pres. Ft. Edward Nat. Bank, Union Cemetery Soc.; mem. exec. com. Glens Falls Ins. Co. Trustee Wesleyan U., 1848—, Round Lake Summer Sch., 1868—. Home: Ft. Edward, N.Y. Died June 3, 1913.

KING, Lida Shaw, univ. dean; b. Boston, 1868; d. late Henry Melville and Susan Ellen (Fogg) K.; A.B., Vassar Coll., 1890; A.M., Brown U., 1894; grad. student Vassar, 1894-95, Radcliffe Coll., 1897-98; Bryn Mawr fellow in Greek, 1899-1900, Agnes Hoppin Memorial fellow, 1900-01, at Am. Sch. Archæology, Athens, Greece; Litt.D., Mt. Holyoke, 1912; LL.D., Western Reserve U., 1913. Fellow and teacher Latin, 1894-95, teacher classics, 1895-97, Vassar; teacher, 1898-99, head classical dept., 1901-02, Packer Collegiate Inst.; dean Women's Coll., 1905-22, asst. prof. classical philology, 1905-09, prof. classical lit. and archæology, 1909—, Brown U. Trustee R.I. Sch. Design; dir. R.I. Hosp. Mem. mng. com. Am. Sch., Classical Studies in Athens. Died Jan. 10, 1932.

KING, Oscar A., neurologist; b. on farm nr. Peru, Ind., Feb. 22, 1851; s. Timothy Lewis and Mary M. (Wright) K.; M.D., Bellevue Hosp. Med. Coll. (New York U.), 1878; m. Minerva Guernsey, 1887. Second and 1st asst. phys. Wis. State Hosp. for Insane, 1879-82; attended lectures U. of Vienna and clinics in Allgemeinen Krankenhausen, 1880-81; spl. studies in neurology and psychiatry under Meynert, Leidersdorf, Weiss and Benedict. Prof. mental and nervous diseases, 1882, and later of neurology, Psychiatry and clin, medicine, sec., 1894, vice dean, 1900—, Coll. Phys. and Surg. (U. of Ill.), Chicago; pathologist and consulting alienist Wis. state charitable and penal instns., 1895; prof. neurology, Post-Grad. Med. Sch.; chief dept. of neurology West Side Free Dispensary; asso. mem. med. staff Cook Co. Hosp. Founded, 1883, the Oakwood Retreat, Lake Geneva, Wis., a private sanitarium for care of the insane, of which became pres. and chief of med. staff; founded, in 1896, Lake Geneva Sanitarium, and in 1901 the two sanitaria were united into one, of which remains dir. In 1896 applied the toxine of erysipelas effectively in the treatment of 23 nearly consecutive cases of mania and melancholia. Home: Lake Geneva, Wis. Died Sept. 11, 1921.

KING, Stoddard, writer; b. Jackson, Wis., Aug. 19, 1889; s. Louis Andrew and Clara Viola (Stoddard) K.; A.B., Yale, 1914; A.M., Whitman Coll., Walla Walla, Wash., 1927; m. Henrietta McColl., Sept. 9, 1915; children— Penelope Jane, Barbara Ann. Reporter Spokesman-Review, Spokane, 1907-10; mng. editor Yale Daily News, 1913-14; asso. editor Harper's Weekly, N.Y. City, 1916; editorial writer and condr. column "Facetious Fragments," Spokesman-Review, 1916—; lecturer. Served as capt., inf., N.G. Wash., 1918-21. Episcopalian. Author (verse): What the Queen Said, 1926; Grand Right and Left, 1927; Listen to the Mocking Bird, 1928; The Raspberry Tree, 1930. Wrote lyrics of songs, "There's a Long, Long Trail," etc. Home: Spokane, Wash. Died June 13, 1933.

KING, Theophilus, mfr., financier; b. Rochester, Mass., Dec. 14, 1844; s. Theophilus and Mary S. K.; acad. edn., Rochester; m. Helen L. Baxter, Dec. 31, 1873; children—Delcevare, Mrs. Zayma Burke. Pres. Granite Trust Co.; asst. treas., dir. Lincoln Mills; pres. Summit Thread Co. Donated trust fund of $16,000 to all organized churches of Quincy for purpose of breaking down inter-denominational lines, fund later increased to over $750,000 to be used in addition for organizations of charitable, philanthropic, religious and civic helpfulness. Home: Quincy, Mass. Died Feb. 1, 1935.

KING, Wilburn Hill, lawyer, farmer, public official; b. Cullodenville, Ga., June 10, 1839; s. Alexander and Mary (Douglas) K.; ed. Americus, Ga., 1846-55; studied medicine and law and practiced law; m. Lucy Furman, Dec. 1867. Served 4 yrs. in C.S.A. as pvt., 1st lt., capt., maj. lt. col., col., brig. gen. and acting maj. gen. Has served as mayor of Sulphur Springs, Tex.; mem. Texas legislature 4 yrs.; adj. gen. of Texas nearly 10 yrs. Democrat. Home: Sulphur Springs, Tex. Died 1910.

KING, William Albert, lawyer; b. Greenfield, Mass., July 22, 1855; s. Patrick and Mary King; A.B., Amherst, 1878; m. Jane S. Cady, Aug. 26, 1889; 1 son, John Hamilton. Admitted to bar, 1879; practiced at Willimantic, Conn. from 1889 until retirement; one of revisers of Connecticut Statutes, 1902; attorney general, Connecticut, 1903-07; mem. Connecticut Ho. of Rep. 4 terms, leader of House sessions, 1901, 19; Rep. candidate for Congress, 2d Conn. Dist., 1912. Conglist. Mason. Home: Willimantic, Conn. Died Aug. 20, 1937.

KING, William Fletcher, college pres.; b. nr. Zanesville, O., Dec. 20, 1830; s. James J. and Mariam (Coffman) K.; A.B., Ohio Wesleyan, 1857, A.M., 1860; (D.D., Ill. Wesleyan, 1870; LLD., State U. of Ia., and Ohio Wesleyan, 1887); m. Margaret McKell, Aug. 3, 1865. Prin. Unionville Acad., Tenn., 1853-54; tutor Ohio Wesleyan, 1857-62; prof. Latin and Greek langs., 1862-63, acting pres., 1863-65, pres., 1865-1908 (emeritus), Cornell Coll., Ia. Del. Gen. Conf. M.E. Ch., 1876, 88, 96, 1904, 08, Ecumenical Conf., London, 1901; mem. Nat. Council Edn., 1886—; mem. Bd. Edn. M.E. Ch., 1895—, Nat. commr. World's Columbian Commn., 1890. Home: Mt. Vernon, Iowa. Died Oct. 23, 1921.

KING, William Frederick, mcht.; b. New York, Dec. 27, 1850; s. Charles and Ellen Elliott K.; pub. sch. edn.; m. Martha Kneeland Danolds, 1883. Mem. firm Calhoun, Robbins & Co., dry goods; dir. Merchants' Assn. (pres.). Home: New York, N.Y. Deceased.

KING, Will(iam) R(ufus), lawyer; b. Walla Walla Co., Wash., Oct. 3, 1864; s. David Rufus and Elizabeth (Estes) K.; student State Agr. Coll., Corvallis, Ore., 1882-85; LL.B., Central Normal Coll., Danville, Ind., 1891; m. L. Myrtle King, Dec. 6, 1892. Practiced law in courts of Ore. and nearby states; mem. Ore. Ho. of Rep., 1892-94, Senate, 1894-98. Dem. nominee for gov. of Ore., 1898; mem. Supreme Court of Oregon, 1907-11; chief counsel U.S. Reclamation Service (Interior Dept.), 1913-20; now gen. practice. Mem. faculty George Washington U., lecturing on mining and irrigation law, 1915-16, also joint author (with E. W. Burr), in work on Irrigation District Laws. Mason. Mem. Dem. Nat. Com., 1912-16, 1924-28; mem. Dem. Nat. Exec. Com., presdl. campaign of 1912; candidate for nomination for U.S. Senate, 1924. Died June 2, 1934.

KING, Willis L., steel mfr.; b. Pittsburgh, Pa., Feb. 14, 1851; s. Hugh Davidson and Eliza Ann (McMasters) K.; Washington and Jefferson Coll., 1867-69; m. Fanny Millard Morris, Oct. 14, 1880; children—Willis L., John M. (dec.), Gordon C. Began with Jones & Laughlin, 1869, v.p., 1902-34, now dir., name of company now Jones & Laughlin Steel Corp. V.p. Am. Iron & Steel Inst. Republican. Presbyterian. Home: Pittsburgh, Pa. Died Dec. 11, 1936.

KINGERY, Hugh Macmaster, college prof.; b. Bethel Parsonage (later Murdoch), O., Mar. 13,

1860; s. Rev. David and Cornelia Ayres (Shields) K.; A.B., U. of Wooster, O., 1884, A.M., 1887, Ph.D., 1892, Litt.D., 1916; L.H.D., Wabash Coll. (Ind.), 1923; m. Mary McMillan, June 24, 1886; children—Hugh McMillan, Helen, Robert, Katharine, Margaret, Mary Frances (dec.). Prof. Latin, Coll. of Emporia, Kan., 1884-91, Wabash Coll., Crawfordsville, Ind., 1891-1916 (emeritus). Republican. Presbysterian. Editor: The Medea of Seneca, 1896, revised edit., 1900; Three Tragedies of Seneca, 1908; Selected Orations and Letters of Cicero, 1910; Pliny, Selected Letters, 1911; Appendix of Proper Names for Latin Dictionary, 1915. Home: Worthington, Ohio. Died Feb. 20, 1927.

KINGMAN, Lewis, civil engr., ry. official; b. Bridgewater, Mass., Feb. 26, 1845; s. Isaac and Sibel (Ames) K.; grad. Hunt's Acad., 1861; studied with J. Herbert Shedd, civ. engr. of Boston, 2 yrs.; m. Alice Newman, Jan. 20, 1887. Engring and developing oil wells, Wilkes-Barré and Oil City, Pa., 1863-68; div. engr. on location surveys, Atlantic & Pacific Ry., 1868-71; on surveys and location, Maxwell Land Grant and U.P. Ry. from Kit Carson, Colo., to Cameron, N.M., 1871-72; on U.S. Govt. serveys under surveyor gen. of N.M., 1873-76; asst. and locating engr. A.,T.&S.F. Ry., 1884-88, at Topeka, and Atlantic & Pacific Ry., West of Albuquerque, N.M., 1881-82; chief engr. Atlantic & Pacific Ry., 1882-83; chief engr. Northern div. Mexican Central Ry. at Chihuahua, Mex., 1883-84; asst. chief engr. A.,T.&S.F. Ry., 1884-88, at Topeka, and constructed 1,348 miles in Kan., Ind. Ty. and Tex.; city engr. of Topeka, 1889-94; chief engr. Mexican Central Ry., 1895-1909; engr. maintenance of way, Nat. Rys. of Mexico. Died Jan. 23, 1912.

KINGSBURY, Frederick John, banker; b. Waterbury, Conn., Jan. 1, 1823; s. Charles Denison and Eliza (Leavenworth) K.; A.B., Yale, 1846, A.M., 1849; (LL.D., Williams, 1893, Yale, 1899); m. Alathea R. Scovill, Apr. 29, 1851. Admitted to Boston bar, 1848; practiced law, Waterbury, 1849-53; identified with banking business, 1850—; cashier, 1853-68, pres. 1868—, Citizens' Nat. Bank; v.p. Scovill Mfg. Co.; asst. treas. Waterbury Savings Bank. Mem. Conn. Ho. of Rep., 1850, 58, 65; pres. Hotchkiss Sch., Lakeville, Conn., 1893-99; commr. Centennial Exhbn., Phila., 1876; mem. Corp. Yale, 1881-99. Republican. Episcopalian. Home: Waterbury, Conn. Died 1910.

KINGSBURY, Joseph Thomas, educator; b. E. Weber, Utah, Nov. 4, 1853; s. Joseph Cordon and Dorcas (Moore) K.; A.B., Ill. Wesleyan, 1892, later A.M., Ph.D.; hon. Sc.D., U. of Utah, 1894, and LL.D., 1916; m. Jane Mair, of Dundee, Scotland, Aug. 7, 1879. Instr. and prof., 1878-92, acting pres., 1892-94, prof., 1894-97, pres., 1897-1916, emeritus, U. of Utah; in charge grad. work, same univ., 1917-24. Mem. State Bd. Edn., Utah, 1897-1931 (emeritus). Home: Salt Lake City, Utah. Died 1937.

KINGSBURY, Kenneth Raleigh, pres. Standard Oil Co. of Calif.; b. Columbus, O., Jan. 22, 1876; s. Francis Homer and Mary Isabella (Wilson) K.; Princeton, 1896; course in Mining Engring., Columbia, 1896-97; m. Mary Bell Gwin Follis, Mar. 14, 1917. Began with Standard Oil Co., in Pa., 1897; elected v.p. Standard Oil Co. (Calif.), 1911, pres., 1919—; dir. Anglo-Calif. Nat. Bank, Del Monte Properties Co. Republican. Presbyn. Mason. Home: San Francisco, Calif. Died Nov. 22, 1937.

KINGSBURY, Nathan Corning, officer corps.; b. Mentor, O., July 29, 1866; s. Selden Bingham and Hulda W. (Corning) K.; ed. Oberlin Coll., 1886-88; Law Dept., Ohio State U., 1898; passed Sup. Ct. examination, for admission to bar; m. Lillian B. Prescott, June 6, 1893. Asst. gen. mgr., Marinette Iron Works, West Duluth, Minn., 1890-97; gen. counsel, Jeffrey Mfg. Co., Columbus, O., 1898-1906; v.p. Mich. State Telephone Co., 1907, pres., 1907-10, now dir.; v.p. Harris Trust & Savings Bank, Chicago, 1910-11, now dir.; 1st v.p., dir., mem. exec. com. Am. Tel. & Tel. Co., New York, Jan. 1, 1911—. Republican. Conglist. Mason. Home: New York, N.Y. Died Jan. 24, 1920.

KINGSBURY, Selden Bingham, judge; b. Camden, Ohio, Oct. 29, 1840; s. Charles Bingham and Betsy (Tennant) K.; A.B., Oberlin Coll., 1864, A.M., 1871; m. Hulda W. Corning, Aug. 17, 1865 (died 1901); m. 2d, Katydid J. Jones, Sept. 25, 1907. Left Oberlin Coll., Apr. 20, 1861, and enlisted in Co. C, 7th Ohio Vol. Inf., reenlisted June 1861, for 3 yrs.; taken prisoner after Battle of Cross Lanes; confined in Libby Prison 1 mo., removed to Parish prison, N.C., then to Salisbury, N.C.; released on parole Aug. 1862; exchanged, 1864. Supt. schs., Flint, Mich., and Constantine, Mich., 8 yrs.; admitted to bar, Coldwater, Mich., 1876; practiced in Constantine and vicinity until 1881, Hailey, Idaho, 1881-93, Boise, 1893-1903; traveled 3 yrs. and settled in Honolulu; judge 2d Circuit, H. Ty., by apptmt. of President Roosevelt, Feb. 9, 1909—. Republican. Conglist. Died Dec. 20, 1915.

KINGSLAND, Mrs. Burton (pseudonym), author; b. New York. Writes for pleasure and contributes proceeds to charity. Author: The Book of Good Manners; The Book of Weddings; The Book of In-door and Out-door Games. Home: New York, N.Y. Deceased.

KINGSLEY, Chester Ward, banker, merchant; b. Brighton (now part of Boston), June 9, 1824; s. Moses and Mary K.; grad. Brighton High Sch.; m. Mary J. Todd, 1846. Began business as messenger, later becoming teller Bank of Brighton; cashier Cambridge Market Bank, 1851-56; mercantile business, 1856-65; from 1865 in coal mining; now part owner Excelsior mine, Northumberland Co., Pa.; pres. Bank of Brighton, 1879-87; has been mem. sch. com., bd. of aldermen and water bd. of Cambridge; mem. Mass. Ho. Reps., 1882, 83, 84, Senate 1888, 89. Has aided Worcester Acad. largely; its "Kingsley laboratories" were named for him; gave it additional $25,000 in 1898, and $25,000 each to Colby Univ., Am. Bapt. Missionary Union, Am. Bapt. Publ. Soc., Am. Bapt. Home Mission Soc., Newton Theol. Instn., Mass. Bapt. Conv. and Brown Univ. Home: N. Cambridge, Mass. Died 1904.

KINGSLEY, Clarence Darwin, ednl. engr.; b. Syracuse, N.Y., July 12, 1874; s. Edwin A. and Emma Howell (Garnsey) K.; student Syracuse High Sch., 1889-92; B.S., Colgate, 1897; M.A., Teachers Coll. (Columbia), 1904; studied summers at Cornell U., Harvard, New York Sch. of Philanthropy; m. H. Elizabeth Seelman, June 26, 1914. Instr. mathematics, Colgate, 1898-1902; teacher Manual Training High Sch., Brooklyn, 1904-12; state supervisor high schs., Mass. Dept. Edn., 1912-23; ednl. engr. specializing on sch. building programs and plans and serving as consultant in various cities, 1923—; teacher ednl. dept. Harvard Summer Sch., 1917-21, U. of Mich. Summer Sch., 1923. Chmn. commn. on reorganization of secondary edn., apptd. by N.E.A., 1912—. Editor of Reports on Commn. on Reorganization of Secondary Edn. (15 separate repts. on different subjects, pub. by U.S. Bur. Edn.). Home: Chicago, Ill. Died Dec. 31, 1926.

KINGSLEY, Darwin Pearl, life underwriter; b. Alburg, Vt., May 5, 1857; s. H. P. and Celia P. (LaDue) K.; A.B., U. of Vt., 1881, A.M., 1884, LL.D., 1904, L.H.D., 1916; m. Mary M. Mitchell, June 19, 1884; 1 son, Walton Pearl; m. 2d, Josephine I. McCall, Dec. 3, 1895; children—Hope, Darwin Pearl, John McCall, Lois. State auditor Colo., 1887-88. V.p., 1898-1907, pres., 1907-31, chmn. bd., 1931—, N.Y. Life Ins. Co. Trustee U. of Vt.; life mem. Am. Mus. of Natural History; pres. Chamber of Commerce, New York, 1920-21. Republican. Home: New York, N.Y. Died Oct. 6, 1932.

KINGSLEY, Elbridge, painter, engraver; b. Carthage, O., Sept. 17, 1842; s. Moses W. and Rachel W. K.; grad. Hopkins Acad., Hadley, Mass.; studied in art schs., Cooper Union, New York; m. Elizabeth W. Cook, 1870. Commenced engraving with Century Co. about 1878; started School of Painter Engraving about 1880, with original work; awarded gold medals, Paris Expn., 1889, Chicago Expn., 1893, Calif. Expn., 1894. Died Aug. 28, 1918.

KINGSLEY, Florence Morse, author; b. nr. Medina, O., July 14, 1859; d. Jonathan Bradley and Eleanor (Ecob) Morse; ed. Wellesley Coll. (was not grad.); m. Charles R. Kingsley, July 12, 1882; children—Charles Rawson, Donald Morse, Mrs. Grace Pouch, James Morse, John Bradley. Author: The Transfiguration of Miss Philura, 1901; The Needle's Eye, 1902; Balm in Gilead, 1907; The Return of Caroline, 1911; Veronica, 1913; The Life of Henry Fowle Durant, Founder of Wellesley College, 1923. Photo plays: An Alabaster Box, To the Highest Bidder, Love's Foreclosure. Home: Westerleigh, S.I., N.Y. Died Oct. 26, 1937.

KINGSLEY, J(ohn) Sterling, biologist; b. Cincinnatus, N.Y., Apr. 7, 1853; s. Lewis and Julia A. (Kingman) K.; A.B., Williams Coll., 1875; Sc.D., Princeton, 1885; U. of Freiburg, 1891-92; m. Mary Emma Read, Jan. 31, 1882. Curator, Peabody Acad. Science, 1876-78; asst., U.S. Entomol. Commn., 1877-80; curator, Worcester Natural History Soc., 1881-82; prof. zoölogy, Ind. U., 1887-89; prof. biology, U. of Neb., 1889-91, Tufts Coll., 1892-1913; prof. zoölogy, University of Ill., 1913-21, now emeritus. Editor of Standard Natural History, 1882-86, Am. Naturalist, 1884-96, Journal of Morphology, 1910-20. Author: Elements of Comparative Zöology, 1896; Vertebrate Zoölogy, 1899; Guides for Vertebrate Dissection, 1907; Comparative Anatomy of Vertebrates, 1912, 3d edit., 1926; Vertebrate Skeleton, 1925. Translator: Hertwig's Manual of Zoölogy, 1902, revised 1912. Home: 2500 Cedar St., Berkeley, Calif. Died Aug. 29, 1929.

KINGSLEY, Norman William, dentist and sculptor; b. St. Lawrence Co., N.Y., Oct. 26, 1829; s. Nathaniel and Eliza (Williams) K.; ed. pub. schs. and acads.; D.D.S., Baltimore Dental Coll., 1870; M.D.S., U. of State of N.Y.; m. Alma W. Shepard, 1850. Began dental practice Owego, N.Y., 1850; removed to New York, 1852; founded, 1866, New York Coll. Dentistry, dean and prof. Pres. State Dental Soc., 1884-85, Dist. Dental Soc., New York, etc. Executed several works of statuary in marble and bronze, including heroic bust of Christ in marble, 1868, portrait bust in bronze of Whitelaw Reid, 1884. Home: Warren Point, N.J. Deceased.

KINGSLEY, Willey Lyon, mfr., banker; b. Rome, N.Y., June 28, 1866; s. Willey J. P. (M.D.) and Georgeanna M. (Vogell) K.; B.A., Yale, 1886; M.D., Harvard, 1891; m. Lucy Stevens, Jan. 22, 1918. Pres. Rome Mfg. Co., 1892-1919, Rome-Turney Radiator Co., 1905-21, Rome Brass & Copper Co., 1908-19, Rome Locomotive & Machine Works, 1916-19, Rome Metal Co., and Rome Tube Co. until merged with Rome Brass & Copper Co.; now chmn. bd. Farmers Nat. Bank & Trust Co.; owner Rome Sporting Goods Mfg. Company, Kingsley Peach Orchard (Pinehurst, N.C.), Kingsley Wheat Ranches (Kansas); also owner Fla. real estate, etc. Chmn. Police Commn. Rome, 1894-1907; chmn. Liberty Loan Com. and Rome War Chest, World War; trustee Jervis Library Assn., Am. Red Cross; hon. pres. Boy Scouts, Rome. V.p. Property Owners' Assn. of Palm Beach, Fla. Donor of Boy Scouts Camp (Rome), club house and grounds of Woman's Gen. Study Club. Home: Rome, N.Y. Died Apr. 6, 1931.

KINKADE, Reynolds Robert, judge, retired; b. in Keokuk Co., Ia., Mar. 3, 1854; s. Eleazer and Hannah (Lyons) K.; studied law at Toledo; m. Addie George, June 15, 1881; children—Arthur (dec.), Mollie (Mrs. C. N. Rakestraw). Admitted to Ohio bar, 1878; in practice at Toledo and Marquette, Mich., 1878-99; judge Court of Common Pleas of Ohio, 1899-1908; judge Circuit Court, 1908-14; judge Court of Appeals, 1914-24; judge Supreme Court of Ohio, 1914-33, retired. Republican. Protestant. Elk. Home: Toledo, O. Died May 25, 1935.

KINKAID, Moses Pierce, congressman; b. in Monongalia Co., W.Va., Jan. 24, 1854; s. John and Amelia K.; LL.B., U. of Mich., 1876 (pres. class of 1876). Practiced in Henry Co., Ill., 1876-80, Pierre, S.D., 1880-81, Holt Co., Neb., 1881—. Mem. Neb. Senate, 1883-85; judge Dist. Ct., 12th Dist., 1887-1900; candidate for justice Supreme Ct., 1896; mem. 58th to 67th Congresses (1903-23), 6th Neb. Dist. Republican. Author of One Section homestead law which has promoted the development of Neb. Home: O'Neill, Neb. Died July 6, 1922.

KINKAID, Thomas Wright, naval officer; b. Cincinnati, O., Feb. 27, 1860; s. William P. and Susan (Monahan) K.; grad. U.S. Naval Acad., 1880; m. Virginia Lee Cassin, Apr. 3, 1883. Promoted asst. engr., June 10, 1882; passed asst. engr., Nov. 11, 1892; transferred to the line as lt., Mar. 3, 1899; lt. comdr., Nov. 2, 1902; comdr., July 1, 1907; capt., Mar. 1, 1911; rear admiral, Oct. 15, 1917. Served on Machias, Spanish-Am. War, 1898; on Oregon, 1901-04; fleet engineer Asiatic Fleet, 1904; duty at Navy Yard, Norfolk, Va., 1904-06; fleet engr. Pacific Squadron, 1906-07; insp. engring. material, Chester, Pa., 1907-08; head of dept. steam engring., Navy Yard, Norfolk, 1908-09; at Engring. Expt. Sta., U.S. Naval Acad., 1909-10; apptd. head of engring., Expt. Sta., Annapolis, Md., Sept. 26, 1910. Home: Annapolis, Md. Died Aug. 11, 1920.

KINKEAD, Edgar Benton, lawyer; b. Beverly, O., Mar. 14, 1862; s. Isaac B. and Hannah A. (Thornburg) K.; student Marietta Coll., 1880-82; m. Nellie M. Snyder, Jan. 20, 1883. Admitted to bar, 1889; prof. law, Coll. of Law, Ohio State U., 1895—; spl. counsel of State of Ohio in important anti-trust litigation, 1897-98; judge Ct. of Common Pleas, Franklin Co., O., 1909-15. Republican. Wrote History of Supreme Court of Ohio for The Green Bag, 1895. Author: Self-Preparation (Kinkead and Black); Code Pleading, 1895, 1898; Kinkead's Common Law Pleading; Kinkead's Instructions to Jury and Judgment Entries; Probate Law and Practice; Kinkead's Practice; Kinkead on Torts; Kinkead's Jurisprudence Law and Ethics. Home: Columbus, O. Died Apr. 9, 1930.

KINKHEAD, John Henry, miner, gov.; b. Smithfield, Pa., Dec. 10, 1826; s. James and Catherine (Bushey) K.; ed. Lancaster (O.) high sch.; m. Lizzie Fall, Jan. 1856. Began business life, 1844, as dry goods clerk in St. Louis; crossed plains to Salt Lake City, 1849; mem. mercantile firm Livingston & Kinkhead, 1849-54; removed to Calif., 1854, and engaged in stock-raising; in mercantile business, Marysville, Calif., 1856-60, Carson City, Nev., 1860; treas. Nev. Ty., 1862-65; mem. 2 constl. convs. which met to organize a State. Was in Alaska, 1867-71; mem. 1st govt. expdn. under Col. J. C. Davis, apptd. postmaster by President Johnson, and was first U.S. official holding civil office in Alaska. Returned to Nev., 1871; engaged as miner and smelter at Unionville, and built other works; founder Washoe City; gov. Nevada, 1879-83; 1st territorial gov. Alaska, 1884-85. Republican. Home: Carson City, Nev. Died 1904.

KINNAN, Alexander Phoenix Waldron, capitalist; b. N.Y. City, Mar. 13, 1856; s. Alexander Phoenix and Margaret Jane (Ostrander) K.; ed. Lawrenceville (N.J.) Sch.; m. Charlotte Ora Morris, Dec. 14, 1887. Pres. Union Dime Savings Bank; treas. and dir. Arrow Realty Co.; dir. City of New York Ins. Co., J. Romaine Brown Co., New York Plate Glass Ins. Co., Tilden Investing Co., Mutual Bank, Met. Life Ins. Co. Trustee Lawrenceville Sch. Republican. Episcopalian. Home: New York, N.Y. Died Jan. 23, 1924.

KINNANE, John E., lawyer; b. Kalamazoo, Mich., Jan. 10, 1862; s. Patrick and Mary Meade (Sullivan) K.; A.B., Kalamazoo Coll., 1885; m. Maud Crosbie,

1897; children—Margaret A., Janet E. Teacher pub. schs. 2 yrs.; county sch. commr., Bay Co., Mich., 1888-93; began practice of law, 1889; pros. atty., Bay Co., 1893-95; Dem. candidate for justice Supreme Court of Mich., 1911; chmn. Mich. Industrial Accident Bd. (administering the state workmen's compensation law), 1912-16; pres. Nat. Assn. Industrial Accident Bds. and Commns., 1913-15; U.S. dist. atty., Eastern Dist. Mich., 1916-22, resigned to resume practice of law. Pres. Board of Commerce of Bay City. Elk. Home: Bay City, Mich. Died Aug. 3, 1936.

KINNE, Edward DeWitt, judge; b. DeWitt Centre, N.Y., Feb. 9, 1842; s. Julius C. and Rachel W. (Wetherby) K.; A.B., U. of Mich., 1864; LL.B., Columbian Law Sch., Washington, 1867; m. Winifred L. Morse, Aug. 21, 1905. Began practice, Ann Arbor, Mich., 1867; recorder of Ann Arbor, 1869; city atty., 1871; mayor, 1876; mem. Mich. Ho. of Rep., 1879; circuit judge 22d Jud. Circuit of Mich., 5 terms, of 6 yrs. each, 1887-1917, declined reëlection. Republican. Pres. 1st Nat. Bank, Washtenaw Gas Co. Episcopalian. Mason. Home: Ann Arbor, Mich. Died July 25, 1921.

KINNE, Helen, prof. domestic science; b. at Norwich, Conn.; d. Henry Clay and Helen (Waterman) K.; diploma, Teachers Coll. (Columbia), 1890; unmarried. Teacher pvt. classes, 1886-88; instr. in domestic science, 1891-97, prof., 1897—, Teachers Coll. (Columbia). Chmn. teaching sect., Lake Placid Home Economics Conf., 1906-09; chmn. on courses of study, Am. Home Economics, 1909-10; pres. N.Y. Assn. for Home Economics 1909-12. Author: Domestic Science Equipment, 1909; Methods of Teaching Domestic Science, 1912; Foods and Household Management, 1913. Home: Woodbury, Conn. Died Dec. 29, 1917.

KINNE, La Vega G., lawyer; b. Syracuse, N.Y., Nov. 5, 1846; s. Æsop K.; ed. high school, Syracuse, N.Y.; grad. law dept. Univ. of Mich., 1868 (LL.D., Western Coll., Toledo, Ia.); m. Mary E. Abrams, Sept. 23, 1869. Judge dist. court, 17th jud. dist., Iowa, for 5 yrs.; judge Supreme Court of Iowa, 1892-97, chief justice, 1897; mem., April 1898—, now chmn. bd. Control State Instns; law lecturer at Univ. of Iowa Law School for 10 yrs.; law lecturer Iowa Coll. of Law, Des Moines, 1897—; mem. for Iowa Commn. on Uniformity of Laws of U.S. Democrat. Author: Kinne's Pleading and Practice. Home: Des Moines, Ia. Died 1906.

KINNEAR, James Wesley, lawyer; b. Tidioute, Pa., Aug. 2, 1859; s. James and Jeannette Stratton (Parshall) K.; A.B., Allegheny Coll., Pa., 1882 (Phi Beta Kappa); student U. of Pa. Dept. of Law, 1884-85; m. Edith M. Rich, May 12, 1886. Admitted to Pa. bar, 1887, and began practice at Pittsburgh; mem. Kinnear, McClockey & Best; 1st v.p. Washington Steel & Ordnance Co., Firth Sterling Steel Company; pres. Wolf Tongue Mining Co. and Am. Stainless Steel Co. Trustee Allegheny Coll., Internat. S.S. Assn., Pa. State Sabbath Sch. Assn.; chmn. exec. com. World's S.S. Assn. Republican. Methodist. Mason. Home: Pittsburgh, Pa. Died Sept. 8, 1922.

KINNEAR, Wilson Sherman, civil engr.; b. Circleville, O., May 25, 1864; s. Richard and Mary Hall (Crow) K.; A.B., U. of Kan., 1884, C.E., 1907; m. Carrie M. Nichols, Nov. 13, 1887; children—Mrs. Carmen Johnston, Lawrence Wilson. In ry. constrn. in Middle West and Chile, S.A., 1884-90; asst. engr., asst. chief engr., asst. supt., asst. gen. supt., chief engr. and asst. gen. mgr., M.C. R.R., 1890-1910; pres. Kansas City Terminal Ry. Co., Sept. 1, 1910-May 1, 1912; pres. U.S. Realty & Improvement Co., New York, 1912-17; sr. partner W. S. Kinnear & Co., cons. engrs., New York, 1918. While asst. gen. mgr. Michigan Central R.R., as chief engr. Detroit River Tunnel Co., built electrically operated tunnel under Detroit River, between Detroit and Windsor, Can., 1¾ miles in length and has largest cross-sectional area of any sub-aqueous tunnel in the world. The method employed in constrn. of river section, ½ mile in length, was so novel and daring that its successful completion marked an epoch in engring. history, tending to revolutionize sub-aqueous tunnel constrn. Awarded Norman medal, Am. Soc. C.E., 1912. Retired. Home: Grosse Pointe, Mich. Died Aug. 8, 1941.

KINNETT, William Ennis, M.D., surgeon; b. Hamilton Co., O., July 3, 1849; s. William Philip and Nancy Ann (Brown) K.; Normal Sch., Taylorville, Ill.; M.D., Eclectic Med. Inst. (now Eclectic Med. Coll.), Cincinnati, O., 1876; m. Mary Elizabeth Cave, Oct. 14, 1875 (died 1886); children—Ira J. (dec.), Stella A. (dec.), Lily D. (Mrs. Alvah L. Hill); m. 2d, Elizabeth Roberts Austin, Sept. 7, 1887. Began practice at Palmer, Ill., 1876; practiced at Yorkville, 1880-1905; settled in Peoria, Ill., 1905; dean Faculty of Teachers of Clinic of Orificial Clinic of Am. Assn. Orificial Surgeons, 1912—; prof. in Sch. of Orificial Surgeons. Republican. Baptist. Mason. Home: Peoria, Ill. Died Feb. 9, 1929.

KINNEY, Abbot, publisher; b. Brookside, N.J., Nov. 16, 1850; s. Franklin Sherwood and Mary (Cogswell) K.; m. Margaret, d. Justice James Dabney Thornton, of San Francisco, Nov. 18, 1884; m. 2d, Mrs. Winifred Harwell Kinney, d. Courtland Harwell, of Kansas City, Mo., March 1913. Went to Calif., 1880; founded city of Ocean Park, Calif., 1894, Venice of America, 1904, pres. 3 mercantile and 1 ry. cos.; propr. and pub. Los Angeles Saturday Post, 1900—. Spl. commr. Mission Indians, with late Helen Hunt Jackson, 1883; officer U.S. Geol. Survey, 1873; chmn. Calif. State Bd. Forestry, 1884-87. Maj. Calif. N.G., 1888-92. Pres. Southern Calif. Acad. Sciences, 1890-1900, Southern Calif. Pomol. Soc., 1882-92, Southern Calif. Forest and Water Soc., 1896-1909; v.p. Am. Forestry Assn. for Calif.; v.p. Water and Forestry Assn. of Los Angeles Co.; pres. Calif. Forestry Soc. Builder and propr. Venice of America Aquarium, for Calif. coast fishes, and Venice Marine Biol. Sta. of U. of Southern Calif. Home: Venice, Calif. Died Nov. 4, 1920.

KINNEY, Bruce, missionary supt.; b. E. Townsend, O., Dec. 12, 1865; s. Edwin and Elizabeth (Godden) K.; A.B., Denison U., 1892, D.D., 1912; B.D., U. of Chicago, 1897; m. Anna Belle Moore, Feb. 19, 1894 (died 1898); children—Edwin Hamilton (dec.), Kathleen Moore (dec.); m. 2d, Mabel Emma Alger, May 31, 1900; children—Dorothy Joy, Marian Alger, Carolyn Elizabeth, Winifred Bruce. Pastor, Fultonham, O., 1890-92; ordained Bapt. ministry, 1893; pastor, Plano, Ill., 1893-94, Windsor Park, Chicago, 1894-97, Sioux Falls, S.D., 1897-98, Albuquerque, N.M., 1898-1902; gen. missionary Am. Bapt. Home Mission Soc., 1902-07; supt. missions and dist. sec. Am. Bapt. Home Mission Soc. for Southwest Dist., 1907-14; gen. supt. for midland div. (10 states W. of Miss. River), 1914-19; joint div. sec. Am. Bapt. Home Mission Soc. and Am. Bapt. Publn. Soc., for states west of the Mississippi, 1919-22; gen. supt. Indian missions for Am. Bapt. Home Missionary Soc., 1922-Jan. 1, 1936 (retired); interim pastor South Hills Bapt. Ch., Cleveland, O., Sept.-Oct. 1936. Author: Mormonism—The Islam of America, 1912; Kingdom Preparedness, 1916; The Pith and Pathos of Frontier Missions, 1917; Frontier Missionary Problems, 1918; also one chapter of The Moccasin Trail, 1932; one chapter of The Gospels from the Mountains, 1936; one devotional of The Upward Look, 1936. Home: Denver, Colo. Died Oct. 15, 1936.

KINNEY, Coates, writer; b. Kinney's Corners, N.Y., Nov. 24, 1826; s. Giles and Myra (Cornell) K.; removed to Ohio, 1840; ed. common schools, acad. and 1 term Antioch Coll.; admitted to bar, 1856; m. Hanna Kelly, 1851; m. 2d, Mary C. Allen, 1862. Edited Xenia Torchlight, Cincinnati Daily Times, Springfield Daily Republic, etc.; was maj. and paymaster U.S.A. during Civil war; mustered out with bvt. rank of lt. col.; mem. Ohio senate, 1881-82. Author: Keuka, 1855; Lyrics, 1888; Mists of Fire and Some Eclogues, 1899. The famous lyric, "Rain on the Roof," is included in this last volume. Home: Xenia, O. Died 1904.

KINNEY, Thomas Tallmadge, pres. Fidelity Trust Co., of Newark, N.J.; b. Newark, N.J., Aug. 12, 1821; grad. Princeton, 1841 (A.M.); m. Estelle Condit, Oct. 1863. Admitted to bar, 1844; editor and propr. Newark Daily Advertiser, 1851-92; delegate to Nat. Rep. conv. and worked for Lincoln's nomination, 1860. Pres. State bd. of agr. of N.J., 1878-82; mem. State bd. of geology; several years pres. N.J. Soc. for Prevention of Cruelty to Animals. Pres. Fidelity Trust Co. from its origin. Home: Newark, N.J. Died 1900.

KINNEY, Troy, artist, author; b. Kansas City, Mo., Dec. 1, 1871; s. William C. and Mary (Troy) K.; A.B., Yale, 1896; studied Yale Sch. of Fine Arts, and Chicago Art Inst.; m. Margaret West, June 9, 1900; 1 son, John West. Etchings and paintings, principally subjects relating to the dance. Historical and analytical articles on the dance in principal Am. and Spanish-Am. mags. With wife, mural paintings, designs, illustrations. Co-author: The Dance, Its Place in Art and Life, 1914; The Etchings of Troy Kinney, 1929; Troy Kinney (Vol. IX, American Etchers), 1930. Associate of Nat. Academy of Design. Home: Falls Village, Conn. Died Jan. 29, 1938.

KINNICUTT, Francis Parker, physician; b. Worcester, Mass., July 13, 1846; s. Francis Harrison and Elizabeth Waldo (Parker) K.; bro. of Leonard Parker K.; A.B., Harvard, 1868, A.M., 1872; M.D., Coll. Phys. and Surg. (Columbia), 1871; univs. of Heidelberg and Vienna, 1871-73; m. Eleonora Kissel, Nov. 19, 1875. Prof. clin. medicine, Coll. Phys. and Surg., 1893—; phys. to Presbyn. Hosp.; cons. physician to St. Luke's, Woman's, Hosp. for Ruptured and Crippled, Babies', Presbyn. and other hosps.; mem. bd. med. dirs. Cancer Hosp. Trustee General Memorial Hosp.; dir. Brearly Sch., Ltd. Pres. Assn. Am. Physicians, 1906-07; dir. Children's Aid Society. Died May 2, 1913.

KINNICUTT, Leonard Parker, chemist; b. Worcester, Mass., May 22, 1854; s. Francis Harrison and Elizabeth Waldo (Parker) K.; bro. of Francis Parker K.; B.Sc., Mass. Inst. Tech., 1875; univs. of Heidelberg and Bonn, 1875-79, Johns Hopkins, 1879-80; D.Sc., Harvard, 1882; m. Louisa Hoar, d. Dr. Henry Clarke, of Worcester, June 4, 1885 (died 1892); m. 2d, Frances Ayres, d. Josiah H. Clarke, of Worcester, July 8, 1898. Instr. chemistry, Harvard, 1880-83; asst. prof. chemistry, 1883-85, prof., 1885—, dir. Chem. Lab., 1890—, Worcester Poly. Inst. Consulting chemist Conn. Sewage Commn., 1903-05. Fellow Am. Acad. Arts and Sciences, A.A.A.S. (v.p. 1904). Home: Worcester, Mass. Died 1911.

KINNICUTT, Lincoln Newton, banker; b. Worcester, Mass., Mar. 14, 1849; s. Francis Harrison and Elizabeth Waldo (Parker) K.; ed. Worcester pub. schs. and in Europe; m. Edith Perley, Oct. 10, 1878. Engaged in father's hardware business, 1867-77; with pvt. banking firm, 1877-84; sr. mem. Kinnicutt & DeWitt, bankers, 1884—; trustee Worcester County Instn. for Savings. Trustee, treas. Worcester Art Mus., 1896—; trustee Worcester Poly. Inst., 1906—. Republican. Wrote: Indian Names in Worcester County; Indian Names in Plymouth County. Author: To Your Dog and to My Dog; King Cole and His Indian Friends. Home: Worcester, Mass. Died Dec. 1921.

KINSLEY, William Wirt, author; b. Buffalo, Oct. 8, 1837; s. William and Caroline K.; A.B., Oberlin Coll., 1861; m. Mary A. Jewell, Oct. 11, 1865. Mem. Co. C, 7th Ohio Vols., 1861; prof. mathematics, Northern Ind. Coll., 1861-64; in auditor gen.'s office, Lansing, Mich., until 1872; entered U.S. Pension Bur., 1872; mem. Bd. of Review, Pension Office, 1881-1909, when resigned; in lit. work, 1909—. Author: Old Faiths and New Facts, 1896; The Bronte Sisters, 1899; Man's Tomorrow, 1911; Does Prayer Avail?, 1911; Was Christ Divine?, 1912; The Three Great Questions, 1912. Home: E. Falls Church, Va. Died July 12, 1923.

KINSMAN, David Nathaniel, physician; b. Heath, Mass., May 3, 1834; s. Bliss and Betsey (Temple) K.; ed. Deerfield (Mass.) Acad.; M.D., Med. Coll. of Ohio, 1863; m. Isabella Stevens, July 20, 1857 (dec.). Practiced at Circleville, O., 1863-66, then at Columbus; prof. diseases of women and children, 1872-74, prof. nervous diseases, 1892-98, Starling Med. Coll.; prof. practice of medicine, Columbus Med. Coll., 1875-92; prof. practice of medicine, Ohio Med. U., 1893-1907. Mem. Ohio Live Stock Commn., 1886-1900; health officer, Columbus, 1893-97. Republican. Conglist. Mason. Home: Columbus, O. Died 1911.

KINSOLVING, George Herbert, bishop; b. Bedford Co., Va., Apr. 28, 1849; s. Rev. Ovid A. and Julia Heiskell (Krauth) K.; ed. U. of Va., 1867-69; grad. P.E. Theol. Sem., Va., 1874; (D.D., U. of the South; S.T.D., Griswold Coll., 1892); m. Grace Jaggar, sister Bishop T. A. Jaggar, Oct. 8, 1879. Deacon, 1874, priest, 1875, P.E. Ch.; asst. at Christ Ch., Baltimore, 1874-75; rector St. Mark's, Baltimore, 1875-78, St. John's, Cincinnati, 1878-81, Ch. of the Epiphany, Phila., 1881-92; elected asst. bishop of Tex., 1892, and succeeded late Bishop Gregg as bishop of Tex., July 11, 1893. Was mem. Standing Com. Diocese of Pa.; overseer P.E. Div. Sch., Phila. Home: Austin, Tex. Died Oct. 23, 1928.

KINSOLVING, Lucien Lee, bishop; b. Loudoun Co., Va., May 14, 1862; s. Rev. Ovid A. and Lucy Lee (Rogers) K.; ed. Episcopal High Sch., Alexandria, Va., and U. of Va.; grad. Va. Theol. Sem., 1889; S.T.D., U. of Pa., 1899; m. Alice Brown, Jan. 7, 1892. Deacon and priest P.E. Ch., 1889; dean of convocation, mem. standing com. and missionary in State of Rio Grande, 1889-98; elected missionary bishop for the Brazilian Episcopal Ch., 1898, consecrated, Jan. 6, 1899; elected missionary bishop of Southern Brazil, 1907. Died Dec. 18, 1929.

KINTER, William Lewis, lawyer; b. nr. Millerstown, Pa., Apr. 19, 1877; s. John Henry and Anne E. (Smith) K.; grad. Chambersburg Acad., 1893; A.B., Lafayette Coll., Easton, Pa., 1897, A.M., 1900; m. Marjorie Boardman, Dec. 20, 1924. Admitted to Pa. bar, 1900, and began practice at Chambersburg; connected with legal dept. of the Reading Co., 1910—, gen. counsel, Mar. 1, 1929—. Republican. Presbyn. Home: Meadowbrook, Pa. Died Dec. 22, 1935.

KINTNER, Samuel Montgomery, elec. engr.; b. New Albany, Ind., Dec. 11, 1871; s. James Peter and Anna (Montgomery) K.; B.M.E., Purdue, 1894, hon. Dr. Engring., 1932; D.Sc., U. of Pittsburgh, 1930; m. Elizabeth Blanchard, Oct. 24, 1895 (now dec.); children—John Benham, Eleanor Magee (Mrs. George Constance); m. 2d, Almira Doherty, Jan. 1, 1916. Engr. Bell Telephone Co. of Ind., 1894-95; asst. prof. and prof., Western U. of Pa., 1895-1903; in research labs., Westinghouse Electric & Mfg. Co., 1903-07, in ry. engring. dept., 1907-11; gen. mgr. Nat. Electric Signaling Co., 1911-17, v.p., 1917-19, pres., 1919; in radio research, Westinghouse Electric & Mfg. Co., 1920-22, dir. research labs., 1922-30, asst. v.p., 1930-31, v.p., 1931—; dir. Westinghouse Electric Elevator Co., Westinghouse Lamp Co. Fellow Inst. Radio Engrs., Am. Phys. Society. Republican. Presbyn. Home: Pittsburgh, Pa. Died Sept. 28, 1936.

KINTZING, Pearce, physician; b. Liberty, Pa., Jan. 31, 1861; s. Tench Cox and Mary Musser (Dunn) K.; B.Sc., Lafayette Coll., 1881; M.D., U. of Pa., 1887; m. Theo. Helen Lorenzen, of Hamburg, Germany, Oct. 1, 1892. Has practiced at Baltimore, 1888—; prof. practice of medicine, Baltimore Polyclinic, 1889-95, anatomy and surgery, Woman's Med. Coll., 1890-97, practice of medicine and diseases of the heart and clin. medicine, Md. Med. Coll., 1899-

1901 and 1904—. Dir. and trustee Md. Med. Coll., Franklin Sq. Hosp., Alliance Française (silver medal from French Govt.). Author: Long Life and How to Attain It, 1908. Home: Baltimore, Md. Died Jan. 30, 1917.

KINYOUN, Joseph James, physician; b. East Bend, N.C., Nov. 25, 1860; s. John H. and Elizabeth (Conrad) K.; M.D., Bellevue Hosp. Med. Coll. (New York U.), 1882; Ph.D., Georgetown U., 1896. In practice of medicine from 1882; in med. corps Marine Hosp. Service, 1886-1902; prof. hygiene and bacteriology, 1890-92, pathology and bacteriology, 1892-99, Georgetown U. Decorated with Order of Bolivar of Venezuela, 1895. Home: Washington, D.C. Died Feb. 15, 1919.

KIP, Leonard, author; b. New York, Sept. 13, 1826; s. Leonard K.; grad. Trinity Coll., Hartford, 1846; (L.H.D., Trinity, 1893; LL.D., Hobart, 1893); admitted to bar; practiced for greater part of life at Albany; pres. Albany Inst., 10 yrs.; retired. Author: California Sketches, 1850; Volcano Diggings, 1851; Ænome, 1866; The Dead Marquis, 1873; Hannibal's Man, 1878; Under the Bells, 1879; Nestlenook, 1880. Home: Albany, N.Y. Died 1906.

KIPP, Charles John, surgeon; b. Hanover, Germany, Oct. 22, 1838; s. Henry and Minna (Dietrich) K.; came to U.S., 1854; ed. Hanover and New York; M.D., Coll. Phys. and Surg. (Columbia), 1861; unmarried. Acting asst. surgeon U.S.A., 1862; asst. surgeon U.S.V., 1863; maj. and surgeon, 1864; bvtd. lt. col. U.S.V., 1865; resigned from U.S.A., 1868. Surgeon Newark Eye and Ear Infirmary, 1880—; pres. bd. mgrs. N.J. Sanatorium for Tuberculous Diseases, 1901-06; pres. Babies' Hosp., Newark; pres. Soc. for Relief of Widows and Orphans of Med. Men of N.J. Pres. Am. Ophthal. Soc., 1907, Am. Otol. Soc., 1908. Home: Newark, N.J. Died 1911.

KIPP, George Washington, congressman; b. Pike Co., Pa., Mar. 28, 1847; s. John and Martha (Conell) K.; pub. sch. edn.; m. Martha A. Kizer, July 15, 1872. Engaged in lumber business, 1865-1900; now engaged in banking, ry. and other enterprises. Co. commr. Wayne Co., Pa., 1880; mem. 60th Congress (1907-09), 14th Pa. Dist. Democrat. Mason. Home: Towanda, Pa. Died 1911.

KIPPAX, John R., physician, author; b. Brantford, Ont., Nov. 5, 1849; s. Robert and Mary (Hargreaves) K.; M.D., Hahnemann Med. Coll., 1869; LL.B., Northwestern Univ., 1872; mem. Coll. Phys. and Surg., Ontario, 1880; m. Martha E. Wood, Oct. 18, 1877. In practice as homœo. physician, Chicago, 1869—. Prof. Hahnemann Med. Coll., 1872-76; pres. and late prof. practice of medicine, clinical medicine and legal medicine, Chicago Homœo. Med. Coll.; one of the founders, same (1876), and prof. there for 25 yrs.; late clinical lecturer and visiting physician, Cook Co. Charity Hosp.; emeritus prof. theory and practice of medicine and of clinical medicine, Hahnemann Med. Coll., 1905. Pres. Homœo. Med. Soc. Chicago, 1900-01. Asso. editor Universal Homœo. Annual, Paris, France, 1894; asso. editor Annual Record of Homœo. Literature, Phila., 1873. Author: Churchyard Literature, 1877; Hand-book of Skin Diseases, 6th edit., 1896; Lectures on Fevers, 1884; Medico-Legal Aspects of the Cremation Problem, 1901. Deceased.

KIRBY, Absalom, naval officer; b. Washington, D.C., Mar. 16, 1837; s. John and Georgianna (Eslin) K.; ed. pub. schs., Washington; m. Sarah Watson Hogg, July 16, 1862. Was engr. of the steamboat "Mt. Vernon," which carried Col. Ellsworth and his regt. to Alexandria the morning he was killed, May 24, 1861; apptd. 3d asst. engr., Oct. 3, 1861; promoted through all the grades; retired Feb. 15, 1898. Chief engr. of ships, Navy Yard, inspr. of machinery and fleet engr. on the blockade, 1861-65; participated in battle of Port Royal, Nov. 7, 1861, battle of Mobile Bay, Aug. 5, 1864; cruised in different parts of the world. Trustee Trinity M.E. Ch., Washington; mem. bd. dirs. Washington City Bible Soc. Republican. Home: Washington, D.C. Died Jan. 23, 1924.

KIRBY, Edmund Burgis, consulting mining engr.; b. Lyme, Conn.; s. Eliab Burgis and Caroline Lydia (Noyes) K.; E.M., Washington U., St. Louis, 1884; unmarried. Engaged in gen. consulting practice, with intervals of mine, mill or smelter management, 1885—. Home: New York, N.Y. Deceased.

KIRBY, Frank E., naval architect; b. Cleveland, O., July 1, 1849; s. Stephen R. and Martha A. (Johnston) K.; ed. pub. schs., Cleveland, and Saginaw, Mich., and Cooper Inst., New York; m. Mary F. Thorp, Oct. 9, 1876; 1 son, Russell T. Began on engring. staff, Allaire Works, New York, constructing machinery for war vessels, 1865; later with Morgan Iron Works; located in Detroit, 1870, and with bro. F. A., built iron ship yards, at Wyandotte, for Capt. E. B. Ward; consulting engr. (with bro.) until 1882, then with Detroit Dry Dock Co.; designed the steamer Frank E. Kirby; the St. Ignace and the St. Marie, 2 ice-crushing steamers plying between St. Ignace and Mackinaw City; all the boats of the Detroit & Cleveland Navigation Co., and hundreds of others. Mem. Detroit Bd. Water Works Commn., 1892-96; expert for U.S. Govt. in selection of ships for transport service, Spanish-Am. War, 1898. Republican. Home: Bronxville, N.Y. Died Aug. 25, 1929.

KIRBY, Fred Morgan, capitalist; b. Brownville, N.Y., Oct. 30, 1861; s. William and Angeline E. (Slater) K.; educated in public schools; m. Jessie Amelia Owen, May 27, 1886 (died 1933); children—Allan Price, Sumner Moore. Was in the employ of Moore & Smith, dry goods, Watertown, 1876-84; removed to Wilkes-Barre, Pa., and asso. with C. S. Woolworth in 5 and 10-cent store; purchased interest of partner, 1887, and became owner of 96 stores, located in nearly every state east of Miss. River; merged interests with F. W. Woolworth Co. and retired Jan. 1, 1912; v.p. F. W. Woolworth Co., New York; dir. Miners Nat. Bank of Wilkes-Barre; pres. Wilkes-Barre Ry. Co. Member board dirs. Wilkes-Barre Hosp., Wyoming Sem., Wilkes-Barre Y.M.C.A.; trustee Lafayette Coll., Easton, Pa., to which has given $100,000 to found Kirby Chair of Civil Rights; also gave $100,000 to Wyoming Sem. to insure the teaching of civil rights there; erected Kirby Hall of Civil Rights, Lafayette College, at a cost of approximately $500,000, 1930; also erected Angeline Elizabeth Kirby Memorial Health Center, Wilkes-Barre, Pa. (cost $2,000,000), 1931. Republican. Episcopalian. Mason. Home: Wilkes-Barre, Pa. Died Oct. 16, 1940.

KIRBY, George Hughes, psychiatrist; b. Goldsboro, N.C., Feb. 9, 1875; s. George L. and Mary C. (Green) K.; B.S., U. of North Carolina, 1896; LL.D., from same univ., 1929; M.D., L.I. Coll. Hosp. Med. Sch., 1899; m. Jeanette Kruszewska, Apr. 29, 1912; 1 dau., Jeanette Vincenta. Specialist in mental and nervous diseases; asst. phys., Worcester (Mass.) State Hosp., 1899-1902; asso. in clin. psychiatry, Psychiatric Inst., New York, 1902-08; dir. clin. psychiatry, Manhattan State Hosp., 1908-17; med. insp. N.Y. State Hosp. Commn., June-Oct. 1917; prof. psychiatry, Univ. and Bellevue Med. Coll., 1914-17; dir. N.Y. Psychiatric Inst., 1917-31; prof. psychiatry, Cornell U. Med. Coll., 1917-27, Coll. Phys and Surg. (Columbia), 1927-32; attending physician New York Hospital. Chief consulting psychiatrist, N.Y. City Dept. of Correction; mem med. advisory com. N.Y. State Hosp. Development Commn. Editor Am. Journal of Psychiatry. Commissioned major, M.C., U.S.A., July 26, 1918; attached to staff of surgeon of Port of Embarkation, New York; later apptd. chief of neuro-psychiatric service, U.S.A. Hosp. 1; assisted in organization of spl. unit for care of returning soldiers suffering from mental or nervous disorders; hon. discharged, Mar. 28, 1919. Consultant in neuropsychiatry U.S. Pub. Health Service, with rank of sr. surg., 1919—; apptd. by sec. of treasury, member Board of Consultants to Develop Hospital Facilities Throughout the Country for Ex-soldiers, 1921; mem. med. council, U.S. Veterans' Bur., Washington, D.C. Home: New York, N.Y. Died Aug. 11, 1935.

KIRBY, John, Jr., mfr.; b. Troy, N.Y., May 16, 1850; s. Peter and Charlotte K.; pub. sch. edn.; m. Merretta Smith Filkins, Oct. 25, 1871. Began at age of 12 in stove works, Waterford, N.Y.; supt. works of Post & Co., Cincinnati, 1875-83; v.p., gen. mgr. Dayton Mfg. Co., 1883-1917, and from then president of same; also pres. of U.S. Headlight Co., 1894—; v.p. Mercantile Metal Milling Co., 1908-13; mem. exec. com. Canadian Car & Foundry Co., in the execution of contracts with Russian Govt. for shell ammunition amounting to $83,000,000, 1915. Inventor and patentee of 88 U.S. patents in his special line. Pres. Dayton Bd. of Trade, 1898-1906; mem. exec. com. Dayton Chamber of Commerce, 1906-10; pres. Dayton Employers' Assn., 1901—, Nat. Assn. Mfrs., 1909-13; mem. administrative council Nat. Metal Trades Assn., 1903-08; an organizer Citizens' Industrial Assn. of America, 1904 (exec. com.); chmn. com. of 100 to erect $500,000 Y.M.C.A. bldg. at Dayton, 1904-09; mem. com. of 100 apptd. at Tariff Commn. Conv., Indianapolis, Feb. 1909 (exec. com.); dir. Nat. Tariff Commn. Assn., 1910—; chmn. Nat. Industrial Council, 1910-22; commr. to Australia and N.Z. for Nat. Assn. Mfrs., 1913; charter mem. Nat. Industrial Conf. Bd., 1916. Republican. Baptist. Home: Oakwood, Dayton, O. Died Dec. 29, 1925.

KIRBY, John Henry, lumberman; b. Peach Tree Village, Tex., Nov. 16, 1860; s. John Thomas and Sarah (Payne) K.; student Southwestern Univ., Georgetown, Tex.; LL.D., Lincoln Memorial University, 1923; read law in office of Sam Bronson Cooper, at Woodville, Tex.; m. Lelia Stewart, Nov. 14, 1883. Admitted to Tex. bar, Dec. 1885. In 1886, became interested in pine timber lands in Eastern Texas, inducing large investments therein by bankers and others of Boston, the management of the properties purchased being committed to his hands; moved to Houston, 1890; in 1893, began construction of Gulf, Beaumont & Kansas City R.R., which he sold to A.,T.&S.F. R.R., 1900; 1901 organized and became pres. the Kirby Lumber Co., with capital of $10,000,000. Pres. Texas World's Fair Commn. of St. Louis Expn., 1903. Mem. Tex. Ho. of Rep., 1912 and 1926; mem. President Harding's Unemployment Conf., 1921; Am. commr. to Brazilian Centennial Expn., 1922; chmn. Southern Com. to Uphold the Constitution, 1935. Mason. Democrat. Home: Houston, Tex. Died Nov. 9, 1940.

KIRBY, R(obert) Harper, financier; b. nr. Hempstead, Tex., Mar. 20, 1861; s. Jared Ellison and Helen Marr (Swearingen) K.; ed. Tex. Mil. Inst., Austin, Tex., 1876-79; Eastman's Business Coll., Poughkeepsie, N.Y., 1879; Vanderbilt U., 1881-82; U. of Tex., 1883; m. Annie E. McAshan, Aug. 28, 1883. Engaged in various lines of business, including land, farming, cattle, city property, timber and oil. Mem. bd. dirs. Am. Endowment Fund of Am. Legion of Tex. Chmn. Men and Religion Forward Movement; state chmn. statewide Prohibition Campaign, Tex., 1919 (traveled 55,000 miles, mostly in automobile, and spent over $100,000); donor of $2,000,000 to religious, charitable, educational philanthropic and other enterprises, among them the Harper and Annie Kirby Theol. Bldg. to Southern Methodist U., Dallas, Tex. Democrat. Fundamentalist (Methodist). Home: Austin, Tex. Died Apr. 16, 1928.

KIRBY, William Fosgate, judge, senator; b. Miller Co., Ark., Nov. 16, 1867; s. Joseph F. and Martha A. (Ferguson) K.; ed. pub. schs., Miller Co., Ark., and Bowie Co., Tex.; LL.B., Cumberland U., Tenn., 1885; m. Ella Kelley, Oct. 19, 1899; 1 son, William J. Practiced law at Texarkana from 1885; mem. Ark. Ho. of Rep., 1893, 1897, Senate, 1899-1901; compiled laws for state, Kirby's Digest Statutes, 1904; atty. gen. of Ark., 1907-08; defeated for Dem. nomination for gov., 1908; asso. justice Supreme Ct. of Ark., term 1910-18. Declined appmt. to U.S. Senate, 1913; elected U.S. senator, Nov. 7, 1916, for unexpired term (1916-21), and resigned from Supreme Court; after Senate service, resumed practice with former Gov. George W. Hays, firm of Kirby & Hays; elected asso. justice Supreme Court of Ark., 1926, for term 1927-35. Died July 26, 1934

KIRBYE, J. Edward; b. Eureka, Mich., Dec. 23, 1873; s. Oliver Perry and Clara Elizabeth (Steffee) K.; ed. Hillsdale Coll. (Mich.); A.B., Piedmont Coll., 1900; grad. student economics and history, U. of Va., 1907-08; D.D., Rollins Coll., Temple Coll. and St. Louis Univ.; m. Izabelle Clark, 1898; children—John E., Mrs. Mariam Schmidt. Pres. and prof. history Drury Coll., 1905-07; v.p. Morris Plan Bank (Des Moines, Ia.), 1914-23; pres. Citizens Industrial Loan Co., 1923; organizer and dir. Citizens Loan and Investment Co. (Milwaukee), 1923; organizer Fond du Lac (Wis.) Citizens Loan and Investment Co., 1924, Eau Claire (Wis.) Citizens Loan and Investment Co., 1924; v.p. Industrial Bank, Detroit. Student and traveler in Europe, 1908-13; minister Plymouth Ch., Des Moines, Ia., 1911-20, United Ch., Raleigh, N.C., 1927-35; Educational and social adviser Resettlement Adminstrn., Washington, D.C., 1935—. Spl. rep. Nat. Near East Relief Com. In Russia, Turkey and Greece, 1921. Trustee Elon (N.C.) Coll. Mason. Home: Memphis, Tenn. Died Nov. 13, 1939.

KIRCHHOFF, Charles (William Henry), editor; b. San Francisco, Calif., Mar. 28, 1853; s. Charles and Virginia (Siemsen) K.; grad. Royal Sch. of Mines, Clausthal, Germany, as mining engr. and metallurgist, 1874. Chemist of Del. Lead Refinery, Phila., 1874-77; asst. editor Metall. Rev., 1877-78, The Iron Age, 1878-81; mng. editor Engring. and Mining Jour., 1881-84; asso. editor, 1884-89, editor-in-chief, 1889-1910, The Iron Age; v.p. and gen. mgr. David Williams Co., New York, until 1910, when retired from business. Spl. agt. U.S. Geol. Survey for collection of statistics of production of lead, copper and zinc, 1883-1906. Home: New York, N.Y. Died July 22, 1916.

KIRCHNER, George H(enry), banker; b. Detroit, Mich., Jan. 1, 1866; s. Sebastian and Mary Ann (Luttenbacher) K.; ed. St. Joseph's Parochial Sch., Detroit; m. Fina Valentin, of Windsor, Ont., Can., June 23, 1892; children—Ralph T., Angus M., George H., Virginia (Mrs. William F. McDonnell), Constance (Mrs. Frank J. Murphy). Began business career as office boy, attorney's office, 1880; messenger for pvt. bank, 1881-85; bookkeeper for contractor, 1885-89; teller City Savings Bank, Detroit, 1889-94; asst. cashier German Am. Bank (name changed to First State Bank, 1917), 1894-1901, cashier, 1901-12, pres., 1912-27; chmn. bd. Griswold-First State Bank, 1927-28; retired Jan. 1, 1929; apptd. conservator Union Guardian Trust Co., Detroit, 1933, pres., 1934—. Catholic. Home: Detroit, Mich. Died Aug. 22, 1938.

KIRCHNER, Otto, lawyer; b. in Germany, July 13, 1846; s. Rudolph and Ottilie K.; came to U.S., 1854; educated mainly by his father; (hon. A.M., U. of Michigan, 1894; LL.D., 1919); m. Isabel Graham Beane, Feb. 17, 1869 (died 1884); 2d, Julia Edmunds, d. late Elijah Wood Meddaugh, Jan. 4, 1887. In practice at Detroit, 1867—; atty. gen. of Mich., 1877-81; prof. law, 1885-86 and 1893-1906, lecturer on legal ethics, 1906-08, U. of Michigan. One of organizers (1914) and pres. Detroit Symphony Soc.; one of organizers, 1916, and pres. Detroit Bureau Governmental Research. Pres. Assn. of Bureaus of Municipal and Governmental Research, 1917—. Home: Detroit, Mich. Died July 21, 1920.

KIRK, Edward Cameron, dentist; b. Sterling, Ill., Dec. 9, 1856; s. Gen. Edward N. and Eliza Marcella (Cameron) K.; ed. Phila. pub. schs.; med. dept. U. of Pa.; D.D.S., Pa. Coll. of Dental Surgery, 1878; Sc.D., Northwestern U., 1903; LL.D., U. of Pa.,

1915; m. Helen Theodora Clements, Oct. 6, 1892. Practiced dentistry at Phila., 1878-96; editor Dental Cosmos, 1891—; prof. dental pathology, materia medica and therapeutics, and dean, The Thomas W. Evans Dental Inst., dental sch. of U. of Pa., 1896-1917, emeritus, 1917—; v.p., S. S. White Dental Mfg. Co., 1920-31, retired. Medalist Société Odontologique de Paris; Officier de l'Académie; sec. gen. 4th Internat. Dental Congress and of Internat. Dental Federation. Republican. Was 2 yrs. pres. Council of Borough of Yeadon. Editor Am. Text-book of Operative Dentistry, 1897. Home: Merion, Pa. Died July 20, 1933.

KIRK, John Foster, author, editor; b. Fredericton, N.B., March 22, 1824; s. Abdiel and Mary K.; academic edn. at Halifax, N.S. (LL.D., Univ. of Pa.); m. 1879, Ellen Warner Olney. Came to U.S., 1842; sec. and asst. to William H. Prescott, the historian, 1847-59; was contbr. to North American Review, etc., and edited Lippincott's Magazine, 1870-86. Lecturer on history, Univ. of Pa., 1885-88. Author: History of Charles the Bold. Editor of Prescott's Works. Home: Chestnut Hill, Philadelphia. Died 1904.

KIRK, John Franklin, clergyman; b. Rowan County, N.C., Feb. 13, 1873; s. William Alexander and Philpena Hannah (Shaver) K.; grad. high sch., Albemarle, N.C., 1893; student Trinity Coll. (now Duke U.), 1893-95; m. Ida Ross, June 28, 1899 (died 1925); m. 2d, Agnes Ellinwood, June 8, 1926. Prin. high sch., Albemarle, 1895-97; headmaster Trinity (N.C.) High Sch., 1897-99; bookkeeper Efird Mfg. Co., Albemarle, 1899-1902; ordained ministry M.E. Ch., S., 1902; pastor Summerfield, N.C., 1902-04, Grace Ch., Winston, 1905, Mocksville, 1906-08, Mount Airy, 1909-10; field sec. Children's Home, Winston-Salem, N.C., 1911; pastor Broad St. Ch., Statesville, 1912-15; presiding elder, Shelby Dist., 1916-18, Salisbury Dist., 1919-20; pastor Salisbury, N.C., 1921-23, W. Market St. Ch., Greensboro, 1924-25; presiding elder, Asheville Dist., 1926-28; pastor Main St. Ch., Thomasville, 1929-30, College Place Ch., Greensboro, Nov. 1933—; exec. secretary Board of Christian Education, Western N.C. Conf., 1930—; mem. bd. mgrs. and ednl. dir., N.C. Methodist Pastors' Sch., Duke University, Durham, N.C., 1930—; dir. Methodist Mutual Fire Insurance Company. Pres. bd. of edn., Western North Conf., M.E. Ch., S., 1913-16, sec., 1910-12. Trustee Duke U., Davenport Coll. (sec. bd.), Jefferson Sch. (pres. bd.); dir. Children's Home, Winston-Salem. Democrat. Mason. Home: Greensboro, N.C. Died Sept. 20, 1934.

KIRK, John R., coll. pres.; b. in Ill., 1851; s. George W. and Mary J. K.; grad. State Normal Sch., Kirksville, Mo., 1878; LL.D., Mo. Wesleyan 1907, Park Coll., 1907; B.S. in edn., State Teachers Coll., Kirksville, 1926; A.M., George Peabody College for Teachers, 1930; m. Rebecca I. Burns, July 1875; children—Robert L., Elsie L., Todd, Victor H., Mary E. (wife of Warner H. Newcomb, M.D.), Laura Pauline. Began teaching, 1871; admitted to bar, 1884, and practiced in Ia. and Mo., 1884-88; city atty, Bethany, Mo., 1888; elementary sch. prin. and high sch. teacher, Kansas City, Mo., 1888-92; supt. Westport (pub.) Sch., Kansas City, 1892-94; state supt. pub. schs. of Mo., and author annual reports Dept. of Edn. of Mo., 1895-99; inspector of schs. for U. of Mo., 1899; pres. State Normal Sch., Kirksville, Mo., June 1899-May 1919; pres. State Teachers Coll., Kirksville, May 1919-Sept. 1925, now pres. emeritus and prof. advanced psychology and philosophy of education; on leave as grad. student Peabody Coll., 1925-26, springs, 1927, 30; student in Paris and London, summer 1902. Teacher George Peabody Coll., summer 1930. Pres. Mo. State Teachers' Assn., 1897. Designed demonstration rural sch bldg., 1907, and demonstration farm cottage, 1915. Mem. N.E.A.; mem. Simplified Spelling Bd., 1912. Home: Kirksville, Mo. Died Nov. 7, 1937.

KIRK, William Frederick, author; b. Mankato, Minn., Apr. 29, 1877; s. David and Caroline (Miller) K.; grad. Chippewa Falls (Wis.) High Sch. Verse and baseball writer; employed in Hearst Service, 1905—. Elk. Author: The Norsk Nightingale, 1905; Right Off the Bat, 1912; Songs of Sergeant Swanson, 1918; The Harp of Fate, 1925; Forever, 1925. Also, songs; (with Gustav Ferrari) The Rainbow of Love; The Harbor of Dreams; Consolation; A Sunset Song; Flag of My Heart; The Other Love; Out of the Current. Home: Chippewa Falls, Wis. Died Mar. 25, 1927.

KIRKHAM, John Henry, lawyer; b. Newington, Conn., Apr. 13, 1865; s. John Stoddard and Harriet Prudence (Atwood) K.; B.A., Yale, 1887; studied law in office of Hyde, Gross & Hyde, Hartford; m. Lilian West, Apr. 29, 1896; children—John West, Lois (Mrs. Stanley Hart). Admitted to Conn. bar, 1889; practiced with firm of Mitchell & Hungerford, New Britain, 1889-98; partner of James E. Cooper, 1898-1918; now senior partner of Kirkham, Camp, Williams & Richardson, partners being John H. Kirkham, Mortimer H. Camp, Margaret Perkins Camp, Harold N. Williams and Carlos A. Richardson. Judge of City and Police courts, New Britain, 1918-20; corporation counsel New Britain, 1920-33. Mem. bd. directors New Britain Institute (libraries and art collections), New Britain Welfare Soc.; class agt. Yale U. Alumni Assn., 1915—. At Yale U. was mem. of lacrosse team, winner of lightweight wrestling for 2 yrs., Univ. chess champion, editor Yale Daily News, and mem. "The Pundits." Republican. Mem. South Congl. Ch. (clk. of the Society). Home: New Britain, Conn. Deceased.

KIRKLAND, Archie Howard, entomologist; b. Huntington, Mass., June 4, 1873; s. Charles Henry and Jane Elizabeth (Parsons) K.; B.S., Mass. Agrl. Coll., 1894, M.S., 1896; unmarried. Asst. entomologist, Mass. Hatch Expt. Station, 1892-94; asst. entomologist, Mass. Bd. Agr., Gypsy Moth Commn., 1894-1900; entomologist Bowker Insecticide Co., 1900-05; state supt. Gypsy Moth work, 1905-09; agt. and expert, U.S. Bur. of Entomology, 1911—. Home: Huntington, Mass. Died 1931.

KIRKLAND, James Hampton, univ. chancellor; b. Spartanburg, S.C., Sept. 9, 1859; s. Rev. William Clarke and Virginia (Galluchat) K.; A.B., Wofford Coll., 1877, A.M., 1878; Ph.D., U. of Leipzig, 1885; LL.D., U. of N.C., U. of Mo., Wesleyan, U. of Pittsburgh, Princeton U., and Baylor U.; D.C.L., U. of the South, 1902; m. Mary Henderson, Nov. 21, 1895; 1 dau., Elizabeth (Mrs. Ben D. Meritt). Prof. Greek and German, Wofford Coll., 1881-83; traveled and studied abroad, 1883-86; prof. Latin, 1886-93, chancellor, 1893-1937, now emeritus, Vanderbilt U. Mem. Tenn. State Geol. Commns., 1909—; mem. Bd. of Forest Conservation, 1923—; chmn. Nat. Conf. Committee on Standards of Colls. and Secondary Schs., 1920-23; mem. Text Book Commission, Tennessee, 1904, 31; mem. Slater Board, 1917—. Trustee Carnegie Foundation (chmn. bd. 1922, 23; sec. of bd. 1920, 21). Founder Assn. Colls. and Secondary Schs. of Southern State, 1895, sec., 1895-1909, pres., 1911-12, 1920-21, pres. emeritus, 1928—. Editor: Satires and Epistles of Horace, 1893. Home: Nashville, Tenn. Died Aug. 5, 1939.

KIRKMAN, Marshall Monroe, author; b. in Central Illinois, July 10, 1842; m. Fannie Lincoln. In service C.&N.W. Ry. Co., 53 yrs., 1857-1910, v.p., 1889-1910, when retired on pension. Writer on ry. subjects, 1877—. Author: The Science of Railways, 1894, revised and republished in 17 vols., 1909; also novels, Romance of Gilbert Holmes, 1900; Primitive Carriers; History of Alexander the Great, 1913; Romances of the Camp and Court of Alexander the Great, The Prince, The King, The Emperor. Home: Evanston, Ill. Died Apr. 18, 1921.

KIRKPATRICK, Andrew, U.S. judge for dist. of N.J., 1896—; b. Washington, Oct. 8, 1844; s. John Bayard and Margaret (Weaver) K.; grad. Union Coll., 1863 (A.M.; also A.M., Princeton). Admitted to bar, 1866; practiced at Newark, N.J.; judge Essex Co., N.J., Court of Common Pleas, 1885-96. Home: Newark, N.J. Died 1904.

KIRKPATRICK, Edwin Asbury, psychologist; b. Peoria, Ia., Sept. 29, 1862; s. Francis Asbury and Catharine (Bradbury) K.; B.S., Ia. State Coll., 1887, M.Ph., 1889, scholar, 1889-90, fellow, 1890-91, Clark U.; m. Florence May Clifford, Aug. 20, 1895; children—Marian Myrna, Clifford, Alice May, Ralph Leonard; m. 2d, Annis Louise Kinsman, May 2, 1927. Assistant in mathematics and English, Iowa State College, 1887-89; instr. Winona (Minn.) State Normal Sch., 1892-97; dir. child study dept., Fitchburg (Mass.) State Normal Sch., 1898-1928. Lecture on edn., Smith Coll., 1905, Columbia, 1906, U. of Chicago, 1907, U. of Va., 1910, Cornell U., 1911, U. of W.Va., 1913, U. of Vt., 1914, and Boston U., 1922. Received gold medal as collaborator of the child-study exhibit made at the St. Louis Expn., 1904. Author: Fundamentals of Child Study, 1903, revised 1929; Genetic Psychology, 1909; The Individual in the Making, 1911; Fundamentals of Sociology, 1916; Studies in Psychology, 1918; Imagination and Its Place in Education, 1919; Conduct Problems, 1930, Set B, 1931; The Sciences of Man in the Making, 1932; Mental Hygiene for Effective Living, 1934. Exchange teacher at Bellingham (Wash.) State Normal Sch., 1916-17. Home: North Leominster, Mass. Died Jan. 4, 1937.

KIRKPATRICK, Elbert W., horticulturist; b. Whitesburg, Tenn., Oct. 12, 1844; s. Jacob M. and Sarah Jane (Campbell) K.; self educated; removed to Collin Co., Tex., 1854; m. Emily T. Clive, Nov. 5, 1874. Took charge of mother's farm at 13; pvt. in C.S.A., 1862-65, Martin's regt. Tex. Brigade, Trans-Miss. Dept.; in 8 battles; wounded at battle of Cabin Creek, Ind. Ty.; taught 1st pub. sch. in Collin Co., 1872; practiced land surveying, 1873, 74; established 1874, and became pres. of the Texas Nursery Co., Whitesboro Orchard & Fruit Co., Nueces Land & Immigration Co.; also farmer and fruit grower. Mem. State Council Defense; co. chmn. Y.M.C.A. War-Fund Com., and Food Conservation Com. Home: McKinney, Tex. Died Mar. 24, 1924.

KIRKPATRICK, William James, composer; b. Duncannon, Pa., Feb. 27, 1838; s. Thompson and Elizabeth (Storey) K.; ed. common schs. and by father; interested in music from boyhood; went to Phila., 1854; thrice married; 1st wife died 1878; m. 2d, Mrs. Sarah Kellogg Bourne, Oct. 23, 1893 (died 1915); m. 3d, Mrs. L. E. (Hinkson) Sweney, Jan. 17, 1917. Joined M.E. Ch., 1855; from then devoted to sacred music; studied singing under T. Bishop, Ettore Barrilli, and Pasquale Rondinella; theory, harmony and composition under Dr. Leopold Meignen; pipe organ under David D. Wood. Fife maj. 91st Pa. Vols., 1861-62; musical director and organist Ebenezer M.E. Church, Phila., 1865-86; musical director Grace M.E. Church, 1886-96. Was editor or asso. editor of over 120 books of music; some of the best known are Songs of Redeeming Love, Nos. 1 and 2, 1882, 86; Songs of Joy and Gladness, Nos. 1 and 2, 1885, 1891; Finest of the Wheat, Nos. 1, 2 and 3, 1890-1904; Organ Score Anthems, 1892, No. 2, 1894; Unfading Treasures, 1893; Infant Praises; Children's Praises; Dew Drops, 1895; Sacred Songs for Little Voices, 1900, 1913; Young People's Hymnal, 1897, No. 2, 1901, No. 3, 1905; The King's Praises, 1907, 1910, 1912; New Christian Hymn Book, 1907; Message in Song, Nos. 1 and 2, 1915; etc. Home: Germantown, Phila., Pa. Died Sept. 29, 1921.

KIRKPATRICK, William Sebring, congressman; b. Easton, Pa., Apr. 21, 1844; s. Newton and Susan (Sebring) K.; A.B., Lafayette Coll., 1863, A.M., 1872; (LL.D., Washington and Jefferson Coll., 1902); studied law with Hon. H. D. Maxwell; admitted to bar, 1865; m. Elizabeth H. Jones, Mar. 20, 1873. Solicitor, Easton, Pa., several yrs.; president judge, 3d Jud. Dist., 1874-75; chmn. Rep. State Conv., 1882; atty. gen. of Pa., 1887-91; mem. 55th Congress (1897-99); lecturer municipal law, 1875-78, trustee since about 1889, acting pres., 1902-03, also pres., 1914-15, Lafayette Coll. Home: Easton, Pa. Died Nov. 3, 1932.

KIRKUS, William, P.E. clergyman, author; b. Yorkshire, England, May 9, 1830; grad. Univ. of London, 1849 (LL.B., 1850; A.M., 1871). Congl. minister in London 16 yrs.; changed to P.E. Ch. Ordered deacon, 1871; ordained priest, 1874. Asst. minister Grace Ch., New York, 20 months; rector St. Michael and All Angels, Baltimore, until 1892. Editor American Literary Churchman. Author: Christianity, Theoretical and Practical, 1854; Miscellaneous Essays, Critical and Theological, 1863; Miscellaneous Essays, 1869; Religion: a Revelation and a Rule of Life, 1886. Home: Brooklyn, N.Y. Died 1907.

KIRKWOOD, Irwin, editor; b. Baltimore, Md., Dec. 30, 1878; s. Robert J. and Caroline (Bradenbaugh) K.; ed. pvt. and pub. schs.; m. Laura, d. William Rockhill Nelson, Nov. 15, 1910. Real estate business until 1914; editor and gen. dir. Kansas City Star, 1915—. Episcopalian. Home: Kansas City, Mo. Died Aug. 29, 1927.

KIRKWOOD, Joseph Edward, prof. botany; b. Cedar Rapids, Ia., Jan. 24, 1872; s. Robert Willis and Phoebe (Hough) K.; A.B., Pacific U., Forest Grove, Ore., 1898; A.M., Princeton, 1902; Ph.D., Columbia, 1903; m. Ella Belinda Hoyt, June 28, 1901; children—Robert Hoyt, Mary Burnett, Edward Russell. Instr. in botany, Syracuse U., 1901-04, asso. prof., 1904-07, prof., 1907; asst. botanist Continental Mexican Rubber Co., Torreon, Mex., 1907-08; investigator, Desert Bot. Lab., Carnegie Inst., Tucson, Ariz., 1908-09; asst. prof. botany and forestry, U. of Mont., 1909-10, prof., 1910-14, prof. botany, 1914—, State U. of Mont., also head dept. of botany, 1910—. Republican. Methodist. Author: Forest Distribution in Northern Rocky Mountains, 1922. Home: Missoula, Mont. Died Aug. 16, 1928.

KISER, Samuel Ellsworth, author, editor; b. Shippensville, Pa.; s. Samuel and Charlotte Kiser; ed. in Pa. and Ohio; m. Mildred M. Palmer; children—Palmer Ellsworth, Howard Spencer. Began writing spl. sketches for Cleveland Leader, 1896; editorial writer Chicago Record-Herald, 1900-14; editor Daily News, Dayton, O., 1917-19. Author: Sonnets of a Chorus Girl, 1909; The Whole Glad Year, 1911; The Land of Little Care, 1913; Glorious Day, 1926; It Is to Laugh, 1927. Home: New Rochelle, N.Y. Died Jan. 30, 1942.

KISSAM, Henry Snyder, architect; b. N.Y. City, Feb. 22, 1866; s. Benjamin Adrian and Sara A. (Snyder) K.; matriculated Coll. City of New York, 1881, but withdrew; studied under pvt. tutor, 1881-82; Ph.B. in Architecture, Sch. of Mines (Columbia), 1886; studied in Paris, France, 1886, 1887; m. Mary Margaret Murray, of Paris, Ont., Sept. 4, 1907. Mem. Kissam & Morris, Tacoma, Wash., 1888-92; N.E. mgr. at New Haven, Conn., for Cady, Berg & See, architects, New York, 1893-94; gen. mgr. for Ernest Flagg, New York, 1895-99; supervising architect Buffalo Expn., 1899-1900; practiced, New York, 1900—; mem. Valentine & Kissam, 1912-16, then alone. Executor Estate of Benjamin A. Kissam; adminstr. Estate of Col. Henry D. H. Snyder. Republican. Episcopalian. Home: New York, N.Y. Died Dec. 26, 1930.

KISSEL, John, congressman; b. Brooklyn, N.Y., July 31, 1864; s. John and Mary (Lutz) K., ed. pub. and pvt. schs.; m. Emma M. Vogt, May 6, 1886. Learned printers' trade; pub. Kings County Republican, 1889-1914. Mem. Rep. County Com., 1886—; mem. Rep. State Com., 1909-11; mem. New York Senate, 1909-10; mem. 67th Congress (1921-23), 3d N.Y. Dist. Organized and conducted at own expense for 15 yrs. the first free labor bur. in U.S. Home: Brooklyn, N.Y. Died Oct. 3, 1938.

KISTLER, John Clinton, church official; b. Penn. Twp., Allegheny Co., Pa., June 5, 1859; s. Josiah Brinker and Margaret Jane (Elliott) K.; student Laird Inst., Parnassus Acad., First Pa. State Normal Sch., Millersville, Pa.; A.B., Westminster (Pa.) Coll., 1886, D.D., 1911; grad. Allegheny Theol. Sem., 1889; m. Maggie C. Alter, Dec. 28, 1886 (died 1927); children—Lizzie Luella (dec.), Raymon M. and Harold C. (both clergymen); m. 2d, Mrs. Nan Rankin Henderson, Apr. 1, 1929. Ordained ministry U.P. Ch., 1889; pastor Buena Vista and Boston, Pa., 1889-1901, Houston, Pa., 1901-22; exec. sec. Bd. of Church Extension, U.P. Ch., 1922-28; asso. sec. Board of Am. Missions, U.P. Church, 1928—. Chairman of U.P. Reunion, Conneaut Lake, Pa., 1892—; moderator Pittsburgh Synod, 1912; mem. U.P. Bd. of Publication and Bd. of Ch. Extension; pres. bd. trustees Westminster Coll. Home: Pittsburgh, Pa. Deceased.

KITCHIN, Claude, congressman; b. Scotland Neck, N.C., Mar. 24, 1869; s. late William H. (mem. 46th Congress) and Maria F. (Arrington) K.; brother of William Walton K.; B.L., Wake Forest Coll., 1888; m. Kate B. Mills, Nov. 13, 1888. Admitted to bar, 1890, and began practice at Scotland Neck, N.C. Mem. 57th to 67th Congresses (1911-23), 2d N.C. Dist.; majority leader 64th and 65th Congresses. Democrat. Home: Scotland Neck, N.C. Died May 31, 1923.

KITCHIN, William Copeman, author; b. St. George, Ont., Sept. 7, 1855; s. Benjamin and Elsie (Copeman) K.; A.B., Syracuse U., 1882, A.M., 1884, Ph.D., 1885; student modern lit. and history of art, grad. dept. Harvard, 1888-92, Sorbonne, Paris, 1894; m. Fanny Carlotta Furbeck, June 23, 1882. Ordained 1882; missionary to Japan, under auspices of M.E. Missionary Soc., 1882-88; prin. of an English sch. at Nagasaki, Japan, 1882-85; prof. English, Keiogi-jiku and Anglo-Japanese Coll., Tokyo, 1885-88; returned to America under contract to prepare a series of textbooks for use in Japanese colls.; instr. Boston U., 1891; prof. Romance langs. and lits., U. of Vt., 1892-1900 (resigned on account of ill health); gen. agt. Conn. Gen. Life Ins. Co., 1900-09; dist. mgr. Northwestern Mut. Life Ins. Co., 1909—. Pres. Epworth League State of Vt., 1888-89. Republican. Editor: English Prose Masterpieces (4 vols.), 1888, 1889. Conductor of European tours, 1911-14. Home: Schenectady, N.Y. Died Jan. 8, 1920.

KITCHIN, William Walton, governor; b. nr. Scotland Neck, N.C., Oct. 9, 1866; s. late William H. (mem. 46th Congress) and Maria F. (Arrington) K.; bro. of Claude K.; A.B., Wake Forest Coll., 1884; m. Musette Satterfield, Dec. 22, 1892. Editor Scotland Neck Democrat, 1885; admitted to bar, 1887; in practice at Roxboro, 1888—; chmn. Dem. Co. Exec. Com., 1890; nominee for State Senate, 1892; mem. 55th to 60th Congresses (1897-1909), 5th N.C. Dist.; gov. of N.C., 1909-13; was mem. Manning & Kitchin, Raleigh; retired. LL.D., U. of N.C. Home: Scotland Neck, N.C. Died Nov. 9, 1924.

KITSON, Samuel James, sculptor; b. Huddersfield, Yorkshire, England, Jan. 1, 1848; s. John and Emma K.; ed. St. Paul's Sch., Armitage Bridge, York, and Lockwood Sch., England; grad. in sculpture (with diplomas and medals), St. Luke's Royal Acad., Rome, Italy; m. Annie Meredith, July 12, 1884. Was principal sculptor for interior William K. Vanderbilt's house, New York; other works include Sheridan monument, Arlington, Va.; north frieze Soldiers' and Sailors' monument arch, Hartford; portrait Gov. Greenhalge, State house, Boston. Died 1906.

KITSON, Theo Alice Ruggles, sculptor; b. Brookline, Mass., 1871; d. Cyrus Washburn and Anna Holmes (Baker) Ruggles; pub. sch. edn., Brookline; pupil of H. H. Kitson and Dagnan-Bouveret, Paris; m. Henry Hudson Kitson, June 29, 1893; children—Dorothy, John, Theo Ruggles. Has exhibited at Paris Expn., 1889 (hon. mention); Paris Salon, 1890 (hon. mention—only Am. woman sculptor to receive hon. mention, Paris Salon); was selected by women of Mich. to make two bronze figures for Chicago Expn. to represent woods of Mich.; has exhibited Mass. Charitable Mechanics' Assn. (2 medals); Soc. Am. Artists, Nat. Acad. Design (New York), Pa. Acad. Fine Arts (Phila.), Boston Art Club, Mus. of Fine Arts (Boston), Art Inst. of Chicago; medal, St. Louis Expn., 1904. Works: The Volunteer, Newburyport, Mass.; Spanish War statues, Minneapolis and Schenectady; Bickerdyke Statue, Galesburg, Ill.; etc.; has erected over fifty public monuments in various parts of U.S., including statue of Gen. Kosciusko, Public Garden, Boston; equestrian statue of Victory, Hingham, Mass., 1929. Home: Framingham Center, Mass. Died Oct. 29, 1932.

KITTELL, James Shepard, clergyman; b. Hamilton, Ont., Can., Mar. 19, 1873; s. John and Jane (Drysdale) K.; Allegheny (Pa.) Coll., 1890-95, Western Theol. Sem., 1896-98; D.D., Rutgers U., 1910; m. Elizabeth Stilwell, May 22, 1895. Came to U.S., 1880; ordained Congl. ministry, 1903; pastor Pilgrim Congl. Ch., Jamestown, N.Y., 1903-05, First Congl. Schenectady, N.Y., 1905-07, First Ref. Ch., Albany, N.Y., 1907-21, Bergen Ref. Ch., Jersey City, N.J., 1922-27; sec. Bd. of Domestic Missions, Ref. Ch., 1927—. Pres. Gen. Synod Ref. Ch. in America, 1913; dir. Theol. Sem. New Brunswick, N.J. Home: Jackson Heights, N.Y. Died Apr. 17, 1937.

KITTLE, Charles Morgan, merchant; b. Elkins, W.Va., Oct. 9, 1880; s. Morgan and Sally (Long) K.; ed. pub. schs.; m. Jane Dabney, Nov. 5, 1921. Began as station clk. W.Va. Central & Pittsburgh R.R. (now part Western Md. Ry.), 1895, later in station and yard service Atlantic Coast Line R.R., Cincinnati, New Orleans & Tex. Pacific Ry., and B.&O. R.R.; became connected with I.C. R.R. Co., 1900, in maintenance of way, mechanical, accounting and transportation depts.; gen. freight claim agt. same rd. and Yazoo & Miss. Valley R.R., 1910-12; asst. to pres. same rds., 1912-16, v.p., 1916-18; federal mgr. same rds., and Gulf and Ship Island R.R., Mississippi Central R.R. and New Orleans Great Northern R.R. during federal control, 1918-20; sr. v.p. I.C. and Yazoo & Miss. Valley rys., Mar. 1, 1920-24; pres. Sears, Roebuck & Co., mail order business, Chicago, Nov. 1924—. Died Jan. 2, 1928.

KITTREDGE, Abbott Eliot, clergyman; b. Roxbury, Mass., July 20, 1834; A.B., Williams Coll., 1854; grad. Andover Theol. Sem., 1859; (D.D., Williams, 1878). Ordained to ministry, 1859; pastor Charlestown, Mass., 1859-63; supply Howard St. Presbyn. Ch., San Francisco, 1864; pastor Eleventh Presbyn. Ch., New York, 1865-70, Third Presbyn. Ch., Chicago, 1870-86, Madison Av. Reformed Ch., New York, 1886-96. Pres. Gen. Synod Reformed Ch. in America, 1903. Home: New York, N.Y. Died Dec. 17, 1912.

KITTREDGE, Alfred Beard, senator; b. Cheshire Co., N.H., March 26, 1861; A.B., Yale, 1882, LL.B., 1885; unmarried. Admitted to bar, 1885, and began practice at Sioux Falls, S.D. Mem. S.D. Senate, 1889-93; mem. Rep. Nat. Com., 1892-1900; apptd. U.S. senator, July 11, 1901, to fill unexpired term (1901-03) of James H. Kyle, deceased; elected for term, 1903-09. Home: Sioux Falls, S.D. Died 1911.

KITTREDGE, George Lyman, university prof.; b. Boston, Mass., Feb. 28, 1860; A.B., Harvard, 1882; LL.D., U. of Chicago, 1901, Johns Hopkins, 1915, McGill Univ., 1921, Brown Univ., 1925; Litt.D., Harvard Univ., 1907, Yale Univ., 1924; D.Litt. Oxford U., 1932; D.C.L., Union U., 1935; m. Frances Gordon, 1886; children—Frances Gordon, Henry Crocker, Dora. Instr. English, 1888-90, asst. prof., 1890-94, prof., 1894-1936, Harvard. Fellow Am. Acad. Arts and Sciences. Author: Words and Their Ways in English Speech (with late James B. Greenough), 1901; Old Farmer and His Almanac, 1905; Advanced English Grammar (with F. E. Farley), 1913; Chaucer and His Poetry, 1915; Shakespeare, 1916; Sir Thomas Malory, 1925; Concise English Grammar (with F. E. Farley), 1918; Dr. Robert Child, the Remonstrant, 1919; Witchcraft in Old and New England, 1929. Editor: Athenæum Press Series of English Classics (with C. T. Winchester), 29 vols., 1890-1905; Albion Series of Anglo-Saxon and Middle English Poetry (with J. W. Bright), 5 vols., 1900-07; English and Scottish Popular Ballads (with H. C. Sargent), 1904; Ballads and Songs, 1917; Complete Works of Shakespeare, 1936; Macbeth, The Tempest, Julius Caesar, As You Like It, Hamlet, 1939; Romeo and Juliet, 1940. Home: Cambridge, Mass. Died July 23, 1941.

KITTREDGE, Henry Grattan; b. Claremont, N.H., Jan. 22, 1845; s. Thomas B. K., of Keene, N.H.; early edn. at Keene, N.H.; spl. tuition at Trinity Coll.; m. Martha S. Hodges, Oct. 12, 1870; m. 2d, Helen Litchfield, July 19, 1883. Formerly woolen mfr.; specialist in industrial journalism; organized textile exhibits Chicago Expn., 1893; Mass. commr. Atlanta Expn., 1896; organized textile exhibit, Paris Expn., 1900; mem. nat. com. of Coal Tar Color Industry Jubilee, 1906; textile technologist for the Century Dictionary and Cyclopedia. Home: Reading, Mass. Died June 5, 1909.

KITTREDGE, Josiah Edwards, clergyman; b. Boston, Mass., Oct. 12, 1836; s. Josiah (M.D.) and Sarah Whiting (French) K.; A.B., Yale, 1860; studied Union Theol. Sem., 1861-62, Andover Theol. Sem., 1862-65; (D.D., New York U., 1884); m. Emma MacNair, June 28, 1871 (died 1898); m. 2d, Nettie S. Long, Dec. 30, 1903. Ordained Presbyn. ministry, 1869; pastor Glastonbury, Conn., 1869-73, Am. Ch., Berlin, Germany, 1874, Am. Union Ch., Florence, Italy, 1874-76, Geneseo, N.Y., 1877-1906, then asst. pastor Central Ch., Rochester, N.Y. Del. from Gen. Assembly Presbyn. Ch. in U.S.A. to Centenary Conf. Missions in China, Shanghai, 1907. Republican. Home: Rochester, N.Y. Died Dec. 21, 1913.

KITTREDGE, Walter, song composer; b. Merrimac, N.H., Oct. 8, 1834; s. Eri and Lucretia K.; grad. Merrimac Normal Inst., 1851; m. Annie E. Fairfield, 1861. Since 1856 has been a song composer, writing words and music of many songs, and giving concerts, singing his own songs, which include Tenting on the Old Camp Ground, 1864; No Night; Golden Streets; Scatter the Flowers Over the Gray and the Blue; Sing the Old War Songs Again. Also engaged in farming. Home: Reed's Ferry, N.H. Died 1905.

KITTREDGE, Wheaton, lawyer; b. Boston, Mass., Sept. 28, 1882; s. of Francis William and Mary Fairchild (Wheaton) K.; A.B., Harvard Univ., 1903, LL.B., 1907; m. Laura McFarlin, June 2, 1908. With legal dept. Boston Elevated Ry. Co., 1907-08; associated in practice with Payson Dana, 1908-17, then alone; dir. Edington & Co., Inc., Groton Realty Corp., H. Dawson & Co., Inc., Starkweather & Shepley, Incorporated. Congregationalist. Republican. Home: Chestnut Hill, Mass. Died Aug. 9, 1936.

KITTRELL, Norman Goree, lawyer; b. Greensboro, Ala., July 28, 1849; s. Pleasant Williams and Mary Frances (Goree) K.; student Washington and Lee Univ., 1868; m. Louisa B. Keyes, Apr. 12, 1875. Admitted to Tex. bar, 1870; atty. for Western Union Telegraph Co. many yrs.; dist. atty. 12th Jud. Dist., Tex., 1884-86; judge same dist., 1886-92 (resigned); practiced in Houston; judge 61st Jud. Dist., Tex., 1903-08 (declined reëlection); resumed practice, Houston; mem. Kittrell & Kittrell; mem. Tex. Ho. of Rep., 1898-99. Democrat. Methodist. Author: A Primer of the Government of Texas, 1910; Texas Illustrated, 1910. Home: Houston, Tex. Deceased.

KIVEL, John, judge; b. Dover, N.H., Apr. 29, 1855; s. Patrick and Catherine K.; A.B., Dartmouth, 1876, A.M., 1879; m. Eva G. Ennis, Oct. 12, 1879. Admitted to N.H. bar, 1879; county solicitor, Strafford Co., 1887-93; mem. State Bd. License Commrs., 1903-13; apptd. justice Superior Court of N.H., May 20, 1913, chief justice, Oct. 4, 1917. Home: Dover, N.H. Died Apr. 1, 1924.

KLAPP, William Henry, head master; b. Phila., Pa., Oct. 13, 1849; s. William Henry K. (M.D.) and Rebecca Plumsted (Devereux) K.; grad. Episcopal Acad., Phila., 1867; A.B., Harvard, 1871; M.D., U. of Pa., 1876 (hon. A.M., 1886); unmarried. Master, 1871-91, head master, 1891-1917, and head master emeritus, 1917—. Episcopal Acad., Phila. Charter mem. Central Com. of U. of Pa., and treas. until 1911. Home: Wayne, Pa. Died Jan. 15, 1924.

KLAUBER, Adolph, theatrical producer; b. Louisville, Ky., Apr. 29, 1869; s. Edward and Caroline (Brahms) K.; prep. edn., high sch., Louisville; student U. of Va., 1896-98; m. Jane Cowl, actress, 1908. Began as reporter New York Commercial Advertiser, 1900; reporter New York Tribune, 1901-04; Sunday editor New York Times, 1904-06, dramatic critic, 1906-18; began as theatrical producer with Eugene O'Neill's "Emperor Jones," 1920; associated with Jane Cowl in presenting "Lilac Time," "Smilin' Through," "Romeo and Juliet," "Pelleas and Melisande" and "Antony and Cleopatra." Home: New York, N.Y. Died Dec. 7, 1933.

KLAUDER, Charles Zeller, architect; b. Phila., Pa., Feb. 9, 1872; s. Louis and Anna Caroline (Koehler) K.; ed. Phila. schs., Sch. Industrial Arts (Pa. Mus.); M.F.A., Princeton, 1921, title of Dr.; m. Fredericka Mathilda Bower, Feb. 27, 1901; children—Elfrieda Marie, Charles Zeller. Entered office F. M. Day & Bro., 1900; mem. Day Bro. & Klauder, 1911-13, Day Bros. & Klauder, 1913-18, now Charles Z. Klauder. Consulting architect Harkness Memorial Dormitories, Yale U.; supervising architect Univ. of Del., Pa. State Coll., Franklin and Marshall Coll., St. Paul's Sch., Southwestern U., Lafayette Coll., Hill Sch.; exec. architect Holder Hall group and other buildings, Princeton U.; Cathedral of Learning, Heinz Memorial Chapel and Stephen Foster Memorial Building, U. of Pittsburgh; also for buildings at various institutions, among them, Brown U., Cornell, U. of Colo., Denver U., U. of Pa., Pa. State Coll., Yale U., Wellesley Coll., Concordia Sem., Mercersburg Acad., Hill School, St. Paul School, Staunton Military Acad., Albion Coll., Drew U., Boy Scout Hdqrs. at Phila. and bank for Drexel & Co., Phila.; chmn. com. cons. architects U.S. Dept. Treasury, 1935-37. Awarded silver medal, T-Square Club, Philadelphia, 1891; medal, Phila. Chapter A.I.A., 1918; gold medal, Archtl. League, New York, 1921; gold medal A.I.A., 1921; Grand Prix, Pan-Am. Congress of Architects, 1927, and silver medal from same; medal in architecture, Olympian Games, Amsterdam, 1928. Associate of Nat. Acad. of Design; fellow A.I.A., 1913. Coauthor: College Architecture in America. Home: Philadelphia, Pa. Died Oct. 30, 1938.

KLAUSER, Karl, author, editor musical works (retired); b. St. Petersburg, Russia, Aug. 24, 1823; s. Joh. V. K.; mainly self-educated; m. Karolina Strasser, Switzerland, 1850. Came to U.S., 1850; from 1855 in Farmington, Conn., musical dir. Miss Porter's Ladies' School. Has edited over 1,000 musical works, classical and modern. Editor: Half Hours (musical selections, in 6 vols.); Famous Composers (6 vols., with Theo. Thomas and Prof. Paine). Arrangement works of Beethoven, Schumann, Liszt, Wagner (for piano), published in German. As photographer, brought out collection of over 400 authentic portraits of musicians, 1880-90. Home: Farmington, Conn. Died 1905.

KLAW, Marc, theatrical mgr.; b. Paducah, Ky., May 29, 1858; s. Leopold and Caroline K.; ed. pub. and high schs., Louisville, Ky.; m. Antoinette M. Morris (dec.). Studied law and was admitted to bar, but from 1881 has been engaged as theatrical mgr.; mem. Klaw & Erlanger; pres. Marc Klaw, Inc.; also officer other corps. In charge mil. entertainment service of War Dept. Commn. on Training Camp Activities. Pres. United Mgrs. Protective Assn. America; trustee Actors' Fund of America. Home: New Rochelle, N.Y. Died June 14, 1936.

KLEBERG, Rudolph, congressman; b. Austin Co., Tex., June 26, 1847; s. Robert and Rosa (von Roeder) K.; ed. pvt. schs.; served in Tom Green's cav. brigade, C.S.A., 1864-65; m. Mathilde E. Eckhardt, 1872. Admitted to bar, 1872; established Cuero Star, 1873; co. atty., 1876-80; mem. Tex. Senate, 1882-84; U.S. atty. for Western Dist. of Tex., 1885-89; elected, April, 1896, to fill vacancy in 54th Congress caused by death of his law-partner, William H. Crain; reëlected 55th to 57th Congresses (1897-1903), 11th Tex. Dist.; Democrat; official reporter, Court of Criminal Appeals, Texas, Feb. 24, 1905—. Home: Austin, Tex. Died Dec. 28, 1924.

KLEIN, Bruno Oscar, composer, pianist; b. Osnabrück, Germany, June 6, 1858; grad. Gymnasium Carolinum there; studied music with his father; later at Royal Music Sch., Munich; m. Emmy Schaefer, pianiste. Compositions include about 75 songs; many motets; 3 masses; 2 suites for piano, concerto and concertstück for piano; a great number of pieces for piano; 2 sonatas for piano and violin; suits for violoncello and orchestra; arias for soprano and orchestra; scènes de ballet and 2 overtures for orchestra; grand opera in 3 acts, "Kenilworth" (prod. at Hamburg, 1895, with Kartharina Klafsky as Amy); quintette for soprano, piano, violin, 'cello and horn; concerto for violin in E minor. Died 1911.

KLEIN, Charles, playwright; b. London, Eng., Jan. 7, 1867; s. Hermann and Adelaide (Soman) K.; brother of Hermann and Charles K. (both q.v.); ed. North London Coll.; m. Lillian Gottlieb, July 10, 1888. Former censor of plays for Charles Frohman. Author: (plays) A Mile a Minute; By Proxy; A Paltry Million; The District Attorney; El Capitan; Heartsease; The Charlatan; The Hon. John Grigsby; Doctor Belgraff; A Royal Rogue; The Red Feather; The Music Master; The Lion and the Mouse; The Daughters of Men; The Stepchild; The Third Degree; The Next of Kin. Home: Rowayton, Conn. Died May 7, 1915.

KLEIN, Frederick Charles, clergyman; b. Washington, D.C., May 17, 1857; s. John M. and Catherine M. (Boutellier) K.; A.B., Western Md. Coll., Westminster, Md., 1880, A.M.; m. Mary Elizabeth Patton, Aug. 16, 1883. Ordained M.P. ministry, 1880; sent to Japan, 1883, as the 1st ordained missionary of M.P. Ch. to foreign field; organizer and 1st pres. Nagoya Coll.; 1st pres. Japan Mission Conf. M.P. Ch.; pastor 1st Ch. Pittsburgh, 1893-94, Trinity Ch., Allegheny, Pa., 1894-95, Laurel, Del., 1895-1901, 1st Ch., Newark, N.J., 1901-05, Mt. Royal Av. Ch., Baltimore, Md., 1905-08; corr. sec.-treas. Bd. of Foreign Missions M.P. Ch., 1908-16; corr. sec. same, 1916—. Del. World Missionary Conf., Edinburgh, Scotland, 1910, World's S.S. Conv., Zürich, Switzerland, 1913; made tour foreign missionary fields, 1919-20. Trustee Western Md. Coll. Democrat. Mason, Odd Fellow. Home: Berwyn, Md. Died Dec. 28, 1926.

KLEIN, Jacob, lawyer; b. Hessen-Darmstadt, Germany, Sept. 1, 1845; s. John Martin and Caroline (Güth) K.; ed. St. Louis pub. schs. and 2 yrs. in high sch.; LL.B., Harvard, 1871; m. Lilly Schreiber, Apr. 17, 1873. Admitted to bar at St. Louis, May 29, 1869; judge of Circuit Ct., City of St. Louis, 1889-1901; mem. Klein & Hough. Counsel of Mercantile Trust Co., Aug. 1901—; pres. Lafayette Mut. Bldg. Assn. Pres. St. Louis Bar Assn., 1901-02, 1903-04; apptd. by President, U.S. del. Universal Congress of Lawyers and Jurists, 1904. Republican. Presbyterian. Home: St. Louis, Mo. Died 1910.

KLEIN, Joseph Frederic, mechanical engr.; b. Paris, France, Oct. 10, 1849; Ph.B., Sheffield Scientific School (Yale), 1871, D.E., 1873; m. Ada Louise Warner, Dec. 30, 1879. Instr. mech. engring., Sheffield Scientific Sch., 1877-81; prof. mech. engring., 1881—, dean, Sept. 1, 1907—, Lehigh U. Author: Elements of Machine Design, 1889; Design of a High-Speed Steam Engine, 1892; Physical Significance of Entropy, 1910. Home: Bethlehem, Pa. Died Feb. 11, 1918.

KLEIN, Manuel, composer; b. London, Eng., Dec. 6, 1876; s. Hermann and Adelaide (Soman) K.; grad. Coll. of Preceptors, London; Oxford local exams.; m. Helen Heartleigh Kaplan, June 1, 1904. Mus. dir. New York Hippodrome, 1904—; conductor Manuel Klein's Orchestra. Composer (comic operas); Mr. Pickwick; The Man From Now; The Top O' the World; The Pied Piper; and all New York Hippodrome productions; also plays, songs, incidental pieces, etc. Home: Douglas Manor, L.I. Died June 1, 1919.

KLEMM, Louis Richard, educationalist, banker; b. Düsseldorf, Ger., Dec. 8, 1845; s. Carl August and Catherine (Schlippert) K.; ed. Düsseldorf; came to U.S., 1866; grad. Normal Sch.; (hon. Ph.D., De Pauw U., 1883); married. Was teacher at Indianapolis and Detroit; asst. supt. schs., Cleveland, O., 1870-80; prin. German Normal Sch., Cincinnati, 1880-84; supt. schs., Hamilton, O., 1884-87; prin. tech. sch., Cincinnati, 1888-89; govt. specialist in foreign edn., 1889-1910; pres. Soc. for Savings, Washington, 1910—. Author; Text-books for the Study of German, 1876; History of German Literature, 1878; Poetry in Home and School, 1879; German by Practice, 1883; European Schools, 1888; Chips from a Teacher's Workshop, 1887; Higher Education of Women, 1891; Public Education in Germany and the United States, 1911. Home: Washington, D.C. Died 1916.

KLEPPER, Max Francis, artist, illustrator; b. Zeitz, Germany, March 1, 1861; came to U.S. with parents, 1876; apprenticed to lithographic firm, Chicago; removed to New York, 1880; m. Emilie von Rhein, 1883. Studied Art Students' League, New York, Royal Acad., Munich, 1887-89, at same time taking a course at Munich Veterinary Coll. Specialty horse subject. Died 1907.

KLIEWER, John Walter, college pres.; b. nr. Berdichiev, Russian Poland, June 8, 1869; s. John and Aganetha (Foth) K.; student Bethel Coll., Newton, Kan., 1893-95; S.T.B., Garrett Bibl. Inst., Evanston, Ill., 1901, D.D., 1925; D.D., Bluffton (O.) Coll., 1925; m. Emma M. Ruth, Oct. 30, 1902; children—Karl G., Ruth L., Paul L. Ordained Mennonite ministry, 1901; sec. Gen. Conf. Mennonite Ch. of North America, 1902-08; pres. Foreign Mission Bd. same ch., 1910-35; pres. Bethel College, 1911-20 and 1925-32 (emeritus); pastor Bethel College Church, 1932-35. Made trip around the world to inspect mission fields, 1920-21; lecturer. Pres. trustees Central Mennonite Coll., Bluffton, O., 1903-11; v.p. Federal Council Chs. of Christ in America, 1913-16. Home: Newton, Kan. Died Feb. 9, 1938.

KLINE, Ardolph L.; b. Sussex Co., N.J., Feb. 21, 1858; s. Anthony and Margaret (Busby) K.; ed. pub. and pvt. schs.; m. Frances A. Phalon, Nov. 25, 1886. In employ W. C. Peet & Co., New York, 1877-86; mem. Bd. of Aldermen, 1904-05, 1906-07, 1912-13 (v.chmn. 1912); reëlected 1914-15, resigned Jan. 5, 1914; mayor of New York under charter provision, Sept. 10-Dec. 31, 1913, to fill vacancy caused by death of William J. Gaynor; has acted as mayor pro tem. on many occasions; tax commr., Jan. 6, 1914-18. Asst. appraiser of mdse., Port of New York, Jan. 1, 1908-July 1, 1911 (resigned); mem. 67th Congress (1921-23), 5th New York Dist.; apptd. New York agent of Sea Service Bureau of U.S. Shipping Board, May 4, 1923. Republican. Bvt. brig. general 14th Regiment N.G.N.Y., Spanish-Am. War, 1898. Pres. Former Officers' Assn. 14th Regt. N.G. N.Y.; life mem. 14th Regt. Camp Spanish-Am. War Vets. Episcopalian. Home: Brooklyn, N.Y. Died Oct. 13, 1930.

KLINE, Charles H., mayor; b. Indiana, Pa., Dec. 25, 1870; s. Wellington B. and Anna Margarete (Custer) K.; student Ind. State Normal Sch. and Kiskiminetas Springs Sch., Saltsburg, Pa.; LL.B., U. of Pa., 1898; m. Katharine Whitesell Johnson, Oct. 24, 1900. Admitted to Pa. bar, 1898, and began practice at Pittsburgh, 1899. Mem. Pa. Ho. of Rep., 1904-05, Senate, 1906-18; apptd. judge Court of Common Pleas of Allegheny Co., 1919, and later in yr. elected to same office for term 1919-29, resigned 1926; mayor of Pittsburgh for terms 1926 to 1934. Trustee Slippery Rock State Normal Sch., Duquesne U., Carnegie Inst. Tech. (ex-officio), U. of Pittsburgh (ex-officio), Carnegie Library, Pittsburgh (ex-officio), St. Francis Hosp. (v.p.), Homeopathic Med. and Surg. Hosp. and Dispensary, Larimer Av. Home of Good Shepherds (pres.). Republican. Presbyn. Mason. Home: Pittsburgh, Pa. Died July 22, 1933.

KLINE, George Milton, psychiatrist; b. Pittsburgh, Pa., Mar. 6, 1878; s. Daniel Zimmerman and Eleanor (Bitler) K.; ed. pub. schs., Grand Rapids, Mich.; M.D., U. of Mich., 1901, hon. M.A., 1931; m. Ethel A. Fry, June 23, 1906; children—Anitra Fry, Nancy Jane. Asst. phys., Worcester (Mass.) State Hosp., 1901-02, Mt. Pleasant (Ia.) State Hosp., 1902-06, State Psychopathic Hosp., Mich., 1906-12; supt. Danvers (Mass.) State Hosp., 1912-16; commr. Mass. Dept. of Mental Diseases, 1916—; dir. Boston Morris Plan Bank. Pres. bd. dirs. Boston Sch. of Occupational Therapy, 1931—. Mem. com. on orgn., 1st Internat. Congress on Mental Hygiene. Decorated Chevalier Legion of Honor (France). Mason. Home: Beverly, Mass. Deceased.

KLINE, George Washington, naval officer; b. Flemington, N.J., Jan. 4, 1864; grad. U.S. Naval Acad., 1885. Promoted ensign, July 1, 1887; lt. jr. grade, Mar. 12, 1896; lt., Mar. 3, 1899; lt. comdr., Sept. 13, 1904; comdr., Aug. 1, 1908; captain July 1, 1912; now retired with rank of rear adm. Served on Annapolis, Spanish-Am. War, 1898; exec. officer, Raleigh, 1904-05; duty Navy Recruiting Sta., N.Y. City, 1905-07; exec. officer Georgia, 1907-09; comd. Castine, 1909-10; insp. ordnance, Phila., Pa., and Camden, N.J., 1910-12; comd. Naval Sta., Guantanamo, Cuba, 1912-13; comd. Idaho, 1913, Vermont, 1913-15; apptd. mem. Bd. Inspection and Survey, Navy Dept., Dec. 24, 1915. Home: Bound Brook, N.J. Died June 28, 1922.

KLINE, Jacob, army officer; b. Lebanon, Pa., Nov. 5, 1840; s. Levi and Bella M. (Ebert) K.; ed. Pa. Coll.; m. Leila Cassell, Oct. 4, 1871. Apptd. from Pa., 1st lt. 16th Inf., Sept. 9, 1861; promoted through grades to brig. gen. vols., May 27, 1898; hon. disch. from vol. service, Mar. 15, 1899; brig. gen. U.S.A., Jan. 23, 1904; retired at own request after 40 yrs.' service, Jan. 24, 1904. Bvtd. capt., Apr. 7, 1862, for battle of Shiloh, Tenn.; maj., Sept. 1, 1864, for Atlanta campaign. Instr. art of war and in dept. of inf., at Inf. and Cav. Sch., Ft. Leavenworth, Kan., 1887-92. Home: Lebanon, Pa. Died 1908.

KLINE, Marcus C. L., congressman; b. in Salisbury Twp., Lehigh Co., Pa.; A.B., Muhlenberg Coll., 1874; m. Clara M. Keller, Oct. 4, 1881. Admitted to bar, June 5, 1876; city solicitor, Allentown, Pa., 1877; dist. atty., Lehigh Co., 1887-90; chmn. Dem. Co. Com., 1895-99; mem. 58th and 59th Congresses (1903-07). Pres. Lehigh Valley Trust & Safe Deposit Co., Jan. 17, 1901—; also pres. Allentown Trust Co. Home: Allentown, Pa. Died 1911.

KLINE, Marion Justus, clergyman; b. Frederick, Md., Oct. 2, 1871; s. William Henry and Mary Ann (Engelbrecht) K.; Frederick Coll.; A.B., Pa. Coll., Gettysburg, 1893, A.M., 1896; grad. Luth. Theol. Sem., Gettysburg, 1896; D.D., N.C. Coll., 1901, Pa. Coll., 1921; m. Annie Plitt Hummel, Apr. 24, 1902. Ordained Luth. ministry, 1896; pastor Bethlehem Ch., Harrisburg, Pa., 1896-1901; gen. sec. and exec. officer Bd. of Foreign Missions, Luth. Ch. in U.S.A., 1901-08; pastor First Ch., Altoona, Pa., June 1908—. Mem. Bd. of Ch. Extension, Gen. Synod, 1899-1902; pres. Pa. Christian Endeavor Union and trustee United Soc. of Christian Endeavor, 1901; editor Luth. Missionary Journal, 1901-07; bd. mgrs. Young People's Missionary Movement (interdenom.), 1907-08; Bd. Edn. Gen. Synod, 1909-18 (v.p. 1909-11, rec. sec. 1911-17, v.p. 1917-18); Bd. Edn. United Luth. Ch. America, 1918-28; Bd. Edn. Alleghany Synod, 1908-14; ordination exam. com., 1914—; Bd. Home Missions, 1914—; Quardi-Centennial Commn. Prot. Reformation, 1913-18. Mem. Exec. Bd. United Lutheran Ch. America, 1930—; mem. bd. Theol. Sem. of Gen. Synod Luth. Ch. in U.S.A. (United Luth. Ch., 1918—), 1913—; pres. bd. dirs. Theol. Sem. United Luth. Ch. in America, 1918-25; v.p. Alleghany Synod Luth. Ch., 1922-24, pres., 1924-25; trustee Pa. Coll., 1917-21. Author: The Genesis of the General Synod of the Lutheran Church in U.S.A., 1918; God and Our Country, 1919; The Protestant Reformation, 1921. Home: Altoona, Pa. Died Sept. 29, 1934.

KLINE, Virgil Philip, lawyer; b. Wayne Co., O., Nov. 3, 1844; s. Anthony and Eliza Jane (Montgomery) K.; A.B., Williams Coll., 1866. Admitted to Ohio bar, 1870, and began practice at Cleveland; sr. mem. Kline, Carr, Tolles & Goff. Mem. bd. edn., 1883-85; twice Dem. candidate for judge Supreme Ct. of Ohio, also candidate for Circuit Ct. and Common Pleas Ct. Mem. Ohio Bd. State Charities. Home: Euclid Heights, Cleveland, O. Died Jan. 18, 1917.

KLINE, William Fair, artist; b. Columbia, S.C., May 3, 1870; s. Theodore David and Ida Eugenia (Holst) K.; ed. pub. schs., Richmond, Va., and Macon, Ga.; studied art at Nat. Acad. Design, New York, and Académie Julien, Paris; asst. to Will H. Low, 1892, Francis D. Millet, Chicago Expn., 1893; awarded traveling scholarship, Nat. Acad., 1889, Jacob H. Lazarus traveling scholarship, 1894; unmarried. Clarke prize, Nat. Acad. Design, 1901, 2d Hallgarten prize, 1903; silver medal, Buffalo Expn., 1901; bronze medal (painting) and gold medal (stained glass window), St. Louis Expn., 1904. Most important pictures: Her Tribute (woman making flag); The Flight Into Egypt; Leda and the Swan; executed Crerar window in Second Presbyn. Church, Chicago, one of largest stained glass windows in the country. A.N.A. Died July 30, 1931.

KLINE, William Jay, editor, publisher; b. Fultonville, N.Y., Nov. 7, 1848; s. William W. and Jane Ann (Booth) K.; A.B., Union Coll., N.Y., 1872, A.M., 1875, L.H.D., 1912; m. Emily Gardiner, Apr. 14, 1875. In office of John H. Starin, New York, 1872-73; purchased Amsterdam Weekly Democrat, 1873; started daily in 1879; bought Amsterdam Recorder and consolidated with Democrat, 1893; now, in company with son, Gardiner, publisher Evening Recorder and Semi-Weekly Recorder Democrat; v.p. Montgomery Co. Trust Co., Amsterdam Savings Bank. Postmaster, Amsterdam, 1877-85. Vice-pres. Amsterdam Free Library; trustee Home for Elderly Women. Mem. U.S. Chamber Commerce. Republican. Presbyn. Mason. Home: Amsterdam, N.Y. Died Nov. 3, 1930.

KLINGAMAN, Orie Erb, educator; b. La Grange Co., Ind., July 7, 1874; s. Jonathan and Jennie (Erb) K.; A.B., Highland Park (Ia.) Coll., 1912; M.A., U. of Ia., 1914; m. Katharine Marley, Feb. 19, 1903; children—Murray Orie, Roger Marley, Halsey Ernest. Prof. and head extension div., State U. of Ia., 1913-23; dir. bureau of research and information, Nat. Retail Dry Goods Assn., 1923-24; personnel mgr. William Filene Sons Co., Boston, 1924-21; dir. store promotion Harris-Emery Co., 1925-26; admitted to Iowa bar, 1927; law practice Des Moines, 1927-29; asst. dir. Davenport Pub. Mus., 1929-34; curator State Hist., Memorial and Art Dept., Des Moines, Ia., 1937-39. President Ia. Housing Assn.; dir. Americanization for Ia., by apptmt. of Sec. of Interior Lane; established Ia. Patriotic League; dir. of physical walfare, Boys' Working Reserve; advisor on clothing Federal

Emergency Relief Adminstrn., Washington, D.C., 1933-34. Democrat. Methodist. Mason. Home: Davenport, Iowa. Died Jan. 25, 1941.

KLIPSTEIN, Ernest Carl, architect; b. St. Louis, Mo., Feb. 4, 1866; s. Christian and Louisa (Zoeckler) K.; prep. edn., Manual Training Sch., St. Louis; student Mass. Inst. Tech. and Polytechnicum, Munich; m. Grace Huiskamp, Nov. 1, 1905; 1 dau., Julia Werth. Teacher drawing and manual training, high sch., Springefild, Mass., 1888-91; instr. of design, U. of Ill., 1895-96; in archtl. offices, 1896-98; began practice at St. Louis, 1898; with Klipstein and Rathman, 1905—; dir. Security Nat. Bank Trust & Savings Co., Semi-Steel Casting Co. Mem. Memorial Plaza Commn. of St. Louis, designers of Court House, Municipal Auditorium and War Memorial. Fellow Am. Inst. Architects. Republican. Unitarian. Home: St. Louis, Mo. Died Nov. 8, 1931.

KLOEBER, Charles Edward, newspaperman; b. Richmond, Va., May 28, 1869; s. Charles Edward and Mary Elizabeth (Smith) K.; ed. pub. and pvt. schs., Va. and Md.; m. Frances Theresa Skelton, Jan. 1894 (died 1898); m. 2d, Helen L. Soule-Ferguson, June 24, 1903. Reporter and Washington corr. various newspapers, 1888-94; joined Washington staff Associated Press, 1897, and became night, and later, day mgr. there; sent to China to report Boxer Rebellion, 1900; apptd. day mgr. New York office, Associated Press, 1901, later gen. news editor; supt. Western div., San Francisco, 1909; chief of news dept., 1912-18; in charge of service western front, World War; corr. in Balkan countries, hdqrs. Vienna, 1919, Tokyo, Japan, 1924; resigned, 1925; asst. to pres. U.S. Daily, Washington, D.C., 1927. Officier de l'Instruction Publique of France. Home: Washington, D.C. Died July 24, 1933.

KLOPP, Edward Jonathan, M.D.; b. Sheridan, Pa., June 10, 1880; s. Aaron Jonathan and Clara Malinda (Pieffer) K.; Pharm.D., Phila. Coll. Pharmacy, 1901; M.D., Jefferson Med. Coll., 1906, hon. B.S., 1925; m. Emma Mabel Riale, Sept. 27, 1911; children—Emily Riale, Sara Carpenter, Mary Elizabeth, Edward Jonathan. Pharmacist at Phila., 1901-02; began practice of medicine at Phila., 1906; prof. surgery, Jefferson Med. Coll.; surgeon Pa. Hosp., Memorial Hosp., Delaware Co. Hosp.; cons. surgeon Girard Coll. Mem. Med. Advisory Bd., Phila., World War; mem. U.S.N.R.F. until 1930. Fellow Am. Coll. Surgeons. Republican. Episcopalian. Home: Philadelphia, Pa. Died Sept. 19, 1936.

KLOPSCH, Louis, journalist; b. Germany, Mar. 26, 1852; public school edn.; m. May E., d. Rev. Stephen Merritt, 1886. Proprietor Daily Reporter, New York, 1877-90; propr. Pictorial Associated Press, 1884-90; propr. Talmage Sermon Syndicate, 1885—; on return from Palestine, in 1890, became interested in The Christian Herald, of which he became propr. in 1892; from then, through his paper, raised and distributed over $3,300,000 in internat. charities; in recognition of his relief operations in the Russian famine of 1892 was received by the Czar of Russia; in 1898 received official thanks of English and Indian Govt. for services in behalf of famine stricken India in 1896, when he sent a cargo of corn, and money, aggregating $400,000; in 1898 apptd. one of 3 U.S. Commrs. charged with the relief of the starving reconcentrados in Cuba, for which purpose he raised nearly $200,000; in spring of 1900, visited famine and cholera fields of India, and to relieve the distress raised through his paper in 6 mos., nearly $700,000, and later guaranteed until Jan. 1908, the support of 5,000 famine orphans in India. In 1901, in response to appeal by cable from Li Hung Chang, raised and sent $80,000 for the starving people in province of Shensi, China; in 1903 went to Finland and Sweden to visit the famine-stricken districts, for relief of which he had cabled nearly $125,000. Was received in pvt. audience by Queen Alexandria, King Christian of Denmark, King and Queen of Sweden and the Dowager Empress of Russia; King Edward conferred on him the Gold Kaiser-I-Hind medal of the first-class, 1904. In 1906 raised $250,000 for relief of famine sufferers in northern Japan and in 1907 sent $300,000 in money and a cargo of flour to relieve famine suffering in central China. Originator of the Red Letter Testament and Red Letter Bible. Decorated Order of the Rising Sun by Emperor of Japan, 1907. Died 1910.

KLOSS, Charles Luther, clergyman; b. New Berlin, Pa., Nov. 7, 1862; s. Daniel and Rebecca Jane K.; B.A., Highland (Kan.) Coll., 1882, A.M., 1886; B.D., Yale, 1885; univs. of Berlin and Heidelberg, 2 yrs.; D.D., Highland, 1905, Drury, 1907; m. Marie Phillips, Nov. 7, 1888; children—Daniel C., Mrs. Sara Hayes, Phillips. Ordained Congl. ministry, 1885; pastor Axtell, Kan., 1888-89, Argentine, 1889-90, Tabernacle Ch., Kansas City, Mo., 1890-97, 1st Ch., Webster Groves, Mo., 1897-1904, Central Ch., Phila., 1904-09, 1st Ch., Webster Groves, 1910-18, Plymouth Ch., Oakland, Calif., 1918-23, San Mateo, Calif., 1923—. Home: San Mateo, Calif. Died Oct. 28, 1931.

KLOTZ, Oskar, pathologist; b. Preston, Ont., Jan. 21, 1878; s. Otto (LL.D.) and Marie (Widenman)

K.; M.B., Univ. of Toronto, 1902; fellow in pathology, McGill U., 1903-05; M.D., C.M., same univ., 1906; student U. of Bonn, 1904-05, U. of Freiburg, 1908; m. Stella M. Scovil, Mar. 4, 1908. Demonstrator and lecturer, McGill U., 1905-10; prof. pathology, and bacteriology, U. of Pittsburgh, 1910-20; prof. pathology, Sao Paulo, Brazil (Rockefeller Foundation), 1920-23; prof. pathology and bacteriology, U. of Toronto, 1923—. Dir. Magee Pathol. Lab., Pathology Labs., Toronto Gen. Hosp., 1923—; cons. pathologist, Hosp. for Sick Children, Toronto, 1923—; hon. consultant in pathology, Dept. of Health, Ontario, 1934—; mem. Yellow Fever Commn., 1926, 28. Author: Arteriosclerosis, 1912. Home: Toronto, Canada. Died Nov. 3, 1936.

KLYCE, Scudder, writer; b. Friendship, Tenn., Nov. 7, 1879; s. Dr. J. R. and C. V. (Binford) K.; student U. of Ark.; grad. U.S. Naval Acad., 1902; post grad. work in engring. at same instn.; m. Etheldreda Hovey, 1908 (died 1917); 1 son, Stephen; m. 2d, Laura Tilden Kent, 1917; children—William (dec.), Dorothy. Commd. lt., U.S.N., May 2, 1907; retired Feb. 15, 1912, to devote attention to investigation of foundations of science. Served in Span.-Am. War and Philippine Campaign. Author: Universe, 1921; Sins of Science, 1925; Dewey's Suppressed Psychology (correspondence with John Dewey), 1928. Home: Winchester, Mass. Died Jan. 28, 1933.

KNABENSHUE, Paul, foreign service officer; b. Toledo, O., Oct. 31, 1883; s. Samuel S. and Salome (Natlaek) K.; grad. high sch., Toledo, 1903; study under pvt. tutors, 1907-08; m. Olive Parr, Aug. 8, 1911; children—Paul Denis, Iona Macdonnell. Partner and gen. mgr. Geroe & Knabenshue, brokers, Toledo, 1903-04; vice-consul, Belfast, Ireland, 1906-11, vice and dep. consul, May-July 1911; vice and dep. consul gen., Cairo, Egypt, 1911-15, vice-consul, 1915-17, consul, 1917-19; consul, Beirut, Syria, 1919-28; consul gen., Beirut, Syria, May-Oct. 1928, Jerusalem, 1928-32; minister resident and consul gen., Bagdad, Iraq, 1932—; E.E. and M.P. to Sultan of Muscat and Oman, 1933, on 100th anniversary of the signing of Treaty of Amity and Commerce with Muscat. Home: Los Angeles, Calif. Died Feb. 1, 1942.

KNABENSHUE, Samuel S., consul general; b. nr. Lancaster, O., Nov. 1, 1845; s. Joseph N. and Nancy (Prentice) K.; ed. pub. schs. followed by pvt. study; m. Salome Matlack, Nov. 28, 1871. Printer, then teacher; prin. grammar sch., Lancaster, 10 yrs.; editor and part propr. the Republican, Mt. Vernon, O., 1876-78; supt. pub. schs., Lancaster, 1878-81; night editor Ohio State Journal, Columbus, 1881-83; polit. writer Toledo Blade, 1884-1905; Am. consul, at Belfast, Ireland, 1905-09; consul gen. at Tientsin, China, 1909-14 (resigned). Home: Los Angeles, Calif. Died Apr. 5, 1926.

KNAPP, Adeline, author, newspaper writer; b. Buffalo, N.Y., Mar. 15, 1860; d. Lyman and Adeline (Maxwell) K. In newspaper work for some yrs.; when last revolution occurred in Hawaii was sent out by San Francisco Call to Honolulu to report; probably the 1st woman ever sent to represent a great daily newspaper in such a crisis. At instance of gen. supt. public instruction went to Philippine Islands, July 1901, and spent 6 mos. traveling and procuring data for history of Filipino people; and 1902 at invitation Insular Dept. Public Health prepared book on hygiene; both books in use in schs. of the archipelago. Editor Household Mag., New York, Dec., 1902-June 1903. Author: The Boy and the Baron, 1902; Well in the Desert, 1908; Iron Pirate, 1911. Deceased.

KNAPP, Bradford, college pres.; b. Vinton, Ia., Dec. 24, 1870; s. Seaman Asahel and Maria E. (Hotchkiss) K.; Ia. Agrl. Coll., Ames, 2 yrs.; B.S., Vanderbilt U., 1892; LL.B., U. of Mich., 1896; D. Agr., Md. Agrl. Coll., 1918; m. Stella White, July 20, 1904; children—Bradford, Marion C. (Mrs. I. E. Hurst), DeWitt L., Roger S., Virginia Stella. Associated with his father in Southern agrl. work several years; practiced law at Clarion, Iowa, 1899-1909; county attorney, Wright County, Iowa, 1907-09; asst. to his father, spl. agt. farmers' coöperative demonstration work, Bur. Plant Industry, Dept. Agr., Nov. 15, 1909, until latter's death, Apr. 1, 1911; apptd. spl. agt. to succeed father, Apr. 11, 1911; chief of Office of Extension Work in the South, States Relations Service, U.S. Dept. Agr., 1915-20; dean Coll. of Agr., U. of Ark., and dir. State Expt. Sta., Jan. 1920-Oct. 1923; pres. Okla. Agrl. and Mech. Coll., 1923-28; pres. Ala. Polytechnic Inst., 1928-32; pres. Texas Technological College, 1932—. Mem. advisory com. on cotton, Federal Farm Bd. Traveled in Europe, invesigating rural finance organization and coöp. marketing for U.S. Dept. Agr., 1913. Fellow Royal Econ. Soc. Democrat. Presbyn. Mason. Rotarian. Home: Lubbock, Tex. Died June 11, 1938.

KNAPP, Charles, philologist; b. New York, June 22, 1868; s. Michael and Mary Josephine (Rennert) K.; A.B., Columbia U., 1887, A.M., 1888, Ph.D., 1890, Litt.D., 1929; m. Therese Isabel Shaw, June 24, 1889 (died 1929); 1 son, Charles Merriam. Prize fellow in classics, Columbia U., 1887-90, tutorial fellow in Latin, 1890-91, instr. Latin and Greek, 1891-1902, adj. prof. classical philology, 1902-06,

prof., 1906-21, prof. Greek and Latin, 1921—, chmn. com. on pub. ceremonies, 1909-19, mem. univ. council, 1923-26. Republican. Episcopalian. Grand Commander of New York United Order of Golden Cross, 1899-1906, 1909-14, 1916—, and mem. Supreme Commandery, 1891— (com. on laws, 1923—; chmn. 1926—; mem. exec. com. 1930—). Editor: Stories from Aulus Gellius, 1895; Selections from Viri Romæ (with Robert Arrowsmith), 1896; The Æneid of Vergil, Books I-VI, selections, VII-XII, 1901, 28; Selections from Ovid, 1922, 2d series, 1925, rev. edit., 1928; Æneid of Vergil, with Selections from Ovid, Metamorphoses, 1928. In charge dept. of classical philology in 2d edit. (1914-16) of New Internat. Ency.; special contbr. on Latin lit., Am. Year Book, 1911-19, on classical philology to New Internat. Year Book, 1907—. Mng. editor The Classical Weekly, 1907—. Author: Bibliography of Charles Knapp, 1893-1923, 1923; General Index to The Classical Weekly, I-XVI, 1924-25. Translator of Latin and Greek poems of John Milton in vol. 1 of Columbia edit. of Milton, 1931. Home: New York, N.Y. Died Sept. 17, 1936.

KNAPP, Charles Luman, congressman; b. Harrisburg, N.Y., July 4, 1847; A.B., Rutgers, Coll., 1869; m. Sarah, d. Hon. Daniel G. Dorvance, of Oneida Castle, N.Y., June 26, 1887. In practice at Lowville, N.Y., 1873—; mem. N.Y. Senate, 1886, 1887; consul-gen. at Montreal, 1889-93; elected to 57th Congress, Nov. 5, 1901, for unexpired term (1901-03), of A. D. Shaw, deceased; reëlected 58th to 61st Congresses (1903-11), 28th Dist. Republican. Home: Lowville, N.Y. Died Jan. 3, 1929.

KNAPP, Charles Welbourne, newspaperman; b. St. Louis, Jan. 23, 1848; s. Col. John and Virginia (Wright) K.; A.B., St. Louis U., 1865, A.M., 1867 (LL.D., 1904); LL.B., U. of Ky., 1867; m. Frances Shackelford, Apr. 22, 1875. Entered service of the Missouri Republican, 1867, of which his father was one of the prin. proprietors; served in various capacities and long had charge of the paper's Washington bureau; in Nov. 1887, became pres. of the corp., "Publishers, George Knapp & Co.," owners of the paper, the name of which was changed to The St. Louis Republic, May 1888. Dir. Associated Press (pres. 1900). Home: St. Louis, Mo. Died Jan. 6, 1916.

KNAPP, Harry Shepard, naval officer; b. New Britain, Conn., June 27, 1856; s. Frederic and Mary Eunice (Burritt) K.; grad. U.S. Naval Acad., 1878; unmarried. Midshipman, 1880; ensign, 1882; lt. jr. grade, 1889; lt., 1894; lt. comdr., 1902; capt., 1909; rear admiral, Aug. 13, 1916. Served on various ships at sea and at Naval Acad. and Naval War Coll.; Army War Coll., winter, 1906-07; chief of staff, Pacific Fleet, 1907-08; comdg. Charleston, 1908-09, Tennessee, 1910-11, Florida, 1911-12; mem. Gen. Bd. of Navy, 1909-10 and 1912-16; mil. gov. Santo Domingo, 1917-18; duty with Peace Conf., 1919; comdr. U.S. Naval Forces in European waters, 1919-20, retired. Conglist. Home: Hartford, Conn. Died Apr. 6, 1923.

KNAPP, Henry Alonzo, lawyer; b. Barker, N.Y., July 24, 1851; s. Peter and Cornelia Eveline (Nash) K.; ed. Binghamton (N.Y.) Acad.; read law in office of Judge John Handley, of Scranton, Pa.; m. Lillie Logan, Mar. 27, 1883. Admitted to Pa. bar, 1875, and began practice at Scranton; judge cts. of Lackawanna Co., by appmt. of Gov. Beaver, July 1887-Jan. 1888; solicitor Scranton Sch. Dist., 1888-98; solicitor Lackawanna Co. many yrs. First lt. and capt., Co. A, Scranton City Guard, 1878-80, which afterward became part of 13th Regt., Pa. N.G.; judge-advocate with rank of maj. 3d Brigade, on staff of Gen. Gobin, 1885-87. Trustee Pa. Sch. for Deaf, West Mountain Sanatorium (Scranton). Republican. Presbyn. Home: Scranton, Pa. Died July 16, 1931.

KNAPP, Herman, physician; b. Dauborn, Prussia, Mar. 17, 1832; s. Johann K. (mem. German Reichsrath, etc.); M.D., U. of Giessen, 1854; studied in Germany, London and Paris. Prof. ophthalmology, Heidelberg, 1864-68; has practiced in New York, 1868—; prof. ophthalmology, New York U. Med. Coll., 1882-88; same chair, Coll. Phys. and Surg. (Columbia), 1888-1902 (emeritus). Founded New York Ophthalmic and Aural Inst., 1869; established Archives of Ophthalmology and Otology, 1869. Home: New York, N.Y. Died 1911.

KNAPP, Herman, educator; b. Poultney, Vt., Dec. 28, 1863; s. Seaman A. (LL.D.) and Maria E. (Hotchkiss) K.; prep. education, Tilford Acad., Vinton, Ia.; Bach. Scientific Agr., Ia. State Coll. Agr. and Mechanic Arts, 1883; m. Mary W. McDonald, Nov. 26, 1885; children—Seaman Arthur, Hermine Marion (Mrs. A. H. Pickford), Jeannette Margaret (Mrs. A. E. Stoddard), Byron McDonald. With Ia. State Coll. Agr. and Mechanic Arts, 1883—; business mgr. and treas. 1887—. Member School Board and Library Board, Ames. Commandant Iowa State College Agriculture and Mechanic Arts, 1898; was captain 55th Iowa N.G.; maj. and adj. gen. First Ia. Brigade, 1901-09; expert rifleman. Republican. Methodist. Red Man. Home: Ames, Ia. Died Mar. 22, 1935.

KNAPP, John Joseph, naval officer; b. St. Louis, Oct. 29, 1857; s. John and Virginia (Wright) K.; grad. U.S. Naval Acad., 1878; m. Lilias Harrison, July 31, 1884. Commd. ensign, June 26, 1884; promoted through the various grades to capt., July 1, 1910. Served on U.S.S. Quinnebaug, 1878-80; Wachusett, 1881-84; New Hampshire, 1884-85; Alert, 1887-90; Baltimore, 1892-93; Patterson, 1896-97; flag lt. to Rear Admiral Howell, on U.S.S. San Francisco, Feb.-Oct. 1898; detached duty and comd. torpedo boat Somers, Mar.-Apr. 1898, and comd. Topeka, Apr.-May 1898, comd. Sylph, July-Sept. 1899; in P.I., 1900-01; on Petrel and comd. Wompatuck; supt. Nautical Sch., Manila, 1901-02; on Solace, 1904-05; comd. Celtic, 1905-06, Cheyenne, 1908-09; hydrographer, Bur. Navigation, Navy Dept., 1910—. Medal for W.I. campaign during Spanish-Am. War; Spanish War and Philippine campaign badges. Home: Washington, D.C. Died Sept. 28, 1915.

KNAPP, Lyman Enos, lawyer; b. Somerset, Vt., Nov. 5, 1837; s. Hiram K.; grad. Middlebury Coll., 1862 (A.M.; also LL.D., Whitman Coll., 1893); m. Martha A. Severance, Jan. 23, 1865. Entered army, 1862, as capt.; engaged in 14 of the historic battles from Gettysburg to the capture of Petersburg; 3 times wounded; bvtd. for gallantry by President Lincoln and retired at close of war as lt. col., comdg. regt. Editor Middlebury, Vt., Register, 1865-78; editorial contributor to Am. Law Register and Chicago Inter Ocean; corr. Associated Press, etc. Practiced law, 1876—. One of clerks Vt. Ho. of Reps., 1872-73; judge of probate, Addison dist., Vt., 1879-89; mem. Vt. Ho. of Reps., 1884-85; gov. of Alaska, 1889-93; engaged in law practice at Seattle, Wash. Home: Seattle, Wash. Died 1904.

KNAPP, Martin Augustine, judge; b. Spafford, N.Y., Nov. 6, 1843; s. Justus Norton and Polly (McKay) K.; A.B., Wesleyan U., Conn., 1868, A.M., 1871 (LL.D., 1892; LL.D., Syracuse, 1911); m. Marian Hotchkiss, Dec. 29, 1869 (died 1904); m. 2d, Mrs. Nellie Maynard Gardner, Aug. 10, 1907 (died 1914). Admitted to New York bar, 1869; was corporation counsel, Syracuse, 1877-83; apptd. Interstate Commerce Commr., Feb. 1891; reapptd., Feb. 1897, and in 1902 and 1908; chmn. of the commn. from 1898, and as ex officio mediator under the Erdman Act participated in numerous negotiations for the settlement of ry. labor disputes; apptd. additional circuit judge and assigned for 5 yrs. to the U.S. Commerce Ct. as presiding judge; assumed the duties of that office Dec. 31, 1910, resigning from the commn. at the same time; later apptd. mediator under amended Erdman Act for 2 yrs. from Mar. 4, 1911; apptd. to Bd. of Mediation and Conciliation created by Newlands Act of 1913, superseding Erdman law; upon dissolution of Commerce Ct., Dec. 31, 1913, assigned by chief justice to Circuit Ct. of Appeals of the 4th Jud. Circuit. Home: Washington, D.C. Died Feb. 10, 1923.

KNAPP, Philip Coombs, physician; b. Lynn, Mass., June 3, 1858; s. Philip Coombs and Sally Harriette (Moore) K.; A.B., Harvard, 1878, A.M., 1883, M.D., 1883; m. Isabel Williams Stebbins, Dec. 12, 1893. Specialist in nervous and mental diseases at Boston, 1884—; visiting phys. diseases of nervous system, Boston City Hosp., 1885—, Boston Dispensary, 1886-88; instr. diseases of nervous system, Harvard Med. Sch., 1888-1913; consulting phys., Mass. State Hosp. for Insane Criminals, 1895—; trustee Boston Insane Hosp., 1897-1902. Pres. Am. Neurol. Assn., 1895, N.E. Soc. of Psychiatry, 1905-08, Boston Soc. of Psychiatry and Neurology, 1901. Author: The Pathology, Diagnosis and Treatment of Introcranial Growths, 1891. Joint author: A System of Legal Medicine, 1894; Textbook of Nervous Diseases by American Authors, 1895. Joint translator and editor: Strümpell's Textbook of Medicine, 1887, 93, 1901, 11. Deceased.

KNAPP, Seaman Asahel, agrl. educator; b. Essex Co., N.Y., Dec. 16, 1833; s. Dr. Bradford and Rhoda (Seaman) K.; A.B., Union Coll., N.Y., 1856; (LL.D., Upper Ia. U., 1882, Baylor U., Tex., 1908; D.Sc., Ia. State Coll. of Agr. and Mech. Arts, 1909); m. Maria E. Hotchkiss, Aug. 6, 1856. Teacher and later asso. mgr. Ft. Edward Collegiate Inst., 1856-63; asso. mgr. Ripley Female Coll., Vt., 1863-65; pres. Ia. State Coll. for Blind, 1869-75; prof. agr., 1879-86, pres., 1883-84, Ia. State Agrl. Coll.; visited Japan, China and the Philippines, 1898, for U.S. Dept. Agr., to report on resources of islands, returning early in 1899; visited Puerto Rico, 1900, on similar mission; visited Japan, China, P.I., Ceylon, India, Burmah and H.I. for U.S. Dept. of Agr., 1901-02; in charge of "Farmers Co-operative Demonstration Work" in Southern states for U.S. Dept. Agr., 1902-10. Home: Washington, D.C. Died 1911.

KNAPP, Thad Johnson, educator; b. Northville, Mich., Apr. 23, 1876; s. John O. and Jennie (Johnson) K.; Ph.B., U. of Mich., 1898, grad. study, 1913-15, M.A., 1927; studied Columbia, various periods, 1901-11; m. Adaline Spalding, June 29, 1905. Teacher, Reed City, Mich., Joliet, Ill., Kearny and Newark, N.J.; prin. high sch., Kearny, N.J.; supt. schs., Highland Park, Mich., 1911-26, Northville, Mich., 1930—, prof. ednl. administration, U. of Mich. Summer Sch., 1920. Mem. N.E.A. (v.p.), Mich. State Teachers' Assn. (pres. 1919-20), Detroit Wayne Co. Ednl. System, U. of Mich. Alumni Assn.; v.p. Mich. State Teachers' Retirement Fund Board. Republican. Presbyn. Accredited with having built up a notable ednl. system at Highland Park and having advanced cause of teachers' salaries in Mich. Home: Northville, Mich. Died Apr. 21, 1933.

KNAPP, William Ireland, educator; b. New York, March 10, 1835; s. Rev. H. R. K.; ed. New York and Colgate univs. (A.M., 1860; Ph.D., 1867; LL.D., 1888; Knight Comdr. of the Order of Isabel la Catolica of Spain, 1877); m. Adeline, d. Capt. Wm. A. Roberts, 1861. Prof. modern languages, Colgate Univ., 1860-65; Vassar Coll., 1865-67; Yale, 1879-92; Univ. of Chicago, 1892-95; in Europe, 1858, 1867-78, 1892; from 1895 has lived in England and France, devoted to literary pursuits. Author: Grammar of the Modern Spanish Language, 1882; Modern Spanish Readings, 1883; Modern French Readings (with notes), 1883; Life Writings and Correspondence of George Borrow, 2 vols., 1899, London and New York. Editor: Las Obras de Juan Boscan, Madrid, 1875; Obras Poéticas de Don Diego Hurtado de Mendoza, 2 vols., Madrid, 1876-77; Lecturas Escogidas de Autores Españoles que Hoy Viven, New Haven, 1880; Borrow's Lavengro and The Romany Rye, London, 1900; Pascual López by Mme. Pardo-Bazán, 1905. Died 1908.

KNAPPEN, Loyal Edwin, judge; b. Hastings, Mich., Jan. 27, 1854; s. Edwin and Sarah M. (Nevins) K.; B.A., U. of Mich., 1873, M.A., 1876, LL.D., 1913; m. Amelia Isabelle Kenyon, Oct. 23, 1876; children—Stuart Edwin, Fred Mason, Mrs. Florence Perry. Admitted to bar, 1875; in practice at Hastings, 1875-88; pros. atty. Barry Co., Mich., 1879-83; U.S. commr., 1880-88; practiced law, Grand Rapids, 1888-1906; U.S. dist. judge Western Dist. of Mich., 1906-10; became U.S. circuit judge, 6th Circuit, 1910. Regent U. of Mich., 1904-11. Died May 15, 1930.

KNAPPEN, Theodore Macfarlane, journalist, economist; b. nr. Poynette, Wis., Oct. 23, 1871; s. Theodore Frelinghuysen and Sarah Letitia (Macfarlane) K.; B.S., Univ. of Minn., 1891; m. Nellie Malura Cross, Aug. 29, 1896; children—Judson Norcross, Theodore Temple, Phoebe Malura, Andrew Macfarlane. Civ. engr. with G. N. and Duluth, S. Shore and Atlantic rys., 1891-93; with Minneapolis Times and St. Paul Call, 1894-95, Minneapolis Journal, 1895-1903, becoming asso. editor; various Fla., Mont., Canadian and Calif. immigration and land settlement enterprises until 1916; industrial corr. New York Tribune, 1917-18, then editor Nat. Lumber Mfrs.' Assn. and asso. editor Magazine of Wall Street (New York). Assistant mgr. campaign of Governor John A. Johnson of Minn. for Dem. nomination for President of U.S., 1908; exec. sec. bur. of clubs, Dem. Nat. Com., 1916. Episcopalian. Author: Wings of War, 1920. Home: Washington, D.C.. Died Oct. 26, 1938.

KNEASS, Strickland Landis, mech. engr.; b. Phila., Jan. 7, 1861; s. Strickland and Margaretta Sybilla (Bryan) K.; grad. Rugby Acad., Phila., 1876; C.E., Rensselaer Poly. Inst., 1880; m. Mary Stewart Edwards, Oct. 22, 1888; children—Strickland, Edward, George Bryan. With William Sellers & Co., Phila., 1883—, became mgr. injector dept., 1895, vice president, 1926—. Awarded diploma, Chicago Exposition, 1893, St. Louis Exposition, 1904; awarded John Scott medal and premium, Franklin Institute, Phila., 1900. Republican. Presbyterian. Author: Practice and Theory of the Injector. Home: Philadelphia, Pa. Died Nov. 24, 1928.

KNEELAND, Stillman Foster, lawyer; b. S. Stukely, Que., Can., May 17, 1845; s. Gardner and Julia (Castle) K.; ed. McGill U., Montreal, and Union Coll.; (LL.D.); served in Union Army during Civil War; wounded in action; m. Mary Stuart Wilson, Nov. 29, 1872. Admitted to bar, 1869; in practice at New York, 1872—; was mem. Kneeland, La Febra & Glaze. Framed and secured the passage, 1886, of an act abolishing perpetual imprisonment for debt in New York; mem. Legislature, 1894; judge-advocate-gen., 1896-98. V.p. dept. painting, Brooklyn Inst. of Arts and Sciences. Author: Law, Lawyers and Lambs; Random Rhymes of a Busy Barrister. Retired. Home: New York, N.Y. Died Aug. 30, 1926.

KNEISEL, Franz, violinist; b. Rumania (of German parentage), Jan. 26, 1865; s. Martin (mus. conductor) and Victoria (Lukas) K.; violin instructor under Grün and Hellmesberger, Vienna; grad. Vienna Conservatory, 1882; (Mus.D., Yale U., 1911, and Princeton U., 1915); m. Marianne Thoma, 1885. Was concertmaster of Hofburg Theatre Orchestra, Vienna; later of Bilse's Orchestra, Berlin; came to America, 1885, to become concertmaster and conductor Boston Symphony Orchestra, with which remained until 1903; also dir. and 1st violin, Kneisel Quartette, 1885—; asso. condr. and condr., Worcester music festivals, 1886-1909; head of violin and string instrument dept., Inst. of Musical Art, New York, 1905—, also head violin and string instrument dept., Kneisel Hall, Blue Hill, Me., summers. Mem. jury, Paris Conservatory, 1907. Compiler: Kneisel Collection (for violin and piano), 3 vols., 1900. Composer: Advanced Studies for the Violin, 1910; concert étude. Died Mar. 26, 1926.

KNIGHT, Albion Williamson, bishop; b. White Springs, Fla., Aug. 24, 1859; s. George Augustine and Martha (Demere) K.; ed. U. of the South, Sewanee, Tenn.; m. Elise Nicoll Hallowes, Aug. 27, 1889; 1 dau., Ada Nicoll (Mrs. Thomas P. Harper); m. 2d, Miriam Powell Yates, April 29, 1919. Deacon, Nov. 27, 1881, priest, 1883, P.E. Ch.; served at Palatka, and Jacksonville, Fla., until 1893; dean of Cathedral, Atlanta, Ga., 1893-1904; consecrated bishop, Dec. 21, 1904; missionary bishop of Cuba, 1904-13; bishop in charge, Panama Canal Zone, 1908-20; chancellor, U. of the South, 1913-22; bishop coadjutor of N.J., 1923; retired. Mem. Gen. Conv. P.E. Ch., 15 times. Alumni trustee U. of the South. Home: Trenton, N.J. June 9, 1936.

KNIGHT, Austin Melvin, admiral U.S. Navy; b. Ware, Mass., Dec. 16, 1854; s. Charles Sanford and Cordelia (Cutter) K.; grad. U.S. Naval Acad., 1873; m. Alice Phinney Tobey, 1878 (died 1879); 1 dau., Alice Austin (Mrs. W. L. Pryor); m. 2d, Elizabeth Harwood Welsh, Apr. 29, 1886 (died 1911); children—Dorothy Knight, Richard Harwood. Commd. ensign, July 1874; promoted through grades to rear admiral, Jan. 29, 1911. Served on board the Tuscarora, Pacific Station, 1873-74; Kearsarge, Palos, and Saco, Asiatic Station, 1874-75; Naval Acad., 1876-78; Quinnebaug, European Station, 1878-79; Galena, European and South Atlantic Stas., 1880-83; ordnance proving ground, Annapolis, Md., 1883-85; in charge same, 1885-89; Flagship Chicago, North Atlantic, European and South Atlantic stas., 1889-92; Naval Acad., 1892-95; Lancaster and Castine, South Atlantic station, 1895-97; Puritan, North Atlantic station, 1897-98; engaged in blockade on north coast of Cuba, and in Puerto Rican expdn. during the Spanish-Am. War; head of dept. of seamanship, Naval Academy, 1898-1901; comd. Newport, summer practice cruise, 1900; War College, summer, 1901; comd. Yankton, surveying on south coast of Cuba, 1901-03; comd. Castine, N. Atlantic Squadron, 1903-04; pres. special board on naval ordnance and pres. joint army and navy board on smokeless powders, 1904-07; comd. Washington, Oct. 7, 1907, to May 1, 1909; pres. special board on naval ordnance and of joint army and navy board on smokeless powders, 1909; later comd. Narragansett Bay (R.I.) Naval Sta.; comdt. same and pres. Naval War Coll., Dec. 1913-Feb. 1917; comdr.-in-chief Asiatic Fleet with rank of admiral, Apr. 1917-Dec. 9, 1918; retired, Dec. 16, 1918. Pres. Board to Award Decorations for War Service, 1918-19. Author: Modern Seamanship, 1901. Home: Washington, D.C. Died Feb. 26. 1927.

KNIGHT, Charles Landon, congressman, pub.; b. Baldwin Co., Ga., June 18, 1867; s. William and Sarah (Landon) K.; A.B., Columbia Coll., 1889, LL.B., 1890; in Europe, 1891-93, studying polit. and social instns.; m. Clara I. Shively, Nov. 22, 1893; children—John Shively, James Landon. On staff Phila. Times, 1896-1900; editor and pub. Beacon Journal, Akron, O., and Massillon (O.) Evening Independent. Mem. Rep. State Central Com., many times; mem. 67th Congress (1921-23), 14th Ohio Dist.; candidate for gov. of Ohio, 1922. Mem. Nat. Advisory Com. Rep. Party, 1924. Commr. of Ohio for Phila. Sesquicentennial, 1926. Episcopalian. Home: Akron, Ohio. Died Sept. 26, 1933.

KNIGHT, Clarence A., lawyer; b. McHenry Co., Ill., Oct. 28, 1853; grad. Cook Co. (Ill.) Normal Sch. Admitted to bar on exam., 1874; asst. city atty., 1879-84, city atty., 1884-88, Chicago, asst. corp. counsel, 1888-89; now sr. mem. Knight, Barbour & Adams. Gen. counsel Lake St. Elevated R.R. Co., 1893—, Union Elevated R.R. Co., and Northwestern Elevated R.R. Co., 1898—. Successfully conducted litigation involving right to construct "Union Loop." Mason. Home: Chicago, Ill. Died 1911.

KNIGHT, Edward Wallace, lawyer; b. Newport, N.H., Apr. 30, 1866; s. Edward Boardman and Hannah Elizabeth (White) K.; A.B., Dartmouth, 1887, A.M., 1925; m. Mary Catherine Dana, Jan. 25, 1893 (died 1935); children—Edward Dana, Elizabeth Swift, Mary Ethel. Admitted to W.Va. bar, 1889; mem. Brown, Jackson & Knight, 1892—; gen. counsel Virginian Ry. Co. and its predecessors, 1902-28, consulting counsel, 1929—; v.p. Central Trust Co. of Charleston. Member City Council, Charleston, 1891-94; vice chmn. West Virginia Constl. Commission, 1929-30. Trustee Dartmouth Coll., 1925-35. Democrat. Presbyn. Mason. Home: Charleston, W.Va. Died Aug. 8, 1939.

KNIGHT, Frederic Harrison, clergyman; b. Saco, Me., Oct. 22, 1859; s. Edward T. and Sarah C. (Boothby) K.; A.B., Dartmouth, 1882, A.M., 1907; B.D., Boston U., 1885, Ph.D., 1895; student Boston U. Sch. of All Sciences, 1892-95, U. of Berlin, 1894-95; m. Marion Butterfield, Sept. 22, 1887. Ordained M.E. ministry, 1882; pastor, Putney, Vt., 1882-83, Wollaston, Mass., 1884-96, Jamaica Plain, Mass., 1887-90, Springfield, Mass., 1891-93, Salem, Mass., 1895-99, Boston, 1900-01; pres. New Orleans

U., 1902-07; supt. N.E. Home for Little Wanderers, Aug. 1907—. Home: Brookline, Mass. Died Oct. 15, 1922.

KNIGHT, Frederick Irving, physician; b. Newburyport, Mass., May 18, 1841; s. Frederick and Ann (Goodwin) K.; grad. Yale, 1862 (A.M., 1865); grad. med. dept., Harvard, 1866; studied afterward in Berlin and Vienna; m. Louisa Armistead Appleton, Oct. 15, 1871 (died 1901). Practice limited to diseases of throat and chest, in which he was instr. and clin. prof., Harvard, for many yrs.; cons. physician, Mass. Gen. Hosp., Sharon Sanatorium and Free Home for Consumptives. Fellow Am. Acad. Arts and Sciences. Died 1909.

KNIGHT, George Alexander, lawyer; b. Worcester, Mass., July 24, 1851; s. George H. and Elizabeth (McFarlan) K.; ed. pub. schs., Eureka, Calif.; grad. Coll. of Calif.; studied law in office of Judge J. E. Wyman, Humboldt, Calif.; m. Fannie H. Wyman, June 1877. Admitted to bar, 1872; dist. atty., Humboldt Co., 3 terms; ins. commr. of Calif.; atty. Calif. State Bd. of Health, 2 terms; judge-advocate with rank of col. on staff Gov. Markham; del. Rep. Nat. convs., 1896 (seconded nomination of McKinley), 1900, 1904, 1908 (seconded nomination of Taft); mem. Rep. Nat. Com., 1908-12. Atty. for U.P. R.R. and for Pacific Steamship Co. at San Francisco; has charge of Charles L. Fair estate of $18,000,000. Home: San Francisco, Calif. Died June 27, 1916.

KNIGHT, George Thomson, theologian; b. S. Windham, Me., Oct. 29, 1850; s. Mark and Emily Jane (Hobbs) K.; A.B., Tufts Coll., 1872, A.M., B.D., 1875; (D.D., Lombard Coll., Ill., 1893); m. Alice Sawyer, June 21, 1877. Ordained Universalist ministry, 1875; instr. rhetoric and ch. history, 1875-83, prof. ch. history, 1883-1900, Christian theology, 1900—, Tufts Divinity Sch. (now Crane Theol. Sch.). Author: The Goodness of God, 1904; The Praise of Hypocrisy, 1906. Died 1911.

KNIGHT, George Wells, univ. prof.; b. Ann Arbor, Mich., June 25, 1858; s. Johnson Wells and Cornelia P. (Hebbard) K.; A.B., U. of Mich., 1878, A.M., 1883, Ph.D., 1884; univs. Berlin, Halle and Freiburg, 1889-90; m. Mariette Amanda Barnes, Jan. 12, 1882; children—Margaret Amanda, Adelaide (dec.). Prin. Lansing High Sch., 1879-81; instr. history, Ann Arbor High Sch., 1883-85; prof. history and polit. science, 1885-98, Am. history and polit. science, 1898-1909, American history, 1909-28 (emeritus), chmn. Graduate School, 1904-08, and dean College of Education, 1914-20, Ohio State U. Vice-pres. Buckeye State Bldg. and Loan Co., 1918—. Mng. editor Ohio Archæol. and Hist. Quar., 1887-89; mem. and sec. Ohio commn., Jamestown Expn., 1907; mem. Ohio Constl. Conv., 1912. Author: History of Higher Education in Ohio (with Prof. John R. Commons), 1891; The Government of the People of Ohio, 1895. Edited with critical and supplementary notes, a new edition of Guizot's History of Civilization in Europe, 1896. Died Feb. 10, 1932.

KNIGHT, Jesse, justice Supreme Court, Wyo.; b. Boonville, N.Y., July 5, 1850; s. Jesse and Henrietta (Guion) K.; ed. common schools Western N.Y.; studied law; m. Mary L. Hezlep, Feb. 14, 1876. Clerk of court 15 yrs.; mem. Constl. Conv., Wyo.; one of 1st dist. judges after statehood; re-elected and resigned; apptd. justice Supreme Court to fill vacancy; elected to same position at last election for term of 8 yrs. Republican. Mason. Home: Cheyenne, Wyo. Died 1905.

KNIGHT, John George David, brig. gen.; b. in Eng., Jan. 24, 1846; s. George Augustus and Louisa (Dockerill) K.; apptd. from Mo., and grad. U.S. Mil. Acad., 1868; m. Gertrude Colden Eltinge, Nov. 22, 1870. Second lt., engrs., June 15, 1868; 1st lt., Jan. 22, 1870; capt., June 15, 1882; maj., Feb. 3, 1895; lt. col., Jan. 23, 1904; col., Mar. 2, 1907; brig. gen. U.S.A., Nov. 30, 1909; retired by operation of law, Jan. 24, 1910. Mem. Common Council of Summit, N.J., 1912-15; engr. commr. of D.C., July 16, 1917—. Died June 9, 1919.

KNIGHT, John Thornton, army officer; b. at "Poplar Hill," Prince Edward Co., Va., Apr. 18, 1861; s. John Hughes and Cornelia (Bland) K.; grad. U.S. Mil. Acad., 1884, Army War Coll., 1910; m. Edith, d. Lt. Gen. Young, of U.S. Army, Sept. 2, 1886; children—Alice Margaret, Sam Young, John Thornton, O'Ferrall, Alexander. Commd. 2d lt. 3d Cav., June 15, 1884; promoted through grades to brig. gen., asst. to q.m. gen., Mar. 8, 1923. Duty with Va. N.G., 1894-96; q.m. in charge constrn. new post at Jefferson Barracks, Mo., 1897-98; depot q.m., Santiago, Cuba, 1898, also chief q.m. Dept. of Santiago, until June 1899; in Philippines, 1899-1900; duty in office Q.M. Gen., Washington, 1906-08; mem. Gen. Staff Corps, 1908-10; duty in office Q.M. Gen., 1910-12; depot q.m. and gen. supt. army transport service, San Francisco, 1912-14; chief q.m. Philippine Dept., Manila, 1914-16; gen. supt. army transport service, San Francisco, 1916-17; q.m. Port of Embarkation, Newport News, Va., Aug. 1917-Sept. 23, 1918; q.m., Brest, France, Base Sect. 5, Oct. 1918 Feb. 1919; asst. to chief q.m. and as chief q.m. A.E.F., Tours and Paris, Feb.-Sept. 26, 1919; asst. to comdg. officer, Army Supply Base, Norfolk, Va., 1919 to 1920; chief of Construction Service, O.Q.M.G., Washington, D.C., Mar. 1923-Apr. 18, 1925 (retired). Christian Scientist. Died Jan. 15, 1930.

KNIGHT, Lucian Lamar, historian, capitalist; b. Atlanta, Ga., Feb. 9, 1868; s. Capt. George Walton and Clara Corinne (Daniel) K.; A.B. (valedictorian and orator), U. of Ga., 1888; studied law at univs., but left before taking degree; M.A., Princeton, 1904; LL.D., U. of Ga., 1917; Litt.D., King College, Bristol, Tenn., 1926; m. Edith M. Nelson, Sept. 4, 1895; children—Frances Walton (dec.), Mary Lamar; m. 2d, Rosa Talbot (Reid). Lit. editor Atlanta Constitution, 1892-1902; resided on Catalina Island on account of ill health, 1906-08; asso. editor Atlanta Georgian, 1908-10; 2d v.p. and lit. editor Martin & Hoyt Co., publishers, Atlanta, 1910—; v.p. John B. Daniel, Inc., wholesale druggists and mfrs., Atlanta, 1915—. Compiler official records of Ga., 1913-19; state historian of Ga., 1919-25; State Historian emeritus, 1925—. Founder Dept. of Archives and History, State of Ga.; founder Ga. Hist. Assn. (1st pres. 1917-19). Author: Woodrow Wilson—the Dreamer and the Dream, 1924; Tracking the Sunset, 1925; Souvenir Book of General Assemblies; The History of Fulton County, 1930; Ency. of Georgia Biography, 1930; Georgia's Bi-Centennial Memoirs and Memories, 1931. Editor: Georgia Colonial, Revolutionary, Confederate and State Records, a series to embrace some fifty volumes; Dictionary of Southern Authors and Historical Sidelights (vols. xv and xvi of the Library of Southern Literature), 1909. Asst. editor: Memoirs of Georgia, 1895; Modern Eloquence, 1899. Home: St Simons Island, Ga. Died Nov. 19, 1933.

KNIGHT, Ora Willis, chemist, geologist; b. Bangor, Me., July 15, 1874; s. George Willis and Nellie Ada (Blood) K.; B.S. (in chemistry), Me. State Coll., 1895; post-grad. work, U. of Me., M.S., 1897; (hon. Sc.D., 1909); m. Minnie Gertrude McDonald, Aug. 11, 1899. Asst. in natural history, Me. State Coll., 1895-97; asst. chemist, Me. Expt. Sta., 1897-1903; state assayer and cons. chemist, 1903—. Chemist, Lackawanna Foundries; expert chemist and microscopist in criminal cases in the courts (in case of State vs. Alexander Terrio, convicted of murder, discovered evidence through which a new trial was granted and Terrio set free—the only new trial ever granted in a murder case in the State of Me.). Republican. Unitarian. Has a nearly complete herbarium of the plants of Me. Home: Portland, Me. Died Nov. 11, 1913.

KNIGHT, (Daniel) Ridgway, artist; b. Phila.; pupil of Gleyre and Meissonier; studied Pa. Acad. Fine Arts and École des Beaux Arts, Paris; m. Rebecca Morris Webster; father of Charles and L(ouis) Aston K. Awarded hon. mention, Paris Salon, 1884; 3d class gold medal, Paris Salon, 1888; gold medal, Munich, 1888; silver medal, Paris Exposition, 1889; Cross, Legion of Honor, France, 1892; Cross, Legion of Honor, Munich, 1892; medal, Chicago Expn., 1893; medal, Antwerp Expn., 1894; grand medal of honor, Pa. Acad. Fine Arts, 1893. Exhibited at Paris Expn., 1900. Cross of Order of Saint Michael of Bavaria; Officer of Legion of Honor by French Govt., 1910. His drawing "The Year's Economies," 1890, was chosen by the British Post Office as New Year's card for all depositors in the British Post Savings Bank; his picture "Bas de laine," or "Woolen Stocking," was selected to serve as propaganda for 3d French war loan and exhibited in every commune in France, 1917. Mem. Com. Am. Relief Clearing House during war. Died Mar. 9, 1924.

KNIGHT, Robert, mfr.; b. Old Warwick, R.I., Jan. 8, 1826; s. Stephen and Weltha (Brayton) K.; student short time at Pawcatuck Acad., Westerly, R.I.; taught dist. sch. one winter; m. Josephine Louisa Webster, Mar. 5, 1849. Employed Cranston, R.I., print works and other cotton factories, 1834-43; clerk in store of brother, Benjamin, Providence, 1843; in 1847, with Z. Parker, leased, and in 1850 purchased John H. Clark's cotton mill and bleachery, Arnold's Bridge; became sole owner, 1851; gave to village and mill name of Pontiac; in 1852 purchased half interest in grain and flour business of brother, Benjamin Brayton K., firm becoming B. B. & R. K.; added to mfg. holdings in Mass. and R.I.; on death of brother, B. B. K., in 1898, became largest individual owner of cotton mills in world, controlling over 20 distinct establishments; dir. 1867, pres. 1884, Nat. Bank Commerce, Providence; dir. 1874, pres. 1884, People's Savings Bank, Providence. Home: Providence, R.I. Died Nov. 26, 1912.

KNIGHT, Stephen Albert, mfr.; b. Cranston, R.I., June 5, 1828; s. Stephen and Weltham (Brayton) K.; removed to Coventry, R.I., 1835; ed. Fruit Hill Acad., 1850-53; m. Ellen, d. Zachariah and Eliza Parker, May 5, 1851. Employed in cotton mill, 1835-46; clerk in a Providence grocery store, 1847; engaged with Parker & Knight, Arnold's Bridge, 1849, as overseer of spinning room. With brothers, Benjamin B. and Robert, purchased cotton mill at Hebronville, Mass., 1853; moved to Providence, 1866, as agent Hebron Mfg. Co., which purchased the Dodgeville Mills, 1866, and Grant Mill, 1870, Mr. Knight being agt. and the business forming part of the system of B. B. and R. Knight. Pres. Hebron Mfg. Co., 1899—; dir. bd. govt., 1895-98, pres. 1898-99, New England Cotton Mfrs. Assn. Died 1907.

KNIGHT, Thomas Edmund, Jr., lt. gov.; b. Greensboro, Ala., June 19, 1898; s. Thomas Edmund and Rebecca (Williams) K.; student U. of Ala., 1914-17; m. Lelia Otts. Began practice of law, Greensboro, 1921; county solicitor, Hale Co., Ala., 1923-25; asst. atty. gen. of Ala., 1925-29, atty. gen., 1930-34; lt. gov., 1934—. Democrat. Methodist. Mason, Elk. Home: Montgomery, Ala. Died May 1937.

KNIGHT, Webster, banker; b. Providence, R.I., Aug. 10, 1854; s. Robert and Josephine L. (Webster) K.; A.B., Brown U., 1876; m. Sarah Waldo Lippitt, Jan. 27, 1881; children—Robert Lippitt, Adelaide. Mem. B. R. & R. Knight, mfrs. sheetings and shirtings, 1897-1921; chmn. bd. Peoples Savings Bank, Phenix Nat. Bank. Mem. staff Gov. Charles Warren Lippitt, rank of col., 1895; asst. q.m. gen. R.I. N.G., 1897-1911. Mem. Warwick (R.I.) Town Council 11 yrs. (pres. 4 yrs.); Rep. presdl. elector, 1904. Trustee Homeopathic Hosp. of R.I. Mem. Providence Chamber Commerce. Episcopalian. Home: Natick, R.I. Died June 30, 1933.

KNIGHT, Wilbur Clinton, geologist; b. Rochelle, Ill., Dec. 13, 1858; s. David A. K.; grad. Univ. of Neb., 1886 (B.Sc., A.M.); asst. territorial geologist, Wyo., 1886; chemist and assayer, Swan Sampling & Testing Co., Cheyenne, 1887; supt. of mines in Colo. and Wyo., 1888-93; prof. mining, 1893, and from 1894 prof. mining and geology, Univ. of Wyo.; also, from 1897, State geologist of Wyo., 1898-99. Fellow Geol. Soc. of America; m. E. Emma Howell, 1889. Home: Laramie, Wyo. Died 1903.

KNIGHT, William Henry, writer; b. Harmony, N.Y., Apr. 19, 1835; s. William and Laura (Jones) K.; ed. Jamestown (N.Y.) Acad., 1848-51; m. Ella J. Waters, June 4, 1868. Compiled Bancroft's Handbook of the Pacific States, 1862-63-64, Bancroft's Map of the Pacific States, 1863; mgr. Bancroft's publishing dept., San Francisco, 1864-69; engaged in business, 1870-96. Writer and lecturer on astron. and other scientific subjects. Pres. Southern Calif. Acad. Sciences, 1894-97, and 1899-1902. Editorial writer, Los Angeles Times, 1905. Home: Los Angeles, Calif. Died May 13, 1925.

KNISKERN, Warren B., ry. official; b. Carlisle, N.Y., July 7, 1851; s. Abram and Margaret K.; ed. in country schs.; m. Margaret Beckham; children—Charles Beckham, Julia Wickliffe. Messenger clerk in gen. pass. dept., I.C. R.R., 1869-73; in charge foreign reports, gen. ticket office, C.&N.W. Ry., 1873-75; chief ticket clerk, New Orleans, Jackson & Northern R.R., 1875-76; in gen. pass. dept., 1876-78, city ticket agt., 1878-85, L.&N. R.R.; asst. gen. pass. agt., 1885-95, gen. pass. and ticket agt., 1895-1901, pass. traffic mgr., 1901-11, C.&N.W. Ry.; retired. Home: East Orange, N.J. Died Feb. 20, 1931.

KNOPF, S. Adolphus, M.D.; b. Halle-on-the-Saale, Germany, Nov. 27, 1857; s. Adolphus and Nanina (Bock) K.; A.B., U. of Paris (Sorbonne) 1890; M.D., Bellevue Hosp. Med. Coll. (New York University), 1888; Faculty of Medicine, Univ. of Paris, 1895; m. Perle Nora Dyar, Oct. 19, 1889 (died 1931); m. 2d, Julia Marie Off, Oct. 6, 1935; children—Gertrude, Lucille, Adolphus. Professor of medicine, department phthisiotherapy, N.Y. Post-Grad. Med. School, Columbia U., 1908-20; sr. visiting phys. Health Department's Riverside Tuberculosis Hosp., 1906-22; hon. dir. Gaylord Farm Sanitorium, Wallingford, Conn.; hon. pres. med. bd. Bruchesi Tuberculosis Inst., Montreal; attending tuberculosis specialist, ranking as maj., U.S.P.H.S., 1920-22; consulting phys. to Riverside Hosp. (N.Y.), St. Gabriel's (N.Y.) Sanatorium for Consumptives, West Mountain Sanatorium, at Scranton, Pa., etc. Fellow N.Y. Acad. Medicine, Assn. Mil. Surgeons U.S., Soc. Med. Jurisprudence, Am. Heart Assn., Am. Soc. for Psychical Research; hon. member Am. Assn. for Thoracic Surgery, Am. Tuberculosis Assn.; hon. vice pres. Brit. Congress on Tuberculosis; govt. del. Internat. Prison Congress, Budapest, Internat. Tuberculosis Congress, Paris; v.p. sect. V of Tuberculosis Congress, Washington, 1908; official del. 4th Internat. Congress on Sch. Hygiene, Buffalo, 1913; laureate French Inst. of Paris, 1896, Coll. Physicians of Phila., 1898, Internat. Congress for study of how best to combat tuberculosis as a disease of the masses, 1900, Institut de France, 1900, Internat. Tuberculosis Congress, Washington, 1908; apptd. rep. U.S. International Union Against Tuberculosis, The Hague, 1932. Founder N.Y. City and Nat. Tuberculosis Assns. Capt. Med. R.C., U.S. Army, 1917; maj. M.O.R.C. Mason. Home: New York, N.Y. Died July 15, 1940.

KNOTT, A(loysius) Leo, lawyer; b. Frederick Co., Md.; s. Edward and Elizabeth Sprigg (Sweeney) K.; A.B., St. Mary's Coll., Baltimore, A.M.; m. Regina M. Kenan, 1873. In practice at Baltimore. Sec. Dem. State Central Com., 1864; mem. Md. Ho. of Dels., 1866 and 1899; state's atty. of Baltimore, 3 terms, 1868-80; mem. Dem. Nat. Exec. Com.,

1872-76; 2d asst. postmaster gen., 1885-89; prof. law, 1900—, dean, 1905—, Baltimore U. Law Sch. Wrote: History of the Redemption of a State. Home: Baltimore, Md. Died Apr. 18, 1918.

KNOTT, James Proctor, governor; b. Washington (now Marion) Co., Ky., Aug. 29, 1830; ed. at home; (LL.D., Centre Coll., Ky., 1885); m. Sarah R. McElroy, June 14, 1858. Admitted to bar, 1851; practiced at Memphis, Mo., 1851-62, Lebanon, Ky., 1862—. Mem. Mo. Ho. of Rep., 1858; atty. gen. of Mo., 1859-61; mem. 40th, 41st (1867-71), 45th to 47th (1877-83) Congresses; gov. of Ky., 1883-87. Democrat. Prof. civics and economics, 1892-94, prof. law and dean law faculty, 1894-1901, Centre Coll. Home: Lebanon, Ky. Died 1911.

KNOTT, Richard Wilson, editor; b. Frankfort, Ky., Sept. 26, 1849; s. Richard and Ann Mary (Roberts) K.; ed. pvt. schs., Louisville, Ky., to 1864; m. Jennie A. Gillmore, June 18, 1891. In retail dry goods business, Louisville, 1864-78; one of 5 who established Evening Post, Louisville, 1878, sold interest, 1880; on staff Louisville Courier-Journal, 1880-93; owner and editor Louisville Evening Post, 1893—; conducted Home and Farm, Louisville, 1880—, and (with Gen. Basil W. Duke) conducted Southern Bivouac, Louisville, 1885-86. Presbyterian. Died Dec. 27, 1917.

KNOTTS, Armanis F.; b. Highland Co., O., Jan. 30, 1856; s. Frank D. and Margaret (Bell) K.; B.S., Valparaiso U., 1882, M.A., 1883, C.E., 1883, LL.B., 1887; m. Mary Hennessy, 1883; children—Mrs. Dolly Bower, Mrs. Eugenie Reinke, Mrs. Marguerete Hulett. Pres. Central Ind. Normal Sch. and Business Coll., 1883-85 inclusive; surveyor of Porter Co., Ind., 1886-87; practiced law at Hammond, Ind., 25 yrs.; mem. Ind. Ho. of Rep., 1899-1900; mayor of Hammond, 1902. Bought the land for City of Gary, Ind., and planned the city for U.S. Steel Co., 1906; started the movement to save the Ind. dunes for a nat. park; organized Nat. Dunes Park Assn. (1st pres.). First pres. Fla. Div. Izaak Walton League. Mason. Recognized as an authority on early history of Indiana, and on Pottawottamie Indians. Now bldg. new town of Yankeetown, Fla., mayor same. Pres. Fla. Inland and Coastal Waterways Assn. Now planning the ideal city of Yankeetown at the gulf terminus of the Cross-Florida Ship Canal. Home: Yankeetown, Fla. Died Oct. 3, 1937.

KNOTTS, Edward C., lawyer; b. nr. Chatham, Ill., Mar. 24, 1863; s. Albion and Mary J. (Peddicord) K.; B.S., Knox Coll., Galesburg, Ill., 1884; A.M., Blackburn U., Carlinville, Ill., 1911; m. Elizabeth A. Routzahn, May 18, 1893; 1 son, Howard C. Admitted to Ill. bar, 1889, and practiced at Girard; state's atty., Macoupin Co., 1892-96; mayor of Girard, 1893-95; removed to Carlinville, 1903; U.S. atty. Southern Dist. of Ill., 1914-22; now mem. Knotts & Knotts. Democrat. Pres. Bd. of Edn., Carlinville, 1907-09. Mason. Home: Springfield, Ill. Died Feb. 11, 1933.

KNOWER, Henry McElderry, anatomist; b. Baltimore, Aug. 5, 1868; s. Capt. Edward C. K. (U.S.A.) and Mary D. (McElderry) K.; A.B., Johns Hopkins, 1890, asst. in biology, 1891-93, Adam T. Bruce fellow, 1895-96, Ph.D., 1896; m. Virginia DuBarry, Feb. 16, 1897; children—Henry DuB., Virginia (wife of William A. Moore). Instructor biology, Williams Coll., 1896-97; instr. anatomy, 1899-1908, asso., 1908-09, Johns Hopkins; lecturer anatomy, U. of Toronto, 1909-10; prof. anatomy, U. of Cincinnati, 1910-25; visiting prof. anatomy, U. of Ga., 1924-26; prof. anatomy, U. of Ala., 1926-29; guest in research, Wistar Inst. Anatomy, Phila., 1929-30; asso. prof. anatomy, Albany Med. Coll., 1930—; research fellow in biology, Yale U., 1932-33, research asso. in biology, 1933-37. Asst. in zoölogy, 1897, librarian, 1910-20, Marine Biol. Lab., Woods Hole, Mass.; one of founders and mng. editor Am. Jour. Anatomy, 1901-22; founder and first editor Anat. Record, 1906. Researches in embryology and anatomy of Termites; lymphatic and vascular systems of frog embryos, by experiment and injections; muscles of human heart. Home: Woods Hole, Mass. Died Jan. 10, 1940.

KNOWLES, Daniel Clark, clergyman; b. Yardville, N.J., Jan. 4, 1836; s. Enoch and Alice Curtis (Hughes) K.; A.B., Wesleyan U., Conn., 1858, A.M., 1860 (D.D., 1886); capt. Co. D, 48th N.Y. Vols., 1861; m. Lucia M. Barrows, Nov. 10, 1863. Ordained M.E. ministry, 1864; prin. Pennington (N.J.) Sem., 1863-67; pastor Lawrence, Mass., 1867-70, Lowell, Mass., 1870-72, Lynn, Mass., 1872-75, Malden, Mass., 1875-78, Lawrence, Mass., 1878-81, Plymouth, N.H., 1882-84; pres., 1885-91, and Ladd prof., 1892—, Tilton Sem. Prohibition candidate for gov. of N.H., 1895. Author: Chapel Talks to Young People, 1909. Home: Tilton, N.H. Died Feb. 13, 1913.

KNOWLES, Ellin J., author; b. Camden, N.J., Oct. 21, 1834; d. Isaiah and Mary Anna (Wallace) Toy; grad. Newark Wesleyan Inst., 1851; m. Rev. Dr. Joseph H. Knowles, Dec. 25, 1856 (died 1898). Writer for ch. publs. from girlhood. Officer Woman's Bd. Foreign Missions M.E. Ch. more than 40 yrs.; pres. Newark Female Charitable Soc.; teacher of woman's Bible class, 1890-1918; pub. speaker. Author: Spirit and Life, 1899; Heart Talks on Bible Themes, 1910. Was mem. original com. called to organize Woman's Christian Temperance Union in America; del. World Ecum. Conf. Edinburgh, 1910; v.p. Woman's Nat. Sabbath Alliance; guest of honor at Woman's Foreign Missionary Nat. Jubilee, M.E. Ch., Boston, Oct.-Nov. 1919. Died Apr. 10, 1929.

KNOWLES, Frederic Lawrence, editor, author; b. Lawrence, Mass., Sept. 8, 1869; s. Rev. Daniel Clark K. (D.D.) and Lucia M. (Barrows) K.; grad. Wesleyan Univ., 1894; (Harvard, A.B., 1896). Edited Cap and Gown Second Series, 1897; Golden Treasury of American Lyrics, 1897; in editorial dept. Houghton Mifflin & Co., Feb.-Sept. 1898; Literary adviser of L. C. Page & Co., 1899-1900, from 1900 of Dana Estes & Co. Unmarried. Author: Practical Hints for Young Writers, Readers and Book Buyers, 1897; A Kipling Primer, 1900; (republished in Eng.); On Life's Stairway (original verse), 1900; A Year Book of Famous Lyrics, 1901; A Treasury of Humorous Poetry, 1902; The Famous Children of Literature Series, 1902. Home: Roxbury, Mass. Died 1905.

KNOWLES, Hiram, judge; b. Hampden, Me., Jan. 18, 1834; s. Freeman and Emily (Smith) K.; grad. Denmark (Ia.) Acad.; student Antioch Coll., Ohio, 1856-57; LL.B., Harvard, 1860; m. Mary Curtis, Apr. 12, 1871. Went to Nev., 1862; pros. atty., Humboldt Co., Nev., 1863; probate judge, 1864; removed to Ida., 1865, to Mont., 1866; asso. justice Supreme Ct. of Mont., 1868-79; mem. Mont. Constl. Conv., 1889; U.S. dist. judge, Dist. of Mont., 1890-1904. Republican. Home: Missoula, Mont. Died 1911.

KNOWLES, Horace Greeley, diplomat; b. Seaford, Del., Oct. 20, 1863; s. Isaac H. D. (M.D.) and Sarah L. (Short) K.; ed. at Del. Coll.; m. Edith E. Wallace, Apr. 20, 1897. Am. consul at Bordeaux, France, 1889-93; E.E. and M.P. to Roumania and Servia and diplomatic agt. in Bulgaria, 1907-09; E.E. and M.P. to Nicaragua, Jan.-Dec. 1909; minister resident and consul-gen. to Dominican Republic, Dec. 1909-June 1910; E.E. and M.P. to Bolivia, June 1910-Aug. 23, 1913. Home: Wilmington, Del. Died Aug. 23, 1913.

KNOWLES, Morris, consulting engr.; b. Lawrence, Mass., Oct. 13, 1869; s. Charles Edwin and Ellen B. (Richardson) K.; S.B., Mass. Inst. Tech., 1891; Dr. Engineering, University of Pittsburgh, 1929; m. Mina P. McDavitt, Apr. 25, 1893. Employed Mass. State Bd. of Health and Met. Water Commn., Boston, 1893-97; investigations, design and construction of filtration system and new water supply, Pittsburgh, Pa., 1897-1910; consulting engring. practice, 1903—; pres. Morris Knowles, Inc., and Morris Knowles, Ltd.; dir. Pittsburgh Aviation Industries Corporation. Designed water works system, T.,C.& I. R.R. Co., Birmingham, Ala., 1909-11; consultant numerous cities and industries on municipal problems and community planning. Mem. Pittsburgh Flood Commn.; mem. Bd. Advisory Engrs. Miami Conservancy Dist., 1914; chief engr., Essex Border Utilities Commn., Ont., Can., 1916-21; superv. engr. Camps Meade and McClellan, 1917; chief engr. Housing Div., U.S. Shipping Bd., 1918-19; mem. Engring. Bd. of Review of Chicago Sanitary Dist., 1924; consultant and adviser to atty. gen. Conn. in case of Conn. vs. Mass. before U.S. Supreme Court, 1928-30; mem. Zoning Commn. U.S. Dept. of Commerce; chmn. com. on utilities, President's Conf. on Home Building and Home Ownership; vice chmn. Pa. Commn. to Study Municipal Consolidation in Counties of Second Class; chmn. City Planning Commn. and chmn. Bd. of Zoning Appeals, Pittsburgh; mem. Pa. State Chamber Commerce; mem. bd. dirs. Pittsburgh Chamber Commerce. Republican. Author: Industrial Housing. Home: Pittsburgh, Pa. Died Nov. 8, 1932.

KNOWLTON, Eliot A., merchant, banker; b. Wardsboro, Vt., Sept. 10, 1844; s. William and Electa Plimpton (Ramsdell) K.; removed with parents to Northfield, Minn., at age of 12; ed. Hamline U. 3 yrs.; m. Ella R. Blake, Mar. 4, 1873 (died 1925); children—George Blake, Clarence Elliott. Served in Co. A, 7th Minn. Vols., in Civil War, 2 yrs. 9 mos. Began as salesman J. D. Blake & Co., Rochester, Minn., 1868, admitted as partner, 1874, title changed to Leet & Knowlton, 1881, now Eliot A. Knowlton Co., of which is pres.; pres. Union Nat. Bank, Rochester, 1891—; also pres. Rochester Bldg. & Loan Assn., Rochester Loan & Trust Co.; v.p. Rochester Milling Co. One of founders, and treas. Southern Minn. Fair Assn. 9 yrs.; pres. Rochester City Sch. Bd. 5 yrs. Republican. Methodist. Treas. Y.M.C.A.; pres. Bd. Trade, 6 yrs. Home: Rochester, Minn. Died Oct. 13, 1927.

KNOWLTON, Frank Hall, botanist, paleontologist; b. Brandon, Vt., Sept. 2, 1860; s. Julius Augustus and Mary Ellen (Blackmer) K.; B.S., Middlebury Coll., 1884, M.S., 1887, hon. Sc.D., 1921; Ph.D., Columbian (now George Washington) U., 1896; m. Annie Stirling Moorhead, Sept. 27, 1887 (died 1890); 1 dau., Margaret; m. 2d, Rena Genevieve Ruff, Oct. 3, 1893; 1 son, Frank Lester. Aid, 1884-87, asst. curator botany, 1887-89, asst. palæontologist, 1889-1900, U.S. Nat. Mus.; palæontologist, 1900-07, geologist, July 1907—, U.S. Geol. Survey, prof. botany, Columbian, 1887-96. Editor The Plant World, 1897-1904 (founder); asst. on Century Dictionary, writing definitions in botany; had whole charge of botany for Standard Dictionary, for which he prepared about 25,000 definitions; assisted in preparing bot. definitions for new edit. (1900) of Webster's Dictionary; prepared bot. matter for The Jewish Encyclopædia. Fellow Geol. Soc. America (v.p. 1917-18), Palæontol. Soc. America (v.p. 1910 and 1915, pres. 1917-18). Author: Catalogue Mesozoic and Cenozoic Plants of North America, 1919; Plants of the Past, 1926. Home: Ballston, Va. Died Nov. 22, 1926.

KNOWLTON, George Willard, banker, mfr.; b. Watertown, N.Y., Aug. 17, 1839; s. George Willard and Elizabeth (Carroll) K.; ed. pub. schs.; m. Frances G. Clarke, 1862 (died 1868); m. 2d, Gertrude S. Ely, 1870. Pres. Watertown Nat. Bank, Knowlton Bros., Inc.; pres. Ontario Paper Co., St. Regis Paper Co. Pres. Jefferson County Orphan Asylum. Republican. Presbyn. Home: Watertown, N.Y. Died Mar. 17, 1931.

KNOWLTON, Helen Mary, artist, writer; b. Littleton, Mass., Aug. 16, 1832; d. John S. C. (editor for 40 yrs. of The Worcester Palladium) and Annie Wheeler (Hartwell) Knowlton; com. and pvt. sch. edn.; studied art in Boston with William M. Hunt and Frank Duveneck; unmarried. Wrote for her father's paper, and with her sisters, edited and published it several yrs. after his death; was on staff Boston Post. Taught art for 30 yrs. in Boston. Compiled William M. Hunt's Talks on Art; wrote Hints to Pupils in Drawing and Painting, 1879; Life of William Morris Hunt, 1899. Home: Needham, Mass. Died May 5, 1918.

KNOWLTON, Hosea Morrill, lawyer; b. Durham, Me., May 20, 1847; s. Isaac Case (D.D.) and Mary Smith (Wellington) K.; grad. Tufts Coll., 1867 (LL.D., 1898) and Harvard Law Sch.; m. Sylvia B. Almy, May 22, 1873. Admitted to Mass. bar, 1870; register in bankruptcy, dist. of Mass., 1872-76; mem. Mass. Ho. Reps., 1876-77, senate, 1878-79; dist. atty. southern dist. Mass., 1879-93; atty. gen. Mass., 1894-1901. Republican. Home: New Bedford, Mass. Died 1902.

KNOWLTON, Marcus Perrin, judge; b. Wilbraham, Mass., Feb. 3, 1839; s. Merrick and Fatima (Perrin) K.; A.B., Yale, 1860 (LL.D., Yale U., 1895, Harvard U., 1900, Williams Coll., 1915); m. Sophia Ritchie, July 18, 1867 (died 1886); m. 2d, Rose M. Ladd, May 21, 1891. Admitted to bar, 1862; pres. Springfield Common Council, 1872-73; mem. Mass. Ho. of Rep., 1878, Senate, 1880-81; justice Superior Ct. of Mass., 1881-87, Supreme Jud. Ct., 1887-1902, chief justice, same, Dec. 1902-Sept. 1911, when resigned. Chmn. bd. of 5 trustees apptd. by the Federal Ct. in 1914, to take over, hold and dispose of a majority of the capital stock of the B.&M. R.R. in the interest of the N.Y.,N.H.&H. R.R. Co. Home: Springfield, Mass. Died May 7, 1918.

KNOWLTON, P(hiletus) Clarke, writer; b. Memphis, Tenn., June 16, 1892; s. Philetus Clarke and Mary (Abbey) K.; prep. edn., Memphis University Sch.; student U. of Tenn., 1 yr.; B.S., U. of Ill., 1914; M.Arch., Harvard, 1917; winner Julia A. Appleton fellowship in architecture (1920-21 spent in Paris, in travel and study, and as visiting student at Am. Acad. in Rome); unmarried. Architectural work, Memphis, Boston and New York, 3 yrs. Served with Am. Field Service with French Army and with U.S.A.A.S., 1917-19, World War. Awarded Croix de Guerre. Home: Memphis, Tenn. Died May 12, 1930.

KNOX, George William, clergyman; b. Rome, N.Y., Aug. 11, 1853; s. William Eaton (D.D.) and Alice Woodward (Jenckes) K.; brother of Mary Alice K.; A.B., Hamilton, 1874; grad. Auburn Theol. Sem., 1877; (D.D., Princeton, 1888; LL.D., Hobart, 1904; D.D., Wesleyan Univ., 1910, Yale Univ., 1911); m. Anna Caroline Holmes, May 11, 1877. Ordained Presbyn. ministry, 1877; was in missionary work in Japan, and prof. homiletics, Union Theol. Sem., Tokio, and prof. philosophy and ethics, Imperial U., Japan; pastor Rye, N.Y.; lecturer on apologetics, 1897-99, prof. philosophy and history of religion, 1899—, Union Theol. Sem., New York. Nathaniel Taylor lecturer, Yale, 1903; lecturer history of religion, 1905-06; Union Seminary lecturer in India, China, Japan, 1911-12. Trustee Hamilton College, 1910—. V.p. Asiatic Soc. of Japan, 1891-92; Order of the Rising Sun, 1908. Author: (in English) A Japanese Philosopher, 1893 (Asiatic Soc. of Japan); Autobiography of Arai Hakuseki, 1902 (Asiatic Soc. of Japan); The Christian Point of View (with Profs. Francis Brown and A. C. McGiffert, 1902; Japanese Life in Town and Country, 1904; The Development of Religion in Japan, 1907; The Religion of Jesus, 1909. Died Apr. 25, 1912.

KNOX, Harry, naval officer; b. Greenville, O., July 2, 1848; s. John Reily and Isabel Southgate (Briggs) K.; grad. U.S. Naval Acad., 1867; m. Mary Gard, Sept. 7, 1875. Promoted ensign, 1868; master, 1870; lt., 1871; lt. comdr., Jan. 1888; comdr., Oct. 1896; capt., Sept. 22, 1901; rear admiral, and retired,

June 20, 1905. Comd. Vesuvius, 1894-95, Thetis, 1895-96, Princeton, 1899-1901, Concord, 1901; comd. Brooklyn, 1903-04. Died Aug. 29, 1923.

KNOX, John Barnett, lawyer; b. Talladega, Ala., Feb. 16, 1857; s. Dr. James C. and Mary Jane (Bowie) K.; ed. pvt. schs.; m. Carrie McClure, 1884; children—Carrie McClure, Mary Lyle (dec.). Admitted to bar, 1878; removed to Anniston, 1888; now sr. mem. firm of Knox, Acker, Sterne & Liles, Anniston, and of Knox, Acker, Dixon & Sims, Talladega, Ala. Del.-at-large Dem. Nat. convs., 1892, 96, 1912; twice chmn. Dem. State Exec. Com.; del.-at-large and pres. Ala. Constl. Conv., 1901; the Va. Constl. Conv. which was also in session 1901, ordered his speech in closing debate on suffrage plan read before it, and followed closely the plan adopted by Ala. Home: Anniston, Ala. Died Feb. 7, 1935.

KNOX, Mary Alice, school prin.; b. Rome, N.Y., Mar. 15, 1851; d. William Eaton (D.D.) and Alice Woodward (Jenckes) K.; sister of George William K.; B.A., Elmira (N.Y.) Coll.; unmarried. Instr. history, Elmira Coll., 1874-84; instr., 1884-86, asso. prof. history, 1887-95, Wellesley Coll.; prin. Emma Willard Sch., Troy, N.Y., 1895-1901; prin. Miss Knox's Sch. for Girls, Briarcliff Manor, N.Y., Oct. 1903—. On leave of absence from Wellesley for coll.-yr. 1886-87, took tour around world; also spent year in travel, 1902-03. Presbyn. Home: Briarcliff Manor, N.Y. Died 1911.

KNOX, Philander Chase, secretary of state; b. Brownsville, Pa., May 6, 1853; s. David S. and Rebekah (Page) K.; A.B., Mt. Union Coll., Ohio, 1872; read law in office of H. B. Swope, Pittsburgh; (LL.D., U. of Pa., 1905, Yale, 1907, Villanova, 1909); m. Lillie, d. Andrew D. Smith, of Pittsburgh, 1880. Admitted to bar, 1875; asst. U.S. dist. atty., Western Dist. of Pa., 1876-77; mem. Knox & Reed (James H.) from 1877. Atty. gen. in cabinets of Presidents McKinley and Roosevelt, Apr. 9, 1901-June 30, 1904; apptd. U.S. senator by Governor Pennypacker, June 10, 1904, for unexpired term of Matthew Stanley Quay, deceased; elected U.S. senator, Jan. 1905, for term, 1905-11; resigned from Senate, 1909; sec. of state in cabinet of President Taft, Mar. 1909-13. Received 68 votes for presdl. nomination in Rep. Nat. Conv., 1908. Reëlected U.S. senator, 1916, for term, 1917-23. Home: Pittsburgh, Pa. Died Oct. 12, 1921.

KNOX, William Elliott, banker; b. Strabane, Ireland, Oct. 27, 1862; s. William and Rachel (Elliott) K.; ed. pub. schs., N.Y. City; m. Robina Watson Bartley, Nov. 11, 1897; children—William Bartley, Robina Watson. Came to U.S., 1872, naturalized citizen, 1884. With G. W. Carleton & Co., pubs., N.Y. City, 1879-85; connected with the Bowery Savings Bank, New York, 1885—, sec., 1906, comptroller, 1908, v.p., 1920, pres., 1922—. Mem. Chamber of Commerce State of N.Y.; del. on U.S. Sect. Inter-Am. High Commn. Republican. Presbyn. Mason. Home: Rochelle, N.Y. Died Feb. 4, 1927.

KNOX, William White, clergyman; b. Utica, N.Y., Dec. 14, 1842; s. Rev. John P., LL.D., and Aletta (Van Doren) K.; A.B., Princeton, 1862, A.M., 1865; grad. Princeton Theol. Sem., 1866; (D.D., Rutgers, 1894); m. A. Maria VanSantvoord, Nov. 16, 1870; children—Susan Varick (dec.), William W. (dec.), Elizabeth Vroom (Mrs. Asher Atkinson), Katharine Veghte (dec.), Anna Romeyn, Evelyn Van Santvoord (Mrs. William Huntington Russell), Cornelius Van Santvoord. Ordained Presbyn. ministry, 1867; pastor Woodhaven, L.I., and stated supply 1st Ch., Springfield, N.Y., 1867-69; pastor 2d Ch., Huntington, L.I., 1869-81, 1st Ref. Dutch Ch., Bayonne, N.J., 1881-93, 1st Presbyn. Ch., New Brunswick, 1893-1917 (emeritus). Trustee Princeton Theol. Sem., N.J. Children's Home Soc. Home: New Brunswick, N.J. Died May 3, 1929.

KOBBÉ, Gustav, author; b. New York, Mar. 4, 1857; s. William A. and Sarah Lord (Sistare) K.; brother of William August K.; Classical Gymnasium and Music, Wiesbaden, Germany, 1867-72; A.B., Columbia University, 1877, LL.B., 1879, A.M., 1880; m. Carolyn Wheeler, Nov. 11, 1882. Engaged in newspaper and magazine work. Founder, 1909, and editor The Lotus, mag. Author: Wagner's Life and Works (2 vols.), 1890; Wagner's Music Dramas Analysed, 1904; Wagner and His Isolde, 1905; Opera Singers, 6th edit., revised, 1913. Home: Garden City, N.Y. Died July 27, 1918.

KOBBÉ, William August, major general U.S.A.; b. New York, May 10, 1840; s. William A. and Sarah Lord (Sistare) K.; ed. N.Y. City until 1854; Wiesbaden, Germany, until 1857; studied mining engring., Freiburg, and Clausthal, Germany, until 1862; grad. U.S. Arty. Sch., 1873; m. Isabella Hoffman, June 26, 1867; children—Ferdinand Walter, Sarah Perry, Rolf (dec.), William Hoffman, Herman, Eric (dec.); m. 2d, Margaret Carnes, 1916. Pvt. Co. K, 7th N.Y. State Militia, June 5-Sept. 5, 1862; pvt. Co. G, 178th N.Y. Inf., May 29, 1863; 1st lt., Oct. 18, 1863; promoted through grades to maj. gen., Jan. 19, 1904; retired at own request after 40 yrs.' service, Jan. 20, 1904. Bvtd. maj. and lt. col. vols., Mar. 13, 1865, "for distinguished and faithful services during the war"; capt., Mar. 2, 1867, "for gallant and meritorious services at battle of Nashville, Tenn."; maj., Mar. 2, 1867, for same at capture of Ft. Blakeley, Ala. Mil. gov. of the Hemp ports, and mil. gov. and dept. commr. of Mindanao and Jolo in P.I.; instr. at U.S. Arty. Sch., 1885-96; comd. Dept. of Dakota, 1902-04. Citations for "gallantry in action" against insurgent forces near Manila, P.I., Feb. 5, 1899, and against insurgent forces at Tulihan River, Luzon, P.I., Mar. 25, 1899. Home: Pasadena, Calif. Died Nov. 18, 1931.

KOBER, George Martin, M.D.; b. Alsfeld, Germany, Mar. 28, 1850; s. Jacob and Dorothea (Behr) K.; ed. Alsfeld; M.D., Georgetown U., 1873, LL.D., 1906, Litt.D., 1923. Acting asst. surgeon U.S.A., 1874-86; prof. hygiene, 1890—, dean Med. Dept., 1901-28 (dean emeritus) and mem. Bd. of Regents, 1928—, Georgetown U.; mem. cons. staff Children's Hosp., Georgetown U. Hosp., and Gallinger Municipal Hosp. Pres. Washington Sanitary Improvement and Housing Cos., 1916—. Mem. President's Home Commn., 1908—; mem. Bd. Charities of D.C., 1906—. Pres. Assn. of Am. Med. Colls., 1906; pres. Sect. IV, industrial and occupational hygiene, 15th Internat. Congress on Hygiene and Demography; chmn. subsect. on social. medicine 2d Pan-Am. Sci. Congress, 1916. Author: Tuberculosis in Relation to Occupation, 1920; Tuberculosis Among the North American Indians, 1921; Industrial Health (Kober and Hayhurst, editors), 1923; Zoning of Cities in Relation to Public Health, 1926; Development of Charitable and Reformatory Institutions in the District of Columbia, 1927; History and Development of the Housing Movement in the City of Washington (3d edit.), 1927. Home: Washington, D.C. Died Apr. 24, 1931.

KOCH, Charles Rudolph Edward; b. Birnbaum, Polish Prussia, Apr. 24, 1844; s. Augustus and Josephine (Von Lutz) K.; brought to America in infancy; student in dental office of Dr. Kennicott, Chicago, until Aug. 1862, when enlisted as pvt. 72d Ill. Inf., serving in Northern Miss. campaign, Yazoo Pass expdn., Vicksburg campaign and siege; detailed chief clk. Gen. Ransom's hdqrs., Nov. 1863; apptd. capt. 49th U.S.C.T.; detailed on staff of Lorenzo Thomas, adj. gen., organizing colored troops in southwest; rejoined command Feb. 1864, serving with it in La. until May 1865; provost marshall, Yazoo City, Miss., May-Aug. 1865, western dist. of Miss., Vicksburg, Aug. 1865-Mar. 1866, when was mustered out; m. Sylvia Bigelow, d. Hon. Otis Adams, of Grafton, Mass., June 25, 1868. Rejoined Dr. Kennicott, 1866, and later his partner in practice of dentistry until 1871, then practiced alone until 1898; sec. dental dept., Northwestern U., Jan. 1904—; lecturer on dentistry. Organized and was capt. of a co. of Union Veterans, serving in labor riots of 1877, and when I.N.G. was organized, enlisted as pvt. in 1st Inf., I.N.G., Aug. 1877; became capt. Co. I, Oct. 1877; maj., Apr. 1886; lt. col., Feb. 1888; col., Apr. 1889; voluntarily retired, Nov. 1893. Organized regt., at breaking out of Spanish-Am. War, 1898, which was accepted by the State and maintained at his own expense over 4 mos., but was finally disbanded and hon. disch. by act of legislature. Mem. George H. Thomas Post No. 5 G.A.R.; pres. Ill. Grand Army Memorial Hall Assn.; past post comdr., past insp. gen., past adj. gen., Dept. of Ill., adj. gen. G.A.R., 1913. Secretary and editor annual publs. of the Chicago Dental Soc., 1871-75; pres. Ill. State Dental Soc., 1877; mil. editor Chicago Inter Ocean, 1880-82; sec. and pres. Ill. State Bd. of Dental Examiners, 1886-91. Received hon. degree D.D.S. from Washington U., 1888. Home: Evanston, Ill. Died July 20, 1916.

KOCH, Felix John, "The Queer Corners Man," writer; b. Cincinnati, O., Jan. 15, 1882; s. Gustav John and Eugenie Matilde (Sarran) K.; grad. Walnut Hills High Sch., Cincinnati, 1900; A.B., U. of Cincinnati, 1904; business courses, Cincinnati Y.M.C.A.; unmarried. Has specialized for many yrs. in articles, illustrated by camera, on strange, odd and curious things, for mags. and newspapers; secured first photos of McKinley assassination for Cincinnati papers, 1901; visited professionally every Balkan state, including Novipazar terror zone; least-known America, Northern Labrador, Newfoundland, Canada Lone Land, Alaska, Panama; attended Presidential notifications, inaugurations; coronation of George V, investiture of Prince of Wales, Mexican Revolution, the Omaha, Dayton and Mississippi River holocausts, Scopes trial, etc.; secured photographic records of Am. home-land activities during World War for Office of Chief of Staff, Washington, and has made a notable collection of photos, etc. (ultimately to pass into possession of the U.S. Govt.); toured U.S., 1930, to bring material up to date. Author of "Little Journeys," textbooks, "Writing for Profit," etc. Home: College Hill, Cincinnati, O. Died Dec. 27, 1933.

KOCH, Theodore Wesley, librarian; b. Phila., Aug. 4, 1871; s. William Jefferson and Wilhelmina (Bock) K.; grad. Central High Sch., Phila., 1888; A.B., U. of Pa., 1892; A.B., Harvard, 1893, A.M., 1894; studied at U. of Paris and Collège de France, 1900-01; m. Gertrude Priscilla Humphrey, Nov. 27, 1907; 1 dau., Dorothy Alden. Engaged 1895-1900 in the preparation of an annotated catalogue of the Dante collection presented by Prof. Willard Fiske to Cornell U. Library; asst., Library of Congress, 1902-04; asst. librarian, 1904-05, librarian, 1905-16, Univ. of Mich.; chief of order div., Library of Congress, 1916-19; librarian, Northwestern U., 1919—. Hon. mem. Dante Soc., London; life mem. Dante Soc., Cambridge, Mass., A.L.A.; mem. Am. Library Inst. (pres. 1930-32). Author: Dante in America (for Dante Soc.), 1896; A Book of Carnegie Libraries, 1917; Books in the War, the Romance of Library War Service, 1919; Notes on the German Book Exhibit, Chicago, 1925; The Florentine Book Fair, 1926; Reading, a Vice or a Virtue?, 1926. Translator of Nodier's Francesco Colonna, 1929; Flaubert's Bibliomania, 1929; Valéry, The Ideal Book, 1930; Fogazzaro's Eden Anto, 1930; Bonnardot's Mirror of the Parisian Bibliophile, 1931; Haarhaus, The Assembly of Books, 1932; Lacroix, My Republic, 1936; Zweig, The Old-book Peddler and Other Tales for Bibliophiles, 1937. Compiler: Cornell University Library Catalogue of the Dante Collection, presented by Willard Fiske, 2 vols., 1898, 1900; Hand-list of Framed Reproductions of Pictures and Portraits Belonging to Dante Collection, 1900; A List of Danteiana in American Libraries, supplementing the Catalogue of the Cornell Dante Collection, 1901. Died Mar. 23, 1941.

KOCKRITZ, (Julius) Ewald, clergyman; b. Napoleonville, La., Jan. 3, 1876; s. Herman and Emma (Winkler) K.; grad. Eden Coll., St. Louis, Mo., 1901; grad. Lane Theol. Sem., Cincinnati, 1908; m. Clara E. Hartmann, Nov. 6, 1901; children—Alwin (dec.), Hubert, Norman (dec.), Ewald, Emma Matilda. Ordained ministry Evang. Synod of N.A., 1901; pastor Clarington, O., 1901-05, St. Luke's Ch., Cincinnati, 1905-10, Salem Ch., New Orleans, 1910-17, Bethel Ch., Evansville, Ind., 1917—; editor Juvenile S.S. Publs., Evang. Synod of N.A., 1907-15. Gen. sec. Evang. Synod of N.A., 1930—. Mem. Denominational S.S. Bd., 1913-21, chmn. Bd. Religious Edn., 1921-29, moderator Evang. Synod of N.A., 1929. Mem. Denom. War Welfare Commn., 1917-18. Dir. Deaconess Hosp. Mem. Evansville Chamber Commerce. Home: Evansville, Ind. Died Mar. 28, 1931.

KOEHLER, Robert, painter; b. Hamburg, Germany, Nov. 28, 1850; s. Ernst and Louise K.; was brought to U.S. 1854; ed. Milwaukee, Wis., and learned lithography, which he practiced in Pittsburgh, Pa., and New York; studied drawing in night classes Nat. Acad. Design; studied painting in Munich; m. Marie Fischer, Sept. 17, 1895. Began to exhibit at Nat. Acad., 1877; organized the Am. dept. of art exhbn., Munich, 1883 and 1888; dir. of Minneapolis School of Fine Arts, 1893—. Prin. paintings: Holiday Occupation; Her Only Support; The Socialist; The Strike; Violet; Judgment of Paris; Love's Secret; The Family Bible; Father and Son; Salve Luna. Home: Minneapolis, Minn. Died Apr. 23, 1917.

KOEHLER, Sylvester Rosa, author; b. Leipzig, Germany, Feb. 11, 1837; came to U.S., 1849; became known as writer of articles on art and as editor American Art Review; apptd. curator print dept. Museum of Fine Arts, Boston, and hon. curator section of graphic arts, U.S. Nat. Museum (Smithsonian Instn.), Washington. Hon. A.M., Harvard; fellow Am. Acad. Arts and Sciences; lecturer on engraving, etc., before Lowell Inst., Boston, Drexel Inst., Philadelphia, and U.S. Nat. Museum, Washington. Author: American Art; Etching; Art Education and Art Patronage in the United States; Catalogue of the Engravings, Dry Points and Etchings of Albert Dürer (pub. by Grolier Club, New York); m. Amelia Susanna Jaeger, Apr. 9, 1859. Died 1900.

KOENIG, Adolph, M.D.; b. Wiggiswyl, Canton Bern, Switzerland, Oct. 30, 1855; s. Christian and Magdalena (Iseli) K.; came to U.S., 1856; ed. Tarentum Acad., Pa., 1872-73; student med. dept. U. of Louisville, 1877-78; M.D., Bellevue Hosp. Med. Coll. (New York U.), 1879; attended summer Sch. of Botany, Harvard, 1886; hon. Pharm.D., Western U. of Pa., 1900; m. Fannie McFarlane Low, Apr. 16, 1889 (died 1890); 1 dau., Fannie Low (dec.); m. 2d, Mary Beatrice Jeffcoat, Feb. 2, 1895 (died 1911); children—Adolphus, Eugene Jeffcoat (dec.), Rhoda Victoria, Beatrice Iseli, Olivia, Frances Mary, Evangeline Angliae et Helvetiae, Theodore Roosevelt, Christian (dec.), Arthur Rudolph, Helen Blakemore, Mary Beatrice (dec.). Resident physician West Pa. Hosp., Pittsburgh, 1879; in gen. practice at Pittsburgh, 1880—; prof. materia medica and botany, 1885-1903, physiology, 1904-11, Pittsburgh Coll. of Pharmacy and Pharmaceutical Dept. of U. of Pittsburgh; asst. surgeon Pa. R.R., 1898-1902; cons. physician West Penn Hosp., 1912. Editor and pub. Pittsburgh Medical Review, 1886-97, Pa. Medical Journal (Pittsburgh), 1897-1904. Twice dir. pub. sch., 4th Ward, Pittsburgh; dir. pub. sch. of Edgewood, 1906-31; asst. sanitary insp. Nat. Board Health, 1882; mem. advisory bd., Dept. of Health of Pa., 1905-23, Board Med. Edn. and Licensure of Dept. Pub. Instrn. of Pa., 1909-27. Republican. Home: Edgewood, Pa. Died Oct. 18, 1932.

KOENIG, George Augustus, chemist; b. Willstätt, Grand Duchy of Baden, Germany, May 12, 1844; s. Johannes and Margaretha (Pfotzer) K.; ed. pub. sch.; progymnasium at Kork, 1854-57; sch. of Moravian Brothers, Lausanne, Switzerland, 1857-59; Poly. Sch., Karlsrühe, 1859-63, degree mech. engr.; U. of Heidelberg, 1863-65, U. of Berlin, 1865-67, A.M., Ph.D., Heidelberg, 1867; Mining Acad., Freiburg, Saxony, 1867-68; m. Wilhelmina Marquart, of Willsbätt, Oct. 7, 1869. Came to U.S., Oct. 1868; manufactured sodium stannate from tin scraps in Phila.; chemist Tacony Chem. Works, Phila., 1868-72; made exam. of old mines in Mexico, winter of 1870-71; asst. prof. chemistry and mineralogy, 1872-79, mineralogy and geology, 1879-92, Univ. of Pa.; prof. chemistry, Mich. Coll. of Mines, 1892—. Discoverer of new minerals: Hydrotitanite, Randite, Leydyite, Alaskaite, Beegerite, Bementite, Footeite, Paramelaconite, Mezapilite, Mohawkite, Keeweenawite, Stibiodomykite, Melanochalcite; has reëxamined many other minerals and discovered diamond in meteoric iron. In 1885 published chromometric methods, a development of blow-pipe analysis, and in 1897 a new way of assaying without muffle; patented an assay furnace to carry out the methods; took out patent, 1881, for chlorination of low-grade silver and gold ores; latest work has been preparation of artificial crystals of arsenides. Author: Chemistry Simplified, 1905. Home: Houghton, Mich. Died Jan. 15, 1913.

KOERNER, William, mining engr.; b. Oregon City, Ore., Feb. 22, 1886; s. Rudolph and Mary (Koehnlein) K.; A.B., Stanford, 1908; m. Della U. Snow, July 18, 1923; children—Katherine, William, Mary. Engr. Ray Consol. Copper Co., 1909, Inspiration Copper Co., 1909-11; supt. Barker Mines Co., 1912-14, Grey Eagle Copper Co., 1916-19; engr. Mason Valley Mines Co., 1921-24; mgr. Flin Flon Syndicate, 1920-21; gen. mgr. Magma Copper Co., 1925—; v.p. and gen. mgr. Magma Ariz. R.R. Co. Dir. William Boyce Thompson Arboretum of Southwest. Home: Superior, Ariz. Died June 30, 1940.

KOERNER, William Henry Dethlep, magazine and book illustrator; b. City of Nünn, Schleswig Holstein, Nov. 19, 1878; s. William Henry Dethlep and Margaret Anna (Williams) K.; brought to U.S. by parents at age of 2 yrs. Home at time of death, Aug. 11, 1938, was 209 Grassmere Av., Interlaken, N.J.

KOESTER, Frank (Franz Köster), engineer, author; b. Sterkrade, Germany, Aug. 28, 1876; s. Johann and Henriette (Trill) K.; ed. in Germany; theoretical and practical training for 10 yrs. in Europe; unmarried. Planned electric central stas. shown at Paris Expn., 1900, for which was awarded gold medal; came to U.S., 1902; was engr. with New York Subway Constrn. Co., J. G. White & Co., Guggenheim Exploration Co., Am. Smelting & Refining Co.; consulting engr. and city planner, 1911—; engring. expert for civic improvements, City of N.Y. Has patented various devices in the field of power plant engring. and other lines. Became naturalized citizen of U.S., 1911. Author: Modern City Planning and Maintenance, 1914. Advisory city planner for Allentown, Bethlehem and Scranton, Pa., etc.; st. lighting expert for Allentown, Scranton, etc. Home: New York, N.Y. Died Oct. 6, 1927.

KOFFKA, Kurt, prof. psychology; b. Berlin, Germany, Mar. 18, 1886; s. Emil and Luise (Levy) K.; Ph.D., U. of Berlin, 1908; student U. of Edinburgh, 1904-05, U. of Freiburg, 1908-09, U. of Würzburg, 1909-10; m. Elisabeth Ahlgrimm (Ph.D.) of Hamburg, Germany, July 21, 1923. Came to U.S., 1928. Asst. U. of Würzburg, 1909-10, Acad. (now Univ.) of Frankfort, 1910-11; privatdozent, U. of Giessen, 1911-18, prof., 1918-27; visiting prof. Cornell U., 1924-25, U. of Wis., 1926-27; William Allan Neilson Research prof., Smith Coll., 1927-32, prof. psychology, 1932—. Fellow Am. Acad. Arts and Sciences. Co-founder, 1922, and editor Psychologische Forschung until 1935; editor Smith Coll. Studies in Psychology. Author: Growth of the Mind, 1924, 2d edit., 1928; also trans. in Spanish, Chinese, Japanese and Russian; Principles of Gestalt Psychology, 1935. Home: Northampton, Mass. Died Nov. 22, 1941.

KOHLBECK, Valentine, abbot; b. Friedrichsthal, Bohemia (Czechoslovakia), Feb. 17, 1864; s. Jacob (James) and Elisabeth (Landshut) K.; classical, philos. and theol. studies, St. Vincent's Coll. and Sem., Beatty, Pa. Came to U.S., 1877; joined Benedictine Order, 1882; ordained priest R.C. Ch., 1887; apptd. pastor St. Vitus Ch., Chicago, 1888, St. Procopius Ch., 1892; mng. editor of the Bohemian daily newspaper, Narod (Nation), Chicago, and the semi-weekly Katolik, 1896-1919; abbot of St. Procopius Abbey, Lisle, Ill., Mar. 1919—; pres. St. Procopius Coll., Lisle. Died Feb. 17, 1937.

KOHLER, Elmer Peter, chemist; b. Egypt, Pa., Nov. 6, 1865; s. Lewis A. and Elizabeth (Newhardt) K.; A.B., Muhlenberg Coll., Allentown, Pa., 1886, A.M., 1889, LL.D., 1918; Ph.D., Johns Hopkins, 1892; unmarried. Asso. in chemistry, 1892-1897, asso. prof., 1897-1900, prof., 1900-12, Bryn Mawr Coll.; prof. chemistry, Harvard, 1912—. Fellow Am. Acad. Arts and Sciences, Nat. Acad. Sciences, Imperial Acad. of Sciences of Halle. Died May 24, 1938.

KOHLER, Fred, mayor; b. Cleveland, O., May 2, 1864; s. Christian and Fredericka K.; ed. pub. schs.; m. Josephine B. Modroch, Aug. 16, 1888. Joined police dept., Cleveland, 1889; chief of police, 1903-13; mayor of Cleveland, term 1922-24; sheriff of Cuyahoga County, 1925-26. Republican. Home: Cleveland, O. Died Jan. 31, 1934.

KOHLER, G. A. Edward, engineer, mfr.; b. Phila., Pa., Feb. 17, 1864; s. Ignatius and Anna C. (Fischer) Kohler; ed. U. of Pa., class 1886; m. Mary Ward Everett, Oct. 11, 1899; children—Franklin W., John Bowen. Moved to Chicago, 1887; in employ of U.S. Construction Co. until 1888; then with Peabody, Daniels & Co.; became sec. and gen. mgr. of a saw mfg. co.; entered electrical business, 1890, and in 1891 organized firm of Kohler Bros., of which became sole propr. in 1910; dir. Kohler Aviation Corporation. Invented and manufactures devices for operating newspaper presses, including magazine reels, known under the name "The Kohler System." Republican. Home: Chicago, Ill. Died Apr. 29, 1932.

KOHLER, Kaufmann, theologian; b. Fürth, Bavaria, Germany, May 10, 1843; s. Moritz and Babette K.; ed. univs. of Munich, Berlin and Leipzig, 1865-69; Ph.D., U. of Erlangen, 1867; m. Johanna Einhorn, 1870. Received a call to pulpit of Beth El Congregation, Detroit, 1869; elected rabbi Sinai Congregation, Chicago, 1871; introduced Sunday lectures there; minister Temple Beth El, New York, 1879-1903, elected hon. minister for life, 1903; pres. Hebrew Union Coll., Cincinnati, 1903-22 (emeritus). Called Rabbinical Conf. at Pittsburgh, at which platform for Reform Judaism in America was adopted, 1885; edited Sabbath Visitor, 1881-82, Jewish Reformer, 1886; one of editors Jewish Ency., dept. theology and philosophy. Author: Der Segen Jacob's (Jacob's Blessing), work on Bible Criticism, 1868; A Guide to Instruction in Judaism, 1899; Hebrew Union College and Other Addresses, 1916; Heaven and Hell in Comparative Religion, with Particular Reference to Dante's Divine Comedy, 1923. Mem. bd. which prepared English transl. of the Bible, pub. by Jewish Publ. Soc., 1917, also of Jewish Classical Com. Hon. pres. Central Conf. Am. Rabbis, 1903—. Home: New York, N.Y. Died Jan. 28, 1926.

KOHLER, Max James, lawyer; b. Detroit, Mich., May 22, 1871; s. Kaufmann and Johanna (Einhorn) K.; B.S., Coll. City of New York, 1890, M.S., 1893; A.M., Columbia, 1891, LL.B., 1893; hon. Dr. Hebrew Law, Hebrew Union Coll., 1925; m. Winifred Lichtenauer, Nov. 6, 1906. Asst. U.S. dist. atty., New York, 1894-98; spl. asst. U.S. atty., 1898-99; independent Democrat. Hon. sec. Baron de Hirsch Fund, 1905—; hon. sec. nat. com. on Celebration of 250th Anniversary of Settlement of Jews in U.S., 1905; mem. Am. Jewish Com. (exec. com.); v.p. Jewish Acad. of Arts and Sciences, 1932—; mem. Joint Council on German Jewish Persecution, 1933—. Apptd. by sec. of Labor, mem. Com. on Ellis Island and Immigrant Relief, 1933. Author: The Registration of Aliens a Dangerous Project, 1925; Some New Light on the Dreyfus Case, 1929; Haym Salomon, the Patriot Broker of the Revolution, 1931; Legal Disabilities of Aliens in the United States, 1930; The United States and German Jewish Persecutions —Precedents for Popular and Governmental Action, 1933; also numerous articles on immigration and Chinese exclusion, diplomatic history, Jewish, and legal subjects. Editor: Settlement of Jews in North America, by Charles P. Daly, LL.D., New York, 1893; Selected Addresses and Papers, by Simon Wolf, 1926; God in Freedom, by Luzzatti, 1930; also editor of dept. "America" in Standard Jewish Encyclopedia, 1926. Home: New York, N.Y. Died July 24, 1934.

KOHLER, Walter Jodok, mfr., chmn. of bd. Kohler Co.; b. Sheboygan, Wis., Mar. 3, 1875; s. John M. and Lilly (Vollrath) K.; educated pub. schs.; hon. M.A., U. of Wis.; LL.D. (hon.), Lake Forest U.; m. Charlotte Schroeder, Nov. 3, 1900; children—John M., Walter J., Carl J., Robert E. Identified from 1890 with the Kohler Co. (founded by his father, 1873), pres., 1905-37; chmn. bd., 1937—; chmn. bd. Kohler Co., Ltd. (London); chmn. bd. Vollrath Co., Sheboygan; pres. Mountain States Supply Co., Salt Lake City; chmn. bd. Security Nat. Bank, Sheboygan, Wis.; trustee and mem. exec. com. Northwestern Mutual Life Ins. Co., Milwaukee; dir. C.&N.W. Ry., C.St.P.,M.&O. Ry. Gov. of Wis., term 1929 and 1930; presdl. elector, 1916. Regent U. of Wis., 6 yrs. (pres. bd. 3 yrs.); trustee Lawrence Coll., Appleton, Wis.; vice chmn. Nat. Industrial Conf. Bd.; pres. Sheboygan Home for Friendless. Participant in making Kohler, Wis., an American industrial garden city. Awarded national service fellowship by Soc. of Arts and Sciences, New York, 1934. Nat. v.p. and dir. Nat. Assn. Mfrs. Republican. Episcopalian. Mason. Home: Kohler, Wis. Died Apr. 21, 1940.

KOHLSAAT, Christian Cecil, judge; b. in Edwards Co., Ill., Jan. 8, 1844; s. Reimer and Sarah (Hall) K.; bro. of Herman Henry K.; ed. common schs., Galena, Ill., and U. of Chicago; (LL.D., Ill. Coll., 1903); m. Frances S. Smith, June 1871. Was law reporter Chicago Journal; minute clerk Co. Ct., 1867; admitted to bar, and practiced at Chicago, 1867-90. Defeated for co. judge, 1881; mem. Bd. of West Park Commrs., 1880-90; probate judge Cook Co., Ill., 1890-99; U.S. dist. judge, Northern Dist., Ill., 1899-1905, U.S. circuit judge, 7th Circuit, 1905—. Trustee Y.M.C.A., Lewis Inst. Pres. Union League Club, 1896. Home: Chicago, Ill. Died May 11, 1918.

KOHLSAAT, Herman Henry, retired editor; b. Albion, Ill., Mar. 22, 1853; s. Reimer and Sarah (Hall) K.; educated common schs., Galena, Ill., and Skinner Sch., Chicago; married. Began business life as cash-boy and later cashier in dry goods store; traveling salesman for two other firms and, 1875-80, for Blake, Shaw & Co., wholesale bakers; became jr. partner, 1880, and had charge of a bakery lunch established by this firm; bought that branch of the business, 1883, and greatly enlarged it, H. H. Kohlsaat & Co. (incorporated) owning several large establishments and also doing large wholesale bakery business; part owner in Chicago Inter Ocean, 1891-93; editor and publisher Chicago Times-Herald, 1894 (amalgamated with Chicago Record, becoming Record-Herald, 1901); also of Chicago Evening Post, 1894-1901; editor Chicago Record-Herald, 1910-12; editor Chicago Inter Ocean, 1913. Presented statue of Gen. Grant to City of Galena, Ill. Author: McKinley to Harding, 1923. Died Oct. 17, 1924.

KOHN, August, newspaperman; b. Orangeburg, S.C., Feb. 25, 1868; s. Theodore and Rosa (Wald) K.; A.B., S.C. Coll., Columbia, 1892; m. Irene Goldsmith, Apr. 1, 1894 (dec.); children—Mrs. Julian Hennig, August, Theodore. Reporter, 1892-94, in charge of the Columbia bureau, 1894-1919, Charleston News and Courier. Pres. Standard Warehouse Co. (Columbia, S.C.); v.p. Nat. Loan and Exchange Bank (Columbia, S.C.), Argus Investment Co., City Development Co., etc. Trustee U. of S.C. (chmn. fin. com.), Hebrew Orphans' Home, Atlanta, Ga. Lt. col. staff of Gov. D. C. Heyward. Pres. S.C. State Press Assn. (2 yrs.). Democrat. Mason. Author: The Cotton Mills of South Carolina, 1908; Water Powers of South Carolina; The Tax Problems in South Carolina. Home: Columbia, S.C. Deceased.

KOHNS, Lee, merchant; b. Columbus, Ga., Sept. 1, 1864; s. Lazarus and Hermine (Straus) K.; B.Sc., Coll. City of N.Y., 1884; m. Clare Elizabeth Elfelt, Nov. 18, 1896; children—Robert Lee, Irene Dorothy, Paul. Began in business, 1884, with father and grandfather—L. Straus & Sons, mfrs. and importers of china and glassware; admitted to firm, 1892, retired 1923, managing partner 15 yrs.; for many yrs. v.p. Abraham & Straus, Inc., dept. store, Brooklyn, retiring 1925; dir. Irving Bank-Columbia Trust Co.; trustee United Hosp. Fund; 1st v.p. Educational Alliance; pres. New York Bd. of Trade and Transportation 7 yrs.; trustee Coll. City of New York, Andrew Freedman Home. An organizer of Democratic League. Home: New York; also Great Neck, L.I. Died Jan. 18, 1927.

KOLB, Louis John, mfr.; b. New York, June 25, 1865; s. John Gotlieb and Sarah Elizabeth (Kaiser) K.; grad. Rugby Academy, Phila.; A.B., U. of Pa., 1887; LL.D., Juniata Coll.; m. Caroline Kaiser, Mar. 20, 1895. V.p. Pa. Sugar Co. and Real Estate Trust Co.; dir. Keystone Telephone Co., Internat. Equities, Phila. Mfrs. Mut. Fire Ins. Co. Lt. col. and a.d.c. on staff Gov. Brumbaugh of Pa. Pres. Hahnemann Hosp.; mem. bd. dirs. Graduate Hosp., U. of Pa., St. Luke's Hosp., Children's Homeopathic Hospital. Republican. Presbyn. Mason. Home: Philadelphia, Pa. Died July 2, 1941.

KOLLE, Frederick Strange, plastic surgeon; b. Hanover, Germany, Nov. 22, 1871; s. John and Bertha (Schaare) K.; common sch. edn. in Germany; M.D., Long Island Coll. Hosp., 1893; (hon. M.E., Nat. Coll. Electro-therapeutics, 1897); m. Loretto Elaine Duffy, 1899. Asst. aural phys. Brooklyn Eye and Ear Hosp., 1892-93; interne Kings Co. Hosp., 1893-94; asst. phys. Contagious Disease Hosp., Brooklyn, 1894; in practice, Brooklyn, 1894—. One of 1st X-ray investigators in U.S., 1896; chief instr. dept. electro-therapeutics, Elec. Engring. Inst., New York, 1896-1900; asso. editor Electrical Age, 1897-1902; radiographer to M.E. Hosp., Brooklyn. Inventor: Radiometer; Kolle X-ray coil switching devices; dentaskiascope; œsophameter; folding fluoroscope; X-ray printing process; Kolle focus tube; direct-reading X-ray meter and many instruments used in plastic surgery, etc. Author: The Recent Roentgen Discovery, 1896; The X-Rays, Their Production and Application, 1896; Medico-Surgical Radiography; Subcutaneous Hydrocarbon Protheses, 1908; Plastic and Cosmetic Surgery; Hakon Jare, 1911. Died May 10, 1929.

KOLLEN, Gerrit John, college pres.; b. in The Netherlands, Aug. 9, 1843; s. Gerrit John and Berendina (Scholten) K.; came to U.S., 1851, locating in Allegan Co., Mich.; A.B., Hope Coll., 1868, A.M., 1871; (LL.D., Rutgers, 1894); m. Mary W., d. Rev. Dr. A. C. Van Raalte (founder City of

Holland, Mich., and Hope Coll.), 1879. Asst. prof. mathematics and natural philosophy, 1871-78, prof. applied mathematics and polit. economy, 1878-93, pres., 1893-1911, pres. emeritus, 1911—, Hope Coll. Mem. Bd. Edn. Reformed Ch. in America. Knight Order of Orange Nassau, 1906. Home: Holland, Mich. Died Sept. 5, 1915.

KOLLER, Paul Warren, ch. official; b. Glen Rock, Pa., July 1, 1872; s. Jesse C. and Alice (Heathcote) K.; B.A., Gettysburg (Pa.) Coll., 1894, A.M., 1897; Gettysburg Theol. Sem., 1894-97; D.D., Hamma Div. Sch., Springfield, O., 1915; m. Mary E. Bollinger, Apr. 24, 1901; 1 dau., Kathrine. Ordained ministry United Luth. Ch. in America, 1897; pastor Messiah Luth. Ch., Cleveland, O., 1897-1900, St. John's Ch., Hudson, N.Y., 1900-10, St. Luke's Ch., Mansfield, O., 1911-21; full time pres. Luth. Synod of Ohio, 1921-28; gen. sec. Bd. of Foreign Missions, United Luth. Ch. in America, 1928—. Mem. com. of reference and counsel, Foreign Mission Conf. of N.A.; mem. Missionary Laymen's Exec. Com., Conf. of Foreign Mission Bds. of Luth. Chs. in America (pres.), Exec. Com. on Coöperation in the Near East. Kiwanian. Home: Baltimore, Md. Died Nov. 11, 1937.

KOLLOCK, Charles Wilson, M.D.; b. Cheraw, S.C., Apr. 29, 1857; s. Cornelius (M.D.) and Mary Henrietta (Shaw) K.; student Cheraw (S.C.) Acad.; grad. Va. Mil. Inst., Lexington, 1877; M.D., U. of Pa., 1881; grad. study London, Paris and Phila. Polyclinic; m. Sarah Irvin, Dec. 11, 1886; children—William Gregg, Henrietta Shaw, Charles Wilson (dec.), Sarah Irvin, Nancy Hicks. Interne Philadelphia Hosp., Children's Hosp. and Wills' Eye Hosp., 1881-84; settled at Charleston, S.C., 1885; prof. rhinology and laryngology, Med. Coll. State of S.C., 1913-30. Capt., Charleston Light Dragoons, 1899-1904; maj. Med. Corps, U.S.A., and flight surgeon, Kelly Field, Tex., World War. Democrat. Episcopalian. Home: Charleston, S.C. Died Sept. 23, 1931.

KONIG, George, congressman; b. North Point, Md., Jan. 26, 1856; s. late George and Caroline (Forrester) K.; self-ed.; m. Margaret A. Schroeder, Dec. 7, 1875. Learned trade of ship calker, at which worked 10 yrs.; gen. mgr. Baltimore Pulverizing Co., 1894—. Mem. City Council, Baltimore, 1903-11; mem. 62d Congress (1911-13), 3d Md. Dist. Democrat. Home: Baltimore, Md. Died May 31, 1913.

KONTA, Alexander; b. Budapest, Hungary, May 11, 1862; s. Joseph J. and Jeannette (Szarvas) K.; grad. Coll. of Pius Brothers, Budapest; m. Annie Laurie Lemp, Oct. 8, 1895. Came to U.S., 1887; founded Modern Historic Records Assn.; commr. Bd. of Parole, N.Y. State Prisons, 1925-27; consul gen. of San Marino at New York. Hon. men. Assn. Grand Jurors N.Y. Co.; hon. pres. Hungarian St. Stephens' Society. Decorated by French govt. with Cross of Merite Agricole, 1908; commander Order of the Crown (Italy), 1930; Chevalier Order of Saint-Lazare of Jerusalem, 1930. Democrat. Elk. Home: New York, N.Y. Died Apr. 27, 1933.

KONTI, Isidore, sculptor; b. Vienna, Austria, July 9, 1862; s. Ignatz Lajos and Rosalie K.; ed. Vienna pub. and high schs.; entered Imperial Acad. at age of 16; won several scholarships and finished studies at Meisterschule of Prof. Karl Kundmann, Vienna; in 1886 won scholarship for 2 yrs.' study in Rome; unmarried. Came to U.S., 1890; worked for Chicago Expn.; executed many decorative monumental and ideal works including group "West Indies" for the colonnade of the Dewey Arch, and "The East and North River," for same arch; groups for Temple of Music; group of playing children for Court of Fountains, and large group symbolizing The Despotic Age, at the Esplanade, Pan-American Expn., Buffalo; memorial to Bishop Horatio Potter, St. John's Cathedral, New York, also fountain in City Park of New Orleans, La.; the marble fountain "Brook" at Greystone, Yonkers, N.Y.; also cascade fountains, the Atlantic and the Pacific Oceans (consisting of over 20 different groups) at St. Louis Expn.; frieze, "Festival Procession" for Gainsborough Studio Bldg., New York; group representing S. America and a hist. relief for the Internat. Bur. of Am. Republics Building, Washington; McKinley Memorial (from sketch models of Charles Lopez), Philadelphia; monument to Kit Carson and Lt. Beal, Nat. Mus. Washington, statues of Justinian and Alfred the Great, Court House, Cleveland, O.; sculpture on Column of Progress, Panama P.I. Expn., 1915; statue of Dr. Morgan Dix, Trinity Ch., N.Y. City; bronze statues "Genius of Immortality," Met. Mus., N.Y.; "Orpheus," Peabody Inst., Baltimore; "Illusion," bought by Italian Govt.; figure on Plaza Fountain, from sketch of the late Karl Bitter, New York; fountain, Audubon Park, New Orleans; monument to heroes of World War; Hudson-Fulton Memorial, and Lincoln Monument, Yonkers, N.Y.; statue of Gov. F. T. Nicholls, Capitol, Baton Rouge, La.; represented in Corcoran Gallery, Washington, D.C., and in museums in Detroit, Newark, St. Louis, etc. Gold medal from St. Louis Expn., 1904, A.N.A., 1906, N.A., 1909. Home: Yonkers, N.Y. Died Jan. 11, 1938.

KOON, Martin B., lawyer; b. Altay, N.Y., Jan. 22, 1841; s. Alanson and Marilla (Wells) K.; A.B., Hillsdale (Mich.) Coll., 1863; m. Josephine Van DeMark, Nov. 18, 1873. Admitted to bar, 1868; practiced at Hillsdale, 1868-78, Minneapolis, 1878—. Co. atty., Hillsdale (Mich.) Co., 1870-74; judge 4th Jud. Dist., Minn., 1883-86. Republican. Pres. Minneapolis Gen. Electric Co.; v.p. Northwestern Nat. Bank, Minn. Loan & Trust Co. Home: Minneapolis, Minn. Died Aug. 20, 1912.

KOONS, John Cornelius, 1st asst. postmaster gen.; b. Patapsco, Md., Feb. 13, 1873; s. Edward E. and Rachel (Micksell) K.; ed. Franklin High School, Reistertown, Md.; m. Ada Florence Childs, Apr. 5, 1898 (died 1905); children—Emily E., Edith M., Dorothy E.; m. 2d, Katie Vernon Haddox, June 14, 1911 (died 1919); 1 son, Edward H.; m. 3d, Bessie Corder Kengla, Apr. 4, 1931. Began in railway mail service, after civil service examination, as substitute clk., Baltimore, Mar. 20, 1895; promoted clk., 1896, and advanced to highest clerical grade; postoffice insp., Kansas City div., 1906-11; div. supt. ry. mail service, Cleveland, O., Apr.-Oct. 1911; supt. Div. Salaries and Allowances, Postoffice Dept., Washington, 1911-15; chief postoffice insp., 1915-16; 1st asst. postmaster gen., Sept. 1, 1916; resigned Mar. 4, 1921; resignation accepted Apr. 7, 1921, and apptd. spl. asst. postmaster gen. same day; resigned June 30, 1921, also as mem. of joint congressional commn. to investigate the postal service. Served as chmn. of com. which developed the parcel post in the U.S.; mem. Wire Control Bd. and had charge of orgn. and administration of telegraph and telephone lines under govt. control, 1918; exec. asst. to pres. Chesapeake & Potomac Telephone Co. and associated cos., July 1, 1921, v.p., Mar. 1923—. Democrat. Episcopalian. Mason. Home: Washington, D.C. Died Apr. 12, 1937.

KOOPMAN, Augustus, artist; b. Charlotte, N.C., Jan. 2, 1869; s. Bernard and Johanna K.; A.B., Central High Sch., Phila., 1886; studied Pa. Acad. Fine Arts and under Bouguereau and Fleury, and at École des Beaux Arts, Paris; m. Louise Lovett Osgood, May 6, 1897. Taught painting in Paris, 1896-99; resident in London, specializing in portraits, 1902-06. Exhibitor at Paris Salons, Munich, London, Venice and Am. exhbns., 1890—. First William Clarke prize Am. Art Assn., Paris, 1899; awards: 2d Wanamaker prize, 1898; bronze and silver medals, Paris Expn., 1900; medal, Buffalo Expn., 1901; medal, St. Louis Expn., 1904, for "Return of Shrimpers"; represented in French and Am. collections, and St. Louis, St. Paul, and Detroit art museums, Phila. Art Club, Brooklyn Inst. Arts and Sciences, portraits and decorations; by etching in Congressional Library; collection of etchings in New York Pub. Library; decoration in U.S. Nat. Pavilion, Paris Expn., 1900. Home: Paris, France. Died Feb. 1914.

KOOPMAN, Harry Lyman, librarian; b. Freeport, Me., July 1, 1860; s. Charles Frederick and Mary Brewer (Mitchell) K.; A.B., Colby Coll., 1880, A.M., 1883, Litt.D., 1908; A.M., Harvard, 1893; m. Helene Luise Mayser, of Ulm, Germany, 1889; children—Mary Fredrika, Karl Henry. Asst. Astor cataloguer, Cornell, Columbia and Rutgers libraries, 1881-86; cataloguer U. of Vt. Library, 1886-92; librarian, 1893-1930, prof. bibliography, 1908-30, Brown U. (emeritus); mem. editorial staff, Providence Jour., 1930—. Asso. editor Brown Alumni Monthly, 1906-17. Mem. advisory council Simplified Spelling Bd.; fellow Am. Library Inst. (pres. 1928-30); pres. Mass. Library Club, 1900-01, R.I. Library Assn., 1904-07; chmn. A.L.A. com. on libraries in nat. parks, 1925-28; member Skyscrapers (amateur astron. soc.), pres., 1934-35; mem. R.I. Historical Soc., Boston Soc. Printers. Author: The Booklover and His Books, 1917; Hesperia, an American National Poem, 2 vols., 1919-24; The Guerdon (poem), 1921; The Narragansett Country, 1927; The Eternal Pilgrim, 1929; Materna (poem), 1930. Editor: Hawthorne's Mr. Higginbotham's Catastrophe, 1931. Writer of monthly column "Planets and Stars." Home: Providence, R.I. Died Dec. 28, 1937.

KOPALD, Louis Joseph, rabbi; b. Cracow, Austria, Apr. 25, 1885; s. Jacob Nachman and Eva (Langer) K.; brought to U.S. in infancy; A.B., U. of Cincinnati, 1906, A.M., 1908; rabbi, Hebrew Union Coll., Cincinnati, 1909; studied U. of Calif., 1909-12; m. Elsa Rheinstrom, Mar. 15, 1920. Rabbi, Temple Israel, Stockton, Calif., 1909-12; rabbi Temple Beth Zion, Buffalo, N.Y., 1912-26, rabbi emeritus, 1926-28; rabbi Chicago North Shore Congregation Israel, Glencoe, Ill., Sept. 1928—. Spl. lecturer Jewish themes, U. of Neb. Summer Sch., 1917. Founder, 1916, and chmn. for 5 yrs. Interdenom. Com. Thanksgiving Service, Buffalo; mem. Buffalo Bd. Edn., 1916-17; mem. Nat. Com. of 100 for Americanization of Immigrants, 1916-19; mem. Am. Blind Relief Com., Am. Jewish Relief Com., Am. Jewish Committee. Active for many yrs. in ednl., civic, patriotic and philanthropic orgns. of Buffalo. Pres. N.Y. State Conf. Charities and Correction, 1919-20. Republican. Died Feb. 4, 1931.

KOPLIK, Henry, M.D.; b. New York, Oct. 28, 1858; s. Abraham S. and Rosalie K.; A.B., Coll. City of New York, 1878; M.D., Coll. Phys. and Surg. (Columbia), 1881; m. Stephanie Schiele, Nov. 1902. Specialist in disease of infancy and childhood; discoverer of an early diagnostic sign in measles, by which a very early diagnosis of the disease is made feasible—sign called "Koplik's spots" by profession generally; also a bacillus of whooping cough. Established 1st milk depot for infants, or gouttes de lait, in U.S.; was attending phys. Good Samaritan Dispensary, St. John's Guild (both N.Y. City); now consulting pediatrist to Mt. Sinai Hosp., Hebrew Orphan Asylum, Hosp. for Deformities, Jewish Maternity Hospital (New York). Member permanent committee of Congress Child Welfare; hon. mem. med societies Vienna and Budapest. Author: Diseases of Infancy and Childhood, 1902 (4th edit.). Died Apr. 30, 1927.

KOPP, William F., congressman; b. Des Moines Co., Ia., June 20, 1869; s. John M. and Mary K.; A.B., Ia. Wesleyan Coll., Mt. Pleasant, 1892; LL.B., U. of Ia., 1894; m. Clara Bird, Dec. 4, 1894. Began practice at Mt. Pleasant, 1894; co. atty., Henry Co., Ia., 1895-99; postmaster, Mt. Pleasant, 1906-14; mem. Ia. Ho. of Rep., 1915-17; mem. 67th to 72d Congresses (1921-33), 1st Ia. Dist.; now in active practice of law in Mt. Pleasant, Ia. Republican. Methodist. Home: Mt. Pleasant, Ia. Died Aug. 24, 1938.

KORBLY, Charles Alexander, congressman; b. Madison, Ind., Mar. 24, 1871; s. Charles Alexander and Mary Antoinette (Bright) K.; student St. Joseph's Coll., 2 terms; admitted to bar, 1892; m. Isabel Stephens Palmer, June 10, 1902; 4 children. Began practice at Madison; became connected with office of father (Smith & Korbly), Indianapolis, 1895, and after death of father, 1900, practiced with surviving partner, Alonzo Greene Smith, and brother Bernard K., until 1902; practiced alone after 1902. Mem. 61st to 63d Congresses (1909-15), 7th Ind. Dist.; receiver gen. of insolvent nat. banks, Washington, 1915-17; on legal staff of alien property custodian during 1918; served with the War Labor Bd. until it dissolved in 1919; with Shipping Bd. until Mar. 1922. Mem. bar D.C. and Marion Co., Ind.; practicing law in Washington, D.C., 1922—. Died July 26, 1937.

KOREN, John, statistician; b. Decorah, Ia., Mar. 3, 1861; s. Vilhelm and Elizabeth K.; A.B., Luther Coll., Decorah, Ia., 1879; S.T.B., Concordia Sem., St. Louis, 1882; also studied abroad; m. Katherine Orne Harnden, 1894. Has lived in Boston, 1884—; engaged in religious work for several yrs.; spl. expert abroad, U.S. Dept. of Labor, 1891; sent to Europe to study Gothenburg system, 1893; in service of com. of 50 to investigate liquor problem, 1894-99; expert spl. agt. U.S. Bur. Census; internat. prison commr. for the U.S. Fellow Am. Statis. Assn. (pres. 1913-14), Royal Statis. Soc. Author: Economic Aspect of the Liquor Problem; The Liquor Problem in Its Legislative Aspects; Alcohol and Society. Died Nov. 9, 1923.

KOREN, Ulrik Vilhelm, clergyman; b. Bergen, Norway, Dec. 22, 1826; s. Paul Skonevik Stub Koren and Henriette Christiane (Rulffs) K.; grad. Cathedral Sch., Bergen, 1844, univ. at Christiania, 1852; (D.D., Concordia Theol. Sem., St. Louis, 1903); m. Else Elisabeth Hysing, of Laurvik, Norway, Aug. 18, 1853. Ordained Lutheran ministry at Christiania, 1853; came to America, 1853, and since pastor nr. Decorah, Ia. Mem. Ch. Council, Synod Norwegian Evang. Luth. Ch. in America, 1861—; pres. Ia. dist. of the Synod, 1876-94; gen. pres. of the synod, 1894—. Comdr. Order of St. Olof. Home: Decorah, Ia. Died 1911.

KORFF, Sergius Alexander, prof. Eastern European history; b. Petrograd, Russia, Mar. 4, 1876; s. Baron Alexander F. and Barbara (Gorstkin) K.; M.A., Petrograd U., 1898, D.C.L., 1910; LL.D., Brown U., 1922; m. Alletta, d. Surgeon Gen. W. K. Van Reypen, U.S.N., June 5, 1905. Prof. Russian history and law U. of Finland, 1907-18; prof. constl. law, Women's U., Petrograd, 1909-18; prof. Foreign Service Sch., Georgetown U., 1921—; prof. Eastern European history, Columbia, 1923—. Lectured in many Am. colls. and univs., auspices Carnegie Inst. Internat. Edn.; Harris lectures, Northwestern, 1922; courses, Johns Hopkins, Wellesley, U. of Mich. Inst. of Politics, Williamstown, Mass.; course on History of Internat. Law at The Hague Acad. Internat. Law, summer, 1923. Author: History of Administrative Justice in Russia, 1910; Dominions of British Empire, 1914—all printed in Russia; Foreign Relations of Russia, 1922; Autocracy and Revolution in Russia, 1923—in English. Home: Washington, D.C. Died Mar. 7, 1924.

KORNEGAY, Wade Hampton, lawyer; b. Dublin County, N.C., Apr. 17, 1865; s. of H. R. and Jeannette (Williams) K.; A.M., Wake Forest (N.C.) Coll., 1884; student U. of Va., summer 1889; LL.B., Vanderbilt U., 1890; m. Hannie L. Stafford, Nov. 1892; children—Jeanette, Clarence Stafford, Wade Hampton, Fay Louise (Mrs. O. M. Confer). Prin. high sch., Richland, N.C., 1885-89; began practice of law at Vinita, Okla., 1891; mem. Supreme Court of Okla., 1931 and 1932; dir. First Nat. Bank, Vinita. Mem. Constl. Conv., Okla. Home: Vinita, Okla. Died Nov. 19, 1939.

KOST, Frederick W., painter; b. New York, N.Y., 1861; student in Nat. Acad. Design, with William S. Macy, and in Munich and Paris. Splty. landscapes; hon. mention Paris Expn., 1900; bronze medal Buffalo Expn., 1901; silver medal St. Louis Expn., 1904. N.A., 1906. Represented in Pa. Acad. Fine Arts by "On the St. John River"; Brooklyn Inst. Arts and Sciences, "Southfield Marshes, Staten Island"; Lotos Club, New York, "The Kelp Gatherers"; etc. Home: Brook Haven, L.I., N.Y. Died Feb. 23, 1923.

KOST, John, physician, educator; b. Carlisle, Pa., 1819; s. John K. Sr.; grad. 1838, Cincinnati; prof. in med. coll. 20 yrs., in Meth. ministry 20 yrs., in scientific researches 20 yrs. Traveled extensively in foreign lands. Now v.p. Mich State Med. Assn. and mem. Mich. State Bd. Registration in Medicine. Founder Univ. of Fla.; chancellor Heidelberg Univ., Tiffin, O. Author: Domestic Medicine, 1844; Practice of Medicine (19 edits.); Materia Medica and Therapeutics, 3 edits.; Obstetrics (2 edits.); Diseases of Women and Children, 2 edits.; Medical Jurisprudence; Philosophy of Death, 1900. Home: Adrian, Mich. Died 1904.

KOSTALEK, John Anton, prof. organic chemistry; b. Prague, Czecho-Slovakia, Sept. 13, 1885; s. Anton and Marie (Koukol) K.; brought by parents to U.S., 1887; B.A., U. of Wis., 1907, M.A., 1908; Ph.D., U. of Ill., 1910; m. Helen Pitcairn, Aug. 23, 1916; children—Mary-Elizabeth, Katharine. Research chemist B. F. Goodrich Rubber Co., 1911-12; instr. in organic chemistry, U. of Ida., 1912-15, asst. prof. same, 1915-18; head of div. analytical and organic chemistry, N.D. Agrl. Coll., 1919; prof. organic chemistry, U. of Ida., 1919—, also dean of Coll. of Letters and Science and dir. Pre-Med. Curriculum, 1931—. Chemist, Chem. Warfare Service, U.S.A., 1918. Democrat. Home: Moscow, Ida. Died Sept. 25, 1937.

KOTANY, Ludwig; b. Szeged, Hungary, Sept. 5, 1860; s. Alexander and Marie Minna (Singer) K.; Ph.D., U. of Vienna, 1884; m. Orie L. Gregg, Oct. 24, 1908 (died 1919). Came to U.S. 1891, naturalized citizen, 1896. Broker in stocks and bonds, St. Louis, many yrs.; sec. Corp. Washington U., 1918-25; student economics. Fellow Royal Economic Soc. (London). Republican. Conglist. Writer on economic topics. Home: St. Louis, Mo. Died May 13, 1930.

KOUDELKA, Joseph Maria, bishop; b. Chlistovo, Bohemia, Austria, Dec. 8, 1852; s. Markus and Anna (Janoushek) K.; ed. coll., Klattau, Bohemia; St. Francis Sem., Milwaukee, Wis. Came to America, 1868; ordained R.C. priest, 1875, by Bishop Mullen; pastor St. Prokopius Parish, Cleveland, O., 1875-82; editor of "Hlas," St. Louis, 1882-83; pastor St. Michael's Parish, Cleveland, 1883-1911; consecrated bishop, Feb. 25, 1908; transferred as auxiliary to Archbishop Messmer, Milwaukee, Sept. 4, 1911; apptd. bishop of Diocese of Superior, Wis., Aug. 1, 1913. Asst. at Pontifical Throne, July 13, 1917. Died June 24, 1921.

KOUNTZ, John S., ins. and real estate; b. Richfield, O., March 25, 1846; s. Michael and Helen K.; common school edn.; m. Sarah Jane Hadnett, Sept. 21, 1868 (died 1875); m. 2d, Agnes Jane Denniston, June 4, 1879. Enlisted Sept. 30, 1861, as drummer, 37th Ohio vol. inf.; lost left leg at battle of Missionary Ridge, Nov. 25, 1863; awarded medal of honor for distinguished gallantry; treas., 1872-74, recorder, 1875-77, Lucas Co., O. Comdr. Dept. Ohio G.A.R., 1881-82; comdr.-in-chief G.A.R., 1884-85; sec. and historian Vicksburg Nat. Mil. Park Commn., apptd. March 1, 1899. Home: Toledo, O. Died 1909.

KOUNTZE, Augustus Frederick, banker; b. Omaha, Neb., Mar. 4, 1870; s. Herman and Elizabeth K.; Ph.B., Sheffield Scientific Sch. (Yale), 1891; m. Davelle Combs, Apr. 17, 1909. In banking business, New York, 1892—; mem. Kountze Bros., bankers; v.p. Merchants Exchange Nat. Bank; dir. H. G. White Engring. Corp. Home: New York, N.Y. Died Mar. 14, 1927.

KOYL, Charles Herschel, engineer; b. Amherstburg, Ont., Aug. 14, 1855; s. Rev. Ephraim Lillie and Frances (Culp) K.; A.B., Victoria Coll., Cobourg, Ont., 1877; post-grad. student Johns Hopkins, 1879-81, fellow in physics, 1881-83; m. Georgiana Thacher Washburn, Nov. 6, 1885; m. 2d, Adèle T. Sanford, Apr. 27, 1901. Physical science master Wesleyan Coll., Stanstead, Que., 1877-79; head dept. mathematics and physics, high sch., Washington, 1885-87; prof. physics, Swarthmore Coll., 1887-89; v.p. Nat. Switch & Signal Co., 1889-91; pres. Nat. Drying Co., 1891-93; scientific asst. to Col. Waring, commr. street cleaning, New York, 1895-96; mgr. Automatic Banjo Co., New York, 1896-99; mgr. Industrial Water Co., 1899-1902; cons. practice; engr. water service G.N. Ry., 1912-19, and of C.,M.&St.P. Ry., 1919—. Delegate to Internat. Congress of Electricians, Phila., 1884. John Scott Legacy Medal, Franklin Inst., for invention of the parabolic semaphore, 1889. Home: Chicago, Ill. Died Dec. 18, 1931.

KRAEMER, Henry, scientist; b. Phila., Pa., July 22, 1868; s. John Henry and Caroline K.; parents died when he was 3 yrs. old; student Girard Coll., 1877-83; Ph.B., Columbia, 1895; Ph.G., Phila. Coll. Pharmacy, 1889; Ph.D., U. of Marburg, 1896; (hon. Pharm.M., Phila. Coll. of Pharmacy, 1912); m. Minnie A. Behm. Instructor in pharmacognosy, Coll. Pharmacy of City of New York, 1890; prof. botany and pharmacognosy, Sch. of Pharmacy, Northwestern U., 1896-97; prof. botany and pharmacognosy and dir. micros. lab., Phila. Coll. Pharmacy, 1897-1917; prof. pharmacognosy, U. of Mich., 1917-20; dir. Kraemer Scientific Lab., 1920—; dir. Era courses in pharmacy, 1921—. Editor Am. Jour. Pharmacy, 1898-1917. Member committee of revision of U.S. Pharmacopœia and chairman sub-committee botany and pharmacognosy, 1900—. Mem. council on pharmacy and chemistry A.M.A., 1913-21; pres. Am. Conf. Pharm. Faculties, 1917, Phila. Author: A Text-book of Botany and Pharmacognosy, 1902, 07, 08, 10; Applied and Economic Botany, 1914, 16; Scientific and Applied Pharmacognosy, 1915, 20. Home: Mt. Clemens, Mich. Died Sept. 9, 1924.

KRAETZER, Arthur Furman, M.D.; b. Brooklyn, N.Y., Apr. 16, 1891; s. Adolph G. and Caroline C. (Bauskett) K.; B.S., Princeton, 1912; M.D., Cornell U. Med. Coll., N.Y. City, 1916; m. Beatrice MacDonald, of St. John, N.B., Can., 1924; separated. Practiced in N.Y. City, 1916—; asso. attending physician Lenox Hill Hosp.; medical director Knickerbocker Hospital; instr. clinical medicine, Cornell U. Med. Coll.; practice limited to internal medicine; radio speaker on diet. Served as 1st lt., U.S. Army M.C., Aug. 1917-Jan. 1919. Republican. Author: Procedure in Examination of the Lungs, 1930; Your Long-Suffering Stomach, 1933. Home: New York, N.Y. Died Mar. 2, 1940.

KRAFFT, Carl R., artist; b. Reading, O., Aug. 23, 1884; s. Rev. Carl F. and Katherine (Meier) K.; ed. Elmhurst (Ill.) College; studied art at Art Inst., Fine Arts Acad. and the Palette and Chisel Club, all of Chicago, Ill.; m. Charlotte Lau, Aug. 21, 1907; children—Hazel Francis, Gladys Charlotte. Landscape and figure painter; exhibited at Art Inst. Chicago, Nat. Acad. Fine Arts (New York), Acad. Fine Arts (Phila.), Carnegie Inst. Exhbn. (Pittsburgh), Herron Art Inst. (Indianapolis), St. Louis Art League and Mus., Kansas City, Omaha, Minneapolis. Represented in many collections. Awards: Englewood prize, Art Inst. Chicago, 1915; Municipal Art League prize, 1916; hon. mention, Artists' Guild, Chicago, 1918; Fine Arts Bldg. prize, Artists' Guild, 1918; Logan medal and $300, Art Inst. Chicago, 1920; bronze medal, Peoria Exhbn., 1920; silver medal, Chicago Soc. Artists, 1921; first Logan medal and $500, Art Inst. Chicago, 1925; Harry A. Frank prize and $150 (figure composition), Art Inst. Chicago, 1925; medal of honor, Allied Artists of America, 1926; also prizes of Chicago Galleries, 1926, 27, 29 and 30. Home: Oak Park, Ill. Died Oct. 18, 1938.

KRAMER, George Washington, architect; b. Ashland, O., July 9, 1847; s. Daniel and Susannah (Baughman) K.; ed. pub. schs.; studied architecture privately, and as contractor 5 yrs.; m. Harriet Estelle Blackman, 1870 (died 1904); children—Ella Estelle (dec.), George Lee, Lora Odessa. Began practice at Ashland, 1873; partner of Jacob Snyder (widely known as designer of churches), 1879-85; mem. Kramer & Weary, 1885-94; removed to N.Y. City, 1894; was mem. George W. Kramer & Son; retired. Architect of over 2,000 chs. and consulting or asso. architect for many more. Prize for model S.S. building plans, World's Fair, Chicago, 1893. Home: East Orange, N.J. Died Oct. 20, 1938.

KRAMER, Harold Morton, author; b. Frankfort, Ind., Apr. 28, 1873; s. Philip Edward and Mary Anne (Choate) K.; grad. Frankfort High Sch., 1891; m. Nora Lee, Sept. 6, 1897. Republican. Methodist. Author: Gayle Langford, 1907; The Rugged Way, 1911; With Seeing Eyes, 1919. Officer in Spanish-Am. War, 1898; served with Y.M.C.A. in France, World War, 1917-18. Home: Frankfort, Ind. Died Mar. 20, 1930.

KRAPP, George Philip, author, univ. prof.; b. Cincinnati, Sept. 1, 1872; s. Martin and Louisa (Adams) K.; A.B., Wittenberg Coll., 1894, A.M., 1897; Ph.D., Johns Hopkins U., 1899; married; 3 children. Instr. English, Horace Mann Sch., New York, 1897-98, Teachers Coll. and Columbia U., 1897-1907; adj. prof. English, Columbia, 1907-08; prof. English, U. of Cincinnati, 1908-10; prof. English, Columbia, July 1910—. Author: The Elements of English Grammar, 1908; Modern English—Its Growth and Present Use, 1909; In Oldest England, 1912; The Rise of English Literary Prose, 1915; Pronunciation of Standard English in America, 1919; Tales of True Knights, 1921; First Lessons in Speech Improvement, 1922; The Kitchen Porch, 1923; America, 1924; The English Language in America, 2 vols., 1925; Comprehensive Guide to Good English, 1927; The Knowledge of English, 1927; Anglo-Saxon Reader, 1929; The Junius Manuscript, 1931. Died Apr. 22, 1934.

KRATZ, Henry Elton, educator; b. Sterling, O., Oct. 14, 1849; s. Jacob and Catharine (Wismer) K.; B.S., Univ. of Wooster, 1874, A.M., Ph.D., 1890; m. Elizabeth M. Deal, July 19, 1876; children—Horace Deal (dec.), Bessie Mae, Arthur Murray, Edward Mars. Taught as high sch. prin. several yrs.; supt. city schs. in Ohio, Mich. and S.D. about 8 yrs.; studied in Eng., 2 yrs.; prof. pedagogy, U. of S.D., 1889-91; supt. schs., Sioux City, Ia., 1891-1902; supt. tp. schs., Calumet, Mich., 1902-10; pres. School and College Bur., Chicago, 1910-20. Mem. Mich. State Commn. on Industrial and Agrl. Edn. to investigate the conditions of elementary industrial and agricultural education in the State of Michigan, 1909. Home: Chicago, Ill. Died Aug. 5, 1929.

KRAUS, Adolf, lawyer; b. Bohemia, Feb. 26, 1850; s. Jonas and Ludmila K.; ed. in Bohemia; came to U.S., 1865; m. Mathilde Hirsh, Jan. 7, 1877; children—Albert, Paula (Mrs. Victor Weil), Harry, Milton. Admitted to bar, 1877, and practiced at Chicago as mem. Kraus, Goodwin, Smietanka & Rickard (retired). Mem. Chicago Bd. Edn., 1881-87 (pres. 1884-86); corp. counsel, Chicago, 1893; pub. and editor Chicago Times, 1894; pres. Civil Service Commn., Chicago, 1897-98. Internat. pres. of B'nai B'rith, 1905—. Home: Chicago, Ill. Died Oct. 22, 1928.

KRAUSE, Allen Kramer, M.D., medical research; b. Lebanon, Pa., Feb. 13, 1881; s. George Derr and Jeanie Julia (Kramer) K.; A.B., Brown U., 1901; grad. student in biology, same univ., 1901-03, A.M., 1902; M.D., Johns Hopkins, 1907; Litt.D. (hon.), Norwich U., 1935; m. Clara Fletcher, Oct. 10, 1906; children—Gregory, Francis, Fletcher. Asst. and instr. pathology, Johns Hopkins, 1907-09; asst. dir. Saranac (N.Y.) Lab., 1909-16; asso. prof. medicine and dir. Kenneth Dows Tuberculosis Research Labs., Johns Hopkins, 1916-29; in charge Tuberculosis Dispensary, Johns Hopkins Hosp., and asso. phys. Johns Hopkins Hosp., 1916-29; pres. The Desert Sanatorium, Tucson, Ariz., 1929-37; clin. prof. medicine, Stanford U., 1929-37; clin. prof. medicine, U. of Southern Calif., 1932-37. Lecturer in medicine, Johns Hopkins. Managing editor Am. Rev. of Tuberculosis, 1916, editor, 1922—; editor Am. sect. of "Tubercle" (London), 1924—; collaborator, Zeitschrift für Tuberkulose (Berlin), Arch. Med.-Chirurg. de l'Appareil Respiratoire (Paris); lecturer Trudeau School of Tuberculosis, 1916-29; counsellor Med. Council U.S. Vets. Bur., 1924—. Awarded Trudeau Medal, 1931. Fellow Am. Coll. Phys., A.A.A.S., American Geographical Soc.; mem. numerous med. societies. Democrat. Protestant. Author: Rest and Other Things, 1922; Environment and Resistance in Tuberculosis, 1923; The Evolution of Tubercle, 1927. Home: Baltimore, Md. Died May 12, 1941.

KRAUSE, Carl Albert, educator; b. Brilon, Germany, Nov. 7, 1872; s. Julius R. and Adelheid (Russ) K.; studied univs. of Marburg and Lausanne; Ph.D., New York U., 1908; m. Margaret Bailey, Dec. 25, 1901; 1 son, Finley Bailey. Began teaching modern langs., 1895; instr. modern langs., Purdue U., U. of Cincinnati and Union Coll., N.Y., 1900-04; instr. High Sch. of Commerce, New York, 1904-09; head of modern lang. dept., Jamaica High Sch., New York, Feb. 1909—. Sent to Europe by New York Bd. of Edn., 1908; lecturer, New York U., 1911-16, summers at U. of Marburg, Germany, 1914, U. of Vt., 1916, U. of Calif. and U. of Southern Calif., 1917, Hunter Coll., N.Y. City, evenings, 1917-18. Author: Gerhart Hauptmann's Treatment of Blank Verse, 1908; The Direct Method in Modern Languages, 1916. Joint author: The Walter-Krause Beginners' German, 1912, 4th revised edition, 1918; First German Reader, 1913; German Songs, 1914; Oral German, 1915; Organization and Administration of a City Vacation High School, 1923. Resident editor of Walter-Krause German Series. Home: Brooklyn, N.Y. Died June 15, 1929.

KRAUSÉ, Lyda Farrington ("Barbara Yechton"), author; b. St. Croix, Danish W.I.; d. Thomas Murray and Mary (Panchen) K.; ed. pvt. schs. On editorial staff The Churchman, New York, 1890-1901, also reader for publishing houses. Republican. Episcopalian. Author: We Ten—or, Story of the Roses, 1896; A Lovable Crank—or, More Leaves from the Roses, 1898; A Young Savage, 1899; Fortune's Boats, 1900; Honor D'Everel, 1903. Home: Princeton, N.J. Died Oct. 31, 1939.

KRAUSKOPF, Joseph, rabbi; b. in Germany, Jan. 21, 1858; s. Hirsch K.; came to America, 1872; B.A., Univ. of Cincinnati, 1883; grad. as rabbi from Hebrew Union Coll., 1883 (D.D., 1885). Rabbi, Kansas City, 1883-87, Reform Congregation Keneseth Israel, Phila., 1887. Founded Jewish Publ. Soc. America; founder and pres. since orgn. of National Farm School in which boys are trained in practical and scientific agr. Apptd. as one of spl. Relief commrs. to Cuba, 1898, of Nat. Relief Commn. sent by U.S. Agrl. Dept. to Paris Expn., summer of 1900, as spl. commr. to report on exhibits of agrl. schs. and to visit European agrl. schs. in general and report to dept. Dir. gen. I. M. Wise Memorial Fund, Hebrew Union Coll., 1903—; pres. Conf. Am. Rabbis, 1904-05. Founder Patriotic Soc. of Phila., 1910. Grand chaplain of Grand Lodge of A.F. and A.M. of Pa. Author: Prejudice—Its Genesis and Exodus; The Service Manual; The Service Ritual; The Kiddush and Seder Service; also 34 vols. of Sunday Lectures, 1887-1921. Rep. of Jewish orgns. in food conservation dept., Washington, 1917-20. Home: Germantown, Phila., Pa. Died June 12, 1923.

KRAUSS, William, M.D.; b. Reichholzmühle, nr. Kaiserslautern, Germany, June 13, 1861; s. William and Barbara (Müller) K.; came to America, 1874; Ph.G., with honors, Md. Coll. Pharmacy (U. of Md.), 1883; Memphis Hosp. Med. Coll., 1886-87; med. dept. Washington U., 1887-88; M.D., Memphis Hosp. Med. Coll., 1889; post-grad. in univs. of Europe and America; m. Mary Louise, d. late Judge Nathaniel Baxter, of Nashville, Dec. 24, 1912 (died Feb. 12, 1914); m. 2d, Margaret Veronica, d. William Curdy, of Phila., Apr. 13, 1918 (died 1928). Specialized in teaching and research. Served as secretary of the Memphis Board of Health, 1890-93; actg. asst. surgeon, U.S. Pub. Health and Marine Hosp. Service, as diagnostician, during yellow fever epidemic, 1897-98 and 1905; vis. pathologist, 1891-1907, visiting phys., 1901-07, pathologist, 1917-19, St. Joseph's Hosp.; consultant in tropical med. Memphis Gen. and Baptist hosps.; asst. demonstrator in anatomy, 1889-91, teacher chemistry, histology, etc., 1891-1903, Memphis Hospital Medical Coll.; an organizer, 1906, and prof. pathology and tropical medicine, 1906-09, Coll. Physicians and Surgeons, Memphis; dean and prof. pathology, clin. branch, med. dept. Univ. of Miss., Vicksburg, 1909-10; prof. tropical medicine and bacteriology, Coll. of Medicine (successor to Coll. Physicians and Surgeons), U. of Tenn., 1910-29 (emeritus); research pathologist Western State Hosp., Bolivar, Tenn., Aug. 1930-Oct. 1932; now dir. Stingity Laboratories, Meridian, Miss. Chmn. Tenn. Pellagra Commn., 1912. Fellow A.M.A., Am. Coll. Physicians. Home: Meridian, Miss. Died Dec. 21, 1935.

KRAUSS, William Christopher, B.S.; physician; b. Attica, N.Y., Oct. 15, 1863; grad. Attica Union School, 1880; Cornell, 1884; Bellevue Hosp. Med. Coll., 1886; Univ. of Berlin, Germany, magna cum laude, 1888; m. Clara Krieger, Sept. 4, 1890. Pres. Am. Micros. Soc., 1898; pres. Buffalo Micros. Club, 1891-92; fellow Royal Micros. Soc., London; pres. Med. Assn. of Central and Western N.Y., 1897-98. Asso. editor Buffalo Medical Journal and of Neurologisches Centralblatt, Berlin. Author of 100 papers on medical subjects and Textbook of Insanity. Home: Buffalo, N.Y. Died 1909.

KRAUTHOFF, Charles Rieseck, army officer; b. St. Louis, Mo., Oct. 6, 1863; enlisted as pvt. in Light Battery F, 2d F.A., Aug. 13, 1884; apptd. 2d lt., 14th Inf., July 31, 1891; grad. Inf. and Cav. Sch., 1895. 1st lt. 14th Inf., Apr. 26, 1898; promoted through grades to brig. gen. Q.M.C., Oct. 1, 1918; retired Dec. 7, 1922. Asst. q.m. gen., July 15, 1919. D.S.M. (U.S.A.); Comdr. Order of the Crown (Belgium); Officer Legion of Honor (France); Officer Order of the Crown (Roumania); Officer Order of the White Eagle (Serbia); Order of St. Sava (Serbs, Croates and Slovenes); medal for bravery (Montenegro). Died Feb. 24, 1936.

KRAUTHOFF, Louis Charles, lawyer; b. St. Louis, Feb. 18, 1858; ed. at Jefferson City, Mo. Admitted to bar when 18 yrs. old; asst. atty. gen. Mo., 1877-81; mem. Mo. Gen. Assembly, 1883; in Kansas City, 1886-99; gen. counsel Armour & Co., Chicago, 1899-1905; residing in New York, 1905—. Author exhaustive discussion of Malice as an Ingredient of a Civil Action, before Am. Bar Assn., 1898; was mem. Nat. (Gold-Standard) Dem. Nat. Com. for Mo., 1896. Died Oct. 26, 1918.

KREBS, Stanley LeFevre, author, lecturer; b. Waynesboro, Pa., Feb. 14, 1864; s. Walter Edmund (D.D.) and Isabella (LeFevre) K.; studied music and composition, Boston Conservatory of Music, 1883; A.B., Franklin and Marshall Coll., 1886, A.M., 1892; Dr. Psychology, Chicago Sch. of Psychology, 1889; graduate Eastern Theology Seminary of Reform Church in U.S., 1890; m. Marjorie Main, Dec. 2, 1921. Ordained ministry Ref. Ch. in U.S., 1890; organized St. Andrew's Ch., Reading, Pa., 1890; pastor First Ch., Greensburg, Pa., 1901; prepared curriculum and textbooks, also lecturer for the Am. Univ. of Trade, founded by John Wanamaker, 1907-11; from 1907 pres. Inst. of Mercantile Art, Inc., conductor of business insts. under auspices city chambers of commerce; admitted to Episcopal orders, 1927. Episcopalian. Author: The Law of Suggestion, 1905; The Buyer's Art, 1912; Salesmanship, 1913; LifiL, 1923; The Cries from the Cross, 1928. Home: New York, N.Y. Died 1935.

KRECH, Alvin William, banker; b. Hannibal, Mo., May 25, 1858; s. E. Wilhelm and Mathilde (Grow) K.; common sch. edn.; m. Angeline S. Jackson, 1895; children—Shepard, Mrs. Angeline J. James, Mrs. Helen Wing, Mrs. Margaret A. Cowles, Gerald. In flour milling business in Minn., 1874-88; ry. contractor, 1888-92; identified with U.P. R.R., 1893-94, Mercantile Trust Co., New York, 1894-1903, Equitable Trust Co., 1903—; now chmn. latter; also chmn. bd. Equitable Safe Deposit Co., Western Pacific R.R. Corp., D.&R.G.W. R.R. Dir. Metropolitan Opera Co.; trustee St. Luke's Hosp.; treas. gen. and dir. Permanent Blind Relief Fund. Chevalier Legion of Honor (French); Commendatore of Crown of Italy; Officer of Order of the Rumanian Crown. Home: New York, N.Y. Died May 3, 1928.

KREHBIEL, Henry Edward, musical critic; b. Ann Arbor, Mich., Mar. 10, 1854; ed. in pub. schs. of Mich. and Ohio; studied law in Cincinnati, 1872-74; (hon. A.M., Yale, 1909); m. Marie Van, Apr. 25, 1896. Musical critic Cincinnati Gazette, 1874-80, New York Tribune, 1880—. Mem. Internat. Jury of Awards, Paris Expn., 1900. Chevalier of Legion of Honor of France, 1901. Author: How to Listen to Music, 1896; Music and Manners in the Classical Period, 1898; Chapters of Opera, 1908; A Book of Operas, 1909; The Pianoforte and Its Music, 1911; Afro-American Folksongs, 1914; A Second Book of Operas, 1917; More Chapters of Opera, 1919. Translator: Carl Courvoisier's The Technics of Violin Playing, 1880. Editor: Annotated Bibliography of Fine Arts (dept. music), 1897; Music and Musicians, by Lavignac. Home: New York, N.Y. Died Mar. 20, 1923.

KREIDER, Aaron Shenk, congressman; b. South Annville Tp., Lebanon Co., Pa., June 26, 1863; s. David and Magdalena (Shenk) K.; ed. Lebanon Valley Coll. (LL.D.); m. Elizabeth B. Horst, Apr. 23, 1885. Established town of Lawn, Lebanon Co., Pa.; established shoe factories at Annville, Elizabethtown, Palmyra, Middletown and Lebanon, Pa.; now pres. The A.S. Kreider Co., Farmers' Trust Co. Member of 63d to 67th Congresses (1913-23), 18th Pa. District. Republican. Pres. bd. mgrs. Mt. Gretna Campmeeting Assn.; pres. trustees Lebanon Valley Coll. Mem. United Brethren Ch. Pres. Nat. Assn. Shoe Mfrs. of U.S., 1913-16. Home: Annville, Pa. Died June 19, 1929.

KREISER, Edward Franklin, organist, conductor; b. New York, Sept. 21, 1869; s. Emile and Amelia (Mills) K.; mus. edn. under Frederick Archer, Chicago, Alexander Guilmant, and Maurice Moszkowski, Paris; m. Mary Alice Henderson, Feb. 28, 1906. Organist and choirmaster, Grand Av. M.E. Ch., 1890-1909, Jewish Temple, 1908—, First Congl. Ch., 1909-10, Independence Boul. Christian Ch., Mar. 1910—, Kansas City, Mo.; conductor Apollo Club. Played more than 200 recitals in Kansas City in one series; played recitals at St. Louis and Jamestown expns. Republican. Methodist. Home: Kansas City, Mo. Died Mar. 3, 1917.

KREMER, J. Bruce, lawyer; b. Louisville, Ky., Sept. 26, 1878; s. Charles Lawrence and Anne Lee (Hendricks) K.; student U. of Va., 1894-95, 1896-97; B.L., U. of Louisville Law Dept., 1898. Admitted to Ky. bar, 1898; practiced Louisville, 1898-1901, Butte, Montana, 1901-33; mem. Kremer, Sanders & Kremer, 1907-33; mem. D.C. bar, 1933, now practicing in Washington, D.C. Mem. (secretary and vice chmn.) Democrat Nat. Committee, 1908-34; sec. Dem. National Conv., 1916, and chmn. Dem. Speakers Bur. western div., nat. campaign, 1916; v. chmn. Dem. Nat. Com., 1919; reëlected 1920; presiding officer at opening Dem. Nat. Conv., San Francisco, 1920; chmn. Mont. delegation Dem. Nat. Conv., New York, 1924; chmn. com. on credentials, Democratic Nat. Conv., Houston, Texas, 1928; chmn. com. on rules, Democratic Nat. Conv., Chicago, 1932. Died July 23, 1940.

KREMERS, Edward, univ. prof.; b. Milwaukee, Wis., Feb. 23, 1865; s. Gerhard and Elsie (Kamper) K.; Ph.G., U. of Wis., 1886, B.S., 1888; Ph.D., U. of Göttingen, 1890; Sc.D., U. of Mich., 1913; Pharm. M. Phila. Coll. of Pharmacy, 1921; m. Laura Haase, July 6, 1892. Instr. pharmacy, 1890-92, prof. phar. chemistry and dir. course in pharmacy, 1892—, Dir. Pharm. Expt. Station, 1913-35, dir. emeritus, U. of Wisconsin. Appointed member of State Board of Pharmacy. Editor of Pharm. Review, 1896-1909; coeditor Standard National Dispensatory. Chmn. committee on volatile oils and related subjects of U.S. Pharmacopœia Revision Com., 1900-10. Author: (English edit.) Gildemeister-Hoffmann-Kremers' The Volatile Oils, 1900, 2d edit., 1913. Died July 9, 1941.

KREMPEL, John P., architect; b. Kreuznach, Germany, Oct. 19, 1861; s. John P. and Susan (Stocker) K.; ed. tech. high sch., Berlin; m. Emilie Kuhrts, Dec. 12, 1896; children—Jack J., Paul W., Lucille S. Settled in Los Angeles, Calif., 1887; head draftsman with Frank J. Capitain, 1888-92, and partner with him, 1893-94; practiced alone, 1894-1911, then with Walter E. Erkes; architect Chino Sugar Factory, Oxnard Sugar Factory, Oxnard Hotel, Maier Brewery, German Hosp., Times Bldg., residence of Gen. Harrison Gray Otis, etc. Mem. State Bd. of Architecture, Calif., 1901—; pres. State Bd. of Architecture, Southern Dist., 1914-16. Republican. Mason. Home: Beverly Hills, Calif. Deceased.

KRESS, Claude Washington, merchant; b. Slatington, Pa., Apr. 4, 1876; s. John Franklin and Margaret (Connor) K.; desc. of Carl Kress who came from Germany and settled in Pa. in 1752; ed. Wyoming (Pa.) Sem.; m. Agatha, d. Cornelius Sheehan, of Atlanta, Ga., 1902; children—Elizabeth, Rosalind. Associated with bro. Samuel H., in mercantile business, at Nanticoke, Pa., 1893, and elected v.p. S. H. Kress & Co., New York, after incorporation, 1907, pres., 1924, company operating chain of 5, 10, and 25 cent stores in 219 cities of U.S. and Hawaii. Home: New York, N.Y. Died Nov. 8, 1940.

KRESS, John Alexander, army officer; b. Tioga Co., Pa., Nov. 4, 1839; s. Benjamin and Margaret Ann (Wilcox) K.; early edn. in schs. of Tioga Co., Pa., and Laporte Co., Ind.; m. Annie A. Muhlenberg, Sept. 1, 1887. Entered U.S. Mil. Acad., 1858; resigned Oct. 31, 1861, to accept apptmt. by Gen. James S. Wadsworth of New York as 1st lt. 25th N.Y. Vol. Inf. and a.-d.-c. to Gen. Wadsworth; maj. 94th N.Y., July 1862; lt. col., Nov. 1862; comd. regt. in battle of Fredericksburg; detailed as insp. gen. 1st div., 1st corps; apptd. 2d lt., ordnance dept., U.S.A., and later chief ordnance Officer, Dept. of the James; lt. col., 117th U.S.C.T., and insp. gen. 25th Army Corps; assigned to Rock Island Arsenal, 1865; U.S. Arsenal, Pittsburgh, 1867; Vancouver, Wash., 1871; San Antonio, Tex., 1882; Indianapolis, 1883; St. Louis Powder Depot, 1886; Benicia, Calif., Arsenal, 1887; St. Louis Powder Depot, 1890; assigned as chief ordnance officer U.S.A., encamped at Chickamauga, Tenn., 1898; served in Cuba as chief ordnance officer 1st army corps, and chief ordnance officer, entire Island of Cuba, on staff Maj. Gen. Brooke; again comdr. St. Louis Powder Depot, 1899, until promoted brig. gen. U.S.A., and retired Aug. 17, 1903. Baptist. Home: Merion, Pa. Died July 4, 1933.

KRETZINGER, George Washington, lawyer; b. in Ohio, 1846; s. Isaac and Elizabeth K.; collegiate edn.; m. Clara Wilson, Aug. 28, 1878. Enlisted in Union Army, 1861, serving through the entire war; admitted to bar; practiced at Knoxville, Ill., until 1873, Chicago, 1873—; sr. mem. Kretzinger, Rooney & Kretzinger. Gen. solicitor Chicago & Ia. Ry., 1887; gen. counsel Louisville, New Albany & Chicago R.R. Co.; gen. counsel Monon Ry., 1891-1910; now atty. Grand Trunk Ry. System, Inc., 1891, and dir. Santa Fe, Prescott — Phoenix Ry. Co. of Ariz. Republican. Home: Chicago, Ill. Died Nov. 17, 1913.

KRIEBEL, Oscar Schultz, clergyman, educator; b. Hereford, Pa., Sept. 10, 1863; s. Andrew S. and Christina (Schultz) K.; A.B., Oberlin Coll., 1889, A.M., 1892; grad. Oberlin Theol. Sem., 1892; U. of Berlin, 1891-92; U. of Pa. (psychology, philosophy and pedagogy), 1901-05; D.D., Franklin and Marshall, 1907; m. Corinne Miller (Oberlin, 1896), June 30, 1891; children—Mrs. Frieda Adams, Mary Miller, Mrs. Louisa Adams. Ordained ministry Schwenkfelder Ch., 1892; pastor Schwenkfelder Ch. of the Upper Dist., 1892-1913, Palm Schwenkfelder Ch., 1913—. Pres. Bd. of Publ. Schwenkfelder Ch.; mem. Bd. of Missions same; prin. Perkiomen Sch., Pennsburg, Pa., 1892—. Republican. Home: Pennsburg, Pa. Died Feb. 6, 1932.

KROEGER, Ernest Richard, musician; b. at St. Louis, Aug. 10, 1862; s. of Adolph E. and Eliza B. A. (Curren) K.; ed. St. Louis; musical studies in St. Louis; m. Laura A. Clark, Oct. 10, 1891; children—Mary Louise, Richard Clark, Eleanor Alice, Beatrice. Director Kroeger Sch. of Music; chmn. bd. examiners Art Publication Soc.; dean School of Music, Washington Univ.; concert pianist and organist; musical lecture recitals; master of programs, Bur. of Music, St. Louis Expn., 1904. Officer of the French Acad. Composer of orchestral works, chamber, piano, organ pieces, songs, ch. music, etc.; writer on musical subjects. Lecturer U. of California, summer session, 1915, Cornell U. summer sessions, 1916-29, Washington U., 1930; organ recitals, Panama-Pacific Expn. Home: St. Louis, Mo. Died Apr. 7, 1934.

KROGER, Bernard Henry, banker, grocer; b. Cincinnati, O., Jan. 24, 1860; s. John Henry and Mary Gertrude (Schlebe) K.; ed. common schs.; m. Mary Emily Jansen, Apr. 28, 1886 (died April 1899); children—Gertrude (Mrs. Irving Wolford Pettengill), Lucille (Mrs. Albert Berne, deceased), Bernard Henry (deceased), Helen (Mrs. Rudolph Homan), Chester Frederick, Gretchen (Mrs. Bruno Graf), Raymond William (dec.); m. 2d, Alice Farrington Maher, March 3, 1928. Began in the grocery business, 1883; formerly chmn. bd. Kroger Grocery & Baking Co.; chmn. bd. Provident Savings Bank & Trust Co.; chmn. bd. First National Bank in Palm Beach, Florida; former director Cincinnati branch Federal Reserve Bank of Cleveland, resigned, 1936. Trustee Charles Fleischmann Endowment Fund, Cincinnati Institute Fine Arts, Cincinnati Bur. Governmental Research; mem. bd. Cincinnati Community Chest and Council of Social Agencies. Donor of ground and buildings for Kroger Hill Camp, for anæmic white children, Kroger Health Camp Co. 2 for anæmic colored children. Active in Red Cross and Community Chest campaigns. World War. Republican. Home: Cincinnati, O. Died July 21, 1938.

KROHN, William Otterbein, M.D.; b. Galion, O., Mar. 23, 1868; s. Benjamin Franklin and Barbara Ann (Smith) K.; B.A., Western (now Leander Clark) Coll., Toledo, Ia., 1887; M.A. and Ph.D., Yale, 1889; European univs., June 1891-Feb. 1892 sr. fellow Clark U., Mar.-Oct. 1892; M.D., North western U., 1905; m. Emma Beardshear, Aug. 26, 1887 (died 1890); children—Gretchen, Stuart Beardshear; m. 2d, Hattie Weaver, Sept. 10, 1892; divorced 1907; m. 3d, Josephine Elliott, 1909. Head dept. of philosophy, psychology and ethics, Adelbert Coll. and Cleveland Coll. for Women, of Western Reserve U., 1889-91; asst. prof. psychology and pedagogy,

1892-93, psychology, 1893-97, U. of Ill.; psychologist, Eastern Hosp. for Insane, Kankakee, Ill., 1897-99. Capt. med. corps, U.S.A., June 1917-Feb. 1918; maj. M.R.C., Feb. 1918. Died July 17, 1927.

KROTEL, Gottlob Frederick, clergyman; b. Ilsfeld, Würtemberg, Germany, Feb. 4, 1826; s. Christopher F. and Louisa Dorothea (Seiz) K.; grad. Univ. of Pa., 1846 (D.D., 1865); LL.D., Muhlenberg Coll.; widower. Clergyman Evan. Luth. Ch. from 1848; served pastorates in Lebanon, Lancaster, and Phila.; in New York, 1868, pastor Evang. Luth. Ch. of the Holy Trinity, 1868-95; from 1896 pastor Ch. of the Advent, New York. Prof. Luth. Theol. Sem., 1864-68. Editor-in-chief The Lutheran, official organ of Gen. Council. Pres. Luth. Ministerium of New York and of Luth. Ministerium of Pa., 1866-68, and 1884-92. One of founders of Gen. Council, and its pres., 1869-70, and 1888-93. Died 1907.

KROUT, Mary Hannah, author; b. Crawfordsville, Ind., Nov. 3, 1857; d. Robert K. and Caroline (Brown) K.; ed. by parents at home; unmarried. Taught, 1872-87; asso. editor Crawfordsville Journal, 1881; editor Terre Haute Express, 1882; 10 yrs. on staff of Chicago Inter Ocean; staff corr. in Hawaii, 1893-94; in New Zealand and Australia, 1884; staff corr. at London, 1895-98; writer of syndicate letters to several leading dailies; spl. letters to New York Tribune from China, Sept. 1899 to May 1900; on staff Denver Times, 1900-01. Traveled in Australia, and made series of addresses, 1906. Author: Alice in the Hawaiian Islands, 1899; Two Girls in China, 1903. Episcopalian. Home: Crawfordsville, Ind. Died May 31, 1927.

KRUEGER, John Frederick, educator; b. Chaibasa, British East India, July 15, 1881; s. John Frederick and Elizabeth (Zippel) K.; A.B., Midland College, Fremont, Neb., 1903, LL.D., 1925; studied Western Theol. Sem., 1904; Ph.D., U. of Neb., 1914; D.D., Bethany Coll., Lindsborg, Kan., 1917; m. Carrie P. Mayer, June 7, 1904; children—Dorothea Elizabeth, Fritz Konrad, Ralph Mayer, Mary Caroline. Came to U.S., 1899, naturalized citizen, 1904. Ordained Luth. ministry, 1903; pastor Fremont, 1903-07, Lincoln, Neb., 1907-11; prof. theology, Western Theol. Sem., 1911-22; pres. Midland Coll. 1922-25; pres. Am. Luth. Mission, Shantung, China, 1925-28; prof. N.T. philology and interpretation, Hamma Div. Sch., Springfield, O., 1928—. Republican. Home: Springfield, O. Died Nov. 13, 1935.

KRUELL, Gustav, artist; b. Düsseldorf, Germany, 1843; s. Ludwig and Franziska K.; m. Clara Kuehn, Sept. 1868. Pupil of R. Brendeamour, Düsseldorf. Awarded honorable mention Expn. Universelle, Paris, 1889; medal at World's Columbian Expn., Chicago, 1893. Exhibited at Paris Expn., 1900; gold medal, St. Louis Expn., 1904. Home: East Orange, N.J. Died 1907.

KRUM, Chester Harding, lawyer; b. Alton, Ill., Sept. 13, 1840; s. Judge John M. and Mary (Harding) K.; B.A., Washington U., 1863; LL.B., Harvard, 1865; m. Elizabeth H. Cutter, Oct. 26, 1866. Admitted to bar, 1864, and practiced in St. Louis; apptd. by Pres. Grant U.S. dist. atty., 1869, and served until elected, 1872, judge of St. Louis Circuit Court; resigned, 1875, and resumed practice. Mem. faculty St. Louis Law Sch., 1873-82; mem. Krum & Madill, 1875-78, J. M. & C. H. Krum, 1877, Krum & Jonas, 1883-87, then alone; spl. master in receivership proceedings of Wabash Railroad, 1912; etc. Unitarian. Home: St. Louis, Mo. Died Oct. 19, 1923.

KRUMWIEDE, Charles, M.D., bacteriologist; b. N.Y. City, Sept. 9, 1879; s. Charles and Johannah (Freese) K.; B.A., Columbia, 1902; M.D., Coll. Phys. and Surg. (Columbia), 1905; m. Ellen Louise Lipps, Nov. 20, 1907; children—Helen Louise, Elma. Began practice in N.Y. City, 1905; asst. dir. Bur. of Laboratories, Dept. of Health, N.Y. City; prof. bacteriology and immunology, Univ. and Bellevue Med. Coll. and New York U. College of Dentistry. Republican. Episcopalian. Home: Bronxville, N.Y. Died Dec. 1930.

KRUSE, Frederick William, judge; b. Mecklenberg-Schwerin, Germany, June 25, 1852; s. John and Sophie (Klötzer) K.; came to America with parents, 1853; ed. Griffith Inst., Springville, N.Y.; LL.D., Alfred U., 1906; m. Julia V. Engle, May 21, 1878; 1 dau., Alice (wife of Judge George A. Larkin). Admitted to bar, 1877; practiced at Olean; mem. N.Y. Assembly, 1884-87; mem. commn. to revise state excise laws, 1888; spl. commr. to investigate federal census frauds, 1890 (reënumerated City of Minneapolis); mem. commn. to prepare gen. charter for 3d class cities in State of N.Y., 1895; co. judge Cattaraugus Co., 1897-1900; justice Supreme Ct. of N.Y., Jan. 1, 1900-Dec. 31, 1922; assigned to Appellate Div., 4th Dept., Jan. 1, 1906; apptd. presiding justice, May 1913, reapptd., 1914; retired. Home: Olean, N.Y. Died Mar. 18, 1939.

KRUTTSCHNITT, Ernest Benjamin, lawyer; b. New Orleans, La., April 17, 1852; s. John and Peninah (Benjamin) K.; ed. Washington Coll. (now Washington and Lee Univ.), 1867-70; studied law, same (LL.D., 1898); admitted to bar, Feb. 1874; unmarried. Mem. bd. dirs. pub. sch., New Orleans, 1884-1903 (pres., 1890-1903); pres. Constl. Conv., La., 1898; chmn. Dem. Exec. Com., 1892-96; chmn. Dem. State Central Com., 1896—. Home: New Orleans, La. Died 1906.

KRUTTSCHNITT, Julius, ry. official; b. New Orleans, La., July 30, 1854; s. John and Peninah (Benjamin) K.; C.E., Washington and Lee U., 1873; m. E. Minna Kock, Feb. 14, 1882. Asst. to Col. William Allan, prin. MacDonough Sch., nr. Baltimore, 1873-78; resident engr. in charge of constrn., 1878-80, roadmaster Western div., 1880-81, asst. chief engr. and gen. roadmaster, 1881-83, chief engr. and supt., 1883-85, Morgan's La. & Tex. R.R.; asst. gen. mgr. S.P. Co.'s Atlantic system (lines east of El Paso, Tex.), 1885-89, gen. mgr. same, 1889-95; gen. mgr. of all lines of S.P. Co., with headquarters at San Francisco, 1895-1904, 4th v.p. same, 1898-1904, asst. to pres. same, 1901-04, and v.p., 1904-11; dir. of maintenance and operation U.P. R.R. Co., Ore. Short Line R.R. Co., Ore. R.R. & Navigation Co. and S.P. Co., headquarters at Chicago, 1904-11, at New York, 1911-13; chmn. exec. com. and dir. S.P. Co., and affiliated cos. operating in Ariz., La. and Tex., and of S.P. R.R. Co. of Mexico; also mem. exec. com. and dir. Western Union Telegraph Co., Erie R.R. Home: New Canaan, Conn. Died June 15, 1925.

KUBEL, Stephen Joseph, engraver; b. Washington, D.C., Apr. 2, 1858; s. Edward and Josephine K.; ed. Gonzaga Coll., Washington, 1865-74; studied music at Washington, and at Scharwenka Conservatory of Music, Berlin, Prussia; studied cartography and map engraving, 1874-78; m. Louise Griffith, July 5, 1884 (died 1924); children—Herbert Graham (dec.), Florence Louise. In Hydrographic Office, Navy Dept., 1878-83; in cartographic div. Prussian gen. staff, Berlin, 1883-85; returned to Hydrographic Office U.S.; chief engraver, U.S. Geol. Survey, 1890-1932 (retired). Has been organist in prominent Catholic chs. in Washington, D.C., 1880—. Died Mar. 2, 1936.

KUBELIK, Jan, violinist; b. Michle, nr. Prague, Bohemia, July 5, 1880; father a market gardener and amateur violinist; began to learn violin at 5 and first played in public at 8; entered Prague Conservatory at 12, continuing 6 yrs.; m. Magyar, d. of Wolfgang Szell de Bessenyei, and divorced wife of Count Czaky. Began giving recitals, 1898; was apptd. violinist Royal Court of Bohemia; first tour in U.S., 1901-02; has played with leading orchestras throughout Europe and America; noted for remarkable feats of virtuosity. Home: Bychor bei Kolin, Bohemia. Died Dec. 5, 1940.

KUERSTEINER, Albert Frederick, college prof.; b. New Orleans, La., Nov. 9, 1865; s. James and Mathilde (Rabel) K.; A.B., U. of Cincinnati, 1888; studied Johns Hopkins, Paris, Madrid, 1894-98; Ph.D., Johns Hopkins, 1904; m. Agnes Christine Duncan, July 6, 1907. Teacher Tech. Sch., Cincinnati, 1887-88; instr. German and French, Wabash Coll., Ind., 1888-90; teacher of Latin and mathematics, Hughes High Sch., Cincinnati, 1890-94; prof. Romance langs., Indiana U., 1898—. Unitarian. Died June 9, 1917.

KUH, Sydney, neurologist, alienist; b. N.Y. City, Mar. 6, 1866; s. Isaac and Mathilda (Kupfer) K.; ed. gymnasium, Bayreuth, Bavaria, 1875-82; Chicago Med. Coll., 1885-86; M.D., U. of Heidelberg, 1890; U. of Vienna, 1890-91; asst. at Univ. Hosp., Heidelberg, 1891-92; studied in Paris and London, 1892. Clin. prof. psychiatry, Rush Medical College (U. of Chicago); prof. neurology and psychiatry, Chicago Policlinic; sr. attending neurologist Michael Reese Hosp.; chief of staff, Cook County Psychopathic Hosp.; attending alienist Seeleth Hosp.; consulting neurologist Lying-in Hosp. Republican. Jewish religion. Home: Chicago, Ill. Died Dec. 27, 1934.

KUHN, Franz Christian, judge; b. Detroit, Mich., Feb. 8, 1872; s. John and Anna C. (Ullrich) K.; B.S., U. of Mich., 1893; LL.B., 1894; m. Mina C. Burton, July 7, 1906; 1 dau., Wilhelmina Ann. Admitted to Mich. bar, 1894, and practiced at Mt. Clemens. Circuit ct. commr., Macomb Co., 1894-98; pros. atty., 1898-1904; probate judge, 1904-10 (resigned); apptd. atty. gen. of Mich. by Gov. Warner, June 1910; elected to same office, Nov. 1910; apptd. mem. Supreme Ct., Mich., by Gov. Osborn, Sept. 1912, to fill vacancy; elected to same office Nov. following to fill unexpired term ending Dec. 31, 1917, and elected Apr. 1917, for full term ending Dec. 31, 1925 (chief justice 1917-18), resigned Dec. 31, 1919; pres. Mich. Bell Telephone Co., 1920—. Republican. Mason. Home: Grosse Pointe, Mich. Died June 16, 1926.

KUHN, Joseph Ernst, army officer; b. Leavenworth, Kan., June 14, 1864; grad. U.S. Mil. Acad., 1885; grad. U.S. Engr. Sch., Willets Point, N.Y., 1888; m. 2d, Helen Squire, Oct. 19, 1917; children—Richard Parker, Joseph Southard (dec.). Commd. 2d lt. Engrs., U.S.A., June 14, 1885; promoted through grades to maj. gen. June 18, 1925. Asst. engr. rivers and harbors, Detroit, 1888-89; instr. civ. engring., U.S. Mil. Acad., 1889-94; asst. engr. rivers, harbors and fortifications, San Francisco, 1894-96; asst. to chief of engrs., Washington, D.C., 1896-1900; engr. bldgs. and grounds, West Point, 1900-03; foreign duty, Philippines, Japan and China, 1903-05; mil. observer Japanese armies, 1904-05; engr. in charge rivers and harbors, Norfolk, Va., 1906-09; dir. mil. engring., Army Staff Coll., Leavenworth, Kan., 1909-12; engr. in charge rivers, harbors and fortifications, Philadelphia, 1912-13; comdr. Engr. Sch. and Depot, Washington, D.C., 1913-14; mil. attaché U.S. Embassy, Berlin, 1915-16, also mil. observer with German armies; pres. Army War Coll., 1917; comdr. 79th Div., World War, 1917-19, Camp Kearney, Calif., 1919-20, Schofield Barracks, Hawaii, 1920-23, Vancouver Barracks, 1923-25; retired, 1925. Awarded Legion of Honor and Croix de Guerre (France). Tech. adviser Copley Press; mem. advisory bd. San Diego branch Pacific States Bldg. & Loan Assn. Chmn. San Diego Chapter Am. Red Cross. Died Nov. 12, 1935.

KUHN, Oliver Owen, editor; b. Crawfordsville, Ind., Feb. 28, 1886; s. Thomas Harvey and Emma (Collins) K.; ed. Butler U. (Indianapolis) and Earlham Coll. (Ind.); m. Leonora Martin-Rivero, Apr. 5, 1915; children—Lois Mary, Eleanor M., Frances. News editor Richmond (Ind.) Palladium, later of the Oklahoman, Oklahoma City, Okla., until 1909; mng. editor Indianapolis Sun, 1909; with Washington newspapers, 1909-11; writer on international affairs, Washington Star, 1911; assigned to cover Peace Conf. for Washington Star, 1919, and continued with the paper as news mgr. and from 1929 as mng. editor. For many yrs. active in civic affairs of D.C. and Md.; pres. and hon. mem. for life of Montgomery County (Mo.) Civic Fedn. Chmn. Asso. Press, Mng. Editors Assn. Mem. Christian (Disciples) Ch. Home: Bethesda, Md. Died July 18, 1937.

KUHN, William Frederick, neurologist; b. Lyons, N.Y., Apr. 15, 1849; s. Frederick and Barbara (Ernst) K.; A.B., Wittenberg Coll., Springfield, O., 1875, A.M., 1878; M.D., Jefferson Med. Coll., Phila., 1884; m. Jessie O. Willson, Oct. 21, 1889. Began practice at Kansas City, Mo., 1888; supt. State Asylum for the Insane, 1905-09; pres. Kansas City Coll. of Pharmacy, 1900-05; adj. prof. psychiatry, U. of Kan. Sch. of Medicine, 1904—. Lutheran. Home: Kansas City, Mo. Died Sept. 1, 1924.

KUHNS, Luther Melanchthon, clergyman, editor; b. Omaha, Neb., Dec. 10, 1861; s. Henry Welty and Charlotta Josepha (Hay) K.; student Newberry (S.C.) Coll., 1878-79, D.D., 1922; student Western Md. Coll., Westminster, 1879-81; student Gettysburg (Pa.) Coll., 1883, A.B. and A.M., 1886, Litt.D., 1918; grad. Gettysburg Theol. Sem., 1886; unmarried. Ordained Luth. ministry, 1886; pastor Freeport and Braddock, Pa., 1886-87; founder, 1887, pastor, 1887-1903 and 1926-28, emeritus pastor, 1931—, Grace Ch., Omaha; gen. sec. Luther League America (charter mem., now life mem.), 1902-16, lit. sec., 1916—. Asso. editor Luther League Review, 1895-1916, editor, 1916-19; also editor "Topics," 1916-19. Pres. Neb. Synod, 1899-1902, historian, 1930—; necrologist del. Gen. Synod, Luth. Ch., 1895, 1917; del. orgn. meeting United Luth. Ch., 1918; sec. traveling sec. com. (missionary) Neb. Synod, 1888-1904; mem. com. for examination of candidates for Luth. ministry several yrs.; pres. Luth. Ministers Union, 1927-28; mem. Com. on Assn. of Young People, United Luth. Ch. Chmn., Neb., welfare work for soldiers and sailors, World War; also same, Polish Relief. Trustee Midland Coll. 3 terms; trustee Masonic Home, Plattsmouth, Neb.; mem. and patron Andhra Christian Coll., India. Charter mem. Neb. Sons of Am. Revolution, past pres. Mason. Author: Luther League Hand Book, 1906; John Huss, 1912; The Church on the Frontier; Life of Constantine, 1916. Traveled around world, 1908-09, establishing Luther Leagues and visiting missions. Home: Omaha, Neb. Died Mar. 18, 1939.

KUHNS, Oscar, univ. prof.; b. Columbia, Pa., Feb. 21, 1856; s. William and Rebecca (Brown) K.; A.B., Wesleyan U., 1885, A.M., 1888; U. of Berlin, 1885-87, also univs. of Geneva, Paris, Rome and Florence; L.H.D., Dickinson, 1904; m. Lillie B. Conn, Apr. 6, 1892; 1 son, Austin Hubbert. Prof. Romance langs., Wesleyan U., 1890—. Author: Selections from Alfred de Musset, 1895; Cuore, by De Amicis, 1896; The Treatment of Nature in Dante's Divina Commedia, 1897; Revised Edition of Cary's Translation of Dante, 1897; Pierre et Virginie, 1898; French Reader, 1899; Cyrano de Bergerac, 1899; The German and Swiss Settlements of Colonial Pennsylvania, 1900; Studies in the Italian Poets, 1901; Studies in Pennsylvania German Family Names, 1903; The Great Italian Poets, 1903; Dante and the English Poets, 1904; Strasbourg (edited), 1905; St. Francis of Assisi, 1906; John Huss, the Witness, 1907; The Sense of the Infinite, 1908; Selections from Boileau, 1908; A Reading Journey Through Switzerland, 1908; Switzerland, Its Scenery, History and Literary Associations, 1910; The Love of Books and Reading, 1910; Notes on the Kuntz (Kuhns) and Brown Families of Lancaster County, Pa., 1909; A One-Sided Autobiography, 1913; The Peaceful Life, 1917. Home: Middletown, Conn. Died Aug. 20, 1929.

KUICHLING, Emil, civil engr.; b. Kehl, Germany, Jan. 20, 1848; s. Louis and Marie (von Seeger) K.; A.B., U. of Rochester, N.Y., 1868, C.E., 1869; student, Carlsruhe (Germany) Poly. Sch., 1870-73;

m. Sarah L. Caldwell, Jan. 28, 1879. Asst. engr., western div. N.Y. State canals, 1869, 1873; asst. engr., 1873-85, chief engr., 1890-1900, Rochester water works; consulting engr. N.Y. State Bd. Health, 1881-91; mem. exec. bd., Rochester, 1885-87; consulting engr., New York, N.Y., 1900—. Died Nov. 9, 1914.

KUMM, H. Karl William, geog. research; b. Hanover, Germany, Oct. 19, 1874; s. H. William and M. W. (Kistenbrugge) K.; grad. Gymnasium Osterode, 1894; studied Harley Coll., London, 1896-98, Heidelberg, 1900, Jena, 1902-03; Ph.D., U. of Freiburg, 1903; also studied Cambridge and Paris, and Arabic in Egypt, and Hausa in Tripoli; m. Lucy Guinness, of Dublin, Ireland, 1900 (died 1906); children—Henry W., Karl Grattan; m. 2d, Frances Gertrude Cato, of Australia; children—Lucy Gertrude, Frederick John. Began as explorer in Africa, 1899; first white man to traverse the north-central African divide between Congo Shari and the Nile; founded missions, schs., hosps., etc.; founder and mng. dir. Bd. for Medical Edn. and Research in Africa, also of Sudan United Mission (22 denominations); made maps for Peace Conf., Paris. Republican. Episcopalian. Author: The Lands of Ethiopia, 1910; African Missionary Heroes and Heroines, 1917. Engaged in hort. experiments with Passifloraceæ in Southern Calif. Home: Pacific Beach, Calif. Died Aug. 22, 1930.

KUNITZER, Robert, physician; b. Szegedin, Hungary, Feb. 10, 1866; s. Emanuel and Johanna (Englander) K.; grad. Gymnasium Vienna; U. of Vienna, 1888; came to U.S., 1889; M.D., U. State of N.Y., 1890; m. Nettie Rosenstraus, Apr. 1918. Prof. practice of medicine, Eclectic Med. Coll., 1892—; visiting phys. Sydenham Hosp., also chief med. dept. Sydenham Hosp. Dispensary; dir. Sydenham Post-Grad. Sch and Hosp. and pres. exec. com. of Med. Bd.; chief med. examiner, Empire State Ins. Co.; examiner for Denver Hosp. for consumptives. Mason. Home: New York, N.Y. Died Sept. 1924.

KUNZ, George Frederick, gem expert; b. New York, Sept. 29, 1856; s. J. G. and Marie Ida (Widmer) K.; ed. pub. schs. and Cooper Union; hon. A.M., Columbia, 1898; Ph.D., U. of Marburg, 1903; Sc.D., Knox, 1907; m. Sophia Hanforth, Oct. 29, 1879 (died 1912). V.p. and gem expert Tiffany & Co., jewelers, 1879—. Spl. agt. U.S. Geol. Survey, 1883-1909; in charge dept. mines, Paris Expn., 1889, Kimberley Expn., 1892, Chicago Expn., 1893; hon. spl. agt. of mines, Atlanta Expn., 1895, Omaha Expn., 1898; on spl. investigation U.S. Fish Commn. on Am. Pearls, 1892-98; hon. spl. agt. to Commr. Gen. U.S., Paris Expn., 1900; del. from U.S. to Internat. Congress, Paris, 1900; radium commr. St. Louis Expn., 1904; spl. agt. in charge of precious stones, 12th U.S. Census. Officer d'Instruction Publique (France), 1889; Officer Legion of Honor (France); Knight Order St. Olaf (Norway); officer of the Rising Sun (Japan). Hon. mem. Chambre Syndicale Pierres Précieuses, Paris; research curator, precious stones, Am. Mus. of Natural History; founder and hon. pres. Museums of the Peaceful Arts (now Mus. of Science and Industry), N.Y. City. Pres. Am. Metric Assn.; hon. pres. New York Bird and Tree Club; pres. Joan of Arc Statue Com. of City of N.Y.. Author: Gems and Precious Stones of North America; The Book of the Pearl (with Charles H. Stevenson), 1908; The Curious Lore of Precious Stones, 1913; E. Roty and His Work, 1914; Magic of Jewels, 1915; Ivory and the Elephant, 1915; Shakespeare and Precious Stones, 1916; The Ring, 1917. Home: New York, N.Y. Died June 29, 1932.

KUNZ, Jakob, prof. mathematical physics; b. Brittnau Aargau, Switzerland, Nov. 3, 1874; s. Jakob and Anna Maria (Weber) K.; B.S., Polytechnicum, Zurich, Switzerland, 1897; Ph.D., U. of Zurich, 1902; m. Anna Bolliger, July 24, 1913; children—Annamarie, Margaret Rosa. Chemist, Gesellschaft für Chemische Industrie, Basel, 1897-1900; instr. and pvt.docent in physics, Polytechnicum, 1900-07; came to U.S., 1908; instr. in physics, U. of Mich., 1908; asst. and asso. prof. physics, U. of Ill., 1909-23, prof. mathematical physics, 1923—. With solar eclipse expdns. to Green River, 1918, Middletown (Conn.), 1925, Lancaster (N.H.), 1932. Served in Swiss Army, 1894-1900. Methodist. Author: Theoretische Physik auf mechanischer Grundlage, 1907. Home: Urbana, Ill. Died July 18, 1939.

KUNZE, Richard Ernest, physician, naturalist; b. Altenburg, Saxony, Apr. 7, 1838; s. John Jacob and Adelaide K.; M.D., Eclectic Med. Coll. of New York, 1868; widower. Practiced in New York until removing to Ariz., 1896; now making studies and investigations in the med. botany and insect fauna of Ariz. Originator of Ariz. cactus farm, and exporter of cacti to the bot. gardens of the world. Pres. N.Y. Therapeutical Assn.; corr. sec. Eclectic Med. Coll. of New York. Home: Phœnix, Ariz. Died Feb. 10, 1919.

KURRIE, Harry Rushworth, ry. pres.; b. Paoli, Ind.; s. Sebastian and Elizabeth (Walls) K.; LL.B., Indiana U., Bloomington, 1895; m. Edna Thompson, Dec. 9, 1909 (died March 19, 1919); children—Harry R., Thompson; m. 2d, Henrietta Brunt, June 1920. Began practice of law at Rensselaer, 1895; became asst. gen. solicitor C.,I.&L. R.R. (Monon Route), of which became pres., 1914, apptd. co-trustee of railroad, Dec. 1935. Republican. Home: Chicago, Ill. Died Dec. 25, 1938.

KURTZ, Charles Lindley, financier; b. Albany, O., May 4, 1854; s. William Wyland and Isabélla (McEllroy) K.; ed. pub. schs.; newsboy and bookseller, 1868-84; m. Annie Jewett, Sept. 11, 1878; children—Ione, Eleanor, Florence (dec.), Charles Jewett; m. 2d, Vivian Ebersole, Nov. 27, 1915. Pres. Columbus Pub. Service Co., Guanajuato Reduction & Mines Co., Keever Starch Co., Scioto Stone Co. Mem. Ohio House of Rep., 1880-84; pvt. sec. to Gov. Foraker, 1886-90; mem. Rep. State Exec. Com., 1885-90 (chmn. 1895-96); contractor pub. works, 1890-95; state insp. oil of Ohio, 1896-1900; state del. Nat. Irrigation Congresses, 1897, 98, 99; mem. Rep. Nat. Com., 1896-1900. Home: Columbus, O. Died Mar. 24, 1929.

KURTZ, Charles M., art director The Buffalo Fine Arts Academy; b. New Castle, Pa., Mar. 20, 1855; s. David B. and Julia Maria (Wilder) K.; grad. Washington and Jefferson Coll., A.B., 1876, A.M., 1879, Ph.D., 1902; student 3 yrs., Nat. Acad. Design, New York; m. Julia Stephenson, Oct. 1, 1885. Was several yrs. connected with the New York Tribune; 9 yrs. editor Nat. Acad. Notes; editor Art Union Mag., 1884; dir. Art Dept. Southern Expn., Louisville, Ky., 1883-86; art editor New York Daily Star, 1889, and also later lit. editor and dir. Sunday Star; asst. chief Dept. Fine Arts, World's Columbian Expn., 1891-93; art dir. for St. Louis Annual Expn., 1894-99, and visited art centers of U.S. and Europe in interests of that expn.; received diploma and medal from Trans-Mississippi Internat. Expn., 1898; asst. dir. fine arts for U.S. commn. to Paris Expn. of 1900; chief, Dept. of Art, La. Purchase Expn., 1901-04; received gold medal, St. Louis Expn., in recognition of services; apptd. Officer of Order of Merit by Prince Ferdinand of Bulgaria, 1905. Home: Buffalo, N.Y. Died 1909.

KURTZ, Robert Merrill, editor; b. Dayton, Pa., Feb. 17, 1871; s. Thomas J. and Sue D. (Patterson) K.; B.A., Allegheny Coll., 1893, M.A., 1896; m. Janet Bryce Laughlin, Oct. 10, 1901; 1 dau., Dorothy L. City editor, Conneaut (Ohio) Evening Post, 1894; asst. editor and editor The Methodist Times, Cleveland, 1895-98; editor Union Gospel News, Cleveland, 1898-1906; sec. publ. dept. Internat. Com. Y.M.C.A., New York, 1906-08; editor, publs. of Biblical Sem. in New York, including The Biblical Review, quarterly, 1912-32. Chmn. publ. com., Am. Tract Soc. Methodist. Home: Tenafly, N.J. Died May 31, 1941.

KUTZ, George Fink, rear admiral U.S.N.; b. Wilkes-Barré, Pa., June 14, 1835; s. Jacob and Rosanna (Fitzgerald) K.; ed. Wilkes-Barré Acad. and Wyoming Sem.; m. Mrs. Katherine Makee Bennett, Oct. 1, 1874. Apptd. 3d asst. engr., June 26, 1856; 1st asst. engr., Aug. 2, 1859; chief engr., Nov. 10, 1861. Served in Frigate Niagara, Atlantic cable expdn., 1857-58; Atlanta, on Paraguay expdn., 1858-59; in Saginaw, Asiatic sta., 1859-62; Pawnee, S. Atlantic sta., 1862; Monongahela, West Gulf squadron, 1862-65; participated in battles of Port Hudson, College Point, Donaldsonville and Mobile Bay; in Ticonderoga, European sta., 1865-69; mem. Examining Bd., 1869-72; in Pensacola and Benicia, Pacific sta., 1872-74; fleet engr. Asiatic sta., 1876-77; at Mare Island Navy Yard, Calif., 1878; fleet engr. Pacific sta., 1881-83; chief engr. of yard, Mare Island, 1883-88; insp. machinery Cramp's Ship Yard, 1888-89, Union Iron Works, San Francisco, 1889-93; chief engr. Mare Island, 1893-96; retired after 40 yrs.' service, June 26, 1896; advanced to rank of rear admiral retired, June 29, 1906, for services during Civil War. Insp. torpedo boats building at Portland, Ore., 1908. Home: Oakland, Calif. Died Aug. 9, 1921.

KVALE, O. J., congressman; b. Decorah, Ia., Feb. 6, 1869; s. Juul T. and Gro (Egge) K.; A.B., Luther Coll., Decorah, 1890; C.T., Luther Sem., Minneapolis, 1893; M.A., U. of Chicago, 1914; m. Ida T. Simley, June 19, 1895 (died Sept. 14, 1926); children—Paul John, Ingolf Theodore, Alfred Joseph, Mildred Gertrude, Walter Frederick, Arthur Lorenz, Robert Eugene. Ordained ministry Luth. Ch., 1893; pastor Orfordville, Wis., 1894-1917, Benson, Minn., 1917-23; mem. 68th to 70th Congresses (1923-29), 7th Minn. Dist., defeating A. J. Volstead by 14,000 votes. Mem. Bd. Edn., Norwegian Synod, 1908-17; mem. Bd. Edn. Norwegian Luth. Ch. America, term 1917-28. Home: Benson, Minn. Died Sept. 11, 1929.

KYLE, D. Braden, laryngologist; b. Cadiz, O., Oct. 11, 1863; s. Samuel W. K.; ed. pvt. sch. and Muskingum (Ohio) Coll.; M.D., Jefferson Med. Coll., Phila., 1891; (hon. A.M., Dickinson Coll., 1904); m. Jeanette E., d. Col. Thomas J. Smith, of Phila., Dec. 19, 1900. In practice at Phila., 1891—; asst. demonstrator pathology, 1891-95, lecturer, 1895-96, prof. laryngology, 1896—, Jefferson Med. Coll.; chief laryngologist, rhinologist and otologist, St. Mary's Hosp., 1891-93; St. Agnes' Hosp., 1893—; bacteriologist, Phila. Orthopedic Hosp. Author: Diseases of the Nose and Throat, 5th edit., 1915. Home: Philadelphia. Died Oct. 23, 1916.

KYLE, Hugh Graham, judge; b. Rogersville, Tenn., Dec. 27, 1849; s. Absalom Arthur and Mary (Graham) K.; A.B., Princeton, 1870 (valedictorian); m. Bertha Glen, Nov. 24, 1879; 1 dau., Margaret Glen (Mrs. James Stone Easley). Editor and pub. Weekly Reporter (only newspaper published in Hawkins Co., Tenn.), 1870-72; mayor of Rogersville; elected judge Chancery Ct., 12th Chancery Div., 1894; reëlected judge 2d Chancery Div., 1902, 1910, retired, 1918. Pres. Citizens Bank of Rogersville; v.p. Guests Mountain Coal & Coke Co. Trustee U. of Tenn.; pres. bd. trustees Rogersville Synodical Coll. Republican. Presbyterian. Home: Rogersville, Tenn. Died July 13, 1927.

KYLE, James Henderson, U.S. senator from S. Dak. from 1891, term expiring, 1903; b. nr. Xenia, O., Feb. 24, 1854; took course in engring. at Univ. of Ill., 1871; grad. Oberlin, 1878, prepared for bar, but later entered Western Theol. Sem., graduating, 1882. While taking theological course taught mathematics and engineering. Later educator and Presbyn. minister in Utah and S. Dak.; became financial sec. Yankton Coll. State senator, 1890. Elected as Independent; usually acts with the Republicans. Home: Aberdeen, S. Dak. Died 1901.

KYLE, John Johnson, physician; b. Aurora, Ind., May 27, 1869; s. Thomas M. and Anna (Johnson) K.; M.D., Miami Med. Coll., 1899; unmarried. Began practice at Marion, Ind., 1892; prof. rhinology, laryngology and otology, Ind. University Med. Coll. (Ind. U.), 1900-12; prof. same, Coll. Physicians and Surgeons, U. of Southern Calif., 1913—. Maj. and surgeon 160th Ind. Inf. in Spanish-Am. War; served in Cuba, 1898-99; commd. maj. Med. R.C., 1917; hon. disch., Jan. 1, 1918. Author: Compend of Diseases of the Ear, Nose and Throat, 1903; Manual of Diseases of the Ear, Nose and Throat, 1911. Home: Los Angeles, Calif. Died Aug. 29, 1920.

KYLE, John Merrill, clergyman; b. Cedarville, O., May 19, 1856; s. James and Maria Jane (Tarbox) K.; A.B., U. of Wooster, O., 1877, A.M., 1880 (D.D., 1892); student Princeton Theol. Sem., 1877-78; B.D., Western Theol. Sem., Pittsburgh, 1880; m. Mary C. Beaton, June 19, 1913. Ordained Presbyterian ministry, 1880; pastor Fredericksburg, O., 1880-82; missionary to Brazil, S.A., under Presbyn. Bd. Foreign Missions, 1882-1907; missionary to the Portuguese, Lowell, Mass., under Congl. Home Missionary Soc., 1909—. Home: Lowell, Mass. Died July 1, 1918.

KYLE, Joseph, theologian; b. nr. Cedarville, O., Nov. 20, 1849; s. Joseph and Hadassah (Kennedy) K.; A.B., Monmouth Coll., Ill., 1872, A.M., 1875; grad. Xenia (O.) Theol. Sem., 1876; (D.D., Westminster Coll., Pa., 1892; LL.D., Monmouth, 1906); m. Marion Lincoln Brown, June 7, 1900. Ordained U.P. ministry, 1877; pastor, Springfield, O., 1877-91, Fourth Ch., Allegheny, Pa., 1891-99; prof. systematic theology, 1899—, pres., May 5, 1912—, Xenia Theol. Seminary. Moderator United Presbyn. General Assembly, 1914. Home: St. Louis, Mo. Deceased.

KYLE, Melvin Grove, clergyman, Egyptologist; b. nr. Cadiz, O., May 7, 1858; s. Samuel W. and Sarah Elizabeth (Grove) K.; A.B., Muskingum Coll., 1881, A.M., 1884; grad. Allegheny Theol. Sem., 1885, D.D., 1893, LL.D., 1909. Clergyman United Presbyn. Ch., 1886—. Egyptologist. Lecturer on Biblical archæology, 1908-15, prof. Bibl. theology and archæology, 1915, Xenia Theol. Seminary (now Pittsburgh-Xenia Theol. Sem.), also pres., 1922-30, now research lecturer. Editor Bibliotheca Sacra, 1921; editor archæol. dept. of S.S. Times, 1911—. L. P. Stone lecturer, Princeton Theol. Sem., 1919; lecturer Am. Sch. Oriental Research, Jerusalem, 1921. Moderator U.P. Ch., 1927. Republican. Author: The Deciding Voice of the Monuments in Biblical Criticism; Moses and the Monuments; The Problem of the Pentateuch; Explorations at Sodom. Made explorations at Sodom and Gomorrah, 1924, at Kirjathi Sepher, 1926-28. Home: Pittsburgh, Pa. Died May 25, 1933.

KYLE, William S., mfr.; b. Quebec, Can., July 12, 1851; s. Alexander and Janet (Laing) K.; ed. pub. and pvt. schs.; m. Abby Morton, 1885; children—Morton, Margaret, and 2 dec. Clk. and partner, wholesale drug business, Portland, Me., 20 yrs.; settled in Plymouth, 1890; owner Bradford-Kyle Co., mfrs. insulated elec. wires; v.p. Plymouth & Middleboro R.R. Co.; trustee Plymouth Savings Bank; mem. Mass. Ho. of Rep., 1898-1900, Senate, 1905-06. Chmn. Com. on Plymouth Tercentenary Celebration, 1920-21; pres. Plymouth Pub. Library; chmn. Sch. Com. 6 yrs.; chmn. Rep. Town Com. 10 yrs.; pres. Plymouth and Bay Conf. 10 yrs.; pres. for 5 yrs. Plymouth Commercial Club (now Chamber Commerce); treas. First Parish of the Pilgrims 30 yrs. Mason (K.T.). Home: Plymouth, Mass. Deceased.

KYNETT, Alpha Gilruth, clergyman; b. Davenport, Ia., Aug. 3, 1858; s. Rev. Alpha Jefferson and Althea Pauline (Gilruth) K.; A.B., Wesleyan U., 1878, A.M., 1881; taught in Rugby Acad. and studied law, 1878-82; B.D., Drew Theol. Sem., 1884; A.M., Ohio Wesleyan U., 1893; D.D., Cornell Coll., Ia., 1897; S.T.D., Wesleyan U., 1918; m. Elizabeth H. Hardy, 1884 (dec.); children—Elizabeth Hardy, Alpha Hardy (dec.), Eleanor Gilruth, Dorothy Dale, Alpha Gilruth (dec.), Katharine Hardy (dec.), Gerald Penfield, Olivia Sterner (dec.), Willard Carpenter; m. 2d, Catharine A. Hardy, 1910 (dec.). Ordained Methodist Episcopal ministry, 1886; pastor in Philadelphia Conf. at Darby, 1884-87, Oxford, 1887-89, Pine Grove, 1889-90, Pottstown, 1890-92, St. Stephen's Ch., Phila., 1892-97, Central Ch., Frankford, Phila., 1897-99, Forty-third St. Ch., Phila., 1899-1901; presiding elder, S. Dist. Phila. Annual Conf., 1901-07; recording and field sec., 1907-16, centenary rep. and asst. treas., 1916-19, asst. in church extension, 1919—, Board of Home Missions and Church Extension of M.E. Ch.; retired 1929. Mem. Bd. Ch. Extension M.E. Ch., 1896-1916, Bd. Missions, 1904-12, Nat. Bd. Temperance, Prohibition and Pub. Morals, 1916-24; del. Gen. Conf. M.E. Ch., 1904, reserve del., 1908, 12, del., 1916, 20; del. Ecumenical Conf., 1912; pres. Phila. Conf. Branch of Retired Ministers Nat. Assn. Mason. Home: Philadelphia, Pa. Died Dec. 26, 1939.

KYSER, William D., lawyer; b. Richmond, Ala., July 17, 1882; s. George W. and Sallie (Patton) K.; B.A., U. of Ala., 1903; LL.B., Cumberland U., Lebanon, Tenn., 1906; m. Tempe Darrow Swoope, June 9, 1917; children—William D. (dec.), Tempe S.D. Began practice at Memphis, Tenn., 1906; formerly mem. Kyser & Allen, now Wilson, Kyser, Armstrong & Allen; pres. and gen. counsel Memphis Power & Light Co., Memphis Street Ry. Co. Assistant U.S. atty., Western Dist. of Tenn., 1914-17, U.S. atty., 1917-21. Democrat. Episcopalian. Home: Memphis, Tenn. Died Feb. 1, 1932.

L

LA BACH, James Oscar, chemist; b. Newcastle, Ind. Apr. 22, 1871; s. James Mayer (D.D.) and Cornelia Esther (Ryker) L.; Carleton Coll., 1 yr.; B.S., U. of Tenn., 1895, M.S., 1897; m. Mary Shepherd Parker, Oct. 10, 1917. Asst. chemist, food nutrition work, U. of Tenn., 1895-97; chemist, Procter & Gamble Co., Cincinnati, O., 1897-1901; chief chemist, Ky. Food and Drug Control Labs., at Ky. Agrl. Expt. Sta., U. of Ky., Lexington, 1901—, also head of food and drug control dept., 1916-18; dir. labs., Ky. State Bd. Health, 1918—. Mem. Lexington Bd. of Health, 1917-19; collaborating chemist, U.S. Bur. Chemistry. Democrat. Presbyn. Home: Lexington, Ky. Died Aug. 31, 1922.

LABAREE, Benjamin, missionary; b. at Columbia, Tenn., Mar. 21, 1834; s. Rev. Dr. Benjamin (pres. Middlebury Coll., Vt.) and Eliza P. (Capen) L.; grad. Middlebury Coll., 1854, Andover Theol. Sem., 1859; (D.D., Marietta and Middlebury, 1887); ordained in Congl. ministry, 1860; m. Elizabeth Edwards Woods, June 5, 1860. Missionary A.B.C.F.M. to Persia from 1860. Father of Rev. Benjamin Woods Labaree, who was murdered by Kurds in Persia, Mar. 9, 1904, whose death was the occasion of important diplomatic transactions between U.S. and Persia. Translated the Four Gospels into Azerbaijan Turkish; supt. mission press; editor Rays of Light and other literature (Syriac); revised Old and New Testament in modern Syriac. Died 1906.

LABBE, Antoine G., mfr.; b. Portland, Ore., July 4, 1881; s. Jean and Angeline (Mathiot) L.; A.B., Williams, 1904; B.S. in M.E., Mass. Inst. Tech., 1907; m. Winifred Loomis, Nov. 30, 1910; children—Elizabeth Beaton, Marguerite Louise. In charge distribution system of Portland Gas Co., 1907-08; became connected with Willamette Iron & Steel Co. as order clk., 1908, and was made asst. manager, 1909, treasurer, 1911, v.p., 1914, pres. from 1921 until dissolution. Republican. Presbyn. Home: Portland, Ore. Died Sept. 25, 1936.

LACEY, Edward Samuel, banker; b. Chili, N.Y., Nov. 26, 1835; s. Edward De Witt and Martha Cornelia (Pixley) L.; ed. Olivet (Mich.) Coll.; m. Annette C. Musgrave, Jan. 1, 1861. Banker at Charlotte, Mich., 1862-89; register of deeds, Eaton Co., Mich., 1860-64; trustee State Insane Asylum, 1874-80, del. Rep. Nat. Conv., 1876; chmn. Rep. State Central Com. of Mich., 1882-84; 1st mayor of Charlotte; mem. 47th and 48th Congresses (1881-85), 3d Mich. Dist.; candidate for U.S. senator, 1886; comptroller of the currency, 1889-92; pres. Bankers' Nat. Bank, Chicago, 1892-1909; chmn. bd. dirs. Commercial Nat. Bank (consolidation of Bankers and Commercial Nat. Banks), Sept. 1, 1909-Aug. 1, 1910; chmn. advisory com., 1910-15, mem. exec. com. and dir., Aug. 1, 1915—, Continental & Commercial National Bank. Home: Evanston, Ill. Died Oct. 2, 1916.

LACEY, James D., timberman; b. Wayne Co., Pa., May 25, 1849; s. Aaron B. and Margaret L.; ed. high sch.; m. Mattie E. Windsor, May 21, 1874. Sr. mem. firm James D. Lacey & Co.; pres. James D. Lacey Securities Corp., Tensas Delta Land Co., La.; dir. Interstate Trust & Banking Co. (New Orleans), Mich. Trust Co. (Grand Rapids). Republican. Episcopalian. Mason (K.T.). Home: Chicago, Ill. Died Jan. 24, 1932.

LACEY, John Fletcher, congressman; b. New Martinsville, Va. (now W.Va.), May 30, 1841; s. John M. and Eleanor (Patten) L.; acad. edn. Pvt. to lt. and asst. adj. gen. U.S.V., 1861-65; bvtd. maj. vols., Mar. 26, 1865, "for faithful and meritorious services during campaign against Mobile"; m. Martha J. Newell, Sept. 19, 1865. Admitted to bar, 1865, and since in practice at Oskaloosa, Ia. Mem. Ia. Ho. of Rep., 1870; mem. city council, 1880-81; city solicitor, 1869; temporary chmn. Rep. State Conv., 1898; mem. 51st Congress (1889-91) and 53d to 59th (1893-1907) Congresses, 6th Ia. Dist.; candidate for U.S. senator from Ia. at Rep. primary, 1908. Author: Lacey's Iowa Digest, 1870; Lacey's Railway Digest, 1875-84. Died Sept. 29, 1913.

LACEY, John Wesley, lawyer; b. Randolph Co., Ind., Oct. 13, 1848; s. Rev. Henry J. and Elizabeth (Thompson) L.; A.B., De Pauw U., 1871, A.M., 1874; LL.D., Denver U., 1914; m. Elizabeth Van Devanter, Oct. 10, 1878. Prof. mathematics, Quincy (Ill.) Coll., 1871-72; prin. schs., Owensville, Ind., 1872-73; supt. pub. schs., Noblesville, Ind., 1873-74; prin. high sch., Pekin, Ill., 1874-75; admitted to bar, 1876; practiced at Marion, Ind., 1876-84; chief justice Supreme Ct. of Wyo. Ty., 1884-86. Mason (33°). Home: Cheyenne, Wyo. Died Feb. 11, 1936.

LACHAISE, Gaston, sculptor; b. Paris, France, Mar. 19, 1882; s. Jean and Marie (Barré) L.; art education, L'École Nationale des Beaux Arts, Paris; m. Isabel Nagle, 1916. Came to U.S., 1906, naturalized citizen, 1916. Exhibited at Bourgeois Gallery, N.Y. City, 1918, 20, Intimate Gallery, 1927, Brummer Gallery, 1928; represented in Cleveland Mus. Art; Newark Mus.; Pa. Mus., Phila.; Morgan Memorial Mus., Hartford, Conn.; Phillips Memorial Gallery, Washington, D.C.; Smith Coll. Art. Mus., and in pvt. collections of Adolph Lewisohn, Scofield Thayer, Alfred Stieglitz, A. E. Gallatin, Mrs. J. D. Rockefeller, Jr., etc.; also decorative frieze Am. Telephone and Telegraph Bldg., New York; decorative sculpture, Rockefeller Center, New York, and entrance to Radio Bldg., A Century of Progress Expn., Chicago, 1933; (portraits) Scofield Thayer, E. E. Cummings, Mrs. O'Donnell Iselin, Edward M. M. Warburg, etc. Published Gaston Lachaise sixteen reproductions in colortype with introduction by E. A. Gallatin. Died Oct. 18, 1935.

LACKAYE, Wilton, actor; b. Loudoun Co., Va., Sept. 30, 1862; s. James and Margaret (Bagnam) L.; ed. Georgetown U.; read law 1 yr.; m. Alice Evans, Sept. 25, 1896 (now dec.); 1 son, Wilton; m. 2d, Katherine Alberta Riley, Mar. 23, 1928. Began with Lawrence Barrett, in "Francesca da Rimini," Star Theatre, New York, 1883; his prin. rôles have been Prince Saviani, in "Joselyn"; Don Stephano, in "Featherbrain"; Jefferson Stockton, in "Aristocracy"; Solomon Strong, in "The Idler"; Svengali, in "Trilby"; Reb Shenwel, in "Children of the Ghetto"; Curtis Jadwin in "The Pit"; Jean Valjean, in "The Law and the Man"; and John J. Haggleton, in "The Battle." Died Aug. 21, 1932.

LACOMBE, Emile Henry, judge; b. New York, N.Y., Jan. 29, 1846; s. Emile Henry and Elizabeth Edith (Smith) L.; pvt. 7th Regt. N.G.S.N.Y., 1862-63; A.B., Columbia, with honors, 1863, LL.B., 1865 (LL.D., 1894); m. Elizabeth Edith Tryon, Oct. 14, 1873. Practiced law at New York, 1865-75; in law dept., New York, 1875-84; corp. counsel, 1884-87; U.S. circuit judge, 2d Circuit, June 1887-1916. Home New York, N.Y. Died Nov. 28, 1924.

LACY, Ernest, college prof.; b. Warren, Pa., Sept. 19, 1863; s. Barnet W. and Martha M. (Maclean) L.; ed. Hasting's Acad., Phila., to 1878, and thereafter under pvt. tutors; (Litt.D., conferred by Bd. of Pub. Edn., Phila., 1903); m. Hattie C. Dugan, June 18, 1885. Taught pvt. pupils, revised plays, and did lit. and newspaper work until 1893; instr., 1893-96, asst. prof., 1896-1900, prof. English lang. and lit., 1900-07, head of dept. of English, 1907—, Central High Sch., Phila. Presbyn. Republican. Author (plays): Chatterton (prod. by Julia Marlowe, 1894); Rinaldo (prod. by Joseph Haworth, 1895); The Ragged Earl (prod. by Andrew Mack, 1899); also Plays and Sonnets (book), 1900; The Bard of Mary Redcliffe (book), 1910. Home: Philadelphia, Pa. Died June 17, 1916.

LACY, William Henry, missionary; b. Milwaukee, Wis., Jan. 8, 1858; s. Walter and Eliza (Woodman) L.; A.B., Northwestern U., 1881, A.M., 1884, D.D., 1906; S.T.B., Garrett Bibl. Inst., 1883; m. Emma Nind (Ph.B., Northwestern, 1880), May 24, 1883. Licensed to preach, 1879; ordained deacon, M.E. Ch., 1883; transferred to Foochow Conf. and ordained elder, 1887; prof. Anglo-Chinese Coll., Foochow, 1887-94; supt. Anglo-Chinese Book Concern, Foochow, 1891-1903; sr. mgr., 1902-06, sole mgr., 1907—, Methodist Pub. House in China (Foochow and Shanghai). Dir. Woman's Coll. of S. China; trustee Anglo-Chinese Coll., Foochow. Chmn. Centenary Conf. S.S. Com., 1907—; pres. China S.S. Union; sec. Central Conf. of China; sec. Foochow Conf. many yrs. Reserve del. Foochow Conf. to Gen. Conf., Cleveland, O., 1896, Minneapolis, 1912, Saratoga Springs, N.Y., 1916. Address: Shanghai, China. Died Sept. 3, 1925.

LADD, Anna Coleman (Mrs. Maynard Ladd), sculptor, author; b. Phila., Pa., July 15, 1878; d. John S. and Mary (Peace) Watts; Mme. Yeatmann's Sch., and pvt. teachers, Paris and Rome, under Profs. Ferrari and Gallori; Charles Grafly, in America; hon. A.M., Tufts Coll., Mass., 1923; m. Maynard Ladd (M.D.), June 26, 1905; children—Gabriella May, Vernon Abbott (Mrs. Gregory Vlastos). Exhibited Rome, Paris Salon, National Sculpture Society, National Academy Design, Art Institute Chicago, Art Museum, Boston, etc. First spl. exhibition 40 bronzes, Gorham's, New York, Jan. 1913; 2d, Corcoran, Washington; 3d, Pa. Acad. Fine Arts. Bronzes: Fenway Court and Pub. Garden, Boston; Palazzo Borghese, Rome; Boston Art Mus.; Studebaker Memorial, South Bend, Ind.; Aldrich Memorial, Grand Rapids; Cathedral of St. John the Divine, New York; Russell Memorial, Andover, Mass.; 4 war memorials, Mass.; portraits of Duse, Pavlowa, Ethel Barrymore, Raquel Meller. Hon. mention, Panama P.I. Expn., 1915. Decorated Chevalier Légion d'Honneur, France, 1934; Order of St. Saba, Servia. Author: (novels) Hyeronymus Rides, 1912; The Candid Adventure, 1912. Home: Boston, Mass. Died June 3, 1939.

LADD, Edwin Fremont, senator; b. Starks, Me., Dec. 13, 1859; s. John and Rosilla (Locke) L.; B.S., U. of Me., 1884, LL.D., 1915; m. Rizpah Sprogie, Aug. 16, 1893. Asst. chemist and chief chemist, N.Y. State Expt. Sta., 1884-90; dean Sch. of Chemistry and Pharmacy and prof. chemistry, N.D. Agrl. Coll., and chief chemist, N.D. Agrl. Expt. Sta., 1890-1916, pres., 1916—; also state chemist. Food commr. of N.D., 1902—; editor the N.D. Farmer, 1899—. Mem. U.S. Senate, term 1921-27. Past pres. Assn. State and Nat. Food and Dairy Depts.; mem. Standards Com. on Food Products for the U.S. Author: Manual of Analysis, 1898; Mixed Paints, 1908; also ann. reports and bulls. Address: Fargo, N.D. Died June 22, 1925.

LADD, Eugene F., army officer; b. Thetford, Vt., Sept. 19, 1859; s. George A. and Louise H. L.; grad. U.S. Mil. Acad., 1884; m. Miss Norman, May 30, 1888; 1 dau., Katharine Louise. Commd. 2d lt. 9th Cav., June 24, 1884; promoted through grades to col. adj. gen., Aug. 17, 1914; retired account of disability in line of duty, Oct. 1, 1915; brig. gen. N.A., Oct. 6, 1917. Home: Cohasset, Mass. Died Apr. 23, 1927.

LADD, George Edgar, econ. geologist; b. Haverhill, Mass., July 23, 1864; s. George W. and Eliza A. (Priest) L.; A.B., Harvard, 1887, A.M., 1888, Ph.D., 1894; studied German univs. 2 yrs.; m. Mary O. Hammond, May 24, 1889. Asst., and asst. geologist, U.S., Mo. and Tex. Geol. surveys, 1887-92; asst. in geology, Harvard, 1892-94; asst. geologist and chemist, Ga. Geol. Survey, 1895-96; dir. and prof. geology and mining, Sch. of Mines and Metallurgy, U. of Mo., 1897-1908; pres. Okla. Sch. of Mines and Metallurgy, 1908-13; pres. N.M. Coll. Agr. and Mech. Arts, 1913-17; economic geologist, Bur. of Pub. Roads, U.S. Dept. Agr., Sept. 1, 1917—. Lecturer on engring. geology, U. of Md., 1921. Died Dec. 23, 1940.

LADD, George Trumbull, univ. prof.; b. Painesville, O., Jan. 19, 1842; s. Silas T. and Elizabeth (Williams) L.; (descendant through father's mother from Elder William Brewster and Gov. William Bradford); A.B., Western Reserve U., 1864, A.M., 1867; grad. Andover Theol. Sem., 1869; (D.D., 1879, LL.D., 1895, Western Reserve; A.M., Yale, 1881; LL.D., Princeton, 1896); m. Cornelia A. Tallman, Dec. 8, 1869; m. 2d, Frances Stevens, Dec. 9, 1895. Preached, Edinburg, O., 1869-71; pastor Spring St. Congl. Ch., Milwaukee, Wis., 1871-79; prof. mental and moral philosophy, Bowdoin Coll., 1879-81, Yale, 1881-1905, emeritus prof., 1905. Lecturer Andover Theol. Sem., 1879-81; lectured at Doshisha and in Summer School in Japan, 1892 and 1899, on invitations from Imperial Ednl. Soc. and Imperial U. of Tokyo; several times lecturer, and conducted Grad. Sem. in ethics, Harvard, 1895-96; lecturer U. of Bombay, and at Calcutta, Madras, Benares, India, 1899-1900; del. World's Congress Psychologists, Paris, 1900; lecturer Western Reserve U. and State U. of Ia., 1906; at Imperial univs., colls., and pvt. univs., Japan, 1907; guest and unofficial adviser of Prince Ito, in Korea, 1907; lecturer in Honolulu, 1907, Coll. for Women, Western Reserve, 1908. Decorated Order Rising Sun, 3d class, 1899, 2d class, 1907; gold medal, Imperial Ednl. Soc. of Japan, 1907 (hon. mem.). Author of many vols. on philos., psychol. and religious subjects. Died Aug. 8, 1921.

LADD, Herbert Warren, gov. R.I., 1889-90, 1891-92; b. New Bedford, Mass., Oct. 15, 1843; s. Warren and Lucy L.; grad. New Bedford High School, 1860 (M.A., Brown Univ.). In wholesale dry goods house, 1860-July, 1861; m. Emma Burrows, May 25, 1870 (died 1889). On staff New Bedford Mercury, 1861; went to field of war, 1862, in N.C. In 1864 entered dry goods house of White, Brown & Co., Boston, but 7 yrs. later formed firm of Ladd & Davis (dry goods), Providence, R.I., incorporated, 1887, as The H. W. Ladd Co., its successor, he being pres. Founded Commercial Club; v.p. Providence Bd. of Trade 2 yrs.; pres. R.I. Soc. for Prevention of Cruelty to Children; pres. R.I. School of Design; one of organizers Providence Congl. Club. Presented fully equipped astron. observatory, erected 1891, to Brown Univ. Republican. Address: Providence, R.I. Deceased.

LADD, Horatio Oliver, clergyman; b. Hallowell, Me., Aug. 31, 1839; s. Gen. Samuel G. and Caroline (Vinal) L.; A.B., Bowdoin, 1859, A.M., 1862; Yale Divinity Sch., 1863; S.T.D., Hobart, 1905; m. Harriett Vaughan Abbott, 1863; children—Mrs. Lillie Vaughan Church, Julia E., Harry Abbott, Maynard. Prin Farmington, Me., Acad., 1859-61; prof. rhetoric and oratory, Olivet Coll., 1868-70; prin. N.H. State Normal Sch., 1873-76; founder, and was pres. U. of N.M., 1881-89; founder Ramona and U.S. Indian schs., Santa Fe. Congl. pastor, Olivet and Romeo, Mich., and Hopkinton, Mass.; entered Episcopal ministry; deacon and priest, 1891; rector Trinity Ch., Fishkill, N.Y., 1891-96, Grace Ch., Jamaica, L.I., 1896-1910. Author of various books on hist. and religious subjects. Home: Jamaica, N.Y. Died Feb. 16, 1932.

LADD, Niel Morrow; b. Brooklyn, N.Y., Apr. 17, 1877; s. Nathaniel Greene and Mary Jane (Irwin) L.; ed. high sch.; m. Agnes L. Nutting, June 15, 1910. Pres. Niel Morrow Ladd Book Co. (Inc.), Ladd & Nichols (Inc.), real estate. Pres. Greenwich Bird Protective Soc., Greenwich Boy Scouts; mem. Linnean Soc. (New York). Republican. Baptist. Author: How to Make Friends with Birds, 1916. Lecturer on Bird Life Conservation and Methods of Bird Protection. Home: Greenwich, Conn. Died May 19, 1940.

LADD, Sanford Burritt, lawyer; b. Milford, Mich., Sept. 11, 1844; s. David M. and Martha A. (Hartwell) L.; A.B., U. of Mich., 1865; studied law, Detroit; m. Clara L. Fuller, July 12, 1870. Admitted to bar, 1869, and began practice at Kansas City, Mo. Instr. law of real property, Kansas City (Mo.) School of Law, 1896-1921, pres. 1930-33; served as special counsel for State of Missouri in railway rate litigation in U.S. Circuit and Supreme Courts, 1905-12; counsel for Kansas City Board of Edn., 1880-1922. Rep. candidate for justice Supreme Court of Mo., 1900. Pres. Mo. and Kansas City bar assns. Episcopalian. Home: Kansas City, Mo. Died June 6, 1936.

LADD, Scott M., judge; b. Sharon, Wis., June 22, 1855; s. John and Sarah (Wilmarth) L.; student Beloit (Wis.) Coll., 1875-77; B.S., Carthage (Ill.) Coll., 1879, M.S., 1881, LL.D., 1897; LL.B., State U. of Ia., 1881, LL.D., 1906; m. Emma Cromer, July 26, 1881; children—Loy, Mrs. Litta Valerius, Mrs. Lora Mills, Mrs. Helen Warren, S. Mason. Practiced at Sheldon, Ia., 1881-87; judge Dist. Court, 4th Jud. Dist., 1887-97; judge Supreme Ct. of Ia., 1897-1920 (chief justice). Republican. Home: Des Moines, Ia. Died Apr. 14, 1931.

LADD, William Mead, banker; b. Portland, Ore., Sept. 16, 1855; s. William Sargent and Caroline A. (Elliott) L.; A.B., Amherst, 1878, A.M., 1923; m. Mary Lyman Andrews, Feb. 24, 1885. As a clerk learned the routine of banking with Ladd & Tilton, founded by his father, became partner 1881, and pres. Ladd & Tilton Bank, upon its incorporation, 1908, later chmn. bd., retired 1925. Mem. Ore. legislature, 1890. Home: Portland, Ore. Died Jan. 1, 1931.

LADD, William Palmer, clergyman; b. Lancaster, N.H., May 13, 1870; s. William Spencer and Mira Barnes (Fletcher) L.; A.B., Dartmouth, 1891; studied at Oxford, Paris and Leipzig, 2 yrs.; B.D., Gen. Theol. Sem., 1897; A.M., Harvard, 1903; D.D., Gen. Theol. Sem., Dartmouth, Wesleyan, 1919; m. Ailsie Taylor, of London, Eng., June 1916; children—John, Edward Taylor, Penelope, Persis Joan. Deacon, 1897, priest, 1898, P.E. Ch.; rector St. Barnabas Ch., Berlin, N.H., 1897-1902; prof. ch. history, Berkeley Div. Sch., 1904—, dean, 1918—. Lecturer in ch. history, Hartford Theol. Sem., 1921-25; chmn. State Child Welfare Commn., 1919-21. Pres. Am. Theol. Soc., 1929. Home: New Haven, Conn. Died July 1, 1941.

LADD-FRANKLIN, Christine, scientist; b. Windsor, Conn., Dec. 1, 1847; d. Eliphalet and Augusta (Niles) Ladd; grad. Vassar College, 1869, LL.D., 1887; studied at Johns Hopkins, 1878-82, under Prof. Sylvester and others, also at Göttingen and Berlin; held fellowships, mathematics, at Johns Hopkins, 1879-82; m. Fabian Franklin, Aug. 24, 1882; 1 dau., Margaret. Her theory of color-vision, published 1892, known as the Ladd-Franklin theory; contributed the doctrine of antilogism to logic. One of asso. editors Baldwin's Dictionary of Philosophy and Psychology, 1901-02; lecturer in logic and psychology, Johns Hopkins, 1904-09, Columbia U., 1910—. Author: Colour and Colour Theories (collected papers), 1928. Home: New York, N.Y. Died Mar. 5, 1930.

LADEW, Edward R., tanner; b. New York, Feb. 18, 1855; s. late Harvey Smith L.; ed. Charlier Inst. and Anthon Grammar Sch.; m. Louise B. Wall, Jan. 20, 1886. Became asst. to his father, then partner in J. B. Hoyt & Co., of which he became mem., 1877; firm name changed to Fayerweather & Ladew, 1884; senior partner, 1889—; v.p. The U.S. Leather Co., etc. Died 1905.

LAEMMLE, Carl, moving pictures; b. Laupheim, Germany, Jan. 17, 1867; s. Julius Baruch and Rebekka (Laemmle) L.; ed. pub. schs.; m. Recha Stern, Flieden, Germany, Aug. 28, 1898; children— Rosabelle, Carl. Came to U.S., 1884; clk. various firms, New York and Chicago; mgr. Continental Clothing House, Oshkosh, until 1906; opened moving picture theatre, Chicago, 1906, founded Laemmle Film Service, 1906; pres. Universal Pictures Corp. until 1936. Mem. B'nai B'rith. Mason. Elk. Home: Beverly Hills, Calif. Died Sept. 24, 1939.

LA FARGE, Bancel, artist; s. John and Margaret M. (Perry) L.; m. Mabel Hooper; children—Louis Bancel, Edward Hooper, Henry Adams, Thomas Sergeant. Painter of figures and landscapes, also of mural decorations; designer of stained glass windows and mosaics. Mem. Nat. Inst. Arts and Letters. Works: Wall paintings, Ch. of the Blessed Sacrament, Providence, R.I.; mosaic decoration of Sanctuary, St. Charles College chapel, Catonsville, Md.; altar pieces, Nat. Shrine of the Immaculate Conception, Washington, D.C.; figure windows, St. Paul (Minn.) Cathedral; mosaic decoration, Trinity Coll. Chapel, Washington, D.C.; two lunettes, New Haven Pub. Library, wall over reredos, St. Aedon's Ch., New Haven. Hon. B.F.A., Yale, 1917. Home: Mt. Carmel, Conn. Died Aug. 14, 1938.

LA FARGE, Christopher Grant, architect; b. Newport, R.I., Jan. 5, 1862; s. John and Margaret (Perry) L.; studied Mass. Inst. Tech., 1880-81, and in office H. H. Richardson, 1892; M.F.A., Princeton, 1921; m. Florence Bayard Lockwood, Sept. 5, 1895; children—Margaret Grant (Mrs. W. H. Osborn), Christopher, Oliver, Francis W. Of firm Heins & La Farge, 1886-1910, architects of: Cathedral of St. John the Divine, interior Ch. of St. Paul the Apostle and Ch. of the Incarnation, ch. and parsonage Fourth Presbyn. Ch., New York; St. Matthew's, Washington; Ch. of the Blessed Sacrament, Providence, R.I.; St. Paul (and parish house), Rochester; Houghton Memorial Chapel, Wellesley, Mass.; R.C. Ch. and rectory, Tuxedo, N.Y.; chapel and parish house St. Michael's, Geneseo; R.C. chapel, West Point, N.Y.; Lorillard, Matthiesen and Bliss mausoleums, Woodlawn, New York; Calvin S. Brice Mausoleum, Lima, O.; alterations and extensions Grace Ch., New York, 1901; accessory bldgs., Cathedral St. John the Divine; R.C. Cathedral, Seattle; Packard Memorial Library, Salt Lake City; all stations, New York subway, built under Rapid Transit Commn.; all buildings, New York Zoöl. Park; also Morgan memorial, Hartford; Williams memorial Trinity Coll.; St. Patrick's Ch., Phila.; U.S. Naval Hosp., Brooklyn (war work); N.Y. Yacht Club Station, Chelsea-Moore Apt. House, New York Geneal. Soc. Bldg.; Gymnasium, Woodstock (Conn.) Acad.; mem. firm La Farge & Son, 1931—. Was investigator, later asist. gen. mgr. U.S. Housing Corp., April-Dec. 1918. Mem. firm La Farge & Morris, 1910-15. A.N.A., 1910; fellow and dir. A.I.A. (past 1st v.p.); past pres. Archtl. League New York, and New York Chapter A.I.A. Trustee and sec. Am. Acad. in Rome. Home: Saunderstown, R.I. Died Oct. 11, 1938.

LA FARGE, John, artist; b. New York, Mar. 31, 1835; s. John Frederic and Louisa Birsse de La Farge; studied architectural decoration; then studied painting with Couture, Paris, and William M. Hunt; (hon. M.A., Yale, 1896, LL.D., 1901; LL.D., Princeton, 1904); m. Margaret M. Perry, 1861. Began painting with religious subjects and decorative work; later mural painting, mostly of religious of ecclesiastical character; maker of stained glass windows for which he invented the new methods known in Europe as "American," changing and reforming entire art of the glass-stainer, from the making of the new glass by new methods to the painting of same. Nat. Academician; mem. Am. Acad. Arts and Letters; pres. Soc. Am. Artists, Soc. Mural Painters. Author: Artist's Letters from Japan, 1887. Home: Newport, R.I. Died 1910.

LAFEAN, Daniel Franklin, commr. banking of Pa.; b. York, Pa., Feb. 7, 1861; s. Charles F. and Charlotte (Kottcamp) L.; ed. common schs.; m. Emma B. Krone, Dec. 26, 1882. Pres. York Telephone & Telegraph Co.; York City Land Co.; v.p. Hoover Wagon Co.; treas. York Card & Paper Co., Keystone Color & Mica Co.; dir. York Rys. Co. Mem. York City Council 6 yrs. (pres. common br. 1 term); mem. 58th to 62d Congresses, 1903-13), 20th Pa. Dist., and 64th Congress (1915-17), Pa. at-large; apptd. commr. of banking of Pa., 1917. Republican. Home: York, Pa. Died Apr. 18, 1922.

LAFFAN, William M., editor New York Sun; b. Dublin, Ireland, Jan. 22, 1848; s. late Michael and Sarah Ellen (Fitz Gibbon) L.; ed. in Dublin, Ireland; m. Georgiana Ratcliffe, 1872. Editor and publisher in U.S., 1867—; pres. Sun Printing & Pub. Assn.; v.p. Lanston Monotype Machine Co.; dir. Harper & Bros. Writer upon fine arts, architecture, ceramics, etc. Home: Lawrence, L.I., N.Y. Died 1909.

LAFFERTY, John James, clergyman; editor Richmond Christian Advocate for 30 yrs.; b. on the Roanoke, Va., 1937; A.M., Emory and Henry Coll.; alumnus U. of Va., Litt.D., Washington and Lee U. Served in Civil war as maj. Confederate cav.; was in leading battles but chiefly operated on the upper waters of the Potomac, outside Confederate lines; State curator Va. Med. Coll. 20 yrs.; inventor and mfr. of a process of milling a white whole wheat flour. Home: Richmond, Va. Died 1909.

LAFFERTY, William Thornton, dean; b. Cynthiana, Ky., Mar. 1, 1856; s. John Aker and Francis Elizabeth (Henry) L.; prep. edn. Cynthiana Acad. and Smith Classical Inst., Cynthiana; student Ky. Agrl. and Mech. College (now U. of Ky.), A.B., 1917 (hon. A.M., 1908); m. Maude Ward, Nov. 20, 1889. Admitted to Ky. bar, 1879; co. atty., Harrison Co., Ky., 1882-86; judge Harrison Co., 1886-94; mem. firm Ward & Lafferty, 1894-99, Lafferty & King until 1908. Was mem. Ky. Ho. of Rep.; organized law dept. U. of Ky., 1908, and dean same; comptroller U. of Ky., 1908-15. Trustee Agrl. and Mech. Coll. of Ky. 5 yrs.; trustee Bible Coll. of Transylvania U. 5 yrs. Democrat. Mem. Christian (Disciples) Ch. Mason, K.P. Home: Lexington, Ky. Died Nov. 9, 1922.

LAFFOON, Ruby, gov.; b. Madisonville, Ky., Jan. 15, 1869; s. John Blesdsoe and Martha (Earle) L.; studied Columbia Law Sch., Washington, D.C.; m. Mary Nisbet, Jan. 31, 1894; children—Laura Isabel (Mrs. C. H. Boyd), Martha Lou (Mrs. W. R. Robinson), Lelia Holeman. Began practice of law at Madisonville, 1892; served as county atty. Hopkins Co., Ky.; judge Circuit Court, 4th Jud. Circuit Ky., 1921-31; gov. of Ky., term 1931-35. Mem. Christian (Disciples) Ch. Mason. Home: Madisonville, Ky. Died Mar. 1, 1941.

LA FLESCHE, Francis, ethnologist; b. on Omaha Reservation, Neb., about 1860; s. Joseph La Flesche, former head chief of Omaha tribe; ed. Presbyn. Mission Sch., Omaha Reservation, Neb.; LL.B., Nat. Univ. Law Sch., Washington, 1892, LL.M., 1893. Clk., Bur. of Indian Affairs, 1881-1910; ethnologist, Bur. of Am. Ethnology, 1910—. Author: The Middle Five, 1900. Joint author: The Omaha Tribe, 1907. Engaged in field study of the Osage tribe. Home: Washington, D.C. Died Sept. 5, 1932.

LA FOLLETTE, Belle Case (Mrs. Robert M.); b. Summit, Juneau Co., Wis., Apr. 21, 1859; d. Anson T. and Mary (Nesbitt) Case; A.B., U. of Wis., 1879, LL.B., 1885 (first woman grad. in law but did not practice); m. Robert M. LaFollette, Dec. 31, 1881. Editor home and edn. dept., LaFollette's Magazine, and contbr. to other mags. and newspapers; active worker for equal suffrage. Home: Madison, Wis. Died Aug. 18, 1931.

LA FOLLETTE, Harvey Marion, mining engr.; b. Dane County, Wis., Sept. 8, 1858; s. Harvey Marion and Susan Catharine (Fullenwider) L.; student Wabash Coll., Wooster U., École des Ponts et Chaussées and École des Mines (Paris); U. of Göttingen, holds scholastic degrees of E.M. and Ph.D.; widower. Prin. and supt. schs. in Ind. until 1887; state supt. pub. instrn., Ind., 2 terms, 1887-91; examining and consulting mining engr., N.Y. City, 1891-98; organizer and pres. for 20 yrs., La Follette Coal & Iron Co., with large holdings at La Follette, Campbell Co., Tenn.; now largely retired from attention to detailed operation; owner of extensive mining interests in Pacific Northwest. Del. to Rep. Nat. Conv., 1904. Republican. Mason, K.P. Owner of one of the largest pvt. libraries in the South. Home: La Follette, Tenn. Died Sept. 19, 1929.

LA FOLLETTE, Robert Marion, senator; b. Primrose, Wis., June 14, 1855; s. Josiah and Mary (Furgeson) L.; B.S., U. of Wis., 1879, LL.D., 1901; admitted to bar, 1880; m. Belle Case, Dec. 31, 1881. Dist. atty. Dane County, 1880-84; mem. 49th to 51st Congresses (1885-91), 3d Wis. Dist.; as mem. Ways and Means Com. took prominent part in framing McKinley Bill; del. Rep. Nat. Conv., 1896, del.-at-large, 1904; elected gov. Wis. for terms, 1901-03, 1903-05, 1905-07; elected U.S. senator, Jan. 25, 1905, for term 1905-10 and resigned governorship; reëlected United States senator 3 terms, 1910-29. Led movement to nominate all candidates by direct vote, adopted by state, 1904; also to tax ry. property by same system and at same rate as other taxable property (adopted 1903); also for the control of ry. rates within state by state commn. (legislature of 1905 enacted such a law); received 25 votes for presdl. nomination, Rep. Nat. Conv., Chicago, 1908. Author: Autobiography—A Personal Narrative of Political Experiences, 1913. Home: Madison, Wis. Died June 18, 1925.

LA FOLLETTE, William L., congressman; b. Boone County, Ind., Nov. 30, 1860; s. Harvey M. and Susan C. (Fullenwider) L.; ed. pub. schs., Ind., until 16, and Ind. Central Normal Coll., 1880; m. Mary Tabor, Sept. 14, 1886. Went to Wash. Ty., 1877; farming, stock raising and fruit growing, 1881—. Mem. Wash. Ho. of Rep., 1899-1901; mem. 62d and 63d Congresses (1911-15), 3d Wash. Dist. and 64th and 65th Congresses (1915-19), 4th Dist. Republican. Address: Colfax, Wash. Died Dec. 20, 1934.

LA FONTAINE, Rachel Adelaide, artist, author; b. Zonnemaire, Holland (Island Zerikzee), 1845; d. John and Martine (Pannekoek) L.; ed. Canandaigua, N.Y.; took course at Art Students' League, New York; afterward studied under Charles Melville Dewey, J. H. Beard, Sr., and Harry Chase, New York; unmarried.

Traveled in England, France and Holland, 1878; splty. sundowns and marines; first exhibited Nat. Acad. Design, 1885, has illustrated several de luxe editions. Traveling missionary and parish visitor. Author: Deck the Altar with Blossoms Fair, 1893, 2d edit., 1913; St. Luke, 1893; The Days and Hours of Raphael, 1905. Editor: The Madonna in Art and Verse, 1893, 4th edit., 1907; The Four Evangelists in Classic Art, 1900, 2d edit., 1910. Deceased.

LA GARDE, Louis Anatole, surgeon U.S.A.; b. Thibodaux, La., Apr. 15, 1849; s. Jules Adolph and Aurelia (Daspit) L.; student Louisiana Mil. Acad., 1866-68; M.D., Bellevue Hosp. Med. Coll., 1872; m. Frances Neely, Mar. 4, 1879. Interne Roosevelt Hosp., New York, 1872-74; apptd. actg. asst. surgeon U.S.A., Apr. 1, 1874; asst. surgeon, June 6, 1878; capt. asst. surgeon, June 6, 1883; maj. surgeon, Nov. 13, 1896; lt. col. dep. surgeon gen., and lt. col., Med. Corps, Mar. 17, 1906; col., Jan. 1, 1910; retired Apr. 15, 1913; recalled to active duty and served during World War. Participated in Sioux Indian War, 1876; comd. Divisional Reserve Hosp., 5th Army Corps, Siboney, Cuba, 1898; in charge evacuation of sick and wounded to Northern hosps.; prof. mil. surgery, New York U., 1900—; comdt. U.S. Army Med. Sch., 1910-13; mem. Nat. Bd. Med. Examiners. Mutter lecturer, Coll. Physicians, Phila., 1902. Author: (text book) Gunshot Injuries, 2d edit., 1916. Has carried on extensive research work with septic bullets and septic powders; demonstrated ineffective material not destroyed by firearms. Home: Washington, D.C. Died Mar. 7, 1920.

LAGERGREN, Carl Gustaf, theologian; b. Östersund, Sweden, June 21, 1846; adopted s. G. P. and Maria L.; A.B., Coll. of Östersund, 1869; instr. in Latin, Swedish lang. and lit. and natural science, Acad. of Sundsvall, and prin. Higher Pvt. Sch., Sundsvall, 1870-71; student U. of Upsala, 1871-73; hon. D.B., Bapt. Union Theol. Sem., Chicago, 1890; D.D., Western U. of Pa., 1907; m. Selma Christina Constantia Vesterlund, June 21, 1873. Pastor Upsala, 1871-83, Sundsvall, 1883-89; prof. systematic theology and pastoral duties, and dean in Swedish dept., Bapt. Union Theol. Sem., 1889-92; prof. systematic theology and dean, Swedish Theol. Sem. (U. of Chicago), 1892-1912; pres. Swedish Bapt. Theol. Sem., Morgan Park, Ill., 1912-14; dean Swedish Bapt. Theol. Sem., St. Paul, 1914—. Author (in Swedish): Strödda Tankar, 1872; Om Små Barns dop, 1874; Om försoningen, 1876; Mose och hans skrifter, 1884; Nytt och gammalt, 1894; Den Kristna församlingen, 1908; De yttersta tingen, 1912; Apostlarnas gärningar, 1914; På upp eller nedgående, 1915. Home: St. Paul, Minn. Died Oct. 27, 1941.

LAGUNA, Theodore de Leo de, coll. prof.; b. Oakland, Calif., July 22, 1876; s. Alexander de Leo de and Frederica Henrietta (Bergner) L.; A.B., U. of Calif., 1896, A.M., 1899; Ph.D., Cornell U., 1901; m. Grace Mead Andrus, Sept. 9, 1905; children—Frederica, Wallace. Asst. prof. edn. U. of Mich., 1905-07; prof. philosophy, Bryn Mawr Coll., 1907—. Author: (with wife) Dogmatism and Evolution, 1910; Introduction to Science of Ethics, 1914; Factors of Social Evolution, 1926. Home: Bryn Mawr, Pa. Died Sept. 22, 1930.

LAIDLAW, Alexander Hamilton, physician, author; b. nr. Lanark, Scotland, July 11, 1828; s. Alexander and Margaret (Hamilton) L.; grad. Phila. Central High Sch., 1845; grad. Hahnemann Homœ. Med. Coll., Phila., 1861; also studied under competent professors and in colleges allopathy, hydropathy, electropathy, eclecticism, and hypnotism; m. Anna Turner Sites, Oct. 28, 1865. In practice of medicine, 1856-1905; prin. Mauch Chunk High Sch., 1851-52, Monroe Grammar Sch., Phila., 1853-60; supt. pub. schs., Hudson County, N.J., 1868-69; pres. Hudson County, N.J. Real Estate Assn., 1870-74; prof. anatomy, New York Homœ. Med. Coll., 1868; retired from practice, 1905. Author: American Pronouncing Dictionary of the English Language, 1859; Curability of Consumption, 1861; Soldier Songs and Love Songs, 1898. Address: New York, N.Y. Died 1908.

LAIDLAW, Alexander Hamilton, Jr., author, playwright; b. Jersey City, N.J., July 7, 1869; s. Alexander Hamilton and Anna Turner L.; ed. Jersey City High Sch.; unmarried. Author: Purgatory, a Story, 1891; How She Married Him and Other Stories, 1892; The Charms of Music (a play), 1892. Unpublished plays (with date of first performance): The Darkest Hour, 1893; An Angel's Sin, 1895; Love as a Tonic, 1895; The Going of the White Swan, 1895; The Game of Three, 1896; A Pair of Misfits, 1899; Phyllis (opera), 1900; His Musical Friend, 1907. Address: New York, N.Y. Died 1908.

LAIDLAW, Walter, clergyman; b. Norval, Ont., Can., Mar. 7, 1861; s. Alexander Robertson (M.D.) and Mary Jane (Patton) L.; B.A., U. of Toronto, 1881, M.A., 1886; U. of Berlin, 1885-86; Ph.D., New York U., 1897; m. Mrs. J. Louise (Childs) Potter, June 6, 1899; 1 son, Robert Wordsworth. Ordained Presbyn. ministry, 1886; pastor Jermain Memorial Ch., Watervliet, N.Y., 1886-92; pres. Fairhaven Coll., Wash., 1892-93; asst. Coll. Ref. Dutch Ch., New York, 1893-95; exec. sec. Federation of Chs., New York, 1895-1921, exec. sec., Cities Census Com., Inc., 1921-32. Consulting engr. Interchurch World Movement survey of New York and Neighborhood. Republican. Editor of Federation. Author: Sermonic. Suggestions to Clergy of the Entire Nation (issued by Treasury Dept. for 1st and 2d Liberty loans). Writer and editor Statistical Sources for Demographic Studies of Greater New York City, 1910, 20; supervisor of tabulation of N.Y. State Census, 1925. Home: New York, N.Y. Died May 20, 1936.

LAIRD, Allison White, lumberman; b. Winona, Minn., Dec. 7, 1863; s. John C. and Charlotte (Jarvis) L.; grad. Winona High Sch., 1882; m. Anna Van Blarcom McCutchen, Oct. 7, 1891; children—Elizabeth (Mrs. C. L. Ainsworth), Charlotte (Mrs. A. D. Decker). Began as messenger 2d Nat. Bank, Winona, 1882, and resigned as cashier, 1905; asst. gen. mgr. Potlatch Lumber Co. (branch of "Weyerhaeuser Syndicate"), 1905-13, gen. mgr. and treas., 1905—; gen. mgr., treas. Wash., Ida. & Mont. Ry. Co.; pres. Potlatch State Bank, Elk River State Bank. Chmn. Sch. Bd., Potlatch; pres. Western Forestry and Conservation Assn., N. Ida. Forestry Assn. Republican. Conglist. Mason. Home: Potlatch, Ida. Died Apr. 30, 1931.

LAIRD, Samuel, clergyman; b. New Castle County, Del., Feb. 7, 1835; s. Samuel and Maria (Kunckel) L.; A.B., Central High Sch., Phila., 1852, later A.M.; A.B., U. of Pa., 1855, later A.M.; began study of law but abandoned it for ministry; D.D., Thiel Coll.; m. Mary Andelucia Easton, Apr. 27, 1865. Ordained Evang. Luth. ministry, Oct. 14, 1861; pastor St. Luke's Ch., Phila., 1861-64, Holy Trinity Ch., Lancaster, Pa., 1864-67, First English Luth. Ch., Pittsburgh, 1867-79, St. Mark's Luth. Ch., Phila., 1879—. Sec. Gen. Council Luth. Ch. in N. America, 1870-79; pres. Lutheran Ministerium of Pa., 1898-1901; treasurer Luth. Theol. Sem., Phila., 1895-1909; trustee German Hosp. of Phila., 1893—; trustee of Mary J. Drexel Home and Phila. Motherhouse of Deaconesses. For some time co-editor of The Lutheran, religious weekly. Del. Internat. Lutheran Conf., Lund, Sweden, 1901. Address: Philadelphia, Pa. Died Dec. 17, 1913.

LAIRY, Moses Barnett, judge, lawyer; b. Harrison Twp., Cass County, Ind., Aug. 13, 1859; s. Thomas and Eliza (Barnett) Thornburgh L.; student Northern Ind. Normal Sch., Valparaiso, Ind.; LL.B., U. of Mich., 1889; m. Nina Justice. Began practice at Logansport, Ind., 1889; judge Cass Circuit Court, 1895-97; judge Appellate Court of Ind., 1911-14; asso. justice Supreme Court of Ind., 1915-21; mem. firm Ralston, Gates, Lairy, Van Nuys & Barnard, Indpls. Democrat. Mason, Elk. Home: Indianapolis, Ind. Died Apr. 9, 1927.

LAIST, Theodore Frederick, architect; b. Cincinnati, Sept. 20, 1869; B.S. in architecture, Cornell, 1888; spl. course, Mass. Inst. Tech.; winner Am. Architect traveling scholarship; studied Paris, Munich; m. Frances Conwell Hays, 1902; 1 dau., Elizabeth Ann (Mrs. Harold Oldham). Practiced at San Francisco, 1894-97; supervising architect's office, Treasury Dept., 1897-1902; chief designer, U.S. Govt. buildings, Pan-American Exposition, San Francisco P.O., etc.; supt. publ. buildings, United States Govt., 1899-1902, Federal Bldg., Cleveland, O., etc.; prof. architecture, in charge dept. George Washington U., 1899-1902; in practice at Chicago, 1910—, also, chief architect and structural engr. Central Dist., div. of valuation, Interstate Commerce Commn., Feb. 1914-17 and 1919; consulting architect and Chicago rep. Nat. Lumber Mfrs'. Assn.; dir. of research in lumber, Antioch Coll., Yellow Springs, O.; consulting engr. Northern Hemlock and Hardwood Mfrs.' Assn., Ohio Assn. Lumber Dealers; lecturer at Polytechnische Hochschule, Dresden, Germany, on Technology of Wood Species of the United States and Building Construction Practices in the U.S.; architect Procurement Div., Treasury Dept. in charge post office construction work. Mem. National Committee on Wood Utilization, Dept. of Commerce. Mem. A.I.A. Served in World War as maj. engrs., Dec. 1917-19, later maj. engrs. R.C.U.S.A. Mason. Home: Yellow Springs, O. Deceased.

LAKEY, Alice, pure food specialist; b. in Ohio; d. Charles D. and Ruth F. (Jaques) L.; ed. pvt. tutelage; studied music in Paris, Florence and London, Eng.; trained as professional singer but abandoned concert stage on account of ill health. Began work of pure food bill, 1903; member of pure food com., 1904-06, insurance adviser, 1928-30, General Federation Women's Clubs; chmn. food investigation com. Nat. Consumers' League, 1905-12; apptd. mem. Street and Highway Safety Com. by Sec. of Commerce Hoover, 1924; exec. sec. Am. Pure Food League; mem. exec. com. of The Consumers and Producers Foundation of America. Delivered many addresses in behalf of pure food legislation before state and nat. orgns. Episcopalian. Charter mem. New York Milk Com.; hon. pres. Cranford Village Improvement Assn. Upon father's decease, 1919, became pub. "Insurance" (bi-weekly). Apptd. chmn., 1921, spl. ins. investigation com., dept. of thrift of Gen. Federation Women's Clubs, to prepare report on the question, Is Insurance Essential to Thrift?, also to prepare a leaflet on insuring the college education of children; insurance specialist Gen. Federation Women's Clubs, 1922-25, later chmn. ins. com.; hon. pres. The League of Ins. Women. Writer and speaker on insurance. Home: Cranford, N.J. Died June 18, 1935.

LAKIN, James Sansome; b. Moundsville, W.Va., Mar. 1, 1864; s. Calvin H. and Catherine (Finney) L.; ed. Fairmont (W.Va.) State Normal Sch., and Ohio Wesleyan U., Delaware; m. Lura Olivia Lakin, Nov. 14, 1889; children—James Offutt, Marion Elizabeth (Mrs. John V. Ray), Florence Katherine (Mrs. Thomas A. Deveny, Jr.). Mem. firm Offutt & Lakin, timber, 1889-1909; pres. S.C.&C. R.R., 1900-05; pres. First Nat. Bank, Terra Alta, W.Va. Republican candidate for Congress, 2d Dist., W.Va., 1905; chmn. Rep. State Exec. Com., 1912; pres. State Bd. of Control (38 state instns. and 5 parks) 1909-17, and 1921-33; chmn. Pub. Service Commn., 1913; state chmn. Com. on Proposed Construction, World War; Four Minute Man during the War; mem. W.Va. "Big Four," Rep. Nat. Conv., Chicago, 1920; mem. W.Va. Mental Hygiene Commn.; mem. Appalachian Forest Research Council, State Crippled Children's Council. Served as 1st lt. Co. M, 1st W.Va. Regt., 1899-1908. Methodist. Mason. Home: Charleston, W.Va. Died Mar. 6, 1934.

LA LANNE, Frank Dale, pres. Nat. Board of Trade; b. Phila., 1849; s. Joseph Peyrigné de La Lanne and Emeline (Warrington) L.; grad. Friends' Sch., Phila., Phila. High Sch., and studied in France; m. Anna Sharpe, 1855. Mem. firm of Frank D. La Lanne & Co., mfrs. dress goods, till 1900 (retired); v.p. and treas. Snow, Church Co., Phila.; dir. Bryn Mawr Trust Co., Bryn Mawr Nat. Bank; also part owner and dir. Schuylkill, Bryn Mawr, Purnell Dale, Power Textile, Lakewood, F. C. Rollman & Co., and S. Phila. Woolen Co. mills. Dir., 1900—, pres., 1906—, Nat. Bd. of Trade of U.S.; v.p. Phila. Bd. of Trade; dir. Nat. Rivers and Harbors Congress; Pa. dir. Atlantic Deeper Waterways. Lived 3 yrs. in France, 3 winters in Rome, Italy; U.S. del. Internat. Commercial Congress of the World, Milan, Italy, 1906, Prague, Bohemia, 1908, London, 1910. Home: Philadelphia, Pa. Died Feb. 1, 1913.

LAMADE, Dietrick, publisher; b. Goelshausen, Baden, Germany, Feb. 6, 1859; s. Johannes Dietrick and Carolina (Suepfle) L.; brought to U.S., 1867; ed. pub. schs.; m. Clara Anne Rhen, May 10, 1881 (died 1919); children—David Wilson, Charles Dietrick, Mrs. Elsie Fleming, Howard John, George Robinson, Ralph Max; m. 2d, Lourena Davidson Coryell, Dec. 30, 1922. Learned printer's trade; organized, 1884, Grit Pub. Co., pub. weekly newspaper, of which is pres. and publisher; dir. West Branch Bank & Trust Co.; trustee Savings Instn., Williamsport Community Trust, Williamsport Hosp.; dir. Y.M.C.A. Lutheran. Mason. Home: Williamsport, Pa. Died Oct. 9, 1938.

LAMAR, Andrew Jackson, clergyman; b. Walton County, Ga., May 29, 1847; s. Andrew J. and Mary A. (Jackson) L.; pvt. Longstreet's corps, C.S.A., 1864-65; student U. of Ga., LL.B., 1872; m. Martha Elsworth; m. 2d, Mary V. Urquhart, 1897. Ordained M.E. Ch., S., ministry; became pub. agt. M.E. Ch., S., 1903. Del. Ecumenical Conf., London, 1891; mem. Gen. Conf. M.E. Ch., S., 1890-1930. Home: Nashville, Tenn. Died Mar. 27, 1933.

LAMAR, Joseph Rucker, jurist; b. Ruckersville, Ga., Oct. 14, 1857; s. James S. and Mary (Rucker) L.; matriculated, U. of Ga., grad. Bethany (W.Va.) Coll., 1877; attended law sch. of Washington and Lee U.; LL.D., Yale, 1911; m. Clarinda Huntington Pendleton, 1879. Admitted to bar, 1878, and practiced at Augusta, Ga., 1880-1903. Mem. Ga. Ho. of Rep., 1886-89; commr. to codify the laws of Ga., 1895; apptd. asso. justice Supreme Ct. of Ga., Jan. 1, 1901, for an unexpired term, and elected same, 1903; resigned, 1905; apptd. asso. justice Supreme Ct. of U.S., Dec. 12, 1910, and assumed duties Jan. 3, 1911. Home: Washington, D.C. Died Jan. 1, 1916.

LAMAR, William Harmong, lawyer; b. Auburn, Ala., Dec. 11, 1859; s. William Harmong (M.D.) and Ann M. (Glenn) L.; A.B., Ala. Polytechnic, Auburn, 1881; LL.B., Georgetown U., D.C., 1884, LL.M., 1885; m. Virginia Longstreet, d. Justice L.Q.C. Lamar of the U.S. Supreme Court, June 21, 1887; children—Mrs. Virginia Longstreet Matthews, Mrs. Gussie Glenn Lyttle, Lucius Q. C., William H. Began practice at Washington, D.C., and Rockville, Md., 1885; mem. Md. Ho. of Rep., 1894; asst. atty., Dept. of Justice (U.S.), 1906-13; asst. atty. gen. and solicitor Post Office Dept., 1913-21; in practice of law with his son, Lucius Q. C. Lamar, firm Lamar & Lamar, 1921—. Capt., U.S.V. Signal Corps, Spanish-Am. War, and served in P.R. campaign. Mem. U.S. Wire Control Bd. while telegraph and telephone properties were operated by Govt., 1918-19. Democrat. Methodist. Author of ann. reports of solicitor, 1913, 14, 15, 16, pub. by Post Office Dept. Home: Rockville, Md. Died Feb. 10, 1928.

LAMB, Daniel Smith, M.D.; b. Phila., May 20, 1843; s. Jacob Matlack and Delilah Mick (Rose) L.; A.B., Central High Sch., Phila., 1859, A.M., 1864; M.D., Georgetown U., Washington, 1867; LL.D., Howard U., 1913, D.Sc., 1923; m. Elizabeth Scott, May 20, 1868 (dec.); children—Mrs. Lillie Fraley Carney, Robert Scott; m. 2d, Isabel Haslup, July 3, 1899; children—Ella (dec.), Delilah (dec.).

Pvt. Co. E, 81st Regt. Pa. Vol., 1861; was on duty in mil. hosps., Alexandria, Va., 1862-65; hosp. steward, 1864-68; acting asst. surgeon U.S.A., on duty at Army Med. Museum, 1868-92, pathologist to Army Med. Mus., 1892-1920. Has been prof. materia medica and then anatomy, Howard U., 1873-1923; prof. gen. pathology, U.S. Coll. of Vet. Surgeons, 1894-1900. Conducted post-mortem examinations of Pres. Garfield, Henry Wilson, Senator Brooks, and the assassin, Guiteau. Mem. leading nat. and local med. socs.; v.p. Assn. of Am. Anatomists (sec.); pres. Assn. of Acting Asst. Surgeons U.S.A. many years, Med. Soc. D.C., 1901, Anthrop. Soc. Washington, 1904-05; v.p. Washington Acad. Sciences, 1904-05. Author of History of Medical Department Howard University, Washington, 1900. Editor Washington Medical Annals, and of History Medical Society of D.C. Home: Poplar Hill, Md. Died Apr. 21, 1929.

LAMB, Edwin Travis, railway pres.; b. Richmond, Va., June 29, 1863; s. Junius and Harriet Anne (Edloe) L.; ed. pvt. sch. to 15; m. Lucy Lane, July 26, 1888. Began as receiving clerk, constrn. dept., Chesapeake & Ohio R.R., at Newport News, Va., 1881; transferred to transportation dept. and later promoted to chief clerk same; chief receiving clerk U.S. & Brazil Mail Steamship Co., New York, 6 mos.; returned to Newport News, 1884, as chief clerk export pier Chesapeake & Ohio R.R. and joint representative U.S. & Brazil Mail Steamship Co., the Ducal Line, and Chesapeake & Ohio R.R.; agent Richmond & Danville R.R. Co., Danville, Va., 1888-90; gen. forwarding agent, Richmond & Danville Deepwater Terminal, at West Point, Va., also joint representative Old Dominion Steamship Co., the Merchants' & Miners' Transportation Co., Clyde Steamship Co., York River Line, and Richmond & Danville R.R. Co., 1890-96; gen. agt. Southern Ry., Norfolk, Va., also gen. agt. Chesapeake Steamship Co. and supt. of constrn. Southern Ry.'s new terminal at Norfolk, 1896-1906; supt. same ry. with jurisdiction over Norfolk div., in addition to duties of former position, 1906-09; gen. mgr. for receivers of Norfolk & Southern Ry. Co., 1909-10; pres. and gen. mgr., June 1910-Aug. 1912, Norfolk & Southern R.R.; receiver and gen. mgr. Atlanta, Birmingham & Atlantic R.R., Aug. 1912, later pres. same; dir. Norfolk Nat. Bank, Norfolk Bank for Savings & Trust; dir. Norfolk Fire Ins. Co. Home: Norfolk, Va. Died Nov. 10, 1919.

LAMB, Frederick Stymetz, artist; b. New York, N.Y., June 24, 1863; s. Joseph and Eliza (Rollinson) L.; student Art Students' League, New York; pupil of Lefebvre, Boulanger and M. Millet, Paris; m. Nellie Albert; children—Harold Albert, Adrian Stymetz. Hon. mention, Chicago Expn., 1893; gold medal, Atlanta Expn., 1895; one of the four glass workers representing U.S. at Paris Expn., 1900, and received gold medal from French Govt. Lecturer and writer on civic art and municipal æsthetics. Pres. Architectural League America; v.p. Architectural League New York; v.p. Met. Parks Assn.; trustee Am. Scenic and Historic Preservation Soc.; sec. Municipal Art Soc., Nat. Soc. Craftsmen. Home: New York, N.Y. Died July 8, 1928.

LAMB, Henry Whitney, mfr.; b. Boston, Mass., Oct. 13, 1853; s. Salem Towne and Elisabeth (Whitney) L.; prepared for Harvard, but did not matriculate; spent 1 term at Mass. Inst. Tech.; unmarried. Clk. in dry goods commn. house, Boston, 1871-80; sr. mem. Lamb & Ritchie Co., mfrs. sheet metal pipe, 1881-1908 (retired); pres. Lamb & Nash Co.; trustee Brookline (Mass.) Savings Bank. Pres. Am. Free Trade League, 1894-1904, Mass. Reform Club, 1912, Young Men's Democratic Club, 1897; dir. Brookline Friendly Soc., Brookline Br. Am. Red Cross; trustee Pub. Library, Brookline. Unitarian. Home: Brookline, Mass. Died Dec. 16, 1926.

LAMB, Isaac Wixom, inventor, clergyman; b. Hartland, Mich., Jan. 8, 1840; s. Rev. Aroswell and Phebe (Wixom) L.; m. 2d, Mrs. Elizabeth Phelps. Invented a machine for braiding whiplashes and patented it in 1859; invented and patented, 1863-65, the Lamb Knitting Machine, which was also patented and introduced into many foreign countries; has since patented many improvements. Was ordained to Bapt. ministry, 1869; in active pastorate up to May 1899. Now pres. and supt. Perry Glove and Mitten Co. Address: Perry, Mich. Died 1906.

LAMB, John Edward, lawyer; b. Terre Haute, Ind., Dec. 26, 1852; s. Michael and Catharine (McGovern) L.; grad. Terre Haute High Sch., 1869; m. Esther Kent, July 2, 1890. Practiced, Terre Haute, 1873—; mem. firm of Lamb, Beasley, Douthitt & Crawford; dir. McKeen Nat. Bank, U.S. Trust Co. Pros. atty., Vigo County, Ind., 1875-79; mem. Congress, 1883-85; U.S. dist. atty., 1886; del. Dem. Nat. Conv., 1892, 96, 1904, 08, 12. Catholic. Address: Terre Haute, Ind. Died Aug. 1914.

LAMB, Peter Oswald, author; b. Kandy, Ceylon, Jan. 20, 1890; s. Peter J. and Lucy (de Soyza) L.; prep. edn., Kingswood Coll., Kandy; student Sch. of Journalism, New York U., 1925; m. Elvira Green Whaley, Oct. 16, 1925; 1 son, Peter Whaley. Came to U.S., 1918, naturalized citizen, 1929. Y.M.C.A. sec., Ceylon and India, 1909-13; reporter Bombay (India) Chronicle, 1913-14; served with Rifle Brig., Brit. Army (Kitchener's First Hundred Thousand), 1914-17; severely wounded in liquid fire attack, and invalided out of service; with War Prisoners' Aid, Switzerland, 1918; editorial asst. to chief scout exec., Boy Scouts America, and asso. editor Boys' Life, 1922-29. Awarded Mons medal, 2 gen. service medals (Eng.). Ind. Democrat. Episcopalian. Author: The Lone Scout of the Sky (with James E. West), 1927; The Boys' Book of Honor, 1931; The Sign of the Buffalo Skull, 1932; He Who Sees in the Dark (with James E. West), 1932. Collaborator with Dan Beard in "Boy Heroes of Today." Home: Bedminster, N.J. Died Nov. 29, 1935.

LAMB, Roland O., life ins.; b. Beverly, Mass., Dec. 20, 1850; s. Samuel T. and Sarah P. (Flagg) L.; ed. pub. schs.; m. Miss James, Dec. 16, 1874. Bookkeeper in mfg. house 5 yrs.; successively bookkeeper, chief clk., sec., John Hancock Life Ins. Co., 1872-1903; dir. and 2d v.p., same, 1895-99; v.p., 1899-1909, pres., 1909—, John Hancock Mut. Life Ins. Co.; dir. Mass. Fire & Marine Ins. Co., N.E. Power Co., Internat. Trust Co. Mason (Past Comdr. De Molay Commandery). Home: Boston, Mass. Died Nov. 14, 1921.

LAMB, William, mcht., soldier; b. Norfolk, Va., Sept. 7, 1835; s. William Wilson Lamb and Margaret Kerr (Wilson) L.; grad. William and Mary Coll., B.P., LL.B., 1855; LL.D., St. Lawrence U., 1899; m. Sarah Chaffee, 1857. Editor Daily Southern Argus, 1856-61; mem. Nat. Dem. Conv., 1856; presidential elector, 1860 on Breckenridge ticket; capt. Woodis Rifles, mil. co. of Norfolk, Va., for several yrs. before war; with his co. joined Va. troops Apr. 1861; served in Confederate army, capt. to col.; had charge defenses at New Inlet on Cape Fear; built and had command Fort Fisher until its fall, Jan. 15, 1865; was wounded and walked on crutches seven yrs. After war in shipping business in Norfolk, leader in building up foreign trade of city; mem. Nat. Dem. Conv., 1876; joined readjusters, 1879; Hancock elector, 1880; headed Harrison and Morton electoral ticket, 1888; chmn. Rep. State Com., 1895-97; del. Rep. Nat. Conv., 1896. Consul for Germany, v.-consul for Sweden at Norfolk. Mayor Norfolk, Va., 1880-86. Pres. Lower Norfolk Coke & Gas Corp. Address: Norfolk, Va. Died 1909.

LAMBDIN, Alfred Cochran, editor; b. Phila., Pa., Jan. 29, 1846; s. James Reid and Mary (Cochran) L.; ed. pvt. schs.; M.D., U. of Pa., 1866; m. Katherine L. McIlwaine, June 11, 1872. Practiced medicine, Germantown, Pa., 1867-75; editor Germantown Chronicle, 1870-75; mng. editor, 1875-96, editor, 1896-1902, Philadelphia Times, which was merged with the Philadelphia Public Ledger, 1902, editor, 1905—. Home: Philadelphia, Pa. Died 1911.

LAMBDIN, Milton Bennett, clergyman, lecturer; b. Baltimore, Md., Feb. 27, 1850; s. John Robert and Elizabeth Hines (Bennett) L.; student Hampden-Sydney Coll., 1882; grad. Union Theol. Sem., 1885; m. Blanche Allen, d. Prof. John M. Dieffenderfer, 1888; children—Allen Bennett, Marjorie (Mrs. Chas. W. Alexander), Raleigh Edwin (dec.), Janet (Mrs. F. H. Sattes), Vera (Mrs. Harry E. Whaley). Ordained to ministry of Presbyterian Church in U.S., 1885; has been pastor successively New Canton, Va., Hancock, Md., Goshen, Va., St. Albans, W.Va., Ft. Worth, Tex., Keyser, W.Va., until 1912, Montgomery, W.Va., 1912-23. Traveled in Syria, Palestine, Egypt and Europe; lecturer on Bibl. archæology and Egyptology, for chautauquas, colleges, chs., etc. Commr. Gen. Assembly Presbyn. Ch. in U.S. 4 times to 1918. Mason. Lecturer: Nineveh, the Magnificent; Babylon, the Golden; Palestine, Gateway to Three Continents; Prehistoric Palestine; Tyre, The Queen of the Seas; Egypt, the Imperial; Triumphs and Trophies of Pick and Spade in Bible Lands; Higher Criticism; A Boy of the Old Dominion; During the Civil War, etc. Home: Victoria, Va. Died May 9, 1940.

LAMBDIN, William Wallace, lawyer; b. Upson County, Ga., Oct. 25, 1861; s. Charles Edwin and Martha (Middlebooks) L.; prep. edn. Gordon Inst. (of which father was founder and pres.), Barnesville; A.B., U. of Ga., 1879 (1st honor); m. Annie M. Smith, Dec. 24, 1883. Teacher pub. schs., later prin. West End Acad., Atlanta, Ga.; began practice of law in Atlanta, 1889; removed to Barnesville, 1899, to Waycross, 1906; U.S. dist. judge, Southern Dist. of Ga., 1915—. Democrat. Methodist. Home: Savannah, Ga. Deceased.

LAMBERT, Alexander, M.D.; b. New York, N.Y., Dec. 15, 1861; s. Edward Wilberforce and Martha M. (Waldron) L.; A.B., Yale, 1884, Ph.B., 1885; M.D., Coll. Phys. and Surg. (Columbia), 1888; m. Ellen W. Cheney, Apr. 23, 1895. Prof. clin. medicine, Cornell U. Med. Coll., 1898-1931; attending physician Bellevue Hosp., 1894-1933; asst. bacteriologist, New York Health Dept., 1894-1901. Col. Med. Auxiliary, U.S.A., and med. head of Am. Red Cross in France, 1917. Mem. A.M.A. (pres. 1919). Address: New York, N.Y. Died May 9, 1939.

LAMBERT, Fred Dayton, botanist; b. Muscatine, Ia., Oct. 28, 1871; s. Daniel Meader and Ellen (Scudder) L.; Ph.B., Tufts Coll., 1894, A.M., Ph.D., 1897; student U. of Freiburg, Germany, winter 1910-11; student Naples Zoöl. Sta., 1911; m. Mary Anna Ingalls, June 6, 1903; 1 dau., Elizabeth Allen. Asst. in biology, 1896-97, instr., 1897-98, Tufts Coll.; submaster Edward Little High Sch., Auburn, Me., 1898-99; instr. natural history, 1899, asst. prof. biology, 1904, prof. botany, 1913—, Tufts Coll. Home: Tufts College, Mass. Died Feb. 21, 1931.

LAMBERT, John, capitalist; b. Hunterdon County, N.J., Jan. 12, 1847; common sch. edn. Removed to Joliet, Ill., 1874; began wire mfg., 1879, as mem. Lambert and Bishop Wire Fence Co.; v.p. and gen. mgr. Consolidated Steel & Wire Co., 1892-99; pres. Am. Steel & Wire Co., 1899-1901, now part of U.S. Steel Corp.; pres. Mines Co. of America, Dolores Mines Co., etc. Apptd. a.d.c. with rank of col. on staff of Gov. Tanner, 1897. Died Mar. 6, 1922.

LAMBERT, Louis A., editor; b. Charleroi, Pa. Apr. 13, 1835; s. William and Lydia (Jones) L.; ed St. Vincent's Coll., Pa., and Archdiocesan Sem., St Louis, Mo.; (LL.D.); ordained R.C. priest, 1859. Asst. pastor Cairo, Ill., and missionary Shawneetown, Ill., 1859-61; chaplain 18th Ill. Inf., 1861-63; pastor Cairo, Ill., 1863-68; taught moral theology and philosophy, Paulist Novitiate, New York; pastor Seneca Falls and Waterloo, N.Y.; founded, 1874, editor, 1874-80, the Catholic Times; editor Philadelphia Catholic Times, 2 yrs.; editor-in-chief New York Freeman's Journal, 1894—. Author: Thesaurus Biblicus, or Hand-Book of Scripture Reference; Notes on Ingersoll; Tactics of Infidels; Reply to Ingersoll's Christmas Sermon Translated; The Christian Father; Instructions on Gospels of the Sundays of the Year. Edited Catholic Belief. Address: Scottsville, N.Y. Died 1910.

LAMBERT, William Harrison; b. Reading, Pa., May 9, 1842; s. James V. and Susanna (Keen) L.; grad. Central High Sch., Phila., 1859; m. Herminia Van Haagen, Oct. 15, 1874. Pvt. 15th Pa. Cav., Aug 22, 1862; 1st lt. and adj. 27th N.J. Vols., Nov. 27, 1862; 1st lt. and adj. 33d N.J. Vols., July 25, 1863; capt., Jan. 16, 1864; bvtd. maj., Mar. 13, 1865; mustered out July 17, 1865; awarded medal of honor. Entered gen. agency Mutual Life Ins. Co. of N.Y. at Phila., 1866; became partner in management, 1872, gen. agt., 1887, mgr., 1901-04, trustee, 1907. Pres. dept. charities and correction, Phila., 1892-99; mem. bd. dirs., city trusts, June 1899 (v.p. 1910—). Author of Lincoln Literature, The Faith of Abraham Lincoln, and other published addresses. Made notable collection of Lincoln and Thackeray literature and manuscripts. Home: Germantown, Pa. Died June 1, 1912.

LAMBERT, Wilton John, lawyer; b. D.C., June 27, 1871; s. Tallmadge A. and Avarilla (Van Riswick) L.; student Princeton, 1892; LL.B., Georgetown U., 1893, LL.M., 1894; m. Elizabeth Gorman, June 24, 1896. Practiced at Washington, D.C.; gen. counsel Munsey Trust Co., Washington Times, Washington & Old Dominion Ry., Washington Herald, Georgetown Gas Light Co., Alexandria & Rosslyn Gas Light Co., Elkins Estate, etc.; of counsel for McLean Estate, Washington Gas Light Co., etc. Home: Washington, D.C. Died July 21, 1935.

LAMBERTON, Benjamin Peffer, rear adm.; b. Cumberland County, Pa., Feb. 25, 1844; s. James Finlay and Elizabeth (Peffer) L.; apptd. from Pa., and grad. U.S. Naval Acad., 1864; m. Lilla Stedman, Feb. 25, 1873. Promoted ensign, Nov. 1, 1866; master, Dec. 1, 1866; lt., Mar. 12, 1868; lt. comdr., Apr. 27, 1869; comdr., June 2, 1885; capt., May 11, 1898; rear adm., Oct. 11, 1903. Summer of 1864 was attached to the America, in pursuit of the Confederate steamers Florida and Tallahassee; comd. Jamestown, 1889-91; at Bur. of Yards and Docks, 1891-94; light house insp. 5th dist., 1894-98; chief of staff of admiral Dewey at battle of Manila Bay, May 1, 1898, and was advanced 7 numbers in rank "for eminent and conspicuous conduct" in this battle; comd. Olympia, Admiral Dewey's flag-ship, 1898-99; mem. Naval Examining and Retiring Bds., 1900; Lighthouse Bd., 1900-03; comdr.-in-chief S. Atlantic Squadron, 1903-04; Naval War Coll., 1904; chmn. Lighthouse Bd., 1905-06; retired, Feb. 25, 1906. Home: Washington, D.C. Died June 9, 1912.

LAMBERTON, James McCormick, lawyer; b. Harrisburg, Pa., May 21, 1856; s. Hon. Robert Alexander (LL.D.) and Annie (Buehler) L.; St. Paul's Sch., Concord, N.H.; A.B. (with honors), Yale, 1878; unmarried. Master, St. Paul's Sch., 1878-81; admitted to Pa. bar, 1880; practiced at Harrisburg, Pa., 1881-87 and 1899—; master St. Paul's Sch., teaching history chiefly, 1887-99. Dir. Harrisburg Bridge Co. Dem. candidate for N.H. Ho. of Rep., 1892; del. Nat. Conf. on Immigration, New York, 1905. Dir. Harrisburg Benevolent Assn.; sec. bd. mgrs. Harrisburg Hosp., Harrisburg Hosp. Training Sch. for Nurses. Class sec. Class of 1878, Yale, 1898—; 1st pres. Ch. Club Diocese of Central Pa. (now Bethlehem); pres. Nat. Conf. Ch. Clubs of U.S., 1909-10. Mason. Episcopalian; deputy Gen. Convs., 1904, 10, 13. Author and editor of legal and Masonic publs., Records of Class of 1878, etc. Home: Harrisburg, Pa. Died 1915.

LAMBERTON, John Porter, librarian; b. Phila., Oct. 22, 1839; s. Robert and Jane (Porter) L.;

A.B., U. of Pa., 1858, A.M., 1861; m. Melvina Vandyke, 1874 (died 1898). Taught in acads., 1859-80; asso. editor American Supplement Encyclopædia Britannica, 1881-90; reviser to Worcester's Dictionary, 1891-95; contributed to Chambers' Cyclopædia, 1893; asst. in library, U. of Pa., 1902—. Editor: (and principal writer) Historic Characters and Famous Events (12 vols.), 1894-96; Literature of All Ages (10 vols.), 1897-99; Literature of the Nineteenth Century, 1900. Asso. editor The Drama (10 vols.), 1904. Author: English Literature, 1905. Compiled the Union List of periodicals in the principal libraries of Phila., 1908, and Supplement to same, 1910. Address: Philadelphia, Pa. Died July 26, 1917.

LAMBERTON, Robert Eneas, mayor; b. South Bethlehem, Pa., Sept. 14, 1886; s. William Alexander and Mary (McCurdy) L.; A.B., U. of Pa., 1906, LL.B., 1910; m. Helen Wight Henderson, Sept. 14, 1911; children—Robert Eneas, William, Laura May, John Porter, Hugh Stirling. Admitted to Pa. bar, 1910, and began practice in Phila.; mem. Common Council of Phila., 1916-20; sheriff of Phila. County, 1920-24; judge Court of Common Pleas of Phila. County, 1931-39; mayor of Phila., 1940—. Trustee Gen. Assembly of Presbyn. Ch. Republican. Presbyterian. Home: Philadelphia, Pa. Died Aug. 22, 1941.

LAMBERTON, William Alexander, univ. prof.; b. Phila., Nov. 26, 1848; s. Robert and Jane (Porter) L.; A.B., U. of Pa., 1866, A.M., 1869 (Litt.D.); m. Mary, d. Daniel McCurdy. Instr. mathematics U. of Pa., 1867-68, Latin and Greek, Lehigh U., 1869-73; instr. mathematics, 1873-78, prof. Greek and Latin langs., 1878-80, Greek, 1880-88, Greek lang. and lit., 1888—, U. of Pa. Edited 6th and 7th books of Thucydides, Harper's Classical Series. Home: Philadelphia, Pa. Died 1910.

LAMBERTSON, Genio Madison, lawyer; b. Franklin, Ind., May 19, 1850; grad. U. of Chicago, 1872; m. Jane Gundry, June 10, 1880; m. 2d, Mary S. Sherwood, Feb. 28, 1895. Practiced law, Lincoln, Neb.; U.S. atty. for dist. Neb., 1878-86; Asst. Sec. Treasury under Pres. Harrison; atty. Interstate Commerce Commn.; argued Counselman case before Supreme Court; atty. receivers U.P. Ry. Co.; candidate for U.S. Senate, 1899. Republican. Address: Lincoln, Neb. Died 1902.

LAMBUTH, Walter Russell, bishop; b. Shanghai, China, Nov. 10, 1854; s. James William and Mary Isabella (McClellan) L. (both Am. missionaries); M.A., Emory and Henry Coll., Va., 1875; M.D., Vanderbilt U., 1877; M.D., Bellevue Hosp. Med. Coll. (New York U.), 1881; post-grad. study Edinburgh and London, 1882; D.D., Emory Coll., Ga., 1892, Randolph-Macon Coll., 1892; m. Daisy Kelley, Aug. 2, 1877. Med. missionary at Shanghai, Soochow and Peking, China, 1877-86; supt. Japan Mission, 1886-91; field sec., 1892-94, gen. missionary sec., 1894-1910, Board of Missions of M.E. Church, South; elected bishop, May 17, 1910. Founded, and in charge Soochow Hosp., 1882-85, M.E. Hosp. Peking, 1885-86; founded Kwansei Gakuin Coll., Japan; one of 6 commrs. who united the leading Meth. bodies of the Empire into the Japan Meth. Ch.; editor Review of Missions, 10 yrs. Del. Ecumenical Conf., Washington, 1892, London, 1902; mem. business com. Ecumenical Missionary Conf., New York, 1900; vice chmn. commn. 11, World Missionary Conf., Edinburgh, 1910. Author: Side Lights on the Orient; Winning the World for Christ, 1915; Medical Missions, 1919. Edited English edit., Discipline of the Japan Methodist Church. Home: Oakdale, Calif. Died Sept. 26, 1921.

LAMME, Benjamin G., elec. engr.; b. Clarke County, O., Jan. 12, 1864; M.E., Ohio State U., 1888; s. James G. and Sarah A. L.; unmarried. With Westinghouse Elec. & Mfg. Co., 1889—, chief engr., 1903—. Pioneer in development of direct current apparatus for ry. lighting and power; widely known for part in development of alternating current apparatus; has taken out many elec. patents. Mem. Naval Consulting Bd., 1915—. Edison medal, 1919. Author: Electrical Engineering Papers, 1919. Awarded Jos. Sullivant medal, Ohio State U., 1923 (first recipient), for engring. work. Home: Pittsburgh, Pa. Died July 8, 1924.

LAMONT, Daniel Scott, Sec. of War of U.S.; b. Cortlandville, N.Y., Feb. 9, 1851; s. John B. and Elizabeth (Scott) L.; ed. McGrawville Union School and Union Coll. (hon. A.M.); m. Juliet Kinney. Engaged in journalism and was, 1885-89, private sec. to President Cleveland. Became prominent in st. ry. interests in New York. Sec. of War U.S., 1893-97. V.p. Northern Pacific Ry. Co. Home: New York, N.Y. Died 1905.

LAMONT, Forrest, operatic tenor; b. Athleston, Can., Jan. 26, 1885; s. Robert and Elizabeth (Outterson) L.; ed. pub. schs., Chicopee, Mass., and business coll.; m. Stella Norelli Nathan, July 10, 1918; m. 2d, Eunice Steen, Apr. 7, 1935. Studied in Italy 3 yrs. and made professional début, in Adriano Theatre, Rome, May 18, 1914, and later sang in principal cities of Italy; joined Chicago Opera Co.; rôles: Aida, Trovatore, Pagliacci, etc. Died Dec. 17, 1937.

LAMONT, Hammond, editor; b. Monticello, N.Y., Jan. 19, 1864; s. Rev. Thomas and Caroline Deuel (Jayne) L.; grad. Harvard, 1886; m. Lillian Mann, May 14, 1891. In journalism in Albany, N.Y., 1887-90; in Seattle, Wash., 1890-92; instr. English, Harvard, 1892-95; asso. prof. rhetoric, Brown, 1895-98; prof. rhetoric, Brown, 1898-1900; mng. editor New York Evening Post, 1900-06; editor The Nation, 1906—. Editor: Specimens of Exposition; Burke's Speech on Conciliation with America. Author: English Composition, 1906. Died 1909.

LA MOTHE, John Dominique, bishop; b. Ramsey, Isle of Man, June 8, 1868; s. John Corlet and Sarah (Banks) L. M.; student King William's Coll., Isle of Man, 1884-85; grad. Theol. Sem. in Va., 1894; D.D., St. John's Coll., Annapolis, Md., 1921, also Theol. Sem. in Va., same yr.; m. Margaret Meade Walker, Aug. 30, 1894; children—John Walker (dec.), Mrs. Margaret Corlet Aaron, Jean M. (dec.), John D. Deacon, 1894, priest, 1895, P.E. Ch.; rector St. Paul's Ch., Hamilton, Va., 1894-1901; asst. Epiphany Ch., Washington, D.C., 1901-02; rector Christ Ch., St. Joseph, Mo., 1903-04; asso. rector Epiphany Ch., Washington, D.C., 1905-07; rector St. Paul's Ch., New Orleans, La., 1907-16, Ascension Ch., Baltimore, Md., 1916-21; consecrated bishop missionary jurisdiction of Honolulu, June 29, 1921. Dep. to Gen. Conv. P.E. Ch., 1910. Mason. Home: Honolulu, T.H. Died Oct. 25, 1928.

LAMOUREUX, Silas Wright, Commr. Gen. Land Office; b. Madison County, N.Y., Mar. 8, 1843; ed. there; went to Wis., 1852; served as capt. in Wis. vols., Civil war; served as State senator one term; county judge, 1879-93; Commr. Gen. Land Office, U.S., 1893-97; pres. Mayville (Wis.) Exchange Bank, 4 yrs. In law practice and mfg. of malleable iron. Address: Beaver Dam, Wis. Died 1909.

LAMPE, Joseph Joachim, clergyman; b. Ratjendorf, Holstein, Germany, May 19, 1837; s. Henry and Cicelia (Wiese) L.; came to America, 1853; A.B., Knox Coll., Ill., 1864, A.M., 1867; Union Theol. Sem., New York, 1864-67; Ph.D., New York U., 1890; D.D., Knox, 1889; m. Emma A. Willard, Sept. 20, 1877 (died 1906); m. 2d, Ideletta (Henry) Willard, July 31, 1907. Ordained Presbyn. ministry, 1867; pastor Brick Ch. Chapel, N.Y. City, 1867-87, Christ Ch., N.Y. City, 1888-95; prof. Hebrew and O.T. lit., 1896-1917, prof. emeritus, 1917—, Presbyterian Theol. Sem., Omaha, Neb. Republican. Home: Omaha, Neb. Died Apr. 21, 1920.

LAMPERT, Floran, congressman. Mercantile business; elected to fill unexpired term of James H. Davidson in 65th Congress, and reëlected 66th to 71st Congresses (1919-31), 6th Wis. Dist. Republican. Home: Oshkosh, Wis. Died July 18, 1930.

LAMPTON, Thaddeus Booth, banker, mcht.; b. Tylertown, Miss., Oct. 23, 1867; s. Benjamin and Mary Jane (Conerly) L.; A.B., U. of Miss., 1889; grad. Eastman's Business Coll., Poughkeepsie, N.Y., and Am. Inst. Banking; m. Mamie D. Terrell, June 10, 1897; children—Adine Terrell (Mrs. George C. Wallace), Lala Helen (Mrs. J. Blake Lowe), Thaddeus B. Pres. Lampton Bros. Co., Tylertown, 1890—; pres. Capital Nat. Bank, Jackson, 1922—; pres. Bank of Wesson, Southern Building and Loan Assn., Masonic Temple Assn.; sec. and treas. Jackson Fertilizer Co. Conducted Mil. Training Camp, Miss., as civilian aide to adj. gen. of U.S., World War. State treas., Miss., 1903-04; federal receiver Miss. Mills, 1906. Trustee Whitworth Coll. (pres. bd.), Millsaps Coll. Mem. Am. Bankers Assn. (exec. council), Miss. Bankers Assn. (pres. 1919-20). Democrat. Methodist. Mason. Home: Jackson, Miss. Died Feb. 8, 1933.

LAMPTON, William James, newspaperman; b. Lawrence County, O.; s. William H. Lampton; ed. Ohio Wesleyan U. and Marietta (O.) Coll.; hon. A.M., Marietta Coll., 1891; unmarried. Began newspaper work as editor of a Republican paper in Ky., 1877-78; consecutively reporter Cincinnati Times, paragrapher Steubenville Herald, on staff Louisville Courier-Journal, editor Merchant Traveler, Cincinnati; staff of Critic and Evening Star, Washington (originated "Shooting Stars" dept., latter), and Detroit Free Press; spl. contbr. of current verse to New York newspapers; mag. writer, prose and verse. Apptd. col. and a.-d.-c. on staff Gov. Willson, of Ky., Mar. 1910. Author: Yawps and Other Things; Confessions of a Husband; The Trolley Car and the Lady, 1908; Mrs. Brown's Opinions, 1886; Jedge Waxem's Pocket Book of Politics, 1908; Tame Animals I Have Known, 1912. Home: New York, N.Y. Died May 30, 1917.

LAMSON, Charles Henry, inventor; b. Augusta, Me., Sept. 17, 1847; s. Joseph S. and Eunice E. (Winslow) L.; ed. Exeter, N.H.; m. Elizabeth H. Cox, July 27, 1874. Engaged in business as watchmaker and optician. Inventor of luggage carriers for bicycles and of novel types of kites and aeroplanes for use in meteorological observations; also of flying machine; was the first to obtain an Am. patent for a method of tilting or warping the wings of kites and aeroplanes for the purpose of balancing the same in flight. Home: Oxnard, Calif. Died May 1930.

LAMSON, Charles Marion, pres. American Bd. Commrs. Foreign Missions, 1897—; b. North Hadley, Mass., May 16, 1843; acad. edn., Williston Sem., Easthampton, Mass.; grad. Amherst (D.D.); m. Helena F. Bridgman, Dec. 25, 1869. Filled various pastorates. Home: Hartford, Conn. Died 1899.

LAMSON, Fred Mason, trustee Christian Science Pub. Soc.; b. Swanzey, N.H., Feb. 23, 1862; s. Isaac and Sarah (Crossette) L.; student Marlboro (N.H.) High Sch., French's Business Coll., Houghton Pvt. Sch., Marlboro, N.H.; m. Helen Foley, Feb. 4, 1913. Private sec. to supt. motive power Fitchburg R.R.; later private sec. to R. D. Evans (pres. Am. Rubber Co.), and Henry L. Higginson (Lee Higginson & Co.); v.p. Old Colony Trust Co., Boston, Mass., 1913-29; v.p. First Nat. Bank, 1929—. Trustee The Christian Science Pub. Soc., Franklin Square House (treas.), Mount Pleasant Home for Old People. Republican. Mem. The First Ch. of Christ Scientist. Home: Marshfield Hills. Died June 15, 1940.

LAMSON, George Herbert, Jr., prof. zoölogy; b. Malden, Mass., Apr. 8, 1882; s. George Herbert and Sarah (Liscombe) L.; B.Agr., Conn. Agrl. Coll., 1902; B.S., Mass. Agrl. Coll., 1903; M.S., Yale, 1905; biology, Wesleyan U., 1903-04; m. Kate Arroll, July 27, 1909; 1 son, Arroll L. With Conn. Agrl. Coll., 1906—, prof. zoölogy, 1910—; dean of division of agricultural science, 1928; economic zoölogist Storrs Expt. Sta. Investigator in applied agrl. science, 1910—. Methodist. Home: Storrs, Conn. Died 1931.

LAMSON-SCRIBNER, Frank, agrostologist; b. Cambridgeport, Mass., Apr. 19, 1851; s. Joseph S. and Eunice E. (Winslow) L.; adopted at age of 3 by family named Scribner, living nr. Augusta, Me.; B.S., Me. State Coll. of Agr., 1873; LL.D., U. of Me., 1920; m. Ella Augusta Newmarch, Dec. 25, 1877; children—Allen, Frank, Louise; m. 2d, Marjorie Fleming Anderson, Aug. 12, 1913. Teacher, public schools, Maine; clerk to secretary Maine State Board of Agriculture 2 yrs.; officer Girard Coll. Phila., 1876-85; taught botany in summer schs. of sciences; spl. agt. in charge mycol. sect., bot. div., U.S. Dept. of Agr., 1885-86, chief sect. of vegetable pathology, 1887-88; prof. botany, U. of Tenn., 1888-94; dir. Tenn. Agrl. Expt. Sta., 1890-94; chief div. of agrostology, U.S. Dept. Agr., 1894-1901; chief Insular Bur. of Agr., P.I., 1901-04. As spl. agt. and expert on exhibits had charge of the preparation and display of exhibits at a large number of fairs and expns. made by the Agrl. Dept., 1904-22, including the St. Louis Expn., 1904; Portland, Ore., 1905; Seattle, Wash., 1909; Buenos Aires, Argentina, 1910; Turin, Italy, 1911; Lethbridge, Can., 1912; Inter. Refrigeration Expn., Chicago, 1913; San Francisco Expn., 1915, at which served as mem. Govt. Exhibit Bd. by presdl. apptmt. Conducted series of war-time exhibits for food conservation in coöperation with the State Fairs throughout the country, 1917-20; apptd. by sec. of state, director of exhibits for U.S. Com. to Brazilian Centennial Expn., Rio de Janeiro, 1922-23; personal asst. to dir. Commercial Museum, Phila., 1924; spl. asst. to U.S. Com. and supervisor of U.S. Govt. Exhibits, Sesquicentennial Expn., Phila., 1926-27; dir. Hist. Museum of Cumberland County Hist. Soc., Carlisle, Pa., 1927-28; advisory mem. science planning com. of "Chicago Century of Progress Exposition 1933." Decorated Chevalier du Mérite Agricole (France), 1889. Author: Weeds of Maine, 1869; Fungus Diseases of the Grape and Other Plants, 1890; Grasses of Tennessee, 1894; American Grasses (3 vols.), 1897-1900. Translator: (with E. A. Southworth) The True Grasses (from the German), 1890. Home: Washington, D.C. Died Feb. 22, 1938.

LANCASTER, Hewes, author; b. Lancaster Lodge, Miss., 1871; s. Charles Dunbar and Carrie Grayson (Hewes) L.; unmarried. Author: Marie of Arcady, 1909; The One and the Other, 1912; The Will, 1914; The Wind in the Garden, 1919; Rainbow Boy, 1925. Home: Cuevas, Miss. Died May 1, 1933.

LAND, Alfred Dillingham, judge; b. Holmes County, Miss., Jan. 15, 1842; s. Thomas Thompson and Mary Eliza (Dillingham) L.; student Centenary Coll., Jackson, La., 1855-57, U. of Va., 1857-59; LL.B., U. of La., 1861; m. Sarah Virginia Lister, Nov. 11, 1869 (dec.). Sergt. Co. H, 7th La. Inf., in Va., and pvt. Co. A, 28th Miss. Cav., and in Harvey's Scouts, C.S.A., 1861-65. Admitted to bar, 1865; practiced at Shreveport, La., 1867-94; judge Dist. Ct., 1894-1903; apptd. asso. justice Supreme Ct. of La., Oct. 1903; elected to succeed himself, Nov. 1912. Democrat. Address: New Orleans, La. Deceased.

LAND, Charles Henry, dentist; b. Simcoe, Ont., Can., Jan. 11, 1847; s. John Scott and Sarah (Hayden) L.; pub. schs., New York and Brooklyn, and pvt. sch. conducted by father, Williamsburg, N.Y.; studied dentistry under Dr. J. B. Meacham, of Brantford, Can., 1864-66, and in offices of Drs. M. B. Sherwood, L. P. Haskell and W. W. Allport, Chicago, 1868-71; m. Evangeline Lodge, Apr. 28, 1875 (died 1919). In dental practice, Detroit, 1871—; inventor of a gold and a porcelain inlay system, and the process of artificially replacing the enamel on defective human teeth; also gas and oil burners and furnaces, incandescent grates and furnaces adapted for the same. Republican. Conglist. Author: Scientific Adaptation of Artificial Dent[illegible], 1885; A Study in Æsthetic Dentistry, 1911. Mem. Detroit Bd. Commerce. Address: Detroit, Mich. Died Aug. 3, 1922.

LAND, Fort Elmo, state supt. schs.; b. Twiggs County, Ga., June 30, 1878; s. Henry Freeman and Mona (Arrington) L.; A.B., Emory Coll., 1901; m. Mrs. Susie Barrow Gurr, Mar. 6, 1912; 1 son, Fort E. Prin. high schs. till 1902; supt. pub. schs., Cordele, Ga., 1903-08, Dawson, 1908-12; state supervisor rural schs., Ga., 1912-20, and of industrial rehabilitation, 1921-22; state dir. vocational edn., 1923-25; state supt. schs., Ga., 1925—. Democrat. Methodist. Home: Atlanta, Ga. Died July 25, 1927.

LANDACRE, Francis Leroy, anatomist; b. Hilliards, O., Feb. 13, 1867; s. Joseph Perry and Sarah Jane (Dobyns) L.; student Ohio Wesleyan U., 1887-91; A.B., Ohio State U., 1895; Ph.D., U. of Chicago, 1914; m. Frances Ward Yeazell, Dec. 17, 1901; children—Katharine Anita, Elizabeth Wade. Prof. embryology, Ohio Med. U., 1896; prof. histology and embryology, Ohio Med. U. and Starling-Ohio Med. Coll., 1902-14; asst. in zoölogy and entomology, 1895-1900, asso. prof., 1902, prof., 1908, prof. anatomy, 1914—, Ohio State U.; lecturer on Neurology, U. of Calif., 1924-27. Conglist. Author: A Laboratory Guide in Zoölogy, 1904; A Laboratory Guide for Vertebrate Dissections, 1918. Home: Columbus, O. Died Aug. 23, 1933.

LANDER, Edward, jurist; b. Salem, Mass., Aug. 11, 1816; s. Edward and Eliza (West) L.; grad. Harvard, 1835, A.M., 1838, LL.B., 1839. Removed to Ind., 1841; was pros. atty. for 8 counties (including Indianapolis); raised company and served 14 mos. as capt. 4th Ind. Vols. in Mexican war; apptd. 1850 by Gov. Wright and at next session legislature elected for full term judge court common pleas; apptd. Mar. 17, 1853, chief justice Supreme Court Wash. Ty. by Pres. Pierce, declined renomination 1857, intending to practice law in San Francisco, but received injury to spine from which he did not recover for yrs.; counsel for Hudson Bay Co. in case before Internat. Commn. at Washington, 1865-70; afterward practiced there. Pres. Harvard Soc. of Washington. Address: Washington, D.C. Died 1907.

LANDER, Jean Margaret, actress; b. Wolverhampton, England, May 3, 1829; at 8 yrs. of age 1st appeared on stage at Richmond, England; played in U.S., 1838-42; starred in England and Holland, 1842-48, as Julia in The Hunchback, and other rôles; dramatic reader, 1848-49; came to U.S., 1849; m. Gen. Frederick West Lander, U.S. Army, Oct. 12, 1860 (died 1862); active in Union Hosp. service during Civil War; returned to stage for a few yrs. after 1865. Home: Washington, D.C. Died 1903.

LANDERS, George Foreman, army officer; b. in Md., Aug. 17, 1865; grad. U.S. Mil. Acad., 1887, Arty. Sch., 1892; Army War Coll., 1916. Commd. 2d lt. 4th Arty., June 12, 1887; 1st lt., Nov. 14, 1893; capt. Arty. Corps, Feb. 2, 1901; maj., Jan. 25, 1907; lt. col. Coast Arty. Corps, Apr. 1, 1911; col., Nov. 2, 1914. Served in Chicago and vicinity during railroad strikes, 1894; recruiting service, 1897; instr. in chemistry, mineralogy and geology, U.S. Mil. Acad., 1897-1901; dist. ordnance officer, Southern Arty. Dist. of N.Y., 1905-07; dist. comdr., Arty. Dist. of Charleston, S.C., 1908; at Naval War Coll., 1916-17. Died Jan. 23, 1939.

LANDES, Henry, geologist; b. Carroll, Ind., Dec. 22, 1867; s. Samuel and Lydia (Duncan) L.; A.B., Indiana U., 1892; A.B. and A.M., Harvard U., 1893; m. Bertha Ethel Knight, Jan. 2, 1894; children—Katherine (dec.), Kenneth. Asst. to state geologist of N.J., 1893-94; prin. Rockland (Me.) High Sch., 1894-95; prof. geology, 1895—, acting pres., 1914-15, also dean Coll. of Science, 1912—, U. of Wash. State geologist of Wash., 1901-21. Editor of and contbr. to Annual Reports and bulletins, Wash. Geol. Survey, 1901, 1902, 1909-21. Home: Seattle, Wash. Died Aug. 23, 1936.

LANDIS, Cary D., lawyer; b. Claypool, Ind., May 10, 1873; s. David and Elizabeth L.; ed. North Manchester (Ind.) Coll., 1889-91, Ind. State Normal Sch., 1891-92; LL.B., U. of Mich., 1899; m. Margaret Weaver, Sept. 4, 1895; children—Erskine, William, Guenevere (dec.). Prin. high sch., Silver Lake, Ind., 1891-92, Flora, Ind., 1892-93, supt. schs., Burlington, Ind., 1894-96; admitted to Ind. bar, 1899, and began practice at Huntington; prof. law, John B. Stetson U., DeLand, Fla., 1901-05; practiced at DeLand, 1905-27; atty. 7th Jud. Dist. of Fla., 1911-13; traveled in America and abroad, 1927-30; mem. Landis, Fish, Hull & Whitchair, DeLand; apptd. atty. gen. of Fla., Mar. 9, 1931, and elected without opposition in 1932 for full four-yr. term. Democrat. Presbyn. Mason, Elk. Home: DeLand, Fla. Died May 10, 1938.

LANDIS, Charles Beary, congressman; b. Millville, O., July 9, 1858; s. Abraham H. and Mary (Kumler) L.; A.B., Wabash Coll., Ind., 1883; m. Cora B. Chaffin, 1887. Editor Logansport (Ind.) Journal, 1883-87, then Delphi (Ind.) Journal. Pres. Ind. Rep. Editorial Assn., 1894-96. Mem. 55th to 60th Congresses (1897-1909), 9th Ind. Dist. V.p. du Pont Engring. Co. and mgr. Washington office E. I. du Pont de Nemours & Co. Address: Washington, D.C. Died Apr. 24, 1922.

LANDIS, Charles Israel, judge; b. Lancaster, Pa., Nov. 18, 1856; s. Jesse and Elisabeth Parke (Daniel) L.; student Franklin and Marshall Coll., Pa., to jr. yr.; m. Jesse A. Witmer, Sept. 5, 1888. Admitted to bar Sept. 8, 1877; city solicitor, Lancaster, 1880, 82; chmn. Rep. County Com., 1884, 85; mem. sch. bd., Lancaster, 6 yrs.; president judge 2d Jud. Dist. of Pa., 1899—. Republican. Episcopalian. Pres. Thaddeus Stevens Industrial Sch., Thaddeus Stevens Home, A. Herr Smith Free Memorial Library; trustee Henry G. Long Asylum; state trustee Millersville Normal Sch.; dir. Peoples' Bldg. Assn. A founder of Lancaster Law Review, 1883. Address: Lancaster, Pa. Died 1932.

LANDIS, Frederick, congressman; b. Seven Mile, O., Aug. 18, 1872; s. Abraham H. and Mary A. (Kumler) L.; LL.B., U. of Mich., 1895; m. Bessie A. Baker, Aug. 12, 1909; children—Kenesaw Mountain, Frederick B., Elizabeth Ann, Frances Katharine, Charles Walter, Lincoln. Began practice at Logansport, Ind., 1893; mem. 58th and 59th Congresses (1903-07), 11th Ind. Dist.; formerly Republican; temporary chmn. Progressive Ind. State Conv., 1912; del. at large Progressive Nat. Conv., Chicago, 1912; Progressive candidate for lt. gov. of Ind., 1912. Author: The Glory of His Country, 1910; The Angel of Lonesome Hill, 1910; Days Gone Dry; (plays) The People Are Coming, 1913; The Copperhead (joint author); The Water Wagon; Montana. Formerly editor Logansport Pharos-Tribune; editor The Hoosier Editor (monthly). Lecturer. Home: Logansport, Ind. Died Nov. 15, 1934.

LANDIS, Henry Robert Murray, M.D.; b. Niles, O., Feb. 3, 1872; s. Henry Gardner and Elizabeth (Hafey) L.; A.B., Amherst, 1894; M.D., Jefferson Med. Coll., Phila., 1897, Sc.D., 1929; m. Margaret Tucker, Apr. 2, 1902. Prof. clin. medicine, U. of Pa. Med. Dept., 1912; dir. clin. and sociol. depts., Henry Phipps Inst. Republican. Episcopalian. Author: (with Dr. G. W. Norris) Physical Diagnosis and Diseases of the Chest, 1917. Address: Philadelphia, Pa. Died Sept. 14, 1937.

LANDIS, John Howard, physician; b. Millville, O., Oct. 10, 1860; s. Dr. Abraham H. and Mary (Kumler) L.; grad. Logansport (Ind.) High Sch., 1879; M.D., Coll. of Ohio, Cincinnati, 1890; m. Daisy M. Graham, June 5, 1894. Interne, Cincinnati Hospital, 1890-91; prof. pathology, Presbyn. and Laura Memorial Coll., 1892-95; mem. staff St. Mary's Hosp., 1907; prof. hygiene, med. dept. U. of Cincinnati (Ohio-Miami Med. Coll.), 1908—; apptd. mem. Cincinnati Bd. of Health, 1909, elected health officer, Jan. 1, 1910. Dir. Visiting Nurse Assn., Council of Social Agencies. Republican. Presbyn. Mem. Commn. on Nat. Milk Standards. Home: Cincinnati, O. Died Aug. 23, 1918.

LANDIS, Josiah Pennabecker, theologian; b. Brickerville, Pa., Oct. 27, 1843; s. Joseph and Caroline (Weiler) L.; served in Union Army, 1862-65; A.B., Otterbein U., 1869, A.M., 1872; student Western Theol. Sem., Pa., 1868-69, Lane Theol. Sem., Ohio, 1869-71, U. of Berlin, 1886; Ph.D., U. of Wooster, 1889; D.D., Otterbein, 1882; m. Addie Belle Kumler, June 6, 1872. Ordained U.B. ministry, 1871; pastor Dayton, O., 1871-74, Miltonville, O., 1874-77, Germantown, O., 1877-80; prof. Hebrew exegesis and O.T. theology, 1880-1909, dean, 1907-09, pres., May 1909-21 (resigned the presidency but continues in chair of O.T. theology and exegesis), Bonebrake Theol. (formerly Union Bibl.) Sem., Dayton, O. Pres. Ohio S.S. Union, 1884-86, Young People's Christian Union, 1890-1902; asst. editor, 1878-85, and elected editor S.S. Lit. of U.B. Ch., 1885, but soon resigned to continue in Sem. Took part in Parliament of Religions, Chicago, 1893, and Methodist Ecumenical Conf., Washington; sec. Tri-Church Council, Congl., U.B. and M.P. chs., Chicago, 1907; sec. U.B. Bd. of Edn., 1909-13; mem. Federal Council of Chs. of Christ in America; mem. Archæol. Congress, Beirut, Syria, and Jerusalem, 1926. Mem. League to Enforce Peace; pres. bd. Dayton Pub. Library. Contbr. to Weaver's "Christian Doctrine." Editor: Sanctuary Hymnal, 1913. Home: Dayton, O. Died Oct. 17, 1937.

LANDON, Judson Stuart, jurist; b. Salisbury, Conn., Dec. 16, 1832; A.M., Union Coll., 1855; LL.D., Rutgers; studied law; practiced at Schenectady until 1873; justice Supreme Court, N.Y., 1873-1901. Pres. ad interim Union Coll., 1885; lecturer on Constitutional law, Albany Law Sch. Author: The Constitutional History and Government of the United States, 1889. Address: Schenectady, N.Y. Died 1905.

LANDON, Melville De Lancey ("Eli Perkins"), humorist; b. Eaton, N.Y., Sept. 7, 1839; s. John and Nancy (Marsh) L.; grad. Union Coll., 1861, A.M.; m. Emily Louise Smith, 1875. Served short time in Treasury Dept., Washington; on staff of Gen. A. L. Chetlain in Civil War; reached rank of maj.; resigned from army, 1864; cotton planter in Ark. and La., 1864-67; traveled in Europe; became sec. U.S. Legation at St. Petersburg; returned to U.S., 1870; lecturer; pres. New York News Assn. Author: Saratoga in 1901, 1870; History of the Franco-Prussian War, 1871; Wit, Humor and Pathos, 1875; Wit and Humor of the Age, 1880; Kings of Platform and Pulpit, 1887; Thirty Years of Wit, 1890; Eli Perkins on Money—Gold, Silver or Bimetallism, 1895. Address: New York, N.Y. Died 1910.

LANDON, Thomas Durland, educator; b. Belvidere, N.J., May 18, 1865; s. Rev. Thompson Hoadley (D.D.) and Sarah (Durland) L.; ed. Centenary Collegiate Inst., Hackettstown, N.J.; Wesleyan Acad., Wilbraham, Mass.; Field Officers' Sch., Fort Sam Houston, Tex.; Army Sch. of the Line, Langres, France; m. Margaret Adams Reese, June 29, 1892. Began, 1885, as asst. to father, Bordentown Mil. Inst., now propr. and pres. Enlisted as pvt. Co. A, 6th Inf. N.G. N.J., Dec. 3, 1885; promoted through grades to col., 1913; capt. and maj. 3d N.J. Inf., Spanish-Am. War, 1898; col. in World War, 3d N.J. Inf., 114th Inf., A.E.F.; comdt. Base Training Schs., 41st Div., and comdr. 163d Inf.; hon. discharged Mar. 11, 1919; col. comdg. 309th Inf., O.R.C.; commd. brevet brig. gen. (Ret.), Nat. Guard N.J., 1933. Decorated Officer Order of Black Star, by President of France, 1919. Republican. Home: Bordentown, N.J. Died Oct. 29, 1934.

LANDON, Thompson Hoadley, clergyman, teacher; b. Lansingburg, N.Y., Nov. 18, 1830; s. Seymour and Phoebe (Thompson) L.; A.B., Wesleyan U., Conn., 1852, A.M., 1855, D.D., 1906; m. Sarah Durland, May 18, 1864 (died 1903). Teacher, Amenia Sem., Amenia, N.Y., and later vice-prin. Pennington (N.J.) Sem.; ordained M.E. ministry, 1860, and mem. N.J. Conf., later Newark Conf.; prin. Bordentown Mil. Inst., 1885—, associating with son Thomas D. as partner and mgr. Prohibitionist. Home: Bordentown, N.J. Died July 30, 1917.

LANDON, Warren Hall, theologian; b. Alburgh, Vt., July 8, 1851; s. Edwin H. and Delia (White) L.; A.B., U. of Vt., 1874, D.D., 1887; Union Theol. Sem., New York, 1879; LL.D., Occidental Coll., 1921; m. Florence E. Phelps, Jan. 22, 1880; children—Mary Augusta, Warren Phelps, Helen Florence. Ordained Presbyn. ministry, 1880; pastor Palmyra, N.Y., 1879-86, Calvary Ch., Portland, Ore., 1887-92; prof. practical theology, 1892-1913, prof. apologetics and missions, 1913—, and pres., Apr. 1910—, San Francisco Theol. Sem. Mem. Jud. Commn. Gen. Assembly Presbyn. Ch., U.S.A., 1910-13, and mem. Bd. of Christian Edn., 1917—. Republican. Vice moderator Gen. Assembly Presbyn. Ch. in U.S.A., 1927-28. Home: San Anselmo, Calif. Died July 14, 1928.

LANDRETH, Burnet, farmer, seed mcht.; b. Phila., Dec. 30, 1842; ed. Episcopal Acad. and Polytechnic Coll., Phila.; married; children—Burnet, Symington Phillips, Frances Hamilton, David. Capt. inf., Army of the Potomac; chief Bur. Agr. Centennial Exhbn.; dir. in chief Am. Exhbn., London; founder and pres. Assn. of Centenary Firms of the U.S.; head of D. Landreth Seed Co., established 1784. V.p. Phila. Soc. of Agr.; pres. Pa. Forestry Soc. Three times decorated Mérite Agricole de France. Author of several vols. on agr. Home: Bristol, Pa. Died Dec. 2, 1928.

LANDRETH, Olin Henry, engineer; b. Addison, N.Y., July 21, 1852; s. Rev. James and Adelia (Comstock) L.; C.E., Union Coll., 1876, A.B., 1877, A.M., 1887, D.Sc., 1905; m. Eliza Taylor, Aug. 20, 1879 (dec.); children—William Comstock (dec.), Olin Henry (dec.), Mrs. Mary Eliza Parker, Helen Adelia, James Taylor (dec.), Robert Nelson. Asst. astronomer, Dudley Obs., Albany, N.Y., 1877-79; prof. engring., 1879-94, dean engring. dept., 1886-94, Vanderbilt U., Nashville, Tenn.; prof. engring., Union Coll., 1894-1917, emeritus prof. engring., 1917—; consulting engr., also chief engr. of Eastern Potash Corp., New York, 1919-21. Consulting engr. N.Y. State Bd. of Health, 1896-1906; mem. N.Y. State Water Storage Commn., 1902, N.Y. State Bay Commn., 1903; mem. Met. Sewerage Commn. of New York. Mech. engr., Ordnance Dept., Washington, 1918-19; consulting practice. Author: Metric Tables; contributor to scientific and tech. jours.; prepared civil engring. terms for new edit. Century Dictionary. Mem. N.Y. Constl. Conv., 1915. Home: Mount Vernon, N.Y. Died Nov. 6, 1931.

LANDRITH, Ira, clergyman; b. Milford, Tex., Mar. 23, 1865; s. Martin Luther and Mary M. (Groves) L.; B.S., Cumberland U., Tenn., 1888, LL.B., 1889; theol. student, same, 1889-90, LL.D., 1903; D.D., Trinity U., Tex., 1906; m. Harriet C. Grannis, Jan. 21, 1891 (died June 24, 1925); children—Grace Grannis, Ira DeWitt (dec.). Asst. editor, 1890-95, editor in chief, 1896-1903, The Cumberland Presbyterian, Nashville; long state chmn. Y.M.C.A. of Tenn.; state sec. Anti-Saloon League, which led in putting saloons out of Tenn.; chmn. "Com. of 100" that reformed civic life of Nashville; gen. sec. Religious Edn. Assn., 1893-94. Presbyn. Brotherhood America, 1907-09. Moderator the last Gen. Assembly Cumberland Presbyn. Ch., during which that denomination was united with the Presbyn. Ch. in the U.S.A., 1906; pres. Internat. Y.M.C.A. Conv., 1913. Pres. Belmont Coll., Nashville, 1904-12, Ward

Sem., 1912-13, Ward Belmont Coll., Nashville 1913-15; mem. Flying Squadron of America, 1914, 15; editor afield Christian Endeavor World and Citizenship; supt. Internat. Soc. of Christian Endeavor, 1915—. Nat. lecturer Anti-Saloon League America and World League Against Alcoholism, 1915-25. Prohibition nominee for v.p. of U.S., 1916. Pres. Intercollegiate Prohibition Assn., Washington, D.C., 1920-27; pres. Nat. Temperance Council, 1928-31; mem. Allied Campaigners for Prohibition Permanency and Enforcement, 1931-32. Address: Pasadena, Calif. Died Oct. 11, 1941.

LANDRUM, William Warren, clergyman; b. Macon, Ga., Jan. 18, 1853; s. Sylvanus (D.D.) and Eliza (Warren) L.; Mercer U., Macon, Ga.; A.B., Brown U., 1872; grad. Southern Bapt. Theol. Sem., Louisville, Ky., 1874; D.D., Washington and Lee, 1875; m. Lottie Baylor, July 15, 1886; children—Grace Warren, Margaret L. (Mrs. F. Watkins), Eliza Marshall (Mrs. Fitzhugh Scott), Baylor, Ida D. (Mrs. W. G. McGowan), Mary K. (Mrs. Stanley B. Johnson). Ordained Bapt. ministry, 1874; pastor Shreveport, La., 1874-76, 1st Ch., Augusta, Ga., 1876-82; 2d Ch., Richmond, Va., 1882-96, 1st Ch., Atlanta, Ga., and Broadway Ch., Louisville, Ky.; prof. philosophy, Bethel College, Russellville, Ky. Served as capt. and chaplain 1st Regt. Cav. Ga. N.G.; brig. gen. Ky. Div. United Boys' Brigades of America. Trustee Southern Bapt. Theol. Sem. Pres. Home Mission Bd. of Southern Bapt. Conv.; sec. Bapt. Edn. Soc. of Ky.; mem. exec. com. Bapt. World Alliance; pres. Bapt. Edn. Commn. of Ga. Democrat. Mason. Author: Use and Abuse of the Baptist Message; Settled in the Sanctuary, 1925. Home: Russellville, Ky. Deceased.

LANDSBERG, Max, rabbi; b. Berlin, Germany, Feb. 26, 1845; s. Meyer and Fanny (Blumenreich) L.; ed. univs. of Göttingen and Breslau; Jewish Theol. Sem., Breslau; Ph.D., U. of Halle, 1866; rabbi, 1870; m. Miriam Isengarten, Feb. 26, 1871; children—Emil, Clara, Rose (Mrs. Benjamin Stolz), Grace Lillian (Mrs. H. Franklin Leiter). Came to America, 1871; minister of Berith Kodesh Congregation, Rochester, N.Y., 1871-1915, rabbi emeritus, 1915—. Governor Hebrew Union Coll., Cincinnati; trustee Reynolds Library, Rochester Gen. Hosps. Pres. 12th N.Y. State Conf. of Charities and Correction, 1911. Published a Ritual for Jewish Worship, 1884, 3d edit., 1910. Address: Rochester, N.Y. Died Dec. 8, 1927.

LANDSTREET, Fairfax Stuart, coal operator; b. Paris, Va., June 17, 1861; s. John and Mary Frances (Swink) L.; ed. high sch.; m. May Davis, Dec. 6, 1886; children—Fairfax Stuart, Mary Davis. Successively supt., gen. mgr. and pres. Davis Coal & Coke Co., 1886-1907; pres. Belgian-Am. Coke Ovens Corp.; chmn. bd. New York Dock Co., Pa. Coal & Coke Corp.; dir. and mem. exec. com. Clinchfield Coal Corp. Del.-at-large Rep. Nat. Conv., 1908. Served with Am. Red Cross in France, World War. Home: New York, N.Y. Died Feb. 5, 1931.

LANE, Albert Grannis, educator; b. Chicago, Mar. 15, 1841; s. Elisha B. and Amanda (Grannis) L.; ed. pub. schs.; prin. Franklin School, Chicago, 1858-69; supt. schools Cook County, Ill., 1869-73; cashier Preston, Kean & Co.'s West Side Bank, Chicago, 1874-77; again county supt. schools, 1877-91; supt. Chicago city schools, 1891-98; asst. supt. same, 1898—. Pres., 1893-94, and later trustee N.E.A.; dir. of its ednl. exhibit, 1887; mem. Nat. Council of Edn.; pres. Ill. State Teachers' Assn., 1899. Active in Methodist Church and Sunday school work; hon. A.M., Dartmouth. Home: Chicago, Ill. Died 1906.

LANE, Charles Homer, agricultural edn.; b. Boston, Mass., July 17, 1877; s. John and Eliza (Wall) L.; grad. Normal Sch., Frederickton, N.B., 1897; U. of New Brunswick, 3 yrs.; B.A., Mt. Allison U., N.B., 1903, M.A., 1908; B.S.A., U. of Tenn., 1909; George Washington U., 1911-12; Ph.D., Research U., 1921; m. Ida West, 1907. Prof. biology, Washington Coll., Tenn., 1905-07; asst. in agronomy and agrl. chemistry, 1907-09, instr. agronomy, 1909-10, in charge dept., 1910-11, U. of Tenn.; asst. in agrl. edn., 1911-12, in charge div. agrl. edn., 1912-17, U.S. Dept. Agr.; with Federal Bd. for Vocational Edn., 1917—, becoming chief agrl. edn. service. Mason. Address: Washington, D.C. Deceased.

LANE, Charles Stoddard; b. Boston, Mass., Jan. 15, 1860; s. George Homer and Sarah (Weeks) L.; grad. Boston Latin Sch., 1876; A.M., Amherst, 1880; grad. Hartford Theol. Sem., 1884; D.D., Wooster, 1912; m. Jessie Carson, May 20, 1885 (died 1926); children—Stoddard, George Homer, Laura Carson (wife of Rev. Ernest Jerome Johanson); m. 2d, Anna Strange, May 28, 1927. Ordained Congl. ministry, 1884; pastor Unionville, Conn., 1884-88, Presbyn. Ch., Mt. Vernon, N.Y., 1888-1910; v.p. Hartford Sch. Religious Edn. (Hartford Sem. Foundation), 1910-28, also prof. ch. history until 1928, prof. emeritus. Address: Hartford, Conn. Deceased.

LANE, Edward Binney, M.D.; b. Melrose, Mass., July 13, 1860; s. Samuel G. and Mary S. (Binney) L.; student Boston U. Coll. Liberal Arts, 1877-78; A.B., Harvard, 1881, M.D., 1885; m. Esther Bridgman, May 29, 1888 (died Jan. 1930); children—Spencer Bridgman, Arthur Binney (dec.), Robert Bridgman, Edward Gordon; m. 2d, Ida N. Southcombe, May 31 1933. Medical house officer, McLean Asylum, July-Sept. 1884; asst. physician, Boston Lunatic Hosp., South Boston, 1884-88; 1st asst. physician Northampton (Mass.) Lunatic Hosp., 1888-89; resident physician, dept. of Boston Lunatic Hosp. at West Roxbury, 1889-95; supt. Boston Insane Hosp., 1895-1905; resident physician Adams Nervine Asylum, 1909-35. Clin. instr. mental diseases, Harvard Med. Sch., 1897-1904; prof. mental diseases, Tufts Coll. Med. Sch., 1903-29 (emeritus). Home: Milton, Mass. Died Sept. 17, 1941.

LANE, Elinor Macartney (Mrs.), author; b. in Md.; d. Nicholas and Elizabeth (Kirkpatrick) Macartney; grad. Washington High Sch., Washington Normal Sch. (specialist in higher mathematics); m. Dr. Francis Ransom Lane, June 23, 1891. Began to write at 16, principally short stories of Southern life; started The Trifler mag., 1901. Author: Mills of God, 1901; Nancy Stair, 1904; All for the Love of a Lady, 1906. Address: Port Deposit, Md. Died 1909.

LANE, Franklin Knight, Secretary of the Interior; b. near Charlottetown, P.E.I., Canada, July 15, 1864; s. Dr. C. S. and C. W. H. L.; removed to Calif. during childhood; ed. U. of Calif., class of 1886; LL.D., U. of Calif., New York U., Brown U. and U. of N.C.; Sc.D., Trinity Coll., Conn.; m. Anne Wintermute, Apr. 11, 1893. Engaged in newspaper work early in life; was reporter and later New York corr. for western papers, and part owner and editor Tacoma Daily News; admitted to the Calif. bar, 1889, and began practice of law at San Francisco; corp. counsel San Francisco, 1897-1902; candidate for gov. of Calif., 1902; party vote of legislature of Calif. for U.S. senator, 1903; mem. Interstate Commerce Commn., 1905-13 (chmn. Jan.-Mar. 1913); Sec. of the Interior in Cabinet of President Wilson, Mar. 5, 1913-Mar. 1, 1920. Democrat. Mem. Permanent Internat. Ry. Commn., representing U.S. Govt.; mem. Am.-Mexican High Commn., 1916; Council Nat. Defense, 1917. V.p. Pan-Am. Petroleum & Transport Co., New York. Address: New York, N.Y. Died May 18, 1921.

LANE, Gardiner Martin, banker; b. Cambridge, Mass., Apr. 30, 1859; s. George Martin (prof. Latin, Harvard) and Frances Eliza (Gardiner) L.; A.B., summa cum laude, Harvard, 1881; m. Emma Louise Gildersleeve, June 1898. Entered office of Lee, Higginson & Co., bankers, as clk., 1881, and after a few yrs. became asst. to Charles Francis Adams, pres. U.P. Ry., and later one of the v.p.s of the co.; resigned, to become partner, Lee, Higginson & Co., in which continues; dir. U.S. Steel Corp., Mass. Electric Cos., Am. Agrl. Chem. Co., L.&N. R.R., Old Colony Trust Co. (Boston), and many others. Pres. Museum of Fine Arts, Boston; treas. of trustees and treas. mng. com. Am. Sch. of Classical Studies at Athens; treas. Boston Soc. Archæol. Inst. of America, etc. Homes: Boston and Manchester, Mass. Died Oct. 4, 1914.

LANE, Harry, senator; b. in Ore., 1855; grad. Willamette U., Salem, Ore., 1876. Practicing physician at Portland, Ore. U.S. senator for term 1913-19. Democrat. Home: Portland, Ore. Died May 23, 1917.

LANE, Henry Marcus, mech. engr.; b. Cincinnati, Aug. 15, 1854; s. Philander Parmelee and Sophia Rebecca (Bosworth) L.; Mass. Inst. Tech., 1873; m. Blanche A. Conkling, Feb. 4, 1903; 1 dau., Geneva. With Lane & Bodley, engine bldrs., Cincinnati, 1878-79; constructing engr. Elm St. Inclined Plane Ry., 1875, Mt. Adams Inclined Plane Ry., 1879-80; built Gilbert Av. Cable Ry. (1st in Ohio), 1885-86, Vine St. (Cincinnati) Cable Ry., 1887, Denver Tramway, 1888 (1st cable ry. in Colo.), Providence Cable Tramway, 1889 (1st and only cable ry. built in N.E.); consulting engr. St. Louis Cable Ry. Co., Western Ry. Co., St. Paul, Boston Tramway Co., 1885-89; pres. Lane & Bodley Co., 1890—. Independent Republican. Presbyn. Home: Cincinnati, O. Died May 15, 1929.

LANE, Isaac, bishop; b. Jackson, Tenn., Mar. 3, 1834; s. Rachel Lane; self ed.; m. Frances Ann Boyce, 1853; m. 2d, Mrs. Mary E. Smith, 1895. Bishop, Colored M.E. Ch., 1873—; trustee, Connectional Property of the Colored M.E. Church, Colored M.E. Pub. House; pres. trustees Lane Coll., Jackson, Tenn. Address: Jackson, Tenn. Died Dec. 6, 1937.

LANE, James H., prof. civil engring. and drawing, Ala. Poly. Inst.; b. Mathews Court House, Va., July 28, 1833; s. Walter G. and Mary A. H. L.; grad. Va. Mil. Inst. and U. of Va.; Ph.D., W.Va. U.; LL.D., Trinity Coll., N.C.; m. Charlotte Randolph Meade, Sept. 13, 1869 (dec.). Before the Civil War was apptd. prof. mathematics and instr. in tactics in Va. Mil. Inst.; prof. of mathematics and commandant in the State Sem. of Fla., at Tallahassee; prof. natural philosophy and instr. in tactics, N.C. Mil. Inst. at Charlotte; served in Civil War as maj. and lt. col. 1st N.C. vols. and col. 28th N.C. troops; apptd. brig. gen. C.S.A. for gallantry; was in all large battles fought by army of Northern Va. and many of the minor ones. Became prof. natural philosophy and commandant in Va. Agrl. and Mech. Coll. after war; prof. mathematics Mo. School of Mines and Metallurgy; supt. Va. Mining and Mfg. Co.; prof. civil engring. and commandant in Ala. Agrl. and Mech. Coll.; later prof. engring. and drawing, Ala. Poly. Inst. Address: Auburn, Ala. Died 1907.

LANE, John Edward, physician; b. Whately, Mass., Feb. 12, 1872; s. Rev. John William and Mary (Haynes) L.; B.A., Yale, 1894, M.A., 1897, M.D., 1903; studied univs. Göttingen, Berlin, Geneva and Paris abt. 2 yrs.; m. Alice Treat Rogers, May 19, 1909. Began practice, New Haven, 1903; specializes in dermatology and syphilology; clin. prof. dermatology, Yale U. Sch. of Medicine, 1920-22 (resigned). Fellow New York Acad. Medicine (chmn. sect. dermatology and syphilis, 1919 and 1920); mem. A.M.A. chmn. sect. dermatology and syphilis, 1924-25), Am. Dermatol. Assn. (v.p. 1922-23), New York Dermatol. Soc. (pres. 1927-28), Conn. State Med. Soc. (sec. 1917-20), New Haven Med. Assn. (pres. 1922), Beaumont Med. Club (pres. 1922-23). Home: New Haven, Conn. Died Oct. 17, 1933.

LANE, Jonathan, lawyer; b. Fayette County, Tex., Oct. 15, 1855; s. Charles Joseph and Ellen E. L.; ed. pvt. schs., Tex.; admitted to bar, 1885; m. Alma Harrison, Dec. 28, 1880. Mem. Tex. Senate, 1887-91. Democrat. Pres. and built 110 miles of Cane Belt R.R., 1899-1903; mem. law firm Lane, Wolters & Storey; pres. Am. Surety & Casualty Co., Guarantee Life Ins. Co., Southern Irrigation Co., Thompson Bros. Lumber Co., Trinity, Texas, Continental Trust Co., Houston, Tex.; dir. Union Nat. Bank, Bankers' Trust Co. Home: Houston, Tex. Died May 27, 1916.

LANE, Levi C., M.D.; ed. Union Coll., N.Y. (A.M., LL.D.); grad. Jefferson Med. Coll., Phila., 1851; mem. Royal Chirurg. Soc., England, 1875; attended European schools and hosps.; founded and endowed, and became prof. surgery in Cooper Med. Coll., San Francisco. Address: San Francisco, Calif. Died 1902.

LANE, Merritt, judge; b. Jersey City, N.J., Jan. 2, 1881; grad. high sch., Jersey City; LL.B., New York Law Sch. Admitted to N.J. bar, 1902, admitted as counselor, 1905; apptd. vice chancellor of N.J., Nov. 8, 1916, to fill vacancy. Home: Jersey City, N.J. Died June 6, 1939.

LANE, Smith Edward, lawyer; b. New York, July 22, 1829; grad. Univ. City of New York, 1848 (A.M.); delivered semi-centennial address at meeting of alumni of that univ., 1898; admitted to N.Y. bar, 1852, and has practiced in New York; identified with politics, 1852—, and for over 30 yrs. has been mem. gen. com. of Tammany Hall. A commr. of parks, New York, 1878-83; mem. 1898-1902, and sec. board commrs. of "New East River Bridge." For services rendered to Venezuela received order El Busto del Libertador, class of Officer 1887, class of Commander 1889; hon. foreign mem. La Academia Naçional de la Historia, Venezuela. Home: New York, N.Y. Deceased.

LANE, Thomas Welsh, clergyman; b. Georgeville, Pa., Sept. 30, 1855; s. Andrew Jackson and Margaret Jane (Welsh) L.; A.B., Mt. Union Coll., Alliance, O., 1876, A.M., 1879; D.D., Dickinson, 1895; m. Emma Keeler, Sept. 19, 1877; children—Essie Blanche, Joseph Jackson, Helen Leona (dec.). Entered M.E. Ministry, 1876, deacon, 1878, elder, 1881; pastor Freeport, O., 1876-78, Edinburg, 1878-80, Rootstown, 1880-82, Bristolville, 1882-85, Girard, 1885-88, First Ch., Bellaire, 1888-92, First Ch., Barnesville, 1892-93, First Ch., Uhrichsville, 1893-96, First Ch., Alliance, 1896-1900; presiding elder, Cleveland Dist., East Ohio Conf., 1900-05; pastor 1st Ch., East Liverpool, O., 1905-07, Fourth St. Ch., Wheeling, W.Va., 1907-10, 1st Ch., Tacoma, Wash., 1910-14, Centenary Ch., Portland, Ore., 1914-18, Pioneer Ch., Walla Walla, Wash., 1918-21, First Ch., Puyallup, Wash., 1921-24. Delegate and assistant sec. Gen. Conf. M.E. Ch., 1900, 04, 24. Trustee Mt. Union Coll., 1888-1910. Mason. Home: Tacoma, Wash. Died Dec. 27, 1927.

LANE, Victor Hugo, prof. law; b. Geneva, O., May 27, 1852; s. Henry and Clotilda Catharine (Sawyer) L.; C.E., U. of Mich., 1874, LL.B., 1878; m. Ida M. Knowlton, Sept. 28, 1876 (died 1921); children—Mrs. Esther Mildred Simpson, Mrs. Charlotte Geraldine McKenzie, Victor Hugo, Henry Knowlton. Practiced at Hudson, Mich., with Jacob C. Sawyer, 1878-84; mem. firm Bean, Underwood & Lane, Adrian, Mich., 1884-88; judge 1st Jud. Circuit of Mich., 1888-97 (resigned); Fletcher prof. law, U. of Mich., 1897—. Republican. Presbyterian. Editor: Cooley's Constitutional Limitations, 1903; Tiffany's Justice Guide, 1905. Home: Ann Arbor, Mich. Died Jan. 24, 1930.

LANE, William Coolidge, librarian; b. Newton, Mass., July 29, 1859; s. William H. and Caroline M. (Coolidge) L.; A.B., Harvard, 1881; m. Bertha Palmer, May 12, 1903; children—Margaret, Rosamond (Mrs. Milton E. Lord). Asst. librarian, Harvard, 1887-93; librarian, Boston Athenæum, 1893-98, Harvard U., 1898-1928; librarian emeritus, 1928—. Pres. A.L.A., 1898-99, Bibliog. Soc. America, 1904-09, sec. and treas. and later chmn. A.L.A. publishing bd., 1886-1907. Sec. Harvard Chapter Phi Beta Kappa, 1889-1919. Home: Cambridge, Mass. Died Mar. 18, 1931.

LANEY, Francis Baker, geologist; b. nr. Springfield, Mo., Apr. 9, 1875; s. John Baker and Jane (Alexander) L.; B.S., Drury Coll., Springfield, 1902; M.A., U. of Wis., 1905; Ph.D. in Geology, Yale, 1908; m. Minnie D. Towner, Sept. 1910; 1 son, Francis T. Began as asst. geologist, N.C., 1903; asst. curator applied geology, Nat. Museum, Washington, D.C., 1908-10; geologist U.S. Geol. Survey, 1914—; microscopist and mineralogist U.S. Bur. Mines, 1914-19; metallographist Central Checking Lab. of Ordnance Dept. U.S. Army, Pittsburgh, Pa., 1917-18; head dept. of geology, U. of Ida., 1920—. Unitarian. Home: Moscow, Ida. Died Apr. 23, 1938.

LANFORD, John Alexander, pathologist; b. Gainesville, Ala., June 19, 1881; s. John Bibb and Maria Adeline (Rogers) L.; Ph.G., Ala. Poly. Inst., 1900; M.D., U. of Ala., 1905; unmarried. Pharmacist (while studying medicine), Mobile, Ala., 1900-05; instr. in surg. pathology, Tulane, 1911-14, asst. prof. pathology and bacteriology, 1914; pathologist Touro Infirmary, New Orleans, La., 1912—; cons. pathologist U.S. Marine Hosp., 1928—; pathologist New Orleans Dispensary, 1926—. Mem. bd. dirs. Am. Soc. for Control of Cancer, 1939—. Served as captain Medical Reserve, U.S.A., 1917; laboratory officer, Justice and Perigueux Hosp. Centers, France, 1918-19; major Medical Reserve Corps, 1919-24, lt. col., 1924-32, col., 1932—; comdg. officer 312th Med. Regt. Res., 1932—. Mem. Southern Med. Assn. (chmn. pathol. sect. 1927), La. State Med. Soc. (chmn. cancer com., 1932—), Orleans Parish Med. Soc. (pres. 1932). Democrat. Methodist. Mason. Home: New Orleans, La. Died July 2, 1940.

LANG, Benjamin Johnson, musician; b. Salem, Mass., Dec. 28, 1837; studied music under his father, an organist and pianoforte teacher, under Francis G. Hill and Gustav Satter, Boston, and under Franz Liszt, Albert Jaell and others, Germany, 1855-58. Pianist, organist, teacher and conductor in Boston; became conductor Apollo Club, 1868; Cecilia Soc., 1874, and Handel and Haydn Soc., 1895; organist Handel and Haydn Soc., 1859; organist of King's Chapel, 1885—. Address: Boston, Mass. Died 1909.

LANG, Charles H., Jr., mfr.; b. Dover, N.H., June 13, 1850; s. Charles H. and Sarah A. (Staples) L.; ed. common schs.; m. May E. Pratt, June 28, 1877. Began as clk. with Cyrus Wakefield, 1872; treas., dir. Wakefield Rattan Co., 1888; treas. Heywood Bros. & Wakefield Co., mfrs. reed and rattan furniture, 1898-1912, pres., 1912—. Home: Melrose, Mass. Deceased.

LANG, Charles Michael Angelo, artist, sculptor; b. Albany, N.Y., Aug. 26, 1860; s. John M. and Anna (Bates) L.; ed. Cooper Union, New York; Royal Acad., Munich, Bavaria, and in Italy, France, and London, Eng.; m. Frances Neville Byrne (died 1923); children—Charles Neville, Frances Madeline, Victoria Adelle, Esther Miriam, Elizabeth Jane. Formerly dir. and prin. Emma Willard Sch. of Art, Troy, N.Y.; dir. George West Museum, Round Lake, N.Y.; dir. Round Lake Summer Sch. of Art; supt. sculpture work of Grand Staircase of the State Capitol, Albany, N.Y., etc. Painted portraits of Theodore Roosevelt, David B. Hill, Roswell P. Flower, Judge Morgan J. O'Brien, Gen. J. B. Carr, Bishop Rooker, John Wanamaker, etc. Awarded prize for painting; also prize for sculpture (monument to Edward Kelsey Apgar, at Cornell U., Ithaca, N.Y.). Mason. Address: Saratoga Springs, N.Y. Died Mar. 15, 1934.

LANG, Henry Roseman, univ. prof.; b. Wartau, Canton St. Gall, Switzerland, Sept. 22, 1853; s. Rev. Dr. H. L. and Constantia (Suter) L.; Ph.D., U. of Strassburg; m. Alice Hubbard Derby, Aug. 29, 1901 (died 1928). Prof. Romance langs. and lit., 1896-1922, Yale, emeritus, 1922—. U.S. del. to Centenary of Spain's War of Independence, at Saragossa, 1908. Silver medals of Saragossa and of Hispanic Soc. America. Fellow Am. Acad. Arts and Sciences. Knight Comdr. Portuguese Order of Santiago. Author: Cancionero del Rey D. Denis, 1892; Liederbuch des Königs D. Denis, 1894; The Descort in Old Portuguese and Spanish Poetry, 1899; Cancionero Gallego-Castelhano, 1902; Zum Cancionero da Ajuda, 1908; also Expert Opinion for American and British Bible Societies on Portuguese Translation of New Testament for Missions in Brazil, 1904. Contributions to the Restoration of the Poema del Cid; Foreword to the Facsimile Reproduction of the Cancionero de Baena. Home: New Haven, Conn. Died July 25, 1934.

LANGDALE, John William, clergyman; b. Newcastle, Eng., Aug. 14, 1874, of American and English parentage, naturalized by father's citizenship; s. John Wilkenson and Anne (Walton) L.; brought to U.S. in infancy; prep. edn., Kiskiminetas Springs Sch.; B.A., Wesleyan U., Conn., 1903, D.D., 1914; LL.D., Simpson Coll., 1934; Litt.D., Emory U., 1935; studied Boston U. Sch. of Theology and Harvard; m. Alice Belle Barnett, Jan. 10, 1905; children—Abram Barnett, Eleanor Katharine. Ordained M.E. ministry, 1905; pastor Meyersdale, Pa., 1905-08, Beaver, Pa., 1908-12, Avondale Ch., Cincinnati, 1912-16, New York Av. Ch., Brooklyn, N.Y., 1916-25; supt. Brooklyn S. Dist., 1925-28; book editor Meth. Ch., 1928—; mem. com. on policy Federal Council Chs.; chmn. Nat. Religious Radio Com. Trustee Wesleyan U., Drew U. Republican. Mason. Author: Citizenship and Moral Reform, 1918. Home: New York, N.Y. Died Dec. 10, 1940.

LANGDELL, Christopher Columbus, lawyer, educator; b. Hillsborough County, N.H., May 22, 1826; studied Harvard, 1848-49; (A.B., A.M., LL.D.); grad. Harvard Law School, 1853; practiced in New York until 1870; became, 1870, Dane prof. law and dean law faculty, Harvard; emeritus. Author: Selection of Cases on the Law of Contracts; Cases on Sales; Summary of Law of Contracts and Equity Pleading; Cases in Equity Pleading; etc. Address: Cambridge, Mass. Died 1906.

LANGDON, Andrew, mfr.; b. New Marlboro, Mass.; s. John Le Droit and Jerusha (Stillman) L.; ed. Lenox (Mass.) Acad.; m. Alice Blunt Woodward, Aug. 29, 1866 (died 1896); m. 2d, Harriet Studebaker, Nov. 25, 1903 (died 1909). V.p. Buffalo Gen. Electric Co.; v.p. and chmn. exec. com. Gen. Ry. Signal Co. (Rochester, N.Y.); dir. Niagara Falls Heat, Light & Power Co., Buffalo Foundry Co., Federal Telephone & Telegraph Co., Frontier Telephone & Telegraph Co., Inter-Ocean Telegraph Co., Commonwealth Trust Co. Park commr. City of Buffalo, 4 yrs.; grade crossing commr. 5 yrs.; v.p. Homœ. Hosp. Pres. Buffalo Hist. Soc., 1893—; v.p. Buffalo Soc. Nat. Sciences. Gave bronze doors to Buffalo Hist. Soc., bronze statue of David, in Delaware Park, Buffalo. Home: Buffalo, N.Y. Died Nov. 11, 1919.

LANGDON, Courtney, university prof.; b. Rome, Italy, Jan. 18, 1861; s. William Chauncy and Hannah Agnes (Courtney) L.; ed. Florence, Italy, Geneva, Switzerland, and Mr. Noble's Sch., Boston; student Harvard, 1878-81; hon. A.B., Brown, 1891; m. Susan Hayward Taft, Aug. 1, 1894. Instr. modern langs., Lehigh U., 1882-84; pvt. tutor Baltimore, 1884-86; instr. Romance langs., Cornell, 1886-90; asst. prof. modern langs., 1890-92, asso. prof. Romance langs. and lits., 1892-99, prof., 1899—, Brown U. Author: Sonnets on the War, 1917; The Divine Comedy of Dante Alighieri, the Italian text with a transl. in English blank verse and a commentary Vol. I, Inferno, 1918, Vol. II, Purgatorio, 1920, Vol. III, Paradiso, 1921. Address: Providence, R.I. Died Nov. 19, 1924.

LANGDON, Frank Warren, M.D.; b. Cincinnati, O., Dec. 1852; s. Oliver Cromwell and Jane Dorsey (Aydelott) L.; ed. pub. schs., and pvt. tutors; M.D., Miami Med. Coll., 1881; post-grad. studies at London and Paris; m. Rhoda Alice Fletcher, 1884; children—Fletcher, Rowena Lan Franco (dec.). Practiced in Cincinnati, O., specializing in consultations in nervous and mental diseases; consultant on staff various hosps.; emeritus prof. psychiatry, Coll. Medicine, U. of Cincinnati. Consultant in neuro-psychiatry, U.S. Veteran's Bur., Dist. 7. Mem. A.M.A. (chmn. sect. nervous and mental diseases, 1902-03), Acad. Medicine Cincinnati (pres. 1907), Neurol. Soc. Cincinnati (pres. 1919-20). Author: The Aphasias and Their Medico-Legal Relations, 1898. Died June 9, 1933.

LANGDON, Loomis Lyman, army officer; b. Buffalo, N.Y., Oct. 25, 1830; s. George W. and Sarah (Russell) L.; pub. and pvt. schs. and grad. U.S. Mil. Acad., 1854. Bvt. 2d lt. 4th Arty., July 1, 1854; 2d lt. 1st Arty., Aug. 31, 1854; 1st lt., July 13, 1860; capt., Aug. 28, 1861; maj. 2d Arty., Mar. 20, 1879; lt. col., Dec. 1, 1883; col. 1st Arty., Jan. 25, 1889; retired by operation of law, Oct. 25, 1894; advanced to rank of brig. gen. retired, by act of Apr. 23, 1904. Bvtd. maj., Feb. 20, 1864, for gallant and meritorious services in battle of Olustee, Fla.; lt. col., Sept. 29, 1864, for same in attack on Ft. Gilmer, Va. Occasional corr. for newspapers; studied painting, Nat. Gallery, London, 1903-04. Author of sketches, stories, etc. Address: Brooklyn, N.Y. Died 1910.

LANGDON, Stephen Herbert, Assyriologist; b. Monroe, Mich., May 8, 1876; s. George Knowles and Abigail Elizabeth (Hassinger) L.; A.B., U. of Mich., 1898; A.M., 1899 (Phi Beta Kappa); B.D., Union Theol. Sem., 1903; Ph.D., Columbia, 1904; internat. fellow, Sorbonne and Collège de France, Paris, 1904-07; studied U. of Leipzig, 1907-08; M.A., Oxford, 1910; m. May Adelaide, d. Thomas Gregory, Nov. 28, 1925. Deacon, Ch. of Eng., Paris, 1905; Shillito prof. Assyriology, Oxford U., Eng., 1908—. Asso. editor Babyloniaca, Paris, 1908-14; curator in Univ. Mus., Phila., Babylonian sect., 1916-18; dir. Oxford and Field Museum Expedition in Mesopotamia, 1923-32. Author: (or editor) Annals of Asurbanipal, 1905; Les Inscriptions du Wadi Brisa, 1905; Babylonia and Palestine, 1906; La Syntaxe du Verbe Sumerian, 1907; Sumerian and Babylonian Psalms, 1909; A Sumerian Grammar and Chrestomathy, 1911; Neu-Babylonische Königsinschriften, 1912; Babylonian Liturgies, 1912; Tammuz and Ishtar, 1914; Sumerian Epical and Liturgical Texts, 1915-17; Le Poeme Sumerian du Paradis, 1919; Sumerian Liturgies and Psalms, 1919; Babylonian Wisdom, 1922; Oxford Editions of Cuneiform Texts, 1923—; Babylonian Epic of Creation, 1924; Excavations at Kish (Vol. 1), 1925; History of Sumer and Accad, in Cambridge Ancient History, Vol. I, 1923; Babylonian Penitential Psalms, 1927; Reisen und Ausgrabungen in Babylonien nach 1914, Alte Orient, 1927; Pictographic Inscriptions of Jemdet Nasr, 1929; Semitic Mythology, 1931; The Poem of Etana, 1931. Lecturer British Acad. and College de France, 1933. Home: Oxford, Eng. Died May 19, 1937.

LANGDON, William Henry, judge; b. Alameda County, Calif., Sept. 25, 1873; s. William and Anne (Moran) L.; grad. San Jose State Normal, 1892; A.B., San Jose State Teachers Coll., 1934; LL.D., Loyola U., Los Angeles, Calif., 1936; m. Myrtle McHenry, Apr. 20, 1908; children—Merl, Lois Ann, Lawton William. Admitted to Calif. bar, 1896, and began practice at San Francisco; supt. pub. schs., San Francisco, 1903-06; dist. atty., San Francisco, 1906-10; pres. Calif. State Bd. of Edn., 1913-16; judge Superior Court, Stanislaus Co., Calif., 1915-19; presiding justice Dist. Court of Appeals, 1919-27; justice Supreme Court of Calif., 1927—; pres. Langdonmerl Co., G. P. Schafer Co. Trustee Fresno State Teachers Coll., 1913-15; mem. Calif. State Land Settlement Bd., 1916-19. Republican. Catholic. As dist. atty. San Francisco conducted graft prosecutions which resulted in removal of mayor and supervisors from office. Home: Hillsborough, Calif. Died Aug. 10, 1939.

LANGDON, Woodbury, merchant; b. Portsmouth, N.H., Oct. 22, 1836; s. Woodbury and Frances C. L.; ed. Portsmouth High Sch.; m. Elizabeth Langdon Elwyn, Sept. 5, 1896. Dry goods mcht., Boston, 1863-68; mem. firm Joy, Langdon & Co., 1868—; pres. and dir. Cannelton Coal Co.; trustee N.Y. Life Ins. Co., N.Y. Trust Co., Title Guarantee & Trust Co.; dir. Nat. Bank of Commerce, German Alliance Ins. Co., German-Am. Ins. Co., Hudson Trust Co., Citizens' Central Nat. Bank, Associated Merchants' Co., Brighton Yarn Co. Served on com. of 70, 1894. Home: New York, N.Y. Died Oct. 24, 1921.

LANGE, Alexis Frederick, educator; b. Lafayette County, Mo., Apr. 23, 1862; s. Alexander and Caroline (Schnegelsiepen) L.; A.B., A.M., U. of Mich., 1885, Ph.D., 1892; U. of Marburg, 1887-88; m. Carolyn Crosby Penny, Sept. 8, 1891. Instr. English, 1888-89, German and Anglo-Saxon, 1889-90, U. of Mich.; asst. prof. English, 1890-97, jr. prof., 1897-1900, prof. English and Scandinavian philology, 1900-07, dean Coll. of Letters, 1897-1909, dean Grad. Sch., 1909-10, dean of faculties (univ. dean), 1910-13, prof. edn., 1907—, and dir. Sch. of Edn., 1913—, U. of Calif. Author: Herbart's Outlines of Pedagogical Doctrine (with Charles de Garmo), 1900; Deloney's Gentle Craft, 1903. Editor: Dekker's Shoemaker's Holiday. Address: Berkeley, Calif. Died Aug. 28, 1924.

LANGERFELDT, Theodore Otto, artist; b. Buckeburg, Schaumburg-Lippe, Germany, Mar. 2, 1841; s. Carl and Augusta L.; studied architecture at Polytechnic School, Hanover; studied and practiced art, 1863-68, in London; in Boston, 1868—. Architectural paintings in water-colors. Address: Boston, Mass. Died 1906.

LANGFITT, William Campbell, army officer; b. Wellsburg, Va., Aug. 10, 1860; s. Obadiah and Virginia (Tarr) L.; grad. U.S. Mil. Acad., 1883, Engr. Sch. of Application, Willetts Point, N.Y., 1886; m. Anne St. John Bemis, Dec. 4, 1886; 1 dau., Dorothy. Commd. 2d lt. engrs., June 13, 1883; brig. gen. N.A., Aug. 5, 1917; maj. gen. N.A., Dec. 17, 1917; major gen. U.S.A., retired, June 21, 1930. Engr. office Dept. of Columbia, 1886-88; river and harbor improvements, Galveston, Tex., 1888-93; improvement of Ohio River and tributaries, 1893-95; instr. Engr. Sch., 1895-98; comd. U.S. forces in H.I., 1898-99; in charge river and harbor improvements, defenses, and engr. 13th Light House Dist., Portland, Ore., 1899-1905; comdr. Engr. Sch. and Depot, Washington Barracks, D.C., 1905-06 and 1907-10; chief engr. Army of Cuban Pacification, 1906-07; river and harbor improvements and water supply, Washington, D.C., 1910-14; river and harbor improvements and div. engr., S.E. Div., Savannah, Ga., 1914-16; chief engr. officer, Southern Dept., including ry. operations, 1916-17; organized 13th Engrs., May-Aug. 1917; joined A.E.F. in France, Aug. 1917; chief of staff, Aug. 24, 1917; apptd. mgr. light rys., Sept. 14, 1917; in charge of all Am. forces on duty with British Army, Oct. 15, 1917; chief of utilities, in charge of transportation, Dept. of Constrn. and Forestry, Dept. of Light Rys. and Roads, and Motor Transportation Dept., Mar. 12, 1918; chief engr. A.E.F., in charge of mil. engring. and engr. supplies, constrn. and forestry, light rys. and roads, July 10, 1918; dist. engr., 2d N.Y. Dist. and Puerto Rico Dist., Aug. 5, 1919; div. engr., N.E. Div., N.Y. City, Aug. 14, 1919-20. D.S.M. (U.S.); Comdr. Legion of Honor (French); Companion Most Honorable Order of the Bath (English); Comdr. Order of Crown (Belgian). Home: Geneva, N.Y. Died Apr. 20, 1934.

LANGFORD, Nathaniel Pitt, banker; b. Westmoreland, N.Y., Aug. 9, 1832; s. George and Chloe (Sweeting) L.; ed. country dist. sch.; m. Emma C. Wheaton, Nov. 1, 1876; m. 2d, Clara Wheaton, Sept. 17, 1884. Left St. Paul, June 16, 1862, for Oregon gold fields; camped on Grasshopper Creek, then in Dak. (now Mont.). When Mont. was organized as territory, May 26, 1864, was apptd. collector internal revenue; held office until Nov. 1868; apptd. by President Johnson, Jan. 1869, gov. of Mont., but not confirmed, senate refusing to confirm any more presidential appmts. during Johnson's term. One of Washburn party, 1870, which discovered geysers of Yellowstone Nat. Park; led in work which resulted in dedication of the park and was its supt., 1872-77; Nat. Bank Examiner for Pacific Coast, 1872-84; dir. Bd. Control, St. Paul. Republican. Grand Master Mont. Masons, 1870. Author: Vigilante Days and Ways, 1890. Address: St. Paul, Minn. Died 1911.

LANGLEY, John Wesley, congressman; b. Floyd County, Ky.; ed. pub. schs.; grad. law depts. of Georgetown, National, and Columbian univs., LL.B., LL.M., D.C.L., Master of Diplomacy; m. Katherine, d. Hon. James M. Gudger, Jr., 1904. Was clerk in Pension Office, mem. bd. pension appeals, and disbursing and appmt. clerk, Census Office; mem. Ky. Ho. of Rep., 2 terms; del. to 3 Rep. nat. convs.; mem. 60th to 68th Congresses (1907-25), 10th Ky. Dist. Home: Pikeville, Ky. Died Jan. 17, 1932.

LANGLEY, Samuel Pierpont, astronomer and physicist, Sec. the Smithsonian Instn., 1887—; b. Roxbury, Boston, Aug. 22, 1834; grad. Boston High School; D.C.L., Oxford; D.Sc., Cambridge, Eng.; LL.D., Harvard, Princeton, Yale, U. of Wis.; U. of Mich.; Ph.D., Stevens Inst. Tech. Practiced architecture and civ. engring.; asst. Harvard Observatory, 1865; later asst. prof. mathematics U.S. Naval Acad.; dir. Allegheny Observatory, 1867, where, 1869, he founded the system of railway time service from observatories, which has since become general, and where he devised the bolometer, now in general use, and other apparatus. Organized expdn. to Mt. Whitney, 1881, where he reëstablished the solar constant and discovered an entirely unsuspected extension of the invisible solar spectrum. Has carried out extended expts. on the problem of mech. flight. Established Astrophysical Observatory and the Nat. Zoöl. Park, Washington. Mem. Nat. Acad. of Sciences. Has been awarded Janssen medal, Inst. of France; Rumford medal of the Royal Soc. of London, and of Am. Acad. Arts and Sciences; Henry Draper medal, Nat. Acad. Sciences, etc., and numerous others. Author: The New Astronomy; Researches on Solar Heat; Experiments in Aërodynamics; Internal Work of the Wind; On the Possible Variation of the Solar Radiation, 1905. Trustee Carnegie Instn. Address: Washington, D.C. Died 1906.

LANGSDORF, William Bell, educator; b. nr. Mechanicsburg, Pa., Feb. 20, 1866; s. A. S. and Wilhelmina (Bell) L.; A.B., Dickinson Coll., 1887, A.M., 1890; U. of Leipzig, 1890-92, 1893; Oxford U., Eng., 1892; Rome and Paris, 1893; grad. Lane Theol. Sem., 1902; Ph.D., Washington and Jefferson Coll., 1897; Litt.D., Hanover Coll., 1897; m. Julia May, d. David S. Tappan, July 11, 1900; children—Wilhelmina, Helen Julia, William Bell, David Stanton. Teacher Asbury Park, N.J., 1887-89; prof. Latin and Greek, Poughkeepsie (N.Y.) Mil. Coll., 1889-90; prof. Latin lang. and lit., Miami U., 1893-1902; ordained Presbyn. ministry, 1902; missionary Presbyn. Bd. Foreign Missions in Japan, 1902-09; dean and prof. Latin lang. and lit., Westminster (Colo.) Coll., 1909-11; pastor Calvary Ch., Los Angeles, Calif., 1911-13. Commr. 107th Gen. Assembly of Presbyn. Ch. (North), 1895. Translator of Seneca's Tranquillity of Mind, and Providence. Editor and propr. of "Fukuin Geppo" (a Japanese monthly), 1903-09. Address: Pasadena, Calif. Died Feb. 8, 1940.

LANGTON, Daniel Webster, landscape architect; b. Kemper County, Miss., May 5, 1864; s. Daniel Webster and Emma (Nelson) L.; grad. U. of Ala., 1882, Ph.D., 1891; m. Berenice Francis, Aug. 17, 1896. Asst. Geol. Survey of Ala., 1883-89; asst. prof. chemistry, U. of Ala., 1889; consulting geologist Chesapeake & Ohio Ry. Co., 1889-93. Author: Report on the Geology of Southeast Alabama, State Geol. Survey, 1890; also geol. papers, Silliman's Jour., 1885-89; Bull. Geol. Soc., America, 1889. Home: Morristown, N.J. Died 1909.

LANGTRY, Albert Perkins, editor; b. Wakefield, Mass., July 27, 1860; s. Joseph and Sarah (Lakin) L.; ed. Newton, Mass.; m. Sarah C. Spear, Aug. 3, 1886. Editor and pub. Springfield (Mass.) Union, 1890—. Dir. Associated Press, 1902—. Mem. Rep. State Com., 1902-10; mem. Mass. Ho. of Rep., 1909-10; sec. Commonwealth of Mass. 8 yrs.; chmn. commn. to build extension to State House, 1913. Republican. Author; Traitors to the Church. Editor of History of Greater Boston. Author of the direct primary law in Mass. Home: Springfield, Mass. Died Aug. 27, 1939.

LANGWORTHY, Charles Ford, chemist; b. Middlebury, Vt., Aug. 9, 1864; s. Charles Parker and Ann Elizabeth (Ford) L.; A.B., Middlebury Coll., 1887, A.M., 1890, D.Sc., 1912; Ph.D., Emperor Wilhelm U., Strassburg, 1893; unmarried. Asst. and instr. chemistry, Wesleyan U., Conn., 1893-95; asso. editor Experiment Station Record, 1895-1924; chief of nutrition investigations, Dept. of Agr., 1905-15; chief of Office of Home Economics, 1915-23, specialist Bur. of Home Economics, 1923, 29, U.S. Dept. of Agr. Author: Digest of Metabolism Experiments (with late W. O. Atwater); Occurrence of Aluminium (with late Peter T. Austen). Writer of and contbr. to bulls. Dept. Agr.; contbr. to New Internat. Ency., 1902-03; Ency. Americana, etc. Home: Washington, D.C. Died 1932.

LANHAM, Samuel Willis Tucker, gov. Texas, 1903-07; b. Spartanburg, S.C., July 4, 1846; s. James Madison and Louisa (Tucker) L.; common school edn.; entered C.S.A. when a boy and served in 3d S.C. regt.; m. Sarah B. Meng, Sept. 4, 1866. Removed to Tex., 1866; admitted to bar, 1869. Was dist. atty. 13th dist.; presidential elector, 1880; mem. Congress, 1883-93, and 1895-1903, 8th Tex. dist. Democrat. Home: Weatherford, Tex. Died 1908.

LANIER, Charles, banker; b. Madison, Ind., Jan. 19, 1837; s. James F. D. and Elizabeth G. L.; ed. Russell's Mil. Sch., New Haven, Conn.; m. Sarah E. Egleston, Oct. 7, 1857 (dec.). Became mem. firm Winslow, Lanier & Co., bankers, at 23, sr. mem., 1860—; pres. Pittsburgh, Ft. Wayne & Chicago Ry. Co., Massillon & Cleveland R.R.; trustee Central Union Trust Co.; dir. Southern Ry Co. Home: New York, N.Y. Died Mar. 7, 1926.

LANIER, Clifford Anderson, author; b. Griffin, Ga., Apr. 24, 1844; s. Robert S. and Mary J. (Anderson) L.; ed. Oglethorpe Coll., Midway, Ga.; m. Wilhelmina Clopton, Nov. 26, 1867. Left coll. at end of sophomore yr. Being too young to be Southern soldier, in 1861, volunteered as Ga. soldier, April 1862; served in Va.; became signal officer of Blockade Runner Talisman, Oct. 1864; wrecked Dec. 1864; went to Bermuda and Cuba; supt. of City of Montgomery schools, 1885; is real estate owner. Author: Thorn Fruit (novel); The Mate's Race with the Banshees; The Doctor's Legend. Wrote: Love and Loyalty at War, and other stories; Dialect Poems, by Sidney and Clifford Lanier (in Poems of Sidney Lanier); Apollo and Keats on Browning, and Other Verses, 1902. Home: Montgomery, Ala. Deceased.

LANING, Harris, naval officer; b. Petersburg, Ill., Oct. 18, 1873; s. Caleb Barrett and Mary Esther (Harris) L.; prep. edn., Peekskill Mil. Acad.; grad. U.S. Naval Acad., 1895; m. Mabel Clare Nixon, July 24, 1900; 1 dau., Hester Marie. Commd. ensign, U.S.N., May 19, 1891; advanced through grades to rear adm. Served on U.S.S. Philadelphia, Oregon and Mohican, 1895-98; served on U.S.S. Monadnock and comdr. U.S.S. Panay, Philippine Insurrection; with dept. English and law, U.S. Naval Acad., 1900-02; on U.S.S. Dolphin, 1902-05; in dept. ordnance and gunnery U.S. Naval Acad., 1905-07; navigation officer U.S.S. Nebraska in cruise around world with Battle Fleet, 1907-10; in charge athletics and head of dept. of navigation, U.S. Naval Acad., 1910-13; comdr. U.S.S. Cassin and Reserve Destroyer Flotilla, 1913-16; with chief of Naval Operations, later in charge officer personnel div., Bureau of Navigation, asst. chief of bureau and acting chief, World War; chief of staff, Destroyer Force, U.S. Fleet, 1919-21; student, later head of dept. of tactics, Naval War Coll., 1921-24; comdr. U.S.S. Pennsylvania, 1924-26, U.S. Naval Training Sta., San Diego, Calif., 1926-27; apptd. chief of staff, U.S. Battle Fleet, 1927; comdr. Battleship Div. Two, U.S. Fleet, 1928-30; pres. U.S. Naval War Coll., 1930-33; comdr. cruisers, U.S. Fleet, with rank of vice admiral, 1933-35, comdr. Battle Force, with rank of admiral, 1935-36; comdt. Third Naval Dist. and comdt. United States Navy Yard, New York, 1936-37; retired, 1937; gov. U.S. Naval Home, Phila., 1937—. Decorated with Navy D.S.C.; campaign medals, Spanish-Am. War, Philippine Campaign, China Relief Expdn., Mexican Campaign, Dominican Campaign, World War (all U.S.); Order of Avis (Portugal); gold medal, as capt. of the United States Rifle Team winning first place in the Olympic Games, Stockholm, 1912. Episcopalian. Mason. Home: Petersburg, Ill. Died Feb. 2, 1941.

LANKFORD, Menalcus, congressman; b. Southampton County, Va., Mar. 14, 1883; s. Dr. Livius and Mary Conway (Burnley) L.; A.B., U. of Richmond, 1904; LL.B., U. of Va., 1906; m. Nancy Waddill, Apr. 14, 1909. Admitted to Va. bar, 1906, and began practice at Norfolk; mem. firm Wolcott, Wolcott & Lankford, 1914—. Rep. candidate for Congress, 1920, 24; mem. 71st and 72d Congresses (1929-33), 2d Va. Dist. Referee in bankruptcy Eastern Dist. Va., 1933—. Ensign Naval Aviation, World War. Baptist. Mason. Home: Norfolk, Va. Died Dec. 27, 1937.

LANMAN, Charles Rockwell, Orientalist; b. Norwich, Conn., July 8, 1850; s. Peter and Catharine (Cook) L.; A.B., Yale, 1871, Ph.D., 1873; grad. student Greek under Hadley, Sanskrit under Whitney; studied Sanskrit under Weber, Berlin, and Roth, Tübingen, and comparative grammar under Curtius and Leskien, Leipzig, 1873-76; LL.D., Yale University, 1902; LL.D., Univ. of Aberdeen, 1906; m. Mary B. Hinckley, July 18, 1888 (died 1936); children—Faith Trumbull (Mrs. T. B. Hine), Thomas Hinckley, Edith Hamilton, Jonathan Trumbull (dec.), Katharine Mary (Mrs. J. Winlock), Esther Cook (Mrs. Robert A. Cushman). Teacher of Sanskrit, Johns Hopkins U., 1876-80; prof. Sanskrit, Harvard, 1880—. Percy Turnbull lecturer on poetry of India, Johns Hopkins, 1898; lecturer Lowell Inst., Boston, 1898; traveled in India, 1889, and acquired valuable books and about 500 manuscripts (Sanskrit and Prakrit) for Harvard. Mem. Philol. Assn. (sec. and editor 5 vols. trans. and proc., 1879-83, pres. 1890), Am. Oriental Soc. (joint editor of jour. and proc. about 15 yrs., corr. sec., 1884-94; v.p. 1897-1907, pres. 1907, reëlected 1919), The Omar Khayyam Club of America (pres. 1921); hon. or corr. mem. many foreign socs. Author: Noun-Inflection in the Veda, 1880; Sanskrit Reader, Vocabulary, Notes, 8 issues, 1884-1927; Rajaçekhara's Karpura Mañjari, Hindu Drama, from Prakrit into English, with Notes, 1900; Beginnings of Hindu Pantheism, 1890. Editor: (with coöperation of various scholars) Harvard Oriental Series (38 vols. printed); Jataka Mala, Buddhist Sanskrit stories (Kern of Leiden); Vijnana Bhikshu's Sankhya Philosophy (Garbe of Tübingen); Buddhism in Translations (Warren of Cambridge, Mass.); Brihad Devata, Myths of Rig-Veda (Macdonell of Oxford); Whitney's Commentary on Atharva-Veda, with transl. (2 vols. revised and completed by Lanman); Little Clay Cart, Sanskrit drama, transl. (Ryder of Berkeley, Calif.); Vedic Concordance (Bloomfield of Johns Hopkins); Kashmirian and Jaina Panchatantra, ancient Hindu tales (Hertel of Leipzig); Bharavi (Cappeller of Jena); Shakuntala (Pischel of Berlin); Yoga System (Woods of Harvard); Black Yajur Veda transl. (Keith of H. M. Colonial Office); Rama's Later History, drama by Bhavabhuti (Belvalkar of Poona, India); Rig-Veda Repetitions (Bloomfield); Rig-Veda Brahmanas (Keith); Vikrama's Adventures (2 vols., Edgerton of U. of Pa.); Buddhist Legends (3 vols., Burlingame of Yale); Religion and Philosophy of Veda and Upanishads (2 vols., Keith); Rig-Veda transl. (3 vols., Geldner of Marburg); Buddha-ghosa's Buddhism (2 vols.); Buddha's Teachings, being the Sutta-Nipata, Pali and English (Lord Chalmers, Master of Peterhouse, Cambridge). Hon. mem. Research Soc. of Bihar (Buddha's native land), 1934. Awarded Japanese Medal, one of 8 bestowed on foreign (non-Japanese) scholars at celebration of 2,500th anniversary of Buddha's birth. Home: Cambridge, Mass. Died Feb. 20, 1941.

LANNING, William Mershon, judge; b. Ewing Tp., Mercer County, N.J., Jan. 1, 1849; grad. Lawrenceville (N.J.) Sch., 1866; m. Jennie Hemenway, Aug. 3, 1881. Taught dist. schs. of Mercer County, 1866-72, in the old Trenton Acad., 1872-78; admitted to bar, Nov. 1880; admitted as counsellor at law, 1883; city solicitor of Trenton, 1883-87; judge City Dist. Ct., Trenton, 1887-91; was mem. of the spl. commn. that framed township laws of N.J.; mem. Constl. Commn., 1894; elected to 58th Congress (1903-05), resigned, June 1904; U.S. dist. judge, Dist. of N.J., 1904-09; U.S. circuit judge, 3d Circuit, 1909—. Republican. Men. bd. mgrs. Trenton Savings Fund Soc.; dir. Mechanics Nat. Bank, Trenton. Trustee Gen. Assembly Presbyn. Ch. in U.S.A.; dir. Princeton Theol. Sem.; trustee Lawrenceville Sch. Author: Help for Township Officers, 1885. Address: Trenton, N.J. Died 1912.

LANSDEN, Dick Latta, judge; b. Bakers Cross Roads, Tenn., May 15, 1869; s. Hugh Hill and Lee Ann (McGee) L.; Doyle (Tenn.) Coll., 3 yrs.; m. Helen Snodgrass, Nov. 16, 1895. Admitted to bar, 1893; practiced at Sparta, Tenn., 1893-97, Crossville, Tenn., 1897-1902; chancellor 4th Jud. Div., Tenn., 1902-10; justice Supreme Ct. Tenn., 1910—, chief justice, 1918—. Democrat. Presbyn. Trustee pub. schs., Cookeville, U. of Harriman. Mason, Odd Fellow, K.P. Home: Nashville, Tenn. Died Aug. 16, 1924.

LANSING, Robert, secretary of state; b. Watertown, N.Y., Oct. 17, 1864; s. John and Maria L. (Dodge) L.; A.B., Amherst, 1886; LL.D., Amherst, 1915, Colgate, 1915, Princeton, 1917, Columbia, 1918, Union, 1918, U. State of N.Y., 1919, Kenyon, 1925; m. Eleanor, d. John W. Foster (sec. of state in cabinet of President Harrison), Jan. 15, 1890. Admitted to bar, 1889; mem. firm Lansing & Lansing, 1889-1907. Asso. counsel for U.S. in Behring Sea Arbitration, 1892-93; counsel for U.S., Behring Sea Claims Commn., 1896-97; solicitor and counsel for U.S. before the Alaskan Boundary Tribunal, 1903; counsel, North Atlantic Coast Fisheries Arbitration at The Hague, 1909-10; agent of U.S., Am. and British Claims Arbitration, 1912-14; counselor for Dept. of State, Mar. 20, 1914-June 23, 1915; secretary of state in cabinet of President Wilson, June 23, 1915-Feb. 13, 1920; mem. firm Lansing & Woolsey, 1920—; counsel for Chinese Govt.; counsel for Chile in Tacna-Arica Arbitration, 1923-25. Mem. Am. Commn. to Negotiate Peace, 1918-19. Trustee (v.p.) Carnegie Endowment for Internat. Peace. Author: Government, Its Origin, Growth and Form in the United States (with Gary M. Jones), 1902; The Peace Negotiations, 1921; The Big Four and Others of the Peace Conference, 1921; Notes on

Sovereignty, 1921. Asso. editor American Journal International Law. Home: Washington, D.C. Died Oct. 30, 1928.

LANSTRUM, Oscar Monroe, editor; b. Galesburg, Ill., Nov. 26, 1869; s. Christian E. and Susan Elizabeth (Crocker) L.; A.B., Knox Coll., 1891, A.M., 1894; M.D., Coll. Phys. & Surg., Chicago, 1894; m. Lillian Gertrude Conrad, Dec. 18, 1897; children—Claude Conrad, Fred Crocker, Philip Monroe. Practiced in Chicago, 1894-95; moved to Marysville, Mont., 1895; mng. editor Montana Daily Record, Helena, 1904—; v.p. Mont. Life Ins. Co. (Helena), Columbia Basin Irrigation League. Mem. Mont. Ho. of Rep., 2 terms, 1903-05; chmn. Rep. Co. Central Com., 1906, State Central Com., 1908; chmn. exec. com. State Central Com., 1910; chmn. Mont. delegation Rep. Nat. Conv., Chicago, 1912; Rep. nominee for U.S. Senate, 1918; mem. Rep. Nat. Com. from Mont. Trustee Knox Coll., Shriners' Hosps. for Crippled Children. Lutheran. Mason. Home: Helena, Mont. Died June 20, 1928.

LANTZ, David Ernest, biologist; b. Thompsontown, Pa., Mar. 1, 1855; s. John King and Margaret (Fry) L.; ed. State Normal Sch., Bloomsburg, Pa.; m. Clara Deen, Mar. 5, 1878. Prin. schs., Mifflintown, Pa., 1876-78; supt. schools, Manhattan, Kan., 1878-83; prof. mathematics, Kan. State Agrl. Coll., 1883-97; prin. Dickinson Co. (Kan.) High Sch., 1898-1900; field agt. Kan. Agrl. Expt. Sta., 1901-04; asst. biologist, U.S. Dept. of Agriculture, 1904—. Methodist. Life mem. Kan. Acad. of Science (sec., 1899-1901, pres., 1898-99). Mason. Home: Washington, D.C. Died Oct. 7, 1918.

LANZA, Gaetano, engineer, b. Boston, Mass., Sept. 26, 1848; s. Gaetano and Mary Ann (Paddock) L.; C.E., 1869, B.Sc., 1870, C.E., M.E., 1870, U. of Va.; m. Jennie D. Miller, Jan. 27, 1891 (died 1923). Asst. instr. mathematics, U. of Va., 1870-72; instr. and asst. prof., 1872-75, prof. theoretical and applied mechanics, 1875-1911, in charge dept. mech. engring., 1883-1911, prof. emeritus, 1911, Mass. Inst. Tech.; special consultant Baldwin Locomotive Works. Fellow Am. Acad. Arts and Sciences. Created Cavaliere dell Ordine dei Santi Maurizio e Lazzaro of Italy, 1907. Author: Applied Mechanics, 1885-1905; Dynamics of Machinery, 1911. Home: Philadelphia, Pa. Died 1928.

LAPHAM, John Raymond, prof. civil engring.; b. West Medway, Mass., Apr. 1, 1886; s. Frank D. and Alfarata (Scott) L.; B.S., Brown U., 1909; M.S., Pa. State Coll., 1916; m. Evelyn M. Ayres, Aug. 16, 1916; children—Evelyn, John R. In construction department N.Y.,N.H.&H. R.R., 1901-11; asst. to instr. in civil engring., Pa. State Coll., 1911-16; asst. prof. civil engring., George Washington U., 1916-19, prof., 1919—, dean Sch. of Engring., 1927—. Home: Washington, D.C. Died Oct. 2, 1939.

LAPHAM, Oscar, congressman; b. Burrillville, R.I., June 29, 1837; s. Duty and Lucinda (Wheelock) L.; first lt., adj. and capt. 12th R.I. Vols. in Civil War; a.d.c. brigade staff; served in Army of Potomac and Dept. of the Ohio, in Ky.; A.B., Brown U., 1864, A.M., 1867; m. Clara Louise Paine, June 20, 1876. Admitted to bar, 1867, and practiced at Providence, R.I. Mem. R.I. Senate, 1887-88; treas. Dem. State Central Com., 1887-91; Dem. candidate for Congress, 1882, 86, 88; elected to 52d and 53d Congresses (1891-95). Col. United Train of Arty. (an ancient mil. organization in R.I.). Trustee Brown U., 1890—(mem. exec. com.); corporator of R.I. and Butler hospitals. Democrat. Home: Providence, R.I. Died Mar. 29, 1926.

LAPLACE, Ernest, surgeon; b. New Orleans, La., July 9, 1861; s. Basil and Eugenie (Sauvage) L.; A.B., Georgetown Coll., 1880, A.M., 1887, LL.D., 1895; M.D., U. of La., 1884, and Faculté de Médécine of Paris, 1886; pupil of Pasteur, Lister, Koch, and Billroth; m. Catherine Borsch, 1902. Prof. surgery, Medico-Chirurg. Coll., Phila., 1892—; prof. surgery, Grad. Sch. of Medicine U. of Pa. Surgeon to Phila., Medico-Chirurg., Polyclinic, and Misericordia hosps.; consulting surgeon State Hosp. for Criminal Insane. Lt. col. Med. R.C. Inventor of first forceps for Intestinal Anastomosis. Officier d' Académie (Palmes Académiques), Paris, 1903; Comdr. Legion of Honor, France; Comdr. Order of Saint Gregory the Great. Address: Philadelphia, Pa. Died May 15, 1924.

LAPSLEY, Robert Alberti, clergyman, editor; b. Selma, Ala., Oct. 18, 1858; s. James Woods and Sara Eliza (Pratt) L.; A.B., Davidson (N.C.) Coll., 1877; Columbia (S.C.) Theol. Sem., 1877-78, 1879-80, Union Theol. Sem., Hampden-Sidney, Va., 1880-81; D.D., Presbyn. Coll. of S.C., 1913; m. Eugenia Browne, Aug. 31, 1881 (died 1901); children—Robert Alberti, Mary Vermelle, James Woods, Horatio Browne, Sara Pratt, Genie Browne, Samuel Norvell; m. 2d, Vermelle McCutchen, Apr. 26, 1905 (died 1918); children—Alberti Fraser, Irene McCutchen, George McIver. Ordained ministry Presbyn. Ch. in U.S., 1881; pastor Lauderdale St. Ch., Memphis, Tenn., 1881-82, Ebenezer Ch., Charleston, S.C., 1882-85, Vine Hill, Ala., 1885-88, Anniston, Ala., 1888-91; evangelist, N. Ala. Presbytery, 1891-92; pastor Bethel Ch., nr. Greenville, Va., 1892-1904, Ashland, 1904-12; editor-in-chief S.S. lesson lit. of Southern Presbyn. Ch., 1903-22; editor Adult Quarterly, and Home Department Quarterly, 1922—. Author: The Songs of Zion, 1925, 26; The Book of the Witnesses for Jesus, 1931. Home: Richmond, Va. Died Mar. 23, 1934.

LARABEE, Frank Sheridan, flour mfr.; b. Ashford, N.Y., Feb. 25, 1864; s. Joseph Delos and Angeline (Oyer) L.; B.A., Hamilton Coll., N.Y., 1886; m. Pearl Bridwell, Dec. 4, 1888. Associated with father and bro. in organizing Farmers State Bank, Stafford, Kan., 1886; with bro., Fred D., entered flour milling business at Stafford, 1888; built first Portland cement plant in Mexico, 1913; wheat raiser on large scale in Kan.; pres. Larabee Flour Mills Corp., Farmers Nat. Bank, Stafford; dir. Highway Oil Refining Co. (Okla.), Farmers State Bank (Belpre, Kan.), Ford County State Bank (Spearville, Kan.). Republican. Home: Kansas City, Mo. Died June 8, 1921.

LARDNER, Ring W., writer; b. Niles, Mich, Mar. 6, 1885; s. Henry and Lena Bogardus (Phillips) L.; grad. Niles High Sch., 1901; Armour Inst. Tech., Chicago, 1901-02; m. Ellis Abbott, June 28, 1911; children—John Abbott, James Phillips, Ring W., David Ellis. Reporter, South Bend (Ind.) Times, 1905-07; successively sporting writer Chicago Inter-Ocean, Chicago Examiner and Chicago Tribune, 1907-10; editor, Sporting News, St. Louis, 1910-11; sporting writer, Boston American, Feb.-Oct. 1911, Chicago American, 1911-12, Chicago Examiner, 1912-13, Chicago Tribune, 1913-19; writer for Bell syndicate, 1919—. Republican. Episcopalian. Author: Bib Ballads, 1915; You Know Me, Al, 1915; Gullible's Travels, 1917; Own Your Own Home, 1917; Treat 'Em Rough, 1918; The Real Dope, 1918; My Four Weeks in France, 1918; The Young Immigrunts, 1919; Symptoms of Being 35, 1921; The Big Town, 1921; How to Write Short Stories, 1924; What of It?, 1925; The Love Nest, 1926; The Story of a Wonder Man; Round Up, 1929; play, June Moon (with George S. Kaufman), 1929. Home: East Hampton, N.Y. Died Sept. 25, 1933.

LARGE, John J., banker; b. Osage, Ia., May 5, 1875; s. Francis A. and Susan (Reifsnider) L.; ed. grade schs.; m. May McQuilkin, Oct. 28, 1896; children—Alice Lucile (Mrs. Kenneth C. Gifford), J. Judson. Asst. cashier First Nat. Bank, La Porte City, 1893-96; cashier First Nat. Bank, Rock Valley, Ia., 1896-1909; nat. bank examiner, 1909-10; v.p. First Nat. Bank, Sioux City, Ia., 1910-15, pres., 1915-24; dir. Terminal Grain Corp., Western Terminal Elevator Co., Sioux City Service Co. (street car co.), Sioux City Building & Savings Assn. Trustee Morningside Coll. (Sioux City), Yankton (S.D.) Coll.; dir. Interstate Fair Assn.; dir. Bur. Social Agencies, Sioux City; treas. and dir. Am. Red Cross, Sioux City. Republican. Conglist. Home: Sioux City, Ia. Died Nov. 3, 1928.

LARIMORE, N(ewel) Greene, farmer; b. Bourbon County, Ky., Aug. 29, 1835; s. Wilson L. and Harriet (Berry) L.; ed. Wyman's Acad., St. Louis, 1849-53, German Coll., Herman, Mo., 1853-54, Jones Commercial Coll., St. Louis, 1854-55; m. Susan Ashbrook, 1855; m. 2d, Mollie E. Jameson, 1867. Pres. St. Louis Warehouse Co., 1865-83, Iron Mountain Bank, 1869-74, Central Elevator Co., 1873-86; v.p. and gen. mgr., 1888—, Elk Valley Farming Co., operating 15,000 acres. Mem. upper house St. Louis City Council, 1878-82; pres. bd. regents State U. of N.D., 1889-93; regent Red River Valley U. (N.D.), 1890-96; trustee Wesley Coll., 1895—; refused nomination for gov. of N.D., 1893. Mem. Trans-Miss. Commercial Congress, 1893—(v.p. 1905, 1st v.p. 1908, 1909); v.p. Nat. Irrigation Congress, 1903—; pres. N.D. Chautauqua Assn., 1900—. Address: Larimore, N.D.; and Los Angeles, Calif. Died Nov. 1913.

LARKIN, Edgar Lucien, astronomer; b. La Salle County, Ill., Apr. 5, 1847; s. Herman I. and Jane L.; ed. La Salle Co., Ill.; m. Alice A. Everman, Apr. 29, 1869. Opened, and dir. New Windsor (Ill.) Obs., 1880-88, Knox Coll. Obs., 1888-95; dir. Lowe Obs., Echo Mountain, Calif., 1900—. Author: Radiant Energy, 1903; Within the Mind Maze, 1911; The Matchless Altar of the Soul, 1916; Popular Studies in Recent Astronomy. Address: Mount Lowe, Calif. Died Oct. 11, 1924.

LARKIN, Francis Marion, clergyman; b. Cincinnati, O., Aug. 15, 1861; s. Joseph Franklin and Julia (Stark) L.; A.B., Ohio Wesleyan U., 1885, D.D., 1915; S.T.B., Boston U., 1888, Ph.D., 1902; Oxford U., Eng., summer 1901; m. Cora Carhart, July 11, 1887; 1 son, Gail Carhart. Ordained M.E. ministry, 1892; pastor Los Angeles, 1892-1900, Grace Ch., San Francisco, 1901-06, Redlands, Calif., 1907-09; dist. supt., Los Angeles, 1909-13; editor Calif. Christian Advocate, 1913-24; exec. sec. Calif. State Ch. Federation, 1924—. Sec. Laymen's Relief Assn., 1906-07; mem. Gen. Conf. M.E. Ch., 5 times between 1912-28; mem. Meth. Ecumenical Conf., London, Sept. 1921; mem. M.E. Ch. Commn. on Church Union (36 members), 1928-32; res. del. to Gen. Conf. M.E. Ch., 1932; mem. Calif. com. The Golden Rule Foundation. Trustee U. of Southern Calif. Republican. Home: San Marino, Calif. Died Jan. 30, 1933.

LARNED, Charles William, army officer; b. New York, N.Y., Mar. 9, 1850; s. Maj. William and Mary (Sherwood) L.; grad. U.S. Mil. Acad., 1870; m. Louise, d. Col. Edmund B. Alexander, Aug. 14, 1884. Promoted 2d lt. 3d Cav., June 15, 1870; transferred to 7th Cav., Oct. 10, 1870; 1st lt., June 25, 1876; reconstruction duty with regt. in South, 1871-73; Stanley expdn. against Sioux Indians and engagement of Big Horn River, 1873; prof. tech. and mil. graphics and applied geometry, U.S. Mil. Acad., and col. U.S.A., 1876—. Author: The Great Discourse, 1890. Address: West Point, N.Y. Died 1911.

LARNED, Josephus Nelson, author; b. Chatham, Ont., May 11, 1836; s. Henry Sherwood and Mary A. (Nelson) L.; ed. pub. schs., Buffalo; m. Frances A. K. McCrea, Apr. 29, 1861. On editorial staff Buffalo Express, 1859-72; supt. edn. Buffalo, 1872-73; supt. Buffalo Library, 1877-97. Pres. A.L.A., 1893-94. Author: Talks About Labor, 1877; History for Ready Reference, 1895, supplementary vol. 6, 1901, vol. 7, 1910; Talk About Books, 1897; History of England for Schools, 1900; A Multitude of Counsellors, 1901; Primer of Right and Wrong, 1902; History of the United States for Secondary Schools, 1903; Seventy Centuries—a Survey, 1905; Books, Culture and Character, 1906; A Study of Greatness in Men, 1911; A History of Buffalo, 1911. Editor: The Literature of American History, 1902. Address: Buffalo, N.Y. Died Aug. 15, 1913.

LARNED, Linda Hull, household economist; b. Little Falls, N.Y., Apr. 4, 1853; d. David Henry and Mary Matilda (Schermerhorn) Hull; ed. Keble Sch., Syracuse, N.Y.; m. Samuel B. Larned, Nov. 4, 1874. Has spoken before many organizations upon the subject of household economics. Official del. Paris Expn., 1900. Mem. exec. bd. of N.Y. State Federation, 1899-1901; mem. Nat. Household Econ. Assn.; school commissioner City of Syracuse, and pres. Board of Education, 1931. Author: The Little Epicure, 1895; The Hostess of Today, 1899; The New Hostess of Today, 1913; One Hundred Salads, 1914; One Hundred Cold Desserts, 1914; One Hundred Luncheon Dishes, 1915; One Hundred Picnic Suggestions, 1915. Home: Syracuse, N.Y. Died June 24, 1939.

LARNED, (William) Trowbridge, writer, editor; b. St. Louis; s. Charles Trowbridge (lt. col. U.S.A.) and Philomena S. (Smith) L.; ed. Freshman yr. Georgetown U., D.C., and under pvt. tutelage; m. Marguerite Langdon Younglove, Jan. 19, 1909. Contbr. verse, essays, short stories, etc., to newspapers and mags.; fence rider English cattle co., Colo.; cowboy Belle Fourche (S.D.) range; farmer and cattle raiser Ozark Mountains, Ark.; on ranch in Zuñi mountains, N.M., 18 mos., 1893-94; reporter, and in various editorial capacities, St. Louis Globe-Democrat, Post-Dispatch, Republic (night city editor and 3 yrs. as dramatic and music editor); news corr. Chicago Tribune, Kansas City Star, etc. In New York, 1906, editor Evening Mail Illus. Supplement, etc. Wrote "The Literary Zoo," for Life, 1907-10; adapted "The Devil" for George Arliss, from Hungarian of Molnar; Fables in Rhyme (La Fontaine); Fairy Tales From France; American Fairy Tales; Arabian Fairy Tales. Died Feb. 9, 1928.

LARNED, Walter Cranston, lawyer; b. Chicago, Nov. 30, 1850; s. Edwin C. and Frances (Greene) L.; A.B., Harvard, 1871; student Harvard Law Sch., 1871-72; in Europe, 1872-74; m. Emma L., d. late Charles Scribner, 1875. Admitted to bar, 1874, and practiced at Chicago. Lecturer on art subjects; was many yrs. art editor Chicago Daily News and Chicago Record. Author: Arnaud's Masterpiece, a Romance of the Pyrenees; Churches and Castles of Mediæval France; Rembrandt, a Romance of Holland. Home: Lake Forest, Ill. Died June 19, 1914.

LARNER, John Bell, lawyer; b. Washington, D.C., Aug. 3, 1858; s. Noble Danforth and Ann Margaret (Keller) L.; LL.B., Columbian (now George Washington) U., 1879, LL.D., 1904; m. Anna E. Parker, Apr. 8, 1891; children—Ruth (Mrs. A. Chambers Oliphant), Margaret (wife of A. S. Wotherspoon, officer U.S.N.), Isabella W. (wife of Charles A. Stott), Anna Southard, Lucy P. Admitted to bar of D.C., 1879, and practiced at Washington; v.p. and gen. counsel, 1889-1917, pres., 1917—, Washington Loan & Trust Co.; pres. and counsel Home Plate Glass Ins. Co.; dir., counsel, v.p., 1929—, Nat. Union Ins. Co. Gen. counsel Young Men's Christian Assn.; gen. counsel to 1916, v.p. Board of Trade; chmn. trustees George Washington U.; trustee Princeton Theol. Sem., Washington Pub. Library, Washington Humane Soc., New York Av. Presbyn. Ch. (pres. bd.), Presbyn. Home for the Aged (treas.; pres. 1928), Columbia Hist. Soc. (v.p.), John Dickson Home for Aged Men (v.p.), Washington Home for Foundlings (pres.), Garfield Memorial Hosp. (dir.); mem. Bd. of Edn., Washington, 1912-19. Mem. Inaugural Com., 1901—; trustee Community Chest, D.C. Pres. Washington Bankers' Assn., 1921-22; v.p. Equitable Coöp. Building Assn. of D.C.; treas. Travelers Aid Soc. Translator: Life of Napoleon (by Alexandre Dumas), 1894. Editor Records of Columbia Hist. Soc., 1905—. Home: Washington, D.C. Died Nov. 9, 1931.

LARNER, Robert Martin, journalist; b. Washington, July 14, 1856; s. Andrew Jackson and Mary Laura L.; ed. pub. schs.; m. H. Adelaide De Freest, Apr. 1896. Page at capitol before serving five yrs. at the case as practical printer; became a newspaper reporter while working at the case; in journalism, 1880—; reporter in Washington, corr. United Press, then on Washington staff Baltimore Sun, and later on New York Sun 5 yrs.; corr. New York Herald and Telegram, Savannah News and Charleston News and Courier. Secured some famous interviews; notably that on a street car with Sir Julian Pauncefote on the Behring Sea dispute. Home: Washington, D.C. Died 1906.

LAROCQUE, Joseph, lawyer; b. New York, Apr. 2, 1831; grad. Columbia, 1849; admitted to bar, 1852. Mem. law firm, Shipman, Larocque & Choate; dir. Am. Cotton Oil Co., Cataract Construction Co., The Celluloid Co., Niagara Falls Power Co., Niagara Development Co., Niagara Junction Ry., Morton Trust Co., Plaza Bank. Chmn. com. of 70, 1894; pres. Assn. Bar City of New York, 1895-96. Home: New York, N.Y. Died 1908.

LaROQUE, George Paul, surgeon; b. Lenoir County, N.C., June 16, 1876; s. Walter Dunn and Annie (Parrott) LaR.; student U. of N.C., 1893-95; M.D., U. of Pa., 1902; m. Eva Page Murdoch, Apr. 19, 1916. Resident and chief resident physician, University Hosp., Phila., 1902-04, asst. surgeon, 1904-05; practiced at Richmond, 1905—; asso. prof. surgery, Med. Coll. of Va., 1910-27, prof. clin. surgery and head of dept. of surgery, 1928—; chief surgeon Memorial, St. Philip and Dooley hosps., 1928. Democrat. Baptist. Home: Richmond, Va. Died 1934.

LARRABEE, Edward Allan, clergyman; b. Chicago, Mar. 31, 1852; s. Charles Rollin and Mary A. (Wood) L.; A.M., Racine Coll., 1873; S.T.B., Gen. Theol. Sem., New York, 1876; D.D., Nashotah House, 1909; unmarried. Deacon, 1876, priest, 1877, P.E. Ch.; in charge St. John's, Quincy, Ill., 1876-79, St. Paul's, Springfield, Ill., 1879-84; rector Ch. of the Ascension, Chicago, 1884-1909; dean Nashotah (Wis.) House, 1909-21; asso. priest, Ch. of the Ascension, Chicago, Oct. 1921—. Superior Gen. Guild of All Souls (Am. branch); deputy to Gen. Conv. from Diocese of Chicago, 1901, 04, 07. Author: Sacramental Teaching of the Lord's Prayer, 1888; The Temple of His Body, 1905; The Calls of the Conqueror, 1907. Home: Chicago, Ill. Died June 13, 1924.

LARRABEE, William, governor; b. Ledyard, Conn., Jan. 20, 1832; s. Capt. Adam and Hannah Gallup (Lester) L.; ed. common schs.; m. Ann M. Appelman, Sept. 12, 1861. Moved to Ia., 1853, and became farmer, is also mfr. and banker. Mem. Ia. Senate, 1868-86 (chmn. Com. on Ways and Means 16 yrs.); gov. of Ia., 1886-90; mem. Bd. of Control of State Instns., 1898-1900. Republican. Ia. State commr. to St. Louis Expn., 1904. Author: The Railroad Question, 1893. Address: Clermont, Ia. Died Nov. 16, 1912.

LARRABEE, William Henry, editor; b. Alfred, Me., Sept. 20, 1829; s. William C. and Harriet (Dunn) L.; A.B., Ind. Asbury (now DePauw) U., 1845, A.M., 1848 (LL.D., DePauw 1888); studied law, admitted to bar, but never practiced; m. Letitia B. Frazier, June 25, 1856 (died 1909). Teaching and farming, 1846-50; clerk in office of supt. pub. instrn., Ind., 1853-59; asst. editor The Methodist, New York, 1862-65, 1870-77; asso. editor Brooklyn Daily Union, 1865-70; translator for and asst. editor The Popular Science Monthly, 1879-1900; dept. contbr. to the Christian Advocate, New York, 1890—; also contbr. to Kiddle & Schem's Cyclopedia of Education, 1877; to Bishop Matthew Simpson's Cyclopedia of Methodism, 1878; contbr. for more than 30 yrs. to Appleton's Annual Cyclopedia (ecclesiastical and spl. articles); contbr. to New International Encyclopædia and Schaff-Herzog Encyclopædia (new edit.). Author: How the World Was Made and Earthquakes and Volcanoes (in Honeyman's Library of the Great World); History of the War in the East (with A. J. Schem), 1877; Education Through the Agency of Religious Organizations (for Pres. N. M. Butler's monographs on edn., edition for St. Louis Expn., 1904). Trustee Plainfield Public Library. Address: Plainfield, N.J. Died May 13, 1913.

LARRAZOLO, Octaviano Ambrosio, governor; b. Allende, Chihuahua, Mex., Dec. 7, 1859; s. Octaviano and Donaciana (Corral) L.; came to U.S., 1870; student St. Michael's Coll., Santa Fe, N.M., 1875-76; m. Rosalia Cobos, 1881 (died 1891); children—Juan B. (deceased), Jose Ma; m. 2d, Maria Garcia, Aug. 4, 1892; children—Octaviano A., Heliodoro A., Maria, Pablo, Rafael, Carlos. Teacher pub. schs., San Elizario, Tex., 1878-84; dep. county and dist. court clk., El Paso Co., Tex., 1884-85; clk. Dist. Court, 34th Jud. Dist. of Tex., 1886-89; dist. atty., same dist., 1890-94; moved to Las Vegas, N.M., 1895; gov. of N.M., 1919-21. Elk. Republican. Catholic. Home: Albuquerque, N.M. Died Apr. 7, 1930.

LARREMORE, Wilbur, lawyer, editor; b. New York, Aug. 8, 1855; s. Richard L. and Caroline E. (Livermore) L.; A.B., Coll. of City of New York, 1875; LL.B., Columbia, 1877; m. Susan Armitage, Dec. 29, 1886. In law practice at New York, 1877—; editor New York Law Journal, 1891—. Extensively engaged as referee. Published vol. of early verse, "Mother Carey's Chickens." Home: New York, N.Y. Died Aug. 11, 1918.

LARSEN, Lauritz, clergyman; b. Decorah, Ia., Nov. 28, 1882; s. Peter Laurentius and Ingeborg (Astrup) L.; A.B., Luther Coll., Decorah, 1902; grad. Luther Theol. Sem., St. Paul, Minn., 1907; S.T.D., Pa. Coll., Gettysburg, Pa., 1919; D.D., Thiel College, Greenville, Pa., 1919; LL.D., Muhlenberg College, Pa., 1921; m. Charlotte Emilie Haugen, June 16, 1908. Prin. pub. schs., Clifford, N.D., 1902-03, Buxton, N.D., 1903-04; teacher English and Latin, State Manual Training Sch., Ellendale, N.D., 1904-05; ordained ministry Norwegian Luth. Ch. America, 1907; pastor Plaza, N.D., 1907-08, Cresco, Ia., 1908-13, Brooklyn, N.Y., 1913-18; sec. Nat. Luth. Commn. for Soldiers and Sailors Welfare, 1917—; sec. Eastern Dists. Norwegian Luth. Ch. America, 1917-19; gen. sec. Nat. Luth. Council, 1920—; sec. Lutheran Foreign Missions Conf. of N.A., 1919—. Editor of Our Friend, 1908-17; editor of Children's Friend, 1917-18. Pres. Norwegian Lutheran Deaconesses Home and Hosp., Brooklyn, 1917—. Author of Annual Report of Nat. Lutheran Council, 3 yrs., 1919-21. Translator: Youth and Christianity (from the Norwegian), 1916. Home: Brooklyn, N.Y. Died Jan. 29, 1923.

LARSEN, Peter Laurentius, educator; b. Christiansand, Norway, Aug. 10, 1833; s. Herman and Marie (Oftedahl) L.; grad. U. of Christiania, Norway, 1850; grad. in theology, same, 1855; D.D., German Luth. Synod of Mo., 1903; m. Karen Neuberg, July 23, 1855 (died 1871); m. 2d, Ingeborg Astrup, Aug. 20, 1872. Came to U.S., 1857; Luth. minister, Pierce County, Wis., 1857-59; Norwegian prof. Concordia Coll. and Sem., St. Louis, 1859-61; pres. Norwegian Lutheran College, Decorah, Ia., 1861-1902, teacher of Hebrew, 1902-11, pres. emeritus, 1911. V.p. Norwegian Luth. Synod, 1876-93; v.p. and part of time acting pres. Synodical Conf., 1879-82. Editor church paper Norwegian Luth. Synod, 1868-89, and 1902-12. Address: Decorah, Ia. Died Mar. 1, 1915.

LARSEN, William Washington, congressman; b. Hagan, Ga., Aug. 12, 1871; s. Peter and Anna Margrada (Petersen) L.; South Ga. Mil. Coll., Thomasville, 1892-93; U. of Ga., 1893-95; m. Dovie Estell Strange, Dec. 18, 1898 (died 1928); m. 2d, Margaret Van Dyke, Apr. 3, 1932. Began practice of law in Swainsboro, 1897. Solicitor, City Court of Swainsboro, 5 yrs.; sec. exec. dept. State of Ga., 2 yrs.; apptd. judge Superior Court, Dublin Circuit, Ga., 1914; mem. 65th to 72d Congresses (1917-33), 12th Ga. Dist., retiring voluntarily at close of 72d Congress. Has large farming interests; regional mgr. Emergency Crop and Feed Loan Sect. Farm Credit Adminstrn., Columbia, S.C. Democrat. Missionary Baptist. Military training 3 years, while at coll.; served as 2d lt. Swainsboro Guards. Trustee State Normal Sch. Bd. State of Ga., also U. of Ga. Mason, Odd Fellow, K.P. Home: Dublin, Ga. Died Jan. 5, 1938.

LARSON, Cora Gunn, teacher; b. (Gunn) Buda, Ill., Sept. 7, 1859; became deaf in childhood from spinal meningitis, but retains power of speech; grad. Ill. State School for the Deaf, Jacksonville, Ill., 1878; taught there 8 yrs.; married Lars Moore Larson, 1893; assisted him in the N.M. School for the Deaf. Address: Santa Fe, N.M. Died 1906.

LARSON, Laurence Marcellus, prof. history; b. nr. Bergen, Norway, Sept. 23, 1868; s. Christian and Ellen Mathilde (Madsen) L.; brought to U.S., 1870; A.B., Drake U., 1894, LL.D., 1925; A.M., U. of Wis., 1900, Ph.D., 1902; LL.D., Augustana Coll., Rock Island, Ill., 1935; m. Lillian May Dodson, Dec. 25, 1895. Prin. Scandinavia (Wis.) Acad., 1894-99; teacher of history, W. Div. High Sch., Milwaukee, 1902-05, E. Div. High Sch., 1905-07; teacher and prof. of history, U. of Ill., 1907—. Trustee Ill. State Hist. Library, 1923—. Author: The King's Household in England before Norman Conquest, 1904; Financial and Administrative History of Milwaukee, 1908; A Syllabus of European History, 1909; Canute the Great, 1912; Short History of England, 1915; A History of England, 1923; also articles in Hoops' Reallexikon, 1913-14. Translator: The King's Mirror, 1917; The Earliest Norwegian Laws, 1935. Home: Urbana, Ill. Died Mar. 9, 1938.

LARSSON, Gustaf, educator; b. Province of Westergötland, Sweden, Dec. 10, 1861; s. Lars Svensson and Inga Maria Jonsdotter; grad. Normal Sch., Nääs, Sweden, 1882; came to America, 1888; m. Greta Sundvall, June 1905. Prin. Sloyd Training Sch. for training teachers of manual training, Boston, since its establishment by Mrs. Quincy A. Shaw, 1888. Over 400 teachers have been sent out from the Sloyd Training Sch. and over 100,000 children are under the instruction of its graduates in America; established 10 centers in Southern India and 6 in Mexico; introduced manual training into pub. schs., Mysore, India, 6 mos., 1907. Editor Sloyd Record. Republican. Mason. Author: Teachers' Sloyd Manual, 1890; Working Drawings of Models in Sloyd, 1895; Handbook of Geometrical Wood Carving, 1895; Elementary Sloyd and Whittling, 1906; Sloyd for Three Upper Grammar Grades, 1907; Working Drawings of Models in Wood-Turning, 1912. Home: Wollaston, Mass. Died July 23, 1919.

LASATER, Ed(ward) Cunningham, farmer, cattle breeder; b. Goliad County, Tex., Nov. 5, 1860; s. Albert H. and Sarah (Cunningham) L.; m. Mary Miller, Oct. 29, 1902. Spent early life in sheep and cow camps in Tex.; owner of ranch of about 100,000 acres in Duval and Brooks counties, Tex.; also owner of the Falfurrias herd of Hereford and Hereford and Brahma crosses of beef cattle, and the Falfurrias Jerseys for dairy purposes (both herds nationally known). Dir. of live stock and farming, U.S. Food Administration, 1917. Progressive Republican. Presbyn. Home: Falfurrias, Tex. Died Mar. 20, 1930.

LA SHELLE, Kirke, author, mgr.; b. Wyoming, Ill., Sept. 23, 1862; s. James R. and Sarah La S.; ed. pub. schs., Wyoming, Ill.; m. Mazie Elizabeth Nodine, June 15, 1893. In newspaper offices, 1876-91, holding positions from apprentice to managing editor on Chicago News, Chicago Mail, Chicago Times and Chicago Post. Theatrical mgr., 1891—. Author (plays): The Ameer (comic opera), Princess Chic (romantic opera); also collaborator on numerous other plays. Home: New York, N.Y. Died 1905.

LASHER, George William, editor; b. Duanesburg, N.Y., June 24, 1831; s. George, Jr. and Adelia D. (Frost) L.; A.B., Colgate, 1857, A.M., 1859; grad. Hamilton Theol. Sem., 1859; D.D., Colgate, 1874; LL.D., Georgetown (Ky.) Coll., 1908; m. Lizzie C. Eaton, Aug. 23, 1860. Ordained Bapt. ministry, 1859; pastor Norwalk, Conn., 1859-61; chaplain 5th Regt. Conn. Vol. Inf., June-Dec. 1861; pastor Newburgh, N.Y., 1862-64, Haverhill, Mass., 1864-68, Trenton, N.J., 1868-72; sec. Bapt. Edn. Soc. State of N.Y., 1872-75; editor Journal and Messenger, 1876; mem. firm of Lasher & Osborne, 1887—. Trustee Denison U., Granville, O., 1877—. Republican. Wrote (pamphlets): Individualism in Religion, 1890; What Did Peter Mean?, 1894; Theology for Plain People, 1906; George W. Eaton, a Memorial, 1913. Home: Cincinnati, O. Died Feb. 1920.

LASSITER, Francis Rives, congressman; b. Petersburg, Va., Feb. 18, 1866; s. Daniel W. and Anna Rives (Heath) L.; ed. public and private schools, Petersburg; U. of Va., 1883-86; grad. same, LL.B.; admitted to Suffolk bar, Boston, Mass., 1887; Va. bar, 1888; m. Fanny Page McGill, Mar. 31, 1891. Mem. Va. State Dem. Com. several times; elected city atty. of Petersburg, 1888; reëlected, 1890-92; presidential elector, 1892; U.S. atty., Eastern dist. of Va., 1893-97; defeated for Dem. nomination for atty. gen. of Va., 1897; supervisor 12th census, 4th dist. of Va., 1899; elected to 56th Congress, 4th Va. Dist., at spl. election, April 1900, and reëlected to 57th, 59th and 60th Congresses. Democrat. Wrote: Arnold's Invasion of Virginia, 1781, Sewanee Rev., 1901. Address: Petersburg, Va. Died 1909.

LATANÉ, James Allen, R.E. bishop; b. Essex County, Va., Jan. 15, 1831; s. Henry Waring and Susannah (Allen) L.; academic edn. and study of law, U. of Va., 1848-53; grad. Va. Theol. Sem., Alexandria; D.D., Hampden-Sidney Coll., Va.; m. Mary Minor Holladay, Nov. 7, 1855. Was pastor Trinity (P.E.) Ch., Staunton, Va., 1857-71; St. Mathew's Ch., Wheeling, 1871-74. In 1874, shortly after R.E. Ch. was organized, gave up P.E. ministry and joined the new denomination; elected bishop, 1879; has charge of missionary jurisdiction of the South; also pastor of a church in Baltimore. Address: Baltimore, Md. Died 1902.

LATANE, John Holladay, univ. prof.; b. Staunton, Va., Apr. 1, 1869; s. Bishop James Allen (R.E. Ch.) and Mary Minor (Holladay) L.; grad. Baltimore City Coll., 1889; A.B., Johns Hopkins U., 1892, Ph.D., 1895; LL.D., U. of Ala., 1913, Washington and Lee U., 1928; m. Mrs. Elinor J. J. Cox, Oct. 17, 1905; 1 dau., Elinor (Mrs. William T. Bissell). Acting prof. history and economics, Baltimore City Coll., 1895-96; master history and English, mil. acad., San Rafael, Calif., 1896-97; first Albert Shaw lecturer in Am. diplomatic history, Johns Hopkins, 1898; prof. history and economics, Randolph-Macon Woman's Coll., 1898-1902; prof. history, Washington and Lee U., 1902-13; prof. Am. history and head of dept. of history, 1913-30, dean coll. faculty, 1919-24, Johns Hopkins U.; mem. research staff of Walter Hines Page Sch. of International Relations, 1930—. Mem. commn. to draft a new charter for city of Baltimore, 1917. Chmn. Ednl. Com. Md. Council of Defense, 1917-19. Mem. bd. trustees St. John's Coll., Annapolis; pres. bd. trustees Roland Park Country Sch., Baltimore. Chevalier Legion of Honor (France). Democrat. Author: Diplomatic Relations of the United States and Spanish America, 1900; America as a World Power, 1907; History of the United States (for high schs.), 1918; From Isolation to Leadership, 1918; The United States and Latin America, 1920; History of American Foreign Policy, 1927. Home: Baltimore, Md. Died Jan. 1, 1932.

LATCH, Edward Biddle, chief engr. U.S.N.; b. Lower Merion Twp., Pa., Nov. 15, 1833; s. Gardiner and Henrietta (Wakeling) L.; ed. pub. schs.; studied mech. engring. Norris Locomotive Works, Phila., 1851-57; unmarried. Began service as asst. engr. U.S.N., Sept. 20, 1858; chief engr. with rank of comdr., Mar. 21, 1870; retired, Nov. 22, 1878. During Civil War was attached to the flagship Hartford (Admiral Farragut); took part in engagements at Fts. Jackson and St. Philip and Confederate fleet Mississippi River, Chalmette, New Orleans, Vicksburg, Port Hudson, Grand Gulf, Warrenton, Grand Gulf and Fts. Morgan,

Gaines and Powell; also with the ram Tennessee at the battle of Mobile Bay. Developed the Mosaic system of chronology. Extensive writer of elucidations of scripture and universal history by the Mosaic system of chronology. Editor The Greater Light (Phila. monthly). Author: A Review of the Holy Bible, 1884; Indications of the Book of Job, 1889; Indications of Genesis, 1890; Indications of Exodus, 1892; also serials in The Greater Light—Indications of Romans, 1900-01; Indications of the Revelation of St. John the Divine, 1901-03; Indications of Leviticus, 1905; Indications of Numbers, 1906-07; etc. Address: Academy P.O., Pa. Died 1911.

LATHAM, Orval Ray, coll. pres.; b. Boone, Ia., Apr. 13, 1890; s. David Harrison and Mary Frances (Wane) L.; grad. high sch., Boone, 1907; A.B., State U. of Ia., 1911, A.M., 1919, Ph.D., 1928; m. Helen Fern Waldron, June 5, 1913; children—Raymond Waldron, Shirley Laurene. Supt. schs., Coggon, Ia., 1911-12, Pomeroy, 1912-17, Ida Grove, 1917-21, Le Mars, 1921-22; asst. supt. schs. and dir. research, Duluth Minn., 1922-24; prof. edn., Ohio U., 1924-26, dir. teacher training, 1926-27; pres. Ia. State Teachers Coll., 1928—. Methodist. Mem. Commn. of 7, apptd. by the Carnegie Foundation for the Survey of Tax-supported Higher Edn. in Calif., 1932; mem. Teacher Edn. Div., Regents Inquiry into the Character and Cost of Edn. in New York, 1936. Home: Cedar Falls, Ia. Died July 9, 1940.

LATHAM, Rex Knight, educator; b. North Loup, Neb., June 19, 1883; s. Norman Wadsworth and Louise Imogene (Knight) L.; grad. high sch., Hanover, Mich., 1900; student Mich. State Normal Coll., Ypsilanti; A.B., Albion (Mich.) Coll., 1908; studied U. of Mich.; m. Florence Alberta Jackson, Sept. 4, 1914; children—Rex Knight, Albert Jackson, James Knight. Instr. Sewanee (Tenn.) Mil. Acad., 1909-12, Western Mil. Acad., Alton, Ill., 1913-14; instr., prin. and asst. supt., Wentworth Mil. Acad., Lexington, Mo., 1914-22; pres. Gulf Coast Mil. Acad., 1923-25; engaged in agrl. development of South Mississippi, 1925-31; asst. supt. Western Mil. Acad., Alton, Ill., 1931—. Episcopalian. Mason. Home: Alton, Ill. Died July 5, 1938.

LATHAN, Robert, editor; b. York, S.C., May 5, 1881; s. Rev. Robert and Fanny (Barron) L.; ed. pub. and pvt. schs.; m. Bessie Agnes Early. Teacher pub. schs., 1898-99; on editorial staff Columbia State, 1900-03; official court reporter and law student, 1903-06; news editor News and Courier, Charleston, S.C., 1906-07; city editor same, 1908-10, editor and mgr., 1910-27; editor Citizen, Asheville, N.C., 1927—; mem. advisory bd. Sch. of Journalism, Columbia. Awarded Pulitzer prize for best editorial in the U.S., 1924. Pres. S.C. Press Assn., 1925-26. Democrat. Visited Europe, 1927, with Carnegie editorial party, studying economics and politics. Episcopalian. Address: Ashville, N.C. Died Sept. 26, 1937.

LATHBURY, Clarence, clergyman; b. Manchester, N.Y., Jan. 21, 1854; s. Rev. John and Betsy Shepherd (Jones) L.; ed. Lodi Acad., Oberlin Coll.; grad. New Ch. Theol. Sch., Cambridge, Mass., 1891; m. Lily A. Tibbals, Dec. 25, 1876; 1 son, Vincent Tibbals. Ordained M.E. ministry, 1887; pastor, Kensington, Conn., 1887-91; entered ministry Church of New Jerusalem, 1891; pastor Fall River, Mass., 1892-95, Elmwood, Mass., 1895-1903; lit. editor Nunc Licet Press, Phila., 1903-05; pastor Elmwood, Mass., 1905-14, Ch. Divine Humanity, Buffalo, N.Y., 1914-17, Ch. of the Holy City, Cleveland, 1917-32. Author: God Winning Us, 1895; A Little Lower han the Angels, 1897; The Code of Joy, 1898; The Being with the Upturned Face, 1904; The Balanced Life, 1905; The Great Morning, 1911. Home: Freeport, N.Y. Died Nov. 10, 1939.

LATHBURY, Mary Artemisia, author; b. Manchester, N.Y., Aug. 10, 1841; d. Rev. John and Betsy Shepherd (Jones) L.; ed. Manchester, N.Y., and Worcester, Mass.; unmarried. After leaving school engaged in teaching art; then editorial work; general literature and illustration, 1874—. Best known through Chautauqua songs and hymns in ch. collections. Editor Picture Lesson Paper. Author and Illustrator: Fleda and the Voice, 1878; Out of Darkness Into Light, 1880; Seven Little Maids, 1882; Ring-Around-a-Rosy, 1884; Twelve Times One, 1885; Idyls of the Months, 1884; From Meadow Sweet to Mistletoe, 1888; Child's Story of the Bible, 1898; etc. Address: E. Orange, N.J. Died Oct. 20, 1913.

LATHE, Herbert William, clergyman; b. Worcester, Mass., June 15, 1851; s. Martin and Mary (Putnam) L.; A.B., Yale, 1873; grad. Andover Theol. Sem., 1877; m. Harriet Preble Thacher, Nov. 14, 1878. Ordained Congl. ministry, 1877; pastor Plymouth Ch., Portland, Me., 1877-81, First Ch., Northampton, Mass., 1882-91, Silverton, Colo., 1892-94, Pasadena, Calif., 1895-1902, Manitou, Colo., 1902-04; without charge at San Diego, Calif., 1904-07; pastor Prescott, Ariz., 1907-14, Newton, Mass., 1914, Lyndeboro, N.H., 1914-20, Cambridge, Mass., 1920—. Author: Chosen of God, 1897; also 6 sermons on Spiritual Life in Its Fullness—The Scriptural Doctrine of Sanctification. Home: Cambridge, Mass. Died Aug. 24, 1932.

LATHERS, Richard, mcht.; b. Georgetown, S.C., 1820, ed. in S.C.; m. Miss A. S. Thurston, 1845. Conducted store at Georgetown, S.C.; was col. 31st regt. S.C. Militia, 1841; commission mcht., New York, 1847; was pres. Great Western Marine Ins. Co. to 1869; Union man during war, raising funds and organizing vols.; gave fund, 1897, to Williams Coll. for gold medal annually for best essay on subject of The Duty of Christians to Government. Address: New York, N.Y. Died 1903.

LATHROP, Bryan, trustee; b. Alexandria, Va., Aug. 6, 1844; s. Jediah H. and Mariana (Bryan) L.; ed. Dinwiddie's Sch., Va., and under pvt. tutors in Germany and France; removed to Chicago, 1865; m. Helen Lynde, d. Judge Asa O. Aldis, Apr. 21, 1875. Engaged in real estate operations, and as mgr. real estate investments for estates, 1865; trustee of estates under wills; pres. Graceland Cemetery Co.; pres. Chicago Symphony Orchestral Assn., founded by Theodore Thomas; pres. Chicago Relief and Aid Soc.; trustee Art Inst. of Chicago, Newberry Library; commr. of Lincoln Park. Republican. Pres. Soc. for Prevention of Blindness. Home: Chicago, Ill. Died May 13, 1916.

LATHROP, Charles Newton, clergyman; b. San Francisco, Calif., Nov. 16, 1871; s. Henry Durant and Sarah (Burrowes) L.; student U. of Calif. 1 yr.; A.B., Harvard, 1896; grad. Western Theol. Sem., 1899; D.D., St. Stephen's Coll., Annandale, N.Y., 1928; m. Helen E. Chappelle, 1918; 1 son, Charles Robert. Ordained deacon, 1900, priest, 1901, P.E. Ch.; curate Ch. of the Advent, San Francisco, 1901-04, rector same, 1904-16; mem. Commn. for Relief in Belgium, in charge of the Province of Liége, 1916-17; dean of All Saints' Cathedral, Milwaukee, Wis., 1917-20; exec. sec. Dept. of Christian Social Service of Nat. Council P.E. Ch., 1920—. Del. to Gen. Conv., P.E. Ch., 4 times, 1910-22; mem. Standing Com. Diocese of Calif., 1911-14. Home: New York, N.Y. Died Jan. 29, 1931.

LATHROP, Francis, artist; b. at sea, nr. Hawaiian Islands, June 22, 1849; s. Dr. George Alfred and Frances M. L.; ed. Dresden, Germany, 1867-70; studied painting in London, England, under Burne-Jones and Madox Brown. Returned to U.S., 1873; painted portraits and decorative pictures, and executed stained glass windows and gen. decorative work. Address: New York, N.Y. Died 1909.

LATHROP, Gardiner, lawyer; b. Waukesha, Wis., Feb. 16, 1850; s. John H. and Frances E. L.; A.B., U. of Mo., 1867, A.M., 1870; A.B., Yale, 1869, A.M., 1872; LL.B., Harvard, 1873; LL.D., U. of Mo., and Washington U., 1907; m. Eva Grant, Jan. 16, 1879. Admitted to bar, 1873, and practiced at Kansas City; sr. mem. firm Lathrop, Crane, Reynolds, Sawyer & Mersereau, formerly Lathrop, Morrow, Fox & Moore; gen. solicitor, 1905-26, spl. counsel, 1926-35, A.,T.&S.F. Ry. System. Pres. Bd. Curators, U. of Mo. Died Jan. 21, 1938.

LATHROP, Henry Burrowes, coll. prof.; b. Gold Hill, Nev., Mar. 22, 1867; s. Henry Durant and Sarah Burrows (McElroy) L.; Cornell U., 1884-86; A.B., Harvard U., 1889; m. Mary Agnes Stinson, June 27, 1890 (died 1926); children—Francis C., Margaret. Asst. prof. English, Hobart Coll., 1889-90; instr. English, Harvard, 1890-92; asst., later asso. prof. English, 1892-96, prof. rhetoric, 1896-1901, Leland Stanford Jr. U.; asso. prof., English, 1901-21, prof., 1921—, U. of Wis. Author: The Art of the Novelist, 1919; Freshman Composition, 1920; also translations from the classics into English, from Caxton to Chapman, 1934. Editor: Malory's King Arthur and His Knights, 1910. Home: Madison, Wis. Deceased.

LATHROP, John, judge; b. Boston, Feb. 8, 1835; s. Rev. John P. and Maria Margaretta (Long) L.; A.B., Burlington (N.J.) Coll., 1853, A.M., 1856; LL.B., Harvard, 1855; LL.D., Williams, 1906; m. Eliza Davis Parker, June 24, 1875. Admitted to bar, 1856; lt. and capt. 35th Mass. Inf., 1862-63; practiced at Boston, 1856-88; reporter decisions Supreme Ct., 1874-88; justice Superior Ct., 1888-91; justice Supreme Jud. Ct. of Mass., 1891-1906; resigned. Lecturer Harvard Law Sch., 1871-73, Boston Law Sch., 1873, 1880-83. Address: Boston, Mass. Died 1910.

LATHROP, John Carroll; b. South Haven, Mich., Apr. 8, 1871; s. Orvis Christy and Laura Virginia (Best) L.; ed. pub. schs., Freeport, Ill.; m. Della S. Benjamin, Oct. 21, 1924. In business in N.Y. City, 1886-96; studied Christian Science with Mary Baker Eddy, at Concord, N.H., 1898, and mem. of her household 18 mos.; practitioner, 1896—; 2d reader to 2d Ch. of Christ, Scientist, New York, 1897-1902, 1st reader, 1906-07; 1st reader The Mother Ch., Boston, 1911-14; pres. same, 1914-15; Christian Science lecturer, 1918-24, 1929. Republican. Home: Brookline, Mass. Deceased.

LATHROP, Julia Clifford; b. Rockford, Ill., 1858; d. William and Sarah Adeline (Potter) Lathrop; Rockford Coll., 2 yrs.; A.B., Vassar Coll., 1880; unmarried. Has spent much time as vol. resident of Hull House, Chicago, 1899—; active worker in various reform movements; has made a spl. study of care of insane, better edn. of children, juvenile ct. laws, etc.; several times visited foreign countries for observation and study of methods. Mem. Ill. State Bd. of Charities, 1893-1909 (intermission by resignation, 4 yrs.); chief Children's Bur., Dept. of Labor, Washington, D.C. Mem. Nat. League of Women Voters; apptd. assessor on Child Welfare Com. of League of Nations, 1925. Author of reports and articles on care of the insane, civil service, child welfare, etc. Address: Rockford. Ill. Died Apr. 15, 1932.

LATHROP, Rose Hawthorne (Mother Mary Alphonsa Lathrop), superioress Dominican Community of Third Order, and directress of Charitable Home; b. Lenox, Mass., May 20, 1851; d. Nathaniel Hawthorne (author); ed. common schs.; m. George Parsons Lathrop (author), 1871. Of late yrs. devoted to betterment of conditions of the poor, especially of cancerous and destitute women; founded St. Rose's Free Home for Cancer, and Rosary Hill Home, 1901. Author: (poems) Along the Shore; Memories of Hawthorne; (with husband) A Story of Courage. Home: New York, N.Y. Died July 9, 1926.

LATHROP, William Langson, artist; b. Warren, Ill., Mar. 29, 1859; s. Byron P. and Isabella (Langson) L.; ed. in acad. at Painesville, O.; self-taught in art; m. Annie Burt, Nov. 1888. Winner of W. T. Evans prize, Webb prize; gold medal, Phila. Art Club; 3d prize, Worcester, Mass.; 3d prize, Carnegie Inst., Pittsburgh; Temple gold medal, Philadelphia Acad. Fine Arts; First Aultman medal, N.A.D. Represented in permanent collections at Carnegie Inst.; Albright Gallery, Buffalo; Minneapolis Art Mus. Gold and silver medals, San Francisco Expn., 1915, St. Louis Art Museum, Rochester Art Museum, Syracuse Art Museum, Phillips Memorial Gallery, Washington, N.A., 1907. Home: New Hope, Pa. Died 1938.

LATIMER, Asbury Churchwell, U.S. senator; b. nr. Lowndesville, S.C., July 31, 1851; s. Clement T. and Frances B. L.; reared on father's farm; common school edn.; m. Sara Alice Brown, June 26, 1877. Took part in campaign of 1876; removed to Belton, Anderson County, 1880, and farmed there; chmn. County Dem. Com., 1890-93; mem. Congress, 1893-1903, 3d S.C. dist.; elected U.S. senator, 1903. Democrat; mem. U.S. Immigration Commn., 1907. Address: Belton, S.C. Died 1908.

LATIMER, (Mary) Elizabeth Wormeley, author; b. London, England, July 26, 1822; d. Rear Admiral Wormeley, of English navy; ed. at home. Published her 1st novel in England, then wrote 2 others and did mag. work until 1856; m. Randolph Brandt Latimer, 1856. Author: Amabel; Our Cousin Veronica; Salvage; My Wife and My Wife's Sister; Princess Amélie; A Chain of Errors; France in the XIXth Century; Russia and Turkey in the XIXth Century; England in the XIXth Century; Europe in Africa in the XIXth Century; Italy in the XIXth Century; Spain in the XIXth Century; My Scrap Book of the French Revolution, 1898; Judea from Cyrus to Titus, 537 B.C.-70 A.D., 1899; Last Years of the XIXth Century, 1901; The Prince Incognito, 1902; Talks of Napoleon at St. Helena with Gen. Gourzand, 1903. Address: St. Denis, Md. Died 1904.

LATIMER, Julian Lane, naval officer; b. Shepherdstown, W.Va., Oct. 10, 1868; s. Thomas Wilmer and Mary Josephine (Quigley) L.; grad. U.S. Naval Acad., 1890; m. Laura Singer Richardson, Dec. 9, 1898; children—Mary Richardson (Mrs. Rupert R. Deese), Laura Towne, Elizabeth Josephine (Mrs. Robert C. Thaxton), Julian Lane. Ensign, July 1, 1892; promoted through grades to rear adm., Nov. 13, 1923. Served on Winslow, Spanish-Am. War, 1898; with Bur. of Ordnance, Navy Dept., 1903-06; on Virginia, 1906-07; comd. Vesuvius, 1907; exec. officer and navigator Montgomery, 1907-09; insp. ordnance and in charge Naval Magazine, Hingham, Mass., 1909-11; comd. Culgoa, 1911-12; exec. officer Vermont, 1912-13; comd. Alabama, 1913-14; insp. engrng. material, Mass. Dist., 1914-16; comd. Rhode Island, 1916-19; at War Coll., 1919-20; comdt. 7th Naval Dist. and Naval Sta., Key West, 1920-21; judge advocate gen. of Navy, 1921-25; comdr. Spl. Service Squadron, 1925-27; comdt. 4th Naval Dist. and Navy Yard, Phila., 1927-30, retired. Home: Clearwater, Fla. Died June 4, 1939.

LATIMER, Margery Bodine, writer; b. Portage, Wis., Feb. 6, 1899; s. Clark Watt and Laura Augusta (Bodine) L.; student Wooster (O.) Coll., U. of Wis. and Columbia; m. Jean Toomer, Oct. 30, 1931. Author: We Are Incredible, 1928; Nellie Bloom and Other Stories, 1929; This Is My Body, 1930; Guardian Angel and Other Stories, 1932. Contbr. book reviews and articles to Century, Bookman, New Masses, New York World, New York Herald-Tribune, etc. Home: Portage, Wis. Died Aug. 16, 1932.

LATIMER, Thomas Erwin, mayor, lawyer; b. Hilliards, O., Apr. 6, 1879; s. Ezekiel and Anna (Van Schoick) L.; student Ohio State U., 1899-1900; A.B., U. of Wash., 1908; A.M., U. of Ill., 1909; LL.B., U. of Minn., 1914; m. Mae Helser, Sept. 1904 (divorced); 1 son, Ira Helser; m. 2d, Elsie Henry, Aug. 10, 1910 (died 1932); m. 3d, Mildred Unger, July 3, 1934. Admitted to Minn. bar, 1919, and practiced in Minneapolis; atty. for Minn. State banking dept., 1933-35; mayor of Minneapolis, 1935—; dir. Triangle Development Co. Mem. Farmer-Labor Party. Methodist. Mason, Odd Fellow, K.P., Eagle. Home: Minneapolis, Minn. Died Nov. 6, 1937.

LATIMER, Thomas Sargent, physician; b. Savannah, Ga., June 17, 1839; s. William Geddes and Mary (Collins) L.; ed. Sherwood Acad., York, Pa., U. of Md., M.D., 1861; unmarried. Pvt. 1st Md. regt., C.S.A., 1 yr., asst. surgeon, same regt., and surgeon, 1864. Engaged in practice, Baltimore. Successively prof. physiology, Baltimore Coll. Dental Surgery; prof. surgery, 1875, diseases of children, 1878, principles and practice of medicine, 1895, Coll. of Phys. and Surg., Baltimore; prof. principles and practice of medicine, Post-Graduate Med. Sch., Baltimore; pres. Baltimore Med. Coll.; now pres. Coll. of Phys. and Surg., Baltimore. Was editor Baltimore Med. Journal, 1871, Journal of Coll. of Phys. and Surg., 1875; editor physiol. part Harris' Dental Surgery. Address: Baltimore, Md. Died 1906.

LATROBE, Ferdinand Claiborne, lawyer; b. Baltimore, Oct. 14, 1833; s. John H. B. and Charlotte Virginia (Claiborne) L.; ed. Coll. of St. James, Md.; m. Louisa Swann; m. 2d, Ellen Penrose. Admitted to bar, 1860, and practiced at Baltimore. Mem. Md. Ho. of Dels., 1869-72 and 1900 (speaker, 1870-72 and extra session, 1901); judge-advocate-gen., gov.'s staff, 1868-79; mayor of Baltimore 7 terms, 1874-95. Pres. Consolidated Gas Co., Baltimore, 1900—. Home: Baltimore, Md. Died 1911.

LATTA, James P., congressman; b. Ashland, O., Oct. 31, 1844; s. John and Mary (White) L.; removed with parents to Eastern Ia. at 2 yrs. of age; dist. sch. edn.; m. Libbie Jonas, Dec. 29, 1870. Took up homestead in Neb., 1863, and engaged in farming and stock raising; organized pvt. bank at Tekamah, Neb. 1880; organized, 1890, and pres. First Nat. Bank of Tekamah. Mem. Neb. Ho. of Rep., 1887, Senate, 1907; mem. 61st Congress (1909-11), 3d Neb. Dist. Democrat. Episcopalian. Address: Tekamah, Neb. Died 1911.

LATTA, Thomas Albert, newspaper editor; b. Park Hill Mission, Indian Ty., Sept. 7, 1872; s. James Eudoris and Harriet Ann (Sheldon) L.; ed. mission schs. and pvt. instrs.; m. Iva Kirkpatrick, Sept. 26, 1900; children—Kirk Edward, Iva, Harriet, Albert Lloyd, Thomas J., Chester A., Alma, Mankie, Dwight M. In newspaper business, 1893—; founder Bartlesville (Okla.) Enterprise; editor Tulsa Daily World, 1919—. Served as pvt. U.S. Vols., Spanish-Am. War. Republican. Presbyn. Mason. Author: Life's Highway, 1928. Home: Tulsa, Okla. Died Apr. 11, 1931.

LATTIMER, George W., wholesale druggist; b. Columbus, O., Dec. 6, 1856; s. Oliver Hallam and Sarah Atherton (Cox) L.; A.B., Amherst, 1879; m. Belle Gardner, 1884 (died 1886); m. 2d, Minnie Williams, 1898. Engaged as wholesale druggist, 1882—, as mfr., 1905—; sec. and treas. The Kauffman-Lattimer Co., The Lattimer-Stevens Co.; sec. The Nye Stove Co., successor to Lattimer Stove Co., of which was pres. 12 yrs. Mem. U.S. Chamber of Commerce, Columbus Chamber of Commerce (mem. 1st bd., 1882, now pres.), Columbus Park Bd. (pres.); represented Ohio Red Cross during floods, 1913; was one of 3 commrs. of Franklin County Conservation Bd. to correct flood dangers; mem. Flood Commn. of Ohio, apptd. by the gov.; mem. State Bd. of Arbitration, Ohio Inst. for Public Efficiency (pres.), Central Philanthropic Council; trustee Associated Charities, Humane Soc. Pres. Nat. Wholesale Druggists' Assn. Awarded medal by Am. Red Cross for work during flood of 1913. Republican. Congregationalist. Home: Columbus, O. Died Feb. 12, 1920.

LATTIMORE, John Compere, school supt.; b. Marion, Ala., Mar. 25, 1862; s. Rev. John Lee and Sarah Catherine (Shivers) L.; grad. Nat. Normal Coll., 1886; B.S., Baylor U., 1895, M.S., 1896; m. Lucy Edens, June 20, 1889. Supt. schs., Falls County, Tex., 1887-90; prin. prep. sch., 1890-92, prof. mathematics, 1892-97, chmn. faculty, 1897-99, Baylor U.; supt. city schs., Waco, Tex., 1899—. Mem. faculty Tex.-Colo. Chautauqua, Boulder, Colo., 1900; mem. Tex. State Bd. of Examiners, 1900-05. Pres. Tex. State Teachers' Assn., 1899. Address: Waco, Tex. Died Mar. 1915.

LATTIMORE, Offa Shivers, judge; b. Marion, Ala., Jan. 10, 1865; s. John Lee and Sarah Catherine (Shivers) L.; A.B., Baylor U., 1887, LL.D., 1927; studied law pvtly.; m. Ermine Field Buck, June 23, 1890; children—Offa Shivers, Halbert Shipp, John Lee, William Buck, Robert Baker, Oliver Carroll, Walter Risher. With Tex. Central Ry. Co., 1883-84; pub. sch. teacher, 1887-89; admitted to Tex. bar, 1889; practiced in Ft. Worth, 1889-1919; asst. state's atty., Tarrant County, 1890-94, state's atty., 1900-04; mem. Tex. State Senate, 1911-19; judge of Court of Criminal Appeals, of Tex., 1919—. Pres. bd. of trustees, Southwestern Bapt. Theol. Sem., Ft. Worth, 1915-28, San Marcos Acad., 1932—; pres. Bapt. Gen. Conv. of Tex., 1920-23. Democrat. Home: Austin, Tex. Deceased.

LATTIMORE, Samuel Allan, univ. prof.; b. Union County, Ind., May 31, 1828; s. Samuel and Mary (Poague) L.; A.B., Ind. Asbury (now DePauw) U., 1850, A.M., 1853 (hon. Ph.D., 1873, and Ia. Wesleyan, 1873; LL.D., Hamilton, 1873); m. Ellen Frances Larrabee, July 28, 1852. Classical tutor, 1850-52, prof. Greek, 1852-60, Ind. Asbury U.; prof. chemistry, Genesee Coll., 1860-67; prof. chemistry, 1867-1908, emeritus prof., 1908, chmn. exec. com., 1886-96, acting pres., 1896-98, U. of Rochester. Commr. annual assay U.S. Mint, 1879, 1900. Chemist N.Y. State Bd. of Health, 1881-83, N.Y. State Dept. of Agr., 1886—. Address: Rochester, N.Y. Died Feb. 17, 1913.

LAUBACH, Charles, geologist, archæologist; b. Durham, Pa., Aug. 29, 1836; s. Anthony L.; ed. in Durham public schools and Collegiate Inst., Easton, Pa. (grad., 1860); studied phrenology; also studied medicine with Dr. H. A. Benton, Saratoga, and obstetrics with Dr. Jacob Ludlow, Easton, Pa.; m. Jane Raub, Mar. 29, 1860. Practiced med. electricity and homœpathy while giving phrenological lectures and delineations of character, and was also engaged in farming; began scientific investigations, 1865, and has devoted prin. attention to them, 1870—. Corr. mem. U. of Pa., archæol. and palæontol. dept.; mem. Anthropol. Club, Phila.; charter mem. Bucks County Hist. Soc. Wrote: History of Durham Township, 1887; Geology of Bucks County, Pa., in Warner's History of Bucks County; Prehistoric Man in the Delaware Valley, 1880. Address: Riegelsville, Pa. Died 1904.

LAUCHHEIMER, Charles Henry, officer U.S. Marine Corps; b. Baltimore, Sept. 22, 1859; s. Meyer Henry and Babette L.; grad. Baltimore City Coll., 1877; grad. U.S. Naval Acad., 1881; LL.B., George Washington U., 1894; unmarried. Officer U.S. Marine Corps, 1883—; promoted through the various grades to rank of brig. gen., Aug. 29, 1916. Also adj. and insp. U.S. Marine Corps. Author: Forms of Procedure for Naval Courts and Boards, 1896, 1902. Died Jan. 14, 1920.

LAUFER, Berthold, anthropologist, Orientalist; s. Max and Eugenie (Schlesinger) L.; b. Cologne, Germany, Oct. 11, 1874; ed. Friedrich Wilhelms Gymnasium, Cologne, 1884-93, U. of Berlin, 1893-95, Sem. for Oriental Languages, Berlin, 1894-95; Ph.D., U. of Leipzig, 1897; LL.D., U. of Chicago, 1931; m. Bertha Hampton. Came to U.S., 1898. Leader Jesup N. Pacific expdn. to Saghalin Island and the Amur region of Eastern Siberia for exploration of ethnology of native tribes, 1898-99; of Jacob H. Schiff expdn. to China for culture-hist. investigations and ethnol. collections, 1901-04; asst. in ethnology, Am. Mus. Natural History, 1904-06; lecturer anthropology, 1905, anthropology and East Asiatic langs., 1906-07, Columbia; asst. curator East-Asiatic Division, 1908—, associate curator of Asiatic ethnology, 1911—, curator of anthropology, 1915, Field Mus. Natural History. Leader Blackstone expdn. to Tibet and China, 1908-10; Marshall Field expdn. to China, 1923. Mem. advisory bd. China Inst. America; mem. Am. Com. of Nat. Council Chinese Cultural and Econ. Inst.; mem. Com. on Promotion of Friendship between America and the Far East; mem. bd. Am. Inst. Persia Art and Archæology. Pres. Am. Oriental Soc., 1930-31. Mem. com. on promotion of Chinese studies and com. on promotion of Japanese studies of Am. Council of Learned Societies. Associate editor American Journal Archæology; spl. corr. Nat. Library, Peiping, China; mem. Advisory Council of Yenching U., Peiping. Author of numerous books and over 200 monographs relating to the ethnology, archæology, art, and philology of Asia, history of cultivated plants and domesticated animals. Collaborator U.S. Dept. of Agr. Made extensive collections of oriental books and mss. for Newberry and John Crerar Libraries, Chicago. Address: Chicago, Ill. Died Sept. 13, 1934.

LAUFER, Calvin Weiss, clergyman; b. Brodheadsville, Pa., Apr. 6, 1874; s. Nathan and Angelina (Weiss) L.; B.A., Franklin and Marshall Coll., Lancaster, Pa., 1897, M.A., 1900; grad. Union Theol. Sem., 1900; D.D., Hastings Coll., 1925; m. Ellen Florinda Metzger, Nov. 28, 1895; 1 son, Edward Basil. Ordained Presbyn. ministry, 1900; pastor Steinway Ref. Ch., Long Island City, N.Y., 1900-05, 1st Presbyn. Ch., West Hoboken, N.J., 1905-14; field rep. Presbyn. Bd. Publn. and S.S. Work, 1914-24; field rep. Presbyn. Bd. Christian Edn., 1924—, also asst. editor of musical publications, 1925—. Mem. Hymn Soc. of New York. Democrat. Author: Keynotes of Optimism, 1911; The Incomparable Christ, 1914; The Bible—Story and Content, 1924; Junior Church School Hymnal, 1927; Songs for Men, 1928; The Church School Hymnal for Youth, 1928; Primary Music and Worship, 1930; Hymn Lore, 1932; The Hymnal, 1933; When the Little Child Wants to Sing, 1935; Handbook to the Hymnal, 1935. Home: Philadelphia, Pa. Died Sept. 20, 1938.

LAUGHINGHOUSE, Charles O'Hagan, M.D.; b. Pitt County, N.C., Feb. 25, 1871; s. Joseph J. and Eliza (O'Hagan) L.; Horner's Mil. Sch., Oxford, N.C.; U. of N.C.; U. of Pa., M.D., 1893; m. Carrie Dail, June 1896; children—Helen, Charles O'Hagan, Haywood Dail. Practiced, Greenville, N.C., 1893—; mem. Bd. Med. Examiners of N.C., 1902-08, inclusive (pres., 1906-08); mem. State Bd. of Health N.C., 1911—; sec. and state health officer of State Bd. of Health, term 1927-33. Member N.C. Sanitary Commn.; coroner and supt. of health for Pitt Co. Commd. maj., Med. O.R.C., May 1917; lt. col., M.C. U.S.A., Aug. 1918; comdg. officer Base Hosp. 85, in France, Sept. 1918-Feb. 1919. Mem. N.C. State Council Defense. Dir. Greenville Banking & Trust Co., Home Bldg. & Loan Assn. Mem. Med. Soc. State of N.C. (pres. 1917), Tri-State Med. Soc. (pres. 1923), Seaboard Med. Soc. (pres., sec.). Democrat. Home: Raleigh, N.C. Died Aug. 26, 1930.

LAUGHLIN, Clara Elizabeth, author; b. New York, N.Y., Aug. 3, 1873; d. Samuel Wilson and Elizabeth (Abbott) L.; grad. North Division High Sch., Chicago, 1890; unmarried. Author: Reminiscences of James Whitcomb Riley, 1916; The Heart of Her Highness, 1917; The Keys of Heaven, 1918; Foch, The Man, 1918; The Martyred Towns of France, 1919; Jeanne-Marie's Triumph, 1922; So You're Going to Paris, 1924; So You're Going to Italy, 1925; So You're Going to England, 1926; So You're Going to France, 1927; So You're Going to Rome, 1928; Where It All Comes True in Italy and Switzerland, 1928; Where It All Comes True in Scandinavia, 1929; Where It All Comes True in France, 1929; So You're Going to Germany and Austria, 1930; So You're Going to Spain, 1931; So You're Going to Ireland and Scotland, 1932; Traveling Through Life, 1934; So You're Going to the Mediterranean, 1935; So You're Going to Scandinavia, 1937; So You're Going to Travel, 1938; So You're Visiting New York, 1939; So You're Seeing New England, 1940. Founder and director of The Clara Laughlin Travel Services; wrote The Clara Laughlin Travel Study Courses. Editor and publisher Clara Laughlin's So You're Going, magazine for travel lovers (monthly). Decorated Chevalier Legion of Honor, 1923. Fellow Am. Geographical Soc., 1932; v.p. Am. Hist. Soc., 1935. Home: Chicago, Ill. Died Mar. 3, 1941.

LAUGHLIN, George Ashton, editor, pub.; b. Wheeling, W.Va., Sept. 28, 1862; s. Samuel and Sydney P. (Ott) L.; ed. Linsly Inst., Wheeling; m. Anna Boettger Bruning, Apr. 5, 1906. Began as sec. Nail City Lantern Co., 1880; pres. Wheeling Intelligencer, 1902-08; editor and pub. Wheeling Evening Telegraph, 1913-25; dir. Wheeling Intelligencer, Wheeling Evening News. Mem. W.Va. Ho. of Dels., 1900, 1931-32; del. at large Rep. Nat. Conv., 1908; dist. delegate Rep. Nat. Convention, 1928. Republican candidate for Congress, 1912; Progressive candidate for Congress, 1913; mem. W.Va. State Capitol Commn. Pres. Wheeling Bd. of Trade, 2 terms. Republican. Presbyn. Mem. Ancient Order United Workmen. Home: Wheeling, W.Va. Died Dec. 7, 1936.

LAUGHLIN, Irwin (Boyle), diplomat; b. Pittsburgh, Pa., April 26, 1871; s. Maj. George McCully and Isabel Bowman (McKennan) L.; B.A., Yale U., 1893; m. Thérese, d. Adrian Iselin, Sept. 18, 1912; children—Gertrude (wife of Hubert Winthrop Chanler, U.S. Navy), Alexander (deceased). Entered office of Jones & Laughlin, Ltd., Pittsburgh, 1894; treas. Jones & Laughlin Steel Co., 1900-03. Pvt. sec. to Am. minister to Japan, 1903-05; 2d sec. Am. Legation at Tokyo, 1905-06; sec. Legation at Bangkok and consul gen. for Siam, 1906-07; 2d sec. Legation at Peking, Mar.-Sept. 1907; 2d sec. Embassy at St. Petersburg, 1907-08; sec. legation to Greece and Montenegro, 1908-09; 2d sec. Embassy at Paris, Aug.-Dec. 1909; sec. spl. Embassy to Sultan of Turkey, Oct.-Nov. 1910; sec. Embassy at Berlin, Dec. 21, 1909-Sept. 1912 (chargé d'affaires June-Oct. 1911); sec. Embassy at London, 1912-17 (chargé d'affaires, Dec. 15, 1912-May 24, 1913, July-Oct. 1916, May-July and Oct.-Dec. 1918), and was counselor of the Embassy, 1916-19, when took extended leave of absence; on duty at Conf. for Limitation of Armament, as sec. to Henry Cabot Lodge, 1921. E.E. and M.P. to Greece, 1924-26; ambassador to Spain, 1929-33. Representative for U.S. on Internat. Commn. for the Advancement of Peace between U.S. and Denmark; mem. bd. regents Smithsonian Instn., 1923-35. Republican. Address: Washington, D.C. Died Apr. 18, 1941.

LAUGHLIN, James Laurence, political economist; b. Deerfield, O., Apr. 2, 1850; s. Harvey and Mary M. (Mills) L.; A.B., Harvard, 1873, A.M. and Ph.D., 1876; Doctor, honoris causa, 300th Jubilee, U. of Giessen, 1906; m. Alice McGuffey, Sept. 1875. Taught in Hopkinson's Classical Sch., Boston, 1873-78; instr. polit. economy, 1878-83, asst. prof., 1883-88, Harvard; pres. Mfrs. Mut. Fire Ins. Co., Phila., 1888-90; prof. polit. economy, Cornell, 1890-92; prof. and head dept. polit. economy, U. of Chicago, 1892-1916, emeritus. Editor Journal of Political Economy, 1892—; lecturer in Berlin on invitation of Prussian Cultus Ministerium, 1906. In 1894-95 prepared for govt. of San Domingo a scheme of monetary reform, which was afterwards adopted; mem. Monetary Commn. created by Indianapolis Monetary Conf., 1897; del. Pan-Am. Scientific Congress, Santiago, Chile, 1909; chmn. exec. com. Nat. Citizens' League for Promotion of Sound Banking System, 1911-13; mem. European commn. of Nat. Industrial Conf. Bd., 1919. Mem. L'Institut Internat. de Statistique, Cobden Club; sec. Political Economy Club. Author: Anglo-Saxon Legal Procedure in Anglo-Saxon Laws, 1876; J. S. Mill's Principles of Political Economy (abridged), 1884; Study of Political Economy, 1885; History of Bimetallism in United States, 1886; Elements of Political Economy, 1887; Gold and Prices Since 1873, 1887; Facts About Money, 1895; Report of Monetary Commission, 1898;

Principles of Money, 1903; Reciprocity, 1903; Industrial America, 1906; Aus dem Amerikanischen Wirtschaftsleben, 1907; Latter-Day Problems, 1909; Credit of the Nations, 1918; Money and Prices, 1919; Banking Progress, 1920; Money, Credit and Prices, 2 vols., 1931. Home: Jaffrey, N.H. Died Nov. 28, 1933.

LAUGHLIN, Julian, lawyer; b. Bath County, Ky., Sept. 27, 1852; s. Tarlton Chiles and Anna (Hopkins) L.; student Transylvania U., 1867-71; admitted to St. Louis bar, 1877; m. Laura E. Vail, June 28, 1898. Author: History of Civilization, 1904. Advocate of a theory of life, theory as to corpuscles and cells forming colonies in human beings, theory as to formation of the solar system, also as to classification of mankind into four races—white, yellow, brown and black. Home: St. Louis Co., Mo. Deceased.

LAUGHTON, George, clergyman; b. Sowerby Bridge, Yorkshire, Eng., June 12, 1875; s. John and Susanna (Brearley) L.; early edn. in England; D.D., Manitoba Coll., Winnipeg, Can., 1926; m. Amelia Pearl Smith, Oct. 28, 1898; 1 dau., Elizabeth Field (wife of Rev. John W. Claxton). Came to U.S., 1897, naturalized, 1915. Ordained Congl. ministry, 1902; held pastorates in N.Y., Mich. and San Francisco, Calif.; pastor First Foreign Ch., Hilo, Hawaii, 1913-17, First Ch., Riverside, Calif., 1917-20, Central Ch., Winnipeg, 1920-26, Montreal, 1926-29, First Ch., Toledo, O., 1929—. Chaplain 2d Regt. N.G., Hawaii, 1917; spl. speaker at mil. camps on Pacific Coast, 1917-18. British interchange preacher and speaker, 1934. Pres. of Toledo Council of Chs., 1938. Wrote pamphlets: The Challenge of Jesus, The Ministry of the Master. Mason. Rotarian. Home: Toledo, O. Died Oct. 12, 1941.

LAUNT, Francis Albemarle Delbretons, clergyman; b. Hamilton, N.Y., June 13, 1864; s. Fitzpatrick and Samantha (van Rensselaer) L.; A.B., Colgate, 1882, A.M., 1890; post-grad. student U. of Oxford, Eng.; studied theology, St. Andrew's Div. Sch.; D.D., Griswold Coll., 1901; D.C.L., U. of King's Coll., 1905. Deacon, 1884, priest, 1886, P.E. Ch.; rector Auburn, N.Y., 1886-91, St. David's, Phila., 1891-1910; examining chaplain to bishop of Pa., 1900-10; rector Holy Trinity Ch., Pueblo, Colo., 1911-14; apptd. lecturer St. Catherine's Coll., Cambridge U., Eng., 1914; abroad, chiefly in lit. pursuits, 1915-18; in Eng. and Italy, 1919-21; spl. preacher, Washington, D.C., and New York, 1924-25. Mason. Author: A Plea for the Prayer Book, 1900; Bartered Birthright, 1901; The Other Cheek; Theological Essays; The Italian Debacle, 1917; Lectures to Masons (Ecclesiastes XII), 1922; Beautiful Bermuda, 1923. Address: Pueblo, Colo.; and Washington, D.C. Deceased.

LAURENTI, Mario, operatic baritone; b. Verona, Italy; ed. as mech. engr., in Verona and Dusseldorf, Germany; studied singing at Verona, Paris, and Dresden, Germany. Joined Met. Opera Co., 1917; principal rôles in Bohème, Lucia, Faust, Carmen, Pagliacci, Cavalleria, Iote Stadt, Manon, Manon Lescaut, Butterfly, and other operas. Home: New York, N.Y. Died Mar. 7, 1922.

LAURIAT, Charles Emelius, bookseller; b. Boston, Mass., Jan. 12, 1842; s. Emelius Anselm and Martha (Foster) L.; grad. Phillips Grammar Sch., Boston; m. Harriet F. Page, Nov. 13, 1867. Began at 20 with W. H. Piper & Co., old booksellers, Boston, continuing 10 yrs.; formed partnership with Dana Estes, as Estes & Lauriat, pubs. and booksellers, 1872, succeeded by Charles E. Lauriat Co., 1898, when became pres.; dir. John Hancock Mut. Life Ins. Co. Republican. Home: Boston, Mass. Died Feb. 12, 1920.

LAURIE, William, clergyman; b. Wigtownshire, Scotland, Aug. 19, 1832; s. William and Jane (Murdoch) L.; came to U.S., 1853; A.B., U. of Pa., 1863; grad. Princeton Theol. Sem., 1866; D.D., Lafayette Coll., Pa., 1886; LL.D., Western U. of Pa., 1897; m. Martha Bailieff, May 8, 1855 (died Aug. 10, 1870); m. 2d, Alice A. Ives, Mar. 5, 1874. Ordained to Presbyn. ministry, 1866; pastor, Stewartsville, N.J., 1866-72, Penn Yan, N.Y., 1872-75, Bellefonte, Pa., 1876-1905. Moderator Synod of Pa., 1897. Address: Bellefonte, Pa. Died 1908.

LAUT, Agnes C., author; b. Ontario, Can., Feb. 11, 1871; grandfather was prin. Queen's U.; taken to Winnipeg in childhood; left Manitoba U. in junior yr. because of ill health; spent summers in Rockies and Selkirks; unmarried. Became editorial writer Manitoba Free Press, Winnipeg, 1895-97; later corr. Am., Canadian and English papers, and mags. in New York. Author: Lords of the North, 1900; Heralds of Empire, 1902; The Story of the Trapper, 1902; Pathfinders of the West, 1904; Vikings of Pacific; Hudson's Bay Company, 1909; Freebooters of the Wilderness, 1910; New Dawn, 1913; Through Unknown Southwest, 1913; Adventures of England on Hudson Bay, 1914; Canadian Commonwealth, 1915; Pioneers of the Pacific Coast, 1915; Conquest of Our Western Empire, 1927; Romance of the Rails, 2 vols., 1928; Overland Trail, 1929; Life of Cadillac, 1931; Pilgrims of the Santa Fe, 1931. Address: Wassaic, N.Y. Died Nov. 15, 1936.

LAUTERBACH, Edward, lawyer; b. New York, Aug. 12, 1844; s. Solon and Mina L.; A.B., Coll. City of New York, 1864, A.M., 1867; LL.D., Manhattan Coll., 1905; admitted to bar, 1866; m. Amanda Friedman, 1870. Mem. law firm Hoadly, Lauterbach & Johnson; active in important ry., telegraph and maritime cases; pres. Baltimore & Southern Ry. Co.; v.p. Am. R.R. Co. of P.R.; dir. various charitable instns.; regent U. State of N.Y.; chmn. bd. of trustees Coll. City of New York. Chmn. Rep. Co. Com., 1895-97. Home: New York, N.Y. Died Mar. 4, 1923.

LAUX, August, artist; b. in the Rhine Pfalz, Bavaria, Dec. 18, 1847; s. Henry and Barbara L.; removed with parents to New York, 1863; studied at Nat. Acad. Design; m. Emilia Heisterhazen, Mar. 9, 1876. Exhibited 1st in spring of 1870 at Nat. Acad.; became notable for decorative work, but devoted his attention to genre and still-life pictures after 1880. Died July 21, 1921.

LAVAL, Jean M., bishop (auxiliary); b. St. Étienne, Loire, France, Sept. 21, 1854; s. François and Catherine (Crozet) L.; studied Mont Brison Little Sem., France; St. Michael Jesuit Coll., St. Etienne; came to U.S., 1872; studied philosophy and theology, New Orleans. Ordained R.C. priest, 1877; asst. pastor, Baton Rouge, La., 1877-84; pastor St. Gabriel's Ch., Iberville, La., 1884-90, St. Francis Ch., Houma, La., 1890-93, St. Joseph's Ch., Baton Rouge, 1893-95, St. John's Ch., New Orleans, 1895-1902, St. Louis Cathedral, New Orleans, 1902-11; apptd. auxiliary bishop of New Orleans, Nov. 28, 1911, also vicar-gen., and pastor Ch. of St. Vincent de Paul. Address: New Orleans, La. Died June 4, 1937.

LAVELLE, Michael J., priest; b. N.Y. City, May 30, 1856; s. Patrick and Rose (Fitzsimons) L.; A.B., Manhattan Coll., 1873, A.M., 1875; grad. St. Joseph's Sem., Troy, N.Y., 1874; LL.D., Manhattan, 1897, Notre Dame, 1920, Fordham, 1929. Ordained R.C. priest 1879; asst., St. Patrick's Cathedral, N.Y. City, 1879-86, rector, 1886—; diocesan consultor, Archdiocese of N.Y. Apptd. vicar gen., New York, 1902; domestic prelate to Pope Pius X, 1903; Prothonotary Apostolic by Pope Pius XII, 1929. Address: New York, N.Y. Died Oct. 17, 1939.

LAW, Arthur Ayer, surgeon; b. Harvard, Ill., Apr. 16, 1872; s. Arthur E. and Eva (Ayer) L.; M.D., U. of Minn., 1894; m. Helen E. Lougee, Nov. 29, 1899; children—Mrs. James G. Fullerton, Mary Ayer. Practiced at Minneapolis, 1894—; asso. prof. surgery, U. of Minn. Med. Sch., 1914—; surgeon Northwestern Hosp.; surgeon and asst. chief University Hosp.; consulting surgeon Glenn Lake Sanatorium. Republican. Episcopalian. Home: Minneapolis, Minn. Died July 9, 1930.

LAW, Charles Blakeslee, judge; b. Hannibal, N.Y., Feb. 5, 1872; s. Eli B. and Mary Louisa (Payne) L.; B.S., Amherst Coll., 1895; m. Ilma Best, Nov. 20, 1901. Admitted to bar, 1897, and practiced at Brooklyn and New York; mem. Rep. County Com., Kings County, N.Y., 1899—; mem. 59th to 61st Congresses (1905-11) 4th N.Y. Dist.; sheriff of Kings County, 1911-13; justice Municipal Ct. of New York, 1916-25. Home: Brooklyn, N.Y. Died Sept. 15, 1929.

LAW, Evander McIver, soldier; b. Darlington, S.C., Aug. 7, 1836; s. E. Augustus and Elizabeth (McIver) L.; grad. S.C. Mil. Acad. of Charleston, 1856; admitted to bar, Yorkville, S.C., 1868; m. Jane E. Latta, Mar. 9, 1863. Prof. history and belles lettres, King's Mountain Mil. Acad., 1857-60; entered C.S.A., Apr. 1861, as lt. col. 4th Ala. Inf.; col. same, Oct. 1861; brig. gen., Oct. 3, 1862; maj. gen., Mar. 20, 1865. Supt. S. Fla. Mil. Inst., 1894-1903. Comdr. Florida Div. U.C.V., 1899-1903, hon. comdr. for life, 1903—. Democrat. Address: Bartow, Fla. Died Oct. 31, 1920.

LAW, James, veterinarian; b. Edinburgh, Scotland, Feb. 13, 1838; ed. burgh schs., Dunbar; vet. and med. schs., Edinburgh; l'École Veterinaire, Alfort, Paris; l'École Veterinaire, Lyons, France; grad. Highland and Agrl. Soc. Vet. Bd., 1857 (V.S.); Royal Coll. of Veterinary Surgeons (M.R.C.V.S., 1863; F.R.C.V.S., 1870). Prof. anatomy and materia medica Edinburgh New Vet. Coll., 1860-65; prof. anatomy Albert Vet. Coll., London, 1865-67; prof. veterinary science, Cornell, 1868-96; dir. and dean, 1896-1908, emeritus, 1908—, N.Y. State Vet. Coll. (Cornell U.). Consulting veterinarian to the N.Y. State Agrl. Soc., 1869-96; chmn. U.S. Treasury cattle commn., 1882-83; field chief of Bur. of Animal Industry for extinction of cattle lung plague in Ill. and N.Y., 1887-88. Author: General and Descriptive Anatomy of Domestic Animals; Farmers' Veterinary Adviser; Text Book of Veterinary Medicine, 5 vols. Address: Ithaca, N.Y. Died May 10, 1921.

LAW, Robert; b. North Platte, Neb., Aug. 17, 1874; s. Robert and Rosetta C. (Michael) L.; student U. of Chicago, 1894-98; m. Frances V. Barnsdall, Apr. 25, 1906; children—Robert Barnsdall, Theodore Newton. Began with C.B.&Q. R.R., 1898; successively engaged in oil production, natural gas production, banking and gen. business; with Barnsdall Corp., petroleum and metal producers, etc., 1919—, pres., 1919-26, later dir.; chmn. bd. Barnsdall Corp., Fairchild Aviation Corp.; dir. Michigan Gas & Oil Co., The Aviation Corp., Small Issues Corp., Bowman Management, Inc., Development Service Corp. Republican. Episcopalian. Home: Port Chester, N.Y. Died Aug. 2, 1932.

LAW, Thomas Hart, clergyman; b. Hartsville, S.C., Aug. 26, 1838; s. Thomas Cassells and Mary Westfield (Hart) L.; grad. S.C. Mil. Acad., 1859; grad. Columbia (S.C.) Theol. Sem., 1862; D.D., Presbyn. Coll. of S.C.; m. Anna Elizabeth Adger, Mar. 16, 1864. Ordained Presbyn. ministry, 1862; pastor, Florence, S.C., 1862-65; (chaplain C.S.A., Ft. Caswell, N.C., 1863); evangelist, Charleston (S.C.) Presbytery, 1867-69; pastor, Spartanburg, S.C., 1869-86; field sec. Am. Bible Soc., 1887-1907; stated clerk and treas. Synod of S.C., 1875-1923; permanent clerk Southern Presbyn. Gen. Assembly, 1904-10; stated clerk and treas. Gen. Assembly, 1910-22. Home: Spartanburg, S.C. Died Dec. 14, 1923.

LAW, William Adger, insurance, banker; b. Hartsville, S.C., Dec. 26, 1864; s. Thomas Hart and Anna Elizabeth (Adger) L.; A.B., Wofford Coll., 1881; m. Lucy Lathrop Goode, Dec. 4, 1889; children—Margaret Lathrop, Mrs. Anna Harris. Pres. Spartanburg Savings Bank, 1891-1903, Central Nat. Bank, Spartanburg, 1893-1903; asst. cashier, cashier, v.p., later pres. Merchants' Nat. Bank, Phila., 1903-10; 1st v.p., 1910-15, pres. 1915-22, chmn. bd., 1922-23, First Nat. Bank, Phila.; pres. Penn Mutual Life Ins. Co., 1922—; dir. First Nat. Bank (Phila.), Fire Assn. (Phila.), Fidelity-Phila. Trust Co., Phila. Electric Co., Reading Co. Mgr. Saving Fund Soc. of Germantown and Its Vicinity; trustee Graduate Hosp. Pres. Am. Bankers Assn., 1914-15. Presbyn.; pres. bd. trustees Gen. Assembly Presbyn. Ch. of U.S.A. Home: Philadelphia, Pa. Died Jan. 21, 1936.

LA WALL, Charles Herbert, pharmacist, chemist; b. Allentown, Pa., May 7, 1871; s. John Jacob and Emma Jane (Boas) La Wall; grad. coll. prep. course, State Normal Sch., Bloomsburg, Pa., 1888; Ph.G., Phila. Coll. Pharmacy, 1893, Ph.M., 1905; hon. Phar.D., U. of Pittsburgh, 1919; Sc.D., Susquehanna U., 1920; m. Millicent Saxon Renshaw, June 5, 1907. Commercial chemist, 1894-1903; instr. pharmacy, 1900-06, asso. prof., 1906-18, prof. of theory and practice of pharmacy, and dean, 1918—, Phila. Coll. Pharmacy and Science. Chemist Pa. Dept. Agr., Bur. of Food, 1904—, Pa. State Pharm. Exam. Bd., 1905-12, 1914—, Pa. Health Dept., 1906-18; food inspection chemist, U.S. Dept. Agr., 1907-12; sec., 1910-18, chmn., 1918-20, sec., 1920—, U.S. Pharmacopœia Revision Com. (chmn. sub-com. inorganic chemicals, 1910; chmn. sub-com. reagents, 1920; chmn. on Volatile oils, 1931); mem. revision com. Nat. Formulary, 1906-29; mem. advisory com. med. supplies, War Industries Bd., World War, 1918-19; pres. Am. Assn. Coll. Pharmacy, 1923. Mem. Internat. com. health and council League of Nations for Studying Opium Assay, 1931—. Republican. Mem. Am. Pharm. Assn. (pres. 1919), Pa. Pharm. Assn. (pres. 1911). Mason. Author: Four Thousand Years of Pharmacy, 1927. Joint Author: Leffmann and La Wall's Organic Chemistry, 1905. Collaborating editor U.S. Dispensatory, 1917—, Remington Practice Pharmacy, 1918—. Recipient of Remington medal for distinguished work in pharmacy, 1928. Home: Philadelphia, Pa. Died Dec. 7, 1937.

LAWLER, Thomas G., comdr.-in-chief G.A.R., 1894-95; b. Liverpool, England, April 7, 1844; brought to Ill. in childhood; enlisted as private, Co. E. 19th Ill. inf., June 1861; became sergt. and was elected 1st lt., but was not commissioned; comd. his co. for 2 months during Atlanta campaign; was col. 3d Ill. inf. 7 yrs.; organized, 1876, Rockford Rifles; postmaster of Rockford, 1877-85, 1889-93 and 1897—. Republican. Coal and lumber mcht. Address: Rockford, Ill. Died 1908.

LAWLOR, William Patrick, judge; b. N.Y. City, Sept. 17, 1854; s. Patrick and Eliza (Maher) L.; left an orphan at 10; ed. parochial and night schs.; worked in cotton and silk mills of Paterson, N.J.; removed to Calif., 1877, and worked in mines; student Hastings Coll. of Law, San Francisco, 1885-87; m. Mary Lee Henry, Nov. 25, 1913. Admitted to Calif. bar, 1898; judge Superior Ct., City and County of San Francisco, 1898-1915; asso. justice Supreme Court of Calif., term 1915-27. Democrat. Catholic. Home: San Francisco, Calif. Deceased.

LAWRANCE, Marion, secretary; b. Winchester, O., Oct. 2, 1850; s. Elonson and Amanda Melvina (Irvin) L.; moved with parents, 1854, to Yellow Springs, O.; ed. Antioch Coll.; m. Flora Gaines, Oct. 15, 1874. Bookkeeper at Syracuse, N.Y., 1871-73; in retail shoe business, Toledo, O., 1873-77; traveling salesman, 1877-83; in fire ins. business, 1883-89; sec. Ohio State S.S. Assn., 1889-99; gen. sec. Internat. S.S. Assn., 1899—; also gen. sec. World's S.S. Assn., May 1910-Mar. 1914. Author: How to Conduct a Sunday School, 1905; Housing the Sunday School, 1911; The Sunday School Organized for Service, 1914. Address: Chicago, Ill. Died May 1, 1924.

LAWRANCE, William Irvin, clergyman; b. Winchester, O., Mar. 3, 1853; s. Elonson and Amanda (Irvin) L.; A.B., Antioch Coll., Yellow Springs, O., 1880; S.T.B., Harvard Div. Sch., 1885; Th.D., Meadville Theol. Sch., 1917; m. Caroline, d. Henry Thomas Butterworth, June 18, 1875; children—Ruth Irvin

(Mrs. H. W. Dutch), Mary, Charles Wm. Ordained ministry Christian Ch., 1875; pastor West Dayton and Bellefontaine, O., until 1880; chaplain and supt. schs., Ohio Reform Sch., 1880-81; acting pres. Miami Valley Coll., Springboro, O., 1881-82; pastor 3d Religious Soc. (Unitarian), Dorchester, Mass., 1885-91; joint dir. Unitarian Mission in Japan, 1891-94; pastor Independent Congl. Ch., Meadville, Pa., 1895-99, Unitarian Ch., Winchester, Mass., 1899-1910; pres. Unitarian S.S. Soc., 1910-25; sec. Dept. of Religious Edn., Am. Unitarian Assn., 1912-25; minister Liberal Community Ch., Hollis, N.Y., 1925-26, First Unitarian Ch., San Jose, Calif., 1926-29, retired; instr. Pacific Unitarian Sch. for the Ministry. Author: The Social Emphasis on Religious Education; A Manual for the Confirmation Class. Home: Berkeley, Calif. Died Oct. 1935.

LAWRENCE, Abraham Riker, lawyer; b. New York, Sept. 19, 1832; s. John L. and Sarah A. L.; ed. pvt. sch.; read law with his father and others and admitted to bar, 1853; m. Eliza W. Miner, Jan. 5, 1860. Mem. Constl. Conv., 1867; Dem. candidate for mayor New York, 1872; justice Supreme Ct. of N.Y., Jan. 1, 1874-Dec. 31, 1901; resumed law practice; official referee to Supreme Ct. of N.Y., Sept. 1911—. Home: New York, N.Y. Died Feb. 14, 1917.

LAWRENCE, Amory Appleton, merchant; b. Boston, Apr. 22, 1848; s. Amos Adams and Sarah E. (Appleton) L.; A.B., Harvard, 1870; m. Emily Fairfax Silsbee, June 1, 1871; m. 2d, Gertrude M. Rice, June 12, 1900. Clk. Lawrence & Co., Boston, 1870-71, partner, 1871—; pres. Salmon Falls Mfg. Co., Ipswich Mills, Gilmanton Mills; v.p. Mass. Hosp. Life Ins. Co., Provident Instn. for Savings; dir. Nat. Union Bank, Boston Mfg. Co., Waltham Bleachery & Dye Works, Dwight Mfg. Co., Cocheco Mfg. Co., N.Y.,N.H.&H.R.R. Co., B.&M. R.R. Co., Me. Central R.R. Co. Overseer of Harvard Coll., 1906—; pres Boston Merchants Assn, 1901-07; v.p. Perkins Inst. for the Blind, Industrial Sch. for Crippled Children; treasurer Boston Episcopal Charitable Soc. Home: Boston, Mass. Died July 6, 1912.

LAWRENCE, Charles Solomon, surgeon; b. Stokes County, N.C., Aug. 1, 1878; s. William A. and Matilda J. (Lawrence) L.; prep. edn., Siloam (N.C.) Acad.; M.D., George Washington U., 1908; m. Mrs. Alice R. Smith, July 29, 1909. Enlisted in U.S. Army, 1897, and served 6 yrs.; with China Relief Expdn. and in Philippines, 1901-03; settled at Winston-Salem, N.C., in practice of surgery, 1908. Commissioned capt. M.C.U.S.A., July 1917; maj., Feb. 1918; lt. col., July 1918; with A.E.F. in France, Aug. 1918-Apr. 1919; comdg. officer Base Hosp. 61; hon. discharged, May 9, 1919. Founder, 1919, and owner Lawrence Hosp., Winston-Salem. Pres. Winston-Salem Lions Club, 1922-23; dist. gov. Lions Clubs of State of N.C., 1922-23. Democrat. Methodist. Mason. Home: Winston-Salem, N.C. Died June 1930.

LAWRENCE, Egbert Charles, clergyman; b. Borodino, N.Y., June 25, 1845; s. Silas Rensselaer and Lucinda (Hull) L.; A.B. (with honors), Union Coll., 1869, A.M., 1872; grad. Princeton Theol. Sem., 1875; post-grad. Auburn Theol. Sem., 1878; post-grad. course in phys. science, Syracuse U.; Ph.D., Nat. U., Chicago, 1889; m. Sarah Jean Burtis, Nov. 27, 1877; m. 2d, Mary Sylvester Dering, Apr. 29, 1896. Ordained Presbyn. ministry, 1875; pastor Grace Ch., Brooklyn, 1875-76. Owasco Outlet, N.Y., 1877-78; instr. Latin and mathematics, 1878-80, adj. prof. history, 1880-82, Union Coll.; pastor Schenectady, N.Y., 1878-80, Alexandria Bay, 1882-86, Vernon, 1886-90, Westhampton, 1890-1902, Schenectady, 1902—. Commr. to Presbyterian General Assembly, 1896; 1913. Corr. sec. L.I. Bible Soc., 1897-1902; life dir. Am. Bible Soc.; treas. Schenectady Co. Hist. Soc., Schenectady Dept. of Mohawk and Hudson River Humane Soc., sec., treas. Schenectady Ministerial Assn. Author: Historical Recreations, 1884; Early Church History of Schenectady. Asst. editor Hudson-Mohawk Genealogical and Family Memoirs, 1911. Assisted Dr. James B. Thomson in preparation of his series of text-books on mathematics. Address: Schenectady, N.Y. Died June 11, 1916.

LAWRENCE, George Pelton, congressman; b. Adams, Mass., May 19, 1859; s. Dr. George C. and Jane E. (Pelton) L.; A.B., Amherst Coll., 1880, A.M., 1886; student Columbia Law School; hon. A.M., Williams, 1899; LL.D., Amherst, 1910. Admitted to bar, 1883, and practiced at N. Adams, Mass. Judge Dist. Ct., Northern Berkshire, 1885-94; mem. Mass. Senate, 1895-97 (pres., 1896-97); elected to 55th Congress, for unexpired term (1897-99) of A. B. Wright, deceased, reëlected 56th to 62d Congresses (1899-1913), 1st Mass. Dist. Republican. Address: N. Adams, Mass. Died Nov. 21, 1917.

LAWRENCE, George Warren, pub. utilities; b. South Gardiner, Me., Sept. 14, 1875; s. James W. and Ellen L.; E.E., U. of Me., 1898; 1 son, H. Warren, by first marriage. Began in testing dept. General Electric Co., Schenectady, N.Y., 1898; then elec. engr. Am. Smelting & Refining Co., Monterey, Mex.; later constrn. foreman Gen. Electric Co., Boston, Mass.; pres. Western Massachusetts Cos.,

1927—; dir. First Nat. Bank & Trust Co. of Greenfield. Served with Signal Corps, U.S.A., Spanish-Am. War. Mason, Odd Fellow. Home: Greenfield, Mass. Died May 28, 1939.

LAWRENCE, Henry Wells, coll. prof.; author; b. Nyack, N.Y., Dec. 2, 1879; s. Henry Wells and Nancy Gertrude (Layman) L.; A.B., Yale, 1906, A.M., 1907, Ph.D., 1910; grad. study U. of Paris, 1909; m. Lillian Gertrude Sutherburg, Sept. 2, 1914; children—Barbara Gordon, Henry Wells, Lincoln Billings. Prof. pro tem. of history, U. of Vt., 1910-11; instr. in history, Dartmouth, 1911-17, asso. dir. summer sch., 1913; asst. prof. history, Middlebury (Vt.) Coll., 1917-18, prof., 1918-20; prof. history and polit. science, Conn. Coll., 1920—; teacher of history, summer sch., Hampton Inst., 1927—. Democrat. Conglist. Author: The Not-Quite Puritans, 1928. Editor: Better Citizenship, 1935. Home: New London, Conn. Died Jan. 23, 1942.

LAWRENCE, Isaac, lawyer; b. in Am. Legation, London (where his father was chargé d'affaires), July 6, 1828; s. William Beach and Esther R. (Gracie) L.; A.B., Columbia, 1847, A.M., 1850; student Harvard Law Sch., class of '48; m. Lee, d. Nicholas Gwynn, Nov. 1, 1883. Asso. editor United States Democratic Review, 1856-59, Nat. Democratic Review, 1860; del. Dem. Nat. Conv., R.I., 1864; U.S. consular agt. at Cobourg, 1862, at Port Hope, Can., 1872-76; Dem. candidate for gov. of R.I., 1878, for 47th Congress, 1880. Lecturer on diplomacy before U.S. Biog. Soc., etc. Editor Lawrence's Wheaton on International Law. Worshipful Master St. John's Lodge F. and A.M., Newport, R.I., 1877; hon. mem. Palestine Commandery of New York. Author: Life of W. B. Lawrence, Governor of Rhode Island, 1895. Pres. Am. Tariff Reform League, 1912-16. Address: New York, N.Y. Died Mar. 21, 1919.

LAWRENCE, James Cooper, univ. dean; b. Columbus, O., Feb. 10, 1890; s. Florus F. and Cora (Peirce) L.; B.A., Ohio State U., 1910; m. Ruth Williamson, 1915. Prof. English, Westminster Coll., New Wilmington, Pa., 1910-11; asst. to gen. sales mgr. B. F. Goodrich Co., 1912-15, asst. treas., 1915-19, dir. of branches, 1919-21; pres. Racine (Wis.) Tire Co., 1921-25; chmn. bd. Commercial Chem. Co. of Tennessee, 1923-27; pres. Faultless Rubber Co., 1925-27; asst. to president, U. of Minn., 1928-31, dean of univ., 1931—. Dir. gen. of Regional Advisors, President's Emergency Com. for Employment, Washington, D.C., 1930-31. Episcopalian. Author: A Theory of a Short Story, 1917; The World's Struggle with Rubber, 1931; The Year of Regeneration, 1932. Home: St. Paul, Minn. Deceased.

LAWRENCE, John Strachan, lawyer; b. Waterford, N.Y., Apr. 15, 1849; s. John and Cornelia Frances (Porter) L.; A.B., Harvard, 1871; unmarried. Began practice of law, Grand Rapids, Mich., 1879; standing master in chancery, U.S. Circuit and Dist. Cts., 1887—; nat. bank receiver, 1888, 93, 96; del.-at-large Nat. Dem. Conv. (gold), 1896; mem. Grand Rapids Police and Fire Commn., 1905-07 (pres. 1906-07); mem. Grand Rapids Library Commn., 1907-15 (pres. 1909-12), Grand Rapids Historical Soc. (pres. 1921—). Episcopalian. Author: Descendants of Moses and Sarah Kilham Porter and Their Ancestry, 1911. Home: Grand Rapids, Mich. Deceased.

LAWRENCE, Margaret (Mrs. Orson D. Nunn), actress; b. Aug. 2, 1889; m. Lt. Comdr. Orson D. Nunn, 1911. First appearance on stage, in "Her Son," at Chicago, 1910; played in New York in "Over Night," 1911; after 7 yrs., reappeared in Belasco Theatre, Washington, D.C., as the wife in "Tea for Three"; toured in "Transplanting Jean," 1920. Died June 8, 1929.

LAWRENCE, Robert Means, M.D.; author; b. Boston, May 14, 1847; s. William Richards and Susan Coombs (Dana) L.; A.B., Harvard, 1869, M.D., 1873; continued studies in Vienna and Paris, 1874-76; m. Katharine Lawrence Cleaveland, June 30, 1870; children—Madeleine, Isabel Cleaveland (Mrs. George B. de Gersdorff), Helen Atherton (dec.), Robert Means (dec.). Physician Boston Dispensary, 1876-86 (bd. mgrs. 1910-12). Asst. surgeon and surgeon 1st M.V.M., 1877-82. Selectman, Lexington, Mass., 1884-86; mem. Sch. Com., 1888-90. Sr. warden, St. Paul's Church, Boston, 1912; trustee of St. Luke's Home for Convalescents; treas. Episcopal Ch. Assn., 1880-93 (pres 1919); mem. Chapter St. Paul's Cathedral, 1914-19. Author: Historical Sketches of Some Members of the Lawrence Family, 1888; The Magic of the Horseshoe, 1898; The Descendants of Major Samuel Lawrence, of Groton, Mass., 1904; Primitive Psychotherapy and Quackery, 1910; Rev. Amos Adams, A.M., Patriot Minister (1728-1775), 1912; The Site of St. Paul's Cathedral, Boston, and Its Neighborhood, 1916; Old Park Street and Its Vicinity, 1922; New England Colonial Life, 1927. Home: Boston, Mass. Died Mar. 7, 1935.

LAWRENCE, Samuel Crocker, merchant; b. Medford, Mass., Nov. 22, 1832; s. Daniel and Elizabeth (Crocker) L.; A.B., Harvard, 1855, A.M., 1858; m. Carrie Rebecca, d. Rev. William and Rebecca Badger, Apr. 28, 1859. In banking business, Chicago, 1856-57; in business with father and brother, Daniel

Lawrence & Sons, Medford, 1858-67, sole propr., 1867-1906; pres. Eastern R.R. Co., 1875 (leased to B.&M., Dec. 2, 1884); dir., 1884—, and mem. exec. com., 1893—, B.&M. R.R.; dir. and mem. exec. com. Me. Central R.R. Co., 1875—. Mem. Mass. Vol. Militia, 1855-64; col. 5th Mass., 1860; wounded 1st Bull Run; brig. gen. Mass. Militia, 1862-64; comdr. Ancient and Hon. Artillery Co., 1869. First mayor City of Medford, 1892-94. Grand Master Masons of Mass., Dec. 1880-83; grand comdr. K.T., Mass. and R.I., 1894-95; active mem. and officer Supreme Council. Home: Medford, Mass. Died 1911.

LAWRENCE, William, jurist, author; b. Mt. Pleasant, O., June 26, 1819; grad. Franklin Coll., 1838; Cincinnati Law School, 1840; A.M., Franklin; LL.D., from 3 Ohio colleges; m. Caroline M. Miller, Mar. 20, 1845. Admitted to bar, 1840; pros. atty. Logan County, 1845-46; mem. legislature, 1846-48; State senator, 1849, 1850, 1854; editor Logan Gazette, 1845-47; reporter Ohio Supreme court, 1851; judge, court of common pleas and district court, 1857-64; one of editors Western Law Monthly. Col. 84th Ohio vols., serving in Md., 1862; mem. Congress, 1865-77; 1st comptroller U.S. Treasury, 1880-85; advocate of and writer on protective tariff; pres. Ohio Wool Growers' Assn., 1891—; pres. Nat. Wool Growers' Assn., 1893—; trustee Ohio Wesleyan U., 1878—; lay delegate to Gen. Conference M.E. Ch., 1872, 1876, 1880 and 1892. Author: Ohio Reports, Vol. 20; Law of Claims Against Governments; Organization of the Treasury Department; Law of Impeachable Crimes; Causes of the Rebellion; Decisions of First Comptroller (6 vols.); Life and Services of John Sherman; The American Wool Interest; Law of Religious Societies; The Treaty Question; Constitutional Law; Memorials to Congress for Wool Tariff (10 vols.); numerous other minor works. Address: Bellefontaine, O. Died 1899.

LAWRENCE, William, bishop; b. Boston, Mass., May 30, 1850; s. Amos Adams and Sarah E. (Appleton) L.; A.B., Harvard, 1871; S.T.B., Episcopal Theol. Sch., 1875, D.D., 1923; S.T.D., Hobart, 1890, Harvard U., 1893; LL.D., Princeton, 1904, Cambridge, 1908, Lawrence, 1910, Boston U., 1923, Harvard, 1931; D.D., Durham, 1908, Yale U., 1909, Columbia, 1911, Trinity Coll., 1925, Williams Coll., 1930; m. Julia Cunningham, 1874 (died 1927); children—Marian (Mrs. Harold Peabody), Julia (Mrs. Morton Fearey), Sarah (Mrs. Charles L. Slattery), Rosamond (dec.), Ruth (Mrs. Lansing P. Reed), William Appleton, Eleanor (Mrs. Lewis Hunt Mills), Frederic Cunningham. Deacon, 1875, priest, 1876, P.E. Ch.; rector Grace Ch., Lawrence, Mass., 1876-84; prof. homiletics and pastoral theology, 1884-93, dean, 1888-93, Episcopal Theol. Sch.; consecrated bishop of Mass., Oct. 5, 1893; resigned office and title of bishop of Mass., May 30, 1926. Trustee Church Pension Fund; chmn. bd. of trustees of Groton School. Author: Life of Amos A. Lawrence, 1889; Proportional Representation in the House of Clerical and Lay Delegates; Visions and Service, 1896; Life of Roger Wolcott, Governor of Massachusetts, 1902; Study of Phillips Brooks, 1903; The American Cathedral, 1921; Fifty Years, 1923; Life of Henry Cabot Lodge, U.S. Senator, 1925; Memories of a Happy Life, 1926; The New American, 1929; Life of Phillips Brooks, 1930. Home: Boston, Mass. Died Nov. 6, 1941.

LAWRENCE, William Mangam, clergyman; b. Washington, May 11, 1848; s. William Spencer and Mary Jane (Mangam) L.; B.P., Colgate, 1870, A.M., 1876; grad. Hamilton Theol. Sem., 1871; D.D., Bapt. Union Theol. Sem., Chicago U., 1881; S.T.D. Colgate, 1921; m. Anna Isabella Hyde, 1871; children—Adelaide (Mrs. L. G. Parker), Fred Hyde (dec.). Ordained Bapt. ministry, 1871; pastor Amsterdam, N.Y., 1871-72, Phila., 1872-80, Second Ch., Chicago, 1880-1904, North Orange Ch., Orange, N.J., Jan. 1, 1905-May 1912. V.p. and pres. divinity sch. trustees and lecturer Divinity School U. of Chicago, 1885-1904; lecturer Chicago Theol. Sem., 1903; pres. bd. trustees Colgate U., 1905-12; professorial lecturer on Christian ethics, Colgate, 1912-27; prof. emeritus, 1927; also prof., pro tempore, pastoral theology, 1915, actg. prof. of homiletics and pastoral theology, 1919-27. Mem. bd. Am. Bapt. Foreign Missionary Soc., 1885-1905, Am. Bapt. Home Missionary Soc., 1905-12; v.p. Bapt. Edn. Soc. N.Y., 1914—. Chaplain Ill. Soc. S.A.R., Ill. Soc. of Colonial Wars. Contbr. to Baptist Ency. Home: Hamilton, N.Y. Died Apr. 11, 1934.

LAWRENCE, William Van Duzer, mcht.; b. Elmira, N.Y., Feb. 12, 1842; s. Robert D. and Catherine (Van Duzer) L.; ed. pub. schs. in Mich.; m. Sarah E. Bates, Aug. 22, 1867. Founded Davis & Lawrence, New York and Montreal, 1867. Founder of Lawrence Park and Lawrence Hosp., Bronxville, N.Y. Home: Bronxville, N.Y. Died May 16, 1927.

LAWS, Annie, humanitarian; b. Cincinnati, O.; d. James H. and Sarah Amelia (Langdon) L.; ed. Miss Appleton's Sch. for Girls and spl. courses under professors in art, lit., music, etc.; hon. A.M., U. of Cincinnati, 1923; unmarried. Pres. Cincinnati Kindergarten Assn., 1900—; chmn. com. of nineteen, Internat. Kindergarten Union; corr. sec. Cincinnati

Orphan Asylum Bd.; mem. Cincinnati Bd. Edn. Mem. Cincinnati Social Hygiene Soc. (v.p.). Home: Cincinnati, O. Died July 1, 1927.

LAWS, Elijah, rear admiral U.S.N.; b. in Pa., Mar. 20, 1833. Apptd. 3d asst. engr. U.S.N., Mar. 19, 1858; 2d asst. engr., Dec. 1, 1860; 1st asst. engr., July 25, 1866; chief engr., 1870; retired Mar. 20, 1895; advanced to rank of rear admiral, June 29, 1906, and given a medal for services during Civil War. Home: Morristown, N.J. Died Sept. 25, 1926.

LAWS, Frank Arthur, elec. engr.; b. Brockton, Mass., May 28, 1867; s. Alfred and Clara Maria (Balch) L.; B.S. in E.E., Mass. Inst. Tech., 1889; Harvard, 1891-92; m. Harriet Patterson Burbank, Aug. 29, 1901. Asst. in physics, 1889-91, instr., 1891-93, instr. in elec. measurements, 1893-97, asst. prof., 1897-1902, asst. prof. elec. testing, 1902-06, asso. prof., 1906-13, prof. elec. engring., 1913-21, prof. elec. measurements, 1921—, Mass. Inst. Tech. Republican. Conglist. Author: Notes for Use in Standardizing, 1906; Electrical Measurements, 1917. Home: Brookline, Mass. Deceased.

LAWS, George William, naval officer; b. Channahon, Ill., Feb. 11, 1870; s. William and Mary (West) L.; grad. U.S. Naval Acad., 1891; Naval War Coll., 1913-14. Asst. engr., July 1, 1893; passed asst. engr., Feb. 16, 1898; trans. to line as lt. jr. grade, Mar. 3, 1899; promoted through grades to rear adm., June 4, 1925. Served on Justin, Spanish-Am. War, 1898; aide on staff comdr. in chief Asiatic Fleet, 1906; head Dept. of Ordnance, Naval Sta., Cavite, P.I., 1906-07; at U.S. Naval Acad., 1907-10; comdr. Dolphin, 1910-13; at Naval War Coll., 1913-14; exec. officer Louisiana, 1915; U.S. Naval Acad., 1915-18; command U.S.S. Michigan, 1918-20; command U.S.S. Wyoming, 1922-24; comdt. 16th Naval Dist., also comdt. Navy Yard, Cavite, 1924-26; comdg. Battleship Div. 2, Scouting Fleet, Oct. 4, 1926-28; comdt. Navy Yard, Mare Island, Calif., 1928-32, 12th Naval Dist., 1932-34; retired Feb. 28, 1934. Deceased.

LAWS, Samuel Spahr, educator; b. Ohio County, Va., Mar. 23, 1824; s. Rev. James and Rachel (Spahr) L.; A.B., Miami U., valedictorian, 1848 (Phi Beta Kappa), A.M., 1851; grad. Princeton Theol. Sem., 1851; LL.B., Columbia, 1870; M.D., Bellevue Hosp. Medical Coll. (New York U.), 1875; LL.D., Westminster Coll., 1871; D.D., Wash. and Lee, 1894; Litt.D., Miami; m. Ann Maria, d. William Broadwell, Jan. 1860. Ordained Presbyn. ministry, 1851; pastor West Ch., St. Louis, 1851-53; prof. phys. science, 1854-55, pres., 1855-61, Westminster Coll., Fulton, Mo.; admitted to N.Y. bar, 1869; pres. U. of Mo., 1876-89, resigned; commd. maj. by Gov. Marmaduke in organizing mil. dept. of Univ.; apptd. visitor to West Point, 1882; Perkins prof. natural science in connection with revelation and Christian apologetics, Presbyterian Theol. Sem., Columbia, S.C., 1893-98. Inventor and introducer of system of simultaneous telegraphing of market reports ("tickers"). Del. Pan-Presbyn. Council, Washington, 1899. Author: The At-onement; The Trinity. Address: Washington, D.C. Died Jan. 9, 1921.

LAWSHE, Abraham Lincoln, 3d asst. postmaster-gen.; b. Somerset, Ind., Oct. 6, 1860; s. Henry D. and Esther A. (Richmond) L.; common and high sch. edn.; m. Anna Sweetser, Oct. 18, 1882 (died 1915); m. 2d, Margaret Delight Sweetser, April 2, 1917. Editor and publisher the Journal, Converse, Ind., 1883-97; postmaster, Converse, 1889-93; del. Rep. Nat. Conv., 1896; deputy auditor Postoffice Dept., 1897-1900; asst. auditor for Cuba, 1900, re-auditing accounts of Cuban Postal Service and investigating the postal frauds; auditor for P.I., 1901-04, 1905-07; mem. and chmn. Philippine Expn. Bd., St. Louis Expn., 1904-05; 3d asst. postmaster-gen., 1907-10. Five yrs. with Hopi, Navajo and Apache Indians of Ariz. Author of various reports on Philippine finances, and U.S. postal affairs. Republican. Mem. Disciples of Christ. Home: Monrovia, Calif. Died Sept. 14, 1919.

LAWSON, Albert Gallatin, clergyman; b. Poughkeepsie, N.Y., June 5, 1842; s. Albert G. and Mary A. (Nichols) L.; ed. Colgate U., hon. A.M., 1876, D.D., 1883; m. Eliza Knight, Sept. 23, 1863. Ordained Bapt. ministry, 1862; pastor Perth Amboy, N.J., 1862-66, Poughkeepsie, N.Y., 1866-67, Brooklyn, 1867-84; sec. Am. Bapt. Missionary Union, Boston, 1884-86; pastor Camden, N.J., 1890-1902, Newark, N.J., 1902-05; gen. sec. Colgate U., 1906-09; pastor Waterbury, Conn., 1909-12, Woodside, N.Y., 1912-18. Instr., Italian dept. Colgate Sem., 1917. Sec. bd. mgrs. Am. Bapt. Missionary Union, 1905-10; served as chmn. Administrative Com. Federal Council Chs. of Christ in America; pres. Bapt. Edn. Soc. State of N.Y., 1921; chmn. Publication Com., Am. Bapt. Publ. Soc., 1922—. Home: Danbury, N.H. Died Mar. 8, 1929.

LAWSON, Ernest, landscape artist; b. San Francisco, Calif., 1873. Exhibited in leading cities of U.S.; paintings on permanent exhibition in principal art galleries; silver medal, St. Louis Exposition, 1904; Sesnan medal, Pa. Academy, 1907; First Hallgarten prize, 1908, Altman prize, 1916, Inness gold medal, 1917, and 1st Altman landscape prize, 1921, N.A.D.; gold medal, San Francisco Expn., 1915; Corcoran silver medal, Washington, 1916; Temple gold medal, Pa. Acad., 1920, first prize, Carnegie Inst., Pittsburgh, 1921; 1st Altman prize, National Acad. Design, 1928, Saltus gold medal, 1930. A.N.A., 1908, N.A., 1917. Mem. Nat. Inst. Arts and Letters. Address: New York, N.Y. Died Dec. 18, 1939.

LAWSON, John Davison, univ. dean; b. Hamilton, Can., Mar. 29, 1852; s. Joseph and Charlotte (Davison) L.; LL.B., Osgoode Hall, 1875; LL.D., U. of Mo., 1892, U. of Toronto, 1919; m. Frances E. Chase, 1879. Practiced law, St. Louis, 1876-85; editor Central Law Journal, St. Louis, 1876-81; judge Civil Ct., 1886-91; prof. contract and international law, 1891-1903, and dean Sch. of Law, 1903-16, U. of Mo. Editor Am. Law Review; asso. editor Journal of Criminal Law and Criminology. Dir. St. Louis Law Library Assn., 1881-85. Mem. Mo. council and com. on penal laws and prison discipline, Am. Bar Assn., 1895-1904; chmn. sect. history of law, Internat. Congress Arts and Sciences, St. Louis, 1904; diploma and medal, St. Louis Expn., 1904; commr. from Mo. on uniform state laws; pres. Mo. Bar Assn., 1904-05 (chmn. exec. com., 1906-09); spl. commr. Am. Inst. Criminal Law and Criminology to investigate administration of criminal law in Great Britain, 1909-10, etc. Author: Contracts of Common Carriers, 1880; Usages and Customs, 1881; The Power of Usage and Custom, 1881; Concordance of Words and Phrases, 1883; Expert and Opinion Evidence, 1883, 1900; Principles of Equity, 1884; Leading Cases Simplified (3 vols.), 1882; Presumptive Evidence, 1885, 1899; Insanity as a Defense, 1884; Defenses to Crime (5 vols.), 1886, 1892; Rights, Remedies and Practice (7 vols.), 1891; American Law of Contracts, 1893, 2d edit., 1905; American Law of Bailments, 1895; Cases on Personal Property, 1896; Cases on Quasi Contracts, 1907. V.p. Internat. Law Assn., Paris, 1912, Madrid, 1913. Editor: American State Trials. Address: Columbia, Mo. Died Oct. 28, 1921.

LAWSON, Publius Virgilius, mfr.; b. Corning, N.Y., Nov. 1, 1853; s. Publius V. and Elizabeth (Fleming) L.; student lit. dept., U. of Wis.; LL.B., U. of Wis., 1878; admitted to state and federal courts, 1877; practiced in Menasha 10 yrs.; m. Florence J. Wright, Aug. 5, 1884. Pres. Menasha Wood Split Pulley Co., 1888—. Court commr., 6th circuit, 1880-88; mayor Menasha 6 terms, 1886, 87, 88, 89, 93, 96; alderman, 1882-83; Rep. candidate for State Senate, 1890; dir. pub. library, 1895-1904; park commr., 1895-1904; v.p. Pub. Library, 1899—; examiner Wis. Civ. Service Commn., 1906-07. Pres. Rep. Club, 1900, Menasha Mus. History and Art Assn., 1889—, Fox River Valley Library Assn., 1900-03, Wis. Library Assn., 1902-04. V.p. Wis. Archæol. Soc., 1902—. Author: Bravest of the Brave, life Charles de Langlade, 1904; Prince or Creole, Mystery of Louis XVII, 1905; Rocks and Minerals of Wisconsin, 1906; Rocks and Minerals of Michigan, 1907; Family Genealogy, 1903; History Winnebago County, 2 vols., 1908; Life of Governor James Duane Doty; Shakespeare and the Worcester Bond (monograph). Mem. Bd. Edn. City of Menasha, 1895, 1915 (pres. bd. 1916—); mem. Wis. Legislature, 1918. Chmn. bldg. com. Council Defense, 1917-19; mem. War Chest Bd., 1917-19. Address: Menasha, Wis. Died Dec. 1, 1920.

LAWSON, Roberta Campbell (Mrs. Eugene B. Lawson), club woman; b. Alluwe, Indian Territory (now Oklahoma); d. J. E. and Emma (Journeycake) Campbell; mother a d. Rev. Charles Journeycake, the last chief of the Delawares; ed. Hardin Coll., Mexico, Mo.; m. Eugene B. Lawson, Oct. 31, 1901 (died 1931); 1 son, Edward Campbell. Pres. Okla. Federation Women's Clubs, 1917-19; dir. Gen. Federation Women's Clubs, 1918-22, chmn. music div., 1926-28, and 1st v.p. Gen. Federation Women's Clubs, 1932-35, pres., 1935-38; nat. women's chmn. Will Rogers Memorial Commn. Chmn. women's com. Council Nat. Defense, World War. Mem. bd. regents Okla. Coll. for Women; v.p. Pan-Pacific Women's Assn., 1937-40. Democrat. Presbyn. Home: Tulsa, Okla. Died Dec. 31, 1940.

LAWSON, Thomas Goodwin, jurist; b. Putnam County, Ga., May 2, 1835; s. Reese and Elizabeth (Keaton) L.; A.B., Mercer U., 1855, A.M., 1858 (LL.D., 1908); m. Mary Frances Reid, Nov. 28, 1860. Admitted to bar, 1857; pvt. C.S.A., 15 months; mem. Ga. Legislature, 1861-66, 1888-89; mem. Ga. Constl. Conv., 1877; judge Superior Cts. of Ga., 1879-87; mem. 52d, 53d and 54th Congresses (1891-97). Engaged in farming, 1887—; dir. Middle Ga. Bank, Middle Ga. Cotton Mills. Trustee Mercer U., Ga. State Sanatorium; mem. State Bd. of Edn. of Ga., 1911-13. Baptist. Democrat. Address: Eatonton, Ga. Died Apr. 16, 1912.

LAWSON, Thomas William, broker, author; b. Charlestown, Mass., Feb. 26, 1857; s. Thomas and Anna Maria (Loring) L.; ed. pub. schs., Cambridge, Mass.; m. Jeannie Augusta Goodwillie, 1878 (died 1907). Banker and broker, 1870—; pres. Bay State Gas Co. of Del., 1907—, Thomas W. Lawson Co., Trinity Copper Co., First Nat. Copper Co. Republican. Prominent as yachtsman. Author: The Krank, 1887; History of the Republican Party, 1888 (spl. edit. of four copies on satin, one presented to President Harrison, one to Vice-President Morton, one to Library of Congress and one retained by author); Secrets of Success, 1888; Collection of Poems and Short Stories from Magazines, 1888; Lawson History of the America's Cup (for pvt. distribution), 1902; Frenzied Finance, 1905; Friday the Thirteenth, 1907; The Remedy, 1912; High Cost Living, 1913; The Leak, 1919. Home: Egypt, Mass. Feb. 8, 1925.

LAWSON, Victor Fremont, editor and pub. Chicago Daily News; b. Chicago, Sept. 9, 1850; s. Iver and Melinda H. L.; ed. Phillips Acad., Andover, Mass.; m. Jessie S. Bradley, Feb. 5, 1880. Took charge of an interest of his father's estate in a printing establishment; bought Chicago Daily News, July 1876, and with his later partner, Melville E. Stone, developed it to success; started morning edition, 1881; bought out Mr. Stone, 1888, and became sole propr. Retained the name Daily News for the evening paper and changed morning issue to the Chicago Record; latter was merged with the Times-Herald, in 1901, under the name of the Record-Herald. Dir. and pres. Associated Press; inaugurated and maintained for many years through his newspapers the movement for the establishment of a govt. savings bank, and has been called the "father of the Postal Savings Bank in America"; established Daily News Fresh Air Fund, which maintains the Lincoln Park Sanitarium; active in other philanthropic work. Home: Chicago, Ill. Died Aug. 19, 1925.

LAWTON, Alexander Rudolf, lawyer; b. Savannah, Ga., Aug. 9, 1858; s. Alexander Robert and Sarah Hillhouse (Alexander) L.; A.B., U. of Ga., 1877 (Phi Beta Kappa); student Eastman Business Coll., 1877, U. of Va. Law Sch., 1878-79, Harvard Law Sch., 1879-80; m. Ella Stanly, d. Bishop Beckwith, Apr. 27, 1882; children—Alexander Robert, Beckwith. Admitted to bar, 1880, and practiced at Savannah; mem. firm Lawton & Cunningham, 1882—; counsel, 1887—, dir., 1896—, v.p., 1904—, Central Ga. Ry. Co.; dir. Ocean S.S. Co., of Savannah (v.p., 1920—). Pres. Central of Ga. Ry. Co. and Ocean Steamship Co., during period of federal control. Served pvt. to col. 1st Regt. Ga. N.G., 1881-1900; col. 1st Ga. Inf., U.S.V., 1898. Mem. Ga. Hist. Soc. (pres. 1907-14 and 1918-20), Am. Bar Assn. (v.p. for Ga., 1919), Ga. Bar Assn. (pres. 1920-21; chmn. ethics com., 1922-27); chmn. Telfair Acad. Arts and Sciences, 1902-19 (pres. 1907-14 and 1919-24; hon. pres. for life 1924); pres. Savannah Board of Trade, 1926-28; v.p. Am. Federation Arts, 1919-24; pres. Savannah Music Club, 1916-19; trustee and pres. Alumni Soc., U. of Ga., 1923-24; mem. Commn. Inter-racial Coöperation; retired from all business, 1928. Home: Savannah, Ga. Died Dec. 18, 1936.

LAWTON, Ezra Mills, consul; b. Ironton, O., Aug. 23, 1864; s. Edward and Mary Louise (Amlin) L.; ed. high sch., Ironton; m. Mary Louise Porter, Nov. 24, 1886. Clk. and mechanic, 1882-87; telephone and elec. construction work, 1887-90; supt. constrn. Cincinnati Electric Light Cos., 1890-95; elec. contracting engr., 1895-1906; went to Mexico as mining engr., 1907; Am. consular agt., Oaxaca, Mexico, 1908-13; Am. consul Tegucigalpa, Honduras, 1914-16; spl. mission to Guatemala, 1914; consul at Nogales, Mexico, 1917-18, Guatemala City, 1919-20, Sao Paulo, Brazil, 1920-23, Sydney, Australia, 1923-29, retired; Spl. assignments at San Jose, Costa Rica and in charge Am. Legation at Tegucigalpa, Honduras, 1919-20. Republican. Presbyn. Mason. Home: Los Angeles, Calif. Died June 26, 1931.

LAWTON, Henry W., maj. gen. U.S.V.; lt. col. U.S.A.; b. Ohio; apptd. to army from Ind.; joined army as sergt. Co. E, 9th Ind. vols., April 1861; discharged July 1861, to enter 30th Ind. regt. as 1st lt.; promoted capt., May 17, 1865; entered regular army as 2d lt. 41st inf., July 28, 1866; captain, March 1879; maj., 188-; lt. col., Feb. 12, 1889. Apptd. maj. gen. U.S. vols., July 8, 1898; afterward on duty in inspector-gen.'s dept. and, in 1899, corps commander in Philippines. Died 1899.

LAWYER, George, prof. law; b. N.Y. City, Sept. 24, 1865; s. James and Eliza (Irwin) L.; B.A., Hamilton Coll., Clinton, N.Y., 1885, M.A., 1887; LL.B., Albany Law Sch., 1887; m. Agnese Pershall, Feb. 9, 1892; children—James Pershall, George Irwin, David Buchanan. Practiced law at Albany, N.Y., 1890—; prof. law, Albany Law Sch., 1906—; judge advocate N.Y.N.G., rank of maj., Feb. 28, 1898-June 20, 1918. Elected surrogate of Albany County, Nov. 8, 1921. Trustee Albany Pub. Library. Democrat. Presbyn.; trustee Presbytery of Albany. Mason, Elk. Editor: Smith on Personal Property (2d edit.), 1908. Home: Albany, N.Y. Died Aug. 14, 1927.

LAY, Julius Gareche, Am. Foreign Service; b. Washington, D.C., Aug. 9, 1872; s. Lt. Col. Richard G. (U.S.A.) and Caroline Y. (Kimball) L.; ed. pub. schs. and by pvt. tutors, and at Columbia Grammar Sch., New York, until 1889; m. Anne Howard, Dec. 10, 1904. Clerk Am. consulate at Ottawa, Can., 1889-91; vice-consul-gen., 1891-96; consul at Windsor, Ont., 1896-99; consul-gen. at Barcelona, Spain, 1899-1904, Canton, China, 1904-06, Cape Town, S. Africa, 1906-10, Rio de Janeiro, Brazil, 1910-14, Berlin,

Germany, June 24, 1914-Feb. 1917; assigned to Dept. of State and served as trade adviser, 1917-20; with Speyer & Co., bankers, New York, 1920-24; consul gen., Calcutta, Ind., 1924-27; counsellor of Embassy, Santiago, Chile, 1927-29; E.E. and M.P. to Honduras, 1930-34; E.E. and M.P. to Uruguay, 1934—; del. to Pan-Am. Commercial Conf., 1935; retired, Aug. 1937. Died Aug. 28, 1939.

LAY, Robert Dwight, life ins.; b. Chicago, Ill., Sept. 30, 1875; s. Charles C. and Fanny M. (Cossitt) L.; grad. Mich. Mil. Acad., Orchard Lake, Mich., 1894; m. Frances Ida Kingcaid, Feb. 2, 1914. Began as office boy for Knickerbocker Ice Co., 1894, resigning as asst. credit man, 1898, to become mgr. of E. A. Shedd & Co.; became identified with the Nat. Life Ins. Co. of the U.S.A., 1902, sec. and dir., 1906-26, pres., 1926-33; dir., sec. and v.p. Hydrox Co. Republican. Episcopalian. Mason. Home: Chicago, Ill. Died Jan. 1, 1940.

LAYCOCK, Charles Wilbur, banker; b. Harveyville, Pa., Oct. 3, 1860; s. Adam Clark and Clarissa Ann (Millard) L., ed. Wyoming Sem., Kingston, Pa.; m. L. Jennie Clapp, June 5, 1890; children—Charles Harold, Robert Clark, Millard Day. Bookkeeper 2d Nat. Bank, Wilkes-Barre, Pa., 1882-90; cashier Anthracite Savings Bank, 1890-1910; with New York and Phila. banking house, 1910-13; cashier Miners Bank of Wilkes-Barre, 1913-15, v.p., 1915-24, pres., 1924—; dir., sec. and treas. Wilkes-Barre Ry. Corp.; dir. Stevens Coal Co. Trustee of Wyoming Sem.; dir. Pa. State Chamber Commerce, Wilkes-Barre-Wyoming Valley Chamber Commerce; treas. Wyoming Hist. and Geol. Soc. Republican. Methodist. Mason. Home: Kingston, Pa. Died Nov. 25, 1940.

LAYLIN, Lewis Cass, lawyer; b. Norwalk, O.; s. John and Mary (Weyburn) L.; ed. Norwalk (O.) High Sch. and under pvt. tutors; m. Frances Latimer Dewey, Nov. 3, 1880. Supt. pub. schs., Bellevue, O., 6 yrs.; admitted to Ohio bar, 1878; practiced law in Norwalk; pros. atty., Huron County, O., 1879-86; mem. Ohio Ho. of Rep., 1888-94 (speaker, 1892-94); sec. of state of Ohio, 1901-07; chmn. Ohio Codifying Commn. 3 yrs.; apptd. asst. sec. interior, Aug. 3, 1912; resigned July 1, 1914, and practiced law at Columbus, O. Formerly chmn. Rep. Exec. Com. of Huron County, chmn. Rep. State Exec. Com. of Ohio. Mason. Home: Columbus, O. Died Nov. 17, 1923.

LAYNG, James D., v.p., Cleveland, Cincinnati, Chicago & St. Louis Ry., 1890—; 2d v.p. West Shore R.R., 1884—; b. Columbia, Pa., Aug. 30, 1833; grad. Western Univ. of Pa., 1849; served, rodman to asst. engr. of construction, O.&Pa. R.R., 1849-51; resident engr. construction Steubenville & Ind. R.R., 1851-53; same, Cleveland & Mahoning R.R., 1853-56; supt. Steubenville & Ind. R.R., 1858-65; supt. Eastern div. Pittsburg, Ft. Wayne & Chicago R.R., 1865-71; asst. gen. mgr., 1871-74; gen. mgr., 1874-81, Pa. Co.'s lines; gen. supt. Chicago & Northwestern Ry., 1881-83; pres. Cleveland, Columbus, Cincinnati & Indianapolis Ry., 1887-90. Home: New York, N.Y. Died 1908.

LAYTON, Caleb Rodney, congressman; b. Frankford, Sussex Co., Del., Sept. 8, 1851; s. Samuel H. and Elizabeth A. L.; A.B., Amherst, 1873; M.D., U. of Pa., 1876; m. Annie E. Sipple, Dec. 28, 1876; m. 2d, Fannie S. Herrington, Oct. 2, 1926. Began practice of medicine at Georgetown, 1876; sec. Union Rep. County Com., Sussex Co., 1876-88; chmn. Rep. County Com., Sussex Co., 1876-1901; sec. of State of Del., by appmt. of Gov. John Hunn, 1901-05; auditor for Dept. of State and other depts., at Washington, D.C., 1906-10 (resigned); mem. Progressive State Com. of Del., 1912-18; mem. 66th and 67th Congresses (1919-23), Del. at large. Editor Union Republican, Georgetown, 1891-1905. Episcopalian. Home: Georgetown, Del. Died Nov. 11, 1930.

LAYTON, Frederick, philanthropist; b. Little Wilbraham, Cambridgeshire, England, May 18, 1827; s. John and Mary (King) L.; ed. pvt. schs., Eng.; m. Elisabeth A. Hayman, Nov. 6, 1851. Came to America, 1842; began active career as partner of father in butchering and meat packing business, Milwaukee, Wis., 1845; associated with John Plankinton, as Layton & Plankinton, same line, 1853-62, Layton & Co., 1863-1900. Founder Layton Art Gallery, Milwaukee, 1888, The Layton Home for Incurables, 1908. Home: Milwaukee, Wis. Aug. 18, 1919.

LAZARO, Ladislas, congressman; b. nr. Ville Platte, La., June 5, 1872; s. Alexandre and Marie Denise (Ortego) L.; M.D., St. Isadore's Coll., New Orleans, 1894; m. Mary Curley; children—Mary (Mrs. E. C. Lake), Elaine (Mrs. South Trimble, Jr.), Heloise (Mrs. Allen H. White), Ladislas. Practiced medicine at Washington, La., 1894-1913; elected mem. La. State Senate, 1908, reëlected, 1912; mem. 63d to 69th Congresses (1913-27), 7th La. Dist. Democrat. Home: Washington, La. Died Mar. 30, 1927.

LAZELLE, Henry Martyn, army officer; b. Enfield, Mass., Sept. 8, 1832; s. Joseph and Roxana L.; grad. U.S. Mil. Acad., 1855. Entered U.S.A. as lt., 1855; served with expdns. against Indians, 1857-59; wounded by Indians through lungs, 1859. In Civil War, 1861-66; prisoner of war, 1861; asst. commissary-gen. for prisoners of war, 1862-63; col. 16th N.Y. Cav., comdg. cav. brig. 22d Army Corps, 1864; on survey of N.P.R.R., 1872-73; on Sioux Expdn., 1878; commandant cadets, West Point, 1879-82; sent to India on spl. service, 1885; editor Records of the Rebellion, 1887-89; retired for disability, 1894; brig. gen. retired, by act of Apr. 23, 1904. Gold Medalist of Military Service Institution, 1883. Author: One Law in Nature, 1872; Matter, Force and Spirit, 1895; also monographs. Died July 21, 1917.

LAZENBY, William Rane, horticulturist, forester; b. Bellona, N.Y., Dec. 5, 1850; s. of Charles and Isabella L.; B. Agr., Cornell, 1874; M.Agr., Ia. Agrl. Coll., 1887; m. Harriet E. Akin, Dec. 15, 1896. Instr. and asst. prof. botany and horticulture, Cornell, 1874-81; prof. botany and horticulture, 1881-92, horticulture and forestry, 1892-1910, prof. forestry, 1910—, Ohio State U. Dir. Ohio Agrl. Expt. Sta., 1882-87, sec. Ohio Medical Univ., 1894-1914; lecturer before farmers' institutes, 1881-1906. Mem. Soc. Promotion Agrl. Science (sec., 1886-91, pres., 1895-97), Am. Pomol. Soc. (v.p., 1905—); pres. Columbus Hort. Soc., 1895—, Ohio Acad. Science, 1902-03, Ohio State Forestry Soc., 1904—; v.p. A.A.A.S., 1896. Mason (33°). Forest engr., Biltmore Forest Sch., 1912. Home: Columbus, O. Deceased.

LEA, Henry Charles, author; b. Phila., Sept. 19, 1825; s. Isaac and Frances Ann (Carey) L.; private edn. (LL.D., U. of Pa., Harvard and Princeton). In publishing business, 1843-80. Author: Superstition and Force, 1866; An Historical Sketch of Sacerdotal Celibacy in the Christian Church, 3 edits.; Studies in Church History, 1869; A History of the Inquisition of the Middle Ages, 1888; Chapters from the Religious History of Spain, 1890; Formulary of the Papal Penitentiary in the Thirteenth Century, 1892; A History of Auricular Confession and Indulgences in the Latin Church, 1896; The Moriscos of Spain: Their Conversion and Expulsion, 1901; History of the Inquisition of Spain (4 vols.), 1906-07. Home: Philadelphia, Pa. Died 1909.

LEA, Homer, author; b. Denver, Nov. 17, 1876; s. Alfred Erskine and Hersa (Coberly) L.; descendant of early Colonial ancestry of Va.; student Occidental Coll., U. of the Pacific, and Stanford U.; unmarried. Undertook relief of Kwang Hsu, Emperor of China, 1900, 1901; raised and comd. 2d Army Div., 1904, holding rank of lt. gen. over these forces. Author: Vermilion Pencil (novel), 1908; The Valor of Ignorance (mil. work in 2 vols.), 1909; The Crimson Spider (drama), 1909. Home: Los Angeles, Calif. Died Nov. 1, 1912.

LEA, John McCormick, lawyer; b. Knoxville, Tenn., Dec. 25, 1818; s. Hon. Luke L.; grad. U. of Nashville, 1837, A.M., 1840; A.M., Bethany Coll., W.Va.; m. Elizabeth B. Overton. Began law practice in Nashville, 1840; U.S. atty. for dist. of Middle Tenn., 1842-44; was circuit judge; declined apptmt. on Supreme Court bench of Tenn.; served as mem. Tenn. Gen. Assembly; pres. Bd. Trustees Univ. of Nashville for many yrs.; pres. Tenn. Hist. Soc. Home: Nashville, Tenn. Deceased.

LEA, Preston, governor; b. Wilmington, Del., Nov. 12, 1841; s. William and Jane Scott (Lovett) L.; ed. Lawrenceville, N.J.; m. Adalaide Moore, Oct. 28, 1870 (died 1888); m. 2d, Eliza Naudain Corbit, 1897. At 18 entered father's mill and after his death, 1876, pres. William Lea & Sons Co.; pres. Union Nat. Bank, 1888—; v.p. Farmers' Mut. Ins. Co.; dir. Phila., Baltimore & Washington R.R.; pres. Equitable Guarantee & Trust Co., Wilmington Ry. Co. Gov. of Del., Jan. 1905-Jan. 1909. Republican. Home: Wilmington, Del. Died Dec. 4, 1916.

LEACH, Abby, college prof.; b. Brockton, Mass., May 28, 1855; d. Marcus and Eliza P. (Bourne) L.; A.B., A.M., Vassar Coll., 1885; student Radcliffe Coll., and U. of Leipzig; the organization of Radcliffe Coll. (Harvard Annex) was partly due to her taking pvt. courses with different professors at Harvard; unmarried. Prof. Greek, Vassar Coll., 1889—. Mem. mng. com. Am. Sch. Classical Studies, Athens, 1888—. Pres. Am. Philol. Assn., 1899-1900; pres. Assn. Collegiate Alumnæ, 1899-1901. Received a gold cup in 1908 from the late Emperor of Japan inscribed with the imperial flower as a token of the "Imperial good will." Home: Poughkeepsie, N.Y. Died Dec. 29, 1918.

LEACH, Albert Ernest, chemist; b. Boston, Mass., Apr. 7, 1864; s. John Brooks and Mary Pamelia (Bellows) L.; S.B., Mass. Inst. Tech., 1886; m. Martha Hughes Thompson, Sept. 2, 1890. Expert in patent causes, 1887-92; asst. analyst, Mass. State Bd. of Health, 1892-99, chief analyst, 1899-1907, having charge of analysis of food and drugs for adulteration; chief U.S. Food and Drug Inspection Lab., Denver, 1907—. Swedenborgian. Author: Food Inspection and Analysis, 1904, 2d edit., 1909. Home: Denver, Colo. Died 1910.

LEACH, Arthur Burtis, banker; b. Detroit, Mich., Sept. 30, 1863; s. Frederick E. and Matilda I. (Shaw) L.; ed. grammar and high schs., Detroit; m. Maud Campbell, Feb. 3, 1887; children—Helen C. (Mrs. Lloyd Robinson), Maud C. (Mrs. J. Carlile Martin), Ferry W., Margaret D. (Mrs. Wm. D. Dana). Began in investment and banking business, at Chicago, 1886; formerly mem. Farson, Leach & Co.; pres. A. B. Leach & Co., Inc., 1913-32; pres. Leach Bros., Inc. Chmn. Liberty Loan Com., N.Y. City, World War. Mem. bd. dirs. Bonnie Brae Farm for Boys, Boys Conservation Bureau. Episcopalian. Mason. Home: South Orange, N.J. Died Jan. 15, 1939.

LEACH, Edward Giles, lawyer; b. Meredith, N.H., Jan. 28, 1849; s. Levi and Susan C. (Sanborn) L.; A.B., Dartmouth, 1871; m. Agnes A. Robinson, Dec. 24, 1874; children—Eugene Wm., Robert Milton. Admitted to bar, 1874; sr. mem. Leach & Stevens, and Leach, Stevens & Crouch, at Concord and Franklin, N.H., 1878—; city solicitor, Franklin, 1894-1906 and 1911—; pres. Mfrs. & Mchts. Mut. Ins. Co. Mem. N.H. Ho. of Rep., 1893-95, Senate, 1900; mem. Gov. McLane's council, 1905-06; co. solicitor, 1880-84; mem. Rep. State Exec. Com., 1880—; mayor of Franklin, 1918-19. Unitarian. Home: Franklin, N.H. Died July 30, 1928.

LEACH, Eugene Walter, writer; b. Excelsior, Minn., Sept. 15, 1857; s. George Washington and Deborah Bianca (White) L.; moved with parents to Racine, Wis., in infancy; ed. high sch.; m. Eva Augusta Roberts, June 22, 1882 (died 1886); children—Alice Eva (Mrs. William Russell Lewis, dec.), Ralph Elmer (dec.); m. 2d, Katharine M. Eager, May 18, 1892. With Racine Advocate, 1875, 76; in employ Racine Hardware Mfg. Co., 1879-94; agt. Aetna Life Ins. Co., 1894-1919. Chmn. registration bd., later sec. and exec. mem. City Hall Draft Bd., Racine, 1917-19. Racine Co. historian and custodian Racine Co. Hist. Rooms. Republican-Prohibitionist. Author: The Methodist Church and Early Racine, 1912; Racine County Militant, 1915; Racine—An Historical Narrative, 1920; Early History of Racine County, 1933. Home: Racine, Wis. Deceased.

LEACH, J(osiah) Granville, lawyer; b. Cape May C.H., N.J., July 27, 1842; s. Joseph S. and Sophia (Ball) L.; LL.B., U. of Pa., 1866; m. Elizabeth T. Whilldin, Oct. 5, 1866. In newspaper work prior to Civil War; sergt., sergt. maj. and lt. 25th N.J. Vols., 1862-63; received first promotion "for gallant conduct at battle of Fredericksburg." In law practice, 1866—; mem. Pa. Legislature, 1876. Republican. Commissary gen. of Pa., with rank of col., 1887-90; appraiser port of Phila., 1889-90. Pres. Geneal. Soc. Pa.; hon. pres. of Pa. Soc. S.R.; pres. Colonial Soc. of Pa.; deputy gov. gen. Soc. Mayflower Descendants. Author and editor various books on geneal. subjects. Home: Philadelphia, Pa. Died May 27, 1922.

LEAHY, Timothy John, lawyer; b. Osage Mission (now St. Paul), Kan., May 6, 1868; s. Edward and Margaret (Lee) L.; A.B., Kan. Normal Coll., Fort Scott, 1889; m. Bertha L. Rogers, Sept. 26, 1896; children—Thomas Rogers, Cora W. (Mrs. H. H. Mundy), Mabel A. (Mrs. Richard T. Edwards, Jr.), Edward Arthur. Admitted to Okla. Ty. bar, 1892; gen. counsel and dir. First Nat. Bank, Pawhuska, 1916—; pres. Price Oil Co., 1917-25; gen. counsel and dir. Peters Petroleum Corp., Tulsa, Okla., 1923—; rep. of Osage Tribe of Indians in litigation involving ownership and taxation oil, gas and coal lands, 1931 (obtained refund of $4,000,000 taxes). Pres. Producers Commn. Assn. of Okla.; dir. Nat. Live Stock Producers Assn. Mem. Okla. Constl. Conv., 1906. Democrat. Served as spl. atty. of Osage Tribe of Indians in various cases pertaining to Federal prosecutions and tribal income tax, etc. Home: Pawhuska, Okla. Died Mar. 3, 1934.

LEAHY, William Augustine, author; b. Boston, Mass., July 18, 1867; s. John and Mary Elizabeth (Driscoll) L.; A.B., Harvard, 1888; 1 yr. post-grad. work, Harvard; unmarried. Teacher Milton (Mass.) Acad., 1889-90; lit. editor Boston Traveler, 1893-94; sec. Music Dept., City of Boston, Jan. 1902-Feb. 1910; sec. to mayor of Boston, 1910-12. Author: The Siege of Syracuse, 1889; The Incendiary (Chicago Record Prize Story), 1896; History of the Catholic Church in New England, 1899; A Little Book for Immigrants, 1921; A Compendium of Reports and Studies Relating to the Commerce and Industries of Boston, 1924. Editor of The story of the Films, 1927; asso. editor Fifty Years of Boston (Tercentenary Memorial Vol.). Home: South Boston, Mass. Died June 4, 1941.

LEAKE, Joseph Bloomfield, lawyer; b. Deerfield, N.J., Apr. 1, 1828; s. Lewis and Lydia L.; removed to Cincinnati, Nov. 1836; A.B., Miami U., 1846, A.M., 1849, LL.D., 1910; m. Cordelia M. Scott, Oct. 4, 1854 (died 1858); m. 2d, Mary P. Hill, Nov. 28, 1865. Admitted to bar, 1850; removed to Davenport, Ia., 1856; mem. Iowa Ho. of Rep., 1861-62; elected state senator, 1862, but resigned after 1st session to become capt. 20th Ia. Vols.; lt. col., 1862-65; bvtd. col. and brig. gen. U.S.V., 1865; elected state senator, 1866, but again resigned; co. atty. Scott Co., Ia., 1866-71; pres. bd. edn., Davenport, 1868-71; moved to Chicago, Nov. 1871; U.S. atty. Northern Dist. of Ill., 1879-84; atty. Bd. Edn., Chicago, 1887-91. Congregationalist. Home: Chicago, Ill. Died June 2, 1913.

LEALE, Charles Augustus, physician; b. N.Y. City, Mar. 26, 1842; s. Capt. William Pickett and Anna Maria (Burr) L.; studied science; received pvt. instruction from Dr. Austin Flint, Sr., Bellevue Med. Coll., in diseases of the heart and lungs, and from Dr. Frank H. Hamilton, in gunshot wounds and surgery; attended med. and surg. clinics in N.Y. City; M.D., Bellevue Hosp. Med. Coll., 1865; m. Rebecca Medwin Copcutt, Sept. 3, 1867; children—Annie (dec.), Lilian, Medwin, Marion, Loyal, Helen (Mrs. James Harper). Apptd. and served full term as med. cadet U.S.A.; later acting asst. surgeon U.S.A. and asst. surgeon U.S. Vols.; took charge of ward for wounded officers and was exec. officer U.S.A., Gen. Hosp., Armory Sq., Washington, 1865; first surgeon to reach President Lincoln after he was shot, Apr. 14, 1865, and was placed in charge of the President by Mrs. Lincoln; prolonged his life and remained continuously with him until he died, Apr. 15, 1865; hon. mustered out of service, Jan. 20, 1866; brevetted capt. U.S. vols.; studied Asiatic cholera in Europe, 1866; in practice, N.Y. City, 1866—. In charge of children's class, Northwestern Dispensary, 1866-71; physician Central Dispensary 2 yrs.; pres. St. John's Guild, 1891, 92; chmn. Floating Hosp. Com.; reorganized Children's and Seaside hosps. President Alumni Assn. Bellevue Hosp. Med. Coll., 1875, Northwestern Med. and Surg. Soc., 1872, New York County Med. Assn., 1885, 86, New York Soc. for Relief of Widows and Orphans of Med. Men, 1895-96. Companion, 1st Class, Mil. Order Loyal Legion; del. London Internat. Med. Congress, 1881; mem. Council Phila. Internat. Med. Congress, 1887; etc. Home: New York, N.Y. Died June 13, 1932.

LEALE, Medwin, M.D.; b. N.Y. City, Aug. 26, 1873; s. Charles A. and Rebecca Medwin (Copcutt) L.; A.B., Columbia, 1894, post-grad. course in philosophy; M.D., Coll. Phys. and Surg. (Columbia), 1896; studied in Europe, 1900; m. Matilda Howard Marvin; children—Bianca Marvin, Rosalind. Interne Roosevelt Hosp., later phys. outpatient dept., same until 1908; adj. attending phys. Children's Hosps. of St. John's Guild, 1912-13; cons. phys. Nassau, North Country Community and St. John's hospitals. Joined Squadron A, N.G.N.Y., 1892; 1st lt. asst. surgeon, 1897; surgeon N.Y. Vol. Cav., Spanish-Am. War, accompanying expdn. to Puerto Rico; surgeon U.S. Cav. in Southern P.R., and attending phys. Gen. Miles' hdqrs.; later capt. surgeon, serving until 1903; mem. exam. bd. for med. officers attached to N.Y. State hdqrs., 1902-03. Episcopalian. Home: New York, N.Y. Died June 30, 1934.

LEAMING, Edmund Bennett, judge; b. Cape May, N.J., May 24, 1857; s. Dr. Jonathan F. and Eliza H. (Bennett) L.; ed. under pvt. tutelage and post-grad. studies, U. of Pa.; studied law in office of late Judge James Buchanan, Trenton, N.J.; m. Edith Hand, June 4, 1907; m. 2d, Alice C. Grey Bergen, Feb. 21, 1925. Admitted to N.J. bar as atty, 1881; vice chancellor of N.J., 1906—. Republican. Baptist. Home: Moorestown, N.J. Died Sept. 23, 1932.

LEAMY, Hugh, editor; b. Dublin, Ireland, June 13, 1899; s. Edmund and Margaret Mary (Hanly) L.; came to U.S., 1909; grad. New Rochelle (N.Y.) High Sch.; m. Doris Montague, Feb. 24, 1928; 1 dau., Antonia. With New York Sun, 1917-24, Boston Herald, 1924-25; asso. editor Collier's Weekly, 1925-29; editor Mentor, 1929-30; with American Magazine, 1930—, mng. editor, 1931—. Democrat. Home: New York, N.Y. Died Feb. 9, 1935.

LEARNARD, Henry Grant, army officer; b. Wright City, Mo., Aug. 19, 1867; s. James E. and Ellen G. (Packard) L.; grad. U.S. Mil. Acad., 1890; m. Florida Lyon, Nov. 7, 1901; children—Henry Grant, Catharine Florida. Commd. 2d lt. inf., U.S.A., June 12, 1890; advanced through grades to col., Apr. 2, 1918; brig. gen., Mar. 21, 1926; retired Aug. 31, 1931. Served with 3d Exploring Expdn., in Alaska, Mar.-Nov. 1899; in Philippines, 1899-1901, except 4 mos. with China Relief Expdn., 1900; wounded in action, June 10, 1898. Awarded D.S.M. "for efficient performance of duty," World War; Silver Star citation "for gallantry in action," at Peking, China, Aug. 14, 1900; awarded Purple Heart. Died Mar. 7, 1937.

LEARNED, Ellin Craven, author; b. N.J.; d. Capt. Tunis Augustus Macdonough (U.S.N.) and Marie Louise (Stevenson) Craven; ed. private schools; studied art at Art Students' League, New York; m. Frank Learned, Apr. 12, 1893. On staff The Churchman, 1890-94, 1896-99; editor Girls' Friendly Magazine, 1904-05. Author: Ideals for Girls, 1905; The Etiquette of New York Today, 1906; Everybody's Complete Etiquette, 1923; Good Manners for Boys and Girls, 1923. Home: New York, N.Y. Died Jan. 8, 1940.

LEARNED, Henry Barrett, historian; b. Exeter, N.H., Mar. 21, 1868; s. John C. and Lucelia (Wakefield) L.; A.B., Harvard, 1890, A.M., 1897; A.M., U. of Chicago, 1894; Ph.D., Yale, 1909; student, U. of Leipzig, under Profs. Marcks and Lamprecht, 1899-1900; m. Emily Cheney, June 14, 1899; children—John, Frank Cheney, Horace Bushnell, Mary Bushnell (dec.), Emily Barrett, Barrett (dec.). Head master pvt. sch., Plymouth, Mass., 1890-92; teacher of history, Univ. Sch., Chicago, 1892-93; in charge dept. of history, Armour Inst. of Tech., Chicago, 1894-96; asst. in history, Harvard, 1897-98; 20 lectures Harvard Summer Sch., 1898; lit. editor Hartford Courant, 1900; instr. in history, Sheffield Scientific Sch. (Yale), 1900-06; lecturer on history, Wesleyan U., 1909-10; in Bur. of Investigation, Dept. of Justice, 1917-19; lecturer and asso. prof. European history, Stamford U., 1920-22, acting prof. history, 1927—. Mem. D.C. Bd. Edn., 1917-21 and, 1925—; del. from Yale and Stanford to 5th Internat. Congress on History (Brussels), 1923; del. to 6th Internat. Congress on History, Oslo, 1928. Author: The President's Cabinet, 1912; Some Aspects of the Cabinet Meeting, 1915; Sketch of W. L. Marcy in American Secretaries of State and Their Diplomacy (Vol. VI), 1928. Editor: Sermons for the New Life (by Horace Bushnell), 1903. Home: Washington, D.C. Died Oct. 12, 1931.

LEARNED, Marion Dexter, univ. prof.; b. nr. Dover, Del., July 10, 1857; s. Hervey Dexter and Mary Elizabeth (Griffith) L.; A.B., Dickinson Coll., 1880, A.M., 1883, L.H.D., 1904; studied in Germany, 1885; Ph.D., Johns Hopkins, 1887; m. Annie Mosser, June 26, 1890; children—Henry Dexter, Mary Rebecca, Anna Carola (Mrs. Robert W. Stuckenrath). Instr. langs., Dickinson Sem., 1880-84; instr., asso. and asso. prof. German, Johns Hopkins, 1886-95; prof. Germanic langs. and lits., U. of Pa., 1895—. Editor Americana Germanica (quarterly), later German American Annals (bi-monthly), 1897—. Organizer and dir. Am. Ethnographic Survey; dir. (with A. C. Myers) Pa. hist. exhibit, Jamestown Expn., 1907; spl. envoy of Carnegie Instn. to study sources of Am. history in German archives, 1909; envoy of Historical Soc. of Pa., 1914, to study sources of German emigration to America. Knight Royal Prussian Order of the Red Eagle. Mem. Am. Philos. Soc., Phi Beta Kappa. Pres. Modern Lang. Assn. America, 1909; sec. German-Am. Hist. Soc.; pres. Deutsch-Amerikanischer Lehrerbund, 1899-1901. Author: The Pennsylvania German Dialect, 1889; The Saga of Walther of Aquitaine, 1892; German Grammar; Herder and America, 1904; German Diaries of the American Revolution (Wiederholdt's Tagebuch, 1902, and Waldeck's Tagebuch, 1905); The Life of Francis Daniel Pastorius, 1908; The Family of Abraham Lincoln, 1909; Guide to the MS. Sources of American History in the German State Archives, 1912. Home: Philadelphia, Pa. Died Aug. 1, 1917.

LEARNED, Walter, banker, author; b. New London, Conn., June 22, 1847; s. Joshua Coit and Jane (Dickerman) L.; grad. high sch.; m. Alice Flagg Beckwith, June 1, 1871. Treas. and v.p. The Savings Bank of New London; pres. New London Gas & Electric Co., Rockville & Willimantic Lighting Co.; dir. Union Bank and Trust Co. Pres. Public Library, and Manual Training and Industrial Sch. (New London). Translator: Coppée's Ten Tales, 1892; Coppée's The Rivals, 1894, Harper's Magazine. Editor: Treasury of Favorite Poems, 1891; Treasury of Favorite American Poems, 1897. Author: Between Times (verse), 1889. Home: New London, Conn. Died Dec. 11, 1915.

LEARNED, William Law, jurist; b. New London, Conn., July 24, 1821; s. Ebenezer and Lydia (Coit) L.; grad. Yale, 1841, LL.D., 1878; admitted to bar, Rochester, N.Y., 1844; settled in Albany; justice Supreme Court N.Y., 1870-91; presiding justice same court, 1875-91; m. Phebe R. Marvin, May 29, 1855; m. 2d, Katharine De Witt, Jan. 15, 1868. Author: Learned Genealogy. Edited: Madam Knight's Journal; Earle's Microcosmography. Home: Albany, N.Y. Died 1904.

LEARY, Peter, Jr., army officer; b. Baltimore, Sept. 15, 1840; s. Cornelius Lawrence Ludlow and Jane Maria (Phillips) L.; ed. in pvt. schs. and acads.; grad. U.S. Arty. Sch., 1880; m. Ellen Morgan, Oct. 23, 1872. Was student of law when Civil War began; entered Alexander's battery, Md. vols., July 1862, as 2d lt. with rank dated from Aug. 11, 1862; promoted 1st lt., Apr. 6, 1865, and hon. mustered out, June 17, 1865; took part in battles of the Gettysburg campaign, 1863, at Berryville, Opequan Creek, Winchester and Stevenson's Sta., Va., and in the Md. campaign, 1864; engaged at Middletown, Frederick and Monocacy, Md.; pvt. sec. and a.d.c. to Gov. Swann, of Md., Jan. 1, 1866-June 30, 1867. Apptd. 2d lt., July 2, 1867; promoted through grades to brig. gen., July 7, 1904. Served in Arapahoe War, Dec. 1869, Modoc War, 1873, Nez Perces War, 1877, and War with Spain, 1898. Bvtd. capt. for gallantry, in Lava Beds campaign, Calif., Apr. 15-16, 1873. First comdr., Md. Commandery, Loyal Legion; pres. Soc. War of 1812 in Md. Republican. Chmn. Sewerage Commn. of Baltimore. Home: Baltimore, Md. Died 1911.

LEARY, Richard Phillips, naval officer; b. Baltimore; grad. Naval Acad., 1860; promoted ensign, Oct. 1863; master, May 1866; lt., Feb. 1867; lt. comdr., Mar. 1868; comdr., June 1882; capt., Apr. 1897. Attached to blockading squadrons off Charleston, S.C., 1863-65; later on various duties and stas.; comd. Adams, Pacific sta., 1888-89; senior officer at Samoa during the revolution of 1888, when Tamasese govt. was overthrown; was voted a gold medal by the Md. legislature for courageous services to govt. at that time; comd. cruiser San Francisco, 1897-98; convoyed the New Orleans, bought from Brazil; was stationed at Boston Navy-Yard after Spanish-Am. war; apptd. capt., Jan. 1899, and was for short time naval gov. Guam. Died 1901.

LEASE, Emory Bair, philologist; b. New Berlin, Pa., Apr. 8, 1863; s. John Henry and Kate A. (Bair) L.; A.B., Ohio Wesleyan U., 1885, A.M., 1888; fellow in Latin, Johns Hopkins, 1892, Ph.D., 1894; research work, Munich, Germany, 1897-98; m. Carrie Lee Essex, Sept. 12, 1894; children—Raymond Essex, Marjorie, B. Murray. Prof. natural sciences and German, Little Rock (Ark.) U., 1885-87; adj. prof. Latin and Greek, U. of Pacific, 1887-91; prof. Latin, Allegheny Coll., 1894-96; asst. prof. Latin, summer, U. of Chicago, 1896; asst. prof. Latin, U. of Mich., 1896-97; with Coll. City of N.Y., 1901—, asst. prof. of Latin, 1918-20, asso. prof. of Latin, Jan. 1920—. Methodist. Author: A Syntactic, Stylistic and Metrical Study of Prudentius, 1895. Editor: T. Livi Ab Urbe Condita, Libri I, XXI, XXII, 1905, 2d edit., 1910; Livy, Books I, XXI and XXII, 1914. Home: New York, N.Y. Died May 19, 1931.

LEASE, Mary Elizabeth, Mrs., lecturer, writer; b. Ridgway, Elk Co., Pa., Sept. 11, 1853; d. Hon. Joseph P. and Mary Elizabeth (Murray) Clyens; grad. St. Elizabeth's Acad., Allegany, N.Y.; removed to Kan. Admitted to Kan. bar, 1885; made first polit. speech before a Union Labor conv., 1888; made 161 speeches in Alliance campaign, 1890, resulting in retirement of Senator John J. Ingalls; apptd. pres. State Bd. of Charities, Kan., being 1st woman to hold such a position in U.S.; had a large following for U.S. senator, 1893; was a v.p. Daughters of Isabella at Chicago Expn. and was orator on Kansas Day; represented Kan. at Nat. Conf. of Charities and Corrections and was also nat. v.p. World's Peace Congress, Chicago, 1893. Author: The Problem of Civilization Solved. Home: New York, N.Y. Died Oct. 29, 1933.

LEATHERWOOD, Elmer O., congressman; b. Waverly, O., Sept. 4, 1872; s. William and America (Hamilton) L.; grad. Kan. State Normal Sch., Emporia, Kan., 1894, completed Latin course, 1896; LL.B., U. of Wis., 1901; m. Nancy Albaugh, Dec. 26, 1896; 1 dau., Margaret Jane. Began practice at Salt Lake City, Utah, 1901; now mem. firm Straup, Nibley & Leatherwood; pres. Western Powder Co., Leary & Warren Stockyard, Olympus Mining & Milling Co. Dist. atty. 3d Jud. Dist. of Utah, 1908-16; mem. 67th to 70th Congresses (1921-29), 2d Utah Dist. Republican. Methodist. Mason (32°). Home: Salt Lake City, Utah. Died Dec. 24, 1929.

LEAVELL, James Berry, clergyman; b. Oxford, Miss., Mar. 1, 1880; s. George Washington and Corra Ball (Berry) L.; B.A., U. of Miss., 1904; Th.B., Southern Bapt. Theol. Sem., 1909; m. Lulu Freeland Bryan, May 29, 1907; children—James Berry, Lulu Lawton, Corra Eleanor, Robert Thomas, Ulleen Elise. Ordained ministry Bapt. Ch., 1905; pastor McComb, Miss., Indianola, Gulfport, Oxford, until 1917, First Ch., Houston, Tex., 1917—; membership over 5,000 in 1926. Trustee Southern Bapt. Theol. Sem., Bapt. Bible Inst., New Orleans. Mason. Home: Houston, Tex. Died Dec. 4, 1933.

LEAVELL, Landrum Pinson, Baptist worker; b. Oxford, Miss., May 10, 1874; s. George W. and Corra (Berry) L.; B.Ph., U. of Miss., 1899; studied in Europe, summer, 1900; D.D., Mississippi Coll., 1921; m. Vara Pulliam, July 23, 1903; children—Marian Frost, Frances Louise. Prof. English (rank of maj.), Jefferson Mil. Coll., Washington, Miss., 1899-1901; field sec. Bapt. S.S. Bd. of Southern Bapt. Conv., July 1903—. Asso. prof. Sunday School pedagogy, Southern Bapt. Theol. Sem., Louisville, Ky. Democrat. Author: B.Y.P.U. Manual, 1907; Division II (Psychology Sect.) of the Convention Normal Manual, 1909; Training in Christian Service; The Intermediate Department of the Sunday School; Pupil Life, with Hints to Teachers; Pilgrim's Progress for the B.Y.P.U. Home: Oxford, Miss. Died June 4, 1929.

LEAVELL, William Hayne, clergyman, diplomat; b. Newberry Dist., S.C., May 24, 1850; s. John Rowland and Elizabeth Jane (Chalmers) L.; ed. Newberry Coll. to 1866; Southern Bapt. Theol. Sem., 1867-70; D.D., Austin Coll., Tex., 1895; LL.D., U. of Miss., 1908; m. Mary George, Dec. 1, 1874; children—James George, Robert Hayne, Selden, Kate George. Ordained ministry, 1870; pastor various chs., 1870-1905; E.E. and M.P. to Guatemala, Sept. 1913-19. Progressive Democrat. Dir. and pres. bd. Presbyn. Theol. Sem., Austin, Tex.; trustee Austin Coll., Sherman, Tex.; commr. of Presbyn. Ch. U.S. to Pan-Presbyn. Council, Liverpool, Eng., 1904. Editor and pub. of George's Political History of Slavery in the United States, 1915. Address: Houston, Tex. Deceased.

LEAVENWORTH, Francis Preserved, astronomer; b. Mt. Vernon, Ind., Sept. 3, 1858; s. Seth M. and Sarah (Nettleton) L.; A.B., Ind. U., 1880, A.M., 1888; m. Jennie Campbell, Oct. 11, 1883; children—Mary Louise, Francis Maury, Richard Ormond. On staff Cincinnati Obs., 1880-82; asst. McCormick Obs., U. of Va., 1882-87; dir. Haverford Coll. Obs., 1887-92; asst. prof. astronomy, 1892-97, prof., 1897-1927, U. of Minn. Author: Double Star Observations, 1888; proc. Haverford Coll. Observatory, 1891; Parallax Lal., 1196, 1892; Photographs of Eros for Solar Parallax, 1902. Home: Minneapolis, Minn. Died Nov. 12, 1929.

LEAVITT, Charles Wellford, civil and landscape engr.; b. Riverton, N.J., Mar. 13, 1871; s. Charles Wellford and Sarah (Allibone) L.; grad. Cheltenham (Pa.) Mil. Acad., 1888; m. Clara Gordon White, Sept. 26, 1899; children—Charles (dec.), Gordon, Kent, Charlotte, Clarissa (dec.), Dundas. Began as asst. engr. E. Jersey Water Co., later in charge constrn. Caldwell Ry., and engr. Town of Essex Fells, N.J.; served as engr. Palisades Inter-State Park Commn.; designed and supervised laying out of race tracks at Saratoga, Sheepshead Bay, Belmont Park, Toronto, Winnipeg, Montreal, etc., and constrn. of estates of William C. Whitney, Foxhall Keene, Daniel S. Lamont, Charles M. Schwab, etc.; made plans for property development for Mrs. Potter Palmer, at Sarasota, Fla.; estate of W. K. Jewett, Pasadena, Calif.; development towns of Grand Marie, Manitoba, Camden, N.J., etc.; cons. engr. Bd. of Water Supply, N.Y. City, and of N. Jersey Dist. Water Commn., Newark, N.J. Pres. Am. Inst. Consulting Engrs. Republican. Episcopalian. Home: Hartsdale, N.Y. Died Apr. 22, 1928.

LEAVITT, Erasmus Darwin, mech. engr.; b. Lowell, Mas., Oct. 27, 1836; s. Erasmus Darwin and Almira (Fay) L.; common sch. edn.; (hon. D.Engring., Stevens Inst., 1884); m. Annie Elizabeth Pettit, June 5, 1867. Served 3 yrs.' apprenticeship in shops Lowell Mfg. Co. and 1 yr. with Corliss & Nightingale, Providence, R.I.; asst. foreman City Point Works, S. Boston, 1858-59, and had charge of building the engine for flagship Hartford; chief draughtsman Thurston, Gardner & Co., Providence, 1860-61; asst. engr. U.S.N., 1861-67; resigned, and resumed practice; splty. pumping and mining machinery; consulting engr. Calumet & Hecla Mining Co., 1874-1904. Has acted as consulting engr. for cities of Boston and Louisville, Henry R. Worthington, of New York, etc. Pres. Am. Soc. Mech. Engrs.; fellow Am. Acad. Arts and Sciences. Home: Cambridge, Mass. Died Mar. 11, 1916.

LEAVITT, Frank McDowell, inventor; b. Athens, O., Mar. 3, 1856; s. Rev. John McDowell (D.D.) and Bithia (Brooks) L.; M.E., Stevens Inst., 1875, E.D., 1921; m. Gertrude Goodsell, Nov. 8, 1893. Designer steam steering-gear, 1876; head draftsman, Bliss & Williams, Brooklyn, N.Y., 1877-81; master mechanic Tex.-Mexican Ry., 1881-82; mgr. Graydon & Denton Mfg. Co., Jersey City, N.J., 1882-84; became asst. supt. E. W. Bliss Co., Brooklyn, N.Y., 1884, later chief engr.; undertook introduction of the Whitehead torpedo into U.S.N., 1890, also installed plant of U.S. Projectile Co. for manufacture shells and other projectiles used in war; invented Bliss-Leavitt torpedo, in use by U.S. Navy, and possessing a range of 12,500 yards; inventor of an automatic can-making machine which practically revolutionized the can business; inventor of a press for producing all kinds of hollow pressed ware; etc. Home: Smithtown, L.I. Died Aug. 6, 1928.

LEAVITT, Julius Adelbert, educator; b. Gouverneur, N.Y., Mar. 4, 1852; s. Halsey C. and Romanda (Leach) L.; A.B., Brown U., 1875; Newton Theol. Instn., 1875-76; D.D., La Grange Coll., Mo., 1896; LL.D., Ewing Coll., 1908; m. Isabella I. Brown, May 30, 1876; m. 2d, Lillie H. Lemen, Dec. 29, 1881. Ordained Bapt. ministry, 1876; pastor Grafton, Vt., 1876-77, Essex, Vt., 1877-80, Beloit, Kan., 1880-82, Leavenworth, Kan., 1882-84; state S.S. supt. for Ill. and financial agt. Am. Bapt. Pub. Soc., 1885-90; pres. Ewing (Ill.) Coll., 1890-1911; supt. Soc. for the Friendless, Neb. Div., 1911—. Conducted Saylor Springs Bapt. Assembly, 1887-91; asso. editor Baptist News, 1896-97; dean Winona Bible Inst., Winona Lake, Ind., 1900. Home: Lincoln, Neb. Died Apr. 3, 1925.

LEAVITT, Mary Greenleaf Clement, teacher, lecturer; b. Hopkinton, N.H., Sept. 22, 1830; d. Rev. Joshua and Eliza (Harvey) Clement; grad. State Normal Sch., W. Newton, Mass. (valedictorian), 1851; m. Thomas H. Leavitt, June 3, 1857 (now deceased). Taught scattered terms of dist. schs. in Vt., N.H. and Mass., 1846-50; taught in Quincy Grammar Sch., 1852-54, Boylston Grammar Sch. (head asst.), 1854-57; established, and conducted pvt. sch. for young ladies and children, Boston, 1867-81. Became interested in Woman's Crusade; helped organize Boston W.C.T.U.; mem. state exec. bd., later Nat. lecturer, and 1882-91 was sec. World's W.C.T.U. and journeyed abroad, organizing W.C.T.U. in Europe, Australia, Asia, Africa, S. America and many islands; hon. life pres. World's W.C.T.U., 1891—. Home: Boston, Mass. Died 1912.

LEAVITT, Sheldon, physician; b. Grand Rapids, Mich., Apr. 9, 1848; s. David Sheldon and Martha Ann L.; M.D., Hahnemann Med. Coll. Chicago, 1877; post-grad. work in Germany, Eng. and France; m. Marcella E. Smith, 1871; children—C. Franklin, Florence Belle. Prof. obstetrics, Hahnemann Med. Coll., 1880-98; prof. gynecology, Chicago Homœ. Med. Coll., 1898-1902. Author: The Science and Art of Obstetrics (text-book), 1882; Psycho-Therapy, 1903; Paths to the Heights, 1908; The Psychic Solution of the Problem of Cure, 1909; Volo-therapy, 1917; Living a Century, 1928. Home: Chicago, Ill. Died Feb. 1, 1933.

LEAYCRAFT, J(ohn) Edgar, real estate; b. N.Y. City, Mar. 15, 1849; s. Anthony D. and Hannah (Thompson) L.; ed. pub. schs.; m. Caroline Crawford, Nov. 25, 1874. In real estate business, N.Y. City, 1872—; dir. J. Edgar Leaycraft Co., Lyncroft Realty Co.; treas., dir. Library Sq. Realty Co.; treas., trustee Franklin Savings Bank; dir. New Netherland Bank. Tax commr. by appmt. Govs. Roosevelt and Odell, 1899-1904; mem. Bd. Examiners and Appraisers, New Barge Canal, by appmt. of Gov. Odell, 1904-08. Pres. N.Y. City Soc. M.E. Ch.; pres. Laymen's Missionary Movement M.E. Ch.; treas. Bd. of Edn. M.E. Ch.; mgr. Bd. of Foreign Missions M.E. Ch.; v.p. Am. Bible Soc.; dir. Y.M.C.A.; trustee Internat. Com. Y.M.C.A., Wesleyan U. (Conn.), Drew Theol. Sem., Peking (China) U.; mem. Gen. Conf. M.E. Ch., 1904, 09, 12. Republican. Mason (32°). Home: New York, N.Y. Died July 3, 1916.

LE BARON, John Francis (Patch); name changed from Patch to Le Baron, 1865, by probate court; engineer; b. Boston, Mass., Sept. 28, 1847; s. John and Margaret Ann Gurley (Poor) Patch; grad. Lawrence Acad., 1866; engring. student 3 yrs. in office of J. Herbert Shedd, Boston and Providence; m. Mary Brown Kinsman; children—Ernest Thacher, Robert Wendell P., Hattie Marie; m. 2d, Mrs. Philomena Euphemia (Brown) Manucy; 1 dau., Joan Frances; m. 3d, Carrie Louise Lakeman, Apr. 29, 1901. Asst. engr. water supply and sewerage for various cities of N.E., 1866-70; asso. engr. City of Charlestown and Middlesex Co., Mass., 1872-76; chief engr. Fitchburg R.R., 1874-77; chief engr. St. John's & Indian River R.R., Fla., 1878-79; asst. engr. U.S.A. and U.S. deputy surveyor, staff of Maj. Gen. Q. A. Gilmore, 1880-83, and Brig. Gen. J. A. Barlow, 1890; in charge Nicaragua Canal surveys and constrn., 1887-90; mem. bd. consulting engrs. Nicaragua Canal, 1888; mem. Maritime Canal Co. of Nicaragua and Nicaragua Govt. Joint Commn., 1889; consulting engr., Jacksonville, Fla., and Cleveland, O., 1891-98; raised Co. L, 10th U.S. Vol. Inf., for Spanish-Am. War, 1898; chief engr. Am. Honduras Co., 1898-1901; consulting engr. New Orleans & Gulf Ry. & Navigation Co., 1903-04; chief and consulting engr. Sumas Development & Reclamation Co., 1908-09; cons. engr. to Bd. of Trade and City of New Westminster, B.C., also to many cos. Original discoverer of immense deposits of phosphate, kaolin and fullers earth in Florida, 1881. Mason. Home: Essex, Mass. Died 1935.

LEBO, Thomas Coverley, army officer; b. Potters Mills, Pa., Nov. 17, 1842; s. Jacob G. and Susannah (Coverley) L.; ed. Phila. pub. schs.; m. Grace F. Hawks, Oct. 8, 1902. Apptd. 2d lt., Apr. 26, 1861; mustered out, July 31, 1861; 2d lt., Nov. 28, 1861; 1st lt., Feb. 12, 1863; capt., Dec. 13, 1864; mustered out, Aug. 7, 1865; apptd. 1st lt., June 12, 1867; advanced through grades to brig. gen., June 22, 1905. Asst. adj. gen. 1st Brigade, 2d Cav. Div., Army of the Potomac, Dec. 1864-June 1865; twice wounded during Civil War; served almost continuously on the frontier, 1867-94, where participated in many of the Indian campaigns and engagements; was thrice mentioned in General Orders "for good judgment, energy and conspicuous gallantry in action with Indians"; comd. 6th U.S. Cav. at battle of San Juan Hill in Spanish-Am. War, where was recommended for a bvt. "for gallantry in action." Home: Albuquerque, N.M. Died 1910.

LE BOEUF, Randall James, lawyer; b. Cohoes, N.Y., Mar. 10, 1870; s. Peter Joseph and Sarah A. (Saunders) L.; LL.B., Cornell, 1892; m. Katharine Washburn, June 3, 1896; 1 son, Randall J. Admitted to N.Y. bar, 1892; corp. counsel, City of Rensselaer, 1897-1901. Apptd. justice Supreme Court N.Y., by Gov. Charles E. Hughes, 1909-10; declined nomination as Pub. Service Commr., 2d Dist. N.Y., 1913; apptd. commr. to revise N.Y. state banking laws, 1913; N.Y. State regional dir. President's Unemployment Conf., 1921-22. Pres. Cornell Law Assn. Republican. Episcopalian. Mason. Home: Albany, N.Y. Died Sept. 14, 1939.

LECKIE, Adam Edward Lloyd, lawyer; b. Ayreshire, Scotland, 1863; s. Samuel and Catherine Stewart (MacClellan) L.; came to America, 1879; LL.B., Georgetown U., 1894, LL.M., 1895; married. In practice at Washington, D.C., 1895—; identified with many important civil and criminal cases. Presbyn. Home: Washington, D.C. Died Oct. 24, 1919.

LECKIE, Katherine, editorial consultant; b. Kingston, Can.; d. William Alexander and Evalyn (McKee) L.; ed. pvt. schs., Chicago. Began as reporter Chicago Chronicle; later with Chicago American and New York Evening Journal; became identified with Munsey publs., 1906; asso. editor Delineator, 1907-08; editor Woman's Magazine, 1908-12, The Housekeeper, 1913. Episcopalian. Dir. press activities, Henry Ford peace expdn., 1915-16; organizer news distribution conservation div., Food Administration, Washington, 1917; dir. publicity, Y.W.C.A. $4,000,000 campaign, 1917, Free Milk for France Com., 1918, $300,000 campaign of New York Assn. for the Blind, 1925. Home: New York, N.Y. Died July 22, 1930.

LE CONTE, Joseph, prof. geology and natural history Univ. of Calif.; b. Liberty Co., Ga., Feb. 26, 1823; grad. Franklin Coll., U. of Ga., 1841; A.M., 1845; Coll. of Phys. and Surg., New York, 1845; Harvard, B.S., 1851; LL.D., U. of Ga., 1879; Princeton, 1896; m. Caroline Elizabeth Nesbit, Jan. 14, 1847. During Civil war in Confederate service, in scientific dept., as chemist of med. laboratory and chemist of the nitre and mining operations. Author: Religion and Science (a course of Sunday lectures); Elements of Geology (text-book for universities); Sight, or Principles of Monocular and Binocular Vision; A Compend of Geology for High Schools; Evolution and Its Relation to Religious Thought; etc. Home: Berkeley, Calif. Died 1901.

LE CONTE, Robert Grier, surgeon; b. Long Branch, N.J., July 17, 1865; s. John Lawrence and Helen (Grier) L.; A.B., U. of Pa., 1885, M.D., 1888; resident phys., Pa. Hosp., 1888-90; studied Berlin, Vienna, Paris and London, 1890-92; married. Assistant surgeon, Pa. N.G., 1893-98; asst. surgeon and ensign U.S.N., 1898; surgeon gen. of Pa., 1903-04; consulting surgeon, Germantown and Bryn Mawr hosps.; surgeon to Pa. Hosp. Trustee U. of Pa., Wistar Inst. of Anatomy, Drexel Institute, Phila., Children's Hosp., Phila. Zoöl. Soc. Pres. Am. Surg. Assn. Comdr. M.C. U.S.N.R.F., in France, 1917. Legion d'Honneur, Navy Cross. Address: Philadelphia, Pa. Died Aug. 6, 1924.

LeCOUNT, Edwin Raymond, pathologist; b. Fond du Lac, Wis., Apr. 1, 1868; student Carroll Coll., Waukesha, Wis., 1887-88; M.D., Rush Med. Coll., 1892; grad. study Johns Hopkins Hosp., 1893-94, Pasteur Inst., Paris, 1896, Berlin, 1905. Prof. pathology, Rush Med. Coll., 1892—; attending pathologist, Cook County, Presbyn., St. Luke's, St. Elizabeth's and St. Anthony's hosps. Pres. Am. Assn. Pathologists and Bacteriologists, Assn. Cancer Research. Home: Chicago, Ill. Died 1935.

LEDBETTER, Walter A., lawyer; b. Warrenton, Tex., Mar. 9, 1863; s. Thomas A. and Almieda (Robison) L.; Sam Houston Normal Sch., Huntsville, Tex., 1881-82; studied law pvtly.; m. Letitia Paranteau, Aug. 17, 1887. Admitted to Tex. bar, 1884, and began practice at Gainesville, Tex.; moved to Ardmore, Okla., 1890, to Okla. City, 1909. Mem. Okla. Constl. Conv., 1906 (chmn. judicial com.); mem. Commn. to Revise Constitution of Okla., 1932. Democrat. Mason. Home: Oklahoma City, Okla. Died Jan. 25, 1934.

LEDERER, Charles, cartoonist; b. Lowell, Mass., Dec. 31, 1856; s. John and Bettina L.; self ed.; m. Bertha Adele Mitchell, of Chihuahua, Colo., Sept. 29, 1907. Cartoonist and illustrator, 1875—, for Frank Leslie's, Harper's, New York World, New York Herald, Chicago Herald and Record-Herald, Chronicle. Writer and illustrator of juvenile books. Home: Chicago, Ill. Died Dec. 13, 1925.

LEDERER, George W., theatrical mgr.; b. Wilkes-Barré, Pa., 1861. First theatrical venture with Sydney Rosenfeld in exploiting the latter's play of Florinel, 1878; several seasons with various attractions on the road; pioneer in America of high class vaudeville; originated the word "vaudeville" as applying to variety performances; also originated the modern style of mus. comedy, lyric farce and fantasy such as "The Belle of New York," and "Madame Sherry"; pioneer producer in America of the so-called Revue, starting with "The Passing Show." Organized in Europe the Herrmann Trans-Atlantique Vaudeville Co., which appeared in leading theatres of U.S.; mgr. of New York Casino, New York Theatre, and various theatres in London; for yrs. mgr. of Lillian Russell and many other leading players. Later mfg. photoplays. Home: New York, N.Y. Died Oct. 8, 1938.

LEDERLE, Ernst Joseph, chemist, sanitarian; b. Staten Island, N.Y., 1865; s. Joseph and Clara J. (Schmidt) L.; Ph.B., Columbia Sch. of Mines, 1886, Ph.D., 1895 (Sc.D., 1904); m. Margaret C. Taylor, June 22, 1895. Chemist New York Health Dept., 1899-1902; commr. of health, 1902-04; pres. and commissioner Dept. of Health of New York, 1910-14. Home: Stamford, Conn. Died Mar. 7, 1921.

LEDLIE, George, newspaper man; b. New York, Jan. 24, 1861; s. Gen. James Hewitt and Katherine (Hees) L.; B.A., Harvard, 1884; unmarried. Reporter and city editor Boston Advertiser, 1884-86; in traffic dept., U.P. and S.L.&S.F. rys., 1886-87; Sunday editor Post Dispatch, St. Louis, 1888-91; with business dept. New York World, 1891—. Episcopalian. Home: New York, N.Y. Died Apr. 16, 1927.

LEDOUX, Albert Reid, mining engr.; b. at Newport, Ky., Nov. 2, 1852; s. Rev. Louis P. and Katharine C. (Reid) L.; ed. Columbia Sch. of Mines, 1870-73; U. of Berlin, 1873-75; A.M., Ph.D., U. of Göttingen, 1875; (hon. M.S., U. of N.C., 1880; m. Annie Van Vorst Powers (died 1918); m. 2d, Mrs. Alice M. Baird, Aug. 26, 1920; father of Louis Vernon L. State chemist and mem. State Board of Health, N.C., 1876-80; since 1880 in practice as consulting engineer, metallurgist, assayer and chemist, and expert in chemistry and engring. cases; for 2 yrs. expert N.Y. Elec. Subway Commn.; receiver Harney Peak Tin Mining Co. 14 yrs.; v.p. Assurance Co. of America; consulting engr. Am. Bur. of Mines; v.p. of Chapultepec Land Co. Pres. Am. Inst. Mining Engrs., 1903. Home: Cornwall-on-Hudson, N.Y. Died Oct. 25, 1923.

LEDOUX, John Walter, hydraulic engr.; b. nr. St. Croix Falls, Wis., Aug. 28, 1860; s. John and Almina (Knox) L.; C.E. (with honors), Lehigh U., 1887; m. Laura A. Ueberroth, July 8, 1888. Consulting engr. for corps. and municipalities, 1927—; designed and built more than 100 water plants in U.S. and other countries, and many special works devices. Home: Swarthmore, Pa. Died Nov. 7, 1932.

LE DUC, William Gates, U.S. commr. of agr.; b. Wilkesville, O., Mar. 29, 1823; s. Henry Savary L.; A.B., Kenyon Coll., 1848; admitted to bar, 1849; settled at St. Paul, Minn., July 1850; m. Mary E. Bronson, 1851. Commr. to World's Fair, New York, 1853; active promoter rys. and immigration; laid out W. St. Paul; projected co. which built Wabasha St. bridge, St. Paul (first to span Miss. River); removed to, and laid out Hastings, Minn., and engaged extensively in farming. Capt. to bvt. brig. gen. U.S. vols. in Civil War. Returned to Minn.; projected and in part constructed Hastings & Dak. Ry. U.S. commr. of agr., 1877-81; established tea-farm, Summerville, S.C., and introduced from foreign countries olives, tea, Japanese persimmons and other plants now acclimated in U.S.; organized what now are the Bur. of Animal Industry and the Div. of Forestry; in service Treasury dept. in N.C., 1890-95. Home: Hastings, Minn. Died Oct. 30, 1917.

LEDWITH, William Laurence, clergyman; b. Brownsville, Pa., Mar. 14, 1850; s. William M. and Jean (Bryce) L.; grad. Princeton, 1874, A.M., 1877; D.D., 1895; grad. Princeton Theol. Sem., 1877; m. Sarah W. Cooper, Oct. 1886. Three pastorates: Bellevue Church, Lancaster Co., Pa., 6 yrs.; South Church, Phila., 9 yrs.; Tioga Ch., Phila., 1892—. Mem. Presbyn. Bd. Publication; twice moderator Presbytery of Phila.; librarian Presbyn. Hist. Soc.; 3 times Commr.-Gen. Assembly Presbyn. Ch. Home: Philadelphia, Pa. Died 1904.

LEDYARD, Erwin, editor; b. Nashville, Tenn.; ed. Acad. of Pinney & Saunders, Mobile; unmarried. Served in Civil war in 3d Ala. regt. C.S.A.; shot in arm and leg at Malvern Hill; in cotton business after war, at Mobile. Began editorial life, 1877, as editor Mobile News; associate editor Mobile Register, 1879-91; associate editor New Orleans Delta, 1893; then editor Mobile Herald; served 2 terms in State legislature. Democrat. Author (with T. C. De Leon): John Holden, Unionist, 1893. Home: Mobile, Ala. Died 1902.

LEDYARD, Henry, lawyer; b. Detroit, Mich., Aug. 7, 1875; s. Henry B. and Mary R. (L'Hommedieu) L.; grad. St. Paul's Sch., Concord, N.H.; A.B., Yale, 1897; LL.B., Harvard, 1900; m. Maude Hendrie, Sept. 5, 1900; children—Augustus Canfield, Henry, Mary H., William H. Admitted to Mich. bar, 1900, and began practice at Detroit; mem. firm Campbell, Bulkley & Ledyard, 1906—. Republican. Episcopalian. Home: Grosse Pointe Farms, Mich. Died Dec. 1, 1932.

LEDYARD, Henry Brockholst, ry. official; b. Paris, France, Feb. 20, 1844; s. Henry and Matilda (Cass) L.; grad. U.S. Mil. Acad., 1865; m. Mary R. L'Hommedieu, Oct. 15, 1867 (died 1895). First lt. 4th U.S. Arty., 1865-70; resigned; clerk, asst. supt. and supt. Eastern div., C.,B.&Q. R.R., 1870-74; asst. gen. supt. and chief engr., 1874-76, gen. supt., 1876-77, gen. mgr., 1877-83, pres., 1883-1905, chmn. bd. dirs., 1906—, M.C. R.R. Home: Grosse Pointe Farms, Mich. Died May 25, 1921.

LEDYARD, Lewis Cass, lawyer; b. in Mich., Apr. 4, 1851; s. Henry and Matilda (Cass) L.; A.B., Harvard, 1872, A.M., LL.B., 1875. In law practice at New York; pres. Northern Finance Corp., Franklin Bldg. Co. Pres. Assn. Bar of the City of New York, New York Pub. Library. Trustee Met. Mus. Art; trustee and v.p. The Frick Collection. Home: New York, N.Y. Died Jan. 27, 1932.

LEDYARD, Lewis Cass, Jr., lawyer; b. N.Y. City, Mar. 7, 1879; s. Lewis Cass and Gertrude (Prince) L.; A.B., Harvard, 1900, LL.B., 1903; m. Ruth L. Emery, Apr. 30, 1906; children—Dorothy, Ruth Emery (Mrs. William V. C. Ruxton), Lewis Cass III, Virginia (dec.). Admitted to N.Y. bar, 1903; pres. Northern Finance Corp.; dir. Melville Bond & Share Corp., M. A. Hanna Co., Gt. Northern Paper Co.; trustee U.S. Trust Company of New York. Trustee and treasurer of the New York Public Library; trustee of Pierpont Morgan Library; dir. Nassau Hospital Assn.; gov. Society of New York Hosp., Soc. of Lying-In Hosp. Home: Syosset, L.I., N.Y. Died May 1, 1936.

LEE, Agnes (Mrs. Otto Freer), author; b. Chicago, Ill.; d. William H. and Harriet H. (Robinson) Rand; ed. in Switzerland; m. 2d, Dr. Otto Freer, May 18, 1911 (died 1932). Author: (verse) The Round Rabbit, 1898; The Border of the Lake, 1910; The Sharing, 1914; Faces and Open Doors (verse), 1922; New Lyrics and a Few Old Ones, 1930. Awarded Guarantor's prize by "Poetry" (mag.), 1926. Home: Chicago, Ill. Died July 23, 1939.

LEE, Albert Lindley, soldier; b. Fulton, Oswego Co., N.Y., Jan. 16, 1834; s. M. Lindley and Ann L.; A.B., Union Coll., 1853. Practiced law at New York, 1855-57; removed to Kan., 1857; judge Supreme Ct. of Kan., 1860-61; maj. 7th Kan. Cav., Oct. 29, 1861; col., May 17, 1862; brig. gen. vols., Nov. 29, 1862; resigned, May 4, 1865. Mem. firm Robert Goodbody & Co., bankers, 1890-1901. Republican. Home: New York, N.Y. Died 1907.

LEE, Andrew Ericson, governor; b. nr. Bergen, Norway, Mar. 18, 1847; s. Eric and Augusta (Johnson) L.; emigrated with parents to Dane Co., Wis., 1851; ed. common and high schs.; m. Annie M. Chappel, 1872. With Charles E. Prentis, in farming and mercantile pursuits, 1869—. Was mayor of Vermilion, S.D.; gov. of S.D., 1896-98, 1898-1900. Populist. Home: Vermilion, S.D. Died Mar. 19, 1934.

LEE, Benjamin, surgeon; b. Norwich, Conn., Sept. 26, 1833; s. Rt. Rev. Alfred and Julia (White) L.; A.B., U. of Pa., 1852; M.D., New York Med. Coll., 1856; Ph.D., U. of Pa., 1876; studied in Europe; surgeon 22d N.Y. Regt., 1862-63; edited Am. Med. Monthly; m. Emma Hale White, Apr. 5, 1859. Prof. orthopedics, Phila. Polyclinic, 1895-96; health officer, Phila., 1898-99; sanitarian Pa. State Bd. of Agr.; sec. Pa. State Bd. Health, 1885-1905; sec. Pa. Quarantine Bd., 1893-1905; asst. to commr. of health of Pa., 1905—. Pres. Am. Acad. Medicine, 1884, Am. Orthopedic Assn., 1891-92, Conf. State and Provincial Bds. of Health of N. America, 1898, Am. Pub. Health Assn., 1898; long treas. Pa. Med. Soc. Author: Correct Principles of Treatment for Angular Curvature of the Spine, 1872; Tracts on Massage (translated from the German), 1885. Home: Harrisburg, Pa. Died July 11, 1913.

LEE, Benjamin Fisler, mfr.; b. Port Elizabeth, N.J., June 30, 1828; s. Hon. Thomas and Rhoda (Murphy) L.; academic edn.; m. Annabella W. Townsend, July 16, 1862. Active in N.J. railroad constrn. and extension; clerk N.J. Sup. Ct., 1872-97, also treas. Dem. State Com.; twice declined Dem. nomination for gov. Pres. Trent Tile Co., Universal Paper Bag Co.; dir. many corps. Pres. bd. mgrs., Home for Feeble Minded Women; pres. State Conf. Charities and Correction. Home: Trenton, N.J. Died 1909.

LEE, Benjamin Franklin, bishop; b. Bridgeton, N.J., Sept. 18, 1841 (of African descent); B.D., Wilberforce U., 1872; m. Mary E. Ashe, Dec. 30, 1872; children—Frances A., Sarah O., Benjamin F., Mary E. Prof. homiletics, etc., 1873-75, pres., 1876-84, Wilberforce U.; editor Christian Recorder, 1884-92; bishop A.M.E. Ch., 1892-June 1924. Del. Conf. of Methodism, 1881, 1901, 11. Home: Wilberforce, O. Deceased.

LEE, Bradner Wells, lawyer; b. East Groveland, N.Y., May 4, 1850; s. David Richard and Elizabeth Northrum (Wells) L.; ed. pub. schs. and by pvt. study; studied law in office of uncle, Col. G. Wiley Wells, Holly Springs, Miss.; m. Helene Farrar, Oct. 16, 1883. Admitted to Miss. bar, 1871; asst. U.S. dist. atty. Northern Dist. of Miss., 1871-79; removed to Los Angeles, 1879; practicing with two sons, Bradner W. and Kenyon F.; identified with much important litigation; served as atty. for executor and estate of E. J. ("Lucky") Baldwin, who died in 1909, final settlement made in 1913; gen. counsel Murphy Oil Co. Declined appmt. judge Superior Court, Los Angeles Co., 1895; chmn. Rep. County Central Com., Los Angeles Co., 1896-1910; mem. Exec. Com. Rep. State Central Com., 1902-04. Trustee Calif. State Library, 1897-1917. Mem. Nat. Conf. of Commrs. on Uniform State Laws, 1916-24; pres. Calif. State Bar Assn., 1919-20. Presbyn. Mason. Home: Los Angeles, Calif. Died Apr. 28, 1925.

LEE, Burton James, surgeon; b. New Haven, Conn., Feb. 4, 1874; s. James Howard and Susan Mar (Hoyt) L.; Ph.B., Yale, 1894; M.D., Coll. of Phys. and Surg. (Columbia), 1898; m. Louise Freeman, Mar. 29, 1919. Clin. prof. surgery, Cornell U. Med. Coll. Commd. capt. M.C., U.S.A., Apr. 1917; maj., June 1918; lt. col., Nov. 1918; active service in France, Aug. 7, 1917-Jan. 25, 1919. Decorated D.S.M. (U.S.); Croix de Guerre (French). Mem. Am. Surg. Assn. Republican. Home: New York, N.Y. Died Nov. 12, 1933.

LEE, David Russell, univ. prof.; b. Hamilton, Ont., Can., Aug. 20, 1869; s. Joseph and Rosanna (Peregrine) L.; early edn. Hamilton Collegiate Inst. with honor matriculation U. of Toronto, 1886; A.B., Albion (Mich.) Coll., 1895, A.M., 1901; U. of Chicago, 1903-04; A.M., Ind. U., 1905; Ph.D., U. of Wis., 1907; studied archæology in British Mus., and Rome, summer, 1905, in Sicily, Greece and Dalmatia, summer, 1908; unmarried. Ordained M.E. ministry, 1897; pastor Robinson, Mich., 1896-98, Pentwater, 1898-1900, Joy Memorial Church, Grand Rapids, 1901-03; instr. Latin, Ind. U., 1904-05; fellow in Latin, 1905-06, asst., 1906-07, U. of Wis.; prof. Greek and Latin, Central Coll., Fayette, Mo., 1907-09; prof. classical lit., 1909-16, dir. Summer Sch., 1912-16, U. of Chattanooga; prof. Greek, Univ. of Tenn., 1916—. Pres. Tenn. Philol. Assn., 1911-12, sec., 1915-18. Mem. Rhodes Oxford Scholarship Com. for Tenn., 1915-16. Author: Child Life, Adolescence and Marriage in Greek New Comedy and in Plautus, 1920. Home: Knoxville, Tenn. Died Oct. 18, 1933.

LEE, Edward Hervey, civil engr.; b. Dayton, O., Jan. 29, 1863; s. John Newton and Julia (Sheldon) L.; ed. Ohio U. and U. of Wooster (O.); m. Ruth Sheldon Brooke, 1916. Asst. engr., prin. asst. engr. and chief engr. with various ry. cos., including Nickel Plate, U.P., E.,J.&E., 1880-98; served as engr., chief engr. and v.p. C.&W.I. R.R., and Belt Railway of Chicago, beginning 1898, pres., 1926-31. Home: Chicago, Ill. Died Jan. 11, 1937.

LEE, E(dward) Trumbull, clergyman; b. New Haven, Conn., Apr. 5, 1855; s. William Brown and Elizabeth Payson (Howe) L.; A.B., Williams Coll., 1879; grad. Union Theol. Sem., 1882; D.D., U. of Colo., 1890; LL.D., Cedarville Coll., Ohio, 1900; m. Mary Catherine Martin, June 7, 1882 (died 1883); m. 2d, Charlotte Josephine Skinner, May 6, 1884. Ordained Presbyn. ministry, 1882; pastor Calvary Ch., Portland, Ore., 1882-86, First Ch., Pueblo, Colo., 1886-95, Second Ch., Cincinnati, 1895-1902, Chambers-Wylie Memorial Ch., Phila., 1902-06, First Ch., Wilkinsburg, Pittsburgh, Pa., 1906—. Author: Sheaf of Wheat; God's Plan of a Christian; Niagara Harnessed; Brief History Presbyterian Church. Home: Pittsburgh, Pa. Died May 5, 1913.

LEE, Elisha, ry. official; b. Chicago, Ill., Sept. 24, 1870; B.S., Mass. Inst. Tech., 1892. Began as rodman, office of div. engr., Tyrone div., Pa. R.R., 1892; with same rd. until 1909; supt. New York, Phila. & Norfolk R.R., 1909-11; asst. to gen. mgr. Pa. Lines East of Pittsburgh and Erie, 1911-16; asst. gen. mgr., same, 1916-17, gen. mgr., Apr. 1, 1917, actg. v.p., 1917-18; federal mgr. of Pa. R.R., Eastern Lines, U.S. R.R. Administration; v.p. in charge Eastern Lines Pa. R.R., 1920-23, v.p. in charge Central Region, 1923, v.p. in charge of operation of Pa. R.R. Co., Nov. 1924-Sept. 1926. Chmn. Conf. Com. of mgrs. of eastern railroads of U.S., 1912-14, later chmn. Nat. Conf. Com. on Negotiations between Rys. and Ry. Brotherhoods. Home: Philadelphia, Pa. Died Aug. 6, 1933.

LEE, Fitzhugh, army officer; b. Clermont, Fairfax Co., Va., Nov. 19, 1835; s. Commodore Sydney Smith L., U.S.N., and Anna Maria (Mason) L.; grad. U.S. Mil. Acad., 1856. Severely wounded in a fight with Indians; instr. of cav., West Point, 1860-61; resigned commission, 1861; was adj. gen. Ewell's brigade, C.S.A., until Sept. 1861; lt. col. and col. 1st Va. cav., participating in all battles of Army of Northern Va., 1861-62; brig. gen., July 25, 1862; maj. gen., Sept. 3, 1863; had 3 horses shot under him and was himself severely wounded at Winchester, Va., Sept. 19, 1864; comd. whole cav. corps Army of Northern Va., Mar. 1865, until he surrendered to Gen. Meade at Farmville; gov. Va., 1886-90. Democrat. U.S. consul to Havana from 1893 until declaration of war with Spain; apptd., May 1898 maj. gen. U.S. vols.; placed in command 7th army corps; after war became mil. gov. Havana, Jan. 1, 1899; later in command dept. of Mo., U.S.A. Home: Richmond, Va. Died 1905.

LEE, Francis Bazley, lawyer; b. Phila., Jan. 3, 1869; s. Benjamin Fisler and Annabella Willson (Townsend) L.; ed. Trenton (N.J.) Inst., and Lawrenceville (N.J.) Classical and Commercial Sch.; grad. N.J. State Model Sch., 1888; spl. course Wharton Sch. Finance and Economy, Phila., 1888-90, English lit. U. of Pa., 1890-91, B.S., 1910; m. Sara Stretch Eayre, June 12, 1894. Studied law in office of Garret D. W. Vroom, Trenton, N.J.; admitted to N.J. bar, 1893. Was mem. Trenton Bd. Health; sec. compilations of Statutes of N.J., 1896, 1906; mem. commn. to exam. operation of penal laws and instns. of N.J. and other states, upon report of which was based N.J. legislation establishing "probation" system. Pres. Trent Tile Co.; receiver and mng. editor Trenton Times, 1897-98; actg. editor Trenton True American, 1905. Episcopalian. Democrat. Sec. of spl. com. on the acquisition of park lands in Trenton; in charge N.J. hist. exhibit, Jamestown Expn., 1907; mem. commn. to preserve pub. records of State of N.J. Author: New Jersey as a Colony and as a State, 1902. Home: Trenton, N.J. Died May 2, 1914.

LEE, Frank, lawyer; b. Stockwell, Ind., Dec. 9, 1861; s. Smith and Rosetta (Skinner) L.; student Stockwell (Ind.) Coll., 1875-79; A.B., Cumberland U., 1886; m. Emma Webster, Jan. 23, 1900. Practiced at Paris, Tex., 1887-1902; moved to Hugo, Ind. Ty., 1902; spl. asst. U.S. atty., Central Dist. Ind. Ty., 1904-07; asst. U.S. atty., Eastern Dist. of Okla., 1907-14, U.S. atty., same dist., 1921—. Sec. Dist. Exemption Bd., World War. Trustee Bapt. Hosp. Republican. Baptist. Home: Muskogee, Okla. Died Oct. 30, 1930.

LEE, Frederic Girard, banker; b. Orange, N.J., June 15, 1873; s. Stephen Girard and Georgiana Gertrude (St. John) L.; grad. Brooklyn (N.Y.) High Sch., 1890; m. Sophie Bohlen Hagedorn, Apr. 16, 1896. Began as clk. Kings Co. Trust Co., Brooklyn, 1890; organizer and sec. Broadway Trust Co., 1902, v.p., 1903-08, later pres.; dir. many corps.; chmn. finance com. Famous Players-Lasky Corp. Episcopalian. Mason. Home: New York, N.Y. Died 1923.

LEE, Frederic Schiller, physiologist; b. Canton, N.Y., June 16, 1859; s. late Rev. John Stebbins (pres. St. Lawrence U.) and Elmina (Bennett) L.; A.B., St. Lawrence U., 1878, A.M., 1881, LL.D., 1918; Ph.D., Johns Hopkins U., 1885; U. of Leipzig, under Ludwig, 1885-86; Sc.D., Columbia U., 1929; m. Laura

Billings, June 5, 1901; children—Julia, Frederick Billings. Instr. biology, St. Lawrence U., 1886-87; instr. and asso. in physiology and histology, Bryn Mawr Coll., 1887-91; demonstrator physiology, 1891-95, adj. prof., 1895-1904, Dalton prof., 1904-20, research prof., 1920-28, prof., 1928—, Jesup lecturer, 1911, mem. Univ. Council, 1913-20, Columbia U. Cutter lecturer Harvard Med. School, 1918; Parker lecturer Union Theol. Sem., 1922. Consulting physiologist, 1917-19, senior physiologist with rank of senior surgeon in reserve corps, 1919-24, U.S. Public Health Service. An editor American Jour. Physiology, 1898-1914, Columbia U. Quarterly, 1900-20. Mem. bd. mgrs. N.Y. Bot. Garden, 1903-27, v.p. 1921-23, pres. 1923-27; trustee Columbia U. Press, 1907-20. Mem. N.Y. Commn. on Ventilation. Spl. mission to Europe to investigate industrial conditions for U.S. Pub. Health Service, 1918. Fellow A.A.A.S. (chmn. sect. K); pres. Soc. for Exptl. Biology and Medicine, 1908-10, Harvey Soc., 1912-14, Am. Physiol. Soc., 1917-19; chmn. Federation Am. Socs. for Exptl. Biology, 1917. Author: Physiology—Vital Processes in Health, in "In Sickness and in Health," 1896; Reproduction, in "An American Textbook of Physiology," 1896; The School of Medicine, in "A History of Columbia University," 1904; Fatigue, in "Harvey Lectures," 1906; The Human Machine in the Factory, in same, 1919; Scientific Features of Modern Medicine, 1911; Fatigue and Occupation, in "Diseases of Occupation and Vocational Hygiene," 1916; The Human Machine and Industrial Efficiency, 1918. Joint Author: Ventilation (The Report of the N.Y. State Commn. on Ventilation), 1923. Translator and Editor: General Physiology, An Outline of the Science of Life (by Max Verworn), 1899. Reviser and Editor: Lessons in Elementary Physiology (by T. H. Huxley), 1900; Harvey's Views on the Use of the Circulation of the Blood (by John G. Curtis), 1915. Home: New York, N.Y. Died Dec. 14, 1939.

LEE, George Washington Custis, univ. pres.; b. Fortress Monroe, Va., Sept. 16, 1832; s. Gen. Robert Edward (C.S.A.) and Mary Ann Randolph (Custis) L.; acad. edn. in Va.; grad. U.S. Mil. Acad., 1854; LL.D., Tulane U., 1887; unmarried. Did important mil. engring. work in Fla. and Calif.; during Civil War was a.d.c. on staff Jefferson Davis; rose to rank of maj. gen. and was captured at Sailor's Creek; prof. civ. and mil. engring., Va. Mil. Inst., 1865; succeeded his father, 1871, as pres. Washington and Lee U., until 1897, pres. emeritus, 1897—. Address: Burke, Va. Died Feb. 18, 1913.

LEE, Gordon, congressman; b. on farm nr. Ringgold, Ga., May 29, 1859; s. James Morgan and Elizabeth (Gordon) L.; A.B., Emory Coll., Oxford, Ga., 1880; m. Olive Berry, June 27, 1900. Is engaged in farming and mfg. Mem. Ga. Ho. of Rep., 1894-96, Senate, 1902-05; mem. state memorial bd.; mem. 59th to 69th Congresses (1905-27), 7th Ga. Dist. Democrat. Home: Chickamauga, Ga. Died Nov. 7, 1927.

LEE, Guy Carleton, publicist; b. 1862; s. Joseph C. Ayer and Caroline E. (Roberts) L.; A.B., Rutherford Coll., N.C., 1889; LL.B., U. of N.C., 1894; A.B., Dickinson Coll., 1895, A.M., LL.M., 1896; Ph.D., Johns Hopkins, 1898; LL.D., Rutherford, 1899; m. Emeline E. Baker, May 1889; 1 dau., Eadgyth Caroline; m. 2d, Hildegarde H. Langsdorf, Jan. 27, 1912; m. 3d, Elizabeth Havilland Herman, Apr. 26, 1923; 1 dau., Caroline Eliza. Admitted N.C. bar, 1894, Pa., 1895, Md., 1897; prof. English history and common law, Dickinson Coll., 1895; scholar, hon. scholar, and fellow, 1896-98, instr. history, 1898-1905, Johns Hopkins; lecturer on comparative politics, George Washington U., 1900-02; lit. editor Baltimore Sun, 1901-08; editor in chief Internat. Lit. Syndicate, 1900-16; staff lecturer in history and lit., Am. Soc. for Extension of Univ. Teaching, 1900-02; mng. dir. Nat. Soc. for Broader Edn., New York, 1909—. Gen. Counsel Pa. State Hotel Assn., 1930—. Pres. Carlisle Chamber Commerce, 1916-20; nat. councilor Chamber Commerce U.S.A., 1916—. Mem. exec. com. of Com. of Pub. Safety, 1917-21. Author: Hincmar—An Introduction to the Study of the Church in the Ninth Century, 1898; Public Speaking, 1899; Historical Jurisprudence, 1900; Source Book of English History, 1900; True History of the War Between the States, 1903; Robert E. Lee, a biography, 1905; Seven Great Hymns, 1909; The Heart of a Child, 1910; The Soul of a Woman, 1910; The Mind of Man, 1911; Social Conscience of the People of the United States, 1931. Editor-in-Chief: The World's Orators (10 volumes), 1900; The History of Woman (10 vols.), 1902-03; The History of North America (20 vols.), 1903-05. Home: Carlisle, Pa. Died Dec. 27, 1936.

LEE, Harry, officer U.S.M.C.; b. Georgetown, D.C., June 4, 1872; s. Jesse Washington and Laura Rose (Collings) L.; ed. pub. schs., Georgetown; m. Henrietta Mercedes Saltmarsh, June 25, 1912; 5 children. Commd. in U.S.M.C., Aug. 2, 1898; promoted through grades to brig. gen., June 5, 1920. Comd. 6th Regt. Marines, June 6, 1918-Aug. 13, 1919; participated in Château-Thierry, Soissons, Mabache sector, St. Mihiel, Blanc Mont, Meuse-Argonne operations and with Army of Occupation, Coblenz bridgehead, Germany. Apptd. comdr. 2d Brig. U.S.M.C., Santo Domingo, D.R., Aug. 8, 1921, military gov. same, 1923-24; later comdg. Marine Barracks, Pariss Island, S.C. Decorated D.S.M., both Army and Navy (U.S.); Officer Legion of Honor and Croix de Guerre with 2 palms (French). Died May 13, 1935.

LEE, Henry Haworth, pres. Pennroad Corp.; b. Pawtucket, R.I., Nov. 3, 1880; s. Frank L. and Clara M. (Haworth) L.; grad. Media (Pa.) High Sch., 1897; m. Edith Carpenter Green, Oct. 9, 1912; children—Henry Haworth, William L. With Pa. R.R., 1898-1929, asst. treas., 1918-24, treas. same and affiliated cos., 1924-29; pres. Pennroad Corp., 1929—; dir. Pa. Co. for Insurances on Lives and Granting Annuities, Pittsburgh & W.Va. Ry. Co., Canton Co., Northern Trust Co. (Phila.); mem. bd. mgrs. Beneficial Savings Fund Soc. Republican. Episcopalian. Home: Moylan, Pa. Died July 30, 1941.

LEE, Hildegarde L. (Mrs. Guy Carleton Lee), physician; b. Centerville, Pa., Mar. 26, 1868; d. William Henry and Lydia R. (Haverstick) Langsdorf; A.B., Dickinson Coll., 1888, A.M., 1891; M.D., Woman's Med. Coll., Phila., 1891; m. Guy Carleton Lee, Jan. 27, 1912. Practiced, Carlisle, Pa., 1892—; on staffs of Harrisburg Insane Hosp., Norristown Insane Hospital, Tewksbury Almshouse. Asst. editor the Pennsylvania Medical Journal. Treasurer Nat. Soc. for Broader Edn. Presbyn. Especially interested in financing charitable orgns.; lecturer on social and economic subjects. Mem. Com. of Pub. Safety, 1917. Home: Carlisle, Pa. Died Apr. 21, 1922.

LEE, Homer, bank note engraver, artist; b. Mansfield, O., May 18, 1856; s. John A. and Elizabeth L.; studied under father and Robert Mackintosh, Toronto, Can.; afterwards studied abroad; m. Charlotte B. Riddle, 1891. Regular exhibitor at Nat. Acad. Design, also in London and Paris; hon. mention, Vienna, 1873; designed Arms of the U.S., which surmounted the entrance to the U.S. Pavilion at Vienna; 1st class medal, State of Ohio, 1887; hon. mention, Paris Expn., 1900. Picture, "Building of the Sky Scraper," was purchased by French govt.; represented in the Lotos and Salmagundi clubs, New York, and elsewhere; exhibited Buffalo Expn., 1901; bronze medal, Charleston, S.C., Expn., 1902, pictures, "Skyscrapers," and St. Louis Expn., 1904. Asst. to commr. of fine arts and the supervising architect, West Indian Expn., Charleston, 1901-02. Was founder and pres. Homer Lee Bank Note Co.; v.p. Franklin Lee Bank Note Co., New York; pres. Hamilton Bank Note Co. Inventor of the Homer Lee rotary steel plate printing system, together with numbering devices used by U.S. Treasury Dept. on govt. bonds and bank notes, and also used abroad; also inventor of the "steelograph" process and of many improvements in linotype composing machines. Apptd. mem. staff gov. of Ohio; col. of Continental Guards; a founder and commr. Hudson-Fulton Celebration, 1909. Mem. com. on liturgy, apptd. by Gen. Assembly Presbyn. Ch. U.S.A. (Los Angeles, Calif.), which produced the Van Dyke prayer book. Mason (32°). A founder of St. John's Guild Floating Hosp. Home: New York, N.Y. Died Jan. 25, 1923.

LEE, Ivy Ledbetter; b. Cedartown, Ga., July 16, 1877; s. James Wideman and Emma Eufaula (Ledbetter) L.; A.B., Princeton, 1898; LL.D., Oglethorpe Univ., Atlanta, Ga., 1931; post-grad. work, Harvard and Columbia univs.; m. Cornelia Bartlett, d. Horace R. Bigelow, 1901; children—Alice Bigelow, James Wideman, Ivy Ledbetter. Newspaper work, New York, 1899-1903; press representative anthracite coal operators, Pa. R.R. and other corps., 1906-07; in charge publicity bur., Pa. R.R., 1908-09; gen. European mgr. for Harris, Winthrop & Co., bankers, 1910-12; exec. asst. Pa. R.R., Dec. 1, 1912-Dec. 31, 1914; mem. personal advisory staff of John D. Rockefeller, Jan. 1, 1915-Apr. 1, 1916. Adviser in pub. relations to Pennsylvania R.R., John D. Rockefeller, Bethlehem Steel Co., and other large interests. Asst. to chmn. Red Cross War Council, 1917-19. Lecturer London Sch. of Economics, 1911-12. Wrote "The Best Administration New York City Ever Had" (used as campaign book by the Citizens' Union, 1903); Memories of Uncle Remus, 1908; Human Nature and Railroads, 1915; Publicity—Some of the Things It Is and Is Not; U.S.S.R.—A World Enigma—1927, 2d edit. (under title Present Day Russia), 1928. Home: New York, N.Y. Died Nov. 9, 1934.

LEE, James Grafton Carleton, brigadier gen. U.S.A.; b. nr. Hamilton, Ont., Aug. 12, 1836; s. Samuel and Anna (Shafer) L.; grad. Victoria U., Cobourg, Can.; m. Sarah J. Loomis, Apr. 25, 1861; m. 2d, Maud Cromelien, Aug. 12, 1902. Apptd. from civil life, Ohio, capt. a.q.m. vols., Nov. 26, 1862; capt. a.q.m. U.S.A., July 2, 1864; maj. q.m., July 2, 1879; lt. col. deputy q.m. gen., Dec. 11, 1892; col. asst. q.m. gen., Feb. 18, 1897; retired, Aug. 12, 1900; advanced to rank of brig. gen. retired, by act of Apr. 23, 1904. Bvtd. maj. and lt. col., July 31, 1865, "for faithful and meritorious services." In Civil War served at headquarters Army of Potomac and at several supply depots in Va., acting chief q.m. during Gettysburg campaign, and in charge depot, Alexandria, Va.; comd. right wing of defenses of Alexandria, Va., 1864; after was in various depts. and duties until retired as chief q.m. Dept. of Lakes; pres. bd. in Cuba to prepare for landing U.S. forces, 1898. Dir. Chicago Inst., 1900-01; mil. instr. Northwestern Mil. Acad., 1901-03. Mason. Address: Hague-on-Lake-George, N.Y.; and Ft. Sam Houston, Tex. Died July 26, 1916.

LEE, James Melvin, educator, editor; b. Port Crane, N.Y., May 16, 1878; s. James Newell and Emma (White) L.; grad. Wyo. Sem., Kingston, Pa., 1896; A.B., Wesleyan U., Conn., 1900; Litt.D., Washington and Lee U., 1925; m. Helen Wellner, May 17, 1908; 1 dau., Cora Virginia. Staff of The Union, Springfield, Mass., 1900; English teacher, Western Reserve Sem., W. Farmington, O., 1901-02; circulation mgr. The Star, Oneonta, N.Y., 1902-03; non-resident mem. staff of Pilgrim, Battle Creek, Mich., 1903-04; circulation mgr., Outing Magazine, 1905-06; editor Bohemian Magazine, 1906-07; lit. editor, The Circle Magazine, 1907-08; asso. editor Leslie's Weekly, 1908; editor Judge, 1908-12. Lecturer on Journalism, New York U., 1910-11; dir. Dept. of Journalism, same, 1911—. Teacher of Journalism, summer, U. of Calif., 1915. Sec. Am. Assn. Teachers of Journalism, 1913-14, pres. 1916-17; sec. Internat. Assn. Schs. of Journalism, 1921—. Editor and part author of "Business Writing," 1920; mem. editorial bd. Blue Pencil; editor in chief of Administration, 1921-23, lit. editor of Editor and Publisher, 1922—, Three Em Dash, 1923—. Exec. sec. Inter-collegiate Newspaper Assn., 1922—. Methodist. Author: How to Be Self-Supporting at College, 1903; Wordless Journalism in America (cartoons), 1915; History of American Journalism, 1917; Newspaper Ethics, 1915; Instruction in Journalism in Institutions of Higher Education, 1918; America's Oldest Daily Newspaper, 1918; Opportunities in the Newspaper Business, 1919; Business Ethics, 1925. Contbr. to Ency. Britannica, 1926, and "Journalism," in Am. Year Book, 1927. Home: New York, N.Y. Died Nov. 17, 1929.

LEE, James Paris, inventor; b. Hawick, Scotland, Aug. 9, 1831; s. George and Margaret (Paris) L.; emigrated to Canada, 1836; ed. Galt, Ont., Can.; m. Caroline Chrysler, 1852 (died 1888). Invented the Lee-Metford, Lee-Enfield, Lee-Straight Pull, and other magazine rifles. Address: Hartford, Conn. Died 1904.

LEE, James Wideman, clergyman; b. Rockbridge, Ga., Nov. 28, 1849; s. Zachary J. and Emily H. (Wideman) L.; ed. at Bawsville Acad., Grantville High Sch. and Emory Coll., Oxford, Ga.; m. Emma Eufaula, d. Rev. L. L. Ledbetter, Dec. 26, 1875; 3 sons and 3 daughters. Ordained to ministry M.E. Ch., S., 1876; pastor ch. at Rockmart, Long Cane, Carrolton, Dalton, Rome and Atlanta, Ga., St. John's Ch., St. Louis, 1893; head of expdn. to Palestine, 1894, sent out in company with artist R. E. M. Bain to secure material for an illustrated book, "Earthly Footsteps of Christ and His Apostles"; presiding elder St. Louis Dist., 1897-1901; pastor St. John's Ch., St. Louis (2d time), 1901-05, Trinity Ch., Atlanta, Ga. (2d time), 1905-09, Park St. Ch. (2d time), 1910, St. John's Ch., St. Louis (3d time), 1911-15; presiding elder St. Louis Dist. (2d time), 1915-16; chaplain, Barnes Hosp., St. Louis, 1917—. Author: The Making of a Man, 1892 (translated into Japanese, 1893, Chinese, 1904, Korean, 1908); Christ the Reason of the Universe (address before the World's Parliament of Religions, Chicago, 1893); The Earthly Footsteps of the Man of Galilee, 1895; Henry W. Grady, Editor, Orator, and Man, 1897; Illustrated History of Methodism, 1900; History of Jerusalem, 1904, revised edit., 1917; The Real Uncle Remus, 1908; Abraham Lincoln, 1909; The Religion of Science, 1912, (transl. into Japanese, 1917); Magnetizing the Commonplace, 1914; Geography of Genius, 1915; Climate and Unity, 1916; Bible and Life (address), 1916; Making of the Flag (address), 1917; A Cathedral of Coöperation (address), 1917; General Robert E. Lee (address), 1918. Edited and illustrated The Self-Interpreting Bible, 1897. Address: St. Louis, Mo. Died Oct. 4, 1919.

LEE, Jesse Matlock, maj. gen. U.S.A.; b. Putnam County, Ind., Jan. 2, 1843; s. John W. and Effey W. L.; ed. Greencastle, Ind.; m. Lucy W. Hathaway, Dec. 23, 1868. Pvt. Co. B, and sergt. 59th Ind. Inf., Nov. 13, 1861; 2d lt., Oct. 13, 1862; 1st lt., Feb. 14, 1863; capt., Aug. 11, 1863; hon. mustered out, July 17, 1865; capt. 38th U.S.C.T., Aug. 23, 1865; hon. mustered out of vols., Jan. 25, 1867; apptd. 2d lt. 39th U.S. Inf., July 28, 1866; 1st lt., Jan. 7, 1867; capt., May 1, 1879; maj., Apr. 26, 1898; col. 10th U.S. Inf. Vols., May 31-July 8, 1898; lt. col. 6th U.S. Inf., Oct. 9, 1900; col. 30th Inf., Nov. 8, 1901; brig. gen., June 17, 1902; maj. gen., Sept. 18, 1906; retired Jan. 2, 1907. Home: Greencastle, Ind. Died Mar. 26, 1926.

LEE, John Clarence, clergyman; b. Woodstock, Vt., Oct. 15, 1856; s. Rev. John Stebbins (pres. St. Lawrence U.) and Elmina (Bennett) L.; A.B., St. Lawrence, 1876, A.M., 1879; A.B., Harvard, 1878; grad. Canton Theol. Sch., 1880; Ph.D., St. Lawrence, 1895; S.T.D., Tufts, 1896; m. Helena Crumett (author), Nov. 25, 1889; children—Cuthbert, Dorothy, Constance, Janet, Roland Stebbins. Ordained Universalist ministry, 1881; pastor, Perry, N.Y., 1889-83, St. Albans, Vt., 1883-84; prof. English lit., 1884-96, pres., 1892, v.p., 1892-96, Lombard U.; pres. St. Lawrence U., 1896-99; pastor Ch. of the Restoration, Phila., 1900-19, Independent Christian Ch., Gloucester, Mass., 1919-29, Stamford (Conn.) Universalist Ch., 1932-33.

Traveled around world, preaching in Fiji Islands, Australia and India, 1929-31. Delegate to Nat. Arbitration and Peace Congress, 1907; del. Internat. Congress for Promotion of Free Christianity, Berlin, 1910. Pres. of Associated Charities, Gloucester; mem. Gloucester Tercentenary Com., 1923. Author: Beginnings of St. Lawrence University, 1913. Address: Stamford, Conn. Died Sept. 16, 1940.

LEE, John Mallory, physician; b. Cameron, N.Y., Sept. 29, 1852; s. Joseph R. and Sarah (Wagener) L.; ed. Penn Yan (N.Y.) Acad., and pvt. tutelage 3 yrs.; M.D., U. of Mich., 1878; Post-Grad. Coll. and Polyclinic, New York diploma, 1889; m. Idella, d. of Dr. Charles E. Ives, Sept. 28, 1876 (died 1897); m. 2d, Carrie M. d. late John Church Thomson, June 20, 1899. Surgeon, consulting surgeon and surgeon-in-chief, Rochester Homœ. Hosp., 1887-98; consulting surgeon of Hahnemann Hosp., 1906-19; consulting surgeon to Gowanda St. Hosp., and proprietor of Lee Private Hosp. State med. examiner under Regents of State of N.Y., 1895-1907; pres. joint board of medical examiners representing the 3 schools of medicine, 1901-07. Dir. Duffy-McInnerney Co., Duffy-Powers Dept. Store (exec. com.). Republican. Baptist. Pres. Am. Inst. Homeopathy, Am. Radium Soc.; hon. alumnus N.Y. Homœ. Med. Coll.; mem. N.Y. State Homœ. Med. Soc. (pres.), Western N.Y. Homœ. Med. Soc. (pres.), Monroe County Homœ. Med. Soc. (pres.). Mason. One of the authors of the Fisher-MacDonald Text Book of Surgery. Address: Rochester, N.Y. Died Dec. 11, 1925.

LEE, John Stebbins, prof. church history and biblical archæology, Canton Theol. Sch., 1869—; b. Vernon, Vt., Sept. 23, 1820; s. Eli and Rebecca S. L.; prep. edn. Deerfield, Mass., Shelburne Falls and Brattleboro acads.; grad. Amherst, 1845, A.M., 1848; studied theology with Rev. Dr. Hosea Ballou, 2d; ordained to Universalist ministry (D.D., Buchtel Coll., Ohio, 1875); m. Elmina Bennett, Feb. 22, 1848. Taught in Mt. Cæsar Sem., Swanzey, Vt., Melrose Sem., Brattleboro, Vt. Liberal Inst., Lebanon, N.H., Green Mountain Inst., S. Woodstock, Vt.; pres. and prof. Greek and Latin, St. Lawrence Univ., Canton, N.Y., 1859-67; visited Europe, Egypt and Palestine, 1868-69. Has lectured extensively on his travels, church history and biblical archæology; has preached regularly in various churches; was asst. editor The Christian Repository over 1 yr. Author: Nature and Art in the Old World; Sacred Cities. Address: Canton, N.Y. Died 1902.

LEE, Joseph, social worker; b. Brookline, Mass., Mar. 8, 1862; s. Henry and Elizabeth Perkins (Cabot) L.; A.B., Harvard, 1883, A.M., LL.B., 1887, LL.D., 1926; m. Margaret C. Cabot, May 20, 1897; children—Mrs. Margaret Lee Woodbury, Susan Mary, Joseph, Amy (Mrs. Charles C. Colt); m. 2d, Marion Snow, Oct. 14, 1930. Admitted to Mass. bar, 1887. Organized, and pres. Mass. Civic League; instrumental in securing much social legislation in Mass.; promoter of playground movement; mem. Boston Sch. Com., 1909-17; mem. Mass. Commn. on Probation, 1908-12; pres. Nat. Recreation Assn., 1910—. Mem. Commn. on Training Camp Activities apptd. by Secs. of War and Navy, 1917-19; pres. War Camp Community Service and of Community Service. Author: Constructive and Preventive Philanthropy, 1902; Play in Education, 1915. Home: Boston, Mass. Died July 28, 1937.

LEE, Leslie Alexander, educator; b. S. Woodstock, Vt., Sept. 24, 1852; s. John Stebbins and Elmina (Bennett) L.; grad. St. Lawrence U., 1872; Ph.D., 1885; grad. student Harvard, 1874; m. Elizabeth Tibbetts Almy, Aug. 28, 1877. Prof. biology and geology, Bowdoin Coll., 1876—. Chief scientific staff on voyage of U.S. Fish Commn. steamer Albatross, from Norfolk, Va., through Strait of Magellan, 1887, collecting for Smithsonian Instn., of which many reports in biology, geology and ethnology were made to and published by U.S. Nat. Museum; dir. Bowdoin Coll. expdn. to Labrador, 1891, when large collections were made and the long-sought Grand Falls (316 feet high) were rediscovered. Organizer and chmn. Topographic Survey Commn. of Me.; State geologist of Me.; pres. Portland (Me.) Soc. Natural History. Address: Brunswick, Me. Died 1908.

LEE, Margaret, author; b. New York; d. Joseph and Mary Georgiana L.; ed. pvt. tutors and later grad. pub. sch.; unmarried. First novel took prize of $1,000 offered by James G. Bennett, of New York Herald. Her "Divorce" was reviewed by Gladstone in Nineteenth Century and published in England as "Faithful and Unfaithful"; wrote memorial for perpetual copyright, numerously signed and presented in U. S. Senate, Dec. 1899. Author: Dr. Wilmer's Love, 1868; Lorimer and Wife, 1881, 1902; Marriage, 1882; Lizzie, 1882; Divorce, 1882; Adriance, 1882; Since First I Saw Your Face, 1883; Missing Marriage Certificate, 1883; A Brighton Knight, 1884; A Brooklyn Bachelor, 1886; The Story of a Story, 1883; One Touch of Nature, 1892, 1902; Separation, 1902; The Master Chivalry, 1903; also serials—A Broken Engagement, 1904; The D'Estimanvilles, 1905; Lovers and Shekels, 1906; Gallatin 1913; The Blot on the Board, 1913; The Wanderer, 1913, etc. Address Brooklyn, N.Y. Died Dec. 24, 1914.

LEE, Peter Martinus (P.A.), farm orgn. exec.; b. Goodhue County, Minn., Dec. 5, 1879; s. Arent Aderson and Beret (Hjelmstad) L.; ed. pub. schs.; m. Lilly Sena Grimsrud, June 25, 1907; children—Arnott Joseph, Kenneth Bernard, Leeward Clay, Valborg Orpha Constance, Lilly Sena, Amidson Lewis, Elaine Margaret. Asst. cashier State Bank of Brocket, N.D., 1905-08; cashier Bank of Pekin, N.D., 1909-17; sec. and treas. Farmers Grain Dealers Assn., 1920—; editor Grainmen's Mirror (monthly mag.). Dir. Greater Grand Forks Traffic Assn. Republican. Lutheran. Mason. Home: Grand Forks, N.D. Died Dec. 19, 1935.

LEE, Porter Raymond, social worker; b. Buffalo, N.Y., Dec. 21, 1879; s. R. Porter and Jennie (Blanchard) L.; A.B., Cornell, 1903; U. of Pa., 1911-12; Columbia, 1912-17; m. Ethel Hepburn Pollock, Jan. 30, 1905; children—Porter R., James P., Margaret T. (dec.), Jean Hepburn, Ruth. Asst. sec. Charity Organization Soc., Buffalo, 1903-09; gen. sec. Phila. Soc. for Organizing Charity, 1909-12; instr. in social case work, New York Sch. of Social Work, 1912—, dir. of the sch., 1917—. Pres. Nat. Conf. Social Work, 1929. Presbyn. Joint-Author: Study of Interrelationship of National Social Agencies, 1923; Social Salvage, 1925; Social Case Work, Generic and Specific, 1929; Mental Hygiene and Social Work, 1929; Social Case Work, 1933. Author: Social Work as Cause and Function, 1937. Mem. President's Emergency Com. for Employment, 1930-31. Home: Englewood N.J. Died Mar. 8, 1939.

LEE, Richard Edwin, chemist; b. Phila., Pa., Sept. 9, 1876; s. Matthias and Sarah Elizabeth (Cook) L.; B.S., Mt. Union Coll., Ohio, 1898; Cornell U., 1901; M.Sc., Mt. Union Coll., 1902; A.M., Harvard U., 1906; Sc.D., New York Univ., 1910; Calif. Inst. of Tech., two semesters, 1931; m. Kathleen Florence Carter, June 7, 1901. Prof. chemistry, Mt. Union Coll., 1902-07; prof. and head dept. of chemistry, Allegheny Coll., 1907—; consulting chemist Nat. Bearing Metals Co., Hookless Fastener Co., Venango Mfg. Co. Lecturer on scientific subjects before chautauquas and teachers' assns. Mem. City Planning Commn. Author: Outline of Qualitative Chemical Analysis, 1910; A Text-Book of Experimental Chemistry, 1908; The Human Body—A Chemically Regulated Organism, 1912; A New System of Qualitative Chemical Analysis (with notes), 1915; Man, the Universe Builder, 1933; Backgrounds and Foundations of Modern Science, 1935; A Technique for Testing Unified Concepts in Science, 1935. Home: Meadville, Pa. Died 1936.

LEE, Robert E., congressman; b. Schuylkill County, Pa.; ed. common schs., Pottsville, Pa. Engaged in business at Pottsville. Mem. 62d and 63d Congresses (1911-15), 12th Pa. Dist. Democrat. Address: Pottsville, Pa. Died Nov. 19, 1916.

LEE, Robert Edward, farmer; b. Arlington House, Va., Oct. 27, 1843; s. Gen. Robert Edward (C.S.A.) and Mary Ann Randolph (Custis) L.; ed. pvt. schs. in Va., and at U. of Va., 1860; m. Juliet Carter, Mar. 8, 1894. Enlisted in Army of Northern Va., C.S.A., Mar. 28, 1862, and served until Apr. 9, 1865, becoming capt.; after Civil War engaged in farming. Episcopalian. Author: Recollections and Letters of General Robert E. Lee, by His Son, 1904. Address: West Point, Va. Died Oct. 19, 1914.

LEE, Samuel Henry, educator; b. Hanover, Conn., Dec. 21, 1832; s. William and Sarah (Storrs) L.; A.B., Yale, 1858, A.M., 1894; grad. Yale Div. Sch., 1862; m. Emma Chloe Carter, Aug. 7, 1861. Ordained Congl. ministry, 1862; pastor, Brockton, Mass., 1862-66; dismissed, 1866; resumed preaching at Greenfield, Mass., Aug. 1866; pastor Second Ch., 1866-72; dismissed, 1872; pastor First Congl. Ch., Cleveland, 1872-78; prof. economics, Oberlin Coll., 1878-83; acting pastor Brattleboro, Vt., 1883-85; introduced Prof. W. R. Harper to Yale Coll. and raised money for his chair; preached in New Haven and Georgetown, Conn., 1885-89; prof. history, 1890-93, pres., July 12, 1893-July 15, 1908, pres. emeritus, 1908—, Am. Internat. Coll., Springfield, Mass. Republican. Address: Springfield, Mass. Died Oct. 20, 1918.

LEE, Stephen Dill, commr. of Vicksburg Nat. Mil. Park, 1899—; b. Charleston, S.C., Sept. 22, 1833; s. Dr. Thomas and Caroline (Allison) L.; grad. West Point, 1854; LL.D., Tulane U., La.; 1st lt. 4th arty., U.S.A., 1854-61, and 3 yrs. regimental q. m. in same; became capt. in C.S.A.; afterward served in C.S.A. as capt., maj., lt. col., col., brig. gen., maj. gen. and lt. gen. Took part in battles around Richmond, 1862; in 2d Bull Run, Sharpsburg, Vicksburg campaign; comd. Confederates at Chickasaw Bayou, Miss., when Sherman was defeated, and in battles of Tupelo, Miss.; Atlanta, Ga.; Jonesborough, Ga.; Franklin, Nashville, etc. Was planter in Miss. after war; m. Regina Lillie Harrison, Feb. 9, 1865. State senator, 1870; mem. Constitutional Conv., Miss., 1890. Chmn. hist. com. Assn. of United Confederate Veterans; lt. gen. comdg. Army of Tenn. Dept. United Confederate Veterans; pres. Miss. Hist. Soc.; pres. Miss. Agrl. and Mech. Coll., 1880-99. Elected gen. comdg., U.C.V., 1904. Address: Columbus, Miss. Died 1908.

LEE, Thomas George, univ. prof.; b. Jacksonville, N.Y., Nov. 27, 1860; s. Horace Cooper and Sarah Lavinia (Shaw) L.; B.S. and M.D., U. of Pa., 1886; U. of Würzburg, 1887; B.S., Harvard, 1892; U. of Munich, 1892; m. Emma Louise Shaw, Dec. 21, 1887. Asst. in histology and embryology, U. of Pa., 1884-86; lecturer on same, and dir. of lab., Yale, 1886-91; asst. in histology, Radcliffe, 1891-92; prof. histology and embryology and dir. of lab., 1892-1909, prof. anatomy and dir. Inst. of Anatomy, 1909-13, prof. comparative anatomy, 1913-29, prof. emeritus, 1929, U. of Minn. Asso. editor Anatomical Record. Republican. Unitarian. Address: Babson Park, Fla. Died Sept. 1, 1932.

LEE, T(homas) G(eorge), pres. Armour & Co.; b. Carrollton, O., Feb. 13, 1878; s. Erasmus W. and Nancy Isabel (Crabb) L.; ed. pub. schs.; m. Harriette Jones, Nov. 8, 1902; children—Jane (Mrs. William E. Graham), Martha. With Armour & Co., packers, Chicago, 1895—, v.p., 1926-31, pres., 1931—. Republican. Episcopalian. Home: Chicago, Ill. Died Nov. 6, 1934.

LEE, Thomas Zanslaur, lawyer; b. Woonsocket, R.I., Sept. 26, 1866; s. Thomas and Eleanor (Monahan) L.; prep. edn., St. Bernard's Acad., LL.B., Boston U., 1888, LL.M., 1908, LL.D. (earned), 1911; m. Flora Provan, June 3, 1920. Clk. R.I. Ho. of Rep., 1888-1902; admitted to R.I. bar, 1888; justice Dist. Court of 12th Jud. Dist., R.I., 1893-99; mem. firm Lee & McCanna. Fellow Boston U. Sch. of Law, 1910-13. Mem. Am. Bar Assn. (gen. council). Rep. Boston U. at Conv. Internat. Law Assn., London, 1910, and at London meeting of Am. and English bar assns., 1924. Home: Providence, R.I. Died Apr. 13, 1931.

LEE, Wallace Howe, educator; b. Brooklyn, N.Y., Aug. 25, 1861; s. William Brown (D.D.) and Elizabeth Payson (Howe) L.; A.B., Williams, 1883, A.M., 1887; D.D., Albany (Ore.) Coll., 1920; m. Elizabeth Fortmiller, June 23, 1887; children—Kate Elizabeth, Edward Howe, Bertha Fortmiller, Helen Rudy. Taught sch. in Conn., 1883-86; mem. faculty, teaching classics, 1886-95, pres., 1895-1905, Albany Coll.; asst. pastor 1st Presbyn. Ch., Seattle, 1905-11; dean Whitworth Coll., Tacoma (now Spokane), 1911-14; head dept. of edn., 1914-15, pres. 1915-20, dean 1920-24, registrar and head dept. ancient langs., 1924—, Albany Coll.; stated clerk Presbytery of Willamette; moderator Synod of Ore., 1932-33. Ordained Presbyn. ministry, 1902. Mason. Home: Albany, Ore. Died Oct. 9, 1936.

LEE, William, publisher; b. Boston, Apr. 17, 1826; s. John and Laura Williams (Jones) L.; m. Anna M. Leavett, Oct. 29, 1861 (died 1883); m. 2d, Mrs. Sarah White Saunders, Nov. 26, 1888. In employ of Samuel G. Drake, bookseller, 1837-40; at school, 1840-42; returned to book trade; clerk, 1845-50, and partner, 1850-57, Phillips, Sampson & Co.; traveled in Europe, 1857-59; mem. Crosby, Nichols, Lee & Co., 1860-61; established, Feb. 1, 1861, firm of Lee & Shepard (with Charles A. B. Shepard, died 1889) and remained at its head until June 1898, when he retired. Address: Brookline, Mass. Died 1906.

LEE, William Granville, labor leader; b. LaPrairie, Ill., Nov. 29, 1859; s. James W. and Sylvesta Jane (Tracy) L.; ed. pub. schs.; m. Mary R. Rice, Oct. 15, 1901. Brakeman and conductor, A.,T.&S.F., Wabash, Mo.P., and U.P. rys., 1879-84; deputy recorder deeds, Ford Co., Kan., 1884-88; conductor, U.P. R.R., 1889-95; 1st v.p., 1895-1909, pres., 1909—, Brotherhood of Railroad Trainmen. Republican. Mason. Home: Cleveland, O. Died Nov. 2, 1929.

LEE, William H., banker. In banking business at St. Louis, Mo., many years; was pres. Merchants Laclede Nat. Bank, and retired from chairmanship of bd., 1926. Was mem. bd. dirs. La. Purchase Expn. Home: Normandy, Mo. Died Mar. 4, 1929.

LEE, William States, engineer; b. Lancaster, S.C., Jan. 28, 1872; s. W. S. and Jennie Lind (Williamson) L.; C.E., The Citadel, Mil. Coll. of S.C., 1894; m. Mary Martin, 1901; children—W. States, Martha, Martin. Pres. and chief engr. Piedmont & Northern Ry. Co.; pres. and cons. engr. W. S. Lee Engring. Corp.; v.p. and chief engr. Duke Power Co., Wateree Power Co., Western Carolina Power Co., Catawba Power Co., Catawba Mfg. & Electric Power Co., Quebec Development Co., Am. Cyanamid Co. Trustee N.C. State Coll. Agr. and Engring., Duke Endowment. Presbyn. Mason. A pioneer in high tension hydro-electric power development; inventor of the Lee pin. Home: Charlotte, N.C. Died Mar. 24, 1934.

LEE, Willis Thomas, geologist; b. Brooklyn, Pa., Dec. 24, 1864; s. John C. and Louesa J. (Garland) L.; Ph.B., Wesleyan U., Conn., 1894, M.S., 1898; fellow in geology, U. of Chicago, 1898-1900, Johns Hopkins, 1902-03; Ph.D., Johns Hopkins, 1912; m. Mary Ingham, 1900; children—Elizabeth Louesa, Dana Willis. Instr. science, R.I. Coll. Agr. and Mechanic Arts, Kingston, R.I., 1894-95; prof. geology and biology, Denver U., 1895-98; prin. high sch., Trinidad, Colo., 1900-02; with U.S. Geol. Survey, 1903—; head dept. geology, U. of Okla., 1919; lecturer in geology, Yale, 1919. Conglist. Died June 16, 1926.

LEECH, Paul Nicholas, chemist; b. Oxford, O., Aug. 12, 1889; s. William David and Ann Cora (Druley) L.; A.B., Miami U., Oxford, O., 1910; Sc.M., U. of Chicago, 1911, Ph.D., 1913; Pharm.M. (hon.), Philadelphia Coll. of Pharmacy and Science, 1937; m. Esther O. Birch, Mar. 10, 1916; children—Esther Doris, Paul Nicholas. Research asst., U. of Chicago, 1911-13; chemist A.M.A., 1913-24; dir. Chem. Lab. same, 1924—, also dir. of scientific exhibit, 1922-30, and editor Ann. Repts.; sec. Council on Pharmacy and Chemistry, 1932—; dir. div. of foods, drugs and physical therapy, 1936—. First lt. Sanitary Corps, Med. Dept. U.S.A., 1918. Mem. Am. Chem. Soc. (chmn.) Chicago sect. 1926-27; chmn. div. med. chemistry 1934; councillor. Home: Winnetka, Ill. Died Jan. 14, 1941.

LEEDS, Samuel Penniman, clergyman; b. New York, Nov. 15, 1824; s. Samuel and Mary Warren (Mellen) L.; A.B., New York U., 1843; grad. Union Theol. Sem., New York, 1846; D.D., Dartmouth, 1870; m. Julia Lockwood, Oct. 3, 1849; m. 2d, Mrs. Emily H. (Wells) Barnes, July 20, 1882. Pastor Congl. Ch., Cuyahoga Falls, O., 1849-55 (a founder of Congl. Assn. of Ohio, 1854); asst. minister to Albert Barnes, Phila., 1855-57; minister in New York City, New Haven, Conn., and Stamford, Conn., 1857-60; minister and pastor, Dartmouth Coll. Congl. Ch., 1860-1900; pastor emeritus, 1900. N.H. del. to Internat. Prison Congress, 1872; mem. Congl. commn. of 25 to prepare a creed, 1880-83. Author: The Christian Philosophy of Life, 1904. Address: Hanover, N.H. Died 1910.

LEEDY, John W., governor; b. Richland County, O., Mar. 8, 1849; tried to enlist at age of 14 in co. leaving for the front, but was rejected. He remained with the co., however, until the war closed, the following spring. Clerk in store, Pierceton, Ind., 1865-68; worked on farm at Carlinsville, Ill., 1868-80; moved to Kan., 1880; became farmer near Leroy, Coffey County, Kan. Originally Republican; became Democrat from 1872 until organization of Populist party, in which he became a leader; mem. Kan. Senate, 1892-96; gov. of Kan., 1896-99; moved to Alaska, 1901; later to Can. Address: Alberta, Can. Died Mar. 24, 1935.

LEEMAN, Paul James, banker; b. Greene, Ia., Feb. 9, 1883; s. Francis A. and Catherine L.; ed. high sch., Kenosha, Wis.; m. Josephine Fisher, Aug. 14, 1903 (dec.); m. 2d, Ruby L. Hackett, July 14, 1920. Began as messenger, First Nat. Bank, Kenosha, 1899; with First Nat. Bank, Minneapolis, Minn., 1902—, v.p., 1917—; v.p. and gen. mgr. First Bank Stock Corp., 1929—; dir. Federal Reserve Bank of Minneapolis, First Bancredit Corp. (St. Paul), First Securities Corp., N.W. Fire & Marine Ins. Co., Twin City Fire Ins. Co., Northern Finance Corp., Western Oil & Fuel Co., Duluth, S. Shore & Atlantic Ry. Co., Agrl. Credit Corpn. Republican. Mason. Home: Minneapolis, Minn. Died Jan. 11, 1934.

LEES, James Thomas, educator; b. Middleton, Lancashire, Eng., Aug. 17, 1859; s. Thomas and Betty (Wrigley) L.; came to U.S., 1870; B.A., Adelbert Coll., Cleveland, O., 1886, M.A., 1889; Ph.D., Johns Hopkins, 1889; m. Anna Belle Murray, Dec. 26, 1889; children—Lucile Betty, Thomas Murray. Head of Dept. of Greek, 1891-1919, provost of the Univ., 1918-23, prof. Greek lang. and lit., 1923—, U. of Neb. Republican. Presbyn. Mason. Author: (brochures) The Rhetorical Element in Euripides; The Metaphor in Æschylus; An Archæological Expedition Through Sicily and Greece. Home: Lincoln, Neb. Deceased.

LEETE, Charles Henry, school prin.; b. Potsdam, N.Y., Mar. 17, 1857; s. Charles Ward and Eliza (Willes) L.; A.B., Yale, 1879; grad. State Normal Sch., Potsdam, 1881; A.M., Ph.D., U. of Leipzig, 1890; m. Isadore A. Kelton, July 26, 1883. Taught in Sachs Collegiate Inst. for Boys, 1881-87; asso. prin., 1891-1907, prin. 1907-11, Sachs Sch. for Girls, New York; prin. Leete Sch., New York, 1911—. Joint author: (Chisholm & Leete) Longman's New School Atlas, 1891; Longman's Text-Book, of Geography, 1891; Longman's Questions on Geography, 1891. Author: Exercises in Geography, 1899. Home: New York, N.Y. Died Jan. 9, 1936.

LEETE, John Hopkin, dir. Carnegie Library; b. Detroit, Mich., Nov. 6, 1868; s. Thomas Towar and Jean (Hopkin) L.; A.B., Colgate U., 1894, Harvard, 1895; D.Sc., Colgate, 1909; m. Edith Payne, Dec. 20, 1895; 1 son, Alexander Payne. Instr. mathematics, 1895-98, asst. prof., 1898-1901, asso. prof. and sec. and registrar, 1901-06, Pa. State Coll.; registrar, 1906, asst. dir., 1907, dean, Sch. of Applied Science, 1908-17, Carnegie Inst. Tech., Pittsburgh; dir. Carnegie Library of Pittsburgh, 1917—. Mem. Morals Efficiency Commn. of Pittsburgh, 1912, 13. Progressive Republican. Episcopalian. Home: Pittsburgh, Pa. Died Oct. 13, 1929.

LEFEVRE, Arthur, businessman; b. Baltimore, Md., June 4, 1863; s. Rev. Jacob Amos and Catherine Louisa (Sauerwein) L.; grad. Baltimore City Coll., 1882; U. of Va., 1882-85; C.E., U. of Tex., 1895; m. Adela Beale Yerby, Nov. 1, 1887; children—Guy (dec.), Arthur, Katharine. Moved to Tex., 1890;

teacher in Ball High Sch., Galveston, 1890-92; supt. schs., Gonzales, 1892-94; instr. mathematics, U. of Tex., 1894-99; supt. schs., Victoria, Tex., 1899-1901; state supt. pub. instrn., Tex., 1901-05; supt. of schs., Victoria, Tex., 1906-08, Dallas, 1908-11; sec. for research of Orgn. for the Enlargement by the State of Tex. of Its Instns. of Higher Edn., 1911-13; with The Texas Co., Houston, 1913—; editor The Texaco Star. Regent Coll. Indust. Arts, Denton, Tex. Mem. Southern Presbyn. Ch. Author: Number and Its Algebra, 1896; The Organization and Administration of a State's Institutions of Higher Education, 1913. Home: Houston, Tex. Died Mar. 4, 1929.

LEFEVRE, Edwin, author; b. Colon, Colombia, Jan. 23, 1871; s. Henry L. (American) and Emilia (de la Ossa) L.; ed. pub. schs. San Francisco, 1880-84, Mich. Mil. Acad., Orchard Lake, Mich., 1884-87; studied mining engring., Lehigh U.; m. Martha Moore, Jan. 22, 1902. In journalism, 1890—. Author: Wall Street Stories, 1901; The Golden Flood, 1905; Sampson Rock of Wall Street, 1907; "H.R.," 1915; The Plunderers, 1916; To the Last Penny, 1917; Simonetta, 1919; Reminiscences of a Stock Operator, 1923. Home: Dorset, Vt. Deceased.

LE FEVRE, Egbert, physician; b. Raritan, N.J., Oct. 29, 1858; s. James (D.D.) and Cornelia (Hasbrouck) L.; A.B., Rutgers Coll., 1880, A.M., 1884; M.D., Univ. Med. Coll. (New York U.), 1883; interne Bellevue Hosp., 1883-85; Sc.D., Rutgers, 1910; LL.D., New York U., 1910; m. mrs. Helen Hasbrouck Trotter, Dec. 12, 1889. Clin. lecturer on practice of medicine, New York U., 1888-90; prof. clin. medicine, 1890-95, adjunct prof. medicine, 1895-98, prof. therapeutics, prof. clin. medicine and dean, Univ. and Bellevue Hosp. Med. Coll., 1898—; visiting phys. to City (Charity) Hosp., 1894-95, Bellevue Hosp., 1898; consulting phys. to Beth-Israel Hosp. Fellow N.Y. Acad. Medicine. Author: Physical Diagnosis, 1902. Home: New York, N.Y. Died Mar. 30, 1914.

LEFEVRE, George, zoölogist; b. Baltimore Md., Sept. 16, 1869; s. Jacob Amos and Catharine Louise (Sauerwein) L.; A.B., Johns Hopkins, 1891, fellow, 1894-95, Bruce fellow, 1895-97, Ph.D., 1896; m. Lelia Childe Deane, Dec. 27, 1898 (died 1900); m. 2d, Julia Faris, Dec. 22, 1914. Asst. in zoölogy and embryology, Johns Hopkins, 1897-98; instr. zoölogy, Marine Biol. Lab., Woods Hole, Mass., 1898-99; prof. zoölogy, U. of Mo., Columbia, 1899—. Mem. staff of Investigation Marine Biol. Lab., 1906—, mem. bd. trustees, 1909—, sec., 1913—; temporary asst. U.S. Bur. of Fisheries, 1907-11. Editor U. of Mo. studies, 1910—. Died Jan. 24, 1923.

LEFFERTS, George Morewood, laryngologist; b. Brooklyn, N.Y., Feb. 24, 1846; s. Marshall and Mary (Allen) L.; ed. Coll. City of New York, 1867; M.D., Coll. Phys. and Surg. (Columbia), 1870; Vienna, 1872-73; hon. A.M., Dickinson, 1869; M.S., Columbia, 1901; m. Annie C. Van Vechten, June 11, 1891. Clin. prof. laryngoscopy and diseases of the throat, 1874-96, laryngology and rhinology, 1896-1904, emeritus prof. laryngology, 1904, Coll. Phys. and Surg.; retired from practice, Nov. 1, 1910. Home: Katonah, N.Y. Died Sept. 21, 1920.

LEFFINGWELL, Albert, author, physician; b. Aurora, N.Y., Feb. 13, 1845; s. Dr. Elisha and Jane E. (Jackson) L.; attended Hamilton Coll., hon. M.Sc., 1894; instr. at Poly. Inst., Brooklyn, several yrs.; M.D., L.I. Coll. Hosp., 1874; resided abroad, engaged in scientific studies and lit. work, 1875-79; traveled in Japan, China and Burma, 1881-82, India, Africa and Spain, 1882, Palestine and Egypt, 1889-90, Russia, 1905; m. Dr. Elizabeth Fear, Dec. 1, 1892; three sons. Founder, and 1st sec. Am. Soc. for Regulation of Vivisection; pres. Am. Humane Assn., 1904-05 (v.p. 1909—); life mem. L.I. Hist. Soc., 1869—; dir. Am. Humane Edn. Soc., 1912—. Am. consul at Warsaw, Russia, 1905-06. Trustee Wells Coll., 1912—. Author: Rambles in Japan Without a Guide, 1892; Illegitimacy and Influence of Seasons Upon Conduct, 1892; Vivisection in America, 1894; The Leffingwell Record, 1895; The Vivisection Question, 1901; The Vivisection Controversy, 1908; The Morality of London, 1908; American Meat, 1910; An Ethical Problem, 1915, 2d edit., 1916. Home: Aurora-on-Cayuga Lake, N.Y. Died Sept. 1, 1917.

LEFFINGWELL, Charles Wesley, clergyman; b. Ellington, Conn., Dec. 5, 1840; s. Lyman and Sara Chapman (Brown) L.; studied at Union Coll. prin. Galveston Acad., Tex., 1859-60; A.B., Knox Coll., 1862, D.D., 1875, LL.D., 1912; v.p. Mil. Sch., Poughkeepsie, N.Y., 1862-65; grad. Nashotah (Wis.) Theol. Sem., 1867; m. Elizabeth Francis, 1862; children—Annie (dec.), Bertha (dec.), Alice (dec.), Charles Warring, Ernest De Koven, Hortense (Mrs. Harlan Wilson), Gertrude (wife of Dr. John Walter Vaughan). Deacon and priest P.E. Ch., 1867; asst. St. James' Ch., Chicago, 1867; founded, 1868, and rector, 1868-1919, St. Mary's Sch., Knoxville, Ill. Rector and founder of St. Alban's Sch. for Boys, 1890. Editor for 21 yrs. of The Living Church, a weekly religious paper, Chicago. Author: Early Days at St. Mary's, Knoxville, Ill. Compiler: Lyrics of the Living Church; English Classics; A Book of Prayers. Home: Pasadena, Calif. Died Oct. 9, 1928.

LEFFINGWELL, William Elderkin, banker; b. Aurora, N.Y., July 10, 1855; s. Dr. Elisha and Jane E. (Jackson) L.; entered Cornell U., 1871, but left before graduation. Registrar and cashier Brooklyn Collegiate and Poly. Inst., 1875-82; reorganized Dansville Sanatorium, 1882, sec.-treas., 1882-85; organized Glen Springs Corp., 1890, and pres., 1890—; pres. Glen Nat. Bank, 1911-22, chmn. bd., 1922—; pres. Jackson Sanatorium, Dansville, N.Y., 1916-18; dir. Watkins Salt. Co.; trustee St. John's Mil. Sch., Manlius, N.Y., 1915-22. Pres. Village of Dansville, N.Y., 1885; mem. bd. trustees, 1899-1901, pres., 1902-05, Village of Watkins, N.Y.; Dem. presidential elector, N.Y., 1904, 12; commr. of water, sewer and electric light, Watkins, N.Y., 1906-10; pres. Watkins Glen Reservation Commn., 1910-15; mem. N.Y. Assembly, 1908, 09. Dir. mil. census, Schuyler Co., and chmn. Dist. Appeal Bd., 1917-18. Democrat. Mason. Home: Watkins Glen, N.Y. Died Oct. 12, 1927.

LEFFINGWELL, William Henry, office management; b. of Am. parents, Woodstock, Ont., Can., June 14, 1876; s. Wendel Phillips and Mary Catherine (Edwards) L.; ed. Union High Sch., Grand Rapids, Mich., 2 yrs.; m. Anna Short, Feb. 12, 1900; children—Evelyn Ethel (Mrs. J. W. Lewis), Dorothy Anna (Mrs. H. F. Scribner), William Henry (dec.). Organized W. H. Leffingwell Co., Chicago, 1918, title changed, 1920, to The Leffingwell-Ream Co., management engrs., then W. H. Leffingwell, Inc., of which was pres. Author: Scientific Office Management, 1917; Office Management Principles and Practice, 1925. Inventor of Leffingwell posture chair for clerks. Home: Westfield, N.J. Died Dec. 19, 1934.

LEFFLER, Charles Doyle; b. Smithland, Ky., Aug. 12, 1868; s. Charles Henry and Mary Frances (Bibb) L.; ed. Horner Sch., Oxford, N.C., U. of the South, Sewanee, Tenn., Eastman Business Coll., Poughkeepsie, N.Y.; m. Hannah May Martin, Feb. 12, 1891; children—Cornelia, Lt. Comdr. Charles Doyle; m. 2d, Mrs. Berenice Horton Houser, June 26, 1935. With Plant Steamship Line until 1892; in retail grocery business, Sanford, Fla., 1892-1900, Miami, 1900-09; commn. agt. Gulf Refining Co. 1908—; pres. Florida Dairies, Linda Lee, Inc., Miami Laundry Co.; dir. Belcher Oil Co. City Commr., 1923-26. Served as 1st lt., U.S.A., Spanish-Am. War; lt. col. Fla. N.G. Served as chmn. Bd. Pilot Commrs. Port of Miami and chmn. Bd. Public Works; mayor of Miami, 1921-23. Mem. Miami Chamber Commerce (pres. 1936-37). Democrat. Home: Miami, Fla. Died Apr. 27, 1939.

LEFFLER, Ray Victor, economist; b. Leipsic, O., Feb. 28, 1892; s. Daniel Monroe and Emma M. (Pfister) L.; A.B., U. of Mich., 1915, A.M., 1917; unmarried. Commercial agt. Mich. State Telephone Co., Detroit, 1915; with Borton & Borton, brokers, Cleveland, 1916; instr. economics, U. of Mich., 1916-19; instr. economics, Dartmouth Coll., 1919-20, asst. prof., 1920-24, prof., 1924—, chmn. of dept., 1927-28 and 1937—; asst. prof. polit. economy, Yale U., 1921-22; visiting prof. economics, U. of Mich., 1928-29; teacher summer sessions, U. of Mich., 1919, Columbia, 1922, State U. of Ia., 1921, 24. Served in U.S. Naval Auxiliary Res., 1918. Independent Republican. Lutheran. Author: Money and Credit, 1935; also spl. studies for Federal Res. Bank of N.Y. and U.S. Chamber of Commerce. Home: Hanover, N.H. Died Apr. 10, 1941.

LEFFMANN, Henry, chemist; b. Phila., Sept. 9, 1847; s. Henry and Sarah Ann (Paul) L.; A.M., Central High Sch., Phila., 1865; M.D., Jefferson Med. Coll., Phila., 1869; D.D.S., Pa. Coll. Dental Surgery, 1884; m. Fannie Frank, Nov. 29, 1876. Asst. prof. chemistry, Central High Sch., 1876-80; port phys., 1884-87 and 1891-92; prof. chemistry, Wagner Free Inst. of Science, 1885—, Woman's Med. Coll. of Pa., 1888-1923. Lecturer on research, Phila. Coll. of Pharmacy and Science. Author: Analysis of Water, 1899; Analysis of Milk and Milk Products, 1888; Select Methods in Food and Analysis, 1905; About Dickens, 1908; States-Rights Fetish, 1913. Home: Philadelphia, Pa. Died Dec. 25, 1930.

LEGARE, George S., congressman; b. Rockville, Charleston Co., S.C., 1870; grad. Porter Acad., Charleston (with honors); student U. of S.C., 2 yrs.; LL.B., Georgetown U., 1892. In law practice at Charleston, 1893—. Corp. counsel, 1898-1903; mem. 58th to 62d Congresses (1903-13), 1st S.C. Dist. Democrat. Home: Charleston, S.C. Died Jan. 31, 1913.

LEGGE, Alexander, pres. Internat. Harvester Co.; b. Dane Co., Wis., Jan. 13, 1866; ed. pub. schs.; widower. Moved with parents to Neb., 1881; entered employment of McCormick Harvester Co., 1891, beginning as collector; appointed collection mgr. of company at Council Bluffs, 1894, branch mgr., 1892 mgr. of domestic sales, Internat. Harvester Co. (successor to McCormick Harvester Co. and other concerns), 1902, asst. gen. mgr., 1906, gen. mgr., 1913, v.p. same yr., pres. 1922-29 and, 1931—; chmn. Federal Farm Bd., July 1929-Mar. 1931. Dollar-a-year man, World War; served as vice chmn. War Industries Bd. and head of Requirements Div. of same, also as mgr. Allied Purchasing Commn. Home: Hinsdale, Ill. Died Dec. 3, 1933.

LEGGETT, Benjamin Franklin, author, educator; b. Chestertown, N.Y., Dec. 29, 1834; s. Joseph W.

and Elizabeth (Mead) L.; B.S., Wesleyan U., Conn., 1863; M.A., Union U., 1866; Ph.D., Cornell U., 1883; studied, U. of Heidelberg, 1875-76; m. Sara Shaw, Aug. 18, 1863. Teacher, Whitewater Coll., Centerville, Ind., 1863; prin. New York Conf. Sem., 1866; teacher, Maplewood Inst., Concordville, Pa., 1867-72, Vt. Methodist Sem., 1872-74, Maplewood Inst., 1874-75, East Greenwich (R.I.) Acad., 1877-79; prin. Ward (Pa.) Acad., 1881-98; engaged in lecturing and lit. work. Prohibitionist. Methodist. Author: A Tramp Through Switzerland; A Sheaf of Song; An Idyl of Lake George; The City of Doom; Out Door Poems; The Cruise of the Half Moon, and Other Poems. Home: Chestertown, N.Y. Died July 18, 1924.

LEGGETT, Eugene Sheldon, govt. official; b. Brantford, Can., December 9, 1902; s. Benjamin Thomas and Mary Elizabeth (Cowan) L.; ed. Brantford Collegiate Inst., 1914-18; m. Dagmar Carlson, Feb. 23, 1924; 1 son, Eugene Sheldon. Began as newspaper reporter with Brantford Courier, 1918, and continued with London Free Press, Brantford Expositor, Toronto Telegram, Detroit Free Press, Owosso (Mich.) Argus-Press, until 1923; Washington corr. Detroit Free Press, 1925—; identified with polit. and economic movements; dir. Nat. Press Building Corp. Acting exec. dir. Nat. Emergency Council. Mem. Press Galleries of Congress, White House Correspondents Assn. Home: Washington, D.C. Died Feb. 19, 1939.

LEGLER, Henry Eduard, librarian; b. Palermo, Italy, June 22, 1861; s. Henry and Raffaela (Messina) L.; ed. in Switzerland and U.S.; m. Nettie M. Clarke, Sept. 4, 1890. Mem. Wis. Assembly, 1889; sec. Milwaukee sch. bd., 1890-1904; sec. Wis. Library Commn., 1904-09; librarian Chicago Pub. Library, Oct. 11, 1909—. Curator Wis. Hist. Soc.; chmn. publishing bd. and mem. exec. council, pres., 1912-13, Am. Library Assn. Author: Chevalier Henry de Tonty, 1896; A Moses of the Mormons, 1897; Leading Events of Wisconsin History, 1897; James Gates Percival, 1901; Early Wisconsin Imprints, 1903; The Genesis of Poe's Raven, 1907; Of Much Love and Some Knowledge of Books, 1912. Died Sept. 13, 1917.

LE GRAS, Gustave, college prof.; b. New York, Jan. 24, 1858; s. Stephen and Jane Marguerite (Martial) L.; B.S., Coll. City of New York, 1879, M.S., 1896; studied law 1 yr.; m. Alice Mary Loëb, Dec. 28, 1904. Tutor and instr., 1883-97, asst. prof., 1897-1906, asso. prof. mathematics, 1906—, Coll. City of New York. Chmn. sub-com. of Internat. Commn. on Teaching of Mathematics. Home: New York, N.Y. Died July 23, 1912.

LEHLBACH, Frederick Reimold, congressman; b. New York, Jan. 31, 1876; s. Paul Frederick and Anna Marie (Jungmann) L.; A.B., Yale, 1897; student N.Y. Law Sch., 1897-98; m. Frances E. Martin, June 10, 1908. Admitted to N.J. bar, 1899. Mem. Newark Bd. of Edn., 1900-03; mem. Gen. Assembly, N.J., 1903, 04, 05; clk. State Bd. of Equalization of Taxes, 1905-08; asst. prosecutor of pleas, Essex Co., N.J., 1908-13; mem. 64th to 72d Congresses (1915-33), 10th N.J. Dist., and 73d and 74th Congresses (1933-37), 12th N.J. Dist. Republican. Mason. Home: Montclair, N.J. Died Aug. 4, 1937.

LEHMAN, Albert Carl, pres. Blaw-Knox Co.; b. Pittsburgh, Pa., Oct. 14, 1878; s. Moses and Fanny (Frank) L.; prep. edn., Stone Sch. of Boston; B.A., Harvard, 1901; married. Connected with Blaw-Knox Co., steel fabricators, Pittsburgh, from 1906, pres., 1915—; pres. Blaw-Knox Constn. Co., Hoboken Land Co.; chmn. bd. Milliken Bros., Blaw-Knox Corp., Nat. Alloy Steel Co.; dir. Bank of Aspinwall. Mem. Bur. Municipal Research; dir. Montifiore Hosp.; dir. Jewish Fedn. of Philanthropies, Nat. Farm Sch. (Phila.), B'nai B'rith Hosp. (Erie, Pa.); trustee Rodef Shalom Congregation. Chmn. for Western Pa. of United Jewish Com. for Foreign Relief; active in sale of Liberty Bonds, and drives for Am. Red Cross and local hosps., World War. Republican. Home: Pittsburgh, Pa. Died July 24, 1935.

LEHMAN, Ambrose Edwin, civil engr.; b. Lebanon, Pa., May 23, 1851; s. Benjamin Bringhurst and Susanna (Mustin) L.; ed. by pvt. tutors and abroad; tech. edn., Paris; m. Emilie Wyonne, d. Capt. M. Koheler, Jan. 28, 1892. Geol. engr. and topographer survey of Pa., 1874-86; was asst. chief engr. Interoceanic Ry., Mexico; chief engr. Gettysburg & Harrisburg R.R., 1882-91, Brooklyn, Bath & Coney Island R.R., 1885-89; consulting engr. Great Falls Water Power Co., N.C., 1889-93; studied European transportation systems, rys. and common roads and highways, 1894-95; mem. civ. service bd. examiners, dept. municipal engring., Phila.; consulting engr. St. Maurice Syndicate, Quebec, exploration and development of mineral deposits, Hudson's Bay region, Transcontinental Ry., Can., 1910—. Mapped the topography and geologic sections of South Mountains, Pa.; numerous expert reports on explorations for iron, coal, copper, etc., in the U.S., Can., Cuba and Mex. Author: Topographic Models and Relief Maps. Home: Philadelphia, Pa. Died Apr. 7, 1917.

LEHMAN, Arthur; b. N.Y. City, June 1, 1873; s. Mayer and Babette (Newgass) L.; prep. edn., Sach Collegiate Sch., N.Y. City; A.B., Harvard, 1894; m. Adele Lewisohn, Nov. 25, 1901; children—Dorothy (Mrs. Richard J. Bernard), Helen (Mrs. Benjamin J. Buttenwieser), Frances (Mrs. John L. Loeb). Early training in banking houses, becoming partner Lehman Bros., 1898; pres. Lehman Corp.; dir. Continental Can Co., Penn-Dixie Cement Corp., Amalgamated Leather Co., General Development Co., Southern States Land & Timber Co., Bing & Bing, Merchants Assn., Am. Internat. Corp., Associated Rayon Corp., Abraham & Straus, Inc., Federated Dept. Stores, Inc., General American Investors Corp., Jewel Tea Co., Radio-Keith-Orpheum Corp., Underwood Elliott Fisher Co. Dir. New Sch. for Social Research. Home: New York, N.Y. Died May 16, 1936.

LEHMAN, Ezra, educator; b. Chambersburg, Pa., Jan. 18, 1871; s. Jacob S. and Mary R. (Stouffer) E.; Ph.B., Bucknell U., 1899, LL.D., 1925; Ph.D., U. of Pa., 1903; Harrison fellow in English, same univ., 1901-03; m. Louise D. Lane, 1900; children—Paul Stouffer, Margaret Kidder. Prin. Huntingdon High Sch., 1892-96; prof. English, Shippensburg (Pa.) State Normal Sch., 1896-1900; asso. editor Lippincott Worcester Dictionary, 1903-06; teacher English Newtown High Sch., N.Y. City, 1906-13; pres. Shippensburg State Teachers Coll., 1913—. Presbyn. Republican. Mason. Rotarian. Editor: George Chapmann's Chabot, Admiral of France, 1906. Home: Shippensburg, Pa. Died June 11, 1931.

LEHMAN, Louis Oliver, college pres.; b. at Sterling, Ill., Sept. 4, 1877; s. Daniel and Amanda (Andreas) L.; A.B., Eureka (Ill.) Coll., 1901; studied U. of Chicago, 1911; m. Ethel Leeper, June 8, 1904. Ordained ministry Disciples of Christ, 1901; pastor Chandlerville, Ill., 1901-03, Havana, 1903-07, Rantoul, 1907-09, Gibson City, 1909-14; successively field sec., sec. treas., Eureka Coll., pres., 1914—. Prohibitionist. Home: Eureka, Ill. Died Mar. 10, 1923.

LEHMANN, Frederick William, lawyer; b. in Prussia, Feb. 28, 1853; A.B., Tabor Coll., Ia., 1873; LL.D., U. of Mo., Franklin and Marshall Coll. and Washington U.; m. Nora Stark, Ia., Dec. 23, 1879; children—Sears, Frederick W., John S. Admitted to bar, 1873; practiced at Nebraska City, Neb., 1873-76, Des Moines, Ia., 1876-90, St. Louis, 1890—; mem. Boyle, Priest & Lehmann, 1895-1905, Lehmann & Lehmann, 1905-10; solicitor gen. of U.S., Dec. 1910-12; resumed practice at St. Louis; gen. counsel U.S. Ry. Wage Commn., 1918. Govt. del. and chmn. com. on plan and scope Universal Congress Lawyers and Jurists, St. Louis, 1904; chmn. coms. on congresses and anthropology, La. Purchase Expn. Co.; pres. St. Louis Pub. Library, 1900-10; chmn. Bd. of Freeholders City of St. Louis, 1909; U.S. del. to A.B.C. mediation at Niagara Falls, 1914; mem. bd. of control City Mus., St. Louis. Home: St. Louis, Mo. Died Sept. 12, 1931.

LEHMER, Derrick Norman, univ. prof.; b. Somerset, Ind., July 27, 1867; s. Derrick Fernstück and Isabel Smith (Peery) L.; A.B., U. of Neb., 1893, A.M., 1896, D.Sc., 1932; Ph.D., U. of Chicago, 1900; m. Clara Eunice Mitchell, July 12, 1910; children—Eunice Elizabeth, Helen Mitchell, Derrick Henry, Stephen McClellan, Alice Sherman. Instr. mathematics, 1900-04, asst. prof., 1904-10, asso. prof., 1910-18, prof., 1918—, U. of Calif. Research asst., Carnegie Instn., Washington. Editor Univ. of Calif. Chronicle. Composer: Seven Songs from the Yosemite Valley; Down the Stream, and other Indian songs; two Indian choruses; Indian Songs from the Northland; The Fingers of the Sun; Indian Songs from the Mesas; Five Songs from the Tundras; two operas based on Indian themes—The Harvest, and the Necklace of the Sun; Fightery Dick and other poems (book of Free Ballads); also music for Indian Mask, given at Bozeman, Mont., June 1927. Home: Berkeley, Calif. Died Sept. 8, 1938.

LEHR, Henry Solomon, educator; b. Oldtown, O., Mar. 8, 1838; s. George John and Salome (Lesig) L.; Mt. Union Coll., Alliance, O., summers, 1856-61, and 1863; m. Albina Johnson Hoover, Oct. 30, 1866. Taught sch. various periods, 1854-66; served 4 mos. in Co. G, 86th Ohio Vol. Inf., 1862; 1 yr. in Co. F, 176th Ohio Vol. Inf. Founded Ohio Northern U. (originally Ohio Normal U.), 1866, and pres. until July 31, 1902. The H. S. Lehr Auditorium of the univ. named in his honor. Organizer and prin. schs., Winona Lake, Ind., 1904-05. Dir. Liberty Bank, Ada Loan Assn. Republican. Mem. Disciples of Christ. Home: Ada, O. Deceased.

LEHY, John Francis, educator; b. S. Royalston, Mass., Nov. 7, 1850; s. Geoffrey and Eliza (Kelly) L.; student Holy Cross Coll., 1872-74; entered Soc. of Jesus, 1874; ordained R.C. priesthood, 1887. Prof. mathematics, Holy Cross Coll., 1879-84, Georgetown U., 1887-88, Woodstock Coll., 1892-93; v.p. Gonzaga Coll., Washington, 1889-90; v.p. 1893-95, pres. 1895-1901, Holy Cross Coll.; at Woodstock Coll., 1901-04; Boston Coll., 1904-06; treas. Holy Cross Coll., Worcester, Mass., 1906—. Died Nov. 19, 1919.

LEIB, Samuel Franklin, judge; b. Fairfield Co., O., Jan. 18, 1848; s. Joseph and Clarissa (Allen) L.; ed. Fairfield County, O.; served in last yr. of Civil War; LL.B., U. of Mich., 1869; m. Lida Campbell Grissim, Dec. 15, 1874. Admitted to bar, 1869; in practice at San José, Calif.; v.p. First Nat. Bank. Judge Superior Ct. of Santa Clara County, 1903. Trustee Leland Stanford Jr. U., 1891—(pres. bd. 7 yrs.). Home: San José, Calif. Died Dec. 26, 1924.

LEIBERT, Morris William, bishop; b. Bethlehem, Pa., Aug. 22, 1855; s. William and Cornelia Matilda (Krause) L.; grad. Moravian Coll., Bethlehem, Pa., 1873, Moravian Theol. Sem., 1875, Union Theol. Sem., 1877; D.D., New York U., 1904; m. Louise Hill, Aug. 22, 1880. Ordained Moravian ministry, 1877; pastor 2d Moravian Ch., New York, 1877-85, Bethlehem, Pa., 1885-1901, Staten Island, N.Y., 1901-04, 1st Ch., New York, 1904—; consecrated bishop, Sept. 13, 1908. Pres. Gen. Synod Moravian Ch., Herrnhut, Saxony, 1899, and mem. Gen. Synods, 1909, 14; pres. various Am. Moravian Provincial and Dist. Synods; pres. Provincial Elders' Conf., 1908-13; mem. gen. exec. bds. Moravian Ch., 1893-1913; mem. exec. com. Federal Council Chs. of Christ in America and of various commns. same; chmn. Moravian Commn. on World Conf. Faith and Order; dir. N.Y. Fedn. Chs. Home: New York, N.Y. Deceased.

LEIDY, Joseph II, M.D.; b. Phila., Pa., Apr. 11, 1866; s. Philip (M.D.) and Penelope Fontaine Maury (Polk) L.; A.B., Phila. Central High Sch., 1884, A.M., 1885; M.D., U. of Pa., 1887; m. Helen Redington Carter; children—Cornelia Carter (Mrs. J. Hamilton Cheston), Philip Ludwell, Carter Randolph, Joseph (dec.). Physician University Hosp., 1887-89, Pa. Gen. Hosp., 1889-91, Pa. Hosp. for Insane; surgeon Howard Hosp., 1891; Hamilton and Phila. Dispensary; phys. to Med. Clinic, Pa. Hosp., 1893-1903; asst. demonstrator pathology, anatomy and morbid histology, U. of Pa., 1892, and of anatomy, 1894. Fellow Coll. of Physicians, A.A.A.S. Acad. Natural Sciences. Official del. from U.S. Govt. and juror on hygiene, Paris, 1900; decorated Officier de l'Instruction Publique, France, 1900; official del. from U.S. Govt. to the Internat. Congress of Hygiene and Demographie, 1900; represented A.A.A.S. at transfer of home of Charles Darwin to British Nation, 1929. Served as lt. col. Med. Corps, U.S.A.; instr. and med. dir. of gas defense, 30th Div., staff officer U.S.A., 1917-19, World War; lt. col. Med. Res. U.S.A. Republican. Home: Philadelphia, Pa. Died July 7, 1932.

LEIGH, Southgate, surgeon; b. Va., May 21, 1866; s. John Purviance and Fannie (Cowdery) L.; M.D., U. of Va., 1888; M.D., Coll. Phys. and Surg. (Columbia), 1889; interne-house surgeon, Mt. Sinai Hosp., New York, 1889-91; spl. work, U. of Vienna, 1892; m. Alice Creekmore, 1905; children—Southgate, Alice, Sallie, Watkins. Practice at Norfolk, Va., 1893—; founder and visiting surgeon and gynecologist, Sarah Leigh Hosp.; cons. surgeon Memorial Hosp.; chief surgeon Virginian Railway; surgeon Norfolk & Western Ry. Co., Pennsylvania R.R., Chesapeake & Ohio and Atlantic Coast Line railways. Was pres. Common Council of Norfolk, Norfolk-Portsmouth Chamber Commerce, Norfolk-Portsmouth Alumni of U. of Va., Tidewater Alumni Columbia U. Mem. Nat. and State Inter-racial Commissions. Fellow Am. Coll. Surgeons (a founder). Awarded Norfolk Distinguished Service Medal, 1929. Home: Norfolk, Va. Died Mar. 5, 1936.

LEIGHTON, Benjamin Franklin, dean law school. Prof. real property and contracts, constl. and statutory law and dean, Law Sch., Howard U., Washington. Was pres. Bar Assn. of Washington, Blackstone Club. Pres. trustees Am. Univ., Washington. Home: Washington, D.C. Died July 5, 1921.

LEIGHTON, George E., capitalist, lawyer; b. in Mass.; s. Eliot L.; ed. in Cincinnati; when 23 yrs. old located as lawyer in St. Louis; m. Isabella, d. Hon. Hudson E. Bridge, Oct. 1862. Served in Union army, 1861-65, under Gens. Lyon, Halleck, Curtis and Schofield, reaching rank of col.; atty. for Mo. Pacific Ry., 1865-73; retired from practice to engage in mfg., banking and other enterprises. Was 4 yrs. pres. Commercial Club, St. Louis; pres. Mo. Hist. Soc. and Univ. Bd., Washington Univ. Delivered speech at Trans-Missouri Congress in opposition to free coinage of silver, of which 150,000 copies were distributed. Apptd. by exec. com. Indianapolis Monetary Conf., 1897, as mem. Monetary Commn. Home: St. Louis, Mo. Died 1901.

LEINBACH, Paul Seibert, clergyman, editor; b. Womelsdorf, Pa., Sept. 21, 1874; s. of Rev. Thomas Calvin and Maria R. (Seibert) L.; A.B., and A.M. (first honor), Franklin and Marshall, 1895; grad. Reformed Ch. Theol. Sem., Lancaster, Pa., 1898; D.D., Heidelburg, 1912; Litt.D., Franklin and Marshall, 1921; m. H. Belle Martin, May 26, 1898 (died 1908); children—Thomas Martin (dec.), Joseph Nevin, Paul Harold; m. 2d, Helen S. DeLong, Aug. 2, 1910; 1 son, John DeLong. Ordained ministry Ref. Ch. in U.S., 1898; pastor Grace Ch., Altoona, Pa., 1898-1900, Trinity Ch., Pittsburgh, 1900-05, 1st Ch., Easton, 1905-13, Hamilton Grange Ref. Ch., New York, 1913-17; editor in chief Reformed Church Messenger, 1917—; exec. sec. Publ. and S.S. Board Ref. Ch., 1925-29; exec. sec. Bd. Christian Education, 1929-30, pres., 1930-38. Pres. Editorial Council Religious Press of America, term 1924-34; editor in chief The Messenger, combined English organ Evang. and Ref. Chs., 1936—. Sec. Gen. Bd. Home Missions Ref. Ch. in U.S., 1905-13; pres. Eastern Synod, 1911-12; 1st v.p. Gen. Synod, 1911-12; editor denominational S.S. lit., 1907-15; pres. bd. of business management of Evang. and Ref. Church, 1940—. Mem. Federal Council of Chs., 1905-41 (exec. and administrative coms.). Mem. Am. Relief Commn. to Near East, 1919; mem. exec. com. and bd. trustees of Internat. Council of Religious Edn.; pres. bd. trustees Am. School for Boys, Baghdad, Iraq. Republican. Mason. Rotarian. Home: Philadelphia, Pa. Died Dec. 7, 1941.

LEIPER, Macon Anderson, prof. English; b. Malvern, Ark., July 25, 1879; s. William Harper and Priscilla (Mason) L.; A.B., Peabody Coll. for Teachers, Nashville, Tenn., 1901, Ph.D., 1926; A.M., Columbia, 1905; studied Princeton, 1906-07; m. Mary Elizabeth Taylor, Nov. 27, 1907; 1 dau., Elizabeth Macon. Instr. in Latin, Beauvoir Coll., 1901-02, Galloway Coll., 1902-03, Maddox Sem., 1903-04, all in Ark.; prof. English, also head dept., Ky. Teachers Coll., 1908—; teacher Peabody Coll., 4 summers; Asheville (N.C.) Normal Sch., summer 1920. Democrat. Presbyn. K.P. Author: Latin Subordinate Clause Syntax, 1913; Language Work in Elementary Schools, 1916; New Idea Speller (with others), 1919; A New English Grammar, 1923; Errors of College Freshmen in Written Compositions, 1926. Lectured widely before teachers' institutes. Home: Bowling Green, Ky. Died June 17, 1936.

LEIPZIGER, Henry Marcus, lecturer, educator; b. Manchester, Eng., Dec. 29, 1854; s. Marcus and Martha (Samuel) L.; came to New York, 1865; A.B., B.S., Coll. City of New York, 1873; LL.B., Columbia, 1875, Ph.D., 1888; LL.D., Union Coll., 1907; admitted to N.Y. bar, 1875; taught in N.Y. pub. schs., 1873-81; traveling, studying and investigating methods of industrial edn., 1881-84; organized Hebrew Tech. Inst., N.Y., and directed same, 1884-91; asst. supt. pub. schs., N.Y., 1891-96; supervisor of lectures, Bd. of Edn., N.Y., 1890—. Organized the system of pub. lectures given by Bd. Edn., N.Y., and dir. same; lecturer on ednl. and ethical topics. Chmn. of library com. of Aguilar Free Library, 17 yrs., which was consolidated in the N.Y. Pub. Library, 1903. Home: New York, N.Y. Died Dec. 1, 1917.

LEISHMAN, John G., ambassador; b. at Pittsburgh, Pa., Mar. 28, 1857; m. Julia Crawford, 1880. Sr. mem. Leishman & Snyder, steel brokers, Pittsburgh, 1881-86; v.p. Carnegie Bros. & Co., Ltd., 1886; pres. Carnegie Steel Co. until 1897; E.E. and M.P. from U.S. to Switzerland, 1897-1900, to Turkey, 1900-06; A.E. and P. to Turkey, 1906-09, to Italy, 1909-11, to Germany, 1911-13. Republican. Home: Pittsburgh, Pa. Died Mar. 27, 1924.

LEIST, Henry Gottlieb, educator; b. Wilton, Ia., Aug. 9, 1871; s. John G. and Henriette (Leveke) L.; A.B., Central Wesleyan Coll., Warrenton, Mo., 1892, A.M., 1895; B.D., Garrett Bibl. Inst. (Northwestern U.), 1895; post-grad. work, U. of Berlin, 1895-97; D.D., Ia. Wesleyan Coll., 1909; m. Lillie Smith, May 8, 1902; children—Florence, John S. Ordained M.E. ministry, 1895; pastor Enterprise, Kan., 1897-98, Denver, Colo., 1898-1900, Cortland, Neb., 1900-02, Kansas City, Mo., 1902-03; prof. German and Bibl. lit., 1903-18, philosophy and religion, 1918—, registrar, 1919-22, dean, 1922-33, continuing as professor of religion and philosophy, acting pres., June-Dec. 1927, Ia. Wesleyan Coll. Pres. German Coll., Mt. Pleasant, Ia., 1908-09. Mem. West German M.E. Conf., 1897, 1924, sec., 1916-24; mem. Ia. M.E. Conf., 1924. Home: Mt. Pleasant, Ia. Died Dec. 13, 1937.

LEITCH, Joseph Dugald, army officer; b. Montague, Mich., Mar. 5, 1864; s. Dugald and Sarah (Furgeson) L.; grad. U.S. Mil. Acad., 1889, Army War Coll., 1914; m. Margaret, d. Col. F. M. Crandal, U.S.A., Oct. 1, 1891. Commd. 2d lt. 24th Inf., June 12, 1889; advanced through grades to col., July 18, 1917; brig. gen. N.A., Feb. 6, 1918; major gen. (temp.), Oct. 1, 1918; maj. gen. regular army, Nov. 6, 1927. Duty at various posts in the Southwest and West until 1898; participated in various engagements at San Juan, and siege of Santiago, Cuba, 1898; in Philippines, 1900-02, 1907-10, and 1916-17; with American expdn. to Vera Cruz, Mem., May 1-Nov. 23, 1914; Gen. Staff, Washington, Jan. 25, 1910-Aug. 31, 1913, and Oct. 1, 1917-Feb. 15, 1918; comd. 15th Brig., Camp Fremont, Calif., Feb. 20-Oct. 5, 1918, 13th Div., Camp Lewis, Wash., Oct. 7, 1918-Mar. 8, 1919; apptd. insp. gen. and chief of staff, A.E.F., in Siberia, 1919-1920; retired Mar. 5, 1928. Decorated D.S.M. (U.S.). Died Oct. 26, 1938.

LEITER, Joseph, capitalist; b. Chicago, Dec. 4, 1868; s. Levi Ziegler and Mary Theresa (Carver) L.; A.B., Harvard, 1891; m. Juliette Williams, 1908. Agt. for his father, 1892-98; in autumn of 1897 bought wheat on Chicago Bd. of Trade to such an extent as to make him, at beginning of 1898, the largest individual holder of wheat in the history of the grain trade. Pres. Zeigler Coal Co.; dir. Am. Security and Trust Co., Washington, D.C. Homes: Chicago, Ill., and Washington, D.C. Died Apr. 11, 1932.

LEITER, Levi Zeigler, capitalist; b. Leitersburg, Md., 1834; ed. there, then clerked in country gen. store until 1854; employed in store at Springfield, O., 1854-55; employee and later partner, Cooley, Wadsworth & Co., dry goods, Chicago, until Jan. 1, 1865, when he and Marshall Field sold their interests in that firm to John V. Farwell and bought controlling interest in dry goods business of Potter Palmer. Firm became Field, Palmer & Leiter, then Field, Leiter & Co., until Jan. 1, 1881, when he sold his interest and retired. Since then has given attention to buying and improving business properties in Chicago; possessed large interests in corporations; m. Mary Theressa Carver, Oct. 1866; 4 children—Joseph, Nancy L. C., Marguerite, Mary Victoria (Lady Curzon of Kedleston). Home: Chicago, Ill. Died 1904.

LELAND, Charles A., asso. justice Supreme Court, N.Mex.; b. Sharon, Nov. 21, 1859; s. Baldwin M. and Rebecca D. L.; m. Cora M. McKee, Dec. 21, 1889. Served 6 yrs. as dist. atty. Noble County, O.; represented same county in legislature 4 yrs.; apptd. asso. justice Supreme Court of N.Mex., 1898. Republican. Home: Socorro, N.M. Deceased.

LELAND, Charles Godfrey ("Hans Breitmann"), author; b. Phila., Aug. 15, 1824; s. Charles and Charlotte (Godfrey) L.; grad. Princeton, 1845 (A.M., Harvard; F.R.L.S.); studied univs. of Heidelberg, Munich and Paris. Studied law; practiced in Phila., 1849-53; entered journalism; editor New York Times, Phila. Evening Bulletin, Vanity Fair; 3 yrs. mng. editor Phila. Press; editor Knickerbocker Mag. and Continental Mag.; from 1869 principally devoted to literature; in London, 1869-80; returned to U.S.; was 1st to establish industrial edn., founded on the minor arts as a branch in the pub. schs., now used in U.S., England, Austria, Hungary, etc.; established, with Mrs. R. Jebb, the British Home Arts and Industries Assn.; one of original founders of Folk-Lore Congress at Paris, 1889; discovered the "Shelta" language, spoken by Celtic tinkers, etc., subsequently verified by Kuno Meyer, from M.S. 1,000 yrs. old, as the famous lost language of the Irish bards. Later yrs. lived in London, England, and Florence, Italy. Author: Hans Breitmann's Ballads; France, Alsace and Lorraine; English Gypsies; Egyptian Sketch Book; Life of Abraham Lincoln; The Minor Arts; Industrial Work in Schools (U.S. Bureau of Education); Practical Education; Legends of Florence; Songs of the Sea and Lays of the Land; One Hundred Profitable Arts; Meister Karl's Sketch Book; Etruscan-Roman Remains; The Gypsies; Algonquin Legends; Anglo-Romany Songs; Legends of Virgil; Have You a Strong Will?. Died 1903.

LELAND, Henry Martyn, mfr.; b. Danville, Vt., Feb. 16, 1843; s. Leander B. and Zilpha (Tifft) L.; D.Eng., U. of Mich., 1920, U. of Vt., 1923; m. Ellen R. Hull, 1867; children—Mrs. Martha Gertrude Woodbridge, Wilfred Chester, Edith Miriam Leland (dec.). Learned machinist's trade at Worcester, Mass.; tool maker in U.S. Armory, Springfield, Mass., 1862-65; with Brown & Sharp, Providence, R.I., 20 yrs., becoming supt. of sewing machine dept.; removed to Detroit, 1890, and engaged as mfr. spl. machinery; organized Leland & Faulconer Mfg. Co., of which was mgr. until merged into Cadillac Motor Car Co., of which was founder 1904, and gen. mgr. until 1909, then pres. and advisory mgr.; founder of Lincoln Motor Co. Founder Detroit Citizens' League (pres. 1911-25). Republican. Presbyn. Home: Detroit, Mich. Died Mar. 26, 1932.

LELAND, Lester, mfr.; b. Boston, Mass., July 20, 1864; s. Lester and Mary E. (Babcock); ed. English High Sch. and business coll.; m. Frances Eugenia Converse, Oct. 25, 1892. Began with C. A. Richards, pres. Met. St. Ry. Co., Boston; later treas. Boston Heating Co.; supt. bldgs. and purchasing agt. Met. Telephone Co., New York; asst. treas., 1893, treas., 1895, Boston Rubber Shoe Co., absorbed, 1898, in U.S. Rubber Co., of which was made dir. and mem. exec. com.; v.p. U.S. Rubber Co., 1901, vice chmn. and mem. exec. com., 1918-24; officer or dir. First Nat. Bank, Old Colony Trust Co., Arkwright Mutual Fire Ins. Co. (Boston), Atlantic Coast Lumber Corp., United Timber Co. (New York). Second lt. Co. C, 5th Mass. Inf., U.S.V., Spanish-Am. War; detailed July 6, 1898, as a.d.c. on staff of Brig. Gen. William A. Bancroft; hon. discharged Aug. 20, 1898. Home: Boston, Mass. Died July 30, 1933.

LEMANN, Isaac Ivan, M.D.; b. Donaldsonville, La., Feb. 8, 1877; s. Bernard and Harriet (Friedheim) L.; A.B., Tulane U., 1895, M.D., 1900; A.B., Harvard, 1896; grad. study, Johns Hopkins Hosp., Baltimore, 1903, U. of Strassburg, 1904-05, U. of Vienna, 1905, U. of Berlin, 1905; m. Stella Hirsch, Oct. 3, 1904; children—Paul Bernard, Richard Berthelot. Began practice at New Orleans, 1900; instr. in medicine, Tulane U., 1903-10, asst. prof. medicine, 1910-14, prof. clin. medicine, 1914—; visiting physician Charity Hosp., 1900-25, consultant in medicine, 1925—, visiting physician Tonor Infirmary, 1907-19, chief of med. service, 1919—. Served as capt. Med. Corps, U.S.A., 1917-19; chief of med. service, Base Hosp. 76, Vichy, France, Oct. 1918-Jan. 1919; formerly lt. col. Med. R.C., chief med. service Tulane unit. Jewish religion. Home: New Orleans, La. Died Sept. 1938.

LEMARE, Edwin Henry, organist, composer; b. Ventnor, Isle of Wight, Eng., Sept. 9, 1866; s. Edwin and Margaret (Wicker) L.; studied under father, an organist; grad. Royal Acad. of Music, London; m. Charlotte S. Bauersmith, Pa., July 1909. Organist and dir. of choristers, Sheffield Cathedral, 1886-92, Holy Trinity Ch., Sloane St., London, 1892, later at St. Margaret's, Westminster. First U.S. tour, 1901; organist and dir. of music, Carnegie Inst., Pittsburgh, 1902-05; made many tours of U.S., Can., Australia, New Zealand and Europe; gave 121 recitals at the P.P.I. Expn., San Francisco, 1915; city organist, San Francisco, 1917-21, Portland, Me., 1921-24, Chattanooga Memorial Auditorium, 1924-29. Composer of more than 200 published works for organ, also ch. music, cantatas, operettas, etc., and 600 orchestra and other transcriptions. Crossed the Atlantic Ocean 55 times in pursuance of professional engagements. Died Sept. 25, 1934.

LEMCKE, Gesine, teacher culinary art; b. Bremen, Germany, Apr. 9, 1841; d. J. Frederick and Frederica Knubel; ed. Bremen; grad. Göttingen, Germany, 1882; spl. courses in music and chemistry under pvt. tutors; m. H. D. Lemcke, Dec. 23, 1862. Contbr. on culinary subjects to New York World, Sunday Journal and American, Press, Mail and Express, Brooklyn Eagle, American Queen, Ledger, Collier's, Demorest's. Author: Desserts and Salads, 1891; American Cuisine, 1895; How to Live on Twenty-five Cents a Day, 1896; Chafing-Dish Recipes, 1897; Preserving and Pickling, 1898. Home: New York, N.Y. Died 1904.

LEMLY, Henry Rowan, major U.S.A.; b. Bethania, N.C., Jan. 12, 1851; s. Henry Augustus and Amanda Sophia (Conrad) L.; grad. U.S. Mil. Acad., 1872; m. Katharine Palmer, Dec. 1, 1874. Apptd. 2d lt. 3d Cav., 1872; transferred to 3d Arty., 1878; 1st lt., 1880; capt. 7th Arty., 1898; retired at own request, over 30 yrs.' service, Apr. 20, 1899. Comd. light Battery C, 7th Arty., in P.R. campaign in Spanish-Am. War. Took part in Indian combats on Tongue River, Rosebud, Slim Buttes and Belle Fourche. Many yrs. dir. Nat. Mil. Sch., Bogotá, Colombia, with local rank of col.; commr.-gen. for Colombia at World's Columbian Expn. Author: Who Was El Dorado?; Among the Arapahoes; The Story of Feather-Head; Santa Fé de Bogotá; A West Point Romance; Padre Anselmo; Uncle 'Man; A Queen's Thoughts; also Spanish trans. of Upton's Infantry Regulations, English trans. of a French Manual of Strategy. Ordered to duty in office of q.m. gen. U.S.A., May 7, 1917; maj. Q.M. Corps, Apr. 22, 1918; retired Mar. 11, 1920. Home: Washington, D.C. Died Oct. 12, 1925.

LEMLY, Samuel Conrad, judge advocate-general U.S.N.; b. Salem, N.C., March 14, 1853; grad. U.S. Naval Acad., 1873; ensign, July 1874; master, Feb. 1880; junior lt., March 1883; lt., Jan. 1886; served on various stas. and duties until apptd. capt. June 5, 1892, and judge-advocate-gen.; reapptd. for 4 yrs. from June 4, 1896, and again, June 4, 1900-04; retired 1904. Died 1909.

LEMMON, John Gill, botanist; b. Lima, Mich., Jan. 2, 1832; s. William and Amila (Hudson) L.; ed. pub. and private schs. and Mich. State Normal Sch.; taught village schs. 8 yrs. and was 4 yrs. school supt.; entered Univ. of Mich.; left before graduation to enter 4th Mich. cav., June 8, 1862; took part in 36 engagements in Ky., Tenn., Ala. and Ga.; captured, Aug. 24, 1864, and remained in Andersonville prison to end of war; m. Sara Allen Plummer, 1880. Moved to Calif., 1866; specialist in forestry; was botanist 4 yrs., Calif. State Bd. Forestry; has added many species of plants, including several kinds of trees, to accepted classifications. Councilman, City of Oakland, 1900-02. Author: Campaigning with Saber and Carbine, 1867; Recollections of Rebel Prisons, 1874; Reports of the Locust Scourge in California, 1878; Discovery of Potato in Arizona, 1881; Ferns of the Pacific Slope, 1884; 2d and 3d Biennial Reports, Calif. Bd. Forestry, 1888, 1890; Handbook of North American Cone-Bearers, 1895, 1900; Botanizing in Apache-land, 1901; How to Tell the Trees, 1902; Native Trees of West America, 1905. Home: Oakland, Calif. Died 1908.

LEMMON, Reuben C., gen. grand high priest, Royal Arch Masons in U.S., 1897—; b. Varick, Seneca Co., N.Y., May 12, 1825; ed. Granville, O.; studied law; admitted to Ohio bar; practiced in Toledo; over 20 yrs. was judge Court of Common Pleas, Toledo. Masonic record: Raised Toledo Lodge, No. 144, Toledo, 1855; exalted Ft. Meigs Chapter, No. 29, 1856; acknowledge Toledo Council, 1860; knighted Toledo Commandery, No. 7, 1857; received various grades A. A. Scottish Rite, 1875, at Cleveland and Cincinnati; crowned with 33d degree, Sept. 16, 1890. Grand Master Grand Lodge, Ohio, 1880-81; grand high priest, Grand Chapter Ohio, 1875-76. Home: Toledo, O. Died 1905.

LE MOYNE, Louis Valcoulon, author; b. Chicago, Jan. 4, 1860; s. John Valcoulon and Julia (Murray)

L.; A.B., Harvard, 1884; admitted to Ill. bar, 1887; studied landscape architecture 3 yrs. in Paris, Italy and Eng.; unmarried. Practiced extensively in various parts of the country. Resident of Hull House for 6 yrs. Episcopalian. Author: Country Residences in Europe and America, 1908. Home: Kenilworth, Ill. Died July 28, 1928.

LE MOYNE, William J., actor; b. Boston, 1831; 1st professional appearance as First Officer in Lady of Lyons, Portland, Me., May 10, 1852; played with G. F. Marchant, E. L. Davenport and others until Civil War began; lt., capt. Co. B, 28th Mass. vol. inf.; wounded at South Mountain and left the service; returned to the stage and acted leading rôles in many dramas, notably old man parts. Died 1905.

LENGFELD, Felix, chemist; b. San Francisco, Calif., Feb. 18, 1863; s. Louis and Henrietta (Honisberg) L.; Ph.G., Coll. of Pharmacy, U. of Calif., 1880; spl. student U. of Calif., 1884-86; grad. student and fellow, Johns Hopkins, 1886-88, Ph.D., 1888; studied Zürich Polytechnicum, U. of Liège, U. of Munich; unmarried. Prof. chemistry and assaying, S.D. Coll. of Mines, 1890-91; instr. chemistry, U. of Calif., 1891-92; instr. chemistry and asst. prof., U. of Chicago, 1892-1901; sec., later pres. Lengfeld's Pharmacy, San Francisco. Jewish religion. Author: Inorganic Preparations. Editor Dept. of Pharmacy and Chemistry, Calif. State Med. Jour. Home: San Francisco, Calif. Died 1938.

LENHER, Victor, chemist; b. Belmond, Ia., July 13, 1873; s. Dr. Levi H. and Susan (Keller) L.; Dickinson Coll., 1889-90; U. of Pa., 1893, Ph.D., 1898; m. May Blood, Aug. 29, 1900; children—George, Sam. Asst. in chemistry, U. of Calif., 1893-96, Columbia, 1898-1900; instr. chemistry, Evening High Sch., New York, 1899-1900; asst. prof. gen. and theoretical chemistry, 1900-04, asso. prof. chemistry, 1904-07, prof., 1907—, U. of Wis. Mem. Bd. of Edn., Madison, Wis., 1905-19, Bd. of Health, 1921-23. Mem. com. Nat. Research Council on uses of selenium and tellurium, 1919-24, chmn., 1921-24. Maj., Chem. Service Sect. N.A.; maj., Chem. Warfare Service, U.S.A.; chief univ. relations, adj. to Maj. Gen. Sibert, chief governmental relations; hon. discharged, Dec. 5, 1918. Author: Laboratory Experiments (3 edits.), 1902; The Electric Furnace (transl. of Moissan), 2 edits., 1904, 20. Discovered the unusual solvent properties of selenium oxychloride, 1919. Home: Madison, Wis. Died June 12, 1927.

LENIHAN, Thomas Mathias, R. C. bishop of Cheyenne, Wyo.; b. May 12, 1845; ed. Bardstown, Ky., Ecclesiastical Sem., Cape Girardeau, Mo., and St. Francis Sem., Milwaukee. Ordained priest, Nov. 19, 1867; pastor St. Benedict's, Decorah, Ia., 1868-70; Corpus Christi Ch., Ft. Dodge, Ia., and adjacent missions; built many new chs.; established new parishes and was made irremovable rector and dean until consecrated bishop, Feb. 24, 1897. Died 1901.

LENKER, John Nicholas, clergyman; b. Sunbury, Pa., Nov. 28, 1858; s. John Bobb and Mary Ann (Gearheart) L.; A. B., Wittenberg Coll., Springfield, O., 1879, A.M., 1880; grad. Hamma Div. Sch. (Wittenberg), 1881, D.D., 1893; studied U. of Leipzig, Germany, 1882; m. Nora Cecelia Walsted, Sept. 18, 1919; 1 dau., Mary Lutherin Walsted. Ordained Evang. Luth. ministry, 1880; pastor Grand Island, Neb., 1882-86; with Bd. of Ch. Extension of Gen. Synod Evang. Luth. Ch. in U.S.A., 1886-94; prof. ch. history, O.T. exegesis, Hebrew and German, Trinity Sem., Blair, Neb., 1900-04; settled in Minneapolis, Minn., 1904; founder of the Luther Press; founder and editor Northern Review, and "The Lutherans in All Lands" (quarterly); pastor Pentecost English Evang. Lutheran Ch. Made extensive research work in Europe, Egypt and Palestine. Pres. Gen. Luth. Missionary Conf.; v.p. Am. Luth. Mission for Russia; organizer and founder students' missionary socs. in Norway, Sweden and Finland. Author: Lutherans in All Lands, 1893; Lutherans in All Lands, Supplement, 1919; Die Lutherische Kirche der Welt, 1901; Three Language Education, 1914. Translator of writings of Martin Luther (13 vols. issued, 7 more translated). Home: Minneapolis, Minn. Died May 16, 1929.

LENNON, John Brown, labor union official; b. Lafayette County, Wis., Oct. 12, 1850; s. John Alexander and Elizabeth Fletcher (Brown) L.; ed. pub. schs.; m. Juna J. Allen, Apr. 5, 1871. Gen. sec. Journeyman Tailors' Union of America, 1886-1910; treas. Am. Fedn. of Labor, Sept. 1889-1917; mem. bd. mediators, U.S. Dept. Labor, 1917—. Editor The Tailor, 1886-1910; apptd. mem. commn. on Industrial Relations, Washington, D.C., 1912; lecturer on social problems. Mem. commn. on social service Federal Council Chs. of Christ in America; v.p. Ill. Anti-Saloon League. Democrat. Presbyn. Mason. Home: Bloomington, Ill. Died Jan. 18, 1923.

LENNON, Thomas J., judge; b. Marysville, Yuba County, Calif., Feb. 25, 1866; s. Michael and Margaret (Kelly) L.; B.S., St. Mary's Coll., San Francisco, 1885; m. Emily Lenhart, June 7, 1893. Admitted to Calif. bar, 1888, and practiced 14 years at San Francisco; judge Superior Court of Marin County, Calif., 1903-11; presiding justice 1st Dist. Court of Appeals, Calif., 1911-19; asso. justice Supreme Court of Calif., term 1919-31. Republican. Catholic. Mem. Native Sons of Golden West, Elks, Moose, Foresters. Home: San Francisco, Calif. Died Aug. 14, 1926.

LENNOX, William, mine operator; b. Iowa City, Ia., Dec. 25, 1850; s. John and Agnes (Houston) L.; student State U. of Ia.; grad. Univ. Business Coll., Iowa City; children—Jessie Beatrice (wife of Col. William G. Fay), Loring Cowgill (dec.), William Gordon, Willabel (Mrs. Kenneth MacGregor). Began mining at Alma, Colo., 1872; pres. Strong Mining Co.; dir. Exchange Nat. Bank. Trustee Colo. Coll. Republican. Methodist. Home: Colorado Springs, Colo. Deceased.

LENOX, John Powell, lecturer-writer; b. N.Y. City, Aug. 22, 1851; s. John F. and Mary A. (Powell) L.; grad. high sch., Chicago, 1869; m. Lucie M. Roberts, Sept. 21, 1897. Sec. Webster Mfg. Co., of Chicago and Tiffin, O., 1882-1911; traveled extensively abroad, and acquired collection of about 4,000 pictures of Christ (prints, engravings, etchings, etc.), upon which lectured; donated this collection, comprised in 17 massive leather vols. with critical notes, to New York Public Library, 1920. Republican. Baptist. Home: Oak Park, Ill. Died Feb. 11, 1926.

LENSKI, Richard Charles Henry, clergyman; b. Greifenberg, Prussia, Sept. 14, 1864; s. William J. and Ernstine F. (Pittelkow) L.; A.B., Capital U., Columbus, O., 1885, later A.M., D.D., 1915; grad. Theol. Sem., Columbus, 1887; m. Marietta Young, Feb. 1, 1888 (died 1923); m. 2d, E. Helen Gruner, May 12, 1924. Ordained Luth. ministry, 1887; successively pastor Baltimore, Trenton, O., Springfield, O., and Anna, O., until 1911; prof. languages and theology, Capital U., Columbus, O., 1916-21, prof. dogmatics, New Testament exegesis and homiletics, 1921-28, became prof. systematic theology, 1928, also dean of Theol. Sem., same univ., 1919, retired as dean emeritus. Editor Lutherische Kirchenzeitung, 1904-24. Author: New Gospel Selections, 1919; The Eisenach Old Testament Selections, 1925; The Active Church Member, 1922; Kings and Priests, 1927; The Sermon, Its Homiletical Construction, 1927; St. John, 1929; The Interpretation of St. John's Gospel, 1931; The Interpretation of St. Matthew's Gospel, 1932; The Interpretation of St. Mark's and St. Luke's Gospel, 1934; The Interpretation of the Acts of the Apostles, 1934; The Interpretation of St. John's Revelation, 1935; The Interpretation of St. Paul's First and Second Epistles to the Corinthians, 1935; The Ancient Church Epistle Selections (exegetical-homiletical), 1935; The Interpretation of St. Paul's Epistle to the Romans, 1936. Died 1936.

LENTZ, John Jacob, life ins.; b. St. Clairsville, O., Jan. 27, 1856; s. Simon and Anna (Myer) L.; grad. Nat. Normal U., Lebanon, O., 1877; student U. of Wooster 1 yr.; A.B., U. of Michigan, 1882; LL.B., Columbia U., 1883; married; 1 son, John Jacob. Was admitted to Ohio bar, 1883, and practiced at Columbus; mem. Nash & Lentz (George K. Nash), 1887, until death of Gov. Nash, 1904; founder Am. Ins. Union, 1894, and became its pres.; retired from practice of law in 1915; elected hon. pres. of the A.I.U. for life, at its silver jubilee, Sept. 21, 1919. Mem. 55th and 56th Congresses (1897-1901), 12th Ohio Dist.; elected hon. v.p. from Ohio by delegation to Dem. Nat. Conv., Denver, Colo., 1908, and chosen to second nominations of both Bryan and Kern. Pres. "Fraternal Day" at Panama-Pacific Expn., San Francisco, 1915; one of founders and continuously a mem. of bd. govs. of "Mooseheart"; mem. Moose war relief commn. to visit war front, 1918; delivered address, "A Free Man, in a Free Nation, in a Free World," at the Colosseum in Rome, Apr. 7, 1918; apptd. mem. Special Immigration Commn. to accompany sec. of labor, making intensive studies of immigration problems of South America, 1924; spent 3 months visiting govts. of 11 European nations, 1928. Author: Thomas Jefferson, the Radical, 1905. Builder of Am. Ins. Union Citadel, Columbus. Home: Citadel, Columbus, O. Died July 27, 1931.

LENTZ, Max Carl Guenther, educator; b. Hathenow, Brandenburg, Prussia, Feb. 27, 1857; s. Carl and Constanze (Ruediger) L.; studied philosophy in Munich 1½ yrs., law, in Zürich, Geneva, Munich and Berlin, 2½ yrs.; came to U.S., 1882; m. Agnes Meinecke, Dec. 26, 1895. Architect, teacher, prin. schs., etc., 1884-1905; acting prof., 1905, asst. prof. Germanic langs., 1906, U. of Me.; prof. Germanic langs., U. of Ark., Sept. 1907-1915. Editor: Stifter, Das Haidedorf, 1895; Heyse, L' Arrabbiata, 1899; Heyse, Anfang und Ende, 1900; Groller, Incognito, 1901; Two German Tales, 1905; Von Perfall's Tejada Spring, 1911. Research work for Carnegie Endowment for Internat. Peace, 1916-18. Home: Tuckahoe, N.J. Died Dec. 21, 1924.

LEONARD, Abiel, P.E. bishop of Salt Lake; consecrated, Jan. 25, 1888; b. Fayette, Mo., June 26, 1848; grad. Dartmouth, 1870; A.M., 1873; grad. Gen. Theol. Sem., 1873 (S.T.D. there; also from Griswold and Bethany colls.); served in ministry of P.E. Ch. in Mo. and Kan. until 1888; m. Flora T. Thompson, Oct. 21, 1875. Residence: Salt Lake City, Utah. Died 1903.

LEONARD, Adna B., clergyman; b. Berlin Tp., Mahoning Co., O., Aug. 2, 1837; s. John and Nancy L.; A.B., A.M., Mt. Union Coll., Ohio; D.D., New Orleans U.; LL.D., Mt. Union; m. Caroline Amelia Kaiser, Feb. 19, 1861. Ordained M.E. ministry, 1860; corr. sec. Missionary Soc. and Bd. Foreign Missions of M.E. Ch., 1888-1912, emeritus, 1912—. Prohibition nominee for gov. of Ohio, 1885. Home: Brooklyn, N.Y. Died Apr. 21, 1916.

LEONARD, Albert, supt. schs.; b. Logan, O., Dec. 21, 1857; s. John and Mahala (Welty) L.; A.B., Ohio U., 1888, A.M., 1891, Litt.D., 1909, Ed.D., 1928; Ph.D., Hamilton Coll., 1894; m. Frances Wright, July 13, 1887; children—Gertrude, Charles Albert. Prin. high sch., Dunkirk, N.Y., 1888-93; Binghamton, N.Y., 1893-97; dean Coll. Liberal Arts and prof. pedagogy, Syracuse U., 1897-1900; pres. normal schs. of Mich., 1900-02; in ednl. dept. of Houghton Mifflin & Co., Boston, 1902-07; supt. schs., New Rochelle, N.Y., 1907—. Editor Journal of Pedagogy, 1891—. Mem. advisory council Simplified Spelling Bd.; pres. N.Y. State Teachers' Assn., 1922-23. Home: New Rochelle, N.Y. Died Dec. 1931.

LEONARD, Alexander Thomas, surgeon; b. Queensfort, Tuam, County Galway, Ireland, Sept. 11, 1858; s. Alexander Thomas and Margaret (Skerrett) L.; student Royal Coll. Surgeons, Ireland, and Queen's Coll., Galway, Ireland; L.R.C.S. and L.R.C.P., Royal Coll. Surgeons, Edinburgh, 1883 (winner Sir Charles Bell medal); hon. M.A., U. of Santa Clara, Calif., 1907; m. Annie Margaret Barry, Oct. 16, 1887 (died 1937); children—Honora Genevieve (Mrs. Bruce Henry McBirney), Alexander Thomas, Marguerite Ann (dec.), Barry William (dec.), Yelverton Vincent (dec.), Eileen Mary (Mrs. John Arthur McInerny), Marie Louise (Mrs. Frederick Lewis Fillmore), Stephen John (dec.), Anita Lucile (Mrs. Howard Albert Clark), Geraldine Claire (dec.), Viola Clarisse (Mrs. Winchester Cooley). Came to U.S., 1883, naturalized, 1896. Resident surgeon, St. Mary's Hosp., San Francisco, 1884-87; chief surgeon, 1887—; staff surgeon and dir. Trinity Hosp., 1917—, and dir. Nurses' Training Sch. of same. Republican. K.C., Knight of St. Patrick. Died July 2, 1939.

LEONARD, Arthur Gray, geologist; b. Clinton, N.Y., Mar. 15, 1865; s. Delavan Levant and Mary Louise (Raymond) L.; A.B., Oberlin, 1889, A.M., 1895; Ph.D., Johns Hopkins, 1898; m. Katherine Gue, Oct. 8, 1901. Spl. asst. Ia. Geol. Survey, 1893-97; prof. geology and related science, Western Coll., Toledo, Ia., 1894-96; asst. state geologist, Ia. Geol. Survey, 1896-97, 1900-03; asst. prof. geology, Mo. State U., 1899-1900; state geologist of N.D., and prof. geology, U. of N.D., 1903—. Asst., U.S. Geol. Survey, 1905-07. Home: Grand Forks, N.D. Died Dec. 17, 1932.

LEONARD, Charles Hall, theologian; b. at Northwood, N.H., Sept. 16, 1822; s. Lemuel and Cynthia (Claggett) L.; ed. Haverhill (Mass.) Acad., Atkinson (N.H.) Acad., Bradford Sem.; grad. Theol. Sch., Clinton, N.Y., 1848; hon. A.M., 1869, LL.D., 1905, Tufts; D.D., St. Lawrence, 1871; m. Phœbe Ann Bassett, 1846 (died 1872). Ordained Universalist ministry, 1848; minister Ch. of the Redeemer, Chelsea, Mass., 1848-71; Goddard prof. homiletics and pastoral theology, 1869, and dean Div. School, 1884, Tufts College (Mass.). Author: Book of Prayer for Church and Home, 1865; Steps in the Religious Life, 1868. Died 1918.

LEONARD, Charles Henri, physician; b. Akron, O., Mar. 28, 1850; s. Charles H. and Ann S. (Gary) L.; A.B., Union Coll., 1872, A.M., 1882; M.D., U. of Wooster, 1874; post-grad. studies, New York; m. Cornelia S. Williams, June 5, 1872; m. 2d, Mrs. Helen (Blakeslee) Mann, Aug. 8, 1918. Prof. med. and surg. diseases women and clin. gynæcology, Detroit Coll. of Medicine, 1880-1910; later emeritus prof. Editor Leonard's Illustrated Medical Journal, nearly 30 yrs.; syndicate writer scientific subjects for papers and mags.; spl. writer, Free Press and Jour. Mem. Detroit Pub. Library Commn., 1896-1901 (pres. 1901). Republican. Author (and publisher): Reference and Dose Book, 1875; Pocket Anatomist, 1876; Manual of Bandaging, 1876; The Hair and Its Diseases, 1879; Materia Medica and Therapeutics, 1891; Physician's Account Books (series of 5); Over 1,000 Prescriptions, 1892. Home: Detroit, Mich. Died July 31, 1925.

LEONARD, Delavan Levant, clergyman; b. Pendleton, N.Y., July 20, 1834; s. Thomas and Betsey (Peck) L.; A.B., Hamilton Coll., —1859; Union Theol. Sem., 1859-63; D.D., Carleton Coll., 1895; m. Mary Louise Raymond, May 6, 1864; children—Arthur Gray, Fred Eugene. Ordained Congl. ministry, 1863; pastor New Preston, Conn., 1863-65, Darlington, Wis., 1865-70, Normal, Ill., 1870-74, Hannibal, Mo., 1874-75, Northfield, Minn., 1875-81; supt. home missions, Utah, Ida., Mont., etc., 1881-87; pastor Bellevue, O., 1888-92; asso. editor Missionary Review of the World, 1893—. Republican. Author: The Story of Oberlin, 1895; A Hundred

Years of Missions, 1895, revised, 1903; Missionary Annals of the Nineteenth Century, 1899; History of Carleton College, 1904. Died Jan. 26, 1917.

LEONARD, Fred Eugene, educator; b. Darlington, Wis., June 2, 1866; s. Delavan Levant and Mary Louise (Raymond) L.; A.B., Oberlin Coll., 1889, A.M., 1892; M.D., Coll. Phys. and Surg. (Columbia), 1892; student summer schs. phys. training, Springfield, Mass., 1888, Chautauqua, 1892, Baron Posse, 1893, Harvard, 1894, 98; student of physical training in Europe, 1900-01 and 1913; hon. grad. Sargent Normal Sch. Phys. Edn., 1907; m. Bertha M. Hopkins, June 27, 1908. Dir. men's gymnasium and prof. hygiene and physical edn., Oberlin Coll., 1892—. Spl. lecturer, Harvard Summer Sch., 1899, 1902, 1908-19, Columbia, summer, 1907; spl. instr. Chicago Inst. and Training Sch. of Y.M.C.A., 1903, 05, 07, 09. Author: Pioneers of Modern Physical Training, 1915. Home: Oberlin, O. Died Dec. 10, 1922.

LEONARD, Jane Elizabeth ("Aunt Jane"), educator; b. nr. Clearfield, Pa., Dec. 27, 1840; d. Robert and Lydia (Wilson) L.; ed. acad., Clearfield, and 1st Pa. State Normal Sch., Millersville; hon. B.S., Indiana Normal Sch. of Pa., 1893; M.A., of Pittsburgh, 1916. Began as teacher pub. schs., Clearfield County, Pa., 1856; teacher 1st Pa. State Normal Sch., 1861-75; preceptress and prof. English lit., Indiana Normal Sch. of Pa., 1875—; for many yrs. speaker at teachers' institutes throughout Pa. Methodist. Home: Indiana, Pa. Died Apr. 6, 1924.

LEONARD, Joel Marvin, clergyman; b. Potsdam, N.Y., July 21, 1852; s. Hiram and Mary Greeley (Butler) L.; A.B., Harvard U., 1874; S.T.B., Boston U., 1877, Ph.D., 1887; U. of Leipzig, 1879-81; D.D., Wesleyan, 1902; m. Ada J. West, 1877; m. 2d, Mary True Mason, Sept. 13, 1883. Ordained M.E. ministry, 1877; pastor, Nashua, Ia., 1877, Anamosa, Ia., 1878-79, Winchester, Mass., 1882-83, Newton, 1884-85, Westfield, 1886-88, Wesley Ch., Salem, 1889-91, Centre Ch., Malden, 1892-95, Melrose, 1896-1900, Baker Memorial Ch., Boston, 1901-02; supt. Lynn dist. (62 chs.), 1903-08; supt. Boston Missionary and Ch. Extension Soc., 1910-13; also asso. pastor Bromfield-Tremont Circuit, Boston, 1912-13; field agt. for retired ministers of N.E. Conf., 1914-15. Trustee Sch. of Expression (Boston), Boston U.; treas. trustees and stewards N.E. Conf. Home: Melrose, Mass. Died Aug. 7, 1916.

LEONARD, John Walter, oil producer; b. N.Y. City, Nov. 17, 1868; s. James Corrigan and Mary Agnes (Coyne) L.; ed. parochial and pub. schs., Titusville, Pa.; m. Caroline McCollum, June 2, 1894; children—Francis Donnelly, James Dennis, John Walter, Jr. Early oil operator in S.W.Pa., W.Va., Ohio, Ky., Ill., Okla., Tex. and Can.; a pioneer operator in Mexico, 1908-14, drilling first oil wells on the Panuco, Tamesi and Tuxpam rivers; an incorporator Mexico Fuel Oil Co. and Penn-Mexico Fuel Oil Co.; an organizer Tropical Oil Co. (later owned by Internat. Petroleum Co., Ltd.); drilled the first producing oil well in Republic of Colombia, 1917-18; pres. Leonard Petroleum Co., Leonard Oil & Gas Co., Leonard Oil Development Co.; dir. Stellar Refining Co., Citizens Nat. Bank (Washington, Pa.). Mem. bd. dirs. Washington (Pa.) Hosp. Republican. Catholic. Elk. Home: Washington, Pa. Died Jan. 25, 1938.

LEONARD, Jonah Fitz Randolph, farmer; b. nr. Waynesburg, Pa., Dec. 10, 1832; s. John and Hannah (Reinhart) L.; ed. common schs. Greene County, Pa.; grad. Chautauqua Lit. and Scientific Circle; m. Margaret A. Sands, Mar. 22, 1870 (died 1911). Went to Kan., 1856; enlisted under Jim Lane in the Kansas war for free state; was in numerous skirmishes; lived Chase County, Kan., 6 yrs.; was co. surveyor, co. supt. schs. and justice of peace; went to Bureau Co., Ill., enlisted Co. C, 93d Ill. Vols., in Civil War; mustered out, 1865; slightly wounded at Vicksburg. Went to Ainsworth, Ia.; mem. M.E. Ch.; was 1st abolitionist, then Republican, Prohibitionist, then United Christian party, which he helped to organize at Davenport, Ia., 1898; was candidate lt. gov., Ia., 1899; nominee for President, United Christian Party, 1900; mem. Nat. Com. same. Home: Stratford, Tex. Deceased.

LEONARD, Joseph Alexander, consul; b. Cambridge, Md., Dec. 24, 1830; s. Rev. William and Harriet (Laverty) L.; M.D., Phila. Med. Coll., 1851; studied law, and admitted to bar, 1858; m. Kate Cowles, Oct. 30, 1861. Practiced medicine in Mich. and Wis., 1852-54; editor Whitewater (Wis.) Gazette, 1854-56, Waukesha (Wis.) Republic, 1857; practiced law, Rochester, Minnesota, 1858-64; postmaster Rochester, 1861-64; captain commissary 1st div. 16th corps; part owner and later owner and editor Rochester (Minn.) Post till 1899; state senator, 1869-70; register U.S. Land Office at Jackson and Worthington, Minn., 1874-75; U.S. consul at Edinburgh, 1881-83; consul-gen. at Calcutta, 1884, at Shanghai, 1889-93; judge of probate, 1897-1903. Comdr. Custer Post, G.A.R., 3 terms; insp. state dept. G.A.R., 1 term; judge advocate same, 1 term. Pres. Minn. Editorial Assn., 1868-69, Minn. Rep. Press Assn., 1896-97. Home: Rochester, Minn. Deceased.

LEONARD, Mary Hall, teacher, author; b. Bridgewater, Mass., Dec. 4, 1847; d. James Madison and Jane N. (Thompson) L.; grad. Bridgewater (Mass.) Normal Sch., 1867; studied in Germany, 1874, U. of Chicago, 1903, various summer schs. Teacher, high sch., Longmeadow, Mass., 1867-68, Bridgewater Normal Sch., to 1885; prin. Winthrop Training Sch. for Teachers, Columbia, S.C., 1886-91; instr. Winthrop Normal Coll. for Teachers, S.C., 1892-94; instr. insts. and summer schs. various times to 1909. Conglist. Author: Story of Portus and Songs of the Southland, 1894; A Code of Honor, 1897; A Discovered Country, 1900; My Lady of the Searchlight, 1905; Mattapoisett and Old Rochester (with others), 1907; Grammar and Its Reasons, 1907; When Youth Met Life, 1911; The Days of the Swamp Angel, 1914. Home: Rochester, Mass. Died Nov. 1921.

LEONARD, Robert Josselyn, educator; b. San Jose, Calif., Feb. 5, 1885; s. Joseph Howland and Ella Isabelle (Clark) L.; grad. State Normal Sch., San Jose, Calif., 1904; B.S., Columbia, 1912, A.M., 1914, Ph.D., 1922; m. Eugenie Ann Andruss, Aug. 13, 1913; children—Eugenie Andruss, Robert Josselyn. Teacher and supervisor elementary and secondary schs., 1904-10; prof. vocational edn., Ind. U., 1914-17; spl. investigator N.Y. Factory Investigation Commn., 1914-15; mem. Ind. Survey Commn., 1916-17; spl. agt. Federal Bd. for Vocational Edn., 1917-18; prof. edn., U. of Calif., 1918-23, also univ. rep. in charge ednl. relations, 1921-23, and acting dean Sch. of Edn., 1922-23; dir. Sch. of Edn. and prof. edn., Teachers Coll. (Columbia), 1923—. Mem. bd. dirs. Nat. Jr. Personnel Service, also of Child Study Assn. of America. Mem. Christian (Disciples) Church. Author: An Investigation of the Paper Box Industry to Determine the Possibility of Vocational Training, 1915; A Study of the People of Indiana and their Occupations, 1915; Some Facts Concerning the People, Industries and Schools of Hammond, Ind., 1915; Vocational Education Survey of Richmond, Indiana, 1916; An Introductory Course on Part-time Education (with others), 1920; Data Sheets for Teachers' Course on Part-time Education, 1920; The Coordination of State Institutions for Higher Education Through Supplementary Curricula Boards, 1923. Dir. surveys of colleges and univs.; lecturer. Home: New York, N.Y. Died Feb. 9, 1929.

LEONARD, Sterling Andrus, author; b. National City, Calif., Apr. 23, 1888; s. Cyreno N. and Eva (Andrus) L.; student Simpson Coll., Indianola, Ia., 1904-07; A.B., U. of Mich., 1908, A.M., 1909; Ph.D., Columbia, 1928; m. Minnetta F. Sammis, Dec. 27, 1913; 1 dau., Barbara Dorrit. Began teaching at U. of Mich., 1908, asst. prof. English, U. of Wis., 1920-25, asso. prof., 1925—. Author: English Composition as a Social Problem, 1917; Essential Principles of Teaching Reading and Literature, 1922; General Language (with Riah Fagan Cox), 1925; The Doctrine of Correctness in English usage (1700-1800), 1928. Editor: Poems of the War and the Peace, 1920; Atlantic Book of Modern Plays, 1922. Made scales of translations from Latin for Classical Investigating Com. Home: Madison, Wis. Died May 15, 1931.

LEONARD, William Andrew, bishop; b. Southport, Conn., July 15, 1848; s. William Boardman and Louisa (Bulkley) L.; ed. Phillips Academy, Andover, Mass.; St. Stephen's Coll., Annandale, N.Y.; grad. Berkeley Div. Sch., Middletown, Conn., 1871; D.D., St. Stephen's Coll., 1870, Washington and Lee U., 1885; LL.D., Kenyon Coll., Gambier, O., 1919; m. Sarah L. Sullivan, Apr. 17, 1873. Deacon, 1871, priest, 1873, P.E. Ch.; asst. Holy Trinity, Brooklyn, 1871-72; rector Ch. of the Redeemer, Brooklyn, 1872-80, St. John's, Washington, 1880-89; consecrated bishop of Ohio, 1889. Chaplain 23d Regt. N.G.S.N.Y., 1876-80, Ohio Soc. of New York, 1889. Mem. Soc. Colonial Wars (chaplain gen.). Author: Via Sacra, or Footprints of Christ, 1875; History of the Christian Church, 1878; A Faithful Life, 1888; New York Church Club Lectures, 1893; Bedell Lectures, "Witness of American Church to Christianity," 1894; Biography of Stephen Bank Leonard, 1909. Died Sept. 21, 1930.

LESEMANN, Louis Frederick William; b. Hoyleton, Ill., Apr. 1, 1869; s. Frederick and Mathilda (Poehler) L.; A.B., Central Wesleyan Coll., Warrenton, Mo., 1892, A.M., 1894, D.D., 1906; S.T.B., Garrett Bibl. Inst., 1897, D.D., 1925; studied Northwestern U., 1898-99; married; children—Maurice T., Wilbur F.; m. 2d, Olive B. Horne, 1933; Ordained Methodist Episcopal ministry, 1896; pastor St. Charles, Mo., 1892-93, Rock Island, Ill., 1893-94, Dolton, Ill., 1895-97, Clyde, 1897-98, South Englewood, 1898-1900, Morgan Park, 1900-04, Trinity Ch., Chicago, 1904-09, La Grange, 1909-12; dist. supt. Chicago Northwestern Dist., 1912-17; pres. Chicago Training Sch. (for city, home and foreign missions), 1917, until affiliated with Garrett Biblical Inst., Evanston, Ill., 1934, then became dir. and prof. Author of Official Membership Manual of M.E. Church, 1914. Died Apr. 22, 1941.

LESH, John Andrew, univ. prof.; b. Snydersville, Pa., Sept. 24, 1879; s. Stogdell Stockes and Mary Elizabeth (Fabel) L.; Ph.B., Taylor U., Ind., 1906; B.D., Drew Theol. Sem., 1908; A.M., U. of Pa., 1909; Ph.D., New York U., 1915; summer sessions Harvard and Columbia; m. Ora Frances Nabring, Sept. 19, 1906; 1 son, Richard Olover (dec.). Head dept. of edn., Ind. State Normal Sch., 1909-11; head dept. history and economics, State Teachers' Coll., Maryville, Mo., 1911-14; head dept. of edn., N.C. State Coll. for Women, Greensboro, N.C., 1915-18; head dept. polit. and social science, 1918-22, head dept. of Am. history and economics, 1922—, Temple U. Methodist. Mason. Home: Philadelphia, Pa. Died Aug. 6, 1939.

LESHER, John V., congressman; b. Union Co., Pa., July 27, 1866; s. Robert and Sarah (Vandling) L.; Bloomsburg State Normal Sch.; B.S., Bucknell U., Lewisburg, Pa., 1897; unmarried. Read law with Hon. Simon P. Wolverton; admitted to Pa. bar, 1900, to Supreme Ct. of Pa., 1903; mem. 63d to 66th Congresses (1913-21), 16th Pa. Dist. Democrat. Presbyn. Home: Sunbury, Pa. Died May 3, 1932.

LESLEY, J Peter ("J" is mere signature), geologist; b. Phila., Sept. 17, 1819; grad. U. of Pa., 1838, LL.D., from same; asst. geol. survey of Pa., 1838-41; studied at Princeton Theol. Sem., 1841-44; licensed to preach by Presbytery of Phila., 1844; studied at U. of Halle following winter; employed by Am. Tract Soc., 1845-47; pastor Congl. Ch., Milton, Mass., 1848-51. His theol. views changing, left pulpit; settled in Phila. as professional expert in geology; sec. Am. Iron Assn., 1855-59; prof. geology and mining and dean scientific faculty U. of Pa., 1872-78; became emeritus prof., 1886; chief geologist in charge of complete resurvey of Pa., begun, 1874; made extensive researches in coal, oil and iron fields in U.S. and Can. Original mem. Nat. Acad. Sciences; sec. and librarian, 1858-85, Am. Philos. Soc.; pres. A.A.A.S., 1883-85; U.S. commissioner to Paris Expn., 1867; m. Susan Inches, d. Hon. Joseph Lyman, Feb. 13, 1849. Author: Man's Origin and Destiny from the Platform of Sciences; Coal and Its Topography; The Iron Manufacturer's Guide; Paul Dreifuss, His Holiday Abroad. Home: Milton, Mass. Died 1903.

LESLEY, Robert Whitman, mfr.; b. Phila., Pa., July 4, 1853; s. James, Jr., and Elizabeth (Thomson) L.; matriculated U. of Pa., 1867; A.M., 1908, as of class of 1871; studied law in office of Benjamin Harris Brewster; m. Eulalia Willcox, 1879. Began with Phila. Ledger, 1868, later asst. editor; admitted to bar (Pa.), 1879. Founded cement firm of Lesley & Trinkle, Phila., 1874, and in early 80's took out a number of patents in connection with mfr. of Portland Cement, which up to that time had been largely imported from Europe; at this period while associated with the late David O. Sayler, of Allentown, Pa., performed an important part in commercial development and introduction of Am. Portland Cement; in recognition of his work was made first pres. Portland Cement Assn., later first hon. member; established Am. Cement Co., a large producer, and later operated as Giant Portland Cement Co., of which was dir.; also dir. Surface Combustion Co., Philadelphia & Camden Ferry Co. Was mem. of concrete ship com. of American Concrete Institute; active in testing and developing new inventions in field of aviation in connection with the Clarke Thomson Research; an organizer Phila. War Chest. Hon. mem. Am. Soc. for Testing Materials, American Concrete Institute; presiding officer cement sect. Internat. Congress of Assn. for Testing Materials, N.Y., 1912. Mem. Franklin Inst. (bd. managers). Republican. Co-author: (with J. B. Lober and G. S. Bartlett) History of Portland Cement Industry in the United States, 1924. Home: Haverford, Pa. Died Nov. 10, 1935.

LESLEY, Susan Inches; b. Northampton, Mass., d. Judge Joseph Lyman; m. Prof. J. Peter L., Feb. 13, 1849; was long actively identified with work of organized charities in Phila. Author: Memoirs of Mrs. Annie J. Lyman (2d edition entitled "Recollections of My Mother"). Home: Milton, Mass. Deceased.

LESLIE, Mrs. Frank (Baroness de Bazus), editor, publisher; b. (Miriam Florence Folline) New Orleans, 1851, of noble French Huguenot family, from whom, when she retired from the pub. business, she took her title of the Baroness de Bazus; m. Frank Leslie, publisher (died 1880). Succeeded to his business, personally managed it and put it on a paying basis. Leased her business to a syndicate and made extended European tour. On her return, syndicate having been unsuccessful, business was put into company, she being pres. and editor of the Popular Monthly, which increased 200,000 copies in 4 months under her management; mag. was subsequently sold and appeared under a new name. Home: New York, N.Y. Died Sept. 18, 1914.

LESLIE, Harry Guyer, gov.; b. Lafayette, Ind., Apr. 6, 1878; s. Daniel and Mary (Burkhardt) L.; B.S., Purdue University, 1905, LL.D., 1932; LL.B., Indiana Law Sch., 1907; m. Martha Morgan, Aug. 16, 1910; children—John Morgan, Richard Foster, Robert Warner. Practiced law, 1907-12; treas. Tippecanoe County, Ind., 1913-17; farmer, 1918-24; v.p. Battle-ground State Bank; mem. Ind. Ho. of Rep., 1923-27 (speaker of House, 1925-27); apptd. div. chief of Income Tax Dept., U.S., 1924; gov. of Ind., term 1929-33. Pres. Standard Life Ins. of Ind. Exec. sec. Purdue Alumni Assn., 1924-28. Mason, Odd Fellow. Republican. Methodist. Home: Indianapolis, Ind. Died Dec. 10, 1937.

LESLIE, John Douglass, church official; b. Statesville, N.C., June 1, 1860; s. Thomas Boston and Jane Melissa (Murdoch) L.; grad. Southwestern Presbyn. U., Clarksville, Tenn. (now Memphis), 1880; grad. Union Theol. Sem., Hampden-Sidney, Va. (now Richmond), 1883; D.D., Austin Coll., Sherman, Tex., 1912, LL.D., 1923; m. Gertrude Mattison, 1885 (died 1896); children—Mattison Douglass, Mrs. Gertrude Mattison Bell (dec.); m. 2d, Alma Le Grand, 1899 (died 1909); children—John Le Grand, Bonnie Louise, Francis Claude; m. 3d, Ella Ragland, 1913. Ordained ministry Presbyn. Ch. U.S., 1883; pastor in Miss. and Tex. until 1921; stated clk. and treas. Presbytery of North Miss., 1886-94, Presbytery of Ft. Worth, Tex., 1895-99, 1911-16, Synod of Tex., 1904-22; permanent clk. Gen. Assembly Presbyn. Ch. U.S., 1910-22, stated clk. and treas., 1922—, also mgr. Bur. of Vacancy and Supply, 1924—. Pres. bd. trustees Daniel Baker Coll., 1904-15. Democrat. Author: The Second Coming of Christ, 1904; Ready Reference Manual for Church Officers and Courts, 1924; Presbyterian Law and Procedure, 1930. Home: Dallas, Tex. Died June 11, 1935.

LESLIE, Preston Hopkins, lawyer, gov.; b. Wayne (now Clinton) County, Ky., March 2, 1819; ed. in neighborhood schools until 1837; 5 months in County Acad., Columbia, Ky.; admitted to bar, Oct. 7, 1840; 2 terms in lower house and 2 terms (8 yrs.) Ky. senate; was speaker of senate; gov. Ky., 1871-75; circuit judge, 1881-86; active mem. Bapt. Ch. from Sept. 1838; gov. Mont. Ty., 1887-89; established law practice at Helena, Mont.; U.S. atty., dist. of Mont., 1894-98. Home: Helena, Mont. Died 1907.

LESTER, Charles Smith, lawyer; b. in Worcester, Mass., March 15, 1824; ed. Washington Acad., Salem, N.Y., A.M., Yale; admitted to N.Y. bar May 1845; m. Lucy Louisa Cooke, Sept. 1849. Was pres. of village of Saratoga Springs; county judge and dist. atty., Saratoga County, and associated with his sons, Charles C. Willard and Col. James W. Lester, in active practice at Saratoga Springs, N.Y. Died 1903.

LESTER, E. F., lawyer; b. Lebanon, Tenn., Aug. 7, 1871; s. Preston S. and Elizabeth (Crutchfield) L.; ed. pub. schs., Nashville, Tenn.; m. Buelah Collier, Apr. 29, 1902; children—Thelman, Doris, Virginia, Fay, Carolynn. Admitted to bar, 1897, and began practice at Whitefield, Indian Ty.; dist. judge 5th dist., Okla., 1918-24; became justice Supreme Court of Okla., 1924, term ending 1933, vice chief justice, 1929-30, chief justice, 1931-32; later in gen. practice of law. Democrat. Mem. Disciples of Christ. Mason, Odd Fellow. Home: Oklahoma City, Okla. Deceased.

LESTER, James Westcott, lawyer, soldier; b. Saratoga Springs, N.Y., Sept. 8, 1859; s. Charles S. and Lucy L. (Cooke) L.; A.B., Union Coll., 1881, L.H.D., same, 1931; law dept. Columbia, 1880-81; m. Bertha N. Dowd, June 13, 1888; children—James Dowd, Charles W., Dudley Gove, Ralph Westcott. Enlisted as pvt. 22d Separate Co., N.G., Nov. 25, 1884; promoted through grades to brig. gen., June 6, 1911; bvt. maj. gen., Jan. 7, 1913. Served as maj. 2d Regt. N.Y. Vols., Spanish-Am. War, May 9-Nov. 25, 1898; in U.S. service as brig. gen. on Mexican border, June 18, 1916-Mar. 7, 1917; also in service, July 18-Aug. 5, 1917; brig. gen. N.A., Aug. 5, 1917; apptd. comdr. 54th Inf. Brigade, Camp Wadsworth, S.C., Sept. 30, 1917; hon. discharged for physical disability, as brig. gen. N.A., Apr. 6, 1918; assigned to duty as brig. gen. N.Y.N.G., Apr. 30, 1919; apptd. comdg. gen. N.Y.N.G., Dec. 17, 1921; resigned and granted hon. discharge, May 28, 1923; then engaged in law practice. Republican. Presbyn. Elk. Home: Saratoga Springs, N.Y. Died Nov. 13, 1932.

LESTER, Rufus E., congressman, lawyer; b. Burke County, Ga., Dec. 12, 1837; s. Ezekiel and Mary (Lewis) L.; grad. Mercer Univ., Ga., 1857; admitted to bar, 1859; served in C.S. army, 1861-65; resumed law practice after war; State senator, 1870-79; pres. State senate, 1876-79; mayor Savannah, 1883-89; mem. Congress, 1889-1907, 1st Ga. dist. Democrat. Home: Savannah, Ga. Died 1906.

LETCHER, John Talbert; b. Shorter, Ala., Dec. 2, 1881; s. Francis Marion and Claudia Caroline (Howard) L.; B.S., Ala. Poly. Inst., Auburn, 1901, M.S., 1902; m. Lillian McCord, Sept. 7, 1911. Admitted to Ala. bar, 1903; practiced in Montgomery; v.p. Montgomery Savings Bank. Alderman, 1909-11; commr. accounts and finances, City of Montgomery, May 1911—. Democrat. Baptist. Mason, K.P., Red Man. Home: Montgomery, Ala. Deceased.

LETCHWORTH, William Pryor, philanthropist, author; b. Brownville, N.Y., May 26, 1823; s. Josiah and Ann L. Mfr. and mcht., Buffalo, N.Y., 1848-69; retired from business, 1869; devoted entire time to charitable work. Mem. State Bd. of Charities, 1873-96 (v.p. 1874-78, pres. 1878-88); pres. Nat.

Conf. of Charities, Oct. 1884; pres. 1st N.Y. State Conf. of Charities and Correction, Nov. 1900; LL.D., U. of N.Y., 1893, "for distinguished services to the state." Secured passage of N.Y. law providing for removal of children from almshouses and other pauper establishments; also devoted much attention to the care of the insane and epileptics, and other reforms; elected pres. Nat. Assn. for the Study of Epilepsy and the Care and Treatment of Epileptics, 1898. In Dec. 1906, gave to the state of N.Y. 1,000 acres of park, including within its boundaries the upper, middle and lower falls of the upper Genesee River, which was accepted by the state, Jan. 1907, on the condition that it should be forever maintained as a public park. Author: The Insane in Foreign Countries, 1889; Care and Treatment of Epileptics, 1900. Home: Glen Iris, Castile, N.Y. Died 1910.

LETTON, Charles Blair, judge; b. Edinburgh, Scotland, Oct. 25, 1853; s. William H. and Agnes (Michie) L.; early edn., Edinburgh and Glasgow; grad. Neb. State Normal Sch., 1879; m. Althera H. Pike, Sept. 2, 1885; children—Henry Pike, William Adam. Admitted to Neb. bar, 1881; mem. firm Letton & Hinshaw, 1888-95; pros. atty., 1886-90; judge 1st Jud. Dist. Neb., 1895-1903; commr. Supreme Court of Neb., 1903-05; asso. justice Supreme Court of Neb., 1905-25; state librarian and clk. Supreme Court of Neb., 1927. Republican. Charter mem. Am. Inst. Law, 1923. Del. Universal Congress Lawyers and Jurists, St. Louis, 1904. Home: Lincoln, Neb. Deceased.

LETTS, Arthur, merchant; b. Holmby, Eng., June 17, 1862; s. Richard and Caroline (Coleman) L.; ed. grammar sch. and under pvt. tutor; m. Florence Philp, Aug. 26, 1886. Came to America, 1883; settled at Los Angeles, Calif., 1896, and established the Broadway Dept. Store, of which was head. Pres. Los Angeles Y.M.C.A.; v.p. Boy Scouts America; trustee State Normal Coll. Mason. Home: Hollywood, Calif. Died May 18, 1923.

LEUPP, Francis Ellington, author; b. New York, Jan. 2, 1849; s. John P. and Emeline M. (Loop) L.; A.B., Williams, 1870, A.M., 1873; LL.B., Columbia U., 1872; LL.D., Williams Coll., 1910; m. Ada Lewis Murdock, Oct. 13, 1874. Asst. editor New York Evening Post, 1874; editor and part owner Syracuse Herald, 1878-85; Washington staff contbr. New York Evening Post, 1885; in charge Washington bur., New York Evening Post, 1889-1904; editor Good Government, official organ Nat. Civil Service Reform League, 1892-95; mem. U.S. Bd. of Indian Commrs., 1895-97; U.S. Commr. Indian Affairs, 1905-09. Author: How to Prepare for a Civil Service Examination, 1898; The Man Roosevelt, 1904; The Indian and His Problem, 1910; Biography of William H. Taft, for Scribner's The Presidents of the United States, 1914; In Red Man's Land, 1914; A Day With Father, 1914; Walks About Washington, 1915. Editor: Memorial volume to William Cullen Bryant, 1878. Home: Tyringham, Mass.; and Washington, D.C. Died Nov. 16, 1918.

LEUTZE, Eugene Henry Cozzens, naval officer; b. Düsseldorf, Prussia, Nov. 16, 1847; s. Emanuel and Julia L.; apptd. to U.S. Naval Acad. by President Lincoln from D.C., 1863, grad. 1867; m. Julia Jarvis McAlpine, Mar. 1873; children—Mary Eugenia (dec.), Trevon Wm., Marion Alice (wife of J. G. Rowcliff, U.S.N.). Promoted ensign, Dec. 18, 1868; master, Mar. 21, 1870; lt., Mar. 21, 1871; lt. comdr., Mar. 26, 1889; comdr., Jan. 5, 1897; capt., Oct. 9, 1901; rear admiral, July 6, 1907. On various ocean survey expdns.; comd. Michigan, 1896-97. Alert, 1897-98, Monterey, May 1898-Dec. 1899, and participated in taking city of Manila; commandant Navy Yard, Cavite, P.I., 1898-1900; supt. naval gun factory, Washington, 1900-02; comd. Maine, 1902-04; mem. Bd. Inspection and Survey, 1904-05; commandant Navy Yard, Washington, and supt. naval gun factory, 1905-10; retired by operation of law, Nov. 16, 1909, but continued on active duty; commandant Navy Yard and Sta., New York, 1910. Died Sept. 15, 1931.

LEVENE, Phoebus Aaron (Theodore), chemist; b. Sagor, Russia, Feb. 25, 1869; s. of Solom and Etta (Brick) L.; M.D., Imperial Military Medical Acad., St. Petersburg, Russia, 1891; special student univs. of Berne, Marburg, Berlin, Munich and Columbia; m. Anna M. Erickson, June 9, 1920. Came to U.S., 1892; asso. in chemistry, State Pathol. Inst., New York, 1896-1905; chemist Saranac Lab. for Study of Tuberculosis, Saranac Lake, N.Y., 1900-02; Herter lecturer in pathol. chemistry, New York U., 1905-06; asst. in chemistry, 1905, mem., 1907-39, member emeritus, 1939—, Rockefeller Institute. Awarded Willard Gibbs medal, Chicago sect. Am. Chem. Soc., 1931; William H. Nichols medal, N.Y. sect. Am. Chem. Soc., 1938. Author of papers on proteins, nucleins, carbohydrates, lipoids, problems of stereo-chemistry, and of monographs, "Hexosamines and Mucoproteins," 1925, "Nucleic Acids," 1931. Home: New York, N.Y. Died Sept. 6, 1940.

LEVENTRITT, David, judge; b. Winnsboro, S.C., Jan. 31, 1845; s. George M. and Betty (Goldberg) L.; A.B., New York Free Acad. (now Coll. City of New York), 1864; LL.B., New York U., 1872; m.

Matilda Lithauer, June 9, 1868. Practiced law, New York, 1872-98; spl. counsel for N.Y. City in important cases; justice Supreme Ct. of N.Y., 1st Dist., 1898-1908; resigned to resume law practice. Democrat. Home: New York, N.Y. Died Jan. 9, 1926.

LEVEQUE, Joseph Mark, journalist; b. Natchitoches, La., Aug. 26, 1868; prep. edn. Collegiate Inst., Baton Rouge, La.; grad. in schs. of English, Latin and Greek, Vanderbilt Univ.; taught in Hubbard Coll., Overton, Tex. Entered newspaper work on Evening Mail, Fort Worth, Tex.; later city editor Fort Worth Gazette and Waco Day; afterward on local staffs New York World, and Morning Advertiser; returned to Fort Worth Gazette, thence to New Orleans, serving 5 yrs. on the Picayune, and 2 yrs. on Times-Democrat. Founded, June 28, 1899, and editor and owner of Harlequin, weekly jour. of comment and opinion. Author: The Swimming Girl, comic opera, produced 1902; King Capital, comic opera (music of both by Henry Wehrmann). Organizing The Morning World, 1907. Home: New Orleans, La. Died 1911.

LEVER, Asbury Francis, congressman; b. Spring Hill, S.C., Jan. 5, 1875; s. Asbury Washington and Elvira (Derrick) L.; A.B., Newberry Coll., 1895; LL.B., Georgetown U., 1899; LL.D., U. of Md., 1920, Newberry Coll., 1937, D.Sc., Clemson Coll., 1937; m. Lucile Scurry Butler, July 5, 1911; children—Mary Catherine, Asbury Francis. Delegate Dem. state conventions, 1896-1900; South Carolina Ho. of Rep., 1900-01 (resigned); elected to 57th Congress for unexpired term (1901-03) of J. William Stokes, deceased; reëlected 58th to 66th Congresses (1903-21), 7th S.C. Dist.; resigned, 1919; mem. Farm Loan Bd., 1919-22; became pres. First Carolinas Joint Stock Land Bank, Columbia, 1922; later field representative of Federal Farm Board; dir. pub. relations Farm Credit Adminstrn., Columbia, S.C. While in Congress was author of Cotton Futures Act, Agrl. Extension Act, Federal Warehouse Act, Act creating Bur. of Markets, Lever Fuel and Food Control Act. Home: Columbia, S.C. Died Apr. 28, 1940.

LEVERE, William C., coll. fraternity executive; b. New Haven, Conn., Oct. 10, 1872; s. Charles F. and Mary (Collin) L.; ed. Northwestern U.; not married. Editor Evanston Index, 1901-05; treas. Evanston, Ill., 1901-03; mem. Ill. Gen. Assembly, 1907-09. Eminent supreme archon of Sigma Alpha Epsilon Fraternity, 1902-06, hon. eminent supreme archon, 1909-10, eminent supreme recorder, 1912—. Pres. Soc. for Erection of Evanston Hist. Tablets; pres. Evanston Hist. Soc. Mason. Author: Imperial America, 1898; 'Twixt Greek and Barb, 1900; The Evanston Poets, 1903; (play) Sharper than a Serpent's Tooth; The Original Minutes, 1904; The Songs of Sigma Alpha Epsilon, 1907; The History of the Sigma Alpha Epsilon Fraternity, 3 vols., 1911; Vivian of Mackinac, 1911; Who's Who in Sigma Alpha Epsilon, 1912; The Directory of Sigma Alpha Epsilon, 1912; Leading Greeks, 1915; Songs of Purple and Gold, 1915; A Paragraph History of Sigma Alpha Epsilon, 1916; My Hut, 1919; A Travel Brochure, 1922. Editor in chief of the Greek Quarterly. Y.M.C.A. sec. in France with A.E.F., Sept. 1917-May 1919; served in Neufchâteau, on the Soissons, Toul and Baccaret fronts, in Germany with the Army of Occupation at Andernach on the Rhine. Medal and Officier d'Académie, France, for services during the war. Home: Evanston, Ill. Died Feb. 22, 1927.

LEVERETT, George Vasmer, lawyer; b. Charlestown, Mass., 1846; s. Daniel and Charlotte (Betteley) L.; A.B., Harvard, 1867, A.M., 1870, LL.B., 1869; m. Mary E. L. Tebbetts, Apr. 3, 1888 (dec.). Practicing lawyer and trustee at Boston, 1871—; associated in practice with Prof. James B. Thayer, of Harvard Law Sch. till his death, 1902; with Am. Bell Telephone Co. and Am. Telephone & Telegraph Co., 1886—, first as official atty., later as gen. counsel and consulting counsel; dir. Conveyancers Title Ins. Co., State St. Trust Co., and other cos. Home: Boston, Mass. Died Oct. 18, 1917.

LEVERING, Albert, illustrator; b. Hope, Ind., 1869; s. Levi Lemuel and Sarah Martha (Youngling) L.; ed. Columbus (Ind.) High Sch.; studied architecture with father, and drawing in Munich; m. Frances Jewell, May 31, 1905. Practiced architecture 8 yrs.; was connected with Minneapolis Times, Chicago Tribune and New York American; on staff of Puck, Life, Harper's Weekly; mem. staff New York Sunday Tribune; illustrator of many humorous books. Home: New York, N.Y. Died Apr. 14, 1929.

LEVERING, Eugene, banker; b. Baltimore, Md., Sept. 12, 1845; s. Eugene and Ann S. (Walker) L.; ed. U. of Md. to 1861; m. Mary E. Armstrong, Jan. 23, 1868 (died 1915); children—Eugene (dec.), Mary A. (wife of Rev. Joseph H. Robinson), Ethel (Mrs. James M. Motley); m. 2d, Harriet S., d. late Frank M. Ellis, 1918. Entered mercantile business July 1861; became mem. firm of E. Levering & Co., sugar and coffee importers, 1866, sr. partner, 1870; organizer, 1886, and sr. partner, firm of Levering & Co., Rio de Janeiro, Brazil; retired from active business, 1900; pres. Nat. Bank of Commerce, Baltimore, 1878-1921, when merged with Merchants Nat. Bank of Baltimore, chmn. bd. of latter. Pres. Baltimore Bapt. Ch. Extension Soc., 1880-1920. Free Pub. Bath Commn., 1895; trustee Johns Hopkins U., 1902. One of incorporators Nat. Red Cross, 1900. Home: Baltimore, Md. Died Aug. 2, 1928.

LEVERING, Joshua, merchant; b. Baltimore, Md., Sept. 12, 1845; s. Eugene and Ann S. L.; ed. pvt. schs., Baltimore; m. Martha W. Keyser, Nov. 1870; m. 2d, Margaret Keyser, sister of 1st wife, 1892; m. 3d, Helen Woods, Apr. 1901. Employe, 1860-66, later partner with father in coffee importing business of E. Levering & Co., Baltimore; retired from active business. Prohibitionist, 1884—; candidate for comptroller of Md., 1891, for gov., 1895; Prohibition nominee for President of U.S., 1896. Was pres. Y.M.C.A., Baltimore, and mem. Internat. Com.; pres. Southern Bapt. Conv. many yrs.; pres. trustees Southern Bapt. Theol. Sem., Louisville, Ky. Home: Baltimore, Md. Died Oct. 5, 1935.

LEVERMORE, Charles Herbert, educator; b. Mansfield, Conn., Oct. 15, 1856; s. Rev. Aaron Russell and Mary Gay (Skinner) L.; A.B., Yale, 1879; Ph.D., Johns Hopkins, 1886; m. Mettie Norton Tuttle, Sept. 4, 1884. Prin. Guilford (Conn.) Inst., 1879-83; univ. fellow in history, Johns Hopkins, 1884-85; instr. history, Hopkins Grammar Sch., 1885-86, U. of Calif., 1886-88; prof. history, Mass. Inst. Tech., 1888-93; prin. Adelphi Acad., Brooklyn, 1893-96; pres. Adelphi Coll., 1896-1912, prof. history, 1912-14; dir. coll. and univ. bur. of World Peace Foundation, Boston, 1913-17; sec. N.Y. Peace Soc., 1917—; also sec. World Court League and League of Nations Union, 1919—. Trustee Hackley Sch. Author: The Republic of New Haven (awarded a John Marshall prize at Johns Hopkins), 1886; Syllabus of Lectures Upon Political History Since 1815, 1889; The Academy Song Book, 1895; The Abridged Academy Song Book, 1898; The Students' Hymnal, 1911; Forerunners and Competitors of the Pilgrim and Puritan, 2 vols., 1912; American Song Book, 1917; Series Year Books of League of Nations, Vols. I, II and III, covering years 1919-22; Life of Samuel T. Dutton, 1922. Winner of Bok $100,000 prize for best plan to preserve peace among nations of world. Home: Brooklyn, N.Y. Died Oct. 21, 1927.

LEVETT, David Maurice, composer; b. New York, Jan. 1, 1844; s. Dr. Maurice and Caroline L.; studied music New York, Germany and France; grad. Conservatory, Leipzig, 1871; m. Kate de Jonge, 1878. Prof. in New Brunswick (N.J.) Conservatory, 1876; in Conservatory at Jacksonville, Ill., 1878-80; at Chicago, 1880-85; afterward at New York; prof. in Stern's Conservatory of Music, Berlin, Germany, 1898-1900, N.Y. Coll. of Music, N.Y. City, 1900—. Author of many compositions for voice, piano and orchestra, produced in U.S. and Europe. Composer: "Harlequinade" and "Memories," two symphonic poems for orchestra; "Romance" and "Serenade," in Italian style, for violin and piano; "Danse Rustique" for orchestra. Died Sept. 26, 1914.

LEVEY, Charles Mack, ry. official; b. Huron County, O., July 27, 1858; s. William Rennox and Mary Julia (McGee) L.; pub. sch. edn.; married. Entered service of C.,B.&Q. Ry. Co. as telegraph operator, 1872, advancing to asst. supt. at Burlington, Ia., 1881; asst. gen. supt. St. Louis, Keokuk & Northwestern R.R., and Chicago, Burlington & Kansas City Ry., 1883-87; gen. supt. same rds. at Keokuk, Ia., 1887-92; supt. Ia. lines, C.,B.&Q. Ry. Co., 1902; gen. mgr. Mo. lines same rd., at St. Louis, 1902-04; asst. to pres. N.P. Ry., 1904-05; 3d v.p. same rd. at St. Paul, 1905-09; v.p. and gen. mgr. Western Pacific Ry., 1909-16, later pres. Western Pacific R.R. Co. (the reorganized Co.), and retired as pres., 1927, but continued as dir. Home: San Francisco, Calif. Died June 24, 1929.

LEVI, Gerson Baruch, rabbi; b. Glasgow, Scotland, Jan. 23, 1878; s. Israel and Miriam (Saltzman) L.; prep. edn., Central High Sch., Phila., Pa.; A.B., U. of Pa., 1899; Ph.D., 1910; rabbi Jewish Theol. Sem., New York, 1904; m. Elsa, dau. of Dr. Emil G. Hirsch, May 20, 1907; children—Julian, Edward, Harry John. Rabbi Temple Beth El, Helena, Ark., 1904-06, Temple Israel, Chicago, 1906-24, Temple Isaiah-Israel, Chicago, 1924—. Asso. editor Reform Advocate, 1910-23, editor, 1923-37. Mem. Common Progress Through Religion, "Century of Progress Expn. Chicago, 1933." Mem. bd. Jewish Charities of Chicago. Republican. Author: Gnomic Literature in Bible and Apocrypha, 1917. Editor: My Religion (sermons by Dr. Emil G. Hirsch), 1925; The Spirit of Thanksgiving and Other Addresses, 1936. Home: Chicago, Ill. Died Feb. 14, 1939.

LEVINE, Manuel, judge; b. Province of Vilna, Russia, May 25, 1881; s. David J. and Michele (Corban) L.; ed. under pvt. tutors; LL.B., Western Reserve Law Sch., Cleveland, O., 1902; m. Jessie Bialosky, Mar. 1910; children—Robert M., Alfred D., Mitzi. Came to U.S., 1897, naturalized citizen, 1902. Admitted to Ohio bar, 1902, and began practice at Cleveland; pros. atty., 1903-07; judge Police Ct., 1908-12; judge Municipal Court, 1912-15; judge Common Pleas Court, 1915-22; judge Court of Appeals, 8th O. Dist., 1922—, became chief justice, 1932, later presiding justice. Trustee Legal Aid Society, Citizens Bureau; mem. Am. Crime Study Commn. Democrat. Mason, K.P. Established the Municipal Court of Cleveland and the first conciliation Court in America; introduced the probation system in Common Pleas Court; established Bur. of Justice for domestic relations cases. Home: Cleveland, O. Deceased.

LEVINSON, Salmon Oliver, lawyer; b. Noblesville, Ind., Dec. 29, 1865; s. Newman D. and Minnie (Newman) L.; A.B., Yale, 1888; LL.B., Lake Forest U., 1891; LL.D., Grinnell Coll., 1929, DePauw U., 1930; m. Helen Bartlett Haire, 1894 (died 1904); children—Horace Clifford, Ronald Bartlett, Helen Winthrop; m. 2d, Ruth Langworthy, 1914; 1 son, John Oliver. Admitted to Ill. bar, 1891, and practiced in Chicago; member Levinson, Becker, Peebles & Swiren; specialized in reorganization of industrials and railroads; reorganized Westinghouse cos., 1908, and George Westinghouse, personal business affairs; St. Louis & San Francisco R.R. Co., 1915; C.&E.I. Ry., 1921. Presented in 1937 to U. of Chicago 50,000 documents depicting growth of outlawry of war idea and telling his personal dealings with Premier Aristide Briand of France, Presidents Wilson, Harding and Coolidge, Senator Borah, Sec. of State Frank B. Kellogg and others; the second large collection given to the univ. 1939. Republican. Liberal Jewish religion. Author of Levinson Plan for readjustment of German reparations, allied and interallied debts, European appeasement and world peace, issued Dec. 1, 1927. Contbr. article on "Aggression, International" In Ency. of Social Sciences, Vol. I, 1928. Writer on outlawry of war. Presented with Rosenberger medal, U. of Chicago, 1931, for outstanding service to humanity. Established W. E. Borah Outlawry of War Foundation of $50,000, U. of Ida. Decorated Croix de Chevalier de la Légion d'Honneur (France), 1934. Home: Chicago, Ill. Died Feb. 2, 1941.

LEVITAN, Solomon, banker; b. Taurrogen, E. Prussia, Nov. 1, 1862; s. Hirsche Mayer and Sarah Gita (Rubenstein) L.; ed. Rabbinical Sch., Kovna, Lithuania, and Rabbinical Coll., Vilna, Poland; m. Dora T. Andelson, Aug. 9, 1887; children—Esther (Mrs. Sidney L. Goldstine), Mortimer, Ethel (Mrs. Albert J. Boner). Came to U.S., 1880, naturalized citizen, 1887. Settled at New Glarus, Wis., 1881; opened store, 1887, later propr. stores in Belleville, Blanchardville and Madison, Wis.; a founder and dir. Commercial Nat. Bank, Madison, 1907, v.p., 1909, pres., 1914, chmn. bd., 1927—; chmn. bd. Madison Trust Co.; pres. Peoples Investment Co. Was justice of the peace, New Glarus; del. Rep. State Conv., various times; alternate del Rep. Nat. Conv., 1912, 16, del., 1920, 24; Rep. presdl. elector, 1912; candidate for state treas., 1918, 1920; elected state treas., 1922, and 6 times reëlected; Wisconsin agent for land bank commr. 1933. Jewish religion. Mason, Odd Fellow, Woodman, Moose, Eagle; past pres. Dist. 6, Grand Lodge B'nai B'rith. Chief of Winnebago and Chippewa Indian tribes. Home: Madison, Wis. Died Feb. 27, 1940.

LEVITAS, Arnold, typographical expert; b. Libau, Latvia, Apr. 6, 1879; s. Isaac and Charlotte (Gelhaar) L.; brought to U.S., 1894; LL.B., New York Law Sch., 1910; B.S., M.A., New York U.; m. Hattie Mayer, 1911; 1 dau., Louise; m. 2d, Charlotte Levy, 1928. Printer and proofreader, 1900-10; served as revising editor Edward Thompson Co. and editorial proofreader Funk & Wagnalls Standard Dictionary; instr. in typography and printing, New York pub. schs., and evening sessions of City Coll., 1913—; originator self-study method of teaching printing and co-related subjects; recognized as an authority in industrial edn. and printing trade edn.; assisted in programs for courses of study for trade schs. of N.Y. State, 1925; lecturer on industrial edn. and printing. Admitted to N.Y. bar, 1910. Democrat. Jewish religion. Author: Proofreading, 1918; Printing and Typography, 1924; Editorial English, 1924; Manual for Teachers of Printing, 1924; Book of Essays, 1926; Commercial English, 1927; Copy Preparation, 1927; Cost-Finding and Estimating, 1927; Commercial Typography, 1928; Advertising Typography, 1928. Home: East Orange, N.J. Died Aug. 1934.

LEVITZKI, Mischa, pianist; b. Kremenchurg, Russia, May 25, 1898 (May 12, Russian calendar); s. Jacob L. and Anna (Smelanski) L.; studied piano with Prof. Michallowsky, Warsaw, 1905-06, Sigismund Stojowski, New York, 1907-11, Erno Dohnanyi, Berlin, 1911-15. Debut at Berlin, Jan. 1914; toured Europe; New York debut, Aeolian Hall, Oct. 1916; toured Australia and New Zealand, 1921, 31, the Orient, 1925. Composer piano pieces. Died Jan. 2, 1941.

LEVY, Edgar M., Bapt. clergyman; b. St. Mary's Ga., Nov. 23, 1822; s. Lewis and Ann (Patterson) L.; parents removed from Ga. to Phila., 1830; ed. in Phila.; A.M., D.D., Bucknell Univ. Was 30 yrs. pastor, Phila.; 10 yrs., N.J. Early identified with anti-slavery cause; strong supporter of Union, by speech and pen, during Civil War; offered prayer at 1st Rep. Nat. Conv., 1856. Author of several religious works. Home: Philadelphia, Pa. Died 1906.

LEVY, Ernest Coleman, sanitarian; b. Richmond, Va., Aug. 11, 1868; s. Abraham and Rachel Cornelia (Levy) L.; M.D., Med. Coll. of Va.; post-grad. work, Coll. Phys. and Surg. (Columbia), Mass. Inst. Tech.; m. Elisabeth Detwiler, June 19, 1912. House phys., Mt. Sinai Hosp., New York, 1890-92; prof. histology, pathology and bacteriology, Med. Coll. of Va., 1897-1900; editor Medical Register, 1897-1900; chief health officer, Richmond, 1906-17; dir. pub. welfare, Richmond, 1919-24; prof. preventive medicine, Medical Coll. of Vienna, 1925; city health officer, Tampa, Fla., 1925-28. Commd. capt. M.C., U.S.A., Aug. 1918; maj., Oct. 1918; hon. discharged, Jan. 1919. Made original investigations in origin of Southern typhoid fever, 1907-08; research in breeding and control of house fly, resulting in invention of the maggot trap, 1911; research in infantile diarrhea. Charter fellow Am. Pub. Health Assn. (pres. 1923); mem. La Société de 40 Hommes et 8 Chevaux; comdr. Richmond (Va.) Post No. 1, Am. Legion, 1925 (resigned). Democrat. Jewish religion. Died Sept. 29, 1938.

LEVY, Jefferson Monroe, congressman; b. N.Y. City; s. Capt. Jonas P. (of Mexican War) and Fanny (Mitchell) L.; LL.B., New York U., 1873; unmarried. Practiced at N.Y. City; mem. 56th (1889-1901) and 62d (1911-13) Congresses, 13th N.Y. Dist., and 63d Congress (1913-15), 14th N.Y. Dist. Leader of Gold Democrats, 56th Congress; author and first to introduce Reserve Bank Bill, 62d and 63d Congresses; obtained increase of wages for postal clks.; advocate of large navy; codified election laws of N.Y.; exposed extravagance of Mayor Mitchel's administration. Inherited "Monticello," Va., the home of Thomas Jefferson. Home: New York, N.Y. Died Mar. 6, 1924.

LEVY, J(oseph) Leonard, clergyman; b. London, Eng., Nov. 24, 1865; s. Rev. Solomon and Elizabeth (Cohen) L.; B.A. (with honors), U. of London, 1884; U. of Bristol, Eng., 1885-86; came to America, 1889; D.D., Western U. of Pa., 1902; m. Henrietta Platnauer, Dec. 26, 1888. Ordained rabbi, 1885; pastor Bristol, Eng., 1885-89, Sacramento, Calif., 1889-93, Temple Keneseth Israel, Phila., 1893-1901, Rodeph Shalom Congregation, Pittsburgh, 1901—. Belonged to radical wing of Jewish Ch.; appeared on lecture platform in nearly every state of the Union, as well as in Eng., Scotland and France, 1909; introduced the interdenominational Thanksgiving Service at Pittsburgh, 1908; founded Phila. Sterilized Milk, Ice and Coal Soc., 1894, and the "Home of Delight" (social settlement), 1895; founder Pittsburgh Peace Soc., 1905. Chaplain Keegan's Brigade, Phila., 1898. Trustee Hebrew Union Coll. (Cincinnati), Nat. Hosp. for Consumptives (Denver), Universal Peace Union, U. of Pittsburgh, Penna. Peace Society, Tuberculosis League. Republican. Author: A Book of Prayer, 1902; A Graduated Text-Book of Religion, 1903; Nineteenth Century Prophets, 1907; Founders of the Faiths, 1908; Old Arrows from New Quivers, 1909; also 16 vols. of sermons. Home: Pittsburgh, Pa. Died Apr. 26, 1917.

LEVY, Louis Edward, photo-chemist; b. Stenowitz, Bohemia, Oct. 12, 1846; s. Leopold and Wilhelmina (Fisher) L.; brought to U.S. in childhood; ed. pub. schs., Detroit, 1855-61; spl. studies in mathematics and physics, U. of Mich., 1866; practical studies in optics under Louis Black, Detroit, 1861-70; m. Pauline Dalsheimer, Jan. 9, 1881. Connected with meteorol. obs., U.S. Lake Survey, Detroit, 1866; made researches in microscopic photography, 1869-70. Publisher and editor The Evening Herald, Independent Dem. daily, Phila., Nov. 1887-90. The Mercury, 1887-91. Lecturer, Franklin Inst., on Techno-Graphic Arts; pres. Graphic Arts Co., Phila., 1908—. Experiments, 1873-74, resulted in his invention in photo-chem. engraving, called the "Levytype," patented, Jan. 1875 (1st patent to Am. citizen in this field); established, 1875, Levytype Co., Baltimore; removed to Phila., 1877. Mem. Com. Science and Arts, and v.p. Franklin Inst.; received 1896 (jointly with brother Max L.), John Scott legacy medal for invention of "Levy line screen," and, 1900, Elliott Cresson gold medal for invention of Levy acid blast—both from Franklin Inst.; medal and diploma, Chicago Expn., 1893, for original discoveries; decoration and diploma Imperial Photographic Soc., Moscow, Russia, 1896; gold medal, Paris, 1900, and St. Louis Expn., 1904, for invention of the acid blast; gold medal, St. Louis Expn., 1904, for invention of etch-powedring machine; Elliott Cresson gold medal for same, Franklin Inst., 1907; silver medal, San Francisco Expn., 1915. Representative of Franklin Inst. at Scientific Congresses of Paris Expn.; v.p. of Congress of Inventors' Assns., Paris, Sept. 1900. Joint founder (1884) and pres. of Assn. for Relief and Protection of Jewish Immigrants, pres. Jewish Community (Kehillah) of Phila. Author: The Jewish Year, 1895; The Russian Jewish Refugees in America, 1895; Business, Money and Credit, 1896; Cause of Business Depressions (with Hugo Bilgram), 1914. Home: Philadelphia, Pa. Died Feb. 17, 1919.

LEVY, Maurice Ambrose, clergyman; b. Townsend, Mass., Sept. 13, 1874; s. Adolph Maximilian and Ellen (Stickney) Léve; A.B., Williams College, 1897,

D.D., 1928; grad. Newton Theol. Instn., 1900; m. L. Mable Deland, June 14, 1899; 1 son, Rev. Maurice Eugene. Ordained Baptist ministry, 1898; pastor First Church, Hingham, Mass., 1898-1901, First Ch., Medford, 1901-07, First Ch., Newton, Newton Center, 1907-14, Greene Av. Ch., Brooklyn, N.Y., 1914-19, First Ch., Pittsfield, Mass., 1919-32, First Church, Williamsport, Pa., 1932—. Mem. bd. mgrs. Am. Bapt. Foreign Mission Soc., 1909-21; rec. sec. Northern Bapt. Conv. and editor Annual, 1912-28; corr. sec. Northern Bapt. Conv., 1928—; mem. bd. mgrs. Conf. of Bapt. Ministers in Mass., 1924-27; recording sec. and dir. Mass. Bapt. Conv., 1929-32, pres., 1927, 28; trustee Newton Theol. Instn., 1909-30, and 1931-33; mem. exec. com. Pa. Council Chs., 1935—; chaplain Ancient and Hon. Arty. Co., Boston, 1913-14; mem. Advisory Council American Bible Soc., 1937—. Pres. Pittsfield Chamber Commerce, 1928-30. Mason, Odd Fellow. Home: Williamsport, Pa. Died Nov. 30, 1939.

LEVY, Max, inventor; b. Detroit, Mar. 9, 1857; s. Leopold and Wilhelmina (Fisher) L.; ed. pub. schs., Detroit; m. Diana Franklin, Sept. 22, 1885. Studied architecture, Detroit, 1875; engaged in photo engraving until 1890; introduced modern screen for half-tone process; prominent in recent advance in half-tone illustration in the development of the theory of the subject. Received from Franklin Inst., Phila., John Scott medal; Royal Cornwall Polytechnic silver medal; gold medals, Chicago, 1893, Paris, 1900, Buffalo, 1901, St. Louis, 1904; medal of honor, San Francisco Expn., 1915. Contbr. to Photographic Soc., Phila., 1896, Paper and Press, 1894-96, Royal Photog. Soc., 1906. Patented Jan. 30, 1917, counting chamber for hæmocytometer, new construction, adopted in army and leading med. instns., and awarded the Edward Longstreth medal, Franklin Inst., Jan. 1918. Engaged in optical instrument program of War Dept., 1917-18. Home: New York, N.Y. Died July 31, 1926.

LEVY, Samuel D(avid), judge; b. N.Y. City, Jan. 10, 1860; s. David and Babetta (Koenigsberger) L.; LL.B., New York U., 1880; m. Millie Irene Berg, Feb. 3, 1889. Began as law clk. with Judge Joachimsen, N.Y. City, 1878; admitted to N.Y. bar, 1881; city magistrate, 1912-16; judge Children's Court, 1916—. Pres. Hebrew Sheltering Guardian Soc. 9 yrs., v.p. 25 yrs.; chmn. N.Y. com. Nat. Jewish Hosp. for Consumptives (non-sect.) of Denver. Democrat. Reform Jewish religion. Mem. Free Sons of Israel, B'nai B'rith and I.O.O.F. Writer of Monographs, Parent and Child; Causative Factors in Stealing; Foster Homes as Against Institutional Care; Religion in its Relation to Delinquency; Causative Factors in Delinquency; Tragedies of the Class Room; Retarded Tenth. Delivered 300 addresses and lectures on various phases of child studies. Home: New York, N.Y. Died Dec. 26, 1940.

LEWELLING, Lorenzo D., governor Kan.; b. Salem, Ia., Dec. 21, 1846; attended school there; worked as railway laborer; drove cattle for quartermaster's dept., U.S. army; later served in bridge-building corps of army at Chattanooga; after war attended Knox Coll. and other institutions; taught school; edited the Salem, Ia., Register (Republican); after that, with his wife, had charge of Ia. State Reform School for Girls 15 yrs.; became prominent as penologist; moved to Kansas, 1887; joined People's Party; gov. Kan., 1893-95. Home: Wichita, Kan. Died 1900.

LEWERS, Robert, educator; b. Franktown, Nev., June 19, 1862; s. Ross and Kate (Taggart) L.; ed. pub. schs. and under pvt. techers; m. Mrs. Louise Blaney, Aug. 20, 1919. Teacher pub. schs., 1881-89; with U. of Nev., 1890—, acting pres. 2 yrs., v.p., 1909—. Mem. State Council of Defense, 1918-19. Trustee Pub. Library, Reno, 17 yrs.; dir. Reno Masonic Temple Assn. Past Grand Master of Masons of Nev.; Past Grand High Priest Royal Arch Masons; Past Grand Comdr. K.T. of Nev.; 33° hon. Scottish Rite; Past Potentate of Shrine. Elk. Democrat. Home: Reno, Nev. Died Jan. 12, 1922.

LEWI, Isidor, newspaper man; b. Albany, N.Y., May 9, 1850; s. Dr. Joseph and Bertha (Schwarz) L.; ed. Albany Acad.; m. Emita Wolff May, Nov. 26, 1902. Formerly on staff Albany Express, and Albany Argus; with editorial dept. New York Herald-Tribune. Author: Isaac M. Wise and Emanu-El; The Tribune, Long Ago. Home: New York, N.Y. Died Jan. 3, 1939.

LEWINTHAL, Isidore, rabbi; b. in Germany, Oct. 17, 1849; s. Rabbi Solomon L.; ed. in Germany; spl. studies in divinity; became Jewish rabbi, 1873; came to U.S.; m. Estelle Block, Aug. 6, 1879. Rabbi of San Antonio, Tex., 1879-88, in Nashville, Tenn., 1888—. Mem. Central Conf. of Am. Rabbis; v.p. Tenn. Bd. State Charities; pres. Fedn. Jewish Charities, Nashville, Tenn. Author: Scriptural Question. Address: Nashville, Tenn. Died May 17, 1922.

LEWIS, Abram Herbert, clergyman; b. Scott, N.Y., Nov. 17, 1836; s. Datus Ensign and Tacy (Maxson) L.; A.B., Alfred U., 1863, A.M., 1866; Union Theol. Sem., 1870-71; D.D., Alfred, 1881, LL.D., 1901; m. Augusta M. Johnson, 1855. Ordained Seventh-Day Bapt. ministry; corr. sec. Am. Sabbath Tract Soc. Editor Sabbath Recorder, Sabbath Outlook, 1882-96; corr. editor Philanthropist. Author: Sabbath and Sunday, Argument and History, 1870; Biblical Teachings Concerning the Sabbath and the Sunday, 1884; A Critical History of the Sabbath and the Sunday in the Christian Church, 1886, 2d edit. 1903; A Critical History of Sunday Legislation from A.D. 321 to 1888, 1888, 1902; Paganism Surviving in Christianity, 1890; Swift Decadence of Sunday; What Next?, 1899; Letters to Young Preachers and Their Readers, 1900. Deceased.

LEWIS, Albert Buell, anthropologist; b. Clifton, O., June 21, 1867; s. Charles Boughton and Anna (McKeehan) L.; student U. of Wooster, O., 1890-93; U. of Chicago, 1894-97, A.B., 1894; Columbia, 1902-06, Ph.D., 1906; m. Gertrude Louise Clayton, Dec. 23, 1915; 1 son, Edgar Bennett. Asst. in biology, summer, 1894, histology, 1895, bacteriology, 1896, U. of Chicago; fellow, 1897-99, instr., 1899-1902, U. of Neb.; asst., 1907-08, asst. curator of Melanesian ethnology, 1908-36, curator, 1937—, Field Museum, Chicago. Head of Joseph N. Field South Pacific Expdn., 1909-13, which visited in interest of anthrop. dept. of Field Mus., Fiji, New Caledonia, New Hebrides, Solomon Islands, Bismarck Archipelago, Admiralty Islands, New Guinea and Dutch Indies. Presbyn. Home: Homewood, Ill. Died Oct. 10, 1940.

LEWIS, Alexander, clergyman; b. Hudson, Wis., Dec. 3, 1864; s. Charles Henry and Katherine (Seeley) L.; B.S., Carleton Coll., Minn., 1887, B.L., 1890; Boston Theol. Sem., 1887-89, Union Theol. Sem., 1889-90; M.S., New York U., 1892, Ph.D., 1894; Oxford U., 1905-06; D.D., Drury Coll., 1907; m. Ella Hatch, Aug. 13, 1890. Ordained Congl. ministry, 1890; asst. pastor Pilgrim Ch., New York, 1890-91; pastor N.E. Ch., Brooklyn, 1891-95, Pilgrim Ch., Worcester, Mass., 1896-1906, First Ch., Kansas City, Mo., Nov. 15, 1906—. Del. and speaker at Internat. Congl. Council, Edinburgh, 1908, Nat. Council, Boston, 1910. Author: Manhood Making, 1902; Sermons Preached in England, 1906; Twenty Years in the Ministry, 1910. Died Mar. 7, 1912.

LEWIS, Alfred Henry ("Dan Quin"), author. Was Washington corr. Chicago Times; in charge Washington bur. New York Journal; founded, 1898, and editor The Verdict (humorous weekly), New York. Author: Wolfville; Episodes of Cowboy Life; Sandburrs, 1900; Wolfville Days, 1902; Wolfville Nights, 1902; Black Lion Inn, 1903; Peggy O'Neal, 1903; The Sunset Trail, 1905; Confessions of a Detective, 1906; Story of Paul Jones, 1906; The Throwback, 1906; When Men Grew Tall, 1907; An American Patrician—Aaron Burr, 1908; Wolfville Folks, 1908; Apaches of New York, 1912; Faro Nell and Her Friends, 1913. Died Dec. 23, 1914.

LEWIS, Bransford, surgeon; b. St. Charles, Mo., Nov. 14, 1862; s. Judge Edward A. and Parthenia A. (Bransford) L.; grad. Smith Acad., St. Louis, 1881; M.D., Mo. Med. Coll., 1884; courses in surgery in London, Paris and Vienna, 1891, Berlin, 1902, Paris and Vienna, 1909; B.Sc., St. Louis U., 1909; m. Jennie Jaynes, Oct. 14, 1896. In practice at St. Louis, 1884—. Jr., sr. and asst. supt. of City and Female hosps., 1884-89; prof. genito-urinary surgery, Marion-Sims Coll. (St. Louis U.); genito-urinary surgeon to St. John's Hosp. and St. Ann's Foundling Asylum. V.p. Pan-American Medical Congress, 1938. Pres. Mississippi Valley Med. Assn., 1905, Am. Urol. Assn., 1907; pres. St. Louis Chess Forum; regional dir. Nat. Chess Fed. U.S.A. Democrat. Methodist. Co-Author: Cystoscopy and Urethroscopy, 1915. Editor: History of Urology. Home: St. Louis, Mo. Died May 18, 1941.

LEWIS, Calvin Leslie, coll. prof.; b. Nineveh, N.Y., May 16, 1868; s. William B. and C. Amelia (Higgins) L.; A.B., Hamilton Coll., 1890; A.M., New York U., 1901; m. Edith Wood Brooks, Dec. 27, 1893; children—William Leslie, Marion Mather, Helen Francis. Teacher in pvt. prep. sch. 4 yrs., in business 3 yrs., in pub. high schs. 8 yrs., to 1908; prof. rhetoric and oratory, Hamilton Coll., 1908—. Dir. Hamilton Coll. Summer Sch. of English, 1914-18; instr. Harvard Summer Sch., 1913; faculty English Sch., summer, Middlebury Coll. Capt. 114th Provisional Infantry N.G.N.Y., 1898. Author: American Speech, 1916. With War Camp Community Service, Phila. and New York, 1918-19. Home: Clinton, N.Y. Died June 13, 1935.

LEWIS, Ceylon Harris, lawyer; b. Tully, N.Y., Dec. 6, 1849; s. Osymandus and Caroline A. (Harris) L.; A.B., Colgate U., Hamilton, N.Y., 1873, and A.M., 1876, LL.D., 1914; m. Jennie M. Heffron, July 6, 1876 (died 1900); children—Robert H., Edmund H. Was admitted to bar, 1877; asst. dist. atty., 1881-83, dist. atty., 1884-86, Onondaga County; practiced at Syracuse, 1877—; mem. Lewis & Crowley; v.p. Merchants Nat. Bank & Trust Co. Mem. N.Y. Constl. Conv., 1894, State Bd. Tax Commrs., 1905, 06, State Bd. Social Welfare, 1915-35. Trustee Colgate U., 1899-1926. Republican. Baptist. Clubs: Citizens', University, Skaneateles Country. Home: Skaneateles Lake (near Syracuse), N.Y. Died Jan. 17, 1939.

LEWIS, Charles Bertrand ("M Quad"), author; b. Liverpool, O., Feb. 15, 1842; grad. Mich. State Agrl. Coll. Began newspaper work on Detroit Free Press; became prominent as humorist and for descriptive writing; most of his work appeared under nom de plume of "M Quad"; engaged in book-writing, syndicate and mag. work. Author: Field, Fort and Fleet; A Sketch Book of the Civil War; The Lime-Kiln Club; Sawed Off Sketches; Mr. and Mrs. Bowser; Quad's Odds; also a number of plays. Home: Brooklyn, N.Y. Died Aug. 21, 1924.

LEWIS, Charles Willard, clergyman, educator; b. New Trenton, Ind., Aug. 30, 1860; s. Nathan and Nancy R. L.; student 2 yrs. in Nat. Normal U.; 1 yr. in De Pauw U., D.D., same, 1899; B.S., Moores Hill Coll., 1890, M.S., 1893. High school prin., Brookville Ind., 1886-89; prof. mathematics, 1890, acting pres., 1897-98, and pres. Moores Hill Coll., 1898—; postgraduate student Harvard, summer of 1895. Mem. Ind. conf. M.E. Ch. and Ind. conf. examining bd.; preacher and lecturer; m. Bertha M. Cruikshank, March 25, 1887. Home: Moores Hill, Ind. Died 1904.

LEWIS, Charlton Miner, university prof.; b. Brooklyn, Mar. 4, 1866; s. late Charlton Thomas and Nancy D. (McKeen) L.; A.B., Yale, 1886, Ph.D., 1898; LL.B., Columbia, 1889; m. Grace H. Robbins, June 16, 1903. Practiced law New York, 1889-94; instr. English, 1895-98, asst. prof. English lang. and lit., 1898-99, Emily Sanford prof., 1899—, Yale U. Author: Foreign Sources of Modern English Versification, 1898; The Beginnings of English Literature, 1900; Gawayne and the Green Knight, 1903; The Principles of English Verse, 1906; The Genesis of Hamlet, 1907. Editor of Yale Series of Younger Poets. Died Mar. 12, 1923.

LEWIS, Charlton Thomas, lawyer; b. West Chester, Pa., Feb. 25, 1834; s. Joseph J. L.; grad. Yale, 1853; Ph.D., Univ. City of New York; m. 1st, Nancy D. McKeen, July 25, 1861; m. 2d, Margaret P. Sherrard, July 1, 1885. Prof. mathematics, State Normal U. of Ill., 1856-57; prof. Greek, 1858-61, Troy Univ.; deputy commr. Internal Revenue, U.S., 1863-64. Practiced law in New York; lecturer on life ins. Harvard and Columbia univs., and on principles of ins., Cornell U. Pres. Prison Assn. of N.Y.; pres. State Charities Aid Assn. of N.J.; chmn. commn. to revise penal laws of N.J.; del. of U.S. to Paris Congress of Prisons, 1895; mem. com. on platform, Nat. Dem. Conv., 1896. Translator of Bengel's Gnomon of the New Testament, 1863. Author: History of Germany, 1871; Harper's Latin Dictionary, 1879; Lewis' Latin Dictionary for Schools, 1889; Lewis' Elementary Latin Dictionary, 1890; Love Letters of Prince Bismarck, 1901. Editor Harper's Book of Facts, 1895. Home: Morristown, N.J. Died 1904.

LEWIS, Claude Isaac, horticulturist; b. Cardiff, Wales, Apr. 12, 1880; s. Isaac and Helen (Hibbard) L.; broughpt to U.S. in infancy; B.S. in Agr., Mass. Agrl. Coll., Amherst, 1902; B.S., Boston U., 1902; M.S.A., Cornell U., 1906; m. Marie A. Berry, Mar. 31, 1905. Chief div. of horticulture, and vice-dir. Expt. Sta. of Ore. Agrl. Coll., 1906-19; orgn. mgr. Ore. Growers Coöperative Assn., Salem, 1919-22. V.p. Corvallis Orchard Co. Mng. editor Am. Fruit Grower (Chicago). Republican. Conglist. Writer of more than 50 bulls. on fruit, orchard economics, etc. Died Jan. 12, 1924.

LEWIS, Daniel, physician; b. Alfred, N.Y., Jan. 17, 1846; s. Alfred and Lucy (Langworthy) L.; served in U.S.N., 1864-65; A.B., Alfred U., 1869, A.M., 1872, Ph.D., 1886; M.D., Coll. Phys. and Surg. (Columbia), 1871; LL.D., Alfred, 1902; m. Achsah D. Vaughan, Oct. 10, 1872. Prof. spl. surgery, Post-Grad. Med. Sch., New York, several yrs. from 1890; commr. of health, State of N.Y., 1892-1904. Pres. Med. Soc. State of N.Y., 1889, New York Co. Med. Soc., 1884-86. Address: Alfred, N.Y. Died Mar. 1919.

LEWIS, Dean (De Witt), surgeon; b. Kewanee, Ill., Aug. 11, 1874; s. L. W. and V. Winifred L.; A.B., Lake Forest (Ill.) U., 1895; M.D., Rush Med. Coll., 1899; D.Sc., U. of Ireland; m. 2d, Norene Kinney, Dec. 26, 1927; children—Julianne, Dean, Mary Elizabeth. Asst. in anatomy, 1900-01, asso., 1901-03, instr. in surgery, 1903-19, asso. prof., 1919-20, prof., 1920-24, Rush Med. Coll.; prof. surgery, U. of Ill., Jan.-July 1925; prof. surgery, Johns Hopkins U., and surgeon in chief to Johns Hopkins Hosp., 1925-39. Editor Archives of Surgery, and Internat. Surgical Digest. Served as lt. col. World War. Awarded D.S.M. Home: Baltimore, Md. Died Oct. 9, 1941.

LEWIS, Ebenezer Ellesville, lawyer; b. Bishop Stortford, Eng., May 1, 1841; s. William and Kezia (Jones) L.; brought to U.S., 1849; ed. pub. schs., Chicago and Ottawa, Ill., and pvt. study; LL.D., Central U., Ia., 1890; m. Del Gracia E., d. Adams Cleghorn, D.D., Aug. 25, 1869. Studied law at Ottawa, Ill., 1858-61, with Gen. W. H. L. Wallace; admitted to Ill. bar, 1861, and practiced at Ottawa, 1861-70; city atty., Ottawa, 1868-70; U.S. commr., Northern Dist. of Ia., 1871-90; master in chancery, U.S. Circuit Court of Ia., 1874—. Pvt. Co. I, 11th Ill. Vols., 4 mos., and 3 mos. in orgn. 4th Ill. Cav. (not enlisted). Trustee Central U., Ia. Republican. Baptist. Mason. Author: Do Your Level Best, 1911;

Great Hymns and Modern Instances, 1917. Home: Sioux City, Ia. Died Sept. 6, 1919.

LEWIS, Edward Morgan, educator; b. Machynlleth, North Wales, Dec. 25, 1872; s. John C. and Jane (Davies) L.; brought to U.S., 1881; B.A., Williams, 1896, M.A. 1899; LL.D., Mass. Agrl. College, 1927, Amherst College, 1927, Marietta (Ohio) College, 1928, Northeastern U., 1931, Williams College, 1932; Litt.D., R.I. State College Agr. and Mech. Arts, 1928; m. Margaret Hallie Williams, July 3, 1896; children—Edward Williams, Gwendolen, John Bascom. Mem. Boston Nat. League Base Ball Team, 1896-1900, American League, 1901; coach Harvard Base Ball Team, 1897 1901; instr. elocution, Columbia, 1901-03; instr. and asst. prof. pub. speaking, Williams Coll., 1903-11; dean, 1911-27, head of dept. langs. and lit., 1913-27, head div. humanities, 1919-27, Mass. Agrl. Coll., also acting pres. 5 yrs. and pres., 1926-27; pres. U. of New Hampshire, 1927—. Instr. Yale Div. Sch., 1904-14, Harvard U. Summer Sch., 1903, 06. Dem. candidate for Congress, 1st Mass. Dist., 1910, 2d Mass. Dist., 1914; chmn. Dem. State Conv., Mass., 1913. Alumni trustee Williams Coll., 1915-27; pres. N.E. Intercollegiate Athletic Assn., 1920-23. Mem. bd. dirs. Nat. Eisteddfod Assn.; mem. exec. com. N.E. School and College Assn.; dir. Northern N.E. Sch. of Religious Edn.; mem. Mass. Fedn. of Chs.; mem. advisory council Chinese Service Bur.; mem. advisory council Yenching U.; v.p. New England Town and Country Ch. Comman. Conglist. Home: Durham, N.H. Died May 24, 1936.

LEWIS, Edward Samuel, clergyman; b. Natick, Mass., Aug. 24, 1855; s. Joseph W. and Dora K. (Heywood) L.; B.A., Boston U., 1877, M.A., 1881; D.D., Little Rock (Ark.) U., 1886; m. Anna C. Sparks, Dec. 25, 1879; children—Anna Carrie (dec.), Edward Rust, Harold Sparks (dec.), Carroll Herbert; m. 2d, Mrs. Nellie D. Sparks, March 28, 1923 (dec.). Professor of physics, Cincinnati Wesleyan Coll., 1881-82; pres. Litle Rock U., 1882-86; pres. Chattanooga U., 1886-90; ordained M.E. ministry, 1884; pastor York St. Ch. and Trinity Ch., Cincinnati, 1890-94, Franklin Av. Ch., Cleveland, 1894-99, First Ch., Columbus, 1899-1908; asso. editor Sunday School Publs. M.E. Ch., 1908-23, in editorial charge of same, 1929-30. Pres. Ohio S.S. Assn., 1892-96; v.p. Internat. S.S. Assn., 1896-1908. Mason (32°, K.T.). Republican. Author: The Senior Worker and His Work, 1910; The Intermediate Worker and His Work, 1911. Home: Cincinnati, O. Died Oct. 14, 1934.

LEWIS, Edwin Herbert, educator; b. Westerly, R.I., Nov. 28, 1866; s. A. Herbert and Augusta (Johnson) L.; A.B., Alfred U., 1887; Ph.D., Syracuse U., 1892; Ph.D., U. of Chicago, 1894; Litt.D., Milton, 1905; LL.D., Alfred U., 1910; m. Elizabeth Loxley Taylor, June 30, 1890 (died 1937); children—Herbert Taylor, Janet Loxley (Mrs. Yvor Winters). Sr. teacher and vice-prin. Plainfield High School, 1887-88, 1889-90; in Italy, 1888-89; prof. Latin, Alfred, 1890-92; asst. in rhetoric, 1893-94; instr. English, 1895-96, U. of Chicago; asso. prof. English, 1896-99, U. of Chicago and Lewis Inst.; prof. English, 1899-1935, dean of coll. students, 1906-13, dean of faculty, 1913-35, Lewis Institute, Chicago, professor and dean emeritus, 1935—. Author: A First Book in Writing English, 1897; A First Manual of Composition, 1899; An Introduction to the Study of Literature, 1899; A Second Manual of Composition, 1900; Specimens of the Forms of Discourse, 1900; Applied English Grammar, 1902; Almost Fairy Children, 1908; Business English, 1910; Those About Trench, 1916; White Lightning, 1923; Sallie's Newspaper, 1924; University of Chicago Poems, 1924. Died June 6. 1938.

LEWIS, Edwin James, Jr., architect; b. Roxbury, Mass., May 1, 1859; s. Edwin James and Sarah Avery (Richards) L.; S.B., Mass. Inst. Tech., 1881; unmarried. In office of Peabody & Stearns, Boston, until 1887, then practiced alone; specializes in rural dwellings and chs.; has designed about 35 chs. in U.S. and Can. Fellow A.I.A.; mem. Boston Soc. of Architects (sec. 10 yrs.). Lecturer on hist. and ecclesiastical topics. Active worker in municipal reform. Home: Milton, Mass. Died Oct. 16, 1937.

LEWIS, Edwin Seelye, ins. counsel; b. Amherst, Mass., July 23, 1868; s. Edwin Rufus and Harriet (Goodell) L.; ed. Collège de Genève, 1878-83; A.B., Wabash Coll., 1888, A.M., 1891; Ph.D., Johns Hopkins, 1892; LL.B., New York U., 1907; m. Elodie Jordan, July 24, 1912. Fellow, 1890-91, asst. in Romance langs, 1891-92, Johns Hopkins; instr., 1892-94, asst. prof., 1894-98, prof. Romance langs., 1898-1907, Princeton; in law practice, New York, 1907-26; life insurance adviser, New York, 1926—; life and business insurance counsel. Editor: Michel Strogoff, 1893; La Tulipe noire, 1900; Doña Perfecta, 1903. Wrote The Dialect of Guernsey, dissertation, 1892. Home: New York, N.Y. Died June 21, 1935.

LEWIS, Ernest Sidney, surgeon; b. New Orleans, Sept. 24, 1840; s. Algernon Sidney and Annette (Tronchet) L.; B.S., U. of La., 1858, M.D., 1862, LL.D., 1922; m. Susan Daggett Phelph McCoy, 1866. Asst. and later acting house surgeon, Charity Hosp., New Orleans, 1862-63; surgeon 3d Ga. Cav., C.S.A., 1863; later brigade surgeon, Crew's brigade, and last 6 months of war chief surgeon of cav. on staff Gen. Joseph Wheeler; prof. materia medica, therapeutics and clin. medicine, 1873-76, prof. obstetrics and diseases of women, 1876-1911, emeritus prof. obstetrics and gynecology, 1911, Tulane U. Served as surgeon-gen. of La. surgeon-gen. Confed. Vets. of La.; v.p. and acting pres. bd. administration, Charity Hosp. (state), 1894-1913; consulting gynecologist, same, 1913—. Pres. Surgeons of Army and Navy of Confederacy; a founder of Internat. Obstet. and Gynecol. Assn. Mem. exec. com. Med. Service Corps of La. Home: New Orleans, La. Died Aug. 12, 1935.

LEWIS, Ernest William, lawyer; b. Indiana, Pa., Dec. 27, 1875; s. George R. and Nancy J. (MacLane) L.; ed. U. of Minn.; m. Ethel May Orme, Feb. 19, 1902; children—Orme, Sylvia MacLane, Robert Porter. Admitted to bar, 1900, and engaged in practice at Phoenix, Ariz.; mem. firm Armstrong, Lewis & Kramer, 1904; counsel for various mining, banking and indust. corps.; reporter Supreme Court of Ariz., 1903-09; asso. justice Supreme Court of Ariz., 1909-12. President's commr. of conciliation during copper strikes in Ariz., 1917. Chancellor of Diocese of Arizona, P.E. Ch. Republican. Mason. Home: Phoenix, Ariz. Died Apr. 3, 1927.

LEWIS, Eugene Howard, lawyer; b. Potosi, Wis., Feb. 7, 1852; s. Simon E. and Mary C. (Harding) L.; ed. pub. schs., Potosi, and Lancaster, Wis., and Beloit Coll.; grad. Yale, 1873; law dept. Columbia Univ., 1875; m. Amy Busby, Mar. 19, 1897. Admitted to bar, 1876, and entered practice at N.Y. City; mem. Assn. of the Bar, New York. Deceased.

LEWIS, Exum Percival, physicist; b. Washington Co., N.C., Sept. 15, 1863; s. Henry Green and Emma (Haughton) L.; B.S., Columbian (now George Washington) U., 1888; Ph.D., Johns Hopkins, 1895; phys. research, U. of Berlin, 1898-1900; m. Louise Sheppard, July 10, 1901; children—Evelyn, John Sheppard. Asst. in physics, Johns Hopkins, 1891-95; instr. physics, 1895-96, asst. prof., 1896-1902, asso. prof., 1902-08, prof., 1908—, U. of Calif. Mem. Crocker eclipse expdn. to South Seas, Jan. 1908, and to Goldendale, Wash., June 1918; mem. 1905-07, pres., 1907-09, Berkeley Bd. of Edn. Editor: The Effect of a Magnetic Field on Radiation, 1900. Contbr. sections on Wave Motion and Light, in Duff's Text-Book of Physics, 1908. Home: Berkeley, Calif. Died Nov. 17, 1926.

LEWIS, F(rancis) Park, M.D., oculist; b. Hamilton, Ont., Can., May 19, 1855; s. John W. and Hannah M. (Gavin) L.; M.D., Pulte Med. Coll., Concinnati, 1876; grad. New York Ophthalmic Hosp., 1877; studied in London, Berlin and Vienna; m. Grace K. Moseley, 1889; children—Katharine Park, Dorothea Park, Frances Park. Practiced in Buffalo, 1876—. Awarded Leslie Dana medal, Am. Acad. Ophthalmology and Oto-Laryngology, 1928; Chancellor medal, U. of Buffalo, 1933. Pres. bd. dirs. N.Y. State Sch. for the Blind; v.p. Nat. Soc. for Prevention of Blindness, Internat. Assn. for Prevention of Blindness. On editorial staff Am. Jour. Ophthalmology. Home: Buffalo, N.Y. Died Sept. 10, 1940.

LEWIS, Franklin Crocker, educator; b. Centreville, Cape Cod, Mass., Feb. 12. 1877; s. Joseph Freeman and Emma Caroline (Hinckley) L.; A.B., Dartmouth, 1900; Harvard, 1901-03, A.M., 1902; m. Ellen Anderson, June 20, 1903. Instr. pedagogy, Dartmouth, 1903-06; asst. supt., Feb.-June, 1906, supt., June 1906—, Ethical Culture Sch., New York. Conglist. Home: New York, N.Y. Died Feb. 13, 1930.

LEWIS, George Albert, banker; b. Phila., July 3, 1829; s. John F. and Eliza (Mower) L.; ed. Friends' Acad. and others; m. Anne Cornelia, d. Rev. Thomas Larcombe, July 1, 1851. Formerly E. India importing mcht.; cashier City Nat. Bank of Phila., 1863-1900. Well known as artist, illustrator and genealogist. Home: Philadelphia, Pa. Died Dec. 23, 1915.

LEWIS, Grant Kirkland, clergyman; b. Steuben Co., Ind., Oct. 13, 1868; s. James and Charity (Laubach) Kirkland; orphaned, and adopted by family named Lewis, whose name assumed; A.B., Tri-State Coll., Angola, Ind., 1890; student Transylvania Coll., Lexington, Ky., 1890-91; Butler Coll., Indianapolis, Ind., 1893-94; A.B., Cotner U., Lincoln, Neb., 1899; m. Emily Kinney, May 25, 1895. Ordained ministry Disciples of Christ, 1891; pastor Decatur, Ind., 1891-93, Alexandria, Ind., 1894-96, Denver, Colo., 1897-99, Pomona, Calif., 1900-03, Long Beach, Calif., 1904-07; sec. Southern Calif. Missionary Soc., 1905-10; sec. and dir. Am. Christian Missionary Soc. (home missionary bd. of Disciples of Christ) from 1910 until it was merged into United Christian Missionary Soc. of which was chmn. div. of home missions, also pres. old holding corp. Pres. and dir. Men and Millions Movement of Disciples of Christ. Republican. Died Feb. 22, 1937.

LEWIS, Henry, clergyman, editor; b. N.Y. City, July 24, 1871; s. Thomas Francis Henry and Ellen (Gostling) L.; B.A., New York U., 1893, A.M., 1895; Ph.D., 1896; grad. Union Theol. Sem., 1896; m. Elizabeth Adelaide Sammond, Apr. 21, 1909. Ordained Congl. ministry, 1896; pastor Schroon Lake, N.Y., 1896-98; editor The American Messenger and other publs. of Am. Tract Soc., 1898-1923, also recording sec. Am. Tract Soc., 1906-23; pastor Congl. Ch., River Edge, N.J., 1902-07, Cresskill, N.J., 1924-28, Oakwood Heights, Staten Island, N.Y., 1929—. Life mem. A.B.C.F.M. Home: Oakwood Heights, Staten Island, N.Y. Died Apr. 23, 1932.

LEWIS, Henry Thomas, asso. justice Supreme Ct, Ga., Dec. 1, 1897-1903; b. Oxford, Ga., Oct. 21, 1847; at time of war was in Ga. Mil. Inst.; from there went into C.S.A. with Ga. cadets and remained until war ended. Grad. Emory Coll., Oxford, Ga., 1870; taught school 2 yrs.; admitted to bar and practiced, 1873-77, Atlanta; 1877-97, at Greensboro, Ga. Mem. Nat. Dem. Convs., 1884 and 1896; in latter placed William J. Bryan in nomination for President. Died 1903.

LEWIS, Ida. See Ida Lewis Wilson.

LEWIS, Irving Jefferson, editor; b. Cleveland, O.; s. I. J. and Harriet M. (Tracy) L.; ed. acad., Painesville, O., and Central High Sch., Cleveland; unmarried. Reporter, Cleveland Plain Dealer, 1889; city editor, Kansas City Globe, 1890; night editor, Chicago Times, 1892-94; cable editor, New York American, 1896-99; mng. editor, New York Morning Telegraph, 1904-24. Odd Fellow. Author: The Chochems Poker Club; John Jackson, Detective; also short stories and motion pictures. Home: Hollywood, Calif. Died Jan. 5, 1927.

LEWIS, Isaac Newton, army officer; b. New Salem, Pa., Oct. 12, 1858; s. James H. and Anne (Kendall) L.; grad. U.S. Mil. Acad., 1884; m. Mary, d. Richard Wheatley, D.D., of N.Y. City, Oct. 21, 1886; children—Richard Wheatley, Laura Anne, George Fenn, Margaret Kendall. Commd. 2d lt. 2d Arty., June 15, 1884; promoted through grades to col., Aug. 27, 1913; retired on account of disability incurred in line of duty, Sept. 20, 1913. Mem. bd. on regulation of coast arty. fire, New York Harbor, 1894-98; recorder Bd. of Ordnance and Fortification, Washington, 1898-1902; instr. and dir. Coast Arty. Sch., Ft. Monroe, Va., 1904-11. Made study of methods of mfr. and supply of ordnance materials, in Europe, 1900, resulting in complete re-armament of field arty. of U.S.; orginator of plan for modern corps orgn. for artillery which was adopted by Congress, 1902. Inventor of the Lewis machine gun which was in general use by all the allies throughout the World War; also inventor of numerous mil. instruments and devices in general use, including the first successful arty. range and position finder, a replotting and relocating system for coast batteries, time interval clock and bell system of signals, quick firing field gun and mount, quick reading mech. verniers, electric car lighting and windmill electric lighting systems, etc. Republican. Methodist. Home: Montclair, N.J. Died Nov. 9, 1931.

LEWIS, James Hamilton, senator, lawyer; b. Danville, Va.; taken to Ga.; ed. Houghton Coll., Ga., and U. of Va.; studied law, Savannah, Ga.; LL.D., Ohio Northern U. and Baylor U.; m. Rose Lawton Douglas, of Ga. Admitted to bar, Seattle; served as mem. Wash. Senate; congressman at large, State of Wash., 1896-1900; chosen by Democracy of Wash. for vice-pres. of U.S., 1900, and endorsed by Pacific Coast States, with U.S. Senator Stephen White, of Calif.; served in Spanish-Am. War; named on staff of Gen. Brooke, in Cuba, as insp. gen.; transferred to staff of Gen. F. D. Grant, Puerto Rico, later Philippines, 1898-1900; was aide to commr. of Joint High Commn. on Can. and Alaska Boundary, at London; commr. to arrange customs regulations between Can. and N.W. U.S. Moved to Chicago, 1903; city atty. and corp. counsel, 1905-07; mem. U.S. Senate, from Ill., for terms 1913-19, 1931-37 and 1937-43; was the last U.S. senator to be elected by a state legislature in the United States; was elected first whip of the Senate in the history of that body and continuously reëlected each session to expiration of senatorial terms; named by primary vote of Democrats and by Dem. State Conv. as choice of Ill. for vice-pres. of U.S., 1920, and unanimously nominated for gov. by Dem. State Conv. of Ill. the following Sept., through compliment of Republicans receiving more than 200,000 votes over Dem. ticket; apptd. U.S. commr. representing Senate at London, to execute treaty laws for safety at sea; commr. for War Dept. and President of U.S., in matters touching prosecution of war; reported in France to Gen. Pershing and later assigned to Gen. George Bell as soldier aide; on return to U.S. on ship Mt. Vernon, in charge of wounded soldiers, torpedoed at sea, put back to Brest, and later resumed his war duties. Tendered ambassadorship to Belgium (declined). Knighted by King of Belgium and King of Greece; made mem. Knights of the Round Table, London, King of England presiding on the occasion. Served in behalf of Am. interests at internat. confs., Genoa, Italy, and Lausanne, Switzerland. Author: (or joint author) Hand Book on Election, 1912; Constitutions, Statutes and Their Construction (with A. H. Putney); Two Great Republics—Rome and the United States; Removal of Causes from State to U.S. Courts; Lewis and Spelling on Injunctions. Home: Chicago, Ill. Died Apr. 9, 1939.

LEWIS, James M., physician; b. Falmouth, Mass., Feb. 24, 1827; grad. Jefferson Med. Coll., Phila.; m.

1st, Jennie Andrews, 1849; m. 2d, Mary C. Wills, 1895. Practiced medicine in Wis. 10 yrs.; apptd. surgeon 2d Wis. vol. inf.; rode into Confederate lines, July 21, 1861, at the battle of Bull Run and surrendered, in order to get to his wounded comrades; later, lt. col. 1st Wis. cav. and afterward col. 28th Wis. inf.; was 4 yrs. commr. of immigration and State lands for Arkansas. Died 1907.

LEWIS, John Beavens, shoe mfr.; b. Wilmington, Mass., Aug. 30, 1841; s. John B. and Sarah (Miller) L.; ed. high sch., Reading, Mass.; m. Hattie A. Bancroft, Aug. 4, 1864 (died 1869); m. 2d, Mary U. Hawes, Jan. 18, 1872 (died 1916); m. 3d, Mrs. Minnie Cora Wilkinson, November 1, 1917. Began at 17 in shoemaker's shop, Reading; later clk. and mgr., John Gilbert, Jr. & Co., grocers, Boston; mem. Co. E, 44th Mass. Inf., 9 mos., 1862-63, until mustered out; in shoe business Shreveport, La., 15 yrs.; removed to Boston, 1880; head of firm J. B. Lewis Co., factories at Abington, Avon, Randolph and Brockton, Mass. (retired, 1900). Candidate for governor of Mass., 1901; mem. Mass. Ho. of Rep., 1907. Mem. bd. mgrs. Nat. Temperance Soc.; mem. exec. com. Mass. Total Abstinence Soc.; life mem. N.E. Sabbath Protective League and various patriotic and reform orgns. Mem. Prohibition Nat. Com. Conglist. Mason. Home: Reading, Mass. Died Nov. 15, 1923.

LEWIS, John Frederick, lawyer; b. Phila., Pa., Sept. 10, 1860; s. S. Weir and Caroline A. (Kalbfus) L.; grad., with first honors, Central High Sch., Phila., 1879; A.M., LL.D., U. of Pa., 1925; studied law under Hon. George M. Dallas; m. Anne H. Rush Baker, May 23, 1895; children—Alfred G. Baker, John Frederick. Admitted to bar, 1882; solicitor Phila. Bourse, Phila. Maritime Exchange; mem. law firm Lewis, Adler & Laws. Spl. lecturer on shipping and admiralty, U. of Pa. Chief sect. 2, U.S. Shipping Bd., charge schs. of navigation and marine engring. bet. Conn. and Norfolk, during war; pres. Am. Acad. of Music, Hist. Soc. of Pa., Mercantile Library of Phila., Acad. of Fine Arts, Art Jury of Phila.; trustee Free Library of Phila. Mason. Home: Philadelphia, Pa. Died Dec. 24, 1932.

LEWIS, John L., lawyer; b. Berkshire, Vt., Mar. 7, 1858; s. Milo G. and Euretta S. (Willard) L.; ed. St. Albans (Vt.) Acad.; m. Georgia E. Harrison, June 25, 1885. Practiced law, then as consulting atty. only; pres. Midland R.R. Co.; v.p. Barton (Vt.) Savings Bank & Trust Co., Farmers' and Merchants' Bank (Georgetown, Ga.), Frontier Elec. Co.; dir. Marl Prod. Co., State Mut. Fire Ins. Co. Mem. Vt. Ho. of Rep., 1904-06. Senate, 1908-10; del.-at-large Rep. Nat. Conv., Chicago, 1912; mem. Rep. Nat. Com., 1912-16. Trustee Norwich U., Northfield, Vt. Episcopalian. Home: North Troy, Vt. Died Oct. 18, 1913.

LEWIS, Joseph H., chief justice Ky.; b. Barren County, Ky., Oct. 29, 1824; became a lawyer; mem. Ky. legislature, 1850-52 and 1869; mem. Congress, 1869-73; later elected to bench of Court of Appeals and becoming chief justice until retired, 1898. Democrat. Home: Frankfort, Ky. Died 1904.

LEWIS, Joseph William, lawyer; b. Kansas City, Mo., Jan. 27, 1868; s. Joseph William and Eliza (Silver) L.; prep. edn., Smith Acad., St. Louis, Mo.; A.B., Princeton, 1890, A.M., 1892; LL.B., Washington U., St. Louis; m. Emily Westwood, Aug. 28, 1902 (dec.); children—William McMillan, Emily Westwood, Joseph William, Hugh Murray French; m. 2d, Frances Allison Tirrill, Jan. 5, 1932. Admitted to Mo. bar, 1894, practicing at St. Louis; mem. firm Lewis, Rice, Tucker, Allen & Chubb, 1908—; chmn. St. Louis Cotton Compress Co.; dir. Laclede Steel Co., Lesser Goldman Co., Security Nat. Bank, Federal Compress & Warehouse Co., Ark. Fertilizer Co., Highway Mfg. Co., Wagner Electric Corp. Trustee Methodist Orphans Home Assn., St. Louis Y.M.C.A. Democrat. Methodist. Home: Clayton, Mo. Died Aug. 6, 1936.

LEWIS, Leon Patteson, lawyer; b. Louisville, Ky., Nov. 21, 1878; s. Adrian Castello and Eliza Duncan (Platt) L.; grad. Louisville Male High Sch., 1895; Ph.B., U. of Chicago, 1902, J.D., 1905; m. Laura Breckinridge McClintock, Mar. 18, 1926. Instr., Stanford Law Sch., 1905-07; prof. Sch. of Law, U. of Louisville, 1908—, dean of Sch. of Law, 1925-30; asst. in city atty's. office, 1908-13; mem. firm Blakey, Quin & Lewis, 1912-18, Blakey, Davis & Lewis, 1919—; pres. Prestonia Bank, Okolona State Bank, Inland Waterways Co.; dir. Am. Barge Line Co., First State Bank, Irvington, Ky. Mem. Ky. Ho. of Rep., 1922-28 inclusive. Democrat. Presbyn. Home: Louisville, Ky. Died May 6, 1932.

LEWIS, Lillian (Mrs. Lawrence Marsden), actress; b. Winona, Minn.; début as the Queen in "Zozo," 1884; shortly afterward began career as a star in "As In a Looking Glass" and "Donsa Sol." Married Lawrence Marsden, playwright, who was her mgr. and author of numerous plays in which she appeared. Died 1899.

LEWIS, Loran Ludowick, lawyer; b. Cayuga Co., N.Y., May 9, 1825; s. John C. and Delecta (Barbour) L.; ed. dist. and pvt. schs., later teaching and studying law, m. Charlotte E. Pierson, June 1, 1852. Admitted to bar, 1848; practiced in Buffalo; identified with many important cases. State senator, 1869-73; justice Supreme Ct. of N.Y., 1883-97; retired from bench and associated with his two sons as counsel (firm Lewis & Lewis). Republican. Pres. Third Nat. Bank of Buffalo. Home: Buffalo, N.Y. Died Mar. 8, 1916.

LEWIS, Lowery Lamon, educator; b. Newport, Tenn., Sept. 3, 1869; s. Samuel Jones and J. (Wood) L.; B.S.A. in Agr., Tex. Agrl. and Mech. Coll., 1892, M.S. in Agr., 1894; D.V.M., Iowa State Coll., 1896; m. Georgiana Holt, Sept. 27, 1903. With Okla. Agrl. and Mech. Coll., 1896—, and dean Sch. Science and Lit. Part Author: Elementary Principles of Agriculture, 1908. Home: Stillwater, Okla. Died Sept. 26, 1922.

LEWIS, Mary Sybil, operatic singer; b. Hot Springs, Ark., Jan. 7, 1900; d. Joseph Lewis and Hattie (Lewis) Kidd; ed. pvt. and pub. schs., Little Rock; m. Michael Franz Bohnen, April 14, 1927; m. 2d, Robert L. Hague, 1931. Was prima donna in Ziegfeld Follies, 1920-23; made her operatic début in "Faust," Vienna Volksopera, Oct. 15, 1923; sang at Monte Carlo, season of 1924, London same yr., and again at Monte Carlo, 1925; sang in Paris 1925; returned to U.S. and appeared in Carnegie Hall, New York, Oct. 27, 1925; début with Metropolitan Opera Co., as Mimi, in "La Bohême," Jan. 28, 1926; sang in Berlin Staatsoper, June 1927. Principal rôles: Thaïs, Juliet, Marguerite, Lauretta, Gilda, Manon, Nedda, Giuletta and Antonia (Hoffmann). Died Dec. 31, 1941.

LEWIS, Merton Elmer, lawyer; b. Webster, Monroe Co., N.Y., Dec. 10, 1861; s. Charles Chadwick and Rhoda Ann (Willard) L.; common sch. edn.; m. Adeline Louise Moody, Jan. 2, 1886 (died 1894); children—Merton E. (dec.), Donald M., Roscoe M.; m. 2d, Eva J. Gates, Nov. 9, 1899; children—Elizabeth (dec.), Margaret, Virginia (dec.). Practiced law, Rochester, N.Y., 1887-1919; was mem. firm Benton, Lewis, McKay & Bown, of Rochester, and Morris, Plante & Saxe, New York, 1919-25; mem. Lewis, McKay, Bown & Johnson, Rochester, N.Y., 1925; mem. firm of Lewis, Bown, Johnson & Tobin. Mem. Common Council, Rochester, 1890-95 (pres. 1893-95); actg. mayor of Rochester, 1895; mem. N.Y. State Constl. Conv., 1894; chmn. Rep. Judiciary Com., 7th Jud. Dist., N.Y., 1896-1914; mem. N.Y. Assembly, 1897, 99, 1900, 01, Senate, 1902-06; candidate for state comptroller, 1906; chmn. exec. com. Rep. State Com., 1912-16. First dep. atty. gen. of N.Y., 1915, and elected atty. gen. by N.Y. legislature, as successor to E. E. Woodbury, resigned; reëlected atty. gen. Nov. 1917, declined renomination, 1918; spl. asst. to atty. gen. of U.S., 1926-30. Mason, K.P. Home: Rochester, N.Y. Died May 2, 1937.

LEWIS, Morris James, M.D.; b. Phila., Pa., Mar. 25, 1852; s. Saunders L.; A.B., U. of Pa., 1871, A.M., M.D., Ph.D., 1874; m. Maria H. Drayton, May 1882. Practiced in Phila., 1874—; emeritus phys. to Pa. Hosp.; phys. to Orthopedic Hosp. and Infirmary for Nervous Diseases. Was trustee U. of Pa.; bd. mgrs. Wistar Inst. Republican. Home: Ambler, Pa. Died Apr. 17, 1928.

LEWIS, Nelson Peter, civil engr.; b. Red Hook, N.Y., Feb. 1, 1856; s. John Neher and Christina Jane (Nelson) L.; A.B., St. Stephen's Coll., Annandale, N.Y., 1875, LL.D., 1911; C.E., Rensselaer Poly. Inst., Troy, N.Y., 1879; m. Minnie Rose MacLean, Oct. 21, 1885. Ry. location and constrn., Colo., La. and Ala., 1879-84 and 1886-89; entered engring. staff, City of Brooklyn, 1884; in charge Bur. of Highways, City and Borough of Brooklyn, 1894-1902; chief engr. Bd. of Estimate and Apportionment, New York, 1902-20; dir. physical survey, Plan of New York and Environs; consultant City Planning Bd., Boston. New York rep. Internat. Road Congresses, Paris, 1908, Brussels, 1910, London, 1913, and Internat. Congress of Cities at Ghent, 1913; visited many European cities, 1910, to examine and report upon care and control of subsurface structures; mem. N.Y. City Improvement Commission and Heights of Bldgs. Commn. Mem. delegation of Am. engrs. visiting France, Dec. 1918, at request of French engrs. and ministers to advise on problems of reconstruction after war. Mem. Franco-Am. Engring. Com. Mem. Dutch Reformed Ch. Mem. visiting com. Sch. of Landscape Architects, Harvard; trustee Poly. Inst. Brooklyn. Author: The Planning of the Modern City, 1916, 22. Home: Brooklyn, N.Y. Died Mar. 30, 1924.

LEWIS, Orlando Faulkland, sociologist; b. Boston, Sept. 5, 1873; s. John Jay and Abbie Goodwin (Davis) L.; A.B., Tufts Coll., 1895; A.M., 1897; U. of Munich, and Sorbonne, Paris; Ph.D., U. of Pa., 1900; m. Edith Schieffelin Sabine, Apr. 20, 1908. Instr., Tufts Coll., 1895-97; prof. modern langs., U. of Me., 1900-05; with Charity Orgn. Soc., New York, 1905-10; gen. sec. Prison Assn. of N.Y., 1910—. Editor The Delinquent (monthly). Instr., New York School Philanthropy, 1906-18; asst. sec. Commn. on Hosps., New York, 1906-08; chmn. Child Labor Com. of N.J., 1907-08; mem. bd. mgrs. N.Y. State Industrial Farm Colony, 1912-16, and Bowery Branch Y.M.C.A.; commissioner Health Dept. of New Rochelle, N.Y., 1915-16, acting pres. New Rochelle Hosp., 1915. Republican. Universalist. Mem. Nat. Conf. Charities and Correction. Am. Prison Assn., Am. Inst. Criminal Law and Criminology; sec. 9th N.Y. State Conf. Charities and Correction, 1908, and pres. 4th N.Y. City Conf. of same. Author: Vagrancy in the United States, 1907. Dir. dept. of community singing, War Camp Community Service, 1918—. Home: New Rochelle, N.Y. Died Feb. 24, 1922.

LEWIS, Paul A., pathologist; b. Chicago, Ill., Apr. 14, 1879; s. Clinton H. and Caroline (Hobart) L.; studied U. of Wis., 1897-98, Wis. Coll. Phys. and Surg., Milwaukee, 1899-1901; M.D., U. of Pa., 1904; m. Louise Durbin, Aug. 6, 1906; children—Janet, Hobart. Resident in pathology, Boston City Hosp., 1904-05; asst. in Antitoxin Lab., Mass. State Bd. of Health, Boston, 1905-08; fellow in comparative pathology, Harvard, 1906-08; asso. in pathology, Rockefeller Inst., N.Y. City, 1908-10; dir. Lab. of Henry Phipps Inst., Phila., 1910-23; prof. exptl. pathology, U. of Pa., 1921-23; asso. mem. Rockefeller Inst. for Med. Research, New York, 1923—. Lt., later comdr. U.S. Naval Reserve, Aug. 1917-21; duty at Naval Hosp., League Island, and Naval Lab., Phipps Inst. (temp. establishment). Home: Princeton, N.J. Died June 30, 1929.

LEWIS, Richard Henry, M.D.; b. near Falkland, N.C., Feb. 18, 1850; s. Richard Henry and Martha Elizabeth (Hoskins) L.; ed. U. of N.C. and U. of Va.; M.D., U. of Md., 1871, became resident physician U. of Md. Hosp.; LL.D., U. of N.C., 1912; m. Cornelia Viola Battle, Feb. 13, 1877 (died 1886); children—Richard Henry, Martha Battle (wife of Dr. Isaac H. Manning), Kemp Plummer, Ivey Foreman; m. 2d, Mary Long Gordon, Apr. 16, 1890 (died 1895); 1 dau., Nell Battle; m. 3d, Mrs. Annie Blackwell Foreman, Oct. 27, 1897 (died 1917). Made specialty of diseases of the eye and ear; practiced at Tarboro, N.C., 1873-74, at Savannah, Ga., 1875-76, and was prof. diseases of the eye and ear Savannah Med. Coll.; in practice at Raleigh, N.C., 1877—; prof. diseases of the eye, ear and throat, Leonard Med. Sch., Raleigh, 1885-1913; prof. diseases of the eye and of hygiene, U. of N.C., 1902-09; sec., treas. N.C. State Bd. Health, 1892-1909. Trustee and mem. exec. coms. U. of N.C., 1891—, St. Augustine Normal Sch. for Colored, 1893—, St. Marys Sch., 1897—; mem. Raleigh Sch. Com., 1885-1918. Episcopalian. Home: Raleigh, N.C. Died Aug. 6, 1926.

LEWIS, Robert, otorhinologist; b. New York City, Mar. 8, 1862; s. Robert and Catherine (Monks) L.; M.D., College of Physicians and Surgeons (Columbia Univ.), 1885; m. Lillie B. Graham, 1892 (died 1929); children—Robert Graham, Hallett Nixon, Gwendolyn (Mrs. John Monks IV). Hosp. interne, clin. work in otology and rhinology, and gen. practice until 1892; became partner of Dr. Albert H. Buck, 1892, and specialized in rhinol. and otol. practice; surgeon New York Eye and Ear Infirmary, aural department, 1901-28; elected consulting surgeon, 1928; prof. clinical otolaryngology, Coll. Physicians and Surgeons, New York, 1908—; cons. otologist N.Y. Soc. for Relief of Ruptured and Crippled, Flushing, St. Francis and Sea View hosps. Mem. Med. Advisory Bd., N.Y. City, World War. Contbr. treatises on otological topics to Reference Handbook of Med. Sciences, The American Practice of Surgery. Died Dec. 20, 1939.

LEWIS, Robert E., judge; b. Cass Co., Mo., Apr. 3, 1857; s. Warner and Sarah M. (Griffith) L.; ed. Westminster Coll., Fulton, Mo.; m. Ella C. Avery, May 13, 1885; children—Mason Avery, Anne, Dorothy Byrd, Meriwether. Admitted to bar, 1880; practiced at Clinton, Mo., 1897—; pros. atty. Henry County, Mo., 1883-87; Rep. candidate for gov. of Mo., 1896; judge 4th Jud. Dist. of Colo., 1903-06; U.S. dist. judge, Dist. of Colo., 1906-21; U.S. circuit judge 8th Jud. Circuit, 1921-29, 10th Jud. Circuit, 1929—. Home: Denver, Colo. Died July 31, 1941.

LEWIS, Thomas Hamilton, clergyman; b. Dover, Del., Dec. 11, 1852; s. Thomas Hamilton and Sabra Ann (Melvin) L.; A.B., Western Md. Coll., Westminster, Md., 1875, A.M., 1878; D.D., Adrian (Mich.) Coll., 1883, Victoria U., Toronto, Can., 1911; LL.D., Washington Coll., Chestertown, Md., 1911; m. Mary Miranda Ward, Dec. 11, 1877; children—Miriam (Mrs. Herbert N. Veasey), Clara Ward (Mrs. Lee H. Richmond), Thomas Hamilton, Marjorie, Hamilton Ward, Elizabeth Ray. Ordained ministry M.P. Ch., 1876; pastor Cumberland, Md., 1875-77, Baltimore, 1878-82; organizer, and pres. Westminster Theol. Sem., 1882-86; pres. Western Md. Coll., 1886-1920; pres. Gen. Conf. M.P. Ch., 1908-12, and 1920—. Author: The Good Life, 1905; Divine Credentials of the Bible, 1907; The Modern Pilgrim, 1923; The Minister and His Own Soul, 1926. Home: Washington, D.C. Died June 14, 1929.

LEWIS, Virgil Anson, author; b. W. Columbia, W.Va., July 6, 1848; s. George W. and Lucy (Edwards) L.; acad. edn.; hon. A.M., W.Va. U., 1893; admitted to bar, 1879, but later abandoned law for ednl. and lit. work; m. Elizabeth Stone, Oct. 31, 1886. Worked in printing office when a boy and became half owner W. Virginia Monitor; founded Southern Historical Magazine, Charleston, W.Va., 1892; editor and pub. W.Va. School Journal, 1892-97; state supt. free schs., 1893-97; mem. State Bd. Pub. Works, 1893-97; commr. of state printing, 1893-97; pres. Bd.

of Regents State Normal Sch., 1893-97; state historian and archivist, 1905—. Del. Southern States Industrial Congress, Asheville, N.C., 1892; mem. and sec. W.Va. commn. Jamestown Expn., 1907. Organized W.Va. Hist. and Antiq. Soc., 1890. Author: History of West Virginia, 1889; Life and Times of Anne Bailey, the Pioneer Heroine, 1891; Graded Course of Study for Country and Village Schools of West Virginia, 1894; History and Government of West Virginia, 1896; Story of the Louisiana Purchase, 1903; Early Education in West Virginia, 1904; Civil Government of West Virginia, 1905. Mason; mem. Grand Lodge of Odd Fellows; Past Grand Chancellor Knights of Pythias. Home: Mason, W.Va. Died Dec. 5, 1912.

LEWIS, Walker, clergyman; b. Washington, Ga., May 11, 1847; s. Josiah and Elizabeth (Moore) L.; hon. A.M., D.D., Emory Coll., Ga.; m. Tallulah Trammell, Ga., Oct. 18, 1872. In Confederate Army 1 yr.; teacher 4 yrs.; ordained M.E. ministry, 1874; served in Macon, Columbus, Americus, Atlanta and Rome, Ga., Nashville, Tenn., Kansas City, Mo., Little Rock, Ark., Montgomery, Ala.; Southern field sec. Crittenton mission. Trustee LaGrange Female Coll. Independent Democrat. Author of Rescue Tracts. Home: Rome, Ga. Deceased.

LEWIS, Wilfred, mech. engr., mfr.; b. Phila., Pa., Oct. 16, 1854; s. Edward and Elizabeth I. L.; grad. Friends' Central Sch., Phila., 1871; B.S. in Mech. Engring., Mass. Inst. Tech., 1875; m. Emily Sargent, Jan. 16, 1895. Mechanic, 1875-78, draftsman, 1879-82, designer, asst. engr. and dir., 1883-1900, William Sellers & Co., Phila.; pres. The Tabor Mfg. Co., 1900—. Inventor and patentee of about 50 patents. Life mem. Am. Soc. Mech. Engrs. (v.p. 1901-03). Republican. Unitarian. Recognized as a world authority on gears, and awarded gold medal of Am. Soc. M.E., 1927, for his contributions to design and construction of gear teeth. Home: Haverford, Pa. Died Dec. 19, 1929.

LEWIS, William Alexander, educator; b. Dwight, Ill., Oct. 12, 1876; s. Lawrence and Anna E. (Oldsen) L.; B.S., Valparaiso (Ind.) U., 1899, A.B., 1910, LL.D., 1914; B.S. in Edn., State Teachers Coll., Warrensburg, Mo., 1901; m. Glennie Coe, Sept. 4, 1904; children—Catherine E., Lawrence, William A. Prof. physics State Teachers College, Warrensburg, Mo., 1901-03; prof. chemistry, Kansas City (Mo.) High Sch., 1903-06, Kansas City Coll. of Pharmacy, 1905-06; prof. chemistry, 1906-10, head dept. farm and home economics, and dir. State Farm, 1910-12, State Teachers Coll., Kirksville; prof. industrial education and dir. State Demonstration Farm, U. of Utah, 1912-13; pres. Fort Hays (Kan.) State Coll., 1913—. Mem. N.E.A. Com. to World Federation of Edn. Methodist. Home: Hays, Kan. Died Oct. 10, 1933.

LEWIS, William Eugene, editor; b. Cleveland, O.; s. I. J. and Harriet M. (Tracy) L.; ed. Painesville (O.) Acad., East High Sch., Cleveland; m. Frances Oviatt. Practiced law Cleveland and Kansas City, 1889-90; mng. editor Kansas City News, 1890-91, Chicago Times, 1893-95; Washington and political corr., 1896-98, war corr., 1898, New York Journal; editor New York Morning Telegraph, 1898-1901; mng. editor Philadelphia North American, 1901-03; editor and gen. mgr. New York Morning Telegraph, 1903—. Dir. Morning Telegraph, Bank of Great Neck, Thomas Engraving Co., Industrial Development Co. Was sec. Bd. of Improvements, Cleveland, O., 1887-89. Home: Great Neck, L.I., N.Y. Died Oct. 28, 1924.

LEWIS, Wilson Seeley, bishop; b. Russell, N.Y., July 17, 1857; s. William H. and Hannah (Turner) L.; A.B., Cornell Coll., Ia., 1889, A.M., 1892; D.D., Upper Ia. U., 1894, Cornell Coll., 1904. Ordained M.E. ministry; supt. schs., Belle Plaine, Ia., 1882-85; prin. Epworth (Ia.) Sem., 1888-97; pres. Morningside Coll., Sioux City, Ia., 1897-1908; bishop M.E. Ch., 1908—. Died Aug. 25, 1921.

LEWIS, Yancey, lawyer; b. Gonzales, Tex., Aug. 24, 1861; s. Everett and Alice Josephine (Strickland) L.; A.B., Emory and Henry Coll., Va., 1881; Ph.B., U. of Tex., 1885, LL.B., 1885; m. Lulie D. Sanford, Jan. 31, 1894. Practiced at Gonzales, 1885-86, at Dallas, 1904—; master in chancery in Choctaw Coal & Railway Co. receivership, Indian Ty., 1893-94, and master commr. to sell the property, 1894; U.S. judge, Central Dist., Ind. Ty., 1894-97; with associates, counsel for Creek Indian Nation, and for Cherokees, 1898-99; leading counsel for Galveston (Tex.) Chamber Commerce, 1908-11. Prof. law, 1900-04, dean law dept., 1902-04, U. of Tex. Home: Dallas, Tex. Died Mar. 10, 1915.

LEWISOHN, Adolph, mining, investments; b. Hamburg, Germany; ed. at Hamburg; came to America. Sr. mem. of Adolph Lewisohn & Sons; pres. Tennessee Corp., General Development Co., Miami Copper Co., S. Am. Gold & Platinum Co. Has made a number of gifts in cause of edn. and philanthropy, including $300,000 to Columbia U. for School of Mines Bldg., the Lewisohn Stadium of Coll. City of N.Y., etc. Pres. Hebrew Sheltering Guardian Soc.; dir. Mt. Sinai Hosp. Hon. mem. Alumni of Coll. City of N.Y. Home: New York, N.Y. Died Aug. 17, 1938.

LEXOW, Clarence, lawyer; b. at Brooklyn, Sept. 16, 1852; s. Rudolph and Caroline (King) L.; acad. edn.; LL.B., Columbia, 1874; Ph.D., U. of Jena; m. Katharine M. Ferris, Feb. 3, 1881. Sr. mem. law firm Lexow, Mackellar & Wells, New York; pres. Antrim Park Realty Co., Star Pub. Co., Tappan Zee Real Estate Co., Cities Development Co.; v.p. Ramapo Trap Rock Co.; dir. Ætna Indemnity Co., Bank of Discount, Cross Island Traction Co., N. River Steamboat Co., Title & Guaranty Co. of Rochester, South Shore Traction Co. Mem. N.Y. Senate, 1893-98; was head of senate com. to investigate city govt. of New York; chmn. joint legislative com. and introducer of bill creating the Greater New York. Republican. Author of report on Municipal Government; Consolidation; Trusts and Unlawful Combinations. Home: Nyack, N.Y. Died 1910.

LEYENDECKER, Frank X., artist; b. Montabour, Germany, Jan. 19, 1879; s. Peter and Elizabeth (Ortseifen) L.; brought to America at age of 6 yrs.; studied painting, Julien Acad., Paris. Studio: New York, N.Y. Died Apr. 19, 1924.

LEYS, James Farquharson, naval officer; b. Delaware County, Pa., Dec. 26, 1867; s. James F. and Rachel (West) L.; M.D., U. of Pa., 1890; m. Gwendoleyne Mary Wigley, 1897; children—Katharine Mary, James Farquharson, Gwendoleyne Mary, Martha Francesca. Apptd. asst. surgeon U.S.N., 1893; promoted through grades to rear adm. and retired for age, Jan. 1, 1932, with advancement to vice adm. for service on construction of Panama Canal, 1907-10, being the first officer of any staff corps in the Navy to attain that rank. Served afloat on U.S.S. Chicago, Alliance, Helena, Vesuvius, Essex, New York and Flagship Wyoming (aide and fleet surgeon); comd. naval hosps. at New port and Boston. Medals: Santiago, Spanish Campaign, Vera Cruz, Panama, Victory (with special commendation). Wrote First Sect., Vol. II, American Practice of Surgery. Collaborator in Reference Handbook of Med. Sciences. Home: Bryn Mawr, Pa. Died Jan. 12, 1938.

LIBBEY, Edward Drummond, mfr.; b. Chelsea, Mass., Apr. 17, 1854; s. William L. and Julia M. (Miller) L.; ed. Boston U.; m. Florence Scott, June 24, 1890. Entered father's glass business as partner, 1874; became sole propr., 1883; organizer and pres. Libbey Glass Co., Toledo Glass Co., Libbey-Owens Sheet Glass Co., The Owens Bottle Co. Home: Toledo, O. Died Nov. 13, 1925.

LIBBEY, Jonas Marsh, editor; b. Ridgewood, N.J., Apr. 8, 1857; s. William and Elizabeth (Marsh) L.; A.B., Princeton, 1877; post-grad. work, U. of Berlin, 1878, U. of Leipzig, 1879, Oxford U., 1885; student New York Law Sch., 1891-93. Editor Princeton Review, 1877-85, as agt. of U.S. Govt., 1885, made investigation of industrial conditions in Eng., giving spl. attention to labor, wages and the cost of production in cotton, woolen, iron, steel and other industries; also made an exhaustive study of various industrial depressions which occurred in Eng. during 19th Century (report pub. in 1st Ann. Report of Commn. of Labor, 1886). Actively interested in municipal improvements. Home: New York, N.Y. Died Feb. 1, 1922.

LIBBEY, Laura Jean, author; b. N.Y. City, d. Thomas H. and Elizabeth L.; ed. pvtly.; m. Van Mater Stilwell, Sept. 23, 1898. Formerly contbr. to New York Ledger, Fireside Companion, and Family Story Paper; editor New York Fashion Bazaar, 1891-94; spl. corr. New York Evening World, 1899-1901. Author: Lovers Once but Strangers Now; That Pretty Young Girl; Miss Middleton's Lover; A Forbidden Marriage; Olive's Courtship; When His Love Grew Cold; and many other novels. Home: Brooklyn, N.Y. Died Oct. 25, 1924.

LIBBEY, William, univ. prof.; b. Jersey City, N.J., Mar. 27, 1855; s. William and Elizabeth (Marsh) L.; A.B., Princeton, 1877, A.M., Sc.D., 1879; m. Mary E. Green, Dec. 7, 1880; children—Mrs. W. Lester Glenney, Mrs. W. Thayer Field. Asst. prof. physical geography, 1882, histology, 1883-98, phys. geography and dir. mus. of geology and archeology, 1883-1923, Princeton, emeritus. Pres. Princeton Savings Bank; v.p. First Nat. Bank. Capt. Co. L, 2d Regt. N.G. of N.J., 1900-06; lt. col. asst. insp. gen. rifle practice, 1906, col., 1917. Maj., Ordnance R.C.U.S.A., Feb. 20, 1918; asst. chief instr., Small Arms Firing Sch., May 13, 1918; lt. col. inf., Sept. 8, 1918; chief rifle demonstrator, Oct. 1, 1918; discharged, Mar. 20, 1919. Officier d'Académie, France. Fellow and foreign sec. Am. Geog. Society. Mem. numerous Am. and fgn. societies. Author: Jordan Valley and Petra (with Dr. Franklin E. Hoskins), 1905. Home: Princeton, N.J. Died Sept. 6, 1927.

LIBBY, Charles Freeman, lawyer; b. Limerick, Me., Jan. 31, 1844; s. James Brackett and Hannah Catharine (Morrill) L.; A.B., Bowdoin Coll., 1864, A.M., 1867 (LL.D., 1902); Columbia Law Sch., 1865-66; m. Alice Bradbury, Dec. 9, 1869. Admitted to bar, 1866; in practice at Portland, 1868—; sr. mem. Libby, Robinson & Ives; pres. Portland R.R. Co., 1904—. Mem. Me. Senate, 1889-92 (pres. 1891-92). Republican. Pres. Overseers of Bowdoin College, 1891-1912. Officier de l'Academie Française, 1907. Home: Portland, Me. Died June 3, 1915.

LIBBY, Edward Norton, M.D., educator; b. Limington, Me., July 17, 1868; s. George Ward and Mary (Cole) L.; A.B., Dartmouth, 1892, M.D., 1895; m. Marjorie Hill, June 1, 1907; children—Mary Louise, Edward Norton. Practiced at Boston, Mass., 1895—; prof. theory and practice of medicine, Tufts Med. Coll.; sr. visiting physician, Boston City Hosp. Republican. Episcopalian. Home: Jamaica Plain, Mass. Died Nov. 5, 1929.

LIBBY, Melanchthon Fennessy, prof. philosophy; b. Port Hope, Ont., Can., Mar. 4, 1864; s. Robert Stephen and Mary (Fennessy) L.; St. Mary's Coll., Ky., 1877-79; Collegiate Inst., Cobourg, Ont., 1879-81; Victoria Coll. (Toronto U.), 1881-83, B.A., 1890; Ph.D., Clark U., Mass., 1901; univs. of Göttingen and Berlin, 3 yrs.; m. Agnes Phillips, of Cobourg, Ont., Dec. 30, 1890. High sch. teacher in Can. (mainly Toronto), 1883-96; fellow and traveling fellow, Clark U., 5 yrs.; prof. philosophy, U. of Colo., 1901—. Widely known account of Denver Saturday lectures, regularly maintained before a gen. audience, 1904—. Episcopalian. Editor: Selections from Wordsworth, 1893; Selections from Tennyson, 1894. Home: Boulder, Colo. Died May 2, 1921.

LICHTENBERG, Leopold, violinist; b. San Francisco, Nov. 22, 1861; began on the violin in early childhood; received instruction at 7 from M. Beaujardin; appeared as soloist in concert; at 12 attracted the attention of Henri Wieniawski, then on visit to San Francisco, and at his invitation became his pupil; spent 3 yrs. at Brussels Conservatoire. Often played before royalty; made tour in Holland as substitute for Wieniawski with great success; soloist at Theodore Thomas concerts, 1877; returned to Europe 3 yrs., playing in prin. cities; returned to U.S.; was mem. Boston Symphony Orchestra; now prin. violin dept. Nat. Conservatory of Music, New York. Home: New York, N.Y. Died May 17, 1935.

LICHTENTAG, Alexander; b. New Orleans, La., Mar. 13, 1868; s. Isaac and Mathilde (Wolff) L.; ed. pub. schs. and by father, grad. Royal U. of Berlin; m. Alice Baumblatt, Oct. 22, 1890; children—Moise, Bertha (Mrs. M. W. Mayer), Alvin P. Inventor of Paragon shorthand system, now in use in many parts of the world, and of "Word Hunt," an ednl. game; pres. Paragon Shorthand Inst.; pres. Paragon Corp.; v.p. and chmn. exec. com. Fidelity Homestead Association. Democrat. Mem. Athenæum, Am. Red Cross, etc. Mason. Author: Paragon Shorthand, 1891-1915; The Word Book; Paragon Shorthand Reader; Word Hunt (syndicated in newspapers of U.S. and other countries). Home: New Orleans, La. Died Jan. 14, 1938.

LICHTY, John Alden, M.D.; b. Meyersdale, Pa., Feb. 26, 1866; s. Jonas and Mary (Miller) L.; Ph.B., Mt. Union Coll., 1890, Ph.M., 1893, Ph.D., 1924; M.D., U. of Pa., 1893; U. of Berlin, 1895-96; m. Cora Lane Stoner (M.D.), Dec. 11, 1894; children—Mrs. Mary Dorothy Lissfelt, Mrs. Marjory Elizabeth Lamb, John Alden, Joseph Stoner. Resident phys., Phila. Hosp., 1893-94; moved to Pittsburgh, 1899; consulting phys., Presbyterian Hosp., phys.-in-chief, Columbia Hosp., 1906, Mercy Hosp., 1910—; asso. prof. medicine, U. of Pittsburgh; supt. Clifton Springs (N.Y.) Sanitarium and Clinic, 1923—. Formerly mem. State Bd. Charities; mem. Com. Lunacy, State of Pa. Trustee Colgate-Rochester Div. Sch., Mt. Union Coll.; regent Am. Coll. Physicians. Republican. Baptist. Mason. Home: Clifton Springs, N.Y. Died May 2, 1932.

LIDDELL, Eva Louise (Barnes), author; b. Boxford, Mass.; d. Phineas Warren and Harriet (Russell) Barnes; graduate Johnson High Sch., North Andover, Mass.; m. Henry Liddell, author, July 13, 1887. Engaged in lit. work from 1889. Editor Sunbeams Little Folks and Sunbeams Young People for several yrs. Author: Polly Perkins' Adventures, 1902. Home: Seaford, L.I., N.Y. Died Mar. 18, 1937.

LIDDELL, Mark Harvey, univ. prof.; b. Clearfield, Pa., Apr. 1, 1866; s. Thomas and Sophronia (Swan) L.; A.B., Princeton U., 1887, fellow in English, 1889; Oxford U., England, 1893-94, 95, 96; Univ. of Berlin, 1894-95; m. Mary Stanley Field, Dec. 30, 1890; children—Mary Gray Patterson (Mrs. Louis B. Wehle), Thomas Mark, Robert Patterson Field. Prof. English, U. of Tex., 1897-1900, U. of Louisville, 1908-11; acting prof. English, Butler U., Indianapolis, 1912-13; instr. English, 1913-14, asst. prof., 1914, asso. prof., 1919, prof., 1921-32, Purdue U., retired 1932. Editor: The Middle English Translation of Palladius de Rustica, Part I—Text, 1896; The Works of Geoffrey Chaucer (with A. W. Pollard, H. Frank Heath and W. S. McCormick), 1898; Chaucer—The Prologue to the Canterbury Tales, The Knight's Tale, The Nonnes Prestes Tale, in Critical Text, with Grammatical Introduction, Notes and Glossary, 1901; The Elizabethan Shakespeare (with critical text in Elizabethan English and Brief Notes illustrative of Elizabethan Life, Thought and Idiom); Macbeth, 1903; The Tempest, 1904. Author: An Introduction to the Study of Poetry, being Prolegomena to a Science of English Prosody, 1902; A Brief Abstract of a New English Prosody, 1914; A New Theory of Sound, 1935. Home: East Orleans, Cape Cod, Mass. Died July 28, 1936.

LIDDON, Benjamin Sullivan, lawyer; b. Jackson Co., Fla., Sept. 7, 1853; s. Benjamin G. and Susan E. (Sullivan) L.; ed. pub. schs. of Ga. and Fla., and for a time at Southern Univ., Greensboro, Ala.; studied law under Judge Allen H. Bush; m. Virginia M. Harvey, Apr. 6, 1880. Admitted to bar, 1875; represented (by spl. apptmt.) State of Fla. in prosecution of C. B. Collins, defaulting State treas., 1897, and in recent proceedings before U.S. Congress of Charles Swayne, U.S. dist. judge; was for several yrs. atty. for State H.R. Commn., resigned, 1902; local counsel for Louisville & Nashville R.R.; dir. and counsel for 1st Nat. Bank of Marianna, Fla. Was supt. pub. schs., Jackson Co., Fla., 1879-80; mayor Marianna, Fla., 4 yrs. in '80s; chief justice, 1894, asso. justice, 1895-97, Supreme Court, Fla.; resigned to resume practice, 1897; chmn. of Commn. for Revision of Statutes of Fla., July 1903—. Mem. M.E. Ch., S. Democrat. Home: Marianna, Fla. Died 1909.

LIE, Jonas, artist; b. Norway, Apr. 29, 1880; s. Sverre and Helen Augusta (Steele) L.; came to America, 1893; grad. Ethical Culture Sch., New York, 1897; art edn., Nat. Acad. Design, Art Students' League, New York; Dr. Fine Arts, Lawrence Coll., 1936. Represented in Metropolitan Mus. of Art, New York; Carnegie Inst., Pittsburgh; Art Inst. Chicago; Memorial Art Gallery, Rochester, N.Y.; Syracuse Mus.; Peabody Inst., Baltimore; Dallas (Tex.) Art Assn.; Lafayette (Ind.) Art Assn.; Luxembourg Museum, Paris; Boston Museum; Brooklyn (N.Y.) Mus.; Albright Gallery, Buffalo, N.Y.; Cleveland (O.) Mus.; Detroit(Mich.) Mus.; R.I. Sch. of Design, Providence, R.I.; Telfair Acad., Savannah, Ga.; Corcoran Gallery, Washington, D.C.; Cedar Rapids (Ia.) Art Assn.; Elmira (N.Y.) Art Assn., Canajoharie (N.Y.) Library; City Hall, Plainfield, N.J.; Library, Saranac Lake, N.Y.; U.S. Mil. Acad., West Point, N.Y.; collection of Crown Prince Olaf of Norway; collection of Addison Mall, Andover, N.H.; Springville (Utah) High Sch. Art Assn.; Ia. State Univ., Iowa City; St. Louis (Mo.) Merchants Club; Engineers Club, N.Y. City; Chicago Norske Club; Whitney Mus., N.Y. City; Norwegian Legation, Washington; Minneapolis Museum; City Art Museum of St. Louis; National Arts Club, N.Y. City. Silver medal, St. Louis Expn., 1904; first Hallgarten Prize, Nat. Acad. of Design, New York, 1914; silver medal, San Francisco Expn., 1915; Greenough memorial prize, Newport, R.I., 1916; gold medal, art week, Phila., 1925; 1st prize, Chicago Norwegian Club, 1925-27; Carnegie prize, Nat. Acad. Design, 1927; 1st prize, Springville (Utah) High Sch. Art Assn., 1927; Maida Gregg memorial prize, Nat. Art Club, 1929; Olympic award, Amsterdam, 1928; prize, Pa. Academy, Phila., 1935; Saltus medal of merit, Nat. Acad. Design, 1936; Obrig prize, Nat. Acad. Design, 1937; Am. Roll of Honor, 1936. Knight of Order of St. Olav (Norway). Mem. Soc. of Medalists, Am. Fedn. of Arts, Nat. Inst. Arts and Letters (v.p.), Art Students League, Am. Nat. Com. on Intellectual Cooperation, Art Commn. Associates. Nat. Academician; pres. Nat. Acad. Design, 1934. Home: New York, N.Y. Died Jan. 10, 1940.

LIEB, John William, mech. engineer; b. Newark, N.J., Feb. 12, 1860; s. John William and Christina (Zens) L.; ed. Newark Acad. and Stevens H.S., Hoboken, N.J.; E.D., M.E., Stevens Inst. Tech., 1880; m. Minnie F. Engler, July 29, 1886. Employed as draftsman, 1880-81; by Mr. Edison put in charge of installation of elec. equipment of old Pearl St., Edison Sta., and assisted in subsequent tests and experiments on this first elec. sta. in U.S., supplying current for incandescent lighting and power from an underground system, and on inauguration of regular service, Sept. 4, 1882, was apptd. first electrician Edison Electric illuminating Co. of New York; next installed mech. equipment, dynamos, and Edison Underground System at Milan, Italy, 1883, for Italian Edison Co.; later installed trolley system in Milan; returned to Edison Elec. Illuminating Co., 1894; now v.p. and gen. mgr. New York Edison Co.; also pres. Elec. Testing Laboratories; dir. in a number of corps. Decorated by King of Italy, Knight Comdr. Order Crown of Italy. Trustee Stevens Institute of Technology. Home: New York, N.Y. Died Nov. 1, 1929.

LIEBER, B. Franklin; b. Phila., Pa., Feb. 17, 1853; s. Benjamin and Rachel (Cromelien) L.; ed. Hamilton's Coll., Phila.; m. Rose, d. David Greenfield, of New York, Nov. 25, 1894. Author of Lieber's Code and other publications, and pres. Lieber Code Co. Home: Kensington, London. Died Nov. 10, 1915.

LIEBER, G(uido) Norman, brig. gen. U.S.A.; b. Columbia, S.C., May 21, 1837; s. Francis L. (Ph.D., LL.D.); A.B., S.C. Coll., 1856; LL.B., Harvard, 1858; m. a d. of Gen. E. B. Alexander, U.S.A. First lt. 11th U.S. Inf., May 14, 1861; promoted through grades to brig. gen. judge advocate gen., Jan. 3, 1895; retired, May 21, 1901. Bvtd. capt., June 27, 1862, "for gallant and meritorious services in battle of Gaines' Mill, Va."; maj., May 28, 1864, for same in Red River, La. campaign; lt. colonel, March 13, 1865, "for faithful and meritorious services during the war." Author: Remarks on the Army Regulations; The Use of the Army in Aid of the Civil Power; etc. Died Apr. 25, 1923.

LIEBLING, Emil, musician; b. Pless, Germany, Apr. 12, 1851; studied piano under Ehrlich and Kullak at Berlin; Dachs at Vienna, and Liszt at Weimar; theory with Dorn at Berlin. In U.S., 1867; at Chicago, 1872—; prominent as concert pianist; also teacher, musical writer, lecturer and composer. Home: Chicago, Ill. Died Jan. 20, 1914.

LIEBMAN, Julius, editor; b. Milwaukee, Wis.; m. Ethel Lewis, Nov. 14, 1911; children—Robert Lewis, William Lewis, Arthur Lewis. Began as reporter Milwaukee Sentinel, 1909, v.p. and editor, 1929—. Republican. Mason. Home: Milwaukee, Wis. Died Jan. 31, 1937.

LIEFELD, (Friedrich Wilhelm) Albert, clergyman; b. Ludwigsfelde, nr. Berlin, Germany, Mar. 14, 1831; s. Daniel Emanuel and Louise (Paul) L.; ed. in Germany; served in 2d Body Regt. Black Hussars under Emperor William I, 1851-55; grad. in divinity, Hermansburg, Hanover, Germany, 1861; Evang. Luth. missionary, S. Africa, 1861-65; came to U.S., Feb. 1866; m. Anna Sophia Braunack, July 27, 1866. Had ministerial charges in Wis., Ill., Ind. and Pa., emeritus. Home: Allegheny, Pa. Died 1907.

LIFE, Andrew Creamor, botanist; b. Grant Co., Ind., July 30, 1869; s. Christian and Ruth Ann (Elliott) L.; A.B., Ind. U., 1896, A.M., 1897; post grad. student Washington U., St. Louis, Mo., 1904-06, U. of Chicago, 1906-07, U. of Calif., 1923-24, also several summers; m. Cora Mae Smith, June 20, 1917. Began as instr. botany, Earlham Coll., 1904; instr. botany, Washington U., 1904-06; asst. prof. botany, U. of Southern Calif., 1907-10, asso. prof., 1910-15, prof., 1915—. Methodist. Mason. Made trip around World for ednl. purposes, 1931. Home: Los Angeles, Calif. Died Sept. 8, 1933.

LIFE, Frank Mann, educator; b. Grant Co., Ind., Sept. 1, 1870; s. Christian and Ruth Ann (Elliott) L.; A.B., Marion (Ind.) Coll., 1891; B.S., DePauw U., 1896; studied U. of Chicago, 1897, 1917; m. Clara Hight, Aug. 18, 1898 (died 1919); 1 son, Harold G.; m. 2d, Mabel Eckstrom, Aug. 17, 1925. Lab. inst., DePauw, 1894-96; instr. science, Soule Coll., Dodge City, Kan., 1896-97; prof. physics and chemistry, Marion (Ind.) Coll., 1897-1907, head dept. of science, 1907-12; dean Muncie (Ind.) Coll., 1914-16; dir. edn., Winona (Ind.) Coll., 1917; instr., asst., asso. prof. and prof. of physics, U. of Ariz., 1919-26; dean Coll. of Letters, Arts and Sciences, 1926-27, head of dept. physics, 1927—. Chief Div. of Imports of Bur. of War Trade Intelligence, War Trade Bd., 1917-19. Rep. state of Ind., Am. Mining Congress, Portland, Ore., 1904. Methodist. K.P. On sabbatical leave, 1929-30, to study in Am. European instns. and complete trip around world. Home: Tucson, Ariz. Died 1933.

LIGGETT, Hunter, army officer; b. Reading, Pa., Mar. 21, 1857; s. James and Margaret (Hunter) L.; grad. U.S. Mil. Acad., 1879; LL.D., U. of Calif., 1921; m. Harriet R. Lane, June 30, 1881. Commd. 2d lt. 5th U.S. Inf., June 13, 1879; promoted through grades to maj. gen., Mar. 6, 1917; retired as maj. gen., U.S.A., Mar. 21, 1921; restored to A.E.F. rank of lt. gen., U.S.A.; retired, 1930. For details of career see Vol. 12 (1922-23). Home: San Francisco, Calif. Died Dec. 30, 1935.

LIGGETT, Walter William, writer; b. Benson, Minn., Feb. 14, 1886; s. Col. William Madison and Mathilda Root (Brown) L.; grad. Central High Sch., St. Paul; student Minn. Agrl. Coll., 1904-05; m. Normal J. Ask, 1909; m. 2d, Edith Fleisher, 1922; children—William Wallace, Marda Molyneux. Newspaper reporter, 1905-08; mng. editor Skagway Alaskan, 1908-10; pub. Pasco (Wash.) Progress, 1911-15; mng. editor Fargo (N.Dak.) Courier-News, 1917-18, New York Call, 1922; worked on New York Times, Post, News and Sun, 1923-25; became free lance writer, 1925; editor Plain Talk, 1930. Dep. commr. of immigration, State of N.Dak., 1919. Author: The Frozen Frontier, 1926; The River Riders, 1927; Pioneers of Justice, 1930; The Rise of Herbert Hoover, 1932. Editor and pub. Austin (Minn.) American and Rochester (Minn.) American. Home: Rochester, Minn. Died Dec. 9, 1935.

LIGGINS, John, clergyman, author; b. Nuneaton, Eng., May 11, 1829; s. John and Elizabeth L.; ed. Episcopal Acad., Phila.; grad. Theol. Sem., Alexandria, Va. Deacon, 1855, priest, 1857, P.E. Ch.; asst. Ch. Ascension, New York, 1855; missionary to China, 1855-59; first Protestant missionary to Japan, 1859-60; returned to U.S. (impaired health); since devoted to literature. Author: One Thousand Familiar Phrases in English and Japanese (pub. in China, U.S., and Japan), 1860; England's Opium Policy, 1883; Missionary Picture Gallery, 1870; Oriental Picture Gallery, 1870; Great Value and Success of Foreign Missions, 1889. Home: Ocean City, N.J. Died Jan. 8, 1912.

LIGHTBURN, Joseph A. J., clergyman; b. Westmoreland Co., Pa., Sept. 21, 1824; common school edn.; m. Oct. 14, 1855, Miss H. E. Whittlesey. Served in U.S.A. 9 yrs.; served through the Mexican and Civil wars; resigned commn. as big. gen. U.S. vols., June 22, 1865; ordained Bapt. minister, 1869. Republican. Home: Lightburn, W.Va. Died 1901.

LIGHTNER, Clarence Ashley, lawyer; b. Binghamton, N.Y., Jan. 24, 1862; s. Rev. Milton C. and Martha (Hurley) L.; B.A., U. of Mich., 1883; studied law in office of Hon. Alfred Russell; m. Frances McGraw, July 20, 1892; children—Theodore A., Clarence H., Alice M. (Mrs. Ernest J. Hope), Martha F. (Mrs. Daniel F. Boone). Admitted to Mich. bar, 1888, and entered practice at Detroit; now mem. Lightner, Crawford, Sweeny, Dodd & Toohy; counsel for Peoples Wayne County Bank; mem. Bd. Law Examiners State of Mich. Episcopalian. Home: Tryon, N.C., and Detroit, Mich. Died Dec. 7, 1938.

LILE, William Minor, dean law sch.; b. Trinity, Ala., Mar. 28, 1859; s. John Allison and Louisa E. (Minor) L.; U. of Va., 1877-78, LL.B., 1882; LL.D., William and Mary Coll., 1901; m. Maud Lee Carson, Jan. 25, 1888; children—Minor Carson, Eleanor (Mrs. Beverley D. Tucker, Jr.), John Allison. Admitted to Va. bar, 1882; began practice at Lynchburg; mem. Kirkpatrick & Blackford, 1885-89, in partnership with R. G. H. Kean, 1891-93; prof. law, Sept. 1893—; dean of Law Sch., 1896—, U. of Va. Dir. Peoples Nat. Bank, Charlottesville, Va. Mem. Gov's. Commn. of Seven to suggest amendments to Va. constitution. Mem. bd. of govs. Woodberry Forest Sch. for Boys, Orange, Va. Mem. vestry St. Paul's Memorial Ch. (Episcopal). A founder, 1895, and asso. editor Va. Law Register, 1895-97, sole editor, 1897-1901, editor-in-chief, 1901-02. Author: Elementary Work on Equity Procedure for Students, 1916. Editor of Bigelow's Bills, Notes and Checks (3d edit.), 1928. Home: University, Va. Died Dec. 13, 1935.

LILIENTHAL, Jesse Warren, lawyer; b. N.Y. City, Aug. 2, 1855; s. Max and Pepi (Nettre) L.; LL.B., Cincinnati Coll. (now U. of Cincinnati), 1872; LL.B., Harvard, 1876; m. Lillie S. Bernheimer, Dec. 14, 1886. Settled in San Francisco, Calif., 1894; now mem. Lilienthal, McKinstry & Raymond; pres. United Railroads Co. of San Francisco, 1913—; dir. Anglo & London Paris Nat. Bank (San Francisco), Anglo-Cal. Trust Co.; chmn. Morris Plan Co., San Francisco. Pres. San Francisco Assn. Prevention of Tuberculosis; pres. San Francisco Council Boy Scouts America; pres. Recreation League of San Francisco; chmn. com. to provide recreation for soldiers and sailors; mem. probation com. of Juvenile Court; mem. finance com. San Francisco Chapter Am. Red Cross. Jewish religion. Home: San Francisco, Calif. Died June 3, 1919.

LILJENCRANTZ, Ottilie Adaline, author; b. Chicago, Jan. 19, 1876; d. Gustave Adolph Mathias and Adaline Charlotte (Hall) Liljencrantz; grad. Dearborn Sem., Chicago, 1893; unmarried. Author: The Scrape that Jack Built, 1896; The Thrall of Leif the Lucky, 1902; The Ward of King Canute, 1903; The Vinland Champions, 1904; Randvar the Songsmith, 1906. Home: Chicago, Ill. Died 1910.

LILLEY, Charles Sumner, lawyer; b. Lowell, Mass., Dec. 13, 1851; s. Charles and Cynthia (Huntley) L.; ed. pub. schs. and pvt. tutors; (hon. A.M., Dartmouth, 1896); m. Clara Bonney, Apr. 14, 1891. Admitted to bar, June 1877, and engaged in practice at Lowell; dir. Lowell Mut. Fire Ins. Co.; trustee Central Savings Bank; pres. Lowell Cemetery Corp. Mem. Mass. Senate, 1880, 81, 86; mem. exec. council, Mass., 1884; justice Superior Ct. of Mass., 1893-1900; resumed practice. Trustee Rogers Hall Sch. Home: Lowell, Mass. Died Apr. 16, 1921.

LILLEY, George, prof. mathematics, Univ. of Ore., 1897—; b. Kewanee, Ill., Feb. 9, 1854; s. William and Harriet (Huntley) L.; ed. Knox Coll., Ill., 1869-73 (M.A.); Univ. of Mich., 1873-75; grad. Ill. Wesleyan Univ., Ph.D., 1882; M.A., 1886; M.A., Washington and Jefferson, 1878; LL.D., Chaddock Coll., 1886; m. Sophia Adelaide Munn, June 11, 1879. Engaged in business, Corning, Ia., 1878-80; pres. S.Dak. Agrl. Coll., 1884-87; prof. mathematics and engring. S.Dak. Agrl. Coll., 1887-90; pres. Washington Agrl. Coll., and School of Science, 1890-93; prin. Park School, Portland, Ore., 1894-96. Home: Eugene, Ore. Died 1904.

LILLEY, George Leavens, congressman, real estate dealer; b. Oxford, Mass., Aug. 3, 1859; s. John Leavens and Caroline W. (Adams) L.; ed. Oxford pub. schs., Worcester High Sch. and Tech. Inst.; m. Anna E. H. Steele, June 17, 1884. Mem. Conn. legislature, 1901; mem. Rep. State Com., 1901—; mem. Congress, Conn., at-large, 1903-09. Republican. Home: Waterbury, Conn. Died 1909.

LILLIBRIDGE, William Otis, author; b. Union Co., S.D., Dec. 18, 1877; s. Walter Germain and Ella Sarah (Hoyt) L.; D.D.S., Coll. of Dentistry, State Univ. of Iowa, 1898; m. Edith Mary Keller, Sept. 1, 1904. Practiced, 1898—. Republican. Author: Ben Blair, 1905; Where the Trail Divides, 1907. Home: Sioux Falls, S.D. Died 1909.

LILLIE, Abraham Bruyn Hasbrouck, officer U.S.N.; b. in N.Y.; entered U.S. Naval Acad. from N.Y., Sept. 24, 1862; grad. 1866. Promoted ensign, Apr. 1868; master, Mar. 26, 1869; lt., Mar. 21, 1870; lt. comdr., Jan. 1887; comdr., Sept. 1895; capt., Mar. 3, 1901. Served on various duties and stations, spending 19 yrs. 3 months at sea, and 18 yrs. and 7 months on shore and other duty, and was commandant U.S. Naval Sta. at Key West, Fla., 1901-03; retired Mar. 6, 1903, with rank of rear admiral. Died 1905.

LILLIE, Gordon William ("Pawnee Bill"), ranchman; b. Bloomington, Ill., Feb. 14, 1860; s. Newton William and Susan A. (Conant) L.; ed. sch. Bloomington, 1866-78; m. Mary Emma Manning, Aug. 31, 1886; 1 son, Gordon William (dec.). Began career as hunter and trapper, 1878, interpreter for Pawnee tribe Indians, ranching nr. Medicine Lodge, Kan.; interpreter and mgr. Pawnee Indians with 1st Buffalo Bill Wild West Show, 1883-86; many yrs. professional showman in U.S. and Europe, known as "Pawnee Bill"; engaged by Bd. Trade, Wichita, Kan., to organize and lead Boomers into Okla., Apr. 1889; partner Buffalo Bill (Col. W. F. Cody), 1908-13; prop. Pawnee Bill's Buffalo Ranch, Oldtown and Indian Trading Post, 1909—; active in work among Pawnee Indians and in perpetuation of the buffalo; v.p. Fern Oil Corp. Pres. U.S. Highway 64 Assn. Nat. supervisor Mounted Troops of America; nat. supervisor Boy Scouts of America; dir. Hist. Soc. of Okla. Republican. Mason. Author: Thirty Years Among the Pawnee Indians, 1928. Co-author: Oklahoma (with Courtney Ryley Cooper), 1926; Blazing Horizon (with Ernest Lynn), 1927; Pawnee Bill The Romance of Oklahoma (with Edwin Mootz), 1928; Stampede Range (with J. R. Johnston), 1928. Home: Oldtown, Pawnee, Okla. Deceased.

LILLIE, Lucy Cecil (Mrs.); b. (White) in N.Y., 1855. Author: Mildred's Bargain; Rolf House; Jo's Opportunity; The Household of Glen Holly; and many others. Deceased.

LILLIS, Thomas F., bishop; b. Lexington, Mo., Mar. 3, 1861; s. James and Margaret (Jordan) L.; A.B., Niagara U.; student St. Benedict's Coll., Kan. Ordained R.C. priest, 1885; pastor Shakelford, Mo., 1885-86, St. Patrick's Ch., Kansas City, Mo., 1887-1904; consecrated bishop of Leavenworth, Dec. 27, 1904; transferred to Kansas City, Mo., Mar. 14, 1910. Died Dec. 29, 1938.

LILLY, D(avid) Clay, clergyman; b. Irvine, Ky., Sept. 17, 1870; s. Henry Clay and Catherine (Tracy) L.; A.B., Central U. of Ky., Richmond, Ky., 1890; D.D., 1900; student Union Theol. Sem., Hampden-Sydney, Va., 1892-93; Edinburg U., 1903; m. Mary D. Guerrant, Sept. 3, 1891; children—Mary Catherine (dec.), Grace Guerrant, Henry Tracy, Edward Guerrant, Anne Elizabeth. Ordained ministry Presbyn. Ch. in U.S., 1894; pastor successively Frankfort, Ky., Tuscaloosa, Ala., First Ch., Winston-Salem, N.C., Grace Street Ch., Richmond, Va., again at Winston-Salem, First Ch., Lexington, Ky., until 1924, Reynolda Ch., Winston-Salem, 1923—. Has held various ch. offices, among them: sec. Gen. Assembly's exec. com. of colored evangelization, 1898-1903; spl. rep. Foreign Mission Com., 1907-10; mem. exec. com. Foreign Missions, 1908-10, 1924-27; mem. Com. of Publ. and S.S. Work, 1911-13; field sec. Internat. Laymen's Missionary Movement, 1913-16; chmn. Gen. Assembly's com. of stewardship, 1920-24; organizer, 1923, and chmn. Reynolda Confs. for the study of present day problems of Christianity; moderator Gen. Assembly of Presbyterian Ch. in U.S., 1937. Trustee Union Theol. Sem. in Va., Peace Inst., Raleigh. Democrat. Mason. Home: Reynolda, N.C. Died May 28, 1939.

LIMA, Manoel de Oliveira, diplomat, publicist; b. Pernambuco, Brazil, Dec. 25, 1867; s. Luiz de Oliveira and Maria Benedicta (de Miranda) L.; grad. Faculty of Letters and Philosophy, Lisbon, Portugal; m. Flora Cavalcanti de Albuquerque, of Pernambuco, Nov. 28, 1891. Diplomatic service of Brazil, various countries of Europe, in Japan and S. America, 1890—; 1st sec. of Embassy at Washington, 1896-1900; visiting prof., Harvard, 1915-16; lectured in European and American univs. Donated library of 40,000 vols. to Catholic U., Washington; prof. internat. law same univ., 1923—. Died Mar. 24, 1928.

LINCOLN, Allen B(ennett), publicist; b. Willimantic, Conn., Aug. 2, 1858; s. Allen and Sallinda (Bennett) L.; grad. Williston Sem., Easthampton, Mass., 1877; B.A., Yale, 1881; m. Caroline Buck, Dec. 18, 1883; children—Marion Buck (Mrs. Elmer E. Yake), Elsie Bennett (Mrs. Alfred Albelli), Barbara Grace, Juliana Armour (Mrs. C. Keith Pevear). Mem. editorial staff Providence (R.I.) Press and Providence Journal, 1882-86; owner and editor New England Home (weekly Prohibition newspaper), 1886-94; spl. agt. Northwestern Mutual Life Ins. Co., 1896—. Mem. Conn. House of Rep., 1925. Independent Republican. Congregationalist. Member Knights of King Arthur; founder and merlin of first all-Italian Castle in America. Editor: Modern History of Windham County, 1920. Author: "New Citizens Pledge," widely used in schools, teaching "the meaning of America" to the foreign born. Home: West Hartford, Conn. Died Sept. 1, 1941.

LINCOLN, Charles Clark, furniture mfr.; b. Marion, Va., Feb. 11, 1866; s. Charles Francis and Harriet (Clark) L.; A.B., King Coll., Bristol, Tenn., 1893; m. Laura M. Dickey, Nov. 22, 1893; children—Charles Clark, Jno. Dickey. In mfg. business at Marion, 1893—; pres. Virginia Table Co., Walker Hotel Operating Co., Lincoln Furniture Mfg. Co., Sugar Grove Lumber Co., Look, Lincoln, Ltd., Central Nat. Bank (Richmond); mem. advisory bd. for Va. of Liberty, Mutual Ins. Co. Trustee Marion Coll. Republican. Presbyn. Kiwanian. Home: Marion, Va. Died Dec. 23, 1928.

LINCOLN, Charles Perez, lawyer; b. Quincy, Mich., Oct. 7, 1843; s. Perez and Harriet Patty (Hopkins) L.; lived on farm in boyhood; ed. Hillsdale (Mich.) Coll.; m. Mary Lawrence Price, 1864 (died 1896); m. 2d, Lizabeth De Vore Allen, May 15, 1899. Orderly sergt. 1st Mich. Inf., Apr. 1861; at Alexandria and Bull Run, Va., May and July 1861; capt. 19th Mich., 1862-64; prisoner of war at Libby, 1863; col. N.G., 1871. Admitted to bar, 1871; asst. assessor internal revenue and chancery court clerk, Granada, Miss., 1871-75; consul at Canton, China, 1875-81; post-grad. Nat. Law U., Washington, 1883; deputy commr. of pensions, U.S., 1889-93; atty. for Kiowa, Comanche and Apache tribes of Indians, 1898-99; now in ins. business at El Reno, Okla. Mayor of El Reno, 1903—. Comdr. dept. of the Potomac, G.A.R., 1888. Home: El Reno, Okla. Died 1911.

LINCOLN, Charles Sherman, army officer; b. Boone, Ia., Feb. 12, 1875; s. James Rush and Priscilla (Hicks) L.; B.E., Ia. State Coll. of Agr. and Mechanic Arts, 1894; grad. Army Sch. of the Line, 1909, Army Staff Coll., 1910; student Army War Coll., 1911 and 1920; m. Cora Thompson, Sept. 15, 1898. Enlisted in U.S. Army, Jan. 5. 1895; commd. 2d lt., Apr. 12, 1898; promoted through grades to brig. gen., Dec. 1, 1931; apptd. chief of staff, Gen. Staff Corps, 1935; now retired. Awarded D.S.C. (U.S.); Legion of Honor (France); Cross of Order of Leopold (Belgium). Episcopalian. Home: Ames, Ia. Died May 18, 1941.

LINCOLN, David Francis, hygienist, author; b. Boston, Mass., Jan. 4, 1841; s. William L.; A.B., Harvard, 1861, A.M., M.D., 1864; unmarried. Acting asst. surgeon U.S.N., 18 months in Civil War. Practiced as specialist in nervous diseases; lecturing and lit. work in connection with Hobart Coll., Geneva, N.Y., some yrs., beginning 1881, having previously relinquished med. practice; resided Boston, 1893—. Author: School and Industrial Hygiene, 1880, 1896; Hygienic Physiology, 1893. Died Oct. 15, 1916.

LINCOLN, James Claiborne, traffic mgr.; b. on farm nr. Liberty, Clay Co., Mo., Apr. 5, 1862; s. Isaac Wells and Martha Louise (Gilkey) L.; ed. pub. and high schs., St. Joseph, Mo.; m. Annie S. Lard, May 23, 1884 (died 1899); m. 2d, Helen Benedict, May 27, 1911 (died 1917). Was successively clerk in office supt. car service and in general freight and pass. depts., St. Joseph & Grand Island R.R., at St. Joseph, Mo., 1876-88; comml. agt. Mo.P. Ry., Atchison, Kan., 1888-90; asst. gen. freight agt., St. Louis, 1890-97, 1st asst. gen. freight agt., 1897-99, gen. freight agt., 1899-1905, asst. freight traffic mgr., same road, Kansas City, Mo., 1905-06; freight commr. Merchants' Exchange, St. Louis, 1906-12; mgr. freight bur. Mchts. Assn. of New York, May 1912—. Also mem. Eastern Freight Traffic Com., under U.S. R.R. Administration, July 1918-20. Democrat. Mem. Christian (Disciples) Church. Pres. Nat. Industrial Traffic League, 1907-11. Home: New Rochelle, N. Y. Died Nov. 1923.

LINCOLN, Jeanie Gould, author; b. Troy, N.Y.; d. late Judge George Gould, N.Y. Court of Appeals; ed. at home by tutors and governesses; m. Nathan Smith Lincoln, Jan. 10, 1877. Author: Marjorie's Quest, 1872; A Genuine Girl, 1896; The Luck of Rathcoole, 1911. Home: Washington, D.C. Died Aug. 8, 1921.

LINCOLN, Leontine, mfr.; b. Fall River, Mass., Dec. 26, 1846; s. Jonathan Thayer and Abby (Luscomb) L.; ed. pub. schs., Fall River and pvt. schs., Providence, R.I.; (A.M., Brown U., 1889); m. Amelia S. Duncan, May 12, 1868. Began in mfg. business at Fall River, 1865; interested in numerous business and public enterprises; pres. Lincoln Mfg. Co., Davis Mills, Luther Mfg. Co., Arkwright Mills, Seaconnet Mills, Parker Mills, Kilburn, Lincoln Machine Co. Pres. Bradford Durfee Textile School from its establishment, 1904. Mem. Mass. State Bd. of Charities, 1894—(chmn. 1898-1919). Author: Leprosy and Its Treatment in Massachusetts. Republican. Home: Fall River, Mass. Died June 1, 1923.

LINCOLN, Mary Johnson (Bailey), household economist; b. S. Attleboro, Mass., July 8, 1844; d. Rev. John Milton and Sarah Morgan (Johnson) Bailey; grad. Wheaton Sem., Norton, Mass., 1864; m. David A. Lincoln, June 21, 1865 (dec.). From 1879 writer and lecturer on household science; first prin. Boston Cooking Sch., 1879-85; culinary editor American Kitchen Magazine, Boston, 1893-1903; lecturer on cookery, in seminaries and large cities of U.S. Author: The Boston Cook Book, 1884; Peerless Cook Book, 1886; Carving and Serving, 1886; The Boston School Kitchen Text-Book, 1888; What to Have for Luncheon, 1904; School Kitchen Text-Book, 1915. Died Dec. 2, 1921.

LINCOLN, Natalie Sumner, author; b. Washington, D.C.; d. late Nathan Smith (M.D., LL.D.) and Jeanie Thomas (Gould) L.; ed. Mrs. Laura A. Flint's private sch., Washington; unmarried. Society editor Washington Herald, 1912-14; editor D.A.R. Magazine, Apr. 1915—. Author: The Trevor Case, 1912; The Man Inside, 1914; The Official Chaperon, 1915; I Spy, 1916; The Moving Finger, 1918; The Three Strings, 1919; The Red Seal, 1920; The Unseen Ear, 1921; The Cat's Paw, 1922; The Meredith Mystery, 1923; The Thirteenth Letter, 1924; The Missing Initial, 1925; The Blue Car Mystery, 1926; P.P.C., 1927; The Dancing Silhouette, 1927; Dead Man's Bluff, 1928; The Fifth Latch-key, 1929; Marked "Cancelled," 1930; No. 13 Thirteenth St., 1932. Contbr. to Smith's, McCall's, All Story, Detective Story mags., and Macfadden publs. Home: Washington. D.C. Died Aug. 31, 1935.

LINCOLN, Robert Todd, secy. of war; b. Springfield, Ill., Aug. 1, 1843; e.s. President Abraham and Mary (Todd) L.; ed. Ill. State U., 1853-59, and Phillips Exeter Acad.; A.B., Harvard, 1864, LL.D., 1893; entered Harvard Law Sch., but left to enter the army, serving until end of war as capt. on staff of Gen. Grant. Admitted to Ill. bar, 1867, and practiced at Chicago; m. Mary, d. James Harlan, of Iowa, Sept. 24, 1868. Del. Rep. State Conv., 1880; presdl. elector, 1880; sec. of war in cabinets of Presidents Garfield and Arthur, 1881-85; U.S. minister to Great Britain, 1889-93. Republican. Was spl. counsel for, and after death of George M. Pullman, became pres. The Pullman Co.; resigned, 1911, and became chmn. bd.; dir. Commonwealth Edison Co., Continental & Commercial Nat. Bank. Home: Washington, D.C. Died July 26, 1926.

LINCOLN, Solomon, lawyer; b. Hingham, Mass., Aug. 14, 1838; s. Solomon and Mehitable L.; grad. Harvard, 1857; studied law (A.M., LL.B., Harvard); m. Feb. 15, 1865, Ellen B. Hayden (died 1897). Tutor Harvard Coll., 1858-63; overseer Harvard and pres. bd., 1890-1902; pres. Bar Assn., City of Boston, 1895-96; pres. bd. trustees, Boston Public Library. Home: Boston, Mass. Died 1907.

LINCOLN, Sumner H., brig. gen.; b. Gardner, Mass., Dec. 21, 1840; s. Rev. Sumner and Gratia (Eliza) L.; ed. Gardner, Mass., Winchendon Acad., Norwich U., Vt.; m. Ruth A. Goodin, Oct. 1, 1874. Enlisted as pvt. Co. B, 1st Vt. Inf., May 2, 1861; disch. Aug. 15, 1861; served as corporal Co. B, 6th Vt. Inf., Oct. 15, 1861-Feb. 21, 1863; 1st lt. adj., 6th Vt. Inf., Feb. 21, 1863-Oct. 28, 1864; maj. 6th Vt. Inf., Nov. 10, 1864; lt. col., Feb. 6, 1865; col. 6th Vt. Vols., June 1865; hon. mustered out, June 26, 1865; apptd. 2d lt. and 1st lt. 17th U.S. Inf., Feb. 23, 1866; promoted through grades to brig. gen. U.S.A., May 29, 1902; retired at own request after 40 yrs.' service, June 9, 1902. Died Apr. 1928.

LINCOLN, Waldo, retired; b. Worcester, Mass., Dec. 31, 1849; s. Daniel Waldo and Frances Fiske (Merrick) L.; A.B., Harvard, 1870; student, Lawrence Scientific Sch., 1 yr.; m. Fanny Chandler, June 24, 1873; children—Merrick (dec.), Josephine Rose, Daniel Waldo, George Chandler, Dorothy (dec.). Engaged in mfg. chemicals and paint, 1873-93; engaged in geneal. and hist. researches, 1893—. Dir. Providence & Worcester R.R. Co. until 1919; treas. and trustee Worcester Poly. Inst., 1883-93. Author: Genealogy of the Waldo Family, 1902; History of the Lincoln Family, 1923. Home: Worcester, Mass. Died Apr. 7, 1933.

LINCOLN, William Henry, shipping merchant; b. Boston, June 13, 1835; s. Henry and Charlotte A. (Lewis) L.; ed. English High and Chauncy Hall schs.; m. Cecelia Frances Smith, Apr. 21, 1863. Clerk in father's shipping office, 1853-56, partner, 1856-61, and as Thayer & Lincoln, 1862, till death of Mr. Thayer, then continued under name of William H. Lincoln & Co.; ship owner and mgr., 1862-1900; mgr. Leyden S.S. Line, Boston to Liverpool, 1876-1902; pres. Brookline Savings Bank, 1877-1904 (now trustee). Mem. Brookline Sch. Com., 1873-95, Brookline Park Commn., 1890-99, Mass. State Nautical Training Sch. Commn., 1892-96 (chmn. 2 yrs.), Corp. Mass. Inst. Tech., 1895—; pres. Boston Commercial Club, 1883-86, Boston Chamber of Commerce, 1900-04. Sec. Y.M.C.A., 1857-61. Trustee Episcopal Theol. Sch., Cambridge, 1895—, Wellesley Coll., 1899—. Home: Brookline, Mass. Died Dec. 2, 1925.

LIND, John, governor; b. Kanna, Smaland, Sweden, Mar. 25, 1854; s. Gustave and Catherine (Jonason) L.; family came to U.S., 1868, and settled at Goodhue, Minn.; ed. pub. schs., 1865-71; taught sch., Sibley Co., Minn., 1872-73; studied U. of Minn., 1875-76; m. Alice A. Shepard, Sept. 15, 1879. Admitted to bar, 1876; began practice at New Ulm, Minn., 1877; now practicing at Minneapolis. Receiver land office at Tracy, Minn., 1881-85; mem. 50th to 52d Congresses (1887-93); 1st lt. and q.m. 12th Minn. Vols. during Spanish-Am. War. Dem. nominee for gov. of Minn., 1896; gov., 1899-1901; defeated for reëlection, 1900; mem. 58th Congress (1903-05), 4th Minn. Dist. Pres. bd. regents U. of Minn. Apptd. by President Wilson as his envoy and personal rep. to Mexico, Aug. 3, 1913; acting as chmn. of Advisory Council to the Sec. of Labor, Washington; mem. Wage Umpire Bd., July 13, 1918. Home: Minneapolis, Minn. Died Sept. 18, 1930.

LINDABURY, Richard Vliet, lawyer; b. Peapack, N.J., Oct. 13, 1850; s. Jacob H. and Mary Ann L.;

ed. pub. schs. and took classical course with Rev. Henry P. Thompson; LL.D., Rutgers College, 1906, Princeton, 1915; m. Littlie V.S. Dinger, July 8, 1892. Admitted to N.J. bar, Feb. 1874; now sr. mem. Lindabury, Depue & Faulks; dir. and gen. counsel Prudential Ins. Co., U.S. Steel Corp.; trustee Howard Savings Bank; pres. N.J. Palisades Interstate Park; trustee Stevens Inst. Tech. Home: Bernardsville, N.J. Died July 15, 1925.

LINDAHL, (John Harald) Josua, zoölogist; b. Kongsbacka, Sweden, Jan. 1, 1844; s. Rev. Johan and Mathilda (Rjoerklander) L.; A.B., Royal U. of Lund, Sweden, 1863, A.M. and Ph.D., 1874; m. Sophie, d. Maj. C. A. Pohlman, 1877 (died 1909). Accompanied Gwyn-Jeffreys and Carpenter as asst. zoölogist in British deep-sea exploring expdn. in H.M.S. Porcupine, 1870; zoölogist in charge of expdn. to Greenland, 1871, in Swedish warships Ingegerd and Gladan; docent in zoölogy, U. of Lund, 1874; sec. Royal Swedish delegation to Internat. Geog. Congress, Paris, 1875; sec. Royal Swedish commn. to Centennial Expn., Phila., 1875-77; prof. natural sciences, Augustana Coll., Rock Island, Ill., 1878-88; curator Ill. State Mus. Natural History, Springfield, 1888-93; dir. Mus. Natural History, Cincinnati, 1895-1906; mgr. Salubrin Lab., 1906—. Officier d'Academie, France, 1876; Knight Ord. of Vasa, Sweden, 1878. Home: Chicago, Ill. Died Apr. 18, 1912.

LINDBERG, Abram Frank, financial adviser; b. Cherokee, Ia., Mar. 29, 1881; s. Rev. Charles and Hannah (Nystrom) L.; B.C.S., New York U., 1907; C.P.A., State of Pa.; m. Katheryn Elizabeth Cahill, Sept. 8, 1909; children—Charles Eric Cahill, Edward Vincent, Elinor Marie, Mary Katheryn, Nancy Therese. Railroad work and mfg. business, to 1905; with Haskins & Sells, certified pub. accountants, 1905-07; asst. auditor of Puerto Rico, 1907-10; financial investigator Bur. Municipal Research, New York and Phila.; auditor Customs Service, later dep. collector gen. of customs of Nicaragua, 1911-17; mem. commn. on Pub. Credit, later of the High Commn., and financial agt. of Nicaragua, 1917-20; asst. mgr. Mercantile Bank of the Americas, 1920-22; v.p. Credit Alliance Corp., New York, 1922-23; comptroller Cross & Brown Co., 1923; mem. Byrne, Lindberg & Byrne, 1924; tech. adviser to Republic of Guatemala, 1924-25; asst. to pres. Am. Brown Boveri Electric Corp., New York, 1926; mng. dir. Compañia Administradora de Rentas, S.A. (tax collecting co.), Lima, Peru, 1927-29; tech. adviser Central Bank of Bolivia and supt. of banks, La Paz, 1930-32; with State Banking Dept. of N.Y. and Federal Deposit Ins. Corp., 1933; consultant Hunter & Weldon, certified pub. accountants, New York, 1934—. Catholic. Co-author: (with William Magowan) The Bolivia National Tax System. Home: Pelham Manor, N.Y. Died Nov. 30, 1934.

LINDBERG, Conrad Emil, theologian; b. Jonkoping, Sweden, June 6, 1852; collegiate edn. in Sweden; grad. Augustana Coll.; came to U.S., 1871; grad. Augustana Theol. Sem., 1872, Phila. Luth. Theol. Sem., 1876; D.D., Muhlenberg Coll., Pa., 1893, LL.D., same, 1910; unmarried. Ordained Luth. ministry, 1874; pastor, Phila., 1876-79, Gustavus Adolphus Ch., New York, 1879-90; prof. theology, Augustana Theol. Sem., 1890—; v.p. Augustana Coll. and Theol. Sem., 1901-10. Pres. N.Y. Conf. Augustana Synod, 1879-89; v.p. Augustana Synod, 1899-1907; mem. Augustana Home and Foreign Mission Bd., 1899-1913; dean Augustana Theol. Sem., 1920—. Order of the North Star, and Commander Royal Order Decorated by King of Sweden, 1901, Knight of Royal Order of the North Star, and Commander Royal Order of Vasa, 1924. Author: Apologetics, 1917, 26; Christian Dogmatics and Notes on History of Dogma, 1922; revised edit., 1928; Syllabus of Lutheran Church Polity, 1927. Chief editor Augustana Theol. Quarterly, 1900-02. Home: Rock Island, Ill. Died Aug. 2, 1930.

LINDBERGH, Charles August, congressman; b. Sweden, Jan. 20, 1860; s. Augusta and Louise L.; brought to U.S., Aug. 1860; ed. Grove Lake Acad., Minn.; LL.B., U. of Mich., 1883; m. Evangeline Lodge Land (B.S., U. of Mich.); 1 son, Charles Augustus. Mem. 60th to 64th Congresses, (1907-17), 6th Minn. Dist. Republican. Author: Banking and Currency, 1913; Why Is Your Country at War, 1917. Home: Little Falls, Minn. Died May 25, 1924.

LINDENKOHL, Adolph, draftsman U.S. Coast and Geodetic Survey; b. Niederkaufungen, Hesse Cassel, March 6, 1833; s. Geo. C. F. and A. E. L.; grad. at Polytechnic School, Cassel, 1852; teacher in U.S., 1852-54; connected with U.S. Coast and Geodetic Survey, 1854—. Author of many articles on geog. exploration and physiog. subjects in Petermann's Mitteilungen, Am. Journal of Science, U.S. Coast Survey Reports, etc. Deceased.

LINDENTHAL, Gustav, civil engr.; b. Brünn, Austria, May 21, 1850; s. Dominik and Franciska (Schmutz) L.; ed. colls. Brünn and Vienna; came to America, 1874; D.Engring, h.c., Polytechnicum, Dresden, 1911, Polytechnicum, Brünn, 1921, Polytechnicum, Vienna, 1926; m. Gertrude Weil, July 10, 1902 (died 1905); m. 2d, Carrie Herndon, Feb. 10, 1910; 1 dau., Franciska. In surveys and constrn. rys. and bridges, Austria and Switzerland, 1870-74; engr. Centennial Expn., Phila., 1874-77; cons. engr. in constrn. western rys. and bridges, office at Pittsburgh, 1877-90; at New York, 1890—; commr. bridges, City of New York, 1902-03; cons. engr. for N.Y. tunnels, Pa. R.R. under Hudson and East rivers; cons. engr. and architect for the Hellgate steel arch bridge over the East River. Pres. North River Bridge Co. Chmn. music festival com. Hudson-Fulton Celebration Commn., 1909. Home: Metuchen, N.J. Died July 31, 1935.

LINDER, Oliver Anderson, editor; b. Gylle, Sweden, Mar. 29, 1862; s. Anders Nilsson and Elna (Martensson) L.; ed. common schs. and under pvt. tutor; m. Therese F. Sennstrom, of Gusslehamm, Sweden, Oct. 10, 1891; children—Cyril Sven, Vera Mathilda (dec.). Reporter, Trelleborgs Allehanda, 1878-90; came to America, 1880; city editor, Svenska Amerikanaren, Chicago, 1884-85; editor, Svenska Romanbladet, 1889; city editor, Svenska Amerikanaren, 1892-1908, managing editor, 1908-36, retired. Lutheran. Author: Glada Grin, 1890-92; I Västerland, 1914. Home: Chicago, Ill. Died Jan. 13, 1939.

LINDERMAN, Frank Bird, author; b. Cleveland, O., Sept. 25, 1869; s. James Bird and Mary Ann (Brannan) L.; ed. pub. schs., Lorain and Elyria, O.; LL.D., U. of Mont., 1927; m. Minnie Jane Johns, Apr. 18, 1893; children—Wilda Jane, Verne Bird, Norma Wenonah (Mrs. Roy Oliver Waller). Successively trapper, cowboy, assayer, newspaper man, sec. Mont. State Mining Assn., state mgr. Germania Life Ins. Co. Mem. Mont. Ho. of Rep., 1903-05; asst. sec. of state, Mont., 1905-07; Rep. nominee for Congress, 1918, for U.S. Senate, 1924; mem. County Bd. of Edn., Flathead Co., Mont., 1924-26. Mem. Mont. State Press Assn. (hon.), Am. Indian Defense Assn., Santa Barbara Art League; mem. by adoption, Chippewa and Cree Indian tribes. Mason. Author: Indian Why Stories, 1915; On a Passing Frontier, 1920; Indian Old-Man Stories, 1920; Bunch-Grass and Blue-Joint, 1921; How It Came About Stories, 1921; Lige Mounts, Free Trapper, 1922; Kootenai Why Stories, 1926; American, Life Story of a Great Indian, 1930; Old Man Coyote, 1931; Red Mother, 1932; Stumpy, 1933; Beyond Law, 1933. Home: Goose Bay, Somers, Mont. Died May 12, 1938.

LINDERMAN, Robert Packer, mfr., coal miner; b. Mauch Chunk, Pa., July 26, 1863; s. Garrett Brodhead and Lucy E. (Packer) L.; grad. Lehigh Univ., Ph.B., 1884. Succeeded, 1885, to the large interests of his father in Lehigh Valley coal mines, iron mfg. and railroads; pres. The Bethlehem Iron Co., Bethlehem Steel Co., and the Lehigh Valley Nat. Bank; dir. in railroad, steamship, mining and financial corporations; head of Linderman & Skeer, coal miners; trustee and mem. exec. com. St. Luke's Hosp., Lehigh Univ., Bishopthorpe School, S. Bethlehem, Pa.; m. Ruth May Sayre, Oct. 15, 1884. Home: Bethlehem, Pa. Died 1903.

LINDGREN, Waldemar, geologist; b. Kalmar, Sweden, Feb. 14, 1860; s. Johan Magnus and Emma (Bergman) L.; ed. in Sweden; M.E., Sch. of Mines, Freiberg, Germany, 1883; D.Sc., Princeton U., 1916, Harvard U., 1935; m. Ottolina Allstrin, of Gothenburg, Sweden, Mar. 8, 1886 (died 1929). Assistant geologist, 1884-95, geologist, 1895-1915, and chief geologist, 1911-12, U.S. Geological Survey; William Barton Rogers professor econ. geology, Mass. Institute of Tech., in charge dept. of geology, 1912-33 (emeritus). Author: Mineral Deposits. Home: Brighton, Mass. Died Nov. 3, 1939.

LINDLEY, Curtis Holbrook, lawyer; b. Marysville, Calif., Dec. 14, 1850; s. Charles and Ann Eliza (Downey) L.; ed. Santa Clara (Calif.) Coll., 1863-65, Eagleswood Mil. Acad., Perth Amboy, N.J., 1865-66, McClure's Mil. Acad., Oakland, Calif., and San Francisco High Sch., 1868-70, Univ. of Calif., 1870-72; (LL.D., Univ. of Santa Clara, 1912, and U. of California, 1917); m. Lizzie Mendenhall, June 19, 1872. Apptd. sec. Calif. Code Commn., 1872; admitted to bar, May 1872, and engaged in practice; city atty., Stockton, Calif., 1883; judge Superior Ct., Amador Co., Calif., 1884-85; now practicing at San Francisco. Hon. prof. dept. of jurisprudence, U. of Calif., 1900—; lecturer, dept. of jurisprudence, Leland Stanford Jr. U., 1900-02; chief counsel U.S. Food Administration, 1917. Democrat. Author: American Law Relating to Mines and Mineral Lands, within the Public Land States, 3 edits., 1897, 1903, 15. Home: San Francisco, Calif. Died Nov. 20, 1920.

LINDLEY, Ernest Hiram, university pres.; b. Paoli, Ind., Oct. 2, 1869; s. Hiram and Laura (White) L.; A.B., Ind. U., 1893, A.M., 1894; fellow Clark U., 1895-97, Ph.D., 1897; LL.D., Indiana University, Baker U., Colo. Coll., State U. of Iowa and U. of Idaho; D.C.L., U. of Delaware; studied at univs. of Jena, Leipzig, Heidelberg, 1897-98, Harvard, 1904-05; m. Elisabeth Kidder, Sept. 18, 1895; children—Ernest Kidder, Stanley Bryan. Instr., 1893-98, asso. prof., 1898-1902, prof. philosophy, 1902-17, Ind. U.; pres. U. of Idaho, 1917-20; chancellor U. of Kansas, 1920-39, chancellor emeritus. Pres. Nat. Assn. of State Univs., 1924-25; mem. Presidents Board of William Rockhill Nelson Trust, 1926-39. Mem. bd. of trustees, Carnegie Foundation; mem. nat. advisory board, Nat. Youth Adminstrn. Presbyn. Republican. Mason. Joint author: (with W. L. Bryan) Arthur Griffith, Arithmetical Prodigy; Compterendu du Quatrième Congrès International de Psychologie, 1900. Died Aug. 21, 1940.

LINDLEY, Hervey, capitalist; b. Belleville, Ind., June 25, 1854; s. Milton and Mary A. (Banta) L.; ed. Minneapolis High Sch. and Minneapolis Commercial Coll. Began in business at Waterloo, Ia., 1873; removed to Pacific Coast, 1886, and engaged in banking and lumber business; now pres. Bowers Timber Company; v.p. United States Trust Co., Seattle, Wash.; dir. First Nat. Bank, Pacific Creosoting Co. Police commr. Los Angeles, Calif., 1888; mem. commn. that purchased Redwood Park, Santa Cruz Co., for State of Calif., about 1892; chmn. Northwest Div. Am. Red Cross during World War. Pres. bd. dirs. Whittier (Calif.) State Sch. Republican. Mason. Home: Seattle, Wash. Died Sept. 21, 1929.

LINDLEY, Paul Cameron, nurseryman; b. Pomona, N.C., Apr. 27, 1877; s. John Van and Sandia (Cook) L.; ed. Guilford (N.C.) Coll. and Cornell U. (no degrees); m. Helen Gunn, June 10, 1913; children—Jack, Paul C., Turner, Henrietta (dec.), J. Thomas, James. In nursery business at Pomona, 1905—; pres. Lindley Nurseries; sec. and treas. J. Van Lindley Nursery Co.; dir. Jefferson Standard Life Ins. Co., Greensboro Fire Ins. Co., N.C. Bank & Trust Co., Atlantic & Yadkin R.R., Odell Hardware Co.; mem. advisory council Eastern Air Transport, Inc. Mayor of Greensboro; chmn. park and recreation com. of City Council, Greensboro; pres. Community Chest of Greensboro; a leader in acquiring 1,000 acres for park at Greensboro; member Nat. Com. for Study of Municipal and County Parks; pres. Greensboro Council, Boy Scouts of America. Trustee Guilford (N.C.) College, Pineland School for Girls, Salemburg, N.C. Quaker. Home: Greensboro, N.C. Died June 10, 1933.

LINDLEY, Walter, physician; b. Monrovia, Ind., Jan. 13, 1852; s. Milton and Mary E. (Banta) L.; ed. high sch., Minneapolis; M.D., L.I. Coll. Hospital, Brooklyn, 1875; Keen's Sch. of Anatomy, Phila.; (LL.D., St. Vincent's Coll., 1903). Engaged in practice from 1875; health officer Los Angeles, 1879; mem. Los Angeles Bd. Edn., 1880-81; supt. Los Angeles Co. Hosp., 1885; dean Med. Dept. U. of Southern Calif., 1902-04; pres. State Bd. Med. Examiners; med. dir. Calif. Hosp.; founded, 1885, and editor and pub. Southern California Practitioner. Pres. bd. trustees Whittier State Sch. Pres. Calif. State Med. Soc., 1889-90; v.p. Nat. Conf. Charities, 1892; dir. Los Angeles Chamber of Commerce. Member Calif. State Bd. Health. Author: California of the South, 1888; The Delinquent Child in Great Britain and France, 1908; The Traducers of Shakespeare, 1908; Irish Dramatists and the Irish Drama, 1914. Trustee Los Angeles City Library. Home: Los Angeles, Calif. Died Jan. 24, 1922.

LINDQUIST, Francis O., congressman; b. Menekaune, Wis., Sept. 27, 1869; s. John O. and I. Marie L.; ed. common schs.; m. Clare Bannister, Nov. 6, 1898. Began as day laborer; now in mail order clothing and mfg. business; pres. Canada Mills Co., Greenville and Muskegon, Mich., and New York. Mem. 63d Congress (1913-15), 11th Mich. Dist. Republican. Methodist. Home: Greenville, Mich. Died Sept. 25, 1924.

LINDSAY, Alexander, Jr., judge; b. Inverkeithing, Fifeshire, Scotland, Oct. 29, 1871; s. Alexander and Isabel (Bonnar) L.; moved with parents to Hawaii at age of 10; LL.B., U. of Mich., 1902; m. Fanny Louise Young, Sept. 13, 1906; children—Elizabeth Young, Richard Faye. Began practice at Honolulu, 1902; dist. magistrate, 1903-05; judge Circuit Court, 1905-09; atty. gen. of Hawaii, 1910-12; asso. justice Supreme Court of Hawaii, 1922—. Republican. Episcopalian. Mason. Home: Honolulu, H.T. Died Sept. 5, 1926.

LINDSAY, George Henry, congressman; b. New York; ed. pub. schs.; engaged in hotel business, Brooklyn, many yrs. Mem. N.Y. Assembly, 7th Dist., 1882-86; coroner, Kings County, 2d Dist., 1886-92; asst. tax commr., New York, 1898; mem. 57th to 62d Congresses (1901-13), 2d N.Y. Dist. Democrat. Home: Brooklyn, N.Y. Died May 25, 1916.

LINDSAY, George Washington, congressman; b. Brooklyn, N.Y., Mar. 28, 1865; s. George Henry and Mary (Beattie) L.; father mem. Congress 14 yrs.; ed. pub. schs.; unmarried. Mem. Dem. State Com., 1919-34; mem. N.Y. State Assembly, 1920; tenement house commr. for Brooklyn and Queens counties, 1921-22; mem. 68th to 73d Congresses (1923-35), 3d N.Y. Dist. Home: Brooklyn, N.Y. Died Mar. 16, 1938.

LINDSAY, Henry Drennan, college pres.; b. Due West, S.C., Oct. 13, 1859; s. Rev. John Oliver and Mary Amanda (Drennan) L.; A.B., Erskine Coll., S.C., 1879; grad. Princeton Theol. Sem., 1884; (D.D., Lafayette Coll., 1896); m. Isabella Wynkoop Williams, Sept. 2, 1884. Ordained Presbyn. ministry, 1884; pastor Brownsburgh, Pa., 1883-84, Wilmington, Del., 1885-88, Easton, Pa., 1889-90, Jamestown, N.Y., 1891-94; Allegheny, Pa., 1894-1906; pres. Pa. Coll. for Women, Pittsburgh, 1906—. Dir. Western Theol. Sem. and Freedman's Bd. of Presbyn. Ch. Home: Pittsburgh, Pa. Died Jan. 18, 1914.

LINDSAY, James Hubert, newspaper pub.; b. Casanova, Va., Dec. 29, 1862; s. Stephen Clarke and Annie (Morgan) L.; student U. of Va., 1908-09; m. Annie Sieg, Dec. 24, 1884; children—Norma Clair (wife of Dr. M. R. Faville), James Gordon, Clarke Epting, Elizabeth (Mrs. M. B. Mount). Founder of weekly newspaper at age 19; founder, 1892, and pub. The Daily Progress, Charlottesville, Va.; dir. Nat. Bank of Charlottesville, Jefferson-Lafayette Theatres, Charlottesville Woolen Mills. Mem. Va. Constl. Convention, 1901-02; mem. School Board of Charlottesville. Trustee Va. Sch. for Deaf and Blind. Democrat. Presbyn. Mason. Author: A Greenhorn in Europe, 1929. Editor: Debates of Virginia Constitutional Convention, 1901-02. Home: Charlottesville, Va. Died Feb. 7, 1933.

LINDSAY, John Douglas, lawyer; b. New York, Dec. 31, 1865; s. William F. (M.D.) and Sarah A. (Vredenburgh) L.; ed. pub. schs., New York, 1875-80; m. Stella, d. Elisha Hall Gregory, M.D., LL.D., of St. Louis, June 3, 1895. Admitted to bar, 1887; deputy asst. dist. atty., New York Co., 1887-94, asst. dist. atty., 1894-98; became mem. Nicoll, Anable & Lindsay, 1898, later Nicoll, Anable, Lindsay & Fuller; mem. Littleton (Martin W.) & Lindsay, N.Y., 1918-21; now in gen. practice alone. Pres. N.Y. Soc. Prevention Cruelty to Children, 1903-20; mem. bd. of mgr. Soc. for the Reformation of Juvenile Delinquents, 1921-25. Democrat. Home: New York, N.Y. Died Oct. 12, 1932.

LINDSAY, John Summerfield, P.E. clergyman; b. Williamsburg, Va., March 19, 1842; s. Thomas and Caroline V. Martin L.; (of Scotch lineage; attended William and Mary Coll. (D.D., 1881), and Univ. of Va.; (D.D., Univ. of the South, 1895; LL.D., Washington and Lee Univ., 1899); m. Caroline Smith. M.E. minister for a few yrs.; chaplain Univ. Va., 1865-67; took orders in P.E. Ch., 1869; asst. Trinity Ch., Portsmouth, Va., 1869-71; rector St. James' Ch., Warrenton, Va., 1871-79; St. John (Georgetown), Washington, 1879-87; chaplain U.S. Ho. of Reps., 1883-85; rector St. John's, Bridgeport, Conn., 1887-89; elected bishop of diocese of Easton, Md., 1887; asst. bishop of Ala., 1890, but declined both; rector St. Paul's, Boston, Mass., 1889—, and archdeacon of Boston, 1897-1900. Mem. gen. convs. P.E. Ch. of 1892, 1895 and 1898, elected gen. sec. Bd. of Missions P.E. Ch., 1899; declined election; pres. standing com. diocese of Mass., 1896—; pres. House of Deputies of gen. conv. P.E. Ch., San Francisco, Oct. 1901. Died 1903.

LINDSAY, John Wesley, clergyman; b. Barre, Vt., Aug. 20, 1820; s. John and Lucy (Nourse) L.; A.B., Wesleyan, 1840, A.M., 1843 (S.T.D., 1861); grad. Union Theol. Sem., 1842; m. Emily Bond, June 16, 1852. Entered M.E. ministry, 1843; prof. Latin and Hebrew, Wesleyan U., 1848-60; pastor, New York, 1860-65; pres. Genesee Coll., 1865-68; dean faculty, Coll. of Liberal Arts, 1873-83, prof. exegetical theology, 1884 (emeritus), Boston U.; prof. exegetical theology, Boston Theol. Sem., 1884; presiding elder Boston and N. Boston dists., N.E. Conf. M.E. Ch., 1888-94. Trustee Wesleyan U. and Boston U. Mem. Bd. of Edn. M.E. Ch., 1868—. Author: Commentary on Deuteronomy, 1891. Home: West Newton, Mass. Died 19—.

LINDSAY, Robert Burns, lawyer; b. Dumfriesshire, Scotland, July 4, 1824; s. John and Elizabeth L.; ed. Univ. of St. Andrews, emigrated to U.S. at 20; settled in N.C.; took charge acad. for young men. Went to Tuscumbia, Ala., 1849; studied law; admitted to bar in Ala.; m. Sarah Miller, sister Gov. John Anthony Winston, 1854. Elected to legislature, 1853; mem. State senate, 1857; presdl. elector, selected by Ala. State Dem. Conv., 1860; refused to support Breckenridge and became an elector on the Douglas ticket; elected State senate, 1866; gov. Ala., 1870-71; elected by Dem. Conservative party. Home: Tuscumbia, Ala. Died 1902.

LINDSAY, Thomas Bond, prof. Latin and Sanskrit, Boston Univ., 1884—; b. New York, April 28, 1853; s. John W. Lindsay; ed. Genessee Wesleyan Sem., 1865-68; Boston Latin School, 1869; grad. Wesleyan Univ., 1874 (A.M.); Phi Beta Kappa (Ph.D., Boston Univ.); m. Ada A. Hubbard, June 25, 1874. Studied in Germany, 1874-77; taught Newton, Mass., High School, 1877-88; asst. prof. Latin and Sanskrit, 1878-84, prof. same, 1884—, Boston Univ. Editor: Cornelius Nepos, 1882, revised, 1885; Easy Latin Lessons (with Mr. Rollins), 1890; Juvenal, 1890; Sight Slips in Latin, 1892; Catullus. Home: West Newton, Mass. Died 1909.

LINDSAY, Thomas Corwin, artist; b. Cincinnati, Sept. 15, 1845; s. Thomas and Elizabeth (Lawrence) L.; ed. in pub. schs.; went abroad, 1867, and studied art in Paris for several yrs.; m. Mary F. Sampson, Jan. 9, 1880. Began as painter, 1860, and has always made his home in Cincinnati; chiefly known as landscape painter, but has also painted animal pictures (especially lions and tigers); pictures chiefly in pvt. collections in Boston, New York, Cincinnati and west to San Francisco. Republican. Home: Cincinnati, O. Died 1907.

LINDSAY, (Nicholas) Vachel, writer; b. Springfield, Ill., Nov. 10, 1879; s. Vachel Thomas and Catharine (Frazee) L.; grad. Springfield High Sch., 1897; student Hiram Coll., Ohio, 1897-1900; Art Inst. Chicago, 1900-03; New York Sch. of Art, under Chase and Henri, 1904-05; m. Elizabeth Conner, May 19, 1925; children—Susan Doniphan, Nicholas Cave. Lectured for West Side Y.M.C.A., New York, winters, 1905-06, 1906-07, 1907-08, Springfield (Ill.) Y.M.C.A., Winter, 1908-09; lecturer for Anti-Saloon League, throughout Central Ill., 1909-10; walked from Ill. to New Mexico, summer of 1912, distributing "rhymes" and speaking in behalf of "The Gospel of Beauty"; tramped through southern states in Spring of 1906, distributing "The Tree of Laughing Bells." Mem. Christian (Disciples) Ch. Author: A Handy Guide for Beggars, 1916; General William Booth Enters Heaven, and Other Poems, 1913; Adventures While Preaching the Gospel of Beauty, 1914; The Congo and Other Poems, 1914; The Art of the Moving Picture, 1915; The Chinese Nightingale and Other Poems, 1917; The Golden Whales of California and Other Poems, 1920; The Golden Book of Springfield (A Sealed Book of Prophecy), 1920; Collected Poems, 1923; Going to the Sun (a book of drawings), 1923; Collected Poems (illustrated by self), 1925; Going to the Stars, 1926; The Candle in the Cabin, 1926; Johnny Appleseed and Other Poems for Children, 1928; The Litany of Washington Street, 1929; Every Soul Is a Circus, 1929; Selected Poems (Modern Readers' Series), 1930. Has recited his poems before the English depts. of many schs. and univs. Pen name "Vachel Lindsay." Home: Springfield, Ill. Died Dec. 5, 1931.

LINDSAY, William, U.S. senator; b. Rockbridge Co., Va., Sept. 4, 1835; s. Andrew and Sallie (Davidson) L.; settled in Clinton, Ky., Nov. 1854; commenced practice of law, 1858; m. Eleanor, d. late Dr. George N. Holmes. Served C.S.A., pvt. to capt., 1861-65; resumed practice; State senator, 1867-70; judge Ky. Court of Appeals, 1870-78; chief justice, 1876-78; then established practice at Frankfort, Ky.; State senator for Frankfort dist., 1889; mem. World's Columbian Commn. from organization to Feb. 20, 1893; declined appmt. on Interstate Commerce Commn.; elected U.S. senator, 1893, to fill vacancy caused by resignation of John G. Carlisle; reëlected, 1894, for term, 1895-1901; U.S. Commr. St. Louis Expn., 1904; mem. law firm Lindsay, Kalish & Palmer, Frankfort, Ky. Trustee Carnegie Instn. Died 1909.

LINDSEY, Daniel Weisiger, lawyer; b. Frankfort, Ky., Oct. 4, 1835; s. Thomas Noble L.; grad. Ky. Mil. Inst., 1854; LL.B., Louisville Law Sch., 1859; (hon. A.M.); m. Katherine McIlvaine Fitch, Jan. 1864. Col. 22d Ky. Inf., U.S.V., during Civil War; led it in campaign of Gen. James A. Garfield in Eastern Ky., winter of 1861-62; in campaign of Gen. Morgan in capture of Cumberland Gap; then up the Kanawa Valley and comd. a brigade of 9th Div., 13th Army Corps, in Vicksburg campaign; resigned 1863. Adj.-gen. Ky., 1863-67; has practiced law at Frankfort, 1867—. Republican. Home: Frankfort, Ky. Died Aug. 4, 1917.

LINDSEY, Joseph Bridgeo, chemist; b. Marblehead, Mass., Dec. 26, 1862; s. Joseph W. and Emily Stuart (Blaney) L.; B.Sc., Mass. Agrl. Coll., Amherst, 1883; Ph.D., U. of Göttingen, 1891; studied Poly. Institute, Zürich, 1892; hon. D.Sc., Mass. State College, 1933; m. H. Frances Dickinson, June 20, 1888; children—Amy Blaney (Mrs. C. E. Goodhue, Jr.), Joseph B. Asst. chemist, Mass. Expt. Sta., 1883-85; chemist to L. B. Darling Fertilizer Co., Pawtucket, R.I., 1885-89; chemist, Mass. Agrl. Expt. Sta., 1892-1907, v. dir. and chemist, 1907—; Goessmann prof. agrl. chemistry, Mass. Agrl. Coll., 1911-33, head of dept. chemistry, 1911-28; retired Dec. 1932. Home: Amherst, Mass. Died Oct. 27, 1939.

LINDSEY, Washington Ellsworth, 3d governor of N.M.; b. Belmont Co., O., Dec. 20, 1862; s. Robert Washington and Julia Anne (Shipman) L.; B.S., Scio (Ohio) Coll., 1886; LL.B., U. of Mich., 1891; m. Amanda C. Haughton, Oct. 1891. Practiced law, Chicago, 1891-1900, then at Portales, N.M. County clk. Roosevelt Co., N.M., 1903-05; asst. dist. atty., 1905-09; mayor of Portales, 1909-10; pres. Bd. of Edn., 1912-16; mem. Constl. Conv., 1910; elected lt. gov., Nov. 1916; sworn in as gov. to succeed late E. C. De Baca, Feb. 19, 1917, for term expiring 1919. Republican. Conglist. Home: Portales, N.M. Died Apr. 5, 1926.

LINDSEY, William, author; b. Fall River, Mass., Aug. 12, 1858; s. William and Maria (Lovell) L.; ed. pub. grammar and high schs.; m. Annie Hawthorne, d. George Sheen, Dec. 16, 1884. Engaged in banking, mfg. and commission business, Fall River, 1876, Boston, 1886-99; at beginning of Boer War he obtained the adoption by the British War Office of a patented equipment for carrying ammunition; established factories in Great Britain, France, and Germany; retired 1904, and returned to Boston. Author: Apples of Istakhar (poems), 1895; Cinder Path Tales (short stories), 1896; The Severed Mantel (novel), 1909; Red Wine of Roussillon (drama in blank verse), prod. under title of "Seremonda," New York, Jan. 12, 1917, also acted in Boston and Chicago. Home: Boston, Mass. Died Nov. 25, 1922.

LINDSEY, William Henry, coal mining; b. Nashville, Tenn., July 6, 1879; s. Alonzo and Etha Jane (Hagan) L.; ed. Nashville pub. schs.; m. Nancy Lee Daugherty, June 30, 1939. Began as sec. to the late Col. E. W. Cole, Dec. 1, 1895, and advanced through official positions in his wide and varied interests, becoming v.p., and later pres. Napier Iron Works and pres. the Crescent Coal Co.; now chmn. bd. Paradise Corp.; pres. Tenn. Mining & Mfg. Co.; v.p. and treas. Ill. Clay Products Co. Democrat. Methodist. Home: Nashville, Tenn. Died July 27, 1940.

LINDSLEY, Charles Augustus, sec. Conn. State Bd. of Health, 1884—; b. Orange, N.J., Aug. 19, 1826; s. John and Eliza L. (Condit) L.; grad. Trinity Coll., Hartford, 1849, A.M., 1852; studied medicine, Coll. of Phys. & Surg., New York, and med. dept. Yale, grad. M.D., 1852; has since practiced at New Haven; prof. materia medica and therapeutics, Yale Med. School, 1860-83; prof. theory and practice of medicine, 1883-97; dean of faculty, 1863-85; lecturer sanitary science, 1898—. Attending physician Conn. State Hosp., 1864-76; sec. Gen. Hosp. Soc., 1865-77; health officer of New Haven, 1874-88. Mem. and has been pres. of med. socs. of his city and State; v.p. and pres. New Haven Dispensary from its origin, 1872-1905. Mem. Conn. State Bd. of Health from its organization, 1878, and sec., 1884—; m. Lydia L. Harrison, Apr. 13, 1852. Home: New Haven, Conn. Died 1906.

LINDSLEY, Henry Dickinson, past nat. comdr. Am. Legion; b. Nashville, Tenn., Feb. 29, 1872; s. Philip and Louise (Dickinson) L.; ed. pvt. schs.; admitted to Tex. bar, 1893. Engaged in banking and many other businesses in Dallas; pres. Southwestern Life Ins. Co., 1908-10; chmn. bd. Dallas Trust & Savings Bank, 1914-18; pres. Citizens Assn. of Dallas, 1905-09; mayor of Dallas, 1915-17; pres. Henry D. Lindsley Co. (New York), 1924-28; dir. City Nat. Bank of Dallas. Commd. maj. U.S. Army, 1917; joined A.E.F., Dec. 1917; commd. col. U.S.A., Aug. 1918; col. O.R.C., 1921—; dir. Bur. War Risk Ins., Washington, D.C., 1919. Permanent chmn. Am. Legion Caucus, St. Louis, Apr. 1919, permanent chmn. 1st Nat. Conv., Minneapolis, Nov. 1919, elected past nat. comdr., Nov. 1919 life mem, exec. com.; vice comdr. in chief Mil. Order of World War; elected v.p. for U.S. of Fedn. Interalliée des Anciens Combattants (FIDAC), 1926, chairman of delegation to annual congress, 1927; designated Initial General Staff Eligible List U.S.A., Dec. 1920. Decorations: D.S.M. (U.S.); Past National Commander's Medal, The American Legion; Officer Public Instruction Order University Gold Palms (France); Officer Legion of Honor (France); Commander Order of the Crown (Belgium). Treas. Am. Republics Corp., 1920-23, retired. Charter founder Roosevelt Memorial Assn., 1919. Democrat. Mason. Home: Dallas, Tex. Died Nov. 18, 1938.

LINDSLEY, Smith M., lawyer; b. Monticello, N.Y., Apr. 11, 1847; s. Rufus B. and Seeny J. (Weed) L.; ed. Monticello Acad., grad. 1866, and 2 yrs. Wyoming Sem., Kingston, Pa.; m. Dorlissa J. Johnston, Apr. 23, 1873. Admitted to bar, 1870; now mem. Lindsley & Mackie. Corp. counsel City of Utica, N.Y., 1872-73; chmn. Civ. Service Commn., 1894, City Audit Bd., 1895, Police and Fire Commn., 1904. Declined nomination for justice Sup. Ct., N.Y., 1906. State grand regent Royal Arcanum, 1879, supreme regent, 1887-88. Mason, etc. Presbyn. Independent Democrat. Home: Utica, N.Y. Died 1909.

LINEBARGER, Charles Elijah, physical chemist; b. Plainfield, Ill., Feb. 21, 1867; s. Isaac and Lucy Ellen (Estes) L.; grad. Northwestern U. Sch. of Music., A.B., Northwestern U., 1888; asst. in chemistry, Chicago Med. Coll., 1888-89; student Tübingen and Paris, 1889-91; teacher of chemistry, North and South Div. high schs., Chicago, 1891-93; student Göttingen and Paris, 1893-95; fellow Clark U., 1895; m. E. Frances Diplock, Oct. 4, 1896; children—Gwendolyn (Mrs. Manfred U. Prescott), Charles Elijah. Teacher, Lake View High Sch., Chicago, 1896—. Editor of Sch. Science, 1901-06; mem. bd. of reviewers Jour. of Phys. Chemistry, 1900-04. Author: Elements of Differential and Integral Calculus (with J. W. A. Young), 1899. Home: Chicago, Ill. Died 1937.

LINEBARGER, Paul Myron Wentworth ("Paul Myron"), lawyer, author; b. Warren, Ill., June 15, 1871; s. Rev. Isaac and Lucy Ellen (Estes) L.; ed. Naperville Coll. and Lake Forest U. until 1889; law student in Paris, France, 1889-92; admitted to bar in Chicago, 1893; lecturer for Congo Annex Soc. throughout Belgium; student U. of Heidelberg, Germany, 1893-95; m. Lillian Bearden Kirk, Feb. 22, 1912; children—Paul Myron, Wayne Wentworth. Began practice at Chicago, 1895; lt. cav. Spanish-Am. War; U.S. judge, 7th Dist., P.I., 1901-07; resigned,

1907 to become legal advisor of Sun Yat Sen, and so served until Dr. Sun's death in 1925; legal advisor Chinese Nationalist Govt., 1930-37. Author: Sun Yat Sen and the Chinese Republic, 1924; Our Common Cause with China Against Imperialism and Communism, 1927; The Maker of Modern China and His Three Principles, 1929; La China Navree, 1931; Es Espana otra China?, 1931; The Gospel of Sun Chung Shan, 1932; The Ocean Men, 1934. Founder and editor Chinese Nationalist. Home: Washington, D.C. Died Feb. 20, 1939.

LINEBAUGH, Daniel Haden, lawyer; b. Camden, Ark., Nov. 4, 1878; s. Rev. Daniel Haden, and Margaret E. (Sweets) L.; ed. pub. schs., Temple, Tex.; m. Della McKinnon, June 1, 1904; children—Margaret Elizabeth, Daniel Haden, John David. Admitted to bar of Oklahoma, 1900; engaged in general practice at Muskogee, Okla. Del. to Dem. Nat. Conv., 1908 (credentials com.), 1920 (presented Senator Robert L. Owen for pres.); chmn. of State Conv., Okla., 1912; U.S. dist. atty. for Eastern Dist. of Okla., 1913-17; spl. asst. atty. gen. of U.S., Washington, D.C., Mar. 23, 1917. Special chief justice Supreme Court of Okla., 1939. Mason. Home: Muskogee, Okla. Died Dec. 17, 1940.

LINEHAN, John C., ins. commr. of N.H., Sept. 28, 1890—; b. Cacroom, County Cork, Ireland, Feb. 9, 1840; s. of John and Margaret (Foley) L.; came to U.S. Oct. 1849; self-ed.; m. Mary E. Pendergast, Jan. 2, 1864. Served in 3d N.H. inf. in Civil war; in mercantile business, 1866-90; mem. governor's council, 1887-88; has held various positions, local, State and Nat., in the G.A.R.; in Concord city govt., 1872-73, 1877-78. Republican. Has written published papers on the Irish Settlers in the Thirteen Colonies; on Gen. John Sullivan, and Hon. Matthew Thornton, of New Hampshire; Matthew Lyon, of Vermont; McClintock's History of New Hampshire; Abbott's History of 1st N.H. Regiment, and Kent's History of the 17th N.H. Regiment; also papers on various subjects for mags. and periodicals, including publs. of the Am.-Irish Hist. Soc., 1898-99; mem. N.H. Hist. Soc., and treas. Am.-Irish Hist. Soc.; pres. bd. of trustees, N.H. State Industrial School, 1884—; trustee Loan & Trust Savings Bank, Concord. Home: Penacook, N.H. Died 1905.

LINES, Edwin Stevens, bishop; b. Naugatuck, Conn., Nov. 23, 1845; s. Henry W. and Harriet (Bunnell) L.; A.B., Yale, 1872; D.D., 1897; grad. Berkeley Div. Sch., 1874, D.D., 1904; D.D., Princeton, 1911, Rutgers, 1917; m. Mary L. Morehouse, May 4, 1880. Deacon and priest, P.E. Ch., 1874; rector Christ Ch., West Haven, Conn., 1874-79, St. Paul's, New Haven, 1879-1903; bishop of Newark, N.J., 1903—. Mem. Nat. Council and various Commissions Episcopal Ch. Trustee Gen. Theol. Sem., Berkeley Div. Sch., Inst. Col. Schs., N.J. Hist. Soc., Newark Museum. Died Oct. 25, 1927.

LINES, George, lawyer; b. Kenosha, Wis., Dec. 16, 1853; s. Henry and Susan D. (Cox) L.; grad. high sch., Oshkosh, Wis.; studied law in office of Finch & Barber, Oshkosh; m. Edessa L. Kunz, Sept. 7, 1907. Admitted to Wis. bar, 1877, Supreme Court of Wis., 1883, Supreme Court, U.S., 1896; began practice at Oshkosh, 1877; practiced, Waupaca, 1878-88, Washington, D.C., 1888-93; associate or mem. Quarles, Spence & Quarles, Milwaukee, 1893-1909; mem. Lines, Spooner, Ellis & Quarles, 1910-17, Lines, Spooner & Quarles, 1917-19; gen. counsel Northwestern Mutual Life Ins. Co., 1919—. Chmn. Draft Bd., 1st div., E. Wis. Dist., 1917-19; mem. com. apptd. by sec. of war to revise selective draft regulations, 1917. Trustee Marquette U. Sch. of Medicine, Milwaukee, 1919—. Republican. Presbyn. Mason. Home: Milwaukee, Wis. Died Dec. 20, 1929.

LINES, H. Wales, builder; b. at Naugatuck, Conn., June 3, 1838; s. Henry Willis and Harriet (Bunnell) L.; ed. com. and high schs., Naugatuck; m. Sarah Congdon, d. Rev. Washington Munger, of Waterford, Conn., June 23, 1861; children—Harriet Louisa (dec.), Henry Washington (dec.), Sarah Lavinia, Clara Belle, Ellie Munger. Began as Perkins & Lines, Meriden, 1864, later H. Wales Lines & Co., and since 1888, The H. Wales Lines Co., of which he is now pres.; pres. Meriden Machine Tool Co.; v.p. Meriden Savings Bank; v.p., treas. New Haven Investment Co.; dir. various corps. Mayor, Meriden, 3 terms; mem. Conn. Ho. of Rep., 1872, Senate, 1879-80; del. Conn. Constl. Conv., 1902; v. chmn. of commn. to build State Library and Supreme Court Bldg., and complete State Capitol, etc. Hon. pres. for life Mayors' Assn. of Conn.; v.p. commn. in charge Ft. Griswold Battle Ground. Mem. Chamber of Commerce, U.S.A., Conn. and Meriden chambers of commerce, Atlantic Deeper Waterways Assn., etc. Mason; mem. bd. mgrs. and chmn. bd. visitors Masonic Home. Home: Meriden, Conn. Died Jan. 11, 1927.

LINGLE, Thomas Wilson, coll. prof.; b. Salisbury, N.C., Dec. 11, 1871; s. Wilson Alex and Martha Jane (Lynch) L.; A.B., Davidson Coll., 1893; grad. student in philosophy, history and philology, Cornell U. and Univs. of Strasbourg and Leipzig, 1894-98, Ph.D., Leipzig, 1898; grad. Princeton Theol. Sem., 1901; student U. of Neuchatel, Switzerland, summer 1910, the Sorbonne, summer 1925; m. Clara Swift Souther, July 2, 1901; children—Sarah Souther, Eustace Everett. Prof. history, Mackenzie Coll., São Paulo, Brazil, 1901-04; pres. Blackburn Coll., Carlinville, Ill., 1904-08; prof. modern langs., Davidson (N.C.) Coll., 1908-27, prof. of European and ancient history, 1927—; prof. European history, summer quarters U. of Va., 1919-24. Welfare service with 10th French Army, around Verdun, Sept. 1917-Dec. 1918; later lecturer French Army on Am. institutions; ednl. work dir. Camp Meade, Md., Mar.-June 1919. Decorated by French minister of war. Raised endowment fund of $370,000 for two colleges; gave pub. addresses in Europe in 3 langs. Trustee Mitchell Coll., Statesville, N.C. Democrat. Engaged in hist. and archeol. study in Near East, 1929. Lecturer on European political, social and economic problems. Home: Davidson, N.C. Died Mar. 26, 1937.

LINGLEY, Charles Ramsdell, prof. history; b. Worcester, Mass., Dec. 31, 1877; s. John Harvey and Catharine (Flanigan) L.; B.S., Worcester Poly. Inst., 1900; A.M., Columbia, 1905, Ph.D., 1910; hon. A.M., Dartmouth, 1919; m. Hattie Bramwell Teasdale, Aug. 29, 1907; 1 son, William S. With Dartmouth Coll., 1907—, prof. history, 1919—, acting dean of freshmen, 1930-31. Executive secretary of War Camp Community Service, 1918; with business dept. War Dept. com. on edn., 1918-19. Trustee Brewster Acad., Wolfeboro, N.H. Conglist. Author: The Transition in Virginia from Colony to Commonwealth, 1910; Since the Civil War, 1920, revised edit., 1926; The American People and Nation (with R. M. Tryon), 1926; The American Nation Yesterday and Today (with R. M. Tryon and F. Morehouse), 1930. Co-editor Tryon and Lingley History Series. Home: Hanover, N.H. Died Jan. 30, 1934.

LINHART, Samuel Black, univ. prof.; b. Irwin, Pa., Nov. 12, 1865; s. Daniel and Elizabeth McCullough (Black) L.; A.B., Coll. of Wooster, O., 1891, A.M., 1894, D.D., 1906; Auburn Theol. Sem., 1893; grad. Western Theol. Seminary, Pa., 1894; LL.D., U. of Pittsburgh, 1934; m. Lora Lovina Adams, June 19, 1894; children—Dorothy Elizabeth (Mrs. Kenneth L. Arnold), Lois Olivia (Mrs. Dayton L. Grabill), Edward Adams. Ordained Presbyn. ministry, 1894; pastor 43d St. Ch., Pittsburgh, 1894-98; pres. Blairsville (Pa.) Coll., 1898-1906; sec. U. of Pittsburgh and prof. history of religion and ethics, 1906—. Republican. Mem. Nat. Council Y.M.C.A. Died Dec. 12, 1936.

LINN, Alonzo, prof. Greek, 1861— (v.p., 1869—), Washington and Jefferson Coll.; b. Butler, Pa., Sept. 26, 1827; s. Dr. George and Elizabeth (Gibson) L.; prep. edn. Monongahela Acad.; grad. Jefferson Coll., Pa., 1849; studied theology, Western Theol. Sem. (Ph.D., Washington and Jefferson Coll.; LL.D., Lafayette Coll.); Presbyn. minister (licentiate); m. Rebecca E. Fulton, Nov. 17, 1858. Tutor Lafayette Coll., 1854-55; adjunct prof. mathematics, 1855-56; prin. Classical School, New Brunswick, N.J., 1856-57; prof. history and polit. economy, Jefferson Coll., 1857-61; prof. of Greek from 1861 in Jefferson Coll., and the united Washington and Jefferson Coll., Washington, Pa. Died 1901.

LINN, Alvin Frank, coll. prof.; b. Springfield, O., Sept. 23, 1864; s. Michael F. and Nancy Jane (Brandle) L.; A.B., Wittenberg Coll., Springfield, 1884, A.M., Ph.D., Johns Hopkins, 1892; m. Mary Harwood Martin, Aug. 10, 1892; children—Frank Harwood, John Martin. Prof. natural science, 1888-91, prof. chemistry and mineralogy, Wittenberg Coll., 1892-1932, prof. of chemistry emeritus, 1932. Fellow A.A.A.S.; mem. Am. Chem. Soc. Republican. Lutheran. Home: Springfield, O. Died May 1939.

LINN, James Weber, univ. prof.; b. Winnebago, Ill., May 11, 1876; s. John M. and Mary C. (Addams) L.; nephew of Jane Addams; A.B., U. of Chicago, 1897; Litt.D., Lake Forest Coll., 1931; m. Mary Howland, Mar. 26, 1904; children—Jane Addams, Elizabeth Howland. Prof. English, U. of Chicago. Sec. Ill. Century of Progress Commn., 1933; dir. Northwest Territory Celebration Commn. for Ill., 1937. Author: The Second Generation (novel), 1902; The Chameleon, 1903; Essentials of English Composition (textbook), 1912; Jane Addams, a Biography, 1935; This Was Life (novel), 1936; Winds Over the Campus (novel), 1936; James Keeley, Newspaperman (biography), 1937. Home: Chicago, Ill. Died July 16, 1939.

LINN, Paul Hinkle, college pres.; b. Huntsville, Mo., Dec. 12, 1873; s. Rev. Ambrose Preston and Anna Eliza (Martin) L.; A.B., Central College, Fayette, Mo., 1894, A.M., 1895 (D.D., 1908); LL.B., Washington U., 1897; m. Daisey Marion Taubman, Sept. 8, 1903. Ordained ministry M.E. Ch., S., 1897; pastor La Plata, Mo., 1897-98, Brookfield, 1898-1902, Maryville, 1902-04; presiding elder St. Joseph (Mo.) Dist.; pastor Central Ch., Kansas City, 1905-09; missionary evangelist for Mo., 1909-10; pastor Scruggs Memorial Ch., St. Louis, 1910-13; pres. Central Coll., Aug. 1913—. Mem. exec. com. Federal Council Chs. of Christ in America; dir. Gen. Bd. Ch. Extension M.E. Ch., S.; mem. Workers' Council, S.S. Publs.; mem. Commn. for Establishing Standards of Edn. in M.E. Ch., S., and dir. Gen. Bd. of Edn.; mem. Commn. of Unification of Am. Methodism; mem. Commn. on Standards in N. Central Assn. of Coll. and Univ. Chautauqua lecturer. Home: Fayette, Mo. Died Feb. 1, 1924.

LINNARD, Joseph Hamilton, naval officer; b. Phila., Sept. 27, 1860; s. Joseph Tauzin and Elvira (Borden) L.; grad. Phila. High Sch., 1877, U.S. Naval Acad., 1881; served at sea, 1881-83; commd. asst. naval constr., July 1, 1883, and sent abroad for course of study in naval architecture, in French Governmental schs.—École Polytechnique, École d'Application du Génie Maritime, grad., ingénieur, 1887; unmarried. Has served at various navy yards and on inspection of war ships in course of constrn. and as asst. in Bur. of Constrn. and Repair, Navy Dept.; retired, Aug. 13, 1910. In active service, Bur. Constrn. and Repair, Navy Dept., 1917-19. Home: Philadelphia, Pa. Died Mar. 31, 1935.

LINNEN, Edward Bangs, United States inspector; b. Le Sueur, Minn., Mar. 21, 1864; s. James and Katherine (Clark) L.; student U. of Minn., 1878-82. Inspector of river and harbor improvements, War Dept., 1882-85; with ry. mail service, 1885-88; insp. Dept. of Interior, 1894-1922, under Secretaries Hitchcock, Garfield, Ballinger, Fisher, Lane, Payne, Fall; now chief insp., operative in charge, U.S. Secret Service, St. Paul, Minn. Editor and pub. Sibley County (Minn.) Independent, 1884-85, Graphic Sentinel, Lake City, Minn., 1885-88. Republican. Mason. Home: Minneapolis, Minn. Died Apr. 1, 1928.

LINNEY, Frank Armfield, lawyer; b. Taylorsville, N.C., June 29, 1874; s. Romulus Z. and Dorcas (Stephenson) L.; student Trinity Coll., Durham, N.C., 1892-95; studied law, Judge A. C. Avery's Law Sch., Morganton, N.C.; m. Hessie Matheson, Jan. 24, 1900; children—Baxter M., Margaret, Kenneth, Mary Francis. Began practice at Taylorsville, 1896; state solicitor (pros. atty.), 1906-14; chmn. Rep. State Exec. Com., 1913-21; candidate for Congress, 1914, 18, for gov. of N.C., 1916; U.S. atty., Western Dist. of N.C. (now Middle Dist.), Aug. 21, 1921—. Organized the White Republican Party of N.C. Trustee U. of N.C., Appalachian Training Sch. Methodist. Mason. Home: Winston-Salem, N.C. Died June 29, 1928.

LINTHICUM, Charles Clarence, lawyer; b. McLean Co., Ill., Nov. 11, 1857; s. Noah Thompson and Hannah (Furr) L.; ed. common schs., teachers' insts. and normal training schs.; LL.B., Northwestern U., 1882; m. Eva Kate Graham, Feb. 27, 1879. Began practice at Chicago, 1882; with Offield & Towle, 1887-91, Offield, Towle & Linthicum, 1891-09, Linthicum, Belt & Fuller, 1909-14; since alone. Prof. patent law, Northwestern U.; formerly pres. Bd. of Edn., Lakeview, Ill. Democrat. Conglist. Home: Evanston, Ill. Died Dec. 12, 1916.

LINTHICUM, George Milton, surgeon; b. Anne Arundel Co., Md., Aug. 17, 1870; s. Sweetser and Laura Ellen (Smith) L.; student St. John's Coll., Annapolis, Md., 1887-89, A.M., 1893; A.B., Johns Hopkins, 1891; M.D., U. of Md., 1893; m. Lillian Noyes Howland, Apr. 12, 1898; children—Howland, Lillian (Mrs. John Scott Keech, dec.). Began practice at Baltimore, 1893; prof. of physiology and proctology, Baltimore Med. Coll., 1895-1907; v.p. med. and chirurg. faculty, 1908-09, pres., 1909-10; prof. diseases of colon and rectum, U. of Md., 1913—; proctologist Univ. of Md., Md. Gen., W. Baltimore Gen. and Baltimore City hosps.; consultant in diseases of colon and rectum, U.S. Vets. Hosp., Hosp. for Consumptives of Md. (chmn. exec. com.), U.S. Marine Hosp.; consultant Baltimore City Health Dept.; medical examiner Fidelity Life Insurance Co. of America. Served as capt. Med. Corps, Md. N.G., Mexican Border, 1916; lt. col. Med. Corps, U.S.A., 1917-19, and comdg. officer U.S. Base Hosp. 113, France; col. Med. R.C. Fellow Am. Coll. Surgeons. Democrat. Episcopalian. Mason. Home: Roland Park, Baltimore, Md. Died July 18, 1935.

LINTHICUM, John Charles, congressman; b. Linthicum Heights, Md., Nov. 26, 1867; s. Sweetser and Laura E. L.; grad. State Normal Sch., Baltimore, 1886; spl. course, Johns Hopkins; LL.B., U. of Md., 1890; m. Helen A., d. late John L. and Harriet Perry. In law practice at Baltimore from 1890, sr. mem. J. Charles Linthicum & Bro. Mem. Md. Ho. of Dels., 1904, Senate, 2 terms, 1905-10; mem. 62d to 72d Congresses (1911-33), 4th Md. Dist. Democrat. Judge advocate-gen. on staff of Gov. A. L. Crothers, 1908-12. Home: Baltimore, Md. Died Oct. 5, 1932.

LINTHICUM, Richard, journalist; b. Libertytown, Md., Mar. 30, 1859; s. Hamilton S. and Sophronia (Gallaher) L.; ed. schs. of Baltimore and Liberty Acad.; m. Mary Alice Van de Venter, Sept. 24, 1882. Served observer U.S. Weather Bureau, 1877-80; engaged in newspaper work and mag. writing, 1883—; contbr. of articles, short stories, etc., to various mags. Author: Boer and Britisher in South Africa, 1900; The War Between Russia and Japan, 1905. News editor Chicago Chronicle, July 1904—. Died Jan. 20, 1934.

LINTON, Edwin, coll. prof.; b. E. Bethlehem, Pa., Mar. 14, 1855; s. Joseph and Naomi (Harry) L.; A.B., Washington and Jefferson Coll., 1879; Ph.D., Yale, 1890; m. Margaret McKnight, d. Rev. James I. Brownson, of Washington, Pa., July 9, 1885; children—Eleanor Acheson (Mrs. Eliot Round Clark), Edwin S. (dec.). Instr. math., 1879-81; grad. student Yale, 1881-82; prof. geology and biology, Washington and Jefferson Coll., 1882-1920, prof. emeritus, 1920; hon. fellow in zoölogy, U. of Mo., 1920-22, parasitology, med. dept. U. of Ga., 1922-26; hon. fellow zoölogy at Univ. of Pa., 1926—. Scientific work for U.S. Fish Commn., at Woods Hole, Mass., summers of 1882-87, 87, 89, 1898-1900, 1903-36, in Yellowstone Nat. Park, summer of 1890; Beaufort, N.C., summers of 1901-02; Bermuda, 1903; Tortugas, 1906-08. Silver medal, Paris Expn., 1900. Died June 4, 1939.

LINTON, William Seelye, congressman; b. St. Clair, Mich., Feb. 4, 1856; s. Aaron and Sarah (McDonald) L.; ed. pub. schs.; m. Ida M. Lowry, Apr. 9, 1878; children—Raymond Aaron, Lawrence Lowry, Elsie Sarah. Lumber mfr., Saginaw, until 1892. Supervisor Bay Co., Mich., 1878-79; mem. Saginaw Common Council, 1883-87; mem. Mich. Ho. of Rep., 1887-88; candidate for lt. gov., 1890; pres. Saginaw Water Bd., 1892; mayor, 1892-94; mem. 53d and 54th Congresses (1893-97); postmaster Saginaw, 1898-1914; candidate in primaries for gov. of Mich., 1913; chmn. State Tax Commn. of Mich. Pres. Northern Nut Growers Assn., Top of Mich. Trail Assn.; pres. Saginaw Bd. of Trade 10 yrs. Republican. Home: Saginaw, Mich. Died Nov. 22, 1927.

LIPMAN, Jacob Goodale, prof. agr.; b. Friedrichstadt, Russia, Nov. 18, 1874; s. Michael G. and Ida (Birkhahn) L.; Baron de Hirsch Agrl. Sch., N.J., 1894; B.Sc., Rutgers Coll., 1898, hon. D.Sc., 1923; A.M., Cornell U., 1900; Ph.D., 1903; hon. Doctor, Catholic U. of Santiago, Chile, 1930; m. Cecelia Rosenthal, Nov. 26, 1902; children—Leonard Herbert, Edward Voorhees, Daniel Hilgard. Asst. chemist, 1898-99, soil chemist and bacteriologist, 1901—, N.J. Agrl. Expt. Sta.; instr. agrl. chemistry, 1902-06, asst. prof. agr., 1906-07, asso. prof., 1907-10, prof. of soil fertility and bacteriology, 1910-13, prof. agr., 1913—, and dean of agr., 1915—, Rutgers Coll.; dir. N.J. Agrl. Expt. Stas., 1911—. Lecturer U. of Ill., 1906, Cornell U., 1906, U. of Tenn., 1909, '10, Ia. Agrl. Coll., 1910, U. of Neb., 1911. Spl. investigator, U.S.A., 1918-19. Editor in chief Soil Science; asso. editor Annales des Sciences Agronomiques, Archiv für Pflanzenbau, Pennsylvania Farmer; editor John Wiley and Sons Agrl. Series. Mem. N.J. State Planning Bd., Internat. Commn. Agrl. Ecology; mem. Czechoslovakia Acad. Agriculture, French Acad. Agr., Swedish Royal Acad. Agr., Reale Academia dei Georgofili di Firenze, Am. Acad. Arts and Sciences; del. Gen. Assembly Internat. Inst. Agr., Rome, 1922, 24, 26; del. 3d Internat. Conf. of Soil Science, Prague, 1922, 4th Conf., Rome, 1924; pres. 1st Internat. Congress of Soil Science, Washington, D.C., 1927; chmn. Am. Delegation to 3d Internat. Congress of Soil Science at Oxford, England; delegate 1st Internat. Nitrogen Conf., Biarritz, 1926; del. World Dairy Congress, London, England, 1928; del. 5th Internat. Tech. and Chem. Congress of Agrl. Industries, Scheveningen, The Netherlands, 1937. Awarded Chandler medal, Columbia U., 1934. Author: Bacteria in Relation to Country Life, 1908; Laboratory Guide of Soil Bacteriology, 1912. Died Apr. 19, 1939.

LIPPINCOTT, Charles Augustus; b. Piedmont, W.Va., July 30, 1865; s. Ebenezer Wood and Annabelle (Weir) L.; A.B., Washington and Jefferson Coll., 1887, D.D., 1912; post-grad. course, Princeton; student Princeton Theol. Sem., 1887-88; Union Theol. Sem., 1888-89; grad. McCormick Theol. Sem., Chicago, 1890; LL.D., U. of Notre Dame, Ind., 1922; m. Anna M. Irwin, Oct. 8, 1890; children—John Irwin, Annabelle, Sarah, Margaret, Elsie, Harlowe H., Mary, Eleanor, Charles A. Ordained Presbyn. ministry, 1890; pastor Joliet, Ill., 1890-95; asso. pastor 2d Ch., Chicago, 1895-99 and acting pastor, 1899-1901; pastor 1st Ch., Flint, Mich., 1901-12, 1st Ch., South Bend, Ind., 1913-19; now mgr. coöp. dept. Studebaker Corp. Moderator Synod of Michigan, 1909; pres. bd. of hosp. mgrs., Flint, 1905-12; pres. Bd. of Commerce, Flint, 1908; dir. McCormick Theol. Seminary. Mason. Home: South Bend, Ind. Died Mar. 14, 1929.

LIPPINCOTT, Craige, publisher; b. Phila., Nov. 4, 1846; s. Joshua Ballinger and Josephine (Craige) L.; bro. of Joshua Bertram L.; ed. U. of Pa.; m. Sallie E. Bucknell, of Phila., Apr. 13, 1871. Entered publishing house of J. B. Lippincott & Co., 1866 (J. B. Lippincott Co., 1885—); pres., 1886. Home: Phila., Pa. Died 1911.

LIPPINCOTT, James, steel mfr.; b. Pittsburgh, Pa., Nov. 19, 1864; s. James and Maria (Davis) L.; ed. pub. schs.; m. Constance Wilmot Morrison, Feb. 15, 1909 (dec.); children—Adele, Mariana, Constance, Louise. Began in steel business with Carnegie Bros. & Co., Ltd., Pittsburgh, 1885; with Kirkpatrick & Co., Ltd., and Chartiers Iron & Steel Co., 1888-1900; organizer, 1897; sec. until 1908, West Leechburg Steel Co., v.p. and gen. mgr., 1908-13, pres. 1913-33, chmn., 1933—. Republican. Presbyn. Home: Sewickley, Pa. Died Sept. 13, 1936.

LIPPINCOTT, Job H., asso. justice supreme court N.J., 1893—; term expires 1900; b. Mt. Holly, N.J., Nov. 12, 1842; ed. public schools, Vincetown (N.J.) Academy and Mt. Holly Inst.; grad. Dane Law School, Harvard, 1865, with the degree of LL.B.; admitted to N.J. bar, 1867; pres. bd. of edn., Hudson City, N.J., 1868-71; counsel bd. of Chosen Freeholders, Hudson Co., 1874-87; U.S. atty. for dist. of N.J., 1885-86; law judge, Hudson Co., N.J., 1886-92. During 1889-91 presided at trials of ballot-box stuffers in Hudson Co., about 70 of whom were convicted and imprisoned. Home: Jersey City, N.J. Died 1900.

LIPPINCOTT, J(oshua) Bertram, publisher; b. Huntingdon Valley, Pa., Aug. 24, 1857; s. Joshua Ballinger and Josephine (Craige) L.; grad. Episcopal Acad., Phila., 1873; U. of Pa., 1 yr., class of '78, hon. B.A., 1907, LL.D., 1935; m. Joanna Wharton, Apr. 21, 1885; children—Joseph Wharton, Marianna (Mrs. Wm. Paul O'Neill), Sarah (Mrs. Nicholas Biddle), Bertram. Entered publishing business, 1875; v.p., 1886-1911, pres., 1911-26, chmn. bd., 1926—, J. B. Lippincott Co.; dir. Farmers & Mechanics Nat. Bank. Dir. of Mercantile Library, Am. Acad. of Music. Republican. Home: Philadelphia, Pa. Died Jan. 19, 1940.

LIPPINCOTT, Sara Jane ("Grace Greenwood"), author; b. Pompey, N.Y., Sept. 23, 1823; d. Dr. Thaddeus and Deborah Clarke; m. Leander K. Lippincott, 1853. For yrs. special corr. in Washington and in Europe for leading New York, Chicago and Calif. papers; has also done much mag. work in addition to writing books—principally for young people. Author: Greenwood Leaves; Countries I Have Seen; Merrie England; Bonnie Scotland; Stories and Legends of Ireland, France and Italy; Stories of Many Lands. Home: New Rochell, N.Y. Died 1904.

LIPPINCOTT, William Adams, poultry husbandman, geneticist; b. Jacksonville, Ill., July 3, 1882; s. Julian Post and Clara Moulton (Adams) L.; A.B., Ill. Coll., Jacksonville, 1903; B.S., Ia. State Coll., 1911; M.S., U. of Wis., 1917, Ph.D., 1920; m. Florence Olivia Humphreys, Aug. 25, 1908; children—Dorothy Adams, William Julian. Asst. prof. animal husbandry, in charge of poultry, Ia. State Coll., 1911-12; prof. poultry husbandry, Kan. State Agrl. Coll., 1912-23; prof. poultry husbandry, Univ. of Calif., 1923—; consulting specialist Bureau of Animal Industry, U.S. Dept. Agriculture, 1929—. Past secretary Kansas Research Council. Author: Poultry Production, 1914. Home: Berkeley, Calif. Died Jan. 5, 1931.

LIPPINCOTT, William Henry, artist; b. Phila., Dec. 6, 1849; s. Isaac and Emily (Hoover) L.; ed. at Friends' Pvt. Sch.; began study of art at Pa. Acad. Fine Arts; became designer of illustrations, later scenic artist; pupil of Léon Bonnât, 1874, remaining at Paris 8 yrs. and regularly exhibiting at Paris salons; m. Mrs. Amolia (Wilson) Chester, 1893. Returned to U.S., 1882; established studio in New York; prof. painting, Nat. Acad. Design, 3 yrs. Paints portraits, figure compositions and landscapes; regular contbr. to Am. art exhibitions; still does some scenic painting. The Duck's Breakfast, Un Jour de Conge, Pink of Old Fashion, Helena, Infantry in Arms, Love's Ambush, and Pleasant Reflections are his most important pictures. A.N.A., 1884, N.A., 1896. Died Mar. 18, 1920.

LIPPITT, Charles Warren, governor; b. Providence, R.I., Oct. 8, 1846; s. Gov. Henry and Mary Ann (Balch) L.; Ph.B., Brown U., 1865; studied under pvt. tutors, 1865-68; traveled in America and Europe; m. Margaret B. Farnum, Feb. 23, 1886. Treas. Silver Spring Bleaching and Dyeing Co., 1871-1903; pres. Social Mfg. Co., 1891-1901, R.I. Nat. Bank, 1896-1901; v.p. United Nat. Bank, 1901-08. Pres. Franklin Lyceum, 1875-76; col. and chief of personal staff of his father, 1875-76. Chmn. R.I. Rep. Conv., 1894; gov. of R.I., 1895-97. Pres. Providence Bd. of Trade, 1881-82; v.p. Nat. Bd. of Trade, 1880; pres. Providence Commercial Club, 1883-84. Home: Providence, R.I. Died Apr. 4, 1924.

LIPPITT, Francis James, lawyer; b. Providence, R.I., July 19, 1812; s. Joseph F. and Caroline S. L.; grad. Brown, 1830 (A.M.). Capt. 1st N.Y. vols. in Mexican war; served in Civil war as col. 2d Calif. inf. and bvt. brig. gen. U.S. vols.; m. Mrs. Pickering Dodge, Sept. 25, 1865. Counsel for U.S. in Dept. of Justice, 1877-82. Was guest of Lafayette at La Grange, 1832; sole survivor of the few who stood by his grave at his burial, 1834; assisted De Toqueville in preparation of La Démocratie aux Etats Unis, 1834; attached to Am. Legation, Paris, 1834-35; mem. (chmn. com. of whole) State Constl. Conv., Calif., 1849. Lecturer at Boston Univ. Law School, 1873-74, before Naval War Coll., Newport, 1896, 1897, 1900. Retired. Died 1902.

LIPPITT, Henry Frederick, senator; b. Providence, R.I., Oct. 12, 1856; s. Henry and Mary (Balch) L.; desc. of John Lippitt, who came to America, 1638; A.B., Brown U., 1878; m. Marie Louise, d. late Tully D. Bowen, Dec. 15, 1881 (died 1911); m. 2d, Mrs. Thomas K. Laughlin, Apr. 1915. After graduation entered cotton mfg. business, beginning as day operator, becoming gen. mgr. The Manville Co.; v.p. Peoples Savings Bank; dir. Mechanics Nat. Bank and other corps. U.S. senator from R.I., 1911-17. Republican. On staff of Gov. Taft of R.I., with rank of col., 1888-89. Pres. N.E. Cotton Mfrs.' Assn., 1889. Home: Providence, R.I. Died Dec. 28, 1933.

LIPPITT, William Donald, pres. Great Western Sugar Co.; b. Denver, Colo., June 28, 1885; s. Frank Harvey and Mary Ellen (Matheson) L.; student Manual Training High Sch., Denver, Colo., 1900-03; m. Charlotte Taylor, June 28, 1909; children—William Frank, Mary Charlotte, Ruth Ann. Began as clk. Great Western Sugar Co., 1904, pres., 1931—; pres. Great Western Ry. Co. With U.S. Food Administration, World War. Vice-pres. bd. dirs. Denver Art Mus.; dir. Colo. Mus. Natural History. Baptist. Mason. Home: Englewood, Colo. Died Feb. 17, 1935.

LIPSCOMB, David, clergyman, editor; b. in Franklin Co., Tenn., Jan. 21, 1831; s. Granville and Ann (Lipscomb) L., cousins; A.B., Franklin Coll., nr. Nashville, Tenn., 1849, A.M., 1851; m. Margaret Zellner, July 23, 1862. Entered ministry Ch. of Christ, 1856; editor Gospel Advocate, 1866-1913; a leader in establishing The Fanning Orphan Sch. for Girls, nr. Nashville, 1881, and the Nashville Bible Sch. for Boys and Girls, 1891; is pres. trustees of both schs. Author: Civil Government, 1889; Life and Sermons of Jesse L. Sewell, 1891; Commentary on Acts of Apostles, 1896; Queries and Answers, 1910; Salvation from Sin, 1912. Home: Nashville, Tenn. Died 1918.

LIPSITZ, Louis, lumber mfr.; b. Detroit, Mich., June 25, 1872; s. Joseph and Rebecca (Lipsitz) L.; ed. high sch., Tyler, Tex., and Eastman Business Coll., Poughkeepsie, N.Y.; unmarried. Began as clk. in retail dry goods business, Tyler, Jan. 1, 1890; became mem. A. Harris & Co., Tyler, 1900; moved to Dallas, Tex., 1907, and organized the Harris-Lipsitz Co., wholesale dry goods, also managing partner Harris Lumber Co., wholesale lumber; discontinued dry goods business, 1914, but continues as mng. partner Harris-Lipsitz Lumber Company; pres. Chronister Lumber Co. (Forest, Tex.), and Lyon-Gray Lumber Co., Trinity Lumber Co., Oak Cliff Lumber Co. (all of Dallas); v.p. Am. Exchange Nat. Bank, dir. Realty Trust Co. Dir. War Savings Campaign for State of Tex., 1918; regional dir. War Industries Bd., 11th Fed. Dist., under Bernard M. Baruch. Mem. U.S. Chamber Commerce (dir.), Dallas Chamber Commerce (dir. 1908—; pres. 1915-17); mem. bd. dirs. Tex. State Fair, 1913—, now 1st v.p. Democrat. Jewish religion. Mason. Home: Dallas, Tex. Died Apr. 1, 1927.

LISCUM, Emerson H., brig. gen. U.S. vols. lt. col. 24th inf. U.S. Army; b. Vt.; served as corporal 1st Vt. vol. inf., May to Aug. 1861; private to sergt. 12th inf., Feb. 1, 1862, to Mar. 22, 1863, when he became 2d lt.; 1st lt., May 4, 1863; later in 30th inf.; capt. 25th inf., Mar. 26, 1867, 19th inf., July 5, 1870; maj. 22d inf., May 4, 1892; lt. col. 24th inf., May 23, 1896. Bvtd. capt., Aug. 18, 1864, for gallant services in battle of North Anna River, Va.; apptd. brig. gen. U.S. vols., 1898, for Spanish-Am. war; disch. from vol. service Dec. 31, 1898. Died 1900.

LISLE, Robert Patton, rear admiral U.S.N.; b. Phila., Aug. 28, 1842. Apptd. acting asst. p.-m. U.S.N., Nov. 2, 1863; asst. p.-m., July 2, 1864; passed asst. p.-m., May 4, 1866; p.-m., Dec. 11, 1867; pay insp., Jan. 19, 1892; pay dir., June 6, 1899; retired Nov. 3, 1903, with rank of rear admiral for services during Civil War. Home: Philadelphia, Pa. Died 1911.

LISMAN, Frederick J., investments; b. Budingen, Germany, July 21, 1865; s. Gerson and Josephine (Gross) L.; ed. abroad; m. Leonora Cohen, June 7, 1892. Came to U.S., 1881; began as bond broker, 1890; mem. New York Stock Exchange and head of firm F. J. Lisman & Co., 1895-1930; dir. Alabama, Tenn. & Northern Railway, etc. Came into prominence, 1891, by exposing poor condition of the Richmond Terminal System, now merged in Southern Ry. Home: New York, N.Y. Died Feb. 14, 1940.

LISSER, Louis, pianist; b. Stettin, Germany, Nov. 29, 1850; s. Emil and Natalie L.; ed. in gymnasium, Stettin; attended lectures, U. of Berlin; grad. Royal Acad. of Arts, Royal High Sch. of Music, Berlin, 1879; (Litt.D., Mills Coll., Calif., 1902); m. Rosa Goldschmidt, June 20, 1882. Appeared first in concerts and made concert tour through Prussian provinces, 1878-79; went to San Francisco, July 1879; dean music dept. and prof. music, Mills Coll., Calif., 1880-1910, prof. emeritus, 1910. Trustee Mills Coll., 1900—. Pres. Musicians' Club of San Francisco, 1893-97 (founder), San Francisco Symphony Soc., 1897-98, San Francisco Guild of Arts and Crafts, 1898. Republican. Trustee 1st Unitarian Ch., 1910-15. Home: San Francisco, Calif. Died Oct. 13, 1919.

LISSNER, Meyer, lawyer; b. San Francisco, Calif., June 16, 1871; s. Louis and Mathilda (Block) L.; ed. pub. grammar and high sch., Oakland, Calif.;

Los Angeles Law Sch., 1898-99; m. Ermine Greenhood, Aug. 12, 1896; children—Louis Meyer, Jay Greenhood, Aline Mathilda. In practice at Los Angeles, 1899—. Organizer and sec. Non-Partisan City Central Com., 1906; an organizer, Lincoln-Roosevelt Rep. League in Calif., 1907 (chmn. Los Angeles County exec. com., 1908, v.p., 1910); organized City Club, Los Angeles, 1907 (pres., 1911); pres. Good Govt. Organization, 1909; organizer, and sec. Good Govt. Fund, 1909-11; mem. exec. com. Direct Legislation League, Calif., 1909-11, Nat. Municipal League, 1909-16, v.p., 1917—. Chmn. Calif. Rep. State Central Com., 1910-11; mem. exec. com. Prog. Nat. Com., 1912-16. Pres. Bd. of Pub. Utilities, City of Los Angeles, 1909-11; mem. Calif. Industrial Accident Commn., 1915-19, and 1928—. Editor California Outlook, 1914-17; mem. U.S. Shipping Bd., June 16, 1921-Dec. 31, 1925 (resigned). Died July 28, 1930.

LIST, Ambrose Shaw, banker; b. Wheeling, W.Va., May 15, 1854; s. Henry K. and Sarah Jane (Shaw) L.; prep. edn., pub. and pvt. schs.; student W.Va. U., 1868-70; unmarried. Began as shipping clk., wholesale grocery, Wheeling, 1871; wool buyer, 1878-86; banking business, 1886—; with Wheeling Dollar Savings & Trust Co., 1918—, now chmn. bd. Republican. Methodist. Elk. Home: Wheeling, W.Va. Died Jan. 10, 1938.

LISTEMANN, Bernhard, violinist; b. Schlotheim, Thüringen, Germany, Aug. 28, 1841; married. Apptd., at 17, court violinist to Prince of Schwartzburg; came to U.S., 1867, and traveled extensively; concertmaster Theodore Thomas orchestra, New York, 1870-74; founded, 1874, Boston Philharmonic Club, and organized, 1879, Boston Philharmonic Orchestra, of which he was dir.; concertmaster Boston Symphony Orchestra, 1881; founded, 1881, The Listemann String Quartette; later head violin dept., Chicago Musical Coll., until 1907; lived at Boston, 1907-09, Chicago, 1909—. Home: Chicago, Ill. Died Feb. 11, 1917.

LISTEMANN, Fritz, violinist; b. Schlotheim, Thüringen, Germany, Mar. 25, 1839; s. Johann F. W. and Marie H. (Kühn) L.; grad. Leipzig Conservatory of Music, also pvt. lessons from Ferdinand David and Wilhelm Ulrich; m. Josephine C. Scharl, 1876. At early age mem. leading orchestras in Europe; came to New York, 1868; became mem. Theodore Thomas Orchestra, and of Boston Symphony Orchestra; also mem. Bernhard Listemann Concert Co.; studied composition with Edward Alexander McDowell for several yrs. Composer: Violin concerts, songs and various smaller pieces. Home: Jamaica Plain, Boston. Died 1909.

LISTER, Ernest, governor; b. Halifax, Eng., June 15, 1870; s. Jeremiah Hartley and Ellen (Hey) L.; came to America, 1884; ed. common schs. and business coll.; m. Alma Thornton, Feb. 28, 1893. Prin. owner Lister Constrn. Co., Tacoma, 1903-12; pres., gen. mgr. Lister Mfg. Co., Tacoma, mfrs. finished wood products; dir. Scandinavian-Am. Bank, Tacoma. Mem. City Council, Tacoma, 1894-96; chmn. State Bd. of Control, Wash., 1897-1903; mem. Charter Revision Commn., Tacoma, 1910; gov. of Wash., terms 1913-17, 1917-21 (both times the only Democrat elected on state ticket). Methodist. Mason. Home: Olympia, Wash. Died June 14, 1918.

LITCHFIELD, Lawrence, M.D.; b. Grand Rapids, Mich., Nov. 8, 1861; s. Gen. Allyne Cushing Litchfield (U.S.V.) and Susan Cornelia Carver (desc. from Robert Carver and William White of the Mayflower); A.B., Harvard, 1885 (Phi Beta Kappa); student Harvard Med. Sch.; M.D., Bellevue Hosp. Med. Coll. (New York U.), 1888; has repeatedly visited med. centers of Europe for study; m. Vienna, Austria, Ethel Herr Jones, June 9, 1898; children—Ethel Carver (wife of Baron van Boetzelaer), Lawrence, Margaret. Practiced at Pittsburgh, 1889—; visiting physician various hosps., also med. consultant. Commd. maj., Med. R.C., 1917; chief of med. service, Base Hosp., Camp Lee, Va., Sept. 1917; med. chief, Base Hosp., Camp Grant, Ill., July 1918; hon. discharged, Dec. 12, 1918. Mem. Pittsburgh Morals Efficiency Committee. Mem. exec. com. Internat. Congress Tuberculosis, and Internat. Union Against Tuberculosis, 1908, Internat. Congress Hygiene and Demography, 1910. Republican. Unitarian. Home: Pittsburgh, Pa. Died Feb. 1930.

LITCHFIELD, William Elias, lumber mcht.; b. Cohasset, Mass., Aug. 4, 1861; s. Joseph W. and Mary J. (Sloan) L.; ed. pub. schs. and Derby (Mass.) Acad.; m. Cordelia Amy Gilbert, Oct. 25, 1883. In lumber business, Boston, 1884—; mem. Litchfield Bros., Boston and North Vernon, Ind.; pres. L. & H. Lumber Co. Trustee charity fund of Mass. Charitable Mechanics' Assn.; dir. Newton Y.M.C.A. Mem. Boston Chamber Commerce, Chamber Commerce U.S.A. (mem. com. visiting prin. cities of Europe, 1911). Republican. Conglist. Home: Newton, Mass. Died Nov. 19, 1921.

LITCHMAN, Charles Henry, mem. U.S. Industrial Commn., June 19, 1900-02; b. Marblehead, Mass., April 8, 1849; s. William and Sarah E. (Bartlett) L.; ed. public schools and 2 yrs. at Marblehead Acad.; studied law 15 months; m. M. Annie Shirley, Feb. 5, 1868. Sec. State and Internat. Grand Lodge Knights of Saint Crispin (Shoemakers), 1875-78; gen. sec. Knights of Labor, 1878-81, and 1886-88; mem. school com. Marblehead, 1873-76; moderator town meeting several yrs.; mem. legislature, Mass., 1879; spl. agt. treasury dept. under Pres. Harrison, 1889-93. Home: Newark, N.J. Died 1902.

LITT, Jacob, theatrical mgr.; b. Milwaukee, 1860; s. I. J. and Henrietta L.; owner of Broadway Theatre, New York; McVicker's, Chicago; Bijou Opera House, Minneapolis; Grand Opera House, St. Paul; Bijou Opera House, Milwaukee. Has produced Shenandoah, In Old Kentucky, Caleb West, Sporting Life, the Club's Baby, The Suburban, The Great Ruby, The Price of Peace, Mistakes Will Happen, Zorah, etc. Home: New York, N.Y. Died 1905.

LITTELL, Isaac William, army officer; b. Elizabeth, N.J., Dec. 5, 1857; s. Isaac William and Elizabeth (Ball) L.; student Stevens Inst. Tech., 2 yrs.; grad. U.S. Mil. Acad., 1883; m. Julia, d. Capt. Gregory Barrett, U.S.A., Jan. 22, 1885. Commd. 2d lt. 10th Inf., June 13, 1883; promoted through grades to brig. gen. Q.M. Corps, Oct. 9, 1917; retired, Feb. 19, 1919. In charge of constrn. of N.A. cantonments and nat. guard camps, 1917; sec. and treas. U.S. Soldiers' Home, Washington, resigned 1922. Episcopalian. Home: Staunton, Va. Died May 1, 1924.

LITTIG, Lawrence William, physician, surgeon; b. Davenport, Ia., July 20, 1858; s. John and Louise (Rogge) L.; A.B., St. Vincent's Coll., Mo., 1880; A.M., 1882; M.D., State U. of Ia., 1883, and U. of Pa., 1884; M.R.C.S., Eng., 1887; 3 years in London, Berlin, Vienna and Paris hosps.; m. Amy Duckett, June 4, 1895. Resident physician, Phila. Hosp., 1884-85; prof. anatomy, 1889-91, theory and practice of medicine, 1891-1902, asst. to chair of surgery, 1889-1902, State U. of Ia.; dir. Univ. Hosp., 1900-02. Fellow Am. Coll. Surgeons (a founder, gov.). Home: Iowa City, Ia. Died July 17, 1918.

LITTLE, Arthur, clergyman; b. Webster, N.H., May 24, 1837; s. Simeon B. and Harriet (Boyd) L.; A.B., Dartmouth, 1860; studied Andover and Princeton Theol. Sems.; (D.D., Dartmouth, 1880); m. L. Elizabeth Frost, Aug. 15, 1863 (died 1883); m. 2d, Elizabeth A. Wales, Feb. 1, 1898. Ordained Congl. ministry, 1863; chaplain 1st Vt. Heavy Arty, 1863-65; pastor Presbyn. Ch., Bedford, N.H., 1866-88, First Congl. Ch., Fond du Lac, Wis., 1868-78, N.E. Congl. Ch., Chicago, 1878-89, Second Congl. Ch., Dorchester, Mass., 1889—. Trustee Ripon (Wis.) Coll., 1869-85; pres. bd. trustees Bradford Acad., 1890—; pres. bd. visitors Andover Theol. Sem., 1897—; corporate mem. A.B.C.F.M.; v.p. Am. Tract Soc. Moderator Nat. Council of Congl. Chs., 1883. Home: Dorchester, Mass. Died Apr. 11, 1915.

LITTLE, Arthur D(ehon), chemical engr.; b. Boston, Mass., Dec. 15, 1863; s. Thomas J. and Amelia (Hixon) L.; ed. pub. and high schs., Portland, Me., Berkeley Sch., New York, Mass. Inst. Tech.; hon. Ch.D., U. of Pittsburgh, 1918; hon. asso., Coll. Tech., Manchester, Eng., 1929; hon. Sc.D., Manchester U., 1929, Tufts, 1930, Columbia, 1931; Perkin medallist, 1931; m. Henrietta Rogers Anthony, Jan. 22, 1901. Chemist and supt. of first mill in U.S. making sulphite wood pulp, 1884-85; chem. engring. practice, Boston, 1886—; pres. Arthur D. Little, Inc., 1909—; dir. Arthur D. Little Industrial Corp. Mem. Corp. Mass. Inst. Tech. (life), pres. Alumni Assn., 1921-22, and founder Sch. of Chem. Engring. Practice. Chmn. Advisory Com. Nat. Exprl. of Chem. Industries; chmn. subcom. on chemistry, Science Advisory Com. of Nat. Research Council, Century of Progress, Chicago, 1933. Organized Natural Resources Survey of Can. for C.P. Ry., 1916-17. During war, in charge of spl. researches on airplane dopes, acetone production, smoke filters, etc., for Signal Corps and Chem. Warfare Service. Inventor processes of chrome tanning, electrolytic manufacture of chlorates, artificial silk, gas and petroleum. Fellow Am. Acad. Arts and Sciences, A.A.A.S., Chem. Soc. (Eng.), Inst. of Fuel (London). Author: Chemistry of Paper Making (with R. B. Griffin); The Handwriting on the Wall; The Fifth Estate. Home: Brookline, Mass. Died Aug. 1, 1935.

LITTLE, Arthur Wilde, clergyman; b. Brooklyn, Oct. 6, 1856; s. William Henry and Caroline Frances (Cobb) L.; bro. of Caroline Frances L.; A.B., Knox Coll., 1877, A.M., 1880; div. at Gen. Theol. Sem., New York, and Berkeley Div. Sch., Middletown, Conn.; (L.H.D., Hobart, 1895; S.T.D., Western Theol. Sem., Chicago, 1905); m. Caroline F. Warren, Oct. 29, 1889. Deacon and priest, P.E. Ch., 1881; rector St. Paul's, Portland, Me., 1881-88, St. Mark's, Evanston, Ill., 1888—. Deputy to Gen. Conv., 1886, 1904; examining chaplain to the bishop, etc. Author: Reasons for Being a Churchman, 1885; The Intellectual Life of the Priest, 1897; The Church Idea, 1906. Died 1910.

LITTLE, Bascom, builder; b. Cleveland, O., Apr. 24, 1879; s. Hiram H. and Laura (Bascom) L.; grad. University Sch., Cleveland, 1897; A.B., Cornell, 1901; m. Florence Cobb, June 2, 1906; children—Bascom, Julie C., Laura B. With Baker Motor Vehicle Co. and Am. Ball Bearing Co. until 1910; pres. Crowell & Little Constrn. Co.; v.p. Cleveland Land & Securities Co. Mem. Charter and Sinking Fund Commns. of Cleveland; pres. Cleveland Taxation Commn., 1915; pres. Cleveland Chamber Commerce, 1915-16; chmn. Nat. Defense Com. Chamber Commerce U.S.A., World War. Commd. col. U.S.A.; awarded D.S.M. Republican. Unitarian. Home: Cleveland, O. Died May 27, 1940.

LITTLE, Charles, clergyman; b. Granville, O., Dec. 1, 1845; s. Rev. Jacob and Ann D. (Thompson) L.; A.B., Marietta (O.) Coll., 1867; Lane Theol. Sem., 1869-72; (D.D., Marietta, 1885; LL.D., Wabash Coll., 1911); m. Annie L. Thurston, Apr. 14, 1879. Ordained Presbyn. ministry, 1873; pastor, Wabash, Ind., Nov. 1, 1872—. Moderator 122d Gen. Assembly, Presbyn. Ch. U.S.A., 1910-11. Trustee Western Coll. for Women, Oxford, O. Home: Wabash, Ind. Died Dec. 28, 1921.

LITTLE, Charles Joseph, theologian; b. Philadelphia, Sept. 21, 1840; s. Thomas Rowell and Ann (Zimmermann) L.; A.B., U. of Pa., 1861, A.M., 1864; studied Berlin, 1870-71; (hon. Ph.D., DePauw, 1882; LL.D., Dickinson, 1885; S.T.D., Northwestern U., 1905); m. Anna Marina Schultze, of Berlin, Dec. 3, 1872. Ordained M.E. ministry, 1862; pastor, Newark, Del., 1862-63, St. James' and Spring Garden St. chs., Phila., 1863-65, Springfield, Pa., 1865-66, Chestnut Hill., Phila., 1866-67; teacher mathematics, Dickinson Sem., Pa., 1867-69; pastor Christ Ch., Phila., 1872-74; prof. philosophy and history, Dickinson Coll., 1874-85; prof. logic and history, Syracuse U., 1885-91; prof. hist. theology, 1891-95, pres., 1895—, Garrett Bibl. Inst., Evanston, Ill. Librarian Pa. State Library, 1882-85; Fernley lecturer to British Conf., 1900. Author: Christianity and the Nineteenth Century, 1900; The Angel in the Flame, 1904. Died 1911.

LITTLE, Charles Newton, prof. civ. engring.; b. Madura, Southern India, May 19, 1858; s. Charles and Susan (Robbins) L.; A.B., Neb. U., 1879, A.M., 1884; Ph.D., Yale, 1885; studied univs. of Göttingen and Berlin; m. Emma R. Funke, Aug. 5, 1886. Instr. mathematics and civ. engring., 1880-84, asso. prof. civ. engring., 1885-90, prof., 1890-93, U. of Neb.; prof. mathematics, Leland Stanford Jr. U., 1893-1901; prof. civ. engring., 1901—, dean Coll. Engring., 1911—, U. of Idaho, Moscow, Ida. Conglist. Died Aug. 31, 1923.

LITTLE, Edward Campbell, congressman; b. Newark, O., Dec. 14, 1858; s. Theophilus, Jr. and Sarah Elliott (Taylor) L.; A.B., U. of Kan., 1883, LL.B., A.M., 1886; admitted to bar, 1886; m. Edna M. Steele, at Topeka, Kan., Nov. 29, 1899. Was diplomatic agent and consul gen. with rank of minister resident to Egypt, 1892-93. Lieutenant colonel 20th Kan. Vols. in P.I., 1898-99; Congressional Spanish War and Filipino campaign medals for services in Philippines. Del. at large Rep. Nat. Conv., 1892; defeated by narrow margin for U.S. Senator, 1897, and for justice Supreme Ct., 1914; mem. 65th to 68th Congresses (1917-25), 2d Kan. Dist.; chmn. Revision of Laws Com. and Codifier of the Federal Statutes. Grand Cordon of the Medjidieh, from Sultan of Turkey for diplomatic service. Home: Kansas City, Kan. Died June 27, 1924.

LITTLE, George, geologist; b. Tuscaloosa, Ala., Feb. 11, 1838; s. John and Barbara (Kerr) L.; A.B., U. of Ala., 1855, A.M., 1856 (LL.D., 1905); Ph.D., U. of Göttingen, 1859; m. Caroline Patillo Doak, May 13, 1869. Prof. natural science, Oakland Coll., Miss., 1860-61; pvt. Lumsden's Battery, Army of Tenn., C.S.A.; capt. arty., ordnance duty on staffs of Generals Clayton, Bate, Brown, Cleburne, Cobb, Hill, Breckenridge, Cheatham, Bragg; lt. col. arty., chief ordnance officer, Hardee's corps until 1865. Prof. geology, U. of Miss., 1866-74, 1881-89; state geologist of Miss., 1870-74, of Ga., 1874-81; geol. expert, Chattanooga, Tenn., 1889-92; druggist, Tuscaloosa, Ala., 1892-1902; geol. reporter on clays, Geol. Survey of Ala., 1903, on mines and railroads, 1904-18. Trustee Pontotoc (Miss.) Presbyn. Collegiate Inst. Democrat. Home: Tuscaloosa, Ala. Died May 15, 1924.

LITTLE, George Thomas, librarian; b. Auburn, Me., May 14, 1857; s. Hon. Edward T. and Lucy Jane (Bliss) L.; A.B., Bowdoin, 1877, A.M., 1880 (Litt.D., 1894); m. Lilly T. W. Lane, Dec. 18, 1884. Teacher of Latin, Thayer Acad., Braintree, 1878-82; teacher of Latin, 1882-85, librarian, 1883—, Bowdoin Coll. Mem. State Library Commn. of Me., 1899—(chmn. 1899-1902). Wrote: Historical Sketch of Bowdoin College, 1794-1894, 1894. Home: Brunswick, Me. Died Aug. 6, 1915.

LITTLE, John Dozier, lawyer; b. Talbotton, Ga., Apr. 17, 1871; s. William Augustus and Sarah Virginia (Dozier) L.; prep. edn., Slade's Sch., Columbus, Ga., 1880-85; A.B., U. of Ga., 1888, LL.B., 1890; m. Ilah Dunlap Jordan, June 16, 1906. Admitted to Ga. bar, 1890, and practiced at Columbus until 1902, Atlanta, 1902—; mem. Little, Powell, Reid & Goldstein. Capt., later maj. Ga. Nat. Guard, 1893-1902. Speaker of Ga. Ho. of Rep., 1898-1901. Home: Leesburg, Ga., and Atlanta. Died Feb. 9, 1934.

LITTLE, John Sebastian, governor; b. Jenny Lind, Ark., Mar. 15, 1853; s. Jesse and Mary E. (Tolman)

L.; ed. Cane Hill Coll., Ark.; admitted to bar, 1874. Dist. atty. 12th circuit of Ark., 1877-84; mem. Ark. Ho. of Rep., 1885; judge Circuit Ct., 1886-90; chmn. State Jud. Conv., 1893; elected to 53d Congress, 1894, to fill unexpired term of Clifton R. Breckenridge; reelected 54th to 59th Congresses (1895-1907); resigned from Congress, Jan. 14, 1907; gov. of Ark., 1907-09. Democrat. Home: Little Rock, Ark. Died Oct. 29, 1916.

LITTLE, J(ohn) Wesley, artist; b. Sullivan Co., Pa., Aug. 24, 1867; s. John P. and Martha Halleck (Edkin) L.; studied at Nat. Acad. of Design, New York, 1888-94, and with Leonard Ochtman; went abroad for travel and study, 1899-1900 and 1905; m. Susan Heim, Dec. 4, 1900. Has exhibited at St. Louis Expn., Pa. Acad. Fine Arts, Art Club, Phila., Am. Water Color Soc., New York Water Color Club, Art Inst. Chicago, Washington Water Color Club, Internat. Exhbn., Montevideo, 1911, Panama P.I. Expn., etc. Silver medal, Am. Art Soc., 1901. Home: Picture Rocks, Pa. Died Sept. 27, 1923.

LITTLE, Joseph James, printer; b. Bristol, Eng., June 5, 1841; s. James and Eunice (Rogers) L.; came to U.S., 1846; ed. dist. schs.; printer's apprentice at Morris, N.Y., 1855-59; employed as compositor, New York, 1859, foreman, 1864; corporal, 1st sergt. and 1st lt. 37th N.Y. Vols., 1862-64; m. Josephine, d. John Robinson of New York, Sept. 25, 1866; father of A. W. Pres. J. J. Little & Co., printers, 1867—, Demorest & Little, 1902—; trustee Excelsior Savings Bank. Pres. Bd. Edn. Greater New York, 1890-91; mem. 52d Congress (1891-93); mem. N.Y. World's Fair Commn., 1893. Democrat. Mason. Home: New York, N.Y. Died Feb. 11, 1913.

LITTLE, Riley McMillan, social worker; b. Cedarville, O., Sept. 15, 1865; s. Robert and Mary Ann (McMillan) L.; B.S., Monmouth (Ill.) Coll., 1890; B.D., Pittsburgh Theol. Sem., 1893; studied U. of Chicago; m. Nannie M. Chamberlin, May 10, 1893; children—Mrs. Mary Ashby, William Clark, Dorothy Josephine, Mrs. Elizabeth Hoadley. Ordained U.P. ministry, 1893; pastor Albany, Ore., 1893-96, Woodlawn Ch., Chicago, 1896-1907, Bellevue Presbyn. Ch., Pittsburgh, 1907-13; gen. sec. Phila. Soc. for Organizing Charity, 1912-16; chmn. U.S. Employees' Compensation Commn., Washington, Mar. 15, 1917-July 1, 1918; dir. Safety Inst. America, 1918-21; dir. Rehabilitation Div. N.Y. Dept. of Edn., 1921—. Presbyn. Home: Albany, N.Y. Died Apr. 26, 1939.

LITTLE, Russell A., insurance; b. Glens Falls, N.Y., Mar. 14, 1849. Began as clk. in local ins. agency, Glens Falls; later spl. agt. Royal Ins. Co.; successively spl. agt. with Glens Falls Ins. Co. (of which father was pres.), gen. agt., sec., v.p., and pres., now retired. Home: Glens Falls, N.Y. Died Dec. 5, 1922.

LITTLE, William Nelson, 2d, rear adm.; b. Newburgh, N.Y., Dec. 31, 1852; s. of William Nelson and Margaret (Thall) L.; grad. U.S. Naval Acad., 1875; m. Kate Sewell, of Brooklyn, Nov. 23, 1876. Commd. asst. engr., 1877; passed asst. engr., 1886; lt. comdr., 1890; chief engr., 1898; comdr., 1904; capt., 1908; rear adm., Mar. 13, 1913; retired Dec. 31, 1914. Served two cruises on N. Atlantic Sta., one on Asiatic Sta.; chief engr. of base at Key West and afloat in Phillippines during Spanish-Am. War, 1898; gen. duties, Philippines, and in China waters during Boxer Rebellion; in two engagements with Philippine insurgents and assisted in searching out and destroying vessels engaged in contrabrand trade with insurgents around the coast of Luzon; insp. of machinery, ordnance and navigation material, 1904-14; inspection duty, Bur. Steam Engring., during World War. Home: Mountain Lakes, N.J. Died Jan. 4, 1925.

LITTLEFIELD, Charles Edgar, congressman; b. Lebanon, Me., June 21, 1851; s. Rev. William H. and Mary (Stevens) L.; acad. edn.; m. Clara H., d. Gen. William Ayer, Feb. 28, 1878. Admitted to bar, 1876, and entered practice at Rockland, Me.; sr. mem. Littlefield & Littlefield. Mem. Me. Ho. of Rep., 1885-89 (speaker, 1887-89); atty. gen. of Me., 1889-93; elected to 56th Congress, June 19, 1899, for unexpired term (1899-1901) of Nelson Dingley, deceased; reëlected 57th to 60th Congresses (1901-09), 2d Me. Dist. Home: Rockland, Me. Died May 2, 1915.

LITTLEFIELD, Eben Northup, banker; b. Pawtucket, R.I., 1854; s. Gov. Alfred H. and Rebecca J. (Northup) L.; ed. English and Classical Sch. of Providence; m. Ida Allen Ballou, 1886; 1 dau., Ida Ballou. Began as clk. in 1st Nat. Bank, Providence; later treas. Littlefield Mfg. Co.; elected v.p. Pawtucket Instn. for Savings, 1902, pres., 1910—; pres. Pawtucket Safe Deposit & Trust Co., Royal Weaving Co.; v.p. Industrial Trust Co. Commr. of sinking funds City of Pawtucket; col. on gov.'s staff, 1880-83; commr. of State Sinking Funds, 1902—. Pres. and trustee Memorial Hosp. Republican. Home: Pawtucket, R.I. Died May 1935.

LITTLEFIELD, George Emery, bookseller; b. Boston, Aug. 29, 1844; s. Jacob and Sarah (Hill) L.; A.B., Harvard, 1866; m. Emily Frances Willis, Feb. 8, 1870. Engaged in the antique book and curio trade, 1868—; authority on hist. Americana and genealogies; collector for great libraries in U.S. Author: Early Boston Booksellers, 1900; Early Schools and School Books of New England, 1904; Early Mass. Press (2 vols.), 1907. Home: Cambridge, Mass. Died Sept. 4, 1915.

LITTLEFIELD, Milton Smith, clergyman; b. N.Y. City, Aug. 21, 1864; s. Milton Smith and Anna Elizabeth (Shull) L.; Johns Hopkins, 1888-89; Union Theol. Sem., N.Y. City, 1889-92; D.D., Washburn Coll., Topeka, Kan., 1915; m. Luella Gardner, Oct. 1, 1895 (dec.); 1 dau., Helen Blauvelt (Mrs. William C. Fuller). Asst. minister Central Presbyn. Ch., N.Y. City, 1892-96; preacher to Hill Sch., Pottstown, Pa., 1897; pastor First Union Presbyn. Ch., N.Y. City, 1898-1907, Bay Ridge Presbyn. Ch., Brooklyn, N.Y., 1907-11; dist. sec. Congl. Edn. Soc., 1911-20; pastor Union Evang. Ch., Corona, L.I., N.Y., 1921—. Conglist. Mason. Author: Hand-Work in the Sunday School, 1908. Compiler: The School Hymnal, 1921; Hymns of the Christian Life, 1925; The Hymnal for Young People, 1927. Home: Corona, L.I., N.Y. Deceased.

LITTLEFIELD, Nathan Whitman, lawyer; b. Bridgewater, Mass., May 21, 1846; s. Rufus Ames and Abigail Russel (Whitman) L.; A.B. (valedictorian), Dartmouth, 1869, hon. A.M., 1909; LL.B., Boston U., 1876; m. Arletta V. Redman, Aug. 13, 1873; m. 2d, Mary Wheaton Ellis, Dec. 1, 1886; children—Nathan Whitman, Alden. Prin. Newport (R.I.) High Sch., 1871-73; prin. high sch. and supt. schs., Westerly, R.I., 1873-74; admitted to Boston bar, 1876, R.I. bar, 1877, and since in practice at Providence; leading counsel for depositors in reorganization of Union Trust Co. of Providence. Mem. R.I. Senate, 1897-98; referee in bankruptcy, Dist. of R.I., 1898-1918; chmn. Sch. Com., Pawtucket, 1898-1901; Dem. candidate for gov. of R.I., 1900; mem. commn. for revising jud. system of the state, 1904-05; mem. commn. for dividing State of R.I. into representative districts, and of com. for drafting laws to carry amendment of state constn. into effect, 1910; judge probate ct., Pawtucket, 1925—. Lecturer on polit, and hist. subjects; Phi Beta Kappa address, Dartmouth, 1910. Pres. Dartmouth Alumni Assn. of R.I. Home: Pawtucket, R.I. Died Dec. 5, 1929.

LITTLEJOHN, Abraham Newkirk, first P.E. bishop of Long Island; consecrated Jan. 27, 1869; b. Florida, N.Y., Dec. 13, 1824; grad. Union Coll., 1845; (D.D., Univ. of Pa., 1856; LL.D., Cambridge, England, 1880; D.C.L., Univ. of the South, 1897); ordered deacon, 1848; ordained priest, 1849; asst. St. Anne's, Amsterdam, N.Y.; St. Andrew's, Meriden, Conn.; rector, 1850-51, Christ Ch., Springfield, Mass.; 1851-60, St. Paul's, New Haven, Conn.; 1860-69, Holy Trinity, Brooklyn. Author: Discourses on Individualism; Christian Dogma Essential; The Christian Ministry at the Close of the Nineteenth Century; etc. Home: Garden City, N.Y. Died 1901.

LITTLEJOHN, Elbridge Gerry, supt. schs.; b. Smith Co., Tex., Sept. 23, 1862; s. Elbridge Gerry Littlejohn and Sara Ann (Jefferies) L.; ed. Peabody Coll. for Teachers, Nashville, Tenn., 1881-82; A.M., Tex. Christian U., Fort Worth, 1899; m. Helen Cullens, Sept. 1, 1887; children—Elfleda, Harry Fendley, Sarah Helen (Mrs. John Keith Torbet), Liska (Mrs. Dan C. McCoy). Teacher city schs., Galveston, Tex., 1883-90, prin., 1890-1924, supt., 1924—. Trustee Galveston Orphans Home. Democrat. Episcopalian. K.P. Author: Texas History Stories, 1903; Geography of Texas, 1913. Asso. editor Texas Journal of Education, 1887-91; lecturer at summer schs., U. of Tex., 1907-23. Home: Galveston, Tex. Died Dec. 2, 1935.

LITTLETON, Frank Leslie, lawyer; b. nr. McCordsville, Ind., Jan. 12, 1868; s. Aaron S. and Mary E. (McCord) L.; Ph.B., De Pauw, 1891, LL.B., 1893, A.M., 1894; unmarried. In gen. practice at Indianapolis, 1893-1907; gen. atty. C.,C.,C.&St.L. Ry. Co., 1907-20; atty. for Indiana, same co., 1920—. Mem. Ind. Ho. of Rep., 1897-1901 (speaker, 1899). Home: Indianapolis, Ind. Died May 27, 1935.

LITTLETON, Jesse M., lawyer; b. Roane Co., Tenn., Mar. 9, 1867; s. Thomas J. and Hannah (Ingram) L.; self-ed.; m. Kathryn Estill, Mar. 10, 1906. Began practice at Winchester, Tenn., 1891; mayor of Winchester, 1903, 05, 07, 09; Rep. nominee for gov. of Tenn., 1904; removed to Chattanooga, 1911; mayor of Chattanooga, 1915-19; Rep. nominee for Congress, 1916; mem. Rep. Nat. Com. from Tenn., 1916—; sr. mem. Littleton, Littleton & Littleton. Episcopalian. Elk, K.P. Home: Chattanooga, Tenn. Died Apr. 23, 1923.

LITTLETON, Jesse Talbot, coll. prof.; b. Portsmouth, Va., Oct. 27, 1856; s. Rev. Oscar and Martha Elizabeth (Bernard) L.; A.M., Randolph-Macon Coll., 1880; Sauveur Còllege des Langues, Amherst, Mass., 1881-82; Litt.D., Ky. Wesleyan Coll., 1902; LL.D., Emory and Henry, 1907; m. Lulie Rosser, Dec. 26, 1882; children—Martha Elizabeth, Jesse Talbot, Leonidas Rosser, Lulie Bernard, Oscar Emory, Wilbur Fisk, Norman Gunnison, Wallace Duncan. Asso. prin. Kanawha Mil. Acad., Charleston, W.Va., 1880-81; prof. modern langs., Wesleyan Female Coll., Murfreesboro, N.C., 1881-83; prof. Greek and German, Wofford Coll., S.C., 1883-86; prin. Belle Haven Acad., 1887-90; prof. modern langs. Danville Coll. for Young Ladies, 1890-93; prof. English, Emory and Henry Coll., Va., 1893-98; prof. modern langs., Southern U., Greensboro, Ala., 1898-1910; prof. modern langs., and dean faculty, 1910-11, prof. English and dean, 1911-13, prof. Romance langs. and dean, 1913, Woman's Coll. of Ala.; pres. Thomas Industrial Inst., 1914-16. Mem. M.E. Ch., South. Democrat. Home: Fort Pierce, Fla. Died Jan. 26, 1929.

LITTLETON, Martin Wiley, lawyer; b. Roane Co., Tenn., Jan. 12, 1872; s. Thomas J. and Hannah B. L.; self ed.; m. Maud Wilson, Dec. 1, 1896. Admitted to bar, 1891; practiced at Dallas, 1893-96, New York, 1896—. Pros. atty., Dallas, 1893-96; asst. dist. atty., Kings Co., N.Y., 1900-04; pres. Brooklyn Borough, 1904-05; del. from N.Y. to Dem. Nat. Conv., 1904, presenting name of Alton B. Parker for presdl. nomination on behalf of State of N.Y.; mem. 62d Congress (1911-13), 1st N.Y. Dist. Home: Plandome, N.Y. Died Dec. 19, 1934.

LITTLETON, William Graham, banking; b. Phila., Pa., Mar. 8, 1868; s. John E. and Mary (Graham) L.; A.B., Central High Sch., Phila., 1884; LL.B., U. of Pa., 1888; m. Annie Newby Kugler, Dec. 1, 1892; children—William Richard, Arthur. Admitted to Pa. bar, 1889; began banking in trust dept. Fidelity Trust Co. (now Fidelity-Phila. Trust Co.), 1889, v.p., 1915—; pres. and dir. Annora Coal Co.; dir. C. H. Boley Co., Robert Buist Co., Heyl Bros. Co., G. A. Bisler, Inc., John & James Dobson, Inc., Smith, Kline & French Laboratories, Central Land & Mining Co., Trustee Presbyn. Hosp. (finance com.), Dunwoody Home; mem. advisory board Women's Homeopathic Hosp. Republican. Presbyn. Home: Bala-Cynwyd, Pa. Died July 11, 1937.

LIVELY, Daniel O'Connell; b. Galveston, Tex., Sept. 14, 1868; s. Dominic and Cecelia (Edwards) L.; self-educated; m. Erna Lazda, June 1921; children—Marjorie, Michael. Farmer, cowboy, laborer, newspaper reporter, agrl. and live stock editor to 1896; connected with stock yards and oil operations to 1904; in wholesale mdse. business, Panama, 1904-08; stock yds. official, Portland, Ore., 1909-12; chief dept. of live stock and commr. to S. America, Panama-Pacific Internat. Expn., 1912-15; active in promoting 3d and 4th Liberty Loans, 1917-18; went to Russia for Am. Red Cross, 1918, trans. to Siberia and served as chmn. Am. Com. for Repatriation of Prisoners of War from Siberia; Far East commr. U.S. Dept. Agr., 1922-23; mgr. State Chamber Commerce, Wash., 1924-28; v.p. White Cross Anti-Narcotic Assn., 1928; nat. dir. China Famine Relief, 1928-31; apptd. nat. dir. Flood Relief in China, Aug. 1931. Republican. Conglist. Home: White Plains, N.Y. Died Nov. 30, 1933.

LIVERIGHT, Horace Brisbin, publisher; b. Osceola Mills, Pa., Dec. 10, 1886; s. Henry and Henrietta (Fleisher) L.; ed. grammar sch., Phila.; m. Lucile Elsas, 1911; children—Herman, Lucy; m. 2d, Elsie Bartlett Porter, 1931. Founder, 1918, and pres. Boni & Liveright, book publishers, New York City; founder and publisher of The Modern Library, 1918-25, comprising works of many living authors. Entered theatrical producing business, and prod. "The Firebrand," 1924, "Hamlet in Modern Dress," 1925, "An American Tragedy," 1926, "Dracula," 1927, "The Dagger and the Rose," 1927; pres. Stonelea Players, Authors' Royalties Co. Mem. exec. com. Com. of 48. Jewish religion. Successful in fight against Justice Ford's Clean Books Bill, before N.Y. Gen. Assembly, 1924. Made Officer French Acad., 1926. Home: New York, N.Y. Died Sept. 24, 1933.

LIVERMORE, Mary Ashton, author, lecturer; b. Boston, Dec. 19, 1820; d. Timothy and Zebiah (Vose) Rice; ed. in public schools and Charlestown (Mass.) Female Sem.; taught school; m. Rev. D. P. Livermore, 1845, Universalist minister (died 1899). Was active in anti-slavery and the Washingtonian temperance movements; went to Chicago, 1857, where her husband became editor and she asso. editor of a Universalist paper; was active in U.S. Sanitary Commn. during Civil war; was 1st pres. Ill. Woman's Suffrage Assn.; editor The Agitator, woman suffrage paper, 1869; merged it into the Woman's Journal, 1870; was editor of latter 2 yrs., removing to Boston. Was 10 yrs. pres. Mass. W.C.T.U.; is pres. Mass. Woman's Suffrage Assn. Has delivered lectures all over the U.S. and in England and Scotland. Author: My Story of the War, 1888; The Story of My Life, 1897. Also "American Women" (edited by late Frances E. Willard and Mary A. Livermore), 1897. Home: Melrose, Mass. Died 1905.

LIVERMORE, Thomas Leonard, financier; pres. N.E. Exploration Co.; v.p. Ashburton Mining Co., Contention Mining Co.; dir. Old Colony Trust Co., Smuggler Union Mining Co. Mem. Corp. Mass. Inst. Tech. Home: Boston, Mass. Died Jan. 9, 1918.

LIVERMORE, William Roscoe, colonel U.S.A.; b. Cambridge, Mass., Jan. 11, 1843; s. George L.; freshman class, Harvard; grad. U.S. Mil. Acad., 1865; m. Augusta Keen, Jan. 18, 1883. First lt. engrs., June 23, 1865; promoted through grades to col. engrs.,

Apr. 23, 1904. Has been connected with fortification work at Key West, Tortugas, Baltimore, Newport and New Bedford; chief engr., Dept. of Tex. and Dept. of the East, survey of N. and N.W. lakes, improvement of Missouri River, river and harbor improvement in Mass., R.I., Conn., N.Y. and N.J.; light house engr., making many improvements in the fog-signal system; mil. attaché Copenhagen and Stockholm, May 1899-June 1902; mem. bd. engrs. for fortifications, 1902-07; retired by operation of law, Jan. 11, 1907; returned to active duty, May 10, 1917, and on spl. duty with Chief of Engrs. U.S.A. With Sir Charles Bright, laid 1st Am. cable from U.S. to Havana, 1868; with Col. A. H. Russell, U.S.A., invented several mag. and automatic guns, including the method of loading by clips, patented 1880; author of "Am. Kriegspiel," a method of practicing the art of war on a map. Fellow Am. Acad. Arts and Sciences. Home: Washington, D.C. Died Sept. 26, 1919.

LIVINGSTON, Crawford, railroad builder; b. New York, May 6, 1848; acad. edn., Albany, N.Y. Purchasing agt. Winona & St. Peter Ry., St. Paul; with Henry Villard built the Little Falls Dak. Ry.; built and was one of the owners of James River Valley Ry., and Duluth-Manitoba R.R.; asso. with A. B. Stickney in building the Minn. Central, and the C.G.W.; was pres. of all the lighting cos. of St. Paul; trustee Minn. Mut. Life Ins. Co. Home: St. Paul, Minn. Died Nov. 16, 1925.

LIVINGSTON, James Duane, banker; b. New York, May 15, 1859; s. Charles James and Charlotte L. (Merry) L.; A.B., Columbia, 1880; LL.B., Transylvania U., Lexington, Ky., 1893; m. Mabel Channing Wright, May 14, 1889. Began in employ 1st Nat. Bank, New York, 1880; with Post, Wales & Co. and Boyd & Livingston, 1883-86; with Austin Corbin, 1886-89; J. Kennedy Tod & Co., 1889-97, in various capacities, particularly as v.p. and gen. mgr. Lexington & Eastern Ry., Lexington, Ky.; trust officer N. Am. Trust Co., 1897-1902; mem. Livingston & Hall, 1902-12; pres. Troy (N.Y.) Trust Co., 1912-15; investment securities, New York, 1915—. Mem. Bd. of Education, Lexington, 1895-97. Trustee Columbia U. Democrat. Episcopalian. Home: Garden City, N.Y. Died May 5, 1936.

LIVINGSTON, Leonidas Felix, congressman; b. Newton Co., Ga., Apr. 3, 1832; pub. sch. edn.; pvt. C.S.A., 1861-65; engaged in farming. Mem. Ga. Ho. of Rep., 2 terms; Senate, 1 term; mem. 52d to 61st Congresses (1891-1911), 5th Ga. Dist. Democrat. V.p. Ga. State Agrl. Soc. 11 yrs. and pres. 4 yrs.; pres. Ga. State Alliance for 3 yrs. Home: Covington, Ga. Died 1912.

LIVINGSTON, Philip, lawyer; b. N.Y. City, Nov. 9, 1861; s. Livingston and Mary Celia (Williamson) L.; A.B., Harvard, 1884; LL.B., Columbia, 1887; m. Juliette Turner Benedict, Jan. 5, 1910; children—Philip, Benedict. Practiced with Davies & Rapallo, later Turner, McClure & Rolston, and the Lawyers Title Ins. Co.; mem. Livingston & Van Amringe, 1896-1900, retired. Member Company K, 7th Regiment, N.G.N.Y., 1885-92; lieut. and capt. 12th Regiment, 1909-11; office of adj. gen., 1917; capt. and insp. small arms practice 12th Regt. and 23d Engrs., maj. Insp. Gen.'s Dept., N.G.N.Y., 1918-20, now on Reserve List. Ex-officer and mem. council Soc. Colonial Wars 15 yrs., S.R. 25 yrs. Republican. Episcopalian. Home: New York, N.Y. Died June 24, 1938.

LIVINGSTONE, John Alexander, newspaper man, lawyer; b. Anson County, N.C., Sept. 6, 1885; s. Walter Woodberry and Lydia (Vick) L.; grad. Pee Dee Inst., Wadesboro, N.C.; student Trinity Coll. (now Duke U.), U. of N.C. and Raleigh (N.C.) Sch. of Law; m. Rosalie Preston Turner, Apr. 30, 1935. Teacher, high schools, 1907-09; asst. principal Brevard (N.C.) Inst., 1909-11; asso. editor Gaston Progress, Gastonia, N.C., 1911-12; reporter, later city editor Wilmington (N.C.) Star, 1913-18 (except 6 mos. with N.C. Div. of Markets); state news editor, also legislative reporter and editorial writer Raleigh News and Observer, 1919-27, Washington corr., 1927-30; admitted to N.C. bar, 1922; asso. editor Commercial Law Journal, Chicago, 1930-31 and 1934-35; became librarian Supreme Court of N.C., 1931. Assistant county food administrator and four-minute speaker, New Hanover County, N.C., 1917-18; with Mil. Intelligence Service, Washington, D.C., 1918. Democrat. Methodist. Mason. Home: Raleigh, N.C. Died May 26, 1937.

LIVINGSTONE, William, banker; b. Dundas, Ont., Can., Jan. 21, 1844. Identified with shipping interests on Great Lakes, 1864—; pres. Lake Carriers' Assn., Dime Savings Bank; chmn. exec. com. Rep. State Central Committee. Pres. Am. Bankers Assn., 1911-12; mem. Detroit Bd. Commerce; pres. Detroit Bd. of Trade. Mem. Mich. Legislature, 1875; pres. Detroit Park and Boul. Commn. Mason. Home: Detroit, Mich. Died Oct. 17, 1925.

LLEWELLYN, Joseph Corson, architect; b. Phila., Pa., July 22, 1855; s. David R. and Huldah S. (Corson) L.; B.S., U. of Ill., 1877; m. Emma Clarinda Piatt, May 1883; children—Ralph Corson, Clarinne, Ruth (Mrs. Fred H. Baird), Vida (Mrs. Henry Livezey). Inst. in U. of Ill., 1877-79; bldg. supt. for J. W. Givens, St. Louis, Mo., 1879-80; supt. Lindell Ry., St. Louis, 1880-86; settled in Chicago, 1893, and began practice as architect; mem. Joseph C. Llewellyn Co., 1908—. Fellow Am. Inst. Architects. Republican. Home: LaGrange, Ill. Died May 15, 1932.

LLEWELLYN, Silas James, iron and steel mfr.; b. Briton Ferry, Wales, Oct. 25, 1860; s. Henry and Elizabeth (Gower) L.; brought to U.S., 1864; ed. pub. schs., Milwaukee, Wis.; m. Mary E. Parkes, June 19, 1884. Entered employ of North Chicago Rolling Mill Co., Milwaukee, 1879, and continued with its successor, Ill. Steel Co., until 1897; became v.p. Inland Iron & Forge Co., 1897, which merged, 1899, into Republic Iron & Steel Co., of which was sec. and mem. exec. com.; in 1900, elected v.p. Plano Mfg. Co., which was merged into the Internat. Harvester Co.; pres. Interstate Iron & Steel Co. from organization, 1905; also pres. Chicago Malleable Castings Co. Mason. Home: Evanston, Ill. Died Sept. 1925.

LLOYD, Alfred Henry, univ. prof.; b. Montclair, N.J., Jan. 3, 1864; s. Henry H. and Anna (Badger) L.; A.B., Harvard, 1886, A.M., 1888, Ph.D., 1893; studied univs. of Göttingen, Berlin and Heidelberg, 1889-91; LL.D., U. of Calif., 1924; m. Margaret E. Crocker, Dec. 28, 1892; children—Alice Crocker, Frederick Thurston, Anna Mary, Putnam Crocker. Instr. philosophy, 1891-94, asst. prof., 1894-99, jr. prof., 1899-1906, prof., 1906—, dean Grad. Sch., 1915—, acting pres. Feb. to Sept. 1925, U. of Mich. Author: Citizenship and Salvation, 1897; Dynamic Idealism, 1898; Philosophy of History, 1899; The Will to Doubt, 1907; Leadership and Progress, 1922. Home: Ann Arbor, Mich. Died May 11, 1927.

LLOYD, Arthur Selden, bishop; b. Alexandria Co., Va., May 3, 1857; s. John Janney and Eliza Armistead (Selden) L.; ed. Potomac Acad., Alexandria, Va., Va. Poly. Inst., U. of Va., and Theol. Sem. of Va.; D.D., Roanoke Coll., 1898, U. of the South, 1915; m. Lizzie Robertson Blackford, June 30, 1880. Deacon, 1880, priest, 1881, P.E. Ch.; record St. Luke's Ch., Norfolk, Va., 1885-1900; gen. sec. Domestic and Foreign Missionary Soc. of the P.E. Ch. in U.S.A., 1900-09; consecrated bishop coadjutor of Va., Oct. 20, 1909; suffragan bishop diocese of N.Y., May 13, 1921. Pres. Bd. of Missions P.E. Ch., 1910-19. Home: New York, N.Y. Died July 22, 1936.

LLOYD, Curtis Gates, botanist, mycologist; b. Florence, Ky., July 17, 1859; s. Nelson Marvin and Sophia (Webster) L.; ed. pvt. schs. Mem. Lloyd Bros., mfg. pharmacists, Cincinnati, 40 yrs. (now retired). Founder and endowed Lloyd Library, containing 52,000 volumes on botany and pharmacy; spl. student on the classification of fungi; instituted the Lloyd Museum, the largest collection of dried fungi ever brought together. Author of 6 vols. miscellaneous writings on fungi subjects, which are privately printed. Died Nov. 11, 1926.

LLOYD, Demarest, journalist, publicist; b. Chicago, Ill., Feb. 19, 1883; s. Henry Demarest and Jessie (Bross) L.; A.B., Harvard, 1904; Harvard Law Sch., 1906-07; m. Katharine Nordell, Dec. 6, 1916; children—Angelica, Demarest, Karen Gallup. Joined F.A. Central Officers Training Sch., Camp Zachary Taylor, Louisville, Ky., Oct. 1918. Pres. Loyal Coalition, Mar. 1920-Jan. 1922; diplomatic corr. of The Christian Science Monitor, 1922-24; European cable editor, at London, 1924-25; editorial representative Christian Science Monitor, at Washington, D.C., 1925-26; dir. Chicago Tribune, 1926-31; chmn. National Immigration Legislative Committee of Patriotic Societies, 1928-29; editor and publisher "Affairs," Dec. 1931—. Vice chmn. bd. Am. Coalition of Patriotic Socs.; mem. Nat. Council of Nat. Economic League; exec. sec. Taxpayers Union; mem. bd. Nat. Rep. Builders, Advisory Council Am. Liberty League. Home: Washington, D.C. Died June 24, 1937.

LLOYD, Frederic Ebenezer John, archbishop; b. Milford Haven, South Wales, June 5, 1859; s. Thomas and Marie (Clay) L.; ed. English schs. and Dorchester Theol. Coll., Oxfordshire; Mus.Doc., Coll. of Ch. Musicians, 1895, later M.A., Litt.D.; D.D., Intercollegiate Univ.; D.D., Rutherford (N.C.) Coll., 1901; m. Mrs. Peabody, widow of Hiram B. Peabody, of Chicago, Feb. 7, 1917; children (by former marriages)—Ethel Mary, Muriel Marie, Lillian Ada, Frederic E. J., Edwyn Clay, Florence Marie Monica, Edythe Ada, Harold Henry, Sallie Beatrice, Mary Frances. Ordained ministry Ch. of England, by the Lord Bishop of Oxford, 1882; emigrated to Can., 1882, and held various pastoral positions; in Labrador many years; came to U.S., 1893, continuing ministerial work; pres. Intercollegiate Univ., Chicago and London; supt. Grace Episcopal Ch. Parish House, Chicago, 4 yrs.; elected bishop coadjutor of Ore., P.E. Ch., 1905, declined; resigned from P.E. ministry, 1906; ordained ministry Am. Catholic Ch., June 18, 1915, consecrated bishop of Ill., Dec. 29, 1915; elected archbishop and primate of America, 1920. Mem. 48th Gen. Assembly of Ill. (1912-14), 3d Senatorial Dist.; was mem. Curran Commn. for investigating home-finding instns. of Ill. Democrat. Editor: Lloyd's Clerical Directory, 1898-1913; Lloyd's Church Musicians' Directory, 1910; Church Life (Ohio diocesan organ, 1901-03. Founder Soc. of St. Philip the Apostle for Mission-preachers, 1902, also founder of the Order of Antioch, 1928. Home: Chicago, Ill. Died Sept. 11, 1933.

LLOYD, Henry, governor; b. Hambrooks Farm, nr. Cambridge, Md., Feb. 21, 1852; s. Daniel and Kitty (Henry) L.; g.s. Edward L. (gov. Md., 1809-11, U.S. senator, 1819-26); ed. pvt. schs. and Cambridge Acad.; m. Mary Elizabeth Stapleforte, Oct. 18, 1886. Admitted to bar, 1873; taught sch. until 1880; in practice at Cambridge, Md., from 1880; pres. Dorchester Nat. Bank, of Cambridge, 1889—. Elected to Md. Senate, 1881 (pres. 1884); gov. of Md. for unexpired term (1885-88) of Robert M. McLane, apptd. minister to France and served as judge Circuit Ct. of Md. Home: Cambridge, Md. Died Apr. 11, 1932.

LLOYD, Henry Demarest, author; b. New York, N.Y., May 1, 1847; grad. Columbia; lecturer on political economy in New York schools; studied law; admitted to New York bar, 1869; sec. Am. Free Trade League. In Chicago, 1872—; on Chicago Tribune, 1872-85, latter portion of time on editorial staff. Author: A Strike of Millionaires Against Miners, 1890; Wealth vs. Commonwealth, 1894; Labor Copartnership, 1898; Country Without Strikes, 1900; Newest England, 1900. Home: Winnetka, Ill. Died 1903.

LLOYD, Hinton Summerfield, clergyman; b. New York, N.Y., Jan. 7, 1833; s. De Witt and Martha Myers (Noll) L.; A.B., Madison (now Colgate) U., 1856; A.M., 1858; grad. Hamilton Theol. Sem., N.Y., 1858; (D.D., Madison, 1880); m. Eliza M. Carr, Aug. 20, 1858; m. 2d, Sara Agnes Worden, June 29, 1903. Ordained Bapt. ministry, 1858; pastor Johnstown, N.Y., 1858-59, Peekskill, 1859-61, Waterford, 1861-63; chaplain 16th N.Y. Vol. Cav., in Va., 1863-65; pastor Port Jervis, N.Y., 1865-69, Waverly, 1869-77; corr. and financial sec. Bapt. Edn. Soc., N.Y., 1877-1915, treas. same, 1892-1907; lecturer on ministerial efficiency, Colgate Theol. Sem., 1890—. Member Bapt. Ministers' Conf. N.Y., Fedn. of Chs. of New York. Home: Hamilton, N.Y. Died Feb. 21, 1918.

LLOYD, Horatio Gates, banker; b. Middletown, Del., Jan. 14, 1867; s. Horatio Gates and Elizabeth (Newell) L.; LL.B., U. of Pennsylvania, 1887, LL.D., same university, 1931; m. Mary Helen Wingate, May 6, 1897; children—Horatio Gates, Richard Wingate. Admitted to Pa. bar, 1888; clk. Phila. Trust Co., 1888-94, asst. sec., 1894-1900; treas. Commercial Trust Co., Phila., 1900, v.p., 1900-02, pres., 1902-10; partner Drexel & Co., 1910—; partner J. P. Morgan & Co., 1912—; mem. Morgan & Cie, Paris; dir. Gen. Asphalt Co., Phila. Electric Co., Phila. Electric Power Co., Susquehanna Power Co., Bell Telephone Co. Chmn. War Chest Campaign Com., during the World War. Pres. bd. commrs. Haverford Twp., Pa., 1912-22. One of founders, 1921, v.p., 1921—, Welfare Federation; chmn. Com. for Unemployment Relief, 1930-31; administrator of Bur. of Unemployment Relief of Dept. of Pub. Welfare, Phila., 1931. Republican. Presbyn. Home: Haverford, Pa. Died Jan. 21, 1937.

LLOYD, John Uri, pharmacist; b. W. Bloomfield, N.Y., Apr. 19, 1849; s. Nelson Marvin and Sophia (Webster) L.; ed. pvt. schs., Florence, Burlington and Petersburg, Ky.; hon. Ph.M., Phila. Coll. of Pharmacy, 1890; Ph.D., U. of Ohio, 1897; LL.D., Wilberforce University; D.Sc., Univ. of Cincinnati, 1916; M.D., Eclectic Med. Coll., Cincinnati, 1921; m. Adeline Meader, Dec. 27, 1876; m. 2d, Emma Rouse, June 10, 1880. Prof. pharmacy, Cincinnati Coll. Pharmacy, 1883-87; prof. chemistry, 1878—, pres., 1896-1904, Eclectic Med. Inst.; asso. editor Pharmaceutical Review to 1909, Eclectic Medical Journal, Eclectic Medical Gleaner; pres. Lloyd Bros., Pharmacists Inc. Outside of profession has investigated dialect, superstition and folk-lore of Northern Ky.; pres. Lloyd Library and Museum. Revised Cleaveland's Pronouncing Med. Dictionary, 1881. Author: Etidorhpa, The End of Earth, 1895; Stringtown on the Pike, 1900; Warwick of the Knobs, 1901; Red Head, 1903; Scroggins, 1904. Has especially investigated plant chemistry and phytochemistry as applied to medicines, alkaloids, glucosids and proximate principles, precipitates in fluid extracts, and phenomena of capilarity. Editor: History of the Vegetable Drugs of the Pharmacopeia of the United States, 1911; A Study of Digitalis, 1912; and of Coca (with J. T. Lloyd), 1913; History of the Discovery of the Alkaloidal Affinities of Hydrous Aluminum Silicate, 1915; Continued Study in Adsorption—Kryptonine, 1916; Echinacea Angustifolia, 1917; A Study in Solvents, 1917; History of the Vegetable Drugs of the U.S. Pharmacopeia, 1920; Felix Moses, the Beloved Jew, 1930; Physics in Pharmacy (with Dr. Wolfgang Ostwald, Leipzig, Germany, 5 parts issued). Four times awarded honor medals by American Pharm. Assn., receiving Remington honor medal, 1920, for research work in colloidal chemistry. Home: Cincinnati, O. Died Apr. 9, 1936.

LLOYD, Marshall Burns, inventor, mfr.; b. St. Paul, Minn., Mar. 10, 1858; s. John and Margaret (Conmee) L.; ed. pub. schs., Meaford, Can.; married. First invention was combination bagholder and scale, for farmers; founded, 1900, at Minneapolis, Minn., later at Menominee, Mich., the Lloyd Mfg. Co., mfrs. bedspring weaving machine; later invented new method and machinery for making thin seamless steel tubing; also new method for producing wicker articles and loom for weaving the wickers; now mgr. Lloyd Mfg. Co.; v.p. Automatic, Seamless Tubing Co. Mayor of Menominee, 1913-17. Republican. K. of P. Home: Menominee, Mich. Died Aug. 10, 1927.

LLOYD, Morton Githens, engr.; b. Beverly, N.J., Sept. 10, 1874; s. Clement E. and Irene Emma (Githens) L.; B.S., U. of Pa., 1896, Ph.D., 1900, E.E., 1908; Harvard, 1897-98; Friedrich Wilhelms Universität, Berlin, 1898-99; m. Ethel Tucker Maurer, June 20, 1907; children—Miriam, Richard Louis. Instr. physics, U. of Pa., 1899-1902; lab. asst., asst. physicist and asso. physicist, Bur. of Standards, Washington, 1902-10; tech. editor, Electrical Review and Western Electrician, Chicago, 1910-16; electrical engr. and chief safety codes sect., Nat. Bur. of Standards, 1917—. Fellow Am. Inst. E.E.; mem. numerous societies. Member Internat. Elec. Congress, St. Louis, 1904, Turin, 1911, Internat. Engring. Congress, San Francisco, 1915; Internat. Congress on Illumination, Saranac, N.Y., 1928. Awarded Edward Longstreth medal, Franklin Inst., 1910. Home: Chevy Chase, Md. Died Apr. 26, 1941.

LLOYD, Nelson McAllister, journalist, author; b. Phila., Dec. 18, 1872; s. Wilson and Sarah (McAllister) L.; ed. Germantown Acad., Phila.; B.S. in elec. engring., Pa. State Coll., 1892; m. Susanne Livingston Green, Apr. 4, 1908 (died 1913). In newspaper work on New York Evening Sun, 1892-1909. Mem. Nat. Inst. Arts and Letters. Author: The Soldier of the Valley, 1904; David Malcolm, 1913. Home: Lawrenceville, N.J. Died Feb. 8, 1933.

LLOYD, Samuel, surgeon; b. Jersey City, N.J., Aug. 4, 1860; s. Gardner Potts and Emma (Disbrow) L.; B.Sc., Princeton, 1882; M.D., U. of Vt., 1884, Coll. Phys. and Surg. (Columbia), 1886; m. Adele Ferrier Peck, June 11, 1888 (dec.); children—Elisabeth (Mrs. Edward H. Wardwell), Augustine A. (Mrs. John Prince Hazen Perry), Samuel. Emeritus prof. surgery, New York Post Grad. Med. Sch.; attending surgeon, Lutheran Hosp. of Manhattan. Col., M.C., U.S.A.; served in France, July 1917-Aug. 1919; A.E.F. rep., U. of Paris (Sorbonne). Officier de l'Instruction Publique, and Officier d'Académie (palms). Fellow Am. Coll. Surgeons. Home: New York, N.Y. Died Dec. 19, 1926.

LLOYD, Stacy Barcroft, banker; b. Camden, N.J., Aug. 1, 1876; s. Malcolm and Anna (Howell) L.; student Lawrenceville Sch., 1892-94; A.B., Princeton, 1898; LL.B., U. of Pa., 1901; m. Eleanor B. Morris, Oct. 25, 1902; children—Ellen Douglas (Mrs. Lloyd Dunham), Stacy Barcroft, Morris. Admitted to Pa. bar, 1901, and asso. with Reed & Pettit, 1901-06; asst. gen. solicitor, later asst. gen. counsel, Pa. R.R., 1906-21; v.p. Phila. Saving Fund Soc., 1921-34, pres., 1934. Asso. counsel for Pa. of the U.S. Food Adminstrn., 1917-18. Commd. maj. judge-advocate, July 1918, and served in France and Italy until June 1919; hon. disch. Aug. 1919. Republican. Episcopalian. Home: Ardmore, Pa. Died July 30, 1941.

LLOYD, Wesley, congressman; b. Arvonia, Kan., July 24, 1883; s. John Q. and Mary Ann (Roberts) L.; student Washburn Coll., Topeka, Kan., 1901-05, Kansas City Law Sch., 1905-06; m. Iva Reedy, Jan. 30, 1910; children—John David (dec.), Mary Jane, David Wendell, Sarah Jean. In practice of law at Tacoma, Wash., 1908—; mem. 73d Congress (1933-35), 6th Wash. Dist. Democrat. Mason. Home: Tacoma, Wash. Died Jan. 10, 1936.

LLOYD, William Henry, prof. law; b. Phila., Pa., Aug. 14, 1870; s. Maj. William H. and Helen (Borden) L.; A.B., U. of Pa., 1890, A.M., 1893, LL.B., 1893, LL.M., 1933; m. Alice Gilpin, April 22, 1920. Practiced at Phila. until 1914; lecturer U. of Pa. Law Sch., 1910-12; asst. prof. law, same, 1912-16, prof., 1916—. Republican. Episcopalian. Author: Early Courts of Pa., 1910; Cases on Civil Procedure, 1916; Cases on Equitable Doctrines, 1917; Cases on Pleading, 1927. Home: Philadelphia, Pa. Died Dec. 31, 1936.

LOAR, James Leazure, Chautauqua mgr.; b. Waynesburg, Pa., Jan. 24, 1864; s. John and Marie (White) L.; ed. pub. schs.; LL.B., U. of Mich., 1887; m. Mildred W. Wood, Aug. 10, 1892; children—Mrs. Constance Greenfield, Mrs. Romaine Alling. Practiced law, Ogden, Utah and Bloomington, Ill., 1888-1920; county atty. Thomas Co., Kan., 1889-92; settled at Bloomington, Ill., 1899; originator and organizer Independent Coöperative Chautauqua plan, 1909; pres. and gen. mgr. Loar Independent Chautauqua Co. Delegate Gen. Conf. M.E. Ch., 1908; pres. Ill. State Epworth League, 1905-06; pres. Laymen's Assn., Ill. Conf. M.E. Ch., 1904-08. Democrat. Mason. Home: Bloomington, Ill. Died Apr. 19, 1927.

LOASBY, Arthur William, banker; b. Rochester, N.Y., Sept. 29, 1876; s. Samuel, Jr. and Emma (Rehberger) L.; ed. pub. schs. and Coll. City of New York; m. Adena, d. Richard Phillips, Oct. 5, 1898; children—Richard Phillips, Marjorie (dec.), Janet. With First Nat. Bank, Syracuse, 1895, serving as loan teller, bond dept. mgr. and asst. cashier, and elected v.p., 1910; pres. Trust & Deposit Co. of Syracuse, 1913-19; negotiated consolidation between First Nat. Bank and the Trust & Deposit Co., under title of First Trust & Deposit Co., of which was pres., 1919-20; v.p. The Equitable Trust Co. of New York, 1920-23, pres., 1923-29, chmn. bd., 1929-30; chmn. bd. First Trust & Deposit Co., Syracuse, 1932—; administrator of Estate Administrations, Inc.; v.p. and dir. Nat. Distillers Products Corp., W. A. Gaines & Co., Hellman Co. Trustee Syracuse U. Republican. Home: Montclair, N.J. Died Nov. 24, 1936.

LOBECK, Charles O., congressman; b. Andover, Ill., Apr. 6, 1852; s. Otto and Anna Lovisa (Gustavson) L.; ed. German Wallace Coll., Berea, O., 1865-66, high sch., Geneseo, Ill., and business coll., Chicago; m. Emma L. Palmer, July 28, 1886. Commercial traveler in Ia. and Neb., 1875-92; in hardware business, Omaha, 1892-95; real estate and ins., 1897-1903. Mem. Neb. Senate, 1893; mem. city council, Omaha, 2 terms, 1897-1903; city comptroller, 3 terms, 1903-10, resigned; mem. 62d to 65th Congresses (1911-19), 2d Neb. Dist. Dem. presdl. elector, 1900. Methodist. Home: Omaha, Neb. Died Jan. 30, 1920.

LOBINGIER, Andrew Stewart, surgeon; b. Laurelville, Pa., Dec. 22, 1862; s. Jacob and Lillias Findley (Stewart) L.; A.B., U. of Mich., 1886, M.D., 1889; m. Kate Reynolds, Nov. 2, 1889; 1 dau., Gladys (wife of Dr. Wm. J. Norris). Practiced Denver, 1889-1902, then at Los Angeles, Prof. bacteriology and pathology, Gross Med. Coll., Denver, 1889-92; prof. pathology, 1892-94, prof. surgery and surgeon to Univ. Hosp., 1894-1902, U. of Colo.; sec., editor proc., Colo. State Med. Soc., 1891-93; lecturer on gen. surgery, Univ. of Southern Calif. Attended clinics and studied with master surgeons in Europe, 1902, 06; mem. staffs Good Samaritan and Hollywood Clara Barton Memorial hosps. Calif. del. nat. conv., Chicago, on Standardization of Am. Hosps., 1917; del. Pan Pacific Surg. Conf., Honolulu, 1929 (chmn. sect. on surgery of upper abdomen); guest lecturer of the Northwest Pacific Medical Assn. Convocation, 1930. Chief examining surgeon for U.S.A. recruiting forces, District No. 12, Aug. 1, 1917-Nov. 10, 1918. Chairman com. for Southern Calif. of Am. Soc. for Control of Cancer, 1913-36; national director Gorgas Memorial Assn. Fellow Am. Coll. Surgeons (founding fellow and member first bd. of govs.), Pacific Coast Surg. Assn. (founding fellow and pres.). Republican. Episcopalian. Joint author of act (now a law) authorizing court to appoint its own expert in civil and criminal cases in Calif. Home: Los Angeles, Calif. Died July 31, 1939.

LOCHER, Casper William, pres. Evang. Synod of N.A.; b. Aburi, Gold Coast, West Africa, June 1, 1866; s. Christopher William and Maria (Diez) L.; brought by parents to U.S., 1869; student Elmhurst (Ill.) Coll., 1882-84, Eden Theol. Sem., St. Louis, Mo., 1884-87, D.D., 1930; m. Lydia J. Walter, June 17, 1890; children—Paul Waldemar (dec.), Rudolf William, Gertrude Matilda. Ordained ministry Evang. Synod of N.A., 1887; pastor St. Paul's Evang. Ch., Elyria, O., 1887-91, Christ Evang. Ch., Chicago, Ill., 1891-94, St. John's Evang. Ch., Lorain, O., 1895-98, St. Mark's Evang. Ch., New Albany, Ind., 1898-1906, St. Matthew's Evang. Ch., Baltimore, Md., 1906-19, Concordia Evang. Ch., Washington, D.C., 1919-24, Zion Evang. Ch., Steubenville, O., 1924-30; pres. Evang. Synod of N.A., 1930—. Home: Webster Groves, Mo. Died Apr. 3, 1934.

LOCHER, Cyrus, senator; b. Putnam Co., O., Mar. 8, 1878; A.B., A.M., Ohio Wesleyan U.; LL.B., Western Reserve Law Sch. Practiced at Cleveland; apptd. asst. city solicitor, 1908, later pros. atty. Cuyahoga County; apptd. commerce dir. by Gov. Donahey, 1923; apptd. U.S. senator, April 1928, for period Apr. 16-Dec. 15, 1928, to succeed Frank B. Willis, dec. Democrat. Home: Cleveland, O. Died Aug. 17, 1929.

LOCHREN, William, judge; b. Co. Tyrone, Ireland, Apr. 3, 1832; s. Michael and Elizabeth L.; parents came to U.S., 1834; reared and ed. in Vt.; admitted to bar, 1856; went to Minn., 1856; pvt. to 1st lt. 1st Minn. Vols., 1861-63; m. Martha A. Demmon, Sept. 6, 1871 (died 1879); m. 2d, Mary E. Abbott, Apr. 19, 1882. Mem. Minn. Senate, 1869-70; judge 4th Jud. Dist. of Minn., 1881-93; U.S. commr. of pensions, 1893-96; U.S. dist. judge, Dist. of Minn., 1896-1908. Democrat. Mason. Home: Minneapolis, Minn. Died 1912.

LOCHRIDGE, P. D., army officer; b. nr. Bexar, Ala., Dec. 2, 1863; s. John and Permelia (Stout) L.; student Miss. Coll., 1880-83; grad. U.S. Mil. Acad., 1887, U.S. Inf. and Cav. Sch., 1893; m. Carlotta Rawolle, Feb. 20, 1889; 1 son, Rawolle. Commd. 2d lt. cav., U.S.A., June 12, 1887, and advanced through grades to col., July 1, 1916; brig. gen. Nat. Army, Dec. 17, 1917; retired for disability in line of duty, Nov. 10, 1919; brig. gen. U.S.A., retired, June 21, 1930. Served in West, Cuba, Puerto Rico, Philippine Islands, Mexican Border, France; mem. Gen. Staff U.S.A., 1915-19; paymaster of Cuban Census and in charge engring. enterprises, 1899-1900. Treas. and dir. Marx & Rawolle, shellac, N.Y. City and Montreal, 1920-26; organizer Calcutta Traders, Ltd., 1921, shellac factories at Purulia and Mirzapur, India, 1922, retired 1926. Awarded D.S.M., Spanish-Am. War, Cuban Occupation and Puerto Rican Occupation medals and Victory Medal (U.S.); Comdr. Legion of Honor (France); Companion Mil. Order of the Bath (England); Comdr. Order of Crown (Italy); Italian War Cross. Home: Washington, D.C. Died June 17, 1935.

LOCKE, Charles Edward, bishop; b. Pittsburgh, Pa., Sept. 9, 1858; s. William Henry (D.D.) and Margaret Ellen (Loor) L.; A.B., Allegheny Coll., 1880, A.M., 1883, D.D., 1892; LL.D., U. of Southern Calif., 1915; m. Mina J., d. Capt. John A. Wood, Dec. 27, 1882; children—Lucile (Mrs. Fletcher White), Ruth Wood (wife of Dr. W. B. Thompson), Lydia Margaret (Mrs. Sidney C. Walker), Dr. Charles Edward (dec.). Ordained M.E. ministry, 1882; pastor Smithfield St. Ch., Pittsburgh, 1888-92, Portland, Ore., 1892-97, San Francisco, 1897-99, Delaware Av. Ch., Buffalo, 1899-1904, Hanson Pl. Ch., Brooklyn, 1904-08, First Ch., Los Angeles, 1908-20; elected bishop, May 1920, and assigned to Philippine Islands; assigned to St. Paul, Minn., May 1924; retired bishop of M.E. Church, May 1932. Elected pres. of Calif. Anti-Saloon League, 1933. Fraternal del. to Centennial New Zealand Methodism, 1922. Conducted funeral of President McKinley, Buffalo, Sept. 1901. Mason. Author: The Typical America, 1902; A Nineteenth Century Crusader, 1902; A Man's Reach, 1914; First Christmas Story, 1915; Daybreak Everywhere, 1919; The Eternal Masculine, 1925; Pray, 1929; The Everlasting Sign, 1929. Home: Santa Monica, Calif. Died Mar. 4, 1940.

LOCKE, Edwin, clergyman; b. Brookville, Ind., Feb. 9, 1857; s. Rev. John W. and Matilda (Wood) L.; DePauw U., 1870-72; A.B., McKendree Coll., 1877, A.M., 1880; (D.D., Taylor U., 1896); m. Evangeline Hogaboom, Dec. 20, 1881 (died 1883); m. 2d, Mary A. Myers, Aug. 19, 1885. Ordained M.E. ministry, 1880; pastor in Kan. at Woodbine, 1880-81, Brookville, 1881-82, Seneca, 1882-83, Sabetha, 1883-85, Centralia, 1885-87, Frankfort, 1887-89, Lyndon, 1889-92, Argentine, 1892-94, Central Av. Ch., Kansas City, 1894-98, Holton, 1898-1903; presiding elder, Topeka Dist., 1903-09; again pastor Central Av. Ch., Kansas City, 1909-11, Euclid Av. Ch., Topeka, 1911-17, London Heights, Kansas City, 1917—. Asst. sec. and sec. Kan. Conf., 1884—; asst. sec. Gen. Conf., 1904, 12, sec., 1916; sec. Meth. Temperance Soc., 1912-16. Trustee Baker U. (Baldwin, Kan.), M.E. Home for Aged (Topeka). Asso. editor Discipline of the M.E. Church, 1916; editor Gen. Conf. Jour., 1916. Home: Kansas City, Kan. Died June 14, 1918.

LOCKE, Frank Lovering, social service; b. Boston, Mass., July 14, 1865; s. James Lovering and Sarah Maria (Swallow) L.; S.B., in civ. engring., Mass. Inst. Tech., 1886; m. Mary Brodhead Kendall, Jan. 16, 1901; children—John Lovering, Eleanor Brodhead, Francis Kendall (dec.), Nancy Lovering. Instr. drawing and civ. engring., Mass. Inst. Tech., 1886-87; in engring. dept., City of Boston, 1887-95; spl. engring. work, asst. supt. and supt., Boston Rubber Shoe Co., 1895-1907; pres. Boston Young Men's Christian Union, 1907-27; personnel dir. Mass. Institute Tech., 1928—. Trustee Norfolk State Hosp.; mem. Corp. Malden Hosp.; term mem. Corp. Mass. Inst. Tech. Enlisted Troop D, 1st Cav. Mass. Vol. Militia, 1885; sergt. and sergt. maj., 1st lt. and adj., 1889-97; col. and asst. insp. gen., 1897-1900, staff of gov. (retired 1901). Mem. Cambridge Industrial Assn. Republican. Unitarian. Home: Boston, Mass. Died Nov. 23, 1934.

LOCKE, Franklin Day, lawyer; b. Gowanda, N.Y., Oct. 8, 1843; s. James and Lucinda Howard (Wheeler) L.; A.B., Hamilton Coll., 1864 (LL.D., 1902); m. Frances Ellen Cooper, May 10, 1866 (dec.); children—Mrs. Sarah L. Richmond, James, Clara Mills (dec.). Admitted to N.Y. bar, 1865, and practiced in Buffalo; now mem. Locke, Babcock, Hollister & Brown; chmn. bd. Kurtzmann & Co., Jewett & Co.; pres. Buffalo Abstract & Title Co. Trustee Hamilton Coll. many yrs. Democrat. Presbyn. Mason. Home: Buffalo, N.Y. Died May 24, 1927.

LOCKE, George Herbert, librarian; b. Beamsville, Ont., Can., Mar. 29, 1870; s. Rev. Joseph H. and Elizabeth (Mackay) L.; B.A., Victoria Coll. (Univ. of Toronto), 1893, M.A., 1896; LL.D., U. of Toronto, 1927; m. Grace Moore, Aug. 1898; 1 son, Macalastair. Acting prof. ancient history, Victoria Coll., 1893-94; fellow in philosophy and edn., U. of Chicago, 1896; lecturer in history of edn., Harvard U. and Radcliffe Coll., 1897-99; editor School Review, asso. prof. edn. and dean Coll. of Edn., U. of Chicago, 1899-1905; asso. in editorial dept. of Ginn & Co., Boston, 1905-07; dean Sch. for Training of Teachers, MacDonald Coll., and acting prof. edn., McGill U., Montreal, 1907-08; chief librarian City of Toronto, Nov. 1908—. Asso. dir. of Pub. Information for Dominion of Can., 1918-19. Mem. Senate, U. of Toronto; mem. Bd. of Regents, Victoria Coll.; pres. A.L.A., 1926-27. Author: When Canada Was New France; Builders of the Canadian Commonwealth. Home: Toronto, Can. Died Jan. 28, 1937.

LOCKE, James, editor; b. Buffalo, N.Y., Nov. 28, 1869; s. Franklin D. and Frances Ellen (Cooper) L.; A.B., Yale, 1890; Ph.D., U. of Heidelberg, Germany, 1895; m. Anna Richards, June 21, 1900; 1 son, John. Instr. chemistry, Yale, 1897-1902; prof. chemistry, Mass. Inst. Tech., 1902-03; retired from teaching on account of ill health, 1903. Contbr. to scientific and popular mags., 1893—; asso. editor Baltimore News, 1911-23, also of Baltimore American, 1920-23 (retired). Author: The Stem of the Crimson Dahlia, 1908; The Plotting of Frances Ware, 1909. Home: New Haven, Conn. Died Feb. 11, 1928.

LOCKE, James Dewitt Clinton, clergyman; b. New York, July 24, 1829; s. James and Mary (Wright) L.; grad. Union Coll., 1849; 2 yrs. at Gen. Theol. Sem., New York; (D.D., Racine Coll., 1864); m. Adele Gleim Douthitt, Jan. 27, 1859. Ordained to P.E. ministry, 1853; rector Grace Ch., Chicago, 1859-94; now dean Chicago Deanery, diocese of Chicago. Author: The Great Western Schism, 1896; Five Minute Talks, 1895. Home: Chicago, Ill. Died 1904.

LOCKE, James William, judge; b. Wilmington, Vt., Oct. 30, 1837; s. Rev. William Sherburne and Caroline Dame (Tibbetts) L.; high sch. and acad. edn.; studied law in office of William Starke, Manchester, N.H., 1857-59; m. Alvina C. Neal, Oct. 5, 1866. Paym. clerk U.S.N., 1861-65, at Naval Sta., Key West, Fla., at close of Civil War; remained and entered practice of law, 1865-68; judge Monroe Co., Fla., 1868-70; mem. Fla. Senate, 1870-72; U.S. dist. judge, Southern Dist. of Fla., Feb. 1, 1872, resigned, July 4, 1912. Republican. Home: Jacksonville, Fla. Died Sept. 5, 1922.

LOCKE, John Staples, author, educator; b. Biddeford, Me., 1836; s. Simon and Mary (Haley) L.; m. Marcia Cleaves, Apr. 26, 1869. Supt. schs. State of Me.; dir. Nat. Edn. Assn.; pres. York Inst., Saco, Me., Me. Ped. Soc., Wardwell Home for Old Ladies, York Co. Hosp. Author: Shores of Saco Bay; The Art of Correspondence, A Brave Struggle (novel); Pleasing Rhymes for Happy Times; Bright Hours; Old Orchard Beach, Maine, 1900. Home: Saco, Me. Died 1906.

LOCKE M(ary) Katherine, publicist, lecturer, writer; b. Sewickley, Pa.; d. Rev. William Henry (D.D., LL.D.) and Margaret Ellen (Loore) L.; lit. edn. under father; M.A. in music, Muskingum Coll., New Concord, O.; studied piano with William Mason, pipe organ with David Wood. Creator "The Katherine Locke Topics," polit. and philos. interpretations of nat. and internat. current interests; founder The Katherine Locke World-Wide Travel Topics; gave first lecture recitals before Brooklyn Inst. Arts and Sciences; gives fortnightly courses in Cleveland, Phila., Pittsburgh, Detroit, Buffalo, New York City, Cincinnati, Chicago, Rochester, Dayton, etc. Methodist. Writer editorials and spl. articles for newspapers and mags. One of few Am. women to climb to the top of Mt. Hood, and one of the first Am. women to make a trip in an aeroplane. On exploration trip in Sahara Desert, 1927. Home: Youngstown, O. Died Nov. 7, 1936.

LOCKE, Robinson, newspaperman; b. Plymouth, O., Mar. 15, 1856; s. David Ross ("Petroleum V. Nasby") and Martha (Bodine) L.; acad. edn. at Zürich, Switzerland, and Paris, France; m. Kate King, July 15, 1886 (died 1894); m. 2d, Mabel Dunham, July 21, 1909. Engaged in newspaper work, 1873—, except 5 yrs. abroad; U.S. consul Newcastle-on-Tyne, Eng., 1883-85; pres. Toledo Blade Co., 1888—; dir. Northern Nat. Bank. Mason. Home: Toledo, O. Died Apr. 20, 1920.

LOCKEY, Mary Ishbel, educator; b. Helena, Mont.; d. Richard and Emily Ellen (Jeffrey) L.; ed. high sch. (Helena), Froebel-Pestalozzi Schule (Berlin), under Frau Schrade 1 yr., Normal Sch. (Helena); A.B., Stanford, 1902. Served as asst. teacher Froebel-Pestalozzi Schule and as substitute teacher, primary to 8th grade, pub. schs., Helena, and teacher of English, high sch., Palo Alto, Calif.; teacher Harker-Hughes Sch., Palo Alto, 2 yrs., Miss Harker's Sch. 1 yr.; founder and prin. Castilleja Sch. (for girls), 1907—. Del. to White House Conf. for Child Health and Protection, 1930. Republican. Baptist. Home: Palo Alto, Calif. Died Mar. 4, 1939.

LOCKHART, Arthur John ("Pastor Felix"), clergyman, author; b. Lockhartville, Kings Co., N.S., May 5, 1850; s. Nathan Albert and Elizabeth Ann (Benzanson) L.; ed. in dist. sch. and printing office; m. Adelaide Beckerton, of St. Andrews, N.B., May 12, 1873. Entered ministry, June 1872, in E. Me. Conf., M.E. Ch., in which has continued. Contbr., under pen-name of "Pastor Felix," of prose and verse to numerous periodicals in U.S. and Canada. Author: The Masque of Minstrels (poems, with brother, Rev. B. W. L.), 1887; Beside the Narraguagus, and Other Poems, 1895; The Papers of Pastor Felix, 1903; The Birds of the Cross, and Other Poems, 1909. Died July 29, 1926.

LOCKHART, James Henry, corp. official; vice-pres. Lockhart Iron & Steel Co.; dir. Mellon Nat. Bank (Pittsburgh), United Engineering & Foundry Co., Union Savings Bank, Union Trust Co., Pittsburgh Steel Foundry Co., and other corps. Died May 16, 1938.

LOCKHART, Malcolm Mabry; b. Augusta, Ga., Sept. 15, 1877; s. Fred Tutt and Elizabeth Milledge (Bothwell) L.; A.B., cum laude, Univ. of Ga., 1896; LL.D., Asbury College, Wilmore, Ky., 1932; m. Bessie Maie Wardlaw, June 12, 1901; children—Elizabeth Wardlaw (Mrs. V. Manget Davis), Helen Coachman (Mrs. Thos. H. Watkins), Malcolm Mabry, Edna Bothwell (Mrs. M. R. Astley), Joseph Wardlaw (dec.). President College Coöperative News Service and of Southern Press Clipping Bureau, both of Atlanta, Georgia. Served as Georgia state Y.M.C.A. war work secretary, 1917-18; financial director for Ga. of United War Work campaign ($1,700,000 subscribed), 1918; asst. nat. dir. Orgn. Near East Relief ($22,000,000), 1919; dir. Agnes Scott Coll. campaign ($825,000), 1920; asso. dir. Ga. Tech. campaign ($1,750,000), 1921; dir. Davidson Coll. campaign ($675,000), 1922-23; dir. Queen's Coll. campaign ($325,000), 1924; field sec. Exec. Com. of Christian Edn., Presbyn. Ch. of U.S., and dir. equipment fund, 1924; pres. William Jennings Bryan Univ., Dayton, Tenn. Died 1940.

LOCKHART, Walter Samuel, lawyer; b. Orange Co., N.C., Nov. 12, 1874; s. Levi Y. and Martha Jane (Breeze) L.; A.B., Trinity Coll., N.C., 1904, LL.B., 1913; student law dept. Harvard, 1911-12; m. Florence Green, Dec. 12, 1917; children—Florence Green, Walter Samuel. Prof. law, Trinity Coll. (now Duke U.), 1912-30; gen. practice at Durham, 1915—. Served at Plattsburg (N.Y.) Camp 1 mo. 1916; U.S. Govt. appeal agt. at Durham, under Selective Service Act. Chmn. Durham County (N.C.) Board of Elections. Democrat. Mem. M.E. Ch., S. Author: A Handbook of the Law of Evidence for North Carolina, 1915, 31. Home: Forest Hills, Durham, N.C. Deceased.

LOCKMAN, John Thomas, lawyer; b. New York, N.Y., Sept. 26, 1834; s. Isaac Paul and Mary (Kennedy) L.; ed. pub. and pvt. schs., New York; LL.B., Columbia, 1867; m. Harriet Hall, Oct. 14, 1862. Apptd. 1st lt. 83d N.Y. Inf., May 27, 1861; capt., Nov. 25, 1861; resigned, Sept. 22, 1862; appt. lt. col., 119th N.Y. Inf., Oct. 16, 1862; col., May 3, 1863; seriously wounded 1st day of Battle of Gettysburg; bvtd. brig. gen. vols., Mar. 13, 1865, "for meritorious conduct in campaign ending with occupation of Atlanta"; hon. mustered out, June 7, 1865. Admitted to bar, 1867, and entered practice at New York; now mem. DeWitt (George G.), Lockman & DeWitt. Officer or dir. in various corps. Home: New York, N.Y. Died Sept. 27, 1912.

LOCKWOOD, Albert, pianist; b. Troy, N.Y., Apr. 3, 1871; s. Charles N. and Albertine (Lewis) L.; musical edn. included 6 yrs. with Reinecke, 3 yrs. with Leschetizky and studies under Buonamici in Florence; grad. at Leipzig Conservatory, 1892. Played with success in London, Paris, Florence and other European cities before returning to U.S.; head of piano dept., Univ. Sch. of Music, Ann Arbor, Mich., 1900—. Home: Ann Arbor, Mich. Died Nov. 9, 1933.

LOCKWOOD, Belva Ann Bennett, lawyer; b. Royalton, N.Y., Oct. 24, 1830; d. Lewis Johnson and Hannah (Green) Bennett; grad. Genessee Coll., Lima, N.Y., 1857; (hon. A.M., Syracuse U., 1871, LL.D., 1908); m. Uriah H. McNall, 1848 (died 1853); m. 2d, Dr. Ezekiel Lockwood, 1868 (died 1877). Taught school, 1857-68. Worked for and secured passage by Congress of bill giving women employes of the govt. equal pay for equal work; B.L., Nat. U., 1873; admitted to D.C. bar; secured passage of a bill admitting women to Supreme Ct. of U.S., 1879; was admitted under it, Feb. 1879; also to U.S. Ct. of Claims; has been engaged in many important law cases, several before Supreme Ct. of U.S.; one of attys. who secured a judgment of $5,000,000 vs. the U.S. for Eastern Cherokees in Ct. of Claims and Supreme Ct., 1906. Prominent in temperance, peace and woman suffrage movements; nominated, 1884 and 1888, by Equal Rights Party for President of U.S.; commd. by State Dept. to represent U.S. at Congress of Charities and Corrections, Geneva, Switzerland, 1896; one of com. apptd. by Fedn. of Women's Clubs which secured law giving equal property rights for women and equal guardianship of their children in D.C. Elected Jan. 18, 1901, pres. Woman's Nat. Press Assn.; pres. D.C. Woman Suffrage Assn.; sec. Am. branch Internat. Peace Bureau. Prepared amendment to statehood bill before Congress, granting suffrage to women in Okla., Ariz. and N.M. Is one of nominating com. for Nobel Peace Prize. Del. Internat. Peace Congress, Milan, Italy, 1906, London, 1908, Rome, 1911; elected atty. gen. Woman's Republic, St. Louis, 1912; presented with oil portrait of herself by women of D.C., Feb. 1913 (portrait now in Art Gallery of Nat. Mus.); dean of 20 ambassadors to Women's Conv., Budapest, Hungary, 1913; elected mem. soc. established in Rome for "creation of a world conscience," 1913; hon. mem. assn. created for heads of internat. socs., Brussels, 1913; elected mem. commn. Internat. Peace Bur., Berne; etc. Died May 19, 1917.

LOCKWOOD, Benjamin Curtis, brig. gen.; b. in Ky., Feb. 28, 1844. Enlisted as pvt. Co. F, 6th Ky. Inf., Oct. 2, 1861; discharged, Apr. 7, 1863; commd. 2d lt. 54th Ky. Inf., Sept. 30, 1864; hon. mustered out, Sept. 1, 1865; 2d lt. 31st U.S. Inf., Mar. 7, 1867; promoted through grades to brig. gen. U.S.A., 1908; retired by operation of law, Feb. 28, 1908. Bvtd. capt., Feb. 27, 1890, "for gallant services in action against Indians at Spring Creek, Mont., Oct. 15 and 16, 1876." Died Jan. 22, 1926.

LOCKWOOD, Charles Daniel, surgeon; b. Effingham, Ill., Jan. 22, 1868; s. John H. and Ruth (Locke) L.; Kan. Wesleyan U.; A.B., Northwestern U., 1893, M.D., 1896; post-grad. work, U. of Vienna, 1906, 11; m. Clara M. Sanford, Sept. 5, 1898. Interne, Chicago Lying-in and Cook Co. hosps., 1896-97; asst. in surgery, Northwestern U. Med. Sch., 1897-99; alternate mem. Calif. State Bd. Med. Examiners, 1901-02; prof. surgery, Coll. of Dentistry U. of Southern Calif., 1902—; sr. surgeon Pasadena Hosp.; attdg. chest surgeon Olive View Sanitarium. Organized Red Cross Ambulance Co. 1, 1916-17; commd. maj. M.C.U.S.A.; in France, Dec. 1917-Jan. 1919, 5 months at the Western front; now lt. col. Med. Reserve, U.S. Army. Mem. Union Liberal Ch. Fellow Am. Coll. Surgeons. Mason. Home: Pasadena, Calif. Died June 11, 1932.

LOCKWOOD, Daniel Newton, lawyer, congressman; b. Hamburg, N.Y., June 1, 1844; s. Harrison and Martha (Phillips) L.; grad. Union Coll., 1865, A.M., 1868. Admitted to Supreme Court bar, N.Y., May 1866; practiced at Buffalo; dist. atty. for Erie Co., N.Y., 1874-77; mem. Congress, 1877-79, 1891-95; U.S. atty. northern dist. N.Y., 1886-89. Democrat. Apptd. pres. bd. gen. mgrs. Pan-Am. Expn., 1901. Senior of Lockwood, Hoyt & Greene. N.Y. State commr. in lunacy, 1902—. Home: Buffalo, N.Y. Died 1906.

LOCKWOOD, George Browning, editor; b. Forest, Ill., Nov. 7, 1872; s. W. W. and Mary (Waite) L.; Ph.B., DePauw U., 1894; m. Anne Lloyd Carlisle, 1897; children—Mary Georgiana, Gordon Browning, John Durbin. Founder, 1894, and first editor, 1894-96, Terre Haute Evening Tribune; pvt. sec. to Col. George W. Steele (M.C., and sec. Nat. Soldiers' Home Bd.), and Washington corr. Am. Press Assn., 1896-1902; supt. press bur. Rep. State Com. of Ind., 1902-08; pvt. sec. Governor Durbin of Ind., 1903-05; col. on staffs of Governors Durbin and Hanly, of Ind.; asst. gen. mgr. Winona Assembly and Schs., 1905-06. Editor and pub. The Shield (official jour. Phi Kappa Psi), 1898-1907, Marion (Ind.) Evening Chronicle, 1906-12, now pub. and editor of Muncie (Ind.) Evening Press. Founder, and editor of The National Republic, Washington, D.C., 1914-28. Secretary to Vice-President C. W. Fairbanks, 1907-09; sec. spl. U.S. commn. to Quebec Tercentenary, 1908; chmn. exec. com. Ind. Rep. State Com., 1912. Sec. Rep. Nat. Com., 1922-24; dir. Washington hdqrs. Hoover-for-President pre-convention campaign, 1928. Trustee Central Ind. Hosp. for the Insane, 1904-07. Hon. life mem. Nat. Shorthand Reporters' Assn.; sec. Ind. State Forestry Assn., 1914-19; pres. Ind. Rep. State Editorial Assn., 1913. Author: The New Harmony Communities, 1902; The New Harmony Movement, 1905; Americanism, 1921. Died Feb. 12, 1932.

LOCKWOOD, George Rae, M.D., educator; b. N.Y. City, Mar. 7, 1861; s. George Rae and Mary Elizabeth (Bigelow) L.; A.B., Coll. City of New York, 1881; M.D., Coll. Phys. and Surg. (Columbia), 1884; m. Louise A. Doble, of Montreal, Can., June 5, 1913. Practiced in N.Y. City, 1884-1922 (retired); prof. clin. medicine, Coll. Phys. and Surg. many yrs.; visiting phys. Bellevue Hosp., 1906-13. Republican. Presbyn. Author: Practice of Medicine, 1896; Diseases of the Stomach, 1913. Home: Washington, D.C. Died Mar. 6, 1931.

LOCKWOOD, Henry, clergyman; b. Albany, N.Y., Jan. 4, 1869; s. Henry and Margaret A. (Kelly) L.; A.B., Rutgers Coll., 1891, A.M., 1894; grad. Reformed Ch. Theol. Sem., New Brunswick, N.J., 1894; D.D., Hope Coll., Mich., 1916; m. Bertha A. Booraem, June 20, 1894 (died 1924); children—Helen Booraem (Mrs. Frank Wilbur Remsen, Jr.), James Kelly. Ordained Reformed Ch. ministry, 1895; pastor Knox and 2d Berne chs., Albany Co., N.Y., 1894-1901, East Millstone, N.J., 1901-25, Hudson Av. Community Ref. Ch., Englewood, N.J., 1925—. Permanent clk. Gen. Synod Reformed Ch., 1907-15, stated clk. same, June 4, 1914—; editor Minutes of Gen. Synod, 1914-31; editor in chief Somerset Church News, 1907-17. Mem. Bd. of Domestic Missions of Ref. Ch., and exec. com. of same. Home: Englewood, N.J. Died June 10, 1932.

LOCKWOOD, Henry Hayes, prof. U.S.N.; retired Aug. 1876; b. Kent Co., Del., Aug. 17, 1814; grad. U.S. Mil. Acad., West Point, 1836; assigned to artillery; m. Annie, oldest dau. Chief Justice Booth of Delaware, Oct. 1845. Served against Florida Indians, 1837; resigned and farmed in Del. until 1841. Apptd., 1841, prof. mathematics U.S. Navy; served at sea with Pacific squadron; took part in capture of Monterey, Calif., Oct. 1842; served at Naval Asylum, Phila., until founding, 1845, of U.S. Naval Acad.; prof. natural philosophy there, 1845; prof. field arty. and inf. tactics, 1845-61; also astronomy and gunnery, 1851-61. In Civil war as col. 1st Del. regt. and, after Aug. 8, 1861, as brig. gen. vols.; commanded at Point Lookout and defenses of lower Potomac; commanded brigade of 12th corps at Gettysburg; later commanded middle dept., with headquarters at Baltimore; mustered out at close of war. Prof. natural philosophy U.S. Naval Acad.,

1865-71; served at Nat. Observatory, 1871-76. Died 1899.

LOCKWOOD, Henry Roswell, P.E. clergyman; b. Honeoye Falls, N.Y., April 8, 1843; s. Henry and Cathalina L. L.; grad. Hobart Coll.; spl. studies in divinity (M.A., S.T.D., Hobart); m. Ellen M. Rich, Nov. 7, 1872. Tutor mathematics, Hobart Coll., 1864-67; ordained to ministry, 1867; missionary Christ Ch., Clayton, N.Y., 1867-73; rector St. Paul's Ch., Syracuse, N.Y., 1873—. Deputy to Gen. Conv. P.E. Ch., Boston, 1877, New York, 1880; trustee Hobart Coll., 1876—. Home: Syracuse, N.Y. Died 1905.

LOCKWOOD, Homer Nichols; b. Victory, N.Y., June 23, 1833; s. Homer and Sally (Benedict) L.; reared on farm; ed. at local acads.; taught sch.; m. Elizabeth Genter, Feb. 13, 1866 (died 1888). Becoming interested in topography, spent many yrs. in Southern States, Cuba and Puerto Rico; published topog. maps in Cuba and Puerto Rico; returned from West Indies, 1865. Mem. N.Y. Legislature, 1866; reëlected, 1867; helped organize and build the Southern Central R.R., now part of Lehigh Valley system. was dir., sec. and auditor until entire road was completed. Retired. Fellow Nat. Geog. Society. Home: Washington, D.C. Died June 23, 1913.

LOCKWOOD, John Alexander, army officer; b. of Am. parents, Dresden, Germany, Oct. 30, 1856; s. John Alexander (surgeon U.S.N.) and Julia (McLane) L.; grad. U.S. Coast Guard Acad., 1879, Inf. and Cav. Sch., U.S.A., 1883; M.S., Mich. State Coll., 1887; unmarried. Commd. 2d lt. inf., U.S.A., 1880; advanced through grades to col. on retired list, 1918. Served in campaign against Sioux Indians, 1890-91, campaign in Philippine Islands, comdg. Troop M, 4th U.S. Cavalry, 1899-1900; retired from active service on account of physical disability incurred in line of duty, 1900; detailed on active duty as prof. military science and tactics, La. State U., 1900-03, Fordham U., 1903-06, also lecturer, N.Y. State Bd. of Edn., 1904-06. Served as adj., Fort Leavenworth, Kan., later asst. to comdg. officer, Plattsburg, N.Y., and comdg. officer S.A.T.C., Hahnemann Med. Coll., Phila., World War. Author: Cadet's Handbook, 1902. Deceased.

LOCKWOOD, Wilton, portrait painter; b. Wilton, Conn., Sept. 12, 1861; s. John L. and Emily (Middlebrook) L.; pupil of John La Farge; also studied 10 yrs. in Paris; m. Ethel Whiton, 1892. Represented in the Carnegie Inst., Pittsburgh, Corcoran Gallery, Washington, Mus. Fine Arts, Boston, Mus. Fine Arts, Worcester, Mass. Hon mention Carnegie Inst., 1897; Temple Fund gold medal, Pa. Acad. Fine Arts, 1898; silver medal, Paris Expn., 1900, Buffalo Expn., 1901, St. Louis Expn., 1904. N.A., 1912. Home: Orleans, Mass. Died Mar. 21, 1914.

LOCY, William Albert zoölogist; b. Troy, Mich., Sept. 14, 1857; s. Lorenzo D. and Sarah (Kingsbury) L.; B.Sc., U. of Mich., 1881, M.Sc., 1884; grad. student in biology, same, 1881-82; fellow in biology, Harvard, 1884-85, U. of Berlin, 1891; hon. fellow U. of Chicago, 1894-95, Ph.D., 1895; (Sc.D., U. of Mich., 1906); m. Ellen Eastman, June 26, 1883. Prof. biology, 1887-89, animal morphology, 1889-96, Lake Forest (Ill.) U.; prof. physiology, Rush Med. Coll., Chicago, 1891; prof. zoölogy, Northwestern U., 1896—. Trustee Marine Biol. Station; investigator, Zoöl. Station, Naples, Oct. 1902-Feb. 1903. Editor in charge of zoöl, articles, and author of several, in new Am. supplement to Ency. Britannica. Author: Biology and Its Makers, 1908; The Main Currents of Zoölogy, 1918. Home: Evanston, Ill. Died Oct. 9, 1924.

LODGE, Henry Cabot, senator; b. Boston May 12, 1850; s. John Ellerton and Anna (Cabot) L.; A.B., Harvard, 1871, LL.B., 1875, Ph.D., (history), 1876; (LL.D., Williams, 1893, Yale, 1902, Clark U., 1902, Harvard, 1904, Amherst, 1912, also Union Coll., Princeton U., and Dartmouth Coll., and Brown, 1918); m. Anna Cabot Mills, d. Rear Adm. Charles H. Davis, U.S.N., June 29, 1871. Admitted to bar, 1876; editor North American Review, 1873-76, International Review, 1879-81; mem. Mass. Ho. of Rep., 1880, 81; mem. 50th to 53d Congresses (1887-93), 6th Mass. Dist.; U.S. senator, 1893—, present term expires, 1929; elected Rep. floor leader of Senate, Aug. 1918. Mem. Alaskan Boundary Tribunal, 1903; mem. U.S. Immigration Commn., 1907; commissioner plenipotentiary for U.S. Internat. Conf. on the Limitation of Armament, which met at Washington, Nov. 12, 1921. Lecturer on American history, Harvard, 1876-79; lecturer Lowell Inst., Boston, 1880. Regent Smithsonian Instn., Washington; trustee Boston Athenæum. Fellow American Academy of Arts and Sciences. Overseer Harvard University, 1911—. Editor: Ballads and Lyrics, 1881; Complete Works of Alexander Hamilton (9 vols.), 1885. Author: Life and Letters of George Cabot, 1877; Short History of the English Colonies in America, 1881; Life of Alexander Hamilton, 1882; Life of Daniel Webster, 1883; Studies in History, 1886; Life of Washington (2 vols.), 1889; History of Boston (in Historic Town Series), 1891; Historical and Political Essays, 1892; Speeches, 1895; Hero Tales from American History (with Theodore Roosevelt), 1895; Certain Accepted Heroes and Other Essays in Literature and Politics, 1897; Story of the Revolution (2 vols.), 1898; Story of the Spanish War, 1899; A Fighting Frigate and Other Essays; A Frontier Town and Other Essays, 1906; Speeches and Addresses, 1910; One Hundred Years of Peace, 1913; Early Memories, 1913; Democracy of the Constitution and Other Essays, 1915; War Addresses, 1917; Senate of the United States, 1921. Home: Nahant, Mass. Died Nov. 9, 1924.

LODGE, Lee Davis, college pres.; b. Montgomery Co., Md., Nov. 24, 1865; s. Rev. James L. and Alice Virginia (Warfield) L.; A.B., Columbian (now George Washington) U., 1885, A.M., Ph.D., 1892; m. Lelia Ella White, Sept. 1, 1887 (died 1895); m. 2d, Mary Louise McClammy, 1897. Tutor Greek, 1884-85, adj. prof. Latin, 1885-87, prof. French, 1887-96, philosophy, 1890-97, polit. science, 1894-99, Columbian U.; pres. Limestone Coll., S.C., 1899—. Established the Winnie Davis School of History as a dept. of Limestone Coll., 1900. Home: Gaffney, S.C. Died Jan. 1, 1923.

LODOR, Richard, brig. gen. U.S.A.; b. New York, Oct. 29, 1832; s. Daniel and Mary Ann (Seyfert) L.; grad. U.S. Mil. Acad., 1856; m. Margaret M. Quintin, Nov. 27, 1856. Bvtd. 2d lt. 4th Arty., July 1, 1856; commd. 2d lt., Oct. 31, 1856; promoted through grades to col. 2d Arty., July 1, 1892; retired by operation of law, Oct. 29, 1896; advanced to rank of brig. gen. retired, by act of Apr. 23, 1904. Bvtd. maj., Dec. 31, 1862, for battle of Stone River, Tenn.; lt. col. and col., Mar. 13, 1865, for services during the war. Instr. in ordnance, gunnery, engring. and law, Arty. Sch., Ft. Monroe, Va. Home: New York, N.Y. Died May 9, 1917.

LOEB, Hanau Wolf, laryngologist, otologist; b. Phila., Aug. 25, 1865; s. Bernhard and Bertha (Myer) L.; A.B., U. of Mo., 1883, A.M., 1886; M.D., Coll. Phys. and Surg. (Columbia), New York, 1888; LL.D., St. Louis U., 1922; m. Grace Sadler, Apr. 12, 1893; 1 dau., Irene (Mrs. Julian B. Cohn). Began practice, St. Joseph, Mo., 1888; moved to St. Louis, 1890; dean St. Louis U. Sch. of Medicine, and prof. ear, nose and throat diseases. Sec. Am. Bd. of Otolaryngology; editor Annals of Otology, Rhinology and Laryngology. Commd. maj. Med. O.R.C., 1917; col., 1919. Author: Operative Surgery of the Ear, Nose and Throat; Military Surgery of the Ear, Nose and Throat. Home: St. Louis, Mo. Died July 6, 1927.

LOEB, Jacques, univ. prof.; b. in Germany, Apr. 7, 1859; grad. Ascanisches Gymnasium, Berlin; studied medicine at Berlin, Munich, Strassburg; M.D., Strassburg, 1884; state exam., Strassburg, 1885; asst. in physiology, U. of Würzburg, 1886-88, U. of Strassburg, 1888-90; biol. sta., Naples, 1889-91; (hon. D.Sc., Cambridge, Eng., 1909; M.D., Geneva, 1909; Ph.D., Leipzig, 1909); m. Anne L. Leonard, 1891. Asso. in biology, Bryn Mawr, 1891-92; asst. prof. physiology and exptl. biology, 1892-95, asso. prof., 1895-1900, prof., 1900-02, U. of Chicago; prof. physiology, U. of Calif.,1902-10; head div. gen. physiology, Rockefeller Inst. for Med. Research, 1910—. Author: The Heliotropism of Animals and Its Identity with the Heliotropism of Plants, Würzburg, 1890; Physiological Morphology, I, 1891, II, 1892; Comparative Physiology of the Brain and Comparative Psychology, 1900; Studies in General Physiology, 1905; Dynamics of Living Matter, 1906; The Mechanistic Conception of Life, 1912; Artificial Parthenogenesis and Fertilization, 1913; The Organism as a Whole, 1916; Forced Movements, Tropisms and Animal Conduct, 1918. Fellow Am. Acad. Arts and Sciences; etc. Home: New York, N.Y. Died Feb. 11, 1924.

LOEB, James, banker; b. New York, Aug. 6, 1867; s. Solomon and Betty (Gallenberg) L.; brother of Morris L.; A.B., Harvard, 1888; unmarried. Mem. Kuhn, Loeb & Co., bankers, New York, 1888-1901; retired. Founder of Loeb Classical Library; published English transl. of Paul Delcharme's Euripides and the Spirit of His Dreams; Maurice Croiset's Aristophanes and the Political Parties at Athens. Mem. English Soc. for Promotion of Hellenic studies. Home: Munich, Bavaria. Died May 28, 1933.

LOEB, Louis, artist, illustrator; b. Cleveland, O.; s. Alexander and Sarah Ehrman L.; studied under Gérôme in Paris; honorable mention Paris Salon, 1895; 3d medal, Paris Salon, 1897; 2 silver medals, Pan-Am. Expn., Buffalo, 1901; 2d Hallgarten prize, Nat. Acad. Design, 1902; Webb prize, Soc. Am. Artists, 1903; 2 silver medals, St. Louis Expn., 1904. A.N.A., 1901. Home: New York, N.Y. Died 1909.

LOEB, Morris, chemist; b. Cincinnati, O., May 23, 1863; s. Solomon and Betty (Gallenberg) L.; bro. of James L.; A.B., Harvard, 1883; Ph.D., U. of Berlin, 1887; student U. of Heidelberg, 1887-88, U. of Leipzig, Germany, 1888; (hon. Sc.D., Union University, 1911); m. Eda Kuhn, Apr. 3, 1895. Asst. to Prof. Wolcott Gibbs, Newport, R.I., 1888-89; docent Clark U., 1889-91; prof. chemistry, 1891—, dir. chem. lab., 1895-1906, New York U. Fellow N.Y. Acad. Sciences, A.A.A.S. Jewish religion. Home: New York, N.Y. Died Oct. 8, 1912.

LOEB, Sophie Irene, newspaper writer, sociologist; b. in Russia, July 4, 1876; d. Samuel and Mary (Carey) Simon; brought to U.S. at age of 6; grad. McKeesport (Pa.) High School; m. Anselm Loeb, Mar. 10, 1896 (divorced). Mem. staff New York Evening World, 1910—. As mem. N.Y. State Commn. for Widows' Pensions studied relation of child and the state in England, Scotland, France, Switzerland, Germany and Denmark; wrote report for N.Y. Legislature, 1914; led campaigns that resulted in N.Y. State Widows' Pension Law; 80-cent gas rate for Brooklyn; motion picture law of N.Y. (making buildings sanitary and fireproof); the guiding force behind investigation of N.Y. Pub. Service Commn., 1916, resulting in appmt. of a new commn.; first woman called as mediator to settle a New York strike, 1917, and settled strike in taxicab industry; secured passage by N.Y. Legislature of bill opening pub. schs. for community forums and civic centers. Pres. Child Welfare Bd. of N.Y. City; apptd. mem. N.Y. State Commn. to examine laws relating to child welfare and estab. first child welfare building in the world, 1921. Author: Epigrams of Eve, 1913; wrote Everyman's Child; Century Fables of Everyday Folks; Epigrams of What Eve Said. Home: New York, N.Y. Died Jan. 18, 1929.

LOEB, William, businessman; b. Albany, N.Y., Oct. 9, 1866; s. William and Louisa (Myer) L.; high sch. edn.; m. Katharine W. Dorr, 1902; 1 son, William. Stenographer, N.Y. Assembly, 1888; later pvt. sec. to various public officials of N.Y.; stenographer N.Y. State Constl. Conv., 1894; grand jury and dist. atty., 1895-98; stenographer and pvt. sec. to Gov. Roosevelt, 1899; sec. to vice-pres. of U.S. (Roosevelt), Mar. 4-Sept. 24, 1901; asst. sec. to the President (Roosevelt), 1901-03; sec. to the President (Roosevelt), 1903-09; collector of the Port of New York, Mar. 9, 1909-Mar. 4, 1913; v.p. Am. Smelting & Refining Co. until Jan. 1, 1934. Republican. Home: Oyster Bay, N.Y. Died Sept. 19, 1937.

LOEFFLER, Charles Martin Tornov, musician, composer; b. Muhlhausen, Alsace, Jan. 30, 1861; educated in Switzerland, Germany, France; Doctor of Music, Yale University, 1926; m. Elise Burnett Fay, Dec. 8, 1910. Came to America, 1881; violinist. Mem. Am. Acad. of Arts and Letters, Nat. Inst. Arts and Letters; Officier de l'Académie and Officier de l'Instruction Publique, and Legion of Honor, of France. Corr. mem. Académie des Beaux Arts. Composer: Les Veillés de l'Ukraine (for orchestra and violin), 1891; Fantastic Concerto (orchestra and violoncello), 1924; Divertimento in A minor (for violin and orchestra), 1895; Symphonic Poem, "The Death of Tintagiles" (for orchestra and viola d'amore), 1897; Divertissement Espagnol (for orchestra and saxophone), 1901; La bonne chanson (symphonic poem); La Villanelle du Diable (symphonic poem); Quartet in A minor (chamber music), 1889; Deux Rapsodies (for oboe, viola and piano), 1901; By the Waters of Babylon (Psalm 137, for female chorus), 1902; For One Who Fell in Battle (chorus for 8 parts), 1906; A Pagan Poem (symphonic poem for orchestra and piano); Hora Mystica (symphony, music for 4 strings; to memory of Victor Chapman); Three Movements; Memories of My Childhood in Russia (symphonic poem); The Canticle of the Sun (by St. Francis of Assisi), for voice and orchestra, 1925; Evocation, for women's voices and modern orchestra, 1930; five Irish fantasies for tenor and orchestra, 1933; etc. Home: Medfield, Mass. Died May 20, 1935.

LOEVENHART, Arthur Solomon, univ. prof.; b. Lexington, Ky., Dec. 29, 1878; s. Henry and Jenny Lind (Goldsmith) L.; B.S., Ky. State U., Lexington, 1898, M.S., 1899; M.D., Johns Hopkins, 1903; m. Minnie Rose Goldsmith, June 16, 1909; children—Elizabeth Jane (dec.), Dorothy Frances (dec.), Janet. Asst., asso. and asso. prof. pharmacology and physiol. chemistry, Johns Hopkins, 1903-08; prof. pharmacology and toxicology, U. of Wis., 1908—. Asso. editor Journal of Pharmacology and Exptl. Therapeutics. Chief pharmacol. sect. research div., Chemical Warfare Service, Am. U., 1918. Home: Madison, Wis. Died Apr. 20, 1929.

LOEW, Marcus, theatres; b. New York City; s. Herman L.; m. Carrie Rosenheim, Mar. 4, 1894. Owner vaudeville and motion picture theatres; now pres. of about 100 corps. Jewish religion. Home: New York, N.Y. Died Sept. 5, 1927.

LOEWE, Dietrich Eduard, mfr.; b. Germany, June 21, 1852; s. Adolph and Charlotte (Schalk) L.; ed. pub. and scientific schs.; came to U.S., 1870; m. Christina Heinzelman, June 21, 1877; children—Charlotte, Mathias C., Ernest E., D. Carl, Melaine C., A. Percival. Learned hatter's trade at Danbury, and became foreman in factory; established D. E. Loewe & Co., 1879. Ordered by hatters' union to unionize shop but refused, leading to one of hardest fought legal battles in history of federal courts, in resistance against boycott announced by United Hatters and A.F. of L.; won case, 1908, establishing principle of the open shop, and the illegality of the boycott. Retired. Republican. Lutheran. Home: Danbury, Conn. Died Sept. 12, 1935.

LOFTON, George Augustus, clergyman; b. Panola Co., Miss., Dec. 25, 1839; s. James Blocker and Olivia

Ann Warburton (Settle) L.; student, Mercer U., Ga., until 1861, A.M., 1871; (D.D., Baylor U., Tex., 1880; LL.D., U. of Nashville, 1900, Carson and Newman Coll., Tenn., 1900); m. Ella E. Martin, Mar. 31, 1864. Served in C.S.A., 1861-65; adj. 9th Ga. Battalion Arty., 1862-65. Prin. Wade Acad., Webster Co., Ga., 1865-67; admitted to bar, 1867, and practiced at Americus, Ga., 1867-68; ordained Bapt. ministry, 1868; pastor country chs., Ga., 1868-69, Dalton, Ga., 1870-72, 1st Ch., Memphis, 1872-77, 3d Ch., St. Louis, 1877-84, Talladega, Ala., 1885-87, Central Ch., Nashville, 1888—. Pres. Southern Bapt. Publn. Soc., Memphis, 1873-76; mem. pub. sch. bd., Nashville, 5 yrs.; pres. State Bd. Missions, 1889—; moderator Nashville Assn. Bapt. Chs.; mem. bd. mgrs. S.S. Bd. Southern Bapt. Conv. Mason. Author: Character Sketches, 1889; Harp of Life, 1897; Baptist Reformation, 1611-1641, A.D., 1899; The Master Wheel, 1902. Home: Nashville, Tenn. Died Dec. 11, 1914.

LOGAN, Albert J., mfr.; b. Pittsburgh, Pa., July 7, 1857; s. James and Lavira (Gill) L.; ed. Pa. Mil. Coll., 1874-76; m. Susan E. Murphy, Nov. 16, 1882. Established, 1882, firm of A. J. Logan & Co., mfrs. of mattresses and bedding, inc., 1908, as A. J. Logan Company, of which was president. Formerly chairman City Planning Commn.; dir. Chamber of Commerce of U.S.A., 1912-13; dir. Chamber of Commerce of Pittsburgh, Western Pa. Hosp. Enlisted in Co. F, 18th Inf. (Duquesne Greys) N.G. Pa., Mar. 1876; promoted through grades to col. 17th Regt., 1898; commissary gen. of Pa., 1902; col. 18th Inf., 1909; brig. gen., in comd. 2d Brig., 1912-17; Mexican border service, June 1916-Jan. 1917; brig. gen. N.A., 1917-18; comd. 56th Inf. Brig., World War, July 15, 1917-Jan. 29, 1918; hon. disch. because of physical disability, Jan. 29, 1918. Mem. Armory Bd. State of Pa.; comdr. Pittsburgh Chapter Mil. Order World War. Republican. Presbyn. Home: Pittsburgh, Pa. Died Dec. 27, 1934.

LOGAN, Frank G(ranger), capitalist, patron of arts; b. Cayuga Co., N.Y., Oct. 7, 1851; s. Simon Ford and Phoebe (Hazen) L.; ed. Ithaca (N.Y.) Acad.; LL.D., Beloit Coll., 1922; m. Josephine Hancock (poet and prose writer), June 15, 1882; children—Rhea (Mrs. Charles A. Monroe, now dec.), Stuart, Howard H. (dec.), Spencer H., Waldo H. Founder Logan & Bryan, grain, stocks and securities, Chicago, retiring 1901. Widely known as an art collector; trustee, benefactor and hon. pres. Art Inst. Chicago. A founder of Am. Coll. of Surgeons; of Research Fund in Pathology, Surgery and Experimental Medicine, U. of Chicago; of Mr. and Mrs. Frank G. Logan Art Inst. medal and prizes; of chair of anthropology and evolution at Beloit Coll., also trustee of Coll. and founder of its Logan Archæol. Mus., sending scientists to Africa, Europe and prehistoric Am. sites, seeking the "cradle of the human race." One of builders of Orchestra Hall, Chicago, and mem. Orchestral Assn.; chmn. of com. that aided in putting through Congress the Non-Partisan Tariff Bill, and the Smith-Lever Agri. Act; one of the 270 founders of Century of Progress Expn. (World's Fair), Chicago, 1933, 34. Mem. Municipal Art Collection Com., apptd. by mayor of Chicago; trustee Ferguson Monument Fund; dir. Am. Red Cross. Awarded decoration, The Palms, by French Acad., for scientific expdns. which he sent to France and into French Africa, and Cross of Legion of Honor, by French Govt., in appreciation of his art interest and influence. Home: Chicago, Ill. Died July 18, 1937.

LOGAN, James, mfr.; b. Glasgow, Scotland, May 6, 1852; s. David and Mary (Kennedy) L.; was brought to America in infancy; mainly self ed.; hon. M.A., Dartmouth, 1904; m. Annie Devereaux Johnson, Dec. 10, 1879. Worked in woolen mill from age of 10 to 16; clerk in dry goods store, 1869-71; bookkeeper in woolen mill, 1871-73, and in book store, 1873-78; salesman in an envelope factory, 1878-83; mem. Logan, Swift & Brigham Envelope Co., Worcester, 1883-98; pres. and gen. mgr. U.S. Envelope Co., Worcester, a consolidation of 10 leading factories, 1898—. Mem. Mass. militia, 6 yrs.; mayor of Worcester 4 terms, 1908-11, inclusive. Republican. Conglist. Trustee Worcester Poly. Institute. Lecturer at Dartmouth, Harvard, Wellesley and Worcester Poly. Institute. Home: Worcester, Mass. Died Nov. 30, 1929.

LOGAN, James Addison, Jr., banker; b. Phila., Pa., Nov. 11, 1879; s. Judge James A. and Elizabeth (Marchand) L.; student Haverford (Pa.) Coll. 1 yr.; grad. Army War Coll., 1912; LL.D., Haverford, 1925; m. Esther Tone Griswold, May 22, 1925. Pvt. Battery A, Pa. Vols., Spanish-Am. War, 1898; capt. vols. Philippine Insurrection, 1899-1900; entered U.S. Army as capt., 1901; chief Am. Mil. Mission with French Army, Sept. 1914-June 1917; col. Gen. Staff, asst. chief of staff G.H.Q., A.E.F. Principal asst. to Herbert Hoover in relief operations in Europe after Armistice; European rep. U.S. Grain Corp., also in charge coördinating operations of tech. advisers to various new states of Central and Eastern Europe; Am. rep. financial sect., Supreme Economic Council, also of communications sect. same; adviser to Am. Relief Administration in connection with Russian Relief, June 1921-June 1923; resigned from Army, July 15, 1922. Asst. Am. unofficial del. to Reparation Commn., Dec. 1919-July 1, 1923; Am. unofficial del. to same, Aug. 1, 1923-May 31, 1925; Am. unofficial rep., London Conf. of Prime Ministers, 1924, Finance Ministers' Conf., Paris, 1925. Associated with Dillon, Read & Co., bankers, June 1925—. Protestant. Home: Bala, Montgomery Co., Pa. Deceased.

LOGAN, James Elmore, M.D.; b. Nicholasville, Ky., Oct. 16, 1861; s. D. W. G. and Mildred T. L.; student U. of Ky., and U. of Mo.; M.D., Bellevue Hosp. Med. Coll. (New York U.), 1884; m. Helen Richards, Oct. 12, 1887. In practice of medicine at Kansas City, Mo., 1884—; pres. faculty and bd. trustees, and prof. diseases of the nose and throat and clin. otology, Univ. Med. Coll., Kansas City, 1885—. Pres. Am. Laryngol., Rhinol. and Otol. Soc., 1905-06, Am. Laryngol. Assn., 1910. Home: Kansas City, Mo. Deceased.

LOGAN, James Parmelee, newspaper editor; b. Springfield, N.J., May 23, 1857; s. James and Jerusha (Clevenger) L.; LL.B., U. of Mich., 1880; m. Emma Ottinger, 1883 (died 1903); children—Eleanor (Mrs. E. Graham Ward), Harold, Constance (Mrs. John F. Clunan), Elisabeth; m. 2d, Mary C. Foley, 1909. In practice law, 1880-83; in newspaper work, 1883—; mng. editor Newark (N.J.) Evening News, 1906-16; editor Newark Sunday Call, 1917-36, retired; dir. Newark Call Printing & Pub. Co.; trustee U.S. Savings Bank. Chief clk. N.J. Assembly, 1888-89; chmn. Passaic Valley Sewerage Commn., 1930—. Home: Montclair, N.J. Died Oct. 27, 1938.

LOGAN, Mrs. John A. (Mary Simmerson Cunningham); b. Petersburg, Boone Co., Mo., Aug. 15, 1838; d. Capt. John M. and Elizabeth H. Cunningham; ed. Convent of St. Vincent, Ky.; m. John A. Logan (afterward Gen. and U.S. senator), Nov. 27, 1855 (died 1886). Since her husband's death has edited The Home Magazine, and 30 yrs. in Washington; on syndicate staff of Hearst news service. Traveled extensively; devoted much time to the perpetuation of Gen. Logan's memory. Has given fine collection of memorials, trophies and souvenirs of her husband and only son, Maj. John A. Logan, Jr., who was killed in battle, Nov. 11, 1899, at San Jacinto, P.I., to the State of Ill. Author: The Part Taken by Women in American History, 1912; Recollections of a Soldier's Wife, 1914; Our National Government, 1919. Home: Washington, D.C. Died Feb. 22, 1923.

LOGAN, John Alexander, Jr., maj. U.S.A., adj. gen.'s dept.; b. in Ill., July 24, 1865 (only son of late Gen. John A. Logan); m. Edith Andrews, Mar. 22, 1887; served through campaign in Cuba on staff of Maj. Gen. J. C. Bates; recommended for promotion to rank of bvt. lt. col. and col. for gallantry in the field. Author: Joyful Russia. Home: Washington, D.C. Died 1899.

LOGAN, John Hubbard, supt. of schools; b. Pike Co., Ala., Dec. 16, 1876; s. Thomas Jefferson and Mathilda (Allen) L.; prep. edn., Mercer Prep. Sch., Macon, Ga.; A.B., Mercer U., 1900; grad. Union Theol. Sem., 1904; A.M., Columbia, 1904; studied univs. of Marburg and Berlin, 2 yrs. and in Italy 1 yr.; m. Alice Barbour, 1927. Teacher history and modern langs., Colgate, 1907-10; acting prof. history, Rutgers, 1910-13, prof., 1913-24, prof. history and polit. science, 1924-25; commr. of edn., N.J., 1925-27; supt. schs., Newark, N.J., 1927—. Mgr. civil relief work, Am. Red Cross, New Brunswick, at outbreak of World War, later asst. dir. Am. Red Cross, Camp Upton, and dir. civil relief, Camp Dix. Trustee Rutgers U. Democrat. Baptist. Home: Newark, N.J. Died Nov. 16, 1936.

LOGAN, Leavitt Curtis, rear adm. U.S.N.; b. Medina Co., O., Jan. 30, 1846; s. Samuel Sheldon and Hannah Hall (Curtis) L.; grad. U.S. Naval Acad., 1867; m. Elizabeth C. Porter, May 9, 1877. Promoted ensign, Dec. 18, 1868; master, Mar. 21, 1870; lt., June 12, 1871; lt. comdr., Dec. 16, 1891; comdr., May 1, 1898; capt., July 11, 1902; rear admiral, Jan. 28, 1908. Served Minnesota, spl. cruise, 1867-68; Pacific Fleet, 1868-70; spl. duty at Navy Dept., Jan.-Sept. 1871; Wabash, flag-ship European Sta., 1871-73; torpedo duty, 1874; Tennessee, Asiatic Squadron, 1875-77; Naval Acad., 1877-80; Powhatan, spl. service, 1880-81; training ships Portmouth, 1881-83, New Hampshire, 1883-84; Naval War Coll., 1884-87; Ossipee, N. Atlantic Sta., 1887-89; recorder Board Inspection, 1889-92; Phila., 1892-94; Training Sta., Newport, R.I., 1894-98; comd. Armeria during Spanish War, Machias, 1898-1900; on duty under Bureau of Equipment, 1900-04; comd. Ohio, 1904-06; comdt., Navy Yard, Pensacola, Fla., Feb. 15, 1907; retired by operation of law, Jan. 30, 1908. Died Nov. 23, 1921.

LOGAN, Marvel Mills, lawyer; b. Brownsville, Ky., Jan. 7, 1874; s. Gillis Franklin and Georgiana (Houchin) L.; ed. pub. and pvt. schs.; m. Della Haydon, Sept. 25, 1896; children—Victor Hubert, Agnes, Leland H., Ralph Hunter. Practiced at Brownsville, 1896-1912; county atty., 1902-03; 1st asst. atty. gen. of Ky., 1912-16; atty. gen. for term 1916-20; resigned June 1, 1917, and was apptd. chmn. Ky. State Tax Commn.; resigned, Dec. 1, 1918, and resumed practice at Louisville; Judge Ky. Court of Appeals, 1926-31, chief justice, 1930-31; U.S. senator from Ky., term 1931-37, re-elected for term 1937-43. Mem. bd. of regents Smithsonian Instn. Democrat. Baptist. Mason. Odd Fellow. Home: Bowling Green, Ky. Died Oct. 3, 1939.

LOGAN, Mercer Patton, clergyman; b. "Dungeness," Va., Oct. 16, 1856; s. James W. and Sarah A. (Strother) L.; Roanoke Coll. Va.; grad. Va. Theol. Sem., 1880; D.D., Washington and Lee U., 1893; m. Elizabeth Kent Caldwell, Oct. 10, 1883; m. 2d, Eliza Huger Dunkin, Sept. 14, 1921. Deacon, 1880, priest, 1881, P.E. Ch.; asst., St. Paul's Ch., Petersburg, Va., 1880-82; rector, Wytheville, Va., 1882-1904, St. Ann's, Nashville, Tenn., 1904-15, St. Paul's Charleston, S.C., 1915-21; dean Du Bose Memorial Church Training Sch., Monteagle, Tenn., 1921—. Dean of Convocation, Southwest Virginia, Diocese of Southern Virginia, 1902-04, of Nashville, Diocese of Tennessee, 1909-11; examining chaplain Diocese of Tenn., 1908-15; mem. Humane Commission, Nashville, 1908-15; mem. Gen. Bd. Religious Edn. P.E. Ch.; mem. com., apptd. by gov. Tenn., to organize Southern Sociol. Congress; v.p. Tenn. Children's Home Soc., 1909-15. Organizer, and pres. Summer Training School for Workers, Sewanee, Tenn., 1910—. Mason. K.P. Home: Monteagle, Tenn. Died Dec. 1, 1928.

LOGAN, Olive, author, actress, lecturer, journalist; b. Elmira, N.Y., Apr. 22, 1839; d. Cornelius Ambrosius and Eliza L.; ed. Methodist Female Sem. and Acad. of Sacred Heart, Cincinnati; became a successful lecturer; m. William Wirt Sikes, 1872 (died 1883), who was apptd. U.S. consul to Cardiff, Wales, by President Grant; had a successful stage career; has written much for leading Am. and foreign journals; m. 2, James O'Neill Logan, 1892. Author: Photographs of Paris Life, 1861; Chateau Frissac, 1865; Women and Theatres, 1869; The Mimic World, 1871; Get Thee Behind Me, Satan, 1872; They Met by Chance; etc.; also the comedy, Surf, or Life at Long Branch, produced by Daly. Died 1909.

LOGAN, Thomas Francis, writer; b. Phila., Pa., Jan. 14, 1881; s. Thomas Francis and Katherine Elizabeth (Murray) L.; student St. Joseph's Jesuit Coll., Phila., 1895-98; m. Mildred Loring, Dec. 23, 1916. Editorial staff Phila. Inquirer, 1898-1908; Washington corr. same, 1908-19, also corr. Am. Economist, Leslie's Weekly and Manufacturers' Record, 1917-19. Vice-chmn. welfare com. of Council Nat. Defense, 1917; spl. shipping commr. of U.S., at Paris, 1918-19; pres. Thomas F. Logan, Inc., advertising, New York, 1919-26; pres. Lord & Thomas and Logan, 1926—. Republican. Home: New York, N.Y. Died Aug. 9, 1928.

LOGAN, Thomas Muldrup, financier; b. Charleston, S.C., Nov. 3, 1840; s. Judge George William L.; grad. S.C. Coll., 1860; joined Washington Light Inf. of Charleston; served with it as pvt. during siege of Fort Sumter, 1861; after fall of Sumter became 2d lt., Co. A, Hampton's Legion; promoted through regular grades until he was commd. brig. gen. C.S.A., Dec. 1864, the youngest of that rank in the C.S. service; was at 1st battle of Manassas; wounded at Gaines' Mill, nr. Richmond, 1862; comd. his co. at 2d Manassas; frequently served on reconnoissance duty to ascertain the enemy's strength; shot from his horse and seriously wounded while endeavoring to delay the Federal advance on the morning that Gen. Grant crossed the Chickahominy; comd. Butler's brigade in Johnston's army until the surrender at Greensboro; m. Kate V. Cox, May 25, 1865. After war studied law; practiced at Richmond, Va., about 12 yrs.; became interested in railroads; organized, 1878, a syndicate of Richmond and New York capitalists which consolidated various Southern railroads into the Richmond & Danville system, now the Southern Ry.; pres. Gray Nat. Telautograph Co.; chmn. Dem. exec. com. of Va., 1879, and of the Gold Dem. party of Va., 1896. Home: Howardsville, Va. Died Aug. 11, 1914.

LOGAN, Walter Seth, lawyer; b. Washington, Conn., Apr. 15, 1847; s. Seth Savage and Serene (Hollister) L.; grad. Yale, 1870; Harvard Law School, 1871; Columbia Law School, 1872; m. Eliza Preston Kenyon, Apr. 13, 1875. Practices in New York; mem., writer and speaker in patriotic, scientific and historical socs. Wrote: Cuautla—The Bunker Hill of Mexico; A Mexican Law Suit. Home: New York, N.Y. Died 1906.

LOGUE, J. Washington, congressman; b. Phila., Pa., Feb. 22, 1863; ed. La Salle Coll., Phila.; married. Admitted to Pa. bar, 1888; practiced, Phila.; mem. 63d Congress (1913-15), 6th Dist., Pa. Democrat. Home: Philadelphia, Pa. Died Aug. 26, 1925.

LOHRE, Nels J., sec. Norwegian Luth. Ch. of America; b. Vermilion, S.D., May 25, 1873; s. John and Gunhild (Tranmel) L.; student U. of Minn.; B.L., Univ. of South Dakota, 1900, M.A., 1912; D.D., Carthage (Ill.) Coll., 1931; m. Carrie A. Eek, 1905; children—Gladys Cordelia, Eleanore Jeanette, Eugene Nels, Carolyn Ruth (dec.). Ordained Luth. ministry, 1897; pastor St. Paul's Ch., Minneapolis, Minn., 1897-1903; part time as student pastor in Univ. of Minn.; sec. and treas. Northern Irrigation Co., 1903-04; pres. Jewell (Ia.) Luth. Coll., 1904-11; pastor Grand Forks, N.D., 1912-18, Mayville, 1917-25. Elected nat. sec. Hauge Norwegian Luth. Synod, 1898, and nat. sec. and statistician of the three Norwegian synods when their union was effected, 1917; elected pres. Inter-Synodical Evang. Luth. Orient-Mission Soc., 1912 (doing pioneer work among the Kurds); exec. sec.-treas. same, 1924-27. Mem. Nat. Jubilee Fund Com. for celebration of Norway's independence, 1914. Author: Handbook for the Norwegian Luth. Ch., 1930. Edited Lents Parish and Synodical Records for Lutheran Ch., 1929. Home: Minneapolis, Minn. Died Dec. 9, 1933.

LOKRANTZ, Sven, M.D., public health adminstr.; b. Stockholm, Sweden, Sept. 22, 1892; s. Axel Wilhelm and Elizabeth (Baroness Von Duben) L.; grad. Unman's School of Swedish Gymnastics, and School of Commerce, Stockholm, Sweden; grad. Coll. Preceptors, 1912, M.D., Tufts Coll., 1918; grad. study Boston Dispensary and U. of Calif.; m. Carolina Anthony Winston, 1923; 1 son, Sven Winston. Came to U.S., 1914, naturalized citizen, 1920. Began practice at Boston, 1918; served as orthopedic surgeon, Boston Dispensary, also as director corrective physical education depts. of same, and at Cambridge Hosp.; lecturer Tufts Coll., 1918; moved to Los Angeles, Calif., 1918; supervisor of the department corrective physical education, city schools, Los Angeles, 1918-24, med. dir. city schs., 1924—; former lecturer U. of Calif.; mem. staff California Hosp., Anita Baldwin Hosp. for Babies, Children's Hosp.; consultant Orthopedic Hosp. Sch.; dir. Lokrantz School of Swedish Gymnastics, Boston, Mass. Lt. comdr. U.S.N. Res. Medical Corps; retired. Founder and chmn. bd. govs. Ling Foundation; med. dir. Tenth Olympic Games; mem. bd. dirs. Am. Red Cross. Knight Order of Vasa, 1st class (Sweden), 1930; Knight Order of the North Star Sweden, 1933; officer Order of Orange Nassau (Holland), 1933. Author: Notes in Corrective Physical Education, 1928; Health Supervision of Kindergarten Children. Died Mar. 11, 1940.

LOMAX, Edward Lloyd, ry. official; b. Fredericksburg, Va., Feb. 25, 1852; s. Presly Thornton and Mildred Henderson (Wellford) L.; ed. Coleman Inst.; m. Georgiana Blackwell, June 11, 1879. Local ticket clerk, Burlington & Mo. R. R.R., 1869-72; chief clerk pass. dept., Central R.R. of Ia., 1872-74; asst.gen. pass. agt. St. Louis & Southeastern Ry., 1874-79; asst. gen. pass. agt., also city pass. and ticket agt., St. Louis, Iron Mountain & Southern Ry., 1879-81; gen. pass. and ticket agt., Toledo, Cincinnati & St. Louis Ry., Mar.-Aug., 1881; chief clerk pass. dept., 1881-85, asst. gen. pass. agt., 1885-87, C.,B.&Q. R.R.; asst. gen. pass. agt., 1887-89, gen. pass. agt., 1889-1910, U.P. R.R.; pass. traffic mgr., Western Pacific Ry., 1910—. Home: San Francisco, Calif. Died Jan. 22, 1916.

LOMAX, Lunsford Lindsay, soldier; b. Newport, R.I., Nov. 4, 1835; s. Maj. Mann Page and Elizabeth (Lindsay) L.; prep. edn. Norfolk, Va.; grad. U.S. Mil. Acad., 1856; m. Elisabeth Winter Payne, Feb. 20, 1873. Served in U.S.A. as 1st lt. U.S. cav., 1856-61; resigned Apr. 22, 1861; entered Confederate service and attained the rank of maj. gen., comdg. div. of cav. Army of Northern Va., until 1865. Home: Warrenton, Va. Died May 28, 1913.

LOMAX, Tennent, lawyer; b. Montgomery, Ala., April 29, 1858; s. Tennent and Carrie (Billingslea-Shorter) L.; grad. Univ. of Ala., A.M., 1878, law dept., 1879; admitted to bar, 1879; began practice in native co., asst. solicitor of jud. circuit, 1880-86; elected solicitor upon erection of Montgomery co. into separate dist., 1886; reëlected, 1892, and 1898. Sec. State Exec. Dem. Com., 1878-88; presided over various convs.; chmn. city com., 1890-96. For 5 yrs. lt. True Blues of Montgomery; hon. mem. of that co. and of Montgomery Greys, also of Lomax Fire Co.; founder and comdr. Holtzclaw camp, Sons of Confederate Veterans; mem. Constl. Conv., Ala., 1901. K.P. Compiler: Lomax's Criminal Digest of Alabama Reports. Home: Montgomery, Ala. Deceased.

LOMBARD, Carole, actress; b. Fort Wayne, Ind., Oct. 6, 1908; d. Frederic and Elizabeth (Knight) Peters; ed. Los Angeles schs.; m. William Powell, June 26, 1931 (divorced 1933); m. 2d, Clark Gable, Mar. 29, 1939. Began in motion pictures with Fox Studios, Hollywood, 1926; later with Max Sennett, Paramount, and other producers; appeared in "Me, Gangster," "Power," "Show Folks," "Big News," "Fast and Loose," "It Pays to Advertise," "Sinners in the Sun," "True Confession," "Nothing Sacred," "Fools for Scandal," "Made For Each Other," etc. Died Jan. 16, 1942.

LOMBARD, Warren Plimpton, coll. prof.; b. Newton, Mass., May 29, 1855; s. Israel and Mary Ann (Plimpton) L.; A.B., Harvard, 1878, M.D., 1881; in Europe, 1882-85, with 2 yrs. research work in Leipzig, under Ludwig; Sc.D., Hobart Coll., N.Y., 1909, Univ. of Mich., 1932; m. Caroline Cook, June 21, 1883 (died 1923). Asst. in physiology, Coll. Phys. and Surg. (Columbia), 1886-89; traveled in Europe, and research work at Turin, Italy, 1889; asst. prof. physiology, Clark U., 1889-92; prof. physiology, U. of Mich., 1892-1923; emeritus prof., 1923. Author: Directions for Laboratory Work in Physiology, 1906. Home: Ann Arbor, Mich. Died July 13, 1939.

LOMBARDI, C(esar) (Maurice), publisher; b. Airolo, Canton Tessin, Switzerland, Aug. 6, 1845; s. Joseph and Clemantina (Lombardi) L.; came to America, 1860; ed. high sch. in Switzerland, and Jesuit Coll., New Orleans; m. Caroline Gaston Ennis, Jan. 16, 1877. Removed to Houston, Tex., 1871; accountant and mgr., 1871-86, mem. firm, 1886-98, William D. Cleveland & Co., wholesale grocers and cotton factors; in wholesale wheat business at Portland, Ore., 1899-1906, and pres. W. A. Gordon Co., 1902-06; v.p. and acting pres., 1906-13, and pres. Dec. 1913—, A. H. Belo & Co., pubs. of Galveston News, Dallas News and Dallas Evening Journal. Trustee William M. Rice Inst., Houston; pres. Houston Sch. Bd., 1886-98. Died June 23, 1919.

LOMEN, Gudbrand J., judge; b. Decorah, Ia., Jan. 28, 1854; s. Jorgen G. and Elizabeth (Brandt) L.; student Luther Coll., Decorah, 1867-73; LL.B., State U. of Ia., 1875; m. Julie E. M. Joys, May 27, 1878; children—George Edward, Carl Joys, Harry, Ralph, Alfred Julian, Helen Mabel. Began practice at Caledonia, Minn., 1875; clk. District Court, Caledonia, 1878-85; mem. Minn. Ho. of Rep., 1891; removed to Nome, Alaska, 1900; mayor of Nome, 1917-19; U.S. atty. 2d Div., Alaska, 1918-21; U.S. dist. judge, 2d Div., Alaska, 1921, reappointed 1925. Chmn. local bd. Selective Service, World War, also chmn. Four Minute Men, Nome. Republican. Lutheran. Knighted by King of Norway, Order of St. Olaf for services rendered Capt. Roald Amundsen and as vice consul of Norway. Home: Nome, Alaska. Died June 12, 1934.

LOMMEN, Christian Peter, educator; b. Spring Grove, Minn., Jan. 30, 1865; s. Peter Johnson and Maria (Rask) L.; B.S., U. of Minn., 1891; studied U. of Berlin and Woods Hole (Mass.) Biol. Lab.; m. Gunhild Solberg, 1892 (died 1914); children—Peter Arnold, Ralph Gerald, Frederick William, Harold Hjalmar; m. 2d, Grace D. Eldridge, Aug. 8, 1923. Prof. biology, U. of S.Dak., 1891—, also organizer, 1907, and dean Sch. of Medicine, same univ. Regent of edn. for United Norwegian Luth. Ch. of America. Republican. Home: Vermilion, S.D. Died July 8, 1926.

LONDON, Alexander Troy, lawyer; b Wilmington, N.C., Feb. 28, 1847; s. Mauger and Rachel (Troy) L.; ed. in N.C.; read law in father's office; m. Mary Parke, Dec. 6, 1892. In C.S.A., from May 1864, pvt., 1st sergt., and afterward adjt. of regt.; paroled April 1865, with Johnston's army; admitted to bar, June 1869; removed to Montgomery, Ala., Nov. 1884; to Birmingham, Jan. 1889, where he engaged in practice. Home: Birmingham, Ala. Died 1908.

LONDON, Jack, author; b. San Francisco, Calif., Jan. 12, 1876; s. John and Flora (Wellman) L.; ed. U. of Calif.; m. Bessie Maddern, Apr. 7, 1900; m. 2d, Charmian Kittredge, Nov. 19, 1905. Left coll. to go to Klondike and never completed course; went to sea before the mast, 1892; went to Japan and seal hunting in Bering Sea, 1893; tramped throughout U.S. and Canada for sociol. and econ. study, 1894; traveled a great deal at various times; journalist and lecturer; war correspondent during the Russo-Japanese War. Navigated his 55-ft. yacht "Snark" in the South Seas, 1907-09. Socialist. Author: The Son of the Wolf, 1900; The God of His Fathers, 1901; A Daughter of the Snows, 1902; The Children of the Frost, 1902; The Cruise of the Dazzler, 1902; The People of the Abyss, 1903; Kempton-Wace Letters, 1903; The Call of the Wild, 1903; The Faith of Men, 1904; The Sea Wolf, 1904; The Game, 1905; War of the Classes, 1905; Tales of the Fish Patrol, 1905; Moon-Face, 1906; Scorn of Women (play), 1906; White Fang, 1907; Before Adam, 1907; Love of Life, 1907; The Iron Heel, 1907; The Road, 1907; Martin Eden, 1909; Lost Face, 1909; Revolution, 1910; Burning Daylight, 1910; Theft, 1910; When God Laughs, 1910; Adventure, 1911; The Cruise of the Snark, 1911; South Sea Tales, 1911; Smoke Bellew Tales, 1912; The House of Pride, 1912; A Son of the Sun, 1912; The Night-Born, 1913; The Abysmal Brute, 1913; John Barleycorn, 1913; The Valley of the Moon, 1913; The Strength of the Strong, 1914; The Mutiny of the Elsinore, 1914; The Scarlet Plague, 1915; The Star Rover, 1915; The Little Lady of the Big House, 1916. Home: Glen Ellen, Calif. Died Nov. 22, 1916.

LONDON, Meyer, congressman; b. in Russia, Dec. 29, 1871. Came to U.S., 1891; admitted to N.Y. bar, 1898; active in socialist and labor movement; mem. 64th and 65th Congresses (1915-19), and 67th Congress (1921-23), 12th N.Y. Dist. Socialist. Home: New York, N.Y. Died June 6, 1926.

LONERGAN, William Ignatius, univ. pres.; b. San Francisco, Feb. 25, 1884; s. Jeremiah Henry and Mary Emily (St. Leger) L.; student St. Ignatius Coll., San Francisco; student Gonzaga U., A.M., 1914, LL.B., 1915; grad. study, Woodstock (Md.) Coll., 1917-21, S.T.D., 1921. Joined Soc. of Jesus (Jesuits), 1904; prof. of classics, U. of Santa Clara (Calif.), 1908-12; prof. of classics, Gonzaga U., 1915-17; ordained priest R.C. Ch., 1920; dean of U. of Santa Clara, 1922-25; asso. editor America (nat. Catholic weekly), 1925-32; pres. U. of San Francisco, 1932—. Author: Campaigning with Christ's Church, 1928. Died Mar. 13, 1936.

LONG, Albert Limerick, v.p. and prof. natural science, Robert Coll., Constantinople; b. Washington, Pa., Dec. 4, 1832; s. Rev. Warner Limerick, of Pittsburgh, Pa.; studied Western Univ., Pa.; grad. Allegheny Coll., 1852 (D.D., same, 1867); grad. in theology, Boston Univ., 1857; joined Pittsburgh Conf., M.E. Ch., 1857; missionary in Bulgaria, 1857-62, editing and translating scriptures in Bulgarian language at Constantinople, 1862-67; superintended electrotyping of edition of Bulgarian New Testament and Ancient Slavic New Testament in parallel pages for Am. Bible Soc. in New York, 1867; prof. Robert Coll., 1872—. Was decorated by Prince Alexander of Bulgaria with cross of Comdr. Order St. Alexander, and by Prince Ferdinand with cross of Comdr. Order of Civil Merit; received vote of thanks, First Bulgarian Nat. Assembly, "for services to the Bulgarian Nation." Died 1901.

LONG, Charles D., justice Supreme Court, Mich., 1887-1907; b. Grand Blanc, Mich., June 14, 1841; ed. in public schools, Flint, Mich.; entered Union army, lost left arm, and received gunshot wound through left hip; came home in 1862; read law; held various co. offices; dept. comdr. Mich G.A.R., 1885. Republican. Home: Lansing, Mich. Died 1902.

LONG, Chester I., senator; b. Perry Co., Pa., Oct. 12, 1860; s. Abraham G. and Mary L.; removed with parents to Daviess Co., Mo., 1865, to Paola, Kan., 1879; acad. edn.; admitted to bar, 1885; m. Anna Bache, Feb. 12, 1895 (died 1919); children—Vera Clemes (Mrs. Roger S. Hurd, foster dau.), Agnes (Mrs. Harry F. Gee, Jr.), Margaret (Mrs. W. E. Stanley). Mem. Kan. Senate, 1889-93; mem. 54th (1895-97) and 56th and 57th (1899-1903) Congresses, 7th Kan. Dist.; reëlected to 58th Congress, but before taking seat was elected U.S. senator for term, 1903-09; member of law firm of Long, Depew & Stanley, Wichita, Kansas; also associated with Long, Chamberlain & Nyce (Washington, D.C.); chmn. Commn. to Revise Gen. Statutes of Kansas. Home: Wichita, Kan. Died July 1, 1934.

LONG, Edward Henry, prin. Peabody School, St. Louis, 1895—; Livonia, N.Y., Oct. 4, 1838; ed. N.Y. Conference Sem., Charlotteville, N.Y., and Genesee Coll., Lima, N.Y.; taught country dist. school winter of 1856-57; for 6 yrs. following taught and attended school alternately. Teacher, 1867-69, and prin., 1869-70, in Buffalo schools; public school prin., 1870-74; asst. supt., 1874-80; supt. public schools, 1880-95, at St. Louis; m. Elvira J. Wilcox, July 13, 1864. Home: St. Louis, Mo. Died 1911.

LONG, Eli, brig. gen. U.S.A., retired Aug. 1867; b. Woodford Co., Ky., June 16, 1837; grad. Frankfort, Ky., Mil. School, 1855; apptd. 2d lt., 1st U.S. cav., 1856; served against Indians; 1st lt. and capt., 1861; col. 4th Ohio cav.; served at Tullahoma, Murfreesboro, Chickamauga and in Atlanta campaign; comd. cav. brigade; comd. div. at Selma, Ala., April 1865, capturing the place; 5 times wounded; bvtd. maj. gen. vols. and U.S.A.; mustered out of vol. service Jan. 15, 1866; retired as maj. gen.; reduced to brig. gen. by Act of March 3, 1875; m. Jane I. Lane, Sept. 5, 1865. Home Plainfield, N.J. Died 1903.

LONG, Eugene Rufus, coll. prof.; b. Sumter Dist., S.C., Dec. 10, 1862; s. Isaac J. and Callie P. (Kennedy) L.; A.B., Ark. Coll.; m. Sallie C. Meek, Dec. 26, 1900. Prof. polit. science, 1883-95, chmn. of faculty, 1891-95, Ark. Coll.; prof. Southwestern Presbyn. U., Clarksville, Tenn., 1895-97; pres. and prof. Bible studies and polit. science, Ark. Coll., Batesville, 1897-1913; prof. Bible and philosophy, Austin Coll., Sherman, Tex., 1913-16, Hampden-Sydney (Va.) Coll., 1916-17; prof. Bible and polit. science, Ark. Coll., 1917—. Del. Pan-Presbyn. Council, Liverpool, 1904; mem. Presbyn. Gen. Assembly, 1903, 23. Mem. City Council, Batesville, Ark., 1906-10 and 1926—; mem. commn. controlling municipal water and light plant, 1910-13. Trustee of Austin Theol. Sem., 1909-13. Home: Batesville, Ark. Died June 29, 1931.

LONG, Henry Fletcher, surgeon; b. 1869; M.D., U. of Md. Sch. of Medicine, 1892. Practiced at Statesville, N.C., 1892—. head of Long's Pvt. Sanitarium. Fellow Am. Coll. Surgeons. Home: Statesville, N.C. Died July 28, 1939.

LONG, Huey Pierce, senator; b. Winnfield, La., Aug. 30, 1893; s. Huey Pierce and Caledonia (Tison) Long; ed. grammar and high schs., Winnfield, and 4 mos. in Shreveport High Sch.; studied law Okla. U. and Tulane U. (non-grad.); m. Rose McConnell, Apr. 12, 1913; children—Rose Lolita, Russell Billiu, Palmer Reid. Admitted to La. bar, 1915, later to practice in all courts of U.S.; practiced, Winnfield, 1915-18, them at Shreveport, La.; mem. Railroad Commn. of La., 1918-21. Mem. La. Pub. Service Commn., 1921-28; candidate for gov., 1924; elected gov. of La., 1928, terms of 4 yrs.; mem. U.S. Senate, 1931-37; practiced law almost continually while holding pub. office; atty. for state in much pub. utility litigation, and for state bodies and depts, while gov.; practiced also in other states. (Two efforts made to impeach him in legislature, one as mem Pub. Service Commn., 1921, and the other as gov., 1929—both efforts abandoned and withdrawn.) Instituted paved road program; drafted free school textbook law; founded Sch. of Medicine of La. State Univ. and Home for Epileptics; instituted program to eradicate illiteracy, legislation for building new State Capitol, for bridging navigable streams, etc. Mem. Dem. Nat. Committee. Baptist. Home: New Orleans, La. Died Sept. 10, 1935.

LONG, John Davis, secretary of the navy; b. Buckfield, Me., Oct. 27, 1838; s. Zadoc and Julia Temple (Davis) L.; A.B., Harvard, 1857; prin. Westford Acad., Mass., 1857-59; studied law in Harvard Law Sch. and pvt. law offices, 1861; (LL.D., Harvard, 1880, Tufts, 1902); admitted to bar, 1861; practiced at Buckfield, Me., 1861-62, then at Boston; m. Mary Woodward Glover, Sept. 13, 1870; 2d Agnes, d. Rev. Joseph D. Pierce, May 22, 1886. Mem. Mass. Ho. of Rep., 1875-78 (speaker 1876-78); lt. gov. of Mass., 1879; gov., 1880-83; mem. 48th to 50th Congresses (1883-89), 2d Mass. Dist.; declined renomination, 1888; was for several yrs. on Statehouse Construction Commn. of Mass. Sec. of the navy, in cabinets of Presidents McKinley and Roosevelt, Mar. 6, 1897-May 1, 1902; resigned. Sr. of law firm of Long & Hemenway, Boston. Pres. Bd. of Overseers Harvard Coll. Fellow Am. Acad. Arts and Sciences, Presented town of Buckfield, Me., the Zadoc Long Free Library, 1901. Author: The Republican Party—Its History, Principles and Policies, 1898, 1900; The New American Navy, 2 vols. Home: Hingham, Mass. Died Aug. 28, 1915.

LONG, John G., consul gen. of U.S. to Cairo, Egypt, Oct. 1900—; b. Wilmington, N.C., Aug. 19, 1846; removed with parents to Fla., 1847; has lived in St. Augustine, 1862—. Asst. postmaster, St. Augustine, 1867; collector of revenues for St. John's Co., 1868-70; States atty. 7th jud. circuit, Fla., 1870-75; later co. solicitor, St. John's Co.; has been mayor of St. Augustine, and has held other local offices. Republican; mem. Rep. Nat. Com. for Fla. Home: St. Augustine, Fla. Died 1903.

LONG, John Harper, chemist; b. nr. Steubenville, O., Dec. 1856; s. John and Elizabeth (Harper) L.; B.S., U. of Kan., 1877; studied at Tübingen, Würzburg, and Breslau, 1877-80; Sc.D., Tübingen, 1879; m. Catherine Stoneman, Aug. 24, 1885. Prof. chemistry, Northwestern U. Med. Sch., 1881—; dean Northwestern U. Sch. Pharmacy, 1913-17. Mem. referee bd. of consulting scientific experts U.S. Dept. Agr.; mem. revision com. U.S. Pharmacopœia. Author: Elements of General Chemistry, 1898, 4th edit. 1906; Text-Book of Analytical Chemistry, 1898, 3d edit. 1906; Laboratory Manual of Physiological Chemistry, 1894; Text-Book of Physiological Chemistry, 1905, 2d edit. 1909. Home: Evanston, Ill. Died June 14, 1918.

LONG, John Luther, author; b. in Pa., 1861. Read law, admitted to bar, and engaged in practice at Phila. Author: Madam Butterfly, 1898; Miss Cherry-Blossom of Tokyo; The Fox-Woman, 1900; The Prince of Illusion, 1901; Naughty Man, 1902; Little Miss Joy-Sing, 1902; Sixty Jane, 1903; Heimweh, and Other Stories, 1905; Billy Boy, 1906; The Way of the Gods, 1906; Felice, 1908; (plays) Madame Butterfly, 1900; The Darling of the Gods (with David Belasco), 1902; Adrea, 1904; The Dragon Fly (with E. C. Carpenter), 1905; Dolce (written for Mrs. Minnie Maddern Fiske), 1907; Kassa (written for Mrs. Leslie Carter), 1910; Baby Grand, 1912; War—or What Happens When One Loves One's Enemy, 1913; Lady Betty Martingale (written for Mrs. Fiske), 1914; Billy Boy, 1915; (cantatas) Yo-Nennen (with Mr. Leps), 1903; Gar-Anlaf (with same), 1905; The Songs of Times (with Dr. Parker), 1911; (operas) Andon (with Mr. Leps), 1904; Hosi-San (with same), 1906; The Unjust Judge, 1916; Seffy, 1907; Crowns (play), 1922; Remembrance (play), with Carpenter, 1909. Home: Elkins Park, Philadelphia, Pa. Died Oct. 31, 1927.

LONG, John Wesley, surgeon; b. 1859; M.D., Vanderbilt U., 1883, U. of Nashville, 1884, New York Polyclinic Med. Sch., 1888. Was prof. gynecology and pediatrics, Med. Coll. of Va.; now surgeon in chief Wesley Long Hosp., Greensboro. Fellow Am. Coll. Surgeons. Home: Greensboro, N.C. Died Aug. 1, 1927.

LONG, Joseph Ragland, prof. law; b. Charlottesville, Va., Dec. 15, 1870; s. John Crallé and Josephine Hardin (Ragland) L.; A.B., Richmond Coll., 1890, LL.D., 1919; B.S., U. of Pa., 1894; LL.B., U. of Va., 1895; m. Talitha Chenault Brinker, Aug. 12, 1902; children—Joseph Ragland, John Chenault, Lucian Massie. Teacher in Alleghany Inst., Roanoke, Va., 1890-92; mem. editorial staff of Edward Thompson Co., pubs. American and English Ency. of Law, Northport, N.Y., 1895-96; in practice at Denver, 1897-1902; prof. law, 1902-23, and dean Sch. of Law, 1917-23, Washington and Lee U.; prof. of law, U. of Colo., 1923—. Baptist. Author: Cases on Domestic Relations, 1915; Government and the People, 1922; Cases on Constitutional Law, 1926. Home: Boulder, Colo. Died Mar. 15, 1932.

LONG, Le Roy, surgeon; b. Lincoln Co., N.C., Jan. 1, 1869; s. William T. and Mary E. L.; studied classics and higher mathematics under pvt. tutors; M.D., Louisville Med. Coll., 1893 (1st honors); m. Martha Downing, Apr. 29, 1896; children—Le Roy Downing, Wendell McLean. Demonstrator genito-urinary diseases, Louisville Med. Coll., 1894-95; dean and prof. surgery, U. of Oklahoma Sch. of Medicine, 1915-31; chief of the Le Roy Long Clinic. Mem. Oklahoma State Bd. Medical Examiners, 1911-15. Major M.R.C., U.S.A., 1918, lt. col., 1923; past comdr. Gen. Hosp. No. 56. Fellow Western Surg. Assn., Am. Coll. Surgeons (gov.). Democrat. Methodist. Home: Oklahoma City, Okla. Died Oct. 27, 1940.

LONG, Lily Augusta, writer; b. St. Paul; d. Rev. Peter and Matilda C. (Tidland) L. Lit. editor St. Paul Pioneer Press, 1913-16. Unitarian. Author: A Squire of Low Degree, 1890; Apprentices to Destiny, 1893; Radisson (a verse drama), 1914; The Singing Place, and Other Poems, 1922. Home: St. Paul, Minn. Died Sept. 8, 1927.

LONG, Maurice Alvin, corp. official; b. Middletown, O., Oct. 25, 1875; s. Eli G. and Elizabeth E. L.; student Middletown (O.) High Sch.; studied architecture and civil engring.; m. Anne May Morris, June 20, 1905. Practicing architect, 1897-99; architect, later chief engr., B.&O. R.R. Co., 1899-1919; organized engring. and contracting firms of The M. A. Long Co., and pres. of same, 1919—; v.p. Md. Slag Co.; chmn. bd. Western Md. R.R.; dir. Equitable Trust Co., Insuranshares Certificates of Md., New Amsterdam Casualty Co., Citizens Savings Bank, Fidelity & Guaranty Fire Ins. Co., Industrial Corp. of Baltimore. Pres. Bapt. Children's Aid Soc. Mem. U.S. Chamber of Commerce (nat. councilor). Baptist (trustee Univ. Ch.). Mason. Home: Baltimore, Md. Died Feb. 27, 1938.

LONG, Oscar Fitzalan, army officer; b. Utica, N.Y., June 16, 1852; s. William W. and Eva E. E.; grad. U.S. Mil. Acad., 1876; m. Amy Requa, 1896; children—Amy, Sally. Apptd. 2d lt. 5th U.S. Inf., June 15, 1876; brig. gen., July 10, 1904. Served against hostile Indians in Mont., and in fight against Sitting Bull and Crazy Horse at Wolf Mountain, Jan. 8, 1877, Lame Deer Creek, May 6, 1877; on Nez Perces Expdn., 1877, and was in fight at Bear Paw Mountain against Chief Joseph, Sept. 30, 1877; received the Congressional Medal of Honor for "most distinguished gallantry" in this action; organized and was gen. supt. of the army transport service in San Francisco during the Spanish-Am. War and Filipino Insurrection; retired at own request, over 30 yrs.' service, July 11, 1904. Pres. Calif. Wire Cloth Co. (Oakland). Home: Piedmont, Calif. Died Dec. 22, 1928.

LONG, Ray, editor; b. Lebanon, Ind., Mar. 23, 1878; s. John H. and Mary A. (Hume) L.; ed. pub. schs., Indianapolis; m. Lucy Virginia Bovie, July 25, 1922; 1 son, Ray. On staff Indianapolis News, 1900-05; mng. editor Cincinnati Post, 1905-08, Cleveland Press, 1908-10; asso. editor Hampton's Mag., 1910-11; editor Hampton-Columbian, 1911-12, Red Book, Blue Book, and Green Book mags., 1912-18. Pres. and editor in chief Internat. Magazine Co. (Hearst's International-Cosmopolitan, Good Housekeeping, Harper's Bazar, Motor, Motor Boating), Jan. 1, 1919-31; chmn. bd. Ray Long & Richard Smith, Inc., 1931—. Home: New York, N.Y. Died July 9, 1935.

LONG, Robert Alexander, lumberman; b. nr. Shelbyville, Ky., Dec. 17, 1850; s. Samuel M. and Margaret K. (White) L.; ed. common and pvt. schs.; m. Ella M. Wilson, Dec. 16, 1875. Began lumber business, Columbus, 1875; now chmn. bd. Long-Bell Lumber Co., of Kansas City, Mo., operating large mfg. plants, 95 retail yards, railroads, etc.; also pres. R. A. Long Properties, owning the R. A. Long Bldg., the first steel skeleton office bldg. of consequence in Kansas City, Mo. Pres. Liberty Memorial Assn., Kansas City. Mem. and speaker Conservation Congress, White House, 1908. Pres. Christian Bd. of Publs., St. Louis, publishers Christian Evangelist, organ Disciples of Christ; trustee Bible Coll. of Mo. Democrat. Home: Lee's Summit, Mo., and Kansas City, Mo. Died Mar. 15, 1934.

LONG, Seely Frederick, surgeon; b. Kingsclear, N.B., Can., Feb. 19, 1855; s. Charles Addington and Joanna Andrew (Hammond) L.; ed. high sch. and normal course in N.B.; went to Calif., 1877; med. student U. of Calif.; M.D., Univ. Med. Coll. (New York U.), 1881; m. S. Ella La Grange, June 28, 1882. In gen. practice at San Francisco, 1881-98; pres., and chief surgeon Buena Vista Sanatorium, 1898—; also pres. Buena Vista Sanatorium and Training Sch. for Nurses. Surgeon gen. with rank of col., Calif. N.G., 1891-95; mem. San Francisco Bd. Health, 1891-95. Home: San Francisco, Calif. Died Sept. 18, 1921.

LONG, Simon Cameron, ry. official; b. nr. Harrisburg, Pa., Sept. 7, 1857; C.E., Lafayette Coll., Pa., 1877; m. Emma Hanes, Nov. 1885. In employ mining cos., Pa., 1877-79; with Phila. & Reading R.R., 1880-81; rodman and transitman, Pa. R.R., 1881-82; in engr.'s office, same, at Altoona, Pa., Apr.-Sept. 1882, asst. supervisor Pittsburgh yard, 1882-83, Walls, Pa., 1883-84, Phila. yard, 1884-85; supervisor Monongahela div., Lancaster, Pa., 1885-89; asst. engr. Delaware div., Phila., Wilmington & Baltimore R.R., 1889-93; asst. engr., Baltimore & Potomac R.R. and Washington Southern Ry., 1893-1901; supt. Bedford div. Pa. R.R., 1901-02; supt. River and Low Grade divs., Buffalo & Allegheny Valley div. same rd., 1902-03; apptd. supt. Pittsburgh div., 1903; apptd. gen. supt. Western Pa. div., 1907; gen. mgr. Pa. R.R. east of Pittsburgh and Erie, Mar. 3, 1911—. Home: Merion, Pa. Died Mar. 25, 1917.

LONG, Simon Peter, clergyman; b. McZena, O., Oct. 7, 1860; s. George and Margaret (Merkling) L.; A.B., Capital U., Columbus, O., 1883, A.M., 1886; theol. course, Columbus and Phila.; studied Shoemaker Oratorical Sch.; (D.D., Wittenberg Coll., 1909, Susquehanna U., 1909); m. Clara Alice Marion, May 12, 1887; children—Margaret Adaline, Clara Martha, Mary (dec.), Naomi Norma, Loy Luther (dec.), Ruth Antoina. Ordained Luth. ministry, 1886; pastor Loudonville, O., 1886-90, Massillon, O., 1890-93, Columbus, 1893-1903; pres. Lima Coll., Ohio, 1898-1903; pastor First Ch., Mansfield, O., 1903-18, Wicker Park Luth. Ch., Chicago, Oct. 1918—. Pres. Wittenberg Synod, 1909. Tendered presidency of Lenoir Coll., Hickory, N.C., and called to First Luth. Ch., Los Angeles, 1915, but his congregation refused to let him accept either position. Pres. Chicago Lutheran Bible School, 1927. Lectured throughout U.S., 1917, in interest of 400th anniversary of the Reformation of 16th Century. Author: Prepare to Meet Thy God, 1894; The Wounded Word, 1903; The Great Gospel, 1904; The Eternal Epistle, 1908; The Way Made, 1908; Prophetic Pearls, 1913; The Crime Against Christ and What I Owe to My Church, 1923; My Lord and My Life (an autobiography including a trip to Jerusalem and 18 countries), 1925. Wrote a reply to R. G. Ingersoll, called "Bob's Bible." Home: Chicago, Ill. Died Jan. 3, 1929.

LONGAN, George Baker, newspaper pub.; b. Holden, Mo., Dec. 11, 1879; s. George Baker and Emma (Lard) L.; educated in the public schools of Kansas City, Mo.; m. Ann Cole, Oct. 9, 1902; children—Mildred Elizabeth (Mrs. Dale Ashby Beronius), Georgette Ann (Mrs. William L. Huggins, Jr.). Reporter on Kansas City Times, Mo., 1898-1900; with Kansas City Star, 1900—; mng. editor, 1926-28, pres. and gen. mgr. Kansas City Star Co., 1928—; dir. The Associated Press, v.p., 1931, 32. Mem. bd. dirs. Kansas City Art Inst., Kansas City Conservatory of Music, Mo. Hist. Soc. Home: Kansas City, Mo. Died Oct. 16, 1942.

LONGDEN, Aladine Cummings, physicist; b. Leesville, O., Feb. 19, 1857; s. Samuel and Adaline (Cummings) L.; A.B., DePauw U., 1881, A.M., 1884; post-grad. work, U. of Chicago, 1897-99; Ph.D., Columbia, 1900; m. Jean I. Humble, Dec. 24, 1884. Instr. mathematics and English, St. John's Mil. Acad., Haddonfield, N.J., 1881-82; prof. mathematics, Riverview Mil. Acad., Poughkeepsie, N.Y., 1882-83, St. James Mil. Acad., Macon, Mo., 1883-84; prof. natural sciences, same, 1884-88; prof. physics and chemistry, State Normal Sch., Westfield, Mass., 1888-97; asst. in physics, U. of Chicago, 1898-99; instr. physics, U. of Wis., 1900-01; prof. physics and astronomy, Knox Coll., 1901-26, emeritus. Comdt. St. James Cadets and capt. N.G., Mo., 1885-88. Republican. Presbyn. Home: Galesburg, Ill. Died July 12, 1941.

LONGFELLOW, A(lexander) Wadsworth, architect; b. Portland, Me., Aug. 18, 1854; s. Alexander Wadsworth and Elizabeth (Porter) L.; A.B., Harvard, 1876; spl. student, Mass. Inst. Tech., 1876-78; École des Beaux Arts, Paris, 1879-81; unmarried. Established, 1887 (offices in Pittsburgh and Boston), Longfellow, Alden & Harlow, designers of the Carnegie Library, Pittsburgh, City Hall, Cambridge, Mass., etc.; firm dissolved, 1895; partnership formed with brother, R. K. Longfellow. Designed: Phillips Brooks House, Semitic Mus. and Arnold Arboretum for Harvard Coll., also 2 memorial laboratories in a proposed Chemical Group for same coll.; Agassiz House and two dormitories for Radcliffe Coll.; Oliver Wendell Holmes and Abraham Lincoln schs., Boston; the original Boston elevated ry. stas.; Memorial Chapel, Mountain Cemetery, Yarmouth, N.S.; etc. Pres. Boston Marine Mus.; trustee Boston Mus. Fine Arts, Boston Athenæum, Boston Co-operative Bldg. Co. Fellow A.I.A., Boston Soc. Architects. Home: Boston, Mass. Died Feb. 16, 1934.

LONGFELLOW, Ernest Wadsworth, artist; b. Cambridge, Mass., Nov. 23, 1845; s. Henry Wadsworth (poet) and Frances (Appleton) L.; S.B., Lawrence Scientific Sch. (Harvard), 1865; studied art in Paris under Hèbert Bonnât and Couture; m. Harriet Spelman, 1868. His best known landscapes and compositions are: Misty Morning; The Choice of Youth; Italian Pifferari; Morning on the Ægean; The Matterhorn; Evening on the Nile; First Love; Portrait of H. W. Longfellow; etc. Home: New York, N.Y. Died Nov. 24, 1921.

LONGFELLOW, William Pitt Preble, architect; b. Portland, Me., Oct. 25, 1836; s. Stephen and Marianne (Preble) L.; and nephew of the poet; A.B., Harvard, 1855; S.B., 1859; m. Emily Daniell, May 26, 1870. Asst. architect, Treasury Dept., 1869-72; original editor The American Architect; adj. prof. architectural design, Mass. Inst. Tech., 1881-82. Trustee Mus. of Fine Arts, Boston; chmn. architectural sect. bd. of judges, Chicago Expn., 1893. Fellow Am. Inst. Architects (sec. for foreign correspondence), Boston Soc. Architects, Royal Soc. Arts, London. Author: Cyclopædia of Architecture in Italy, Greece and the Levant, 1895; Applied Perspective, 1901. Died 1913.

LONGLEY, Edmund Waters; b. Chelmsford, Mass., Mar. 30, 1863; s. Edmund and Mary A. M. (Reed) L.; ed. Salem (Mass.) High Sch.; m. Anna True Peabody, Apr. 23, 1895. Engaged in telephone business, 1881-1928; began as clk. N.E. Telephone & Telegraph Co.; later mgr. of exchange and in accounting dept.; sec. and auditor of the co., 1902-12, sec. and gen. auditor, 1912-13, v.p. 1917-28; pres. Boston Acceptance Co., Inc. Chmn. Salem Rebuilding Commn., by appmt. of Gov. Walsh, after great fire of June 25, 1914, term of 3 yrs. Asst. exec. mgr. and treas. Mass. Com. Pub. Safety, 1917-18. Republican. Unitarian. Mason. Home: Brookline, Mass. Died May 14, 1941.

LONGLEY, W(illiam) H(arding), prof. biology; b. Paradise, N.S., Can., Oct. 27, 1881; s. Israel Manning and Ermina Judson (Morse) L.; A.B., Acadia U., Wolfville, N.S., 1901, D.Sc., 1931; grad. study, Provincial Normal Sch., Truro, N.S., 1902; A.B., Yale, 1907, A.M., 1908, Ph.D., 1910; m. Hazel Fowler Baird, Sept. 12, 1908; children—William Harding, Elizabeth Fowler Baird, John Prescott (dec.), James Baird. Came to U.S., 1906, naturalized citizen, 1925. Instr. in biology, Yale, 1910; asso. prof. botany, Goucher Coll., 1911-14, prof., 1914-17, prof. biology, 1917—; exec. officer Tortugas (Fla.) Marine Biol. Lab., Carnegie Instn. of Washington, 1923—; collaborator marine invertebrates U.S. Nat. Museum. Home: Baltimore, Md. Died Mar. 10, 1937.

LONGNECKER, Edwin, naval officer; b. Cumberland Co., Pa., Feb. 19, 1844; grad. U.S. Naval Acad., 1865; married. Promoted ensign, Dec. 1, 1866; master (lt. jr. grade) Mar. 12, 1868; lt., Mar. 26, 1869; lt. comdr., Aug. 30, 1881; comdr., Oct. 2, 1891; capt., Mar. 3, 1899; rear admiral, July 8, 1905; retired by operation of law, Feb. 19, 1906. Served on America during Civil War; on Richmond, 1890-91; comd. Passaic, 1892; comd. Ranger, 1892-94; Navy Yard, Washington, D.C., 1895; Naval War Coll., Newport, R.I., 1895; insp. ordnance, Navy Yard, League Island, 1895-99; comd. New Orleans, 1899-1900; Navy Yard, Boston, 1900-01; Naval Sta., Port Royal, S.C., 1901-03, serving as commandant, Apr. 12, 1902-June 14, 1903; comdt. Naval Sta., Charleston, 1903-04; Navy Yard, Norfolk, 1904; Navy Yard, League Island, 1904-06; retired on account of age, Feb. 19, 1906, and as rear admiral of sr. nine in recognition of service during Civil War. Home: Wernersville, Pa. Died Nov. 13, 1923.

LONGSHORE, Hannah E., physician; b. Montgomery Co., Md., May 30, 1819; d. Samuel and Paulina Myers. At early age moved with parents to Washington, remaining there until her 14th yr., when family went to Ohio; m. Thomas E. Longshore, March 26, 1841. Mem. 1st class of students of the Female Med. Coll. (now Woman's Med. Coll.), opened in 1850, in Phila., grad. 1851. Gave several courses of lectures to women on physiology and hygiene. After graduation apptd. demonstrator of anatomy, Woman's Med. College. Home: Philadelphia, Pa. Died 1901.

LONGSTREET, James, soldier, U.S. commr. of Pacific railroads, Nov. 2, 1897—; b. in Edgefield Dist., S.C., Jan. 8, 1821; s. James L.; grad. West Point, 1842; served in Mexican, Indian and Civil wars; won title of major at battle of Molino del Rey, Sept. 8, 1847; served in C.S.A. as brig. gen. and maj. gen.; as lt. gen. comd. 1st corps Army of Northern Va. in 1862-65; a short period in the Army of Tenn. under Bragg; returned to Lee's army in 1864. Comd. in many battles, and was wounded by the fire of his own troops at the Wilderness, May 1864; was included in the surrender at Appomattox, April 9, 1865. After war became a Republican; was apptd. surveyor of customs at New Orleans by President Grant; later was supervisor of internal revenue; postmaster at Gainesville, Ga.; U.S. minister to Turkey, and U.S. marshal for dist. of Ga.; m. Helen Dortch, Sept. 8, 1897. Home: Washington, D.C. Died 1904.

LONGWORTH, Nicholas, congressman; b. Cincinnati, O., Nov. 5, 1869; s. Nicholas and Susan (Walker) L.; A.B., Harvard, 1891; student Harvard Law Sch., 1893; LL.B., Cincinnati Law Sch., 1894; LL.D., New York U., 1926, U. of Michigan, 1927, University of Pennsylvania, 1929; m. Alice Lee, d. President Roosevelt, at White House, Feb. 17, 1906; 1 dau., Paulina. Admitted to bar, 1894; mem. Bd. Edn., Cincinnati, 1898; mem. Ohio Ho. of Rep., 1899-1901, Senate, 1901-03; mem. 58th to 62nd Congresses (1903-13) and reëlected 64th to 71st Congresses (1915-31), 1st Ohio Dist.; mem. Ohio Rep. State Com., 1900—; mem. exec. com. Rep. Congressional Com.; Rep. floor leader Nat. Ho. of Rep., 1923-25, speaker of 69th, 70th and 71st Congresses, 1925-31. Home: Cincinnati, O. Died Apr. 9, 1931.

LONGYEAR, John Munro, capitalist; b. Lansing, Mich., Apr. 15, 1850; s. John Wesley and Harriet (Munroe) L.; ed. prep. dept. Olivet (Mich.) Coll., and Georgetown Coll., D.C., Cazenovia (N.Y.) Sem.; m. Mary Hawley Beecher, Jan. 4, 1879. Largely interested in mineral and lumber lands of Northern Mich. and in Spitzbergen coal mines; pres. Marquette (Mich.) Nat. Bank. Mayor of Marquette, 1890-91. Mem. bd. of Control Mich. Coll. Mines, 1888-1913; mem. Corp. Mass. Inst. Tech. Home: Brookline, Mass. Died May 28, 1922.

LÖNNQUIST, Carl Adolph, clergyman; b. Frederydsocken, Smaland, Sweden, Sept. 27, 1869; s. Johan Reinhold and Johanna (Carlson) Lönn; ed. U. of Upsala, Sweden, 1889-90; Augustana Theol. Sem., Rock Island, Ill., 1891-93; D.D., Augustana Coll., Rock Island, 1919; m. Esther Cedilia Magnuson, Sept. 27, 1893. Ordained Swedish Evang. Luth. ministry, 1893; pastor Stromsburg, Neb., 1893-96, Bethany Ch., Axtell, Neb., 1896-1921; supt. and treas. Bethphage Mission, 1921—; dir. Augustana Book Concern, Rock Rock Island, Ill., 1921—. Statistician Neb. Conf., 1893-1900, sec., 1894-97. Mem. bd. dirs. Luther Coll., Wahoo, Neb., 1914-20; dir. Bethphage Inner Mission, 1915. Author: Dikter of Teofilus (poems), 1906; Pastorn o. den kristl. bildn. i församl, 1909; Kantat för jubelsynoden, 1910; Fyrväplingen (poems), 1911; Sundet vid Treskär o.a. Dikter af Teofilus, 1913; On Eagle Wing (music), 1915; F. N. Swanberg (in memoriam), 1915; Vildros, poems, 1916; Efter 40 år, 1916; Och jag såg det nya Jerusalem (sermons), 1917; The Christ (a sonnet sequence), 1935. Editor of Guldax (monthly), of The Bethphage Messenger (quarterly), Bethphage Hymnal, 1923, Melodies (music), 1925; Melodies II, 1929. Home: Axtell, Neb. Died June 15, 1937.

LOOKER, Thomas Henry, rear admiral; b. Cincinnati, O., Nov. 23, 1829; s. James H. and Rachel H. L.; ed. U.S. Naval Acad. and by tutors; m. Lucilia S. Brigham, May 19, 1857. Apptd. midshipman to Naval Acad., Nov. 6, 1846; resigned Nov. 24, 1852; apptd. purser U.S.N., Aug. 31, 1853; promoted pay dir., Mar. 3, 1871; retired, June 29, 1906, with rank of rear admiral, for creditable services during Civil War. Asst. to Sec. of Navy, Mar. 16, 1877; in charge navy pay office, Washington, 1883-88; gen. insp. pay corps, 1889-90; p.m. gen. U.S.N., Mar.-May 1890. Home: Washington, D.C. Died 1910.

LOOMIS, Archibald Gilbert, banker; b. Hartford, Conn., June 20, 1848; s. Pascal and Martha Jones (Greenfield) L.; ed. pub. grammar and high schs., Hartford; m. Cordelia Gertrude Harwood, Nov. 11, 1869 (died 1873); 1 son, Archie Harwood; m. 2d, Mary Walz, Nov. 20, 1878 (died 1886); m. 3d, Ellen Seymour Hanson, May 18, 1892; children—Madeleine Seymour, Stillman Wadsworth. Clerk Ætna Nat. Bank, Hartford, 1865-87, cashier, 1887-91, pres. same, 1891-99; v.p. and dir. Nat. City Bank of New York, 1899-1905; with N. W. Halsey & Co., bankers and brokers, San Francisco, 1905-07; v.p. Union Trust Co., Providence, 1907-15; asst. treas., June-Aug. 1917, treas., Sept. 1, 1917—, C.,M.&St.P. Ry. Co., Chicago; federal treas. same, Aug. 1, 1918. Conglist. Republican. Home: Chicago, Ill. Died Dec. 3, 1927.

LOOMIS, Benjamin Bloomfield, clergyman; b. Bridgewater, N.Y., Oct. 6, 1836; s. Benjamin P. and Sarah (Bloomfield) L.; A.B., Union Coll., 1863; A.M., Ph.D., Syracuse U., 1887 (D.D., 1893); m. Sophia O. Witt, June 9, 1863. Ordained M.E. ministry, 1863; pastor Troy (N.Y.) Conf., at Hoosick Falls, 1863-65, Green Island, 1866-67, Keeseville, 1868-69, Mechanicville, 1870-71, Ballston Spa, 1872-74, Albany, 1875-77, Plattsburgh, 1878-80; presiding elder Cambridge Dist., 1881; pastor Troy, 1882-84, Albany, 1885-87, Watervliet, 1888-90, Lansingburgh, 1891-93, Canajoharie, 1894-95, Cambridge, 1896-98; pres. Round Lake Summer Inst., 1901-03; pastor Scotia, 1902-05, Delmar, 1906-07, Fonda, 1908; retired, 1909. Dir. Ocean Grove Assembly, 1884-1902; editor New Jersey Methodist, 1901. Author: Studies in the Book of Acts, 1897. Died May 10, 1917.

LOOMIS, Charles Battell, author; b. Brooklyn, N.Y., Sept. 16, 1861; s. Charles Battell and Mary (Worthington) L.; brother of Harvey Worthington L.; ed. Poly. Inst. of Brooklyn, acad. dept.; was not grad.; in business as clerk, 1879-91; m. Mary Fullerton, Feb. 14, 1888. Public reader. Author: Cheer Up, 1906; A Bath in an English Tub, 1907; Poe's "Raven" in an Elevator (3d edit. of More Cheerful Americans), 1907; The Knack of It, 1908; A Holiday Touch, 1908; Just Irish, 1909; Little Maude, 1909. Home: Leonia, N.J. Died 1911.

LOOMIS, Chester, painter; b. near Syracuse, N.Y., Oct. 18, 1852; s. Chauncey C. and Lucy E. L.; ed. in Syracuse, N.Y., and 1868-71, Cornell; studied painting under Harry Thompson, then 2 yrs. pupil of Léon Bonnât, Paris; m. Sarah S. Dana, Aug. 23, 1883. Lived 11 yrs. in France, returned to U.S., 1885; exhibited at 6 salons in Paris. Built house and studio at Englewood, N.J., 1890; has painted many portraits there and in New York; picture, "Christopher Sly" bought by Indianapolis Art Assn.; is represented by figure and landscape paintings in many private collections; gold medal, Mass. Charitable and Mechanics' Inst. for "A Normandy Milkmaid," A.M.A., 1906. Home: Englewood, N.J. Died Nov. 12, 1924.

LOOMIS, Dwight, jurist; b. Columbia, Conn., July 27, 1821; s. Elam and Mary (Pinneo) L.; grad. Yale Law School, 1847, LL.D.; admitted to bar, 1847, settling at Rockville, Conn.; mem. Congress, 1859-63; judge superior court, Conn., 1864-75; judge Supreme Court, Conn., 1875-91, retiring upon reaching constitutional limit of age. Apptd. by the legislature of Conn., 1891, a State referee for trial of causes referred to him, which office he still holds. In 1895 he was apptd. presiding judge State Bd. of Arbitration, but subsequently resigned the office; was, 1892-94, prof. in law dept., Yale; m. Mary E. Bill, Nov. 26, 1848 (died 1864); m. 2d, Jennie E. Kendall, Beloit, Wis., May 28, 1866 (died 1876). Home: Hartford, Conn. Died 1903.

LOOMIS, Eben Jenks, astronomer; b. Oppenheim, N.Y., Nov. 11, 1828; s. Nathan and Waite Jenks (Barber) L.; ed. Lawrence Scientific Sch. (Harvard); m. Mary Alden Wilder, July 13, 1853; father of Mabel Loomis Todd. For 50 yrs. asst. in Nautical Almanac (senior asst., 1859-1900); retired; mem. U.S. eclipse expdn. to the West Coast of Africa, 1889. Author: An Eclipse Party in Africa, 1896; A Sunset Idyl, and Other Poems, 1903. Home: Amherst, Mass. Died Dec. 2, 1912.

LOOMIS, Edward Eugene, ry. pres.; b. Herkimer Co., N.Y.; s. Chester and Esther L.; LL.D., Lafayette Coll.; m. Julia Olivia Langdon, Nov. 29, 1902; children—Olivia Langdon, Virginia Langdon (Mrs. Bayard Schieffelin). Entered railroad service in law dept. Denver & Rio Grande R.R.; became supt. Tioga Div., Erie R.R., 1894; also supt. in charge of bituminous and lumber interests of Blossburg Coal Co.; gen. supt. N.Y., Susquehanna & Western R.R. and Wilkes-Barre & Eastern R.R., 1898; supt. coal mining dept. D.L.&W. R.R., 1899, sr. v.p., 1902; elected pres. L.V. R.R., 1917; officer many other corporations. Mem. National Industrial Conf. Board; chmn. Com. Pub. Relations of Eastern Railroads. Home: New York, N.Y. Died July 11, 1937.

LOOMIS, Elmer Howard, physicist; b. Vermillion, N.Y., May 24, 1861; s. Hiram Warren and Adaline Sabra (Sayles) L.; A.B., Madison (now Colgate) U., 1883; student Göttingen and Strassburg univs., 1890-93, Ph.D., Strassburg, 1893; hon. Sc.D., Colgate, 1910; m. Mary E. Bennett, July 23, 1885 (died 1904); 1 son, Robert B.; m. 2d, Grace Eaton Woods, Oct. 12, 1911. Teacher physics and chemistry, Colgate Acad., Hamilton, N.Y., 1883-90; instr., asst. prof. and prof. physics, Princeton U., 1894-1929. Dir. N.J. Sanitarium for Tuberculosis, McKinley Hosp., Trenton; dir. N.J. Anti-Tuberculosis Assn. Mem. Simplified Spelling Bd. (advisory council). Devised important improvement in methods of determining the freezing points of dilute solutions. Home: Princeton, N.J. Died Jan. 22, 1931.

LOOMIS, Frederic Brewster, coll. prof.; b. Brooklyn, Nov. 22, 1873; s. Nathaniel H. and Julia R. (Brewster) L.; B.A., Amherst Coll., 1896; asst. in biol. lab., Amherst, 1896-97; student U. of Munich, 1897-99, Ph.D., 1899; m. Florence C. Calhoun, Sept. 7, 1904; children—Newell Calhoun, Frederic Brewster. Instr. biology, 1891-1903, asso. prof., 1903-08, prof. comparative anatomy, 1908-17, prof. geology, 1917—, Amherst. Dir. Amherst exploring expeditions to Big Bad Lands, S.D., Wasatch Basin, Wyo., Converse Co., Wyo., Sioux Co., Neb., Maine shell heaps, Patagonia, N.E. Colo., New Mexico and Fla. Fellow Am. Acad. Arts and Sciences, Geol. Soc. America. Author; Hunting Extinct Animals in the Patagonian Pampas, 1913; The Deseado Formation of Patagonia, 1915; Common Rocks and Minerals, 1923; Evolution of the Horse, 1926. Home: Amherst, Mass. Died July 28, 1937.

LOOMIS, Harvey Worthington, composer; b. Brooklyn, Feb. 5, 1865; s. Charles Battell and Mary (Worthington) L.; Brooklyn Poly. Inst.; awarded $900 free scholarship by Dr. Antonin Dvorâk; studied music in different branches at National Conservatory of Music; studied piano with Mme. Madeline Schiller. Composed four comic operas, "The Maid of Athens," "The Burglar's Bride," "Going Up?" "The Bey of Baba"; also grand opera, "The Traitor Mandolin" (book by Edwin Star Belknap); also chamber music and music for dramatic productions, "The Tragedy of Death," Empire Theatre, New York; "The Coming of the Prince," Boston, etc. Composer; Fairy Hill, cantata for children; Song Flowers for Children to Gather, 2 vols.; Toy Tunes (text by composer); The Lyric Song Book, for high schools; Sandalphon, a musically accompanied recitation; songs and piano compositions; Lyrics of the Red Man; Lectures on Indian Music; After the Lesson (24 miniature piano duets); Pedagogic and Kindergarten Music; also "The Foresman System," piano (with Arthur Edward Johnstone); All at Sea (operetta for high schs.); Magic Music Lessons (with Elizabeth L. Gallagher). Editor C. C. Birchard & Co., pubs. Home: Roxbury, Mass. Died Dec. 25, 1930.

LOOMIS, Henry P., physician; b. New York, Apr. 20, 1859; s. Alfred L. and Sarah J. (Patterson) L.; grad. Princeton, 1880, med. dept. Univ. of New York (1st in class of 500), 1883; student in Berlin (with Prof. Koch), Heidelberg and Vienna 1 yr.; m. Julia J. Stimson, Feb. 1887. Apptd. visiting physician to Bellevue Hosp., 1887; prof. pathology Univ. of City of New York, 1887-95; apptd. visiting physician to New York Hosp., 1896; cons. pathologist, New York Bd. of Health, 1897; prof. therapeutics and clinical medicine, Cornell Univ., 1898. Died 1907.

LOOMIS, Lafayette Charles, author, educator; b. N. Coventry, Conn., July 7, 1824; s. Silas and Esther

(Case) L.; grad. Wesleyan Univ., Conn., 1844 (A.M.); grad., M.D., Georgetown Coll., D.C.; m. Esther L. Lincoln, 1847; m. 2d, Mary Williams, 1870. Was co-founder of Adelphian Acad., Brockton, Mass.; later pres. of colleges at Wilmington, Del., and Wheeling, W.Va.; afterward prof. med. dept. Howard Univ., Washington; retired. Author: Index Guide to Travel and Art Culture in Europe, 1880; Myself, 1894. Died 1906.

LOOMIS, Leverett Mills, ornithologist; b. Roseville, O., Oct. 13, 1857; s. Rev. Samuel and Maria Rebecca (Hamilton) L.; unmarried. Curator dept. of ornithology, 1894-1912, dir. mus., 1902-12, Calif. Acad. Sciences. Fellow Am. Ornithologists' Union. Author: A Review of the Albatrosses, Petrels, and Diving Petrels, 1918. Home: San Francisco, Calif. Died Jan. 12, 1928.

LOOMIS, Nelson Henry, lawyer; b. Highgate, Vt., June 28, 1862; s. of Noah W. and Ellen Bradbury (Hungerford) L.; pub. and high sch. edn., Chicago and Evanston, Ill.; LL.D., Missouri Valley Coll., Mo., and from Hastings (Neb.) Coll.; m. Mary Campbell, Sept. 23, 1885 (died 1888); 1 son, Alexander Campbell; m. 2d, Christie Campbell, Aug. 12, 1891; children—John Usher, Robert Henry. Admitted to Kan. bar, 1883; entered law dept. U.P. Ry., at Lawrence, Kan., 1885, as stenographer and law clerk; asst. gen. atty. U.P. Ry. for Kan. and Mo., at Topeka, 1891-1902, gen. atty. for Kan. and Mo., 1902-08, gen. solicitor, May 1, 1908-July 16, 1918, and from Mar. 1, 1920, U.P. R.R.; corp. counsel U.P. System, July 16, 1918-Mar. 1, 1920. Republican. Home: Omaha, Neb. Died May 8, 1933.

LOOMIS, Samuel Lane, clergyman; b. Littleton, Mass., Aug. 16, 1856; s. Elihu and R. Augusta (Lane) L.; A.B., Amherst, 1877, D.D., 1899, student Yale Div. Sch., 1877-78; grad. Andover Theol. Sem., 1880; spl. studies Berlin and London, 1885-86; m. Marion Lippincott, Aug. 23, 1887; 1 son, Henry Sprague. Ordained Congl. ministry, 1880; pastor York St. Ch., Newport, Ky., 1880-85; in Europe, 1885-86, 1907, 1927, lecturer Andover Theol. Sem., 1886-87; asst. pastor Tompkins Av. Ch., Brooklyn, 1887-90; pastor Belleville Av. Ch., Newark, N.J., 1890-96, Union Ch., Boston, 1896-1907, Westfield (N.J.) Ch., 1909-16; asso. sec. Am. Missionary Assn., New York, 1917-24; editor Am. Missionary Mag., 1923-28. Pres. Class of 1877, Amherst. Author: Modern Cities and Their Religious Problems, 1887. Home: Larchmont, N.Y. Deceased.

LOOMIS, Seymour Crane, lawyer; b. Suffield, Conn., Nov. 12, 1861; s. George Wells and Mary Ellen (Norton) L.; grad. Conn. Literary Instn., 1878 (valedictorian); A.B., Yale, 1882, LL.B., cum laude, 1884; m. Catherine Canfield Northrop, Apr. 20, 1892. Has practiced at New Haven, 1884—, principally in cases involving the rights and liabilities of employers and employees and common carriers, the law of ins. and of trusts and trustees. Asst. city clk., and acting city clk. of New Haven, 1885, 1886; exec. sec. State of Conn., 1893, 1894. Compiler and editor City Year Books of New Haven, 1885, 1886. Dir. Organized Charities. Rep. of Provost Marshal Gen. and govt. appeal agt. in selective draft, 1917, 18. Republican. Home: New Haven, Conn. Died Oct. 9, 1921.

LOOMS, George, author; b. Louisville, Ky., Nov. 22, 1886; s. George W. and Kate (Farrell) L.; B.Litt., Princeton, 1908; m. Laura C. Doub, May 17, 1921; 1 dau., Katherine. Dramatic critic Denver Express, 1922-23; music critic Rocky Mountain News, 1924; book editor same, 1925. Enlisted in U.S. Army, Aug. 26, 1917; commd. 1st lt. Inf., Nov. 27, 1917; capt., Sept. 1918; no overseas service. Author: Stubble, 1922; John-no-Brown, 1923; The Caraways, 1925. Home: Denver, Colo. Died Dec. 24, 1926.

LOOP, Jennette Shepherd, artist; b. New Haven, Conn., Mar. 5, 1840; d. James and Charlotte (Lynde) Harrison; studied with Louis Bail at New Haven and later with Henry Augustus Loop, N.A., whom she married (died 1895). She studied in Paris and Italy, 1867; became asso. Nat. Acad., 1875. Home: Saratoga Springs, N.Y. Died 1909.

LOOS, Isaac Althaus, univ. prof.; b. Upper Bern, Pa., Dec. 6, 1856; s. John and Sarah (Althaus) L.; A.B., Otterbein, 1876, A.M., 1879; B.D., Yale, 1881; studied Paris and Leipzig, 1882-84; (D.C.L., Penn Coll., Ia., 1898; LL.D., Ia. Coll., 1901); m. Laura Resler, 1882 (died 1886); m. 2d, Mary Alice, d. Bishop Dickson, of Chambersburg, Pa., Dec. 25, 1889. Prof. history and German, Western (now Leander Clark) Coll., Toledo, Ia., 1884-89; prof. polit. science, 1890-1900, dir. Sch. of Polit. and Social Science and Commerce, which became Sch. of Commerce, Sept., 1914, and head prof. polit. economy and sociology, 1900-Sept. 1915, now prof. polit. economy, State U. of Ia. Author: Studies in the Politics of Aristotle and Plato, 1899. Died Apr. 1919.

LOPEZ, Charles Albert, sculptor; b. Matamoras, Mex., Oct. 19, 1869; s. Pedro Manuel and Concepcion (de Castro) L.; ed. by pvt. tutors and in sculpture pupil of J. Q. A. Ward, of Anton Falguiére at École des Beaux Arts, Paris, and at Nat. Acad. Design, New York; m. Marion Kean, Nov. 22, 1898. Professionally engaged as sculptor, 1884—; silver medal, Charleston Expn., 1902, gold medal, La. Purchase Expn., St. Louis, 1904. Died 1906.

LOPP, William Thomas, educator, explorer; b. Valley City, Ind., June 21, 1864; s. Jacob Conrad and Lucy (Trotter) L.; B.A., Hanover (Ind.) Coll., 1888, A.M., 1911, LL.D., 1925; m. Ellen Louise Kittredge, Aug. 22, 1892; children—Lucy Alaska (dec.), Dwight Thomas, Sara Louise, Katharine Kittredge, Weyana, Irene Frances, Mary, Alice Marguerite. Prin. pub. schs., Valley City, Ind., 1884-85, 1887-88; asst. prin. high sch., Winchester, Ind., 1888-89; prin. pub. schs., New Amsterdam, Ind., 1889-90; missionary teacher, Cape Prince of Wales, Alaska, 1890-92; supt. U.S. Teller Reindeer Sta., Port Clarence, Alaska, 1893-94; missionary teacher and reindeer supt., Cape Prince of Wales, 1894-95, 1896-1902; supt. govt. schs. (native) and reindeer, Northern Dist. of Alaska, 1904-05, 1906-09; chief Alaska Div. U.S. Bur. Edn., 1910-23, and supt. of edn. of natives of Alaska, 1923-25; reindeer expert for Hudson's Bay Co., 1925-27, covering Baffin Land and Norway; made survey of Eskimo Reindeer Industry in N.W. Alaska for Indian Rights Association, summer 1936. Was in charge of deer herd in Pt. Barrow relief expdn., under Capt. Jarvis, 1897-98; with aid of 7 Eskimos drove 400 reindeer from Cape Prince of Wales to Pt. Barrow, 750 miles, route lay across treacherous ice of Kotzebue Sound (50 miles wide) and wind-swept Arctic Coast; has traveled over entire coast region from Pt. Barrow to Pacific Ocean with reindeer, and greater part of interior of Alaska with dogs; author of "endless chain" plan for distribution of reindeer, resulting in the natives of Alaska becoming owners of more than 600,000 reindeer, valued at $2,000,000. Conglist. Author: White Sox (a story of the domestication of reindeer). Home: Seattle, Wash. Died Apr. 10, 1939.

LORAM, Charles Templeman, prof. edn.; b. Pietermaritzburg, S. Africa, May 10, 1879; s. Albert and Alice (Hipkiss) L.; B.A., U. of Cape of Good Hope, 1900; M.A., LL.B., Cambridge U. (Eng.); Ph.D., Columbia, 1916; grad. study U. of Cape Town, 1922-24; Ed.D., U. of Colo., 1937; m. Hilda Vautier Amy, July 3, 1908; children—Hilda Margaret, Joan Marion, Ian Craig, Cynthia Margery, Mary Patricia. Came to U.S., 1931. Teacher Pietermaritzburg Coll., S. Africa, 1896-1900; inspector schs., Natal, S. Africa, 1906-17, chief inspector native edn., 1917-20; mem. Union of S. Africa Native Affairs Commn., 1920-29; chief inspector of edn., Natal, 1929-30, supt. of edn., 1930-31; Sterling prof. of edn., Yale, from 1931 and chmn. and dir. studies, dept. of culture contacts and race relations, Grad. School, Yale, 1933—. Asso. fellow Silliman College, Yale, 1940. Member Phelps Stokes Edn. Commn. to Africa, 1922, E. Africa, 1925; mem. S. African Native Coll. and Lovedale Inst., 1921-31; dir. Yale U. Summer Seminar on Edn. and Culture Contracts, 1934; co-dir. Hawaii-Yale Seminar Conf. on Edn. in Pacific Areas, Honolulu, 1936; lecturer summer sch., Columbia, 1926, Colo. U., 1932, 37, U. of Calif., 1939, Cornell, 1940; co-dir. U. of N.C., Yale, Hampton Institute, Seminar Conf. on Edn. of Am. Negro and African Native, 1937; co-dir. Univ. of Toronto-Yale Seminar Conf. on The North American Indian Today. Life trustee Natal Tech. Coll.; trustee Yale-in-China, Am. Colonization Soc.; Phelps Stokes Fund. Episcopalian. Author: Education of the South African Native, 1919. Home: Hamden, Conn. Died July 9, 1940.

LORD, Arthur, lawyer; b. Sept. 2, 1850; s. William H. and Persis (Kendall) L.; A.B., Harvard, 1872; LL.D., Dartmouth, 1921; Litt.D., Brown, 1921; m. Sarah Shippen, Oct. 2, 1878. Practiced, Plymouth and Boston, 1874—; pres. Silver, Burdett & Co., pubs., 1910-14. Mem. Mass. Ho. of Rep., 1885 and 1886 (chmn. judiciary com.); mem. Civil Service Commn. of Mass., 1888-89; mem. bd. mgrs. Jamestown Expn., 1907; pres. The Pilgrim Soc., 1917—; fellow Am. Acad. Arts and Sciences. Mem. Pilgrim Tercentenary Commn.; chmn. Public Safety Committee in 1917. Republican. Unitarian. Home: Plymouth, Mass. Died Apr. 10, 1925.

LORD, Augustus Mendon, clergyman; b. San Francisco, Feb. 7, 1861; s. Daniel Sackett and Theresa (Mendon) L.; A.B., Harvard, 1883, A.M., S.T.B., 1887; D.D., Brown U., 1906; m. Frances Augusta Lord, June 29, 1892; 1 son, Robert Mendon. Ordained Unitarian ministry, 1887; minister Arlington, Mass., 1887-90, First Congl. (Unitarian) Ch., Providence, R.I., 1890-1931, emeritus. Pres. Ministers' Inst., 1906, Unitarian Ministerial Union, 1927; trustee Providence Pub. Library; mem. bd. visitors, Brown U.; preacher to Harvard, 1921. Author: A Book of Verses, 1886; The Touch of Nature; Little Stories of Great People, 1904. Home: Providence, R.I. Died Sept. 14, 1941.

LORD, Austin Willard, architect; b. Rolling Stone, Minn., June 27, 1860; s. Orville M. and Martha Elizabeth (Deming) L.; grad. State Normal Sch., Winona, 1881; in architects' offices at Winona, Minneapolis and St. Paul, 1881-84; spl. course Mass. Inst. Tech., 1884-85; took Rotch scholarship, 1888 (2 yrs. abroad); dir. Am. Sch. at Rome, 1894-96; m. Margaret Elizabeth Gage, Jan. 4, 1887. Architect to Isthmian Canal Commn., 1912; prof. architecture and dir. Sch. of Architecture, Columbia U., 1912-15. Mem. Lord & Hewlett, New York, N.Y. Died Jan. 19, 1922.

LORD, Bert, congressman; b. Broome County, N.Y.; s. James A. and Henrietta (Hawkins) L.; ed. Afton (N.Y.) High Sch. and Acad.; m. Lilian Kniskers. Formerly engaged in lumbering and mercantile business; now farming; supervisor Afton 1905-15; mem. N.Y. Assembly, 1915-22 and 1924-29; motor-vehicle commr. State of N.Y., 1921-23; mem. N.Y. Senate, 1929-35; mem. 74th and 75th Congresses (1935-39), 34th N.Y. District. Republican. Mason, Redman. Home: Afton, N.Y. Died May 24, 1939.

LORD, Chester Sanders, editor; b. Romulus, N.Y., Mar. 18, 1850; s. Rev. Edward and Mary J. (Sanders) L.; student Hamilton Coll., 1869-70, hon. A.M., 1894; LL.D., St. Lawrence, 1898, Hamilton, 1925; m. Katherine M. Bates, 1871 (died 1910); children—Chester (dec.), Edward Roy (dec.), Kenneth, Richard Sanders; m. 2d, Elizabeth S. Riggs, 1926 (died 1931). Associate editor of the Oswego (N.Y.) Advertiser, 1871-72; on staff New York Sun, 1872-1913, managing editor, 1880-1913. Regent Univ. of State of New York, 1897-1904, and, 1900—; chancellor U. of State of N.Y., 1921—. Home: Garden City, N.Y. Died Aug. 1, 1933.

LORD, Daniel Miner; b. Newton Corner, Mass., Sept. 29, 1844; s. Rev. Daniel Miner and Eliza Ann (Hardy) L.; bro. of Herbert Gardiner L.; ed. common schs.; m. Alice Barbee Tullis, Sept. 21, 1887. Was engaged in shipping business, New York, until close of Civil War; went to Chicago, 1868; entered newspaper business, 1870; sr. mem. Lord & Thomas until Feb. 1, 1904; officer or dir. in other corps. Home: Chicago, Ill. Died May 27, 1930.

LORD, Frederick Taylor, M.D.; b. Bangor, Me., Jan. 16, 1875; s. Samuel Veazie and Kate Eva (Taylor) L.; A.B., Harvard, 1897, M.D., 1900; m. Mabel Delano Clapp, Nov. 25, 1901; 1 dau., Mrs. Harry Butler. House officer, Mass. Gen. Hosp., 1900-1901; physician to out-patients, same, 1903, visiting phys., 1912-35, mem. bd. of consultation, 1935—; asst. in clin. medicine, 1905-09, instr., 1909-30, clinical prof. of medicine, 1930-35 (emeritus), Harvard Medical School. Mem. Am. Red Cross Commission to Serbia, 1917. Republican. Unitarian. Author: Diseases of the Bronchi, Lungs and Pleura, 1915, 25; Pneumonia, 1922, 29; Lobar Pneumonia and Serum Therapy (with Dr. Roderick Heffron), 1936, Pneumonia and Serum Therapy (with Dr. Roderick Heffron), 1938. Home: Boston, Mass. Died Nov. 4, 1941.

LORD, Henry, ship broker; b. Bangor, Me., May 7, 1847; s. Charles Edwin and Caroline Lydia (Weston) L.; ed. Bangor pub. schs. and Bucksport Sem.; m. Emma C. Saunders, Feb. 20, 1872 (dec.); children—Anne, Harry (dec.), Charles, Alice, Frederick (dec.). Ship brokerage and commn. business, Bangor, 1868—; firm of Henry Lord & Co., Henry and Edwin Lord, 1889—. Pres. Bangor Common Council, 1873-74; mem. sch. com. 5 yrs.; mem. Me. Ho. of Rep., 1877-78 (speaker, 1878), Senate, 1887-91 (pres. 1889-91). Pres. Bangor Bd. of Trade, 1881-94, Me. State Bd. of Trade, 1889-1903; trustee U. of Me., 1891-1908 (pres. bd. 1892-1908); pres. trustees Westbrook Sem., 5 yrs.; pres. Universalist State Conv. of Me. 3 yrs.; mem. bd. of mgrs. Home for Aged Women, Bangor, 1888—; commr. for Me. for Vessel Owners' and Captains' Nat. Assn., 6 yrs. Mem. Bangor Hist. Soc. (v.p. 1889-1906, pres. 1906—). Del. 5th Nat. Rivers and Harbors Congress, 1908, 6th Atlantic Deeper Waterways Conv., 1913. Republican. Deceased.

LORD, Henry Curwen, astronomer; b. Cincinnati, Apr. 17, 1866; s. Henry Clark and Eliza Burnet (Wright) L.; Ohio State U., 1884-87; B.S., U. of Wis., 1889; m. Edith L. Hudson, June 22, 1898. Asst. in mathematics and astronomy, 1891-94, asso. prof. astronomy, 1894-1900, prof., 1900—, dir. Emerson McMillin Obs., 1894—, Ohio State U. Fellow Royal Astron. Soc. Appointed instr., U.S. Army, Sch. of Mil. Aeronautics at Ohio State U., May 1917. Deceased.

LORD, Herbert Gardiner, univ. prof.; b. Boston, Mass., Mar. 29, 1849; s. Rev. Daniel Miner and Eliza Ann (Hardy) L.; A.B., Amherst, 1871, hon. A.M., 1900; grad. Union Theol. Sem., 1877; m. Mally Graham Coatsworth, Oct. 20, 1887; children—Herbert Gardiner, Mally Graham (Mrs. James Taylor Kemp), Lucy (Mrs. Brenton Welling), Thomas Coatsworth. Tutor Latin, Knox Coll., 1871-72; prin. high sch., Holliston, Mass., 1872-73; ordained Presbyterian ministry, 1878; pastor Ch. of the Redeemer, Buffalo, 1877-95; prof. philosophy, Sch. Pedagogy, Univ. of Buffalo, 1895-98; prin. Franklin Sch., Buffalo, 1899-1900; prof. philosophy, Columbia, 1900-21 (retired). Author: Psychology of Courage. Joint author: Essays Philosophical and Psychological in Honor of William James; Studies in the History of Ideas. Home: New York, N.Y. Died Mar. 12, 1930.

LORD, Herbert Mayhew, army officer; b. Rockland, Me., Dec. 6, 1859; s. Sabin and Abbie (Swett) L.; A.B. from Colby Coll., Me., 1884, A.M. from same coll., 1889, LL.D., 1920; LL.D., Tufts Coll., 1929; m. Annie Stuart Waldo, Sept. 9, 1885. Newspaper work, and served as clerk, ways and means com. of Ho. of Rep., Washington, D.C., until 1898; apptd. maj. add. p.-m. vols., May 17, 1898; hon. discharged, May 7, 1901; capt. p.-m., U.S.A., Feb. 5, 1901; promoted through grades to brig. gen. U.S.A., July 15, 1919; retired June 30, 1922. Apptd. asst. to Maj. Gen. Goethals, title dir. of finance, Oct. 1918; chief of finance, U.S.A., July 1, 1920; served as Army Liberty Loan officer during World War; dir. Bur. of the Budget July 1, 1922-May 31, 1929. Awarded D.S.M., "for exceptionally meritorious and conspicuous service" as asst. to q.-m. gen. and as dir. of finance. Republican. Christian Scientist. Home: Washington, D.C. Died June 2, 1930.

LORD, James Brown, architect; b. April 26, 1858; s. J. Cowper and Margaretta (Brown) L.; ed. St. Paul's School and Princeton; m. Miss Nicoll, June 1879. Designer and architect court house, New York, etc. Home: Tuxedo Park, N.Y. Died 1902.

LORD, J(ere) Williams, dermatologist; b. Portland, Me., Feb. 5, 1864; s. John D. and Jannett R. (Williams) L.; A.B., Johns Hopkins, 1884; M.D., U. of Pa., 1887; m. Evelyn Pope, June 8, 1898; children—Llewellyn Williams, Jannett Williams, Jere Williams. Apptd. clin. prof. dermatology, Johns Hopkins, 1898 (emeritus); dermatologist to Johns Hopkins Hosp. and Dispensary, 1889—. Home: Baltimore, Md. Died Apr. 23, 1933.

LORD, John King, coll. prof.; b. Cincinnati, O., Oct. 21, 1848; s. John King and Laura Esther (Smith) L.; A.B., Dartmouth, 1868, A.M., 1871, Ph.D., 1893; LL.D., Dartmouth, and U. of Me., 1908; m. Emma Fuller Pomeroy, Jan. 20, 1873; children—John King, Frederic Pomeroy, Laura Woolsey (Mrs. Robert Leighton Scales), Arthur Hardy. Taught Appleton Acad., New Ipswich, N.H., 1868-69; tutor Latin, 1869-72, asso. prof. Latin and rhetoric, 1872-80, Evans prof. oratory and belles lettres, 1880-82, asso. prof. Latin lang. and lit., 1882-92, Daniel Webster prof., 1892-1916, prof. emeritus, 1916—, acting pres., 1892-93, and acting pres. of the faculty, 1893-1909, trustee, 1917—, Dartmouth College. Editor: Cicero, Lælius, 1883, revised, 1897; Livy, books XXI, XXII, 1890, book I, 1896; Chase's History of Dartmouth College, 1891. Author: History of Dartmouth College, Vol. II, 1913; Atlas of the Geography and History of the Ancient World, 1902. Translator: Hertzberg's Geschichte der Römer im Alterthum (in History of All Nations), 1902. Home: Hanover, N.H. Died June 26, 1926.

LORD, John Prentiss, surgeon; b. Dixon, Ill., Apr. 17, 1860; s. John L. and Mary Louise (Warner) L.; M.D., Rush Med. Coll., Chicago, 1882; post-grad. study, New York Post-Grad. Coll., 1886; m. Minnie L. Swingley, Oct. 20, 1886; children—Frances Louise, Upton Prentiss. Practiced at Creston, Ill., 1882-86; settled at Omaha, 1886; surgery, exclusively, 1893—; prof. anatomy, 1892, prof. surgery, 1893-1913, Creighton Med. Coll.; prof. orthopedic surgery, Med. Dept. U. of Neb., 1913—; orthopedic surgeon to Clarkson U., Methodist and St. Catherine's hosps.; attending orthopedic surgeon, Lord Lister Hosp.; chief surgeon of Neb. Orthopedic Hosp.; cons. orthopedic surgeon Convalescing Home for Crippled Children; dist. surgeon I.C. Railroad; cons. surgeon of C.,R.I.&P. Railway. Pres. Omaha Midwest Clin. Assn., 1935. Fellow Am. Coll. Surgeons; mem. numerous professional societies. Dir. Y.M.C.A. Maj. M.C., U.S.A.; chief instr. mil. orthopedic surgery, Med. Officers Training Camp, Ft. Riley, Kan., 1918. Conglist. Home: Omaha, Neb. Died Mar. 3, 1940.

LORD, Livingston C., normal sch. pres.; b. Killingworth, Conn., Aug. 27, 1851; s. Benjamin and Antoinette (Case) L.; grad. State Normal Sch., New Britain, Conn., 1871; LL.D., U. of Ill., 1904; A.M., Harvard U., 1912; Dr. of Edn., Miami U., 1927; m. Mary E. Cook, 1874. Prin. Terryville (Conn.) High Sch., 1871-74, Winnebago City (Minn.) schs., 1874-78, Union Sch., Mankato, Minn., 1878-79; supt. schs., St. Peter, Minn., 1879-88; pres. State Normal Sch., Moorhead, Minn., 1888-99; pres. Eastern Ill. State Normal Sch., Charleston, Ill., 1899—. Conglist. Republican. Lecturer. Home: Charleston, Ill. Died May 15, 1933.

LORD, Nathaniel Wright, prof. metallurgy and mineralogy Ohio State Univ.; b. Cincinnati, Dec. 26, 1854; s. Henry C. and Eliza (Wright) L.; grad. Columbia Coll. School of Mines, E.M., 1876; chemist and engr. Monte Grande Gold Mining Co., 1879; chemist, 1883-88, now cons. chemist, Ohio Geol. Survey; is chemist in charge analysis of fertilizers for Ohio State Bd. of Agriculture. Author: Notes on Metallurgical Analysis. Wrote: Iron Manufacture of Ohio, vol. 5, and Natural and Artificial Cements, vol. 6, Ohio Geol. Survey. Dir. chem. laboratory, U.S. Fuel Testing Plant, St. Louis Expn., 1904. Home: Columbus, O. Died 1911.

LORD, Rivington David, clergyman; b. Hillsdale, Mich., Aug. 13, 1858; s. Rev. David H. (M.D.) and Annette (Merrill) L.; A.B., Hillsdale (Mich.) Coll., 1877, A.M., 1880, LL.D., same college, 1934; graduate Union Theol. Seminary, 1883, post-grad. studies, 1883-84; D.D., Hillsdale, 1895; D.D., Bates College, Lewiston, Me., 1933; m. Etta Lillian Chesley, Jan. 27, 1885. Ordained Free Bapt. ministry, by Central Assn. of N.Y., Jan. 18, 1885; stated supply, and pastor First Ch., Brooklyn, 1884—. Pres. Gen. Conf. of Free Baptists, 1898-1904, Gen. Conf. Bd. of Free Baptists, 1910—; mem. bd. mgrs. Am. Bapt. Home Mission Soc. (chmn. bd. 1926-32; pres. 1932—); rec. sec. Federal Council of Chs. of Christ in America. Pres. Gen. Alumni Assn. of Union Theol. Sem., 1933-34. Home: Brooklyn, N.Y. Died July 18, 1938.

LORD, William Paine, governor; b. Dover, Del., 1838; A.B., Fairfield Coll., N.Y., 1860; LL.B., Albany Law Sch., 1866, Capt. 1st Del. Inf., Sept. 8, 1862; maj., Apr. 18, 1864; hon. mustered out of vol. service, June 26, 1865; 2d lt. 2d U.S. Arty., Sept. 4, 1867; resigned, May 28, 1868. Practiced law at Salem, Ore.; was city atty.; mem. Ore. Senate, 1878; justice Supreme Ct., 14 yrs.; gov. of Ore., 1895-99; E.E. and M.P. to Argentine Republic, 1899-1903. Republican. Home: Salem, Ore. Died 1911.

LORD, William Sinclair, author; b. Sycamore, Ill., Aug. 24, 1863; s. Frederic A. (M.D.) and Emily (Bull) L.; public sch. edn. In mercantile business, 1886—. Author: Verses, 1882; Beads of Morning, 1888; Blue and Gold, 1895; Jingle and Jangle, 1898; This Is for You, 1902; The Rockaby Book, 1905. Editor: Best Short Poems Nineteenth Century, 1899. Home: Evanston, Ill. Died Sept. 24, 1925.

LORD, William Wilberforce, P.E. clergyman; b. Madison Co., N.Y., Oct. 28, 1819; at (defunct) Western N.Y. Univ.; grad. Princeton Theol. Sem., 1845; Boudinot fellow Princeton (D.D., Univ. of Ala.); was tutor at Amherst, 1847; ordered deacon P.E. Ch., 1848; ordained priest, 1850; rector in the South and Southwest; chaplain in C.S.A. during Civil War. Author: (poems) Christ in Hades; Andre: a Tragedy. Home: Cooperstown, N.Y. Died 1907.

LORE, Charles Brown, judge; b. Odessa, Del., Mar. 16, 1831; s. Eldad C. and Priscilla (Henderson) L.; A.B., Dickinson Coll., June 1852 (LL.D., 1894; LL.D., Delaware Coll., 1896); m. Rebecca A. Bates, July 7, 1862. Admitted to bar, 1861; practiced law, Wilmington, Del., until 1893; attorney general of Delaware, 1869-74; presidential elector, 1880, 92; mem. 48th and 49th Congresses (1883-87); chief justice Supreme Ct., Del., 1893-1909. Democrat. Retired. Pres. bd. trustees Delaware College. Home: Wilmington, Del. Died 1911.

LOREE, Leonor Fresnel, ry. pres.; b. Fulton City, Ill., Apr. 23, 1858; B.S., Rutgers, 1877, M.S., C.E., LL.D.; Dr. Engring., Rensselaer Polytech. Inst., 1933. Entered ry. service, 1877, as asst. in engr. corps Pa. R.R.; transitman, engr. corps U.S.A., 1879-81; leveler, transitman and topographer, preliminary survey, Mexican Nat. Ry., from Rio Grande River to Saltillo, Mex., 1881-83; with Pa. R.R. Co. as asst. engr. Chicago div. 1883-84, engr. maintenance of way, I.&V. div., 1884-86, engr. m. of w., Chicago div., 1886-88, engr. m. of w., Cleveland and Pittsburgh div., 1888-89, supt. Cleveland & Pittsburgh div., 1889-96, gen. mgr., 1896-1901, 4th v.p. Pa. Lines W. of Pittsburgh, Jan. 1-June 1, 1901; pres. Baltimore & Ohio R.R. Co., June 1, 1901-Jan. 1, 1904; pres. Rock Island Co. of N.J. and chmn. exec. com. C.,R.I.&P. Ry. Co. and S.L.&S.F. Ry. Co., Jan. 1-Oct. 4, 1904; chmn. exec. com., 1906-36, chmn. bd. dirs., 1909-36, Kansas City Southern Ry. Co.; pres., chmn. exec. com. and mem. bd. mgrs. Del. & Hudson Co., 1907-38; dir. various corps. Trustee Rutgers Univ., Brackett mem. of Princeton Engring. Assn.; trustee and 1st v.p. N.Y. Geneal. and Biog. Soc.; v.p. Chamber Commerce of State of N.Y., 1922-28, pres., 1928-30, mem. exec. com., 1931—; mem. Royal Commn. on Rys. and Transportation (Can.). Judge of transportation, Chicago Expn., 1893. Apptd. mem. Nat. War Labor Bd., Washington, D.C., Apr. 1918. Home: West Orange, N.J. Died Sept. 6, 1940.

LORENZ, Richard, artist; b. Voigtstaedt, Germany, Feb. 9, 1858; s. Carl and Emilie (Lorenz) L.; pupil of Brendel, Thedy and Hagen, 1874-86; Carl Alexander prize, 1884; unmarried. Was awarded Osborne prize for best genre painting of Am. subject, 1906. Lutheran. Mem. Society Western Artists. Home: Milwaukee, Wis. Died Aug. 3, 1915.

LORIGAN, William George, judge; b. Melbourne, Australia, Feb. 12, 1855; s. Bartholomew and Mary (Moran) L.; brought to U.S., 1860; A.B., Santa Clara Coll., Santa Clara County, Calif. (LL.D.); m. Annie F. Burgis, Feb. 14, 1880. Admitted to Calif. bar, 1879; practiced in San Jose, Calif.; judge Superior Court, Santa Clara Co., 1890-1903; asso. justice Supreme Court of Calif., 1903—. Republican. Catholic. Mem. Elks, Foresters of America. Home: San Jose, Calif. Deceased.

LORILLARD, Pierre, capitalist; b. New York, Jan. 28, 1860; s. Pierre and Emily (Taylor) L.; m. Caroline J. Hamilton, 1881. Long connected with P. Lorillard Co., tobacco. Pres. Tuxedo Park Assn. Home: Tuxedo Park, N.Y. Died Aug. 6, 1940.

LORIMER, George Claude, clergyman; b. Edinburgh, Scotland, 1838; came to U.S., 1856; ed. Georgetown Coll., Ky.; ordained to Bapt. ministry, 1859. Pastor successively of chs. at Harrodsburg, Paducah and Louisville, Ky.; Boston and Chicago; lately at Boston as pastor of Tremont Temple; now pastor Madison Av. Bapt. Ch., New York. Author: Isms Old and New; The Great Conflict; Jesus the World's Saviour; Studies in Social Life; Christianity and the Social State; Christianity in the XIX Century; Messages of Today to the Men of Tomorrow; The Master of Millions, 1903. Died 1904.

LORIMER, George Horace, editor; b. Louisville, Ky., Oct. 6, 1868; s. Rev. Dr. George C. and Belle (Burford) L.; ed. Mosely High Sch., Chicago; college course at Colby and Yale; Litt.D., LL.D.; m. Alma V., d. Judge Alfred Ennis, of Chicago, June 6, 1892. Editor in chief Saturday Evening Post, 1899—; v.p. Curtis Pub. Co., 1927-32; pres. until 1934, chmn., 1934—. Decorated Chevalier de la Légion d'Honneur; Comdr. Order of Crown of Italy. Mem. Com. on Conservation and Administration of Pub. Domain. Aide to gov. of Ky., rank of colonel, 1923. Author: Letters from a Self-Made Merchant to His Son., 1902; Old Gorgon Graham, 1904; The False Gods, 1906; Jack Spurlock—Prodigal, 1908. Home: Wyncote, Pa. Died Oct. 22, 1937.

LORIMER, William, senator; b. Manchester, Eng., Apr. 27, 1861; s. William and Sarah (Harley) L.; at age of 5 came with parents to U.S., and in 1870 to Chicago; m. Susan Mooney, July 1884. At 10 he became sign-painter's apprentice; later worked in packing houses and for a street railroad co.; entered real estate business, 1886, and later mem. of Murphy & Lorimer in bldg. and brick mfg. business; mem. Lorimer & Gallagher, contractors, 1900—; pres. Federal Improvement Co., 1907—. Supt. water-main extensions and later supt. water dept., City of Chicago, 1887-93; defeated for clerk Superior Ct., 1892; mem. 54th to 56th Congresses (1895-1901), 2d Ill. Dist. and 58th to 61st Congresses (1903-11), 6th Dist.; mem. coms. on Agr. and Rivers and Harbors; elected U.S. senator, May 26, 1909, for term 1909-15; resigned from Ho. of Rep. and took seat in U.S. Senate, June 18, 1909. Republican. Validity of election challenged in Senate, Jan. 9, 1911; by vote of 46 to 40, Mar. 1, 1911, challenge was not sustained; Senate decided to reopen investigation June 1, 1911; majority of Com. reported election not brought about by corrupt means; by vote of 55 to 28, July 14, 1912, Senate sustained a resolution declaring that corrupt methods and practices had been employed in the election and that his election was invalid. Was pres. La Salle St. Trust & Savings Bank, 1910-15. Home: Chicago, Ill. Died Sept. 13, 1934.

LORIMER, Wright, actor; b. near town of Athol, Mass., Mar. 10, 1874; entered Colgate U.; went to Eng. and took spl. course in psychology and English literature, Oxford U. After return to U.S. was offered professorship in English lit. and psychology in several univs., but decided to follow strongest inclinations and became a mem. of Dearborn Stock Co. in Chicago as utility man; has continued on the stage and is now at head of own co. in own production, "The Shepherd King," under direction of William A. Brady. Died 1911.

LORING, Albert Carpenter, flour mfr.; s. of Charles M. and Emily S. (Crosman) L.; ed. U. of Minn.; m. Adelaide Ingalls. Has been identified from early youth with milling interests, his father having been one of the pioneer merchant millers of Minneapolis. Now pres. Pillsbury Flour Mills Co. Mem. Chamber of Commerce. Home: Mound, Minn. Died Dec. 11, 1932.

LORING, Augustus Peabody, trustee, lawyer; b. Boston, Mass., Dec. 7, 1856; s. Caleb William and Elizabeth S. (Peabody) L.; A.B., Harvard, 1878, LL.B., 1881; m. Ellen Gardner, June 3, 1884; children—Augustus P., Caleb, Ellen Gardner Vaughan (dec.). Trustee Albany Trust, Beacon Chambers Trust, Bedford Trust. Mem. Mass. Senate 2 terms. Regent Smithsonian Institution. Republican. Unitarian. Author: A Trustee's Handbook, 1898. Home: Beverly, Mass. Died Mar. 18, 1938.

LORING, Charles Greely, dir. Museum of Fine Arts, Boston; b. Boston; s. Charles G. L.; grad. Harvard, 1848 (A.M.); m. Mary Hopkins. Commissioned capt., Dec. 1861; lt. col. and asst. insp. gen. 9th army corps, July 22, 1862; resigned July 1865; trustee Museum Fine Arts, 1873, exec. officer, 1876—. Fellow Am. Acad. Arts and Sciences. Breveted maj. gen. U.S. Volunteers. Died 1902.

LORING, Charles Harding, chief engr. U.S.N., with rank of capt.; b. Boston, Dec. 26, 1828; s. William Price and Eliza (Harding) L.; ed. Boston, 1833-41; entered U.S.N. as engr. officer, Feb. 26, 1851; m. Ruth D. Malbon (dec.). Was engr. of the fleet, N. Atlantic squadron, in early yrs. of Civil War, taking part in capture of Fts. Hatteras and Clark, and in battle between the Monitor and Merrimac, March 8 and 9, 1862. Apptd. engr.-in-chief of navy in 1884; retired for age, 1890. Died 1907.

LORING, William Caleb, judge; b. Beverly, Mass., Aug. 24, 1851; s. Caleb William and Elizabeth Smith (Peabody) L.; A.B., Harvard, 1872, LL.B., 1874, A.M., 1875, LL.D., 1901; m. Susan Mason Lawrence, Sept. 25, 1883. Asst. atty. gen. Mass., 1875-78; gen. solicitor and later gen. counsel N.Y.&N.E. R.R., 1882-86; mem. Ropes, Gray & Loring, 1878-99; asso. justice Supreme Jud. Court of Mass., 1899-1919 (resigned); lecturer on practice of law, Harvard

Law Sch., 1920-29. Pres. Mass. Humane Soc., 1921—; pres. trustees Am. Sch. of Classical Studies (Athens), 1911-28. Knight Comdr. Royal Order of George I (Greece), 1922. Fellow Am. Acad. Arts and Sciences. Vestryman Trinity Ch., Boston. Home: Boston, Mass. Died Sept. 18, 1930.

LOSEY, Frederick Douglas, coll. prof.; b. Conesus, N.Y., Nov. 28, 1866; s. Jesse Bradford and Elizabeth Frances (Knapp) L.; A.B., U. of Rochester, 1891; B.E., Nat. Sch. of Oratory, 1893; grad. student in English, Harvard, 1898-1900, A.M., 1899; Litt.D. from Syracuse U., 1927; m. Marie L. Hale, May 25, 1890. Pub. reader, 1889—; instr. English, 1900-01, asso. prof. English, 1901-04, head of dept. of rhetoric and pub. speaking, 1904-06, Syracuse U.; prof. rhetoric and pub. speaking, U. of Ala., 1907-16; lecturer, Columbia, summers, 1916, 17. Lecturer, Brooklyn Inst., 1918-19. Pub. lectures and recitals, Shakespearean and modern drama; pub. speaker on lit., ednl. and social topics. Ednl. lecturer Y.M.C.A. and Army Ednl. Corps with A.E.F., in France and Germany, 1919. Methodist. Editor The "Losey" Shakespeare, 1926. Died June 5, 1932.

LOTHIAN, Marquess of (Philip Henry Kerr), British ambassador to U.S.; b. London, England, Apr. 18, 1882 (11th Marquess of Lothian); s. Maj. Gen. Lord Ralph and Lady Anne (Howard) Kerr; ed. The Oratory Sch., Birmingham, and New Coll., Oxford U.; unmarried. Asst. sec. Inter-Colonial Council of Transvaal and Orange River Colony and also of Ry. Com. of Central South African Rys., 1905-08; sec. Transvaal Indigency Commn., 1907-08; editor of The State, South Africa, 1908-09; editor The Round Table, 1910-16; sec. to prime minister, 1916-21; dir. United Newspapers, Ltd., 1921-22; sec. Rhodes Trust, 1925-39; chancellor, Duchy of Lancaster, 1931; parliamentary under-sec., India Office, 1931-32; chmn. Indian Franchise Com., 1932; Brit. ambassador to U.S., Aug. 30, 1939—; privy councillor, 1939. Decorated Companion of Honor. Liberal in politics. Christian Scientist. Home: Aylsham, Norfolk, England; Monteviot, Ancrum, Roxburghshire, England. Died Dec. 12, 1940.

LOTHROP, Amy, author. See Anna Bartlett Warner.

LOTHROP, Harriett Mulford ("Margaret Sidney"), author; b. New Haven, Conn.; d. Sidney M. and Harriett (Mulford) Stone; m. Daniel Lothrop (founder pub. house D. Lothrop & Co.), Oct. 4, 1881. Founder, nat. pres., 1895-1901, hon. pres. for life, 1901—, Nat. Soc. Children Am. Revolution. Author: Five Little Peppers and How They Grew; Five Little Peppers Midway; Five Little Peppers Grown Up; Phronsie Pepper; Stories Polly Pepper Told; Adventures of Joel Pepper, Who Told It to Me; Little Paul; Rob and the Frisbie School; Two Modern Little Princes; The Gingham Bag; Our Town; Five Little Peppers Abroad; Half Year at Bronckton; How They Went to Europe; Hester and Other New England Stories; An Adirondack Cabin; Whittier with the Children; Dilly and the Captain; Old Concord, Her Highways and Byways; A Little Maid of Concord Town; The Judge's Cave, a Romance of the Days of the Regicides, 1661; Sally; Five Little Peppers at School; Five Little Peppers and Their Friends; Ben Pepper; Two Little Friends in Norway; Five Little Peppers in the Little Brown House, 1907; A Little Maid of Boston Town, 1910; Our Davie Pepper, 1916. Home: Concord, Mass. Died Aug. 2, 1924.

LOTHROP, Howard Augustus, surgeon; b. Sharon, Mass., Dec. 31, 1864; s. Horace A. and Sarah Gorham (Swain) L.; A.B., Harvard, 1887, A.M., 1890, M.D., 1891; unmarried. House officer Mass. Gen. Hosp., 1890-92; surgeon in chief Boston City Hosp.; consulting surgeon Symmes Arlington Hosp., City Hosp.; asst. in anatomy, 1896-1901, 1903, 08, asst. prof. surgery, 1908—, Harvard Med. School. Fellow Am. Coll. Surgeons. Home: Boston, Mass. Died June 4, 1928.

LOTHROP, Marcus Thompson, metallurgist, engineer; b. Buffalo, N.Y., Oct. 2, 1884; s. Benjamin L. (M.D.) and Maria (Thompson) L.; B.Sc., U. of Mich., 1906; m. Margaret Frank, June 15, 1921; children (adopted)—Margaret, John Henry. Chief metallurgist and asst. chief engr. H. H. Franklin Mfg. Co., Syracuse, N.Y., 1906-07; metallurgist and chief mech. engr. Halcomb Steel Co., Syracuse, 1907-11; with Timken Roller Bearing Co., mfrs. tapered roller anti-friction bearings, Canton, O., 1911—; pres. Timken Steel & Tube Co.; pioneer in mfr. of tapered roller bearings. Trustee Aultman Hosp., Canton. Republican. Episcopalian. Home: Hills and Dales (Canton), O. Died May 23, 1935.

LOTHROP, Thornton Kirkland, lawyer; b. Dover, N.H., June 3, 1830; s. Samuel Kirkland and Mary (Buckminster) L.; A.B., Harvard, 1849, A.M., LL.B., 1853; m. Anne M., d. Samuel Hooper, of Boston, Apr. 30, 1866. Admitted to bar, 1853, and entered practice at Boston. Mem. Corp. Mass. Inst. Tech.; trustee Boston Athenæum, Mus. Fine Arts. Author: Life of William H. Seward (Am. statesman series). Died Nov. 2, 1913.

"LOTTA," (Charlotte Crabtree), actress; b. New York, 1847. First stage appearance when 6, at Petaluma, Calif.; 10 yrs. later made her New York début at Nibio's Garden, followed by a Western starring tour with her parents. Played in Eng. and U.S. for 30 yrs.; as the Marchioness in "Little Nell," and in "Firefly," "Topsy," "Musette," "Bob," "Nitouche," "The Little Detective," etc., met with great success, and retired with a fortune. Never married. Has lived in New York for many years. Died Sept. 23, 1924.

LOTTE, Edward F. L., silk dyer; b. Phila., Pa., Sept. 18, 1868; s. Edward A. and Pauline (Gerbon) L.; student Temple U., Phila., 2 yrs.; grad. Pa. Mus. and Sch. Industrial Art, 1892; m. Mary Viola Collom, Apr. 19, 1893; children—Charles Walter, Marguerite Teresa. Pres. Lotte & Mazeres Co., skein silk dyers, Phila. and Allentown, 1895-1903; pres. Lotte Bros. Co., Allentown, 1903-09; gen. mgr. and dir. Nat. Silk Dyeing Co., 1909—; dir. U.S. Testing Co., U.S. Trust Co. (Paterson, N.J.). Apptd., 1920, by Dept. of State, as mem. dyes and chemicals advisory com. of the Textile Alliance, Inc., representing silk industries of U.S. Trustee Bucknell U. (Lewisburg, Pa.), Y.M.C.A. (Paterson); mem. bd. of corporators, The Peddie School, Hightstown, N.J. Republican. Baptist. Home: Paterson, N.J. Died Sept. 24, 1931.

LOTTRIDGE, Silas A., naturalist, author; b. Columbus, N.Y., Oct. 17, 1863; s. Henry and Bessie (Fenton) L.; ed. New Berlin, N.Y., Union Sch., and St. Lawrence U., Canton, N.Y.; m. Alice D. Myers, Aug. 25, 1886. Author: Animal Snapshots, 1905; Familiar Wild Animals, 1906. Home: East Orange, N.J. Died Feb. 12, 1940.

LOUD, Eugene Francis, congressman, merchant; b. Abington, Mass., March 12, 1847; went to sea and to Calif. at age of 13; served as pvt. in Union cav., 1862, until close of war; returned to Calif. Studied law; was in the customs service; afterward followed mercantile business. Mem. Calif. legislature, 1884; cashier and tax collector of city and co. of San Francisco; mem. Congress, 5th Calif. dist., 1891-1903; chmn. com. on postoffices and post roads. Republican. Home: San Francisco. Died 1908.

LOUD, Frank Herbert, astronomer; b. Weymouth, Mass., Jan. 26, 1852; s. Francis Eliot and Mary Tolman (Capen) L.; descendant of Elder William Brewster of the Mayflower; A.B., Amherst, 1873; student Clark U.; A.M., Harvard, 1899; Ph.D., Haverford, 1900; m. Mabel Wiley, July 13, 1882 (died 1923); children—Francis Martin, Mrs. Mary Thorne, Paul D. (dec.), Harriet, Norman Wiley, William Brewster. Walker instr. mathematics, Amherst, 1873-76; prof. mathematics and astronomy, Colorado Coll., 1877-1907; retired on Carnegie foundation, 1907. In charge of sta. for stellar photography, 1885-1923. Fellow British Esperanto Assn.; sec. Western Assn. for Stellar Photography. Republican. Conglist. Author: An Elementary Geometry on the Analytic Plan, 1878. Home: Colorado Springs, Colo. Died Mar. 2, 1927.

LOUD, George Alvin, congressman; b. Bracebridge, O., June 18, 1852; s. Henry M. and Villetta (Kile) L.; grad. Ann Arbor High Sch., 1869; m. Elizabeth Glennie, Dec. 5, 1888. Engaged as lumberman ever since leaving sch.; mem. H. M. Loud's Sons Co.; v.p. and gen. mgr. Au Sable & Northwestern R.R., 1898. Paymaster U.S. revenue cutter McCullough, when it participated in battle of Manila Bay. Mem. 58th to 62d Congresses (1903-13), and 64th Congress (1915-17), 10th Mich. Dist. Republican. Home: Bay City, Mich. Deceased.

LOUD, Henry Martin, merchant; b. Westhampton, Mass., Dec. 11, 1824; s. Austin and Mehetable (Bartlett) L.; attended school 3 months in year, and studied nights while working days on his father's farm; licensed to exhort at 18, and later to preach in M.E. Ch.; joined Erie Conf. at 26; filled pastorates at Hartford and Braceville, O.; attended Methodist Theol. School, Concord, N.H., 1853-56; resumed ministry, 1856-65, filling pastorates at Watertown, Lowell, Fitchburg and Medford, Mass.; then took supernumerary relation; became lumberman at Au Sable, Mich., where he established an extensive business, of which he was the head for over 30 yrs., until 1898; m. Vilitta J. Kile, May 25, 1845 (died 1880); m. 2d, Mrs. Nancy P. Miller, Nov. 29, 1883. Has been mayor of Au Sable; was pres. Bay View Assembly, where he built Loud Hall; was trustee Albion Coll.; endowed there a chair in history; also endowed a lectureship with the Wesleyan Guild at Ann Arbor, for the students of Mich. Univ. Was largely interested in fruit raising in Southern Calif.; retired, 1898. Home: Au Sable, Mich. Died 1905.

LOUDEN, William, inventor, mfr.; b. Cassville, Pa., Oct. 16, 1841; s. Andrew and Jane (Speer) L.; of Scotch-Irish descent; settled in Fairfield, Ia., 1842; ed. pub. schs. and Axline U. (now defunct), Fairfield, Ia.; m. Mary Jane Pattison, Jan. 2, 1868; children—Helen Craig (dec.), Agnes May, Arthur Claire, Robert Bruce. Founder Louden Machinery Co., Fairfield, with branches in various parts of U.S. and Can., and v.p. from incorporation, 1892; pres. Ia. Malleable Iron Co., Tribune Printing Co., Fairfield; v.p. Thoma & Son, Inc., Fairfield; dir. Perry-Fry Co., St. Paul, Minn.; patentee farm and factories devices; awarded 118 patents, 1866—. Pres. Fairfield Chautauqua Assn. Home: Fairfield, Ia. Died Nov. 5, 1931.

LOUDENSLAGER, Henry Clay, congressman; b. Mauricetown, N.J., May 22, 1852; s. S. Paul and Sarah L.; ed. common schs.; m. Kate L. Salisbury, Dec. 9, 1872. In produce commn. business, Phila., 1872-82. Co. clerk, Gloucester Co., N.J., 1882-92; mem. 53d to 61st Congresses (1893-1911), 1st N. J. Dist.; chmn. Com. on Pensions, 55th to 61st Congresses; mem. Com. Naval Affairs. Sec. Rep. Nat. Congressional Com.; sec. Rep. Caucus, Ho. of Rep. Mason. Home: Paulsboro, N.J. Died 1911.

LOUDERBACK, Harold, judge; b. San Francisco, Jan. 30, 1881; s. Davis and Frances Caroline (Smith) L.; A.B., U. of Nev., 1905; LL.B., Harvard, 1908. Admitted to Mass. and Calif. bars, 1908, and began practice with Mastick & Partridge, San Francisco; gen. practice alone, 1911-17, 1919-21; judge Superior Court, City and County of San Francisco, 1921-28; judge U.S. Dist. Court, Northern Dist. of Calif., 1928—. Served as 1st lt., C.A.C., U.S.A., 1917-18, capt., 1918. Republican. Mason, Odd Fellow. Home: Berkeley, Calif. Died Dec. 11, 1941.

LOUDERBACK, William Johnson; b. Hamilton, N.Y., Sept. 16, 1864; s. Alfred and Sarah (Wilson) L.; grad. Episcopal Acad., Phila., 1880; m. Jane Darragh, 1897; children—William Johnson, Elizabeth Darragh, Sarah, Jane. Clerk for Western Union Telegraph Co., Chicago, 1880-81; with Central Union Telegraph Co., until 1885; with Pullman Co., 1886-87; cashier Chicago, Santa Fe & Calif. R.R., until 1889; afterward with Norman Williams, in charge of estates; became mem. King, Hodenpyl & Co., and their successors, John C. King & Co., then spl. partner of Babcock, Rushton & Louderback, until 1909; now pres. Miami Corp. Treas. of The John Crerar Library. Republican. Episcopalian. Home: Highland Park, Ill. Died Nov. 27, 1926.

LOUGEE, Willis Eugene, philanthropic worker; b. Chelsea, Vt., May 2, 1857; s. John C. and Marcia (Hood) L.; ed. Gilmanton (N.H.) Acad.; hon. A.M., Bates Coll., Me., 1911; m. Ella Florence Reed, Mar. 17, 1885 (died 1921); m. 2d, Annie C. Howland, Apr. 19, 1922. Was sec. Y.M.C.A., New Bedford, Mass., 1886-95, pres., 1926-29; sec. Internat. Com. Y.M.C.A., 1895-1907; asso. sec., 1907-10, treas., 1910-13, Congl. Home Missionary Soc. Treas. and chmn. finance com. N.Y. Christian Home for Intemperate Men; trustee Jerry McAulay Mission; sec. and trustee Madura Coll.; mem. exec. com. Presbyn. Union; organizer and sec. Grenfell Assn. America. During past 10 years has raised about $5,000,000 for various religious and philanthropic socs. Eastern rep., dir. and trustee, Billings (Mont.) Poly. Inst.; elected pres., same, 1923, hon. pres. for life, 1925. Home: New Bedford, Mass. Died Nov. 3, 1935.

LOUNSBURY, George Edward, gov. of Conn.; b. Poundridge, N.Y., May 7, 1838; s. Nathan and Delia (Scofield) L.; removed to Ridgefield, Conn., when a few months old; grad. Yale, 1863, Berkeley Divinity Sch., Conn., 1866; m. Frances J. Whedon, Nov. 29, 1894. State senator, Conn., 1894-98; gov. Conn., 1899-1901. Republican. Home: Ridgefield, Conn. Died 1904.

LOUNSBURY, Phineas Chapman, governor; b. Ridgefield, Conn., Jan. 10, 1844; s. Nathan and Delia A. (Scofield) L.; acad. edn.; (LL.D., Wesleyan U.); m. Jane Wright, June 12, 1867. Mem. Conn. Ho. of Rep., 1874; gov. of Conn., 1887-89; v.p. Preferred Accident Ins. Co. of New York, Atwood Fire Ins. Co.; treas. Worcester Salt Co. Served in 17th Conn. Inf., Civil War. Republican. Methodist. Home: Ridgefield, Conn. Died June 22, 1925.

LOUNSBURY, Ralph Reed, lawyer, coll. prof.; b. Meriden, Conn., Nov. 3, 1871; s. Cooke and Isabella (Spalding) L.; A.B., Yale, 1894; LL.B., Chicago-Kent Coll. of Law, 1900; m. Helen Beeks, Oct. 15, 1902; children—Richard Cooke, James Breckinridge. State editor Hartford Courant, 1894; asso. editor Bridgeport Standard, 1895-97; news editor Chicago Daily News, 1897; admitted to Ill. bar, 1900; practiced at Chicago, 1900-18, New York, 1918-30; former mem. Lounsbury, Ely & Fain; former corp. officer and counsel, also counsel several nat. trade orgns.; prof. govt. and polit. science and dir. Inst. of Statesmanship, Rollins Coll., Winter Park, Fla., 1930—. Rep. speaker, nat. and state campaigns, 1896—; mem. Rep. County Com., Westchester Co., N.Y., 1922-30; mem. Williamstown (Mass.) Inst. Politics, 1925, 26, and of Inst. Pub. Affairs, U. of Va., 1929, 31. Lecturer. Conglist. Home: North Tarrytown, N.Y. Died Oct. 16, 1933.

LOUNSBURY, Thomas Raynesford, univ. prof.; b. Ovid, N.Y., Jan. 1, 1838; s. Rev. Thomas and Mary Janette (Woodward) L.; A.B., Yale, 1859; A.M., 1877; (LL.D., Yale, 1892, Harvard, 1893, Aberdeen, 1906; L.H.D., Lafayette Coll., 1895, Princeton, 1896); m. Jennie D. Folwell. Engaged on American Cyclopædia, 1860-62; 1st lt. 126th N.Y. Vols., 1862-65; instr. English, 1870-71, prof. English lang. and lit., 1871—, librarian Sheffield Scientific Sch., 1873-1906, emeritus prof., 1906, Yale. Edited Chaucer's Parliament of Foules, 1877. Mem. Am. Acad. Arts and Letters. Author: History of the English Language, 1879, 1894; Life of James Fenimore Cooper, 1882; Studies in Chaucer (3 vols.),

1891; Shakespeare as a Dramatic Artist, 1901; Shakespeare and Voltaire, 1902; The Standard of Usage in English, 1908; English Spelling and Spelling Reform, 1909. Edited complete writings of Charles Dudley Warner, with biographical sketch, 1904; Tab Book of American Verse, 1912. Died Apr. 9, 1915.

LOURIE, David A., lawyer; b. Lithuania, June 23, 1878; s. Haskell and Rebecca (Port) L.; was brought to U.S. in childhood; grad. English High Sch., Boston, 1895; LL.B. cum laude, Boston U., 1899; m. Annie Florence Richmond, June 24, 1902; children—George B., Ruth L., Joseph Richmond, Hazel Esther. Began practice, 1899; apptd. asso. justice Municipal Court, Boston, Aug. 1922; asso. justice, by apptmt., of Superior Court of Mass., Oct. 1924—. Trustee Blackstone Savings Bank. Hon. pres. Home for Jewish Children; hon. dir. Hebrew Free Loan Assn. of Boston, Jewish Consumptives Relief Soc. of Denver; mem. bd. mgrs. Federated Jewish Charities of Boston (life); mem. Am. Jewish Com.; dir. Beth Israel Hosp.; mem. exec. com. United Synagogue of America. Hon. pres. N.E. Zionist Region; v.p. Boston Bur. Jewish Education; mem. advisory council Boston U. Law School. Home: Boston, Mass. Deceased.

LOVE, Alfred Henry, merchant; b. Phila., Sept. 7, 1830; s. William H. and Rachel (Evans) L.; A.B., Central High Sch., Phila., 1847; m. Susan Henry Brown, Jan. 13, 1853. Package woolen commn. mcht., Phila., 1853—; sr. mem. A. H. Love & Co. Editor Bond of Peace, The Voice of Peace, The Peacemaker, and Court of Arbitration, 1866—; co-editor and late editor Prison Journal. An organizer, 1866, and from then pres. Universal Peace Union; organized, and was pres., and hon. pres., 1875—, Am. Lit. Union; v.p. Pa. Abolition Soc.; patron Internat. Council of Women; official visitor of prisons 43 yrs. Home: Philadelphia, Pa. Died June 29, 1913.

LOVE, Don Lathrop, mayor; b. Janesville, Wis., Mar. 7, 1863; s. Horace and Gratia Ann (Ashton) L.; B.A., State Univ. of Ia., 1886; m. Julia Larrabee, Aug. 20, 1890. Practiced law in Lincoln, Neb., 1888-1909; since given attention to politics and financial matters; treas. Lincoln Joint Stock Land Bank. Acting county judge, 1896-97; pres. Liberty Life Ins. Co. of Lincoln; pres. Board of Edn., Lincoln, 1907-08; mayor of Lincoln, 1909, 10; mem. and treas. Rep. State Com., Neb., 1912; chmn. Draft Bd., Lincoln, during the war; again mayor of Lincoln, 1929-32. Pres. Neb. Art. Assn., 1910—, Neb. State Hist. Soc., 1919—. Unitarian. Mason. Home: Lincoln, Neb. Died Sept. 12, 1940.

LOVE, Frank Samuel, coal operator; b. Tarentum, Pa., Feb. 2, 1874; s. George H. and Anna B. (Logan) L.; A.B., Washington & Jefferson Coll., 1895; m. Rebecca Ludwick, Apr. 4, 1916; 1 dau., Rebecca Frances. In coal business, 1902—; pres. Union Collieries Co., Pittsburgh, 1922—; pres. First Nat. Bank (Russellton, Pa.); v.p. Bessemer Coal & Coke Co.; organizer and formerly dir. Union Nat. Bank. Trustee Washington and Jefferson Coll. Presbyn. Home: Pittsburgh, Pa. Died Sept. 26, 1933.

LOVE, Robertus, writer; b. nr. Irondale, Mo., Jan. 6, 1867; s. Thomas Shelby (D.D.) and Nancy Eveline (McFarland) L.; A.B., McCune Coll., Louisiana, Mo., 1884; Lincoln (Ill.) Univ., 1885-86; m. Catherine Heck, Dec. 31, 1901 (died Mar. 30, 1926). Became local editor Louisiana (Mo.) Press, 1886; city editor Wichita (Kan.) Daily Journal, 1887; editor Daily Press, Asbury Park, N.J., 1892-95; founder and editor Seashore Life, 1895; coast corr. New York Sun, 1895; founder and editor Asbury Park Daily Star, 1896; mng. editor The Day, New London, Conn., 1896-99; staff writer St. Louis Post-Dispatch, 1900-03; editor Gen. Press Bur., St. Louis Expn., 1903-04; editor The Valley Magazine, St. Louis, 1904; editorial writer Portland Oregonian, 1905; mng. editor, General Press Bur., Lewis and Clark Expn., 1905; spl. feature writer, asst. mng. editor Am. Press Assn., 1906-11; on editorial staff St. Louis Post-Dispatch, 1911-13; spl. feature and humorous writer, St. Louis Republic, 1913-16; Sunday editor Tulsa (Okla.) Democrat, 1917-18; editor of Daily Ardmoreite, Ardmore, Okla., 1918-20; editorial staff Kansas City Post, 1921; on editorial staff St. Louis Post-Dispatch, 1922—, lit. editor, Sept. 1925-June 1926; on editorial staff St. Louis Globe-Democrat, Nov. 1926—, lit. editor, 1928—. Author: Poems All the Way from Pike, 1904; The Rise and Fall of Jesse James, 1925. Home: Webster Groves, Mo. Died May 7, 1930.

LOVE, Smoloff Palace, lawyer; b. Lincoln Co., Ky., May 10, 1826; ed. Fulton Acad., Fulton, Mo.; clerked in store; taught school; served in 1st Mo. inf., 1846-48, in Mexican war; returned to Ky., 1848, settling in Muhlenberg Co., 1840; taught school until 1861; served in Union army, raising 11th Ky. inf. and becoming its col., 1861-65, fighting at Shiloh, Perryville, Stone River, Bowling Green and other battles under Gens. Buell, Burnside and Sherman. Admitted to Ky. bar; co. judge, Muhlenberg Co., 1866-74; resumed practice until 1894; retired; m. Jane McConnell, July 15, 1850. Home: Greenville, Ky. Died 1903.

LOVE, Stephen Hunter; b. Salt Lake City, Utah, Jan. 15, 1865; s. David and Margaret (Hunter) L.; ed. pub. schs.; m. Eleanor Wilding, Feb. 8, 1883. Began as clk. in retail store, later in business on own account and in county recorder's office, Salt Lake Co.; became identified 1887, with Zion's Coöperative Instn. as traffic mgr.; sales and traffic manager, 1915—, of the Utah-Idaho Sugar Co.; pres. Security Storage Co., Traffic Service Bureau of Utah. Member sugar distributing com. of Federal Food Administration, World War, also mem. San Francisco Traffic Com. during federal control of rys. Pres. U.S. Beet Sugar Assn. Mem. Utah Senate, 1901-09 (pres. 2 sessions); mem. Bd. of Regents, U. of Utah; mem. Bd. of Edn., Salt Lake Co., 10 yrs. Mem. Troop C, Utah N.G., 3 yrs. Republican. Mormon. Home: Salt Lake City, Utah. Died Feb. 22, 1937.

LOVE, William De Loss, clergyman; b. New Haven, Conn., Nov. 29, 1851; s. Rev. William De Loss and Matilda (Wallace) L.; A.B., Hamilton Coll., 1873, A.M., 1877, Ph.D., 1894; grad. Andover Theol. Sem., 1878; m. Ada Minerva Warren, July 6, 1878 (died 1881); 2d, Mary Louise, d. Gov. Samuel W. Hale, of Keene, N.H., Oct. 30, 1884. Ordained Congl. ministry, 1878; pastor Lancaster, Mass., 1878-81, Keene, N.H., 1882-83; in commercial and railroad business, Boston, 1883-84; pastor Farmington Av. Ch., Hartford, 1885-1910. Park commr. Hartford, 1894-1909. Author: The Fast and Thanksgiving Days of New England, 1895; Samson Occom and the Christian Indians of New England, 1900; The Colonial History of Hartford, 1914. Home: Hartford, Conn. Died Apr. 12, 1918.

LOVEJOY, Francis Thomas Fletcher; b. Baltimore, July 21, 1854; s. William Alexander and Mary J. (Robinson) L.; ed. Washington, O.; learned telegraphy while attending sch.; m. Jane Clyde, d. Robert James Fleming, June 22, 1892. Served at Washington, Pa., and Pithole, Pa., as telegrapher, etc., 1870-80; employed by Am. Union Telegraph Co., Pittsburgh, 1880-81; entered service Carnegie steel interests as clerk and telegrapher; became auditor Apr. 1889, Carnegie Bros. & Co., Ltd., and Carnegie, Phipps & Co., Ltd., also mem. and stockholder same; elected sec. Carnegie Bros. & Co., June 1889; elected mem. bds. mgrs. of both assns., 1891; took active part in their consolidation, becoming, July 1, 1892, sec. and a mgr. of the Carnegie Steel Co., Ltd.; resigned all positions, 1900, refusing to take part in attack by majority stockholders upon Mr. Frick, chmn. bd. of mgrs.; conducted compromise negotiations, and Mar. 19, 1900, wrote agreement under which new co. was to be formed; apptd. one of com. to carry out provisions of agreement. In 1902-03, took up gold mining. Home: Pittsburgh, Pa. Died Dec. 7, 1932.

LOVEJOY, George Edwards, clergyman; b. Bradford, Mass., June 30, 1843; s. John H. and Sally (Grout) L.; studied theology at Andover Theol. Sem.; m. Mary L. Sinclair, May 1, 1867. Enlisted, Aug. 12, 1862, in Co. H, 22d Regt., Mass. Vols., serving as pvt. and corporal to close of war; participated at Antietam, Shepardstown, Chancellorsville, Gettysburg, Rappahannock Station, Poplar Grove Church, Petersburg, etc. Ordained Congl. ministry, 1873; pastor Candia, N.H., 1873-77, Bedford, Mass., 1877-80, Franklin, 1880-91, Oak Park Ch., Minneapolis, 1891-93, Stoneham, Mass., 1893-97, Pittsfield, N.H., 1897-1903, South Ch., Lawrence, Mass., Feb. 1903—. Republican. Mason. Chaplain-in-chief, G.A.R., 1912-13. Home: Lawrence, Mass. Died Dec. 25, 1916.

LOVEJOY, Thomas E., ins. pres.; b. Spaulding, Ga., Sept. 16, 1875; s. P. H. and Henrietta (McKenzie) L.; ed. commercial coll. and by courses of study in Georgia, Baltimore and New York; m. Fannie Brown, Nov. 9, 1897 (died 1910). Began asst. cashier Planters Bank, Hawkinsville, Ga., 1896; v.p. First Nat. Bank, Hawkinsville, 1905-09; pres. Montgomery (Ala.) Bank & Trust Co., 1909-13; pres. Manhattan Life Ins. Co. of New York, May 1913—; v.p. and trustee Manhattan Savings Instn., New York; mem. advisory bd. Chemical Bank & Trust Co., Plaza Office, New York. Home: New York, N.Y. Died Dec. 12, 1939.

LOVELAND, Francis William, businessman; b. Brighton, Ill., July 24, 1859; s. William A. H. and Miranda Ann (Montgomery) L.; removed to Denver, 1860; A.B., U. of Mich., 1880; LL.B., U. of Denver, 1894; m. Adele Beebe, Dec. 19, 1883. Sec. and treas. Rocky Mountain News Co., pub. Denver Daily News, 1879-86; sec. and treas. Denver Circle R.R. Co., 1882-87; treas. Denver, Lakewood & Golden R.R. Co., 1894-1910; pres. Rex Coal Mining Co., Loveland Ranch Co., Century Realty & Securities Co., Mountain Blaugas Co.; treas. Denver & Inter-Mountain R.R. Co.; sec. and treas. Louisville (Colo.) Coal Mining Co., etc. Episcopalian. Home: Denver, Colo. Died Mar. 18, 1921.

LOVELL, John Harvey, biologist; b. Waldoboro, Me., Oct. 21, 1860; s. Harvey Hinckley and Sophronia Caroline (Bulfinch) L.; A.B., Amherst, 1882, A.M., 1899; m. Lottie Evangeline Magune, Oct. 24, 1899; children—Harvey Bulfinch, Ralph Marston. Has devoted many yrs. to original observations on floroecology of Northern plants, their manner of pollination, insect visitors, distribution of flower colors, etc.; specialist in photography of flowers, natural size. Republican. Conglist. Author: The Flower and the Bee; Plant Life and Pollination, 1918; The Honey Plants of North America, 1926. Biol. editor ABC of Bee Culture, issued triennially; contbr. daily illustrated articles on New England plants to the Boston Globe, and to other N.E. newspapers, 1926—. Home: Waldoboro, Me. Died Aug. 2, 1939.

LOVELY, John A., asso. justice Supreme Court, Minn., elected 1898; b. Burlington, Vt., Nov. 18, 1843; admitted to bar, Milwaukee, Wis., 1865; practiced at Albert Lea, Minn., 1867—; co. atty., Freeborn Co., Minn., 1876-82; has been city atty. Albert Lea; pres. State Bar Assn., 1886-90. Home: St. Paul, Minn. Died 1907.

LOVEMAN, Robert, author; b. Cleveland, O., Apr. 11, 1864; s. David R. and Esther (Black) L.; acad. edn., Dalton, Ga.; (hon. A.M., U. of Ala.); unmarried. Has traveled and studied abroad. Author: Songs from a Georgia Garden, and Echoes from the Gates of Silence, 1905; The Blushful South and Hippocrene, 1909; On the Way to Willowdale, 1912; Sonnets of the Strife, 1917. Home: Dalton, Ga. Died July 10, 1923.

LOVERING, Henry Bacon, congressman, shoemaker; b. Portsmouth, N.H., Apr. 8, 1841; s. John Gilman and Mary Ann (Martin) L.; ed. pub. schs., Lynn, Mass.; m. Abby Jane Clifford, Dec. 25, 1864. Began at shoemaking, 1853; served pvt. in Co. D, 8th Mass. Inf., and Co. C, 3d Mass. Cav., 1863-65; wounded in battle at Winchester, Va., Sept. 19, 1864, resulting in amputation of left leg. Mem. Mass. Ho. Reps., 1872-74; gen. bd. of assessors, Lynn, 1879-80; mayor of Lynn, 1881-82; mem. Congress, 1883-87; Dem. nominee for gov. of Mass., 1887; U.S. marshall, dist. of Mass., 1888-91; warden Mass. State prison, 1891-93; U.S. pension agt., Boston, 1894-98; sealer of weights and measures, Boston, 1902-05. Democrat. Home: Boston, Mass. Died 1911.

LOVERING, William C., congressman, cotton mfr.; b. R.I., 1837; ed. Cambridge High School and Hopkins Classical School, Cambridge, Mass.; engaged in mfg. as pres. and chief mgr. Whittenton Mfg. Co., Taunton, and dir. and mgr. of many other factories; served for a short time in Civil War as engr. at Fortress Monroe; retired because of ill health; State senator, Mass., 1874-75; del. to Nat. Rep. Conv., 1880; mem. Congress, 1897-1903, 12th Mass. dist. and 1903-09, 14th dist. Republican. Home: Taunton, Mass. Died 1910.

LOVETT, Robert H., asst. atty. gen. of U.S.; b. Brimfield, Ill.; s. Robert B. and Adaline (White) L.; ed. State Normal Sch., Normal, Ill.; m. Laura Gilson, Sept. 16, 1886. Admitted to Ill. bar, 1885, and began practice at Peoria; co. judge, 11 yrs.; U.S. master in chancery and commr. many yrs.; apptd. asst. atty. gen. of U.S., in charge of litigation involving claims, Apr. 1921. Republican. Christian Scientist. Mason. Home: Peoria, Ill. Died Aug. 23, 1926.

LOVETT, Robert Scott, ry. pres.; b. San Jacinto, Tex., June 22, 1860; s. William and Susan (Hardy) L.; ed. Houston (Tex.) High Sch., followed by pvt. instrn. and self-edn.; m. Lavinia Abercrombie, Oct. 29, 1890; 1 son, Robert Abercrombie. Admitted to bar, Houston, Tex., Dec. 22, 1882; atty. for Houston, East & West Tex. Ry. Co., 1884-89; asst. gen. atty Tex. & Pacific Ry. Co., Dallas, 1889-91; gen. atty. Tex. & Pacific Ry. Co., 1891-92; mem. Baker, Botts, Baker & Lovett, Houston, Tex., and gen. atty. and counsel for all Southern Pacific lines in Tex., 1892-1903; gen. counsel for U.P. R.R. Co. and S.P. Co. and affiliated lines, commonly known as the Harriman System, 1904-09; chmn. exec. com. and pres. U.P. and S.P. R.R. systems, 1909-13; chmn. exec. com. U.P. System, 1913-18; priorities commr. and mem. War Industries Bd., Aug. 1917-Mar. 1918; dir. div. of capital expenditures under U.S. ry. administrator, Mar.-Dec. 31, 1918; pres. Union Pacific System, 1919-20, chmn. bd., Mar. 1, 1920—; dir. I.C. R.R., Y.&M.V. R.R., Western Union Telegraph Co. Democrat. Home: Locust Valley, L.I. Died June 19, 1932.

LOVETT, Robert Williamson, physician; b. Beverly, Mass., Nov. 18, 1859; s. John Dyson and Mary Elizabeth (Williamson) L.; A.B., Harvard, 1881, M.D., 1885; (D.Sc., U. of Cincinnati, 1920); m. Elizabeth Moorfield Storey, 1895. In practice at Boston, 1886—; specialist in orthopedic surgery; prof. orthopedic surgery, Harvard Univ.; consulting orthopedic surgeon to N.Y. State Dept. of Health. Maj. M.C.U.S.A., Jan. 1918-19. Home: Boston, Mass. Died July 2, 1924.

LOVETT, William Cuyler, clergyman, editor; b. Screven Co., Ga., Nov. 28, 1852; s. Robert Watkins and Elisabeth (Mason) L.; A.B., Emory Coll., Ga., 1874; (D.D., Southern U., 1893); m. Miss M. A. H. Smith, Dec. 28, 1878; 2d, Eva Edwards, Dec. 28, 1898. Ordained ministry, M.E. Ch., S., 1874; editor, Wesleyan Christian Advocate, 1900—. Pres. trustees South Ga. Coll.; trustee Wesley Memorial Hosp. Democrat. Home: Atlanta, Ga. Died July 1, 1940.

LOVETTE, Oscar Byrd, congressman; b. Greene Co., Tenn., Dec. 20, 1871; s. John Dickson and Mary

Emily (Woolsey) L.; B.S., Tusculum Coll., 1893, also A.B. and M.A.; m. Lillie Fowler, Dec. 23, 1896 (died 1923); children—Leland P., Frank H., Marianna, Lois Byrd; m. 2d, Mabel Rogan Stein, July 16, 1927. Admitted to Tenn. bar, 1927, and began practice at Greenville; mem. Lovette, Berry & Easterly. Mem. Tenn. Ho. of Rep., 1895-97; atty. gen. 1st Judicial Circuit of Tenn., 1918-26; mem. 72d Congress (1931-33), 1st Tenn. Dist. Trustee Tusculum Coll. Republican. Presbyterian. Mason. Rotarian. Home: Greenville, Tenn. Died July 6, 1934.

LOVEWELL, Joseph Taplin, chemist; b. Corinth, Conn., May 1, 1833; s. Nehemiah and Martha (Willis) L.; A.B., Yale, 1857, Ph.D., 1874; m. Margaret L. Bissell, Sept. 3, 1863; m. 2d, Caroline F. Barnes, of Topeka, Kan., June 30, 1885. Prin. Prairie du Chien (Wis.) Coll., 1859-63; prin. high sch. and supt. of city schs., Madison, Wis., 1863-64; prof. mathematics, Wis. State Normal Sch., Whitewater, 1870-73; prof. chem. and physics, State Coll., Pa., 1875-77, Washburn Coll., Kan., 1878-99; sec. and librarian, 1902-16, emeritus sec., 1916, Kan. Acad. Science (pres. 2 yrs., editor 5 vols. Trans.). Republican. Conglist. Home: Topeka, Kan. Died Sept. 11, 1918.

LOVING, Starling, physician; b. Russellville, Ky., Nov. 13, 1827; s. Willis and Susanna Jane (Starling) L.; ed. Russellville (Ky.) Academy.; M.D., Starling Med. Coll., 1849; post-grad. work Bellevue Hosp., New York, 1849-53; m. Margaret D. Noble, Apr. 22, 1856; m. 2d, Annie F. Hurlbutt, 1883 (both dec.). Engaged in med. practice, 1849—. Maj. surgeon 6th Ohio Inf., 1861. Prof. materia medica, 1857, theory and practice of medicine, 1875, dean, 1884, Starling Med. Coll. Phys.-in-chief St. Francis Hosp., Columbus, 1866; cons. physician Mt. Carmel Hosp., 1900, Lawrence Hosp. for Women, 1903—; trustee Children's Hosp. Republican. Home: Columbus, O. Died 1911.

LOW, Sir A. Maurice, author and journalist; b. London, Eng., 1860; ed. King's Coll., London, and in Austria; M.A., Dartmouth Coll. Chief Am. corr. of London Morning Post. Investigated for U.S. Dept. of Labor certain phases of English labor legislation, 1900, English trade unions and industry, 1903. Knighted for services to British Government. Chevalier Order of Leopold; Imperial Order of the Rising Sun; Order of the Redeemer, Greece. Author: The Supreme Surrender, 1901; Protection in the United States, 1904; American Life in Town and Country, 1905; A Short History of Labor Legislation in Great Britain, 1907; The American People, A Study in National Psychology, 1909, Vol. II, 1911; Woodrow Wilson, An Interpretation, 1918. Died June 17, 1929.

LOW, Albert Howard, chemist, educator; b. Chelsea, Mass., June 27, 1855; s. Albert Burrell and Mary Jane (Gilman) L.; B.S., Mass. Inst. Tech., 1876; D.Sc., Colo. Sch. of Mines, 1922; m. Helen A. Jones, June 12, 1888; 1 son, Albert Estabrook (dec.). Consulting practice, Denver, 1885; head chemistry dept., Colo. Sch. of Mines, 1919-26; conducting petroleum research, 1926-28. Charter mem. Colo. Scientific Society. Republican. Author: Technical Methods of Ore Analysis, 1905; Notes on Technical Ore Analysis, 1923. Home: Denver, Colo. Died 1936.

LOW, Benjamin Robbins Curtis, lawyer, author; b. Fairhaven, Mass., June 22, 1880; s. William Gilman and Lois Robbins (Curtis) L.; B.A., Yale, 1902; LL.B., Harvard, 1905; m. Virginia Wagner, Feb. 15, 1922; children—Caroline Davison, Malcolm Scollay. Began practice at New York, 1905; mem. Hoes, Low & Miller, 1923-28; gen. counsel Home Life Ins. Co. Commd. capt. O.R.C., July 12, 1917; maj. U.S.A., Feb. 18, 1918; served at Washington, D.C., equipment and procurement divs., Ordnance Dept.; hon. disch. Dec. 20, 1918. Republican. Episcopalian. Author: The Pursuit of Happiness, 1919; Broken Music, 1920; Darkening Sea, 1925; Winged Victory, 1927; To the Funeral Pyre of Shelley, 1929; Roland, 1930; Child on Bronze Horse, 1931; Off Soundings, 1932; King Philip, 1933; Brooklyn Bridge, 1933; Turn of the Road, 1933; Seth Low (biography), 1925; Symphony in D Minor, 1937. New York, N.Y. Died June 22, 1941.

LOW, Berthe (Eugénie Marie), Julienne (Mrs), writer; b. Caen, France, June 7, 1853; d. Arthur Numa and Marie Madeleine, (Quesnel) Julienne; ed. in convent of St. Sauveur, Caen; m. Will H. Low, artist, 1875. Translator into French (from Stevenson): Le cas étrange du Dr. Jekyll et M. Hyde, 1888. Author: French Home Cooking, Adapted to American Households, 1904. Home: Bronxville, N.Y. Died 1909.

LOW, Frederick Rollins, editor; b. Chelsea, Mass., Apr. 3, 1860; s. James Liswell Hawkes and Martha Hale (Rollins) L.; ed. pub. schs.; m. Adeline Frances Giles, Sept. 23, 1881. With Boston Journal of Commerce, 1880-88; editor "Power" (pub. by McGraw-Hill Co.), 1898-1931; mech. engring. practice. Served as mem. Bd. of Health, councilman, councilman at large and mayor, of Passaic, N.J. Unitarian. Mason. Author: Steam Engine Indicator, 1898; Power Catechism, 1906; Condensers, 1906; The Compound Engine, 1906. Home: Passaic, N.J. Died Jan. 22, 1936.

LOW, Marcus A., lawyer; b. Guilford, Me., Aug. 1, 1842; s. Frederick P. and Mary J. (Robinson) L.; ed. Auburn (Me.) Acad., and Law Sch., U. of Mich., 1866-67; (LL.D., Bethany Coll., Kan., 1901); m. Diantha L. Hovey, Feb. 14, 1867. Engaged in practice of law, 1867—; pres. St. Joseph & Ia. Ry. Co., 1886-87 (gen. solicitor, 1887-92), Chicago, Kan. & Neb. Ry. Co., 1887-92, Chicago, Rock Island & Tex.. Ry. Co., 1892-1900, Chicago, Rock Island & Gulf Ry. Co., and of Chicago, Rock Island & Mexico Ry. Co., 1902-03. Gen. atty., C.,R.I.&P. Ry. Co., 1892-Aug. 1912, when retired on pension. Republican. Pres. Bd. Park Commrs., Topeka, Kan. Pres. Topeka Public Library Assn. Home: Topeka, Kan. Died July 19, 1921.

LOW, Seth, educator, publicist; b. Brooklyn, Jan. 18, 1850; s. Abiel Abbot and Ellen Almira (Dow) L.; A.B., Columbia, 1870; (LL.D., Amherst, 1889, U. State of New York, Harvard, U. of Pa. and Trinity, 1890, Princeton, 1896, Yale, 1901, U. of Edinburgh, Scotland, 1910); m. Annie Wroe Scollay, d. Judge Benjamin R. Curtis, Dec. 9, 1880. Clerk, and later partner, in his father's tea-importing house. Mayor of Brooklyn, 1881-85, elected on independent ticket; unsuccessful candidate for mayor Greater New York, 1897; pres. Columbia Univ., 1890-1901 (trustee, 1881-1914); mayor of Greater New York, Jan. 1, 1902-Dec. 31, 1903. Del. Peace Conf. at The Hague, 1899; trustee Carnegie Instn., Washington. Home: New York, N.Y. Died Sept. 17, 1916.

LOW, Will Hicok, artist; b. Albany, N.Y., May 31, 1853; pupil of Gérome and Carolus Duran, Paris, France, 1873-77; m. Berthe Eugenie Marie Julienne, of Paris, France, 1875; m. 2d, Mary Louise Fairchild, Nov. 4, 1909. His works include decorative paintings, stained glass and ideal groups and portraits; has done much illustrating; silver medal for drawings, Paris Expn., 1889; medal, Chicago Expn., 1893; silver medal, Buffalo Expn., 1901. Designed diploma of awards for Chicago Expn., 1893, and St. Louis Expn., 1904; mem. Internat. Jury Awards, St. Louis Expn. Painted ceiling in reception room, Waldorf Hotel, 1892; 4 decorative panels for music room of C. T. Yerkes' residence, New York, 1896; and 20 panels for the concert hall and ballroom of the Astoria Hotel, New York, 1897; 4 lunettes in residence of A. N. Brady, Albany, N.Y., 1906; panel in Essex Co. (N.J.) Court House, Newark, 1907; mural paintings in Luzerne Co. Court House, Wilkes-Barre, Pa., 1908, Federal Bldg., Cleveland, 1910, St. Paul's P.E. Ch., Albany, 1910. Has had charge of life classes in schs. of Cooper Union, 1882-85, in Nat. Acad. Design, 1889-92; gave exhibit of his work and course of instruction, Art Inst. Chicago, 1902, and delivered 5th ann. course of Scammon lectures, 1910; finished series of 32 mural paintings for rotunda of New York State Edn. Bldg. depicting "The Aspiration of Man and the Results of His Achievement," and in 1915 installed frieze in the Legislative Library, N.Y. State Capitol, Albany; war picture, "Victory," Earl Hall, Columbia Univ., 1920; "The Poet and His Muse—R. L. Stevenson at Fontainebleau, 1875," based on sketch from life and shown at Centennial Exhbn. of Nat. Acad. Design, 1925. Mem. Nat. Inst. Arts and Letters; N.A., 1890; founder mem. Soc. Am. Artists, 1878. Author: A Chronicle of Friendships, 1908; A Painter's Progress, 1910. Home: Bronxville, N.Y. Died Nov. 27, 1932.

LOW, William Gilman, lawyer; b. Brooklyn, N.Y., Apr. 9, 1844; s. William Henry and Anne Davison (Bedell) L.; A.B., Columbia, 1865, LL.B., 1867, A.M., 1868; admitted to bar, 1867; m. Lois Robbins, d. Judge Benjamin R. Curtis, of Boston, Jan. 15, 1873; children—William G., Anna C. (Mrs. Herbert A. Grant Watson), Lois Curtis, Benj. Robbins Curtis, Rosamond Curtis (wife of Rev. John H. Chapman), Harriette, Esther Hope (wife of Rev. Francis K. Little). Pres. Hospital Saturday and Sunday Assn. of Brooklyn; v.p. N.Y. Civil Service Reform Assn., and of Legal Aid Soc. Fellow Am. Society. Wrote: The Balance of the Geneva Award, International Review, May 1881; A Law Primer, A. A. Low and Bros. Fleet of Clipper Ships: A Genealogical Quest; Some Recollections for My Children and Grandchildren. Home: Brooklyn, N.Y. Died June 28, 1936.

LOWBER, James William, clergyman; b. Chaplin, Ky., Aug. 30, 1847; s. Joseph P. and Elizabeth Lowber; A.B., Butler Coll., 1871, A.M., 1874; grad. Div. Coll. of Ky. U., 1880; Ph.D., Syracuse U., 1880; Sc.D., U. of Wooster, 1897; m. Maggie P. De Baun, July 4, 1882. Ordained Disciples of Christ ministry, 1868; pastor Pittsburgh, 1872-73, Scranton, Pa., 1874-77; prin. Quaker St. Lit. Inst., New York, 1877-80; pres. Columbia Coll., Ky., 1880-81; pastor Lancaster, Ky., 1882-84, Louisville, 1884-86, Paducah, Ky., 1886-88, Ft. Worth, Tex., 1888-93, Galveston, Tex., 1893-97, Austin, Tex., 1897—. Editor Apostolic Church, 1883-87; chancellor Tex. Christian U., 1892-97; lecturer at colls. and univs. Fellow Royal Geog. Soc., Royal Astron. Society, Royal Soc. of Arts, North British Acad. (councillor), Royal Scottish Geog. Soc., Royal Soc. Antiquaries, Scotland, Ednl. Inst. of Scotland, A.A.A.S., Am. Geog. Society. Author: Struggles and Triumphs of the Truth, 1888, 3d edit., 1909; Devil in Modern Society, 1888, 10th edit., 1918; Macrocosmus, or Hints Toward the Greatest Problems, 1902; Highest Culture and Christianity, 1915; The Philosophy of Human Progress, 1925. Knight Comdr. of the Court of Honor, Supreme Council Scottish Rite Masonry. Home: Austin, Tex. Died Dec. 5, 1930.

LOWDERMILK, Patricia Cannales, verse writer, entertainer; b. Arcadia, Wis.; d. Andrew and Susan Frances (Cannales) Flynn; ed. high sch., Ellsworth, Minn., Ia. Business Coll., Des Moines, Ia., Kan. State Teachers Coll.; m. Dr. R. C. Lowdermilk, July 3, 1907; children—Richards Claude, Margaret Rosemary. Teacher pub. schs. 3 yrs.; teacher verse technique, 1926—; poetry editor The Van; public reader and entertainer. Pres. Equal Suffrage Assn. during campaign for adoption of equal suffrage in Kan., 1912. Republican. Catholic. Home: Galena, Kan. Died Mar. 18, 1928.

LOWE, Arthur Houghton, mfr.; b. Rindge, N.H., Aug. 20, 1853; s. John and Sarah (Mead) L.; ed. pub. schs. of Fitchburg; m. Anne Elizabeth, d. John Parkhill, of Fitchburg, Mass., Dec. 11, 1878. Established 1879, Parkhill Mfg. Co., cotton goods, inc., 1881, of which is treas.; also established Lowe Mfg. Co., Huntsville, Ala.; pres. Amoskeag Mfg. Co.; v.p. Fitchburg Savings Bank. Alderman of Fitchburg, 1888; mayor, 1893; mem. Governor's Council, 1902-03; mem. Mass. Constl. Conv. Trustee Baldwinsville Hosp. Cottages for Children, Cushing Acad., Murdock Sch. Fund. Home: Fitchburg, Mass. Died Oct. 27, 1932.

LOWE, Ephraim Noble, geologist; b. Utica, Miss., May 5, 1864; s. Edmund F. and Emily M. (Peyton) L.; Ph.B., U. of Miss., 1884; post-grad. work, in absentia, same univ., 1 yr., 1890; M.D., Tulane U., 1892; studied U. of Chicago, summers 1905, 06, 07; m. Sarah Yeager, Nov. 28, 1895 (died 1898); children—Marguerite Emily, Edmund Peyton; m. 2d, Laura Edna Haley, May 14, 1904; 1 dau., Edna May (dec.). Engaged in pvt. geol. and biol. work in Colo., 1887-89; practiced medicine in Miss., 1892-93, in Colo., 1893-1902, also geol. work; asst. in geology and biology, 1905-07, actg. prof., 1907-08, prof., 1908-09, U. of Miss.; dir. Miss. Geol. Survey, 1909—; head of Dept. of Geology, U. of Miss., 1924—. Fellow A.A.A.S., Am. Geog. Soc. Democrat. Mem. M.E. Ch., S. K.P. Author: Plants of Mississippi; Economic Geography of Mississippi. Home: University, Miss. Died Sept. 12, 1933.

LOWE, John, naval officer; b. Liverpool, Eng., Dec. 11, 1838; s. John and Mary (Blinston) L.; ed. Liverpool and Columbus, O.; studied engring.; m. Josephine L., d. George B. Dyer, of Washington, Nov. 5, 1867. Enlisted pvt. 2d Ohio Regt., 1861 (No. 15 on Ohio's roll); apptd. to U.S.N., Aug. 1861, by Hon. S. S. Cox, M.C.; wounded in 1st battle Bull Run; served through Civil, Corean and Spanish wars; mem. Greely Relief Expdn., 1884, and on various stas. and duties in peace times; in 1898 was 1st naval officer of any nationality to have submarine service in submarine torpedo boat, and made 1st report ever presented to sec. of the navy upon that topic; retired, Dec. 11, 1900. In Oct. 1901, participated in decisive experiment, with 6 other men, in a submarine torpedo boat, submerged to the bottom of Peconic Bay for 15 hours. Medal conferred by Act of Congress for "meritorious service." Home: Washington, D.C. Died Aug. 28, 1930.

LOWE, Martha Perry, author; b. Keene, N.H., Nov. 21, 1829; d. Gen. Justus Perry; ed. at Mrs. Sedgewick's School, Lenox, Mass.; m. Rev. Charles Lowe, deceased. Author: (verse) The Olive and the Pine; Love in Spain; Story of Chief Joseph; Bessie Gray; also Memoir of Rev. Charles Lowe. Home: Somerville, Mass. Died 1902.

LOWE, Thaddeus S. C., scientist, inventor; b. Jefferson, N.H., Aug. 20, 1832; s. Clovis and Alpha Green L. (Pilgrim ancestry); ed. common schs.; spl. studies in chemistry; m. Leontine A. Gachon, of Paris, France, 1855. Constructed balloons as an aid to study of atmospheric phenomena, 1856 and 1858-59, securing instruments from govt., invented and made other instruments for investigating upper air currents, including an Altimeter for quickly measuring latitude and longitude without a horizon; built, 1859-60, the largest aerostat that was ever made, made trip from Cincinnati to a point 900 miles distant, nr. S.C. coast, in 9 hours, Apr. 20, 1861. Entered govt. service as chief of aeronautic corps, which he organized, rendering valuable service to Army of the Potomac, from Bull Run to Gettysburg, by observations and timely warnings. In 1862 invented system of signaling to comdr. of field batteries from high altitudes—largely used in Peninsula campaign, and later by Brazilian Govt., to which he sold his outfit after Civil War. Invented compression ice machine, 1865, making first artificial ice in U.S.; built regenerative metall. furnaces for gas and petroleum fuel, 1869-72; invented and built water-gas apparatus, 1873-75, and later other machines; from 1897 inventing and putting into operation New Lowe Coke Oven system, for simultaneously producing gas and metall. coke, known as "Lowe

Anthracite." Built Mt. Lowe Ry., 1891-94, and established Lowe Observatory in Sierra Madre Mountains. Home: Pasadena, Calif. Died Jan. 1913.

LOWE, Walter Irenaeus, educator; b. Ilion, N.Y., Jan. 30, 1867; s. Irenaeus H. and Jane A. (Griffith) L.; A.B., Yale, 1890, Ph.D., 1897; m. Catherine Young Caskey, June 6, 1894; children—Catherine Caskey, Elizabeth Pritchard. Instr. history, Sheffield Scientific Sch., Yale, 1892-1900; prof. history and polit. science, Wells Coll., 1900-20; prof. history, Colgate U., 1920—; leave of absence for travel and study in Europe, 1911-12, also 1st semester 1925-26, for trip around the world, lecturing. In France, 1918-19, with Y.M.C.A., as div. dir. 7th Div. and mem. faculty of history, A.E.F. Univ., at Beaune. Republican. Baptist. Mason. Home: Hamilton, N.Y. Died Feb. 21, 1929.

LOWELL, Amy, author; b. Brookline, Mass., Feb. 9, 1874; d. Augustus and Katharine Bigelow (Lawrence) L.; ed. pvt. schs.; (Litt.D., Baylor Univ., 1920; Phi Beta Kappa, Columbia, 1920; Phi Beta Kappa poet, Tufts Coll., 1918, Columbia, 1920). Lecture courses at Brooklyn Inst. Arts and Sciences, 1917-18; Francis Bergen foundation lecturer, Yale, 1921; Marshall Woods lecturer, Brown, 1921. Author: A Dome of Many-Coloured Glass, 1912; Sword Blades and Poppy Seed, 1914; Six French Poets, 1915; Men, Women and Ghosts, 1916; Tendencies in Modern American Poetry, 1917; Can Grande's Castle, 1918; Pictures of the Floating World, 1919; Legends, 1921; (with Florence Ayscough) Fir-Flower Tablets—Poems Translated from the Chinese, 1921; A Critical Fable, 1922. Home: Brookline, Mass. Died May 1, 1925.

LOWELL, Daniel Ozro Smith, retired head master; b. Denmark, Me., Apr. 13, 1851; s. Daniel and Mary A. (Smith) L.; A.B., Bowdoin, 1874, A.M., 1877, Litt.D., 1909; M.D., Med. Sch. of Me., 1877; m. Emma Woodman Jordan, Dec. 2, 1878 (died 1914); 1 dau., Muriel Emma (adopted); m. 2d, Anna M. Jordan, Dec. 23, 1916. After brief med. practice became teacher; taught in schools and acads. in Me. until 1884; master in Roxbury Latin Sch., Boston, 1884-1909, headmaster, 1909-21. Examiner in English, College Entrance Exam. Bd., 1907-09; local hon. sec. Egypt Exploration Fund, 1909-21. Mem. bd. mgrs. N.E. Home for Little Wanderers, 1918-25. Trustee Hanson Pub. Library, 1923-25; mem. Hanson Sch. Com., 1924-25. Royal Arch Mason, Odd Fellow. Author: Jason's Quest, 1893, 1904; A Munsey-Hopkins Geonealogy, 1920; Esperanto for Beginners, 1923. Editor: The Roger de Coverley Papers, 1896. Co-translator: (with Grinstead and Anderson) St. John's Gospel into Esperanto, 1910. Asso. editor Amerika Esperantisto, 1911-12. Home: Malden, Mass. Died Mar. 2, 1928.

LOWELL, Delmar Rial, clergyman; b. South Valley, N.Y., Nov. 29, 1844; s. Reuben and Catherine (Seeber) L.; A.B., Wesleyan U., 1873, A.M., 1876; (D.D., Ohio Wesleyan, 1888); pvt. Co. G, 121st N.Y. Inf., 1864-65; lost right arm at Battle of Sailor's Creek, Va., Apr. 6, 1865; m. Irene E. Maynard, Jan. 26, 1876; 2d, Harriet A. Davis, June 26, 1879. Ordained M.E. ministry, 1874; pastor Albany, N.Y., 1874-75, Richmondville, N.Y., 1876, Hart's Falls, N.Y., 1877-78, Fairhaven, Vt., 1879-81, Rutland, Vt., 1882-84, Albany, N.Y., 1885-87, Rutland, Vt., 1888-89; post chaplain U.S.A., Apr. 19, 1890; retired, Sept. 18, 1897; advanced to rank of maj. retired, by act of Apr. 23, 1904. Chaplain Conn. Ho. of Rep., 1901-03; alderman Middletown, Conn., 1902. Mem. G.A.R. (chaplain Vt. and Conn. depts.; chaplain-in-chief, 1892-93; a.-d.-c. on staff comdr.-in-chief, 1893, 1910-11; pres. 1st conv. of the Blue and Grey, St. Louis Expn., 1904; charter mem., first registrar and chaplain Utah Soc. S.A.R., Conn. State Army and Navy Union). Author: The Historic Genealogy of the Lowells in America. Died Feb. 1, 1912.

LOWELL, Francis Cabot, judge; b. Boston, Jan. 7, 1855; s. George G. and Mary Ellen (Parker) L.; A.B., Harvard, 1876; studied Harvard Law Sch., 1877-79; m. Cornelia Prime Baylis, Nov. 27, 1882. Admitted to bar, 1880, and practiced in Boston until apptd. judge; mem. Boston Common Council, 1889-92; Mass. Ho. of Rep., 1895-98; U.S. dist. judge, Dist. of Mass., 1898-1905; U.S. circuit judge, 1st Circuit, Feb. 23, 1905—. Fellow corp. Harvard. Fellow Am. Acad. Arts and Sciences. Author: Joan of Arc, 1896. Home: Boston, Mass. Died 1911.

LOWELL, Guy, architect; b. Boston, Aug. 6, 1870; s. Edward Jackson and Mary W. (Goodrich) L.; A.B., Harvard, 1892; B.S., Mass. Inst. Tech., 1894; grad. École des Beaux Arts, Paris, 1899; m. Henrietta Sargent, May 17, 1898. Began practice, Boston, 1900. Architect, Museum Fine Arts, Boston, Mass.; New York County Court House; Cumberland Co. Court House, Portland, Me.; N.H. Hist. Soc. Bldg., Concord, N.H.; also numerous ednl., commercial and residential bldgs. Lecturer on landscape architecture, Mass. Inst. Tech., 1900-13. Trustee Simmons Coll., Boston; sole trustee Lowell Observatory, Flagstaff, Ariz. Dir. dept. mil. affairs, Am. Red Cross, in Italy, 1917-19. Decorations: Italian War Cross (2 citations); silver medal for valor; Order SS. Mauritius and Lazarus; Order Crown of Italy. Home: Brookline, Mass. Died Feb. 4, 1927.

LOWELL, James Arnold, judge; b. Newton, Mass., Feb. 5, 1869; s. John and Lucy Buckminster (Emerson) L.; A.B., Harvard, 1891, LL.B., 1894; m. Mary Wharton Churchman, Dec. 2, 1897 (died 1920); children—James A., Wharton. Began practice in Boston, with father and brother, 1894; mem. Mass. Ho. of Rep., 1904-06; chmn. Commn. on Workmen's Compensation, Mass., 1910-12; chmn. Bd. of Labor and Industries, Mass., 1913-14; mem. Mass. Constl. Conv., 1917-18; mem. Mass. Commn. to Consolidate the Laws, 1917-20; apptd. U.S. Dist. Judge, Mass., Sept. 1922. Unitarian. Editor: Lowell on Bankruptcy, 1898. Home: Newton, Mass. Died Nov. 30, 1933.

LOWELL, John, lawyer; b. Boston, May 23, 1856; s. John and Lucy B. (Emerson) L.; grad. Harvard, 1877; Harvard Law Sch. till 1879; m. Mary Emlen Hale, Oct. 24, 1883. Admitted to bar, 1880, and began practice at Boston; now sr. mem. Lowell & Lowell; dir. Waltham Bleachery & Dye Works, Mass. Hosp. Life Ins. Co.; mem. advisory bd. and general counsel Employers' Liability Assurance Corp., Ltd., London. Treas., trustee Harvard Loan Fund; sinking fund commr. City of Newton; trustee Mass. Soc. Promoting Agr., Mass. Gen. Hosp., McLean Hosp. Convalescent Home (Waverly); pres. Boston Poultry Assn. Unitarian. Home: Chestnut Hill, Mass. Deceased.

LOWELL, Josephine Shaw, author, humanitarian; b. (Shaw) West Roxbury, Mass., Dec. 16, 1843; ed. in Europe, New York and Boston; m. Charles Russell Lowell, col. 2d Mass. cav. regt., who was killed at battle of Cedar Creek, Oct. 1864, 1863. She was one of the commrs. of N.Y. State bd. of charities, 1877-89. Author: Public Relief and Private Charity; Industrial Arbitration and Conciliation. Now engaged in charitable work. Died 1905.

LOWELL, Percival, astronomer; b. Boston, Mar. 13, 1855; s. Augustus and Katharine Bigelow (Lawrence) L.; bro. of A(bbott) Lawrence L.; A.B., Harvard, 1876; (LL.D., Amherst, 1907, Clark U., 1909); m. Constance Savage Keith, June 10, 1908. Went to Japan 1883, and lived there from time to time till 1893; counsellor and foreign sec. to Korean Spl. Mission to U.S. Established Lowell Obs., 1894; undertook eclipse expdn. to Tripoli, 1900; sent expdn. to the Andes to photograph planet Mars, 1907. Received Janssen medal of French Astron. Soc., 1904, for researches on Mars; gold medal for work on Mars from Sociedad Astronomica de Mexico, 1908; has made discoveries on the planets Mercury, Venus, Saturn, and especially Mars; apptd. non-resident prof. astronomy, Mass. Inst. Tech., 1902. Fellow Am. Acad. Arts and Sciences. Author: The Soul of the Far East, 1886; Noto, 1891; Occult Japan, 1894; Mars, 1895; The Solar System, 1903; Mars as the Abode of Life, 1908; The Evolution of Worlds, 1909. Home: Boston, Mass. Died Nov. 13, 1916.

LOWELL, Sherman James, U.S. tariff commr.; b. Lamberton, N.Y., May 28, 1858; s. James Willoughby and Jane (Selleck) L.; ed. pub. schs.; m. Martha Louisa March, Nov. 27, 1889; children—Fred Albert, Clyde Marsh. Mgr. Pomfret Fruit Co., 1900-10; organizer N.Y. State Grange Exchange, 1917, succeeded by Grange League Federation Exchange, of which was director; organizer Nat. Grange Mutual Liability Assn., 1922, then dir.; apptd. mem. U.S. Tariff Commn. by President Coolidge, July 6, 1926. Mem. N.Y. State Food Supply Commn., 1917, Wood Fuel Commn., 1918, Reconstruction Commn., 1919. Served as lecturer N.Y. State Grange 4 yrs., overseer 4 yrs., master 4 yrs.; chmn. exec. com. Nat. Grange 3 yrs., master 4 yrs. Mason. Home: Fredonia, N.Y. Died Feb. 3, 1940.

LOWENSTEIN, Solomon, social work; b. Phila., Pa., Mar. 3, 1877; s. Levi and Dina (Newmayer) L.; B.A., U. of Cincinnati, 1898; rabbi Hebrew Union Coll., Cincinnati, 1901, D.H.L., 1926; m. Linda Berger, Jan. 27, 1904; children—Leonore (Mrs. John Pollak), Nathan, Judith (Mrs. A. R. Cohen), Rebecca. Headworker of Jewish Settlement, Cincinnati, 1900; supt. United Jewish Charities, Cincinnati, 1901-04; asst. mgr. United Hebrew Charities, N.Y.C., 1904; supt. Hebrew Orphan Asylum, N.Y. City, 1905-20; exec. dir. Fedn. for Support of Jewish Philanthropic Societies of N.Y. City, 1920—, exec. vice-pres., 1935—. Dep. commr. Am. Red Cross Commn. to Palestine, 1918-19; pres. Nat. Conf. of Jewish Social Work, 1922, N.Y. State Conf. of Social Work, 1923, N.Y. City Conf. of Social Work, 1932, 33, Nat. Conf. of Social Work, 1937-38; apptd. mem. Temporary Emergency Relief Adminstrn., N.Y. State, 1934, N.Y. State Bd. of Social Welfare, 1936. Trustee Am. Jewish Com., Am. Jewish Joint Distribution Committee, Bureau Jewish Social Research (sec.), Vocational Service for Juniors (mem. advisory bd.), Am. Friends of Hebrew U. in Palestine (v.p.), etc. Jewish religion. Home: New York, N.Y. Died Jan. 20, 1942.

LOWETH, Charles Frederick, civil engr.; b. Cleveland, Mar. 3, 1857; s. Daniel and Mary A. P. (Brown) L.; student Oberlin Coll., 1877-78; hon. C.E., U. of Wis., 1915; Dr. Engring., Rose Poly. Institute, 1926; m. Carrie T. Curtis, Feb. 15, 1881; children—Mary Grace, Margaret, Frederick Curtis, Robert Charles. Began as rodman on survey for Cleveland, Loraine & Wheeling Ry., in Ohio; civil engr., 1880—, principally in ry. service; successively chief engr. Davenport, Rock Island & Northwestern Ry., and consulting engr. N.P. Ry., M.,St.P.&S.Ste. M. Ry., M.&St.L. Ry., and others; engr. and supt. bridges and bldgs., 1901-10, chief engr., 1910—, C.M.St.P&P. R.R. Republican. Presbyn. Home: Chicago, Ill. Died May 15, 1935.

LOWMAN, Seymour, asst. sec. U.S. Treasury; b. nr. Chemung, N.Y., Oct. 7, 1868; s. John and Fanny (Bixby) L.; grad. high sch., Bainbridge and Lowell's Business Coll., Binghamton; studied law while serving as stenographer in law office, Elmira; m. Kate H. Smith, Sept. 7, 1893; children—Abner M., Gratia (Mrs. Arthur L. Stiles), Fanny (Mrs. John A. Schwab), Caroline (wife of Raymond V. Marron, U.S. Coast Guard), Katherine (Mrs. Jacob R. Schlager). Admitted to N.Y. bar, 1891, and began practice at Elmira; pres. Elmira Savings Bank, 1933—; pres. Lowman Constrn. Corp., U.S. Cut Flower Co.; interested in farming in Chemung County. Chamberlain City of Elmira, 1900-07; mem. N.Y. Assembly, 1909, 10, State Senate, 1918-24; lt. gov. of N.Y., 1925-26; asst. sec. U.S. Treasury, Aug. 1, 1927-Mar. 15, 1933. Rep. leader southern tier N.Y. counties. Sec., treas. N.Y. State Reformatory 10 yrs.; trustee Elmira Coll. Episcopalian. Mason, K.P., Elk. Home: Elmira, N.Y. Died Mar. 13, 1940.

LOWMAN, Webster B., physician; b. Mar. 25, 1841; ed. at Burlington (N.J.) Coll.; grad. Jefferson Med. Coll., Phila., 1867. Served in Civil war, pvt. to capt. Pa. vols.; later capt. battery D, 5th Pa. arty. Since graduation has practiced at Johnstown, Pa.; surgeon to Pa. R.R., Cambria Iron Co., etc.; elected, May 1898, pres. State Med. Soc. of Pa.; dir. in banks; etc.; m. July 3, 1857. Home: Johnstown, Pa. Died 1904.

LOWNDES, Arthur (Edward Gilbert), clergyman; b. London, Eng., June 13, 1858; s. Arthur and Marion (Waller) L.; ed. King's Coll., London, London U., Lycée de St. Germains, Paris; (D.D., Hobart Coll., 1896; S.T.D., Western Theol. Sem., 1906); widower. Came to America, 1880; deacon and priest, Ch. of England, 1884, at Cathedral, Fredericton, N.B.; rector, Prince William, N.B., 1884-89, Bishop Doane Memorial Ch., S. Amboy, N.J., 1889-91, St. Mark the Evangelist, Philmont, N.Y., 1891-94; chaplain, Peekskill, N.Y., in St. Gabriel's Sch., 1894-98; rector Ch. of the Transfiguration, Freeport, N.Y., 1898-1900; editor of the Church Eclectic, 1900-08; editor Archives of the General Convention. Sec. Christian Unity Foundation. Author: Vindication of Anglican Orders (2 vols.), 1899, 3d edit., 1911. Home: New York, N.Y. Died Jan. 2, 1917.

LOWNDES, Lloyd, capitalist; b. Clarksburg, W.Va., Feb. 21, 1845; grad. Allegheny Coll., Meadville, Pa., (LL.D.); gov. Md., 1895-99; pres. 2d Nat. Bank, Cumberland, Md., and Union Mining Co., Allegheny Co., Md.; dir. Fidelity & Deposit Co., Baltimore, and New York Mining Co. Republican. Home: Cumberland, Md. Died 1905.

LOWNEY, Walter M., manufacturer; b. Sebec, Me., Sept. 2, 1855; s. William and Eliza Jane (Weston) L.; ed. pub. schs., Bangor, Me.; m. Nettie Bolton, Jan. 25, 1877. Began mfg. chocolate bonbons at Boston, 1883, inc., 1890, as The Walter M. Lowney Co., of which is pres.; also pres. The Walter M. Lowney Co. of Can., Ltd., chartered, 1905, factory at Montreal. Dir. First Nat. Bank, Mansfield, Mass.; pres. Mansfield Realty Assn. Overseer Bunker Hill Boys' Club, Charlestown, Mass.; dir. Boys' Club Federation. Mason. Home: Mansfield, Mass. Died Apr. 4, 1921.

LOWRIE, John Cameron, Presbyterian clergyman; b. Butler, Pa., Dec. 16, 1808 (son of Walter Lowrie, U.S. senator from Pa., 1819-25); grad. Jefferson Coll., Pa., 1829 (D.D.); prepared for ministry at Western Theol. Sem. and Princeton Theol. Sem.; licensed to preach, June 21, 1832; apptd. missionary to India, 1833; returned, 1836, because of failing health; became asst. sec., and later sec., Presbyn. Missionary Bd.; now sec. emeritus. Was pastor 42d St. Presbyn. Ch., New York, 1845-50; moderator gen. assembly Presbyn. church, 1865. Author: Two Years in Upper India; Memoirs Hon. Walter Lowrie; Manual of Foreign Missions; Missionary Papers; Presbyterian Missions; m. Louisa Wilson, 1833 (died in India); m. 2d, Elizabeth Boyd, 1838. Home: East Orange, N.J. Died 1900.

LOWRIE, Samuel Thompson, clergyman; b. Pittsburgh, Feb. 8, 1835; s. Walter H. (late chief justice of Pa.) and Rachel (Thompson) L.; A.B., Miami U., 1852, A.M., 1854; Western Theol. Sem., Pa., 1852-56; U. of Heidelberg, 1856-57, Berlin, 1863; (D.D., Washington and Jefferson, 1875); m. Sarah A. Hague, Sept. 6, 1860 (died 1862); m. 2d, Elizabeth A., d. Rev. H. S. Dickson, of W. Chester, Pa., Mar. 5, 1867 (died 1907); father of Walter L. Ordained to the Presbyterian ministry, 1858; pastor, Alexandria, Pa., 1858-63, Bethany Church, Phila., 1865-69, Abington, Pa., 1869-74; prof. N.T. lit. and exegesis, Western Theol. Sem., 1874-78; pastor

Ewing, N.J., 1879-85; chaplain Presbyn. Hosp., Phila., 1886-89; asso. pastor Wylie Memorial Ch., Phila., 1891-96. Dir. Princeton Theol. Sem., 1893-1910. (Declined re-election, May 1910.) Corr. sec. Presbyterian Hist. Soc., 1893-1906; v.p. Presbyn. Bd. of Relief, 1900-12. Co-translator, Numbers and Isaiah, Lange-Schaff Bible-Work. Translator: Beyond the Grave (from German of Dr. Hermann Cremer), 1886. Died Sept. 22, 1924.

LOWRY, Horace, rapid transit official; b. Minneapolis, Minn., Feb. 4, 1880; s. Thomas and Beatrice M. (Goodrich) L.; B.Sc., U. of Minn., 1900; m. Kate S. Burwell; Mar. 18, 1909; children—Thomas, Goodrich. With Twin City Rapid Transit Co., 1900—, successively as electrician, chief clk. auditor's dept., supt. Minn. div., 1908, 12, v.p. and gen. mgr., 1912-16, pres., 1916—; also pres. Arcade Investment Co.; dir. Duluth-Superior Traction Co., Northwestern National Bank, Minn., etc. Trustee Minn. Inst. Fine Arts. Republican. Elk. Universalist. Home: Minneapolis, Minn. Died Aug. 22, 1931.

LOWRY, Robert, clergyman-hymn writer; b. Philadelphia, March 12, 1826; grad. Lewisburg, Pa., 1854 (D.D., 1875); entered Baptist ministry; pastor successively at West Chester, Pa., New York, Brooklyn, Lewisburg, Pa., and Plainfield, N.J.; pres. N.J. Baptist Sunday School Union, 1880-86; has written numerous Easter and Christmas services and single songs; edited a large number of hymn and Sunday school song collections. Prof. belles lettres, Lewisburg (now Bucknell) Univ., Pa., 1869-75; chancellor, 1876-82; edited Poems of Fanny J. Crosby, 1898; speaker at the Robert Raikes Centennial, London, 1880. Died 1899.

LOWRY, Robert, lawyer, gov. Miss.; b. S.C., 1830; common school education and law studies; m. Maria M. Gammage, Sept. 9, 1849. Entered C.S.A., 1861, pvt. Co. B 6th Mississippi regiment; an organization elected maj., later col. and 1864, promoted to brig. gen.; was at Shiloh and all battles in campaign of Ga., Columbia, Franklin, Nashville, Tenn., Corinth, Port Gibson, Baker's Creek, Miss., and others; twice wounded. Served both branches legislature; gov. Miss., 2 terms, 1882-90. Home: Jackson, Miss. Died 1910.

LOWRY, Thomas, financier; b. Logan Co., Ill., Feb. 27, 1843; s. Samuel R. and Rachel (Bullock) L.; ed. common schs. and 1 yr. Lombard Univ., Galesburg, Ill.; m. Beatrice M. Goodrich, Dec. 14, 1870. Admitted to bar, 1867; practiced at Minneapolis; several yrs. later bought and improved the entire st. ry. systems of St. Paul and Minneapolis, now owned by the Twin City Rapid Transit Co., of which he is pres. Also pres. Minneapolis, St. Paul & Sault Ste. Marie R.R. Home: Minneapolis, Minn. Died 1909.

LOWTHER, Granville, author, editor; b. Doddridge Co., W.Va., Jan. 19, 1848; s. Jesse and Hannah (Leeson) L.; ed. pub. schs., West Union, W.Va., and under pvt. tutors; D.D., Baker U., Kan., 1899; m. Elizabeth Ann Boyce, Dec. 22, 1869; children—Ada May (Mrs. Horace S. Wilkinson), John Franklin, Charles Centennial, Lola Edith, Mabel Elizabeth (Mrs. W. T. Schwarz). Agriculturist until 1874; minister in M.E. Ch. in Ill. and Kan., 1874-1902; presiding elder Winfield Dist., Kan., 1894-1900. Teacher psychology, sociology, Southwest Kansas College, acting pres. Southwest Kansas Coll., 1896-98; teacher of ancient and modern religions. Moved to Yakima, Wash., 1905, and engaged in fruit growing; discovered causes and remedies of various fruit diseases, notably apple rosette. Editor Fancy Fruit Magazine, 1908-12; hort. editor Northwest Farm Trio, Spokane, Wash., 1914—. Mem. governor's advisory bd., Wash., 1916-18. Minister Congregational Church. Mason. Author: Encyclopedia of Practical Horticulture, 4 vols., 1914; Poems, 1922. Home: Seattle, Wash. Died Sept. 9, 1933.

LOWY, Alexander, coll. prof.; b. New York, N.Y., Mar. 31, 1889; s. David and Fanny (Weiss) L.; B.S., Columbia, 1911, A.M., 1912, Ph.D., 1915; m. Dora Landberg, Dec. 23, 1915; children—Evelyn F., Muriel A., Alexander D. Asst. in electrochemistry, Columbia U., and teaching in N.Y. City until 1918; prof. of organic chemistry, U. of Pittsburgh, 1918—; holder of numerous U.S. patents on chem. research discoveries. Vice-pres. Am. Electrochemical Soc, 1930-33 and 1938-41; chmn. of its publ. com., 1931-41. Jewish religion. Author: Introduction to Organic Chemistry, 1922; Study Questions in Organic Chemistry, 1923; Laboratory Methods in Organic Chemistry, 1926; Industrial Organic Chemicals and Dye Intermediates, 1935. Home: Pittsburgh, Pa. Died Dec. 25, 1941.

LOY, Matthias, theologian; b. Cumberland Co., Pa., Mar. 17, 1828; s. Matthias and Christina (Reaver) L.; ed. Harrisburg Acad.; grad. Theol. Sem., Columbus, O., 1849; (hon. A.M., Capital U., 1853; D.D., Muhlenberg Coll., 1885); m. Mary Willey, Dec. 25, 1853. Ordained Luth. ministry, 1849; pastor Delaware, O., 1849-65; prof. theology, Capital U., 1865—. Editor Lutheran Standard, Columbus, O., 1864-91 Columbus Theol. Magazine 1881-88, and still regular contbr. Pres. Evang. Luth. Synod of Ohio, 1860-78, 1880-94. Author: The Doctrine of Justification, 1869; Sermons on the Gospels, 1888; The Christian Church, 1898; Story of My Life, 1905; Sermon on the Mount, 1909; Sermons on the Epistles. Translated: Life and Deeds of Dr. Martin Luther, by Rev. Herman Fick, 1878. Address: Columbus, O. Died Jan. 26, 1915.

LOYALL, George Robert, ry. pres.; b. Shadwell, Va., Dec. 3, 1867; s. John Henry and Lucy Caroline (Dabney) L.; ed. pub. and pvt. schs.; m. Lura Bradley Fulkerson. Telegraph operator and station agt. C.&O. Ry.; train dispatcher, chief dispatcher and master of trains, E. Tenn., Va. and Ga. Ry.; supt. Southern Ry., at Louisville, Ky., 1894-98; supt. same rd., at Asheville, N.C., 1898-1903; supt. same rd., Eastern dist., at Charlotte, 1903-06, and gen. supt. Middle dist., at Knoxville, Tenn., 1907-17; asst. v.p. Southern Ry. System, in charge of operation, at Washington, D.C., 1917 to period of federal control; then asst. federal mgr. Southern Ry. Lines, Carolina, Clinchfield & Ohio, Piedmont & Northern, and Ala. & Vicksburg Rys., and asst. regional dir. in charge of operation all railroads Southern region, at Atlanta, Ga.; asst. v.p. in charge of operation Southern Ry. System, at Washington, D.C., 1920-21; pres. and dir. Norfolk Southern R.R., at Norfolk, Va. Died Jan. 19, 1941.

LUBBOCK, Francis Richard, gov. of Texas; b. Beaufort, S.C., Oct. 16, 1815; s. Henry W. and Susan Ann (Saltus) L.; ed. Beaufort and Charleston, S.C.; m. Adele Baron, Feb. 5, 1835; 2d, Mrs. A. A. Porter, née Sarah E. Black, Dec. 1883; 3d, Lue Scott, Aug. 12, 1903. Began mercantile life quite young; went to Texas, 1836; has held offices of comptroller and other offices under republic of Texas; lt. gov., 1856, and gov. of Texas, 1861-63 (and known as the "War Governor"); state treas. for 12 yrs.; has held other offices under the state govt. Democrat. After term as gov. entered C.S.A.; was lt. col. and col. cav.; a.d.c. to President Davis; captured with him; imprisoned at Ft. Delaware nearly 8 months in solitary confinement. Author: Six Decades in Texas, Austin, 1900. Home: Austin, Tex. Died 1905.

LUBECK, Henry, clergyman; b. Sydney, N.S.W., Australia, Feb. 2, 1856; s. Peter Henry and Louisa (Collins) L.; came to U.S., 1883; LL.B., Albany (N.Y.) Law Sch., 1884; M.A., Hobart College, Geneva, N.Y., 1887; M.A., Bishop's Coll., Canada, 1892, D.C.L., same, 1894; B.C.L., D.C.L., Trinity U., Toronto, Ontario, 1896; LL.D., Hobart Coll., 1893; m. Emma Rose, June 25, 1884. Deacon, 1881; priest, 1882, Ch. of Eng. in Australia; missionary at Walgett and incumbent at Glen Innes, Australia, 1882; missionary at Fonda, N.Y., 1883-85; rector Grace Ch., Lyons, N.Y., 1885-88, St. Timothy's Ch., New York, 1888-90, Ch. of Zion and St. Timothy, New York, 1890-1918; canon Cathedral of SS. Peter and Paul, Washington, D.C., 1924—. Died Sept. 4, 1933.

LUBIN, David, merchant; b. 1849. In mercantile business at Sacramento, Calif. Suggested the founding, and U.S. del. to Internat. Inst. of Agr., Rome, for world crop, import and export reports, etc.; treaty ratified by 53 nations; to this project King of Italy gave a bldg. and an annual income of $60,000. Introduced the rural credits question in the U.S., also the nat. marketing proposal on the lines of the German Landwirtschaftsrat; secured introduction in Congress of proposal for an internat. conv. for the establishment of an internat. commerce commn. on merchant marine (passed by Congress Sept. 1, 1914); secured presentation in Congress, 1916, of measure for improving the parcels post service, to promote direct dealing between producers and consumers. Pres. Calif. Mus. Assn., Sacramento. Author: Let There Be Light. Home: Sacramento, Calif. Died Jan. 1, 1919.

LUBIN, Simon Julius, merchant; b. Sacramento, Calif., Nov. 27, 1876; s. David and Louise (Lyons) L.; A.B. magna cum laude, Harvard, 1903; m. Rebecca Cohen, Dec. 9, 1905; children—David J., Ruth H., Miriam J. In charge New York office of Weinstock, Lubin & Co. of Sacramento, 1904-06; sec. same corpn., 1906-16, v.p., 1916-20, pres., 1920-30, chmn. board, 1931-33. Now dir., Bureau of Commerce of State of Calif. Founder and pres. State Commn. of Immigration and Housing of Calif., from orgn., 1913 until Oct. 1923. Pres. from foundation, July 1926 to Jan. 1931, Sacramento Region Citizens Council, for economic and social development of 21 northern Calif. counties; pres. First Pan Am. Reciprocal Trade Conf., Sacramento, 1930; pres. Pan Am. Inst. of Reciprocal Trade. Republican. Jewish religion. Apptd. spl. commr. by Nat. Labor Bd. to investigate agrl. disturbances in Imperial Valley, Calif. Home: San Francisco, Calif. Died Apr. 15, 1936.

LUBOMIRSKI, Prince Casimir, diplomat; b. Cracow, Poland, July 16, 1869; s. Prince Georges and Countess Cecilia (Zamoyska) L.; ed. in law, univs. of Cracow, Munich and Vienna; in politics, École des Sciences politiques, Paris; in forestry, École forestiere, Nancy, France; m. Therese, Countess Wodzicka, of Poland, Apr. 19, 1902. Mem. legislative body of Austrian Poland, 12 yrs.; largely interested in farming and lumber industry; E.E. and M.P. of Republic of Poland to U.S., Sept. 1919—. Died Dec. 16, 1930.

LUBY, James, newspaperman; b. Dublin, Ireland; s. Thomas Clarke and Letitia (Fraser) L.; ed. St. Lawrence's School, Dublin, until 14; A.B., College of the City of New York; m. Emily Louise Huber (died 1916); m. 2d, Grace Louise Farrant. Began newspaper work in New York, 1877; asst. city editor Phila. Times, 1881; city editor New York Herald, 1887-89; editor Jersey City (N.J.) News, 1889-1903; cable editor New York Sun, 1905-12, London corr. in charge of European news service, June-Sept., 1912; mng. editor New York Evening Sun, Sept. 17, 1912; mng. editor The Sun, in succession to Chester S. Lord (resigned), Feb. 23, 1913; editor Evening Sun, Feb. 4, 1915-21; mng. editor Jour. of Commerce, 1921-22; editorial writer The Evening Mail, 1923—. Lecturer. Trustee Free Pub. Library, Jersey City, 1897-1904. Catholic. Cleveland Democrat. Author: The Black Cross Clove, 1910; One Who Gave His Life, 1923. Home: Brooklyn, N.Y. Died May 30, 1925.

LUCAS, Anthony Francis, mining engr.; b. Trieste, Austria, Sept. 9, 1855; s. Capt. Francis Stephen and Giovanna (Giovanizio) L.; ed. Poly. Acad., Gratz, Austria, 1874-77; post-grad. course in mining engring.; m. Carolina Weed Fitzgerald, Sept. 22, 1887. Has discovered various deposits of rocksalt occurring in Domes and to great depth, 3,000 feet and over, and by drilling a discovery well on Spindle-Top near Beaumont, Tex., Jan. 10, 1901, with initial capacity of 100,000 barrels of petroleum per day, established by original work an economic precedent for the production of petroleum, sulphur and rock salt on the Coastal Plains of La., Tex. and Mex. heretofore considered barren, thus establishing his Dome theory of oil concentration about salt Domes. Home: Washington, D.C. Died Sept. 2, 1921.

LUCAS, Daniel Bedinger, jurist; b. Charlestown, Va., Mar. 16, 1836; s. William and Virginia (Bedinger) L.; student Univ. of Va.; (LL.D., Univ. of W.Va., 1883); on staff Gen. H. A. Wise, in Civil War; m. Lena T., d. Henry L. Brooke, of Richmond, Va., Oct. 7, 1869. Presdl. elector, 1872, 1876, 1884, 1896; mem. W.Va. legislature, 1884-87; U.S. senator under gov.'s apptmt., 1887-88; pres. Sup. Ct. of Appeals of W.Va., 1888-93; resumed law practice; nat. elector, 1896, on the Bryan ticket. Author: Memoir of John Yates Beall, 1865; Poems and Madrigals, 1884; Nicaragua and the Filibusters, 1895; Hour Glass Series; etc. Home: Charlestown, W.Va. Died 1909.

LUCAS, Frederic Augustus, museum dir.; b. Plymouth, Mass., Mar. 25, 1852; s. Augustus Henry and Eliza (Oliver) L.; pub. sch. edn.; Sc.D., U. of Pittsburgh, 1909; m. Annie J. Edgar, Feb. 13, 1884; children—Jannette May, Ann Edgar. Asst., Ward's Natural Science Establishment, Rochester, N.Y., 1871-82; osteologist, 1882-87, asst. curator div. comparative anatomy, 1887-93, curator, 1893-1904, U.S. Nat. Mus.; curator-in-chief museums of Brooklyn Inst. of Arts and Sciences, 1904-11; dir. Am. Mus. of Natural History, New York, 1911-23, hon. dir., Jan. 1924—. Mem. commn. to investigate condition of fur seal herd of Pribilof Islands. Fellow Am. Ornithologists' Union, N.Y. Acad. Sciences. Author: Animals of the Past, 1901; Animals Before Man in North America, 1902. Home: Flushing, N.Y. Died Feb. 9, 1929.

LUCAS, John Henry, clergyman, educator; b. Pittsburgh, Pa., May 13, 1861; s. Henry and Elizabeth (Lowe) L.; ed. Hamiltonian Inst., Uniontown, Pa.; Adrian (Mich.) Coll., 1877-81; (D.D., Kansas City U., 1904, LL.D., 1914); m. Martha E. Scott, Sept. 17, 1884. Ordained ministry M.P. Ch., 1885; pastor Waynesburg, Pa., 1883-85, Kittanning, 1 yr., 1885-86, Springdale, 1886-90, Trinity Ch., Brooklyn, 1890-93, 1st Ch., Pittsburgh, N.S., 1893-1902, People's Temple, Fairmont, W.Va., 1902-05; sec. treas. Bd. Home Missions, M.P. Ch., 1905-08; pastor 1st Congl. Ch., Pittsburgh, Pa., 1908-11, Squirrel Hill M.P. Ch., Pittsburgh, 1911-14; chancellor Kansas City U., July 1, 1914—. Pres. Pittsburgh Conf. M.P. Ch., 1913-14; mem. Bd. Publn. M.P. Ch. Trustee Adrian Coll. 8 yrs. Died Sept. 1, 1919.

LUCAS, Thomas John, army officer; b. Lawrenceburg, Ind., Sept. 9, 1826; s. Frederick and Letitia (Netherly) L.; ed. Lawrenceburg, Ind.; m. Ann Eliza Munson, Sept. 24, 1848. Learned jewelry trade with father and engaged in business. Served, pvt. to adj., Co. C, 4th Ind. vols., in Mexican war, participating in battles of Broken Bridge, Cerro Gordo, Huamantha, Ecliso, Pueblo, etc. In Civil war helped raise 2 cos.; raised 3d, becoming capt.; col. 16th Ind. vols., which met Kirby Smith at Richmond, Ky., losing 200 men; fought under Grant in all the operations about Vicksburg; regt. joined 13th army corps and captured Arkansas Post; later took part in all battles in and around Vicksburg until surrender; promoted brig. gen. and entered on Mobile campaign; bvtd. maj. gen., and at head of independent command, under Canby, raided Western Fla.,

Ga. and Ala., destroying railroads and munitions of war; after war in New Orleans until mustered out, Jan. 1866. Was in internal revenue service 4 yrs.; postmaster of Lawrenceburg, 1881-85, 1889-93; was candidate for Congress, 1886, defeated. Republican. Home: Lawrenceburg, Ind. Deceased.

LUCCOCK, George Naphtali, clergyman; b. Kimbolton, O., Mar. 31, 1857; s. Samuel W. and Elizabeth W. (Day) L.; A.B., U. of Wooster, 1878, A.M., 1881 (D.D., 1904); grad. Western Theol. Sem., 1881; m. Emma Bingham, Sept. 3, 1882. Ordained Presbyterian ministry, 1881; in home missionary work, Kossuth, Emmett Dickinson and Greene counties, Ia., and Westminster Ch., Des Moines, 1881-91; pastor First Ch., Bloomington, Ind., 1891-94, Met. Ch., Washington, D.C., 1894-1903, 1st Ch., Oak Park, Ill., Aug. 1903—. Del. World's Missionary Conf., Edinburgh, 1910; mem. Gen. Assembly's Com. to prepare new Intermediate Catechism; chmn. Gen. Assembly's com. on vacancy and supply; mem. bd. dirs. Training Sch., Chicago; pres. Bd. Ch. Extension, Chicago; trustee German Theol. Sch., Dubuque, Ia. Republican. Presbyn. Died Feb. 23, 1943.

LUCCOCK, Naphtali, bishop; b. Kimbolton, O., Sept. 28, 1853; A.B., Ohio Wesleyan U., 1874, A.M., 1877; Ph.D., Western U., of Pa. (now U. of Pittsburgh), 1886; (D.D., Syracuse U., 1886); m. Etta Anderson, Sept. 27, 1877. Was pastor M.E. chs., Pittsburgh and Erie, Pa.; prof. Allegheny Coll., Meadville, Pa., 1885-88; pastor Union M.E. Ch., St. Louis, and editor American Illustrated Methodist Magazine; later pastor Hyde Park Ch., Kansas City, Mo., to 1912; elected bishop M.E. Ch., 1912. Author: Christian Citizenship; Living Words from the Pulpit; (in collaboration) Illustrated History of Methodism, 1901; Royalty of Jesus (sermons), 1905. Home: Helena, Mont. Died Apr. 1, 1916.

LUCE, Cyrus Gray, farmer, gov. Mich., 1887-91; b. Windsor, O., July 2, 1824; ed. country schools and 3 terms at Northwestern Ind. Collegiate Inst., Ontario, Ind.; defeated by 11 votes as Whig candidate for Ind. legislature, 1848; removed to Branch Co., Mich., 1848, and engaged in farming there; supervisor Gilead Tp., 12 yrs.; mem. legislature, 1854-56; co. treas., 1858-62; State senator, 1865, 1867; mem. constl. conv., 1867; State oil insp., 1879-83; mem. commn. to locate instn. for feeble-minded, 1894; prominent in agrl. organizations; m. Julia A. Dickinson, 1849 (died 1882); m. 2d, Mary E. Thompson, Nov. 8, 1883. Home: Coldwater, Mich. Died 1905.

LUCE, Harry James, mcht.; b. Monroe, Mich., June 16, 1861; s. William Euston and Sophia (Hayes) L.; student U. of Mich., 1885-86; m. Katherine Moxley, 1889. Began as clk. Globe Tobacco Co., Detroit, 1887; later with Powell Smith & Co. to 1901; pres. Acker, Merrall & Condit Co., grocers, 1902—; dir. Henry Maillard, Inc., Faber Coe, Gregg, Inc. Home: New York, N.Y. Died Aug. 17, 1929.

LUCE, Stephen Bleecker, rear admiral; b. Albany, N.Y., Mar. 25, 1827; s. Vinal and Charlotte (Bleecker) L.; apptd. midshipman from N.Y., Oct. 19, 1841; served on many stations and circumnavigated the globe; served on the Pacific coast during Mexican War; went to Naval Acad. for promotion to passed midshipman, 1848; promoted master, Nov. 15, 1855; lt., Sept. 16, 1855; lt. comdr., July 16, 1862; comdr., July 25, 1866; capt., Dec. 28, 1872; commodore, Nov. 25, 1881; rear admiral, U.S.N., Oct. 5, 1885. During Civil War was lt. of frigate Wabash, comdr. of monitor Natucket and the double-ender Sonoma, the Canandaigua and the Pontiac; served in N. Atlantic Blockading Squadron; in active service after war until retired, Mar. 25, 1889. Founded Naval War Coll., 1884; was mainly instrumental in establishment of naval training system. Commr. gen., Columbian Hist. Expn., Madrid, 1892. Author: Naval Songs, 1889; Seamanship, 1898, 1905. Home: Newport, R.I. Died July 28, 1917.

LUCEY, Dennis Benedict, lawyer; b. Boston, Mass., Aug. 17, 1860; s. Dennis Joseph and Ellen (Goggin) L.; grad. Potsdam (N.Y.) Normal Sch., 1883; m. Mary Agnes Tuck, June 30, 1891. Practiced at Ogdensburg, 1888—; associated in practice with George R. Malby from 1890 until his death, 1912; mayor Ogdensburg, 1895, 96, 97; served as chmn. Dem. County Com., St. Lawrence Co., also del. to N.Y. State and nat. convs.; U.S. dist. atty., by appmt. of President Wilson, 1916; reappointed by same, 1920; resigned, 1921. Trustee St. Lawrence Co. Savings Bank. Pres. Bd. of Edn., Ogdensburg. Mem. N.G.N.Y., 1885-99; 1st lt. Co. H, 203d Regt. U.S. Vol. Inf., Spanish-Am. War, 1898. Home: Ogdensburg, N.Y. Died Oct. 6, 1929.

LUCKENBILL, Daniel David, univ. prof.; b. nr. Hamburg, Pa., June 21, 1881; s. Benjamin Franklin and Mary Jane (Berger) L.; A.B., U. of Pa., 1903; studied U. of Berlin, 1905; Ph.D., U. of Chicago, 1907; Am. Sch. of Archæology at Jerusalem, 1908-09; m. Florence Parker, Feb. 24, 1914. Asso. in Semitic langs. and lits., 1907-09, instr., 1909-15, asst. prof., 1915-19, asso. prof., 1919-23, prof., 1923—, U. of Chicago. Advisory editor Journal of Religion; coöperating editor Am. Journal Semitic Languages and Literatures. Curator Assyrian collections in Haskell Mus.; mem. U. of Chicago Oriental Expdn., 1919-20; British Museum Expdn., autumn 1924. Republican. Mem. Ref. Ch. in U.S. Author: The Annals of Sennacherib, 1924. Home: Chicago, Ill. Died June 5, 1927.

LUCKEY, George Washington Andrew, educator; b. on farm near Decatur, Ind., Feb. 11, 1855; s. George W. and Druzilla (Arnold) L.; B.S., Northern Indiana Normal School, 1883; A.B., Stanford, 1894; A.M., Clark, 1895; Ph.D., Columbia, 1900; student biology, Hopkins Seaside Lab., Pacific Grove, Calif., summers, 1893, 94; fellow in psychology, Clark U., 1894-95; fellow in edn., Teachers' Coll. (Columbia), 1899-1900; graduate student Göttingen Univ., 1912-13; m. Bertha M. Musson, Dec. 26, 1882; children—Bertha Musson, George Paul. Teacher rural and village schs., 1872-79; co. supt. schs., Adams Co., Ind., 1879-83; prin. high sch. and city supt. schs., Decatur, Ind., 1883-87; supervisory prin. schs., Beaumont, Calif., 1887-88; supt. schs., Ontario, Calif., 1888-92; asso. prof. and organized dept. edn., 1895-96, prof., 1896-1906, head prof. edn., 1906-18, and dean Grad. Sch. of Edn., 1914-18, U. of Neb.; specialist in foreign ednl. systems, U.S. Bur. of Education, 1920-25. Travel and study, Europe, 1906-07, 1912-13. Chmn. exec. com., Neb. Child Study Assn., 1896-1907. Author: The Essentials of Child Study, 1917; Education, Democracy, and League of Nations, 1919; Outlines of Education Systems and School Conditions in Latin America, 1923; The International Education Research Council and World Bureau of Education, 1925; Longevity of Eminent Individuals, 1929; Longevity of Eminent Poets, Scientists, and Educators Compared, 1931. Editor child study dept., Northwestern Monthly, 1896-99; edited Child Study and Physical Child numbers, Northwestern Monthly, July 1896 and 1897. Home: Lincoln, Neb. Died Mar. 30, 1933.

LUCKEY, James S., educator; b. Short Tract, N.Y., Aug. 1, 1867; s. James and Pollyanne (Davis) L.; A.B., Oberlin, 1904, A.M., 1905; A.M., Harvard, 1908; Pd.M., Albany Normal Coll., 1898; LL.D., Wheaton Coll., Wheaton, Ill., 1933; m. Edith Sarah Bedell, June 28, 1894; children—James Harold, Ruth Evangeline, Robert Raphael. Prin. Union Sch., Millerton, N.Y., 1898-1902; instr. Oberlin Coll., 1905-07; pres. Houghton Sem., 1908-23; pres. Houghton Coll., 1923—. Republican. Wesleyan Methodist. Home: Houghton, N.Y. Died Apr. 7, 1937.

LUCKING, Alfred, congressman; b. Ingersoll, Ont., Dec. 18, 1856; s. Joseph and Margaret (Ford) L.; ed. Mich. State Normal Coll.; LL.B., U. of Mich., 1878; m. Vie Loree Rose, Feb. 3, 1881; children—William Alfred, Dean Loree. Practiced at Jackson, Mich., 1878-80; mem. Maybury, Lucking, Emmons & Helfman, 1903-10; head of firm Lucking, Helfman, Lucking & Hanlon, 1910—. Temporary chairman Dem. State Convention, 1900, permanent chmn., 1902 and 1908; mem. 58th Congress (1903-05), 1st Mich. Dist.; primary nominee of Dem. party for U.S. senator, 1912, and received entire vote of the party in the legislature; chmn. Dem. State Conv., 1924; mem. resolutions com. and author of plank of platform for referendum on League of Nations. Was gen. counsel Ford Motor Co. and Henry Ford interests for many yrs.; v.p. Nelson Baker & Co.; pres. Detroit-Vancouver Timber Co. Home: Detroit, Mich. Died Dec. 1, 1929.

LUDDEN, Patrick Anthony, bishop; b. nr. Castlebar, Ireland, 1836; studied at St. Jarlath's Coll., Tuam, Ireland, and Grand Séminaire, Montreal, Can.; ordained R.C. priest, 1864. Asst. Immaculate Conception Cathedral, Albany, N.Y.; pastor, Malone, N.Y., rector Albany Cathedral, and vicar-gen. of diocese, 1877-80; pastor St. Peter's Ch., Troy, N.Y., 1880-87; consecrated 1st bishop of Syracuse, May 1, 1887. Was present at Ecumenical Council, Rome, 1869. Died Aug. 6, 1912.

LUDERS, Gustav Carl, composer; b. Bremen, Germany, Dec. 13, 1865; s. Dr. Gustav Heinrich and Louise Clementine (Precht) L.; ed. Gymnasium, Sondershausen; served 1 yr. in German Army; studied violin, piano, and composition under Henry Petri, now royal concert-meister at Dresden; came to America, 1888; m. Grace Gorseline, Feb. 3, 1901. Lutheran. Author (comic operas): The Burgomaster; King Dodo; Prince of Pilsen; Woodland; The Shogun; Mlle. Napoleon; The Grand Mogul; Marcelle; The Fair Coëd; The Old Town. Home: New York, N.Y. Died Jan. 24, 1912.

LUDINGTON, Arthur Crosby, polit. reform work; b. New York, Mar. 6, 1880; s. Charles Henry and Josephine Lord (Noyes) L.; A.B., Yale, 1902; U. of Heidelberg, 1907-08; Columbia, 1909-11; unmarried. With bond house, New York, 1903-05; instr. and asst. to the pres. (Woodrow Wilson) of Princeton U., 1905-07; supervisor U.S. Indian Schs., Dept. Interior, Washington, short time, 1912, to write report on Indian policy of U.S. Government. Author: American Ballot Laws, 1888-1910, 1911. Home: New York, N.Y. Died Nov. 4, 1914.

LUDINGTON, Charles Henry, publisher; b. N.Y. City, Aug. 9, 1866; s. Charles Henry and Josephine Lord (Noyes) L.; prep. edn., St. Paul's Sch., 1878-83; B.A., Yale, 1887; M.A., 1889; m. Ethel Mildred Saltus, Apr. 24, 1895 (died 1922); children—Charles Townsend, Wright Saltus, Nicholas Saltus. Admitted to N.Y. bar, 1891, and practiced 10 yrs. with Anderson & Howland, later with Cary & Whitridge; was sec. U.S. Debenture Corp., Ltd., and pres. Continental Filter Co.; moved to Phila., 1901, as sec. and treas. The Curtis Pub. Co., now v.p. and treas. V.p. Phila. Congress of Arts; trustee Pa. Mus. and Sch. Industrial Art; trustee and treas. Bryn Mawr Presbyn. Ch. Home: Ardmore, Pa. Died Nov. 13, 1927.

LUDINGTON, Marshall Independence, major general; b. Smithfield, Pa., July 4, 1839; s. Zalmon and Lovila (Hagans) L.; m. Harriet Foote Marvin, Oct. 18, 1871. Commd. capt. asst. q.m. vols., Oct. 20, 1862; maj. q.m., Aug. 2-Oct. 23, 1864; col. q.m., Oct. 24, 1864-Jan. 1, 1867; bvtd. maj., lt. col. and col. vols., Mar. 13, 1865, "for faithful and meritorious services during the war," and brig. gen. vols., Mar. 13, 1865, and lt. col. U.S.A., Mar. 2, 1867, "for faithful and meritorious services in q.m. dept. during the war." Apptd. from Pa., maj. q.m. U.S.A., Jan. 18, 1867; lt. col. deputy q.m. gen., Mar. 15, 1883; col. asst. q.m. gen., Dec. 31, 1894; brig. gen. q.m. gen., Feb. 3, 1898; maj. gen., Apr. 12, 1903; retired at own request after 40 yrs'. service, Apr. 13, 1903. Home: Skaneateles, N.Y. Died July 29, 1919.

LUDLAM, Reuben, M.D.; b. Camden, N.J., Oct. 7, 1831; grad. med. dept., Univ. of Pa., 1852; studied in Europe; settled in Chicago as homœopathic physician; connected with Hahnemann Med. Coll. and hospital from organization, 1860, becoming dean and clinical prof. surgical diseases of women. Pres. Am. Inst. Homœopathy, 1870; pres. Chicago Acad. of Medicine, 1873; member Ill. State bd. of health, 1877-87. Author: Clinical Lectures on Diphtheria; Clinical and Didactic Lectures on Diseases of Women; etc. Home: Chicago, Ill. Died 1899.

LUDLOW, Arthur Clyde, clergyman; b. Chardon, O., June 4, 1861; s. Linnaeus Charles and Helen Augusta (Stafford) L.; A.B., Adelbert Coll. (Western Reserve U.), 1884, A.M., 1887; Lane Theol. Sem., Cincinnati, 1884-85; B.D., Union Theol. Sem., 1887; D.D., Wooster, 1901; m. Jennie Gould, May 17, 1888 (died 1890); 1 son, Carroll Gould; m. 2d, Rosa Elizabeth Roeder, Mar. 28, 1893 (died 1918); m. 3d, Miss Lillian S. Prall, June 20, 1923. Ordained Presbyn. ministry, 1887; pastor Miles Park Ch., Cleveland, 1886-1923, now pastor emeritus. Stated clk. Cleveland Presbytery; permanent clk. Synod of Ohio; moderator of Synod, 1913. Author: History of Cleveland Presbyterianism, 1896; Centennial History of the Old Stone (First Presbyterian) Church, Cleveland, Ohio, 1920; Centennial History of Western Reserve University, 1926. Home: Cleveland Heights, O. Died Apr. 16, 1927.

LUDLOW, Edwin, mining engr.; b. Oakdale, L.I., N.Y., Mar. 12, 1858; s. William Handy and Louise (Nicoll) L.; ed. Flushing (N.Y.) Inst., 1868-75; M.E., School of Mines (Columbia), 1879; m. Anna Wright, Nov. 22, 1893. Asst. engr. on river and harbor works, Phila., 1879-81; asst. supt. and supt. Mineral R.R. & Mining Co., Shamokin, Pa., 1881-89; supt. mines, Choctaw, Okla. & Gulf R.R., Hartshorne, Okla., 1889-99; gen. mgr. Mexican Coal & Coke Co., Las Esperanzas, Mex., 1899-1911; v.p. New River Collieries Co., Eccles, W.Va., 1911-12; v.p. Lehigh Coal & Navigation Co., Lansford, Pa., 1912-19; consulting mining engr., New York, July 1, 1919—. Democrat. Episcopalian. Died Feb. 10, 1924.

LUDLOW, George C., asso. justice supreme court N.J.; b. Milford, N.J., April 6, 1830; grad. Rutgers Coll., 1850; admitted to bar, 1853; established practice at New Brunswick, N.J. Became active in politics as a Democrat; State senator, 1876-80; pres. senate, one session; gov. N.J., Jan. 1881 to Jan. 1884; resumed practice until apptd. to supreme bench. Home: New Brunswick, N.J. Died 1900.

LUDLOW, Henry Gilbert, inventor, mfr.; b. Nassau, N.Y., March 28, 1823; grad. Union Coll., 1843; spent some time with gas co. in Phila., in order to learn profession of gas engring.; later, with friends, engaged in constructing gas works. Invented the Ludlow straight-way slide-stop valve and engaged in its manufacture, incorporating the Ludlow Valve Mfg. Co., now the largest valve mfg. co. in the world; retired from the business, 1891, but still has an interest in it; m. Harriet M. Shattuck, 1854. Home: Troy, N.Y. Died 1904.

LUDLOW, Jacob Lott, engineer; b. Spring Lake, N.J., Dec. 20, 1862; s. Samuel and Nancy (Johnson) L.; C.E., Lafayette Coll., Easton, Pa., 1885, later M.S.; m. Myra M. Hunt, Jan. 5, 1887. Began practice at Winston-Salem, N.C., 1890; pres. The Ludlow Engrs., Inc.; mem. and cons. engr. N.C. State Bd. of Health, 1890-1920; mem. Engring. Bd. of Review, Sanitary Dist. of Chicago, 1924, 25. Has served as cons. engr. various Southern cities, on water supply and sewerage projects, valuation of pub. utilities, etc. Col. and chief of engrs., N.C.N.G., 1908-16; supervising engr. on constrn. camp cantonments, World War, also supervising sanitary engr. U.S. Shipping Bd. for S. Atlantic and Gulf states. Democrat. Presbyn. Home: Winston-Salem, N.C. Died Aug. 18, 1930.

LUDLOW, James Meeker, clergyman; b. Elizabeth, N.J., Mar. 15, 1841; s. Ezra and Deborah (Crane) L.;

A.B., Princeton, 1861; grad. Princeton Theol. Sem., 1864; D.D., Williams, 1872; L.H.D., Princeton, 1888; m. Emma J., d. David Orr, July 5, 1865. Ordained Presbyn. ministry, 1864; pastor First Ch., Albany, 1865-69, Collegiate Ch., New York, 1869-77, Westminster Ch., Brooklyn, 1877-85, Munn Av. Ch., E. Orange, N.J., 1886-1900, pastor emeritus. Trustee Union Theol. Sem., Whittier House Social Settlement, Jersey City. Author: Captain of the Janizaries, 1886; A King of Tyre, 1890; That Angelic Woman, 1890; Deborah, 1901; Incentives for Life, 1902; Sir Raoul, 1905; Jesse Ben David, 1907; Judge West's Opinion, 1908; The Discovery of Self, 1910; Avanti!, 1913; Along the Friendly Way, 1919. Home: East Orange, N.J. Died Oct. 4, 1932.

LUDLOW, Nicoll, rear admiral U.S.N.; b. Riverside Islip, L.I., N.Y., Sept. 11, 1842; s. Gen. William H. and Frances Louisa (Nicoll) L.; apptd. from N.Y., and grad. U.S. Naval Acad., 1863; m. Frances Mary Thomas, May 1870; m. 2d, Mary McLean Bugher, Feb. 1897. Promoted ensign, Oct. 1, 1863; advanced through grades to rear adm., Nov. 1, 1899; retired. Served on Wachusett, Brazilian Squadron, 1863-64; participated in capture of Confederate cruiser Florida in Harbor of Bahia, Brazil, Oct. 7, 1864; served on monitor Dictator, 1865; Monadnock, 1865-66, making passage from New York to San Francisco; Iroquois, Asiatic Squadron, 1867-70; Naval Acad., 1870-73; exec. officer Monongahela, 1873-75; Brooklyn, 1876; torpedo duty, 1876-77; exec. officer Trenton, European Squadron, 1877-80; insp. ordnance, West Point Foundry, South Boston Iron Works and Midvale Steel Works, 1880-83; comd. Quinnebaug, European sta., 1883-86; spl. duty, New York, 1886-87; light house insp., 12th dist., 1887-90, 9th dist., 1891-92; insp. ordnance, Navy Yard, Mare Island, 1892; comd. Mohican, Bering Sea Squadron, 1893; leave 1894; Naval War Coll., 1895; comd. Monterey, Pacific Squadron, 1896; mem. Naval Retiring Bd., Jan.-July 1897; comd. Terror, Atlantic Fleet, 1897-98, Massachusetts, Atlantic Fleet, 1898-99; retired, Nov. 1, 1899; gov. Naval Home, Phila., 1904-07. Died Dec. 9, 1915.

LUDLOW, William, brig. gen. U.S.A., Jan. 21, 1900; b. Riverside, Islip, L.I., N.Y., Nov. 27, 1843; s. William Handy and Frances Louisa (Nicoll) L.; ed. Burlington Coll., N.J., and N.Y. Univ., 1853-60; grad. West Point, June 20, 1864; commissioned 1st lt., corps of engrs.; m. Genevieve Almira Sprigg, 1866. Chief engr. 20th army corps, under Gens. Hooker and Slocum, in Atlanta campaign, 1864; chief engr., left wing Gen. Sherman's army in Savannah, and the Carolinas campaign, 1864-65; comdg. Co. E, engr. battalion, Jefferson barracks, Mo., 1865-67; capt. engrs. U.S.A., March 7, 1867; chief engr., Dept. of Dak., in Black Hills and Yellowstone expdns.; in charge of various works of fortifications, rivers and harbors, on Atlantic coast from New York to St. Augustine, Fla.; chief engr. Phila. water dept. by election of city councils and spl. joint resolution of Congress, 1883-86; maj. engrs., June 30, 1882; engr. sec. light house bd., Washington, 1882; engr. commr. of D.C., 1886-88; charge river and harbor and light house work on Great Lakes, 1888-93; mil. attaché U.S. Embassy, London, 1893-96; lt. col. engrs., Aug. 13, 1895; pres. U.S. Nicaragua Canal Commn., 1895; brig. gen., U.S.V., May 4, 1898; chief engr. armies in the field, May, 1898; comdg. 1st brigade, 2d div., Shafter's corps, Santiago campaign; battles of Caney and San Juan and investment of Santiago June-Sept., 1898; maj. gen. U.S.V., Sept. 7, 1898; pres. bd. to organize Army Sea Transport Service, Sept.-Oct., 1898. Mil. gov. Havana, Dec. 12, 1898, to May 1, 1900; comdg. dept. Havana, Dec. 1898-May 1, 1900; pres. War Coll. Bd., May 1, 1900—. Died 1901.

LUECK, Martin Lawrence, lawyer; b. Juneau, Wis., July 24, 1872; s. Frederick W. and Phillipine (Scheuer) L.; ed. pub. schs.; LL.B., U. of Wis., 1894; m. Hedwig Kuentzel, May 4, 1904; children—Ruth H., Dorothy C., Mae C. Admitted to Wis. bar, 1894, and began practice at Juneau; dist. atty. Dodge Co., Wis., 1899-1903; mayor of Juneau, 1906-07; circuit judge, 13th Jud. Circuit, Wis., 1907-21; mem. Dem. Nat. Com., Wis., 1924—. Mem. German Ref. Ch. Home: Beaver Dam, Wis. Died July 18, 1926.

LUECKE, Martin, college pres.; b. Sheboygan Co., Wis., June 22, 1859; s. Christian and Emily (von Henning) L.; grad. prep. sch., Concordia Coll., Ft. Wayne, Ind., 1878, Concordia Theol. Sem., St. Louis, 1881; m. Sina Mansholt, 1882; children—Martin Paul Emil, Martha (dec.), Elisabeth, John, Christian, Walter, Wilbur. Ordained Evang. Luth. ministry, 1881; pastor Bethalto, Ill., 1881-84, Troy, Ill., 1884-92, Springfield, Ill., 1892-1903, also holding several positions in Synod of Mo., Ohio and other States; pres. and prof. N.T. Greek and religion, Concordia Coll., Ft. Wayne, 1903—. Founded Springfield (Ill.) Hospital and Training Sch., 1897. Author: Synopsis of the Holy History of Old and New Testaments, 1906; Short Life of Christ, 1911. Home: Ft. Wayne, Ind. Died Apr. 13, 1926.

LUEDEKING, Robert, physician; b. St. Louis, Nov. 6, 1853; s. Carl and Elise (Dauber) L.; grad. St. Louis High Sch., 1871; studied medicine univs. of Heidelberg and Strassburg, Germany, 1872-76, M.D., Strassburg, 1876; post-grad. work Vienna, 1876-77, in Berlin, 1887, 1899, 1903, 1905; m. Elise Biebinger, Oct. 18, 1879. Dispensary physician and sec. St. Louis Bd. of Health, 1877-83; acting supt. City and Female hosps., 1880; lecturer, 1882-83, prof. pathol. anatomy, 1883-92, St. Louis Med. Coll.; prof. medicine and diseases of children, 1892—, dean med. dept., 1902—, Washington Univ.; mem. staff Jewish Hosp., St. Luke's Hosp., Bethesda Founding Home; mem. St. Louis Milk Commn. Home: St. Louis, Mo. Died 1908.

LUFKIN, Elgood Chauncey, corp. officer; b. Springfield, Mass., Feb. 5, 1864; s. Chauncey Forbush and Rachel (Barr) L.; B.Sc., Mass. Inst. Tech., 1886; m. Lula Moulton, Oct. 15, 1890; children—Mrs. Florence Hunsiker, Chauncey Forbush, Elgood Moulton. Engr. The Holly Mfg. Co., Lockport, N.Y., 1886-89; chief engr. Ind. Pipe Line Co., Lima, O., 1889-95; v.p., gen. mgr. Snow Steam Pump Works, Holly Mfg. Co., Buffalo, N.Y., 1895-1908; v.p. The Texas Co., Houston, Tex., 1909-11, of New York, 1911-13, pres. of latter, 1913-20, chmn. bd. and exec. com., 1920-26; chmn. bd. Rye (N.Y.) Trust Co.; dir. Houston Properties Corp.—all of N.Y.; retired from business, 1926. Served as mem. sub. com. on oil, of com. on raw materials and metals, Council of Nat. Defense, World War; v. chmn. Nat. Petroleum War Service Com. Republican. Presbyn. Mason. Home: Rye, N.Y. Died Oct. 9, 1935.

LUFKIN, Wilfred W., congressman; b. Essex, Mass., Mar. 10, 1879; s. Alvin P. and Ida (Herrick) L.; ed. pub. schs.; m. Georgia Story, Nov. 7, 1914; children—Wilfred W., Constance G., Edith, Elizabeth. Formerly newspaper corr.; served as pvt. sec. to Congressman Augustus P. Gardner; after resignation of Mr. Gardner from Congress, May 15, 1917, elected to 65th Congress for his unexpired term (1917-19), 6th Mass. Dist.; reëlected to 66th and 67th Congresses (1919-23); resigned June 30, 1921, to accept apptmt. as collector of port of Boston. Republican. Mem. Mass. Constl. Conv., 1917; chmn. Sch. Bd., Essex, 1901-07 and 1922-26. Universalist. Mason. Home: Essex, Mass. Died Mar. 28, 1934.

LUKE, Arthur Fuller, banker; b. Cambridge, Mass., Jan. 28, 1853; pub. sch. edn.; m. Eliza W. Brown, Dec. 17, 1878. Entered bank as clk., 1870; asst. nat. bank examiner, Boston, 1878-80; cashier Nat. Bank of N. America, 1880-90; asst. treas. Nat. Tube Works Co., 1890-92, treas., 1892-99; treas. Nat. Tube Co., 1899-1901; treas. U.S. Steel Corp., Apr. 1901-Jan. 1902; mem. Luke, Banks & Weeks, New York, N.Y. Died Sept. 29, 1917.

LUKEMAN, (Henry) Augustus, sculptor; b. Richmond, Va., Jan. 28, 1871; studied Nat. Acad. Design, New York, École des Beaux Arts, Paris; L.H.D., Dickinson Coll. Important work: Statues of William McKinley, for Adams, Mass., and Dayton, O.; of "Manu" for court house, N.Y.; sculpture for Pan-American Expn., Buffalo, 1901, St. Louis Exposition, 1904; portrait busts and bas reliefs; architectural sculpture for buildings in Pittsburgh and in New York; 4 colossal statues in marble for Royal Bank Bldg., Montreal; 4 colossal statues for Brooklyn Inst.; war memorial, Pittsfield, Mass., and Wilmington, Delaware; Masonic war memorial, Elizabethtown, Pa.; soldiers' monument for Somerville, Mass.; statue of Prof. Joseph Henry for Princeton U.; equestrian statue of Kit Carson, for Trinidad, Colo.; of Francis Asbury, Washington, D.C.; equestrian statue of Francis Asbury, Drew Theol. Sem., Madison, N.J.; of General Gregg, Reading, Pa.; statue of Columbus, Custom House, New York; Women of the Confederacy monument, Raleigh, N.C.; U.S. Grant memorial, San Diego, Calif.; Franklin Pierce monument, Concord, N.H.; Straus memorial fountain, New York; Gen. William Shepard monument, Westfield, Mass.; Brooklyn's Honor Roll and Soldiers' Memorial, Prospect Park; Red Hook Park Soldiers' Monument, Brooklyn; memorial fountain, Elizabethtown, Pa.; statues of Senator J. Z. George and Jefferson Davis for Statuary Hall, Washington, D.C.; heroic bas-relief portrait of Daniel Boone, for Paris, Ky.; heroic portrait bust of Jefferson Davis, for Transylvania Coll., Lexington, Ky.; portrait statue of Elisha Yale, Gloversville, N.Y.; heroic bronze portrait statue of James Kennedy Patterson, 1st pres. U. of Ky., Lexington, Ky. Medal, St. Louis Exposition, 1904; Stone Mountain Confederate memorial with Memorial Mall, Stone Mountain, Ga. A.N.A., 1909. Home: New York, N.Y. Died Apr. 3, 1935.

LUKS, George Benjamin, painter; b. Williamsport, Pa., Aug. 13, 1867; s. Emil Charles and Bertha (von Kraemer) L.; ed. Pa. Acad. Fine Arts; Düsseldorf (Germany) Acad.; studied Paris and London. War corr. and artist for Philadelphia Bulletin in Cuba, 1895-96. Awarded Temple gold medal by Pa. Acad. Fine Arts; Logan medal, Chicago Art Inst.; Hudnut water color prize, New York; Corcoran Art Gallery prize, Washington, D.C.; Gold medal, Locust Club, Phila., 1926. Studio: New York, N.Y. Died Oct. 29, 1933.

LUMMIS, Charles Fletcher, Americanist, author, explorer; b. Lynn, Mass., Mar. 1, 1859; s. Henry and Harriet Waterman (Fowler) L.; ed. Harvard, class of 1881; (Litt.D., Santa Clara Coll., 1903); A.B. Harvard U., 1906; married 3 times; children—Bertha, Turbesé, Amado (dec.), Quimu Jordan, Keith. Edited newspaper in Ohio, 1882-84; in 1884 walked from Cincinnati to Los Angeles, Calif., by roundabout route, purely for pleasure, 3,507 miles, 143 days. City editor Los Angeles Daily Times, 1885-87; lived 5 yrs. in Indian pueblo of Isleta, N.M., learning Indian languages and customs; traveled all over Southwest on horseback; also in Mexico, Central and S.A.; has explored continent from Canada to Chile. Founder, and editor, 1894-1909, Out West Mag.; librarian Los Angeles Pub. Library, June 21, 1905-Apr. 1, 1910. Founder and pres. Landmarks Club (to preserve historic landmarks, Calif.), 1895; has preserved Missions San Juan Capistrano, Pala and San Fernando; founder, 1902, and chmn. exec. com. Sequoya League (to make better Indians); pres. Warner's Ranch Indian Commn., which secured better homes for 300 evicted Indians. Founder and sec. Southwest Soc. Archæol. Inst. America, 1903; one of incorporators, 1906, and life mem. Archæol. Inst. America; founder The Southwest Museum, 1907, and its unique 125-ft. tower named, "Lummis Caracol Tower"; hon. mem. Davenport (Ia.) Acad. of Sciences; mem. Nat. Inst. Arts and Letters; charter regent Mus. of N.M., till 1912; mem. mng. bd. and exec. com. Sch. of Am. Research; an incorporator Modern History Records Assn., First life mem. Hidalgos of America; 1st hon. mem. Hispanic Society of Calif.; corr. mem. Royal Acad. of Spain; knighted by King of Spain, 1915, for researches in Spanish-Am. history, as comendador con placa de la Real Orden de Isabel la Catolica; Socio de Honor, Casa de España en Puerto Rico. Has made phonographic records of 550 old Spanish songs of Southwest, and 425 Indian songs in 37 langs. Author: Birch Bark Poems, 1879 (on real bark); A New Mexico David, 1891; A Tramp Across the Continent, 1892; The Land of Poco Tiempo, 1893; The Spanish Pioneers, 1893, 16th edit. (Spanish transl. 1915); The King of the Broncos, 1897; The Awakening of a Nation, Mexico To-day, 1898; My Friend Will, 1911; Spanish Songs of Old California, 1923, 2d book, 1928; Mesa, Cañon and Pueblo, 1925. Home: Los Angeles, Calif. Died Nov. 25, 1928.

LUMPKIN, Alva Moore, judge; b. Milledgeville, Ga., Nov. 13, 1886; s. William Wallace and Annie Caroline (Morris) L.; mem. notable Lumpkin family of Ga.; ed. Columbia (S.C.) High Sch., U. of S.C., LL.B., 1908; m. Mary Sumter Thomas, Nov. 14, 1912; children—Mary Waties, Alva Moore. Admitted to S.C. bar, 1908, and began practice in Columbia; partner Thomas, Lumpkin & Cain until 1939; appointed U.S. judge for Eastern and Western districts of S.C., May 22, 1939; asst. secretary S.C. State Senate, 1906-08; mem. S.C. Gen. Assembly, 1911-15; spl. asst. atty. gen. S.C., 1918-20; mem. S.C. Bd. Pardons, 1922-23; apptd. acting asso. justice Supreme Ct. of S.C., 1926 and 1934; formerly dir. Equitable Trust Co., Standard Bldg. & Loan Assn., Columbia. Mem. Conciliation Commn. for Advancement of Peace between U.S. and Uruguay. Democrat. Episcopalian. Mason. Home: Columbia, S.C. Died Aug. 1, 1941.

LUMPKIN, Joseph Henry, judge; b. Athens, Ga., Sept. 3, 1856; s. William Wilberforce and Maria Louisa (King) L.; A.B., U. of Ga., 1875; (LL.D., Univ. of Ga., 1914); unmarried. Admitted to bar, 1877; asst. reporter, 1877-82, reporter, 1882-88, Supreme Ct. of Ga.; judge Superior Ct., Atlanta Circuit, 1893-1905; asso. justice Supreme Ct. of Ga., Apr. 10, 1905—. Democrat. Home: Atlanta, Ga. Died Sept. 6, 1916.

LUMPKIN, Samuel, jurist; b. Lexington, Ga., Dec. 12, 1848; grad. Univ. of Ga., July 1866 (A.M.; also LL.D., Southwestern Bapt. Univ., Jackson, Tenn.); admitted to bar; solicitor gen., northern jud. circuit of Ga., 1872-76; State senator, 1878-80; judge Superior Court, northern jud. circuit, 1885-90; asso. justice Supreme Court, Ga., 1891—; presiding justice, 2d div., Jan. 1, 1897—. Home: Atlanta, Ga. Died 1903.

LUMSDON, Christine Marie, portrait painter; b. Brooklyn, N.Y.; d. Wilhelm Christian Franz Heinrich and Emma (Seabrook) Voss; ed. Adelphi Acad., Brooklyn, and Normal Coll., New York; studied art under Carolus Duran, Paris, also under Henry Mosler and Childe Hassam; m. John W. Lumsdon, Apr. 19, 1890 (dec.). Instr. in painting landscape and portrait, Carnegie Hall. Exhibited Paris Salon, 1904; Pa. Acad. Fine Arts; Art Inst. Chicago; Omaha Expn.; Acad. Design and Architectural League, New York; Corcoran Art Gallery of Washington, D.C., 1935. Works: Ideal head of Christ, which has won world-wide fame, "La Mandolinist," Paris Salon; "Angel," Architectural League; "Cœur et Fleur," Art Inst. Chicago; portraits of E. W. Bliss and Col. Richard Lathers, Portrait Show, Acad. Design, also "Bavarian Peasant," 1933, "Zemenia"—lady with peacock; "Love's Messenger"—symphony in green, design for church windows; etc. Winner Henry Mosler prize. Founder of Health Culture Club for women. Life fellow Nat. Acad. Design. Episcopalian. Lecturer. Studio: New York, N.Y. Died Apr. 8, 1937.

LUNA, Solomon; mem. Rep. Nat. Com. from N.M. Pres. N.M. Conservation Commn., etc. Home: Los Lunas, N.M. Died Aug. 30, 1912.

LUNDEEN, Ernest, senator; b. Beresford, S.D.; s. Rev. Charles Henry and Christine (Peterson) L.; B.A., Carleton Coll., Minn., 1901; law dept., U. of Minn., 1901-04; m. Norma Ward, Feb. 5, 1919; children—Ernest Ward, Joan Jessie. Admitted to bar, 1906, and began practice in Minneapolis; admitted to Supreme Court of the U.S., 1916; mem. Minn. House of Rep. two terms, 1910-14; mem. 65th Congress (1917-19), 5th Minn. Dist.; voted against entering war, against conscription for foreign service; conducted 1st Congressional referendum on war; mem. 73d Congress (1933-35), Minn. at large, and 74th (1935-37), 3d Minn. District; elected U.S. senator for term 1937-43. Served as pvt. Co. B, 12th Minn. Vols., Spanish-American War, held commn. Minn. N.G. Mason. Methodist. Home: Wayzata, Minn. Died Aug. 31, 1940.

LUNDIE, John, consulting engr.; b. Arbroath, Scotland, Dec. 14, 1857; s. James and Anne (Honeyman) L.; B.Sc., U. of Edinburgh, 1880, D.Sc., 1902; m. Iona Oakley, d. Capt. J. C. Gorham, of St. Louis, and grand-niece of Gov. Sterling Price, of Mo., July 6, 1906 (died 1925); m. 2d, Mrs. Alice Eddy Snowden (A.M., Columbia U.), July 15, 1929. Harbor work, Dundee, Scotland, 1873-77; railroad work, Ore. and Wash., 1880-84; municipal work, Chicago, 1884-90; bridge work, 1890-93; pvt. practice after 1893. Developed method for determination of yield of artesian water areas during investigation of water supply system of Memphis, Tenn.; designed the first combined electric hoist and traveler (the "telfer"); investigated and reported on electrification of I.C. R.R., Boston Elevated R.R., Brooklyn Elevated R.R., Manhattan lines, New York, Met. Underground, London, Eng., etc. Investigated costs of freight movement on U.S. Steel Corp. railroads; officer in charge of Birmingham Southern R.R. Co.; v.p. and gen. mgr. Panama-Am. Corp. in Panama; developed Lundie formula for train resistance; designed the Lundie rheostat, Lundie tie plate, Lundie duplex rail anchor, etc.; co-designer Lundie-Durham rail. Pres. The Lundie Engring. Corp. Mason. Home: New York, N.Y. Died Feb. 9, 1931.

LUNDIN, Carl Axel Robert, optical expert; b. Venersborg, Sweden, Jan. 13, 1851; s. C. F. and U. H. (Anderson) L.; ed. high sch., Faluh, Sweden; (hon. M.A., Amherst, 1905); m. Hulda M. Hansen, Apr. 3, 1875. Has taken an active and prin. part in the work done by Alvan Clark & Sons (now Alvan Clark & Sons Corp.) 1874—, including the 30-inch objective for Pulkowa Obs., 1883 (which was taken over and installed by him under spl. decree of Russian Govt.), the 36-in. objective of the Lick Obs., 1887, and the 40-inch objective for the Yerkes Obs., 1895; completed 24-inch objective for Lowell Obs., 1895; made 16-inch objective for U. of Cincinnati, 1904, and 18-inch objective for Amherst Obs., 1905; from 1896 in entire charge of the optical work of the concern, and has devised and put into operation several important optical tests. Home: Cambridgeport, Mass. Died Nov. 28, 1915.

LUNG, George Augustus, naval officer; b. Canandaigua, N.Y. Dec. 21, 1862; s. Rev. A. H. and Catherine (Deck) L.; A.B., U. of Rochester, 1883, A.M., 1891; M.D., U. of Pa., 1886; m. Helen Van Courtland de Peyster, Apr. 28, 1908. Apptd. asst. surgeon U.S.N., Aug. 18, 1888; passed asst. surgeon, Aug. 18, 1892; surgeon, Nov. 1900; rank of lt. comdr., Apr. 9, 1908; medical director, June 1917. Served with Sampson's squadron during war in Cuba; afterward in U.S.S. Philadelphia in annexation of Hawaii, and Samoan difficulty, in which his courageous conduct was commended by the Sec. of Navy; with China Relief Expdn., 1900; senior med. officer with 1st Regt. U.S. Marines to Peking and return, Oct. 1900; dist. surgeon Peninsula of Cavite, P.I., 1901; spl. duty Washington, 1902-03; comdg. U.S. Naval Hosp., Brooklyn, Oct. 1916—. Died July 26, 1921.

LUNGER, John B., life ins.; b. Asbury, N.J., Apr. 5, 1864; s. Amos and Emma (Baylor) L.; ed. Centenary Collegiate Inst., Hackettstown, N.J.; m. Jane Estelle Burnett, 1896. Began as clk. in statis. dept. Prudential Ins. Co., Newark, N.J., 1880, later became actuary of the company; mng. actuary New York Life Ins. Co., 1897-1902; v.p. Travelers Ins. Co., 1902-12; v.p. Equitable Life Assurance Soc. of U.S., 1912—. Home: New York, N.Y. Died June 12, 1919.

LUNSFORD, William, clergyman; b. Roanoke, Va., May 22, 1859; s. Charles and Julia (Preston) L.; attended U. of Va.; Southern Bapt. Theol. Sem., 1898; D.D., Wake Forest Coll., 1906; m. Nannie P. Preston, Dec. 31, 1885; children—Preston, Dr. Chas. Julian, Dr. Bruce, Campbell, Julia, Gordon. Ordained ministry Southern Bapt. Ch., 1897; pastor Jefferson St. Ch., Roanoke, 1897-98; 1st Ch. Bowling Green, Ky., 1898-1903, Waco, Tex., 1903-04, Asheville, N.C., 1904-09, Edgefield Ch., Nashville, Tenn., 1909-18; cor. sec. Relief and Annuity Bd. of Southern Bapt. Conv., 1918—. Home: Dallas, Tex. Died May 24, 1927.

LUNT, Horace Gray, lawyer; b. Chicago, Aug. 13, 1847; s. Orrington and Cornelia (Gray) L.; A.B., Harvard, 1870; (hon. A.M., Northwestern, 1878); m. Caroline K. Isaacs, Sept. 3, 1874. Practiced, Chicago, 1873-86; since at Colorado Springs, except when serving, 1895-99, as judge Dist. Court, 4th Jud. Dist., Colo. Republican. Home: Colorado Springs, Colo. Deceased.

LUPTON, Charles Thomas, geologist; b. nr. Mt. Pleasant, O., Feb. 28, 1878; s. Benjamin C. and Anna (Thomas) L.; A.B., Oberlin, 1907; LL.B., Nat. U. Law Sch., Washington, D.C., 1915, LL.M., 1915; m. Addie White Bradshaw, Nov. 25, 1914; children—Martha, Charles T., Jr., Frantz Russell, Bradshaw Babb. With U.S. Geol. Survey, Washington, D.C., 1907-16; geologist in charge Rocky Mountain operations of Cosden Oil & Gas Co., 1916-19; chief geologist Frantz Corp., 1919-20; consulting practice, Denver, Colo., 1920—. Mem. Coal Classification Bd., U.S. Geol. Survey, 1909-11; chmn. Com. on Estimates of Oil Reserves in Rocky Mountain States, 1921. Republican. Conglist. Home: Denver, Colo. Deceased.

LUPTON, John Thomas, manufacturer; b. nr. Winchester, Va., Mar. 6, 1862; s. Jonah J. and Rebecca Catherine (Lee) L.; A.B. and A.M., Roanoke Coll., Salem, Va., 1882; LL.B., U. of Va., 1886; LL.D., Oglethorpe U., Atlanta, Ga., 1922; m. Elizabeth Olive Patten, Nov. 14, 1889; 1 son, Thomas Cartter. Admitted to Tenn. bar, 1886, and began practice at Chattanooga, 1887; v.p. and treas. Chattanooga Medicine Co., 1891-1906; an organizer Volunteer State Life Ins. Co., 1904; founder, 1920, now chmn. bd. Dixie Mercerizing Co.; chmn. bd. First Nat. Bank of Chattanooga; pres. The Coca-Cola Bottling Co.; v.p. and treas. Stone Fort Land Co. Pres. Baylor Sch.; trustee Peabody Coll., Agnes Scott Coll., Oglethorpe U., U. of Chattanooga. Democrat. Presbyn. Elk. Home: Chattanooga, Tenn. Died July 31, 1933.

LUQUER, Lea McIlvaine, educator; b. Brooklyn, N.Y., 1864; s. Rev. Lea and Eloise Elizabeth (Payne) L.; early edn. at home and at pvt. boarding sch.; grad. Columbia Sch. of Mines, C.E., 1887, Ph.D., 1894; m. Anne Low Pierrepont, 1896. In faculty of Columbia Univ. from 1887, becoming adj. prof. mineralogy. Author: Minerals in Rock Sections, 1898. Home: New York, N.Y. Died Jan. 20, 1930.

LUQUIENS, Frederick Bliss, college prof.; b. Auburndale, Mass., Dec. 10, 1875; s. Jules and Emma (Clark) L.; B.A., Yale, 1897, Ph.D., 1905; m. Elizabeth Koll, June 23, 1904. Asst. prof. Spanish, Yale U., 1906-14, prof., Sept. 1914—, Street prof. modern languages, 1935—. Curator Latin Americana, Yale U. Library, 1930—. Sec. commn. of financial advisers to Colombian Govt., 1923. Author: An Introduction to Old French Phonology and Morphology, 1909; Elementary Spanish American Reader, 1917. Gen. editor Macmillan Spanish Series, 1916-25; Irreducible Minimum of Spanish Grammar, 1926; Spanish American Literature in the Yale University Library, 1939. Home: New Haven, Conn. Died Apr. 17, 1940.

LURTON, Horace Harmon, jurist; b. Newport, Ky., 1844; s. Lycurgus L. and Sarah (Harmon) L.; ed. pub. schs., Douglas and Cumberland univs.; served 3 yrs. in C.S.A.; L.B., Cumberland U., Tenn., 1867; (D.C.L., U. of the South, 1899; LL.D., U. of Pa., 1912); admitted to bar, 1867; m. Frances Owen, Sept. 1867. Chancellor 6th Div., Tenn., 1875-78; justice Supreme Ct. of Tenn., 1886-93 (chief justice, Jan.-Apr. 1893); U.S. circuit judge, 6th Jud. Circuit, 1893-1910; asso. justice Supreme Ct. of U.S., Jan. 3, 1910—. Prof. constl. law, 1898-1910, and dean law dept., 1905-10, Vanderbilt U. Home: Nashville, Tenn. Died July 12, 1914.

LUSE, Claude Zeph, judge; b. Stoughton, Wis., Feb. 23, 1879; s. Louis K. and Ella (Bartholomew) L.; B.Litt., U. of Minn., 1901; LL.B., U. of Wis., 1903; m. Gertrude W. Baker, Sept. 20, 1904. Mem. Luse, Powell & Luse, Superior, Wis., 1904-21; U.S. dist. judge, Western Dist. of Wis., Apr. 9, 1921—. Republican. Conglist. Mason. Died May 28, 1932.

LUSK, Frank Stillman, banker, stockman; b. Buffalo, N.Y., Apr. 27, 1857; s. James W. and Cornelia M. (Stillman) L.; grad. East Cleveland (O.) High Sch., 1871; m. Louise Buchanan Findley, Apr. 25. 1894. Entered live stock business in Colo., 1876, and still continues; identified with banking, 1886—; r.r. contractor, 1887-1907; lived at Lusk, Wyo., 30 yrs., at Missoula, Mont., 1907—; pres. First Nat. Bank of Missoula, 1909-19; pres. Gen. Securities Co., etc. V.-chmn. Mont. Expn. Commn.; chmn. Mont. State Text Book Commn.; mem. Missoula Pub. Library Bd. Republican. Home: Missoula, Mont. Died Aug. 6, 1930.

LUSK, Graham, physiologist; b. Bridgeport, Conn., Feb. 15, 1866; s. Dr. William T. and Mary Hartwell (Chittenden) L.; Ph.B., Columbia, 1887; Ph.D., Munich, 1891; hon. A.M., Yale, 1896, Sc.D., 1908; LL.D., U. of Glasgow, 1923; hon. M.D., U. of Munich, 1929; m. May W. Tiffany, Dec. 20, 1899; children—William T., Louise (Mrs. Collier Platt), Louis T. Instr. physiology, 1891-92, asst. prof., 1892-95, prof., 1895-98, Yale; prof. physiology, Univ. and Bellevue Hosp. Med. Coll., 1898-1909; prof. physiology, Cornell U. Med. Coll., New York, 1909—; mem. Inter-Allied Scientific Food Commn., 1918; scientific director Russell Sage Inst. of Pathology. Fellow Royal Soc. of Edinburgh; corr. fellow Imperial Soc. of Physicians of Vienna. Author: Elements of the Science of Nutrition, 4th edit., 1928. Home: New York, N.Y. Died July 19, 1932.

LUSK, James Loring, army officer; b. Pittsburgh, Pa., Feb. 1, 1855; s. Amos (M.D.) and Agnes Sterret (Clow) L.; grad. West Point, 1878; m. Mary E. Webster, Oct. 16, 1883. Apptd. 2d lt. June 14, 1878, 1st lt. June 14, 1881, capt. June 15, 1888, maj. July 5, 1898, corps of engrs., U.S.A.; lt. col. and chief engr., U.S. Vols., May 9, 1898, to Dec. 7, 1898. Served in various duties of corps engrs., and as asst. instr. and instr. mil. engring. at West Point. Mem. U.S. Bd. Geographic Names, Mar. 21, 1899—; asst. to Chief of Engrs., U.S.A., Sept. 19, 1898—. Died 1906.

LUSK, Willard Clayton, newspaper pub.; b. McConnells, Ill., Nov. 6, 1869; s. George Franklin and Harriet (Spatz) L.; B.S., S.D. State Coll., 1893, Ia. State Coll., 1893; student U. of Wis., 1893-94; m. Alma Victoria Davies, Feb. 20, 1897; children—Martin Willard, Edward Franklin, Robert Davies, Stowell Warmington (dec.), Elizabeth (Mrs. Russell F. Lundy); m. 2d, H. Clara Darrow, Oct. 31, 1938. Began as teacher, 1888, and publisher country newspapers, 1896; pub. Press and Dakotan, 1897-1928; postmaster, Yankton, S.D., 1914-15; pres. Lusk-Mitchell Newspapers, 1928—, Yankton Printing Co., 1904—; chmn. bd. First Dakota Nat. Bank and Trust Co.; pres. Dakota Finance Co., Yankton, Norfolk and Southern R.R.; v.p. Rapid City, Black Hills and Western R.R. Pres. bd. edn., Yankton; mem. S.D. State and Federal Com. Unemployment; mem. bd. for dist. of S.D., N.D. and Minn., NRA; mem. S.D. Debt Conciliation Board under Sec. of Treasury Morgenthau. Trustee Yankton Coll.; vice chmn. S.D. Welfare Commn.; spl. liaison officer, 9th Region Federal Housing Administration. Republican. Conglist. Mason. Home: Yankton, S.D. Died July 7, 1940.

LUSTRAT, Joseph, prof. Romance langs.; b. Vichy, Allier, France, Sept. 23, 1858; s. Christophe Pierre and Jeanne (Busson) L.; Lycée de Moulin, Allier, 1869-74; Lycée de Clermont-Ferrand, Puy de Dôme, France, 1874-77; Bachelier ès Lettres, University of France, 1877; Dr. of Letters, U. of Ga., 1922; m. Eléonore Maria Moure, of Vichy, Allier, Oct. 7, 1880. Came to U.S., 1892, naturalized citizen, 1903. Prof. Romance langs., Shorter Coll., Rome, Ga., 1893-97; prof. same, U. of Ga., and State Normal Sch., Athens, 1897—. Officier d'Académie. Catholic. Author: Formation and Simple Tenses of French Verbs, Regular and Irregular. Home: Athens, Ga. Died Feb. 4, 1927.

LUTHER, Edwin Cornelius, mining engr.; b. Pottsville, Pa., Nov. 30, 1878; s. Roland Cornelius and Theresa (Yuengling) L.; grad. Hill Sch., Pottstown, Pa., 1898; C.E., Princeton, 1902, E.M., Columbia, 1904; m. Anna A. Henning, Apr. 17, 1912; children—Roland Cornelius, Edwin Cornelius, John (dec.), Isabel Therese. Mining engr. with Phila. & Reading Coal & Iron Co., 1904-08, with Estate of P. W. Sheafer, 1908-16; consulting practice, anthracite and bituminous coal mining, 1916—, also agt. for large coal estates; pres. and treas. Peerless Coal & Coke Co.; pres. Powhatan Coal & Coke Co., Pottsville Community Hotel Co., Safe Deposit Bank, Pottsville; v.p. Pottsville Water Co. Trustee Pottsville Public Library. Republican. Episcopalian. Mason. Home: Pottsville, Pa. Died Aug. 8, 1935.

LUTHER, Flavel Sweeten, college pres.; b. Brooklyn, Conn., Mar. 26, 1850; s. Flavel Sweeten and Jane (Lillie) L.; A.B., Trinity Coll., 1870, A.M., 1873; hon. Ph.D., 1896, LL.D., 1904, Trinity; LL.D., Tufts, 1905, Wesleyan, 1906; m. Isabel Blake Ely, Nov. 2, 1871. Deacon P.E. Ch., 1871; prof. mathematics, Racine Coll., 1876-81; teacher Gambier, O., 1881-82; prof. mathematics, Kenyon Coll., 1882-83; Seabury prof. mathematics and astronomy, 1883—, pres., 1904-19, Trinity Coll. Mem. Conn. Senate, 1907-11. Home: Pasadena, Calif. Died Jan. 4, 1928.

LUTKIN, Peter Christian, musician; b. Thompsonville, Wis., Mar. 27, 1858; s. Peter Christian and Hannah Susanna Define (Olivarius) L.; ed. Chicago pub. schs., pvt. sch.; mus. edn., Mrs. Regina Watson (piano), Clarence Eddy (organ), and Frederick Grant Gleason (theory), Chicago; also piano under Oscar Raif (Berlin) and Moritz Moszkowski (Paris), organ, August Haupt, theory, Waldemar Bargiel, Berlin; student Hochschule für Musik, Berlin, 1881-83, Leschetizky Piano Sch., Vienna, 1883; (hon. Mus.Doc., Syracuse U., 1900); m. Nancy Lelah Carman, Oct. 27, 1885; 1 son, Harris Carman. Organist, Cathedral SS. Peter and Paul, Chicago, 1871-81, St. James' Ch., Chicago, 1891-96; dir. theoretical dept., Am. Conservatory of Music, Chicago, 1888-95; prof. music, 1891—, dean, 1897-1928, Sch. of Music, Northwestern U. Conductor Evanston Mus. Club, 1894—, Ravenswood Mus. Club, 1896-1904, Chicago North Shore Festival Assn., 1909—. Episcopalian. Independent Republican. Joint mus. editor of official hymnal of M.E. Ch. and M.E. Ch., S.; mus. editor Methodist Sunday School Hymnal; mem. commn. for revision of hymnal of P.E. Ch., author of Music in the Ch.; composer of ch. music and part songs. Lectured on ch. music, Western Theol. Sem., Chicago, and Garrett Bibl. Inst., Evanston, Ill. Pres. Music Teachers Nat.

Assn., 1911-12, 1919-20. Home: Evanston, Ill. Died Dec. 27, 1931.

LUTZ, Frank J., surgeon; b. St. Louis, Mo., May 24, 1855; s. John T. and Rosina (Miller) L.; A.B., St. Louis U., 1873; M.D., St. Louis Med. Coll., 1876; m. May Silver, 1884. Practiced, St. Louis, 1876—; surgeon-in-charge, Josephine Hosp.; attending surgeon, Barnard Free Skin and Cancer Hosp.; prof. surgery, Medical Dept., Washington U., 1911—. Fellow Am. Coll. Surgeons. Home: St. Louis, Mo. Died Mar. 24, 1916.

LUYTIES, Carl Johann, physician; b. St. Louis, Mo., Sept. 15, 1860; s. Diedrich Reinhard (M.D.) and Anna Lucia (Ruyter) L.; grad. Mound City Commercial Coll., 1877; Ph.G., St. Louis Coll. Pharmacy, 1881; M.D., Mo. Med. Coll., 1884; M.D., Hahnemann Med. Coll., Phila., 1885; post-grad. work in clinics and hosps., Vienna, Austria; m. Ella Evangeline Augst, Oct. 29, 1892. Practiced in St. Louis, 1884—; resident physician St. Louis Child's Hosp., 1885-88; mem. visiting staff same, 1898-1909; mem. visiting staff City Hosp., 1910-14; prof. chemistry, Homœ. Med. Coll. of Mo., 1885-88; prof. diseases of children, same coll., 1898-1909. Republican. Lutheran. Home: St. Louis, Mo. Died Dec. 23, 1916.

LYALL, James, mfr.; b. Auchterardar, Scotland, Sept. 13, 1836; came to U.S. when 3 yrs. old; ed. public schools; worked in father's shop, making Jacquard looms; served 12th N.Y. inf. in defense of Washington early in Civil war; invented, 1863, a mixture for enameling cloth which was approved by Govt.; received large contract for supplying knapsacks and haversacks for army. Invented Lyall positive-motion loom, 1868; established large trade in supplying it; afterward established mills for mfg. cotton and jute goods, of which he became the head; m. Sept. 8, 1864, Margaret Telford. Home: New York, N.Y. Died 1901.

LYBRAND, Archibald, congressman; b. Tarlton, O., May 23, 1840; s. Archibald and Jemima L.; removed to Delaware, O., 1857; ed. Ohio Wesleyan U.; m. Martha C. Jones, Oct. 9, 1883. Pvt. to capt., 4th and 73d Ohio Vols., in Civil War, taking part in many battles; wounded at Peach Tree Creek and again at Dallas, Ga.; returned to Delaware, O.; mayor, 1869; admitted to bar, 1871; became partner, 1863, in Delaware Chair Co.; postmaster of Delaware, O., 1881-85; mem. 55th and 56th Congresses (1897-1901), 8th Ohio Dist. Republican. Home: Delaware, O. Deceased.

LYDECKER, Charles Edward, lawyer; b. New York, May 26, 1851; s. John A. and Julia (Kent) L.; B.S., Coll. City of New York, 1871; LL.B., Columbia, 1873. Instr. Coll. City of New York, 1875-80; pub. administrator, N.Y. City, 1889-93; active practice of law, corp. work, will contests, administration of estates, reference and counsel duties. Printed and distributed ballot securing vote for State Constl Convention, 1894. Major 7th Infantry, N.G. New York, 1901-09; bvt. lt. col. N.G. New York; mem. council U.S. Mil. Service Inst., 1903—; pres. Nat. Guard Assn., 1906; a founder Nat. Security League (elected president 1918). Trustee Coll. City of New York, 1913—. Democrat. Home: New York, N.Y. Died May 7, 1920.

LYDECKER, Garrett J., brig. gen. U.S.A.; b. Englewood, N.J., Nov. 15, 1843; s. John R. and Elizabeth (Ward) L.; student Coll. City of New York; grad. U.S. Mil. Acad., 1864; m. Delia W. Buel, Sept. 21, 1869. Commd. 1st lt. engrs., June 13, 1864; promoted through grades to col., Apr. 3, 1901; brig. gen. and retired by operation of law, Nov. 15, 1907. Bvtd. capt., Apr. 2, 1865, "for gallant and meritorious services in siege of Petersburg, Va." Has been engaged in river and harbor work at Galveston, Michigan City, Ind., New Orleans, Chicago, Detroit, etc. Died July 9, 1914.

LYDSTON, G(eorge) Frank, surgeon; b. Tuolumne, Calif., 1858; s. George N. and Lucy A. L.; M.D., Bellevue Hosp. Med. Coll. (New York U.), 1879; m. Josie M. Cottier, 1884. House staff Charity Hosp., New York, 1879-81; resident surgeon N.Y. State Emigrant Hosp., 1881; lecturer genito-urinary diseases, 1882, and formerly prof. genito-urinary surgery and venereal diseases, Med. Dept. U. of Ill., Chicago. Fellow Chicago Acad. Medicine, etc. Author: Stricture of Urethra; Text Book on Genito-Urinary and Venereal Diseases; Varicocele and Treatment; The Surgical Diseases of the Genito-Urinary Tract; The Diseases of Society; Panama and the Sierras; Over the Hookah; Poker Jim, Gentleman, 1907. Home: Chicago, Ill. Died May 14, 1923.

LYFORD, James Otis, lawyer; b. Boston, June 28, 1853; s. James and Mary I. (McLane) L.; ed. Boston pub. schs. and Tilton (N.H.) School; LL.D., U. of New Hampshire, 1922; m. Susan Ayer Hill, May 2, 1882. Editor "People" newspaper, Concord, 1877-79; admitted to bar, 1880; practiced law Tilton, N.H., 1880-82; clerk depot q.-m.'s office, Washington, 1882-87; chmn. N.H. Savings Bank Commn., 1887-95; city auditor, Concord, N.H., 1896-98; mem. N.H. Legislature, 1893, 95, 97, 1915, 23; naval officer dist. of Boston and Charlestown, Mass., 1898-1913; editor Nashua Telegraph; sec. Concord Bd. of Trade, 1914. Sec. N.H. Rep. Com., 1896; mem. N.H. constl. convs., 1876, 1902, 12, 18. Chmn. N.H. Savings Bank Commn., 1915—. Trustee Tilton Sem. Editor History of Concord, N.H., 1903. Home: Concord, N.H. Died Sept. 19, 1924.

LYFORD, Oliver Smith, railway v.p.; b. Mt. Vernon, Me., June 19, 1823; s. Dudley and Betsey L.; high sch. edn.; m. Lavinia A. Norris, Sept. 27, 1852; father of Will Hartwell L. Watchman, asst. baggagemaster, ticket agt., and pass. conductor, Boston & Lowell R.R., 1846-51; shop clerk and pass. conductor, Erie R.R., Dunkirk, N.Y., 1851-55; joint sta. agt. Erie & Atlantic and Great Western rys., Salamanca, N.Y., 1860-63; div. and asst. gen. supt. Atlantic & Great Western Ry., 1863-71; div. supt., Buffalo and Rochester divs. Erie Ry., 1871-72; gen. supt. Hannibal & St. Joseph R.R., 1872-73; gen. supt. Kan. Pacific Ry., 1874-76; supt., 1878-86, gen. mgr., 1886-87, v.p. and gen. mgr., 1887-90, and v.p. C.&E.I. R.R. Co., 1890-July 1, 1913, when retired. Home: Chicago, Ill. Died Oct. 12, 1914.

LYFORD, Will Hartwell, lawyer; b. Waterville, Me., Sept. 15, 1858; s. Oliver Smith and Lavinia A. (Norris) L.; A.B., Colby College, Maine, 1879, also A.M., and LL.D.; m. Mary Lee MacComas, Apr. 28, 1886 (died 1931); children—Gertrude Wells (Mrs. Edwin Ruthven Boyd), Calhoun T.; m. 2d, Saidee D. MacComas, Dec. 31, 1932. Asst. engr., 1879-80, stenographer for gen. supt., 1881-82, chief clerk to gen. mgr., 1882-83, claim agt., 1883-84, C.&E.I. R.R.; admitted to bar, 1884; asst. gen. solicitor, 1884-87, atty. in charge law dept., 1887-89, gen. solicitor, 1889-92, gen. counsel, Mar. 15, 1892-1913, gen. counsel for receivers, 1913-21, v.p. and gen. counsel, Jan. 1, 1922—, C.&E.I. Ry. Co. Home: Chicago, Ill. Died May 16, 1934.

LYLE, Benjamin Franklin, M.D.; b. Georgetown, Ky., Mar. 3, 1861; s. John M. (M.D.) and Mary (Phillips) L.; ed. pub. schs., Cincinnati; M.D., Med. Coll. of Ohio, 1882; m. Alice Johnson, Sept. 1891; children—Alice F., Donald J., Herbert P. Engaged in med. practice, Cincinnati, 1882—; phys. to Cincinnati Branch Hosp. for Consumptives, 1897-1907, 1908-09; med. insp. Ohio State Bd. Health and Cincinnati Bd. Health, 1901-07; dir. bur. for the prevention of tuberculosis, Cincinnati Bd. Health, 1921-28; clin. prof. diseases of chest, U. of Cincinnati. Presbyn. Republican. Home: Clifton, O. Died Sept. 9, 1939.

LYLE, Hubert Samuel, clergyman, educator; b. Dandridge, Tenn., Mar. 1, 1873; s. William Harris and Sarah Porter (Mathes) L.; B.A., Maryville (Tenn.) Coll., 1899, M.A., 1908, D.D., 1913; student Auburn Theol. Sem., 1901-04; m. Millicent Candee Robinson, Sept. 14, 1904; children—Gordon Robinson, Barbara Beagle. Prin. Grassy Cove (Tenn.) Acad., 1899-1901, also pastor under Bd. of Home Missions Presbyn. Ch.; ordained Presbyn. ministry, 1904; pastor Youngstown, N.Y., 1904-07; prof. New Testament, Maryville Coll., 1907-11; pastor New Providence Ch., Maryville, Tenn., 1911-17; pres. Arkansas Cumberland Coll. (now Coll. of the Ozarks), 1917-23; pres. Washington Coll. (self-help sch. for boys and girls), Tenn., July 1923—. Died Mar. 21, 1931.

LYLE, William Thomas, civil engr.; b. Utica, N.Y., Jan. 10, 1875; s. Rev. Albert Franklin (LL.D.) and Louisa (Thomas) L.; grad. Newark (N.J.) Acad., 1892; C.E., Princeton, 1896; m. Mertie A. Daykin, July 17, 1897; children—Thomas Howland, Mary. With engr. corps Essex Co. (N.J.) Park Commn., 1897-1900; municipal contracting, 1901-02; instr. and asst. prof. civ. engring., U. of Pa., 1902-07; asst. prof. municipal engring., Lafayette Coll., 1907-10, prof., 1910-18; civ. engr. Taylor-Wharton Iron & Steel Co., 1918-19; lecturer Rice Inst., Houston, Tex., 1919-21; prof. civ. engring. and head of dept., Washington and Lee U., 1921—. Offered gen. plan for development of City of Houston. Democrat. Presbyn. (elder). Mason. Author: Parks and Park Engineering, 1916; The Thomas Family as Descended from David and Anna Noble Thomas, 1907. Home: Lexington, Va. Died Oct. 30, 1933.

LYMAN, Albert Josiah, clergyman; b. Williston, Vt., Dec. 24, 1845; s. Josiah and Mary L. (Bingham) L.; grad. Union Theol. Sem., 1868; resident licentiate, Yale Theol. Sem., 1869; (D.D., Amherst, 1891); m. Ella Stevens, June 1, 1870 (died 1893); 2d, Annie Elizabeth Hills, June 26, 1902. Ordained Congl. ministry, 1870; pastor First Ch., Milford, Conn., 1869-73, South Ch., Brooklyn, Jan. 1, 1874. Pres. council Brooklyn Inst. Arts and Sciences, 1899-1904. Author: A Plain Man's Working View of Biblical Inspiration, 1907. Died Aug. 22, 1915.

LYMAN, Alexander Steele, lawyer; b. New Orleans, Apr. 8, 1860; s. Joseph Bardwell and Laura Elizabeth (Baker) L.; grad. Chamberlain Inst., Randolph, N.Y., 1880; A.B., New York U., 1884; LL.B., cum laude, Columbia, 1886; m. Bertha Bidwell, d. Dr. E. D. Burton, of E. Cleveland, O., Sept. 17, 1891. In office of Judge Horace Russell, New York, 1886-90; with Davies & Rapallo, and successors, Davies, Short & Townsend, and Davies, Stone & Auerbach, 1890-97; mem. Blair, Phelps & Lyman, 1897-99; counsel for receiver, Brooklyn Elevated R.R. Co., 1898-99; in charge claim dept., Brooklyn Rapid Transit Co., 1899-1901; mem. Blair, Price & Lyman, 1902-05; asst. to gen. atty., 1905-07; apptd. gen. atty., Jan. 1, 1908, N.Y.C. R.R. Co.; valuation counsel New York Central Lines, 1925—. Republican. Home: Mamaroneck, N.Y. Died Mar. 7, 1930.

LYMAN, Arthur Theodore, mfr.; b. Boston, Dec. 8, 1832; s. George Williams and Anne (Pratt) L.; A.B., Harvard, 1853, A.M., 1857; m. Ella, d. John Amory and Elizabeth Cabot (Putnam) Lowell, of Boston, Apr. 8, 1858. Engaged in E. India trade, Boston, 1856-60; became associated in cotton mfg., 1860; treas. Appleton Co., 1860-63, Hamilton Mfg. Co., 1860-63, Hadley Co., 1866-89, Lowell Mfg. Co., 1881-1900; partner, J. W. Paige & Co., selling agts., for textile mills, 1862-63; pres. Pacific Mills, Bigelow Carpet Co., Mass. Cotton Mills (Lowell), Mass. Mills in Ga., Merrimack Mfg. Co. (Lowell), Boston Mfg. Co. (Waltham); Whittenton Mfg. Co. (Taunton), Waltham Bleachery & Dye Works, Essex Co., Mass. Hosp. Life Ins. Co.; propr. of locks and canals on Merrimac River; pres. Provident Instn. for Savings in Boston. Overseer of Harvard U., 1892-99; formerly mem. Corp. of Mass. Inst. Tech.; pres. Boston Athenæum. Home: Boston, and Waltham, Mass. Died Oct. 24, 1915.

LYMAN, Benjamin Smith, geologist, mining engr.; b. Northampton, Mass., Dec. 11, 1835; s. Samuel Fowler and Almira (Smith) L.; A.B., Harvard, 1855; École des Mines, Paris, 1859-61; Royal Acad. Mines, Frieberg, 1861-62; unmarried. Asst. geologist of Ia., 1858; spent yrs. in pvt. geol. work; mining engr. under public works dept., govt. of India, 1870 (surveying oil fields); chief geologist and mining engr., Japanese Govt., 1873-79; asst. geologist of Pa., 1887-95. Has traveled over U.S., British America, Europe, India, China, Japan, Philippines, etc., making geol. researches; common councilman, Northampton, Mass., 1885-86; resided in Phila., 1856-72, and since 1887. Patented a solar transit, 1871. Home: Philadelphia, Pa. Died Aug. 30, 1920.

LYMAN, Charles, govt. official; b. Bolton, Conn., Apr. 10, 1843; s. Jacob and Dorcas C. (Chapman) L.; acad. edn.; served 14th Conn. Vols. in Civil War; LL.B., Nat. U., 1874, LL.M., 1908; m. Mrs. Cornelia F. Clarke, Oct. 4, 1910. Clerk and asst. chief of div., Treasury Dept., 1869-78; chief clerk, U.S. Treasurer's office, 1878-83; chief examiner, U.S. Civil Service Commn., 1883; mem. U.S. Civil Service Commn., 1886-93 (pres. 1889-93); chief div. appointments, Treasury Dept., 1898—. Commr. to Gen. Assembly Presbyn. Ch., 4 times; pres. Y.M.C.A., Washington; pres. Reform Bur. for Promotion of Christian Reforms. Died **1913.**

LYMAN, Charles Baldwin, surgeon; b. Rockford, Ill., Sept. 20, 1863; s. Jabez Baldwin and Lucy (Depue) L.; prep. edn. high schs., Rockford, and Salem, Mass.; M.D., cum laude, Harvard, 1886; m. Ella M. Miller, June 23, 1906. Practiced at Denver, 1887—; surgeon to Union Pacific Hosp., 1887-97; prof. surgery, U. of Colo., 1908, also head of clin. surgery; med. dir. Mountain States Telephone and Telegraph Co.; chief of surg. staff Colo. Gen. Hosp., Denver Gen. Hosp.; visiting surgeon St. Joseph's and Children's hosps. Fellow Am. Coll. Surgeons. Republican. Conglist. Mason. Home: Denver, Colo. Died Aug. 24, 1927.

LYMAN, Chester Wolcott, paper mfr.; b. New Haven, Conn., May 25, 1861; s. Chester Smith and Delia Williams (Wood) L.; B.A., Yale, 1882, M.A., 1895; spl. courses in naval architecture; m. Marguerite Buhler Couleru, of Paris, France, Feb. 26, 1915. Began in mfr. of paper, N.Y. City, 1885; became connected with Herkimer (N.Y.) Paper Co., 1890, later dir. and mgr. same; asst. to pres. Internat. Paper Co., N.Y. City, 1898-1916, v.p., dir. and mgr. of sales, 1916-23, sec.-treas. Am. Paper & Pulp Assn., 1898-1900; pres. Umbagog Paper Co.; v.p. Am. Realty Co.; treas., dir. Continental Paper & Bag Mills, Falls Mfg. Co.; dir. Am. Paper Exports, Inc., etc. Republican. Conglist. Home: New York, N.Y. Died Apr. 7, 1926.

LYMAN, David Brainerd, lawyer; b. Hilo, Hawaii, Mar. 27, 1840; s. Rev. David B. and Sarah (Joiner) L. (parents being missionaries of A.B.C.F.M.); came to U.S., 1860; A.B., Yale, 1864, A.M., 1874; LL.B., Harvard, 1866; m. Mary E., d. F.D. Cossitt, of LaGrange, Ill., Oct. 5, 1870. Admitted to Mass. bar, 1866; became sr. mem. Lyman, Lyman & O'Connor, Chicago; pres. Chicago Title & Trust Co., 1895-1902. Home: LaGrange, Ill. Died Apr. 8, 1914.

LYMAN, Elias, businessman; b. Burlington, Vt., Oct. 22, 1849; s. Elias and Cornelia J. (Hall) L.; A.B., U. of Vt., 1870, A.M., 1873 (LL.D., 1911); m. Harriet E. Phelps, Oct. 20, 1880; m. 2d, Alice M. Henry, Nov. 29, 1916. Began in coal business at Burlington, 1875; president Elias Lyman Coal Company, Burlington Traction Co., Baldwin Refrigerator Co., Burlington Venetian Blind Co., Magnesia Talc Co., Queen City Cotton Co., Military Post St. Ry. Co.; v.p. Howard Nat. Bank, City Trust Co., O. L. Hinds Co. Acting pres. U. of Vt., Dec. 1910-Oct. 1911, now trustee. Mem. Vt. Senate, 1894. Republican. Episcopalian. Mason. Home: Burlington, Vt. Died Mar. 31, 1923.

LYMAN, Elmer Adelbert, educator; b. Manchester, Vt., July 27, 1861; s. Thomas Robert and Angeline Mary (Moore) L.; A.B., U. of Mich., 1886; LL.D., Berea (Ky.) Coll., 1918; m. Effie Elizabeth Polhamus, Dec. 28, 1887; m. 2d, Florence Lyon, Aug. 6, 1926. Began teaching, U. of Mich., 1890; prin. Mich. State Normal Coll., 1899-1902; head dept. of mathematics, Mich. State Normal Coll., 1898—. Trustee Alma (Mich.) Coll., Berea Coll. Republican. Presbyn. Author: Plane and Spherical Trigonometry, 1899; Advanced Arithmetic, 1905; Plane and Solid Geometry, 1908; Elementary Algebra, 1918; Elementary Algebra, First Course, 1923; Elementary Algebra, Second Course, 1926. Home: Ypsilanti, Mich. Died Oct. 9, 1934.

LYMAN, Frederick Wolcott, drug merchant; b. Plymouth, Conn., June 18, 1849; s. Rev. Ephraim and Hannah D. (Richards) L.; ed. pub. schs., Washington, Conn., and Northampton, Mass., and Gunnery Sch., Washington, Conn.; m. Elizabeth Huntington Clark, May 9, 1876 (died 1913); children—Katharine Hart, Jennie Huntington (dec.), Margaret Foster (Mrs. Charles Boden Green), Frederick Clark. In wholesale drug business at Minneapolis, 1875, retired, 1905; dir. several financial corps. One of founders, 1885, of Rollins Coll., Winter Park, Fla., and first pres. of the corp.; trustee Pomona Coll., Claremont, Calif. Home: Minneapolis, Minn. Died Dec. 22, 1931.

LYMAN, George Richard, plant pathologist; b. Lee Center, Ill., Dec. 1, 1871; s. George Alexander and Mary Eliza (Jones) L.; A.B., Beloit (Wis.) Coll., 1894; A.B., Harvard, 1897, A.M., 1899, Ph.D., 1906; m. Frances E. Badger, June 23, 1903; 1 dau., Mavis Katherine. Instr. botany, 1901-04, asst. prof., 1904-15, Dartmouth; pathologist in charge plant disease survey, U.S. Dept. Agr., 1916-23; dean W.Va. Coll. of Agr., 1923—. Mem. war emergency bd. Am. Plant Pathologists, 1918, and chmn. advisory bd. of same, 1919-21; mem. Nat. Research Council, 1919-22. Republican. Conglist. Home: Morgantown, W.Va. Died June 7, 1926.

LYMAN, George Richards, merchant; b. Plymouth, Conn., Dec. 27, 1844; s. Rev. Ephraim and Hannah D. (Richards) L.; ed. The Gunnery, Washington, Conn., until 1860; Williston Sem., Easthampton, Mass., 1860-62; Phillips Acad., Andover, Mass., 1863-64; Yale Scientific Sch., 1864-66; m. Marietta P. Ives, Aug. 10, 1875; children—Mabel Ives (Mrs. Chas. F. Flocken), Florence Richards (Mrs. J. C. Brainard), George Huntington (dec.), Marietta (Mrs. C. R. McCollom), Alice (Mrs. H. H. Abbott), Henry DeForest, Marjorie (Mrs. John W. Snyder). Head of wholesale drug business, 1868-1905. Trustee Carleton College, 1894-1916; pres. Minneapolis Y.M.C.A., 1891-95. Home: Minneapolis, Minn. Died Jan. 14, 1935.

LYMAN, Hart, journalist; b. Plymouth, Conn., Dec. 8, 1851; s. Rev. Ephraim and Hannah D. (Richards) L.; A.B., Yale, 1873; studied univs. of Berlin and Heidelberg, 1874-75; studied law Minneapolis, 1875-76; m. Marion Torrey, Nov. 16, 1881; children—Katharine Stele, Marion Stebbins, Huntington. Was editor Yale Literary Magazine; taught sch., Stockbridge, Mass., spring term, 1874; on editorial staff, New York Tribune, 1876-1913, succeeding Whitelaw Reid as editor-in-chief, Mar. 10, 1905; resigned Mar. 1, 1913. Died Oct. 30, 1927.

LYMAN, Henry Darius, suretyship; b. Parkman, O., Apr. 12, 1852; s. Darius and Betsey Collins (Converse) L.; common sch. edn.; m. Mrs. Louise C. Judson Davis, June 7, 1907. Spl. agt. U.S. Postoffice Dept., 1878; chief clerk contract office, Postoffice Dept., 1881-84; 2d asst. postmaster gen., 1884; sec., 1885-86, v.p., 1886-99, pres., 1899-1912, chmn. bd., Jan. 17, 1912—, Am. Surety Co. Home: New York, N.Y. Died Feb. 27, 1921.

LYMAN, Henry Munson, physician; b. Hawaii, Nov. 26, 1835; grad. Williams Coll., 1858 (A.M.), and med. dept. Columbia Coll. For many yrs. practiced in Chicago; attending physician Presbyn. Hosp.; prof. principles and practice of medicine and senior dean of faculty Rush Med. Coll., Chicago. Author: Artificial Anæsthesia and Anæsthetics; Insomnia and Other Disorders of Sleep; A Text Book of the Practice of Medicine. Died 1904.

LYMAN, James, engineer; b. Middlefield, Conn., Sept. 1, 1862; s. David and Catherine (Hart) L.; Ph.B., Yale, 1883; M.E. and M.M.E., Cornell U., 1895; m. Anna J. Bridgman, June 6, 1891; 1 son, Oliver B. Engr. with The Edison Co., 1883-86, Metropolitan Mfg. Co., 1886-93, General Electric Co., Schenectady, N.Y., 1895-99; engr., western dist. Gen. Electric Co., Chicago, 1902-11; mem. Sargent & Lundy, Inc., mech. and elec. engrs., Chicago, 1911—, v.p., 1920—. Fellow Am. Inst. E.E. (life). Home: Evanston, Ill. Died Mar. 29, 1934.

LYMAN, Joseph, artist; b. Ravenna, O., July 17, 1843; s. Joseph and Mary (Clark) L.; grad. Cleveland High Sch.; studied art in New York; unmarried. After 4 years' travel and study in Europe settled as a landscape and coast painter in New York. Bronze medal, St. Louis Expn., 1904. A.N.A. Home: New York, N.Y. Died Mar. 5, 1913.

LYMAN, Robert Hunt, newspaperman; b. Huntington, Mass., Mar. 3, 1864; s. Samuel T. and Augusta H. (Kirkland) L.; A.B., Yale, 1884; m. 2d, Harriet L. Munson, Sept. 27, 1904; 1 dau., Susan Elizabeth. On staff Springfield (Mass.), Republican, 1884-87, New York Herald, 1887-91, as reporter, legislative corr. and night editor; mng. editor London edition Herald, 1889-90; mng. editor New York Recorder, 1891-92. Joined editorial staff New York World, 1893, night editor, asst. mng. editor and acting mng. editor; editor The World Almanac, May 1922—. Decorated Officier de l'Instruction Publique (French), 1919. Home: New York, N.Y. Died Sept. 3, 1937.

LYMAN, Sarah E. educator; ed. Oberlin Coll.; left college to begin teaching; m. Arthur Essex Lyman. Prin. Laurel Sch., Cleveland, 1906—. Built a large country day school with eleven acres of playing fields. Home: Shaker Heights, Cleveland, Ohio. Deceased.

LYMAN, William Denison, college prof.; b. Portland, Ore., Dec. 1, 1852; s. Horace and Mary (Denison) L.; B.S., Pacific U., Ore., 1873; A.B., Williams Coll., Mass., 1877, A.M., 1880; m. Mattie Clark, June 15, 1882. Prof. English lit., history, and economics, Pacific U., 1877-87; prof. same, 1889-1907, professor history, 1907—, Whitman College, Walla Walla, Wash. Supt. public instruction, Washington Co., Ore.; mountain climber and amateur photographer. Thrice a del. to Rivers and Harbors Congress at Washington, D.C. Democrat. Congregationalist. Author: History of Walla Walla County, 1901; History of Snohomish and Skagit Counties, 1906; The Columbia River, 1909. Advocate of river and harbor improvement, and organizer and lecturer for Rivers and Harbors Congress, 1910-11; dir. Rivers and Harbors Congress for State of Wash., 1911—; pres. Columbia River Waterway Assn., 1912-13. Died June 21, 1920.

LYMER, Elmer E., educator; b. Millbrook, Pa., Apr. 28, 1862; s. John and Elizabeth (Jaques) L.; B.S., Amity Coll., College Springs, Ia., 1879, M.S., 1886; grad. student, U. of Denver, 1895-96 and 1905; Boston U., 1903-04; S.T.D., Simpson Coll., Indianola, Ia., 1897; LL.D., Iowa Wesleyan Coll., 1917; m. Elizabeth Turner, June 21, 1882; 1 dau., Ethel (dec.). V.p., 1890-97, pres. and prof. philosophy, 1897-99, Black Hills (S.D.) Coll.; dean and prof. philosophy Morningside Coll., Sioux City, Ia., 1901-04; mem. of faculty, Ia. Wesleyan Coll., 1904-16, dean, 1909-16, and prof. philosophy and edn.; pres. Gooding (Ida.) Coll., 1916-18; actg. prof. philosophy, Morningside Coll., 1918-19; v.p. same, 1919-20; v.p. Ia. Wesleyan Coll., 1920-22 (emeritus). Served as pastor of M.E. chs. at Ida Grove and Spirit Lake, Ia. Home: San Diego, Calif. Deceased.

LYMER, William Barker, lawyer; b. Clarinda, Ia., Aug. 22, 1882; s. Richard H. and Sarah Ann (Bagnall) L.; A.B., Amity Coll., College Springs, Ia., 1901; LL.B., Harvard, 1907; m. California Lucas, Aug. 6, 1913. Prin. schs., Montecito, Calif., 1902-03; reporter Boston American, 1905; admitted to Colo. bar, 1907, Calif. bar, 1908, H.T. bar, 1909; dep. atty. gen. of Hawaii, 1910; in pvt. practice, Honolulu, 1910-25; atty. gen., Hawaii, 1925-28; U.S. dist. judge, Dist. of Hawaii, 1928-34. Adviser to Hawaiian Legislative Commn. to Washington, 1925; rep. of H.T. in securing federal road aid from U.S. Dept. Agr., 1925; in pvt. law practice, July 1934—. Republican. Home: Kahala, Honolulu, H.T. Deceased.

LYNCH, Charles Wesley, judge; b. nr. South Clarksburg, Va. (now W.Va.), Mar. 11, 1851; s. James and Catharine Jane (Stout) L.; A.B., W.Va. Univ., 1874, A.M., 1877; LL.D., W.Va. Wesleyan Coll.; m. Mary Virginia Robinson, Mar. 8, 1888. Teacher and supt. schs., Burning Springs and Clarksburg to 1882; admitted to W.Va. bar, 1882; mem. W.Va. Ho. of Dels., 1882-83, 1891-92; pros. atty. Harrison Co., W.Va., 1885-89 and 1893-97; judge Circuit Ct., 13th Jud. Circuit, W.Va., 1905-12; asso. justice Supreme Court of W.Va., 1913-21; mem. Lynch & Lynch. Mem. Commn. to Revise and Recodify Laws of W.Va. Pres. trustees W.Va. Wesleyan Coll. Mason. Republican. Home: Clarksburg, W.Va. Deceased.

LYNCH, Frederick (Henry), clergyman, editor; b. Peace Dale, R.I., July 21, 1867; s. Capt. Thomas B. and Jane G. (Gough) L.; A.B., Yale, 1894, B.D., 1897; m. Elizabeth Standish Deming, Apr 21, 1899; m. 2d, Maude Barrows Dutton, Apr. 12, 1909. Ordained Congl. ministry, 1899; asst. pastor United Ch., New Haven, Conn., 1896-98; pastor First Ch., Lenox, Mass., 1898-1903, Pilgrim Ch., N.Y. City, 1903-08; editor Christian Work, 1906-26; editorial staff Yale Divinity Quarterly, 1920-24, Am. Scandinavian Rev., 1921-29, Christian Century, 1926-27, Christian Union Quarterly, and Presbyn. Advance, 1927-29, etc. Sec. Commn. on Internat. Justice and Good Will of Federal Council Chs., 1909-11; pres. Am. Scandinavian Foundation, 1910-18; sec. Ch. Peace Union, 1914-26; a founder, and sec. World Alliance for Internat. Friendship, 1914-26; treas. Fund for Starving in Europe, 1916-26; a founder, and mem. exec. com. Near East Relief, 1916-20, trustee, 1916-29; treas. Internat. Serbian Ednl. Com., 1926-29; sec. Ch. Touring Guild, 1928-29; mem. or officer many other orgns. Has spent every summer in Europe since World War, attending internat. confs. Exchange preacher U.S. to Gt. Britain, 1919. Decorated Order of King George of Greece, 1924; Order of St. Sava (Serbia), 1927; knighted, King of Sweden, 1926. Republican. Author: The Peace Problem, 1911; Through Europe on the Eve of War, 1914; The Last War, 1915; The Christian in War Time (with others), 1917; One Great Society—A Book of Recollections, 1918; Mobilizing for Peace, 1924; Christian Unity in the United States (lectures). Home: New York, N.Y. Died Dec. 19, 1934.

LYNCH, James Kennedy, banker; b. San Francisco, Calif., Sept. 7, 1857; s. James and Alice (Kennedy) L.; grad. Boys' High Sch., San Francisco, 1876; m. Genevieve Soulé, Sept. 3, 1884. Began, 1877, in San Francisco, with First Nat. Gold Bank (name changed to First National Bank, 1884), cashier, 1894-1904, v.p., 1904-17; gov. Federal Reserve Bank of San Francisco, Aug. 7, 1917—. Pres. Am. Bankers' Assn., 1915-16, Calif. Bankers' Assn., 1901-03. Republican. Unitarian. Home: Alameda, Calif. Died Apr. 28, 1919.

LYNCH, James Mathew, industrial commr.; b. Manlius, N.Y., Jan. 11, 1867; s. James and Sarah (Caulfield) L.; ed. Manlius graded sch., 1874-81; began printing trade, Aug. 1881; m. Letitia C. McVey, June 28, 1899. Pres. Syracuse Trade Assembly 7 terms; 1st v.p., 1899-1900, pres., 1900-Jan. 1914, Internat. Typographical Union; mem. N.Y. State Industrial Commn., 1914-21. Home: Syracuse, N.Y. Died July 16, 1930.

LYNCH, Jeremiah, capitalist; b. Fall River, Mass., Mar. 18, 1849; s. Daniel and Bridget (Callaghan) L.; ed. pub. schs., Fall River, Mass., Fond du Lac, Wis., Shasta, Calif., and San Francisco High Sch.; unmarried. Moved with parents to California, 1858; engaged in baking powder business with uncle, 1870; became mem. San Francisco Stock and Mining Exchange, 1874; went to Dawson, Klondike, 1898, remained 3 yrs. Mem. Calif. Senate, 1882-86; largely instrumental in driving C. F. Buckley, the "Boss Tweed" of California, out of the state. Democrat. Agnostic. Author: Three Years in the Klondike, 1904; A Senator of the Fifties, 1911. Deceased.

LYNCH, John A., banker; b. Chicago, Ill., June 11, 1853; s. Thomas and Ann (Flanagan) L.; ed. pub. schs. and business coll.; m. Clara M. Schmahl, Jan. 21, 1896. Began with distilling firm of H. H. Shufeldt & Co., but later sold out interest and turned attention to banking; an organizer Nat. Bank of the Republic, and pres. and chmn. respectively, 1892, until it was merged into Central Republic Bank & Trust Co., 1931. Home: Chicago, Ill. Died Oct. 2, 1938.

LYNCH, John Fairfield, lawyer; b. Harrington, Me., May 9, 1845; s. John and Maria Louise (Moore) L.; ed. pub. schs. and Cherryfield Acad., studied law 3 yrs. with William Freeman, Jr., Cherryfield; m. Mary E. Lewis, Dec. 9, 1872 (died 1881); m. 2d, Abbie Ella Putnam, July 24, 1895. In practice at Machias, Me., 1868—. Enlisted in Co. A of the Coast Guards, Me. Vols., summer of 1864, and served at Ft. McClarey, Kittery, Me., 60 days, when term of service expired (Hannibal Hamlin, then vice-president of U.S., was a mem. of the co. and served during the term); mem. Me. Ho. of Rep., 1876; commissary gen. with title of col., on staff of Gov. Alonzo Garcelon, 1879; Dem. candidate for Congress, 4th Dist. of Me., 1884, 1886; U.S. collector of customs, 1886-90; candidate for U.S. Senate after death of Senator William P. Frye, 1911, and received support of eastern part of state. Author: The Advocate—An Autobiography and Series of Reminiscences, 1916. Home: Machias, Me. Died May 1, 1923.

LYNCH, John Roy; b. Concordia Parish, La., Sept. 10, 1847; s. Patrick and Catharine L.; m. Ella W. Somerville, Dec. 18, 1884; m. 2d, Mrs. Cora E. Williamson, 1911. Lived in Adams County, Miss., 1863; mem. Miss. Ho. of Rep., 1869-73 (speaker 1871-73); mem. 43d and 44th Congresses (1873-77) and 47th Congress (1881-83), 6th Miss. Dist.; chmn. Rep. Exec. Com. of Miss., 1871-89; 4th auditor Treas. Dept., 1889-93; del. Rep. Nat. Convs., 1872, 84, 88, 92, 1900 (temporary chmn. 1884); one of leading colored Republicans in the South. Apptd. maj. p.m. U.S.V., July 1898, and served through Spanish-Am. War after which apptd. capt. and p.m. U.S.A.; promoted maj. and p.m., Sept. 13, 1906; retired Sept. 10, 1911. Admitted to bar in Miss., 1896, D.C., 1897, Ill., 1919. Home: Chicago, Ill. Died Nov. 2, 1939.

LYNCH, Matthew Christoper, prof. law; b. Napa, Calif., Nov. 2, 1882; s. Peter and Mary (Donnelly) L.; B.L., U. of Calif., 1906, J.D., 1908; studied law dept. U. of Chicago; m. Jean Maria Cunningham, Dec. 15, 1915; children—Robert Cunningham, Richard Carey, Matthew Christopher. Began practice at San Francisco, 1908; instr. in law, 1910-13, asst. prof., 1913-15, asso. prof., 1915-18, prof., 1918—, U. of Calif.; asst. to pres., U. of Calif., 1918; asst. fed. reserve agt., Fed. Reserve Bank of San Francisco, 1919; counsel City of Berkeley, 1924. Order of the Coif, Order of Golden Bear. Republican. Home: Berkeley, Calif. Died Nov. 14, 1931.

LYNCH, Robert Newton; b. Sharpsville, Pa., Dec. 18, 1875; s. Isaac Newton and Maria (Caufield) L.; under-grad. State Normal Sch., Chico, Calif., 1894; Th.G., Southern Bapt. Theol. Sem., Louisville, Ky., 1899, Th.B., 1900; Regent's Park Coll., London, 1900-03, A.T.S., 1902; m. Elizabeth Riley, Apr. 18, 1907;

children—Elizabeth Ann, Maria, Robert Newton. Ordained Bapt. ministry, 1903; pastor Petaluma, Calif., 1903-12; v.p. and mgr. Calif. Development Bd., 1910-16, San Francisco Chamber of Commerce, 1912—. Commr. of Calif. to Internat. Expn., Turin, Italy, 1911, Ghent, 1913; studied immigration problems in Europe. Decorated Knight Crown of Italy, 1911. Visited Japan, 1919, by invitation of Japanese Chambers of Commerce, as mem. Japanese Relations Com. Mem. Inst. Pacific Relations, 1925-27. Republican. Home: San Francisco, Calif. Died June 4, 1931.

LYNDE, Francis, author; b. Lewiston, N.Y., Nov. 12, 1856; s. William Tilly and Elizabeth (Need) L.; acad. education; Litt.D., University of the South, 1926; m. Mary Antoinette Stickle, Jan. 17, 1888. In ry. service to 1893; engaged in literary work, 1893—. Author: The Price, 1911; The Honorable Senator Sage-Brush, 1913; After the Manner of Men, 1916; Stranded in Arcady, 1917; David Vallory, 1919; The Wreckers, 1920; The Girl, a Horse and a Dog, 1920; The Fire Bringers, 1921; The Donovan Chance, 1921; Dick and Larry—Freshmen, 1922; Pirates' Hope, 1922; The Golden Spider, 1923; Mr. Arnold, 1923; The Fight on the Standing Stone, 1925; Mellowing Money, 1925; The Cruise of the Cuttlefish, 1925; The Tenderfoots, 1926; The Flight of the Gray Goose, 1927; Blind Man's Buff, 1928; Young Blood, 1929; Silver Wings, 1929. Home: Chattanooga, Tenn. Died May 16, 1930.

LYNDE, Samuel Adams, lawyer; b. Rock Island, Ill., Dec. 14, 1855; s. Cornelius and Mary (Adams) L.; A.B., Harvard, 1877; studied law at Rock Island and was admitted to Ill. bar, 1881; m. Nannie B. Pleasants, Aug. 27, 1879. Engaged in gen. practice at Chicago, 1881-1901; gen. atty., 1901-10; v.p., 1910—, C.&N.W. Railway Co. Died May 16, 1930.

LYNDON, Lamar, consulting engr.; b. Newnan, Ga., Aug. 12, 1871; s. Edward Smith and Anna (Brown) L.; B.Engring., U. of Ga., 1893; spl. work, Stevens Inst. Tech.; Cornell, 1892-94; m. Sara Elizabeth Rucker, June 27, 1895; children—Elizabeth Rucker (dec.), Moselle (Mrs. Hobert Haviland); m. 2d, Grace Hudson, Apr. 1927. Engaged in engring. installations; operated gas and electric systems, Athens, Ga.; went to Yokohama, Japan, 1896, as engr. Am. Trading Co.; then to Kobe to cover Shanghai, Korean and Japan offices of the co. and to Hongkong, Singapore, Java, Burmah, India on engring. work, and Egypt, thence to London for Am. Trading Co.; designed mech. and elec. equipment, Kobe Pier Co., steam pumping equipment of Tandjong Pagar Dock Co. (Singapore), steam power plant for Internat. Cotton Spinning Co. (Shanghai), traction system (Calcutta), equipment for Imperial Chinese Tech. Schools (Tientsin), etc.; returned from London to N.Y. City as chief engr., Am. Trading Co., 1898; joined Electric Vehicle Co., Baltimore, 1900; practiced in New York, 1902-07; mem. Duncan (Dr. Louis) & Lyndon, 1907-10; associated with Gen. Arsene Perrilliat of New Orleans, offices in New York and New Orleans, 1916-20; mem. Bd. of Spl. Problems, U.S. Naval Consulting Bd., World War; lived in Paris, 1920-22; resided in Los Angeles, 1929—. Made engring. investigations, Santo Domingo, 1903; 1st power survey, Grand Canyon of Ariz., 1908; designed and built dam and power plant on Colorado River, at Austin, Tex., 1911-15; referee for Thomas A. Edison in regard to disaster of U.S. Submarine E-2, 1916, and cons. engr. for Edison, 1916-19; made pub. utility and economic municipal investigations for Harrisburg (Pa.), Lynchburg (Va.), Atlanta (Ga.), Houston (Tex.), etc. Fellow Am. Inst. E.E. Democrat. Author: Storage Battery Engineering (transl. in French), 1903; Hydro-Electric Power (2 vols.), 1916; Rate-Making for Public Utilities, 1923. Has made about 40 inventions in electrical, hydraulic and structural arts; developed new formulæ, now standard, for computing engring. problems, including backwater curve, thickness of gravity dams, windings for variable voltage dynamos, electrolyte density in storage cells, etc. Died May 4, 1940.

LYNE, Wickliffe Campbell, insurance mgr.; b. Richmond, Va., Sept. 22, 1850; s. D. Robert Baylor and Mary (Edwards) L.; A.B., Bethany (W.Va.) Coll., 1870; Litt.D., Grove City (Pa.) Coll.; m. Mary Vowell Winters, Aug. 1878; children—Wickliffe Bull, Sarah Harmon, Robert Addison, Virginia Brown. Successively head of acad., normal sch., high sch., and supt. edn., 1871-76; mgr. Nat. Life Ins. Co. of Vt., 1884-1907; resident mgr. Union Central Life Ins. Co., Pittsburgh, Pa., 1907—. Served as organizer and dir. First Nat. Bank of Wilkinsburg, also of Wilkinsburg Trust Co. Lecturer on literature, history and methods of instruction, Curry Univ., Pittsburgh, 1882-84; chmn. Pa. delegation, Armistice Day, 1920, Washington, D.C., honoring burial of unknown soldier; chmn. Pittsburgh's celebration, Sept. 17, 1922, observing birthday of Am. Constitution; chmn. Thomas Jefferson Memorial Foundation, 1926. Trustee Bethany Coll., Pittsburgh Acad., Carnegie Library (Wilkinsburg), Carnegie Art Soc. Mem. exec. council Four-Minute Men, World War. Republican. Presbyn. An organizer East End Christian Ch., Pittsburgh, and chmn. bd. trustees, 1880-90. Died Nov. 8, 1933.

LYON, A. Maynard, philanthropist; b. Brandon, Vt., Aug. 29, 1818; s. Esbon E. and Sarah (Knight) L.; ed. high sch., Brandon, Vt. For 40 yrs. a real estate dealer in New York, with A. T. Stewart, John Jacob Astor and other noted men as regular clients; later an underwriter in stocks until his 92d yr. Prin. builder and 1st pres. Jacksonville, St. Augustine and Halifax, R.R. (which he financed); an extensive traveler. Mgr., for 56 yrs., pres. 1865-72, and from 1890, Northwestern Med. Dispensary of New York; mem. New York City Assn. for Improving the Condition of the Poor, 1850-68, and chmn. and treas. 22d ward com. same. Mem. New York City Union Defense Com. to disburse city fund of $3,500,000 to families of needy Union soldiers. For many yrs. an official of 42d St. Presbyn. Ch. Author: "Holy Waves," "Jewels," "The Tolling Bell," "Unusual Patriotic Anthem," "Celestial Morn," "Why Bide I by the Sea," "War Song," "Victory"; and fugitive poems and hymns published in religious periodicals. Died Oct. 14, 1916.

LYON, Cecil Andrew, lumberman; b. Boston, Ga., Nov. 29, 1869; s. Oliver Thomas and Lydia Doris (Dupon) L.; ed. Austin Coll., Sherman, Tex., 1882-84, State Agrl. and Mech. Coll., Coll. Sta., Tex., 1884-86; grad. Pa. Mil. Coll., Bachelor of Architecture, 1890 (ranking capt. cadet corps); m. Claudia Du Pont, June 12, 1900. V.p. and gen. mgr. Hardeman Co. Irrigation Co.; pres. Lyon-Gray Lumber Co.; dir. Great Southern Life Ins. Co. Col. 4th Inf., Tex. N.G.; mem. Rep. State Exec. Com., 1890-1900; chmn. Rep. Com., 1900-12; mem. Rep. Nat. Com., 1904-12; del.-at-large, 1904, 08, 12; assisted in organizing Progressive party, 1912; chmn. Prog. State Com., Tex., 1912—; mem. Prog. Nat. Com., 1912—. Home: Sherman, Tex. Died Apr. 4, 1916.

LYON, David Gordon, univ. prof.; b. Benton, Ala., May 24, 1852; s. Dr. Isaac and Sarah Caroline (Arnold) L.; A.B., Howard Coll., Ala., 1875; Ph.D., Leipzig, 1882; S.T.D., Harvard, 1901; m. Tosca Woehler, of Leipzig, Germany, July 24, 1883 (died 1904); m. 2d, Mabel Everett Harris, August 17, 1910 (died 1931); 1 son, David Gordon. Hollis professor divinity, 1882-1910. Hancock professor Hebrew and other Oriental langs., 1910-22, prof. emeritus, 1922—, 1st curator Semitic Mus., 1891-1922, acting curator, 1922-31, hon. curator, 1922—, Harvard U. Dir. Am. School for Oriental Study and Research, Palestine, 1906-07. Fellow Am. Acad. Arts and Sciences. Author: Keilschrifttexte Sargons Königs von Assyrien, 1883; An Assyrian Manual, 1886; Harvard Excavations at Samaria, 1908-10 (with others), 2 vols., 1924; articles in Journal of American Oriental Society, etc. Editor: Studies in the History of Religions (with George F. Moore), 1912. Home: Cambridge, Mass. Died Dec. 4, 1935.

LYON, Edmund, humanitarian; s. Harrison A. and Fannie Minerva (Gale) L.; A.B., A.M., U. of Rochester; LL.B., Columbia, 1880; m. Carolyn Hamilton Talcott, June 2, 1896. Began law practice at Rochester, 1880; also in real estate and mining business; a founder of E. Rochester, 1897; mng. dir. North East Electric Co., Rochester; dir. Lincoln Nat. Bank; pres. Riverside Cemetery. Instr., lecturer and writer on teaching the deaf, 1890-1900; sec. N.Y. State Bd. Charities, 1895-96; pres. Am. Assn. to Promote Teaching Speech to the Deaf, dir., 1893—; state examiner schs. for deaf, 1895-98; mgr. N.Y. State Industrial and Agrl. Sch.; pres. Western N.Y. Sch. for the Deaf; treas. Rochester Mechanics Inst.; v.p. Rochester Dental Dispensary, Rochester Friendly Home, Infants Summer Hosp.; trustee U. of Rochester. Author: The Lyon Phonetic Manual, 1891. Home: Rochester, N.Y. Died Apr. 24, 1920.

LYON, Eldridge Merick; b. Chicago, Ill., Nov. 14, 1853; s. Isaac Lewis and Maria Delia (Merick) L.; A.B., Yale, 1874; grad. Goldsmith & Bryant Business Coll., 1874; m. Clara S. Grout, 1878 (died 1901); children—Alice Grout (Mrs. Donald C. Scott), Ruth (Mrs. Sidney Locock Lasell); m. 2d, Mabel deCloston Salter, 1907. In timber business, 1874-82; admitted to Mich. bar, 1883; practiced at Detroit, 1883-86; began orange growing, Redlands, Calif., 1891; entered orange packing business, 1894; mem. I. L. Lyon & Sons, 1902—, pres. Sunny Mt. Orange Co., Redlands & Yucaipa Land Co.; vice pres. Bear Valley Water Co., Crafton Water Co. Pres. Calif. Citrus League, Redlands Asso. Charities, Redlands br. Am. Red Cross, Redlands Community Hosp. (dir.), A. K. Smiley Pub. Library. Republican. Home: Redlands, Calif. Died Sept. 28, 1935.

LYON, Elias Potter, physiologist; b. Cambria, Mich., Oct. 20, 1867; s. Nelson J. and Mary (Hebard) L.; B.S., Hillsdale Coll., 1891, A.B., 1892; Ph D., Univ. of Chicago, 1897; hon. M.D., St. Louis Univ., 1910, LL.D., 1920; hon. D.Sc., Hillsdale College, Mich., 1924, Univ. of Southern Calif., 1930; m. Nellie P. Eastman, Sept. 1, 1897. Instr. Hillsdale Coll., 1890-92, Harvard Sch., Chicago, 1892-96, Bradley Poly. Inst., Peoria, Ill., 1897-1900; asst. prof., Rush Med. Coll., 1900-04; asst. prof. physiology and asst. dean, U. of Chicago, 1901-04; prof. physiology, 1904-13, dean, 1907-13, St. Louis U. Med. Sch.; prof. physiology and dean, U. of Minn. Med. Sch., 1913—. Biologist, Cook Greenland expdn., 1894; investigator U.S. Bur. of Fisheries, 1908-11; investigator, Marine Biol. Laboratory various summers; trustee of same, 1921; trustee Hillsdale Coll., 1925. Lt. col., U.S.A. Reserve, Sanitary Corps, retired. Home: Minneapolis, Minn. Died May 4, 1937.

LYON, Ernest Neal, teacher; b. Greenfield, Mass., Oct. 26, 1873; s. Rev. A. Judson and Mary (Wheaton) L.; grad. Colgate Univ., 1897; m. Amelia Stamm, 1904. Prof. English literature, Marion (Ala.) Mil. Inst., 1897-1900; head English dept., Mt. Hermon Sch., Northfield, Mass., 1900-02; instr. English, Manual Training High Sch., Brooklyn, 1905—. Republican. Home: Brooklyn, N.Y. Deceased.

LYON, George Armstrong, rear adm.; b. Erie, Pa., Dec. 23, 1837; s. Rev. George A. and Mary (Sterrett) L.; ed. Dartmouth Coll., class of 1858; admitted to bar of Pa., 1861; m. Rose Vincent, June 21, 1877. Apptd. asst. p.-m. U.S.N., June 11, 1862; promoted p.-m., Jan. 23, 1866; pay insp., Sept. 15, 1888; pay dir., Mar. 15, 1898; retired, Dec. 23, 1899, with rank of rear adm. for services during Civil War. Died Mar. 6, 1914.

LYON, George F., judge; b. in town of Barker, Broome Co., N.Y., July 13, 1849; s. Harry and Pamelia A. (Livermore) L.; A.B., Hamilton Coll., 1872, LL.D., 1904; m. Elizabeth R. Mather, Apr. 9, 1884. Admitted to bar, 1875; mem. Chapman & Martin, 1876-77, of Chapman & Lyon, 1877-90; mem. N.Y. Constl. Conv., 1894; elected justice Supreme Court of N.Y., 1895; reëlected on Rep. and Dem. tickets, Nov. 1909; designated a mem. of Appellate Div. for 3d Jud. Dept., Jan. 1912; official referee, Jan. 1920—. Republican. Home: Binghamton, N.Y. Died May 21, 1940.

LYON, Henry Ware, rear admiral U.S.N.; b. in Mass. Grad. U.S. Naval Acad., 1866; promoted ensign, Apr. 1868; master, July 26, 1869; lt., Mar. 21, 1870; lt. comdr., Nov. 1884; comdr., Oct. 1, 1893; capt., Mar. 27, 1900; rear admiral, Feb. 19, 1906. First sea service, 1866-67, was with the Sacramento, which was lost off the coast of India; comd. U.S.S. Olympia, 1901; commandant Navy Yard, Mare Island, Calif., 1906-07; retired, Nov. 8, 1907. Home: Paris, Me. Died Nov. 22, 1929.

LYON, John Denniston, banker; b. Pittsburgh, Pa., Jan. 24, 1861; s. Alexander Parker and Eliza Thaw (Denniston) L.; grad. Lawrenceville, N.J., Sch., 1878; m. Maude Fleming Byers, Feb. 18, 1896; 1 dau., Martha Byers (Mrs. H. Nelson Slater). Began with William R. Thompson & Co., Pittsburgh, 1890; with N. Holmes & Sons, 1900-05; elected v.p. Union Nat. Bank, 1905, and dir. Safe Deposit & Trust Co. (now Peoples Pittsburgh Trust Co.), of which became pres., 1913. Federal director National War Savings Com., World War. Republican. Presbyn. Home: Sewickley, Pa. Died Aug. 14, 1939.

LYON, LeRoy Springs, army officer; b. Petersburg, Va., Oct. 15, 1866; s. John and Margaret M. (Springs) L.; A.B., Richmond Coll., 1886 (LL.D., 1919); grad. U.S. M.A., 1891, Coast Arty. Sch., Ft. Monroe, Va., 1898, Sch. of Submarine Defense, Ft. Totten, N.Y., 1903; m. Harriette Amsden, Dec. 1, 1902. Commd. 2d lt. 7th Cav., June 12, 1891; promoted through grades to col. May 15, 1917; brig. gen. N.A., Aug. 5, 1917; major general N.A., Apr. 12, 1918. A.d.c. to Gen. Royal T. Frank, 1898-99, serving at Chickamauga Park, Ga., Anniston, Ala., and hdqrs. Dept. of Gulf; with light battery and 2d Arty., in Cuba, 1899-1900; dist. arty. engr., Ft. Barrancas, Fla., 1903-06; in P.I., 1906-07, participating in expdn. against hostile Moros; served in Canal Zone, 1916-17; at El Paso, Tex., Aug. 1917; comd. 65th Field Arty. Brigade, Camp Kearny, Calif., Aug. 25, 1917-May 1918; comd. 31st (Dixie) Div., Camp Wheeler, Ga., and in France, May-Nov. 1918, 90th Div., Nov.-Dec. 1918; in France, Sept. 29, 1918-May 13, 1919; participated in Meuse-Argonne offensive, Oct. 11-Oct. 18, 1918; comd. Camp Bowie, Tex., May-July 15, 1918; returned to regular rank of col. F.A., July 15, 1918, comd. Field Arty. Basic School, Camp Taylor, Ky., July 26, 1919—. Died Feb. 23, 1920.

LYON, T(homas) Lyttleton, agronomist; b. Pittsburgh, Pa., Feb. 17, 1869; s. James B. and Anna M. (Lyon) L.; B.S.A., Cornell, 1891, Ph.D., 1904; studied agrl. chemistry, U. of Göttingen, 1893-94; m. Bertha L. Clark, 1899; children—John Lyttleton, George Clark. Instr. chemistry, 1891-95, prof. agr., 1895-1906, U. of Neb.; asso. dir. Nebr. Agrl. Experiment Sta., 1899-1906; prof. agronomy, Cornell U., 1906-37, prof. emeritus, 1937—. Potts medal, Franklin Inst., 1911; Chilean nitrate soda research award. Author: Soils and Fertilizers; Principles of Soil Management (with E. O. Fippin); Soils, Their Properties and Management (with E. O. Fippin and H. O. Buckman); Nature and Properties of Soils (with H. O. Buckman). Home: Ithaca, N.Y. Died Oct. 7, 1938.

LYON, William Henry, clergyman; b. Fall River, Mass., Dec. 23, 1846; s. Henry and Julia Ann (Wilbur) L.; A.B., Brown U., 1868; S.T.B., Harvard, 1873; (D.D., Brown, 1896); m. Louise Dennison, Apr. 5, 1893. Ordained Unitarian ministry, 1873; minister First Soc., Ellsworth, Me., 1873-78, Mt. Pleasant and All Souls' chs., Roxbury, Mass., 1880-96, First Parish, Brookline, Mass., 1896— (now sr. minister). Councillor Hungarian Unitarian Synod; sec. Nat. Unitarian Conf.; pres. Unitarian S.S. Soc., Brookline Edn. Society. Author: A Study of the Sects, 1891; Early Old Testament Narratives, 1893; Later Old Testament Narratives, 1905. Died Dec. 20, 1915.

LYON, William Penn, judge; b. Chatham, N.Y., Oct. 28, 1822; s. Isaac and Eunice (Coffin) L.; ed. in dist. schools of native town; studied law at intervals; admitted to bar, 1846; (LL.D., U. of Wis., 1873); m. Adelia Caroline Duncombe, of St. Thomas, Ont., Nov. 18, 1847. Dist. atty. Racine Co., Wis., 1853-59; mem. and speaker Wis. Assembly, 1859-60; capt. Co. K, 8th Wis. Vols., 1861; col. 13th Wis. Vols., 1862-65; bvtd. brig. gen., 1865. Judge 1st circuit, Wis., 1866-71; justice Supreme Ct., 1871-94 (chief justice, 1892, 1893); mem. 1896-1903, pres. 1898-1903, State Bd. of Control of State Charitable, Penal and Reformatory Institutions. Republican. Died Apr. 4, 1913.

LYONS, Albert Brown, chemist; b. Waimea, Hawaii, Apr. 1, 1841; s. Rev. Lorenzo and Lucia Garratt (Smith) L.; desc. William Lyon, Roxbury, Mass., 1635; spent early life at a remote mission sta. in H.I.; ed. at home, and, 1857-63, at Oahu Coll.; A.B., Williams, 1865; M.D., U. of Mich., 1868; m. Edith M., d. Rev. Zachary Eddy, of Detroit, Apr. 25, 1878; children—Lucia Eddy, Albert Eddy. Prof. chemistry, Detroit Med. Coll., 1868-80; consulting chemist for Parke, Davis & Co., Detroit, 1881-86; 1st editor Pharmaceutical Era, 1887-88; head of Science Dept. Oahu Coll., also govt. chemist for Hawaii, 1888-95; chemist, 1897—, Nelson, Baker & Co., Detroit. Mem. Com. of Revision of U.S. Pharmacopœia, 1900-20. Author: Manual of Pharmaceutical Assaying, 1887; Practical Assaying of Drugs and Galenicals, 1899; Plant Names, Scientific and Popular, 1900, enlarged edit., 1907; The Lyon Families of New England, 1905, 1907, 1908; Standardization by Chemical Assay of Organic Drugs, 1920. Home: Detroit, Mich. Died Apr. 13, 1926.

LYONS, Chalmers J., prof. oral surgery; b. Martinsburg, O., Apr. 30, 1874; s. John P. and Manilla (White) L.; ed. Central Mich. Normal Sch., Mt. Pleasant, Mich.; D.D.S., U. of Mich., 1898, D.D.Sc., 1911; m. Grace B. Driggs, 1909; 1 son, Richard Hugh. Practiced at Adrian, Mich., 1898-1907; moved to Jackson, Mich., 1907, and asso. in practice with Dr. J. W. Lyons; instr. oral surgery, 1907-15, prof. 1915—, U. of Mich. Republican. Episcopalian. Mason. Author: Fractures and Dislocations of the Jaws, 1919, revised, 1926. Home: Ann Arbor, Mich. Died May 18, 1935.

LYONS, Charles William, clergyman, educator; b. Boston, Mass., Jan. 31, 1868; s. Patrick Ambrose and Mary Cecelia (Hagerty) L.; prep. edn., English High Sch., Boston; scientific lit., philos. and theol. courses, Frederick Novitiate and Woodstock Coll., Md. Joined Soc. of Jesus, 1890; ordained priest R.C. Ch., 1904; teacher metaphysics and polit. economy, St. Francis Xavier Coll., New York, 1905-07, Boston Coll., 1907-08; pres. Gonzaga Coll., Washington, D.C., 1908-09, St. Joseph's Coll., Phila., 1909-14, Boston Coll., 1914-18; pres. Georgetown U., Oct. 1, 1924—. Mem. Mil. Commn. of Mass., 1915-16; mem. Advisory Bd. of State Bd. of Edn., Mass., 1916-17. Mem. U.S. Bunker Hill Sesquicentennial Commn., 1925. Decorated Comdr. Order of the Star, Roumania. Died Jan. 31, 1939.

LYONS, Dennis Francis, lawyer; b. Danvers, Mass., Feb. 15, 1880; s. John and Bridget Maria (Sullivan) L.; A.B., Dartmouth, 1902 (Phi Beta Kappa); LL.B., U. of Minn., 1906; m. Anna Gall, July 14, 1908; children—Kathleen, William Hart. Admitted to Minn. bar, 1906, and began practice at St. Paul; with N.P. Ry. Co., 1911—, gen. counsel, July 1, 1925—. Democrat. Catholic. Home: St. Paul, Minn. Died June 12, 1937.

LYONS, Judson Whitlocke, lawyer; b. in Burke Co., Ga., Aug. 15, 1860; LL.B., Howard U., 1884; m. Jane Hope, 1890. Admitted to bar, 1884, and practiced at Augusta, Ga.; register U.S. Treasury, 1898-1906. Formerly mem. Rep. Nat. Com. for Ga. Trustee and pres. Haines Normal Inst., Augusta. Home: Augusta, Ga. Died June 22, 1924.

LYONS, Julius J., lawyer, amateur musician; b. New York, Oct. 7, 1843; s. Rev. Jacques J. (rabbi) and Grace L.; ed. Univ. Grammar Sch., New York; admitted to bar, 1866; m. Constance Hendricks, 1872 (died 1906). Counsel, incorporator and dir. State Bank of New York from its organization until 1909; 12 yrs. dir. and hon. sec. Montefiore Home for Chronic Invalids; dir. and 10 yrs. sec. Mt. Sinai Hosp.; dir. and sec. Hebrew Tech. Inst. for several yrs.; judge advocate 2d Brigade, on Gen. Vilmea's staff, with rank of maj., 1875-76. Long prominent in musical matters, writer on staff Sunday Herald on religious and musical subjects; also musical editor Daily News. Wrote the music of the opera "The Lady and the Tiger," produced by McCaull's and later by DeWolf Hopper's co.; founded and was pres. and conductor of Met. Amateur Orchestra (90 instrumentalists), which for 7 yrs. gave entertainments, devoting entire receipts to charitable and ednl. purposes. Retired. Home: Chatham, N.J. Died June 1920.

LYONS, Katharine, dramatic critic; b. Boston, Mass., Oct. 11, 1889; d. Joseph Talbot and Ellen (Noonan) Lyons; ed. pub. schs.; m. Herman O. Bletzer, Feb. 21, 1924; 1 dau., Katharine Anne. Began newspaper work with Boston Herald-Traveler, 1908; dramatic editor and critic of the Traveler (evening paper), 1918—. Home: Brookline, Mass. Died Jan. 3, 1933.

LYONS, Thomas Richard, judge; b. Bendigo, Australia, Mar. 19, 1867; s. Thomas and Anne (Tuohy) L.; brought to U.S., 1870; prep. edn. Whitman Coll., Wash.; Ottawa Coll., Can.; LL.B., U. of Mich., 1892; m. Rose E. Dovell, June 20, 1906. Practiced law in Ore., 1892-97; trustee for townsite entries of land at Juneau, Alaska, 1897-1900; asst. U.S. atty., 1900-03; temporary U.S. atty., 1st Div. of Alaska, Jan.-May 1903; asst. U.S. atty., May 1903-June 1905; U.S. dist. judge, Alaska, May 4, 1909-May 21, 1913; now mem. Lyons & Orton. Republican. Catholic. Home: Seattle, Wash. Died Jan. 4, 1941.

LYONS, Timothy Augustine, capt. U.S.N.; b. in Ireland, Mar. 25, 1845; grad. U.S. Naval Acad., 1865; m. Marie Blanche Humbert, Sept. 14, 1871. Promoted through the various grades to comdr.; retired on account of disability, May 15, 1897; advanced to rank of capt.; retired, June 29, 1906. Served on various ships of N. Atlantic, European, Pacific and Asiatic squadrons, 1865-92, with intervals of duty at Naval Acad., Navy Dept. and New York; comd. U.S.S. Monongahela, 1892-93, U.S.S. Alliance, 1893-94. Author: Meteorological Charts of North Pacific Ocean, 1878; The Magnetism of Iron and Steel Ships, 1884; Treatise on Electro-magnetic Phenomena and on the Compass and Its Deviations Aboard Ship (2 vols.), 1901-03. Home: New York, N.Y. Died 1919.

LYSTER, Theodore Charles, M.D., surgeon; b. Fort Larned, Kan., July 10, 1875; s. William John and Martha Guthrie (Doughty) L., grad. high sch., Detroit, Mich., 1893; Ph.B., U. of Mich., 1897, M.D., 1899; m. Lua Withenbury, Jan. 10, 1907; children—Russell Withenbury, Theodore Charles. Pvt. and acting hosp. steward, Hosp. Corps, U.S.A., June 1898-Feb. 1899; served with Med. Corps, U.S.A., advancing from 1st lt. to col., 1900-19; asst. surgeon, Manhattan Eye and Ear Hosp., New York, 1901-04; chief of eye, ear, nose and throat, Ancon Hosp., Canal Zone, 1904-09; chief of eye service, Philippine Univ., Manila, 1911; chief health officer, Vera Cruz, Mexico, during Am. occupation, 1913; chief of aviation and professional services, Surgeon-General's Office, 1917-18, in France, winter 1917-18; retired as col., 1919 (brig. gen., retired, spl. act of Congress, Aug. 16, 1930); a dir. of yellow fever elimination, Rockefeller Foundation, 1918-22; in practice at Los Angeles, Calif., mem. firm Lyster and Jones, 1920—. Fellow Am. Coll. Surgeons, Am. Laryngol., Rhinol. and Otol. Society. Awarded D.S.M. "for exceptionally meritorious and conspicuous service," 1919. Republican. Episcopalian. Home: Los Angeles, Calif. Died Aug. 5, 1933.

LYTE, E(liphalet) Oram, school prin.; b. nr. Bird-in-hand, Pa., June 29, 1842; s. Louis Clarkson and Rebecca (Martin) L.; served pvt. in inf. regt. and commd. officer in light arty. during Civil War; B.S., Pa. State Normal Sch., 1868, M.S., 1876; (hon. A.M., 1878, Ph.D., 1887, Franklin and Marshall Coll.); m. Mary McJunkin, Mar. 26, 1872. Prof. pedagogy and English grammar, 1887-86, prin. and prof. psychology and logic, 1887—, First Pa. State Normal Sch., Millersville, Pa. Lecturer on ednl. and lit. subjects; chmn. group and dept. juries on edn. and mem. Superior Jury of Awards, St. Louis Expn., 1904. Author: Elementary English, 1898; Elements of Grammar and Composition, 1898; Advanced Grammar and Composition, 1898; State Normal Schools of the United States, 1903. Died Jan. 3, 1913.

LYTER, Jean Curtis, M.D., diagnostician; b. Berry, Ky., Oct. 7, 1883; s. Alonzo D. and Annette M. (Terry) L.; grad. Smith's Sch., Cynthiana, Ky., 1903; M.D., St. Louis U. Sch. of Medicine, 1907; m. Lena Ingram, 1911 (now dec.); 1 dau., Martha Cecile; m. 2d, Mildred Luedinghaus, Aug. 28, 1930. Began practice St. Louis, 1907; asst. prof. medicine, St. Louis U. Sch. of Medicine, 1916—; phys. in chief to St. Anthony's Hosp., St. Louis; visiting physician to Mo. Bapt. Sanitarium, Jewish Hosp.; consulting phys. to St. Louis Co. Hosp. Capt., Med. Corps, U.S.A., World War. Home: St. Louis, Mo. Died Oct. 9, 1937.

M

MAAS, Anthony J., college pres.; b. Bainkhausen, Westphalia, Germany, Aug. 23, 1858; s. John and Elizabeth (Peetz) M.; ed. pvt. schs., Hellefeld, Westphalia, 1869-72, Stockum, 1872-74, Gymnasium, Arnsberg, 1874-77, Manresa, N.Y., 1877-79, Woodstock Coll., Md., 1880-83, 1884-88, Manresa, Spain, 1893-94. Ordained R.C. priest; entered Soc. of Jesus, 1877; prof. Latin and Greek, Frederick, Md., 1883-84; prof. Hebrew, 1885-1902, librarian, 1888-1902, prof. Scripture, 1891-1902, prefect of studies, 1897-1905, pres. 1907-12, Woodstock (Md.) Coll.; provincial of Md.-N.Y. Province of Soc. of Jesus, 1912-18; prof. ascetical theology, Novitiate of St. Andrew, Poughkeepsie, N.Y., 1918—. Author: Life of Christ, 1891; Enchiridion, etc., 1892; Day in the Temple, 1892; Christ in Type and Prophecy, Vol. I, 1893, Vol. II, 1896; Commentary of Gospel of St. Matthew, 1898. Address: Poughkeepsie, N.Y. Died Feb. 1927.

MABERY, Charles Frederic, chemist; b. New Gloucester, Me., Jan. 13, 1850; s. Henry and Elizabeth A. (Bennett) M.; S.B., Lawrence Scientific Sch. (Harvard), 1876, Sc.D., 1881; m. F. A. Lewis, Nov. 19, 1872. Asst. in chemistry, Harvard, 1874-83; prof. chemistry Case Sch. Applied Science, 1883-1911, emeritus. Researcher in organic chemistry; especially in investigations of the composition of Am. petroleum, lubricants and lubrication. Address: Cleveland, O. Died June 26, 1927.

MABIE, Hamilton Wright, editor; b. Cold Spring, N.Y., Dec. 13, 1846; s. L. J. and Sarah C. M.; A.B., Williams, 1867, later A.M.; LL.B., Columbia, 1869; L.H.D., Williams, 1890; LL.D., Union, 1899, Western Reserve, 1904, Washington and Lee, 1906; m. Jeannette Trivett, Oct. 11, 1876. Asso. editor The Outlook. Author: Norse Stories Retold from the Eddas, 1882; Nature in New England, 1890; My Study Fire, 1st series, 1890; Short Studies in Literature, 1891; Under the Trees and Elsewhere, 1891; Essays in Literary Interpretation, 1892; My Study Fire, 2d series, 1894; Nature and Culture, 1897; Books and Culture, 1897; Work and Culture, 1898; The Life of the Spirit, 1899; William Shakespeare—Poet, Dramatist and Man, 1900; Works and Days, 1902; Parables of Life, 1902; Backgrounds of Literature, 1903; Myths Every Child Should Know, 1905; Fairy Tales Every Child Should Know, 1905; The Great Word, 1905; Heroes Every Child Should Know, 1906; Legends Every Child Should Know, 1906; Christmas Today, 1908; Introductions to Notable Poems, 1909; American Ideals, Character and Life, 1913; Japan, Today and Tomorrow, 1914. Home: Summit, N.J. Died Dec. 31, 1916.

MABIE, Henry Clay, clergyman; b. Belvidere, Ill., June 20, 1847; s. Daniel and Harriet (Saxton) M.; A.B., U. of Chicago, 1868; B.D., Bapt. Theol. Sem., Chicago, 1875; D.D., Chicago, 1882; LL.D., Baylor, 1912; m. Edith S. Roe, Sept. 14, 1869. Ordained Bapt. ministry, 1869; pastor State St. Church, Rockford, Ill., 1869-73, Oak Park, Ill., 1873-75, Brookline, Mass., 1876-79, First Ch., Indianapolis, 1879-83, First Ch., Belvidere, Ill., 1883-85, First Ch., St. Paul, 1885-88, Central Ch., Minneapolis, 1888-90; corr. sec. Am. Bapt. Missionary Union, 1890-1908; visited missions in Asia, Japan, China, India, etc., 1890, 1913, 14; active in advocacy of foreign mission work. Represented Am. Bapt. Missionary Union at the Morrison Centenary Conf., Shanghai, 1907. Address: Boston, Mass. Died Apr. 30, 1918.

MABURY, Margaret Ellis (Mrs.), composer; ed. pub. schs., Cambridge, young ladies' sch., Winchester; convents in Providence and Brighton, St. John's Episcopal Sch., New York; m. Henry Nelson Mabury, June 1897. Engaged in writing and composing songs and pianoforte music, 1897—. Has played original compositions at many pvt. musicals, also in Chickering Hall, Boston, and at many ednl. clubs, 1903-04. Songs: To a Nightingale; Go, Lovely Rose; Pity My Sorrow; O, the Blue Hills; Daffodils. Pianoforte Compositions: Aquarelle; A Water-Wheel; Mazurka; Nocturne Mignonne; Mazurka II. Home: Cambridge, Mass. Died 1909.

See also **Mc** spellings, pages 794-824 inclusive.

MAC AFEE, John Blair, banker; b. St. John, N.B., July 4, 1861; s. Robert and Catharine Isabella (Stevens) M.; LL.B., U. of Pa., 1882; hon. Dr. Engring., U. of Ky., 1910; m. Clara Brinton, d. Granville B. Haines, Dec. 9, 1886. Admitted to bar, 1882; discontinued practice of law, 1890; consulting engr. Chandler Bros. & Co., New York, Phila. and Boston, 1901—, and in charge foreign business of the co., 1911; chmn. MacAfee & Co., Ltd., bankers, London. Was pres. New York and Phila. Traction Co., Central Jersey Traction Co. and Paritan Constrn. Co., which were merged into the Public Service Co.; also Central Ky. Traction Co., Lexington Ry. Co., Norfolk & Portsmouth Traction Co., Lexington Utilities Co., Blue Grass Traction Co., Pomeroy & Middletown Electric Co. Pres. Am. Engring. Co., 1898-1900, Mich. Traction Co., 1899-1900; v.p. Railways Co. General, 1899-1901; also officer in other corps.; dir. Ohio River Electric Ry. & Power Co., Ky. Traction & Terminal Co., Pomeroy & Middleport Electric Co., Utilities Securities, Ltd.; dir. and chmn. finance com. Am. Chamber of Commerce, London. Republican. Episcopalian. V.p. English Speaking Union. Home: Ardmore, Pa. Died Jan. 11, 1921.

MAC ALISTER, James, educator; b. Glasgow, Scotland, Apr. 26, 1840; s. John and Agnes (Robertson) M.; came to U.S., 1850; A.B., Brown U., 1856 (A.M., by spl. vote, 1890, LL.D., 1890); LL.B., Albany Law Sch., 1864; m. Lucretia Brayton, June 24, 1866. Supt. pub. schs., Milwaukee, 1874-81; regent normal schs., Wis., 1878-83; 1st supt. of pub. schs., Phila., 1883-91; pres. Drexel Inst., Phila., 1891—. Lecturer Johns Hopkins, 1893, Coll. City of New York, 1894. Trustee U. of Pa., 1885-97. Officier d'Académie, Paris, 1890. Mem. bd. Fairmount Park Art Assn., 1893—. Author: Manual of Primary Instruction, 1884; Manual of Instruction in United States History and Civil Government, 1887; Catalogue of Pedagogical Library, with Bibliographical Notes, 1887; Manual Training in the

Public Schools of Philadelphia, 1890; Art Education in the Public Schools, 1893. Home: Philadelphia, Pa. Died Dec. 11, 1913.

MAC ALPINE, Robert John, clergyman; b. Cedarville, Ont., Can., Aug. 25, 1874; s. Alexander and Isabella (Morison) MacA.; grad. in Pharmacy, U. of Toronto, 1892, B.A., 1899, M.A., 1900; studied theology, Knox Coll., 1901; D.D., Maryville (Tenn.) Coll., 1919; m. Mary Margaret, d. T. J. Stewart, Feb. 4, 1903; children—Stewart Alexander, Robert Knox (dec.), Edith Marie (adopted). Ordained Presbyn. ministry, 1902; pastor Owen Sound, Ont., 1902-07, North Ch., Cleveland, O., 1907-09, Boulevard Ch., Cleveland, 1909-14; Central Ch., Buffalo, N.Y., 1914—, ch. membership built up from 500 to 2,650. Mem. Gen. Assembly's Com. for consolidation and reconstruction of all bds. of Presbyn. Ch. U.S.A., 1920-23. Republican. Mason. Author: Bible Readings and Prayers, 1918; What Is True Religion?, 1923; There Is No Death. Home: Buffalo, N.Y. Died Sept. 5, 1926.

MAC ARTHUR, Archibald, contractor; b. Mt. Morris, N.Y., June 15, 1834; s. John R. and Mary MacA.; acad. edn., followed by course in civ. engring.; m. Keturah Pratt, 1856. Learned contracting business under father; with brothers, William and James, established, 1857, the firm of MacArthur Bros.; headquarters of firm moved to Chicago, 1873; became pres. MacArthur Bros. Co. upon incorporation, 1903; has executed many contracts in the U.S., involving construction of railroads, also large contracts for U.S. Govt.; chmn. of the W. & A. MacArthur Co., Ltd., of Cheboygan, Mich. (lumber business). Home: Chicago, Ill. Died 1908.

MAC ARTHUR, Arthur, lt. gen. U.S.A.; b. Springfield, Mass., June 2, 1845; s. Arthur and Aurelia (Belcher) M.; ed. pub. schs., Milwaukee, and pvt. tutors; m. Mary Pinkney Hardy, May 19, 1875. Commd. 1st lt. adj. 24th Wis. Inf., Aug. 4, 1862; maj., Jan. 25, 1864; lt. col., May 18, 1865; hon. mustered out, June 10, 1865; apptd. from Wis. 2d lt. and 1st lt. 17th U.S. Inf., Feb. 23, 1866; transferred to 26th Inf., Sept. 21, 1866; capt. 36th Inf., July 28, 1866; assigned to 13th Inf., July 5, 1870; maj. a.-a.-g., May 26, 1896; brig. gen. vols., May 27, 1898; maj. gen., Aug. 13, 1898; brig. gen. U.S.A., Jan. 2, 1900; maj. gen., Feb. 5, 1901; lt. gen., Sept. 15, 1906. Bvtd.: lt. col. vols., Mar. 13, 1865, for battles of Perryville, Ky., Stone River, Missionary Ridge and Dandridge, Tenn.; col. Mar. 13, 1865, for battle of Franklin, Tenn., and Atlanta campaign; awarded Congressional Medal of Honor, June 30, 1890, "for seizing colors of regt. at critical moment and planting them on captured works on the crest of Missionary Ridge, Nov. 25, 1863." Participated in battles of Perryville, Stone River, Dandridge, Missionary Ridge, Resaca, Adairsville, New Hope Ch., Kenesaw Mountain (wounded), Peach Tree Creek, Jonesboro, Lovejoy's Sta., Atlanta, Franklin (wounded); comd. brigade, independent div., 8th Army Corps, June 12, 1898, and 3d expdn. to Manila, June-July, 1898; comd. 1st Brigade, 1st Div., 8th Army Corps, in advance on Manila, July-Aug., and battle of Manila, Aug. 13, 1898; comd. 2d Div., 8th Army Corps, Aug. 1898-Feb. 1899, Dept. of Northern Luzon, Apr. 1, 1899-May 5, 1900, Div. of the Philippines, and mil. gov., May 5, 1900-July 4, 1901; comd. Dept. of Colo., Dec. 30, 1901-Mar. 27, 1902, Dept. of the Lakes, Mar. 29-July 19, 1902, Dept. of the East, July 21-Nov. 8, 1902, Dept. of the Lakes, Nov. 10, 1902-Mar. 23, 1903, Dept. of Calif., Apr. 1, 1903, Pacific Div., Jan. 15, 1904-Apr. 30, 1907; retired by operation of law, June 2, 1909. Address: Milwaukee, Wis. Died Sept. 5, 1912.

MAC ARTHUR, Arthur, newspaper pub.; b. Troy, N.Y., July 24, 1850; s. Charles Fafayette and Susan (Colegrove) M.; grad. Troy Acad., 1868; Rensselaer Poly. Inst., Troy, 1868-72; m. Ella Elizabeth Griffin, Jan. 9, 1877 (died 1907). Pub. Troy Northern Budget, 1875—; sole surviving partner of C. L. MacArthur & Son; dir. Union Nat. Bank. County treas. Rensselaer County, 1906-11; trustee Troy Acad., Troy Pub. Library, Y.M.C.A. Served as mem. Citizens' Corps, Troy; was mem. staff Maj. Gen. J. B. Carr, N.G.N.Y., staffs of Gov. Levi P. Morton, with rank of col. and Gov. Frank S. Black, as asst. p.-m.-gen. Republican. Presbyn. Mason (33°); Grand Comdr. of K.T., State of N.Y., 1888; Grand Master of Grand Encampment, K.T., U.S.A., 1913-16; has had many offices in the order. Home: Troy, N.Y. Died Dec. 27, 1914.

MAC ARTHUR, Arthur Frederic, engineer, contractor; b. Oramel, N.Y., Oct. 24, 1860; s. Archibald and Keturah (Patt) M.; A.B., Harvard, 1882; Bryant & Stratton Business College, Chicago, 1882; m. Mary Seymour Barnum, June 24, 1889. Began as supt. MacArthur Bros. Co., St. Paul, 1883, became general mgr., Chicago, 1892, v.p., 1903, pres. same co., New York, 1908—; pres. U.S. Equipment Co., MacArthur Bros. Co.; Ltd., MacArthur-Hanger Co., West Coast Constrn Co.; v.p. Mason-Hanger-MacArthur Bros., Inc.; chmn. bd. W. & A. MacArthur, Ltd., Construction & Engring. Finance Co. Upon entry of U.S. into the war declined a commn. in the army, and took personal charge in the field for MacArthur Bros. Co., of entire constrn. of Camp Merritt, the Port of Newark Terminals, the constrn. and operating of Woodbury Bag Loading Plant, the construction of 1,000 houses for U. S. Shipping Bd., and reconstrn. of a double track trolley line bet. Phila. and Wilmington, Del. Address: New York, N.Y. Died Dec. 1, 1926.

MAC ARTHUR, James, litterateur; b. Glasgow, Scotland, Feb. 18, 1866; ed. there; married. Came to U.S., 1888. Joint editor The Bookman (with Prof. Harry Thurston Peck), 1894-1900; also reader and gen. lit. adviser for Dodd, Mead & Co. Has been with Harper & Bros. in the same capacity, 1901—. Dramatized Ian MacLaren's Bonnie Brier Bush; also joint author, with Max Pemberton, in The Masque of the White Rose and Kronstadt; with W. F. Payson in Captain Debonnaire, and with Rex Beach, in the Spoilers. Has also dramatized Bunyan's Pilgrim's Progress. Died 1909.

MAC ARTHUR, John R., contractor, engr.; b. Mt. Morris, N.Y., July 24, 1862; s. Archibald and Keturah (Pratt) M.; A.B., Harvard, 1855; student law sch., Harvard, 1887-89; studied at École des Sciences Politiques, Sorbonne and Collège de France, Paris; m. Pauline, d. Judge William H. Arnoux, June 27, 1889. Actively identified with MacArthur Bros. Co., 1900, becoming v.p.; Construction & Engring. Finance Co., MacArthur Bros. Co., Ltd., U.S. Equipment Co., W. & A. MacArthur Co., Ltd., West Coast Constrn. Co.; treas. MacArthur-Hanger Co. In diplomatic service 4 yrs.; sec. U.S. Legation, at Madrid, Spain, 1897; apptd. spl. asst. sec. in office of Sec. of State, 1898; asst. sec. U.S. Commn. that negotiated treaty of peace with Spain, 1898, and sec. to first Philippine Commn., 1899; mem. Am. Industrial Commn. to France, Aug.-Dec. 1916. Home: 175 E. 78th St., New York, N.Y. Deceased.

MAC ARTHUR, Robert Stuart, clergyman; b. Dalesville, Que., Can., July 31, 1841; s. Archibald and Margaret (Stuart) M.; A.B., U. of Rochester, 1867; grad. Rochester Theol. Sem., 1870; D.D., Rochester, 1880, Acadia College, 1910; LL.D., Columbian U., 1896; McMaster U., 1911; m. Mary Elizabeth Fox, Aug. 4, 1870. Ordained Baptist ministry, 1870; pastor Calvary Ch., New York, May 15, 1870-Sept. 1911. For yrs. was corr. of Chicago Standard; long editorially connected with Christian Enquirer and Baptist Review; lecturer on foreign travel. Author: Old Testament difficulties; The Question of the Centuries, and Other Sermons, 1905; Quick Truths in Quaint Texts, 2d series, 1907; Advent, Christmas, Easter and Other Sermons, 1907; The Christic Reign, 1908; Royal Messages of Cheer and Comfort, 1909; The True Scala Santa, 1910; Famous Johns of Christendom, 1915; The Baptists—Their Principle, Their Progress, and Their Prospects, 1920; The Question of the Centuries—What Think Ye of Christ?, 1921; also many others before 1900. Pres. Bapt. World Alliance. Address: New York, N.Y. Died Feb. 23, 1923.

MACARTNEY, Thomas Benton, Jr., coll dean; b. New Castle, Va., Aug. 16, 1875; s. Thomas Benton and Emily Frances (Carper) M.; A.B., Milligan Coll., Tenn., 1895, A.M., 1900; M.A., Ph.D., U. of Va., 1902; LL.D., Transylvania Coll., 1922; grad. student, U. of Chicago, 1909, 23; travel and study in Rome and Greece, summer 1911; Columbia U., autumn 1925; m. Weta Smith, June 9, 1897. Instr. Latin and Greek, Milligan Coll., 1895-97; prin. New Castle Acad., 1897-98; licentiate in Latin, U. of Va., 1899-1902; head master in Latin, Rawlings Inst., Charlottesville, Va., 1901-02; asst. prof. Greek and prin. Acad., 1902-06, dean of coll. and prof. Greek, 1906-25, prof. sociology, 1925—, acting pres., 1906-08 and 1921-22, Transylvania Coll. Lecturer in State Summer Sch. of Va., 1906. Mem. Ky. Crime Commn., World Conf. on Narcotic Edn. Author: The Use of Pronouns in Oratio Obliqua, 1902. Address: Lexington, Ky. Died Sept. 11, 1929.

MACAULEY, Charles Raymond, cartoonist; b. Canton, O., Mar. 29, 1871; s. John K. and Abbie (Burry) M.; ed. pub. schs., Canton, O.; m. Clara Halter, 1893; 1 dau., Clara; m. 2d, Emma Worms, Apr. 16, 1897; m. 3d, Edythe Belmont Lott, 1914. Adopted career as cartoonist after winning $50, 1st prize, Cleveland Press, 1891; political cartoonist Cleveland World, Cleveland Plain Dealer, Cleveland Leader until 1894; removed to N.Y. City, 1894; contributed cartoons to leading met. papers and periodicals until 1899; with Philadelphia Inquirer, 1899-1901; engaged in lit. work, 1901-04; editorial cartoonist New York Morning World, 1904-14; then with Brooklyn (N.Y.) Daily Eagle; later with Daily Mirror, New York, N.Y. Awarded the Pulitzer prize for best cartoon pub. in 1929. Author: (and illustrator) Fantasmaland, 1904; The Red Tavern, 1914; Whom the Gods Would Destroy; Keeping the Faith; The Man Across the Street; The Optimistic Spectacles (photoplays). Address: New York, N.Y. Died Nov. 24, 1934.

MACBETH, George Alexander, mfr.; b. Urbana, O., Oct. 29, 1845; s. James Reed and Frances Ann (Bayard) M.; ed. common schs. of Urbana; m. Katharine Duff, 1880. Druggist, 1862-72; mfr. of glass, 1872—; pres. Macbeth-Evans Glass Co., Charleroi (Pa.) Savings and Trust Co., First Nat. Bank of Charleroi. Made first optical glass in America, 1891; awarded medals for exhbn. of glass at Centennial Expn., Phila., 1876, Paris, Expn., 1889; medal, Chicago Expn., for 1st exhbn. of optical glass made in America. Pa. del. to World's Columbian Expn. Pres. Pittsburgh Art Soc.; v.p. Pittsburgh Acad. Arts and Science; life trustee Carnegie Free Library and chairman library committee since its formation. Member of New Church (Swedenborgian). Independent in politics. Made the first lighthouse lenses made in U.S., increasing efficiency and conforming to modern sources of light. Home: Pittsburgh, Pa. Died Feb. 11, 1916.

MACBRIDE, Thomas Huston, educator; b. Rogersville, Tenn., July 31, 1848; s. Rev. James Bovard and Sarah (Huston) M.; A.B., Monmouth Coll., 1869, A.M., 1873, LL.D., 1914; U. of Bonn, 1891; Ph.D., Lenox Coll., 1895; LL.D., Coe Coll., 1915; m. Harriet Diffenderfer, Dec. 31, 1875; children—Elizabeth (dec.), Ruth (dec.), Jean Philip Douglas. Prof. mathematics and modern langs., Lenox Coll., 1870-78; asst. prof. natural sciences, 1878-84, prof. botany, 1884-1914, pres., 1914-16, pres. emeritus, 1916—, State U. of Ia. Spl. student of fungi. Mem. Am. Forestry Assn. Author: Botany (textbook), 1895, 1900; North American; Slime Moulds, 1899, 1923; On the Campus, 1916, 2d series, 1925; In Cabins and Sod-houses, 1928; many chapters in reports of the Iowa Geol. Survey, and many pub. lectures and addresses. Home: Iowa City, Ia. Died Mar. 27, 1934.

MacCALLA, Clifford Sherron, pub. utilities; b. Wallingford, Pa., Mar. 31, 1876; s. Clifford P. and Helen (Arrison) MacC.; prep. edn., Friends Central Sch., Phila.; E.E., Lehigh U., 1896; m. Anne Lanter, June 7, 1922; children—Sylvia, Willard Arrison. Inspector, Phila. Electric Co., 1896-97; successively draftsman, constrn. boss and gen. foreman, Brooklyn (N.Y.) Edison Co., 1897-1901; asst. engr. foreign dept., Gen. Electric Co., Schenectady, N.Y., 1901-03; successively asst. to gen. mgr., asst. gen. mgr., v.p. and gen. mgr., chief engr., Washington Water Power Co., Spokane, 1903-18; works mgr. Gen. Electric Co., at Rochester, N.Y., 1918-20; v.p. and gen. mgr. Virginian Power Co., Charleston, W.Va., 1920-23; pres. and gen. mgr. Pa. Power Co. and Youngstown (O.) Municipal Ry. Co., 1923—; v.p. and gen. mgr. Pa.-Ohio Power & Light Co., 1923—; pres. Ohio River Edison Co.; vice-pres. and division mgr., Ohio Edison Co. Republican. Presbyn. Home: Youngstown, O. Died Feb. 4, 1935.

MAC CAMERON, Robert, portrait painter; b. Chicago, Jan. 14, 1866; pupil of Gerôme, Beaux Arts, Paris. Represented in permanent collections of Memorial Mus., Phila., Corcoran Art Gallery, Washington, Met. Mus. Art, New York; ann. exhibitor, Paris, London, and prin. exhbns. in U.S. Hors concours Société des Artists Française (Paris). A.N.A., 1910. Home: Rochester, N.Y. Died Dec. 29, 1912.

MAC CAULEY, Clay, clergyman, publicist; b. Chambersburg, Pa., May 8, 1843; s. Isaac H. and Elizabeth (Maxwell) M.; A.B., Princeton, 1864, A.M., 1867; grad. Theol. Sem. of Northwest, Chicago, 1867; U. of Heidelberg, 1873; hon. alumnus, Keio U., Japan, 1911; D.D., Meadville Theol. Sch., 1916, Princeton, 1923; m. Annie Cleveland, d. Dr. Josiah Deane, July 25, 1867 (died 1887). Lt. Co. D, 126th Pa. Vols. and on staff Gen. S. D. Sturgis, 1862-63; prisoner of war, Libby Prison, Richmond, Va., May 1863; mem. Christian Commn. in U.S.A., 1864-65. Ordained Unitarian ministry, 1868; pastor Waltham, Mass., 1869-72, All Souls Ch., Washington, 1876-81; collaborator Bur. Am. Ethnology, 1880-81; dir. Unitarian Mission to Japan, 1890-1900 and 1909-20; pres. and prof. philosophic and historic theology, Coll. for Advanced Learning, Tokyo, Japan, 1891-99; lecturer on Japan, 1904-09. Decorated with Order of the Rising Sun, Japan, 1909; Order of the Sacred Treasure, 1918; delegate from Japan to 8th Internat. Geog. Congress, 1904, 5th Internat. Zoöl. Congress, 1906. V.p. Asiatic Soc. of Japan; pres. Am. Peace Soc. of Japan; v.p. Internat. Press Assn. of Japan; councillor American Association of Tokyo; hon. v.p. America-Japan Society, Tokyo. Author: Christianity in History, 1891 (also in Japanese); Introductory Course in Japanese, 1896, 1905; Hynakunin-Isshu (Single Songs of a Hundred Poets), metrical transls. from Japanese, 1899-1917; Japanese Literature, 1899; A Day in the Very Noble City, Manila, 1899; also several translations from Japanese—all published in Japan; Religious Problem of Japan—How Solve It?, 1894; Florida Seminoles, 1884; Present Religious Conditions of Japan, 1902; Unitarian Mission to Japan, 1909; A Daughter of the Samurai, 1910; Thought and Fact for Today (also in Japanese), 1911; The Memorial Most Worthy of Our Patriot Dead, 1911; The English Language in the New Georgean Era, 1911; Charles Dickens, an Appreciation, 1912; The Faith of the Incarnation, 1913; Memories and Memorials, 1914; The American-Japanese Problem as a Race Question, 1915; Hohenzollern Dynasty, 1916; Measure of the True American, 1916; Krause's League for Human Right and Thereby World Peace, 1917; Looking Before and After (war-time essays), 1919. Edited Japanese Unitarian Magazine "Shukyo" (religion), 1890-95; regular Japan correspondent Boston Transcript, 1890-1900, and contbr. to Japan Mail and Advertiser, Tokyo. Address: Boston, Mass. Died Nov. 15, 1925.

MAC CLINTOCK, William Darnall, univ. prof.; b. Elizaville, Ky., July 28, 1858; s. Alexander and Cornelia (Darnall) M.; A.B., Ky. Wesleyan, 1878, A.M., 1882; Johns Hopkins, 1880-82; Union Theol. Sem., 1883-85; British Mus., London, 1889, 1892, 1894; m. Lucia Porter Lander, July 7, 1886; children—Lander, Paul, Hilda (wife of Capt. J. D. Brown, U.S.A.), Elizabeth (Mrs. Walther Lieber). Prof. English, 1881-98, sec., 1888-89, Chautauqua Coll., Plainfield, N.J.; prof. English, Wells Coll., 1889-91; asst. prof. English lit., 1892, asso. prof. and dean Jr. Coll., 1892-1909, prof. English lit., 1900-25, dean Univ. Coll., 1900-05, prof. emeritus, 1925—, U. of Chicago; dean Ill. Coll., 1926-27. Address: Chicago, Ill. Died Apr. 21, 1936.

MAC COLL, James Roberton, mfr.; b. Glasgow, Scotland, Apr. 2, 1856; s. Hugh and Janet (Roberton) M.; ed. acad., high sch. and tech. coll., Glasgow; m. Agnes Bogle, Apr. 15, 1884. With Henry Fyfe & Son, Glasgow, 1871-78, partner Thomson & Mac Coll, 1878-82; agent, 1882-96, treas., 1896-1920, pres., 1920—, Lorraine Mfg. Co., cotton and worsted goods; pres. Ponemah Mills, Morris Plan Co. of R.I., Moshassuck Valley R.R. Co.; v.p. Industrial Trust Co. of Providence; executor, trustee F. A. Sayles Estate; dir. Providence Gas Co., Mfrs. Mutual Fire Ins. Co., Mathieson Alkali Works, and other corporations. Pres. N.E. Cotton Mfrs.' Assn., and Nat. Assn. Cotton Mfrs., 1905-07; pres. Internat. Conf. Cotton Growers and Mfrs., Washington, 1906, Atlanta, Ga., 1907; pres. Home Market Club, Boston, 1908-09, R.I. Anti-Tuberculosis Assn., 1907-11; dir. Chamber of Commerce of U.S.A., 1914-20. Republican. Congregationalist. Home: Providence, R.I. Died Nov. 23, 1931.

MAC COLL, William Bogle, textile mfr.; b. Pawtucket, R.I., Oct. 26, 1886; s. James Roberton and Agnes (Bogle) M.; grad. St. Paul's Sch., Concord, N.H., and New Bedford Textile School, 1905; m. Mabel Coats, Oct. 16, 1923; children—Jean, William B. With Lorraine Mfg. Co., Pawtucket, 1908-10, gen. supt., 1910-12, asst. treas., 1912-19, treas. and sec. 1919-32, pres., 1932—; treas. Lortex Co., Lorraine Mfg. Co. of N.Y.; dir. Slater Trust Co., Industrial Trust Co., Mfrs. Mutual Fire Ins. Co.; trustee Peoples Savings Bank. Commd. maj. U.S. Q.M.C., and served as asst. chief purchasing officer, Paris, World War. Pres. R.I. Boy Scouts of America, 1926-27; pres. Pawtucket and Blackstone Valley Community Chest; regional dir. Liberty Mutual Ins. Co., Mill Associates. Decorated Order of Leopold (Belgium), 1918. Republican. Episcopalian. Home: Bristol, R.I. Died Nov. 7, 1941.

MacCOLL, William Hamilton, educator; b. Hamilton, Ont., Can., Sept. 5, 1873; s. John Alexander and Mary Anne (MacColl) MacC.; brought to U.S., 1875, naturalized, 1896; A.B., Princeton, 1895; D.Sc., Washington and Jefferson, 1925; m. Anna Belle Jones, Aug. 1, 1901; children—Jean Stuart (Mrs. Arthur Horton), John Duncan (dec.), Betty Sutherland, William Alexander. Began teaching, 1895; admitted to partnership Kiskiminetas Springs School, Saltsburg, Pa., 1903, v.p., 1913, pres., 1930—. Presbyn. Home: Saltsburg, Pa. Died Dec. 26, 1937.

MAC CONNELL, Charles Jenkins, naval officer; b. Falls Twp., Bucks County, Pa., Dec. 14, 1837; s. William and Ann S. (Jenkins) M.; grad. Model Inst. and State Normal Sch., Trenton, N.J.; m. Louisa B. Small, Dec. 13, 1863. Served apprenticeship in Phila. as mech. engr. and builder; prof. drawing and civil engring., State Normal Sch., Trenton; served in Co. A, N.J.N.G. for 3 mos. at outbreak of Civil War; apptd. from N.J. by Pres. Lincoln, 3d asst. engr. U.S.N., Oct. 29, 1861; 2d asst. engr., Sept. 1863; 1st asst. engr., Oct. 1866; chief engr., Dec. 5, 1885; comdr., June 5, 1896; capt., Aug. 10, 1898; retired, Jan. 19, 1899, on account of disabilities received in line of duty; promoted to rank of rear admiral retired, June 29, 1906. Served on Miss. River on Gulf coast and on Atlantic coast during Civil War, and in principal parts of the world later; participated as fleet engr. N. Atlantic Sta., on flagship New York, in naval operations of Spanish-Am. War; received war medal for conspicuous conduct and bravery in battle; consulting engr. for various mining cos., etc. Home: Brooklyn, N.Y. Died 1909.

MAC CORD, Charles William, mech. draftsman; b. Northeast, N.Y., Mar. 18, 1836; s. Rev. William J. and Lorinda L. (Tapping) M.; A.B., Princeton, 1854, A.M., 1857; hon. Sc.D., 1881; m. Evelyn Holden, June 23, 1863. Chief draftsman for Capt. John Ericsson, 1859-68; prof. mech. drawing and designing, 1871-1906, emeritus prof., 1906, Stevens Inst. Tech. Author: Kinematics, or Mechanical Movements, 1883; Mechanical Drawing, Progressive Exercises and Practical Hints, 1888; Elements of Descriptive Geometry, 1895; Velocity Diagrams, 1901. Address: Hoboken, N.J. Died Apr. 13, 1915.

MacCORKLE, Emmett Wallace, clergyman; b. Lexington, Va., Aug. 28, 1855; s. William Henry and Virginia (Wilson) MacC.; B.Ph., Washington and Lee U., 1874, D.D., 1895; B.D., Union Theol. Sem. in Va., 1878; m. Mamie Bryant, Nov. 22, 1899; 1 son, Emmett Wallace. Ordained ministry Presbyn. Ch. in U.S., 1881; organizer and pastor Clifton Forge Ch., 1880-1903; pastor Nicholasville, Ky., 1903-11, Bethesda Ch., Rockbridge Baths, Va., from 1911 until 1928. Rep. to General Assembly Presbyn. Ch. in U.S. 5 times; to World Alliance, London, Liverpool and Cardiff, Wales; mem. World Alliance Presbyn. Chs.; chmn. Foreign Missions Com. Synod of Va., and of Presbytery of Lexington; mem. Victoria Institute of London, England. Asst. chaplain gen. U.C.V. Democrat. Mason, Odd Fellow, K.P. Wrote: The Spirit of Progress in the Westminster Symbols, 1900; The Scotch Irish of Virginia, 1905. Home: Ashland, Ky. Died Apr. 21, 1938.

MAC CORKLE, William Alexander, governor; b. Lexington, Va., May 7, 1857; s. William and Mary (Morrison) M.; B.L., Washington and Lee U., 1879, LL.D., 1907; LL.D., U. of W.Va., 1893, D.C.L., 1918; m. Isabelle Goshorn, Oct. 19, 1881; children—William Goshorn, Isabel Brooks. Admitted to bar, 1878; practiced at Charleston, W.Va., 1879—; mem. firm Chilton, MacCorkle & Chilton, 1897—. Pros. atty. Charleston, W.Va., 1880-89; gov. of W.Va., 1892-97; mem. Va. Senate, 1910-14. Democrat. In charge Liberty Loan campaigns, 1917-18. Author: Some Southern Questions, The Monroe Doctrine, The Book of the White Sulphur, The Personal Genesis of the Monroe Doctrine, Recollection of Fifty Years of West Virginia, etc. Address: Charleston, W.V. Died Sept. 24, 1930.

MacCORMACK, Daniel William, banker; b. Wick, Scotland, Apr. 9, 1880; s. John G. and Sara (McCann) MacC.; came with parents to U.S., 1889; ed. prep. depts., Boston (Mass.) Coll., Robert Gordon's Coll., Aberdeen, Scotland, and St. Laurent's Coll., ~~Montreal~~, Can.; m. Mary Hyde, d. Dr. Christopher Seymour, Dec. 23, 1920. Served with 26th Inf., U.S.A., Philippine Insurrection, 1899-1901; with Panama Canal orgn., 1905-17, staff div. meteorology and river hydraulics, later supt. mfg. plants and acting gen. mgr. commissary dept.; capt., later lt. col. Transportation Corps, U.S.A., World War, serving as asst. exec. officer Army Transport Service, Port of N.Y., exec. officer Shipping Control Com., and gen. insp. in charge reorgn. Army Transport Service in France; on mission to Russia for Peace Conf., 1919; resigned as capt. Q.M.C., regular army, 1922; mem. Am. Financial Mission to Persia, 1922-27, serving as dir. internal revenue of Persian Govt., dir. alimentation during famine period, 1925-27; mem. Russo-Persian Tariff Commn., and assigned to visit capitols of Europe to increase Persian exports; represented Persia in council and assembly of League of Nations, 1927; organized and administered receivership dept., Irving Trust Co., N.Y. City, Jan. 1929-June 1930; pres. Fiduciary Trust Co. of New York and The Fiducary Corp., June 1930-Mar. 1933; commr. gen. of immigration, Apr.-Aug. 1933; commr. of imimgration and naturalization, Dept. of Labor, Washington, 1933—. Comdr. Order of Crown of Italy; Officer Order of the Black Star (France). Mem. advisory bd. Yorkville Music Sch. Democrat. Catholic. Home: Washington, D.C. Died Jan. 1, 1937.

MAC CRACKEN, Henry Mitchell, chancellor; b. Oxford, O., Sept. 28, 1840; s. Rev. John Steele and Eliza (Hawkins-Dougherty) M.; A.B., Miami U., 1857; U.P., Theol. Sem., Xenia, O., 1860-62, Princeton Theol. Sem., 1862-63; univs. of Tübingen and Berlin, 1867-68; D.D., Wittenberg, 1878; LL.D., Miami, 1887, New York, 1910; m. Catherine Hubbard, July 2, 1872. Teacher and supt. schs. in Ohio, 1857-61; ordained to the Presbyn. ministry, 1863; pastor Westminster Ch., Columbus, 1863-67, First Ch., Toledo, 1868-81; prof. philosophy and chancellor, Western U. of Pa. (now U. of Pittsburgh), 1881-84; prof. philosophy, 1884—, vice-chancellor, 1885-91, chancellor, 1891-1910, New York U. Del. Gen. Assembly, Free Church of Scotland and of Irish Presbyterian General Assembly, 1867; committeeman for life of the Hall of Fame, organized by him, 1900. Author: Tercentenary of Presbyterianism, 1870; Leaders of the Church Universal (3 volumes), 1879; Cities and Universities, 1882; The Scotch-Irish in America, 1884; John Calvin, 1888; A Metropolitan University, 1892; Educational Progress in the United States, 1893; The Three Essentials, 1901; The Hall of Fame, 1901; Urgent Eastern Questions, 1912. Address: New York, N.Y. Died Dec. 24, 1918.

MAC DANIEL, Frank, educator; b. Frosburg, Md., Aug. 18, 1872; s. Humphrey Carroll and Mary Ann (Leech) M.; student Shepherd Coll., Shepherdstown, W.Va., 1887-90, M.E.L., 1890; A.B., Dickinson Coll., Pa., 1894, A.M., 1897, D.D., 1911; B.D., Drew Theol. Sem., 1897; post-grad. work, N.Y.U.; traveled in Europe; m. Louise Nora Hocker, Feb. 27, 1900; children—Mary Louise, Margaret B. Pastor Summerfield Ch., Newark, N.J., 1st Ch., Orange, 1st Ch., Passaic, to 1910; headmaster Pennington (N.J.) Sch. for Boys, 1910-21; elected 1915, pres. W.Va. Wesleyan Coll. (declined); endowment sec. Methodist Ch. of N.J., 1921; pres. Genesee Wesleyan Sem., Lima, N.Y., 1922—; pres. Secondary Schs. of Methodism; mem. Newark Conf. M.E. Ch., Coll. Assn. M.E. Ch. Mem. Hosp. and Homes Assn. of M.E. Church. Republican. Mason. Lecturer. Home: Lima, N.Y. Died Dec. 25, 1932.

MAC DILL, David, prof. apologetics Xenia Theol. Sem., 1885—; m. Morning Sun, O., Aug. 10, 1826; grad. Centre Coll., Danville, Ky., 1849; hon. A.M., LL.D., Centre Coll., Ky.; D.D., Monmouth Coll., Ill.; m. Miss M. E. Gordon, Sept. 21, 1853. Licensed to preach, 1852; ordained, 1853; pastor United Presbyn. Ch., Cherry Fork, O., 1853-76; prof. philosophy, Monmouth (Ill.) Coll., 1876-85. Author: The Bible a Miracle; The Mosaic Authorship of the Bible; Premillennialism Discussed. Address: Xenia, O. Died 1903.

MACDONALD, Alexander, conservation commr.; b. Nova Scotia, Can., Sept. 13, 1867; s. Alexander and Catherine (MacAulay) MacD.; came to U.S., 1879; A.B., Middlebury Coll., 1892, A.M., 1900; m. Edith O'Neil, June 15, 1900. Prin. high sch., St. Regis Falls, 1892-99; sch. commr. Franklin County, N.Y., 1900-09; mem. N.Y. Ho. of Rep., 1910-16 (com. on conservation); dep. conservation commr. of N.Y., 1916-22, became conservation commr., Feb. 15, 1922. Trustee State Coll. of Forestry. Republican. Presbyn. Home: St. Regis Falls, N.Y. Deceased.

MAC DONALD, Arthur, anthropologist; b. Caledonia, N.Y., July 4, 1856; s. Angus and Virginia (Dibble) M.; A.B., U. of Rochester, 1879, A.M., 1883; studied law, 1879; Princeton Theol. Sem., 1880; grad. Union Theol. Sem., 1883; post-grad. courses in philosophy, metaphysics, etc., Harvard, 1883-85; apptd. fellow in psychology, Johns Hopkins, but declined appmt. in order to pursue studies, 1885-89, at Berlin, Leipzig, Paris, Zürich and Vienna, in medicine (full course), psycho-physics, and spl. courses in insanity, hypnotism and criminology; m. Margaret J. Porterfield, Sept. 29, 1904. Docent (a distinct advance beyond the doctorate) in criminology, Clark U., 1889-91; with U.S. Bur. of Edn., 1892-1904, as specialist in edn. as related to the abnormal and weakling classes. U.S. del. to 3 Internat. Psychol. and Criminol. congresses; hon. pres. 3d Internat. Congress of Criminal Anthropology of Europe; studied Am. and European prisons, insane and inebriate asylums, slums, etc., for U.S. Bur. of Edn. Author: Abnormal Man, 1893; Criminology, 1894; Education and Patho-Social Studies, 1896; Le Criminel-Type, 1895; Emile Zola, 1899; Experimental Study of Children, 1899; Hearing on the Bill to Establish a Laboratory for the Study of the Criminal Pauper and Defective Classes, 1902; Plan for the Study of Man, etc., 1902; Statistics of Crime, Suicide and Insanity, 1903; Man and Abnormal Man, 1905; Juvenile Crime and Reformation, 1908; Senate Documents; Mentality of Nations and Social Pathology, 1912, and contbns. to Am. and European publications on criminology, human abnormalities, hypnotism, etc.; also articles on criminology in Ency. Americana and Nelson's Ency., and spl. articles: A Study of the United States Senate, Scientific Political Training of President Coolidge, Old Age in Man, Death in Man, Study of Man After Death, Education and Psychoanalysis, Education and Eugenics, Legislative Anthropology, etc. Home: Washington, D.C. Died Jan. 17, 1936.

MACDONALD, Carlos Frederick, psychiatrist; b. Niles, O., Aug. 29, 1845; s. John and Caroline (Barber) M.; Iron City Coll., Pittsburgh, 1865-66; M.D., Bellevue Hosp. Med. Coll. (New York U.), 1869, LL.D., 1917; hon. A.M., Union College, 1894; m. Alice M. Hardy, Mar. 24, 1874. Served in 6th Ohio Cav. during Civil War; asst. physician Kings County Hosp. and visiting physician Kings County Smallpox Hosp. and Almshouse, 1869-70; asst. physician, 1870-73, acting resident physician, 1871-83, med. supt., 1873-75, Kings County Lunatic Asylum; mgr. and cons. physician, N.Y. State Inebriate Asylum, 1877-79; med. supt. Binghamton Asylum for Insane, 1879-80, State Asylum for Insane Criminals, 1881—. Prop. Dr. MacDonald's Sanitarium for mental and nervous diseases, Central Valley, N.Y. Pres. N.Y. State Commn. in Lunacy, 1889-96; prof. mental diseases, Bellevue Hosp. Med. Coll., 1888-97, Univ. and Bellevue Hosp. Med. Coll., 1897-1906, emeritus prof., 1906. Lecturer insanity, Albany Med. Coll., 1892-94; cons. physician Manhattan State Hosp. for Insane; cons. alienist Hackensack (N.J.) City Hosp. Called to Buffalo by Erie County Bar Assn. to determine mental condition of Czolgosz, assassin of President McKinley; med. counsel to Dist. Atty. Jerome in the trial of Harry K. Thaw, 1907. Pres. Am. Psychiatric Assn., 1913-14. Home: Central Valley, N.Y. Died May 29, 1926.

MACDONALD, Charles, civil engr.; b. Gananoque, Can., Jan. 26, 1837; s. William Stone and Isabella (Hall) M.; ed. Queen's U., Kingston, Ont. (LL.D., 1894); C.E., Rensselaer Poly. Inst., Troy, N.Y., 1857; m. Sarah L. Willard, Aug. 5, 1861. Asst. engr. on constrn. Grand Trunk Ry., in Mich., and in charge of surveys and constrn. Phila. & Reading Rd., 1863-68; removed to New York, 1868, and engaged in bridge constrn.; mem. Union Bridge Co., 1884-1900; assisted in building Hawksburg Bridge (Australia), The Leavenworth (Kan.) Bridge, Poughkeepsie Bridge, Merchants' Bridge (St. Louis), etc. Trustee Rensselaer Poly. Inst., Troy, N.Y. Pres. Am. Soc. C.E., 1908-09. Home: Brooklyn, N.Y. Died 1928.

MACDONALD, George Alexander, lawyer, capitalist; b. New York, N.Y., May 11, 1869; s. Alexander Forbes and Janet (Campbell-Erskine) M.; B.S., New York U., 1891, LL.B., 1892; studied Columbia Law Sch.; Columbia Sch. Polit. Science; unmarried. Admitted to N.Y. bar, 1892, to practice in U.S. cts., 1899; formerly asso. with Charles L. Buckingham in litigation involving many important corp. interests; counsel for many large corps.; has large real estate holdings in downtown sect. of New York. Apptd. by Supreme Court of Can. to take testimony in New York. Campaign speaker for Rep. party, 1896—. Pres., dir. Mut. Warehouse Co., Hursley Real Estate Co. Presbyn. Mason; mem. Masonic Bd. Relief. Author: How Successful Lawyers Were Educated, 1896. Wrote a history of New York University. Home: Brooklyn, N.Y. Died July 5, 1936.

MACDONALD, Gordon, banker; b. Gananoque, Ont., Can., Jan. 1, 1856; s. William Stone and Isabella (Hall) M.; ed. Model Sch., Toronto, and Collegiate Inst., Kingston, Ont.; m. Emilie Iselin, May 23, 1882. Went to New York, 1871; with house of Maitland, Phelps & Co., 1872-1884; with Kessler & Co., bankers, 2 yrs.; v.p. Continental Trust Co., 1891-1901; mem. firm of Speyer & Co., bankers, 1901—; dir. Bank of Long Island, Bank of New York (N.B.A.), Frankfort-Am. Ins. Co., New York Trust Co., Rapid Transit Ferry Co., Speyer Building (pres.). Democrat. Episcopalian. Home: Morristown, N.J.; and New York, N.Y. Died 1908.

MACDONALD, James Allan, capitalist; A.B., Columbia, 1863, A.M., 1866; B.S., Yale, 1866, hon. Ph.B., 1892. Formerly partner in mining of Senator W. A. Clark, of Mont.; dir. Queen Ins. Co. of America, Commercial Trust Co. of N.J., Royal Indemnity Co. of N.Y.; mem. New York bd. of management Royal Ins. Co. of England. Home: Flushing, L.I., N.Y. Died Apr. 15, 1929.

MACDONALD, John William, surgeon; b. Antigonish, N.S., June 25, 1844; s. John and Christina M.; acad. edn. St. Francis Xavier's Coll.; M.D., U. of Edinburgh, 1871. Went to Minn., 1887; prof. surgery, 1887-98, emeritus prof., 1898, Hamline U.; surgeon St. Barnabas' Hosp., City Hosp. F.R.C.S., Edinburgh. Author: Surgical Diagnosis and Treatment, 1897. Home: Minneapolis, Minn. Died Mar. 4, 1913.

MACDONALD, Neil Carnot, educator; b. County Grey, Ont., Can., Mar. 17, 1876; s. Neil and Isabelle (MacLeod) M.; grad. State Normal Sch., Mayville, N.D., 1896; B.A., State U. of N.D., 1900, M.A., 1908; post-grad. work at Harvard, Edinburgh, U. of Chicago and Stanford; traveled and studied in Europe; Ed.D., Harvard, 1921; m. Katrine C. Belanger, June 14, 1904. Came to U.S., 1885; teacher and administrator for more than 20 yrs., including experience as city and county supt. of schs., state sch. insp. and state supt. pub. instrn. (4 terms), also instr. and lecturer in normal schs. and univs.; prof. sch. administration, Sch. of Edn., Ohio State U., 1921—. Past pres. State Bd. of Edn. (N.D.), Nat. Assn. State Sch. Inspectors, State Edn. Assn. Presbyn. Mason. Address: Columbus, O. Died Sept. 8, 1923.

MAC DONALD, William, author, journalist; b. Providence, R.I., July 31, 1863; s. Rev. William and Frances (Jordan) M.; A.B., Harvard, 1892; hon. Ph.D., Union, 1895; LL.D., U. of N.B., 1900; m. Harriet B. Haskell, Nov. 24, 1887; 1 son, John Haskell. Prof. history and economics, Worcester Poly. Inst., 1892-93; prof. history and polit. science, Bowdoin, 1893-1901; prof. history, Brown U., 1901-17; lecturer on govt., U. of Calif., 1917-18; lecturer Am. history, Yale, 1924-26. Spl. foreign corr. in Europe and asso. editor, The Nation, 1918-20, acting lit. editor, 1929, editorial writer, 1930-31; same for The Freeman (New York), 1923-24, Commercial and Financial Chronicle (New York), 1924—. Chmn. Pub. Archives Commn. of Am. Hist. Assn., 1900-02. Editor: Select Documents Illustrative of the History of the U.S., 1898; Select Charters and Other Documents Illustrative of American History, 1899; Johnston's High School History of the United States, 1901; Select Statutes and Other Documents Illustrative of the History of the United States, 1903; Burke on Conciliation, 1904; Documentary Source Book of American History, 1908, 3d edit., 1926; Parkman's Oregon Trail, 1911. Author: History and Government of Maine, 1902; Jacksonian Democracy, 1905; Larger History of the United States (with T. W. Higginson), 1905; From Jefferson to Lincoln, 1913; A New Constitution for a New America, 1921; Reconstruction in France, 1922; Three Centuries of American Democracy, 1923; The Intellectual Worker and His Work, 1923; The Menace of Recovery, 1934. Contbr. to Ency. Brit., Nelson's Cyclo., Cyclo. of Am. History and Govt., Dictionary of Am. Biography, Ency. of the Social Sciences, etc. Wrote Essay on Henry Adams in American Writers on American Literature, 1931. Home: New York, N.Y. Died Dec. 15, 1938.

MACDONALD, William H., opera singer, mgr.; b. Steubenville, O.; early developed musical talent; studied with leading masters in England, Germany and Italy; début in latter country in "Il Trovatore"; continued in Italian opera until he became a mem. of Emma Abbott Co.; joined Boston Ideals, 1880; with Tom Karl and H. C. Barnabee organized, 1887, the Bostonians. Died 1906.

MACDONALD, Willis Goss, surgeon; b. Cobleskill, N.Y., Apr. 11, 1863; s. Sylvester M.; grad. Cobleskill Free Acad., 1878, and N.Y. State Normal Sch.; student Cornell; M.D., Albany Med. Coll., 1887; U. of Berlin, 1889-90; unmarried. Resident surgeon, 1887, surgeon, 1891, Albany Hosp.; lecturer on surgery, 1892, adj. prof. surgery, 1895, Albany Med. Coll.; surgeon Albany Hosp., 1896; prof. abdominal surgery and gynecology, Albany Med. Coll., 1900. Maj. and surgeon U.S. Vols., 1898, and in charge of surgical div. of depot hosp. at Ft. McPherson, Ga., during Spanish-Am. War; mem. N.Y. State Tuberculosis Commn., 1900—; pres. bd. trustees N.Y. State Hosp. for Treatment of Incipient Pulmonary Tuberculosis. Republican. Mem. Pan-Am. Med. Congress, 10th, 11th, 12th Internat. Med. Congresses. Home: Albany, N.Y. Died 1910.

MACDONALL, Angus (Peter), painter, illustrator; b. St. Louis, Apr. 7, 1876; s. John A. and Virginia C. (Van Steenkist) M.; ed. Christian Bros. Coll., St. Louis Sch. of Fine Arts; m. Catherine Agnes Walsh, Oct. 24, 1900; children—Lucille Blair, Patricia Claire, Frances Helen, Donald Angus. Worked in architects' offices, St. Louis, and with various engraving cos. to 1900; illustrator and cartoonist for Life, Scribner's American, Red Cross Mag., Ladies' Home Journal, Harper's, etc., also illustrator of books and lecturer on art. Catholic. Home: Westport, Conn. Died Dec. 19, 1927.

MAC DOUGALL, Clinton Dugald, soldier; b. Glasgow, Scotland, June 14, 1839; s. Dugald and Margaret (MacKendrick) M.; grad. Jordan Acad., 1853; m. Eva Sabine, Jan. 23, 1867 (died 1875); m. 2d, Marianna Cook, Nov. 28, 1878. Capt. 75th N.Y. Inf., Sept. 16, 1861; lt. col. 111th N.Y. Inf., Aug. 20, 1862; col., Jan. 3, 1863; bvtd. brig. gen. vols., Feb. 25, 1865, "for gallant and meritorious services"; hon. mustered out, June 4, 1865; comd. brigade and div. Army of Potomac; comd. 1st Div., 2d Army Corps, at Grand Review, Washington, May 1865. Postmaster Auburn, N.Y., 1869-73; mem. 43d and 44th Congresses (1873-77); U.S. marshal, Northern Dist., New York, 1877-85; offered, 1878, by President Hayes, choice of consul general positions at London or Paris—declined both; presdl. elector, 1888; declined treasurership of U.S. and positions of commr. internal revenue and commr. of patents in 1876; U.S. marshal, Northern Dist. of N.Y., 1901-11; retired. Republican. Address: Auburn, N.Y. Died May 25, 1914.

MAC DOUGALL, Robert, coll. prof.; b. Dewittville, Que., Can., June 12, 1866; s. William and Christina (MacPherson) M.; B.A., McGill U., Montreal, 1890; A.M., Harvard, 1893, Ph.D., 1895; U. of Berlin, 1895-96, The Sorbonne, Paris, 1896; m. Carita Atwill Chapman, June 23, 1898; children—Marjorie (dec.), Robert Gordon, Constance. Home missions, Presbyn. Ch. of Can., 1890; field staff, Canadian Geol. Survey, 1891-92; instr. philosophy, 1896-97, asso. prof. pedagogy, 1897-98, Western Reserve U., Cleveland; instr. philosophy and asst. dir. psychol. lab., Harvard, 1898-1901; became prof. psychology, 1901, New York U., now retired. Ednl. dir. Belvoir, Camp Humphreys, Va., 1918, Camp Holabird, Md., 1918-19; rep. Civil Service Commn., Camp Holabird, 1919. Author of General Problems of Psychology. Home: Montclair, N.J. Died Oct. 31, 1939.

MACDOWELL, Edward Alexander, composer and pianist; b. New York, Dec. 18, 1861; s. Thomas F. and Frances M. M.; studied in Paris, 1876-79, and at Frankfort-on-Main, 1879-81. Became first piano teacher at Darmstadt Conservatory, 1881; resided in Wiesbaden, 1884-88; in Boston, 1888-96; in New York, 1896— (hon. Mus. Doc., Princeton, 1896, and U. of Pa., 1902). Prof. music, Columbia, 1896-1904; dir. Mendelssohn Glee Club of New York, 1896-98; pres. Am. Soc. of Musicians and Composers, 1897-98; v.p. Inst. Arts and Letters, 1904-05; mem. Acad. in Rome. Orchestral works have been given in all important cities of America and Europe. Composer: 2 orchestral suites, 2 piano concertos, 4 symphonic poems for orchestra, 4 piano sonatas, 12 virtuoso studies, 6 idyls after Goethe, 6 poems after Heine, over 50 songs, Sea Pieces, Woodland Sketches, New England Idyls, Fireside Tales, etc. Address: Peterboro, N.H. Died 1908.

MACDUFFIE, John, school prin.; b. Cambridge, Mass., May 16, 1861; s. John and Hannah Elizabeth (Givens) M.; A.B., cum laude, Harvard, 1884; post-grad. Harvard, Columbia; Ph.D., Lombard U., 1895; m. Abby, d. Rev. James Challis Parsons, Aug. 10, 1886. Prin. Kingston (Mass.) High Sch., 1886; asso. prin. Prospect Hill Sch., Greenfield, Mass., 1887; founder, 1890, prin. MacDuffie Sch. for Girls, 1890-1937. Address: Springfield, Mass. Died Sept. 21, 1941.

MACE, Frances Laughton, author; b. (Laughton) Orono, Me., Jan. 15, 1836; grad. Bangor, Me., High School, 1852; m. Benjamin H. Mace, 1855. Wrote the hymn, "Only Waiting," 1854. Removed to Calif., 1885. Became paralyzed, 1891. Author: Poems, Legends, Lyrics and Sonnets; Under Pine and Palm. Address: Los Gatos, Calif. Died 1899.

MACE, William Harrison, univ. prof.; b. nr. Lexington, Ind., Nov. 27, 1852; s. Ira and Nancy (Johnson) M.; grad. State Normal Sch., Terre Haute, Ind., 1876; B.L., M.L., U. of Mich., 1883; A.M., Indiana Univ., 1889; grad. student Cornell, 1890-91; Ph.D., U. of Jena, 1897; LL.D., Syracuse U., 1916; m. Ida Dodson, Sept. 10, 1878; 1 dau., Mrs. Deirdré Gowing. Prin. ward sch., Logansport, Ind., 1876-77; supt. pub. schs., Winamac, Ind., 1877-79; McGregor, Ia., 1883-85; prof. history, DePauw U. Normal Sch., 1885-90; William Griffin prof. history and polit. science, Syracuse U., 1891-1916. Univ. extension lecturer on Am. history to regents of U. State of N.Y., 1892—, to Am. Soc., 1899, Cambridge, Eng., Summer Sch., 1893, summer, U. of N.C., 1898, summer, S. Knoxville, Tenn., 1903-04. Author: A Working Manual of American History, 1895; Method in History, 1897; A School History of the United States, 1904; Stories of Heroism, 1907; Old Europe and Young America (with Dr. E. P. Tanner), 1919; American History for Schools (with Dr. George Petrie), 1919; History of the United States (with Prof. Frank S. Bogardus), 1921; Am. Hist. for High Schs., 1925; Lincoln, the Man of the People, and Washington, a Virginia Cavalier, in Little Lives of Great Men; Lincoln and Douglas (brochure), 1933. Home: Syracuse, N.Y. Died Aug. 10, 1938.

MacFADYEN, Alexander, pianist, composer; b. Milwaukee, Wis., July 12, 1879; s. Archibald and Jennie Louise (Carter) MacF.; ed. pub. schs. and under pvt. tutors; studied music under Julius Klauser and Wm. Borchert, Milwaukee, and Rudolph Ganz, Arthur Friedheim, Felix Borowski, Herman Devries and Dr. Louis Falk, Chicago; Mus.B., Chicago Musical Coll., 1905; winner Marshall Field diamond medal for post-grad. work; Mus.D., Chicago Conservatory of Music, 1932; unmarried. Début at Auditorium, Chicago, as piano soloist, 1905; was soloist with orchestra conducted by Hans von Schiller and toured with Leonora Jackson Concert Co.; appeared as soloist with Chicago Symphony Orchestra under Frederick Stock, and has toured as soloist widely in U.S.; served as mem. faculty Internat. Conservatory (New York) and Chicago Conservatory; teacher of piano, Wis. Coll. of Music, 1922-29; pres. Badger Music Pub. Co. Republican. Presbyterian. Composer of more than 100 songs, piano pieces, etc.; best known songs, Inter. Nos, Love Is the Wind, Spring Singing, Cradle Song and Day Break. Sonata, composed by him, performed by Josef Hofmann, in his All-American program, in Carnegie Hall, N.Y. City. Home: Milwaukee, Wis. Died June 6, 1936.

MacFARLAND, Finlay Leroy, businessman; b. Richmond, Mo., Sept. 16, 1862; s. Oscar Alexander and Kathryne Margaret (Hubbell) MacF.; ed. pub. schs.; m. Ellen Phillips, June 11, 1913; children—John Wellington (dec.), Janet (dec.). In retail mercantile business, Longmont, Colo., 1878-84; wholesale produce, Denver, 1884-93; coffee grower in Mexico, 1893-1903; engaged in asphalt street paving, Denver, 1903-12; founder, 1906, and pres. MacFarland Auto Co. until 1925 (retired); pres. The MacFarland Co., investments; dir. U.S. Nat. Bank. Pres. Denver Water Bd., 1918-23; pres. Colo. State Chamber of Commerce, 1929-30; a founder of Denver's Mountain Parks; dir. Denver Chamber Commerce (pres.); head of local sale of Liberty Bonds, World War. Mem. Colo. Scientific and Hist. Soc. Mason, Elk. Chmn. Local Board, NRA, Denver Dist. Home: Denver, Colo. Died June 16, 1937.

MACFARLAND, Henry Brown Floyd; b. Phila., Pa., Feb. 11, 1861; s. Joseph and Isabelle (Floyd) M.; grad. Rittenhouse Acad., Washington, 1876; read law and attended lectures Law School, Columbian (now George Washington) U.; m. Mary Lyon Douglass, Oct. 1888. Pres. bd. commrs. of D.C., 1900-10; mem. law firm Kenyon & Macfarland, Washington, Jan. 1910—. Chmn. Citizens' Com., Nat. Capital Centennial, 1900; delivered Centennial address, White House, Dec. 12, 1900, D.C. day, Buffalo Expn., Sept. 3, 1901, St. Louis Expn., Oct. 19, 1904, Jamestown Expn., June 11, 1907. Republican. Pres. Internat. Conv. Y.M.C.A., 1904. Mem. of Internat. Y.M.C.A.; chmn. Red Cross War Fund for D.C., 1917-18; mem. com. on labor Council Nat. Defense, 1917-19; mem. Near East Relief, Nat. Council Boy Scouts, Gen. Bd. Edn. Presbyn. Ch.; pres. Nat. Parks Assn., 1919. Home: Washington, D.C. Died Oct. 14, 1921.

MACFARLANE, Peter Clark, author; b. St. Clair County, Mo., Mar. 8, 1871; s. James Clark and Mary Elizabeth (Sperry) M.; Fla. Agrl. Coll., Lake City, 1885-87; Berkeley Bible Sem., 1902-05, diploma, 1905; m. Emma D. Garfield, Mar. 8, 1891 (died 1908); m. 2d, Florence E. Judson, Oct. 24, 1909. With gen. frt. dept., A.,T.&S.F., R.R., Los Angeles, 1892-1900; actor in various stock cos. on Pacific Coast, 1900-01; pastor 1st Ch. (Disciples of Christ), Alameda, Calif., 1902-08; gen. sec. Men's Brotherhood of Disciples of Christ, Kansas City, Mo., 1909-11, traveling 50,000 miles a yr.; lit. work and lecturing, 1911—. Went to Europe for Saturday Evening Post, Apr. 1918, 3 months at Queenstown, Ireland, with trips to sea upon American destroyers; with U.S.A. in France, Aug.-Nov. 1918, and went into Germany with 2d Div. Author: The Quest of the Yellow Pearl, 1908; The Centurions' Story, 1910; Those Who Have Come Back, 1914; Held to Answer, 1916; The Crack in the Bell, 1918; Exploits of Bilge and Ma, 1919; Man's Country, 1923; Tongues of Flame, 1924. Lectured on "Us Americans" for Chautauquas, 1921-22, and on "Stories I Couldn't Print," in Lyceum Courses, 1922-23. Home: Pine Dunes, Pacific Grove, P.O., Calif. Died June 9, 1924.

MACFEELY, Robert, brig. gen. U.S.A., retired, July 8, 1890; b. July 8, 1828; grad. West Point, 1850; served as inf. lt. against hostile Indians in Oregon; staff capt., May 11, 1861; commissary for State of Ind., then of the Army of Ohio, and later of Army of Tennessee; maj., Feb. 9, 1863; received two brevets in May 1865 for faithful service; advanced after war to chief commissary of subsistence, with rank of brig. gen. Died 1901.

MAC GAHAN, Barbara, journalist; maiden name Elagine, of family of landed proprs., govt. of Tula, Russia; m. J. A. MacGahan, Am. war corr. (died 1878). Russian corr. New York Herald, 1876-80; New York Times, 1883; resident corr. Sidney (Australia) Herald at St. Petersburg, 1878-80. Sent as spl. corr. to U.S. by political daily, Golos (St. Petersburg), to describe presidential campaign of 1880; Am. resident corr. of Russkya Viedomosti, Moscow, 1883-89; Novosti, St. Petersburg, 1883-93; Moskovskya Viedomosti, 1899—; corr. New York Sunday Sun, 1895; contributor to Am. Press Assn. Contributor of Russian letters to syndicate, 1894, including New York Times, Brooklyn Eagle, Pittsburgh Dispatch, Knickerbocker Press, etc. Hon. mem. Slavonic Benevolent Soc. (political), St. Petersburg, 1880; mem. Mutual Aid Soc. of Russian Authors, St. Petersburg, 1898. Contbr. to Russian mags. on political and economic subjects. Translated stories of Bret Harte, Mark Twain and Edgar A. Poe into Russian for Novoye-Vremia, St. Petersburg; wrote fiction in Viestnik Europy under nom de plume, Vlad Kashirin. Author: Xenia Repnina (novel in English), 1889. Address: New York, N.Y. Died 1904.

MAC GILLIVRAY, Alexander Dyer, entomologist; b. Inverness, O., July 15, 1868; s. John Henry and Elizabeth (Adams) M.; Ph.B., Cornell, 1900, Ph.D., 1904; m. Fanny M. Edwards, Sept. 17, 1891. Asst., 1890-1900, instr. entomology, 1900-06, asst. prof. entomology and invertebrate zoölogy, 1906-11, Cornell; asst. prof. systematic entomology, 1911-13, asso. prof., 1913-17, prof. 1917—, U. of Ill. Specialist Me. Agrl. Expt. Sta., summer, 1913. Fellow Entomol. Soc. America (2d v.p. 1911, sec.-treas. 1911-16). Wrote: The Coccidæ. Address: Urbana, Ill. Died Mar. 24, 1924.

MAC GILVARY, Paton, engineer; b. Berkeley, Calif., June 28, 1896; s. Prof. Evander Bradley and Elizabeth Allen (Paton) M.; B.S. in E.E., U. of Wis., 1916; unmarried. Chief engr. and supt. gas. works, Waukesha (Wis.) Gas & Electric Co., 1916; power specialist, Milwaukee Electric Ry. and Light Co., 1917; pres. and gen. mgr., Curtiss Airplane Co. of New England, 1919—; dir. Curtiss Northwest Airplane Co. Joined Air Service, U.S. Army, May 1917; went abroad, July 1917, training in Italy; successively chief pilot, adjutant and comdg. officer, Camp Ovest, Foggia; engr. attached to representative in Italy of Joint Army and Navy Aircraft Bd.; on Italian Front, June 1918 till close of war, as adj. of Combat Div.; hon. discharged, Dec. 30, 1918. Decorated by King of Italy with Croce di Guerre; awarded Bronzino and two citations while at the front. Republican. Home: Boston, Mass. Died May 10, 1921.

MAC GINNISS, John, copper miner, banker; b. Homer, Ia., Oct. 10, 1867; s. John and Mary B. M.; ed. at Chicago; m. Eloise Sylvester, Feb. 26, 1908. Engaged in mining and smelting, 1890—; owner of large copper and coal properties in Mont., Mexico, and British Columbia; pres. Interstate Utilities Co., Spokane, Wash., Mo. Oxide & Chem. Co., Joplin, Mo.; pres. Gibraltar Gold Mines Co., Beatty, Nevada, MacGinnis Realty Co., Butte, Mont. Dir. Trans-Pacific Latin-America Assn., Los Angeles. Defeated for U.S. Senate by 2 votes, 1901; mem. Dem. Nat. Com. Died May 28, 1936.

MAC GOWAN, Granville, surgeon; b. Davenport, Ia., Apr. 12, 1857; s. Davis Garrett and Ellen von der Weyden (Nugent) M.; Millersville (Pa.) State Normal Sch.; M.D., U. of Pa., 1879; post-grad. univs. of Berlin, Paris, Vienna, 1880-84; m. Lillie May Briggs, June 16, 1890; children—Hilliard Vincent, Mary Eleanor. Practiced, New York, 1884, 85; moved to Los Angeles, 1886; specialist in diseases of skin and genital and urinary organs, 1892-1900, genito-urinary surgery, 1900—; prof. genito-urinary surgery, U. of Calif. and U. of Southern Calif. Organizer of Los Angeles Health Dept., serving as health commr. 4 yrs., and as mem. Bd. of Health, 4 yrs. Mem. Am. Urol. Assn. (pres. 1912-13). Home: Los Angeles, Calif. Died Jan. 31, 1935.

MAC GOWAN, John Encil, journalist; b. in Mahoning County, O., Sept. 30, 1831; s. Samuel MacG.; ed. pub. schs., Mahoning County, O., and Mt. Union and Hiram colls.; m. Maria Malvina Johnson, 1854 (died 1896). Entered U.S.A., 1861, as pvt. and was mustered out as col. 1st U.S. arty. vols. at Chattanooga, March 31, 1866. Read law and practiced in Ohio and Ind. before war, and in Tenn. after war; then engaged in newspaper work. Address: Chattanooga, Tenn. Died 1903.

MAC GRATH, Harold, author; b. Syracuse, N.Y., Sept. 4, 1871; s. Thomas H. and Lillian Jane M.; ed. in Syracuse; m. Alma Kenyon 1905. Engaged in journalism, 1890—. Author: Arms and the Woman, 1899; The Puppet Crown, 1901; The Grey Cloak, 1903; The Man on the Box, 1904; The Princess Elopes, 1905; Enchantment, 1905; Hearts and Masks, 1905; Half a Rogue, 1906; The Watteau Shepherdess (operetta), 1906; The Best Man, 1907; The Enchanted Hat, 1908; The Lure of the Mask, 1908; The Goose Girl, 1909; A Splendid Hazard, 1910; The Carpet from Bagdad, 1911; Place of Honeymoons, 1912; Parrot & Co., 1912; Deuces Wild, 1913; Pidgin Island, 1914; Voice in the Fog, 1915; The Luck of the Irish, 1917; Girl in His House, 1918; Private Wire to Washington, 1919; Yellow Typhoon, 1919; Man with Three Names, 1920; The Drums of Jeopardy, 1920; The Pagan Madonna, 1921; The Ragged Edge, 1922; The World Outside, 1923; The Green Stone, 1924; The Cellini Plaque, 1925; The Sporting Spinster; We All Live Tro' It; The Changing Road; The Wolves of Chaos; Impromptu; The Green Complex; The Dance of Dead Leaves; The Other Passport. Home: Syracuse, N.Y. Died Oct. 29, 1932.

MAC GREGOR, Henry Frederick; b. Londonderry, N.H., Apr. 25, 1855; s. Lewis Aiken and Augusta Watts (Blodgett) M.; Pinkerton Acad., Derry, N.H.; grad. Bryant and Stratton Commercial Coll., Manchester, N.H., 1871; m. Elizabeth Stevens, Dec. 10, 1885. Removed to Tex., 1873; in various positions until 1879; sec. Galveston City R.R. Co., 1879-83; v.p. and gen. mgr. Houston Ry. System, 1883-1903; real estate and other investments, 1903—; v.p., dir. State Land Oil Co., Bay & Bayou Co.; dir. South Tex. Commercial Nat. Bank, Houston Printing Co.; treas., dir. Glen Park Co. Chmn. Rep. State Exec. Com., 1894-96; Rep. nominee for Congress, 1904; Tex. mem. Rep. Nat. Com., 1912—. Presbyn. Pres. trustees Hermann Hosp. Estate; v.p. Home Market Club. Home: Houston, Tex. Died Sept. 3, 1923.

MACHEN, J(ohn) Gresham, theologian; b. Baltimore, Md., July 28, 1881; s. Arthur Webster and Minnie (Gresham) M.; A.B., Johns Hopkins, 1901; grad. student same, 1901-02; M.A., Princeton, 1904; B.D., Princeton Theol. Sem., 1905; studied univs. of Marburg and Göttingen, 1905-06; D.D., Hampden-Sydney Coll., 1921; Litt.D., Wheaton (Ill.) College, 1928; unmarried. Instr. in N.T. Princeton Theol. Sem., 1906-14, asst. prof. N.T. lit. and exegesis, 1914-29; prof. New Testament, Westminster Theol. Sem., 1929—; ordained Presbyn. ministry, 1914. Sprunt lecturer Union Theol. Sem. in Va., 1921; Smyth lecturer Columbia Theol. Seminary, 1927. Y.M.C.A. work with French Army and A.E.F., in France and Belgium, Jan. 1918-Mar. 1919. Independent Democrat. Author: The Origin of Paul's Religion, 1921; Christianity and Liberalism, 1923; New Testament Greek for Beginners, 1923; What Is Faith?, 1925; The Virgin Birth of Christ, 1930. Home: Philadelphia, Pa. Died Jan. 1, 1937.

MAC INNIS, John Murdoch, clergyman; b. P.E.I., Can., Aug. 6, 1871; s. Angus and Mary (Mac Pherson) M.; ed. high sch.; Moody Bible Inst., Chicago; B.A., Ia. Christian Coll., 1913, M.Litt., 1904, Ph.D., 1914; B.D., Temple U., 1911; D.Litt., Syracuse U., 1920; m. Ida E. Coffin, Oct. 20, 1897; children—David Sutherland, Florence Stearns, Mary Ruth, William Montague, Gordon Alexander, John Morgan. Ordained Presbyn. ministry, 1898; pastor Hallock, Minn., 1898-1900, Macalister Coll. Chapel, St. Paul, 1900-01, Santa Clara, Calif., 1901-03, Montrose, Pa., 1903-08, Gaston Ch., Phila., 1908-10, Park St. Ch., Halifax, N.S., 1910-13, South Ch., Syracuse, N.Y., 1913-22; dean Bible Inst., Los Angeles, Calif., 1925-28; representative of Los Angeles Presbytery in Christian edn. work. Dir. and sec. Montrose Bible Conf., 1914-23; mem. bd. trustees and com. on edn. of Religious Conf. at U. of Calif. in Los Angeles. Made tour of China, speaking before schs., colleges, and at student and missionary confs. Republican. Wrote: Peter the Fisherman Philosopher; The Church as Teacher; Historical Outline of The Old Testament; The Deacon and the Church Today; The Trustee and the Church Today. Home: Pasadena, Calif. Died May 6, 1940.

MAC INTOSH, John Alexander, clergyman, educator; b. Halifax, N.S., Apr. 11, 1868; s. James Campbell and Rebecca (Davies) M.; B.A., Dalhousie U., Halifax, N.S., 1892; studied Columbia, 1893-94; grad. Union Theol. Sem., 1895; D.D., Dubuque (Ia.) Coll. and Sem., 1914; LL.D., Lake Forest U., 1925; m. Sara Elizabeth Archibald, June 29, 1897; children—Archibald, Mildred, Marion, Ruth. Ordained Presbyn. ministry, 1895; pastor John Knox Ch., Jersey City, N.J., 1895-97, 1st Ch., Malone, N.Y., 1897-1912, 1st Ch., Ithaca, 1912-19; prof. philosophy of religion and ethics, McCormick Theol. Sem., 1919—. Lecturer in philosophy and ethics, Columbia, summer 1921. Pres. Union Sem. Alumni Assn., 1920-21; mem. Presbyn. Bd. of Christian Edn., 1922—. Mason. Home: Chicago, Ill. Died Jan. 22, 1927.

MacISAAC, Fred(erick), novelist; b. Cambridge, Mass., Mar. 22, 1886; s. John and Katherine (Skerry) M.; student Harvard, 1904-06; m. Ethel Brown Marshall, Dec. 2, 1916 (divorced, 1926); 1 son, Frederick Marshall; m. 2d, Violet Palmer, concert pianist, 1929. Author: Tony Sarg Marionette Book, 1921; Tin Hats, 1926; Hole in the Wall, 1927; Vanishing Professor, 1927; Mental Marvel, 1931; The Yellow Shop, 1936; also Nothing But Money (comedy), produced 1937; novels, Hot Gold, Dead Men Do Tell Tales, Murder C.O.D., published by Methuen's, London, 1938, Murder Special, 1939; novels, Devil Was Kind, The Alligator Ring. Home: Hollywood, Calif. Died May 5, 1940.

MACK, Andrew, actor; b. Boston, Mass., July 25, 1863; ed. pub. schs. Began on variety stage; subsequently with Peter Dailey in "A Country Sport" and played Sir Lucius O'Trigger in the all-star burlesque of "The Rivals"; starred 4 seasons in legitimate Irish comedy, presenting "Myles Aroon," "An Irish Gentleman," and "The Ragged Earl"; visited Australia, 1905 and 1907; played Nanki-Poo in revival of "The Mikado," 1910; etc. Address: New York, N.Y. Died May 21, 1931.

MACK, Isaac Foster, editor; b. Monroe County, N.Y., Aug. 1, 1837; s. Isaac Foster M.; A.B., Oberlin, 1862, A.M., 1871; served in 7th Ohio Vols. in Civil War; m. Mary L. Foote, Oct. 12, 1864. Admitted to bar, 1864; editor Sandusky Register, 1869-1909; retired. Prominent in founding State Soldiers' and Sailors' Home, Sandusky, and Soldiers' Orphans' Home of Ohio. Comdr. Dept. of Ohio G.A.R., 1892-93; pres. Ohio Soc. S.A.R., 1904-06. Address: Sandusky, O. Died Apr. 18, 1912.

MACK, John Givan Davis, mech. engr.; b. Terre Haute, Ind., Sept. 5, 1867; s. William and Amanda Jane (Davis) M.; B.S., Rose Poly. Inst., Terre Haute, 1887; M.E., Cornell U., 1888; m. Laura Abby Davis, Nov. 24, 1903. In gen. engring. practice, 1888-93; instr. engring., 1893-95; asst. prof. machine design, 1895-1903, prof., 1903-15, Coll. of Engring., U. of Wis.; state chief engineer of Wis., 1915—. Chief mech. dept. R.R. Commn. of Wis., 1905-12 (except 1 yr.); made first valuations of rolling stock and other equipment of all railroads in state of Wis. Mem. Engring. Soc. of Wis. (pres. 1913-14). Vice-chmn. and engring. rep. Wis. State Council Defense, 1917-19; mem. and sec. Wis. Deep Waterways Commn.; dir. Nat. Rivers and Harbors Congress. Mem. Minn.-Wis. Boundary Commn. Mason. Home: Madison, Wis. Died Feb. 24, 1924.

MACK, John M., contractor; b. Phila., Aug. 15, 1852; s. John and Mary M.; ed. pub. schs. Began business as contractor, 1876, founded and managed Mack Paving Co., Pa. Asphalt Co., and Southern Elec. Light & Power Co., and Mack Mfg. Co., of Pittsburgh; reorganized the various asphalt cos. into Asphalt Co. of America; arranged the merging of the entire street ry. system of Phila. into one co.; was pres. and dir. Barber Asphalt Paving Co., Gen. Asphalt Co., Uintah R.R. Co., and dir. in various other cos.; retired. Home: Torresdale, Pa. Died Jan. 26, 1915.

MACK, John Sephus, pres. G. C. Murphy Co.; b. Indiana County, Pa., Mar. 9, 1880; s. John McCrory and Sarah Ellen (Murphy) M.; ed. pub. schs., Indiana County, Pa., and business coll., Johnstown, Pa.; hon. L.H.D., Westminster College, 1939; m. Margaret L. Gordon, Jan. 31, 1907; children—John Gordon, James S. Began as stockroom clk. McCrory Stores Corp., Johnstown, Pa., 1899, advancing to gen. mgr., 1908; with G. C. Murphy Co., McKeesport, Pa., 1911—, pres. and chmn. bd., 1912—; v.p. and dir. Mack Realty Co. Trustee Indiana (Pa.) Hosp. Republican. Presbyterian. Elk. Home: McKeesport, Pa. Died Sept. 27, 1940.

MACK, Norman Edward, newspaperman; b. July 24, 1858; pub. sch. edn.; m. Harriet B. Taggart, Dec. 22, 1891; children—Mrs. Norma Metz, Mrs. Harriet Welch. Engaged in business pursuits; established Sunday Times in Buffalo, 1879, and the Daily Times, 1883, of which was editor and publisher until May 1929 (retired). Del. Dem. Nat. Conv. 6 times between 1892 and 1912. N.Y. mem. Dem. Nat. Com., 1900—, chmn., 1908. Home: Buffalo, N.Y. Died Dec. 26, 1932.

MACKALL, Leonard Leopold, bibliographer; b. Baltimore, Md., Jan. 29, 1879; s. Leonard Covington and Louisa Frederika (Lawton) M.; grad. Lawrenceville (N.J.) Sch., 1896; A.B., Johns Hopkins, 1900; student Harvard Law Sch., 1900-02, U. of Berlin, 1902-04; Johns Hopkins fellow, 1906; U. of Jena; unmarried. First and only librarian De Renne Georgia Library, Savannah, Ga., 1916-18; editor Notes for Bibliophiles, in "Books" (lit. supplement New York Herald-Tribune) since its first number, Sept. 21, 1924. First v.p. Bibliog. Soc. of America, 1935—. Editor: Goethe's Correspondence with Americans (for the Goethe-Schiller Archiv., at Weimar, Germany), 1904. Co-editor: Goethe's Collected Conversations (Leipzig), 5 vols., 1909-11; Osler's Yale Lectures on Evolution of Modern Medicine, 1921; Osler Library

Catalogue, 1929; Catalogue of the W. J. DeRenne Georgia Library (3 vols.), 1931. Consultant in bibliography to N.Y. Acad. of Medicine, 1930—. Home: Savannah, Ga. Died May 19, 1937.

MACKALL, Louis, physician; b. Washington, D.C., Nov. 25, 1867; s. Louis and Margaret Whann (McVean) M.; student U. of Va., 1885-87; M.D., Columbian (now George Washington) U. Dept. of Medicine, 1890; post-grad. work in Europe; m. Lucy Haw Matthews, Nov. 15, 1899. Practiced in Washington, 1890—; clin. prof., George Washington U., 1913—. Dir. Federal Nat. Bank, Oak Hill Cemetery; trustee Peabody Library Inst. Episcopalian. Address: Washington, D.C. Died July 27, 1930.

MACKAY, Clarence Hungerford, capitalist; b. San Francisco, Apr. 17, 1874; s. John W. and Marie Louise (Hungerford-Bryant) M.; m. Katherine Alexander Duer, May 17, 1898 (divorced); children—Katherine (Mrs. Kenneth O'Brien), Ellin (Mrs. Irving Berlin), John William; m. 2d, Anna Case, concert soprano, July 18, 1931. Chmn. bd. Postal Telegraph Cable Co.; pres. Commercial Cable Co., Commercial Pacific Cable Co., Mackay Cos., Cuban All America Cables; dir. Internat. Telephone & Telegraph Corp. Chmn. bd. Philharmonic Soc., St. Vincent's Hosp.; dir. Metropolitan Opera Co. Treas. Lincoln Farm Assn. which raised funds for purchase of Lincoln farm in Ky. and preservation of log cabin in which Lincoln was born. Home: Roslyn, L.I., N.Y. Died Nov. 12, 1938.

MACKAY, Donald Sage, clergyman; b. Glasgow, Scotland, Nov. 20, 1863; s. Rev. W. Murray and Christian (Sage) M.; grad. Glasgow U., M.A. (philosophy), 1885, New College, Edinburgh, 1889; D.D., Rutgers Coll., 1895; LL.D., Hope Coll., Mich., 1906; m. Helen L., d. Gov. J. Gregory Smith, of Vt., July 23, 1890. Came to U.S., 1890; ordained to Congl. ministry, 1890; pastor 1st Congl. Ch., St. Albans, Vt., 1890-94, N. Reformed Ch., Newark, N.J., 1894-99, Collegiate Ch. of St. Nicholas, 1899—. Pres. Gen. Synod Reformed Ch. in America, 1906—. Author: Collegiate Sermons, 1906. Home: New York, N.Y. Died 1908.

MACKAY, John William, capitalist; b. Dublin, Ireland, Nov. 28, 1831; moved with family to New York, 1840; learned shipbuilding trade; went to Calif., 1851; to Nev., 1860; engaged in mining; had two-fifths share in "Bonanza" mines of the Comstock lode, which made him one of the richest men in the world. Established (with Messrs. Flood and Fair) Nevada Bank, San Francisco, becoming its pres.; established (with James Gordon Bennett) the Commercial Cable Co.; pres. Postal-Telegraph Cable Co. Home: San Francisco, Calif. Died 1902.

MACKAY, William Andrew, artist; b. Phila., Pa., July 10, 1876; s. Frank F. and Elizabeth J. Sneathen (Bond) M.; student Coll. City of N.Y., Academie Julian, Paris, and Am. Acad. in Rome, 1906-07; pupil of Benjamin Constant and Jean Paul Laurens. Worked as apprentice under Frank Millet, Columbian Expn., Chicago, 1893; painter of murals and decorations; decorated ceiling of U.S. Senate Reading Room; represented by his work in Federal Bldg., Cleveland, Civic Opera House, Chicago, Minn. Capitol Bldg., Baltimore Customs House; Murals in N.Y. State Roosevelt Memorial Bldg., New York. Chief Camouflage artist 2d Dist., U.S.A., World War. Episcopalian. Mason. Home: Coytesville, N.J. Died July 26, 1939.

MACKAY, William Eshorne, executive; b. Phila., Pa., Jan. 9, 1865; s. William Eshorne and Charlotte Elizabeth (Richardson) M.; prep. edn., Trinity Sch., Del., 1877-79, Rugby, 1879-81; grad. U.S. Naval Acad., 1885; m. Helen E. Baker, Jan. 21, 1891; children—Wilson Eshorne, Woodbury Eshorne. Engr. Boston Gas Light Co., 1887-1905, Boston Consol. Gas Co., 1905-10; with N.E. Gas & Coke Co., 1910-27, as v.p., later pres. and trustee; pres. N.E. Mfg. Co., 1915-33; pres. Beacon Oil Co., 1919-24; chmn. bd. Mystic Iron Works, 1924—; pres. N.E. Fuel & Transportation Co., Mystic Steamship Co., N.E. Coke Co.; sr. v.p. Mass. Gas Cos.; dir. N.E. Coal & Coke Co., C. C. B. Smokeless Coal Co., Castner, Curran & Bullitt; trustee Eastern Gas & Fuel Associates. Lt. Naval Brig., Mass. Vol. Militia, 1896-98, capt. and chief of brig., 1900; lt. U.S.N., 1898. Trustee Mass. Nautical Sch. (chmn. bd. 1928-31; commr. 1910-31). Republican. Episcopalian. Home: Boston, Mass. Died Mar. 1935.

MACKAY-SMITH, Alexander, bishop; b. New Haven, Conn., June 2, 1850; A.B., Trinity Coll., Conn., 1872; studied in Eng. and Germany; D.D., Trinity, 1889; S.T.D., Hobart, 1889. Deacon, 1876, priest, 1877, P.E. Ch.; asst. All Saints, Worcester, Mass., 1876-77, Grace Ch., S. Boston, 1877-80, St. Thomas', New York, 1880-86; 1st archdeacon New York, 1887-93; rector St. John's, Washington, 1893-1902; consecrated coadjutor bishop of Pa., 1902. Declined election as coadjutor bishop of Kan., 1886. Address: Philadelphia, Pa. Died 1911.

MACKAYE, Harold Steele, author; b. Paris, France, Mar. 10, 1866; s. Steele and Mary Keith (Medbery) M.; C.E., Columbia, 1887; LL.B., and LL.M., Georgetown U., 1891; m. Helen Lyle Lane, June 2, 1892. Admitted to bar, 1892, and engaged in patent practice at N.Y. City; mem. firm Wilkinson, Fisher, Witherspoon & Mackaye, 1912-17; private practice, 1917—. Author: The Panchronicon, 1903; The Winged Helmet, 1904. Home: Yonkers, N.Y. Died June 1928.

MacKAYE, James, author, educator; b. New York, Apr. 8, 1872; s. (James) Steele and Mary Keith (Medbery) M.; B.S., Harvard, 1895; A.M., Dartmouth, 1932; m. Mary de Veber Morse, 1906. Lecturer philosophy, Rollins Coll., Winter Park, Fla., 1931-32; prof. philosophy, Dartmouth, 1932—. Author: The Economy of Happiness, 1906; The Politics of Utility, 1906; The Happiness of Nations, 1915; Americanized Socialism, 1918; The Logic of Conduct, 1924; The Dynamic Universe, 1931; Thoreau—Philosopher of Freedom, 1931. Home: Hanover, N.H. Died Jan. 22, 1935.

MACKENZIE, Alexander, major gen. U.S.A.; b. Potosi, Wis., May 25, 1844; s. Donald Alexander and Mary Ann (Conner) M.; ed. Platteville (Wis.) Acad., grammar and high schs., Dubuque, Ia.; grad. U.S. Mil. Acad., 1864; Sc.D., U. of Pa., 1906; widower. Apptd. 1st lt. engrs., June 13, 1864; capt., Mar. 7, 1867; maj., Apr. 5, 1882; lt. col., Feb. 3, 1895; col., May 3, 1901; brig. gen. chief of engrs. U.S.A., Jan. 23, 1904; maj. gen., 1908. Bvtd. captain, Mar. 13, 1865, "for gallant and meritorious services during the war." Served as asst. engr., Dept. of Ark., 1864-65; as asst. engr. on various improvements, 1865-66; harbor improvement of Lake Mich., 1866-68; comd. engr. co. Willetts Point, N.Y., 1868-74; asst. engr. on Louisville and Portland canal, etc., 1874-77; on works under Maj. Weitzel, 1874-79; in charge river and harbor improvement, Miss. River, 1879-95; mem. Mo. River Commn., 1884-95; 1st asst. to chief of engrs., 1895-1903; mem. Lighthouse Bd., 1895-1904; mem. Bd. Ordnance and Fortification from 1904, bd. commrs. of Soldiers' Home from 1904; retired by operation of law, May 25, 1908. Active duty, 1917-19. Home: Washington, D.C. Died Feb. 23, 1921.

MACKENZIE, A(lexander) Cameron, D.D., LL.D.; pres. Elmira Coll., 1897—. Address: Elmira, N.Y. Died Mar. 24, 1915.

MACKENZIE, Cameron, publisher; b. Wilkes-Barre, Pa., Sept. 7, 1882; s. James Cameron and Ella (Smith) M.; grad. Lawrenceville Sch., N.J., 1899; Yale, 1899-1901; LL.B., New York Law Sch., 1906; m. Elizabeth McClure, April 2, 1907. On staff New York Sun, 1901-06; assistant managing editor, 1906; mng. editor, 1907-09, gen. mgr. and pub., 1909-11, McClure's Magazine; with Frederick L. Collins bought controlling interest in mag., also acquiring Ladies' World; resigned vice presidency McClure publication, 1915, to engage in writing. During the war was spl. corr. of London Chronicle on Gen. Pershing's staff; after armistice spl. corr. in Warsaw for Paris and N.Y. Herald. Presbyn. Author: Mr. and Mrs. Pierce; The Prussian, and Other Stories. Home: Brook Haven, L.I., N.Y. Died Mar. 18, 1921.

MacKENZIE, Frederick William, editor; b. Black Earth, Wis., July 11, 1883; s. John Benjamin and Annie (Johns) M.; A.B., U. of Wis., 1906; m. Nellie Howard Dunn, Feb. 9, 1916. Polit. reporter Milwaukee Journal, 1906; asst. sect. Mchts.' and Mfrs.' Assn., Milwaukee, 1907; univ. editor, U. of Wis., 1908; mng. editor La Follette's Magazine, Madison, Wis., 1909-17; dir. publicity Am. Assn. for Labor Legislation; asso. editor Am. Labor Legislation Review. Died May 24, 1928.

MACKENZIE, James Cameron, educator; b. Aberdeen, Scotland, Aug. 15, 1852; s. Alexander and Katherine M.; A.B., Lafayette Coll., 1878, Ph.D., 1882; student Princeton Theol. Sem., 1882; m. Ella Smith, Oct. 5, 1880; children—Cameron (dec.), Alexander, George Miner, James Cameron, Richard, Anna (Mrs. Snell Smith), Jean (Mrs. Kenneth E. Walser), Margaret (Mrs. Hermann Betz). Founded Wilkes-Barre Acad., 1882; ordained Presbyn. ministry, 1885; organizer, 1882, and first headmaster, 1882-99, Lawrenceville (N.J.) Sch.; reorganizer, 1899, dir., 1899-1901, Tome Inst., Port Deposit, Md.; founder, and head of Mackenzie Sch., Monroe, N.Y., 1901-26; lit. work and preaching, 1926—. One of 3 organizers Headmasters' Assn. (pres. 1897); pres. Assn. Colls. and Prep. Schs. of the Middle States and Md., 1898; chmn. Internat. Congress of Secondary Edn., Chicago, 1893; chmn. advisory bd. St. Luke's Sch., New Canaan, Conn.; mem. advisory council Simplified Spelling Bd.; mem. Com. of Ten, 1891. Home: New York, N.Y. Died May 10, 1931.

MACKENZIE, Jean Kenyon, missionary; b. Elgin, Ill., Jan. 6, 1874; d. Rev. Robert and Lydia A. (McLeod) Mackenzie; spl. courses U. of Calif. and U. of Paris, France; hon. M.A., Smith Coll., 1927. Author: Black Sheep, 1916; An African Trail, 1917; African Adventures, 1917; The Story of a Fortunate Youth, 1920; African Clearings (essays), 1924; The Venture (poems), 1925; Friends of Africa, 1928; The Trader's Wife, 1930. Home: Riverdale on Hudson, N.Y. Died Sept. 1936.

MACKENZIE, John Noland, laryngologist; b. Baltimore, Oct. 20, 1853; s. John C. and Eleanor (Noland) M.; A.B., U. of Va., 1874, M.D., 1876; M.D., Univ. Med. Coll. (New York U.), 1877; house surgeon Bellevue Hosp., New York; interne Rotunda Hospital, Dublin, 1879; univs. of Munich and Vienna; chief of staff Golden Sq. Hosp., London. Prof. laryngology, U. of Md., 1887-97; clin. prof. laryngology and rhinology, Johns Hopkins U., 1889-1912; laryngologist, Johns Hopkins Hosp.; surgeon Baltimore Eye, Ear and Throat Charity Hosp. Editor Md. Med. Journal, Journal Laryngology and Rhinology. Corr. fellow British and French socs. of Laryngology, Rhinology and Otology; pres. Am. Laryngol. Assn., 1889-90. Address: Baltimore, Md. Died May 21, 1925.

MACKENZIE, Kenneth Alexander J., surgeon; b. Cumberland House, Manitoba, Can., Jan. 13, 1859; s. Roderick and Jane M.; Nest Acad., Jedburgh, Scotland; high sch., Montreal, Can.; Upper Can. Coll., Toronto; M.D., C.M., McGill U., 1881; L.R. C.P. and L.R.C.S., Edinburgh, 1882; also studied univs. of London, Berlin, Paris, Vienna; m. Cora Hardy Scott, 1885 (died, 1901); m. 2d, Marion Higgins Brown, Apr. 1905. In practice at Portland, Ore., 1882—; prof. theory and practice of medicine, 1887-1907, operative and clin. surgery, 1907—, U. of Ore. Surgeon St. Vincent's Hosp., 1883—; chief surgeon in Ore. and Wash. of Ore. R.R. & Navigation Co., 1895—; 1st lt. U.S.A. Medical Reserve Corps. Dir. U.S. National Bank. Head of relief corps of physicians and nurses under auspices of Citizens Relief Com. of Portland, San Francisco, 1906; organized and in charge Harbor View relief sta., under Gen. Torney, U.S.A.; dir. and med. dir. Lewis and Clark Expn.; dir. Portland Free Dispensary; dean Med. Dept., U. of Ore. Republican. Episcopalian. Fellow Am. Surg. Assn., Portland Acad. Medicine (pres. 1909-10); v.p. A.M.A., 1906-07. Mason. Home: Portland, Ore. Died Mar. 16, 1920.

MACKENZIE, Morris Robinson Slidell, rear admiral U.S.N.; b. N.Y.; grad. U.S. Naval Acad., 1866. Promoted ensign, Apr. 1868; master, Mar. 26, 1869; lt., Mar. 21, 1870; lt. comdr., Dec. 1884; comdr., Apr. 16, 1894; capt., July 1, 1900; rear admiral, May 13, 1906. Served on the various stas. and duties; comd. Prairie, 1898-1900, U.S.S. New York, 1901, Navy Yard, Portsmouth, N.H., 1903; insp. in charge, 3d light house dist., 1905; retired, June 28, 1906. Address: Morristown, N.J. Died Jan. 16, 1915.

MACKENZIE, Murdo, stockman; b. County Ross, Scotland, Apr. 24, 1850; s. David and Jessie (Mackenzie) M.; grad. Royal Acad. Tain, Scotland, 1869; m. Isabella Stronach MacBain, Jan. 14, 1876; children—Alexander M., David G. (dec.), Mrs. T. G. Chittenden, Mrs. F. R. Button, John. Came to U.S., 1885; mgr. Prairie Cattle Co., Ltd., 1885-90; mgr. Matador Land & Cattle Co., Ltd., 1891-1911, gen. mgr., 1922-37. Pres. Cattle Raisers' Assn. of Tex., 1901-02; pres. Am. Nat. Live Stock Assn., 1904-11; mgr. Brazil Land, Cattle & Packing Co., Sao Paulo, Brazil, 1911-19; dir. Denver Br. Federal Reserve Bank, Dist. No. 10, 1923-35. Republican. Mason. Home: Denver, Colo. Died May 30, 1939.

MACKENZIE, Robert, clergyman; b. Cromarty, Scotland, Nov. 5, 1845; s. John and Isabella (Allan) M.; came to America, 1866; ed. U. of Chicago (spl. course); grad. McCormick Theol. Sem., Chicago, 1873; D.D., Centre Coll., Kentucky, 1883; LL.D., U. of Wooster, Ohio, 1905, Lafayette Coll., Pa., 1915; m. Lydia Ann McLeod, Apr. 9, 1873. Ordained Presbyterian ministry, 1873; pastor, Decatur, Ill., 1873-76, Lafayette, Ind., 1876-79, Howard Ch., San Francisco, 1879-85, First Ch., San Francisco, 1886-1901, Rutgers Ch., New York, 1901-09; pres. San Francisco Theol. Sem., 1909-10; exec. sec. Coll. Bd. Presbyn. Ch., 1910-18 (pres. same, 1904-09). Republican. Author: The Loom of Providence, 1904. Address: New York, N.Y. Died Sept. 15, 1925.

MACKENZIE, Roderick Dempster, artist; b. London, Eng., Apr. 30, 1865; s. John Dempster and Isabella (McClean) M.; brought by parents to U.S., 1872; prep. edn., Barton Acad., Mobile, Ala.; student under Otto Grundeman, Robert Vonnoh, Frederick Crowninshield and Longfellow, Boston Mus. Fine Arts, scholarship, 1884-85; studied at Julian Acad. and L'Ecole des Beaux Arts, Paris, under Lefebvre, Constant, Jean Paul Laurens in painting, Charles Chapu in sculpture; m. Charlotte Elizabeth Barnes, 1891 (died 1920). Maintained studio at Mobile, 1885-89 and 1913—; engaged in painting tigers of India, 1893-96, Afghans and Baluchis of northwest Indian frontier, 1898-1900; official painter of state entry into Delhi (painting is 18 ft. long, 11 ft. high and contains 1000 figures), accession of Edward VII as emperor of India, 1902; commd. to make model for restoration of Chitor elephants, Delhi Gate; painted series of 43 pastels of furnaces at Ensley Steel Works, Birmingham, Ala.; made 8 murals and 4 panels in relief for rotunda and dome of Ala. State Capitol, 1926-30. Awarded Curzon gold medal, 1898; elected to Ala. Hall of Fame, 1925. Lecturer and writer on India and big game hunting. Has exhibited at McLean Gallery, Haymarket, London, Brooklyn Mus., Grand Central Galleries, N.Y. City, Grand Central Palace, Southern Expn., 1924, etc. Studio: Mobile, Ala. Deceased.

MACKENZIE, William Douglas, theologian; b. Fauresmith, Orange River Colony, S. Africa, July 16, 1859; s. John M. (missionary) and Ellen (Douglas) M.; ed. Watson's Coll. Sch., 1875; M.A., U. of Edinburgh, 1881, D.D., 1910; Congl. Theol. Hall., Edinburgh, 1880-82; U. of Göttingen, 1886; U. of Marburg, 1895; D.D., Beloit Coll., 1896, Wesleyan U., 1906, Yale, 1907, Knox Coll., Toronto, 1915; LL.D., Princeton, 1906; Th.D., Giessen, Germany, 1926; Litt.D., Trinity Coll., Hartford, Conn., 1928; m. Alice, d. T. B. Crowther, Apr. 27, 1883 (died 1926). Ordained Congl. ministry, 1882; prof. systematic theology, Chicago Theol. Sem., 1895-1903; pres. Hartford Sem. Foundation, 1904-30, emeritus, 1930—. was also prof. of systematic theology, 1904-30. Author: Ethics of Gambling, 1893; The Revelation of the Christ, 1896; Christianity and the Progress of Man, 1897; South Africa—Its History, Heroes and Wars, 1900; John Mackenzie, South African Missionary and Statesman, 1902; The Final Faith, 1910; Galatians & Romans (in Westminster N.T.), 1912; Christian Ethics in the World War, 1918; The Christ of the Christian Faith, 1933; Paternoster Sheen, or Light on Man's Destiny, 1933; Man's Consciousness of Immortality (Ingersoll lecture), 1933. Also article on Jesus Christ in Hastings' Encyclopedia of Religion and Ethics, 1914. Editor of Transplanted Heather, by J. M. Campbell, 1929. Home: Hartford, Conn. Died Mar. 29, 1936.

MACKEY, Charles William, lawyer; b. Franklin, Pa., Nov. 19, 1842; s. Charles W. and Julia Ann (Fagundus) M.; ed. in schs. of Franklin; learned printer's trade and published a newspaper when a boy; began study of law, 1860; served in "Venango Grays" (Co. C, 10th Pa. Reserve Vols.), 1861-63, and took part in numerous battles from Dranesville to Gettysburg; spl. agt. U.S. Treasury for Eastern Va. and N.C. Dist., 1863-65; admitted to Pa. bar, Aug. 1865; m. Lauretta B., d. Cyrus Paige Fay, May 9, 1867. Head mem. of law firm of Mackey & Hughes, Franklin, Pa.; personally counsel for numerous ry. and industrial cos.; pres. or dir. Jacksonville (Ill.) Water Works Co., Franklin Steel Co., Russ Automatic Labeling Co., Rey del Oro Mining Co., Almada Sugar Co., Franklin Drug & Chemical Co., Franklin Rolling Mill & Foundry Co. Organized Nat. Lead Co., Nat. Saw Co., Columbia Spring Co., Am. Axe & Tool Co., Firth-Sterling Steel Co., Columbia Gas Light & Fuel Co. and many other ry., industrial and financial corps. Rep. candidate for Congress, 27th Pa. Dist., 1884; del. Rep. Nat. Conv., 1888; councilman and solicitor, City of Franklin, Pa., several terms, mayor, 1872-73. Capt. Pa. N.G., 1872-73. Past commander G.A.R. Home: Franklin, Pa. Died May 25, 1917.

MACKEY, Harry A(rista), mayor; b. Susquehanna, Pa., June 26, 1873; s. George W. and Isadore (MacCollum) M.; A.B., Lafayette Coll., Easton, Pa., 1890; LL.B., U. of Pa., 1893; m. Ida Boner, Feb. 1, 1900; 1 dau., Lorna. Admitted to Pa. bar, 1893, and began practice at Phila. with Hon. W. W. Porter; mem. firm J. G. Gordon, 1898-1902; practiced alone, 1902—; dir. H. A. Mackey Bldg. & Loan Assn. Dir. dept. health and charities, Phila., 1905-07; mem. Common Council, 1908-10; became dir. Dept. Pub. Works, 1911; chmn. Pa. Workmen's Compensation Bd., 1915-23; city treas., Phila., 1925-27; mayor of Phila., term 1928-31 inclusive. Republican. Episcopalian. Mason, Elk, Eagle, Red Man, Forester. Home: Philadelphia, Pa. Died Oct. 17, 1938.

MACKINNON, Allan P(armelee), lawyer; b. Brockville, Ont., Can., Feb. 28, 1880; s. Tristram A. and Margaret A. (Cardell) M.; B.L., Dartmouth, 1902; LL.B., Harvard, 1905; m. Amy S. Higgins, Nov. 2, 1907; children—Tristram A., Allan P. Admitted to Mass. bar, 1905, and began practice at Boston; asst. to gen. solicitor B.&M. R.R., 1905-07, asst. solicitor, 1907-09, solicitor, 1909-14, asst. gen. solicitor, 1914-18, gen. solicitor, 1918-30, gen. counsel, 1930—; dir. Conn. & Passumpsic Rivers R.R. Co., Troy Union R.R., Vt. Valley R.R., Massawippi Valley Ry. Co., Boston & Lowell R.R. Corp., Lake Champlain & St. Lawrence Junction R.R., North Station Hotel Bldg., Inc. Republican. Episcopalian. Home: Winchester, Mass. Died Aug. 7, 1880.

MacKINNON, George V., hat mfr.; b. Dundee, Scotland, Jan. 4, 1882; s. Samuel and Agnes (Valentine) MacK.; brought to U.S., 1888; ed. Central High Sch., Phila., Pa., 1896-97; grad. Peirce Sch. of Business Administration, 1900; m. Imogene Derbyshire, Mar. 16, 1910; 1 dau., Alice I. (dec.). Began as errand boy, J. P. Twaddell & Co., retail shoes, Phila., 1897; clk., Thos. Cocker & Co., brush mfrs., 1897-99, Welsbach Commercial Co., 1899-1900; with John B. Stetson Co., hat mfrs., 1900—; clk., bookkeeper, chief accountant to 1917, treas. until 1924, v.p. in charge finance, 1924-28, pres., 1928—; pres. John B. Stetson Co., Ltd. (Canada), John B. Stetson Bldg. & Loan Assn.; treas. Goodwill Industries of Phila.; dir. Fidelity-Phila. Trust Co., Phila. Mfrs. Mutual Fire Ins. Co., Fidelity Mutual Life Ins. Co. dir. Philadelphia Chamber of Commerce; pres. and dir. Stetson Hosp. of Phila.; dir. S.E. Pa. chapter Am. Red Cross. Trustee Methodist Episcopal Orphanage. Republican. Methodist. Home: Jenkintown, Pa. Died June 17, 1939.

MacKINNON, Lee Warner, educator; b. London, O., Dec. 8, 1878; s. John Wesley and Clara Emeline (Wallace) MacK.; grad. high sch., London, 1895; A.B., Wittenberg Coll., 1899, A.M., 1905; A.M., U. of Chicago, 1922; m. Annie L. Locke, Mar. 11, 1901; children—Wallace LeRoy, John Godfrey. Prin. high sch., Plain City, O., 1899-1900; teacher high sch., Fostoria, O., 1900-01, Washington C.H., 1901-02; prin. high sch., Hillsboro, O., 1902-05; supt. schs., Granville, O., 1905-07; prin. high sch., Gallipolis, O., 1907-12, Marietta, 1912-17; prin. Central High Sch., Akron, O., 1917-21; dir. Junior Coll., Univ. of City of Toledo, 1923-31, v.p. of univ., 1926—. dean of administration, 1930—. Republican. Presbyn. Home: Toledo, O. Died Feb. 15, 1935.

MACKINTOSH, George Lewis, college pres.; b. N.S., Can., Jan. 1, 1860; s. John and Elizabeth (Bruce) M.; A.B., Wabash Coll., Ind., 1884, A.M., 1887; Baldwin prize in oratory, Ind. State Oratorical Assn.; 2d prize, Interstate Oratorical Assn.; D.D., U. of Wooster, 1903; LL.D., Hanover Coll., 1908; m. Bertha Garfield Stowe, Sept. 11, 1902; m. 2d, Jean Mitchell, June 17, 1912. Ordained Presbyn. ministry, 1889; pastor Fourth Ch., Indianapolis, 1891-1907; lecturer in philosophy, 1905-07, pres., 1907-26, Wabash Coll. Address: Crawfordsville, Ind. Died Feb. 29, 1932.

MACKLIN, James Edgar, brigadier gen. U.S.A.; b. in N.Y., Oct. 18, 1846. Served as pvt. and corporal Co. B, 16th Ind. Inf., Apr. 22, 1861-May 23, 1862; pvt. Co. K, 16th Ind. Inf., June 1, 1862; discharged, Aug. 18, 1862; commd. 2d lt. 16th Ind. Inf., Aug. 19, 1862; 1st lt., Mar. 1, 1863; capt., Dec. 20, 1864; hon. mustered out, June 30, 1865; apptd. from Ind., 2d lt. 31st U.S. Inf., Aug. 9, 1867; assigned to 22d Inf., July 14, 1869; 2d lt. 11th Inf., Jan. 12, 1877; 1st lt., Apr. 24, 1886; capt. 11th Inf., Feb. 25, 1891; maj. 24th Inf., Oct. 19, 1899; transferred to 11th Inf., Feb. 17, 1900; lt. col. 3d Inf., Apr. 20, 1903; col. 4th Inf., May 8, 1906; brig. gen. U.S.A. and retired at own request, over 40 yrs.' service, Dec. 2, 1906. Died Dec. 16, 1925.

MACKUBIN, Florence, artist; b. Florence, Italy, May 19, 1861; d. Charles Nicholas and Ellen M. (Fay) M.; pupil Louis Deschamps and Julius Rolshoven, Paris; Prof. Herterrich, Munich, and in miniatures, Mlle. J. Devina, Paris; unmarried. Exhibited Chicago Expn., 1893, Tenn. Expn., 1897 (medal and diploma for miniatures), Paris Expn., 1900, Buffalo Expn., 1901, Charleston Expn., 1902. Apptd. by Gov. Smith and Bd. of Pub. Works, of Md., 1900, to paint portrait of Queen Henrietta Maria (after whom Md. was named) to hang in State House (portrait after Vandyck's painting in Warwick Castle, Eng.); exhibited 3 miniatures at St. Louis Expn., 1904; painted portraits of govs. Lloyd (1809), Winder (1812), Ridgely (1815), Swann (1865), and Lowndes (1900), to be hung in exec. chamber in Md. State House; represented by 3 miniatures and portrait in Md. Bldg., at Jamestown Expn., 1907; painted portraits of 1st and 2d barons of Baltimore (founders of Md.), at Windlestone, Hall, Eng., for Baltimore Club, 1908; portrait of Prof. Basil Gildersleeve, for U. of Va.; miniature of Cardinal Gibbons, and "A Study in Yellow," bought for Walter's Gallery, Baltimore; portrait of Sir Charles Drury, admiralty House, Chatham, Eng.; of Sir William Van Horne, of Can., 1913; of Francis Scott Key, with flag presented to Francis Scott Key Sch., Baltimore, 1913; portraits of Govs. Calvert and Eden, of Md., for State House, etc. Address: Baltimore, Md. Died Feb. 7, 1918.

MACLACHAN, David Cathcart, clergyman; b. Barrhead, Renfrewshire, Scotland, Mar. 16, 1869; s. Ivie Macrae and Jean Louise (McCulloch) M.; M.A., Glasgow U., 1889, also passing in all subjects for B.L.; studied Free Ch. Hall, Glasgow, 1889-90; D.D., Richmond U., 1918; m. Margaret Graves Wolverton, June 7, 1904. Came to U.S., 1894, naturalized citizen, 1903. Ordained ministry Christian (Disciples) Ch., 1904; pastor Shelbyville, Ky., 1901-07, Richmond, Va., 1908—. Pres. Juvenile Protective Assn. of Va., 1912-16; mem. exec. bd. Va. Industrial Sch. for Girls (reformatory); a founder and mem. exec. com. Sch. of Social Work and Pub. Health, Richmond; an organizer Juvenile Court of Richmond. Served as chmn. War Camp Community Service of Richmond, World War; mem. Draft Bd., Y.M.C.A. Selection Bd., etc. Democrat. Mason. Home: Richmond, Va. Deceased.

MacLACHLAN, Daniel A., oculist, aurist; b. Aylmer, Ont., Can., Nov. 10, 1852; s. Archibald and Mary (Robertson) M.; pub. sch. edn., Aylmer; M.D., Homœ. Med. Coll. (U. of Mich.), 1879; passed exams. Coll. Phys. and Surg., Toronto; visited hosps. of London, Heidelberg, Vienna and Paris, 1889, London and Edinburgh, 1892; m. Bertha Hadley, Dec. 15, 1881. Prof. theory and practice of medicine, 1885-89, ophthalmology, otology and pædology, 1889-95, Homœ. Med. Coll., U. of Mich.; in practice at Detroit, 1895—; dean and prof. ophthalmology, otology and laryngology, Detroit Homœ. Coll., 1899-1912; mem. staff Grace Hosp.; asso. editor Medical Counselor; mem. Mich. State Bd. Health, 1899-1905. A founder Am. Ophthal., Otol. and Laryngol. Soc.; pres. Mich. State Homœ. Med. Soc., 1895-97; mem. Am. Inst. Homeopathy (1st v.p., 1896; hon. pres., 1921-22). Mason. Home: Detroit, Mich. Died Feb. 8, 1938.

MAC LACHLAN, Lachlan, furniture designer; b. Stirling, Scotland, Jan. 25, 1874; s. Andrew and Dorothy (McCulloch) MacL.; ed. high sch.; studied art in various countries of Europe; m. Gertrude Eleanor McDonald, Apr. 1907. Came to U.S., 1905, naturalized citizen, 1923. Dir. studio of W. and J. Sloane, New York, 1909-14; apptd. art dir. Berkey & Gay Furniture Co., Grand Rapids, Mich., 1915, later v.p.; dir. Wallace Furniture Co., Consolidated Furniture Corp. Trustee Art and Museum Commn., Grand Rapids. Republican. Christian Scientist. Mason. Home: Grand Rapids, Mich. Deceased.

MacLAFFERTY, James Henry, congressman; b. San Diego, Calif., Feb. 27, 1871; s. Rev. B.S. and Antha (Taylor) MacL.; ed. pub. schs.; married; children—James Henry, Mrs. Antha Goemmer. Formerly in lumber business; representd J. W. Butler Paper Co., of Chicago, on Pacific Coast several yrs. from 1899; established 3 wholesale paper houses on the coast. Elected to 67th Congress to fill vacancy occasioned by death of John A. Elston, and to 68th Congress (1923-25), 6th Calif. Dist.; then asst. to Sec. of Commerce Hoover. Republican. Mason, Elk. Home: Oakland, Calif. Died June 9, 1937.

MAC LANE, Mary, author; b. Winnipeg, Man., May 2, 1883; d. James W. and Margaret L. Mac Lane; grad. high sch., Butte, Mont., 1899. Left Butte, 1902, to do feature writing for New York World; engaged in spl. writing for newspapers at intervals, 1902-12; later as feature star in motion pictures. Author: Story of Mary MacLane, 1902; My Friend Annabel Lee, 1903; I, Mary MacLane, 1917. Died Aug. 6, 1929.

MAC LAREN, Archibald, surgeon; b. Red Wing, Minn., Apr. 16, 1858; s. Robert N. and Anna (McVean) MacL.; B.S., Princeton, 1880; M.D., Coll. Phys. and Surg. (Columbia), 1883; m. Katherine Dean, Dec. 12, 1891. Interne Woman's Hosp., New York, 1883-85; settled in St. Paul, 1885; mem. firm MacLaren, Ritchie & Daugherty; prof. surgery U. of Minn. Med. Sch.; chief of staff St. Luke's Hosp.; asso. attending surgeon University Hosp. Presbyterian. Home: St. Paul, Minn. Died Oct. 12, 1924.

MACLAURIN, Richard Cockburn, educator; b. Lindean, Scotland, June 5, 1870; s. Robert Campbell and Martha Joan (Spence) M.; prep. edn., Auckland Grammar Sch., New Zealand; M.A., U. of Cambridge, Eng., 1897; Smith's Prizeman in mathematics, 1897, and Yorke Prizeman in law, 1898, U. of Cambridge; LL.D., U. of Cambridge, 1904, Wesleyan U., 1909, Harvard U., 1910, Denison, 1914, Sc.D., Cambridge, 1908, Dartmouth, 1909; m. Alice Young, Dec. 27, 1904. Mem. Honorable Soc. Lincoln's Inn; elected fellow St. John's Coll., Cambridge, 1897; prof. mathematics, 1898-1905, dean faculty of law, 1905-07, New Zealand U.; fellow U. of New Zealand, 1899-1907; elected prof. math. physics, Columbia, 1907; pres. Mass. Inst. Tech., 1909—. Author: Title to Realty, 1900; The Theory of Light, 1909; Lectures on Light, 1909; also various scientific memoirs pub. by the Royal Soc. of London, the Cambridge Philos. Soc., The Philosophical Magazine, La Revue Scientifique, etc. Home: Cambridge, Mass. Died Jan. 15, 1920.

MACLAY, Isaac Walker, civil engr., real estate dealer; b. New York, May 14, 1841; s. Dr. Archibald and Julia Anne (Walker) M.; ed. Univ. Grammar Sch. and U. City of New York to 1860; grad. U.S. Mil. Acad., 1864; m. Laura Amelia Havemeyer, Nov. 1869. Commd. 2d lt., 1st U.S. Arty., 1864; served in Civil War, 1864-66; was at Ford's Theatre when President Lincoln was assassinated, assisted in carrying the President to the Peterson house, and, at request of Mrs. Lincoln, brought Dr. Stone to bedside. Promoted 1st lt. Ordnance Corps, U.S.A.; served as ordnance officer in various arsenals, 1864-73; resigned. Asst. topog. engr., Dept. Pub. Parks, New York; later chief engr. L.I. R.R.; apptd. a city surveyor engaged in practice of engring. with William E. Davies as Maclay & Davies until 1892; since then in real estate business. Pres. Maclay & Davies Real Estate Co., Yonkers Wharf & Warehouse Co.; v.p. Pelhamdale Land Co.; trustee People's Savings Bank, Yonkers. An incorporator and charter mem. New York Zoöl. Soc., Underwriters' Club, New York, Md. Soc. of N.Y. Trustee Va. Union U.; mem. bd. mgrs. Am. Bapt. Home Mission Soc.; mem. exec. com. Andrew H. Green Memorial Assn. Del. to Internat. Sunday Rest Congress and mem. Internat. Congress Arts and Science at St. Louis Expn., 1904. Author: Henry Sater (1690-1754), 1897; Life of Rev. Archibald Maclay, D.D. (1776-1860), 1902. Home: Yonkers, N.Y. Died 1909.

MACLAY, James, prof. mathematics; b. Troy, N.Y., Nov. 6, 1864; s. William and Elizabeth McNeile) M.; C.E. Columbia, 1888, tutorial fellow in mathematics, 1888-91, Ph.D., 1899; U. of Berlin, 2 yrs.; m. Winifred Roosa Craine, Sept. 1, 1904. Tutor in mathematics, 1891-95, instr., 1895-1901, adj. prof., 1901-05, prof., 1905—, Columbia U. Home: New York, N.Y. Died Nov. 28, 1919.

MACLAY, Otis Hardy, M.D.; b. Oakland, Calif., July 9, 1873; s. Rev. William J. and Alvira (Hardy) M.; student U. of Mich., 1894-96; B.S., Northwestern U., 1897, M.D., 1901; m. Urma Connell, June 1902; children—Josephine Roxbury, Hardy King. Practiced at Chicago, 1901—, specializing in treatment of nose, throat and ear; attending laryngologist, Wesley Memorial Hosp.; asst. prof. laryngology and rhinology, Northwestern U. Med. Sch.; mem. Chicago Laryngol. and Otol. Soc. (sec. 1911-16; pres. 1916). Republican. Home: Chicago, Ill. Died Sept. 5, 1936.

MACLAY, Robert Samuel, clergyman, author; b. Concord, Pa., Feb. 7, 1824; s. Robert and Arabella (Erwin) M.; grad. Dickinson Coll., 1845, D.D., 1861; entered ministry M.E. Ch., 1846; sailed as missionary to Foochow, China, Oct. 13, 1847; m. Henrietta Caroline Sperry, July 10, 1850; m. 2d, Sarah Ann Barr, June 6, 1882. Mem. com. which translated New Testament into Foochow dialect; supt. and treas. Foochow mission, 1852-72; transferred to Japan and apptd. supt. and treas. Japan mission, 1872; mem. com. which translated New Testament into Japanese; delegate from Japan, Ecumenical Meth. Conf., London, 1881; aided in founding Anglo-Chinese Coll., Foochow, 1881; went to Korea, 1884, and procured King's permission to commence work of Christian missions in Korea; aided in establishing, 1883 (pres., 1883-87), Anglo-Japanese Coll., and, 1884 (dean 1884-87), Philander Smith Biblical Inst., both at Tokyo, Japan; ministerial del. from Japan to gen. conf. M.E. Ch., New York, 1888; dean Maclay Coll. of Theology, San Fernando, Calif., 1888-93. Author: Life Among the Chinese, 1861; Dictionary of the Chinese Language in the Dialect of Foochow (with Rev. C. C. Baldwin, D.D.), 1871. Wrote sketch of Japan M.E. Mission, in Reid's History of Methodist Missions; "Shintooism," in Reid's "Doomed Religions," published 1882. Address: San Fernando, Calif. Died 1907.

MacLEAN, Angus Dhu, lawyer; b. Maxton, N.C., July 12, 1877; s. John Allan and Mary Virginia (Brown) M.; prep. edn. N.C. pvt. schs.; student U. of N.C., 1894-98; m. Annetta Everett, Oct. 24, 1900; children—Angus Duart (dec.), Mary Virginia (Mrs. Alexander T. Jeanette), Martha Lawrence, Annetta Everett, Jane Duart. Admitted to N.C. bar, 1898, practiced in Washington, N.C., until 1933; mem. N.C. Ho. of Rep., 1927-32; state senator, 1933 (author of state-wide sch. legislation); asst. solicitor gen. of U.S., 1933-35; asst. atty. gen. U.S., 1935; resigned to resume law practice at Raleigh, N.C. as sr. partner MacLean, Pou & Emanuel; also asso. partner MacLean & Rodman (Washington, N.C.); mem. Brewster & MacLean (Washington, D.C.); Democrat. Presbyn. Address: Raleigh, N.C. Died Sept. 1, 1937.

MacLEAN, Annie Marion, sociologist; b. P.E.I., Can.; d. Rev. John Anderson and Christina (MacDonald) MacLean; A.B., Acadia Coll., N.S., 1893, A.M., 1894; Ph.M., U. of Chicago, 1897, Ph.D., 1900; Litt.D., honoris causa, Acadia Coll., 1923; unmarried. Prof. sociology, Adelphi Coll., 1906-16; prof. sociology, Nat. Training Sch. of Y.W.C.A., New York, 1903-16; extension asst. prof. of sociology, U. of Chicago, 1903—, conducted nat. investigation of labor of women for Nat. Bd. of Y.W.C.A., 1907-09; lecturer on sociol. subjects. Baptist. Author: Wage Earning Women, 1910; Mary Ann's Malady, 1913; Women Workers and Society, 1916; Cheero, 1918; Some Problems of Reconstruction, 1921; Our Neighbors, 1922; This Way Lies Happiness, 1923; Modern Immigration, 1925. Also many mag. articles. Home: Pasadena, Calif. Died May 1, 1934.

MACLEAN, Charles Fraser, judge; b. New Hartford, N.Y.; s. Charles and Anne (Waters) M.; A.B., Yale, 1861, Ph.D., 1866; J.U.D., U. of Berlin, 1869; m. Marie Mott. Police commr., 1879-80 and 1888-94 (pres. of bd. 1889-90); park commr., 1880-83; health commr., 1889-90; justice Supreme Ct. of N.Y., 1896-1909. Democrat. Lecturer on pub. and private internat. law, Columbia, 1873-74, on principles of criminal law, New York U., 1885-97. Home: New York, N.Y. Died Mar. 20, 1924.

MacLEAN, Charles Thomas Agnew, editor; b. Ballymena, Ireland, Sept. 2, 1880; s. John H. and Elizabeth (Agnew) MacL.; brought to U.S. at age of 5; ed. Boys' High Sch., Brooklyn, N.Y.; N.Y. Law Sch., 1901-02; m. Grace Anita Thomas, Oct. 1905 (died 1918). Editorial staff New York Sun, 1896-98, New York Times, 1898-1901; gen. editorial work, Street & Smith, pubs., 1901-05; editor Popular Magazine and Smith's Magazine, 1905—; mng. editor Street & Smith Corp.; cons. editor Outline of Christianity, 1925—. Served in 1st Cav., N.G. N.Y. (then Troop C, Brooklyn), 1899-1902. Mason. Author: The Mainspring, 1912; Here's to the Day, 1914. Home: Brooklyn, N.Y. Died June 17, 1928.

MacLEAN, George Edwin, educator; b. Rockville, Conn., Aug. 31, 1850; s. Edwin W. and Julia H. (Ladd) M.; A.B., Williams, 1871, A.M., 1874, L.L.D., 1895; B.D., Yale, 1874; Ph.D., U. of Leipzig, 1883, golden jubilee diploma, 1937; U. of Berlin and Oxford, 1882; LL.D., Syracuse, 1909, U. of Wales, 1921, U. of Manchester, 1922, U. of Glasgow, 1924; Litt.D., Ia. State U., 1936; m. Clara S. Taylor, May 20, 1874 (died 1922). Ordained Congl. Council and Presbytery, New Lebanon, N.Y., Sept. 21, 1874; pastor New Lebanon, 1874-77, Memorial Presbyn. Ch., Troy, N.Y., 1877-81; prof. English lang. and lit., U. of Minn., 1883-95; chancellor U. of Neb., 1895-99; pres. State U. of Ia., 1899-1911; U.S. bur. specialist in higher edn., 1913; visiting univs. and colls. of Gt. Britain and Ireland, 1914-16; dir. for univs. and colls. in United Kingdom, U.S.A. Ednl. Commn., 1918-19; dir. British Div. Am. Univ. Union in Europe, 1919-23. Decorated Officier de l'Instruction Publique (France). Author: A Chart of English Literature, with References, 1892; Old and Middle English Reader, with Introduction, Notes and Glossary, 1893; A Decade of Development in American State Universities, 1898; The Next Stages in the Educational Development of Nebraska, 1898; Bureau of Education bull. Present Standards of Higher Education in U.S., 1913; Studies in Higher Education in England and Scotland, with Suggestions for Universities and Colleges in U.S., 1916; Similar Studies in Ireland and Wales, 1917; Opportunities for Graduate Study in Great Britain, 1921; The New International Era, 1923; History of Great Barrington, Mass., 1928; also addresses, articles and reviews. Editor: Ælfric's Anglo-Saxon Version of Alcuini Interrogations Sigewulfi Presbyteri in Genesin, 1883; An Old and Middle English Reader, by Zupitza, 1889; An Introductory Course in Old English, prepared by Prof. Wilkin and K. C. Babcock, 1888; The Spell (by Charlotte Bronte, with an introduction), 1931. Address: Washington, D.C. Died May 5, 1938.

MacLEAR, Anne Bush, author; b. Wilmington, Del.; d. Henry C. and Martha (Yates) MacLear; prep. edn. The Misses Hebb's Sch., Wilmington; B.S., Teachers Coll. (Columbia), 1901; A.M., Columbia, 1906, Ph.D., 1908. Teacher in elementary schs., 1901-05, in secondary schs., 1906-10; instr. in history, Hunter Coll., 1910-14, asst. prof., 1914-18, asso. prof., 1918-29, prof., 1929—. Republican. Presbyn. Author: Early New England Towns, 1909. Contbr. to Dictionary Am. Biography. Address: New York, N.Y. Died 1938.

MACLEISH, Andrew, dry goods mcht.; b. Glasgow, Scotland, June 28, 1838; s. Archibald and Agnes (Lindsay) M.; grad. high sch., Glasgow; came to Chicago, 1856; m. Lillias Young, 1858; m. 2d, M. Louise Little, 1880; m. 3d, Martha Hillard, 1888. Entered firm J. B. Shay & Co., 1863; entered firm Carson, Pirie, Scott & Co., and started its retail dept., 1867. Trustee U. of Chicago, Rush Medical Coll. Republican. Home: Chicago, Ill. Died Jan. 13, 1928.

MACLENNAN, Francis, opera singer; b. Bay City, Mich., Jan. 7, 1879; s. Thomas J. and Mary Louise (Marsac) M.; ed. high sch. and business coll., Bay City; studied music in N.Y. City and London, Eng.; m. Florence Easton, May 15, 1904; children—Thomas John, Vilma Mary (dec.). Began as ch. singer, Bay City; later sang in chs. in N.Y. City, and in concerts and oratorios, London; début in opera, 1902, in "Faust," Covent Garden Opera House, London; with Henry W. Savage English Grand Opera Co.; in America, 1904-06, Royal Opera, Berlin, 1906-12, Hamburg Opera, 1912-15; during same period sang guest performances in prin. cities in Germany, concerts in Belgium, 2 seasons Covent Garden, London, 3 seasons in Wagner and Strauss festivals, Edinburgh, Glasgow, Manchester; Wagnerian tenor, Chicago Opera Co., seasons 1915-16, 1916-17; toured U.S. in recitals with wife, 1918; with the Scotti Grand Opera Co., 1919-20; sang in Germany and England, 1921-25; with The American Singers in New York, 1925; sang Wagnerian rôles in England, 1926. Teacher of voice production, N.Y. City, 1931—. Home: Port Washington, L.I., N.Y. Died July 17, 1935.

MacLENNAN, Frank Pitts, newspaperman; b. Springfield, O., Mar. 1, 1855; s. Kenneth and Adelia M. (Bliss) M.; B.S., U. of Kan., 1875, M.S., 1887; m. Anna Goddard, May 29, 1890 (died 1922); 1 dau., Mary (Mrs. James A. Farrell); m. 2d, Madge Overstreet Wright, May 18, 1925. On staff, 1877-80, part owner, 1880-85, Emporia (Kan.) Daily News; prop. and editor Topeka State Journal, 1885—. Pres. Kansas Hotel Co.; v.p. Hotel Kansas Operating Co. V.p. Associated Press, 1910, 11, dir., 1919—. Pres. and one of organizers Kan. Reserve State Bank. Author: A Kansan in New York, 1918; Four Weeks with the Navy, 1924; A Tale of the Great Sea, 1925. Home: Topeka, Kan. Died Nov. 18, 1933.

MACLEOD, Frederick Joseph, judge; b. Dunstaffnage, P.E.I., Can., June 30, 1870; s. Hector and Melinda (Douglas) M.; Prince of Wales Coll., P.E.I., 1882-86; B.A., Dalhousie Coll., Halifax, N.S., 1890; A.B., Harvard, 1891, A.M., 1892, LL.B., 1899; m. Elizabeth Gwendolen Conner, June 21, 1910; children—Graham, Janet. Practiced law, Boston, 1899-1922. Mem. Mass. Senate, 1906, 07; chmn. Dem. State Com., 1909, 10; chmn. Mass. R.R. Commn., Aug. 16, 1911-July 1, 1913; chmn. Mass. Pub. Service Commn., July 1, 1913-Dec. 1, 1919; apptd. justice Superior Court of Mass., July 12, 1922. Unitarian. Mason. Home: Brookline, Mass. Died Oct. 18, 1935.

MACLEOD, John James Rickard, physiologist; b. Dunkeld, Scotland, Sept. 6, 1876; s. Rev. Robert and Jane (McWalter) M.; M.B., Ch.B., U. of Aberdeen, 1898; U. of Leipzig, 1898-99; D.P.H., U. of Cambridge, Eng., 1902; m. Mary Watson McWalter, July 1903. Prof. physiology, Western Reserve Med. Coll., Cleveland, 1903—. Lt. (with captain's certificate) in Ambulance Corps of 19th Middlesex Rifles, 1900-03. Presbyn. Fellow A.A.A.S. (v.p. Sect. K). Author: Practical Physiology (jointly), 1902; Recent Advances in Physiology (jointly), 1905; Organic Chemistry (jointly), 1907; Diabetes, Its Pathological Physiology, 1913; Fundamentals of Physiology, 1917. Home: Cleveland, O. Died Mar. 16, 1935.

MacLEOD, Malcolm James, clergyman; b. P.E.I., Can., May 24, 1865; s. Donald A. and Ann (McKenzie) M.; B.A., Dalhousie College, Halifax, N.S., 1887; M.A., Princeton, 1890; graduate Princeton Theol. Sem., 1890, McCormick Theol. Sem., 1890; D.D., Williams College, 1914, Rutgers U., 1933; S.T.D., New York U., 1936; m. Edith Norton Wilson, June 30, 1898; children—Malcolm James, Jean. Ordained Presbyn. ministry, 1890; pastor Third Ch., Chester, Pa., 1893-99; prof. N.T. Exegesis, Lincoln U., 1899-1900; pastor Pasadena, Calif., 1900-10, Collegiate Reformed Church, New York, 1910—. Pres. Clergy Club of N.Y. City. Author: Heavenly Harmonies, 1901; Earthly Discords, 1903; Culture of Simplicity, 1905; A Comfortable Faith, 1909; The Unsearchable Riches, 1911; Fragrance of Christian Ideals, 1912; Letters to Edward, 1913; What God Hath Joined Together, 1915; Songs in the Night, 1919; Revival of Wonder, 1923; When the Morning Wakens, 1926; The Challenge of the Changing, 1930; Seen from My Pulpit, 1935. Address: Bronxville, N.Y. Died Oct. 5, 1940.

MACLOSKIE, George, biologist; b. Castledawson, Ireland, Sept. 14, 1834; s. Paul and Mary (McClure) M.; A.B., Queen's U., Ireland, 1857, A.M., 1858; LL.B., U. of London, 1868, LL.D., 1871; D.Sc., Queen's U., 1887; hon. A.M., Princeton U., 1896; m. Mary C. Dunn, Aug. 18, 1863 (died 1907); 2d, Mrs. Lila M. Campbell, June 19, 1909. Ordained Presbyn. ministry, 1861; pastor Ballygoney, Ireland, 1861-72; prof. biology, 1875-1906, emeritus prof., 1906, Princeton. Author: Elementary Botany, 1887; Flora of Patagonia, 1905. Address: Princeton, N.J. Died Jan. 4, 1920.

MACMILLAN, Kerr Duncan, college pres.; b. Mt. Forest, Ont., Can., Mar. 17, 1871; s. John and Catherine (Walker) M.; Upper Can. Coll.; B.A., U. of Toronto, 1894; B.D., Princeton Theol. Sem., 1897; U. of Berlin, Germany, 1900-03; S.T.D., Hobart, 1913; m. Cornelia Chesebro Lash, June 6, 1905. Instr. O.T., 1897-1900, instr. Semitic langs., 1903-07, instr. ch. history, 1907-13, Princeton Theol. Sem.; pres. Wells Coll., Aurora, N.Y., 1913—. Presbyn. Author: Protestantism in Germany, 1917. Address: Aurora-on-Cayuga, N.Y. Died Mar. 13, 1938.

MAC MILLAN, Thomas C.; b. Stranraer, Wigtownshire, Scotland, Oct. 4, 1850; s. James H. and Susan (Cumming) M.; to U.S. with parents, 1857; grammar and high schs.; partial course at old Chicago Univ.; A.M., Ill. Coll., 1885; LL.D., Knox Coll., Ill., 1911; m. Mary C. Goudie, Jan. 24, 1883. On staff Chicago Inter Ocean, 1873-95, and editor ten ann. numbers of "Notes and Queries," pub. by that journal; clerk U.S. District Court, Northern Dist. Ill., Dec. 1895-June 30, 1919. Mem. Cook County (Ill.) Bd. Edn., 1879-82; dir. Chicago Pub. Library, 1882-87; mem. Ill. Ho. of Rep., 1885-89, Senate, 1889-93; mem. commn. which drafted Chicago Sanitary Dist. Act, and chmn. state senate com. on waterways which secured its passage; chmn. senate com. on World's Fair, which secured $800,000 appropriation from the state for the Expn.; author of first woman's school suffrage act in Illinois, passed 1891; mem. bd. mgrs. Ill. State Reformatory, Pontiac, 1897; pres. La Grange (Ill.) Sch. Bd., 1909-14; trustee Ill. Coll., Jacksonville, 15 yrs. Life member A.B.C.F.M.; moderator Ill. State Congl. Assn., 1899; pres. Ill. Congl. Home Missionary Soc., 10 yrs.; pres. Chicago Congl. Club, 1900-01; 1st pres. Am. Congl. Deaconess Assn.; chmn. 7 yrs. polit. action com. Chicago Civic Federation; pres. Cook Co. Child Saving Conf.; 1st v.p. Third Internat. Congl. Council, Edinburgh, 1908; pres. Ill. St. Andrew Soc., 1906-08; moderator Nat. Council Congl. Chs., 1907-10; mem. Chicago Charter Conv. Author: The Scots and Their Descendants in Illinois, in Trans. Ill. Hist. Soc., 1919. Home: La Grange, Ill. Died Dec. 13, 1935.

MacMONNIES, Frederick (William), sculptor; b. Brooklyn, Sept. 28, 1863; s. William and Juliana Eudora (West) M.; admitted to studio of Augustus Saint-Gaudens, 1880; worked 4 yrs. studying at night in life classes of Acad. Design and Art Students' League; completed art edn. abroad at Munich and in atelier of Falguière in École des Beaux Arts; also in private studio of Falguière; m. Mary Fairchild, Sept. 20, 1888; m. 2d, Alice, d. John P. Jones, Mar. 23, 1910. Received 1st prize, Nat. Acad. Design, 1884;

prix d'atelier, highest prize open to foreigners, Écoles des Beaux Arts, Paris, 1886, 87. Established own studio, Paris, 1887; hon. mention, 1st figure, "Diana," Paris Salon, 1889; 2d medal, Salon, 1891 (1st time conferred on an American), for statues of Nathan Hale (New York), and J. S. T. Stranahan (Brooklyn); 1st class gold medal, Antwerp, 1894; grand prize of honor, Paris Expn., 1900; medals also expns. Atlanta, Buffalo, Phila., Boston; hon. mention, Paris Salon, 1902, also hon. mention in 1903, and awarded 3d medal for painting 1904. Decorated Chevalier Legion of Honor, French Govt., 1896; Chevalier Order St. Michael of Bavaria-Munich, 1897. N.A., 1906. Mem. Am. Acad. Arts and Letters. Works: Central bronze doors and statue of Shakespeare, Congressional Library, 1898; army and navy groups for soldiers' and sailors' arch and quadriga for Brooklyn Arch, Prospect Park, Brooklyn, 1900; two groups of horses, Prospect Park, Brooklyn, 1900; equestrian statue of General Slocum, Brooklyn, 1900; equestrian statuette of Theodore Roosevelt, 1905; equestrian statue of General G. B. McClellan, Washington, 1906; 2 fountains, Knickerbocker Hotel, New York, 1906; Princeton Battle Monument, "Washington at Princeton," 1918; pioneer monument for Denver; colossal group, representing "Civic Virtue," City Hall Fountain, New York, 1919, Marne monument (colossal group, erected on the battlefield of the Marne, France), 1926; busts of Whistler, Motley, Hastings, Brisbane, Mrs. Brisbane, Frank V. Storrs; medal of Lindbergh, and distinguished visitors' medal, for N.Y. City. Decorated Comdr. Legion of Honor, French Govt., 1933. Home: New York, N.Y. Died Mar. 22, 1937.

MAC NEILL, Charles Mather, capitalist; b. Oak Park, Ill., Nov. 25, 1871; s. Joseph Edward and Mary A. R. (Amerman) Mac N.; ed. pub. schs.; m. Mrs. Marion Parsons Irwin, 1910. Began as cashier of a smelting co. in Colo., at 19; has devoted attention chiefly to ore reduction and copper developments and allied operations; an incorporator, 1904, and pres. Union Copper Co., of Salt Lake City, Utah; pres. Chino Copper Co., of Santa Rita, N.M., from its organization, 1909; pres. Bingham & Garfield R.R., of Utah; officer or dir. Ray Consolidated Copper Co., Nev. Consolidated Copper Co., Nev. Northern Ry. Co., Granite Gold Mining Co., Cresson Gold Mining Co.; dir. First Nat. Bank (Denver), First Nat. Bank (Colorado Springs), Cripple Creek Central Ry. Co., Replogle Steel Co., of N.J. Served as col. Colo. N.G., on staff of gov. of Colo., 1903, during Colo. labor troubles. Home: New York, N.Y. Died Mar. 17, 1923.

MACOMB, David Betton, rear admiral U.S.N.; b. in Fla., Feb. 27, 1827. Apptd. 3d asst. engr., U.S.N., Jan. 11, 1849; 2d asst. engr., Feb. 26, 1851; 1st asst. engr., June 26, 1856; chief engr., Sept. 21, 1860; retired list, Feb. 27, 1889; advanced to rank of rear admiral retired, June 29, 1906, for services during Civil War. Served in Civil War on spl. duty and on Canonicus; fleet engr. N. Atlantic Fleet, May 17-Dec. 16, 1871; pres. bd., Navy Yard, Portsmouth, N.H., Sept. 15, 1882-July 26, 1883. Died 1911.

MACOMB, Montgomery Meigs, brigadier gen. U.S.A.; b. Detroit, Oct. 12, 1852; s. John Navarre and Nannie (Rodgers) M.; grad. Hughes High Sch., Cincinnati, 1869; Yale, 1 yr.; apptd. cadet Sept. 1, 1870, from Ill., and grad. number 4 in class, U.S. Mil. Acad., 1874; grad. Arty. Sch., 1886; m. Mrs. Caroline Luce Walter, Oct. 7, 1908. Commd. 2d lt. 4th Arty., June 17, 1874; 1st lt. Sept. 6, 1879; capt. 7th Arty., Mar. 8, 1898; maj. Arty. Corps, Nov. 4, 1901; lt. col., Mar. 26, 1906; col. Apr. 5, 1907; assigned to 6th Field Arty., June 6, 1907; brig. gen. U.S.A., Nov. 15, 1910. Served frontier duty, Ft. Wrangel, Alaska, Jan.-June 1875; on duty in Europe, a.-d.-c. to Gen. M. C. Meigs, 1875-76; with U.S. geog. explorations west of 100th meridian (Wheeler Survey), 1876-83; at Arty. Sch. and duty with regt., 1884-87; instr. in mathematics and asst. prof. drawing, U.S. Mil. Acad., 1887-91; on special duty under Intercontinental Railway Commission in charge surveys and explorations in Central America and making report on same, 1891-96; duty with regt., Ft. Riley, Kan., 1896-98; comdg. Light Battery M, 7th Arty., in Puerto Rico, Spanish-Am. War; and in Philippines, 1900-02; mem. bd. reporting upon defense of prin. harbors of P.I., 1902; recalled to U.S. Aug., 1902, and detailed as mem. Ordnance Bd. and Bd. of Ordnance and Fortification; mem. War Dept. Gen. Staff, Aug. 15, 1903-Mar. 26, 1906, and May 23, 1908-Nov. 14, 1910; mil. attaché with Russian armies in Manchuria during Russo-Japanese War, 1904-05, and present at battles of Liaoyang, Sha River and Mukden; comdg. Arty. subpost Ft. Riley, Kan., Oct. 1, 1906-June 15, 1908; also pres. Field Arty. Examining Bd. and of bd. to determine best type of field-guns and field-works; organized 6th Regt. Field Arty. (Horse), June 1907, and commanded same to June 15, 1908; comdg. District of Hawaii, Jan. 12-Sept. 30, 1911; comdg. Dept. of Hawaii, Oct. 1, 1911-Feb. 14, 1913, and Hawaiian Dept., Feb. 15-Apr. 3, 1913, also Jan. 23-Mar. 12, 1914; comdg. 1st Hawaiian Brigade, Feb. 15, 1913-Feb. 25, 1914; mem. bd. of officers on defense of Oahu, 1912-14; pres. Army War Coll., Apr. 23, 1914-Oct. 12, 1916, and mem. Gen. Staff, June 3-Oct. 12, 1916; retired by operation of law, Oct. 12, 1916. On active duty, Oct. 30, 1917-Mar. 22, 1918; comdg. post, Fort Sill, Okla., Nov. 1, 1917-Mar. 19, 1918. Episcopalian. Home: Washington, D.C. Died Jan. 19, 1924.

MACOMBER, William, lawyer; b. Oakfield, N.Y., Nov. 4, 1857; s. William and Maritta Mary (Pratt) M.; A.B., U. of Rochester, 1885; studied law in Buffalo; passed state exam. and admitted to bar, 1887; m. Augusta Woodruff, May 18, 1887. Practiced gen. law, 1887-90, patent, copyright and trademark law, 1890—. Lecturer on law of patents, Buffalo Law Sch., 1890-1902, Cornell U. Coll. of Law and Sibley Coll., 1910—. Republican. Baptist. Author: The Fixed Law of Patents, 1910, 2d edit., 1913; Engineer's Handbook on Patents, 1913. Home: Buffalo, N.Y. Died Feb. 1920.

MACON, Robert Bruce, congressman; b. nr. Trenton, Ark., July 6, 1859; s. Robert Berton and Mary J. (Swan) M.; has always lived in Phillips County, Ark.; an orphan at 9 without resources; worked on farm and attended local schs., adding home studies; admitted to bar, 1891; mem. Ark. Ho. of Rep., 1883-87; clerk Circuit Ct., 1892-96; pros. atty., 1st Jud. Circuit, 1898-1902; mem. 58th to 62d Congresses (1903-13), 1st Ark. Dist. Democrat. Address: Helena, Ark. Died Oct. 13, 1925.

MAC QUEARY, Thomas Howard, teacher; b. nr. Charlottesville, Va., May 27, 1861; s. Thomas H. and Sarah J. (Garland) M.; grad. Episcopal Theol. Sem., Alexandria, Va., 1886; A.B., U. of Minn., 1897, A.M., 1898; grad. student history and economics, U. of Chicago, summers 1897, 1899 and session 1900-01; m. Emma Clarkson, d. Hon. John T. Harris, Jan. 14, 1892. Deacon, 1885, priest, 1886, P.E. Church; pastor Fairmont, W.Va., and Canton, O., 1887-91; tried by ecclesiastical court at Cleveland, O., Jan. 1891, for denial of miracles; suspended from P.E. ministry for 6 months; resigned, Sept. 1891, and entered Universalist ministry, but finally resigned; engaged in sociol. work; founded Unity House Social Settlement, Minneapolis, and taught in Morgan Hall Acad., Minneapolis, 1899; v.prin. Northwestern Mil. Acad., Highland Park, Ill., 1899-1900; supt. Parental Sch., Chicago, 1900-06; head assistant, Yeatman High Sch. and Soldan High Sch., St. Louis, 1906—. Chautauqua lecturer. Author: The Evolution of Man and Christianity, 1889; Topics of the Times, 1891. Address: St. Louis, Mo. Died July 1930.

MAC QUEEN, Peter, lecturer; b. Wigtonshire, Scotland, Jan. 11, 1865; s. Hugh and Janet (MacHarg) M.; came to America, 1881; student Hamilton Coll., N.Y., 1883; A.B., Princeton, 1887 (hon. A.M., 1903); grad. Union Theol. Sem., 1890. Ordained to ministry, 1890; pastor Bronxville, N.Y., 1890-93, Day St. Ch., West Somerville, Mass., 1893-1900, Harvard Ch., Charlestown, 1900-07; lecturing on travel, 1898—. Has traveled over 250,000 miles in various countries; was corr. Spanish-Am. War, 1898, Philippine campaign, 1899, S. African War, 1900; traveled in Russia on pass from the Czar, 1901; was in Battle of Marne, 1914, with Gen. Foch and 9th French Army; corr. for Leslie's Weekly with French Army, 1915; corr. Nat. Magazine and Leslie's Weekly at Peace Conf., Paris, 1919. Republican. Chaplain 5th Regt. Mass. Vol. Militia, 1905—; mem. Mil. Order of Pretoria, Hellenic Brotherhood, Spanish War Vets. (honorary). Author: Around the World with the Flag, 1889; Campaigning in the Philippines, 1900; in Wildest Africa, 1909; The New South America, 1914. Home: East Boothbay, Me. Died Jan. 11, 1924.

MAC RAE, James Cameron, jurist; b. Fayetteville, N.C., Oct. 6, 1838; s. John and Mary (Shackleford) M.; grad. Donaldson Acad., N.C., 1854; LL.D., U. of N.C., 1883; m. Fannie Hinsdale, Oct. 31, 1867. Admitted to bar and began practice, Aug. 1859; served pvt. to maj. and asst. adj. gen., C.S.A., 1861-65; resumed practice, 1865; mem. N.C. legislature, 1874-75; judge Superior Court, N.C., 1882; asso. justice Supreme Court, N.C., 1892; prof. law and dean Law Sch., U. of N.C., 1899—. Democrat. Several of his addresses have been published. Address: Chapel Hill, N.C. Died 1909.

MacRAE, William Alexander, bank mgr.; b. Stornoway, Scotland, Dec. 31, 1856; s. Charles Mackenzie and Annabella J. M.; ed. Free Ch. Sch., Stornoway; m. Janet Henshelwood, May 8, 1889. With City of Glasgow Bank, 1870-76; with London & San Francisco Bank, 1876-1905; at London until 1879, San Francisco, 1879-96, Tacoma, 1896-1900, Portland, 1900-05; mgr. Bank of California Nat. Assn., Portland branch, 1905—. Republican. Presbyn. Home: Portland, Ore. Died June 30, 1927.

MacVEAGH, Charles, diplomat, lawyer; b. West Chester, Pa., June 6, 1860; s. Wayne and Letitia Miner (Lewis) M.; A.B., Harvard, 1881; LL.B., Columbia, 1883; m. Fanny Davenport Rogers, June 15, 1887; children—Rogers, Lincoln, Ewen Cameron, Charles (dec.), Francis Wayne, Charlton. Practiced at N.Y. City, 1883—; mem. firm Bangs & Stetson and its successors, Bangs, Stetson, Tracy & MacVeagh, then Stetson, Jennings & Russell, and Davis, Polk, Wardwell, Gardiner & Reed; gen. solicitor and asst. gen. counsel U.S. Steel Corp., 1901-25; Am. ambassador to Japan, Oct. 8, 1925-Dec. 9, 1929. Vice-pres., sec., counsel and mem. exec. com. Fatherless Children of France, Inc., during World War, also pres. Immediate Relief to Italy Fund, Inc. Episcopalian. Home: Washington, D.C.; and Dublin, N.H. Died Dec. 4, 1931.

MacVEAGH, Franklin, sec. of the treasury; b. on farm in Chester County, Pa.; s. Major and Margaret (Lincoln) M.; A.B., Yale U., 1862; LL.B., Columbia U., 1864; LL.D., Yale, 1912, George Washington U., 1920; m. Emily Eames. Admitted to bar, 1864, and engaged in practice at New York, 1864-66; abandoned practice because of ill health; went to Chicago, 1866; established firm of Franklin MacVeagh & Co., wholesale grocers, of which remained the head until Mar. 1909, again pres., 1925-31; was also interested in other business, mfg. and banking enterprises. Dem. nominee for U.S. senator, 1894, and canvassed the state, but was defeated in legislature; Republican, 1896—; Sec. of Treasury in cabinet of President Taft, Mar. 5, 1909-Mar. 1913. Pres. Citizens' Assn., Chicago, 1874, in which inaugurated many important municipal reforms; pres. Chicago Bur. Charities, Municipal Art League; mem. exec. com. Nat. Civic Federation; v.p. Am. Civic Assn., 1905. Home: Chicago, Ill. Died July 6, 1934.

MAC VEAGH, (Isaac) Wayne, Attorney-Gen. of U.S.; b. nr. Phœnixville, Chester Co., Pa., Apr. 19, 1833; s. Maj. John and Margaret (Lincoln) M.; A.B., Yale, 1853; LL.D., Amherst, 1881, U. of Pa., 1897, Harvard, 1901; m. Letty Miner Lewis, May 22, 1856; m. 2d, Virginia Rolette Cameron, Dec. 27, 1866. Admitted to bar, 1856; dist. atty., Chester County, Pa., 1859-64; capt. of inf., 1862, and of cav., 1863, when invasions of Pa. were threatened; chmn. Rep. State Com. of Pa., 1863; U.S. minister to Turkey, 1870-71; mem. Pa. Constl. Conv., 1872-74; head of "MacVeagh Commn." sent to La., 1877, by President Hayes to amicably adjust disputes of contending parties there; Atty.-Gen. of U.S. in cabinet of President Garfield, 1881, but resigned on accession of President Arthur, resuming law practice at Phila. Was chmn. Civ. Service Reform Assn. of Phila., and of Indian Rights Assn. Supported Cleveland for President, 1892; ambassador to Italy, 1893-97; chief counsel of U.S. in the Venezuela arbitration before The Hague Tribunal, 1903. Address: Bryn Mawr, Pa. Died Jan. 11, 1917.

MACY, Arthur, supt. The Bradstreet Co., Boston; b. Nantucket, Mass., Feb. 25, 1842; s. Oliver and Phebe F. M.; ed. at Manchester, N.H., Nantucket, Mass., and Detroit; served in Civil War; wounded 3 times at Gettysburg and taken prisoner; m. Mary T. Winchell, June 30, 1868. Mem. Papyrus Club; one of the incorporators of the Omar Khayyam Club of America. Home: Boston, Mass. Died 1904.

MACY, Jesse, college prof.; b. Henry County, Ind., June 21, 1842; s. William and Phœbe (Hiatt) M.; A.B., Ia. (now Grinnell) Coll., 1870, A.M., 1873; LL.D., Brown U., 1898, Grinnell Coll., 1911, Oberlin Coll., 1915; m. Maude M. Little, July 25, 1872 Prin. acad. of Iowa Coll., 1871-85; acting prof. history and polit. science, 1883-85, prof. polit. science, 1885-1912, prof. emeritus, 1912, Ia. (now Grinnell) Coll. Harvard Foundation lecturer in French provincial univs., 1913. Author: Civil Government in Iowa, 1881; Institutional Beginnings in a Western State, 1883; Our Government, 1886; A Government Text-Book for Iowa Schools, 1887; The English Constitution, 1897; Political Parties in the United States, 1846-61, 1900; Party Organization and Machinery, 1904; Political Science, 3 vols. (in The Woman Citizen's Library), 1913; Comparative Free Government (with J. W. Gannaway), 1915; The Anti-Slavery Crusade, 1917. Address: Grinnell, Ia. Died Nov. 2, 1919.

MACY, John (Albert), author; b. Detroit, Mich., Apr. 10, 1877; s. Powell and Janet Foster (Patten) M.; A.B., Harvard, 1899, A.M., 1900; m. Anne Mansfield Sullivan, May 2, 1905. Instr. in English, Harvard, 1900-01; asso. editor Youth's Companion, 1901-09; sec. to mayor of Schenectady, N.Y., May-Sept. 1912; lit. editor, Boston Herald, 1913-14; literary editor The Nation, 1922-23. Author: Life of Poe (in Beacon Biographies), 1907; Guide to Reading, 1909; The Spirit of American Literature, 1913; Socialism in America, 1915; Walter James Dodd, a Biography, 1918; The Critical Game, 1922; The Story of the World's Literature, 1925; About Women, 1930; (with Blanche Colton Williams) Do You Know English Literature?, 1930. Editor: Supplementary Account in Helen Keller's Story of My Life, 1903; Between Dawn and Sunrise, by James Branch Cabell, 1930; American Writers on American Literature, 1931. Died Aug. 26, 1932.

MACY, V(alentine) Everit, capitalist; b. New York, Mar. 23, 1871; s. Josiah, Jr. and Caroline (Everit) M.; Ph.B., Coll. of Architecture, Columbia U., 1893, but never practiced profession; m. Edith W. Carpenter, Feb. 18, 1896. Dir. Title Guarantee & Trust Co., Seamans Savings Bank, etc.; trustee Provident Loan Soc. Was chmn. Ship-building Adjustment Bd. and umpire to the War Labor Bd. Trustee Met. Mus. of Art, Teachers Coll. Home: Scarborough-on-Hudson, N.Y. Died Mar. 21, 1930.

MADDEN, Martin Barnaby, congressman; b. Darlington, Eng., Mar. 20, 1855; s. John and Elizabeth (O'Neill) M.; ed. pub. sch., night sch. and business coll., beginning work at age of 10 in stone business; m. Josephine Smart, May 16, 1878; 1 dau., Mrs. Mabel Henderson. Pres. Western Stone Co.; dir. Met. Trust & Savings Bank. Pres. Quarry Owners' Assn. of U.S., 1885-89, Ill. Mfrs. Assn., 1901-02; v.p. Builders' and Traders' Exchange of Chicago, 1886-87; del. Nat. Builders' convs. 5 times. Chmn. Rep. City Com., Chicago, 1890-96; mem. Rep. County Com., 1890-1904; temporary chmn. Rep. State Conv., 1896; del. Rep. Nat. convs., 1896, 1900 (on com. on resolutions and wrote Isthmian plank, 1900); mem. Chicago City Council, 1889-97 (presiding officer, 1891-93); mem. 59th to 69th Congresses (1905-27), 1st Ill. Dist. Home: Chicago, Ill. Died Apr. 27, 1928.

MADDOX, Fletcher, lawyer; b. Washington, Dec. 23, 1860; s. Thomas Harris and Marion Elizabeth (Fletcher) M.; Germantown (Pa.) Acad., 1870-75; grad. Cheltenham (Pa.) Acad., 1878; read law, Helena, Mont., 1882-84; m. Jessie Coburn, Mar. 31, 1887; children—Coburn Fletcher, Marion Frances (Mrs. Harry S. Dulin). Admitted to bar, 1884; practiced at White Sulphur Springs, 1884-96, Great Falls, Mont., 1897-1908. Reporter Supreme Court, 1889-97; mem. Mont. Senate, 1902-06 (chmn. jud. com.); solicitor internal revenue, Dept. Justice, June 1908-13. Mem. firm Maddox & Church. Del. territorial and state Rep. convs., 1884-1910; chmn. Rep. State Central Com., 1906; speaker in state campaigns, 1902-14; Rep. nominee for Congress, 1914; dir. Speakers Bur. Rep. Nat. Hdqrs., Chicago, 1916. Mason. Home: Great Falls, Mont. Died Mar. 9, 1931.

MADDOX, Samuel T., justice Supreme Ct. of N.Y., 2d Dist. for term expiring Dec. 31, 1923. Republican. Address: Brooklyn, N.Y. Died Mar. 12, 1916.

MADDOX, William Arthur, college pres.; b. Richmond, Va., Feb. 24, 1883; s. Samuel Franklin and Rosa G. (Tayman) M.; A.B., William and Mary Coll., Williamsburg, Va., 1904, LL.D., 1926; A.M., Teachers Coll. (Columbia U.), 1911, Ph.D., 1917; m. Susie Ware Warner, Dec. 15, 1909. Asst. in philosophy and edn., Coll. of William and Mary, 1902-03; prin. grammar sch., Portsmouth, Va., 1904-06; prin. County High Sch. and Training Sch., Portsmouth, 1906-07; supt. schs., Henrico County, Va., 1907-10; prof. psychology and prin. Training Sch., State Normal Coll., Farmville, Va., 1910-13; research scholar, Columbia, 1912-13; dir. teacher training, State Normal Sch., Oswego, N.Y., 1913-16; asst. prof. edn., Teachers Coll. (Columbia), 1916-19; pres. Rockford Coll., 1919—. Pres. Fed. Ill. Colls., 1925-26. Episcopalian; mem. Bishop's Council, Chicago Diocese; senior warden, Episcopal Ch. Mason, K.P., Elk. Author: The Free School Idea in Virginia Before the Civil War, 1918; chapter, Development of Method in Twenty-five Years of American Education, 1924. Address: Rockford, Ill. Died Aug. 10, 1933.

MADEIRA, Louis Childs, coal operator; b. Phila., June 2, 1853; s. Louis Cephas and Adeline Laura (Powell) M.; B.S., U. of Pa., 1872, LL.D., 1926; m. Marion, d. E. W. Clark, Oct. 16, 1890. Civ. engr. with Wilmington & Northern R.R., 1872-74, Bound Brook R.R., 1874-77; mem. Louis C. Madeira & Sons, ins. agts., Phila., 1877—; mem. Madeira, Hill & Co., colliery properties; v.p. Madeira, Hill & Co., Standard Ice Co.; dir. Harleigh-Brookwood Coal Co., Colonial Colliery Co.; mgr. Savings Fund Soc. of Germantown. Trustee U. of Pa. Republican. Episcopalian. Home: Philadelphia, Pa. Died Oct. 31, 1930.

MADISON, Edmond H., congressman; b. Plymouth, Ill., Dec. 18, 1865; s. James W. and Frances (Doty) M.; ed. common schs.; m. Lou Vance, Dec. 12, 1900. Admitted to bar, 1888; county atty., Ford County, Kan., 1889-93; judge 31st Jud. Dist. of Kan., 1900-07; mem. 60th and 61st Congresses (1907-11), 7th Kan. Dist. Republican. Presbyn. Address: Dodge City, Kan. Died 1911.

MADISON, Lucy Foster, author; b. Kirksville, Mo., Apr. 8, 1865; d. Judge George W. and Almira (Parker) Foster; left orphan in early teens; grad. Louisiana (Mo.) High Sch., followed by spl. instruction in music, art, Latin, French; m. Winfield Scott Madison, June 11, 1890. Contbr. of short stories and serials to various publs.; Inst. and Chautauqua assembly worker in Mo., Kan. and Neb. Author: A Maid of the First Century, 1899; A Maid at King Alfred's Court, 1900; A Colonial Maid, 1902; A Daughter of the Union, 1903; In Doublet and Hose, 1904; A Maid of Salem Towne, 1906; Peggy Owen, 1908; Peggy Owen, Patriot, 1910; Peggy Owen at Yorktown, 1911; Peggy Owen and Liberty, 1912; Bee and Butterfly: A Tale of Two Cousins, 1913; Time's Follower, 1914; A Life of Joan of Arc, for young people, 1918; A Life of Lafayette, for young people, 1920; A Life of Washington; Captain Kitty—A Little Maid of Knickerbocker New York; The Story of Abraham Lincoln—an American Epic, 1927. Home: Hudson Falls, N. Y. Died Mar. 16, 1932.

MAES, Camillus Paul, bishop; b. Courtrai, Belgium, Mar. 13, 1846; grad. Coll. of Courtrai, 1864, Am. Coll., Louvain, 1868. Ordained R.C. priest, Dec. 19, 1868; came to U.S., 1869; pastor Mount Clemens, and Monroe, Mich., 1869-80; sec. Diocese of Detroit, 1880-85; consecrated bishop of Covington, Ky., Jan. 25, 1885. Mem. bd. dirs., Catholic U. of America, and Catholic Extension of U.S. of A.; permanent pres. Eucharistic Congresses. Founder of Emanuel, organ of the Eucharistic League. Author: Life of Father Nerinckx, 1880. Address: Covington, Ky. Died May 10, 1915.

MAGEE, Christopher Lyman, State senator, Pa.; propr. Pittsburgh Times, 1884—; b. Pittsburgh, Pa., Apr. 14, 1848; acad. edn.; m. Eleanor L. Gillespie. Cashier city treasurer's office, 1869-71; city treasurer, 1871-77; mem. State senate, 1896—; prominent in political circles; sec. State committee many years; del. to Republican National convs. of 1876, 1880, 1884, 1888, 1892 and 1896; one of the 306 at Chicago convention, 1880, who held out for Grant under Conkling's leadership; largely interested in banking, insurance and electrical industries. Address: Pittsburgh, Pa. Died 1901.

MAGEE, Walter Warren, congressman; b. Groveland, N.Y., May 23, 1861; s. Col. John and Mariet (Patchin) M.; A.B., Harvard, 1889; m. Sarah Genevieve, d. Brig. Gen. Palmer G. Wood, Nov. 1895. Admitted to N.Y. bar, 1891, and practiced in Syracuse. Mem. Bd. of Supervisors Onondaga County, N.Y., 1892-93; corp. counsel, Syracuse, 1904-14; mem. 64th to 69th Congresses (1915-27), 35th N.Y. Dist. Republican. Presbyterian. Home: Syracuse, N.Y. Died May 25, 1927.

MAGEE, William Addison, mayor; b. Pittsburgh, May 4, 1873; s. Edward Simpson and Elizabeth (Sees) M.; pub. and high sch. edn.; unmarried. Admitted to bar, 1895, and practiced at Pittsburgh. Mem. Common Council, 1898-1901, 1934-38; mem. Pa. Senate (to fill vacancy), 1901-04; mayor of Pittsburgh, 1909-14 and 1922-26. Republican. Appointed mem. Public Service Commn. of Pa., May 20, 1915, resigned July 15, 1917. Catholic. Address: Pittsburgh, Pa. Died Mar. 25, 1938.

MAGELSSEN, William Christian, consular service; b. Rushford, Minn., Oct. 19, 1873; s. Kristian and Sara (Stockfleth) M.; student Luther Coll., Decorah, Ia.; m. Winifred Townend, Jan. 25, 1910. Asst. city assessor Sioux Falls, S.D., 2 terms; clk. Am. Consulate, Beirut, Turkey, 1898-99; v. and dep. consul, Beirut, 1899-1905; v. and dep. consul gen., same, 1905-06; consul at Bagdad, 1906-09, Colombo, Ceylon, 1909-11, Melbourne, Australia, 1911—. Lutheran. Died Oct. 17, 1919.

MAGIE, William Jay, judge; b. Elizabeth, N.J., Dec. 9, 1832; s. Rev. David and Ann Frances (Wilson) M.; A.B., Princeton, 1852, A.M., 1855, LL.D., 1891; m. Sarah Frances Baldwin, Oct. 1, 1857; 1 son, William Francis. Admitted to bar, 1856, and practiced at Elizabeth, N.J., 1856-80; prosecutor of pleas, Union County, N.J., 1866-71; mem. N.J. Senate, 1876-78; asso. justice, 1880-97, chief justice, 1897-1900, Supreme Ct. of N.J.; chancellor of N.J., 1900-08. Republican. Trustee Princeton U. Address: Elizabeth, N.J. Died Jan. 15, 1917.

MAGILL, Edmund Charles, educator; b. Kingman, Kan., Nov. 8, 1889; s. Charles Arthur and Evangeline Constance (Ward) M.; B.S. in Horticulture, Kansas State Coll., 1912, grad. student, 1912-13; grad. student, Cornell U., summer 1919; M.S. in Agrl. Edn., Va. Poly. Inst., 1924; m. Mildred Barr, June 30, 1915; children—Walter Barr, Charles Arthur, Mildred. Teacher of agr., Wayzata, Minn., 1913-16; mng. partner Parkhead Orchard Co., Big Pool, Md., and mem. bd. dirs. Potomac Valley Fruit Growers, Cumberland, Md., 1916-18; garden specialist, agrl. extension div., Va. Poly. Inst., 1918-19; asso. prof. of agr., 1919-23, itinerant teacher trainer, 1923-24, prof. and head of dept. of agr. edn., 1924-34, prof. and head vocational edn., 1934—; mng. partner Gilbrae (orchard). Awarded Va. Planter by State Assn. Future Farmers of America. Democrat. Mason. Author of bulletins on lessons in gardening, potato growing and others on vocational edn. in agr. Home: Blacksburg, Va. Died June 20, 1940.

MAGILL, Edward Hicks, educator; b. Solebury, Pa., Sept. 24, 1825; grad. Brown U., 1852, A.M.; LL.D., Haverford Coll.; m. Sarah W. Beans, 1852 (died 1898); m. 2d, Sarah Elizabeth Gardner, 1902. Prin. classical dept., High Sch., Providence, 1852-59; sub-master Boston Pub. Latin Sch., 1859-67; foreign travel, 1867-69; prin. prep. dept., Swarthmore Coll., Pa., 1869-70; pres. Swarthmore, 1870-89; foreign study and travel, 1889-90; prof. French, 1890-1902, emeritus prof. and lecturer on French literature, Swarthmore. Author: French Grammar; Intermediate French Reader; French Prose and Poetry; Reading French Grammar; Modern French Series (4 vols.); Sixty-five Years in the Life of a Teacher, 1907. Address: Swarthmore, Pa. Died 1907.

MAGILL, Robert Edward, business man; b. Chickamauga Park, Ga., Sept. 23, 1861; s. A. N. and Jane (Wilson) M.; ed. pub. schs., Calif. and Tenn.; m. Elizabeth Lund, Dec. 22, 1890; children—Mrs. Cornelia Whittet, Mrs. Elizabeth Keesler. In mfg. business at Nashville, 1883-1903. Sec. and treas. Presbyn. Com. of Publ. (S. Presbyn. Ch.), Richmond, Va., 1903-34. Mem. World's Sunday Sch. Assn.; exec. com. International S.S. Council Religious Edn., John Milton Foundation for the Blind; commr. to the Near East for Am. Com. for Armenian and Syrian Relief. Trustee Montreat Assn., Inc. Home: Montreat, N.C. Died May 4, 1939.

MAGILL, Samuel Edward, consul; b. Erie, Pa., Feb. 18, 1861; s. William E. and Louisa (Jones) M.; A.B., Lafayette Coll., Easton, Pa., 1881; m. Julia Groves, June 30, 1887. Clerk in consulate at Cardenas, Cuba, 1881-82; engaged in coal and real estate business, Chicago, 1882-97; consul at Tampico, Mex., 1897-1907; consul-gen. at San Salvador, 1907-08; consul at Guadalajara, Mex., 1908—. Home: Chicago, Ill. Died Jan. 30, 1913.

MAGINNIS, Martin, congressman; b. Wayne County, N.Y., Oct. 27, 1841; s. Patrick and Winifred (Devine) M.; Jesuit Coll., LaSalle, Ill., and Hamline U., Minn., 1856-61; pvt. 1st Minn. Inf., Apr. 18, 1861; 2d lt., Aug. 1861; 1st lt., Sept. 1862; capt., July 1863; maj. 11th Minn. Inf., Sept. 1, 1864; engaged in all battles of Army of Potomac; twice promoted for gallantry; one of the 47 survivors of the famous charge of the 1st Minn. at Gettysburg; m. Louise E. Mann, Mar. 11, 1868. Removed to Mont., 1866; editor Helena Daily Gazette; later in mining and real estate business. Mem. 43d to 48th Congresses (1873-85); in 1890, when 2 rival legislatures each elected 2 U.S. senators, he was one of the Democratic senators, but the senate, then Republican, seated his opponent; also received votes for U.S. senator, 1899; apptd. U.S. senator by Gov. Smith, May 1900, until legislature met. Was mem. Dem. Nat. Com., 30 yrs., and del. and chmn. Mont. delegation to most of nat. convs. during that period; active in nat. campaign, 1912; pres. board mgrs. Mont. Soldiers' Home; pres. Mont. Pioneers' Assn., 1913. Address: Helena, Mont. Died Mar. 27, 1919.

MAGINNIS, Samuel Abbot, lawyer; b. Zanesville, O., Oct. 23, 1885; s. William Lyman and Letie (Abbot) M.; grad. St. Mary's (Kan.) College, 1904; m. Margaret McKenna, Apr. 29, 1914 (died 1933); children—William Lyman, Mary Elizabeth, James Stafford; m. 2d, Gwendolyn Brownlee, Aug. 12, 1936. Admitted to Utah bar, 1909, mem. firm Warner & Maginnis, Salt Lake City, 1913-15, Moore, Mitchell & Maginnis, 1916-18, Mitchell & Maginnis, 1918-19; later mem. law firm of Maginnis & Maginnis; E.E. and M.P. to Bolivia, Sept. 23, 1919-Jan. 8, 1922. Served as maj. judge advocate Utah N.G.; dir. Gen. Civilian Com., in charge Citizens' Mil. T.C., Ft. Douglas, Utah, 1916; sec., later chmn. Pub. Safety Com., Salt Lake County, 1917-18. Admitted N.Y. bar, Nov. 1923, and practiced at N.Y. City and Washington, D.C. Spl. asst. to atty. gen., Anti-Trust Div., Dept. of Justice, 1938—. Democrat. Elk (past exalted ruler). Address: Washington, D.C. Died Sept. 25, 1941.

MAGNER, John F., journalist; b. St. Louis, Oct. 18, 1855; s. Richard and Margaret (Leech) M.; grad. Coll. Christian Brothers, St. Louis, A.M., 1876; m. Julia S. Downs, Aug. 6, 1904. After graduation was prof. English and Greek, Coll. of Christian Brothers, St. Louis. Entered newspaper business, 1883; city editor St. Louis Post-Dispatch, 1885, mng. editor, 1887; dramatic editor St. Louis Globe-Democrat until Apr. 4, 1893; editor St. Louis Star, 1893—. Roman Catholic. Independent in politics. Home: St. Louis, Mo. Died 1907.

MAGNUSSON, Carl Edward, electrical engr.; b. (Magnalpha) Harris, Minn., Sept. 29, 1872; s. Sven and Christina Maria (Stendahl) M.; B.E.E., U. of Minn., 1896, M.S., 1897, E.E., 1905, scholar in physics, 1896-97; fellow U. of Wis., 1899-1900, Ph.D., 1900; studied under Dr. Steinmetz, Schenectady, N.Y., 1911-12; m. Elva Cooper, 1913; children—Philip Cooper, Edward Fenimore. Prof. physics, U. of N.M., 1901-03, N.M. Sch. of Mines, 1903-04; asso. prof., 1904-06, prof. and head of dept. elec. engring., 1906—, dean Coll. Engring., 1917-29, U. of Wash.; dir. Engring. Expt. Sta., same, 1917—. Consulting engr. Am. Nitrogen Products Co., Seattle, 1917-18; mem. Am. com. First World Power Conference, London, 1924, 3d Conference, Washington, 1936; tech. adviser Washington State Planning Council, 1934—. Democrat. Congregationalist. Fellow and life mem. American Inst. E.E. (v.p. 1920-21). Author: Alternating Currents, 1916; Electric Transients, 1926; Direct Currents, 1929; Electric Figures Formed in Magnetic Fields, 1932; Hydro-Electric Power in Washington, 1936; International Boundary Waters, 1937; Electric Power Markets, 1938. Home: Seattle, Wash. Died July 10, 1941.

MAGONE, Daniel, lawyer; b. Oswegatchie, N.Y., Jan. 26, 1829. Admitted to bar, 1853; practiced Ogdensburg, N.Y., 1859-71; mem. State Canal Commn., 1875; collector port of New York, 1886; chmn. N.Y. State Dem. Com., 1876; del. to Nat. Dem. Conv., 1876, 1884. Home: Ogdensburg, N.Y. Died 1904.

MAGONIGLE, H(arold) Van Buren, architect; b. Bergen Heights, N.J., Oct. 17, 1867; s. John Henry and Katherine Celestine (Devlin) M.; ed. pub. schs.; studied architecture in offices of Vaux & Radford,

Charles C. Haight, McKim, Mead & White, Rotch & Tilden, until 1894; gold medal, Architectural League, New York, 1889; won Rotch traveling scholarship, 1894, and traveled 1894, 95, 96; Dr. Architecture, U. of Neb., 1931; m. Edith Marion Day, 1900. Practiced in partnership to 1904, alone, 1904—. Instr. in decorative design, Cowles Art Sch., Boston, 1893-94; architect McKinley nat. memorial, Canton, O.; nat. Maine monument, New York; nat. watergate in memory of Robert Fulton; firemen's memorial, New York; Gates Av. Court House, Brooklyn; Liberty Memorial, Kansas City, Mo.; U.S. Embassy and Consulate, Tokyo; Arsenal Tech. Schs., Indianapolis, Ind.; also sculptor of colossal figures for Liberty Memorial, Kansas City, Mo., etc., and landscape architect for same and McKinley Memorial, Canton, O., etc.; also architect for many pvt. residences, clubs, schs. and other bldgs. Served as 1st lt. and batt. adj. 109th Regt., N.G.N.Y. Republican. Fellow A.I.A., also mem. New York Chapter A.I.A. (pres.); mem. Am. Federation of Arts (dir.); Nat. Sculpture Soc. (v.p. 1925-27). Awarded gold medal of honor, New York Chapter A.I.A., 1930-31, A.N.A., 1925. Author: Architectural Rendering in Wash.; The Renaissance; The Nature, Practice and History of Art; etc. Home: New York, N.Y. Died Aug. 29, 1935.

MAGOON, Charles E., governor; b. Steele County, Minn., Dec. 5, 1861; s. Henry C. and Mehitable W. (Clement) M.; ed. high sch., Owatonna, Minn., U. of Neb.; LL.D., Monmouth, 1905; unmarried. Admitted to bar, 1882, and practiced at Lincoln, Neb., 1882-99; judge advocate with rank of maj. Neb. N.G.; law officer of Bur. of Insular Affairs, War Dept., 1899-1904; gen. counsel, Isthmian Canal Commn., July 1, 1904-Apr. 1, 1905; mem. Isthmian Canal Commn., 1905-06; gov. Canal Zone, May 25, 1905-Oct. 12, 1906; E.E. and M.P. to Panama, July 7, 1905-Oct. 12, 1906; provisional gov. of Cuba, Oct. 12, 1906-Jan. 28, 1909. Republican. Congregationalist. Author: The Law of Civil Government Under Military Occupation, 1902. Home: Lincoln, Neb. Died Jan. 14, 1920.

MAGOUN, Henry A., marine engr.; b. Bath, Me., July 24, 1863; s. John W. and Harriet (Hatch) M.; student Mass. Inst. Tech., 1883; m. Amy Hawthorne, Feb. 1889; children—Katherine Hawthorne, John Warren, Priscilla, Mary Young (dec.), Harriet Hatch, Ruth Neal. Became connected with shipbuilding at Bath, Me., 1881; entered service Md. Steel Co., Sparrows Point, Md., as draftsman, 1889, and advanced to supt.; sr. v.p. New York Shipbuilding Corp., Camden, N.J., 1906-26; retired. Hon. v.p. Soc. Naval Architects and Marine Engrs. Republican. Episcopalian. Home: Bath, Me. Died Oct. 25, 1931.

MAGRATH, George Burgess, M.D.; b. Jackson, Mich., Oct. 2, 1870; s. Rev. John Thomas and Sarah Jane (Herrick) M.; A.B., Harvard, 1894, M.D., 1898, A.M., 1899; unmarried. Asst. in pathology, Harvard, 1898-1905; also pathologist Long Island Hosp., Boston, 1898-1905, and Carney Hosp., 1900-05; asst. to sec. Mass. Bd. of Health, 1905-07; asst. in hygiene, Harvard, 1905-07; med. examiner Suffolk County, Mass., 1907-35; instr. in legal medicine, Harvard, 1907-31, prof., 1931-37, emeritus; lecturer Lowell Inst., 1932—. Maj. Mass. State Guard, World War. Mem. rowing com. Olympic Games, 1932. Republican. Co-author: Studies in Variola and Vaccinia (with W. T. Councilman and others), 1903. Assisted in discovery of Cytoryctes Variolæ, 1903. Home: Boston, Mass. Died Dec. 10, 1938.

MAGRUDER, Benjamin Drake, judge; b. Jefferson County, Miss., Sept. 27, 1838; A.B., Yale, 1856, LL.D., 1906; LL.B. (valedictorian), U. of La., 1858; m. Julia M. Latham, June 1864. Practiced law, Memphis, Tenn., 1859-61, Chicago, 1861-85; master in chancery, 1868-85; asso. justice Supreme Ct. of Ill. many yrs. from 1885. Republican. Home: Chicago, Ill. Died 1910.

MAGRUDER, David Lynn, brigadier gen. U.S.A.; b. Frederick, Md., Apr. 23, 1825; s. Jonathan Wilson and Mary Galloway (Lynn) M.; ed. acad. Cumberland, Md., Coll. of St. James nr. Hagerstown, Md.; M.D., U. of Md., 1849; m. Mary Cuthbert Larkin, Oct. 15, 1863. Apptd. from Va. asst. surgeon U.S.A., Feb. 1, 1850; capt. asst. surgeon, Feb. 1, 1855; maj. surgeon, Apr. 16, 1862; lt. col. surgeon, June 30, 1882; col. surgeon, July 26, 1886; retired by operation of law, Apr. 23, 1889; advanced to rank of brig. gen. retired, by act of Apr. 23, 1904. Bvtd. lt. col., Mar. 13, 1865, "for faithful and meritorious services during the war." Served in N.M., 1850-54, Fts. Pierre, Lookout and Randall, Dak., 1854-60; in charge Infirmary Hosp., Washington, to June 1861; med. dir. Gen. McDowell's army, 1861-62 (present at battle of Bull Run); at Phila., to Feb. 1863; med. dir. Dept. of Mo., to Oct. 1893; chief med. purveyor of the West, at Louisville, 1863-66; med. dir. Dept. of the Platte, Mar.-June 1866; surgeon at various posts, 1866-73; med. dir. Dept. of Ariz., 1873-77, at St. Louis, 1877-80; med. dir. Dept. of Mo., Ft. Leavenworth, Kan., 1880-84; attending surgeon, Phila., 1884-89. Episcopalian. Home: Bryn Mawr, Pa. Died 1910.

MAGRUDER, George Lloyd, physician; b. Washington, Nov. 1, 1848; s. Thomas C. and Elizabeth O. (Morgan) M.; A.B., Gonzaga Coll., Washington, 1868; M.D., Georgetown U., 1870, A.M., 1871; m. Belle, d. Gen. W. W. Burns, U.S.A., Nov. 22, 1882. Prof. chemistry, Gonzaga Coll., 1871-73; prosector to prof. anatomy, 1870-73, for a number of yrs. prof. materia medica and therapeutics and dean, Sch. of Medicine, Georgetown U. One of the originators, Central Dispensary and Emergency Hosp., 1871, and later mem. consulting staff; also of Georgetown U. Hosp.; mem. consulting staff, Providence Hosp.; mem. bd. visitors, Govt. Hosp. for Insane over 9 yrs. Address: Washington, D.C. Died Jan. 28, 1914.

MAGRUDER, Julia, author; b. Charlottesville, Va., Sept. 14, 1854; d. Allan B. and Sarah Magruder; private edn. Author: Across the Chasm, 1885; A Magnificent Plebeian; The Princess Sonia, 1895; The Child Amy; Child Sketches from George Eliot; Labor of Love; The Violet; Dead Selves; Miss Ayr of Virginia; A Realized Ideal; A Heaven-Kissing Hill; Struan; A Beautiful Alien; A Manifest Destiny; The Thousandth Woman, 1905. Address: Washington, D.C. Died 1907.

MAGRUDER, Thomas Pickett, naval officer; b. Yazoo County, Miss., Nov. 29, 1867; s. Lawson William and Jessie M. (Kilpatrick) M.; grad. U.S. Naval Acd., 1889, Naval War Coll., Newport, R.I., 1916; m. Rose Boush, May 29, 1893; 1 dau., Adele (wife of S. O. Greig, U.S. Navy). Ensign, July 1, 1891; lt. jr. grade, Oct. 9, 1898; lt., Mar. 3, 1899; lt. comdr., July 1, 1905; comdr., July 1, 1910; capt., Aug. 6, 1915; temp. grade rear adm., Apr. 25, 1920; perm. rear adm., June 5, 1921. Was wrecked on Kearsarge, Roncador Reef, Feb. 4, 1894; served on Nashville, Spanish-American War, 1898; advanced 5 numbers "for gallantry" at Cienfuegos, Cuba, May 11, 1898; duty U.S. Naval Acad., 1905-06; navigator of Iowa, 1906-07; exec. officer Alabama, 1907-09; insp. machinery, Phila., Pa., 1909-11; duty at Naval Sta., Cavite, P.I., 1911-13; comd. Albany, 1913, Raleigh, 1913-15; in charge Div. Naval Affairs, Navy Dept., 1916-17; apptd. comdr. Squadron Four, Patrol Force, Atlantic Fleet, Aug. 1917; wrecked on Guinevere, west coast of France, Jan. 25, 1918; comd. U.S.S. Nevada, 1919; naval attaché Am. Embassy, Paris, 1920-21; special duty, 1921; comdt. 8th Naval Dist. and Naval Sta., New Orleans, La., Dec. 1921-Jan. 1, 1924; comdr. light cruisers Scouting Fleet, 1924-26; comdt. 4th Naval Dist. and Navy Yard, Phila., to Nov. 5, 1927; became comdr. Base Force of U.S. Fleet, Aug. 1929; retired from active service. Guarded Army World Flight, Scotland to Boston, 1924; rescued Italian aviator, Locatelli, near Greenland, Aug 25, 1924; comd. light cruisers on visit of U.S. Fleet to Australia, 1925. Commended for gallantry on U.S.S. Charleston, at San Francisco, Calif., May 11, 1890; presented a gold mounted sword by fellow citizens of Vicksburg, Miss., after Spanish-Am. War. Awarded D.S.M. (U.S.); Comdr. Legion of Honor (France); Commenda Mauriziana (Italy). Presbyn. Home: Greenville, Miss. Died May 26, 1938.

MAGRUDER, William Thomas, mech. engr.; b. Baltimore, Apr. 22, 1861; s. William Thomas (U.S.A., C.S.A.) and Mary Clayton (Hamilton) M.; ed. Trinity Sch., New York, St. John's Sch., Sing Sing, N.Y., Peekskill Mil. Acad.; M.E., Stevens Inst. Tech., 1881 (Priestly prize, 1880), E.D., 1921; grad. student in mathematics and chemistry, Johns Hopkins, 1886-87; m. Ellen Fall Malone, June 18, 1891; children—William Thomas, Thomas Malone. Draftsman and designer, Campbell Printing Press & Mfg. Co., Taunton, Mass., 1881-86; chief chemist B.&O. R.R., Mt. Clare, Baltimore, 1887; instr., 1887-88, adj. prof. mech. engring., 1888-96, Vanderbilt U.; chief of machinery, Tenn. Centennial Expn., 1896; prof. mech. engring., Ohio State U., 1896-1933; emeritus, 1933; also consulting mech. engr. Mem. Am. Soc. Mech. Engrs. (v.p. 1925-27), A.A.A.S. (sec. Sect. D, 1899-1900 and 1902-07), Engrs. Club of Columbus (pres. 1904-05), Ohio Soc. Mech. Engrs. (pres. 1905-07); mem. Soc. Promotion Engring. Edn. (councillor 1899-1902 and 1907-11, v.p. 1905-06, sec. 1906-07, pres. 1912-13), Am. Assn. Univ. Profs. (councillor, 1915-16). In charge of dept. of engines, U.S.A. School of Mil. Aeronautics, Columbus, 1917-18. Home: Columbus, O. Died June 21, 1935.

MAHAN, Alfred Thayer, rear admiral U.S.N.; b. West Point, N.Y., Sept. 27, 1840; s. Prof. Dennis Hart and Mary Helena (Okill) M.; grad. U.S. Naval Acad., 1859; D.C.L., Oxford, Eng., 1894; LL.D., Cambridge, Eng., 1894, Harvard U., 1895, Yale U., 1897, McGill U., 1900, Columbia U., 1900; m. Ellen Lyle Evans, June 11, 1872. Promoted to midshipman, June 9, 1859; lt., Aug. 31, 1861; lt. comdr., June 7, 1865; comdr., Nov. 20, 1872; capt., Sept. 23, 1885; retired at own request after 40 yrs.' service, Nov. 17, 1896; advanced to rank of rear admiral retired, June 29, 1906. Served on Congress, 1859-61; Pocahontas, S. Atlantic Blockading Squadron, 1861-62; Naval Acad., 1862-63; Seminole, W. Gulf Blockading Squadron, 1863-64; James Adger, S. Atlantic Squadron, 1864-65; Muscoota, Gulf squadron, 1865-66; ordnance duty, Navy Yard, Washington, 1866; Iroquois, Asiatic Squadron, 1867-69; comd. Aroostook, Asiatic Squadron, 1869; Navy Yard, New York, 1870-71; Worcester, 1871; spl. duty Navy Yard, New York, 1871; receiving-ship at New York, 1872; comd. Wasp, 1873-74; Navy Yard, Boston, 1875-76; Naval Acad., 1877-80; Navy Yard, New York, 1880-83; comd. Wachusett, 1883-85; Naval War Coll., 1885; pres. Naval War Coll., 1886-89; pres. commn. to select site for navy yard on northwest coast, 1889; spl. duty, Bur. of Navigation, 1889-92; pres. Naval War Coll., 1892-93; comd. Chicago, 1893-95; spl. duty in connection with Naval War Coll., 1895-1896; mem. Naval War Bd., during war with Spain, 1898; spl. duty, 1906. Del. to Hague Peace Conf., 1899. Pres. Am. Hist. Assn., 1902-03. Author: The Gulf and Inland Waters, 1883; Influence of Sea Power Upon History, 1890; Influence of Sea Power Upon French Revolution and Empire, 1892; Life of Admiral Farragut, 1892; Life of Nelson, 2 Vols., 1897; The Interest of the United States in Sea Power, 1897; Lessons of Spanish War, 1899; The Problem of Asia, 1900; The South African War, 1900; Types of Naval Officers, 1901; Retrospect and Prospect, 1902; Sea Power in Its Relations to the War of 1812, 1905; From Sail to Steam, 1907; Some Neglected Aspects of War, 1907; Naval Administration and Warfare, 1908; The Harvest Within, 1909; Interest of America in International Conditions, 1910; Armaments and Arbitration, 1912; Major Operations of the Navies in the War of American Independence, 1913. Address: Quogue, N.Y. Died Dec. 1, 1914.

MAHAN, Dennis Hart, commodore U.S.N.; b. West Point, N.Y., Mar. 28, 1849; s. Prof. Dennis Hart and Mary Helena (Okill) M.; student Burlington Coll., N.J.; grad. U.S. Naval Acad., 1869; m. Jeannette Katherine Murat Brodie, Nov. 24, 1875. Promoted ensign, 1870; master, 1873; lt., 1877; lt. comdr., 1898; comdr., 1901; capt., July 1, 1905; retired as commodore, July 1, 1909. Served in Philippine campaign, 1899-1900 on U.S.S. Brooklyn; at Kingston, Jamaica, during earthquake rescue, comdg. U.S.S. Indiana. Episcopalian. Returned to active duty, Apr. 1917, and assigned in charge censorship at Honolulu, T.H.; remanded to retired list, June 1, 1919. Home: Warrenton, Va. Died May 29, 1925.

MAHAN, George Addison, lawyer; b. Marion County, Mo., Aug. 6, 1851; s. George A. B. and Jennie (Griffith) M.; student Bethel Coll., Palmyra, Mo., 1868, Washington and Lee U., 1870; LL.B., Indiana U., 1872; LL.D., Culver-Stockton Coll., Canton, Mo., 1930; m. Ida Dulany, May 24, 1883 (died 1930); 1 son, Dulany. In practice of law at Hannibal, Mo., 1873—; mem. Mahan, Mahan & Fuller, 1923—; city atty., Hannibal, 1877; state's atty., Marion County, 1880-86; mem. Mo. Ho. of Rep., 1887-88; dir. Miss. Valley Trust Co. (St. Louis), Hannibal Nat. Bank, Hannibal Bridge Co., Hannibal Mutual Bldg. & Loan Co., Hannibal Connecting R.R. Co., Atlas Transportation Co. Mem. State Hist. Soc. of Mo. (pres. 1927—). Mem. Christian (Disciples) Ch. Mason. Bought the Mark Twain home at Hannibal and gave it to the City as a memorial, and erected monument to Tom Sawyer and Huck Finn as tribute to Mark Twain. Home: Hannibal, Mo. Died Dec. 16, 1936.

MAHAN, Patrick Joseph, univ. prof.; b. St. Louis, Mo., Aug. 25, 1880; s. Michael and Mary (O'Rourke) M.; A.M., St. Louis U. Sch. of Philosophy and Divinity, 1906; LL.D., Loyola, 1931. Ordained priest R.C. Ch., 1914; joined Soc. of Jesus (Jesuits), 1899; instr. St. Ignatius High Sch., Chicago, 1906-09, Loyola High Sch., Chicago, 1909-10, St. Mary's (Kan.) High Sch., 1910-11, St. Ignatius High Sch., Chicago, 1916-18; regent Loyola U. Sch. of Medicine, 1918-31; pres. Creighton U., Omaha, Neb., 1931-37; asst. prof. of philosophy, St. Louis (Mo.) U., 1937—; v.p. Catholic Hosp. Assn., 1919-26; dir. of hosps., Catholic Archdiocese of Chicago, 1919-31. Democrat. Mem. K.C. Address: Omaha, Neb. Died Aug. 6, 1938.

MAHANY, Rowland Blennerhassett, congressman; b. Buffalo, N.Y., Sept. 28, 1864; s. Kean and Catherine (Reynolds) M.; student Hobart Coll., 1882-84, Union Coll., 1887; A.B., summa cum laude, Harvard, 1888 (elected first marshal, Harvard Phi Beta Kappa, 1888, but resigned in favor of William A. Leahy, who was then chosen). Asso. editor Buffalo Express, 1888; instr. history and lit., Buffalo High Sch., 1889-90; sec. Am. Legation in Chile, 1890; E.E. and M.P. to Ecuador, 1892; candidate for Congress, 1892; returned to Ecuador and concluded Santos treaty, 1893; mem. 54th and 55th Congresses (1895-99), from the then 32d N.Y. Dist.; harbor commr. of Buffalo, 1899-1906; gen. counsel Polish Patriotic Congress of U.S., Rome and Europe, 1903; editor Buffalo Enquirer, 1910-11; U.S. commr. of conciliation, 1914-18; interdepartmental commr., 1918-19; asst. to sec. of labor, 1918-19; mem. Foreign Trades Relation Com. of Dept. of State, 1919; apptd. by President Wilson one of the ten federal umpires for the Nat. War Labor Bd., 1919; mem. bd. dirs. U.S. Housing Corp., 1919; solicitor Dept. of Labor, and acting sec. of labor, 1920-21; rep. of U.S. to Internat. Commn. on Immigration and Emigration, Geneva, Switzerland, 1921; practiced law at Washington, D.C. Del. to Democratic Nat. Conv., 1924, 28; counsel for Japanese Empire in successful adjustment of Japan's claims for War Zone shipping services to U.S., 1926. Episcopalian. Author: Tuscany and Other Poems, 1909. Home: Buffalo, N.Y. Died May 2, 1937.

MAHER, George Washington, architect; b. Mill Creek, W.Va., Dec. 25, 1864; s. Theo. Daniel and Sarah (Landis) M.; studied architecture in offices in Chicago and later in Europe; m. Elizabeth Brooks, Oct. 25, 1894. Began practice, 1888; developed a specialty in original residence and monumental work, and in shaping architecturally cities and towns. Fellow A.I.A.; pres. Ill. Chapter A.I.A., 1918 (chmn. municipal art com. and town planning com.). Chmn. Restoration Com. Fine Arts Palace, Jackson Park, Chicago. Republican. Presbyn. Home: Kenilworth, Ill. Died Sept. 12, 1926.

MAHER, James Denis, clerk Supreme Ct. U.S.; b. West Point, N.Y., Oct. 1, 1854; s. Denis and Bridget (Fennon) M.; ed. pub. and pvt. schs.; unmarried. Clk. Supreme Ct. of U.S., 1913—. Catholic. Home: Washington, D.C. Died June 3, 1921.

MAHER, Stephen John, M.D.; b. New Haven, Conn., Apr. 12, 1860; s. Michael and Johanna (Gorman) M.; St. Charles' Coll., Ellicott City, Md., 1875-81; M.D., with honors, Yale, 1887; post-grad. work in hosps., Eng. and Ireland; hon. M.A., Manhattan Coll., New York, 1895; unmarried. In gen. practice, New Haven, 1888-99; has devoted much time to study of tuberculosis in labs. and clinics, 1900—; consulting physician to St. Raphael Hosp.; mem. Bd. of Health, New Haven, 2 yrs. Mem. State Commn., apptd. by Gov. Woodruff, to investigate tuberculosis conditions in Conn., 1906; mem. board dirs. Gaylord Farm Tuberculosis Sanatorium, and mem. Tuberculosis Commn. in charge of 5 Conn. instns., 1911— (chmn. 1913—). Mem. inner council Internat. Tuberculosis Conf., 1914; pres. N.E. Conf. on Tuberculosis, 1915; pres. Conn. State Med. Soc., 1915; mem. bd. Nat. Tuberculosis Association, 1922—, Framingham Tuberculosis Expt., 1916—; official rep. U.S. Govt. at Internat. Tuberculosis Conf., Rome, 1928, Oslo, 1930, Lausanne, 1924, Amsterdam, 1932, and Lisbon, 1937. Awarded Laetare medal, U. of Notre Dame, 1932. Wrote, "Told in the Priest's House," a novelette which has been widely quoted, describing loss of life from tuberculosis in Catholic convents; and during the war "The Sister of a Certain Soldier," and a few poems and essays. Address: New Haven, Conn. Died June 6, 1939.

MAHIN, Frank Webster, retired foreign service officer; b. Muscatine, Iowa, Nov. 6, 1851; s. Jacob and Elizabeth (Hare) M.; student Ia. Wesleyan U., Mt. Pleasant, Ia., 1869-71, Harvard U. Law Sch., 1876-77; LL.B., Columbia University, 1878; m. Abbie A. Cadle, May 29, 1879; children—Anna Cadle (Mrs. Alexander R. Tweedie), Frank Cadle. Practiced law, 1878-81; editor and manager Clinton (Ia.) Daily Herald, 1881-97; postmaster, Clinton, 1890-94; trustee Ia. State Normal Sch., 1888-90; regent State U. of Ia., 1894-97; col. 1st Regt. Ia. N.G., 1891-98. Consul at Reichenberg, Bohemia (now Czechoslovakia), 1898-1902, Nottingham, Eng., 1902-10, Amsterdam, Netherlands, 1910-13; retired Dec. 1913. Engaged in lit. work, contributing to North American Review and other periodicals, until Feb. 1915; apptd. consul to Amsterdam, serving there through the World War and until July 1, 1924; retired from active foreign service; resumed lit. work. Officer Royal Order of Orange Nassau (Netherlands), 1929. Mem. English-Speaking Union, Art and Archeol. League, etc. Mason. Home: Clinton, Ia. Died May 6, 1936.

MAHIN, John Lee, advertising; b. Muscatine, Ia., Dec. 14, 1869; s. John and Anna (Lee) M.; Wayland Acad., Beaver Dam, Wis.; night sch. course, Chicago Coll. of Law, 1 yr.; m. 2d, Jean Dillard, Dec. 20, 1928. City editor and mgr. father's paper, Muscatine Journal, 1887-90; entered the adv. dept. Chicago Daily News, 1891, later adv. mgr. The Interior; pres. Mahin Advertising Co., Chicago, 1898-1916; dir.-at-large, Federal Advertising Agency, N.Y. City, 1916-25; v.p. Street Railways Advertising Co. and Barron G. Collier, Dec. 1, 1925-Jan. 1, 1929; reëngaged in advertising agency business in own name, May 1, 1929. Republican. Presbyn. Author: Mahin Advertising Data Book; Advertising—Selling the Consumer, 1916; Breaking In; Why Advertise. Has lectured before U. of Chicago, U. of Wis., Northwestern U., etc. Home: New York, N.Y. Died Nov. 9, 1930.

MAHL, William, ry. official; b. Germany, Dec. 19, 1843. Began in mech. dept. L.&N. R.R., 1860, advancing to chief clk. same dept.; auditor and purchasing agt., Louisville, Cincinnati & Lexington Ry., 1864-72; auditor, purchasing agt. and financial agt., Tex. & Pacific Ry., 1872-74; auditor Louisville, Cincinnati & Lexington Ry., 1874-80; gen. supt. same road, 1880-82; with Collis P. Huntington, 1882, until his death, 1900, as gen. agt. or asst. to pres. or controller various rys.; controller Southern Pacific Co. and proprietary cos. and Pacific Mail S.S. Co., 1891-1909; v.p. and controller same cos., 1909-13; v.p. and controller U.P. R.R. and proprietary cos., 1901-Feb. 1, 1913; also controller C.&A. R.R., K.C. Ry., 1891-1906. Retired v.p. and controller S.P.Co., Apr. 7, 1913. Home: New York, N.Y. Died May 14, 1918.

MAHON, Wilfred John, lawyer; b. Cleveland, O., Jan. 5, 1880; s. John and Mary Frances (Walsh) M.; LL.B., George Washington U., 1906; unmarried. Admitted to Ohio bar, 1906, and practiced at Cleveland until 1928; 1st asst. U.S. atty., Cleveland, 1928-29, U.S. atty., 1929—; sec. and dir. North Am. Fibre Products Co.; treas. and dir. The Dobeckmun Co. Mem. Ohio Naval Reserve, 1908-09. Mem. advisory bd. St. John's Hosp., Cleveland. Republican. Mem. K.C. Home: Lakewood, O. Died Sept. 22, 1933.

MAHONEY, Bernard Joseph, bishop; b. Albany, N.Y., July 24, 1875; s. Daniel and Honora (O'Connor) M.; A.B., Mt. St. Mary's Coll., Md., 1899, A.M., 1901; S.T.D., North Am. Coll., Rome, 1912. Ordained priest R.C. Ch., 1904; asst. pastor St. Peter's Ch., Troy, N.Y., 1904-09; spiritual dir. North American Coll., Rome, 1909-22; consecrated bishop of Sioux Falls, S.D., June 29, 1922. Home: Sioux Falls, S.D. Died Mar. 20, 1939.

MAHONEY, Caroline Smith, asso. editor Sunny South Mag. several yrs.; b. Spartanburg County, S.C.; d. Dr. Robert Marion Smith, prominent politician; ed. Reidville and Greenville Female Coll.; m. J. P. Mahoney, Atlanta, Ga. Contributor to Am. periodicals and foreign journals; mem. Soc. Am. Authors; prominent and enthusiastic club woman. Home: Atlanta, Ga. Died 1909.

MAHONEY, Edward R., editor; b. Milwaukee, Wis., July 18, 1881; s. George Richard and Katherine Allan (Coughlin) M.; ed. high sch. and Spencerian Coll., Milwaukee; student Webster Coll. of Law, Chicago, LL.B., 1920; admitted to Ill. bar, 1920; m. Blanche Ramsay Young, 1921. Reporter Milwaukee Sentinel, 1902-04; night city editor Chicago Examiner, 1904-07; asst. city editor Inter-Ocean, Chicago, 1907-10; city editor Chicago Journal, 2 yrs., Chicago American, 5 yrs.; later mng. editor Boston American, Boston Daily Advertiser and Boston Sunday Advertiser until 1929; asso. editor New York Journal, 1929-33; editor Wisconsin News, 1933; sec. Milwaukee Pub. Co.; sec. Wis. News Co. Chief of Efficiency Bur. Civil Service Commn. of Cook Co., Ill., 1911-12; comptroller Sanitary Dist. of Chicago, 1913-15; pres. Northeastern Pub. Co., Boston, 1926-27. Col. a.d.c. to comdr. in chief Wis. N.G. Democrat. Mason, Elk, Moose. Home: Whitefish Bay, Wis. Died Dec. 1, 1937.

MAHONEY, William Frank, congressman; b. Chicago, Feb. 22, 1856; pub. sch. edn.; m. Jennie A. Gleason. Mem. city council, Chicago, 2 yrs.; engaged in wholesale trade; mem. Congress, 5th Ill. dist., 1901-03, and 8th dist., 1903-05. Democrat. Home: Chicago, Ill. Died 1904.

MAHONY, Emon Ossian, lawyer; b. Eldorado, Ark., Sept. 4, 1874; s. Edmund and Mary Rosina (Klopher) M.; student U. of Ark., 1895; m. Pattie Floride Wright, Jan. 27, 1898. Admitted to Ark. bar, 1896; county judge, Union County, Ark., 1898-1903; judge 7th Chancery Dist., 1903-09; pros. atty., 13th Jud. Circuit of Ark., 1912-16; apptd. U.S. atty., Western Dist. of Ark., Sept. 30, 1917. Democrat. Baptist. Odd Fellow, K.P., Elk. Home: Eldorado, Ark. Died Aug. 28, 1920.

MAHONY, Michael Joseph, clergyman, educator; b. New Burgess, County Tipperary, Ireland, Sept. 29, 1860; s. Michael and Mary (Fennessy) M.; A.B., Royal U., Dublin, 1885; studied Mungret Coll., 1881-86, Woodstock (Md.) Coll., 1888-90, Milltown Park, Dublin, 1898-99; Ph.D., Fordham, 1919; LL.D., Marquette U., Milwaukee, Wis., 1931. Joined Soc. of Jesus (Jesuits), 1886; ordained priest R.C. Ch., 1898. Prof. Latin, Greek and English, St. Francis Xavier Coll., N.Y. City, 1890-93, St. John's Coll. (Fordham), 1893-95, 1899-1905, Holy Cross Coll., Worcester, Mass., 1905-11; prof. logic and metaphysics, St. John's Coll. (Fordham), 1911-20; prof. history of modern thought and sociology, Grad. Sch. of Fordham, 1916-20. Mem. K.C. Author: Formal Logic, 1917; Epistemology, 1923; Cartesianism, 1925; Modern Thought—The English, Irish and Scotch Schools, 1933; also various brochures and pamphlets on philos., ednl., ethical and sociol. subjects. Address: Fordham, N.Y. Died Mar. 13, 1936.

MAHOOL, John Barry, mayor; b. Phœnix, Md., Sept. 14, 1870; s. Col. James and Fannie (Hammond) M.; ed. pub. schs.; m. Mary Frame, Oct. 19, 1893; children—George F. (dec.), J. Barry. Entered grain commn. business, 1884; mem. firm Frame, Knight & Co., 1891—; v.p. Eureka (Md.) Assurance Corp., Bonded Mortgage Co. Mem. (pres., 1905-07) City Council, 1903-07; mayor of Baltimore, 1907-11; mem. Bd. of Pub. Improvement, 1921. Pres. League of Am. Municipalities, 1907-08. Home: Baltimore, Md. Died July 29, 1935.

MAILLER, William Henry, shipping mcht.; b. Cornwall, N.Y., Feb. 4, 1823; s. Coleman M.; m. Julia Frances Davis, 1846. Became clerk in Wall St. house at age of 13, attending school nights; agt. New York and Baltimore Packet Line, 1844; established in shipping and commission trade; partner, 1853, in a firm which established a line of sail vessels (afterwards steamers), from New York to Australia and New Zealand; sold the ships after Civil war began; received indemnity out of Geneva award for losses of vessels and cargoes during war; since 1844 head of Mailler & Quereau in Australia and New Zealand trade, 1844—. Home: New Brunswick, N.J. Died 1903.

MAILLY, William, editor; b. Pittsburgh, Nov. 22, 1871; s. James and Mary M.; ed. common schs., Lennoxtown, Scotland, and Liverpool, Eng.; m. Bertha Howell, May 15, 1903. Asso. editor Birmingham Labor Advocate, 1895-96; editor Nashville Journal of Labor; organizer Social Dem. Party, New York, 1898; editor Haverhill (Mass.) Social Democrat, 1899-1900; asso. editor The Worker, New York, 1901 and 1906-07; mng. editor New York Evening Call, 1908-09. State sec. United Mineworkers of Ala., 1894; del. Am. Federation of Labor, New York, 1895. One of organizers of Social Dem. (now Socialist) party at Chicago, 1898; sec. Nat. Socialist Party Conv., Indianapolis, 1901; organizer and sec. Socialist Party of Mass., 1902; Nat. sec. Socialist Party, 1903-05; mem. Nat. Exec. Com. Socialist Party, 1905-06. Address: New York, N.Y. Died Sept. 4, 1912.

MAIN, Arthur Elwin, theologian; b. Adams Centre, N.Y., Aug. 23, 1846; s. Daniel C. and Harriet R. M.; A.B., U. of Rochester, 1869, A.M., 1870; grad. Rochester Theol. Sem., 1872; D.D., Milton Coll., Wis., 1885; L.H.D., Salem Coll., W.Va., 1910; m. Lucie E. Carr, Oct. 6, 1875; children—(by first marriage) George T. (dec.), (by second marriage) Daniel Carr, George Arthur. Ordained Seventh Day Bapt. ministry, 1871; pastor Ashaway, R.I., 1871-80; corr. sec. Seventh Day Bapt. Missionary Soc. and editor missionary periodicals, 1879-93; pres. Alfred U., 1893-95; missionary southern R.I., 1895-96; pastor at Plainfield, N.J., 1896-1901; dean and prof. theology, Alfred Theol. Sem., 1901—. Founded the Helping Hand, 1885; editor Jubilee Papers, 1892. Author: Bible Studies on the Sabbath Question, 1910; The Book of Job; The New Psychology, Behaviorism, and Christian Experience, 1931. Address: Alfred, N.Y. Died Jan. 29, 1933.

MAIN, Herschel, chief engr., U.S.N., retired; b. in Ill., July 6, 1845; s. Prof. James Main; ed. Washington, 1851-57; Phillips Exeter Acad., N.H., 1858-61; grad. Naval Acad., 1866; spl. studies marine engring.; m. Charlotte A. Bradbury, June 1, 1875. Third asst. engr. U.S.N., Oct. 10, 1866; chief engr., U.S.N., Nov. 11, 1892; retired Sept. 10, 1895. Address: Washington, D.C. Died 1909.

MAIN, Hubert Platt, composer, editor; b. Ridgefield, Conn., Aug. 17, 1839; s. Sylvester and Susan (Lobdell) M.; ed. pub. schs., Ridgefield; m. O. Louise De Groff, Sept. 18, 1865. Has composed over one thousand songs, hymn tunes, and anthems, compiled and edited song collections for church, Sunday school and other devotional use, 1854—. Author: (with others) The Victory, 1870; The Coronation, 1872; Christian Songs, 1872; Temple Anthems, 1873; Winnowed Hymns, 1873; Book of Praise, 1875; Songs for Little Folks, 1875; Imperial Harmony, 1876; Glee Circle, 1879; Sterling Gems, 1880; The Alleluia, 1880, 1884, 1886; Church Praise Book, 1881; Little Pilgrim Songs, 1883; Our Treasury of Song, 1883; Hymns of Praise, 1884; Sterling Anthems, 1886; New Organ Folio, 1887; Select Songs No. 2, 1893; Harvest Gems, 1896; Gems of Song for the Sunday School, 1901; Leo Hoonani (Sandwich Islands), 1902; Devotional Songs, 1903; Songs of Alpha Phi, 1904; Hamilton College Songs, 1915; Songs of Liberty, 1919; also numerous services and carols for Thanksgiving, Christmas, Easter, etc. Asst. in the compilation of Christian Praise, a collection for church worship, by Rev. M. W. Stryker, D.D., LL.D., also in compilation of over 500 publs. of the Biglow & Main Co. One of editors of Standard Hymns and Spiritual Songs, 1917. Home: Newark, N.J. Died Oct. 27, 1925.

MAIN, John Hanson Thomas, college pres.; b. Toledo, O., Apr. 2, 1859; s. Hezekiah Best and Margaret (Costello) M., A.B., Moores Hill Coll., Ind., 1880, A.M., 1883; Ph.D., Johns Hopkins, 1892; LL.D., Oberlin, 1911, Ia. State U., 1912, Grinnell (Ia.) College, 1916, Harvard U., 1926; L.H.D., Colorado Coll., 1927; m. Emma Myers, June 18, 1881. Prof. ancient langs., Moores Hill Coll., 1880-89; asst. Greek and Latin, Woman's Coll. of Baltimore, 1890-91; sr. fellow in Greek, Johns Hopkins, 1891-92; Carter prof. Greek lang. and lit., 1892-1900, acting pres., 1900-02, dean faculty, 1902-06, pres., 1906—, Iowa (now Grinnell) Coll. Trustee Carnegie Foundation for Advancement of Teaching, 1924—. Mem. Am. Relief Commn. to the Near East. Address: Grinnell, Ia. Died Apr. 1, 1931.

MAIN, William Holloway, clergyman; b. Adams Center, N.Y., Aug. 7, 1862; s. Isaac Sheldon and Lucy A. (Holloway) M.; studied law; grad. theol. dept. Colgate U., 1887; m. Hattie A. Gramm, July 1, 1884; 1 dau., Lucy Carolyn. Ordained Bapt. ministry, 1885; pastor Waterford, Buffalo, and Syracuse, N.Y., Hartford, Conn., Memorial Ch., Phila. (2 pastorates), First Ch., Chicago; with Am. Bapt. Publication Soc.,

1922—, later exec. sec. and mem. bd. mgrs. Trustee Internat. Bapt. Sem., Orange, N.J.; Edn. Bd. of Pa. Bapt. Gen. Conv.; Pa. Bapt. Gen. Conv.; George Nugent Home (Phila.); mem. Bd. Missionary Coöperation Northern Bapt. Conv. Republican. Mason. Wrote: Our Bible, Evangelism, etc.; also writer for Sunday sch. periodicals. Lecturer on popular and religious subjects. Home: Wyncote, Pa. Died Jan. 4, 1933.

MAINS, George Preston, publishing agt.; b. Newport, N.Y., Aug. 7, 1844; s. William D. P. and Charlotte (Brown) M.; served in U.S.N., 1864-65, in N. Atlantic Squadron under Admiral Porter; A.B., Wesleyan U., Conn., 1870, A.M., 1873, D.D., 1889, LL.D., 1914; studied theology, New York; D.D., Syracuse U., 1889; m. Mary A. Curtiss, Aug. 4, 1870 (died 1907) children—William Curtiss (dec.), Jessie May (wife of Dr. A. E. Strong), George Preston (dec.), Mary Pearl (Mrs. Clarence L. Howland); m. 2d, Mary K. Calder, Dec. 9, 1909 (died 1923). Ordained Methodist Episcopal ministry, 1870; pastor Ansonia, Conn., 1871-72, West Chapel St. Ch., New Haven, Conn., 1873-75, New Britain, Conn., 1876-78, Bristol, 1879, Grace Ch., Brooklyn, 1880-82, First Ch., Waterbury, Conn., 1883; presiding elder, New York East Dist., 1884; pastor Brooklyn, 1885-91; supt. Brooklyn Ch. Soc., 1892-95; pastor Mt. Vernon, N.Y., 1896; pub. agt. M.E. Ch., 1896-1916, retired. Sec. N.Y. East Conf., 8 yrs., 1889-97; del. Gen. confs., 7 times; mem. bd. mgrs. M.E. Missionary Soc., 1896—; treas. Episcopal Fund, 1896—; pres. New York Wesleyan Club, 1890-91, New York Preachers' Meeting, 1890-91. Mem. bd. mgrs. M.E. Hosp., Brooklyn; trustee Syracuse U. and N.Y. East Conf. Author: Life of Francis Asbury, 1909; Modern Thought and Traditional Faith, 1911; Some Moral Reasons for Belief in the Godhood of Jesus Christ, 1912; Christianity and the New Age, 1914; Divine Inspiration, 1915; Religious Experience; Life of James Monroe Buckley, 1917; Premillennialism, 1919; United States Citizenship, 1921; Life's Westward Windows, 1925; Science, Christianity and Youth, 1926; Mental Phases in a Spiritual Biography, 1928; Occasional Musings, 1928. Home: Altadena, Calif. Died Sept. 6, 1930.

MAISCH, Henry Charles Christian, chemist; b. Brooklyn, Sept. 29, 1862; s. Prof. John M. and Charlotte J. M.; ed. private and public schools of Phila., leaving high school, 1881; grad. Phila. Coll. of Pharmacy, 1885; studied chemistry and botany, U. of Göttingen, Ph.D., 1889; m. Sarah A. P. H. C. Elwert, Dec. 31, 1889. Assisted Prof. A. Michael, 1889-90 in chem. research in Worcester, Mass.; lectured on botany and materia medica at Chicago Coll. of Pharmcy, 1890-91, and in Medico Chirurg. Coll., dept. pharmacy, Phila., 1898-1900; chemist to Stetson Laboratory of Hygiene, 1895-97; chemist of analytical dept., Hance Bros. & White, mfg. pharmacists, Phila., 1899—. Author: Maisch's Manual of Materia Medica, 1895; materia medica portion of the National Dispensatory, 1894. Address: Philadelphia, Pa. Died 1901.

MAJOR, Charles, see Edwin Caskoden.

MAJOR, David R., psychologist; b. Frankport, Ind., Mar. 26, 1866; s. Thomas and Almeda (Allen) M.; B.S., Wabash Coll., 1890; Ph.D., Cornell U., 1896; diploma in edn., Columbia U., 1899; LL.B., Indiana Law School, 1916; m. Mary Randolph Campbell, Jan. 8, 1901. Supt. and prin. pub. schs., 1890-98; prof. pedagogy, U. of Neb., 1899-1900, Teachers Coll. (Columbia U., 1900-01; prof. psychology edn., Ohio State U., 1901-14. Practicing law. Author: Teleology in the Critical Philosophy of Kant, 1897; First Steps in Mental Growth, 1906; The Elements of Psychology, 1913. Home: Columbus, O. Deceased.

MAJOR, Samuel C., congressman; b. Fayette, Mo., July 2, 1869; ed. Central Coll., Fayette, and St. James Mil. Acad., Macon, Mo.; m. Elizabeth M. Simpson, Dec. 17, 1895. Admitted to Mo. bar, 1890; served as pros. atty. Howard County; mem. Mo. Senate, 1907-11; mem. 66th Congress (1919-21), also 68th to 70th Congresses (1923-29), 7th Mo. District. Democrat. Home: Fayette, Mo. Died July 28, 1931.

MAKINSON, George Albert, consular service; b. San Francisco, Calif., Mar. 18, 1887; s. George Henry and Mary (Saul) M.; grad. Lowell High Sch., San Francisco; studied under pvt. tutors in Europe, 1908-14; m. Mary Taft Atwater, Mar. 29, 1921; children—Robert Taft, Mary Snowden. Machinist's apprentice 3 yrs.; salesman, asst. foreman machinist, Bur. of Navigation, Manila, P.I., 1907; asst. sec. Am. Assn. Commerce and Trade, Berlin, Germany, 1908-09; apptd. consular agt., at Sorau, Germany, Dec. 23, 1909; dep. consul, Tampico, Mexico, 1914-15; vice consul, 1915-16; consular agt. Amapalpa, 1916; consular asst., 1916; consular agt. Santa Fe, Isle of Pines, 1918, Nueva Gerona, 1918, Cardenas, 1918-19; vice consul Santo Domingo, 1919-22; consul at Valparaiso, Chile, 1922-25; consul in charge of Consulate Gen., at Callao-Lima, Peru, 1925-30; in charge of consulate, Birmingham, Eng., 1930—. Mem. Calif. Naval Militia, 1903-06. Conglist. Home: San Anselmo, Calif. Deceased.

MAKUEN, G(eorge) Hudson, laryngologist; b. Goshen, N.Y., July 16, 1855; s. George and Ellen G.

(Magennis) M.; A.B., Yale, 1884; M.D., Jefferson Med. Coll., Phila., 1889; m. Nancy Baker Dyer, Dec. 20, 1900. Instr., Centenary Collegiate Inst., N.J., 1879-80, Nat. Sch. Elocution and Oratory, 1884-86, Jefferson Med. Coll., 1889-92; prof. defects in speech, Phila. Polyclinic, 1896—; laryngologist and otologist to Chester Hosp. Fellow Am. Acad. Medicine (pres. 1900-01), Am. Laryngol. Assn. (pres. 1915), Am. Laryngol., Rhinol. and Otol. Soc. (pres. 1912); mem. A.M.A. (pres. sect. laryngology and otology, 1902-03). Home: Newfield, N.J. Died Feb. 21, 1917.

MALBY, George R., congressman; b. Canton, N.Y., Sept. 16, 1857; M.S., St. Lawrence U.; married, 1883. Admitted to bar, and practiced at Ogdensburg, N.Y.; sr. mem. firm Malby & Lucey. Mem. N.Y. Assembly, 1890-95 (speaker, 1894), Senate, 1895-1907; mem. 60th to 62d Congresses (1907-13), 26th N.Y. Dist. Republican. Address: Ogdensburg, N.Y. Died July 6, 1912.

MALCOLMSON, Charles Tousley, mech. engr.; b. St. Thomas, Ont., Can., 1874; s. Henry Chalmers and L. V. (Tousley) M.; B.S., Armour Inst. Tech., Chicago, 1897, E.E., 1901; m. Margaret Ewing Wilkinson, 1905. Engr., Anaconda Copper Mining Co., 1897-99; chief engr., U.S. Commn., Paris Expn., 1899-1901; chief engr., S.C. Inst. and West Indian Expn., 1901-02; supt. machinery, St. Louis Expn., 1902-03; gen. supt. Lanyon Zinc Co., 1903-05; engr. in charge U.S. Testing Plant, 1905-08; briquetting engr. R.I. Coal Co., 1908-09, Roberts & Schaefer Co., 1909-12; pres. Malcolmson Engineering and Machine Corp., 1912—. Home: Chicago, Ill. Died Jan. 10, 1922.

MALCOLMSON, James W(addell), consulting engr.; b. Dover, Kent, Eng., Oct. 9, 1866; s. James and Cherrie (Mercer) M.; student Inst. Civ. Engrs., 1886-91; grad. Royal Coll. Science, London, 1889; m. Katherine Haden Krause, Dec. 22, 1888. Asst. mining and mech. engr., Michoacan Ry. & Mining Co., Mexico, 1893; mining engr., Consolidated Kansas City Smelting & Refining Co., 1893-98; mgr. mining dept. Am. Smelting & Refining Co., 1898-1902; gen. consulting practice, 1902—. Democrat. Presbyn. Dir. Am. Mining Congress, 1906. Home: Kansas City, Mo. Died Dec. 26, 1917.

MALKIEL, Leon Andrew, lawyer; b. Moscow, Russia, Aug. 1, 1866; s. Andrew and Elizabeth M.; classical edn. at 5th and 6th gymnasiums at Moscow and gymnasium of Tiflis (Asia Minor), Russia; came to U.S., 1881; in real estate business, 1888-96; LL.B., New York U., 1896; m. Theresa Serber, July 7, 1900; 1 dau., Henrietta. Admitted to bar, 1898, and practiced at New York. Mem. Nat. Exec. Com. and recording sec. Socialist Labor party, 1896-1900; left the Socialist Labor party, 1900, and joined the Social Dem. party; mem. of city exec. com. 2 yrs.; nominated for Justice Supreme Court of N.Y., 1903 and 1906, for atty. gen., 1904; del. state conv., 1904; mem. State Com., 1906-07; sec. Co. Com. Westchester Co. Socialist party, 1907-09; candidate for dist. atty. N.Y. Co., 1917; candidate for asso. justice Court of Appeals, 1920. Dir. N.Y. Call. Home: New York, N.Y. Deceased.

MALL, Franklin Paine, anatomist; b. Belle Plaine, Ia., Sept. 28, 1862; s. Francis and Louise (Miller) M.; prep. edn. pub. and pvt. schs.; M.D., U. of Mich., 1883; student Heidelberg, Leipzig and Johns Hopkins; hon. A.M., U. of Mich., 1900; LL.D., U. of Wis., 1904; Sc.D., U. of Mich., 1908; LL.D., Washington U., St. Louis, 1915; m. Mabel Stanley Glover, Mar. 28, 1895. Fellow, 1886-88, instr. pathology, 1888-89, Johns Hopkins; adj. prof. vertebrate anatomy, Clark U., 1889-92; prof. anatomy, U. of Chicago, 1892-93; prof. anatomy, Johns Hopkins U., 1893—. Dir. dept. of embryology, Carnegie Instn. of Washington, 1915. Mem. Commn. for Neurol. Research of Internat. Assn. of Acads., 1903—; mem. Soc. Am. Naturalists (v.p. 1900, chmn. 1904); pres. Assn. Am. Anatomists, 1905-07; mem. Institute International d'Embryologie. Trustee of Marine Biol. Lab., Woods Hole, Mass. Author: Causes Underlying the Origin of Human Monsters; On the Fate of the Human Ovum in Tubal Pregnancy. Joint editor of Handbuch der Entwicklungsgeschichte des Menschen; co-editor and one of founders Am. Journal of Anatomy, and the Anatomical Record; asso. editor Journal of Morphology; editor Studies from the Anatomical Laboratory of Johns Hopkins U. Address: Baltimore, Md. Died Nov. 17, 1917.

MALLALIEU, Willard Francis, bishop; b. Sutton, Mass., Dec. 11, 1828; s. John and Lydia (Emerson) M.; A.B., Wesleyan U., Conn., 1857, A.M., 1860; D.D., E. Tenn. Wesleyan U., 1874; LL.D., New Orleans U., 1891; m. Eliza Frances Atkins, Oct. 13, 1858. Entered N.E. Conf., M.E. Ch., 1858; pastor Grafton, Mass., 1858-59, Mt. Bellingham, Chelsea, 1860-61; First Ch. Lynn, 1862-63; Monument Sq., Charleston, 1864, Bromfield St., Boston, 1865-67, Walnut St., Chelsea, 1868-70, Trinity, Worcester, 1871, Broadway, South Boston, 1872-74; trip to Europe for study and observation, 1875; pastor Bromfield St., Boston, 1876-78; Walnut St., Chelsea, 1879-81; presiding elder Boston Dist., 1882-84; elected bishop, 1884. Del. Gen. Conf., 1872, 1880, 1884; pres. and chmn. exec. com. of Gen. Conf. Commn. on Aggressive Evangelism; v.p. Bd. Foreign Missions;

mem. Bd. Home Missions; pres. Mass. Anti-Saloon League; chmn. bd. dirs. Mass. Total Abstinence Soc., dir. Twentieth Century Pledge Signing Crusade, N.E. Sabbath Protection League; v.p. Prevention of Cruelty to Animals. Trustee Boston U., Wesleyan Acad., Wilbraham, Mass., E. Greenwich (R.I.) Acad. (pres. bd.), Am. U., New Orleans U. Pres. Boston Bible Club; trustee Mass. Bible Soc.; v.p. N.E. Meth. Hist. Soc.; life mem. N.E. Hist.-Geneal. Soc.; dir. Boston Evang. Alliance. Author: The Why, When and How of Revivals, 1901; The Fullness of the Blessing of the Gospel of Christ, 1903; Words of Cheer and Comfort. Address: Auburndale, Mass. Died 1911.

MALLARY, R(aymond) De Witt, clergyman; b. Fulton, N.Y., Sept. 28, 1851; s. Lyman and Theresa (French) M.; A.B., Amherst Coll., 1872, A.M., 1875; studied law 1 yr.; grad. Union Theol. Sem., 1876; D.D., Howard U., Washington, 1895; m. Alice M. Davis, 1879 (died 1881); m. 2d, Lucy Adam Walker, 1883. Ordained Congl. ministry, 1876; pastor, Williamsport, Pa., 1876-78, Detroit, Mich., 1878-79, Lenox, Mass., 1880-89; in literary and ednl. work at Lenox, 1889-1900; pastor, Housatonic, 1900-08; pres. Am. Internat. Coll., July 15, 1908—. Author: Lenox and the Berkshire Highlands, 1902. Composer of a number of ch. hymns. Address: Springfield, Mass. Deceased.

MALLET, John William, chemist; b. Dublin, Ireland, Oct. 10, 1832; s. Robert and Cordelia (Watson) M.; A.B., Trinity Coll., Dublin, 1853; Ph.D., U. of Göttingen, 1852; M.D., U. of La., 1868; LL.D., Coll. of William and Mary, 1872, U. of Miss., 1872, Princeton, 1896, Johns Hopkins, 1902, U. of Pa., 1906; came to U.S., 1853, but is a British subject; m. Mary E., d. Judge John J. Ormond, of Ala., 1857; m. 2d, Mrs. Josephine Burthe, of La., 1888. Asst. prof. analytical chemistry, Amherst, 1854; chemist to geol. survey, Ala., 1855-56; prof. chemistry, U. of Ala., 1855-60; officer on staff Gen. Rodes, C.S.A., 1861; transferred to arty., 1862, and placed in general charge of ordnance laboratories of Confed. States; paroled as lt. col. arty., 1865; prof. chemistry, med. dept., U. of La., 1865-68; prof. analytical, industrial and agrl. chemistry, 1868-72, gen. and industrial chemistry, 1872-83 and 1885-1908, emeritus prof. chemistry, 1908, U. of Va. Lecturer, Johns Hopkins, 1877-78; prof. chemistry and physics and chmn. faculty, U. of Tex., 1883-84; prof. chemistry, Jefferson Med. Coll., Phila., 1884-85; mem. U.S. Assay Commn. 3 times. Mem. Am. Chem. Soc. (pres. 1882). Address: University, Va. Died Nov. 6, 1912.

MALLETT, Wilbert Grant, educator; b. Topsham, Me., Apr. 10, 1867; s. Isaac Emery and Mary (Purington) M.; A.B., Bowdoin, 1891, hon. A.M., 1921; m. Ella Longfellow, Nov. 29, 1893; children—Ann Burpee, Emery Longfellow, Richard Purington. With State Normal Sch., Farmington, Me., 1891—, prin., 1909—. Pres. Franklin County Savings Bank. Republican. Conglist. Home: Farmington, Me. Died Jan. 12, 1942.

MALLINCKRODT, Edward, mfr.; b. St. Louis, Jan. 21, 1845; s. Emil and Eleanore Didier (Luckie) M.; ed. pub. and pvt. schs., and chem. edn. in Germany; m. Jennie, d. Charles R. Anderson, June 7, 1876. Began, 1867, as mem. firm of G. Mallinckrodt & Co., mfrs. of chemicals, which was succeeded by Mallinckrodt Chem. Works, Inc., 1882, with works at St. Louis and Jersey City, N.J., pres., 1882— Organizer, 1889, and pres. Nat. Ammonia Co., St. Louis; dir. 1st Nat. Bank, St. Louis Union Trust Co. Dir. Washington U., etc. Republican. Home: St. Louis, Mo. Died Feb. 1, 1928.

MALLOCH, Douglas, author; b. Muskegon, Mich., May 5, 1877; s. Charles Frederick and Sarah Elizabeth (Baum) M.; common sch. edn.; m. Bertha Keillor, May 5, 1898; children—Dorothy May (Mrs. Vilas Matheson Swan), Douglas Keillor (dec.), Donald Herbert, Amy Jean. Reporter Muskegon Daily Chronicle, 1886-1903; mem. editorial staff American Lumberman, 1903—; asso. editor, 1910—. Republican. Pres. Press Club, Chicago, 1912-13; master Writers Guild, Chicago, 1917-18; pres. Soc. Midland Authors, 1927-29. Author: In Forest Land, 1906; Resawed Fables, 1911; The Woods, 1913; The Enchanted Garden, 1915; Toteroad and Trail, 1917; Come on Home, 1923; Little Hop-Skipper, 1926; Be the Best of Whatever You Are, 1926; The Heart Content, 1927. Home: Chicago, Ill. Died July 2, 1938.

MALLORY, Clifford Day, shipping; b. Brooklyn, N.Y., May 26, 1881; s. Henry Rogers and Cora (Pynchon) M.; student Lawrenceville (N.J.) Sch., 1896-1900; m. Rebecca Sealy, Jan. 3, 1911; children—Margaret Pynchon, Clifford Day, Barbara. Began as clk., C. H. Mallory & Co., 1900; sec. Mallory S.S. Co., 1907-13; v.p. same and Clyde S.S. Co., 1913-17; asst. dir. operation U.S. Shipping Bd., 1917-19; pres. C.D. Mallory & Co., shipping, 1919—; pres. Malston Co., Mallory Transport Lines, Lehigh & Lackawanna Corp., Ardmore Steamship Co., Inc., C. D. Mallory Corp.-Seminole S.S. Corp.; pres. and dir. C. D. Mallory Brokerage, Inc.; v.p. and dir. Imperial Lifeboat Equipment Corp.; dir. The Putnam Trust Co., Hasler & Co., Inc., Vamar Steamship Co., Inc., Seatrain Lines, Inc., Am. Protection & Indemnity Assn., Inc., Waterways Operating Co., Inc., P. R. Mallory Co. Dir.

Navy League of U.S.; trustee Webb Inst. Naval Architecture. Republican. Presbyn. Home: Greenwich, Conn. Died Apr. 7, 1941.

MALLORY, Hugh, lawyer; b. Dallas County, Ala., Oct. 30, 1874; s. Hugh S. D. and Jacqueline Louisa (Moore) M.; A.B., U. of Ala., 1895; LL.B., Cumberland U., Lebanon, Tenn., 1897; m. Claude Howze Melvin, Nov. 19, 1902; children—Hugh, Martha Melvin. Admitted to Ala. bar, 1897, and began practice at Selma; mem. firm Mallory & Mallory, 1897-1933. Trustee Selma Pub. Sch. System, Ala. Bapt. Hosp. (hon.), Judson Coll. (pres. bd.). Baptist. Mason. Home: Selma, Ala. Died Nov. 1, 1937.

MALLORY, Hugh Shepherd Darby, lawyer; b. Talladega County, Ala., Feb. 6, 1848; s. James and Ann Maria (Darby) M.; A.B., U. of Ala., 1865; LL.B., U. of Va., 1868; LL.D., Howard Coll., 1911; m. Jacqueline Louisa Moore, Oct. 15, 1872. In practice at Selma, Ala., 1869—; sr. mem. Mallory & Mallory, Mayor of Selma, 1886-88; mem. Sch. Bd.; mem. Dem. State Exec. Com. (chmn. 4 yrs.). Pres. Ala. Bapt. State Conv.; v.p. Southern Bapt. Conv.; pres. Interdenominational State S.S. Conv. of Ala.; pres. trustees Dallas Acad., Selma; trustee Ala. Girls' Tech. Inst., Louisville (Ky.) Theol. Sem., Bapt. Theol. Sem. Pres. Bar of Dallas Co., State Bar Assn. Ala. Past Grand Master of Masons Ala.; Past Grand Dictator Knights of Honor Ala. (Past Supreme Rep.). Home: Selma, Ala. Deceased.

MALLORY, Stephen Russell, U.S. senator, Fla., 1897-1909; b. Fla., Nov. 2, 1848; s. Stephen R. M., U.S. senator from Fla., 1851-61; entered C.S.A., fall of 1864; entered C.S.N., as midshipman, spring of 1865; grad. Georgetown Coll., D.C., 1869; taught a class there until July, 1871; admitted to bar, 1873; removed to Pensacola, 1874, and began law practice. Mem. State legislature, 1876; State senator, 1881-89; mem. Congress, 1891-95. Democrat. Home: Pensasola, Fla. Died 1907.

MALM, Gustav Nathanael, author; b. Jönköpings Län, Sweden, Jan. 20, 1869; s. Rev. Per August and Mathilda (Petterson) M.; ed. Elementary Coll. of Jönköping, to 1884; came to America, 1889; studied landscape, figure and water color painting at Bethany Coll., Kan., 1894-96; m. Mathilda Wredberg, Jan. 3, 1893; children—Viola Gertrude, Alba Margarete, Amrah Augusta. Mem. firm of Malm Bros. & Co., decorators, Lindsborg; mural decorations of firm in many chs. and pub. bldg. of Kan.; designer interior decoration with Acme White Lead & Color Works, Detroit, Mich. Lutheran. Recording sec. and historian Bethany Oratorio Soc., Lindsborg, 1897—. Author: Charley Johnson (a study of the Swedish immigrant), 1909; Härute (a play), 1919. Home: Lindsborg, Kan. Died Feb. 12, 1928.

MALONE, Dana, lawyer; b. Arcade, N.Y., Oct. 8, 1857; s. James C. and Mary E. M.; pub. sch. edn., student Harvard Law Sch.; m. Margaret Bradford Robbins, Dec. 15, 1908. Admitted to bar, 1881; trial justice Franklin County, Mass., 1890-96; mem. Mass. Ho. of Rep., 1893, 1894 (chmn. Judiciary Com.), Senate, 1895, 1896 (chmn. Judiciary Com.); mem. Rep. State Com., 1897-1905; dist. atty. Northwestern Dist. of Mass., 1902-05; atty. gen. of Mass., 1906, 07, 08, 09, 10. Resumed practice. Jan. 1911. Home: Boston, Mass. Died Aug. 13, 1917.

MALONE, J. Walter, clergyman; b. Clermont County, O., Aug. 11, 1857; s. John C. and Mary Ann (Pennington) M.; student Earlham (Ind.) Coll.; grad. Chickering Inst., Cincinnati, O., 1877; m. Emma Brown, Jan. 18, 1886; children—Carroll B., J. Walter, Mrs. Esther M. Waterbury, Mrs. Ruth M. Osborne, Mrs. Margaret M. Crobaugh, Franklin P. Founder, and pastor 25 yrs. (emeritus) First Friends Ch., Cleveland; organized 4 other chs. in Cleveland and vicinity; founder, and pres. 25 yrs. Cleveland Bible Inst. now pres. bd. trustees and chmn. exec. com. Supt. of Ohio yearly meeting of Friends Ch. 12 yrs. Author: Gospel in Jonah, 1900; The Christian Sabbath, 1904; also corr. course on New Testament (12 books), 1922. Home: Cleveland, O. Died Dec. 30, 1935.

MALONE, James Thomas, judge; b. Norwich, Conn., Jan. 9, 1865; s. James and Beatrice (Donnelly) M.; grad. Phillips Exeter Acad., N.H., 1885; A.B., Harvard, 1889; Harvard Law Sch., 1890; LL.D., Villanova Coll., 1910; m. Mary Frances Reilly, Sept. 4, 1895. Admitted to N.Y. bar, 1891; practiced in New York, 1891-1908; asst. corp. counsel, City of New York, 1894-1908; judge Ct. of Gen. Sessions, N.Y., term 1908-22. Democrat. Catholic. Address: New York, N.Y. Died Dec. 1, 1920.

MALONE, John Wesley, teacher, clergyman; b. Atlanta, Ga., July 10, 1856; s. Jeremiah Dumas and Mary (Hale) M.; A.M., Hiwassee Coll., Madisonville, Tenn., 1881, D.D., 1901; studied Vanderbilt U., 1883-84; m. Lillian Kemp, June 15, 1887; children—Raiford Kemp, Dumas Hale, John Wesley (dec.), Miles Sturdivant, Lillian, Mary Elizabeth, Sara Heath (Mrs. Rogers Post Sharp), Virginia. College pres. 27 yrs. to 1925; reëstablished Grenda (Miss.) Coll., 1889-94, with Andrew Coll., Cuthbert, Ga., 1906-18, Centenary Coll., Cleveland, 1918-25, retiring as pres. Pastor M.E. Ch. S., Brunswick, Ga., 1902-06; pastor Rural Retreat, Va. Trustee Millsaps Coll., Grenada Coll., Centenary Coll. Home: Rural Retreat, Va, Died Aug. 17, 1930.

MALONE, Richard Harwell, business man; b. La Grange, Tenn., Mar. 23, 1857; s. Richard Henry and Mary (Cossitt) M.; ed. Denver High Sch., 1873-75; Beloit (Wis.) Coll., 1875-76; m. 2d, May Thomson, Apr. 6, 1910. With F. W. Crocker & Co., Denver, 1876-90; mem. Am. Biscuit & Mfg. Co., 1890-98, Nat. Biscuit Co., 1898-1901; dir. Federal Reserve Bank, Kansas City, 1914-22; in real estate business on own account. Rep. of U.S. Govt. on securities com. for $1,000,000 to move crops, 1913. Pres. Denver Chamber Commerce, 1902. Active mem. in Colo. of The Order of De Molay. Democrat. Presbyn. Mason. Home: Denver, Colo. Died Feb. 18, 1937.

MALONE, Thomas Henry, lawyer; b. Nashville, Tenn., Mar. 7, 1872; s. Thomas Henry and Ellen (Fall) M.; prep. edn., Montgomery Bell Acad., Nashville; A.B., Vanderbilt, 1892, A.M., 1893, LL.B., 1896; grad. study, U. of Berlin, 1893; m. Mary Cornelia Gibson, Jan. 26, 1916; 1 son, Thomas Henry III. Admitted to Tenn. bar, 1896, and practiced at Nashville; spl. judge, Supreme Court, Tenn., 1917, 23; prof. equity jurisprudence, Vanderbilt, 1923—. Pres. Tenn. State Bar Assn., 1923, Nashville Bar Assn., 1929. Democrat. Episcopalian. One of counsel for defense in Scopes fundamentalist trial, Tenn., 1925. Home: Nashville, Tenn. Died Mar. 1941.

MALONE, Walter, judge, author; b. De Soto County, Miss., Feb. 10, 1866; s. Franklin Jefferson and Mary Louisa M.; Ph.B., U. of Miss., 1887; unmarried. Practiced law, Memphis, Tenn., 1887-97; in lit. pursuits, New York, 1897-1900, resumed law practice, Memphis; judge 2d Circuit Ct., Shelby County, Tenn., 1905—. Author: Claribel, and Other Poems, 1882; The Outcast, and Other Poems, 1885; Narcissus, and Other Poems, 1892; Songs of Dusk and Dawn, 1894; Songs of December and June 1896; The Coming of the King (short stories), 1897; Songs of North and South, 1900; Poems, 1904; Songs of East and West (poems), 1906. Address: Memphis, Tenn. Died May 18, 1915.

MALONE, William Battle, M.D., surgeon; b. Brownsville, Tenn., July 4, 1874; s. William Battle and Ella Kate (Barbee) M.; A.B., Vanderbilt, 1896; M.D., U. of Tenn., 1899; m. Jeanne Hyde, Oct. 17, 1901. Began practice at Memphis, 1900; div. surgeon I.C. R.R. and Yazoo & Miss. Valley R.R.; local surgeon N., C.&St.L. Ry.; surgeon Southern R.R.; consulting surgeon Frisco R.R.; appointed prof. surgery, U. of Tenn., 1913; chief of staff, Methodist Hosp., 1921—. Served as maj. Med. Corps, U.S.A., 1917-19; awarded D.S.M. Mem. Am. Assn. Ry. Surgeons (pres. 1917), Southern Surg. Assn. (v.p. 1923), Tenn. State Med. Assn. (pres. 1928), Memphis and Sheby Co. Med. Soc. (pres.). Democrat. Methodist. Home: Memphis, Tenn. Died Sept. 4, 1939.

MALTBIE, William Henry, lawyer; b. Toledo, O., Aug. 26, 1867; s. Silas Benjamin and Angie M. (Van Deman) M.; A.B., Ohio Wesleyan, 1890, A.M., 1892; Ph.D., Johns Hopkins, 1895; LL.B., U. of Md., 1908; m. Kate A. S. McCurley, Dec. 19, 1903 (died 1914); 1 dau., Margaret McCurley; m. 2d, Dorothy Sippel, June 14, 1922; 1 son, William Henry. Prof. mathematics, Hedding Coll., Ill., 1890-91; instr., Feb.-Sept. 1895, asso. prof., 1895-99, prof. mathematics, 1899-1910, Woman's (now Goucher) Coll., of Baltimore; in law practice, 1908—. Was asst. to, later acting, and finally federal food administrator for Md., 1917-19. Author: Theory and Practice of Public Utility Valuation, 1924. Home: Baltimore, Md. Died Jan. 23, 1926.

MALTER, Henry, rabbi; b. Zabno Galicia, Mar. 23, 1867; s. Solomon and Rosa (Malter) M.; student of Berlin, 1889-94; Ph.D., cum laude, U. of Heidelberg, 1894; rabbi, Hochschule für die Wissenschaft des Judentums, Berlin, 1898; Feitel-Heine-Ephraim'sche Lehranstalt, Berlin, 1890-98, under the famous bibliographer, M. Steinschneider; m. Bertha Freund, Sept. 30, 1900. Prof. Judaeo-Arabic philosophy, Hebrew Union College, Cincinnati, 1900-07; prin. Hebrew School of Hebrew Orphan Asylum, New York, 1907-09; prof, rabbinical lit., Dropsie Coll., Phila., 1909—. Sec. American Academy for Jewish Research; hon. v.p. Federation of Am. Zionists. Author; Abhandlung des Abû Hâmid al-Gazzâlî, 1896; Sifrut Israel ("Jewish Literature"), 1897-1900; Saadia Gaon—His Life and Wks., 1921. Contbr. numerous articles to revs., mags., Jewish Ency. and Hastings' Ency. of Religion and Ethics. Home: Philadelphia, Pa. Died Apr. 5, 1925.

MALTZAN, Adolf Georg Otto (Ago) Freiherr Von (Baron Maltzan), diplomat; b. Klein-Varchow, Mecklenburg-Schwerin, Germany, July 31, 1877; s. Ulrich Freiherr and Adelheid (Bierbaum) Von M.; ed. univs. legation, Peking, China, 1912; rep. of Foreign Office to Estland and Letland, 1919-21; ministerial dir. at Foreign Office, Berlin, 1921-22; sec. of state at Foreign Office, 1922-25; A.E. and P. from Germany to of Bonn and Breslau; m. Edith Gruson, Apr. 4, 1914; 1 dau., Edith Carola Adelheid. Apptd. counselor of U.S., 1925—. Lutheran. Died Sept. 23, 1927.

MAN, Alrick Hubbell, lawyer, real estate operator; b. N.Y. City, May 4, 1858; s. Albon Platt and Mary Elizabeth (Hubbell) M.; A.B., Coll. City New York, 1877; LL.B., Columbia, 1879; m. Lucy Edwards Russell, Oct. 28, 1891; children—Alrick Hubbell, Mary Elizabeth (Mrs. Wayne A. Sarcka), James Nelson. Admitted to N.Y. bar, 1879, and began practice at N.Y. City; mem. firm Man & Man; treas. New York & Sea Beach Ry. Co., 1883-84, mng. dir. and pres., 1885-97; pres. Norton Point Land Co., 1892-96; pres. Kew Gardens Corp., 1912—; pres. South Richmond Hill Land Co., Long View Realty Corp., Borough Edge Corp., Kew Club Realty Corp., Kew Gardens Hotel Bldg. Corp., 23 W. 10th Street Corp., O'Gorman's Island Corp.; chmn. bd. Seawane Corp.; v.p. Kew Hall Corp.; sec. and treas. East Richmond Hill Land Co. Pres. Richmond Hill Sch. Dist., 1891-94; pres. Village of Richmond Hill., 1894-96; mem. Bd. of Edn., N.Y. City, 1902-15; mem. Zoning Commn. City New York, 1913-16. Pres. Queens Council Boy Scouts of America, 1915-30 (hon. pres.); pres. Fed. Councils Boy Scouts America in City New York, 1915-18. Trustee Normal Coll. of City of New York (now Hunter Coll.), chmn. bd. 1902-15; trustee Boy Scout Foundation of Greater N.Y., New York Geneal. and Biog. Soc. Republican. Episcopalian. Home: Kew Gardens, L.I., N.Y. Deceased.

MAN, Ernest A., consul; b. in Pa., 1849; ed. pvt. schs. Admitted to N.Y. and N.J. bars; planter in Fla., 1883-87. Consul at Gothenburg, Sweden, 1887-90, at Bergen, Norway, 1896-98; consular agt. at Schiedam, Netherlands, 1898-1901; consul at Breslau, Germany, 1901-06; consul gen. at Copenhagen, Denmark, 1906-07; consul at Leghorn, Italy, 1907-11; resigned. Address: St. Petersburg, Fla. Died Dec. 15, 1917.

MANAGAN, William Henry, lumber mfr.; b. Covington, Pa., Sept. 22, 1864; s. Thomas Jefferson and Harriet Amanda M.; ed. Pa. State Normal Sch., Mansfield, Pa., and Williamsport Commercial Coll.; m. Martha Matilda East, Oct. 2, 1889; children—William Henry, Clarence Mortimer, Ralph Edward, Luther Carswell, Lucille (Mrs. F. T. McCollum). Began in lumber business, Westlake, La., 1889; v.p. Krause & Managan Lumber Co., Krause & Managan, Inc., Sabine & Neches Valley R.R. Co.; sec. and treas. Houston River Canal Co.; sec. Christie & Eastern R.R. Co.; dir. Peavy Byrnes Lumber Co., Peavy Wilson Lumber Co., Peavy Moore Lumber Co., Hopkins Bros. Co., Murray Brooks Hardware Co. Trustee Bapt. Bible Inst., New Orleans, La., Southern Bapt. Sem., Louisville, Ky. Pres. bd. trustees La. Bapt. Conv., La. Retail Bldg. Material Assn. Democrat. Mem. Woodmen of World. Home: Lake Charles, La. Died May 1934.

MANAHAN, James, congressman; b. Chatfield, Minn., Mar. 12, 1866; s. Joseph and Catherine (McCarthy) M.; grad. Winona Normal Sch., 1886; law dept. U. of Minn., 1889; m. Mary Z. Kelly, Sept. 20, 1893. Practiced law in St. Paul, 1889-95, Lincoln, Neb., 1895-1905, Minneapolis and St. Paul, 1905—; took prominent part in railroad rate litigation before Interstate Commerce Commn., notable cases won beging the Pullman rate case (Loftus vs. Pullman Co.) and the general express investigation (Sundberg vs. American Express Co. et al.); mem. 63d Congress (1913-15), Minn. at-large. Republican. Catholic. Address: St. Paul, Minn. Died Jan. 9, 1932.

MANATT, J(ames) Irving, univ. prof. b. Millersburg, O., Feb. 17, 1845; s. Robert and Jemima (Gwin) M.; pvt. 46th Ia. Inf., 1864; A.B., Ia. (now Grinnell), Coll., 1869, A.M., 1872; Ph.D., Yale, 1873; U. of Leipzig, 1876-77; LL.D., Ia. Coll., 1886, U. of Neb., 1902; m. Arletta Winifred Clark, June 28, 1870. Prof. Greek, Denison U., 1874-76, Marietta Coll., 1877-84; chancellor U. of Neb., 1884-89; U.S. consul at Athens, 1889-93; prof. Greek lit. and history, Brown U., 1892—. Mng. com. Am. Sch. at Athens; del. First Internat. Congress of Archæology at Athens, 1905. Author: The Mycenæan Age (with Dr. Tsountas), 1897; Ægean Days, 1913. Editor: Xenophon's Hellenica (with commentary), 1888. Home: Providence, R.I. Died Feb. 14, 1915.

MANCHESTER, Charles Howard, pub. utility exec.; b. Bristol, R.I., Jan. 22, 1865; s. John Howard and Emily Frances (Greene) M.; ed. high sch., Bristol; m. Lois Burnham, April 7, 1886; 1 son, Howard Norcott. Clk., later cashier First Nat. Bank, Bristol, 1881-98, also treas. Bristol Instn. for Savings; with Industrial Trust Co. of Providence, 1900-12, successively as mgr. Bristol br., mgr. Mechanics br., and as sec. and credit mgr.; treas., 1912-14, v.p., 1914-18, pres., 1918—, Providence (R.I.) Gas Co.; pres. and gen. mgr. Bristol & Warren Water Wks., Barrington Water Co., Drownville Water Co.; treas. Providence Dyeing, Bleaching and Calendering Co.; dir. Federal Reserve Bank, Boston. Treas. Providence Community Fund. Republican. Episcopalian. Mason. Home: Providence, R.I. Died June 25, 1930.

MANDEL, John Alfred, chemist; b. Stockholm, Sweden, Oct. 18, 1865; s. Phillip H. and Agnes C. (Lundberg) M.; came to U.S., 1870; ed. Boston; Sc.D., New York U., 1901; D.Agr., U. of Berlin, 1923; m. Paula H. Heinrich, Aug. 3, 1891. Asst. in chemistry, 1884-97, adj. prof. physiol. chemistry, 1897-98, Bellevue Hosp. Med. Coll.; prof. chemistry and physiol. chemistry, Univ. and Bellevue Hosp. Med. Coll., 1898—; prof. chemistry, New York Coll. Vet. Surgeons, 1894-97; asst. prof. chemistry and physics, Coll. City of New York, 1897-98. Home: Yonkers, N.Y. Died May 5, 1929.

MANDELL, George Snell, newspaper editor; b. Boston, Mass., July 25, 1867; s. Samuel Pierce and Ann E. (Dutton) M.; A.B., Harvard, 1889; m. Emily Proctor, Apr. 30, 1896; 4 children. With Boston Transcript, 1889—; chmn. bd. Boston Transcript Co. Address: Boston, Mass. Died Aug. 11, 1934.

MANDERSON, Charles Frederick, senator; b. Phila., Pa., Feb. 9, 1837; s. John and Katharine M.; ed. Phila. High Sch. Removed, 1856, to Canton, O.; admitted to bar, 1859; city atty., Canton, 1860-61; in Union Army, 1861-65; enlisting as pvt., filled all grades, including brig. gen., resigning, Apr. 1865, after participating in all the battles of Middle West, because of severe wounds received in charge at Lovejoy's Station, Ga.; m. Rebekah S. Brown, Apr. 11, 1865. Resumed law practice in Stark County, O.; twice elected pros. atty. of Stark Co.; removed to Omaha, Neb., 1869. Mem. Neb. Constl. convs., 1871, 74; city atty. Omaha over 6 yrs.; U.S. senator, 1883-95; pres. pro tem of Senate in 51st and 52d Congresses. Gen. solicitor Burlington system, West of Missouri River, 1895—. Author: The Twin Seven Shooters, 1902; also many speeches and addresses on polit., legal and war topics. Pres. Am. Bar Assn., 1900-01. Address: Omaha, Neb. Died 1911.

MANDEVILLE, Giles Henry, clergyman Reformed (Dutch) Ch. in America, 1851—; b. New York, N.Y., Dec. 12, 1825; s. Thomas and Hester Bailey (Secor) M.; grad. Rutgers Coll., 1848; Theol. Sem., New Brunswick, N.J., 1851; A.M., D.D., Rutgers; LL.D., Hope Coll., Mich.; m. Rachel Jacobus, July 29, 1851. Pastor, Flushing, N.Y., 1851-69; Newburg, N.Y., 1859-69; Harlem, New York (City), 1869-81; corr. sec. Bd. of Edn., Reformed Ch., in America, 1884-99, treas., 1886—; pres. Hope Coll., Mich., 1887-88. Author: Flushing Past and Present, 1860. Address: New York, N.Y. Died 1904.

MANDEVILLE, John Appleton, cotton mfr.; b. Carrollton, Ga., July 7, 1882; s. LeRoy Clifton and Carrie Louise (Richardson) M.; grad. high sch., Carrollton, 1899; student Ga. Sch. of Technology, Atlanta, 1899-1900; grad. U.S. Naval Acad., 1905; m. Lula T. Calloway, Apr. 19, 1910; children—John Appleton, Grace, Jane, Anne Howard. Pres. and treas. Mandeville Mills; pres. Carroll Realty & Ins. Co. Commd. ensign U.S.N., 1905; served on U.S.S. Maryland, also on Concord and Illinois, 1905-09. Former mem. and chmn. Sch. Bd. and mem. Water and Light Commn., Carrollton. Presbyn. Mason. Home: Carrollton, Ga. Died Oct. 5, 1941.

MANGUM, Charles Staples, coll. prof.; b. Greensboro, N.C., July 14, 1870; s. Adolphus Williamson and Laura Jane (Overman) M.; A.B., U. of N.C., 1891; student U. of N.C. Med. Sch., 1891-92; M.D., Jefferson Med. Coll., Philadelphia, 1894; m. Laura Rollins Payne, Oct. 24, 1900; 1 son, Charles Staples. In practice of medicine at Audenried, Pa., 1894-96; prof. physiology and materia medica, U. of N.C., 1896-1900, prof. pharmacology and demonstrator of anatomy, 1900-05, prof. anatomy, 1905—, dean School of Medicine, 1933-37; dir. State Hosp. for Mental Diseases. Home: Chapel Hill, N.C. Died Sept. 29, 1939.

MANHART, Franklin Pierce, theologian; b. Catawissa, Pa., Aug. 30, 1852; s. George and Elizabeth (Bates) M.; grad. Missionary Inst., Selinsgrove, Pa., 1875; A.B., Pa. Coll., Gettysburg, 1877, D.D., 1899; M.A., U. of Pa., 1896; LL.D., Wittenberg Coll., Springfield, O., 1925; m. Catharine, d. Prof. P. Born, Sept. 5, 1889; children—George Born, Sarah Born. Ordained Luth. ministry, 1878; pastor Bloomsburg, Pa., 1881-89, Phila., 1889-93; supt. Missionary Inst., and pres. Susquehanna U., 1893-95; head of Deaconess Motherhouse, Baltimore, 1896-1904; dean theol. dept., Susquehanna U., 1904—. Sec. Gen. Synod of Lutheran Church in the U.S., 1909-22 and 1926—, pres., 1922-26; pres. Susquehanna Synod of Central Pa., 1923-24; pres. Susquehanna Summer Assembly, 1920—; v.p. Inner Mission Bd., 1913-18; dir. Luth. Publ. Board, 1892-1930. Pres. Luth. Hist. Soc. U.S. and Luth. Hist. Acad., 1911—, Snyder Co. Hist. Soc., 1913—. Del. to World Conv. of Lutherans, Copenhagen, Denmark, 1929. Author: Present Day Lutheranism, 1910 (4 edits.); Lutheranism and Episcopacy; History of Susquehanna Synod. Home: Selinsgrove, Pa. Died Sept. 13, 1933.

MANIERRE, Alfred Lee, lawyer; b. New York, N.Y., May 4, 1861; s. Benjamin F. and Caroline (Flynn) M.; A.B., Columbia, 1883; m. Cornelia Putnam Lockwood, Nov. 10, 1897. Admitted to bar, 1892; active in Prohibition party; candidate for mayor, New York, 1900 and 1909, for gov. N.Y., 1902. Treas. Red Cross Hosp.; trustee Nat. Temperance Soc. Home: New York, N.Y. Died 1911.

MANIGAULT, Gabriel Edward, prof. natural history and geology, Coll. of Charleston; b. Charleston, S.C., Jan. 6, 1833; grad. Coll. of Charleston, S.C., 1852; Med. Coll. of S.C., 1854; did not practice medicine, but fitted himself, while completing his medical studies at Paris, 1854-56, for curatorship of Museum of Natural History, Coll. of Charleston, which position he has held, 1873—; conducted rice plantation on Cooper River, S.C., 1857-73; in Confederate army, 1861-65. Address: Charleston, S.C. Died 1899.

MANLEY, Joseph Homan, pres. Me. Farmer Pub. Co.; b. Bangor, Me., Oct. 13, 1842; grad. Little Blue Abbott Acad., Farmington, Me., 1858; grad. Albany Law School, 1862. Is treas. Augusta Waterworks Co.; pres. Augusta Savings Bank; dir. 1st Nat. Bank, Kennebec Light and Heat Co., Edwards Mfg. Co., Maine Central R.R., Knox & Lincoln R.R., Portland, Mt. Desert & Machias Steamboat Co.; was chmn. Rep. State Com. for 20 yrs.; resigned Jan. 1901; delegate Rep. Nat. Conv., 1876, 80, 84, 88, 1900; mem. Rep. Nat. Com. and of the exec. com. Mem. Me. legislature, 1887, 88, 89, 90, 99, 1900, 01; speaker Ho. of Reps., 1901; senator, 1903-04. Address: Augusta, Me. Died 1905.

MANLEY, Thomas Henry, physician, surgeon; b. Tewksbury, Mass., Mar. 1, 1851; s. Patrick R. and Catherine (Jordon) M.; grad. med. dept., U. of New York, 1875; interne Park Hosp., New York, 1875-76; practiced at Lawrence, Mass., 1876-81, New York, 1881—; m. Olivia Mott Brennan; visiting surgeon to Blackwell's Island, Harlem Hosp., Metropolitan Hosp. and Dispensary, and other hosps.; prof. surgery, New York School of Clinical Medicine. Author: Operations for Hernia, 1890; Local Anaesthetics, 1893. Address: New York, N.Y. Died 1905.

MANLY, Charles, clergyman; b. Charleston, S.C., May 28, 1837; s. Rev. Basil and Sarah Murray (Rudulph) M.; A.B., U. of Ala., 1855, A.M., 1859; grad. Princeton Theol. Sem., 1859; D.D., William Jewell Coll., 1872; m. Mary Esther Hellen Matthews, Nov. 16, 1864; children—John Matthews, Charles Matthews, Basil Maxwell. Ordained Baptist ministry, 1859; pastor Tuscaloosa, Ala., 1859-71; v.p. Ala. Central Coll., 1862-71; pres. Union U., and pastor Murfreesboro, Tenn., 1871-73; pastor Staunton, Va., 1873-80, Greenville, S.C., 1880-81; pres. Furman U., Greenville, S.C., 1881-97; pastor Belton, S.C., 1882-98, Brushy Creek and Rocky Creek, S.C., 1882-86, Seneca, S.C., 1886-98, Lexington, Mo., 1898-1903, Lexington, Va., 1903-14. Home: Chicago, Ill. Died May 1, 1924.

MANLY, Charles Matthews, mech. engr.; b. Staunton, Va., Apr. 24, 1876; s. Charles and Mary Esther Hellen (Matthews) M.; grad. Master Mathematics and Mech. Philosophy, Furman U., Greenville, S.C., 1896; M.E., Cornell, 1898; m. Grace Agnes Wishart, June 9, 1904 (died 1921); children—Charles Wishart, John Frederick. Chief asst. to Dr. Samuel P. Langley in aviation development work, Smithsonian Instn., 1898-1905; v.p. and chief engr. Manly Drive Co., New York, 1905—; mem. Manly & Veal, cons. engrs., N.Y. City; cons. engr. to British War Office, on development of large aeroplanes in America, June-Sept. 1915; cons. engr. to Curtis Aeroplane & Motor Corp., Buffalo, N.Y., 1915-19; asst. gen. mgr. same N.Y. City, 1919-20; cons. engr. various industrial corps.; mem. firm Manly & Veal. Mem. U.S. Commn. to Internat. Aircraft Standards Conference, London, Feb.-Mar. 1918; mem. automotive advisory com. to U.S. Ordnance Board. Mem. Soc. Automotive Engineers (pres. 1919, rep. on Am. Engring. Standards Com.). Baptist. Author: (with S. P. Langley) Langley Memoirs on Mechanical Flight (No. 3, Vol. 27, Contbns. to Knowledge, Smithsonian Instn.), 1911. Built and piloted the historic Langley aeroplane, in its tests, 1903, the work being stopped by lack of funds before complete tests could be made; same machine flown in 1914 by G. H. Curtiss, "demonstrating that it was the first aeroplane." Inventor some 50 patents on automotive transportation, power generation and transmission. Home: Kew Gardens, L.I., N.Y. Died Oct. 17, 1927.

MANLY, George C., lawyer; b. Uniontown, O., Nov. 21, 1863; s. Robert Woolf and Mary Jane (Starkey) M.; A.B., U. of Denver, 1885 (1st prize Colo. intercollegiate oratorical contest, in 1885, and represented Colo. in interstate oratorical contest, 1885); A.M., LL.B., U. of Mich., 1887; LL.D., U. of Denver, 1933; m. Allie Vera Blake, May 12, 1891; children—Esther Louise (dec.), Mrs. Marion Agnes Mitchell. Admitted to Colo. bar, 1887, and practiced at Denver; mem. firm of Manly & Moore, 1888-92; gen. counsel Nev. Southern Ry. Co. and allied corps., 1892-96; atty. for Citizens' Alliance, 1904-08; pres., 1905-08; atty. for the Master Builders' Assn., Gen. Contractors' Assn., Independent Employers' Assn., etc., 1904-08; Colo. counsel Marland Oil Co. of Colo., 1925-29; dir. Employers Mutual Ins. Co.; gen. counsel Oakdale Coal Co., Alamo Coal Co., Barbour Coal Co., and metal mining and oil cos.; member of Colorado State Senate, 1930-34. Prof. law, 1892—, dean of law dept., 1910-26, dean emeritus, 1926—, U. of Denver. Republican. Methodist. Mem. Am. Bar Assn. (gen. council, 1908-12), Colo. Bar Assn. (pres. 1921), Denver Bar Assn. (pres. 1913). Mason. Home: Denver, Colo. Deceased.

MANLY, John Matthews, univ. prof.; b. Sumter County, Ala., Sept. 2, 1865; s. Charles and Mary (Matthews) M.; A.M., Furman U., 1883; A.M., Harvard, 1889, Ph.D., 1890; LL.D., Furman, 1912; L.H.D., Brown U., 1914, U. of N.C., 1924; Litt.D., U. of Wis., 1923, Yale, 1925; unmarried. Engaged in teaching, 1884—; asso. prof. and prof. English, Brown U., 1891-98; prof. English, 1898-1929, Sewall L. Avery distinguished service prof. English, 1929-33; also head of dept. of English, 1898-1933, U. of Chicago, prof. emeritus; engaged in making critical text of Chaucer's Canterbury Tales, 1926—; Chicago exchange prof. of Göttingen, 1909; lecturer at Lowell Inst., 1924, at British Acad. (Wharton lecture on poetry), 1926, at Royal Soc. of Lit., 1927. Granted leave of absence for duration of the war; enlisted in U.S.A. for 5 yrs.; commd. capt., Oct. 27, 1917; assigned to Military Intelligence Div., General Staff; chief sect. 8, same, Aug. 1918-May 1919; discharged and commd. maj., O.R.C., July 1919. Mem. Modern Lang. Assn. America (pres. 1920), Modern Humanities Research Assn. (pres. 1922-23); fellow Medieval Acad. America (pres. 1929-30); v.p. English Assn. Great Britain. Contbr. to Cambridge History of English Literature, Encyclopedia Britannica (11th edition), the Shakespeare Memorial Volume (1916), and to various periodicals. Editor: Macbeth, 1896; Specimens of the Pre-Shakespearean Drama, 1897; English Poetry, 1907; English Prose, 1909; English Prose and Poetry, 1916, 26; Chaucer (Canterbury Tales), 1928. Author: A Manual for Writers (with J. A. Powell), 1914; The Writing of English (with E. Rickert), 1919, 23, 29; The Writer's Index (with same), 1923; Contemporary British Literature (with Edith Rickert), 1921, 29, 35; Contemporary Am. Literature (with same), 1922, 29, 34; Some New Light on Chaucer, 1926; Chaucer and the Rhetoricians, 1926; The Text of the Canterbury Tales, 8 vols. (with Edith Rickert and others), 1940. Awarded Sir Israel Gollancz biennial prize by British Acad. for The Text of the Canterbury Tales, 1939. Home: Tucson, Ariz. Died Apr. 2, 1940.

MANLY, William Hester, banker; b. Tuscaloosa, Ala., June 2, 1875; s. Richard Fuller and Elizabeth (Hester) M.; ed. Barton Acad., and high sch. Mobile, Ala.; m. Edith Johnston, Oct. 27, 1909; children—Martha, Edith, Nannie, William H. Connected with the Birmingham Trust & Savings Co., 1895—; successively clk. until 1898, sec. 1898-1902, cashier, 1902-23, v.p., 1923—; mem. State Banking Bd. of Ala., 1919-23. V.p. Birmingham Pub. Library; served as state treas. Y.M.C.A. War Fund in Ala.; treas. Jefferson County Chapter Am. Red Cross. Pres. Ala. State Bankers Assn., 1912-13. Trustee Southern Bapt. Theol. Sem., Louisville, Ky.; deacon First Bapt. Ch. Democrat. Home: Birmingham, Ala. Died Nov. 28, 1938.

MANN, Albert, diatomist, botanist; b. Hoboken, N.J., June 30, 1853; s. Albert and Lydia Helen (Everett) M.; A.B., A.M., Wesleyan U., Conn., 1879, Sc.D., 1924; Ph.D., Munich, 1894; m. Jennie F. Yard, Oct. 6, 1880; 1 son, Albert. Prof. botany, Ohio Wesleyan U., 1894-1900; expert U.S. Dept. Agr., 1906-19; prof. botany, George Washington U., 1907-09; with Carnegie Instn., 1919—. Republican. Presbyn. Home: Washington, D.C. Died Feb. 1, 1935.

MANN, Arthur Teall, surgeon; b. New York, 1866; s. Samuel Rexford and Georgianna (Teall) M.; S.B., U. of Minn., 1888; M.D., Harvard, 1896; interne Channing Hosp., Brookline, Mass., 1895-96; house surgeon Boston City Hosp., 1896-98; resident Mass. State Hosp., 1898-99; post-grad. study, Boston, 1902, Germany and Austria, 1904 and 1914; m. Winona B. Orff, 1904; 1 dau., Margaret Butler. Asst. in surgery, Sch. of Medicine, U. of Minn., 1899-1902; instr., same, 1902-06, clin. prof., 1906-13; asso. prof. of surgery, U. of Minn. Med. Sch.; consulting surgeon Minneapolis City Hosp., 1922—. Republican. Presbyn. Mem. Minneapolis Med. Club (pres.), Western Surg. Assn. (pres.), Minneapolis Pathol. Soc. (sec.), Am. Acad. Medicine; fellow Am. Coll. Surgeons (gov.). Maj. M.C. U.S.A., 1918-19; surg. consultant U.S. Pub. Health Service, 1919-23. Home: Minneapolis, Minn. Died Apr. 15, 1935.

MANN, B(enjamin) Pickman, examiner U.S. Patent Office; b. W. Newton, Mass., Apr. 30, 1848; s. Hon. Horace and Mary (Peabody) M.; A.B., Harvard, 1870; m. Louisa van de Sande, July 12, 1878. Entomologist to Brazil, 1870-71, entomol. counsellor, 1872-86; instr. botany, Bowdoin Coll., 1877; asst. entomologist, U.S. Dept. Agr., 1881-86; asst. examiner U.S. Patent Office, 1887—. Was mem. Board of Children's Guardians, District of Columbia, 1892-1914 (sec. 1893-1904, pres. 1905-14); trustee People's Ch., Washington, 1892— (pres. various times, 1893—; treas. 1899-1904, 1922—). Life mem. Cambridge Entomol. Club (sec. and treas. 1874-81, pres. 1883); mem. Esperanto Assn. N.A. (treas. 1919—), Universala Esperanto-Asocio, Kolumbia Esperanto-Asocio (pres. 1920—), Single Tax Assn. of the D.C. (treas. 1920—). Editor of "Psyche," 1874-85. Compiler of Mann's Reference Indexes and specialist in preparation of bibliog. lists. Editor of a catalogue of the phænogamous plants of the U.S., etc. Home: Washington, D.C. Died 1922.

MANN, Cameron, bishop; b. New York, Apr. 3, 1851; s. Rev. Duncan Cameron and Caroline Brother (Schuyler) M.; A.B., Hobart, 1870, A.M., 1874; grad. General Theol. Sem., 1873; S.T.D., Hobart, 1888, Gen. Theol. Sem., 1902, U. of the South, 1914; LL.D., Rollins Coll., 1927; m. Mary Le Cain, June 14, 1882; children—Justine (Mrs. William Edgar Fisher), Dorothea (Mrs. Clinton M. Harbison), Duncan Cameron (dec.), Le Cain (dec.). Deacon, 1873, priest, 1876, P.E. Ch.; missionary in charge, Branchport, N.Y., 1873; curate St. Peter's, Albany, N.Y., 1875; rector St. James', Watkins, N.Y., 1875-82, Grace Ch., Kansas City, 1882-1901; consecrated bishop of N.D., Dec. 4, 1901; translated to the bishopric of South Florida, Oct. 1913. Author: October Sermons, Five Discourses on Future Punishment, 1888; Comments at the Cross, 1893; The Longing of Circe and Other Poems, 1922; A Concordance to the English Poems of George Herbert, 1927. Address: Winter Park, Fla. Died Feb. 8, 1932.

MANN, Charles Holbrook, lecturer; b. Syracuse, N.Y., Sept. 11, 1839; s. Seth Hunt and Mary (Holbrook) M.; A.B., Beloit Coll., 1860, A.M., 1863; m. Clausine Borchsenius, Mar. 14, 1867; 1 son, Charles Riborg. In q.m.'s dept. U.S.A., 1862-65; chief clerk post at Winchester, Va.; entered Swedenborgian ministry, 1865. Editor New-Church Messenger, New York City, 1878-1902; resigned from the ministry, 1914. Traveled through Germany, Switzerland, Italy, Egypt, Palestine, Syria, Greece, Austria, Denmark, Norway, Sweden and England, 1895-96. Author: Interior Spiritual Living, 1887; Sermons on Marriage, 1895; What God Hath Cleansed, 1895 (revised edit. 1914); The Christ of God, 1898; Psychiasis, or Healing Through the Soul, 1899; God and Man in the Bible, 1900; The Life Within Life, 1904; Spiritual Sex-Life, 1914. Address: New York, N.Y. Died Apr. 10, 1918.

MANN, Edward Ames, judge; b. Beatrice, Neb., Mar. 12, 1867; s. Rev. Henry P. (M.E.) and Marie Louise (Minard) M.; attended Belle Plaine (Tex.) Coll., but not grad.; studied law in office of L. H. Thompson, Norton, Kan.; m. Lena Beard Newell, June 9, 1896 (died 1905); m. 2d, Lucy O'Manson, June 26, 1907. Admitted to Kan. bar, Feb. 14, 1891; pros. atty. Scott's Bluff County, Neb., 1900-02; removed to N.M., 1903; asso. justice Supreme Ct. of N.M., June 1, 1904-June, 1909; resumed practice at Albuquerque, N.M., July 1, 1909. Republican. Address: Albuquerque, N.M. Died Nov. 19, 1915.

MANN, Frank Irving, farmer; b. Marshall County, Ill., May 8, 1854; s. William Henry and Elizabeth D. (Abraham) M.; B.L., U. of Ill., 1876; m. Fannie Judson, Apr. 25, 1878; children—Charles Judson, Mary Elizabeth (Mrs. N. W. Hepburn), Deborah Frances; m. 2d, Lena Stevenson, Dec. 26, 1913. Engaged in farming, 1878—. Dir. Ill. State Farmers Inst., 1895—; mem. advisory com. U. of Ill., 1910—. Pres. bd. edn. Gilman (Ill.) Community High Sch. Methodist. Author: Frank Mann's Soil Book, 1912; also many articles on agrl. problems appearing in Prairie Farmer, etc. Soil fertility editor Prairie Farmer, 1905-29. Home: Gilman, Ill. Died Oct. 4, 1937.

MANN, George Douglas, newspaperman; b. Goderich, Ont., Can., June 8, 1879; s. Frederick Richard and Mary (Woodsworth) M.; brought by parents to U.S., 1881; grad. high sch., St. Paul, Minn.; A.B., U. of Minn., 1903; twice married; one dau., Edith Eleanor, by first marriage; m. 2d, Stella Irene Hilleboe, Mar. 20, 1928. Began as reporter St. Paul Pioneer Press, 1903, political editor, 1903-06; editor Minot (N.D.) Optic, 1906-08; political editor St. Paul Dispatch, 1910-13, city and news editor, 1913; editor and pub. Bismarck (N.D.) Daily Tribune, 1917—. Republican. Methodist. Mason, Elk. Home: Bismarck, N.D. Died Mar. 26, 1936.

MANN, Henry, soldier, author, editor; b. Glasgow, Scotland, Mar. 25, 1848; s. Alexander and Amelia (Carney) M.; ed. Eng. and Scotland, until 15 yrs. of age; came to U.S.; served, 1864-65, in 82d and 59th N.Y. Vols. in Civil War; in 13th and 31st U.S. Inf. against Indians in Northwest; m. Ellen J. Angell, Nov. 14, 1870; m. 2d, Emma C. Lindstrom, Jan. 8, 1887. Reported many famous trials for New York Sun; has been editorial writer New York Sun, Providence Journal, New York Press, New York Times, and editor-in-chief Providence Telegram; Key West corr. Christian Herald and Brooklyn Eagle in Spanish-American War. Was justice of the peace, 6th Jud. Dist., R.I., also mem. town council and Court of Probate, N. Providence, 1886-87. Editor Home and Country, mag., 1895-96; asst. editor Success, mag., 1898-99; with lit. bur. Rep. Nat. Com., 1908-12, and with Municipal Fusion Com., 1913; editor-in-chief Columbian Mag., 1909-11. V.p. 82d Regimental Assn., 1911, pres. 1912-14; a.d.c. to N.Y. department commander G.A.R., 1911. Compiled Trust Problems for Nat. Civic Federation, 1911-12; mem. com. of citizens of New York, apptd. by Mayor Gaynor, on celebration of One Hundredth Anniversary of Peace Among English Speaking Peoples. Author: Ancient and Mediæval Republics, 1879; Features of Society in Old and New England, 1885; English Free Trade, 1888 (Rep. State Com., R.I.); Handbook for American Citizens, 1895; The Land We Live In, 1896; Turning Points in History, 1895; Story of the Declaration of Independence, 1901; Adam Clarke—A Story of the Toilers, 1905. Editor Crown Encyclopedia, 1903; on editorial staff Encyclopedia Americana, 1904. Am. editor Sir Alfred Harmsworth's Self-Educator. Home: New York, N.Y. Died Nov. 16, 1915.

MANN, Horace Borchsenius, architect; b. Orange, N.J., Apr. 4, 1868; s. Charles Holbrook and Clausine C. R. (Borchsenius) M.; Ph.B., Sch. of Mines (Columbia), 1890; unmarried. Awarded Columbia traveling fellowship in architecture, 1892, and studied in France and Italy; asso. in practice with Snelling & Potter, New York, 1895-1901; became partner Mann & MacNeille, 1902; in gen. practice of architecture—commercial bldg., schs., chs., apartment houses and residences; cons. architect in industrial housing, 1917 and 1918 for the U.S. Shipping Bd. and U.S. Army. Republican. Swedenborgian. Address: New York, N.Y. Died July 16, 1937.

MANN, Horace L., pub. utilities; b. Middleburgh, N.Y., June 3, 1872; s. Charles W. and Harriet (Eckerson) M.; ed. pub. schs. of Middleburgh, and business coll., Albany, N.Y.; m. Grace Albro, Oct. 21, 1903. Pub. accountant until 1909; treas. Buffalo Gen. Electric Co. (now Buffalo Niagara Electric Corp.), 1909-30, pres., 1930—; v.p. and dir. Buffalo, Niagara and Eastern Power Corp., Niagara Falls Power Co.; dir. Niagara Hudson Power Corp., Niagara, Lockport and Ontario Power Co., Liberty Bank of Buffalo; pres. and dir. Utilities Mut. Ins. Co. Trustee Millard Fillmore Hosp. Republican. Methodist. Mason. Home: Buffalo, N.Y. Died Feb. 10, 1942.

MANN, Isaac Thomas, capitalist; b. Ft. Spring, W.Va., July 23, 1864; s. Matthew and Elizabeth (Curry) M.; ed. under pvt. tutors; m. Vernie Meyers, Mar. 2, 1899; children—William Thomas, Mrs. Alice Owen. Began as bank teller, 1883; cashier Bank of Bramwell, W.Va., 1889, later pres.; pres. Pocahontas Fuel Co. Delegate at large from W.Va. to Rep. Nat. Conv., Chicago, 1908. Address: Washington, D.C. Died May 18, 1932.

MANN, James Robert, congressman; b. on farm nr. Bloomington, Ill., Oct. 20, 1856; s. William Henry and Elizabeth Dabney (Abraham) M.; moved to Iroquois County, 1867; grad. U. of Ill., 1876, M.L., 1892, LL.D., 1903; LL.B., Union College of Law, Chicago, 1881; admitted to bar, 1881, and practiced at Chicago; m. Emma Columbia, May 30, 1882. Mem. Oakland sch. bd., Village of Hyde Park (now in Chicago), 1887; atty. village of Hyde Park, 1888; upon annexation to Chicago became alderman 32d Ward, Chicago, 1893-96; temporary chmn. Rep. State Conv., 1894; chmn. Cook Co. Rep. convs., 1895, 1902; master in chancery, Superior Ct. of Cook Co., 1892-96; gen. atty. South Park Bd., Chicago, 1895; mem. 55th to 57th Congresses (1897-1903), 1st Ill. Dist., and 58th to 67th Congresses (1903-23), 2d Dist. Minority leader 62d to 65th Congresses. Home: Chicago, Ill. Died Nov. 30, 1922.

MANN, James Walter, building contractor; b. Wilcox County, Ga., May 30, 1872; s. David Crockett and Louise (Johnson) M.; ed. pub. sch.; m. Mattie Owens, of Vicksburg, Miss., Dec. 11, 1906; 1 dau., Frances. With Flagler Hotel Co., 1892-96; entered constrn. business, 1896; pres. The Mann Co.; builder and owner 18-story office bldg., Oklahoma City. Mem. Associated Gen. Contractors America (dir.; pres. Okla. br.). Democrat. Methodist. Mason. Home: Oklahoma City, Okla. Died Oct. 1930.

MANN, Louis, actor playwright; b. New York, Apr. 20, 1865; s. Daniel and Carolina M.; m. Clara Lipman. First appearance on stage at 3 yrs. of age in a children's production of "Snowflake," a Christmas pantomime, at Old Stadt Theatre, N.Y. City; ed. N.Y. pub. schs. and partial course U. of Calif.; did not complete coll. course but joined McCullough & Barrett Stock Co. and played boy parts; on Sundays appeared with General Stock Co. Appeared with Booth, Salvini, Marie Prescott and Lewis Morrison in all their repertoires; in 1883 at the Union Square Theatre played "Page" in the late Oscar Wilde's first play, "Vera, the Nihilist"; played with the late D. E. Bandmann in "Dr. Jekyll and Mr. Hyde"; headed own co. as Robert Audley in "Lady Audley's Secret" and an extensive repertoire; played Dick Winters in "Incog"; was original caricaturist of Svengali in "Merry World"; took own co. to Pacific Coast and back, co-starring with Clara Lipman in "The Laughing Girl," also starring with her in "Girl from Paris," "The Telephone Girl," "Girl in the Barracks," and "Julie Bon Bon" which she wrote. Starred alone in "Elevating a Husband," "Man Who Stood Still," "The Bubble"; achieved greatest success as Carl Pfiefer in "Friendly Enemies," 1918; played in "Nature's Nobleman," comedy-drama, season 1921-22, "Give and Take," 1923-24, as Milgrim in "Milgrim's Progress," 1924; and co-starred with wife in "That French Lady," 1926. Mem. Actors' Fidelity League (v.p.), Broadway Assn., Grand Street Boys' Assn. (v.p.). Mason. Co-author of "The Bubble," also of "Thieves Paradise" and starred in latter, 1927; adapter and translator of "The Cheater." Home: Montrose on the Hudson, N.Y. Died Feb. 15, 1931.

MANN, Matthew Derbyshire, gynecologist; b. Utica, N.Y., July 12, 1845; s. Charles A. and Emma (Bagg) M.; A.B., Yale, 1867, A.M., 1871; M.D., Coll. Phys. and Surg. (Columbia), 1871; studied in Europe, 1871-73; m. Elizabeth Pope, Nov. 11, 1869. Practiced New York, 1873-79; Hartford, Conn., as specialist in diseases of women, 1879-82; clin. lecturer on gynecology, Yale, 1880-82; prof. obstetrics and gynecology, U. of Buffalo, 1882-1910; consulting gynecologist and obstetrician Buffalo Gen. Hosp. Pres. Am. Gynecol. Soc., 1894. Author: Manual of Prescription Writing, 1879; etc. Editor: American System of Gynecology, 1888. Address: Buffalo, N.Y. Died Mar. 3, 1921.

MANN, Newton, clergyman; b. Cazenovia, N.Y., Jan. 16, 1836; s. Darwin H. and Cordelia (Newton) M.; ed. Cozenovia Sem.; m. Eliza J. Smith, Aug. 8, 1857 (died 1908); m. 2d, Dr. M. Rowena Morse, Aug. 20, 1912. Ordained Unitarian ministry, 1865; pastor Kenosha, Wis., 1865-68, Troy, N.Y., 1868-70, Rochester, N.Y., 1870-88, Omaha, Neb., 1889-1910. Author: A Rational View of the Bible, 1879; Evolution of a Great Literature, 1905, 2d edit., 1906. Import and Outlook of Socialism, 1910. Address: Chicago, Ill. Died July 25, 1926.

MANN, Parker, artist; b. Rochester, N.Y., July 6, 1852; s. Alexander and Caroline (Parker) M.; ed. U. of Rochester; studied at École des Beaux Arts, Paris (Atelier Alex. Cabanel); m. Julia Mullany, June 29, 1884 (died 1910); m. 2d, Miss Lee, d. late J. M. Miller, Dec. 14, 1911. Engaged as landscape painter in Washington most of time, 1887-98; in New York, 1899-1906. Spent several years painting in England, France, Holland, Switzerland, Italy and Spain. Died Dec. 14, 1918.

MANN, Seth, lawyer; b. Randolph, Mass., June 29, 1860; s. Levi and Abby (Allen) M.; A.B., U. of Calif., 1881; m. Maud L. Daulton, June 24, 1890; children—Dorothy (Mrs. Innes Randolph), William Daulton. Admitted to Calif. bar, 1883; admitted to U.S. Supreme Court and U.S. Circuit Court, 9th Circuit; atty. of traffic bureau San Francisco Chamber Commerce, 1915—; chmn. Dem. State Central Com., Calif., 1898-1900; personal rep. of President Wilson on excursion to Alaska, June, July, 1913. Assisted in framing pub. utility laws of Calif. Mem. Western Frt. Traffic Com. of U.S. R.R. Administration, July 1918-Mar. 1920. Home: San Francisco, Calif. Died Mar. 4, 1935.

MANN, William Abram, army officer; b. in Pa., July 31, 1854; grad. U.S. Mil. Acad., 1875; Army War Coll., 1905; married. Commd. 2d lt., 17th Inf., June 16, 1875; promoted through grades to brig. gen., Jan. 20, 1915; retired, July 31, 1918; promoted maj. gen. retired, June 21, 1930. Died Oct. 8, 1934.

MANN, William D'Alton, editor; b. Sandusky, O., Sept. 27, 1839; s. William R. and Eliza (Ford) M.; ed. as civ. engr.; m. Sophie Hartog, 1902. Entered Union Army at outbreak of Civil War; commd. capt. 1st Mich. Cav.; organized 1st Mounted Rifles, afterwards 5th Mich. Cav., and Daniels' Horse Battery, 1862; organized 7th Mich. Cav. and Gunther's Horse Battery (these troops composing Mich. Cav. Brigade); commd. col., 1862; devised improvements in accoutrements of troops, used in U.S. Army, and Austrian Army. Settled in Mobile, Ala., after the war; pioneer mfr. cotton-seed oil; several yrs. propr. Mobile Register; 1st Dem. candidate for Congress, under Reconstruction, from Mobile Dist. (elected to 41st Congress but not seated); invented and patented the boudoir car, 1871, and introduced it throughout Europe; founded the Compagnie Internationale des Wagons-Lits; organized Mann Boudoir Car Co., New York, 1883 (later bought out by Pullman Co.); pres. and editor Town Topics, 1891—; founder and mgr. The Smart Set. Author: The Raiders, 1876. Home: New York, N.Y. Died May 17, 1920.

MANN, William Hodges, governor; b. Williamsburg, Va., 1843; ed. Brownsburg (Va.) Acad. Deputy clk. Nottoway County, 1859-61, pvt. Co. E, 12th Va. Inf., 1861; obliged to retire from service on account of injury; acted as scout in operations around Petersburg; admitted to bar, 1867; county judge Nottoway County, 1870-92, resigned; for many yrs. active campaign speaker; mem. Dem. State Exec. Com.; mem. Va. Senate, 1899; chmn. com. on revision laws of Va.; gov. of Va., 1910-14. Author of Mann law, which closed about 800 saloons in the country districts where there was no police protection, and patron in the Senate of the high school bill, passed in 1906 and under which some 350 high schools have been erected. Presbyterian. Address: Richmond, Va. Died Dec. 12, 1927.

MANNERS, J(ohn) Hartley, dramatist; b. London, Eng., Aug. 10, 1870; ed. under pvt. tutors; m. Laurette Taylor, actress, 1912. An actor, 1898-1905; first appearance Bijou Theatre, Melbourne, Australia; in U.S., 1902—. Roman Catholic. Author: (Plays) A Queen's Messenger; As Once in May; The Girl in Waiting; The Crossways; Zira; The House Next Door; The Woman Intervenes; Peg O'My Heart; A Marriage of Reason; The Panorama of Youth; The Day of Dupes; The Harp of Life; Out There; Wreckage; Happiness; The Wooing of Eve; Hate with a Will to Victory; One Night in Rome; The National Anthem, etc. Died Dec. 19, 1928.

MANNEY, Henry Newman, rear adm. U.S.N.; b. La Porte, Ind., Jan. 22, 1844; apptd. to U.S. Naval Acad., from Minn., 1861, grad. 1866. Promoted ensign, Mar. 12, 1868; master, Mar. 26, 1869; lt., Mar. 21, 1870; lt. comdr., Oct. 7, 1886; comdr., May 10, 1895; capt., Mar. 2, 1901; retired as rear adm. of senior grade, Jan. 22, 1906. On board Macedonian, in the summer of 1864, in pursuit of the Confederate steamers Florida and Tallahassee; served on Resaca, 1866-69; Swatara, 1870-72; Michigan, 1872-73; receiving ship Independence, 1873; Tuscarora, 1873-74; Kearsarge, 1875; Yantic, 1876; Alaska, 1878-81; Naval Acad., 1881-84; Powhatan, 1884; Lancaster, 1884-87; Hydrographic Office, 1888; Naval Home, Phila., 1889-91, 1892-95, 1898-99; exec. officer Newark, 1891-92; comd. Alliance, 1895-97; Navy Yard, New York, 1889-1901; comd. Massachusetts, 1901-03; spl. duty with General Bd. of the Navy, 1903-04; chief Bur. of Equipment, with the rank of rear adm., 1904-06; spl. duty Navy Dept., 1906-07; spl. duty on Pacific Coast in connection with constrn. of coal depot at California City Point, Calif., 1907-08; rep. Bur. of Equipment, Navy Dept., and charged with the disposition of all chartered colliers, providing the fleet, 1908-09; assumed charge naval coaling sta., being constructed at San Diego, Calif., Feb. 10, 1909; retired from active duty, Nov. 20, 1909. Del. Internat. Conf. on Wireless Telegraphy, Berlin, 1906. Address: Point Loma, Calif. Died Oct. 25, 1915.

MANNING, Charles Henry, engineer; b. Baltimore, Md., June 9, 1844; s. Joseph Cogswell and Rebecca Parkman Jarvis (Livermore) M.; B.S., Lawrence Scientific Sch. (Harvard), 1862; m. Fanny Bartlett, Jan. 17, 1871. Apptd. engr. U.S. Navy, Feb. 19, 1863; served through Civil War; instr. U.S. Naval Acad., 1870-75, 1878-81; mem. 1st advisory bd. to build new navy, 1881-82; advanced to chief engr., 1906, retired, June 14, 1884; chief engr. Key West Naval Sta. during Spanish-Am. War. Gen. supt. Amoskeag Mfg. Co., 1883-1913. Designer of Manning boiler, in gen. use in textile mills. Address: Manchester, N.H. Died Apr. 1, 1919.

MANNING, George H(enry), newspaper corr.; b. London, Eng., Dec. 8, 1883; s. George H. and Pittman S. (Dixon) M.; came with parents to U.S., 1896; ed. pub. schs., Washington, D.C.; m. Alice May Franks, Sept. 5, 1903; children—George H., Helen May, Alice P. Began as reporter for Internat. News Service, 1910; began as Washington corr. for number of newspapers and trade jours., 1912; organizer, 1925, and editor and pres. Gen. Press Assn., rep. newspapers and trade papers in Washington. Episcopalian. Home: Washington, D.C. Died Nov. 4, 1934.

MANNING, James Hilton, mayor; b. Albany, N.Y., Sept. 22, 1854; s. Daniel (Sec. of the Treasury, 1885-87) and Mary (Little) M.; grad. Albany Free Acad., 1873; m. Emma J. Austin, Oct. 22, 1879. Editor and mgr. Albany Argus, 1873-93; pres. Weed-Parsons Printing Co., Albany, 1893-1913, Nat. Savings Bank, 1904—; dir. Nat. Commercial Bank and Trust Co., Consolidated Car Heating Co., New York Telephone Co., Title Guarantee & Trust Co., of New York. Mayor of Albany, 2 terms, 1890-94. Democrat. Connected with N.G.S.N.Y., 1875—. Home: Albany, N.Y. Died July 4, 1925.

MANNING, James Smith, lawyer; b. Pittsboro, N.C., June 1, 1859; s. John and Louisa (Jones) M.; A.B., U. of N.C., 1879; studied law U. of N.C. Law Sch.; m. Julia Tate Cain, Dec. 12, 1888. Formerly practiced at Durham; mem. law firm Manning & Manning, Raleigh, N.C. Chmn. Dem. County Exec. Com. and mem. Dem. State Exec. Com. for many yrs.; candidate for judge Superior Court, 1896; mem. N.C. Ho. of Rep., 1907, Senate, 1909; became justice of Supreme Court of N.C., 1909; atty. gen. of N.C., 1917-25. Home: Raleigh, N.C. Died July 29, 1938.

MANNING, Mary Margaretta Fryer; b. Albany, N.Y.; d. William J. and Margaret Livingston (Crofts) Fryer; ed. at Albany; m. Daniel Manning (Sec. of the Treasury, 1885-87). Nov. 19, 1884 (died 1887). By joint resolution of Congress and appmt. of the President, commr. to Paris Expn., 1900, and to represent U.S. and D.A.R. at unveiling of statue of Lafayette, July 4, 1900, in Paris; and on July 3, 1900, assisted in unveiling statue of Washington, gift of the women of U.S. to France. Pres. bd. of Lady Mgrs. St. Louis Expn., 1904. Decorated with Cross of Legion of Honor by Pres. Loubet, and received decoration of Officier de l'Instruction Publique, France, and Chevalier de l'Ordre de Léopold, Belgium. Hon. v.p. Fédération de l'Alliance Française; hon. pres.-gen. D.A.R. (served two terms as pres.-gen.). Apptd. by Gov. Alfred E. Smith mem. bd. trustees Schuyler Mansion, Nov. 8, 1926. Address: Albany, N.Y. Deceased.

MANNING, Richard Irvine, governor; b. Homesley Plantation, S.C., Aug. 15, 1859; s. Richard Irvine and Elizabeth Allen (Sinkler) M.; prep. edn. Kenmore U. High Sch., Amherst, Va.; matriculated in U. of Va. (withdrew in 1879); m. Lelia Bernard Meredith, Feb. 10, 1881. Engaged in farming, Sumter County, 1880—; pres. Am. Products Export and Import Corp., Cotton Warehouse Co., Nat. Bank of Sumter, Bank of Mayesville, S.C., Cotton Warehouse Co., S.C. Land & Settlement Assn.; dir. Sumter Telephone Co., Telephone Mfg. Co., Magneto Mfg. Co., Palmetto Fire Ins. Co., N.Y. Life Ins. Co., Union-Buffalo Mills Co., Clifton Mfg. Co.; chmn. bd. Peoples State Bank of South Carolina. Mem. S.C. Ho. of Rep., 1892-96, Senate, 1898-1906; gov. of S.C., terms 1915-17, 1917-19. Democrat. Episcopalian; mem. Nat. Council of P.E. Ch. Life trustee Clemson Coll., S.C. Mason, K.P. Home: Columbia, S.C. Died Sept. 11, 1931.

MANNING, Van(noy) H(artrog), petroleum engr.; b. Horn Lake, Miss., Dec. 15, 1861; s. Van H. and Mary Z. (Wallace) M.; U. of Miss., 1878-81; D.Engring., U. of Pittsburgh, 1919; m. Emily S. Stevens, 1898; children—Vannoy H., Oscar Stevens. Civ. engr. with U.S. Geol. Survey, 1886-1910; with Bur. of Mines, Dept. of Interior, 1910, asst. dir., 1911-14, dir., 1914-20; dir. research, Am. Petroleum Inst., 1920-24; petroleum engr. Pan Am. Petroleum and Transportation Co., 1924-25; cons. petroleum engr., 1926-28; dir. engring. and tech. research, Petroleum Research Corp., 1928-30; cons. engr. U.S. Bur. Mines; also cons. petroleum engr., Republic of Cuba. Mem. central petroleum com., Nat. Research Council. Democrat. Episcopalian. Mason. Home: Forest Hills, N.Y. Died July 13, 1932.

MANNING, Walter Webster, editor, pub.; b. Worcester, Mass., May 23, 1875; s. Charles Walter and Eva Webster (Parker) M.; ed. grade schs. and Boston Latin Sch.; m. Mabel Porter Conant, June 12, 1900; children—Conant, Gordan P., Richard. Eastern mgr. Alburger Stoer & Co., Phila., Pa., 1903-10; advertising mgr. McClure Publs., N.Y. City, 1910-14, Woman's World of Chicago, at N.Y. City, 1914-17; pres., owner, editor, pub. same, at Chicago, 1917—. Pres. Manning Assn. of America, 1925. Republican. Mason. Author: Handbook of National Distribution, 1915; Guide to Profitable Distribution, 1917; County Handbook of National Distribution, 1922. Compiler: Library of Needlework, 1924; Library of Cookery, 1925. Home: Highland Park, Ill. Died Feb. 16, 1931.

MANNING, Warren Henry, landscape designer; b. Reading, Mass., Feb. 7, 1860; s. Jacob Warren and Lydia (Chandler) M.; grad. Reading High Sch.; m. Henrietta H. Pratt, June 2, 1885; 1 son, Warren Harold. Began active career in his father's nursery, and later was a student under Frederic Law Olmstead, Sr., for 8 years, also served as his aid; has designed and planned over 1,600 landscapes and regional plan undertakings in 40 states, 1896—, including numerous parks and park systems; was pres. Warren H. Manning Offices, Inc. One of organizers Am. Park and Outdoor Art Assn. (now Am. Civic Assn.); an organizer and charter mem. Am. Soc. Landscape Architects (pres. 1914-15); v.p. Federated Socs. on Planning and Parks; mem. President Hoover's Conf. on Home Building and Home Ownership; mem. Com. on Federal National Resources. Engaged in nat. planning studies and is mem. nat. planning com. of Am. Civic Assn. and of Am. Soc. Landscape Architects. Organized Manning Assn. of America (sec.), 1900. Home: North Billerica, and Waltham, Mass. Died Feb. 5, 1938.

MANNING, William T., journalist; b. San Francisco, Calif., Oct. 2, 1865; s. Thomas and Ellen M.; ed. pub. schs. and coll., San Francisco; m. Annie E. Caswell, Oct. 1895. Began career as printer, afterwards became publisher and editor; editor Los Angeles Telegram, 1890-91, San Francisco Weekly Sun, 1884-89, The Manhattan, New York, 1894-96; polit. editor New York Recorder, 1893-96; polit. corr. various papers under nom de plume of "John Marthol"; founded the Cosmographic, newspaper syndicate, 1898. Author: Political History of the United States (2 vols.), 1899. Home: New York, N.Y. Died 1908.

MANSFIELD, Archibald Romaine, clergyman; b. Spring Valley, N.Y., Jan. 3, 1871; s. Romaine Stiles and Emelia (Moore) M.; grad. St. John's Sch., Ossining, N.Y., 1888; A.B., St. Stephen's Coll., Annandale, N.Y., 1892, D.D., 1915; grad. Gen. Theol. Sem., 1896; m. Ella Louise Huntington, June 14, 1899; children—Richard Huntington, Archibald Romaine, Bissell Stiles, Margaret Louise, Helen Huntington, George Herbert. Deacon, 1896, priest, 1897, P.E. Ch.; with Seamen's Ch. Inst. of New York, as chaplain, 1896-1904, superintending chaplain, 1904-09, supt., 1909—. Trustee Am. Merchant Marine Library Assn. Republican. Home: New York, N.Y. Died Feb. 1934.

MANSFIELD, Burton, lawyer; b. Hamden, Conn., Apr. 4, 1856; s. Jesse Merrick and Catharine Betsey (Warner) M.; Ph.B., Yale, 1875, LL.B., 1878; D.C.L., Trinity, 1924, Berkeley Divinity Sch., Middletown, Conn., 1925; m. Anna Rosalie Mix, Oct. 16, 1900. Admitted to Conn. bar, 1878, and began practice at New Haven; pres. Conn. Savings Bank, 1896—; dir. Merchants Nat. Bank, Security Ins. Co., New Haven Water Co., West Haven Buckle Co., Pilot Reinsurance Co. of New York. Conn. state ins. commr., 1893-95, 1911-23. Trustee Morgan Memorial, Wadsworth Atheneum, Hartford New Haven Colony Hist. Soc. Chmn. State Commn. of Sculpture, Conn., and Municipal Art Commn., New Haven; mem. nat. council P.E. Ch.; v.p. Am. Ch. Building Fund. Fellow Nat. Acad. Design. Democrat. Episcopalian. Owner of notable collection paintings. Author of various pamphlets on insurance and on matters pertaining to P.E. Ch. Home: New Haven, Conn. Died Oct. 4, 1932.

MANSFIELD, Henry Buckingham, rear admiral U.S.N.; b. Brooklyn, N.Y., Mar. 5, 1846; s. Capt. Charles and Eliza Maria (Buckingham) M.; ed. pub. sch., Sheffield, Mass., Hudson River Inst.; grad. U.S. Naval Acad., 1867; m. Harriet Sheldon, Oct. 23, 1872. Promoted ensign, 1868; master, 1870; lieut., 1871; lieut. comdr., 1890; comdr., May 1897; captain, 1902; rear admiral and retired, June 15, 1905. While midshipman served in Marion, Macedonian, Winnepec, and Minnesota; spl. service, 1867-68; served on Mohongo and Mohican, Pacific fleet, 1869-70; eclipse expdn. to Siberia, 1869; comd. 2d launch from Mohican, in expdn. which cut out and burned piratical steamer Forward in Tecupan River, Mex.; on various duties, chiefly coast survey and hydrographic work and comdg. coast survey steamers, 1871-93; receiving-ship Vermont, 1893-97; comd. Fern, 1897-98; light house insp., Apr.-May 1898; comd. U.S.S. Celtic, N. Atlantic Squadron, May-Sept. 1898; at Navy Yard, N.Y., Sept.-Dec., 1898; light house insp. to Dec. 1899; comdg. U.S.S. Lancaster, Dec. 1899-1901; in charge recruiting rendezvous, New York, Nov. 1901-03, Naval War Coll., Apr.-Oct. 1903; naval examining and retiring bd. to Nov. 1903; comdg. battleship Iowa to Jan. 1905; on duty at New York Navy Yard, 1905. Home: Brooklyn, N.Y. Died July 17, 1918.

MANSFIELD, Howard, lawyer; b. Hamden, Conn., July 2, 1849; s. Jesse Merrick and Julia (Tuttle) M.; A.B., Yale, 1871, hon. A.M., 1913; LL.B., Columbia, 1874; m. Nellie Coolidge Tuttle (Todd), Sept. 12, 1895. Admitted to bar, Oct. 1874; mem. firm Lord, Day & Lord, 1901—. Author: Descriptive Catalogue of Etchings and Dry-points of Whistler, 1909. Home: New York, N.Y. Died Aug. 14, 1938.

MANSFIELD, Richard, actor; b. Heligoland, 1857; studied for East Indian civil service, but came to Boston and opened a studio; studied art in England and later entered theatrical profession. Played small parts in comic opera; came to U.S. again and appeared at Standard Theatre, New York, as Dromez in Les Manteaux Noirs. Has been successful in a wide repertoire from Koko in Mikado, to Richard III. Head of his own company, and has created such parts as Beau Brummel, Baron Chevrial, and the titular rôles in Dr. Jekyll and Mr. Hyde. Appeared as Cyrano de Bergerac in 1899, and has played Shylock, Henry V., Beaucaire and Brutus in Julius Cæsar; m. Beatrice Cameron, his leading woman. Author. (poems) Blown Away, a nonsense-book for grown-up children; (plays) Monsieur, Ten Thousand a Year, and Don Juan. Address: New York, N.Y. Died 1907.

MANSFIELD, Robert E., consul gen.; b. in Ind., June 13, 1866; s. Robert Goble and Margaret (Thornburg) M.; pub. sch. edn.; m. Fanny Gowdy, Apr. 17, 1906. Asso. editor New Castle (Ind.) Courier, 1884-90; state editor Indianapolis Journal, 1891; city editor Muncie (Ind.) Times, 1892-95; owner and editor Marion (Ind.) News, 1897-1900. Consul at Zanzibar, 1899-1901, at Valparaiso, Chile, 1901-06, at Lucerne, Switzerland, 1906-08, at St. Gall, Switzerland, 1908-09; consul gen. at Zürich, Switzerland, 1909-13, at Vancouver, 1913—. Author: Country Life in Chile. Home: Marion, Ind. Died Sept. 18, 1925.

MANSFIELD, Samuel Mather, brig. gen. U.S.A.; b. Middletown, Conn., Sept. 23, 1839; s. Maj. Gen. Joseph King Fenno and Louisa (Mather) M.; grad. U.S. Mil. Acad., 1862; m. Mrs. Anna Baldwin Wright, Apr. 16, 1874 (dec.). Promoted 2d lt., corps engrs., June 17, 1862; promoted through grades to brig. gen. U.S.A., Feb. 20, 1903. In Civil War, col. 24th Conn. Inf., Nov. 18, 1862-Sept. 30, 1863. Bvtd. capt., June 14, 1863, "for gallantry at Port Hudson, La."; maj. and lt. col., Mar. 13, 1865, "for gallant and meritorious services during the war." Has been in charge of constrn. of many fortifications; engr., 9th, 10th and 11th light house dists., and many other works; pres. commn. to run and mark the boundary lines between portion of Ind. Ty. and Texas, 1885-87; pres. Calif. debris commn. to regulate hydraulic mining, 1898-99; pres. Yosemite Nat. Park Commn., 1899; div. engr., Pacific div., Nov. 7, 1898, Northwestern div., May 3, 1901, Eastern div., July 4, 1901; retired at own request, over 40 yrs.' service, Feb. 21, 1903. Mass. harbor and land commr., July 23, 1906-July 17, 1912. Address: Boston, Mass. Died Feb. 18, 1928.

MANSON, Marsden, civil engr.; b. Leewood, Va., Feb. 14, 1850; s. Robert E. and Sophia A. (Smith) M.; grad. Va. Mil. Inst., Lexington, 1870, B.S. and C.E., 1877; Ph.D., U. of Calif., 1893; m. Samuella L. Chase, Sept. 12, 1883 (died 1913); m. 2d, Julia D. E. Wright, Jan. 1916; children—Julia Alexandria Wright, Marsden Wright. Asst. engr., U.S. Engr. Dept., 1873-75; asst. prof. physics and chemistry, Va. Mil. Inst., 1876-77; asst. engr., State Engring. Dept., Calif., 1879-81; asst. engr., U.S. Engr. Dept., 1881-82; chief engr., Bd. State Harbor Commn., San Francisco, 1883-92; mem. bd. engrs., San Francisco drainage, 1893-94; consulting engr., commr. pub. works, Calif., 1895-99; pres. dept. highways, Calif., 1896-99; commr. pub. works, San Francisco, 1900-03; cons. engr., 1904-07; city engr. San Francisco, 1908-12. Democrat. Episcopalian. Author: The Evolution of Climates; Geologic and Present Climates. Home: Berkeley, Calif. Died Feb. 21, 1931.

MANSUR, Zophar M., collector of customs; b. Morgan, Vt., Nov. 23, 1843; s. Warren and Jane A. (Morse) M.; ed. Derby Acad., Vt.; admitted to

Vt. bar, 1879; m. Ellen L. Newhall, Aug. 16, 1868. Pvt. Co. K, 10th Vt. Regt., 1862-65; lost right arm at Opequan Creek, Va., Sept. 19, 1864; apptd. postmaster, Island Pond, Vt., 1867; mem. Vt. Ho. of Rep., 1886, Senate, 1888; state's atty. Essex County, 1886-88; elected lt. gov. Vt., 1894; apptd. collector of customs for Dist. of Memphremagog, Oct. 1, 1897; pres. Nat. Bank of Derby Line. Republican. Dept. comdr. G.A.R., 1890; pres. Vt. Soc. S.A.R., 1894. Address: Newport, Vt. Died Mar. 29, 1914.

MANTELL, Robert Bruce, actor; b. Irvine, Ayrshire, Scotland, Feb. 7, 1854; s. James and Elizabeth M.; m. 2d, Marie Booth Russell (died 1911). Professional début Rochdale, Eng., as the Sergeant in "Ar-rah-na-Pogue," Oct. 21, 1876; came to U.S. and played juvenile rôles with Mme. Modjeska, 1878; returned to England, for 3 yrs. supported Miss Wallis (now Mrs. Lancaster) as leading man. Later appeared in New York as Loris Ipanhoff in "Fedora" with Fannie Davenport; afterward became a star and has been at the head of his own company in classic and romantic plays including Hamlet, Othello, Richard III, Macbeth, Romeo and Juliet, Richelieu, Lady of Lyons, Corsican Brothers, Monbars, Dagger and Cross; appeared at Princess Theatre, New York, as Richard III, 1904; played revivals of King Lear and Macbeth, 1905; later played Julius Cæsar, The Merchant of Venice, etc. Address: New York, N.Y. Died June 27, 1928.

MANTLE, Lee, U.S. senator; b. Birmingham, Eng., Dec. 13, 1851; s. Joseph H. and Mary Susan M.; came to U.S., 1864, with mother, his father having died before he was born; went west to Utah; later moved to Idaho, and in 1877 to Montana; married; 1 son, Lee. He worked on farm until 16 years old; was telegrapher at Pleasant Valley, Idaho, 1872-77; agent Wells Fargo Express Co. at Butte, Mont., 1877-80; established and owned Daily Inter-Mountain, 1881, conducted it until 1901. Has been alderman and mayor of Butte; 3 terms mem. and 1 term speaker territorial legislature; 1st pres. Mineral Land Assn. of Mont.; apptd. U.S. senator, 1893, but Senate decided appmt. unconstitutional; elected 1895 for term ending 1899. Pres. Mont. commn. St. Louis Expn., 1904, Portland Expn., 1905; chmn. Mont. State Rep. Central Com., 1892, 1894, 1904. Address: Los Angeles, Calif. Died Nov. 18, 1934.

MANTON, Walter Porter, physician; b. Providence, R.I., Aug. 3, 1858; s. Walter Bartlett M.; private edn. in U.S. and Germany, fitting for coll., but poor health prevented acad. course; M.D., Harvard, 1881; 3 yrs. post-grad. studies abroad; practiced at Detroit; m. Cara M. Williamson, 1879. Emeritus prof. and dir. dept. obstetrics Detroit Coll. of Medicine and Surgery; formerly gynecologist to Eastern and Northern asylums for insane and cons. gynecologist to St. Joseph's Retreat; pres. med. bd. Women's Hosp.; gynecologist emeritus to Harper Hosp.; formerly directing consultant maternity dept. Herman Keifer Hosp. Fellow Am. Assn. Obstetricians and Gynecologists, of which was v.p. 1921 (resigned). Author: A Cyllabus of Lectures on Human Embryology; Helps to Natural History Series (6 manuals); Epitome of Obstetrics, 1903, 13. Wrote chapters in Jewett's Obstetrics and Peterson's Obstetrics; also more than 150 spl. articles. Asso. editor 5 yrs. Sajous' Am. Universal Med. Sciences; formerly editor The Microscope. Retired, 1922, and moved to Pasadena, Calif. Died Sept. 24, 1925.

MANZANARES, Francisco Antonio, mcht., delegate in Congress; b. Abiquiu, Rio Arriba County, N.M., Jan. 25, 1843; ed. by private tutor and in schools at St. Louis and New York; m. Antonia Baca, 1871. Spent a yr. in a wholesale grocery house, Kansas City, completed course at commercial coll. in New York; followed by a short time in a banking house; established as mcht. at terminus of Kansas Pacific Ry. during construction, moving westward with the road until it reached Kit Carson; then continued in the same line along the Atchison, Topeka & Santa Fe R.R.; finally established, 1879, at Las Vegas, N.Mex., with branch at El Paso, Tex.; also interested in banks, etc. Delegate in Congress from N.M., 1893-95. Democrat. Address: Las Vegas, N.M. Died 1904.

MAPES, Carl Edgar, congressman; b. Eaton County, Mich., Dec. 26, 1874; s. Selah W. and Sarah Ann (Brooks) M.; A.B., Olivet Coll., 1896; LL.B., U. of Mich., 1899; m. Julia Pike, Aug. 14, 1907; children—Robert W., John P., Jane E. Began practice of law, Grand Rapids, 1899. Mem. Mich. Ho. of Rep., 1905-07, Senate, 2 terms, 1909-13; mem. 63d to 75th Congresses (1913-39), 5th Mich. Dist. Republican. Home: Grand Rapids, Mich. Died Dec. 12, 1939.

MAPES, Charles Victor, agrl. chemist; b. New York, July 4, 1836; A.B., Harvard, 1857; m. Martha Meeker Halsted, 1863; 1 son, Victor M. Became expert in agrl. chemistry—especially in fertilizers; introduced spl. crop manures in U.S. by preparing a fertilizer adapted for growth of Irish potatoes; was associated in soil tests, with Prof. W. O. Atwater, of the Nat. Expt. Sta., at Washington; founder and pres. The Mapes Formula and Peruvian Guano Co., New York; became pres. New York Chemical and Fertilizer Exchange at its organization. Home: New York, N.Y. Died Jan. 23, 1916.

MAPHIS, Charles Gilmore, educator; b. nr. Edinburg, Va., Feb. 12, 1865; s. John Miley and Elizabeth Ann (Coffelt) M.; grad. Peabody Coll., 1886; Ped.D., Davidson Coll., 1923; LL.D., Roanoke Coll., 1923; m. Bessie Dold, Oct. 14, 1890; children—Charles Craig (dec.), Elliott Dold (dec.) and Edwin Willis (twins). Prin. Strasburg (Va.) High Sch., 1886-87, Harrisonburg High Sch., 1887-90; mem. Va. State Bd. Sch. Examiners, 1905-11 (pres. 1908-11); registrar, 1905-11, dir., 1911-19, dean, 1920—, U. of Va. Summer Quarter; prof. secondary edn., 1911-19, dir. univ. extension, 1920-25, U. of Va.; sec. Va. Edn. Commn., 1910 (mem. 1918-20); organizer, 1927, dir. Inst. of Pub. Affairs at U. of Va., and exec. dean of third University World Cruise, 1929-30. Dir. personnel work, Southeast Div., S.A.T.C. Com. on Edn. and Spl. Training, War Dept. Mem. exec. com., Co-operative Edn. Assn. Va.; pres. Assn. Colls. and Secondary Schs. of Southern States, 1916-19; sec.-treas. Assn. Va. Colls., 1915-20, pres. 1921-22; pres. Va. State Teachers' Assn., 1916; pres. Nat. Univ. Extension Assn., 1922-23; chmn. finance com. Southern Woman's Ednl. Alliance, 1924; member Va. Commn. for the Blind, 1926—; pres. Assn. of Deans and Dirs. of Summer Sessions, 1933-34. Awarded Parchment of Distinction, N.Y. Southern Soc., 1934. Democrat. Presbyn. Author pamphlets and articles in periodical press. Address: University, Va. Died May 15, 1938.

MAPOTHER, Wible Lawrence, ry. pres.; b. Louisville, Ky., Sept. 28, 1872; s. Dillon H. and Mary P. (Cruise) M.; pub. and pvt. schs., Louisville; spl. com. course, St. Mary's (Ky.) College, 1886-88; m. Amelia F. Porter, July 9, 1895. Began as office boy with L.&N. R.R., 1888, and successively chief clerk in executive dept., 1902, asst. to pres., 1904, 1st v.p. 1905, dir. 1914, same rd.; apptd. federal mgr. U.S. R.R. Administration, June 8, 1918, with jurisdiction over L.&N. System, L.,H.&St.L., N.,C.& St.L., Tenn. Central, and Birmingham & Northern rys., and certain terminal properties; apptd. federal mgr. Atlanta & West Point Ry. and Western Ry. of Ala., Nov. 26, 1919; exec. v.p. L.&N. R.R., March 1, 1920, pres. Mar. 17, 1921—; also v.p. Louisville, Henderson & St. L. Ry. Co.; dir. Nashville, Chattanooga & St. L., Atlanta & West Point, Western Ry. of Ala., Fruit Growers Express Co., etc. Democrat. Home: Louisville, Ky. Died Feb. 3, 1926.

MARBLE, Annie Russell, author; b. Worcester, Mass., Aug. 10, 1864; d. Isaiah Dunster and Nancy Maria (Wentworth) Russell; A.B., Smith Coll., 1886, A.M., 1895; m. Charles Francis Marble, Nov. 18, 1890; children—Anna Bell, Paul Francis. Author: Books That Nourish Us, 1900; Thoreau—His Home, Friends and Books, 1902; Books in Their Seasons, 1905; Heralds of American Literature, 1907; The Women Who Came in the Mayflower, 1920; Women of the Bible, 1923; Nobel Prize Winners in Literature, 1925, 32; Study of the Modern Novel Since 1900, 1928; Pen Names and Personalities, 1930; From Boston to Boston, 1930; Builders and Books, 1931; From Prentice to Patron, 1935. Editor: Heroes and Hero-Worship, 1897; Nature Picture by American Poets, 1899; The Marble Faun, 1901; Thoreau Calendar, 1909; Whittier Year-Book, 1910; The Optimist's Year-Book, 1911; The Story of Leatherstocking, 1927. Contributor to literary journals, etc. Compiled pageants: Heroines of Literature, 1915; The Children's Quest, 1919; Thrift and Spendthrift, 1919; Faith of Our Fathers, 1920; Boys and Girls of Hebrew History, 1922; In the Days of the Judges, 1922; Founders of the Faith, 1923; For Home and Country, 1928; Merchants of Light, 1931; also dramatization, Standish of Standish, 1919. Address: Worcester, Mass. Died Nov. 23, 1936.

MARBLE, Charles Baldwin, editor; b. Methuen, Mass., Jan. 8, 1875; s. William Crawford and Sarah Ellen (Barker) M.; grad. Methuen High Sch., 1893; m. Mary Flowers, June 30, 1908. Salesman with William S. Cooper Brass Works, Phila, Pa., 1896-1904; entered adv. business, 1904, with H. B. Humphrey Co., Boston; connected with The Priscilla Co. (pubs. The Modern Priscilla), 1907—, successively as promotion mgr. in charge of publicity, asst. business mgr., asst. gen. mgr., v.p. and mng. editor. Republican. Christian Scientist. Mason. Home: Boston, Mass. Died Sept. 30, 1927.

MARBLE, Edgar M., patent lawyer. Was admitted to bar and engaged in practice of law in Mich. until 1877, when became asst. atty. gen. of U.S. until 1880; U.S. commr. of patents, 1880-84; engaged in practice in New York, 1884—. Address: New York, N.Y. Died 1908.

MARBLE, Fred Elmer; b. Honeoye Falls, N.Y., June 21, 1861; s. Albert B. and Frances Elizabeth (Hunt) M.; A.B., U. of Rochester, 1887; grad. Rochester Theol. Sem., 1890; Ph.D., Yale, 1897; student U. of Berlin, 1897-98; Harvard Summer School of Theology, 1902, 07; m. Adeline Louise Morris, Dec. 3, 1891. Ordained Bapt. ministry, 1890; pastor successively First Ch., Wallingford, First Ch., Brattleboro, Vt., North Av. Ch., Cambridge, Mass., 1911; with Bureau of University Travel, Boston, 1913-17; in charge of the Far East and Round the World business of the Am. Express Travel Dept., New York, 1919-21; ednl. dir. world cruises, 1922, 23, 25, 28, Mediterranean cruise, 1925. Mason (K.T.). Author: Marble's Round the World Travel-Guide, 1925. Home: New Haven, Conn. Deceased.

MARBLE, George Watson, newspaper pub.; b. Fort Scott, Kan., Oct. 9, 1870; s. Edward Livingston and Carrie G. (Smith) M.; ed. pub. schs.; m. Manette Doud, Nov. 14, 1900; children—Manette, George Watson, Rachel Carolyn. In newspaper business at Ft. Scott, 1902—; pub. Tribune-Monitor; pres. and mgr. Tribune-Monitor Co., past pres. Nat. Editorial Assn. Active in development of dairy industry in Southern Kan. Mem. bd. regents, U. of Kan., 2 terms. Presbyn. Mason. Home: Ft. Scott, Kan. Died Mar. 15, 1930.

MARBLE, John Hobart, lawyer; b. Ashland, Neb., Feb. 26, 1869; s. Andrew and Sarah Matilda (Brush) M.; ed. pub. schs., Dak. and Neb., and U. of Neb.; m. Mattie Louise O'Bryan, 1893. Admitted to bar, 1903; practiced at San Francisco, 1903-06; atty., in charge div. inquiry, Interstate Commerce Commn., 1906-12; sec. Interstate Commerce Commn., Feb. 1912—. Atty., U.S. Senate Com. on Privileges and Elections, in matter of investigation of election of William Lorimer as senator from Ill., June 1911-12. Home: Washington, D.C. Died Nov. 21, 1913.

MARBLE, Manton, publicist; b. Worcester, Mass., Nov. 16, 1834; s. Joel and Nancy Chapin (Coes) M.; ed. by father; Albany Acad., 1853; U. Rochester, 1855. Asst. editor Boston Jour., 1855-56; editor Boston Traveler, 1856-57; on staff N.Y. Evening Post, 1858-60; propr. and editor New York World, 1862-76. Wrote Dem. state platform, 1874, Dem. nat. platform, 1876, and most of that of 1884. Spl. envoy (1885) to govts. of Great Britain, France, and Germany; after conf. with Prince Bismarck, Mr. Gladstone, Lord Iddesleigh and Mr. Goschen, MM. Freycinet and Carnot, and also with Cernuschi, the classic authority upon internat. bimetallism, advised President Cleveland that coöperation of United Kingdom, for which neither Liberal nor Tory leaders were prepared, was the condition precedent of German or French resumption of Free Bimetallic Coinage, and that U.S. Treasury purchases of silver should cease. Author: Letter to Abraham Lincoln, 1864; The Presidential Counts, 1877; A Secret Chapter of Political History, 1878; Memoir of Alex. G. Mercer, D.D., prefacing his Notes of an Outlook on Life, 1899; etc. Address: Bedford, N.Y. Died July 24, 1917.

MARBLE, William Allen, mfr.; b. Woonsocket, R.I., Mar. 4, 1849; s. Russel and Phebe (Almy) M.; grad. Moses Brown Sch., Providence, 1867; m. Catharine Alice Cain, July 1, 1873; children—William E., James McNab (dec.). Salesman, 1867-88; mem. firm Roth & Goldschmidt, corset mfrs., 1888-97; became v.p. and gen. mgr. R.&G. Corset Co., New York, 1897, later pres., retired. Republican. Mem. Soc. of Friends. Mem. Merchants Assn. (pres. 1913), S.A.R. (pres.-gen. 1910-11), Founders and Patriots America (registrar-gen.). Home: New York, N.Y. Deceased.

MARBURG, Edgar, civil engr.; C.E., Rensselaer Poly. Inst., Troy, N.Y., 1885; Sc.D., LL.D.; m. Fanny Dulany, Aug. 14, 1893. Prof. civil engring., U. of Pa. Mem. Engring. Com. of Nat. Research Council, 1917—. Sec. Am. Soc. for Testing Material. Author: Framed Structures and Girders. Home: Philadelphia, Pa. Died June 27, 1918.

MARBURY, Elisabeth, author; b. N.Y. City, June 19, 1856; d. Francis F. and Elisabeth (McCoun) M.; ed. by father and in pvt. schs. Author's representative for many yrs. Twice decorated by French Govt. for services rendered to French authors; decorated by U.S., Belgium and Italy for services in World War. Author: My Crystal Ball (reminiscences), 1923. Translator: Faith of France (by Maurice Barrès), 1918. Home: New York, N.Y. Died Jan. 22, 1933.

MARBURY, William L., lawyer; b. Prince George's County, Md., Dec. 26, 1858; s. Fendall and Catherine Taylor (Marshall) M.; spl. course, Johns Hopkins, 1878-79, A.M., 1902; B.L., U. of Md. Law Sch., 1882; LL.D., St. John's Coll., Annapolis, Md.; m. Silvine Von Dorsner Slingluff, Oct. 10, 1894; children—Valerie Von Dorsner (Mrs. Barroll), Fendall, Silvine Von Dorsner, William Luke, Robert I. Taylor, Francis Cross. Began practice in office of uncle, Col. Charles Marshall, Baltimore, 1882; U.S. atty., Dist. of Md., by appmt. of President Cleveland, 1904-98; mem. Marbury, Gosnell & Williams, 1903—. Democrat. Episcopalian. Home: Baltimore, Md. Died Oct. 26, 1935.

MARBUT, Curtis Fletcher, geologist; b. Lawrence County, Mo., July 19, 1863; s. Nathan T. and Jane (Browning) M.; B.S., U. of Mo., 1889; A.M., Harvard, 1895; studied in Europe, 1899-1900; LL.D., U. of Mo., 1916; m. Florence Martin, Dec. 17, 1891 (dec.); children—Louise, Thomas Fiske, William Martin, Helen, Frederick Browning. Inst. geology and mineralogy, 1895-97, asst. prof., 1897-99, prof. and curator Geol. Mus., 1899-1913, U. of Mo.; dir. Soil Survey of Mo., 1905-13; spl. agt. Bur. of Soils, U.S. Dept. Agr., 1909-10; in charge Soil Survey, U.S. Dept. Agr., 1910—. Democrat. Unitarian. Address: Washington, D.C. Died Aug. 25, 1935.

MARCH, Daniel, clergyman; b. Millbury, Mass., July 21, 1816; ed. Millbury Acad.; grad. Yale, 1840; Yale Theol. Sem.; A.M., Yale; D.D., Western Univ., Pa. Congl. pastor in Nashua, N.H., Phila., and Woburn, Mass.; now pastor emeritus 1st Ch. Woburn. Author: Night Scenes in the Bible; Walks and Homes of Jesus; Our Father's House; Home Life in the Bible; The First Khedive; Morning Light in Many Lands; From Dark to Dawn. Address: Woburn, Mass. Died 1909.

MARCH, Francis Andrew, philologist; b. Millbury, Mass., Oct. 25, 1825; s. Andrew Patch and Nancy (Parker) M.; A.B., Amherst, 1845, A.M., 1848; LL.D., Princeton, 1870, Amherst, 1871; L.H.D., Columbia, 1887; D.C.L., Oxford, Eng., 1896; Litt.D., Cambridge, Eng., and Princeton, 1896; admitted to N.Y. bar, 1850; m. Mildred Stone Conway, 1860; children—Francis Andrew, Jr., Peyton Conway, Alden, John Lewis. Prof. English lang. and comparative philology, Lafayette Coll., 1856-1906; Carnegie hon. emeritus prof., 1907. Pioneer in philol. study of English classics and hist. study of English lang. Pres. Am. Philol. Assn., 1873-74, 1895-96, Spelling Reform Assn., 1876-1905, Modern Lang. Assn. America, 1891-93; mem. Internat. Congress Arts and Sciences, St. Louis Expn., 1904. Has been chmn. Commn. of State of Pa. on Amended Orthography; dir. Am. Workers for Hist. English Dictionary of Philol. Soc., London. Consulting editor Standard Dictionary. Author: Method of Philological Study of the English Language, 1865; A Parser and Analyzer for Beginners, 1869; Comparative Grammar of the Anglo-Saxon Language, 1870; Anglo-Saxon Reader, 1870; An A-B-C Book, 1880; also many addresses and articles in encyclopædias, periodicals, and the transactions of learned socs. on philos. and philol. subjects (particularly Anglo-Saxon) and on lit. (especially Shakespeare and Am. lit.), and Spelling Reform. Editor: Latin Hymns, with English Notes; Eusebius; Tertullian; Athenagoras; being vols. I-IV, Douglass series, Christian, Greek and Latin Classics, 1874-76; A Thesaurus-Dictionary of the English Language (with his son, F. A. March, Jr.), 1903. Address: Easton, Pa. Died 1911.

MARCH, Francis Andrew, Jr., philologist; b. Easton, Pa., Mar. 2, 1863; s. Francis Andrew and Mildred Stone (Conway) M.; A.B., Lafayette Coll., 1881, later A.M. and Ph.D.; m. Alice Youngman, Sept. 4, 1889; children—Mrs. Katharine Thomas, Francis Andrew, U.S.A., Robert Peyton. Tutor modern langs., 1882-84, adj. prof., 1884-91, prof. English lit., 1891-1905, prof. English Lang., 1905—, Lafayette Coll. Asst. in etymol. dept., Century Dictionary; editor in charge etymol. dept. Standard Dictionary; editor-in-chief (with his father) the Thesaurus-Dictionary. Mayor of Easton, Pa., 1905-09. Mason, Elk. Author: History of the World War, 1918; America in the World War (with R. J. Beamish), 1919; Athletics at Lafayette College, 1926. Home: Easton, Pa. Died Feb. 28, 1928.

MARCH, Thomas Stone, educator; b. Easton, Pa., Feb. 26, 1868; s. Francis Andrew and Mildred Stone (Conway) M.; A.B., Lafayette, 1889, A.M., 1892, Ph.D., 1899; m. Jennie Baldridge Bridge, June 20, 1893. Prin. acad., Parksburg, Pa., 1889-90; prin. schs., Clearfield, 1890-96, Honesdale, 1896-1902, Susquehanna, 1902-04; supt. schs., Greensburg, 1904-11; state insp. of schs., Pa., 1911-18; supt. of schs., Greensburg, Pa., 1918-34. Presbyn. Mason. Author: A History of Pennsylvania, 1915. Editor: Pennsylvania Arbor Day Manual, 1913; Pennsylvania Bird Day and Arbor Day Manual, 1917. Address: Greensburg, Pa. Died Jan. 13, 1939.

MARCIAL-DORADO, Carolina, author; b. Toledo, Spain, 1889; d. José and María M.; A.B., Instituto Cisneros, Madrid, 1907; came to U.S., 1907; post-grad. work, Wellesley, Columbia and U. of Pa.; M.A., U. of Pa., 1920. Instr. Spanish, Wellesley, 1907-11; asst. prof. Spanish, U. of Puerto Rico, 1911-17; instr. Spanish lit., Bryn Mawr, 1918-20; asso. in Spanish, Barnard Coll., 1920-24, asst. prof., 1924-40, asso. prof., 1940—. Middlebury Coll. Summer Sch., 1918; summer session U. of Calif., 1919; summer session Teachers' Coll., Columbia, 1921; dean summer sch. U. of Barcelona, 1922, 23. Dir. Spanish Residence, Columbia U., 1938—. Spanish editor Ginn & Co., 1917-24; dir. Bur. Pro-España and gen. publications mgr. Internat. Telephone and Telegraph Co., 1924-34. Decorated by Spanish Govt. with Gran Cruz de Alfonso XII, and the Cruz de Plata de Mérito Civil. Author: España Pintoresca, 1917; Primeras Lecciones de Español, 1918; Primeras Lecturas en Español, 1919; Segundas Lecciones de Español, 1922; Geografía Moderna, 1923; Chispitas (6 short Spanish plays), 1926, Pasitos, 1935. Editor of Blasco Ibañez' Vistas Sudamericanas, 1920; Libro Tercero de Lectura, 1928; Libro Cuarto de Lectura, 1934. Co-editor Trozos Modernos, 1922. Address: New York, N.Y. Died July 25, 1941.

MARCONI, (Guglielmo) William, elec. engr.; b. Bologna, Italy, Apr. 25, 1874 (mother Irish-born); ed. Leghorn and U. of Bologna; LL.D., Glasgow, Aberdeen, U. of Pa.; D.Sc., Oxford; m. Hon. Beatrice O'Brien, Mar. 16, 1905. Began, 1890, on his father's estate, experiments to test the theory that the electric current is capable of passing through any substance, and, if started, in any given direction, of following an undeviating course without need for a wire or other conductor. He invented an apparatus for wireless telegraphy which attracted attention of Sir William Henry Preece, engr. and electrician-in-chief English Postal Telegraph, who tested the apparatus, with success, in England; soon afterward succeeded in sending messages from Spezia to a steamer 15 kilometers distant; also sent messages from Queen Victoria ashore to Prince of Wales on royal yacht, 1897; came to U.S., 1899; used his method in reporting election, 1900; succeeded in establishing wireless telegraphic communication across Atlantic Ocean, 1902; daily ocean news service by wireless telegraphy inaugurated by him on trans-Atlantic liners, 1904. Invented directive method of wireless telegraphy, 1905, and continuous-wave system, 1906. Awarded one-half of the Nobel Prize, for physics, 1909. Home: Bologna, Italy. Died July 19, 1937.

MARCOSSON, Sol, violinist; b. Louisville, Ky., June 10, 1869; s. Louis and Helene (Newmark) M.; ed. pub. schs., Louisville; began mus. studies under Henry Burck, Louisville; student Royal Hochschule, Berlin, Germany, 1887-92; pupil of Heinrich de Ahna and Joachim; m. Dorothy Frew, Oct. 5, 1903; children—John, Diana Ruth, Dorothy June, Frederick Frew. First violinist with Mendelssohn Quintette Club, Boston, 1892-93, New York Philharmonic Club, 1893-94; concert master, Cleveland Symphony Orchestra, 1895-96, later Chicago Symphony Orchestra; dir. violin dept., Chautauqua (N.Y.) Institution and of Lake Erie Coll. for Women; dir. Marcosson Music Sch., Cleveland, and 1st violin, Philharmonic Quartet. Studio: Cleveland, O. Died Jan. 10, 1940.

MARCUS, Louis, mayor; b. Brooklyn, N.Y., Jan. 9, 1880; s. Eleazor Albert and Diana (Gumpel) M.; prep. edn., pub. schs., Dover, Del., and York, Pa., until 1895; student Bucknell U., 1895-96; m. Gertrude Levin, Jan. 16, 1912; 1 son, Louis Howard. Learned trade of electrical machinist, in Phila., Pa., and worked at it until 1907; removed to Salt Lake City, 1907, and engaged in motion picture business as operator, exchange mgr. and owner of film exchange and theatres; disposed of theatre interests, 1929; repurchased an interest in motion picture theatres; pres. United Realty Co., real estate investments; dir. Tracy Loan & Trust Co., Walker Bank & Trust Co. Mayor of Salt Lake City; retired Dec. 31, 1935. Mason, Elk; mem. B'nai B'rith. Republican. Jewish religion. Home: Salt Lake City, Utah. Died July 27, 1936.

MARCUS, Louis William, judge; b. Buffalo, May 18, 1863; s. Leopold and Amelia M.; ed. Williams Acad. and Central High Sch., Buffalo; LL.B., Cornell, 1889; m. Ray R. Dahlman, Nov. 19, 1889. Admitted to bar, 1889; surrogate, Erie County, N.Y., 1895-1905; apptd. justice Supreme Ct. of N.Y., 8th Dist., Nov. 11, 1905; elected to same, Nov. 1906, for term 1907-20; reëlected, for term 1920-34. Republican. Mason. Home: Buffalo, N.Y. Died Aug. 18, 1923.

MARCY, Erastus Edgerton, M.D.; b. Greenwich, Mass., Dec. 9, 1815; grad. Amherst, 1834; Jefferson Med. Coll., 1837; practiced, Hartford, Conn., 1837-47; became convert to homœopathy; practiced in New York after 1847; founded, 1852, and edited until 1865, North Am. Jour. of Homœopathy. Author: Theory and Practice of Medicine; Homœopathy vs. Allopathy; Theory and Practice of Homœopathy; Christianity and Its Conflicts; Life Duties; etc. Address: New York, N.Y. Died 1900.

MARCY, George Edward, grain mcht.; b. Lockport, Ill., Aug. 14, 1863; s. William W. and Mary (Dowse) M.; ed. pub. schs. of Chicago; m. Carrie E. Emery. Began with H. W. Rogers & Bro., grain, 1879; became identified, 1889, with Armour & Co., grain, and Armour Grain Co., becoming pres. Armour Grain Co., 1907; dir. Union Trust Co., Erie R.R. Home: Chicago, Ill. Died Aug. 25, 1939.

MARCY, Henry Orlando, surgeon; b. Otis, Mass., June 23, 1837; s. Smith and Fanny (Gibbs) M.; ed. Wilbraham Acad. and Amherst Coll.; M.D., Harvard, 1863; hon. A.M., Amherst, 1870; LL.D., Wesleyan, 1887; m. Sarah E. Wendell, Oct. 14, 1863. Asst. surgeon 43d Mass. Vols., Apr. 1863; surgeon 35th U.S.C.T., Nov. 1863; med. dir. of Fla., 1864; med. dir. on Sherman's staff, Carolina campaign; made sanitary renovation of Charleston, S.S.; practiced Cambridge, Mass., 1865-69; studied at U. of Berlin, and in London and Edinburgh, 1869-70; was 1st Am. pupil of Dr. Lister, Edinburgh, and later introduced Lister's methods to America. Returned to U.S. and devoted his attention to laboratory and practical study of antiseptic methods of wound treatment; has conducted pvt. hosp. in Cambridge for treatment surgical diseases, 1880—. Was asst. to Dr. Henry J. Bowditch, Boston, and after his death chief dir. in renovation Charles River Basin; built Harvard Bridge, completed Cambridge Esplanada Parkway, and placed M.I.T. on Cambridge front, the site of which he chiefly owned; a leader in development of the Parkway reservation. President A.M.A., 1892, Am. Acad. Medicine, 1884. Author: The Reproductive Process (transl. from G. B. Ercolani's work, 2 vols.), 1884; The Anatomy and Surgical Treatment of Hernia; The Radical Cure of Hernia, 1889; The Perineum, Its Anatomy and Surgical Treatment, 1889. Active in surg. service during entire period of the World War. Home: Boston, Mass. Died Jan. 2, 1924.

MARCY, Oliver, prof. geology Northwestern U.; b. Colrain, Mass., Feb. 13, 1820; grad. Wesleyan U., Middletown, Conn., 1846; hon. A.M., Wesleyan; LL.D., U. of Chicago, 1873; m. Elizabeth Eunice Smith, July 2, 1847. Taught, 1846-62, Wilbraham Acad.; prof. in Northwestern U., 1862—, acting pres., 1876-81. Address: Evanston, Ill. Died 1899.

MARDEN, Charles Carroll, univ. prof.; b. Baltimore, Dec. 21, 1867; s. Jesse and Anna Maria (Brice) M.; A.B., Johns Hopkins, 1889, Ph.D., 1894; m. Mary Talbott Clark, Dec. 2, 1897; children—John Clark, Charles Carroll, Nicholas Brice, Mary Talbott Clark. Instr. modern langs., Norfolk (Va.) Acad., 1889-90; instr. French, U. of Mich., 1890-91; instr., asso., asso. prof., Romance langs., 1894-1900, asso. prof. Spanish, 1900-05, prof., 1905-17, Johns Hopkins U.; prof. Spanish, Princeton U., 1917—. Mng. editor Modern Language Notes, 1911-15; chief examiner in Spanish for Coll. Entrance Exam. Bd., 1922-24; Carnegie visiting prof. to Spanish universities, 1928. Mem. exec. council Modern Lang. Assn. America, 1924-26, pres., 1932; Knight Comdr. Order of Isabel la Católica. Author: Phonology of the Spanish Dialect of Mexico City, 1896; Bibliography of American Spanish, 1911, 26; A First Spanish Grammar (with F. C. Tarr), 1926. Editor: Poema de Fernan Gonzalez, 1904; Libro de Apolonio, 1917; Cuatro Poemas de Berceo, 1928; Berceo, Veintiún Milagros de Nuestra Señora, 1929; Martirio de San Lorenzo, 1930. Home: Princeton, N.J. Died May 11, 1932.

MARDEN, George Augustus, asst. treasurer U.S. at Boston, 1899—; b. Mt. Vernon, N.H., Aug. 9, 1839; s. Benjamin F. and Betsey (Buss) M.; grad. Dartmouth, 1861; m. Mary P. Fiske, Dec. 10, 1867; entered army, Dec., 1861, in 2d regt. Berdan's U.S. Sharpshooters, later in 1st regt. Berdan's Sharpshooters, serving as q.m. and as acting asst. adj. gen. 3d brigade, 3d div., 3d army corps; mustered out, Sept., 1864; studied law; became connected with Concord Monitor, Boston Daily Advertiser; editor and a propr. of Lowell Daily Courier, 1867—; also Lowell Morning Citizen; mem. Mass. legislature, 1873; clerk same, 1874-82. Speaker, same, 1883-84; mem. Mass. senate, 1885; treas. and receiver gen. of Mass., 1889-93. Home: Lowell, Mass. Died 1906.

MARDEN, Orison Swett, editor, author; b. Thornton, N.H., about 1850; s. Louis and Martha (Cilley) M.; B.S., Boston U., 1877, Bachelor of Oratory and A.M., 1879, LL.B., 1882; M.D., Harvard, 1881; m. Clare L. Evans, May 1905. Founded, 1897, and was editor of the Success Magazine. Author: The Making of a Man, 1905; Choosing a Career, 1905; Every Man a King, 1906; The Power of Personality, 1906; Success Nuggets, 1906; The Optimistic Life, 1907; He Can Who Thinks He Can, 1908; Why Grow Old?, 1909; Peace, Power and Plenty, 1909; Do It To a Finish, 1910; Not the Salary But the Opportunity, 1910; Getting On, 1910; Be Good to Yourself, 1910; The Miracle of Right Thought, 1910; Self Investment, 1911; The Joys of Living, 1913; The Exceptional Employee, 1913; The Progressive Business Man, 1913; Training for Efficiency, 1913; Keeping Fit, 1914; I Had a Friend, 1914; Hints for Young Writers, 1914; The Crime of Silence, 1915; Woman and Home, 1915; Making Life a Masterpiece, 1916; The Victorious Attitude, 1916; Selling Things, 1916; Everybody Ahead, 1917; Thrift, 1918; How to Get What You Want, 1917; Love's Way, 1918; Ambition and Success, 1919; You Can, But Will You?, 1919; Success Fundamentals, 1920; Masterful Personality, 1921; also many others prior to 1905. Edited Consolidated Encyclopedic Library (10 vols.), 1901. Home: Sea Cliff, L.I., N.Y. Died Mar. 10, 1924.

MARDEN, Oscar Avery, judge; b. Palermo, Me., Aug. 20, 1853; s. Stephen P. and Julia A. (Avery) M.; ed. Westbrook Sem., Deering, Me.; LL.B., Boston U., 1876; m. May T. Ball; children—Edgar A. (dec.), Oscar H. (dec.); m. 2d, Caroline A. Avery, Jan. 24, 1896. Began practice, Boston, 1877; trial justice Norfolk Co., 1877-91; judge Dist. Court of Southern Norfolk, 1891—; mem. appellate div. of Dist. Courts, 1922-31. Mem. Sch. Com., Stoughton, 17 yrs. Liberal Democrat. Universalist. Mason (Dist. Dep. G.M. 22d Masonic Dist., 1907, 08); Grand Patriarch of Grand Encampment of Mass., I.O.O.F., 1893. Govt. appeal agt. Div. 35, Mass., 1917-18. Home: Stoughton, Mass. Died Aug. 27, 1932.

MARDEN, Robert Fiske, newspaper editor; b. Lowell, Mass., June 14, 1876; s. George Augustus and Mary (Porter) M.; A.B., Dartmouth, 1898; m. Ella B. Pote, June 12, 1901; children—Dorothy Fiske (Mrs. Charles Francis Fairbanks II), Barbara. Solicitor life insurance, 1898-1905; began as reporter with Lowell (Mass.) Courier-Citizen, 1905, later editor; partner Marden & Murphy, real estate brokers; pres. Marden & Murphy, Inc., Lowell Ice Co.; dir. and clk. Courier-Citizen Co., Courier-Citizen Newspaper Co.; dir. Appleton Nat. Bank (Lowell); trustee Lowell Instn. for Savings. Served as pvt. Mass. Vol. Militia, 1903-06; 2d lt. Mass. State Guard, 1918-20; mem. Mass. Com. Pub.

Safety and Lowell Pub. Safety Com., 1918-19. Trustee McCollum Inst., Mt. Vernon, N.H. Republican. Conglist. Mason. Home: Lowell, Mass. Died Mar. 13, 1935.

MAREAN, Emma Endicott, writer; b. Boston, Mass., Jan. 20, 1854; d. Henry and Agibail Hastings (Browning) Endicott; ed. Cambridge, Mass., and Hanover and Dresden, Germany, 1871-73; m. Joseph Mason Marean, Jan. 20, 1876; children—Edith E. (Mrs. Roderick Stebbins), Henry E., Parker E., Browning E., Endicott. Lived in Chicago 12 yrs.; editor the Christian Register, Boston, 1897-1918. Author: Eighteen (poems), 1894; Now and Then (poems), 1928. Home: Cambridge, Mass. Died Oct. 17, 1936.

MAREAN, Josiah Taylor, judge; b. Maine, N.Y., Apr. 30, 1842; s. Chester and Arvilla (Taylor) M.; grad. State Normal Sch., Albany, 1862; studied law in office of Emerson, Goodrich & Knowlton; m. Elizabeth Richards. Admitted to bar, 1866; practiced law, Brooklyn, 1867-99; elected dist. atty. Kings County, 1897; justice Supreme Ct. of N.Y., for term Jan. 1, 1899-Dec. 31, 1912; later official referee of Supreme Court. Democrat. Home: Brooklyn, N.Y. Died Feb. 8, 1922.

MAREAN, Willis Adams, architect; b. Woodhull, N.Y., May 24, 1853; s. Ransom and Clarissa Jane (Adams) M.; ed. Middlebury Acad., Wyoming, N.Y.; State Normal Sch., Geneseo, N.Y.; m. Charlotte Terese Hemeranger, Dec. 19, 1891. Began as architect, Denver, 1880; partner F. E. Edbrooke, 1881-95; mem. firm of Marean & Norton from 1895 until retired. Home: Denver, Colo. Died Feb. 9, 1939.

MARGOLIS, Max Leopold, philologist; b. Merech, govt. Vilna, Russia, Oct. 15, 1866; s. Rabbi Isaac and Hinde (Bernstein) M.; ed. Merech and Warsaw, 1873-83; grad. Leibniz Gymnasium, Berlin, 1889; A.M., Columbia, 1890, Ph.D., 1891; m. Evelyn Kate, d. Philip N. Aronson, June 20, 1906. Lecturer on Jewish lit., Glenmore Sch. for Culture Sciences, Keene, N.Y., 1892; asst. prof. Hebrew and Bibl. exegesis, Hebrew Union Coll., Cincinnati, 1892-97; asst. prof. Semitic langs. and lits., 1897-98, asso. prof., 1898-1905, U. of Calif.; prof. Bibl. exegesis, Hebrew Union Coll., 1905-07; visited European libraries, 1907-08; editor in chief Bible translation for Jewish Publication Soc. of America, 1908-09; prof. Bibl. philology, Dropsie Coll. for Hebrew and Cognate Learning, Phila., 1909—; ann. prof., Am. Sch. of Oriental Research, and prof., Hebrew U., Jerusalem, 1924-25. Author: Commentarius Isaacidis quatenus ad textum talmudicum investigandum adhiberi possit tractatu Erubhin Ostenditur (thesis for Ph.D.), 1891; The Columbia College Manuscript of Meghilla, 1892; An Elementary Text-Book of Hebrew Accidence, 1893; The Theological Aspect of Reformed Judiasm, 1904; The Holy Scriptures with Commentary on Micah, 1908; A Manual of the Aramaic Language of the Babylonian Talmud, 1910; The Story of Bible Translations, 1917; The Hebrew Scriptures in the Making, 1922. Editor Journal of Am. Oriental Soc., 1922—. Home: Oak Lane, Pa. Died Apr. 2, 1932.

MARINDIN, Henri Louis François, asst. U.S. Coast and Geodetic Survey, 1863—; b. Lausanne, Switzerland, July 2, 1843; s. François Louis Frederic and Marianne (Trabaud) M.; common school edn. there; ed. as civil engr., 1860-63, Owego, N.Y.; topog. engr. with army in front of Richmond, 1863-64; coast survey mem. Isthmus of Darien Commn., 1870; mem. Mississippi River Commn. (for improvement navigation); field officer U.S. Coast and Geodetic Survey comdg. U.S.S. Eagle, etc.; m. Eliza Eliot Ritchie, 1885. Has written papers pertaining to physical hydrography in official reports. Home: Woodside, Md. Deceased.

MARIX, Adolph, rear admiral U.S.N.; b. Dresden, Saxony, May 10, 1848; s. Henry and Frederica (Meyer) M.; grad. U.S. Naval Acad., 1868; m. Grace Filkins, May 31, 1896. Commd. midshipman, June 1, 1868; promoted through various grades to capt., Mar. 21, 1903; rear admiral, July 4, 1908. Served on European and Asiatic stas.; was judge advocate of Maine court of inquiry; capt. of port of Manila, 1901-03; comd. U.S.S. Scorpion during Spanish-Am. War, and was promoted for conspicuous bravery; chmn. Lighthouse Board, 1907-10; retired, May 10, 1910. Address: New York, N.Y. Died July 12, 1919.

MARK, Clayton, mfr.; b. Fredericksburg, Pa., June 1858; s. Cyrus and Rebecca (Strohm) M.; ed. pub. schs.; m. Anna L. Griffith, Sept. 1880 (died 1915); children—Clarence, Alice (Mrs. McMicken Hanchett), Clayton, Lydia (Mrs. Arthur T. MacDonald), Phyllis (Mrs. Everett L. Wyman), Cryus, Scytha (Mrs. Alvin M. Ehret, Jr.), Griffith, Anna (Mrs. Avery Rockefeller). Began with Chicago Malleable Iron Co., co. succeeded by Nat. Malleable Castings Co., of Cleveland, of which was dir., 1894, 2d v.p., 1902, and resident v.p. until 1917; pres. Mark Mfg. Co. until 1919, company merging into The Steel and Tube Co. of America, of which was chmn. bd. until sold to The Youngstown Sheet Tube Co., 1923; pres. Clayton Mark & Co. Pres. Bd. of Edn. of City of Chicago; pres. Civic Federation of Chicago, 1907-09 and 1923—. Republican. Mason. Home: Lake Forest, Ill. Died July 8, 1936.

MARKBREIT, Leopold, pres. and mgr. Cincinnati Volksblatt Co., 1875—; b. Vienna, Austria, 1842; s. Leopold and Johanna (Abele) M.; came to Cincinnati, 1848; ed. in Sandusky, O., Phila., and Cincinnati; studied law; admitted to bar; partner for short time of Rutherford B. Hayes (later President of U.S.); served sergt. to capt. and asst. adj. gen. in 28th Ohio inf., under Gens. Moore, Crook, Roberts, Cox and Averell; captured Dec. 1863, by Confederates; confined in Libby prison for many months; released Feb. 1865, with health shattered; held city office; col. on staffs Govs. Cox and Hayes; U.S. minister to Bolivia, 1869-73; went to Brazil, Bolivia, Uruguay, Chile, Peru and Ecuador on business mission, 1873-74; asst. treas. U.S. at Cincinnati, 1882-86; mem. Cincinnati, 1882-86; mem. Cincinnati Water Works Commn., 1896—; mayor of Cincinnati, 1908-10. Home: Cincinnati, O. Died 1909.

MARKELL, Charles Frederick, author; b. Frederick, Md., Oct. 16, 1855; s. Frederick and Catherine Sue (Thomas) M.; classical edn.; LL.B., Columbian (now George Washington) U., 1876; m. Sue Markell Rogan, Jan. 28, 1902. Admitted to practice Supreme Ct., D.C.; practiced profession in native town, at same time owning and editing a daily Republican newspaper; mem. Md. House of Delegates, 1884-85, 1896-97; sec. of legation to Brazil, 1892; chargé d'affaires, 1893; induced Brazilian Govt. to remove expediente tax on wheat flour from U.S. Author: Chamodine and Other Poems; The Chaskell Papers; Ypiranga—A Love Tale of the Brazils. Has spent many yrs. abroad, residing in all the leading capitals of Europe. Address: Birmingham, Ala. Died July 5, 1941.

MARKENS, Isaac, writer; b. New York, N.Y., Oct. 9, 1846; s. Elias and Rosetta (Friedlander) M.; ed. pub. schs.; m. Rachel Benjamin, Sept. 3, 1873; children—Elias, Rose, Edward Wasgate, Walter Henry. In shipping and commn. business, 1862-67; commercial traveler, 1867-73; stenographer, 1873-77; pvt. sec. to Albert Fink, organizer of Trunk Line Commn., 1877-81; asst. mgr. United Press Assn., 1881-82; on staff N.Y. Commercial Advertiser, 1882-83, Mail and Express, 1883-94; commercial editor New York Star, 1887-89. Past Sr. Grand Deacon Masonic Grand Lodge of Fla. Author: Hebrews in America, 1888; Abraham Lincoln and the Jews, 1909; President Lincoln and the Case of John Y. Beall, 1911; Why President Lincoln Spared Three Lives, 1911; Lincoln's Masterpiece, 1913; Manassas, an Israelite of Colonial Days, 1917; Origin of Famous Lincoln Sayings, 1918. Authority on Abraham Lincoln. Home: Newark, N.J. Died Aug. 14, 1928.

MARKHAM, Charles Henry, ry. pres.; b. Clarksville, Tenn., May 22, 1861; s. Daniel and Mary (Redden) M.; ed. pub. schs., Addison, N.Y., 1873-77; m. Anna E. Smith, Feb. 18, 1884. Began ry. service as section laborer on A.,T.&S.F. Ry., 1881; station laborer and clerk at Deming, N.M., station agt., Lordsburg, N.M., Benson, Ariz., and Reno, Nev., 1881-97; agt. and dist. freight and pass. agt., Fresno, Calif., gen. freight and pass. agt. of Ore. Lines, Portland, 1897-1901, asst. freight traffic mgr., San Francisco, Sept. 1-Dec. 28, 1901, Southern Pacific Co.; v.p. Houston & Tex. Central R.R., 1901-04; v.p. and gen. mgr., Apr. 1-Nov. 1, 1904, Southern Pacific Co.; gen. mgr. Guffey Petroleum Co., of Beaumont, Tex., 1904-09; pres. Gulf Refining Co. and Gulf Pipe Line Co., Pittsburgh, 1909-11; pres. Ill. Central R.R. Co., 1911-18; also pres., then chmn. bd. Ocean Steamship Co. and Central of Ga. Ry., 1911-18. Apptd. regional dir. of rys., Southern region, Atlanta, Ga., by Dir. Gen. McAdoo, Jan. 1918; regional dir. Allegheny region, Phila., June 1, 1918-Sept. 30, 1919; pres. Ill. Central R.R. Co., 1919-26, chmn. bd., 1926—, also chmn. bd. Central of Ga. Ry. Co. and Ocean Steamship Co., Oct. 1, 1919—. Home: Chicago, Ill. Died Nov. 24, 1930.

MARKHAM, Edwin, poet lecturer; b. Oregon City, Ore., Apr. 23, 1852; s. Samuel and Elizabeth (Winchell) M.; went to Calif., 1857, worked at farming, blacksmithing, herded cattle and sheep during boyhood; ed. San Jose Normal Sch. and two Western colls.; spl. studies in ancient and modern literature; Litt.D., Baylor; L.H.D., Syracuse U., 1924; Litt.D., New York U., 1930, St. Lawrence U., Canton, N.Y., 1933; m. Anna Catherine Murphy, 1898; 1 son, Virgil. Was prin. and supt. of schs. in Calif. until 1899. Has written poems since early boyhood in Calif. papers and received recognition of best Eastern mags. Wrote: "The Man with the Hoe," a poem, 1899, which received world-wide attention, being hailed by many as "the battle-cry of the next thousand years." Author: The Man with the Hoe, and Other Poems, 1899; The Man with the Hoe, with Notes by the Author, 1900; Lincoln, and Other Poems, 1901; The Shoes of Happiness and Other Poems; California the Wonderful, 1915; Gates of Paradise (poems), 1920; The Ballad of the Gallows Bird, 1926; New Poems —Eighty Songs at Eighty, 1932; The Star of Araby, 1937. Has been engaged in selecting and editing Remarkable Pages from Thomas Lake Harris. Wrote: The Social Conscience, as a baccalaureate sermon, Stanford University, 1897; also The Hoe-Man in the Making, a series of magazine articles covering the whole problem of child labor (series published in book form called The Children in Bondage). Editor: Foundation Stones of Success (4th edit.), 1925; The Book of Poetry (2 vols. covering 1,000 yrs. of European and American poetry), 1927; California in Song and Story, 1930; Poetry of Youth (anthology) 1935. Made recordings of interpretations of his principal poems, under title Edwin Markham, Himself, 1938. Address: Port Richmond, S.I., N.Y. Died Mar. 7, 1940.

MARKHAM, Henry Harrison, governor; b. Wilmington, N.Y., Nov. 16, 1840; s. Nathan B. and Susan (McLeod) M.; ed. pub. and pvt. schs.; worked on farm until 1861; removed to Wis.; served in Union Army; was with Sherman on march to the sea; severely wounded at battle of Whippy Swamp, Feb. 3, 1865; studied law; admitted to practice Wis. and U.S. courts; m. Mary A. Dana, May 17, 1876. Practiced at Milwaukee, 1867-78; removed to Pasadena, Calif., 1878; engaged in gold and silver mining; mem. 49th Congress (1885-87); gov. of Calif., 1891-95; mem. bd. mgrs. Nat. Home for Disabled Vol. Soldiers. Republican. Address: Redondo Beach, Calif. Died Oct. 9, 1923.

MARKHAM, William Guy, farmer; b. Rush, N.Y., Sept. 2, 1836; s. Guy and Eliza (Williams) M.; ed. Genesee Wesleyan Sem., Lima, N.Y.; m. Josephine Foote, May 28, 1885. Breeder of registered cattle and sheep, 1860—; sec. Nat. Wool Growers' Assn., 1876-83, 1885-1901; sec. N.Y. State Sheep Breeders' and Wool Growers' Assn., 1876, pres., 1877-84; pres. N.Y. State Am. Sheep Breeders' Assn., 1879-85; v.p. State Bank of Avon; dir. Rochester & Genesee Valley R.R., Pfaudler Co. (chem. bd.), Livingston County Trust Co., etc. Pres. Rochester Humane Soc., 1885-86. Author: New York American Merino Register (the first individual pedigrees of sheep), 1876; American Merino Flock Record, 1877. Personally delivered 200 sheep to Japanese Govt., 1879; exported Merino sheep extensively to Australia, New Zealand, Cape Town, S. Africa, and Buenos Aires, 1882-91. Visited China, Mongolia, Italy, France and Germany, 1880, in interest of improved sheep, also Australia, New Zealand and Tasmania, 1888. Home: Avon, N.Y. Died May 16, 1922.

MARKLE, Alvan, corp. official; b. Hazleton, Pa., Aug. 29, 1861; s. G. B. and Emily A. (Robinson) M.; A.B., Fafayette, 1882; m. Mary Dryfoos, 1887; children—Mrs. Emily Bannard, Alvan Donald, Eckley B., John II. Pres. Wilkes-Barre & Hazleton Ry. Co., Markle Banking & Trust Co., Lehigh Telephone Co., Lehigh Traction Co. Republican. Address: Hazleton, Pa. Died Mar. 19, 1931.

MARKLE, John, coal operator; b. Hazleton, Pa., Dec. 15, 1858; s. G. B. and Emily A. M.; grad. Lafayette Coll. (mining engring. course), 1880; m. Mary E. Robinson, Apr. 22, 1884. Apptd. gen. supt. of mines of G. B. Markle & Co., 1880, and upon his father's retirement succeeded him, was pres. of Jeddo-Highland Coal Co., successor to G. B. Markle Co., one of largest "independent" cos. in the anthracite coal industry, also pres. and chief engr. Jeddo Tunnel Co., retired. Was one of the leading figures and represented the independent operators in the negotiations with President Roosevelt, and in the inquiry by the President's commn. in connection with the anthracite coal strike, 1902. Trustee Lafayette Coll., Pa., Knickerbocker Hosp., N.Y. City. Home: New York, N.Y. Died July 10, 1933.

MARKLEY, Alfred Collins, brig. gen. U.S.A.; b. Doylestown, Pa., Apr. 18, 1843; s. John Sorver and Eliza (Collins) M.; ed. pvtly. to 1854, Penn Grammar Sch., 1854-56, and Central High Sch., Phila., 1856-58; m. Rebecca Conrad Morgan, Apr. 23, 1868; 1 son, Edward Browning (dec.). With Browning & Bros., mfrs. Phila., 1861-63; pvt. 25th Pa. Inf., 1862; corporal 52d Pa. Inf. (State Militia), 1863, both in active service in Pa. and Md., sergt. 197th Pa. Vols., 1864, 2d lt. 127th U.S. Colored Inf., Sept. 1864; 1st lt. and adj., Mar. 1865; mustered out, Oct. 1865; apptd. 2d lt., 41st U.S. Inf. (regular army), July 28, 1866; promoted through grades to brig. gen. U.S.A., Mar. 2, 1907. Served in Antietam and Gettysburg campaigns, also in operations before Richmond, Va., 1864-65; siege and capture of Petersburg, Va., Mar. 1865; pursuit of Lee's army to surrender at Appomattox, April 1865; with "Army of Observation" on Rio Grande (to drive French Army out of Mexico), under Gen. Sheridan, May-Oct. 1865; frontier service against Indians, 1867-80; campaign in Cuba, June-Aug. 1898, battle of San Juan Hill, comdg. 24th Inf., after wounding of lt. col., July 1; participated in capture and occupation of Ft. San Juan, which comd. until July 9, 1898 (cited with silver star for gallantry at Santiago, July 1898, 1924); comdg. officer 24th Inf., July 1-Aug. 26, that volunteered, at Santiago, to go to yellow fever camp at Siboney to nurse the sick and bury the dead and do other hosp. service requiring great courage and self-sacrifice, ultimately resulting in death to about one-fourth of the officers and men of the regt.; comd. regt. and other troops, 4,000 men, and depot of supply for army at Siboney, Cuba; comd. Fort D. A. Russell, Wyo., and Vancouver Barracks, Wash., to Dec. 1899, when ordered to Philippines; comd. dist. of 13 towns and system of supply to troops in Caraballo Mountains; returned to U.S.

July 1902; comd. Ft. McDowell, 1902-05; went to P.I., Oct. 5, 1905, comd. Fort Wm. McKinley, Manila; retired by operation of law, Apr. 18, 1907; returned to U.S., June 9, 1907. Home: Alton, Ill. Died Aug. 24, 1926.

MARKLEY, Joseph Lybrand, coll. prof.; b. E. Nantmeal Tp., Chester County, Pa., Oct. 6, 1859; s. Napoleon Bonaparte and Ellen Ann (Liggett) M.; grad. West Chester (Pa.) Normal Sch., 1881, scientific course, 1883; A.B., Haverford (Pa.) Coll., 1885, A.M., 1886; A.M., Harvard, 1887, Ph.D., 1889; U. of Göttingen, 1895-97; m. Mary Elizabeth Butler, July 6, 1893. Instr. mathematics, Harvard, 1889-90; instr. mathematics, 1890-95, asst. prof., 1895-1904, jr. prof., 1904-07, prof., 1907—, chmn. math. dept., 1922—, U. of Mich. Address: Ann Arbor, Mich. Died Apr. 19, 1930.

MARKOE, Thomas Masters, physician and surgeon; b. Phila., Sept. 13, 1819; s. Francis and Sarah (Caldwell) M.; grad. Princeton, 1836; Coll. of Phys. & Surg., New York, 1841; prof. anatomy Castleton Med. Coll., Vt.; prof. path. anatomy med. dept. Univ. of City of New York, 1852-54; adjunct prof. surgery, 1860-70, prof. surgery, 1870-79, prof. principles of surgery, 1879-90, med. dept., Columbia Coll., retired 1899. Author: Diseases of the Bone; etc. Address: New York, N.Y. Died 1901.

MARKS, Avery C., Jr., editor; b. Greenville, Mich., Feb. 16, 1887; s. Avery Cornelius and Alice Gertrude (Riley) M.; grad. Manual Training Sch., Muskegon, Mich.; student U. of Chicago, Yale; hon. B.S., Northern Ill. Coll., 1909; m. Harriet H. Ennis, Aug. 1914. Began as reporter, Grand Rapids (Mich.) News, 1911; mng. editor, Washington Times, 1919-28; became mem. exec. staff Nat. Broadcasting Co., 1928; v.p. Radio Associates, 1931—. Mason. Home: New York, N.Y. Died Dec. 15, 1935.

MARKS, Bernard; b. Bromberg, Germany, Sept. 19, 1833; brought to America at age of 3; mainly self-educated; m. Cornelia Dorman Barlow, 1860. Arrived in San Francisco, Feb. 23, 1853; successfully identified for a number of yrs. with gold mining in Calif.; prin. Spring Valley Grammar Sch., 6 yrs., Lincoln Grammar Sch., San Francisco, 4 yrs.; began farming in Fresno County, 1875, and established large colony, later established colonies in Merced, Sacramento, and other counties; recognized as a leading irrigationist of Calif. Address: Sacramento, Calif. Died Dec. 28, 1915.

MARKS, Mrs. L. S., author; see Josephine Preston Peabody.

MARKS, Marcus M., merchant; b. Schenectady, N.Y., Mar. 18, 1858; s. David and Leontine M.; ed. public sch. and College City of New York, class of 1877; LL.D., Lincoln Memorial U.; m. Esther Friedman, May 21, 1890. Started retail business, Passaic, N.J., 1877, and with father wholesale clothing firm of David Marks & Sons; retired. Organized Nat. Assn. of Clothiers, and its pres. 10 yrs.; one of founders of Merchants Assn., Ednl. Alliance (hon. dir.), and of conciliation dept. of Nat. Civic Federation; served as mediator and arbitrator on numerous industrial disputes; retired from business to devote whole time to above mentioned activities. Elected pres. Borough of Manhattan, N.Y., on Fusion Com. ticket, 1913. Mem. exec. com. Nat. Civic Federation; mem. President Roosevelt's "Nobel Prize" com. of 9 on industrial peace; organizer and pres. of Tuberculosis Preventorium for Children; established the first 3 open pub. markets in N.Y. City, 1914; also new form Joint Trial Bd. for trial of civil service employees; initiated welfare work among municipal employees, etc. Trustee Church Peace Union. Writer on subjects of labor and conciliation and on commercial coöperation. Introduced the movement for "Daylight Saving" in U.S., 1915; organizer and pres. Nat. and N.Y. Daylight-Savings assns.; organized Com. on Foreign Study and Travel, 1924. Home: New York, N.Y. Died Aug. 26, 1934.

MARKS, Solon, physician and surgeon; b. Stockbridge, Vt., July 14, 1827; ed. pub. schs. Stockbridge, Randolph and Bethel, and at Royalton Acad.; M.D., Rush Med. Coll., Chicago, 1853; widower. Surgeon 10th Wis. Inf., Sept. 27, 1861; detached on staff Gen. Sill, as brigade surgeon, until capture of Huntsville, Ala., Apr. 11, 1862; in charge mil. hosps., Huntsville, Ala., until Oct. 1862; accompanied Gen. Sill's brigade until Oct. 8, 1862; then chief surgeon Gen. Rosseau's div. until the organization of the Army of the Cumberland; then chief surgeon of the 1st Div. 14th Army Corps until term of service expired. Is prof. mil. surgery, fractures and dislocations, Wis. Coll. Phys. and Surg.; chief surgeon C.,M.&St.P. R.R. Co., 1870-1902; chief surgeon St. Mary's Hosp., 1866—; mem. from orgn. and many yrs. pres. Wis. State Bd. Health. Home: Milwaukee, Wis. Died Sept. 29, 1914.

MARKS, William Dennis, engineer; b. St. Louis, Mo., Feb. 26, 1849; s. Dennis and Elmira (Bacon) M.; Ph.B., Yale, 1870, C.E., 1871; spl. study as civ. and mech. engr.; m. Jeannette Holmes Colwell, 1874; (died 1894); father of Jeannette M. Engaged in practical engring. on various rys., gas works, iron works, etc., 1873; instr. mech. engring. Lehigh U., 1876; Whitney prof. dynamic engring., U. of Pa., 1877; supt. Internat. Elec. Exhbn., of Franklin Inst., 1884; engr. and pres. of the Edison Electric Light Co., Phila., 1887. Author: The Relative Proportions of the Steam Engine, 1880; Revised edition of Nystrom's Mechanics' Pocket Book, 1885; The Finances of Gas and Electricity Mfg. Enterprises, 1902. Home: Westport, N.Y. Died Jan. 1914.

MARKWARD, Joseph Bradley, clergyman; b. Jacksonville, Pa., Mar. 25, 1869; s. George Grove and Mary Ellen (Hale) M.; student Chambersburg (Pa.) Acad., 1885-87; A.B., Gettysburg (Pa.) Coll., 1891, A.M., 1895; Gettysburg Theol. Sem., 1892-95; D.D., Midland Coll., Fremont, Neb., 1909; m. Ivy Lorella Eggers, June 8, 1899; 1 dau., Florence Marjorie. Ordained ministry United Luth. Ch., 1895; asst. pastor Trinity Luth. Ch., North Side, Pittsburgh, Pa., 1895-99; pastor Calvary Luth. Ch., Wilkinsburg (Pittsburgh), 1899-1909, Bethlehem Luth. Ch., Harrisburg, Pa., 1909-19, First Luth. Ch., Springfield, O., 1919—. Pres. Bd. of Am. Missions of United Luth. Ch. in America. Dir. Wittenberg Coll., Springfield. Home: Springfield, O. Died June 30, 1933.

MARKWART, Arthur Hermann, engring. exec.; b. Du Quoin, Ill., Feb. 13, 1880; s. Hermann and Sarah (Beck) M.; grad. Calif. Sch. Mech. Arts, San Francisco, 1899; B.S., U. of Calif., 1904; m. Marie Louise Chesebrough, May 26, 1908; children—Arthur Hermann, Henry Chesebrough, John, Philip Gordon, Elizabeth. Employed as engr., 1904-06; chief engr., mgr. Syndicate Water Co., Oakland, Calif., 1906-07; partner Howard & Galloway, architects and engrs., San Francisco, 1907-08, Galloway & Markwart, cons. engrs., 1908-12, 1915-17 and 1919-20; chief of constrn. Panama Pacific Internat. Expn., San Francisco, 1912-15; cons. engr., 1917-19; dir. engring. Pacific Gas & Electric Co., 1920-22; v.p. in charge engineering, 1922—; member board dirs. North Am. Investment Corp., Commonwealth Investment Co., San Francisco Remedial Loan Assn., Tacoma Mill Co.; pres. Calif. Sch. Mech. Arts. Republican. Protestant. Home: Piedmont, Calif. Died Jan. 25, 1940.

MARLER, Herbert Meredith, diplomat; b. Montreal, Que., Can., Mar. 7, 1876; s. William de Montmollin and Josephine Charlotte (Howard) M.; B.C.L., McGill U., 1898; LL.D., U. of Brit. Columbia, 1932; m. Beatrice Isabel Allan, of Montreal, April 9, 1902; children—George Leonard, Howard Meredith, Adelaide Edythe (Mrs. Cecil Jackson North, Jr.). Asso. in practice of law with father in Can., 1898-29; mem. Council of Edn., P.Q., 1918-27; fuel adminstr., P.Q., 1917-18; mem. Canadian House of Commons, 1921-25; mem. Prime Minister's Cabinet, 1925; served as E.E. and M.P. from Dominion of Can. to Japan, 1929-36; apptd. Minister to U.S., 1936. Created Knight Comdr. of St. Michael and St. George, 1935; awarded cross of merit, Red Cross Soc. of Japan, 1934. Mem. Anglican Ch. Home: Montreal, Que., Can. Died Jan. 31, 1940.

MARLIN, Harry Halpine, clergyman, writer; b. Shelocta, Pa., Aug. 19, 1869; s. Thomas Jefferson and Elizabeth (Hutchison) M.; A.B., Tarkio (Mo.) Coll., 1894; grad. Pittsburgh Theol. Sem., 1897; D.D., Monmouth, 1919; m. Norma Henrietta Fenderich, May 20, 1915. Ordained ministry U.P. Ch., 1897; pastor 11th Ch., Pittsburgh, 1897-1900, 4th Ch., East End, Pittsburgh, 1900-24, 4th Ch., East End, Cleveland, O., 1925-28. Member editorial staff United Presbyterian, 1917—, contributing 2 pages weekly under "Current Events and Comment." Secretary Social Service Com. of U.P. Ch. many yrs.; mem. Commn. on the Ch. and Social Service of Federal Council Chs. of Christ in America, 1913-25. Newspaper columnist. Home: New Castle, Pa. Died Sept. 5, 1939.

MARLING, Alfred Erskine, real estate; b. Toronto, Can., Oct. 5, 1858; s. Francis H. (D.D.) and Marina C. (Macdonald) M.; ed. Collegiate Inst., Toronto; m. Harriet W. Philips, Jan. 10, 1884. Chmn. bd. Horace S. Ely & Co., real estate brokers and mgrs., New York; trustee Fulton Trust Co., Mut. Life Ins. Co., Bank of New York & Trust Co., Bank for Savings; v.p. and dir. Woodlawn Cemetery. Trustee Columbia U. Pres. Real Estate Exchange, 1896, pres. Chamber of Commerce of State of N.Y., 1918-20. Republican. Presbyn. Home: New York, N.Y. Died May 29, 1935.

MARLOW, Thomas A., banker, mcht.; b. St. Louis, Mo., Mar. 9, 1861; s. Parmenio and Emily (Wilson) M.; ed. pub. schs., Palmyra, Mo.; m. Louise Miltz, Sept. 20, 1906. Began in employ of post trading firm at Ft. McGinnis, Mont., 1882, admitted as partner, 1885; established firm of McNamara & Marlow, Big Sandy, Mont., 1888; pres. First Nat. Bank & Trust Co. (Helena). Mem. Rep. Nat. Com., 1908-20. Elk. Home: Helena, Mont. Died Mar. 28, 1938.

MARMION, Robert Augustine, med. dir. U.S.N.; b. Harper's Ferry, Va., Sept. 6, 1844; s. Nicholas and Lydia Ingraham (Hall) M.; ed. pvt. schs. of native place, until 13 yrs. old, Mt. St. Mary's Coll., Emmitsburg, Md., A.B., 1861, A.M., 1863, Univ. of Pa., M.D., 1868; m. Beatrice Paul, Oct. 7, 1885. Apptd. from W.Va. asst. surgeon, U.S.N., Mar. 26, 1868; promoted past asst. surgeon Mar. 26, 1871, surgeon, June 3, 1879; med. insp., June 15, 1895, med. dir., Oct. 1899. Served in various depts. of sea and shore service, at hosps., navy yards, etc., trip with Juniata around the world, Jan. 1886-Mar. 1889; on spl. duty Smithsonian Instn., 1894; fleet surgeon S. Atlantic Sta., July 1894-June 1896; etc. Naval del. to Am. Med. Assn., 1900, 02, 03, 04; comdg. U.S. Naval Mus of Hygiene and Med. Sch., Sept. 1902—. Mem Anatomical Bd., D.C. Catholic. Home: Washington, D.C. Died 1907.

MARMON, Jeff Berry, life ins. mgr.; b. Hickory Flat, Miss., Apr. 15, 1861; s. Peter Menter and Lou (Berry) M.; ed. pub. and high schs. in Miss.; m Hilda F. Monroe, Sept. 28, 1892; children—Jeff A. Kathleen Hutcheson, Hilda M. Entered life ins. business, 1891; mgr. for Memphis, Mut. Life Ins. Co. of New York, 1912-32 (retired). A leader in Men and Religion Forward Movement, 1912; was conf. leader in Meth. Ch., Memphis conf.; widely known in South as speaker on religious and reform topics. Democrat. Mason. Home: Memphis, Tenn. Died Mar. 10, 1933.

MARNELL, Robert Overton, banker; b. Hannibal, Mo., Aug. 31, 1869; s. James E. and Katharine (Hawkins) M.; ed. pub. schs.; m. Georgia Hawke, June 2, 1896; 1 dau., Sue (Mrs. Frank D. Lowrey). Various occupations and clk. post office, Nebraska City, until 1886; entered employ Merchants Nat. Bank, 1886, asst. cashier, 1894, cashier, 1897—, dir., 1907—; dir. Omaha Br. Federal Reserve Bank of Kansas City, 1917—. Democrat. Home: Nebraska City, Neb. Died Mar. 7, 1933.

MAROT, Helen, editor, writer; b. Phila., Pa.; d. Charles Henry and Hannah (Stuart) Marot; ed. pub. schs. Phila. Began with Univ. Extension Soc., Phila., 1893; librarian Wilmington (Del.) Library, 1896, Library of Economics and Polit. Science, Phila., 1897; investigator for U.S. Industrial Commn., 1901, New York Child Labor Com., 1903; sec. Pa. Child Labor Com., 1904-05, Women's Trade Union League, New York, 1906-14; mem. U.S. Industrial Relations Com., 1914-16; on staff the Masses, New York, 1916; mem. editorial bd. Dial, 1917-19. Author: Handbook of Labor Literature, 1898; American Trade Unions, 1913; Creative Impulse in Industry, 1918. Home: New York, N.Y. Died June 3, 1940.

MARQUAND, Allan, archeologist; b. New York, N.Y., Dec. 10, 1853; s. Henry G. and Elizabeth L. (Allen) M.; A.B., Princeton, 1874; U. of Berlin, 1877-78; Ph.D., Johns Hopkins, 1880; (L.H.D., Hobart, 1888); m. Eleanor Cross, June 18, 1896. Tutor and lecturer, 1881-83, prof. archeology and history of art, 1883-1905, prof. art and archeology, 1905—, dir. Mus. of Historic Art, 1890-1921, Princeton. Prof. archeology Am. Sch. of Classical Studies at Rome, 1896-97; asso. editor American Jour. Archeology, 1885—. Joint author and editor: Iconographic Encyclopedia, Vol. III, 1896. Joint author: History of Sculpture, 1896-99. Author: Greek Architecture, 1909; Della Robbias in America, 1912; Luca Della Robbia, 1914; Robbia Heraldry, 1919; Giovanni Della Robbia, 1920; Benedetto and Santi Buglioni, 1921; Andrea della Robbia (2 vols.), 1922. Fellow Am. Acad. Arts and Sciences. Home: Princeton, N.J. Died Sept. 24, 1924.

MARQUAND, Henry Gurdon, capitalist; b. New York, N.Y., April 11, 1819; ed. Pittsfield, Mass.; for 20 yrs. mgr. large real estate interests of his brother, Frederick Marquand (died 1882); banker in New York 10 yrs.; one of purchasers, 1868, and v.p., and later pres. Iron Mountain & Southern R.R.; has made gifts and loans to Metropolitan Museum of Art (pres. of the museum); presented a chapel and (with Robert Bonner) a gymnasium to Princeton Univ.; he and his brother gave a pavilion to Bellevue Hosp. Home: New York, N.Y. Died 1902.

MARQUESS, William Hoge, theologian; b. Sparta, Tenn., Feb. 22, 1854; s. William Henry and Anne Lacy (Hoge) M.; A.B., Westminster Coll., Mo., 1873, A.M., 1876; (D.D., L.H.D., LL.D.); m. Maggie A. Buckner, Oct. 7, 1880. Formerly pres. Westminster Coll.; then prof. Hebrew Lit. and English Bible, Presbyn. Theol. Sem. of Ky., Louisville; now prof. English Bible, Bible Teachers' Training School, New York, N.Y. Died Apr. 10, 1921.

MARQUIS, David Calhoun, theologian; b. Lawrence Co., Pa., Nov. 15, 1834; s. Andrew and Lydia (Morehead) M.; A.B., Jefferson Coll., Cannonsburg, Pa., 1857; student Western Theol. Sem., Pa., and Northwestern Theol. Sem., Chicago, 1860-63; (D.D., Washington and Jefferson Coll., 1875; LL.D., Westminster Coll., Mo., 1891, Westminster Coll., Pa., 1892, Washington and Jefferson, 1902); m. Anna M. Kennedy, Oct. 8, 1863; m. 2d, Helen M. Pearson, July 16, 1879; m. 3d, Emeline E. Vaughn, Oct. 10, 1898 (died 1901). Licensed to preach, 1862; ordained Presbyn. ministry, 1863; pastor Decatur, Ill., 1863-66, Chicago, 1866-70, Baltimore, 1870-78, St. Louis, 1878-83; prof. N.T. lit. and exegisis, 1883-1903, N.T. interpretation, 1903-09, emeritus prof. N.T. lit. and exegesis, 1909, McCormick Theol. Sem. Moderator Presbyn. Gen. Assembly, 1886; mem. Pan-Presbyn. Council, Edinburgh, 1877, Glasgow, 1896. Home: Chicago, Ill. Died Oct. 8, 1912.

MARQUIS, Don(ald Robert Perry), author and playwright; b. Walnut, Bureau Co., Ill., July 29, 1878; s. James Stewart and Virginia Elizabeth (Whitmore) M.; m. Reina Melcher, June 8, 1909 (died 1923); m. 2d, Marjorie Vonnegut, Feb. 2, 1926. Author: Danny's Own Story, 1912; Dreams and Dust, 1915; Cruise of the Jasper B., 1916; Hermione, 1916; Prefaces, 1919; The Old Soak, 1921; Carter and Other People, 1921; Noah an' Jonah an' Cap'n John Smith, 1921; Poems and Portraits, 1922; Revolt of the Oyster, 1922; Sonnets to a Red Haired Lady, 1922; The Old Soak's History of the World, 1924; The Dark Hours, 1924; Out of the Sea, 1927; The Almost Perfect State, 1927; Archy and Mehitabel, 1927; Love Sonnets of a Cave Man, 1928; When the Turtles Sing, 1928; Variety of People, 1929; Archy and Mehitabel, 1930; Off the Arm, 1930; Master of the Revels, 1934; Chapters for the Orthodox, 1934; Archy Does his Part, 1935. Died Dec. 29, 1937.

MARQUIS, George Paull, M.D.; b. Allegheny, Pa., Sept. 12, 1868; s. Rev. David C. and Anna (Kennedy) M.; A.B., Washington and Jefferson Coll., 1889, A.M., 1892; M.D., Northwestern U. Med. Sch., 1892; post-grad. work Berlin and Vienna; m. Emily Chamberlain, 1899 (died 1919); 1 dau., Anna (Mrs. Arthur Dixon, III). Practiced at Chicago, 1892—; attdg. laryngologist and otologist, St. Luke's Hosp.; formerly attdg. laryngologist and otologist Cook Co., St. Joseph's and Columbus hosps., also asst. prof. laryngology and rhinology Northwestern U. Med. Sch. and asso. prof. otology, Chicago Polyclinic. Chief surgeon 2d Ill. Vols., Spanish-Am. War; served in Cuba. Fellow Am. Coll. Surgeons. Republican. Presbyn. Home: Chicago, Ill. Died Dec. 22, 1933.

MARQUIS, John Abner, educator and clergyman; b. at Dinsmore, Pa., Dec. 27, 1861; s. James T. and Mary C. (Bucher) M.; A.B., Washington and Jefferson Coll., 1885, LL.D., 1910; grad. Western Theol. Sem., Pa., 1890; D.D., Coe Coll., 1902; m. Martha Miller Neilson, Sept. 1, 1896; children—Sarah, James Taggart (dec.), John Neilson, Elisabeth. Prof. Greek and mathematics, Blairsville (Pa.) Coll. for Women, 1885-87; ordained Presbyn. ministry, 1891; asso. pastor First Ch., Greensburg, Pa., 1890-91; pastor Westminster Ch., Greensburg, 1892-1902, First Ch., Redlands, Calif., 1902-05, First Ch., Beaver, Pa., 1905-09; pres. Coe Coll., Cedar Rapids, Ia., 1909-20. Gen. sec. Bd. Home Missions Presbyn. Ch., U.S.A., 1917-23; gen. sec. Bd. Nat. Missions Presbyn. Ch., U.S.A., 1923-30. Asso. editor Presbyterian Banner, Pittsburgh, 1899-1909. Trustee Washington and Jefferson Coll., 1898-1909; dir. Presbyn. Banner Pub. Co., 1899-1917, Destern Theol. Sem., 1907—; moderator Gen. Assembly Presbyn. Ch., U.S.A., 1916; chmn. Administration Com. of Federal Council Chs. of Christ in America, 1924—; del. to World Conf. on Christian Life and Work, Stockholm, 1925, and to World Conf. on Faith and Order, Lausanne, 1927. Author: Learning to Teach from the Master Teacher, 1913; Christian Conception of Property, 1916. Home: Montrose, N.Y. Died July 5, 1931.

MARQUIS, Robert Lincoln, coll. pres.; b. Goliad, Tex., Jan. 4, 1880; s. Alexander and Emma (Webster) M.; A.B., Tex. Christian U., Ft. Worth, Tex., 1901; B.S., U. of Tex., 1902; M.S., U. of Chicago, 1903; grad. student, U. of Tex., 1909; LL.D., Austin Coll., Sherman, Tex., 1925; m. Lulu Mae Parkey, June 2, 1907; children—Robert and Richard (twins). Teacher of science, Christian Coll., Thorp Spring, Tex., 1903-04; teacher of science, John Tarleton Coll., Stephenville, Tex., 1904-08; prof. biology, Sam Houston State Teachers' Coll., Huntsville, Tex., 1908-09; West Tex. State Teachers' Coll., Canyon, Tex., 1910-18, North Tex. State Teachers' Coll., 1918-20; pres. Sul Ross State Teachers' Coll., Alpine, Tex., 1920-23, North Tex. State Teachers' Coll., 1923—. Pres. Assn. of Colls. and Secondary Schs. of Southern States, 1929. Democrat. Mem. Disciples of Christ. Mason. Rotarian. Home: Denton, Tex. Died Apr. 15, 1934.

MARQUIS, Rollin Ruthwin, clergyman; b. Murray, Ind., Dec. 28, 1853; s. Robert Crawford and Martha (Riddile) M.; Hanover (Ind.) Coll., 1875-77; A.B., Wooster U., 1880, A.M., 1883, D.D., 1905; B.D., Western Theol. Sem., 1883; m. Clara J. McCormick, May 8, 1883 (died 1892); m. 2d, Ida Irene Shumaker, Feb. 18, 1896; children—Rollin Howard, Leone Irene, Dean Wilson, Donald George, Robert Irwin. Ordained Presbyn. ministry, 1883; pastor Northfield, O., 1883-86, Sedan, Kan., 1888-89, Osage City, Ia., 1889-91, Sedalia, Mo., 1891-97, Quincy, Ill., 1897-99, Cedar Falls, Ia., 1900-02, Winterset, Ia., 1902-06, Irwin, Pa., 1906-10, Lawrenville, Ill., 1911-18, Wickliffe, O., 1919-23, Pierce, Fla., 1926-27, Vincennes, Ind., 1929-32. Commr. Gen. Assembly Presbyn. Ch. in U.S.A., 1893, 1905, 16, 24; moderator Synod of Ill., 1913-14, chmn. exec. commn. V.p. Mo. Christian Endeavor Union, 1893-94; supt. Mo. State Chautauqua, 1893-95; Western sec. Chautauqua Alumni Assn., 1892-1912; mem. exec. com. Ill. Christian Endeavor Union, 1898-1900. Mason. Republican. Author: Textual Index of the Bible, 1900. Home: Winona Lake, Ind. Died Mar. 18, 1935.

MARQUIS, William Stevenson, clergyman; b. Kenton, O., Oct. 2, 1853; s. James Edgar and Mary (DuBois) M.; A.B., Ill. Wesleyan U., Bloomington, Ill., 1876, A.M., 1879; grad. Princeton Theol. Sem., 1879; D.D., Knox Coll., Galesburg, Ill., 1895; m. Adelaide M. Bell, Dec. 21, 1881; children—Helen Adelaide (dec.), Laura Betta, William Bell, Stewart Dent. Ordained Presbyn. ministry, 1879; pastor Minonk, Ill., 1879-84, Broadway Ch., Rock Island, June 1884-1913, and pastor emeritus same, 1913—. Elected commr. to Gen. Assembly Presbyn. Ch. U.S.A., 4 times; moderator Synod of Ill., 1905; chmn. of com. on foreign missions, Synod of Ill., for 22 consecutive yrs.; del. to World's Missionary Conf., Edinburgh, Scotland, 1910; rep. Presbyterian Ch. U.S.A. to General Synod of Waldensian Ch., Switzerland, 1910; del. to Council of Chs. holding Reformed Faith, Aberdeen, Scotland, 1913. Dir. Geneseo (Ill.) Collegiate Inst., Winona Assembly and Bible Conf. Western rep. of Presbyn. Gen. Assembly's Com. for the Every Member Plan, 1914-18; asso. sec. New Era Movement of Presbyn. Ch. U.S.A., 1918—; chmn. Gen. Council staff, and operating com. of Gen. Council of Presbyn. Ch., U.S.A., 1924-26 (dir. emeritus). Died Aug. 19, 1929.

MARQUIS, William Vance; b. Mt. Vernon, O., May 1, 1828, of French Huguenot and Scotch-Irish family, settling in U.S., 1720; common school edn.; m. Annie Sterritt, Nov. 13, 1861; m. 2d, Mrs. Helen M. Guy, Mar. 31, 1880; m. 3d, Adelaide G. Swift, May 12, 1883; m. 4th, Margarette E. Parks, July 14, 1892. Postmaster, 1853-61; mayor 1 term; member city council 10 years; bd. edn., 15 years, Bellefontaine, O. Lt. gov. Ohio, 1890-92; pres. Columbus Northwestern R.R. Home: Bellefontaine, O. Died 1899.

MARR, Carl, artist, educator; b. Milwaukee, Wis., Feb. 14, 1858; s. John and Bertha (Bodenstein) M.; ed. in German and English Acad., Milwaukee, and at acads. of Fine Arts at Weimar, Berlin and Munich; D.Litt. from the U. of Wisconsin, 1929. Professionally engaged as painter, 1877—; professor of painting, Academy Fine Arts, Munich, 1893—; dir. same acad. until retired, 1925. Prin. works: Icarus; Heavenward; Madonna; The Old Song; The Dying Day. Mem. acads. at Berlin, Munich and Athens. Decorated Order of St. Michaels, 2d Class, Bavaria; Order of the Prussian Crown, 3d Class; knighted, 1909; Order of the Bavarian Crown; Order of the Italian Crown. Mem. Nat. Inst. Arts and Letters. Died July 10, 1936.

MARRINER, Theodore, U.S. diplomatic service; b. Portland, Me., May 17, 1892; s. James Elmer (died 1925) and Harriet Cram (Thorpe) M.; A.B., Dartmouth, 1914; A.M., Harvard, 1915, Ph.D., 1918; unmarried. Asst. in English, Harvard, 1916-18; 3d sec. Legation, at Stockholm, 1918-21; 2d sec. Legation, Bucharest, 1921-23; attached to Spl. Embassy, coronation of King and Queen of Rumania, Oct. 1922; 1st sec. Embassy on duty in Western European Div., Dept. of State, 1923-26; sec. of Am. Legation, Berne, and sec. Am. Delegation to Preparatory Commn. on Reduction and Limitation of Armaments, Geneva, Oct. 1926-Apr. 1927; chargé d'affaires in Switzerland and acting head Am. Representation on Subcommittee B of Disarmament Commn., Nov. 1926-Mar. 1927; mem. Am. Mission to Paris for signature of gen. pact of renunciation of war, Aug. 1928; chief Div. of Western European Affairs, Dept. of State, 1927-31; adviser Am. delegation, London Naval Conf., 1930; apptd. counselor of Embassy, Paris, Apr. 1931; adviser Am. delegation, London Financial Conf., Aug. 1931; designated to accompany Prime Minister Laval on his visit to Washington, Oct. 1931; adviser Am. delegation, Gen. Disarmament Conf., Geneva, 1932. Home: Cape Elizabeth, Me. Died Oct. 12, 1937.

MARRIOTT, Abraham Robert, banker; b. on farm, Ill., May 26, 1860; s. William and Kittie (Gresham) M.; ed. pub. schs., Wheaton, Ill., and Chicago Coll. of Law; m. Minnie Cooper, Oct. 19, 1882 (died 1910); children—Ida Elizabeth (Mrs. Robert A. McClevey), Arthur Cooper, Robert William, Thomas Benton; m. 2d, Mabel Rogerson; children—Rogerson, Elizabeth Jane, David Francis. Clerk with Haddock, Coxe & Co. and Haddock, Vallette & Rickcords (abstracts of title), 1875-91; supt. of Haddock, Vallette & Rickcords Co., 1891-95; vice-pres. Security Title & Trust Co., 1895-1901; v.p. Chicago Title & Trust Co., 1901-29, pres., 1929—; pres. Allman-Gary Title Co. (Gary, Ind.), Du Page Title Co. (Wheaton, Ill.). Republican. Mason. Home: Oak Park, Ill. Died May 20, 1931.

MARRIOTT, W(illiams) McKim, pediatrist; b. Baltimore, Md., Mar. 5, 1885; s. James Hamilton Wilson and Lucretia E. (Williams) M.; B.S., U. of N.C., 1904; M.D., Cornell U. Med. Sch., 1910; m. Elizabeth Devereux Robinson, 1911; children—Elizabeth Devereux, McKim. Asst. in chemistry, U. of North Carolina, 1903-04; asst. in biochemistry, Cornell U., 1904-07; instr. biol. chemistry, Washington U., 1910-14; asso. in pediatrics, Johns Hopkins, 1914-17; asso. pediatrician Johns Hopkins Hosp., 1915-17; prof. pediatrics, Washington U., 1917-36, dean Sch. of Medicine, 1923-36; dean and prof. of research medicine, U. of Calif. Sch. of Medicine, San Francisco, 1936—. Trustee John Burroughs Sch., McMillan Eye, Ear, Nose and Throat Hosp., Good Teeth Council, St. Louis Smoke Abatement League. Devised methods for chem. examination of the blood, methods for infant feeding, etc. Fellow Am. Coll. Physicians (vice-pres.; regent 1926-29). Author: Recent Advances in Chemistry in Relation to Medical Practice, 1928; Infant Nutrition, 1930. Died Nov. 11, 1936.

MARRS, Starlin Marion Newberry, supt. schs.; b. Gauley Bridge, W.Va., Jan. 2, 1862; s. Francis Marion and Catherine Lloyd (Paddleford) M.; B.S., Nat. Normal U., Lebanon, O., 1884; m. Annie Ross Heslep, Aug. 18, 1886 (died 1904); children—Reginald Heslep, Cecil Douglas, Starlin Marion, Mary Catherine; m. 2d, Ina Caddell, June 9, 1909. Supt. schs. in Tex., at Stephenville, 1885-88, Hamilton, 1888-90, Cleburne, 1890-93, Terrell, 1893-98; chief clk. Tex. State Dept. Edn., 1898-99; supt. schs., Terrell, 1899-1919; chief supervisor state high schs., 1919-21; 1st asst. state supt. schs., 1921-23; state supt. schs., Jan. 1923—. Mem. State Bd. Examiners, 1905-10; condr. many summer normal schools. Democrat. Baptist. Home: Austin, Tex. Died Apr. 18, 1932.

MARSH, Benjamin F., farmer; b. Wythe Tp., Hancock Co., Ill., 1839; took 4 yrs.' course in Jubilee Coll.; admitted to bar; established practice at Warsaw, 1860; in U.S.A., 1861-66, becoming col. 2d Ill. cav.; resumed practice of law. Mem. Congress, 1877-83; defeated for re-election; became farmer and stock-raiser; railroad and warehouse commr., Ill., 1889-93; again mem. Congress, 1893-1901, and 1903-05, 14th Ill. dist.; chmn. Com. on Militia, 54th and 55th Congresses. Republican. Home: Warsaw, Ill. Died 1905.

MARSH, C(harles) Dwight, physiologist; b. Hadley, Mass., Dec. 20, 1855; s. J. Dwight and Sarah (Ingram) M.; A.B., Amherst Coll., 1877, A.M., 1880, Sc.D., 1927; Ph.D. from University of Chicago, 1904; m. Florence Lee Wilder, Dec. 27, 1883; children—Hadleigh, Charles Wilder. Prof. of chemistry and biology, 1883-1889, biology, 1889-1904, dean of faculty, 1900-04, Ripon (Wis.) College; prof. biology, Earlham Coll., 1904-05; physiologist in charge field investigations of poisonous plants, Bur. of Plant Industry, Dept. Agr., 1905-15, transferred to Bur. of Animal Industry, 1915, in charge poisonous plant investigations; retired, 1931. Hon. curator fresh water copepoda, U.S. Nat. Mus. Ex-officio mem. commrs. Wis. Geol. and Natural History Survey, sec. bd., 1897-99; biologist on Geol. and Natural History Survey, Wis.; lecturer in biology, Milwaukee Med. Coll., 1903-04. Conglist. Author: Limnetic Crustacea of Green Lake; The Plankton of Lake Winnebago and Green Lake; A Revision of the North American Species of Diaptomus; A Revision of North American Species of Cyclops; The Loco Weed Disease of the Plains; Stock-Poisoning Plants of the Range; sr. joint author of Zygadenus or Death Camas; Larkspur Poisoning of Live Stock; Lupines as Poisonous Plants. Home: Washington, D.C. Died 1932.

MARSH, Edward Clark, publisher; b. Portland, Mich., Feb. 19, 1875; s. Rev. Augustus and Martha Scott (Hewitt) M.; A.B., Alma, Mich., Coll., 1896; studied U. of Chicago, 1898-99; A.M., U. of Mich., 1900; m. Helen, d. Col. Nathan Church, of Ithaca, Mich., Sept. 13, 1901. Journalist and editor, contbr. short stories, and reviews of books, music and plays in various periodicals, 1900-06; with The Macmillan Co. as head of editorial dept., also v.p. and head of publ. dept., 1906-20; lit. adviser, Harper & Bros., 1921—. Editor: The Wisdom of Carlyle, 1910. Home: Little Chasm, Pawling, N.Y. Died Sept. 25, 1922.

MARSH, Frank Burr, prof. ancient history; b. Big Rapids, Mich., Mar. 4, 1880; s. Edwin Johnson and Alma Lucia (Burr) M.; A.B., U. of Mich., 1902, Ph.D., 1906; grad. study U. of Paris, 1902-03; unmarried. Asst., later instr. in history, U. of Mich., 1903-10; instr. in ancient history, U. of Tex., 1910-16, adj. prof. ancient history, 1916-23, asso. prof., 1923-26, prof., 1926—. Fellow Royal Hist. Soc. (London). Democrat. Author: English Rule in Gascony (1199-1259), 1912; The Founding of the Roman Empire, 1922, rev. edit., 1927; The Reign of Tiberius, 1931; A History of the Roman World from 146 to 30 B.C., 1935. Editor: Tacitus—Selections from His Works (with H. J. Leon), 1936. Died May 31, 1940.

MARSH, Joseph William, banker, mfr.; b. N.Y. City, May 21, 1858; s. Peter and Katharine (Hoffman) M.; ed. pub. schs., and Iron City Coll., Pittsburgh; m. Rose Ingraham, June 20, 1883; children—Rose Guthrie (wife of J. S. Payton, D.D.), James Ingraham, Sarah Elizabeth (Mrs. E. F. W. Salisbury), Katharine Modisette (Mrs. William Clark Fuellhart). Began as clerk in country store, Ohio, later teacher in Iron City College; became stenographer and priv. sec. to Richard S. Waring, founder of Standard Underground Cable Co., 1881; sec. Standard Underground Cable Co., 1882, asst. gen. mgr., 1889, v.p. and gen. mgr., 1891, pres., 1909—. Vice chmn. bd. Gen. Cable Corp. Trustee Christ M.E. Ch. Mason. Home: Pittsburgh, Pa. Died Jan. 31, 1936.

MARSH, Tamerlane Pliny, clergyman, educator; b. Orland, Ind., July 30, 1845; s. Madison and Hannah Paulina (Hudson) M.; grad. Wesleyan Univ., Conn., 1869 (A.M., Wesleyan Univ.; D.D., Mount Union Coll.; LL.D., Allegheny Coll.); m. Harriet M. Newhall, sister of Prof. Fales H. Newhall of Wesleyan

Univ., Sept. 6, 1870. Eighteen yrs. in regular M.E. pastorates in Rock River Conf. in 5 Chicago chs., chs. in the Chicago suburbs of Austin and Oak Park, and at Rockford, Ill.; pres. Mt. Union Coll., 1888-98; retired July, 1898. Built chs. at Austin and Oak Park, Ill.; supt. Lake Bluff Assembly, Lake Bluff, Ill. Home: Alliance, O. Died 1903.

MARSHALL, Albert Brainerd, theologian; b. Bryan, Pa., July 10, 1849; s. John and Matilda Catherine (Findley) M.; A.B., Princeton, 1871, A.M., 1874; grad. Princeton Theol. Sem., 1874; D.D., U. of Wooster, 1894; LL.D., Macalester Coll., 1911; m. Jane B. Hervey, Sept. 1, 1875; m. 2d, Mary E. Hallock, June 12, 1915. Ordained Presbyn. ministry, 1874; pastor, Morris, Ill., 1875-78, Lisbon, O., 1879-87, 1st Ch., E. Liverpool, O., 1887-94, Central Ch., Des Moines, Ia., 1894-1903, 1st Ch., Minneapolis (oldest religious orgn. in Minn.), 1903-10; pres. Presbyn. Theol. Sem., Omaha, 1910-20; pastor, Clarinda, Ia., Sept. 1, 1920-Sept. 1, 1925; lecturer, in Theol. Dept., Yenching U., Peking, China, 1925-26; pastor Presbyn. Ch., Bellevue, Neb., Oct. 1926—. Republican. Home: Bellevue, Neb. Died Oct. 29, 1931.

MARSHALL, Alfred; b. Flatbush, N.Y., Sept. 3, 1868; s. Henry George and Jessie (Jardine) M.; ed. Poly. Inst. Brooklyn; m. Georgie Martin, Nov. 25, 1895. In machinery business, New York, 1885-92; mgr. Chicago office Prentiss Tool & Supply Co., 1892-98; pres. Marshall & Huschart Machinery Co., Chicago, 1898-1916; asso. with Carnegie Inst. Natural History and Nat. Geog. Soc. in planning and financing expdn. into interior and across Labrador Peninsula to establish northern range of bird migration, and took active part in expdn.; presented collection of birds to Linnæan Soc. and now in possession of Am. Mus. Natural History. Asst. to War Trade Bd., Washington, 1917-18; financed city improvement and flood protection work, Columbus, O., 1918; now engaged in reclaiming delta of San Antonio and Guadalupe rivers, Tex. Republican. Episcopalian. Home: Montrose, Ala. Deceased.

MARSHALL, Charles, lawyer; b. Warrenton, Va., Oct. 3, 1830; grad. Univ. Va., 1849; prof. mathematics, Univ. of Ind., 1849-52; practiced law Baltimore. Served in C.S.A. as asst. adj. gen. and inspector-gen. on staff of Gen. Robert E. Lee; after war resumed law practice in Baltimore, Md. Died 1902.

MARSHALL, Charles Clinton; b. Poughkeepsie, N.Y., June 19, 1860; s. Edwin and Hetty (Vincent) M.; grad. Law Sch., Columbia U., 1882; m. Abby A. Story, Oct. 9, 1889; children—Hetty Vincent (Mrs. Roswell Forman Barratt), Charles Russell, Alicia S. (Mrs. Lamont Dominick), Muriel (Mrs. Donald Jones), Rufus S. Admitted to New York bar, 1882; bar of Supreme Court of U.S., Jan. 9, 1895; mem. Shipman, Larocque & Chote, N.Y. City, 1889-1900, Marshall, Moran & Williams, 1901-1911; retired, 1911. Episcopalian. Author: The Roman Catholic Church in the Modern State, 1928; Governor Smith's American Catholicism, 1928. Writer of "An Open Letter to the Hon. Alfred E. Smith," pub. Atlantic Monthly, April 1927; Report to Hague Congress of Internat. Acad. of Comparative Law on "The Historical Relation of Law and Religion in its American Aspect," 1932; also in controversy with Hilaire Belloc, "The Catholic Church in the Modern State," Atlantic Monthly, Mar. 1930; "The Basic Facts in the Mexican Question." Died June 9, 1938.

MARSHALL, Charles Edward, microbiologist; b. on farm, Port Clinton, O., Oct. 6, 1866; s. Lavinas and Lurena (Crandall) M.; Ph.B., U. of Mich., 1895, Ph.D., 1902; Jorgensen's Lab., Copenhagen, Denmark, 1898; Pasteur Inst., Paris; Ostertag's Lab., Berlin, 1903; Inst. f. Infektionskrankheiten (Robert Koch), Berlin, 1913; m. Maud Alice Skidmore, July 7, 1896. Asst. in bacteriology, U. of Mich., 1893-96; asst. in bacteriology, 1896-98, bacteriologist, 1898-1912, scientific and v. dir. Expt. Sta., 1908—, prof. bacteriology and hygiene, 1902-12, Mich. Agrl. Coll.; dir. of Grad. Sch. and prof. microbiology, Mass. Agrl. Coll., 1912—. Pres. Sch. Bd. of East Lansing, Mich. Editor: Microbiology, 1911. Died Mar. 20, 1927.

MARSHALL, Clarence James, veterinarian; b. Rome, Pa., Mar. 13, 1864; s. James E. and Margaret Ann (Swetland) M.; grad. Susquehanna Collegiate Inst., Towanda, Pa., 1889; V.M.D., U. of Pa., 1894; Sc.D., U. of Pa.; m. Augusta Stevens, Nov. 19, 1896. House surgeon, U. of Pa. Vet. Dept., 1894, 1895; pvt. practice, 1895-1910; prof. vet. medicine, U. of Pa., 1910—; state veterinarian of Pa., 1911-19. Mem. advisory council of State Bd. of Health, 1911-21. Maj., Vet. Corps N.A., Oct. 5, 1917, lt. col., Feb. 6, 1918; disch., Feb. 20, 1919. Distinguished Service Order (British), 1919. Hon. mem. Royal Coll. Vet. Surgeons of Great Britain; mem. and pres. Am., Pa. State and Keystone vet. med. assns. Republican. Universalist. Mason. Home: Philadelphia, Pa. Died Oct. 29, 1938.

MARSHALL, (Davis) Edward, author; b. Enfield Center, N.Y., May 31, 1869; s. Davis Chester and Algiana Rebecca (Osborn) M.; ed. Benedict's Prep. Sch., Rochester; m. 2d, Margaret Davies, London, 1916; 1 dau. (by 1st marriage), Edna Noble (dec.). News editor Am. Press Assn., Buffalo and New York, 1885-89; Sunday editor New York Press, 1890-95; European corr. Bancheller & Johnson Newspaper Syndicate, 1896; Sunday editor, New York Journal, 1897; European corr. and Sunday editor New York World, 1897-98; war corr. New York Journal, 1898 (shot at Las Guasimas, June 24); editor McClure's Newspaper Syndicate, 1900; corr. first Peace Conf. at The Hague; Sunday editor New York Herald, 1901. Newspaper and mag. writer on tenement house reform in Europe and New York; sec. N.Y. State Tenement House Commn., 1894; lecturer on Spanish-Am. War, the Army, Paris, etc.; corr. Columbian Mag., Mexican insurrection, 1911; interviews for New York Times and Sunday newspapers throughout the country, 1910-14; organized Edward Marshall Newspaper Syndicate (Inc.), 1914, which purchased Curtis Brown News Bureau, London, 1916, establishing newspaper service in Europe and America; dir. committee on Productions, Films, Inc.; dir. De Forest Phonofilm, Inc., 1923-24; corr. in England, France, Italy and Belgium during European War; passenger on S.S. Sussex when torpedoed; Am. corr. Sunday Observer, London; consulting editor Aero Digest. Dir. Nat. Paper Process Co. Author: Story of the Rough Riders, 1898; Lizette, 1902; The Middle Wall, 1904; The Writing on the Wall, 1909; In Old Kentucky (with Charles T. Dazey, author of the play), 1910; The Old Flute-player (with Charles T. Dazey), 1911; The Spendthrift (with Porter Emerson Browne, author of the play), 1911; The Family (with Robert Hobart Davis, author of the play), 1911; Bat: An Idyl of New York, 1912; Master of the House, from Edgar James' play, 1912; Broadway Jones, from George M. Cohan's play, 1913. Co-author, with Earl Mayo, dramatization of "Cape Cod Folks," 1902. Home: New York, N.Y. Died Feb. 25, 1933.

MARSHALL, Edwin Jessop, capitalist; b. Baltimore, Md., Mar. 18, 1860; s. Henry Vincent and Amanda C. (Jessop) M.; ed. pub. schs.; m. Sally McLemore, June 7, 1892. Became clk. in ry. office, St. Louis, 1887, later asst. master of transportation, Gulf, Colo. & Santa Fe R.R.; cashier, later pres. for 12 yrs., First Nat. Bank, Lampassas, Tex., also engaged in ranching business; assisted in organizing the Hogg-Swayne oil syndicate, after discovery of oil at Beaumont, Tex., 1900, subsequently associating with John W. Gates and others in the Texas Co.; closed out oil interests and removed to Los Angeles, Calif., 1904, as v.p. Southwestern Nat. Bank; now pres. Torrance, Marshall & Co., bonds; dir. First Nat. Bank of Los Angeles; large land owner in Calif. and principal owner of 2,000,000 acre ranch—the Palomas—in Mexico; breeder of thoroughbred Hereford cattle. Republican. Episcopalian. Home: Los Angeles, Calif. Died Mar. 4, 1937.

MARSHALL, Harold, clergyman; b. Kingston, N.H., June 8, 1866; s. James F. and Mary Miranda (George) Marshall; special student at Tufts Coll., D.D., 1920; m. Bertha, d. Thomas Hills, of Boston, Sept. 11, 1893; 1 dau., Elisabeth. Ordained Universalist ministry, 1891; pastor Beverly, Mass., 1891, Swampscott, Mass., 1897, Melrose, Mass., 1903-17; mgr. Universalist Pub. House and The Christian Leader, Boston, 1917—. Lecturer on Am. history and civics. Founder Boston Flower Mission. Mason. Joint author: Democracy in the Making, 1915. Home: Melrose, Mass. Died July 14, 1932.

MARSHALL, Henry Rutgers, architect; b. New York, July 22, 1852; s. Henry Perry and Cornelia E. (Conrad) M.; A.B., Columbia, 1873, A.M., 1876; L.H.D., Rutgers, 1903; D.Sc., Hobart, 1910; m. Julia R. Gilman, May 18, 1881 (died 1888). In practice as architect, 1878—. Lecturer on æsthetics, Columbia U., 1894-95, Yale U., 1906-07, Princeton U., 1915-17; mem. Art Commn., City of N.Y. (exec. sec.). Fellow A.I.A. (pres. New York chapter 1902-04). Author: Pain, Pleasure and Æsthetics, 1894; Æsthetic Principles, 1895; Instinct and Reason, 1898; Consciousness, 1909; War and the Ideal of Peace, 1915; Mind and Conduct, 1919; The Beautiful, 1924. Home: New York, N.Y. Died May 3, 1927.

MARSHALL, James Rush, architect; b. Carlisle, Pa., Oct. 30, 1851; s. James William and Jane (Stevenson) M.; ed. Rutgers Coll. to end of junior yr., class of 1871; unmarried. In office of supervising architect, Treasury Dept., 1871-83; mem. Hornblower & Marshall, 1883—. Architect U.S. Custom House (Baltimore), U.S. Nat. Mus. and Army and Navy Club bldgs., Washington, etc.; majority of work pvt. dwellings. Fellow A.I.A. Home: Washington, D.C. Died June 2, 1927.

MARSHALL, John, chemist; b. Reading, Pa., Feb. 9, 1855; s. John Gloninger (M.D.) and Susan A. (Kline) M.; student Pa. Coll., Gettysburg, 1873-76; M.D., U. of Pennsylvania, 1878; studied U. of Göttingen, 1879, Tübingen (grad. Nat. Sc.D.), 1882, Christiania, Norway; (LL.D., Pa. Coll., 1899); m. Mary W., d. Prof. Theo. G. Wormley, of Phila., Apr. 24, 1884. Asst. demonstrator of practical chemistry, 1878-79, demonstrator, 1879-89, asst. prof. chemistry, 1889-97, prof. chemistry and toxicology, 1897-1922, emeritus prof. chemistry and toxicology, 1922, med. dept. U. of Pa.; dean of faculty of Vet. Medicine, 1889-97, dean faculty of medicine, 1892-1902. U. of Pa. Author: A Course for Systematic Qualitative Testing (with G. E. Abbott), 1879; Chemical Analysis of the Urine (with Edgar F. Smith), 1881. Home: Philadelphia, Pa. Died Jan. 5, 1925.

MARSHALL, John, judge; b. Logansport, Ind., Apr. 11, 1858; s. Humphrey and Margaret (Rice) M.; U. of Kan., 1880-82; m. Addie Jenks, 1882. Began practice at Howard, Kan., 1883; mayor of Howard, 1887-88, city atty., 1885-1900; co. atty. of Elk Co., 1895-99; city atty. of Winfield, Kan., 1905-07; asst. atty. gen. of Kan., 1907-11; atty. of Pub. Utilities Commn. of Kan., 1911-13; justice Supreme Court of Kan., 1915—. Mem. Bd. of Edn. of Howard, Kan., 1892-1914. Republican. Methodist. Author: Kansas Trial Brief, 1905; Kansas Probate Law, 1906. Home: Topeka, Kan. Died Mar. 26, 1931.

MARSHALL, John Patten, musician, educator; b. Rockport, Mass., Jan. 9, 1877; s. John White and Mary Louise (Knowlton) M.; pub. sch. edn.; studied music in Boston with Edward Alexander MacDowell, Benjamin Johnson Lang, George Whitfield Chadwick and Homer Albert Norris, 1895-1900; hon. Mus. Doc., Holy Cross College in 1927; hon. fellow Trinity Coll. of Music, London, 1933; m. Emily Geiger, Nov. 24, 1903; 1 son, John Geiger; m. 2d, Miriam Brooke Smith, July 25, 1930. Organist St. John's Church, Boston, 1896-1903; Boston Symphony Orchestra, 1909-18, First Ch., 1909-26; prof. music Boston U., 1902—; dir. music, Middlesex Sch., Concord, Mass., 1902-12; lecturer on music, Harvard Summer Sch., 1908-11, Univ. Extension, 1911—. Capt. U.S.A., 1919; development specialist in music, Gen. Staff, U.S.A., 1920-22; lecturer on music Holy Cross Coll., 1925-29; dean Coll. of Music, Boston U., 1928—. Dean N.E. Chapter Am. Guild Organists, 1925-29; master of music, American section, Anglo-Am. Music Conference, Lausanne, Switzerland, 1931. Republican. Author: Syllabus of History of Music, 1906; Syllabus of Music Appreciation, 1911; Musical Instruction for Army Bandsmen (U.S. War Dept.). Home: Boston, Mass. Died Jan. 17, 1941.

MARSHALL, Louis, lawyer; b. Syracuse, N.Y., Dec. 14, 1856; s. Jacob and Zilli (Strauss) M.; Syracuse pub. and high schs.; Law Sch., Columbia U.; LL.D., Syracuse U., 1913; L.H.D., Hebrew Union Coll., 1920; L.H.D., Jewish Theol. Seminary, 1927; m. Florence Lowenstein, May 6, 1895 (died 1916). Began practice at Syracuse, 1878; now mem. Guggenheimer, Untermyer & Marshall; has argued many important causes in the higher courts, especially constl. and corp. law. Mem. Constl. convs., N.Y., 1890, 1894, 1915; mem. commn. apptd. by Mayor Low, 1902, to investigate East Side conditions; chmn. N.Y. State Immigration Commn., apptd. by Gov. Hughes, 1908; counsel for Gov. Sulzer in his impeachment trial, and for Leo M. Frank in the U.S. Sup. Court. Chmn. bd. and chmn. exec. com. Jewish Theol. Sem. of America; pres. Am. Jewish Com.; pres. of Temple Emanuel; founder Jewish Protectory and Aid Soc.; dir. Ednl. Alliance, Dropsie Coll., Phila.; pres. Am. Jewish Com., Am. Jewish Relief Com., which with kindred organizations, collected more than $75,000,000 for relief of Jewish war sufferers. Mem. N.Y. District Board, 1917-19. Pres. Comité des Délégations Juives auprès de la Conference de la Paix, whose efforts resulted in the treaties with Poland, Rumania, Jugo-Slavia, Czecho-Slovakia and other countries, which guarantee equal rights to all racial, religious and linguistic minorities. Trustee Syracuse U., from 1910, to which has presented law library; pres. N.Y. State Coll. of Forestry; for 20 yrs., chmn. com. on amendment of law of Assn. Bar City of N.Y. (com. revision of N.Y. corp. laws). Republican. Active in settlement of differences of opinion regarding articles appearing in the Dearborn Independent concerning alleged attempt of Jews to control the finances of the world. Home: New York, N.Y. Died Sept. 11, 1929.

MARSHALL, Robert Eliot, clergyman, educator; b. Roxbury, Boston, Mass., June 1, 1883; s. Andrew and Emily Ann (Hentz) M.; student Harvard, 1900; A.B., Dartmouth, 1904; B.D., Gen. Theol. Sem., 1910; unmarried. Teacher, Kenyon Mil. Acad., Gambier, O., 1904-06, Ridge Sch., Washington, D.C., 1906-07; deacon, 1910, priest, 1911, P.E. Ch.; asst. St. Mary's Ch., Bronx, N.Y., 1910-11; minister Trinity Ch., Hartford, Conn., 1911-20; rector St. Matthew's Ch., Bedford, N.Y., 1920-22, Holderness Sch., Plymouth, N.H., 1922-28, St. Mark's Ch., Dorchester, Boston, 1928-30, Ch. of Our Redeemer, Lexington, Mass., 1930—. Mem. Conn. N.G., 1917-19. Republican. Episcopalian. Died Sept. 21, 1937.

MARSHALL, Roujet De Lisle, judge; b. Nashua, N.H., Dec. 27, 1847; s. Thomas and Emeline M.; parents settled at Delton, Sauk Co., Wis., 1854; ed. Delton Acad., Baraboo (Wis.) Collegiate Inst., and Lawrence U.; (LL.D., Lawrence, 1904, U. of Wis., 1905); m. Mary E. Jenkins, 1869. Admitted to bar, 1873; judge co. ct., 1876-82; regent, U. of Wis., 1884-86; judge Circuit Ct., 1889-95; justice Supreme Ct. of Wis., Aug. 1895—. Republican. Home: Chippewa Falls, Wis. Died May 22, 1922.

MARSHALL, Thomas, field sec. Bd. Foreign Missions, Presbyn. Ch. of U.S.A., 1890—; b. E. Weare, N.H., April 14, 1831; s. Moody and Sarah (Beard) M.; grad. Dartmouth, 1857, A.M., 1871, D.D., 1902; Union Theol. Sem., New York, 1864; (D.D., Gale Coll., 1891); m. Mrs. Louise Goodheart Schneck, d. Daniel Stichter, Lebanon, Pa., Oct. 1871. Prin. Wilson Acad. and teacher in sem., Wilson, N.C., 1857-60; teacher civil engring. dept. Cooper Union, New York, 1862-63; ordained by 4th Presbytery, New York, Dec. 18, 1864. Pastor First Presbyn. Ch., Mankato, Minn., 1865-69; High St. Presbyn. Ch., 1869-72, and Glasgow Av. Presbyn. Ch., 1874-81, St. Louis. Synodical missionary of Mo., 1881-88; traveled around the world, visiting Japan, Korea, China, Siam, Straits Settlements of Malacca, Burma, India, Egypt, Palestine, Syria, Europe and the British Isles, 1888-89; elected life mem. Asiatic Soc. of Japan, 1868. Died 1903.

MARSHALL, Thomas, lawyer; b. Washington, Ky., Aug. 25, 1834; ed. Kenyon Coll., Gambier, O.; m. Sarah J. Hughes, 1855. Studied law with Judge Thomas A. Marshall, Lexington, Ky.; admitted to St. Louis bar; located in Salt Lake City, Utah, 1866; atty. Central Pacific R.R. Co., and its successor, Southern Pacific R.R. Co., 1869; admitted to bar of U.S. Supreme Court, 1872; served 1 term in Territorial council; filled other public offices. Home: Salt Lake City, Utah. Died 1903.

MARSHALL, Thomas Frank, congressman; b. Mar. 7, 1854; s. George W. and Sarah E. (Hefflebower) M.; ed. State Normal Sch., Platteville, Wis.; m. Eva E. Grigsby, Dec. 4, 1878. Is banker and surveyor. Mayor of Oakes, N.D., 1888-92; del. Rep. Nat. Conv., 1892; mem. N.D. Senate, 1896-1900; candidate for U.S. senator, 1899; mem. 57th to 60th Congresses (1901-09), N.D. at-large. Republican. Mem. Rep. Nat. Com., 1912-16. Home: Oakes, N.D. Died Aug. 20, 1921.

MARSHALL, Thomas Maitland, prof history; b. Lansing, Mich., Oct. 25, 1876; s. Orville (M.D.) and Sarah Eliza (Metlin) M.; B.L., U. of Mich., 1900; M.L., U. of Calif., 1910, Ph.D., 1914; post-grad. student, Stanford, 1910-11; m. Vesta Woodbury, Sept. 17, 1907; children—Willis Woodbury, Leroy Maitland. Teacher pub. schs. of Wis. and Calif. until 1915; acting asst. prof. Am. history, Stanford U., 1915-16; asso. prof. history, U. of Ida., 1916-17; asst. prof. history, U. of Colo., 1917-19, asso. prof., 1919-20; prof. history, Washington U., 1920-35. Lecturer, U. of Texas Summer Sch., 5 summers, U. of Washington, 1922, Harvard U., 1923, U. of California, 1929, U. of Mich., 1931. Fellow Tex. State Hist. Assn.; hon. mem. Mich. Acad. Science, Arts and Letters. Author: A History of the Western Boundary of the Louisiana Purchase, 1819-1841, 1914; St. Vrain's Expedition to the Gila in 1826 (in Pacific Ocean in History), 1917; Report on the Archives of Idaho, 1920; Colonization of North America, 1492-1783 (with Herbert E. Bolton), 1920; Life and Papers of Frederick Bates (2 vols.), 1926; American History, 1930. Editor Early Records of Gilpin County, Colorado, 1859-1861. Home: Campbell, Calif. Died Apr. 12, 1936.

MARSHALL, Thomas Riley, 28th Vice President of the United States; b. North Manchester, Ind., March 14, 1854; s. of Daniel M. and Martha A. (Patterson) M.; A.B., Wabash Coll., 1873, A.M., 1876 (LL.D., 1909; LL.D., Notre Dame U., 1910, U. of Pa., 1911, U. of North Carolina, 1913, Univ. of Maine, 1914, Washington and Jefferson Coll., Pa., 1917; J.D., Villanova Coll., Pa., 1918); m. Lois I. Kimsey, Oct. 2, 1895. Admitted to bar, 1875; practiced at Columbia City, Ind.; mem. Marshall & McNagny, 1876-92, Marshall, McNagny & Clugston, 1892-1909; gov. of Ind., 1909-13. Nominated for Vice-President of the United States in Dem. Nat. Conv., Baltimore, 1912, on ticket with Woodrow Wilson, and elected, Nov. 4, 1912, for term Mar. 4, 1913-Mar. 4, 1917; reëlected Vice-President for term Mar. 4, 1917-Mar. 4, 1921. Mem. U.S. Coal Commn., 1922. Trustee Wabash Coll. Presbyn. Mason. Home: Indianapolis, Ind. Died June 1, 1925.

MARSHALL, Waldo H., banker; b. June 7, 1864; ed. pub. schs. Asst. supt. motive power, C.&N.W. Ry., May 1897-June 1899; supt. motive power, 1899-1902, gen. supt., Feb. 1902-July 1, 1903, gen. mgr., 1903-06, L.S.&M.S. Ry.; pres. Am. Locomotive Co., New York, 1906-17. Was also pres. Richmond Locomotive Works; dir. Am. Brake Shoe & Foundry Co., Bucyrus Co., Chatham & Phenix Nat. Bank of N.Y.; with J. P. Morgan & Co., bankers, New York, 1917. Apptd. chief of Production Div. of Ordnance Dept. U.S.A., Jan. 1918. Formerly mem. Naval Consulting Board. Home: New York, N.Y. Died Aug. 22, 1923.

MARSHALL, William A., life insurance; b. N.Y. City, Apr. 1, 1847; s. William S. and Henrietta (Wolven) M.; ed. schs. of N.Y. and Conn.; m. Julia Marshall, 1869. Entered employ Home Life Ins. Co., Apr. 6, 1866, actuary, 1877, v.p., 1904, pres., 1919, now advisory dir.; dir. Nyack Nat. Bank. Charter mem. Actuarial Soc. America, N.E. Society. Republican. Presbyterian. Deceased.

MARSHALL, William Alexander, naval officer; b. Lancaster, Pa., Oct. 17, 1849; grad. U.S. Naval Acad., 1871; married. Promoted ensign, July 14, 1872; advanced through grades to rear admiral, Mar. 17, 1910. Assisted in fitting out Mosquito Fleet during Spanish-Am. War; served Navy Yard, Boston, 1901-02; insp., 15th Light House Dist., 1902-03; comdr. Vicksburg, 1903-04; comdr. Raleigh, 1904-05; insp. 2d Light House Dist., 1905-06; Navy Yard, Boston, 1906-08; comd. North Carolina, 1908-09; comdt., Navy Yard, Norfolk, 1909-11; retired on account of age, Oct. 7, 1911. Home: Washington, D.C. Died July 10, 1926.

MARSHALL, William Louis, brig. gen.; b. Washington, Ky., June 11, 1846; s. Col. Charles A. and Phœbe A. (Paxton) M.; ed. Kenyon Coll., Ohio, 1859-61; pvt. Co. A, 10th Ky. Cav., Aug. 16, 1862-Sept. 17, 1863; grad. U.S. Mil. Acad., 1868; m. Elizabeth Hill Colquitt, d. late A. H. Colquitt, U.S. senator from Ga., June 2, 1886. Bvtd. 2d lt. engrs., June 15, 1868; promoted through grades to brig. gen. chief of engrs. U.S.A., July 2, 1908. Acting asst. prof. natural and exptl. philosophy, U.S. Mil. Acad., 1870-71; in charge Colo. sect. "Explorations West of 100th Meridian," 1872-76; discovered "Marshall Pass" across Rocky Mountains, 1873, also gold placers of Marshall Basin, San Miguel River, Colo., 1875; in charge constrn. of levees in Miss., La., and Ark., and improvements of Mississippi River in 3d dist., 1881-84; of harbors on Lake Michigan, 1884-1900, and also of improvement of Calumet, Chicago, Illinois and Rock rivers, Ill., and Fox and Wisconsin rivers, Wis.; in charge of construction Hennepin Canal, 1890-1900; mem. Missouri River Commn., 1898-1902; engr. in charge construction of fortifications at eastern and southern entrances to New York harbor, and improvements of main channels of New York harbor, 1900-08; constructed new 40-ft. channel (Ambrose) entrance to New York harbor; in command of the Corps of Engrs. U.S.A. and in charge of river and harbor and fortification works of the U.S. from July 2, 1908; retired, June 11, 1910. Consulting engr. to sec. of the interior, July 2, 1910—. Mem. bds. of engrs. on dam for storage reservoir in Sacramento River, Calif., at Red Bluff, for irrigation and power; on development of hydro-electric power at the Dalles, Columbia River, 1913; engr. in charge protection Imperial Valley, Calif., against overflow of Colorado River, 1914-15; mem. central bd. of review of reclamation project costs, 1915-16. Inventor automatic movable dams, lock gates and valves. Home: Washington, D.C. Died July 2, 1920.

MARSTEN, Francis Edward, clergyman; b. Jersey City, N.J., Sept. 12, 1855; s. Cornelius and Eliza A. (Ballard) M.; A.B., Amherst, 1874, A.M., 1880; student, Andover Theol. Sem., class 1876 (D.D., U. of Wooster, O., 1894); m. Ida M. Freeman, June 7, 1879. Ordained Presbyn. ministry, Oct. 5, 1878; pastor 1st Ch., Boston, 1878-82, Old First Ch., Columbus, O., 1883-87, Broad St. Ch., Columbus (founder), 1887-98; asso. editor New York Evangelist, 1899, Saturday Lit. Rev., New York, 1900—; pastor Bethany Ch., New York, 1903-13; corr. sec. Mass. Bible Soc., Boston, 1913—. Mason. Author: A Short History of Presbyterianism, 1895; Songs of Life, 1897; The Freedom of Christ, 1898; Art and Social Well Being, 1901; The Mask of Christian Science, 1910. Died Aug. 22, 1915.

MARSTON, Edgar Lewis, banker; b. Burlington, Ia., Mar. 8, 1860; s. Sylvester W. and Susan H. (Carpenter) M.; A.B., La Grange Coll., 1878; LL.B., Washington Univ., St. Louis, Mo., 1881; m. Jennie C. Hunter, June 4, 1884; m. 2d, Mrs. Ann M. Ellis, 1925. Practiced law in partnership with Edmund T. Allen, St. Louis, from 1881; acted as representative of Eastern capitalists, making investments in the Southwest; organized Tex. & Pacific Coal Co., 1888; from 1887 resident New York; became mgr. bond dept., Blair Co., May 1890, member firm, 1893—; chmn. bd. Tex. Pacific Coal & Oil Co.; dir. Interstate Co., Clinchfield Coal Co., Ponds Extract Co., Citizens Nat. Trust & Savings Bank, Los Angeles. Baptist; trustee Bishop Baptist Coll., Brown University. Retired. Deceased.

MARSTON, George W., musician and teacher; b. Sandwich, Mass., May 23, 1840; academic edn.; began study of music at 12; at 16 was church organist; taught pianoforte; settled in Portland, Me.; later removed to Boston. Composer of numerous ballads, including Marguerite, and Douglas, Tender and True; cantatas, Te Deums, anthems, piano compositions, etc. Home: Boston, Mass. Died 1901.

MARSTON, Percival Freeman, clergyman; b. Gorham, Me., Oct. 14, 1863; s. Samuel Freeman and Annie (Varney) M.; A.B., Bowdoin, 1888; grad. Andover Theol. Sem., 1894; (D.D., Bates, 1907); m. Maybelle H. Haynes, Apr. 11, 1888. Ordained Congl. ministry, 1894; pastor Cambridge, N.Y., 1894-96, Lancaster, N.H., 1896-1902, Pine St. Ch., Lewiston, Me., 1902-08, N.E. Ch., Chicago, 1908-11, 1st Ch., Grinnell, Ia., 1911-15. Trustee N.H. Home Missionary Soc., 1898-1902, Me. Home Missionary Soc., 1904-08; corporate mem. A.B.C.F.M., 1912—. Democrat. Mason. Home: Concord, N.H. Died Feb. 19, 1916.

MARTENS, Frederick Herman, author; b. N.Y. City, July 6, 1874; s. Carl G. and Josephine (Weeks) M.; ed. under pvt. tutors, specializing in history and modern langs.; studied theory of music with Max Spicker, piano with Henry C. Timm and W. H. Barber; unmarried. Writer on musical topics, 1907—, contributing to Musical Quarterly, Musical America, Vanity Fair, Vogue, London Chesterian, Sackbut. Contributing editor, Art of Music, Singing (1925). Author: Violin Mastery, 1919; Art of the Prima-Donna; String Mastery; Fairy Tales from Far Away; Fairy Tales from the Orient, 1923; Wonder Tales of Far Away, 1924; One Thousand and One Nights of Opera; Book of the Opera and Ballet, 1925; operettas, choral works, songs. Republican. Episcopalian. Home: Mountain Lakes, N.J. Died Dec. 18, 1932.

MARTIN, Abe. See Frank McKinney Hubbard.

MARTIN, Alfred Wilhelm, lecturer, author; b. Cologne, Germany, Jan. 21, 1862; s. Charles and Bertha (Herx) M.; A.B., McGill U., 1882; S.T.B., Harvard, 1885, A.M., 1886; m. Lillie Frothingham, July 3, 1892. Ordained Unitarian ministry, 1888; pastor Chelsea, Massachusetts, 1888-92; founder and pastor of an independent ch., Tacoma, Wash., 1892-1907, also at Seattle, Wash., 1899-1907; asso. leader Ethical Culture Soc., Oct. 1907—. Univ. extension lecturer, Columbia U.; lecturer Brooklyn Inst. Arts and Sciences, lecturer League for Polit. Edn., New York. Author: The Dawn of Christianity, 1914; Faith in a Future Life, 1916; A Critique of Christian Science, 1922; Psychic Tendencies of To-day, 1918; A Philosophy of Life and Its Spiritual Values, 1923; Comparative Religion and the Religion of the Future, 1925; A Fellowship of Faiths, 1927; Seven Great Bibles, 1929; Consolations, 1930. Home: New York, N.Y. Died Oct. 15, 1932.

MARTIN, Alvah Howard; b. Mt. Pleasant, Va., Sept. 20, 1858; s. Col. James G. and Bettie L. (Gresham) M.; ed. Webster Inst., Norfolk, Va.; studied law; m. Mary E. Tilley, Jan. 6, 1881. County clk., Norfolk Co., 1881—; prominent for many yrs. in state and nat. Rep. councils; mem. Rep. Nat. Com., 1908-12, 1912-16, 1916-20. Pres. Merchants' and Planters' Bank (Norfolk), Chesapeake Bldg. Assn. Dir. gen. Jamestown Expn., Oct. 6-Nov. 30, 1907, and later chmn. bd. of receivers same. Pres Ragged Island Gunning Assn. Home: Norfolk, Va. Died July 6, 1918.

MARTIN, Artemas, mathematician; b. Steuben Co., N.Y., Aug. 3, 1835; s. James Madison and Orenda Knight (Bradley) M.; was a short time in Franklin Select Sch., and Franklin Acad., 1852-55; (hon. A.M., Yale, 1877; Ph.D., Rutgers, 1882; LL.D., Hillsdale Coll., 1885); unmarried. As a boy worked at farming summers, chopped wood winters and later taught district sch. and drilled oil wells, devoting all spare time to math. studies and contributing problems and solutions to math. jours.; ran a market garden, 1871-85; since then employed in U.S. Coast and Geod. Survey Office. Editor and pub. Mathematical Magazine and Mathematical Visitor. Home: Washington, D.C. Died Nov. 7, 1918.

MARTIN, Benjamin Ellis, author; b. New York. Author: About England with Dickens; Old Chelsea; In the Footprints of Charles Lamb; The Stones of Paris in History and Letters, 1899 (with Charlotte M. Martin). Home: New York, N.Y. Died 1909.

MARTIN, Bradley, capitalist; b. Albany, N.Y., Dec. 18, 1841; s. Henry Hull and Anne (Townsend) M.; grad. Union U., A.M., 1863, later LL.B.; m. Cornelia, d. Isaac Sherman, of New York; father of Bradley M., Jr. Admitted to bar; served short time in Civil War as 1st lt. 93d Regt., N.G.S.N.Y.; col. and a.d.c. on staff Governor Fenton, N.Y., 1865-68; for some yrs. has lived in London. Died Feb. 5, 1913.

MARTIN, Burton McMahan, clergyman; b. McMinn Co., Tenn., Oct. 25, 1866; s. Robert Edwin and Eliza Ellen (Blackburn) M.; ed. Hayesville (N.C.) Male and Female Coll., 1888-91, Theol. Sch., Grant U. (now U. of Chattanooga), 1892-95; D.D., U. of Chattanooga, 1913; m. Zona Haggard, May 27, 1896. Deacon, M.E. Ch., 1896, elder, 1898; pastor Pikeville, Tenn., 1895, Highland Park, Chattanooga, 1896, Rockwood, 1897, Pikeville, 1898, Morristown, 1899-1901, Maryville, 1902-06, Athens, 1906-11; dist. sup. Harriman Dist., 1911-16; agt. Preachers' Aid Soc., 1917-18; pastor 2d Ch., Knoxville, 1918-20; sec. Missionary Centenary, Chattanooga Area, 1920—. Dir. Chattanooga Goodwill Industries, Inc.; trustee U. of Chattanooga. Republican. Mason. Lecturer Summer Sch. for Rural Pastors, Athens, Tenn. Home: Chattanooga, Tenn. Deceased.

MARTIN, Celora E., judge of the N.Y. Court of Appeals, 1896-Dec. 31, 1904; b. Newport, N.Y., Aug. 23, 1834; s. Ellis and Lucetta (Brayton) M.; ed. in Newport, N.Y., 1839-49; at Fairfield and Holland Patent, 1849-53; studied law at Newport, N.Y.; admitted to bar, July 1856; m. Almanza R. Barney, Sept. 23, 1857; m. 2d, Ada L. Mills, Sept. 4, 1901. Practiced Whitney's Point, Broome Co., 1857-67, Binghamton, 1867-77; apptd. 1877 and later same year elected justice Sup. Court; re-elected 1891; in 1887 designated as justice of general term and acted as such until Dec. 31, 1895. Republican. Home: Binghamton, N.Y. Died 1909.

MARTIN, Chalmers, theologian; b. Ashland, Ky., Sept. 7, 1859; s. Edwin Welles and Narcissa (McCurdy) M.; A.B., Princeton, 1879, A.M., 1882, D.D., 1901; grad. Princeton Theol. Sem., 1882; m. Lillian Allen, Sept. 25, 1883; children—Ruth, Edwin Allen, Dorothy (Mrs. H. H. Ormond), Stuart McCurdy. Ordained Presbyn. ministry, 1883; missionary Laos tribes, Northern Siam, 1883-86; pastor, Moorestown, N.J., 1888-91, Port Henry, N.Y., 1891-92; instr. Hebrew, Princeton U., and Elliott F. Shepard instr. O.T., Princeton Theol. Sem., 1892-1900; pres. Pa. Coll. for Women, 1900-03; prof. O.T. history and literature, College of Wooster, 1903-29 (emeritus). Students' lecturer on missions, Princeton Theol. Seminary, 1894-95 and 1900-01. President Middle West sect., Coll. Bible Teachers Assn., 1920-21. Author: Apostolic and Modern Missions, 1898. Home: Wooster, O. Died Feb. 28, 1934.

MARTIN, Charles Cyril, civil engr.; b. Springfield, Pa., Aug. 30, 1831; grad. Rensselaer Poly. Inst., Troy, 1856; asst. in geodesy there 1 yr.; entered on engring. practice; held several positions; was connected with water works, bridge-building and other engring. operations in Brooklyn; engr. Prospect Park there; later 1st asst. engr. until May 1883, then chief engr. and supt. New York and Brooklyn Bridge; cons. engr. to dept. of bridges, New York, Feb. 1, 1902—. Died 1903.

MARTIN, Daniel Strobel, geologist; b. New York, June 30, 1842; s. Benjamin Nicholas and Louisa Caroline (Strobel) M.; A.B., New York U., 1863, A.M., 1866; grad. Union Theol. Sem., 1866; (hon. Ph.D., Regents, U. State of N.Y., 1881); unmarried. Prof. geology and related branches, Rutgers Female Coll., New York, 1868-95; regents' examiner in English studies for law students, 1882-87; asso. with geol. work at various times in Cooper Union, N.Y. Acad. Sciences, Brooklyn Inst. Arts and Sciences; prof. geology, College for Women, Columbia, S.C., 1898-1904; hon. curator geology and mineralogy, Charleston (S.C.) Mus., 1906—. Lecturer on geology, Chicora Coll., Greenville, S.C., 1908—. Pres. trustees Cuban Home Training Sch., Brooklyn. Address: Brooklyn, N.Y. Died 1925.

MARTIN, David B., mgr. passenger traffic Baltimore & Ohio R.R., Apr. 15, 1897—; b. Mount Joy, Pa.; began R.R. service with "Bee Line," Oct. 1867, serving with it and its successor, the "Big Four" (C.,C.,C.&St.L. Ry.), until Apr. 1897, from cashier in the Dayton, O., office to gen. passenger agt.; served throughout the Civil war. Mason. Died 1909.

MARTIN, Dempster Disbrow, clergyman, educator; b. Sumpter, Mich., Apr. 1, 1862; s. Winslow Packard and Emerett Alida (Disbrow) M.; B.D., Hillsdale (Mich.) Coll., 1891, D.D., 1904; post-grad. work, Allegheny Coll., U. of Chicago; m. Ora Adel Van Horn, Apr. 23, 1884; children—Eathel Agnes, James Morris. Ordained minister M.E. Ch., 1889; pastor Sherwood, Mich., 1888-90, Reading, 1890-94, St. Johns, 1894-98, First Ch., Battle Creek, 1898-1903; dist. supt. Albion Dist., Mich., 1903-08; ednl. sec. Albion Coll., Mich., 1908-10; prof. Christian missions and comparative religion, and dir. Sch. of Missions, Gammon Theol. Sem., Atlanta, Ga., 1910-32; trustee Atlanta Sch. of Social Service, Inc.; gen. sec. Stewart Missionary Foundation for Africa, and editor The Foundation (monthly). Republican. Home: Albion, Mich. Died Apr. 5, 1935.

MARTIN, Earle, newspaper editor; b. Edinburg, Ind., Sept. 12, 1874; s. John Henry and Clara Josephine (Hansell) M.; grad. Moores Hill (Ind.) Coll., 1894; Litt.D., Evansville Coll., 1927; m. Florence Roseberry, Aug. 21, 1897; 1 dau., Mary Elizabeth (Mrs. Royale C. Wise). Began as reporter Indianapolis News, 1894; mng. editor Cincinnati Post, 1899, Indianapolis News, 1900-03; editorial dir. Indianapolis Star, Muncie Star, Terre Haute Star, 1904-05; editor Cleveland Press, 1905-13; editor in chief Scripps-McRae League of Newspapers, 1913-21; pres. and gen. mgr. Newspaper Enterprise Assn., 1921-23; editor Cleveland Press, 1924-25; editor and pub. Cleveland Times, 1926-27; commissioner Cleveland Industrial Development Com., 1928-32; editor Cleveland News, 1932—. Republican. Unitarian. Home: South Euclid, O. Died May 5, 1938.

MARTIN, Eben Wever, congressman; b. Maquoketa, Ia., Apr. 12, 1855; s. Capt. James W. and Lois Hyde (Wever) M.; A.B., Cornell Coll., Ia., 1879, A.M., 1882, LL.D., 1904; law student U. of Mich., 1879-80; m. Jessie A. Miner, June 13, 1883; children—George M. (dec.), Mrs. Lois W. Finger, Paul E., Charl E., Mrs. Jessie A. Allen. Admitted bar, 1880. Mem. Dak. Territorial Legislature, 1884-85; pres. Deadwood Bd. Edn., 1886-1900; mem. 57th to 59th Congresses (1901-07) and elected to 60th Congress for unexpired term (1908-09) of William H. Parker, deceased; reëlected to 61st and 62d Congresses (1909-13), S.D. at-large, and 63d Congress (1913-15), 3d Dist. Republican. Home: Hot Springs, S.D. Died May 1932.

MARTIN, Edgar Stanley, editor, educator; b. Gorham, N.Y., Mar. 8, 1873; s. William and Elizabeth (McIntyre) M.; grad. Keuka Coll., N.Y., 1894; N.Y. State Normal Coll., Albany, N.Y., 1898; spl. courses sociology and education univs. of Chicago, Pittsburgh and Ohio State; B.A., Central U., 1901; m. Gertrude Bishop, Dec. 24, 1898; children—Clinton Stanley, Margaret Elizabeth, Ruth Alice. Prin. high sch., Tully, N.Y., 1898-1901; prin. John G. McMynn Sch., Racine, Wis., 1901-10; sec. Dept. of Recreation, Columbus, O., 1910-11, also commr. Franklin Co. (O.) Council Boy Scouts America; supt. play grounds of D.C., also commr. and scout exec., 1911-15; mem. Nat. Council Boy Scouts of America, 1910-15, sec. editorial board, 1915-31, editor of Scouting, 1927—, nat. dir. of publs., 1931—. Pres. Am. Swimming Assn., 1923-25; instructor in scoutmastership at Columbia U., 1925-28. Republican. Methodist. Mason. Home: Orange, N.J. Died Aug. 9, 1940.

MARTIN, Edward, surgeon; b. Phila., 1859; s. J. Willis and M. (Register) M.; A.B., Swarthmore Coll., 1878, A.M., 1882; M.D., U. of Pa., 1883, LL.D., 1919; Sc.D., Swarthmore Coll., 1920; LL.D., Temple U., 1935; m. Anna Withers, 1887. Clin. prof. surgery, Woman's Med. College of Pa., 1902—; prof. clin. surgery, 1903-10, John Rhea Barton prof. surgery, 1910-18, U. of Pa.; surgeon to University and Howard hosps.; consulting surgeon, Bryn Mawr Hosp., Norristown State Hosp. for Insane and Wernersville State Hosp. for Insane, Welada General Hospital; dir. Public Health and Charities, Phila., 1903-05; mem. Bd. of Education, 1911— (v.p.); commr. of health, State of Pa. Consulting surgeon 5th Army Corps, Spanish-Am. War; lt. col. World War; col. 364th Med. Regt. O.R.C. Now prof. surg. physiology, U. of Pa. Mem. bd. mgrs. Swarthmore Coll., 1895—. Fellow Am. Coll. Surgeons. Home: Media, Pa. Died Mar. 17, 1938.

MARTIN, Edward Hamilton, physician; b. Matthews Co., Va., Feb. 28, 1865; s. Joseph Edward (D.D.) and Mary Elizabeth (Hamilton) M.; Lincoln (Ill.) U., 1877-81; Purdue U., Ind., 1881-82; M.D., Med. Coll. of Ohio, Cincinnati, 1887; m. Virginia Louise Walker, Nov. 7, 1889. Taught sch., Ind., 18 mos.; practiced at Sunflower Landing (now Green Grove), Miss., 1887-98, Clarksdale, Miss., 1898-1906, Hot Springs, Ark., 1906—. Democrat. Episcopalian. Mason, Elk, K.P. Home: Hot Springs, Ark. Died May 5, 1921.

MARTIN, Edward Sandford, author; b. Willowbrook, N.Y., Jan. 2, 1856; s. E. T. Throop and Cornelia (Williams) M.; A.B., Harvard Univ., 1877, hon. A.M., 1916; Litt.D., U. of Rochester, 1917; LL.D., Lafayette College, 1924; admitted to bar, Rochester, New York, 1884; m. Julia, d. George J. Whitney, of Rochester, Sept. 2, 1886; children—George Whitney, Mary (Mrs. Paul A. Degener), Lois Whitney (Mrs. E. S. Blagden). A founder of Harvard Lampoon, 1876; founder and first editor of Life, 1883, editorial writer for that paper, 1887-1933; writer for Harper's Weekly, asst. editor, 1893-1913; writer of "The Easy Chair," Harper's Mag., 1929-35. Chevalier of Legion of Honor (France), 1919. Mem. Nat. Inst. Arts and Letters. Author: Cousin Anthony and I, 1895; Lucid Intervals, 1900; Poems and Verses, 1902; The Luxury of Children, and Other Luxuries, 1904; The Courtship of a Careful Man, 1905; In a New Century, 1908; Reflections of a Beginning Husband, 1913; Unrest of Women, 1913; Abroad with Jane, 1918; The Life of J. H. Choate, 1920; What's Ahead, and Meanwhile, 1927. Home: New York, N.Y. Died June 13, 1939.

MARTIN, Edwin Moore, clergyman; b. Tiffin, O., Feb. 15, 1872; s. Jefferson McC. and Eliza Jane (McFaddin) M.; A.B., Park Coll., Parkville, Mo., 1896; grad. McCormick Theol. Sem., Chicago, 1899; m. Jennie May Stewart, May 10, 1899; children—Loyal Stewart, Kent Edwin. Ordained ministry Presbyn. Ch. in U.S.A., 1899; pastor Richland Center, Wis., 1899-1904, Shawano, Wis., 1904-06, Mattoon, Ill., 1906-09, Grand Ridge, 1909-13, Westwood, Cincinnati, 1913-21, Price Hill, Cincinnati, 1921-30. Moderator Madison (Wis.) Presbytery, 1903, Cincinnati Presbytery, 1918. Mason. Author: They Knew Jesus, 1929. Home: Cincinnati, O. Died Oct. 12, 1935.

MARTIN, Ernest Gale, physiologist; b. Minneapolis, Minn., Nov. 16, 1876; s. John Wesley and Mary Esther (Bullard) M.; Ph.B., Hamline U., 1897; Ph.D., Johns Hopkins Univ., 1904; m. Ruby A. Ticknor, Aug. 31, 1904; 1 daughter, Lois Ticknor. Fellow and assistant in physiology, Johns Hopkins, 1902-04; instr. physiology, Purdue U., 1904-06; instr. physiology, 1906-10, asst. prof., 1910-16, Harvard, also lecturer Sargent Sch. for Physical Edn., 1906-14; asst. prof. physiology, Radcliffe Coll., 1914-16, and physiologist, Vt. State Bd. of Health, 1915-16; prof. physiology, Stanford U., 1916—. Scientific asst. (physiologist) U.S. Pub. Health Service; mem. sub-com. on industrial fatigue, Advisory Commn. to Council Nat. Defense, 1917-18; mem. com. on physiology of Nat. Research Council, 1917-18. Capt. Sanitary Corps, U.S.A., Sept. 10, 1918-Jan. 22, 1919; div. nutrition officer 10th Div., Nov. 7, 1918-Jan. 22, 1919. Fellow Am. Acad. Arts and Sciences, A.A.A.S. (v.p. Pacific Div., 1927-31). Conglist. Author: The Measurement of Induction Shocks, 1912. Revised 9th, 10th and 11th edits. of The Human Body (by Henry N. Martin), 1910; vol. on physiology (Collier's Popular Science Library), 1921. Joint author of General Biology (with Burlingame, Heath, and Peirce); Elements of Physiology (with Weymouth), 1928. Died Oct. 17, 1934.

MARTIN, Everett Dean, coll. prof.; b. Jacksonville, Ill., July 5, 1880; s. Buker E. and Mollie (Field) M.; B.A., Ill. Coll., Jacksonville, 1904, Litt.D., 1929; grad. McCormick Theol. Seminary, 1907; m. Esther W. Kirk, 1907 (divorced 1915); children—Mary, Margaret, Elizabeth; m. 2d, Persis E. Rowell, 1915 (divorced); 1 son, Everett Eastman; m. 3d, Daphne Crane Drake, 1931. Ordained Congl. ministry, 1907; pastor 1st Ch., Lombard, Ill., 1906-08, Peoples Ch., Dixon, Ill., 1908-10, Unitarian Ch., Des Moines, Ia., 1910-14; writer on philos. subjects, 1914-16; lecturer on social philosophy, Peoples Inst., N.Y., 1916-36; asst. dir. and sec., 1917-22, and dir., 1922-38; dir. Cooper Union Forum, the largest center for free discussion of polit. and ednl. subjects in America, head of its dept. social philosophy, 1918-38; prof. of social philosophy, Cooper Union, 1934-38, Graduate School, Claremont (Calif.) Colleges, 1936—; mem. of Faculty Graduate School of Banking, 1938—; lecturer social psychology, New School for Social Research, 1922; instructor in social psychology, Brookwood Workers Coll., Katonah, N.Y., 1922-23; traveling lecturer and prof. of social philosophy, during second half of each academic year, for assn. of Am. Colls. under grant of Carnegie Corp., 1939. Chmn. Nat. Bd. of Review of Motion Pictures, 1919-22; Culver lecturer, Brown University, 1930. Author: The Behavior of Crowds; The Mystery of Religion; Psychology; Psychology and Its Uses; The Meaning of a Liberal Education; Liberty; The Conflict of the Individual and the Mass; Civilizing Ourselves; Farewell to Revolution; Philosophical Backgrounds of Current Economic and Social Problems; Some Principles of Political Association; The Nature of the State. Home: Claremont, Calif. Died May 10, 1941.

MARTIN, Fernando Wood, chemist; b. Volga, W.Va., May 5, 1863; s. Washington and Matilda (Cool) M.; B.S., Chaddock Coll., 1886; Ph.D., Syracuse U., 1893; Univ. of Leipzig, 1897 and 1897-98; m. Emma Herron, June 26, 1889. Prof. natural science, Chaddock Coll., 1886-90; lecturer on chemistry and toxicology, Quincy (Ill.) Med. Coll., 1889-90; prof. natural science and vice president, Ft. Worth (Tex.) University, 1890-92; professor chemistry, 1893-1929, v.p., 1894-1907, Randolph-Macon Woman's Coll., prof. emeritus, 1929. Methodist. Author: Qualitative Analysis with the Blow Pipe, 1903; Text-Book on Inorganic Chemistry, 1904; Qualitative Analysis, 1907; Introduction to Anthropology, 1913; Essentials of Organic Chemistry, 1915. Home: Lynchburg, Va. Died Mar. 22, 1933.

MARTIN, Frank Joseph, insurance; b. nr. Bloomington, Ind., June 25, 1865; s. F. J. and Lavina (Sanders) M.; ed. pub. schs.; m. Isabella, d. Dr. V. V. Johnson, of McMinnville, Ore., 1888. Began in fire ins. business at McMinnville, Ore.; founded Ore. Fire Relief Assn., 1894; founded, 1901, and became pres. Northwestern Mut. Fire Assn., Seattle, Wash.; pres. Instantaneous Alarm Co., Rockwood Sprinkler Co., Martin Gen. Agency, Improved Risk Mutuals, N.Y. City, Nat. Assn. Mutual Ins. Cos. Home: Hunt's Point, Seattle P.O., Wash. Died Mar. 18, 1929.

MARTIN, Frank Lee, educator; b. Benedict, Neb., July 7, 1881, s. Lee and Anna Grace (Crownover) M.; A.B., U. of Neb., 1902; m. Martha Maria Hall, Sept. 25, 1907; children—Martha Anne (wife of Ralph P. Swofford, Jr., U.S.A.), Frank Lee. Reporter Kan. City Star, 1902-06, asst. telegraph editor, 1906-07, asst. city editor, 1907-09; asst. prof., School of Journalism, U. of Missouri, 1909-12, asso. professor, 1912-16, professor, 1921-30, asso. dean, 1930-35, dean, 1935—; news editor Japan Advertiser, Tokyo, 1915-16; editor Quill, 1917-22; exchange prof. journalism, Yenching U., Peiping, China, 1931-32. Convention chmn. World Press Congress, 1931—; dir. Mo.-Yenching Foundation; mem. bd. govs. Am. Press Soc.; mem. governing council and pres. Walter Williams Memorial Journalism Foundation. Author: The Practice of Journalism (with Walter Williams). Asso. editor Journalism Quarterly, 1929—. Home: Columbia, Mo. Died July 18, 1941.

MARTIN, Franklin H., surgeon; b. Ixonia, Wis., July 13, 1857; s. Edmond and Josephine (Carlin) M.; ed. pub. schs. and acads. of Wis.; M.D., Chicago Med. Coll. (now medical dept. of Northwestern U.), 1880; LL.D., Queen's Univ., Belfast, Ireland, U. of Wales and U. of Pittsburgh; D.P.H., Detroit Coll. of Medicine and Surgery; D.Sc., Northwestern Univ.; m. Isabelle, d. John H. Hollister, M.D., of Chicago, 1886. Prof. gynecology, Polyclinic, Chicago, 1886-88; organized, with Dr. W. F. Coleman, Post-Grad. Med. Sch., Chicago, 1888; gynecologist, Woman's Hosp. many yrs.; organized Charity Hosp.; founded Surgery, Gynecology and Obstetrics (med. jour.), 1905, editor in chief same, and added Internat. Abstract of Surgery, 1913; organized clin. Congress Surgeons of N.

America (now Clin. Congress of Am. Coll. Surg.), 1910, dir. gen. same; organized Am. Coll. Surg., 1913, dir. gen. and mem. bd. regents, same, pres., 1928-29; asso. editor Am. Jour. Obstetrics and Gynecology. Chmn. bd. Gorgas Memorial Inst. Tropical and Preventive Medicine. Mem. Advisory Commn. of Council National Defense, 1916-21, chmn. Gen. Med. Bd., 1917-19; col. M.C., U.S.A., 1917-19; hon. adviser U.S. Army Industrial Coll., 1925—. Was trustee Northwestern U. Decorated D.S.M. (U.S.); Companion Order of St. Michael and St. George (British); Commander of the Order of the Crown of Italy. Author: Treatment of Fibroid Tumors of the Uterus, 1897; Treatise on Gynecology, 1903; South America from a Surgeon's Point of View, 1923; (monograph) Australia and New Zealand, 1924; The Joy of Living—An Autobiography, 1933. Home: Chicago, Ill. Died Mar. 7, 1935.

MARTIN, Frederick Townsend, author; b. Albany, N.Y., Dec. 6, 1849; s. Henry Hull and Anne (Townsend) M.; ed. Albany Boys Acad.; LL.B., Albany Law Sch. (Union U.), 1872; unmarried. Engaged in studying labor questions. Dir. Met. Trust Co. Trustee Night Camp of Tuberculosis Hosp., New York. Entered Zouave Cadets, 10th Regt. N.G.S.N.Y., as pvt.; became judge advocate with rank of col. on staff Maj. General Carr. Author: The Passing of the Idle Rich, 1911; My Personal Experiences of Meeting Snobs, 1911; The Reminiscences of My Life, 1911. Home: New York, N.Y. Died Mar. 8, 1914.

MARTIN, George, editor, writer; b. Falls City, Neb., Aug. 26, 1889; s. Francis and Helen (Pepper) M.; ed. pub. schs. and St. Benedict's Coll., Atchison, Kan.; m. Florence Mauran. Asso. editor Philadelphia Evening Times, 1913; city editor Omaha Daily News, 1914; staff editor United Press Assn., 1915-18; with Office of Information, U.S. Food Administration, 1917-18; asso. editor Every Week Mag., 1918; editor Farm and Fireside Magazine, 1918-29; also chief editorial writer Collier's Weekly, 1919-21; devoting full time to radio and lecture work, 1929. Republican. Home: New York, N.Y. Died Jan. 19, 1938.

MARTIN, George Ellsworth, teacher; b. Falls City, Neb., Mar. 19, 1872; s. Elza and Eliza Anna (Holland) M.; grad. State Normal Sch., Peru, Neb., 1909; A.B., U. of Neb., 1914; A.M., Columbia, 1919; m. Alice Kriger, June 12, 1895; children—Alice Inez, Ruth E. (dec.), Frances Wesna, Kathryn Anna. Prin. pub. schs., Dawson, Neb., 1899-1903; prin. high sch., Nebraska City, 1903-08, supt. schs., 1908-15; with State Normal Sch., Kearney, 1915—, pres., 1919—. Republican. Methodist. Joint author: Studies in Reading, 1910. Home: Kearney, Neb. Died July 18, 1936.

MARTIN, G(eorge) Forrest, surgeon; b. Mason, O., Dec. 10, 1862; s. of John Douglass and Caroline T. (Thompson) M.; M.D., New York Homœ. Med. Coll. and Flower Hosp., New York, 1890; m. Gertrude Darling Hunter, May 21, 1890; children—Marion, Donald (dec.). In gen. practice, Skaneateles, N.Y., 1890-94; surg. and spl. work, Lowell, Mass., 1894—; senior surgeon Lowell Gen. Hosp. (pres. of staff; trustee, 1913—). Trustee Central Savings Bank. Mem. Lowell Sch. Com., 1894-95; appointed member Lowell Bd. of Health, 1909 (chmn. 1910). Republican. Universalist. Fellow Am. Coll. Surgeons; pres. Alumni Assn. New York Homœ. Med. Coll., 1911. Exec. mem. Com. of Safety, 1917. Trustee Mass. State Infirmary (chmn. 1923—); chmn. Lowell Cancer Com., 1926—. Mason. Home: Lowell, Mass. Died Nov. 4, 1934.

MARTIN, George Henry, educationist; b. Lynn, Mass., Aug. 16, 1841; s. George and Clarissa (Weston) M.; grad. State Normal School, Bridgewater, Mass.; (hon. A.M., Amherst, 1879; Litt.D., Tufts, 1905); m. Angie P. Woodbury, Dec. 3, 1867. Teacher Bridgewater Normal Sch., 1864-82; agt. Mass. Bd. Edn., 1882-92; supervisor of schs., Boston, 1892-1904; sec. Mass. Bd. Edn., 1904-09, treas. same, 1909-11. Author: The English Language, 1890; Evolution of the Massachusetts Public School System, 1892; Martin's Civil Government, 1875; Hints on Teaching Civics, 1895. Home: West Lynn, Mass. Died Mar. 25, 1917.

MARTIN, George Riley, ry. official; b. Evans Mills, N.Y., July 3, 1864; s. James Riley and Amelia (Walradt) M.; LL.B., U. of Minn., 1902, LL.M., 1903; m. Laura Owen, Jan. 26, 1918; children—(by first marriage), Paul W., Hugh W., (by second marriage) George Riley, Richard Owen M. (adopted nephew). With C.&N.W. Ry., 1885-86, M.,St.P.& S.S.M. Ry., 1887-90; with G.N. Ry., 1890-1933, advancing to gen supt., comptroller, June 1, 1911, v.p. accounting dept., Sept. 1, 1916, v.p. exec. dept., Mar. 1, 1920, also dir. and v.p. subsidiary lines; comptroller for trustees G.N. Iron Ore Properties, and comptroller subsidiary cos. (retired 1933). Republican. Home: Minneapolis, Minn. Died June 20, 1938.

MARTIN, George Washington, editor; b. Hollidaysburg, Pa., June 30, 1841; s. David and Mary (Howell) M.; ed. common schs. and in printing office; (hon. A.M., Baker U., 1909); m. Lydia Coulson. 1863 (died 1900); m. 2d, Mrs. Josephine Blakely, Oct. 10, 1901. Began in printing business, Junction City, Kan., 1862; register U.S. Land Office, Junction City, 1865-66, 1869-70; state printer of Kan., 1873-81; sec. Kan. State Hist. Soc., Dec. 1899—. Republican. Presbyn. Editor Kansas Historical Collections, Vols. VI-XII. Odd Fellow. Home: Topeka, Kan. Died Mar. 27, 1914.

MARTIN, Guy H., jurist; b. Lancaster, Ia., Aug. 31, 1866; s. Edward M. and Eliza A. (Goss) M.; ed. dist. sch. and high sch., Haraln, Ia.; m. Alma L. Austin, June 9, 1894; 1 dau., Ione. Admitted to Ia. bar, 1892, and began practice at Spencer; served as local atty. C.,M.&St.P. Ry. and C.,R.I.&P. Ry.; dist. atty. Clay Co., Ia., 1894-99. Admitted to bar, Wash. and Ida., 1907, and practiced at Sandpoint, Ida., until 1923; dist. atty. Canal Zone, 1923-24; U.S. dist. judge for Canal Zone, 1924-29; spl. asst. to atty. gen., 1929-31; atty. Court of Claims Div., 1931—. Republican. Episcopalian. Mason. Home: Washington, D.C. Died Mar. 20, 1933.

MARTIN, Helen Reimensnyder, author; b. Lancaster, Pa., Oct. 18, 1868; d. Rev. Cornelius and Henrietta (Thurman) Reimensnyder; spl. student English subjects, Swarthmore Coll., Pa., and Radcliffe Coll., Cambridge, Mass.; m. Frederic C. Martin, Sept. 5, 1899; children—Frederic Thurman, Helene Thurman. Contbr. short stories of Pennsylvania Dutch life to mags. Author: Tillie, A Mennonite Maid (dramatized), 1904; Sabina, A Story of the Amish, 1905; The Crossways, 1910; The Parasite, 1913; Barnabetta, 1914 (dramatized as "Erstwhile Susan" and played by Mrs. Fiske); Maggie of Virginsburg, 1918; The Snob, 1924; Challenged, 1925; Ye That Judge, 1926; Sylvia of the Minute, 1927; The Lie, 1928; Wings of Healing, 1929; Yoked with a Lamb (short stories), 1930; Tender Talons, 1930; Porcelain and Clay, 1931; Lucy Anderson, 1932; From Pillar to Post, 1933; The Whip Hand, 1934; Deliverance, 1935; House on the Marsh, 1936; Emmy Untamed, 1937. Home: Harrisburg, Pa. Died June 29, 1939.

MARTIN, Herbert Spencer, corp. official; b. New York, 1883; s. Max and Matilda (Newgass) M.; A.B., Harvard, 1903; married. Entered business of father, M. Martin & Co., mfrs. of women's garments, 1902, becoming pres., 1913, and acquiring all other interests; turned over business to associates, July 1923, now chmn. bd.; formerly v.p., treas., Ambassador Hotels Corp., pres. and treas., Jan. 1, 1925—; pres. Lester Livingston, Inc.; chmn. bd. M. Martin & Co.; v.p and dir. S. W. Straus & Co., Straus Nat. Bank & Trust Co. Was mem. arbitration com. in settlement of strike in cotton factories. Mem. bd. dirs. Fedn. of United Hosp. Fund, Montefiore Hosp., Bedford Sanatorium. Formerly mem. 7th Regt. Home: New York, N.Y. Died Jan. 14, 1930.

MARTIN, James, newspaperman; b. Dundee, Scotland, Dec. 16, 1862; s. Peter and Margaret M.; ed. pub. schs. in Scotland; m. Helen T. B. Welsh, of Dundee, Scotland, June 25, 1889. Connected with New York Tribune, 1895—; news editor, 1899-1905, mng. editor, Mar. 10, 1905—. Active in promoting cause of honest government in N.J.; persistent advocate of non-partisanship in municipal affairs. Home: East Orange, N.J. Died 1910.

MARTIN, James Loren, judge; b. Landgrove, Vt., Sept. 13, 1846; s. James and Lucy (Gray) M.; grad. Marlow (N.H.) Acad., 1867; LL.B., Albany Law Sch., 1869; (hon. A.M., Dartmouth, 1882); m. Delia E. Howard, Nov. 19, 1869 (died 1881); m. 2d, Jessie Lilley Dewey, Jan. 10, 1884. Admitted to bar, 1869; practiced at Londonderry, 1869-82, Brattleboro, Vt., from 1882. State's atty., 1874-76; mem. Vt. Ho. of Rep., 1874-82 and 1892 (speaker 1878-82); commr. of state taxes, 1888, 1890, 1892, 1894; U.S. atty. for Vt., 1898-1906; U.S. dist. judge, Dist. of Vt., Oct. 23, 1906—. Republican. Home: Brattleboro, Vt. Died Jan. 14, 1915.

MARTIN, John, senator; b. in Wilson Co., Tenn., Nov. 12, 1833; s. Matt and Mary A. (Penn) M.; ed. common country schs.; worked on farm until 18 yrs. old; clerked in stores and studied law; widower. Moved to Kan., 1855; asst. clerk Territorial Ho. of Rep., 1855; co. clerk and register of deeds, 1855-57; admitted to bar, 1856; postmaster Tecumseh, 1857-58; co. atty., Shawnee Co., 1858-59; deputy U.S. atty., 1859-61; established as lawyer in Topeka, 1861; mem. Kan. Legislature, 1874 and 1875; Dem. nominee for gov., 1876; renominated in 1882, but declined; elected judge 3d Dist., 1883; defeated for Congress, 1886; again nominee for gov., 1888; worked for Dem. endorsement of Populist State ticket, 1892, with result of success in the election; selected U.S. senator, 1893-95, to fill unexpired term of Senator Plumb (deceased); clerk Supreme Ct. of Kan., 1897-1900. Mem. Dem. State Central Com., 1864-84 (chmn. 1870-84); retired. Died Sept. 3, 1913.

MARTIN, John Andrew, congressman; b. Cincinnati, O., Apr. 10, 1868; ed. pub. schs.; studied law, 1895-96. Farming and railroad worker, 1884-94; editor La Junta Times, 1895-96; admitted to Colo. bar, 1896; in practice at Pueblo; mem. Colo. Gen. Assembly, 1901-02; city atty., Pueblo, 1905-07, 1915-17; mem. 61st and 62d Congresses (1909-13), 2d Colo. Dist., and 73d to 75th Congresses (1933-39), 3d Colo. Dist. Recruited a vol. batt., World War, enlisted as pvt., later commd. major. Democrat. Home: Pueblo, Colo. Died Dec. 23, 1939.

MARTIN, John Calvin, coal operator; b. Millersville, Pa., Nov. 13, 1845; s. Barton B. and Catherine C. (Roher) M.; ed. pub. and pvt. schs.; m. Emilie Doolittle. Enlisted in the Union Army at 17, 1st lt. Co. D, 175th Pa. Vols.; hon. disch. for disability at Fairfax C.H., Va., 1864. Mfr. of lumber and miner of coal in 1869; owner of large coal properties in Cambria Co., Pa.; pres. Martin Coal Co., Martin Realty Co., Martindale Water Co.; treas. Penn Realty Co. Actively engaged in philanthropic work; founded, 1889, the John C. Martin Ednl. Fund, to promote Christian edn. in U.S. and its insular possessions; founded at Portage, Pa., 1908, The Emilie D. Martin Hosp. and Training Sch. for Nurses, etc. Presbyn. Republican. Trustee Soc. for Suppression of Vice, New York. Died Sept. 3, 1912.

MARTIN, John Irwin, lawyer; b. St. Louis, May 24, 1848; s. William and Frances (Irwin) M.; ed. St. Louis pub. schs.; m. Clara E. LaBarge, June 11, 1871. Elected to Mo. Legislature, 1871, and twice reëlected (speaker 1875); admitted to Mo. bar, 1876, Supreme Ct. of U.S., 1879; in practice at St. Louis and Chicago. Many yrs. been mem. of state and city Dem. coms.; speaker in every nat. campaign from 1876; sergt.-at-arms of Dem. Nat. Committee, 1892—, and managed nat. convs. at Chicago, 1896, Kansas City, 1900, St. Louis, 1904, Denver, 1908; reëlected for com. and conv., 1912; sergt.-at-arms Nat. Rivers and Harbors Congress; v.p. Upper Miss. River Improvement Assn.; chmn. com. on statutory legislation Mo. Fraternal Congress (composed of leading fraternal ins. assns.). Brigade insp. rifle practice, Mo. N.G., with rank of col. Presbyterian. Died Aug. 3, 1923.

MARTIN, John James, theologian; b. Carnkie, Cornwall, Eng., Feb. 10, 1870; came to America, 1891; s. Thomas and Elizabeth (Cock) M.; A.B., Albion (Mich.) Coll., 1900, D.D., 1922; B.D., Chicago Theol. Sem., 1903; Ph.D., Halle-Wittenberg, Germany, 1905; m. Harriett Hewitt, May 3, 1905; children—Robert Hewitt, Paul Thomas, Elizabeth, John Arthur, Dorothea. Ordained Congl. ministry, 1905; instr. Chicago Theol. Sem., 1905-06; pastor 1st Ch., Austin (Chicago), 1907-10, Calvary Ch., Montreal, P.Q., 1910-13; Buck prof. Christian theology, Bangor (Me.) Theol. Sem., 1913—; sch. pastor Oak Grove (Girls') Sch., Vassalboro, Me. Home: Bangor, Me. Died Sept. 5, 1934.

MARTIN, Larkin Morris, ry. official; b. Mason Co., W.Va., Dec. 6, 1853; s. George W. and Louisa A. M.; ed. common schools of Iowa; m. Sarah Ellen Cox, Nov. 22, 1873. Commenced railroading as telegraph operator, 1871; later became gen. mgr. Des Moines, Northern & Western Ry., v.p. and gen. mgr. St. Louis, Des Moines & Northern Ry., pres. Iowa Central & Western Ry., and gen. mgr. Iowa Central Ry.; also v.p. Santa Fé & Grand Cañon Ry. Del. at large Dem. Nat. Conv., Chicago, 1892, Indianapolis, 1896; mem. Nat. Com. from Iowa and chmn. Nat. Campaign Com., Gold Standard Democracy, 1896-1900; now engaged in constrn. of electric rys. Home: Des Moines, Ia. Died 1909.

MARTIN, Louis Adolphe, Jr., engineer, teacher; b. Hoboken, N.J., Nov. 5, 1880; s. Louis Adolphe and Pauline Justine (Feuerstein) M.; M.E., Stevens Inst. Tech., 1900; A.M., Columbia, 1903, post-grad., 1903-05; m. Alwynne Elaine Buttlar, June 30, 1904; 1 dau., Lois. Instr. mathematics, physics and chemistry, Hoboken Acad., 1900-02; instr., 1903-06, asst. prof. mathematics and mechanics, 1906-08, prof. mechanics, June 1908—, also dean, 1910-28, Stevens Inst. Tech. Author: Text-Book of Mechanics, Vol. I, Statics, 1906, Vol. II, Kinematics and Kinetics, 1907, Vol. III, Mechanics of Materials, 1911, Vol. IV, Applied Statics, 1913, Vol. V, Hydraulics, 1914, Vol. VI, Thermodynamics, 1916. Home: Hoboken, N.J. Died Aug. 16, 1938.

MARTIN, Martha Evans, author; b. Terre Haute, Ind.; d. John and Margaret E. (Briggs) Evans; ed. DePauw Univ. (hon. A.M., 1910); m. Edwin C. Martin. Taught in pub. schs. 1 yr.; court reporter, Richmond, 3 yrs.; asso. editor, with husband, of Richmond Daily Telegram, 1886-91; editor Demorest's Magazine, 1896-1900. Author: The Friendly Stars, 1907; The Ways of the Planets, 1912. Exec. chmn. ednl. propaganda dept. of Woman's Com. of Council of Nat. Defense, Feb. 1918—. Address: Watchung, N.J., and New York, N.Y. Died Jan. 6, 1925.

MARTIN, Melvin Albert, psychologist; b. Petersburg, Va., Oct. 18, 1871; s. Melvin Anthony and Alberta Goodwin (Robertson) M.; B.A., U. of Richmond, 1898; grad. student U. of Chicago, 1898-1900; A.M., Columbia, 1905, Ph.D., 1915; m. Ruth Nelson Bowers, June 25, 1896. Prof. mathematics, Woman's Coll., Richmond, Va., 1896-98; headmaster Mossy Creek (Va.) Acad., 1900-01; dean Southside Female Inst., 1901-02; prof. physics and chemistry, Woman's Coll., 1902-04; prof. psychology and edn., and dean, 1905-13, same coll.; prof. psychology, U. of Va., 1911-15; asst. to head of dept. of psychology, Columbia, 1914-16; head of dept. of psychology and edn., Converse Coll., Spartanburg, S.C., 1916-23;

prof. of psychology, Asheville (N.C.) Summer Sch., 1919-20; head dept. of psychology, Newcomb Coll. (Tulane U.), 1923—; prof. of psychology, Tulane U. Summer Sch., 1923—. Lecturer U.S.T.C. for women, Asheville, N.C., 1920-22; lecturer at The Manor, Asheville, N.C., 1922; lecturer Monteagle Assembly, Tenn., 1923, 27. Author: Transfer-Effects of Practice, 1915. Home: New Orleans, La. Died Mar. 27, 1936.

MARTIN, Paul Curtis, lawyer; b. Springfield, O., Aug. 16, 1876; s. Oscar Thaddeus and Mary (MacCoy) M.; student Wittenberg Acad., Springfield, O., 1891-94; A.B., Princeton, 1898; student Cincinnati Law Sch., 1899-1900; LL.D., Wittenberg Coll., 1929; m. Bessie Black, Apr. 9, 1901. Admitted to Ohio bar, 1901, and began practice at Springfield, O.; sr. mem. Martin & Corry. Pres. Bd. of Edn., Springfield, 1904-09; mem. Permanent Judicial Commn., Presbyn. Ch., U.S., 1931. Life trustee Princeton U.; trustee Princeton Theol. Seminary, Western Coll., Wittenberg Coll. Republican. Presbyn. Mason. Home: Springfield, O. Died Oct. 15, 1939.

MARTIN, Robert Grant, prof. English; b. Orange, N.J., Feb. 16, 1882; s. Robert Mitchell and Helen (Grant) M.; A.B., Brown U., 1904; A.M., Harvard, 1905, Ph.D., 1910; unmarried. Teacher St. George's Sch., Newport, R.I., 1905-07; instr. English, 1911-13, asst. prof., 1913-19, asso. prof., 1919-24, Northwestern U.; prof. Occidental Coll., 1924—. Abroad, 1910-11, as holder Sheldon traveling fellowship from Harvard. Commd. capt. Mil. Intelligence Div., Gen. Staff, June 28, 1918; hon. disch., July 30, 1919. Republican. Editor: A Book of English Literature (with F. B. Snyder), 1916; Representative English Plays (with J. S. P. Tatlock), 1916. Home: Pasadena, Calif. Died Sept. 14, 1931.

MARTIN, Robert Hugh, newspaperman; b. Mt. Jackson, Va., Mar. 26, 1858; s. Albion and Anne Gillespie (Koontz) M.; grad. high sch., Woodstock, Va.; student Washington and Lee U., 1878-79; m. Maggie Belle Hughes, Dec. 22, 1885 (dec.); 1 dau., Margaret June; m. 2d, Mary Etta Echard, June 24, 1896; children—Elizabeth Gillespie, Carolyn Virginia, John Thompson. Teacher pub. sch., Woodstock, 1877-79; prin. graded sch., Mt. Jackson, 1880-81; prin. schs., Woodstock, 1882-83; editor and owner The Virginian, Woodstock, 1885-90; co-editor Virginian and News, Woodstock, 1890-91; editor Strasburg (Va.) News, 1891-92; founder Shenandoah County Record, Woodstock, 1892; mng. editor Staunton (Va.) Daily News, 1893-96, editor, 1896; one of founders Augusta County Record, Staunton, 1897; mng. editor Charleston (W.Va.) Daily Mail Tribune, 1898-1900; in charge Bellaire, O., br. Wheeling Intelligencer, 1900; mng. editor Charleston Daily Mail, 1901-13, chief editorial writer same, 1913-32; retired voluntarily for disability. Republican. Presbyn. Home: Charleston, W.Va. Died Jan. 17, 1939.

MARTIN, Samuel Albert, college prof.; b. at Cannonsburg, Pa., Nov. 1, 1853; s. William and Mary (Houston) M.; A.B., Lafayette Coll., Pa., 1877; grad. Western Theol. Sem.; studied Edinburgh, Scotland; (D.D., Lafayette, 1892); m. Kate K., d. Rev. T. C. Porter, of Easton, Pa., Feb. 1881; m. 2d, Mary A., d. E. D. Ricker, of St. Louis, Dec. 1900. Ordained Presbyn. ministry, 1881; pastor Christ Ch., Lebanon, Pa., 1881-85; prof. homiletics, Lincoln U., 1855-95; acting prof. homiletics, Princeton Theol. Sem., 1902-03; pres. Wilson Coll., 1895-1902, Pa. Coll. for Women, 1903-06; prin. Pa. State Normal Sch., Shippensburg, Pa., 1907-13; prof. philosophy, Lafayette Coll., Easton, 1913—. Acting prof. homiletics, Princeton Theol. Sem., 1913-14. Author: The Man of Uz, 1891; The Oracles of God, 1916; Philosophy of Conduct, 1917. Died Mar. 26, 1921.

MARTIN, Sylvester Mitchell, evangelist; b. Antioch, O., Aug. 16, 1857; s. Enoch and Nancy (Huffman) M.; ed. normal schs. at Antioch and Stafford, O.; M.D., Barnes U. Med. Coll., St. Louis, 1905; hon. A.M., Plattsburg (Mo.) Coll., 1899; m. Mary Catherine Barnes, Dec. 23, 1876 (died 1922); children—Mrs. Nina Hatcher (dec.), Mrs. Lela Thatcher, Mrs. Minnie Shuey. Began teaching sch. at 15 and taught 15 yrs.; prin. high sch. 4 yrs.; teacher at Ohio U., Athens, 1882-84; v.p. and prof. science and German, Bowling Green (Mo.) Coll., 2 yrs., 1884-86; specialized in elocution and penmanship. Ordained ministry Christian (Disciples) Ch., 1885; state evangelist of Christian chs. of Mo., 1888-91; gen. evangelism, 1891—; has conducted over 295 revivals. Republican. Prohibitionist. Mason. Author: Thirty Years on the Firing Line, 1920. Home: Seattle, Wash. Died Sept. 27, 1937.

MARTIN, Thomas Commerford, editor; b. London, Eng., July 22, 1856; s. Thomas and Catharine (Commerford) M.; ed. in acad., Gravesend, Eng., and by pvt. tutor; later student in divinity; m. Elizabeth Gould, 1880; m. 2d, Carmelita Beckwith, 1910. Associated with Thomas A. Edison in lab. work and elec. development, 1877-79; editorial work, 1879—; editor Elec. World, 1883-1909; advis. sec. Nat. Elec. Light Assn., 1909—; staff editor, Science and Industrial Information Bureau. Decorated by French Govt. Officer of Pub. Instruction, 1907. Special expert for U.S. Census Office, 1900-15. Republican. Has lectured at Royal Instn. of Engrs., Société Internationale des Electriciens, Paris, U. of Neb., Columbia U., Lehigh U., Delaware Coll., New York bd. of Edn. Mem. conf. com., organized by engring. socs. to expend the gift of Mr. Carnegie of $1,500,-000, for a united engring. bldg. and the Engineers' Club in New York; mem. numerous professional societies. Author: The Electric Motor and Its Applications, 1886; Inventions, Researches and Writings of Nikloa Tesla, 1893; Edison—His Life and Inventions (with Frank L. Dyer), 1910; The Story of Electricity (with Stephen L. Coles), 1919. Home: Larchmont Manor, N.Y. Died May 17, 1924.

MARTIN, Thomas Staples, senator; b. Scottsville, Va., July 29, 1847; has resided on farm two miles from Scottsville, 1853—; cadet, Va. Mil. Inst., 1864-65; much of that time in Confederate service; student U. of Va., 1865-67. Admitted to bar, 1869; U.S. senator, 1895— (4th term will expire Mar. 3, 1919). Democrat. Home: Charlottesville, Va. Died Nov. 12, 1919.

MARTIN, Victoria Claflin Woodhull, editor, author; b. Homer, O., Sept. 23, 1838; d. Reuben, and Roxanna (Hummel) Claflin; m. Dr. Canning Woodhull; m. 2d, John Biddulph Martin (died 1897); mother of Zula Maud Woodhull. Was banker in New York; editor Woodhull and Claflin's Weekly, New York; memorialized Congress for woman suffrage, 1870; lectured in favor of woman suffrage, scientific and religious improvement of human race, etc., through U.S.; nominated for president of U.S. by Equal Rights Party, 1872; has lectured and spoken extensively in U.S. and Europe. Author: The Origin, Tendencies and Principles of Government; Social Freedom; Pharmacy of the Soul; Aristocracy of Blood; Garden of Eden; Stirpiculture; Rapid Multiplication of the Unfit; The Human Body the Temple of God; Arguments for Woman's Electoral Rights, etc. Died June 10, 1927.

MARTIN, Whitmell Pugh, congressman; b. Assumption Point, La., Aug. 12, 1867; s. Robert Campbell and Margerite Chism (Littlejohn) M.; B.S., La. State U., 1888; student U. of Va. Law Sch., 1891; m. Amy Williamson, Apr. 14, 1896 (died 1923); children—Mrs. Amy Williamson Tabor, Whitmell Pugh (dec.), Marshall Leigh, Robert Campbell. Prof. chemistry, Ky. Mil. Inst., 1889-90; chemist, Sugar Land Refinery, Tex., 1890-91; removed to Thibodaux, La., 1892, and admitted to La. bar; supt. of edn., Parish of Lafourche, La., 1894-1900; dist. atty. 20th Dist., La., 1900-06; judge 20th Jud. Dist., La., 1906-14; mem. 64th to 69th Congresses (1915-27), 3d La. Dist.; elected to 64th and 65th Congresses as a Progressive, 66th to 70th as a Democrat. Episcopalian. Mason. Home: Thibodaux, La. Died Apr. 6, 1929.

MARTIN, William Alexander Parsons, missionary; b. Livonia, Ind., Apr. 10, 1827; A.B., Ind. U., 1846; studied theology at Presbyn. Sem., New Albany, Ind.; (D.D., Lafayette, 1860; LL.D., New York U., 1870, Princeton, 1899); m. Jane Vansant, 1849 (died 1893); father of Winfred Robert M. Missionary to Ningpo, China, 1850-60; acted as interpreter for William B. Reed, U.S. minister, in negotiating treaty with China, 1858; missionary at Peking, 1863-68; pres. and prof. internat. law, Tung Wen Coll., Peking, 1868-94; 1st pres. Imperial U. of China, 1898-1900; was in siege of legation at Peking. Adviser of Chinese authorities on matters of internat. law in several internat. disputes with European powers; made a mandarin of the 3d class, 1885, and of the 2d class, 1898. Author: Lore of Cathay; Siege in Peking; A Cycle of Cathay; Chinese Legends, and Other Poems; Awakening of China, 1907; also works in Chinese on Evidences of Christianity, Natural Philosophy, International Law, etc. Died Dec. 18, 1916.

MARTIN, Winfred Robert, librarian; b. Ningpo, China, Mar. 22, 1852; s. William Alexander Parsons and Jane (Vansant) M.; A.B., Princeton, 1872, A.M., 1875; LL.B., New York U., 1878; Ph.D., U. of Tübingen, 1887; (LL.D., Trinity Coll., 1907; Caballero de la Real Orden de Isabe lla Católica, 1911); unmarried. Prof. Oriental langs., Trinity Coll., 1888-1907; instr. Sanskrit in mission courses, Hartford Theol. Sem., 1902-07; librarian Hispanic Soc. of America, N.Y. City, Mar. 1907—. Died 1915.

MARTINDALE, Thomas, author; b. Ling Riggs, Weardale, Durham Co., Eng., Dec. 15, 1845; s. Joseph and Annie (Watson) M.; ed. pub. schs. short time; chiefly self-ed.; m. Rosie Crum, Oct. 25, 1870. In wholesale and retail grocery business, Oil City, Pa., 1869-74, Phila., 1875—; head Thomas Martindale & Co. Republican. Second v.p. Chamber Commerce; pres. Poor Richard Club. Mason. Author: Sport Royal, 1897; Heat, Storms and War, 1898; Wildwood Ways and Down East Wilds, 1905; Sport Indeed, 1906; With Gun and Guide, 1910; Hunting in the Upper Yukon, 1913. Home: Philadelphia, Pa. Died Sept. 13, 1916.

MARTINE, James Edgar, senator; b. New York, Aug. 25, 1850; s. Daniel and Anna Maria (Neber) M.; ed. pub. schs.; m. Julie Edgar Rodman, g.d. Jacob Lorillard, of New York, Oct. 1903. Engaged in farming at Plainfield, N.J.; also in real estate and building. Has been candidate for N.J. Ho. of Rep. and Senate and for other offices; U.S. senator from N.J., term 1911-17. Democrat. Home: Plainfield, N.J. Died Feb. 26, 1925.

MARTINEAU, John Ellis, gov.; b. Clay County, Mo., Dec. 2, 1873; s. Gregory and Sarah Hettie (Lamb) M.; A.B., U. of Ark., 1896, LL.B., 1899; m. Mabel Erwin Thomas, May 1, 1919. Admitted to Ark. bar, 1899, and began practice at Little Rock; mem. Ark. Ho. of Rep., 1903-05; chancellor 1st Chancery Circuit, Ark., 1907-27; gov. of Ark., 1927-28; U.S. dist. judge Eastern Dist. Ark., 1928—. Methodist. Mason. Died Mar. 6, 1937.

MARTINEZ, Felix; b. Taos Co., N.M., Mar. 29, 1857; s. Felix and Reyes (Cordova) M.; ed. St. Mary's Coll., Mora, N.M., and at pvt. sch., Denver, Colo.; m. Virginia Buster, Sept. 24, 1880. Began in gen. mercantile business, at El Moro, Colo., 1877, later at Las Vegas; sold out, 1886, and began building homes for settlers; removed to El Paso, Tex., 1897, and since prominently identified with irrigation and real estate projects; in charge of the irrigation system of the El Paso Valley, known as the Rio Grande Project; v.p. Southwestern Portland Cement Co.; dir. 1st Nat. Bank, El Paso. Served as mem. both branches Territorial legislature of N.M.; chmn. N.M. delegation to Dem. Nat. Conv., 1892; Dem. candidate for 1st U.S. senator from N.M. Died 1916.

MARTINY, Philip, sculptor; b. Alsace, then France, May 19, 1858; boyhood in France working in various studios; pupil of St. Gaudens. Principal works: McKinley Monument, Springfield, Mass.; statue of Garret A. Hobart, Paterson, N.J.; doors for St. Bartholomew's Ch., New York; Soldiers and Sailors' Monument, Jersey City, N.J.; two groups in N.Y. Chamber of Commerce Bldg.; group of Allies, Flatiron Bldg., N.Y.; 2 soldiers Monuments in N.Y. City; etc. A.N.A. Home: Bayside, N.Y. Died Jan. 25, 1927.

MARTYN, (William) Carlos, clergyman; b. New York, Dec. 15, 1841; s. Rev. Job H. and Sarah Towne (Smith) M.; grad. Union Theol. Sem., 1869; (DD., LL.D.); m. Mercedes, d. Don Fermin Ferrer, pres. of Nicaragua, 1866. Ordained Congl. ministry, 1869; pastor St. Louis, 1869-71, Portsmouth, N.H., 1871-76, New York, 1876-90, Newark, N.J., 1890-92, Sixth Presbyn. Ch., Chicago, 1892-94; lecturer and occasional supply, 1894-1905; pastor Noroton, Conn., 1906—. Lit. dir. The Abbey Press, New York, 1897-1903; edited American Reformers' series, 1890-96. Author: John Milton, 1866; Life of Martin Luther, 1866; History of the English Puritans, 1867; History of the Huguenots, 1868; The Dutch Reformation, 1869; The Pilgrim Fathers of New England, 1870; Wendell Phillips—the Agitator, 1890; William E. Dodge, 1891; John B. Gough, the Apostle of Cold Water, 1893; Christian Citizenship, 1896; Sour Saints and Sweet Sinners (novel), 1898. Home: Noroton, Conn. Died Aug. 4, 1917.

MARTYN, Chauncey White, lawyer; b. Canton, N.Y., July 17, 1865; s. Albert T. and Mary S. (Clark) M.; B.S., St. Lawrence U., Canton, 1885; LL.B., Union Coll. of Law, Chicago, 1890; m. Anna D. Thompson, 1894 (died 1921); 1 son, Chauncey White; m. 2d, Mary V. Carr, Apr. 29, 1922. Admitted to bar, 1890, practicing at Chicago; atty. with Standard Oil Co. of Ind. from 1904, gen. atty., 1915-18, gen. counsel, 1918-28; retired. Home: Lakeside, Mich. Died Oct. 24, 1939.

MARVEL, Ik. See Donald Grant Michell.

MARVIN, Dwight Edwards, clergyman, author; b. Greenwich, N.Y., Feb. 22, 1851; s. Rev. Uriah and Margaret J. (Stevens) M.; grad. Alexander Inst., White Plains, N.Y., 1869; grad. Auburn Theol. Sem., 1880; studied Union Theol. Sem., 1881; Ph.D., Franklin Coll., New Athens, O., 1900; m. Ida N. Whitman, Sept. 17, 1874; children—Charles Ingalls, Caroline Whitman, Dwight Marvin, Rowland Whitman (dec.). Ordained Congl. ministry, 1882; pastor 1st Ch., East Albany, N.Y., 1881-84, Plymouth Ch., Utica, 1884-88, 1st Ch., Germantown, Phila., 1888-1900, Flatbush Presbyn. Ch., Brooklyn, 1902-10. Author: The Antiquity of Proverbs, 1922; The Passing of the Caravans, 1924; The Wonderful City, 1924; The Castle of the Soul, 1924; The Chariot of God, 1925; The Wings of Time, 1929; Knowing God, 1931; Devotional Lyrics and Other Poems, 1933; In the Splendor of His Presence, 1934; Vanished Barriers, 1935; Abba Father, 1936; When and Where, 1937; Home and the Children, 1937; Nearness to God, 1939; also The Looming Cross; Cloud Islands; Highlands of the Sky; Historic Child Rhymes. Compiler: Curiosities in Proverbs, 1916. Home: Summit, N.J. Died Feb. 1940.

MARVIN, Frank Olin, engineer; b. Alfred, N.Y., May 27, 1852; s. James and Armina (Lesuer) M.; A.B., with science honor, Allegheny Coll., 1871, A.M., 1874; studied engring. with practical work in the field on ry. irrigation, sanitary and city work; m. Josephine B. March, Dec. 31, 1901. Has taught in U. of Kan., 1875—, except when prin. Lawrence High Sch., 1876-77; asst. in mathematics and physics to 1883, prof. engring., 1883—, dean Sch. of Engring., 1891-1913, advisory dean, Sept. 1, 1913—, U. of Kan.; consulting engr., Kan. State Bd. of Health. Died Feb. 6, 1915.

MARVIN, Fred Richard, editor; b. Garden City, Minn., Dec. 22, 1868; s. William Rose and Jean (Willson) M.; ed. pub. schs. and 1 yr. at U. of Wis.; m. Helen McCurdy, June 21, 1903; 1 son, Richard Gose. Began as reporter Spokane (Wash.) Spokesman-Review, 1894; sec. to Congressman W. C. Jones, 1897-99; editor Dayton (Wash.) Daily Courier-Press, 1899-1900, Walla Walla Daily Statesman, 1900-01; publicity agent, Wash., Pan-Am. Expn., 1901; sec. to Senator George Turner, 1901-02; publicity agt., Wash., St. Louis Expn., 1903; editor Las Animas (Colo.) Democrat, 1910-12, Pueblo Morning Chieftain, 1910-14; founder, 1917, editor until 1923, Mountain States Banker and Mountain States Mineral Age; editor in chief New York Daily Commercial, 1925-28; sec. Am. Coalition, 1929-33; ednl. dir. Com. on Am. Edn., 1933—. Republican. Writer of "Are These Your Friends?"; "My Country 'Tis of Thee"; "Underground with the Reds"; "Ye Shall Know the Truth"; The Marvin Lectures on Government; "Fool's Gold." Died July 13, 1939.

MARVIN, Frederic Rowland, clergyman; b. Troy, N.Y., Sept. 23, 1847; s. Rev. Uriah and Margaret Jane M.; M.D., Coll. Phys. and Surg. (Columbia), 1870; grad. Theol. Sem. Reformed Ch. in America, New Brunswick, N.J., 1878; m. Persis A. Rowell, May 28, 1874. Ordained Congl. ministry, 1879; pastor First Ch., Middletown, N.Y., 1879-83, First Ch., Portland, Ore., 1883-86, First Ch., Great Barrington, Mass., 1887-95; traveled and studied in Europe several yrs. Author: The Companionship of Books and Other Papers, 1905; A Book of Quatrains, 1909; Poems and Translations, 1907; Excursions of a Book-Lover, 1910; Love and Letters, 1911; A Free Lance, 1912; Fireside Papers, 1915. Died July 22, 1919.

MARVIN, Joseph Benson, physician; b. Monticello, Fla., Aug. 3, 1852; s. Joseph M. and Mary Louise (Linton) M.; grad. Va. Mil. Inst., 1870, B.S., 1871; M.D., Hosp. Coll. of Medicine, Louisville, Ky., 1875; (LL.D., Georgetown Coll., 1898); m. Juliette H. Norton, Apr. 30, 1879. Asst. prof. chemistry and physics, Va. Mil. Inst., 1870-73; prof. chemistry and microscopy and diseases of nervous system, Hosp. Coll. of Medicine, 1875-82; prof. practice of medicine, Ky. Sch. of Medicine, 1882-98; was prof. medicine and pres. Med. Dept. Ky. U.; now prof. medicine and neurology, U. of Louisville; phys. to Bapt. Orphans' Home, and Louisville City Hosp.; pres. med. staff, Norton Infirmary. Home: Louisville, Ky. Died Sept. 2, 1913.

MARVIN, William Glenn, lawyer; b. Aberdeen, O., Nov. 16, 1892; s. Gwynne Leabon and Elizabeth Field (Taylor Leggett) M.; grad. Steele High Sch., Dayton, O., 1909; Litt.B., University of California, 1913; LL.B., Hastings College of Law, San Francisco, 1916; m. Charlotte Linden (M.D., Stanford U., 1916), July 3, 1916; children—Dorothy Christine, Wm. Glenn, Elizabeth Anne, Barbara June. Worked way through high school and college; prof. public speaking Wash. State Coll., 1 yr.; practiced law in San Francisco, 1916-17; served as gen. counsel Federal Land Bank, Berkeley, Calif.; with Nat. City Bank, New York, 1919-21, advancing to head of legal dept.; mem. Rosenberg, Ball & Marvin, 1921-22; organizer and head of Marvin & Bergh, internat. lawyers, 1922; gen. counsel Am. Mfrs.' Export Assn.; gen. counsel and mng. dir. Am. Mfrs.' Foreign Credit Exchange; chmn. legal adv. com. Div. of Commercial Laws of U.S. Dept. Commerce; gen. counsel Am. Chamber Commerce, London; Am. counsel Am. Chamber Commerce in Germany and Cuba; pres. Am.-Russian Chamber Commerce; etc.; chmn. Aviation Advisory Com. City of San Francisco; chmn. bd. Ellery A. Baker & Co., New York; president Realty Finance Corporation. Enlisted as private Air Service, U.S.A., and served as lt. until close of World War, retiring as chief of tech. staff, Wilbur Wright Field, Dayton, O. Mem. Rep. State Com., Calif. Baptist. Author: The Defensive Side of Banking, 1926. Home: Los Altos, Calif. Died Jan. 5, 1932.

MARVIN, Winthrop Lippitt, steamship official; b. Newcastle, N.H., May 15, 1863; s. Thomas E. O. and Anne (Lippitt) M.; A.B., Tufts, 1884 (Litt.D., 1903); m. Nellie Meloon, June 17, 1885. Reporter and night editor Boston Advertiser, 1884-86; N.E. news editor, 1886-87, editorial writer, 1887-95, asso. editor and chief editorial writer, 1895-1903, Boston Journal; mem. Mass. Civ. Service Commn., 1901-04; sec. U.S. Merchant Marine Commn., Washington, 1904-05; connected with ocean shipbuilding and shipowning interests, 1905-09; sec.-treas. Nat. Assn. of Wool Mfrs., 1909-19, and also sec.-treas. Woolen Goods Exchange, New York, and secretary joint committee of wool mfrs., coöperating with Council Nat. Defense; v.p. and general manager Am. Steamship Assn., 1919—; pres. and treas. Marine Jour. Co., 1923—. Author: The American Merchant Marine, 1902. Republican. Home: New York, N.Y. Died Feb. 3, 1926.

MARX, Charles David, civil engr.; b. Toledo, O., Oct. 10, 1857; s. Joseph Eugen and Johanna (Pulster) M.; B.C.E., Cornell U., 1878; C.E., Karlsruhe Polytechnicum, 1881, Dr. Engring., Karlsruhe, 1925; m. Harriet Elisabeth Grotecloss, July 18, 1888; children—Roland G., Mrs. Dorothy Sherwood, Stephanie (dec.), Alberta (Mrs. Harland B. Graham). U.S. asst. engr. Mo. River improvement, 1882-84; asst. prof. civ. engring., Cornell, 1884-90; prof. civ. engring., U. of Wis., 1890-91, Stanford, 1891-1923, emeritus. Hon. mem. Am. Soc. C.E. Home: Palo Alto, Calif. Died Dec. 31, 1939.

MARX, Oscar B., mayor; b. Detroit, July 14, 1866; s. Stephan and Eleanore (Busch) M.; ed. pub. schs. and German Am. Sem., Detroit; m. Lydia Darmstaetter, Feb. 4, 1897. Assisted father on farm and in dairy until 25; with Mich. Optical Co., 1891—, pres. 1913. Estimator-at-large, Detroit, 1894-95; alderman, 1895-1903; city assessor, 1911-13; mayor of Detroit 3 terms, 1913-19. Republican. Home: Detroit, Mich. Died Nov. 23, 1923.

MARYE, George Thomas, ambassador; b. Baltimore, Md., Dec. 13, 1849; s. George Thomas and Helen (Tucker) M.; studied in Italy, Germany, France and Spain; LL.B., U. of Cambridge, Eng., 1872 (1st honors); m. Marie Alice Doyle, June 28, 1904; 1 dau., Helen Martha. Admitted to Calif. bar, 1875, and practiced in San Francisco; later abandoned law, and asso. with father in banking business, San Francisco and Virginia City, Nev., 1876-92. Chmn. exec. com. Dem. State Central Com. of Calif., 1888-93; Dem. presdl. elector, 1888; A.E. and P. to Russia, 1914-16. Decorated by Emperor of Russia with the Order of St. Alexander Nevsky. Former regent U. of Calif.; pres. Mercantile Library, San Francisco; was mem. Bd. of Freeholders to draft a charter for City and County of San Francisco. Mem. Ch. of England. Home: Washington, D.C., and Burlingame, Calif. Died Sept. 2, 1933.

MARZO, Eduardo, musician; b. Naples, Italy, Nov. 29, 1852; s. Carlo and Angiola (Bertolè-Viale) M.; ed. Naples, Italy; m. Clara L. Philbin, 1882; children—Albert Stephen, Mrs. Maria Josephine Flanagan, Clarence Philbin, Rita E. Came to U.S. in boyhood; returned to Naples long enough to finish his studies in composition under Pappalardo; returned to New York as musical dir. with Gazzaniga, Ronconi, Patti, di Murska, Titjens, etc.; for past 40 yrs. teacher of vocal music, organist and composer; specially distinguished for sacred compositions. Mem. Royal Acad. of St. Cecilia, Rome, 1892; Knight of the Crown of Italy, 1884; Knight Order of San Sylvester by Pope Benedict XV, 1914. Composed 15 masses, 4 vespers and many songs for the Catholic Ch.; also several Te Deums, anthems and songs for Protestant chs.; orchestral preludes, piano pieces, secular songs and duets; operettas and cantatas for children's voices, etc. Editor: Songs of Italy, 1905; The Art of Vocalization; 3 books, Carols of all Nations. Died June 7, 1929.

MASCHKE, Maurice, lawyer; b. Cleveland, O., Oct. 16, 1868; s. Joseph and Rosa (Salinger) M.; grad. Phillips, Exeter Acad., Exeter, N.H., 1886; A.B., Harvard, 1890; m. Minnie Rice, June 5, 1903; children—Helen Rice, Maurice. Admitted to Ohio bar, 1891, and began practice at Cleveland; mem. Orgill, Maschke & Wickham, 1925—. Recorder of Cuyahoga County; collector of customs, Federal Dist. of Ohio; mem. Ohio State Rep. Nat. Com. Republican. Jewish religion. Mason. Home: Cleveland Heights, O. Died Nov. 19, 1936.

MASON, Alfred Bishop, lawyer, author; b. Bridgeport, Conn., Feb. 23, 1851; s. Hon. R. B. (mayor of Chicago, 1870-72) and Harriet Lavinia (Hopkins) M.; desc. from Capt. Levi Mason, Revolutionary Army, and Stephen Hopkins, a signer of Declaration of Independence; A.B., Yale, 1871 (Skull and Bones, Phi Beta Kappa), A.M., 1874; m. Mary Elizabeth Murdoch, 1872 (died 1912); 2d, Mary Knight Wood, Apr. 7, 1914. Editorial writer, Chicago Tribune, 1872; admitted to bar, 1875; v.p. Jacksonville, Tampa & Key West R.R., 1883-89, Am. Cotton Oil Co., 1892; pres. Vera Cruz & Pacific R.R., Mex., 1898-1902, Cauca R.R., Colombia, S.A., 1905-07. Democrat. Author: Primer of Political Economy, 1875, 13th edit., 1914; Tom Strong, Washington's Scout, 1911; Tom Strong, Boy Captain, 1913; Tom Strong, Junior, 1915; Tom Strong, Tihrd, 1916; Tom Strong, Lincoln's Scout, 1919; A Duchess and Her Daughter, 1929; Horace Walpole's England, 1930. Translator and editor: Von Holst's Constitutional History of the United States, 1876; Constitutional Law of the United States, 1887. Died Jan. 26, 1933.

MASON, Alfred De Witt, clergyman editor; b. Brooklyn, Mar. 21, 1855; s. Theodore L. (M.D.) and Katharine V. V. (De Witt) M.; A.B., Amherst, 1877, A.M., 1880; grad. New Brunswick Theol. Sem., 1880; (D.D., Hope Coll., Holland, Mich., 1909); m. Elizabeth Swain, Oct. 18, 1883. Ordained minister Reformed Ch. in America, 1880; pastor, Locust Valley, L.I., N.Y., 1880-82, South Ch., Brooklyn, 1882-91, Boonton, N.J., 1891-94; sec. Young Peoples Work, Mission Bd. of Ref. Ch., 1894-1906; editor Mission Field, 1894-1909; editor Christian Intelligencer, 1908-17. Lecturer on history of missions, Union Missionary Training Inst., Brooklyn, 1904. Mem. Federal Council Chs. of Christ in America, 1921—; chmn. permanent com. on public morals, Gen. Synod Reformed Ch. in America, 1914—; mem. Presbyn. Alliance, 1909-14; acting supt. Brooklyn City Mission and Tract Soc., 1918-20. Author: Outlines of Missionary History, 1912, revised edits., 1915, 1921; Modern Methods in Sunday-School Work, 1913. Home: Brooklyn, N.Y. Died Jan. 26, 1923.

MASON, Amelia Gere, author; b. Northampton, Mass.; d. Frederick and Ruth Sheldon (Warner) Gere; grad. Mt. Holyoke Coll.; spl. studies in music, New York and Boston; m. Alverin Armington Mason, Dec. 18, 1872 (died 1904). Spent 7 yrs. in Europe gathering material for her books in foreign libraries. Author: The Women of the French Salons, 1891; Woman in the Golden Ages, 1901; Memories of a Friend, 1919. Died Aug. 11, 1923.

MASON, Augustus Lynch, lawyer; b. Bloomington, Ind., Feb. 10, 1859; s. William Fisher and Amanda D. (Lynch) M.; student Northwestern Christian U., Indianapolis, 1873-75; Ph.B., De Pauw U., 1879, A.M., 1882; m. Annie D., d. Gov. Albert G. Porter, of Indianapolis, Jan. 25, 1893. Studied law, 1879-82, with U.S. Senator J. E. McDonald and John M. Butler, Indianapolis; mem. McDonald, Butler & Mason, 1883-87; from 1883 engaged in practice of corp. law, chiefly foreclosure and reorganization of steam railroads, organization of interurban, street ry. cos., etc. Pres. Citizen' St. Ry. Co., Indianapolis, 1893-97. Dean De Pauw U. Law Sch., 1890-93; lecturer on r.r. law, Ind. Law Sch., U. of Indianapolis, 1899-1905. Methodist. Independent Republican. Author: Pioneer History of America, 1884; Trusts and Public Welfare, 1901; Corporations and Social Changes, 1908; Govt. of Indianapolis, 1910; Guiding Principles for American Voters, 1920. Home: Indianapolis, Ind. Died Feb. 13, 1939.

MASON, Caroline Atwater, author; b. Providence, R.I., July 10, 1853; d. Stephen and Mary (Weaver) Atwater; parents mems. Soc. of Friends; attended Friends' schs.; studied in Germany; m. Rev. John H. Mason, May 29, 1877; children—Mary A., Ruth Little, Helen C. (dec.). Author: A Titled Maiden; A Wind Flower; A Lily of France (trans. into Dutch and French), 1901; The Little Green God, 1902; The White Shield (trans. into Dutch), 1904; The Binding of the Strong, 1908; The Spell of Italy, 1909; The Mystery of Miss Motte, 1909; The Spell of France, 1912; The Spell of Southern Shores, 1914; Jesus Christ's Men, 1914; World Missions and World Peace, 1916; Conscripts of Conscience, 1919; Wonders of Missions, 1922; The High Way (trans. into Dutch), 1924; Royton Manor (trans. into Dutch), 1928; Challenged, 1932. Home: Danvers, Mass. Died May 2, 1939.

MASON, Cassity E. (Miss), educator; b. Florence, Ala.; d. Joseph D. (M.D.) and Eliza M. (Bigelow) M.; grad. Memphis Conference Collegiate Inst., hon. LL.M., 1895; spl. work at Am. colls. and in Europe; made several surveys in foreign countries. Prin. St. James Hall (diocesan sch. of Episcopalian Ch. of W. Tenn.), 1891, Brooke Hall Sem., Media, Pa., 1892-95; founded, 1895, and became prin Miss Mason's Sch., The Castle, Inc., Tarrytown-on-Hudson, N.Y. Knighted, 1921, by King Alexander of Serbia (Chevalier Order of St. Saba), and also, 1923, by King Manual of Montenegro, made Grand Officer of Knights of Danilo. Home: Tarrytown-on-Hudson, N.Y. Died Aug. 24, 1933.

MASON, David Hastings, editor, author; b. Phila., Jan. 8, 1829; s. David H. and Elizabeth A.M.; academic edn.; studied 2 yrs. at Yale (non-grad.); m. Margaretta E., d. late Thomas G. Woodward, editor Journal and Courier, New Haven, Conn., June 10, 1851. Connected editorially with Chicago dailies, 1867-82; best known as tariff editor of the Inter Ocean; clerk Bureau of 2d Class Matter, Chicago Post-office, Aug. 7, 1900—. Author: How Western Farmers Are Benefited by Protection, 1875; A Short Tariff History of the United States, 1884. Died 1903.

MASON, Edward Campbell, lawyer; b. Ravenna, O., Nov. 17, 1864; s. Edward Beecher and Myra (Campbell) M.; A.B., Harvard, 1888, LL.B., 1892; m. Martha Sprague, Oct. 6, 1892. Instr. polit. economy, Harvard, 1890; began practice with Ralph A. Kellogg, at Buffalo, N.Y., 1891; moved to Boston, 1904; has specialized in corp. work; dir., sec. Dorchester Mut. Fire Ins. Co.; trustee, sec. Mass. Utilities Associates; sec. and gen. atty. N.E. Power Assn.; trustee Central Mass. Light & Power Co. Mem. bd. mgrs. Nat. Congress of Parents and Teachers, also trustee Endowment Fund of same. Republican. Conglist. Author: The Veto Power, 1890. Home: Winchester, Mass. Died Mar. 31, 1937.

MASON, Edward Tuckerman, author; b. New York, N.Y., Apr. 10, 1847; s. Prof. Cyrus and Hannah Parkman (Tuckerman) M.; ed. pvt. schs. and pvt. tutor, New York, 1859-67; m. Frances Mason Tompkins, May 3, 1870. Began lit. career with some work in theatrical criticism on New York World, 1866; did considerable work in book reviewing and theatrical criticism on several New York weekly and monthly publs., 1870-73. Episcopalian. Author: Samuel Johnson, His

Words and Ways, 1879; Selections from the Poems of Robert Browning, 1883; Personal Traits of British Authors, 4 vols., 1885; Humorous Masterpieces of American Literature, 1886; British Letters, 1888; Songs of Fairy Land, 1889; The Othello of Salvini, 1890. Home: Ossining, N.Y. Died 1911.

MASON, Emily Virginia, author; b. Lexington, Ky., Oct. 15, 1815; d. John T. and Eliza B. (Moir) M.; (sister Stevens Thomson Mason, first gov. State of Mich., 1835-39); ed. Troy, N.Y., Female Sem.; for 15 yrs. before war resided in Fairfax Co., Va., and when war began she left Alexandria and volunteered in C.S. hosp. service. Was matron successively of hosps. at Greenbrier, White Sulphur Springs, Charlottesville, Lynchburg and Richmond, Va.; after war 15 yrs. in Paris; was asst. prin. of an Am. sch. for young ladies. Author: Life of General Robert E. Lee, 1871. Editor: Southern Poems of the War, 1867; Journal of a Young Lady of Virginia in 1798, 1871. Home: Georgetown, D.C. Died 1909.

MASON, Frank Holcomb, consul gen.; b. Niles, O., Apr. 24, 1840; s. Dean E. and Bertha M. (Holcomb) M.; ed. at pub. schs., Niles, and at Hiram Coll.; was not grad.; served as pvt. 42d Ohio Inf. from July 1861; promoted capt. and a.d.c. July 1863, at Vicksburg; mustered out as capt. 12th Cav., Nov. 25, 1865; m. Jennie V. Birchard, Sept. 26, 1866. Successively reporter, editorial writer and mng. editor Cleveland Leader until 1880; Am. consul at Basle, Switzerland, 1880-84, at Marseilles, 1884-89; consul gen. at Frankfort-on-the-Main, 1889-99, at Berlin, 1899-1905, at Paris, Mar. 6, 1905-Jan. 24, 1914. Chmn. Am. Ambulance Hosp., Paris, Jan. 1914. Died June 21, 1916.

MASON, Frank Stuart, musician; b. Weymouth, Mass., Oct. 21, 1883; s. Frank Hale and Lucretia Augusta (Chipman) M.; grad. with highest honors, N.E. Conservatory of Music 1907; studied piano in Paris with Isidor Philipp, Raoul Pugno and André Wormser, composition with André Gédalge; m. Margaret C. Mason, Dec. 24, 1925; 1 son, William Chipman II. Début as pianist with Boston Orchestral Club, 1910; soloist Boston Symphony Orchestra, 1921; guest conductor same, 1923; condr. People's Symphony Orchestra, 1919-27; prof. piano playing and lecturer on history of music N.E. Conserv. of Music, also for dept. of edn. of Mass.; asst. prof. Coll. of Music, Boston U. Officier d'Académie, 1922, and Officier de l'Instruction Publique, 1929 (both of France). Mason. Composer: Rhapsody (on a Persian air); Bergerie (suite for orchestra). Home: Boston, Mass. Died Oct. 25, 1929.

MASON, Henry Freeman, judge; b. Racine, Wis., Feb. 17, 1860; s. Lemuel B. and Lucy (Cole) M.; grad. U. of Wis., 1881; m. Elizabeth Wilkinson, Nov. 26, 1891 (died 1909); m. 2d, Lucy S. Greene, July 16, 1910. Worked in newspaper office, Black River Falls, Wis., 1881-86, meanwhile studying law; moved to Garden City, Kan., 1886, and practiced law there until Jan. 1903. Co. atty. Finney Co., Kan., 1889-93; mem. Kan. Ho. of Rep., 1899, 1901; justice Supreme Court of Kan., 1903—, present term expires, 1927. Lecturer on constl. law, Washburn Coll. Unitarian. Republican. Home: Garden City, Kan. Died May 4, 1927.

MASON, James Tate, surgeon; b. Lahore, Va., May 20, 1882; s. Dr. Claiborne Rice and Mary Moore (Woolfolk) M.; M.D., U. of Va., 1905; m. Laura DeWolfe Whittlesey, Jan. 3, 1912; children—James Tate, Mary Virginia, Frederick DeWolfe. Surgeon, Phila., Pa., and Franklin, Wash., 1906-09; in practice, Seattle, 1909—; surgeon and supt. King Co. Hosp., 1916-20; surgeon-in-chief Mason Clinic and pres. Virginia Mason Hosp., 1920—; cons. surgeon U.S. Marine Hosp., Am. Mail Line, Alaska S.S. Co., N.P. Ry. Co. Trustee Lakeside Sch. Fellow Am. Coll. Surgeons. Home: Seattle, Wash. Died June 20, 1936.

MASON, James Weir, prof. pure mathematics, Coll. City of New York, 1879-1903; mem. Actuarial Soc. of America; b. New York, N.Y., April 22, 1836; s. Rev. Ebenezer M. and Sarah Locke (Weir) M.; grad. Coll. City of New York, 1855 (A.M.); prin. Albany Acad., 1863-68; actuary Mass. Mut. Life Ins. Co., 1869-72; actuary Penn. Mut. Life Ins. Co., 1872-79; unmarried. Home: New York, N.Y. Died 1905.

MASON, John (Hill Belcher), actor; b. Orange, N.J., Oct. 28, 1858; s. Daniel Gregory and Susan W. (Belcher) M.; ed. pvt. schs., Frankfort Gymnasium, and Columbia U.; m. Marion Manola (actress); m. 2d, Katherine Grey (actress). First appearance at 20 in Walnut St. Theatre, Phila.; played in Boston, 1879-89, except 2 seasons with A. M. Palmer's Union Sq. Theatre Co., New York; played "Simeon Strong," in The Idler, London, 1890; starred with Marion Manola, 1891-94; in vaudeville, 1894-96; toured U.S. in Mason-Manola Co., 1898; leading man in Frohman's Lyceum Theatre Co., 2 seasons; later with Jacob Litt; with Elsie DeWolfe, in The Way of the World; with Annie Russell, in Mice and Men; leading man with Minnie Maddern Fiske, 1905-06; starred as "Jack Brookfield," in The Witching Hour, 1907-08; starred in None so Blind, and A Son of the People; first appeared with own co. at New Theatre, New York, 1910; starred in As a Man Thinks, 1911-12. Home: Bayport, L.I., N.Y. Died Jan. 12, 1919.

MASON, John Henry, clergyman; b. West Swanzey, N.H., May 29, 1850; s. David Green and Roxana (Little) M.; A.B., Brown U., 1872, A.M., 1875, D.D., 1904; grad. Rochester (N.Y.) Theol. Sem., 1877; D.D., U. of Rochester, 1903; m. Caroline Atwater, May 29, 1877; children—Mary Atwater, Ruth Little, Helen Carol (dec.). Ordained Bapt. ministry, 1877; pastor Sennett, N.Y., 1877-81, Brockport, N.Y., 1881-89, 1st Ch., New Haven, Conn., 1889-96, 1st Ch., Batavia, N.Y., 1898-1904; prof. English Bible, Rochester Theol. Sem., 1903-13; lecturer, Gordon Bible Coll., Boston, 1914-19; pres. Boston Browning Soc., 1924-27. Home: Brookline, Mass. Died June 24, 1928.

MASON, John William, judge; b. Monongalia Co., Va. (now W.Va.), Jan. 13, 1842; s. John McLure and Susan B. (Hutchinson) M.; ed. Monongalia Acad., Morgantown, W.Va.; m. Rebecca E. Wallace, Sept. 6, 1870. Served as sergt. in Battery F, 1st Regt., W.Va. Light Arty. Vols., 1861-64; began practice at Grafton, W.Va., 1868; U.S. commr. internal revenue, Washington, D.C., 1889-93; judge Circuit Court, 2d and 14th Circuits, W.Va., 1900-13; chmn. Va. Debt Commn., 1914-16; judge Supreme Court of Appeals of W.Va., Nov. 1915-Dec. 31, 1916. Republican. Presbyn. Mason. Home: Fairmont, W.Va. Died Apr. 23, 1919.

MASON, Joseph Warren Teets, newspaper corr., author; b. Newburgh, N.Y., Jan. 3, 1879; s. John A. and Georgiana L. (Niver) M.; prep. edn., Barnard Sch., New York; student Coll. City of New York; m. Edith Hannah, d. Capt. Frederick Halbert of British Mercantile Marine, Feb. 24, 1903; 1 dau., Margaret E. H. Reporter Harlem (N.Y.) Local Reporter, 1898; London editor, later European mgr. Scripps-McRae and Publishers' Press assns. of America, 1899-1907; European mgr. United Press, 1907-08; New York corr. London Daily Express, 1908-31, spl. corr., 1931—; war critic United Press, 1914-18, and United Press writer on foreign affairs, 1918-30; writer on foreign affairs for La Prensa, Buenos Aires, 1925—; New York corr. La Lucha, Havana, 1915-27. Traveled extensively on foreign assignments; made spl. study of Occidental and Oriental philosophies and religions; lectured in India, China and Japan on oriental and western cultures. Officer Order of the British Empire, 1920; Order of the Rising Sun, 4th Class (Japan), 1934. Mem. advisory com., Columbia U., on Japanese Studies. Author: Creative Freedom, 1926; The Creative East, 1928; Kami Nagara No Michi (in Japanese, translated by Shinichiro Imaoka), 1933; Sozo-No Nihon (in Japanese, compiled by Rev. Kyugo Kano), 1934; The Meaning of Shinto, 1935; Shintogan Mita Obei, 1935; The Spirit of Shinto Mythology, 1939. Died May 13, 1941.

MASON, L. Walter, clergyman; b. Franklin, Pa., Nov. 24, 1861; s. Joseph and Eugenia (Anderson) M.; Utica Acad., Edinboro, Pa.; grad. Meadville (Pa.) Theol. Sch., 1886; D.D., Buchtel, 1908; m. Caroline Wilkins, June 23, 1886; children—Charles Wilkins, Joseph John (dec.), Shirley Lowell, Eugenia Chapin (dec.), Elizabeth Holbrook. Ordained Unitarian ministry, 1886; pastor, Brookfield, Mass., 1886-90, 1st Church, Gloucester, Mass., 1890-1900, 1st Ch., Pittsburgh, Nov. 27, 1900—. Trustee Meadville Theol. Sch. Del. Congress of Religious Liberals, Paris, 1913. Author: State Parent-hood of Dependent Children; The Way to World Peace; The Fellowship of Religions On the Verge of War, and other sermons. Home: Pittsburgh, Pa. Deceased.

MASON, Lewis Duncan, physician; b. Brooklyn, N.Y., June 21, 1843; s. Theodore Lewis (M.D.) and Katherine Van Vliet (DeWitt) M.; special diploma, New York U., 1863; M.D., L.I. College Hosp., Brooklyn, 1866; m. Mrs. Mary Frances Dickson, d. Isaac D. Witherspoon, of Yorkville, S.C., Dec. 20, 1883. Attending surgeon, adj. surgeon and chief of surg. clinic, 1866-75, surgeon on hosp. staff and instr. surgery, 1875-82, L.I. Coll. Hosp.; visiting physician, 1866-82, cons. physician, 1882-94, Kings Co. (Brooklyn) Inebriates' Home. Pres. Brooklyn City Bible Soc.; dir. Am. Bible Soc.; hon. dir. Brooklyn City Mission Society. Fellow New York Acad. Medicine, etc. Home: Brooklyn, N.Y. Died June 12, 1927.

MASON, Madison Charles Butler, clergyman; b. Houma, parish of Terrebonne, La., Mar. 27, 1859; s. Alfred and Julia M.; A.B., New Orleans U., 1888, A.M., 1891; grad. Gammon Theol. Sem., 1891; (D.D., New Orleans U., and Wiley U., 1893); m. Mary E. Mason, Dec. 17, 1878. Ordained M.E. ministry, 1883; pastor New Orleans, 1883-88, Atlanta, Ga., 1889-91; field agt., 1891-93, asst. corr. sec., 1893-96, corr. sec. from 1896, Freedmen's Aid and Southern Edn. Soc. of M.E. Church. Author: The Gospel Message, 1905. Home: Cincinnati, O. Died July 30, 1915.

MASON, Otis Tufton, ethnologist; b. Eastport, Me., Apr. 10, 1838; s. John and Rachel Thompson (Lincoln) M.; grad. Columbian, 1861 (A.M., 1862; Ph.D., 1879; LL.D., 1898); in charge prep. sch. Columbian Univ., 1861-84; from 1884 curator ethnology Nat. Museum, and head curator, dept. anthropology, 1902—. Hon. and corr. mem. many Am. and European scientific socs. Author: The Hupa Indian Industries; Woman's Share in Primitive Culture, 1894; Origin of Inventions, 1895 (London); Primitive Transportation; The Land Problem; Cradles of the North American Indians; The Antiquities of Guadeloupe; Aboriginal American Basketry (2 vols.), 1904. Home: Washington, D.C. Died 1908.

MASON, Rufus Osgood, physician, author; b. Sullivan, N.H., Jan. 22, 1830; s. Rufus and Prudence (Woods) M.; grad. Dartmouth, 1854 (A.M.); Coll. Physicians & Surgeons, N.Y., 1859; m. Marian Isabel Goodwin, July 3, 1871; m. 2d, Charlotte Van Der Veer Quick, Apr. 27, 1886. Acting asst. surgeon U.S. Navy, 1861-64. Author: Sketches and Impressions, Musical, Theatrical and Social, Including a Sketch of the Philharmonic Society of New York, 1887; Telepathy and the Subliminal Self, 1897; Hypnotism and Suggestion in Therapeutics, 1901. Home: New York, N.Y. Died 1903.

MASON, Silas Boxley, contractor, horse breeder; b. Orange Co., Va., Oct. 22, 1879; s. Horatio Pleasants and Samuella Bolling (Annthony) M.; grad. Univ. Sch., Charlottesville, Va., 1897; student Princeton, 1897-98, Washington and Lee U., Lexington, Va., 1899; m. Rosa Johnston Tucker, June 9, 1906; m. 2d, Susanne Burnett, Apr. 26, 1932. Joined Mason & Hoge Co., N.Y. City, contractors, founded by grandfather Claiborne R. Mason, his father being then pres., 1900; treas. of succeeding Mason & Hanger, 1906-25, pres., 1925—; chmn. bd. dirs. Mason & Hanger Co., Silas Mason Co., Mason & Walsh Co., Mason-Walsh-Atkinson-Kier Co. (all contracting cos.); pres. Mason Foundation Co., Mason-Hagan, Inc.; breeder of thoroughbred horses on Ky. estate; engaged in building Mid Town Tunnel (N.Y. City), Grand Coulee Dam (Mason City, Wash.), Ft. Peck (Mont.) Diversion Tunnels. Home: Lexington, Ky. Died Apr. 14, 1936.

MASON, Silas Cheever, horticulturist; b. East Greensboro, Vt., Apr. 19, 1857; s. Elkanah Phillips and Adaline (Cheever) M.; B.S., Kan. State Agricultural College, 1890, M.S., 1893; hon. D.Sc. from same college, 1928; m. May V. Quinby, Jan. 1, 1884. Teacher pub. schs. 3 yrs.; asst. prof. horticulture and forestry Kan. State Agrl. Coll., 1890, prof., 1894-97; prof. horticulture and forestry, Berea (Ky.) Coll., 1897-1906; arboriculturist (under new classification horticulturist) U.S. Dept. Agr., 1907-31. Detailed by sec. of agr. to study date palm culture in Egypt and Sudan, and secure offshoots of valuable varieties, 1913-14; again in Egypt, 1920, in Algeria, 1921-22; leave of absence, 1924-25, as consulting expert on date culture, to Sudan Govt. Discovered the identity, history and geog. range of the Saidy date of the oases of the Libyan Desert, securing 7,000 offshoots for U.S. Dept. Agr., for planting in Southern Calif. Methodist. Home: Riverside, Calif. Died Oct. 19, 1935.

MASON, Victor Louis, railroads; b. Washington, Dec. 9, 1870; s. James M. and Laura Elizabeth (Pepin) M.; B.S., Columbian (now George Washington) U., 1897; m. Daisy Comstock Simons, Mar. 3, 1891. Pvt. sec. to Secretaries R. A. Alger and Elihu Root, 1897-99; asso. with Gen. Alger in Detroit, 1899-1902; apptd. mem. N.Y. and N.J. Interstate Bridge Commn., 1906, 1908; chmn. N.J. Commn., 1909-10; asst. sec. Rep. Nat. Com. in charge of Eastern div., campaign of 1908. Pres. N.C. Transcontinental Construction Co., Jan. 1911—. Pres. Passaic (N.J.) Bd. of Trade, 1906-11. Episcopalian. Home: Passaic, N.J. Died 1912.

MASON, Walt, humorist, poet; b. Columbus, Ont., May 4, 1862; s. John and Lydia Sarah (Campbell) M.; self-educated; came to U.S., 1880; m. Ella Foos, of Wooster, O., Feb. 15, 1893. Connected with Atchison Globe, 1885-87, later with Lincoln (Neb.) State Journal and other papers; editorial paragrapher Evening News, Washington, 1893; asso. with William Allen White on Emporia (Kan.) Gazette, 1907—. Prose poems are pub. daily in more than 200 newspapers in the U.S. and Can. Author: Uncle Walt, 1910; Walt Mason's Business Prose Poems, 1911; Rippling Rhymes, 1913; Horse Sense, 1915; Terse Verse, 1917; Walt Mason, His Book, 1918. Home: La Jolla, Calif. Died June 22, 1939.

MASON, William, pianist; b. Boston, Jan. 24, 1829; s. Dr. Lowell, musician (1792-1872), and Abigail M.; studied in Germany under Moscheles, Moritz Hauptmann, Dreyschock and finally Liszt. (Mus. Doc., Yale, 1872); made several tours as pianist in Europe and U.S.; from 1854 has been principally engaged in teaching; established, 1855 (with Carl Bergmann, Theodore Thomas, Joseph Mosenthal, Geo. Matzka and F. Bergner) the Mason and Thomas recitals of chamber music in New York, which continued until 1868. Author: Two Pianoforte Methods (with Eli S. Hoadley); Pianoforte Technics (with William S. B. Mathews); Touch and Technics; Memories of a Musical Life, 1901. Home: New York, N.Y. Died 1908.

MASON, William Ernest, congressman; b. Franklinville, N.Y., July 7, 1850; s. Lewis J. and Nancy (Winslow) M.; removed with parents to Bentonsport, Ia., 1858; acad. edn.; taught sch., 1866-70, last 2 yrs. at Des Moines, Ia.; m. Edith Julia White, June 11, 1873. Admitted to Ill. bar, 1872; mem. Ill. Gen. Assembly, 1879, Senate, 1881-85; mem. 50th and 51st Congresses (1887-91); U.S. senator, 1897-1903; mem. 65th and 66th Congresses (1917-21), Ill. at-large. Republican. Senior mem. Mason & Mason, Chicago.

Author: John the Unafraid, 1910. Home: Chicago, Ill. Died June 16, 1921.

MASON, William Pitt, chemist; b. New York, Oct. 12, 1853; s. James and Emma (Wheatley) M.; C.E., Rensselaer Poly. Inst., 1874, B.S., 1877; M.D., Union Univ., 1881, Sc.D., 1917; studied bacteriology, Pasteur Inst., Paris; LL.D., Lafayette Coll., Pa., 1908; m. Emilie E. Harding, 1886; children—George Harding (dec.), William Pitt; m. 2d, Margaret D. Betts, 1908. Asst. in chemistry, 1875-82, prof. analytical chemistry, 1882-93, prof. chemistry, 1893—, Rensselaer Poly. Inst. Mem. U.S. Assay Commn., 1896. Fellow A.A.A.S. (chmn. Chem. Sect., 1897). Author: Examination of Potable Water, 1890; Water Supply, 1896; Notes on Qualitative Analysis, 1896; Examination of Water, 1899. Home: Troy, N.Y. Died 1937.

MASON, William Woodman, banker; b. Limerick, Me., Aug. 25, 1851; s. Jeremiah Miller and Martha Weeks (Woodman) M.; desc. of Amos Mason, of York Co., Me.; ed. Limerick Acad., and Eastman Business Coll., Poughkeepsie, N.Y.; m. Mary Cleaves, May 1891. Learned business and financial management under father; cashier Limerick Nat. Bank (of which father was pres.) many yrs.; elected v.p. Portland Nat. Bank, 1889, pres. many yrs., now dir.; dir. Union Safe Deposit & Trust Co. (pres. 1925); mem. Me. Ho. of Rep., 1885. Odd Fellow. Republican. Home: Portland, Me. Died Jan. 14, 1938.

MASQUERAY, Emmanuel Louis, architect; b. Dieppe, France, September 1861; s. Charles Emmanuel and Louise (De Lamare) M.; ed. École des Beaux Arts, Paris (Deschaume prize, 1879; Chaudesaigues prize, 1880; gold medal, Salon 1883); unmarried. Came to America, 1887, to St. Paul, 1905; chief of design at the St. Louis Expn., 1904, erecting there The Cascades, Colonnade of States and Pavilions, Transportation, Agrl., Hort., Fisheries and Forestry bldgs.; also La. Purchase monument and 12 bridges; has also erected many important structures in various parts of the country, including L.I. College Hosp., Brooklyn, Cathedral of St. Paul, Pro-Cathedral of Minneapolis; also cathedral at Wichita, Kansas; Cathedral and St. Joseph's Coll., Dubuque, Ia.; capitol grounds at Des Moines, Ia.; Ch. of St. May, Winnipeg, Man., etc. Died May 26, 1917.

MASSEY, George Betton, M.D.; b. Massey, Md., Nov. 15, 1856; s. Benjamin Hemsley Clinton and Bersheba (Betton) M.; ed. Galena, Md., and by pvt. tutors at Tallahassee, Fla.; M.D., U. of Pa., 1876; m. Harriet Louise Stairs, Mar. 25, 1885. Established practice, 1876; since 1880 engaged specially in electro-therapeutic practice; has advocated electro-therapeutics in gynecology and treatment of cancer in various nat. med. gatherings. Asst. phys. State Hosp. for Insane, Danville, Pa., 1876-79; asst. phys. Infirmary for Nervous Diseases, Phila., 1879-87, electro-therapeutist, same, 1881-87; phys. gynecol. dept., Howard Hosp., Phila., 1887-98; attending surgeon Am. Oncologic Hospital, Phila., 1904-12. Judge of awards, Internat. Elec. Exhbn., Franklin Inst., Phila., 1884. Former pres. and fellow Am. Electro-Therapeutic Assn. Author: Electricity in the Diseases of Women, 1888; Conservative Gynecology and Electro-Therapeutics, 1898; Ionic Surgery in Cancer, 1910; Practical Electrotherapeutics and Diathermy, 1923. Died Mar. 29, 1927.

MASSEY, George Valentine, lawyer; b. West Whiteland Tp., Pa., Dec. 16, 1841; s. Isaac and Mary (Robinson) M. Engaged in practice Dover, Del., 1865-95; solicitor Phila., Wilmington & Baltimore R.R., 1876-95; asst. gen. solicitor, 1895-1902, gen. counsel, Nov. 26, 1902-Dec. 31, 1911, Pa. R.R. Co.; retired. Home: Philadelphia, Pa. Died Oct. 21, 1924.

MASSEY, Wilbur Fisk, horticulturist; b. Accomac Co., Va., Sept. 30, 1839; s. Rev. James A. and Anne (Parker) M.; prep. edn. Washington Coll., Md., and Dickinson Coll., Pa., 1856-57; (Sc.D., N.C. State Coll. Agr. and Engring., 1917); m. Sarah E. M. Phoebus, May 4, 1861; m. 2d, Aurilla J. Phoebus, sister of first wife, Apr. 4, 1876. Engaged in railroad constrn. in the West in 1858 on N.Mo. R.R.; returned to Va. at outbreak of war. After war, in Kent Co., Md., was 1st sec., examiner and treas. of new pub. sch. system, Kent Co.; at same time, engaged in a nursery and florist business, which was later transferred to Baltimore. Engaged in agrl. and hort. edn., 1st at Miller School, Albemarle, Va., 1885—; prof. horticulture and botany, N.C. Coll. Agr. and Mechanic Arts, 1889-1905; also station investigator, Agrl. Expt. Sta. of N.C.; now agrl. and hort. expert. Asso. corr. editor of Southern Planter (Richmond, Va.), Progressive Farmer (Raleigh, N.C.), Southern Farm Gazette (Starkville, Miss.), Market Growers' Journal (Louisville, Ky.), Practical Farmer, Philadelphia, Pa. Registered Farmers' Inst. lecturer, U.S. Dept. Agr. Democrat. Author: Practical Farming for American Farmer, 1907; Massey's Garden Book for the South, 1918. Home: Salisbury, Md. Died Mar. 30, 1923.

MASSEY, William Alexander, senator; b. Oakland, O., Oct. 7, 1856; ed. Union Christian Coll., Merom, Ind., and Asbury (now DePauw) U., Greencastle, Ind. (non-grad.). Admitted to Ind. bar, 1877; practiced at Sullivan, Ind.; moved to Nev., 1888, and engaged in prospecting and mining; resumed practice at Elko, Nev.; served as dist. atty., mem. Nev. Ho. of Rep. and justice Supreme Ct. of Nev. (resigned from latter position 1902); apptd. mem. U.S. Senate to fill vacancy occasioned by death of Hon. George S. Nixon, period July, 1912-Mar. 4, 1913. Republican. Home: Reno, Nev. Died Mar. 5, 1914.

MASSIE, David Meade, lawyer; b. Chillicothe, O., Feb. 26, 1859; s. Henry and Susan Burton (Thompson) M.; A.B., Princeton, 1880, A.M., 1883; LL.B., Cincinnati Law Sch., 1882; m. Juliet Matthews, Nov. 6, 1883. Admitted to Ohio bar, 1882; elected Ohio Senate, 1887, 89; trustee Ohio State U., 1888-1907; commr. to take testimony in Cuba under Spanish Treaty Claims Commn., 1902-09. Pres. First Nat. Bank of Chillicothe, Ohio; v.p. Valley Savings Bank and Trust Co.; sec., treas. The Marcus Boggs Estate Co. Mem. Nat. Agrl. Advisory Com., 1918. Republican. Presbyn. Home: Chillicothe, O. Died Sept. 3, 1927.

MASSIE, Eugene Carter, lawyer; b. Orange Co., Va., May 27, 1861; s. Henry and Susan Elizabeth (Smith) M.; acad. of Maj. Horace W. Jones, Charlottesville, Va.; U. of Va., 1876-83; m. Laura Roy Ellerson, Nov. 11, 1897. Admitted to Va. bar, 1884; mem. firm of Pleasants & Massie (James Pleasants) until death of partner, July 16, 1898, then practiced alone. Mem. Va. militia many yrs.; chief of staff, rank of col., under Gov. Claude A. Swanson, 1906-10. Mem. Va. Ho. of Dels., 1906-10; commr. from Va. on uniform state laws under Governors Swanson, Mann, Stuart, Davis and Trinkle; former chmn. exec. com. and v.p. Nat. Conf. Commrs. Uniform State Laws. Pres. Retreat for the Sick, Richmond; chmn. "Four Minute Men," 1917-18. Pres. Va. Soc. S.A.R. Episcopalian. Author of Manual of the Uniform Land Registration Act in Virginia. Home: Richmond, Va. Deceased.

MASSIE, Robert Kinloch, clergyman; b. Charlottesville, Va., Feb. 4, 1864; s. Nathaniel Hardin and Eliza Kinloch (Nelson) M.; grad. U. of Va., 1888; Theol. Sem. in Va., 1891; M.A., Columbian (now George Washington) U., 1902; D.D., Washington and Lee U., 1906; m. Harriet Ross Milton, July 8, 1891; children—Robert Kinloch (dec.), Francis Milton. Deacon and priest, P.E. Ch., 1891; missionary in China, 1891-95, also prof. St. John's Coll., Shanghai; prof. eccles. history, Theol. Sem. in Va., 1898-1912; dean Christ Church Cathedral, Lexington, Ky., 1913-29 (dean emeritus); dep. Gen. Conv., P.E. Church, 1913-28. Chmn. Vice Commn. and mem. Bd. Asso. Charities, Lexington; pres. Ky. Conf. Charities and Correction, 1916-18; charter mem. Welfare League of Lexington; mem. Ky. Inter-Racial Commn., Ky. Com. for Mothers and Babies; mem. bd. dirs. Margaret Coll., Versailles, Ky. Democrat. Episcopalian. Mason. Home: Lexington, Ky. Died Apr. 1, 1932.

MASSIE, Robert Kinloch, Jr., educator; b. of Am. parents, Shanghai, China, May 21, 1892; s. Robert Kinloch and Harriet Ross (Milton) M.; brought to U.S., 1895; grad. Episcopal High Sch., Alexandria, Va., 1911; B.A., U. of Va., 1914, M.A., 1916; unmarried. Founder Massie Sch., Lexington, Ky., 1919; school incorporated, 1923, and moved to Versailles; pres. and headmaster same since organization. Grad. Ft. Sill (Okla.) Sch. of Arms, as asst. div. instr., 1918; served as 2d lt., 1st lt., and capt. Inf. U.S.A., 1917-18; maj. O.R.C., 1925. Mem. Southern Assn. Colls. and Secondary Sch., Lexington Y.M.C.A. Democrat. Episcopalian. Home: Versailles, Ky. Died Apr. 7, 1930.

MASSINGALE, Sam Chapman, congressman; b. Quitman, Miss., August 2, 1870; s. George Mordecai and Martha (McGowan) M.; ed. pub. schs., Quitman, and U. of Miss. (non-grad.); studied law pvtly.; m. Anna Canaday, Dec. 17, 1903; children—Margaret (Mrs. Ralph W. Hippen), Sam (dec.), Betty Lou (Mrs. J. H. Nelson), Jane. Began practice of law at Cordell, Okla., 1900; elected mem. Territorial Legislature, 1902; mem. 74th to 76th Congresses (1935-41), 7th Okla. Dist. Served as pvt. Co. D, 2d Tex. Inf., Spanish-Am. War, 1898. Democrat. Mason. Rotarian. Home: Cordell, Okla. Died Jan. 17, 1941.

MASSLICH, Chester Bentley, lawyer; b. Union City, Ind., Mar. 24, 1872; s. Bentley and Lucia (Farson) M.; grad. high sch., Union City, 1889, Northwestern Acad., Evanston, Ill., 1890, A.B., Northwestern U., 1894 (Phi Beta Kappa); diploma, Chicago Coll. of Law, 1897; m. Lucy Shuman, Sept. 15, 1903; 1 dau., Marjorie. Admitted to Ill. bar, 1897; mgr. bond buying dept., Farson, Leach & Co., Chicago, 1898-1900; gen. atty. same, 1900-06; gen. atty. A. B. Leach & Co., 1906-10; moved to New York, 1910; mem. Hubbard & Masslich, 1910, Caldwell, Masslich & Reed, 1911-15, Caldwell & Masslich, 1915-19; practiced alone, 1919—. Home: Pelham, N.Y. Died Jan. 17, 1933.

MASSON, Thomas L. (Tom Masson), editor; b. Essex, Conn., July 21, 1866; s. Thomas L. and Malvina M. M.; ed. pub. schs., New Haven; m. Fannie Zulette Goodrich, of Hartford, Conn., Oct. 24, 1893. Literary and mng. editor of Life, New York, 1893-1922; mem. editorial staff New York Times, 1924; asso. editor Saturday Evening Post, 1922-30. Author: Yankee Navy, 1899; A Corner in Women, 1905; The Von Blumers, 1906; A Bachelor's Baby, and Some Grown-ups, 1907; The Best Stories in the World, 1913; Humorous Masterpieces of American Literature, 1904; In Merry Measure, 1905; The New Plato, 1905; Humor of Love in Verse and Prose, 1906; Short Stories from Life, 1916; Best Short Stories, 1918; Well Why Not?, 1921; Our American Humorists, 1922; Listen to These, 1922; That Silver Lining, 1923; Why I Am a Spiritual Vagabond, 1925; The City of Perfection, 1926; Tom Masson's Compendium of Wit and Humor, 1927; In Tune with the Finite, 1928; Ascensions, 1929; Within, 1931. Died June 18, 1934.

MASTERSON, William Wesley, consul; b. Carrollton, Ky., Feb. 9, 1861; ed. Henry Coll.; studied law, Cincinnati Law Sch.; practiced in Carrollton, 1885-98; consul at Aden, Arabia, 1885-88 (resigned); reëntered practice of law at Carrollton, also edited newspaper; consul at Aden, 1903-06, Batun, 1906-08, Harput, 1908-14, Durban, Apr. 24, 1914—. Died May 10, 1922.

MASTIN, William McDowell, surgeon; b. Mobile, Ala., July 3, 1853; s. Claudius Henry (M.D.) and Mary E. (McDowell) M.; M.D., U. of Pa., 1874; LL.D., St. Joseph's Coll., Mobile, 1905; m. Margaret L. Crawford, Nov. 1822; 1 dau., L. C. Practiced at Mobile, 1877—; surgeon Mobile City Hosp. and Providence Infirmary, 1895—. Fellow Am. Surgical Assn., A.C.S., Southern Surg. and Gynecol. Assn. Home: Mobile, Ala. Died Feb. 3, 1933.

MATCHETT, Charles Horatio, socialist; b. Needham, Mass., May 15, 1843; s. Horatio and Clarissa Clifford (Batchelder) M.; ed. high sch., Boston. Sailor 4 yrs.; in U.S.N., 1861-62; was in mercantile house in Chicago; 1 yr. in grocery store, Boston; worked in shoe factory, and at carpenter's trade, later becoming an electrician; was mem. Knights of Labor; was active in Socialist Labor Party; joined Socialist movement in 1885; has been nominee for mayor of Brooklyn, gov. of N.Y., pres. and v.p. U.S.; was presidential nominee, 1896; candidate for asso. justice Ct. of Appeals, 1903, for chief justice, 1904. Died Oct. 23, 1919.

MATEER, Calvin Wilson, missionary; b. Mechanicsburg, Pa., Jan. 9, 1836; s. John and Mary A. (Diven) M.; A.B., Jefferson (now Washington and Jefferson) Coll., 1857, A.M., 1860; studied Western Theol. Sem.; (D.D., Hanover Coll., Ind., 1880; LL.D., Worcester Univ., O., 1889, Washington and Jefferson Coll., 1892); m. Julia A. Brown (dec.), Delaware, O., Dec. 23, 1862; m. 2d, Ada Haven, Chefoo, China, Sept. 23, 1890. Prin. Beaver (Pa.) Acad., 1857-59; ordained to Presbyn. ministry, 1861; pastor Delaware, O., 1861-63; settled in Tengchow, Shantung, China, 1863; preached throughout the Eastern part of province; founded Tengchow Coll.; writer of text-books in Mandarin and authority in the language; chmn. com. in translating the Bible into Mandarin, 1893—. Author: Practical Arithmetic (3 vols.), 1875; Course of Algebra (2 vols.), 1880; Complete Geometry (2 vols.), 1882; Review of Methods of Mission Work, 1888; A Course of Mandarin Lessons, 1891; Primary Lessons in Mandarin, 1900; The Meaning of the Word Shen (God), 1900; Analysis of 2,118 Chinese Characters, 1895. Died 1908.

MATHER, Alonzo Clark, pres. Mather Stock Car Co.; b. Fairfield, N.Y.; s. William and Mary Ann (Buell) M.; ed. Fairfield Prep. Sch. After leaving sch. obtained employment at Utica, N.Y.; moved to Quincy, Ill., and in 1875 to Chicago; engaged in business; patentee of many inventions, among them the Mather Palace Stock Car for the humane transportation of horses and cattle, for which received a gold medal from Am. Humane Soc.; president Mather Stock Car Co. Was one of the first members of 1st Regiment, I.N.G. Home: Chicago, Ill. Died Jan. 25, 1941.

MATHER, Fred, author, fish-culturist; b. Green bush, N.Y., Aug. 2, 1833; ed. at acad. in Albany, N.Y., 1854-57; hunter and trapper in Wis., 1857-59; was in the Kan. war, 1862; private 113th N.Y. vols.; then sergt. to capt. 7th N.Y. arty. until discharged, May 1865; lt. col. Albany Rangers, 1898; fish-culturist, 1868; asst. U.S. Fish Commn., 1873; supt. N.Y. Fish Commn., 1883-95; invented hatching cone for shad and other apparatus; had charge Am. exhibit, Fisheries Exhbn., Berlin, 1880; m. Elizabeth McDonald (died 1861), 1854; m. 2d, Adelaide Fairchild, 1877. Author: Men I Have Fished With; Fish-culture; Icthyology of the Adirondacks. Lecturer. Home: Brooklyn, N.Y. Died 1900.

MATHER, Frederic Gregory, journalist, author; b. Cleveland, O., Aug. 11, 1844; s. late Samuel Holmes (LL.D.) and Emily W. (Gregory) M.; A.B., Dartmouth, 1867, A.M., 1870; studied law, Cleveland, 1867-70; m. Cornelia Heyer Olcott, Oct. 10, 1871; m. 2d, Alice Evelyn Yager, Nov. 11, 1880; m. 3d, Lilian Thompson, Jan. 12, 1921. Editor-in-chief of Binghamton (N.Y.) Republican, 1874-79; spl. rep. in Canada of U.S. Bur. of Edn., 1874-75; editorial writer Albany Evening Journal, 1879-80; spl. Albany corr. of various newspapers, 1880-97. Editor and compiler: New York in the Revolution, 1898; editor supplement same, 1901. Author: Refugees of 1776 from Long Island to Connecticut, 1913. Mem. various historical societies. Vestryman, St. John's Ch., Stamford. Home: Stamford, Conn. Died Aug. 31, 1925.

MATHER, Margaret Morgan Herbert; b. (Herbert) Monmouth Co., N.J., (desc. of the English earls of Pembroke and Powis); ed. by governess and (grad.) Miss Hale's Sem.; m. De Witt Clinton Mather, Oct. 24, 1866. V.p., for N.J., Nat. Mary Washington Memorial Assn.; life member Va. Hist. Soc.; a Colonial Dame; one of 5 founders Daughters Am. Revolution in N.J. Collected and edited (under pen-name "Morgan Herbert") poems of Frank Forester (late Henry William Herbert) with sketch of his life; trustee Evelyn Coll., Princeton, N.J. Author: History of Polo; Hunting Then and Now; Biography of Fox, a Celebrated Polo Pony. Home: Bound Brook, Somerset County, N.J. Died 1900.

MATHER, Robert, lawyer, ry. official; b. Salt Lake City, Utah, July 1, 1859; s. James and Margaret (Holt) M.; A.B., Knox Coll., Ill., 1882, A.M., 1885 (LL.D., 1907); m. Alice Caroline, d. Horatio Jell, Apr. 23, 1892. Admitted to Ill. bar, at Chicago, 1886; apptd. local atty. C.,R.I.&P. Ry. Co., 1889; asst. gen. atty., 1894, gen. atty., 1894-1902, gen. counsel, 1902-09; pres. the Rock Island Co., 1904-09; chmn. bd. dirs. Westinghouse Electric & Mfg. Co., 1909—; also dir. C.,R.I.&P. Ry. Co.; v.p. St.L.&S.F. R.R. Co.; gen. counsel C.&A. R.R. Co. Republican. Episcopalian. Trustee Knox College. Home: New York, N.Y. Died 1911.

MATHER, Samuel; b. Cleveland, O., July 13, 1851; s. Samuel Livingston and Georgiana Pomeroy (Woolson) M.; ed. Cleveland pub. schs. and St. Mark's Sch., Southborough, Mass.; m. Flora A. Stone, Oct. 19, 1881 (died 1909); children—Samuel Livingston, Amosa Stone, Constance, Philip Richard. Sr. mem. Pickands, Mather & Co., miners and dealers in iron ore and coal and mfrs. of pig iron. Pres. Lakeside Hosp.; v.p. and trustee Western Reserve U. and Adelbert Coll.; trustee Cleveland Mus. of Art. Protestant Episcopal; warden Trinity Cathedral. Home: Cleveland, O. Died Oct. 18, 1931.

MATHER, Stephen Tyng; b. San Francisco, Calif., July 4, 1867; s. Joseph W. and Bertha J. (Walker) M.; B.Litt., U. of Calif., 1887; LL.D., George Washington U., 1921, U. of Calif., 1924; m. Jane T. Floy, Oct. 12, 1893. On staff of New York Sun, 1887-93; Chicago mgr. Pacific Coast Borax Co., 1894-1903; now pres. Sterling Borax Co.; asst. to sec. of the interior, Jan. 22, 1915-Mar. 22, 1917; dir. nat. park service, Dept. of the Interior, May 16, 1917—. Episcopalian. Home: Chicago, Ill. Died Jan. 22, 1930.

MATHER, William Tyler, univ. prof.; b. Amherst, Mass., Sept. 2, 1864; s. Richard Henry and Elizabeth (Carmichael) M.; A.B., Amherst, 1886, A.M., 1891; Ph.D., Johns Hopkins, 1897; m. Mabel Elizabeth Nevins, June 30, 1892; children—Richard Nevins, Helen Marquis, Edward Otis, Dorothy Georgia. Instr. Leicester (Mass.) Acad., 1886-87, Williston Sem., 1887-93; practicing chemist, Boston, 1893-94; univ. scholar, 1895-96, fellow in physics, 1896-97, asst., 1897, Johns Hopkins; asso. prof. physics, 1898-1907, prof., 1907—, U. of Texas. Independent Democrat. President Anti-Vice League of Austin; elder Univ. Presbyn. Ch.; mem. bd. dirs. Univ. Y.M.C.A., from 1910 (pres.); mem. State Com. Y.M.C.A. Died June 14, 1937.

MATHESON, Alexander E.; b. Eagle, Wis., July 11, 1868; s. John and Mary A. (Bentley) M.; Ph.B., Beloit (Wis.) Coll., 1890 (valedictorian), M.A., 1893; LL.B., U. of Wis., 1894; m. Georgia L. Hubbard, Sept. 26, 1894; children—Marion Barbara (Mrs. Walter H. Green), John Hubbard. Admitted to Wis. bar, 1894, and began practice at Janesville; mem. Whitehead & Matheson until 1924, then alone; lecturer on internat. law, Beloit Coll., 1896-1900; mem. Wis. Ho. of Rep., 1921-25; postmaster of Janesville, 1924; resigned to become county judge of Rock Co., Wis. Chmn. exec. com. Selective Service Bd., Rock Co., Wis., World War. Trustee Beloit Coll. Moderator Wis. State Conf., 1927-28. Republican. Conglist. Mason; Grand Master of Masons, Wis., 1911-12; Grand Comdr. K.T., 1914; pres. Wis. Masonic House for Adults. Home: Janesville, Wis. Died Nov. 11, 1931.

MATHESON, James Pleasant, M.D.; b. Taylorsville, N.C., Nov. 20, 1879; s. William Bogle and Mary (Ayers) M.; A.B., Davidson (N.C.) Coll., 1899, D.Sc., 1926; M.D., N.C. Med. Coll., 1902, U. of Md., 1905, studied U. of Vienna, 1912; unmarried. Began practice at Charlotte, N.C., 1905; specialist in otolaryngology, Charlotte Eye, Ear and Throat Hosp., 1905—; dir. Industrial Loan and Investment Bank. Served as maj., Hosp. Unit O, Base Hosp. 6, overseas 1917-19. Trustee Davidson Coll. Fellow Am. Coll. Surgeons. Democrat. Presbyn. Home: Charlotte, N.C. Died Aug. 5, 1937.

MATHESON, Kenneth Gordon, college pres.; b. Cheraw, S.C., July 28, 1864; s. John F. and Mary E. (Graham) M.; prep. edn. S.C. Mil. Coll. (The Citadel), 1882-85; M.A., Stanford, 1897; studied at U. of Chicago, summer 1899, Columbia, 1903-04; LL.D., Washington and Lee U., 1906, U. of Ga., 1918; Sc.D., U. of Pa., 1923; m. Belle Seddon Fleet, Dec. 27, 1898; children—Belle Seddon, Kenneth Gordon, Frederick Graham, Mary. Commandant cadets, Ga. Mil. Coll., 1885-88; comdt. cadets and asst. prof. English U. of Tenn., 1888-90; comdt. cadets and prof. of English, Mo. Mil. Acad. (with one intermission), 1890-96; prof. English, Ga. Sch. Tech., Atlanta, 1897-1905, chmn. of faculty, 1905-06, pres., 1906-22; pres. Drexel Inst., Phila., 1922—. Y.M.C.A. div. chief, Langres area, France, Mar.-Sept. 1918. Democrat. Presbyn. Mason. Trustee Thomas W. Evans Mus. and Dental Inst., U. of Pa.; trustee Presbyn. Hosp. of Phila., Princeton Theol. Seminary. Home: Philadelphia, Pa. Died Nov. 30, 1931.

MATHESON, William John, businessman; b. Elkhorn, Wis.; s. Finlay and Anna Meigs (Lighthall) M.; ed. St. Andrews, Scotland; LL.D., U. of St. Andrews, 1920; m. Harriet Torrey, 1881; children—Mrs. Willis D. Wood, Hugh M., Malcolm. Began, 1876, as chemist in application of coal tar dyes, later officer or dir. various large corps.; now v.p. Corn Products Refining Co.; trustee Bank of New York & Trust Co. Home: Coconut Grove, Miami, Fla., Huntington, L.I., and New York, N.Y. Died May 15, 1930.

MATHEWS, Albert, lawyer, author; b. New York, N.Y., Sept. 8, 1820; s. Oliver and Mary (Field) M.; grad. Yale, 1842; studied law at Harvard Law School and New York City, 1842-45; admitted to bar, N.Y., 1845; m. Louise Mott Strong (died 1857), 1849; m. 2d, Cettie Moore Gwynne (died 1884), 1861. Author: (under pen-name of Paul Siegvolk) Walter Ashwood: A Love Story, 1859; A Bundle of Papers, 1879; Thoughts on Codification of the Common Law, 1881; Memorial of Bernard Roelker, 1889; Ruminations—The Ideal American Lady and Other Essays, 1893; Incidental Protection a Solecism; A Few Verses, 1896. Home: New York, N.Y. Died 1903.

MATHEWS, Alfred, editor; b. Painesville, O., Sept. 11, 1852, s. Samuel Huntington (M.D.) and Huldah (Ford) M.; ed. pub. sch. and pvt. study. Unmarried. Served all-around apprenticeship in journalism on Cleveland Leader and other papers. Later editorial attaché of book publishing houses (mostly in Phila.); spl. writer, book reviewer for eastern jours., etc. Author: Ohio and the Western Reserve, 1902. Home: Philadelphia, Pa. Died 1904.

MATHEWS, Charles Thomson, architect; b. Paris, of Am. parentage, Mar. 31, 1863; s. Charles Drelincourt and Rebecca Bacon (Thompson) M.; arrived in America with parents in infancy; B.A., Yale, 1886, M.A., 1892; Ph.B. in Architecture, Columbia, 1889; studied Coll. of Phys. and Surg. (Columbia); traveled for 5 yrs. in Europe, Asia, and Northern Africa, studying architecture; unmarried. In practice at New York, 1890—; won competition for remodeling Ch. of the Holy Trinity, New York, 1891; exhibited drawings at Chicago Expn., 1893; won internat. competition for remodeling east end of St. Patrick's Cathedral, New York, 1901. Fellow Am. Inst. Architects. Episcopalian. Author: The Renaissance under the Valois, 1893; The Story of Architecture, 1896. Home: New York, N.Y. Died Jan. 11, 1934.

MATHEWS, Clarence Wentworth, prof. horticulture; b. Lawrence, Mass., Feb. 10, 1861; s. Ezekiel Wentworth and Eunice Chase (Small) M.; B.S. in Agr., Cornell U., 1891; post-grad. work Cornell and U. of Chicago; m. Henrietta Safford, Dec. 29, 1891; children—Ruth Elliot (dec.), Eleanor Safford (dec.), Ruth Elizabeth, George Frederick, Paul Wentworth. Prof. botany and horticulture, U. of Ky., 1892-1910, prof. horticulture, U. of Ky., 1910—. Presbyn. Home: Lexington, Ky. Died Aug. 26, 1928.

MATHEWS, Delancey North, banker, mcht.; b. Hurley, N.Y., Nov. 29, 1849; s. Egbert R. and Sarah Elizabeth (North) M.; ed. dist. schs.; m. Sarah M. Dart, Oct. 13, 1870 (died 1899); m. 2d, Carry Eloise Smith, May 15, 1901. With State of N.Y. Nat. Bank, Kingston, 1886—, pres., 1903—; v.p. Kingston Grain Co., Kingston Savings Bank; treas. Olive Coöperative Ins. Co. Active in Red Cross work, World War. Trustee Home for the Aged, Kingston Hosp., Kingston Industrial Home. Liberal patron of ch. and charitable instns. Republican. Baptist. Mason. Home: Kingston, N.Y. Died Oct. 3, 1935.

MATHEWS, F(erdinand) Schuyler, author, illustrator; b. New Brighton, S.I., N.Y., May 30, 1854; s. Ferdinand Schuyler and Frances (Coffin) M.; ed. pub. schs. and Cooper Inst., New York, and other instns.; traveled in Italy for art edn.; m. Caroline A., d. Prof. George W. Maynard, of Morristown, N.J., Nov. 17, 1886. Connected for many yrs. with L. Prang & Co., lithographic art pubs., Boston, as a spl. artist; splty. decorative design. Author: Familiar Flowers of Field and Garden; Familiar Trees and Their Leaves; The Fieldbook of American Wild Flowers, 1902; Fieldbook of Wild Birds and Their Music, 1904; Fieldbook of Trees and Shrubs, 1914; Book of Birds for Young People, 1921; Book of Wild Flowers for Young People, 1923. Home: Cambridge, Mass. Died Aug. 20, 1938.

MATHEWS, Frank Stuart, surgeon; b. Washington, Pa., Nov. 14, 1869; s. William J. Mathews and Frances (Pelletreau) M.; M.D., Coll. Phys. and Surg. (Columbia), 1893; m. Julia E. King, Dec. 27, 1899. Practiced at N.Y. City, 1893—; clin. prof. surgery, Coll. Phys. and Surg.; attending surgeon St. Luke's Hosp., St. Mary's Free Hosp. for Children; cons. surgeon Home for Incurables, New York Hosp. for the Ruptured and Crippled, Lawrence Hosp. (Bronxville). Fellow Am. Coll. Surgeons. Republican. Presbyn. Home: New York, N.Y. Died Feb. 17, 1936.

MATHEWS, George Martin, bishop; b. Cincinnati, Aug. 22, 1848; s. John and Milchi Ann (Mathews) M.; B.S., Otterbein U., Ohio, 1870; student Lane Theol. Sem., 1879-80, Union Bibl. Sem., Dayton, O., 1881-82; (D.D., Lane U., Kan., 1896; LL.D., Otterbein, 1912); m. Clara Belle Hopper, Dec. 25, 1872. Ordained to U.B. ministry, 1882; pastor Cleves, O., 1880-81, Dayton, O., 1881-89 and 1894-98; presiding elder Miami Conf., 1889-94; editor U.B. Quarterly Review, 1893-99; asso. editor Religious Telescope, 1899-1902; bishop U.B. Ch., 1902—. Mem. exec. com. Federal Council of Chs. of Christ in America; dir. of edn. Home and Foreign Mission Bds. U.B. Ch.; v.p. Nat. Anti-Saloon League of America; pres. Otterbein Orphanage Home, Lebanon, O. Home: Dayton, Ohio. Apr. 3, 1921.

MATHEWS, James Abram, newspaperman; b. Indianapolis, Ind., July 19, 1881; s. John C. and Emma (Kivel) M.; ed. high sch. and Butler Coll., Indianapolis; m. Muriel Marie Ross, Jan. 27, 1903. Messenger with Associated Press, 1896-1903; with Indianapolis News, 1904-09; supt. Successful Farming, Des Moines, Ia., 1910-11; with Oklahoma and Times, Oklahoma City, 1912-22, Scripps-Howard newspapers, 1923, Hearst newspapers, 1924, St. Paul Pioneer Press-Dispatch, 1925-27; editor and pub. Aberdeen (S.D.) Evening News and Aberdeen Morning American, 1928—. Pres. S.D. state exec. com. Boy Scouts America. Republican. Methodist. Mason. Home: Aberdeen, S.D. Died Dec. 23, 1933.

MATHEWS, James Edward; b. Olney, Ill., Jan. 29, 1876; s. James Edward and Martha (Antle) M.; grad. U.S. Naval Acad., 1899; m. Caroline Myers, June 4, 1905 (died 1920). Resigned from U.S.N., 1901; entered employ of Bethlehem Steel Co., ordnance dept., 1901; in charge of European business of the company, at London, Eng., 1908-13; called to Bethlehem as head of ordnance dept., 1913; retired from steel business, 1919; chmn. bd. First Nat. Bank & Trust Co. Republican. Episcopalian. Home: Bethlehem, Pa. Died June 11, 1935.

MATHEWS, Joanna Hooe, author; b. New York, 1849; grad. Madame Reichard's School, New York. Not married. Author: The Bessie Books; Sunbeams; Flowerets; Haps and Mishaps; Rutherford series; Kitty Books; also other books for children (making 50 in all); Guy Hamilton (novel); Edith Murray (novel). Home: Summit, N.J. Died 1901.

MATHEWS, John Alexander, metallurgist; b. Washington, Pa., May 20, 1872; s. William Johnston and Frances (Pelletreau) M.; B.S., Washington and Jefferson Coll., 1893, M.S., 1896, Sc.D., 1902; A.M., Columbia, 1895, Ph.D., 1898; Royal Sch. Mines, London, 1900-01; m. Florence Hosmer King, Jan. 29, 1903; children—Margaret King, John Alexander. Asst. in assaying, 1896-97, tutor chemistry, 1898-1900, Columbia; Barnard Fellowship for Encouragement of Scientific Research, 1900, 1901, 1902; Andrew Carnegie Research Scholarship of Iron and Steel Inst. of Great Britain, 1901; received first award of "Andrew Carnegie Gold Medal for Research" from Iron and Steel Inst., 1902; Robert W. Hunt gold medal, A.I.M. and M.E., 1928. Mem. U.S. Assay Commn., 1900, 05, 11; metallurgist and asst. mgr. Sanderson works, Crucible Steel Co. of America, 1902-08; gen. mgr. Halcomb Steel Co., Syracuse, N.Y., 1908-15, and pres., 1915-20; v.p. and director of research, Crucible Steel Company of America. Trustee Washington and Jefferson College. Served on several tech. committees during World War. Home: Scarsdale, N.Y. Died Jan. 11, 1935.

MATHEWS, John Lathrop, journalist; b. Evanston, Ill., Jan. 10, 1874; s. William Smith Babcock and Flora E. (Swain) M.; bro. of Albert Prescott M.; student U. of Ill., 1891, U. of Chicago, 1892, 1894, Mass. Inst. Tech., 1893; A.B., Harvard, 1896; m. Gertrude Singleton, Sept. 10, 1900. Reporter Chicago News, 1898, Chicago Tribune, 1900; spl. writer Chicago Sunday Tribune, 1901; spl. writer mags., using pen name "John Swain" (later discarded), 1902; editor New Orleans Item, 1903; asst. editor Youth's Companion, 1903-07. Student of Miss. waterway development; spl. commr. Sanitary Dist. of Chicago, 1900-01; corr. Boston Transcript, 1904—. Author: Remaking the Mississippi, 1909; Conservation of Water, 1910; The Log of the Easy Way, 1911; Economic series, Harper's Monthly, 1913. Home: Normandie, Mo. Died May 27, 1916.

MATHEWS, S(amuel) Sherberne, clergyman; b. Salisbury, Mass., June 3, 1847; s. Rev. Samuel Sherberne and Elisabeth Smith (Babcock) M.; took coll. studies pvtly.; Hartford Theol. Sem., 1868-69; Geneva and Lausanne, Switzerland, 1870-71; grad. Andover Theol. Sem., 1874; U. of Berlin, 1905-06; (D.D., Redfield Coll., 1903); m. Anna Elvira Wright, Apr. 25, 1870 (died 1886). Ordained Congl. ministry, 1874; pastor Wilmington, Mass., 1874-75, Maynard,

1876-78, Boylston St. Ch., Jamaica Plain, 1878-87, Olivet Ch., Wichita, Kan., 1887-88; sec. New West Edn. Commn., 1888-93; pastor Hanover St. Ch., Milwaukee, Wis., 1895-99, Danielson, Conn., 1899-1905; dean and treas. Weston Sch. for Girls, Boston, 1906—. Ednl. sec. People's Palace, Boston; univ. sec. U. of Humanity, New York, 1909— (training sch. for officers of the Salvation Army); pres. bd. trustees H. M. Weston Trust. President Wis. State S.S. Conv., and mem. Internat. S.S. Com., 1897-99; del. from Conn. to Nat. Council Congl. Chs., Des Moines, Ia., 1904, etc. Republican. Author of Manuals of Union Congl. Ch., Maynard, and Boylston Congl. Ch., Boston, Hanover Congl. Ch., Milwaukee, etc.; sermons, "Elijah," "Mormonism," "Ebenezer." From 1896 engaged in original investigations on "The Making of the Bible." Home: Roxbury, Mass. Died 1910.

MATHEWS, William, author; b. Waterville, Me., July 28, 1818; s. Simeon and Clymena (Esty) M.; grad. Waterville Coll. (now Colby Univ.), 1835 (LL.D., 1868); studied law in office and at Harvard Law School 4 yrs.; LL.B., Harvard, 1839; admitted to Kennebec Co., Me., bar, 1838; began practice at Waterville, 1841; soon after started a newspaper, The Watervillonian, afterward changed to The Yankee Blade. Moved to Gardiner, Me., 1843; to Boston, 1847, and, in 1856, it was sold and united with The Portfolio. Removed to Chicago, 1856; librarian Young Men's Assn. there, 1859-62; prof. rhetoric and English, Univ. of Chicago, 1862-75; thereafter wholly devoted to literature, residing in Boston; m. Mary Elizabeth Dingley, 1845; m. 2d, 1850, Isabel I. Marshall; m. 3d, 1865, Harriet N. Griggs. Author: Oratory and Orators, 1879; Literary Style and Other Essays, 1881; Nugæ Literariæ, or, Brief Essays on Literary, Social and Other Themes, 1896; Conquering Success, 1903. Died 1909.

MATHEWS, William Smith Babcock, editor; b. Loudon, N.H., May 8, 1837; ed. in N.H.; studied music in Boston (Mus. Doc., Highland U., Ill.); m. Flora E. Swain, 1857; m. 2d, Blanche Dingley, 1902; father of Albert Prescott and John Lathrop M. Practical teacher of music, 1853—; was adj. prof. music, Wesleyan Female Coll., Macon, Ga.; organist Centenary M.E. Ch., 1867-93; editor Musical Independent, 1869-71; on editorial staff Chicago Herald, Record, and Tribune, 1877-87. Established, 1891, and edited Music (mag.), merged in Philharmonic, Jan. 1903. Author: How to Understand Music (2 vols.), 1880, 1888; Primer of Musical Forms, 1890; Music and Its Ideals, 1897; The Great in Music, 1900; Dictionary of Musical Terms, 1895; Primer of Music (with Dr. William Mason), 1895; The Masters and Their Music, 1898; Great in Music (3 vols.), 1900-03; Popular History of Music, 1901; many collections of music for pedagogic purposes; also spl. edited collections of Schumann, Chopin, etc. Revised Mason's Technics, 1905; Complete School of Pedals, 1904. Editor-in-chief of musical publs. of Columbian Conservatory of Music, Dallas, Tex. Home: Denver, Colo. Died Apr. 1, 1912.

MATHEWSON, Charles Frederick, lawyer; b. Barton, Vt., May 3, 1860; s. Azro B. and Amelia (Sias) M.; A.B. (valedictorian), Dartmouth, 1882 (hon. A.M., 1907); LL.B., Columbia, 1885; (LL.D., Middlebury, 1912); m. Jeanie Campbell Anderson, Dec. 8, 1886. With Turner, Lee & McClure, 1885-87; mem. Root (Hon. Elihu) & Strong, 1887-90, Strong & Mathewson, 1890-91, Strong, Harmon & Mathewson, 1891-98, Harmon & Mathewson, 1898-1909, Krauthoff (Louis C.), Harmon (Benjamin S.) & Mathewson, 1909—; chief counsel for Consolidated Gas Co. in the "80-cent gas case"; gen. counsel Caledonian Ins. Co. of Edinburgh (in America), Caledonian-Am. Ins. Co. (New York), New York & Queens Electric Light & Power Co., N.Y. & Queens Gas Co., etc.; dir. Colo.-N.M. Coal Co., Caledonian-American Insurance Co. (finance com.) Trustee Dartmouth Coll., 1894—. Republican. Home: New York, N.Y. Died Mar. 24, 1915.

MATHISON, Edward Thomson, clergyman; b. Old Town, Me., June 21, 1870; s. Robert Lauder and Catharine Susan (Roberts) M.; A.B., Yale, 1893; grad. Berkeley Div. Sch., Middletown, Conn., 1895; m. Elizabeth Hull Colburn, Feb. 16, 1898. Deacon, 1895, priest, 1896, P.E. Ch.; rector St. Andrew's Ch., Marbledale, Conn., 1895-96, Immanuel Ch., Ansonia, 1896-1900, St. Michael's Ch., Brattleboro, Vt., 1900-06, St. Timothy's Ch., Massillon, O., 1906-09, Grace Ch., Oak Park, Ill., 1909-12; asso. rector, 1912-14, rector, 1914-15, Shattuck Sch., Faribault, Minn.; rector St. John's Ch., Rockville, Conn., Sept. 1, 1915—. Mem. Bd. of Missions Diocese of Ohio, 1908-09, of Chicago, 1909-12, of Conn., 1918; mem. Cathedral Chapter of Christ Ch. Cathedral, Hartford, Conn.; archdeacon Hartford Archdeaconry; alternate del. to Gen. Conv., 1909; mem. exec. council Diocese of Conn. Mason. Home: Clinton, Conn. Died Apr. 1930.

MATILE, Léon Albert, brig. gen. U.S.A.; b. Neuchatel, Switzerland, Sept. 28, 1844; s. George A. and Marie Eugenia (Schaffter) M.; ed. pvt. schs., Princeton, N.J., and Phila.; m. Katherine Agnes Fletcher, Apr. 10, 1875. Entered mil. service in U.S.A., Dec. 3, 1863, and continuously in same until retired, Aug. 17, 1903; wounded in battle of Atlanta, Aug. 1864; participated in campaigns against Comanche, Kiowa, Cheyenne and Sioux Indians; served in Alaska and the Philippines; recommended for brevet in battle against insurgents, Manila, Feb. 4, 5, 1899; in command of 14th U.S. Inf. at battle of Zapota River, June 13, 1899; promoted brig. gen. and retired, Aug. 17, 1903. Died Apr. 10, 1938.

MATSON, Courtland Cushing, congressman; b. Brookville, Ind., Apr. 25, 1841; s. John Allen and Margaretta Melvina (Woelpper) M.; A.B., Asbury (now DePauw) U., 1862 (enlisted in Union Army, Apr. 14, 1861; at close of jr. yr., and in 1870 by vote of trustees was graduated as of class of 1862); m. Mary Nelson Farrow, Dec. 12, 1871 (died 1893). Pvt. to lt. Co. K, 16th Ind. Vols., Apr. 1861-June 1862; apptd. post adj. Camp Dick Thompson, Terre Haute, Ind., and helped to organize 3 regts.; apptd. lt. col. 71st Ind. Vols. (later 6th Ind. Cav.), Dec. 1862, after all the field officers of the regt. had been killed at battle of Richmond, Ky., and served in that position until near close of war, when was promoted col. 5th and 6th Ind. Cav., consolidated. Pros. atty. various courts in Ind., 1868, 70, 72; mem. 47th to 50th Congresses (1881-89); Dem. candidate for gov. of Ind., 1888; mem. State Bd. of Tax Commrs. of Ind., 1909-13. Methodist. Home: Greencastle, Ind. Died Sept. 4, 1915.

MATSON, Frederick Eugene, lawyer; b. Pennsville, Ohio, June 1, 1869; s. George M. and Mary C. (Dodds) M.; A.M., Muskingum College, New Concord, Ohio, 1893, LL.D., 1937; LL.B., U. of Michigan, 1895; m. Mabelle M. McKitrick, Oct. 3, 1894; 1 son, Frederick George. Teacher, country sch., 1886-87; admitted to Ind. bar, 1895, and began practice at Indianapolis; mem. Ind. State Senate, 1900-04; corp. counsel City of Indianapolis, 1906-10; mem. Matson, Ross, McCord & Ice; author Indiana Sanitary Dist. Law (1917), Park Dist. Law (1919) and Grade Separation Law (1929). Bond counsel for Indiana municipalities, R.F.C. and Federal Emergency Administration of Pub. Works. Republican. Presbyn. Home: Indianapolis, Ind. Died June 14, 1941.

MATSON, George Charlton, geologist, engr.; b. Strang, Neb., Feb. 4, 1873; s. Thomas and Susannah (Charlton) M.; B.S., Doane Coll., Crete, Neb., 1900; studied U. of Neb., 1900-01; A.M., Cornell U., 1903; Ph.D., U. of Chicago, 1920; m. Beulah Edwards, 1913; children—Thomas Edward, Mary Barbara, George Charlton. Asst. in geology, Cornell U., 1901-03; instr. geology, U. of Ill., 1903-04; fellow in geology, U. of Chicago, 1904-06; geologist U.S. Geol. Survey, 1906-16, Mexican Gulf Oil Co., 1916-17, Gulf Refining Co., of La., 1917; Gypsey Oil Co. and S. American Gulf Oil Co., 1917-21; consulting geologist, 1921—; vice-pres. Schermerhorn Oil Co., 1922-29; independent oil operator, 1929—. Writer on geol. topics. Home: Tulsa, Okla. Died Jan. 3, 1940.

MATSON, Henry, author, clergyman; b. Ellsworth, O., June 23, 1829; ed. Oberlin Coll. (A.M.); grad. Oberlin Theol. Sem., 1861; filled various pastorates, Mass. and Ohio, 1861-72; librarian Oberlin Coll., 1874-87; unmarried. Author: References for Literary Workers, 1892; Knowledge and Culture, 1895. Home: Oberlin, O. Died 1901.

MATSON, Roderick Nathaniel, lawyer; b. on farm, Town of Ira, N.Y., Nov. 1, 1871; s. William Townsend and Sarah Jane (Brackett) M.; A.B., Franklin Coll., New Athens, O., 1894, A.M., 1897; studied law in office of Waters, McLennan & Waters, Syracuse; LL.B., Syracuse U., 1897, LL.D., 1927; m. Alice May Warkley, Dec. 18, 1917. Admitted to N.Y. bar, 1897, and began practice at Syracuse as mem. Matson & Kennedy; firm moved to Cheyenne, Wyo., 1901; mem. Wyo. Ho. of Rep., 1903-05; apptd. judge 1st Jud. Dist. of Wyo., by Gov. Bryant B. Brooks and elected to same office, 1906, for term of 6 yrs.; again mem. Matson & Kennedy, 1913-21, alone, 1921-28; mem. Matson & Swainson, 1928—; alternate del. from N.Y. to Rep. Nat. Conv., 1900, del. at large from Wyo., 1924; v.p. and chmn. for Wyo., Nat. Hoover-Curtis Lawyers Assn., 1928. Apptd. commr. of U.S. to Internat. Expn., at Seville, Spain, 1926. Trustee Wyo. State U., 1922-23. Fellow Am. Geog. Soc. Republican. Mason, Elk. Home: Cheyenne, Wyo. Died Feb. 14, 1933.

MATSON, Smith Corbin, lawyer; b. Greencastle, Ind., Sept. 13, 1872; s. Courtland Cushing and Mary Nelson (Farrow) M.; student DePauw U., Greencastle, 1889-92; m. Nancy Jane Gwin, June 7, 1911. Began practice at Greencastle, 1893; pros. atty. 13th Jud. Circuit, Ind., 1900-05; removed to Ardmore, Okla., 1906; asst. county atty., Carter Co., Okla., 1907-10; asst. atty. gen. of Okla., 1910-17; judge Criminal Court of Appeals, Okla., 1917-25; resumed practice of law; asst. attorney gen. of Okla., 1931—. Democrat. Mason, Elk. Home: Oklahoma City, Okla. Died Feb. 9, 1936.

MATSON, William; b. in Sweden, Oct. 18, 1849; ed. in Sweden. Went to sea for 1 yr. at age of 10, and later adopted a seafaring life; has been identified with shipping business at San Francisco, 1863—; built a vessel to operate between San Francisco and the Hawaiian Islands, 1882, the business developing into the Matson Navigation Co., San Francisco, of which is pres.; also pres. Honolulu Consolidated Oil Co., Commercial Petroleum Co., Wonder Water Co. Died Oct. 11, 1917.

MATTESON, Charles, judge; b. Coventry, Kent Co., R.I., Mar. 21, 1840; s. Asahel and Julia (Johnson) M.; A.M., Brown U., 1861 (LL.D., 1891); law student, Harvard, 1862-63; m. Belle Himes, Aug. 22, 1872. Admitted to bar, 1864; mem. R.I. Senate, 1870-71, 1871-72; asso. justice, 1875-91, chief justice, 1891-1900, Supreme Ct. of R.I.; resigned. Pres. R.I. Humane Edn. Soc., 1914—. Dir. Centreville Nat. Bank of Warwick, Jan. 10, 1871—, v.p. Jan. 20, 1913—. Home: Providence, R.I. Died Aug. 14, 1925.

MATTESON, Frank Willington, trustee; s. George W. R. and Emily Robinson (Kent) M.; Ph.B., Brown U., 1892; m. Mary W. Fleming; 1 son, Kent Fleming. Pres. Shawmut Iron Co., Prov., Warren & Bristol R.R. Co., Prov. Terminal Co.; v.p. Providence Instn. for Savings; treas. Butler Hosp., Narragansett Land Co., Brown Land Co., Gilman Land Co., dir. Blackstone Mfg. Co., R.I. Hosp. Trust Co., Providence Gas Co., etc. Trustee Brown U. (treas.). Republican. Home: Providence, R.I. Died Mar. 19, 1933.

MATTHEW, William Diller, paleontologist; b. St. John, N.B., Can., Feb. 19, 1871; s. George Frederic and Katherine Mary (Diller) M.; A.B., U. of N.B., 1889; Ph.B., Columbia, 1893, A.M., 1894, Ph.D., 1895; m. Kate Lee, July 15, 1905; children—Elizabeth Lee, Margaret Mary, William Pomeroy. Asst., 1895-98, asst. curator, 1898-1902, asso. curator, 1902-10, curator, 1911-25, curator-in-chief, Div. I, 1922-27, Am. Mus. Natural History; prof. paleontology, U. of Calif., 1927—. Fellow N.Y. Acad. Sciences, Geol. Soc. America, Paleontol. Soc., A.A.A.S., N.Y. Zoöl. Soc., Royal Soc. (London). Home: Berkeley, Calif. Died Sept. 24, 1930.

MATTHEWMAN, Lisle de Vaux, journalist; b. Barnsley, Yorkshire, Eng., Feb. 23, 1867; s. Charles and Jane (Exley) M.; ed. England and Continent (Inst. Delessert, Switzerland, and Univ. of Berlin); unmarried. In journalism, 1892—; Sept. 1900 to Sept. 1902, lit. editor, dramatic critic, leader and spl. writer Phila. Evening Telegraph. Author: Crankisms, 1901; Brevities, 1903; Rips and Raps, 1903. Home: New York, N.Y. Deceased.

MATTHEWS, (James) Brander, author; b. New Orleans, La., Feb. 21, 1852; s. Edward and Virginia (Brander) M.; A.B., Columbia, 1871, LL.B., 1873, A.M., 1874, LL.D., 1904; D.C.L., U. of South, 1899; Litt.D., Yale, 1901; LL.D., Miami, 1909; m. Ada S. Smith, of London, Eng., May 10, 1873. Admitted to bar, 1873, but turned to lit.; prof. lit., 1892-1900, dramatic lit., 1900-24, Columbia. One of founders of Authors and Players Clubs; one of organizers Am. Copyright League, Dunlap Soc.; chancellor Am. Acad. Arts and Letters, 1922-24; pres. Modern Lang. Assn. America, 1910, Nat. Inst. of Arts and Letters, 1913-14, Dunlap Soc., 1914—. Trustee of Columbia University Press. Legion of Honor from French Govt., 1907, officer, 1922. Author: The Theatres of Paris; French Dramatists of the Nineteenth Century; In Partnership (with H. C. Bunner); Margery's Lovers (a comedy); The Last Meeting (a story); A Secret of the Sea and Other Stories; A Gold Mine (a comedy, with G. H. Jessop); Pen and Ink; A Family Free, and Other Stories; On Probation (a comedy, with G. H. Jessop); With My Friends; In the Vestibule Limited; A Tale of Twenty-Five Hours; Tom Paulding; Americanisms and Briticisms; The Decision of the Court (a comedy); The Story of a Story; Studies of the Stage; Vignettes of Manhattan; The Royal Marine; This Picture and That; His Father's Son; Bookbindings, Old and New; Introduction to the Study of American Literature; Tales of Fantasy and Fact; Aspects of Fiction; Outlines in Local Color; Peter Stuyvesant, a comedy (with Bronson Howard); A Confident To-Morrow; The Action and the Word; The Historical Novel; Parts of Speech; Development of the Drama; Recreations of an Anthologist; Inquiries and Opinions; The American of the Future; A Study of the Drama, 1910; Molière, 1910; A Study of Versification, 1911; Shakespeare as a Playwright, 1913; A Book About the Theater, 1916; These Many Years, 1917; Principles of Playmaking, 1919; Essays on English, 1921; Playwrights on Playmaking, 1923. Died Mar. 31, 1929.

MATTHEWS, Edmund Orville, rear adm. U.S.N.; b. Baltimore, Oct. 24, 1836; s. John and Mary Righter (Levering) M.; apptd. to U.S. Naval Acad. from Mo., 1851, grad. 1855; m. Hattie R. Hammond, of Newport, R.I., May 20, 1878. Promoted passed midshipman, Apr. 15, 1858; advanced through grades to rear adm., June 19, 1897. Served on Potomac and Saratoga, Home Squadron, 1855-58; Macedonian, Mediterranean Squadron, 1858-60; Naval Acad., 1860-61; Wabash, May-Nov. 1861; capture of forts at Hatteras Inlet; Naval Acad., 1861-64; S. Atlantic Blockading Squadron, 1864-65; comd. naval light arty. at Honey Hill, S.C., Nov. 30, 1864; participated in battle at Tullifinny Cross Roads, Dec. 1864; on staff of Admiral Dahlgren, Jan.-July 1865; comd. Savannah, Aug.-Nov. 1865; Naval Acad., 1865-69; head of torpedo corps, 1869-73; comd. Ashuelot, 1874-77; insp. ordnance, Navy Yard, New York, 1878-81; comd. Powhatan, 1881-83, training-ship New

Hampshire, 1883-84; mem. of Gun Foundry Bd., 1883-85; comd. Brooklyn, 1885-87; capt. of yard, Navy Yard, Boston, 1887-90; comd. receiving-ship Wabash, 1890-91; mem. Bd. of Inspection and Survey, 1891-94; chief Bur. of Yards and Docks, 1894-98; pres. Examining and Retiring Bds., 1898-99; retired, Oct. 24, 1898. Home: Cambridge, Mass. Died 1911.

MATTHEWS, Franklin, editor; b. St. Joseph, Mich., May 14, 1858; s. J. H. and Mary (Force) M.; A.B., Cornell U., 1883; followed by 1 yr. post-grad. work, but not for degree; m. Mary Crosby, 1886. Traveled as lecture agt. for J. B. Pond, with Beecher, Mark Twain, Carl Schurz, and others, 1883-86; reporter and editor Philadelphia Press, 1886-90; editor, reporter, The Sun, New York, 1890-1909; corr. The Sun on U.S. Atlantic Fleet's cruise around the world, Dec. 1907-Feb. 1909; asst. Sunday editor, 1912, night city editor, 1913—, New York Times. Associate in journalism, 1912-14, asso. prof., 1914—, Columbia University. Trustee, Cornell U., 1913. Author: Philadelphia, 1889 (printed for private circulation among Pan-Am. delegates); Our Navy in Time of War, 1899; The New-Born Cuba, 1899; With the Battle Fleet, 1908; Back to Hampton Roads, 1909. Compiler of Casual Essays of The Sun, 1905. Home: Woodhaven, L.I., N.Y. Died Nov. 26, 1917.

MATTHEWS, George Edward, editor; b. Westfield, N.Y., Mar. 17, 1855; s. James N. and Harriet (Wells) M.; A.B., Yale, 1877; m. Elizabeth Burrows, of Buffalo, N.Y., July 11, 1887. Editor Buffalo Express, 1889—, succeeding his father; also head The Matthews-Northrup Works, printers and publishers. Home: Grand Island, Erie Co., N.Y. Died 1911.

MATTHEWS, J(oseph) Merritt, chemist; b. Phila., June 9, 1874; s. Joseph Merritt and Blanche (Fowler) M.; B.Sc., U. of Pa., 1895, Ph.D., 1898; m. Augusta Spalding Gould, May 15, 1903. Head dept. chemistry and dyeing, Phila. Textile Sch., 1898-1907; mgr. of dyeing dept. of N.E. Cotton Yarn Co., 1907-10; consulting chemist, and expert in textile chemistry and dyestuffs, 1910—. Editor of Color Trade Jour., 1917—. Member National Research Council, etc. Author: Vol. III, Part I, on Dyestuffs, Allen's Commercial Organic Analysis, 1900; Textile Fibres, 1924; Laboratory Manual Dyeing and Textile Chemistry, 1909; Application of Dyestuffs, 1920; Bleaching Technology, 1921. Translator: Alexieff's General Principles of Organic Syntheses, 1906. Home: San Diego, Calif. Died 1931.

MATTHEWS, Mark Allison, clergyman; b. Calhoun, Ga., Sept. 24, 1867; s. Mark Lafayette and Malinda Rebecca (Clemmons) M.; acad. edn. at Calhoun; D.D., 1900; LL.D., Whitman Coll., 1908, Huron Coll., 1912; m. at Seattle, Grace Owen, d. Rev. Owen Jones, of Wales, Aug. 24, 1904. Began preaching at 19; ordained Presbyn. ministry, 1887; pastor First Ch. (which he built), Calhoun, Ga., 1888-93, Dalton, Ga., 1893-96, Jackson, Tenn., 1896-1902, First Ch., Seattle, 1902—. Admitted to bar June 1900. Trustee Whitman College, Walla Walla, Wash., Whiteworth Coll., Spokane, Wash., San Francisco Theol. Sem., Seattle Chamber of Commerce. Mem. Federal Council of Chs. and Ministers' Assn. Mason. Moderator Gen. Assembly Presbyn. Ch., Louisville, 1912. Home: Seattle, Wash. Died Feb. 5, 1940.

MATTHEWS, Nathan, lawyer; b. Boston, Mar. 28, 1854; s. Nathan and Albertine (Bunker) M.; A.B., Harvard, 1875, LL.B., 1880, LL.D., 1909; m. Ellen B., d. Col. Lucius Manlius Sargent, Apr. 5, 1883. In practice at Boston, 1880—. Mayor, 4 terms, 1891-95; chmn. Boston Finance Commn., 1907-09. Lecturer dept. of govt., Harvard, 1909-10 and 1911-12. Pres. Franklin Foundation; chmn. Salem and Beverly Water Supply Bd., 1913-23; chmn. trustees Mass. State Library. Spl. counsel U.S. R.R. Administration, 1918-19; chmn. Boston Com. on the Budget System, 1916; chmn. Boston Com. on New Sources of Revenue, 1920-21. Democrat. Author: The City Government of Boston, 1895; Municipal Charters, 1914. Home: Boston, Mass. Died Dec. 11, 1927.

MATTHEWS, Nelson Edwin, congressman; b. Ottawa, O., Apr. 14, 1852; s. John K. and Catherine (Row) M.; ed. pub. schs.; m. Grace C. Pugh, Dec. 20, 1877. Entered employ of C. H. Rice & Co., now the Putnam County Banking Co., Ottawa, 1872; became partner, 1878, later pres.; retired, 1911; dir. Putnam Telephone Co., Ottawa. Mem. Ohio Constl. Conv., 1912; mem. 64th Congress (1915-17), 5th Ohio Dist. Pres. Business Men's Club, Ottawa, 1910—. Presbyn. Mason. Home: Defiance, O. Died 1917.

MATTHEWS, Washington, physician, maj. U.S.A., retired, Sept. 25, 1895; b. Killiney, nr. Dublin, Ireland, July 17, 1843; s. Dr. Nicholas Blaney and Anna (Burke) M.; came to U.S. in infancy; lived in Wis., later in Iowa; ed. in common schools; grad. Univ. of Iowa (med. dept.), 1864 (LL.D., 1888). Acting asst. surgeon U.S.A., 1864-65; re-entered mil. service, 1865; asst. surgeon, U.S.A., 1868; capt. and asst. surgeon, 1871; maj. and surgeon, 1889; retired from active service on account of disability contracted in line of duty. Was on duty at Army Med. Museum, 1884-90. Has made notable investigations in ethnology and philology of the Navajo Indians and other native American races. Author: Navajo Silversmiths, 1883; Navajo Weavers, 1884; The Mountain Chant, a Navajo Ceremony, 1887; Navajo Legends, 1897; The Night Chant, a Navajo Ceremony, 1902. Home: Washington, D.C. Died 1905.

MATTHEWS, William Baynham, lawyer; b. Lynchburg, Va., July 1850; s. James M. and Ellen B. M.; bro. of George Bagby M.; deputy clerk of Essex Co., Va., 1866-70; took law course, U. of Va., 1870-71, B.L., 1873; LL.M., Columbian (now George Washington) U., 1882; m. Alice P., youngest d. Carolinus Turner of Belle Grove, Va., Jan. 12, 1875. Chief preëmption div. U.S. Gen. Land Office, 1883-89; editor and publisher National Domain, 1888; atty. for State of Idaho, 1892-96; Washington atty. Rio Grande Western Ry. Co., 1898—. Author: Matthews' Forms of Pleading, etc., 1873; Guide for Executors and Administrators, 1872; Digest Land Decisions, 1888; Matthews' Guide, 1889, 1895. Deceased.

MATTICE, Burr, jurist; b. Jefferson, N.Y., July 10, 1856; s. George and Dellissa (Pickett) M.; grad. Oneonta High Sch., 1876; studied law; m. Charlotte L. Johnson, Oct. 20, 1880. Admitted to N.Y. bar, Sept. 1880; dist. atty. Otsego Co., 1889-92; co. judge Otsego Co., 1893-95; apptd. justice Supreme Court, 6th jud. dist. N.Y., Dec. 31, 1895; to succeed Judge Martin, and elected, 1896, for full term expiring Dec. 31, 1910. Republican. Home: Oneonta, N.Y. Deceased.

MATTINGLY, William Francis, lawyer; b. in D.C., 1837; Ph.B. Columbian (now George Washington) U., 1857 (hon. A.M., 1862, LL.D., 1901). Mem. Bar Assn. of D.C., etc.; del. Universal Congress Lawyers and Jurists, St. Louis, 1904. Home: Washington, D.C. Died Oct. 7, 1918.

MATTISON, Fitch Champlin Edmonds, M.D., surgeon; b. Louisville, Ky., May 4, 1861; s. Samuel J. and Catherine (Jennings) M.; prep. edn., Z. T. Pindells' Acad., Annapolis, Md., and Md. Inst., Baltimore; M.D., Coll. Phys. and Surgeons, Chicago, 1888; m. Helen Blake, Dec. 28, 1890 (dec.); 1 dau., Bess (Mrs. Ernst Behr). Began practice at Chicago, 1888; moved to Pasadena, Calif., 1898; chmn. staff and chmn. med. bd. Los Angeles Gen. Hosp.; dir. 1st Nat. Bank, 1st Trust & Savings. Chmn. and treas. Los Angeles County Med. Milk Commn. Fellow Am. Coll. Surgeons. Mem. bd. regents Pacific Geog. Society. Mason. Home: Pasadena, Calif. Deceased.

MATTISON, Richard Vanselous, mfr.; b. Solebury Tp., Pa., Nov. 17, 1851; s. Joseph Jones and Mahala (Vanselous) M.; Ph.G., Phila. Coll. of Pharmacy, 1873; M.D., U. of Pa., 1879; m. Esther Dafter, Nov. 4, 1874 (died 1919); children—Richard Vanselous, Royal; m. 2d, Mary E. Cottrell Seger, Apr. 27, 1920. Established as mfg. chemist, 1873; chmn. Keasbey & Mattison Co., mfrs. of magnesia and asbestos products, also mfrs. Bromo-Caffeine and other pharm. preparations; chmn. Ambler Asbestos Shingle Sheathing Co.; pres. Ambler Spring Water Co., Upper Dublin Water Co. Home: Ambler, Pa. Died Nov. 18, 1936.

MATTOCKS, Charles Porter, soldier; b. Danville, Vt., Oct. 11, 1840; s. Henry and Martha (Porter) M.; A.B., Bowdoin, 1862; A.M., 1865; served in 17th Me. Inf. as lt., Aug. 2, 1862; capt., Dec. 4, 1862; maj., Dec. 22, 1863; col., May 15, 1865; comd. 1st U.S. Sharpshooters in winter and spring of 1864. Bvtd.: col. vols., Apr. 9, 1865, "for gallant and meritorious services during campaign ending with surrender of Gen. R. E. Lee"; brig. gen. vols., Mar. 13, 1865, "for faithful and meritorious services"; awarded Congressional Medal of Honor, May 29, 1899, "for extraordinary gallantry at Little Sailor's Creek, Va.," Apr. 6, 1865. LL.B., Harvard, 1867, and from then in practice at Portland; m. June 27, 1871. County atty. Cumberland Co., Me., 1869-72; mem. Me. Ho. of Rep., 1880-84; mem. exec. commn. for Me., Chicago Expn., 1893; probate judge 1900-07. Republican. Brig. gen vols., June 8-Oct. 31, 1898, Spanish-Am. War. Home: Portland, Me. Died 1910.

MATTOON, Arthur Martyn, astronomer; b. Maxtown, O., Sept. 12, 1855; s. Henry Martyn and Julia Ledyard (Hempstead) M.; A.B., Marietta (O.) Coll., 1880, A.M., 1883; U. of Cambridge, Eng., 1903-04; m. Eliza Alberta Bailey, Aug. 2, 1882. Instr. mathematics, Albany (Ore.) Coll., 1880-83, Coll. of Mont., 1883-87; prin. Bozeman (Mont.) Acad., 1887-89; prof. mathematics, Blackburn Coll., Carlinville, Ill., 1889-90; prin. Elgin (Ill.) Acad., 1890-91; prof. mathematics and astronomy and dir. Charles Smith Scott Obs. of Park Coll., Parkville, Mo., 1892-1912, prof. emeritus, 1912-17; prof. mathematics and astronomy, Albany (Ore.) Coll., 1917—. Author: Essentials of Plane and Spherical Trigonometry, 1895 (3d edit., 1907); Introduction to the Theory of Equations, 1906. Died Jan. 7, 1924.

MATZ, Nicholas, bishop; b. Münster, Alsace-Lorraine, Apr. 6, 1850; ed. in Petit Seminaire, Finstingen; came to U.S., 1868; prepared for priesthood in old Mt. St. Mary's Sem. of the West, Cincinnati. Ordained R.C. priest, 1874; asst. pastor cathedral, Denver, Colo., 1874-77; pastor Georgetown, Colo., 1877-85; later of St. Anne's, E. Denver, till consecrated titular bishop of Telmessa and coadjutor, Oct. 28, 1887, bishop of Denver, July 10, 1889. Died Aug 9, 1917.

MATZ, Philip Benjamin, pathologist; b. Baltimore, Md., Aug. 25, 1885; s. Oscar and Freda (Kaplan) M.; Litt.B., Mather Coll., Kansas City, Kan., 1911; M.D., Coll. of Medicine, L.I. Coll. Hosp., 1908; m. Eleanor Crampton, Nov. 20, 1913. Has specialized in pathology and clin. investigation; served as chief of lab. service, Base Hosp., Camp Travis, Tex., World War; commissioned as surgeon (Res.) U.S.P.H.S., 1920, and served as chief lab. service various hosps. of the U.S. Pub. Health Service; chief of Med. Research Subdivision, Veterans' Adminstrn., 1925—. Fellow Am. Soc. Clin. Pathologists, Am. Coll. Physicians. Home: Washington, D.C. Died June 25, 1938.

MATZ, Rudolph, lawyer; b. Chicago, Dec. 11, 1860; s. Otto H. and Mary E. (Lewis) M.; A.B., Williams Coll., 1882; LL.B., Northwestern U., 1886; m. Florence H. Henderson, Nov. 19, 1890. Mem. law firm Matz, Fisher & Boyden, Chicago; dir. Chicago Savings Bank & Trust Co., United Shoe Machinery Co., Chicago Auditorium Assn. Pres. Legal Aid Soc. Chicago; trustee Civic Federation; mem. exec. com. Western Soc. for Suppression of Vice; trustee Winnetka Congl. Ch. Republican. Home: Hubbard Woods, Ill. Died Mar. 15, 1917.

MATZEN, Herman N., sculptor; b. Denmark, July 15, 1861; s. Nicolai Edinger and Henrietta (Rasch) M.; came to U.S. in boyhood; grad. German-Am. Sem., Detroit, Royal Acad. Fine Arts, Berlin (medal of 2d class, 1896); m. Emma Hale (died 1897); m. 2d, Blanche Dissette, July 11, 1908. Engaged in sculpture, 1893—; executed groups "War" and "Peace," Indianapolis Soldiers' and Sailors' Monument; also Schiller Monument, Detroit, and other patriotic monuments; Burke mausoleum, figures Moses and Gregory, Cleveland Ct. House; figures Law and Justice, Akron (O.) Ct. House; Richard Wagner monument; memorial to Tom L. Johnson, Pub. Sq., Cleveland; Haserot Memorial, Cleveland; City Hall sculptures, Cleveland. Awarded medal Great Berlin Expn. Unitarian. Home: Cleveland, O. Died Apr. 22, 1938.

MATZKE, John Ernst, university prof.; b. Breslau, Germany, Oct. 20, 1862; s. Rev. H. M. M.; A.B., Hope Coll., Mich., 1882; Ph.D., Johns Hopkins, 1888; m. Edith Virginia Hedges, June 26, 1895. Prof. French, Bowdoin Coll., 1889-90; prof. Romanic langs., Ind. U., 1890-91; asso. in Romanic langs., Johns Hopkins, 1891-93; prof. Romanic langs., Leland Stanford Jr. U., 1893—. Advisory editor Modern Philology, 1903—. Died 1910.

MAUCHLY, Sebastian Jacob, physicist; b. Swanton, O., July 9, 1878; s. John William and Mary Jane (Ziegler) M.; A.B., U. of Cincinnati, 1911, Ph.D., 1913; studied U. of Chicago; m. Rachel Elizabeth Scheidemantel, Dec. 27, 1905; children—John William, Helen Elizabeth. Prin. and instr. physics, Hartwell High Sch., Cincinnati, 1905-11; Hanna research fellow, dept. of physics, U. of Cincinnati, 1911-13; head dept. of physics Woodward High Sch., Cincinnati, 1913-14; apptd. asso. physicist, Dept. Terrestrial Magnetism Carnegie Instn. of Washington, Nov. 1, 1914; asst. chief obs. div. same, 1917-18, and chief of sect. terrestrial electricity same, Jan. 1, 1919—. Fellow Am. Physical Soc., A.A.A.S. Presbyn. Mason. Co-author of Vol. V, Researches Dept. of Terestrial Magnetism (Carnegie Instn., Washington), 1926. Research in earth currents and in elec. conduction in gases, including atmospheric electricity. Home: Chevy Chase, Md. Died Dec. 24, 1928.

MAUCK, Joseph William, college pres.; b. Cheshire, O., Aug. 17, 1852; s. Joseph and Adaline (Sigler) M.; A.B., Hillsdale (Mich.) Coll., 1875, A.M., 1877; LL.D. Hillsdale Coll., 1895, and U. of South Dakota, 1927; partial post-grad. course Johns Hopkins; m. Mary Frances Ball, Dec. 25, 1884; children—Mrs. Ruth Viola Walrath, Mrs. Joy Katherine Hayes, Mrs. Doris Lucina Friedrichs, Willfred O. Prof. Greek, 1876-79, Latin, 1881-83, Hillsdale Coll.; in pub. and banking business, Chicago and Minneapolis, 1883-91; pres. U. of S.D., 1891-97; in mfg. and railroading, Chicago, 1897-1902; pres. Hillsdale Coll., 1902-22, emeritus. Pres. Gen. Conf. Free Baptists, 1904—; mem. Federal Council of Chs. from its orgn.; pres. Mich. Sch. Masters' Club, 1915-16; del. to Universal Christian Conf., Stockholm, 1925, and to World Conf. on Faith and Order, Lausanne, 1927; v.p. Am. Bapt. Publication and Hist. societies. Republican. Mason. Kiwanian. Home: Hillsdale, Mich. Died July 7, 1937.

MAULDIN, Frank Gratin, army officer; b. in Pickens County, S.C., Aug. 16, 1864; s. Joab and Deborah Reed (Hollingsworth) M.; grad. U.S. Military Acad., 1890; LL.B., Columbian (now George Washington) U., 1893; grad. Sch. of Submarine Defense, Ft. Totten, N.Y., 1904; unmarried. Commd. additional 2d lt. 3d Arty., June 12, 1890; promoted through grades to brig. gen. N.A., Aug. 5, 1917. Instr. law and history, U.S. Mil. Acad., 4 yrs.; served under Gen. Shafter in Cuba, 1898; comdr. of one of U.S.A. mine planters 4 yrs.; with Insp. General's Dept., 1910-13; later comdr. the Presidio, Calif., and Recruit Depot, Ft. Slocum, N.Y.; assigned as comdr. 59th Field Arty. Brigade, Camp Cody, N.M., Sept. 1917. Died Jan. 25, 1940.

MAURAN, John Lawrence, architect; b. Providence, R.I., Nov. 19, 1866; s. Frank and Mary Louise (Nichols) M.; student Mass. Inst. Tech., 1885-89; traveled and studied in Europe, 1889-90; in office of Shepley, Rutan & Coolidge, architects, Boston, 2 yrs., then in their Chicago office working on the Chicago Public Library and Chicago Art Inst.; rep. same firm at St. Louis, 1893, later becoming St. Louis partner; m. Isabel, d. J. G. Chapman, of St. Louis, 1896; children—Isabel Lawrence (Mrs. William V. V. Warren), Elizabeth Chapman (Mrs. Charles Mullikin). Mem. Mauran, Russell & Garden, 1900, Mauran, Russell & Crowell, 1911—. Principal works: St. Louis Union Trust Co., New Bank of Commerce Bldg., Butler Bros. bldgs. (St. Louis and Dallas), Ry. Exchange, St. Louis Country Club, Galvez Hotel (Galveston), Rice Hotel (Houston), Skin and Cancer, and Children's hosps., Federal Reserve Bank, Southwestern Bell Telephone Office Bldg. Mem. Pub. Library Bd., 1906 (v.p. 1926—); dir. Mercantile Library, 1906 (pres. 1908-09); dir. Mercantile Trust Co., 1924—; dir. Skin and Cancer Hosp., 1909—; bd. control St. Louis Mus. Fine Arts, 1906-10; advisory bd. Home for Friendless, 1912—. Presdl. elector, 1908; mem. Fine Arts Commission, 1908, Nat. Commn. Fine Arts, 1930; apptd. chmn. Public Buildings Commn. St. Louis, 1904; pres. St. Louis Grand Opera Com., 1910-12; chmn. "Made in St. Louis" Carnival, 1915; mem. exec. com. St. Louis Community Council, 1924-29; pres. Plaza Commn., 1925—; U.S. del. 6th Internat. Congress Architects, Madrid, 1904; fellow A.I.A. (treas. 1913-15, pres. 1916-18); sec. St. Louis Chapter A.I.A., 1900-02, pres., 1902-04; mem. corp. Mass. Inst. Tech., 1925-29. Dir. St. Louis Chapter Am. Red Cross (mem. exec. com. 1917-28, chmn. of same, 1922-28); mem. sub-com. industrial safety War Industries Bd., 1917-18, com. on contracts, Council Nat. Defense, 1917-18; sec. commn. on contracts, Construction Div., U.S.A., 1918; chmn. canteen and mil. relief coms., St. Louis Chapter A.R.C., 1918-19; chmn. purchasing com., Hosp. Unit 21, 1917-19; mem. Mil. Intelligence U.S.A., 1918. Pres. trustees Ch. of the Messiah (Unitarian), 1900-20. Mem. Republican State Com., 1926-29. Home: St. Louis, Mo. Died Sept. 23, 1933.

MAURER, William Allen, lawyer; b. Altoona, Pa., Oct. 25, 1872; s. George and Eliza (McCartney) M.; ed. pub. schs.; m. Hettie D. Evans, Dec. 30, 1897; children—Neal E., William Allen. Began practice at El Reno, Okla., 1894; city atty., 1899-1901; county judge, Canadian Co., 1911-15, 1919-22; U.S. dist. atty., by apptmt. of President Harding, Oct. 25, 1921. Presbyterian. Mason. Home: Oklahoma City, Okla. Died Apr. 23, 1929.

MAURITZSON, Jules Göte Ultimus, coll. prof.; b. Balkåkra, Sweden, July 19, 1868; s. Anders Vilhelm and Gustava Louise (Lagerlöf) M.; student Holsingborg Coll. and U. of Lund (Sweden), and Luth. Theol. Sem. (Chicago); B.D., Augustana Theol. Sem., Rock Island, Ill., 1899; post-grad. work U. of Upsala (Sweden), Copenhagen (Denmark), and Christiania (Norway); m. Maria Thorsson, June 23, 1899; children—Anna, Tyra, Elsa, Anders Vilhelm, Gunhild. Prof. Swedish lang. and lit., Augustana Coll., 1901—, and dean, 1921—. Mem. Soc. Advancement Scandinavian Study (pres. 1913-15), etc. Lutheran. Decorated by King of Sweden, Knight Royal Order North Star, 1924. Author: Swedish Orthography, 1908. Home: Rock Island, Ill. Died Feb. 7, 1930.

MAURY, Carlotta Joaquina, paleontologist; b. Hastings-on-Hudson, N.Y., Jan. 6, 1874; d. Mytton and Virginia (Draper) M.; studied at Radcliffe Coll., Columbia, U. of Paris; Ph.B., Cornell U., 1896, Schuyler fellow, 1898, Ph.D., 1902, Sarah Berliner fellow, 1916. Asst. in dept. of paleontology, Columbia, 1904-06, La. Geol. Survey, 1907-09; lecturer on geology, Barnard Coll. (Columbia), 1909-12; paleontologist, Venezuelan Geol. Expdn., 1910-11; prof. geology and zoölogy, Huguenot Coll. (U. of Cape of Good Hope), S. Africa, 1912-15; organized Maury expdn. to Dominican Republic, 1916; cons. paleontologist Royal Dutch Shell Petroleum Co.; paleontologist Brazilian Govt.; has made a specialty of study of Antillean, Venezuelan and Brazilian stratigraphy and fossil faunas. Fellow Geol. Soc. America, A.A.A.S., Am. Geog. Soc. Author: Eocene of Trinidad, 1912; Dominican Type Sections and Fossils, 1917; Mollusca Gulf of Mexico, 1922; Miocene of Trinidad, 1925; Tertiary and Cretaceous of Brazil, 1925; Silurian of Santa Catharine, 1927; Silurian of Para, 1929; Puerto Rican, Dominican, and Soldado Stratigraphy and New Formational Names, 1929-31; Cretaceous of Parahyba do Norte, 1930; Bartonian and Ludian Upper Eocene in the Western Hemisphere, 1931; Cretaceous of Sergipe, Brazil; Triassic and Cretaceous of Northeastern Brazil, 1934; Lovenilampas, A New Echinoidean Genus from the Brazilian Cretaceous, 1934; New Genera and New Species of Fossil Terrestrial Mollusca from the States of Rio de Janeiro and São Paulo, Brazil, 1935. Home: Yonkers, N. Y. Died Jan. 3, 1938.

MAURY, Dabney Herndon, author, soldier; b. Fredericksburg, Va., May 21, 1822; grad. Univ. of Va.; and at West Point, 1846; entered Mounted Rifles, June 1846; served in Mexico; marched from Point Isabel to Monterey, thence to Vera Cruz; seriously wounded and bvtd. for gallantry at Cerro Gordo; became instr. in belles lettres at West Point; later regimental adjutant and supt. cavalry instruction, Carlisle Barracks; in 1861 was capt. and adj. gen., Dept. of New Mexico, but resigned upon secession of Va. Was col. Confederate army; promoted to brig. gen. for conduct in Elkhorn campaign; held Grant in check at Grenada during Van Dorn's raid, 1864. With Stephenson and Stephen D. Lee defeated Sherman's army before Vicksburg, Dec. 28, 1864. Later in command of Dept. of Tenn., then of Dept. of Gulf until May 24, when he was paroled prisoner of war with his forces. U.S. minister to United States of Colombia, 1885-89. Author: System of Tactics in Single Rank (published 1859 and now universally used); Recollections of a Virginian; History of Virginia. Home: Richmond, Va. Died 1900.

MAURY, Dabney Herndon, consulting engr.; b. Vicksburg, Miss., Mar. 9, 1863; s. Dabney Herndon and Nannie Rose (Mason) M.; grad. Va. Mil. Inst., 1882; M.E., Stevens Inst. Tech., 1884; m. Mary McCaw, Apr. 26, 1893; 1 son, Dabney H. Civ. and mining engr. in Colombia, S.A., 1887-92; in practice of engring., Peoria, Ill., 1893-1912; consulting engr. on hydraulic and sanitary work, Chicago, 1917-27 (retired). Adv. engr. on water supply to constrn. div. of the Army, May 1917-June 1919; commd. maj., Engr. R.C., 1917; lt. col., Q.M.C., 1918; hon. discharged, May 31, 1919. Episcopalian. Home: Chevy Chase, Md. Died May 11, 1933.

MAURY, Mytton, clergyman; b. Liscard, opposite Liverpool, Eng., Jan. 18, 1839; s. William and Sarah Mytton (Hughes) M.; came to America, 1849; B.A., Columbia, 1857, M.A., 1860; Berkeley Div. Sch., Middletown, Conn., 1861-63; spl. course in biology, Mass. Inst. Tech., 1889-90; spl. course Cornell, 1896-97; (D.D., New York U., 1868); m. Virginia, elder d. John William Draper, of Hastings-on-Hudson, 1865; father of John William Draper. Deacon, 1861, priest, 1865, P.E. Ch.; rector St. Mary's-in-the-Highlands Ch., Cold Spring, N.Y., 1865-72, St. James', Fordham, N.Y., 1872-75, St. Thomas', New York, 1875; acting prof. physics and analyt. chemistry, U. of New York, 1883-85; rector St. James', Goshen, N.Y., 1885-88, St. Paul's, Halifax, N.S., 1892-93, St. John's, Rockland, N.Y., 1904—. Obtained, 1887, a writ of certiorari against Henry C. Potter, bishop of New York, and judgment against him with costs in Supreme Ct. of N.Y., Feb. 1888, establishing the fact that the Supreme Ct. is the court of appeal for a clergyman against a bishop. Editor: Maury's Geographical Series, 1875-95; Famous Men of Greece, Middle Ages and Modern Times, 1903-04. Home: Hastings-on-Hudson, N.Y. Died Aug. 4, 1919.

MAURY, Richard Brooke, physician; b. Georgetown, D.C., Feb. 5, 1834; s. Richard Brooke and Ellen (Magruder) M.; U. of Va.; M.D., U. of Va. Med. Sch., 1857, Univ. and Bellevue Hosp. Med. Coll. (New York U.), 1858; m. Jennie Poston, Oct. 10, 1876. In practice with Dr. R. W. Mitchell for 37 yrs.; retired; surgeon, 4 yrs. in Confederate army; prof. theory and practice of medicine, Memphis Med. Coll., 1869-72; prof. gynecology, Memphis Hosp. Med. Coll., 1885-97. Episcopalian. Home: Memphis, Tenn. Died Mar. 17, 1919.

MAURY, William Arden, lawyer; LL.B., Harvard, 1853; (LL.D., Columbian U., 1880). Asst. atty. gen. under President Harrison, 1889-93; now mem. Spanish Treaty Claims Commn. Prof. common law pleading, federal procedures, evidence, and ins., George Washington U. Mem. Washington Nat. Monument Soc.; mem. bd. visitors Govt. Hosp. for the Insane. Died June 15, 1918.

MAUS, L(ouis) Mervin, army officer; b. Burnt Mills, Montgomery Co., Md., May 8, 1851; s. Isaac Rhodes and Mary Malvina (Greer) M.; St. John's College, Annapolis, Md.; post graduate, Pasteur Inst., Paris, and medical clinics in Europe, 1890-91; M.D., U. of Maryland, 1874; m. Anna Page Russell, Jan. 5, 1876; children—Mary Thruston (wife of E. A. Fry, U.S.A.), Anna Louise (wife of L. Halstead, U.S.A.). Commd. 1st lt. asst. surgeon U.S.A., Nov. 10, 1874; advanced through grades to col. asst. surgeon gen., May 10, 1907. Served in South, 1874-77; on the plains, 1877-93; participated in several Indian campaigns and was recommended for medal of honor for exceptional bravery, Nov. 5, 1877; chief surgeon 7th Army Corps in Cuba during Spanish-Am. War; 1st commr. pub. health of P.I. under William H. Taft, then gov.; made changes in sanitary conditions reducing mortality of native population from 88 per 1000 to 32 per 1000; eradicated bubonic plague from Manila in 1902; in charge Asiatic cholera epidemic and by vaccination practically eliminated smallpox among the natives; chief surgeon, Central Division, 1911; department surgeon, Department of the East, 1912-15; retired from active service, May 8, 1915; Secretary Kentucky Tuberculosis Commn., Sept. 8, 1915-Jan. 1, 1917; placed on active duty, June 18, 1917, and assigned to the Council of Nat. Defense; dept. surgeon, Western Dept., San Francisco, Calif., 1917-19. Awarded D.S.M. Mason. Author: Army Officer on Leave in Japan, 1911; Glengyle Manor, 1937. Died Aug. 3, 1939.

MAUS, Marion Perry, brig. gen.; b. Burnt Mills, Montgomery Co., Md., Aug. 25, 1850; grad. U.S. Mil. Acad., 1874; m. Lindsay Poor, June 1899. Second lt. 1st Inf., June 17, 1874; promoted through grades to col. 20th Inf., Jan. 24, 1904; brig. gen. U.S.A., June 27, 1909. Had many yrs. service in campaigns against the Sioux, Apache, Cheyenne, Nez Perces, and other Indians; in action with Sioux Indians in the Black Hills, Dak., with the Nez Percés at Bear Paw Mountains, Mont.; with Apaches in Ariz., and Old Mexico, in the Sierra Madre Mountains; in the campaign at Pine Ridge against the Sioux, 1890, awarded Congressional Medal of Honor, Nov. 27, 1894, "for most distinguished gallantry in action against hostile Apache Indians in Sierra Madre Mountains, N.M., Jan. 11, 1886." Went with Gen. Miles to observe the Græco-Turkish War, to represent the govt. at the Queen's Jubilee in England, 1897; and also to witness the manœuvres of Russia, Germany and France; served throughout Spanish-Am. War as insp. gen.; present during last days of siege and during negotiations for surrender of Santiago, Cuba; accompanied expdn. to Puerto Rico, remaining there until signing of protocol for peace; later on duty as insp. gen. Dept. of Calif. and the Columbia; a.d.c. on staff lt. gen. comdg. the army July 1, 1901-03; served in P.I., 1903-06; on duty at San Francisco during earthquake, Apr. 1906; comd. Presidio of Monterey, Pacific Div., Dept. of Calif., etc., 1906-09; comdg. Dept. of the Columbia, 1909; retired. Died Feb. 9, 1930.

MAUZÉ, Joseph Layton, clergyman; b. Montevideo, Va., Feb. 2, 1873; s. Joseph Nicholas and Margaret (Yancy) M.; student Augusta Mil. Acad., Fort Defiance, Va., 1889-90, Hampden-Sidney (Va.) Coll., 1893-96; grad. Union Theol. Sem., Richmond, Va., 1899; D.D., Westminster Coll., Fulton, Mo., 1913; m. Eleanor Harmon, Dec. 11, 1900; children—George Watts, Eugene Harmon, Eleanor Cameron, Joseph Layton, Margaret, Charles Warwick. Ordained ministry Presbyn. Ch. of U.S., 1899; pastor successively Timber Ridge and Fairfield chs., Va., 1899-1902, Central Ch., St. Louis, 1902-17, First Ch., Huntington, W.Va., 1917-28, Central Ch., Kansas City, Mo., Sept. 1928—. Trustee Synodical Coll. (Fulton, Mo.), Greenbrier Coll. (Lewisburg, W.Va.). Mem. Federal Council Chs. Died Apr. 25, 1937.

MAVER, William, Jr., electrical engr.; b. Forfar, Scotland, Oct. 12, 1851; s. William and Mary McNicol (Alexander) M.; brought to Montreal, Can., by parents, 1857; ed. private school; holds veteran's medal, Fenian raid campaign, 1865-66; fifer, 5th Royals, Montreal, Can.; m. Maryannie MacTavish, Nov. 22, 1876. Came to New York, 1873; capt. of Am. Athletic Club, 1877-79; elec. expert Western Union Telegraph Co., 1880-84; elec. engr. B.&O. Telegraph Co., 1884-87; with elec. dept. Western Union Telegraph Co., 1888; elec. engr. Safety Insulated Wire & Cable Co., 1889-90; electrician Consol. Telegraph & Electrical Subway Co., New York, 1889-96; elec. expert New York Heat, Light & Power Co., 1893-97; expert in much elec. patent litigation. Propr. Maver Pub. Co. Fellow Am. Inst. E.E. Mason. Presbyn. Author: The Quadruplex and Other Articles on Telegraphy, 1884; Practical Systems of Electrical Telegraphy, 1888; American Telegraphy and Encyclopedia of the Telegraph, 1892, revised edit., 1912 (used as text book in colls. and by Signal Corps, U.S.A.); Maver's Wireless Telegraphy and Telephony, 1903, 4th edit., 1910; Progress in Wireless Telegraphy, 1905. Home: Jersey City, N.J. Died Aug. 8, 1928.

MAXCY, Carroll Lewis, coll. prof.; b. Norristown, Pa., May 28, 1865; s. Eaton Whiting and J. Eliza (Lewis) M.; B.A., Williams Coll., 1887, M.A., 1892; m. Louise Hawley, June 26, 1895. Prof. English, 1898-1911, Morris prof. rhetoric, 1911—(emeritus 1935—), dean, 1917-19, v. chmn. faculty, 1920—, Williams Coll. Home: Williamstown, Mass. Died Aug. 7, 1936.

MAXEY, Edward Ernest, M.D.; b. Irvington, Ill., Aug. 21, 1867; s. Dr. W. C. and Sarah G. (Lane) M.; M.D. from Coll. Phys. and Surg., Chicago (gold medal), 1891; post-grad. study at Baltimore, Phila., New York, and 1 yr. in European clinics; m. Edna Horn, Dec. 19, 1900; children—Marie, Edward. Splty. eye, ear, nose and throat. Fellow Am. Coll. Surgeons, A.M.A. Commd. capt. Med. R.C., 1917, and in active service; maj., Feb. 1918. Home: Aberdeen, Wash. Died Aug. 31, 1934.

MAXEY, Thomas S., judge; b. Brandon, Miss., Sept. 1, 1846; s. Robert and Harriet Virginia M.; served in C.S.A., 1864-65; student U. of Miss., 1865-67; LL.B., U. of Va., 1869; (LL.D., U. of Miss., 1888, Tulane U., 1897); m. Lizzie Coffee, Oct. 12, 1871; m. 2d, Mary Frances Campbell, Sept. 25, 1878. Mem. Miss. Ho. of Rep., 1870; resigned; practiced at Jefferson, Tex., 1870-77, at Austin, 1877-88; U.S. dist. judge, Western Dist. of Tex., June 1888-Dec. 14, 1916, resigned. Democrat. Home: Austin, Tex. Died Dec. 5, 1921.

MAXFIELD, Ezra Kempton, prof. English; b. Winthrop, Me., Apr. 23, 1881; s. Benjamin Horace and

Laverna (Kempton) M.; grad. Coburn Classical Inst., Waterville, Me., 1900; A.B., Colby Coll., Waterville, 1905; spl. study U. of Pa., 1907-08; A.M., Harvard, 1911, Ph.D., 1920; m. Jane Ernisse Crowe, July 24, 1912; children—David Kempton, Susan Ernisse. Prin. high schs., Waldoboro, Me., 1905-06; teacher of science, Friends Central High Sch., Philadelphia, 1906-08; instr. in English, Del. State U., 1909-10, Haverford (Pa.) Coll., 1911, Simmons Coll., Boston, Mass., 1911-12; asst. prof. English, Colby Coll., 1912-16, U. of Rochester, 1916-17; prof. English Northeastern Coll., Boston, 1917-18; asst. in English, Harvard, 1919-20; prof. and head of dept. English, Washington and Jefferson Coll., 1920—. Republican. Quaker. Home: Washington, Pa. Died Jan. 8, 1941.

MAXIM, Hiram Percy, inventor, mech. engr.; b. Brooklyn, N.Y., Sept. 2, 1869; s. Sir Hiram Stevens and Louisa Jane (Budden) M.; grad. Sch. of Mechanic Arts of Mass. Inst. Tech., 1886 (youngest student in class); D.Sc., Colgate; m. Josephine, d. Gov. Hamilton of Md., Dec. 21, 1898; children—Hiram Hamilton, Percy (dau.). Elec. engr. Ft. Wayne (Ind.) Jenney Electric Co., 1886-87, W. S. Hill Electric Co., Boston, 1887-88, Thomson Elec. Welding Co., Lynn, Mass., 1888-90; supt. Am. Projectible Co., Lynn, 1890-95; chief engr. Electric Vehicle Co., Hartford, Conn., 1895-1907; pres. Maxim Silencer Co. (Hartford). Inventor elec. devices and ordnance, Columbia automobiles, the Maxim silencer, etc. Pres. Am. Radio Relay League, Internat. Amateur Radio Union. Republican. Unitarian. Lt. comdr. U.S.N.R. Author: Life's Place in the Cosmos, 1933. Home: Hartford, Conn. Died Feb. 17, 1936.

MAXIM, Hiram Stevens, inventor; b. Sangerville, Me., Feb. 5, 1840; s. Isaac Wetson and Harriet M.; common sch. edn.; scientific knowledge obtained by study and attending lectures; 4 yrs. apprentice to coach-building; worked in various iron works; m. Louisa Jane Budden; 2d, Sarah Haynes; father of Florence and Hiram Percy M. Has patented numerous inventions in U.S.; went to England, 1881; has patented many elec. inventions, including incandescent lamps, self-regulating current machines, etc.; invented the Maxim gun, automatic system of firearms, which makes the recoil of the gun serve as the power for reloading; also other ordnance inventions, "Cordite," a smokeless powder, and more recently has devoted much time and invention to aërial navigation; consulting engr. Vicker's Ltd. Knighted by Queen Victoria, 1901. Died Nov. 24, 1916.

MAXIM, Hudson, inventor, mech. engr.; b. Orneville Co., Me., Feb. 3, 1853; s. Isaac and Harriet Boston (Stevens) M.; ed. Me. Wesleyan Sem., Kent's Hill, Me.; D.Sc., Heidelberg, 1913; LL.D., St. Peters, 1918; m. Jane Morrow; m. 2d, Lilian Durban, Mar. 26, 1896. In printing and subscription pub. business, Pittsfield, Mass., 1883; took up bus. of ordnance and explosives, 1888; was 1st to make smokeless powder in U.S., and 1st to submit samples to U.S. Govt. for trial; built at Maxim, N.J. (named for him), 1890, dynamite factory and smokeless powder mill; in 1897 sold smokeless powder inventions to E. I. du Pont de Nemours & Co., Wilmington, Del., and is now consulting engr. and expert in development dept. of that co. U.S. Govt. adopted his smokeless powder; in 1901 sold to U.S. Government formula of "Maximite," first high explosive to be fired through heavy armor plate; has perfected "Stabillite," a smokeless powder producing much better ballistic results than any other; inventor of U.S. service detonating fuse for high explosive armor-piercing projectiles; of "motorite," a new self-combustive material for driving automobile torpedoes; of process and apparatus for mfg. multi-perforated powder grains; of improvements in smokeless powder grains, etc.; has many U.S. patents now pending. Past pres. Pan-Am. States Assn., Aeronautical Soc. of N.Y.; mem. Mil. Service Instn. Mem. Naval Consulting Bd., Sept. 1915—. Author: The Science of Poetry and the Philosophy of Language, 1910; Defenseless America, 1915; Dynamite Stories, 1916. Home: Landing P.O., N.J. Died May 6, 1927.

MAXON, William Densmore, clergyman; b. Schenectady, N.Y., Oct. 23, 1857; s. George G. and Ann Maria (Wood) M.; B.A., Union Coll., Schenectady, 1878, M.A., 1886, D.D., 1894; student Gen. Theol. Sem., N.Y. City, and Berkeley Div. Sch., Middletown, Conn.; m. Annie Cuyler Lush, Oct. 26, 1881; children—Margaret (Mrs. Warren F. Draper), Paul, Richard L. Deacon, 1881, priest, 1882, P.E. Ch.; missionary, Fonda, N.Y., 1881; asst. minister St. George's Ch., Schenectady, 1882; acting prof. logic and rhetoric, Union Coll., 1882; successively rector Grace Ch., Waterford, N.Y., Trinity Ch., Utica, Calvary Ch., Pittsburgh, Pa., until 1898, Christ Ch., Detroit, 1899-1933 (rector emeritus). Chaplain Base Hosp. 36, France, Nov. 15, 1917-Aug. 13, 1918. Pres. standing com. Diocese of Mich., 1919-32; v.p. diocesan exec. council, 1924-31; dep. Gen. Conv. P.E. Ch., 11 times to 1934; chmn. com. on canons, Gen. Conv., 1925, 28, 31-34. Home: Grosse Pointe Farms, Mich. Died Oct. 3, 1940.

MAXWELL, Allison, physician; b. Bloomington, Ind., Sept. 24, 1848; s. Dr. James Darwin and Louisa Jane (Howe) M.; A.B., Ind. U., 1868, A.M., 1871; M.D., Miami Med. Coll., Cincinnati, 1876; m. Cynthia A. Routh, May 31, 1883. Began practice at Indianapolis, Ind., 1876; professor practice of medicine, Ind. U. Sch. of Medicine; med. dir. State Life Ins. Co. of Indianapolis; mem. Indianapolis Bd. Pub. Health 2 terms; mem. and pres. Indianapolis Bd. Sch. Commrs. 3 yrs. Republican. Presbyn. Home: Indianapolis, Ind. Died Jan. 16, 1915.

MAXWELL, Augustus Emmett, jurist; b. Elberton, Ga., Sept. 21, 1820; ed. in Ala. and in Univ. of Va.; practiced law at Eutaw, Ala., 1843-45; removed to Tallahassee, Fla., 1845; mem. Fla. legislature, 1847; State senate, 1849; was also sec. of State and atty. gen. of Fla.; mem. Congress, 1853-57; in Confederate senate, 1862-65; judge Supreme Court, Fla., 1866; judge circuit court, 1877-85; chief justice Supreme Court, 1887-91; was also, 1885, mem. State Constl. Conv. Retired. Home: Pensacola, Fla. Died 1903.

MAXWELL, Charles Robert, educator; b. Fayston, Vt., Jan. 19, 1878; s. John and Eliza (Ferris) M.; student Norwich U., Northfield, Vt., 1894-96. Dartmouth, summer 1903; B.S., Teachers Coll. (Columbia), 1905; A.M., Columbia, 1906; m. Ella Worthen, Dec. 28, 1909; 1 son, Charles R. Prin. pub. schs., Waitsfield, Vt., 1898-1902; supt. schs. Fayston, 1902-03; prin. high sch., Quincy, Ill., 1907-12; supervisor Training Sch., State Normal Sch., Whitewater, Wis., 1913-19; dean Coll. of Edn. and dir. Summer Sch., U. of Wyo., Sept. 1919—; prof. of sch. administration, Ohio State U., summer 1929. Author: Observation of Teaching, 1917; Selection of Textbooks, 1921; High School Administration (with L. R. Kilzer), 1936. Home: Laramie, Wyo. Died Sept. 13, 1939.

MAXWELL, George Holmes, patent atty.; b. New Woodstock, N.Y., Apr. 16, 1864; s. Rev. Joseph and Elizabeth (Holmes) M.; A.B., Syracuse U., 1888, A.M., 1891, LL.D., 1928; LL.B., Columbian (now George Washington) U., 1892, LL.M., 1893; m. Mrs. Carrie A. Baker Peek, Sept. 1, 1904. Examiner in U.S. Patent Office, Washington, D.C., 1889-95; admitted to practice in state and federal courts and Supreme Court of U.S., 1893, courts of Mass., 1896; practiced at Boston, 1895-1917; inventor and mfr. shoe machinery; pres. Lacene Mfg. Co., Manchester, N.H., North Am. Chemical Co. (Boston), Phoenix Investment & Trust Co. Established and endowed chair of U.S. Citizenship at Boston U., Sch. of Citizenship and Pub. Affairs at Syracuse U.; endowed Retired Ministers' Fund of Central N.Y. Conf. M.E. Ch.; established Nurses Home, Clifton Springs (N.Y.) Sanitarium, also lectureship at American U. Trustee Boston (life), Syracuse and Am. universities. Pres. Syracuse in China Assn. (life mem.); mem. Pasadena Art Inst. (life), Phoenix (Ariz.) Y.M.C.A. Republican. Methodist. Home: Boston, Mass.; Pasadena, Calif.; Phoenix, Ariz. (legal residence). Died Sept. 16, 1932.

MAXWELL, Guy Everett, educator; b. Forest City, Ill., Sept. 10, 1870; s. Henry Clay and Mary Barnett (Ewers) M.; A.B., Hamline U., St. Paul, 1893, Ed.D., 1929; Columbia, 1898-1900, A.M., 1899; Pd.D., Miami Univ., 1920; m. Jeannette R. Evans, June 24, 1896; children—Robert Evans, Richard Barnett, Eugene Everett. Principal Herman (Minn.) village schs., 1893-95; prin. Marinette (Wis.) High Sch., 1895-98; prin. Elementary Dept., 1900-04, pres., 1904—, Winona State Teachers College; pres. (3 times) Am. Assn. Teachers Coll., and its predecessors; mem. nat council Y.M.C. Assns. of U.S., 1924, 27; life mem. N.E.A. Republican. Methodist. Mason. Home: Winona, Minn. Died Jan. 3, 1939.

MAXWELL, John Rogers, capitalist. Chairman exec. com. Central R.R. of N.J.; mem. Maxwell & Graves, bankers and brokers; pres. and dir. Atlas Portland Cement Co., N. American Portland Cement Co., Northampton & Bath R.R.; mem. bd. mgrs. D.,L.&W. R.R. Co.; dir. numerous corporations. Home: New York, N.Y. Died 1910.

MAXWELL, Lawrence, lawyer; b. Glasgow, Scotland, May 4, 1853; s. Lawrence and Alison (Crawford) M.; B.S., U. of Mich., 1874, hon. A.M., 1893, LL.D., 1904; LL.B., Cincinnati Law Sch., 1875; m. Clara Barry Darrow, Dec. 27, 1876; children—Mrs. Marjorie Graydon, Mrs. Jean Schmidlapp. Admitted to bar, 1875, and began practice at Cincinnati. Solicitor-gen. of U.S., 1893-95; prof. law, Cincinnati Law Sch., 1896-1912; non-resident lecturer, law dept. U. of Mich., 1909-16. Chmn. bar com. on revision of the equity rules of the Supreme Court, 1911. Mem. gen. council Alumni Assn. of U. of Mich.; pres. Cincinnati Alumni Assn. U. of Mich.; pres. Cincinnati Musical Festival Assn. Commemoration orator at 75th anniversary of founding of U. of Mich., 1912. Home: Cincinnati, O. Died Feb. 18, 1927.

MAXWELL, Samuel, congressman, jurist; b. Lodi, N.Y., May 20, 1826; ed. in common schools and under private tuition; removed to Mich., 1844; taught school, farmed and held local offices; went to Neb., 1855-56, and pre-empted 160 acres Govt. land, which he improved; returned to Mich., 1858; completed law studies; admitted to bar, 1859; returned to Neb., and began law practice. Delegate to first Rep. Territorial Convention; mem. Territorial legislature, 1860-65; mem. State constl. conv., 1864, 1871 and 1875; mem. State legislature, 1866; mem. several State commissions; judge supreme court Neb., 1872-94; member Congress, 1897-99; Fusionist. Prominent as free-coinage advocate. Author: Practice in Justice Courts; Pleading and Practice; Criminal Procedure; Code Pleading. Home: Tremont, Neb. Died 1901.

MAXWELL, William Cochrane, ry. official; b. Keokuk, Ia., Feb. 20, 1865; s. John and Elizabeth M.; m. Persis Taylor Cochrane, 1891; 1 dau., Elinor. Connected with traffic dept., C.,B.&Q. System, 1881-1905; asst. gen. traffic mgr., 1905-08, gen. traffic mgr., 1908-15, v.p., 1915—, Wabash Ry. Episcopalian. Home: St. Louis, Mo. Died Aug. 4, 1936.

MAXWELL, William Henry, supt. of schs.; b. Stewartstown, Co. Tyrone, Ireland, Mar. 5, 1852; s. Rev. John and Maria M.; A.B., Queen's U., Ireland, 1872, A.M., 1874; (hon. Ph.D., St. Lawrence, 1890; LL.D., Columbia, 1901); came to U.S., 1874; m. Marie A. Folk, Dec. 2, 1877. Asst. supt. schs., Brooklyn, 1882-87, supt. same, 1887-98; supt. pub. schs., Greater New York, 1898, emeritus. Pres. N.E.A., 1905, State Council of Supts., 1893, Nat. Dept. of Supts., 1895; mem. advisory council Simplified Spelling Bd. Author: Elementary English Grammar; School Grammar, and other endl. works. Home: Flushing, N.Y. Died May 3, 1920.

MAY, David William, agriculturist; b. Platte Co. Mo., Apr. 22, 1868; s. Benjamin L. and Mary (Nicol) M.; ed. State Normal Sch., Warrensburg, Mo., 1888; student U. of Mo., 1890-91 and 1892-96, B.Agr., 1894, M.Agr., 1896; m. Lena Harrison, Dec. 24, 1896. Asst. agriculturist, Mo. Expt. Sta., in charge of field expts., 1896-99; asst. in agr. U.S. Dept. Agr., Washington, 1899, and did editorial work and work in plant physiology; apptd. animal husbandman, Ky. Expt. Sta., Lexington, 1901; apptd. spl. agt. in charge of Puerto Rico Expt. Station, Mayaguez, P.R., 1904. Presbyterian. Died 1937.

MAY, Edna, actress; b. (Edna May Pettie) Syracuse, N.Y., 1878; d. E. C. Pettie; m. Frederick Titus; m. 2d, Oscar Lewisohn, June 4, 1907 (died 1917). Début in "Santa Maria," New York; appeared as Violet Gray, in "The Belle of New York," in New York and London; starred in "An American Beauty," "Three Little Maids," "The School Girl," "The Catch of the Season," etc.; retired from stage, 1907. Died Dec. 13, 1917.

MAY, Edward, naval officer; b. Leicester, Mass., Jan. 20, 1838; s. Samuel and Sarah (Russell) M.; ed. pvt. schs. and Leicester Acad.; m. Mary Mignot Blodgett, Oct. 4, 1871 (died 1901). Apptd. asst. pay master, U.S.N., Sept. 6, 1861; promoted p.m., Apr. 14, 1862; pay insp., Sept. 25, 1875; pay dir., Dec. 24, 1883; retired Jan. 20, 1900, with rank of rear admiral for services during Civil War. Home: Jamaica Plain, Mass. Died Feb. 5, 1917.

MAY, Ernest H., banker; b. Washington, D.C., Oct. 16, 1859; s. Joseph J. and Annie E. (Heath) M.; ed. pub. schs., Washington, D.C.; m. Virginia McD. Lyon, Dec. 4, 1884 (died 1917); 1 son, Ernest Crawford. Connected with Joseph Rippard's Sons, importers, New York, 1876-80; in office of 1st comptroller of the treasury, Washington, D.C., 1880-85; became connected with First Nat. Bank, Pasadena, Calif., as clk., 1886, and retired as pres., 1911; cashier, later pres. Pasadena Savings & Trust Co.; organizer, 1912, and pres. Security Nat. Bank, until 1925, chmn. bd., 1925-26 (retired). Republican. Episcopalian. Mason. Home: Pasadena, Calif. Died June 21, 1935.

MAY, Julia Harris, teacher, author; b. Strong, Me., Apr. 27, 1833; d. Rev. William and Delia Maria (Johnson) M.; grad. Mt. Holyoke Coll., 1856 (hon. M.A., 1906); unmarried. Taught in various schs., 1848-92; teacher of classes in art and lit. from 1897, in Auburn and Lewiston, Me. Conglist. Lecturer before women's clubs. Author: Songs from the Woods of Maine (poems), 1894; Looking for the Stars (poems), 1903; Pictures Framed In Song, 1907. Home: Auburn, Me. Died May 6, 1912.

MAY, Max, banker; b. Germany, July 3, 1861; s. Gotschall and Betty (Lorch) M.; ed. in Germany; m. Sarah Rosenberg, June 24, 1890; children—Walter H., Mrs. Edna Livingston, Mrs. Dorothy Goldstein. Foreign exchange business, Darmstadt and Karlsruhe, 1878-83; came to U.S., 1883, naturalized citizen, 1888; successively with Union, Atlas and First Nat. banks, Chicago, 1883-1904; with Guaranty Trust Co., New York, 1904-18, Foreign Trade Banking Corp., 1918-20; foreign exchange business on own account, 1920-22; dir. and mem. bd. Russian Commercial Bank, Moscow, Russia, 1922-July 1925. Retired. Home: New York, N.Y. Deceased.

MAY, Max Benjamin, judge; b. Cincinnati, O., July 21, 1866; s. Benjamin and Emily (Wise) M.; B.Litt., U. of Cincinnati, 1888; M.A., Harvard, 1890; studied Harvard Law Sch.; m. Jean Cahn Wolf, Apr. 29, 1908 (died 1914); m. 2d, Aimee Mack Benswanger, Mar. 16, 1917. Began practice in Cincinnati, 1890; elected judge Court of Common Pleas,

Hamilton Co., O., term 1913-19. Democrat. Jewish religion. Author: Isaac Mayer Wise, Founder of American Judaism, 1916. Wrote prize essays, 1900 and 1901, offered by Ohio Soc. S.R. Home: Avondale, Cincinnati, O. Died Oct. 2, 1929.

MAY, Thomas, cartoonist; b. Detroit, June 30, 1860; s. Thomas and Margaret (Shannon) M.; pub. sch. edn., Detroit; (hon. A.M., U. of Mich., 1910); m. Maria L. Hollings, 1888. Cartoonist Detroit Evening News, 1886-92, Detroit Journal, 1892-1912, Detroit Times, 1912—. Home: Detroit, Mich. Died Dec. 2, 1927.

MAY, William Andrew, officer corps.; b. Hollidaysburg, Pa., Dec. 3, 1850; s. Lewis and Louisa (Haines) M.; A.B., Williamsport Dickinson Sem., 1873; C.E., Lafayette Coll., 1876, A.M., 1879; m. Emma L. Richards, June 5, 1878. Began as rodman on engring. corps, and advanced to chief engr. several coal companies; became supt. Hillside Coal & Iron Co., 1883; with many coal companies in charge of operations, etc.; pres. Pa. Coal Co., Feb. 1913—; pres. Hillside Coal & Iron Co., New York, Susquehanna & Western Coal Co., Northwestern Mining & Exchange Co., Blossburg Coal Co.; pres. Scranton Board of Trade Bldg. Co. Pvt. Co. D, 13th Regt. N.G. Pa., 1878; resigned as capt., 1888. Mem. Select Council, City of Scranton, 2 terms; mem. Bd. Control, Scranton City Schs., 1898-1902. Pres. Scranton Bd. Trade, 1893-97; v.p. Nat. Bd. Trade, 1893-97. Dir. Williamsport Dickinson Sem.; trustee Lafayette Coll. Republican. Methodist. Mason. Home: Scranton, Pa. Died June 1, 1923.

MAYBURY, William Cotter, mayor of Detroit, 1897-1905; b. Detroit, Nov. 20, 1849; s. Thomas and Margaret (Cotter) M.; ed. pub. schs., Detroit, and Univ. of Mich., B.A., 1870, M.A., 1880. Admitted to bar, 1871; city atty., 1875-80; mem. Congress, 1883-87, 1st Mich. dist.; prof. jurisprudence, Mich. Coll. of Medicine, 1881-82; mem. Maybury, Lucking, Emmons & Helfman. Chevalier Legion of Honor, July 25, 1901. Democrat. Home: Detroit, Mich. Died 1909.

MAYER, Constant, artist; b. Besancon, France, Oct. 4, 1832; studied at École des Beaux Arts and under Leon Cogniet, Paris; had his studio there until 1857; then in New York for many yrs.; now divides his time between New York and Paris. Asso. Nat. Acad. Design, 1866—; Knight of the Legion of Honor of France; mem. Soc. of French Artists. Has painted notable portraits including those of Gens. Grant and Sherman; as well as life-sized genre paintings, including Maud Muller, The Song of the Shirt, The First Communion, Evangeline, The Witch's Daughter, Trilby, The Lord's Day, etc. Died 1901.

MAYER, Emil, laryngologist; b. N.Y. City, May 23, 1854; s. David and Henrietta (Rosenbaum) M.; student Coll. City of N.Y., 1868-70; Pharm. G., Coll. of Pharmacy, 1873; M.D., Univ. Med. Coll. (New York U.), 1877; m. Louise Blume, 1883. Lecturer diseases of nose and throat, New York Poly. Inst., 1895; surgeon and chief of clinic throat dept., New York Eye and Ear Infirmary, 1893-1904; attending laryngologist, Mt. Sinai Hosp., and chief of clinic, throat and ear dept., Mt. Sinai Dispensary, 1904-19; cons. laryngologist. Rep. for U.S. Med. Intelligence Bur., Am. Red Cross, 1917, 18; vol. Am. Med. Service Corps, 1918. Fellow Am. Laryngol. Assn. (pres. 1922), Phila. Laryngol. Assn. (hon.). Home: New York, N.Y. Died Oct. 20, 1931.

MAYER, Julius M., judge; b. New York, Sept. 5, 1865; s. J. Daniel and Fannie (Marshuetz) M.; A.B., Coll. City of New York, 1884; LL.B., Columbia Law Sch., 1886, LL.D., 1921. Was mem. Mayer & Gilbert. Counsel for Excise Bd., New York, 1895-96, City Bldg. Dept., 1897-98; justice Ct. of Spl. Sessions, 1902-04; atty. gen. State of N.Y., 1905-07; apptd. by President Taft judge Dist. Ct., Southern Dist. of N.Y., Feb. 15, 1912; apptd. U.S. circuit judge, 2d Circuit, Oct. 5, 1921. Mason. Home: New York, N.Y. Died Nov. 30, 1925.

MAYER, Levy, lawyer; b. Richmond, Va., Oct. 23, 1858; s. Henry D. and Clara (Goldsmith) M.; grad. Chicago High Sch., 1874; took spl. studies at Yale and at law dept., Yale, 1876. Asst. librarian of Chicago Law Inst., 1876-81, and while so engaged prepared its first catalogue and edited and revised MS. of Judge David Rorer's works on interstate or pvt. internat. law, and on jud. and execution sales, and contributed to legal mags. In practice, 1881—; sr. mem. Mayer, Meyer, Austrian & Platt. Mem. Constl. Conv. of Ill., 1920-22; mem. Ill. State Council of Defense, and chmn. com. on law and legislation. Home: Chicago, and Manomet, Mass. Died Aug. 14, 1922.

MAYES, Edward, lawyer; b. in Hinds Co., Miss., Dec. 15, 1846; s. Daniel and Elizabeth (Rigg) M.; pvt. 4th Miss. Cav., C.S.A., 1864-65; A.B., U. of Miss., 1868, LL.B., 1869; (LL.D., Miss. Coll., 1890); m. Frances Eliza, d. late L. Q. C. Lamar, May 11, 1869. Prof. law, 1877-92, chmn. faculty, 1886-89, chancellor, 1889-92, U. of Miss.; prof. law and dean law faculty, Millsaps Coll., 1895—; mem. Mayes & Mayes. Mem. Miss. Constl. Conv., 1890; presdl. elector, 1900. Democrat. Home: Jackson, Miss. Died Aug. 9, 1917.

MAYES, Robert Burns, judge; b. Gallatin, Miss., June 28, 1867; s. Herman Bowmar and Charity (Barlow) M.; ed. pub. and pvt. schs., Hazlehurst, Miss., and attended U. of Miss.; LL.B., same, 1890; m. Lelia Hart Beaty, Feb. 21, 1900. Began practice of law, Hazlehurst, Miss., 1890; mem. Miss. Senate, 1892-93; spl. agt. in U.S. Treasury Dept., 1893-95; resumed law practice at New York, 1895-97; returned to Miss. and practiced at Hazlehurst, 1898-1903; judge Chancery Ct., 1903-06; apptd. asso. justice Supreme Ct., Miss., May 10, 1906; chief justice, Apr. 16, 1910-Aug. 12, 1912, resigned; dist. counsel I.C. R.R. Co. and Yazoo & Miss. Valley R.R., Jackson, Miss., 1912—. Methodist. Democrat. Home: Jackson, Miss. Died Feb. 18, 1921.

MAYES, William Harding, feature writer; b. Mayfield, Ky., May 20, 1861; s. Robert Chappell and Fredonia Charlotte (Stephens) M.; ed. Paducah Dist. Methodist Coll., Milburn, Ky.; Norton's English and Classical Sch., Union City, Tenn.; Vanderbilt U., Nashville, 1880-81; LL.D., Daniel Baker Coll., Brownwood, Tex., 1914; m. Jessie Wise, Nov. 26, 1886 (died 1899); children—Ethridge, Tyty, William H., Wendell W.; m. 2d, Anna Marshall, Aug. 2, 1900; children—Lewis Ousley, Isabelle, Robert C. Admitted to Ky. bar, 1881, to Tex. bar, 1882; practiced in Mayfield, Ky., 1881-82, in Brownwood, Tex., 1882-86; atty., Brown Co., Tex., 1882-83; editor and pub. Brownwood Bulletin, 1887-1914; lt. gov. of Tex., 1913-14; prof. journalism, U. of Tex., 1914-27; devoting attention to writing. Pres. Assn. of Am. Schs. and Depts. of Journalism, 1920-21; exec. vice pres. Tex. Centennial Com. Democrat. Methodist. Mason. Rotarian. Home: Austin, Tex. Died June 26, 1939.

MAYFIELD, James Jefferson, judge; b. Mar. 22, 1861; s. James Jefferson and Amanda (South) M.; A.B., U. of Ala., 1885, LL.B., 1888; m. Susie Martin, June 1897. Began law practice at Tuscaloosa, Ala., 1888; mem. Ala. Ho. of Rep., 1894-96; elected judge City Court, Tuscaloosa, 1897; asso. justice Supreme Court, Ala., 11 yrs.; resigned to make code of 1924 for state of Ala. Spl. counselor to Govs. Kilby and Brandon. Presdl. elector, 1896; candidate for U.S. Senate to succeed O. W. Underwood. Codified the laws of Ala., code of 1907; digested decisions of the Supreme Court of Ala., 7 vols., and decisions of Supreme Court of U.S.; annotated the Constitutions of 1875 and 1901 of Ala.; annotated the Constitution of U.S.; compiled Scrap-book on Constitutional Government; also Mayfield's Form Book. Home: Montgomery, Ala. Died Jan. 1, 1927.

MAYNARD, Charles Johnson, naturalist; b. West Newton, Mass., May 6, 1845; s. Samuel and Emeline M.; ed. common schs.; married; 1 dau.; worked on his mother's farm, and studied nature from earliest youth. V.p., 1875, Nuttall Ornith. Club, Cambridge, Mass.; originator and editor Nuttall Bulletin (ornithological); one of original mems., and pres. 1891, Newton Natural History Soc.; made notable investigations of vocal organs of birds; discovered vocal organs of American bittern; spl. studies on the land shells of the West Indian genus Strophia (now Cerion). Instr. in econ. bird study, Mass. Agrl. Coll., Amherst, 1910-19. Author: Contributions to Science (3 vols.); Nature Studies No. 2—"Sponges"; Manual of Taxidermy; Methods in Moss Study; Field Directory to the Birds of Eastern North America; Atlas to the Directory of the Birds of Eastern North America; Records of Walks and Talks with Nature, 12 vols.; Field Ornithology; Plates to Field Ornithology; Migration of Birds and Other Animals; Vocal Organs of Talking Birds and of Other Species, 1918, 2d edit., 1922; Notes on Life History of Cerions, 1919. Home: West Newton, Mass. Died Oct. 15, 1929.

MAYNARD, George Colton, curator; b. Ann Arbor, Mich., Oct. 23, 1839; s. Charles Moseley and Sophronia (Colton) M.; ed. pub. schs. and under pvt. tutors; m. Lucy Julia Warner, Apr. 10, 1879. Began as telegraph operator in Mich., 1855; removed to Washington, D.C., 1864; with U.S. Army telegraph service, 1864-66, U.S. Signal Service (telegraph), 1870-76; entered pvt. elec. business, 1876; with Bell Telephone Co., 1878-83; apptd. custodian elec. collections, Nat. Mus., 1896, curator, 1911—. Republican. Conglist. Home: Washington, D.C. Died July 28, 1918.

MAYNARD, George William, mining engr.; b. Brooklyn, N.Y., June 12, 1839; s. George Washington and Caroline Augusta (Eaton) M.; A.B., Columbia, 1859, A.M., 1864; U. of Göttingen and Royal Mining Acad., Clausthal, Germany, 1860-63; m. Fannie Atkin, June 12, 1865. Had charge of metall. works in Ireland, 1863-64; engaged as mining engr. in Colo., 1864-67; prof. mining and metallurgy, Rensselaer Poly. Inst., 1868-72, also cons. engr. to various iron and steel works; cons. engr. for iron, steel and copper works in Eng. and Germany, 1873-79; cons. mining and metall. engr., 1879—. Has had charge of constrn. of various mills and reduction plants in Ireland, Colo., Russia, etc.; aided in the development of the Thomas Basic Steel Process in Eng. and introduced it in the U.S. and finally sold it to the Bessemer Assn. Home: New York, N.Y. Deceased.

MAYNARD, George Willoughby, artist; b. Washington, D.C., Mar. 5, 1843; s. Edward and Ellen Sophia (Doty) M.; studied at Royal Acad. of Fine Arts, Antwerp; m. Louise Brownell, Dec. 26, 1907. Had studio at Paris, 1878, but later located in New York. N.A., 1885. Home: New York, N.Y. Died Apr. 5, 1923.

MAYNARD, James, manufacturer; b. Knoxville, Tenn., July 15, 1853; s. Horace and Laura Ann (Washburn) M.; A.B., U. of Tenn., 1872, A.M., 1875; A.B., Amherst, 1874; LL.B., George Washington, 1885; LL.M., 1892; m. Caroline Jones Taylor, Apr. 10, 1879 (died 1909); children—James (dec.), Horace (dec.); m. 2d, Andasia R. Purnell, Dec. 16, 1911. Committee clerk on Banking and Currency, Ho. of Rep., Washington, 1874-75; commr. to take testimony for Southern Claims Commn., 1875-76; marshal to Consular Courts in Turkey, 1876-80; in postal service, Washington, 1880-94; practiced law, Knoxville, 1894-98; lecturer on internat. law, U. of Tenn., 1897-98; manufacturer, 1898—; pres. and dir. Brookside Mills; dir. Mechanics Bank & Trust Co., 1896-1922. Pres. bd. trustees Knox Co. Industrial Sch., 1895—; trustee U. of Tenn., 1896-1919 (treas. 1900-14), Lawson McGhee Library, 1915—; mem. Bd. State Charities of Tenn., 1905—; Rep. mem. State Bd. of Election Commrs., 1909-13. Episcopalian. Republican. Home: Knoxville, Tenn. Died Apr. 14, 1926.

MAYNARD, John Walter, clergyman; b. Worcester, Mass., June 7, 1859; s. John Quincy and Maria Louise (Capron) M.; prep. edn., Wesleyan Acad., Mass.; B.A., Wesleyan U., Middletown, Conn., 1883, D.D., 1908; B.D., Drew Theol. Sem., 1886; grad. study, Yale; m. Susan Maria Peck, Oct. 31, 1886; children—Marjorie Blair (Mrs. Kenneth D. Cranstoun), John Paul. Ordained ministry M.E. Ch., 1886; pastor New Haven, Conn., 1908-12, Brooklyn, N.Y., 1913-19; spl. speaker, Y.M.C.A., 1918; chaplain, rank of 1st lt., U.S.A., 1918-19; pastor American Ch., Rome, Italy, 1919—; v.p. Collegio Internazionale Monte Mario, Rome, 1925-29, pres., 1929-32; rep. Board of Foreign Missions, Rome, 1936-37. Counsellor and treas. M.E. Ch., Italy; del. to Ecumenical Conf. M.E. Ch., London, 1920. An organizer Rome Post, Am. Legion, also Am. Legion Dept. of Italy; served as post chaplain, dept. adj. and dept. chaplain; twice del. to meeting of nat. com. of Am. Legion, Indianapolis. Awarded gold medal, Am. Legion; medal, war com. Federal Council Chs. of Christ in America. Republican. Mason. Home: Stratford, Conn. Died June 10, 1939.

MAYNARD, La Salle Almeron, editor; b. Hancock, N.Y., Feb. 18, 1857; s. M. H. and Marie Antoinette (Fletcher) M.; ed. pub. schs., Hancock, N.Y.; m. Mary C. Macrum, 1886. Taught dist. and pvt. schs., Mich. and Ill., 1870-80; studied law, 1880-81; editor Criterion, 1881-83; asso. editor New York Observer, 1884-88; mng. editor New York Mail and Express, 1888-89; mng. editor Christian Work, 1889-98; asso. and lit. editor Leslie's Weekly, 1898—. Owner and mgr. Maynard's Press Agency, 1895—. Home: Oneonta, N.Y. Died 1906.

MAYNARD, Samuel Taylor, horticulturist; b. Hardwick, Mass., Dec. 6, 1844; s. William and Sarah (Nourse) M.; grad. Mass. Agrl. Coll., 1872, and became connected with the college and the Mass. Expt. Sta.; prof. botany and horticulture, Mass. Agrl. Coll., 1879—; botanist and pomologist Mass. State Bd. of Agr.; dir. hort. div., Mass. Expt. Sta. Sec. Mass. Fruit Growers' Assn.; mem. sch. bd. of Amherst, 8 yrs. Author: Practical Fruit Grower, 1886; Landscape Gardening as Applied to Home Decoration, 1899; Successful Fruit Culture, 1902; The Small Country Home, 1907. Asso. editor Suburban Life, Boston. Hort. specialist and landscape gardener, 1907—. Home: Northboro, Mass. Died 1923.

MAYNARD, Walter Effingham; b. N.Y. City, Nov. 17, 1871; s. Effingham and Helen Maria (Hollister) M.; A.B., Harvard, 1893; m. Eunice Ives, Apr. 19, 1903. Pres. Dranyam Realty Corp.; dir. Met. Trust Co., Detroit, Hillsdale & S.W. R.R. Co., etc. Active in civic movements in N.Y. City. Trustee Beaux Arts Inst., New York Orthopedic Dispensary and Hosp., Fifth Av. Assn. Chevalier Legion of Honor (French). Republican. Protestant. Home: Jericho, L.I., and New York, N.Y. Died Mar. 4, 1925.

MAYNARD, Washburn, rear admiral U.S.N.; b. Knoxville, Tenn., Dec. 5, 1844; s. Horace and Laura Ann (Washburn) M.; bro. of James M.; grad. U.S. Naval Acad., 1866; widower. Promoted to ensign, Apr. 1868; master, Mar. 26, 1869; lt., Mar. 21, 1870; lt. comdr., Sept. 27, 1884; comdr., Sept. 27, 1893; capt., Mar. 9, 1900; rear admiral and retired, Nov. 1, 1902. Has from 1866 served consecutively on naval vessels: Susquehanna, Franklin, Frolic, Seminole, California, Saranac, Richmond, Wyandotte, Coast Survey, Tennessee, Brooklyn and Pinta, and comd. Nashville during Spanish-Am. War, Apr.-Aug. 1898; light house insp., 1899-1900; Naval Examining Bd., Oct. 1900-Mar. 1901; naval sec. Lighthouse Bd., Mar. 1901-Nov. 1902. Died Oct. 24, 1913.

MAYNE, Dexter Dwight, educator; b. Beetown, Wis., May 14, 1863; s. Nicholas and Mary Elizabeth (Treloar) M.; grad. State Normal Sch., Platteville, Wis., 1883; spl. courses in different instns.; m. Nella

G. Coman, Dec. 14, 1887 (dec.); children—James Coman, Mac Hudson, Dexter Charles, Nella. Principal of schs., Fennimore, Wis., 1883-84, Elkhorn, Wis., 1884-89, Ft. Atkinson, 1889-93; prin. and supt. schs., Janesville, Wis., 1893-1901; supt. schs., Ishpeming, Mich., 1901-02; prin. Sch. of Agriculture of U. of Minn., 1903—. Mason. Author: Modern Business Speller, 1899; Office Methods and Practical Bookkeeping, 1900; First Principles of Agriculture (with E. S. Goff), 1904; Mayne's Sight Speller, 1906; Modern Business English (with C. J. Smith), 1906; High School Agriculture (with K. L. Hatch), 1913; A Business Spelling Book, 1913; Farm Shop Work (with George M. Brace), 1915. Home: St. Paul, Minn. Deceased.

MAYO, Amory Dwight, clergyman, educator; b. Warwick, Mass., Jan. 31, 1823; s. Amory and Sophronia M.; ed. Deerfield Acad. and Amherst Coll. (A.M., Amherst; LL.D., Berea, Ky., Coll.); taught in common schools of Mass., 1839-44; prof. and lecturer, Meadville, Pa. (Unitarian), Theol. School, 1868-98; minister Universalist Ch., Gloucester, Mass., 1846-54; Independent Christian Ch., Cleveland, O., 1854-56; Division-St. Ch., Albany, N.Y., 1856-63; Ch. of the Redeemer (Unitarian), Cincinnati, 1863-72; Ch. of the Unity, Springfield, Mass., 1872-80; has since devoted his attention to the cause of edn. in the South, lecturing in 30 States; chief editorial writer in New England and National Jour. Education, 1880-86. Author: Graces and Powers of the Christian Life; Southern Women in the Recent Educational Movement in the South; History of the American Common School; etc. Home: Washington, D.C. Died 1907.

MAYO, Charles Horace, surgeon; b. Rochester, Minn., July 19, 1865; s. William Worrall (M.D.) and Louise Abigail (Wright) M.; prep. edn., Rochester High Sch., Niles Acad.; M.D., Northwestern U., 1888, M.A., 1904; post-grad. study, N.Y. Polyclinic, N.Y. Post-Grad. Med. Sch.; LL.D., U. of Md., 1909, Kenyon Coll., 1916, Northwestern, 1921, U. of Edinburgh, 1925, Queen's U. (Belfast), 1925, U. of Manchester, 1929, Hamline U., 1930, Carleton Coll., 1932, U. of Minnesota, 1935, U. of Notre Dame, 1936, Villanova Coll., 1937; D.Sc., Princeton, 1917, U. of Pa., 1925, U. of Leeds, 1929; M.Ch., U. of Dublin, 1925; D.P.H., Detroit Coll. Medicine and Surgery, 1927; M.D., U. of Havana, 1930; B.S., Yankton Coll., 1937; F.A.C.S., 1913; F.R.C.S., England, 1920; F.R.C.S., Ireland, 1921; F.R.S.M., London, 1926; m. Edith Graham, 1893; children—Margaret (dec.), Dorothy, Charles William, Edith (Mrs. Fred W. Rankin), Joseph Graham (dec.), Louise (Mrs. George T. Trenholm), Rachel (dec.), Esther (Mrs. John B. Hartzell). Practiced surgery at Rochester, 1888—; with brother, W. J., donated $2,800,000 to establish Mayo Foundation for Med. Edn. and Research at Rochester, in affiliation with U. of Minn.; with brother, in 1919, founded the Mayo Properties Assn., to hold all the properties, endowments and funds of the Mayo Clinic and to insure permanency of the instn. for public service; now surgeon and associate chief of staff Mayo Clinic; surgeon to St. Mary's, Colonial and Worrall hosps.; professor surgery Med. Sch., U. of Minn., 1919-36, and prof. surgery Grad. Sch., U. of Minn. (Mayo Foundation), 1915-36, emeritus. Member State Bd. of Health and Vital Statistics, Minn., 1900-02; health officer, Rochester, 1912-37; v.p. Rochester School Bd., 1915-23. Apptd. 1st lt. Med. R.C., Army of U.S., 1913; served as maj., later col., 1917-19; chief consultant (alternating with brother William J.) for all surg. services, Office of Surgeon Gen., 1917-19; rec'd hon. discharge from army, Feb. 28, 1919; apptd. brig. gen. Med. O.R.C., Army of U.S., 1921; brig. gen. Med. Dept., Army of U.S., 1926, and brig. gen. Auxiliary Army of U.S., 1931. Awarded certificate Council of Nat. Defense, 1919; D.S.M. (U.S.), 1920; Officier l'Ordre Nat. de la Légion d'Honneur (France), 1925; Officer l'Instruction Publique et des Beaux Arts (France), 1925; Cross Comdr. Royal Order Crown of Italy, 1932; letter of commendation, Minn. State Med. Assn., 1934; and from Northwestern U. Alumni Assn., in recognition of worthy achievement, 1934; citation for distinguished service given by nat. orgn. Am. Legion; commemorative plaque presented by Pres. of United States in person, 1934; certificate in recognition of service to U. of Minn. and to State as prof. of surgery, 1936; bronze medal presented by Interstate Post Grad. Med. Assn. of North America for contributions to scientific medicine, 1936. Fellow or mem. numerous scientific and non-scientific organizations in U.S. and fgn. countries. Services to scientific and non-scientific periodicals—Anales de Cirugia la Habana, Cuba (fgn. collaborator), Archives of Clin. Cancer Research (editorial bd. 1924-32), Gaceta Medica Española (del. in U.S. 1926-30; internat. patron in U.S., 1931—), Internat. Clinics (collaborating editor 1907-33), Narkose Und Anaesthesie (contbr. 1928), Nosokomien (editorial bd.), The Ency. Britannica (mem. advisory bd.). Trustee Carleton Coll., Northwestern U. Ind. Democrat. Mason. Home: Rochester, Minn. Died May 26, 1939.

MAYO, Henry Thomas, rear adm.; b. Burlington, Vt., Dec. 8, 1856; s. Henry and Elizabeth (Elrie M. Wing, Mar. 1881; children—Chester G., George. Advanced through various grades and promoted rear adm., June 15, 1913; advanced to admiral on retired list, June 1930. Served on various vessels of U.S. Navy, also on both naval and coast survey; was comdt. Mare Island Navy Yard; aid for personnel at Navy Dept., Washington; comdr. 4th Div., Atlantic Fleet, Dec. 18, 1913; comdg. battleship squadrons of Atlantic Fleet with rank of vice admiral, June 10, 1915; promoted admiral, 1916, and apptd. comdr.-in-chief Atlantic Fleet, on Pennsylvania. Demanded apology from Mexican comdr. and firing of nat. salute of 21 guns to U.S. flag, to make amends for arrest of paymaster and crew of dispatch boat Dolphin, at wharf in Tampico, Mex., while loading gasoline into whaleboat, Apr. 9, 1914. Comdr.-in-chief Atlantic Fleet during entire period of war, the command including all vessels in the Atlantic and European waters; represented U.S. at naval conf. of allied nations, London, Sept. 1917; made inspection trip to all U.S. naval activities in Great Britain, France and Italy, 1918; command designated as U.S. Fleet, Jan. 1919; hauled down flag as comdr.-in-chief U.S. Fleet, June 30, 1919, whereupon the fleet was divided into the Atlantic and Pacific fleets; reverted to permanent rank of rear adm. and assigned to duty on Navy Gen. Bd.; retired for age, Dec. 1920; gov. U.S. Naval Home, Phila., 1924-28. Home: Burlington, Vt. Died Feb. 23, 1937.

MAYO, Katherine, author; b. Ridgeway, Pa.; d. James Henry and Harriet Elizabeth (Ingraham) M.; ed. pvt. schs., Boston and Cambridge, Mass. Episcopalian. Author: Justice to All, 1917; The Standard Bearers, 1918; That Damn Y, 1920; Mounted Justice, 1922; Isles of Fear, 1925; Mother India, 1927; Slaves of the Gods, 1929, Volume Two, 1931; Soldiers—What Next?, 1934; The Face of Mother India, 1935; General Washington's Dilemma, 1938. Home: Bedford Hills, N.Y. Died Oct. 9, 1940.

MAYO, Robert William Bainbridge, M.D., b. Fortress Monroe, Va., Dec. 23, 1883; s. Rev. Charles J. S. and Mary Reynolds (Webber) M.; A.B., U. of Md., 1903, M.S., 1904; M.D., Johns Hopkins, 1908; m. Florence Stabler, Nov. 6, 1922. Supt. Gulf Coast Sanitarium, 1908-09; interne, Church Home and Infirmary, Baltimore, 1909; resident surgeon Woman's Hosp., Baltimore, 1909-12; asso. in medicine, Coll. Physicians and Surgeons, 1912-15; instr. in clin. medicine, Johns Hopkins, 1915-22; med. dir. Home for Incurables, 1922—; pres. Med. Arts Bldg. Corp.; pvt. practice as consultant in internal medicine. Mem. Med. Advisory Bd., Baltimore, and chief examiner Am. Red Cross, World War; contract surgeon U.S.A., 1918. Republican. Episcopalian. Home: Guilford, Baltimore, Md. Died Oct. 21, 1937.

MAYO, William James, surgeon; b. Le Sueur, Minn., June 29, 1861; s. William Worrall (M.D.) and Louise Abigail (Wright) M.; prep. edn. Rochester High Sch. and Niles Acad.; M.D., U. of Mich., 1883, hon. A.M., 1890; Certificated N.Y. Post Grad. Med. Sch., 1884; M.D., N.Y. Polyclinic, 1885; F.R.C.S., Edinburgh, 1905, Eng., 1913, Ireland, 1921; F.R.S.M., Eng., 1926; LL.D., U. of Toronto, 1906, U. of Md., 1907, U. of Pa., 1912, McGill U., 1923, U. of Pittsburgh, 1924, Carleton Coll., 1928, U. of Manchester, 1929, Temple U., 1930, U. of Aberdeen, Scotland, 1933, U. of Minn., 1935, U. of Notre Dame, 1936, Villanova Coll., Pa., 1937; D.Sc., U. of Mich., 1908, Columbia, 1910, U. of Leeds, 1923, Harvard, 1924, Marquette and Northwestern, 1929, Yankton Coll., S.D., 1937; M.D. in Surgery, U. of Dublin and Trinity College, 1923, U. of Havana, 1929; m. Hattie M. Damon, Nov. 20, 1884; children—Carrie L. (wife of Dr. D. C. Balfour), Phoebe G. (wife of Dr. H. Waltman Walters). Engaged in practice of surgery, Rochester, Minn., 1883—; surgeon Mayo Clinic (St. Mary's Hosp.), 1889—, and asso. chief of staff. With brother donated $2,800,000 to establish Mayo Foundation for Med. Edn. and Research, at Rochester, in affiliation with U. of Minn. First lt. Med. R.C., 1912, maj. Med. O.R.C., 1917; col. M.C. U.S.A., and chief consultant for surg. service, 1917-19; col. M.R.C., 1919, brig. gen. M.O.R.C., 1921; brig. general Auxiliary Res., 1926-31. Awarded gold medal Nat. Inst. Social Sciences, 1918; D.S.M. (U.S.), 1919; certificate Council Nat. Defense, 1919; Henry Jacob Bigelow gold medal of Boston Surg. Soc., 1921; Comdr. Royal Order of Northern Star (Sweden), 1927; Finlay Congressional D.S.M. (Republic of Cuba), 1929; gold medal A.M.A., 1930; Cross of Royal Order of Knight Commander of the Crown of Italy, 1932; special award for distinguished service to science, Sigma Xi (chapter U. of Minn.), 1933; letter of commendation, Minn. State Med. Assn., 1934; citation for distinguished service presented by Nat. Comdr. Am. Legion; commemorative plaque presented by President of U.S. in person, 1934; Scroll of Distinguished Service, Gen. Alumni Assn. U. of Minn., 1935. Regent U. of Minn., 1907—; elector, Hall of Fame, 1920—. Mem. numerous Am. and foreign scientific societies. Home: Rochester, Minn. Died July 28, 1939.

MAYO, William Kennon, commodore U.S.N.; b. Drummondtown, Va., May 29, 1829; was apptd. from Braden, June 14, 1888. Superintendent schs., Carrolldredge) M.; grad. U.S. Naval Acad., 1876; m. Car-Va. a midshipman in the navy, Oct. 18, 1841; served in various stations, then through the Mexican war, taking part in blockade of Tampico and Vera Cruz, etc. Went to Naval Acad.; passed midshipman, Aug. 1847; master, Sept. 14, 1855; lt., Sept. 15, 1855; instr. seamanship and naval tactics, Naval Acad., 1854-57; asst. prof. ethics, same, 1859-60; lt. commander, July 16, 1862; comdr., July 25, 1866; capt., Dec. 12, 1873; commodore, July 1882; retired, 1886, on own application, after 40 years' service. Because of adherence to Union, was by vote of Va. Convention, July 1861, declared an alien enemy and forever banished from the State. During Civil war executive officer steamsloop "Housatonic," blockade off Charleston, S.C.; then comdr. "Kanawha" in Western Gulf squadron, having engagements with riflemen and field batteries, Mobile Point, and a fight with Fort Morgan, Oct. 1863. Later engaged in blockade of Charleston, S.C., in command of a monitor; after war on duty at several stations, comdg. Naval Station, Norfolk, Va., 1882-85. Died 1900.

MAYO-SMITH, Richmond, prof. political economy, Columbia, 1883—; b. Ohio, 1854; grad. Amherst, 1875; hon. fellow Royal Statistical Soc. of Great Britain; mem. Nat. Acad. of Sciences. Author: Emigration and Immigration, 1890; Sociology and Statistics, 1895; Statistics and Economics, 1899. Died 1901.

MAYOR, Alfred Goldsborough, zoölogist; b. Frederick, Md., Apr. 16, 1868; s. Prof. Alfred M. and Katherine Duckett (Goldsborough) M.; M.E., Stevens Inst. Tech., 1889; S.D., Harvard, 1897; m. Harriet Randolph, d. late Prof. Alpheus Hyatt, of Cambridge, Mass., Aug. 27, 1900. Asst. to Dr. Alexander Agassiz, 1892-1900; in charge radiates, Mus. Comparative Zoölogy, Harvard, 1895-1900; curator of natural sciences and curator-in-chief, 1900-04, hon. curator, 1904—, Brooklyn Inst. Museum; dir. Marine Lab., Carnegie Instn., Tortugas, Fla., 1904-05; dir. dept. of marine biology, Carnegie Instn., Washington, 1905—. On scientific expdns. as asst. to Dr. A. Agassiz, Bahamas, 1892-93, Australia, 1896, Fiji Islands, 1897; cruise of "Albatross" through tropical Pacific, 1899-1900; Dry Tortugas, Fla., 1897, 98, 99, 1902, 08; Torres Straits, and New Guinea, 1913; Samoa, 1917-20; Naples Zoöl. Sta. Lecturer biology, Princeton U., 1913. Fellow and patron New York Zoöl. Society. Author: Medusæ of the World, 3 vols., 1910; Navigation illustrated by diagrams, 1918. Home: Princeton, N.J. Deceased.

MAYTAG, Frederick L(ouis), manufacturer; b. Elgin, Ill., July 14, 1857; s. Daniel W. and Amelia (Tonebohn) M.; ed. rural schs.; LL.D., Parsons Coll., 1926; m. Dena Bergman, Sept. 20, 1882; children—Lulu (Mrs. William H. Smith), Freda Louise, Elmer Henry, Lewis Bergman. Engaged in farming until 1880; implement salesman, 1880-90; in lumber business, 1890-93; began in mfg. business, 1893; mfr. washing machines as The Maytag Co., 1907—, now chmn. bd.; chmn. bd. Jasper County (Ia.) Savings Bank; pres. Maytag Acceptance Corp.; mem. Ia. State Senate, 1902-12; mayor of Newton, 1923-25; 1st dir. Ia. State Budget, 1925. Republican. Mason, Odd Fellow, K.P., Elk. Awarded gold medallion, 1926, by The Home Appliance Merchants of America. Donated $250,000 to Newton Y.M.C.A., many thousands of dollars to colleges, and on 70th birthday distributed $132,000 among his employes. Home: Newton, Ia. Died Mar. 26, 1927.

MAZE, Matthew T., bishop; b. Lewisville, Ind., Nov. 16, 1857; s. Wesley A. and Sarah B. (Pratt) M.; ed. normal sch., Danville, Ind.; m. Katie Goar, Sept. 8, 1881; children—Emery E., Mrs. Nellie Broderson. Teacher pub. schs., Ind.; went to Neb., 1883, on account of ill health; entered ministry Evang. Ch., 1888; various pastorates, also presiding elder, 1896-1903 and 1906-14; supt. missions, Kan. and Okla., 1902-03; field sec. Western Union Coll., Lemars, Ia., 1916-18; elected bishop, Oct. 1918 and for 4th term, 1930, designated bishop emeritus, 1934. Pres. Bd. of Publication and Bd. of Church Extension, Board Home and Foreign Missions; mem. Federal Council of Chs. in America (administrative and policy coms.), chmn. Commn. on Union of United Evang. Ch. (negotiations resulted in union of Evang. and United Evang. assns.), 1922; pres. Pa. State Council of Churches, 1933—. Republican. Home: Lincoln, Neb. Died Oct. 28, 1940.

See also **Mac** spellings, pages 758-766 inclusive.

McADAM, David, asso. justice Supreme Court, N.Y., 1896-1904; b. New York, Oct. 6, 1838; s. Thomas and Janet McAdam; public school edn.; studied law and admitted to bar, 1859; married 1860. Justice marine court, 1874-82; chief justice City court, 1882-90; justice Superior Court, 1891-95. Democrat. Author: Marine Court Practice, 1868, 1872; Landlord and Tenant, 1875, 1882, 1900; etc. Home: New York, N.Y. Died 1901.

McADAM, Dunlap Jamison, educator; b. Moorefield, O., Aug. 2, 1843; s. John and Susan (Dunlap) M.; Athens (O.) Coll., 1862; pvt. Co. C, 126th Ohio Inf., 1862-63; A.B., Washington and Jefferson Coll., Pa., 1868, A.M., 1874 (LL.D., 1913); Harvard Obs., 1872; m. Kate Wishart, July 8, 1875; m. 2d, Rebecca

ton, O., 1870-72; prof. Latin, 1872-73, mathematics, 1873-1914, Washington and Jefferson Coll.; also consulting engr. Democrat. Presbyn. Author: Land Surveying; Einstein's Relativity—a Criticism; Coal—Government Ownership or Control. Home: Washington, Pa. Died Feb. 15, 1925.

McADAM, George Harrison, lawyer; b. New York, May 3, 1854; s. James Graham and Phebe Janet (Titus) M.; A.B., Coll. City of New York, 1875. In law practice at New York, 1878—; federal election marshal, 1885; mem. N.Y. Assembly, 1887; declined Dem. nom. for N.Y. Senate, 1888. Editorial writer and author "Bourbon Column," New York Ledger; Commercial Law, in Am. Penman; legal editor New York Daily News, 1901-06; editor N.Y. World Almanac. Universalist. Mason. Home: New York, N.Y. Died Nov. 2, 1925.

McADAMS, Clark, writer, editor; b. Jersey Co., Ill., Jan. 29, 1874; s. William and Annie E. (Curtis) M.; ed. pub. schs. and Shurtleff Coll., Ill.; m. Laura S. Baker, July 12, 1904. In charge of editorial page, St. Louis Post-Dispatch. Apptd. by sec. of agr. mem. advisory bd. in relation to migratory bird treaty act, 1913-32. Instr. in journalism, Washington U. (St. Louis), 1929-30. President St. Louis Artists Guild, Little Theatre of St. Louis. Home: St. Louis, Mo. Died Nov. 29, 1935.

McADOO, William, congressman; b. Rathmelton, Co. Donegal, Ireland, Oct. 25, 1853; s. Joseph and Elizabeth M.; came to U.S. in early boyhood; ed. public schools; (LL.D., New York U., 1915); m. Eva Lee Tardy, 1885. At age of 20 became law student in office of late I. W. Scudder, Jersey City, occupying leisure hours with reporting for local newspaper; admitted to bar and was apptd. atty. Hudson Co. (N.J.) Bd. of Health; became mem. N.J. Assembly; mem. 48th to 51st Congresses (1883-91), 7th N.J. Dist.; asst. sec. of the navy, 1893-97; engaged in law practice in New York; police commr. of New York, 1904-05; chief city magistrate, July 1, 1910—. Author: When the Court Takes a Recess, 1924; The Procession to Tyburn, 1927. Home: New York, N.Y. Died June 7, 1930.

McADOO, William Gibbs, chmn. bd. Am. President Lines; former U.S. senator, former sec. of Treasury; b. nr. Marietta, Ga., Oct. 31, 1863; s. Judge William Gibbs (LL.D.) and Mary Faith (Floyd) M.; ed. U. of Tenn.; hon. A.M., Hamilton Coll., 1909; LL.D., U. of N.C., 1916, U. of Southern Calif., 1923, Mercer U., 1927, Tusculum Coll., 1927; D.H.L., Lincoln U., 1929; m. Sarah Houstoun Fleming, Nov. 18, 1885 (died Feb. 1912); children—Harriet F. (Mrs. Clayton Platt, Jr.), Francis H., Nona H. (Mrs. Nona M. Taylor), William G., Sally F. (Mrs. Brice Clagett); m. 2d, Eleanor Randolph Wilson, d. of President Woodrow Wilson, May 7, 1914, in the White House; children—Ellen Wilson, Mary Faith; m. 3d, Doris I. Cross, Sept. 14, 1935. Was appointed deputy clerk of the U.S. Circuit Court for the Southern Division, Eastern District of Tenn., May 1882; admitted to bar, 1885; practiced at Chattanooga until 1892, when moved to New York. For a number of years, and until 1903, was partner with William McAdoo in practice of law. Was pres. and dir. Hudson & Manhattan R.R. Co., operating Hudson River tunnel system, which completed, Mar. 8, 1904, the first tunnel under the Hudson River; the first Hudson River tunnels (between Hoboken, N.J., and 6th Av. and 19th St., New York City), were opened for traffic, Feb. 25, 1908; 4th tunnel under the Hudson completed, Mar. 11, 1909. Vice chmn. Dem. Nat. Com., 1912, and acting chmn. for greater part of campaign, 1912; sec. of the treasury in cabinet of President Wilson, Mar. 6, 1913; chmn. Federal Reserve Bd.; also chmn. ex officio Federal Farm Loan Bd., and of U.S. sect. of Internat. High Commn.; dir. gen. of U.S. railroads and Coastwise and intercoastal shipping, Dec. 28, 1917; resigned as sec. of the Treasury, Dec. 16, 1918, and as dir. gen. of rys., Jan. 10, 1919; in Dem. Nat. Conv. at San Francisco, 1920, developed greatest strength as nominee for President on many ballots, although had requested that name be not presented to the Convention; in Dem. Nat. Conv. at New York, 1924, was the leading candidate, but conv. was deadlocked under the two-thirds rule for more than 100 ballots, resulting in nomination of John W. Davis; chmn. Calif. delegation to Dem. Nat. Conv., Chicago, 1932; cast the vote of Calif. on the 4th ballot for Franklin D. Roosevelt, resulting in his nomination on that ballot; chmn. Calif. delegation to Dem. Nat. Conv., Phila., 1936; mem. Dem. Nat. Com., 1932—. U.S. senator from California, term 1933-39; chmn. bd. dirs. Am. President Lines (steamships), 1939—. Episcopalian. Author: The Challenge—Liquor and Lawlessness versus Constitutional Government, 1928; Crowded Years (autobiography), 1931. Home: Santa Barbara, Calif. Died Feb. 1, 1941.

McAFEE, Lapsley Armstrong, clergyman; b. Ashley, Mo., Mar. 31, 1864; s. John Armstrong and Anna W. (Bailey) M.; grad. Park Coll. Acad., Parkville, Mo., 1878; A.B., Park Coll., 1882, A.M., 1885; grad. Presbyn. Theol. Sem. of Northwest (now Presbyn. Theol. Sem., Chicago), 1885, D.D., 1899; m. Ella Taylor, Aug. 17, 1887; children—H. Bailey, Mrs. Robert W. Macdonald, L. Ray, Wallace T. Ordained Presbyn. ministry, 1889; pastor Parkville, 1888-98, Phoenix, Ariz., 1898-1905, Berkeley, Calif., 1905-31 (retired); made pastor at large of Berkeley Ch. Moderator Platte Presbytery, 1890, Presbytery of Ariz., 1900, Oakland Presbytery, 1907, San Francisco Presbytery, 1917-19, Synod of N.M., 1904, Synod of Calif., 1923; pres. San Francisco Presbytery Ch. Extension Bd., 1916-25; commr. to Presbyn. Gen. Assembly 7 times. Y.M.C.A. sec. Spruce Production Div., World War. Trustee San Francisco Presbyn. Theol. Sem., Mt. Hermon Assn. Republican. Home: Berkeley, Calif. Died Jan. 18, 1935.

McAFEE, Lowell Mason, college pres.; b. Fulton, Mo., June 6, 1860; s. John Armstrong (pres. Park College) and Anna Waddle (Bailey) M.; bro. of Cleland Boyd M. and Joseph Ernest M.; A.B., Park College, 1880, A.M., 1885; student McCormick Theol. Sem., 1883, U. of Chicago, 1897; (LL.D., Knox Coll., 1903); m. Carrie E. Canfield, Sept. 28, 1887 (died 1912); 2d, Clara Malden Haynie, Nov. 12, 1913. Exec. head Park Coll., Parkville, Mo., 1890-1913; pres. Parsons Coll., Fairfield, Ia., 1913-16. Sec. Presbyn. Coll. Union, 1901-16. Home: Parkville, Mo. Deceased.

McALESTER, Andrew Walker, surgeon; b. Rocheport, Mo., 1841; A.B., U. of Mo., 1865, M.D., 1866, A.M., 1868 (LL.D., 1897); studied abroad, 1873, 1885; m. Sallie McConathy, 1873. Prof. surgery, 1873-1910, dean dept. medicine, 1880-1910, emeritus dean and prof. surgery, 1910, U. of Mo. Supt. Parker Memorial Hosp., 1901-05; pres. State Bd. Health, 1901-05. Home: Columbia, Mo. Died Nov. 2, 1922.

McALEXANDER, Ulysses Grant, army officer; b. Dundas, Minn., Aug. 30, 1864; s. C. P. and Margaret McAlexander; grad. U.S. Mil. Acad., 1887, Army War Coll., 1907, Gen. Staff Coll., 1920; LL.D., Oregon State Coll., 1930; widower (Aug. 20, 1935). Commissioned second lt. 25th Inf., June 12, 1887; promoted through grades to brig. gen. (temp.), Aug. 16, 1918; brig. gen. (perm.), Mar. 5, 1921, maj. gen., July 21, 1924; retired on account of physical disability, July 22, 1924. Prof. mil. science and tactics, Ia. Wesleyan U., Mt. Pleasant, Ia., 1891-95; in the field, Santiago Campaign, Cuba, Apr.-Aug. 1898; recommended for promotion "for gallantry under fire" in battles in front of Santiago; in charge office Chief Q.-M., Dept. of the East, Nov. 14, 1898-Feb. 17, 1899; with regt. in Philippines, 1900-02; a.d.c. to Maj. Gen. Weston, in Philippines, 1906; mem. Gen. Staff Corps, 1906-07; prof. mil. science and tactics, Oregon Agrl. Coll., 1907-11, 1915-16; with regt. in Philippines, 1912-15; insp.-instr. Ore. N.G., 1916-17; arrived in France, June 26, 1917; comd. 18th Inf., July-Dec. 1917; insp. gen. Base No. 1, Jan.-May 1918; comd. 38th U.S. Inf. in 2d Battle of the Marne, July 15, 1918; at Jaulgonne, July 22, on the Vesle, Aug. 2-10, 1918; comd. 180th Inf. Brigade (Tex. Brigade), Aug. 1918-June 1919; participated, 1918, campaigns, Aisne, Champagne-Marne, Marne defensive, Aisne-Marne, St. Mihiel and Meuse-Argonne; broke last great German offensive on Marne, July 15, 1918; known as "The Rock of the Marne"; wounded, July 16 and July 23, 1918. Life size portrait presented to State of Texas by Texas Brigade. Comdg. 6th brig., 3d Div., Oct. 1921; at Ft. Douglas, Utah, June 7, 1922-July 21, 1924. Awarded D.S.M., D.S.C., and cited "for distinguished valor" (U.S.); Officier Légion d'Honneur and Croix de Guerre (twice) with palm (French); Croce di Guerra (Italian). Hon. life pres. "Rock of the Marne Post" No. 138, Vets. Foreign Wars, N.Y. City, also of Salt Lake Post, V.F.W.; life mem. Soc. Santiago de Cuba. Author: History of the Thirteenth Regiment, 1905. Lectures on Second Battle of the Marne, and on Leadership. Home: Portland, Ore. Died Sept. 18, 1936.

McALISTER, William King, judge; b. Nashville, Tenn., July 4, 1850; s. William K. and Frances Rhea (Anderson) M.; A.B., Bethany (W.Va.) Coll., 1869; B.L., U. of Nashville, 1871; m. Laura Dortch, Nov. 14, 1872. City atty., Nashville, 1874-83; judge Circuit Ct., 1886-93; justice Supreme Ct. of Tenn., 1893-1910. Democrat. Home: Nashville, Tenn. Died May 16, 1923.

McALLISTER, Charles Albert, engineer; b. Dorchester, N.J., May 29, 1867; s. William and Abagail Ann (Shute) M.; M.E., Cornell U., 1887; m. Adelaide Kenyon, Mar. 6, 1907; 1 dau., Clara A. Apptd. 2d asst. engineer, U.S.R.C.S., June 30, 1892; commd. 1st asst. engineer, June 6, 1895, chief engr., Apr. 13, 1902, engineer-in-chief, Mar. 9, 1916, U.S. Coast Guard; retired, July 12, 1919. V.p. Am. Bur. of Shipping, 1919-26, president, 1926—. Passed assistant engr. U.S.N., on board U.S. Flagship Philadelphia, in Spanish-Am. War. Mem. jury awards, machinery, San Francisco Expn., 1915. Episcopalian. Author: The Professor on Shipboard, 1902; McAndrew's Floating School, 1913. Delegate to Internat. Conf. on Safety at Sea, London, 1929. Home: New York, N.Y. Died Jan. 6, 1932.

McALLISTER, David, Ref. Presbyn. clergyman; b. New York, Aug. 25, 1835; s. David McA.; grad. Union Coll., 1860; theol. edn. at Allegheny Ref. Presbyn. Sem. and Union Sem., New York; (D.D., Muskingum Coll., 1884; LL.D., Franklin Coll., 1884); entered ministry, 1863; m. Margaret A. King, Nov. 25, 1863. Editor Christian Statesman, 1867-1902, propr. and pub., 1895-1902. Gen. sec. Nat. Reform Assn., 1871-76, treas. 1884-1900, mem. exec. com., 1871—; editor and pub. Christian Reformer and Dissenter, 1892-96; prof. polit. science, Geneva Coll., Pa., 1883-87. Author: Manual Christian Civil Government, 1871; Poets and Poetry of the Covenant, 1894; The Organic Unity of the Church of Christ, 1896; The Constitutionality of Reading the Bible in Our Public Schools, 1902. Home: Allegheny, Pa. Died 1907.

McALLISTER, Joseph Thompson, lawyer; b. Malden, W.Va., Feb. 27, 1866; s. Abraham Addams and Julia Ellen (Stratton) M.; bro. of Addams Stratton and J(ames) Gray M.; B.A., Hampden-Sidney Coll., 1889; LL.B., U. of Va., 1891; m. Virginia Richards Anderson, Mar. 18, 1893; children—Joseph Thompson (dec.), Jean Graham (Mrs. O. R. Randolph); m. 2d, Marjorie Roosevelt Leaycraft, Apr. 8, 1916; children—Meriel Roosevelt, Marjorie Stratton, Julian Berkeley. Admitted to the Virginia bar, 1891; counsel for Virginia Hot Springs Co., 1891—, and for various corps. in Bath Co., Va.; pres. Hot Springs Valley Investment Co., Alleghany Land Co. Trustee Hampden-Sidney Coll., 1896-1910; organizer and trustee Va. Hot Springs Library (pres.). Democrat. Presbyn. Mason. Rotarian. Author: Historical Sketches of Hot Springs and Bath County, Va., 1908; Humor in Ebony, 1911; Virginia Militia in the Revolution—McAllister's Data, 1913; Appalachian Tours in the Virginias, 1913. Has made a large collection of material on Va. soldiery in the Revolutionary War; assisted sec. Wis. Hist. Soc. in publ. "The Dunmore War." Home: Hot Springs, Va. Died June 13, 1927.

McALLISTER, Ward, lawyer; b. Newport, R.I., July 27, 1855; s. Ward McA.; ed. Princeton; grad. Albany Law School; admitted to N.Y. bar; studied at Harvard Law School 4 yrs.; removed to Calif.; U.S. atty., 1882-84; 1st U.S. dist. judge, dist. of Alaska, from July 5, 1884, to Aug. 28, 1885; returned to San Francisco; apptd. spl. commr. in Chinese habeas corpus cases; resigned and became counsel Pacific Mail Steamship Co. Home: San Francisco, Calif. Died 1908.

McALONEY, Thomas Simpson, educator; b. Co. Antrim, Ireland, June 26, 1869; s. James and Elizabeth (Simpson) McA.; student South Kensington Science and Art Inst., Belfast, 1886-89; Gallaudet College, Washington, D.C. (normal dept.), 1892-93; hon. A.M., Gallaudet, 1927; studied Columbia University; LL.D., Colo. Coll., 1927; m. Mary B. Holt, Nov. 2, 1898; children—Elizabeth Holt, Samuel Holt. Came to U.S., 1892, naturalized citizen, 1897. Teacher, Ulster Instn. for Deaf and Blind, Belfast, 1885-92, Ontario (Can.) Sch. for Deaf, 1893-94, Ala. Sch. for Deaf, 1894-99; head teacher, Ky. Sch. for Deaf, 1899-1900; supt. Mont. Sch. for Deaf and Blind, 1900-06, also organizer Mont. Sch. for Feeble-minded; supt. West Pa. Sch. for Blind, 1906-22, Colo. Sch. for Deaf and Blind, 1922—. Mem. Ala. N.G., 1894-98. Pres. Nat. Commn. on Uniform Type for the Blind, 1910; mem. Colo. Conf. of Social Work (v.p. 1927); mem. bd. Associated Charities, Colorado Springs, Colo., 1924; mem. bd. Colo. Springs Chamber Commerce. Trustee Am. Printing House for Blind, 1900—. Mem. Nat. Conf. of Executives of Schools for the Deaf (exec. com.). Republican. Christian Scientist. Mason. Editor of Colorado Index. Home: Colorado Springs, Colo. Died Aug. 2, 1932.

McALPIN, Benjamin Brandreth; b. N.Y. City, Oct. 4, 1871; s. Gen. Edwin Augustus and Annie (Brandreth) McA.; A.B., Princeton, 1893; LL.B., New York Law Sch., 1895; m. Alice Townsend Martin, Nov. 10, 1897; children—Benj. B., Donald Martin, Townsend Martin. Dir. Interflash Signal Corp., Tao Tea Co., Woman's Hotel Co., Greeley Square Hotel Co.; pres. of Bay Pond, Inc. An organizer of Republican Coll. League, 1892. Mem. Co. I, 7th Regt., N.Y.N.G., 1893-1908; capt. 1902-08; insp. gen., rank of lt. col., 1908-11; mem. several yrs. 7th Regt. shooting team, victors against Queen's Westminster Regt. shooting at Creedmore, 1906. Home: New York, N.Y. Died Jan. 17, 1931.

McALPIN, Edwin Augustus, clergyman; b. Ossining-on-Hudson, N.Y., July 29, 1874; s. Edwin Augustus and Annie (Brandreth) M.; B.A., Princeton, 1898; grad. Union Theol. Sem., 1901; M.A., Columbia, 1901; D.D., Dubuque, 1916, Alma, 1916; m. Emily Benedict Pickard, Apr. 27, 1904; children—Marjorie, Edwin Augustus, Charles Williston, Emily Benedict. Ordained Presbyn. ministry, 1901; asst. headworker, Union Settlement, New York, 1902-03; asst. pastor 1st Ch., Binghamton, N.Y., 1903-05; pastor Babcock Memorial Ch., Baltimore, Md., 1905-13, Presbyn. Ch., Madison, N.J., 1913-27 (resigned). Formerly dir. Prisoners' Aid Soc. of Md., Lawrence House Social Settlement, etc.; pres. College Bd. of Presbyn. Ch. U.S.A., 1915—; sec. Gen. Bd. of Edn. Presbyn. Ch. U.S.A., 1917—; mem. Bd. of Christian Edn. Presbyn. Ch. U.S.A., 1923—. Author: Faith, Health and Common Sense, 1926; Old and New Books as Life Teachers, 1928. Home: Madison, N.J. Died June 27, 1936.

McALVAY, Aaron Vance, judge; b. Ann Arbor, Mich., July 19, 1847; s. Patrick Hamilton and Sarah (Drake) M.; A.B., U. of Mich., 1868, LL.B., 1869 (LL.D., 1910); m. Barbara Bässler, Dec. 9, 1872. In practice at Manistee, Mich., 1871-1905; nonresident prof. law, U. of Mich., 1898-1903. Judge 19th Jud. Circuit, Mich., 1878-79, 1901-05; justice Supreme Ct. of Mich., Jan. 1, 1905—; reëlected, 1907. Republican. Conglist. Home: Lansing, Mich. Died July 9, 1915.

McANDREW, James William, army officer; b. in Pa., June 29, 1862; grad. U.S. Mil. Acad., 1888; honor grad. Army Sch. of the Line, 1910; grad. Army Staff Coll., 1911; Army War Coll., 1913. Commd. 2d lt. 21st Inf., June 11, 1888; promoted through grades to brig. gen. N.A., Aug. 5, 1917; maj. gen. N.A., Apr. 16, 1918; brig. gen. U.S.A., Nov. 8, 1918; maj. gen., Mar. 5, 1921. Was in Sioux Indian Campaign, 1890-91; in Battle of El Caney, Cuba, July 1, 1898, and in investment of Santiago, until its surrender, July 16, 1898; duty in Philippines, 1899-1902; with regt. in Alaska, 1905-06; mem. Gen. Staff Corps, 1916, 17; service in France, June 26, 1917-June 6, 1919; chief of staff, A.E.F., May 6, 1918-May 26, 1919; now comdt. Gen. Staff Coll., Washington. Awarded D.S.M., 1918; Legion of Honor and Croix de Guerre with two palms (French); K.C.M.G. (British); Grand Officer Order of Crown (Belgian); Order of Santi Maurizio and E. Lazzaro (Italian); Montenegran decorations, Panama La Solidaredad. Died Apr. 30, 1922.

McANDREW, William, editor; b. Ypsilanti, Mich., Aug. 20, 1863; s. William and Helen (Walker) McA.; graduate State Normal College, Ypsilanti, Mich., 1916; A.B., U. of Mich., 1886 (Phi Beta Kappa); m. Susan Irvine Gurney, June 28, 1893; children—Helen (Mrs. John William Hill), Mary (Mrs. George Stonehill), John. Teacher, later prin. Hyde Park High Sch., Chicago, 1889-91; supt. schs. St. Clair, Mich., 1886-88; dist. passenger agt. G.N. Ry., St. Paul, 1891-92; prin. Pratt Inst. High Sch., Brooklyn, N.Y., 1892-98; organized Washington Irving High Sch., N.Y. City, and prin. until 1914; asso. supt. schs. N.Y. City, 1914-24; supt. of schools, Chicago, 1924-28; editor Educational Review, School and Society, 1928—. Democrat. Unitarian. Mason. Home: Mamaroneck, N.Y. Died June 27, 1937.

McANEENY, William Joseph, pres. Hudson Motor Car Co.; b. Newport, Herkimer Co., N.Y., Nov. 21, 1872; s. John McA.; ed. country schs.; m. Susan Eugenia Peck, Dec. 22, 1904; children—John, Elizabeth Marie. Began, 1899, as purchasing agt. Riker Motor Vehicle Co., later successively in same capacity with Electric Vehicle Co., Chalmers Motor Co. and Hudson Motor Car Co.; apptd. factory mgr. Hudson Motor Co., 1910; later sec. Hudson Motor Car Co., v.p., 1918-29, became pres., 1929, now chmn. bd.; pres. Essex Motors; dir. First Nat. Bank, Detroit. Served as pvt., corpl. and sergt. 47th N.Y. Inf., Spanish-Am. War; participated in Puerto Rico Expdn. Democrat. Home: Detroit, Mich. Died Mar. 24, 1935.

McARTHUR, Clifton Nesmith, congressman; b. The Dalles, Ore., June 10, 1879; s. Lewis Linn and Harriet (Nesmith) McA.; B.A., U. of Ore., 1901; m. Lucile Smith, June 25, 1913. Admitted to Ore. bar, 1906, and practiced in Portland; extensively interested in farming and breeding registered Jersey cattle. Sec. Ore. Rep. State Central Com., 1908; pvt. sec. to Gov. Frank W. Benson, 1909-11; speaker Ore. Ho. of Rep., 1909-13; mem. 64th to 67th Congresses (1915-23), 3d Ore. Dist. Republican. Episcopalian. Mason, Elk. Home: Portland, Ore. Deceased.

McARTHUR, John, mfr.; b. parish of Erskine, Scotland, Nov. 17, 1826; ed there; learned blacksmith's trade; m. Christina Cuthbertson, of his native parish, 1848. Settled in Chicago, 1849; became boiler mfr.; entered Civil War as col. 12th Ill. vols.; brig. gen., March 21, 1862, and bvt. maj. gen. Had command 2d div., 17th army corps, in operations against Vicksburg; distinguished himself in several battles. Was commr. Public Works of Chicago and pres. of bd. during Chicago fire, 1871; postmaster, Chicago, 1873-77. Home: Chicago, Ill. Died 1906.

McARTHUR, Lewis Linn, surgeon; b. Boston, Jan. 23, 1858; s. Maj. Joseph H. (U.S.A.) and Julia (Woodworth) M.; ed. Lake Forest (Ill.) Acad., 1873-74, Santa Clara (Calif.) Coll., 1875; M.D., Rush Med. Coll., Chicago, 1880; house surgeon, Cook Co. (Ill.) Hosp., 1880-81; post-grad. studies Universities of Heidelberg and Vienna, 1882-83; m. Mamie Walker, Feb. 25, 1885 (died 1932); children—Selim, Emilie Constance (dec.), Lewis Linn, Billings. Served as attending surgeon, St. Luke's and Michael Reese hosps., 1886—. Fellow Am. Surg. Assn. (pres. 1923), Am. Coll. Surgeons. Commd. maj., Med. R.C., 1917; dir. Base Hosp. No. 14. Chevalier Order of Leopold of Belgium. Home: Chicago, Ill. Died Nov. 5, 1934.

McARTHUR, William Taylor, surgeon; b. Moorefield, Ont., Can., Dec. 31, 1866; s. Duncan and Elizabeth (Taylor) McA.; grad. Owen Sound (Ont.) Collegiate Inst., 1891; M.B., Toronto U., 1895; post-grad. study London and Edinburgh; m. Mary Delia Smith, June 16, 1904; children—Elizabeth, Mary Beauchamp, William Taylor, Duncan Donald. Came to U.S., 1895; naturalized citizen, 1904. Began practice at Los Angeles, Calif., 1895; attending surgeon Los Angeles Gen. Hosp., 1914-19; prof. surg. anatomy, Los Angeles dept. U. of Calif., 1907-11; lecturer, artistic anatomy, Los Angeles Sch. of Art and Design; dir. "Better Health," pub. of Calif. Hosp.; mem. staff Calif. Lutheran Hosp. Examiner for pensions, Brit. Govt. and for U.S. Draft Bd., World War. Fellow Am. Coll. Surgeons, Royal Coll. Surgeons, Edinburgh. Republican. Presbyn. Mason. Home: Los Angeles, Calif. Died Mar. 12, 1930.

McATEE, John Lind, jurist; b. Smithsburg, Md.; s. William Brady and Anne (Boyd) M.; ed. Coll. of St. James, Md., and Princeton Coll., A.M., 1867; grad. law dept. Univ. of Md., 1878; m. Mary Ella McMurray, Oct. 5, 1870 (died 1893). Nominated, 1894, and renominated, 1900, as asso. justice Supreme Court of Okla. Republican. Resigned office and resumed practice of law, Apr. 1902. Home: Oklahoma City, Okla. Died 1904.

McAULIFF, Cornelius, newspaperman; b. in Ireland, 1850; s. Cornelius and Hannah M.; came to U.S. at 14; ed. in pub. schs., and law dept. U. of Mich.; m. Mary Hanlan, 1883. Engaged at various times in editorial positions on Chicago Morning News and Chicago Times; one of founders of Chicago Evening Mail; first mng. editor of Chicago Evening Post, 1890-95; mng. editor Chicago Times-Herald, now the Record-Herald, 1895—. Home: Chicago, Ill. Died 1911.

McAVOY, Charles D., lawyer; b. Danboro, Pa., Nov. 11, 1878; s. Dennis and Mary (Nolan) M.; B.A., Villanova Coll., 1898, M.A., 1901, LL.D., 1918; m. Alice McDermott, Nov. 16, 1907; children—Charles D., Mary Katherin, John Daniel. Began practice at Norristown, 1902; U.S. atty. Eastern Dist. of Pa., Mar. 4, 1920-Aug. 1, 1921 and from Sept. 13, 1913; as U.S. atty., investigated, indicted and convicted the Bergdolls and others associated with them on a charge of conspiracy to evade draft. Trustee Villanova Coll. Democrat. Catholic. Home: Norristown, Pa. Died Feb. 28, 1937.

McAVOY, John Vincent, judge; b. N.Y. City, July 11, 1878; s. Thomas F. and Mary A. (Fealey) M.; A.B., Manhattan Coll., 1897; LL.B., New York Law Sch., 1899; m. Marian Newcomb, Jan. 18, 1904; children—Clifford Thomas, Virginia, John, Richard, Marian Rebecca, Ann. Justice City Court of New York, 1908-18; justice Supreme Court of N.Y., 1st Dist., term 1918-31 (apptd. asso. justice Appellate Div., Jan. 1, 1923); reëlected to Supreme Court, 1931, for term ending 1945. Democrat. Home: New York, N.Y. Died Apr. 12, 1937.

McBAIN, Howard Lee, univ. prof.; b. Toronto, Can., July 20, 1880; s. William and Mary Catherine (Warden) M.; B.A., Richmond (Va.) Coll., 1900, M.A., 1901, LL.D., 1932; student University of Chicago, 1904; M.A., Columbia, 1905, Ph.D., 1907, LL.D., from same in 1929; m. Agnes Bartlett, Dec. 17, 1910; children—Bartlett, Mary. Asst. prin. Richmond High Sch., 1901-04; lecturer constl. history, U. of Va. Summer Sch., 1905; scholar, constl. law, 1904-06, hon. fellow, 1906-07, Columbia; instr. polit. science, 1907-09, dean College of Polit. Sciences, 1909-10, George Washington U.; asso. prof. polit. science, U. of Wis., 1910-13; asso. prof. municipal science and administration, 1913-17, Eaton prof., 1917-25, Ruggles prof. constl. law, 1925—, and dean of the graduate faculties, 1929—, Columbia U. Spl. counsel for City of N.Y. before State Constl. Conv., 1915. Member Bd. of Edn. City of N.Y., 1916-18; mem. and sec. N.Y. Charter Commn., 1921-23. Author: DeWitt Clinton and the Origin of the Spoils System, 1907; The Law and the Practice of Municipal Home Rule, 1916; Government and Politics in Virginia, 1916; American City Progress and the Law, 1917; The New Constitutions of Europe (with L. Rogers), 1922; The Living Constitution, 1927; Prohibition, Legal and Illegal, 1928. Homes: N.Y. City; Warsaw, N.Y. Died May 7, 1936.

McBEE, Silas, editor; b. Lincolnton, N.C., Nov. 14, 1853; s. V. A. M.; ed. U. of the South, Sewanee, Tennessee, 1876 (D.C.L., 1919). Editor of The Churchman, 1896-1912; founder and editor The Constructive Quarterly. Author: An Eirenic Itinerary. Home: Great Neck, L.I. Died Sept. 3, 1924.

McBRAYER, Louis Burgin, M.D.; b. Buncombe Co., N.C., Dec. 27, 1868; s. Adolphus and Lou (Case) M.; student Judson Coll., Hendersonville, N.C., 1883-86; M.D., U. of Louisville, Ky., 1889; m. Lillian Cordie Deaver, July 1890; children—Reuben A., Mrs. Sadie McCain, Louis B. Practiced at Asheville, 1889-1914; coroner Buncombe Co., N.C., 1901-07; health officer, Asheville, and mem. Bd. of Health, Buncombe Co., 1909-14; supt. N.C. Sanatorium for Treatment of Tuberculosis, 1914-24, organizing the state for fight against tuberculosis; mng. dir. N.C. Tuberculosis Assn., 1915—; surgeon Mission Hosp. Pres. State Bd. Med. Examiners, N.C., 1908-14. Pres. Sandhill Fruit Growers' Assn., 1922. Fellow Am. Coll. Physicians, A.M.A., Medical Society State of N.C. (pres. 1915; sec., treas., 1921—; editor ann. trans. 1918—). Democrat. Baptist. Grand Marshal Sovereign Grand Lodge, I.O.O.F., 1933, 34. Editor sect. on state medicine, in Southern Medicine and Surgery, 1920. Home: Southern Pines, N.C. Died Apr. 1, 1938.

McBRIDE, George Wickliffe, senator; b. Yamhill Co., Ore., Mar. 13, 1854; student Christian Coll., Ore., 2 yrs.; married. Admitted to bar, but never practiced; mcht. 10 yrs. Mem. Ore. Ho. of Rep., 1882 (speaker); sec. of state, Ore., 1887-95; U.S. senator from Ore., 1895-1901. U.S. commr. St. Louis Expn., 1901-05. Republican. Home: Portland, Ore. Died 1911.

McBRIDE, Henry, governor; b. Utah, Feb. 1856; student Trinity Coll., Conn., 3 yrs.; m. Alice Garrett, 1884. Admitted to bar, 1884; pros. atty., Skagit Co.; Wash., 1888; judge Superior Ct., 1891-96; elected lt.-gov., Wash., 1900, becoming gov. for unexpired term (1901-05) of Gov. John R. Rogers, deceased. Republican. Mem. law firm McBride, Stratton & Dalton. Home: Seattle, Wash. Died Oct. 6, 1937.

McBRIDE, James Harvey, M.D.; b. La Fayette, Ore., Jan. 23, 1849; s. James and Mahala (Miller) M.; student McMinnville Coll., Ore.; M.D., Bellevue Hosp. Med. Coll. (New York U.), 1873; service at Charity Hosp., Blackwell's Island, New York; m. Evangeline Ackley, Sept. 21, 1887; children—James Ackley (dec.), Emily (Mrs. Perigord). Asst. physician Northern Hosp. for Insane, Oshkosh, Wis., 1874-76; lecturer mental diseases, med. dept. U. of Pacific (now Cooper Med. Coll.), San Francisco, 1877-79; supt. Hosp. for Insane, Milwaukee, Wis., 1880-84; founder and med. dir. Milwaukee Sanitarium for Nervous Diseases, 1884-95; prof. neurology, Chicago Polyclinic, 1890-95; pres. Am. Acad. Medicine, 1909-10; chmn. Sect. Nervous and Mental Diseases A.M.A., 1905; pres. Am. Neurol. Assn., 1919. Mem. Calif. Commn. of Immigration and Housing; trustee Throop Elementary Sch., Pasadena. Republican. Home: Pasadena, Calif. Deceased.

McBRIDE, Robert W., lawyer; b. Richland Co., O., Jan. 25, 1842; s. Augustus and Martha Ann (Barnes) M.; pub. schs., Ohio and Ia. and Kirkville (Ia.) Acad.; m. Ida S. Chamberlain, Sept. 27, 1868. Admitted to bar, Apr. 1867; practiced at Waterloo, 1867-90 (except when on bench), at Indianapolis from 1893. Judge Circuit Ct., 35th Jud. Circuit, 1882-88; justice Supreme Ct. of Ind., Dec. 17, 1890-Jan. 2, 1893. Republican. Dir. counsel loan dept. State Life Ins. Co. Mem. Union Light Guard of Ohio (Abraham Lincoln's body guard); capt., lt. col. and col. 3d Regt. Ind. N.G. Mason. Author: History of the Union Light Guard Cavalry of Ohio; Abraham Lincoln's Body Guard, Personal Recollections of Abraham Lincoln. Adj. gen. G.A.R., 1917. Home: Indianapolis, Ind. Died May 15, 1926.

McBRIDE, Thomas Allen, judge; b. Yamhill Co., Ore., Nov. 15, 1847; s. James and Mahala (Miller) M.; brother of James Harvey M.; student McMinnville Coll., Ore.; m. Mary E. Merrill, Feb. 7, 1874. Admitted to bar, 1870; practiced at La Fayette, Ore.; mem. Ore. Ho. of Rep., 1877; dist. atty., 5th Jud. Dist., Ore., 1882-92; circuit judge, same dist., 1892-1909; asso. justice Supreme Ct. of Ore., 1909—(now chief justice). Republican. Mem. Christian (Disciples) Ch. Home: Deer Island, Ore. Died Sept. 10, 1930.

McBRIEN, Jasper Leonidas, educator; b. Newton Co., Mo, Mar. 19, 1867; s. William and Hetty (Henry) M.; student Campbell Normal U., Holton, Kan., 1886; B.E., State Normal Sch., Peru, Neb., 1900; A.M., U. of Neb., 1908; m. Eva Forbes, Dec. 29, 1891; children—Dean D., Rufus O., Ruth Beverley, Laura Betty, Richard L. Co. supt. schs., Johnson Co., Neb., 1890-93; dean Orleans Coll., 1893-97; supt. schs., Geneva, Neb., 1897-1901; dep. state supt. pub. instrn., Neb., 1901-05, state supt. pub. instrn., 1905-09; dir. Extension Div., U. of Neb., 1909-11; supt. schs., Harvard, Neb., 1913; sch. extension specialist, U.S. Bur. Edn., 1913-21; head dept. rural edn., Indiana State Normal School, Terre Haute, Ind., 1921-24; prof. rural edn. and dir. of community activities, Central State Teachers' Coll., Edmond, Okla., 1925-33; supervisor in secondary schs. and character education, State of Nebraska, 1933—. Special supervisor at large in the Indian Edn. Service, 1916; selected by Secretary Lane to direct 3rd Liberty Loan drive for the Dept. of Interior, 1918, raising $2,325,000; mem. Neb. State Bd. Edn., 1905-09; sec. Neb. State Bd. Health, 1905-09; sec. State Bd. Charities and Correction, 1905-09. Mason. Author: America First, a Patriotic Reader, 1916. Home: Lincoln, Neb. Died Mar. 24, 1935.

McBRYDE, James Bolton, chemist; b. Buckingham Co., Va., Sept. 2, 1866; s. John McLaren and Cora (Bolton) M.; bro. of John McLaren M., Jr.; A.B., S.C. Coll., 1886; C.E., U. of S.C., 1888; m. Mary Read Comfort, Aug. 8, 1905. Asst. chemist, S.C. Agrl. Expt. Stas., 1888-91; asst. chemist, 1891-94, and chemist, 1894-1901, Tenn. Agrl. Expt. Sta.; asst. prof. chemistry, 1905-07, prof., 1907—, head of dept., 1915—, Va. Poly Inst. Author (with

W. H. Beall): The Chemistry of the Cotton Plant. Home: Blacksburg, Va. Died July 2, 1925.

McBRYDE, John McLaren, educator; b. Abbeville, S.C., Jan. 1, 1841; s. John and Susan (McLaren) M.; studied U. of S.C., and U. of Va., 1860; (LL.D., Southwestern Presbyn. U., 1884, and U. of South Carolina, 1920; Ph.D., Univ. of Tenn., 1887; Sc.D., Va. Poly. Inst., 1907); officer C.S.A., 1861-63; in Confederate treasury dept., 1863-65; m. Cora Bolton (sister of Benjamin M. Bolton), Nov. 18, 1863; father of John McLaren, Jr., James Bolton and Charles N. McB. Farmed in Virginia; active in farmers' organizations; prof. botany and agr., U. of Tenn., 1879-82; prof. botany and pres., S.C. Coll., 1883-87; elected pres. U. of Tenn., 1887, but declined; dir. S.C. Agrl. Expt. Stas. and pres. U. of S.C., 1887-91; pres. Va. Poly. Inst., 1891-1907, pres. emeritus. Received hon. appmt. on Carnegie Foundation for Advancement of Teaching, 1907. Mem. Miller bd. trustees, U. of Va., 1876-79. Declined position U.S. asst. sec. agr., 1893; dir. Va. Agrl. Expt. Sta., 1891-1904; elected pres. U. of Tenn., 1887, pres. Sweet Briar Inst., 1903, and pres. U. of Va., 1904, but declined all three. McMaster medalist, U. of S.C., 1912. Home: Blacksburg, Va. Died Mar. 20, 1923.

McBURNEY, Charles, surgeon; b. Roxbury, Mass., Feb. 17, 1845; s. Charles and Rosine (Horton) M.; A.B., Harvard, 1866, A.M., 1869; M.D., Coll. Phys. and Surg. (Columbia), 1870; m. Margaret W. Weston, Oct. 8, 1874. Asst. and demonstrator anatomy, 1872-89, also lecturer anatomy of nerves and surgery, 1878-82, prof. surgery, 1889-92, clin. surgery, 1892-1907, emeritus prof. surgery, 1907, Coll. Physician and Surgeons; visiting surgeon, St. Luke's Hosp., 1875-79, Bellevue Hosp., 1888-1900; sole visiting surgeon, Roosevelt Hosp., 1889-1901; consulting surgeon, New York, Presbyn., St. Luke's, St. Mark's and Orthopedic hosps., and to Hosp. for Ruptured and Crippled (N.Y. City). Hon. fellow Royal Coll. Surgeons, Edinburgh, Coll. Physicians of Philadelphia. Died Nov. 7, 1913.

McCABE, Charles Cardwell, M.E. bishop, 1896—; b. Athens, O., Oct. 11, 1836; s. Robert and Sarah (Robinson) M. C.; ed. Ohio Wesleyan Univ., Delaware, O.; entered Ohio Conf., M.E. Ch., 1860. Became, in autumn of 1862, chaplain 122d Ohio inf.; captured at battle of Winchester; was in Libby Prison 4 months; rejoined his regt., but soon after went into service of the Christian Commn., for which he raised large sums; after war became pastor at Portsmouth, O., and financial agt. Ohio Wesleyan Univ.; in 1868 agt., and later asst. corr. sec. Bd. of Ch. Extension, M.E. Ch.; 1884 sec. Missionary Soc. M.E. Ch. His work as sec. added half a million dollars to the annual income of that society. Elected chancellor Am. Univ., Washington, Dec. 10, 1902. Died 1906.

McCABE, Harriet Calista (Clark), Christian worker; b. Sidney, N.Y., Jan. 19, 1827; d. Arvine and Eliza (Higgins) Clark; ed. chiefly at home by pvt. tutors and at Elmira Acad., N.Y.; preceptress Dickinson Sem., Williamsport, Pa., 1851-57; m. L. D. McCabe, D.D., LL.D., of Ohio Wesleyan U., July 19, 1857 (dec.). Was chmn. of state com. which organized the Woman's Temperance Crusade in Ohio, 1873-74; was 1st pres. W.C.T.U., wrote original charter and gave organization its name. Editor Woman's Home Missions, organ Woman's Home Missionary Soc. M.E. Ch., 1884-1902, and was also v.p. and in charge of the Indian Bur. of the society. Home: Delaware, O. Died Sept. 25, 1919.

McCABE, Lida Rose, author; b. Columbus, O., Mar. 3, 1865; d. Bernard and Delia (Molloy) McCabe; grad. Columbus High Sch.; student at Sorbonne and Convent rue Notre Dame de Sion, Paris, Columbia U. Paris corr. Am. Press Assn., 1889-90, New York Tribune, 1890; spl. writer New York Herald, Times and Sun; staff New York Press, 1902-03. Opened ethical lecture course to women at St. Xavier's Coll., New York. Author: Occupation and Compensations of Women; Don't You Remember? (vol. of hist. sketches of Ohio); The American Girl at College. Died Dec. 9, 1938.

McCABE, W(illiam) Gordon, educator; b. Richmond, Va., Aug. 4, 1841; s. Rev. John Collins (poet and antiquarian) and Sophia Gordon (Taylor) M.; (g.g.d. George Taylor, Signer of Declaration of Independence); gold medalist twice Hampton (Va.) Acad., 1858; grad. U. of Va., 1861; (hon. A.M., William and Mary, 1868, LL.D., 1906; A.M., Williams, 1885; Litt.D., Yale, 1897); served pvt. to capt. arty., 3d corps, in Army of Northern Va., 1861-65; m. Jenny Pleasants Harrison Osborne, Apr. 9, 1867 (died 1912); m. 2d, Gillie Armistead Cary, Mar. 16, 1915. Established and conducted, 1865-1901, University Sch., Petersburg and Richmond. Visitor, 1888-92, vice-rector, 1892-96, Univ. of Va. Commr. and dir. Jamestown Expn., 1905-07. Pres. Va. Hist. Soc.; pres. S.R. in Va., 1907-09; historian-gen. Gen. Soc. S.R., 1908-11; pres. Soc. Descendants of the Signers; pres. Soc. of Cincinnati in Va.; col. comdg. A. P. Hill Camp U.C.V., 1880, 1890-95; mem. Va. Gettysburg Monument Commn.; president Pegram Battalion Assn. Vets. Author: A Grammar of the Latin Language, 1884; Latin Reader, 1886; Cæsar's Gallic War, 1886; Virginia Schools Before and After the Revolution, 1890; Memoir of Joseph Bryan, 1909; The First University in America, 1619-1622, 1911. Home: Richmond, Va. Deceased.

McCAGG, Ezra Butler, lawyer; b. Kinderhook, N.Y., Nov. 22, 1825; studied law, Hudson, N.Y.; practiced in Chicago, 1847—; was mem. U.S. Sanitary Commn. and pres. Northwestern Sanitary Commission during Civil war; pres. many yrs. bd. trustees Ill. Hosp. for Insane; 1st pres. Lincoln Park trustees; has large library and art collection. Home: Chicago, Ill. Died 1908.

McCAIN, George Nox, journalist, author; b. Pittsburgh, Pa., Jan. 27, 1856; s. Robert Galbraith and Elizabeth Griffin (Rockefeller) M.; ed. Classical and Scientific Inst., Mt. Pleasant, Pa.; hon. A.M., Bucknell U., 1897; Litt.D., Ursinus Coll., 1922; m. Mary V. Overholt, Jan. 21, 1879. Publisher Times and Mining Journal, Mt. Pleasant, 1878-79; city editor, 1880-86, New York corr., 1886-87, Pittsburgh Dispatch; Washington correspondent, with proprietary interest in the Pittsburgh Gazette, 1887-89; on editorial staff Philadelphia Press, 1889-1902 and 1904-Dec. 1906. Editor and pub. Colorado Springs (Colo.) Daily Gazette, 1902-04. Spl. corr. Phila. Press in interior Venezuela during British boundary excitement, 1896; editorial staff Evening Public Ledger, 1919-23, Morning Public Ledger, 1924-26, Philadelphia Evening Bulletin, 1927-28; foreign correspondent. Pa. commr. Trans-Mississippi and Internat. Expn., Omaha, 1898; mem. Phila. Relief Expdn. to P.R. on U.S.S. Panther, 1899; spl. agt. U.S. P.O. Dept., investigating mail routes on the Yukon, 1901. Mem. Exec. Council and dir. press news for Pa. Federal Food Administration during World War. Lecturer on and traveler in Balkans, Far East, Barbary States, Central and South America, Alaska, etc., 1906-13. Delivered Sesquicentennial address at Valley Forge, on occasion of celebration of Washington's encampment there. Lieutenant colonel military staff Governor Hastings of Pa., 1895-99. Decorated Order of the Liberator by Govt. Venezuela, 1896. Republican. Mason. Author: Through the Great Campaign; The Crimson Dice; Farm Homes (U.S. Dept. of Agr.); War Rations for Pennsylvanians; Little Songs of Travel (verse). Home: Philadelphia, Pa. Died Dec. 11, 1934.

McCAIN, Henry Pinckney, army officer; b. in Carroll Co., Miss., Jan. 23, 1861; s. W. A. McC.; grad. U.S. Mil. Acad., 1885; m. Emeline De Moss, Nov. 14, 1888. Commd. 2d lt. 3d Inf., June 14, 1885; promoted through grades to col., Apr. 23, 1904; brig. gen. the adj. gen., Aug. 27, 1914; maj. gen. the adj. gen., Oct. 6, 1917; maj. gen. Nat. Army, Aug. 27, 1918; maj. gen. regular army, retired, July 22, 1921. Served in Montana and Minn. until 1889; prof. mil. science and tactics, La. State U., 1889-91; acting asst. adj. gen. in Alaska, and in divisions of 8th Army Corps in Philippines, 1898; actg. chief commissary and actg. judge advocate, Dept. of the Columbia, 1899-1900; mem. Gen. Staff Corps and chief of staff, Dept. of Mindanao and of Southwestern Div., Mar. and Apr. 1904; adj. gen. Philippine Div., 1912-14; adj. gen. U.S.A., 1914-18; comdg. 12th Div., Camp Devens, Mass., Aug. 1918. Awarded D.S.M., 1919. Died July 25, 1941.

McCALEB, Ella, educator; b. Mt. Pleasant, Pa., Apr. 23, 1856; d. John Dickey and Sarah Beidler (Sherrick) McCaleb; A.B., Vassar Coll., 1878; unmarried. Teacher, Foster School, Clifton Springs, N.Y., 1878-81, Detroit (Mich.) Home and Day Sch., 1881-85; sec. Vassar Coll., 1885, dean, 1913-23. Trustee Penn. Sch., St. Helena Island, S.C., 1927—. Presbyterian. Died Jan. 9, 1933.

McCALEB, John Bell, lawyer; b. Evening Shade, Ark., Oct. 24, 1856; s. James Haywood and Frances Ann M.; ed. academy, Evening Shade; m. Allie Abernathy, Jan. 10, 1883. Admitted to Ark. bar, 1881; practiced, Evening Shade, 7 yrs., as partner Hon. Sam H. Davidson; moved to Batesville, 1906, and practiced with Hon. Lyman F. Reeder, as McCaleb & Reeder, until 1918; in practice with son as McCaleb & McCaleb. Judge 16th Jud. Circuit of Ark., 3 terms, 1891-1902; state capitol commr., 1903-09 (chmn. bd.); del. Ark. Constl. Conv., 1917. Democrat. Mason. Home: Batesville, Ark. Died Aug. 2, 1931.

McCALL, Edward Everett, judge; b. Albany, N.Y., Jan. 6, 1863; s. John and Catherine M.; ed. Albany High Sch., and New York U.; LL.B., New York U., 1884; (LL.D., Manhattan Coll. and N.Y. U., 1904); m. Ella Frances Gaynor, Sept. 29, 1886. Admitted to bar, 1884, and practiced at New York, 1884-1902; justice Supreme Ct. of N.Y., 1st District, 1902-13; Dem. candidate for mayor, Nov. 1913. Died Mar. 12, 1924.

McCALL, John A., pres. New York Life Ins. Co., 1892—; b. Albany, N.Y., 1849; ed. there; became clerk in Albany State Currency Assorting House; then was in service of Conn. Mut. Life Ins. Co. until 1869; served in N.Y. State Ins. Dept. as clerk, 1869-76; deputy supt., 1876-83, supt. Ins. of N.Y., 1883-86; comptroller Equitable Life Assurance Soc., 1887-92; m. Mary I. Horan. Pres. Berkshire Cotton Mfg. Co.; trustee Continental Trust Co., N.Y. Security & Trust Co.; dir. Nat. City Bank, Central Nat. Bank, First Nat. Bank of City of New York, etc. Home: New York, N.Y. Died 1906.

McCALL, John Etheridge, judge; b. Clarksburg, Tenn., Aug. 14, 1859; s. Henry and Rebecca Frances (Bowlin) M.; A.B., U. of Tenn., 1881; m. Addie Timberlake, Oct. 14, 1885. Admitted to bar, 1882; editor Tennessee Republican, 1882; mem. Tenn. Ho. of Rep., 1887-90; asst. U.S. atty., Western Dist. of Tenn., 1890-91; mem. 54th Congress (1895-97); candidate for gov. of Tenn., 1900; collector internal revenue, 1902-05; U.S. dist. judge for West Tenn., Jan. 17, 1905—. Methodist. Home: Memphis, Tenn. Died Aug. 8, 1920.

McCALL, Samuel Walker, governor; b. East Providence, Pa., Feb. 28, 1851; s. Henry and Mary Ann (Elliott) M.; A.B., Dartmouth, 1874, Phi Beta Kappa; (LL.D., Dartmouth, 1901, Oberlin, 1908, Tufts, 1914, U. of Maine, 1915, Trinity, Columbia, Williams, 1916; Dalhousie, 1918, U. of Rochester, 1919); m. Ella Esther Thompson, May 23, 1881. Admitted to Mass. bar, in practice at Boston; was editor-in-chief Boston Daily Advertiser. Del. Rep. Nat. Conv., 1888, del. at-large, 1900, 16 (seconded nomination of Gen. Gresham for presidency, 1888); mem. Mass. Ho. of Rep., 1888, 89, 92; mem. 53d to 62d Congresses (1893-1913), 8th Mass. Dist.; mem. Ways and Means Com. 14 yrs.; gov. of Mass., 1916, 17, 18. Mem. President's 2d Industrial Conf.; mem. Lincoln Memorial Commn. Fellow Am. Acad. Arts and Sciences, Nat. Inst. Social Sciences. Author: Life of Thaddeus Stevens (Am. Statesmen Series), 1899; The Business of Congress (the Blumenthal lectures, Columbia U.), 1911; Life of Thomas B. Reed (Am. Statesmen Series), 1914; The Liberty of Citizenship (Dodge lectures, Yale U.), 1915. Cole lecturer at Bowdoin; Phi Beta Kappa orator at Harvard, Dartmouth and Tufts. Home: Winchester, Mass. Died Nov. 4, 1923.

McCALLA, Albert, mfr.; b. Bloomington, Ind., Dec. 1, 1846; s. Thomas and Marianne (Davisson) M.; A.B., Monmouth (Ill.) Coll., 1867, A.M., 1870, Ph.D., 1883; student McCormick Theol. Sem., Chicago, 1868-69; B.D., Union Theol. Sem., New York, 1870; m. Eleanor N. Hamill, May 16, 1871. Ordained Presbyn. ministry, 1871; pastor Emporia, Kan., 1871-73; prof. natural sciences, Parsons Coll., Fairfield, Ia., 1875-86; prof. mathematics and astronomy, Lake Forest (Ill.) U., 1886-89; pres. Merced (Calif.) Collegiate Inst., 1890-93; instr. biology, N. Div. High Sch., Chicago, 1893-95; pres. McCalla-Wilson Co., later McCalla-Ross Co., Chicago, 1898-1907, Calumet Car Co., 1898—; v.p. and mgr. McCalla-Reichert Co.; sec., dir. Calumet Advertising Co.; dist. mgr. for Northern Ill. of Keystone View Co. Republican. Home: Chicago, Ill. Died June 6, 1918.

McCALLA, Bowman Henry, rear admiral U.S.N.; b. Camden, N.J., June 19, 1844; s. Auley and Mary Duffield (Hendry) M.; apptd. from N.J., and grad. U.S. Naval Acad., 1864; m. Elizabeth Hazard Sargent, Mar. 3, 1875. Promoted ensign, Nov. 1, 1866; advanced through grades to rear adm., Oct. 11, 1903. Summer of 1864 on board the yacht America, in pursuit of Confederate steamers Florida and Tallahassee; served on Susquehanna, 1865-66; Brooklyn, 1866-67; Sabine, 1867-68; Tuscarora, 1868-71; Wabash, 1871-74; Wachusett, 1874; Naval Acad., 1874-78; exec. officer Powhatan, 1878-81; asst. to Bur. of Navigation, 1882-87; comd. Enterprise, 1887-90; Navy Yard, Mare Island, 1893-97; Naval War Coll., 1897; comd. Marblehead, N. Atlantic Sta., 1897-98, during the war with Spain; "for eminent and conspicuous gallantry in battle during the Spanish War," was advanced 6 numbers in rank; on duty Navy Yard, Norfolk, 1898-99; comd. Newark, Asiatic Sta., 1899-1901; during the Boxer uprising in China, in June, 1900, comd. the landing party from U.S. Asiatic Fleet which formed a part of the column under Vice Admiral Seymour of the British Navy, in an attempt to relieve the legations in Peking. For this service was advanced 3 numbers in rank "for eminent and conspicuous gallantry in battle;" comd. Kearsarge, 1901-02; commandant, Naval Training Sta., San Francisco, 1902-03, Navy Yard, Mare Island, Calif., 1903-06; retired, June 19, 1906. Recipient of 2 Congressional medals for battle of Cienfuegos and at Guantanamo; and 1 Congressional Medal for "specially meritorious service other than in battle," during Spanish War. Decorated with Order of the Red Eagle, by Emperor of Germany; China War Medal, by the King of England, in recognition of service during Boxer uprising in China in 1900. Home: Santa Barbara, Calif. Died 1910.

McCALLEY, Henry, chief asst. State geologist of Ala., 1890—; b. Madison Co., Ala., Feb. 11, 1852; s. Thomas Sanford and Caroline Matilda McC.; grad. Univ. of Va., B.S., C.E., M.E., 1875 (A.M., causa honoris, Univ. of Ala., 1878); unmarried. Farmed, 1876; taught school, Demopolis, Ala., 1877; asst. prof. chemistry, Univ. of Ala., 1878-83; surveyed the Warrier River, above Tuscaloosa, Ala., under auspices of War Dept., 1879; chemist to Geol. Survey of Ala. and asst. State geologist, 1883-90. Treas. Ala. Industrial and Scientific Soc., 1890—; fellow Geol. Soc. of America. Home: University, Ala. Died 1904.

McCALLIE, Samuel Washington, geologist; b. Sevier Co., Tenn., Aug. 2, 1856; s. Andrew Jackson and Theodosia Adeline (Cunningham) McC.; Ph.B., Wesleyan U., Athens, Tenn., 1882; grad. study Johns Hopkins, 1888-90; m. Elizabeth Macfarlane Hanleiter, Dec. 25, 1899; children—Edith Emeline, Mrs. Elizabeth Snoots. Instr. in geology, U. of Tenn., 1891-93; asst. state geologist, Ga., 1893-1908, state geologist, 1908—. Served with Signal Corps, U.S.A., 1882. Mem. advisory bd., Ga. Nat. Defense, World War. Democrat. Presbyn. Author: Mineral Resources of Georgia, 1910, 26; Handbook of Mineral Resources of Georgia, 1911, 3d edit., 1923; Drainage Investigations in Georgia, 1911; Agricultural Drainage in Georgia, 1917. Home: Atanta, Ga. Died Oct. 26, 1933.

McCALLIE, Thomas Spencer, clergyman; b. Chattanooga, Tenn., Jan. 7, 1869; s. Thomas Hooke and Ellen Douglas (Jarnagin) McC.; prep. edn., Bingham Sch., N.C.; student King Coll., Bristol, Va., 1884-85, Central U. of Ky., 1886-87, U. of Chattanooga, 1888-89; D.D., King Coll., 1916; LL.D., U. of Chattanooga, 1932; m. Bessie D. Crane, Apr. 19, 1894; 1 son, Thomas Crane. Ordained ministry Presbyn. Ch. in U.S., 1896; pastor successively East Lake Ch., Chattanooga, 1896-1909, Central Ch., Chattanooga, 1909— (new bldg. and equipment, 1921). Chmn. Home Mission, Presbytery of Knoxville, 1914, Chattanooga Red Cross, 1917—; dir. Chattanooga Community Chest, Chattanooga Social Service Bur. Chaplain, maj. R.O.T.C. of Chattanooga, World War; organized, operated Soldiers' Recreation Centre, Chattanooga, World War; apptd. "Chaplain of Chattanooga" for life by City Commn., 1927; moderator of the Synod of Apalachia, 1929-30. Trustee King Coll. (Bristol, Tenn.), Stonewall Jackson Coll. (Abingdon, Va.); pres. McCallie Sch. for Boys; founder Orphans' Home for Mountain Children of Tenn. Democrat. Mason, K.P. Home: Chattanooga, Tenn. Died Sept. 22, 1936.

McCAMMON, Joseph Kay, lawyer; b. Philadelphia, Oct. 13, 1845; s. David Chambers and Josephine Kay McC.; grad. Princeton, 1865 (A.M.); studied law in Phila.; m. Catherine McKnight, Sept. 22, 1870. Register in Bankruptcy, 1870; spl. counsel of U.S. in Washington, 1871; pres. bd. to investigate Indian service, 1877; asst. atty. gen. U.S., 1880-85; U.S. commr. of railroads, 1881; apptd. by Pres. Garfield to treat with Bannock and Shoshone Idians, 1881, by Pres. Arthur with Flatheads and affiliated Indians, 1882. Author: Report on Indian Service, 1878; Report of Councils with Bannock and Shoshone Indians, 1881; Report Councils with Flathead and Other Indians, 1882; Arguments in Cases Affecting Pacific and Other Railroads. Home: Washington, D.C. Died 1907.

McCAMPBELL, Eugene Franklin, physician; b. Marysville, O., Apr. 15, 1880; s. of James and Flora Jeanette (Ryan) McC.; Ohio State U., 1899-1902; S.B., U. of Chicago, 1906, Ph.D., 1910; M.D., Rush Medical Coll., 1912; m. Katharine Scott, June 14, 1906; children—Jean Katharine, Barbara. Instr. bacteriology, Ohio Med. U., 1903-04; asst. in bacteriology, U. of Wis., 1905-06; asst. in pathology, U. of Chicago, summers, 1908-11; asst. prof. of bacteriology, 1906-10, prof., 1910-12, prof. of preventive medicine, 1912-27, Ohio State U. Pathologist, Columbus State Hosp., 1909-11; sec. and exec. officer Ohio State Bd. of Health, 1912-16; dean Coll. of Medicine, Ohio State U., 1916-27. Lt. col. M.C., U.S.A., 1917-19; col. M.O.R.C., 1922. Fellow Am. Coll. Physicians. Methodist. Mason. Author: General Bacteriology (with Frost), 1910; Laboratory Methods for Study of Immunity, 1910. Home: Columbus, O. Died May 8, 1937.

McCANDLESS, David Alexander, judge; b. Hart Co., Ky., Mar. 2, 1865; s. William Vaughn and Sarah Bell (Thurman) McC.; ed. acads.; B.L., Cumberland U., Lebanon, Tenn., 1894; m. Elizabeth Moneypenny, June 20, 1894; children—Belle (Mrs. W. H. Fulton), David A., Frances (wife of Allen Roby, officer of the U.S. Army). Began practice at Munfordville, 1894; county judge, Hart Co., Ky., 1897-1900; commonwealth atty., 10th Ky. Jud. Dist., 1906-10; circuit judge 10th Ky. Jud. Dist., 1916-23, elected judge Court of Appeals, Nov. 1922, for term beginning Jan. 1, 1923; retired from appellate bench Nov. 1, 1929; practicing at Louisville. Democrat. Baptist. Mason. Home: Louisville, Ky. Died Mar. 2, 1939.

McCANDLESS, John Andrew, capitalist; b. Indiana, Pa., June 11, 1853; s. Thomas McCarthy and Eliza Anna (Newman) McC.; ed. pub. schs.; m. Ella Thompson, 1877 (dec.); children—Frances Madge, dec. (Mrs. H. M. Hepburn), James Crystal (dec.); m. 2d, Stella Hymson, Sept. 20, 1927. Engaged in oil well drilling until 1881, artesian well drilling, Honolulu, 1881—; mem. McCandless Bros., well drillers; pres. John A. McCandless & Co.; v.p. Oahu Sugar Co., Pioneer Mill Co. Active in Hawaiian revolutions of 1887 and 1893; mem. Com. of 13 which overthrew the kingdom; Hawaiian senator, Republic of Hawaii; supt. pub. works, Hawaii, 1 yr. Republican. Mason. Home: Honolulu, T.H. Died Jan. 30, 1930.

McCANDLESS, Lincoln Loy, territorial delegate; b. Honolulu, T.H., Sept. 18, 1859; s. Thomas McCartney and Eliza Ann (Newman) McC.; ed. pub. schs., W.Va.; m. Elizabeth Janet Cartwright, May 24, 1904; 1 dau., Elizabeth Loy (Mrs. A. Lester Marks). Was engaged in oil and mining business, W.Va. and Colo.; later engaged in constrn. artesian wells, T.H.; operator cattle ranches, T.H., 1887—; resident commr. from T.H. to 73d U.S. Congress (1933-35). Democrat. Home: Honolulu, T.H. Died Oct. 5, 1940.

McCANN, Alfred W(atterson), author; b. Pittsburgh, Pa., Jan. 9, 1879; A.B. and D.Litt., Duquesne U.; LL.D., Fordham; studied U. of Chicago; m. May C. Carmody, 1905; children—Frances M., Muriel M., Alfred W., Rosemary, Justin Carmody. Author: Starving America, 1913; Vital Questions and Answers, 1913; Thirty-Cent Bread, 1917; This Famishing World (later issued under title Science of Eating), 1919; God—or Gorilla, 1922; The Science of Keeping Young, 1925; Greatest of Men—Washington, 1927. Home: Yonkers, N.Y. Died Jan. 19, 1931.

McCANN, George, judge; b. Elmira, N.Y., June 23, 1864; s. James and Helen L. (Neish) M.; B.S., Cornell U., 1886, LL.B., 1888; m. Florence Fillingham, Apr. 6, 1893 (died 1915); m. 2d, Mrs. Florence J. Farr, May 27, 1919. Admitted to N.Y. bar, 1888, and practiced at Elmira; judge and surrogate, Chemung Co., N.Y., 1903-14; justice Supreme Court of N.Y., 6th Dist., term Jan. 1914-Dec. 31, 1927; assigned to appellate div., 1923. Republican. Home: Elmira, N.Y. Died Dec. 1, 1932.

McCANN, Rebecca, writer, illustrator; b. Quincy, Ill.; d. John A. and Ada May (Keller) McCann; ed. pub. schs., Ill., and Chicago Acad. Fine Arts (winner of 1st scholarship for women there, 1913). Began, 1914, writing and illustrating a daily newspaper feature, "The Cheerful Cherub," for the Chicago Evening Post; this feature syndicated throughout the country, 1914—. Author: The Adventures of Annabel (vols. I and II), 1918; About Annabel, 1922; The Cheerful Cherub, 1923. Home: New York, N.Y. Died Dec. 22, 1927.

McCANN, William Penn, commodore U.S.N., retired May 1892; b. Paris, Ky., May 4, 1830; apptd. to U.S.N., Nov. 1848; grad. U.S. Naval Acad., June 15, 1854—passed midshipman; lt., Sept. 16, 1855; lt. comdr., July 16, 1862; comdr., July 25, 1866; capt., Sept. 21, 1876; commodore, Jan. 26, 1887. In blockading and other active duty during Civil war; drove off Confederate battery attacking Franklin's corps, May 2, 1862, at West Point, Va.; captured, July 4, 1862, Confederate gunboat Teaser, with plans of batteries, torpedoes and defenses of Richmond; later in numerous engagements with batteries; captured several blockade runners; took part in battle of Mobile Bay, etc. After war served on many stas.; acting rear admiral comdg. S. Pacific Sta., 1891. With 5 cruisers at Iquique, Chile, June 4, 1891, enforced the surrender of steamer Itata, with arms and ammunition smuggled out of San Diego, Calif., and transferred to the Itata at Santa Catalina Island. Sent the ship and arms back to San Diego and received thanks and commendation of Navy Dept. Mem. bd. for exam. and promotion of officers, 1891-92; during war with Spain, 1898, served as pres. on courts of inquiry, and courts martial, and as prize commr. Southern dist. of N.Y. Home: New Rochelle, N.Y. Died 1906.

McCARL, John Raymond, former comptroller general of U.S.; b. near Des Moines, Ia., Nov. 27, 1879; s. of John Henry and Sarah (Gosslee) McCarl; LL.B., U. of Nebraska, 1903; m. Ethel Barnett, Nov. 26, 1905. Mem. law firm Cordeal & McCarl, McCook, 1903-14; pvt. sec. to U.S. Senator George W. Norris, 1914-18; exec. sec. Nat. Rep. Congressional Com., 1918-21; comptroller gen. of U.S., 1921-36. Methodist. Home: McCook, Neb. Died Aug. 2, 1940.

McCARREN, Patrick H., politican; b. East Cambridge, Mass.; removed to Brooklyn, with parents, when 8 yrs. old; ed. in pub. schs. Mem. N.Y. Assembly, 3 terms; State senator, 1895—. Active Democratic leader in Brooklyn many years. Home: Brooklyn, N.Y. Died 1909.

McCARROLL, William, merchant; b. Belfast, Ireland, May 1851; s. Rev. William and Mary A. (McCreery) M.; ed. Russell's Acad., Belfast, Brookville Acad., Royal Academical Instn., Belfast; came to America, 1869; m. Jennie Allen, Sept. 12, 1872 (died 1901); children—Joseph A., Mary Clyde (Mrs. Henry A. Mark), Irene M., Jennie Frances (wife of Rev. Dr. F. Boyd Edwards), William R., Estelle S.; m. 2d, Grace J. Johnston, May 1911. Entered business in New York as Wm. McCarroll & Co., 1878; organizer, 1882, v.p. and gen. mgr. Am. Leather Co.; organized Am. Leather Co. of New York, and was its president until retired; v.p. Munson Inland Water Lines; trustee and v.p. Dime Savings Bank, Brooklyn; pres. Nat. Bond & Mortgage Insurance Co., 1912-16; mem. advisory com. Bedford Branch Brooklyn Trust Co. Mem. N.Y. Pub. Service Commn. (1st dist.), 1907-12; commr. State of N.Y. Barge Canal Survey Committee. Pres. Morocco Mfrs. Nat. Assn., N.Y. Bd. Trade & Transportation (dir.); v.p. Nat. Immigration Restriction League; v.p. Chamber Commerce, New York; v.p. Brooklyn-Queens Y.M.C.A. Trustee Adelphi Coll. Republican. Presbyn. Home: New York, N.Y. Died Aug. 14, 1933.

McCARTER, James W.; b. Jarvis, Ont., Can., July 29, 1872; s. John McCarter and Sarah Jane (Craig) McC.; came to U.S., 1890; LL.B., Valparaiso (Ind.) U., 1899; m. Matilda Jane Jacobson, May 18, 1902; children—Sarah Jane C. (Mrs. S. M. Stockdale), Marie E., Opia A. Began practice at Bowdle, 1900; state's atty., Edmunds Co., S.D., 1901, 02, county judge, 1910-13; Dem. nom. for gov. of S.D., 1914; asst. register of Treasury, Washington, D.C., 1915-20; resumed law practice, 1920; state's atty. Edmunds Co., term 1927 and 28, inclusive; county judge, Edmunds County, 1929—. Candidate for Congress, 2d S.D. Dist., 1918. Pres. of S.Dak. Good Roads Assn., Apr. 1935—. Home: Ipswich, S.D. Died Dec. 22, 1939.

McCARTER, Margaret Hill, author; b. Charlottesville, Ind.; d. Thomas Thornburg and Nancy (Davis) Hill; grad. State Normal Sch., Terre Haute, Ind.; hon. A.M., Baker; Litt.D., Washburn, also Litt.D., Coll. of Emporia; m. William Arthur McCarter, D.D.S.; children—Katharine Davis (Mrs. John R. Dean), Jessie Isabel (Mrs. Charles L. Baker), William Hill. Taught in Ind. pub. schs., later head English Dept., Topeka High Sch.; lecturer on lit. and ednl. subjects. Mem. Kan. State Illiteracy Commn. V.p. Woman's Rep. Nat. Com., 1920. Methodist. Author: The Cottonwood's Story, 1903; Cuddy's Baby, 1907; In Old Quivira, 1908; Cuddy and Other Stories, 1908; The Price of the Prairies, 1910; The Peace of the Solomon Valley, 1911; A Wall of Men, 1912; Master's Degree, 1913; Winning the Wilderness, 1914; The Corner Stone, 1915; Vanguards of the Plains, 1917; The Reclaimers, 1918; Paying Mother, 1920; Homeland, 1922; Widening Waters, 1924; The Candle in the Window, 1925. Home: Topeka, Kan. Died Aug. 31, 1938.

McCARTER, Robert Harris, lawyer; b. Newton, N.J., Apr. 28, 1859; s. Thomas N. and Mary Louise (Haggerty) M.; A.B., Princeton, 1879, LL.D. honoris causa, 1904; LL.B., Columbia, 1882; LL.D. honoris causa, N.J. Law Sch., 1935; m. Mary Bouvier Peterson, Oct. 12, 1886; children—George W. C., Mrs. Eleanor Young. Admitted to bar, 1882, and began practice at Newark, N.J.; sr. mem. McCarter & English. Atty.-gen. of N.J., 1903-08. Trustee Newark Museum Assn. Republican. Presbyn. Home: Rumson (P.O. Red Bank), N.J. Died May 30, 1941.

McCARTER, Thomas Nesbitt, lawyer; b. Morristown, N.J., Jan. 31, 1824; s. Robert Harris and Eliza Nesbitt McC.; grad. Princeton, 1842 (hon. LL.D., 1875); m. Mary Louise Haggerty, Dec. 4, 1849 (died 1896). Admitted to N.J. bar, 1845; commenced practice at Newton, N.J.; removed to Newark, June 1865; was apptd., 1863, Chancery reporter of N.J., and published 2 vols. chancery reports (14 and 15 N.J. Equity Reports); delivered annual address, 1868, at commencement at Princeton before the 2 literary socs., as representative of Am. Whig Society. Republican. Honorary corporator at Dickinson Coll., Pa.; N.J. v.p. of Scotch Irish Soc. of America; hon. mem. Am. Geog. Soc.; trustee Princeton Univ., elected June 1879. Home: Newark, N.J. Died 1902.

McCARTER, Uzal H., banker; b. Newton, N.J., July 5, 1861; s. Thomas H. and Mary L. (Haggerty) M.; A.B., Princeton, 1882; m. Jane Meeker Lewis, Jan. 30, 1889; 1 dau., Isabelle (Mrs. Roger Young). With Kidder, Peabody & Co., investments, 1882-87, Lamboro Investment Co., 1887-89; exec. mgr. Fidelity Union Trust Co., Newark, 1889-1907, pres., 1907—; chmn. bd. Fidelity Union Mortgage Co.; dir. Pub. Service Corp. of N.J. and its subsidiaries and Newton Trust Co. Republican. Presbyn. Home: Red Bank, N.J. Died Aug. 15, 1931.

McCARTHY, Charles, librarian, lecturer; b. Brockton, Mass., 1873; s. John and Katherine (O'Shea) M.; Ph.B., Brown U., 1896; scholar in history, U. of Wis., 1900, fellow in history, 1901, Ph.D., 1901; (Litt.D., Brown, 1913); m. Lucile Schreiber, 1901. Legislative librarian for Wis., 1901—; originator of legislative reference dept. in state libraries for the drafting of laws at request of legislators. Author: Anti-Masonic Party, 1902 (winner Justin Windsor prize, Am. Historical Assn.); The Wisconsin Idea, 1912. Was mem. U.S. Commn. on Industrial Relations (resigned, 1915). Was asst. to Mr. Hoover in U.S. Food Administration, Washington, and was sent to Europe on a mission for that dept. and for War Labor Bd. Home: Madison, Wis. Died Mar. 26, 1921.

McCARTHY, Charles James, governor; b. Boston, Mass., Aug. 4, 1861; s. Charles and Joana (McCarthy) M.; ed. pub. schs. and Pacific Business Coll., San Francisco; m. Margaret Teresa Morgan, of Honolulu, Jan. 16, 1889; children—Eileen Catherine, Mary Louise, Pearl Lydia, Virginia, Margaret. Settled in Honolulu, 1881; mem. Ho. of Nobles, Kingdom of Hawaii, 1890; sec. Hawaiian Legislature, 1892; senator Territorial Legislature, 1907-11; harbor commr., 1911-18; treas. City and County of Hawaii, 1913-14; treas. Ty. of Hawaii, 1914-18; gov. of Hawaii, June 22, 1918, for term ending June 22, 1922, retired July 5,

1921; Washington rep. Honolulu Chamber Commerce, 1921—; gen. mgr. Honolulu Water Works. Served in N.G. of Hawaii, pvt. to lt. col. Odd Fellow, K.P., Elk. Democrat. Catholic. Home: Honolulu, H.I. Died Nov. 26, 1929.

McCARTHY, Daniel Edward, army officer; b. Albany, N.Y., Apr. 14, 1859; grad. U.S. Mil. Acad., 1881, Inf. and Cav. Sch., Ft. Leavenworth, Kan., 1887, Army War Coll., Washington, 1917; m. Laura Fendrich, Oct. 13, 1892. Commd. 2d lt. 12th Inf., June 11, 1881; 1st lt., Jan. 2, 1888; capt. a.-q.-m., Oct. 14, 1896; maj. q.-m. vols., Dec. 3, 1900; hon. disch. from vols., May 1, 1901; maj. q.-m. U.S. Army, Oct. 2, 1902; lt. col. dep. q.-m. gen., Apr. 13, 1910; col. Q.-M. Corps, Mar. 5, 1913. Served in Indian campaigns in Ariz. and N. and S.D.; in Cuba during Spanish-Am. War, later in Philippines; apptd. chief q.-m. on staff of Gen. Pershing and served with him in France until invalided home, Sept. 1917. Catholic. Elk. Author: Manual for Quartermasters Serving in the Field (Govt. Printing Office), 1900. Home: Chicago, Ill. Died 1922.

McCARTHY, Denis Aloysius, poet, journalist; b. Carrick-on-Suir, Co. Tipperary, Ireland, July 25, 1870; s. Denis and Margaret (Connolly) M.; ed. Christian Brothers' Sch., Carrick-on-Suir and private study in U.S., to which he came at the age of fifteen; LL.D. from Boston Coll., 1922; m. Ruphine Antonia Morris, Oct. 16, 1901. Spl. editorial writer Boston Herald and other publs. Chautauqua and forum lecturer and reader of own poems; lecturer for Mass. Dept. of Edn. in Americanization work, and for Boston and New York pub. sch. centers; asso. with Knights of Columbus Com. on War Activities, Washington, D.C., 1918-19. Mem. first Mass. Pilgrim Tercentenary Commn., 1913-14; hon. mem. Boston Sch. Principals' Assn. Mem. bd. trustees Boston Floating Hosp.; mem. board of dirs. Charitable Irish Society. Former trustee pub. library, Winthrop, Mass. Asso. editor Sacred Heart Rev., Boston, 1900-16; first editor North Am. Teacher, 1917; staff contbr. Catholic Sch. Jour., and Jour. of Edn. Editorial adviser for Ginn & Co. Author: A Round of Rimes, 1900, 09; Voices from Erin, 1906, 10; Heart Songs and Home Songs, 1916; Songs of Sunrise, 1917; Ould Father Toomey, 1927; The Harp of Life, 1929. Wrote "The Sowers" (for Boston Celebration of 150th Anniversary of Am. Revolution), "The Land Where Hate Should Die," "A Song for the Flag," and other patriotic poems widely used in the schools. Home: Arlington, Mass. Died Aug. 18, 1931.

McCARTHY, Eugene, author; b. Syracuse, N.Y., June 3, 1857; s. Robert and Eliza J. (Pierce) M.; grad. Georgetown Univ., 1876; m. Mary R. O'Hara, Apr. 11, 1899. Hardware mcht., 1877—; contbr. to mags., newspapers and newspaper syndicates, principally on the subject of fishing, hunting and kindred subjects. Author: Leaping Ouananiche; A Tale of Lake St. John; Familiar Fish. Home: Syracuse, N.Y. Died 1903.

McCARTHY, James Frederick, mining; b. St. Clair, Pa., Jan. 30, 1867; s. William J. and Joanna (Sullivan) McC.; ed. pub. schs., St. Clair, and night sch., Cooper Inst.; m. Anna Rose Langton, Feb. 12, 1896; children—Anita Maria (Mrs. Leo J. Hoban), Joseph Langton, James Frederick. Clerk prothonotary's office, Pottsville, Pa., 1882-88; salesman, 1889; with New York Metall. Works, 1889-92; with Dos Hermanos Mining Co., Montserrat Mining Co. and New York Honduras Rosario Mining Co., Honduras, C.A., 1892-96, Mammoth Mining Co., Wallace, Ida., 1897-1903; with Hecla Mining Co., 1903—, becoming pres. and manager. Republican. K.C., Elk. Home: Wallace, Ida. Died Mar. 6, 1940.

McCARTHY, Michael Henry, lumberman; b. LaSalle, Ill., Aug. 13, 1853; s. James and Hanora (Hayes) McC.; grad. high sch. and commercial coll.; m. Annie Dunn, Feb. 18, 1879. Began as teacher pub. schs., Ia.; entered lumber business with J. M. and Charles W. Robison, Dubuque, Ia.; treas. and associated mgr., Standard Lumber Co., Dubuque, 1881—; pres. and treas. Standard Lumber Yard Co., Highland Lumber & Coal Co.; v.p. and treas. Central Lumber & Coal Co. Actively identified for many yrs. with large lumber mfg. enterprises. Democrat. Roman Catholic. Died Dec. 6, 1920.

McCARTHY, P(atrick) H(enry), mayor; b. Killoughteen, Newcastle West, Co. Limerick, Ireland, Mar. 17, 1863; s. Patrick and Eileen McC.; ed. in pub. schs. of native co.; learned carpenter's trade; came to America, 1880; resided at Chicago, and St. Louis, and went to San Francisco, 1886; m. Jeanette H. Saunders, of City of Cork, Ireland, Jan. 15, 1905. Aided in organizing United Brotherhood of Carpenters and Joiners of America, and elected mem. exec. bd., 1904; organizer, 1894, and pres. Building Trades Council of San Francisco 29 consecutive yrs.; organizer, and pres. State Building Trades Council of Calif. 22 consecutive yrs.; organizer, and pres. Building Trades Temple Assn. of San Francisco 15 yrs., running cojointly with the City and State building trades councils; resigned these three positions in 1923. Was mem. Freeholders Conv. that framed charter of San Francisco and one of first civil service commrs. under said charter; Union Labor candidate for mayor of San Francisco, 1909, and elected for term of 2 yrs.; engaged in investment banking business. Republican. Catholic. Home: San Francisco, Calif. Died June 30, 1933.

McCARTY, Orin Philip, ry. official; b. Massillon, O., Nov. 19, 1848; s. Alfred Clay and Agnes (Mabon) M.; ed. pub. and pvt. schs.; m. Elva Deborah Barney, Dec. 23, 1869. Entered gen. ticket office, Cincinnati-Chicago Air Line, at Richmond, Ind., June 1, 1864; transferred to Chicago & Great Eastern part of system, Chicago, May 1, 1865; sent to Indianapolis, 1867, with Columbus & Ind. Central Ry., later merged with Chicago & Great Eastern and Pan Handle or Pa. lines; transferred to gen. pass. office, Columbus, O., and later auditor's office, Steubenville, O., 1869; chief clk. gen. pass. office, Indianapolis, Bloomington & Western Ry., at Urbana, Ill., and Indianapolis, 1870-80; chief clk. pass. dept. and asst. gen. pass. agt., U.P. Ry., Omaha, 1880-87; chmn. Trunk Line Pass. Rate Com., New York, 1887-88; chief clk. gen. pass. office, B.&O. R.R. Co., Baltimore, 1888-89; asst. gen. pass. agt., same rd., Columbus, O., 1889-90; gen. pass. agt., B.&O.S.W. R.R. Co., Cincinnati and St. Louis, 1890-94; asst. gen. pass. agt., S.P. Co., New Orleans, 1894-97; gen. pass. agt., B.&O.S.W. R.R. Co., 1897-1911; jurisdiction extended also over C.,H.&D. R.R.; pass. traffic mgr. B.&O. R.R. Co., Sept. 1, 1911—. Republican. Methodist. Mason. Home: Baltimore, Md. Died Dec. 7, 1925.

McCARTY, Thomas J., clergyman; b. Manchester, Ia., Oct. 30, 1863; s. Laurence and Eliza (Clinton) McC.; Creighton Coll., Omaha, Neb., 1884; St. Joseph's (now Columbia) Coll., Dubuque, Ia., 1888-89; St. Francis Sem., Milwaukee, Wis., 1889-92. Ordained priest R.C. Ch., 1892; temp. appointments at St. Mary's Ch., Marshalltown, Ia., and St. Mary's Ch. (now Cathedral of the Epiphany), Sioux City, Ia., until Dec. 1892; pastor Eagle Center, Ia., 1892-93, Holy Cross Ch., Dubuque Co., Ia., 1893-1903; chancellor Diocese of Sioux City, 1903-12; pastor St. Joseph's Ch., Carroll, Ia., 1912-20, Epiphany Cathedral, 1920—; apptd. domestic prelate (monsignor), Sept. 19, 1927; vicar gen. Diocese of Sioux City, Apr. 16, 1931—. Died May 27, 1933.

McCARTY, William Murdock, judge; b. Alpine, Utah, May 15, 1859; s. James Hardwich and Lydia Margaret (Craygun) M.; during boyhood worked on farm, at sawmills and cattle ranches during spring, summer and autumn months, attending country schs.; taught in log houses, during winter; attended acad. 16 weeks, winter of 1881-82; m. Lavinia L. Murray, Oct. 7, 1893. Left farm, 1876; went to mining camps, chopped cordwood, drove team, worked in smelters, quartz mills and mines; began to read law in Monroe, Utah, 1882; admitted to bar, Sept. 22, 1887; apptd. asst. U.S. dist. atty., 1889; elected co. atty. Sevier Co., Utah, 1892, reëlected 1894; on admission to statehood, 1895, elected dist. judge 6th Jud. Dist., reëlected 1900; asso. justice Supreme Ct. of Utah, 1902— (chief justice 1907, 1908, 1913-14); present term expiring 1920. Republican. Home: Salt Lake City, Utah. Died Dec. 19, 1919.

McCASKEY, Hiram Dryer, geologist; b. Fort Totten, Dak. Ty. (now N.D.), Apr. 10, 1871; s. Major General William Spencer and Eleanor Forsythe (Garrison) M.; B.S. in mining, Lehigh U., Bethlehem, Pa., 1893; M.S. in geology, same univ., 1907; m. Mary Louise Fuller, June 7, 1913. Chemist, Boston & Mont. Smelter, Great Falls, Mont., 1893-95; instr. mathematics, 1895-96, headmaster and instr. English, 1896-98, St. Thomas Hall, Miss.; instr. mathematics and English, St. Matthew's Sch., Calif., 1898-1900; mining engr., Mining Bur., Manila, P.I., 1900-03; chief of the Mining Bur. and of Div. of Mines, Bur. of Science, Manila, 1903-06; fellow in geology, Lehigh U., 1906-07; asst. geologist, 1907-10, geologist, 1911—, chief sect. of metal resources, 1912-19, geologist in charge Div. Mineral Resources, 1915-19, U.S. Geol. Survey. Del. from P.I. to 10th International Geol. Congress, Mexico City, 1906. Exploratory field work in P.I. Reorganized Mining Bur. in P.I.; asstd. in reorgn. of work of U.S. Geol. Survey in metallic mineral resources of U.S. and in charge Nov. 1912-Jan. 1919. U.S. del. Internat. Engring. Congress, San Francisco, 1915, Pan-Am. Scientific Congress, 1917. Home: Central Point, Ore. Died Apr. 26, 1936.

McCASKEY, William Spencer, major gen. U.S.A.; b. Lancaster Co., Pa., Oct. 2, 1843; s. William and Margaret Eckert (Piersol) M.; bro. of John Piersol M.; ed. pub. schs., Lancaster, Pa., until 1858; m. Eleanor Forsyth Garrison, Nov. 20, 1867. Was one of first 75,000 men enrolled as vols. in Civil War; pvt. Co. F, 1st Pa. Inf., Apr. 20-July 26, 1861; 1st sergt. Co. B, 79th Pa. Inf., Sept. 5, 1861-Oct. 8, 1862; promoted through grades to maj. gen., Apr. 15, 1907. Engaged in all battles of Army of the Cumberland; was on Sherman's marches to the Sea and through the Carolinas to Washington; in Grand Review, Washington, May, 1865; comd. 20th Inf., Cuban campaign, 1898, in battle of El Caney and Santiago; in Philippines, Mar. 1899-Feb. 1902; at Ft. Sheridan, Ill., Mar. 23, 1902-Nov. 20, 1903; comd. 1st brigade and post of Manila, P.I.; later comd. depts. of the Colo., Tex., and Dak.; retired Oct. 2, 1907. Home: Pacific Grove, Calif. Died Aug. 10, 1914.

McCASKILL, Virgil Everett, educator; b. Knox Co., Ill., May 3, 1866; s. Archibald Turner and Sarah Ellen (Nelson) M.; A.B., Ohio Wesleyan, 1893, A.M., 1894; Ph.D., U. of Chicago, 1902; m. Della Temple, June 18, 1896. Teacher in rural schs., Mo., 4 yrs.; prin. commercial dept., Ohio Wesleyan U., 1893-94; chair of biology, State Normal Sch., Stevens Point, Wis., 1896-1902; state inst. conductor, Superior, Wis., 1902-07; pres. State Normal Sch., Superior, Wis., Apr. 1907—. Republican. Methodist. Mason. Died May 2, 1922.

McCAUGHAN, William John, clergyman; b. Moycraig, Ballycastle, Co. Antrim, Ireland, Dec. 4, 1859; s. Nehemiah Craig and Mary Jane (Taggart) M.; C.A., Magee Coll., Londonderry, Ireland, 1879; studied div. New Coll., Edinburgh; m. Sara A. Cooper, Apr. 9, 1890. Ordained Presbyn. ministry, 1884; pastor Ballymena, Ireland, 1884-85; Mountpottinger Ch., Belfast, 1885-97, St. Andrew's Ch., Toronto, Can., 1897-98, Third Ch., Chicago, 1898-1907, May Street Ch., Belfast, Ireland, 1907—. High chief ranger of Ireland, Independent Order of Foresters, 1893-97, of Ill., 1903-05. Editor Presbyterian Quarterly Visitor, 1894-97; asso. editor Independent Forester, 1896-99. Died 1910.

McCAULEY, Calvin Hudson, lawyer; b. Elk Co., Pa., July 10, 1850; student Bucknell U., Lewisburg, Pa.; m. Juliet A. McGibney, Dec. 25, 1871. Admitted to the bar, 1872, and began practice at Ridgway, Pa.; mem. McCauley & Whitmore; solicitor Buffalo, Rochester & Pittsburgh Ry. Co.; local atty. Pa. R.R. Co., and Erie R.R. Co.; pres. and gen. solicitor Allegheny & Western Ry. Co., Allegheny Terminal Co., Mahoning Valley R.R. Co.; gen. solicitor Elk Tanning Co., Central Pa. Lumber Co. Episcopalian. Home: Ridgway, Pa. Died 1910.

McCAULEY, Lena May, writer, art editor; b. "Palmyra Farm," Hagerstown, Md., May 2, 1859; d. James and Lena (Rowland) McCauley; grad. Dearborn Sem., Chicago, 1878; spl. work in lit. and science, U. of Chicago, 4 yrs.; U. of Ill. and U. of Wis. 1 yr. each; unmarried. Teacher, later asst. prin., Chicago pub. schs., 1882-1900; asst. lit. editor, 1900-02, art editor, 1902-30, Chicago Evening Post; art correspondent American Art News and Christian Science Monitor, 1920—. Illinois state chairman of art, Ill. Fedn. of Women's Clubs. Episcopalian. Author: Etchers of Architecture, 1904; (Ten) Monographs of Etchers, 1905-07; The Joy of Gardens, 1912; The Painters of Illinois, 1932. Home: Evanston, Ill. Died Nov. 27, 1940.

McCAULEY, William Fletcher, clergyman; b. nr. West Salem, O., Dec. 6, 1858; s. David and Lucinda (Leasure) M.; studied at U. of Wooster; A.B., Lebanon U., 1883; grad. Lane Theol. Sem., 1886; (Litt.D., Lebanon, 1893); m. Mary Eliza Wherry, June 14, 1887. Ordained Presbyn. ministry, June 1, 1886; minister Park and Wayne Av. chs., Dayton, O., Fifth, Toledo, O., Third, Cincinnati, O., First, McKeesport, Pa. (1911—). President-elect of Lebanon (Ohio) U., 1908. On staff Standard Pub. Co., Cincinnati. Mem. exec. com. Ohio S.S. Assn., 1890-94, Ohio Christian Endeavor Union (pres. 1891-95, subsequently v.p. World's Christian Endeavor Union); mem. Gen. Assembly Presbyn. Ch., 1893, 1906; trustee Ohio Anti-Saloon League, 1894-1904; moderator Presbyteries of Dayton, Maumee, Mahoning, Cincinnati and Chillicothe. A leader in successful opposition to ritualistic movement in Presbyn. Church. Author: Next Steps, 1897; The Bible in Story, 1902. Home: McKeesport, Pa. Died Mar. 13, 1915.

McCAW, Walter Drew, army officer; b. Richmond, Va., Feb. 10, 1863; s. James Brown and Delia (Patteson) McC.; ed. pvt. schs., Richmond; M.D., Med. Coll. of Va., 1882; M.D., Coll. Phys. and Surg. (Columbia), 1884, D.Sc., 1932; unmarried. Commd. asst. surgeon U.S.A., 1884; capt. asst. surgeon, 1889; maj. surgeon, Feb. 2, 1901; lt. col. Med. Corps, Jan. 1, 1909; col., May 9, 1913; brig. gen. asst. surgeon general U.S.A., Mar. 5, 1919, retired, Feb. 10, 1927. In volunteer service as major brig. surgeon, June 4, 1898; major surgeon, 42d U.S. Vol. Inf., Aug. 17, 1899. Was in campaign of Santiago de Cuba, 1898; in P.I., 1900-01, during insurrection; has served in Depts. of Mo., the Platte, East Tex. and Calif.; on duty in Washington, 1902-13; librarian, surgeon gen.'s office in charge of mus. and library div.; prof. mil. hygiene, 1902-05, prof. mil. and tropical medicine, 1904-13, Army Med. Sch., Washington; chief surgeon Div. of the Philippines, 1914; comdg. Div. Hosp., Manila, 1915; dept. surgeon, Southern Dept., Ft. Sam Houston, Tex., 1916-17; on duty chief surgeon's office, A.E.F., Mar.-Oct. 1918; chief surgeon A.E.F., Oct. 1918-July 15, 1919. D.S.M. (U.S.), also awarded Silver Star medal by U.S., 1932; Comdr. Legion of Honor (French); Companion of the Bath (C.B.) (British); Officer Order of Saints Maurice and Lazarus (Italian). Fellow Am. Coll. of Surgeons; asso. fellow Coll. Physicians Phila.; hon. mem. Royal Soc. Medicine, Va. Soc. of the Cincinnati. Home: Woodstock, N.Y. Died July 7, 1939.

McCAWLEY, Charles Laurie, officer U.S. Marines; b. Boston, Mass., Aug. 24, 1865; s. Charles Grymes and Elizabeth Mary (Colegate) M.; ed. pvt. schs.; LL.B., Columbian (now George Washington) U., 1893; m. Sarah Helen Frelinghuysen Davis, July 24, 1906. Apptd. capt. a.-q.-m., U.S. Marine Corps, June 27, 1897; bvtd. maj., June 11, 1898, for "distinguished conduct in the presence of the enemy"; promoted lt. col., May 13, 1908; col. q.-m., June 2, 1913; brig. gen. q.-m. Marine Corps, Aug. 29, 1916. At hdqrs. Marine Corps, Washington, until Apr. 1898; at Key West, Fla., and Guantanamo, Cuba, until Aug. 1898; participated in engagements in defense of Camp McCalla, Guantanamo, and in attack on Manzanillo, 1898; with 1st Batt. of Marines, Cavite, P.I., 1899; in charge depot of supplies, Phila., Pa., 1900-02; at headquarters Marine Corps, and on duty with the President, 1902-10; in charge Quartermaster's Department, Marine Corps, 1910-13; appointed q.-m. Marine Corps, June 2, 1913; retired Aug. 24, 1929. Holds West India campaign medal of Spanish-Am. War, Spanish War and Philippine campaign badges, D.S.M., and Brevet medal (Navy), and Victory medal. Died Apr. 29, 1935.

McCAY, Leroy Wiley, chemist; b. Rome, Ga., Aug. 9, 1857; s. Robert T. and Susan L. (Wiley) M.; A.B., Princeton, 1878, A.M., 1881, D.Sc., 1883; studied at Freiberg Sch. of Mines, and U. of Heidelberg. Asst. in analytical chemistry, 1883-86, instr., 1886-89, asst. prof., 1889-92, prof. inorganic chemistry, 1892-1928, emeritus prof., 1928—, Princeton. Chief subjects of research, cobalt, nickel and iron pyrites, methods for determining arsenic, the nonexistence of sulpharsenic acid, the sulphoxyarsenic acids and their salts, the separation of the metals of the tin group, use of hydrofluoric acid in ordinary and electro-chem. analysis, use of mercury as a reducing agent. Home: Princeton, N.J. Died Apr. 13, 1937.

McCHESNEY, Calvin Stewart, lawyer; b. Pittstown, N.Y., Dec. 15, 1857; s. Nelson and Sarah Stewart (Barry) M.; grad. Peekskill (N.Y.) Mil. Acad., 1877; B.A., Yale, 1881, LL.B., 1884; m. Caroline Lindsley, Oct. 25, 1899. Began practice, Troy, N.Y., 1886; mem. McChesney & Betts, 1893-96 and 1902-06, McChesney & Gillet, 1909-12; surrogate of Rensselaer Co., 1914-20. Enlisted in 6th Separate Co. (Troy Citizens' Corps), N.G.N.Y., Apr. 13, 1890; q.-m. sergt. same, Oct. 20, 1893; enlisted in Co. A, 2d N.Y. Vol. Inf., May 17, 1898; q.-m. sergt. same co., May-June, 1898; 2d lt. in field, June-Oct. 1898; hon. discharged, Nov. 30, 1898; judge-advocate United Spanish War Vets., 1913-14. Home: Troy, N.Y. Died Feb. 1, 1924.

McCHESNEY, Dora Greenwell, author; b. Chicago, Oct. 1, 1871; d. Prof. Joseph Henry and Elizabeth (Studdiford) McChesney; ed. chiefly by mother, in a life of wide and most unmethodical travel and reading; unmarried. Made acquaintance with German literature, Italian art and Roman antiquity, and, seeing Sir Henry Irving act Charles I in 1891, was led to a spl. study of the English civil war, which caused her to become the chronicler of Lord Strafford and Prince Rupert. Author: Kathleen Clare, Her Book, 1637-1641, 1895; Miriam Cromwell, Royalist, 1897; Beatrix Infelix, 1898; Rupert, by the Grace of God, 1899; Cornet Strong of Ireton's Horse; Yesterday's Tomorrow; Wounds of a Friend, 1908. Died July 5, 1912.

McCHESNEY, Elizabeth Studdiford ("L. Studdiford McChesney"), author; b. Monroe, Mich., Apr. 29, 1841; d. William Van Horn Studdiford; mother of Dora Greenwell McChesney; ed. Monroe Sem., Buffalo Sem., Elmira Coll.; later studied in Germany; m. Prof. Joseph Henry McChesney, of Univ. of Chicago, July 18, 1865 (died 1895). Has spent many yrs. in England, 2 yrs. in Rome and traveled much upon the continent. Author: Under Shadow of the Mission: A Memory of Santa Barbara, 1897. Died 1906.

McCHORD, Charles Caldwell, lawyer; b. Springfield, Ky., Dec. 3, 1859; s. Robert Caldwell and Laura (Hynes) M.; ed. Center Coll. (now Central U.), Danville, Ky.; m. Nellie Grundy, Jan. 8, 1888. Admitted to Ky. bar, 1882, and practiced in Kentucky; mem. McChord, Hines & Norman until Jan. 1, 1911; pros. atty. Washington Co., Ky., 1886-92; chmn. Ky. R.R. Commn., 1892-95 and 1899-1907; mem. Ky. Senate, 1895-99; mem. Interstate Commerce Commn., Washington, 1911-Jan. 1, 1926; was chmn. of Commn. various periods from 1915; resigned to practice law. Democrat. Author of McChord ry. rate bill enacted by Ky. legislature; spl. counsel for Ky. in numerous ry. rate cases. Mem. Ry. Wage Commn. and arbitrator War Labor Bd., 1918, 19. Pres. Nat. Assn. Ry. Commrs., 1906-07. Home: Washington, D.C. Deceased.

McCLAIN, Edward Lee, mfr.; b. Greenfield, O., May 30, 1861; s. William Page and Margaret Ann (Parkinson) M.; ed. pub. schs., Greenfield; m. Lulu Johnson, Dec. 17, 1885; children—Edward Lee, Mrs. Helen St. Clair Young, Donald Schofield. Founded mfg. business at Greenfield, 1881, incorporated July 1, 1903, as The Am. Pad & Textile Co., branches at Chillicothe, O., and Chatham, Ont., Can.; founded, 1905, The Am. Textile Co., at Atco, Bartow Co., Ga.; also founder or co-founder of various other industries. Donated to Greenfield, 1915, the land, building and equipment of Edward Lee McClain High Sch.; in 1924 donated a separate building, furnishings and equipment for vocational purposes, also an athletic field. Republican. Methodist. Home: Greenfield, O. Died May 1934.

McCLAIN, Emlin, judge; b. Salem, O., Nov. 26, 1851; s. William and Rebecca (Harris) M.; Ph.B., State U. of Ia., 1871, A.B., 1872, LL.B., 1873, A.M., 1882 (LL.D., 1891, and Findlay Coll., 1891); m. Ellen, d. Capt. H. H. Griffiths, of Des Moines, Ia., Feb. 19, 1879. Practiced law at Des Moines, 1873-81; prof. law, 1881-87, vice-chancellor of law dept., 1887-90, chancellor, 1890-1900, State U. of Ia.; judge Supreme Ct. of Ia., 1901-12 (chief justice, 1906, 12); prof. law, Leland Stanford Jr. U., 1913—. Republican. Ia. commr. on uniform legislation, 1894; mem. Ia. Code Commn., 1894-97; prepared annotations for new code, published by state of Ia., 1897, and for supplement to same, 1902, 07, 13. Author: McClain's Annotated Statutes of Iowa, 1880; Outlines of Criminal Law and Procedure, 1884; A Treatise on the Criminal Law as Now Administered in the United States, 1897; A Selection of Cases on Constitutional Law, 1900, new edit., 1909; Constitutional Law in the United States (Am. Citizen Series), 1905, 2d edit., 1910. Died May 25, 1915.

McCLANAHAN, Harry Monroe, pediatrist; b. Norwood, Ill., Aug. 17, 1857; s. John Porter and Margaret Jane (Jones) M.; Monmouth (Ill.) Coll., 1872-75; M.D., Jefferson Med. Coll., Phila., 1878; A.M., by examination, U. of Neb., 1924; m. Nellie E. Holloway, Sept. 6, 1883 (died Oct. 19, 1921); 1 dau., wife of Dr. J. A. Henske. Resident phys., Jefferson Med. Coll. Hosp., 1878-79; practiced at Alexis, Ill., 1879-80; agency phys., Ft. Belknap, Mont., 1880-81 (resigned); practiced at Woodhull, Ill., 1881-89, Omaha, Neb., 1889—; prof. pediatrics, Omaha Med. Coll. (now U. of Neb. Coll. of Medicine), 1892—. Republican. Presbyn. Home: Omaha, Neb. Died Nov. 20, 1929.

McCLARY, Nelson Alvin, gas official; b. Albany, Vt., Aug. 17, 1856; s. Orson Ricker and Lucy Philinda (Smith) M.; A.B., Dartmouth Coll., 1884; m. Emily Becknell Rood, Sept. 13, 1889; children—Orson Rood, George Brewer. In book business at Hanover, N.H., 1876-83; gas business, 1885—; gen. mgr. Ogden Gas Co., 1895-1901; pres. North-western Gas Light & Coke Co., 1901-13; pres. De Kalb County Gas Co., and sec. Sterling Gas & Electric Light Co., 1900-12; dir. Nat. Gas & Water Co.; also owner Apple Orchard Enterprise, Empire, Mich., 1914—. Pres.-gen. Nat. Soc. S.A.R., 1907 (pres. Ill. Soc. 1905). Mem. bd. edn., Oak Park, Ill., 1899-1905; chmn. local exemption bd. No. 5, for Cook County, 1917-19. Republican. Presbyn. Home: Empire, Mich. Died Apr. 9, 1936.

McCLATCHY, Carlos Kelly, newspaper editor; b. Sacramento, Calif., Mar. 2, 1891; s. Charles Kenny and Ella (Kelly) McC.; B.S., Columbia, 1911; m. Phebe Briggs, Jan. 17, 1918; children—James Briggs, William Ellery, Charles Kenny. Began as reporter Sacramento Bee, 1911; editor Fresno Bee, 1922—; gen. mgr. Sacramento Bee and Modesto (Calif.) News Herald; v.p. McClatchy newspapers. Served as capt. Inf., U.S.A., World War. Home: Fresno, Calif. Died Jan. 17, 1933.

McCLATCHY, Charles Kenny, editor; b. Sacramento, Calif., Nov. 1, 1858; ed. in pub. schs. and at Santa Clara Coll.; m. Ella Kelly, 1885. Succeeded his father, James McClatchy, the veteran Calif. editor, as editor of the Sacramento Bee, Jan. 1884, sole owner of it and Fresno Bee, 1923—; also sole owner Modesto News-Herald. Advocate of many governmental reforms; pioneer in nation-wide crusade for amendment to nat. constn. that hereafter amendments to that document shall be ratified only by majority vote of all the people at the polls regardless of states; pioneered newspaper opposition to Am. entrance into League of Nations. Died Apr. 27, 1936.

McCLATCHY, Valentine Stuart, newspaperman; b. Sacramento, Calif., Aug. 29, 1857; s. James and Charlotte (McCormack) M.; B.S., Santa Clara (Calif.) Coll., 1877; m. Adaline Hanifin, Feb. 9, 1881; children—Edna (Mrs. J. Everett Johnson), H. J., J. V., Valentine (Mrs. Ira Woodhouse), Ralph I., Claire, Leo A., Marion (Mrs. Butler Jack). Pub. and half owner Sacramento Bee, 1893-1923; established Fresno (Calif.) Bee as half owner, 1922; sold interest both papers 1923. Sec. and gen. mgr. Pacific Associated Press, 1894-1900; dir. Associated Press, 1910-23; pres. Calif. State Reclamation Bd. in charge state portion Sacramento River Flood Control Project, 1912-17. Secured coöperation of Congress, Navy Dept. and Manila newspapers in installation 1,000 word daily news report by Navy Radio between Manila, Honolulu and San Francisco, 1919. Exec. sec. Calif. Joint Immigration Com., 1923—; hon. pres. Am. Coalition Patriotic Socs., 1934—. Home: Sacramento, Calif. Died May 15, 1938.

McCLAUGHRY, Robert Wilson, warden; b. Fountain Green, Ill., July 22, 1839; s. Mattehw and Mary M.; A.B., Monmouth Coll., 1860 (LL.D., 1906); m. Elizabeth C. Madden, June 17, 1862 (died 1914); m. 2d, Emma F. Madden, Apr. 8, 1915. Private 118th Illinois Inf., Aug. 15, 1862; capt., Nov. 7, 1862; maj., Dec. 8, 1862; served in Army of the Tenn. until May 1864; transferred to pay dept., as maj. and additional p.-m. vols.; mustered out, Oct. 13, 1865. Co. clerk Hancock Co., Ill., 1865-69; warden Ill. State Penitentiary, 1874-88; gen. supt. Pa. Industrial Reformatory, 1888-91; chief of police, Chicago, 1891-93; gen. supt. Ill. State Reformatory, 1893-97; warden Ill. State Penitentiary, 1897-99, U.S. Penitentiary, Leavenworth, Kan., July 1, 1899-July 1, 1913. Home: Joliet, Ill. Died Nov. 9, 1920.

McCLEARY, James Thompson, congressman; b. Ingersoll, Ont., Feb. 5, 1853; s. Thompson and Sarah (McCutcheon) M.; ed. at high sch. and McGill U., Montreal; m. Mary Edith Taylor, June 4, 1874. Co. supt. schs., Pierce Co., Wis., 1879-81; state inst. conductor, Minn., 1881-92; prof. history and civics, State Teachers' College, Mankato, 1881-92. Mem. 53d to 59th Congresses (1893-1907), 2d Minn. Dist.; 2d asst. postmaster-gen., 1907-08. Republican. Sec. Am. Iron and Steel Inst., New York, 1911-20; pres. Minn. Ednl. Assn., 1891. Author: Studies in Civics, 1888; Manual of Civics, 1894. Home: Washington, D.C.; and St. Paul, Minn. Died Dec. 17, 1924.

McCLELLAN, Elisabeth, author; b. Phila., Oct. 30, 1851; d. Dr. John Hill Brinton and Maria (Eldredge) M.; ed. pvt. schs., Phila. Asst. librarian, The Library Co., of Philadelphia, 1880—. Translator: Schiller and His Times (Scherr), 1880. Author: Historic Dress in America, 1607-1800, 1904; Historic Dress in America, 1800-1870, 1910. Home: Germantown, Pa. Died Dec. 3, 1920.

McCLELLAN, George Brinton, publicist; b. Dresden, Saxony (where his parents were on a visit), Nov. 23, 1865; s. Gen. George Brinton (U.S.A.) and Ellen M. (Marcy) M.; A.B., Princeton, 1886, A.M., 1889, LL.D., 1905; LL.D., Fordham, 1905, Union U., 1906; m. Georgianna L. Heckscher, Oct. 30, 1889. Was reporter and on staffs of New York dailies; treas. New York & Brooklyn Bridge, 1889-92; admitted to bar, 1892; pres. bd. of aldermen, New York, 1893-94; mem. 54th to 58th Congresses (1895-1903); member Com. on Ways and Means; mayor New York, 1903-09. Hon. chancellor, Union U., 1906; Stafford Little lecturer on pub. affairs, Princeton U., 1908-10, university lecturer public affairs, 1911-12, prof. econ. history, 1912-31, prof. emeritus, 1931—; also lecturer at Cornell, Rutgers, Washington and Jefferson, Washington and Lee, U. of N.C., etc. An incorporator, trustee and vice-pres. Am. Acad. in Rome; chmn. exec. com. Smithsonian Gallery of Art Commn. Maj., Ordnance Dept., U.S.R., Apr. 16, 1917; lt. col., U.S.A., Jan. 13, 1918; served in U.S. and overseas, Meuse-Argonne Battle Clasp; hon. disch., Apr. 18, 1919; now col. inactive, U.S. Army. Hon. mem. Am. Inst. of Architects; awarded medal of Beaux Arts Soc. of Architects, 1909; patron Am. Mus. of Natural History; fellow in perpetuity Met. Mus. of Art. Grand officer Order Crown of Italy. Democrat. Episcopalian (sr. warden St. John's Ch., Washington); trustee of Church Charities and Diocesan Church Funds, Diocese of Washington). Author: The Oligarchy of Venice, 1904; The Heel of War, 1915; Venice and Bonaparte, 1931; Modern Italy, 1933. Home: Washington, D.C. Died Nov. 30, 1940.

McCLELLAN, Henry Brainerd, prin. of Sayre Female Inst., 1870—; b. Phila., Oct. 17, 1840; s. Samuel McC. (M.D.); grad. Williams Coll., 1858 (A.M.); m. Katherine M. Matthews. Taught school in Va., 1858-61; served 4 yrs. in C.S.A. in Northern Va., and was, 1863-65, maj. and asst. adjt. gen. and chief of staff of the cav. corps, successively, under Gens. J. E. B. Stuart and Wade Hampton. Author: The Life and Campaigns of Major General J. E. B. Stuart, 1886. Home: Lexington, Ky. Died 1904.

McCLELLAN, John, army officer; b. Chicago, Ill., Apr. 11, 1847; s. Col. John and Jane Josephine (Walker) M.; ed. pvt. schs., St. Paul, Detroit, and in Germany; grad. U.S. Mil. Acad., 1867; grad. Arty. Sch., 1888; m. Miss A. R. L. Wüppermann, of Hamburg, Germany, 1885; children—Frederic W., Rose Lee (wife of Charles W. Exton, U.S.A.), Josephine F. J.; m. 2d, Miss E. A. Halstead, of Honolulu, T.H., Jan. 3, 1905; 1 son, John Halstead. Apptd. 2d lt. 5th U.S. Arty., June 17, 1867; 1st lt., Jan. 5, 1870; capt., Oct. 25, 1894; maj. chief ordnance officer vols., July 18, 1898; hon. discharged from vol. service, May 12, 1899; maj., U.S. Arty. Corps, Feb. 28, 1901; lt. col., Aug. 11, 1903; col., Mar. 16, 1906; brig. gen., June 1, 1906; retired at own request, over 40 yrs.' service, June 9, 1906. Served as officer of weather bur. of War Dept., 1875-81; received the thanks of the State Dept. for "valuable services," 1883; in charge ordnance depots 7th Army Corps, at Jacksonville, Fla., Savannah, Ga., and Havana, Cuba, 1898-99; on staff of Gen. Fitzhugh Lee, Aug. 1898-Jan. 1899; on staff of Gen. Brooke at Havana, Jan.-Apr. 1899. Home: San Diego, Calif. Died Nov. 24, 1928.

McCLELLAN, John Jasper, organist, dir.; b. Payson, Utah, Apr. 20, 1874; s. John Jasper and Eliza Barbara (Walser) M.; studied music at U. of Mich.

and under Ernst Jedliczka, Alberto Jonas and Xaver Scharwenka, of Berlin, Germany; m. Mary Douglas, July 15, 1896. Asst. to Prof. A. A. Stanley, organist at the World's Fair, Chicago, 1893; teacher, Mich. Sch. of Music, Ann Arbor, 1894-97; prof. music, Brigham Young U., Provo, Utah, 1900-01; organist Mormon Tabernacle, Salt Lake City, 1900—. Conductor Salt Lake Opera Co., 1902-10; dir. Salt Lake Symphony Orchestra, 1906-12; founder, 1911, and dean and head of piano dept., Utah Conservatory of Music; has appeared as concert organist in many leading cities of U.S.; gave organ recitals at St. Louis Expn., 1904, Jamestown Expn., 1907, San Francisco and San Diego expns., 1915. Home: Salt Lake City, Utah. Died 1926.

McCLELLAN, Thomas Cowan, lawyer; b. Athens, Ala., Jan. 11, 1873; s. Robert Anderson and Aurora (Pryor) M.; U. of Ala., 1889-92; grad. law dept. Cumberland U., Lebanon, Tenn., 1893; m. Sue Ruth Phillips, July 16, 1902; 1 dau., Ruth. Admitted to bar, 1893; practiced at Athens, Ala.; mayor, 1896-98; asso. justice Supreme Court, Ala., 1906-23, resigned 1923, to resume practice of law. Trustee U. of Ala., 1899-1923. Democrat. Home: Birmingham, Ala. Died July 28, 1929.

McCLELLAN, Thomas Nicholas, chief justice Supreme Court, Ala., Nov. 1898—; b. Limestone County, Ala., Feb. 23, 1853; ed. Oak Hall, Tenn.; grad. Cumberland Univ., Lebanon, Tenn., LL.B.; began practice of law when 19 yrs. old (Sept. 1872), at Athens, Ala.; unmarried. State senator, 1880-84; atty. gen. Ala., 1884-89; asso. justice Supreme Court, 1889-98. Democrat. Home: Montgomery, Ala. Died 1906.

McCLELLAND, Charles Samuel, clergyman; b. Roxbury, Pa., Sept. 16, 1852; s. Joseph and Mary Holmes (Maclay) M.; A.B., U. of Wooster, 1877, A.M., 1881, D.D., same, 1895; D.D., U. of Pittsburgh, 1919; m. Mary Rebecca Parry, Sept. 28, 1880. Ordained Presbyn. ministry, 1880; traveled around the world, 1880-83; missionary at Petchaburi, Siam, 1880-83; pastor Bethel Ch., Inverness, O., 1883-89, Herron Ave. Ch., Pittsburgh, 1889-98, Mt. Washington Ch., Pittsburgh, 1898-1923. Permanent clk., Presbytery of Pittsburgh, 1893-94, stated clk., 1894-1923. Trustee U. of Wooster, 1905-12. Pres. Pittsburgh Presbyn. Ministerial Assn., 1918-19, v.p. Presbyn. Union of Pittsburgh, 1919-20, pres., 1920-21. Republican. Home: New Cumberland, Pa. Died Mar. 23, 1933.

McCLELLAND, Thomas, college pres.; b. Quilly, Co. Derry, Ireland, May 1, 1846; s. William and Margaret (Smiley) M.; A.B., Oberlin, 1875, A.M., 1883; Oberlin Theol. Sem., 1876-77, Union Theol. Sem., New York, 1877-88; grad. Andover Theol. Sem., 1880; (D.D., Tabor Coll., 1891; LL.D., U. of Illinois, 1905; LL.D., Grinnell College, Ia., 1915); m. Harriet C. Day, Aug. 19, 1880. Prof. philosophy, Tabor Coll., 1880-91; pres. Pacific U., Ore., 1891-1900, Knox Coll., 1900-17 (emeritus). Trustee Carnegie Foundation for Advancement of Teaching, 1905-17. Home: Galesburg, Ill. Died Jan. 29, 1926.

McCLELLAND, T(homas) Calvin, clergyman; b. New York, June 10, 1869; s. William and Elizabeth (Farrell) M.; student Coll. City of New York, 3 yrs.; A.B., New York U., 1889, A.M., 1891, Ph.D., 1892; grad. Union Theol. Sem., 1892; (D.D., New York U., 1906); m. Mary Louise Allason, July 12, 1892. Ordained Presbyn. ministry, 1892; pastor Bushwick Ref. Ch., Brooklyn, 1892-93, North Ref. Ch., Brooklyn, 1893-96, United Congl. Ch., Newport, 1896-1905, Memorial Presbyn. Ch., Brooklyn, 1905-11. Moderator and stated clerk Presbytery of Brooklyn; trustee Berkeley Institute. Author: The Cross-Builders, 1903; The Mind of Christ, 1909. Home: Brooklyn, N.Y. Died Oct. 24, 1917.

McCLEMENT, John Hall, banker; b. Phila., Pa., May 27, 1862; s. John Wesley and Mary Ann (Hall) M.; A.B., Central High Sch., Phila., 1879, and A.M., 1884; m. Miss Lena Morgan, June 1, 1892. Clerk at Port Richmond, Phila. & Reading R.R. Co., 1879; clerk Pa. R.R., auditor of disbursements, 1879-81; chief clerk to comptroller D.&R.G., Mexican Nat. Rys., and Colo. Coal & Iron Co., N.Y. City, 1881-83; comptroller Northern Pacific Terminal Co., Portland, Ore., 1883-85; asst. sec. and treas. Buffalo, N.Y. & Phila. R.R., 1886-87; comptroller Edison Electric Light Co., and Edison Gen. Electric Co., 1887-90; pres. of numerous elec. companies, 1890-99; asst. to chmn. in reorgn. of Northern Pacific R.R., 1894-97; comptroller Chicago Terminal Transfer R.R., 1897-99; v.p. and comptroller St. Louis, Peoria & Northern R.R., 1897-99; v.p. and chmn. Colo. Fuel & Iron Co., 1904; mem. George P. Butler & Bro., 1899-1908; pres. and chmn. bd. Empire Engring. Co. Republican. Mason. Home: Brooklyn, and Westhampton Beach, L.I. Died May 16, 1924.

McCLENAHAN, Howard, scientist; b. Port Deposit, Md., Oct. 19, 1872; s. John Megredy and Laura Jane (Farrow) M.; E.E., Princeton U., 1895, M.S., 1897; LL.D., Washington Coll., Md., 1907, Swarthmore, 1929; Litt.D., Franklin and Marshall, 1929; Sc.D., Union Coll., Schenectady, N.Y.; D.Sc., U. of Pa., 1931; m. Bessie L. Lee, Nov. 1, 1899; children—John Megredy, Richard Lee, Elizabeth Lee. Instr. physics, 1897-1902, asst. prof., 1902-06, prof., 1906-12, dean of the Coll., 1912-25, Princeton; sec. Franklin Inst. State of Pa., May 1925—; editor Jour. of Franklin Inst., 1925—; dir. Benjamin Franklin Memorial and Franklin Inst. Mus., 1930—. Pres. Assn. Colls. and Prep. Schs. of Middle States and Md., 1919; chmn. Coll. Entrance Exam. Bd., 1919-23. Trustee Lincoln U.; asso. trustee for grad. study and research, U. of Pa. Officier de l'Ordre de la Couronne (Belgian), 1919; awarded gold medal Sesquicentennial Exhbn. for services on Internat. Jury of Awards, 1926. Author: Laboratory Directions in Experimental Physics, 1906. Died Dec. 17, 1935.

McCLENCH, William Wallace, insurance pres.; b. Chicopee, Mass., Apr. 6, 1854; s. Joseph U. and Mary A. (Johnson) M.; A.B., Tufts Coll., 1875, LL.D., 1922; m. Katharine A. Hill, Dec. 8, 1880. After graduation taught at Hitchcock Free Acad., Brimfield, Mass.; was prin. high sch., Ware, Mass., until 1878; admitted to bar, 1878; gen. practice, 1878-98; pres. Mass. Mut. Life Ins. Co.; trustee, v.p. Springfield Inst. for Savings. Mayor Chicopee, Mass., 1892; pres. Springfield Bd. Trade. Unitarian. Republican. Home: Springfield, Mass. Died Nov. 16, 1928.

McCLERNAND, Edward John, army officer; b. Jacksonville, Ill., Dec. 29, 1848; s. Maj. Gen. John Alexander (comdr. 13th Army Corps in Civil War) and Sarah (Dunlap) M.; ed. Jacksonville and Springfield, Ill., 1856-66; grad. U.S. Mil. Acad., 1870; m. Sarah Pomp, Nov. 14, 1888. Apptd. 2d lt. 2d Cav., June 15, 1870; promoted through grades to brig. gen., Aug. 27, 1912. Breveted first lieut., Feb. 27, 1890, "for gallantry in pursuit of Indians and in actions against them at Bear Paw Mountains, Mont., Sept. 30, 1877"; awarded Congressional Medal of Honor, Nov. 27, 1894, "for most distinguished gallantry in action against Nez Percés Indians." Served in Santiago Campaign, Spanish-Am. War, later in Philippines; retired from active service, Dec. 29, 1912. Home: Easton, Pa. Died Feb. 9, 1926.

McCLERNAND, John A., lawyer, veteran general; b. Breckenridge Co., Ky., May 30, 1812; on his father's death, 1816, his mother removed to Shawneetown, Ill.; brought up on farm; admitted to bar, 1832; served in war against Sacs and Foxes, 1832; mem. Ill. legislature, 1836-42; edited Shawneetown Democrat, and practiced law. Mem. Congress, 1843-51 and 1859-61; resigned to enter army; raised McClernand Brigade and served as brig. gen. and maj. gen. vols.; commanded the right of the line at Fort Donelson; a division at Shiloh; relieved Gen. Sherman in Vicksburg expedition, Jan. 1863; led at capture of Arkansas Post; comd. 13th army corps until relieved, July 1863; resigned from army, Nov. 30, 1864; resumed practice at Springfield, Ill. Home: Springfield, Ill. Died 1900.

McCLINTIC, Howard H(ale), bridge builder; C.E., Lehigh U., 1888; m. Margaret McCulloch; children—Howard H., Robert H., Stewart, Margaret W. (Mrs. George H. Love). Vice president Union Shipbuilding Co., Hughes-Foulkrod Company; dir. Fidelity Trust Co. (Pittsburgh); trustee Koppers Co. of Mass. Trustee Lehigh Univ., Carnegie Hero Fund Commn. Home: Pittsburgh, Pa. Died Aug. 5, 1938.

McCLINTOCK, Andrew Hamilton, lawyer; b. Wilkes-Barre, Pa., Dec. 12, 1852; s. Andrew Todd and Augusta Bradley (Cist) M.; A.B., Princeton, 1872, A.M., 1875; m. Eleanor Welles, Dec. 1, 1880 (died 1910). Practiced, Wilkes-Barre, 1876—; pres. Wyo. Nat. Bank; dir. Lehigh & Wilkes-Barre Coal Co., Lehigh Luzerne Coal Co., etc. Trustee Home for Friendless Children, Osterhout Free Library, First Presbyn. Church. Democrat. Home: Wilkes-Barre, Pa. Died Oct. 7, 1919.

McCLINTOCK, Emory, actuary; b. Carlisle, Pa., Sept. 19, 1840; s. John M. (D.D., LL.D.); A.B., Columbia, 1859, A.M., 1862; (hon. Ph.D., U. of Wis., 1884; LL.D., Columbia, 1885, Yale, 1899); m. Isabella Bishop, 1890. Tutor mathematics, Columbia, 1859-60; U.S. consular agt. at Bradford, Eng., 1863-66; actuary Asbury Life Ins. Co., New York, 1867-71, Northwestern Mutual Life Ins. Co., Milwaukee, 1871-89; actuary, 1889-1911, v.p., trustee, 1905-11, consulting actuary and trustee, 1911—, Mut. Life Ins. Co., New York. Hon. fellow Am. Acad. Arts and Sciences; fellow Inst. Actuaries, London. Home: Bay Head, N.J. Died July 10, 1916.

McCLINTOCK, James Harvey, writer; b. Sacramento, Calif., Feb. 23, 1864; s. John and Sarah Ann (Brittingham) M.; m. Dorothy Goodson Bacon, June 15, 1900. Formerly teacher pub. schs. and editor in Ariz.; postmaster, Phoenix, 1902-14, 1928-33; state historian Ariz., 1919-23; Rep. candidate for U.S. Senator, 1922. Captain 1st U.S. Vol. Cav. (Rough Riders), Spanish-Am. War; severely wounded in Cuba; col. 1st Regt. Inf., N.G. Ariz., 1902-10; actg. adj. gen., 1908. Mem. Ariz. Folk Lore Soc. (pres.), Ariz. Archæol. Soc. (pres.), Rough Riders' Assn. (pres.), United Spanish War Vets. (former dept. comdr.); former treas. State Rep. Com.; former chmn., treas., Maricopa County Rep. Com. Unitarian. Author: McClintock's History of Arizona, 1916; Mormon Settlement in Arizona, 1921. Home: Phoenix, Ariz. Died May 10, 1934.

McCLINTOCK, John Calvin, Presbyn. clergyman; b. Carmichaels, Pa., Aug. 20, 1843; s. Rev. Dr. John and Mary (Orr) McC.; grad. Washington Coll., Pa., 1862 (A.M., 1865; D.D., Monmouth, Ill., 1886); m. Mary E. McKean, Oct. 4, 1865. Pastor 1st Presbyn. Ch., Mt. Pleasant, Ia., 1865-71; 1st Presbyn. Ch., Burlington, Ia., 1871-96; 1st Presbyn. Ch., Sioux City, Ia., 1896—; stated clerk synod of Iowa, 1890—; weekly contbr. to The Interior, 1888—; dir. Omaha Theol. Sem. Author: Love Never Faileth, 1903. Home: Sioux City, Ia. Died 1903.

McCLINTOCK, Mary Law, educator; b. Newberry, S.S.; d. Ebenezer Pressley and Elizabeth Jane (Young) M.; B.A., Goucher Coll., 1895; M.Ph., U. of Chicago, 1902. Head dept. English, U. of Fla., 1896-1901; asst. prin., Ward's Sem., Nashville, Tenn., 1902-03; prin. Miss McClintock's School, Boston, 1908. Presbyn. Home: Boston, Mass. Died Jan. 1925.

McCLINTOCK, Norman, lecturer; b. Pittsburgh, Pa., June 13, 1868; s. Oliver and Clara Courtney (Childs) M.; B.A., Yale, 1891; m. Ethel M. Lockwood, Feb. 14, 1906. Mem. faculty U. of Pittsburgh, title of photo naturalist, 1925—. Has developed to a high degree the application of telephotography in securing natural history motion pictures; maker motion pictures of ecol. and zoöl. subjects. Photo-biologist to Koppers Research Corp., Pittsburgh, 1930-31; photo-naturalist ad spl. lecturer, Rutgers U., 1931—. Republican. Episcopalian. Lectures on wild birds, animal life and plant life, illustrated with motion pictures. Specialist in time-lapse motion pictures of plant movements. Home: New Brunswick, N.J. Died Feb. 26, 1938.

McCLINTOCK, Oliver; b. Pittsburgh, Oct. 20, 1839; s. Washington and Eliza (Thompson) M.; B.A., Yale, 1861, M.A., 1864; m. Clara Courtney Childs, June 7, 1866. Head of Oliver McClintock Co. (predecessors established 1807), 1863, inc. 1897 and made pres.; co. dissolved, 1914. Pres. trustees, Pa. College for Women, Pittsburgh; dir. Shady Side Acad., Western Theol. Sem. Republican. Presbyn. Mem. exec. council Nat. Municipal Yeague (v.p.). Retired. Home: Pittsburgh, Pa. Died Oct. 10, 1922.

McCLISH, Eli, clergyman; b. Warren Co., Ind., Oct. 3, 1846; s. James and Elizabeth (West) M.; served in Union Army under Gen. Sherman, 1863-65; A.B., Northwestern U., 1874, A.M., 1876; B.D., Garrett Bibl. Inst., 1877; (D.D., Northwestern, 1887); m. Louisa A. Clarke, Dec. 24, 1872. Entered M.E. ministry, 1877; pres. Grand Prairie Sem., 1884-91; declined presidency U. of the Pacific, 1891; pastor Grace Ch., San Francisco, 1891-95; pres. U. of the Pacific, 1896-1906; pastor W. Adams Ch., Los Angeles, 1906-09, First Ch., San Bernardina, Calif., 1909-13, Central M.E. Ch., San Diego, Calif., 1913-15; chaplain Pacific Branch Nat. Home for Disabled Vol. Soldiers Oct. 1, 1915—. Home: Soldiers Home, Calif. Died Feb. 7, 1918.

McCLOSKEY, George V(ictor) A(ndronicus), lawyer, author; b. N.Y. City, Jan. 27, 1883; s. George Bracknell and Cecilia (Bassié) McC.; A.B., Coll. City of N.Y., 1902; LL.B., New York U., 1906, J.D., 1907. Practiced in N.Y. City, 1907—; specializes in admiralty law; mem. firm House, Holthusen & McCloskey. Republican. Catholic. Author: Lyrics, 1919; The Flight of Guinevere and Other Poems, 1921, 2d edit., 1928; St. Joan of Arc (epic). Editor 5th edit. Benedict on Admiralty. Home: New York, N.Y. Died Mar. 29, 1933.

McCLOSKEY, William George, R.C. bishop of Louisville (Ky.), 1868—; b. Brooklyn, Nov. 10, 1823; ed. St. Mary's Coll., Emmitsburg, Md.; ordained priest, 1852; spent a year in mission work in New York; then apptd. to a chair in St. Mary's; became 1857-59, prof. moral theology and sacred scripture there; 1st pres. Am. Coll., Rome, 1859-68, under apptmt. by Pope Pius IX. Died 1909.

McCLOUD, Charles A., banker; b. Moravia, Ia., May 14, 1860; s. William E. and Ann M. (Sears) McC.; ed. Centerville (Ia.) Normal Sch., Ia. Wesleyan U. and Bryant & Stratton Commercial Coll., St. Joseph, Mo.; m. Flora S. Bowman, Nov. 28, 1883; 1 dau., Elsie M. (Mrs. Wm. T. Conley). Began as cashier Citizens State Bank, York, Neb., 1886; right of way agt. for C.&N.W. Ry., 1887, 1888; in loan and real estate business, 1889-1905; pres. First Nat. Bank, York, 1912—; pres. First Trust Co., First State Savings Bank, York Hotel Co., York Mutual Bldg. & Loan Assn., First Nat. Bank, Bradshaw, First Nat. Bank, Benedict, Bank of Lushton, Blue River Bank, McCool, Thayer Bank (Thayer, Neb.), Farmers & Traders Bank, Waco, Lincoln Investment & Safe Deposit Co. (all of Neb.). Dep. county treas., York Co., 1881-85; supervisor York Co., 1887-92; mayor of York, 1902-06; chmn. Rep. State Com., Neb., 1920-22; member Rep. Nat. Com., 1924—. Chmn. bd. trustees York College. Conglist. Mason. Home: York, Neb. Died Mar. 21, 1937.

McCLUNG, Calvin Morgan, merchant; b. St. Louis, May 12, 1855; s. Franklin Henry and Eliza Ann

(Mills) M.; bro. of Lee M.; B.A., U. of Tenn., 1874, M.A., 1877; Ph.B., Yale, 1876; m. Annie McGhee, Mar. 3, 1881 (died 1898); 2d, Barbara Adair, Mar. 16, 1905. Began business with father, 1877; bought controlling interest in wholesale hardware firm in Knoxville, 1882; incorporated it as C. M. McClung & Co., 1905, and became pres.; dir. E. Tenn. Nat. Bank, Knoxville Cotton Mills. Trustee Lawson McGhee Library. Home: Knoxville, Tenn. Died Mar. 1919.

McCLUNG, Hugh Lawson, judge; b. Russellville, Tenn., June 2, 1858; s. Hugh Lawson and Anna (Gillespie) McC.; B.A., U. of Tenn., 1877; m. Ella Gibbins, Dec. 15, 1892; 1 dau., Ellen Lawson (Mrs. Thomas H. Berry). Admitted to Tenn. bar, 1879, practicing at Knoxville; mem. Webb & McClung, later Webb, McClung & Baker; apptd. spl. judge Supreme Ct. of Tenn. by Gov. McMillan; chancellor Knoxville Chancery Div., 1909, 10, retired. Trustee U. of Tenn. 23 yrs.; trustee and chmn. bd. East Tenn. Inst. for Girls many yrs.; trustee and pres. bd. Robert N. Strong Home; trustee Knoxville Pub. Library; dir., pres. for 5 yrs., Holston Nat. Bank. Democrat. Presbyn. Home: Fountain City, Tenn. Died Apr. 25, 1936.

McCLUNG, (Thomas) Lee, treasurer of the United States; b. Knoxville, Tenn., Mar. 26, 1870; s. Franklin Henry and Eliza Ann (Mills) M.; bro. of Calvin Morgan M.; A.B., Yale, 1892; (hon. A.M., 1905); unmarried. Traveled in Europe and U.S., 1892-93; p.m. St. Paul & Duluth R.R. Co., at St. Paul, 1894-98; with Southern Ry. Co., 1898-1901; asst. to 2d v.p. Southern Ry. Co., Washington, 1901-02; asst. freight traffic mgr., same, at Louisville, Ky., 1902-04; treas. Yale U., 1904-09; treas. of the U.S., Nov. 1, 1909-Nov. 22, 1912 Dir. Marion (Ala.) Inst.; nat. councilman Boy Scouts of America. Home: Washington, D.C. Died Dec. 19, 1914.

McCLURE, Alexander Kelly, editor-in-chief Philadelphia Times, 1873 to April 1901; b. Sherman's Valley, Perry Co., Pa., Jan. 9, 1828; s. Alexander and Isabella (Anderson) M.; reared on farm; ed. at home; (LL.D., Washington and Lee Univ.); apprenticed to tanner's trade, 1843-46; m. Matilda S. Gray, Feb. 10, 1852; m. 2d, Cora M. Gratz, Mar. 19, 1879. Edited and published Mifflin Sentinel, 1846-50, Chambersburg Repository, 1850-56 and 1862-64; on staff Gov. Johnston with rank of col., 1849; U.S. marshal, Juniata Co., Pa., 1850; admitted to bar, 1856; Whig candidate for auditor gen. of Pa., 1853; mem. of conv. that organized Rep. party, Pittsburgh, 1855; state supt. Erie & N.E. R.R., 1856; mem. legislature, 1857-58 and 1864; state senator, 1859; asst. adj. gen. U.S.V., 1862. Del. Nat. Rep. convs., 1856, 64, 68; practiced law, Phila., 1868-73; chmn. Pa. delegation to Liberal Rep. Conv., 1872; chmn. Rep. State Com., 1860, chmn. Liberal Rep. State Com., 1872; State senator, 1872; independent candidate for mayor of Phila., 1874; defeated by small plurality; prothonotary Sup. Court, Pa., 1904—. Author: Lincoln and Men of War Times, 1892; Recollections of Half a Century; To the Pacific and Mexico, 1901; Old Time Notes of Pennsylvania, 1906. Home: Philadelphia, Pa. Died 1909.

McCLURE, James Gore King, theologian; b. Albany, N.Y., Nov. 24, 1848; s. Archibald and Susan Tracy (Rice) M.; A.B., Yale, 1870; grad. Princeton Theol. Seminary, 1873; D.D., Lake Forest Univ., 1888, Princeton, 1906, Yale, 1906; LL.D., Illinois College, 1904; LL.D., Lake Forest U., 1929; m. Annie P., d. Nathan F. Dixon, of Westerly, R.I., Nov. 19, 1879; children—Annie Dixon (Mrs. Dumont Clarke), James G. K., Harriet (Mrs. R. Douglas Stuart), Archibald, Nathan Dixon. Ordained Presbyn. ministry, 1874; pastor New Scotland, N.Y., 1874-79; traveled in Europe, Egypt, Holy Land, Turkey and Greece, 1879-80; pastor Lake Forest, Ill., 1881-1905; pres. Lake Forest U., 1897-1901; pres. McCormick Theol. Sem. (now Presbyn. Theol. Sem.), Chicago, 1905-28, pres. emeritus. Deputy gov. gen. Soc. of Mayflower Descendants in United States (gov. Ill. Society). Author: Possibilities, 1896; Environment, 1899; Grandfather's Stories, 1926; Grandfather's Stories II, 1928; The Story of England's First Library, 1929; History of Presbyterian Theological Seminary, Chicago, 1929. Home: Lake Forest, Ill. Died Jan. 18, 1932.

McCLURE, Meade Lowrie, banker; b. Clarion Co., Pa., May 6, 1863; s. Hugh Lowrie and Rhoda (Lowrie) McC.; ed. Callinsburg (Pa.) Acad.; Carrier Sem., Clarion, Pa.; Nat. Normal U., Lebanon, O.; m. Oma Reynolds, May 28, 1887; 1 son, Lowrie Ellis. Asst. cashier Citizens Nat. Bank, Harper, Kan., 1883-86, Bank of Kiowa, Kan., 1886-96; cashier Stock Exchange Bank, Caldwell, Kan., 1896-99; mgr. later pres. Drumm Commn. Co., live stock loans, Kansas City, St. Louis and Chicago, 1899-1921; pres. and mgr. Stock Growers' Financial Corp., a $50,000,000 bankers' pool to relieve live stock credits, 1921-25; dir. Federal Reserve Bank of Kansas City, Mo., 1914—, now chmn. bd. and federal reserve agt.; sec. and dir. Double Circle Cattle Co. (breeding cattle in Ariz.). Pres. Nat. Live Stock Exchange 2 yrs.; dir. Kansas City Agency of War Finance Corp. and mem. Live Stock Industrial Com., World War. Trustee Andrew Drumm Inst. of Kansas City (sch. and home for boys). Republican. Presbyn. Mason. Home: Kansas City, Mo. Died Dec. 5, 1934.

McCLURG, Alexander Caldwell, bookseller and publisher; b. Philadelphia, Pa., about 1834; grad. Miami Univ., 1853 (A.M., Yale, 1893). Went to Chicago and entered as clerk the bookselling house of S. C. Griggs & Co. Enlisted, Aug. 15, 1862, as private; later became capt. 88th Ill. vols. and afterward promoted lt. col. in adj. gen.'s dept. Later chief of staff 14th army corps, and bvtd. col. and brig. gen.; participated in battles and campaigns of Perryville, Stone River, Chickamauga, Missionary Ridge, Atlanta and the March to the Sea. After war became a partner in the firm of S. C. Griggs & Co., afterward Jansen, McClurg & Co., succeeded later by A. C. McClurg & Co., booksellers and publishers, of which he became the head. On Feb. 12, 1899, this establishment, with all its rare and valuable contents, was destroyed by fire. The temptation to retire to a life of ease and literary leisure was strong, but the demand in Chicago and the West that the old bookstore should be re-established on the old lines, and the interests of many competent and faithful assistants, finally induced General McClurg to join in the reorganization of the old concern as a stock company (pres. new company). Home: Chicago, Ill. Died 1901.

McCLURG, Walter Audubon, naval officer; b. Landenberg, Pa., Feb. 4, 1852; s. John Russell (M.D., U.S.V.) and Ruth Ann (Higgins) McC.; ed. Cleveland (O.) Mil. Acad., 1862-64; Kennett Sq. (Pa.) Acad., 1865-68; Millersville (Pa.) State Normal Sch., 1869; M.D., Jefferson Med. Coll., Phila., 1872; m. Edmonia Phelps Mason, d. Rear Admiral T. S. Phelps, Oct. 10, 1906. Commd. asst. surgeon U.S.N., Feb. 8, 1874; promoted passed asst. surgeon, Nov. 2, 1877; surgeon, Jan. 25, 1889; med. insp., Nov. 19, 1900; med. dir., June 16, 1907; voluntarily retired after 34 years' active service, Sept. 1, 1908. Served on fifteen ships, 17 yrs.; duty Bur. Medicine and Surgery, Navy Dept., 1889-93; fleet surgeon N. Atlantic Fleet, 1902-03. Republican. Presbyterian. Deceased.

McCLURKIN, John Knox, clergyman; b. Sparta, Ill., Nov. 23, 1853; s. Rev. John Johnson and Maria S. M.; A.B., Westminster Coll., Pa., 1873, A.M., 1876 (D.D., 1887, LL.D., 1919); Princeton Theol. Sem., 1877; R.P. Theol. Sem., Allegheny, Pa., 1878-81; unmarried. Ordained R.P. ministry, 1881; instr. Latin, Westminster Coll., 1874; prof. Greek, Geneva Coll., 1875; prof. Greek, 1876-82, acting pres., 1883, pres.-elect, 1884, Westminster Coll., Pa.; pastor 2d Ref. Presbyn. Ch., Phila., 1884-87; prof. systematic theology, homiletics and ch. history, Reformed Presbyn. Theol. Sem., Allegheny, 1887-91; pastor Shadyside U.P. Ch., Pittsburgh, Pa., 1891—. Moderator 48th Gen. Assembly of U.P. Ch., 1906; dir. Pittsburgh Theol. Sem., Westminster Coll., Pa. Coll. for Women, Pittsburgh U.; trustee Cairo (Egypt) U. Died Nov. 9, 1923.

McCLUSKEY, Thomas Joseph, univ. prof.; b. New York, N.Y., July 31, 1857; s. Arthur J. and Mary C. (Jones) M.; grad. De La Salle Inst., New York, 1871; A.B., with highest honors, Manhattan Coll., 1874, A.M., 1881; philos. and theol. studies, St. Joseph's Sem., Troy, N.Y., Collegium Maximum, Woodstock, Md. Ordained priest R.C. Ch., 1880; asso. at St. Leo's Ch., New York, 1881-87; vice-rector New York Cathedral, 1887-89 inclusive; entered Soc. of Jesus, 1889; asst. rector St. Ignatius' Ch., New York, 1894-97; pastor St. Francis Xavier's Ch., 1897-1901; prof. classics, Boston Coll., 1902-06; v.p. Woodstock Coll., 1906-07; pres. St. Francis Xavier Coll., New York, 1907-11, Fordham U., 1911-15; prof. philosophy, Boston Coll., 1915-25; head dept. of philosophy, Boston Coll., 1920-25; prof. philosophy, Fordham, 1925—. Died July 13, 1937.

McCOLL, Jay Robert, engineer; b. Webster, Mich., Mar. 24, 1867; s. Robert and Sophia McC.; grad. engring. dept. Mich. State Coll., 1890; post-grad. student there and at Cornell; m. Belle Gertrude Baldwin, Jan. 3, 1900; 1 dau., Jennette Baldwin. Adj. prof. mech. engring., U. of Tenn., 1890-1902; asso. prof. thermodynamics, Purdue U., 1902-03; asso. prof. steam engring. in charge dept., same univ., 1903-05; chief engr. Am. Blower Co., Detroit, 1905-10; dean engring. dept., U. of Detroit, 1910—; mem. McColl, Snyder & McLean, consulting engrs. Mem. bd. of rules, Dept. Bldg. and Safety Engring., Detroit, 1918—; mem. Mich. State College Board, 1922-34. On editorial staff Michigan Architect and Engineer. Republican. Conglist. Home: Detroit, Mich. Died Oct. 30, 1936.

McCOLLESTER, Sullivan Holman, clergyman; b. Marlboro, N.H., Dec. 18, 1826; s. Silas and Achsah (Holman) M.; A.B., Norwich U., 1850, A.M., 1853; student Harvard Div. Sch. 1863; (D.D., St. Lawrence U., N.Y., 1873; Litt.D., Buchtel Coll., Ohio, 1908); m. Sophia Fanny Knight, Nov. 23, 1852 (dec.); m. 2d, Emma Parker, Nov. 17, 1903 (dec.); m. 3d, Elizabeth E. Randall, Dec. 15, 1905; father of Lee Sullivan M. Prin. Walpole (N.H.) Acad., 1850-53, Mt. Cæsar Sem., Swanzey, N.H., 1853-58, Valley Sem., N.H., 1858-62; ordained Universalist ministry, 1853; pastor, Westmoreland and W. Chesterfield, N.H., 1857-61; prin. Westbrook Coll. and Sem., 1862-69; pastor Nashua, N.H., 1869-73; pres. Buchtel Coll., Akron, O., 1873-78; pastor Bellows Falls, Vt., and Dover, N.H., until 1885; from then devoted attention mainly to travel, lit. and missionary work and sch. supervision. Extensive traveler. Mem. N.H. Ho. of Rep., 1889-90; pres. N.H. Universalist State Conv. Republican. Author: Round the Globe in Old and New Paths, 1893; Mexico, Old and New—A Wonderland, 1899; Leaves from Mapleside. Home: Marlboro, N.H. Died May 20, 1921.

McCOLLOM, John Hildreth, physician; b. Pittston, Me., May 6, 1843; s. James Tomb and Elizabeth Phillips (Hildreth) M.; grad. Phillips Acad., Andover, Mass., 1861; M.D., Harvard Med. Sch., 1869; (hon. M.S., Dartmouth, 1910); m. Susan Cartée, July 5, 1875. Has practiced at Boston, 1871—; hosp. steward 30th Regt., Mass. Vol. Inf., 1862-65; asst. supt. U.S. Marine Hosp., Chelsea, Mass., 1870-71; city phys., Boston, 1881-95; resident phys., South Dept., infectious service, Boston City Hosp., 1895—; phys. for infectious diseases, 1900—, supt. and med. dir., 1909—, Boston City Hosp.; asst. prof. contagious diseases, 1903-08, prof., 1908—, Harvard Med. Sch. Episcopalian. Died June 14, 1915.

McCOMAS, Francis John, artist; b. Fingal, Tasmania, Oct. 1, 1874; s. Richard Newton and Julia (Davies) M.; ed. Sydney Tech. Coll.; m. Marie Louise Parrott, June 28, 1905; m. 2d, Gene Frances Baker, Oct. 31, 1917. Came to U.S., 1898. Exhibited in New York, Boston, Chicago; San Francisco, Phila., London and Paris. Awarded Phila. water color prize; Dana gold medal, Phila.; Hudnut prize, Am. Water Color Soc. Works on exhibition at Met. Mus., New York; San Francisco Mus.; Portland Mus.; Mills Coll. Art Gallery; mural decorations Del Monte Hotel and Pebble Beach Lodge, Calif. Mem. Jury of Award, San Francisco Expn. Episcopalian. Home: Pebble Beach, Calif. Died Dec. 27, 1938.

McCOMAS, Louis Emory, justice Court of Appeals, D.C., 1905—; b. Washington Co., Md., Oct. 28, 1846; s. Frederick C. and Catharine (Angle) McC.; ed. Saint James Coll., Md.; grad. Dickinson Coll., Carlisle, Pa., 1866; LL.D., Dickinson, 1898, Georgetown Univ., 1901; m. Leah M. Humrichouse, Sept. 23, 1875. Admitted to bar, 1868; mem. Congress, 1883-91. Republican. Apptd., 1892, asso. justice Supreme Court of D.C. and served until 1899; U.S. senator, Md., 1899-1905. Was several yrs. prof. internat. law, Georgetown Univ. Law Sch. Home: Williamsport, Md. Died 1907.

McCOMB, William Andrew, clergyman; b. Perry Co., Miss., Nov. 8, 1860; s. Hugh Howard and Menervia Jane (Jenkins) McC.; A.B., Miss. Coll., Clinton, Miss., 1888, A.M., 1904, D.D., 1914; student Bapt. Theol. Sem., Louisville, Ky., 1888-89, Rochester Theol. Sem., 1889-90; Ph.D., Morgan Park Sem. (now Div. Sch. U. of Chicago), 1891; m. May Willis, Aug. 29, 1895; children—Catherine Evers (Mrs. Carl Lobitz), Agnes May (Mrs. Robert A. Kimbrough, Jr.). Ordained ministry Baptist Church, 1886; pastor Corinth, Miss., 1891-93, Eureka Springs, Ark., 1893-95, Plano, Tex., 1895-99, Crystal Springs, Miss., 1899-1903, Gloster, Miss., 1903-07, Alexandria, La., 1907-08, Baton Rouge, La., 1917-23, Gulfport, Miss., 1923-31, Flora, Miss., 1931-37, Long Beach, Mississippi, 1937—. Evangelist Home Mission Bd., Southern Bapt. Conv., 1908-12; financial sec., Miss. Coll., Clinton, Miss., 1912-14; assisted Foreign Mission Bd., Southern Bapt. Conv., in raising $1,250,000, 1914-16; financial sec. Tri-State Bapt. Memorial Hosp., Memphis, Tenn., 1916-17. Trustee Miss. Coll.; mem. exec. com. and dir. Southern Bapt. Conv., 1895-1931; dir. Home Mission Bd., State Mission bds. of Tex., La. and Miss. Mason. Home: Gulfport, Miss. Died Oct. 14, 1939.

McCOMBS, William Frank, lawyer; b. Hamburg, Ark., Dec. 26, 1875; s. William Faulkner and Mary Frances (Pugh) M.; A.B., Princeton, 1898; LL.B., Harvard Univ., 1901; (LL.D., Lincoln Memorial U. and U. Ark.). Practiced, New York, 1901—; mgr. nat. campaigns which resulted in nomination and election of Woodrow Wilson as President, 1912; chmn. Dem. Nat. Com., 1912-16; tendered ambassadorship to France, Mar. 1913 (declined). Trustee Coll. City of New York, Lincoln Memorial U. Died Feb. 22, 1921.

McCONAUGHY, James, editor; b. Gettysburg, Pa., Mar. 30, 1857; s. David and Leana (Mathews) M.; B.A., Pennsylvania Coll., Gettysburg, Pa., 1875, M.A., 1878, Litt.D., 1917; Union Theol. Sem., 1880-83; m. Eleanor Underhill, Apr. 16, 1884 (died 1926); children—Louise (dec.), James Lukens, Donald, Eleanor (dec.), Katharine (Mrs. Williams D. Bailey). In office Internat. Y.M.C.A., New York, 1875-76; general sec. Harrisburg Y.M.C.A., 1876-80; sec. Harlem Branch Y.M.C.A., New York, 1880-83; jr. gen. sec. New York Y.M.C.A., and sec. 23d St. Branch, 1883-91; head of dept. English Bible, Mt. Hermon Sch., 1891-1912; mng. editor, 1912-15, editor, Mar. 1, 1915—, Am. S.S. Union. Y.M.C.A. religious work dir., Camp Meade, Md., 1918. Author: Union Bible Pictures; Sunday-School Teaching and Management, 1916. Home: Germantown, Phila., Pa. Died Dec. 6, 1934.

McCONAUGHY, Robert, physician, surgeon; b. Mt. Pleasant, Pa., Apr. 6, 1852; s. James (M.D.) and Harriet (Shallenberger) M.; Lafayette Coll., 1870-72; M.D., Jefferson Med. Coll., Phila., 1875; m. Mary

Miriam Rice, Sept. 26, 1888; m. 2d, Mary Floy Lawrence, Oct. 5, 1892. Div. surgeon, Pa. R.R., at Mt. Pleasant and Scottdale, Pa., 1876-85; removed to York, Neb., 1885; local surgeon Fremont, Elkhorn & Mo. Valley Ry. Co., 1887-92, C.,B.&Q. R.R. Co., 1902—; physician and health officer, city of York. Sec. U.S. Bd. Pension Examiners, 1887-1914; sec. Med. Advisory Bd. for York Co.; mem. Bd. of Edn., York, 1901-02, 1904-16; sec. bd. Chautauqua Assn., York; dir. Presbyn. Theol. Sem., Omaha; sec. and dir. bd. Y.M.C.A. Republican. Presbyn. Mason. Home: York, Neb. Died Dec. 18, 1923.

McCONNELL, Fernando Coello, clergyman; b. Clay Co., N.C., Aug. 2, 1856; s. William Ross and Jane Christine (Jameson) M.; B.A., Mercer U., Macon, Ga., 1888, (D.D., 1894); grad. Southern Bapt. Theol. Sem., Louisville, Ky., 1882; m. Emma England, Jan. 12, 1876; children—Mrs. Myrtle McBee, Strubbe, Mrs. Christine Rousseau, Lucius Willingham, Fernando Coello, Carter Jameson. Ordained Bapt. ministry, 1880; pastor Gainesville, Ga., 1888-94, Lynchburg, Va., 1894-1901; sec. Home Mission Bd., Southern Bapt. Conv., 1901-03; pastor Calvary Ch., Kansas City, Mo., 1903-09, 1st Ch., Waco, Tex., 1909-15, Druid Hills Ch., Atlanta, Ga., Jan. 1, 1915—. Mem. Home Mission Bd.; mem. exec. bd. Ga. Bapt. Conv.; dir. Christian Index. Home: Atlanta, Ga. Died Jan. 12, 1929.

McCONNELL, Ira Welch, civil engr.; b. Schell City, Mo., Oct. 17, 1871; s. James Calvin and Cecelia Elizabeth (Welch) M.; C.E., Cornell U., 1897; m. Grace Lucille Bowerman, Sept. 22, 1903; children—John Waldo, Charles Edwin. Instr. civ. engring., Cornell U., 1899-1900; contractor's supt., Chicago and New Orleans, 1901-03; prof. civ. engring., Mo. Sch. of Mines, Rolla, 1903; project engr., 1903-07, supervising engr., 1907-09, U.S. Reclamation Service; chief irrigation engr., J. G. White & Co., Inc., New York, 1909-10; v.p. and gen. mgr. Idaho Irrigation Co., Ltd., 1910-12; hydraulic engr., 1912-17, chief engr., 1917, Stone & Webster, div. of constrn. and engring.; asst. gen. mgr., Am. Internat. Shipbldg. Corp., Hog Island Shipyard, 1918; v.p. United Engineers & Constructors, Inc. (Phila.), Dwight P. Robinson & Co., Inc., New York. Conglist. Mason, Elk. Home: Hastings-on-Hudson, N.Y. Died Jan. 6, 1933.

McCONNELL, James Eli, clergyman; b. St. Clairsville, O., Feb. 29, 1860; s. James C. and Susannah (Morgan) M.; B.A., Oberlin, 1884; B.D., Union Theol. Sem., 1887; D.D., Carleton Coll., Northfield, Minn., 1906; m. Marion Vincent Ellis, May 1, 1889; children—Ellis Huntington (dec.), Florence Marion, Elizabeth. Ordained Congl. ministry, 1887; pastor Churchville, N.Y., 1887-90, Northfield, Minn., 1890-1905, Union Ch., Providence, R.I., 1905-20; emeritus secretary Commn. on Missions, Congl. Ch. Independent Republican. Author: President McKinley's Services to the Country and the World, 1901; Samson's Riddle, 1904; The Apostles of Home Missions, 1904; How a Church Can Help Its Pastor, 1910; Evil Communications and Good Manners, 1913. Home: Kew Gardens, L.I., N.Y. Deceased.

McCONNELL, James Moore, state commr. edn.; b. Armstrong Co., Pa., May 28, 1868; s. William and Rebecca Dickey (Moore) M.; grad. State Normal Sch., Edinboro, Pa., 1889; studied law, Warren, Pa., 1890-92; A.B., Carleton Coll., Minn., 1910; m. Margaret Jeannette Graham, July 19, 1893. Began as teacher rural schs., Pa.; supt. schs., Heron Lake, Minn., 1895-98, Winnebago, 1900-04, Mankato, 1904-09; prof. Am. history and govt., State Normal Sch., Mankato, 1909-18; apptd. by gov., state supt. of edn., 1919; commr. of edn. under act of legislature creating State Bd. of Edn., Aug. 1919—. Republican. Episcopalian. Mason. Home: St. Paul, Minn. Died Apr. 29, 1933.

McCONNELL, Joseph Moore, prof. history; b. McConnellsville, S.C., Nov. 29, 1875; s. John Daniel and Sarah Amanda (Jaggers) McC.; B.A., Davidson Coll., 1899; M.A., U. of Va., 1903, Ph.D., 1907; m. Eliza Howard Riggs, Aug. 3, 1905; children—Joseph Howard, Elisha Riggs, John Daniel. Asso. prin. Pantops Acad. (now defunct), 1903-05; with Davidson Coll., 1905—, successively asso. prof. Latin and mathematics, 1905-07, prof. history and economics, 1907-20, prof. history, 1920—, also dean of faculty, 1928—; prof. of European history, U. of Virginia, summers 1909-16; prof. Am. history, State Normal Sch., Farmville, Va., summer 1910; mem. bd. trustees graded schs., Davidson, 15 yrs.; pres. Davidson Building & Loan Assn. Moderator Presbyterian Synod of N.C., 1933-34. Democrat. Presbyn. Author: Southern Orators, 1909. Home: Davidson, N.C. Died May 16, 1935.

McCONNELL, Lincoln, lecturer, evangelist; b. Maryville, Tenn., June 6, 1867; s. Moses Lamar and Margaret (Clemens) M.; ed. Maryville Coll. through jr. year; LL.D., State U. of Ky., 1913; D.D. Simmons U., Abilene, Tex., 1925; m. Maimie White, Dec. 24, 1889; children—J. Edwin, Mrs. Ethel Jean Larkin, Lincoln, Robt. E. Lee. Mem. Atlanta Police and Detective Dept., 1890-93; asst. to solicitor Criminal Court of Atlanta, 1894-95; began evangelistic work, 1896; first pastor Wesley Memorial Instnl. Ch., Atlanta, 1901-02; resigned to resume evangelistic work and lecturing, 1903; pastor Bapt. Tabernacle Ch., Atlanta, 1913-14, First Ch., Oklahoma City, 1924-27, First Ch., St. Petersburg, Fla., May 1928—. Author: Who Was Jesus?; The Philosopher's Riddle; Will the Old Book Stand?; Is Faith a Philosophic Fact or a Foolish Fancy?; The Meaning of Easter; The Acid Test; Was Jesus Mistaken?; The Amusement Question; The Greatest Romance of all History; The Divine Message of the Stone Miracle. Home: St. Petersburg, Fla. Died May 5, 1930.

McCONNELL, Samuel David, clergyman; b. Westmoreland Co., Pa., Aug. 1, 1845; s. David and Agnes (Guthrie) M.; A.B., Washington and Jefferson Coll., 1868; D.D., U. of Pa., 1887; D.C.L., Hobart, 1897; LL.D., Washington and Jefferson, 1902; m. Anna Bliss, Sept. 3, 1873 (dec.); children—Ellicott (dec.), Guthrie (dec.), Chrystie. Deacon, 1872, priest, 1873, P.E. Ch.; rector St. John's Ch., Erie, Pa., 1872-73, Watertown, Conn., 1873-76, Middletown, Conn., 1876-82, St. Stephen's, Phila., 1882-96, Holy Trinity Ch., Brooklyn, 1896-1902, All Souls Church, N.Y. City, 1902. Archdeacon of Conn., 1876-82, Brooklyn, 1898. Author: History of American Episcopal Church, 1890, Sermon Stuff (1st and 2d series), 1888, 1895; A Year's Sermons, 1896; Christ; Christianity; Confession of an Old Priest; Immortability. Home: Easton, Md. Died 1939.

McCONNELL, Samuel Parsons, lawyer; b. Springfield, Ill., July 5, 1850; s. Gen. John and Elizabeth C. (Parsons) M.; A.B., Lombard Coll., Ill., 1871; m. Sarah, d. Judge John G. Rogers, of Chicago, 1876; children—Mrs. Julia Follansbee, James Rogers, Mrs. Eleanor Truitt; m. 2d, Mayo Methot, 1902; children—Elizabeth, Patsy, Mrs. F. G. Albright, John S. Admitted to Ill. bar, 1872; practiced in Chicago; judge Circuit Ct., Cook Co., Ill., 1889-94. Democrat. Pres. George A. Fuller Co., bldg. contracting corp., New York, 1899-1904. Home: Los Angeles, Calif. Died Apr. 1935.

McCONNELL, William J., governor; b. Commerce, Mich., Sept. 18, 1839; s. James and Nancy (Coulter) M.; ed. dist. schs. and acads. in Mich.; m. Louisa Brown, Sept. 15, 1866. Went to Calif., 1860, to Ore., 1862, and taught sch., 1862-63; walked from Ore. to Boisé City, Ida. Ty., 1863; deputy U.S. marshal, Ida. Ty., 1865-67; returned to Calif. and engaged in business in Humboldt Co., 1867-72; returned to Ore. and established business there and in Ida.; became mem. and, in 1882, pres. Ore. Senate; moved to Ida., engaging in business as mcht. and banker; was mem. Ida. Constl. Conv., 1890; one of its 1st U.S. senators, drawing the short term, 1890-91; gov. 1893-96; U.S. Indian inspector, 1897-1901; immigrant inspector, 1909—. Author: Early History of Idaho, 1913; Episodes of Pioneer Life, 1919. Home: Moscow, Ida. Died Mar. 29, 1925.

McCONWAY, William, b. County Derry, Ireland, Feb. 14, 1842; s. John and Isabella (Kissic) McC.; m. Josephine A. Eaton, 1880. Pres. McConway & Torley Co.; dir. Westinghouse Electric & Mfg. Co., Westinghouse Machine Co.; pres. Allegheny Cemetery; trustee Carnegie Inst., Elizabeth Steel Magee Hosp. Home: Pittsburgh, Pa. Died July 28, 1925.

McCOOK, Alexander McDowell, soldier; b. Columbiana Co., O., April 22, 1831; s. Daniel McC.; early edn. in public school, Carrollton, O.; grad. West Point, July 1, 1852; m. Kate Phillips, Jan. 23, 1863; m. 2d, Annie M. Colt, Oct. 8, 1885. Apptd. bvt. 2d lt. 3d Inf., June 30, 1852; promoted through grades to maj gen. U.S.A., Nov. 9, 1894; retired from active service under the law, April 22, 1895. Bvtd. in regular service for gallant and meritorious services during Civil war as maj., July 21, 1861 (Bull Run); lt. col., March 3, 1862 (capture of Nashville, Tenn.); col., April 7, 1862 (Shiloh); brig. gen., March 13, 1865 (Perryville, Ky.); maj. gen., March 13, 1865, for gallant and meritorious services in field during the war. Represented U.S. at coronation of Czar of Russia, Moscow, May 1-24, 1896; mem. commn. apptd. by President to investigate War Dept., during war with Spain, Sept. 23, 1898 to Feb. 10, 1899; Presbyterian. Died 1903.

McCOOK, Anson George, soldier; b. Steubenville, O., Oct. 10, 1835; s. Dr. John and Catharine Julia (Sheldon) M.; bro. of Edward Moody, Henry Christopher and John James M.; pub. sch. edn.; crossed plains to Calif., 1854, returning, 1860; admitted to bar, 1861; capt. 2d Ohio Inf., Apr 17, 1861; maj., Aug. 6, 1861; lt. col., Jan. 1, 1863; col., Jan. 20, 1863; bvtd. brig. gen. vols., Mar. 13, 1865, "for meritorious services"; hon. discharged, Oct. 21, 1865; served in Army of the Cumberland and with Sherman in Atlanta campaign; m. Hettie B. McCook, June, 1886. U.S. assessor internal revenue, Steubenville, O., 1866-72; removed to New York, 1873; mem. 45th to 47th Congresses (1877-83), 8th N.Y. Dist.; sec. U.S. Senate, 1884-93; city chamberlain, New York, 1895-97. Republican. Home: New York, N.Y. Died Dec. 30, 1917.

McCOOK, Edward Moody, soldier, gov.; b. Steubenville, O., June 15, 1833; s. Dr. John and Catharine Julia (Sheldon) M.; pub. sch. edn.; m. Mary Thompson; m. 2d, Mary McKenna. Removed to Pike's Peak, 1859; mem. Kan. legislature, 1860; U.S. Govt. vol. secret agt. previous to Civil War; entered Union Army, 2d lt. 1st U.S. Cav., May 8, 1861; 1st lt., July 17, 1862; in vol. service was maj., lt. col. and col. 2d Ind. Vol. Cav.; brig. gen. vols., Apr. 27, 1864; hon. mustered out of vol. service, Jan. 15, 1866. Bvtd. 1st lt., Apr. 7, 1862, for battle of Shiloh; capt., Oct. 8, 1862, for battle of Perryville, Ky.; maj., Sept. 20, 1863, for battle of Chickamauga; lt. col., Jan. 27, 1864, for cav. operations in E. Tenn.; col., Mar. 13, 1865, for capture of Selma, Ala.; brig. gen., Mar. 13, 1865, for gallant and meritorious services in the field during the war; maj. gen. vols., Mar. 13, 1865, for gallant and meritorious services during the war; resigned from regular army, May 9, 1866. U.S. minister to Hawaii, 1866-69; gov. Colo. Ty., 1869-75. Home: Riverside, Conn. Died 1909.

McCOOK, Henry Christopher, clergyman; b. New Lisbon, O., July 3, 1837; s. Dr. John and Catharine Julia (Sheldon) M.; bro. of Edward Moody, Anson George, John James M.; A.B., Jefferson (now Washington and Jefferson) Coll., 1859; Western Theol. Seminary, 1860-63; (D.D., 1880, ScD., 1888, Lafayette College; LL.D., Washington and Jefferson, 1902)); m. Emma C. Herter, Sept. 11, 1860 (died 1897); m. 2d, Mrs. E. D. S. Abbey, June 27, 1899. Ordained Presbyn. ministry, 1861; home missionary, Ill. and Mo.; assisted in organizing 41st Ill. Vols. of which was 1st lt. and chaplain, 1861-62; pastor Clinton, Ill., 1862-64; city missionary, St. Louis, 1864-69; pastor, 1870-1903, pastor emeritus, 1903, Tabernacle Presbyn. Ch., Phila. Chaplain Pa. Commandery, Loyal Legion; chaplain (May, 1898) 2d Regt. Pa. Vols. in Spanish-Am. War; founder of Nat. Relief Commn. in Spanish-Am. War. Prominent as entomologist. Pres. Am. Entomol. Soc.; v.p. Acad. Natural Sciences, Phila.; pres. Am. Presbyn. Hist. Soc. Author: American Spiders and Their Spinning-work (3 vols., folio, 900 illustrations, 35 hand-colored plates); Tenants of an Old Farm; Old Farm Fairies (all scientific books); The Gospel in Nature; Object and Outline Teachings; Teachers' Commentary on the Life of Christ, Vols. I, II; Nature's Craftsmen, 1907; Ant Communities and How They Are Governed, 1909. Died 1911.

McCOOK, John James, clergyman; b. New Lisbon, O., Feb. 2, 1843; s. Dr. John and Catharine Julia (Sheldon) M.; student Jefferson Coll., 1858-60; studied law, 1860-61; A.B., Trinity Coll., 1863, A.M., 1866; Coll. Phys. and Surg. (Columbia), 1863-64; Berkeley Div. Sch., 1866, D.D., 1901, LL.D., 1910, Trinity Coll.; m. Eliza Sheldon Butler, June 7, 1866; children—John Butler, Eliza Lydia (wife of Rt. Rev. Logan H. Roots), Mary Catherine (dec.), Philip James, George Sheldon (dec.), Frances Agnes, Anson Theodore, Lucy Eleanor. Second lt. 1st Va. Inf. U.S.V., 1861. Deacon, 1866, priest, 1867, P.E. Ch.; rector St. John's Detroit, 1867-68, St. John's, East Hartford, Conn., 1866-67, and 1869—. Editor Church Weekly, 1872; prof. modern langs., Trinity Coll., 1883-1923, now prof. emeritus; sec. bd. fellows Trinity College from 1882, pres., 1915; mem. Hartford High School Com., 1901-13, chmn. 1913-15; pres. bd. dirs. Conn. Reformatory, 1895-97; twice apptd. by gov. on commns. for penol. legislation; com. coordination, State Council Defense, 1917. Trustee Trinity Coll. Writer reports on poor-law administration and prison reform. Home: Hartford, Conn. Died Jan. 9, 1927.

McCOOK, John James, lawyer; b. Carrollton, O., May 25, 1845; s. Daniel and Martha (Latimer) M.; youngest of Ohio family known as "the fighting McCooks"—consisting of father and his nine sons, who, with five cousins, were all officers in the Civil War; enlisted in 52d Ohio Inf.; commd. 1st lt. 6th Ohio Cav., and capt. and a.-d.-c. U.S. Vols., June 18, 1863-Oct. 13, 1864; served in campaigns of Perryville, Stone River Tullahoma, Chattanooga and Chickamauga with Western armies, and in Gen. Grant's campaign with Army of Potomac; severely wounded, Shady Grove, Va., May, 1864; mustered out, bvt. lt. col. vols.; A.B., Kenyon Coll., 1866, A.M., 1869; LL.B., Harvard, 1869; (hon. A.M., Princeton, 1873; LL.D., U. of Kan., 1890, Lafayette, 1893); m. Janetta Alexander, Feb. 17, 1876. Practiced at New York, 1871—; sr. mem. Alexander & Green (one of the oldest legal firms in U.S.). Was invited to place in President McKinley's 1st cabinet; chmn. Army and Navy Christian Commn. of the Y.M.C.A. during war with Spain, 1898. Trustee Kenyon Coll.; dir. Princeton Theol. Seminary. Home: New York, N.Y. Died 1911.

McCOOK, Willis Fisher, lawyer; b. Lisbon, O., Jan. 1851; A.B., Yale, 1873; studied law at Columbia Law Sch. Admitted to bar, 1875; atty. for Henry Clay Frick, 1878—; organized H. C. Frick Coke Co., 1882; atty. Pittsburgh Steel Co., Western Pa. Expn. Soc., U.S. Glass Co. and other corps. Dir. Pittsburgh Steel Co., Duquesne Nat. Bank. Trustee St. Joseph's Protectory for Boys, Mercy Hosp. Home: Swissvale, Pa. Died Aug. 5, 1923.

McCORD, George, Herbert, landscape and marine painter; b. New York, Aug. 1, 1848; s. George and Matilda McC.; ed. at Quackenbos Collegiate School and New York and Hudson River Inst., Claverack, N.Y.; in art was a pupil of Prof. Moses Morse, and studied in England, Scotland, Canada, Holland and France. Received silver medal and diploma, New

Orleans Expn.; bronze medal and diploma, Charitable Mechanic Assn., Mass.; Shaw prize Salmagundi Club, for black and white drawing, 1901; life mem. Lincoln Club, Brooklyn, for picture, "Haven Under the Hill"; bronze medal, St. Louis Expn., 1904. Has painted pictures which are in leading public and private collections; notably studies in Fla. and on the N.E. coast A.N.A. Studio: New York, N.Y. Died 1909.

McCORD, Myron Hawley, gov. Ariz.; b. Ceres, Pa., Nov. 26, 1844; s. Myron and Ann Eliza M.; ed. Richburgh (N.Y.) Acad.; removed to Wis., 1864; mem. Wis. legislature 1873-74, 1880-82; mem. Congress, 1889-91; removed to Phoenix, Ariz., 1893; mem. territorial Bd. of Control, Ariz., 1895-96; gov. Ariz., 1897-98; resigned to become col. of 1st Territorial Regt. U.S. Vol. Inf., Aug. 1, 1898 and continued in commond of regt. until it was mustered out, Feb. 15, 1899; U.S. marshal for Ariz., 1901-05, then collector of customs for dist. of Ariz. Republican. Home: Nogales, Ariz. Deceased.

McCORMACK, George Bryant, coal operator; b. Plattin, Mo., Apr. 4, 1859; s. Reed and Lucinda Catherine (Kindrick) M.; Carleton Inst., Farmington, Mo., 2 yrs.; m. Leonora Augustus Lichtenstadt, Aug. 21, 1881. Telegraph operator and station agt., 1876-80, clk. to asst. treas., 1880-88, supt. to gen. mgr., 1888-1901, Tenn. Coal, Iron & R.R. Co.; chmn. Ala. By-Products Corp.; mem. Goodall, Brown & Co. (dry goods), Ala. Grocery Co.; pres. Cedartown Iron Co.; v.p. Globe Coal Co. Mem. exec. com. Ala. Coal Operators' Assn. Democrat. Mason. Home: Birmingham, Ala. Died Nov. 1925.

McCORMACK, Joseph Nathaniel, physician; b. Nelson Co., Ky., Nov. 9, 1847; s. Thomas and Elizabeth (Brown) M.; ed. pub. schs.; M.D., Miami Med. Coll., 1870, and med. dept. U. of Louisville, 1873; served in Cincinnati Hosp., 1870-71; (LL.D., Central U., 1893); m. Corinne Crenshaw, Sept. 14, 1871. Practiced Nelson Co., Ky., 1871-75, then in Bowling Green. Mem. from 1879, sec. 1883-1913 and from 1914, state sanitary inspector for State Board of Health of Ky.; was mem. Internat. Quarantine Commn., 1892. Home: Louisville, Ky. Died May 1922.

McCORMACK, Thomas Joseph, editor; b. Brooklyn, May 28, 1865; s. Thomas and Eleanor (Burke) M.; A.B., Princeton, 1884, A.M., 1887; LL.B., Chicago Law School, 1890; admitted to bar but never practiced; studied history and philosophy at Leipzig and Tübingen, Germany; hon. M.S., Princeton, 1919; LL.D., Northwestern U., 1930; m. Nancy Montrose Hume, July 5, 1893 (died 1928); children—Joseph Hume, Thomas Hume, Jessie Hume, Ned Hume; m. 2d, Evelyn Keith, July 28, 1930. One of editors of the Open Court and Monist, Chicago. Prin. La Salle-Peru Tp. High Sch. and director La Salle-Peru-Oglesby Junior Coll. Editor: Series of Philosophical Classics; Mathematical Series; Memoirs of Gustave Koerner, 2 vols., 1909. Translator: Binet's Psychic Life of Micro-Organisms, 1889; Binet's Double Consciousness, 1890; Mach's Science of Mechanics, 1893; Mach's Popular Scientific Lectures, 1895; Weismann's Germinal Selection, 1896; Eimer's Orthogenesis, 1898; La Grange's Lectures on Elementary Mathematics, 1898; Schubert's Mathematical Essays and Recreations, 1893; Topinard's Science and Faith, 1899; Delitzsch's Babel and Bible, 1902; Cumont's Mysteries of Mithra, 1902; Mach's Space and Geometry, 1907. Home: Peru, Ill. Died 1932.

McCORMICK, Albert M(ontgomery) D(upuy), naval officer; b. Berryville, Va., Mar. 27, 1866; s. Edward and Ellen Lane Jett (Virginia) M.; prep. edn. Potomac Acad., Alexandria, Va.; M.D., U. of Md., 1888; m. Edith Lynde Abbot, Oct. 25, 1894; children—Lynde Dupuy, Mrs. Edith Beardall, Mrs. Cora Clark, Ellen Jett. Apptd. asst. surgeon, rank ensign, July 23, 1888; promoted through grades to rear adm. (temp.), July 1, 1918; perm. rank of rear adm., Jan. 1, 1921. Served on Panther and ashore at Guantanamo, Spanish-Am. War, 1898; fleet surgeon, Atlantic Fleet, 1910; duty at U.S. Naval Acad., 1910-19; insp. med. dept. activities, U.S.N., Pacific Coast, July 1, 1919; comdr. Med. Supply Depot, Mare Island; became pres. Bd. of Med. Examiners and pres. Naval Retiring Bd. and Naval Examining Bd., 1923; retired, Mar. 27, 1930. Awarded Sampson medal, Spanish campaign medal, Victory medal with silver star for meritorious conduct during World War; Order of the Busto del Libertado conferred by the Gov. of Venezuela. Fellow Am. Coll. Surgeons. Episcopalian. Home: Berryville, Va. Died Apr. 20, 1932.

McCORMICK, Alexander Agnew, journalist; b. Phila., Pa., Feb. 21, 1863; s. Alexander Agnew and Katherine (McQuiston) M.; ed. in pub. schs., Phila.; m. Maud Warner, June 1, 1895. A. C. McClurg & Co., Chicago, 1888-95; gen. mgr. Evening Post and Times-Herald, Chicago, 1895-1901, of Record-Herald, 1901-03; editor and publisher Chicago Evening Post, 1904-Jan. 1, 1906; editor and publisher The Indianapolis Star, the Terre Haute Star, The Muncie Star, Jan. 1, 1906-09; pres. Board of Commrs. Cook Co., Ill., 1912-14; alderman 6th Ward, Chicago, 1915-21. Pres. Civil Service Reform Assn.; trustee Ill. Coll., Jacksonville; sec. Sunset Club, 1892; v.p. Am. Newspaper Publishers' Assn., 1903-04 (chmn. labor com., 1900-07). Republican. Home: Chicago, Ill. Died Nov. 26, 1925.

McCORMICK, Alexander Hugh, rear admiral U.S.N.; b. in D.C., May 9, 1842; s. Alexander and Eliza (Van Horn) M.; apptd. to U.S. Naval Acad. from Tex., 1859; resigned May 22, 1861; reinstated June 3, 1861; m. Isabella Howard, Feb. 9, 1864. Promoted ensign, Dec. 22, 1862; lt., Feb. 22, 1864; lt. comdr., July 25, 1866; comdr., Sept. 30, 1876; capt., Apr. 3, 1892; rear admiral, Sept. 9, 1899. Served on Quaker City, 1861; Norwich, S. Atlantic Blockading Squadron, 1862-63; participated in bombardment of Ft. Pulaski and fort on Winyaw Bay, S.C., 1862; served on Iroquois, spl. service, 1864-65; Chattanooga, 1866; Naval Acad., 1866-69; Lancaster, 1869-72; Naval Acad., 1872-75; exec. officer Pensacola, 1875-76; spl. ordnance duty, 1877-81; comd. Essex, 1881-85; Navy Yard, Washington, 1885-88; Bur. of Ordnance, 1888-89; insp. of ordnance, New York, 1889-92; comd. Lancaster, 1892-94; Navy Yard, Norfolk, 1894-97; mem. armor and personnel bds., 1897-98; comd. Oregon, 1898; comdt., Navy Yard, Washington, 1898-1900; retired, Mar. 26, 1900. Home: Annapolis, Md. Died Aug. 21, 1915.

McCORMICK, Andrew Phelps, judge; b. Brazoria Co., Tex., Dec. 18, 1832; s. Joseph Manson and Louisa Agnes (McKenzie) M.; A.B., Centre Coll., Ky., 1854; m. Mary Copes, Sept. 8, 1859 (died 1870); m. 2d, Lula Bell, Mar. 1, 1871. Admitted to bar, 1855, and practiced at Brazoria, Tex.; judge of probate, 1865-66; mem. Tex. Constl. Conv., 1866, 68; judge Dist. Ct. of Tex., 1871-76; mem. Tex. Senate, 1876-79; apptd. U.S. dist. atty., Eastern Dist. of Tex., Jan., 1879, but did not qualify; U.S. dist. judge, Northern Dist. of Texas, 1879-92; U.S. circuit judge, 5th Circuit, Mar. 17, 1892—. Republican. Home: Waco, Tex. Died Nov. 2, 1916.

McCORMICK, Charles Wesley, clergyman; b. New Prospect, N.J., Dec. 14, 1856; s. William Henry and Josephine Lafayette (Force) M.; A.B., Wesleyan U., Conn., 1881, A.M., 1884; A.M., New York U., 1894, Ph.D., 1898; (D.D., Syracuse U., 1897, Wesleyan, 1910); m. Edith C. Mirteenes, Oct. 5, 1881. Ordained M.E. ministry, 1880; pastor Mount Hope, N.J., 1881, Stapleton, N.Y., 1882, Ogdensburg, N.Y., 1883-85, Lowville, N.Y., 1886-87, Watertown, N.Y., 1888-92, Boonton, N.J., 1893-94, Newark, N.J., 1895-97, Hackettstown, N.J., 1898-99; pres. Centenary Collegiate Inst., Hackettstown, N.J., 1900-01; pastor 1st Ch., Hartford, Conn., 1902-08, Nostrand Av. Ch., Brooklyn, 1908-12, Grace Ch., Brooklyn, 1912-16; supt. New York Dist. N.Y. East Conf., 1916—. Author: The Heart of Prayer. Home: Stamford, Conn. Died Oct. 19, 1920.

McCORMICK, Cyrus Hall, mfr.; b. Washington, D.C., May 16, 1859; s. Cyrus Hall (inventor of reaping machine) and Nettie (Fowler) M.; Princeton, class of 1879, hon. A.M., 1887; LL.D., Lafayette Coll., 1915; m. Harriet Bradley Hammond, March 5, 1889 (died 1921); children—Cyrus, Elizabeth (dec.), Gordon; m. 2d, Alice M. Hoit, April 22, 1927. With McCormick Harvesting Machine Co., 1879—; was president same from time of father's death, 1884, until 1902; pres. Internat. Harvester Co., 1902-19, chmn. bd., 1919-35, now director and mem. exec. committee. Member special diplomatic mission of U.S. to Russia, 1917. Trustee War Fund, Y.M.C.A. (U.S.); trustee Princeton University, Field Mus. Natural History, Elizabeth McCormick Memorial Fund; dir. Presbyn. Theol. Seminary. Died June 2, 1936.

McCORMICK, Edith Rockefeller; b. Cleveland, O., Aug. 31, 1872; d. John Davison and Laura Celestia (Spelman) Rockefeller; educated under private tutelage; m. Harold Fowler McCormick, Nov. 26, 1895 (divorced 1921); children—Fowler, Muriel (Mrs. Elisha D. Hubbard), Mathilde (Mrs. Max Oser). Resided abroad 15 yrs.; one of two founders of John McCormick Institution of Infectious Diseases; original promoter of civic opera in Chicago; founder Chicago Zoölogical Gardens; patroness of opera in English for American audiences. Member League of Women Voters, Ohio Society, D.A.R., Friends of Opera, Drama League. Home: Chicago, Ill. Died Aug. 25, 1932.

McCORMICK, Edmund Burke, college dean; b. Normal, Ill., Nov. 24, 1870; s. Henry and Numantia B. (Kinyon) M.; grad. Ill. State Normal U., 1889; S.B. in mech. engring., Mass. Inst. Tech., 1897; m. Jeanette Maxey, Dec. 26, 1899. Machinist with C.&A. R.R., 1889-93; instr. mech. engring., 1898-99, asst. prof., 1899-1901, Mont. State Coll.; prof. mech. engring., 1901-10, dean div. of engring., 1908-13, dir. Engring. Expt. Sta., 1910-13, Kan. State Agrl. Coll.; consulting engr., 1907-13, mech. engr., 1913-15, chief div. rural engring., 1915-20, chief equipment div., July 1, 1920—, Bur. of Public Roads, U.S. Dept. Agriculture. Consulting editor Agricultural Engineering Series, McGraw-Hill Book Co. Republican. Mason. Home: Alameda, Calif. Died Jan. 15, 1926.

McCORMICK, Ernest O., ry. official; b. Lafayette, Ind.; grad. high sch., Lafayette. Began in operating dept. L.E.&W. R.R., 1879; freight dept. Louisville, New Albany & Chicago R.R. (Monon Route), at Lafayette; gen. agt. Great Eastern Freight Line, at Louisville, Ky.; city ticket and pass. agt. at Louisville and Chicago, gen. Northwestern pass. agt. at Chicago, and gen. pass. and ticket agt. at Chicago, to 1889, Monon Route; gen. pass. and ticket agt. C.,H.&D. Ry., 1889-93; pass. traffic mgr., C.,C.,C.&St.L. Ry., 1893-99; pass. traffic mgr. S.P. Co., at San Francisco, 1899-1904; asst. traffic dir. U.P. and S.P. systems, Ore. Short Line Ry., and Ore. R.R. & Navigation Co., at Chicago, 1904-10; v.p. S.P. Co., Mar. 10, 1910—. Home: San Francisco, Calif. Died Nov. 1, 1923.

McCORMICK, Harold Fowler, mfr., capitalist; b. Chicago, Ill., May 2, 1872; s. Cyrus Hall (inventor of the reaper) and Nettie (Fowler) M.; A.B., Princeton, 1895; m. Edith, d. John D. Rockefeller, Nov. 26, 1895; children—John Rockefeller (died 1901), Harold Fowler, Muriel (Mrs. Elisha Dyer Hubbard), Editha (died 1904), Mathilde (Mrs. Max Oser); m. 2d, Mme. Ganna Walska, Aug. 11, 1922; m. 3d, Adah Wilson, May 31, 1938. V.p., 1902-19, treas., 1906-16, pres., 1918-22, chmn. exec. com., 1922, chmn. finance com., 1932-35, chmn. bd., 1935—, Internat. Harvester Co.; dir. First Nat. Bank. Dir. Chicago Orchestral Assn.; hon. chmn. Chicago Grand Opera Co., 1934—. Home: Chicago, Ill. Died Oct. 16, 1941.

McCORMICK, Harriet Hammond; b. Monmouth, Eng.; d. Capt. George W. and Emma (Young) Hammond; ed. Chicago and in Europe; m. Cyrus Hall McCormick, Mar. 5, 1889. Promoter and financial backer of Child Welfare Exhibit, Chicago, 1911; actively interested in promotion of civic and social welfare. Episcopalian. Home: Chicago, Ill. Died Jan. 17, 1921.

McCORMICK, Henry Buehler, trustee; b. Harrisburg, Pa., June 12, 1869; s. late Col. Henry and Annie (Criswell) McC.; B.A., Yale U., 1892; m. Mary Boyd, June 13, 1895. Admitted to Pa. bar, 1895; pres. Lawrence Iron Co.; sec. and treas. Patriot and Evening News; dir. Dauphin Deposit Trust Co., Harrisburg Bridge Co.; trustee Estate of Henry McCormick. Elder Pine St. Presbyn. Ch. Home: Harrisburg, Pa. Died Dec. 27, 1941.

McCORMICK, John Newton, bishop; b. Richmond, Va., Feb. 1, 1863; s. John and Virginia (Newton) M.; A.B., Randolph-Macon Coll., 1883, grad. in theology, 1883; post-grad. Johns Hopkins, 1886-88; D.D., U. of the South, 1903; m. Bessie Chapman Tucker, Oct. 9, 1889; children—James Donald, John Brian (dec.), Augustine, Virginia, Douglas. Ordained M.E. Ch., S., ministry, 1884; pastor Frederick, Md., 1884-85, Arlington, Md., 1885-87, Trinity Ch., Baltimore, 1888-89, Winchester, Va., 1890-91; became deacon, 1893, priest, 1894, P.E. Ch.; rector St. Paul's, Suffolk, Va., 1893-95, St. Luke's, Atlanta, Ga., 1895-98, St. Mark's, Grand Rapids, Mich., 1898-1906; consecrated bishop coadjutor, diocese of Western Mich., Feb. 14, 1906; became bishop of the diocese, Mar. 19, 1909, on death of Bishop Gillespie; bishop in charge Am. chs. in Europe. Represented War Commn. of P.E. Church in France, 1917-19, and maj. in Am. Red Cross, in charge of Red Cross Chaplain's Bur.; maj., chaplain, lt. col. O.R.C., U.S.A. Chmn. Mich. State Welfare Commn. Deputy to gen. convs., 1901, 04. Author: Distinctive Marks of the Episcopal Church, 1902; The Litany and the Life, 1904; Pain and Sympathy, 1907; Good News From a Far Country, 1910; A Small Part, 1933. Home: Grand Rapids, Mich. Died Nov. 26, 1939.

McCORMICK, Leander Hamilton, author; b. Chicago, Ill., May 27, 1859; s. Leander J. and Henrietta (Hamilton) McC.; B.S., Amherst, 1881; student law dept. Columbia, 1881-83, also studied architecture; m. Constance, d. Edward Plummer, of Canterbury, Eng., Feb. 15, 1887. Lived in London 17 yrs.; traveler, inventor, sculptor, art collector; author of over 100 inventions, including aeroplanes, aerial torpedo, motorcycles, a watch which records time the world over, etc.; art collection embraces early English and old Dutch schs. Presbyterian. Author: Characterology, 1920; Students Course in Characterology, 1921. Home: Chicago, Ill. Died Feb. 2, 1934.

McCORMICK, Leander J., inventor-capitalist; b. Walnut Grove, Va., Feb. 8, 1819; m. Henrietta Maria Hamilton, 1845. Became connected with the pioneer reaper mfg. industry with his father (Robert McCormick, inventor of the reaper) and his brother (Cyrus Hall McCormick) and in 1847 went to Cincinnati and engaged with his brother in the manufacture of 100 machines; moved with family to Chicago, 1848; became partner with his brother as mfrs. of reapers, 1849. Had active supervision of mfg. dept. until business was incorporated as McCormick Harvesting Machine Co., 1879, and in 1889 he retired from active business; made many valuable inventions of improvements in reapers; has large real estate and other interests in Chicago. Presented to Univ. of Va., 1871, a large 24-inch refracting telescope and the observatory now known as the McCormick Observatory. Home: Chicago, Ill. Died 1900.

McCORMICK, Marshall, lawyer; b. Clarke Co., Va., June 29, 1849; s. Province and Margaretta Holmes (Moss) M.; student U. of Va., 1867-69; Va. Mil. Inst., 1869-70; m. Rosalie A. Taylor, June 12, 1872. Admitted to Va. bar, 1871, and practiced in Berryville and Roanoke; counsel for Norfolk &

Western Ry.; pros. atty., Clarke Co., 1879-88; mem. Va. Senate, 1883-87; author Anderson-McCormick election law. Democrat. Episcopalian. Home: Berryville, Va. Died May 15, 1918.

McCORMICK, (Joseph) Medill, U.S. senator; b. Chicago, May 16, 1877; s. of Robert Sanderson and Katharine Van Etta (Medill) M.; brother of Robert Rutherford M.; A.B., Yale U., 1900; LL.D. from Monmouth (Ill.) College, 1923; m. Ruth, d. late Senator M. A. Hanna, of Cleveland, June 10, 1903. Was publisher Chicago Daily Tribune. V. chmn. Prog. Nat. Com., 1912-14; twice elected to Ill. Gen. Assembly; mem. 65th Congress (1917-19), Ill. at-large; U.S. Senator from Ill., term 1919-25. Feb. 25, 1925.

McCORMICK, Paul, stockman; b. Rexville, Steuben Co., N.Y., June 14, 1845; s. James and Margaret M.; ed. Alfred (N.Y.) U., 1864-66; m. Mary Spear, Mont., Feb. 23, 1879. A pioneer of Mont., 1866; organizer and leader of expdn. into the lower Yellowstone country (then occupied by hostile Indians), known as the Ft. Pease Expdn., 1875; pres. McCormick Mercantile Co., Junction City, Mont., 1882-92; pres. Custer Cattle Co., 1892—. McCormick Cattle Co., 1910—; pres. Donovan-McCormick Co., gen. mdse., Billings, 1898-1908; pres. Billings State Bank, 1900-06; mgr. Buffalo Ranch. Mem. Mont. Territorial Legislature, 1879; served both as Roosevelt and Taft elector from Mont. Catholic. Home: Billings, Mont. Died Jan. 26, 1921.

McCORMICK, Richard Cunnigham, journalist; b. New York, May 23, 1832; classical edn.; became broker in New York, 1850; war corr. in Crimea, 1854-55; edited Young Men's Magazine, 1858-59; in editorial dept. Evening Post, 1860; war corr. of New York papers, 1861-62; chief clerk U.S. Dept. Agr., 1862-63; sec. Arizona Ty., 1863-66; gov. Ariz., 1866-69; del. in Congress from Ariz., 1869-75; mem. Congress from 1st New York dist., 1895-97; m. dau. Hon. A. A. Thurman, of Ohio, 1873. Established The Arizona Miner, Prescott, 1864, and The Arizona Citizen, Tucson, 1870; commr. to Centennial Exbn., 1876; Asst. sec. Treasury, U.S., 1877-78; commr. gen. to Paris Expn., 1878; comdr. Legion of Honor of France, 1878. Edited: Reports U.S. Commrs. to Paris Expn. (6 vols.). Home: Jamaica, L.I., N.Y. Died 1901.

McCORMICK, R(obert) Hall, capitalist; b. Rockbridge Co., Va., Sept. 6, 1847; s. Leander J. and Henrietta M. (Hamilton) M.; g.s. Robert M., inventor, McCormick reaper; went to Chicago, 1848; ed. old Chicago U.; m. Sarah Lord Day, June 1, 1871. During 1875-76, experimented personally with the self-binder in the field from Texas to Minn., and was in charge of the field trials exhibit of the McCormick Binder at Centennial Expn., Phila., 1876, which was the introduction of the self-binder to public as the greatest labor-saving device of the age; made improvements on reaper and binder which were patented; trustee Leander J. McCormick estate. Has made a spl. study of British sch. of art; has examples of many of leading artists of that sch. in his collection; published an illustrated catalogue of the collection, which is in prin. art galleries of U.S. and Europe; interested in yachting and automobiling and was one of the first to introduce coaching in the West. Trustee Art Inst.; hon. life mem. Copley Soc. (Boston). Chmn. Rivers and Lakes Commn., 1911—. Home: Chicago, Ill. Died Mar. 14, 1917.

McCORMICK, Robert Laird, lumberman, banker; b. Clinton Co., Pa., Oct. 29, 1847; s. Alexander and Jane Hayes (Laird) M.; ed. high sch., Lock Haven, Pa., and Saunders Inst., Phila.; m. Anna E. Goodman, Sept. 11, 1870. In lumber business, Minn. and Wis., 1874-1902, and during this period became interested in grain, timber and iron properties; moved to Tacoma, Wash., July, 1903, as sec. Weyerhaeuser Timber Co., capital $12,500,000; also pres. Pacific Nat. Bank, Tacoma. Mem. Minn. Senate, 1880-82; Wash. mem. Rep. Nat. Com., 1908-12. Home: Tacoma, Wash. Died 1911.

McCORMICK, Robert Sanderson, diplomat; b. Rockbridge Co., Va., July 26, 1849; s. William Sanderson (mem. reaper firm) and Mary Ann (Grigsby) M.; ed. prep. dept. U. of Chicago, and U. of Va.; m. Katherine Van Etta Medill, June 8, 1876; father of (Joseph) Medill and Robert Rutherford M. Secretary of Am. Legation at London, 1889-92; official representative World's Columbian Expn. in London, 1892-93; E.E. and M.P., Mar. 1901 to July 1902, first ambassador, July to Dec. 1902, to Austria-Hungary; Am. ambassador to Russia, 1902-05, to France, May 1, 1905-Mar. 2, 1907. Decorated with Order of the First Class of the Rising Sun, Japan, 1907. Home: Chicago, Ill. Died Apr. 16, 1919.

McCORMICK, Samuel Black, educator; b. Westmoreland Co., Pa., May 6, 1858; s. Dr. James Irwin and Rachel L. (Black) M.; A.B., Washington and Jefferson Coll., 1880, A.M., 1883, D.D., 1897, LL.D., 1902, same; also LL.D., William and Mary Coll., 1913, Allegheny Coll., 1915, U. of Pa., 1916, U. of Pittsburgh, 1921; m. Ida May Steep, Sept. 29, 1882; children—James Irwin, Mrs. Gertrude Smith, Samuel Black, Rachel. Taught in Canonsburg Acad., 1880; prof. Washington and Jefferson Coll., 1881-82; admitted to bar, 1882; practiced at Pittsburgh, 1882-83, Denver, Colo., 1883-87; student Western Theol. Sem., Pa., 1887-90; ordained Presbyn. ministry, 1890; pastor Central Ch., Allegheny, 1890-94, First Ch., Omaha, Neb., 1894-97; pres. Coe Coll., Ia., 1897-1904; chancellor U. of Pittsburgh (formerly Western Univ. of Pa.), 1904-21, now chancellor emeritus. Dir. Western Theol. Sem. Mem. revision com., Presbyn. Ch., 1901-02. Died April 18, 1928.

McCORMICK, William, editor, social worker; b. Harrisburg, Pa., Apr. 24, 1866; s. James and Mary Wilson (Alricks) M.; A.B., Yale, 1887; unmarried. Reporter, Boston Post, Phila. Record, Bethlehem (Pa.) Times; taught sch. 1 yr. at Burnham Industrial Farm, Canaan, N.Y.; founder and editor Allentown (Pa.) Leader; editor and owner Reading Herald, 1895-1920; pub. News-Times and Herald-Telegram, 1920—. Founded Olivet Boys' Club, 1898, erected bldg. for it, 1910; prin. mover in establishing Olivet Playgrounds and Gardens (14 acres), 1905. Presbyn. Author: The Boy and His Clubs, 1912; Fishers of Boys, 1915. Editor and pub. Work With Boys, bi-monthly mag., to June 1920. Home: Reading, Pa. Died Feb. 1923.

McCORMICK, Willoughby M., importer, mfr.; b. Dover, Va., July 12, 1864; s. Robert Burns and Katherine (Raynolds) McC.; ed. pvt. acad.; m. Estelle Bancroft Tyler, 1895 (died 1903); m. 2d, Helen Cobb, July 7, 1906. President McCormick & Company, importers of spices, teas and drug specialties, 1889—; an organizer, and pres. 6 yrs. Baltimore Commercial Bank; dir. Baltimore Steam Packet Co., Md. Casualty Co., First Nat. Bank, Cinder Block Corp., Industrial Corp., etc. Mem. Chamber Commerce U.S.A. (dir. 1912-16). Organizer, 1916, and pres. Bapt. Home of Md.; organizer and pres. Bapt. Childrens Aid Soc., The Virginians of Md. Democrat. Mason. Home: Baltimore, Md. Died Nov. 4, 1932.

McCORNACK, (Robert) John Knox, banker; b. Eugene, Ore., Apr. 4, 1863; s. Andrew and Maria (Eakin) McC.; student U. of Ore., 1882, Heald's Business Coll., San Francisco, Calif., 1884; m. Mary F. DeHuff, Jan. 25, 1888. Engaged in land office work and surveying, 1882-86; banking business, The Dalles, 1886-89, Palouse City, 1889-1910; pres. First Nat. Bank, Wenatchee, Wash. Pres. Camp Fire Council, Spokane. Republican. Presbyn. Odd Fellow, K.P. Home: Spokane, Wash. Died Mar. 1937.

McCORT, John J., bishop; b. Phila., Pa., Feb. 16, 1860; s. James and Sarah C. (McCrystal) McC.; ed. La Salle Coll. (Phila.), St. Charles Sem., (Overbrook, Pa.). Ordained priest R.C. Ch., 1883; prof. mathematics, St. Charles Sem., and subsequently of ecclesiastical history and liturgy, 1883-99; apptd. permanent rector Our Mother of Sorrows Ch., Phila., 1899; diocesan atty., 1905; vicar gen., 1910; consecrated titular bishop of Azotus and auxiliary bishop of Phila., Sept. 17, 1912; apptd. coadjutor bishop of Altoona (Pa.), Jan. 26, 1920, bishop of Altoona, Oct. 22, 1920. Died Apr. 21, 1936.

McCORVEY, Thomas Chalmers, univ. prof.; b. Monroe Co., Ala., Aug. 18, 1851; s. Murdock and Lydia (Ranaldson) M.; A.B., U. of Ala., 1873, LL.B., 1875, A.M., 1878, LL.D., 1906; m. Netta L., d. late Dr. Henry Tutwiler, of Ala., July 22, 1880; children—Jean Campbell, Gessner Tutwiler, Eleanor Packer (Mrs. George Doherty Johnston), Thomas Chalmers (dec.). Teacher in U. of Ala. from graduation, prof. history and polit. science, 1888-1923; granted retiring allowance by Carnegie Foundation, 1923. Mem. bd. of visitors, U.S. Mil. Acad., 1886; mem. Ala. Centennial Commn., 1919. Author: The Government of the People of the State of Alabama, 1895; Alabama's Brood, and Other Historical Poems. Home: Tuscaloosa, Ala. Died Apr. 2, 1932.

McCOSH, Andrew J., surgeon; b. Belfast, Ireland, 1858; s. James and Isabella (Guthrie) M.; A.B., Princeton, 1877, A.M.; M.D., Coll. of Phys. and Surg., New York, 1880; post-grad. study, Univ. of Vienna, 1882; (LL.D., Columbia, 1905, Princeton, 1906). Practiced at New York, 1883—; surgeon to Presbyterian Hosp., 1889—; prof. clin. surgery, Columbia Univ. Fellow Am. Surg. Assn., etc. Died 1908.

McCOY, Daniel, banker; b. Phila., July 17, 1845; s. John and Mary Ann M.; ed. pub. schs., Phila.; m. Gail Lyon Ayer, Oct. 19, 1869. In grain and produce and lumber business, 1866-92; since then banking. Pres. State Bank of Mich., Imperial Furniture Co., The Baxter Co.; dir. Herkner Jewelry Co. Republican; formerly pres. village of Clam Lake, Mich., and mayor Cadillac, Mich.; State treas., Mich., 1900-04. Episcopalian. Author: Old Fort St. Joseph, 1907. Home: Grand Rapids, Mich. Died 1908.

McCOY, Henry Bayard, mining man; b. Carlinville, Ill., Aug. 5, 1866; s. Asa Shinn and Lydia (Chamberlin) M.; student Ill. Wesleyan U., 1885-87; m. May Ludlow Dorland. Served in P.I. throughout Spanish-Am. War; lt. col. 1st Colo. Vols., May 1-Aug. 13, U.S. Vols., Sept. 1899-July 1, 1901. Dep. collector of customs, P.I., 1901-09; collector of customs, 1909-1898; col., Aug. 13, 1898-Sept. 12, 1899; maj. 44th 13; mem. Rep. Nat. Com., 1904—. An organizer of mining in P.I.; pres. and gen. mgr. Colorado Mining Co. Methodist. Home: Manila, P.I. Died Oct. 1, 1923.

McCOY, James Henry, bishop; b. Blount Co., Ala., Aug. 6, 1868; s. William Clarke (D.D.) and Annie (Vaughan) M.; B.A., Southern U., Greensboro, Ala., 1888, M.A., 1889 (D.D., 1906); m. Annie Bradley, Dec. 31, 1895. Entered N. Ala. Conf. M.E. Ch., S., 1889; pastor, Ensley Circuit, 1889-90, New Decatur, 1890-91, Dadeville and Alexander City, 1891-93, Birmingham, 1893-94, Tuscaloosa, 1894-96, Huntsville, 1896-1900; editor Ala. Christian Advocate, 1900-01; pastor, Birmingham, 1902-06; pres. Birmingham Coll., 1906-10; elected bishop, May 17, 1910. Pres. Epworth League of M.E. Ch., S., 1910—; mem. Ednl. Commn. of M.E. Ch., S.; v.p. trustees Emory U., Atlanta, Ga.; trustee Meth. Training Sch., Nashville. Democrat. Died Mar. 22, 1919.

McCOY, Walter Irving, judge; b. Troy, N.Y., Dec. 8, 1859; s. James and Cornelia (Beach) M.; Princeton U., 1877-79; A.B., Harvard, 1882, LL.B. and A.M., 1886; m. Kate Philbrick Baldwin, Oct. 17, 1888; children—Percy B., George Baldwin (dec.), Philbrick, Catherine B., Eleanor Holman. In law practice at New York, 1886-1914; trustee Village of S. Orange, N.J., 1893-95, 1901-05, 1910; v.p. Essex Co. (N.J.) Dem. Com.; mem. 62d Congress (1911-13), 8th N.J. Dist., and 63d Congress (1913-15), 9th Dist.; chief justice Supreme Court of D.C. until 1929. Retired. Home: Washington, D.C. Died July 17, 1933.

McCRACKAN, William Denison, author; b. Munich, Germany (of Am. parents), Feb. 12, 1864; grad. Trinity Coll., Conn., 1885, A.M.; m. 1887. Mem. Christian Science Publication Com., 1901-04. Author: The Rise of the Swiss Republic, 1892; Romance and Teutonic Switzerland, 1894; Swiss Solutions of American Problems; Little Idyls of the Big World, 1895; The Huntington Letters, 1897; Fair Land Tyrol, 1905; The Italian Lakes, 1907; Christian Science, Its Discovery and Development, 1912. Asso. editor The Christian Science Journal and Christian Science Sentinel, 1916-19; editor Jerusalem News, 1920. Died June 12, 1923.

McCRACKIN, Josephine Clifford, author; b. Petershagen Castle, Prussia, Nov. 25, 1838; d. George Ernst and Charlotte, Baroness Ende (von Wolfsprung) Woempner; came to America with parents, 1846; ed. Sacred Heart Externat and pvt. sch., St. Louis; m. Lt. J. A. Clifford (U.S.A.), Jan. 1864 (died 1867); m. 2d, Jackson McCrackin, of S.C. (speaker Ho. of Rep., 1st Legislature of Ariz.), 1882 (died 1904). Began as writer in Overland Monthly, 1869, later on Californian and wrote for Western Monthly, Lakeside Monthly, Harper's Magazine, etc. Lived on ranch, 25 yrs.; connected with Santa Cruz Sentinel, 1905—. Correspondent of San Jose Mercury-Herald. Began movement in behalf of conserving the redwoods, 1900; founder Ladies' Forest and Song Bird Protective Assn., 1901; 1st woman mem. and 4th v.p. Calif. Game and Fish Protective Assn.; sec. Santa Cruz Humane Soc.; v.p.-at-large Sempervirens Club of Calif. Catholic. Author: Overland Tales, 1877; Another Juanita, 1893; The Woman Who Lost Him and Tales of the Army Frontier (collection), 1913. Home: Santa Cruz, Calif. Deceased.

McCRADY, Edward, lawyer, author; b. Charleston, S.C., Apr. 8, 1833; s. Edward McC., lawyer and theologian; grad. Charleston Coll.; admitted to S.C. bar, May 1855; m. Mary F. Davie, Feb. 24, 1863. Took part as capt. vol. co., State service, in the taking of Castle Pinckney, Charleston harbor, Dec. 27, 1860; was present at battle of Ft. Sumter, Apr. 12-13; entered C.S.A. as capt. of 1st co. raised in S.C. for the whole war, June 27, 1861; maj. and lt. col. 1st S.C. vols.; severely wounded at Manassas, Aug. 30, 1862; seriously injured in camp by falling tree Jan. 27, 1863; disabled for field service and transferred to command of camp of instruction, Madison, Fla., Mar. 1864; surrendered May 5, 1865, subsequently maj. gen. State volunteer troops; mem. Ho. of Reps., State legislature, 1880-90; pres. Hist. Soc. of S.C., trustee Charleston Library Soc., trustee Med. Coll. of S.C. Author of Election and Registration Laws of S.C., known as the eight box law; chmn. vestry of St. Philip's Ch., Charleston. Democrat. Author: The History of South Carolina under the Proprietary Government, 1670-1719, 1897; The History of South Carolina Under the Royal Government, 1719-1776, 1899; The History of South Carolina in the Revolution, 1775-1780, 1901; The History of South Carolina in the Revolution 1780-83, 1902. Home: Charleston, S.C. Died 1903.

McCRAE, Thomas, physician; b. at Guelph, Ont., Can., Dec. 16, 1870; s. David and Janet (Eckford) M.; A.B., U. of Toronto, 1891, M.B., 1895, M.D., 1903; studied U. of Göttingen, 1899; D.Sc. from U. of Toronto, 1927; m. Amy Gwyn, of Dundas, Ont., Sept. 16, 1908. Fellow biology, U. of Toronto, 1892-94; asso. in medicine, Johns Hopkins Hosp., 1904-12; asso. prof. medicine, Johns Hopkins U., 1906-12; prof. medicine, Jefferson Med. Coll., Phila., 1912—; phys. to Jefferson and Pa. Hosps., 1912—. Fellow Royal Coll. Physicians (London), also Lumleian lecturer, same, 1924. Author: Cancer of the Stomach (with Sir William Osler), 1900. Editor: Osler's System of Medicine (3d edit.); Osler's Practice of Medicine (11th edit.), 1930. Home: Philadelphia, Pa. Died June 30, 1935.

McCRAY, Warren T., governor; b. Newton Co., Ind., Feb. 4, 1865; s. Greenberry Ward and Martha Jane (Galey) M.; ed. pub. schs.; m. Ella M. Ade, d. John and Adaline Bush Ade and sister of George Ade, of Kentland, Ind., June 15, 1892. Farmer and extensive grain shipper; owner Orchard Lake Stock Farm, Kentland, noted for its Hereford cattle; pres. Discount & Deposit State Bank, Kentland, founded by father, 1874; gov. of Ind., term 1921-25. Republican. Presbyn. Mason. Home: Kentland, Ind. Died Dec. 19, 1938.

McCREA, Annette E., landscape architect; b. New York; widow. First woman landscape architect in America, began at Kalamazoo, Mich., 1892; at various times consulting landscape architect for C.&N.W. Ry., C., M.&St.P. Ry., C.,B.&Q. Ry., Illinois Central Ry., S.P. Ry., etc. Episcopalian. Home: Chicago, Ill. Died Sept. 20, 1928.

McCREA, James, ry. pres.; b. Phila., May 1, 1848; s. James Alexander and Ann B. (Foster) M.; ed. Pa. Poly. Coll. Entered ry. service, June 1865, as rodman and asst. engr. Connellsville & Southern Pa. R.R. until 1867; rodman on constrn., Wilmington & Reading R.R., 1867-68; asst. engr. Allegheny Valley R.R., 1868-71; with Pa. R.R., 1871-82, consecutively as asst. engr. and div. supt.; mgr., gen. mgr. and 4th v.p. Pa. Lines west of Pittsburgh, 1882-90; 2d v.p., 1890-91; 1st v.p., 1891-1907; dir. June 9, 1899—, and pres. Pa. R.R. Co., Jan. 2, 1907—; also pres. Pa. Co., P.,C.,C.&S.L. Ry. Co., Phila., Baltimore & Washington R.R. Co., Northern Central Ry. Co., West Jersey & Seashore R.R. Co., Cumberland Valley Ry. Co. Home: Ardmore, Pa. Died Mar. 28, 1913.

McCREA, James Alexander, ry. official; b. Phila., Pa., May 26, 1875; s. James and Ada (Montgomery) McC.; father was pres. Pa. R.R.; Ph.B., Sheffield Scientific Sch. (Yale), 1895; m. Mabel Clarke, Dec. 15, 1897. Began as rodman Pa. Lines West of Pittsburgh, Nov. 5, 1895; on engr. corps, Phila. div., Pa. R.R., at Phila., 1897-98; asst. engr. maintenance of way, Eastern div., Pa. Lines West of Pittsburgh, 1898-99; engr. maintenance of way, same div., 1899-1901; supt. Cincinnati div., Pa. Lines, at Cincinnati, 1901-06, also supt. Cincinnati, Lebanon & Northern Ry.; gen. supt., 1906-11, gen. mgr., 1911-17, Long Island R.R.; apptd. gen. mgr. Railroad Transportation Corps in France, title of col., Oct. 29, 1917; v.p. Pa. System, in charge central region. Home: Woodmere, L.I., N.Y. Died Oct. 17, 1923.

McCREA, Tully, brig. gen.; b. Natchez, Miss., July 23, 1839; s. John and Mary McC.; apptd. from Ohio, and grad. U.S. Mil. Acad., 1862; m. Harriet Hale Camp, May 20, 1868. Second lt. 1st Arty., June 17, 1862; promoted through grades to col. 6th Arty., July 15, 1900; brig. gen. U.S.A., Feb. 21, 1903. Served in Civil War in Army of Potomac, taking part in battles of Antietam, Fredericksburg, Chancellorsville, Gettysburg, etc.; later in dept. of South; wounded severely at battle of Olustee, Feb. 20, 1864. Bvtd.: first lt., Sept. 17, 1862, for Antietam; capt., July 3, 1863, for Gettysburg; maj., Feb. 20, 1864, for Olustee. Retired at own request after 40 yrs.' service, Feb. 22, 1903. Died Sept. 5, 1918.

McCREARY, George Deardorff, congressman; b. York Springs Village, Pa., Sept. 28, 1846; s. John B. and Rachel F. (Deardorff) M.; ed. U. of Pa. to jr. yr.; m. Kate R. Howell, June 18, 1878. Held position in Honey Brook Coal Co., Phila., of which his father was pres., 1867-70; mem. firm of Whitney, McCreary & Kemmer, 1870-79, retiring, 1879, to take charge of his father's estate. Became interested in municipal affairs in Phila., 1882; an original mem. Com. of 100; treas. city and co. of Phila., 1892-95; inaugurated the present financial system of the city; mem. 58th to 62d Congresses (1903-13), 6th Pa. Dist. Republican. Officer in and dir. of several financial, mining and business cos.; also in ch. and philanthropic instns. Died July 26, 1915.

McCREARY, James Bennett, governor; b. Madison Co., Ky., July 8, 1838; s. E. R. and S. B. M.; A.B., Centre Coll., Ky., 1857 (LL.D., 1879); LL.B., Cumberland U., Tenn., 1859; maj. and lt. col. of cav., C.S.A., under Gens. Morgan and Breckenridge, 1862-65; m. Kate Hughes, 1867 (died 1908). Admitted to bar, 1859, and entered practice at Richmond, Ky. Mem. Ky. Ho. of Rep., 1869, 71, 73 (speaker, 1871-73); gov. of Ky., 1875-79; mem. 49th to 54th Congresses (1885-97); U.S. senator, 1903-09; again gov. of Ky., term 1911-15. Del. Dem. Nat. convs., 1868, 1900, 04, 08, 12; del. Internat. Monetary Conf., Brussels, 1891-92; mem. Pan-Am. Com. of U.S. Home: Richmond, Ky. Died Oct. 8, 1918.

McCREERY, Fenton Reuben, diplomat; b. Flint, Mich., Apr. 21, 1866; s. Col. William Barker and Ada Birdsall (Fenton) M.; ed. Mich. Mil. Acad. and U. of Mich., class of 1888; unmarried. Clerk in U.S. Consulate, Valparaiso, Chile, 1890-91; sec. legation Santiago, Chile, 1891-93 (chargé d'affaires about 4 mos.); sec. legation and embassy, Mexico City, 1897-1906 (chargé d'affaires, 1905-06); apptd. minister resident and consul gen. to Dominican Republic, Jan. 10, 1907; E.E. and M.P. to Honduras, 1909-11; associated in advisory capacity with subcommittee U.S. Senate Com. on Foreign Relations investigating Mexican affairs, Aug. 3, 1912-Feb. 10, 1913; traveled in Egypt, Palestine, Greece, Feb.-Aug. 1913; lectured on Mexico and ancient races of America, 1915-16; capt. Am. Red Cross, attached to office of commr. for Europe (Paris), Jan.-May 1918; speaker in Ohio and Mich. in 2d Red Cross drive, May 1918; commd. maj., N.A., June 24, 1918; detailed as mil. attaché to Am. Embassy, Rio de Janeiro, Brazil; served on Gen. Staff, mil. intelligence div., Washington, Sept. 3-Oct. 29, 1919, hon. discharged. Traveled in Baltic States and Russia, 1929. Hon. vice chmn. at large Am. Peace Centenary Com., 1914-15; del. to Fourth Pan-Am. Conf., Washington, 1931. Mem. exec. council Am. Soc. Internat. Law, 1923-26; mem. Mich. State Com. Y.M.C.A., 1925; nat. counsellor Flint Chamber of Commerce. Elk. Vestryman P.E. Church; lay dep. from Diocese of Mich. to 48th Triennial Conv. P.E. Ch., 1925. Given vote of thanks by Peace Conf., Honduras, 1911, "for opportune and efficient services." Home: Flint, Mich. Died Oct. 6, 1940.

McCREERY, James W., lawyer; b. Indiana Co., Pa., July 13, 1849; s. William G. and Mary H. M.; grad. State Normal Sch., Indiana, Pa.; studied law with Silas M. Clark, Indiana, Pa.; m. Mary M. Arbuckle, Aug. 27, 1883. Admitted to bar, Dec. 6, 1880; began law practice Greeley, Colo., June 1, 1881; specialties, irrigation and corporation laws. Mem. Colo. Senate, 1888-92, 1896-1900; mem. bd. trustees Colo. State Normal Sch., Greeley, Colo., 1892-99 (pres. bd. 1895-99); lecturer on irrigation and water rights, U. of Colo. Republican. Home: Greeley, Colo. Died Feb. 20, 1923.

McCUE, C(harles) A(ndrew), agrl. educator; b. Cass City, Mich., May 29, 1879; s. Charles E. and Catherine Sariah (Campbell) McC.; grad. high sch., Cass City, 1897; B.S., Mich. Agrl. Coll., 1901; post-grad. work, same coll., 1903-04, U. of Pa., 1910-12, 1913-14; m. Florence E. Beebee, June 1906 (died 1907); 1 son, John Beebee; m. 2d, Essie B. Willis, Mar. 1912. With U.S. Forest Service, 1901-03; instr. horticulture, Mich. Agrl. Coll., 1904-07; with U. of Del., 1907—, prof. horticulture until 1920; dir. Delaware Agrl. Expt. Station, 1920-39, also director Agrl. Extension and dean Sch. of Agr., U. of Del. Republican. Methodist. Mason. Editor of Proceedings of Association of Land-Grant Colleges and Universities, 1928-34. Home: Newark, Del. Died Jan. 12, 1942.

McCULLOCH, Champe Carter, Jr., medical officer U.S.A.; b. Waco, Tex., Sept. 10, 1869; s. Champe Carter (mayor of Waco) and Emma Maria (Basset) M.; A.B., Baylor U., Tex., 1885; C.E., Agrl. and Mech. Coll. of Tex., 1890; M.D., U. of Va., 1891; M.D., Columbia, 1892, A.M., 1904; m. Mary Azalete, d. Davis Gurley, of McLennan Co., Tex., Oct. 23, 1889; children—Mary (wife of Dr. William James), Champe Carter (dec.), Louisa Earle (dec.), Roderick Roy, Sarah Champe (Mrs. Alfred Powis). Apptd. asst. surgeon U.S.N., Mar. 26, 1892; asst. surgeon U.S. Army, May 5, 1892; promoted through grades to col., May 15, 1917, retired Nov. 30, 1922. Dep. state health officer Western Maryland (Cumberland). Died Oct. 14, 1928.

McCULLOCH, Duncan, clergyman, educator; b. Staten Island, N.Y., Sept. 15, 1853; s. John Sears and Anna (Austen) McC.; deacon, 1881, priest, 1882, Theol. Sem. of Va.; m. Mary Sterett Carroll, Dec. 29, 1887; children—Mary W. C., Duncan, Ann (Mrs. George Watts Hill). In charge Lynnhaven Parish, Va., 1881-82; rector Christ Ch., Richmond, Va., 1882-84, St. Paul's Ch., Pleasant Valley, N.Y., 1884-86, Immanuel Parish, Baltimore Co., Md., 1886-1913; pres. and treas. Oldfields Sch., Inc. (established by mother, 1866), Glencoe, 1909—. Home: Glencoe, Md. Died Nov. 20, 1932.

McCULLOCH, Edgar Allen, federal trade commr.; b. Trenton, Tenn., Aug. 21, 1861; s. Dr. Philip Doddridge and Lucy Virginia (Burrus) M.; ed. pub. schs.; m. Hattie Louise Hassel, Nov. 30, 1887. Admitted to bar, July 1883; practiced law at Marianna, Ark., 1883-1904; was mem. McCulloch and McCulloch. Justice Supreme Court of Ark., Oct. 31, 1904, for term expiring 1928, chief justice, 1909 until resignation, 1927; mem. Federal Trade Commn., Feb. 11, 1927—. Democrat. Presbyn. Served as chmn. Ark History Commn. Home: Washington, D.C. Died Jan. 23, 1933.

McCULLOCH, James Edward, sociologist; b. Montgomery Co., Va., July 29, 1873; s. Benjamin and Elizabeth (McDonald) M.; A.B., Randolph-Macon College, Va., 1898; B.D. from Vanderbilt University, Nashville, 1901; m. Minerva Annette Clyce, Sept. 3, 1903; children—Elizabeth Allen, Donella Margaret, Edith Isabelle. Missionary sec. Young People's Socs. M.E. Ch., S., 1901-02; Southern sec. Student Vol. Movement for Foreign Missions, 1902-03; studied in instns. in Europe engaged in the training of religious and social workers, 1903-04; pres. Methodist Training Sch. for Religious Workers, 1905-11; gen. sec. Southern Sociol. Congress, 1911-19; edul. sec. Am. Sociol. Congress, 1920—; gen sec. Southern Coöperative League for Edn. and Social Service, 1921; dir. Home Betterment League, 1925; exec. sec. Vanderbilt University School of Religion, 1927-33; was organizer and exec. secretary of the Charleston Educational Center. Author: The Open Church for the Unchurched, 1905; Mastery of Love, 1910; Home—The Savior of Civilization, 1923. Editor: Call of the New South, 1912; Challenge of Social Service, 1913; Human Way, 1913; South Mobilizing for Social Service, 1913; Battling for Social Betterment, 1914; The New Chivalry—Health, 1915; Democracy in Earnest, 1918; Distinguished Service Citizenship, 1920. Home: Silver Spring, Md. Died Jan. 25, 1939.

McCULLOCH, Richard, street ry. official; b. St. Louis, Mo., June 3, 1869; s. Robert and Emma (Paxton) M.; M.E., Washington U., 1891 (hon. A.M., 1905); m. Mary Grace Beggs, 1906; children—John I. B., Robert Paxton, Mary Sue. Chief engr. Nat. Ry. Co., St. Louis, 1893-99; constrn. electric rys. in France and Switzerland, 1899-1901; asst. gen. mgr. Chicago City Ry. Co., 1901-04; apptd. asst. gen. mgr. United Rys. Co. of St. Louis, 1904; elected v.p. same co., 1907, pres. 1915, also gen. mgr. of company; trustee of Beggs Estate; pres. East Coast Development Co., Beggs Investment Co., Clarksville Coal Co., Montana Ry. Co. Mason. Home: St. Louis, Mo. Died Aug. 28, 1940.

McCULLOCH, Robert, farmer; b. Albemarle Co., Va., Nov. 23, 1820; s. Robert and Patsey (Mills) McC.; moved with family to Cooper Co., Mo., 1835; m. Louisa Weight, Jan. 27, 1852. Served in C.S.A., 1861-65; comd. brigade of cav. under Gen. Nathan Bedford Forrest; resumed farming after war; collector Cooper Co., Mo., 1872-78; sheriff, 1878-80; State register of lands, 1880-92. Democrat. Home: Clark's Fork, Cooper Co., Mo. Died 1905.

McCULLOH, Allan, lawyer; b. Ossining, N.Y., Sept. 27, 1858; s. James W. and Isabella Steel (Walker) M.; LL.B., Columbia, 1878. Practiced at New York, 1879—; mem. Alexander & Green, counsel for Equitable Life Assurance Soc., Pullman Co., L. V. R.R.; treas. and dir. Homestake Mining Co.; dir. Equitable Life Assurance Soc., Cerro de Pasco Copper Corp. Apptd. by A. Mitchell Palmer as mem. advisory com. on alien fire ins. cos., Sept. 1918. Independent Democrat. Presbyn. Home: New York, N.Y. Died May 5, 1932.

McCULLOH, Charles Sears, accountant; b. Riverdale, N.Y., July 1, 1856; s. James William and Isabella Steel (Walker) McC.; ed. Hackensack (N.J.) Acad. and Greylock Inst., S. Williamstown, Mass.; m. Kate M. Mayo, Apr. 22, 1889 (died 1918); 1 dau., Katharine Mayo (Mrs. Grant Elbert Scott); m. 2d, Jessie O. Burton, Oct. 30, 1926. Began as clk. Universal Life Ins. Co. of N.Y. City, 1875; with Equitable Life Ins. Soc., 1877-81; practiced on own account, 1881-1936; granted certificate as pub. accountant, state of N.Y., 1901, later in 7 other states, also registered in Ill. and in Treasury Dept. U.S., Washington, D.C.; now mem. F. W. Lafrentz & Co., New York; treas. and gen. mgr. Guaranty Building Co., Kansas City, Mo. Mem. N.Y. State Bd. of Pub. Accountant Examiners, 1910-26 (sec. and pres.). Presbyn. Home: New York, N.Y. Died Dec. 26, 1940.

McCULLOUGH, Ernest, civil engr.; b. Staten Island, N.Y., May 22, 1867; s. James and Caroline (McBlain) M.; grad. high sch., Wyandotte (now Kansas City), Kan., 1883; Inst. of Technology, Chicago, 1884-85; degree of C.E. from Van der Naillen Sch. of Engineering, San Francisco, 1887; m. Elizabeth Townsend Seymour, 1891 (died 1918); children—George Seymour, Caroline McBain (wife of Col. Paul C. Galleher), Elizabeth Howland (dec.), James David; m. 2d, Therese Claquin, of Tours, France, 1919. In engring. practice, San Francisco, 1887-98, Lewiston, Ida., 1898-1903, Chicago, 1903-17, Syracuse, N.Y., 1920-21, N.Y. City, 1921—. Registered architect, Illinois; registered engineer, New York and New Jersey. Editor Engineer and Contractor, San Francisco, 1893-96; asso. editor Engineering-Contracting, Chicago, 1909, Railway Age Gazette, Chicago, 1910, Am. Architect, New York, 1921-22; editor Building Age and National Builder, New York, 1925-28. Served in Ida. N.G. as capt. inf.; in Ill. N.G. as lt. engrs. and lt. F.A. In World War, maj. Engrs. O.R.C., promoted lt. col. Chem. Warfare Service; wounded near Cambrai, Nov. 1917; chief engr. Am. Red Cross, France; chief gas officer, 1st Corps; also chief gas officer, Army Arty., 1st Army; asst. chief and later chief, arty. sect. Chem. Warfare Service; constrn. engr., R.R. and C. Service, June 1917-Aug. 1919 in France; asst. comdt. Lakehurst Proving Ground, N.J., and dir. C.W.S. Officers' Sch., Aug. 1919-July 1920; lt. col. C.W.S., O.R.C., July 1920-Jan. 1926. Mason. Republican. Episcopalian. Author: Reinforced Concrete, 1908; Engineering as a Vocation, 1911; Practical Surveying, 1915, 22; Practical Structural Design, 1917, 3d edit., 1926; Everybody's Money, 1923; La Vie Chère et les Crises Monétires, 1926; Class Warfare, 1927. Home: Long Island City, N.Y. Died Oct. 1, 1931.

McCULLOUGH, Hiram R., ry. official; b. Elkton, Md., Oct. 7, 1850; s. Hiram M.; ed. Washington and Lee U.; m. Martha M., d. Marvin Hughitt; 1 dau., Belle (Mrs. Chauncey Blair Borland). With gen. freight dept. I.C. R.R., 1873-79; div. freight agt. C.&N.-W. at Winona, Minn., 1880-82, Chicago, 1883-85; asst. gen. freight agt. at Chicago, 1885-86, gen. freight agt., 1887-95, gen. traffic mgr., 1896-97, 3d v.p., 1898-1906, v.p. Jan. 23, 1906, C.&N.-W. Ry. Co.; retired. Died Oct. 7, 1932.

McCULLOUGH, John Griffith; governor; b. on Welsh Tract, nr. Newark, Del., Sept. 16, 1835; s. Alexander and Rebecca (Griffith) M.; A.B., Delaware Coll., 1855; LL.B., U. of Pa., 1858; (LL.D., Middlebury, 1900, U. of Vt., 1904, Norwich U., 1905); m. Eliza Hall Park, Aug. 30, 1871. Went to Calif., 1859; mem. Ho. of Rep., 1861, Senate, 1862; atty. gen. of Calif., 1863-67; practiced law at San Francisco, 1867-73; removed to Bennington, Vt., 1873; v.p., 1874-83; pres., 1883-88, Panama R.R.; v.p., 1877-83, pres., 1883-1900, Bennington & Rutland R.R.; pres. First Nat. Bank of N. Bennington, Vt., 1883—, Chicago & Erie R.R., 1890—; dir. Erie R.R. Co., 1884—, Central Vt. Ry., 1898—, A.,T.&S.F. Ry. Co., 1900—, Pere Marquette R.R. Co., Lackawanna Steel Co., Nat. Life Ins. Co., Bank of New York, Standard Trust Co. of New York. Mem. Vt. Senate, 1898; gov. of Vt., 1902-04. Home: North Bennington, Vt. Died May 29, 1915.

McCULLOUGH, Joseph Allen, lawyer; b. Greenville Co., S.C., Sept. 9, 1865; s. Rev. Allen Cleveland and Anne (Rebecca) Stepp; student Wofford Coll., Spartanburg, S.C., 1881-82; A.B., South Carolina Coll., Columbia, S.C., 1883, LL.B., 1887, LL.D., 1905; m. Maud d'Alvigny, June 3, 1890 (died 1914); children—James d'Alvigny, Chas. Frederic, Elizabeth McCullough (dec.), Maud McCullough (dec.), Joseph A. (dec.); m. 2d, Mrs. Emma Lumpkin Clark, Jan. 3, 1916 (died 1923). Adopted on account of mother's ill health and brought up by maternal uncle, Col. James McCullough; admitted to S.C. bar, 1887, and practiced at Greenville as mem. various firms; moved to Baltimore, Md., 1918; mem. S.C. Ho. of Rep. 8 yrs.; active in securing passage of first child labor law in S.C., the first compulsory edn. law and an appropriation of $850,000 for good roads; frequently called upon to act as spl. judge in the courts; chief atty. for U.S. Fidelity & Guaranty Co., Baltimore, 1918-28; in gen. practice of law, 1928—. Mem. bd. govs. Med. Gen. Hosp., Franklin Sq. Hosp.; trustee Emory U.; was mem. commn. apptd. by Gen. Conf. M.E. Ch., S., to represent interests of Vanderbilt Univ., and for many yrs. mem. Court of Appeals of same denom. Democrat. Mason. Home: Honea Path, S.C. Deceased.

McCULLOUGH, Myrtle Reed, author; b. Chicago (Norwood Park), Sept. 27, 1874; d. H. V. and Elizabeth A. Reed; grad. West Div. High Sch., Chicago, 1893; m. James Sydney McCullough, Oct. 22, 1906. Author: Love Letters of a Musician, 1899; Later Love Letters of a Musician, 1900; The Spinster Book, 1901; Lavender and Old Lace, 1902; Pickaback Songs, 1903; The Shadow of Victory, 1903; The Master's Violin, 1904; The Book of Clever Beasts, 1904; At the Sign of the Jack o' Lantern, 1905; A Spinner in the Sun, 1906; Love Affairs of Literary Men, 1907; Flower of the Dusk, 1908; Old Rose and Silver, 1909. Home: Chicago, Ill. Died 1911.

McCULLOUGH, Theodore Wilson, journalist; b. Kirksville, Ia., Sept. 26, 1861; s. Samuel Clinton and Annie (Wilson) M.; ed. pub. schs. and pvt. study; m. Alice May Shaw, Sept. 26, 1888; children—(Mrs. H. K. Owen), Roger Shaw, Philip Morgan. Became connected with newspaper business at 12; locomotive fireman, C.,B.&Q. R.R., out of Burlington, 1878-80; returned to newspaper work in spring of 1881; removed to Omaha, from Black Hills, 1889; city editor Omaha Herald; night editor Omaha World-Herald, 1890; night editor Omaha Bee, 1891-97, asst. mng. editor, 1897, city editor, 1898; city editor, Denver Times, 1899; rejoined Bee, 1900, mng. editor, 1906-17; became asso. editor, 1917; chief editorial writer, Omaha Bee-News, 1927—. Served in N.G. of Ia., N.M. and Neb.; lt. col. Neb. N.G., 1904-08. Republican. Mem. U. S. Express Profits Tax Advisory Bd., 1917-18. Pres. Neb. Forestry Assn. Home: Omaha, Neb. Died Dec. 8, 1937.

McCUMBER, Porter James, senator; b. Crete, Ill., Feb. 3, 1858; s. Orlin and Anne E. M.; pub. sch. edn.; LL.B., U. of Mich., 1880; m. Jennie Shorning, May 29, 1889. Sr. mem. law firm of McCumber & Bogart, Wahpeton, N.D., 1881-1900. Mem. Territorial Ho. of Rep., 1885-89; state's atty., Richland Co., 1896-97; U.S. senator, 4 terms, 1899-1923; chmn. Senate Finance Com., Jan. 1922-Mar. 1923; mem. McCumber & Sullivan, 1923-26, McCumber & Brand, Washington, D.C., 1926—. Mem. Internat. Joint Commn., 1925—. Republican. Died May 18, 1933.

McCUNE, Samuel L., banker; b. Athens, O., June 30, 1875; s. John K. and Maria A. (Pickering) McC.; B.A., Ohio U., Athens, 1896, M.A., 1913; m. Marguerite Dwinell, Nov. 6, 1907. Nat. bank examiner, 1902-11; clearing house examiner, Cincinnati, 1911-14; sec. Maynard H. Murch Co., Cleveland, 1915-21; pres. Ohio-Pa. Joint Stock Land Bank, Cleveland, 1921-29; pres. Cleveland Securities Corp., New York Joint Stock Land Bank (Rochester, N.Y.). Active in promoting Liberty Loan campaigns, World War. Trustee Ohio University, Athens, O. Republican. Methodist. Mason. Home: Cleveland, O. Died Aug. 24, 1936.

McCURDY, Irwin Pounds, clergyman, univ. prof.; b. Westmoreland Co., Pa., Mar. 23, 1856; s. Alexander Jackson and Sarah (Pounds) M.; student State Normal schs., Edinboro and Indiana, Pa., 1874-77, Washington and Jefferson Coll., 1877-78, U. of Wooster, 1878-79, Lafayette Coll., 1879-80, Princeton Theol. Sem., 1880-82; grad. student Lafayette, 1880-90, Princeton, 1880-82, Johns Hopkins, 1882-83; non-res. grad. student Wooster, 1882-85, and 10 other colls. and univs., 1885—; received 22 degrees from various ednl. institutions, 17 the doctor's degree, 18 on examination; awarded by Lafayette "the highest honor of the college for greatest proficiency in English philology," and by Princeton, on recommendation of President McCosh, a special certificate "for superior philosophic ability"; m. Rachel Long, d. William Ewing, of Irwin, Pa., Nov. 29, 1877. Teacher, prin., and law student, 1873-78; prof. Greek and higher mathematics, Frederick Female Sem. (now Hood Coll.), 1881-84; instr. of students for the ministry, Phila., 1885-92; financial sec., Lafayette Coll., 1891-92; dean Oriental U., 1909-12; prof. science and religion, Theol. Dept., Temple U., 1910—. Ordained presbyn. ministry, 1881; pastor First Ch., Frederick City, Md., 1881-84, Southwestern Ch., Phila., 1884-95 (hon. pastor for life); pastor-elect St. Andrew's Ch., Boston, 1896; First Ch., Shrewsbury, N.J., 1897; pastor Fifth Ch., Kansas City, Mo., 1897-1900; stated supply Hope Ch., Phila., 1903-07, Mariner's Ch., Phila., 1908-09; pastor-elect, 1909-10, pastor, 1910—, First Ch., Lansford, Pa. Del. Pan-Presbyn. Council, London, 1888; sec. Presbyn. General Assembly Centennial, 1887-88; mem. Presbyn. Bd. Edn., 1887-98; pres. bd. mgrs. Phila. Evang. Alliance, 1889-94; acting stated clerk Synod of Pa., 1893. Author: A Philological Discussion of the Works, Style and Language of Edgar Allan Poe, 1880; The Successful Teacher, 1881; Sacra Trinitas, 1881; Charter and Constitutions, 1886; Evangelistic Work, 1888; Centennial Hymns, 1888; Lovely Lafayette and Other Poems, 1889; The Saxon and Norman Elements in our Language and Literature, 1890; The Causes of the Intellectual Development of the Elizabethan Age, 1890; Christmas Carols and New Year Hymns, 1892; Our Country's Glory, 1901; Patriot Poems, 1907; Regina-Saquehanna, 1907. Home: Lansford, Pa. Deceased.

McCURDY, James Huff, physical dir.; b. Princeton, Me., Dec. 2, 1866; s. John and Augusta Evelyn (Heath) M.; grad. Princeton High Sch., Princeton, Me., 1885; M.D., Univ. Med. Coll. (New York U.), 1893; student in physiology of exercise, Harvard Med. Sch., 1896, 1900; hon. grad. Sargent Normal Sch., 1907, Master Physical Edn., Internat. Y.M.C.A. Coll., 1907; A.M., Clark U., 1909; m. Persis Baker Harlow, July 17, 1895; children—Hugh Graham, Elizabeth Evelyn. Asst. sec. Bangor (Me.) Y.M.C.A., 1887; physical dir. Auburn (Me.) Y.M.C.A., 1888; athletic and aquatic dir. New York Y.M.C.A., 1891-94; physical and med. dir., 23d St. Branch Assn., New York, 1893-95; med. and physical education dir., Internat. Y.M.C.A. Coll., 1895-1935, dir., 1906—; research worker, organic efficiency problems, 1935—. Special collaborator U.S. Bureau Edn. on hygiene and physical edn., 1915. Dir. Y.M.C.A. div. of athletics, hygiene and health, for A.E.F. in France, 1917-18. Author: Physiology of Exercise, 1939. Joint Author: Decimal Classification of Physical Training, 1901; Calisthenic Nomenclature, 1916. Editor Am. Physical Edn. Rev., 1906-29. Home: Springfield, Mass. Died Sept. 4, 1940.

McCURDY, Richard Aldrich, capitalist; b. New York, Jan. 29, 1835; s. late Robert H. M.; LL.B., Harvard, 1856; practiced law in New York with Lucius Robinson, who afterward became gov. N.Y.; married. Apptd. atty. Mutual Life Ins. Co., 1860, elected v.p., 1865, pres., 1885-1906; resigned; retired. Home: Morristown, N.J. Died Mar. 6, 1916.

McCURDY, Stewart LeRoy, surgeon; b. Bowerston, O., July 15, 1859; s. Peter and Mary A. (Bower) M.; M.D., Ohio State U., 1881; M.D., New York Post-Grad. Med. Sch. and Hosp., 1885; hon. A.M., Scio Coll., 1894; m. Susan Rigg Street, Sept. 1, 1887. Prof. anatomy and oral surgery, dental dept. U. of Pittsburgh, 1896—; asst. prof. surgery, med. dept. U. of Pittsburgh; surgeon Pa. R.R.; orthopædic surgeon Columbia hosp. Author: Manual of Orthopædic Surgery, 1898; Oral Surgery, 1901; Anatomy in Abstract; Emergencies in Abstract; Arthrosteopedic Surgery, 1909. Oral Surgery, 1912; Dissector in Abstract. Home: Wilkinsburg, Pa. Died Sept. 8, 1931.

McCURDY, Thomas Alexander, clergyman; b. Lewisville, Pa., Jan. 18, 1839; s. John and Sarah (Ewing) M.; A.B., A.M., Washington and Jefferson Coll., Pa., 1862; grad. Western Theol. Sem., 1865; (D.D., Wittenberg, 1878; LL.D., Washington and Jefferson, 1902); m. Elizabeth S. Woodend, 1866 (died 1905); m. 2d, Eva J. G. Simpers, 1909. Ordained Presbyn. ministry, 1865; pastor Wellsville, O., 1865-68, 1st Ch., Steubenville, O., 1868-74, Wooster, O., 1874-89; pres. Macalester Coll., Minn., 1884-90; pastor 1st Ch., Peoria, Ill., 1890-96, Central Ch., Wilmington, Del., 1896-97, Mandan, N.D., 1908—. V. moderator permanent jud. commn. Gen Assembly Presbyn. Ch. in U.S.A.; trustee Jamestown (N.D.) Coll.; trustee Wooster U. Home: Mandan, N.D. Died Mar. 1, 1915.

McCUTCHEN, Edward Johnson, lawyer; b. San Jose, Calif., Nov. 10, 1857; s. William and Amanda (Henderson) McC.; student St. Mary's Coll., San Francisco, 1871-73, Hastings Coll. of Law, 1878-79; m. Elizabeth E. Requa, Aug. 9, 1883. Admitted to Calif. bar, 1879, and since practiced at San Francisco; now mem. McCutcheon, Olney, Mannon & Greene; pres. Hobart Estate Co., Calif. Pacific Title Ins. Co. Mem. council Am. Law Inst. Protestant. Democrat. Home: Los Altos, Calif. Died June 22, 1933.

McCUTCHEON, Ben Frederick ("Benjamin Brace"), author; b. Lafayette, Ind., May 31, 1875; s. John Barr and Clara (Glick) M.; brother of John Tinney and George Barr M.; student Purdue U.; m. Anna Barnes, June 5, 1900. Commercial editor Chicago Tribune, 1905—. Author: Sunrise Acres, 1905; The Seventh Person, 1906. Home: Chicago, Ill. Died Aug. 27, 1934.

McCUTCHEON, George Barr, author; b. Tippecanoe Co., Ind., July 26, 1866; s. John Barr and Clara (Glick) McC.; ed. Purdue U.; m. Marie Van Antwerp Fay, Sept. 26, 1904. Became reporter Lafayette Journal, 1889; city editor of Lafayette Courier, 1893. Author: Graustark, 1901; Castle Craneycrow, 1902; The Sherrods, 1903; Brewster's Millions, 1903; The Day of the Dog, 1904; Beverly of Graustark, 1904; Nedra, 1905; Purple Parasol, 1905; Cowardice Court, 1906; Jane Cable, 1906; The Flyers, 1907; The Daughter of Anderson Crow, 1907; The Husbands of Edith, 1908; The Man from Brodney's, 1908; The Alternative, 1909; Truxton King, 1909; The Butterfly Man, 1910; The Rose in the Ring, 1910; What's-His-Name, 1911; Mary Midthorne, 1911; Her Weight in Gold, 1912; The Hollow of Her Hand, 1912; A Fool and His Money, 1913; Black Is White, 1914; The Prince of Graustark, 1914; Mr. Bingle, 1915; From the House Tops, 1916; The Light That Lies, 1917; Green Fancy, 1917; Shot with Crimson, 1918; The City of Masks, 1918; Sherry, 1919; Anderson Crow, Detective, 1920; West Wind Drift, 1920; Quill's Window, 1921; Yollopp, 1922; Viola Gwyn, 1922; Oliver October, 1923; East of the Setting Sun, 1924; Romeo in Moon Village, 1925; Kindling and Ashes, 1926; The Inn of the Hawk and Raven, 1927. Died Oct. 23, 1928.

McCUTCHEON, Otis Eddy, lawyer; b. Dryden, N.Y., Aug. 8, 1845; s. Rensellaer and Elvira (Bishop) M.; A.B., Albion (Mich.) College, 1873; was admitted to the bar, 1872; m. Mary Ella Gough, Nov. 15, 1872; children—Helen D., Otis E., Grace B., Robert B. Practiced law, Oscoda, Mich., 1872-92, Saginaw, Mich., 1892-1902, Idaho Falls, Ida., 1902-11, 1913-19. Pros. atty. Iosco Co., Mich., 1872-76; circuit court commr., 1874-76; mem. Mich. Ho. of Rep., 2 terms, 1878-82; mem. Ida. Senate, 1907-09, Ida. Ho. of Rep., 1909-11; dean Coll. of Law, U. of Ida., 1911-13. Trustee Ida. Insane Asylum; regent U. of Ida., 1908-11. Republican. Mason, Elk. Home: Idaho Falls, Ida. Died Mar. 22, 1926.

McDANIEL, George White, clergyman; b. Grimes County, Tex., Nov. 30, 1875; s. Francis Asbury and Letitia Anne (White) McD.; A.B., Baylor, 1898; Th.B., Southern Bapt. Theol. Sem., 1900; D.D., Richmond Coll., 1905; LL.D., Baylor, 1920; m. Martha Douglass Scarborough, March 20, 1898; children—Mrs. Mary Parker, John Harrington. Ordained Bapt. ministry, 1900; pastor Temple, Tex., 1900-02, Gaston Av. Ch., Dallas, 1902-04, 1st Ch., Richmond, Va., 1904—. Trustee Southern Bapt. Theol. Sem.; dir. Bapt. Orphanage of Va. (pres. bd.); mem. Bapt. Edn. Bd. of Va.; pres. Bapt. Gen. Assn. of Va.; pres. Southern Bapt. Conv. Democrat. Author: Our Boys in France; The People Called Baptists; The Churches of the New Testament; A Memorial Wreath; Seeing the Best; The Supernatural Jesus. Died Aug. 18, 1927.

McDANIEL, Henry Dickerson, governor; b. Monroe, Ga., Sept. 4, 1836; s. Ira Oliver and Rebecca J. (Walker) M.; A.B., Mercer U., 1856, A.M., 1859; LL.D., U. of Ga., 1907. Admitted to bar, 1857; mem. Ga. Secession Conv., 1861; 1st lt., capt. and maj. 11th Ga., C.S.A., 1861-65; m. Hester, d. Stephen Felker, Dec. 20, 1865. Mem. Ga. Constl. Conv., 1865; disability to hold office removed by U.S. Congress, July 1872; mem. Ga. Ho. of Rep., 1873-74, Senate, 1874-83; gov. of Ga., 1883-86. Democrat. Home: Monroe, Ga. Died July 25, 1926.

McDANIEL, Reuben E., clergyman; b. Parke Co., Ind., Apr. 12, 1846; s. Henry and Mariah Barbara (Sappenfield) M.; Wabash Coll., Crawfordsville, Ind., 1865-66; Ind. U., 1867-68; Wittenberg Coll., Springfield, O., 1869-70; grad. Luth. Theol. Sem., Phila., 1873; Ph.D., Curry U., Pittsburgh, Pa., 1893; (hon. A.M., Wabash and Wittenberg, 1887; D.D., Potomac U., 1904, S.T.D., 1905); m. Julia F. McFadden, May 19, 1874. Ordained Evang. Luth. Ministry, 1873; pastorates Colburn, Ind., 1876-81, Toledo, O., 1881-82, Vandalia, Ill., 1882-88, Verona, Pa., 1889-1902, Corry, Pa., 1902-07; Edinboro, Pa., 1907-10, Moundsville, W.Va., 1911—. Prof. theology, Potomac U. A promoter Luther League of America; pres. Ind. Synod Luth. Ch., 1879-80. Democrat. Died Apr. 11, 1920.

McDANIEL, Sanders, lawyer; b. Monroe, Ga., Sept. 19, 1867; s. Henry Dickerson and Hester (Felker) M.; Monroe Acad.; A.B., U. of Ga., 1886; m. Anne Henderson, May 14, 1895; children—Harriet, Marshall. Practiced, Atlanta, 1895—; mem. McDaniel, Neeley & Marshall; v.p. and gen. counsel Southeastern Express Co.; div. counsel for Ga. for Southern Ry. Co.; pres. Central Bank Block Assn. Trustee U. of Ga.; pres. Atlanta Bar Assn. Democrat. Home: Atlanta, Ga. Died May 2, 1934.

McDANIELS, Joseph Hetherington, college prof.; b. Dennis, Mass., Oct. 25, 1840; s. John and Ann (Hetherington) M.; A.B., Harvard, 1861, A.M., 1872; (LL.D., Griswold, 1891, Hobart, 1911). Prof. Greek lang. and lit., Hobart Coll., 1868-1911 (emeritus). Independent. Episcopalian. Editor: Letters and Memorials of Wendell Phillips Garrison, 1908. Home: Geneva, N.Y. Died July 22, 1938.

McDAVITT, Thomas, M.D.; b. St. Louis, Mo., May 15, 1857; s. Virgil (M.D.) and Caroline (McGinnis) M.; M.D., Chicago Med. Coll., 1879; m. Hattie Easton, June 25, 1884. Practiced at St. Paul, Minn., 1891—; specializes in treatment of the eye and ear; oculist and aurist St. Joseph's hosp.; sec. Minn. State Bd. of Med. Examiners, 1912—. Fellow Am. Coll. Surgeons. Mason. Home: St. Paul, Minn. Died Mar. 4, 1926.

McDERMOTT, Allan Langdon, congressman; b. S. Boston, Mass., Mar. 30, 1854. Corporation atty., Jersey City, N.J., 1879-83; dist. court judge, 1883-86; pres. Jersey City bd. of finance and taxation, 1883-86; mem. State bd. of taxation, 1884-86; mem. State assembly, 1880-81; State senate, 1899-1900; chmn. N.J. State Dem. com., 1885-95; mem. commn. to revise constitution, N.J., 1894; corp. counsel, Jersey City, 1897—; candidate for U.S. senator, 1895. Elected to 56th Congress to fill vacancy caused by death of Hon. Wm. D. Daley; reëlected to 57th Congress, 1901-03, 7th N.J. dist., and 1903-07, 10th dist. Democrat. Home: Jersey City, N.J. Died 1908.

McDERMOTT, Charles J(ames), lawyer; b. Borough Bronx, N.Y., June 15, 1867; s. James W and Mary E. (Hill) McD.; prep. edn., Adelphi Acad., Brooklyn, N.Y.; LL.B., Columbia, 1889; LL.D., St. Lawrence U., 1931; m. Mary E. Thornton, Nov. 26, 1895; children—Marian T. (Mrs. Edward V. Manico), Charles J. Began practice at N.Y. City, 1888; mem. McDermott & Turner; member advisory board Hamilton Trust Branch Chase National Bank. Judge County Court, Kings County, New York, 1917-21; former member Board of Higher Education, N.Y. City. Trustee Washington and Lee University. Democrat. Episcopalian. Mason. Home: Brooklyn, N.Y. Died Dec. 20, 1941.

McDERMOTT, Edward John, lawyer; b. Louisville, Ky., Oct. 29, 1852; s. William and Catherine (Byrne) M.; A.B., U. of Louisville, 1871; student Queen's Coll., Belfast, Ireland, 1 yr., U. of Göttingen, 1 yr.; LL.B., Harvard, 1876; LL.D., Ky. State U., 1913, also Notre Dame U., Ind., 1917; m. Susan Rogers, d. Hon. John W. Barr, Oct. 15, 1895; children—Susan Barr (Mrs. Raymond Gordon Clarke), Edward J., Catherine Watson. In practice at Louisville, 1876—; mem. Ky. Ho. of Rep., 1880; presdl. elector, 1880; mem. Constl. Conv., 1890; U.S. chief supervisor of elections for Ky., 1888; chmn. com. of 3 that prepared present charter of Louisville, 1892; lt. gov. of Ky., term 1911-15; prof. law U. of Louisville, 1919—. Democrat. Mem. exec. bd. Am. Inst. Criminal Law and Criminology, 1913, 14, 15. Grand Knight of K. of C. Home: Louisville, Ky. Died May 1, 1926.

McDERMOTT, Frank, educator; b. N.Y. City, Sept. 10, 1877; s. Bernard and Delia (Hassett) McD.; grad. Cooper Inst., N.Y. City, 1897; m. Grace Bird, June 3, 1903; children—Grace Bird, Nadine Bird, B. Clinton. Public accounting practice, 1897-1912; treas. Cheltenham Advertising Agency, 1912-17, Sherman & Bryan, Inc., adv. agency, 1917-24; pres. New York Elec. Sch., 1924—. Democrat. Catholic. Home: New Rochelle, N.Y. Deceased.

McDERMOTT, George Robert, naval architect; b. Glasgow, Scotland, Oct. 28, 1860; s. Neil and Jane (Campbell) M.; ed. acad. and Tech. Inst., Glasgow; m. Jeanie Lennox Rolland, July 1880; children—George Rolland, Marion Dall (dec.), Jean. In shops and drafting offices, 1880-83, chief scientific and designing staff, 1884-86, naval architect and asst. to shipyard mgr., 1887-89, Clydebank Shipbuilding and Engring. Co. (John Brown & Co.), Clyde, Scotland; naval archt. and asst. to gen. mgr. Southampton (Eng.) Naval Works, 1890-91; asst. prof. naval architecture, 1892-1904, prof. naval architecture in charge Dept. Naval Architecture and Marine Engring., 1904-29, Sibley Coll., Cornell U.; prof. emeritus Cornell U., 1929. On leave from univ., apptd. engr.-in-chief in organization and construction of Naval Repair Station of Lloyd Brazileiro (Brazilian Govt.), Ilha de Mucangue, Rio de Janeiro, 1910-12. On leave from univ., apptd. May 4, 1917, by Gen. George W. Goethals, as dist. officer, U.S. Shipping Bd., Emergency Fleet Corp., and apptd. Oct. 30, 1917, as agt. of same by E. N. Hurley, chmn.; apptd. chmn. U. S. Govt. com., Atlantic & Gulf coast div. on loadlines of mercantile vessels, July 1921. Ind. Republican. Author: Screw Propeller Computer and Text-book on Screw Propellers, 1903. Home: Ithaca, N.Y. Died May 26, 1937.

McDERMOTT, George Thomas, judge; b. Winfield, Kan., Oct. 21, 1886; s. James and Tirzah (Henderson) McD.; Ph.B., Southwestern Coll., Winfield, 1906, LL.D., 1932; Ph.B., U. of Chicago, 1908, J.D., 1909; LL.D., Washburn Coll., 1929; m. Katharine Stewart, Dec. 28, 1914; children—Jane, Mary, James. Admitted to Kan. bar, 1910, and began practice at Topeka. Judge U.S. Dist. Court, Kan., 1928-29; judge U.S. Circuit Court, 10th Jud. Circuit, May 1, 1929—. Served as 1st lt. 339th F.A., U.S.A., 1917-19. Republican. Presbyn. Home: Topeka, Kan. Died Jan. 19, 1937.

McDEVITT, Philip R., clergyman; b. Phila., Pa., July 12, 1858; s. Richard and Mary A. (Dinneney) M.; grad. La Salle Coll., Phila., 1877, St. Charles Borromeo Theol. Sem., Overbrook, Pa., 1885; LL.D., Notre Dame, 1925. Ordained R.C. priest, July 14, 1885; supt. parish schs., Phila., May 1, 1899-1916; created Domestic Prelate, with title of monsignor, July 16, 1910; bishop of Harrisburg, July 10, 1916—. Pres. Am. Catholic Hist. Soc., 1910. Died Nov. 11, 1935.

McDIARMID, Errett Weir, coll. prof.; b. Toronto, Ont., Dec. 31, 1877; s. Hugh and Mary (Campbell) M.; A.B., Bethany (W.Va.) Coll., 1895, A.M., 1896; A.M., Hiram (O.) Coll., 1897; studied U. of Neb., 1898-99, summers, Harvard, 1906, U. of Chicago, 1918; m. Allie May McCorkle, June 18, 1903; children—Archie Campbell (dec.), Florence, Errett Weir, John, James King (dec.). Teacher, Fairfield (Neb.) Coll., 1897-1908, Hazel Green (Ky.) Acad., 1899-1900, Morehead Normal Sch., 1900-06; prof. Latin, Bethany Coll., 1906-08; prin. Beckley Inst., 1908-13; pres. Milligan (Tenn.) Coll., 1913-14; pres. Hamilton Coll., Lexington, Ky., 1914-18; prof. philosophy, Tex. Christian U., Sept. 1918—. Mem. Disciples of Christ. Mason. Home: Ft. Worth, Tex. Died Sept. 5, 1937.

McDILL, John Rich, surgeon; b. Plover, Wis., July 20, 1860; s. Alexander Stuart (M.D.) and Eliza Jane (Rich) M.; M.D., Rush Med. Coll., Chicago, 1885; interne Cook Co. Hosp., 1885-87; studied univs. Berlin and Munich, 1890-92; m. Josephine Neale, Jan. 27, 1903; children—Alexander Stuart, John Harcourt, Jane Rich. Practiced, Milwaukee, 1887-98 (except when abroad); capt. and surgeon, Wis. N.G., 1893-98; maj. and surgeon vols., Spanish-Am. War, 1898, and until 1903, serving as brigade surgeon and chief operating surgeon in the field in Cuba for 7th Army Corps and as chief operating surgeon in Manila, 1900-03; organized and became chief surgeon Woman's Hosp., Manila, 1902, and of St. Paul's Hosp., 1905-10; prof. surgery and head of dept., U. of Philippines, 1906-12; chief surgeon Philippine Gen. Hosp., 1910-12; resumed practice at Milwaukee, Sept. 1912. Asso. prof. surgery, Rush Med. Coll. (U. of Chicago). In med. and surg. relief work in Germany, 10 mos., 1916-17; maj., Med. Corps, U.S.A., 1917; surg. chief Base Hosp., 40th Div., Camp Kearny, Calif., Sept. 1917-July 1918; consultant in reconstruction, Surgeon Gen.'s Office, Aug. 1918-Mar. 1919; chief med. officer, Federal Bd. for Rehabilitation of Disabled Soldiers, with rank of asst. surg. gen. (R.) U.S. Pub. Health Service, 1919-21; chief med. consultant U.S. Veterans' Bur., 1922-23; med. officer in charge U.S. Vets'. Hosp., Waukesha, Wis., 1925, 1932. Surgeon gen. and life mem. Vet. Army of Philippines; lt. col. Med. Aux., U.S.A. Fellow Am. Coll. Surgeons (founder), A.M.A. Mason. Author: Tropical Surgery; Lessons from the Enemy; How Germany Cares for Her War-Disabled, 1918. Home: Cornwall-on-Hudson, N.Y. Died Sept. 15, 1934.

McDOEL, William Henry, ry. pres.; b. Goffstown, N.H., Mar. 28, 1841; s. Joseph and Ann (Clogston) M.; ed. common schs.; m. Rebecca Lucas, Sept. 12, 1865; m. 2d, Katherine R. Neff, of Kenosha, Wis., Dec. 27, 1898. Clerk and agt. Great Western R.R. of Ill., 1861-63; agt. at State Line, Ind., 1864-65. gen. agt., Keokuk, Ia., 1865-75. Toledo, Wabash & Western Ry.; Western agt. "Blue Line," 1875-77; gen. freight agt. Hannibal & St. Joseph R.R., 1878-84; Southwestern freight agt. C.,B.&Q. R.R., at Kansas City, 1884; from July 1884, with Louisville, New Albany & Chicago Ry. and its successor, the Chicago, Indianapolis & Louisville Ry., as gen. freight agt., 1884-86, traffic mgr., 1886-91, gen. mgr., 1891-94, v.p. and gen. mgr., 1894-96, receiver, 1896-97. v.p. and gen. mgr., 1897-99, pres. and gen. mgr., 1899-1909. Home: Chicago, Ill. Died Apr. 26, 1916.

McDONALD, Alexander; b. in Murrayshire, Scotland; came to U.S., 1851, and located in Chillicothe, O., where he remained until 1857, when he engaged in business in Cincinnati. Pres. Standard Oil Co. of Ky., and connected with a number of financial, ednl. and charitable instns. in Cincinnati. Home: Clifton, Cincinnati, O. Died 1910.

McDONALD, Charles Sanford; b. Cromwell, Ia., Sept. 17, 1879; s. Charles Walker and Dora May (Cochrane) McD.; student State U. of Ia., 1897-1900; m. Alice E. Keenan, Apr. 26, 1906; children—Charles John, Marion Maud. In real estate, bond and ins. business, Sioux Falls, 1906—; pres. Chas. S. McDonald Co.; mem. S.Dak. Ho. of Rep., 1923-25 (speaker of House, 1925); mem. State Senate, 1926-27. Republican; state chmn. Hoover-Curtis Club, 1928; chmn. Rep. State Central Com., 1930-34. Civilian aide to sec. of war for State of S.Dak. Presbyn. Elk, Moose. Home: Sioux Falls, S.Dak. Died Nov. 15, 1934.

McDONALD, Howard, educator; b. Duncan Falls, O., Apr. 11, 1876; s. Emesiah and Martha Ann (Cline) M.; A.B., Muskingum Coll., Ohio, 1901; A.B., Princeton, 1902; A.M., U. of Mich., 1914, Ph.D., 1916; m. Katharine Miller, May 21, 1908; children—Winifred Carol, Marian Christine, Malcolm Edwin. Prof. Greek and Latin, Knoxville Coll., 1902-03; prof. Greek and philosophy, Muskingum Coll., New Concord, O., 1903-09; clerk of Common Pleas Court, Muskingum Co., O., 1909-13; dean and prof. polit. science, Muskingum Coll., 1915-18; dean and prof. history and economics, 1918-22, pres., 1922—, Parsons Coll., Fairfield, Ia. Died July 9, 1927.

McDONALD, Hunter, civil engr.; b. Winchester, Va., June 12, 1860; s. Angus W. and Cornelia (Peake) M.; student Washington and Lee U., 1878-79; m. Mary Eloise Gordon, Feb. 8, 1893. Asst. engr. L.& N. R.R., Aug.-Dec. 1879, Nashville, Chattanooga & St. Louis Ry., 1879-89; supt. Huntsville, Fayetteville and Columbia div., same rd., 1889-91; resident engr. Western & Atlantic R.R., Atlanta, Ga., 1891-92; chief engr. Nashville, Chattanooga & St. Louis Ry., 1892-1931; consulting practice. Chief engr. N.C.& St.L. Ry., Tenn. Central R.R. and Birmingham & Northwestern R.R. under federal operation, 1918-20. Episcopalian. Edited and published A Diary with Reminiscences of the War and Refugee Life in the Shenandoah Valley, 1860-1865 (by his mother), 1935. Home: Nashville, Tenn. Died Aug. 24, 1937.

McDONALD, James Richard, publisher; b. Brunswick, Me., June 18, 1867; s. Thomas and Elinor (Butler) M.; lived at Pepperell, Mass., 1877-1889; A.B., from Williams College, 1889; m. Etta Austin Blaisdell, Aug. 3, 1899. News editor Springfield Republican, 1889-90, Boston Daily Advertiser, 1891, Hartford Courant, 1892-93; with Allyn & Bacon, book pubs., Boston, 1894-96, The Macmillan Co., 1896-1902 (estab. Boston office, 1897, ednl. mgr., New York, 1902), Lothrop Pub. Co., Boston, 1903; editor and ednl. mgr., Little, Brown & Co., Boston, 1904—(estab. schoolbook business), now dir. and sec. of corp. Pres. bd. trustees Lawrence Acad., Groton, Mass. Home: West Medford, Mass. Died Nov. 8, 1933.

McDONALD, Jessie Claire, educator; b. Indianapolis, Jan. 24, 1869; d. Ezekiel M. and Lydia P. (Tousey) M.; prep. edn. McDonald-Ellis Sch., Washington, D.C.; B.S., Wellesley Coll., 1888; M.S., Columbian (now George Washington) U., 1894; studied Sorbonne (U. of Paris), U. of Pa.; unmarried. Prin. National Cathedral School, Washington, D.C., July 1, 1913—. Former trustee Wellesley College. Died Aug. 12, 1928.

McDONALD, John B., railroad contractor and builder; b. in Ireland, Nov. 7, 1844; s. Bartholomew and Mary M.; ed. pub. schs., New York; m. Georgia A. Strang, 1869. Builder Vanderbilt tunnels north of 42d St., New York; High Bridge branch of N.J. R.R.; Georgian branch of Canadian Pacific R.R.; B.&O. R.R. from Baltimore to Phila.; I.C. R.R. from Elgin, Ill., to Dodgeville, Wis.; Baltimore Belt R.R. to connect the B.&O. lines by a tunnel under city of Baltimore, 1891-94; contractor for the construction of the rapid transit railroad in New York. Pres. Interstate Tunnel Ry. Co.; v.p. Interborough Met. Co., Oakland Bayside Realty Co. Home: New York. Died 1911.

McDONALD, John Bacon, army officer; b. in Ala., Feb. 8, 1859; grad. U.S. Mil. Acad., 1881; Army War Coll., 1913. Commd. 2d lt. 5th Inf., June 11, 1881; promoted through grades to brig. gen. N.A., Dec. 17, 1917. Commandant cadets, Agrl. and Mech. Coll., Auburn, Ala., Sept. 1888-91; prof. mil. science and tactics and comdt. cadets, S.C. Mil. Acad., 1897-98; mustering officer, State of Ala., Sept.-Nov. 1898; in Philippine Islands, 1900-01; wounded in battle at Borongabong, Apr. 27, 1901; comdr. Ft. Ethan Allen, Vt., 1907-08; duty Insp. Gen.'s Dept., 1914-17; brig. gen., in comd. 181st Inf. Brig., 91st Div., in France and Belgium, 1918-19; participated in St. Mihiel, Meuse-Argonne and Ypres-Lys offensives; comd. Presidio, San Francisco, 1919; comd. U.S. Disciplinary Barracks, Alcatraz, Calif., 1920-21. Awarded D.S.M. and D.S.C.; Officer Legion of Honor, Croix de Guerre with Palm (French); Belgian Croix de Guerre and Italian War Cross. Died Mar. 15, 1926.

McDONALD, John Samuel, judge; b. Ontario, Can., Feb. 8, 1865; s. Samuel and Annie McD.; student Victoria U., 1887-88; LL.B., U. of Mich., 1890; m. Adelia J. Duncan, Nov. 27, 1895; 1 son, John Duncan. Came to U.S., 1888; admitted to Mich. bar, 1890; pros. atty. Kent Co., Mich., 1907-08; circuit judge 17th Jud. Circuit, 1908-22; apptd. asso. justice Supreme Court of Mich. to fill vacancy, 1922; elected same, 1922, and reëlected 1925 for term ending 1933; now mem. McDonald & McDonald. Republican. Methodist. Mason. Home: Grand Rapids, Mich. Died July 6, 1941.

McDONALD, Morris, ry. official; b. New Albany, Ind., Aug. 20, 1865; ed. pub. schs. Began with engring. corps, Ky. & Ind. Bridge Co., 1883; paymaster, asst. treas., chf. clk. to supt., trainmaster and supt. transportation, Louisville, Evansville & St. Louis Ry., 1885-92; chf. clk. to supt. and asst. trainmaster in charge Savannah div., Central R.R. of Ga., 1893-94; sec. to gen. mgr., 1896-97, gen. supt., 1897-1908, v.p. and gen. mgr., 1908-13, Me. Central R.R.; pres. B.&M. and Me. Central rys., 1913-14; pres. Me. Central R.R. and subsidiary cos., 1914-32; retired Sept. 1, 1932. Home: Portland, Me. Died May 19, 1938.

McDONALD, Thomas Edward, prof. law; b. Erin, Tex., Sept. 3, 1893; s. James Alfred and Sarah Leona (Wigley) McD.; grad. Sam Houston Normal Inst., Huntsville, Tex., 1916; A.B., Stanford U., 1922, J.D., 1924; Carnegie scholar, The Hague, 1937; m. Dorothy Eaton, Dec. 23, 1920; children—Barbara Louise, Dorothy Standish. Teacher pub. schs., Jasper Co., Tex., 1912-15; supt. pub. schs., Roganville, 1915-17; county supt. schs., Jasper Co., 1919-20; admitted to Calif. bar, 1924, and practiced in San Mateo, 1924-25; admitted to Tex. bar, 1932; prof. law, Baylor U., Waco, Tex., 1925-35, de facto dean, Baylor U. Law Sch., 1935-37, dean, 1937—. Served as sergt. 143d Inf., U.S. Army, 1917-18; 2d lt. 363d Machine Gun Batt., 1918-19, World War. Democrat. Baptist. Mason. Woodman. Home: Waco, Tex. Died Dec. 7, 1939.

McDONALD, William, M.E. clergyman; b. Belmont, Me., March 1, 1820; s. of Joseph and Mary (Wilson) McD.; ed. in common schools, Belfast, Me. (D.D., Upper Iowa Univ., 1887); entered ministry, 1840; united with Maine Conf., M.E. Church, 1843. Among his pastorates were: South Berwick, Portland and Biddeford, Me.; Appleton, Wis.; Lawrence, Chelsea, New Bedford and Boston, Mass.; Providence, R.I., and Brooklyn, N.Y. Editor Advocate of Bible Holiness, 1870-83, and The Christian Witness. Was 16 yrs. v.p. and 12 yrs. pres. Nat. Camp Meeting Assn. Made evangelistic tour to England and India, visiting the Holy Land, 1880-81; to England again, 1892. Author: Scripture Way of Holiness; Saved to the Uttermost, Wesley and His Doctrine; Another Comforter; The People's Wesley. Home: West Somerville, Mass. Died 1901.

McDONALD, William C., governor; b. Jordanville, N.Y., July 25, 1858; s. John and Lydia Marshall (Biggs) M.; ed. W. Winfield Acad., Richfield Springs Acad., Cazenovia (N.Y.) Sem.; m. Frances J. McCourt, Aug. 31, 1891. Admitted to bar, Ft. Scott, Kan., 1880, and same yr. removed to Lincoln Co., N.M.; civ. and mining engr., 1881-90; mgr. Carrizozo Cattle Ranch Co., 1890-1912, El Capitan Live Stock Co., 1910-12. Apptd. U.S. surveyor, 1891; assessor Lincoln Co., 1885-86; mem. N.M. legislature, 1891-92; chmn. Bd. Co. Commrs., Lincoln Co., 1895-96; mem. Cattle Sanitary Bd. N.M., 1906-12; chmn. Dem. Territorial Com., Dec. 1911-Oct. 1912; elected first state gov. N.M., Nov. 7, 1911, term expiring, Jan. 1917. Home: Carrizozo, N.M. Died Apr. 11, 1918.

McDONALD, William Jesse, state revenue agt., Texas; b. Kemper Co., Miss., Sept. 28, 1852; s. Enoch and Eunice (Durham) M.; ed. pub. schs., Henderson, Tex., and Soule's Commercial Coll., New Orleans; m. Rhoda Carter, 1876 (died 1906). In grocery and lumber business until 1883; ranching, 1883—. Deputy sheriff Wood and Hardeman cos., Tex., and deputy U.S. marshal Northern Dist. of Tex. and Southern Kan., until 1901; capt. Tex. Rangers, until he became state revenue agt., Jan. 19, 1907. Home: Austin, Texas. Died Jan. 15, 1918.

McDONALD, Witten, capitalist; b. Wyoming Co., W.Va., June 4, 1846; moved to Mo., 1857; ed. St. Paul's (P.E.) Coll., Palmyra, Mo. Engaged in lumber and banking business at Carrollton, Mo., Wausau, Wis., Kansas City, 1868-85; afterward in other banks; organized and was v.p. First Nat. Bank, Kansas City, 1886-88, v.p. Kansas City Hydraulic-Press Brick Co., 1889-96; pres. Midland Nat. Bank, 1888-93; owner Kansas City Times, 1893-96; propr. Mammoth Springs Cotton Mills, 1896-99; not in active business, 1899-1904; pres. Kansas City Cotton Mills Co. and Kansas City Cotton Seed Products Co. Home: Kansas City, Mo. Died 1910.

McDONNELL, Charles Edward, bishop; b. New York, Feb. 1, 1854; ed. Christian Brothers and by Jesuits of St. Francis Xavier's Coll.; at Am. Coll., Rome, 1872-78 (D.D., 1878). Ordained R.C. priest, 1878; asst. St. Mary's Ch., New York, 1878, St. Stephen's, 1879; master of ceremonies New York Cathedral, 1879-84; sec. to Cardinal McCloskey, 1884-85, to Archbishop Corrigan, and chancellor, 1885-92; one of pvt. chamberlains to Pope Leo XIII, 1890-92; consecrated bishop of Brooklyn, Apr. 25, 1892. Died Aug. 8, 1921.

McDONNELL, Thomas Francis Irving, lawyer; b. Providence, R.I., June 11, 1868; s. Patrick and Ellen (Irving) McD.; A.B., Brown U., 1891, hon. A.M., 1923; m. Mary Stanton Kenyon, May 28, 1913. Practiced at Providence from 1893 until retired. Served as judge advocate First Light Infantry Regiment, 1909-10; vice chmn. Providence Chapter Am. Red Cross, World War, also chmn. speakers' bur. same, and dir. of four-minute men for R.I. Secretary and mem. exec. com. Voters' League of R.I. Pres. Providence Chamber of Commerce, 1922-23. Order of Vasa conferred by King Oscar of Sweden, 1907. Catholic. Home: Providence, R.I. Died Jan. 29, 1939.

McDONOUGH, John Henry, machinery mfr.; b. Meade Co., Ky., Nov. 9, 1858; s. John M. and Priscilla (Peak) McD.; ed. Woodlawn Country Sch., Ky.; m. Mary C. Kirby, May 20, 1890; children—Grace, Kirby, Clare. Engaged in farming, Meade Co., Ky., until 1881; clk., ry. mail service, 1886-93; machinery salesman for Keating Implement & Machine Co., 1893-97; pres. and gen. mgr. The Murray Co., mfrs. cotton ginning and cotton seed oil machinery, 1901—. Democrat. Catholic. Home: Dallas, Tex. Died Feb. 2, 1938.

McDONOUGH, John James, lawyer; b. Fall River, Mass., Mar. 15, 1857; s. Michael and Ellen (Hayes) M.; A.B., Holy Cross Coll., Worcester, Mass., 1880 (LL.D., 1908); post-grad. course in philosophy at Sem. of St. Sulpice, Montreal, Can.; LL.B., Boston U. Law Sch., 1884; m. Elizabeth Frances McCarthy, Nov. 6, 1890. Began practice of law at Fall River, 1884. Mem. Mass. Ho. of Rep., 1889-90; mem. State Dem. Com., 1890; justice 2d Dist. Ct. of Bristol Co., 1893—. Trustee Fall River Pub. Library, 1900—. Lecturer and essayist. Mem. Catholic Knights of America. Home: Fall River, Mass. Died 1912.

McDOUGALL, Alexander, shipbuilder; b. in Scotland, Mar. 16, 1845; s. Dougall and Ellen (MacDougall) M.; came to America, 1854, to Minn., 1870; ed. country schs.; m. Emmeline Ross, Jan. 1878. Sailed for 21 yrs. on the Great Lakes and for 35 yrs. has been closely identified with lake shipbuilding and lake transportation; pres. McDougall-Duluth Co., shipbuilders, Northern Power Co. of Wis.; dir. Great Northern Power Co. (Minn.), City Nat. Bank (Duluth), Northeastern Power Co. (Me.). Inventor of the only method devised for making merchantable the vast deposits of sand iron ores in Minn. Inventor of "whaleback" ships. Home: Duluth, Minn. Died May 23, 1923.

McDOUGALL, William, psychologist; b. Lancashire, Eng., 1871; s. I. S. and R. (Smalley) McD.; ed. Owens Coll., Manchester; St. Thomas Hosp., London; M.B., Cambridge U.; M.A., Oxford U.; studied Göttingen; Dc.Sc., British Soc. Psychical Research (pres.); m. A. A. Hickmore, of Brighton, Eng., 1899; children—Mrs. Paul Brown, Duncan Shimwell, Angus Dougal, Kenneth Dougal, Janet Aline (dec.). Fellow St. John's Coll., Cambridge, 1898; reader, University Coll., London; reader in mental philosophy and fellow, Corpus Christi Coll., Oxford; prof. psychology, Harvard, 1920-27; professor of psychology, Duke University, 1927—. Maj. Royal Army M.C., 1914-19. Unitarian. Author: Physiological Psychology, 1905; Social Psychology, 1908; Pagan Tribes of Borneo, 1911; Psychology, 1912; Body and Mind, 1912; Group Mind, 1920; Is America Safe for Democracy?, 1921; Outline of Psychology, 1923; Ethics and Some Modern World Problems, 1924; Outline of Abnormal Psychology, 1926; Janus, 1927; Character and the Conduct of Life, 1927; Modern Materialism and Emergent Evolution, 1929; World Chaos—the Responsibility of Science, 1931; Energies of Men, 1933. Home: Durham, N.C. Died Nov. 28, 1938.

McDOWELL, Alexander, congressman; b. Franklin, Pa., Mar. 4, 1845; s. Parker and Lavinia (Titus) M.; common sch. edn.; m. Clara Blekley, Sept. 26, 1866. Served 3 yrs. in 121st Pa. Vols. in Civil War. Entered banking business at Sharon, Pa., 1870; pres. McDowell Nat. Bank; treas. Protected Home Circle, etc. Mem. 53d Congress (1893-95), Pa. at-large; clerk Ho. of Rep., 54th to 61st Congresses (1895-1903); mem. sch. bd. of Sharon, 1871-1911. Republican. Home: Sharon, Pa. Died Sept. 30, 1913.

McDOWELL, Arthur Roscoe, college dean; b. Yuba Co., Calif., Jan. 8, 1890; s. James and Ellen (Dunning) M.; student Wilkins Normal Sch., Marysville, Calif., 1908; D.D.S., Coll. Phys. and Surgeons, San Francisco, 1917; m. Helen Bertha Kramer, Nov. 26, 1922; children—Alan Rae, Coleen Dunning. Teacher Calif. grade schs., 1910-14; teacher dentistry, Coll. Phys. and Surgeons, 1917, instr. head and neck anatomy, demonstrator operative dentistry, 1917-21, jr. dean dental faculty, 1921-23, dean and prof. operative dentistry, 1923-28, dean and prof. dental ethics and econ., 1928—. First lt. Officers Dental Res. Corps, U.S.A., 1918-20. Pres. Am. Assn. Dental Schs., 1935-36 (fgn. relations com.); mem. Nat. Bd. Dental Examiners, Golden Gate Internat. Dental Congress (zd. dirs.), Pacific Coast Dental Conf.; sec. bd. trustees Coll. of Phys. and Surgeons. Fellow Am. Coll. of Dentists (v.p. 1937). N.Y. Acad. Dentistry; life mem. Alumni Assn. Coll. of Phys. and Surgeons (exec. com.); hon. mem. Ore. State Dental Assn., Golden Gate Study Club. Republican. Mason. Editor Jour. Calif. State Dental Assn., 1919-20. Home: San Francisco, Calif. Died May 14, 1938.

McDOWELL, George Stanley, newspaper editor; b. Doylestown, Pa., Sept. 29, 1855; s. George and Amanda (Matthews) McD.; grad. Doylestown English and Classical Sem., 1872; m. Emma Matthews Scott, Aug. 9, 1881 (dec.); children—George Scott, Robert, James Duffel, Kenneth. Began as "devil" in office of Intelligencer, Doylestown, 1872; successively reporter, city editor, mng. editor Cincinnati (O.) Commercial Tribune, 1880-1904; financial editor Cincinnati Enquirer, 1904-26, also mng. editor, 1926—. Admitted to Pa. and Ohio bar. Republican. Baptist. Elk. Home: Cincinnati, O. Died Aug. 28, 1932.

McDOWELL, Henry Burden; b. San Antonio, Tex., Apr. 29, 1857; s. late Maj. Gen. Irvin (U.S.A.) and Helen (Burden) M., of Troy, N.Y.; A.B., Harvard, 1878; studied law, same univ., 1879-80; student of Oriental langs., especially Sanskrit and Chinese; m. Maude Appleton, d. Charles E. Fuller, of Boston, June 1, 1892; children—Madeleine Fuller, Irvin (dec.). Began as chemist, Burden Iron Co., Troy, N.Y., 1882, later consulting engr., N.Y. City, for Gen. Electric Co., Otis Elevator Co., Barber Asphalt Co., etc. Editor and propr. San Francisco Ingleside (newspaper), 1883-85; mem. editorial staff San Francisco Examiner, 1885; legal expert of "reform" grand jury, San Francisco, 1886; in charge of publicity, Citizens' Union Campaign against Mayor Grant, New York, 1888; organized Roosevelt Club, Cambridge, Massachusetts, 1912; assisted in securing 50,000 signatures at Chicago, 1912, for principles maintained by Theodore Roosevelt; speaker in Progressive campaign, Michigan, 1914, later in Massachusetts, and in New York for Charles E. Hughes; raised over $1,000,000 in small subscriptions in N.Y. City for Liberty Loan, 1917. Univ. extension lecturer, Cambridge and Boston, 1908—. Unitarian. Made extensive researches in Chinese mythology and religion and author of the "Chaldæo-Chinese hypothesis"; published maps of prehistoric irrigating ditches of Salt River Valley, Ariz., leading to building of Roosevelt Dam; delivered address before Engineers' Club, New York, 1901, pointing out that proposed applications of liquid air were in wrong direction, and predicting greater use for nitrogen than for oxygen. Home: Cambridge, Mass. Died Feb. 1, 1928.

McDOWELL, Henry Clay, judge; b. Louisville, Aug. 24, 1861; s. Henry Clay and Anne (Clay) M.; A.B., Yale, 1884; LL.B., U. of Va., 1887; m. Louise Clay, July 5, 1893. Practiced law, Lynchburg, Va., 1885-1901; U.S. dist. judge, Western Dist. of Va., Nov. 14, 1901—. Republican. Home: Lynchburg, Va. Died Oct. 8, 1933.

McDOWELL, John, clergyman; b. Dalry, Scotland, Sept. 24, 1870; s. William and Margaret (Beggs) M.; student Mt. Hermon Sch., Mass., 1885-90; Princeton U., 1890-94, Princeton Theol. Sem., 1896; D.D., Coll. of Wooster, 1915, Princeton, 1916; LL.D., Occidental Coll., Los Angeles, 1933; m. Minnie M. Fowler, June 2, 1897. Ordained Presbyn. ministry, 1896; pastor Steelton, Pa., 1896-90, Second Av. Ch., Detroit, 1899-1905, Park Ch., Newark, N.J., 1905-15, Brown Memorial Ch., Baltimore, 1915-19; sec. Bd. Nat. Missions of Presbyn. Ch., U.S.A., 1919—, also sec. of com. on social and industrial relations of same bd.; pres. Home Missions Council, 1930-32. Y.M.C.A. religious work dir. for war industries, 1917-18. Moderator Gen. Assembly, Presbyn. Ch., U.S.A., 1933-34. Author: Dwight L. Moody, the Discoverer of Men and Maker of Movements, 1915; Christian Essentials, 1928; Fellowship of Toil, 1930. Home: East Orange, N.J. Died Nov. 13, 1937.

McDOWELL, John Sherman, editor, pub.; b. McArthur, O., Nov. 29, 1868; s. John S. and Mahala J. McD.; ed. high sch., Vallejo, Calif.; m. Myra L. Frierson, Nov. 9, 1904; children—W. Clifford, John S. Began as reporter San Francisco Chronicle, 1887; reporter, later business mgr., Oakland (Calif.) Tribune, 1890-1906; pub. Alameda Daily Argus, 1906-08, Alameda Times-Star, 1908—; pres., gen. mgr. Times-Star Co.; treas. Alameda Community Hotel Corp. Mem. Calif. State Bd. Harbor Commrs., 1926-27. Mem. Alameda Chamber Commerce (pres.). Republican. Elk. Home: Alameda, Calif. Died Nov. 11, 1931.

McDOWELL, Mary E., settlement worker; b. Cincinnati, O., Nov. 30, 1854; d. Malcolm and Jane Welch (Gordon) M.; pub. and pvt. schs. Mem. faculty U. of Chicago; became dir. and head U. of Chicago Settlement, stock yards district, 1893, head resident emeritus; mem. exec. com. Chicago Urban League (succeeding Frederick Douglas Center); executive of Chicago br. of Nat. Assn. for Advancement of Colored People; dir. Chicago Immigrants' Protective League; dir. Council Meth. Fedn. for Social Service; v.p. Ill. Woman's Trade Union League; chmn. com. Ill. League of Women voters, com. on Internat. Cooperation for the Prevention of War; chmn. sub-com. of foreign-born women, and mem. exec. com. on women in industry of Advisory Council of Council Nat. Defense. Commr. of Public Welfare, Chicago, 1923. Awarded Order of the White Lion "for distinctive service," by Czechoslovak Republic; Order of the Grand Duke Gediminas, by Lithuanian Govt., for services rendered Lithuanians in Stockyards dist. of Chicago, 1931. Home: Chicago, Ill. Died Oct. 14, 1936.

McDOWELL, Ralph Walker, surgeon, capt. Med. Corps U.S.N.; b. Altoona, Pa., Feb. 4, 1883; s. Robert and Ida May (Kolley) McD.; M.D., Jefferson Med.

Coll., Phila., Pa., 1905; grad. U.S. Naval Med. Sch., 1909; post-grad. study, U. of Pa., New York Post-grad. Med. Sch.; resident phys. Phila. Gen. Hosp.; m. Ruth, d. Theodore W. Noyes, Feb. 17, 1913; children—Mary, Dean, Theodore Noyes. Commd. med. officer, U.S.N., 1908, and promoted through grades to capt. Med. Corps, 1931. Served as med. officer afloat and ashore, 1908-17; regtl. surgeon with U.S. Marines, A.E.F., France, 1918-19; chief of surg. service, U.S. Naval Hosp., San Diego, Calif., 1919-22; surgeon U.S.S. Relief, hospital ship with U.S. Battle Fleet, 1923-25; chief surgeon, U.S. Naval Hosp., Philadelphia, 1926-29; exec. officer and surgeon, U.S. Naval Hosp., Pearl Harbor, T.H., 1929-31; chief surgeon, U.S. Naval Hosp., Washington, D.C., 1931—; instr. in surgery, U.S. Naval Med. Sch., Washington, D.C. Fellow Am. Coll. Surgeons; D.S.M. (U.S.); Legion of Honor (France). Republican. Presbyn. Mason. Home: Washington, D.C. Died Feb. 22, 1935.

McDOWELL, William Fraser, bishop; b. Millersburg, O., Feb. 4, 1858; s. David A. and Rebecca (Fraser) M.; A.B., Ohio Wesleyan, 1879, Ph.D., 1893; S.T.B., Boston U., 1882; D.D., Ohio Wesleyan, 1894, Wesleyan, 1903; LL.D., U. of Denver, 1904, Northwestern, 1904, American U., 1934; L.H.D., U. of Vt., 1914; m. Clotilda Lyon, Sept. 20, 1882 (died 1930); 1 dau., Olive V. (dec.). Ordained M.E. ministry, 1882; pastor Lodi, O., 1882-83, Oberlin, O., 1883-85, Tiffin, O., 1885-90; chancellor U. of Denver, 1890-99; corr. sec. Bd. Edn., M.E. Ch., 1899-1904; elected bishop, May 1904; resident bishop at Chicago, 1904-16, at Washington, D.C., 1916-32 (retired). Cole lecturer, Vanderbilt U., 1910; Lyman Beecher lecturer, Yale, 1917; Mendenhall lecturer, De Pauw U., 1922; Merrick lecturer Ohio Wesleyan U., Earl lecturer Pacific School of Religion, 1926; alumni lecturer Gammon Sch. of Theology, 1927; Wilkin lecturer Wesley Foundation, U. of Ill., 1928; Drew lecturer Drew Univ., 1933. Chmn. Washington office Federal Council of Chs. Officially visited India, China, P.I., and Japan, 1910-11. Author: In the School of Christ, 1910; A Man's Religion, 1913; Good Ministers of Jesus Christ, 1917; This Mind, 1922; Making a Personal Faith, 1924; That I May Save Some, 1927; Them He Also Called, 1929; "Father and Brethren" Lectures on Christian Biography, 1933. Home: Washington, D.C. Died Apr. 26, 1937.

McDOWELL, William George, bishop; b. Lexington, Va., Aug. 2, 1882; s. William George and Ruth Conway (Prichard) McD.; B.A., Washington and Lee U., 1902; B.D., Va. Theol. Sem., 1909, D.D., 1922; D.D., U. of the South, 1923, Washington and Lee U., 1923; m. Mary Meade Phelps, May 25, 1915; children—William George, Richard Edward, Robert (dec.), John Meade, Alan, Douglas Randolph, Mary Meade. Deacon and priest, P.E. Ch., 1909; rector Meherrin Parish, Va., 1909-13, Emmanuel Ch., Staunton, Va., 1913-18; 1st lt. chaplain U.S.A., 1918-19; student pastor Ala. Poly. Inst., 1919-22; bishop coadjutor of Ala., 1922; bishop of Ala., 1928. Trustee U. of the South. Home: Birmingham, Ala. Died Mar. 20, 1938.

McEACHRON, Duncan Lendrum, educator; b. S. Argyle, N.Y., Oct. 20, 1863; s. John A. and Jeanette (Lendrum) M.; A.B., Washburn Coll., Kan., 1894; grad. student U. of Chicago, 1896-97; Litt.D., Monmouth Coll., Ill., 1906; LL.D., Washburn Coll., Kan., 1916; m. Ella Campbell Scott, Aug. 3, 1899; children—Lendrum Scott, John Douglas, Jean. Instr. Franklin (Neb.) Acad., 1894-96; prin. Washburn Coll. Acad., 1897-1900; chmn. faculty, 1900-02, dean and prof. English, 1902-20, sec., July 1, 1911-13, v.p., July 1, 1913—, Washburn Coll. Home: Topeka, Kan. Died May 15, 1937.

McELDOWNEY, Henry C., banker; m. Annabel Doyle. Pres. Union Savings Bank, Union Trust Co., both Pittsburgh; dir. Mellon Nat. Bank, Nat. Union Fire Ins. Co., P.&L.E. R.R. Co., Pittsburgh, McKeesport & Youghiogheny R.R., Pittsburgh Steel Co., Union Fidelity Title Ins. Co., Bankers Trust Co. of New York, etc. Trustee, Homeo. Hosp., Peoples Inst. (Salvation Army), U. of Pittsburgh, Y.M.C.A. of Pittsburgh. Home: Pittsburgh, Pa. Died Mar. 9, 1935.

McELMELL, Jackson, naval officer; b. Phila., June 4, 1834. Apptd. 3d asst. engr. U.S.N., Aug. 2, 1855; 2d asst. engr., July 21, 1858; 1st asst. engr., Mar. 25, 1861; chief engr., Feb. 2, 1862; retired June 4, 1896; chief engr., Feb. 2, 1862; retired June 4, 1896; advanced to rank of rear admiral retired, June 29, 1906, for services during Civil War. Served on various vessels during Civil War; pres. Naval Examining Bd. at Phila., 1888-96. Home: Philadelphia, Pa. Died 1908.

McELROY, Clarence Underwood, lawyer; b. Lebanon, Ky., Nov. 27, 1847; s. A.B. and Eliza (Skiles) M.; grad. Centre Coll., Danville, Ky.; m. Litie H. Trigg, Oct. 15, 1884. Admitted to bar, 1870, and entered practice at Bowling Green, Ky. Presdl. elector, 1876; mem. Ky. General Assembly, 1877-85; Dem. nominee for Congress, 1894; trustee Ky. U., 1893-95; in the Orient, 1908; mem. Ky. Tax Commn., 1909—; Ky. mem. Lakes-to-Gulf Deep Waterway Commn.; chmn. Bd. Examiners on Admission to the bar, July 1918—. Home: Bowling Green, Ky. Deceased.

McELROY, George Wightman, naval officer; b. Henry, Ill., Mar. 19, 1858; s. George B. and Mary (Good) M.; grad. U.S. Naval Acad., 1878; unmarried. Asst. engr. June 20, 1880; promoted through grades to rear adm., Aug. 29, 1916. Served on Gloucester, Spanish-Am. War, 1898; in charge engring. dept., Wisconsin, 1901-04; insp. machinery and engring. material, Thurlow, Pa., 1904; in charge dept. steam engring., Naval Sta., Cavité, P.I., 1905-06; insp. machinery, Bath Iron Works, 1906. Babcock & Wilcox Co., Bayonne, N.J., 1906-09; insp. engring. material, Eastern N.Y. and N.J. dists., 1909-11, New York Shipbuilding Co., Camden, N.J., 1911-13; insp. engring. material, Pittsburgh Dist., 1913-15; apptd. insp. machinery and ordnance, Fore River Shipbuilding Co., Quincy, Mass., Mar. 19, 1915; later insp. engring. material, Brooklyn Dist.; retired Mar. 19, 1922. Advanced 3 numbers in rank "for eminent and conspicuous conduct in battle during Spanish-Am. War." Home: Adrian, Mich. Died Jan. 6, 1931.

McELROY, Henry F., city manager; b. Amboy, Ill., Aug. 17, 1865; s. B.E. and Anne McE.; ed. pub. schs., Dunlap, Ia.; married, Oct. 7, 1906 (wife dec.); children—Mary, Henry F. Began as salesman country store, 1880; later operated real estate business, now city manager, Kansas City, Mo. Democrat. Mason. Home: Kansas City, Mo. Died Sept. 15, 1939.

McELROY, John, editor; b. Greenup Co., Ky., Aug. 25, 1846; s. Robert and Mary (Henderson) M.; common sch. edn.; m. Elsie Pomeroy, Feb. 1866 (dec.); children—Karl Pomeroy, Elsie Pomeroy (Mrs. H. D. Slater); m. 2d, Isabel Worrell Ball, May 16, 1925. Learned printing trade and worked at St. Louis and Chicago; enlisted in McClernand Body Guards, Oct. 1862, and became acting sergt.-maj., 16th Ill. Cav.; was taken prisoner at Jonesville, Va., Jan. 3, 1864, and confined in Andersonville and other prisons until close of war; reporter on Chicago papers, 1868-74; editor Toledo Blade, 1874-84; mng. editor National Tribune, 1884—. Author: Andersonville, 1879; Army of the Cumberland, 1906; Economic Functions of Vice, 1907; Army of the Tennessee, 1907; Army of the Potomac, 1908; The Struggle for Missouri, 1909. Comdr. Kit Carson, G.A.R., 12 times; comdr. Dept. of Potomac G.A.R., 3 times; sr. vice comdr. in chief G.A.R., 1901. Home: Washington, D.C. Died Oct. 12, 1929.

McELROY, Mary Arthur; b. Greenwich, N.Y., 1842; d. Rev. William and Malvina (Stone) Arthur; sister of Chester Alan Arthur, 21st President of the United States; ed. Emma Willard's Female Sem., Troy, N.Y.; m. John E. McElroy, 1861. During her brother's term as President (he being a widower) she presided as mistress of the White House. Home: Albany, N.Y. Died Jan. 8, 1917.

McELROY, William H., lecturer; b. Albany, N.Y.; s. William and Jane (McMullen) M.; A.B., Union Coll., 1860 (LL.D.); m. Ella Robinson, 1871 (died 1892); 2d, Mary Livingston McDonnell, 1898. Associated with late Charles Emory Smith in editing Albany Journal; later on staff New York Tribune, and Mail and Express; editor Rochester Post-Express, 1895-98. Republican. Author: Matthew Middlemas' Experiment, 1888; An Overture to William Tell, 1892; An Old War Horse to a Young Politician; A Brazilian Wedding. Deceased.

McELVEEN, William Thomas, clergyman; b. New York, Oct. 3, 1867; s. James and Mary (Bradford) M.; A.B., Coll. City of New York, 1887; Ph.D., U. of New York, 1892; grad. Union Theol. Sem., 1890; m. Eva Lilian Montross, Oct. 1890; 1 dau., Mrs. Eva L. Krumsick; m. 2d, Helen L. Thomas, June 1929. Ordained Congl. ministry, 1890; pastor North Ch., New York, 1890-96, New England Ch., Brooklyn, 1896-99, Shawmut Ch., Boston, 1899-1908, First Ch., Evanston, Ill., 1908-18, Manhattan Congl. Ch., N.Y. City, 1918-19, First Ch., Portland, Ore., 1919-23, Plymouth Ch., St. Paul, Minn., 1923-26, Pilgrim Ch., Chicago, 1926-28, Pilgrim Ch., Evanston, 1928-30, Congl. Christian Ch., Atlanta, 1930—. Home: Atlanta, Ga. Died June 19, 1933.

McENERY, Samuel Douglas, senator; b. Monroe, La., May 28, 1837; s. Henry O'Neil and Caroline (Douglas) M.; ed. Spring Mill Coll., nr. Mobile, Ala., U.S. Naval Acad. and U. of Va.; LL.B., State and Nat. Law Sch., Poughkeepsie, N.Y., 1859; served as lt. in C.S.A.; after war engaged in law practice; m. Elizabeth Phillips, June 27, 1878. Elected lt. gov. of La., 1879, becoming gov. Oct. 1881, on death of Gov. Wiltz; elected gov. for term, 1884-88; asso. justice Supreme Ct. of La., 1888-97; Dem. nominee for gov., 1891; U.S. senator, 1897-1903, 1903-09, 1909-15. Democrat. Died 1910.

McEVOY, James, lawyer; b. Baltimore, Md., Dec. 12, 1874; s. James and Nannie (Sowers) McE.; ed. pvt. schs., Baltimore; LL.B., U. of Md., 1900; m. Anna G. Lippincott, Oct. 30, 1907 (died 1927); children—Anne L. (Mrs. Cyril H. Moore), James, John K., Mary R.; m. 2d, Ruth M. Morgan, May 15, 1932. Admitted to Md. bar, 1900; in gen. practice, Baltimore, 1900-16, New York, 1916-20; dir. patent sect., Gen. Motors Corp., 1920—. Pres. Detroit Board of Commerce, Detroit Community Fund. Episcopalian. Home: Detroit, Mich. Died Feb. 12, 1941.

McEWAN, William Leonard, clergyman; b. Frankfort, Ky., Oct. 17, 1859; A.B., Centre Coll., Ky., 1882; grad. Princeton Theol. Sem., 1885; D.D., Central U., Danville, Ky., 1894, U. of Pittsburgh, 1895; LL.D., Maryville Coll., Tenn., 1919, U. of Wooster, 1919; m. Eleanor Fulton. Ordained Presbyn. ministry, 1885; pastor Rodney St. Ch., Wilmington, Del., 1886-92, Webster Groves, Mo., 1892-94, Third Church, Pittsburgh, 1894-1931 (emeritus). Pres. bd. trustees Princeton Theol. Sem., Presbytery of Pittsburgh, Am. Hussite Soc., Rochester Home for Epileptics; v.p. bd. of trustees Am. Tract Soc., Grove City Coll.; trustee Western Theol. Sem., Beaver Coll., Pa. Coll. for Women, Washington Coll., Maryville Coll. Home: Pittsburgh, Pa. Died Nov. 4, 1937.

McFADDEN, George, merchant; b. Apr. 30, 1873; s. George H. and Emily B. (Kennedy) M.; B.A., U. of Pa., 1893; m. Josephine Burton McIlvain, Apr. 27, 1906; children—Caroline Burton, George H., Emily B., Alexander B. Mem. Geo. H. McFadden & Bro., 1895—, now sr. mgr. partner; trustee Penn Mut. Life Ins. Co. Representative in France, hdqrs. Paris, of U.S. Food Admn., Blockade U.S. War Trade Bd.; also associated by the Treasury Dept., with Asst. Sec. Oscar Crosby, for consideration of financial questions; hon. 1st sec. of embassy; an economic adviser during peace negotiations in Paris and one of the two civilian Am. members of the Armistice Commn. Awarded D.S.M. by General Pershing, 1919, "for exceptionally meritorious and distinguished services in many matters of vital importance to the A.E.F." Presbyn. Home: Villa Nova, Pa. Died Jan. 5, 1931.

McFADDEN, George H., merchant; b. Phila., Pa., July 24, 1847; s. George and Charlotte (Elliott) M.; ed. Friends' Central High Sch., Phila.; m. Emily B. Kennedy, Apr. 20, 1871. In mercantile business, Phila., 1868—; now sr. mem. George H. McFadden & Bro. Trustee Hosp. of U. of Pa., Merchants' Fund. Presbyn. Home: Philadelphia, Pa. Died Oct. 16, 1926.

McFADDEN, Louis T., congressman; b. Troy, Pa., July 25, 1876; s. Theodore L. and Julia (Babb) M.; ed. pub. schs. and commercial coll.; m. Helen Westgate, Oct. 12, 1898. Began at 16 as office boy, First Nat. Bank, Canton, Pa.; elected cashier, 1899, and pres., Jan. 11, 1916. Mem. 64th to 73d Congresses (1915-35), 15th Pa. Dist.; chmn. Com. on Banking and Currency, 1920-32. Republican. Presbyn. Mason. Home: Canton, Pa. Died Oct. 1, 1936.

McFADEN, Frank Talbot, clergyman; b. Salisbury, Md., Feb. 5, 1864; s. Rev. Joseph Alexander and Mary Anna (Duke) McF.; A.B., B.Litt., Hampden-Sydney (Va.) Coll., 1886; B.D., Union Theol. Sem. Va., 1889; D.D., Washington and Lee, 1902; m. Mary Minge Friend, Apr. 10, 1890; children—Mary (Mrs. L. C. Caldwell), Natalie Friend (wife of Dr. W. B. Blanton), Frances Talbot (wife of Rev. E. D. Witherspoon), Frank Talbot. Ordained ministry of the Presbyterian Ch. in U.S., 1889; pastor successively Marion, Va., First Ch., Lynchburg, First Ch., Richmond, until 1922; pres. Gen. Training Sch., Gen. Assembly Presbyn. Ch. in U.S., 1922-23 (pres. bd.); pastor First Ch., Winchester, 1923—. Col. and chaplain on staff of Gov. Trinkle; maj. asst. chaplain gen. Va. Div., U.C.V. Trustee Union Theol. Sem., Hampden-Sydney Coll., Mary Baldwin Coll. Mason. Home: Winchester, Va. Died Aug. 5, 1933.

McFARLAND, George Austin, coll. pres.; b. Chagrin Falls, O., Apr. 8, 1858; s. Johnston and Isabel (Watson) M.; B.S., Hiram Coll., Ohio, 1883, M.S., 1886, A.M., 1905; LL.D., Fargo Coll., N. Dak., 1922; m. Duella Harris, Aug. 7, 1884; children—Elsie Winona (Mrs. J. A. McLean), Genevieve (Mrs. E. B. Cox), Eugene Harris, Robert Kenneth, Dorothy Bruce (Mrs. H. U. Thomas), Pauline Harris (Mrs. H. H. Fisher), Superintendent of schools, Scotland, S.D., 1884-87; founder and editor Dakota Educator (now South Dakota Educator), 1887-90; prof. psychology and history, State Normal Sch., Madison, S.D., 1890-91; pres. State Normal School, Valley City, N.D., 1892-1918; asst. supt. pub. instrn., Jan. 1-Sept. 1, 1919; supt. sch., Williston, N.D., 1919-22; pres. State Teachers Coll., Minot, N.D., 1922—. Mem. and sec. Territorial Bd. of Edn., Mar. 1887-May 1889; mem. N.D. Ednl. Commn. for adjustment of the higher ednl. instns. of the state; mem. N.D. State Bd. Edn., 1915-17. Conglist. Home: Minot, N.D. Died June 17, 1938.

McFARLAND, John Thomas, clergyman; b. Mt. Vernon, Ind., Jan. 2, 1851; s. Sylvanas and Elizabeth (Ginn) M.; student Ia. Wesleyan U.; A.B., Simpson Coll., Ia., 1873; B.D., Boston U., 1878; (D.D., U. of Southern Calif., 1886; LL.D., Simpson, 1894); m. Mary Burt, Aug. 19, 1873. Ordained M.E. ministry, 1873; pastor Millersburg, Ia., 1873-75, Sweetland Center, Ia., 1875-76; Portsmouth, R.I., 1876-78, Eddyville, Ia., 1878-79, Elmwood, Ill., 1879-80, First Ch., Peoria, Ill., 1880-82; v.p., 1882-84, pres., 1884-91, Ia. Wesleyan U.; pastor Grace Ch., Jacksonville, Ill., 1891-96, New York Av. Ch., Brooklyn, 1897-99, First Ch., Topeka, Kan., 1899-1904; editor S.S. literature of M.E. Ch., June 1904—. Republican. Author: Preservation vs. the Rescue of the Child; The Book and the Child; Etchings of the Master. Home: Maplewood, N.J. Died Dec. 22, 1913.

McFARLAND, Robert White, mathematician; b. Champain Co., O., June 16, 1825; s. Robert and Eunice (Dorsey) M.; A.B., Ohio Wesleyan U., 1847, A.M., 1850 (LL.D., 1884); m. Mary A. Smart, Mar. 19, 1851. Teacher of mathematics, Greenfield Sem., 1848-51; supt. pub. schs., Chillicothe, O., 1851-53; prof. mathematics, Madison Coll., Ohio, 1853-56, Miami U., 1856-73, Ohio State U., 1873-85; pres. Miami U., 1885-88; emeritus prof. civ. engring., Ohio State U., 1902—. Computed the eccentricity of the earth's orbit and the longitude of the perihelion for 4,500,000 yrs., at intervals of 10,000 yrs. (Am. Jour. Science, 1880-3, Vol. XX.) Capt. Co. A, 86th Ohio Inf., 1862; lt. col., 1863-64. Editor 6 books of Virgil, 1849. Home: Oxford, O. Died 1910.

McFARLAND, Silas Clark, consul-gen.; b. Mt. Pleasant, Ia., June 3, 1859; s. Samuel and Mary A. (Woolson) M.; ed. Cornell Coll., Mt. Vernon, Ia., and Wesleyan Univ.; m. Marie Eiboeck, Sept. 1 1886. Editor and pub. Marshalltown (Ia.) Times, 1883-99; consul at Nottingham, 1899-1902, at Reichenberg, 1902-07; consul-gen. at St. Gall, Mar. 30, 1907—. Home: Marshalltown, Ia. Died 1908.

McFARLAND, Thomas Bard, jurist; b. Mercersburg, Pa., Apr. 19, 1828; s. John and Eliza (Parker) McF.; grad. Marshall Coll., Mercersburg, Pa.; studied law with Robert M. Bard, Chambersburg, Pa.; admitted to bar, 1849; m. Susie Briggs, 1861. Dist. judge, Nevada and Placer Cos., Calif., 1862-70; register U. S. land office, Sacramento, Calif., 1874-78; judge Superior Court, Sacramento, Co., Calif., 1882-86; mem. Calif. constl. conv., 1879; justice Supreme Court Calif., 1886—. Republican. Home: San Francisco, Calif. Died 1908.

McFARLAND, Walter Martin, engineer; b. Washington, D.C., Aug. 5, 1859; s. John M. and Sarah J. (Slater) M.; grad. U.S. Naval Acad., 1879; unmarried. Served on various naval vessels; asst. prof. mech. engineering, Cornell, 1883-85; twice asst. (once prin. asst.) to Admiral Melville, engr.-in-chief U.S. Navy; mem. bd. to reorganize personnel of U.S.N., 1897; chief engr. U.S.N., 1898; lt. U.S.N., Mar. 3, 1899; resigned, 1899; acting v.p. Westinghouse Electric & Mfg. Co., 1899-1910; mgr. marine dept., Babcock & Wilcox Boiler Co., 1910-31. Sec. div. marine engring. Internat. Engring. Congress, 1893; pres. Soc. Naval Architects and Marine Engrs., 1922-24; v.p. Am. Soc. Mech. Engrs., 1907-08. Lecturer at Cornell, Columbia, Johns Hopkins, U.S. Naval War Coll. and Post Grad. Sch., of U.S. Navy, on engring. and econ. subjects. Pres. trustees Webb Inst. of Naval Architecture, 1926-31; pres. Naval Acad. Graduates Assn., New York, 1928, sr. mem. council, 1928—. Died 1935.

McFAUL, James Augustine, bishop; b. nr. Larne, Co. Antrim, Ireland, June 6, 1850; s. James and Mary (Hefferman) M.; ed. St. Vincent's Coll., Westmoreland Co., Pa.; Coll. of St. Francis Xavier, New York; grad. Seton Hall. S. Orange, N.J., 1873; (D.D., 1894, LL.D., 1898, Seton Hall; LL.D., St. Francis Xavier, 1909). Ordained priest, May 26, 1877; sec. to Bishop O'Farrell, Trenton, N.J., 1882-84; pastor Long Branch, N.J., 1883-90; chancellor, diocese of Trenton, 1890-92; vicar-gen., 1892-94; consecrated bishop of Trenton, Oct. 18, 1894. Has lectured and written on Christian edn., etc. Died June 16, 1917.

McFIE, John Robert, lawyer; b. Washington Co., Ill., Oct. 9, 1848; s. John and Elisabeth (Borland) M.; acad. edn., Randolph Co., Ill.; m. Mary Steele, Oct. 9, 1876. Pvt. Co. E, 30th Ill. Vet. Vol. Inf., Feb. 1864; practiced in Ill. 13 yrs.; mem. Ill. Ho. of Rep., 31st and 33d Gen. Assemblies; register U.S. Land Office, Las Cruces, N.M., 1884-85; asso. justice Supreme Ct. of N.M., 1889-93, and 1897-1912. Now sr. mem. McFie, Edwards & McFie, Santa Fe and Gallup, N.M. Pres. bd. regents Agrl. and Mech. Coll., 7 yrs.; pres. bd. regents Archæol. Sch. and Mus. of N.M., Santa Fe; pres. N.M. Archæol. Soc. Past dept. comdr. G.A.R. Home: Santa Fe, N.M. Died July 19, 1930.

McGAFFIN, Alexander, clergyman; b. Banbridge, Co. Down, Ireland, Feb. 15, 1870; s. Alexander and Elizabeth (Geary) McG.; came to U.S., 1885; grad. Mt. Herman (Mass.) Sch., 1889; B.A., Princeton, 1894, M.A., 1897; grad. Princeton Theol. Sem., 1897; D.D., Western Reserve, 1911; m. Anna Sternberg DeYoe, Aug. 3, 1904; 1 dau., Elizabeth Anna DeYoe. Ordained Presbyn. ministry, 1897; pastor Mt. Sterling, Ill., 1897-99, 2d Ch., Brooklyn, N.Y., 1899-1902, Lockport, N.Y., 1904-08, Euclid Av. Ch., Cleveland, O., 1908-20, Ch. of the Covenant, Cleveland, 1920—. Home: Hewitt, N.J. Died Aug. 13, 1929.

McGARRAH, Gates W., banker; b. Monroe, N.Y., 1863; m. Elizabeth Wallace. Clk. Goshen (N.Y.) Nat. Bank, 1881; cashier and pres. to 1904, Leather Mfrs. Nat. Bank of N.Y.; chmn. exec. com. Chase Nat. Bank, 1926-27; chmn. bd. and federal reserve agent, Federal Reserve Bank of N.Y., until 1930; pres. Bank for Internat. Settlements, Basle, Switzerland, 1930-33. Pres. N.Y. Clearing House Assn., 1917-19, chmn. Clearing House Com., 1917, 22, 23; apptd. by Reparations Commn. Am. mem. Gen. Council, Reichsbank, Berlin, Germany, 1924. Dir. Am. Express Co., Bankers Trust Co., Del. & Hudson Co., D.&H. R.R. corp.; trustee Mercantile Stores, Greenwich Savings Bank. Home: New York, N.Y. Died Nov. 5, 1940.

McGARRY, William James, clergyman; b. Hamilton, Mass., Mar. 14, 1894; s. Edward Leslie and Julia Agnes (Burns) McG.; A.B., Woodstock Coll., 1917, A.M., 1918, S.T.D., 1926; Ph.D., Fordham U., 1922, hon. Litt.D., 1938; S.S.Lic., Pontifical Biblical Inst., Rome, Italy, 1930; hon. LL.D., Holy Cross U., Worcester, Mass., 1938. Mem. Soc. of Jesus, 1911—; ordained priest Roman Cath. Ch., 1925. Prof. of mathematics and philosophy, Fordham U., 1918-22; prof. of sacred scriptures, Weston Coll., 1930-35, prof. dogmatic theology, 1935-37, dean of philosophy, 1930-33, dean of studies, 1934-37; pres. Boston Coll., Chestnut Hill, Mass., 1937-39; editor Theological Studies, 1939—. Author: The Biblical Commission, 1931; Anthropology and Knowledge of God, 1932; Mystical Body, 1935; Paul and the Crucified, 1939. Died Sept. 23, 1941.

McGARVEY, John William, theologian; b. Hopkinsville, Ky., Mar. 1, 1829; s. John and Sallie Ann (Thomson) M.; A.B., Bethany Coll., W.Va., 1850, A.M., 1853 (LL.D., 1881); m. Ottie Hix, Mar. 23, 1853. Ordained Christian (Disciples) ministry, 1852; pastor, Fayette, Mo., 1851-53, Dover, Mo., 1853-62, Lexington, Ky., 1862-74; prof. sacred history, 1865—, pres. Coll. of the Bible, 1895—, Ky. U. Connected with religious newspapers as corr. and editor for 50 yrs. Author: Commentaries on Acts of Apostles, 1863, 1893, and on Matthew and Mark, 1875; Lands of the Bible, 1881; Text and Canon of New Testament, 1886; Credibility and Inspiration of the New Testament, 1891; McGarvey's Sermons, 1894; Jesus and Jonah, 1897; Authorship of Deuteronomy, 1902. Home: Lexington, Ky. Died 1911.

McGARVEY, William, clergyman; b. Phila., Aug. 14, 1861; s. Alexander and Mary Jane (Colwell) M.; educated private tutors; B.D., Gen. Theol. Sem., New York, 1887; (D.D., Nashotah Sem., Wis., 1904). Ordained P.E. ministry, Aug. 22, 1886; curate Ch. of the Evangelists, Phila., 1886-96; rector St. Elizabeth's Ch., Phila., 1896-1908; withdrew from P.E. Ch., May 10, 1908, and received into Catholic Ch., May 27, 1908. Master Congregation of the Companions of the Holy Saviour (soc. of Episcopalian clergymen), 1890-1908; chaplain gen. of Episcopalian Sisters of St. Mary in U.S., 1902-08; at St. Charles' Sem., Overbrook, Pa., and Catholic U., Washington, 1908-10; ordained priest, Dec. 17, 1910; asst. priest, Ch. of the Holy Child, Phila., 1911-12, St. James' Ch., 1912-20; apptd. pastor Holy Infancy Ch., Bethlehem, Pa., 1919; made domestic prelate by late Pope Benedict XV, Mar. 17, 1921. Author: Catechetical Instruction, 1893; The Council of Nicaea, 1894; Liturgiæ Americanæ, 1895; The Doctrine of the Church of England and of St. Thomas on the Real Presence, 1900; The Ceremonies of Low Mass, 1905. Home: Bethlehem, Pa. Died Feb. 27, 1924.

McGAUGH, Elmer Thomas, M.D.; b. Richmond, Mo., Jan. 2, 1872; s. George Washington and Sarah Ann (Brown) McG.; B.L., U. of Mo., 1897, A.M., 1898, M.D., 1899; m. Lucy Hart, Jan. 2, 1903 (died 1920); m. 2d, Nan Jo Stalcup, June 24, 1924. Supt. State Hosp., Fulton, Mo., 1927-30; mayor of Richmond, 1931-32; mem. State Bd. of Health, Mo., 1926-30; apptd. state health commr. of Mo., May 1, 1933, term of 4 yrs., also mem. State Bd. of Health; partner Richmond Drug Co. Mem. Mo. State Dem. Com., 1931-34. Mason, Elk. Home: Jefferson City, Mo. Deceased.

McGAW, George Keen, merchant; b. Harford Co., Md., Jan. 8, 1850; s. John and Mary Bartol (Keen) M.; ed. Bel Air and West Nottingham acads., Md.; m. Margaret A. Warden, Jan. 16, 1877. Entered grocery business, 1875; mem. Hopper, McGaw, & Co., McGaw, Davis & Co. Trustee Johns Hopkins Hosp., Tome Inst., Egerton Home, Baltimore Free Dispensary. Democrat. Presbyn. Mason. Pres. St. Andrew's Society. Home: Baltimore, Md. Died Sept. 9, 1919.

McGEACHY, Archibald Alexander, clergyman; b. Robeson Co., N.C., Mar. 3, 1869; s. Neill R. and Sarah (McFayden) McG.; A.B., Davidson (N.C.) Coll., 1891; B.D., Union Theol. in Va., 1894; D.D., Austin (Tex.) Coll., 1906; m. Irving Harding, July 14, 1910. Ordained ministry Presbyn. Ch. in U.S., 1894; pastor successively Pleasant Hill, and Fulton, Mo., and Sherman, Tex., until 1908, 2d Ch., Charlotte, N.C., 1908— (2,000 members). Organized first men's club in Southern Presbyn. Ch., 1919. Pres. bd. Queen's Coll., State Home and Industrial Sch. for Girls and Women (founder), Home for Delinquent Boys of Mecklenburg County (unit of Stonewall Jackson Tr. Sch.); trustee Davidson Coll. Democrat. Home: Charlotte, N.C. Died Sept. 24, 1928.

McGEE, James Ellington, clergyman; b. Washington, Ark., Jan. 3, 1868; s. Michael Macduffie and Carrie (Lowry) M.; student Vanderbilt U., 1888-89; Ohio Wesleyan U., 1897-1901; A.B., Boston U., 1902, A.M., 1903, Ph.D., 1912; m. May Genevieve De Silva, Oct. 23, 1889. Pastor 1st Ch., Bonne Terre, Mo., 1889-92, 1st Ch., Fredericktown, Mo., 1892-95, Park View Ch., Portsmouth, Va., 1902-04, Pleasant Ridge Ch., Cincinnati, O., 1904-08, Trinity Ch., Dayton, O., 1908-11, Worthington, O., 1911-14, 1st Ch., Marietta, O., 1914-16, Hamline Ch., Steubenville, O., 1916-19, 1st M.E. Ch., Massilon, O., 1919-21. Author: The Religion of a Person, 1912. Home: Columbus, O. Died Aug. 11, 1925.

McGEE, John Bernard, physician; b. Boston, July 3, 1853; s. Peter and Mary A. (Donnelly) M.; grad. pub. schs., Boston; M.D., Western Reserve U., 1878; m. Mary Lavina Rogers, Oct. 1884 (died 1885); 2d, Elizabeth Dieter, Sept. 17, 1892. Formerly prof. therapeutics, and sec. Cleveland Coll. of Phys. and Surg., and asso. prof. therapeutics, Western Reserve U. Home: Cleveland, O. Died Feb. 10, 1923.

McGEE, John Franklin, lawyer; b. Amboy, Ill., Jan. 1, 1861; s. Hugh Henry and Margaret (Heenan) M.; grad. Amboy High Sch., 1881; read law with Hon. Vespasian Warner; m. Elizabeth L. Ryan, Sept. 14, 1884. Admitted to Ill. bar, 1882, Dak. Ty. bar, 1883, and practiced at Devil's Lake; removed to Minneapolis, 1887; counsel for C.,G.W. Ry., 1887-97, and from 1902; apptd. judge 4th Jud. Dist. of Minn., 1897; elected to same office, 1898, for term of 6 yrs.; resigned, 1902, and reëntered pvt. practice, specializing in corp. law; apptd. by gov., 1913, mem. com. of 30 to formulate plan for more economical and efficient govt. of Minn. Federal fuel adminstr. for Minn., Oct. 7, 1917-Apr. 1, 1919; mem. Commn. of Pub. Safety, 1917—; U.S. dist. judge, Minn., 1923—. Republican. Catholic. Home: Minneapolis, Minn. Died Feb. 15, 1925.

McGEE, W. J., anthropologist, geologist, hydrologist; b. Dubuque Co., Ia., Apr. 17, 1853; s. James and Martha (Anderson) M.; self ed.; (LL.D., Cornell Coll., Ia., 1901); m. Anita, d. late Simon Newcomb, 1888. While at farm work, 1863-73, studied Latin, higher mathematics, astronomy and surveying; also read law; in land surveying and justice-court practice, 1873-75; invented, patented and mfd. agrl. implements, working at forge and bench, 1874-76; studied geology and archæology, 1875-77; made geologic and topographic survey of Northeastern Iowa —most extensive ever executed in America without public aid, 1877-81; examined and reported upon building stones of Iowa for 10th Census, 1881-82; became attached to U.S. Geol. Survey, and in 1885 assumed charge of important div.; surveyed and mapped 300,000 sq. miles in Southeastern U.S.; compiled geologic maps of U.S. and of New York; investigated Charleston earthquake, 1886; explored, 1894-95, Tiburon Island, home of a savage tribe never before studied. Ethnologist in charge Bur. of Am. Ethnology, 1893-1903; resigned July 1903, to become chiew dept. of anthropology, St. Louis Expn., 1904, bringing together an unprecedented assemblage of the world's peoples; dir. St. Louis Pub. Mus., 1905-07; U.S. commr. Inland Waterways Commn., 1907—; expert U.S. Dept. of Agr., 1907. Lecturer; U.S. commr. Am. Internat. Commn. of Archæology and Ethnology, from 1902; chmn. organizing com. for Internat. Geographic Congress, 1904; senior speaker dept. of anthropology, World's Congress of Arts and Sciences, 1904; sec. Conf. of Governors in White House, 1908. Leading founder Columbian Hist. Soc.; pres. Am. Anthrop. Assn.; pres. Anthrop. Soc. Washington; acting pres. A.A.A.S., 1897-98; pres. Nat. Geog. Soc., 1904-05; v.p. Archæol. Inst. America, 1902-05. Author: Pleistocene History of Northeastern Iowa, 1891; Geology of Chesapeake Bay, 1888; The Lafayette Formation, 1892; The Portable Waters of Eastern U.S., 1894; The Siouan Indians, 1897; Primitive Trephining in Peru, 1898; The Seri Indians, 1900; Primitive Numbers, 1901; Outlines of Hydrology, Bull. Geol. Soc., America, 1908; Soil Erosion, 1911; The Agricultural Duty of Water, 1911. Editor dept. anthropology, Internat. Encyclopedia. Died Sept. 4, 1912.

McGEEHAN, William O., newspaperman; b. San Francisco, Calif., Nov. 22, 1879; s. Hugh and Theresa (O'Connell) M.; m. Sophie Treadwell, Jan. 27, 1910. Began as reporter San Francisco Call, 1900; was city editor, later mng. editor San Francisco Post; moved to New York, 1914; sport editor New York Tribune, 1915-20, mng. editor, 1921-22; sport editor New York Herald, 1922, then same, with New York Herald Tribune. Served with 1st Calif. Vols., Spanish-Am. War and Philippine Insurrection, 1898-99; capt. Inf., U.S.A., 1917-18; maj. Inf. R.C. Home: New York, N.Y. Died Nov. 29, 1933.

McGEHEE, Lucius Polk, dean law sch.; b. on father's estate, "Woodburn," Person Co., N.C., May 14, 1868; s. Montford and Sarah Polk (Badger) M.; A.B., U. of N.C., 1887; studied law U. of N.C., 1890, 1891; m. Julia Leslie Covert, Jan. 28, 1903 (died 1903). Admitted to N.C. bar, 1891, N.Y. bar, 1894; prof. law, U. of North Carolina, 1904-08, dean Law Sch. same, Sept. 1, 1910—. Contbg. editor on Staff Am. and English Ency. of Law, 1894; asso. gen. editor same, 1895-1904. Mem. Commn. to Revise Pub. Laws of N.C., 1917. Democrat. Episcopalian. Author: Due Process of Law, 1906. Died Oct. 11, 1923.

McGIFFERT, Arthur Cushman, theologian; b. Sauquoit, N.Y., Mar. 4, 1861; s. Rev. Joseph Nelson and Harriet Whiting (Cushman) M.; A.B., Western Reserve, 1882, A.M., 1885; grad. Union Theol. Sem., 1885; student U. of Berlin, 1885-86; U. of Marburg, 1886-87; France and Italy, 1887-88; Ph.D., Marburg, 1888; D.D., Western Reserve, 1892, Harvard, 1906,

Presbyn. Coll., Halifax, 1920, St. Andrews, 1922; LL.D., Gettysburg, 1917, Queen's U., Kingston, 1919; m. Eliza Isabelle King, June 9, 1885 (died 1887); 1 dau., Elizabeth (wife of Rev. Dwight F. Mowery); m. 2d, Gertrude Huntington Boyce, Nov. 12, 1891; children—Arthur Cushman, Katharine Wolcott (Mrs. John K. Wright). Ordained Presbyn. ministry, 1888; became Conglist., 1899; instr. and prof. church history, Lane Theol. Sem., Cincinnati, 1888-93; prof. church history, 1893-1927 (emeritus), and pres., 1917-26, Union Theol. Seminary. Author: Translation of Eusebius' Church History (with prolegomena and notes), 1890; A History of Christianity in the Apostolic Age, 1897; The Apostles' Creed, 1902; The Christian Point of View (with Francis Brown and G. W. Knox), 1902; Protestant Thought Before Kant, 1911; Martin Luther, the Man and His Work, 1911; The Rise of Modern Religious Ideas, 1915; The God of the Early Christians, 1924; A History of Christian Thought, vol. 1, 1931, vol. 2, 1932. Address: Dobbs Ferry-on-Hudson, N.Y. Died Feb. 25, 1933.

McGIFFIN, Malcolm, banker; b. Corsica, Pa., June 14, 1872; s. John and Anna Mary (McCormick) McG.; prep. edn., Washington and Jefferson Prep. Sch.; A.B., Washington and Jefferson Coll., 1897; studied law with Patterson, Sterrett & Acheson, Pittsburgh, 1899-1902; unmarried. Admitted to Pa. bar, 1902, and practiced at Pittsburgh, 1902-03; trust officer Equitable Trust Co. of Pittsburgh, 1904-05; asst. trust officer Fidelity Trust Company, 1905-15, trust officer, 1915-18, dir., 1917, pres., 1918—; pres. John F. Scott Co.; v.p. Union-Fidelity Title Ins. Co., Citizens Traction Co.; resident v.p. Am. Surety Co. of New York. Trustee Children's Service Bur. (treas.), Kingsley Assn., Elizabeth Steel Magee Hosp. (chmn. exec. com.); dir. Legal Aid Soc., Travelers Aid Soc.; mem. advisory bd. Protestant Home for Incurables, Home for Aged Protestant Women. Republican. Presbyn. Mason. Home: Pittsburgh, Pa. Deceased.

McGILL, Andrew Ryan, gov., lawyer; b. Saegerstown, Pa., Feb. 19, 1840; s. Charles D. and Angeline (Martin) M.; common sch. and academic edn., Sagerstown, Pa.; studied law in Minn.; m. Mary E. Wilson, Oct. 1, 1880. Gov. Minn., 1887-89; postmaster St. Paul, 1900—. Home: St. Paul, Minn. Died 1905.

McGILL, David Frazier, clergyman; b. West Alexander, Pa., Mar. 22, 1857; s. James L. and Christiana (Sights) M.; A.B., Washington and Jefferson, 1881, A.M., 1884; grad. Allegheny Theol. Sem., 1884; D.D., Muskingum Coll., 1892; LL.D., Washington and Jefferson Coll., 1916; m. Hattie J. Weddle, June 12, 1884; 1 son, James Stewart. Ordained U.P. ministry, 1885; pastor Sixth U.P. Ch., Allegheny, Pa., Jan. 1, 1885-Oct. 9, 1911, U.P. Ch., Ben Avon, Pa., Oct. 24, 1911-Nov. 7, 1915; prof. ecclesiastical history and ch. govt., Pittsburgh Theol. Sem., 1915—. Asso. editor, United Presbyterian, 1891-1914. General sec. of Young People's Christian Union of U.P. Ch., 1897-1900; prin. clerk Gen. Assembly U.P. Ch. of N. America, May 1903—; mem. 9th Gen. Council, and of exec. commn. of the Alliance of Reformed Chs. throughout the World holding the Presbyn. System; treas. Council of Reformed Chs. in America Holding Presbyn. System. Trustee Allegheny Theol. Sem., 1890-1915, Westminister Coll., 1897—. Home: Bellevue, Pa. Died Apr. 26, 1931.

McGILL, J. Nota, lawyer; b. in D.C., Jan. 8, 1867; s. John D. and Mary J. M.; ed. pub. and pvt. schs.; LL.B., Georgetown U., 1887, LL.M., 1888; m. Frances Maloy, Sept. 27, 1897. In patent law practice at Washington, 1887—; register of wills, D.C., 1895-99; lecturer on patent law, Georgetown U. Law Sch., 1898—. Pres. bd. trustees, Nat. Training Sch. for Girls; v.p. Union Trust Co., D.C. Home: Washington, D.C. Died 1915.

McGILL, John Dale, surgeon; b. Allegheny City, Pa., Dec. 23, 1846; s. Alexander T. (D.D., LL.D.) and Ellen Acheson (McCulloch) M.; A.B., Princeton, 1867, A.M., 1870; M.D., U. of Pa., 1870; m. Josephine Emma Robinson, May 17, 1883 (died 1888). In practice at Jersey City, 1871—; med. dir. St. Francis' Hosp., 1887—; surgeon-gen. N.J.N.G., 1886—. Pres. Hudson Co. Nat. Bank, 1901—. Fellow N.J. State Med. Society. Home: Jersey City, N.J. Died Nov. 26, 1912.

McGILL, Thomas Julian, pres. Twin City Rapid Transit Co.; b. Leesburg, Va., Aug. 21, 1876; s. Samuel and Elizabeth Randolph (Fauntleroy) McG.; m. Minnie Shores, June 24, 1903; children—Virginia Randolph, Janet Shores, Ann Fauntleroy. Sales mgr. Siemers & Halske Electric Co. of America, 1896-98; dist. mgr. Westinghouse Electric & Mfg. Co., 1902-21; v.p. st. rys., Minneapolis and St. Paul, 1921—; pres. Twin City Rapid Transit Co., 1931—; pres. Minneapolis St. Ry. Co., St. Paul City Ry. Co., Minneapolis & St. Paul Suburban R.R. Co., Transit Supply Co. Democrat. Episcopalian. Home: Minneapolis, Minn. Died Oct. 10, 1936.

McGILLICUDDY, Daniel John, congressman; b. Lewiston, Me., Aug. 27, 1859; s. John and Ellen (Byrnes) M.; A.B., Bowdoin Coll., 1881; m. Minnie M. Sprague, July 5, 1898. Admitted to bar, 1883, and entered practice at Lewiston. Mem. Me. Ho. of Rep., 1884-85; mayor, Lewiston, 1887, 1890, 1902; Dem. candidate for Congress, 2d Me. Dist., 1906, 1908; elected 62d to 64th Congresses (1911-17), 2d Dist. Mem. Dem. Nat. Com., 1912-32. Home: Lewiston, Me. Died July 30, 1936.

McGINLEY, Daniel Eugene, educator, consular officer; b. Saxonville, Mass., Jan. 3, 1846; s. Daniel and Ann (Sheridan) M.; ed. pub. schs., Saukville, Wis., 1854-58, after that self-educated; unmarried. Lived on backwoods farm, 1851-63; enlisted Oct. 1, 1863, in 16th Wis. vols.; was in all of Gen. Sherman's campaigns from May 1864, to end of war; lumberman, 1868-73; pub. sch. teacher, 1875-92; wrote for press, 1878-97. Sec. Ozaukee Co. Agrl. Soc., 1887-98; pres. Co. Teachers' Assn., 1879-81, 1895-98; sec. Wis. State Fair Mgrs. Assn., 1892-96; U.S. consul at Athens, Greece, Jan. 6, 1898—. Home: Cedarburg, Wis. Died 1904.

McGINNESS, John Randolph, brig. gen. U.S.A.; b. nr. Dublin, Ireland, Sept. 17, 1840; s. Francis and Anne (Hartford) M.; grad. U.S. Mil. Acad., 1863; unmarried. Apptd. 1st lt. ordnance, June 11, 1863, took part in Civil War, becoming chief ordnance officer Dept. of the South, Apr. 1864, and afterward on various duties; bvtd. capt. and maj. for gallant and meritorious services before Charleston; promoted capt., Feb. 10, 1869; maj., June 1, 1881; lt. col., July 7, 1898; col., June 14, 1902; chief ordnance officer P.I., Dec. 31, 1898-Apr. 1, 1901, Dept. Calif., 1901-02, Dept. Lakes, 1902-04; brig. gen. and retired, Sept. 17, 1904. Died Dec. 17, 1918.

McGINNIS, Edwin, surgeon; b. Orland, Cook Co., Ill., Aug. 20, 1877; s. James W. and Anna Stacia (Bremner) McG.; A.B., U. of Mich., 1901; M.D., Northwestern U. Med. Sch., 1904; m. Jane Cool, Dec. 26, 1914. Practiced in Chicago, 1904—; asso. oto-laryngologist Children's Memorial Hosp.; asso. laryngologist, Presbyn. Hosp.; clin. asst. prof. otology, Rush Med. Coll.; attending bronchoscopist Edward Hines Hospital. Fellow Am. Coll. Surgeons. Home: Chicago, Ill. Died 1933.

McGINNIS, William F., clergyman; b. Brooklyn, N.Y., Dec. 28, 1867; s. James and Mary A.M.; A.B., St. John's Coll., Brooklyn, 1887, LL.D., 1920; D.D., North Am. Coll., Rome, 1892. Ordained priest R.C. Ch., 1891; pastor St. Brigid's Ch., Westbury, N.Y., 1904-22; rector St. Thomas Aquinas Ch., Brooklyn, 1922. Founder, and pres. Internat. Catholic Truth Soc., 1899—, and editor in chief of Truth (mag.). Pres. Pub. Sch. Bd., Westbury. Home: Brooklyn, N.Y. Died May 16, 1932.

McGINNIS, William Hereford, judge; b. Raleigh Co., W. Va., Dec. 29, 1855; s. James Hereford and Mary (Williams) McG.; ed. common schs.; m. Sallie E. Holroyd, July 16, 1891. Began practice at Beckley, W.Va., 1881; pros. atty. Raleigh Co., 1892-96; mem. W.Va. Senate, 1902-06; chmn. Dem. Exec. Com. of Raleigh Co. many terms, also mem. State Exec. Com.; judge Supreme Court of Appeals, W.Va., Dec. 16, 1922-Dec. 31, 1924. Mem. M.E. Ch., S. Home: Beckley, W.Va. Died Aug. 12, 1930.

McGINTY, George Banks, sec. Interstate Commerce Commn.; b. Monroe Co., Ga., Sept. 8, 1878; s. John Thomas and Louise Marion (Banks) M.; ed. high sch., Forsyth, Ga. and Emory Coll., Oxford, Ga.; m. Leone Elizabeth Spletzer, June 13, 1923; children—Sawtelle, Geo. F. Served as pvt. sec. to v.p. and gen. mgr. Southern Ry. Co. and traveling passenger and freight agt. West Point Route, Montgomery, Ala.; with Interstate Commerce Commn., Nov. 1908—, atty.-examiner, 1911-12, asst. sec., 1912-13, sec., Mar. 10, 1913. Democrat. Methodist. Mason. Home: Washington, D.C. Died Feb. 16, 1937.

McGLANNAN, Alexius, surgeon; b. Baltimore, July 24, 1872; s. Alexius W. and Agnes Veronica (Gallagher) M.; A.B., Calvert Hall, Baltimore, 1887; Ph.G., Md. Coll. Pharmacy, 1890; M.D., Coll. Phys. and Surg., Baltimore, 1895; LL.D., Loyola Coll., 1924; m. Sally Porter Law, July 2, 1910. Prof. surgery, U. of Md. Med. Sch., and Coll. Physicians and Surgeons, Baltimore. Consulting surgeon Mercy Hopsital. Author: Laboratory Manual of Physiological Chemistry, 1900; Simon's Chemistry (collaborator), 1901; Manual of Physics and Inorganic Chemistry, 1903; Manual of Organic and Physiological Chemistry, 1903. Collaborator, Kelly-Musser Therapeutics, also of Tice's System and Lewis' System of Surgery. Home: Baltimore, Md. Died Feb. 25, 1940.

McGLAUFLIN, William Henry, clergyman; b. Charlotte, Me., Oct. 2, 1856; s. Thomas and Alice (McCabe) M.; ed. St. Lawrence U., N.Y.; grad. div. sch., same, 1882; courses in Bibl. langs. under Prof. William R. Harper, 1884-85; spl. studies Am. U., Harriman, Tenn., 1894-95; A.M., 1895; D.D., Am. U., 1896, St. Lawrence U., 1907; m. Lucy Culver Sibley, 1887 (died 1897); m. 2d, Alice Gertrude Coe, 1912. Ordained Universalist ministry, 1882; pastor Friendship, N.Y., 1882-87, Rochester, Minn., 1887-91, Harriman, Tenn., 1891-96, Atlanta, Ga., 1896-1904; tri-state supt. of chs., Minneapolis, 1904-07; gen. supt. Universalist Ch. of America, Jan. 20, 1907-Dec. 1916; pastor Scranton, Pa., 1916—. Past Chancellor K.P., Minn., 1890. Chaplain Good Templars, Ga., 1898-1900; jr. v.comdr. Ala. and Tenn. divs. Sons of Vets., 1901-04; comdr. Pa. Camp 500, S. of Va., 1920-22; hon. chaplain 143d Pa. Regt. G.A.R., 1922; chaplain New England Soc. of Northeastern Pa., 1924—. Pres. Scranton Pub. Forum, 1918-19. Lecturer in colls., high schs., etc., 1903-13; mem. permanent com. on temperance, Universalist Gen. Conv., 1900-08; mem. Am. Council World Alliance for Internat. Friendship Through the Chs.; mem. Pa. Com. on Penal Affairs. Editor Tri-State Messenger, 1904-07. Author: Faith with Power, 1912. Home: Scranton, Pa. Died Mar. 8, 1927.

McGLENNON, Cornelius A., congressman; b. East Newark, N.J., Dec. 10, 1878; A.B., Seton Hall Coll., South Orange, N.J., 1899, A.M., 1901. Pub. and high sch. prin. 15 yrs.; admitted to N.J. bar, 1916; served as mem. N.J. Senate, and as mayor of Newark; mem. 66th Congress (1919-21), 8th New Jersey Dist. Democrat. Mem. Knights of Columbus, Elks. Home: East Newark, N.J. Died June 13, 1931.

McGLOTHLIN, William Joseph, coll. pres.; b. nr. Gallatin, Tenn., Nov. 29, 1867; s. William James Alexander and Elizabeth Ellen (King) M.; A.B., Bethel Coll., Ky., 1889, A.M., 1891; Th.M., Southern Bapt. Theol. Sem., Ky., 1894; Ph.D., U. of Berlin, 1901; D.D., Bethel, 1898; LL.D., Furman U., 1909, Wake Forest Coll., 1914, Baylor U., 1915; m. May Belle Williams, June 8, 1897 (died 1926); children—Bessie May (dec.), Kathryn, Mary Louise, William Joseph, James Harrison. Teacher public schools of Tennessee at intervals, 1884-88; asst. instructor in natural science, Bethel Coll., 1888-89; ordained Baptist ministry, 1891; instructor in mathematics and English, Bardstown (Ky.) Male and Female Inst., 1889-91; tutor in Hebrew and O.T., 1893-94, instr., 1894-96, asst. prof., 1896-99, prof., 1900-19, and dir. correspondence work, 1915-19, Southern Bapt. Theol. Sem.; pres. Furman U., 1919—. Representative of Southern Baptists in Fed. Food Administration, 1917. Author: A Guide to the Study of Church History, 1908; Baptist Confessions of Faith, 1910; A Vital Ministry, 1913; Infant Baptism in History, 1915; The Course of Christian History, 1917; History of Furman University, 1926. Pres. Southern Bapt. Conv., 1930—. Home: Greenville, S.C. Died May 28, 1933.

McGLYNN, Edward, R.C. clergyman; b. New York, Sept. 27, 1837; ed. at Coll. of Propaganda, Rome; pastor St. Stephen's Ch., New York, 1866. Removed for opposing establishing of parochial schools and for advocating single-tax doctrines of Henry George. Refusing to obey a summons to the Vatican he was excommunicated. One of the founders, 1887, and pres. Anti-Poverty Society. Restored to church and priesthood, 1893, and went to Rome; later resumed pastoral labors in New York. Died 1899.

McGOLRICK, James, bishop; b. Tipperary, Ireland, 1841; s. Felix and Bridget (Henry) M.; ed. for priesthood, All Hallows Coll., Dublin. Ordained R.C. priest, 1867; came to U.S. as asst. pastor Cathedral, St. Paul, Minn., 1867-88; pastor Ch. Immaculate Conception, 1868-89; consecrated 1st bishop of Duluth (Minn.), Dec. 27, 1889. Died Jan. 23, 1918.

McGONAGLE, William Albert, railway pres.; b. Conshohocken, Pa., Mar. 28, 1861; s. Joseph and Agnes (McKeeman) M.; B.S., U. of Pa., 1881; m. Sarah L. Sargent, Oct. 5, 1887; children—Joseph Sargent, Robert Emerson, Mrs. Mary Tibbetts, William Albert (dec.). Began active career as transitman in locating the Little Falls & Dakota branch of N.P. Ry.; asst. engr. same, 1881-82; asst. engr., 1882-90, resident engr. and supt. bridges and bldgs., 1890-1901, asst. chief engr., 1901-02, Duluth & Iron Range R.R.; asst. to pres., 1902-03, 1st v.p. and gen. mgr., 1903-09, pres., Mar. 20, 1909—, Duluth, Missabe & Northern Ry. Mason. Second member Duluth Hall of Fame. Home: Duluth, Minn. Died Aug. 2, 1930.

McGOODWIN, Henry Kerr, architect; b. Bowling Green, Ky., Apr. 5, 1871; s. I. D. and Virginia (Wooten) M.; B.S., Ogden Coll., Bowling Green, 1891; B.S. in architecture, Mass. Inst. Tech., 1894; m. Harriet Ford Smith, June 27, 1906. Practiced, Bowling Green and Louisville, 1894-99, Charleston, S.C., 1899-1901; instr. architecture, U. of Pa., 1901-04, Washington U., St. Louis, 1904-06; prof. architecture, Carnegie Inst. of Tech., Pittsburgh, 1906-19; resumed practice at Phila. Apptd. prof. architecture (in charge dept.) and chmn. of faculty of Coll. of Fine Arts, Carnegie Inst. of Tech., Pittsburgh, 1923. Fellow of A.I.A. and mem. Pittsburgh Chapter. Author: Architectural Shades and Shadows, 1904. Deceased.

McGOVERN, John, author; b. Troy, N.Y., Feb. 18, 1850; s. James and Marion (Carter) M.; m. Kate C. Van Arsdale, 1877. Compositor, proofreader and night editor Chicago Tribune, 16 yrs.; from 1880 engaged in lit. work; editor various periodicals, Current, Graphic, Ill. World's Fair, etc.; for 3 yrs. lit. expert for Samuel Eberly Gross, author of The Merchant Prince of Cornville vs. Edmond Rostand, author of Cyrano de Bergerac (both being dramas);

in this case 707 exhibits were prepared, one of which alleged 1,200 parallels of Rostand's French sentences with the English sentences of Gross, written 20 yrs. earlier; decree of U.S. court at Chicago, May 21, 1902, forbade representation of Cyrano de Bergerac in America, because of piracy of play right. Lecturer on Andrée, Rousseau, Shakespeare, Marie Antoinette, Lincoln, Carlyle's "French Revolution," and "The United Brethren—Wilbur and Orville." Author: Hospitality. Owner and author (with Jesse Edson Hall) of dramas: David Lockwin; Burritt Durand; Lord of Como; Joan of Arc; Patrick Henry. Home: Chicago, Ill. Died Dec. 17, 1917.

McGOWAN, John, rear admiral U.S.N.; b. Port Penn., Del., Aug. 4, 1843; s. John and Catherine (Caldwell) M.; ed. Phila. pub. schs., 1848-53; pvt. schs., Elizabeth, N.J., 1853-59; m. Evelyn Manderson, Oct. 1871. Acting master's mate U.S.N., Mar. 8, 1862; acting master, May 8, 1862; master (regular service), Mar. 1868; lt., Dec. 1868; lt. comdr., May 1870; comdr., Jan. 1887; capt., Feb. 1899; rear admiral, retired, Apr. 1901. Home: Washington, D.C. Died Aug. 13, 1915.

McGOWAN, Samuel, naval officer; b. Laurens, S.C., Sept. 1, 1870; s. Homer L. and Julia Ann (Farrow) M.; B.A., U. of S.C., 1889, LL.B., 1891 (LL.D., 1918); unmarried. Apptd. asst. p.m. U.S.N., Mar. 15, 1894; passed asst. p.m., Mar. 30, 1895; p.m., May 5, 1899; pay insp., May 11, 1906; p.m. gen. of the Navy and chief Bur. Supplies and Accounts with rank of rear admiral, July 1, 1914; promoted to permanent rank of rear admiral, Aug. 29, 1916. Paymaster general of the navy and chief supply officer throughout the World War; voluntarily retired, Dec. 31, 1920. Awarded Navy D.S.M. (U.S.); Comdr. Legion of Honor (France); Royal Order of the Redeemer (Greece). Presbyn. Mason. Home: Laurens, S.C. Died Nov. 11, 1934.

McGRADY, Thomas, author, lecturer; b. Lexington, Ky., June 6, 1863; completed classical course at St. Joseph's Coll., Bardstown, Ky.; finished theol. studies at Kankakee, Ill.; ordained R.C. priest, at Galveston, Tex., Apr. 12, 1887. Served at Cathedral, Galveston, 7 months; pastor St. Patrick's, Houston, 1888-90; transferred to Dallas; later located at Lexington and Cynthiana, Ky.; pastor St. Anthony's Ch., Bellevue, Ky., 1895-1902. As author and lecturer his social and economic views subjected him to severe criticism, and his case was presented to the highest ecclesiastical authorities. Resigned pastorate, Dec. 8, 1902. No longer connected with the ch. and has abandoned the creed; now in law practice and lecturing. Author: The Mistakes of Ingersoll, 1898; The Two Kingdoms, 1899; Beyond the Black Ocean, 1900; City of Angels, 1901; A Voice from England, 1902; The Clerical Capitalist, 1902. Home: Newport, Ky. Deceased.

McGRANAHAN, James, composer, conductor, Gospel singer, hymn writer; b. Adamsville, Pa., July 4, 1840; s. George and Jane (Blair) M.; ed. schs. and acads., Adamsville, Pa.; studied music under Carlo Bassini, New York, Dr. George F. Root, Chicago, Carl Zerrahn, Boston, Dr. William Mason, New York, and others; m. Addie Vickery, 1863. Composer of many Gospel songs. Joint editor: The Choice, 1875; The Harvest of Song, 1878 (both singing school books); The Gospel Male Choir, No. 1, 1878, No. 2, 1883, Gospel Hymns, No. 3, 1878, No. 4, 1881, No. 5, 1887, No. 6, 1891; Songs of the Gospel, 1881; Gospel Male Chorus Book, 1883; Christian Choir; Gospel Choir No. 1, 1885, No. 2, 1895; Sacred Songs No. 1, 1896, No. 2, 1899; Church Hymns and Gospel Songs, 1898; Hymns, Psalms and Gospel Songs, 1904. Home: Kinsman, O. Died 1907.

McGRANAHAN, Ralph Wilson, missionary sec.; b. Adamsville, Pa., Feb. 26, 1862; s. John and Rebecca (Gray) McG.; A.B., Monmouth (Ill.) College, 1887; A.M., 1890; D.D., Westminster Coll., 1899; m. Sarah M. Marshall, June 30, 1892; 1 dau., Isabel (Mrs. William F. Donaldson). Prin. Sunbury (Pa.) Acad., 1887-89; prof. Latin, Westminster Coll., 1889-93; ordained U.P. ministry, 1892; pastor Tenth Ch., Allegheny, Pa., 1893-99; pres. Knoxville (Tenn.) Coll., 1899-1918, also acting pres. during leave of pres., 1935-36; exec. sec. Bd. of Freedmen's Missions of United Presbyn. Ch., 1918-28; asso. sec. Bd. of Am. Missions of U.P. Ch., 1928—. Author: Historical Sketch of Freedmen's Missions, 1904; At Work in the Homeland, 1930. Home: Beaver, Pa. Died Apr. 13, 1936.

McGRATH, Benjamin R(obert), surgeon; b. Jo Daviess County, Ill., May 17, 1873; s. Robert and Esther (Weir) McG.; grad. high sch., Savanna, Ill., 1890; student Marion Sims Coll., St. Louis, 2 yrs.; MD., U. of Ill. Coll. of Medicine, 1902; m. Susan E. Williamson, May 30, 1905; children—William M., Esther L., Benjamin R., James R.; m. 2d, Dessie P. Shaffer, May 31, 1928; 1 son, Harvey C. Began practice at Grant, Neb., 1902; moved to Grand Island, 1908; pres. Bd. of Edn., Grand Island, 1908-17. Served as capt. Med. Corps, U.S.A., Aug. 1917-Feb. 1919; surgeon in charge of Operating Team No. 35, A.E.F. Fellow Am. Coll. Surgeons. Republican. Mason Home: Grand Island, Neb. Died Nov. 18, 1940.

McGRATH, Justin, newspaperman; b. St. Louis, Feb. 18, 1867; s. Major John P. and Mary Jane (Finney) M.; ed. St. Louis U., 1880-86; m. Lucile Mansford, Aug. 10, 1897; children—Justine (Mrs. Robert Hanesworth), Lucile (Mrs. William A. Watson), Mansford. Joined staff of St. Louis Post-Dispatch, 1886, city editor, 1889-95; Washington corr. St. Louis Globe-Democrat, 1895-99; Albany corr., New York Times, 1900-05; joined staff of Hearst's New York American, 1905, and served as city editor 6 yrs., mng. editor 1 yr., chief of editorial staff 1 yr.; mgr. Washington Bur. and editorial contbr. Hearst papers, Dec. 1914-July 1915; mng. editor San Francisco Examiner, 1915-19; in charge news service for all Hearst papers and Universal Service, Peace Conf., Paris; Washington editorial corr. all Hearst and Universal Service papers, 1919; organizer, and dir. foreign and domestic news and feature service of Catholic papers for Nat. Catholic Welfare Council, March 1920—. Home: Washington, D.C. Died May 17, 1931.

McGRAW, James J., banker; b. Leavenworth, Kan., Aug. 21, 1874; s. Thomas and Anna (Gilmore) McG.; ed. pub. schs.; m. Frances Agnes Donahue. Settled at Tulsa, Okla., 1920; pres. Exchange Nat. Bank of Tulsa, 1921—; pres. McGraw-Baughman-Bearly Lumber Co.; Rep. Nat. Com., 1916-20. Decorated Legion of Honor (French); Knight of St. George (Belgian), K.C. Home: Tulsa, Okla. Died Mar. 3, 1928.

McGRAW, John Harte, governor; b. Penobscot Co., Me., Oct. 4, 1850; s. Daniel and Catherine (Harte) M.; ed. pub. schs., Me.; m. May L. Kelley, Oct. 12, 1874. Went to Wash. Ty., 1876; admitted to bar, 1886; pres. First Nat. Bank, Seattle, 1890-97; investment broker, 1900—. Sheriff King Co., 1882-90; gov. of Wash., 1893-97. Pres. Seattle Chamber of Commerce, June 1905—. Home: Seattle, Wash. Died 1910.

McGRAW, John Thomas, lawyer; b. Grafton, W.Va., 1856; s. Thomas and Mary B. M.; student St. Vincent's Coll., W.Va.; LL.B., Yale, 1876; (LL.D., Mt. St. Mary's Coll., Md.); unmarried. Pros. atty., Taylor Co., 1881-85; collector internal revenue Dist. of W.Va., 1885-89; govt. distributing agt. for W.Va. during Cleveland's 2d administration; a.-d.-c. with rank of col., on staff Govs. Jackson and Fleming; was chmn. Congressional Exec. Com., 2d Dist., W.Va.; mem. Dem. State Exec. Com., 12 yrs.; Dem. candidate for Congress, 2d W.Va. Dist., 1898, 1904; mem. Dem. Nat. Com. for W.Va., 1896—; Dem. candidate for U.S. senator, 1899, and after Nathan B. Scott was declared elected by 1 vote contested the seat, but contest was decided against him; also candidate, 1901, 03. Home: Grafton, W.Va. Died Apr. 29, 1920.

McGRAW, Theodore Andrews, surgeon; b. Detroit, Nov. 11, 1839; s. Alexander C. and Susana (Walker) M.; A.B., U. of Mich., 1859 (LL.D., 1905); M.D., Coll. Phys. and Surg. (Columbia), 1863; m. Alice Simpson, July 10, 1866. Asst. surgeon U.S.A., 1863-65; in practice at Detroit, 1865-1912 (retired); prof. surgery, Detroit Coll. Medicine, 1869-1912. Republican. Mem. Detroit Bd. of Commerce. Home: Detroit, Mich. Died Sept. 6, 1921.

McGREGOR, James Clyde, coll. prof.; b. Wheeling, W.Va., July 10, 1883; s. Harlan Page and Lucy (Baggs) M.; student U. of Va., 1901; B.S., Washington and Jefferson Coll., 1905, A.M., 1908; Ph.D., U. of Pa., 1913; studied constl. law, Columbia, 1916; m. Grace N. Gilleland, July 10, 1917; children—Robert Harlan, Eleanor Lucy, Margaret Nancy. Prof. history and polit. science, Washington and Jefferson Coll., 1913—. Author: The Disruption of Virginia, 1922. Home: Washington, Pa. Died Feb. 15, 1940.

McGREGOR, Thomas, brig. gen. U.S.A.; b. Paisley, Scotland, June 26, 1837; s. Thomas and Agnes M.; ed. Paisley and Edinburgh; m. Jennie M. S. Woodburne, June 8, 1864. Served as pvt., corporal, sergt., and 1st sergt., Co. A, 1st Dragoons, Apr. 8, 1858-Oct. 1, 1862; apptd. 2d lt. 1st Cav., July 17, 1862; promoted through grades to col. 9th Cav., July 15, 1898; retired by operation of law, June 26, 1901; advanced to rank of brig. gen. retired, by act of Apr. 23, 1904. Bvtd. capt., May 6, 1864, for battle of Todd's Tavern, Va.; maj., Feb. 27, 1890, for action against Indians at Santa Maria Mountains, Ariz., May 6, 1873. Home: Benicia, Calif. Died Feb. 4, 1921.

McGREGOR, Tracy W.; b. Berlin Heights, O., Apr. 14, 1869; s. Thomas and Elizabeth (Taitt) McG.; student Oberlin Coll. 2½ yrs. (non-grad.); LL.D., U. of Detroit; D.Litt., Coll. City of Detroit, 1933; m. Katherine Whitney, Nov. 20, 1901. Pres. Whitney Realty Co., LaSalle Land Co., Provident Loan & Savings Soc. Pres. Merrill-Palmer Sch., McGregor Fund; trustee Good Will Farm Sch. (Hinckley, Me.), Am. Hist. Assn.; dir. Nat. Probation Assn.; pres. Detroit Community Fund, Wayne County (Mich.) Training Sch. for Feeble Minded. Republican. Conglist. Home: Detroit, Mich. Died May 6, 1936.

McGREGORY, Joseph Frank, univ. prof.; b. Wilbraham, Mass., Apr. 11, 1855; s. Joseph and Emeline (Fuller); A.B., Amherst, 1880, A.M., 1883, D.Sc., 1905; studied chemistry and mineralogy at univs. of Göttingen and Heidelberg, 1880-81, 1883-84, 1890-91, 1896, 1910-11; m. Emma E. J. Hodgkins, July 12, 1883 (died 1917). Instr. chemistry, Amherst, 1881-83; prof. chemistry, Colgate U., 1883-1929, also mineralogy, 1885-1909, prof. emeritus, 1929—, Colgate U. Fellow Chem. Soc. of London, A.A.A.S. K.T. Author: Lecture Notes on General Chemistry, 1894, 1902; Qualitative Analysis, 1903; Inorganic Chemistry, 1909. Home: Hamilton, N.Y. Died Oct. 1934.

McGREW, George Harrison, clergyman; b. Kingwood, Va., May 19, 1846; s. James Clark and Persis (Hagans) M.; B.A., Wesleyan U., Conn., 1870, M.A., 1873 (D.D., 1891); LL.B., Harvard, 1873; B.D., Drew Theol. Sem., 1876; m. Anna Julia Lore, Sept. 11, 1876. Missionary M.E. Ch., in India, 1875-85; pastor, Meriden, Conn., 1886-89, St. Paul's Ch., New York, 1890-92; united with P.E. Ch., 1892; asst. St. Bartholomew's Parish, New York, 1892-97; rector St. Paul's Parish, Cleveland, 1897-1906, Silver Spring Parish, Diocese of Washington, D.C., 1907—. Examining chaplain, hon. canon, Cathedral of St. Peter and St. Paul; pres. Archdeaconry of Washington. Pres. of Ecclesiastical Court. Scout in the Union Army, 1863; actg. chaplain 42d Highland Regt. ("The Black Watch"), Cawnpore, India, 1882-85. Mason. Author: Outlines of Systematic Theology (3 edits.), 1880; Old Testament History (3 grades), 1895; History of the Apostolic Church, 1896; The Negro Problem in the United States, 1907. Home: Silver Spring, Md. Died Aug. 15, 1917.

McGUGIN, Dan E., lawyer; b. Tingley, Ia., July 29, 1879; s. Benjamin Franklin and Mellissa Almeda (Critchfield) McG.; A.B., Drake U., 1901; LL.B., U. of Mich., 1904; m. Virginia Louise Fite, Dec. 6, 1905; children—Lucy Ann, Dan E., Leonard F. Admitted to Mich. bar, 1904, and began practice at Detroit; moved to Nashville, 1909; mem. Anderson, Aust, McGugin & Evans, gen. counsel Tenn. Mfg. Assn. and attys. for Tenn. Electric Power Co., Tenn. Road Builders Assn.; teacher of engring. contracts and constl. law, Vanderbilt, 1909-13, head football coach, 1904—, athletic dir., rank of full prof., 1921—, also in charge student military activities of Vanderbilt Univ., World War. Trustee Fisk Univ., Nashville. Pres. American Football Coaches Association; mem. Nashville Chamber Commerce. Mem. Christian (Disciples) Ch. Mason. Home: Nashville, Tenn. Died Jan. 19, 1936.

McGUIRE, Edgar Robinson, surgeon; b. Mt. Forest, Ont., Can., Aug. 13, 1877; s. George and Henrietta (Gardner) McG.; grad. Mt. Forest High Sch., 1895; M.D., U. of Buffalo, 1900; married; children—Edgar, Annette. Practiced at Buffalo, 1900—; prof. surgery, U. of Buffalo, 1917—, surgeon in chief Buffalo City Hosp.; attending surgeon Buffalo Gen. Hosp. Fellow Am. Surg. Assn., Am. Coll. Surgeons. Home: Buffalo, N.Y. Died Apr. 22, 1931.

McGUIRE, George Alexander, patriarch; b. Antigua, B.W.I., Mar. 26, 1866; s. Edward Henry and Henrietta (George) McG.; grad. Mico Coll., Antigua, 1886; grad. Theol. Sem., St. Thomas, 1888; M.D., Jefferson Med. Coll., Phys. and Surg., Boston, 1910; m. Ada Eliza Roberts, Dec. 20, 1892; children—Georgette (dec.), Mrs. Ada May Higgins. Ministerial service, P.E. Ch., West Indies and U.S., until 1913; minister and phys., B.W.I., 1913-19; withdrew from P.E. Ch. and carried on independently, 1919-21; organized African Orthodox Ch., and consecrated bishop and primate same, Sept. 28, 1921; elected archbishop, Sept. 1924; elected patriarch, Sept. 1927. Editor Negro Churchman. Author: Constitution and Canons of the African Orthodox Church, 1921; The Divine Liturgy of the African Orthodox Church, 1923. Home: New York, N.Y. Died Nov. 10, 1934.

McGUIRE, Hunter Holmes, surgeon; b. Winchester, Va., Oct. 11, 1835; ed. Winchester Acad.; grad. Winchester Med. Coll., 1855; Med. Coll. of Va., 1858 (LL.D., Univ. of N.C., 1888; Jefferson Med. Coll., 1889); med. director Stonewall Jackson's army, 1861; m. Mary Stuart, Dec. 19, 1866. Pres. Univ. Coll. of Med., Richmond; surgeon St. Luke's Hosp. and Va. Hosp.; pres. Am. Med. Assn., Am. Surgeons Assn., Southern Surg. and Gynecol. Assn., etc. Home: Richmond, Va. Died 1900.

McGUIRE, James Clark, civil engr.; b. nr. Ellicott City, Md., Sept. 21, 1867; s. Joseph D. and Anna (Chapman) McG.; C.E. Rensselaer Poly. Inst., 1888; unmarried. With U.S. Geol. Survey, later asst. engr. Nicaragua Canal, engr. with Phoenix Bridge Co., Phoenixville, Pa., and in Supervising Architect's Office, Washington, D.C.; settled at N.Y. City, 1894; pres. James C. McGuire & Co., engrs. and contractors, N.Y. City; pres. Porterfield Constrn. Co., Brookfield Constrn. Co.; etc. Pres. Knickerbocker Hosp., New York. Maj. engrs. O.R.C., U.S.A., World War. Died Dec. 7, 1930.

McGUIRE, Joseph Deakins, lawyer; b. Washington, Nov. 26, 1842; s. James C. and Margaret (Deakins) M.; ed. Georgetown Coll., 1856-59; entered Princeton, class of 1863, left at beginning of war, April 19, 1861; studied languages 1 yr. in France, 2 yrs. in Germany; (hon. A.M., Princeton, 1901); m. Anna Chapman, Dec. 19, 1866. Admitted to bar, Sept. 1, 1876; state's atty., Howard Co., Md., 1884-1900. Writer on Am. Archæology and ethnology. Hon.

collaborateur Smithsonian Institution. Died Sept. 6, 1916.

McGUIRE, Ulysses Melville, clergyman; b. Jennings Co., Ind., Apr. 7, 1856; s. William Edward and Nancy Violetta (Deputy) McG.; student Hanover (Ind.) Coll., Southern Bapt. Theol. Sem.; D.D., Franklin (Ind.) Coll., 1921; m. Elba Graham, Mar. 7, 1880 (died 1914); children—Ella May (Mrs. Joseph Todd Randolph, now dec.), Mary Agnes (Mrs. Walter F. Wood), Arthur Graham, Elbert Clive, Clarence Vane, Paul Raymond, Edith Fern (Mrs. John Barnett). Ordained ministry Bapt. Ch., 1881; pastor various village chs. until 1892; then successively pastor Anderson, Sullivan, Washington, Lawrenceburg, Princeton, Sullivan and Greencastle—all of Indiana. Editor The Baptist Observer 5 yrs.; editor The Baptist to 1931. Chmn. many yrs. of social service coms. Ind. Baptist Convention until 1917, also of Northern Bapt. Convention; president of Chicago Bapt. Ministers' Conf.; organization and relief work among Chicago unemployed, 1931-32. Mason, Woodman. Lecturer; specialist in adult education. Home: South Bend, Ind. Died July 5, 1939.

McGUIRE, William Anthony, writer; b. Chicago, Ill., July 9, 1887; s. Daniel and Jane Louise (Simms) McG.; student University Sch., Chicago, and Notre Dame, Ind.; married. In candy and advertising business for several years; writer from 1907. Catholic. Author: (plays) The Devil, The Servant and the Man; The Heights; The Divorce; Everyman's Castle; Six Cylinder Love; It's a Boy; Kid Boots; Whoopee; Three Musketeers; Rosalie; Follies of 1922-23; 12 Miles Out; If I Were Rich; (motion pictures) She Wanted a Millionaire; Disorderly Conduct; Kid from Spain; Roman Scandals; Okay America; Out All Night; Little Man, What Now; The Great Ziegfeld; Siegfeld Girl. Produced and wrote: Rosalie; Girl of the Golden West; Lillian Russell. Died Sept. 16, 1940.

McHARG, Henry K., banker; b. Albany, N.Y., Feb. 6, 1851; s. John and Martha Whipple (Patch) M.; ed. Albany Acad., Walnut Hill (boarding) Sch., and Rev. Thomas C. Reed, Geneva, N.Y. Bank clerk, 1866-71; mem. New York Stock Exchange, 1872—; dir, 1882—, v.p., 1893—, Manhattan Co.; pres. Detroit & Mackinac Ry. Co.; dir. N.Y., Ontario & Western Ry. Co., Stamford Trust Co. Home: Stamford, Conn. Died Jan. 28, 1941.

McHENRY, John Geiser, congressman; b. Benton Tp., Columbia Co., Pa., Apr. 26, 1868; s. Rohr and Caroline (Geiser) M.; ed. Orangeville Acad., Pa.; m. Mary E. Wolfe, 1894. Engaged in banking, mfg. and farming; pres. Columbia Co. Nat. Bank, Rohr McHenry Distilling Co.; treas. Northwestern Lumber Co. State supt. grange nat. banks of Pa.; mem. 60th, 61st and 62d Congresses (1907-13), 16th Pa. Dist. Democrat. Home: Benton, Pa. Died Dec. 27, 1912.

McHUGH, William Douglas, lawyer; b. Galena, Ill., Sept. 10, 1859; s. John and Harriet (Murphy) M.; ed. pub. schs., and Ill. State Normal Sch., 1 yr.; m. Caroline E. Jones, Sept. 9, 1886. Admitted to bar, 1883; practiced at Galena, 1883-88, Omaha, from 1888; U.S. dist. judge, Dist. of Neb., 1896-97; gen. counsel Internat. Harvester Co., Chicago, Apr. 1920—. Home: Chicago, Ill. Died Dec. 26, 1923.

McILHENNEY, Charles Morgan, artist; b. Phila., Apr. 4, 1858; s. James L. and Margaret A. McI.; ed. there; m. 1888, Ada Ingersoll. Studied painting under Frank Briscoe and anatomy in Phila. Acad. of Fine Arts, 1877. Regular exhibitor at Nat. Acad. of Design, of which he is an asso. mem., 1882—. Spent 1878-81 on a sketching tour in S. Pacific. Received W. T. Evans prize, Am. Water-Color Soc., 1892; 1st Hallgarten prize, Nat. Acad., 1893; medals at World's Columbian Expn., 1893; hon. mention, Paris Expn., 1900; bronze medal, Pan-Am. Expn., Buffalo, 1901. Home: Shrub Oak, N.Y. Died 1904.

McILHENNY, Francis Salisbury, lawyer; b. Columbus, Ga., Oct. 3, 1873; s. John and Bernice (Bell) M.; A.B., U. of Pa., 1895, LL.B., 1898; m. Marie Louise Hoopes, Nov. 7, 1908; children—Francis Salisbury, Louise, Alan. Practiced in Phila., 1898—; v.p. Sun Oil Co.; dir. Crucible Steel Casting Co., Phila. Commn., The Counties Gas & Electric Co., Am. Meter Co. Mem. Pa. Senate, 1907-15. Pres. The Am. Foundation, Inc.; trustee Thomas W. Evans Museum and Dental Inst., Chestnut Hill Acad.; dir. Germantown Y.M.C.A. Asso. chief sec. and treas., in London, of Am. Y.M.C.A. for United Kingdom, Oct. 1918-Mar. 1919. Republican. Presbyterian. Home: Chestnut Hill, Pa. Died May 1927.

McILHENNY, John D., mfr.; b. Columbus, Ga., Oct. 7, 1866; s. John and Bernice (Bell) M.; B.A., Phila. High Sch., 1885; m. Frances Galbraith Plumer, June 15, 1898. Began in business at Phila., 1888; now mem. Helme & McIlhenny, gas meters; mng. dir. Portsmouth (Va.) Gas Co.; mem. bd. mgrs. Saving Fund Soc. of Germantown. Pres. Pa. Mus. and Sch. of Industrial Art; trustee Fairmount Park Art Assn.; dir. Art Alliance of Phila. Republican. Presbyn. Home: Germantown, Phila., Pa. Died Nov. 23, 1925.

McILHINEY, Parker Cairns, chemist; b. Jersey City, N.J., Oct. 9, 1870; s. James and Martha (Cairns) M.; Ph.B., Columbia, 1892, A.M., 1893, Ph.D., 1894; m. Clarissa Ann Walker, Nov. 5, 1895. Hon. asst. in assaying, 1893-94, asst. in metallurgy, 1894-98, hon. asst. same, 1898-1900, Columbia; asso. with Louis C. Tiffany, in artistic glass, jewelry and enamel mfg., 1894—; cons. chemist, 1898—. Silver and bronze medals, Paris Expn., 1900. Home: Great Neck, L.I., N.Y. Died June 21, 1923.

McILVAINE, Charles ("Tobe Hodge"), author; b. Springton Farm (Penn Manor of Springton), Chester Co., Pa., May 31, 1840; s. Hon. Abraham Robinson McI. (congressman 7th Pa. dist., 1842-46); ed. country schools, Chester Co., Pa., until 1851; Northwest Grammar School, Phila., 1851-53; studied engring.; civ. engr. div. engr., East Brandywine & Waynesburg R.R., 1859-61; m. Sarah G. McIlvain, Oct. 20, 1864. Raised co. of vols. under war dept., which he attached to 97th regt., Pa. vols.; mustered in as capt., Oct. 1861; apptd. capt. 19th inf., U.S.A., Nov. 1861; judge advocate, dept. South, 1862; chief of ordnance, staff Maj. Gen. Alfred H. Terry, Maj. Gen. Joseph R. Hawley; apptd. maj. 1st S.C. cav. (col.), 1863; declined; held important positions upon the staffs of several of our noted generals; resigned on account of ill health, 1863; traveled in Europe, 1873-74; chief engr. Jamesville & Washington R.R., 1888-89; inventor of copyable printing ink. Republican. Pres. Phila. Mycol. Center; prin. School of Mycology, N.Y. Chautauqua. Author: A Legend of Polecat Hollow, 1884; 1,000 American Fungi, 4to, 705 pp. (fully illustrated by the author), 1900, 02; Outdoors, Indoors and Up the Chimney, 1906. Home: Cambridge, Md. Died 1909.

McILVAINE, James Hall, clergyman; b. Utica, N.Y., 1846; s. Joshua Hall (D.D.) and Sarah (Dutton) M.; A.B., Princeton, 1866; grad. Princeton Theol. Sem., 1873 (D.D., 1889); m. Grace P. Biddle, Mar. 11, 1873. Ordained Presbyn. ministry, 1873; pastor Beverly, N.J., 1872-79, Summit, N.J., 1879-83, Union Ch., Providence, 1883-87, Ch. of the Covenant, N.Y., 1887-95, Brick Ch., New York, 1895-97; entered P.E. ministry, 1898; rector Calvary Ch., Pittsburgh, 1900—. Author: Modern Thought and Christian Evidences; St. Francis of Assisi, 1902. Home: Pittsburgh, Pa. Died Mar. 14, 1921.

McILWAINE, Henry Read, librarian; b. Farmville, Va., July 12, 1864; s. Joseph Finley and Sarah Embra (Read) M.; A.B., Hampden-Sydney Coll., Va., 1885; Ph.D., Johns Hopkins, 1893; unmarried. Prof. English and history, and librarian, Hampden-Sydney Coll., 1893-1907; librarian Va. State Library, July 6, 1907—. Editor of Va. State Library's edition of Jours. of the House of Burgesses and of Journals of the Council of Colonial Virginia. Author: The Struggle of Protestant Dissenters for Religious Toleration in Virginia. Mem. Am. Library Assn. Dir. Va. of Am. Library Assn.'s library war service; mem. Va. State Council Defense, War History Commission of Va. Democrat. Presbyn. Home: Richmond, Va. Died Mar. 16, 1934.

McILWAINE, William Baird, lawyer; b. Petersburg, Va., Oct. 4, 1854; s. Robert Dunn and Lucy Atkinson (Pryor) McI.; A.B., Hampden-Sydney Coll., Va., 1873; m. Jane Maury Pegram; 1 son, Richard (dec.); m. 2d, Sarah Joseph Alston Claiborne, Dec. 28, 1882; children—(a dau.) Joseph Alston Claiborne (Mrs. Edgar S. Bowling), Wm. Baird, Lucy Atkinson, Anne Claiborne (Mrs. Wm. Taliaferro Thompson), Hibernia (dec.), Elizabeth Herbert (dec.). Admitted to Va. bar, 1878, and entered practice at Petersburg; Va. counsel Atlantic Coast Line R.R. Co.; pres. Petersburg Telephone Co.; formerly pres. Am. Bank & Trust Co. Mem. City Council several terms; mem. Va. Ho. of Delegates, 1891-93, Va. Senate 12 yrs.; presdl. elector at large, 1896; mem. Bd. Visitors U. of Va. 1 term. Mason. Home: Petersburg, Va. Died Aug. 11, 1930.

McINTIRE, Albert Washington, governor; b. Pittsburgh, Pa., Jan. 15, 1853; s. Joseph Phillips and Isabel (Wills) McI.; A.B., Yale, 1873, LL.B., 1875; twice married. Removed to Denver, 1876; judge County Court, Conejos Co., Colo., 1883-86; dist. judge 12th Jud. Dist., Colo., 1891-94; gov. of Colo., 1895-97. Home: Denver, Colo. Deceased.

McINTIRE, Charles, physician; b. Philadelphia, Aug. 30, 1847; s. Charles and Eliza (Cook) M.; A.B., with honor, Lafayette, 1868, A.M., 1871; M.D., U. of Pa., 1873; m. Ella, d. Traill Green, M.D., LL.D., May 19, 1881. Asst. in chemistry, 1868-70, adj. prof., 1870-74, lecturer sanitary science, 1880-1905, Lafayette Coll. Mem. advisory council Simplified Spelling Bd. Home: Easton, Pa. Deceased.

McINTIRE, Warren Wallace, educator; b. Wooster, O., July 13, 1869; s. William Henry and Sarah Alice (King) M.; Ph.B., Coll. of Wooster, 1896, Ph.M., 1899; A.M., Columbia, 1912; m. Nettie Ellen Lautenschlager, 1892. School book pub. business, Cincinnati, O., 1896-1902; teacher Norwood High Sch., Cincinnati, 1902-03, prin., 1903-20; dean Coll. of Edn., Ohio U., Sept. 1920—. Mem. retirement bd. of Ohio State Teachers' Retirement System, and chief author Ohio teachers' retirement law. Republican. Presbyn. Mason. Home: Athens, O. Died July 9, 1922.

McINTOSH, Henry Payne, banker; b. Cleveland, O., Oct. 27, 1846; s. Alexander and Agnes (Nicol) McI.; ed. pub. sch.; m. Olive A. Manfull, Jan. 19, 1871 (died 1915); children—Frances (Mrs. John Sherwin), Alexandrine (Mrs. R. D. Beatty), Ralph Edward (dec.), Olive Marie (Mrs. E. H. Brown), Henry Payne, John Manfull. Telegraph operator, later bookkeeper; identified with business interests of Henry B. Payne and Oliver H. Payne, Cleveland, 1876-1901; pres. Guardian Savings & Trust Co., 1901-17, chmn. bd., 1917—. Trustee Adelbert Coll. (Western Reserve U.). Presbyn. Mason. Home: Cleveland Hts., Cleveland, O. Died Dec. 24, 1935.

McINTOSH, James Henry, lawyer; b. nr. Salineville, O., Dec. 10, 1858; s. John Calder and Jane (McLennan) McI.; A.B., magna cum laude, Harvard, 1884; m. Claire Rustin, Apr. 28, 1890 (died 1925); children—Kenneth, Rustin, Marjorie. Began practice at Omaha, 1887; removed to New York, 1903, as gen. counsel New York Life Ins. Co., resigned Sept. 1, 1922; mem. Alexander & Green, Jan. 1925—. Republican. Episcopalian. Home: New York, N.Y. Died Feb. 25, 1941.

McINTYRE, Hugh Henry, osteopathic physician; b. Randolph, Vt., Aug. 10, 1844; s. James and Charlotte (Blodgett) McI.; ed. Orange Co. grammar school; grad. Georgetown Med. Coll., Washington, 1868; Am. School of Osteopathy, Kirksville, Mo., 1899; studied Post Graduate Med. Coll., New York, 1899-1900; m. Emma, d. Hon. Crosby Miller, Jan. 31, 1871. In Civil war, 10th Vt. vols., 1862; U.S.A. Signal Corps, 1864-65; in U.S. Treasury dept., sec.'s office, 1866-68; U.S. special treasury agt. for Alaska, 1869-70; supt. seal fisheries of Alaska, 1871-90; spl. agt. U.S. State Dept. in connection with Paris Arbitration of 1892-93. Home: Randolph, Vt. Died 1906.

McINTYRE, Oscar Odd, newspaper writer; b. Plattsburg, Mo., Feb. 18, 1884; s. Henry Bell and Fanny (Young) McI.; ed. acad., and Bartlett's Coll., Cincinnati; m. Maybelle Hope Small, Feb. 18, 1908. Reporter Gallipolis Journal, 1902; feature writer East Liverpool (O.) Tribune, 1904-05; polit. writer, later mng. editor Dayton (O) Herald, 1906; telegraph editor, city editor and asst. mng. editor Cincinnati Post, 1907-11; asso. editor Hampton's Mag., 1912; dramatic editor New York Evening Mail, 1913; writing daily article "New York Day by Day," 1912—, syndicated in 550 newspapers. Author: White Light Nights, 1924; Twenty Three Selected Stories, 1929; Another Odd Book, 1931; The Big Town, 1935. Home: New York, N.Y. Died Feb. 14, 1938.

McINTYRE, Robert, bishop; b. Selkirk, Scotland, Nov. 20, 1851; s. Charles and Elizabeth (Anderson) M.; student Vanderbilt U., Tenn., 1877; (D.D., U. of Denver); m. Ella Chatten, Dec. 31, 1877. Ordained M.E. ministry, 1878; pastor at Easton, Marshall, Charleston, Urbana and Chicago, Ill., Denver, and First Ch., Los Angles, until 1908; bishop M.E. Ch., 1908—. Author: Poems—At Early Candle Light, 1899; A Modern Apollos, 1900. Home: Oklahoma City, Okla. Died Aug. 31, 1914.

McIVER, Charles Duncan, educator; b. Moore Co., N.C., Sept. 27, 1860; descendant of Scotch Presby'ns, early settlers of Cape Fear dist., N.C.; grad. Univ. of N.C., 1881 (Litt.D., 1893; LL.D., 1904); m. Lula V. Martin, 1885. Assisted in organizing pub. schs. of Durham and Winston; joined faculty Peace Inst., Raleigh, 1886; State Inst. conductor, 1889-92, and conducted teachers' insts. in nearly every co. of State. Has been supt. summer Normal schs.; pres. N.C. Teachers' Assembly; mem. exec. com. bd. trustees Univ. of N.C.; chmn. of com. of Teachers' Assembly which secured, 1891, the establishment and an ann. appropriation for N.C. State Normal and Industrial Coll., which he organized in 1892 and of which he became president; mem. Southern Edn. Bd. and chairman campaign com.; pres. Southern Edn. Assn., 1905; mem. Nat. Council of N. E. A. Home: Greensboro, N.C. Died 1906.

McIVER, Henry, jurist; b. nr. Society Hill, S.C., Sept. 25, 1826; grad. S.C. Coll., 1846 (A.M., 1848); m. Caroline H. Powe, June 7, 1849. Began law practice at Cheraw, S.C., 1848; was solicitor (pros. att'y for the State) from Dec., 1853, to July, 1868, when displaced by reorganization of the State govt.; officer C. S. A., 1861-65; twice severely wounded on same day, May 28, 1864, but served until close of war. Asso. justice, 1877-91, and from 1891 chief justice Supreme Court of S.C. Home: Cheraw, S.C. Died 1903.

McIVER, Joseph, neuropsychiatry; b. Madison Co., Tex., Sept. 27, 1886; s. Walter and Jennie (Searcey) McI.; M.D., U. of Tex., 1912; m. Regina McManus, Sept. 2, 1916 (died 1932). Began practice at Phila., 1913; chief of visiting staff Phila. General Hosp.; neurologist to Misericordia Hosp. Served in U.S.N. R.F., U.S. Naval Hosp., League Island, Phila., 1917-19. Republican. Catholic. Home: Philadelphia, Pa. Died Sept. 7, 1940.

McIVOR, Nicholas Williams, lawyer; b. Cheraw, S.C., Apr. 30, 1860; s. Francis Marion and Henrietta

Kelsall (Robbins) M.; Burlington (N.J.) Coll.; A.B., Trinity Coll., Conn., 1882; Harvard Law Sch., 1882-85; m. Elizabeth Greene, Sept. 6, 1890. Began practice at Cedar Rapids, 1885; corp. counsel, Cedar Rapids, 1891-92; adj. gen. of Ia., 1892-93; U.S. consul gen. and judge of U.S. Ct., Yokohama, Japan, 1893-97; holder of protecorate over Chinese in Japan during Chino-Japanese War, 1894-95; counsel and dir. various Am., English, Continental and Japanese corps. Democrat. Episcopalian. Decorated Chinese Order of the Double Dragon. Died Feb. 9, 1915.

McIVOR-TYNDALL, Alexander James, metaphysician; b. Leicestershire, England; s. Alexander (M.D.) and Agnes Stuart Sampson McI.; ed. English pub. schs., Wellingbrough, Market Harborough, and pvt. tutors in Edinburgh, Scotland; M.D., St. Bartholomew's Hosp. Med. Coll., 1888; m. Margaret Logan, Sept. 3, 1896; m. 2d, Laura Hudson Wray, June 13, 1917; children—Victoria, Margaret. Came to U.S., 1889, naturalized, 1893. Began theosophic lectures in Canada, 1890; founded Calif. Internat. Psychic Science Alliance, 1903; editor of the Swastika Magazine, 1906-11; writer Denver Post (Colo.), 1906-07; pres. internat. New Thought Fellowship, 1912; lecturer on psychology, metaphysics, and spiritualism in U.S., Canada, and England, 1919-38; ordained minister of Nat. Spiritualist Assn., 1923, created prelate, 1923; prelate Gen. Assembly Spiritualists, 1923; dean of Los Angeles Scientific Psychical Research Soc., 1937-40. Author: Cosmic Consciousness; The Man-God Whom We Await, 1911; Sex—The Unknown Quantity, 1916; How Thought Can Kill, 1917; Survival—Life After Death, 1918; writes under nom de plume Ali Nomad, also Dr. John Lockwood. Home: Los Angeles, Calif.; and Detroit, Mich. Died Dec. 10, 1940.

McKAY, Ambrose Noble, newspaper pub.; b. Ontario Co., Can., May 5, 1868; s. Donald and Alice (Noble) McK.; B.A., U. of Toronto, 1890; m. Mary E. Cope, Oct. 23, 1897. Came to U.S., 1890, and worked on newspapers in Cheyenne, Salt Lake City and Denver; mng. editor Salt Lake Herald, 1898-1909; gen. mgr. Salt Lake Tribune, Jan. 1, 1911—. Mem. Associated Press, 1911—, v.p., 1919-20. Presbyn. Mason, Elk. Home: Salt Lake City, Utah. Died Nov. 18, 1924.

McKEAN, Horace Grant, coll. prof.; b. Hammonton, N.J., Dec. 13, 1864; s. Edward Thomas and Mary Louisa (Grant) McK.; grad. Colgate Acad., 1885; A.B., Colgate U., 1889, A.M., 1892, Litt.D., 1916; student Crozer Theol. Sem., Chester, Pa., 1889-90; m. Elizabeth Kennedy Bergfels, Sept. 21, 1892. Ordained Bapt. ministry, 1890; pastor Phila. Pa., and Arlington, N.J., 1890-95; prof. English lang. and lit., Pa. Mil. Coll., Chester, Pa., 1895-99; headmaster Colby Acad., New London, N.H., 1899-1905; prof. rhetoric and pub. speaking, Union Coll., Schenectady, N.Y., 1905—. Republican. Baptist. Died Jan. 9, 1927.

McKEAN, Thomas, author, playwright; b. Phila., Apr. 29, 1869; s. Thomas and Elizabeth (Wharton) McK.; B.S., Trinity Coll., Conn., 1892; m. Katharine Johnstone Bispham, Nov. 25, 1896. Author: The Mermaid, 1907; The Master Influence, 1907; The Punishment, 1909; The Mercy of Fate, 1910; The Wife Decides, 1911. Home: Philadelphia, Pa. Died Feb. 7, 1942.

McKEAN, William Vincent, editor; b. Phila., Oct. 15, 1820; s. William and Ellen McK.; ed. private schools, Phila.; studied law with James C. Van Dyke, of Phila.; m. Hannah Rudolph, Feb. 1, 1841. Asso. editor of Pennsylvanian, with John W. Forney, 1850-52; chief clerk Ho. of Reps. 1853-55, part of 1856; asst. examiner U.S. Patent Office; private sec. to James Buchanan, pending his election to the presidency, part of 1856; prin. editorial writer Phila. Inquirer, 1860-64; editor-in-chief Phila. Public Ledger, Dec., 1864, to Sept., 1891, when he asked the proprs., George W. Childs and Anthony J. Drexel, to relieve him from his heavy duties, which was done, with a continuance of his salary for the rest of his life; retired. Independent Democrat. Editor Nat. Almanac Record for 1864, published in Phila., London, Paris. Wrote: Report favoring Money Order System for the United States, 1858; What the Navy Has Done During the War, U.S. Journal, April 1864; General McClellan's Campaign, U.S. Journal, May 1864; Centennial of American Independence. Home: Philadelphia, Pa. Died 1902.

McKEE, Alexander Ellsworth, newspaper editor; b. Sullivan, Ind., Feb. 8, 1862; s. Addison and Louvina (Butner) McK.; ed. pub. schs.; m. Fannie Leslie Knight, June 7, 1888 (died 1918); children—Leonard Knight (dec.), Addison Lee; m. 2d, Clara Joan Culver, Jan. 15, 1920. Began as reporter Kansas City (Mo.) Journal, 1891; political writer same, 1893-99, Kansas City World, 1899-1900; financial writer Cleveland (O.) Press, 1900-03, Cleveland Plain Dealer, 1903-06; branch bank mgr., Cleveland Trust Co., 1906-11; political writer Cleveland Plain Dealer, 1911-17; editor Ohio State Journal, Columbus, 1920—. Mem. Ohio State Bd. of Clemency, 1917-20. Trustee White Cross Hosp., Columbus. Republican. Presbyn. Elk. Home: Columbus, O. Died Mar. 19, 1934.

McKEE, David Ritchie, newspaperman; b. Wheeling, Va., Sept. 17, 1842; s. Redick and Eliza (Ritchie) M.; grad. San Francisco High Sch., 1859; m. Frances E., d. Gen. W. McKee Dunn, U.S.A., May 11, 1871. Mem. engring. party engaged 2 yrs. in locating r.r. lines that formed beginning of transcontinental system; chief dep. U.S. marshal for Calif. 2 yrs.; with Tallant & Co., bankers, San Francisco, 2 yrs.; travel and study of langs. in Europe 1½ yrs.; became Washington corr., 1867, San Francisco Bulletin (to which regularly contributed letters over signature of "Ritchie," 15 yrs.); also entered employ Associated Press, 1867, and was in charge its Congressional reports to May 1882, when apptd. mgr. of its Washington bureau, including supervision of reports from the South; retired Jan. 1, 1893. Mem. Bd. Washington Nat. Monument Soc. Republican. Presbyn. Home: Washington, D.C. Died June 13, 1924.

McKEE, William James, merchant, soldier; b. Madison, Ind., Dec. 12, 1853; s. Robert S. and Celine L. M.; Sheffield Scientific Sch., Yale; m. Fannie B. McKinney, Feb. 20, 1878. Engaged in commercial pursuits; identified with N.G. of Ind., in which he became brig. gen. comdg. in Mar., 1893, and maj. gen., Apr., 1905; apptd. brig. gen. U.S.V., May 27, 1898; served until Mar. 15, 1899; comdg. 2d Div., 1st Army Corps; 2d Brigade, 2d Div., 1st Corps; 3d Brigade, 1st Div., 1st Corps, and 2d Separate Brigade, 2d Army Corps. Home: Indianapolis, Ind. Died Dec. 24, 1925.

McKEE, William Parker, clergyman, educator; b. Indianola, Ill., Aug. 8, 1862; s. Melvin and Hattie (Parker) M.; A.B., Wabash Coll., 1883; B.D., Bapt. Union Theol. Sem., 1887; grad. student in history, U. of Minn., 1895-97, A.M., 1897; B.D., U. of Chicago, 1887; married, 1887; 1 son, Howard Harper; m. 2d, Florence Turney, June 1901; 1 daughter, Mrs. Margaret Damon. Ordained Baptist ministry, 1887; pastor Olivet Ch., Minneapolis, Minn., 1887-97; pres. Francis Shimer Sch., 1897-1930 (retired). Republican. Home: Urbana, Ill. Died Aug. 10, 1933.

McKEEHAN, Charles Louis, judge; b. Phila., Pa., Mar. 29, 1876; s. Charles Watson and Mary Anna (Givin) McK.; A.B., U. of Pa., 1897, LL.B., 1900; unmarried. Practiced at Phila., 1900-23; judge U.S. Dist. Court, Eastern Dist. of Pa., Feb. 19, 1923—. Commd. maj. Ordnance Corps, U.S.A., Nov. 9, 1917; lt. col., Jan. 12, 1918; with A.E.F., July 1918-Mar. 1919. Republican. Episcopalian. Home: Philadelphia, Pa. Died Mar. 23, 1925.

McKEEN, James, lawyer; b. Brunswick, Me., Dec. 5, 1844; s. Joseph and Elizabeth F. M.; A.B., Bowdoin, 1864, A.M., 1867 (LL.D., 1900); m. Miss M. E. Lewis, Apr. 29, 1871. Admitted to bar, 1867; in practice at New York, 1870—; mem. McKeen, Brewster & Morgan; counsel for Armstrong Com., 1905, Mut. Life Ins. Co., 1907. Overseer Bowdoin, 1886—; pres. and mem. bd. mgrs. N.Y. State Colonization Soc.; trustee Brooklyn Pub. Library, Packer Collegiate Inst. Home: Brooklyn, N.Y. Died 1910.

McKEEVER, Chauncey, col. U.S.A.; retired Aug. 31, 1893; b. in Md., 1828; grad. West Point, 1849; assigned to arty.; 1st lt., Dec. 24, 1853; capt. of staff and asst. adj. gen., Aug. 3, 1861. Took part in Bull Run and other battles in Civil War; reached bvt. rank of brig. gen. After war promoted through grades to colonel. Died 1901.

McKEEVER, Franklin Garrett, clergyman; b. Oxford, Pa., Dec. 24, 1852; s. Samuel and Elizabeth (Lockard) M.; A.B., Brown U., 1881, A.M., 1889; grad. Rochester Theol. Sem., 1884; (D.D., Brown, 1906); m. Clara Frances Butts, Feb. 3, 1885. Ordained Bapt. ministry, 1884; pastor, Medina, N.Y., 1884-88, Providence, R.I., 1888-93, New London, Conn., 1893-1908; lit. work, 1909-12; pastor Newport, R.I., 1912-18; engaged in literary work, 1918—. Special lecturer Bucknell Univ., 1898. Newton Theol. Institution, 1907; studying and preaching in Europe, 1897 and 1903. Trustee, 1st v.p. Conn. Bapt. Conv.; trustee and sec. R.I. Bapt. Conv.; trustee Conn. Bapt. Edn. Soc., Newton Theol. Instn., Conn. Lit. Inst. Author: Centennial History of the First Baptist Church of New London, Conn. Home: Providence, R.I. Died Dec. 1, 1922.

McKEEVER, William Arch, author, lecturer; b. Jackson Co., Kan., Apr. 12, 1868; s. Archibald and Elvira (Means) M.; A.M., U. of Kan., 1898; Ph.M., U. of Chicago, 1904; spl. philos. course, Harvard; LL.D., Berea Coll., Ky., 1917; m. Edith E. Shattuck, Dec. 25, 1895 (died 1929); children—Harold James, Warren Wendell, Fergus Sunshine; m. 2d, Ollie M. Jenkins, June 3, 1931. Prof. philosophy, Kan. State Agrl. Coll., 1900-13; head dept. child welfare, U. of Kan., 1913-20; dir. Sch. of Psychology, Oklahoma City, Okla. Originator of "Home Training Bulletins," circulated among English-speaking people. Originator Juvenile Welfare Inst.; dir. Better City Campaign; mem. com. Internat. S.S. Assn.; mem. N.E.A. Author: Psychologic Method in Teaching, 1909; Farm Boys and Girls, 1912; Training the Boy, 1913; Training the Girl, 1914; Outlines of Child Study, 1915; Man and the New Democracy, 1919; The Child and the Home, 1923; The Creative Mind, 1925; Leaves of Healing, 1927; Side Stepping Divorce, 1927; You and Your Life, 1930; Love's Fulfillment, 1931; Living a Century, 1935; Campaign Against Old Age, 1937; Create Your Own Job, 1939. Home: Oklahoma City, Okla. Died July 8, 1940.

McKELWAY, Alexander Jeffrey, social work; b. Sadsburyville, Pa., Oct. 6, 1866; s. John Ryan and Catherine Scott (Comfort) M.; family removed to Charlotte Co., Va., 1867; A.B., Hampden-Sidney Coll., Va., 1886; grad. Union Theol. Sem., Va., 1891; (D.D., Davidson Coll., N.C., 1900); m. Ruth Smith, July 15, 1891. Ordained Presbyn. ministry, 1891; home missionary, Johnston Co., N.C., 1891; pastor Fayetteville, N.C., 1892-97; editor Presbyterian Standard, 1898-1905, Charlotte News, 1903-04; sec. for Southern States Nat. Child Labor Com., 1904—. Chmn. Com. of 40 on Popular Govt. for D.C.; v.p. Nat. Reform Assn.; v.p. Nat. Training Sch. for Girls. Democrat. Home: Washington, D.C. Died Apr. 16, 1918.

McKELWAY, St. Clair, editor; b. Columbia, Mo., Mar. 15, 1845; s. Dr. Alexander J. and Mary A. (Ryan) M.; family removed to N.J., 1853; ed. by pvt. tutors; (hon. A.M., Colgate, 1883; LL.D., Syracuse, 1890; L.H.D., Union, 1897; D.C.L., St. Lawrence, 1898; LL.D., U. of Mo., 1904, Princeton, 1904, N.Y. U., 1913); m. Eleanor Hutchison, 1867 (died 1884); 2d, Virginia Brooks Thompson, 1888. Admitted to N.Y. bar, 1866, but never practiced; writer for several papers; joined staff Brooklyn Eagle, 1868, became asso. editor, 1883, editor-in-chief, 1885—. Regent U. of State of N.Y., 1883—, vice-chancellor, 1900-13, acting chancellor, 1905-12, chancellor, 1913—. Home: N.Y. Died July 16, 1915.

McKENNA, Charles Francis, chemical engr.; b. New York, June 4, 1861; s. William and Mary E. M.; A.B., St. Francis Xavier Coll., New York, 1879, A.M., 1880; Ph.B., Columbia, 1883, Ph.D., 1894; m. Laura O'Neill, 1885 (died 1900); m. 2d, Julia Harlin, 1903. Employed as chemist, 1885-93; dir. Lab. of Phys. Testing, N.Y. City, 1893-95; chemist, Passaic Zinc Co., 1895-97; consulting chemist, 1897—, specializing in qualities of materials. Chemist member Municipal Explosives Commn., New York, 1902-04. Mem. State Bd. of Probation, N.Y. (v.p. 1907), Bd. of Parole, New York City. Chmn. sub-com. chmn. engring. Council Nat. Defense, 1918. Republican. Catholic. Home: New York, N.Y. Died Apr. 25, 1930.

McKENNA, Edward William, ry. official; b. Pittsburgh, Oct. 24, 1848; ed. St. Vincent's Coll., Latrobe, Pa.; m. Columbia C. Conduitt, Oct. 22, 1872 (died 1893); 2d, Retta Johnston, Feb. 15, 1905. Was telegraph messenger and operator Pa. R.R., 1862-64; served in Civil War in U.S. mil. telegraph, 1864-65; frt. clk. to gen. supt., P.,C.&St.L. Ry.; train dispatcher, 1870-71, supt., 1871-80, Indianapolis & Vincennes R.R.; supt. Jeffersonville, Madison & Indianapolis R.R., 1880-85; in spl. service under gen. mgr., Pa. lines west of Pittsburgh, 1886-87; chief clk. to gen. mgr. N.Y.,L.E.&W. R.R., Feb.-June, 1887; supt. Prairie du Chien and Mineral Point divs., C.,M.&S.P. Ry., 1887-88; supt. LaCrosse and Wis. Valley divs., 1888-89; asst. gen. supt., C.,M.& St.P. Ry., 1890-94; gen. supt. Eastern dist., G.N. Ry., at St. Paul, 1894-95; pres. McKenna Steel Working Co., Joliet, Ill., 1895-1903; asst. to the pres., C.,M.&St.P. Ry., 1904-05, 2d v.p., 1905-09, v.p. in charge operation and construction, Sept. 23, 1909, and mem. conf. com., 1914. Dir. Kansas City, Mexico & Orient Ry., U.S. Industrial Alcohol Co. Republican. Deceased.

McKENNA, Joseph, jurist; b. Phila., Pa., Aug. 10, 1843; s. John and Mary (Johnson) M.; attended St. Joseph's Coll., Phila., until 1855; moved with parents to Benicia, Calif.; attended pub. schs. and grad. Benicia Collegiate Inst., 1865; admitted to bar, 1865; m. Amanda F. Borneman, June 10, 1869 (died 1924). Dist. atty. Solano Co., Calif., 1866-68; mem. Calif. Ho. of Rep., 1875-76; candidate for Congress, 1876, 1878; mem. 49th to 52d Congresses (1885-92), 2d Calif. Dist.; resigned from 52d Congress, Mar. 28, 1892; U.S. circuit judge, 9th Circuit, 1892-97; atty. gen. in Cabinet of President McKinley, Mar. 1897-Jan. 25, 1898; asso. justice Supreme Court of U.S., Jan. 26, 1898-Jan. 5, 1925 (resigned). Died Nov. 21, 1926.

McKENNAN, Thomas McKean Thompson, neurologist; b. Washington, Pa., July 13, 1859; s. Dr. Thomas and Margaret (Stockton) M.; A.B., Washington and Jefferson Coll., 1879; M.D., U. of Pa., 1882; m. Sallie Louise Ruff, Apr. 17, 1889; m. 2d, Eleanor Lee Wallace, Apr. 30, 1912. In practice at Pittsburgh, 1882-83, Minneapolis, 1883-84, Pittsburgh, 1884—; prof. diseases of nervous system, U. of Pittsburgh, 1900—; neurologist to St. Francis Hosp. Home: Pittsburgh, Pa. Died Feb. 16, 1935.

McKENNEY, James Hall, clerk Supreme Ct. of U.S., 1880—; b. Hartford Co., Md., July 12, 1837; s. John and Mary Jane M.; ed. Bel Air Acad., Md., Rugby Acad., Washington; m. Virginia Dorcas Walker, May 15, 1862; father of Frederic Duncan M. Clerk in clerk's office, Circuit Ct. of D.C., 1853-58, Supreme Ct. of U.S., 1858-80. Home: Washington, D.C. Died Oct. 13, 1913.

McKENNY, Charles, coll. pres.; b. Dimondale, Mich., Sept. 5, 1860; s. Albert and Angeline (Torry) M.; B.S., Mich. Agrl. Coll., 1881; A.B., Olivet Coll., 1889, A.M., 1892; A.M., U. of Wisconsin, 1904; LL.D., Olivet, 1912; D.Ed., Miami University, 1928; m. Minnie E. Alderman, June 25, 1890; children—Charles Arthur, Laurence A., Marion Louise. Taught at Charlotte, and Vermontville, Mich., 1882-87; instr. English and history, Olivet Acad., 1889-95; prof. history, Olivet Coll., 1895-96; prin. State Normal Sch., Mt. Pleasant, Mich., 1896-1900; pres. State Normal Coll., Ypsilanti, July 1912—. Conglist. Author: The Personality of the Teacher, 1910. Lecturer; editor Am. Schoolmaster; asso. editor Mich. Edn. Jour. Home: Ypsilanti, Mich. Died Sept. 23, 1933.

McKENZIE, Alexander, clergyman; b. New Bedford, Mass., Dec. 14, 1830; s. Daniel and Phebe Mayhew (Smith) M.; A.B., Harvard, 1859, A.M., 1862; grad. Andover Theol. Sem., 1861; (D.D., Amherst, 1879; S.T.D., Harvard, 1901); m. Ellen Holman Eveleth, Jan. 25, 1865; father of Kenneth M. Ordained Congl. ministry, 1861; pastor South Ch., Augusta, Me., 1861-67, First Ch., Cambridge, Mass., 1867, 1910, pastor emeritus, 1910. Lecturer, 1882-83, preacher, 1886-89, Harvard U. (overseer, 1872-84, sec. bd., 1875-1901); lecturer Andover Theol. Sem., 1881-82 and 1894-97. Emeritus pres. bd. trustees Wellesley Coll.; trustee Phillips Acad., Andover, Mass., Hampton Inst., Va. Pres. Boston Seaman's Friend Soc., 1890, Boston Port Soc. Author: The Divine Force in the Life of the World, 1898; A Door Opened, 1898; Now, 1899; Getting One's Bearings, 1903. Home: Cambridge, Mass. Died Aug. 6, 1914.

McKENZIE, George, surgeon; b. Port Huron, Mich., May 30, 1871; s. Hugh and Anna (Robinson) M.; M.D., Rush Med. Coll., Chicago, 1893; m. Fannie Vaughn, Aug. 25, 1897. Practiced at Victor, Colo., 1894-1908, Reno, Nev., 1908—. Fellow Am. Coll. Surgeons. Mason, Elk. Home: Reno, Neb. Died Feb. 4, 1924.

McKENZIE, James A., farmer, congressman, diplomat; b. in Christian Co., Ky., Aug. 1, 1840; ed. as lawyer, but turned to farming; mem. Ky. legislature, 1867-71; presdl. elector, 1872; mem. Congress, 1877-83; U.S. minister to Peru, 1893-97; grand master Masons Ky., 1890-91; Ky. commr. to World's Columbian Expn., 1891-93. Democrat. Home: Oak Grove, Ky. Died 1904.

McKENZIE, John Charles, congressman; b. Woodbine Tp., Jo Daviess Co., Ill., Feb. 18, 1860; s. Donald and Sarah (Atchison) M.; ed. pub. schs.; read law in offices of Judge W. T. Hodson, Galena, Ill.; married; 1 dau., Jean. Admitted to Ill. bar, 1890, and began practice at Elizabeth, Ill.; dir. Elizabeth Exchange Bank. Mem. Ill. Ho. of Rep., 2 terms, 1892-96; mem. Ill. State Commn. of Claims, 1896-1900; mem. Ill. Senate, 3 terms, 1900-11 (pres. pro tem. 1 term), resigned, 1911; mem. 62d to 68th Congresses (1911-25), 13th Ill. Dist.; chmn. Muscle Shoals Inquiry, reporting Nov. 14, 1925. Republican. Methodist. Mason, Odd Fellow, K.P. Home: Elizabeth, Ill. Died Sept. 17, 1941.

McKENZIE, John Heyward, clergyman; b. Bourneville, O., May 31, 1862; s. Henry B. and Ella A. (Gregg) M.; A.B., Mt. Union Coll., 1883; A.M., Boston U., 1884; (L.H.D., Kenyon College, 1905; D.D., Nashotah House, 1910); unmarried. President Hillsboro College, 1888-90; pres. Belmont College and Ohio Mil. Inst., College Hill, O., 1890-94; deacon, 1892, priest, 1893, P.E. Ch.; rector Howe (Ind.) Sch., 1895—; rector St. Mark's Ch., Howe, Ind., 1895—; dean Cathedral, Indianapolis, 1897. Deputy Gen. Conv., P.E. Ch., 1898, 1901, 04, 07, 10, 13, 16; examining chaplain Diocese of Michigan City; trustee Nashotah (Wis.) House, Akeley Hall, Grand Haven, Mich., Howe Sch. Mem. Gen. Bd. Religious Edn., New York, 1915—; pres. N. Academic Assn.; pres. Diocesan Bd. Religious Edn.; hon. sec.-treas. Jerusalem and East Mission Fund, etc. Home: Howe, Ind. Died Aug. 3, 1920.

McKENZIE, Robert Tait, M.D., sculptor; b. Almonte, Ont., Can., May 26, 1867; s. Rev. William and Catherine (Shiells) M.; ed. Ottawa Collegiate Inst.; A.B., McGill, 1889, M.D., 1892, LL.D., 1921; diploma Harvard Summer Sch. Physical Edn., 1891; M.P.E., Springfield (Mass.) Training Coll., 1913; m. Ethel O'Neil, of Hamilton, Ont., Aug. 18, 1907. House phys., Montreal Gen. Hosp., 1893; surgeon Beaver Line steamer Liverpool to Montreal, 1893; house phys. to gov.-gen. Can., 1895; demonstrator, then lecturer anatomy, 1895-1904, med. dir. physical training, 1896-1904, McGill U.; lecturer artistic anatomy, Montreal Art Assn., 1901, Harvard Summer Sch., 1901, Olympic lecture course, St. Louis, 1904; prof. and dir. dept. physical edn., U. of Pa., 1904-30, research prof. of physical education, 1931—. Temporary major R.A.M.C., 1915, 16; insp. physical training Kitchener's armies, med. officer in charge Heaton Park Command Depot, 1916. Has exhibited at Salon, Royal Acad. and elsewhere; sculptor of the Sprinter, Athlete, Competitor and heroic statues of the Youthful Franklin and Rev. George Whitefield on the campus of U. of Pa.; Victory Memorial, Cambridge, England; Scottish American War Memorial, Edinburgh, 1927; General Wolfe Statue, Greenwich, 1930; Alma Mater, Girard College, Phila., 1932; Delano Nurses Memorial, Washington, D.C., 1933; war memorials in Parliament Bldg., Ottawa; etc. Author: Exercise in Education and Medicine; Treatment of Convalescent Soldiers by Physical Means; Reclaiming the Maimed. Home: Philadelphia, Pa. Died Apr. 28, 1938.

McKENZIE, Roderick Duncan, prof. sociology; b. Carman, Manitoba, Can., Feb. 3, 1885; s. John and Katherine (Stevenson) McK.; A.B., U. of Manitoba, 1912; Ph.D., U. of Chicago, 1921; m. Eva Irene Bissett, of Winnipeg, Can., Nov. 28, 1916. Came to U.S., 1913, naturalized citizen, 1922. Instr. in sociology, Ohio State U., 1915-19; asso. prof. sociology, W.Va. U., 1919-20; prof. sociology, U. of Wash., 1920-29; spl. investigator urban problems, President's Research Com., 1929-30; prof. sociology and chmn. dept., U. of Mich., 1930—. Dir. civilian relief, Am. Red Cross, Camp Sherman, 1918; investigator U.S. Food Administration, O., 1919. Fellow Albert Kahn Foundation (foreign travel of Am. teachers), 1925-26. Author: The Neighborhood, 1921; Oriental Exclusion, 1927; L'Evolution Economique du Monde, 1928; The Metropolitan Community, 1933. Died May 6, 1940.

McKENZIE, William P., trustee, dir.; b. Almonte, Can.; s. Rev. William and Catherine (Shiells) McK.; ed. Upper Can. Coll.; A.B., Toronto U., 1884; spl. corr. The Mail, during the N.W. campaign to put down Riel's Insurrection, 1885; grad. Knox College, Toronto, Can., 1889; post-grad. student Auburn (New York) Theol. Sem., 1890; became a naturalized citizen of the U.S., 1901; m. Daisette Dudley Stocking, Aug. 1, 1901; 1 son, G. Stuart. Pastor 1st Presbyn. Ch., Avon, N.Y., 1891-94; instr. English lit. and rhetoric, U. of Rochester, 1892-95; elected a "first mem." of The First Ch. of Christ, Scientist, in Boston, 1894; apptd. by Mrs. Eddy on com. preparing lesson sermons for use in all the churches, 1896; joined with other first mems. in accepting Mrs. Eddy's gift to The Mother Ch., of the Pub. House, 1898; trustee Christian Science Pub. Soc., 1898-1917; mem. Bd. of Lectureship, 1898-1915; pres. of Ch., 1899, 1906, 10, 17; elected editor Christian Science Jour., Sentinel, etc., July 26, 1917; resigned Mar. 12, 1920, in protest against conditions during an injunction; when litigation ended appointed a trustee of the Christian Science Pub. Soc. by decree of the Supreme Judicial Court of Mass., Jan. 28, 1922; elected mem. Christian Science Bd. of Dirs., Sept. 1, 1932, and apptd. a trustee under the Will of Mary Baker Eddy, Sept. 30, 1932. Author: Heartsease Hymns; The Sower; Fields of Bloom; The Auld Fowk, Some Verses in Scots. Home: Cambridge, Mass. Died Sept. 8, 1942.

McKEOGH, Arthur, editor; b. Troy, N.Y., Jan. 27, 1890; s. J. T. J. and Mary L. (Callaghan) McK.; A.B., Coll. of St. Francis Xavier, 1911; LL.B., Fordham, 1915; m. Elsie Garretson Finch, June 4, 1921. Reporter N.Y. Evening Sun, 1912-14; editorial staff N.Y. Sunday World, 1914-17; admitted to N.Y. bar, 1917; asso. editor and art editor Sat. Eve. Post, Phila., 1919-23; editorial rep. Internat. Mag. Co., N.Y. City, 1923-25; editor Cosmopolitan Mag. and Cosmopolitan Book Corp., 1925; editor McClure's Mag., 1925-27; New York editor Red Book Mag., 1927-29; mng. editor of Good Housekeeping Mag., 1929—. Commd. 2d lt. inf., Plattsburg, Aug. 1917; student Sch. of Trench Warfare, Harvard; served with 308th Inf., 77th Div., A.E.F.; 1st lt. Sept. 1918; divisional liaison instr. 95th Div., Camp Sherman, O., and editor Govt. mil. history, Washington; disch., Mar. 1919; reapptd. capt. M.I.O.R.C., 1922; promoted maj., 1928; retired 1933. Awarded D.S.C. (U.S.). Author: The Victorious 77th, 1919; Over the 77th War Grounds, 1929; The Real Calvin Coolidge (in collaboration with Mrs. Grace G. Coolidge), 1934-35. Editor: History of the 308th Infantry, 1927. Home: New York, N.Y. Died June 15, 1937.

McKIBBEN, Frank Pape, civil engr.; b. Ft. Smith, Ark., Nov. 13, 1871; s. Frank Read and Minnie Elizabeth (Pape) McK.; student of Ark. U., 1887-90; B.S., Mass. Inst. of Tech., 1894; m. Arabelle Almy, Jan. 1899 (died 1921); 1 son, Elliot S.; m. 2d, Ariana K. Elder, Apr. 1923. Instr. civ. engring., later prof., Mass. Inst. Tech., 1894-1907; prof. civ. engring., Lehigh U., 1907-19; same, Union Coll., 1919-1926. Asst. engr. Boston Elevated Ry. Co., 1899-1901, Mass. R.R. Commn., 1901-07; consulting engr. Pa. Water Supply Commission, 1914-15; v.p. People's Trust Co., 1915-19; supervisor tech. training Emergency Fleet Corp., 1918, city engr., Schenectady, 1924-26; cons. engr. Gen. Electric Co., 1927-32, also cons. engineer City of Rochester and engineer of design and construction on two bridges; engineer examiners Pub. Works Adminstrn., 1933—. Republican. Presbyn. Part author: Taylor and Thompson's Concrete, Plain and Reinforced, 1903; American Civil Engineers' Pocket Book, 1912. Home: Fayetteville, Pa. Died Nov. 27, 1936.

McKIBBEN, Paul Stilwell, anatomy; b. Granville, O., Mar. 14, 1886; s. George Fitch and Elizabeth Thresher (Stilwell) McK.; B.S., Denison University, Granville, O., 1906, Sc.D., 1936; Ph.D., U. of Chicago, 1911; LL.D., U. of Western Ont., Can., 1928; m. Elizabeth Kendall, Feb. 20, 1919; children—Paul Stilwell, Richard Kendall, Elizabeth Thresher, John Hansford. Fellow, asst. and instr. in anatomy, U. of Chicago, 1907-13; prof. anatomy, Faculty of Medicine, U. of Western Ont., 1913-27, also dean, 1917-27; asso. prof. and prof. anatomy, U. of Mich., 1927-29; prof. anatomy, U. of Southern Calif. Sch. of Medicine, 1929—, dean Sch. of Medicine, 1931—. Served as 1st lt. Sanitary Corps, U.S. Army, 1918-19, attached to Army Neuro-Surgical Lab., Johns Hopkins Med. School. Democrat. Episcopalian. Home: Los Angeles, Calif. Died Nov. 11, 1941.

McKIBBIN, Chambers, brig. gen. U.S.A.; b. Pittsburgh, Nov. 2, 1841; s. Chambers and Jane (Bell) M.; ed. at Andover, Mass.; m. Mary Gaines Sibley, Nov. 3, 1869. Enlisted as pvt., gen. service, U.S.A., Sept. 22, 1862; disch. Sept. 24, 1862; commd. 2d lt. 14th Inf., Sept. 22, 1862; promoted through grades to brig. gen. vols., July 8, 1898; col. 12th Inf., U.S.A., Apr. 1, 1899; hon. disch. from vol. service, May 12, 1899; transferred to 24th Inf., Aug. 12, 1901; brig. gen., Oct. 2, 1902; retired, at own request, after 40 yrs'. service, Oct. 3, 1902. Bvtd. capt., Aug. 18, 1864, for battle of North Anna River, Va., and operations on Weldon R.R. Participated in battle of Santiago, and was mil. gov. Santiago de Cuba; comd. 2d Brigade, 2d Div., 5th Army Corps; comd. 1st Brigade, 1st Div., 2d Army Corps, Sept. 22, 1898-Apr. 1, 1899; comd. Dept. of Tex., 1899. Home: Washington, D.C. Died May 1919.

McKIBBIN, William, theologian; b. Pittsburgh, Pa., May 24, 1850; s. William C. and Jane Denny (Brackenridge) M.; A.B., Princeton, 1869, later A.M.; grad. Western Theol. Sem., Pa., 1873; D.D., U. of Wooster, 1889, LL.D., 1904; m. Nancy McCulloch Patterson, Sept. 10, 1874. Ordained Presbyn. ministry, May 20, 1873; pastor 7th Ch., Pittsburgh, 1873-74, Central Ch., St. Paul, 1874-79, Second Ch., Pittsburgh, 1880-88, First Ch., Walnut Hills, Cincinnati, 1888-1904; pres. and prof. systematic theology, Lane Theol. Sem., Cincinnati, 1904-25 (pres. emeritus.). Home: Cincinnati, O. Died Dec. 20, 1931.

McKIM, Charles Follen, architect; b. Chester Co., Pa., Aug. 24, 1847; s. James Miller and Sarah Allibone (Speakman) M.; student Lawrence Scientific Sch., Harvard, 1866-67, École des Beaux Arts, Paris, 1867-70; (hon. A.M., Harvard, 1890, Bowdoin, 1894). Began practice, 1872, joined in partnership by Wm. R. Mead, 1877, and by late Stanford White in 1879 as McKim, Mead & White; among notable bldgs. erected by firm are: Columbia Univ., State Capitol, R.I., Brooklyn Inst. Arts and Sciences, Walker Art Gallery (Bowdoin Coll.), Dept. of Architecture (Harvard), Music Hall, Pub. Library (Boston), Agrl. Bldg., N.Y. State bldgs. (World's Columbian Expn.), Newport Casino, University, Harvard, Century clubs (New York), etc. Mem. congressional commn. for improvement of Washington park system; mem. New York Art Commn. Hon. mem. Am. Inst. Architects (pres.); N.A., 1907. Awarded Royal gold medal by King Edward for promotion of architecture, 1903. Home: New York, N.Y. Died 1909.

McKIM, John, bishop; b. Pittsfield, Mass., July 17, 1852; s. James and Mary Ann (Dunbar) M.; student Griswold Coll., Davenport, Ia., 1866-69; grad. Nashotah Theol. Sem., 1879; D.D., 1893; D.D., Trinity, 1893, Oxford U., 1908; m. Ellen Augusta, d. Rev. A. D. Cole, of Nashotah, Wis., Sept. 16, 1879 (died Oct. 7, 1915); m. 2d, Mrs. John E. Baird, May 4, 1924. Deacon, 1878, priest, 1879, P.E. Ch.; missionary in Japan, 1880-93; consecrated bishop of Tokyo, June 14, 1893. Decorated Order of Sacred Treasure, Japan, 1924. Died Apr. 4, 1936.

McKIM, Randolph Harrison, clergyman; b. Baltimore, Apr. 15, 1842; s. John S. and Catharine L. (Harrison) M.; A.B., U. of Va., 1861; (D.D., Washington and Lee, 1871; LL.D., George Washington U., 1904; D.C.L., U. of the South, 1908); m. Agnes G. Phillips, 1863; m. 2d, Mrs. A. M. C. Brooke, 1890. Served in C.S.A., 1861-65. Deacon, 1864, priest, 1866, P.E. Ch.; asst., Emanuel Ch., Baltimore, 1865, rector, St. John's, Portsmouth, Va., 1866-67, Christ Ch., Alexandria, Va., 1867-75, Holy Trinity Ch., Harlem, New York, 1875-86, Trinity Ch., New Orleans, 1886-88, Epiphany Ch., Washington, 1889—. Elected dean Theol. Sem. of Va., 1897; pres. House of Deputies, 1904, 1907, 1910. Author: A Soldier's Recollections, 1910; Numerical Strength of the Confederate Army, 1912; The Soul of Lee, 1918; For God and Country, 1918. Ex-chaplain gen. S.R.; pres. D.C. Soc. S.R., 1912-13. Died July 15, 1921.

McKIM, William Duncan, M.D., author; b. Baltimore, Md., Feb. 14, 1855; s. Haslett and Sally (Birckhead) M.; A.B., Columbia, 1875, A.M., 1878, M.D., 1878; studied abroad, 1879-81, 1892-95; Ph.D., Leipzig, 1895; m. Rogé Coolidge, Nov. 22, 1882; m. 2d, Martha Moran Jones, Apr. 26, 1900; m. 3d, Leonora Jackson (violinist), Oct. 12, 1915. Began practice at N.Y. City, 1878; retired 1892; moved to Washington, D.C., 1900. Republican. Author: Heredity and Human Progress, 1900; Study for the Times, 1920. Home: Washington, D.C. Died Apr. 10, 1935.

McKINLEY, Abner, lawyer; b. Ohio; s. William and Nancy Campbell (Allison) McK.; bro. late President William McKinley. Admitted to Ohio and N.Y. bars; practiced law, Canton, O., until 1897, New York, N.Y., 1897—. Died 1904.

McKINLEY, Albert Edward, coll. prof.; b. Phila., Sept. 11, 1870; s. Albert Barnes and Margaret (Johnson) M.; Ph.B., U. of Chicago, 1896; Ph.D., U. of Pa., 1900; m. Jessie S. Willits, Dec. 29, 1903; children—Albert E., Alfred Willits, Margaret, C. Scott. Prof. history, 1896-1915, dean Coll. Liberal Arts and Sciences, 1904-15, Temple U., Phila.; prof. of history, U. of Pa., 1915—. Editor History Teacher's Mag., and Histor. Outlook, 1909—; sec. Pa. War History Commn., 1918-21; pres. Pa. Federation of Hist. Socs., 1921; pres. Nat. Council for Social Studies, 1921. Republican. Baptist. Author: Public Archives of Philadelphia (with Herman V. Ames), 1902; Suffrage Franchise in English Colonies, 1905; Island Possessions of U.S. (Vol. 20 of Lee & Thorpe's History of North America), 1907; School History of the Great War (with C. A. Coulomb and A. J. Gerson), 1918; Collected Materials for the Study of the War, 1918; What Europe Gave to America (with C. A. Coulomb and H. White), 1927; World History in the Making (with A. C. Howland and M. Dann), 1927; World History Today (with same), 1927; Workbooks for the Same, 1930. Home: Germantown, Phila., Pa. Died Feb. 26, 1936.

McKINLEY, Carlyle, journalist; b. Newnan, Ga., Nov. 22, 1847; s. Charles G. and Frances C. (Jackson) McK., grad. Presbyn Theol. Sem., Columbia, S.C., 1874; m. Miss E. H. Bryce, 1875. Editorial writer Charleston News and Courier, 1884—. Author: Appeal to Pharaoh, 1889 F2. Monographs, etc.: The Cyclone of 1885, Year Book City of Charleston, 1885; The Charleston Earthquake, 1886, same, 1886, and 9th Annual Report U.S. Geol. Survey. Home: Mt. Pleasant, S.C. Died 1904.

McKINLEY, Earl Baldwin, bacteriologist; b. Emporia, Kan., Sept. 28, 1894; s. Joseph Baldwin and Mary Elizabeth (Griffith) McK.; A.B., U. of Mich., 1916, M.D., 1922; fellow Nat. Research Council, Pasteur Inst., U. of Brussels, 1924-25; m. Leola Edna Royce, June 23, 1917; children—Elsbeth Janet, Royce Baldwin. Instr. in bacteriology and biochemistry, U. of Mich. Med. Sch., 1919-22; asst. prof. medicine, Coll. Medicine, Baylor U., 1922-23, prof. hygiene and bacteriology and chmn. dept., 1923-24; asst. prof. bacteriology, Coll. Phys. and Surgeons, Columbia, 1925-26, asso. prof., 1926-27; field dir., Manila, P.I., Rockefeller Foundation, 1927-28; mem. advisory com. to gov. gen. for control of leprosy, and lecturer, U. of Philippines, 1927-28; prof. bacteriology, Coll. Phys. and Surgeons, Columbia, and dir. Sch. of Tropical Medicine, U. of Puerto Rico (under auspices of Columbia), 1928-31; dean Coll. of Medicine and prof. bacteriology, George Washington U., 1931—. Intelligence officer U.S.A., World War. Fellow A.M.A., Am. Coll. Physicians, Royal Soc. Tropical Medicine and Hygiene (London); mem. numerous scientific societies. Author: Filterable Virus and Rickettsia Diseases, 1929; a Geography of Disease, 1935; Agents of Disease and Host Resistance (with others), 1935. Died July 29, 1938.

McKINLEY, Ida Saxton; b. Canton, O., June, 1847; d. James Asbury and Catherine (Dewalt) Saxton; ed. in schs. of Cleveland and at Brook Hill Sem., Media, Pa.; visited Europe for 6 mos. in 1869, and soon after her return became cashier in her father's bank in Canton; m. Maj. William McKinley, Jan. 25, 1871. Their first child, Ida, b. Dec. 25, 1871, lived to the age of 4, and their second child, Catherine, died in infancy. Shock resulting from the death of her children and of her mother resulted in a nervous disease which made her an invalid for life. She resided in Washington during her husband's service in Congress, 1877-91, in Columbus while he was gov. of Ohio, 1892-96, and in the White House while he was president, and notwithstanding her invalided condition successfully dispensed the hospitality due to her position. She was at Buffalo with President McKinley when he visited the Pan-Am. Expn., and was the chief object of his solicitude when his final hour came. Lived in retirement at her home from time of husband's death. Home: Canton, O. Died 1907.

McKINLEY, James F., army officer; b. San Francisco, Calif., Feb. 22, 1880; s. James and Eliza Howe (Fuller) McK.; grad. high sch., Canton, O., 1898, Army Sch. of the Line, 1911; m. Margaret Disosway, Sept. 18, 1912; children—Margaret, William, James. Served as pvt. 8th Vol. Ohio Inf., Spanish-Am. War, June-Nov. 1898; commd. 2d lt. Cav., U.S. Army, Feb. 3, 1899; advanced through grades to col., May 9, 1921; apptd. asst. to the adj. gen., rank of brig. gen., 1929; maj. gen., the adjutant general, June 1933, term of 4 yrs.; retired with rank of maj. gen., Oct. 31, 1935; now pres. Nat. Bank of Ft. Sam Houston, San Antonio. Awarded 2 silver star citations for gallantry in action; holder of campaign badges for Spanish-Am. War, Cuban Pacification, Cuban Occupation, Philippine Insurrection, Mexican border and World War victory; on Gen. Staff eligible list. Methodist. Died Jan. 17, 1941.

McKINLEY, William, President of the United States; b. Niles, O., Jan. 29, 1843; s. William and Nancy Campbell (Allison) McK.; ed. at public schools, Poland Acad. and Allegheny Coll. Taught in public schools; enlisted, pvt., 23d Ohio vol. inf., 1861; commissary sergt., 1862; 2d lt., 1862; 1st lt., 1863; capt., 1864; served on staffs of Gens. R. B. Hayes, George Crook and Winfield S. Hancock; bvtd. maj. U.S. vols. by President Lincoln for gallantry in battle, March 13, 1865; detailed as acting asst. adjt. gen., 1st div., 1st army corps, until mustered out, July 26, 1865; m. Ida, d. James A. Saxton, 1871. Studied law in Mahoning Co., O.; took a course at Albany (N.Y.) Law School, 1867; admitted to Ohio bar, 1867, and settled at Canton, O., which has since been his home. Pros. att'y Stark Co., O., 1869; mem. Congress, 1876-91, and as chmn. Com. on Ways and Means reported the tariff bill of 1890, known as the "McKinley Bill"; especially known in Congress as advocate of high protective tariff. His dist., having been changed by Dem. legislature, he was defeated for Congress at Nov. election, 1890. Elected gov. Ohio, 1891; re-elected, 1893. Delegate at large to Rep. Nat. Conv., and mem. Com. on Resolutions, 1884, and supported James G. Blaine; to that of 1888 (supporting John Sherman), and was chmn. Com. on Resolutions; delegate at large to conv., 1892, and was made its chmn.; received 182 votes for President, but refused to allow his name to be considered, supporting renomination of Benjamin Harrison. Nominated for President at Rep. Nat. Conv., St. Louis, June 18, 1896, receiving 661 out of a total of 905 votes; elected in Nov., 1896, by popular plurality of 600,000 votes, and received 271 electoral votes as against 176 for William J. Bryan. On June 21, 1900, unanimously renominated by Rep. Nat. Conv., Phila., and re-elected in Nov., the leading opposing candidate again being William J. Bryan. Popular plurality, 849,000 votes; received 292 electoral votes against 155 for Mr. Bryan. Died 1901.

McKINLEY, William Brown, senator; b. Petersburg, Ill., Sept. 5, 1856; s. George and Hannah (Finley) M.; student U. of Ill., 2 yrs.; m. Kate Frisbee, Feb. 1881. Partner in banking and mortgage loan business of J. B. & W. B. McKinley since 1877; building and operating pub. utilities since 1885. Mem. 59th to 62d Congresses (1905-13) and 64th to 66th Congresses (1915-21), 19th Ill. Dist.; U.S. senator, term 1921-27. Trustee U. of Ill., 1902-05. Republican. Home: Champaign, Ill. Died Dec. 7, 1926.

McKINLOCK, George Alexander, manufacturer; b. Oswego, New York, Dec. 27, 1857; s. John and Margaret Ann (McCormick) M.; m. Marion Wallace Rapelye, Dec. 2, 1890; 1 son, George A., Jr. (D.S.C.), 2d lt., U.S.A., killed in action in France, July 21, 1918. Moved to Chicago, 1887, an organizer and long president of the Central Electic Company. Retired. Republican. Home: Lake Bluff, Ill. Died Dec. 16, 1936.

McKINNEY, Alexander Harris, clergyman, author; b. New York, July 28, 1858; s. James and Sarah (Harris) M.; B.A., Coll. City of New York, 1881, M.A., 1887; grad. Union Theol. Sem., 1886; Ph.D., New York U., 1891; D.D., Bloomfield Theol. Sem., 1916; m. Adele Miller Van Tassell, June 27, 1888. Ordained Presbyn. ministry, 1886; pastor Romeyn Chapel, New York, 1886-87, Olivet Memorial Ch., New York, 1887-99; supt. N.Y. State S.S. Assn., 1899-1903; lecturer on S.S. pedagogy, 1903-04; editorial work, 1901-05; pastoral work, 1905-09; asst. supt., 1910-12, supt., 1912-29, New York City Mission Soc. Author: The Child for Christ, 1902; After the Primary, What?, 1904; Practical Pedagogy for the Sunday School, 1911; The Sunday School Teacher at His Best, 1915; Guiding Boys Over Fool Hill, 1918; Guiding Girls, 1920; Average Boys and Girls, 1925; A Top-Notch Teacher, 1925; Human Nature in Christian Work, 1928; Triumphant Christianity, 1932. Home: Jamaica, N.Y. Died April 1941.

McKINNEY, Buckner Abernathy, banker; b. McKinney, Tex., Jan. 16, 1872; s. Thomas C. and Katherine (Abernathy) McK.; ed. pub. schs.; studied law pvtly.; m. Lucile Geers, Sept. 12, 1906; (died 1935); children—Buckner Abernathy, Frances. Admitted to Tex. bar, 1902, and practiced at Bonham, Tex., until 1906; vice president and cashier Durant (Okla.) Nat. Bank, 1906-20; dir. Federal Reserve Bank of Dallas, Tex., 1914-22, gov., 1922-25, also 1931-36, pres., Mar. 1, 1936—; was vice pres. Am. Exchange Bank, Dallas, 1920-22 and 1925-29; 1st v.p. First Nat. Bank Dallas, 1929-31; mem. Federal Advisory Council Federal Reserve Bd., 1925-31, pres. of Council, 1930-31 (resigned as pres. upon election as gov. of bank). Home: Dallas, Tex. Died Apr. 2, 1939.

McKINNEY, David, clergyman; b. at Phila., May 20, 1860; s. William and Margaret (Ritchie) M.; U. of Pa., 1878-80; grad. R.P. Theol. Sem., Phila., 1884; (D.D., Wittenberg Coll., 1895; LL.D., Franklin Coll., O., 1908); m. Carrie H. Chapin, June 3, 1891; children—David Earl, Robert Stevenson, Anne Carolyn. Ordained Reformed Presbyn. ministry, 1884; pastor, Elgin, Ill., 1884-86, 1st Ref. Presbyn. Ch., Cincinnati, 1888-1914, 1st Presbyn. Ch., Cincinnati, 1914-26 (emeritus); was also president Cedarville (O.) Coll., 1894-1915 (emeritus); dean R.P. Theol. Sem., 1913-14. Trustee R.P. Theol. Sem., Phila., Cedarville Coll. Moderator Gen. Synod R.P. Ch., 1892. Sec. Com. of 500, Cincinnati, 1888-90; pres. Ohio State Sabbath Assn., Municipal Reform League, Cincinnati; prominently identified with social and municipal reform movements in Cincinnati. Home: Cincinnati, O. Died Apr. 26, 1934.

McKINNEY, James, congressman; b. Oquawka, Ill., Apr. 14, 1852; s. John and Mary (Stewart) M.; A.M., Monmouth Coll., 1874 (LL.D., 1913); m. Mary O. McDonald, Nov. 6, 1878. Pres. Aledo Bank, 1892-1907. Mem. Ill. Rep. State Com., 1894-1906; chmn. exec. com. same, 1900-04, in charge presdl. campaign in Illinois; mem. Ill. Warehouse Commn., 1901-02; elected to 59th Congress, Nov. 7, 1905, to fill unexpired term (1905-07) of Hon. B. F. Marsh, deceased; reëlected to 60th, 61st and 62d Congresses (1907-13), 14th Ill. Dist. Home: Aledo, Ill. Died Sept. 29, 1934.

McKINNEY, Philip Watkins, gov. Va.; b. Buckingham Co., Va., May 1, 1832; grad. Hampden-Sidney, 1851; studied law; admitted to bar, 1858; was capt. in 4th Va. cav., Confederate army, until incapacitated by wounds received at Brandy Station; after that on post duty at Danville; mem. legislature, 1858-65; Democratic candidate for Congress, 1872; twice presdl. elector; Commonwealth's atty. several terms; del. to Nat. Democratic conventions, 1884 and 1888; candidate for atty. gen., 1881; gov. Va., 1890-94. Home: Farmville, Va. Died 1899.

McKINNEY, Robert C., manufacturer; b. Troy, N.Y., Jan. 20, 1852; s. Robert and Mary (Smyth) M.; ed. Cornell U., class of 1876; m. Eleanor Beckett, Oct. 15, 1879. Pres. Niles-Bement-Pond Co., Pratt & Whitney Co., of Hartford, Conn. Home: New York and Greenwich, Conn. Died Oct. 3, 1916.

McKINNEY, Thomas Emery, mathematician; b. Hebron, W.Va., Apr. 26, 1864; s. Joseph Morris and Margaret (Carlin) M.; B.A., Marietta Coll., O., 1887, M.A., 1890; post-grad. work, Johns Hopkins, 1889-90, 1895-96; fellow in mathematics, U. of Chicago, 1896-97, Ph.D., 1905; m. Mary Margaret Penrose, Dec. 23, 1893; 1 dau., Margaret Jane. Instr. in mathematics, 1887-89, prof. mathematics and Lee lecturer on astronomy, 1890-1906, Marietta Coll.; asso. prof. mathematics and head of dept., Wesleyan U., Conn., 1906-08; prof. mathematics and astronomy, U. of S.D., 1908-28. Mem. Lick eclipse expdn. to Spain, 1905. Author: War-Time Talks and Essays; Life and Education, and Other Essays; Essays and Addresses. Died April 12, 1930.

McKINSEY, James O., chmn. bd. Marshall Field & Co.; b. Gamma, Mo., June 4, 1889; s. James Madison and Mary Elizabeth (Logan) McK.; Pd.B., State Teachers Coll., Warrensburg, Mo., 1912; LL.B., U. of Ark., 1913; Ph.B., U. of Chicago, 1916, A.M., 1919; m. Alice Louise Anderson, June 12, 1920; children—Robert, Richard (twins). Mem. faculty U. of Chicago, 1917—, prof. business policies, 1926-35, lecturer on accounting, Columbia, 1920-21; C.P.A., Ill., 1919; sr. partner James O. McKinsey & Co., 1925-35; chmn. bd. Marshall Field & Co., 1935—; dir. Chicago Corp., Kroger Grocery & Baking Co., Selected Shares Corp. Dir. Woodlawn Hosp. Served as pvt., later lt., Ordnance Dept., U.S.A., 1917-19. Mem. bd. trustees Armour Inst. Tech.; mem. bd. mgrs. Chicago Y.M.C.A., mem. bd. dirs. Central Y.M.C.A. Coll.; mem. transportation com. Chicago Assn. of Commerce. Author: Bookkeeping and Accounting, 1920; Budgetary Control, 1922; Managerial Accounting, 1924; Business Administration, 1925; Accounting Principles, 1929. Home: Chicago, Ill. Died Nov. 30, 1937.

McKINSTRY, Addis Emmett, president Internat. Harvester Co.; b, nr. Eaton, O., Jan. 27, 1870; s. M. H. and Katherine (Waldron) McK.; ed. pub. schs.; m. Elizabeth Minot, Jan. 1, 1896; 1 son, Ross Waldron. Began in employ of Wm. Deering & Co., Chicago, 1886; division mgr. Internat. Harvester Co., 1916-20, v.p. and dir., 1920-32, 1st vice pres. and dir., 1932-33, president, 1933-35, chmn. exec. com. and dir, 1935—. Republican. Mason. Home: Hinsdale, Ill. Died Mar. 21, 1941.

McKINSTRY, Grace E., artist; b. Fredonia, N.Y.; d. Archibald W. and Ellen E. (Putnam) McK.; ed. Art Students' League, New York; Art Inst., Chicago; Académie Julian and Académie Colarossi, Paris; pvt. pupil of Raphael Collin; also studied in Spain and Holland. Portrait painter and lecturer on art and travel topics. Portraits on permanent exhbn. at Army and Navy Club, Washington, D.C.; Beloit (Mich.) Coll.; Lake Erie Coll.; Pomona Coll.; U. of Minn.; Carleton Coll.; Woman's Club of Minneapolis; Shattuck Sch.; Cornell U.; Seabury-Western Theol. Sem., Evanston. Republican. Conglist. Studios: Minneapolis, Minn. and Washington, D.C. Died Nov. 26, 1936.

McKISSICK, Anthony Foster, cotton mfr.; b. Union, S.C., June 10, 1869; s. Isaac Going and Sarah Agnes (Foster) McK.; B.S. and A.M., U. of S.C., 1889; M.M.E., Cornell U., 1895; m. Margaret Adger Smyth, Dec. 17, 1891; children—Ellison Smyth, Sarah Foster (dec.). Teacher elec. engring., Ala. Polytechnic, 1891-99; chief eng. Pelzer Mfg. Co., 1899-1901; pres. Grendel Mills, Greenwood, S.C., 1901-18, "Ninety Six" Cotton Mills, 1906-17; v.p.

Alice Mills, Easley, 1923—; dir. P.&N. Ry., C.&W.C. Ry., Norwood Nat. Bank; mem. Port Commn., Charleston, S.C., 1922— (chmn. bd. 1923-24); mem. Dist. Exemption Bd., 1917-19, World War; mem. S.C. Ho. of Rep., 1922-26. Mason. Home: Greenville, S.C. Died Apr. 8, 1938.

McKITTRICK, William James, clergyman; b. Greenport, N.Y., May 13, 1854; s. William and Isabella (Wasson) M.; A.B., Princeton, 1876; grad. Union Theol. Sem., 1879; (D.D., Westminster Coll., Mo., 1903; LL.D., Mo. Valley College, 1909; m. Julia Humphrey Seward, Oct. 3, 1889. Ordained Presbyn. ministry, 1880; pastor Hope Chapel, New York, 1878-88, Florida, N.Y., 1888-91, First Ch., Batavia, N.Y., 1891-95, Cavalry Ch., Buffalo, N.Y., 1895-99, First Ch., St. Louis, Mo., 1899—. Trustee Westminster Coll., Mo., Lindenwood Coll., Mo. V.p. Religious Edn. Assn. Died Dec. 13, 1916.

McKNIGHT, Alexander Hearne, lawyer; b. nr. Melrose, Tex., Oct. 25, 1874; s. Daniel Milton and Octavia (Hearne) McK.; student Southwestern U., Georgetown, Tex., 1893-94 and 1896; LL.B., U. of Tex., 1900; m. Ada Elizabeth Chambers, Oct. 29, 1902; children—Alexandra Elizabeth (dec.), Adrian Hearne; m. 2d, Mrs. Madelyn Hamilton, June 16, 1928. Teacher public schools, Center and Garrison, Tex., 1897-98; admitted to Tex. bar, 1900, bar Supreme Court of U.S., 1912; mem. Bryarly & McKnight, Center, 1901-02; mayor of Center, 1901-02; asso. with Alexander & Thompson, Dallas, 1903-05; with legal dept. M.K.T. Lines in Tex., Apr. 1, 1905—, asst. gen. solicitor, Sept. 1917—. Asso. editor Tex. Law Review. Democrat. Episcopalian. Home: Dallas, Tex. Died Nov. 30, 1929.

McKNIGHT, Charles, banker, steel mfr.; b. Sewickley, Pa., Sept. 2, 1863; s. Charles and Jeannie (Bair) McK.; m. Eliza C. Wilson, Oct. 31, 1888. Pres. Western Nat. Bank (Pittsburgh), Carbon Steel Co. Home: Pittsburgh, Pa. Died Jan. 28, 1926.

McKNIGHT, Harvey Washington, educator; b. McKnightstown, Pa., Apr. 3, 1843; s. Capt. Thomas and Margaret Fleming (Stewart) M.; A.B., Pa. Coll., Gettysburg, 1865; grad. Theol. Sem., Gettysburg, 1867; (D.D., Monmouth Coll., 1883; LL.D., Lafayette Coll., 1889); sergt. to capt. Pa. vols., 1862-65; m. Mary C. Welty, Nov. 12, 1867. Ordained Luth. ministry, 1867; pastor Newville, Pa., 1867-70; disabled by sickness, 1870-72; pastor St. Paul's Ch., Easton, Pa., 1872-80; First English Luth Ch., Cincinnati, 1880-84, Trinity Ch., Hagerstown, Md., a few months, 1884; pres. Pa. Coll., 1884-1904, instr. intellectual and moral science, 1904-06, pres. emeritus, 1910. Mem. Gettysburg Battlefield Memorial Assn., 1888-95; pres. Gen. Synod Luth. Ch. of U.S., 1889-91; a founder Pa. Chautauqua; mem. Coll. and Univ. Council, State of Pa., 1903-07; v.p. Evang. Alliance of U.S. Died May 29, 1914.

McLACHLAN, James, congressman; b. Argyllshire, Scotland, Aug. 1852; s. James and Jean (McKellar) M.; came to U.S., 1855; A.B., Hamilton Coll., 1878; m. Minnie J. Jones, Dec. 26, 1887; children—Mrs. Anita Jean Reynold, Mrs. Gladys Kathrine Towne, Mrs. Marjorie Janet Bissell, James Douglas; m. 2d, Nellye Orletta Becker, Sept. 1, 1931. Admitted to bar, 1880; practiced at Ithaca, N.Y., 1881-88, Pasadena, Calif., 1888—. Sch. commr., Tompkins Co., N.Y., 1877; dist. atty. Los Angeles Co., Calif., 1890; mem. 54th (1895-97) and 57th (1901-03) Congresses, 6th Calif. Dist., and 58th to 61st Congresses (1903-11), 7th Dist. Mem. Nat. Monetary Commn., 1910-11. Republican. Home: Pasadena, Calif. Died Nov. 21, 1940.

McLAIN, John Scudder, newspaperman; b. Brown Co., O., May 26, 1853; s. James Robinson and Nancy (Anderson) M.; A.B., Wabash Coll., 1877 (hon. A.M., 1892); m. Caroline E. Thomson, Apr. 19, 1881 (died 1924); 1 dau., Linda (Mrs. L. D. Hawkridge); m. 2d, Mrs. Margaret Conklin Roberts, Aug. 1927. City and mng. editor Kansas City Journal, 1878-81; gen. advertising agt. A.,T.&S.F. R.R., Topeka, 1881-85; v.p. and editor Minneapolis Journal, 1885-1908; editor of St. Paul Dispatch, and Pioneer Press, 1909-12; editor of the Minneapolis Tribune, 1915-21. Republican. Author: Alaska and the Klondike, 1905. Died Nov. 17, 1931.

McLAIN, John Speed, physician; b. D.C., Aug. 9, 1848; s. Rev. Wm. McL., D.D.; ed. in private schools, Washington; grad. M.D., Columbian Univ., 1871; unmarried. Acting asst. surgeon U.S.A., 1878-84, in New Mexico, Colo., and Texas, in various Indian campaigns and yellow fever epidemic, 1881; pres. bd. supervisors, Washington; pres. bd. med. examiners, Dist. Columbia. Died 1907.

McLANE, James Woods, physician; b. New York, Aug. 19, 1839; s. James Woods (D.D.) and Ann Huntington (Richards) M.; A.B., Yale, 1861; M.D., Coll. Phys. and Surg. (Columbia), 1864; m. Adelaide Lewis Richards, Oct. 10, 1866. Lecturer materia medica, 1867-88, prof. materia medica and therapeutics, 1868-72, adj. prof. obstetrics, diseases of women and children and med. jurisprudence, 1872-79, prof. obstetrics and diseases of children, 1879-91, gynecology, 1882-85, obstetrics, 1891-98, emeritus prof., 1898, dean med. faculty, 1891-1903, pres., 1889-91, Coll. Phys. and Surg.; pres. Roosevelt Hosp., 1905—; cons. physician to New York and Sloane Maternity hospitals, New York, N.Y. Died Nov. 25, 1912.

McLANE, John, governor; b. Lennoxtoun, Scotland, Feb. 27, 1852; ed. in pub. schs., Manchester, N.H.; m. Ellen L. Tuck, Mar. 10, 1880. Learned trade of cabinet maker; engaged from 1876 as mfr. of postoffice furniture and equipments, and now head of McLane Mfg. Co.; also pres. Souhegan Nat. Bank; dir. N.H. Fire Ins. Co. Mem. N.H. Ho. of Rep., 1885, Senate, 1891, 1893, and pres. Senate both sessions; gov. of N.H., 1905-06. Republican. Mason, Conglist. Mem. Amoskeag Veterans. Home: Milford, N.H. Died 1911.

McLANE, William Ward, clergyman; b. Lewisville, Pa., Nov. 13, 1846; s. John and Julia A. (Fisher) M.; A.B., Blackburn Coll., 1871, A.M., 1874; grad. Western Theol. Sem., Pa., 1874; Ph.D., Yale, 1889; D.D., Blackburn, 1882; m. Frances Robinson, Nov. 18, 1880. Ordained Presbyn. ministry, 1874; pastor Presbyn. Ch., Brownsville, Pa., 1874-78, Second Presbyn. Ch., Steubenville, O., 1878-83, Plymouth Congl. Ch., New Haven, Conn., 1884-1912, Leominster, Mass., 1912—. Author: The Cross in the Light of Today, 1883; Evolution in Religion, 1892; A Scientific Study of Christianity (also transl. into Japanese); The Secret of Successful Life, 1918. Home: Leominster, Mass. Died June 4, 1931.

McLAREN, Donald, rear admiral U.S.N.; b. Caledonia, N.Y., Mar. 7, 1834; s. Rev. Donald Campbell and Jane (Stevenson) M.; A.B., Union Coll., 1853; grad. Princeton Theol. Sem., 1857; (D.D., U. of Wooster, 1882); m. Elizabeth Stockton Green, July 14, 1858. Ordained Presbyn. ministry, 1857; pastor Tennent Ch., Monmouth, N.J., 1857-62. Commd. by Pres. Lincoln chaplain U.S.N., Mar. 10, 1863; retired, 1896; promoted, for creditable record during Civil War, rear admiral retired, Jan. 1907. Agt. Am. Bible Soc. in P.R., 1902-04; for W.I. (hdqrs. Havana), 1905-06; for Va., 1906-07; establishing Pacific agency of the Am. Bible Soc., 1907-08, at San Francisco. Republican. Died May 27, 1920.

McLAREN, William Edward, P.E. bishop; b. Geneva, N.Y., Dec. 13, 1831; grad. Jefferson Coll., 1851 (A.M., 1854; S.T.D., Racine Coll., 1873; D.C.L., Univ. of the South, 1884; LL.D., Washington and Jefferson Coll., 1902. Engaged in teaching and editorial work until 1857; entered Presbyn. ministry, 1860; embraced Episcopal faith, 1871; ordered deacon, 1872; ordained priest, 1872, in Detroit; rector in Cleveland, O., 1872-75; consecrated bishop of Ill., 1875; title changed to Bishop of Chicago, 1883. Two new dioceses were erected in Ill. in 1877. Founded Western Theol. Sem., Chicago, 1883, and Waterman Hall for Girls, Sycamore, Ill., 1885; pres. trustees St. Mary's School, Knoxville, Ill.; primus Province of Ill. Author: The Practice of the Interior Life, 1897; The Holy Priest, 1899; The Essence of Prayer, 1901; etc. Died 1905.

McLAUGHLIN, Chester Bentine, judge; b. Moriah, N.Y., Feb. 10, 1856; s. Lyman and Harriet (Chapman) M.; grad. U. of Vt., 1879; studied law, 1879-81; LL.D., Middlebury Coll., 1901, U. of Vt., 1904; m. Lucy Warner, Apr. 22, 1886; children—Warner, Chester B., Donald G. Practiced law at Port Henry, 1881-96; co. judge and surrogate Essex Co., N.Y., 1891-95; del. N.Y. Constl. Conv., 1894; justice Supreme Ct. of N.Y. for terms 1896-99, 1910-Dec. 31, 1923; designated by gov. as asso. justice Appellate Div., 1st Dept., Jan. 1, 1898; resigned from Supreme bench, Feb. 1, 1917, and apptd. judge Ct. of Appeals, N.Y., for term ending Jan. 1, 1918; elected to same for term Jan. 1, 1918-Dec. 31, 1931; retired from Court of Appeals, Jan. 1, 1927, and as a retired judge of the Court of Appeals became official referee for State of N.Y.; gen. counsel firm of McLaughlin & Rogers. Republican. Home: Albany, N.Y. Died Apr. 12, 1929.

McLAUGHLIN, George Asbury, clergyman; b. Nashua, N.H., Oct. 13, 1851; s. John and Mary Abbey (Towle) M.; A.B., Wesleyan U., Conn., 1873, A.M., 1875; (D.D., Taylor U., 1903); m. Mary Ella Henshaw, Oct. 27, 1875 (died 1910); children—Mary Hendley, Grace Irene; m. 2d, Mrs. Jennie Reeves Walker, Oct. 20, 1914; step-dau., Mary Grace. Ordained M.E. ministry, 1875; pastor Franklin Falls, N.H., 1875-77, Whitefield, N.H., 1877-79, Littleton, N.H., 1879-82, 1st Ch., Haverhill, Mass., 1882-85, Laconia, N.H., 1885-88, Exeter, N.H., 1888-92; in evangelistic work, Chicago, 1892-1912; pres. Central Holiness U., University Park, Ia., 1911-17; prof. theology and homiletics, Calif. Bible Coll., Los Angeles, 1918-22; prof. Christian doctrine, Training School for Christian Workers, Huntington Park, Calif., 1919-29, pres., 1924-27, again prof. Pastor Trinity Mission Ch., Los Angeles, 1919-22; editor Christian Witness, Chicago, 1891—. Prohibitionist. Author: Commentary on St. Matthew, 1909; on St. Mark, 1910; on St. Luke, 1911; on St. John, 1913; Acts, 1915; Romans, 1925. Home: Walnut Park, Calif. Died Mar. 10, 1933.

McLAUGHLIN, Hugh; b. Brooklyn, Apr. 2, 1827; ed. public school; learned rope-making trade; engaged in lighterage and later in fish business; master mechanic Brooklyn Navy Yard, 1857-61; defeated for sheriff Kings Co., 1860; register Kings Co. from 1861 for 3 terms; for many yrs. Dem. leader in Brooklyn; was active in promoting construction of Brooklyn Bridge and Prospect Park. Home: Brooklyn, N.Y. Died 1904.

McLAUGHLIN, James, U.S. inspector Interior Dept.; b. Avonmore, Ont., Can., Feb. 12, 1842; s. Felix and Mary (Prince) McL.; ed. common schs.; m. Mary L. Buisson, Jan. 28, 1864. Entered U.S. Indian Service, July 1, 1871, as an employe at Devil's Lake Agency, then Dakota Ty., now N.D.; apptd. U.S. Indian agt., same agency, and reapptd. June 8, 1880; while agt. at Devil's Lake abolished the Indian sun dance on that reservation; transferred as agt. to Standing Rock Agency, N.D., June 27, 1881; apptd. U.S. Indian insp., Mar. 31, 1895. While at Standing Rock had charge of about 6,000 Sioux Indians, including about 3,500 late hostile Sioux returned from Canada, who were formerly followers of Sitting Bull; procured authentic history of the battle of the Little Big Horn (Custer's defeat) from Sioux participants; suppressed ghost dance movement in 1890 on the Standing Rock reservation, and prevented uprising of the Sioux under Sitting Bull. Friend of Sioux chiefs John Grass, Red Cloud, Gall, Crow King, Two Bears, Mad Bear, Hump, and Rain-in-the-Face; procured personal history of Chief Joseph, famous Nez Perce leader; concluded more than 40 agreements between Indians and the U.S. Govt.; chmn. commn. to determine eligibility of allotted Indians for citizenship; said to have greater personal acquaintanceship with Indians than any other living American. Roman Catholic. Author: My Friend the Indian, 1910. Home: McLaughlin, S.D. Died July 28, 1923.

McLAUGHLIN, James Campbell, congressman; b. Beardstown, Ill., Jan. 26, 1858; s. David and Isabella (Campbell) M.; brother of Andrew Cunningham M.; student U. of Mich., 1878-79, LL.B., 1883. In practice at Muskegon, Mich., 1883—; pros. atty. Muskegon Co., 1887-91; mem. Mich. Bd. State Tax Commrs. and Bd. Assessors, 1901-06; mem. 60th to 72d Congresses (1907-33), 9th Mich. Dist. Republican. Home: Muskegon, Mich. Died Nov. 29, 1932.

McLAUGHLIN, James W., architect; b. Cincinnati, Nov. 1, 1834; s. William and Mary Ann (Robinson) M.; ed. pub. schs., Cincinnati; m. Olive Amelia Barbe, Sept. 27, 1862. Began as architect, Cincinnati, 1855; designed Art Mus., Art Acad., Pub. Library, Shillito, Pogue, The Fair and Mabley & Carew dept. stores, bldgs. in Zoöl. Gardens, many pvt. residences, Cincinnati; Hamilton Co. (O.) Court House; Wayne Co. (Ind.) Court House; library, Northampton, Mass., etc. Apptd. Sept. 1861, 1st lt. Benton Cadets, bodyguard of Gen. John C. Fremont and served in Mo. until Gen. Fremont was superseded; spl. artist Frank Leslie's Weekly in Army of the Southwest, 1862, bombardment of Island No. 10, Ft. Pillow and other engagements on Miss. River. Presbyn. Fellow Am. Inst. Architects. Home: New York, N.Y. Died Mar. 4, 1923.

McLAUGHLIN, Joseph, congressman; b. Burt, County Donegal, Ireland, June 9, 1867; ed. nat. schs. of Ireland; m. Eleanor Driscoll. Settled in Philadelphia, 1889; formerly engaged in real estate business; now editor National Hibernian and nat. pres. Ancient Order of Hibernians; mem. 65th and 67th Congresses (1917-19, 1921-23), Pa. at-large. Republican. Died Nov. 21, 1926.

McLAUGHLIN, Mary Louise, artist; b. Cincinnati; d. William and Mary (Robinson) McLaughlin; unmarried. Began making porcelain called Losanti war, 1898, exhibited first in Paris Expn., 1900; silver medal for decorative metal work, Paris Expn., 1889; hon. mention for china painting, Chicago Expn.; gold medal, Atlanta; silver medal, Nashville Expn.; bronze medal for Am. porcelain, Buffalo Expn., 1901. Author: China Painting; Pottery Decoration; Suggestions to China Painters; Painting in Oil; The Second Madame; An Epitome of History, 1923. Home: Cincinnati, O. Died Jan. 17, 1939.

McLAUGHLIN, Melvin Orlando, congressman; b. Osceola, Ia., Aug. 8, 1876; s. William D. and Jane (Creger) McL.; student Omaha Normal U., 1895-96, Peru (Neb.) Normal Sch., 1897-98; B.D., Union Bibl. Sem., Dayton, O., 1907; A.B., Oskaloosa (Ia.) Coll., 1907; A.M., Omaha U., 1914; (D.D., Leander Clark Coll., 1914); m. Elma Pierson, Aug. 4, 1897. Teacher pub. schs. 7 yrs.; ordained U.B. ministry, 1903; pastor Panama, Neb., 1900-03, Dayton, O., 1904-07, Omaha, Neb., 1907-13; pres. York (Neb.) Coll., 1913-19; mem. 66th to 69th Congresses (1919-27), 4th Neb. Dist. Republican. Mason. Died June 18, 1928.

McLAUGHLIN, Robert William, clergyman; b. New Haven, Conn., Aug. 5, 1866; s. Robert William and Emily Louise (Meredith) McL.; B.D., Oberlin Div. Sch., 1895; D.D., Olivet Coll., 1905; D.D., U. of Vt., 1923; m. Annie Oggel, Sept. 11, 1899; children—Robert W., Mary Louise, Adelaide, Maud. Ordained Congl. ministry, 1895; pastor Ashland, Wis., 1895-97, Kalamazoo, Mich., 1897-1902, Grand Rapids, 1902-08, Brooklyn, N.Y., 1908-21, Piedmont Ch., Worcester, Mass., Oct. 1, 1921-29. Author: Washington and Lincoln, 1911; Caleb Matthews, 1913; The Spiritual Element in History, 1926; The Overlooked Chapter in American History, 1928; Fishing for Fish Not in the Pond (essays), 1930. Home: Newagen, Me. Died Mar. 20, 1936.

McLAURIN, Anselm Joseph, U.S. senator from Miss., terms 1901-13; b. Brandon, Miss., Mar. 26, 1848; s. Lauchlin and Ellen (Tullus) M.; reared on farm in Smith Co., Miss.; ed. neighborhood schs., and at age of 16 attended Summerville Inst. a half session; entered C.S.A., Aug. 1864; at close of war re-entered Summerville Inst., remaining to finish in junior class; m. Laura Rauch, Feb. 22, 1870. Admitted to Miss. bar, July 1868, locating at Raleigh; elected dist. attorney, Nov. 1871; moved to Brandon, 1876; elected to legislature, 1879; presdl. elector, 1888; mem. Constl. Conv., 1890; elected U.S. senator, Feb. 7, 1894, for unexpired term, ending Mar. 4, 1895; elected gov. Miss., 1896-1900; again U.S. senator, 1901-07, 1907-13. Democrat. Home: Brandon, Miss. Died 1909.

McLAURIN, John Lowndes, senator; b. Red Bluff, S.C., May 9, 1860; s. Philip B. and Tommie Jane (Weatherly) M.; ed. at various acads. and U. of Va.; m. Nora Breeden, Feb. 19, 1883; children—Thomas B., John B., Mrs. Elizabeth Mills, Mrs. Emma Drake, Mrs. Nora Matheson, Mrs. Sara Sligh. Admitted to bar, 1882, and practiced at Bennettsville. Mem. Gen. Assembly, 1890; atty. gen. of S.C., 1891; elected 52d Congress, 1892, for unexpired term (1892-93) of Eli T. Stackhouse, deceased; reëlected 53d to 55th Congresses (1893-99), 7th S.C. Dist.; resigned May 1897; apptd. U.S. Senator, May 27, 1897, and elected, 1897, for unexpired term (1897-1903) of Joseph H. Earle, deceased; mem. S.C. Senate, 1913, 14; state warehouse commr. of S.C., 1914-17. Cotton planter, 1903—. Secured passage of state warehouse law for cotton from S.C. legislature, 1914; established the plan now practiced in every cotton state for warehousing cotton and borrowing on the receipts. Democrat. Home: Bennettsville, S.C. Died July 29, 1934.

McLAUTHLIN, Herbert Weston, M.D.; b. Plympton, Mass., Sept. 23, 1854; s. Simeon Weston and Frances Adelia (Bradford) M.; A.B., Amherst, 1877, A.M., 1887; M.D., Harvard, 1882; m. Emma Luella Stranger (died 1901); children—Alden Bradford, Herbert Francis, Carl Addison; m. 2d, Marguerite Jeanne McGill, Oct. 27, 1908. In practice at Denver, 1882—. Prof. pathology and histology, 1884-85, obstetrics and diseases of women and children, 1885-93, materia medica, therapeutics and clin. medicine, 1893-94; principles and practice of medicine, 1894-96, U. of Colo.; prof. materia medica and therapeutics, Colo. Coll. Dental Surgery (U. of Denver), 1897-1930. Health commr., Denver, 1885-87; co. physician, Arapahoe Co., Colo., 1886-91. Mason. Republican. Conglist. Home: Denver, Colo. Died Apr. 30, 1939.

McLEAN, Andrew, journalist; b. Scotland, Aug. 7, 1848; s. Andrew and Mary; ed. in Scotland and Brooklyn; m. Ida L. Thomson, May 10, 1876. In newspaper work, 1868—; editor-in-chief Brooklyn Eagle 2 yrs.; editor-in-chief Brooklyn Daily Citizen. Democrat. Lecturer. Home: Brooklyn, N.Y. Died Dec. 5, 1922.

McLEAN, Angus, surgeon; b. St. Clair, Mich., Apr. 4, 1862; s. Donald and Catherine (McDonald) McL.; grad. Ontario Collegiate Inst., 1880; M.D., Wayne U. Med. Sch., 1886; grad. study U. of Edinburgh, 1895; m. Rebecca Scotten, Apr. 9, 1907. Practiced in Detroit from 1888; formerly prof. anatomy, Wayne U. Med. Sch., now emeritus prof. surgery. Served with A.E.F. in France, World War. Decorated by U.S.; also by Italy Knight Commander Order of the Crown of Italy (Nov. 11, 1936), and by other foreign countries. Fellow Am. Coll. Surgeons, A.M.A. Home: Detroit, Mich. Died Apr. 11, 1939.

McLEAN, Angus Wilton, governor; b. Robeson Co., N.C., Apr. 20, 1870; s. Archibald Alexander and Caroline (Purcell) M.; grad. McMillan Mil. Sch., 1884; high sch., 1885-89; B.L., U. of N.C., 1892; LL.D. from U. of North Carolina, 1926; m. Margaret French, Apr. 14, 1904; children—Angus W., Margaret F., Hector. Began practice at Lumberton, 1892; co. atty., Robeson Co., 1892-1904; sr. mem. McLean, Varser & McLean; pres. Bank of Lumberton, 1898-1914; now pres. Nat. Bank of Lumberton, Robeson Development Co., McLean Trust Co.; v.p. Lumberton Cotton Mills, Jennings Cotton Mills. Chmn. Dem. Exec. Com. Robeson Co., 1892; chmn. presdl. campaign com., 1912, 16; mem. Dem. Nat. Com., 1916-24; elected gov. of N.C., term 1925-28, inclusive, by largest majority ever given any candidate in the state. Dir. War Finance Corp., Washington, 1918-20; mng. dir., 1920-21; asst. sec. of Treasury, 1920-21; mem. ry. loan advisory com. U.S. Treas., 1920-21; mem. Selective Service Advisory Com.; gen. counsel in N.C. for alien property custodian; organized Robeson Co. Chapter Am. Red Cross; chmn. co. Liberty Loan Com. Pres. trustees Flora MacDonald Coll.; trustee Union Theol. Sem., Richmond, Va., 1920—, U. of N.C., 1912—. Presbyn. K.P. Home: Lumberton, N.C. Died June 21, 1935.

McLEAN, Archibald, clergyman; b. P.E.I., Dec. 26, 1850; s. Malcolm and Alexandra (McKay) M.; A.B., Bethany (W.Va.) Coll., 1874. Ordained Disciples of Christ ministry, 1874; sec., 1882-1900, pres., 1900—, Foreign Christian Missionary Soc. Author: Where the Book Speaks, 1908; Alexander Campbell as a Preacher; Thomas and Alexander Campbell, 1910; Epoch Markets of Modern Missions, 1912; History of the Foreign Christian Missionary Society. Pres. Men and Millions Movement. Home: Cincinnati, O. Died Dec. 15, 1920.

McLEAN, Donald, lawyer; b. Rahway, N.J., Sept. 19, 1852; s. George Washington and Rebecca Jackson (McCormick) M.; ed. Bel Air (Md.) Acad., and pvt. tutors; LL.B., Columbia, 1873; m. Emily Nelson Ritchie, Apr. 24, 1883. In law practice at New York, 1873—; alderman, 1881; U.S. gen. appraiser, 1889-92; candidate for judge City Ct., 1892; Progressive. Dir. Guanajuato Consol. Mining & Milling Co. Del. Universal Congress Lawyers and Jurists, St. Louis, 1904. Episcopalian. Home: New York, N.Y. Deceased.

McLEAN, Edward Beale, newspaper propr.; b. Washington, D.C.; s. John Roll and Emily (Beale) McL.; educated under pvt. tutors; m. Evelyn L., d. late Thomas F. Walsh, of Washington, D.C. Succeeded father as propr. Washington Post and Cincinnati Enquirer. Home: Cleveland Park, D.C. Died July 27, 1941.

McLEAN, Emily Nelson Ritchie, patriotic worker; b. Frederick, Md., Jan. 28, 1859; d. Judge John and Betty Ritchie; grad. Frederick Sem. (now Woman's Coll.), 1873; post-grad. courses, lang., history and mathematics; m. Donald McLean, Apr. 24, 1883. Charter mem. D.A.R.; regent New York City Chapter 10 yrs.; pres. gen. Nat. Soc. D.A.R. several yrs. from 1905, now hon. pres. gen. Scholarship bearing her name established, 1898, in Barnard Coll. by D.A.R., N.Y. Chapter; Emily Nelson Ritchie McLean course of lectures on Am. history established, 1909, to be delivered in Memorial Continental Hall, Washington. Commr. from N.Y. to Cotton States and Internat. Expn., 1895-96, to S.C. Expn., 1901-02, to Jamestown Expn., 1907. Home: New York, N.Y. Died May 19, 1916.

McLEAN, George Payne, senator; b. Simsbury, Conn., Oct. 7, 1857; s. Dudley B. and Mary (Payne) M.; grad. Hartford High Sch., 1877; hon. A.M., Yale U., 1904; LL.D., Trinity College, Conn., 1929; m. Juliette Goodrich, Apr. 10, 1907. Admitted to bar, 1881, and since in practice at Hartford, Conn. Mem. Conn. Ho. of Rep., 1883 (chmn. Com. on State Prisons and prepared bill creating bd. of pardons); clerk Bd. of Pardons of Conn., 1884-1901; mem. commn. to revise statute laws of Conn., 1885; mem. Conn. Senate, 1886; U.S. atty. for Conn., 1892-96, and during same period was also counsel for the state comptroller and state treas.; gov. of Conn., 1901-03; U.S. senator, Conn., 3 terms, 1911-29; voluntarily retired. Republican. Home: Simsbury, Conn. Died June 6, 1932.

McLEAN, John Knox, theologian; b. Jackson, N.Y., Mar. 31, 1834; s. Thomas K. and Mary (Perine) M.; A.B., Union Coll., 1858; grad. Princeton Theol. Sem., 1861; (D.D., Knox Coll., 1876; LL.D., U. of Calif., 1913); m. Sarah M. Hawley, June 26, 1861. Ordained Congl. ministry, 1861; pastor Fairhaven, Conn., 1861-62, Framingham, Mass., 1863-67, Springfield, Ill., 1867-72, First Ch., Oakland, Calif., 1872-95; pres. Pacific Theol. Sem., Berkeley, Calif., Mar. 31, 1894-1911. Corporate mem. A.B.C.F.M.; dir. for Calif. of Religious Edn. Assn.; mem. advisory council Internat. Com. of Moral Training; mem. Calif. State Bd. of Charities and Corrections from its beginning, 1903 (pres. 1906—); pres. Calif. Oriental Mission. Home: Berkeley, Calif. Died Feb. 16, 1914.

McLEAN, John Roll, journalist; b. Cincinnati, Sept. 17, 1848; s. Washington and Mary L. M.; ed. in pub. and pvt. schs., Cincinnati, and at Harvard; bought interest of his father in Cincinnati Enquirer; became sole owner, 1881; also owner Washington Post; candidate for U.S. Senate, 1885; candidate for gov. of Ohio, 1899; Ohio mem. Dem. Nat. Com. for many years. Home: Washington, D.C. Died June 9, 1916.

McLEAN, Ridley, naval officer; b. Pulaski, Tenn., Nov. 10, 1872; s. Thornton and Sallie (Ridley) M.; student, U. of Tenn., 1888-90; grad. U.S. Naval Acad., 1894; m. Olive Gale, Nov. 8, 1916; step-children (adopted)—Olive Beatrice, Gale. Commd. ensign, July 1, 1896; promoted lt. (jr. grade), July 1, 1899; lt., Aug. 7, 1901; lt. comdr., July 1, 1907; comdr., July 1, 1913; judge adv. gen. with rank of capt., Nov. 5, 1913; capt., Aug. 31, 1917. Served on bd. protected cruiser San Francisco, 1894-95, later on battleships Indiana, Oregon, and other vessels; on gunboat Marietta during Reyes Rebellion in Nicaragua, 1898; served on ammunition ship Armeria, during Spanish-Am. War; on staff of Rear Admiral Kempff during Boxer rebellion in China, 1900; and Philippine insurrection, 1901-02; specialized in gunnery work, being asst. insp. target practice, 1903-06, and fleet gunnery officer on staff of commander-in-chief, Atlantic Fleet, 1906-09; Gen. Bd., Navy Dept., 1909-11; navigator, 1st lt., and exec. officer Battleship Florida, 1911-13; judge adv. gen. U.S.N., Nov. 5, 1913-Dec. 2, 1916; comd. U.S.S. Columbia, Dec. 1916-Aug. 1917; chief of staff Battleship Force One, Aug. 1917-Oct. 1918; comd. Battleship New Hampshire, Oct. 1918-Nov. 1919, engaged as escort for convoys until armistice and afterward on transport duty return of expeditionary force to the U.S.; comd. Battleship Arkansas, 1922-24; apptd. dir. naval communications, 1924; promoted to rear admiral June 2, 1927; comdr. Submarine Divisions, Battle Fleet, 1927-29; budget officer Navy Dept., 1929—. Unitarian. Author: Bluejacket's Manual, 1902. Died Nov. 12, 1933.

McLEAN, Thomas Chalmers, rear admiral U.S.N.; b. New Hartford, N.Y., Oct. 25, 1847. Apptd. from N.Y., and grad. U.S. Naval Acad., 1868; ensign, Apr. 19, 1869; promoted through grades to rear admiral, July 19, 1908. Served on S. Pacific Squadron in the Tuscarora, 1868-69; Benicia, 1869-71; torpedo duty, 1872-73; exptl. battery, 1873-75; Tennessee, 1875-76; torpedo duty, 1876-77; Navy Yard, Washington, 1878-79; Constellation, 1879-81; spl. duty abroad, 1881-82; Vienna Expn., 1883; Dolphin, 1884-88; torpedo sta., Newport, 1889-93; exec. officer of Detroit, 1893-96; Bur. of Navigation, Navy Dept., 1896-97; torpedo Sta., Newport, 1897-99; comd. Don Juan de Austria, 1899-1901, Castine, 1901, Cincinnati, 1901-02; in charge recruiting sta., Baltimore, 1902-03; capt. of yard, Navy Yard, League Island, 1903-05; comd. Pennsylvania, 1905-07; on duty at Naval War College; pres. Bd. Inspection and Survey, 1907-09; retired by operation of law, Oct. 25, 1909. Home: Utica, N.Y. Died Aug. 29, 1919.

McLEAN, Walter, rear admiral; b. Elizabeth, N.J., July 30, 1855; s. George Washington and Rebecca J. (McCormick) M.; grad. U.S. Naval Acad., 1876; short course, Naval War Coll., full course Army War Coll.; m. Emma Bowne Jarvis, Dec. 8, 1887. Apptd. at large by Pres. U. S. Grant, to U.S. Naval Acad., 1872; grad., 1876; ensign U.S.N., Feb. 26, 1878; promoted through grades to rear admiral, Mar. 10, 1914. Served on Asiatic Station, 1878-82; made trip across Siberia and Russia from Nagasaki, Japan, to Moscow, June-Sept. 1882; sr. aid on staff of Commodore George Dewey, 1898, in comd. dispatch vessel Zafiro until return to U.S., 1899; commanding 4th Div. Atlantic Fleet, 1914-15; comdt. Navy Yard and Sta., Norfolk, Va., and 5th Naval Dist., 1915; retired. Has taken active part in development of modern ordnance, especially in development of armor from wrought iron to Krupp armor; was mem. bd. to determine cost of armor plate and armor plant, 1905. Republican. Episcopalian. Part author of Observations upon the Korean Coast, Japanese-Korean Ports and Siberia (U.S. Govt. publ.), 1883. Home: Lutherville, Md. Died Mar. 20, 1930.

McLEAN, William L., newspaper pub.; b. Mt. Pleasant, Pa., May 4, 1852; s. Robert C. and Augusta D. (Voigt) M.; ed. pub. schs.; m. Sarah B., d. late William G. Warden, of Phila., Nov. 9, 1889. In business dept., Pittsburgh Leader, 1872-78; business mgr., Phila. Press, 1878-95; pres. and pub. Evening Bulletin, Phila. (established 1847), 1895—. Dir. Associated Press, 1896-1924, Am. Newspaper Pubs.' Assn., 1899-1905. Home: Germantown, Pa. Died July 30, 1931.

McLEAN, William Swan, Jr., judge; b. Wilkes-Barre, Pa., Dec. 17, 1877; s. William Swan and Anne Stephenson (Roberts) McL.; student Harry Hillman Acad., 1889-94, A.B., Lafayette Coll., Easton, Pa., 1898, A.M., 1900; m. Frances Leigh Ricketts, Jan. 27, 1921; 1 dau., Elizabeth Swan. Admitted to Pa. bar, 1901, solicitor Luzerne Co., Pa., 1911-19, mem. County Bd. for Revision of Taxes, 1919-21; elected judge, Common Pleas Court, 11th Jud. Dist., Pa., 1921, pres. judge, 1928—. Dir. First Nat. Bank of Wilkes-Barre. Brig. gen. Pa. N.G., comdg. 53d F.A. Brig.; served on Mexican border, 1916, Mexico, 1916-17, France and Belgium, World War. Awarded Croix de Guerre (Belgian), Polonia Restituta (Polish). Trustee Wilkes-Barre Institute, Lafayette College, Bucknell U., Wyoming Seminary. Democrat. Presbyn. (elder). Mason. Home: Wilkes-Barre, Pa. Died Nov. 17, 1938.

McLEARY, James Harvey, judge; b. Smith Co., Tenn., July 27, 1845; s. Samuel D. and Sarah A. (Weller) M.; served in C.S.A., 1861-65; A.B., Washington and Lee U., 1868, LL.B., 1869; m. Miss King, July 11, 1906. Asst. prof. English, Washington Coll., 1868-69; practiced law at San Antonio, Tex., 1869-98; mem. Tex. Legislature, House and Senate, 1874-77; atty. gen. of Tex., 1881-82; justice Supreme Ct. of Mont., 1886-88; maj and insp. gen. U.S.V., in war with Spain, in Cuba, 1898; alcalde Santiago de Cuba, 1898; asst. sec. of Puerto Rico, 1901; asso. justice Supreme Ct. of P.R., Oct. 8, 1901—. Mason. Home: San Juan, P.R. Died Jan. 5, 1914.

McLELLAN, Archibald, editor; b. Moncton, N.B., Nov. 10, 1857; s. Norman and Christiana (Murray) M.; pub. schs., Boston; LL.B., Kent Coll. of Law, Chicago, 1895; m. Jeannette M. Reid, June 3, 1885. Editor The Christian Science Journal, and Christian Science Sentinel, 1902—, Der Herold der Christian Science, 1903—; editor-in-chief Christian Science Monitor, Nov. 1908-June 1914. Dir. First Ch. of Christ, Scientist, Boston. Mason. Home: Brookline, Mass. Died July 18, 1917.

McLELLAN, Isaac, poet-sportsman, Greenport, N.Y.; b. Portland, Me., May 21, 1806; prepared at Phillips

(Andover) Acad., where in 1822 Nathaniel P. Willis was his roommate, and Oliver Wendell Holmes was a fellow student; grad. Bowdoin, 1826 (H. W. Longfellow, Nathaniel Hawthorne and George B. Cheever were in the next class); practiced law in Boston for several years; removed to New York, 1851; devoted to field sports and literary work, principally poetry. Author: The Year, and Other Poems; The Fall of the Indian; Poems of the Rod and Gun; Haunts of Wild Game; War Poems (in press); etc. Home: Greenport, L.I., N.Y. Died 1899.

McLEMORE, Jeff, congressman; b. nr. Spring Hill, Maury Co., Tenn.; s. Robert Anderson and Mary Hargood (McEwen) McL.; ed. common sch.; m. May Clark, Dec. 27, 1916; 1 dau., May Clark. Left Tenn. for Tex., 1878; became a cowboy and went up the trail to Kan., 1879; prospected for gold and silver in Colo., N.M. and Mex., 4 yrs.; returned to Tex. in fall of 1883 and followed newspaper work. Mem. Texas Ho. of Rep., Corpus Christi Dist., 1892-96; mem. City Council, Austin, 1896-98; sec. State Dem. Exec. Com., 1900-04; elected to 64th and 65th Congresses (1915-19), Tex. at large; author of resolution (defeated) in the 64th Congress, object of which was to keep American citizens off of the armed boats of the belligerent nations. Democrat. Home: Laredo, Tex. Died Mar. 4, 1929.

McLENEGAN, Charles Edward, librarian; b. Beloit, Wis., Jan. 23, 1858; s. Henry Hall and Sarah Frances (Reigart) M.; B.A., Racine (Wis.) Coll., 1882, M.A., 1884; (hon. M.A., Beloit Coll., 1895); m. Clara Rogers, July 22, 1886. Instr. Kenyon Mil. Acad., 1884, Racine Coll., 1885-86; head master Markham Acad., Milwaukee, 1886-87; head of English dept., Milwaukee High Sch., 1887-94, Boys' High Sch., Brooklyn, 1895; prin. West Div. High Sch., Milwaukee, 1896-1910; librarian, Pub. Library, Milwaukee, Nov. 15, 1910—. Democrat. Episcopalian. Mason. Home: Milwaukee, Wis. Died Mar. 17, 1920.

McLENNAN, Grace Tytus, magazine writer; b. Ossining, N.Y., Sept. 9, 1875; d. Louis Philip and Alice (Seeley) Henop; ed. Brearley Sch., N.Y. City, and under tutors in Eng., France and Germany; m. Robb de Peyster Tytus, Egyptologist, 1903 (died 1913); children—Mildred Mordaunt, Victoria Stuart; m. 2d, Senator John Stewart McLennan, of Canada, 1915; 1 son, John Stewart. Excavated, with Mr. Tytus, the palace of Amenhotep III, at Thebes, Egypt, 1904; speaker for Canadian Food Administration, World War; lecturer on civic and polit. subjects. Formerly pres. Ottawa Woman's Canadian Club and mem. Council of Proportional Representation Soc. Fellow Royal Geog. Soc., London. Mem. Anglican Ch. Home: Tyringham, Mass. Died Oct. 29, 1928.

McLENNAN, Peter Baillie, judge; b. Lyndon, N.Y., Dec. 3, 1850; s. Colin and Ann (Frazer) M.; Ph.B., Alfred U., 1873, Ph.D., 1886 (LL.D., 1902); m. Belle Barron, Dec. 1, 1881. Admitted to bar, 1876; justice Supreme Ct. of N.Y. for terms 1892-1906, 1907-20; judge Appellate Div., 4th Dept., 1898-1903, presiding justice, Jan. 1, 1904—. Republican. Home: Syracuse, N.Y. Died May 8, 1913.

McLEOD, Thomas Gordon, governor; b. Lynchburg, S.C., Dec. 17, 1868; s. William James and Amanda (Rogers) McL.; A.B., Wofford Coll., Spartanburg, S.C., 1892; degree of LL.D. conferred by same college, 1926; m. Elizabeth Alford, Dec. 31, 1902; children—McDonald Alford, Thomas Gordon, Lucy Mood, Yancey Alford. Admitted to S.C. bar 1896; mem. McLeod & Dennis, Bishopville, 1905—; extensively engaged in farming; a pioneer in promotion of cooperative marketing among Southern farmers. Mem. S.C. Ho. of Rep., 1901-02, Senate, 1903-06; lt. gov. of S.C., 1907-10; gov. of S.C., 2 terms, 1923-27. Chmn. Exemption Bd., Lee Co., World War. Mem. M.E. Ch., S. Mason, K.P., Woodman. Died Dec. 11, 1932.

McLOUTH, Lawrence Amos, univ. prof.; b. Ontonagon, Mich., Jan. 19, 1863; s. Dr. Lewis and Sarah A. (Doty) M.; A.B., U. of Mich., 1887; univs. of Leipzig, Heidelberg and Munich, 1890-92; m. Martha Linne Robinson, Dec. 31, 1888; 1 dau., Carol. Prin. Danville (Ill.) High Sch., 1887-90; instr. German U. of Mich., 1892-95; prof. Germanic langs. and lits., New York U., 1895—; exchange prof., Peking, China, 1920-21. Author: Verses, 1910. Home: New York, N.Y. Died Feb. 24, 1927.

McMAHAN, Anna Benneson, author; b. Quincy, Ill., July 24, 1846; d. Robert Smith and Electa Anne (Park) Benneson; grad. Rockland Inst., Nyack, N.Y., 1864; m. Dr. Robert D. McMahan, Nov. 19, 1868. Editorial contbr. to Chicago Tribune, 1893-94, identified with study class work; lecturer. Editor: Best Letters of Horace Walpole, 1890; Best Letters of William Cowper, 1893. Author: Florence in the Poetry of the Brownings, 1904; With Shelley in Italy, 1905; With Byron in Italy, 1906; With Wordsworth in England, 1907; Shakespeare's Christmas Gift to Queen Bess, 1907; Shakespeare's Love Story, 1909. Home: Bryn Mawr, Pa. Died Nov. 1919.

McMAHON, James, univ. prof.; b. Armagh Co., Ireland, Apr. 22, 1856; s. Robert and Mary (Hewitt) M.; A.B. (2 gold medals), U. of Dublin, 1881, A.M., 1890; D.Sc., 1918; m. Katharine A. Crane, June 26, 1890. Examiner mathematics, 1883-84, instr., 1884-90, asst. prof., 1890-96, asst. prof. 1st grade, 1896, prof. mathematics, 1904-21, prof. emeritus, 1921—, Cornell Univ. Asso. editor Annals of Mathematics, 1891-97. Joint author: Higher Mathematics, 1896; Cornell Mathematical Series, 1898; Plane Geometry, 1903. Died June 1, 1922.

McMAHON, John A., lawyer; b. Frederick Co., Md., Feb. 19, 1833; s. John V. L. and Elizabeth (Gouger) M.; A.B., St. Xavier's Coll., Cincinnati, 1849; m. Mary R. Sprigg, Jan. 23, 1861. In practice at Dayton, O., 1854—; pres. Peoples Railway Co. Mem. 44th, 45th and 46th Congresses (1875-81), 3d Dist. of Ohio. Democrat. Home: Dayton, O. Died Mar. 8, 1923.

McMAHON, John Eugene, army officer; b. Buffalo, N.Y., Dec. 8, 1860; s. Col. John E. and Esther (Bryan) M.; A.B., Fordham U., 1880; grad. U.S. Mil. Acad., 1886, Arty. Sch., 1898; m. Caroline Bache, May 12, 1888. Commd. 2d lt. 4th Arty., July 1, 1886; promoted through grades to maj. gen. N.A., Dec. 17, 1917. Instr. modern langs., U.S. Mil. Acad., 1890-91; a.d.c. to Maj. Gen. A. McD. McCook, 1891-95; adj. gen. 2d Brigade Provisional Div., 5th Army Corps, June-July, 1898; adj. gen. 2d Brigade, 2d Div., 4th Army Corps, Oct.-Nov. 1898; adj. gen. U.S. forces, Puerto Principe, Jan.-May 1899; in Philippines, 1901; pres. Field Arty. Bd., 1907; duty Gen. Staff, 1911-14; apptd. comdr. 160th Field Arty. Brigade, Camp Custer, Battle Creek, Mich., Sept. 1917, 5th Div. U.S.A., Dec. 28, 1917. Home: Utica, N.Y. Died Jan. 30, 1920.

McMAHON, John Joseph, bishop; b. Hinsdale, N.Y., Sept. 27, 1875; s. Martin and Margaret (Maroney) McM.; prep. edn. Belfast (N.Y.) Sem. and Union High School, Belfast, N.Y.; A.B., St. Bonaventure's Coll., Alleghany, N.Y., 1895, LL.D., 1919; studied Urban Coll. de Propaganda Fide, Rome, 1896-1900. Ordained priest R.C. Ch., 1900; asst. rector SS. Peter and Paul's Ch., Jamestown, N.Y.; trans. to St. Bridget's Ch., Buffalo, 1900; acting pastor St. Peter's Ch., Leroy, 1901; pastor St. Bridget's Ch., Newfane, 1902-03; adminstr. Nativity Parish, Buffalo, and asst. to vicar gen., 1903; asst. supt. schs., Buffalo Diocese, 1904-06; organized Parish of Our Lady of Mt. Carmel, later Parish of St. Mark; apptd. dir. Holy Name Soc., Diocese of Buffalo, 1919, diocesan visitor to religious communities of nuns, same diocese, 1924; consecrated bishop of Trenton (N.J.), May 10, 1928. Died Dec. 31, 1932.

McMAHON, Joseph H., clergyman; b. New York, Nov. 18, 1862; s. James and Alicia (O'Callaghan) M.; A.B., Manhattan Coll., New York, 1880, A.M., 1881; Ph.D., St. Francis Xavier's Coll., N.Y., 1900; LL.D., Manhattan Coll., New York, 1923. Ordained R.C. priest, Troy, N.Y., June 19, 1886; asst. at St. Patrick's Cathedral, 1886-1901; founder and pastor Our Lady of Lourdes Parish, New York, Sept. 1, 1901—. Dir. Cathedral Library of New York, 1888; chief of Cathedral Free Circulating Library until merged with New York Pub. Library, 1902; mem. circulation com. New York Pub. Library; founder, dir. and lecturer Catholic Library Reading Circles, later merged into Catholic Library Assn. (dir.); one of organizers Catholic Summer Sch. America. Apptd. domestic prelate of the Papal Court by Pope Benedict XV, 1921. Home: New York, N.Y. Died Jan. 6, 1939.

McMAHON, Martin Thomas, judge Court of General Sessions of the Peace, New York Co., for term Jan. 1, 1896, to Dec. 31, 1909; b. La Prairie, Canada, March 21, 1838; grad. St. John's Coll., Fordham, N.Y., 1855 (A.M., 1857; LL.D., 1866); established in law practice; m. Louise Claire Hargous, April 1872 (died 1872). Served through Civil war; was chief of staff 6th army corps; participated in all great battles of Army of Potomac; bvtd. to rank of maj. gen.; received from Congress medal of honor for distinguished bravery at Battle of White Oak Swamp; resigned from army, 1866. Corporation atty. New York, 1866-88; U.S. minister to Paraguay, 1869. Receiver of taxes for city of New York, 1873-85; U.S. marshal, 1885-89; mem. of assembly, 1890; State senator, 1891-95. Democrat. Mgr. Nat. Home for Disabled Vol. Soldiers, elected by Congress, 1880, 1886, 1892, 1898, sec. bd. of mgrs., 1880-1898; now pres. same. Home: New York, N.Y. Died 1906.

McMASTER, John Bach, univ. prof.; b. Brooklyn, June 29, 1852; s. James and Julia (Bach) M.; A.B., Coll. City of New York, 1872; Litt.D., U. of Pa., 1894, Princeton, 1925; LL.D., Washington and Jefferson, 1901, U. of Toronto, 1907; m. Gertrude Stevenson, Apr. 14, 1887; children—Julia Bach (dec.), John Bach (dec.), Philip Duryée. Civ. engr., 1873-77; instr. civ. engring., Princeton, 1877-83; prof. Am. history, U. of Pa., 1883-1920, prof. emeritus, 1920—. Author: A History of the People of the United States (8 vols. published), 1883-1912; Benjamin Franklin as a Man of Letters, 1887; A School History of the United States, 1897; A Primary School History of the United States, 1901; Daniel Webster, 1902; Brief History of the United States, 1907; Chapters IX, XI, XII, Vol. 7, Cambridge Modern History, 1903; Life and Times of Stephen Girard, 1917; The United States in the World War (2 vols. published), 1918-20; A History of the People of the United States during the Administration of Abraham Lincoln, 1927. Joint editor Am. Historical Review, 1896-99. Home: Philadelphia, Pa. Died May 22, 1932.

McMASTER, John Stevenson, lawyer; b. Pocomoke, Md., Dec. 29, 1859; s. John Thomas Bayly and Elizabeth Grace (Stevenson) M.; Delaware Coll., 1877-78; A.B., Lafayette Coll., Pa., 1883, A.M., 1886; studied law, U. of Va., 1885; m. Louisa Jane Dennis, May 15, 1894; children—John Dennis, Alfred Dennis. Teacher, high school, Pocomoke, 1878-80; teacher mathematics and natural sciences, Morris Acad., Morristown, 1883-88; admitted to N.J. bar, 1888, later apptd. spl. master in chancery and Sup. Ct. commr.; practiced at Dover with Hon. Mahlon Pitney (justice U.S. Supreme Ct.); removed to Jersey City, 1889; pvt. sec. to Gov. George T. Werts, 1893-96; devotes attention largely to Court of Chancery, and to management of estates; now associated in practice with son, John D. Pres. Children's Friend Soc. of Jersey City. Democrat. Elder 1st Presbyn. Church. Pres. Clan MacMaster of America; life mem. Assn. for Preservation of Va. Antiquities. Founder of Old Home Prize. Home: Jersey City, N.J. Deceased.

McMATH, Francis Charles; b. St. Louis, Mo., Jan. 29, 1867; s. Robert Emmett and Frances (Brodie) McM.; B.S. in Engring., Washington U., St. Louis, 1887; m. Josephine Cook, June 26, 1890 (died 1914); children—Robert R., Neil C., Marian H.; m. 2d, Madeline Davenport King, 1916. Began with Detroit Bridge & Iron Works, 1887, and became chief engr., 1899; pres. Canadian Bridge Co., 1900-21 (dir.); dir. Grosse Ile Bridge Co., Motors Metal Mfg. Co., Essex Real Estate Co., Essex Terminal Ry. Co. Mem. bd. trustees Detroit Bur. of Governmental Research, 1924—. Republican. Home: Detroit, Mich. Died Feb. 13, 1938.

McMECHAN, Francis Hoeffer, M.D., editor; b. Cincinnati, O., Jan. 16, 1879; s. James C. and Mary A. (Hoeffer) McM.; A.B., St. Xavier Coll., Cincinnati, 1896, A.M., 1898; M.D., U. of Cincinnati Med. Coll., 1903; m. Laurette van Varseveld, of Paris, France, June 5, 1905. Founder Quarterly Supplement of Anesthesia and Analgesia of Am. Jour. of Surgery, 1914, also of Internat. Anesthesia Research Soc., and Current Researches in Anesthesia and Analgesia, 1922, now editor-sec. gen. of all three; sec. Asso. Anesthetists of U.S. and Can., 1916; asso. editor British Jour. Anesthesia, Schmerz, Narkose und Anæsthesie. Fellow Internat. Coll. of Anesthetists. Democrat. Catholic. Home: Rocky River, O. Died June 29, 1939.

McMEEN, Samuel Groenendyke, consulting engr.; b. Eugene, Ind., Nov. 28, 1864; s. James McEwen and Ann (Groenendyke) M.; ed. Purdue U., Ind., 1883-84; m. Myra Dale Dutton, Nov. 1, 1888; children—Maurice James, Mrs. Catherine Dale Clark; m. 2d, Auta Judith Proctor, Dec. 23, 1897. Central Union Telephone Co., 1885-1902, assistant engr., 1893-96, chief engineer, 1896-1902; with the Western Electric Co., 1902-04; mem. McMeen & Miller, 1904-18; pres. sundry public utility cos., 1912-20; pres. Columbus (O.) Ry., Power & Light Co., 1912-19; v.p. E. W. Clark & Co. Management Corp., 1913-20; chmn. bd. North Electric Mfg. Co., 1918-22. Editor of Archery mag. Fellow Am. Inst. E.E.; hon. life mem. Nat. Archery Assn. Joint Author: Telephony (with Kempster B. Miller); American Handbook for Electrical Engineers; American Archery (with Dr. R. P. Elmer). Home: Pasadena, Calif. Died June 22, 1934.

McMICHAEL, Clayton, journalist; b. Phila., June 30, 1844; s. Hon. Morton McM.; ed. private schools; served 2d lt. to bvt. maj. U.S.A., April, 1861, to Sept. 1865; m. Anna Fotterall, April 24, 1867. Editor of The North American (daily newspaper), 1866-98; prop. same, 1879-98; commr. Internat. Expn., Vienna, 1873; U.S. marshal of D.C., 1882-85; city treas. Phila., Jan., 1898, for terms of 3 yrs.; postmaster of Philadelphia, Jan. 10, 1902—. Home: Philadelphia, Pa. Died 1906.

McMICHAEL, Thomas Hanna, coll. pres.; b. Bellbrook, O., July 7, 1863; s. Jackson Burgess and Mary N. (Hanna) M.; A.B., Monmouth Coll., 1886, A.M., 1889; B.D., Xenia Theol. Sem., 1890; D.D., Westminster Coll., 1903; LL.D., Coll. of Wooster, 1928, Westminster, 1929, Augustana Coll., 1935, Muskingum Coll., 1937; L.H.D., Monmouth, 1937; m. Minnie E. MacDill, May 21, 1890 (died 1929); children—Mary Lois (wife of Rev. Dr. George C. Vincent), David M. (business mgr. Monmouth Coll.). Ordained U.P. ministry, 1890; pastor Spring Hill, Ind., 1890-92, First Ch., Cleveland, O., 1892-1903; pres. Monmouth Coll., 1903-36 (emeritus). Moderator Gen. Assembly U.P. Ch., 1915. Republican. Home: Monmouth, Ill. Died June 23, 1938.

McMILLAN, Charles, university prof.; b. Moscow, Russia, Mar. 24, 1841; s. Alexander and Elizabeth (Platt) M.; ed. at Moscow until 1854, Hamilton, Can., 1855-56; C.E., Rensselaer Poly. Inst., 1860; (hon. A.M., Princeton). Asst. engr. Brooklyn Water Works, 1860, Croton Water Works, New York,

1861-65; prof. geodesy and road engring., Rensselaer Poly. Inst., 1865-71; prof. civ. and mech. engring., Lehigh U., 1871-75; prof. civ. engring. and applied mathematics. Princeton, 1875-1914; retired. Editor of Smith's Topographical Drawing, 1885—. Died Sept. 19, 1927.

McMILLAN, Duncan J(ames), clergyman; b. Gemini Fontes, Tenn., June 2, 1846; s. Rev. Edward and Mary Ann (Brown) M.; A.B., S.T.B., Blackburn Coll., Ill., 1870, A.M., 1873; D.D., Washington and Jefferson Coll., 1883; m. Emily Kent Johnston, June 18, 1879; children—Harran Haskell (dec.), Clarence, Florence. Regtl. orderly 32d Ill. Inf., 1862; pvt. Co. K, 7th Ill. Inf., 1865. Supt. city schools, 1870-72. Ordained Presbyterian ministry, 1872; pastor Walnut Grove Ch., Carrollton, Ill., 1872-75; supt. Presbyn. Mission Schs. and Ch. Work, Utah, Ida. and Mont., 1875-84; pres. Coll. of Mont., 1883-90; corr. sec. Presbyn. Bd. Home Missions, 1890-98; pastor New York Presbyn. Ch., New York, 1899-1911; corr. sec. Presbyn. Bd. of Ch. Erection, 1911-13; gen. sec. N.Y. Sabbath Com., 1915-33. Republican. Home: New York, N.Y. Died June 27, 1939.

McMILLAN, James, U.S. senator from Mich., 1889—; present term expires 1907; b. Hamilton, Ont., May 12, 1838; removed to Detroit, 1855; prominently identified with the manufacturing, commercial, transportation and banking interests of that city. Was elected to U.S. senate in 1889, 1895 and 1901, each time being the unanimous choice of the Rep. members of the legislature. Was chmn. Rep. State Com., 1885-96; presdl. elector, 1884. Home: Detroit, Mich. Died 1902.

McMILLAN, James Winning, mem. bd. of review U.S. Pension Office; b. Clark Co., Ky., 1825; s. Robert McMillan, a son of Col. James McMillan, staff of Gen. George Washington; ed. in country schools of Ky. and Ill.; family lived neighbors with the Lincoln family for many yrs.; m. Minerva Foote, 1860. Commissioned col. by Pres. Lincoln, 1861; served through war; bvtd. maj. gen., March, 1864; comd. 1st and 2d brigade, 19th army corps; served with Butler in Gulf campaign; captured blockade runner "Fox," one of the richest prizes captured during the Civil war; wounded 5 times; is also a veteran of the Mexican war. Died 1903.

McMILLAN, Neil Alexander, banker; b. Coosa Co., Ala.; s. Archibald A. and Scotta H. (McKenzie) McM.; ed. pub. schs. and commercial coll.; m. Mattie Caruth, Apr. 2, 1890. In wholesale and retail grocery business, Waxahachie, Tex., 1880; organized pvt. bank of Patrick, McMillan & Co., 1881; organized, and cashier First Nat. Bank of Waxahachie, 1882-86; an organizer, and cashier Nat. Exchange Bank, Dallas, Tex., 1887-97; treas. Union Trust Co., St. Louis, 1897, until its merger, 1902, into St. Louis Union Trust Co., of which was v.p., 1902-09, pres., 1909-19; exec. mgr. First Nat. Bank (consolidation of St. Louis Union Trust Co., Mechanics Am. Nat. Bank and Third Nat. Bank), July 1919—. Democrat. Home: St. Louis, Mo. Died Sept. 5, 1927.

McMILLAN, Philip Hamilton, capitalist; b. Detroit, Mich., Dec. 28, 1872; s. James and Mary L. (Wetmore) M.; A.B., Yale, 1894; Harvard Law Sch., class of 1898; m. Elizabeth Anderson, June 7, 1899. Trustee of family estate, 1902—; pres. Detroit & Cleveland Navigation Co.; dir. Detroit Savings Bank, First and Old Detroit Nat. Bank, Detroit Hotel Co., Detroit Free Press, Monarch Steel Castings Co., Packard Motor Car Co., Detroit Creamery Co. Trustee Grace Hosp. and Y.M.C.A. Republican. Home: Grosse Pointe Farms, Mich. Died Oct. 4, 1919.

McMILLAN, Thomas Sanders, congressman; b. Ulmers, S.C., Nov. 27, 1888; s. James Carroll and Mary (Cave) McM.; B.A., U. of S.C., 1912, LL.B., 1913; m. Clara Gooding, Dec. 14, 1916; children—Thomas Sanders, James Carroll, William Gooding, Edward Webb, Robert Hampton. Admitted to S.C. bar, 1913, and began practice at Charleston; mem. S.C. Ho. of Rep., 1916-24 inclusive (speaker pro tem, 1921-22, speaker 1923-24); mem. 69th to 75th Congresses (1925-30), 1st S.C. Dist. Mem. bd. visitors Clemson (S.C.) Coll., 1921. Democrat. Baptist. Mason. Home: Charleston, S.C. Died Sept. 29, 1939.

McMILLAN, William Charles, capitalist, mfr.; b. Detroit, Mich., Mar. 1, 1861; s. James and Mary L. (Wetmore) M.; ed. pub. schs. and tutors, Detroit, Yale Coll., A.B., 1884; m. Marie Louise Thayer, July 15, 1884. Sec. Mich. Car Co., 1884; in 1886 became gen. mgr. Mich. Car Co., Detroit Car Wheel Co., Mich. Forge & Iron Co.; sec. Detroit Iron Furnace Co., and Detroit R.R. Elevator Co.; in 1891 dir. and chmn. exec. com. Detroit Citizens' R.R. Co., also pres. Detroit Gas Co.; dir. State Savings Bank, 1st Nat. Bank and 1st v.p. Union Trust Co.; sec. Detroit-Cleveland Steam Navigation Co., and other corps.; in 1892 mng. dir. Mich. Peninsular Car Co. Now chmn. exec. com. Mich. Telephone Co., Union Trust Co.; pres. and gen. mgr. Detroit & Cleveland Navigation Co.; treas. and gen. mgr. Detroit & Buffalo Steamboat Co.; pres. Mich. Malleable Iron Co., Detroit Seamless Tubes Co. Presbyn. Republican. Home: Detroit, Mich. Died 1907.

McMILLAN, William H., clergyman; b. Iberia, O., Dec. 18, 1837; s. Thomas and Elizabeth M.; A.B., Washington Coll., Ia. (now Monmouth Coll., Ill.), 1860; U.P. Theol. Sem., Monmouth, Ill., 1860-61; Xenia Theol. Sem., Ohio, 1862-63; (D.D., Monmouth, 1879; hon. Ph.D., U. of Wooster, 1901; LL.D., Muskingum, 1902); m. Mary M. Conden, June 30, 1864. Ordained U.P. ministry, 1863; pastor Second Ch., Allegheny, Pa., 1873—. Controller Allegheny City pub. schs., 1876-91. Pres. Bd. Missions to the Freedmen, 1890—; trustee United Soc. Christian Endeavor, 1894—; moderator Gen. Assembly U.P. Ch., 1883; dir. Allegheny Theol. Sem., 1876—. Home: Allegheny, Pa. Died Sept. 13, 1911.

McMILLAN, William Linn, planter; b. Hillsboro, O., Oct. 18, 1829; ed. there; grad. Starling Med. Coll., 1852; practiced medicine in Ohio until July 1862; m. Mrs. Elizabeth I. King, d. William Neil, Columbus, O., April 18, 1861. Surgeon Russian army in Crimean war; surgeon 1st Ohio vols., 1861; surgeon gen. Ohio, 1861-62; col. 95th Ohio vol. inf., 1862-65. Moved to La., 1866, and engaged in planting cotton. Mem. Constl. Conv., 1868; State senator, 1870-72; chosen, 1872 and 1873, U.S. senator from La. by the McEnery legislature, but was not admitted to a seat; postmaster New Orleans under Hayes; surveyor of port under Harrison. Republican. Home: New Orleans, La. Died 1902.

McMILLEN, Alonzo Bertram, lawyer; b. Van Wert Co., O., Mar. 15, 1861; s. James J. and Harriet (Gililland) McM.; student Ohio Northern U.; LL.B., U. of Mich., 1886; m. Florence O. Prentice, Dec. 14, 1887; children—Eileen (Mrs. L. F. Lee), Dorothy (Mrs. Pearce C. Rodey), Katherine (Mrs. R. P. Woodson, Jr.). Began practice at Paulding, 1886; moved to Albuquerque, N.M., 1893; pres. Occidental Life Ins. Co., Jemez Land Co., Fernandez Co. (land, cattle and sheep), San Mateo Land Co.; dir. and gen. atty. First Nat. Bank, First Savings Bank & Trust Co.—both of Albuquerque. Presbyn. Mason. Home: Albuquerque, N.M. Died Aug. 12, 1927.

McMILLIN, Benton, governor; b. Monroe Co., Ky., Sept. 11, 1845; acad. edn.; read law and admitted to bar; began practice at Celina, Tenn., 1871; now at Carthage, Tenn. Mem. Ho. of Rep., 1874; commd. by gov. to treat with State of Ky. for purchase of territory, 1875; presdl. elector, 1876; spl. judge Circuit Ct., 1877; elected 46th to 55th Congresses (1879-99); resigned from 55th Congress, Jan. 16, 1899; gov. Tenn., 2 terms, 1899-1903; engaged in insurance business in Nashville, Tenn.; apptd. E.E. and M.P. to Peru, July 2, 1913. Democrat. Died Jan. 8, 1933.

McMILLIN, Emerson, banker; b. Ewington, O., Apr. 16, 1844; ed. dist. schs. Served in Civil War, 18th Ohio Inf. and 2d W.Va. Cav.; after war in merchandising, then in employ of contracting firm, building gas works at Ironton, O., of which he became mgr. after their completion. In 1875 became interested in iron mfg. and coal mining; lived 13 yrs. at Columbus, O.; one of first presidents of Columbus Bd. of Trade; removed to New York and opened banking house of Emerson McMillin & Co., making a specialty of gas, electric and street ry. stocks; chmn. bd. Am. Light & Traction Co.; pres., dir. Detroit City Gas Co., Grand Rapids (Mich.) Gas Light Co., St. Joseph (Mich.) Gas Co., Southern Light & Traction Co., Western Gas Co., San Antonio Gas & Electric Co., San Antonio Traction Co. Home: Darlington, Mahwah, N.J. Died May 31, 1922.

McMILLIN, Francis Briggs, mfr. hydraulic machinery; b. Mount Gilead, O., Nov. 30, 1868; s. Rev. Milton and Nannie (Mercer) McM.; ed. pub. schs., Mount Gilead; m. Alice K. Struble, Mar. 25, 1891 (dec.); children—Ruth (dec.), Howard F.; m. 2d, Martha A. Terry, Apr. 7, 1927. Shoe mcht., Mount Gilead, 1889-1902; president and gen. mgr. The Hydraulic Press Mfg. Co., 1902—; pres. Mt. Gilead Short Line Ry., 1911—. Judge, Probate Court, Morrow Co., O., 1900. Chmn. Morrow Co. War Savings Com., 1918-19, making national record. President Nat. Assn. State Chambers Commerce, 1929, Ohio Chamber of Commerce, 1925-34, Hydraulic Machinery Mfrs. Assn., 1928-29, Mfrs. Assn. Central Ohio, 1924-25. Mem. Gen. Bd. Edn., Presbyn. Ch. U.S.A., 1917-23, Bd. Aid for Colls., 1923-29; sec. Westminster Foundation Bd. for Promotion of Religious Edn. in State Colls. and Univs. in Ohio, 1911-28; elder 27 yrs., S.S. supt. 25 yrs., ch. treas. 13 yrs. Republican. Mason. Home: Mt. Gilead, Ohio. Died Sept. 8, 1938.

McMILLIN, Frederick Nelson, clergyman; b. Mt. Gilead, O., Oct. 14, 1872; s. Rev. Dr. Milton and Nancy (Mercer) McM.; A.B., Coll. of Wooster, 1895, M.A., 1898, D.D., 1911; B.D., McCormick Theol. Sem., 1898; m. Mabel Henrietta Saybolt, Sept. 20, 1898; children—Frederick Nelson, Allison Saybolt. Ordained Presbyn. ministry, 1898; pastor Memorial Ch., Dayton, O., 1898-1910 (built Patterson Memorial Presbyn. Ch.), First Ch., Walnut Hills, Cincinnati, 1910—; has broadcast Sunday evening sermons over WLW for 8 yrs.; in 29 yrs. received over 3,000 members into ch. Chmn. Ch. Extension Bd., Presbytery of Cincinnati, 1912-26. Chaplain A.E.F. in France and Eng., Oct. 1918-May 1919; maj., chaplain 147th Inf., Ohio N.G. Trustee Cedarville Coll. (Ohio), Deacones- Hosp. Republican. Lecturer on "Optimism" and "Everybody's Business." Home: Cincinnati, O. Died Apr. 26, 1937.

McMULLEN, Hugh Aloysius, banker, merchant; b. Westernport, Md., Dec. 9, 1859; s. Hugh and Eliza (Ryan) McM.; ed. parochial and pub. schs., Westernport; m. Anna M. Mulledy, June 18, 1889; children—Mary (Mrs. Luther P. Shaffer), Daniel F., Catherine (wife of John R. Gloninger, U.S. Army), Hugh A. (dec.), Alice (wife of Wm. E. Delaney, M.D.), Helen (widow of Wm. C. Jacob), Josephine (widow of Henry A. Mackey), John J. Mem. McMullen Bros. Dept. Store, Cumberland, 1896—; pres. Liberty Trust Co., 1920-23, chmn. exec. com., 1923—; sec. and treas. Merchants Finance Corp. Comptroller of the treasury, Md., 1916-20; mem. exec. com. Md. State Council Defense, 1918; apptd. chief of dilution of labor, U.S. Dept. of Labor, 1918. Democrat. Catholic. Home: Cumberland, Md. Died Nov. 6, 1937.

McMURRAY, Charles Backman, banker; b. Troy, N.Y., Dec. 1, 1865; s. Alfred Warner and Augusta E. (Fake) McM.; grad. Troy Acad., 1883; A.M., L.H.D., Union Coll., 1887; m. Eleanor Beattie, Apr. 4, 1888; children—Augusta E., Isabel Beattie. Vice-pres. and trustee Troy Trust Co., 1923—. Pres. Leonard Hosp.; trustee Emma Willard Sch., Russell Sage Coll., Albany Med. Coll., Union Coll. Republican. Home: Troy, N.Y. Died Jan. 25, 1940.

McMURRAY, James Henry, college pres.; b. Tuscarawas, O., Mar. 26, 1871; s. Ebenezer Gordon and Lydia Ann (Van Lehn) M.; A.B., Oberlin, 1897; A.M., Harvard, 1901; (hon. Ph.D., James Millikin U., Decatur, Ill., 1908); m. Kathryn Belle Romig, Aug. 25, 1897. Prof. science, 1897-1902, pres., 1902-05, Central Coll., Huntington, Ind.; pres. Lincoln (Ill.) Coll., 1905-18; field dir. Am. Red Cross, Camp Taylor, Ky., 1918—. Republican. Presbyn. Home: Oberlin, O. Died Apr. 6, 1938.

McMURRAY, William Josiah, physician; b. Williamson Co., Tenn., Sept. 22, 1842; s. John M. and Mary Jane (Still) M.; grad. Nolensville Acad., 1867, Univ. of Nashville, M.D., 1869; m. Frances Marion McCampbell, Oct. 22, 1872. Served in 20th Tenn. vol. inf. in Civil war. In practice as physician, 1869—; pres. Tenn. State Bd. of Health; pres. Tenn. Confederate Soldiers' Home. Surgeon Gen. on staff Lt. Gen. Stephen D. Lee, United Confederate Veterans. Democrat. Home: Nashville, Tenn. Died 1905.

McMURRY, Charles Alexander, educator; b. Crawfordsville, Ind., Feb. 18, 1857; s. Franklin Morton and Charlotte (Underwood) M.; grad. Ill. Normal U., 1876; at U. of Mich., 1876-80; Ph.D., Halle, 1887; m. Emily K. LeCrone, July 19, 1888; children—Donald LeCrone, Ruth Emily, Kenneth Charles, Marjorie (Mrs. Dwight Anderson), Dorothy. Taught in Ill., Colo. and Minn.; prin. Practice Sch., Northern Ill. Normal Sch., 1892-99; prin. Practice Sch., Ill. State Normal U., and lecturer Teachers' Coll., U. of Chicago, 1899, 1900; prof. elementary edn., George Peabody Coll. for Teachers, Nashville, Tenn., 1915—. Author: Method of the Recitation (with F. M. McMurry), 1898; Special Method in Reading, 1898; Special Method in Literature and History, 1898; Special Method in Geography, 1898; Special Method in Natural Science; Course of Study in the Eight Grades; Teacher's Manual in Geography; Special Methods in Manual Arts; Special Method in Arithmetic; Special Method in Language; Pioneer History Stories, 3 vols.; William Tell; Conflicting Principles in Education and Handbook of Practice for Teachers; Teaching by Projects, 1919; How to Organize the Curriculum, 1923. Editor: Year-Books of the National Herbart Society, also 3 vols. of Type Studies in Geography and Practical Teaching. Died Mar. 24, 1929.

McMURRY, Frank Morton, coll. prof.; b. nr. Crawfordsville, Ind., July 2, 1862; s. Franklin Morton and Charlotte (Underwood) M.; student U. of Mich., 1881-82, univs. of Halle and Jena, 1886-89, Ph.D., Jena, 1889; Geneva and Paris, 1892-93; m. Elizabeth Lindley, Dec. 20, 1894; children—Katherine, Margaret. Prin. schs., 1883-86; prin. of sch., Chicago, 1889-90; prof. pedagogics, State Normal Sch., Normal, Ill., 1891-92; prof. pedagogy, U. of Ill., 1893-94; prin. Franklin Sch., Buffalo, 1894-95; prof. pedagogics and dean Teachers Coll., U. of Buffalo, 1895-98; prof. elementary edn., Teachers Coll. (Columbia U.), 1908-26 (emeritus). Presbyn. Author: Tarr and McMurry Common School Geographies (with Ralph S. Tarr), 1900; Method of the Recitation (with C. A. McMurry), 1903; How to Study and Teaching How to Study, 1909; Elementary School Standards; McMurry and Parkins Common School Geographies (with A. E. Parkins), 1921; Living Geography (with E. Huntington and C. B. Benson), 1932. Asso. editor: The Student's Reference Work, 1909; McMurry and Benson Social Arithmetics, 1926. Home: Yonkers, N.Y. Died Aug. 1, 1936.

McMURRY, William Fletcher, bishop; b. Shelby Co., Mo., June 29, 1864; s. Rev. William Wesley and Mary Elizabeth (Williams) M.; ed. St. Charles Coll., Mo., 1880-82, Central Coll., Fayette, Mo., 1882-85; D.D., Emory and Henry Coll., Va., 1902; LL.D., Ky. Wesleyan Coll., Centenary Coll., Shreveport, La., Central Coll., Fayette, Mo., all 1921; m. Frances Byrd Davis, Oct. 9, 1888; children—Claudia, Bernice (dec.), William Fletcher, Frances, Wesley (dec.). Ordained

M.E. Ch., S., ministry, 1886; pastor various chs. in Mo., 1886-97; presiding elder, 1897-1902; pastor Centenary Ch., St. Louis, 1902-06; corr. sec. Bd. of Ch. Extension M.E. Ch., S., 1906-18; elected bishop, May 1918. Official visit to mission fields of S. America, 1910, to the Orient, 1918; pres. Bd. of Finance, of M.E. Ch. S., St. Louis, Bd. of Ch. Extension, M.E. Ch., S., Louisville, and mem. Gen. Conf. Commn. to Write Constitution of M.E. Ch., S.; mem. Joint Commn. on Unification of M.E. Ch., S., and M.E. Ch.; apptd. del. to Ecumenical Conf., London, 1901, 21, 31; pres. Central Coll., Fayette, 1924-30. Home: Fayette, Mo. Died Jan. 17, 1934.

McMURTRIE, William, chemist; b. Belvidere, N.J., Mar. 10, 1851; s. Abram and Almira M.; E.M., Lafayette Coll., 1871, M.S., 1874, Ph.D., 1875; m. Helen M. Douglass, Apr. 5, 1876. Asst. and chief chemist, 1872-79, spl. agt. in agrl. technology, 1879-82, U.S. Dept. Agr.; prof. chemistry, U. of Ill., 1882-88; chemist New York Tartar Co., 1888—; consulting chemist Royal Baking Powder Co., 1899—; consulting prof. gen. tech. chemistry, Poly. Inst., Brooklyn, 1905—; also 2d v.p. Royal Baking Powder Co., 1908—. Chemist Ill. State Bd. Agr., 1884-88, Ill. Agrl. Expt. Sta., 1886-88. Agt. Dept. Agr. at Paris Expn., 1878; chmn. com. on wools, Bur. Awards, Chicago Expn., 1893. Chevalier du Mérite Agricole, France, 1883. Author: Culture of the Beet and Manufacture of Sugar Therefrom, 1880; The Culture of Sumac, 1880; Grape Culture in the United States, 1883; Wools and Other Animal Fibres, 1886, 1901. Home: New York, N.Y. Died May 24, 1913.

McMURTRY, Lewis S., surgeon; b. Harrodsburg, Ky., Sept. 14, 1850; s. Lewis R. and Amanda (Reid) M.; A.B., Centre Coll., Ky., 1870, A.M., 1875; M.D., Tulane U., 1873 (LL.D., 1909); m. Mary E. Ball, Sept. 16, 1879 (died 1880). Prof. gynecology and abdominal surgery, med. dept. U. of Louisville; surgeon Louisville City Hosp. Fellow British Gynecol. Soc., Obstet. of Edinburgh, Am. Surg. Assn. Now pres. faculty and prof. abdominal surgery and gynecol., U. of Louisville. Home: Louisville, Ky. Died Feb. 2, 1924.

McNABB, Samuel W., lawyer; b. Andrew, Ia., Dec. 18, 1868; s. James and Mary (Hogg) McN.; ed. grade schs. and high sch., Maquoketa, Ia.; m. 2d, Alice L. Thompson, June 16, 1916; children—(by 1st marriage) Mary Vera (Mrs. Paul N. McCloskey); (by 2d marriage) James Wylie. Admitted to Calif. bar, 1909, and began practice at San Bernardino; mayor of San Bernardino 3 terms of 2 yrs. each, between 1909-25; U.S. dist. atty. for Southern Dist. of Calif., Feb. 16, 1925-33; U.S. referee in bankruptcy for Los Angeles County, Mar. 1, 1933—. Republican. Conglist. Mason, Elk. Home: South Pasadena, Calif. Died Dec. 4, 1940.

McNAIR, Fred Walter, college pres.; b. Fennimore, Wis., Dec. 3, 1862; s. Hugh A. Wilson and Mary Jane (Dorland) M.; B.S., U. of Wis., 1891; student U. of Chicago, winter, 1893; (Sc.D., Lafayette College, 1907; Sc.D., Rhode Island State College, 1919); m. Berta Philbrick, June 30, 1886. Asst. prof. mathematics, Mich. Agrl. Coll., 1892-93; prof. mathematics and physics, 1893-99, pres., 1899—, Michigan Coll. of Mines. Fellow A.A.A.S. (v.p. Sect. D, 1904-05, sec. council, 1905-06, gen. sec., 1906-07); pres. Am. Soc. Promotion Engrng. Edn., 1904-05 (v.p., 1902-03; mem. Bd. of Investigation and Coördination, 1922—); v.p. Lake Superior Mining Inst., 1904-05. Consulting engr. physicist, U.S. Bur. of Standards, 1918-20, mem. Bd. of Visitors, 1920—. Home: Houghton, Mich. Died June 30, 1924.

McNAIR, Frederick Vallette, rear admiral U.S.N.; b. Pa., Jan. 13, 1839; entered navy, acting midshipman, Sept. 21, 1853; grad. midshipman U.S. Naval Acad., June 10, 1857; passed midshipman, June 25, 1860; master, Oct. 24, 1860; lt., Apr. 18, 1861; lt. comdr., Apr. 20, 1864; commander, Jan. 29, 1872; capt., Oct. 30, 1883; commodore, May 10, 1895; rear admiral, 1898. During Civil war participated in much active war service, including engagements and passage of Forts Jackson and St. Philip, Chalmette batteries, and capture of New Orleans, and in the opening up of the Mississippi River and passage of the Vicksburg batteries, etc., engagements and surrender of Fort Fisher. After war served on many stations and assignments; commanded U.S. naval force on Asiatic Station, Dec. 1895, to Jan. 1898. From July 1898, supt. U.S. Naval Academy. Home: Annapolis, Md. Died 1900.

McNAIR, William Sharp, army officer; b. Tecumseh, Mich., Sept. 18, 1868; s. David and Lucinda M. (Sharp) McN.; grad. U.S. Mil. Acad., 1890, Arty. Sch., 1896, Army War Coll., 1914; m. Louise Bestor Potts, Dec. 26, 1894; children—Mary Louise (Mrs. Edward Arthur Sterling, Jr.), Dorothy, William Douglas, Norma Bestor. Commd. add. 2d lt. arty., U.S.A., June 12, 1890, and advanced through grades to col., July 1, 1916; brig. gen., Dec. 14, 1930. Brig. gen. N.G.N.Y., 1916-17; comdr. F.A. of 1st Div., A.E.F., later 151st Arty. Brig.; participated in Argonne Meuse offensive and advance to Sedan; chief of Arty., 1st A.my, 1918-19; comd. 4th Coast Arty. Dist.; retired, Sept. 30, 1932. Awarded D.S.M. (U.S.), silver star citation. Presbyn. Home: San Antonio, Tex. Died Apr. 6, 1936.

McNALLY, Frederick George, publisher; b. Chicago, Dec. 20, 1865; s. Andrew and Delia (Hyland) McN.; ed. Highland Mil. Acad., class of 1884; m. Lydia L. Wyles, 1884. Began connection with house of Rand, McNally & Co. as bill clerk, 1884, and from that position steadily advanced until became v.p. and auditor, 1898, and from that, in 1904, succeeded his father as pres. of Rand, McNally & Co., publishers. Dir. Chicago Nat. Bank, Home Savings Bank, Equitable Trust Co.; pres. and dir. Prairie Farmer Pub. Co., Farm Life Co., Vindermere Ranch Co., Neff Laboratory Co. Episcopalian. Mason. Home: Chicago, Ill. Died 1907.

McNALLY, James Clifford, consul; b. Stratfordshire, Eng., May 12, 1865; s. Thomas and Mary (Moran) M.; brought to U.S., 1868; student, Holy Ghost Coll., Pittsburgh; A.M., St. Vincent's Coll., Latrobe, Pa.; student, St. Laurent's Coll., Montreal; LL.B., U. of Mich., 1891; m. Agnes Keane, July 7, 1891. Practiced law, Salt Lake City, 1891-93; U.S. commr., 1893-94; served as probate judge by appmt. of Pres. Cleveland, 1894-96; sec. Am. Legation and consul gen. at Bogota, Colombia, 1898-99 (was chargé d'affaires, 4 months), at Guatemala City, Guatemala, 1899-1900; consul gen. at Guatemala City, 1900-02; consul at Liége, Belgium, 1902-07, at Nanking, China, 1907-10, at Tsingtau, China, Apr. 15, 1910-Apr. 1914; vice and deputy consul, Kehl, Germany, 1915-16, Hamburg, 1916-17; consul gen. Zurich, Switzerland, May 8, 1917—. Republican. Catholic. Home: Pittsburgh, Pa. Died Aug. 5, 1920.

McNAUGHT, Francis Hector, surgeon; b. Hobart, N.Y., Jan. 1854; s. John S. and Helen (Hoy) M.; common and pvt. schs.; M.D., Coll. Phys. and Surg. (Columbia), 1878; m. Helen Cowan, 1879. In practice at Denver, 1891—; chief surgeon Colo. & Southern Ry. Co.; acting surgeon C.,B.&Q. Ry. Co.; emeritus prof. obstetrics, med. dept., U. of Colo.; mem. surg. staffs, St. Luke's and St. Joseph's hosps.; consulting surg. staff, Children's Hosp. and Denver Gen. Hospital. Lt. Col. Med. R.C., U.S.A. Republican. Presbyn. Home: Denver, Colo. Died Mar. 6, 1940.

McNAUGHTON, John Hugh, author, composer; b. Caledonia, N.Y., July 1, 1829; ed. in public schools and Temple Hill Acad., Geneseo, N.Y. Writer and composer of Faded Coat of Blue, Belle Mahone, Blue and the Gray. Author: Treatise on Music; Babble Brook Songs; Ounalinda (a metrical romance). Home: Caledonia, N.Y. Deceased.

McNEAL, Joshua Vansant, ry. official; b. Baltimore, June 11, 1846; s. James and Sarah J. (Golibart) M.; ed. Loyola Coll., Baltimore, 1860-62; m. May Preston, May 19, 1873 (died 1913). In fire and marine ins. business, Baltimore, until 1871; with B.&O. R.R. Co., 1871—; clk. gen. freight office and traveling auditor, 1871-72; chief clk. auditor's office, 1872-80; auditor Indianapolis, Decatur & Western R.R., 1880-93; asst. treas., 1893-99, treas., 1899-1904, 4th v.p. and treas., Aug. 1, 1904—, B.&O. R.R. Co.; also treas. Washington Terminal Co., Akron (O.) Union Passenger Depot Co., Staten Island Rapid Transit Co., B.&O. Chicago Terminal R.R. Co., Sharpsville R.R. Co. Democrat. Catholic. Home: Baltimore, Md. Died Sept. 26, 1917.

McNEIL, (Henry) Everett, author; b. nr. Stoughton, Wis., Sept. 28, 1862; s. David and Eunice Ann (Barlow) M.; B.S., Milton (Wis.) Coll., 1887; unmarried. Served as pvt. Co. I, 9th N.Y. Regt. Vols., Chickamauga Park, Ga., Spanish-Am. War. Unitarian. Author: (juveniles) The Lost Treasure Cave, 1905; The Boy Forty-Niners, 1908; In Texas with Davy Crockett, 1908; With Kit Carson in the Rockies, 1909; Fighting with Fremont, 1910; The Cave of Gold, 1911; The Totem of Black Hawk, 1914; The Lost Nation, 1918; Buried Treasure, 1919; Tonty of the Iron Hand, 1925; Daniel du Luth, or Adventuring on the Great Lakes, 1926; For the Glory of France, 1927; Fighting Under Frontenac, 1928. Also photoplays. Home: Brooklyn, N.Y. Died Dec. 14, 1929.

McNEIL, Hiram Colver, chemist; b. Emerald (Winchester), O., Oct. 2, 1866; s. Samuel and Elizabeth H. (Cory) M.; B.S., Denison U., 1896, M.S., 1900; student Harvard Coll. Summer Sch., 1896, U. of Chicago, 1898-99, and summer, 1901; Ph.D., George Washington U., 1905; m. Sarah M. Hooper, Sept. 4, 1901; children—Robert Hooper, Ernest Samuel, Harold Osman. Taught in pub. schs., Ohio, and N. Liberty (O.) Acad., 1889-93; instr. chemistry, Denison U., 1896-98; research chemist with Mariner & Hoskins, Chicago, 1899; prof. chemistry and head dept. of science, Shurtleff Coll., 1899-1904; research chemist on "The Constitution of the Natural Silicates," U.S. Geol. Survey, under F. W. Clarke, 1904-05; research chemist with Columbus Pharmacal Co., 1905-06; asst. chemist, Bur. of Chemistry, Washington, 1907-14; asso. chemist, Bur. of Standards, 1914-18; asst. prof. chemistry, 1910, prof., 1918—, head of dept., 1918-26, George Washington U. Baptist. Died 1937.

McNEILL, George Edwin, labor writer, trades-union organizer, etc.; b. Amesbury, Mass., Aug. 4, 1837; s. John and Abigail Todd (Hickey) McN.; ed. public and private schools; worked at shoe bench, in woolen mill and at many other occupations; treas. and gen. mgr. Accident Insurance Co., 1883—; m. Adeline J. Trefethen, Dec. 24, 1859. Sec. Grand Eight-Hour League, Boston, 1863-64; founder New England Labor Reform League, 1865; unpaid agt. Daily Evening Voice, workingman's paper, 1865-67; founder and pres., 1867-69, Workingmen's Inst.; pres. Boston Eight-Hour League, 1869-74; deputy chief Bureau of Statistics of Labor, Mass., 1869-73; asso. founder Order of the People, 1870; pres. New England 10-Hour League, 1874-76; mem. school com., Cambridge, Mass., 1872-75; apptd. officer to enforce laws regulating edn. of children of Mass., 1875. Author of Declaration of Principles later accepted by Knights of Labor. Founder and pres. Internat. Workingmen's Union, 1876-79; State sec. Sovereigns of Industry, 1875; asso. editor Labor Standard, Paterson, N.J., and Fall River, Mass., and editor Home Journal, Paterson, N.J., 1880-82; sec.-treas. Dist. 30 (State of Mass.), Knights of Labor, 1883-86; pres. Order of Co-operators, 1885; pres. Co-operative Printing Co., Boston, 1885; editor and propr. Labor Leader, Boston, 1886-87; delegate to Am. Fedn. of Labor, 1886-98, fraternal delegate same to England, 1898; founder and nat. sec. Order of Columbia, 1888-92; commr. for State of Mass. upon manual training, 1893-94; commr. same on taxation, 1897-98; commr. same on uniform laws, 1902—; asso. founder and dir. Anti-Tenement House League, 1891. Author: Eight-hour Primer; The Slave of Fortune (novel); The Story of a Silver Dollar, 1900; A Study of Accidents and Accident Insurance, 1900; Book of Verses—Unfrequented Paths, 1903. Home: Somerville, Mass. Died 1906.

McNEILL, George Rockwell, supt. city schools, Dothan, Ala., 1900—; b. Fayetteville, N.C., July 1, 1854; s. Rev. George and Maggie (Gilbert) McN.; grad. Davidson Coll., N.C., 1874 (A.M.; Ph.D., Ala. Normal Coll., 1892); m. Dec. 23, 1875, Mrs. Julia V. Marlin. Prin. private school, Rowan Co., N.C., 9 yrs., co. supt., and pres. State Assn. of County Supts.; prin. Male Acad., Reidsville, N.C., 1883-89; pres. LaFayette Coll., Ala., 1889-95; pres. Ala. Ednl. Assn., 1895; pres. Isbell Female Coll., Talladega, Ala., 1895-98; pres. LaFayette Coll., Ala., 1898-1900 (2d time); spent summer 1900 in Europe studying history and geography, visiting Italy, Spain, Switzerland, Germany, Belgium, France, England, Scotland and Ireland. Home: Dothan, Ala. Died 1901.

McNEILL, John Charles, writer; b. in Scotland Co., N.C., July 26, 1874; s. Duncan and Euphemia (Livingston) M.; A.B., Wake Forest Coll., 1898, A.M., 1899; admitted to bar, 1900; unmarried. Mem. N.C. legislature, 1903-05; spl. newspaper writer, 1904—; awarded Patterson cup by N.C. Lit. and Hist. Assn., 1905, for having done best lit. work of any writer in the State, presented by President Roosevelt. Author: Songs, Merry and Sad, 1906. Home: Charlotte, N.C. Died 1907.

McNEIR, George, carpet mfr.; b. Washington, D.C., June 29, 1860; s. Thomas Shepherd and Emily (Schwarar) McN.; LL.B., Georgetown U., 1881, LL.M., 1882, LL.D., 1920; m. Meda, d. Senator J. C. Burrows, of Mich., Oct. 12, 1881; children—Burrows, Thomas S. Became page in U.S. Senate, 1870; in practice of law, Minneapolis, 1883-94; mgr. House of W. & J. Sloane, 1894-1922; chmn. bd. Mohawk Carpet Mills, Amsterdam, N.Y., 1920—; trustee The Bowery Savings Bank. Regent Georgetown U. Republican. Episcopalian. Home: New York, N.Y. Died June 14, 1941.

McNICHOLS, John Patrick, clergyman, educator; b. St. Louis, Mo., Feb. 24, 1875; s. Henry and Mary (O'Neil) M.; A.B., St. Louis U., 1896, A.M., 1898, Ph.D., 1905; studied St. Louis U. and St. Stanislaus Sem., Mo. Joined Soc. of Jesus (Jesuits), 1891; instr. classics and English, St. Xavier Coll., Cincinnati, O., 1898-1903 and 1908-12, prof., 1912-13; prof. classics and English, Campion Coll., Prairie du Chien, Wis., 1913-15; prof. English, 1915-19, dean Coll. Arts and Science, 1919-21, Marquette U.; pres. U. of Detroit, 1921—. Author: Fundamental English, 1908; Teachers' Handbook, 1908. Home: Detroit, Mich. Died Apr. 26, 1932.

McNIECE, Robert Gibson, college dean; b. Topsham, Vt., Jan. 10, 1839; s. John and Lydia (Divoll) M.; A.B., Dartmouth Coll., 1867, A.M., 1869; grad. Princeton Theol. Sem., 1877; (D.D., Wabash Coll., 1883, Knox Coll., 1883); m. Sara J. Irwin, Aug. 4, 1881. Prin. Ft. Wayne (Ind.) High Sch., 1867-70; editor Ft. Wayne (Ind.) Daily Gazette, 1870-73; ordained Presbyn. ministry, 1877; pastor First Ch., Salt Lake City, Utah, 1877-97; dean of faculty of Westminster Coll., Salt Lake City, Apr. 1, 1897—. Home: Salt Lake City, Utah. Died Oct. 3, 1913.

McNULTA, John, lawyer; b. New York, Nov. 9, 1837; went West, 1852; settled in Attica, Ind.; traveling salesman, 1856, partner, 1858, Dick & Co., wholesale tobacco dealers; settled in Bloomington, Ill., March 1859; capt. Co. A, 1st Ill. cav., May 3, 1861; lt. col. 94th Ill. Inf., Aug. 20, 1862; took command of regt. a few days after it was mustered in; promoted col. and bvtd. brig. gen. for gallant and meritorious services in battle; mustered out, Aug. 9, 1865; m. Laura Pelton, Jan. 15, 1862. Admitted to Ill. bar, 1866, to Supreme Court U.S., 1873; elected State senator, 1868; member Congress, 1873-75; renominated but defeated for succeeding Congress; master in chancery, 1881-85. Receiver of what is now the Toledo, St. Louis & Kansas City Ry., June, 1885; receiver Wabash Ry., April 1887, of the Whisky Trust, Feb. 1895, of the Calumet Electric Street Ry. Co., Jan. 3, 1898, of the Nat. Bank of Illinois, Jan. 4, 1898; moved to Chicago, Jan. 1895. Died 1900.

McPHEETERS, William Marcellus, theologian; b. St. Louis, Mo., Apr. 8, 1854; s. Rev. Samuel Brown (D.D.) and Eliza Cassandra (Shanks) M.; A.B., Washington and Lee U., 1874; grad. Union Theol. Sem. in Va., 1878; D.D., Presbyn. Coll. of S.C., and Washington and Lee U., 1889; LL.D., Davidson Coll., N.C., 1905; m. Emma Gold Morrison, Oct. 10, 1878. Ordained ministry Presbyn. Ch. in U.S., 1879; pastor Liberty, Va., 1878, Rockymount, Va., 1879-85, Marion, Va., 1886-88; prof. O.T. lit. and exegesis, Presbyn. Theol. Sem., Columbia, S.C., 1888—. Editor The Bible Student, 1900-04; Stone lecturer Princeton Theol. Sem., 1912; lecturer at Wilbur W. White Bible Sch., at Montclair, N.J., 1900. Moderator Synod of S.C., Presbyn. Ch. of U.S., 1896. Trustee Presbyn. Coll. of S.C., Clinton, S.C., and Chicora Coll. for Women, Columbia. Home: Decatur, Ga. Died Aug. 14, 1935.

McPHERSON, John Bayard, judge; b. Harrisburg, Pa., Nov. 5, 1846; s. William C. and Elizabeth (Wallace) M.; A.B., Princeton, 1866, A.M., 1869; (LL.D., Princeton, U. of Pa., and Franklin and Marshall, 1899); m. Annie C., d. Judge David W. Patterson, of Lancaster, Pa., Dec. 29, 1879 (died 1907). Admitted to bar, 1870, and practiced at Harrisburg; dist. atty., 1874-77; judge Ct. Common Pleas, 1882-99; U.S. dist. judge, Eastern Dist. of Pa., Mar. 13, 1899-Apr. 8, 1912; U.S. circuit judge, 1912—. Republican. Presbyn. Mem. Shakspere Society. Home: Philadelphia, Pa. Died Jan. 20, 1919.

McPHERSON, John Edward, insurance; b. Blue Rapids, Kan., July 15, 1872; s. John and Emma Amanda (Reed) McP.; A.B., U. of Kan., 1898; LL.B., Kansas City (Mo.) Sch. of Law, 1905; unmarried. Began as sec. John A. Prescott & Co., investment bankers, Kansas City, 1899, exec. sec., 1901-13; sec. Maxwell Investment Co., farm mortgage bankers, 1913-19; sec., trust officer, dir. and mem. exec. com. Guaranty Trust Co., 1919-24; exec. mgr. R. B. Jones & Sons, gen. ins., 1924-26; controller Business Men's Assurance Co. of America, 1926-31, treas., 1931—. Served as v. chmn. accounting com. 2d Red Cross drive, gen. sec. 4th Liberty Loan and Victory Liberty Loan campaigns, World War. Sec. financial section Am. Life Conv., 1935. Life trustee Liberty Memorial Assn. (sec., 1920—); gen. sec. Liberty Memorial and Allied Charities campaign. Republican. Home: Kansas City, Mo. Died 1937.

McPHERSON, Logan Grant, economist; b. Circleville, O., Aug. 11, 1863; s. Daniel Workman and Frances Louise (Kinnear) M.; pub. school edn. Newspaper reporter, 1879; in service of Pa. lines, 1880-91; held various positions in coal industry, Pittsburgh, 1892-1901; in service B.&O. R.R. Co., 1902; sec. and asst. treas. Consolidation, Fairmont, and Somerset Coal cos., 1903; statistician Rock Island System, 1904; asst. to late Samuel Spencer in his capacity as representative of associated rys. of U.S., 1905-06; engaged in economic investigation of railroad freight rates, 1906-09; accompanied Nat. Waterways Commn. to Europe as traffic expert, 1909; organized Bureau of Ry. Economics, at invitation of com. of ry. presidents, 1910, and its director until 1914. Lecturer on transportation, Johns Hopkins U., 1906-14. Author: Transportation in Europe, 1910; How the World Makes Its Living, 1916; The Flow of Value, 1919; Human Effort and Human Wants, 1923. Home: New York, N.Y. Died Mar. 23, 1925.

McPHERSON, Ross, M.D.; b. Cambridge, Mass., May 31, 1876; s. Ewen Ross and Esther Elizabeth (Ball) M.; A.B., Harvard, 1898, M.D., 1902; m. Virginia Wisschusen, Oct. 1, 1907. House surgeon, Carney Hosp., Boston, 1902-03; attending surgeon New York Lying-In Hosp., 1904-24; prof. gynecology and obstetrics, New York Polyclinic Med. Sch. and Hosp.; attending gynecologist and obstetrician same; cons. obstetrician Hackensack (N.J.), United Portchester and Caledonian hosps., Holy Name Hosp., Teaneck, N.J.; cons. obstetrician and gynecologist Long Beach Hosp.; cons. obstetrician Dobb's Ferry Hosp. Republican. Episcopalian. Home: New York, N.Y. Died Aug. 16, 1935.

McPHERSON, Simon John, headmaster; b. Mumford, N.Y., Jan. 19, 1850; s. John F. and Jeannette (Fraser) M.; A.B., Princeton, 1874, A.M., 1877; grad. Princeton Theol. Sem., 1879; (D.D., Knox Coll., 1883, and Princeton, 1896); m. Lucy Belle Harmon, May 15, 1879. Ordained Presbyn. ministry, 1879; pastor First Ch., E. Orange, N.J., 1879-82, Second Ch., Chicago, 1882-99; headmaster Lawrenceville (N.J.) Sch., Sept. 1, 1899—. Univ. preacher, Harvard, 1897. Dir. McCormick Theol. Sem. and Presbyn. Hosp., Chicago, 1883-1900; trustee Princeton, 1897—; mem. Chicago Ednl. Commn., 1897-98; formerly trustee Lake Forest (Ill.) U., and John Crerar Library, Chicago. Died Jan. 9, 1919.

McPHERSON, Smith, judge; b. nr. Mooresville, Ind., Feb. 14, 1848; s. O. H. and Polly (Matthews) M.; pub. sch. edn.; LL.B., State U. of Ia., 1870; m. Frances H. Boyer, Oct. 2, 1879. Practiced at Red Oak, Ia., 1870-1900; dist. atty. 3d Jud. Dist., 1874-80; atty. gen., 1881-85; elected to 56th Congress (1899-1901), 9th Ia. Dist.; resigned, June 6, 1900; U.S. dist. judge, Southern Dist. of Ia., June 7, 1900—. Republican. Home: Red Oak, Ia. Died Jan. 17, 1915.

McPHERSON, William Lenhart, journalist, author; b. Gettysburg, Pa., May 23, 1865; s. Edward and Annie (Crawford) M.; A.B., Pa. Coll. (now Gettysburg Coll.), 1883; Litt.D., 1923; A.B., Harvard, 1884, A.M., 1885; m. Mrs. Jessie Cuthbert McDonald, June 5, 1909; children—Janet Cuthbert, Jessie Middleton. On editorial staff, 1885-89, attached to Washington bur., 1889-1902, corr. in Cuba, 1899, New York Tribune; editorial writer Washington Times, 1902-03, New York Tribune, 1903—. Editor The Tribune Almanac, 1903—; Am. editor Whitaker's American Almanac, 1913-16; mil. critic; writer of "Military Comment" in Tribune and other newspapers, April-Nov. 1918; translator of French and German short stories. Author: Tales of Wartime France (translations of French war stories), 1918; The Vandal of Europe (transl. of Dr. Wilhelm Mühlon's diary), 1918; The Strategy of the Great War, 1919; A Short History of the Great War, 1920. Translator of Germany After the Armistice, by Maurice Berger, 1920. Home: New York, N.Y. Died Nov. 8, 1930.

McPIKE, Henry H., lawyer; b. Vallejo, Calif.; s. Andrew Jackson and Elizabeth (Halladay) M.; m. Amelia Wilson, 1898; 1 son, Halladay Wilson. Admitted to Calif. bar, 1893, later to bars of U.S. Dist. and U.S. Supreme cts.; became U.S. dist. atty., Calif., 1933. Chmn. Dem. Com. of Alameda Co., 1912-26, Dem. State Central Com., 1926-30. Home: San Francisco, Calif. Died July 1940.

McQUAID, Bernard John, first R.C. bishop of Rochester (N.Y.) consecrated July 12, 1868; b. New York, N.Y., Dec. 15, 1823; studied at Chambly Coll., nr. Montreal, Can., and St. John's Coll., Fordham, N.Y.; finished classical course, 1843, and was tutor there 3 yrs.; studied theology; ordained priest, Jan. 16, 1848; was pastor in N.J.; founder and pres. 10 yrs. Seton Hall Coll. and Sem., and part of the time also rector Newark Cathedral. Died 1909.

McQUEEN, Henry Clay, banker; b. Lumberton, N.C., July 16, 1846; s. Edmund (M.D.) and Susan Ann (Moore) M.; ed. Bingham Sch., Oaks, N.C.; Hillsboro Mil. Acad.; m. Mary Agnes Hall, Nov. 9, 1871 (died 1904); children—Sue Moore, Mrs. Agnes Emerson. Served as pvt. Co. D, 1st Battalion Heavy Arty., N.C. Vols., C.S.A., 1863-June 1865; wounded and made prisoner at Ft. Fisher, N.C., Jan. 1865. In banking business, Wilmington, 1893—; chmn. bd. Peoples Savings Bank. Chmn. Bd. of Navigation and Pilotage of Cape Fear River; commr. of sinking fund, Wilmington, many yrs.; pres. Produce Exchange, Wilmington. Chmn. Wilmington Chapter Am. Red Cross, 1917-18. Democrat. Presbyn. Home: Wilmington, N.C. Died Oct. 31, 1935.

McQUEEN, Stewart, clergyman; b. Scotch Glen, Fla., Oct. 15, 1857; s. James Archibald and Virginia (Douglas) M.; A.B., A.M., U. of the South, 1878, B.D., 1881; m. Virginia Dunbar, Nov. 1, 1883. Deacon, 1881, priest, 1882, P.E. Ch.; rector Decatur, Ala., 1881-83, Marion, Ala., 1883-87, Georgetown, S.C., 1887-92, Durham, N.C., 1892-94, Goldsboro, N.C., 1894-97, Ch. of the Holy Comforter, Montgomery, Ala., 1897—. Pres. Standing Com. Diocese of Ala., 1903-17; deputy to Gen. Conv. P.E. Ch., 1904—. Died Oct. 5, 1923.

McQUIGG, John Rea, lawyer, banker; b. nr. Dalton, O., Dec. 5, 1865; s. Samuel and Jane (McKinney) McQ.; A.B., U. of Wooster (now Wooster Coll.), 1888; student Cornell Law Sch., Ithaca, N.Y., 1888-89; LL.B., Nat. Law Sch., Washington, D.C., 1890; m. Gertrude W. Imgard, Feb. 16, 1892; children—Pauline, Donald. Admitted to Ohio bar, 1890, to U.S. courts, 1893; mem. Riley & McQuigg, 1890—; mayor of East Cleveland 3 terms, 1907-13; pres. and gen. counsel Windermere Savings & Loan Co.; v.p. Am. Realty Co.; dir. Derbyshire Realty Co. Cadet captain at Wooster University; served as 1st lieut. infantry Ohio National Guard, 1890-91; mem. Cleveland Grays, 1892-98; captain 10th Ohio Vol. Inf., Spanish-Am. War, 1898-99; capt., maj., lt. col. engrs. Ohio N.G., 1899-1916; served on Mexican border, 1916; col. engrs., Ohio N.G., July 11, 1917; col. engrs., U.S.A., Aug. 5, 1917; assigned as comdr. 112th U.S. Engrs., 37th Div.; mobilized regt. at Camp Sheridan, Ala.; went overseas, June 1918; served with regiment in Baccarat sector and in Argonne; hon. disch., Jan. 17, 1919; recommissioned col. engrs., Apr. 28, 1920; apptd. brig. gen. Ohio N.G. and federally recognized, May 10, 1921; dept. comdr. Am. Legion of Ohio, 1920-21; elected nat. comdr. Am. Legion, 1925; v.p. Am. Legion Endowment Fund Corp. Chmn. bd. trustees First U.P. Ch. Republican. Mason. Home: East Cleveland, Ohio. Died Oct. 26, 1928.

McQUILLIN, Eugene, lawyer; b. Lee County, Ia., Dec. 14, 1860; s. B. and Hannah (Shane) McQ.; ed. pub. and normal schs., pvt. acads. and college of Iowa; LL.B., Keokuk Coll. of Law, 1883, LL.D., 1916. Admitted to bar, 1881; settled in St. Louis, 1884; spl. atty. for first St. Louis Smoke Abatement Assn., 1895-97; spl. atty. for St. Louis in Mullamphy Charity (established for poor immigrants and travelers), 1897-1900; spl. atty. for St. Louis in preparation of Municipal Code, 1898-1901; circuit judge, 1909-15; mem. Mo. Pub. Service Commn., 1915-17. Lecturer on equity jurisprudence and pub. corps., 1909-34, Benton Coll. of Law, St. Louis. Mem. Nat. Conf. of Commrs. on Uniform State Laws. Pres. of organized legal aid service in St. Louis in army enlistment, World War. Republican. Author, compiler or editor: Treatise on the Law of Municipal Ordinances, 1904; The Law of Instructions to Juries in Civil Cases, with approved forms, 1905; Missouri Civil Practice (2 vols.), 1907; Code Pleading Forms, 1909; The Law of Municipal Corporations (6 vols.), 1911-13, 2d edit. (7 vols.), 1928, supplement, 1934, revision of vol. 6, 1936; Failures of Urban Democracy, 1931; Chaos of Urban Democracy, 1932; Evolution and Future of Urban Democracy, 1933; The American City of Today, 1934; The Municipal Corporation in Epitome, 1935; The Evolution of the Municipal Corporation, 1936; The Constitution and Its Critics, 1936; Principles and Precedents, or The Case Doctrine in Construction, 1936. Home: St. Louis, Mo. Died Dec. 10, 1937.

McRAE, Austin Lee, educator; b. McRae, Ga., Oct. 25, 1861; s. John Colin and Elizabeth Jane (Clements) M.; B.S., U. of Ga., 1881; S.D., Harvard, 1886; m. Minnie Wood, June 15, 1893. Atmospheric electricity investigations, U.S. Signal Service, 1886-89; organized Mo. State Weather Service, 1889-91; asst. prof. Physics, U. of Mo., 1889-91; prof. physics, U. of Mo. School of Mines, Rolla, 1891-94; asso. prof. physics, U. of Texas, 1894-96; cons. engr., St. Louis, 1896-99; prof. of physics, 1899-1920, dir., 1915-20, emeritus prof., 1920—, School of Mines, Rolla. Served as capt. Co. B, U. of Ga. Cadets; chmn. Phelps Co. (Mo.) br. Am. Red Cross, also chmn. Phelps Co. br. Council Nat. Defense; mem. advisory com. for Mo. for Explosives Act. Mason. Democrat. Episcopalian. Home: Rolla, Mo. Died Mar. 18, 1922.

McRAE, Bruce, actor; b. in India, English parents, Jan. 15, 1867. Début in "Thermidor," 1891; with Marie Burroughs in repertoire, 1895; with Julia Marlowe as Captain Trumbull, in "Barbara Frietchie," 1900; appeared in "The Lily," at Stuyvesant Theatre, New York, 1909; several seasons in stock co., Denver; in "Nearly Married," Chicago, 1914. Home: New York, N.Y. Died May 7, 1927.

McRAE, James Henry, army officer; b. Lumber City, Ga., Dec. 24, 1863; s. Daniel F. and Marion (McRae) M.; grad. U.S. Mil. Acad., 1886, Army War Coll., 1911; m. Florence, d. Lt. Col. Geo. W. H. Stouch, U.S.A., Dec. 14, 1887; children—Donald Marion, Dorothy (wife of Lewis C. Beebe, U.S.A.), Mildred (wife of Archibald M. Mixson, U.S.A.); m. 2d, Mrs. Helen Burgar Stouch, Feb. 24, 1926. Commd. 2d lt. 3d Inf., July 1, 1886; promoted through grades to col., July 1, 1916; brig. gen. N.A., Aug. 5, 1917; maj. gen. N.A., Apr. 12, 1918; brig. gen. regular army, Jan. 1, 1920; maj. gen. regular army, May 10, 1922. Participated in Santiago campaign and Battle of El Caney, Spanish-American War; in Philippine Insurrection, various campaigns and engagements; recommended for bvt. of captain, July 1, 1898, "for gallantry in Battle of Santiago"; to be maj., "for distinguished gallantry in action on Mt. Dumandan, Jan. 17, 1900." Mem. Gen. Staff, 1905-08; adj. gen., 1913-17; apptd. comdr. 158th Depot Brigade, Camp Sherman, Chillicothe, O., Sept. 1917; comd. 9th Brig., 5th Div., U.S.A., Dec. 1917, 78th Div., Apr. 18, 1918-June 1919; asst. chief of staff, 1921-22; comdg. 5th Corps Area, 1922-24; comdg. Filipino Div., Mar.-Nov. 1924; comdg. Philippine Dept., 1924-26; comdg. 9th Corps Area, Feb.-Nov. 1926; comdg. 2d Corps Area, 1926-27; retired Dec. 24, 1927. Participated in St. Mihiel and Meuse-Argonne operations. Awarded D.S.M. and Silver Star (oak-leaf cluster), U.S.; Companion Order of Bath (British); Comdr. Legion of Honor, also Croix de Guerre with palm (French). Home: Berkeley, Calif. Died May 1, 1940.

McRAE, Milton A., newspaper pub., mfr.; b. Detroit, Mich., June 13, 1858; s. D. B. and Helen M. (Stevenson) McR.; academic edn.; med. student one yr.; m. Victoria Wallis, of Toronto, Ont., Can., Aug. 11, 1880; children—Mrs. Richmond Temple, Mrs. Helen Henderson, Lindsay S., Mrs. Edith Scripps (dec.). Stockholder and one of founders of Scripps-McRae League of newspapers, consolidated with and now managed and directed by Scripps-Howard Newspaper Syndicate; stockholder in other daily newspapers in U.S.; largest stockholder and dir. General Brass Co., Detroit, mfrs. brass goods. Pres. Detroit Bd. of Commerce; pres. and now v.p. Boy Scouts of America (New York); pres., now trustee Harper Hosp., Detroit; v.p. Scripps Memorial Hosp. and Scripps Metabolic Clinic, San Diego, Calif. Presbyn. Author: Forty Years in Newspaperdom. Died Oct. 10, 1930.

McRAE, Thomas Chipman, governor; b. Mount Holly, Ark., Dec. 21, 1851; s. Duncan L. and Mary Ann (Chipman) M.; ed. pvt. schs.; grad. Soulé Business Coll., New Orleans, 1869; LL.B., Washington and Lee U., 1872; m. Amelia A. White, Dec. 17, 1874; children—Mrs. Ethel Bemis, Herbert Christopher (dec.), Mrs. Mary Montgomery, Alice (dec.), Corrie Scott (dec.), Thomas Christopher, Norvelle White (dec.), Duncan L., Mrs. Mildred Barlow. In practice at Rosston, Ark., 1873-77, Prescott, Ark., since 1877. Mem. Ho. of Rep., 1877-79; presdl. elector, 1880; chmn. Dem. state convs., 1884, 1902; mem. Dem. Congressional Co., 1888-1902, Dem. Nat. Com., 1896-1900; mem. 49th to 57th Congresses (1885-1903), 3d Ark. Dist. Voluntarily retired from Congress; governor of Ark., 2 terms 1921-25; now in practice of law at Prescott; pres. Bank of Prescott. Mem. Ark. Constl. Conv., 1918. Home: Prescott, Ark. Died June 2, 1929.

McREYNOLDS, Peter Wesley, college pres.; b. Kokomo, Ind., Mar. 16, 1872; s. Raven and Nancy (Orem) M.; Central Normal Sch., Danville, Ind.; Union Christian Coll., Ind.; A.B., Hiram Coll., Ohio, 1893; B.D., Union Christian Coll., 1896; A.M., Defiance Coll., Ohio, 1901; m. Crea Mae Kennedy, June 26, 1905. Ordained Christian ministry, 1896; pastor Marshall Ch., March, Mich., 1896-02; pres. Defiance (Ohio) Coll., 1902—. Trustee Defiance Pub. Library. Democrat. Died Oct. 3, 1917.

McREYNOLDS, Samuel Davis, congressman; b. Pikeville, Tenn., Apr. 16, 1872; s. Isaac Stephens and Virginia Adeline (Davis) McR.; ed. Peoples Coll., Pikeville, Tenn., and Cumberland U.; m. Mary Caldwell Davenport, Mar. 9, 1910; 1 dau., Margaret Henriette. Admitted to Tenn. bar, 1893, and began practice at Pikeville; moved to Chattanooga, 1895; apptd. judge Criminal Court, 6th Circuit of Tenn., 1903, and elected to same office three times without opposition; resigned Feb. 1, 1923; mem. 68th to 75th Congresses (1923-39), 3d Tenn. Dist.; del. to Monetary and Economic Internat. Conf., London, 1933. Democrat. Mem. M.E. Ch., S. Mason. Home: Chattanooga, Tenn. Died July 11, 1939.

McSHANE, Andrew James, mayor; b. New Orleans, 1864; s. Bernard and Rosa (Fitzpatrick) McS.; ed. parochial schs.; m. Agnes Bruns, Apr. 4, 1918; 1 dau., Rose Mary. Began, 1873, in employ of Fitzpatrick & Hall, wholesale hides and wool, New Orleans; name of firm changed, 1883, to H. F. Hall & Co., of which became owner 1886, and has since operated as Andrew J. McShane; mayor of New Orleans, 1920-25. Democrat. Catholic. Home: New Orleans, La. Died Apr. 17, 1936.

McSWAIN, John Jackson, congressman; b. Cross Hill, S.C., May 1, 1875; s. Eldredge T. (M.D.) and Janie (McGowan) M.; A.B., and L.L., summa cum laude, S.C. Coll., 1897; LL.D., S.C. Mil. Coll., Charleston, 1935; LL.D., John Randolph Neal Coll. of Law, Knoxville, Tenn., 1936; m. Sarah C. McCullough, Apr. 26, 1905. Admitted to S.C. bar, 1899, and began practice at Greenville, 1901. Referee in bankruptcy, 1912-17; trustee city schs. many yrs.; mem. 67th to 74th Congresses (1921-37), 4th S.C. Dist. Enlisted 1st O.T.C., May 1917; commd. capt. Co. A, 154th Inf.; sailed for France, 154th Inf., Aug. 4, 1918; overseas service about 6 mos.; hon. disch., Mar. 6, 1919. Democrat. Methodist. Mason, Odd Fellow, K. of P., Elk. Home: Greenville, S.C. Died Aug. 6, 1936.

McSWEENEY, Miles Benjamin, gov. S.C., 1899-Jan., 1903; b. Charleston, S.C., April 18, 1855; father died of yellow fever in Charleston when the son was 4 yrs. old; at 10 he sold newspapers, and later clerked in a book store and attended night school; served apprenticeship as a job printer, and worked on newspapers in Charleston and Columbia. Won scholarship in Washington and Lee Univ. offered to Charleston Typographical Union; but, because of lack of means to meet outside expenses, only attended a short time. In 1877 moved to Ninety-Six, Abbeville Co., S.C., and published The Ninety-Six Guardian until 1879; then publisher of The Hampton County Guardian; was chmn. Co. Dem. Com., 1884-94; mem. S.C. legislature, 1894; lt. gov., 1896-99, succeeding as gov. on death of Gov. Wm. H. Ellerbe; elected gov., 1900-02. Home: Columbia, S.C. Died 1909.

McVEA, Emilie Watts, coll. pres.; b. Clinton, La., Feb. 17, 1867; d. Judge John and Emilie Rose (Watts) M.; grad. St. Mary's Sch., Raleigh, N.C., 1884; student, Cornell U., 1900; A.B., George Washington U., 1902, A.M., 1903; Litt.D., U. of Cincinnati, 1916; LL.D., U. of N.C., 1921. Teacher and prin. St. Mary's Sch.; instr. English, U. of Tenn., 1903-04; asst. prof. English, 1906-16, dean of women, 1909-16, U. of Cincinnati; pres. Sweet Briar (Va.) Coll., 1916-25, pres. emeritus; spl. work in English, Rollins Coll. (Fla.), 1926—. Sec.-treas. Southern Assn. of College Women, 1903, 1904; pres. Cincinnati Woman's Club, 1911; mem. Woman's Civic Commn., 1912; mem. Commn. on College Admissions of Assn. of Colleges in Southern States, 1923-26; mem. State Bd. Charities and Corrections, 1922; mem. Bd. of Visitors U. of Va. Lecturer for Nat. Y.W.C.A. and Federal Food Administration, 1918-19. Episcopalian. Independent Democrat. Home: Sweet Briar, Va. Died July 26, 1928.

McVEY, William E., M.D.; b. Waverly, Ill., June 30, 1864; s. Richard E. and Nancy (Harris) M.; B.S., Ill. Coll., 1883; M.D., Kansas City Med. Coll., 1888; m. Annabelle Josephine Bauer, Sept. 12, 1893; children—Maud Annabelle (Mrs. W. J. Burns), Pauline Josephine (Mrs. Evan Browne, Jr.). Prof. diseases of nose, throat and chest, 1892-1913, dean Apr. 1909-13, Kan. Medical Coll. (Washburn U.), Topeka, Kan. Founded, edited and published Kansas Medical Journal, 1889-99; editor Medical Monograph, 1899-1900; editor, Kan. Med. Society Jour., 1914— (sec., pres. soc.). Home: Topeka, Kan. Died Oct. 21, 1931.

McVICKAR, William Neilson, bishop; b. New York, Oct. 19, 1843; s. John A. (M.D.) and Charlotte (Neilson) M.; A.B., Columbia, 1865, A.M., 1868; grad. Gen. Theol. Sem., 1868; (D.D., Kenyon, 1885, U. of Pa., 1898; S.T.D., Columbia, 1898; LL.D., Brown, 1904). Deacon, 1867, priest, 1868, P.E. Ch.; rector Holy Trinity, Harlem, New York, 1868-75, Holy Trinity, Phila., 1875-97; consecrated coadjutor bishop of Rhode Island, Jan. 27, 1898; succeeded as bishop of R.I., on death of Bishop Clark, Sept. 7, 1903. Deputy to Gen. Convs., 1883-95; was pres. Southwest Convocation and mem. diocesan bd. missions and bd. mgrs. Gen. Missionary Society. Died 1910.

McWADE, Robert Malachi, journalist, author; b. Belfast, Ireland; s. James D. and Susan Rae (Campbell) M.; St. Aloysius Coll., Glasgow, Scotland, 1864-65; St. Malachy's Diocesan Coll., Vicinage, Belfast, 1866-71; Jefferson Med. Coll., Phila., 1882; m. Glasgow, Scotland, Rosina Lennox, May 12, 1872 (died 1899); m. 2d, Isabel Anne Roantree, Jan. 12, 1900. Phila. corr. for Boston trade jours. and Chicago Times, and Tribune, 1872-76; city editor Phila. Press, 1875-76; on staff Public Ledger, Phila., night city editor and city editor, 1876-94; pres. Universal Automatic Fire Extinguisher Co., Phila., 1897-1900; U.S. consul, at Canton, China, 1900-02, consul-gen., 1902-04; mgr. Washington bur. Lewis Pub. Co., St. Louis, 1905-12; dean, Coll. Journalism, People's U., St. Louis, 1910-12. Founded Philadelphia Leader, 1883, Delaware Co. Citizen, 1889; sec. Irish Famine Relief Com., 1879; organized Citizens' Permanent Relief Com. Phila., 1879. Was corr. in China of London Telegraph; Washington corr., Am. Can., English and other foreign newspapers. Arranged treaty between foreign missionaries, Chinese Govt. and resident foreign consuls which ended troubles between Christian converts and other natives; twice decorated by Chinese Empress Dowager. Author: The Uncrowned King, 1887; The Great Irish Struggle, 1889; also transl. of Demosthenes' De Corona, Virgil's works, Tacitus, etc. U.S. commr. of conciliation, Aug. 19, 1914—. Home: Philadelphia, Pa. Deceased.

McWANE, James Ransom, pres. McWane Cast Iron Pipe Co.; b. Wytheville, Va., Aug. 15, 1869; s. Charles Philip and Eliza Hoge (Dudley) McW.; student Milligan (Tenn.) Coll., 1884-85; Transylvania U., 1885-86; A.B., Bethany (W.Va.) Coll., 1891; m. Ella Mae McCartney, Dec. 23, 1895; 1 son, William. Minister Disciples of Christ, 1891-94; gen. mgr. McWane Plow Works, 1894-96; v.p. later pres. Lynchburg (Va.) Plow Co., 1896-1903; pres. Am. Steel Casting Co., Birmingham, Ala., 1903-04; coal and coke brokerage, 1904-07; v.p. and pres. Am. Cast Iron Pipe Co., 1907-22; pres. McWane Cast Iron Pipe Co., 1922—; pres. Pacific States Cast Iron Pipe Co., Provo, Utah, 1926—. Maj. Ordnance Dept., U.S.A. 1918; staff asst. to v.p. Emergency Fleet Corp., July-Nov. 1918. Mem. bd. trustees Pension Fund, Disciples of Christ, also of Berry Sch., Mt. Berry, Ga. Home: Birmingham, Ala. Died June 24, 1933.

McWHINNEY, Thomas Martin, educator, author; b. in Ohio, Nov. 16, 1823; s. Matthew and Temperance (Hendrick) M.; reared on farm; worked his way through sch. and coll.; (D.D., LL.D.); m. A. M. Stark, Nov. 12, 1846. Non-resident prof. Christian ethics and applied psychology, Christian Biblical Inst., New York, Union Christian Coll., Ind., Defiance Coll., Ohio, and Palmer Coll., Iowa. Author: Reason and Revelation; Ethical Science; Christ Our Creed; Chinese Problem; Church Federation. Home: Yellow Springs, O. Died 1909.

McWHIRTER, Felix T., banker; b. Lynchburg, Tenn., July 17, 1853; s. Dr. Samuel H. and Nancy C. (Tyree) M.; A.B., E. Tenn. Wesleyan (now Grant Memorial) U., 1873, A.M., 1876; Ph.D., De Pauw, 1885; student Johns Hopkins U., 1885-86; m. Luella Frances Smith, Nov. 18, 1878. Editor of the Athens (Tenn.) News, 1873-76; mayor of Athens, 1877-78; instr. and asso. prof. rhetoric and English lit., De Pauw, 1884-88; real estate broker, Indianapolis, 1888-1900; pres. Peoples State Bank, Dec. 1, 1900—. Mem. Prohibition Nat. Com., 1892-12 (treas. 1906-12, exec. com., 1905-12); chmn. Ind. State Prohibition Com., 1893-94, 1896-98. Prohibition candidate for gov. Ind., 1904; 1st v.p. Ind. Children's Home Finding Soc., 1909-11. Home: Indianapolis, Ind. Died June 5, 1915.

McWHORTER, Ashton Waugh, educator; b. Bachelor's Hall, Va., June 18, 1877; s. James Kyle and Virginia Lee (Millan) McW.; A.B., Roanoke Coll., Salem, Va., 1895; A.M., 1902; Ph.D., Johns Hopkins, 1905; m. Bessie Belle Gammon, June 15, 1921; children—Elizabeth Lee, Ashton Waugh. Principal of schools, South Carolina, 1895-98; prof. Latin and English, Presbyn. Coll. of S.C., 1899-1903; prof. Latin and modern langs., Thornwell Sem., Clinton, S.C., 1899-1903; fellow in Greek, Johns Hopkins, 1904-05; instr. Greek and Latin, George Washington U., 1905-06; classical master, Sewanee Grammar Sch. (U. of the South), 1906-07; prof. English and history, 1907-18, librarian, 1907-18, treas., 1914-19, acting pres., 1917-19, prof. Greek, 1918-23, dean, 1920-23, Hampden-Sydney Coll.; prof. Latin and Roman archeology, U. of Tenn., 1923-33, prof. of classical languages and literatures, 1933—. Prof. Latin, 7 summers, history, 1919, govt., 1923; Coll. of William and Mary; prof. Latin, U. of Va., summer 1928. Democrat. Presbyterian. Home: Knoxville, Tenn. Died Nov. 17, 1938.

McWHORTER, Henry Clay, lawyer; b. Marion Co., O., Feb. 20, 1836; s. Fields and Margaret (Kester) M.; enlisted in Union Army, as pvt., Sept. 16, 1861; mustered Sept. 30, as 2d lt.; promoted capt., Mar. 2, 1862; resigned on account of wound, Sept. 17, 1863; in provost marshal's enrollment office, chief clerk, 1863-65; m. Mary Hardmann, Dec. 16, 1857 (died 1878); m. 2d, Eliza F. McWhorter, May 8, 1879 (died 1881); m. 3d, Lucy M. Clark, Jan. 8, 1885 (died 1900); m. 4th, Mrs. Caroline M. Gates, May 18, 1904. Admitted to bar, 1866; mem. W.Va. Ho. of Delegates, 4 terms, 1865-68 (chmn. jud. com.) and 1885, 1887 (speaker 1868); pros. atty., 1869-73; postmaster Charleston, W.Va., 1891-93; judge Supreme Ct. Appeals of W.Va., 1897-1908 (presiding judge 3 yrs.). Mem. Gen. Conf. M.E. Ch., 1880, 1908. Elector for Hall of Fame, Syracuse U., 1905; pres. bd. trustees W.Va. Wesleyan Coll., June 1897—. Mason. Home: Charleston-Kanawha, W.Va. Died Apr. 15, 1913.

McWILLIAMS, Clarence A., surgeon; b. Brooklyn, N.Y., Jan. 29, 1870; s. Daniel Wilkin and Helen (Marquand) McW.; grad. Poly. Inst. Brooklyn, 1888; A.B., Princeton, 1892, A.M., 1895; M.D., Coll. Phys. and Surg. (Columbia), 1895; unmarried. Practiced at N.Y. City; attending surgeon New York Skin and Cancer Hosp.; asso. surgeon Fifth Av. Hosp.; prof. clin. surgery New York Polyclinic Hosp., N.Y. City. Served as lt. M.C., Spanish-Am. War; maj. M.C., with A.E.F. in France 2 yrs., World War. Fellow Am. Coll. Surgeons. Decorated Officier de l'Instruction Publique (France). Republican. Presbyn. Died Jan. 20, 1927.

McWILLIAMS, Thomas Samuel, clergyman, educator; b. Shelbyville, Ky., Nov. 22, 1865; s. Samuel and Martha (Harrington) M.; A.B., Centre Coll., Ky., 1886, A.M., 1889, D.D., 1899; grad. Princeton Theol. Sem., 1899; Columbia, 1915-17; m. Susan Probasco Nipgen, Dec. 5, 1889; 1 son, John Probasco. Ordained Presbyn. ministry, 1889; pastor Chillicothe, O., 1889-92, Am. Presbyn. Ch., Montreal, 1892-1902, Calvary Ch., Cleveland, O., 1902-14; prof. comparative religions, Western Reserve U., 1917—. Home: Cleveland, O. Died Dec. 8, 1937.

McWILLIE, Thomas Anderson, lawyer; b. Kirkwood, Miss., July 18, 1849; s. William and Catherine Morris (Anderson) M.; ed. U. of Miss., 1866-68; m. Elizabeth Webb, Apr. 15, 1875 (dec.). Admitted to bar, Jan. 1875; mem. Nugent & McWillie, 1875-96, McWillie & Thompson, Mar. 1897—; atty. and dir. Ala. & Vicksburg Ry. Co.; atty. Pullman Co. Mem. lower house Miss. Legislature, 1880-81; reporter Supreme Ct. of Miss., 1895—; trustee Deaf and Dumb Inst. of Miss., 1896-1904. Episcopalian. Democrat. Home: Jackson, Miss. Died 1911.

MEAD, Albert Edward, governor; b. Manhattan, Kan., Dec. 14, 1861; s. William Banks and Harriet (Carlton) M.; grad. Southern Ill. Normal U., Carbondale, 1882; jr. law course Union Coll. of Law, Chicago, 1883-84; twice married (1st wife died); m. 2d, Mina J. Pifer, of Vancouver, B.C., May 5, 1899. Admitted to bar, Ill. Supreme Ct., 1885; practiced law in Wichita Co., Kan., until removed to Wash., 1889; mayor of Blaine, Wash., 1892-93; mem. Wash. Ho. of Rep., 1893-95; co. atty. Whatcom Co., 1899-1901; gov. of Wash., 1905-09; resumed law practice at Bellingham, Wash., 1909; mem. Mead & Whitcomb. Home: Billingham, Wash. Died Mar. 19, 1913.

MEAD, Charles Larew, bishop; b. Vienna, N.J., July 20, 1868; s. Joshua and Alice A. (Hough) M.; A.B., New York U., 1896; D.D., Syracuse, 1907, Univ. of Colo., 1927; LL.D., U. of Denver, 1920; m. Eleanor M. Smith, June 10, 1896; children—Winifred Marcena, Eleanor Charlene, Marion Salome, Charles L., Robert Smith. Ordained M.E. ministry, 1895; pastor Rutherford, N.J., 1895-99, Hoboken, N.J., 1899-1904, Newark, 1904-08, Hoboken, 1908-09, Baltimore, Md., 1909-13, N.Y. City, 1913-14, Trinity Ch., Denver, Colo., 1914-20; bishop M.E. Ch., May 20, 1920—, Denver Area, 1920-32, Kansas City Area, 1932-39; bishop South Central Jurisdiction, Meth. Ch., 1939—. Served with Y.M.C.A. in France 6 mos., World War. Mason. Died May 17, 1941.

MEAD, Charles Marsh, clergyman; b. Cornwall, Vt., Jan. 28, 1836; s. Rufus and Anna (Janes) M.; A.B., Middlebury Coll., 1856, A.M., 1859; grad. Andover Theol. Sem., 1862; univs. of Halle and Berlin, 1863-66; Ph.D., Tübingen, 1866; (D.D., Middlebury, 1881, Princeton, 1896; LL.D., Middlebury, 1906); m. Caroline Thayer, Aug. 2, 1867. Ordained Congl. ministry, 1866; prof. Hebrew, Andover Theol. Sem., 1866-82; lived in Germany, 1882-92; prof. Christian theology, Hartford Theol. Sem., 1892-98. Mem. Am. Bible Revision Com., 1872—. Author: Exodus, in Lange's Commentary, 1876; The Soul Here and Hereafter, 1879; translation (in part) of Dorner's Christian Ethics, 1886; Supernatural Revelation, 1889; Romans Dissected (under pseudonym E. D. McRealsham); Christ and Criticism, 1893; Irenic Theology, 1905. Home: New Haven, Conn. Died 1911.

MEAD, Edward Campbell, author; b. Newton, Mass., Jan. 12, 1837; s. Rev. Zachariah and Anna Maria (Hull) M.; ed. Ridgeway Acad., Albemarle Co., Va.; m. Nov. 1861. Made a voyage to Australia and East Indies, 1858-59; engaged in business in Richmond, Va., 1860; took up farming in 1862, account of failing health. Author: Genealogical History of the Lee Family of Virginia and Maryland, 1866; Biographical Sketch of Anna M. Chalmers, 1893. Has conducted the geneal. column of Baltimore Sun and Richmond Times-Dispatch, 1903—. Home: Keswick, Va. Died 1908.

MEAD, Edwin Doak, author, lecturer; b. Chesterfield, N.H., Sept. 29, 1849; s. Bradley and Sarah (Stone) M.; acad. edn.; m. Lucia True Ames, Sept. 29, 1898. Spent boyhood on a farm and in village store; in 1866 entered employ of Ticknor & Fields, Boston publishers; in English and German univs., 1875-79; then engaged in lecturing and lit. work: editor New England Magazine, 1889-1901. Several yrs. pres. Mass. Good Citizenship Soc., Am. Free Religious Assn., and 20th Century Club of Boston, and dir. Old South hist. work in Boston, editing the Old South Leaflets and other publs.; editor International Library. Dir. World Peace Foundation; del. Am. Peace Soc. to congresses of Glasgow, Rouen, Lucerne, Munich and London; chmn. exec. com. 13th Internat. Peace Congress, Boston, 1904. Author: Martin Luther—A Study of Reformation; The Philosophy of Carlyle; The Roman Church and the Public Schools; Organize the World; The Influence of Emerson; The Principles of the Founders, etc. Home: Brookline, Mass. Died Aug. 17, 1937.

MEAD, Elizabeth Storrs, educator; b. Conway, Mass., May 21, 1832; d. Charles Eugene and Sarah Williston (Storrs) Billings; ed. at sem. in Ipswich, Mass.; (hon. A.M., Oberlin, 1890; L.H.D., Smith, 1900); m. Rev. Hiram Mead, Aug. 5, 1858 (died 1881). Conducted a family sch., Andover, Mass., with sister, 1852-58; instr. English composition, Oberlin Coll., 1881-83; teacher Abbott Acad., Andover, 1883-89; pres. Mt. Holyoke Coll., 1890-1900; resigned. Home: Oberlin, O. Died Mar. 25, 1917.

MEAD, Elwood, engineer; b. Patriot, Ind., Jan. 16, 1858; s. Daniel and Lucinda M.; B.S., Purdue, 1882, M.S., 1884, E.D., 1904; C.E., Iowa State U., 1883; LL.D., U. of Mich., 1925; m. Florence Chase; children—Tom C., Lucy F., Arthur E.; m. 2d, Mary Lewis; children—Catherine, Sue, John. Asst. engr., U.S. Engrs., 1882-83; prof. Colo. Agrl. Coll., 1883-84, 1886-88; territorial and state engr., Wyo., 1888-99; chief irrigation and drainage investigation, U.S. Dept. Agr., 1897-1907; prof. institutions and practice of irrigation, U. of Calif., 1898-1907; chmn. State Rivers and Water Supply Commn., Victoria, Australia, 1907-15; prof. rural instns., U. of Calif., 1915, and chmn. Land Settlement Bd.; commr. of reclamation, Apr. 1924—; mem. Com. Conservation and Administration of Pub. Domain. Consulting engineer for various irrigation and water works companies. Author: Irrigation Institutions; Helping Men Own Farms. Home: Washington, D.C. Died Jan. 26, 1936.

MEAD, Frederick Sumner; b. Boston, Mass., July 25, 1866; s. Sumner Rust and Ada (Lawrence) M.; A.B., Harvard, 1887, hon. A.M., 1926; m. Katharine Rand, June 11, 1890. Mem. F. S. Mead & Co., stock-brokers, 1891-1901; comptroller Harvard U., 1920-26. Editor: Harvard Alumni Directory, 1917-21; Harvard's Military Record in the World War, 1921. Home: Brookline, Mass. Died Oct. 7, 1935.

MEAD, George Herbert, univ. prof.; b. S. Hadley, Mass., Feb. 27, 1863; s. Rev. Hiram and Elizabeth Storrs (Billings) Mead; A.B., Oberlin Coll., 1883; pvt. tutor, 1883-87, A.B., Harvard, 1888; univs. Leipzig and Berlin, 1888-91; m. Helen Kingsbury Castle, Oct. 1, 1891 (died 1929); 1 son, Henry C. A. Instr. philosophy, 1891-93, asst. prof., 1893-94, U. of Mich.; asst. prof. philosophy, 1894-1902, asso. prof., 1902-07, prof., 1907—, U. of Chicago. Died Apr. 26, 1931.

MEAD, John Abner, governor; b. Fairhaven, Vt., Apr. 20, 1841; s. Roswell Rowley and Lydia Ann (Gorham) M.; pvt. 12th Vt. Vols., 1862-63; A.B., Middlebury (Vt.) Coll., 1864; M.D., Coll. Phys. and Surg. (Columbia), 1868; (LL.D., Norwich U., Middlebury Coll., U. of Vt.); m. Mary Madelia Sherman, Nov. 30, 1872. Practiced medicine, Rutland, Vt., until 1888; surgeon-gen. of Vt., 1878-79; was treas. Rutland R.R. Co., 1880-86; pres. Vt. State Trust Co., 1881-86; treas. Addison R.R., 1880-86, etc.; pres. Howe Scale Co., 1888—, Baxter Nat. Bank, 1904—. Secured 1st charter for City of Rutland, Vt., and elected 1st mayor, 1893; Vt. commr. Chicago Expn., 1893, Mexican Nat. Expn., 1895. Mem. Vt. Senate, 1892, Ho. of Rep., 1906; lt. gov. of Vt., 1908-09; gov. for term 1910-12. Republican. Conglist. Home: Rutland, Vt. Died Jan. 12, 1920.

MEAD, Kate Campbell Hurd, M.D.; b. Danville, Prov. Quebec, Can., Apr. 6, 1867; d. Edward Payson and Sarah Elizabeth (Campbell) Hurd; came with parents to U.S., 1870; M.D., Woman's Med. Coll. of Pa., Phila., 1888; studied New England Hosp., Boston, various med. schs. in Europe and Johns Hopkins Med. Sch.; m. William Edward Mead, June 21, 1893. Hospital practice, 1888-90; med. dir. Bryn Mawr Sch., Baltimore, 1890-93; practiced, Middletown, Conn., 1893-1925; cons. gynecologist, Middlesex Hosp., 1907-25; research on history of Med. Women, Europe, 1925-29; practiced at Haddam, Conn., 1929—. Organizer Middletown Dist. Nurse Assn., 1900, Middletown Hosp. Aid Soc., 1907, Middletown Hosp. Nurses' Training Sch., 1907; pres. Pub. Health Assn., Haddam, 1931-36. Mem. Vol. Med. Service Corps, Council of Nat. Defense, 1917-19, also lecturer on Speakers' Bur. and teacher classes Am. Red Cross. Republican. Author: American Medical Women Pioneers, 1933; A History of Women in Medicine, vol. I, 1938. Home: Haddam, Conn. Died Jan. 1, 1941.

MEAD, Larkin Goldsmith, sculptor; b. Chesterfield, N.H., Jan. 3, 1835; s. Larkin Goldsmith and Mary Jane (Noyes) M.; bro. of William Rutherford M.; ed. pub. schs., Brattleboro, Vt.; m. Marietta Di Benvenuti, of Florence, Italy, Feb. 26, 1866. Hardware clerk at 15; studied drawing and sculpture 2 yrs. under Henry K. Brown; produced several noteworthy works; went to Italy; was attached to the U.S. Consulate at Venice, where his brother-in-law, W. D. Howells, was consul. During Civil War was 6 months in camp as artist for Harper's Weekly. Among his works are the National Lincoln Monument at Springfield, Ill.; the Soldiers' Monument at St. Johnsbury, Vt.; statutes of Ethan Allen in Nat. Art Gallery, Washington, and in State Capitol, Montpelier, Vt.; also the pediment, 60 feet long, representing "The Return of Proserpine from the Realms of Pluto," over main entrance Agriculture Bldg., Chicago Expn, and many ideal works; a large group representing the Stanford family, to be placed in Stanford U., Calif.; also a colossal statue of The Mississippi River, at Minneapolis Ct. House, colossal marble group representing Columbus appealing to Isabella, Sacramento, Calif.; high relief portraits in bronze of Henry James, William D. Howells and John Hay. Professore Corrispondente dell' Accademia di Belle Arti. Died 1910.

MEAD, Leonard Charles, alienist; b. Hampden, Wis., Jan. 18, 1856; s. Ezra and Sylvia (Barber) M.; U. of Wis., 1874-76; M.D., Rush Med. Coll., Chicago, 1881; post-grad. work, New York Polyclinic Med. Sch. and Hosp.; (LL.D., U. of S.D., 1918); m. Matilda Fraser Gardner, June 25, 1886. Practiced at Good Thunder, Minn., 1881-82, Elk Point, S.D., 1882-90; asst. supt. and supt. S.D. State Hosp. for Insane, Yankton, S.D. 1891—. Republican. Conglist. Mason. Home: Yankton, S.D. Died Jan. 13, 1920.

MEAD, Lucia True Ames, author; b. Boscawen, N.H., May 5, 1856; d. Nathan P. and Elvira Ames; m. Edwin Doak Mead, Sept. 29, 1898. Conducted adult classes in studies in Nineteenth Century Thought, Boston, and lectures on internat. arbitration and economic and social questions; especially active in the movement for a League of Nations. Author: Great Thoughts for Little Thinkers, 1890; Memoirs of a Millionaire, 1890; To Whom Much Is Given, 1898; Milton's England, 1902; Primer of the Peace Movement; Patriotism and the New Internationalism, 1907; Swords and Ploughshares, 1912; Law or War, 1928. Home: Brookline, Mass. Died Nov. 1, 1936.

MEAD, William Rutherford, architect; b. Brattleboro, Vt., Aug. 20, 1846; s. Larkin Goldsmith and Mary Jane (Noyes) M.; A.B., Amherst, 1867, LL.D., 1902; Doctor of Fine Arts, U. of Pa., 1921; studied architecture with late Russell Sturgis, New York; studied abroad 2 yrs.; m. Budapest, Hungary, Olga Kilenyi, Nov. 13, 1884. Mem. McKim, Mead & White, 1879—; firm are architects of Boston Public Library, Columbia U., Coll. City of New York, U. of Va., Metropolitan, University and Century clubs, New York Herald Bldg., Madison Sq. Garden, Knickerbocker Trust Co., Nat. City Bank, Tiffany Bldg., Gorham Bldg., Bellevue Hosp., Pa. Sta., new U.S. Post Office and Municipal Office bldgs., New York, Brooklyn Inst. Arts and Sciences, R.I. Capitol, Bank of Montreal, War Coll., Washington, etc. Awarded gold medal of honor, Nat. Inst. Arts and Letters. Knight comdr. Crown of Italy, 1922. Mem. Am. Acad. Arts and Letters; fellow A.I.A.; pres. Am. Acad. in Rome; N.A., 1910. Home: New York, N.Y. Died June 20, 1928.

MEAD, William Whitman, naval officer; b. Burlington, Ky., Feb. 8, 1845; s. Sackett and Anna A.M.; grad. U.S. Naval Acad., 1865; m. Julia B. Watts, of Ky. Promoted ensign, Dec. 1, 1866; advanced through grades to rear adm., July 1, 1905. Was lt. in command of a steam launch, in 1st day's fight with Corean forts; when expdn. landed for capture and destruction of the forts comd. light arty. from flagship; comd. U.S.S. Machias during latter part of war with Spain; comd. U.S.S. Brooklyn in spring 1899, U.S.S. Phila., Feb. 20, 1900-Jan. 1902; mem. Bd. of Inspection, Mar.-Aug. 1902; comdt. Naval Training Sta., Newport, R.I., Sept. 1902-July 1904, Navy Yard, Portsmouth, N.H., 1904-07; retired by operation of law, Feb. 8, 1907. Home: Wayne, Pa. Died Mar. 13, 1930.

MEADE, Richard Kidder, chemical engr.; b. Charlottesville, Va., Nov. 28, 1874; s. Rev. Francis Alexander and Mattie (Mosby) M.; grad. U. of Virginia, 1893; hon. M.S., Lafayette Coll., 1908; m. Fannie Louise Thomas, Dec. 20, 1900; children—Martha Haskins (Mrs. George E. Baughman), Francis Alexander. City editor Independent-Herald, Hinton, W.Va., 1894; chemist Longdale Iron Co., Allegheny Co., Va., 1895-96; asst. in chemistry, Lafayette Coll., 1897-1902; chief chemist, Edison Portland Cement Co., 1902, Northampton Portland Cement Co., 1903. Dexter Portland Cement Co., 1904; founder and editor The Chemical Engineer, 1904; dir. Meade Testing Laboratories, Allentown, Pa., 1908-11, gen. mgr. Tidewater Portland Cement Co., Baltimore, 1911-12; in consulting practice, Baltimore, 1912—. Consulting chem. engr. to many Portland cement plants; inventor of numerous processes and appliances of use in the Portland cement industry. Author: The Chemists' Pocket Manual, 1900; The Chemical and Physical Examination of Portland Cement, 1901; Portland Cement, 1906; The Design and Equipment of Small Chemical Laboratories, 1907; Tables for Determination of Economic Minerals, 1907; The Technical Analysis of Brass, 1911. Home: Roland Par, Md. Died Oct. 13, 1930.

MEADE, Richard Worsam; b. Cold Spring-on-Hudson, N.Y., Feb. 7, 1870; s. Rear Adm. Richard W. (U.S.N.) and Rebecca (Paulding) M.; grad. high sch., Washington, D.C., 1888; m. Helena Rutherfurd Ely, 1905; children—Richard Worsam, Helena Rutherfurd, John Paulding. Ry. secretarial positions until 1898; in Navy, Spanish-Am. War (Santiago Campaign); with N.Y.C. R.R., and Met. St. Ry., New York, 1899-1904; pres., gen. mgr. New York Transportation Co., etc., 1904-18, established first taxicab and motor bus services in America, 1906; pres., gen. mgr. Detroit Motorbus Co., 1919-21; pres., gen. mgr. People's Motorbus Co. of St. Louis, 1923-31; now in cons. practice. Home: Mt. Kisco, N.Y. Died Dec. 3, 1933.

MEADE, Robert Leamy, officer U.S. Marine Corps; b. Washington, Dec. 26, 1841; s. Capt. Richard W. (U.S.N.) and Clara Forsyth (Meigs) M.; ed. Mt. St. Mary's Coll., Emmitsburg, Md., and U.S. Naval Acad.; m. Mary, d. Admiral H. Paulding, U.S.N., Feb. 6, 1865. Apptd. acting midshipman, U.S.N., Sept. 30, 1856; resigned, Dec. 2, 1858; watch officer U.S. coast survey steamer Bibb, 1858-61; commd. 2d lt. U.S. Marine Corps, 1862; promoted through grades to col., Mar. 3, 1899; brig. gen. and retired, Jan. 29, 1906. Bvtd. brig. gen. for battle of Tientsin, China; received W. I. campaign medal (congressional), Comd. co. of marines during draft riots in New York, July, 1863; captured, Aug. 8, 1863, and held prisoner of war for 15 mos.; on cruise in U.S.S. Shenandoah, in India, China, Japan and Korea, 1865-69; fleet marine officer of Admiral Sampson's Fleet during Spanish-Am. War; participated in Chinese expdn., 1900. Home: Lexington, Mass. Died 1910.

MEADOR, Chastain Clark, clergyman, editor; b. Bedford Co., Va.; s. Jeremiah and Rachel M.; ed. common schs. and Columbian Coll., A.B., A.M., LL.D.; m. Ann C. Shield, Aug. 1857 (died 1900). Joined the Bapt. Ch., 1844, in which he has obtained distinction as pastor; founded, 1857, and from then pastor, 5th Bapt. Ch., Washington; studied in the Columbian Univ., Washington; editor and propr. of the Baptist Beacon, 1881—, Washington, D.C. Died 1905.

MEADOWCROFT, William Henry; b. Manchester, Eng., May 29, 1853; s. Henry and Elizabeth Hannah (Roberts) M.; ed. common and high schs., Manchester, Eng.; m. Phoebe Canfield, Dec. 11, 1878 (died 1918); children—William Miron, Charles Harry. Came to U.S., 1875; in employ law firm of Carter & Eaton, N.Y. City, 1875-81; admitted to N.Y. bar, 1881; connected with Thomas A. Edison enterprises, 1881—; assistant and confidential secretary to Mr. Edison, 1910, until Mr. Edison's decease in 1931, and continues at Edison Laboratory in historical and other work. First exploiter of miniature electric lamp; originator of application of electricity to display signs; early experimenter with X-ray and with liquid air. Founder, mem., and historian, Edison Pioneers (pres. 1927); hon. v.p. Thomas Alva Edison Foundation, Inc. Republican. Mem. Dutch Ref. Ch. Author: A B C of Electricity, 1888; A B C of the X-Ray, 1897; The Boy's Life of Edison, 1911, 28; collaborator (with Dyer and Martin); Edison—His Life and Inventions, 1911, 29. Home: Boonton, N.J. Died Oct. 15, 1937.

MEAGHER, James Francis, lawyer; b. Brooklyn, Jan. 26, 1858; s. James F. and Mary (Nagle) M.; came to Chicago in early childhood; ed. pub. schs.; read law in offices at Chicago; m. Pauline Hayes, Feb. 28, 1889. Admitted to bar, 1881, and since in practice at Chicago; mem. Meagher, Whitney, Ricks & Sullivan, Jan. 1, 1916—. Gen. counsel, 1902-15, v.p., 1906-13, pres., Oct. 1913-July 1915, Peoples Gas Light & Coke Co., Chicago. Republican. Home: Chicago, Ill. Died Oct. 30, 1917.

MEAGHER, James Luke, clergyman, author; b. Drangan, Tipperary Co., Ireland, Aug. 14, 1848; s. John and Bridget (Connelly) M.; brought to America, 1850; full course (11½ yrs.), Montreal (Can.) Coll. and Sem.; (D.D., by Pope Leo XIII, 1903). Ordained R.C. priest, 1875; subdeacon and deacon under Archbishop Fabre, Montreal, 1875-77; with St. Joseph's Ch. and Cathedral, Albany, N.Y., 1876-79; asst. 6 yrs., pastor 10 yrs., Cazenovia Diocese of Albany. Incorporated, 1894, the Christian Press Assn., 1895, the Christian Lit. Union, and became pres. both orgns. Author: Christ's Kingdom on Earth; The Temples of the Eternal; The Protestant Churches; What is Man?; etc. Home: Long Island City, N.Y. Died May 8, 1920.

MEAKIN, L. H., painter, etcher; b. Newcastle, Staffordshire, Eng.; brought to U.S. as a child; studied old Sch. of Design, now Art Acad. of Cincinnati; studied at Munich and Paris and worked in various parts of France, Germany, Italy, Holland, etc. Received several awards; exhibited Paris Expn., 1900; silver medal, St. Louis Expn., 1904, Appalachian Expn., 1911; Chicago Fine Arts Bldg. Corp. prize ($500), 1911. Instr. drawing and painting, Cincinnati Art Acad.; curator of painting, Art. Mus. of Cincinnati. Represented in various pub. collections, A.N.A. Home: Cincinnati, O. Died Aug. 14, 1917.

MEANS, David MacGregor, lawyer; b. Groton, Mass., May 1, 1847; s. Rev. James and Elizabeth Phebe (Johnson) M.; brother of Emily Adams Means; A.B., Yale U., 1868; studied divinity, Andover, Mass., and New Haven, Conn.; L.H.D., Hobart, 1912; m. Laura Haven, Apr. 5, 1877. Tutor, Yale, 1876; fellow Johns Hopkins, 1877; prof. economics, Middlebury, 1877-80; admitted to bar, 1881, and entered practice at New York. Author: The Boss, 1894; Industrial Freedom, 1897; The Methods of Taxation, 1909. Home: Middlebury, Vt. Died Apr. 24, 1931.

MEANY, Edmond Stephen, univ. prof.; b. East Saginaw, Mich., Dec. 28, 1862; s. Stephen and Margaret Ann (English) M.; B.S., Territorial U. of Wash., 1885; M.S., U. of Wash., 1899; Litt.M., U. of Wisconsin, 1901; LL.D. from the College of Puget Sound, 1926; m. Sarah Elizabeth Ward, May 1, 1889; children—Elizabeth Lois (dec.), Thomas Mercer (dec.), Margaret (Mrs. J. Arthur Younger), Edmond S. Prof. history, Univ. of Wash., 1897—. Member Wash. Legislature, 1891-93. Active worker in erection of statues of distinguished Americans and hist. monuments in Wash. Chevalier Legion of Honor (French). Scout commr. Boy Scouts of America, Seattle. Conglist. Republican. Author: History of the State of Washington, 1909; United States History for Schools, 1911; (co-author) The State of Washington, 1893; Washington's First Constitution, 1919; Origin of Washington Geographic Names, 1923; Newspapers of Washington Territory, 1923; Washington From Life, 1931; The Ulster County Gazette, 1931; Lincoln Esteemed Washington, 1933. Editor: Diary of Wilkes in the Northwest, 1926, also of Washington Historical Quarterly from its beginning in 1906. Died Apr. 22, 1935.

MEANY, Edward P., lawyer, financier; b. Louisville, Ky., May 13, 1854; s. Edward A. and Maria Lavina (Shannon) M.; ed. Public schs.; studied law under father; m. Rosaline Behr. Admitted to bar, 1878; counsel Am. Telephone & Telegraph Co. many yrs. Became judge advocate gen. of N.J., 1905, with rank of brig. gen. Home: New York, N.Y. Died Nov. 24, 1938.

MEARA, Frank S., M.D.; b. Salem, Mass., May 6, 1866; s. Sherman Timothy and Eugenia Eliza (Norton) M.; A.B., Yale, 1890, Ph.D., 1892; M.D., Coll. Phys. and Surg. (Columbia), 1895; m. Alice M. Sykes, Dec. 9, 1897. Asst. physiol. chemistry, Yale, 1890-92; instr., materia medica, Coll. Phys. and Surg., 1903-04, in pediatrics, 1904-09; asst. attending phys. in charge children's med. service, 1904-09, asst. attending physician and attending phys., 1909-20, Bellevue Hosp., now cons. physician; asso. attending physician St. Luke's Hosp., 1907; prof. therapeutics, Cornell U. Med. Coll., N.Y. City, 1909-20, then prof. clin. medicine; consulting phys. to various hospitals. Republican. Congregationalist. Author: Treatment of Acute Infectious Diseases, 1916, 1921. Home: New York, N.Y. Deceased.

MEARNS, Edgar Alexander, lt. colonel U.S.A.; b. Highland Falls, N.Y., Sept. 11, 1856; s. Alexander and Nancy R. (Carswell) M.; M.D., Coll. Phys. and Surg. (Columbia), 1881; m. Ella Wittich, 1881. Apptd. 1st lt. asst. surgeon, Dec. 3, 1883; capt. asst. surgeon, Dec. 3, 1888; maj. brigade surgeon vols., June 4, 1898; maj. chief surgeon, Jan. 7, 1899; hon. discharged from vol. service, Mar. 22, 1899; maj. surgeon, Feb. 2, 1901; lt. col. retired, Jan. 1, 1909. In charge of the naturalists of the Smithsonian African Expdn. sent out under the direction of Col. Theodore Roosevelt, 1909; field naturalist of Childs-Frick African expdan., 1911-12; asso. in zoölogy, U.S. Nat. Museum, Washington. Patron Am. Mus. Natural History, New York. Author: Mammals of the Mexican Boundary of the United States, 1907. Died Nov. 1, 1916.

MEARS, David Otis, clergyman; b. Essex, Mass., Feb. 22, 1842; s. David and Agibail (Burnham) M.; bro. of Leverett M.; A.B., Amherst, 1865, A.M., 1868; full theol. course under direction of Rev. E. N. Kirk, D.D., Boston; (D.D., Ia. [now Grinnell] Coll., 1882); m. Fannie J. Bentley, Sept. 11, 1867; m. 2d, Mary C., d. Hon. J. B. Grinnell, of Grinnell, Ia., Sept. 6, 1882. Ordained to ministry, 1867; pastor North Av. Congl. Ch., Cambridge, Mass., 1867-77, Piedmont Congl. Ch., Worcester, Mass., 1877-93, Calvary Presbyn. Ch., Cleveland, O., 1893-95, Fourth Presbyn. Ch., Albany, N.Y., 1895-1910, pastor emeritus, 1910. Asso. editor Golden Rule (now Christian Endeavor World), Boston, 1879-80. Author: Life of Edward Norris Kirk, D.D., 1877; The Deathless Book, 1888; Oberlin Lectures, 1892; Inspired Through Suffering, 1895. Edited Lectures on Revivals, by E. N. Kirk, D.D., 1875. Died Apr. 29, 1915.

MEARS, Frederick, engineer; b. Ft. Omaha, Neb., May 25, 1878; s. Frederick and Elizabeth (McFarland) M.; prep. edn. Shattuck Sch., Faribault, Minn.; distinguished grad. U.S. Inf. and Cav. Sch., 1904; U.S. Staff Coll., 1905; m. Jennie, d. late Maj. J. P. Wainwright, U.S.A., Apr. 6, 1907. With G.N. Ry., advancing to resident engr., 1897-99; enlisted U.S.A. as pvt., Oct. 1, 1899; commd. 2d lt., 5th Cav., July 1, 1901; 1st lt., 11th Cav., Sept. 20, 1906; capt., July 1, 1916; col., Jan. 1918; lt. colonel engineer corps, Oct. 18, 1920. Served in Philippine Islands until July 1903; duty, Isthmian Canal Commn., 1906-14; surveyed location for new high level ry., 1906-07; res. engr. and engr. constrn. New Panama R.R., 1907-09; chief engr., same rd., 1909-14, also gen. supt., 1913-14; mem. Alaskan Engring. Commn., 1914-17; col. 31st Engrs., Jan. 16, 1918; sailed for France, June 6, 1918; asst. gen. mgr. (Aug. and Sept.) and gen. mgr. Sept. 1918-May 1919, R.R. Dept., S.O.S., France; returned to U.S., May 21, 1919; chmn. and chief engr. Alaskan Engring. Commn., 1919-23; retired as col., July 19, 1923; chief engr. St. Paul Union Depot Co., St. Paul, Minn., 1923-25; asst. chief engr., G.N. Ry., May 1925—. Awarded D.S.M. (U.S.); Officer Legion of Honor (French), 1919. Episcopalian. Home: Seattle, Wash. Died Jan. 11, 1939.

MEARS, Helen Farnsworth, sculptor; b. Oshkosh, Wis., 1878; d. John H. and Elizabeth (Farnsworth) M. (whose pen-name was "Nellie Wildwood"); sister of Mary M. M.; ed. State Normal Sch., Oshkosh, Wis.; studied New York and Paris; unmarried. First success "Genius of Wisconsin," exhibited Chicago Expn., 1893; executed "The Fountain of Life," 1904; marble statue of Frances E. Willard, 1905, placed in the Capitol, Washington; portrait bust of George Rogers Clark; also bust of William L. G. Morton, M.D., placed in Smithsonian Instn.; portrait reliefs of Augustus St. Gaudens, Louise Collier Willcox, Edward A. McDowell. Exhibited, New York, Chicago; awarded medal, St. Louis Expn., 1904. Died Feb. 17, 1916.

MEARS, Leverett, chemist; b. Essex, Mass., May 19, 1850; s. David and Abigail (Burnham) M.; bro. of David Otis M.; A.B., Amherst, 1874; Ph.D., U. of Göttingen, 1876; (hon. A.M., Williams, 1888); m. Mary V. Brainerd, July 9, 1878 (died 1907); m. 2d, Elizabeth Addis, June 9, 1909. Instr. chemistry, Amherst Coll., 1876-81; prof. physics and chemistry, 1881-88, chemistry, 1888—, Williams Coll. Mem. U.S. Assay Commn., 1898, 1907-08. Author: Lecture Notes on Chemistry, 1912; Qualitative Analysis, 1909. Home: Williamstown, Mass. Died June 22, 1917.

MEBANE, Robert Sloan, cotton mfr.; b. Mebane, N.C., Sept. 12, 1868; s. Cornelius and Julia (Sloan) M.; ed. pub. and pvt. schs., and under pvt. tutors in chemistry in Baltimore, New York and Washington; m. Cora A. Holt, Oct. 25, 1899 (died 1904); 1 son, Robert Sloan; m. 2d, Myra Ruff, Jan. 22, 1919; 1 dau., Myra Sloan. Began in cotton mfg. at Graham, 1898; moved to Great Falls, 1909; now pres. Republic Cotton Mills, Bank of Great Falls; dir. numerous mfg. and other corps. in S.C. and N.Y. City. Republican. Presbyn. Mason. Home: Blowing Rock, N.C. Deceased.

MECHEM, Floyd Russell, univ. prof.; b. Nunda, N.Y., May 9, 1858; s. Isaac J. and Celestia (Russell) M.; ed. high schs., Battle Creek, Mich., and Titusville, Pa.; hon. A.M., U. of Mich., 1894, LL.D., 1912; m. Jessie P. Collier, Dec. 4, 1884; children—John Collier, Philip Russell. Admitted to bar, 1879; practiced at Battle Creek, 1879-87, Detroit, 1887-93; prof. and dean, Detroit Coll. of Law, 1891-92; Tappan prof. law, U. of Mich., 1892-1903; prof. law, U. of Chicago, 1903—. Mem. Mich. State Bd. Law Examiners, 1895-1903; pres. U. of Chicago Settlement, 1906-19. Author: (law books) Agency, 1889, 2d edit., 1914; Public Officers, 1890; Mechem's Hutchinson on Carriers, 1891; Cases on Agency, 1893; Cases on Partnership, 4th edit., 1924; Elements of Partnership, 2d edit., 1920; Sales of Personal Property (2 vols.), 1901; Outlines of the Law of Agency, 3d edit., 1923; Mechem and Gilbert's Cases on Damages, 1909; also many articles in law publs. Mem. District Appeal Bd. No. 1, Northern Dist. Ill., 1917-18; mem. summer session law faculty, Columbia U., 1919, 20, U. of Colo., 1922, Stanford U., 1923. Reporter on agency for Am. Law Institute. Died Dec. 11, 1928.

MEDARY, Milton Bennett, architect; b. Phila., Pa., Feb. 6, 1874; s. Milton Bennett and Mary Emma (Cregar) M.; student U. of Pa., 1890-91, Dr. Fine Arts, 1927; m. Hannah Leech Stadelman, Dec. 27, 1900; children—Hannah Stadelman, M. Bennett, Henriette Rachel, Richard Young, John Van Dyck (dec.). Mem. Field & Medary, 1895-1905, M. B. Medary, Jr., 1905-10, Zantzinger, Borie & Medary, 1910—. Mem. Nat. Commn. of Fine Arts, apptd. by President Harding, 1922; mem. Nat. Capital Park and Planning Commn., by apptmt. of President Coolidge, 1926; mem. Bd. Archtl. Consultants U.S. Treasury Dept., by apptmt. of Secretary Mellon, 1927; served as chmn. com. of U.S. Housing Corp. of U.S. Dept. of Labor to design and construct working men's villages at Neville Island, Pittsburgh, and Bethlehem, Pa., 1918; cons. architect Cornell U., Mount Vernon on Potomac, Roosevelt Memorial Assn. Dir. Foundation for Architectural and Landscape Architecture, Lake Forest, Ill. Mem. Am. Inst. Architects (pres.). Awarded gold medal Art Club of Phila., 1927. Mem. bd. mgrs. Glen Mills Schs. Episcopalian. Democrat. Home: West Park, Philadelphia, Pa. Died Aug. 7, 1929.

MEDBURY, Charles Sanderson, clergyman; b. Warren, O., Nov. 19, 1865; s. Sheldon and Melinda (Sanderson) M.; ed. pub. schs., and Eureka (Ill.) Coll.; (D.D., Drake U., 1910); m. Anna Laura Pickrell, Dec. 30, 1890; children—Margaret (Mrs. James C. Blackburn), Sheldon Pickrell. In insurance business, Cleveland, Erie, Pa., and Chicago, 1883-88; with Christian Oracle, Chicago, and preaching at Crystal Lake, Ill., 1889-90; ordained Ch. of Christ (Disciples) ministry, 1894; pastor, El Paso, Ill., 1893-96, Angola, Ind., 1897-1903, University Ch., Des Moines, Ia., 1904—. Chautauqua and lyceum lecturer; conv. speaker Men and Religion Forward Movement; chaplain of 157th Regt. Ind. Vols., Spanish-Am. War; trustee Drake U. (chaplain 1905-17); lecturer in army camps for League to Enforce Peace and Y.M.C.A., 1917-18. Pres. Christian Endeavor Union of Ind., 1901-03; mem. bd. dirs. Christian Bd. of Publ., St. Louis; pres. Am. Christian Missionary Soc., Centennial Conv., Pittsburgh, Oct. 1909. Mem. state bd. of Ia. Christian Missionary Soc., 1915-25; mem. exec. com. United Christian Missionary Soc., 1922-25. Author: Standard Sunday School Commentary, 1904; From Eden to the Jordan, 1908; From the Jordan to the Throne of Saul, 1909; From the Throne of Saul to Bethlehem, 1910; Christian Bible School Commentary (co-author), 1912. Awarded Evening Tribune trophy "for most distinguished community service in Des Moines," 1923. Home: Des Moines, Ia. Died Apr. 24, 1932.

MEE, William, banker; b. Monmouth Co., N.J., Jan. 1, 1861; s. Martin and Honora (Hurley) M.; student Sterling (Ill.) Acad., 1877-78, Graves Acad., Iowa City, Ia., 1884-85, Cornell Coll., Mt. Vernon, Ia., 1885-87; m. Mabel M. Wescott, July 1894; children—William, Herbert M., Bernice, Mary, Charles Harry. Asst. cashier Grundy County Nat. Bank, Grundy Center, Ia., 1888-91; pres. 1st Nat. Bank, Gladbrook, 1900-08; pres. Security Nat. Bank, Oklahoma City, 1907-25; chmn. exec. com. Am.-First Nat. Bank, 1925—; dir. Oklahoma Br., Fed. Reserve Bank of Kansas City; treas. Okla. R.R. Co. Home: Oklahoma City, Okla. Died Dec. 18, 1932.

MEEHAN, Thomas, nurseryman; b. in England, March 21, 1826; s. Edward and Sarah M.; chiefly self-educated. Botanist of Pa. State Bd. of Agriculture from its formation; was for 30 yrs. editor of the Gardener's Monthly; now editor Meehan's Monthly. Author: The American Handbook of Ornamental Trees, 1853; Gardener's Monthly, 1861; The Flowers and Ferns of the United States, serial, Meehan's Monthly, 1878-91; etc. Home: Germantown, Philadelphia. Died 1901.

MEEK, Benjamin Franklin, prof. English language and literature, U. of Alabama; b. Tuscaloosa, Ala., Sept. 20, 1836; grad. Univ. of Ala., 1854 (A.M., same; LL.D., Univ. of Miss.); prof. ancient languages, Florence Wesleyan Univ., 1869-71; delegate of M.E. church, South, to Ecumenical Meth. Council, London, England; pres. Ala. Ednl. Assn.; m. Nettie Hemphill, Sept. 4, 1889. Author: Students' Guide to Composition and Reading. Died 1899.

MEEK, John Henry, lawyer; b. Louisa, Ky., Sept. 8, 1877; s. Edward and Amy (Kirk) M.; prep. edn., Oakview Acad., Wayne, W.Va.; LL.B., W.Va. U., 1899; m. Charlie Burgess, Nov. 14, 1901; children—John Burgess, Amy Kirk, Howard Ferguson. Admitted to W.Va. bar, 1899, and began practice at Wayne as mem. Naper & Meek; pros. atty. Wayne Co., 1902-03; mem. Meek & Renslow, Huntington, W.Va., 1915-20, now Vinson, Thompson, Meek & Scherr; dir. First Huntington Nat. Bank. Republican. Mason. Home: Huntington, W.Va. Died Nov. 22, 1940.

MEEK, Seth Eugene, zoölogist; b. Hicksville, O., Apr. 1, 1859; s. Hiram and Mary (Batchelor) M.; B.S., Ind. U., Bloomington, 1884, A.M., 1886, Ph.D., 1891; fellow Cornell, 1885-86; m. Ella Tourner, Dec. 25, 1886. Prof. natural science, Eureka (Ill.) Coll., 1886-87, Coe Coll., Cedar Rapids, Ia., 1887-92; asst. prof. zoölogy and geology, U. of Ark., 1892-96; asst., U.S. Fish Commn., 1896-97; asst. curator zoölogy, Field Mus. Natural History, Chicago, 1897—. Lecturer dental anatomy, Sch. Dentistry, U. of Ill., 1901—. Ichthyologist, Biol. Survey of Panama, 1911—. Explorations of streams of Central and Western U.S., Mexico, Guatemala, Nicaragua, Costa Rica and Panama. Author: Fishes of Mexico North of the Isthmus of Tehuantepec, 1904. Home: Chicago, Ill. Died July 6, 1914.

MEEKER, Claude, stockbroker; b. Columbus, O., Dec. 20, 1861; s. George W. and Harriet (Hatch) M.; desc. of Abner Meeker, from Eng. to New Haven, Conn., 1639; student Neb. Coll., 1872-75; m. Elizabeth Parks, 1891; children—Marjorie, Marion, Campbell. Began as newspaper writer at Columbus, at age of 21, later connected with Cincinnati News-Journal, Cincinnati Enquirer, the Post, the Times-Star and New York World; served as chief polit. writer of Enquirer; sec. to Gov. James E. Campbell, 1890-91; U.S. consul at Bradford, Eng., 1893-97; engaged in stock brokerage business, 1897—. Episcopalian. Author: Haworth the Home of the Brontes, 1895. Home: Bexley, Columbus, O. Died Dec. 6, 1929.

MEEKER, Ezra, author; b. Huntsville, O., Dec. 29, 1830; s. Jacob Redding and Phoebe (Baker) M.; self-ed.; m. Eliza Jane Sumner, May 13, 1851. Crossed over Oregon Trail, with ox-team to the Northwest, 1852; returned with ox-team to Washington, D.C., 1906; farmer in Washington 50 yrs. Pres. Pioneers of America, New York. Republican. Unitarian. Author: The Oregon Trail, 1907; Uncle Ezra's Pioneer Stories for Children—Eighty-five Years of a Busy Life, 1916; Seventy Years of Progress in Washington, 1921; Ox Team Days, 1922; Kate Mulhall, 1926. Home: Seattle, Wash. Died Dec. 3, 1928.

MEEKER, Jacob Edwin, congressman; b. Fountain Co., Ind., Oct. 7, 1878; s. Theodore Marston and Julia (McKnight) M.; A.B., Union Christian Coll., Merom, Ind., 1900; B.D., Oberlin, 1904; student Benton Coll. of Law, St. Louis, 1912-13; m. Ora Maude Larr, June 13, 1900. Ordained ministry Christian Ch., 1900, Congl. Ch., 1903; farmer and preacher in Ind., 1901-02; home mission work Eldon, Mo., 1904-06; pastor Compton Hill Ch., St. Louis, 1906-12 (resigned); admitted to Mo. bar, 1914; mem. 64th and 65th Congresses (1915-19), 10th Mo. Dist. Republican. Active and aggressive opponent of Prohibition and Anti-Saloon League, 1909—. Home: St. Louis, Mo. Died Oct. 16, 1918.

MEEKER, Jonathan Magie, clergyman; b. Elizabeth, N.J., Sept. 20, 1850; s. Jonathan Magie and Mary Elizabeth (Deleger) M.; A.B., Wesleyan U., Conn., 1873; B.D., Drew Theol. Sem., N.J., 1880; Ph.D., New York U., 1888; (D.D., Wesleyan, 1908); m. Fannie Storer Denman, Sept. 3, 1873. First state sec. Y.M.C.A. in N.J., 1876-79; ordained M.E. ministry, 1879; pastor in N.J. at Raritan, 1879, South Orange, 1880, Bound Brook, 1881-83, Cross St. Ch., Paterson, 1884-85, Emory Ch., Jersey City, 1886-88, Roseville Ch., Newark, 1889-92, Hackettstown, 1893, St. Paul's Ch., Cincinnati, O., 1894-96, St. Paul's Ch., Newark, N.J., 1897, First Ch., Orange, 1898, Market St. Ch., Paterson, 1899-1903, Park Av. Ch., East Orange, 1904-05; presiding elder Newark Dist., 1906-08; pres. Centenary Collegiate Inst., Hackettstown, N.J., June 1908—. Republican. Died Jan. 1, 1917.

MEEKINS, Lynn Roby, editor, author; b. Salem, Md., Nov. 14, 1862; s. George J. M. (12 yrs. treas. of Dorchester Co., Md.); grad. Western Md. Coll., Westminster, 1882 (A.M.); m. Kate Owings, d. Rev. Dr. Augustus Webster, Nov. 5, 1891; 1 son, Lynn Webster. Lit. editor Baltimore American 17 yrs. prior to May 1899; mng. editor Saturday Evening Post, Phila., 1899-1901; chief editor Baltimore Herald, 1903-06, pres. and pub. 1907; editor Baltimore Star, 1908-11; sec. Atlantic and Pacific Transport Co., 1911; on editorial staff Phila. Ledger, 1913-14; editor Hershey (Pa.) Press, 1914-17; sec. Md. Council of Defense, 1917-20; on editorial staff the News, Baltimore, 1920-27. Sec. Chesapeake and Delaware Canal Commn.; sec. Md. Commn. Jamestown Expn., 1907; one of the organizers of Atlantic Deeper Waterways Assn.; Md. del. to Conservation Cong.; corr. sec., mem. exec. com. Nat. Star-Spangled Banner Centennial, 1914; mem. gen. com. Baltimore Bi-centennial, 1929; apptd. by gov. of Md. mem. commn. to reform the penal laws of state, 1914; v.p. Eastern Shore Soc.; trustee Western Md. Coll. Author: The Robb's Island Wreck, 1894; Some of Our People, 1898; Adam Rush, 1902. Home: Baltimore, Md. Died Nov. 8, 1933.

MEERSCHAERT, Theophile, bishop; b. Russignies, nr. Renaix, Belgium, Aug. 24, 1847; ed. in Coll. of Renaix, 1859-64; Coll. of Audenarde, 1864-68; Am. Coll. of Louvain, Belgium, 1868-72, where he was ordained R.C. priest, Dec. 23, 1871. Came to U.S., 1872; went to Natchez, Miss. Took yellow fever at Ocean Springs, Oct. 1875, after nursing the sick for 8 weeks; assisted yellow fever patients again, 1878. Apptd. vicar-gen. Diocese of Natchez, 1887, administrator, 1888, again vicar-gen., 1889, until apptd., 1891, 1st vicar apostolic of the Ind. Ty., comprising Okla. and Ind. Ty., with the title of bishop of Sidyma; made bishop of Okla. with the see permanently located at Oklahoma City, 1905. Officer Order of the Crown (Belgium), 1914; created Roman count and asst. at Pontifical Throne, 1916. Died Feb. 21, 1924.

MEES, Arthur, musical dir.; b. Columbus, O., Feb. 13, 1850; s. Rev. Konrad and Elise (Adam) M.; brother of Theophilus Martin Konrad and Carl Leo M.; A.B., Concordia Coll., Ind., 1870; studied music under Theodore Kullak S. and C. F. Weitzmann, Heinrich Dorn, at Berlin; also at Leipzig; (Mus. Doc., Alfred U., 1901); m. Susan Marguerite Howell, Jan. 28, 1897. Conductor Cincinnati May Festival Chorus; asst. conductor American Opera and Chicago Orchestra (Theodore Thomas, conductor); conductor New York Mendelssohn Glee Club, Albany Musical Assn., Worcester Co. (Mass.) Festival, Cecilia Soc., Boston, Bridgeport Oratorio Soc. Author: Choirs and Choral Music. Wrote: Annotated programs, New York Philharmonic Soc., 1887-96, and of Chicago Orchestra, seasons 1896-97 and 1897-98. Home: New York, N.Y. Died Apr. 26, 1923.

MEES, Carl Leo, coll. pres.; b. Columbus, O., May 20, 1853; s. Rev. Konrad and Elise (Adam) M.; student Ohio State U., 1874-75; M.D., Starling Med. Coll., Columbus, 1874; post-grad. studies at U. of Berlin and South Kensington, Eng., Ph.D., 1892; unmarried. Asst. chemist, Ohio Geol. Survey, 1871-74; prof. physics, Male High Sch., Louisville, Ky., 1876-80; in Europe, 1880-81; prof. physics, Ohio U., Athens, 1882-87; prof. physics, 1887—, pres., 1895-1919, pres. emeritus, 1919, Rose Poly. Inst., Terre Haute, Ind. Died Apr. 20, 1932.

MEES, Theophilus (Martin Konrad), coll. prof.; b. Columbus, O., July 13, 1848; s. Rev. Konrad and Elise (Adam) M.; bro. of Arthur and Carl Leo M.; ed. Lutheran Coll., Fort Wayne, Ind., 1865-68; grad. St. Louis Theol. Sem., 1872; spl. studies philology and theology; Berlin and Leipzig, 1872-74; (hon. Ph.D., Capital U., 1898; D.D., 1917); m. Jennie Brauer, July 1, 1875. Ordained Luth. ministry, 1875; prof. Latin and Hebrew, Capital U., 1875-88; pres. Teachers' Sem., Woodville, O., 1888-1903; prof. mental and moral science, Capital U., and prof. in theol. sem., Columbus, 1903—. Asst. pastor Luth. St. Paul's Ch., Columbus, 1874-88; editor Journal of Pedagogy, 1900, Theol. Mag., 1912—. Traveled extensively in Europe and America, 1872-74. Author: Doctrinal History of Predestination from 1517 to 1580, 1891; School Government and Methods, 1895. Died July 25, 1923.

MEESE, William Henry, industrialist; b. Michigan City, Ind., Sept. 3, 1883; s. William M. and Harriet (Cook) M.; B.S. in E.E., U. of Mich., 1905; LL.D., Washington Coll., 1933; L.H.D., Md. Coll. for Women (in absentia), 1934; D.Sc., Temple U., 1935; Master Engring., U. of Mich., 1935; m. Nellie Rogers, Sept. 12, 1907 (died 1933); children—Mrs. William Pollard, Elizabeth Grace. With Western Electric Co. from 1905 in this country and abroad, v.p. of the co. from Dec. 1928, and works mgr. at Point Breeze, Baltimore, Jan. 1, 1929—; co-receiver and co-trustee United Rys. & Electric Co., Baltimore, 1933-35; v.p. Industrial Corp.; dir. and mem. exec. com. Hopkins Place Savings Bank; mem. bd. dirs. Central Fire Ins. Co. Pres. Community Fund of Baltimore and exec. chmn. 1932 and 1933 campaigns; mem. Nat. Com. and chmn. Fifth Fed. Res. Dist. of Com. on Industrial Rehabilitation; mem. construction and civic development dept. com. U.S. Chamber Commerce; mem. bd. Gen. German Orphan Assn.; trustee Municipal Com. on Govt. Efficiency and Economy; mem. ednl. com. Baltimore Y.M.C.A. Schs., etc. Methodist; mem. official bd. First M.E. Ch. Pianist and linguist. Home: Baltimore, Md. Died Mar. 26, 1939.

MEESER, Spenser Byron, theologian; b. Phila., Pa., Feb. 16, 1859; s. William Henry and Josephine Hoover (Shermer) M.; grad. Girard Coll., Phila., 1874; Ph.B., Bucknell U., Lewisburg, Pa., 1883; grad. Crozer Theol. Sem., Chester, Pa., 1886; (D.D., Brown, 1901); m. Lillian Burk, Dec. 14, 1886; children—Carol Cooke (Mrs. Eugene Edmond Ayres), Burk Shermer (dec.). Ordained Bapt. ministry, 1886; pastor 1st Ch., Paterson, N.J., 1886-93, 2d Ch., Wilmington, Del., 1893-96, 1st Ch., Worcester, Mass., 1896-1902, Woodward Av. Ch., Detroit, 1902-07; abroad 1 yr.; acting pastor Emmanuel Ch., Brooklyn, 1908-09; prof. systematic theology, Crozer Theol. Sem., 1909-30. Sec. and exec. officer Citizens' State League of N.J., 1892-93; aided in securing legislative act raising age of consent in Delaware. College preacher, Vassar, 1904; univ. preacher, U. of Chicago, 1906. Corr. sec. Gen. Conv. Baptists of N.A., 1907—; pres. Am. Bapt. Hist. Soc., 1916-31; editor of The Crozer Quarterly. Home: Pittsburgh, Pa. Died May 7, 1939.

MEGRUE, Roi Cooper, playwright; b. N.Y. City, June 12, 1883; s. Frank Newton and Stella Georgiana (Cooper) M.; A.B., Columbia, 1903; unmarried. Republican. Episcopalian. Author: (plays) An Unlucky Star (1-act), prod. 1912; Under Cover, 1913; (with Walter Hackett) It Pays to Advertise, 1914; Under Fire, 1915; (with Montague Glass) Potash and Perlmutter in Society, 1915; Seven Chances, 1916; (with Irvin S. Cobb) Under Sentence, 1916; Where Poppies Bloom, 1918; Tea for Three, 1918; Honors Are Even, 1920; Venice for Two (from the French of Sacha Guitry), 1925. Home: New York, N.Y. Died Feb. 27, 1927.

MEIER, Fred Campbell, plant pathologist; b. Riggston, Ill., Apr. 5, 1893; s. William Herman Dietrich and Lizzie B. (Campbell) M.; B.S., Harvard, 1916, M.S., 1917; m. Agnes Walton Eastman, Oct. 23, 1920. With U.S. Dept. Agr., 1915—, prin. pathologist, Bur. Plant Industry, 1930-34; sr. scientist Extension Service, 1934—. Sec. treas. Am. Phytopathol. Soc., 1929-34 and vice-pres., 1935; business mgr. of Phytopathology (internat. jour. of Am. Phytopathol. Soc.), 1930-34; fellow A.A.A.S. Research on dissemination of micro-organisms by upper air currents with govt. aviation units and commercial airlines, 1929—. Lindbergh North Atlantic flight, 1933, Century of Progress stratosphere flight, 1933, Nat. Geog. Army Air Corps stratosphere flights, 1934, 35, aerial collections over Caribbean Sea, 1935; chmn. com. on aerial dissemination of pathogens and allergens, Nat. Research Council, 1937—. Presbyterian. Home: Chevy Chase, Md. Died July 29, 1938.

MEIER, Julius L.; b. Portland, Ore., Dec. 31, 1874; s. Abraham and Jeanette (Hirsch) M.; ed. pub. schs., Portland; LL.B., U. of Ore., 1895; m. Grace R. Mayer, Dec. 25, 1901; children—Jean Ellen (Mrs. Joseph Ehrman, Jr.), Elsa Frances (Mrs. Fred Ganz) Julius L., Jr. In mercantile business, 1896—; pres. of the Meier & Frank Co., department store; elected governor of Oregon for term, 1931-35. A leader in Liberty Loan drive, World War; Northwest regional dir. Council Nat. Defense; active in rehabilitation of devastated France. One of original promoters, with Samuel Hill, of Columbia River Highway. Republican. Jewish religion. Mason. Home: Corbett, Ore. Died July 14, 1937.

MEIER, Walter Frederick, lawyer; b. Lancaster County, Neb., Sept. 12, 1879; s. Francis William and Susan Elizabeth (Harris) M.; A.B., U. of Nebraska, 1903, LL.B., 1903; m. Anna L. Jones, Aug. 12, 1908; children—Ronald Wilson, Lois Elizabeth, Kenneth Walter. Admitted to Neb. bar, 1903, Washington bar, 1905, practicing in Seattle, 1905-15; chief dep. pros. atty., King Co., 1915-16; 1st asst. corp. counsel, Seattle, 1916-18, corp. counsel, 1918-23; mem. Meier & Meagher, 1923—. Republican. Conglist. Grand Exalted Ruler B.P.O. Elks, 1933-34. Mason (33°; Grand Patron, O.E.S., 1922-23; Grand Master, F.&A.M., 1926-27; Grand Patron, O. of A., 1929-30; Grand Master, R.&S.M., 1934-35 in the state of Washington; Gen. Grand Captain of the Guard in Gen. Grand Council, R.&S.M., of the U.S.A., 1939-42). Author: Decisions of the General Grand Chapter, O.E.S., 1924; Decisions of the Grand Chapter of Washington, O.E.S., 1924; The Heart of Elkdom, 1925; Decisions of the Grand Forum, B.P.O. Elks, 1928. Home: Seattle, Wash. Died July 19, 1940.

MEIGHAN, Thomas, actor; b. Pittsburgh, Pa., Apr. 9, 1879; m. Frances Ring, actress. First appearance on stage with Henrietta Crosman, in "Mistress Nell"; played at Manhattan Theatre, New York, as Col. Gorda in "Her Majesty, the Girl Queen of Nordenmark," 1900; appeared in the all-star cast of "The Two Orphans" and as Billy Bolton in "The College Widow"; début in London, in same part, 1908, and reappeared there as Robert Wallace in "Broadway Jones," 1914; devoted mainly to moving pictures from 1916, among them "M'liss," "Out of a Clear Sky," "The Miracle Man," "Male and Female," "Don't Change Your Wife," etc. Died July 8, 1936.

MEIGS, Arthur Vincent, physician; b. Philadelphia, Pa., Nov. 1, 1850; s. Dr. John Forsyth and Ann Wilcocks (Ingersoll) M.; brother of William Montgomery M.; ed. Classical Acad., Phila.; M.D., U. of Pa., 1871; m. Mary R. Browning, Oct. 16, 1878. Physician to the Pa. Hosp. Pres. Coll. Physicians, Phila., 1904-06. Author: Milk Analysis and Infant Feeding, 1885; The Origin of Disease, 1899; A Study of the Human Blood-Vessels in Health and Disease, 1907. Home: Philadelphia, Pa. Deceased.

MEIGS, John, headmaster; b. Pottstown, Pa., Aug. 31, 1852; s. Matthew and Mary (Gould) M.; prep. edn. The Hill Sch., Pottstown; A.M., Ph.D., Lafayette Coll.; (hon. A.M., Yale, 1908); m. Marion Butler, June 1, 1882. Instr. and asst. prof. in Lafayette Coll., 1872-76; headmaster The Hill Sch., Pottstown, Pa., 1876—. Dir. Union Theol. Sem., New York. Home: Pottstown, Pa. Died 1911.

MEIGS, Montgomery, U.S. civil engr.; b. Detroit, Mich., Feb. 27, 1847; s. Gen. Montgomery Cunningham (q.m. gen. U.S.A.) and Louisa (Rodgers) M.; 2 yrs. at Lawrence Scientific Sch., Harvard; 2 yrs. Royal Poly. Sch., Stuttgart, Germany, ending in 1869; m. Grace C. Lynde, Jan. 3, 1877 (dec.); children—

Mrs. Mary A. Atwater, Mrs. Louise R. Green, Mrs. Grace L. Crowder, Mrs. Alice McK. Orr, Cornelia L., Mrs. Emily F. Fales. On surveys of N.P. R.R., as resident engr., 1870-73; from 1874 employed on improvements of Miss. River from St. Paul to mouth of Mo. River; from 1882 at Keokuk, Ia., in charge U.S. Des Moines Rapids canal; at Keokuk, Ia., 1882-1926; retired under pension law, after 53 yrs.' service. Inventor of a "canvas cofferdam" for foundation work and like constructions; constructed U.S. dry dock at Keokuk. In 1898 proposed a new method of improving country roads by using oil with a sprinkler to make a watertight surface and lay dust, which attracted wide attention. Builder and designer of many steamboats and steam dredge tenders for the U.S. Local engr. for U.S. in constrn. of the great lock, dry dock and power developments in Miss. River at Keokuk, Ia., 1910-13. Home: Keokuk, Ia. Died Dec. 9, 1931.

MEIGS, William Montgomery, lawyer; b. Phila., Pa., Aug. 12, 1852; s. Dr. John Forsyth and Ann Wilcocks (Ingersoll) M.; A.B., U. of Pa., 1872, A.M., M.D., 1875; unmarried. Admitted to bar, 1879, and entered in practice at Philadelphia. Author: Life of Josiah Meigs, 1887; Life of Charles Jared Ingersoll, 1897; The Growth of the Constitution, 1900; Life of Thomas Hart Benton, 1904; Life of John C. Calhoun, 1917; The Relation of the Judiciary to the Constitution, 1919. Home: Philadelphia, Pa. Died Dec. 30, 1929.

MEIKLEJOHN, George De Rue, assistant sec. of war; b. Weyauwega, Wis., Aug. 22, 1857; s. Peter M.; reared on farm; ed. State Normal Sch., Oshkosh, Wis.; prin. high schs., Weyauwega, Wis., and Liscomb, Ia.; LL.B., U. of Mich., 1880. Practiced law at Fullerton, Nance Co., Neb., from 1880; co. atty. 3 yrs.; mem. Neb. Senate, 1884-88 (pres. 1886-88); chmn. Rep. State Conv., 1887; lt. gov. of Neb., 1889-91, and as such presided over famous joint conv. to canvass election returns of 1891, in which Supreme Court sustained him; mem. 53d and 54th Congresses (1893-97); asst. sec. of war, Apr. 16, 1897-Mar. 14, 1901, resigned; candidate for U.S. Senate, 1901; resumed practice of law at Omaha; also interested in mining. Decorated by King Oscar of Sweden, Feb. 27, 1899, a Knight of the Royal Order of the Sword. Home: Omaha, Neb. Died Apr. 19, 1929.

MEINRATH, Joseph; b. Boston, Mass., Feb. 22, 1857; s. Samuel and Leah (Engel) M.; grad. Boston Latin Sch., 1874; student Harvard, 1874-77; m. Helena Marie Susmann, Nov. 16, 1887. In Postal Service, Boston, 1878-81; secretarial work Pickert, DeButts & Co., Boston, wholesale salt and canned fish, 1881-83; in brokerage business, Kansas City, Mo., beginning 1883; a founder and for many yrs. pres. Meinrath Brokerage Co., wholesale merchandise brokers, specializing in refined sugar and food products; retired, 1921. From 1918 actively interested in patriotic civic and political causes; patron of arts and music. Awarded membership in Am. Civic Assn., Washington, D.C., "for distinguished service in the establishment of historical monuments"; medal of honor from U.S. Commn. George Washington Bicentennial. Mem. bd. of govs. Patriots' and Pioneers' Memorial Foundation, Kansas City, Mo. Home: Kansas City, Mo. Died May 14, 1941.

MELBA, Mme. Nellie, prima donna; b. (Helen Porter Mitchell) at Richmond, nr. Melbourne, Australia, May 19, 1866; d. David and Isabella (Dow) Mitchell; father, Scotch, and mother of Spanish descent; ed. Presbyn. Ladies' Coll., Melbourne; began to learn piano under mother at age of 3 and appeared in concert, singing to own accompaniment on piano, at 6; later studied under teachers in Melbourne, and under Mme. Marchesi, Paris, France, 1886-87; m. Capt. Charles Nesbitt Frederick Armstrong, 1882. Début as Gilda, in "Rigoletto," at Théâtre de la Monnaie, Brussels, Belgium, Oct. 15, 1887, adopting nom de théâtre of "Melba"; success was immediate, and same season appeared as Lakmé, Violetta and Ophélie; London début as Lucia in "Lucia di Lammermoor," 1888; first appeared in New York, in 1893, and has since frequently toured U.S.; greatest triumph was on return to Australia, 1903, when she was publicly received by the heads of the colonial govts. and sang to immense audiences; prima donna assoluta at the Royal Opera, Covent Garden, London. Repertoire includes leading Italian and French rôles. Recipient of numerous decorations and gifts from sovereigns and others. Created Dame of the British Empire, 1918, for war work. Home: Victoria, Australia. Died Feb. 23, 1931.

MELCHER, Frank Otis, ry. official; b. Damariscotta, Me., June 14, 1864; s. Franklin Ben and Harriet Newell (Harrington) M.; grad. Tufts Coll., 1887, C.E., 1895; m. Edna Elizabeth Lane, Oct. 1, 1895. Instrumentman, asst. engr., chief engr., 1887-97, div. supt., 1897-98, gen. supt., 1898-1900, Fitchburg R.R.; supt. Fitchburg div. B.&M. R.R., 1900-02; supt. Ill. div., 1902-04, gen. supt. Choctaw dist., 1904-05, gen. mgr. central and northern dists., June 15, 1905—, C.,R.I.&P. Ry. Home: Winnetka, Ill. Died 1912.

MELCHERS, Gari, artist, painter; b. Detroit, Mich., Aug. 11, 1860; s. Julius and Marie (Bangertor) M.; gen. edn. in Detroit; studied at Acad., Düsseldorf, Germany, 1877-80, and in Paris at École des Beaux Arts and under Lefèbvre and Boulanger; LL.D., U. of Mich., 1913; m. Corinne Lawton Mackall, 1903. Gold medal, Paris Salon, 1886; grand medal of honor, Berlin, 1891, Antwerp, 1894; grand medal of honor, Salon, 1889; grand gold medals in Amsterdam, Munich, Vienna, Dresden, Phila., Buffalo, 1901, St. Louis, 1904. Pictures: Maternity (Musée de Luxembourg); The Family (Nat. Gallery, Berlin); etc.; mural decorations, Peace and War (Congressional Library, Washington); portrait of Charles Hutchinson (Art Inst. Chicago); portrait of President Roosevelt (Freer collection, Smithsonian Instn.); etc. Officer Royal Bavarian Order of St. Michael; knight, 1895, officer, 1903, Légion d'Honneur de France; Officer Royal Prussian Order of the Red Eagle, 1907. N.A., 1906. Officer grand ducal order The White Falcon of Saxony, 1911. Mem. Am. Acad. Arts and Letters. Home: Falmouth, Va. Died Nov. 30, 1932.

MELCHOR, Oliver Hoffman, clergyman; b. Bucks Co., Pa., Dec. 23, 1848; s. Tobias and Susanna (Hoffman) M.; prep. edn. Doylestown (Pa.) English and Classical Sem.; student Lafayette Coll.; A.B., Pa. Coll., Gettysburg, 1876, A.M., 1879; grad. Luth. Theol. Sem., Gettysburg, 1879; m. Mary E. Montfort, Oct. 14, 1880. Ordained Luth. ministry, 1879; pastor Springtown, Pa., 1879—. Pres. Eastern Conf. Gen. Synod Luth. Ch., also treas.; twice del. to Gen. Synod; pres. Bucks Co. S.S. Assn. 13 yrs. Democrat. Celebrated 48th anniversary of his first and only pastorate, July 12, 1927. Home: Springtown, Pa. Died Sept. 7, 1928.

MELDRIM, Peter W., lawyer; b. Savannah, Ga., Dec. 4, 1848; s. Ralph M. and Jane (Fawcett) M.; A.B., U. of Ga., 1868, LL.B., 1869, A.M., 1871, LL.D., 1913; m. Frances P. Casey, June 30, 1881. Began practice at Savannah, 1869. Was mem. Ga. Ho. of Rep., and Senate, and mayor of Savannah; now judge Eastern Judicial Circuit of Ga. Chmn. Ga. delegation Dem. Nat. Conv., Denver, 1908. Col. comdg. 1st Regt. Ga. Cav.; now brig. gen. Ga. Nat. Guard, retired. Organized and commanded Ga. State Guard during World War; maj. gen. commanding Ga. Div. Confed. Veterans. Trustee U. of Ga., Confederate Memorial Assn., Confederate Soldiers Home. Home: Savannah, Ga. Died Dec. 13, 1933.

MELDRUM, Andrew Barclay, clergyman; b. Kirkcaldy, Fifeshire, Scotland, Sept. 9, 1857; s. Capt. Robert and Agnes Ness (Grant) M.; student Knox Coll., Can., 1878-83, U. of Toronto, 1878-82; grad. San Francisco Theol. Sem., 1884; D.D. Hanover (Ind.) Coll., 1894; m. Laura Rison, June 18, 1885 (died 1903); m. 2d, Ella H. Herrick, Jan. 10, 1907 (died 1914). Ordained Presbyn. ministry, 1884; pastor St. John's Ch., San Francisco, 1884-87, Central Ch., Rock Island, Ill., 1887-89, Grace Ch., Evansville, Ill., 1889-95, Central Ch., St. Paul, Minn., 1895-1902, Old Stone Ch., Cleveland, O., 1902-25 (emeritus). Chaplain Cleveland Grays (mil. orgn.), 1904—. Republican. Mason. Died Aug. 26, 1928.

MELENEY, Clarence Edmund, educator; b. Salem, Mass., Dec. 8, 1853; s. Henry Edmund and Eliza A. (Innis) M.; A.B., Colby, 1876, A.M., 1879 (LL.D., 1903); courses in edn. at Harvard and Columbia; m. Carolyn E. Coit, May 20, 1885. Prin. high and grammar schs. in Me., Mass., N.Y. and N.J., until 1883; supt. schs., Paterson, N.J., 1883-8. Somerville, Mass., 1888-93; prin. Horace Mann Sch. and prof. edn., Teachers Coll. and Columbia U., 1893-96; asst. supt. schs., N.Y. City, 1896-03, asso. supt., 1903—. Lecturer on edn., Poly. Inst. of Brooklyn, Adelphi Coll. and Dartmouth Coll., 1905-13; dir. Marthas Vineyard Summer Sch. Inst.; trustee Colby Coll., 1903-6. Mason. Home: Brooklyn, N.Y. Died Mar. 26, 1938.

MELINE, James Florant, asst. treasurer U.S.; b. in Ohio, June 3, 1841; s. Florant M. and Ellen M. (Reilly) M.; entered army as pvt. 6th Ohio Vol. Inf., April 19, 1861; served until June 23, 1864, becoming 1st lt.; wounded at Stone's River, Jan. 2, 1863; 3 mos. clerk in Treasury Dept.; returned to army as capt. 2d regt., U.S. Veteran Inf., Hancock's corps; left army March 26, 1866. Bvt. maj. of vols., June 13, 1865. Again clerk Treas. Dept. Advanced to asst. treasurer U.S., 1893-1907. Died 1908.

MELL, Patrick Hues, college pres.; b. Penfield, Ga., May 24, 1850; s. Patrick Hues and Lurene Howard (Cooper) M.; A.B., U. of Ga., 1871, M.E., 1872, Ph.D., 1880; (LL.D., S.C. Coll., 1905); m. Annie R., d. William N. White, of Athens, Ga., June 15, 1875. State chemist of Ga., 1874-77; prof. geology and botany, Ala. Poly. Inst., 1878-1902; pres. S.C. Agrl. and Mech. Coll. (Clemson Agrl. Coll.) 1902-10. Dir. Ala. Weather Service, 1884-93, Ala. Agrl. Expt. Sta., 1898-1902. Invented system of weather signals now used by U.S. Weather Bur. Declined presidency of Mercer U. (Ga.), 1893, of North Ga. Agrl. Coll., 1897, of Fla. U., 1904. Medal, Paris Expn., 1900. Treas. Bd. Missions Southern Bapt. Conv., 1913; pres. coll. sect. Am. Assn. Colls. and Stations, 1909. Comdr. Ala. div. Sons of Confed. Veterans, 1898. Author: Improvement of Cotton Plant by Crossing, 1894; Botanical Laboratory Guide, 1895; Revision of Mell's Parliamentary Practice, 1896; Revision of White's Gardening for the South, 1901; Biological Laboratory Methods, 1902. Home: Atlanta, Ga. Died Oct. 15, 1918.

MELLEN, Charles Sanger, ry. official; b. Lowell, Mass., Aug. 16, 1851; s. George K. and Hannah M. (Sanger) M.; ed. pub. grammar and high schs., Concord, N.H.; (hon. A.M., Yale, 1906); m. Marion Beardsley Foster, Sept. 23, 1875; m. 2d, Katharine Lloyd Livingston, Nov. 15, 1893. Began ry. service Sept. 22, 1869, as clk. in cashier's office Northern N.H. R.R.; clk. to chief engr. Central Vt. R.R., 1872-73; supt.'s clk., later chief clk. and asst. treas., Northern N.H. R.R., 1873-80; asst. to mgr. Boston & Lowell R.R., 1880-81; auditor, 1881, supt., 1883, gen. supt., 1884-88, Boston & Lowell, and Concord rys.; gen. purchasing agt., 1888, asst. gen. mgr., 1888-89, gen. traffic mgr., 1889-92, U.P. System; gen. mgr. N.Y.&N.E. R.R. at Boston, 1892; 2d v.p. N.Y., N.H.&H. R.R., 1892-96; pres. N.P. Ry. Co., 1896-1903, N.Y., N.H.&H. R.R. Co., 1903-13; pres. B.&M. R.R. Co., 1910-13. Home: Concord, N.H. Died Nov. 17, 1927.

MELLEN, Chase, lawyer; b. Cincinnati, O., Sept. 21, 1863; s. William Proctor and Ellen Seymour (Clark) M.; prep. depts. Colorado Coll. and Swarthmore Coll.; B.A., Brasenose Coll., Oxford U., Eng., 1887; Columbia U. Law Sch., 1889-91; m. Lucy Cony Manley, June 7, 1893. Admitted to N.Y. bar, 1892, and began practice in N.Y. City; admitted to U.S. Supreme Court, 1900; asst. corp. counsel, New York, 1895-97, 1900-03; dir. The Hayward Co., James H. Dunham & Co. Republican. Died Mar. 31, 1939.

MELLEN, George Frederick, writer; b. Clarke Co., Miss., June 27, 1859; s. Seth S. and Susan H. (Bush) M.; A.M., U. of Ala., 1879, A.M., Ph.D., U. of Leipzig, 1890; m. Mary B. Baldwin, July 7, 1885; children—Seth Baldwin, Helen Vandergraft (Mrs. Wallace McClure), George Frederick, Cornelia Daniel. Prin. schs., Gainesville, Livingston and Demopolis, Ala.; prof. Greek and French, 1891-98, prof. Greek and history, 1898-1900, U. of Tenn.; mem. Tenn. Ho. of Rep., 1905-07. Trustee Martha Washington Coll., Abingdon, Va., 1909-18; trustee Lawson McGhee Library of Knoxville (Old Board). Mem. M.E. Ch. S. Democrat. Author: Early History of Knoxville. Home: Knoxville, Tenn. Died June 4, 1927.

MELLIN, Carl Johan, mechanical engr., inventor; b. Westergotland, Sweden, Feb. 17, 1851; s. Sven and Maria Elizabeth (Bjorn) M.; coll. and tech. edn. in Sweden; apprentice in ry. offices and gen. machine works and 3 yrs.' tech. course at Gothemburg to 1873; draftsman Gothemburg, 1873-77; mech. engr. and naval architect in Sweden and with Robert Napier & Son, Scotland, the Caledonian Locomotive Works, and with Erickberg and Atlas Works, Sweden; came to America, 1887; m. Gertrude Alice Levie, Dec. 31, 1889. Mech. engr., New York, 1889-94; chief engr. Richmond (Va.) Locomotive Works, 1894-1902; cons. engr. Am. Locomotive Co., 1902—. Home: Schenectady, N.Y. Died Oct. 15, 1924.

MELLISS, David Ernest, engineer; b. New York, Mar. 11, 1848; s. David M. and Mary D. M.; ed. Columbia Univ. Sch. of Science and univs. of Göttingen and Vienna; A.M., Ph.D., Göttingen, 1870; m. Frances Pauline Botton, Sept. 4, 1890 (died 1901). Constantly engaged as consulting and constructing engr. on important works, mining and civil, in U.S., Central and S. America and Mexico. Decorated with Order Bust of Bolivar, of Venezuela. Home: San Rafael, Cal. Died Mar. 24, 1913.

MELLON, Andrew William, industrialist; b. Pittsburgh, Mar. 24, 1855; s. late Judge Thomas and Sarah (Negley) M.; ed. Western Univ. of Pa. (now U. of Pittsburgh), Class of 1873; LL.D., Cambridge U., Eng., 1931; m. Nora McMullen, 1900. Was pres. Mellon Nat. Bank, and officer or dir. various financial and industrial corps., also engaged in development of coal, coke and iron enterprises; resigned as pres. Mellon Nat. Bank, Mar. 1, 1921; sec. of the Treasury in cabinet of President Harding, Mar. 4, 1921, remaining in that office under President Coolidge and President Hoover until confirmed by U.S. Senate as ambassador to Great Britain, Feb. 5, 1932, resigned, Mar. 17, 1933. Served as chmn. ex-officio Federal Reserve Bd., Farm Loan Bd., U.S. Sect. Pan-Am. High Commn., also dir. gen. U.S. R.R. Administration and mem. bd. Reconstruction Finance Corp. Awarded (with brother Richard B.) chemistry medal 1931, by Am. Inst. of Chemists, as a pioneer patron of science. Home: Pittsburgh, Pa. Died Aug. 26, 1937.

MELLON, James R., banker; b. Pittsburgh, Pa., Jan. 14, 1846; s. Judge Thomas and Sarah Jane (Negley) M.; A.B., Jefferson Coll., Pa., 1863; m. Rachel H., d. Gen. William Larimer, June 3, 1867. Pres. City Deposit Bank, Ligonier Valley Railroad. Pres. Western Pennsylvania Hosp.; trustee Athalia Daly Home for Working Girls; pres. Allegheny Co. Juvenile Court Farm; pres. trustee East Liberty Presbyn. Ch. Republican. Home: Pittsburgh, Pa. Died Oct. 20, 1934.

MELLON, Richard Beatty, banker; b. Pittsburgh, Pa.; s. late Judge Thomas and Sarah Jane (Negley)

M.; m. Jennie, d. Alexander and Sarah Cordelia (Smith) King. Began with Ligonier Valley R.R. of which later served as pres.; now pres. Mellon Nat. Bank, Pittsburgh; dir. Federal Reserve Bank of Cleveland, Dec. 17, 1917—. Home: Pittsburgh, Pa. Died Dec. 1, 1933.

MELLON, Thomas, banker; b. Lower Castleton, County Tyrone, Ireland Feb. 3, 1813; came to U.S. in infancy; reared at Greensburg, Pa.; grad. at Western Univ., 1837 (LL.D., 1907). Practiced at Pittsburgh; law judge court of common pleas, 1859-70; became wealthy from investments; from 1870 head of Thomas Mellon & Sons, bankers. Home: Pittsburgh, Pa. Died 1908.

MELLOR, Charles Chauncey, piano and music dealer; b. Pittsburgh, Sept. 26, 1836; s. John H. and Julia A. (Hillier) M.; ed. pub. and pvt. schs.; m. Laura Reinhart, June 20, 1867. Intended to become professional musician (pianist), and in youth studied to that end, but on death of father, took up his business (established, 1831), as piano and music dealer, and has continued it ever since. Mem. bd. trustees Carnegie Inst., and chmn. Mus. Com., 1896—; mem. bd. trustees, Carnegie Hero Fund. Home: Edgewood Park, Allegheny Co., Pa. Died 1909.

MELLOR, Walter, architect; b. Phila., Pa., Apr. 25, 1880; s. Alfred and Isabella (Latham) M.; grad. Haverford (Pa.) Sch., 1897; B.S., Haverford Coll., 1901; B.S. in Architecture, U. of Pa., 1904; m. Elizabeth Wharton Mendelson, Oct. 11, 1919; 1 dau., Louise. In office of T. P. Chandler, 1904-06; mem. Mellor & Meigs, 1906-17, Mellor, Meigs & Howe, 1917-28, Mellor & Meigs, 1928—; firm architects for branch banks, Phila. Saving Fund Soc.; auditorium for Bryn Mawr Coll.; memorial to U.S. Coast Guard Service, Arlington, Va.; chapel at Bony, France, and monument at Ypres, for Am. Battle Monuments Commission; Phi Gamma Delta fraternity houses, Phila., Pa. State Coll. and Seattle; Gymnasium Bldg., Pa. Inst. for the Deaf; Hilles Lab. of Applied Science and Strawbridge Observatory, Haverford Coll.; residences in Phila. for F. S. McIlhenny, Casper W Morris, etc., also residences for Col. Henry Dupont, Arthur E. Newbold, Jr., Melville G. Curtis (Bala, Pa.), etc. Dir. Kestner Evaporator Co.; trustee The Cummington Sch. Fellow Am. Inst. of Architects. Firm awarded ann. medal Phila. chapter A.I.A., 1922; gold medal, Archtl. League of New York, 1925. Republican. Quaker. Home: Philadelphia, Pa. Died Jan. 11, 1940.

MELONEY, William Brown, author; b. San Francisco, Calif., June 6, 1878; s. James and Adelaide (Jackman) M.; ed. pub. and pvt. schs.; spl. student U.S. history, U. of Calif., 1901; m. Marie Mattingly, editor, June 6, 1904; 1 son, Wm. Brown. On staff San Francisco Chronicle, 1896-97, Examiner, 1897-99, Bulletin, 1899-1901; reporter, staff corr. and day city editor, New York World, 1901-08; contbg. editor Butterick Pub. Co., 1919-21; on editorial staff New York Tribune, 1921. Exec. sec. mayor of New York, 1910-11; attended Plattsburg Mil. Training Camp, 1915, 16, O.R.T.C., Ft. Oglethorpe, Ga., 1917; commd. capt. F.A., Aug. 3, 1917; maj., Dec. 31, 1917; served in England and France with 81st and 6th divs., Aug. 1918-Mar. 1919; participated Meuse-Argonne offensive, Oct. 26-Nov. 11, as comdg. officer 6th Ammunition Train; hon. discharged, Mar. 15, 1919; maj. F.A. O.R.C. U.S.A., May 5, 1923; lt. col. F.A., Apr. 1, 1925. Author: The Girl of the Golden Gate, 1913; The Heritage of Tyre, 1916; Where Do We Go From Here?, 1919; Graft (4-act play, prod. Phila., 1911); Knave of Hearts (1-act, prod. N.Y., 1912). Lived at New York, N.Y. Died Dec. 7, 1925.

MELTON, William D., univ. pres.; b. nr. Lewis Turnout, Chester Co., S.C., May 26, 1868; s. William C. D. (M.D.) and Mary Jane (Poag) M.; grad. U. of Va., 1890; LL.B., U. of S.C., 1892, LL.D., 1922; LL.D., Presbyn. Coll. of S.C., 1924; m. Caro Belser, May 10, 1898 (died 1903); children—Caroline (wife of Dr. Walter J. Bristow), Gulielma (Mrs. Harry Kamines, Jr.), William Davis; m. 2d, Netta Loeb, Sept. 17, 1911; 1 dau., Henrietta. Began practice at Chester, S.C., moved to Columbia, 1893; mem. Melton & Belser; pres. U. of South Carolina, July 1, 1922—; served as atty., dir. Nat. Loan & Exchange Bank, Columbia Savings Bank & Trust Co., S.C. Ins. Co., Homestead Building & Loan Co., Columbia Real Estate & Trust Co., etc.; alderman and chmn. ways and means com. City of Columbia, 1900-06; chmn. State Bd. Law Examiners, 1910-19; state chmn. four-minute men, World War; state chmn. United War Work Campaign. Moderator Synod Presbyn. Ch. of S.C., 1922-23; dean S.S. Conv., Richland County, S.C., 1923; mem. Internat. Com. Y.M.C. Assn. Democrat. Mason. Died May 3, 1926.

MELTZER, Charles Henry, dramatist, critic; b. London, Eng.; s. Diedrich Herman and Julie Marie M. (Russian-born, naturalized British); ed. at London and Paris; m. Anne Harris Hamlen, of Bristol, Eng.; children—Alice Marie, Gwendoline Margaret, Dorothy, Phyllis, Harold. Was Paris corr. Chicago Tribune, spl. and regular corr. New York Herald, Paris, Rome, London, Spain, Berlin, Cairo, etc.; came to U.S., 1888; dramatic and musical critic New York Herald; dramatic reviewer New York World, 1893-96; asst. and sec. to Maurice Grau, 1902, and Heinrich Conried, 1903; N.Y. corr. London Daily Chronicle, 7 years; was music critic and special writer New York American and Cosmopolitan Magazine. Was asso. as lit. adviser and dir. with various dramatic art schemes. Author: (plays) The Story of Rodion, the Student (dramatization) of Dostoiewsky's Crime and Punishment, prod. by Richard Mansfield; English versions of Hannele (Hauptmann); Mme. Sans-Gêne (Sardou and Moreau); Le Collier de la Reine (Decourcelle), and L'Arlesienne (Daudet); The Sunken Bell (adapted from Hauptmann), prod. by E. H. Sothern; His Honor the Mayor, original farce (with A. E. Lancaster), prod. by W. H. Crane; Manon Lescaut (original—prod. Milwaukee); Salome (with Armand Silvestre and Pierne; prod. Paris); The First Duchess of Marlborough (original—prod. 1901, Trenton, and played throughout the West). Has made many English singing versions of French, German and Italian grand opera librettos. Home: New York, N.Y. Died Jan. 14, 1936.

MELTZER, Samuel James, physiologist; b. in Russia, Mar. 22, 1851; gen. edn. Königsberg, Prussia; studied philosophy and medicine at U. of Berlin, 1875-82, M.D., 1882; (LL.D., U. of Md., 1906, St. Andrews U., Scotland, 1912, and Washington U., St. Louis, 1914). Came to U.S., 1883, and since in practice at New York; head dept. of physiology and pharmacology, Rockefeller Inst. for Med. Research, 1906—; cons. physician Harlem Hosp. Maj., Med. O.R.C., 1917. Fellow A.A.A.S., N.Y. Acad. Sciences, N.Y. Acad. Medicine. Home: New York, N.Y. Died Nov. 7, 1920.

MELVILLE, Frank, Jr., merchant; b. N.Y. City, June 4, 1860; s. Francis and Mary A. (Bamman) M.; ed. Lockwood Acad., Brooklyn, N.Y.; m. Jennie Florence Macconnell, Jan. 18, 1886; 1 son, Ward. Began as salesman with Eugene Ferris, N.Y. City, 1890; founder, 1892, since chmn. bd. Melville Shoe Corp., chain of retail stores; founder and chmn. bd. John Ward Men's Shoes, Inc., Rival Shoe Co., Thom McAn Shoe Co., R-W Realty Co., Frank Lee Corp. Democrat. Episcopalian. Home: Stony Brook, L.I., N.Y. Died Feb. 25, 1935.

MELVILLE, George Wallace, rear admiral U.S.N.; b. New York, Jan. 10, 1841; s. Alexander and Sarah M.; ed. common schs. and Brooklyn Poly. Inst.; (hon. D. Eng., Stevens Inst. Tech., 1898, Georgetown U., 1899; M.S., Columbia, 1899; LL.D., Georgetown, 1899); twice married; m. 2d, Estella Smith Polis, Oct. 1907 (died 1910). Apptd. to navy as asst. engr., July 29, 1861; served through Civil War; later on various stas. and at navy yards; sailed, 1879, with DeLong in the Jeannette, from San Francisco; comd. the boat's crew which escaped from the wastes of the Lena Delta; later headed the expdns. which recovered the records of the Jeannette expdn. and recovered the remains of DeLong and his companions; made 3 Arctic voyages altogether; gold medallist and advanced 15 numbers by spl. act of Congress, Sept. 1890, for bravery in Arctic; apptd., Aug. 1887, and reapptd. Jan. 1892, and Jan. 1896, engr. in chief of navy; rear admiral from Mar. 4, 1899. During his term designs have been gotten out for 120 ships and 700,000 horsepower. Greatest professional success, probably the triple-screw flyers Columbia and Minneapolis; retired, Jan. 10, 1903. Inventor of many mech. appliances. Decorated with Order of St. Stanislaus, Mil. Order of the First Class (Russia). Home: Philadelphia, Pa. Died Mar. 17, 1912.

MELVILLE, Henry, lawyer; b. Nelson, N.H., Aug. 25, 1858; s. Josiah Henry and Nancy Rebecca (Nesmith) M.; A.B., Dartmouth, 1879; A.M., and LL.B., cum laude, Harvard, 1884. Admitted to bar, 1885, and since in practice at New York; associated with Senator Roscoe Conkling, 1885-88. Capt. Co. A, 8th N.Y. Vols., Spanish-Am. War, 1898. Pres. State Bd. Mgrs. Elmira Reformatory. Author: Ancestry of John Whitney, 1896, etc. Home: New York, N.Y. Died Oct. 21, 1930.

MELVIN, Alonzo Dorus, veterinary surgeon; b. Sterling, Ill., Oct. 28, 1862; s. Addison Smith and Cordelia (McKinney) M.; ed. sch. and bus. coll., then 4 yrs. on stock farm; D.V.S., Chicago Vet. College, 1886; m. Ella Herriman, of Bootle, England, January 5, 1892. Entered service United States Department of Agriculture, 1886; transferred to Baltimore, 1887; sent to Liverpool to inspect animals and vessels from U.S., 1890; in charge meat inspection at Chicago, 1892; chief inspection div., 1895-99, asst. chief Bur. of Animal Industry, Washington, D.C., 1899-1905, chief, Dec. 1, 1905—. Mem. advisory bd. of Hygienic Lab., U.S. Pub. Health and Marine Hospital Service. Died Dec. 7, 1917.

MELVIN, Henry Alexander, judge; b. Springfield, Ill., Sept. 28, 1865; s. Samuel Houston (M.D.) and Sarah Amanda (Slemmons) M.; Ph.B., U. of Calif., 1889; LL.B., Hastings Coll. of Law (Univ. of Calif.), 1892; m. Sarah Louise Morse, June 14, 1893. Asst. dist. atty. Alameda Co., Calif., 1893-94; pros. atty., City of Oakland, 1894-99; chief deputy dist. atty., Alameda Co. (excepting 3 mos. when acting as dep. atty.-gen. Calif.), 1899-1901; judge of Superior Ct., Alameda Co., 1901-08; justice Supreme Ct. of Calif., Sept. 28, 1908—; term expires Jan. 1923. Prof. legal medicine, Oakland Coll. of Medicine and Surgery, 1906—. Republican. Episcopalian. Home: San Francisco, Calif. Died Apr. 23, 1920.

MEMMINGER, Allard, M.D., author; b. Charleston, S.C., Sept. 30, 1854; s. C. G. Memminger (sec. of the treasury, C.S.A.) and Mary Withers (Wilkinson) M.; grad. U. of Va., and M.D., S.C. Med. Coll., 1880; m. Margaret Aloysius Coleman (Past Great Pocahontas of S.C., Degree of Pocahontas, I.O.R.M.), of Charleston, S.C., December 10, 1913. Dean and prof. chemistry and hygiene and clin. urinary diagnosis, S.C. Medical Coll., and dean and prof. gen. and applied chemistry, Coll. of Pharmacy of S.C.; member State Bd. Pharm. Examiners of S.C.; chairman Charleston City Bd. of Health, and made scientific examination of waters of Charleston for U.S. Govt.; co-framer with Dr. S. C. Baker, of Sumter, S.C., of laws governing practice of medicine and surgery in S.C.; state chemist of S.C.; was chemist many phosphate and fertilizer cos.; a pioneer in development of marble industry in N.C. Awarded gold medal and diploma of honor by Académie Parisienne Française des Inventeurs (hon. corr.). Delivered address, at Richmond, Va., May 13, 1905, before the Confederate Memorial Lit. Soc., presenting portraits of 3 members of the cabinet of the Confederate States—the sec. of navy, the atty. gen., and the sec. of the treasury. Mem. Vol. Med. Service Corps, World War. Author: Diagnosis by the Urine (3 edits.); Qualitative Chemical Analysis (2 edits.); Science in the Field (manual guide for the farmer); Stop and Think, or Reasons for the Decadence of Aristocrats, 1913. Home: Charleston, S.C. Died Jan. 16, 1936.

MEMMINGER, Christopher Gustavus, mining engr.; b. Charleston, S.C., Aug. 10, 1865; s. Robert Withers and Susan (Mazyck) M.; student U. of Va., 1882-86; m. Mary Lee King, Jan. 6, 1887; 1 dau., Christine Gustava. Began in mining engring., Colo., 1887; engaged in development of phosphate mining industry, Fla., 1893—; pres. State Bank of Lakeland (Fla.), 1908-12; cons. mining engr., New York, 1900—; pres. Coronet Phosphate Co., 1916—; pres. Diamond Sand Co. Pres. Bd. of Commrs., Lakeland, 1908-10; pres. Fla. State Bd. of Health, 1908; spl. trade commr. sent to Europe by U.S. Dept. Commerce, 1919. Republican. Episcopalian. Home: Asheville, N.C. Died Aug. 1930.

MENCKEN, Sara Powell Haardt, author; b. Montgomery, Ala., Mar. 1, 1898; d. John Anton and Venetia (Hall) Haardt; A.B., Goucher Coll., Baltimore, 1920; student Johns Hopkins U., 1922-25; m. Henry Louis Mencken, Aug. 27, 1930. Teacher Margaret Booth Sch., Montgomery, Ala., 1920-22, Goucher Coll., Baltimore, 1922-24. Democrat. Author: The Making of a Lady, 1931. Home: Baltimore, Md. Died May 31, 1935.

MENDEL, Lafayette Benedict, physiological chemist; b. Delhi, N.Y., Feb. 5, 1872; s. Benedict and Pauline (Ullman) M.; A.B., Yale, 1891, Ph.D., 1893; Larned fellow, Yale, 1891-94; research student, univs. of Breslau and Freiburg, 1895-96; hon. Sc.D., U. of Mich., 1913, Rutgers Coll., 1930; LL.D., Western Reserve University, 1932; m. Alice R. Friend (A.B., U. of Wis.). Teaching at Yale, 1892, asst. prof., 1897-1903, prof. physiol. chemistry, 1903-21, Sheffield Scientific Sch. (Yale); Sterling prof. physiol. chemistry, Yale U., 1921—, also member governing bd. Sheffield Scientific Sch., Grad. Sch. of Yale and Sch. of Medicine, Yale. Hitchcock lecturer, Univ. of Calif., 1923. Dir. Russell Sage Institute of Pathology; mem. advisory board J. S. Guggenheim Memorial Foundation; research asso. Carnegie Instn. of Washington. Mem. numerous Am. and foreign scientific societies. Gold medalist Am. Institute of Chemists, 1927. Author: Nutrition—The Chemistry of Life; Changes in the Food Supply and Their Relation to Nutrition. Editor Journal of Biological Chemistry, also Journal of Nutrition, and of chem. monographs of Am. Chem. Soc. Home: New Haven, Conn. Died Dec. 9, 1935.

MENDELL, Seth, publisher; b. Acushnet, Mass., Nov. 6, 1845; s. Ellis and Catherine (Allen) M.; ed. Rochester (Mass.) Acad.; m. Elizabeth M. Ballou, Aug. 24, 1881. Pres. Perry Mason Co., pubs. The Youth's Companion, many yrs. to 1912; then dir. Republican. Conglist. Home: Brookline, Mass. Died July 27, 1922.

MENDELSOHN, Charles Jastrow, philologist; b. Wilmington, N.C., Dec. 8, 1880; s. Rev. Dr. Samuel and Esther (Jastrow) M.; grad. Episcopal Acad., Phila., Pa., 1896; A.B., U. of Pa., 1900, Ph.D., 1904. Began as tutor in Greek, Coll. City of New York, 1905, instr., 1907, in history dept., 1920—. Granted leave of absence during World War; engaged in foreign language work, postal and newspaper censorship, 1917-18; commd. capt. Mil. Intelligence Div. of Gen. Staff, U.S.A., July 17, 1918; in charge decipherment of German codes; hon. disch., Aug. 1, 1919; continued research in codes and prepared studies in diplomatic code for U.S. Govt. Harrison Scholar in Classics, 1900-01, fellow, 1901-03, research fellow,

1904-05, U. of Pa. Author: Studies in the Word-Play in Plautus, 1907; Universal Trade Code (with H. O. Yardley), 1921. Home: New York, N.Y. Died Sept. 27, 1939.

MENDELSOHN, Samuel, rabbi; b. in Russia, Mar. 31, 1850; s. Feiwel and Jetta M.; ed. in Vilna, Russia, Berlin, Germany, and Phila.; m. Esther Jastrow, May 11, 1879. Rabbi Congregation Beth-El, Norfolk, Va., 1873-76, Temple of Israel, Wilmington, N.C., Apr. 1876—. Dir. Associated Charities of Wilmington; supreme pres. U.S. Benevolent Fraternity; grand ruler Jurisdiction No. 9, and supreme rep.-at-large, Fraternal Mystic Circle; grand chaplain Jurisdiction of N.C., Royal Arcanum. Author: The Criminal Jurisprudence of the Ancient Hebrews, 1891. Home: Wilmington, N.C. Died Sept. 30, 1922.

MENDELSSOHN, Louis, capitalist; b. Germany, Aug. 12, 1854; s. Maurice and Pauline (Hill) M.; brought to U.S. in infancy; ed. pub. schs., Detroit and under pvt. tutors; studied art in France 2½ yrs.; m. Lydia Benda, Sept. 1881 (died 1901); children—Gordon, Paxton C.; m. 2d, Evelyn Dumas, June 10, 1903; 1 dau., Lydia Evelyn. Asst. tech. draftsman, car and locomotive dept. M.C. Ry., 1871-73; asso. with Mortimer L. Smith in practice of architecture, 1873-80; head of own archtl. and engring. orgn. in the west, 1880-96; in Europe studying mfg., 1896-1901; partner, mgr. and treas. Modern Match Co., 1901-09; dir., treas., chmn. bd. Fisher Body Corp., Detroit, 1909-26 (corp. taken over by Gen. Motors Corp.). Retired. Mem. Detroit Mus. of Art. Home: Grosse Pointe Shores, Mich. Died Mar. 28, 1935.

MENDENHALL, Charles Elwood, physicist; b. Columbus, O., Aug. 1, 1872; s. Thomas Corwin M. and Susan Allan (Marple) M.; B.S., Rose Poly. Inst., Terre Haute, Ind., 1894; Ph.D., Johns Hopkins, 1898; m. Dorothy M. Reed, Feb. 14, 1906; children—Thomas Corwin, John Talcott. Instr. physics, U. of Pa., 1894-95, Williams Coll., 1898-1901; asst. prof. physics, 1901-03, asso. prof., 1903-05, prof., 1905—, U. of Wis. Chmn. div. of physical sciences, Nat. Research Council. Commd. maj., Signal R.C., 1917, and in active service, 1917-19. Republican. Home: Madison, Wis. Died Aug. 18, 1935.

MENDENHALL, Harlan George, clergyman; b. Coatesville, Pa., Apr. 12, 1851; s. Washington B. and Susan A. (Harlan) M.; A.B., Lafayette Coll., 1874, A.M., 1880, D.D., 1894; S.T.D., University of Debreczen, Hungary, 1930; grad. Western Theol. Sem., Pittsburgh, 1874; m. Mary L. Brewer, Oct. 12, 1882 (died 1883); m. 2d, Lillian H. Peck, 1904. Asso. editor Springfield (Mass.) Republican, 1869. Ordained Presbyn. ministry, 1875; pastor 3d Ch., Ft. Wayne, Ind., 1874-77, 6th Ch., Pittsburgh, 1878-80, Mercersburg, Pa., 1880-83, Grand Forks, N.D., 1884-89; pres. Jamestown (N.D.) Coll., 1889-90; pastor Greene Av. Ch., Brooklyn, 1890-95, 1st Ch., Kansas City, Kan., 1895-1900, Perth Amboy, N.J., 1900-04, West 23d Street Church, New York, 1906-15. President Presbyn. Ministers' Assn., New York, 1911-13; pres. Presbyn. Union, New York, 1918; moderator synod of New York, 1916-17, Presbytery of New York, 1916-22, and stated clk. same, 1922-32, emeritus, 1932—; commr. to Gen. Assembly, Presbyn. Ch. in U.S.A. 9 times between 1882 and 1919. Decorated by King of Greece with Order of the Redeemer, 1919. Home: Litchfield, Conn. Died May 15, 1940.

MENDENHALL, Thomas Corwin, physicist; b. Hanoverton, O., Oct. 4, 1841; s. Stephen and Mary (Thomas) M.; pub. sch. edn.; (hon. Ph.D., Ohio State U., 1878; Sc.D., Rose Poly. Inst.; LL.D., U. of Michigan, 1887, Western Reserve U., 1912); m. Susan Allen Marple, July 12, 1870; father of Charles Elwood M. Professor physics and mechanics, Ohio State U., 1873-78; prof. physics, Imperial U. of Japan, 1878-81, Ohio State U., 1881-84, emeritus prof., 1884; prof. U.S. Signal Corps, 1884-86; pres. Rose Poly. Inst., 1886-89; supt. U.S. Coast and Geod. Survey, 1889-94; pres. Worcester Poly. Institute, 1894-1901; in Europe, 1901-12. Supt. United States weights and measures, 1889-94; member U.S. Light House Board, 1889-94; mem. 1st Bering Sea Commn., 1891; U.S. and Great Britain Boundary Line Survey Commn., 1892-94; chmn. Mass. Highway Commn., 1896-1901; U.S. del. Internat. Elec. Congress, 1893; medal, Paris Expn., 1900. Hon. fellow Am. Geog. Soc. (gold medal, 1901), Nat. Geog. Soc., Franklin Institute (gold medal, 1918); fellow Am. Acad. Arts and Sciences. Decorated Order The Sacred Treasures, 2d class, Japan, 1911; gold medal, Nat. Ednl. Soc. of Japan, 1911. Trustee Ohio State U., 1919—. Author: A Century of Electricity. Home: Ravenna, O. Died Mar. 23, 1924.

MENDES, Frederick de Sola, rabbi; b. Montego Bay, Jamaica, W.I., July 8, 1850; s. Rev. Abraham Pereira and Eliza (de Sola) M.; A.B., U. of London, 1869; Univ. of Breslau, and Jewish Theological Seminary, Breslau, 1870-73; Ph.D., University of Jena, 1871; preacher New Synagogue, Great St. Helen's, London, 1873; came to U.S., 1873; m. Isabel Frances Cohen, Feb. 14, 1877. Rabbi Shaaray Tefillah (now West End Synagogue) Congregation, Jan. 1, 1874-Nov. 1920, elected for life Dec. 21, 1904, rabbi emeritus, 1920—. Founded, 1879, editor, 1879-85, the American Hebrew; revising editor and chief translation bureau, until Sept. 1902, Jewish Encyclopedia; asso. editor (with Dr. M. Jastrow and Dr. K. Kohler) of New Bible Translation, 1903; mem. Schiff Com. on Jewish Classics, 1923; contbr. Johnson's Ency., Ency. Americana, etc. Author: A Hebrew's Reply to the Missionaries, 1876; (Jewish school books): Child's First Bible, 1880; Outlines of Scripture History, 1884. Home: Pelham, N.Y. Died Oct. 26, 1927.

MENDES, Henry Pereira, rabbi; b. Birmingham, Eng., Apr. 13, 1852; s. Abraham Pereira and Eliza (de Sola) M.; ed. Univ. Coll., London, and Northwick Coll. (rabbinics); M.D., New York University, 1885; D.D., New York Jewish Theol. Seminary; m. Rosalie Piza, of New York, Oct. 15, 1890; children—A. Piza, S. Pereira. Minister Spanish and Portuguese Congregation, Manchester, Eng., 1874-77, Shearith Israel (Spanish and Portuguese), New York, 1877-1920; minister emeritus Shearith Israel, 1920—. One of 2 founders, 1886, sec. advisory bd., and prof. history and acting pres. of faculty, Jewish Theol. Sem., New York; professor homiletics, Rabbinical College, N.Y. A founder New York Bd. Jewish Ministers (sec. 1881-1901, pres. 1901-05); pres. Union Orthodox Jewish Congregations of the U.S. and Canada; Past Grand Chaplain for State of N.Y. of F. and A.M.; hon. v.p. Inst. for Improved Instrn. of Deaf Mutes. Founder Sch. for Jewish Crippled Children, also Sch. for Jewish Deaf Mute Children; initiator of movement to found Institution in honor of Sir Moses Montefiore, now functioning under name of Montefiore Hospital. Author: Jewish History Ethically Presented, 1895; The Jewish Religion Ethically Presented, 1904; The Pentateuch Ethically Presented; Ethical Presentation of Daily Duties, 1917; Derech Hayim or Prayers and Meditations, 1934. Home: New York, N.Y. Died Oct. 20, 1937.

MENEES, Thomas, physician; b. nr. Nashville, Tenn., June 26, 1823; s. Benjamin Williams and Elizabeth M.; grad. Transylvania Univ. (med. dept.), 1846; practiced, Springfield, Tenn., 1846-65; after that at Nashville; mem. Tenn. senate, 1857, and of Confederate Congress during Civil War; prof. Univ. of Nashville, 1874-75; prof. obstetrics, 1875-98, and dean med. dept. Vanderbilt Univ., 1875-96; retired, 1898; emeritus prof. Home: Nashville, Tenn. Died 1905.

MENGEL, Levi Walter, dir. museum; b. Reading, Pa., Sept. 27, 1868; s. Matthias and Amelia M. (Soder) M.; Pharm.D., Phila. Coll. of Pharmacy; Sc.D., Bucknell Univ., Lewisburg, Pa., 1932; LL.D., Albright Coll., Reading, 1934; unmarried. Teacher natural sciences, 1895-1905; chemistry teacher, 1905-15; dir. of Reading Museum, 1915—. Mem. bd. trustees Reading Pub. Library. Republican. Quaker. Mason. Author: Synonymic Catalogue of the Family Erycinidæ, 1905. Home: Reading, Pa. Died Feb. 3, 1941.

MENOCAL, Aniceto G., civil engr. U.S.N., 1872—; b. Island of Cuba, Sept. 1, 1836; ed. in schools at Havana; C.E. Rensselaer Poly. Inst., 1862; sub-chief engr. Havana water works, 1863-69; engr. dept. public works, New York, 1870-72. Has been chief engr. of all U.S. Govt. surveys for establishing practicability of a ship canal from the Atlantic to the Pacific at Nicaragua and Panama, and of the Maritime Canal Co. of Nicaragua; has made final plans and estimates of cost for a ship canal through Nicaragua. Apptd. delegate to Paris Canal Congress, 1879; decorated by President Grevy, Chevalier Legion of Honor. Has published several official reports on Nicaragua Canal, etc. Mem. commn. to select site for prin. naval station in Philippine Islands, 1900-01; mem. bd. to prepare plans and estimates of cost for naval sta. at Olongapo, Subig Bay, P.I., 1901-02; in 1902 directed by Navy Dept. to select site for coaling sta. on coast of Liberia, Africa; engaged in important drainage work in Cuba, 1906-07. Home: New York, N.Y. Died 1908.

MENOHER, Charles Thomas, army officer; b. in Pa., Mar. 20, 1862; grad. U.S. Mil. Acad., 1886, Arty. Sch., 1894; Army War Coll., 1907; m. Nannie Pearson; children—Charles C. (dec.), Pearson, Darrow, William; m. 2d, Elizabeth Painter. Commd. 2d lt. 1st Arty., July 1, 1886; promoted through grades to col., July 1, 1916; brig. gen., N.A., Aug. 5, 1917; maj. gen. N.A., Nov. 28, 1917; brig. gen., U.S.A., Nov. 7, 1918, maj. gen., Mar. 8, 1921. A.d.c. to Brigadier General E. B. Williston, U.S. Vols., 1898; with Light Arty. Brigade, 2d Corps, Chickamauga Park, Ga., July-Dec. 1898; at Havana, Cuba, 1898-99; adj. gen. to provost marshal gen., and of Separate Brigade, Provost Guard, Manila, P.I., 1899-1901; comd. 28th Battery, Field Arty. (mountain), 1901-03; duty Gen. Staff, 1903-07; provost marshal and asst. to chief of staff, Army of Cuban Pacification, 1907. Comd. 5th F.A., Sept. 1916-Aug. 26, 1917, and provisional brig. F.A., El Paso, Tex., Sept.-Nov. 1916; comd. Sch. of Instrn., F.A., Saumur, France, Sept. 5-Dec. 14, 1917; comd. 42d (Rainbow) Div., Dec. 19, 1917-Nov. 10, 1918; comd. 6th Corps, Nov. 10-Dec. 17, 1918; dir. Air Service, 1919-21; comdg. Hawaiian Div., 1922-24, Hawaiian Dept., 1924-25, 9th Corps Area, 1925; retired Mar. 20, 1926. Participated in operations in Luneville and Baccarat sectors, Feb. 17-June 21, 1918, Champagne-Marne defensive, July 15-18, attack above Château Thierry, July 24-Aug. 2, attack on St. Mihiel salient, Sept. 12-14, and in occupation of the sector to Oct. 1, 1918; attack in Argonne, Oct. 12-Nov. 8, 1918. Awarded D.S.M., 1919; decorated by the French, Belgian and Italian Govts. Home: Washington, D.C. Died Aug. 11, 1930.

MÉRAS, Albert Amédée, author, educator; b. N.Y. City, May 15, 1880; s. Baptiste and Louise (Laffont) M.; B.A., Coll. City of New York, 1900; M.A., New York U., 1904, Ph.D., 1908; unmarried. Successively teacher pub. schs., N.Y. City; lecturer French lang. and lit., New York U.; asst. prof. Romance langs., Teachers Coll. (Columbia), and asso. prof. French, same; visiting prof. U. of Paris, 1922-24. Served as maj. inf., U.S.A., with A.E.F. Democrat. Mason. Author: Petit Vocabulaire, 1913; Le Premier Livre, 1914; Le Second Livre, 1915; Petits Contes de France, 1915; El Pequēno Vocabulario, 1916; Ein Wartschortz, 1917; La France Éternelle, 1920. Died Mar. 1, 1926.

MERCER, Alfred Clifford, M.D.; b. Syracuse, N.Y., July 5, 1855; s. Alfred and Delia (Lamphier) M.; M.D., Syracuse U., 1878; student, St. Thomas' Hosp., London, 1878-80, Great Ormond St. Hosp. for Sick Children, London, 1891-92; unmarried. Instr., lecturer and curator, Syracuse U., 1880-86, prof. pathology, 1886-93, clin. pediatrics, 1893-1904, pediatrics, 1894-1926 (emeritus); health officer Syracuse, 1883-85; cons. staff Syracuse Free Disp. and Hosp. of House of the Good Shepherd; phys. Children's Pavilion, of Syracuse Memorial Hosp. Pres. bd. mgrs. Onondago (Co.) Sanatorium for Tuberculosis, 1914-19. Mem. tuberculosis advisory board to N.Y. State Dept. of Health. Life fellow Royal Micros. Soc. (London). Author: Revision and part V, How to Work with the Microscope, by Lionel S. Beale, F.R.S., 5th edit., 1880; An Experimental Study of Aperture as a Factor in Microscopic Vision, 1896. Home: Syracuse, N.Y. Died Apr. 10, 1927.

MERCER, David Henry, congressman; b. Benton Co., Ia., July 9, 1857; s. John J. and Elizabeth M.; B.L., U. of Neb., 1880; LL.B., U. of Mich., 1882; m. Birdie Abbott, June 6, 1894. Practiced at Brownville, Neb., 1882-85, Omaha, 1885—. Was city clerk and police judge of Brownville, Nebraska; secretary Republican State Central Com., 1884-85; chmn. Rep. City Com., Omaha, 1887-90, Rep. Co. Com., 1890-92; sec. Rep. Nat. Congressional Com., 1896; chmn. Rep. State Central Com., 1897-98; mem. 53d to 57th Congresses (1893-1903). Spl. counsel State Council Defense, 1917. Pres. Douglas Co. Pioneer Assn., 1918. Home: Omaha, Neb. Died Jan. 7, 1919.

MERCER, Henry Chapman, anthropologist; b. Doylestown, Pa., June 24, 1856; s. William Robert and Mary Rebecca (Chapman) M.; A.B., Harvard U., 1879; Sc.D., Franklin and Marshall Coll., 1916. Curator of Am. and prehistoric archæology, Univ. of Pa., 1894-97. Hon. mem. U.S. Archæol. Commn., Madrid, 1893; editor for anthropology in Am. Naturalist, 1893-97. Found remains of extinct animals, tapir, mylodon, peccary and fossil sloth in Am. caves; compared remains of ancient man in drift gravels and flint workings of America and Europe; explored caverns of Yucatan, fixing geol. date for the peninsular ruins; found several new species of extinct animals in bone cave, Port Kennedy, Pa.; examined artistic remains of the Pa. German settlers, and experimented upon and developed their processes of making and decorating pottery, inventing, 1899, a new method of mfg. tiles for mural decoration, and, 1902, a new process of making mosaics; invented process of printing large designs in color on fabrics and paper, 1904. Grand prize, St. Louis Expn., 1904. Craftsmanship medal, Am. Inst. Architects, 1921. Author: Lenape Stone, 1885; Hill Caves of Yucatan, 1896; Researches Upon the Antiquity of Man in the Delaware Valley and the Eastern United States, 1897; Tools of the Nation Maker, 1897; Bible in Iron, 1915; Ancient Carpenters' Tools, 1925. Made a collection of utensils and implements illustrating the industrial history of the colonial U.S., to preserve and exhibit, which he built and endowed a museum at Doylestown, Pa., 1916. Home: Doylestown, Pa. Died 1930.

MERCER, William Fairfield, prof. biology; b. Eddyville, N.Y., Jan. 22, 1864; s. James C. and Emmertt (Ballard) M.; grad. Chamberlain Inst., Randolph, N.Y., 1885; Ph.B., Hillsdale (Mich.) Coll., 1890, Ph.M., 1894; Ph.D., Cornell U., 1900; m. Belle C. Eddy, Sept. 6, 1886. Instr. mathematics, Hillsdale Coll., 1886-90; prin. acad. and supt. pub. schs., Waterford, Pa., 1891-94; prof. nat. science, Chamberlain Inst., 1895-98; prof. biology, Ohio U., Athens, O., 1900—. Republican. Methodist. Mason. Author: Laboratory Guide, 1910. Home: Athens, O. Died July 29, 1929.

MERCUR, Rodney Augustus, lawyer; b. Towanda, Pa., Sept. 29, 1851; s. Chief Justice Ulysses and Sarah Simpson (Davis) M.; ed. Hopkins Grammar Sch., New Haven, Conn.; grad. Phillips Exeter Acad., Exeter, N.H.; student Harvard U., 1871-72; m. Mary Ward, June 12, 1879; children—Louise Ward (dec.), Sarah Davis, Amy Hart and Mary Ward (twins, both dec.), Rodney Augustus. Admitted to Bradford Co.

bar, 1875, U.S. Dist. Court, 1876, Supreme Court of Pa., 1878, Supreme Court of U.S., 1905; register in bankruptcy, Western Dist. of Pa., 1877-79. Trustee Robert Packer Hosp., Sayre, Pa. Pa. commr. to Chicago Expn., and treas. state commn.; U.S. del. Universal Congress Lawyers and Jurists, St. Louis, 1904; lay deputy General Conv., P.E. Ch., 1886-1931; chancellor Diocese Bethlehem, Pa., 23 years. Episcopalian. Republican. Home: Towanda, Pa. Deceased.

MEREDITH, Edwin Thomas, secretary of agr.; b. Avoca, Ia., Dec. 23, 1876; s. Thomas Oliver and Minnie Minerva (Marsh) M.; ed. Highland Park Coll., Des Moines, Ia., 1893-94; m. Edna C. Elliott, Jan. 8, 1896. Pub. Farmers' Tribune, Des Moines, 1896-1902; started Successful Farming, 1902; past dir. Chicago Fed. Reserve Bk., Iowa Trust & Savings Bank. Candidate for U.S. senator, 1914, for gov., 1916; apptd. mem. Bd. Excess Profit Advisors, Nov. 1917; apptd. mem. Industrial Conf., Oct. 1919; sec. of agr. in cabinet of President Wilson, Jan. 1920-Mar. 4, 1921. Democrat. Methodist. Founder of Jefferson Highway. Mason. Died June 17, 1928.

MEREDITH, Joseph Carroll, civ. engr.; b. Rushville, Ind., Mar. 23, 1856; s. William Gray and Caroline (Barrett) M.; B.M.E., Ia. State Coll., 1878; student Stevens Inst. Technology, 1879-81; m. Ella Lane, 1891. U.S. asst. engr., Mo. River improvement, 1881-87; asst. engr., 1888-93, div. engr., 1893-96, Mo. River Commn.; engr. pvt. corps., 1896-1900; asst. engr. Tampico (Mex.) harbor improvements, 1900-04; constructing engr., Florida East Coast Ry., at Miami, 1904—. Democrat. Died 1909.

MEREDITH, Virginia Claypool; b. Fayette Co., Ind., Nov. 5, 1848; d. Austin B. and Hannah (Petty) Claypool; grad. Glendale (O.) Coll., 1866; m. Hon. Henry Clay Meredith, 1870 (died 1882). On death of husband took active management of the homestead in Wayne Co., Ind., and became successful breeder of Shorthorn cattle and Southdown sheep. Was spl. lecturer at State Farmers' Insts.; pres. Ind. Union of Lit. Clubs, 1893; apptd. 1891, mem. bd. lady mgrs. Chicago Expn., and as chmn. of its com. on awards had charge of selection and appmt. of over 100 women judges from the leading nations. Prof. home economics, Coll. of Agr., U. of Minn., 1897-1902. Home: Cambridge City, Ind. Died Dec. 10, 1936.

MEREDITH, William Henry, clergyman; b. Bristol, Eng., Mar. 28, 1844; s. Charles and Elizabeth (Timmins) M.; acad. edn., Bristol, Eng.; came to U.S., 1870; spl. student Coll. Liberal Arts, Boston U.; grad. Boston Univ. Sch. of Theology, 1875; (Litt.D., Moores Hill Coll., Ind., 1905; S.T.D., Syracuse U., 1908); m. Susan Barrett, of Bristol, Eng., Sept. 21, 1867. Deacon, 1871, elder, 1873, M.E. Ch.; pastor at Topsfield, 1875-76, Salem, 1877-79, Winchester, 1880-81, Northampton, 1882-83, Lowell, 1884-86, Lynn, 1887-89, Stoneham, 1890-91, Springfield, 1892-94, Everett, 1895-98, Lowell, 1899-1900, Boston, 1901-02, Southbridge, 1903, Lynn, 1904-06, Framingham, Mass., 1907—; instr. in Boston Deaconess Training Sch., 1903—; spl. lecturer, Boston Univ. Sch. of Theology, 1905—. Author: The Real John Wesley, 1903; John Wesley, His Courage and Ambition, 1904; Jesse Lee, a Methodist Apostle, 1909. Home: Framingham, Mass. Died 1911.

MERICA, Charles Oliver, educator, editor; b. St. Paris, O., July 3, 1864; s. William and Catharine (Snyder) M.; B.A., De Pauw U., 1891; M.A., Ia. Wesleyan U., 1892; (LL.D., Lawrence Coll., Appleton, Wis., 1907); m. Alice White, 1888. Pres. Dakota Wesleyan U., Mitchell, S.D., 1891-94; prof. economics, 1894-97, sociology, 1903-07, Lawrence Coll.; supt. Wis. Industrial Sch. for Boys, Waukesha, Wis., 1897-1903; pres. U. of Wyo., May 1, 1908-Aug. 1, 1912; supt. Minn. State Training Sch., Red Wing, 1912-14; editor The News-Sun, Kendallville, Ind., 1914—. Died July 24, 1918.

MERIWETHER, Colyer, teacher; b. Clark's Hill, S.C.; s. Nicholas and Emily (Collier) M.; student Furman U., S.C., 1877-78, 1880-81, Vanderbilt U., 1881-82; A.B., Johns Hopkins, 1886, Ph.D., 1893; m. Elizabeth S. Quynn, Feb. 23, 1893 (died Aug. 1, 1903); 2d, Mona Nelson, Sept. 16, 1915. Educationally employed by Japanese Govt. at Sendai, Japan, 1889-92; head geography dept., Business High Sch., Washington, 1903—. Author: Our Colonial Curriculum, 1907; Life of Raphael Semmes, 1913. Home: Takoma Park, D.C. Died Aug. 26, 1920.

MERIWETHER, Elizabeth Avery, author; b. (Avery) Bolivar, Tenn., 1824; d. Nathan (M.D.) and Rebecca R. Avery; m. Minor Meriwether, lawyer, Jan. 5, 1852 (died, 1910); mother of Lee Meriwether. Author: The Master of Red Leaf; Black and White; The Ku Klux Klan; My First and Last Love: Facts and Falsehoods Concerning the War on the South of 1861 and 1865 (under pen name "George Edmonds"), 1904; the Sowing of Swords, 1910. Home: St. Louis, Mo. Died Nov. 4, 1917.

MERLE-SMITH, Wilton, clergyman; b. Elmira, N.Y., Apr. 18, 1856; s. Judge H. Boardman and Ellen (Hays) Smith; A.B., Princeton, 1877 (D.D., 1889); grad. Auburn (N.Y.) Theol. Sem., 1881; m. Zaidee Van Santvoord, Nov. 19, 1885. Ordained Presbyn. ministry, June 16, 1881; pastor, Cazenovia, N.Y., 1881-84; asso. pastor First Ch., Cleveland, 1884-89; pastor Central Ch., New York, 1889-1920. Pres. Presbyterian Bd. Home Missions. Home: New York, N.Y. Died Oct. 3, 1923.

MERONEY, William Penn, sociologist; b. at Plano, Tex., Jan. 7, 1881; s. of William Lowndes and Lucete (Howard) M.; student Agrl. and Mech. Coll. of Tex., 1896-97, 1897-98; grad. Howard Payne Coll., Brownwood, Tex., 1903; A.B., Baylor, 1907; Th.B., Southwestern Bapt. Theol. Sem., Ft. Worth, Tex., 1912; Th.M., Southern Bapt. Theol. Sem., Louisville, Ky., 1917, Th.D., 1919; A.M., U. of Chicago, 1922; m. Ada Kathreen Reid, Feb. 10, 1904; children—Howard Maxwell, Charles Arthur, William Albert. Ordained Bapt. ministry, 1903; missionary, Mills Co., Tex., 1903-04; pastor Manor, Tex., 1904-05; student pastor country chs., 1905-07; pastor Walters, Okla., 1907-08, Groesbeck, 1908-09, Hamlin, 1910-11, Bellevue, 1911-13, Turner St. Ch., Waco, 1914-16, Horse Cave, Ky., 1916-20, Marion, 1920, 21; teacher, Bethel Coll., Russellville, Ky., 1918-19; prof. sociology, Baylor U., 1922—, also head dept. of sociology. Formerly chmn. Tex. Commn. on Inter-racial Coöperation, Waco-McLennan County Chapter Am. Red Cross; pres., now scout commr. Heart of Texas Council of Boy Scouts of America. Democrat. Mason. Author: Introductory Studies in Sociology, 1925, revised edit., 1928. Home: Waco, Tex. Died Dec. 25, 1938.

MERRELL, John Porter, naval officer; b. Auburn, N.Y., Sept. 7, 1846; s. John Camp and Jane A. (Allen) M.; grad. U.S. Naval Acad., 1867; m. Sarah Frances Tyler, Jan. 22, 1872. Promoted ensign, Dec., 1868; advanced through grades to rear adm., Mar. 19, 1907. Served with European Fleet, 1867-70; signal duty, Washington and Darien Surveying expdn., 1870-71; Torpedo sta., Newport, R.I., 1872-75; Swatara, N. Atlantic Fleet, 1875-77; in charge naval ordnance proving grounds, 1877-79; "Marion," N. Atlantic, and S. Atlantic fleets, 1879-81, "Shenandoah," S. Atlantic Fleet, 1881-82; instr. mathematics, mechanics, physics, chemistry, U.S. Naval Acad., 1882-87; flagships Pensacola, Quinnebaug and Lancaster (on staff comdr.-in-chief) European sta., 1887-89; Naval Acad. (head dept. applied mathematics last 3 yrs.), 1889-93; Baltimore, Asiatic sta., 1893-95; mem. State Dept. Commn. to investigate anti-foreign riots in the province of Szechuen, China, 1895-96; insp. 13th light house dist., 1896-98; on staff Naval War Coll., Jan.-May, 1898; Scipio and Glacier, N. Atlantic Fleet, May-Oct., 1898; equipment officer Navy Yard, New York, 1898-99; U.S.S. Montgomery, S. Atlantic Squadron, 1899-1900; equipment officer Navy Yard, Norfolk, Va., 1900-01; comdt., naval station, New Orleans, 1901-03, Naval War Coll., June-Oct., 1903; comdt. New Orleans, 1903-04, U.S.S. Oregon, Asiatic Fleet, 1904; pres. U.S. Naval War Coll., and mem. Gen. Bd., May 24, 1906-Oct. 9, 1909; mem. Joint Army and Navy Bd., 1909; retired by operation of law, Sept. 7, 1908. Home: Washington, D.C. Died Dec. 8, 1916.

MERRIAM, Alexander Ross, theologian; b. Goshen, N.Y., Jan. 20, 1849; s. Henry and Ann Eliza (Reeve) M.; A.B., Yale, 1872; grad. Andover Theol. Sem., 1877; D.D., Olivet Coll., 1906; S.T.D., Syracuse U., 1907; m. J. May Gore, July 16, 1879; children—Edmund Sawyer, Alma May, Elizabeth Caroline (Mrs. Raymond A. Beardslee), Helen Louise (Mrs. Roger W. Davis), Margaret Isabelle (dec.). Ordained Congl. ministry, 1877; pastor of Payson Church of Easthampton, Mass., 1877-84, First Ch., Grand Rapids, Mich., 1884-91; prof. homiletics, pastoral care and sociology, 1893-1917, prof. emeritus Jan. 1, 1918, Hartford (Conn.) Theol. Sem. Trustee Williston Sem., Easthampton, Mass., 1881-84, Olivet (Mich.) Coll., 1883-84, Good Will Club; dir. Conn. Bible Soc., Charity Organization Soc. Home: Hartford, Conn. Died Dec. 26, 1928.

MERRIAM, Carroll Burnham, banker; b. Johnson, Vt., Nov. 15, 1870; s. Everett B. and Sarah Partridge (Dillingham) M.; ed. Washburn Coll., Topeka, Kan., 1890-93; m. Marguerite Bradley, July 1, 1897; 1 son, John Everett. Began as clk. with T. E. Bowman & Co., Topeka, 1897, admitted to partnership, 1899; treas. Merriam Mortgage Co., 1900-20; with Central Trust Co., 1920—, chmn. bd., 1930—; v.p. Central Nat. Bank. Dir. Federal Home Loan Bank, R.F.C., June 1933—. Served with Am. Red Cross, World War, becoming dir. personnel. Mem. exec. com. of bd. trustees Nat. Foundation for Infantile Paralysis. Mem. bd. dirs. Soc. for Crippled Children of Kan., Topeka Pub. Library; mem. bd. regents Kan. State Ednl. Instns., 1925-31; trustee Washburn Coll. Republican. Episcopalian. Home: Topeka, Kans. Died Dec. 9, 1941.

MERRIAM, Edmund Franklin, editor; b. Winthrop, Me., Jan. 26, 1847; s. Franklin and Eunice Clarke (Ward) M.; A.B., Colby Coll., Me., 1868, D.D., 1901; grad. Newton Theol. Instn., Mass., 1879; m. Abby Frances Baker, Aug. 2, 1876. In produce business, New York, 1868-76; ordained Bapt. ministry, 1879; pastor Livermore Falls, Me., 1879-80; editor and sec. Am. Bapt. Missionary Union, Boston, 1880-1901; editor the Watchman, Boston, 1901-13; mng. editor the Watchman-Examiner, 1913-16 (retired). Trustee, Newton Theol. Instn.; visitor Brown U.; etc. Author: The American Baptist Missionary Union and Its Missions; History of American Baptist Missions. Died Nov. 21, 1930.

MERRIAM, George Spring, author; b. Springfield, Mass., Jan. 13, 1843; s. George and Abby (Fiske) M.; A.B., Yale, 1864, A.M., 1867; tutor there and studied theology, 1866-68; m. Mrs. Fanny Smith Post, 1868 (died 1878); 2d, Susan Adela Clapp, 1897. Office editor Christian Union, 1870-75. Author: Reminiscences and Letters of Caroline C. Briggs, 1897; The Negro and Nation, 1906; The Man of Today, 1911. Home: Springfield, Mass. Died Jan. 22, 1914.

MERRIAM, Henry Clay, major gen. U.S.A.; b. Houlton, Me., Nov. 13, 1837; s. Lewis and Mary (Foss) M.; A.B., A.M., Colby Coll., 1867 (LL.D., 1908); read law; m. McPherson McNeil, June 4, 1876. Capt. 20th Me. Inf., Aug. 29, 1862; resigned Jan. 7, 1863; capt. 80th U.S.C.T., Mar. 11, 1863; lt. col. 85th U.S.C.T., May 21, 1864; transferred to 73d U.S.C.T., June 3, 1864; hon. mustered out, Oct. 24, 1865; maj. 38th U.S. Inf., July 28, 1866; lt. col. 2d Inf., June 10, 1876; col. 7th Inf., July 10, 1885; brig. gen. U.S.A., June 30, 1897; maj. gen. vols., May 4, 1898-Feb. 24, 1899; retired, Nov. 13, 1901; advanced to rank of maj. gen. retired, Feb. 19, 1903. Bvtd. col. vols., Mar. 26, 1865, "for faithful and meritorious services during campaign against Mobile"; lt. col., Mar. 2, 1867, for same at Antietam; awarded Congressional Medal of Honor, June 28, 1894, "for conspicuous gallantry at Ft. Blakely, Apr. 9, 1865." Served in numerous expdns. against Indians; also in defense of Am. citizens on both sides of Rio Grande during revolutionary uprisings, 1873-76; comd. depts. Columbia and Cal., and organized, equipped and forwarded troops for Philippine expdn., 1898; comd. Dept. of the Colo., 1900-01. Inventor of the Merriam infantry pack. Died Nov. 18, 1912.

MERRIAM, William Rush, governor; b. Wadham's Mills, Essex Co., N.Y., July 1849; s. John L. and Mahala (de Lano) M.; A.B., Racine (Wis.) Coll., 1871; m. Laura E. Hancock, Oct. 2, 1873. Began as clk. Merchants Nat. Bank, St. Paul, 1871, became pres. 1882; pres. Shenandoah Iron & Coal Co., Liberty Furnace Co. (Va.), Tabulating Machine Co. (Washington, D.C.). Formerly mem. Minn. Ho. of Rep. (speaker of House, 1886); gov. of Minn., 1889-92; dir. U.S. Census, 1898-1903. Republican. Home: Washington, D.C. Died Feb. 18, 1931.

MERRICK, Edwin Thomas, lawyer; b. in Point Coupee Parish, La., Oct. 27, 1859; s. Edwin Thomas and Caroline Elizabeth (Thomas) M.; Vanderbilt U., 1878-80; m. Katharine Lombard, May 15, 1889; children—Laura (Mrs. Alfred Loveland), Susan (Mrs. Jackson A. Dykman). In practice at New Orleans, 1882—; mem. Merrick, Schwarz, Guste, Barnett & Redmann; atty. for New Orleans Clearing House, National Bank of Commerce, Philip Werlein, Ltd., Federal Reserve Bank of Atlanta, Newman, Saunders & Co. Chairman com. appointed by Circuit Court of Appeals, Fifth Circuit, to suggest amendments to equity rules of Supreme Court of U.S. adopted in 1912. Chmn. Law Examining Com. for the State of La. Democrat. Methodist. Author: Merrick's Civil Code, 1925. Home: New Orleans, La. Died June 21, 1935.

MERRICK, George Peck, lawyer; b. Manteno, Ill., Oct. 4, 1862; s. Dr. George C. and Mary (Peck) M.; B.L., Northwestern, 1884, hon. LL.M., 1909; read law in office of Hon. Elbridge Hanecy; m. Grace Thompson, Jan. 21, 1885; children—Clinton, Grace (Mrs. John Breyspraak), Thompson. Admitted to Ill. bar, 1886; asst. atty. A.T. & S.F. Ry., Chicago, 1886-89; mem. firm of Hanecy & Merrick, 1889-93, later Merrick, Evans & Whitney, now Bayley, Merrick, Webster & Gregory. Trustee Northwestern U. Republican. Methodist. Mason. Home: Evanston, Ill. Died Nov. 2, 1938.

MERRICK, Harry L., editorial paragrapher Washington Post; b. Xenia, O., Jan. 26, 1859; s. Charles R. and Mary A. M.; ed. Xenia, O. An editor of the Washington (D.C.) Post, 1889—; writer of short editorial paragraphs; contributor to mags. and newspapers. Died 1903.

MERRICK, John Vaughan, mech. engr.; b. Philadelphia, Aug. 30, 1828; s. Samuel Vaughan and Sarah M.; grad. Central High Sch., 1843; engring. edn. in works at Phila.; m. Oct. 23, 1855, Mary Sophia Wagner (died 1897). Senior and engring. partner Merrick & Sons, Phila., 1849-70. Mgr. from 1872 and v.p. from 1886, Zoöl. Soc. of Phila.; mem. bd. experts Phila. water supply, 1883; mem. bd. experts U.S. Navy Dept., 1867; pres. from 1873 Free and Open Church Assn., founder St. Timothy's Memorial Hosp., Roxborough, Phila.; trustee Univ. of Pa., 1870—; mem. Franklin Inst. (pres. 1867-70). Died 1906.

MERRIFIELD, Fred, clergyman, educator; b. Amboy, Ill., Jan. 18, 1874; s. Albert Henry and Lucie D. (Tooker) M.; A.B., U. of Chicago, 1898, B.D., 1901; m. Anna Holcombe Marshall, Sept. 6, 1907; children—Fred Marshall, Charles Warren, Margaret Comfort, Dudley Bruce, Marcia Helen. Gen. sec.

Y.M.C.A., U. of Chicago, 1898-1900; asso. pastor Memorial Bapt. Ch., Chicago, 1900-01; ordained Bapt. ministry, 1901; pastor Scribner St. Bapt. Ch., Grand Rapids, Mich., 1901-04; teacher and coach of baseball, Tokyo, Japan, 1904-07; dir. Bapt. Students' Guild, Ann Arbor, Mich., 1907-11; instr. N.T. history and interpretation, 1911-16, asst. prof., 1916-33, U. of Chicago; coach of baseball, U. of Chicago, 1920-21; minister All Souls Liberal Ch., Chicago, 1922-32; asso. editor World Unity, 1927-33. Pres. Liberal Ministers' Assn., 1924-25; chmn. Social Service Ind. Com. for Polit. Action, 1931-34; mem. com. of Governor's Commn. on Unemployment and Relief. Dean of Jackson Park Community Center. Republican. Author: The Rediscovery of Jesus, 1929. Editor: Modern Religious Verse and Prose, 1925; asso. editor Supplementary Bible, 1927. Home: Chicago, Ill. Died Feb. 6, 1935.

MERRIFIELD, Webster, university pres.; b. Williamsville, Vt., July 27, 1852; s. John A. and Louisa W. M.; A.B., Yale, 1877 (hon. A.M., 1892; LL.D., U. of N.D., 1909); m. Elizabeth McBride Bull, June 26, 1902. Tutor Yale, 1879-83; prof. Greek, 1884-91, polit. and social science, 1891-1905, pres. 1891-1909, U. of N.D. Some time pres.-elect. U. of Montana. Home: Pasadena, Calif. Died Jan. 1916.

MERRILL, Abner Hopkins, brig. gen. U.S.A.; b. in N.Y., Jan. 19, 1843; grad. U.S. Mil. Acad., 1866. Commd. 2d lt. 1st Arty., June 18, 1866; 1st lt., May 1, 1870; grad. Arty. Sch., 1878; capt., Aug. 14, 1887; maj. 3d Arty., Feb. 23, 1899; lt. col. corps, Aug. 1, 1901; col., Apr. 14, 1903; brig. gen. and retired at own request, over 40 yrs.' service, Mar. 16, 1906. Home: Poughkeepsie, N.Y. Died Feb. 25, 1923.

MERRILL, Charles White, publisher; b. Indianapolis, Feb. 15, 1861; s. Samuel and Emily Frances (White) M.; A.B., Wabash Coll., Crawfordsville, Ind., 1882, A.M., 1887, (Litt.D., 1908); m. Celine Lodge McKee, May 18, 1891. Identified with The Bobbs-Merrill Co., 1882—, and treas., 1895—; also pres. Hollenbeck Press; sec. Gen. Securities Co. Republican. Home: Indianapolis, Ind. Died Feb. 18, 1920.

MERRILL, Cyrus Strong, ophthalmologist; b. Bridport, Vt., Sept. 21, 1847; s. Edward W. and Sarah W. (Strong) M.; A.B., Amherst, 1867, A.M., 1870; M.D., Coll. Phys. and Surg. (Columbia), 1871; spl. studies U. of Switzerland, and at Zürich, Vienna, Heidelberg, Paris, and London; m. Mary E. Griffin, Oct. 12, 1875. Prof. diseases of eye and ear, Albany Med. Coll. (med. dept. Union U.), 1876—; ophthalmic and aural surgeon to Albany Hosp., and The Child's Hosp. Pres. Ticonderoga Pulp & Paper Co., Thomson Pulp & Paper Co. Home: Albany, N.Y. Died Mar. 16, 1926.

MERRILL, Edward Bagley, lawyer; b. New Bedford, Mass., Jan. 25, 1835; s. Edward and Mary (Converse) M.; A.B., Bowdoin Coll., 1857, A.M., 1860; m. Mary Elizabeth Gibbs, Sept. 12, 1861. Practices in New York. Mem. bd. of mgrs. N.Y. State Colonization Soc.; mem. N.Y. Prison Assn. Home: New York, N.Y. Died 1920.

MERRILL, Elmer Truesdell, univ. prof.; b. Millville, Mass., Jan. 1, 1860; s. Rev. Charles Atwood and Mary (Truesdell) M.; B.A., Wesleyan U., Conn., 1881, M.A., 1889; grad. study, Wesleyan, 1881-82, Yale, 1885-86, U. of Berlin, 1886-87, various periods in research work in Europe; LL.D., U. of St. Andrews, Scotland, 1911; Litt.D., Kenyon Coll., 1924, Wesleyan U., 1926; D.D., Trinity Coll., Hartford, Conn., 1926; m. Edith Valentine, June 19, 1890; children—Doris (dec.), Robert Valentine, Cedric Valentine. Instr. classics, Mass. State Normal Sch., Westfield, 1882-83; tutor in Latin, Wesleyan, 1883-86; prof. Latin, U. of Southern Calif., 1887-88; Robert Rich prof. Latin lang. and lit., Wesleyan U., 1888-1905; prof. Latin lang. and lit., Trinity Coll., Hartford, 1905-08; professor Latin, U. of Chicago, 1908—; emeritus, 1925. Deacon, 1894, priest, 1895, P.E. Ch.; mem. mng. com., 1895-1901, of exec. com., sec. and actg. chmn., 1899-1900, chmn., 1900-01, Am. Sch. Classical Studies in Rome, and prof. in the sch., 1898-99. Asso. editor and editor Classical Philology many years. Author (or editor): Catullus, 1893; Fragments of Roman Satire, 1897; Selected Letters of the Younger Pliny, 1903, 1919; C. Plini Cæcili Secundi Epistularum Libri Decem, 1922; Catulli Veronensis Liber, 1923; Essays in Early Christian History, 1924. Died Apr. 19, 1936.

MERRILL, Frederick James Hamilton, geologist; b. New York, Apr. 30, 1861; s. Hamilton Wilcox and Louisa (Kauffman) M.; Ph.B., Columbia Sch. of Mines, 1885, Ph.D., 1890; m. Winifred Edgerton, Sept. 1, 1887. Asst. on Geol. Survey of N.J., 1885-89; asst. state geologist of N.Y., 1890-93; asst. dir., 1890-94, dir., 1894-1904, N.Y. State Mus.; state geologist of N.Y., 1899-1904; pvt. practice as mining geologist, 1904—; field asst. Calif. State Mining Bur., 1913—. Dir. scientific exhibit of N.Y. State at Chicago Expn., 1893, Buffalo Expn., 1901, St. Louis Expn., 1904. Home: Los Angeles, Calif. Died Nov. 29, 1916.

MERRILL, George Earnest, architect; b. St. Paul, Minn., July 17, 1870; s. Daniel David and Alice Almira (King) M.; student Mass. Inst. Tech., 1889-90, 1891-93; student U. of Minn., 1890-91; hon. Sc.D., Kalamazoo Coll., 1929; m. Grace Gassin Mortimer, Apr. 23, 1895 (died 1896); 1 dau., Grace Mortimer; m. 2d, Lulu Belle Orcutt, Feb. 6, 1900; children—Mary Alice (Mrs. John M. Budinger), George Earnest (dec.), David Orcutt. With W. S. Sampson & Co., contractors, Boston, 1894-96; represented Ernest Flagg, architect, in the building of U.S. Naval Acad., Annapolis, 1898-1908, as v.p. and gen. mgr. of Noel Construction Co.; dir. building operations at Naval Training Sta., North Chicago, Ill., and Chicago City Hall Bldg., 1908-12; asso. with Mr. Flagg in practice, 1914-16; assisted in erecting powder plant for U.S. Govt., at Nitro, W.Va., 1917-18; sec. in charge Dept. of Architecture, The Am. Bapt. Home Mission Soc., 1920—. Trustee Bapt. Internat. Sem., East Orange, N.J. Republican. Baptist. Mason. Author: (with Henry E. Traile) Planning Church Buildings, 1921; Building for Religious Education, 1926. Home: Montclair, N.J. Died Nov. 22, 1933.

MERRILL, George Edmands, pres. Colgate Univ., 1899—; b. Charlestown, Mass., Dec. 19, 1846; grad. Harvard, 1869 (A.M., 1872); Newton Theol. Instn., 1872 (D.D., Colby Univ., 1895; LL.D., Univ. of Rochester, 1901); pastor Baptist churches, Springfield, Mass., 1872-77, Salem, Mass., 1877-85, Colorado Springs, Colo., 1885-87, Immanuel Ch., Newton, Mass., 1890-99. Author: Crusaders and Captives, 1890; The Reasonable Christ, 1893; The Parchments of the Faith, 1895; also Song of Solomon, in Am. Commentary on the Old Testament, 1905. Home: Hamilton, N.Y. Died 1908.

MERRILL, George Perkins, geologist; b. Auburn, Me., May 31, 1854; s. Lucius and Anne Elizabeth (Jones) M.; B.S., U. of Me., 1879, M.S., 1883, Ph.D., 1889; student Wesleyan U., 1879-80; Johns Hopkins U., 1886-87; Sc.D., George Washington U., 1917; m. Sarah P. Farrington, Nov. 1883 (died 1894); m. 2d, Katherine L. Yancey, 1900. Asst. chemist, Wesleyan U., 1879-80; asst. in geol. dept. U.S. Nat. Mus., 1881; head curator dept. geology, U.S. Nat. Mus., 1897—; prof. geology and mineralogy, George Washington (formerly Columbian) U., 1893-1915. Expert spl. agt. of 12th Census in stonequarry statistics. Hon. corr. mem. A.I.A. J. L. Smith gold medal, Nat. Acad. Sciences, for researches in meteorites. Author: Stones for Building and Decoration, 1891, 1897, 1903; Rocks, Rock-weathering and Soils, 1897, 1907; The Non-Metallic Minerals—Their Occurrence and Uses, 1904, 1910; also contributions to a History of American Geology, 1905, and History of American State Geological and Natural History Surveys, 1920; Catalogue and Handbook Meteorite Collection in the U.S. Nat. Museum, 1915; Handbook of Gems and Precious Stones (with others), 1922; The First 100 Years of American Geology, 1924. Home: Washington, D.C. Died Aug. 15, 1929.

MERRILL, Henry Ferdinand, commr. Chinese Customs Service; b. White River, Vt., June 15, 1853; s. Josiah and Henrietta (Converse) M.; A.B., Harvard, 1874; m. Emma Burnett Hill, Oct. 17, 1890; 1 dau., Helen B. (Mrs. Everitt G. Smith). Apptd. to Chinese Customs Service, 1874; apptd. acting commr. customs Takow, Formosa, 1884, serving during Franco-Chinese War; was chief commr. of customs in Corea, 1885-90 (organized service there); commr. of customs in China, 1892-97; assisted in establishing Imperial postoffices in various parts of China, 1899-1904; commr. of customs at Tientsin, 1906-08; detached for duty in America as dir. Chinese Govt. students, 1908-09; commr. customs and dir. Conservancy Bd., Shanghai, 1909-13; commr. of customs, Canton, 1915-16; retired and returned to America. Decorated Imperial Order Double Dragon, and Civ. Rank, 2d Class, China; patent of nobility 2d Class, Corea, 1891; Chinese Order of Chia Ho, 1915. Hon. v.p. Board of Revenue, Corea. Home: West Newton, Mass. Died July 10, 1935.

MERRILL, James Andrew, educator, geologist; b. in Rockcastle Co., Ky., Apr. 6, 1861; s. Andrew H. and Ann Eliza (Eastin) M.; student William Jewell Coll., Liberty, Mo., 1879-80; grad. State Normal Sch., Warrensburg, Mo., 1887; S.B., Harvard U., 1893; LL.D., Mo. Valley College, 1923; m. Nellie A. Lowen, Dec. 23, 1896; children—Robt. Lowen (dec.), George Lowen, Helen Elizabeth. Teacher of natural sciences, Warrensburg (Mo.) State Normal Sch., 1887-97; same, Manual Training Sch., Kansas City, Mo., 1897-1900; prof. geology and geography, State Teachers' College, Superior, Wis., 1900-22, 1925-37, pres., 1922-25, pres. emeritus, 1936—. Assistant U.S. Geological Survey, 1890; investigated oil structures of Peace River region, Alberta, Can., summer 1921. Author: Industrial Geography of Wisconsin, 1909; Wisconsin—A Geographical Reader, 1931; Wonderland of Lake Superior, 1936. Conglist. Mason. Home: Superior, Wis. Died June 23, 1938.

MERRILL, James Cushing, surgeon U.S.A., June 26, 1875—; b. Cambridge, Mass., Mar. 26, 1853; s. James C. M.; grad. Univ. of Pa., M.D., 1874; m. Mary P. Chase, Nov. 16, 1892. Now on duty at Army Med. Museum. Contributor of ornithology to different journals. Home: Washington, D.C. Died 1902.

MERRILL, James Griswold, clergyman; b. Montague, Mass., Aug. 20, 1840; s. Rev. James H. and Lucia (Griswold) M.; bro. of William Fessenden M.; A.B., Amherst, 1863; student Princeton Theol. Sem., 1863-64; grad. Andover Theol. Sem., 1866; (D.D., Shurtleff, 1887, Amherst, 1903); m. Louisa W. Boutwell, Oct. 11, 1866 (died 1919). Ordained Congl. ministry, 1867; pastor Mound City, Kan., 1866-68, Topeka, Kan., 1868-69; supt. missions in Kan., 1869-72; pastor Davenport, Ia., 1872-82, First Ch., St. Louis, 1882-89, Payson Memorial Ch., Portland, Me., 1889-94; editor Christian Mirror, Portland, 1894-99; acting pres., 1899-1901, pres., 1901-08, Fisk U.; pastor Somerset, Mass., 1909-12, Lake Helen, Fla., 1912-17; retired First Asst. Moderator Nat. Congl. Council, Cleveland, O., 1907. Author: Children's Sermons, 2 vols., 1876-78; From Servitude to Service. Home: Andover, Mass. Died Dec. 22, 1920.

MERRILL, Leon Stephen, agriculturist; b. Solon, Me., Dec. 22, 1864; s. Stephen and Perusha Caroline (Dean) M.; prep. edn. Solon High Sch.; M.D., Medical School of Maine (Bowdoin), 1889; Sc.D. from U. of Maine, 1922; m. Alice Estelle Wilson, Aug. 12, 1885; children—Gladys Helen, Earl Stephen. Druggist, 1889-1900; mgr. Solon Creamery Co., 1900-08; state dairy instr., 1907-10; prof. agrl. extension, U. of Me., 1910-30, and dean Coll. of Agr., Mar. 1, 1911—. Federal Food Administrator for Me., 1917-19. Republican. Conglist. Old Fellow (Grand Sire, 1927-28). Home: Orono, Me. Died Sept. 3, 1933.

MERRILL, Lucius Herbert, chemist; b. Auburn, Me., Oct. 1, 1857; s. Lucius and Anne Elizabeth (Jones) M.; B.S., Me. State Coll., 1883; hon. Sc.D., U. of Me., 1908; m. Lydia Maria Buffum, June 24, 1893 (died 1907); 1 dau., Katharine Buffum; m. 2d, Annie Clifford Moore, June 15, 1910; children—Lucius Robert, Edward Osgood. Asst. in dept. of lithology and physical geology, U.S. Nat. Mus., 1885-86; chemist Me. Agrl. Expt. Sta., 1886-1908; instr. biol. chemistry, 1897-98, prof., 1898-1906, prof. biol. and agrl. chemistry, 1907-30, U. of Me., also served as state geologist of Maine (retired). Home: Orono, Me. Died Jan. 27, 1935.

MERRILL, Payson, lawyer; b. Stratham, N.H., Dec. 7, 1842; s. Phinehas and Abigail M.; B.A., Yale, 1865, M.A., 1907; LL.B., Columbia, 1868; m. Emma H. Strong, Apr. 28, 1879. Admitted to bar, 1868, and began practice at New York; now sr. mem. Merrill & Rogers. Trustee U.S. Savings Bank; v.p. and dir. Union Mortgage & Realty Co.; dir. Lawyers' Title Ins. & Trust Co. Fellow Corp. of Yale U., 1905—. Home: New Canaan, Conn., and New York, N.Y. Died Oct. 15, 1933.

MERRILL, Samuel, publisher; b. Indianapolis, May 30, 1831; s. Samuel and Lydia Jane (Anderson) M.; A.B., Wabash Coll., Ind., 1851, A.M., 1854; m. Emily White, July 19, 1859. Began as pub. and bookseller in Indianapolis, 1852. Served as 2d lt., capt., maj., lt. col., bvt. col., comdg. 70th Ind. Vol. Inf., Civil War. Consul-gen. at Calcutta, India, 1889-93; Whig and Republican. Presbyn. Quartermaster-gen. Dept. of Indiana, G.A.R., 1866; comdr. Dept. of Calif. and Nev., 1908, 09. Retired. Author: The Seventieth Indiana Volunteer Infantry in the War of the Rebellion, 1900. Home: Long Beach, Calif. Died Sept. 3, 1924.

MERRILL, Samuel, author; b. Charlestown, N.H., Jan. 1, 1855; s. Gyles and Eliza Watson (Newsbury) M.; A.B., Dartmouth, 1876; studied in Europe, 1877-79; LL.B., Columbia, 1880. Editorial staff Boston Globe, 1882—. Pres. Mass. Rifle Assn., 1909-11; life mem. N.H. Historic-Geneal. Soc.; mem. New Hampshire Hist. Soc., Boston Soc. Natural History, Mass. Fish and Game Assn. Many yrs. a hunter of big game. Author: Newspaper Libel, 1888; The Moose Book, 1916, revised edit., 1920; A Merrill Memorial, 1917-28; Dartmouth, 1876 — Biographical Sketches, 1926. Home: Cambridge, Mass. Died Jan. 11, 1932.

MERRILL, Selah, Am. consul; b. Canton Centre, Conn., May 2, 1837; s. Daniel and Lydia (Richards) M.; entered Yale, class of 1863; left before graduation (A.M., Yale; D.D., Iowa Coll., 1875; LL.D., Union, 1884); student New Haven Theol. Sem.; ordained Congl. ministry, 1864; chaplain 49th U.S. colored inf., Vicksburg, 1864-65; preached, LeRoy, N.Y., and San Francisco; studied in Germany, 1868-70; taught Hebrew, Andover Theol. Sem.; m. 1875, Adelaide Brewster Taylor. Archæologist. Am. Palestine Exploration. Soc., 1874-77; discovered and excavated the Second Wall of Jerusalem outside of which Christ was crucified; made large collections of Palestinian coins, utensils, birds, mammals, etc.; now curator of Biblical Mus., Andover Theol. Sem. Am. consul at Jerusalem, 1882-85, 1891-93, 1898-1907; at Georgetown, Guiana, 1907—. Author: East of the Jordan (2 edits.), 1881-83; Galilee in the Time of Christ, 1881; Greek Inscriptions Collected in the Years 1875-77 in the Country East of the Jordan; The Site of Calvary, 1885; Ancient Jerusalem, 1906. Home: Andover, Mass. Died 1909.

MERRILL, Stephen Mason, M.E. bishop, 1872—; b. Jefferson Co., O., Sept. 16, 1825; s. Joshua M.;

m. July 18, 1848, Anna Bellmire (D.D., Ohio Wesleyan, 1868; LL.D., Northwestern, 1886); entered M.E. ministry in Ohio Conf., 1846; editor Western Christian Advocate, 1868-72. Author: Christian Baptism; Aspects of Christian Experience; Digest of Methodist Law; Union of American Methodism. Home: Chicago, Ill. Died 1905.

MERRILL, William Bradford, newspaper man; b. Salisbury, N.H., Feb. 27, 1861; s. Rev. Horatio and Sarah B. (Whitman) M.; ed. Boston Latin Sch., 1874-76; finished edn., in Paris, France, 1876-78; studied art in Paris short time; m. Sara Louise Taylor, Sept. 12, 1882 (died 1913); children—Bradford (dec.), Elizabeth (dec.), Dorothy Susan (Mrs. Aaron Davis); m. 2d, Josephine H. Bissell, 1922. Began as reporter Philadelphia North American, 1879; staff corr., 1879, telegraph editor, 1880, dramatic and Sunday editor, 1881-85, mng. editor, Philadelphia Press, 1886-91; mng. editor New York Press, 1891-95; mng. editor, 1896-1901, financial mgr., 1901-07, New York World; mgr. New York American, 1908-17; gen. mgr. Hearst newspapers, Sept. 1917—. Home: Manhasset, L.I. Died Nov. 26, 1928.

MERRILL, William Fessenden, civil engr.; b. Montague, Mass., June 14, 1842; s. James H. and Lucia (Griswold) M.; bro. of James Griswold M.; A.B., Amherst, 1863; student Lawrence Scientific Sch. (Harvard), 1865-66; m. Eliza G. Fessenden, Oct. 17, 1872. Civ. engr. on C.B.&Q. R.R., 1866-73; resident engr. Erie Ry. at Buffalo, N.Y., 1873-75; asst. engr. and supt. Toledo, Peoria & Western Ry., 1875-80; gen. supt. Chicago and Ia. div. Wabash R.R., 1880-82; gen. supt. C.&A. R.R., 1882-83; supt. Iowa lines C.,B.&Q. R.R., 1883-87; gen. mgr. Hannibal & St. Joseph, and Kansas City, St. Joseph & Council Bluffs R.R., 1887-90; gen. mgr. C.,B.&Q. R.R., 1890-96; 2d v.p. Erie R.R., 1896-1900; 1st v.p. N.Y.,N.H.&H. R.R., 1900-03; cons. engr., 1903—. Home: Plainfield, N.J. Died Feb. 3, 1922.

MERRILL, William Fessenden, pres. Remington Rand, Inc.; b. Davenport, Ia., Mar. 19, 1877; s. James Griswold and Louise Wilder (Boutwell) M.; prep. edn., Phillips Acad., Andover, Mass.; A.B., Amherst Coll., 1899; m. Edith Blackburn Sheraton, 1904; 1 son, Frederick Thayer. With Library Bur., successively works mgr., mdse. mgr., gen. mgr. east div., dir., 1899-1913; pres. Mfrs. Equipment Co., Ames Plow Co. and Framingham Machine Works, 1914-16; pres., gen. mgr. and mem. exec. com. The Lamson Co., 1916-27; pres. Am. Pneumatic Service, 1923-27; pres., gen. mgr. and mem. exec. com. Remington Rand, Inc., 1928—; pres., dir., mem. exec. com. Remington Rand Business Service, Remington Typewriter Co.; pres. and dir. Remington Rand Internat., Ltd., Am. Writing Machine Co.; vice pres. Dalton Adding Machine Co., Remington Accounting Machine Corp. Republican. Conglist. Home: New York, N.Y. Died Oct. 7, 1933.

MERRILL, William Henry, editor (in charge editorial page) New York World under Joseph Pulitzer, 1888—; b. New York, 1840; editor Western New Yorker, 1861-75; mem. State Constitutional Conv., 1867; editor Golden Rule, Boston, 1875-80; leading editorial writer Boston Herald, 1880-86; m. Flora A. Judd, 1863 (died 1880); m. 2d, Julia M. Briggs, 1883. Home: New York, N.Y. Died 1907.

MERRIMAN, Daniel, clergyman; b. Manchester, Vt., Dec. 3, 1838; s. Addison and Prudence (Adams) M.; A.B., Williams, 1863; 1st lt. and adj. 132d Ill. Inf., 1864; grad. Andover Theol. Sem., 1868; (D.D., Ripon, 1881, Williams, 1881, Yale, 1898); m. Helen Bigelow, Sept. 1, 1874. Ordained Congl. ministry, 1868; pastor Broadway Ch., Norwich, Conn., 1868-75, Central Ch., Worcester, Mass., 1878-1901, emeritus pastor, 1901. Trustee Williams Coll.; pres. and trustee Worcester Art Mus., Memorial Hosp., Abbot Acad. Republican. Died Sept. 1912.

MERRIMAN, Mansfield, civil engr.; b. Southington, Conn., Mar. 27, 1848; s. Mansfield and Lucy (Hall) M.; Ph.B., Sheffield Scientific Sch. (Yale), 1871, C.E., 1872, Ph.D., 1876; Sc.D., U. of Pa., 1906; LL.D., Lehigh U., 1913. Asst. engr. U.S. Engr. Corps, 1872-73; instr. civ. engring., Sheffield Scientific Sch., 1875-78; asst. on U.S. Coast and Geod. Survey, 1880-85; prof. civ. engring., Lehigh U., 1878-1907; cons. civ. and hydraulic engr., 1907—. Author: Mechanics of Materials, 1885; Treatise on Hydraulics, 1889; Roofs and Bridges (with H. S. Jacoby), 1890; Higher Mathematics (with R. S. Woodwarth), 1896; Strength of Materials, 1897; Precise Surveying and Geodesy, 1899; Elements of Sanitary Engineering, 1906. Asso. editor Appleton's Universal Cyclopedia, 1895; editor in chief American Civil Engineers' Pocket Book, 1911. Home: New York, N.Y. Died June 7, 1925.

MERRIMAN, Myra Hunt Kingman; b. Tremont, Ill., Nov. 2, 1873; d. Lysander Philip and Susan Wilde Pettes (Hunt) Kingman; ed. Miss Fenner's Sch. (Tremont, Ill.), Ill. State Normal School; also studied journalism, civics and philanthropy; m. George Alonzo Miller, June 26, 1895 (died 1916); m. 2d, Dr. Josiah C. Merriman, Aug. 6, 1921. Was mem. staff Peoria (Ill.) Transcript, Chicago Chronicle; traveling corr. in South and Central America, for Chicago Record; settled in Calif., 1894; mem. staff Long Beach (Calif.) Tribune, later staff of Telegram; editor Sierra Magazine, 1908. Pres. College Women's Club, of Long Beach, Calif., 1912-15; del. to biennial Nat. Fedn. of Coll. Women, San Francisco, 1915 (v.p. 1916, and pres., 1917-18-19); apptd. by Sec. Labor Wilson mem. bd. dirs. Bur. of Registration for Woman's Service, 1917; mem. advisory com. Woman's Liberty Loan Com., advisory com. Woman's Com. Nat. Council of Defense; etc. Mem. nat. com. D.A.R. On editorial and lecture staffs Community Motion Picture Bur., N.Y.; chmn. Foreign Film Reconstruction Unit, 1919; exec. sec. Nat. Fedn. Better Film Workers; sec. Nat. Council of Women of U.S.A., 1920-21; del. Internat. Council of Women, 1921. Home: New York, N.Y. Died June 28, 1922.

MERRIMAN, Thaddeus, civil engr.; b. New Haven, Conn., Apr. 6, 1876; s. Mansfield and Wanda (Kubale) M.; C.E., Lehigh U., 1897; hon. Dr. Engring., same university, 1930; m. Margaret Mather, Jan. 12, 1904; children—Margaret Mather, Mansfield. Began as asst. engr. New Britain (Conn.) Water Works, 1897; on surveys U.S. Nicaragua Canal Commn., 1897-99; chief of survey party, U.S. Isthmian Canal Commn., 1899-1900; with N.Y. Continental Jewell Filtration Co. on design Little Falls, N.J., water filtration plant, 1900-01; insp. in U.S. for Guayaquil & Quito Ry. Co., 1901-02; with Jersey City Water Supply Co. as asst. engr. constrn. Boonton Dam, later div. engr. E. Jersey, Passaic & Acquackanonk Water cos., 1902-05; with Bd. of Water Supply City of New York, surveys, plans, designs and constrn. Catskill Water Supply System, from 1905, successively asst. engr., asst. to chief engr., dept. engr., deputy chief engr., and, June 1922-Nov. 1933, chief engr. same, continuing with plans for new project for supply from Delaware River, this plan was approved by U.S. Supreme Ct. in 1913; in private practice as cons. engr., 1933-36; now cons. engr. Bd. of Water Supply on construction Delaware River Aqueduct for N.Y. City. Lecturer on hydraulics and water supply, Lehigh U. Consulting engr. to War Dept. on Ft. Peck project in Mont. and on flood control project in Los Angeles and Orange Counties, Calif.; cons. engr. to Tenn. Valley Authority. Editor in chief Am. Civil Engrs. Handbook. Home: New York, N.Y. Died Sept. 26, 1939.

MERRITT, Edwin Atkins; b. Sudbury, Vt., Feb. 26, 1828; removed to St. Lawrence Co., N.Y., 1841; became surveyor-engr.; held successively several local offices; elected to legislature, 1859; reëlected, 1860; at beginning of war was q.m. of 60th N.Y. Regt.; served with Army of Potomac and Sherman's Ga. campaign; apptd. capt. and commissary of subsistence, U.S. vols.; q.m.-gen. of N.Y., 1865-69; also supt. Soldiers' Home in N.Y. City; established free agencies for collections of bounties, back pay and pensions that were due N.Y. soldiers; del. Constl. convs., 1867, 1868; naval officer, port of New York, 1869-70; unsuccessful candidate state treasurer, 1875; surveyor port of New York, 1877; collector, same, 1878-82; U.S. consul-gen., London, 1881-85. Pres. bd. trustees St. Lawrence U., local bd. Potsdam State Normal and Training Sch.; mem. bd. trustees Thomas I. Clarkson Memorial Sch. Home: Potsdam, N.Y. Died Dec. 26, 1916.

MERRITT, Frank, civil engineer; b. Scituate, Mass., June 11, 1856; s. C.E., Tufts Coll., 1879, M.Sc., 1929, from same college. Began, 1881, as axman on location Atchison, Topeka & Santa Fe RR., and advanced to track engr.; in city and hydraulic engring. 3 yrs.; with G.,C.&S.F. Ry. Co., successively levelman, transitman, on maintenance of way 3 yrs., construction 8 yrs., reconnaissance and location 5 yrs., resident engr., at Cleburne, Tex., until 1909, chief engr., at Galveston, Nov. 10, 1909—. Died Aug. 3, 1930.

MERRITT, Leonidas, capitalist; b. Chautauqua Co., N.Y., Feb. 20, 1844; s. Lewis Howell and Hephzibeth (Jewett) M.; ed. pub. schs. and Grand River Inst., Ashtabula Co., O.; m. Elizabeth E. Wheeler, May 8, 1873 (died 1902). Various lines of business until 1879; began prospecting for pine lands, 1879, also for ore bodies; discovered and located principal mines on Missabe Range, 1888-91; built Duluth, Missabe & Northern Ry.; discovered and opened up copper and gold mines in the West and in Mexico; an organizer and 1st pres. Lake Superior Consol. Iron Mines; owner Mountain Iron (Minn.) Bank. Served as pvt. Co. B, Brackett's Batt. of Minn. Cav., Civil War. Mem. Minn. Ho. of Rep., 1893, 94 (author of Braydon Bill, saving all mineral on school lands for benefit of Minn. schs.); commr. Pub. Utilities, Duluth, 1914-17; commr. of Finance, 1921-25. Methodist. Home: Duluth, Minn. Died May 9, 1926.

MERRITT, (Edward) Percival, author; b. Boston, Mass., Mar. 28, 1860; s. George Washington and Almira (Curtis) M.; A.B., Harvard, 1882; m. Elisabeth Birdseye, Oct. 6, 1886. Began as pvt. banker, Boston, 1882; with Blake Bros. & Co., 1882-86; partner Adams, Blodget & Co., 1886-92; mem. Blodget, Merritt & Co., 1893-1910 (retired). Mem. visiting com. dept. of English, Harvard, Boston Pub. Library. Episcopalian. Author: An Account of Strawberry Hill Catalogues, 1915; The Parochial Library of the 18th Century in Christ Church, Boston, 1917; Piozzi Marginalia, 1925; True Story of the So-Called Love Letters of Mrs. Piozzi, 1927. Home: Boston, Mass. Died Apr. 16, 1932.

MERRITT, Robert Clarence, lawyer; b. McKinney, Tex.; s. William Washington and Virginia (Compton) M.; Agrl. and Mech. Coll. of Tex., 1891-93; m. Leslie Pearson. Admitted to Tex. bar, 1895; began practice with Judge H. M. Garnett as Garnett & Merritt, firm later Garnett, Smith & Merritt; county atty., Collin Co., Tex., 1902-06; chmn. Dem. Exec. Com., Collin Co., 6 yrs.; del. Dem. Nat. Conv., 1912, 20; U.S. dist. atty. for Eastern Dist. of Tex., July 1, 1914; reappointed July 1, 1918; resigned Mar. 1, 1920, to enter private practice; mem. Merritt, Leddy & Harty, Dallas, Tex., 1920—. Mem. Christian (Disciples) Ch. Mason, Odd Fellow, Elk. Home: Dallas, and McKinney, Tex. Died Apr. 28, 1927.

MERRITT, Wesley, army officer; b. New York, June 16, 1836; s. John W. and Julia Anne M.; grad. U.S. Mil. Acad., assigned to dragoons; promoted to 1st lt., May 13, 1861; capt., Apr. 5, 1862; promoted for bravery to bvt. maj. gen. U.S.A., Mar. 13, 1865, and rank of lt. col., July 28, 1866; commd. brig. gen. vols., June 29, 1863; maj. gen. vols. Apr. 1, 1865. Since war regularly promoted from lt. col. to maj. gen. U.S.A. Served in Army of the Potomac until June 1864; participated in all its battles and earned 6 successive bvt. promotions for gallantry at Gettysburg, Yellow Tavern, Hawes' shop, Five Forks, etc. Afterward accompanied Gen. Sheridan on cavalry raid toward Charlottesville, and engaged in battle of Trevilian's Sta.; comd. cav. div. in Shenandoah campaign, Aug. 1864 to Mar. 1865; was engaged in battles of Winchester, Fisher's Hill, etc.; comd. corps of cav. in Appomattox campaign; one of three comdrs. from Nat. Army to arrange with Confederate comdrs. for surrender of Army of Northern Va. After war served in various depts., participated in several Indian campaigns; supt. U.S. Mil. Acad., 1882-87; comd. Dept. of the Atlantic until assigned, May 1898, to command of U.S. forces in the P.I., continuing there until summoned to the aid of the Am. Peace Commrs. in session in Paris, Dec. 1898; returned to U.S.; on duty in command of Dept. of the East, Governor's Island, until retirement, June 16, 1900. Died 1910.

MERRY, John Fairfield, rear admiral U.S.N.; b. Edgecomb, Me., Mar. 5, 1940; s. John and Sarah A. M.; ed. pub. schs., Edgecomb; m. Nancy J. Winslow, Aug. 11, 1862. Entered navy, Oct. 15, 1862, and served through the Civil War; served also in the Spanish-Am. War; has served in all the foreign and home stas., in the grades of ensign, lt., lt. comdr., comdr., capt. and rear admiral; last duty comdt. U.S. Naval Sta., Honolulu, H.I.; retired at age limit, Mar. 5, 1902. Chmn. Mass. Nautical Sch. Bd., 1911-13. Home: Somerville, Mass. Died May 30, 1916.

MERRY, William Lawrence, diplomat; b. New York, Dec. 27, 1842; s. Thomas Henry and Candida Isbina (Xavier) M.; acad. edn.; m. Blanche, d. William S. Hill, of Scarsdale, N.Y. (now widower). Went to sea; became comdr. of steamships on Atlantic and Pacific oceans in Calif. trade under Am. flag.; resigned from Pacific Mail Steamship Co., 1874, at San Francisco, and established residence there. Was 3 yrs. gen. agt. Central Am. Transit Co., and N. Am. Steamship Co., on the Nicaraguan Isthmus; 1 yr. agt. U.S. Mail Steamship Co. on the Panama Isthmus. Pres. North Am. Navigation Co. on Pacific coast; 2 terms pres. San Francisco Chamber of Commerce, and several yrs. trustee; consul-gen. for Nicaragua on Pacific Coast of U.S.; E.E. and M.P. to Nicaragua, San Salvador and Costa Rica, 1897-1907, to Nicaragua and Costa Rica, 1907-08, to Costa Rica, 1908—. Active and influential supporter of Nicaragua Canal project, of increased naval force, and of maritime development of Pacific coast ports. Author: The Nicaragua Canal the Gateway Between the Oceans; The Problem of Cheap Transportation. Home: San Francisco, Calif. Died 1911.

MERRYMAN, Andrew Curtis, lumberman; b. Bowdoin, Me., Dec. 22, 1831; learned ship carpenters' trade and became shipbuilder at Middle Bay, nr. Portland, Me. Went to Fond du Lac, Wis., 1855, and established saw mill; helped organize, 1866, what is now the Hamilton & Merriman Co., with large mills at mouth of Menominee River; also has interests in Chicago banks, paper mills, flouring mills, etc. Prominent Prohibitionist; has been Prohibition candidate for gov. of Wisconsin. Home: Marinette, Wis. Died 1909.

MERRYWEATHER, George Edmund, mechanical engr.; b. Avondale, Cincinnati, O., Aug. 28, 1872; s. George Neave and Ellen Lusanna (Beaman) M.; B.Sc., Mass. Inst. Tech., 1896; m. Laura Esselborn, Dec. 21, 1908; children—Janet, George Esselborn, Constance, Hubert Orr, Laura. Machine tool merchant, Cleveland, O., from 1904; was pres. The Motch & Merryweather Machinery Co.; dir. Central Nat. Bank. Chief of machine tool sect. War Industries Bd., 1917-19. Home: Gates Mills, O. Died June 8, 1930.

MERSELES, Theodore Frelinghuysen, pres. Johns-Manville Corp.; b. Jersey City, N.J., Aug. 17, 1863; s. Theodore Frelinghuysen and Charlotte (Thompson) M.; ed. pub. and pvt. schs.; m. Elizabeth Rich, Oct. 24, 1888; children—Herbert E., Henry R. (dec.), Theodore I. Clk. Pa. R.R. Co., Jersey City, and Trunk Line Assn., N.Y. City, 1881-93; mgr. and v.p. Western Wheel Works, bicycle mfrs., Chicago, 1893-99; with Col. Albert A. Pope and A. G. Spalding, assisted in organizing Am. Bicycle Co. of New York and was its v.p., 1899-1903; v.p. and gen. mgr. Nat. Cloak & Suit Co., mail order house, N.Y. City, 1903-21; pres. Montgomery Ward & Co., Chicago, 1921-27 (now chmn. exec. com.); pres. Johns-Manville Corp., Canadian Realty Corp.; trustee Mutual Life Ins. Co. (New York). Republican. Conglist. Home: Bronxville, N.Y. Died Mar. 6, 1929.

MERTZ, Albert, naval officer; b. Dodge Co., Wis., Mar. 26, 1851; s. Leonard and Katinka M.; ed. high sch., Beaver Dam, Wis.; grad. U.S. Naval Acad., 1872; m. Mary E. Germain, July 11, 1878. Promoted through grades to rear adm., Oct. 20, 1910; retired Mar. 26, 1913. Served on monitor Amphitrite in Cuban campaign, 1898, and in supply ship Glacier, Philippine campaign; commanded 6 lighthouse vessels, Dept. Commerce and Labor, in voyage from New York to San Francisco via Straits of Magellan, the voyage being consummated in 124 days—Sept. 21, 1908-Jan. 24, 1909; highly commended by Dept. Commerce and Labor and Lighthouse Bd., Washington; comdg. U.S. naval stas. at Cavite and Olongapo, P.I., Nov. 1, 1909 to Feb. 4, 1912; gov. Sailors' Home, Phila., Mar. 25, 1912 to May 20, 1913. Medals for service in Cuban and Philippine campaigns, Spanish-Am. War. Home: Bonita, Calif. Died July 21, 1936.

MERWIN, Henry Childs, lawyer; b. Pittsfield, Mass., Aug. 5, 1853; s. Elias M.; A.B., Harvard, 1874; m. Anne Amory Andrews, Apr. 22, 1884. Formerly lecturer Boston U. Law Sch. and Lowell Inst. Pres. Boston Work Horse Relief Assn.; sec. Pine Tree Humane Soc.; dir. Red Acre Farm (home for horses); dir. Animal Rescue League. Author: Patentability of Inventions, 1884; Road, Track and Stable, 1893; Life of Aaron Burr, 1899; Life of Thomas Jefferson, 1901; Dogs and Men, 1910; Life of Bret Harte, 1911; The Horse, 1916. Editor: Merwin's Equity, Curtis' Jurisprudence of Federal Courts. Home: Boston, Mass. Died Jan. 21, 1929.

MERWIN, Milton Hervey, judge; b. Leyden, N.Y., June 16, 1832; s. Alanson and Amanda (Kimball) M.; A.B., Hamilton Coll., 1852 (LL.D., 1878); m. Helen E. Knapp, Nov. 1858. Admitted to bar, July 1853; surrogate, Jefferson Co., N.Y., 1860-64; mem. N.Y. Constl. Conv., 1867-68; justice Supreme Ct. of N.Y., 1874-1903; assigned to gen. term, 1888-95; Appellate Div., 1895-1900. Republican. Home: Utica, N.Y. Died Oct. 16, 1916.

MERWIN, Samuel, author; b. Evanston, Ill., Oct. 6, 1874; s. Orlando H. and Ellen (Bannister) M.; ed. Northwestern University; m. Edna Earl Fleshiem, June 25, 1901; children—Bannister (dec.), Samuel Kimball, John (adopted, dec.). Author: The Short Line War (with Henry Kitchell Webster), 1899; Calumet K (with same), 1901; The Road to Frontenac, 1901; The Whip Hand, 1903; His Little World, 1903; The Merry Anne, 1904; The Road Builders, 1905; Comrade John (with same), 1907; Drugging a Nation, 1908; The Citadel, 1912; The Charmed Life of Miss Austin, 1914; Anthony the Absolute, 1914; The Honey Bee, 1915; The Trufflers, 1916; Temperamental Henry, 1917; Henry Is Twenty, 1918; The Passionate Pilgrim, 1919; Hills of Han, 1920; In Red and Gold, 1921; Goldie Green, 1922; Old Concord—Seen Through Western Spectacles, 1922; Silk, 1923; Moment of Beauty, 1924; Entertaining Angel, 1926; Anabel at Sea, 1927; Lady Can Do, 1929; Bad Penny, 1933. Associate editor Success magazine, 1905-09, editor, 1909-11. Traveled in China, Jan.-July 1907, to study the opium question. Died Oct. 17, 1936.

MERWIN, Samuel Edwin, pres. Yale Nat. Bank; pres. New Haven Savings Bank; b. Brookfield, Conn., Aug. 23, 1831; s. Samuel Edwin M.; academic edn.; m. Lucy Emily Beers, 1854. State senator, 1876; adj. gen. Conn., 3 yrs.; lt. gov. Conn., 1890-94. Home: New Haven, Conn. Died 1907.

MESERVE, Charles Francis, educator; b. North Abington, Mass., July 15, 1850; s. Charles and Susanna (Blanchard) M.; A.B., Colby Univ., 1877, A.M., 1880 (LL.D., 1899); m. Abbie Mary Whittier, Nov. 19, 1878; children—Alice Whittier, Meserve; m. 2d, Julia Frances Philbrick, May 16, 1900. Prin. high sch., Rockland, Mass., 1877-85, Oak St. Sch., Springfield, Mass., 1885-89; supt. Haskell Inst., U.S. Indian industrial training sch., Lawrence, Kan., 1889-94; pres. Shaw U., 1894-1920, pres. emeritus, 1920—, also trustee. Frequently gives public addresses on the Negro and Indian problems. In 1896, as agt. Nat. Indian Rights Assn. of Phila., facilitated the work of the Dawes Commn. in Indian Ty. by a personal investigation and a favorable report. Elected pres. Me. Meserve Family Assn., 1922, reëlected for life, 1920. Baptist. Republican. Died April 20, 1936.

MESERVE, Harry Chamberlain, sec. Nat. Assn. Cotton Mfrs.; b. Quincy, Ill., July 12, 1868; s. Harry and Nancy Lucenia (Chamberlain) M.; grad. Lowell (Mass.) High Sch., 1886; B.D., Yale, 1894; post-grad. study, Yale, 1895; m. Bertha Francis Murkland, May 23, 1894. Ordained Congl. ministry, 1894; pastor Faith Ch., Springfield, Mass., 1893-1900, Plymouth Ch., Indianapolis, 1900-03, First Ch., Danbury, Conn., 1903-14, Rye, N.Y., 1914-17. Captain, chaplain 68th Coast Arty., A.E.F., 1917-19; maj. M.I.O.R.C. Lecturer Nat. Industrial Conf. Bd., 1920-21; sec. Nat. Assn. Cotton Mfrs., 1921—. Mem. Loyal Legion. Republican. Mason. Home: Brookline, Mass. Deceased.

MESSENGER, North Overton, newspaperman; b. Tuscumbia, Ala., May 12, 1865; s. North Allan and Lillian Teresa (Rozell) M.; ed. pub. schs., Washington, D.C.; hon. A.M., George Washington Univ., 1921; m. Eudora Alden Goldsborough, June 22, 1892 (died 1917). Has been Washington correspondent for various newspapers, 1885—; now representative of Washington Evening Star; writer on polit., financial, Congressional and nat. affairs. Republican. Episcopalian. Home: Washington, D.C. Died June 1925.

MESSER, Alpha, farmer, editor; b. Rochester, Vt., 1842; s. Lyman and Mary (Morse) M.; academic edn. at Barre, Vt.; taught school, 1860-71; since then engaged in general farming; m. Lizzie P. Bond, 1871. Became master Vt. State Grange, Patrons of Husbandry, 1886-95; lecturer Nat. Grange, 1893-99. Began publication of The Patron's Rural, 1882, merged into Rural Vermonter, 1886, and that in turn consolidated with Vermont Watchman, 1888. Been mem. of editorial staff New England Farmer and Grange Homes, 1889—; mem. Vt. State Bd. of Agr. and Cattle Commn., 1896-98. Home: Rochester, Vt. Died 1902.

MESSER, Edmund Clarence, artist; b. Skowhegan, Me., Feb. 18, 1842, s. Benjamin Edmund and Mary Burt (Holt) M.; ed. studio of Peter Baumgras, Washington, 1863; Acad. of Design, Cooper Inst. and Cummings Acad., New York, 1864-65; Phila. Acad. Art, 1865-66; Acad. of Design, Chicago, 1870; Colorossi and Rollin studios, Paris, under Collin, Courtois and Aime Morot, Paris; m. Emma B. North, Sept. 16, 1880. Mem. 1st Minn. Inf., 3 mos., 1861. Prin. Sch. of Washington Art Club, 1879-85; instr. Students' Art League, most of time, 1886-1901; prin. Corcoran School of Art, 1892—. Christian Scientist. Home: Washington, D.C. Died Feb. 9, 1919.

MESSER, L(oring) Wilbur, general sec. Y.M.C.A. of Chicago; b. Somersworth, N.H., Mar. 1, 1856; s. Charles and Emily A. (Leathers) M.; pub. sch. edn.; (A.M., Northwestern U., 1908; H.M., Internat. Y.M.C.A. Coll., Springfield, 1909); m. Elizabeth I. Garcelon, Sept. 14, 1887. With B.&M. R.R., Boston, 1872-74; in dry goods business with Copeland & Bowser, Reading, Mass., 1874-81; gen. sec. Y.M.C.A., Peoria, Ill., 1881-83, Cambridge, Mass., 1883-88, Chicago, Apr. 1888—. Mem. State exec. com. Y.M.C.A.; trustee and instr. Y.M.C.A. College, Chicago; trustee Internat. Y.M.C.A. Coll., Springfield, Mass.; mem. exec. com. Nat. War Work Council of Y.M.C.A.'s Republican. Methodist. Address: Chicago, Ill. Died July 15, 1923.

MESSINGER, Charles Raymond, farm equipment; b. New Haven, Conn., Oct. 27, 1883; s. Charles Frederick and Helen (Beecher) M.; prep. edn., Dwight Sch. and Boardman High Sch., New Haven; Ph.B., Sheffield Scientific Sch. (Yale), 1906; m. Mildred Hart, Apr. 25, 1911; children—John Beecher, William Clifford, Grant Hart, Jane Hart. Salesman, Harbison-Walker Refractories Co., 1906-09; v.p. and gen. mgr. Sivyer Steel Casting Co., 1909-28, pres., 1928-29, chmn. bd., 1929—; v.p. and gen. mgr. Chain Belt Co., 1917-23, pres. and gen. mgr., 1923-31, chmn. bd. Chain Belt Co., 1931-34; pres. Oliver Farm Equipment Co., 1931-34, chmn. bd., 1934—; pres. Chain Belt Co. Asst. chief of Ordnance, Chicago District. Dir. Milwaukee Co. Community Fund; dir. Columbia Hosp. Trustee Milwaukee Art Inst.; dir. Milwaukee Country Day Sch.; mem. exec. com. Yale Alumni Bd.; mem. and v.p. Yale Engring. Assn. Republican. Episcopalian. Home: Milwaukee, Wis. Died Feb. 4, 1941.

MESSITER, Arthur Henry, organist; b. Frome, Somersetshire, Eng., Apr. 1834; s. George and Marian M.; ed. at pvt. classical sch. in Eng.; studied music, 1850-55; (hon. Mus. Doc. St. Stephen's Coll., Annandale, N.Y.); m. Margaret, d. Jacob Bergen Gaddis, of Jersey City, N.J., Oct. 1871. Organist and choirmaster of Trinity Ch., New York, 1866-97; retired. Author: History of the Choir and Music of Trinity Church, New York, 1907. Home: New York, N.Y. Died July 2, 1916.

MESSMER, Sebastian Gebhard, archbishop; b. Goldach, Switzerland, Aug. 29, 1847; s. Sebastian Gebhard and Rosa (Baumgartner) M.; ed. St. George Coll., St. Gall, Switzerland, 1861-66; U. of Innsbruck, Austria, 1866-71; D.D., from Pope Leo XIII, 1885; D.C.L., Appollinare U., Rome, 1890. Ordained R.C. priest, July 23, 1871; prof. theology, Seton Hall Coll., S. Orange, N.J., 1871-89; prof. canon law, Catholic U. Washington, 1890-92; consecrated bishop of Green Bay, Wis., Mar. 27, 1892; apptd. archbishop of Milwaukee, Dec. 10, 1903. Author: Praxis Synodalis, 1883; Canonical Procedure, 1886; Spirago's Method, 1901; Outlines of Bible Knowledge, 1910. Editor: Devivier's Christian Apologetics, 1903; Bishop England's Works (7 vols.), 1908. Died Aug. 4, 1930.

MESTREZAT, Stephen Leslie, judge; b. Mapletown, Pa., Feb. 19, 1848; s. Jean Louis Guillaume and Mary Ann (Hartley) M.; A.B., Waynesburg College, 1869, A.M., 1873; LL.B., Washington and Lee U., 1871; (LL.D., Waynesburg, 1901, Washington and Jefferson, 1913); m. Eliza Willson Ewing, Aug. 1, 1888. Dist. atty. Fayette Co., Pa., 1878-81; judge 14th Jud. Dist., 1894-99; justice Supreme Ct. of Pa., 1900-21. Counsel for Connellsville Coke & Iron Co., H. C. Frick Coke Co., B.&O. R.R. Co., and other corps. prior to elevation to bench. Democrat. Presbyn. Trustee Waynesburg Coll. Homes: Uniontown, Pa., and Philadelphia, Pa. Died Apr. 29, 1918.

METCALF, Frank Arthur, educator, pub.; b. Acworth, N.H., Dec. 14, 1873; s. Frank M. and Jennie E. (Mitchell) M.; grad. Kimball Union Acad., 1896; A.B., Dartmouth, 1900; m. Jennie Louise Bryant, Aug. 7, 1901. Registrar The Home Correspondence Sch., Springfield, Mass., 1900-04, pres. and mng. dir., 1904-35; founder and mng. editor The Writer's Monthly. Democrat. Has organized many courses of study and planned and projected many successful publs., including The Writer's Library. Home: Springfield, Mass. Died Apr. 23, 1939.

METCALF, Henry Brewer, mfr.; b. Boston, Apr. 2, 1829; ed. Boston public schools; m. May 4, 1854, Elizabeth Freeman (died 1902). Apprentice, 1844, in wholesale dry goods business, in which he continued in Boston until 1872, then engaged in mfr. in Mass. and R.I.; treas. of several mfg. corporations and of Providence Co. Savings Bank. Prominent in Universalist Ch.; over forty yrs. Sunday School supt.; many yrs. trustee and from 1898 pres. corporation of Tufts Coll.; mem. of R.I. senate, Republican, 1885-86; now Prohibitionist. Prohibition candidate for v.p. of U.S., 1900. Home: Pawtucket, R.I. Died 1904.

METCALF, Henry Harrison, editor, pub.; b. Newport, N.H., Apr. 7, 1841; s. Joseph P. and Lucy (Gould) M.; Mt. Caesar Sem., Swanzey, N.H.; LL.B., U. of Mich., 1865; studied law with Hon. Edmund Burke, Newport, N.H.; hon. A.M., Dartmouth, 1913; m. Mary Jane Jackson, Dec. 18, 1869; children—Harry Bingham, Edmund Burke, Laura Prucia (Mrs. Harlan C. Pearson). Admitted to bar, 1866; editor White Mountain Republic, Littleton, 1867-68, The People, Concord, 1868-72; purchased White Mountain Republic and conducted it, 1872-74; established the Democratic Press, Dover, N.H., editing same, 1874-79; editor Manchester Daily Union, 1879-82, Concord People and Patriot, 1882-92; founded the Granite Monthly at Dover, 1877, later moved it to Concord and published same until 1919. Del. to every Dem. State Conv. of N.H., 1867— (pres. 1900); sec. Dem. State Com., 1869-70; candidate for Congress, 1910; del. N.H. Constl. Conv., 1919-23. State historian of N.H., 1913—. Lecturer, N.H. State Grange, 1897-1903. V.p. N.H. Universalist State Conv., 1906-15 (trustee 1918-24; elected life mem.). Secretary Concord Board of Trade, 1892-1901, 02, 13, N.H. Bd. Trade, 1907-16. Pres. N.H. Old Home Week Assn., 1914-29; sec. N.H. Sunday Law Com., 1920-21, N.H. Ter-Centenary Com., 1921-23, Sesqui-Centennial Com., 1925-26. Editor: New Hampshire Women, 1895; New Hampshire Agriculture, 1897; Harry Bingham Memorial, 1910; One Thousand New Hampshire Notables, 1919; New Hampshire in History, 1922; Sullivan County Recollections, 1926; New Hampshire Democrat, 1924; Granite Monthly, 1927. Home: Concord, N.H. Died Feb. 4, 1932.

METCALF, Irving Wight, businessman; b. Bangor, Me., Nov. 27, 1855; s. Eliab Wight and Eliza Maria (Ely) M.; A.B., Oberlin Coll., 1878; student Andover Theol. Sem., 1879-80; B.D., Oberlin Theol. Sem., 1881; m. Flora Belle Mussey, May 20, 1885; children—Edith Eastwood, Harold Mussey. Ordained Congl. ministry, Jan. 31, 1882; pastor Eastwood Ch., Columbus, O., 1881-89, Hough Av. Ch., Cleveland, 1889-94; asso. pastor Pilgrim Ch., Cleveland, 1894-97; in business at Lawrence, Kan., 1897-99; Elyria, O., 1899-1902, and at Oberlin, 1902—. Sec. Congregational City Missionary Soc., Cleveland, 1892-97, and Ohio Congl. Bd. Ministerial Relief; moderator Congl. Assn. Ohio, 1902; chmn. ch. property com. Nat. Council Congl. Chs., 1898-1913; trustee Oberlin College, 1900-26; also trustee Thessalonica Agrl. and Industrial Inst., Salonica, Greece, 1904—; corporate mem. A.B.C.F.M., 1904—. Home: Oberlin, O. Died Feb. 12, 1938.

METCALF, Joel Hastings, astronomer; b. Meadville, Pa., Jan. 4, 1866; s. Lewis Herbert and Anna (Hicks) M.; grad. Meadville Theol. Sch., 1890; student, Harvard Div. Sch., 1890; Ph.D., Allegheny (Pa.) Coll., 1892; Manchester Coll. (U. of Oxford), 1903; D.D., Meadville Theol. School, 1920; m. Elizabeth S. Lochman, Sept. 22, 1891. Ordained Unitarian ministry, 1890; minister, Burlington, Vt., 1893-1903, First Congl. Ch., Taunton, Mass., 1904-10, Unitarian Ch., Winchester, Mass., 1910-20, First Parish of Portland, Me., 1920—. Interested in astronomy and has discovered about 41 minor planets, several variable stars and 6 comets (2 periodic). Has made several telescopes as a recreation, his last one the largest at Harvard Obs. (16 in. double). Chmn. visiting com. Harvard Obs.; mem. visiting com. Ladd Obs. Awarded 5 medals, Astron. Soc. of the Pacific, and gold medal, Astron. Soc. Mexico. Author: World Stories, 1909. Y.M.C.A. overseas sec., 1918-19, with 3d Div., 7th Inf.; divisional citation for work at Chateau Thierry. Home: Portland, Me. Died Feb. 21, 1925.

METCALF, Leonard, civil engr.; b. Galveston, Aug. 26, 1870; s. Joseph Houghton and Emma Augusta (Leonard) M.; B.S. in C.E., Mass. Inst. Tech., 1892; unmarried. Consulting engr., Boston, 1897; mem. firm of Metcalf & Eddy. Mem. Corp. M.I.T. Trustee Concord Free Pub. Library. Unitarian. Mem. various societies. Past chmn. Council of Affiliated Tech. Socs. of Boston. Home: Concord, Mass. Died Jan. 29, 1926.

METCALF, Lorettus Sutton, editor; b. Monmouth, Me., Oct. 17, 1837; s. Mason Jerome and Hannah Elizabeth (Welch) M.; ed. in Monmouth and Boston pub. schs.; (A.M., Bates Coll., 1889; LL.D., Ia. Coll., 1890); m. Amanda Ames Lemont, Sept. 2, 1861. Editor several weekly jours. published in combination in Mass., 1871-76; mng. editor North American Review, 1876-85; founded, 1886, and edited The Forum, 1886-91; founded, 1893, and edited Florida Daily Citizen, Jacksonville, 1893-97. Home: Los Angeles, Calif. Died Jan. 15, 1920.

METCALF, Maynard Mayo, zoölogist; b. Elyria, O., Mar. 12, 1868; s. Eliab Wight and Eliza Maria (Ely) M.; A.B., Oberlin Coll., 1889; Ph.D., Johns Hopkins, 1893; Sc.D., Oberlin, 1914; m. Ella M. Wilder, Sept. 10, 1890; children—Fern Wilder (dec.), Mildred Ella (Mrs. William P. Beetham). Asso. prof. and prof. biology, Women's Coll., Baltimore, 1893-1906; prof. zoölogy, Oberlin Coll., 1906-14 (leave of absence for zoölogical study in Germany and Naples, 1906-08); research associate and professor zoölogy, Johns Hopkins, 1925—; collaborator marine invertebrates, United States National Mus. Trustee Marine Biol. Lab., Nat. Research Council (chmn. in biology and agr., 1924-25). Mem. numerous scientific societies. Author of zoological memoirs in American and German journals, chiefly upon Protozoa, Tunicata and Mollusca and numerous papers on geog. distribution of animals since the Triassic, and of "An Outline of the Theory of Organic Evolution" also of articles upon economic theory. Home: Waban, Mass. Died Apr. 1940.

METCALF, Ralph, editor, mfr.; b. Providence, R.I., Nov. 2, 1861; s. Alfred and Rosa Clinton (Maloy) M.; A.B., U. of Mich., 1883; LL.D., College of Puget Sound, Tacoma, Wash.; m. Edith O., d. V. Simpson, of Winona, Minn., Apr. 20, 1887; 1 dau., Mrs. E. M. Fogg. Editor Winona (Minn.) Herald, 1885-89, Tacoma (Wash.) Morning Globe, 1889-94; sec. and treas. Metcalf Shingle Co., 1894-1910. Sec. Bd. Pub. Works, Tacoma, 1890-94; chmn. Rep. City Com., 1904-06; mem. Wash. State Senate, 1907-39, pres. pro tem. of Senate, 1927-29. Member Am. Rural Credit Commission to Europe, 1913; sec. Internat. Trade Commn. to Europe, 1922, 24, 25; vice chmn. and sec. Commercial Commn. to Scandinavia, 1923; vice chmn. Commercial Commission to Cuba, 1924. Episcopalian. Mason, Elk, Woodman. Wrote: Direct Primary Legislation, 1907; Rural Credits in Germany, 1914; Rural Credit, Coöperation and Agricultural Organization in Europe, 1915; also various repts. Home: Tacoma, Wash. Died Apr. 14, 1939.

METCALF, Victor Howard, secretary of the navy; b. Utica, N.Y., Oct. 10, 1853; s. William and Sarah P. M.; grad. Utica Free Acad., 1871, Russell's Mil. Acad., New Haven, Conn., 1872; entered Yale, academic, 1872; LL.B., Yale, 1876; m. Emily Corinne Nicholson, Apr. 11, 1882. Admitted to Conn. bar, 1876, N.Y. bar, 1877; practiced at Utica, N.Y., 1877-79, Oakland, Calif., 1879-1904; mem. 56th to 58th Congresses (1899-1904), 3d Calif. Dist.; resigned from 58th Congress, July 1, 1904; sec. Dept. Commerce and Labor, July 1, 1904-Dec. 16, 1906; sec. of the navy, Dec. 17, 1906-Dec. 1, 1908, in cabinets of President Roosevelt. Republican. Home: Oakland, Calif. Died Feb. 20, 1936.

METCALF, Wilder Stevens; b. Milo, Me., Sept. 10, 1855; s. Isaac Stevens and Antoinette Brigham (Putnam) M.; A.B., Oberlin, 1878; LL.B., U. of Kan. Sch. of Law, 1897; m. Mary Eliza Crosier, July 30, 1878 (died 1914); m. 2d, Alice L. Bullene, Jan. 8, 1916. With Crosier & Sheldon, mfrs. of cheese and butter, at Wellington, O., 1878-87; mem. Russell & Metcalf, Lawrence, Kan., 1887-98, alone from 1898; pres. Douglas County Building & Loan Assn.; dir. Liberty Life Ins. Co. (Topeka), Lawrence Nat. Bank; chmn. bd. Federal Home Loan Bank, Dist. 10, Topeka. U.S. pension agt., Topeka, 8½ yrs.; commissioner of pensions, Washington, D.C., Mar. 28, 1925-July 1, 1925 (resigned). Pvt. to lt. 5th Ohio N.G.; pvt. to brig. gen. Kan. N.G. (now on retired list); maj. and col. 20th Kan. Inf., U.S.V., 1898-1899; served in Philippines; bvtd. brig. gen. vols. by Pres. McKinley; mem. Nat. Militia Bd., apptd. by Sec. of War, 8 yrs. Commd. col. U.S.A., Aug. 5 1917; brig. gen., Aug. 29, 1917; Comdg. 77th Inf. Brig., Camp Beauregard, Alexandria, La.; hon. discharged on account of age, May 25, 1918. Del.-at-large Rep. Nat. Conv., Phila., 1900; mem. sch. bd., Lawrence, 17 yrs., pres., 10 yrs.; state senator, 1915-19. Conglist. Congressional medal for service in Philippines. Home: Lawrence, Kan. Died Feb. 1, 1935.

METCALF, Willard Leroy, artist; b. Lowell, Mass., July 1, 1858; s. Greenleaf Willard and Margaret Jane (Gallop) M.; ed. pub. schs., Mass.; apprenticed to wood engraver, Boston, 1875, then to George L. Brown, landscape painter, S. Boston, 1876-77; student Lowell Inst., Boston Normal Art Sch., Boston Art Mus. Sch., Academie Julien, Paris, under Boulanger and Lefebvre, 1883; m. Henriette A. McCrea, 1911. Represented in the permanent collections of Smith College, Art Mus., Boston, Cincinnati Mus., Nat. Gallery and Corcoran Gallery of Art, Washington, Pa. Acad. Fine Arts, Worcester Art Mus., Detroit Mus. Art, Art Inst. Chicago, Memorial Art Gallery, Rochester, N.Y., Hackley Gallery of Art, Muskegon, Mich., Carnegie Inst., Pittsburgh, St. Louis Mus. Fine Arts, Albright Gallery, Buffalo. Honorary mention, Paris Salon, 1888; medal, Chicago Expn., 1893; Webb prize, Society American Artists, 1896; hon. mention, Paris Expn., 1900; silver medal, Buffalo Expn., 1901; silver medal, St. Louis Expn., 1904; Temple gold medal, Pa. Acad. Fine Arts, 1907; Corcoran gold medal and first prize, Corcoran Art Gallery, Washington, 1907; Harris silver medal and prize, Chicago Art Inst., 1910; gold medal, Internat. Expn., Buenos Aires, 1910; gold medal of honor, Pa. Acad. Fine Arts, 1911; Sesnan gold medal, same, 1912; gold medal of honor, Panama P.I. Expn., 1915. Home: New York, N.Y. Died Mar. 9, 1925.

METCALF, William, engr., steel mfr.; b. Pittsburgh, Sept. 3, 1838; grad. Rensselaer Polytechnic Inst., Troy, N.Y., 1858; in charge manufacture of heavy Rodman and Dahlgren guns at Fort Pitt Foundry, Pittsburgh, 1860-65; steel mfr., 1868—. Mem. and past pres. Am. Soc. Civ. Engrs., and Am. Inst. Mining Engrs. Home: Pittsburgh, Pa. Died 1909.

METCALFE, George Richmond, editor; b. Brooklyn, N.Y., Feb. 4, 1865; s. George and Elizabeth Talbot (Root) M.; student Brooklyn Poly. Inst., 1879-81; M.E., Stevens Inst. Tech., 1886; m. Grace Darling Brown, Nov. 8, 1899; children—Richmond (dec.), Winthrop, Donald, George, Grace Elizabeth. Elec. engr. with Edison United Mfg. Co., Daft Electric Co., Sprague Electric Ry. & Motor Co. and Edison Gen. Electric Co. until 1892; editor Electricity, New York, 1893-97; tech. editor Electric Ry. Review, Chicago, 1899-1904; and electrical engr. Woods Motor Vehicle Co., 1903-04; editor Technical World, 1904-05, also editor textbooks for Am. Sch. of Correspondence, Chicago; editor publ. dept. Westinghouse Electric & Mfg. Co., Pittsburgh, 1905-10; editor Am. Inst. Elec. Engrs., New York, 1910-33 (retired). Edited tech. articles in Internat. Cyclo., 1904-05, Procs. Inst. Radio Engrs., 1926-27. Democrat. Episcopalian. Home: Hewlett, N.Y. Died Feb. 7, 1938.

METCALFE, James Stetson, dramatic critic; b. Buffalo, N.Y., June 27, 1858; s. James H. and Erzelia (Stetson) M.; A.B., Yale, 1879, A.M., 1891; m. Edith Williams, Aug. 27, 1896; m. 2d, Elizabeth Tyree, July 14, 1904. Editor and pub. The Modern Age, 1883-84; editorial writer Buffalo Express; 1884-85; editor People's Pictorial Press, 1886; mgr. Am. Newspaper Publishers' Assn., 1886-89; dramatic editor of Life, 1889-1920 (lit. editor, 1890-95, art editor, 1919); mng. editor Cosmopolitan Mag., 1895; art and dramatic editor Judge, 1920-21; dramatic editor and critic Wall Street Jour., 1923. Dem. candidate for assembly, 1903. Chevalier Legion of Honor (France), 1919. Author: Mythology for Moderns, 1900; The American Slave, 1900; Another Three Weeks, 1908; The Diary of a District Messenger, 1909; Jane Street, 1921. Established Metcalfe dramatic prize, Yale U., 1915. Home: New York, N.Y. Died May 26, 1927.

METEYARD, Thomas Buford, artist; b. Rock Island, Ill., Nov. 12, 1865; s. Capt. Thomas C. and Marion (Lunt) M.; ed. pub. and pvt. schs., Chicago, 2 yrs. at Harvard; studied art in Europe; m. Isabel Montagu Barber, of London, Eng., July 9, 1910; 1 son, Robert Thomas Buford. Exhibited pictures at Paris, Salon, Chicago Expn., Soc. Am. Artists, New York, Pa. Acad., Phila., St. Louis Expn., 1904, and other exhibitions in U.S. Decorator for Songs from Vagabondia (by Bliss Carman and Richard Hovey), and numerous other books. Vol. musketry instr. (Old Boys Corps, pub. schs. and univs. men, 3d Batln. Co. of London Regt. Vols.) since early in the war. Home: Fernhurst, Sussex, England. Died Mar. 17, 1928.

METZ, Herman A., mfr.; b. N.Y. City, Oct. 19, 1867; ed. high sch. and Cooper Union Evening Sch.; hon. Sc.D., Union Coll., Schenectady, N.Y., 1911; LL.D., Manhattan Coll., 1914. Pres. H. A. Metz Co. (mfrs. dyestuffs and chemicals), H. A. Metz Laboratories, Gen. Aniline Works, Inc., Ettrick Realty Co., Consolidated Color & Chem. Co., Gen. Dyestuff Corp., Advance Solvents & Chemical Corp.; v.p. and treas. Am. I. G. Chem. Corp.; dir. Interborough Rapid Transit Co., Fulton Savings Bank, Bank of the Manhattan Co. Was comptroller City of New York, 1906-10; was mem. Bd. of Edn., Brooklyn and City of New York, and commr. State Bd. of Charities; mem. 63d Congress (1913-15), 10th N.Y. Dist. Trustee Adelphia Coll. Col. comdg. Q.M. Corps, N.G.N.Y. Democrat. Home: New York, N.Y. Died May 17, 1934.

MEYER, Adolph, congressman; b. Oct. 19, 1842; grad. Univ. of Va., 1862; served, 1862-65, in C.S.A. on staff of Gen. John S. Williams; after war engaged in culture of cotton and sugar; connected with financial and commercial interests in New Orleans. Elected col. 1st regt., La. State Nat. Guard, 1879, and in 1881 apptd. brig. gen.; mem. Congress from 1st La. dist., 1891-1909. Democrat. Home: New Orleans, La. Died 1908.

MEYER, Adolphus William, coll. pres.; b. Adelaide, South Australia, July 20, 1860; s. Christian Frederick and Emelie (Nolte) M.; came to U.S. at 16; grad. Concordia Coll., Ft. Wayne, Ind., 1882, Concordia Sem., St. Louis, 1885; D.D., St. Louis Concordia Sem., 1927; m. Dorothea Haeckel, Sept. 12, 1886; children—Agnes Magdalene (wife of Rev. Geo. Jacobsen), Arthur John, Herbert Wm., Irene Elizabeth (wife of Rev. Henry Blanke), Adolf Fred, Dorothy Adelaide, Edith Ellanora. Ordained ministry Luth. Ch., 1885; pastor successively Conway, Mo., St. Martin's Ch., Winfield, Kan., St. Andrew's Ch., Pittsburgh, Pa., until 1895; pres. St. John's Coll., Winfield, Kan., 1905-27; asst. pastor Trinity Luth. Ch., Long Island City, N.Y., 1927—. Editor Lutheran Guide 8 yrs.; pres. English Synod of Mo. 2 terms; life mem. Mo. Synod. Republican. Home: Long Island City, N.Y. Died May 26, 1937.

MEYER, Arthur John, univ. prof.; b. Milwaukee Co., Wis., June 24, 1878; s. John and Sophia (Rohr) M.; grad. short course in agr., U. of Wis., 1902; A.B., U. of Mo., 1915; m. Illma Rohr, Sept. 4, 1911; children—Donald Arthur, John Harold, Philip Howard. Teacher rural schs., Wis., 5 yrs.; asst. in agronomy, Wis. Coll. Agr., 1902-04; asso. editor Wis. Agriculturist, Racine, Wis., 1906-07; supt. short course and asst. to dean, Coll. of Agr., U. of Mo., 1911-14; dir. agrl. extension service, same univ., 1914—, also giving spl. courses in methods of extension teaching. Mem. Com. on Agr. and Food Production, Mo. Council of Defense, World War, also spl. agt. U.S. Food Administration. Methodist. Mason. Home: Columbia, Mo. Died Sept. 19, 1930.

MEYER, Christian Frederick Gottlieb, druggist; b. Halden, Prussia, Dec. 9, 1830; s. John W. M.; came to U.S. 1847; ed. in private schools of Ft. Wayne, Ind. Learned drug trade; m. Francesca Schmidt, July 1854. Went to St. Louis; established there, 1865, a wholesale drug house, now Meyer Brothers Drug Co., of which he is president. Home: St. Louis, Mo. Died 1905.

MEYER, Edward Barnard, utilities engr.; b. Newark, N.J., Oct. 22, 1882; s. John H. and Katie (Schroeder) M.; grad. Newark Tech. Sch., 1901, Pratt Inst., Brooklyn, 1903; m. Anna E. Benner, May 29, 1907; children—Grace (Mrs. Erving E. Bradley, dec.), Elizabeth (Mrs. K. Price). Engring. asst. Pub. Service Corp. of N.J., 1903-06, field engr., 1906-09, asst. engr., 1909-12, asst. to chief engr., 1912-19, asst. chief engr., 1919-22; chief engr. Pub. Service Production Co., 1922-29, v.p., 1929-30; v.p. and chief engr. United Engrs. & Constructors, Inc., 1930-35; chief engr. electric engring. dept. Pub. Service Electric & Gas Co., 1935—; pres. Willow Island Assn. Republican. Presbyn. Author: Transmission and Distribution. Home: South Orange, N.J. Died Jan. 1937.

MEYER, George Homer, author; b. San Francisco, Jan. 31, 1858; s. Lewis and Annie Eliza (Wilson) M.; student Christian Coll., Santa Rosa, Calif., 1876-77; m. Belle Menefee, June 14, 1883; children—Mrs. Isabel Annie Vinson, Edwin Marion George Harold. Began newspaper work, 1883; later on staff various papers; with San Francisco Bd. of Edn., 1914—. Author: Lamara and Other Poems, 1878; The Nine Swords of Morales, 1906. Editor San Francisco Municipal Blue Book, 1912. Home: Burlingame, Calif. Died Feb. 1926.

MEYER, George von Lengerke, sec. of the navy; b. Boston, June 24, 1858; s. George A. and Grace Helen (Parker) M.; A.B., Harvard, 1879 (LL.D., 1911); m. Alice Appleton, June 25, 1885. In business as merchant and trustee, 1879-99. Mem. Boston Common Council, 1889-90, Bd. of Aldermen, 1891; mem. Mass. Ho. of Rep., 1892-97 (speaker, 1894-97); chmn. Mass. Paris Expn. mgrs., 1898; mem. Rep. Nat. Com., 1898-1904; ambassador extraordinary and plenipotentiary to Italy, 1900-05, to Russia, 1905-07; Postmaster gen. in cabinet of President Roosevelt, Mar. 4 1907-Mar. 6, 1909; sec. of the navy in cabinet of President Taft, Mar. 6, 1909-Mar., 1913.

Overseer of Harvard U., 1911—. Home: Hamilton, Mass. Died Mar. 9, 1918.

MEYER, Herman Henry Bernard, bibliographer, librarian; b. N.Y. City, Oct. 17, 1864; s. Charles Henry Herman and Freuda Margaret Henrietta (v. Kroog) M.; E.M., Columbia, 1885; Pratt Inst., Library Sch., 1901-02; Litt.D., Howard U., 1922; m. Helen Harris Spalding, Sept. 3, 1894. Engineer Oregon Iron Works (gas light engring.), New York, 1885-97; constr. engr. Brooklyn Union Gas Co., 1897-1901; with Library of Congress from 1905 as chief of periodical div., 1905-06, chief of order div., 1906-08, chief bibliographer, 1908-23, dir. legislative reference service, July 1921—, retired Nov. 1935. Episcopalian. Compiler of many bibliographies on social, economic and political questions, 1909-21; Handbook of the Libraries of the District of Columbia, 1914; Brief Guide to the Literature of Shakespeare, 1915; The United States at War, Organizations and Literature, 1917; European War (check list), 1918; Scientific Management, 1920. Has collected a private library of over 10,000 vols. on fine printing in America, and first editions of English and Am. authors. Home: Washington, D.C. Died Jan. 16, 1937.

MEYER, Joseph F., banker; b. Germany, Mar. 17, 1851; s. Frank and Emilia M.; brought to U.S. 1855; ed. pub. schs., Memphis, Tenn.; m. Rebecca Baker, Feb. 1884. Engaged in wagon material business many yrs.; formerly pres. Houston Nat. Bank. Democrat. Home: Houston, Tex. Died Mar. 4, 1935.

MEYER, Lucy Rider, principal training sch.; b. New Haven, Vt.; d. Richard D. and Jane (Child) Rider; A.B., Oberlin, 1872, A.M., 1880; Woman's Med. Sch. of Pa., 1873-75; Boston Sch. Tech., 1877-78; M.D., Woman's Med. Coll. (Northwestern U.), 1887; grad. student Div. Sch. U. of Chicago, 1907; m. J. S. Meyer, May 23, 1885. Founder, 1885, and since prin. Chicago Training Sch., an instn. for Bible, social service and mission training; founder, 1887, Deaconess Order M.E. Ch. of America; sec. Meth. Deaconess Assn. Twice elected mem. Gen. Conf. M.E. Ch.; mem. Ecumenical Conf. of Methodism, Toronto, Can., Oct., 1911. Author: Children's Meetings, 1885; Deaconesses, 1889; Mary North (purpose novel), 1902. Home: Chicago, Ill. Died Mar. 16, 1922.

MEYER, Martin A., rabbi; b. San Francisco, Jan. 15, 1879; s. Charles and Louisa B. (Silverstein) M.; B.A., U. of Cincinnati, 1899; B.D., Hebrew Union Coll., Cincinnati, 1901; fellow Am. Sch., Jerusalem, 1901-02; Ph.D., Columbia, 1906; m. Jennie May Haas, June 19, 1905. Rabbi, Albany, N.Y., 1902-06, Brooklyn, 1906-10, Temple Emanu El, San Francisco, Jan. 1, 1910—. Dir. 1st Hebrew Congregation, Berkeley; lecturer, U. of Calif., Jan. 1911—; pres. Pacific Coast Br. Jewish Chautauqua Soc., hon. pres. Young Men's Hebrew Assn.; mem. Calif. Commn. Charities and Correction, 1911-20; chmn. N. Calif. br. Jewish Board Welfare Work; v.p. Jewish Publ. Society of America; etc. Overseas Am. Red Cross, 1918-19. Author: History of the City of Gaza, 1906; Jew and Non-Jew, 1913; Methods of Teaching Post Biblical History and Literature, 1915. Died June 27, 1923.

MEYER, Rudolph J., clergyman; b. St. Louis, Nov. 8, 1841; s. George Henry and Anna Mary (Kemper) M.; ed. St. Louis U., Boston Coll., Georgetown Coll. and Woodstock (Md.) Coll. Entered the Society of Jesus, July 11, 1858; ordained priest R.C. Ch., 1873; in Europe 1874-75; minister and prefect of studies, St. Xavier Coll., Cincinnati, 1876-77; prefect of studies, St. Ignatius Coll., Chicago, 1877-79; pres. St. Francis Xavier's College, Cincinnati, 1879-81; pres. St. Louis U., 1881-85; provincial of Mo., 1885-89; commissary or visitor of the Cal. Mission Soc. Jesus, 1889; prefect of studies and later rector, Marquette Coll., Milwaukee, Wis., 1890-92; delegated to assist at the Gen. Congregation, S.J., Loyola, Spain, 1892; asst. for English speaking provinces of S.J., 1893-1906; superior of Buffalo Mission Soc. Jesus, whose colleges and houses he annexed to the Am. provinces of the order, 1906-07; provincial of Mo., 1907—. Author: First Lessons in the Science of the Saints, 1902; The World in Which We Live, 1908. Died Dec. 2, 1912.

MEYER, Theodore Frederick, wholesale druggist; b. in Ft. Wayne, Ind., June 4, 1857; s. of Christian F. G. and Franciska Therese (Schmidt) M.; A.B., Concordia Coll., Ft. Wayne, Ind., 1876; B.S. in Pharmacy, U. of Mich. Sch. of Pharmacy, 1878; m. Eda Hampmann, June 20, 1888. Entered employ of Meyer Bros. & Co., Ft. Wayne, Ind., 1878; transferred to house of Meyer Bros. & Co., Kansas City, Mo., 1879, to Meyer Bros. & Co., St. Louis, 1883; in charge of Dallas, Tex., br., 1887-89; v.-p. and mgr. Meyer Bros. Drug Co., 1889-1906, pres., 1906—. Home: St. Louis, Mo. Died Mar. 30, 1916.

MEYER, Willy, surgeon; b. Minden, Westphalia, Germany, July 24, 1858; M.D., U. of Bonn, Germany, 1880; asst. to surg. clinic, U. of Bonn, 1881-84; came to U.S., 1884; m. Lilly O. Maass, Apr. 29, 1885. Prof. clin. surgery, Woman's Med. Coll., New York, 1886-93; instr. and prof. surgery, N.Y. Post-Grad. Med. Sch. and Hosp., N.Y. City, 1887—. Died Feb. 24, 1932.

MEYERCORD, George Rudolph, mfr.; b. Washington Heights, Ill., May 23, 1875; s. of Philip and Marie Caroline (Seiff) Meyercord; ed. pub. schs. of St. Louis, and Armour Inst., Chicago; m. Agnes Adams, Aug. 23, 1905; children—Agnes Marie, Margaret Elizabeth, George, Edward Bernard, Helen. Organized, 1894, The Meyercord Co., mfrs. of decalcomania transfer ornaments, now its pres.; organized the Vitrolite Co. of Parkersburg, W.Va., mfrs. of Vitrolite ("Better than Marble"), of which was pres. until 1935; pres. Haskelite Mfg. Corp., Am. Mfrs.' Foreign Credit Underwriters. Mem. bd. mgr. Am. Tariff League, New York. Republican. Methodist. Home: Chicago, Ill. Died Feb. 22, 1941.

MEYERS, George Julian, naval officer; b. Council Bluffs, Ia., April 10, 1881; s. Ferdinand and Emma (Fuss) M.; grad. U.S. Naval Acad., 1902, U.S. Naval War Coll., 1922, U.S. Army War Coll., 1923; completed course mech. engring. U.S. Naval Post Grad. Sch., 1912; m. Elizabeth Worthington Clagett, Dec. 4, 1904; 1 son, George Julian. Entered U.S. Navy, May 23, 1898; advancing through grades to capt., Nov. 22, 1924, rear adm., Dec. 1935; spent 20 years in sea service; now comdt. 16th Naval Dist., P.I. Mem. U.S. Naval Institute. Awarded Navy Cross for service in World War. Mason. Author: Steam Turbines, 1917; Strategy, 1928. Home: Council Bluffs, Ia. Died Dec. 7, 1939.

MEYERS, Robert C. V., author; b. Philadelphia, May 1, 1858; s. Henry and Caroline M.; pvt. edn.; unmarried. Author: Mistress Margery's Roses, 1895; The Colonel's Christmas Morning, 1900; Victoria, Empress and Queen, 1901; Battles and Heroes of the American Navy, 1902; Theodore Roosevelt, 1904; A Hero, 1909. Home: Philadelphia, Pa. Deceased.

MEYERS, William John, statistician; b. Caledonia, Mich., June 27, 1869; s. James M. and Esther (Kinsey) M.; B.S., Mich. Agrl. Coll., 1890; LL.B., U. of Mich., 1900; m. Marian B. Swain, Oct. 11, 1905; children—Sarah, Esther. Statistician, Pub. Service Commn., 2d Dist., N.Y., Sept. 1907-Sept. 1, 1910; statistician, Interstate Commerce Commn., Sept. 1, 1910-July 1917; sec. United Electric Light and Power Co., N.Y. City, July 1917—; chmn. coms. on uniform classification of accounts, Nat. Electric Light Assn. and Am. Gas Assn., 1919-23, and 1925. Home: Westfield, N.J. Died Mar. 13, 1928.

MEZES, Sidney Edward, coll. pres.; b. Belmont, Calif., Sept. 23, 1863; s. S. M. and Juliet (Johnson) M.; B.S., U. of Calif., 1884; A.B., Harvard, 1890, A.M., 1891, Ph.D., 1893; LL.D., Southwestern, 1911, U. of Calif., 1912, New York U., 1915, U. of Cincinnati, 1915; m. Annie O. Hunter, Dec. 10, 1896. Adj. prof. philosophy, 1894-97, asso. prof., 1897-1900, prof., 1900-08, dean, 1902-08, pres., 1908-14, U. of Tex.; pres. Coll. City of New York, 1914-27. Dir. The Inquiry, 1917-18; dir. Territorial Sect. of Am. Commn. to Negotiate Peace, 1918-19; mem. Central Territorial Commn. of Paris Peace Conf., 1919. Author: The Conception of God (co-author), 1897; Ethics, Descriptive and Explanatory, 1901; What Really Happened in Paris (part author), 1921. Died Sept. 11, 1931.

MICHAEL, Arthur, chemist; b. Buffalo, N.Y., Aug. 7, 1853; s. John and Clara M.; ed. pvt. and pub. schs., Buffalo, univs. of Berlin and Heidelberg, École de Médecine de Paris; hon. A.M., Tufts, 1882, Ph.D., 1890, LL.D., 1910; LL.D., Clark U., 1909; m. Helen C. Abbott, June 1889. Prof. chemistry, Tufts Coll., 1882-89 and 1894-1907, prof. emeritus, 1907-12; prof. organic chemistry, Harvard, 1912-36, emeritus. Mem. Nat. Acad. Sciences. Home: Newton Center, Mass. Died Feb. 8, 1942.

MICHAEL, Elias, merchant; b. Eschau, Bavaria, Germany, Sept. 28, 1854; s. Simon and Sarah (Ottenheimer) M.; ed. in pub. schs. of Memphis, Tenn.; m. Rachel Stix, June 17, 1886. Began in employ of Rice, Stix & Co., wholesale dry goods, Memphis, 1869; became buyer for firm and admitted to full partnership, 1885, after removal of business to St. Louis; successively sec., v.p. and pres. Rice-Stix Dry Goods Co., 1906—; pres. Premium Mfg. Co. Mem. Bd. of Edn., St. Louis, 1904-10; apptd. by Mayor Wells, as vice-chmn. Bridge and Terminals Commn. Mem. bd. of dirs. of Jewish Charitable and Ednl. Union of St. Louis; trustee St. Louis Provident Assn., Self-Culture Hall Assn.; mem. exec. bd. Hospital Saturday and Sunday Assn. Was mem. bd. dirs. La. Purchase Expn. Home: St. Louis, Mo. Died Sept. 15, 1913.

MICHAEL, Helen Abbott, chemist, writer; b. Phila.; d. James and Caroline Montelius Abbott; ed. by private teachers; m. Arthur Michael, 1889. Special studies in music, medicine (2 yrs. Woman's Med. Coll. Phila., passing final exams. in chemistry, anatomy, physiology); worked in chem. laboratories, Coll. of Pharmacy, 1884-88, since then Tufts Coll.; lectured winter lecture course, Franklin Inst., Phila., 1887; Nat. Museum Course, Washington, 1887; writer on chem. subjects and in gen. literature. Has published researches in plant chemistry and organic chemistry in trans. and proc. Am. Philos. Soc., Berichte, Journal Practical Chemistry, Franklin Inst. Journal, Am. Journal Chemistry. Died 1904.

MICHAEL, William Henry, consul-gen.; b. Marysville, O., July 14, 1845; s. Munson Hoyt and Nancy Kinkaid (Kezerta) M.; grad. Bacon's Coll., Cincinnati, 1863; irregular course at U. of Iowa, 1866-69; m. Emily J. Quinn, Nov. 15, 1871. Enlisted as pvt. Co. B, 11th Ia. Inf., 1861; hon. disch., 1862, after injury in battle of Shiloh; apptd. master's mate U.S.N., 1863; promoted for gallant conduct, 1864; resigned 1866. City editor Sioux City (Ia.) Journal, 1873; mail service, 1874; editor and owner Nebraska newspapers, 1875-81; admitted to bar, 1880; practiced law till 1887; Washington corr. 3 newspapers, 1887-90. Alternate presdl. elector, 1876; clerk printing records, U.S. Senate and compiler Congressional Directory and editor of messages and documents, 1887-96; chief clerk Dept. of State, 1897-1905; consul-gen. at Calcutta, Nov. 16, 1905-12. Compiler and editor govt. literature: History of the Mississippi Squadron, 1886; History of the Declaration of Independence, 1895; U.S. tariff laws, 1778-1897; laws relating to the navy and marine corps, 1898; History of the Department of State, 1903; Better Dead Than Homeless, Tariff in Story, 1888, 1900; Homesteader's Daughter, 1900. Rep. of Dept. of State on U.S. bd. of Omaha, Buffalo, Charleston, St. Louis and Portland expns. Home: Washington, D.C. Died May 16, 1916.

MICHAELIS, Richard C., journalist; b. Genthin, Germany, Sept. 1, 1839; s. Carl G. W. and Wilhelmine (Pilegard) M.; academic edn.; m. Clara Leist, Berlin, July 2, 1867; served in Austro-Prussian war, 1866. Author: Looking Further Forward: An Answer to Bellamy's Looking Backward; Die Ansieder am Cottonwood River; Somewhat Sensational Reminiscences of a Publisher; was editor of The Chicago Freie Presse and Illinois Staats Zeitung, and gen. mgr. Ill. Pub. Co., publishers of the papers; retired. Home: Medford, Wis. Died 1909.

MICHAUD, John Stephen, R.C. bishop of Burlington, Vt.—consecrated June 29, 1892; b. Burlington, Vt., Nov. 24, 1843; s. Stephen and Catherine (O'Rogan) M.; studied at Montreal Coll., P.Q.; grad. Holy Cross Coll., Worcester, Mass., 1870; and theol. studies at St. Joseph's Sem., Troy, N.Y.; ordained priest, June 7, 1873. Died 1908.

MICHAUD, Regis, college prof.; b. Montélimar, France, May 1, 1880; s. Marius and Reine Marie (Voyron) M.; student Sorbonne, Coll. of France and École des Hautes Études, Paris; A.M., U. of Paris, 1905; came to U.S., 1906; m. Jennie Wells Chase, 1907; children—Regis, Marie Louise. Asst. prof. French, Princeton, 1907-14; asso. prof. French, Smith Coll., Northampton, Mass., 1907-19; prof. French, U. of Calif., 1919—, also chmn. of dept., 1923-25 and 1926-27; visiting prof. Romance langs., U. of Ill., 1930—. Decorated Chevalier Legion of Honor (France). Catholic. Author: Mystiques et Réalistes anglo-saxons, 1918 (French Academy prize, 1920); Autour d'Emerson, 1924; The American Novel To-day, 1928; Emerson, the Enraptured Yankee, 1930; Panorama de la littérature Américaine, 1928; L'Ame Américaine, 1929; Modern Thought and Literature in France, 1934. Died Feb. 7, 1939.

MICHEL, Richard Fraser, physician; b. Charleston, S.C., Feb. 15, 1827; s. William and Eugenia Ash (Fraser) M.; grad. Acad. of Alexander Spring, Charleston, S.C., 1844; studied medicine Phila., 1845-46; grad. Charleston, S.C., 1847; m. Annie Rivers, Feb. 1854. Prof. materia medica, Charleston, S.C., 1848-60; surgeon C.S.A., Gen. Evans' brigade, 1860-65; from close of war at Montgomery, Ala., in active practice of medicine. Founder and ever since pres. Social Med. Club, Montgomery; mem. several Masonic fraternities; counsellor of Med. Assn. of S.C., 1859-60; v.p. Am. Med. Assn., 1872. Home: Montgomery, Ala. Died 1907.

MICHELSON, Albert Abraham, scientist; b. Strelno, Germany, Dec. 19, 1852; s. Samuel and Rosalie (Przlubska) M.; grad. U.S. Naval Acad., 1873; midshipman U.S.N., 1873; instr. physics and chemistry, U.S. Naval Acad., 1875-79; Nautical Almanac Office, Washington, 1880; student at univs. of Berlin, 1880, Heidelberg, 1881, Collège de France and École Polytechnique, 1882; hon. Ph.D., Western Reserve, 1886, Stevens Inst. Tech., 1887; Sc.D., U. of Cambridge, 1899; LL.D., Yale, 1901, Franklin Bicentenary U. of Pa., 1906; Ph.D., Leipzig, 1909, Göttingen, 1911; LL.D., McGill U., 1921; m. 2d, Edna Stanton, Dec. 23, 1899. Professor of physics, Case Sch. Applied Science, Cleveland, 1883-89, Clark U., 1889-92; prof. and head of dept. of physics, U. of Chicago, 1892-1929, "distinguished service" prof., same, 1925—; Lowell lecturer, 1899; exchange prof., U. of Göttingen, summer 1911, Université de Paris, 1920. Rumford Medal, 1889; Grand Prix, Paris Expn., 1900; Mattencci Medal, Soc. Italiana, Rome, 1904; Copley Medal, Royal Soc., London, 1907; awarded Nobel Prize, for Physics ($40,000), by Swedish Acad. Sciences, 1907; Elliott Cresson medal, 1912, Draper medal, 1916. Fellow Am. Acad. Arts and Sciences, A.A.A.S.; mem. numerous scientific socs. Author: (brochure) Velocity of Light, 1902; Light Waves and Their Uses, 1903. Home: Chicago, Ill. Died May 9, 1931.

MICHELSON, Albert Heminway, consul; b. Annapolis, Md., Jan. 16, 1878; s. Albert Abraham M. and

Margaret M. (Heminway) M.; student École Mansart, Paris, 1892-93; grad. Worcester (Mass.) Acad., 1897; B.S., Harvard, 1901; unmarried. Am. consular agt. at Charleroi, Belgium, 1901-06; consul at Turin, Italy, 1906-12, at Hanover, Germany, Aug. 22, 1912—. Am. commr. to Internat. Expn. Industry and Labor, Turin, 1911; Am. del. Internat. Expns. Conf., Berlin, 1912. Mem. Philharmonic Acad. (Turin). Died June 9, 1915.

MICHELSON, Truman, ethnologist; b. New Rochelle, N.Y., Aug. 11, 1879; s. Albert Abraham and Margaret McLean (Heminway) M.; A.B., Harvard, 1902, A.M., 1903, Ph.D., 1904; studied univs. of Leipzig and Bonn, 1904-05; studied pvtly. with Prof. Boas, of Columbia, 1909, 10; m. Katherine Harrison, July 18, 1903. Parker fellow, Harvard, 1904-05; instr. Latin, U. of Mo., 1905-06; pvt. research, 1906-09; clk. with U.S. Immigration Commn., 1909; ethnologist, Bur. Am. Ethnology, Washington, June 1, 1910—; prof. ethnology, George Washington U., 1917-32; exec. officer dept. anthropology, 1927-32; taught anthropology, Columbia, summer 1924. Expdns. to Algonquin tribes every season, 1910-32; to Algonquian Indians and Eskimos of James' and Hudson's Bays, 1935, 36, to Algonquin Indians of Northern shore of St. Lawrence River, 1937. Author: Kickapoo Tales (with William Jones), 1915; The Autobiography of a Fox Indian Woman, 1925; Notes on Fox Mortuary Customs and Beliefs, 1925; Contributions to Fox Ethnology, 1927; Buffalo Head Dance of Thunder Gens of Fox Indians, 1928; Thunder Dance of Bear Gens of Fox Indians, 1929; Notes on the Fox Wâpanowiweni, 1932; Fox Miscellany, 1937. Made first scientific classification of Algonquin tribes on a linguistic basis. Deceased.

MICHENER, Louis Theodore, lawyer; b. Fayette Co., Ind., Dec. 21, 1848; s. William and Mary Ann (Blake) M.; student Brookville (Ind.) Coll., 1867-68; admitted to bar, 1871; m. Mary E., d. Thomas B. Adams, of Brookville, Ind., May 30, 1872; children—Mrs. Nora Mohun, Mrs. Helen Halstead. Del. Nat. Ednl. Conv., Louisville, Ky., 1883; polit. mgr. Gen. Benjamin Harrison, 1884-92; chmn. of the Harrison nominating coms. in nat. convs. of 1888-92; sec. Republican State Com. of Ind., 1884-86; atty.-gen. of Ind., 1886-90; chmn. Rep. State Com. of Ind., 1889-90. Mason. Grand Master Grand Lodge Odd Fellows, Ind., 1888. Died Feb. 10, 1928.

MICHIE, Peter Smith, prof. natural and experimental philosophy, U.S. Mil. Acad., Feb. 14, 1871—; b. Brechin, Scotland, Mar. 24, 1839; went to Cincinnati in boyhood; grad. West Point, 1863; (Ph.D., Princeton, 1871; A.M., Dartmouth, 1873; LL.D., Union Coll., 1893); m. Maria L. Roberts, June 21, 1863. Commissioned 1st lt. engrs., June 11, 1863; capt., Nov. 23, 1865; reached bvt. rank brig. gen. vols.; participated in siege of Charleston, and in Fla. and Va. campaigns, becoming chief engr., army of the James. Author: Elements of Wave Motion Relating to Sound and Light; Life and Letters of Maj. Gen. Emory Upton; Personnel of Sea Coast Defense; Elements of Analytical Mechanics; Elements of Hydro-Mechanics; Practical Astronomy. Member bd. overseers, Thayer School Civil Engineering, Dartmouth Coll., 1871—; mem. Military Commn. to Europe, 1870. Died 1901.

MICHIE, Robert Edward Lee, army officer; b. "Bel Air," Albemarle Co., Va., June 1, 1864; s. Dr. J. Augustus and Susan R. (Jackson) M.; grad. U.S. Mil. Acad., 1885, Army War Coll., 1905; m. Gray Beachy, Jan. 19, 1887. Commd. 2d lt. 2d Cav., June 14, 1885; promoted through grades to col. cav., U.S.A., July 1, 1916; brig. gen. N.A., Aug. 5, 1917. Duty at mil. posts in Ida., Ariz., N.M. and Kan. until 1897; adj. gen. Dept. of Province of Havana and Pinar Del Rio, Cuba, 1899-1900; adj. gen. Dept. of Mo., 1900-01; in Philippines, 1903-04, 1910-11; duty Gen. Staff, Washington, 1905-07; witnessed German Army maneuvers, 1908; duty on Mexican border, various periods, 1912-14; mem. Gen. Staff, 1914-17; with U.S. Commn. to Russia, 1917; apptd. comdr. 53d Inf. Brigade, Camp Wadsworth, Spartanburg, S.C., Sept. 1917. Died June 5, 1918.

MICKEY, John Hopwood, governor; b. on farm nr. Burlington, Ia., Sept. 30, 1845; s. Oliver Perry and Betsey Ann (Davison) M.; student Ia. Wesleyan U., 1866-67; served in Co. D, 8th Ia. Cav., 1863-65; m. Marinda McCray, Sept. 10, 1867 (dec.); m. 2d, Flora C. Campbell, Dec. 8, 1888. Banker, 1879—; mem. Neb. Ho. of Rep., 1881-82; gov. of Nebraska, 2 terms, 1903-07. Republican. Mem. Gen. Conf. M.E. Ch., Cleveland, 1896, Chicago, 1900; pres. bd. trustees Neb. Wesleyan U. Home: Osceola, Neb. Died 1910.

MICKLE, William English, adjutant gen. U.C.V.; b. Columbia, S.C., Oct. 31, 1846; s. Capt. Joseph Thomas and Nancy (Gandy) M.; ed. at large prep. sch. in Noxubee Co., Miss.; left sch. in 1864, to enlist in Co. A, 3d Ala. Inf., of Army of Northern Va.; severely wounded twice battle Cedar Creek, Oct. 19, 1864, and retired at Petersburg, Va., Feb. 17, 1865, by medical board for nine months for disability from wounds; m. Ellie Squire Woodhull, Oct. 8, 1867. Teacher after war; became prin. Boys' Senior Grammar Sch., Mobile; later in business in Mobile. One of charter mems. Raphael Semmes Camp, U.C.V., of Mobile; several yrs. asst. adj. gen., and from Jan. 19, 1903, adj. gen. U.C.V. For a number of yrs. pension examiner of Mobile Co., Ala. Sec. Mobile Fair Assn., 1880-84. Presbyn. Democrat. Home: Mobile, Ala. Died Feb. 18, 1920.

MICOU, Richard Wilde, theologian; b. New Orleans, June 12, 1848; s. William Chatfield and Anna Davenport (Thompson) M.; ed. univs. of Ga., Ala., Erlangen, Bavaria, Edinburgh, Scotland, Gen. Theol. Sem., New York; (hon. M.A., Trinity Coll., 1892; D.D., Kenyon Coll., 1897); m. Mary Dunnica, May 16, 1872. Deacon, 1870, priest, 1872, P.E. Ch.; pastor Franklin, La., 1870-74, Kittanning, Pa., 1874-77, Trinity Ch., Waterbury, Conn., 1877-92; prof. systematic divinity, Phila. Div. Sch., 1892-98; prof. fundamental theology and systematic divinity, Va. Theol. Sem., 1898—. Died June 4, 1912.

MIDDLEBROOK, Louis Francis, author; b. Trumbull, Conn., May 28, 1866; s. James Robert and Frances Adelia (Brinsmade) M.; ed. Conn. Lit. Inst., Suffield, 1881-84; m. Lillian W. Goodale, Oct. 27, 1891 (died 1932); children—Marion Calhoun (Mrs. Robert K. Smith), Katherine (dec.), John (dec.), Louis F.; m. 2d, Margaret A. Dütting, Jan. 31, 1933. Began 1885, as clk. with The Hartford Steam Boiler Inspection and Ins. Co. and has continued with same co., sec., Oct. 25, 1921—. Served as ensign U.S.N., 1898. Republican. Episcopalian. Author: History of Maritime Connecticut During Revolutionary War, 1925; Seals of Maritime New England, 1926; The Frigate South Carolina, 1926; The Loomis Journal, 1926; Capt. Gideon Olmsted, Conn. Privateersman, 1933; Salisbury Conn. Cannon Revolutionary War, 1935. Editor and compiler of Middlebrook Family Register, 1907. Home: West Hartford, Conn. Died Feb. 1, 1937.

MIDDLETON, Arthur D., baritone; b. Logan, Ia., Nov. 28, 1880; s. Wiley and Julia Ann (Lockling) M.; grad. high sch., Missouri Valley, Ia., 1899; student Simpson Coll., Indianola, Ia., 6 yrs., specializing in music and literature; hon. Mus.D. from Simpson College; m. Eva Frances Hill, Sept. 10, 1902. Became asst. vocal instr. in coll. after 1 yr. there, and toured middle west in concert and oratorio; teacher of voice, Des Moines Music Coll., 1905-06, Chicago Music Coll., 1906-11; joined Met. Opera Co., New York, 1914, appearing 35 times first season. Has sung with Apollo Club, Chicago; Handel and Haydn Soc., Boston; Denver Choral Assn.; St. Paul Orchestra; Syracuse Festival; New York Symphony Orchestra; Minneapolis Symphony Orchestra, etc. Reportory includes leading rôles in "Lohengrin," "Fidelio," "Carmen," "Aïda," "Rheingold," "Parsifal," "Faust," etc. Republican. Presbyn. K.P., Elk. Home: New York, N.Y. Died Feb. 8, 1929.

MIDGLEY, John William, traffic expert; b. Leeds, Eng., Dec. 24, 1843; s. John and Mary (Ellison) M.; m. Luella Wheeler, Oct. 8, 1873. Stenographic sec. to gen. supt. I.C. R.R., 1868-71, to pres., 1871-72; similar positions on C.&N.-W. Ry., 1872-76; sec. Southwestern R.R. Rate Assn., 1876-78; commr. same, 1878-87; commr. Colo. Traffic Assn., 1881-87; later chmn. Associated Southwestern, Colo., Utah and Pacific Coast lines, and chmn. Western Freight Assn. Organized Bur. of Car Performances, Apr. 1901, and led agitation resulting in adoption of per diem mode of payment for use of freight cars in U.S., Canada and Mexico; also conducted investigation of abuses incident to the operation of pvt. freight cars, which resulted in popular demand for railroad legislation, in response to the President's message to Congress, Dec. 1904; during 1906-07, promoted sentiment which led to formation of Am. Ry. Clearing House; retired, 1908. Home: Evanston, Ill. Died Apr. 4, 1922.

MIELATZ, Charles Frederick William, etcher; b. Breddin, Germany, May 24, 1860; s. Charles and Wilhelmine (Wolff) M.; ed. in schs. in Chicago; studied drawing at Chicago Sch. of Design, and painted with the elder F. Rondel; m. Mary Stuart McKinney, Feb. 25, 1903. Mem. Internat. Jury of Awards for etchings and engravings, St. Louis Expn., 1904; instr. etching, the Nat. Acad. Design, A.N.A. Home: New York, N.Y. Died June 2, 1919.

MIELZINER, Leo, portrait painter; b. N.Y. City, Dec. 8, 1869; s. Dr. Moses and Rosetta (Lewald) M.; ed. Cincinnati Art Acad.; École des Beaux Arts, Paris; acads. Julian and Colarossi, Paris, with Kroyer, Copenhagen; m. Ella MacKenna Friend, 1896; children—Leo, Jo. Instructor Art Students' League, New York, 1913-15; writer and lecturer on art. Represented in the Met. Art Mus., New York, Boston Art Mus., Worcester Art Mus., Brooklyn Art Mus., Cincinnati Art Mus., Univ. of Del., State Dept. and at Columbia Univ., with portraits of Harlan Stone, John Bassett Moore, and Nathan Abbott; oil portrait of Woodrow Wilson at Democratic Club, New York. Home: Truro, Mass. Died Aug. 11, 1935.

MIELZINER, Moses, prof. Talmudical literature, Hebrew Union Coll., 1879—; b. Schubin, Germany, Aug. 12, 1828; s. Rabbi Benjamin and Rosa M.; studied at Univ. of Berlin, 1879-92; (Ph.D., Univ. of Giessen, Germany; D.D., Hebrew Union Coll.); m. Rosette Levald, of Copenhagen, Denmark, 1861. Rabbi of a congregation in Waren, Germany; later prin. of a theol. school in Copenhagen; rabbi of a large congregation in New York, 1865-73; prin. of an ednl. inst., 1873-79. Author: The Jewish Law of Marriage and Divorce, 1884; Selections from the Book of Psalms, 1884; Slavery Among the Ancient Hebrews, 1894; Introduction to the Talmud, 1894; Legal Maxims and Fundamental Laws of the Civil and Criminal Code of the Talmud, 1898; Rabbinical Law of Hereditary Succession, 1900. Home: Avondale, Cincinnati, O. Died 1903.

MIERS, Robert Walter, congressman; b. Decatur Co., Ind., Jan. 27, 1848; s. Thomas S. M.; B.S., Ind. U., 1870, LL.B., 1871. Admitted to bar, 1872, and began practice at Bloomington, Ind. Pros. atty. 10th Jud. Circuit, 1875-79; mem. Ind. Ho. of Rep., 1879; judge 10th Jud. Circuit, 1883-96; mem. 55th to 58th Congresses (1897-1905), 2d Ind. Dist. Democrat. Trustee Ind. U., 1881-93. Home: Bloomington, Ind. Died Feb. 20, 1930.

MIFFLIN, George Harrison, publisher; b. Boston, May 1, 1845; s. Charles and Mary (Crowninshield) M.; A.B., Harvard, 1865; m. Jane Appleton Phillips, Oct. 24, 1877. Became connected with the pub. house of Hurd & Houghton, 1867, and with the Riverside Press; admitted to the firm, 1872, and has continued as partner of the succeeding firm of Houghton, Osgood & Co., 1878-80, and Houghton, Mifflin & Co., of Boston, 1880-1908; pres. of Houghton, Mifflin Co., 1908—; also pres. The Riverside Press, Cambridge, Mass. Unitarian. Republican. Home: Boston, Mass. Died Apr. 5, 1921.

MIFFLIN, Lloyd, author; b. Columbia, Pa., Sept. 15, 1846; s. J. Houston M. (portrait painter) and Elizabeth Anne Bethel (Heise) M.; educated Washington Classical Inst. and by pvt. tutors; studied art under his father and under T. Moran, 1868-69, in Germany under H. Herzog, and in Italy, 1871-72; (Litt.D., Franklin and Marshall Coll., 1903, U. of Pa., 1908); unmarried. Exhibited paintings in U.S.; health failing applied himself to literature; lectured on Conversation as a Fine Art. Author: At the Gates of Song, 1897-1901; Year Book, with quotations, 1897; Memorial Day Ode, 1897; The Slopes of Helicon, and Other Poems, 1898; Echoes of Greek Idyls, 1899; The Fields of Dawn and Later Sonnets, 1900; Castalian Days, 1903; The Fleeing Nymph and Other Verse, 1905; Collected Sonnets of Lloyd Mifflin, 1905; My Lady of Dream, 1906; Toward the Uplands, 1908; Flower and Thorn, 1909; As Twilight Falls, 1916. Home: Columbia, Pa. Died July 16, 1921.

MIGHELS, Philip Verrill, author; b. Carson City, Nev., Apr. 19, 1869; s. Henry Rust and Lucy Ellen (Verrill) M.; ed. pvt. sch. and Carson City High Sch.; studied law in office of Trenmore Coffin, Carson City. Admitted to bar by Supreme Ct. of Nev., Jan. 10, 1890; journalist in San Francisco, 1892-93, New York, 1894; from 1895, exclusively devoted to authorship. Spent 4 yrs. in London, beginning Sept. 1897. Author: Bruvver Jim's Baby, 1904; The Ultimate Passion, 1905; Chatwit, the Man-Talk Bird, 1906; Dunny, 1906; Sunnyside Tad, 1907; The Pillars of Eden, 1909, and dramatization of same; also dramatization of Bruvver Jim's Baby, and other plays. Home: New York, N.Y. Died 1911.

MILBURN, Arthur W., president and chmn. exec. committee The Borden Co. (milk and food products); dir. Borden, Ltd. (Can.), Borden Realty Corp. and officer or dir. various other corps. Died Oct. 11, 1937.

MILBURN, George Roszelle, judge; b. Washington, Nov. 15, 1850; s. Benedict and Martha (Page) M.; A.B., Yale Coll., 1872; LL.B., Nat. Law Sch., Washington, 1880; m. Eugenie Prentiss, d. D. W. Bliss, M.D., of Washington, Dec. 7, 1875 (wife dec.). In Indian service, 1880-85; while spl. Indian agt. in 1884, built Crow agency on the Little Big Horn; admitted to Mont. bar, 1886; co. atty. Custer Co., Mont., 1886-88; judge 7th Dist. Mont., 1889; reelected 1892; asso. justice Supreme Ct. of Mont., 1901-07; now practicing law. Democrat. Home: Miles City, Mont. Died 1910.

MILBURN, John George, lawyer; b. nr. Sunderland, Eng., Dec. 13, 1851; ed. in pvt. schs. in Eng.; came to U.S., 1870; studied law at Batavia, N.Y.; LL.D., Princeton and Alfred univs. Admitted to bar, Apr. 1874; practiced in Buffalo; mem. Carter, Ledyard & Milburn, New York, 1904—. Pres. Pan-Am. Expn., Buffalo, 1901. Pres. McKinley was taken to his house after fatal assault and died there. Dir. Am. Express Co., Chase National Bank; trustee New York Life Ins. Co., N.Y. City, 1907—. Mem. Bd. Commrs. of Statutory Consolidation, which consol. all gen. statutes of N.Y. from 1777. Trustee Columbia, Barnard Coll. (chmn. bd.), New York Pub. Library. Died Aug. 11, 1930.

MILBURN, William Henry, chaplain U.S. Senate; b. Phila., Sept. 26, 1823; ed. at Phila., 1838-41; at Jacksonville, Ill., 1838-41; was in Ill. Coll., 1841-43, but his health failed, and he was not graduated; (A.M.; D.D., Ill. Coll.); m. 1846 (wife deceased). Lost sight of one eye totally, and other in great measure, when 5 yrs. of age. Has been wholly blind for many yrs. Elected chaplain of Congress first in 1845, second in 1853, then of Ho. of Reps. in 1885, and of senate in 1893. Author: Rifle, Axe and Saddle-Bags; Ten Years of Preacher Life; Lance, Cross and Canoe; etc. Died 1903.

MILES, Basil; b. Phila., Pa., June 20, 1877; s. Frederick B. and Gertrude E. (Woodworth) M.; grad. St. Mark's Sch., Southboro, Mass., 1893; A.B., U. of Pa., 1897; B.Litt., Balliol Coll. (Oxon, Eng.), 1905; m. Mrs. Peabody Savell, née von Braun, of Budapest, Mar. 23, 1925. Apprentice, Bement, Miles & Co., Phila., 1897-99; master St. Mark's Sch., 1899-1902; sec. to U.S. Ambassador George von L. Meyer, and 3d sec. of Embassy, Petrograd, Russia, 1905-07; 3d sec. of Embassy, Berlin, 1907-08; in charge foreign mail service, P.O. Dept., 1908-13; with Chamber Commerce, U.S.A., 1913-16; spl. rep. of U.S., with rank of minister plenipotentiary, in charge German and Austro-Hungarian prisoners of war in Russia, 1916-17; sec. spl. diplomatic mission to Russia (Root Mission), 1917; in charge Russian affairs, Dept. of State, 1917-19; served as acting editor Nation's Business; mgr. and asst. sec. gen. 1st Pan-Am. Financial Conf.; mem. com. that devised postal savings system in U.S.; sec. Com. on Nat. Preparedness of Chamber Commerce U.S.A., 1915; mem. Central Com. of Officers' Training Camps Assn., 1915-16; exec. sec. Washington Conf. on Limitation of Armament, 1921-22, and sec. Am. Delegation; Am. administrative commr. to Internat. Chamber Commerce, 1922—. Officier Légion d'Honneur (France). Republican. Episcopalian. Died June 14, 1928.

MILES, Daniel Curtis, farmer, banker; b. Westminster, Mass., June 1, 1827; s. Daniel and Mary (Curtis) M.; bro. Lt. Gen. Nelson Appleton M. and desc. of Rev. John Myles, b. in Wales, 1621, and came to N.E., 1663; ed. pub. and high schs., Westminster Acad.; m. Lucy Ann Puffer, May 22, 1851. Taught sch. at Lancaster, Westminster and Gardner, Mass., 12 yrs.; extensively engaged as a mfr. and lumber mcht. for many yrs.; pres. Worcester Bapt. Assn. Prominent owner of real estate in Southern Calif. and cattle ranch, Miles City, Mont. Has been auditor, selectman, assessor, mem. Sch. Com., and collector, Town of Westminster; pres. Mass. Agrl. Soc., Worcester North Agrl. Soc.; U.S. bank examiner 8 yrs.; supt. Bapt. Sunday Sch., 21 yrs.; pres. Worcester Bapt. Assn. Prominent for many yrs. in promoting and establishing good roads in Mass., and in philanthropy has been most generous, giving thousands of dollars to benevolent objects. Went to field after some of greatest battles of Civil War and nursed the wounded; after battle of Chancellorsville conveyed his brother, who was desperately wounded, to his home in Mass. Has traveled in every state of U.S., provinces of Canada, and in Europe. Died Feb. 22, 1912.

MILES, Evan, army officer; b. McVeytown, Pa., Mar. 28, 1838; s. Richard and Hannah (Van Cleve) M.; m. Martha A. Stitzel, Dec. 17, 1874. Apptd. from Pa., 1st lt. 12th U.S. Inf., Aug. 5, 1861; capt., Jan. 20, 1865; transferred to 21st Inf., Sept. 21, 1866; maj. 25th Inf., Apr. 24, 1888; lt. col. 20th Inf., Apr. 25, 1892; transferred to 22d Inf., Sept. 11, 1895, to 1st Inf., Nov. 4, 1895; col., May 4, 1897; brig. gen. vols., Oct. 6, 1898; disch. from vol. service, Jan. 10, 1899; retired on account of disability in line of duty, Apr. 19, 1899; advanced to rank of brig. gen. retired, by act of Apr. 23, 1904. Bvtd. capt., Aug. 18, 1864, for gallantry during operations on Weldon R.R., Va.; maj., Feb. 27, 1890, for gallantry in actions against Indians in Idaho and Oregon. Died 1908.

MILES, Joshua Weldon, lawyer, banker; b. Somerset Co., Md., Dec. 9, 1858; s. Southey F. and Christina (Roach) M.; A.B., Western Md. Coll., 1878, A.M., 1880; student Md. U. Sch. of Law, also in law offices; m. Lillian Maria Rider, Feb. 4, 1884. In practice at Princess Anne, July 1880—; now mem. Miles & Myers; solicitor New York, Phila. & Norfolk R.R., 1894—; pres. Bank of Somerset, Princess Anne; dir. Continental Life Ins. Co., Wilmington, Del. State's atty., Somerset Co., 1883-87; mem. 54th Congress (1895-97). Trustee Western Md. Coll. Collector internal revenue, Dist. of Md., 1915-21. Presbyterian. Home: Princess Anne, Md. Died Mar. 4, 1929.

MILES, Nelson Appleton, lt. gen. U.S.A.; b. Westminster, Mass., Aug. 8, 1839; s. Daniel and Mary (Curtis) M.; academic education; (LL.D., Harvard U., 1896, Brown U., 1901, Colgate U., 1910); m. Mary Hoyt Sherman, June 30, 1868. First lt. 22d Mass. Inf., Sept. 9, 1861; promoted through grades to brig. gen. U.S.A., Dec. 15, 1880; maj. gen., Apr. 5, 1890; lt. gen. U.S.A., June 6, 1900. Bvtd.; maj. gen. vols., Aug. 25, 1864, "for highly meritorious and distinguished conduct throughout campaign and particularly for gallantry and valuable services at battle of Reams Sta., Va."; brig. gen., Mar. 2, 1867, "for gallant and meritorious services at Chancellorsville"; maj. gen., Mar. 2, 1867, for same at Spottsylvania; awarded Congressional Medal of Honor, July 23, 1892, "for distinguished gallantry at Chancellorsville (severely wounded). Comd. an army corps of 26,000 men at twenty-five years of age; conducted several campaigns against hostile Indians on Western frontier, notably that against Sitting Bull, Crazy Horse, Chief Joseph, Geronimo and Natchez; commanded United States troops at Chicago, during railroad strike troubles, 1894; represented U.S.A. at seat of Turco-Grecian War, and also at Queen Victoria's Diamond Jubilee, 1897; sr. officer, comdg. U.S.A., 1895-1903, comdg. U.S. Army during Spanish-Am. War. Retired Aug. 8, 1903. President Jefferson Memorial Assn. Commanded Mass. Militia, 1905. Author; Personal Recollections, or From New England to the Golden Gate, 1896; Military Europe, 1898; Observations Abroad, or Report of Maj. Gen. Nelson A. Miles, Commanding U.S. Army, of His Tour of Observation in Europe, 1899; Serving the Republic, 1911. Home: Washington, W.C. Died May 15, 1925.

MILES, Robert Parker, lecturer; b. Burnley, Lancashire, Eng., July 11, 1866; s. Harrison and Sarah (Parker) M.; St. Stephen's Coll., Annandale, N.Y., 1885-88; Union Theol. Seminary, New York, 1892; m. Lena B. Coburger, Nov. 12, 1899; children—Mrs. Dorothy M. Colwill, Mrs. Elsie R. Thorp, Mrs. Gertrude V. Hostetter, Robert B., Mrs. Isabelle M. Draeger. Ordained Presbyterian ministry, 1892; assistant pastor Rutherford, N.J., 1892-96; pastor Ravenswood Ch., New York, 1896-97; religious editor New York Evening Journal, 1897-99; traveled extensively as newspaper and mag. corr.; has lectured in U.S., Can. and English-speaking countries, 1901—; prin. lectures "Tallow Dips" (given over 7000 times), "Sparks" and "Dawn." Republican. Mason. Mem. Internat. Lyceum Assn., Eulexion Soc. (St. Stephen's Coll.). Author: Three Men and a Woman, 1901; also wrote several chapters of character sketches in "New Metropolis," 1898, and sketch of George Francis Train; Thumb Nail Sketches of Lyceumites. Home: Lakewood, O. Dec. 28, 1940.

MILES, Willard Wesbery, judge; b. Albany, Vt., Feb. 6, 1845; s. Orin and Eunice (Clark) M.; ed. common schs., acad., and pvtly. in Greek and Latin; m. Ellen M. Dow, Sept. 29, 1872. Prin. Albany Acad. and supt. schs., 1867-68; admitted to bar, 1872; supt. schs., Craftsbury, Vt., 1876; town clerk, Craftsbury, 1874-81; mem. Vt. Ho. of Rep., 1872, 1878-79, 1904-05; Senate, 1894-95; state atty., Orleans Co., 1890-94; judge Supreme Court of Vt., Nov. 25, 1905-Dec. 1, 1906; superior judge and chancellor, Dec. 1, 1906-Feb. 1, 1917; asso. justice Supreme Court Ct., 1917-23, retired. Republican. Home: Barton, Vt. Died May 13, 1926.

MILES, William Porcher, sugar planter; b. in S.C., July 4, 1822; grad. Charleston Coll.; studied law; became prof. mathematics Charleston Coll.; later mayor of Charleston; mem. U.S. Congress; mem. Confederate Congress; later col. in Confederate army on staff of Gen. Beauregard. After war pres. Univ. of N.C. His wife inherited 13 sugar plantations in La., and Col. Miles resigned from university position to manage them; became second largest sugar producer in U.S.; now pres. W. P. Miles Planting and Mfg. Co. Home: Burnside, La. Died 1899.

MILFORD, Morton Marshall, newspaperman; b. Lafayette, Ind., June 20, 1883; s. Arthur Bartlett and Harriet Louise (Chase) M.; A.B., Wabash Coll., 1904; m. Florence Bell Moffett, Sept. 6, 1921; 1 son, Arthur Lee. Member of the editorial staff Indianapolis Sentinel, 1904-06, Memphis News-Scimitar, 1906-07; police reporter Memphis Commercial Appeal, 1907-09; editorial staff Indianapolis News, 1909-10; asst. Washington corr. same, 1910-15; Washington corr. Louisville Times, and Courier-Journal, 1915-19; mem. President Wilson's party on League of Nation's trip to Pacific Coast, Sept. 1919; asst. to publicity dir. of Dem. Nat. Com. in New York, 1920; owner and pub. Fort Myers (Fla.) Press, Nov. 1919-May 1924; editor in chief Miami (Fla.) Daily News, 1924-30, Washington corr., 1901; publicity and pub. relations counsel, New York, 1932; spl. asst. to chief adminstr. in charge of pub. relations and press information, Federal Emergency Relief Administration, Civil Works Adminstrn., Federal Surplus Relief Corp., Nat. Youth Adminstrn., and Works Progress Adminstrn, May 1933—. Democrat. Presbyn. Mason. Elk. Home: Chevy Chase, Md. Died July 18, 1938.

MILHOLLAND, John Elmer, businessman, writer; b. Lewis, N.Y., May 30, 1860; s. John and Mary Ann (Moore) M.; student New York U.; m. Jean Torry. Was with New York Tribune 12 yrs. as reporter, corr., polit. adviser, business rep. and editorial writer. Organized 1st Nat. Conv. for placing primary elections under the law; settled strike difficulty between New York Tribune and the typographical unions after 15 yrs. duration; an organizer of the McKinley League and the Hughes League; with others established International Union Club, London, 1898, which championed the Boers' cause; speaker and writer in presenting measures for defense of negroes' constitutional rights, prison reform, federal aid to edn., cutting down of Southern representation in Congress; etc. Active in World's Race Congress, London, 1911; helped to inaugurate Saturday half holiday in America; built systems which carried first mail and parcels underground in New York and other cities; started movement that led to the saving and rebuilding of old Ft. Ticonderoga. Supervising insp. of immigration at New York under President Harrison. Republican. Presbyn. Home: New York City and Lewis, N.Y. Died June 29, 1925.

MILLAR, Alexander Copeland, clergyman; b. McKeesport, Pa., May 17, 1861; s. William John and Ellen (Caven) M.; A.B., Central Coll. Mo., 1885, A.M., 1889; (D.D., Wesleyan Coll., Winchester, Ky., 1907; LL.D., U. of Ark., 1922); m. Elizabeth Harwood, June 27, 1887 (died May 22, 1924); children—Ethel Key, Paul Harwood, George, Dana; m. 2d, Susie McKinnon, Oct. 15, 1925. Ordained M.E. Ch., S., ministry, 1888; prof. English and German, Grove's High Sch., Dallas, Tex., 1885-86; pres. and prof. Latin and philosophy, Neosho (Mo.) Collegiate Inst., 1886-87; pres. Central Collegiate Inst., Altus, Ark. (which later moved to Conway, Ark., and became Hendrix Coll.), 1887-1902; prof. history and economics, Central Coll., 1902-04; presiding elder Little Rock dist., 1906-10; pres. Hendrix Coll. (2d time), 1910-13; pres. Okla. Meth. Coll., Muskogee, Okla., 1913-14; asso. editor Western Methodist (now the Ark. Methodist), 1904-14, and editor-in-chief, 1914—; presiding elder of the Arkadelphia District, 1932. Head of the good roads movement which resulted in the adoption, 1899, of an amendment to Constitution of Ark., authorizing counties to levy road tax. Led movement to secure legislation regulating coll. charters and degrees. Del. Ecumenical Conf. on Foreign Missions; mem. Gen. Bd. of Edn. of M.E. Ch., S., 1898-1902, Edn. Commn., 1903-06; mem. Ark. History Commn., 1909-13 and 1927—; spl. investigation of Ark. Penitentiary, 1908. Del. Gen. Conf. M.E. Ch., 5 times to 1930; sec. Ark. Hon. Forestry Commn., 1924—; pres. Ark. Anti-Saloon League, 1923—; pres. Western Meth. Assembly, Fayetteville, 1922-23, v.p., 1933—; v.p. Judicial Council (Supreme Court) M.E. Ch., S., 1934-39; reserve mem. Judicial Council Meth. Church, 1939—. Author: Twentieth Century Educational Problems, 1901; (poem) Together? Yes, Together (a response to the English laureate's "Together"); (song) My Own Loved Arkansas (adopted by State Teachers' Assn. for use in the pub. schs.); words and music of song, America, Our Fatherland, 1937. Home: Little Rock, Ark. Died Nov. 9, 1940.

MILLAR, Edward Alexander, army officer; b. in Ky., June 25, 1860; grad. U.S. Mil. Acad., 1822; grad. Arty. Sch., 1886; Army War Coll., 1909. Commd. 2d lt. 3d Arty., June 13, 1882; promoted through grades to col. 2d Field Arty., Dec. 1, 1911; trans. to 6th Field Arty., June 13, 1913, to 2d Field Arty., Jan. 27, 1914, to 3d Field Arty., 1916. Asst. instr. engring. and arty., Arty. Sch., Ft. Monroe, Va., 1891-96; a.d.c. to Gen. Edward B. Williston, 1898-99; with regt. in Philippine Islands, 1899; duty on Mexican border, 1917; comdr. 6th Brigade F.A., 6th Div., 5th Army Corps, A.E.F. in France, July 1918. Died Jan. 31, 1934.

MILLAR, William Bell, clergyman; b. Lake Mills, Wis.; s. Rev. William Thomas and Isabella (Buchanan) M.; A.B., Lawrence College, Appleton, Wis., 1889, D.D., 1920; m. Lella Frances McKesson, July 15, 1889; children—Laura McKesson, Muriel Waite, William Buchanan, Florence Isabelle. Gen. sec. Y.M.C.A., La Crosse, Wis., 1889; sec. 23d St. Y.M.C.A., New York, 1890-96; sec. Internat. Com. Y.M.C.A., 1896-1910; gen. sec. Laymen's Missionary Movement of U.S. and Can., 1910-20; asso. gen. sec. Interch. World Movement of N.A., 1919-20; gen. sec. Greater N.Y. Fedn. of Chs., 1921-34; sec. Motion Picture Foundation of U.S.A., 1934—. Organized Army and Navy Dept. of Y.M.C.A., 1898, and sr. sec. same until 1910, securing permanent bldgs., and funds of more than $2,000,000; traveled widely throughout N. America, Europe and Asia; visited Far East, 1904, and aided in opening way for work in Japanese Army, in Russo-Japanese War; organized World's Conf., held in Germany, 1909, promoting Christian and welfare work in armies and navies of the world. Trustee Dew University, Golden Rule Foundation, Near East Relief, etc. Mem. N.Y. Conf. M.E. Ch. Republican. Home: New York, N.Y. Died May 30, 1939.

MILLARD, Bailey, editor, author; b. Markesan, Wis., Oct. 2, 1859; s. George S. and Phœbe J. M.; ed. State Teachers Coll., Mankato, Minn.; wife dec.; children—Elmer Sherman, Mrs. L. W. Dwiggins. City editor San Francisco Call, 1891-92, city editor San Francisco Examiner, 1892-93, lit. editor same, 1895-1902; editor Cosmopolitan Magazine, May 1905-Oct. 1907; special writer for The Los Angeles Times, 1924—. Author: Fettered Commerce, 1892; Great American Novel (essays), 1899; She of the West (short stories), 1900; Songs of the Press, 1902; The Lure o' Gold (novel), 1904; The Difficult Islands (mag. serial), 1907; The Sea Hawk, 1910; Schoolma-am Island, 1912; Sunland Song, 1933. Mng. editor Munsey's Mag., 1912-14; editor Orchard and Farm, 1916-18; mng. editor San Francisco Evening Bulletin, 1918-19. Wrote series of articles on land conditions in Calif. which have effected agrarian reforms in that State; also History of the San Francisco Bay Region, for the Am. Hist. Society. Home: Eagle Rock City, Calif. Died Mar. 20, 1941.

MILLARD, Everett Lee, lawyer; b. Chicago, Apr. 28, 1877; s. Sylvester M. and Amelia Chapin (Collins) M.; A.B., Harvard, 1898; LL.B., Northwestern U., 1900; m. Elizabeth Boynton, June 17, 1908; children—Everett Lee, Elizabeth, Malcolm. Admitted to Ill. bar, 1900, and since practiced in Chicago;

pres. Chicago Suburban Gas & Electric Co., North Shore Gas Co.; v.p. North Shore Coke & Chem. Co., Denver Ice & Cold Storage Co. Commr. Art Commn. of Chicago (pres.); v.p. Eli Bates Settlement, Highland Park Hosp.; dir. Chicago Galleries Assn. Republican. Presbyn. Leader in securing bill-board regulation in Chicago; initiated State Art Commn. Act, now in force in Ill.; active in securing passage of Ill. Forest Preserve Act. Chevalier Order of the Crown, Belgium. Home: Highland, Park, Ill. Died Mar. 21, 1933.

MILLARD, Joseph Hopkins, senator; b. Hamilton, Can., Apr. 1836; s. J. K. and Elizabeth (Hopkins) M.; (parents temporarily residing in Can.); ed. common schs.; m. Caroline Grover Barrows, 1860 (died 1901). Resident of Omaha, 1856—; founded, 1866, pres., 1867-1920, now chmn. bd. Omaha Nat. Bank. Mayor of Omaha; govt. dir., 6 yrs., and dir., 7 yrs., U.P. R.R.; U.S. senator, 1901-07. Republican. Home: Omaha, Neb. Died Jan. 13, 1922.

MILLER, A. Blanchard, farming and land development; b. Richlands, N.C., Sept. 5, 1878; s. Joseph K. and Eliza (Blanchard) M.; ed. Pomona Coll., Claremont, Calif.; unmarried. Pres. Fontana Farms Co., ranchers and subdividers; president Fontana Union Water Co., Fontana Domestic Water Co., Fontana Power Co., B. B. Co. Regent U. of Calif. Republican. Elk. Home: Fontana, Calif. Died Apr. 13, 1941.

MILLER, Albert Edward, lawyer; b. Ypsilanti, Mich., Sept. 21, 1861; s. Albert and Olive (Tyler) M.; A.B., U. of Mich., 1883; m. Bessie G. Wilkinson, Nov. 11, 1896; children—James W., Edwin W. Was admitted to Mich. bar, 1885; has been with Duluth, S. Shore & Atlantic Ry., 1888—; successively atty., asst. to gen. counsel, and gen. solicitor, 1918-38, was also gen. solicitor Mineral Range R.R.; sr. of law firm Miller, Eldredge & Eldredge, Marquette, Mich., 1918-38, in practice alone, 1938—. Episcopalian. Republican. Home: Marquette, Mich. Died Jan. 23, 1939.

MILLER, Alexander Macomb, lt. col. corps of engrs., U.S.A.; b. Washington; s. Gen. Morris S. M., g.s. Gen. Alexander Macomb; apptd., March 2, 1861; grad. West Point, June 23, 1865, as 1st lt. engrs.; capt., Feb. 22, 1869; maj., April 16, 1883; lt. col., 1898; has been engaged in many engring. works; now in charge office of Washington aqueduct. Home: Washington, D.C. Died 1904.

MILLER, Alfred Brashear, pres. emeritus and acting prof. of the philos. sciences, Waynesburg Coll.; b. Brownsville, Pa., Oct. 16, 1829; prep. edn. in various academies; grad. Waynesburg Coll. (the 1st class grad. by coll.) 1853; D.D. (Adrian Coll.); LL. D. (Univ. Lebanon, Tenn.); prof. Mathematics Waynesburg Coll., 1853-58; pres. same, 1858-99. Clergyman Cumberland Presbyn. Ch., and was 10 yrs. pastor Waynesburg Ch. Author: Doctrines and Genius of the Cumberland Presbyterian Church, etc. Home: Waynesburg, Pa. Died 1902.

MILLER, Alfred Stanley, mining engr.; b. Normal, Pa., Oct. 20, 1856; s. Stephen and Mary E. C. (Riddle) M.; grad. Keystone State Normal Sch., 1880, M.E., 1882; A.B., Stanford, 1895, A.M., 1895; Ph.D. (pro merito), Heidelberg U. (Ohio), 1895; E.M., The A. Van der Naillen Sch. of Engring., 1898. Prin. high sch. and supt. schs., E. Mauch Chunk, Pa., 1880-82; prof. natural science, 1889-92, pres., 1892-93, Wichita (Kan.) U.; grad. student Stanford, 1893-95; with Nev. Metall. Works, 1896; mining engr., Auburn, Calif., 1897; in research work U. of Calif., 1897; prof. mining, metallurgy, and geology, U. of Ida., 1897-1905. Author: Manual of Assaying, 1900; The Cyanide Process, 1903. Home: Moscow, Idaho. Died Aug. 23, 1928.

MILLER, Andrew Joyce, investments; b. Washington, D.C., Oct. 22, 1867; s. William J. and Frances Marion (Joyce) M.; ed. Georgetown U.; m. Grace Converse Saunders, Apr. 20, 1904; 1 dau., Frances Marion. Partner Hallgarten & Co., 1926—; dir. Anaconda Copper Mining Co., Chile Copper Mining Co., Kansas City Southern Ry., Atlantic Gulf & West Indies S.S. Co., etc. Catholic. Home: New York, N.Y. Died Oct. 30, 1937.

MILLER, Arthur McQuiston, geologist; b. Eaton, O., Aug. 6, 1861; s. Robert and Margaret Ann (McQuiston) M.; U. of Wooster, 1880-82; A.B., Princeton, 1884, A.M., 1887; studied U. of Munich, 1891-92; unmarried. Prin. schs., Morning Sun, O., 1884-85; prin. high sch., Eaton, O., 1885-88; fellow in biology, Princeton, 1888-89; prof. natural history, Wilson Coll., Chambersburg, Pa., 1889-91; prof. geology, U. of Kentucky, 1892—, also dean Coll. Arts and Sciences; resigned deanship, 1917, and granted leave of absence as consulting and field geologist, Federal Oil Co., June 1917-June 1918; retired as prof. emeritus of geology, June 30, 1925. Democrat. Presbyn. Wrote: The Lead and Zinc Bearing Rocks of Central Kentucky, 1905; Coals of Western Border of Eastern Coal Field in Kentucky, 1910; Geology of the Georgetown Quadrangle, 1913; Geology of Franklin County, Kentucky, 1914; Geology of Kentucky, 1919; Geology of Woodford Co., 1925 (all pub. by Ky. Geol. Survey). Home: Asheville, N.C. Died Oct. 28, 1929.

MILLER, Augustus Samuel, lawyer, mayor; b. Plainfield, Conn., Aug. 13, 1847; s. Simon Williams and Anne (Lawton) M.; prep. edn. Mowry & Goff's Classical Sch., Providence, R.I.; grad. Brown Univ., A.B., 1871, later A.M.; m. Elizabeth Le Moine Davis, Feb. 17, 1881. Admitted to R.I. bar, Apr. 2, 1874; later to U.S. Circuit and to U.S. Supreme Court; engaged in gen. practice. Pres. Am. Enamel Co. Mem. Providence city council, 1885-87 (pres. 1887), R.I. Ho. Reps., 1884-85, 1889-91 (speaker 1889-91); State senator, 1893-94; mem. commn. to revise constn. of R.I., 1897; elected mayor of Providence, 1902, 1903, 1904; present term expires Jan 1, 1906. Democrat. Chmn. State Commn. on Harbor Improvement. Home: Providence, R.I. Died 1905.

MILLER, Benjamin Kurtz, lawyer, retired; b. Milwaukee, June 6, 1857; s. Benjamin Kurtz and Isabella (Peckham) M.; A.B., Pa. Coll., Gettysburg, Pa., 1877; studied law in offices of Finches, Lynde & Miller, 1877-80; unmarried. Admitted to Wis. bar, 1880; member Finches, Lynde & Miller, 1886-90, Miller, Noyes & Miller, 1890-98, Miller, Noyes, Miller & Wahl, 1898-1900, Miller, Noyes & Miller, 1900-Feb. 1906, retired. Trustee Northwestern Mut. Life Ins. Co., 1898— (finance com., 1899-1907, exec. com., 1904-07). Democrat. Was mem. Legal Advisory Board and chief Am. Protective League, Milwaukee. Author: Unabridged Table of Citations of Cases in Wisconsin Reports up to and Including the 126th Wisconsin, 1906; Foreign Citations in the Wisconsin Reports (58-140), 1910; J. N. Kurtz, Life and Genealogy, 1925. Home: Milwaukee, Wis. Died Mar. 17, 1929.

MILLER, Bloomfield Jackson, mathematician; b. Newark, N.J., Dec. 31, 1849; s. Elias Newton and Sarah M. Coates M.; ed. Newark Acad., Rutgers Coll., scientific class of 1868; m. Jeannie Ogden Miller, Nov. 5, 1880. Entered math. dept. Mutual Benefit Life Ins. Co., 1867; apptd. actuary, 1871, mathematician, 1882, 2d v.p., 1894, v.p. and mathematician, 1902—, dir., 1894—. Charter mem. and pres. Actuarial Soc. of America. Home: Perth Amboy, N.J. Died 1905.

MILLER, Byron E., physician; b. Dundee, N.Y., Mar. 17, 1855; s. John B. and Cynthia (Baker) M.; M.D., Cleveland Homœ. Hospital Coll., 1883; post-grad. work New York Polyclinic Sch. of Medicine and Surgery, 1889, N.Y. Post-Grad. Med. Sch. and Hosp., 1891 and 1898; spl. courses in microscopy and urinalysis and surgery, Vienna, Austria, 1901-03; m. Jessie A. Burbank, July 25, 1888. Began practice, Doylestown, O., 1882; located in Portland, Ore., 1884; surgeon-in-chief homœ. staff diseases of women, Portland Hosp., 1900-04; phys. to I.O.O.F. Home of Ore.; med. dir. Am. Life Ins. Co. of Ore.; mem. and sec. State Bd. Med. Examiners of Ore., 1895-08 (pres. 1908-09); specializes in surgery and diseases of women. Mason, Odd Fellow. Home: Portland, Ore. Died Feb. 25, 1925.

MILLER, Charles, merchant, soldier; b. Oberhoffen Alsace, France, June 15, 1843; common sch. edn. (A.M., Bucknell U.); came to U.S., 1854. Entered oil bus., 1869, and was pres. Galena-Signal Oil Co. many yrs., now chmn. bd. Chmn. bd. Am. Steel Foundry Co., Am. Locomotive Co., and dir. about 40 other corps.; pres. Lake Erie, Franklin & Clarion R.R. Co. Mayor of Franklin, Pa., 2 terms; mem. Pa. State Board of Charities 6 years; maj.-gen. Pa. N.G. 5 years. Supt. 1st Baptist S.S. of Franklin from 1872 and conducts Bible class of more than 600 pupils; has maintained at own expense, at Franklin, the Miller Night Sch., 1890—. Decorated by French Govt. as Chevalier of Legion of Honor for eminent services to industry and commerce. Home: Franklin, Pa. Died Dec. 20, 1927.

MILLER, Charles Armand, clergyman; b. Shepherdstown, W.Va., Mar. 7, 1864; s. Rev. J. I. and Lida (Hulls) M.; A.B., Roanoke Coll., Va., 1887, A.M., 1892; grad. Theol. Sem. of Evang. Luth. Ch., Phila., 1889; B.D., Chicago Theol. Sem. 1903; (D.D., Roanoke Coll., 1904); m. Mary M. Sherman, June 25, 1889. Ordained Evang. Luth. ministry, 1889; pastor Coll. Ch., Roanoke Coll., 1888-96, Ch. of the Holy Trinity, New York, 1896-1908, St. John's Charleston, S.C., 1908-12, St. Mark's, Phila., June 1912—. Author: Ad Astra, and Other Verses on Sacred Themes, 1898; The Way of the Cross, 1899; A Book of the Bible Texts (transl. from the German), 1901; The Perfect Prayer, 1902; The Sacramental Feast, 1911. Home: Philadelphia, Pa. Died Sept. 10, 1917.

MILLER, Charles C., apiarist, writer; b. Ligonier, Pa., June 10, 1831; s. Johnson J. (M.D.) and Phebe (Roadman) M.; A.B., Union College, Schenectady, N.Y., 1853; M.D., Med. Dept., U. of Mich., 1856; m. Mrs. Helen M. White, Aug. 12, 1857 (died 1880); 2d, Miss Sidney J. Wilson, Nov. 15, 1881. Began keeping bees at Marengo, 1861; had at one time 400 colonies of bees. Writer for bee and agrl. journals; dept. editor Gleanings of Bee Culture, 1890—; asso. editor Am. Bee Journal, 1894—. Prohibitionist. Presbyn. Author: A Book—By P. Benson, Sr., 1874; A Year Among the Bees, 1886; Forty Years Among the Bees, 1902; Fifty Years Among the Bees, 1911. Editor "Apiary Terms" in Standard Dictionary. Home: Marengo, Ill. Died Sept. 4, 1920.

MILLER, Charles Ervine, univ. pres. emeritus; b. nr. Massillon, O., Feb. 24, 1867; s. Peter and Angeline M.; A.B., Heidelberg U., 1886, A.M., 1890, D.D., 1900; LL.D., 1911; grad. Heidelberg Theol. Sem., 1888; Union Theol. Sem., 1889-90; U. of Chicago, summer, 1897; m. Laura G. Garver, Dec. 12, 1894. Ordained Reformed Ch. in U.S. ministry, 1890; pastor Dayton, O., 1890-99; prof. practical theology, Heidelberg Theol Sem., 1900-02; pres., prof. ethics, æsthetics and evidences of Christianity, Heidelberg Univ., 1902-37 (emeritus). Editor Christian World, Dayton, O., 1898-1901. Pres. Ohio Christian Endeavor Union, 1895; v.p. Ohio S.S. Assn., 1898-1902. Home: Rocky River, O. Died Jan. 10, 1939.

MILLER, Charles Henry, landscape painter; b. New York, N.Y., Mar. 20, 1842; s. Jacob M.; ed. there and at Royal Acad. of Bavaria; m. Mrs. Elizabeth Dorothea Mosback, Oct. 3, 1900. First exhibited his paintings at Nat. Acad. of Design, 1860; noted for his paintings of Long Island scenes; has exhibited at all important nat. and internat. expns. of fine arts, 1876—; has received numerous medals. N.A., 1875. Home: Queens, New York, N.Y. Died Jan. 21, 1922.

MILLER, C(harles) Jeff(erson), surgeon; b. Winchester, Tenn., Feb. 9, 1874; s. Charles Jewett and Elizabeth (Johnston) M.; Terrill Coll., Tenn.; U. of the South, Sewanee, Tenn.; M.D., U. of Tenn., 1893; m. Ada Parker, Jan. 30, 1896; 1 dau., Elizabeth. Prof. gynecology, Tulane U., 1911; prof. gynecology Tulane Post-Grad. Med. Sch.; visiting surgeon, Charity Hospital; also chief in gynecology, Touro Infirmary. President Howard Memorial Library, New Orleans; mem. bd. of control Leper Home of La. Fellow Am. Coll. Surgeons (pres. 1930). Mem. Med. R.C., U.S. Army. Home: New Orleans, La. Died Mar. 21, 1936.

MILLER, Charles R., governor; b. Chester Co., Pa., Sept. 30, 1857; B.L., Swarthmore Coll., 1879; LL.B., U. of Pa., 1881; LL.D., Delaware Coll., 1917; m. Abigail Morgan Woodnutt, Dec. 11, 1884. Admitted to Phila. bar, 1881; engaged as officer and dir. for 30 yrs. in ry. mfg., mining, gas, electric light and water power corps. in various parts of U.S.; retired from active management, 1910 and 1911; still dir. in many cos. Elected, 1910, mem. Del. State Senate for term of 4 yrs.; resigned Aug. 24, 1912, to accept nomination for gov.; apptd. water commr. City of Wilmington, July 1, 1911, resigned to assume office of gov. of Del., term 1913-17. Mem. Rep. Congressional Com. (exec. com.), Am. Bankers Assn. (exec. com. and federal legislative com.), Pa. Soc. of New York; trustee and pres. finance com. Delaware Coll., Newark. Sr. Warden Immanuel Episcopal Ch.; pres. Del. Hosp.; pres. Del. Bldg. and Loan Assn. Republican. Home: Wilmington, Del. Died Sept. 18, 1927.

MILLER, Charles Ransom, editor; b. Hanover, N.H., Jan. 17, 1849; s. Elijah T. and Chastina (Hoyt) M.; A.B., Dartmouth, 1872 (LL.D., Dartmouth Coll., 1905; Litt.D., Columbia Univ., 1915); m. Frances Daniels, Oct. 10, 1876. On staff Springfield Republican, 1872-75; on New York Times, 1875—, editorial writer, 1881-83, editor-in-chief, 1883—. V.p. and dir. New York Times Co.; dir. Tidewater Paper Co. Chevalier Legion of Honor (France); Order of Leopold (Belgian), Commander Royal Order of George I (Greek). Home: New York, N.Y. Died July 18, 1922.

MILLER, Charles Russel, lawyer; b. Canton, O., Oct. 1, 1858; s. William K. and Sarah B. M.; ed. Canton High Sch., and Canton Acad.; m. Alice Evelyn Rose, May 9, 1883. Admitted to bar, Dec. 3, 1879; presdl. elector, 1896; pres. Commercial Law League, 1899; maj. and asst. adj. gen., 1898-99; judge advocate gen. Spanish War Vets., 1900-01; comdr.-in-chief United Spanish War Vets., 1906-07. Republican. Home: Cleveland, O. Died Dec. 18, 1916.

MILLER, Charles Wesley, lawyer; b. Galena, Ind., Feb. 4, 1863; s. Jacob B. and Isabelle (Smith) M.; student Southern Ind. Normal Sch. 2 yrs., Central Ind. Normal Sch. 2 yrs.; LL.B., U. of Mich., 1884; m. Sarah Elizabeth Perkins, June 1, 1887. Practiced at Greenfield, Ind., 1884-85, Goshen, Ind., 1885-1909, Indianapolis, 1909—; mem. Miller & Dowling. Director National City Realty Co., Farmers Trust Co. (Indianapolis), and the National City Bank. Mayor of Goshen, 1888-90; presdl. elector-at-large for Ind., 1900; atty. gen. of Ind., 1903-07; U.S. atty. for Ind., Apr. 6, 1909-Jan. 1, 1914; conducted prosecution dynamite conspiracy case. Methodist. Mason. Died Feb. 17, 1923.

MILLER, Charles William Emil, univ. prof.; b. Richmond, Va., Jan. 14, 1863; s. Charles William and Margarethe (Klatte) M.; grad. Baltimore City Coll., 1880; A.B., Johns Hopkins, 1882, Ph.D., 1886; m. Sue Farwell Parsons, Aug. 12, 1889; children—Emil Eliphalet, Harold Warner, Edith Virginia, Helen Mar. Instr., Milton Acad., Baltimore, 1885-88; prof. Latin and Greek, Peoria (Ill.) High Sch., 1888-90; prof. Latin and English, Walther Coll., St. Louis, 1890-91; spl. asst. to prof. Gildersleeve, at Johns Hopkins, 1891-92; asso. in Greek, 1892-97, asso. prof. Greek, 1897-1915, prof. Greek, 1915-25, Francis White prof.

Greek, 1925-33, prof. emeritus and lecturer in Greek, 1933—, sec. Bd. of Univ. Studies, 1915-26, mem. Acad. Council, 1925-30, Johns Hopkins Univ. In Europe on leave of absence, Feb.-Sept. 1913. Democrat. Part author: Syntax of Classical Greek from Homer to Demosthenes, Part I, 1900, Part II, 1911. Editor: Selections from the Brief Mention of Basil Lanneau Gildersleeve, 1930. Asst. editor, 1916-18, mng. editor, 1918-20, editor, 1920-34, Am. Journal of Philology. Died Aug. 7, 1934.

MILLER, Cincinnatus Heine ("Joaquin Miller"), author; b. in Wabash Dist., Ind., Nov. 10, 1841. Removed with parents to Ore., 1850; mined in Calif.; returned to Ore., 1860; studied law; express messenger in Idaho, 1861; edited, 1863, the Eugene (Ore.) Democratic Register, a weekly, which was suppressed on charges of disloyalty; practiced law Cañon City, Ore., 1863-66; co. judge Grant Co., Ore., 1866-70; went to London and published his first book of poems, which met with a favorable reception; several yrs. in newspaper life at Washington; from 1887 has been resident of Oakland, Calif.; corr. New York Journal in Klondike, 1897-98. Author: Songs of the Sierras; Pacific Palms; Songs of the Sunland; The Ship of the Desert; Life Among the Modocs; First Families of the Sierras; The One Fair Woman; The Danites in the Sierras; Shadows of Shasta; Memorie and Rime; Baroness of New York; Songs of Far-Away Lands; The Destruction of Gotham; The Building of the City Beautiful, a Poetic Romance; '49, or, the Gold-Seekers of the Sierras; Chants for the Boer, 1900; True Bear Stories, 1900. Plays: The Danites; The Silent Man; '49; Tally-Ho; etc. Mem. Nat. Inst. Arts and Letters. Home: Dimond, Calif. Died Feb. 17, 1913.

MILLER, Clarence B., congressman; b. in Goodhue Co., Minn., Mar. 13, 1872; s. Benjamin Grant and Sally Esther (Perkins) M.; A.B., U. of Minn., 1895, LL.B., 1900; m. Effie Jack, June 8, 1904; m. 2d, Gertrude V. Pattison, Aug. 2, 1913. Supt. pub. schs., Rushford, Minn., 1895-98; practiced law in Duluth several yrs.; sec. Rep. Nat. Com., Jan. 1920. Mem. Minn. Ho. of Rep., 1907; mem. 61st to 65th Congresses (1909-19), 8th Minn. Dist. Home: Washington, D.C. Died Jan. 10, 1922.

MILLER, Clyde Winwood, insurance exec.; b. Osage City, Kan., June 30, 1875; s. Hiram B. and Eva I. (Lapham) M.; A.B., U. of Kan., 1895, LL.B., 1897; m. Grace E. Colwell, Oct. 27, 1897; children—Margaret Irene (Mrs. John K. Kline), Eva Colwell (Mrs. Wm. W. Payne), Marjorie Virginia (Mrs. Ned N. Fleming), Marian Lucile (Mrs. Creston Alexander). Began in insurance business at Topeka, 1907; pres. Preferred Risk Fire Ins. Co., Miller Live Stock & Investment Co., Investors Security Co., Miller-Colwell Investment Co.; apptd. receiver Federal Life Ins. Co., Kansas City, Kan., 1937. Dir. Kan. State Chamber of Commerce; dir. Kan. Univ. Endowment Assn.; dir. Kan. Pioneers Memorial Corp.; dir. Regional Agrl. Credit Corp. (govt. bank), Wichita, Kan., serving states of Kan., Okla., N.M. and Colo.; dir. Topeka Hotel Co. Republican candidate for Congress, 1916; sec. to Gov. Paulen, 1925-26. Pres. bd. trustees, Kan. Vocational Coll., 1912-16. Presbyn. Mason. Home: Topeka, Kan. Died Apr. 16, 1940.

MILLER, Crosby Parke, brig. gen.; b. Pomfret, Vt., Oct. 20, 1843; s. Crosby and Orpha (Hewitt) M.; ed. pub. schs. and West Point; m. Frances Laura Haskin, May 28, 1874. Enlisted as corporal Co. G, 16th Vt. Vol. Inf., Sept. 4, 1862; disch. Mar. 12, 1863; apptd. U.S. Mil. Acad., July 1, 1863; commd. 2d lt. 4th U.S. Arty., June 17, 1867; promoted through grades to col. q.m. vols., July 12, 1898-Mar. 2, 1899; lt. col. deputy q.m. gen. U.S.A., Oct. 2, 1902; brig. gen., Mar. 30, 1906; retired at own request, over 40 yrs.' service, Mar. 31, 1906. Home: Burlington, Vt. Died Mar. 20, 1927.

MILLER, Daniel Long, bishop; b. nr. Hagerstown, Md., Oct. 5, 1841; s. Abram and Kathrine (Long) M.; attended subscription and dist. schools in Maryland; taught school, at Rockdale, Maryland, and in Franklin County, Pa., 1865-66; (LL.D., Mt. Morris Coll., 1898); m. Elizabeth Talley, Feb. 6, 1868. In grain and grocery business, several yrs.; became business mgr. Mt. Morris (Ill.) Coll., 1879; took up publishing business, 1882; elected pres. Mt. Morris Coll., 1881; studied Halle, Germany, 1884. Editor of Gospel Messenger, 1885; elected to ministry of Ch. of The Brethren, 1887; ordained bishop, 1890; world-wide traveler. Chmn. Missionary and Tract Board of Church of the Brethren. Author: Girdling the Globe, 1897; Eternal Verities, 1902; The Other Half of the Globe, 1906; Some Who Led, 1912. Home: Mt. Morris, Ill. Died June 8, 1921.

MILLER, Darius, ry. pres.; b. Princeton, Ill., Apr. 3, 1859; s. J. S. and Elizabeth H. M.; ed. Princeton, Ill.; m. Sue C. Brown, Oct. 19, 1882. Began ry. service as stenographer in gen. freight office M.C. R.R., 1877-80; clerk gen. freight office St. Louis, Iron Mountain & Southern Ry., 1880-81; chief clerk to gen. mgr., 1881-83, gen. freight and ticket agt., 1883-87, Memphis & Little Rock R.R.; gen. freight and pass. agt., 1887-89, traffic mgr., 1889-90, St. Louis, Ark. & Tex. Ry.; traffic mgr. "Queen & Crescent" route, 1890-93; traffic mgr., 1893-96, v.p., Nov. 1896-Oct. 1898, M.,K.&T. Ry.; 2d v.p. G.N. Ry., Oct. 1898-Jan. 1, 1902; 1st v.p., Jan. 1, 1902-Jan. 31, 1910, pres., Feb. 1, 1910—, C.,B.&Q. R.R. Co.; also pres. C.&S. Ry. Co., Feb. 1, 1910—. Home: Chicago, Ill. Died Aug. 23, 1914.

MILLER, Dayton Clarence, physicist; b. Strongsville, O., Mar. 13, 1866; s. Charles W. D. and Vienna (Pomeroy) M.; A.B., Baldwin U., 1886, A.M., 1889; D.Sc., Princeton, 1890, Miami, 1924, Dartmouth, 1927; LL.D., Western Reserve, 1927, Baldwin-Wallace Col., 1933; D.Eng., Case, 1936; m. Edith C. Easton, June 28, 1893. Prof. natural science, Baldwin U., 1888-89; asst. in mathematics and physics, 1890-93, prof. physics, 1893—, Case Sch. Applied Science, Cleveland, O. Fellow Am. Phys. Soc. (sec. 1918-22, v.p. 1923-24, pres. 1925-26), A.A.A.S. (sec. sect. physics, 1903-07, v.p. 1908, gen. sec. 1910), Am. Acad. Arts and Sciences, Ohio Acad. Sciences; mem. numerous scientific socs. Awarded Longstreth medal, 1917; Elliott Cresson gold medal, Franklin Institute, 1926; A.A.A.S. prize, 1925; Cleveland Distinguished Service medal, 1927. Trustee Baldwin-Wallace Coll., 1899—, sec. bd., 1913-26, chmn. bd., 1936—. Lowell lecturer, 1914. Author: Laboratory Physics, 1903; Boehm on The Flute and Flute-Playing, 1908; The Science of Musical Sounds, 1916; Bibliography of the Flute, 1935; Anecdotal History of Sound, 1935; Sound Waves, Shape and Speed, 1937; Sparks, Lightning, Cosmic Rays, 1939. Died Feb. 22, 1941.

MILLER, (Jahu) Dewitt, lyceum lecturer; b. Cross River, Westchester Co., N.Y., Mar. 1, 1857; s. John and Phœbe (Seymour) M.; ed. Fort Edward (N.Y.) Collegiate Inst. and Pennington (N.J.) Sem.; unmarried. Life mem. Bibliog. Soc., London. Home: Forest Glen, Md. Died 1911.

MILLER, Edmund Howd, chemist, educator, author; b. Fairfield, Conn., Sept. 12, 1869; s. George M. M.; grad. Columbia, 1891; took course in chemistry School of Mines, Columbia, 1887-91 (A.M., 1892; Ph.D., 1894, Columbia); m. June 11, 1898. Engaged in teaching chemistry, 1891—; adj. prof. analytical chemistry and assaying, 1901-04, prof. analytical chemistry, 1904—, Columbia. Fellow Chem. Soc., London, A.A.A.S. Author: Notes on Assaying (with Prof. Ricketts), 1897; Calculations of Analytical Chemistry, 1900; Quantitative Analysis for Mining Engineers, 1904. Died 1906.

MILLER, Edward Furber, engineer; b. Somerville, Mass., Jan. 18, 1866; s. William Gibbs and Sarah (Furber) M.; S.B., Mass. Inst. Tech., 1886; D.Sc., R.I. State Coll., 1921; m. Mary Willard Reed, Sept. 11, 1900. Teacher of mech. engring., 1886-92, prof. steam engring., 1892—, Mass. Inst. Tech., also in charge dept. mech. engring., 1911—; dean of army officers, Mass. Inst. Tech., 1922—. Col. Auxiliary Reserve; asst. dist. chief of ordnance, 1930—. Universalist. Author: Steam Boilers (with Cecil H. Peabody), 1897; Problems in Thermodynamics and Heat-Engineering (with C. W. Berry and J. C. Riley), 1911; Notes on Power Plant Design (with James Holt), 3d edit.; Notes on Heat Engineering, 1931. Home: Newton Center, Mass. Died June 12, 1933.

MILLER, Edward Terhune, lawyer; b. Keytesville, Mo., Dec. 29, 1870; s. John Caskie and Ann Almeria (Hawes) M.; prep. edn., Wentworth Mil. Acad., Lexington, Mo.; B.S., Westminster Coll., Fulton, Mo., 1889, M.S., 1892; m. Bess Townsend, Jan. 20, 1904; children—Edward Howes, Townsend. Admitted to Mo. bar, 1892, and began practice at Keytesville and Brunswick; moved to St. Louis, 1903; mem. legal staff St.L.&S.F. Ry. Co., 1908-32; v.p. and gen. solicitor, 1925-32, became gen. counsel for receivers, Nov. 1932; mem. law firm, E. T. and E. H. Miller. Trustee Sch. of Ozarks. Presbyterian. Mason. Home: St. Louis, Mo. Died Aug. 11, 1938.

MILLER, Edward Waite, clergyman; b. Montgomery, N.Y., Aug. 29, 1865; s. Peter Eager and Margaret Bruyn (Waite) M.; A.B., Union U., Schenectady, N.Y., 1887, A.M., 1891, D.D., 1902; grad. Auburn Theol. Sem., 1891; student U. of Berlin, 1 yr.; m. Lorraine Bailey Taylor, June 10, 1917; children—Edward Waite, Charles Taylor, Hasbrouck Bailey. Ordained ministry Presbyn. Ch., 1891; pastor Syracuse, N.Y., 1892-95; prof. ch. history, Auburn Theol. Sem., 1895-1908; pastor Albany, N.Y., 1908-13; sec. Bd. Foreign Missions Ref. Ch. in America, 1913-17; pastor Locust Valley, N.Y., 1917-21, Gloversville, N.Y., 1921—; stated clerk and treasurer Presbytery of Albany, 1928—. Republican. Author: Life and Writings of Wessel Gansfort (2 vols.), 1917; Lyrics of the Camp, 1928. Editor: The Parsons Memorials, 1932. Home: Gloversville, N.Y. Died Feb. 6, 1939.

MILLER, Edwin Lillie, educator, author; b. Aurora, Ill., Jan. 9, 1868; s. Robert and Mary (Lillie) M.; A.M., U. of Mich., 1890, A.M., 1891; m. Gertrude Margaret Doyle, July 19, 1920. Principal high sch., Hancock, Mich., 1891-92; teacher Englewood High Sch., Chicago, 1892-1907; head English dept. and asst. prin., Detroit Central High Sch., 1907-14; prin. Northwestern High Sch., Detroit, 1914-20; prin. Northern High Sch., Detroit, 1920; supervising prin. Detroit high schs., 1922; asst. supt. schs., Detroit, 1925. Mem. bd. dirs. Detroit Bd. of Commerce, 1918-20. Republican. Mason. Author: Practical English Composition (books I-IV), 1914-16; English Literature—A Guide to the Best Reading, 1917; New English Composition (books I-IV), 1927-30; Explorations in Literature—American Writers, 1933. Gen. editor Lippincott's English Classics. Home: Detroit, Mich. Died Aug. 21, 1934.

MILLER, Elizabeth Smith, reformer; b. "Hampton," nr. Geneseo, N.Y., Sept. 20, 1822; d. Gerrit and Anne Carroll (Fitzhugh) Smith; ed. by home governesses, and at Manual Labor Sch., Clinton, N.Y., and Friends Sch., Phila.; m. Col. Charles Dudley Miller, banker, Oct. 18, 1843. Designed, in 1851, the "Bloomer" costume, which took its name from the editor of "The Lily," Mrs. Amelia Bloomer, who adopted it; an early advocate of suffrage for women; hon. pres. Geneva (N.Y.) Polit. Equality Club. Dormitory of William Smith Coll., Geneva, named in her honor. Author: In the Kitchen (receipt book); Chimes Calendar, 1885. Home: Geneva, N.Y. Died 1911.

MILLER, Emerson R., chemist; b. Bascom, O., June 2, 1862; s. George and Charity Ann (Hook) M.; National Normal U., Lebanon, O., 1883; Wittenberg College, Springfield, 1884-87; Ph.C., U. of Michigan, 1892, Phar.M., 1893, B.S., 1894, M.S., 1895; U. of Marburg, 1901-02; Ph.D., U. of Minn., 1918; m. Mary Adda White, June 22, 1892. Prin. high sch., Arkansas City, Kan., 1888-91; asst. in qualitative analysis, U. of Mich., 1894-95; adj. prof. pharmacy, Ala. Poly. Inst., 1895-96, prof., 1896-1905; chief chem. dept., Expt. Sta., Santiago de Las Vegas, 1905-06; prof. pharm. chemistry, Ala. Poly. Inst., 1906-13; actg. asst. prof. plant chemistry, and chemist, Pharmaceut. Expt. Sta., Wis., 1913-17; prof. of chemistry, and research chemist, Ala. Poly. Inst., 1918—. Home: Auburn, Ala. Deceased.

MILLER, Emily (Clark) Huntington, author; b. Brooklyn, Conn., Oct. 22, 1833; d. Dr. Thomas and Paulina (Clark) Huntington; A.B., Oberlin Coll., 1857 (hon. A.M., 1893; L.H.D., Northwestern U., 1909); m. John E. Miller, Sept. 5, 1860 (died 1882). Editor Little Corporal (children's mag.), afterward combined with St. Nicholas, 1867-75; dean of women, Northwestern U., 1891-98. Author: The Kirkwood Series; What Tommy Did; The House that Johnny Rented; A Summer at Riverside Farm; Fighting the Enemy; The King's Messengers; Thorn Apples; Helps and Hindrances; A Little Maid (poem); Highways and Hedges; Kathie's Experience; For the Beloved (poems); Songs from the Nest (poems). Home: St. Paul, Minn. Died Nov. 2, 1913.

MILLER, E(mma) P(ark) Smith, educator; b. Burlington, N.Y.; d. Rev. Henry A. and Emeline L. (Kendall) Smith; grad. Hamilton (N.Y.) Sem., 1862; m. H. Thane Miller, Feb. 1881 (died 1895). Prin. the H. Thane Miller Sch. for Girls and Young Ladies (founded 1856). Baptist. Mem. Mt. Auburn Lit. Soc., Cincinnati Br. Am. Folk-Lore Society. Home: Cincinnati, O. Deceased.

MILLER, Ephraim, univ. prof.; b. Carrollton, O., Apr. 25, 1833; s. John and Mary (Miller) M.; A.B., Allegheny Coll., Pa., 1855, A.M., 1858, hon. Ph.D., 1895; m. Miss Elisabeth Campbell, July 10, 1855 (died 1860); m. 2d, Anna A. Hoge, June 5, 1862; children—Mrs. L. J. Richards (dec.); Mrs. M. O. Stanley, Lloyd W., Mrs. Mary E. Barnes. Supt. of schs., Youngstown, O., 1855-56, Findlay, O., 1859-70, Lawrence, Kan., 1870-74; prof. mathematics and astronomy, 1874-1910 (emeritus), dean Coll. Liberal Arts and Sciences, 1895-1903, U. of Kansas. Republican. Presbyn. Author: Plane and Spherical Trigonometry, 1891. Home: Pasadena, Calif. Died Nov. 21, 1930.

MILLER, Ernest Henry; b. La Rue, O., Apr. 9, 1888; s. Joseph and Julia (Keache) M.; prep. edn., high sch., Marion, O.; student New York U.; m. Beatrice May, Jan. 5, 1912. Treas. Universal Auto Co., taxicabs, East Orange, N.J., 1909-12; organizer and pres. Yellow Cab Co., Newark, N.J.; one of organizers, 1921, pres., 1926-29, Yellow Taxi Corp., N.Y. City; chmn. bd. and pres. Parmalee Transportation Co., 1929—; pres. Transportation Management Corp., E. H. Miller, Inc.; v.p. Checker Cab Mfg. Corp. Home: New York, N.Y. Died Dec. 24, 1932.

MILLER, Eugene Harper, banker; b. South Bend, Ind., Jan. 30, 1869; s. William and Mary (Groff) M.; grad. high sch., South Bend; m. Anne Archbold, Aug. 10, 1896; children—Dama Hunnison (dec.), Eugene Harper, Janet (dec.), Richard Archbold. Began with Citizens Nat. Bank, South Bend, 1893; began with Am. Trust Co., South Bend, 1904, becoming pres., 1919; now pres. Quick Action Ignition Co. Chmn. bankers com. Liberty Loan campaign, South Bend, World War. Pres. Camp Fire Girls (South Bend). Republican. Mason. Home: South Bend, Ind. Died Feb. 23, 1940.

MILLER, Francis Garner, forester; b. Lanark, Ill., June 2, 1866; s. Isaiah and Isabel Jane (Moffett) M.; M. Didactics, Ia. State Normal Sch., 1893; B.Ph., State U. of Ia., 1900; B.S. Agr., Ia. State Coll., 1901; post-grad. work, degree Master Forestry, Yale, 1903; m. Evelyn Depew Miller, Sept. 15, 1906; 1 dau., Frances Depew (dec.). Supt. pub. schs. in Ia., 1893-99; prof. forestry, U. of Neb., 1903-07; prof. forestry and dean Coll. of Forestry, U. of Wash.,

1907-12; prof. and head of dept. forestry, Wash. State Coll., 1915-17; prof. forestry and dean Sch. of Forestry, U. of Ida., 1917—. Forest asst., Forest Service, U.S. Dept. Agr., 1903-12. Home: Moscow, Idaho. Died Mar. 8, 1934.

MILLER, Frank Augustus, hotel keeper; b. Tomah, Wis., June 30, 1857; s. Christopher Columbus and Mary A. (Clark) M.; ed. at home by mother; m. Isabella Demorest Hardenberg, June 8, 1880 (died 1907); m. 2d, Marion Louise Clark, Dec. 8, 1910. Removed to Calif. with parents, 1873; with his parents founded Glenwood Mission Inn, 1875, and with them continued to own and operate it while they lived, rebuilding it in Spanish architecture, 1901, and making later additions, including chapel dedication, 1932, to St. Francis of Assisi; has collected Spanish and Oriental art objects, making the Inn a museum of architecture and art; widely known as "Master of the Inn"; has secured many important meetings at Riverside; pres. Glenwood Hotel Co.; builder, 1890, and mgr. 15 yrs. Loring Opera House; builder, 1898, and mgr. 15 yrs. Riverside & Arlington Electric Ry. Leader in securing location U.S. Govt. Indian Sch., U.S. Aviation Sch., U. of Calif. Grad. Sch. of Sub Tropical Agr.; established Riverside Civic Center (10 grouped pub. bldgs. in Spanish Colonial style), etc. Republican. Conglist. Decorated Order Rising Sun by Emperor of Japan, 1928, in recognition of work for internat. friendship; assisted in founding So. Calif. Japanese Cherry Blossom Festival, 1929; decorated by French Govt. as an art connoisseur, 1930. Home: Riverside, Calif. Died June 15, 1935.

MILLER, Frank Ebenezer, M.D.; b. Hartford, Conn., Apr. 12, 1859; s. Ebenezer B. and Mayette (Deming) M.; A.B., Trinity Coll., Conn., 1881; M.D., Coll. Phys. and Surg. (Columbia), 1884; m. Emily Weston, Apr. 28, 1892. Interne New York and Charity Hosps., 6 mos., St. Francis Hosp., 2 yrs., sanitary insp. Bd. of Health, N.Y. City, 1886-89; served as asst. to various specialists in treatment of nose, throat and ear; began practice, 1896; chief throat surgeon to Bellevue Hosp., 1886, Vanderbilt Clinic, 1890-93; now consulting phys. to St. Francis and St. Joseph's hosps. Tenor singer; made scientific study of the voice and originated "vocal art-science," a method of voice production. Republican. Baptist. Author: Observations in Vocal Art Science, 1909; The Voice, Its Production, Care and Preservation, 1910; Vocal Art-Science, 1917; The Banner of Universal Harmony, 1919. Home: New York, N.Y. Died Apr. 15, 1932.

MILLER, Frank Harvey, lawyer; b. Augusta, Ga., Oct. 13, 1836; s. Andrew Jackson and Martha Burt (Olive) M.; ed. Acad. of Richmond Co., pvt. schs., and two yrs. Univ. of Ga.; m. Julia Dyer Kitchen, July 6, 1859. Admitted to bar, Nov. 1855; was asst. to dist. atty. Confederate States; adj. 9th regt. Ga. State troops. Pres. and trustee Acad. of Richmond Co.; chmn. trustees Masonic Hall; v.p. Augusta Orphan Asylum; chancellor diocese of Ga., P.E. Church. Home: Augusta, Ga. Died 1908.

MILLER, Frank Justus, univ. prof.; b. Clinton, Tenn., Nov. 26, 1858; s. Rev. James W. and Lydia Ann (Butler) M.; A.B., Denison U., 1879, A.M., 1882; Ph.D., Yale, 1892; attended lectures univs. of Halle, München and Jena, 1902-03; LL.D., Denison, 1909; m. Lida Willett, July 10, 1883; children—Winifred Fisk (Mrs. John Maurice Clark), Raymond Philbrook. Prof. Latin, Clinton Coll., 1880-81; vice-prin. high sch., Plainfield, N.J., 1881-87; instr. Latin, Worcester (Mass.) Acad., 1887-90; asst. and examiner affiliations, 1892-98, dean of affiliations, 1898-1904, examiner for secondary schs., 1904-11, dean in Colleges, 1911-23, U. of Chicago; also instr. Latin, 1892-94, asst. prof., 1894-1901, asso. prof., 1901-09, prof. 1909-25; emeritus, 1925—, U. of Chicago; visiting U. of Ia., 1925—, U. of Missouri, 1929-30, U. of Illinois, 1933; mem. staff of Vergilius Cruise, 1930. Editor Classical Journal, 1908-28. Decorated Commendatore Crown of Italy, 1930. Editor: Selected Works of Vergil, with commentary, 1892; Selected Works of Ovid, with Commentary, 1898; A Second (year) Latin Book, 1902. Author: Dido, an Epic Tragedy, 1901; Studies in Roman Poetry, 1901; The Tragedies of Seneca in English Verse, 1907; Two Dramatizations from Vergil, 1908; In the Loeb Classical Library; Translation, with Text, Metamorphoses of Ovid; Translation (prose), with text, Tragedies of Seneca, 1915. Home: Denver, Colo. Died Apr. 23, 1938.

MILLER, Franklin Thomas, publisher; b. Newton, Mass., Apr. 15, 1873; s. Edward Frederick and Olive Sanford (Burke) M.; B.S. in naval architecture, Mass. Inst. Tech., 1895; m. Lois Mabel Sawyer, June 4, 1901; 1 son, Richard Franklin. Sec. F. W. Dodge Co., pubs., 1895, treas., 1912, pres., 1915, chmn. bd. Sweets Catalogue Service, Inc., Architectural Record Co., Record and Guide Co., Am. Contractor Pub. Co., 1920. Dir. div. constrn. and development U.S. Dept. of Labor, World War, also as asst. to U.S. Senate Com. on Reconstruction and as asst. to Sec. of Commerce. Mem. President's Emergency Com. for Employment. Trustee Mass. Inst. Tech., 1920-25. Retired. Republican. Methodist. Home: Auburndale, Mass. Died Jan. 29, 1940.

MILLER, Fred J., industrial engr.; b. Yellow Springs, O., Jan. 3, 1857; s. John Z. and Elizabeth (Woodhurst) M.; ed. pub. schs.; m. Julia Kindelberger, 1876; children—Katherin C., Grace E. With Am. Machinist, 1887-1907, as editor and last 10 yrs. as editor-in-chief; gen. mgr. factories of Union Typewriter Co., 1909-18; pub. service commr. of Pa., Mar. 1924-Apr. 1925. Served as maj. Ordnance Dept., U.S.A., Jan. 4, 1918-Feb. 21, 1919. Trustee Simplified Spelling Bd. Awarded Gantt medal, by joint action of Am. Soc. M.E. and Inst. of Management, 1929. Home: New Hope, Pa. Died Nov. 26, 1939.

MILLER, George Carter; b. Cincinnati, O., Mar. 25, 1878; s. George C. and Eliza Davidson (Wise) M.; ed. Cincinnati Inst. of Technology and U. of Cincinnati; m. Nellie Baumes, May 12, 1902; children—Elizabeth W., John B., George C., Robert, Helen. Was connected with various cos. as mech. and industrial engr.; supt. Charles Williams Stores, New York, 1913-15; formerly gen. mgr. Montgomery Ward & Co., Chicago; pres. Tillotson Mfg. Co., Pittsfield, Mass., and New York, and v.p. George W. Goethals & Co.; pres. Dodge Mfg. Corp., Mishawaka, Ind., 1923—; pres. Mishawaka Housing Corp., Penn Finance and Building Co. Republican. Presbyn. Home: Mishawaka, Ind. Died May 10, 1939.

MILLER, George E., newspaperman; b. Beavertown, Pa.; s. Elisha Peter and Elizabeth Pennypacker (Grimm) M.; Adrian (Mich.) Coll., 1880-83; m. Grace Willett, Apr. 11, 1892 (died 1909); children—Tom A., Karl W., Helen W., Alma E.; m. 2d, Grace V. Bailey, 1918. With Adrian Daily Times until 1887; with Detroit News, 1887—, successively as city editor and news editor until 1896, Washington corr., 1896-1900, editor morning edition (Detroit Tribune), 1900-05, head of Washington bur. Nov. 1, 1905-Feb. 1, 1918; editor Detroit News, Feb. 1, 1918—. Pres. North Am. Newspaper Alliance, 1922—. Home: Detroit, Mich. Died Jan. 14, 1934.

MILLER, George Lee, ranchman, showman; b. Baxter Springs, Kan., Sept. 9, 1881; s. George Washington and Mollie A. (Carson) M.; student Lutheran Coll., Winfield, Kan., and Eastman Business Coll., Poughkeepsie, N.Y.; married; 1 dau., Margaret. One of proprietors Miller Bros. 101 Ranch, comprising 110,000 acres, also part owner Wild West show; engaged in ranching, stock raising, oil operating and refining. Mem. Okla. State Council of Defense, 1920. Mason. Home: Ponca City, Okla. Died Feb. 2, 1929.

MILLER, George Macculloch; b. Morristown, N.J., May 4, 1832; s. Hon. Jacob W. and Mary (Macculloch) M.; A.B., Burlington (N.J.) Coll., 1850; law student, Harvard, 1852-53; m. Elizabeth Hoffman, Oct. 15, 1857. Admitted to bar, N.J., 1853, N.Y., 1854; practiced corp. law; retired from business, 1902. Trustee Central Trust Co., Greenwood Cemetery, etc. Trustee from 1869, pres., 1890—, St. Luke's Hosp.; original trustee and sec., 1873—, of corporation of P.E. Cathedral of St. John the Divine; founder Hospital Saturday and Sunday Assn., New York, and pres., 1880-1910; pres. Church Club, 1900-06. Home: New York, N.Y. Died Nov. 14, 1917.

MILLER, George Morey, prof. English; b. Cope, Ind., Sept. 17, 1868; s. William Clinton Thompson and Mary Elizabeth (Carroll) M.; A.B., Ind. U., 1892; A.M., Harvard, 1898; Ph.D., U. of Heidelberg, 1911; m. Ethel Douglas Scrogin, Dec. 21, 1907; children—John Smith, George Morey, Jr. Head of English dept. and asst. prin. and prin. high schs., Peru and Noblesville, Ind., 1892-97; instr. English, U. of Cincinnati, 1898-99; asst. in English, Radcliffe Coll., 1899-1900; acting prof. English, Wash. State Coll., 1900-01; instr. English, U. of Wis., 1901-02; asst. prof. English, U. of Cincinnati, 1902-07, asso. prof., 1907-13; prof. English lang. and lit., Wabash Coll., 1913-17; prof. English, U. of Ida., 1917—, also head of department. Episcopalian; dir. Nat. Council Brotherhood of St. Andrew, 1925-28. Author: The Dramatic Element in the Popular Ballad, 1904; State Course of Study in English for the High Schools of Idaho, 1920, 3d edit., 1926; Theory and Practice Outline for Freshman English, 1926; Anthology of English Literature, the Victorian Period, 1929. Home: Moscow, Ida. Died Jan. 15, 1937.

MILLER, George Noyes, business rep. Oneida Community, Ltd.; b. Putney, Vt., Sept. 13, 1845; s. John R. and Charlotte Augusta (Noyes) M. (who was a sister of John Humphrey Noyes, founder of Oneida Community); early edn. at Oneida Community, Oneida, N.Y.; grad. Yale Coll., scientific dept., Ph.B., 1872; m. Annie Elizabeth Kelly, Nov. 27, 1875. Author: The Strike of a Sex, 1890; Zugassent's Discovery, 1893. Home: New York, N.Y. Died 1904.

MILLER, Gerrit Smith, farmer, cattle breeder; b. Cazenovia, N.Y., Jan. 30, 1845; s. Charles Dudley and Elizabeth (Smith) M.; prep. edn., Epes Sargent-Dixwell Sch., Boston, Mass., 1860-65; student Harvard, 1865-66 (withdrew on account of ill-health); hon. M.A., same univ., 1924; m. Susan Hunt Dixwell, Wil-21, 1867; children—Gerrit Smith, Basil Dixwell, William Fitzhugh (dec.). Importer and breeder of Holstein-Friesian cattle; founder, 1869, Kreimhild Herd (oldest Holstein herd in America); editor Holstein Herd Book, 1878; mem. N.Y. Assembly, 1880; mem. bd. of control Expt. Sta., for Agr., Geneva, N.Y., 1883-87. Mem. 28th Unattached Militia, Boston, 1863-64; excise commr., Peterboro, 1867-80; supervisor Town of Smithfield, 1867-68, trustee George Jr. Republic, 1897-1907; trustee Home for Homeless Children of Madison Co., N.Y., 1872-83, Evans Acad. (now Peterboro Union Sch.), 1872—. Vice-pres. Asso. Breeders Thoroughbred Holstein Cattle, 1878-79, pres., 1880-81. Republican. Unitarian. Founder of the Oneida Football Club, Boston, Mass., 1862; tablet to team unveiled on Boston Common, 1923. Author: Holstein Cattle in America, 1887. Home: Peterboro, N.Y. Died Mar. 10, 1937.

MILLER, Grace Moncrieff, teacher, author; b. St. Louis, Mo., Mar. 12, 1875; d. Robert Finlay and Virginia (Dunand) M.; ed. in Europe and at Radcliffe College. Formerly principal Brookline (Mass.) Culture Courses, and instr. French, Brookline High Sch.; originator Miller System of Correct English (oral classes and corr. courses). Republican. Methodist. Author: Correct Pronunciation, 1916; Miller System of Correct English, 1918; English for Everybody, 1924. Radio broadcaster. Home: Boston, Mass. Died Nov. 6, 1933.

MILLER, Gustavus Hindman, merchant, mfr., author; b. on ranch nr. present site of Coryell, Tex., Sept. 4, 1857; s. Franklin Lubbock and Emily (McGee) M.; ed. common schs.; m. Nancy Tennessee Jameson, Jan. 23, 1879. Began as clk. in country store, Christiana, Tenn., 1877, later at Waco, Tex.; started gen. mdse. store at Burrustown, Tenn., 1879; in business at Bell Buckle, Tenn., 1883-89; moved to Chattanooga, 1889, and entered department store bus., Miller Bros. Co., adding wholesale dept., 1895; pres. United and Buster Brown's Hosiery Mills, 1907-23; pres. Miller Bros. Co.; v.p. Hamilton Nat. Bank, Standard-Coosa-Thatcher Co. Republican. Unitarian. Author: Lucy Dalton, 1883; Is Marriage a Failure?, 1895; Tribute to His Brother, 1921; The Jew, 1921. Died Dec. 12, 1929.

MILLER, Harriet Mann. See Olive Thorne Miller.

MILLER, Harry Edward, prof. economics; b. Boston, Mass., Oct. 10, 1897; s. Charles and Jennie (Hurwitz) M.; A.B., Boston U., 1919; A.M., Harvard, 1920, Ph.D., 1923; m. Rosabelle Miller Winer, June 13, 1935. Assistant instr. economics, Harvard, 1921-23; asst. prof. economics, Clark U., Worcester, Mass., 1923-24; asst. prof. econs., Brown, 1924-27, asso. prof., 1927-30, Eastman prof. polit. economy, 1930—. Private U.S.A., World War. Chmn. R.I. Spl. Commn. on Liquor Legislation, 1931; dir. Jewish Family Welfare Soc.; mem. Providence County Consumers Council. Author: Banking Theories in the United States Before 1860, 1927. Home: Providence, R.I. Died Nov. 14, 1937.

MILLER, Harry Irving; b. Cleveland, O.; s. John F. and Almira (Grizzell) M.; attended Russell's Mil. Coll., New Haven, Conn., Mt. St. Mary's Coll., Emmitsburg, Md., and Cornell U.; LL.D., Mt. St. Mary's, 1909; m. May Burbank; m. 2d, Florence Neff; 1 son, Harry Irving. Insp. masonry and later asst. engr. Pa. lines, 1882-85; engr., Pa. lines, Indianapolis to Columbus and Richmond to Logansport, 1885-88; completed constrn. Cincinnati & Richmond R.R., Apr.-Sept. 1888; div. supt. Pa. lines, Richmond, Ind., 1888-90, Louisville, Ky., 1890-94; supt. Vandalia line, 1894-1901, gen. mgr. same, June 10, 1901-Dec. 15, 1903; gen. mgr. Rock Island system, Dec. 1903-Mar. 1, 1905; v.p., Mar. 1, 1905-Nov. 15, 1906, pres., Nov. 15, 1906-Nov. 30, 1909, C.&E.I. R.R., Evansville & Terre Haute R.R. Evansville & Indianapolis R.R.; receiver Buffalo & Susquehanna Ry., May 1910-Dec. 1915; v.p. Mex. N.W. Ry.; pres. Madeira Co., Ltd., Sept. 1911-Dec. 1916; v.p. and gen. mgr. Automatic Straight Air Brake Co. Decorated Order of Sacred Treasure, Japan, 1909. Home: New York, N.Y. Died Apr. 22, 1930.

MILLER, Henry, stockman; b. Brackenheim, Württemberg, July 21, 1827; came to U.S., 1847; m. Sarah Wilmarth Sheldon, July 10, 1860. Was butcher in Washington Market, New York, 1847-50; went to San Francisco, 1850; worked in meat market, 1850-51; started on his own account, 1851; with Charles Lux, started in cattle business, 1857; they acquired 800,000 acres in Calif., beside other lands in Ore. and Nev., and at one time had 80,000 cattle and 100,000 sheep; Mr. Lux died, 1887, and the business was incorporated, Mr. Miller retaining large interests. Home: San Francisco, Calif. Died Oct. 14, 1916.

MILLER, Henry (John), actor and manager; b. London, Eng., Feb. 1, 1860; s. John and Sophia (Newton) M.; came to America, 1871; pub. sch. edn.; m. Helen Stoepel, Feb. 1, 1884. Made first appearance in a stock company, Toronto, in "Amy Robsart," at 19; joined Modjeska's co., 1878, and was with Adelaide Neilson 2 seasons; made appearance in Daly's Theatre, New York, in "Odette," 1882; later performed part of Herbert in "Young Mrs. Winthrop" at Madison Square Theatre; was leading man for Minnie Maddern, leading juvenile of original Lyceum Theatre Co., and Kerchival West in "Shenandoah"; under Charles Frohman appeared as leading man of Empire Theatre stock co. Appeared as star in original production of "Heartsease," 1896; starred in "The Master," 1898, and created leading rôle in "The Only Way," 1899; opened,

Princess Theatre, with "The Great Divide," 1906; prod. and created rôle of John Belden, in "Her Husband's Wife," at Garrick Theatre, New York, 1910; leading man in "The Havoc," 1911; prod. "The Rainbow," with Ruth Chatterton, at Liberty Theatre, New York, 1911, and "Daddy Long Legs," with same, 1913, opened Henry Miller's Theatre, New York, with "Fountain of Youth," 1918; later prod. "A Marriage of Convenience," with Billy Burke, later appearing with Ruth Chatterton as the Comtesse; prod. "Molière," playing leading rôle, Dec. 1919; prod. "The Famous Mrs. Fair," with Blanche Bates in title rôle, creating rôle of Mr. Fair, and playing it until Apr. 1922; prod. "La Tendresse," with Ruth Chatterton as co-star, 1922; appeared in title rôle of "Pasteur," 1923; prod. and played in "The Changelings," 1923. Home: North Stamford, Conn. Died May 9, 1926.

MILLER, Henry, ry. official; b. Hannibal, Mo., Feb. 24, 1863; s. Philip and Katherine M.; grad. Hannibal High Sch.; m. Margaret Brady, Nov. 26, 1886. Began as boilermaker's apprentice, Hannibal & St. Joseph Ry., 1880; successively switchman, yardmaster, trainmaster, supt. and gen. supt., C.,B. &Q. Ry. Co., to 1905; v.p. and gen. mgr., Wabash Ry., 1905-15; pres. Mo. & Ill. Bridge & Belt R.R., 1915-17; pres. Terminal R.R. Assn. of St. Louis, 1920—. Dir. Am. Credit Indemnity Co. V. chmn. Am. Advisory Ry. Commn. to Russia, 1917. Home: St. Louis, Mo. Died Apr. 9, 1926.

MILLER, Henry B., educator; b. Sidney, O., Apr. 11, 1854; s. Albert Stuart and Cecilia (Harris) M.; grad. high sch., Toledo, O., 1873, and Heald's Bus. Coll., San Francisco, 1874; m. Mary L. Kelly, Nov. 24, 1875. Bridge engr., contractor and in lumber business, Ore., 1879-95; pres. Ore. Agrl. Coll., Corvallis, 1897-98; pres. State Bd. of Horticulture, 1899-1900; Am. consul at Chungking, China, 1900; consul-gen. at Newchwang, 1901-04, Yokohama, 1905-09, Belfast, Ireland, 1910; dir. U. of Ore. Sch. of Commerce, 1914—. Mem. bd. Senate, 1885-89, Ho. of Rep., 1891-92; mem. bd. mgrs. trade and commerce bur. Portland Chamber of Commerce. Chinese Red Cross decoration for services as pres. Chinese Refugee and Aid Soc. in Manchuria during Russo-Japanese War. Republican. Presbyn. Mason. Home: Portland, Ore. Died Nov. 28, 1921.

MILLER, Henry Watkins, ry. official; b. Raleigh, N.C., Aug. 8, 1868; s. Henry M. and Elizabeth (Collins) M.; ed. pub. schs.; m. Elizabeth Taylor, Oct. 25, 1899. Began as delivery clk. Richmond & Danville R.R., at Raleigh, N.C., Oct. 1, 1885, advancing through various positions to sec. to 3d v.p.; asst. to 1st v.p. Southern Ry., at Raleigh, 1901-10; asst. to pres. same rd., 1910-15, also asst. to v.p. Mobile & Ohio R.R., and asst. to v.p. Ala. Gt. Southern R.R., 1901-15; v.p. Southern Ry. and affiliated lines, at Atlanta, Ga., 1915-20, and at Washington, D.C., Mar. 1920; v.p. in charge of operation, Southern Ry., Jan. 10, 1921—; v.p. Ga. Southern & Fla. R.R., Ala. Gt. Southern R.R., Cincinnati, New Orleans & Texas Pacific R.R., New Orleans & Northeastern R.R., etc. Episcopalian. Home: Washington, D.C. Died Oct. 20, 1933.

MILLER, Horace Alden, musical educator; b. Rockford, Ill., July 4, 1872; s. Horace Gillette and Mary (Alden) M.; grad. Cornell Coll., Mt. Vernon, Ia., 1896; Mus.B., Oberlin (O.) Conservatory of Music, 1904; studied theory and piano in Berlin, 1911-12; theory under Charles Kitson, composition under Herbert Howells, London, 1925-26; studied organ under George Andrews and Clarence Eddy; Mus.D., Cornell College, Mt. Vernon, Ia., 1937; m. Luella Matson Albrook, July 20, 1909. Began as teacher of theory and organ, Cornell College Conservatory of Music, 1904, later prof. organ, harmony and composition, also orchestra leader; manager Cornell Music Publishing Co., Altadena, Calif. Republican. Methodist. Mason. Rotarian. Author: New Harmonic Devices, 1930. Composer: Four Indian Themes; Moon Series; Melodic Views of Indian Life; Negro spirituals for organ—Were You There?, Steal Away, Please Don't Let This Harvest Pass, O Zion, Go Chain the Lion Down; for violin—An Old Dave Song; for organ—The Indian Flute, Barbaric Splendor, Largo (after New World); Songs—I Told the Rose My Love, Fulfilment, Starlight, To the Lea, Even Today. Died July 25, 1941.

MILLER, Humphreys Henry Clay, lawyer; b. New York, Oct. 17, 1845; s. George and Isabella M.; located in Ill., 1855; A.B., U. of Mich., 1868, A.M., 1871; m. Harriet S. Lewis, Dec. 27, 1870. Supt. pub. schs., Morris, Ill., 1870-75; admitted to bar, 1875, and began practice at Chicago; now sr. mem. Miller, Oppenheim, Little & Miller. Pres. bd. edn., 1883—, mayor, 1887-90, pres. bd. civ. service commrs., 1894-1907, Evanston, Ill.; trustee Northwestern U. (v.p. of bd.); col. on staff Gov. Yates, 1901-05. Republican. V.p. State Bank of Evanston. Home: Evanston, Ill. Died 1910.

MILLER, Jacob F., lawyer; b. Claverack, N.Y., Nov. 25, 1837; s. Samuel M. and Elizabeth M.; ed. dist. schools, Claverack Acad. and Hudson River Inst.; grad. Williams Coll., 1859; m. Laura Augusta Chace, Oct. 31, 1861. Admitted to bar, 1861; entered practice at New York; mem. N.Y. assembly, 1883; mgr. House of Refuge, New York; trustee Wartburg Orphan Farm Sch.; trustee George Jr. Republic. Home: New York, N.Y. Died 1906.

MILLER, J(acob) Jay, judge; b. Somerset, Pa., Aug. 22, 1857; s. Jacob D. and Barbara (Saylor) M.; grad. Indiana (Pa.) State Normal Sch., 1879; studied U. of Va., Law Sch., 1885-86; LL.D., U. of Pittsburgh, 1907; m. Annie M. Clark, May 29, 1894; 1 son, Clark. Teacher, pub. schs., until admission to bar, 1884; was active in Dem. politics for many yrs.; judge Orphans' Ct., Pittsburgh, 3 terms 1903-34. Lecturer on wills, trusts, decedents' estates and legal ethics, U. of Pittsburgh, 1907—. Judge advocate, rank of maj., N.G. Pa., 6 yrs. Trustee Pa. Coll. for Women, Shadyside Acad., Diocese of Pittsburgh (P.E. Ch.); mem. Carnegie Hero Fund Commn. Mason. Home: Pittsburgh, Pa. Died Feb. 10, 1929.

MILLER, Jacob William; b. Morristown, N.J., 1847; s. Jacob W. and Mary L. M.; grad. U.S. Naval Acad., 1867; m. Katharine Wise, 1873. Pres. and dir. Newport & Wickford R.R. & Steamboat Co.; v.p. and gen. mgr. N.E. Steamship Co.; gen. mgr. Costa Rica Development Co.; dir. Signal & Control Co. Served U.S.N., 1863-84; capt. N.Y. Naval Mililtia. Dir. Navy League of U.S. Home: New York, N.Y. Died 1918.

MILLER, James, brig. gen.; b. in Mass., Feb. 11, 1844. Served pvt. Co. B, 50th Mass. Inf., Sept. 11, 1862-Aug. 24, 1863; 2d lt. 4th Mass. Cav., Jan. 2, 1864; 1st lt., Feb. 8, 1864; hon. mustered out, Nov. 14, 1865; 2d lt. 16th U.S. Inf., Feb. 23, 1866; 1st lt., July 28, 1866; transferred to 2d Inf., Apr. 17, 1869; capt., June 7, 1879; maj. 20th Inf., Apr. 26, 1898; transferred to 22d Inf., Sept. 10, 1900; lt. col. 19th Inf., Nov. 13, 1900; col. 22d Inf., Nov. 11, 1901; brig. gen. U.S.A., Aug. 11, 1903; retired at own request, over 40 yrs.' service, Aug. 12, 1903. Home: Temple, N.H. Died Dec. 11, 1916.

MILLER, James Collins, univ. prof.; b. Wellington Co., Ont., Can., June 18, 1880; s. James and Ann (Collins) M.; student U. of Calif., summers, 1905-07; B.S., Throop Coll. of Tech., Pasadena, Calif., 1907; A.M., Teachers Coll. (Columbia), 1910; Ph.D., Columbia, 1913; m. Ida B. Zener, Sept. 23, 1925. As exec. officer Govt. of Alberta, Can., established its 2d provincial normal sch.; organized and put into operation the 1st university summer session in western Can.; organized and established a system of tech. edn. for Province of Alberta; dist. vocational officer of Mil. Hosp. Commn. of Can., 1916-19; lent to Govt. of U.S., 1918, to aid in orgn. of work of vocational rehabilitation, Washington, D.C.; returned to Canada, Sept. 1919, to aid in expansion of tech. edn. in Ontario; prof. edn., Ind. U., 1921-25; prof. ednl. administration, U. of Pennsylvania, Sept. 1925—. Presbyn. Author: Rural Schools in Canada, 1913; Vocational Rehabilitation of Disabled Soldiers in Alberta, 1918; National Government and Education in Federated Democracies—Dominion of Canada, 1940. Died Oct. 1, 1940.

MILLER, James Russell, clergyman; b. Harshaville, Pa., Mar. 20, 1840; s. James A. and Eleanor C. M.; A.B., Westminster Coll., Pa., 1862 (D.D., 1880); m. Louise E. King, June 22, 1870; father of Russell King M. Ordained Presbyn. ministry, 1867; pastor Bethany Ch., Phila., 1869-78, Broadway Ch., Rock Island, Ill., 1878-80, Hollond Memorial Ch., Phila., 1880-98, St. Paul's, Phila., 1900—. Editorial supt. Presbyn. Bd. of Publication and S.S. Work, 1880—. Author: Week Day Religion, 1880; Home Making, 1882; In His Steps, 1885; Wedded Life, 1886; Silent Times, 1886; The Marriage Altar, 1888; Practical Religion, 1888; Bits of Pasture, 1890; Making the Most of Life, 1891; Girls—Faults and Ideals, 1892; Young Men—Faults and Ideals, 1893; Glimpses Through Life's Windows, 1893; Building of Character, 1894; Secrets of Happy Home Life, 1894; Life's Byways and Waysides, 1895; Blessing of Cheerfulness, 1895; Things to Live For, 1896; Personal Friendships of Jesus, 1897; By the Still Waters, 1897; The Ministry of Comfort, 1901; In Perfect Peace, 1902; The Face of the Master, 1903; Our New Edens, 1904; Manual for Communicants' Classes, 1905; Beauty of Kindness, 1905; The Best Things, 1907; Glimpses of the Heavenly Life; The Beauty of Self-Control, 1911. Home: Philadelphia, Pa. Died 1912.

MILLER, Joaquin. See Cincinnatus Heine Miller.

MILLER, John, grain merchant, gov.; b. Dryden, N.Y., Oct. 29, 1843; s. Archibald and Isabel M.; ed. public schools and Dryden Acad.; boyhood on farm; then engaged in merchandising at Dryden until 1880; removed to Dakota Ty.; became interested in wheat growing on large scale and in real estate operations. Elected to Dakota Territorial council, 1888; in 1889 elected first gov. of the new State of N.Dak.; refused re-election. While gov. the La. lottery tried to gain a foothold in N.Dak., but he opposed it successfully. In 1896 removed to Duluth. Now pres. The John Miller Co., grain commn. merchants. Home: Duluth, Minn. Died 1908.

MILLER, John Barnes, chmn. Southern Calif. Edison Co., Ltd.; b. Port Huron, Mich., Oct. 23, 1869; s. John Edgar and Sarah Amelia (Barnes) M.; grad. Ann Arbor (Mich.) High Sch., 1888; U. of Mich., 1888-90, hon. M.A., 1923; studied law, 1890; m. Carrie Borden Johnson, Apr. 17, 1895. Planter in La., 1892-94; domestic and steamboat fueling business, Mich., 1894-96; went to Southern Calif. and engaged in amalgamation of small light and power cos. and development of water power for long distance transmission, resulting in orgn. of Southern Calif. Edison Co., Ltd., and its predecessors, of which has been head, 1901—; chmn. bd. Claude Neon Elec. Products, Inc.; pres. Landowners Co., San Joaquin & Eastern R.R. Co. Trustee Harvard Military Sch., Los Angeles; dir. Hosp. of Good Samaritan. Mem. bd. of Incorporators Am. Red Cross, also trustee of its Endowment Fund, advisory com. Pacific Div. and vice chmn. Los Angeles chapter. Republican. Episcopalian. Mason. Home: Pasadena, Calif. Died Apr. 14, 1932.

MILLER, John Calvin, clergyman; b. Sept. 12, 1844, Apple Creek, O.; s. Samuel and Maria (Clayton) M.; A.B., U. of Wooster, 1871, A.M., 1874 (D.D., 1893); grad. Union Theol. Sem., 1874; m. Agnes Sloan, Apr. 30, 1874. Ordained Presbyn. ministry, 1874; pastor Garnett, Kan., 1874-78, 2d Ch., Topeka, 1878-85, 1st Ch., Winfield, 1885-95, 1st Ch., Newton, 1895-98; pres. Coll. of Emporia (Kan.), 1898-1905; pastor, Osborne, Kan., 1905-12; Parkville, Mo., 1912-15. Served as pvt. Co. H, 89th Ind. Vols., Civil War, 1862-65. Home: Concord, Calif. Died Nov. 29, 1923.

MILLER, John Eschelman, merchant; b. Cumberland Co., Pa., Aug. 2, 1857; s. John and Lucetta (Culver) M.; ed. pub. schs.; hon. M.A., U. of Neb., 1925; m. Grace Edna Walters, Sept. 25, 1883; children—John Haldeman (dec.), Margaret Culver (dec.), Dorothy Tibbetts (Mrs. Robert Erle Campbell), Donald Walters. Settled in Lincoln, Neb., 1879, and began as clk. in gen. mercantile store of J. W. Winger, later admitted as partner; entered business with Dr. B. L. Paine, 1885, now title of Miller & Paine, Inc., of which is pres.; dir. Omaha Br. Federal Reserve Bank of Kansas City; mem. Neb. Senate, 1909, 10; mayor City of Lincoln, 1917-20 inclusive; regent U. of Neb., 1915-20. Democrat. Methodist. Presented with Kiwanis medal "for distinguished public service," 1924. Home: Lincoln, Neb. Died Mar. 15, 1938.

MILLER, John Franklin; b. Port Perry, Pa., Feb. 28, 1859; s. George Torrence and Mary Jane (Craig) M.; student Western U. of Pa. (now U. of Pittsburgh); A.B., Wooster (O.) Coll., 1881; m. Mary Louise Paull, Sept. 22, 1887; 1 dau., Rebecca Paull (Mrs. Allen Stewart Davison); m. 2d, Mrs. Clara L. Westinghouse (widow of Henry Herman Westinghouse), Apr. 5, 1937. Began with B. & O. R.R., 1880; assistant sec. Westinghouse Air Brake Co., 1899-1902, sec., 1902-05, v.p., 1905-16, pres., 1916-19, vice chmn. bd., 1919—; vice chmn. bd. Pittsburgh Screw & Bolt Co.; chmn. bd. First Nat. Bank of Wilmerding. Decorated Order of Rising Sun (Japan). Presbyn. Home: Pittsburgh, Pa. Died Sept. 17, 1939.

MILLER, John Franklin, congressman; b. nr. South Bend, Ind., June 9, 1862; s. Isaac Newton and Martha Emmeline (Ritter) M.; LL.B., U. of Valparaiso, 1887; m. Mary E. Stewart, Feb. 12, 1889; children—Leah (wife of Capt. William O. McKay), Stewart F. Settled in Seattle, Wash., 1888; dep. pros. atty., King Co., 3 yrs., pros. atty., 4 yrs.; mayor of Seattle, 1908-10; mem. 65th to 71st Congresses (1917-31), 1st Wash Dist. Republican. Mason, Elk, Odd Fellow. Died May 28, 1936.

MILLER, John Henderson, clergyman; b. Mansfield, O., May 11, 1845; s. John K. and Ellen (Weise) M.; A.B., Wittenberg Coll., 1868, A.M., 1871; grad. Princeton Theol. Sem., 1871 (D.D., Highland, Kan., U., 1885); m. Emma Frances Orr, Nov. 11, 1879. Ordained Presbyn. ministry, 1872; pastor Olathe, Kan., 1871-72, Sedalia, Mo., 1872-76, Junction City, Kan., 1877-81; supply Second Ch., Kansas City, Mo., 1881-82; pastor Fourth Ch., Kansas City, 1883-88, Rich Hill, Mo., 1889-98, Nevada, Mo., 1898-1907, Prospect Av. Ch., Kansas City, Mo., 1911-15. Stated clerk, Presbytery of Kansas City, 1887-1905; permanent clerk, 1884-91, stated clerk, 1891—, Presbyn. Synod of Mo. Commr. to Gen. Assembly Presbyn. Ch. U.S.A., 1891, 1896, 1900. Fraternal corr. of Grand Chapter Royal Arch Masons of Mo., 1909—(grand chaplain, 1896-97); Grand Chaplain of Grand Lodge A.F. & A.M. of Mo., 1895—; Grand Prelate of the Grand Commandery K.T. of Mo., 1897—; chaplain at conv. of Grand Masters of Grand Lodges of Masons of U.S., Mex. and Can., St. Louis, May, 1914. Author: Review of the Presbyterian Synod of Missouri; Masonic Stories and Sermonettes. Home: Kansas City, Mo. Died Apr. 19, 1923.

MILLER, John Henry, lawyer; b. Lynchburg, Va., Aug. 26, 1854; s. William A and Margaret (Henry) M.; A.M., Richmond College, Va., 1874; LL.D. from U. of Richmond, 1927; went to California, 1875; studied law, and admitted to bar, 1879; m. Susie Jones, Nov. 28, 1906. Has practiced in patent causes from 1885 and has conducted much important litigation in many states, representing many large corps.; admitted to bar Sup. Court U.S., 1888. Mason. Home: San Francisco, Calif. Died Sept. 4, 1935.

MILLER, John Rulon, Jr., pres. Empire Construction Co.; b. Riverton, N.J., Mar. 11, 1883; s. John Rulon and Margaret Hansell (French) M.; prep. edn., St. Paul's Sch., Concord, N.H., and in Switzerland and Germany; A.B., Princeton, 1905; m. Anna Richmond Taylor, Apr. 29, 1909; children—John Rulon III, Berkeley Taylor, Richmond, Robert, Amey Richmond. Began with Empire Constrn. Co. and affiliated cos., 1907; pres. Empire Constrn. Co. (Baltimore), 1923—; pres. George W. Rogers Constrn. Corp., and Empire Engring. Co., both of New York; v.p. C. H. Reeves & Co. (Baltimore), The Little Empire Co. (New York). Republican. Home: Baltimore, Md. Died July 18, 1931.

MILLER, John Stocker, lawyer; b. Louisville, N.Y., May 24, 1847; s. John and Jane (McLeod) M.; A.B., St. Lawrence U., 1869; law student there, 1869-70; admitted to N.Y. bar, 1870; m. Annie Gross, Dec. 12, 1887. Prof. mathematics, 1871-72, Latin and Greek, 1872-74, St. Lawrence U.; in law practice at Chicago, 1874—; mem. Miller, Starr, Brown, Packard & Peckham; dir. Morris Plan Bank. Argued in behalf of City of Chicago the celebrated lake front case against I.C.R.R. Co. Corp. counsel, Chicago, 1891-93. Republican. Episcopalian. Home: Chicago, Ill. Died Feb. 6, 1922.

MILLER, Joseph Dana, editor and pub.; b. New York, July 1, 1864; s. Edmund Butler and Harriet Zillah (Smith) M.; ed. pub. schs. and under pvt. tutelage; unmarried. Founder 1901, and propr. Land and Freedom (formerly Single Tax Review, bi-monthly mag.). Mem. "Fossils." Single Tax candidate for pres. Bd. of Aldermen, New York, 1919, and for mayor of New York, 1921. Author: Verses from a Vagrant Muse, 1894; Thirty Years of Verse Making, 1926. Editor and pub. Single Tax Year Book, 1917. Home: Jersey City, N.J. Died May 8, 1939.

MILLER, Joseph Leggett, M.D.; b. Kewanee, Ill., Nov. 24, 1867; s. James and Jane (Leggett) M.; reared on farm; B.S., U. of Mich., 1893; M.D., Northwestern U. Med. Sch., 1895; married, 1901. Engaged in practice at Chicago, from 1895; formerly attending phys. Cook County Hosp.; now attending phys. St. Luke's Hosp.; prof. clin. medicine, U. of Chicago. Commd. maj., M.C., U.S.A., Sept. 1917; lt. col., Aug. 1918. Home: Chicago, Ill. Died Aug. 6, 1937.

MILLER J(oseph) Maxwell, sculptor; b. Baltimore, Dec. 23, 1877; s. Joseph Henry and Elizabeth Catherine (Maxwell) M.; ed. Md. Inst. Sch. of Art and Design, 1893-97 (medal of honor); Charcoal Club, 1898-1900, and Rinehart Sch. of Sculpture, 1897-1900 (both of Baltimore); winner Rinehart Scholarship to Paris, 1901-05; Académie Julian, 1901 (concour medals); pupil of Verlet, 1902-04; m. Mary Catharine, d. J. Ross Diggs, of Baltimore, Sept. 22, 1900; 1 dau., Mary Elizabeth. Hon. mention, Salon des Artistes Français, Paris, 1902; silver medal, St. Louis Expn., 1904; Officier d'Académie Française, 1912; hon. mention for medals, Panama Expn., 1915. Dir. Rinehart Sch. of Sculpture, 1923—; instr. in sculpture, Corcoran Sch. of Art, Washington, D.C., 1930—. Home: Baltimore, Md. Died Feb. 20, 1933.

MILLER, Joseph Nelson, naval officer; b. Springfield, O., Nov. 22, 1836; apptd. acting midshipman, U.S. Naval Acad., from Ohio, 1851, grad. 1856; m. Nov 22, 1866; 2d, Nov. 13, 1877. Promoted passed midshipman, Nov. 22, 1856; advanced through grades to rear admiral U.S.N., Mar. 21, 1897. Served on Independence, 1854-56; instr. Naval Acad., 1857-58; on Preble, 1858-60; comd. Perry and served on Cambridge, at Naval Acad., on Pocahontas and Passaic, Sacramento and Sangamon, 1860-63; was present at attacks on Forts McAllister and Sumter; on Monadnock, 1864-67; took part in both attacks on Ft. Fisher; Powhatan, 1867-69; chief of staff Southern Squadron, Pacific Fleet, 1870-72; Hydrographic Office, 1873, 1874-75; comd. Ajax, 1873-74, Tuscarora, 1875-76; Bureau Yards and Docks and lighthouse duty, 1876-80; spl. duty at Washington, 1880-81, comd. receiving-ship Wabash, 1881, Tennessee, 1882; spl. duty and comdg. Tennessee, 1883-84; comd. receiving-ship Wabash, 1885-88; Navy Yard, New York, 1888-91; comd. Chicago, 1891-92, receiving-ship Vermont, 1892-94; comdt. Navy Yard, Boston, 1894-97; naval representative at Queen Victoria's jubilee, 1897, with Brooklyn as flagship; comdr.-in-chief Pacific Fleet, 1897-98; retired Nov. 22, 1898. Died 1909.

MILLER, Joseph Torrence, pub. utility exec.; b. Port Perry, Pa., Aug. 21, 1871; s. George Torrence and Mary Jane (Craig) M.; prep. edn., Newell's Inst., Pittsburgh, Pa., Turtle Creek Acad. and prep. depts. Western U. and Columbian Coll. (now George Washington U.); student Coll. of Wooster (O.) 1889-91; law study Columbian Coll., 1892; m. Mary Margaret Stewart, Sept. 22, 1898 (died 1916); children—Jane Craig (Mrs. John Bemis Veach), Nancy Irwin (Mrs. Lawrence Crofton Bemis); m. 2d, Mary Lizbeth Bucknam, Apr. 21, 1920. With Municipal Engring. Corps, Wilmerding and Edgewood, Pa., 1893, with Allegheny (Pa.) Heating Co. at Pittsburgh, 1894, Philadelphia Co., 1895-99, E. Pittsburgh Improvement Co., 1899-1902; with Pa. Water Co. and subsidiaries, 1902—, becoming treas., sec. and purchasing agt. Asst. fuel administrator Pittsburgh Dist., World War. Pres. League of Borroughs, Tps. and Cities of 3d class of Allegheny Co. Republican. Presbyn. Home: Edgewood, Pa. Died July 18, 1938.

MILLER, Kempster Blanchard, consulting engr.; b. Boston, Aug. 14, 1870; s. Joseph K. and Eliza (Blanchard) M.; E.E., Cornell U., 1893; m. Antha Knowlton, July 3, 1897; children—Dorothea Knowlton, Antha, Ruth Blanchard. Asst. examiner, U.S. Patent Office, Washington, 1893-96; chief engr. Western Telephone Construction Co., Chicago, 1896-98; elec. engr., Scranton, Pa., 1898-99; engr. of Kellogg Switchboard & Supply Co., Chicago, 1899-1904; engaged in practice as mem. McMeen & Miller, 1904-18. Chief engr. Central Union Telephone Co. (Ill., Ohio and Ind.), 1913-18; varied practice as consulting, constructing and operating engineer, principally in telephone field in United States and Can.; has served as expert in many court suits relating to telephone and as arbitrator in controversies concerning public utility properties; designed and built several hydro-electric plants in Ore. and Calif.; designed recently completed fire-alarm telegraph system for City of N.Y. Fellow Am. Inst. E.E. Author: American Telephone Practice, 1904; Telephone Theory and Practice, 1930. Joint author: Telephony, 1912. Home: Pasadena, Calif. Died Nov. 22, 1933.

MILLER, Leslie William, artist; b. Brattleboro, Vt., Aug. 5, 1848; s. N. and Hannah (Works) M.; ed. pub. schs.; student art 3 yrs. in Sch. of Drawing and Painting of the Boston Mus. of Fine Arts; grad. Mass. Normal Art Sch., Boston, 1875; Dr. Fine Arts, U. of Pa., 1920; LL.D., Temple U., 1920; m. Maria Persons, Oct. 29, 1874; children—Percy Chase, Arthur Persons. Prin. Sch. of Industrial Art, Phila., 1880-1920, prin. emeritus, 1920—. Lecturer on Art, Swarthmore Coll.; sec. Fairmont Park Art Assn.; v.p. Art Jury, Phila. Gold medal, Art Club of Phila., 1920. Author: The Essentials of Perspective, 1887. Home: Oak Bluffs, Mass. Died Mar. 7, 1931.

MILLER, Leverett Saltonstall, ry. exec.; b. N.Y. City, May 23, 1865; s. George Macculloch and Elizabeth (Hoffman) M.; C.E., Rensselaer Poly. Inst., 1885; m. Susan Goldthwaite Rose, Mar. 1913. Began as engr. of maintenance, Denver, Utah & Pacific R.R., 1885; successively engr. Colo. Ry., chief engr. Ala. Eastern R.R., asst. resident engr. Thames River Bridge, asst. supt. New York, Providence & Boston R.R., chief engr., later asst. gen. mgr., St. Paul & Duluth R.R., gen. mgr. Seattle & Internat. R.R., asst. to pres. Erie R.R., gen. mgr. Tenn. Central R.R., gen. mgr. Tenn. Constrn. Co., gen. mgr. Central N.E. Ry. Co., until 1909; pres. New York, Westchester & Boston Ry., 1909—; pres. Westchester Street Ry. Co., 1918-20, receiver, 1920; pres. New York & Stamford Ry. Co., 1918—; pres. County Transportation Co., 1926; pres. Kearny Land Co., Soundview Transportation Co., Port Chester-Glenville Bus Co.; dir. Utilities Mut. Ins. Co. Home: New York, N.Y. Died Mar. 21, 1931.

MILLER, Marcus P., brig. gen. U.S.A., Feb. 15, 1899—; b. in Mass.; entered Mil. Acad., Sept. 1, 1854; bvt. 2d lt. 4th arty., July 1, 1858; commd. 2d lt., Sept. 26, 1859; 1st lt., May 14, 1861; capt., May 11, 1864; lt. col., 1st arty., Oct. 10, 1894; col. 3d arty., Apr. 30, 1897. Apptd., May 27, 1898, brig. gen. U.S. vols.; comd. brigade in Manila, 1898-99. Bvtd. capt., July 1, 1862, for gallantry at Malvern Hill; maj., Mar. 13, 1865, for gallantry in cav. campaign from Winchester to Richmond, Va.; lt. col., Mar. 31, 1865, for gallantry at Dinwiddie Court House, Va.; col., Feb. 27, 1890 for gallantry and ability in Indian campaigns in Lava Beds, Calif., Apr. 17, 1873, and at Clearwater, Ida., July 1877. Retired Mar. 27, 1899. Died 1906.

MILLER, Maude Murray; b. Marion, Ala.; d. James Wimberly and Frances (Pattilo) Cook; desc. of Francis Cook of the Mayflower; A.B., Judson College, Marion, Ala.; m. John P. Murray, 1884 (died 1902); children—Herbert Cook Murray and Wallace Smith Murray; m. 2d, Albert C. Miller, 1906 (dec.). Mem. editorial staff Columbus (Ohio) Dispatch (retired); three times apptd. mem. Ohio Bd. Motion Picture Censors; apptd. by gov., mem. Bd. Women Visitors to State Instns.; state chmn. Woman's Chamber of Commerce; woman asso. mem. Dem. Nat. Com. for Ohio. Trustee Children's Hosp. Mem. and v.p. Columbus branch Nat. League Am. Pen Women; mem. English-Speaking Union, O.E.S. Christian Scientist. Home: Columbus, O. Died Mar. 28, 1935.

MILLER, Merrill, rear admiral U.S.N.; b. Bellefontaine, O., Sept. 13, 1842; s. Henry and Mary M.; apptd. from Ohio, and grad. U.S. Naval Acad., 1862; m. Sarah Katharine Lynch, July 11, 1865. Promoted ensign, Oct. 13, 1862; lt., Feb. 22, 1864; lt. comdr., July 25, 1866; comdr., Nov. 25, 1877; capt., Feb. 25, 1893; rear admiral, July 1, 1900. Served on Potomac, Atlantic and Gulf coast and Santee, 1861-62; Miss. Squadron, 1862-63; participated in battles of Arkansas Post, 1862, and Haines' Bluff, 1863; in charge of mortar boats at siege of Vicksburg, 1863; served N. Atlantic Blockading Squadron, 1863-65; expdn. up James River, 1864; both attacks on Ft. Fisher; Monadnock, 1865-66; Naval Acad., 1866-69; Lancaster, 1869-72; receiving-ship Sabine, 1872-73; exec. officer Worcester, 1873-74; Naval Acad., 1874-79; comd. Yantic, 1880-81; light house insp. 6th dist., 1881-85; comd. Marion, 1885-87; Navy Yard, Portsmouth, 1888-89; Naval Home, Phila., 1890-92; light house insp. 1st dist., 1892-93; comd. receiving-ship Franklin, 1893-94, Raleigh, 1894-97, receiving-ship Vermont, 1897-1900; commandant, Navy Yard, Mare Island, 1900-03, Pacific naval dist., 1903-04; retired by operation of law, Sept. 13, 1904. Home: Berkeley, Calif. Died Aug. 5, 1914.

MILLER, Milton A.; b. Linn Co., Ore., 1862; s. Robert C. and M. J. (Irvine) M.; pub. schs., and U. of Ore.; m. Flora M. McCalley (died 1908). Mem. Ore. Ho. of Rep., 2 yrs.; Ore. Senate, 12 yrs.; mem. State Text Sch. Bd.; regent U. of Ore., 1905—; mem. Dem. Nat. Com. Dem. candidate for U.S. Senate, 1924; collector internal revenue, Dist. of Ore., 1913-20; collector of customs for Ore., Sept. 1, 1933—. Home: Portland, Ore. Deceased.

MILLER, Olive Thorne (Harriet Mann Miller), author, lecturer on birds; b. Auburn, N.Y., June 25, 1831; d. Seth Hunt and Mary (Holbrook) Mann; sister of Charles Holbrook Mann; ed. pvt. schs.; m. Watts Todd Miller, 1854. Author: Little Folks in Feathers and Fur, 1879; Little People of Asia, 1882; Bird Ways, 1885; In Nesting Time, 1888; Four Handed Folk, 1890; Little Brothers of the Air, 1890; Bird-Lover in the West, 1894; The First Book of Birds, 1899; The Second Book of Birds, 1901; True Bird Stories, 1903; Kristy's Queer Christmas, 1904; Kristy's Surprise Party, 1905; Kristy's Rainyday Picnic, 1906; What Happened to Barbara, 1907; The Bird Our Brother, 1908; The Children's Book of Birds, 1915. Home: Los Angeles, Calif. Died Dec. 25, 1918.

MILLER, Oscar Phineas, banker; b. Chautauqua Co., N.Y., May 15, 1850; s. Phineas Johnson and Sylvia (Winship) M.; ed. pub. and pvt. schs.; m. Ellen M. Fowler, Dec. 25, 1870; children—Clarena J., Mrs. Jessie Peck, Arthur G., Oscar P. Druggist, 1870-77; cashier Citizens Bank and its successor, the Citizens Savings Bank, Elgin, Ia., 1875-80; postmaster, Elgin, 1876-80; sr. partner Miller & Thompson, owners Lyon Co. Bank, Rock Rapids, 1880-1904; pres. Lyon Co. Nat. Bank (successor to Lyon Co. Bank), 1904—; organizer, and pres. Doon Savings Bank, and pres. of its successor, 1st Nat. Bank of Doon, 1903—; an organizer of Rock Co. Bank (Luverne, Minn.), 1881, Pipestone Co. Bank, 1882, State Bank of Slayton, 1st nat. banks at Jasper, Iona and Woodstock, Minn.; pres. Miller & Thompson Land & Loan Co., Rock Rapids. Trustee Cornell Coll., Mt. Vernon, Ia., 1885— (pres. bd. during the coll. yr., 1917 and 18); del. Gen. Conf. M.E. Ch., 5 times, reserve del., 1916; treas. General Conf., 1904—; trustee and treas. bd. Northwest Ia. Conf. M.E. Ch.; mem. Bd. Pension and Relief (formerly Conf. Claimants), Chicago, 1908—. Republican. Mason. Home: Rock Rapids, Ia. Died Dec. 26, 1928.

MILLER, Perry B., lawyer; b. Logan Co., Ky., Feb. 15, 1867; s. William Henry and Sarah Elizabeth (Price) M.; A.B., Bethel Coll., Russellville, Ky., 1886; m. Camille R. Waggener, Apr. 29, 1891; children—Mary Willis (Mrs. Arthur F. Shuey), Henry. Admitted to Ky. bar, 1890, and practiced at Morganfield alone till 1911; mem. Allen & Miller, 1911-14. City atty., Morganfield, 1894-96, mayor, 1896-1900; U.S. atty. Western Dist. of Ky., 1914-19; engaged in gen. practice, 1919—; mem. faculty of law dept., U. of Louisville. Home: Louisville, Ky. Died July 7, 1939.

MILLER, Ransford Stevens, foreign service; b. Ithaca, N.Y., Oct. 21, 1867; s. Ransford Stevens and Adaline A. (Taber) M.; B.A., Cornell U., 1888; m. Lily Murray, Aug. 23, 1895; children—Lilian May, Harriet Hartman. Interpreter Am. Legation at Tokyo, Japan, 1895-1906; Japanese sec. to embassy, Tokyo, 1906-09; chief of Div. of Far Eastern Affairs, Dept. of State, Washington, 1909-13; consul gen. at Seoul, Korea, 1913; detailed to Dept. of State, Aug.-Oct. 1917, on occasion of Ishii spl. mission; detailed to Am. Embassy, Tokyo, Jan.-June 1918; chief of Div. of Far Eastern Affairs, Sept. 1918-19; reapptd. consul gen. at Seoul, Korea, 1919; assigned to the Div. of Far Eastern Affairs, Dept. of State, Dec. 20, 1929. Episcopalian. Home: Ithaca, N.Y. Died Apr. 26, 1932.

MILLER, Reed, singer; b. Anderson, S.C., Feb. 29, 1880; son of George W. M.; ed. Clemson Coll., S.C.; student voice with masters; m. Nevada Van der Veer, contralto, 1909. Played cornet in band 1st S.C. Regt., Spanish-Am. War; tenor soloist Calvary M.E. Ch., New York, 1902-05, Plymouth Ch., Brooklyn, 1905-08, Brick Presbyn. Ch., New York, 1908—; soloist St. Thomas' P.E. Ch., 1910—. Sings with orchestras and choral socs. and in joint recitals with wife. Democrat. Episcopalian. Mason, Elk. Home: New York, N.Y. Died Dec. 29, 1923.

MILLER, Richard E., artist; b. St. Louis, Mar. 22, 1875; s. Richard L. and Essie (Story) M.; student St. Louis Sch. of Fine Arts, 1885-89; studied Julien Academy, Paris, France, 1899-1901; m. Harriet, d. of Joshua Adams, of Providence, R.I., Nov. 1907. First picture exhibited, Paris, France, awarded gold medal, Salon, 1901; second gold medal, Salon, 1904; awarded medal, Buffalo Expn., 1901, St. Louis Expn., 1904, Liége, Belgium, 1905. Portland (Ore.) Expn., 1905; Temple gold medal, Pa. Acad. Fine Arts, 1911; Potter Palmer gold medal and $1,000 prize, Art Inst. Chicago, 1914; Thomas B. Clarke prize, N.A.D., 1914; medal of hon, San Francisco Expn., 1915. French Govt. purchased Salon pictures, 1903 and 1909, for the Luxembourg Galleries. Prof. École Colarossi, Paris. Knight Legion of Honor, 1906. N.A., 1915. Home: New York, N.Y. Deceased.

MILLER, Robert Johnson, clergyman, editor; b. Hanover, Pa., Feb. 1, 1853; s. James A. and Eleanor (Creswell) M.; A.B., Muskingum Coll., 1873; grad. Xenia Theol. Sem., 1878, D.D., 1888, LL.D., 1923; m. Anna E. Shepherd, June 13, 1878; children—Henry Russell, Earl Dalton, Raymond Shepherd. Ordained ministry U.P. Ch., 1878; pastor Sidney, O., 1878-80, 8th Ch., Allegheny, Pa., 1886-90, Good Hope Ch., 1894-1902, McNaugher Memorial Ch., 1902-21, Good Hope Ch., 1921—. Editor Bible Teacher, 1880-1918; editor Christian Union Herald, Youth's Evangelist, Olive Plants. 1880—, Slowa Zywota (Polish), 1899—, Christian Instructor, 1913-16. Trustee Gen. Assembly U.P. Ch., 1890-1924; dir. Pittsburgh Theol. Sem., 1914-15. Republican. Author: The Rod That Budded, 1903; Fundamentals of Protestantism, 1917; Harnessed for Service, 1925. Home: Pittsburgh, Pa. Deceased.

MILLER, Robert Talbott, mcht.; b. Neville, O., May 4, 1834; s. John and Eliza (Kain) M.; pub. sch. edn. principally; (LL.D., Ohio Wesleyan U., 1906); m. Eliza H. Hamilton, May 12, 1864. In retail and wholesale drug business, 1857-75, lubricating, illuminating and ry. oils, 1876-1900. Retired. Treas. Champaign Co., Ill., 1862-66. Trustee Woman's Coll. (Baltimore). Elizabeth Gamble Deaconess Assn. (Cincinnati), M.E. Ch.; mem. Gen. Confs. M.E. Ch., 1896, 1900, 04, 08, 12; mem. Book Com. M.E. Ch., 1894—; mem. commn. on federation of the Meth. Chs., and commn. on jud. procedure, 1896—. Mason. Home: Avondale, Cincinnati, O. Died Apr. 23, 1914.

MILLER, Roswell, railroad pres.; b. Harford, Pa., Oct. 28, 1843; ed. in pub. schs. and acad.; m. Mary L. Roberts. Entered ry. service on Cairo & Vincennes R.R., of which he was sec. and later supt. until 1882; 2d v.p. and treas. Chicago & Indiana R.R., 1882-83; asst. to gen. mgr., 1883-84, asst. gen. mgr., 1884-85, gen. mgr., 1885-88, pres. and gen. mgr., 1888-90, pres., 1890-99, chmn. bd. dirs., 1899—, C.,M.& St.P. Ry. Co. Home: New York, N.Y. Died Jan. 3, 1913.

MILLER, Rufus Wilder, editor; b. Easton, Pa., May 12, 1862; s. Thomas Thompson and Emma (Meixsell) M.; A.B., Lafayette Coll., 1883, A.M., 1886; Union Theol. Sem., 1883-84; grad. Eastern Theol. Sem., Ref. Ch., 1886; (D.D., Heidelberg U., Ohio, 1902, Lafayette Coll., 1907); m. Katharine McCauley, May 9, 1888 (died 1918). Ordained Reformed Ch. ministry, Sept. 1886; asso. pastor 2d Ch., Reading, Pa., 1886-92; pastor Hummelstown, Pa., 1892-94; sec. and editor publ. and S.S. work Ref. Ch. in U.S., 1894—; Founder of Brotherhood of Andrew and Philip, 1888, and hon. pres. of its internat. council; founder, 1902, Pocono Pines Assembly; 1st sec. and organizer S.S. Bd. of Ref. Ch.; editorial supervision of 30 periodicals. Trustee United Soc. C.E. Exec. com. Federal Council Chs. of Christ in America (v. chmn. administrative com.); pres. Eastern Synod of the Ref. Ch., 1909-10; mem. joint com. of union between Presbyn. and Ref. chs.; gen. sec. Philip Schaff Memorial Com.; pres. Pa. Bible Soc.; mem. Internat. S.S. Lesson Com., Internat. Sunday School Exec. Com. V.p., dir. Parkway Trust Co. Republican. Author: The Primary and Junior Hymnal, 1902; Standard Songs, 1905; Treasured Hymns, 1908; The Minister as a Man, 1915; Daily Devotions, 1920. Home: Philadelphia, Pa. Died Oct. 11, 1925.

MILLER, Russell King, composer, organist; b. Phila., May 10, 1871; s. Rev. James Russell and Louise E. (King) M.; student Princeton U. to sophomore yr.; musical edn., Phila. and New York; m. Emily Meyer Wilson, 1899; 1 dau., Louise King (Mrs. Raymond W. Clawson). Teacher of music, and has served as organist in Holland Presbyn. Ch., 1893, First Presbyn. Ch., Germantown, 1898, First Bapt. Ch., 1900, Temple Keneseth Israel, 1902—, all in Phila. Compositions: (organ) Symphonic Scherzo, 1895; Nocturne, 1897; Epilogue, 1897; Festival March (awarded prize as best organ composition by Am. Guild of Organists), 1903; Concert Overture, 1909; Festival Postlude, 1904; Impromptu, 1904; Cortège, 1904; Elegy, 1905; Chanson Pastorale, 1907; Berceuse, 1908; Serenade, 1908; for tenor and organ, recit. and arietta, What Is Man?, 1909; A Christmas Idyl, for solo voices, chorus and organ, 1933; Three Hymns of the Ancient Church, 1934; also many compositions for piano, songs and church music. Prof. composition and theory of music, Combs College of Music, Philadelphia, 1923—. Died May 3, 1939.

MILLER, Samuel Duncan, lawyer; b. Ft. Wayne, Ind., Sept. 25, 1869; s. William Henry Harrison (U.S. atty. gen. 1889-93) and Gertrude Amelia (Bunce) M.; prep. edn., Indianapolis (Ind.) Classical Sch.; A.B., Hamilton Coll., Clinton, N.Y., 1890; student Columbia Law Sch.; LL.B., Nat. Univ. Law Sch., 1892; m. Helen Karcher, July 24, 1892 (dec.); 1 son, Sidney Stanhope; m. 2d, Amelia E. Owen, Oct. 23, 1907; children—William H. H. (dec.), Laura Owen. Admitted to Ind. bar, 1893, and began practice at Indianapolis; now member Miller, Miller & Bredell; mem. bd. James Whitcomb Riley Hosp. for Children; mem. bd. of corporators Crown Hill Cemetery. Pvt. sec. to Secs. of War Redfield Proctor and Stephen B. Elkins, 1891-93. Republican. Presbyn. Home: Indianapolis, Ind. Died Sept. 1939.

MILLER, Samuel Haas, banker; b. Northumberland Co., Pa., Aug. 7, 1869; s. Simon and Salome (Haas) M.; ed. pub. schs.; LL.D., Juniata Coll., Huntingdon, Pa., 1922; m. Valeria Minium, Sept. 3, 1891. With Chase Nat. Bank, New York, June 30, 1889—, asst. cashier, 1900-08, cashier, 1908-10, v.p., Jan. 12, 1910—, dir., Oct. 18, 1916—; v.p. and dir. First Nat. Bank, Bound Brook, New Jersey; dir. many corps. Conglist. Home: Bound Brook, N.J. Died June 22, 1929.

MILLER, Samuel Warren, army officer; b. in Pa., Feb. 10, 1857; grad. U.S. Mil. Acad., 1879. Commd. 2d lt. 5th Inf., June 13, 1879; 1st lt., Mar. 7, 1885; capt., Jan. 26, 1898; maj. 46th U.S. Inf., Aug. 17, 1899; hon. mustered out vols., May 31, 1901; maj. 19th Inf., July 30, 1902; insp. gen., May 25, 1906; lt. col. 25th Inf., Apr. 2, 1910; col. of inf., Nov. 2, 1912; assigned to 10th Inf., Apr. 25, 1914; col., Nov. 12, 1912; brig. gen. N.A., Aug. 5, 1917. Prof. mil. science and tactics, Purdue U., Lafayette, Ind., 1894-98; at Tampa, Fla., during Spanish-Am. War; chief mustering officer, State of Pa., 1899; organized 46th Inf., U.S. Vols., and served with regt. in Philippine Islands, 1899-1900; acting and insp. gen. 1st and 2d brigades, Dept. Southern Luzon, 1901; again in P.I., as insp. gen. and asst. insp. gen., 1906-08; apptd. comdr. 160th Depot brigade, Camp Custer, Battle Creek, Mich., Sept. 1917. Died Apr. 22, 1940.

MILLER, Shackelford, judge; b. Greene Co., Mo., Feb. 28, 1856; s. John A. and Barbara A. (Nevill) M.; grad. Male High Sch., Louisville, Ky., 1877; LL.B., U. of Louisville, 1879; (LL.D., Kentucky State Univ., 1911); m. Mary Floyd Welman, Nov. 12, 1888. Began practice at Louisville, 1879; chancellor Louisville, 1896-1911, resigned; judge Ct. of Appeals of Ky., for term 1911-19 (chief justice 1915-16). Democrat. A founder, 1905, and dean Jefferson Sch. Law. Trustee Louisville Presbyterian Orphanage, and Kentucky Presbyn. Theol. Seminary. Home: Louisville, Ky. Died Oct. 17, 1924.

MILLER, Sidney Trowbridge, lawyer; b. Detroit, Mich., Jan. 4, 1864; s. Sidney Davy and Katherine Sproat (Trowbridge) M.; B.A., Trinity Coll., Conn., 1885, M.A., 1888, LL.D., 1923; Harvard Law Sch., 1886-87; m. Lucy Trumbull Robinson, Nov. 20, 1889. Admitted to practice in Supreme Court of Mich., 1887; mem. Miller, Canfield, Paddock & Stone; dir. and counsel Detroit Trust Co., U.S. Radiator Corp., Detroit Bank, Detroit Fire & Marine Ins. Co., Wyandotte Savings Bank. Pres. trustees Detroit Coll. Medicine and Surgery; pres. St. Luke's Hospital; was mem. Detroit Library Commission 30 yrs.; former member Detroit Gas Commission. Democrat. Episcopalian; mem. Standing Com. Diocese of Michigan. Trustee of Trinity Coll., Conn.; pres. Trinity Coll. Alumni Assn. of Mich.; state chmn. Am. Red Cross, World War; v.p. Detroit Bureau of Govtl. Research. One of the organizers Detroit Naval Reserve. A founder and dir. Detroit Symphony Society. Home: Grosse Pointe Farms, Mich. Died May 19, 1940.

MILLER, Thomas Marshall, lawyer; b. Port Gibson, Miss., Jan. 19, 1847; s. William T. and Emily (Van Dorn) M.; ed. Elliott's Acad. and other schs. in Miss.; under tutors in France, and eclectic course, U. of Virginia, grad. LL.B., 1869; m. Letitia Dabney, Apr. 11, 1872. Admitted to Miss. bar, Nov. 1869; atty. gen. of Miss., 1886-93, when resigned and removed to New Orleans, where engaged in practice; sr. mem. Miller, Miller & Fletchinger. Member bar of Supreme Ct. of U.S. Episcopalian. Democrat. Home: New Orleans, La. Died Aug. 31, 1920.

MILLER, Warner, senator; b. Hannibal, N.Y., Aug. 12, 1838; reared on farm; A.B., Union Coll., 1860 (LL.D.; LL.D., Syracuse U., 1891); prof. Greek and Latin, Ft. Edward Collegiate Inst., 1860-61; pvt., sergt. maj. and lt. colonel 5th N.Y. Cav., Civil War; m. Caroline Churchill, 1864. Established as paper mfr. in Herkimer, N.Y. Mem. N.Y. Assembly, 1874-76; elected to 46th and 47th Congresses (1879-81); elected U.S. senator for term 1881-87, and resigned from 47th Congress. Has been prominent in Nicaragua Canal project. Home: Herkimer, N.Y. Died Mar. 21, 1918.

MILLER, Webb, newspaper corr.; b. Pokagon, Mich., Feb. 10, 1892; s. Jacob H. and Charlotte (Alexander) M.; grad. Dowagiac (Mich.) High Sch., 1910; m. Marie Alston, in London, Eng., 1920; 1 son, Kenneth. Taught rural school, 1910-11; began newspaper work, Dowagiac, 1911; staff Chicago American, 1912-16; corr. United Press Assn., 1916—; corr. Pancho Villa and Am. Punitive Expdn., Mexico, 1916; Chicago, New York and Washington offices, 1916-17; London staff, 1917, covering Sinn Fein outbreak in Ireland and Brit. front in Flanders; corr. with A.E.F. at Ourcq, Vesle, Argonne; mgr. London office, 1919, Paris bureau, 1920-25; corr. for French occupation of Ruhr; corr. Riff War in Morocco, 1923-24; corr. South America, 1926; asst. European mgr., London, 1926; made 15,000 mile air trip to India to cover Gandhi salt riots, 1930; corr. Italian Army in Ethiopia, 1935 (awarded hon. mention in Pulitzer prize for 44 minute scoop on commencement of war); corr. Franco armies in Spanish War; flew Atlantic on first trip of Zeppelin "Hindenburg," 1936; corr. for abdication of King Edward VIII, coronation of George VI, wedding Duke of Windsor (witnessed all 3 events); corr. European War, 1939; corr. Brit. Army in France, 1939, Finnish Army, 1939. Author: I Found No Peace (autobiography), 1936. Died May 7, 1940.

MILLER, William, engraver; b. New York, N.Y., Dec. 3, 1850, of German parents; m. New York, Apr. 1881. Started engraving on wood at Frank Leslie's publishing house, 1868; studied drawing, etc., in Germany, 1871-73; asso. with Frederick Juengling, 1877-89. Exhibited in New York, Munich Salon, Paris Expn., 1900. Medal, Chicago Expn., 1893, Buffalo Expn., 1901. Mem. Am. Fedn. of Arts, Nat. Geog. Society. Home: New York, N.Y. Died Jan. 10, 1923.

MILLER, William Henry Harrison, attorney gen.; b. Augusta, N.Y., Sept. 6, 1840; s. Curtis and Lucy (Duncan) M.; reared on farm; A.B., Hamilton Coll., 1861 (LL.D., 1889); m. Gertrude A. Bunce, Dec. 23, 1863. Lt. 84th Ohio Vols., May-Sept. 1862; admitted to bar, 1865; practiced at Ft. Wayne, Ind., 1866-74, Indianapolis, 1874-89, in partnership with Gen. Benjamin Harrison; atty. gen. of U.S., 1889-93, in cabinet of President Harrison; practicing law, Indianapolis, 1893—. Republican. Trustee Hamilton Coll., 1893-98. Home: Indianapolis, Ind. Died May 25, 1917.

MILLER, William Niswonger, judge; b. Uniopolis, O., Oct. 18, 1855; s. Charles and Sarah Ellen (Niswonger) M.; A.B., Otterbein U., 1879, A.M., 1881, LL.D., 1921; read law in office of Wyman L. Cole; admitted to bar, 1882; m. Anna A. Bright, Sept. 3, 1883; m. 2d, Mrs. Maud B. Dawson, widow of Gov. William M. O. Dawson, June 25, 1921. Practiced at Parkersburg, W.Va., first as mem. Cole & Miller, alone after 1885. Judge advocate gen. on staff of gov., 1901-07; apptd. judge Supreme Ct. of Appeals by Gov. Dawson, July 28, 1907, for unexpired term of Hon. Frank Cox, resigned; Rep. nominee as own successor, 1908, and elected for term ending Jan. 1, 1917; reëlected for term 1917-29. Was judge adv. gen. W.Va. N.G. under Govs. White and Dawson. Home: Charleston, W.Va. Died Aug. 7, 1928.

MILLER, William Snow, anatomist; b. Stirling, Mass., Mar. 29, 1858; s. William and Harriet Emily (Snow) M.; M.D., Yale, 1879; fellow Clark U., 1890-92; U. of Leipzig, 1895-96; fellow Johns Hopkins, 1905-06; Sc.D., U. of Cincinnati, 1920, and from University of Wis., 1926; m. Carrie M. Bradley, Oct. 14, 1881 (died 1901); m. 2d, Alice L. Burdick, Aug. 6, 1912. Pathologist, City and Memorial hosps., Worcester, Mass., 1889-92; instr. vertebrate anatomy, 1892-95, asst. prof. anatomy, 1895-1904, prof., 1904-24, prof. emeritus, 1924—, U. of Wis. Lecturer in medicine, med. dept. Johns Hopkins, 1918-19. Mason. Conglist. Author: The Lung, 1937. Received Trudeau medeal, 1934. Home: Madison, Wis. Died Dec. 26, 1939.

MILLER, William Wilson, lawyer; b. Washington, D.C., May 14, 1870; s. William J. and Frances Marion (Joyce) M.; LL.B., Nat. U., Washington, 1891, LL.M.; LL.D., hon. A.M., Princeton, 1900. Began practice of law at New York, 1891; member Miller, Owen, Otis and Bailly; dir. Otis Elevator Co., Carolina, Clinchfield & Ohio R.R. Co., Houbigant, Inc., Cheramy, Inc. Home: New York, N.Y. Died July 16, 1941.

MILLET, Francis Davis, artist; b. Mattapoisett, Mass., Nov. 3, 1846; s. Asa and Huldah Allen (Byram) M.; drummer 60th Mass. Vols., 1864; acting asst. contract surgeon, Army of the Potomac, 1864; A.B., Harvard, 1869, A.M., 1872; m. Elizabeth Greeley Merrill, Mar. 11, 1879. At Royal Acad. Fine Arts, Antwerp, 1871-72; sec. Mass. Commn. to Vienna Expn., 1873; corr. New York Herald, London Daily News and London Graphic in Russo-Turkish war, 1877-78. Dir. of decoration, 1892-93, and dir. of functions, 1893, Chicago Expn. Spl. corr. London Times, and Harper's Weekly at Manila, July-Sept. 1898. Chmn. U.S. Niagara Falls Com.; chmn. advisory com. Nat. Mus.; sec. Am. Acad. in Rome, Am. Fedn. of Arts; vice-chmn. U.S. Commn. of Fine Arts; U.S. commr. gen. to Tokyo Expn. Has decorations of mil. crosses St. Anne and St. Stanislaus, Russia; Rumanian Iron Cross; war medals of Russia and of Rumania; medal at Paris, 1889; New Orleans, Chicago; Chevalier Legion of Honor, Paris, 1900; first-class Order of the Sacred Treasure, Japan. N.A., 1885; mem. Am. Acad. Arts and Letters; hon. mem. Am. Inst. Architects. Author: Capillary Crime and Other Stories, 1892; The Danube, 1891; Expedition to the Philippines, 1899. Died Apr. 15, 1912.

MILLIGAN, Alexander Reed, university prof.; b. Washington, Pa., Dec 21, 1842; s. Robert and Eleanor Blaine (Russell) M.; student Bethany Coll., W.Va., 1854-59; A.B., Ky. U., 1861, A.M., 1864 (LL.D., 1902; Litt.D., Milligan Coll., Tenn., 1910); unmarried. Tutor, 1861-65, adj. prof. Greek and Latin, 1865-69, prin. Acad., 1866-67, adj. prof. English and mathematics, 1869-70, prof. Latin, 1870-77 and 1878-1911, chmn. faculty of liberal arts, 1897-1900, acting pres., 1900-01, Transylvania U.; resigned, 1911. Home: Lexington, Ky. Died Apr. 30, 1913.

MILLIGAN, Edward, insurance official; b. Haddonfield, N.J., June 1, 1862; s. William C. and Jane E. (Simons) M.; ed. pub. and pvt. schs.; unmarried. Clerk in ins. agency office of J. B. Kremer & Durbin, Phila., 1879-84; surveyor, office of Aetna Ins. Co., Phila., 1884-88; spl. agt. Phoenix Ins. Co. of Hartford, at Phila., 1888-96; sec., 1896-1907, v.p., 1907-13, pres., 1913—, same co.; pres. Conn. Fire Ins. Co., Phoenix Securities Co., Equitable Fire & Marine Ins. Co., of Providence; pres. Reliance Ins. Co. of Can.; dir. numerous companies. Mem. Hartford Pub. Library; permanent trustee Trinity Coll., Hartford. Fellow Am. Geog. Soc. Republican. Conglist. Home: Hartford, Conn. Died Apr. 30, 1937.

MILLIGAN, Ezra McLeod, author; b. N.Y. City, Sept. 9, 1858; s. Rev. John Calvin Knox (D.D.) and Rachel Ward (Farrington) M.; ed. Geneva Coll., Pa., and under pvt. teachers; grad. Reformed Presbyn. Theol. Sem., Pittsburgh, 1889; D.D., Muskingum and Westminster colls., 1907; m. Ada Rachel Milligan, Mar. 1889; children—Rachel Eleanor (dec.), John Calvin Knox, Alexander McLeod, Frederick Eugene, James Ritchie (dec.), Gregg Irvine. Ordained ministry Ref. Presbyn. Ch., 1889; pastor Ref. Presbyn. Ch., Parnassus, Pa., 1889-90, First U.P. Ch., Steubenville, O., 1891-95, Sewickley, Pa., 1895-1913; gen. mgr. U.P. Bd. of Publn., Pittsburgh, 1913—. Moderator 1st U.P. Synod of the West, 1896; dir. (Sewickley, Pa.) pub. schs., 1905-14; mem. bd. Westminster Coll., 1906-20. Republican. Author: The Two Messages of the Gospel, 1922; Is the Kingdom Age at Hand?, 1925; Science and the Bible, 1925. Home: Pittsburgh, Pa. Died May 27, 1935.

MILLIGAN, Robert Wiley, naval officer; b. Phila., Apr. 8, 1843; s. James and Mary (Thornton) M.; ed. pub. and high schs., Phila.; m. Sarah Ann Du Bois, Feb. 17, 1870. Entered U.S.N., as 3d asst. engr., Aug. 3, 1863; 2d asst. engr., July 25, 1866; passed asst. engr., Mar. 25, 1874; chief engr., Feb. 20, 1892; comdr., Mar. 3, 1899; capt., Nov. 7, 1902; advanced to rank of rear adm. and retired, Apr. 8, 1905. Served on U.S.S. Mackinaw in N. Atlantic Blockading Squadron during Civil War, participating in both battles of Ft. Fisher, fall of Wilmington, N.C., and fall of Petersburg and Richmond, Va.; on duty later in N. and S. Atlantic and Pacific Squadrons and as instr. U.S. Naval Acad.; chief engr. battleship Oregon on her run from Pacific to Atlantic coast and engr. same vessel in battle of Santiago; fleet engr. N. Atlantic Fleet, on flagship New York, for 1 yr.; chief engr. Norfolk Navy Yard, 1899-1905. Episcopalian. Republican. Home: Norfolk, Va. Died 1909.

MILLIGAN, William Edwin; b. Fingal, Ont., Can., Apr. 8, 1867; s. James and Mary Jane (Hunt) M.; grad. Collegiate Inst., St. Thomas, Ont., 1890; married Jan. 19, 1914. Mem. firm Milligan Bros., fire insurance. Mem. Rep. Nat. Com., S.D., 1924—. Episcopalian. Mason. Home: Aberdeen, S.D. Died Sept. 5, 1930.

MILLIKEN, Joseph Knowles, textile mfr.; b. Salem, Mass., July 5, 1875; s. Charles Dodge and Helen Doane (Knowles) M.; grad. Friends Acad., New Bedford, Mass., 1892; A.B., Harvard, 1896; m. Carrie E. Dodds, June 3, 1903 (died 1933); children—Robert Dodds, Helen Doane (Mrs. William Gordon Hughes), Joseph Knowles, Ruth Knowles (Mrs. Joseph Harold FitzGerald); m. 2d, Gertrude E. Cornish, Dec. 21, 1935. Clk. Dunnell Mfg. Co., Pawtucket, R.I., 1895-99; bookkeeper Hathaway Mfg. Co., New Bedford, 1899-1901; treas. and gen. mgr. Mt. Hope Finishing Co., bleachers and dyers of cotton and rayon fabrics, N. Dighton, Mass., 1901—; treas. Dighton Mfg. Co.; chmn. Machinists Nat. Bank. Dir. House in the Pines Sch., Bristol County Agrl. Sch.; chmn. finance com. Town of Dighton, Mass. Member various chemical socs. Republican. Unitarian. Mason. Regarded a leader in textile industry; has come into pub. view as leader in betterment labor relations. Home: North Dighton, Mass. Died Feb. 14, 1938.

MILLIKEN, Seth Mellen, capitalist; b. Poland, Me., Jan. 7, 1836; s. Josiah and Elizabeth (Freeman) M.; ed. pub. schs. and Hebron and Yarmouth acads.; m. Margaret L. Hill, Oct., 1874. Began commercial life, Minot, Me., 1856; with William Deering, founded Deering, Milliken & Co., 1866, of which was many years sr. mem.; largely interested in N.E. and Southern mfg. cos. Rep. presdl. elector, 1892. Home: New York, N.Y. Died Mar. 5, 1920.

MILLIKIN, Benjamin L., ophthalmologist; b. Trumbull Co., O., Dec. 24, 1851; s. Christopher and Mary M.; A.B., Allegheny College, 1874, A.M., 1877; M.D., U. of Pa., 1879; post-grad. work hosps. of Europe; m. Julia W. Severance, 1891. Resident phys. and surg., U. of Pa. Hosp., 1879-80, Children's Hosp., Phila., 1880-81; resident surgeon, Wills Eye Hosp., Phila., 1881-82; apptd. visiting ophthalmologist, Charity Hosp., Cleveland, 1884; visiting ophthalmologist, 1892-1912, sr. visiting ophthalmologist, 1912—, Lakeside Hospital; apptd. prof. diseases of the eye, med. dept. Western Reserve U., 1893, and became sr. prof. ophthalmology same; dean and exec. officer med. faculty, Western Reserve U., 1900-12. Republican. Presbyn. Home: Cleveland, O. Died Jan. 4, 1916.

MILLINGTON, Charles Stephen, congressman; b. Norway, N.Y., Mar. 13, 1855; s. Stephen R. (M.D.) and Harty (Lambertson) M.; acad. edn.; m. Allie Webster, Mar. 6, 1878 (died, 1902). Organizer, and cashier, 1872-94, Bank of Poland, which he organized into a nat. bank, 1880; v.p., 1894, pres., 1895, Herkimer Bank, and pres. of its successor, Herkimer Nat. Bank, 1895—; also pres. First Nat. Bank of Dolgeville; v.p. Mohawk Valley Real Estate Co. Mem. 61st Congress (1909-11), 27th N.Y. Dist.; asst. treas. of U.S. at New York, June 19, 1911—. Trustee Herkimer Free Library. Home: Herkimer, N.Y. Died Oct. 25, 1913.

MILLION, John Wilson, college pres.; b. nr. Maryville, Mo., Mar. 6, 1863; s. Edward Jackson and Nancy (Broyles) M.; A.B., William Jewell Coll., 1889, A.M., 1891, LL.D., 1909; Johns Hopkins, 1891-92, U. of Chicago, 1892-93, 1893-94, 1895, U. of Berlin, summer, 1894; m. Helen Louise Lovell, Dec. 23, 1896; children—Margaret Lovell, Edward Henry, John Willson, Helen Harrison. Instr. English and mathematics, prep. dept., William Jewell Coll., 1888-91; prof. history and polit. economy, 1895-97, pres., 1897-1918 and 1919-21, financial sec., 1918-19, Hardin Coll., Mexico, Mo.; pres. Des Moines Univ., June 1, 1921—. Democrat. Baptist. Author: State Aid to Railways in Missouri, 1897. Died Sept. 5, 1941.

MILLIS, Wade, lawyer; b. Wheatland, Mich., June 3, 1868; s. Walter and Jane Clark (Carlow) M.; LL.B., U. of Mich., 1898; m. Beulah Bowen, Aug. 22, 1894; children—Dorothy (Mrs. Wm. R. Hamilton II), John Bowen. Practiced law at Detroit, 1898—; admitted to practice U.S. Supreme Ct., 1910; chmn. bd. Addison Savings Bank; chmn. Legal Advisory Bd., Selective Service Act, 14th Draft Dist., 1917-19; commr. to promote uniformity of legislation in U.S., by apptmt. of gov. of Mich., 1921—; chmn. com. drafting Uniform Incorporation Act. U.S. Asso. counsel for U.S. Senate Com. on Investigation of Veterans' Bur., 1923; commr. for Can. in courts of U.S. by apptmt. of gov. gen. of Can., 1915—; Mich. del. Nat. Council Legal Edn., Washington, 1922. Fellow Am. Geog. Society. Lt. col., judge advocate gen. (Res.); Gen. Staff, War Dept.; civilian aide to secretary of war for Mich., 1925-27. Mem. U.S. Infantry Assn. Republican. Episcopalian. Mason. Author: Notes on Workmen's Compensation Act; A Spy Under the Common Law of War; The First Trial of the Constitution; Defense Day Address; A Monument to the American Sense of Justice; Truth Beareth Away the Victory; A Tribute to General Gouverneur K. Warren; A Forgotten Hero; The Caravan Moves On; Sesquicentennial of American Independence. Home: Detroit, Mich. Died Apr. 14, 1939.

MILLS, Abbot Low, banker; b. Brooklyn, Jan. 13, 1858; s. Ethelbert Smith and Ellen Porter (Low) M.; Brooklyn Poly. Inst., 1868-73; A.B., Harvard, 1881; m. Evelyn Scott Lewis, June 29, 1891. With Goodrich & Benson, tea brokers, New York, 1873-74; with J. C. Phillips & Co., tea importers, New York, 1874-76; sr. mem. Mills & Samuels, tea mchts., Richmond, Va., Jan.-Nov. 1876; with W. A. & A. M. White, New York, 1881-82; mem. Mills & Howe, stock raisers, Ore., 1882-85; mem. Perkins & Mills, bankers, Colfax, Wash., 1885-90; v.p. Security Savings & Trust Co., Portland, 1890-1903; pres. First Nat. Bank, Portland, Apr. 9, 1903—; also pres. Ore. Life Ins. Co.; v.p. Security Savings & Trust Co. Pres. Portland Open Air Sanatorium for Consumptives; dir. Nat. Assn. Study and Prevention Tuberculosis (pres. Ore. Br.). Chmn. Bd. Pub. Works, Portland, 1901-03; mem. Ore. Ho. of Rep., 1904-05 (speaker, 1905). Republican. Unitarian. Home: Portland, Ore. Died Aug. 11, 1927.

MILLS, Albert Leopold, army officer; b. New York, May 7, 1854; s. Abiel Buckman and Anne (Warford) M.; grad. U.S. Mil. Acad., 1879; m. Alada Thurston, d. Rt. Rev. John Adams Paddock, of Brooklyn, Nov. 15, 1883. Commd. 2d lt. 1st Cav., June 13, 1879; 1st lt., Jan. 23, 1889; capt. asst. adj. gen. vols., May 12, 1898; hon. disch. from vol. service, Sept. 24, 1898; capt. 6th U.S. Cav., Oct. 24, 1898; transferred to 1st Cav., Aug. 9, 1899, to 10th Cav., Feb. 1, 1904; brig. gen. U.S.A., May 7, 1904. Awarded Congressional Medal of Honor, July 28, 1902, "for distinguished gallantry in action nr. Santiago de Cuba, July 1, 1898, in encouraging those nr. him by his bravery and coolness after being shot through the head and entirely without sight." Supt. U.S. Mil. Acad., with rank of col., 1898-1906; comdg. Dept. of the Visayas, Jan. 16, 1907-Mar. 1, 1908, Dept. of Luzon, P.I., Mar. 3, 1908-Apr. 6, 1909, Dept. of the Gulf, Atlanta, Ga., May 28, 1909-Jan., 1912; pres. Army War Coll., Jan.-Sept. 1912; chief, Div. of Militia Affairs, Gen. Staff, Sept., 1912—. Home: Washington, D.C. Died Sept. 8, 1916.

MILLS, Alfred Elmer, lawyer; b. Morristown, N.J., July 22, 1858; s. Alfred and Katharine Elmer (Coe) M.; A.B., Coll. of N.J. (now Princeton U.), 1882, A.M., 1885; unmarried. Admitted to N.J. bar as atty., 1886, counselor, 1889, associating in practice with father; counsel for Town of Morristown, 1892-94; prosecutor of the pleas for Morris Co., 1898-1903; pres. judge Court of Common Pleas for Morris Co., 1903-13; now practicing at Morristown; mem. bd. mgrs. Morris County Savings Bank; dir. Nat. Iron Bank. Pres. Washington Assn. of N.J.; apptd. mem. Washington Crossing Commn., by Gov. Fort, 1910; a trustee of Morristown Library; a trustee Morristown Green. Republican. Jr. Warden St. Peter's P.E. Ch. Home: Morristown, N.J. Died Dec. 1, 1929.

MILLS, Anson, brig. gen.; b. on farm in Boone Co., Ind., Aug. 31, 1834; s. James P. and Sarah (Kenworthy) M.; cadet at West Point, 1855-57; m. Hannah Cassel, Oct. 13, 1868. Engaged in engring. and land surveying in Tex.; laid out first plan of the city of El Paso and in 1859 was surveyor to boundary commn. establishing boundary between N.M., Ind. Ty. and Tex.; left Tex., Mar. 1861; became 1st lt. 18th U.S. Inf., May 14, 1861; capt., Apr. 27, 1863; transferred to 3d Cav., Jan. 1, 1871; maj. 10th Cav., Apr. 4, 1878; lt. col. 4th Cav., Mar. 25, 1890; col. 3d Cav., Aug. 16, 1892; brig. gen. U.S.A., June 16, 1897; retired at his own request, June 22, 1897. During Civil War was never absent, either on leave or from sickness, but was present in all engagements of his regt., participating in most of the Indian wars since, and comdg. U.S. troops at the battle of Slim Buttes, Dak., Sept. 9, 1876; mem. bd. of visitors U.S. Mil. Acad., 1866; mil. attaché to the Paris Expn., 1878. Invented the woven cartridge belt (and loom for its manufacture), now exclusively used in U.S. army and navy and by the British army. Mem. Mexican Boundary Commn., Oct. 26, 1893—. Died Nov. 5, 1924.

MILLS, Benjamin Fay, evangelist; b. Rahway, N.J., June 4, 1857; s. Thornton A. M. (D.D.) and Anna C. M.; A.B., Lake Forest (Ill.) U., 1879, A.M., 1881; (D.D., Ia. Coll., declined); m. Mary Russell, d. Hon. Henry Hill, of Minn., Oct. 31, 1879. Ordained to Congl. Ch., 1878; pastor Rutland, Vt.; evangelist, 1886-97; withdrew from orthodox ch. on account of liberal views, 1897; conducted independent religious movement in Boston Music Hall and Hollis St. Theatre, 1897-99; minister First Unitarian Ch., Oakland, Calif., 1899-1903; founder and 1st permanent minister, Los Angeles Fellowship, a new religious organization, 1904-11; founder and leader of The Chicago Fellowship, Jan. 1911-14. Reentered evangelical ministry and enrolled by the Presbytery of Chicago as a Presbyterian minister, 1915, later engaged in interdenominational evangelistic work. Author: God's World, and Other Sermons, 1893; Twentieth Century Religion, 1899; The Divine Adventure, 1905. Home: Grand Rapids, Mich. Died May 1, 1916.

MILLS, Charles Francis, editor; b. Montrose, Pa., May 29, 1843; s. Bartlet Hinds and Delia (Halsey) M.; bro. of Henry Edmund M.; g.s. of Josiah Mills, Revolutionary patriot; ed. Shurtleff College, Upper Alton, Ill.; entered Union Army during senior yr. and before graduation, as pvt. Co. C, 124th Ill. Vols., promoted, 1863, to hosp. steward U.S.A., which held until end of war; student Bryant & Stratton Commercial Coll. after war; studied medicine and practiced in army to limited extent; (L. H.D., Blackburn Coll., Carlinville, Ill.); m. Mary Elizabeth Bennett, May 26, 1869 (dec.). After war farmer and breeder improved stock; editor and pub. The Farm Home, Springfield, Ill., 1890—. Served as sec. Sangamon Co. (Ill.) Fair; chief clerk, asst. sec. and sec. Ill. State Fair; sec. Am. Live Stock Assn., sec. Am. Fat Stock Show; sec. Ill. Dept. Agr.; chief clerk (sec.) Live Stock Show, Chicago Expn., 1893; sec. and chief Dept. Live Stock, St. Louis Expn., 1904; chmn. advisory com. Live Stock Dept. Panama Expn., 1915; sec. and pres. Am. Berkshire Assn.; sec. Am. Clydesdale Assn.; pres. Am. Ancestral Assn. Mason, Odd Fellow. Drafted bill and secured passage of law creating Ill. Farmers' Inst. and was state sec. of same for yrs.; organizer, and sec. commn. of the Ill. Farmers' Hall of Fame; organizer and secretary Nat. Top Notch Farmers' Club; sec. Universal Corn Convention. Mem. Ill. N.G., capt. and adj. 5th Inf., maj. and q.-m. 2d Brigade, colonel and asst. adj-gen. I.N.G.; sec. Illinois Veterans Club, G.A.R.; pres. Grant Memorial Assn. Presbyterian. Republican. Editor Year Books of Am. Clydesdale Assn. (8 vols.), Am. Berkshire Assn. (10 vols.), Ill. Dept. Agr. (4 vols.), The American Live Stock Industry (4 vols.), and reports of other socs. and of live stock shows of world's fairs, 1893 and 1904. His portrait was installed, 1913, in Hall of Fame, Ill. Dept. Agr.,

State House, Springfield, Ill. Home: Springfield, Ill. Died Dec. 9, 1915.

MILLS, Charles Henry, musician, director; b. Nottingham, Eng., Jan. 29, 1873; s. Charles and Sarah Ann (Selby) M.; Guildhall Sch. of Music, London; Mus.B., U. of Edinburgh, Scotland, 1904 (medalist); Mus.D., McGill U., Montreal, Can., 1911; studied pvtly. under Dr. Ebenezer Prout, Prof. F. Niecks and other masters; m. Caroline Louise Bell Miller, of Edinburgh, Aug. 17, 1908; 1 son, Charles Selby. Concert tour in America as pianist 1892-93; organist various chs. in Eng., Wales and Scotland, 1894-1907; condr. Aberdeen Operatic Soc., 1898-1900; city organist, Aberdeen, 1900; borough organist, Salford, Manchester, Eng., 1906-07; prof. history, and theory of music, Syracuse (N.Y.) U., 1907-08; prof. music and dir. Sch. of Music, U. of Ill., Sept. 1908-14, of U. of Wis. Sch. of Music, 1914—. Mem. Ch. of England. Asso. Royal Coll. of Music, London, 1898; fellow Royal Coll. Organists, London, 1905, Am. Guild Organists (dean Wis. Chapter); mem. Internat. Musical Soc., Wis. Music Teachers' Assn. (pres.). Composer: Magnificat in F for chorus and soli, 1910; mus. setting of Dryden's Ode to St. Cecilia, for double chorus, soli and full orchestra; festival overture for full orchestra; various songs; Wreck of the Hesperus; ballad for chorus and orchestra. Author: Syllabus of Music History (with E. Benham). Home: Madison, Wis. Died July 22, 1937.

MILLS, Charles Karsner, neurologist; b. Phila., Dec. 4, 1845; s. James and Lavinia Ann (Fitzgerald) M.; ed. Central High Sch., Phila., 1860-64; M.D., U. of Pa., 1869, Ph.D., 1871, LL.D., 1916; m. Clara Elizabeth Peale, Nov. 6, 1873. Prof. diseases of mind and nervous system, Phila. Polyclinic, 1883-98; clin. prof. nervous diseases, Women's Med. Coll. of Pa., 1891-1902; prof. mental diseases and med. jurisprudence, 1893-1901, clin. prof. nervous diseases, 1901-03, prof. neurology, 1903-15, emeritus prof. neurology, 1915, U. of Pa. Med. witness in numerous medico-legal cases. Fellow Coll. Physicians of Phila.; corr. mem. Sect. of Neurology of Royal Soc. of Medicine of England. Author: A Treatise on the Nervous System and Its Diseases, 1898. Home: Philadelphia, Pa. Died May 28, 1931.

MILLS, Darius Ogden, banker, financier; b. N. Salem, N.Y., Sept. 25, 1825; s. James and Hannah (Ogden) M.; ed. at N. Salem Acad. and at Mt. Pleasant Acad., Sing Sing, N.Y.; m. Jane Templeton, d. James Cunningham, New York, Sept. 5, 1854. Was a clerk in New York; cashier Merchants' Bank of Erie Co., Buffalo, 1847-49; went to Calif. in 1849; became merchant and dealer in exchange, Sacramento, and founded bank of D. O. Mills & Co.; pres. Bank of Calif., San Francisco, 1864-7; after it was wrecked by his successor again took charge of it until 1878, placing it on a sound basis. Regent and treas. Univ. of Calif., 1868-80, and founded Mills professorship of moral and intellectual philosophy; one of first trustees of Lick estate and Lick Observatory, Calif. Since 1880 in New York; built Mills Bldg., New York; also system of hotels where meals and lodgings are furnished respectable men at nominal prices; training sch. for male nurses, etc.; chmn. exec. com. Fordham Home for Incurables; trustee Carnegie Instn. (Washington), Tribune Fresh Air Fund, Met. Mus. of Art, Am. Mus. Natural History, Am. Geog. Society; pres. N.Y. Bot. Garden. Home: New York, N.Y. Died 1910.

MILLS, Edmund Mead, clergyman; b. Ottawa, Can., July 17, 1848; s. Andrew and Caroline D. M.; A.B., Wesleyan U., 1872, A.M., 1875, D.D., 1888; Ph.D., Syracuse U., 1877, Litt.D., 1918; m. Emily Rexford Adams, Aug. 23, 1875 (dec.); m. 2d, Mrs. Sadie Brown Albright, Mar. 11, 1908. Ordained M.E. ministry, 1872; pastor Elbridge, N.Y., 1872, Lafayette, N.Y., 1872-74, Brown Memorial Ch. (which he built), Syracuse, 1874-77, Wolcott, N.Y., 1877-80, Pen Yan, N.Y., 1880-83, First Ch. (which he built), Elmira, N.Y., 1883-86, First Ch., Syracuse, 1886-87, State St. Ch., Ithaca, N.Y., 1887-90, First Ch., Elmira, 1890-95; presiding elder Elmira Dist., 1895-99; sec. 20th Century Thank Offering Commn., 1899-1903; presiding elder, 1905; field sec. Ednl. Soc. of M.E. Ch., 1907-08; pastor Towanda Ch., 1909; supt. Syracuse East District. Sec. Gen. Conf. M.E. Ch., 1920-24; mem. board control Epworth League, 1889-1900 (v.p., 1896-1900); trustee Wesleyan U.; mem. commn. apptd. by bishops to consolidate M.E. Book Concerns, 1905; sec. Gen. Conf. M.E. Ch., 1920-24 (sec. emeritus). Pres. emeritus Am. Rose Soc., Syracuse Rose Soc. Mason. Author: As He Thinketh (M.E. Pulpit Series), 1905; Only a Profession, and Other Sermons, 1905. Home: Santa Ana, Calif. Died Mar. 15, 1933.

MILLS, Enos A., lecturer, author; b. nr. Kansas City, Kan., Apr. 22, 1870; s. Enos and Ann (Lamb) M.; self-educated; m. Esther A. Burnell, Aug. 1918. Went to Rocky Mountains early in life; established home in cabin on Long's Peak, Colo., 1886; has extensively explored the Rocky Mountains, alone on foot and without firearms; guide on Long's Peak, which he has climbed over 250 times; Colo. "snow observer" for Govt., 1907, 1908. Through articles and addresses has urged bird, wild flower and scenery protection and development of nat. parks. Author: The Story of Estes Park, 1905; Wild Life in the Rockies, 1909; The Spell of the Rockies, 1911; In Beaver World, 1913; The Story of a Thousand Year Pine, 1914; Rocky Mountain Wonderland, 1915; The Story of Scotch, 1916; Your National Parks, 1917; The Grizzly, Our Greatest Wild Animal, 1918; The Adventures of a Nature Guide, 1919; Waiting in the Wilderness, 1921; Watched by Wild Animals, 1922; "Father of the Rocky Mountain National Park" (1915). Died Sept. 21, 1922.

MILLS, Harriette Melissa, educator; b. Burlington, Conn.; d. Leavit Dunbar and Melissa (St. John) Mills; ed. New Britain State Normal Sch., 1877-78; diploma Columbus (O.) Kindergarten Training Sch., 1896; diploma Teachers Coll. (Columbia), 1904; studied Clark U. Summer Schs., 1898, 99. Kindergarten teacher, pub. schs., Columbus, 1894-96; prin. Model Sch. (Kindergarten Assn.), Columbus, 1896-1902, also asst. prin. Kindergarten Training Sch., and instr. in kindergarten edn.; critic teacher Speyer Sch. (Teachers Coll., Columbia), 1902-06; instr. in kindergarten edn., Teachers Coll., 1903-06; head dept. of kindergarten edn., N.Y. Froebel Normal Sch., 1906-09; instr. same, New York U., Summer Sch., 1906-16; prin. Harriette Melissa Mills Kindergarten and Primary Training Sch. (affiliated with New York U.), 1909; instr. in extra mural div., New York U., 1910-21; lecturer Sch. of Pedagogy and Sch. of Edn., same univ., 1910-24. Protestant. Joint author: Nature Songs and Stories (song book for children), 1898. Home: New York, N.Y. Died July 23, 1929.

MILLS, Hiram Francis, hydraulic engr.; b. Bangor, Me., Nov. 1, 1836; s. Preserved B. and Jane (Lunt) M.; ed. pub. schs., Bangor, Me.; C.E., Rensselaer Poly. Inst., 1856; (hon. A.M., Harvard, 1889); m. Elizabeth Worcester, Oct. 8, 1873. Asst. engr. Bergen Tunnel, 1858, Brooklyn Water Works, 1859; water measurements, Cohoes, N.Y., 1859; with J. B. Francis, C.E., Lowell, Mass., 1860-63; on important ry. and hydraulic work until 1867 (Hoosac tunnel, Deerfield dam, water power on Penobscot River at Bangor, etc.); hydraulic engr., Boston, 1867-9; chief engr. Essex Co., controlling water power of Merrimac River at Lawrence, 1869—; cons. engr. on hydraulic work in 10 states and Mexico, 1868—; consulting engr. of Proprs. Locks and Canals on Merrimac River at Lowell, 1893, and chief engr. same, 1894-1917. Has had charge of investigations of Mass. State Bd. Health on purification of water supplies and of sewage by filtration and otherwise, 1886-1914; designed and built Lawrence City filter, 1892-3; chmn. com. state bd. in originating and designing met. sewerage system and met. water supply; cons. engr. Wachusett dam and reservoir. Mem. Mass. State Bd. Health and chmn. com. on water supply and sewerage, 1886-1914; cons. engr. Met. Water and Sewerage Bd., 1901—. Fellow Am. Acad. Arts and Sciences. Mem. corp. Mass. Inst. Technology, 1885—. Mem. New Jerusalem Ch. Republican. Home: Hingham, Mass. Died Oct. 4, 1921.

MILLS, Isaac Newton, judge; b. Thompson, Conn., Sept. 10, 1851; s. Isaac and Susan Elizabeth (Arnold) M.; A.B., Amherst, 1874, LL.D., 1911; LL.B., Columbia, 1876; m. Cara Maria Burnett, Dec. 18, 1876. Admitted to bar, 1876, and practiced at Mt. Vernon and New York, 1876-1906; judge Co. Court, Westchester Co., 1884-95; mem. N.Y. Senate, 1900, 1901; justice Supreme Court of N.Y., 9th Dist., terms 1907-21; asso. justice Appellate Div., 2d Dept., 1915-21; official referee, 1921—. Republican. Home: Mt. Vernon, N.Y. Died June 15, 1929.

MILLS, J. Warner, lawyer; b. Lancaster, Wis., July 6, 1852; ed. Beloit Coll., 2 yrs.; grad. Univ. of Wis., A.B., 1875; studied law with father; admitted to bar, 1876; practiced law, Lake City, Colo., 1877-86, Denver, 1886—; m. Mrs. S. Adelia Crump, 1881. Pres. Mills Pub. Co.; was Populist party candidate for judge Supreme Court, Colo.; prepared bill passed by Colo. legislature, 1893, giving right of suffrage to women. Mem. conv. that organized Nat. Direct Legislation League, St. Louis, 1896; pres. Colo. Direct Legislation League. Author: Mills' Constitutional Annotations; Mills' Annotated Statutes of Colorado (3 vols.), 1901-04; Mills' Colorado Digest, 1901; Mills' Annotated Code, 1905; Mills' Annotated Negotiable Instruments Law. Editor Colorado Decisions (annotated). Died 1907.

MILLS, Job Smith, bishop U.B. Church, 1893—; b. nr. Plymouth, O., Feb. 28, 1848; s. Lewis and Ann M.; prep. edn. Bartlett Acad., Plymouth, O.; grad. Ill. Wesleyan Univ., Ph.B.; ed. for ministry under private teachers; (A.M., Otterbein Univ., 1884; D.D., Westfield Coll. and Lebanon Valley College, 1890; Ph.D., Illinois Wesleyan U., 1893; LL.D., Lebanon Valley Coll., 1904); m. Sarah Ann Metzger, 1870; m. 2d, Mary Keister, 1876. Pastor of Otterbein Univ., 1874-80, 1885-87; prof. of English literature and rhetoric 3 yrs.; of philosophy 1 yr., pres. and prof. philosophy 2 yrs., Western Coll., Toledo, Ia., 1887-93. Visited the univs. of Berlin, Leipzig, Halle, Jena, Oxford and Cambridge, 1897; traveled in Europe, Africa and Asia, 1903-04. Author: Mission Work in West Africa, 1898; Manual of Family Worship, 1900; Holiness, 1902. Home: Annville, Pa. Died 1909.

MILLS, John Sedwick; b. Uniontown, Md., Mar. 30, 1856; s. Bernard (M.D.) and Mary Cecilia (Gore) M.; student Western Md. Coll., Westminster, 1870-72; m. Mary Elizabeth Scott, Sept. 17, 1913; children—John Kenneth, Edith Margaret. Learned printer's trade in office of Democratic Advocate, Westminster; later reporter, editor and mag. writer; entered Govt. Printing Office, Washington, D.C., 1876; transferred to Treasury Dept., as editor and expert, 1897; later editor and chief Div. of Printing; also represented Treasury Dept. on U.S. Geog. Bd. Presbyn. K.T. Died: Dec. 15, 1928.

MILLS, Luther Laflin, lawyer; b. North Adams, Mass., Sept. 3, 1848; s. Walter N. and Caroline J. (Smith) M.; family removed to Chicago, 1849; ed. public schools and Univ. of Mich.; admitted to bar, 1871; m. Ella J., d. Joseph M. Boies, Nov. 15, 1876. State's atty. Cook Co., Ill., 1876-84. Republican. During term and afterward prosecuted many important cases, notably the Sturlata and Cronin murder cases, the Chicago "boodle" trials and the Columbus, O., tally-sheet forgeries; also well known as orator. Pres. Chicago Tract Soc., Chicago Boys' Club. Home: Chicago, Ill. Died 1909.

MILLS, Ogden, capitalist; b. Sacramento, Calif., 1856; s. Darius Ogden and Jane Templeton (Cunningham) M.; A.B., Harvard, 1878; m. Ruth Livingston, Apr. 11, 1882 (died 1920). Pres. Mills Estate, Inc., Va. & Truckee Ry.; v.p. Met. Opera & Real Estate Co.; Mergenthaler Linotype Co.; dir. Chicago Transfer & Clearing Co., City & Suburban Homes Co., Farmers Loan & Trust . Mem. Trust Co., N.Y.C. R.R. Co., Niagara Falls Power Co., S.P. Co. Home: New York, N.Y. Died Jan. 1929.

MILLS, Ogden Livingston, secretary of treasury, lawyer; b. Newport, R.I., Aug. 23, 1884; s. Ogden and Ruth T. (Livingston) M.; A.B., Harvard, 1904, LL.B., 1907; m. 2d, Dorothy Randolph Fell, Sept. 2, 1924. Admitted to N.Y. bar, 1908, and practiced in New York City; treas. Rep. Co. Com., New York Co., 1911-26; Rep. candidate for Congress, 1912 (defeated), for governor of N.Y., 1916; elected mem. of State Senate, 1914 and 1916. Trustee Provident Loan Soc., Am. Mus. Natural History, Metropolitan Mus. Art; pres. Home for Incurables. Commd. capt. U.S.A., July 1917; with A.E.F. in France, Jan. 1918-Mar. 1919. Mem. 67th to 69th Congresses (1921-27), 17th N.Y. District; under secretary of treasury, 1927-32; secretary of the treasury, Feb. 1932-Mar. 4, 1933. Episcopalian. Home: New York, N.Y. Died Oct. 11, 1937.

MILLS, Roger Quarles, senator; b. Todd Co., Ky., Mar. 30, 1832; s. Charles H. and Tabitha B. M.; moved to Tex., 1849; m. Caroline R. Jones, Jan. 7, 1858. Admitted to bar (by act of legislature) at 20, and began practice at Corsicana, Tex. Mem. Tex. Ho. of Rep., 1859; was at battle of Wilson's Creek (Oak Hill), Aug. 10, 1861; later col. 10th Tex. Inf., C.S.A., which comd. in battles of Arkansas Post, Jan. 11, 1862, Chickamauga, Sept. 19-20, 1863, until fall of Gen. James Deshler, when he took command of the brigade; comd. regt. at battles of Missionary Ridge, Nov. 24-25, 1863 (wounded), New Hope Ch., May 27, 1864, and Atlanta, July 22, 1864 (twice wounded). Mem. 43d to 52d Congresses (1873-93); resigned from 52d Congress, Mar. 29, 1892, having been elected U.S. senator for unexpired term (1892-93) of Horace Chilton; reëlected for term, 1893-97. Democrat. Home: Corsicana, Texas. Died 1911.

MILLS, Samuel Myers, officer U.S.A.; b. Pottsville, Pa., Dec. 15, 1843; entered Mil. Acad. from Pa., graduating 1865; grad. Arty. Sch., Ft. Monroe, Va., 1882. Commd. 2d lt. 19th Inf., June 23, 1865; promoted through grades to col. Apr. 14, 1903; brig. gen. and chief of arty., 1905. Served on reconstruction of Southern States; honorably mentioned and congratulated in orders for successful arrest and delivery to U.S. marshal of certain desperadoes, 1866; was in signal service, 1882-85, becoming 2d ranking officer in that service and frequently acting as chief signal officer; instr. at Arty. Sch., Ft. Monroe, Va., 1885; and filled many and varied duties. Died 1907.

MILLS, Sebastian Bach, pianist; b. Cirencester, England, March 13, 1839; appeared in concerts as a boy; studied in Germany, 1856-59; came to U.S., 1859, settling as piano teacher in New York, also well known as concert pianist and composer of music for piano. Composition include Murmuring Fountain; Polonaise; Fairy Fingers; Recollections of Home; two Etudes de Concert; Saltarello; etc. Deceased.

MILLS, Stephen Crosby, officer U.S.A.; b. New Hartford, N.Y., May 8, 1854; s. Henry Abiran and Julia (Crosby) M.; ed. pub. schs., Mt. Carroll, Ill., Syracuse, N.Y., Ann Arbor, Mich.; grad. U.S. Mil. Acad., 1877; m. Lilian Lee, Apr. 10, 1894. Apptd. 2d lt. 17th Inf., June 15, 1877; 2d lt. 12th Inf., June 30, 1877; 1st lt., May 28, 1884; capt., Dec. 16, 1894; maj. insp. gen. vols., May 12, 1898; hon. disch. from vols., July 28, 1898; maj. insp. gen. U.S.A., July 25, 1898; lt. col. insp. gen., Feb. 2, 1901; col. insp. gen., Apr. 12, 1903. Bvtd. 1st lt., Feb. 27, 1890, "for gallant services in action against Indians in the San Andreas Mountains, N.M., Apr. 7, 1880, and in the Las Animas Mountains, N.M., Apr. 28, 1882." Served on plains, 1877-82; abroad collecting information, 1890-91; recorder of commn. apptd. to investigate conduct of War Dept. in Spanish-Am. War; chief of staff, Div. of the Philippines, 1907-09, Dept. of the Lakes, 1909-10; chief of staff, Dept. of the East, 1910-11; insp. gen., Eastern Div., Aug. 15, 1911—. Died Aug. 3, 1914.

MILLS, Susan Lincoln, educator; b. Enosburg, Vt., Nov. 18, 1826; d. John and Elizabeth Tolman; grad. Mt. Holyoke Sem., 1845; (Litt.D.); teacher under Mary Lyon, Mt. Holyoke, 1845-48; m. Cyrus T. Mills, D.D., 1848 (died 1884). After marriage went to Ceylon and was associated with her husband in Batticotta Coll. 6 yrs.; removed to H.I., 1860, husband pres. Oahu Coll., where she was instr. 4 yrs.; removed to California, 1865, and husband purchased the oldest Protestant sch. for girls, which was chartered as a coll., 1885, as Mills Coll., the only coll. for women in Calif., of which was pres., 1884-1909. Died Dec. 12, 1912.

MILLS, Thomas Brooks; b. Manchester, Wis., Oct. 12, 1857; s. Hugh Brooks and Mary (Rogers) M.; grad. Racine (Wis.) Acad., 1881; studied law dept., Columbia U., 1889; unmarried. Mem. T. B. & J. H. Mills, real estate, Superior, Wis., 1887—; v.p. Jackson Land & Lumber Co., The Mills Co. Mem. Wis. Ho. of Rep., 1885-90 (speaker, 1887-90), Wis. Senate, 1895-98; U.S. collector of customs, Superior, Wis., 1897—. Republican. Pres. Douglas Co. Humane Soc.; dir. Pub. Welfare Assn. Mason. Member B.P.O.E. (Grand Exalted Ruler, 1912-13). Died Mar. 19, 1930.

MILLS, Thornton Allen, clergyman; b. Indianapolis, Ind., Sept. 19, 1855; s. Thornton Anthony and Anna Cook (Mills) M.; A.B., Wooster (O.) U., 1878, Ph.D., 1892; grad. McCormick Theol. Sem., Chicago, 1882; m. Cornelia Mary Safford, May 9, 1879 (died 1912); m. 2d, Clara B. Clark, widow of Rev. Theodore B. Williams, June 22, 1916. Ordained Congl. ministry, 1877; while stated supply at Maine, Minn., joined Presbytery, 1879; stated supply Northwood, Ia., 1879-80, Bacon Hill, N.Y., 1880-81, Essex, 1881-82, Champlain, 1883; pastor Flanders, N.J., 1885-87, Asbury, N.J., 1887-89, Providence, R.I., 1889-92, Wilkes-Barre, Pa., 1892-1902, San Jose, Calif., 1902-07, Schenectady, N.Y., 1907-12; asso. missionary in Korea, 1912-13; pastor Lake George, N.Y., 1914-18, Flanders, N.J., Dec. 1918. Died July 1, 1922.

MILLS, Thornton Anthony, clergyman; b. Lead City, S.D., May 28, 1881; s. Benjamin Fay and Mary Russell (Hill) M.; ed. Tufts Coll. and U. of Calif. (non-grad.); m. Ruth Elliot Ticknor, June 30, 1908. Ordained Congl. ministry, 1902; minister Peoples Ch., Santa Rosa, Calif., 1902-03; supply, Unitarian Ch., San Jose, 1903-06; asso. minister Ch. of the Divine Paternity, New York, 1906-07; minister Ch. of Christian Union, Rockford, Ill., 1907-12, 1st Congl. Ch., Battle Creek, Mich., 1912-18, New England Ch. (Congl.), Chicago, 1921—. Commd. maj. U.S.A., 1918, and assigned to counteract the influence of the I.W.W.; an organizer of Loyal Legion of Loggers and Lumbermen, of the Northwest; after the war assisted in organizing the Legion on a permanent civilian basis; maj. R.C., U.S.A., 1919—. Home: Chicago, Ill. Died Mar. 14, 1929.

MILLS, William C., museum director; b. Pyrmont, Montgomery Co., O., Jan. 2, 1860; s. Joshua and Mary (Mundhenk) M.; B.Sc., Ohio State U., 1898, M.Sc., 1902; m. Olive Buxton, Oct. 7, 1885; 1 dau., Helen Marie. Curator and librarian, Ohio State Archæol. and Hist. Soc. and curator Ohio State U. Museum, 1898—. Librarian Ohio Acad. Science, 1899—; asst. editor Ohio Naturalist, 1900—. In charge Ohio State Archæol. and Hist. Socs. exhibit, Buffalo Expn., 1901; hon. supt. archæology, St. Louis Expn., 1904; supt. archæology, Jamestown Expn., 1907. Republican. Conglist. Author: Archæological Atlas of Ohio, 1914; Map and Guide to Fort Ancient, 1920; Ohio Archæological Exhibit at the Jamestown Exposition, 1907; Certain Mounds and Village Sites in Ohio, Vol. I, 1907, Vol. II, 1911, Vol. III, 1922. Home: Columbus, O. Died Jan. 17, 1928.

MILLS, William Howard, journalist; b. Bangor, Me., Apr. 18, 1839; s. William Howard, Sr., and Sarah Ann Hastings M.; grad. High Sch., Bangor; widower. Apptd. 1st lt. 14th inf., Mar. 6, 1862, capt., Dec. 23, 1865; bvt. capt., July 3, 1863, bvt. maj., Apr. 9, 1865; resigned Dec. 12, 1868. Writer on subjects of war history; active among those bringing about the good feeling now existing between the men who fought each other in the Civil war. Home: Washington, D.C. Died 1904.

MILLS, William Joseph, governor; b. Yazoo City, Miss., Jan. 11, 1849; s. William and Harriet (Beale) M.; LL.B., Yale, 1877; m. Alice Waddingham, Jan. 14, 1885. Practiced law at New Haven, Conn., 1877-85, in New Mexico, 1886-93, New Haven again, 1894-98. Mem. Conn. Ho. of Rep., 1878, Senate 1881-82; chief justice Supreme Ct. of N.M. and judge 4th Jud. Dist., 1898-Feb. 28, 1910; gov. of New Mexico, Mar. 1, 1910-Jan. 15, 1912. Republican. Home: East Las Vegas, N.M. Died Dec. 24, 1915.

MILLS, William Webster, banker; b. Marietta, O., Jan. 27, 1852; s. John and Dorothy (Webster) M.; A.B., Marietta Coll., 1871, LL.D., 1921; m. Betsey Gates, Oct. 12, 1875. Was with Elston & Co., bankers, Crawfordsville, Ind., 1873-87; pres. First Nat. Bank, Marietta, 1887—; also pres. First State Bank, Belpre, Ohio. Sec. and treas. bd. Marietta Coll.; corporate mem. and auditor A.B.C.F.M. Chmn. Marietta Chapter Am. Red Cross. Republican. Conglist. Home: Marietta, O. Died Mar. 16, 1931.

MILLSAPS, Reuben Webster, banker; b. Copiah Co., Miss., May 30, 1833; s. Reuben and Lurenia (Clower) M.; student Hanover (Ind.) Coll., 2 yrs.; A.B., Asbury (now DePauw) U., 1854; LL.B., Harvard, 1858; m. Mrs. Mary F. Younkin, Dec. 19, 1869. Practiced law at Pine Bluff, Ark., 1858-61; pvt. to lt. col. 9th Ark. Regt., C.S.A., 1861-65; wounded in battles of Shiloh and Nashville; in merchandise business, Brookhaven, Miss., 1869-81; wholesale grocery and cotton commn. mcht., St. Louis, 1881-84; traveled in Europe 1 yr. and then settled at Jackson, Miss.; pres. Capital State Bank, Citizens' Savings Bank & Trust Co., Merchants' and Planters' Bank (Hazelhurst, Miss.), Bank of Forest, Miss.; v.p. Capital Nat. Bank (Jackson). Founder and trustee Millsaps Coll., Jackson; trustee Vanderbilt U. Republican. Methodist. Home: Jackson, Miss. Died June 30, 1916.

MILLSPAUGH, Charles Frederick, botanist; b. Ithaca, N.Y., June 20, 1854; s. John Hill (artist) and Marion E. (Cornell) M.; studied Cornell, 1872-73; M.D., New York Homœ. Med. Coll., 1881; m. Mary Louisa Spaulding, Sept. 19, 1877 (died 1907); m. 2d, Clara Isobel Mitchell, 1910. Practicing phys., Binghamton, N.Y., 1881-90, Waverly, N.Y., 1890-91; botanist, W.Va. Univ., 1891-93; curator dept. botany, Field Mus. of Natural History, Chicago, 1894—; prof. med. botany, Chicago Homœ. Med. Coll., 1897—; professorial lecturer econ. botany, U. of Chicago, 1895—. Mem. Pan-Am. Com. on Med. Botany; hon. mem. N.Y. Homœ. Med. Soc., Faculty of Medicine Mexico, Faculty of Medicine Brazil, Binghamton Acad. Science; fellow Am. Acad. Arts and Sciences. Explored in Mexico, 1887, 1894, 1898, 1900, West Indies, 1887, 1894, 1898, 1900, Brazil, 1888, a number of uninhabited Bahamian islets, 1904, 05, 07, 11, in interest bot. science; spl. field of botanic work, The Antillean region. Editor Homœopathic Recorder, 1890-92. Author: American Medical Plants (illustrated), 1887; Weeds of West Virginia, 1892; Flora of West Virginia, 1892; Plantæ Utowanæ; Flora of St. Croix; Flora Sand Keys of Florida; Prænunciæ Bahamenses; Plantæ Yucatanæ; Flora of West Virginia, 1891, 95, 1913; revised and enlarged MacIlvaine's "1,000 American Fungi," 1911. Home: Chicago, Ill. Died Sept. 16, 1923.

MILLSPAUGH, Frank Rosebrook, bishop; b. at Nichols, N.Y.; s. Cornelius and Elvira (Rosebrook) M.; grad. Shattuck Sch., Faribault, Minn., 1870; B.D., Seabury Div. Sch., 1873 (D.D., 1895); m. Mary C. Clarkson, Oct. 20, 1882. Deacon, 1873, priest, 1874, P.E. Ch.; missionary in Minn., 1873-76; dean Omaha Cathedral, 1876-86; rector St. Paul's, Minneapolis, 1886-94; dean Grace Cathedral, Topeka, Kan., 1894-95; consecrated bishop of Kan., Sept. 19, 1895. Pres. standing com. Diocese of Neb. and deputy to Gen. convs. from Neb., 1876-86; mem. standing com. of Diocese of Minn. Home: Topeka, Kan. Died Nov. 1916.

MILLSPAUGH, Jesse Fonda, educator; b. Battle Creek, Mich., June 18, 1855; s. Jacob and Mary Ann (Decker) M.; B A., U. of Mich., 1879 (hon. M.A., 1904); M.D., U. of Pa., 1883; m. Mary Clark Parsons, Aug. 17, 1886. Prin. Frankfort (Ind.) High Sch., 1879-81; prin. Salt Lake Collegiate Inst., 1883-90; supt. pub. schs., Salt Lake City, 1890-99; mem. Utah State Bd. Edn., 1895-99; pres. Winona (Minn.) State Normal Sch., 1899-1904; pres. Los Angeles (Calif.) State Normal School, 1904-17, and pres. emeritus, 1917-19; dean Southern Br. of U. of Calif., 1919—. Mem. Calif. State Bd. Edn., 1904-12. Republican. Conglist. Home: Los Angeles, Calif. Died Dec. 12, 1919.

MILNE, Caleb Jones, Jr.; b. Philadelphia, Pa., Mar. 6, 1861; s. Caleb Jones and Sarah Margaretta (Shea) M.; ed. pvt. schs. and Episcopal Acad., Phila.; m. Lenore Bonwill, Oct. 24, 1882; children—Caleb Jones III, Marguerite, Warren. Began with father, mfr. cotton and woolen goods, Phila., 1879; partner C. J. Milne & Sons, 1885-1924; pres. United Security Trust Co., 1921-23. Mgr. Grad. Hosp., U. of Pa. Trustee Chapin Memorial Home for Aged Blind (v.p.); pres. Howard Hosp., 1915; elected mgr. Pa. Retreat for Blind Mutes and Aged and Infirm Blind Persons, 1930; mem. of the bd. of mgrs. Pa. Working Home for Blind Men; mem. advisory bd. Phila. Home for Incurables (mem. finance com.), Hahnemann Hosp.; mem. Pa. Historical Commission, 1933—. Republican. Episcopalian. Home: Philadelphia, Pa. Died May 23, 1941.

MILNE, David, mfr.; b. Phila., Pa., July 24, 1859; s. Caleb Jones and Sarah Margaretta (Shea) M.; B.A., U. of Pa., 1881, M.A., 1883, Ph.B., 1885; m. Margaret Love, d. Rear Admiral Jospeh S. Skerrett, U.S.N., Apr. 29, 1896; children—Norman Forbes, Sidney Wentworth, Gordon Fairfax, David Dudley. Sr. mem. C. J. Milne & Sons, textile mfrs. until 1924; dir. United Security Trust Co.; trustee U. of Pa. and Evans Inst.; mem. bd. mgrs. Howard and Polyclinic hosps. and Grad. Hosps. U. of Pa.; mem. Com. of Henry Phipps Inst.; mem. advisory bd. mgrs. Hahnemann Med. Coll. and Hosp., Sanitarium Assn. of Phila.; pres. Pa. Retreat for Blind Mutes and Aged and Infirm Blind Persons, also of Pa. Working Home for Blind Men. Republican. Episcopalian. Home: Germantown, Pa. Died Jan. 24, 1929.

MILNE, James M., lawyer; b. in Scotland, 1850; s. William D. and Mary A. M.; grad. Rochester Univ., 1880 (Ph.D., Colgate Univ.); studied at Heidelberg Univ.; m. Susan M. Schermerhorn, 1881. Prin. academic dept., 3 yrs., and prof. Latin and Greek, 12 yrs., Cortland, N.Y., Normal School; prin. State Normal School, Oneonta, N.Y., 9 yrs.; institute lecturer. Admitted to bar, 1901. Has been pres. N.Y. State Ednl. Assn. and pres. Normal Dept. Nat. Ednl. Assn. Author: An English Grammar. Died 1904.

MILNER, Duncan Chambers, clergyman; b. Mt. Pleasant, O., Mar. 10, 1841; s. David N. and Mary Ann (Chambers) M.; sergt. maj., 1st lt. and adj. 98th Ohio Inf.; wounded at Chickamauga, Sept. 20, 1863; A.B., Washington and Jefferson Coll., 1866; Union Theol. Sem., 1866-68; D.D., Coll. of Emporia, Kan., 1883; m. Lucie M. Reid, May 19, 1868; children—Mrs. Wilma Reid White, Madeleine Wade, Paul C., Ella (dec.), Rachel. Ordained Presbyn. ministry, 1868; pastor Osceola, Mo., 1868-71, Third Ch., Kansas City, 1871-75, Ottawa, Kan., 1875-82, Atchison, Kan., 1882-87, Manhattan, Kan., 1887-92, Armour Mission, Chicago, 1893-98, Joliet, Ill., 1899-1905, Logan Square Church, Chicago, 1905-07; associate minister Ravenswood Presbyn. Ch., Chicago, 1915—. Delegate U.S. Christian Commission, 1864; pres. Ottawa (Kan.) Chautauqua Assembly, 1882-99; pres. Kan. State Temperance Union, 1893-94; moderator Synod of Kan., 1883-84; editor Kansas Presbyter; chaplain, Ill. Commandery Loyal Legion. Republican. Dir. Chicago Law and Order League; pres. Provident Hosp. and Training Sch. Author: Lincoln and Liquor. Home: Chicago, Ill. Died Mar. 18, 1928.

MILNER, Henry Key; b. Greenville, Ala., Sept. 25, 1866; s. Maj. Willis J. and Gustrine (Key) M.; M.E., U. of Ga., 1887; post-grad. work, Sch. of Mines (Columbia); m. Helen Bishop, Feb. 14, 1889 (died 1910); children—Martha, Gustrine; m. 2d, Susie G. Martin, June 2, 1915. Began as asst. engr. Birmingham Water Works Co.; mining engr. Milner Coal & R.R. Co.; later one of organizers, sec. and treas. Milner & Kettig Co. (sold to Crane Co. in 1905); founder, 1912, and pres. Milner Land Company; also pres. Warrant Compress & Warehouse Co., Birmingham-Mobile Investment Corp.; vice-pres. Port of Birmingham Co. Served as v.p. and exec. com. Ala. Good Roads Assn., and chmn. Terminal and Transport Com.; pres. Ala. State Harbor Commn., 1921-23. Chief of Am. Protective League, World War. Democrat. Episcopalian. Home: Birmingham, Ala. Died Dec. 26, 1939.

MILROY, Charles Martin, judge; b. Northwood, O., Dec. 5, 1867; s. William and Isabella (McCracken) M.; B.S., Northern Ohio U., Ada, 1890; LL.B., U. of Mich., 1897; m. Mary Hallaran, Oct. 12, 1904; 1 son, Richard H. Began practice at Toledo, 1897; asst. city solicitor, 1903-05; pros. atty. Lucas Co., O., 1913, 14; mayor of Toledo, 1916, 17; judge Court of Common Pleas, Lucas Co., 2 terms, 1921-33. Dir. and trustee Toledo U. 8 yrs. Republican. Conglist. Mason. Home: Toledo, O. Died Dec. 1931.

MILTENBERGER, George Warner, physician; b. Baltimore, Mar. 17, 1819; ed. U. of Virginia; M.D., Univ. Md., 1840; m. Sarah E. Williams, May 2, 1850. Taught 50 yrs. at Univ. of Md.; as demonstrator of anatomy, 1840-52; prof. path. anatomy, 1847-52; prof. materia medica, 1852-58; prof. obstetrics, 1858-90, and after 1855 dean of the faculty. Home: Baltimore, Md. Died 1905.

MILTON, George Fort, editor and pub.; b. Macon, Ga., July 16, 1869; s. Harvey Oliver and Sarah Floyd (Fort) M.; grad. Chattanooga High Sch., 1885; student Chattanooga U., 1886, U. of the South, 1887-89; (hon. B.Litt., U. of the South, 1915); m. Caroline McCall, Feb. 8, 1893 (died 1897); m. 2d, Abby Crawford, Sept. 19, 1904. Established The Taxpayer (monthly), Chattanooga, 1894; became editor Knoxville Sentinel, 1895, and owned controlling interest, 1899-12; bought controlling interest in Chattanooga News, 1909; pres. Chattanooga News Co. First lt. 6th U.S. Vol. Inf., 1898, Spanish-Am. War. Mem. com. resolutions, Tenn. Dem. state convs., 1904, 06, 08, 10, Special Tax Commn. of Tenn., 1915, "Ford Peace Party" which visited Europe, Dec. 1915 and Jan. 1916. Author: The Constitution of Tennessee, 1896; Compulsory Education in the South, 1908. Home: Chattanooga, Tenn. Died Apr. 23, 1924.

MILTON, John Brown, naval officer; b. Lexington, Ky., Oct. 20, 1848; s. Bushrod T. and Mary A. M.; grad. U.S. Naval Acad., 1870; m. Harriet B. Steele, Oct. 20, 1880. Promoted ensign, July 13, 1871; master (lt., jr. grade), Nov. 19, 1874; lt., Sept. 14, 1881; lt. comdr., Mar. 3, 1899; comdr., Sept. 26, 1900; capt., June 6, 1906; rear admiral, Jan. 9, 1910. Served on various vessels during Spanish-Am.

War; insp. 12th Light House Dist., 1901-04; comd. Monterey, 1904; at Naval Sta., Cavite, 1904-05; Naval War Coll., Newport, 1906-07; comd. West Virginia, 1907; capt. of yard, Navy Yard, Mare Island, 1907-08; comd. Independence, 1908-10; Naval Training Sta., San Francisco, 1910; retired on account of age, Oct. 20, 1910. On duty at U.S. Naval Sta., New Orleans, La., 1917. Home: Annapolis, Md. Died Jan. 7, 1931.

MILTON, William Hall, senator; b. Jackson Co., Fla., Mar. 2, 1864; s. Maj. William Henry and Lucy Hall (Hearn) M.; ed. Agrl. and Mech. Coll., Auburn, Ala.; admitted to bar, 1890; m. Sarah S. Baker, Nov. 23, 1893. City clerk, Marianna, 1885-93; mem. Fla. Ho. of Rep., 1889; Dem. presdl. elector, 1892; apptd. U.S. surveyor-gen. of Fla. by Pres. Cleveland, 1894; mayor of Marianna, 1898-99; pres. bd. of mgrs. State Reform Sch., Marianna, 1897-1913; apptd. U.S. senator, Mar. 27, 1908, for unexpired term (1908-09) of William James Bryan, deceased. U.S. commr., 1923—. Was mem. Fla. Repeal Convention. V.p. Ga. Soc. of the Cincinnati. Episcopalian. Mem. local exemption bd., Jackson Co. Mem. State Welfare Bd. of Fla. Sec.-treas. Marianna Federal Savings and Loan Assn. Home: Marianna, Fla. Died Jan. 4, 1942.

MIMS, Livingston, underwriter; b. Edgefield, S.C., 1833; s. Henry and Susan (Burr) M.; ed. in Miss.; studied law; m. Sue Harper, 1866. Admitted to Miss. bar before 20 yrs. of age; clerk Superior Court Chancery of Miss.; senator from Jackson and Hinds Co.; presdl. elector on Breckinridge and Lane ticket, 1860; joined first co. of Miss. troops enlisted for the war, 1861; assigned to duty staff of Gen. William Barksdale; apptd. by President Davis chief q.m. dept. Miss. and E. La., with rank of maj.; served on staffs of Gens. Pemberton and Joseph E. Johnston. After war in partnership with Gen. Joseph E. Johnston in ins. business; now mgr. for South, N.Y. Life Ins. Co. Mayor Atlanta, 1901-02; many yrs. pres. Southeastern Tariff Assn. Democrat. Home: Atlanta, Ga. Died 1906.

MINARY, Thomas Jay, street ry. official; b. Versailles, Ky., Aug. 19, 1850; s. John Sloan and George Ann (Stone) M.; ed. pub. schs., Versailles, and pvt. sch. of Col. William H. Henry, Woodford Co., Ky.; m. Amelia Stephens, June 12, 1876; children—James Stephens, Thomas Helm, Alfred D. Sec.-treas. Central Passenger R.R., 1872-76, gen. mgr., 1876-88; gen. mgr. Louisville Ry. Co., 1888-98, pres., 1898-1920, chmn. bd., 1920—; dir. Louisville Railway Co., Nat. Bank of Ky., Louisville Trust Co., Banco Kentucky; trustee Bank of Ky. and Louisville Trust Co. Consol. Trustee Christian Edn. Soc. Mem. Christian (Disciples) Ch. Elk. Home: Louisville, Ky. Died Aug. 1, 1935.

MINER, Asher, miller; b. Wilkes-Barré, Pa., Nov. 14, 1860; s. Charles Abbott and Eliza Ross (Atherton) M.; ed. Williston Sem., Mass., and grad. Wilkes-Barre (Pa.) Acad., 1879; m. Hettie McNair Lonsdale, Nov. 6, 1889. Pres. Miner-Hillard Milling Co., Pa. Millers' Mutual Fire Insurance Co. Enlisted in Co. D, 9th Regt., N.G.P., 1884; promoted through various grades and apptd. gen. insp. rifle practice with rank of col., 1895; on staff of Gov. Hastings, 1895-98; col. 7th Regt., N.G. Pa., 1898-99; col. 9th Inf., N.G. Pa., 1907-12; apptd. col. Field Arty., N.G. Pa., and assigned to 3d Pa. Field Arty., Aug. 16, 1916; Mexican border service, Aug. 17, 1916-Mar. 29, 1917; commd. in federal service, Aug. 5, 1917; col. 109th Field Arty. with A.E.F. in France, May-Dec. 1918; participated in Fismes-Vesle and Meuse-Argonne offensives; wounded in face and leg necessitating amputation of left leg, Apremont, France, Oct. 4; apptd. brig. gen. Pa. N.G. Comdg. 53d F.A. Brig.; retired with rank of maj. gen., 1923; awarded D.S.C. and D.S.M. Republican. Presbyn. Home: Wilkes-Barre, Pa. Died Sept. 2, 1924.

MINER, George Roberts, editor; b. Manchester, Vt., Aug. 17, 1862; s. Ahiman Lewis and Susan Sarah (Roberts) M.; grad. Burr & Burton Sem., Vt., 1879; B.S., Norwich U., 1883, C.E., 1883, M.A., 1886, M.S., 1887; m. Mary S. Upton, June 10, 1886. Reporter New York Herald, 1883-96; editor Paris edit. New York Herald, 1896; editor Cosmopolitan Mag., 1896-1900; Sunday editor, Phila. Press; editor and propr. Bangor Daily News; Sunday editor and news editor of New York World, 1900; Sunday editor New York Herald, 1902-08; London corr., Herald, 1908-12; Sunday editor New York Sun, 1912-15. Mgr. Whitney Theatre, London, 1912. Served as 1st lt. and capt. N.G. Vt.; a.-d.-c. on staff of gen. comdg.; maj. and instr. mil. tactics, Vt. Inst., Burlington. Democrat. Episcopalian. Author: Looping North America. Home: New York, N.Y. Died 1918.

MINER, Harlan Sherman, chemist; b. Chester, Vt., June 29, 1864; s. John Jay and Lurena Betsey (Hoar) M.; grad. Vt. Acad., Saxton's River, 1884; B.S., Lehigh U., Pa., 1888, Sc.D., 1922; Sc.D., U. of Pa., 1919; m. Emma Estelle Mayers, Nov. 11, 1891; children—Lurena C., Dorothy (dec.), Harlan (dec.). Asst. chemist, 1888-98, chief chemist, 1898—, Welsbach Co., Gloucester. Gold medal and diploma, St. Louis Expn., 1904. Mem. Bd. Health, Gloucester, 25 yrs. (pres. 23 yrs.); trustee Pennington Sem., N.J., 10 yrs.; hon. alumni trustee Lehigh U. 3 yrs. Asso. mem. Naval Cons. Bd. of U.S., 1917. Republican. Methodist. Home: Gloucester, N.J. Deceased.

MINER, James A., jurist; b. Marshall, Mich., Sept. 9, 1842; s. Alvin G. and Betsey (Latham) M.; ed. Mich. common schs. and Lyons Inst.; studied law; m. Sept. 1, 1867. Elected to Supreme bench as asso. justice; was chief justice Supreme Court, Utah. Home: Salt Lake City, Utah. Died 1907.

MINER, Luella, educator; b. Oberlin, O., Oct. 30, 1861; d. Daniel Ireneus and Lydia Jane (Cooley) M.; B.A., Oberlin, 1884, M.A., 1897; hon. Litt.D., 1914. Missionary, A.B.C.F.M., in China, 1887—; teacher Luho Acad. for Boys, Tungchow, 1888-90; teacher, N. China Union Coll., Tungchow, 1889-1902; prin. Bridgman Acad. for Girls, Peking, 1903-13; founder, 1905, and pres. until 1920, N. China Union Women's Coll., now Women's Coll. of Peking Univ., title of Yenching Coll., of which was dean until 1922; dean of women and prof. of religious edn. in Sch. of Theology, Shantung (China) Christian Univ., 1923—. Pres. Soc. for Protection of Women and Children, 1914-15; fgn. adviser Peking Women's Red Cross Soc.; mem. exec. com. of Nat. Christian Council of China; mem. editorial bd. of Ednl. Review of China; mem. council on religious edn. of the China Christian Ednl. Assn. Author: Two Heroes of Cathay, 1902; China's Book of Martyrs, 1902; Textbook of Geology (in Chinese), 1911. Died Dec. 3, 1935.

MINER, William Harvey, journalist, author; b. New Haven, Conn., Mar. 5, 1877; s. William R. and Carrie L. (Pardee) M.; spl. lit. course Yale, 1896, Columbian (now George Washington) U., 1899; m. Ada Martha, d. J. J. Odgers, of Cleveland, O., Aug. 27, 1907; children—William Harvey, John Odgers, Robert Camp, Luther Ernest, Eugene Denton. Traveled in middle and far west, Can., C.A. and Europe. Pres. The William Harvey Miner Co., Inc., pubs. Author: The Iowa Indians, 1911; Bananas, A Trip to the Tropics, 1914; History of the American Indians, North of Mexico, 1917. Home: Kirkwood, St. Louis, Mo. Died Feb. 10, 1934.

MINIER, George Washington, Christian (Disciples) minister; b. Ulster, Bradford Co., Pa., Oct. 8, 1813; s. John and Rachel (Brown) M.; ed. common schools there; academic edn. at Athens, Pa., 1834-35; went to Ill.; m. Sarah Ireland, Jan. 1, 1839 (dec.). Preached 51 yrs. for the Ch. of the Disciples and during most of that time conducted farm in Tazewell Co., Ill. Retired. Charter mem. and pres. Am. Forestry Assn.; for many yrs. has been associated with Ill. State Agrl. and Hortl. Socs.; life dir. of the Bible Union; mem. Universal Peace Union; 1st man in U.S. nominated for Congress on Prohibition ticket. Home: Austin, Ill. Died 1902.

MINNIGERODE, Lucy, supt. nurses U.S.P.H.S.; b. Leesburg, Va., Feb. 8, 1871; d. Charles and Virginia Cuthbert (Powell) M.; nursing diploma, Training Sch. for Nurses, Bellevue Hosp., New York, 1899; registered nurse, New York, 1905. Private nurse, 1901-10; administration work in hosps., Washington and Savannah, Ga., until 1912; with Am. Red Cross in Russia, 1914-15, Columbia Hosp., Washington, 1915-17; again with Am. Red Cross, 1917-19; with U.S.P.H.S., 1919—, now supt. of nurses. Mem. Nat. Com. on Nursing Service, Am. Red Cross; chmn. Govt. nursing sect. of Am. Nurses Assn.; chmn. Delano Memorial Com. Organizer nursing service for disabled ex-service men, 1919-22. Decorated Russian Gold Cross of St. Anne, 1915; Florence Nightingale medal, 1925. Democrat. Episcopalian. Home: Alexandria, Va. Died Mar. 25, 1935.

MINOR, Benjamin Blake, lawyer, educator; b. Tappahannock, Essex Co., Va., Oct. 21, 1818; s. Dr. Hubbard Taylor and Jane (Blake) M.; grad. U. of Virginia, 1838; William and Mary, LL.B., 1839 (LL.D., Univ. of Mo.); m. Virginia Maury, d. James H. Otey, D.D., P.E. bishop of Tenn., May 26, 1842. Lawyer in Petersburg and Richmond, Va., from 1840; editor Southern Literary Messenger, 1843-47; v.p. Commercial Conv., Memphis, Tenn., 1845; prin. Va. Female Inst., Staunton, 1847; founded, 1848, Home School for Young Ladies' Richmond; practiced law, Richmond, 1848-60; pres. State Univ. of Mo., 1860; prin. Female Sem., St. Louis, 1865; later for some yrs. in life ins. business; after 1870 lectured on astronomy and the Bible; returned to Richmond, 1889. Edited new editions of "Wythe's Chancery Reports" (with memoir), and of Hening and Munford's "Virginia Reports." Life mem. Va. Hist. Soc.; sec. Va. African Colonization Soc.; now sec. Va. Soc. Sons Am. Revolution. Also engaged in study and in literary writing for the press. Home: Richmond, Va. Died 1904.

MINOR, Charles Launcelot, M.D.; b. Brooklyn, May 10, 1865; s. Dr. James Monroe and Ellen Josephine (Pierrepont) M.; Episcopal High Sch. of Va., U. of Va., and M.D., U. of Va., 1888; house surgeon St. Luke's Hosp., New York, 1888-90; in Vienna hospitals, 1890-92; LL.D., U. of North Carolina; m. Mary McDowell Venable, Dec. 10, 1890. Began practice at Washington, 1892; removed to Asheville, N.C., 1895. Mem. various med. societies. Cleveland Democrat. Episcopalian. Wrote sect. on "Symptoms and Diagnosis" for Klebs' "Tuberculosis," 1909. Home: Biltmore, N.C., and Asheville, N.C. Died Dec. 26, 1928.

MINOR, Edward S., congressman; b. Jefferson Co., N.Y., 1840; s. Martin and Abigail J. (St. Ores) M.; removed with parents to Wis., 1845; acad. edn., pvt. to 1st lt. 2d Wis. Cav., 1861-64; m. Tillie E. Graham, Aug. 6, 1867. Engaged in mercantile pursuits, 1865-84; supt. Sturgeon Bay & Lake Michigan Ship Canal, 1884-91; owns marine property; is licensed master of steam vessels. Mem. Wis. Assembly, 1877-82, Senate, 1883, 1885; mem. Wis. Fish Commn., 4 yrs.; mayor Sturgeon Bay, Wis.; mem. 54th to 59th Congresses (1895-1907); postmaster, Sturgeon Bay, Wis., Apr. 1, 1911—. Republican. While in Congress served on the Merchant Marine Commn. Home: Sturgeon Bay, Wis. Died July 25, 1924.

MINOR, George Henry, lawyer, ry. official; b. Deposit, N.Y., Sept. 27, 1866; s. James S. and Mary E. (Burrows) M.; A.B., Hamilton Coll., 1890, A.M., 1893; law dept., Lake Forest U., Chicago, Ill., 1895; m. Sara Porter Strong, Aug. 12, 1913; children—George Henry, Mary Porter, William Strong. Prof. mathematics, Park Coll., Parkville, Mo., 1890-92; instr. mathematics, Northwestern U., 1892-95; admitted to Ill. bar, 1895, N.Y. bar, 1896; practiced at Buffalo, N.Y., 1896-1903; became connected with law dept. Erie R.R., N.Y. City, 1903, land and tax agt. for the co. at Cleveland, O., 1904-05, asst. gen. solicitor at N.Y. City, 1905-19, v.p. and sec. same rd. and its allied subsidiary cos. (about 60), 1919—, also dir. in most of them. Republican. Presbyn. Author: The Erie System, Its Organization and Corporate History, 1911. Home: Shaker Heights, O., and Deposit, N.Y. Died Mar. 21, 1937.

MINOR, Raleigh Colston, lawyer; b. University, Va., Jan. 24, 1869; s. John B. and Anne Fisher (Colston) M.; B.A., U. of Va., 1887, M.A., 1888, LL.B., 1890; m. Natalie Embra Venable, June 8, 1897. Admitted to Va. bar, 1890; practiced at Richmond, Va., 1890-93; asst. prof., 1893-95, adj. prof., 1895-99, prof. law, 1899—, U. of Virginia. Democrat. Author: Law of Tax Titles in Virginia, 1898; Conflict of Laws, 1901; Law of Real Property, 1908; Minor and Wurts on Real Property (with John Wurts), 1909; Notes on Government and States Rights; A Republic of Nations, 1918. Died June 14, 1923.

MINOR, Robert Crannell, landscape painter; b. New York, N.Y., 1840; s. Israel and Charlotte (Crannell) M.; studied painting under H. Boulanger and Joseph Van Luppen in Belgium and under Diaz at Barbizon, France. Has received various honors and medals and has furnished works to notable collections. Is mem. Nat. Acad. of Design; pres. Salmagundi Club of New York. Home: New York, N.Y. Died 1904.

MINOR, Thomas Chalmers, physician; b. Cincinnati, O., July 6, 1846; s. Thomas H. and Rebecca (Baldridge) M.; ed. Chickering's Acad., Cincinnati; M.D., Ohio Med. Coll., 1867; m. Alice Carneal, Nov. 26, 1878. Mem. bd. of health, Cincinnati, 4 yrs.; health officer, Cincinnati, 1878-79; dir. U. of Cincinnati, 6 yrs.; chief surgeon Cincinnati police and fire depts., 1902-10; police commr. Cincinnati, 1886-91, 1901-02. Mem. bd. of elections, Cincinnati, 4 yrs.; U.S.A. examining surgeon for recruits, Cincinnati, 15 yrs. Democrat. Author: Scarlatina Statistics of United States, 1875; Notes on the Epidemiology of Ohio, 1877; Report on Yellow Fever in Ohio, 1878; also two copyrighted opera librettos—"Don Juan" and "Frasquita," etc. Translator Sciences Occultes et Physiologie Psychique, by Dupouy, 1903. Home: Cincinnati, O. Died Feb. 18, 1912.

MINOT, Charles Sedgwick, anatomist; b. W. Roxbury, Boston, Mass., Dec. 23, 1852; s. William and Katherine (Sedgwick) M.; B.S., Mass. Inst. Tech., 1872; univs. of Leipzig, Paris and Würzburg, 1873-76; S.D., Harvard, 1878; (LL.D., Yale U., 1899, U. of Toronto, 1904, St. Andrew's U., Scotland, 1911; Sc.D., Oxford U., 1902); m. Lucy Fosdick, June 1, 1889. Lecturer on embryology and instr. oral pathology and surgery, 1880-83, instr. histology and embryology, 1883-87, asst. prof., 1887-92, prof., 1892-1905, James Stillman prof. comparative anatomy, 1905, dir. of Anat. Labs., 1912, Harvard Med. School. Harvard exchange professor at univs. of Berlin and Jena, 1912-13. Invented 2 forms of automatic microtomes. Fellow A.A.A.S. (gen. sec. 1885, pres. 1900), Am. Acad. Arts and Sciences. Author: Bibliography of Vertebrate Embryology, 1893; A Laboratory Text-Book of Embryology, 1903, 2d edit., 1910; Age, Growth and Death, 1908; Die Methode der Wissenschaft, 1913; Moderne Probleme des Biologie, 1913 (also translated into English). Died Nov. 19, 1914.

MINOT, William, lawyer; b. in Mass., 1849; practices in Boston. Author: Taxation in Massachusetts; Local Taxation and Municipal Extravagance. Home: Boston, Mass. Died 1900.

MINOT, William, trustee, real estate management; b. Wareham, Mass., Aug. 15, 1885; s. William and Elizabeth Vredenburgh (Van Pelt) M.; A.B., Harvard, 1907; m. Lucy Greenleaf Woodworth, June 23, 1908 (died 1920); m. 2d, Elizabeth Howard Chapman, May 29, 1922. Associated with Laurence Minot, trustee, upon entering the bar; became head of Minot office upon death of Laurence Minot, June 4, 1921; pres. City Land Co., Port Wentworth Co., Boston Storage Warehouse Co., Conveyancers' Title Ins. and Mortgage Co.; clk. of corp., dir. Boston Wharf Co.; trustee, treas. Boston Block Trust (Minneapolis), Western & Southern Associates, Bay State Associates, Western Real Estate Trustees, Boston Ground Rent Trust; treas. Woodbourne Co., Cape Cod Ship Bldg. Corp., Boston Personal Property Trust; trustee Rivers Sch., Municipal Real Estate Trust, Weeks Real Estate Trust, Dwelling House Associates. Republican. Unitarian. Home: Boston, Mass. Died Mar. 15, 1937.

MINTON, Henry Collin, clergyman; b. Prosperity, Pa., May 8, 1855; s. Matthias and Margaret (Hanna) M.; A.B., Washington and Jefferson Coll., 1879, A.M., 1882 (D.D., 1892, LL.D., 1902); grad. Western Theol. Sem., Pa., 1882; m. Claire Louise Smith, Feb. 4, 1891. Ordained Presbyn. ministry, 1882; pastor First Ch., Duluth, Minn., 1882-83; pastor-elect Second Ch., Baltimore, 1883-84; pastor First Ch., San José, Calif., 1884-91; Stuart prof. systematic theology, San Francisco Theol. Sem., 1892-1902; pastor First Ch., Trenton, N.J., 1902-18. Traveled around the world, 1888-89; moderator Gen. Assembly of Presbyn. Ch. in U.S.A., 1901; chmn. Com. on Creed Revision, 1901-02; Stone lecturer Princeton Theol. Sem. for 1901; lecturer in theology, Auburn Theol. Sem., 1901-02; N.J. mem. Inter-State Divorce Congress, 1906; pres. Nat. Reform Assn., 1911—; pres. trustees Christ's Mission, New York, 1914—; mem. administration com. Federal Council Chs. of Christ in America, 1916—. Author: Christianity Supernatural, 1900; The Cosmos and The Logos, 1902. Home: San Rafael, Calif. Died June 14, 1924.

MINTURN, James Francis, judge; b. Hoboken, N.J., July 16, 1860; s. John and Annie M.; ed. Martha Inst., Columbia U., and under tutelage of Prof. Louis Barton; LL.B., Columbia, 1880; LL.D., Seton Hall Coll., 1908; m. Minnie T. Foley, Dec. 6, 1903. Corp. atty., Hoboken, 1884-1904; mem. N.J. Senate, 1904-07; judge Circuit Court, 1907-08; justice Supreme Court of N.J., 1908-29, retired; now dean John Marshall Coll. of Law, Jersey City, N.J.; also advisory master in chancery. While practicing was atty. in many important cases, notably the Hutchins' Will Case, involving bequest of large amount of money for circulation of works of Henry George. Judge-advocate old 2d Regt., N.G.N.J., 1884-91. One of organizers of Free Pub. Library, Hoboken, State Charities Aid Assn., Soc. for Prevention of Cruelty to Children. Democrat. Roman Catholic. Home: Hoboken, N.J. Died Nov. 16, 1934.

MITCHAM, Orin Burlingame, army officer; b. in Va., July 25, 1853; grad. U.S. Mil. Acad., 1874. Commd. 2d lt. 4th Arty., June 17, 1874; promoted through grades to col. ordnance, Jan. 21, 1909. Asst. Rock Island (Ill.) Arsenal, 1894; inspector of powder and in charge mfr. smokeless powder, 1899-1902; comdg. U.S. Powder Depot, Dover, N.J., and insp. powder and high explosives, 1902-07; apptd. comd. New York Arsenal, Governors Island, also armament officer and insp. ordnance, 1907. Died Aug. 20, 1934.

MITCHEL, Frederick Augustus, staff editor Am. Press Assn.; b. Cincinnati, O., Dec. 4, 1839; s. Maj. Gen. Ormsby MacKnight M.; A.M., Brown U., 1860. Second lt. 21st N.Y. Inf., Aug. 27, 1861-Sept. 24, 1862; capt. a.d.c. vols., Sept. 3, 1862; 2d lt. 16th U.S. Inf., Mar. 25, 1863; resigned, Aug. 17, 1863. Author: Ormsby MacKnight Mitchel, Astronomer and General (biography); also War Romances—Chattanooga; Chickamauga; etc. Home: East Orange, N.J. Deceased.

MITCHEL, John Purroy, mayor; b. Fordham, N.Y., July 19, 1879; s. Capt. James and Mary (Purroy) M.; St. John's Coll., Fordham; A.B., Columbia, 1899; LL.B., New York Law Sch., 1901; (LL.D., Columbia, 1917, also N.Y.U. and U. of Rochester); m. Olive, d. Franklin D. Child, of Boston, April 3, 1909. Admitted to N.Y. bar, June 1901; spl. counsel to City of New York, Dec. 1906-Apr. 1907; commr. of accounts of New York, Apr. 22, 1907-09; pres. Bd. of Aldermen, 1909-13 (acting mayor, Aug.-Sept. 1910); collector Port of New York, June 7-Dec. 1913; mayor of New York, term Jan. 1, 1914-Dec. 31, 1917. Commd. major Aviation Corps, U.S.A., Jan. 11, 1918. Democrat. Catholic. Home: New York, N.Y. Died July 6, 1918.

MITCHELL, Albert Graeme, M.D., prof. pediatrics; b. Salem, Mass., Feb. 22, 1889; s. Fred Albert and Marie (Graham) M.; grad. Central High Sch., Philadelphia; M.D., U. of Pa., 1910; m. Adele Wentz, Oct. 2, 1920; children—Marie Graham, Kathryn Wentz. Began practice at Philadelphia, 1912; asst. pediatrician, Children's Hosp., Phila., 1912; instr. in pediatrics, U. of Pa., 1919-21, asso. in pediatrics, 1921-24; prof. pediatrics, U. of Cincinnati (O.), 1924—; dir. pediatrics and contagious diseases, Cincinnati Gen. Hosp.; chief of staff and med. dir. Children's Hosp., Cincinnati; dir. Children's Hospital Research Foundation. Served as lt., later capt., Med. Corps, U.S.A., med. dir. Am. Hosp. for Civilians, Neufchâteau, France, later with 149th Machine Gun Bn., World War. Med. dir. Babies Milk Fund Assn. of Cincinnati; mem. White House Conf. on Child Care; mem. White House Conf. on Children in a Democracy. Chmn. Sect. on Pediatrics of Am. Med. Assn., 1935; v.p. Pan-Am. Assn. Sect. on Pediatrics, 7th Cruise Congress, Jan. 1938. Republican. Presbyn. Co-author: (with J. P. C. Griffith) Diseases of Infants and Children (2 vols.), 1927, (1 vol.), 1933, 2d edit. in one vol., 1937; Pediatrics and Pediatric Nursing (with Echo Upham and Elgie Wallinger), 1939. Pediatric editor The Cyclopedia of Medicine; asso. editor Am. Jour. of Diseases of Children. Home: Cincinnati, O. Died June 1, 1941.

MITCHELL, Albert Roscoe, surgeon; b. Cambridge, Ill., Apr. 5, 1856; s. John Burl and Alcina (Hawley) M.; ed. high schs., Kewanee, Ill., and by pvt. study; M.D., Rush Med. Coll., Chicago, 1879; m. Sophie Schwab, June 14, 1882; 1 dau., Helene (Mrs. Glen H. Foe). Practiced at Lincoln, 1879—; first dean Neb. U. Coll. of Medicine, 1883-87; sr. surgeon St. Elizabeth's Hosp.; med. dir. Banker's Life Ins. Co.; local surgeon C.,R.I.&P. Ry., North Western R.R. Co.; cons. surgeon C.,B.&Q. Ry.; dist. surgeon U.P. R.R. Co. Surgeon gen. Neb. N.G., Spanish-Am. War; mem. Med. Advisory Bd., Lincoln, World War. Fellow Am. Coll. Surgeons, Am. Medical Assn. (mem. war com., World War; now mem. bd. trustees). Elk. Home: Lincoln, Neb. Died May 25, 1933.

MITCHELL, Alfred, physician; b. N. Yarmouth, Me., Mar. 17, 1837; s. Tristram Gilman and Elizabeth Buckman (Chandler) M.; A.B., Bowdoin, 1859, A.M., 1862; M.D., Coll. of Phys. and Surg. (Columbia), 1865; (LL.D., Bowdoin, 1907); m. Abby E. Swett, Dec. 26, 1865. Asst. surgeon 9th Me. Regt. in Civil War; has practiced in Brunswick, Me., 1865—; lecturer on pathology, 1869-72, prof. obstetrics and diseases of children, 1872-75, prof. obstetrics and diseases of women and children, 1875-94, of obstetrics and diseases of children, 1894-97, of internal medicine, 1898-1911, sec. and dean of faculty, 1873-1911, Med. School of Maine; cons. physician Me. Gen. Hosp., and Central Me. Gen. Hosp. Mem. bd. overseers Bowdoin Coll. Home: Brunswick, Me. Died June 19, 1915.

MITCHELL, Charles Andrews, educator; b. Norwalk, O., Apr. 5, 1857; s. William and Katharine (Haller) Mitchell; graduated B.A., cum laude, Harvard U., 1881; m. Elizabeth Watkin Smith, July 9, 1894. Formerly teacher of classics, Cleveland High Sch., St. Paul's School, Concord, N.H.; asst. prin. Univ. School, Cleveland, 1890-1900; became prin., and asso. owner of Asheville (N.C.) Sch. for Boys, Sept. 1900; retired. Republican. Home: Easton, Pa. Died Apr. 19, 1921.

MITCHELL, Charles Dennis, alienist; b. Pontotoc, Miss., Oct. 29, 1866; s. Charles Bawlyn and Virginia (Dennis) M.; student U. of Miss.; M.D., Memphis Hosp. Med. Coll. (now U. of Tenn. Coll. Medicine), 1888; post-grad. study, N.Y. Post-Grad. Sch. and N.Y. Polyclinic Med. Sch.; m. Mary Herron, Dec. 12, 1888; children—Charles B., Thomas H. Began practice at Pontotoc, 1888; moved to Jackson, Miss., 1918; supt. Miss. State Insane Hosp., 1918—; cons. psychiatrist U.S. Vets. Home, Biloxi, Miss. Pres. Miss. State Bd. Health, 1912-16; pres. bd. Chickasaw Female Coll., Pontotoc; mem. Hosp. Bldg. Commn., 1926—. Democrat. Presbyn. Mason. Odd Fellow, K.P. Home: Jackson, Miss. Died Jan. 25, 1941.

MITCHELL, Charles Edward, diplomatic service; b. St. Michaels, Md., May 3, 1870; s. Edward and Amelia (Chambers) M.; ed. pub. and high schs., Boston Commercial Coll. and Internat. Business U. (Detroit); certified pub. accountant, W.Va., 1911; m. Elizabeth Murray, Aug. 31, 1905. Began as stenographer, 1904; business mgr. W.Va. State Coll. (colored), 1904-31, also teacher of business W.Va. Collegiate Inst.; pres. Mutual Savings & Loan Co., Charleston, W.Va., 1920-31; dir. Prudential Bank (Washington, D.C.), Mut. Savings & Loan Co. (Charleston, W.Va.); apptd. E.E. and M.P. to Liberia, 1931; retired, Mar. 22, 1933. Mem. Virgin Island Commn. under President Coolidge; mem. Rep. State Com. W.Va. 8 yrs., 1921-29; chmn. colored div. Rep. State Com. W.Va., 1916, and of colored div. Nat. Com., 1924, v. chmn., 1928; now mem. N.Y. State and County Rep. coms. Served in U.S. Navy 4½ yrs. Episcopalian. Mason. Odd Fellow, K.P., Elk. Home: New York, N.Y. Deceased.

MITCHELL, Charles Elliott, lawyer; b. Bristol, Conn., May 11, 1837; s. George H. and Lurene (Hooker) M.; Ph.B., Brown U., 1861; LL.B., Albany Law Sch., 1864; m. Cornelia A. Chamberlain, Dec. 13, 1866. Began practice of patent law, New Britain, Conn., 1864, New York, after 1891. City atty. New Britain, 1870-71; mem. Conn. Ho. of Rep., 1880-81; U.S. commr. of patents, 1889-91, resigned. Pres. Stanley Rule & Level Co. Home: New Britain, Conn. Died 1911.

MITCHELL, Clifford, M.D.; b. Nantucket, Mass., Jan. 28, 1854; s. Francis Macy and Ellen M.; A.B., cum laude, Harvard, 1875; studied Chicago Med. Coll., 1876-77; M.D., Chicago Homœ. Med. Coll., 1878; m. Susan P. Lillie, May 1878 (dec.); m. 2d, Anna L. Proctor, Sept. 2, 1908 (dec.); m. 3d, Sarah Celeste Dorland, June 24, 1912. Practice limited to urinology and diseases of the kidneys; formerly prof. clin. urinology and renal diseases, Chicago Homœ. Med. Coll., Hahnemann Med. Coll. and Gen. Med. College. Author: Manual of Urinary Analysis, 1897-1902; Renal Therapeutics, 1898; Diseases of the Urinary Organs, 1903; Modern Urinology, 1911. Mem. Vol. Med. Service Corps, U.S.A., 1918. Co-discoverer with Frederick G. Germuth of reagent for detection of uranium. Home: Chicago, Ill. Died Oct. 19, 1939.

MITCHELL, Donald Grant ("Ik Marvel"), author; b. Norwich, Conn., April 1822; s. Rev. Alfred M.; ed. Judge Hall's Ellington School, 1830-37; grad. Yale, 1841 (LL.D.); m. Mary F. Pringle. Studied law in New York; U.S. consul to Venice, 1853-54; lived on his farm of Edgewood. Author: Reveries of a Bachelor, 1850; Dream Life, 1852; My Farm of Edgewood, 1863; Seven Stories with Basement and Attic, 1864; Dr. Johns, 1866; Bound Together, 1884; Out-of-Town Places, 1884; English Lands, Letters and Kings, 1889; American Lands and Letters, 1897. Home: New Haven, Conn. Died 1908.

MITCHELL, Edmund, author, journalist; b. Glasgow, Scotland, Mar. 19, 1861; s. John and Margaret (Milne) M.; M.A. (gold medal for English literature), Aberdeen U., 1881; m. Ada Sophia, d. late William Jones, sculptor, of London, 1886. Engaged in journalism as editorial writer on staff of the Glasgow Herald, the Times of India, Melbourne (Australia) Age, and Los Angeles (Calif.) Times. Senior lt. Bombay Vol. Arty., 1888-89. Has traveled as spl. corr. over Europe, Morocco, the Canary Islands, Egypt, India, Ceylon, Java, Indo-China, China, Japan, Australia, New Zealand, the Pacific Islands, Canada and U.S.; attended as special correspondent internat. expns. at Chicago, 1893, Antwerp, 1894, Paris, 1900, St. Louis, 1904, Portland, Ore., 1905. Author: The Temple of Death, 1894; Towards the Eternal Snows, 1896; Chickabiddy Stories, 1899; Plotters of Paris, 1900; The Lone Star Rush, 1901; Only a Nigger, 1901; The Belforts of Culben, 1902; The Despoilers, 1904; In Desert Keeping, 1905; El Moko, Story of a Burro, 1909; Captain of His Soul, 1912; Tales of Destiny, 1913; also The Telephone, one-act comedy, prod. London, 1901. German translations of foregoing novels published Stuttgart, 1908-14. Home: Los Angeles, Calif. Died Mar. 31, 1917.

MITCHELL, Edward Cushing, pres. Leland Univ., 1885—; b. East Bridgewater, Mass., Sept. 20, 1829; grad. Waterville Coll. (now Colby Univ.), Me., 1849; Newton, Mass., Theol. Sem., 1853; resident graduate, same, 1853-54; ordained Baptist minister. Pastor Calais, Me., 1854-56; Brockport, N.Y., 1857-58; Rockford, Ill., 1858-63; prof. Biblical interpretation, Alton, Ill., 1863-70; prof. Hebrew and O.T. lit., Baptist Union Sem., Chicago, 1870-77; prof. Hebrew, Regents Park Coll., London, England, 1876-77; pres. Baptist Theol. School, Paris, France, 1878-82; pres. Roger Williams Univ., Nashville, Tenn., 1884-85. Editor: Benjamin Davies Hebrew Lexicon; Gesenius's Hebrew Grammar. Author: The Critical Handbook—a Guide to the Authenticity, Canon and Text of the Greek New Testament; Les Sources du Nouveau Testament; Hebrew Introduction; etc. Home: New Orleans, La. Died 1900.

MITCHELL, Edward Page, editor; b. Bath, Me., Mar. 24, 1852; s. Edward H. and Frances A. (Page) M.; A.B., Bowdoin, 1871, Litt.D., 1907; Litt.D., Columbia U., 1919; m. Annie Sewall Welch, Oct. 29, 1874 (died 1909); children—Edward Sewall, Dana, Frank Stockbridge, Robert; m. 2d, Ada M. Burroughs, July 22, 1912; 1 son, Burroughs. Entered journalism on Boston Advertiser, 1871; continuously engaged on editorial staff New York Sun, 1875-1920, editor in chief 1903-20; on consolidation of Morning Sun and New York Herald, 1920, became mem. editorial staff of the Herald; pres. Sun Printing & Pub. Co., 1909-11. Overseer, Bowdoin Coll. Author: Memoirs of an Editor, 1924; Centennial Address, Longfellow-Hawthorne Celebration, Bowdoin College, 1925. Home: Kenyon, R.I. Died Jan. 22, 1927.

MITCHELL, Edwin Knox, theologian; b. Locke, Ohio, Dec. 23, 1853; s. Spencer and Harriet Newell (Howard) M.; A.B., Marietta (Ohio) Coll., 1878, A.M. same, 1881, D.D., 1896; taught in Columbus (O.) High Sch., 1879-81; B.D., Union Theol. Sem., New York, 1884; univs. of Berlin and Giessen, 1884-86; m. Hetty Marquand Enos, Jan. 20, 1887; children—Spencer Trask, Rev. E. Knox, Frederica. Ordained Presbyterian ministry, 1886; pastor Memorial Ch., St. Augustine, Fla., 1886-90; studied in Berlin and traveled in Orient, 1890-91; prof. Græco-Roman and Eastern ch. history, Hartford Theol. Sem., 1892-1925, grad. prof., 1925-28, prof. emeritus, 1928—. Mem. Federal Council Chs. of Christ in America, Com. on Interch. Relations of Nat. Council Congl. Chs., Ch. Unity League, Foreign Policy Assn. Chmn. Hartford World Court Com.; mem. Hartford Bd. Park Commrs., 1914-27; pres. Hartford Council Chs., 1914-30; dir. Watkins School, Yaddo Corp., Horace Bushnell Memorial Foundation, Charity Organization Soc. Fellow Am. Geog. Society. Author: Life and Character of Christ According to St. Paul, 1894; Creeds and Canons, 1905. Home: Hartford, Conn. Died Oct. 5, 1934.

MITCHELL, Guy Elliott, librarian U.S. Geol. Survey; b. Woodward, Pa., Apr. 11, 1870; s. Frederick William and Caroline Cooper (Grimwood) M.; student Mich. State Coll., 1889-1890; m. Madeleine Blandy, Aug. 22, 1899; children—Dorothy Elliott (Mrs. Maxwell Laing Johnston), Margaret Blandy. Sec. to U.S. senator, John B. Allen, state of Wash., 1888; in natural history exploration to Nicaragua, 1891-92; farmer, 1892-96, in newspaper work, 1897-1900; sec. Nat. Irrigation Assn. and editor and pub. of Nat. Irrigation and Nat. Homemaker, 1900-06; chief exec. div. U.S. Geol. Survey, Washington, 1907-29, librarian, 1930—. Conglist. Mason. Died Dec. 5, 1939.

MITCHELL, Harry Dawson, clergyman; b. Baltimore, Md., Aug. 22, 1863; s. Zachariah and Priscilla (Logie) M.; A.B., Western Md. Coll., 1890 (D.D., 1908); m. Nellie Grant Horn, Apr. 15, 1890. Ordained M.E. ministry, 1888; pastor various chs. at Baltimore; pastor Metropolitan Memorial Ch. ("The National Methodist Church"), Washington, D.C., 1916—. Hon. mem. Naval Vets. Assn., Md., and G.A.R. of D.C. Republican. Mason. Deceased.

MITCHELL, Harry Walter, M.D.; b. Plymouth, N.H., Nov. 6, 1867; s. Harris Blair and Frances (Blair) M.; Peacham (Vt.) Acad.; M.D., U. of Vt., 1896, hon. Sc.D., 1931; m. Mary Paulsell, Aug. 16, 1902. Asst. phys., State Farm, Bridgewater, Mass., 1896-99; asst. phys., Danvers (Mass.) State Hosp., 1899-1907; supt. Eastern Me. Insane Hosp., 1907-10, Danvers State Hosp., Mass., 1910-12, Warren State Hosp., Warren, Pa., 1912—. Unitarian. Home: Warren, Pa., Died June 13, 1933.

MITCHELL, Henry, engr.; b. Nantucket, Mass., Sept. 16, 1830; s. William M. (astronomer); ed. private schools (A. M., Harvard, 1867); asst. to commrs. on harbor encroachments of New York, 1859; consulting engr. U.S. commn. on Boston harbor; later mem. of commn., now mem. advisory council, to bd. harbor commrs. of Boston. Has been prof. Am. Inst. of Technology, mem. U.S. advisory councils on harbors of Portland, Me., Providence, R.I., Norfolk and Portsmouth, Va., and Phila.; in 1874 apptd. by President Grant to represent Coast and Geodetic Survey in bd. of engrs. for improvement of mouth of Mississippi; later mem. Mississippi River commn. Mem. Nat. Acad. Sciences; fellow Am. Acad. of Sciences of Boston. Home: Nantucket, Mass. Died 1902.

MITCHELL, Henry, physician; b. Norwich, N.Y., Aug. 6, 1845; s. Henry and Mary (Bellamy) M.; ed. Catskill (N.Y.) Acad. and Phillips Exeter Acad.; M.D., Bellevue Hosp. Med. Coll. (New York U.), 1866; m. Elizabeth Roberts, Nov. 14, 1866. Practiced in Norwich, N.Y., 1866-69, Jersey City, N.J., 1869-79; removed to Asbury Park, 1879; pres. Bd. of Health, Asbury Park, 1880-94; mem. and exec. officer N.J. State Bd. of Health, 1894-1908. Trustee Pub. Library, Asbury Park. Surgeon, 103d Regt. N.Y. Vols., 1868; mem. Bd. Commrs., Asbury Park, 1886. Republican. Home: Asbury Park, N.J. Died Jan. 31, 1919.

MITCHELL, Hinckley Gilbert (Thomas), theologian; b. Lee, Oneida Co., N.Y., Feb. 22, 1846; s. James and Sarah Gilbert (Thomas) M.; A.B., Wesleyan, Conn., 1873, A.M., 1876; S.T.B., Boston U., 1876; Ph.D., U. of Leipzig, 1879; (D.D., Mt. Union, 1888, Wesleyan, 1901); m. Alice Stanford, June 29, 1880. M.E. pastor Fayette, N.Y., 1879-80; instr. Latin and Hebrew, Wesleyan U., 1880-83; prof. Hebrew and O.T. exegesis, 1883-1905, instr. Semitic langs. and lit., 1905-06, Boston U.; engaged in exegetical work, 1906-10; prof. Hebrew and exegesis, Tufts College, 1910—. Refused confirmation by the Bd. of Bishops of the M.E. Ch. for denying the historicity of the early chapters of Genesis, 1905. Dir. Am. Sch. for Oriental Study and Research in Palestine, 1901-02. Transferred to N.H. Conf., 1909, to N.E. Conf., 1913. Lecturer, Harvard Summer Sch. of Theology, 1899, 1910; substitute prof., U. of Chicago, summer, 1914. Author: Hebrew Lessons, 1885; Isaiah, a Study of Chapters I-XII, 1897; The World Before Abraham, 1901; Tales Told in Palestine (with J. E. Hanauer), 1904; Genesis, 1909; Commentary on Haggai and Zechariah ("International"), Ethics of the Old Testament, 1912. Home: Boston, Mass. Died May 19, 1920.

MITCHELL, James, editor Arkansas Democrat; b. Washington Co., Ark., May 8, 1833; ed. common schools and Cane Hill Coll.; taught school in Ark., 1859-60; mem. Ark. legislature, 1860; pvt. to capt., C.S.A., 1861-65; taught in Texas; prof. in Cane Hill Coll., Ark., 1868-74; prof. English literature Ark. Industrial Univ. (Fayetteville), 1874-76; editor Arkansas Gazette, 1876-78; part owner and editor Arkansas Democrat, 1888, and from 1890 pres. Arkansas Democrat Co.; postmaster Little Rock, 1893-97. Home: Little Rock, Ark. Died 1902.

MITCHELL, James Alfred, prof. geology, mineralogy and physics Mount St. Mary's Coll., Emmitsburg, Md., lecturer on natural science, St. Joseph's Acad., same place; s. M. and Jane (Petrie) M.; grad. Royal School of Mines, England; studied astronomy and meteorology at Lord Ross's Observatory, Birr Castle, Ireland; carried on further researches in geology and chemistry at Harvard, and in paleontology at Johns Hopkins; (A.M., Mt. St. Mary's Coll., 1888; Ph.D., Niagara Univ., 1894); m. Margaret J. Willson, 1889. Worked on reports for State Geol. Survey and U.S. Weather Bureau; 1st to discover fossilferous footprints in the Newark system of the Jura Trias in Maryland. Mem. of the Washington Acad. Sciences; mem. of the faculty of Mt. St. Mary's Coll. for past 13 yrs. Home: Emmitsburg, Md. Died 1902.

MITCHELL, James Tyndale, author; b. Belleville, Ill., Nov. 9, 1834; A.B., Harvard, 1855, A.M., 1857; LL.B., U. of Pa., 1858; (LL.D., Jefferson Med. Coll., Phila., 1872, Harvard, 1901, U. of Pa., 1902); unmarried. Admitted to Phila. bar, 1857; asst. city solicitor, Phila., 1860-63; judge Dist. Ct., 1871-75; judge Ct. of Common Pleas, 1875-88; justice, 1889-1903, chief justice, 1903-09, Supreme Ct. of Pa. Editor-in-chief Am. Law Register, 1862-87. Chmn. of commrs. apptd. to report on the acts of the Colonial Assembly not printed, and to edit and publish the statutes at large from 1681 to 1800. Author: History of the District Court, 1875, Mitchell on Motions and Rules, 1879; Fidelity to Court as Well as Client, 1900; Address on John Marshall Day, 1901; History of the Law Association of Philadelphia, 1902; Hints on Practice in Appeals, 1904. Now prothonotary Supreme Ct. of Pa. Home: Philadelphia, Pa. Died July 4, 1915.

MITCHELL, John, labor official; b. Braidwood, Will Co., Ill., Feb. 4, 1870; s. Robert and Martha (Halley) M.; ed. Braidwood, from 6 until 10 yrs. of age; subsequent edn. obtained by night study; studied law 1 yr.; read on economic questions; gathered information on questions of organization, etc., by connection with organized labor from 16 yrs. of age; m. Katherine O'Rourke, June 1, 1891. Worked in coal mines 1882; joined Knights of Labor, 1885; traveled in the West, mining coal, 1885-90; sec.-treas. sub-dist. of United Mine Workers of America, 1895; organizer, 1897—, nat. v.p., 1898, apptd. acting nat. pres., Sept. 1898, pres., 1899-1908, United Mine Workers of America; chmn. Trade Agreement Dept. of Nat. Civic Fedn., 1908-11; on lecture platform, subject trade unionism, 1911-13; 2d v.p. A.F. of L., 1900-14 (4th v.p. 1898-1900); directed strikes of anthracite mine workers, 1900, 1902; mem. State Workmen's Compensation Commn., N.Y., 1914-15; chmn. N.Y. State Industrial Commn., 1915—. Pres. N.Y. State Food Commn., chmn. Federal Food Bd. for N.Y. State, pres. N.Y. State Council of Farms and Markets, and mem. Federal Milk Commn. for Eastern States, 1917—. Home: Mt. Vernon, N.Y. Died Sept. 9, 1919.

MITCHELL, John Ames, editor; b. New York, Jan. 17, 1845; s. Asa M.; fitted for coll. at Exeter, N.H.; studied at Lawrence Scientific Sch. (Harvard); studied architecture in Boston and at École des Beaux Arts, Paris, 1867-70; married. Practiced as architect, Boston, 1870-76; after that engaged in artistic and decorative work; studied drawing and painting in Paris, 1876-80; artist, illustrator, writer, New York, 1880-83; founder, Jan. 3, 1883, and from then editor of Life. Author: Amos Judd, 1895; That First Affair, 1896; Gloria Victis, 1897; The Pines of Lory, 1901; The Villa Claudia, 1904; The Silent War, 1906; Dr. Thorne's Idea, 1910; Pandora's Box, 1911; Drowsy, 1917. Mem. Nat. Inst. Arts and Letters. Home: New York, N.Y. Died June 29, 1918.

MITCHELL, John H., U.S. senator from Ore.; b. Washington Co., Pa., June 22, 1835; ed. Witherspoon Inst.; studied law; admitted to Pa. bar; went to Calif.; practiced San Luis Obispo and San Francisco; removed to Portland, Ore., 1860; m. Mattie E. Price, Feb. 25, 1862. Corporation atty., 1861; State senator, 1862-66; pres. State senate, 1864; has been lt. col. Ore. militia; U.S. senator from Ore., 1873-79 and 1885-97; reëlected, Feb. 25, 1901, to U.S. senate for term 1901-07. Republican. Practiced law at Portland, Ore., 1897—. Prof. med. jurisprudence Willamette Univ., Salem, Ore., 1867-71. Home: Portland, Ore. Died 1905.

MITCHELL, John Inscho, a judge Superior Court of Pa. for term 1900-10, U.S. senator; b. Tioga, Pa., July 28, 1838; ed. in township schools and, 1857-59, at Lewisburg Univ., Pa.; was not graduated; m. Jeannette Baldwin, Oct. 1860 (died 1869); 2d, Mary Alice Archer, Feb. 1871. Admitted to bar Sept. 1864; dist. atty., Tioga Co., 1869-72; mem. Pa. legislature, 1872-76; mem. Congress, 1877-81; U.S. senator, 1881-87. Republican. Pres. judge, 1899; judge Superior Court, Pa., Jan. 1900—. Home: Wellsboro, Pa. Died 1907.

MITCHELL, John J., banker; b. Alton, Ill., Nov. 3, 1853; s. William H. and Mary A. M.; ed. pub. schs. and at Kent's Hill, Me.; m. Mary Louise Jewett, Feb. 11, 1890; children—Gwendolyn (Mrs. Robert E. Hunter), William H., John J., Clarence B., Louise J. Entered employ Ill. Trust & Savings Bank as messenger boy, 1873, of which was pres., 1880-1923, and pres. of its successor, the Ill. Merchants Trust Co., 1923—. Trustee and mem. advisory com. Am. Surety Co. of New York; trustee Mut. Life Ins. Co. of New York. Dir. Art Inst. Chicago. Home: Chicago, Ill. Died Oct. 29, 1927.

MITCHELL, John Joseph, congressman; b. Marlboro, Mass., May 9, 1873; s. Edward and Bridget (McKeon) M.; Boston Coll., and Albany Law Sch.; unmarried. Mem. Mass. Ho. of Rep., 1903-06, Senate, 1907, 1908; mem. 61st Congress, Dec. 1, 1910-Mar. 4, 1911, and 63d Congress, Apr. 15, 1913-15, 13th Mass. Dist., to succeed John W. Weeks (elected to U.S. Senate). Democrat. Catholic. Home: Marlboro, Mass. Died Sept. 13, 1925.

MITCHELL, John Kearsley, physician; b. Philadelphia, July 13, 1859; s. S(ilas) Weir and Mary Middleton (Elwyn) M.; brother of Langdon Elwyn M.; Harvard, 1877-80 (A.B., 1904); M.D., U. of Pa., 1883; m. Anne Keppele Williams, 1889. Resident phys. Children's Hosp., 1883, Episcopal Hosp., 1883-85; demonstrator, 1886-92, lecturer, 1893-98, U. of Pa. Med. Sch.; now physician to Phila. Infirmary for Nervous Diseases; cons. neurologist Pa. Instn. for Feeble-Minded. Episcopalian. Author: Fat and Blood (with Dr. S. Weir Mitchell), 8th edit., 1898; Remote Consequences of Injuries of Nerves, 1895; Mechano-therapy, Massage and Physical Education, 1904. Home: Philadelphia, Pa. Died Apr. 10, 1917.

MITCHELL, John Lendrum, U.S. senator; b. Milwaukee, Wis., Oct. 19, 1842; ed. in public schools, mil. school, Hampton, Conn., and at Dresden, Munich and Geneva; served in Wis. vols. as lt., 1861-64; State senator, Wis., 1872-73 and 1875-76; pres. Milwaukee school bd., 1884-85; pres. Wis. State Agrl. Soc.; pres. Northwestern Trotting-Horse Breeders' Assn.; mem. bd. of mgrs. Nat. Home for Disabled Vol. Soldiers, 1886— (v.p., 1895); v.p. Marine Nat. Bank, Northwestern Nat. Ins. Co.; was mem. Nat. Dem. Com. 4 yrs. and chmn. Dem. Congressional Com., 1892; mem. Congress, 1891-93; U.S. senator, 1893-99. Democrat. Home: Milwaukee, Wis. Died 1904.

MITCHELL, John Murray, congressman, lawyer; b. New York, March 18, 1858; grad. Columbia, 1877 (A.M., 1880); Columbia Law School, 1879; admitted to bar, 1879; traveled in Europe, 1879-80; law clerk, 1880-82; has practiced, 1882—; mem. Congress, 8th N.Y. dist., 1895-99; defeated, 1898, for 56th Congress. Republican. Home: New York, N.Y. Died 1905.

MITCHELL, John R., judge; b. Halifax Co., Va., Jan. 31, 1861; s. John A. and Mary F. (Pringle) M.; ed. common schs. of Va.; studied law pvtly. and at U. of Va. (non-grad.); m. Hallie Price, Apr. 22, 1891; 1 son, Richard Sharp. Settled at Olympia, Wash., 1888; admitted to Wash. bar, 1894; pros. atty. Thurston Co., Wash., 1897-99; practiced with Thomas M. Vance, 1901-08; judge of Superior Court, Thurston and Mason cos., 3 terms, 1908-20; apptd. asso. justice Supreme Court of Wash., to fill vacancy, May 1918, elected for terms ending 1925, 31, 37; chief justice, 1929-31; retired Jan. 1937. Baptist. Mason, K.P., Woodman. Home: Olympia, Wash. Died Mar. 24, 1939.

MITCHELL, John Raymond, banker; b. Franklin, Pa., Jan. 9, 1868; s. John L. and Harriet (Raymond) M.; Ph.B., Yale, 1889; m. Mary E. Lamberton, Jan. 29, 1896 (died 1909); m. 2d, Adelia Sanders Anderson, Nov. 14, 1919. Began as v.p. Winona Deposit Bank, 1897; pres. Capital Nat. Bank, St. Paul, 1906-20; apptd. mem. Federal Reserve Bd., term 1921-31, resigned May 12, 1923; apptd. federal reserve agent and chmn. bd. Federal Reserve Bank, Minneapolis, by Federal Reserve Board, 1924. Republican. Presbyn. Home: Minneapolis, Minn. Died Jan. 31, 1933.

MITCHELL, John William, clergyman, editor; b. Franklin Co., Va., May 5, 1856; s. James Randolph and Nancy Mariah (Wright) M.; student Richmond (Va.) Coll., 1883-85; grad. Crozer Theol. Seminary, Chester, Pa., 1888; D.D., Georgetown (Ky.) Coll., 1906; m. Jennie Kate Moorhead, Sept. 24, 1888; children—Jennie Kate, John William, James Franklin, Theodosia, Mattie. Ordained ministry Baptist Church, 1880; pastor successively at Wytheville, Va., and South Street Ch., Portsmouth, until 1902; co-editor Religious Herald, Richmond, Va., 1902-07; editor Baptist Banner, Parkersburg, W.Va., 1907-18, Florida Baptist Witness, 1918-28; pastor Liberty Bapt. Ch., Jacksonville, Fla. Democrat. Mason. Home: Jacksonville, Fla. Died Nov. 13, 1933.

MITCHELL, Langdon Elwyn, playwright; b. Phila., Feb. 17, 1862; s. S(ilas) Weir and Mary Middleton (Elwyn) M.; ed. St. Paul's Sch., Concord, N.H., and studied abroad for 3 yrs.; law student Harvard, 2 yrs., Columbia, 1 yr.; admitted to New York bar, 1886; m. Marion Lea, 1892. From 1883 playwright and author; pen-name "John Philip Varley." Author: Sylvian, and Other Poems, 1884; Poems, 1894; Love in the Backwoods, 1896; "Becky Sharp" (play); "The New York Idea" (play); and other plays; (book) Understanding America, 1927. Mem. Nat. Inst. Arts and Letters. Home: New York, N.Y. Deceased.

MITCHELL, Leander Perry, U.S. official; b. Henry Co., Ind., Feb. 5, 1849; s. Charles and Mary (Black) M.; LL.B., Ind. U., 1872; B.S., Northwestern Christian (now Butler) U., Indianapolis, 1873; m. Gertrude L. Mitchell, Jan. 6, 1879. Pvt. 139th Ind.

Vols., 1864; practiced law New Castle, Ind., 1872-98; Rep. presdl. elector, 1888; mem. Rep. State Central Com., 1896; asst. comptroller U.S. Treasury, Jan. 1898—. Home: New Castle, Ind. Died Dec. 6, 1912.

MITCHELL, Maggie, actress; b. New York, 1832. Began her life on stage as a baby; afterward taking child parts before she was 5 yrs. old; début, Burton's Chambers St. Theatre, New York, as Julia in "The Soldier's Daughter." Famous in title rôle of Fanchon, first produced at New Orleans, 1860; and later in Mignon, Lorie, The Pearl of Savoy, Nan the Good for Nothing, Jane Eyre, and other plays; retired; m. Henry Paddock, Oct. 15, 1868; 2d, Charles Abbott. (Real name, Margaret Julia Mitchell.) Home: New York, N.Y. Died Mar. 22, 1918.

MITCHELL, Mason, consul; b. Hamilton, N.Y., Feb. 26, 1859; s. David J. M.; ed. St. John's Sch., Manlius, N.Y., and Phillips Acad., Exeter, N.H.; m. Edna M. Ellis, Nov. 25, 1905. Went on stage at 18, becoming mem. of co. at old Broadway Theatre, New York; was support of Edwin Booth, Lawrence Barrett and John McCullough, and leading man with Mme. Modjeska; accompanied Mary Anderson and played with her during her engagement through Great Britain, 1883-85. Chief of scouts under Canadian Govt. through Riel Rebellion, 1885, promoted for gallantry in action. Traveled through S. America and South Sea Islands, writing and illustrating articles of travel in those countries for various mags., and was for some time in Samoa with Robert Louis Stevenson. Became mgr. Garrick Theatre, New York, for Richard Mansfield, and supported Mrs. James Brown Potter; leading man and bus. rep. with Dion Boucicault, 1896. Enlisted in Roosevelt's Rough Riders, 1898, and wounded at battle of Santiago; spoke through gubernatorial campaign of Theodore Roosevelt; Am. consul at Zanzibar, 1902-05, at Chungking, China, 1905-08, at Apia, Samoa, 1908-20, at Queenstown, Ireland, 1920-21, at Malta, Maltese Island, 1921—. Was shot and slightly wounded by a lunatic while consul at Malta in December 1922. On outbreak of European war took over British and French interests in German Samoa, Aug. 8, 1914, and Aug. 29, the colony being captured by British and the German officials being deported to Auckland, N.Z., assumed representation of German interests. Was the first to shoot the "Takin," which has been named after him (Budorcas taxicolor Mitchelli); also a new species of lynx (Felis temencki Mitchelli). Died June 16, 1930.

MITCHELL, Oscar, lawyer; b. on farm Greene Co., Ill., Aug. 10, 1863; s. Jackson Gates and Elizabeth (Hubbell) M.; ed. pub. and pvt. schs.; LL.B. honoris causa, U. of Mich., 1925 as of class of 1891; m. Mary Wildey, July 7, 1892; children—Constance Moffett (Mrs. Irving D. Fish), Wildey Hubbell, Margaret Elizabeth, Oscar. Began as country sch. teacher, 1885; prin. high sch., Salem, Mo., 1888-89; admitted to Minn. bar, 1892, and began practice at Duluth; partner Mitchell, Gillette, Nye & Harries; pres., dir. and gen. counsel, Stone Ordean Wells Co.; dir. and gen. counsel Minn. Power & Light Co., Duluth-Superior Transit Co., First & Am. Nat. Bank of Duluth (also mem. exec. com.). Trustee Carleton Coll., Northfield, Minn.; chmn. Bd. of Directors of Trusts, City of Duluth. Republican. Home: Duluth, Minn. Died Feb. 17, 1937.

MITCHELL, Robert, mfr.; b. nr. Enniskillen, County Fermanagh, Ireland, Nov. 15, 1811; came with family to U.S., 1824; settled on farm in Ind.; apprenticed to cabinetmaker; in 1836, with Robert M. Moore, established small cabinet shop; started to use machinery, 1844; for years pres. Robert Mitchell Furniture Co., Cincinnati, O., a large business. Died 1899.

MITCHELL, Samuel S., clergyman; b. Clinton, N.Y., Aug. 16, 1839; s. Armstrong and Jane (Mitchell) M.; A.B., Princeton, 1861 (D.D., 1875); grad. Princeton Theol. Sem., 1864; m. Thresa Wierman, June 25, 1868. Ordained Presbyn. ministry, 1864; pastor Pine St. Ch., Harrisburg, Pa., 1864-69, New York Av. Ch., Washington, D.C., 1869-78, Ref. Dutch Ch., Brooklyn, N.Y., 1878-80, 1st Ch., Buffalo, N.Y., 1881-1904. Died Jan. 7, 1919.

MITCHELL, Samuel Thomas, pres. Wilberforce Univ., 1884—; b. Toledo, O., Sept. 24, 1851; is of Negro race; attended public schools of Cleveland and Cincinnati; grad. Wilberforce Univ., 1873 (A.M., 1881; LL.D., State Univ. of Ky., 1889); taught at Wilmington, O., 2 yrs.; was prin. Lincoln Inst., Jefferson City, Mo., 3 yrs.; was 1st pres. Colored State Teachers' Assn., Jefferson City, Mo. Licensed to preach, 1875; prin. in Springfield, O., 5 yrs., on 10 yrs.' certificate. Was a v.p. Ednl. Congress at World's Columbian Expn. Home: Wilberforce, O. Died 1901.

MITCHELL, Sidney, mfr.; b. Chicago, Ill., Feb. 12, 1876; s. Joseph Sidney and Helen (Leeds) M.; ed. Armour Inst. Chicago; unmarried. Began as clk. A. L. Dewar & Co., Chicago, 1895; mgr. Milmine Bodman & Co., 1899-1905; partner Milmine Bodman Grain Co., 1906-08; pres. Am. Strawboard Co., 1907-12, United Boxboard & Paper Co., 1907-13, Queen City Paper Co., 1907-12; pres. United Paper Board Co., Benton & Fairchild Ry. Co., Leedsmere Corp. Mem. Metropolitan Museum Art (New York). Home: New York, N.Y. Died Feb. 26, 1938.

MITCHELL, S(ilas) Weir, neurologist; b. Phila., Feb. 15, 1829; s. John Kearsley and Matilda (Henry) M.; ed. in grammar sch. and U. of Pa., but was not grad. because of illness during sr. yr.; M.D., Jefferson Med. Coll., 1850; (hon. M.D., Bologna, 1888; LL.D., Harvard, 1886, Edinburgh, 1895, Princeton, 1896, Toronto, 1906, Jefferson Med. Coll., Phila., 1910); m. Mary Middleton Elwyn; 2d, Mary Cadwalader, 1875; father of John Kearsley and Langdon Elwyn M. Established practice in Phila.; prominent as physiologist and especially as neurologist. Fellow Am. Acad. Arts and Sciences, Coll. Physicians, Phila. Trustee U. of Pennsylvania, Carnegie Instn., Washington. Author: Nurses and Their Education, 1902; The Evolution of the Rest Treatment, 1904; Rest Treatment and Psychic Medicine, 1908; Collected Poems, 1896; Hugh Wynne, 1898; Adventures of Francois, 1899; Autobiography of a Quack, 1900; Youth of Washington, 1904; The Red City, 1907. Home: Philadelphia, Pa. Died Jan. 4, 1914.

MITCHELL, Walter, P.E. clergyman; b. Nantucket, Mass., Jan. 22, 1826; grad. Harvard, 1846 (A.M., Trinity); admitted to bar, Bristol Co., Mass., 1849); candidate for ministry, 1856; deacon, 1859; priest, 1860. Successively rector St. John's Ch., Stamford, Conn.; St. Mark's, Phila.; Holy Trinity, Rutland, Vt.; Holy Trinity, Middletown, Conn.; Christ Ch., Rye, N.Y.; chaplain Kenyon Coll., Gambier, O.; retired from active pastorate. Married. Author: Two Strings to His Bow (novel); Bryan Maurice (novel); The Mocking Bird (poem); etc. Home: New York, N.Y. Died 1908.

MITCHELL, Walter Scott, banker; b. Somerset, Pa., Mar. 17, 1857; s. Chauncey Forward and Mary (Plowman) M.; ed. pub. schs., Greensburg and Pittsburgh, Pa.; m. Anne Chalfant, Sept. 2, 1915. With T. Mellon & Son's Bank, Pittsburgh, 1871-1902; cashier Mellon Nat. Bank, 1902-16, v.p., 1916—; sec. McClintic-Marshall Corp. and subsidiaries; mem. Pittsburgh Stock Exchange. Republican. Home: Pittsburgh, Pa., and Sewickley, Pa. Died Sept. 25, 1930.

MITCHELL, William, justice supreme court of Minn., March, 1881—; b. Welland Co., Ont., Nov. 19, 1832; grad. Jefferson Coll., Pa., 1853. Admitted to bar in Va., 1857; same year settled in Winona, Minn.; practiced law, 1857-73; judge 3d judical dist., Jan. 1, 1874 to March, 1881. Home: St. Paul, Minn. Died 1900.

MITCHELL, William, army officer, stock raiser, farmer; b. of Am. parents temporarily sojourning abroad, Nice, France, Dec. 29, 1879; s. U.S. Senator John Lendrum and Harriet Danforth (Becker) M.; attended Racine (Wis.) Coll.; A.B., George Washington U., 1899; distinguished grad. Army Sch. of the Line, 1908; grad. Army Staff Coll., 1909; m. Elizabeth Trumbull Miller, Oct. 11, 1923; children—Lucy Trumbull, William. Enlisted as pvt., Co. M, 1st Wis. Inf., May 14, 1898; advanced through all grades, including brig. gen.; served in Spanish-Am. War, Philippine Insurrection, during construction of telgraph lines in Alaska, Army of Cuban Pacification, on Mexican Border and in World War. Instr. Army Staff Coll., and on Gen. Staff. Comdr. Air Forces, A.E.F., during entire campaign, and later dir. of Military Aviation, U.S. Army; participated in 14 major enagagements in World War. Resigned commn. in U.S. Army, Feb. 1, 1926. Awarded grade of Mil. Aviator for service against enemy, also D.S.C. and D.S.M. (U.S.); Croix de Guerre with 5 palms and Comdr. Legion of Honor (French); Companion Order of St. Michael and St. George (British), Commendatore S.S. Maurizio e Labbaro, Medal for Merit in War and Grand Officer Crown of Italy (Italian). Episcopalian. Author: Our Air Force, 1921; Winged Defense, 1925; Skyways, 1930. Home: Middleburg, Va. Died Feb. 19, 1936.

MITCHELL, William Samuel, clergyman; b. Bloomfield, Ia., Sept. 27, 1877; s. William Samuel and Emma (King) M.; A.B., Ia. Wesleyan Coll., 1900, A.M., 1903, D.D., 1929; S.T.B., Boston U. Sch. of Theology, 1904; D.D., Grove City Coll., 1915, Allegheny Coll., 1915; m. Axie E. Lute, Sept. 27, 1905; children—Alan Lute, William Samuel. Licensed to preach, 1900; ordained M.E. ministry, 1906; asst. pastor Epworth Memorial Ch., Cleveland, O., 1905-08; pastor Stone Ch., Meadville, Pa., 1907-11, Grace Ch., Oil City, Pa., 1911-15, Plymouth Ch., Buffalo, N.Y., 1915-19; prof. evangelism and head of dept., Boston U. Sch. of Theology, 1919-20; pastor Calvary Ch., Phila., 1920-23, Wesley M.E. Ch., Worcester, Mass., 1923-33, Centre Ch., Malden, Mass., 1933—. Was chaplain and capt. 16th Inf. N.G. Pa. Mem. and founder Beth Resh Mem (Hebrew letter frat. for theol. students). Republican. Mason. Author: Elements of Personal Christianity, 1921; also wrote A Seven Day Church at Work; Christ and Our Changing World. Died Sept. 17, 1936.

MITCHELL, William Whittier, capitalist; b. Hillsdale, Mich., June 3, 1854; s. Charles Tennant and Harriet Skinner (Wing) M.; Hillsdale Coll., 1872-73; m. Ella Yost, Oct. 2, 1876. Engaged in lumber business, 1873—; large mfr. of maple flooring, wood alcohol and charcoal iron; owner of timber lands in Ore. and Mich.; pres. Cobbs & Mitchell, Inc., Mitchell Bros. Co., Mitchell-Diggins Iron Co., Cadillac Chem. Co.; trustee Traverse City State Hosp. Republican. Presbyn. Home: Cadillac, Mich. Died Nov. 9, 1915.

MITTEN, Thomas Eugene, street ry. pres.; b. Brighton, Sussex, Eng., Mar. 31, 1864; came to U.S. with parents, 1877; on farm in Newton Co., Ind. until 19. Began ry. career as telegraph operator and joint agt. for C.&E.I. R.R., and Big Four, at Wyndham, Ind.; local agt. at Attica, Ind., 1887-90; in minor positions with D.&R.G. R.R., Rock Island, and the Rio Grande Western R.R., 1890-93; gen. supt. Denver, Lakewood & Golden R.R., 1890-95; supt. and gen. mgr. Milwaukee Elec. Ry., 1895-1900; gen. supt., 1901-04, gen. mgr., 1904-05, Internat. Ry. Co., Buffalo; v.p., later pres. Chicago City Ry. Co., 1905-11; was also v.p. and mng. dir. Internat. Ry. Co., Buffalo; chmn. exec. com. Phila. Rapid Transit Co., 1911—, pres., 1914-23, now chmn. bd., also pres. Mitten Men & Management Bank & Trust Co., Philadelphia, Pa. Died Oct. 1, 1929.

MIX, Charles Louis, M.D.; b. Byron, Ill., Dec. 3, 1869; s. Ernest and Louise (Misick) M.; A.B., Harvard, 1890, A.M., 1891, M.D., 1894, U. of Vienna, 1896-97; U. of Berlin, 1897; LL.D., Loyola U., Chicago, 1921; m. Jeannette Elise Caldwell, Dec. 27, 1894. Began practice, 1897; specialist in nervous diseases and internal medicine; prof. anatomy, Northwestern U., Woman's Med. Sch., 1899, prof. Dental Sch. of same, 1901; asst. prof. anatomy, 1900-03, prof. physical diagnosis, Sept. 1903-14, clin. prof. medicine, 1914-20, Northwestern U. Med. Sch., Chicago, prof. general medicine, Post-Grad. Med. Sch., 1900-05; prof. medicine and head Dept. of Medicine, Loyola U. Med. Sch., 1920-29 (prof. emeritus); cons. internist I.C. R.R. until 1929; senior attending physician, Mercy Hosp., Chicago, until 1929. Commd. maj., Med. R.C., 1917; med. chief Base Hosp., Camp Mills, N.Y., Apr. 1918-June 1918; lt. col. Med. R.C., 1910-29. Retired from active practice 1929. Republican. Baptist. Editor-in-chief Practical Medical Series. Died Nov. 21, 1935.

MIX, Tom; b. El Paso Co., Tex., Jan. 6, 1880; s. Edward E. and Elizabeth (Smith) M.; m. Victoria Forde, actress, 1917; children—Ruth (by former marriage), Thomasina; m. 3d, Mabel Hubbell Ward, Feb. 16, 1932. Cowboy in Tex., Ariz., Wyoming and Mont.; served in U.S.A. in Philippines, Spanish-Am. War, and in Boxer trouble in China, receiving medal and citation; served with British in Boer War, S. Africa, at Siege of Ladysmith. Was sheriff of Montgomery Co., Kan., and Washington Co., Okla.; dep. U.S. marshal and enforcement officer, Eastern Dist. of Okla., later with Tex. Rangers 3 yrs.; livestock foreman Miller Bros. "101" Ranch, Bliss, Okla., 1906-09; with the Sells Floto Circus, season of 1929. Won national riding and roping contest, Prescott, Ariz., 1909, Canon City, Colo., 1911, etc. Identified with motion pictures, 1910—; best pictures: "Dick Turpin," "The Lucky Horse-Shoe"; with the Sells Floto Circus, 1930 and 1931; motion pictures, and vaudeville tours, 1932 and 1933; with Tom Mix Circus and Wild West Show, 1933—. Made personal appearance tour of Europe, 1938, 39. Mem. Spanish War Vets., World War Vets. Mason. B.P.O.E. (life). Home: Pacoima, Calif. Died Oct. 12, 1940.

MIXER, Albert Harrison, educator; b. Forestville, N.Y., Sept. 8, 1822; s. Nathan and Rhoda (Frink) M.; ed. Fredonia (N.Y.) Acad., Madison (now Colgate) Univ., A.B., 1848, Madison Theol. Sem., B.D., 1850, A.M., Univ. of Rochester, 1851, LL.D., Colgate Univ., 1898; m. Jennie L. Morse, Aug. 5, 1857. Tutor in Greek and history, Univ. of Rochester, 1850-52; student univs. of Berlin and Munich, 1853-54; prof. modern langs., Univ. of Rochester, 1855-58; opened first Univ. of Chicago, 1858; prof. modern langs., 1858-60, prof. Greek, 1860-66, Univ. of Chicago; studied in France and Italy, 1866-67; prof. modern langs., U. of Rochester, 1868—. During yrs. 1863-66 was engaged in financial work for Univ. of Chicago, raising $25,000 for equipment of Dearborn Observatory and $80,000 for erection of the main bldg. Baptist. Republican. Author: Manual of French Poetry, 1874; Manual of French Pronunciation, 3d edit., 1901. Home: Rochester, N.Y. Died 1908.

MIXTER, Samuel Jason, surgeon; b. Hardwick, Mass., 1855; s. William and Mary (Ruggles) M.; S.B., Mass. Inst. Tech., 1875; M.D., Harvard, 1879; m. Wilhelmina Galloupe, 1879; children—William Jason, Charles Galloupe, George, Samuel. Began practice at Boston, 1879; consulting surgeon Mass. Gen. Hosp. and to Mass. Charitable Eye and Ear Infirmary. Lt. col., Med. R.C., 1919. Home: Eau Gallie, Fla. Died Jan. 19, 1926.

MIXTER, William Gilbert, chemist; b. Dixon, Ill., Sept. 23, 1846; s. George and Susan Elizabeth (Gilbert) M.; Ph.B., Sheffield Scientific Sch. (Yale), 1867, A.M., 1887; m. Ada Louise Webber, Aug. 26, 1875. Asst. in chemistry, 1868-70, instr., 1870-72,

1874-75, prof., 1875-1913, prof. emeritus, 1913, Yale U. Author: An Elementary Text-Book of Chemistry, 1889. Home: New Haven, Conn. Died Mar. 9, 1936.

MIZNER, Henry Rutgeras, brig. gen.; b. Geneva, N.Y., Aug. 1, 1827. Apptd. from Mich., capt. 18th Inf. U.S.A., May 14, 1861; col. 14th Mich. Inf., Dec. 22, 1862; hon. mustered out of vol. service, July 18, 1865; transferred to 36th Inf., Sept. 21, 1866; maj. 20th Inf., Feb. 22, 1869; transferred to 12th Inf., Mar. 15, 1869, to 8th Inf., May 14, 1877; lt. col. 10th Inf., Dec. 15, 1880; col. 17th Inf., Jan. 2, 1888; retired by operation of law, Aug. 1, 1891; advanced to rank of brig. gen. retired, by act of Apr. 23, 1904. Bvtd.: maj., Dec. 31, 1862, for battle of Murfreesboro, Tenn.; lt. col., Sept. 1, 1864, for Atlanta campaign and battle of Jonesboro, Ga.; brig. gen. vols., Mar. 13, 1865, for services during the war. Home: Detroit, Mich. Died Jan. 4, 1915.

MIZNER, Wilson, dramatist; b. Benecia, Calif., May 19, 1876; s. Lansing Bond and Ella (Watson) M.; went with father (Am. minister to Central America) to Guatemala, 1889; ed. Nat. Inst. of Guatemala, 1889-91; Santa Clara (Calif.) Coll., 1892-94; unmarried. Went to Alaska for Alaska Fur Co., 1897, and was among the first dozen men on the Klondyke; returned to the states in 1902 and prospected in Nev.; in New York, 1903—. Author (plays): The Only Law (with G. Bronson Howard), prod. Hackett's Theatre, New York, 1909; The Deep Purple (with Paul Armstrong), prod. Princess Theatre, Chicago, 1910; The Greyhound (with latter), prod. Astor Theatre, New York, 1912. Home: New York, N.Y. Died Apr. 3, 1933.

MOALE, Edward, brigadier gen. U.S.A.; b. in Md., Jan. 29, 1840. Apptd. from Md., 1st lt. 19th Inf., May 14, 1861; capt., Sept. 13, 1864; lt. col. a.-a.-g. vols., Mar. 21, 1865; transferred to 37th U.S. Inf., Sept. 21, 1866, to 3d Inf., Aug. 11, 1869; maj. 1st Inf., Feb. 1, 1887; lt. col. 3d Inf., Dec. 4, 1891; col. 15th Inf., Feb. 4, 1897; retired at own request after 40 yrs.' service, Jan. 31, 1902; advanced to rank of brig. gen. retired, by act of Apr. 23, 1904. Bvtd.: maj., Dec. 2, 1864, for battle of Spottsylvania and campaign before Richmond; lt. col., Apr. 2, 1865, for service in front of Petersburg, Va.; col. vols., Mar. 13, 1865, for services during the war. Died Sept. 27, 1913.

MODJESKA, Helena (Mme. Chlapowski), actress; b. Cracow, Poland, Oct. 12, 1844; début, Bochnia, Poland, 1861; soon became leading actress in her native country; m. Charles Bozenta Chlapowski, compatriot, 1868. First appearance in English, San Francisco, 1877, in Adrienne Lecouvreur, followed by a starring tour through U.S. Returned here after two London engagements and played leading Shakespearean parts, Camille, Mary Stuart, etc. Died 1909.

MODJESKI, Ralph, civil engr.; b. Cracow, Poland, Jan. 27, 1861; s. Gustav and late Helena (Opid) Modrzejewski; came to U.S. with mother, 1876; name changed to Modjeski for Am. naturalization, his mother being the celebrated tragedienne, Helen Modjeska; grad. Coll. des Ponts et Chaussées, Paris, at head of class, with honors; D.Eng., U. of Ill., 1911, Pa. Mil. Coll., 1927, Polytechnic Inst. of Lwow (Poland), 1930; m. Felicie Benda, of Cracow, Poland, Dec. 28, 1885 (divorced); m. 2d, Mrs. Mary T. Giblyn, July 7, 1931. Cons. bridge engr. at Chicago, 1892-1940. Mem. firm Modjeski & Noble, chief engrs. of bridge over Mississippi River at Thebes, Ill.; designed and built new govt. bridge, Rock Island, Ill., as well as many ry. bridges; consulting engr. for city of Chicago and Sanitary District on their bascule bridges; in charge of reconstruction of Bismarck Bridge and others for N.P. Ry.; designed and built the Columbia and Willamette River bridges for Portland & Seattle Ry.; chief engr. McKinley Bridge at St. Louis; Broadway Bridge, Portland, Ore.; Columbia River Bridge, Celilo, Ore.; Cherry St. Bridge, Toledo, O. Mem. bd. engrs. Quebec Bridge (reconstruction), new Memphis (Tenn.) Bridge; chief engr. Delaware River Bridge (Phila.), Mid-Hudson Bridge, New Orleans Bridge; chief engr. Huey P. Long Bridge over Mississippi River at New Orleans, Iowa-Ill. Memorial Bridge, Davenport, Calvert St. Bridge, Washington, D.C.; chmn. bd. cons. engrs. Trans-Bay Bridge, San Francisco. Awarded John Scott medal (Phila.), 1924; John Fritz medal, 1930; Washington Award, 1931; Knight Legion of Honor (France). Died June 26, 1940.

MOELLER, Henry, archbishop; b. Cincinnati, Dec. 11, 1849; s. Bernard and Teresa (Witte) M.; student St. Xavier's Coll., Cincinnati, 1863-69; studied philosophy and theology, Rome; D.D., Propaganda, Rome, 1876. Ordained at Rome, Italy, June 10, 1876; pastor St. Patrick's Ch., Bellefontaine, O., 1876-77; prof., Mt. St. Mary's Sem., 1877-79; sec. temporarily to Bishop Chatard, Indianapolis, to July 1880; sec. and chancellor of archdiocese of Cincinnati to Aug. 25, 1900; consecrated bishop of Columbus, Aug. 25, 1900; promoted to Archiepiscopal See of Areopolis and made coadjutor archbishop of Cincinnati with right of succession, Apr. 27, 1903; became archbishop of Cincinnati, Oct. 31, 1904; invested with pallium, Feb. 15, 1905. Died Jan. 5, 1925.

MOELLER, Louis (Charles), artist; b. New York, Aug. 5, 1855; s. Charles and Helene M.; served 3 yrs.' apprenticeship to his father, a decorative painter; then studied art at Cooper Inst. and Acad. Design, New York, later in Munich; m. Marianne Haining (dec.). Returned to New York. Genre painter. Awarded Hallgarten prize. Represented in Corcoran Gallery, Washington; etc. A.N.A., 1884, N.A., 1895. Home: Weehawken, N.J. Died Nov. 11, 1930.

MOELLRING, George H., lawyer; b. Columbus, Ill., Nov. 14, 1878; s. Daniel C. and Christiana (Peters) M.; LL.B., Highland Park Law Coll., Des Moines, 1901; m. Nelle Wiley, June 28, 1905; children—Vivian (Mrs. Kent R. Whitlock), Genevieve Leone, Lela Lorraine, Justin Hubert George. In practice in N.D., 1901-20; judge 5th jud. dist. N.D., 1921-33; asso. justice Supreme Court of N.D., 1933-34; asst. atty. gen., 1935—. Mem. N.D. Bar Bd., 1919-20. Dir. N.D. Tuberculosis Assn.; mem. adv. bd. Florence Crittenden Home, Children's Home, Fargo, N.D. Democrat. Methodist. Odd Fellow, Woodman, K.P., A.O.U.W. Author: The Neutral's Portion (a polit. novel written under the nom de plume Elwin Lorraine), 1916. Home: Bismarck, N.D. Died May 31, 1935.

MOENCH, Charles L., bishop; b. Lititz, Pa., Feb. 20, 1855; s. William N. and Louisa (Schneider) M.; B.A., Moravian Coll. and Theol. Sem., Bethlehem, Pa., 1873, B.D., 1875, D.D.; studied Union Theol. Sem., 1877-78; m. Gertrude Naomi Shultz, June 10, 1879 (died 1920). Ordained Moravian Ch. ministry, 1878; pastor Blairstown, Ia., 1878-81, Hopedale, Pa., 1881-86, 2d Ch., Phila., 1886-89, Lititz, Pa., 1889-1901, 1st Ch., Phila., 1901-08; mem. and sec. Provincial Elders' Conf. (exec. bd.) Northern Province, Moravian Ch. in America, 1908-13, pres. of bd., 1913—; consecrated bishop, Sept. 18, 1898, retired 1925. Pres. bd. trustees Moravian Coll. and Theol. Sem.; ex-officio mem. bd. trustees Moravian Coll. for Women, Bethlehem, Linden Hall Sem. (Lititz, Pa.), Nazareth (Pa.) Hall Mil. Acad. Republican. Home: Ardmore, Pa. Died May 7, 1927.

MOERDYKE, Peter, clergyman; b. Biervliet, Netherlands, Jan. 29, 1845; s. James and Maria C. (Faas) M.; brought to U.S., 1849; A.B., Hope Coll., Holland, Mich., 1866, A.M., 1869; grad. Western Theol. Sem., 1869; D.D., Heidelberg U., Tiffin, O., 1889; m. Fannie J. Guy, 1869 (died 1880); m. 2d, Maria Perry, June 4, 1883. Ordained ministry Ref. Ch. in America, 1869; pastor Macon and South Macon, Mich., 1869-71, 1st Ch., Grand Rapids, 1873-91, Trinity Ch., Chicago, 1891-1907, 1st Ch., South Bend, Ind., 1907-14; stated supply Federated Presbyterian and U.P. chs., Martin, Mich., 1915. Prof. Latin and Greek, Hope Coll., Holland, Mich., 1871-73; instr. N.T. Greek and exegesis, Western Theol. Sem., 1884-86. Stated clk. Bd. Supts. Western Theol. Sem., 1884—; stated clk. Particular Synod of Chicago, 1885; pres. Gen. Synod Ref. Ch. in America, 1916-17. Trustee Hope Coll., Western Theol. Sem. Home: Pasadena, Calif. Died July 18, 1923.

MOEUR, Benjamin Baker, M.D., governor; b. Decherd, Tenn., Dec. 22, 1869; s. John Baptist and Esther Kelly (Knight) M.; M.D., Ark. Industrial U. (now U. of Ark.), 1896; m. Honor G. Anderson, June 15, 1896; children—John Kelly, Vyvyan Bernice (Mrs. Ralph Gardner Parmelee), Jessie Belle (Mrs. James Monroe Hamilton), Benjamin Baker. Began practice at Tempe, Ariz., 1896; gov. of Ariz. for terms, 1933-35 and 1935-37. Was mem. Ariz. State Constl. Conv.; sec. bd. edn. Ariz. State Teachers Coll. 12 yrs. Democrat. Mason, Modern Woodman, Woodman of the World, Elk. Home: Tempe, Ariz. Died Mar. 16, 1937.

MOFFAT, David Halliday, banker; b. Washingtonville, N.Y., 1839; s. David H. and Katherine (Gregg) M.; ed. at Washingtonville until 1854; m. Fannie A. Buckhout, Dec. 11, 1861. Was messenger boy New York Exchange Bank, 1854-55; became clerk with A. J. Stevens & Co., bankers, Des Moines, Ia., 1855; cashier First Nat. Bank, Denver, 1865; cashier, 1866, later becoming pres. First Nat. Bank, Denver; pres. D.&R.G. R.R., 1884-91; built, largely at his own expense, Florence & Cripple Creek R.R., connecting Cripple Creek mines with D.&R.G. system. Home: Denver, Colo. Died 1911.

MOFFAT, Frederick G., banker; b. Albany, N.Y., June 19, 1861; s. Frederick Woodworth and Mary (Whitney) M.; nephew of late David H. Moffat, of Denver, Colo.; student Columbian (now George Washington) U. Dept. of Medicine, also Columbia U.; m. Charlotte Selden, Oct. 31, 1895. Mem. engring. corps in charge of completion of Washington Monument, and constrn. of State, War and Navy Dept. bldgs., Washington, D.C., until 1890; connected with 1st Nat. Bank, N.Y. City, many years following 1890; later engaged in numerous business enterprises in Denver, Colo. Republican. Episcopalian. Mason. Died Mar. 14, 1930.

MOFFAT, James David, college pres.; b. New Lisbon, O., Mar. 15, 1846; s. Rev. John and Mary A. (McNeelan) M.; A.B., Washington and Jefferson Coll., Pa., 1869; student Princeton Theol. Sem., 1869-71; D.D., Hanover Coll., Ind., 1882, Princeton, 1883; LL.D., Western U. of Pa., 1897, U. of Pa., 1901, Mo. Valley Coll., 1906; m. Elizabeth Dalzell Crangle, Sept. 6, 1876. Ordained Presbyn. ministry, May 8, 1873; pastor Second Ch., Wheeling, W.Va., 1871-82; pres. Washington and Jefferson Coll., 1882-1915, retired, pres. emeritus. Asst. editor Presbyterian Banner, Pittsburgh, 1893-1905. Moderator Presbyn. Assembly, Winona Lake, Ind., 1905. Home: Washington, Pa. Died Nov. 4, 1916.

MOFFAT, John Little, ophthalmologist; b. Brooklyn, June 14, 1853; s. Reuben Curtis (M.D.) and Elizabeth Virginia (Barclay) M.; B.S., Cornell U., 1873; M.D., New York Homœ. Med. Coll., 1877; post-grad. work New York Ophthalmic Hosp.; degree O. et A. Chir., 1881; m. Elizabeth M., d. late George M. Rhodes, of Antigua, W.I., Apr. 8, 1893. Specialized in ophthalmology, 1881-1911; consulting ophthalmic surgeon, Cumberland St. Hosp., New York. Editor Journal of Ophthalmology, Otology and Laryngology, 1901-14; editor Homœopathic Eye, Ear and Throat Journal, 1905-10. Republican. Swedenborgian. Mem. Am. Inst. Homœopathy (a sr.), Am. Homœ. Ophthal., Otol. and Laryngol. Soc. (v.p. 1905, 08), and other socs. Home: Ithaca, N.Y. Died Feb. 18, 1917.

MOFFETT, Cleveland (Langston), author, newspaperman; b. Boonville, N.Y., Apr. 27, 1863; s. William H. and Mary (Cleveland) M.; A.B., Yale, 1883; m. Mary E. Lusk, 1899. Was on European staff, 1887-91, on New York staff, 1891-92, New York Herald; foreign editor New York Recorder, 1893-94; subsequently in mag. work; Sunday editor New York Herald, 1908-09. Author: Real Detective Stories, 1898; Careers of Danger and Daring, 1901; A King in Rags, 1907; The Battle, 1909; Through the Wall, 1909; The Bishop's Purse (in collaboration with Oliver Herford), 1913; The Mysterious Card, 1913; The Hand of Mystery, 1913; The Conquest of America, 1916; How to Live Long and Love Long, 1917; The War Beautiful, 1917; Possessed, 1919; Glint of Wings (in collaboration with Virginia Hall); also prose poems, A Woman's Creed, The Litany of the Men, A Vision of Christmas, 1917, Glorious France. Plays: Money Talks, prod. 1906; Playing the Game, prod. 1907; The Battle, prod. 1908; For Better for Worse, prod. 1910; Greater Than the Law, 1912. Translator: Cosmopolis (Paul Bourget), 1894. Trustee Am. Defense Soc. Died Oct. 14, 1926.

MOFFETT, Samuel Austin, missionary; b. Madison, Ind., Jan. 25, 1864; s. Samuel Shuman and Maria J. (McKee) M.; B.S., Hanover (Ind.) Coll., 1884, M.A., 1888, D.D., 1901; grad. McCormick Theol. Sem., 1888; post-grad. Princeton Theol. Sem., 1907; m. Mary Alice Fish, M.D., June 1, 1899 (died 1912); children—James McKee, Charles Hull; m. 2d, Lucia Hester Fish, June 30, 1915; children—Samuel Hugh, Howard Fergus, Thomas Fish. Ordained to ministry of Presbyn. Church, 1888; stated supply, Appleton City and Montrose, Mo., 1888-89; became missionary in Korea, Presbyn. Bd. U.S.A., 1889. Pastor Central Ch., Pyengyang, Korea, 1893-1907, 5th Ch., Pyengyang, Korea, 1909-25; mem. faculty Presbyn. Theol. Sem. of Korea, 1902-35, pres., 1902-24; pres. Union Christian Coll., 1918-28. First moderator of Presbyn. Ch. of Korea, 1907, and moderator Gen. Assembly, 1919; del. World's Missionary Conference, Edinburgh, 1910; chmn. exec. com. Korea Presbyn. Mission 3 times to 1933; del. Jerusalem Conf., 1928. Recipient govt. gen. empire day honor "for distinguished services in the cause of edn. in Korea," 1925; gold medal from Imperial Education Assn., 1935; representative from Korea to Evaluation Conf., China, 1926. Author of a number of text-books and tracts in Korean. Died Oct. 24, 1939.

MOFFETT, Samuel Erasmus, writer; b. St. Louis, Nov. 5, 1860; s. William A. and Pamela A. (Clemens) M.; spl. studies U. of Calif.; A.M., Ph.D., Columbia; m. Mary Emily Mantz, Apr. 13, 1887. Editorial work, San Francisco Post, San Francisco Examiner and New York Journal, 1885-1902, except when Washington corr. Examiner, 1891-93. Mng. editor Cosmopolitan Mag., 1902; editorial writer New York World, 1902-04; editorial staff Collier's Weekly, 1904—. Author: The Tariff—What It Is and What It Does, 1892; Chapters on Silver, 1893 (serially in San Francisco Examiner); Suggestions on Government, 1894. Died 1908.

MOFFETT, William Adger, naval officer; b. Charleston, S.C., Oct. 31, 1869; s. George Hall and Elizabeth (Simonton) M.; grad. U.S. Naval Acad., 1890; m. Jeannette Beverly Whitton, July 26, 1902; children—Janet Whitton, George Hall, William Adger, Elizabeth Simonton, Charles Simonton, Anna Beverly. Promoted through grades to rear adm., July 25, 1923. Served under Admiral Dewey, on board Charleston, capture of Manila, 1898; comd. Chester, at Vera Cruz, and at Tampico, Mex., when demand was made for salute of Am. flag by Admiral Mayo, 1914; comd. Chester at taking of Vera Cruz, Apr. 22, 1914; comdt. U.S. Naval Training Sta., Great Lakes, Ill., 1914-18; comdt. 9th, 10th and 11th naval dists.; chief Bur. of Aeronautics, rank of rear adm., Sept.

1921; tech. adviser Washington Limitation of Armaments Conf., 1921-22; reappointed chief Bur. of Aeronautics, Mar. 1925; again apptd. Mar. 1929; tech. adviser Limitation of Armaments Conf., at London, 1930. Awarded Congressional Medal of Honor "for eminent and conspicuous conduct in battle" (capture of Vera Cruz); D.S.M. "for exceptionally meritorious service in a position of great responsibility in the World War." Home: Washington, D.C. Died Apr. 4, 1933.

MOFFETT, William Walter, judge; b. Culpeper County, Va., July 19, 1854; s. John and Sarah William (Brown) M.; ed. Rappahannock Male Acad.; m. Jessie Mary Dudley, Feb. 22, 1883; children—Mrs. Willie Gates Jones, John Daniel (dec.), Fannie Dudley (Mrs. B. N. Eubank), Sarah A. (Mrs. W. N. Walters), Mary Lois. Read law with uncle, Horatio G. Moffett; admitted to bar, 1877; began practice in Rappahannock County; removed to Salem, 1891. Mem. Dem. State Central Com. several yrs. from 1883; mem. Va. Ho. of Rep., 1883-85; judge Roanoke County Court, 1893-1904; judge 20th Va. Circuit, terms 1906-16, 1916-24, resigned Feb. 1923; judge Law and Chancery Court of Roanoke City, 1923-27; trustee and chmn. Bapt. Orphanage; pres. Bapt. Gen. Assn., 1903-04. Home: Roanoke, Va. Died Aug. 25, 1926.

MOHLER, A. L., railway official; b. Ephrata, Pa., 1850; s. George and E. R. M.; ed. common sch.; m. Jennie M. Smith, Feb. 7, 1877. Entered ry. service, 1868, as clerk C.&N.W. Ry.; held numerous positions on various roads and in 1882 became gen. freight agt. St. Paul, Minneapolis & Manitoba Ry., and after intermediate promotions became asst. gen. mgr. G.N. Ry., 1888-89; gen. mgr. same and Mont. Central Ry., 1889-93; gen. mgr. Minneapolis & St. Louis Ry., 1894-97; pres. and gen. mgr. Oregon R.R. & Navigation Co., 1897-1904; also pres. Portland & Asiatic Steamship Co., and of Ilwaco Ry. & Navigation Co.; v.p. and gen. mgr. U.P. R.R. Co., 1904-11, U.P. and Oregon Short Line R.R. cos., 1911-12; pres. U.P. R.R. Co., 1912-16; retired. Home: Omaha, Neb. Died June 6, 1930.

MOHLER, Henry Keller, M.D., med. dean; b. Ephrata, Pa., Apr. 2, 1887; s. William K. and Amanda K. Mohler; Pharm.D., Phil Coll. of Pharmacy, 1907; M.D., Jefferson Med. Coll., 1912; hon. D.Sc., LaSalle Coll., 1939; m. Nellie Whiteley, Feb. 21, 1918; 1 dau., Alicia Whiteley. Interne, Jefferson Hosp., 1912-13; asso. with Jefferson Med. Coll., 1913—, in charge lab. of clin. medicine, 1913-14, instr. in medicine, 1913-22, demonstrator of medicine, 1922-25, asso., 1925-29, asst. prof., 1929-32, asso. prof., 1932-38, clin. prof. of therapeutics, 1936-38, dean and Sutherland M. Prevost prof. of therapeutics, 1938—; med. dir. Jefferson Med. Coll. Hosp., 1914-38, asst. physician, 1932-38, attending physician, 1938—, also physician in charge dept. of electrocardiology; private practice, Phila., 1915-41. Served as capt. Med. Corps, U.S. Army, World War; asst. and chief med. service Gen. Hosp., 38, Nantes, France; lt. col. Med. O.R.C., resigned 1938. Mem. bd. dirs. Children's Heart Hosp. Fellow Am. Coll. Hosp. Adminstrs. (charter mem.), Am. Coll. Physicians, Phila. Coll. Physicians. Co-author Cyclopedia of Medicine. Home: Merion, Pa. Died May 16, 1941.

MOHLER, John Frederick, physicist; b. Boiling Springs, Pa., Oct. 30, 1864; s. Samuel and Elizabeth (Williams) M.; A.B., Dickinson Coll., Pa., 1887, A.M., 1890; Ph.D., Johns Hopkins, 1897; m. Sarah Loomis, June 24, 1892; children—Frederick Loomis, Samuel Loomis, Nora May. Instr. mathematics and science, Wilmington Conf. Acad., Dover, Del., 1887-90; instr. mathematics, Wesleyan Acad., Wilbraham, Mass., 1890-94; prof. of physics, Dickinson Coll., Carlisle, Pa., 1896—. Republican. Methodist. Author: Practical Physics, 1897 (5 edits). Died Jan. 28, 1930.

MOHN, Thorbjorn Nilson, pres. St. Olaf Coll., 1874—; b. in Norway, July 15, 1844; emigrated to U.S., 1853; ed. pub. schools Wis. and Minn.; grad. Luther Coll., Decorah, Ia., 1870; grad. in theology, Concordia Sem., St. Louis, 1873; Lutheran clergyman in Chicago 1 year, then in St. Paul 6 months; m. Anna Elizabeth Ringstad, July 15, 1875. Home: Northfield, Minn. Died 1899.

MOHR, Charles, physician; b. Phila., May 2, 1844; s. Carl and Katherine M.; grad. Hahnemann Med. Coll., 1875; m. Eliza J. Hulfish, Aug. 1, 1866. Chief of staff, Hahnemann Coll. dispensary, 1877-82; senior visiting physician, Hahnemann Hosp., 1882-1901; lecturer on pharmacy, Hahnemann Med. Coll., 1879-81; lecturer on hygiene for New Century Club of Phila., 1882; prof. clinical medicine and physical diagnosis, Hahnemann Med. Coll., 1882-85, and prof. materia medica and therapeutics, 1885—. Sec. Homœ. Med. Soc., 1878-84, and pres., 1894-96; pres. Pharmacol. Soc. of the Hahnemann Med. Coll. and Gen. Director Hahnemann Hosp. Home: Philadelphia, Pa. Died 1907.

MOHR, Charles (Carl) Theodor, botanist; b. in Esslingen, Würtemberg, Germany, Dec. 28, 1824; s. Louis M.; ed. Pædagogium Esslingen, Volksschule Denkendorf, private tuition; studied chemistry and natural sciences, Polytechnical School, Stuttgart, 1842-43; Ph.D., Univ. of Ala., 1890; m. Sophia Roemer, Mar. 12, 1852. Accompanied A. Kappler on exploring expdn. of Dutch Guiana, 1845; one of pioneers Calif. gold fields, 1849; pharmacist, Louisville, Ky., 1853-57, Mobile, Ala., 1857-92; explored forests of Gulf states for 10th census, 1880-81; retired from business to engage in forestry and bot. work exclusively, 1892; botanist Geol. Survey of Ala., 1884—; agt. Div. Forestry, U.S. Dept. Agr., 1889—. Author: The Timber Pines of the Southern United States, 1896, 1897; Plant Life of Alabama, 1901. (Contributions U.S. Nat. Herbarium, Vol. VI.) Wrote: The Forests of Alabama and Their Products, the Grasses and Other Forage Plants of Alabama, in Handbook of Alabama, by Saffold Berney. Died 1901.

MOHUN, Barry, lawyer; b. Washington, Sept. 27, 1873; s. Francis B. and Martha V. (Laub) M.; ed. Lehigh U.; LL.B., Georgetown U., 1896, LL.M., 1897; m. Nora Michener, Jan. 30, 1905. Admitted to bar, 1897; practiced law at Washington, D.C., 1900—. Assisted in drafting uniform law relating to warehouse receipts for the Conf. of Commrs. on Uniform State Laws. Scout commr. D.C. Council of Boy Scouts of America, 1924—. Democrat. Author: Mohun on Warehousemen, 1904, 2d edit., 1913. Home: Washington, D.C. Died Apr. 16, 1931.

MOIR, Henry, life insurance; b. Midlothian, Scotland, Feb. 22, 1871; s. James and Margaret (Weir) M.; ed. George Watson's Coll. for Boys, Edinburgh; m. Janet Ballantine Niven, of Edinburgh, July 1, 1899; children—Thomas Niven, Margaret, Janet Ballantine. Came to U.S., 1901. With Scottish Life Assurance Co., Ltd., of Edinburgh, until 1901; actuary Provident Savings Life Assurance Soc. of New York, 1901-08; actuary and v.p. Home Life Ins. Co. of New York, 1909-22; pres. U.S. Life Ins. Co., 1922—; dir. Morris Plan Ins. Soc., Eagle Fire Ins. Co., Norwich Union Indemnity Co. Mem. Advisory Com. War Risk Ins., 1917. Trustee Hartford Sem. Foundation. Fellow or mem. numerous actuarial socs. Presbyn. Editor: Principles and Practice of Life Insurance, 7th edit., 1910. Also wrote Life Assurance Primer and Agency Arguments. Home: Upper Montclair, N.J. Died June 9, 1937.

MOIR, John Troup, sugar plantation mgr.; b. Scotland, Dec. 21, 1859; s. Francis and Julia (Troup) M.; ed. pub. sch.; m. Louisa Silver, of Kincardineshire, Scotland, July 20, 1889; children—Frances Julia (wife of Dr. Gurdon Potter), Louisa Agness, John Troup, William Whitmore Goodale, Hector McDonald. Came to U.S., 1888, naturalized citizen, 1900. Railroading, 1875-80, farming, 1880-88; sugar plantation overseer, Waiakea, H.T., 1888, with Hilo Sugar Co., 1889-91, with Onomea Sugar Co., 1891-96; mgr. Honomu Sugar Co., 1896-98; mgr. Onomea Sugar Co., 1898—; pres. First Trust Co. of Hilo, Hawaiian Ins. & Guaranty Co. Served as lt. col., H.T.N.G. Mem. Hawaiian Sugar Planters Assn. Republican. Mason, Elk. Home: Papaikou, H.T. Deceased.

MOLDEHNKE, Edward Frederick, clergyman; b. Insterburg, East Prussia, Aug. 10, 1836; grad. Sept. 1853, coll. at Lyck, East Prussia; Ph.D., Univ. of Rostock, Germany; D.D., Muhlenberg Coll., Pa. Instr. in coll. at Lyck, 1859-61; sent to Wis. and Minn., 1861, as traveling missionary; was the first prof. in Luth. Coll. at Watertown, Wis., and in its Theol. Sem.; published the church paper of the Wis. Synod at Watertown, 1865-66. Lutheran pastor at New York, 1869—, and 1895-1899 pres. gen. counsel of the Luth. Ch. in N. America. Has edited several church papers, and published several works in German. Died 1904.

MOLDENKE, Charles Edward, author; b. Lyck, East Prussia, Oct. 10, 1860; s. Edward F. and Elise (Harder) M.; A.B., Columbia, 1879, A.M., 1883; Ph.D., U. of Strassburg, 1885; m. Sophia M. Heins, Sept. 26, 1894; children—Theodore Victor, Harold Norman. Ordained Luth. ministry, 1885; pastor St. John's, Jersey City, N.J., 1885-90, St. Peter's, New York, 1890-96, St. Paul's, Mt. Vernon, N.Y., 1897-1900. Specialist in Egyptology and pupil of the European savant Dümichen. Author: The Egyptian Origin of Our Alphabet, 1886; The Trees of Ancient Egypt, 1886; The New York Obelisk, 1891; The Tale of the Two Brothers, 1898; Egyptian Classics, 1900. Address: Watchung, N.J. Died Jan. 18, 1935.

MOLDENKE, Richard (George Gottlob), metallurgist; b. Watertown, Wis., Nov. 1, 1864; E.M., Columbia, 1885, Ph.D., 1887; m. Anne. d. John D. Heins, of New York, Sept. 18, 1891. Specialist on metallurgy of cast iron and expert in malleable castings. Author: The Production of Malleable Castings, 1911; The Principles of Iron Founding, 1917. Extensive writer on the metallurgy of iron and steel. Address: Watchung, N.J. Died Nov. 17, 1930.

MOLINEUX, Edward Leslie, manufacturer, soldier; b. London, Eng., Oct. 12, 1833; came to U.S. in boyhood; ed. Mechanics' Soc. Sch., New York. When Civil War began was lt. col. 23d N.G.N.Y.; in war as col. 159th N.Y. Vols.; comd. brigade, 19th Army Corps, in campaigns against Port Hudson, Red River and Petersburg, and in the Shenandoah Valley; bvtd. brig. gen. and maj. gen. vols.; apptd. 1880, brig. gen. 11th Brigade, N.G.S.N.Y., and, 1885, maj. gen. 2d div. of same. Comdr. Mil. Order Loyal Legion, 1886. Dir. F. W. Devoe & T. C. Raynolds Co., paint mfrs. Died June 10, 1915.

MOLITOR, Frederic Albert, civil engr.; b. Detroit, Apr. 1868; s. Albert and Lucille I. (Goodell) M.; ed. Trinity Sch., New York, 1881-83, Cornell U. to 1886; m. Katherine Jefferies, 1896. Served in minor capacities on various Eastern R.R. engring. depts., 1886-89; prin. asst. engr. Ky. Central R.R., 1889; engr. maintenance of way, C.&O. R.R., 1890; asst. engr. Phila. & Reading R.R. and engr. Phila. Belt Line R.R., 1891-94; engr.-in-charge of constrn. L.I. R.R., 1895; chief engr. Choctaw, Oklahoma & Gulf R.R., and of allied cos. in charge of constrn. of 900 miles of new road, 1896-1903; gen. mgr., chief engr. and dir. Midland Valley R.R., 1903-06; also chief engr. Cherokee Constrn. Co., 1904-06; supervising ry. expert for the govt. in P.I., 1906-08; pvt. practice, New York, 1908-33, retired. Mem. spl. Panama Canal Commn., 1921; chmn. Bd. of Economics and Engring., Nat. Assn. Owners of R.R. Securities, 1922; study of terminal and post facilities of New York; rept. for receiver Brazil Ry. Co.; investigation proposed low grade line, N.Y., Pittsburgh & Chicago R.R.; mem. Arbitration Bd. St. Paul Union Depot; confidential rept. New York Rapid Transit situation; chmn. and mem. Commn. on Valuation of Damages Nat. Rys. of Mexico; cons. railroad engr. Bd. of Hudson River Regulating Dist., etc. Col. engrs. U.S.A., 1917-19; in charge of all engring. supplies at time of signing Armistice. Episcopalian. Republican. Author: Manual for Constructing Engineers, 1902. Home: New York, N.Y. Died 1938.

MOLLENHAUER, Emil, musician; b. Brooklyn, Aug. 4, 1855; s. Frederick and Margaret (Pugh) M.; ed. Russell's Acad., New York; m. Mary E. Laverty, Apr. 1, 1884. Mem. Booth's Theatre Orchestra at age of 14; at 16, mem. Theodore Thomas Orchestra as one of 1st violins; was mem. New York and Brooklyn Philharmonic socs.; located in Boston, 1884; mem. Boston Symphony Orchestra 4 yrs.; conductor Germania Orchestra, and conductor Municipal Concerts until 1903; conductor of Handel and Haydn Soc., Boston, Lynn, Brockton, Newburyport and Salem oratorio socs., Apollo Club, Boston, and Boston Festival Orchestra, Boston Band; conductor, St. Louis Expn., 1904, San Francisco Expn., 1915. Died Dec. 10, 1927.

MÖLLER, Mathias Peter, pipe organ mfr.; b. Bornholm, Denmark, Sept. 29, 1855; s. Nels Jorgen and Anna Katrina Hildebrand (Peterson) M.; ed. in Denmark; hon. Mus.D., Susquehanna U., 1926; m. Julia Maybelle Greenlund, 1892; children—Mathias Peter, Mrs. Maybelle Louise Wagaman, Mrs. Mary Dagmar Hanson, Mrs. Martha Elizabeth Daniels. Came to U.S., 1872. Began in organ factory, Erie, Pa.; built first organ at Warren, Pa., 1875; settled in Hagerstown, Maryland, 1880, where he established M. P. Möller Organ Works, of which became pres.; pres. M. P. Möller Motor Car Co., Kinetic Engring. Co., Home Builders Bldg. & Loan Assn., Hagerstown Trust Co.; owner of Hotel Dagmar; dir. Potomac Edison Co. Elected to Md. Synod of Luth. Ch. 18 times, Gen. Conv. Luth. Ch., 8 times; del. to World Luth. Conv., Copenhagen, 1929. Trustee Susquehanna U., Tressler Orphan's Home, Hagerstown Y.M.C.A. (pres. bd.). Decorated Knight Order of Dannebrog (Denmark). Mason. Home: Hagerstown, Md. Died Apr. 13, 1937.

MOLYNEAUX, Joseph West, judge; b. Bellevue, Ky., Dec. 12, 1863; s. James Kennedy and Harriet E. (West) M.; student Miami U., Oxford, O.; grad. Law Sch., U. of Cincinnati, 1882; m. May Louise Schomberg, June 6, 1900; children—Harold Joseph, Richard Frederic, Louise West, John Kennedy. Admitted to Minn. bar, 1884, and began practice at Minneapolis; judge, Dist. Court, Minneapolis, 1913-25; U.S. dist. judge, Dist. of Minn., 1925-38; retired. Republican. Home: Minneapolis, Minn. Died Jan. 24, 1940.

MOMBERT, Jacob Isidor, author; b. Cassel, Germany, Nov. 6, 1829; s. Dr. J. L. and Joanna M.; acad. edn. in Germany and Eng.; D.D., U. of Pa., 1866; m. Emma Elizabeth Muhlenberg, July 5, 1860. Deacon, 1856, priest, 1857, P.E. Ch.; asst. Trinity Ch., Quebec, Can., 1857-59; rector St. James', Lancaster, Pa., 1859-70, St. John's, Dresden, Germany, 1870-76, Christ Ch., Jersey City, N.J., 1877-79, St. John's, Passaic, N.J., 1879-82; devoted to literature, 1882—. Translator: Tholuck's Psalms; The Catholic Epistles in Lange's Commentary. Editor: Tyndale's Five Books of Moses, 1884. Author: Authentic History of Lancaster County, Pa., 1869; Faith Victorious (Life of Ebel), 1882; Great Lives, 1886; Charles the Great, 1888; Handbook of English Versions of the Bible, 1890, 1907; Short History of the Crusades, 1894; Raphael's Sistine Madonna, 1895. Home: Paterson, N.J. Died Oct. 7, 1913.

MONAELESSER, Adolph, M.D., surgeon; b. Laxey, Isle of Man, June 22, 1855; s. Maurice and Emilie (Schyar) M.; prep. edn., pub. sch., Manchester, Eng.; student Coelnisches Gymnasium, Berlin, Germany, 1869-73, Greifswald U., Germany, 1873-75, U.

of Berlin, 1875-76, Breslau and Bonn, Germany, 1876-77, U. of Paris, 1877-79; M.D., Eclectic Med. Coll., 1882; M.D., Coll. City New York, 1886; Sc.D., Lincoln Memorial U., 1930; m. Bettina Hofker (who served as sister-in-chief of Am. Nat. Red Cross during Spanish-Am. War), Aug. 6, 1887; 1 son, Mozart. Came to U.S., 1879, naturalized citizen, 1922. Asso. curator to Dr. N. M. Miller, City Hosp., N.Y. City, 1884-87; attending surgeon St. Elizabeth's Hosp., N.Y. City, 1887—; surgeon in chief Am. Red Cross (served in Cuba, Spanish-Am. War), 1893-1903; pathologist to Commn. for Investigation of Crime, Am. Bar Assn., 1923. Fellow A.M.A., New York Acad. Medicine, New York Acad. Sciences, New York Micros. Soc., Institut Pasteur (Paris). Mem. Free Unitarian Congregation. Author: Medical Service During the Cuban Insurrection and Spanish American War, 1899; Effets du venim de cobra modifie sur les tumeurs cancereuses, 1930. Research in therapeutic value of snake venom in nerve affections and malignant growths. Died Mar. 27, 1936.

MONAGHAN, James Charles, publicist; b. Boston, Oct. 11, 1857; s. James and Mary A.M.; prep. for Brown in Mowry's Acad., and Sch. of Christian Brothers; A.B., Brown, 1885, A.M., 1903, studied langs., lit. law and economics in Mannheim, Heidelberg, Berlin, Leipzig and Chemnitz, Germany, 1885-1900; m. Dorothy T. Ryan, June 12, 1892. Mem. Providence City Council (while student at Brown), 1884-85; consul at Mannheim, Germany, 1885-89, at Chemnitz, Germany, 1893-1900; editor The Manufacturer, 1899-1900; prof. theory and practice domestic and foreign commerce, U. of Wis., 1900-03; chief div. consular reports, Bur. Statistics, Dept. Commerce and Labor, 1903-06; prof., U. of Notre Dame, 1907-08; U.S. consul at Kingston, Jamaica, 1914—. Campaigned for Cleveland, 1884, 1892; lecturer on consular service, George Washington U.; del. World's Commercial Congress, 1899. Recipient of Lætare Medal, 1908. Sec. Nat. Soc. for Promotion of Industrial Edn.; nat. lecturer for Knights of Columbus; pres. Columbus Travel Soc. Home: Bayonne, N.J. Died Nov. 12, 1917.

MONAGHAN, John James, bishop; b. Sumter, S.C., May 23, 1856; s. Thomas and Margaret (Bogin) M.; took classical course at St. Charles Coll., Md., 1872-76; theol. studies at St. Mary's Sem., Baltimore. Ordained R.C. priest, Dec. 19, 1880; asst. priest in Charleston, S.C., first at St. Joseph's and then at St. Patrick's; rector Greenville, S.C., 1882-87; pro-rector at Cathedral, Charleston, S.C., and chancellor of the diocese, 1887-88; assistant to vicar gen. at St. Patrick's Ch., Charleston, 1888-97; consecrated bishop of Wilmington, Del., 1897, resigned 1925; titular bishop of Lydda, 1925—. Died Jan. 7, 1935.

MONAHAN, Michael, editor; b. County Cork, Ireland, Apr. 6, 1865; s. Jeremiah and Ellen (McElligot) M.; ed. by father, who was a classical teacher; m. Anastasia Bowes, Dec., 1889. Entered newspaper career as reporter, Albany, 1887; became editor Albany Press, news editor Albany Argus, spl. writer for Dem. Nat. Com., 1892; journalistic work New York and Denver, 1892-93; sec. to mayor of Albany, 1896-1900; founded the Papyrus mag., Mt. Vernon, N.Y., 1903, and later conducted same as the Phœnix, S. Norwalk, Conn. Lecturer. Author: Benigna Vena, 1904; Palms of Papyrus, 1908, 1909; Heinrich Heine, Adventurer in Life and Letters, 1910; Nova Hibernia, At the Sign of the Van, 1914. Died Nov. 22, 1933.

MONCRIEF, John Wildman, university prof.; b. Wirt, Ind., Sept. 10, 1850; s. Jeptha and Grace M.; A.B., Denison U., 1873; tutor in history and Greek, Franklin Coll., 1873-75; studied U. of Leipzig, 1875-76; A.M., Franklin, 1876; D.D., Denison, 1904; m. Lucy L. Wood, Dec. 12, 1878. Prof. Greek, Franklin Coll., 1876-79; prin. prep. dept., Denison U., 1879-81; prof. history, Franklin, 1881-94; asst. prof. ch. history, 1894-97, asso. prof., 1897—, U. of Chicago. Author: Short History of the Christian Church, 4th edition. Died Mar. 28, 1936.

MONDELL, Frank Wheeler, lawyer; b. St. Louis, Nov. 6, 1860; s. Ephraim W. and Nancy (Gould) M.; common sch. edn., also special courses, and under private tutors; LL.D., George Washington U., 1921, U. of Wyoming, 1934; m. Ida Harris, May 13, 1899; 5 children. Located in Wyo., 1887; mayor Newcastle, 1888-95; elected to 1st State Senate, 1890 (pres. 1892); asst. commr. Gen. Land Office, 1897-99; mem. 54th (1895-97) and 56th to 67th Congresses (1899-1923), Wyo. at-large; majority floor leader, 66th and 67th Congresses; dir. War Finance Corp., 1923-25. Del. to Rep. Nat. Conv. 7 times between 1892 and 1924, permanent chmn. 1924. President Dry Farming Congress, 1910-15. Mason. Author: My Story (autobiography). Home: Newcastle, Wyo. Died Aug. 6, 1939.

MONELL, Ambrose; commd. col. Aviation Sect., Signal Corps, 1917; resigned as pres. Internat. Nickel Co., 1917, to enter army; was dir. Am. Internat. Corp., Midvale Steel & Ordnance Co., Internat. Motor Co., Liberty Nat. Bank of N.Y., Am. Bank Note Co., Haskell & Barker Car Co., etc. V.p. Soc. for Relief of French War Orphans. Mem. Am. Inst. M.E., Inventors Guild. Home: New York, N.Y. Died May 2, 1921.

MONEY, Hernando de Soto, senator; b. Holmes Co., Miss., Aug. 26, 1839; s. Peirson and Tryphena (Vardaman) M.; LL.B., U. of Miss., 1860; m. Claudia Boddie, Nov. 5, 1863 (died 1907). Served in C.S.A., 1861-64, retiring Sept. 24, 1864, because of defective eyesight. Elected 44th to 48th Congresses (1875-85) and 53d and 54th Congresses (1893-97), 4th Miss. Dist.; elected U.S. senator, Jan., 1896, for term beginning Mar. 4, 1899; apptd. U.S. senator, Oct. 8, 1897, to fill vacancy caused by death of James Z. George, and elected, Jan., 1898, for remainder of the term expiring Mar. 4, 1899, when his term by previous election began; term expired, 1911. Democrat. Home: Mississippi City, Miss. Died Sept. 18, 1912.

MONFORT, Elias Riggs, postmaster; b. Greensburg, Ind., Mar. 2, 1842; s. Joseph Glass (D.D.) and Hannah Congar (Riggs) M.; A.B., Hanover (Ind.) Coll., 1865, A.M., 1874, LL.D., 1884; LL.B., Cincinnati Law Sch., 1867; m. Emma A. Taylor, Sept. 4, 1867. Pvt. Co. A (Guthrie Grays), Ohio Inf., June-Oct. 5, 1861; 2d lt. to capt., 75th Ohio Inf., Oct. 5, 1861-Jan. 3, 1864; in battles of Philippi, Bealington, Laurel Hill, Carrick's Ford, McDowell, Shaw's Ridge, Shenandoah Mountain, Franklin, Cross Keys, Cedar Mountain, Straussburg, Freeman's Ford, Sulphur Springs, Waterloo Bridge, Warrenton, 2d battle of Bull Run, Fredericksburg, Chancellorsville, and Gettysburg; discharged, Jan. 2, 1864, on account of wounds received at Gettysburg, July 2, 1863. Began practice of law at Greensburg, 1867; removed to Cincinnati, 1875; sr. mem. firm of Monfort & Co., pubs. Herald and Presbyter 1874—; editorial writer for many yrs.; pres. Mamolith Carbon Paint Co. Mem. Cincinnati Sch. Bd., 1890-99 (pres. last 3 yrs.); county clerk Hamilton Co., O., 1896, 1897; postmaster of Cincinnati, 1899-1915. Pres. Bd. of Trustees, Hamilton Co. (O.) Soldiers' and Sailors' Memorial Assn. (built $250,000 memorial bldg.); pres. trustees, Presbytery of Cincinnati; v.p. and trustee Lane Theol. Sem., Cincinnati, 1879—; trustee Hanover Coll., 1878—. Comdr. G.A.R. Dept. of Ohio, 1900; comdr. Ohio Commandery Loyal Legion, 1907; comdr.-in-chief G.A.R., 1915-16. Died July 29, 1920.

MONFORT, Joseph Glass, clergyman; b. Warren County, O., Dec. 9, 1810; grad. Miami Univ., 1834; D.D., Hanover Coll., LL.D., Central Coll., Ky., 1853; studied theology, Ind. Sem., 1835-36; a founder and editor Louisville (Ky.) Presbyterian Herald 1836-37; licensed to preach, Sept., 1837; pastor Hamilton, O., and Greensburg and Sandy Creek, Ind., 1837-55; became editor Presbyterian of the West, 1855, changing its name to The Presbyter, which, in 1869, was united with the Presbyterian Herald (new school organ) as The Herald and Presbyter. Afterward joined by his son, Francis C. Monfort, in firm of Monfort & Co. Apptd. by gen. assembly, 1866, mem. joint com. on the reunion of the two branches of the church; held many prominent positions in the church. Home: Cincinnati, O. Died 1906.

MONIN, Louis Célestin, college prof.; b. in Switzerland, Nov. 9, 1857; s. Louis Célestin and Marie Magdalena Euphrosina (Hool) M.; grad. Gymnasium, St. Gall, Switzerland, 1878; student U. of Leipzig, 1878-79, U. of Zürich, 1879-81; prin. high sch., Canton Glarus, Switzerland, 1881-83; student and tutor, Milan, Italy, 1883-85; student U. of Zürich, 1885-86, U. of Heidelberg, 1886-88; came to U.S., 1888; teacher University and Harvard (pvt.) schs., Chicago, 1890-92, and at same time took post-grad. course in Lake Forest U., Ph.D., 1892; m. Cathinka Elizabeth Weiss of Germany, 1887; m. 2d, Elise Rose Urfer, of Switzerland, 1922. Docent in philosophy, U. of Chicago, 1982-94; with Armour Inst. Tech., 1893—, successively prof. modern langs. and instr. philosophy, prof. economics and philosophy and dean cultural studies, and, 1922—, dean Coll. of Engring. Was prin. Armour Scientific Acad., 1899, asst. prof. edn. summer quarter U. of Chicago, 1900. Home: Chicago, Ill. Died Nov. 8, 1931.

MONKS, John Austin Sands, artist; b. Cold Spring-on-Hudson, N.Y., Nov. 7, 1850; s. John and Sarah Catherine (Jolly) M.; ed. Hudson River Inst., Claverack, N.Y.; studied wood engraving and etching, 1869; pupil in painting of George Innness, 1875; m. Olive Betty Young, Sept. 20, 1877. Engaged in art work, 1874—; specialty painting sheep. Mem. Copley Soc., Boston. Home: Medfield, Mass. Died Mar. 1917.

MONKS, Leander John, judge; b. Winchester, Ind., July 10, 1848; s. George Washington and Mary Ann (Irvin) M.; ed. Ind. State U.; LL.D., Wabash Coll., 1907; m. Elizabeth White, Aug. 2, 1869 (died 1908). Admitted to bar, 1869; practiced until 1878; judge 25th Jud. Circuit of Ind., 1878-94; justice Spreme Court of Ind., 1895-1913 (chief justice 1904). Republican. Home: Winchester, Ind. Died Apr. 19, 1919.

MONKS, Lester Hawthorne, banker; b. Brookline, Mass., Apr. 27, 1870; s. Frank Hawthorne and Elizabeth Oakley (Crowell) M.; A.B., Harvard, 1898; m. Caroline Townsend Cox, June 5, 1917. Formerly mem. firm Warren & Monks; treas. R. E. Paget Co.; partner William H. Randall & Co.; pres. W. A. Harriman & Co.; chmn. bd. Lester H. Monks; v.p. Warren Export Coal Co.; dir. Monks, Goodwin & Shaw, Coastwise Transportation Co., Am. Ship & Commerce Corp., Atlantic Coast Fisheries Co., Shawmut Steamship Co. Contbr. to Atlantic Monthly. Died Sept. 9, 1927.

MONNETTE, Mervin Jeremiah, banker; b. Marion County, O., Aug. 24, 1847; s. Abraham and Catharine (Braucher) M.; ed. pub. schs.; m. Olive Adelaide Hull, Jan. 5, 1869 (dec.). Began in live stock business, Chicago, 1868; pres. 2d Nat. Bank, Bucyrus, O., 1881-91; stockbroker, Cripple Creek, Colo., 1897-98; ranch owner and cattleman in Neb., 1898-1905, later becoming part owner Mohawk mine, Goldfield, Nev.; removed to Los Angeles, Calif., 1907; v.p. and exec. officer, Citizens Nat. Bank; dir. and mem. bd. Citizens Trust & Savings Bank until 1922; vice pres. Bank of America, Los Angeles, 1922-29; mem. regional bd. Bank of Italy Nat. Trust & Savings Assn. An organizer Los Angeles-Nev. Mining Stock Exchange, Monnette Mining & Milling Co. Republican. Methodist. Home: Los Angeles, Calif. Died Mar. 29, 1931.

MONNETTE, Orra Eugene, banker, lawyer; b. nr. Bucyrus, O., Apr. 12, 1873; s. Mervin Jeremiah and Olive Adelaide (Hull) M.; B.A., Ohio Wesleyan U., 1895; LL.D., Lincoln Memorial U., 1930; m. Ella Elizabeth Crim, Oct. 5, 1891; m. 2d, Carrie Lucile Janeway, Nov. 6, 1895; m. 3d, Helen Marie Kull, Dec. 15, 1917; 1 dau., Helen Hull. Admitted to Ohio bar, 1896, and practiced at Bucyrus, later at Toledo; continued practice Los Angeles, 1907; was pres. and dir. Citizens Trust & Savings Bank; founder and organizer, 1923, Bank of America (was also pres.), Los Angeles, and Lincoln Mortgage Co. of Calif.; the original Bank of America consolidated, 1924, with Bank of Italy; later changed to Bank of Italy Nat. Trust and Savings Assn., then Bank of America of which was v.p.; chmn. bd. Ameri-commercial Corp., 1927, now dir. and vice chmn. bd.; treas. Prudential Building and Loan Assn. of Los Angeles. Mem. Municipal Annexation Commn. of Los Angeles; pres. bd. Los Angeles Library 21 yrs.; mem. City Planning Commn.; mem. Bd. of Freeholders of Los Angeles, adopting City Charter, 1924; pres. Business Men's Co-op. Assn.; officer Calif. State Chamber Commerce; dir. Chamber Commerce of U.S., 1931-33; pres. League of Western Writers' Inc., 1934; v.p. La Fiesta de Los Angeles. Mem. State Council of Defense (Calif.), World War; capt. Team 25, Liberty Loan Campaign. Trustee Lincoln Memorial U.; pres. annual meeting trustees sect. Am. Library Assn., 1931. Republican. Methodist. Mason, K.P., Elk. Author: Monnet Family Genealogy, a Huguenot Lineage, 1911; California Chronology, 1915; Red Shining Star (verse), 1926; First Settlers of Piscataway and Woodbridge, New Jersey, 1929. Home: Los Angeles, Calif. Deceased.

MONOHAN, John M., banker; b. St. Matthews, Ky.; s. Edward S. and Alice (O'Farrell) M.; ed. Georgetown U.; m. Sadie Apperious, Nov. 20, 1907; children—Mary Ellen, John M., Alice, Henry. Began as clk., with Ky. Title Co., 1908; with 1st Nat. Bank, 1910—, pres., 1929—; pres. Ky. Title Trust Co. Knight of Columbus, Elk. Home: Matthews, Ky. Died Dec. 6, 1931.

MONROE, Charles Fraser, agriculturist; b. Greene, Ia., Nov. 18, 1884; s. John and Clara (Glenn) M.; B.S.A., Ia. State Coll. Agr. and Mech. Arts, 1908, M.Agr., 1920; m. Gladys Leona Grubbe, June 16, 1914. Successively instr., asst., asst. prof. and asso. prof. animal husbandry, Wash. State Coll., 1911-15; county agrl. agt., Grays Harbor Co., Wash., 1915-18; asst. county agt. leader, Pullman, Wash., 1918-19; county agt. leader, State Coll. N.M., 1919; dir. extension, same coll., 1919-26; dir. extension, N.D. Agrl. Coll., 1926—. Sec. extension sect. Assn. Land Grant Colls. and Univs., 1922, chmn., 1923; chmn. extension com. on range livestock improvement, Western Agrl. Colls., 1923-26; chmn. Drouth Relief Commn., N.D., 1931; dir. Agrl. Adjustment Program, N.D., 1933; mem. Nat. Bd. of Review on wheat allotment contracts, Agrl. Adjustment Adminstrn., 1933; sec. St. Paul Bank for Coöperatives, Farm Credit Adminstrn., 1933—. Rotarian. Home: St. Paul, Minn. Died Oct. 25, 1935.

MONROE, Frank Adair, judge; b. Annapolis, Md., Aug. 30, 1844; s. Victor and Mary Townsend (Polk) M.; ed. pvt. schs. and, 1860-61, Kentucky Mil. Inst.; left latter at beginning of sophomore yr., and entered C.S.A.; served 4 yrs. in Co. E, 4th Ky. Inf., and Co. C, 1st La. Cav.; wounded and captured nr. Somerset, Ky., Mar. 1863; exchanged, Oct. 1863; paroled at Abbeville, S.C., 1865; m. Alice, d. Jules A. Blanc, Jan. 3, 1878; children—Frank Adair, Jules Blanc, Alice (Mrs. S. S. Labouisse), Kate Adair (Mrs. G. R. Westfeldt), Gertrude (Mrs. T. M. Logan), Winder Polk (dec.), Adèle (Mrs. Geo. E. Williams), Marion (Mrs. John T. Chambers), William Blanc, James Hill. Admitted to bar, 1867; practiced in New Orleans; elected judge 3d Dist. Court, Parish of Orleans, Nov. 1872; dispossessed of office after a month's service; took part with White League in action of Sept. 14, 1874, which overturned "Packard" govt.; reëlected judge, Nov. 1876; apptd. judge Civil Dist. Court, Parish of Orleans, 1880; reapptd., 1884 and 1892; took active part in anti-lottery campaign, 1892; mem. La. Constl. Conv., 1898; apptd. asso. justice Supreme Court of La., Mar. 1899; elected without opposition, for terms 1908-20, 1920-32; became chief justice, Apr. 6, 1914; retired, Jan. 2, 1922, after 45 years' service on the bench; counsel with law firm Monroe & Lemann. Was member law faculty, Tulane U. of La., 20 yrs. Was pres. Assn. Army of Tenn. (Camp No. 2, U.C.V.); many yrs. mem. bd. of govs. (Confed.) Memorial Hall at New Orleans. Democrat. Home: New Orleans, La. Died Jan. 16, 1927.

MONROE, Harriet, author; b. Chicago; d. Henry S. and Martha (Mitchell) M.; grad. Visitation Academy, Georgetown, D.C.; Litt.D., Baylor U., Waco, Texas, 1920; L.H.D., Rockford (Ill.) College, 1935; in March 1891, was requested by the committee on ceremonies of Chicago Exposition to write poem for the dedication; her "Columbian Ode" was read and sung at the dedicatory ceremonies on 400th anniversary of the discovery of America, Oct. 21, 1892; recovered $5,000 damages from New York World for prematurely publishing same. Founder and editor of Poetry: a Magazine of Verse, endowed from Oct. 1912, by over one hundred persons. Author: Valeria and Other Poems, 1892; The Columbian Ode, 1893; John Wellborn Root—a Memoir, 1896; The Passing Show—modern plays in verse, 1903; You and I (poems), 1914; The Difference and Other Poems, 1924; Poets and Their Art (prose essays), 1926; Chosen Poems, a Selection from My Book of Verse, 1935. Edited (with Alice Corbin Henderson) The New Poetry, an Anthology of Twentieth-Century Verse, 1917, enlarged edit., 1932; (with M. D. Zabel) Poems for Every Mood, 1933. Home: Chicago, Ill. Died Sept. 26, 1936.

MONROE, Harriet Earhart, author; b. Indiana, Pa., 1842; d. Rev. David and Mary (Patton) Earhart; acad. edn. under pvt. teachers; widow. Pres. Atchison (Kan.) Collegiate Inst., 1870-75; lived in Phila., 1888-1901; lecturer on hist. and travel subjects (with stereopticon). Author: The Art of Conversation; Heroine of the Mining Camp; Historical Lutheranism (translated into 13 languages); Washington, Its Sights and Insights; History and Dramatization of the Life of Gustavus Adolphus; Twice-Born Men in America, 1914. Corr. The Lutheran, Phila. Engaged in social service work, Washington. Home: Washington, D.C. Died July 16, 1927.

MONROE, Jay Randolph, mfr.; b. South Haven, Mich., Jan. 6, 1883; s. Lyman Sylvester and Caroline Jane (Curtiss) M.; student Stetson U., 1893-1900, Kalamazoo (Mich.) Coll. Prep. Sch., 1900-01, Kalamazoo Coll., 1901-03; LL.B., U. of Mich., 1906; m. Betty Belle Baughman, Aug. 22, 1908 (dec.); children—Jay Randolph (dec.), Marjorie Belle, Malcolm, Marilyn; m. 2d, Edith House Montgomery, June 19, 1926 (dec.); m. 3d, Ethlyn Wheeler, May 12, 1931. Clk. Western Electric Co., Chicago, 1906, acting head of voucher dept., 1906-07, vacation man, Pittsburgh, 1907-10, gen. chief clk., N.Y. City, 1910-11, in legal dept., 1911-12; pres. Monroe Calculating Machine Co., 1912—; pres. Defiance Mfg. Co., Calculator Equipment Corp.; dir. Savings Investment & Trust Co. Republican. Mason. Home: South Orange, N.J. Died Apr. 29, 1937.

MONROE, Will S(eymour), psychologist, author; b. Hunlock, Pa., Mar. 22, 1863; s. Ransom and Emeline (Womelsdorf) M.; A.B., Stanford, 1894; univs. of Jena, Paris, Leipzig, 1894-95, Leipzig and Grenoble, 1900-01; unmarried. Teacher and prin. schs., Luzerne County, Pa., 1881-87; supt. schs., Nanticoke, Pa., 1887-88, Pasadena, Calif., 1889-92; prof. psychology, Mass. State Normal Sch., Westfield, 1896-1908, N.J. State Normal Sch., Montclair, 1909-25, retired 1925. Lecturer, U. of Ill., 1903, Columbia, 1904, U. of Chicago, 1908, U. of Vt., 1914-20, U. of Sofia (Bulgaria), 1926. Mem. Internat. Jury of Education, St. Louis Expn., 1904; del. to several foreign congresses and expns. Hon. mem. Assn. Med. Officers of Am. Instns. for Idiotic and Feeble-Minded Persons. Mem. peace inquiry of U.S., organized by President Wilson for study of spl. problems of the Peace Conf., 1918-19. Silver medal of Merit from City of Prague, Bohemia; Order of Commander's Cross from King Boris III of Bulgaria. Licensed judge of the American Kennel Club. Author: Poets and Poetry of the Wyoming Valley, 1887; Educational Labors of Henry Barnard, 1893; Comenius' Sch. of Infancy, 1896; Bibliography of Edn., 1897; Child Study Outlines, 1898; Die Entwickelung des Sozialen Bewusstseins der Kinder, 1899 (also transl. into Swedish, Flemish and Bulgarian); Comenius and the Beginnings of Ednl. Reform, 1900; History of the Pestalozzian Movement in the U.S., 1905; Turkey and the Turks, 1907; In Viking Land, 1908; Sicily, the Garden of the Mediterranean, 1909; new edit. title, The Spell of Sicily, 1922; Bohemia and the Czechs, 1910; Our Country and Its People, Europe and Its People (with Anna Buckbee), 1911, 12; Bulgaria and Her People, 1914; Spell of Bohemia, 1929; Edward Carpenter—An Appreciation, 1931. Asso. editor Monroe's Cyclopedia of Edn., 1911-13. Builder of the Monroe skyline, a section of the Long Trail of the Green Mountain Club, Vt., extending from Winooski Gorge to Middlebury Gap (48 miles). Home: Waterbury, Vt. Died Jan. 29, 1939.

MONSARRAT, Nicholas, railway pres.; b. London, Can., Mar. 1, 1839; s. Charles and Elizabeth M.; B.A., U. of Toronto, 1859; m. Corinne Blanche Henry, Oct. 26, 1870. In the ry. service in various official positions, 1872—; pres. Hocking Valley Ry. Co., 1899—. Home: Columbus, O. Died 1910.

MONSEN, Frederick Imman, explorer; b. Bergen, Norway, July 8, 1865; s. Hans and Anna Sophia (von Branneberg) M.; ed. under pvt. tutors; Ph.D., U. of Christiania, 1910; studied art; came to America, 1880; m. Harriet Van Anden, Jan. 15, 1892 (died 1903); children—Frederick Courtenay, Hans Shavenau. Engaged in western exploration, geol. survey, 1887; Salton Sea expdn., 1891; explored Lower Calif., 1892, Death Valley, and other Calif. deserts, 1893; made investigations among N.M. Indians, 1894-95; artist and topographer Yosemite Nat. Park Boundary Survey, 1896, Alaska Coast Survey, 1897, Yukon Exploration, 1898; investigations among Indian tribes of Ariz., N.M., Calif., and Mex., 1896—. Engaged in Mexican, Central and S. Am. travels and exploration, 1906-09; travels and observations in W.I. and the Orinoco River, Venezuela, 1909-11, Sonora and Chihuahua Deserts, Mexico, 1914. Fellow Royal Geog. Soc., Eng., Am. Nat., and Phila. Geog. Socs.; mem. A.A.A.S., Am. Anthrop. Assn. Professional lecturer on Am. history and exploration, and on ethnol. and History of the Indians of Southwestern United States; geog. subjects; artist; author and artist Ethnographic author and illustrator of many reports and mag. articles on exploration and travel among primitive people and in little known lands. Died Nov. 10, 1929.

MONSON, George S., dentist, lecturer; b. St. Paul, Minn., Mar. 20, 1869; s. F. William and Margaret (Sterrett) M.; grad. U. of Minn., Coll. of Dentistry, 1893; m. Bertha Clement Gordon, 1894. Studied portrait painting; began practice of dentistry at St. Paul, 1893; has specialized in prosthetic dentistry; clin. demonstrator before colls., state and city dental socs.; has conducted post-grad. dental schs. in Chicago, St. Louis, Des Moines, etc. Founder Monson Clinic Club of St. Paul. Inventor of instrument for reproducing the movements of the human jaws. Died May 27, 1933.

MONTAGUE, Andrew Jackson, congressman; b. Campbell Co., Va., Oct. 3, 1862; s. Robert Latané and Gay (Eubank) M.; grad. Richmond (Va.) Coll., 1882; LL.B., U. of Va., 1885; LL.D., Brown U., 1903; LL.D., U. of Pa., 1923; m. Elizabeth Lyne Hoskins, Dec. 11, 1889; children—Mrs. Chas. Beatty Moore, Mrs. Wm. J. Nunnally, Robert L. (U.S. Marine Corps). Began law practice, Oct. 1885; U.S. dist. atty. for Western Dist. of Va., 1894-98; atty. gen. of Va., 1898-1902; gov. of Va., 1902-06; dean Law Sch. of Richmond Coll., 1906-09; resumed practice, Richmond, 1909; del.-at-large Dem. Nat. Conv., 1904; mem. 63d to 74th Congresses (1913-37), 3d Va. Dist. U.S. del. Pan-Am. Conf., Rio de Janeiro, 1906, to 3d Internat. Conf. on Maritime Law, Brussels, 1909-10. Trustee Carnegie Instn. Washington, and Carnegie Endowment for Internat. Peace, 1910. Pres. Am. Soc. Jud. Settlement of Internat. Disputes, 1917; pres. Am. Peace Soc., 1920-24; pres. Am. group Interparliamentary Union, 1930-35. Author: Life of John Marshall, Secretary of State (in Am. Secretaries of State and Their Diplomacy), Vol. II. Home: Richmond, Va. Died Jan. 24, 1937.

MONTAGUE, Andrew Philip, college pres.; b. Essex County, Va., Sept. 27, 1854; s. Howard W. and Mildred Columbia (Broaddus) M.; grad. U. of Va., 1875; A.M., Columbian (now George Washington) U., 1879, Ph.D., 1888; LL.D., Richmond Coll., 1896; m. May Christian, Nov. 3, 1881; 1 dau., Maud Augusta (Mrs. M. B. Hawkins); m. 2d, Florence Wood, May 8, 1907; 1 son, Howard Christian. Tutor Latin, 1875-79, adj. prof., 1879-82, prof., 1882-97, prin. prep. sch., 1884-93, dean, 1895-97, Columbian U.; pres. Furman U., 1897-1902, Howard Coll., Ala., 1902-12, Columbia Coll., Lake City, Fla., 1912-19; prof. Latin and public speaking, 1919—, dean, 1923-24, vice-pres., 1924—, acting pres., 1927, Mercer U., Macon, Ga. Pres. Fla. Edn. Assn., 1915. Editor: Selected Letters of Cicero, 1890; Selected Letters of Pliny, 1893. Home: Macon, Ga. Died Dec. 3, 1928.

MONTAGUE, Dwight Preston, manufacturer; b. Chester, O., July 20, 1853; s. Theodore Langdon and Catherine (Stivers) M.; student Cornell U., 1872-74; m. Genevieve Allan, Sept. 21, 1882. Engaged in mfg., Chattanooga, Tenn., 1875—; propr. Montague & Co., 1875-1905; pres. New Soddy Coal Co., 1892-1910, Fox Coal Co., 1895-1910; pres. Chattanooga Sewer Pipe & Fire Brick Co., 1905-15; pres. Richmond Cotton Oil Co., Roane Iron Co.; dir. Hamilton Nat. Bank; pres. Stonegap Colliery Co. Republican. Presbyn. Died May 25, 1921.

MONTAGUE, James Jackson, newspaper writer; b. Mason City, Ia., Apr. 16, 1873; s. J. V. W. and Martha (Jackson) M.; ed. high sch., Portland, Ore.; m. Helen L. Hageny, Aug. 18, 1898 (died 1937); children—Richard, Doris, James Lee. Was reporter and asst. editor Portland Oregonian; nat. conv. and Washington corr. Universal News Service, 1912-16; reported Peace Conf., Paris, France, for newspaper syndicate, 1918-19; widely known as writer of verse. Author: More Truth Than Poetry, 1920. Home: New Rochelle, N.Y. Died Dec. 16, 1941.

MONTAGUE, Richard Ward, lawyer; b. Charles City, Ia., Feb. 11, 1862; s. John Vose Wood and Martha Washington (Jackson) M.; grad. high sch., Mason City, Ia., 1878; B.Ph., State U. of Ia., 1883, LL.B., 1884; hon. A.M., U. of Ore., 1919; m. Ellen Amelia Barton, June 5, 1889; children—Margaret (Mrs. B. B. Payne), John Richard, Caroline Content (Mrs. George J. Beggs). Admitted to Ia. bar, 1884, and practiced at Mason City until 1888; chamber counsel and asst. sec. Equitable Mortgage Co., New York, 1888-90; moved to Portland, Ore., 1890; mem. Wood, Montague, Matthiesen & Rankin. Examiner, Emergency Fleet Corp., U.S. Shipping Bd., and counsel Ore. Food Administration and civil br. Am. Red Cross, Ore., 1917-18. Mem. charter comms., Portland, 1901, 08, 11, 13; chmn. Ore. State Commission on Govt. Simplification, 1927-29. Vice-pres. Portland Library Assn.; trustee of Reed Coll., Portland. Author: Oregon Digest, 1905-16. One of compilers Lord's Oregon Laws, 1910. Was mem. editorial council Nat. Municipal Review; was lecturer on equity, law dept., U. of Ore. Home: Portland, Ore. Died July 17, 1935.

MONTAGUE, William Lewis, educator, linguist; b. Belchertown, Mass., Apr. 6, 1831; s. Ephraim and Laura (Sabin) M.; grad. Amherst Coll., 1855; Ph.D., Ill. Wesleyan U.; licensed Congl. preacher; traveled and studied in Europe; m. Rebecca W. Pope, Aug. 19, 1858. Teacher Latin and Greek, Williston Sem., 2 yrs.; instr. Latin and French, Amherst, 6 yrs.; prof. modern languages, Amherst, 1864-95; also librarian, 1864-78, and registrar, 1860-80; resided in Paris, 1896-1900. Director of Amherst Summer Sch. Languages, 1884-96. Author: Comparative Spanish Grammar, 1873; Manual of Italian Grammar, 1887; Introduction to Italian Literature, 1875. Editor: Biographical Record of the Alumni and Non-Graduate Members of Amherst College, 1821-71, 1885, same, 1871-1896 (vol. II), 1901; History and Genealogy of the Montague Family in America (with George W. Montague), 1886; Modern Italian Readings, 1893; La Fille de Roland (Bornier), 1895; Half Century Record of the Class of Fifty-Five, Amherst College, 1905. Died 1908.

MONTEZUMA, Carlos, physician; b. of Apache Indian parents, in Ariz., 1867; s. Co-lu-ye-vah; captured by Pima Indians and sold for $30 to C. Gentile; ed. pub. schs., Chicago and Galesburg, Ill., Brooklyn, N.Y., and under pvt. tutors, Urbana, Ill.; B.S. (at age of 17), U. of Ill., 1884; M.D., Chicago Med. Coll., 1889; m. Mary Keller, Sept. 19, 1913. Phys. and surg. Interior Dept., 1889-96, serving at various Indian agencies; associated with Dr. Fenton B. Turck, in his clinic (stomach and intestinal diseases), at Post-Grad. Med. Sch., Chicago, 1896-1914; med. instr. Coll. Phys. and Surg., Chicago, 1904-06; instr. in medicine, Chicago Medical School. Baptist. Mason. Author: The Indian of Today and of Tomorrow, 1906; Let My People Go, 1914; Abolish the Indian Bureau, 1919. Editor of Indian mag., "Wassaja." Home: Chicago, Ill. Died Jan. 31, 1923.

MONTGOMERY, Edmund Duncan, biologist, philosopher; b. Edinburgh, Scotland, Mar. 19, 1835; ed. pvt. tuition in Eng., France and Germany; univs. of Heidelberg, 1852-56, Berlin, 1855, Bonn, 1856, Würzburg, 1857; M.D., Prague, 1858; Vienna, 1859; M.R.C.P., London, 1861; m. at Madeira, Elisabet Ney, sculptress, 1865 (died 1907). Resident phys. German Hosp., London, 1860-61; med. attendant Bermondsey Dispensary and Poor District, 1861-62; pathologist St. Thomas' Hosp., London, 1861-64; practiced Madeira, Mentone and Rome, 1865-70; resided in Texas, 1872—. Author: Die Kantsche Erkenntniplehre vom Standpunkt der Empirie, 1871; The Vitality and Organization of Protoplasm, 1904; Philosophical Problems in the Light of Vital Organization, 1907. Home: Hempstead, Tex. Died 1911.

MONTGOMERY, Edward Emmet, M.D.; b. Newark, O., May 15, 1849; s. Henry A. and Mary (Lemert) M.; B.S., Denison U., 1871, LL.D., 1901; M.D., Jefferson Med. Coll., 1874; m. Helen M. Buckley, Dec. 27, 1876; children—Susan Lukens (wife of Dr. P. Brooke Bland), Mary Ellen (dec.); m. 2d, Alice Jayne, Feb. 6, 1917. Interne Phila. Hosp., 1874-75; obstetrician, same, 1878-94; prof. gynecology, 1886-91, obstetrics and gynecology, 1891-92, Medico-Chirurg. Coll.; prof. clin. gynecology, 1892-98, gynecology, 1898-1921, prof. emeritus, 1921—, Jefferson Med. Coll., Phila.; gynecologist St. Joseph's Hosp., 1890—; retired from practice, 1923; traveled extensively until 1925. Asst. editor Universal Medical Annual and Sajous' Annual and Analytical Cyclopædia of Practical Medicine. Contbr. to Keating and Coe's Practical Gynecology, Am. Text-Book of Gynecology, Keen's Surgery, Vols. V and VI. Author: Practical Gynecology, 4th edit., 1911; Care of the Patient, Before, During and After Operation in

Gynecology and Abdominal Surgery, 1917. Died Apr. 17, 1927.

MONTGOMERY, Edward Louis, educator; b. South Manchester, Conn., July 25, 1874; s. Charles P. and Lina Pease (Luce) M.; East Greenwich (R.I.) Acad.; B.S., Wesleyan U., Conn., 1898; studied Yale, 1906-07, 1908-09; m. Mabel V. Lawton, Nov. 23, 1904; children—Marjorie Lawton, Lyman Charles (dec.). Instr. history, Central Grammar Sch., New Britain, Conn., 1899-1900; head dept. mathematics, Mt. Pleasant Acad., Ossining, N.Y., 1900-02, Cartaret Acad., Orange, N.J., 1902-03; asst. prin. Meriden (Conn.) High Sch., 1903-13; prin. Morse High Sch., Bath, Me., 1913-14; Natick (Mass.) High Sch., 1914-18, Holton High Sch., Danvers, Mass., 1918-19; asso. prin. Mt. Ida Sch., Newton, Mass., 1919-23; prin. and owner Fairmount Sch., Washington, D.C., 1923—; founder, 1915, and dir. Eggemogin Camp for Girls, East Harpswell, Me. Mem. 1st Regt. Conn. Vol. Inf., 1898. Republican. Conglist. Home: Washington, D.C. Deceased.

MONTGOMERY, Frank Hugh, physician; b. Minn., Jan. 6, 1862; s. Albertis and Mary Louisa M.; ed. St. Cloud High School and Univ. of Minn.; grad. Rush Med. Coll., 1888; post-grad. work in Vienna, London and Paris; m. Caroline L. Williamson, Jan. 11, 1897. Asso. prof. skin and genito-urinary diseases, Rush Med. Coll.; dermatologist to St. Elizabeth and Presbyn. hosps. Author: A Practical Treatise on Diseases of the Skin (with Dr. James Nevins Hyde), 7th edit., 1904; A Manual of Syphilis and the Venereal Diseases (with Dr. James Nevins Hyde), 2d edit., 1900. Home: Chicago, Ill. Died 1908.

MONTGOMERY, George, coadjutor archbishop of San Francisco; b. Daviess County, Ky., Dec. 30, 1847; s. Pius and Harriet M.; ed. common school in Ky., Cecilian Coll., Ky., St. Charles Coll., Md., and St. Mary's Sem., Baltimore. Ordained priest, Baltimore, Dec. 1879; spent about 15 yrs. in San Francisco as a R.C. priest; consecrated coadjutor bishop of Los Angeles, Apr. 8, 1894; became coadjutor archbishop, of San Francisco, Apr. 1903. Died 1907.

MONTGOMERY, Helen Barrett; b. Kingsville, O., July 31, 1861; d. Rev. A. Judson and Emily (Barrows) Barrett; A.B., Wellesley, 1884, LL.D., 1925; A.M., Brown, 1917; D.H.L., Franklin Coll., 1922; LL.D., Denison U., 1922; m. William A. Montgomery, Sept. 6, 1887; 1 dau., Edith (Mrs. G. F. Simson). Teacher Rochester Free Acad., 1884-85, Wellesley Prep. Sch., Phila., 1885-87; licensed as minister Bapt. Ch., 1892; pres. Woman's Am. Bapt. Foreign Mission Soc., 1913-24; pres. Nat. Fed. Woman's Bds. of Foreign Missions, 1917-18; mem. Am. sect. World Alliance for Internat. Friendship; head of Woman's Bible Class (200 members) of Lake Av. Baptist S.S.; pres. Northern Bapt. Conv., 1921; was pres. N.Y. State Fed. Women's Clubs. Has lectured extensively on foreign missions, citizenship, etc. Made trip around the world to study conditions in non-Christian countries. Author: The Island World of the Pacific, 1906; Western Women in Eastern Lands, 1910; Following the Sunrise, 1913; The King's Highway, 1915; The Bible and Missions, 1920; Prayer and Missions, 1924; The Story of Jesus as Told by His Friends, 1927; The Preaching Value of Missions, 1929. Translator of entire New Testament out of the original Greek, 1924. Home: Rochester, N.Y. Deceased.

MONTGOMERY, James Eglinton, retired; b. Dutchess County, N.Y., Sept. 20, 18—; s. John Crathorne and Elizabeth (Philips) M.; grad. Princeton, 1845; twice married; m. 2d, Florence Miller, Nov. 15, 1904. Studied law; civ. engr. Pa. R.R., 1847-51. Served as asst. adj. gen. 6th, 13th, 22d corps U.S.A., 1861-66; wounded thrice; sec. to Admiral Farragut on visit to European govts., 1867-68; consul at Geneva, 1877-79, at Leipzig, 1879-82, at Brussels, 1882, at Trieste, 1882; resigned on account of ill health. Republican. Episcopalian. Author: Our Admiral's Flag Abroad, 1870. Home: Pasadena, Calif. Died 1909.

MONTGOMERY, John Harold, religious edn.; b. Woodstock, Ont., Can., of Am. parents, Sept. 28, 1874; s. Jabez and Lucy (Carrington) M.; B.S., U. of Mich., 1897, M.S., 1898, E.E., 1907; post-grad. work, U. of Southern Calif., and Northwestern U.; m. Edith Irene Clark, Sept. 2, 1903; children—Harold Clark, Verner Lee. Various positions in elec. engring., 1898-1903; engr. Mich. State Inspection Bur., 1903-10; prof. physics and elec. engring., U. of Southern Calif., 1912-16, registrar, 1915-24, prof. religious edn., 1916—; visiting prof. Northwestern U. 3 summers to 1927. Trustee Palm Hall Sch. for Girls, Los Angeles, Calif.; dir. Southern Calif. Bapt. Conv. Author: Electric Wiring Specifications, 1914; Social Message of Jesus, 1923. Home: Los Angeles, Calif. Died Jan. 9, 1929.

MONTGOMERY, J(ohn) Knox, coll. pres.; b. Belfast, Tenn., Aug. 4, 1861; s. Rev. Andrew Spence and Lavinia Grace (Tate) M.; student Enfield (Ill.) Coll., Ind. State U., 1879-84; B.D., Xenia (O.) Theol. Sem., 1887; D.D., Sterling Coll., 1904; LL.D., W Va. Wesleyan U., 1922; m. Emma Zetta Patton,

Dec. 25, 1889; children—Mary Grace, John Knox, Don Patton, Geneva Kathleen, Robert Nathaniel, Paul Spence. Ordained to U.P. ministry, 1887; pastor Harshaville, O., 1887-90, Sparta, Ill., 1890-95, Cincinnati, 1895-99, Chicago, 1900-01, Charlotte, N.C., 1901-04; pres. Muskingum Coll., 1904—. Editor The Evangel, 1894-1902; dept. editor, Christian Union Herald, Pittsburgh, 1898-1914; dept. editor Christian Instructor, Phila., 1900-05; dept. editor Reformed Presbyterian, Due West, S.C., 1903-04. Gen. Sec. of Young People's Work in South, 1903-04; chmn. evangelistic work, 1903-04, and elected synodical evangelist for Ohio, 1896; pres. of AllHealing N.C. Bible Conf., 1903-05. Lecturer. Prohibitionist candidate for sec. of state of Ohio, 1900. Spl. preacher in army camps under Nat. War Work Council; dir. Muskingum Bible Conf. and Training Sch.; advisory mem. Ohio Civil Service Commn.; pres. Ohio Anti-Saloon League, 1914—; pres. Ohio and Nat. Anti-Cigaret Alliance; sec. spiritual life dept. of New World Movement, United Presbyn. Ch. Was Y.M.C.A. war sec. Home: New Concord, O. Died Dec. 30, 1931.

MONTGOMERY, John Rogerson, lawyer; b. Chicago, Ill., Mar. 8, 1866; s. William A. and Ellen S. (Smith) M.; A.B., Beloit (Wis.) Coll., 1887; LL.B., Union Coll. of Law, Chicago, 1889; LL.D. Yankton (S.D.) College, 1931; m. Marion Howard, Feb. 11, 1896 (died 1910); children—Mrs. Ellen Crawley, William A. (dec.), John R., Marion Corkran; m. 2d, Marion Vidaud Hunter, Dec. 28, 1912 (died 1934). Practiced at Chicago, 1889—; mem. Montgomery, Hart, Pritchard & Herriott. Trustee Beloit Coll.; chmn. bd. Chicago Theol. Sem. Republican. Home: Hubbard Woods, Ill. Died Mar. 5, 1937.

MONTGOMERY, Oscar Hilton, judge; b. Seymour, Ind., Apr. 27, 1859; s. Theophilus Wylie and Susan Harriet (Close) M.; A.B., Hanover (Ind.) Coll., 1881, A.M., 1886; m. Ida E. Harding, Oct. 27, 1886; children—Madge E. T. Harlan, Merrill M., Harriet E. Admitted to Ind. bar, 1884; practiced law, 1884-1904; city atty., Seymour, 10 yrs.; judge Supreme Court of Ind., 1905-11; resumed practice at Seymour, Jan. 1911; mem. Indiana Constl. Conv., 1933, to ratify 21st Amendment to Constitution of United States. V.p. and trustee 1st Nat. Bank of Seymour. Del. Rep. Nat. Conv., 1896, 1912. Trustee Hanover Coll. (pres. bd.). Home: Seymour, Ind. Died May 5, 1936.

MONTGOMERY, Robert, newspaper editor, pub.; b. Quarryville, Pa., May 25, 1872; s. Robert and Margaret (Kerr) M.; student Octorara Acad., Georgetown, Pa.; 1887-90; B.S., Whitworth Coll., Spokane, Wash., 1896; m. Agnes E. Cook, Oct. 13, 1903; children—Thomas Sterling, Margaret Agnes. Was daily newspaper reporter, 1890; editor Sumner Herald, 1896-1903; editor and pub. Puyallup Valley Tribune, 1903—; pres. Snow Lumber & Shingle Co. Mayor of Sumner, 1899-1903. Apptd. mem. Bd. of Regents, U. of Wash., 1933. Democrat. Unitarian. Mason, Elk. Author of Life of Washington, Life of Jackson, Life of Lincoln, Life of Robert E. Lee, also (brochures) Robert Burns, Lord Byron, Among the Stars, Thoughts on Evolution, Motherhood, Life's Sweetest Relation, West of Fifty-Four. Awarded Schoenfeld silver trophy for having written most constructive community-building editorials of any newspaper editor in State of Wash. Home: Puyallup, Wash. Died May-3, 1936.

MONTGOMERY, Robert M., judge; b. Eaton Rapids, Mich., May 12, 1849; s. Johnson and Elvira (Dudley) M.; ed. pub. and high schs.; m. Theodosia Wadsworth, Dec. 1873. Admitted to bar, 1870; practiced at Pentwater, and Grand Rapids; pros. atty., 1874; asst. U.S. dist. atty., 1877; circuit judge, Kent County. Mich., 1881-88; justice Supreme Ct. of Mich., 1892-1910; presiding judge U.S. Ct. of Customs Appeals, Mar. 1910—. Republican. Home: Lansing, Mich. Died June 28, 1920.

MONTGOMERY, Roselle Mercier, author; b. Crawfordville, Ga.; d. William Nathaniel, and Emma Esther (Smith) Mercier; ed. Mary Baldwin Sem., Staunton, Va., Harvard Summer Sch. and Columbia U.; D.Litt. from Oglethorpe U., Atlanta, Ga., 1927; m. John Seymour Montgomery; children—John Seymour, Roselle Mercier. Chmn. Red Cross, at Riverside, Conn., World War; chmn. literature and poetry, N.Y. City Fedn. Women's Clubs; vice chmn. poetry, League of Am. Pen Women. Author: Ulysses Returns and Other Poems; Many Devices (verse). Home: Riverside, Conn. Died Sept. 16, 1933.

MONTGOMERY, Samuel Thomas, b. in Mo., Nov. 6, 1860; s. George Washington (D.D.) and Sarah Ann (Rankin) M.; prep. edn., Lees Acad., Loxa, Ill.; student Waynesburg (Pa.) Coll., 1887-90; S.T.B., Western Theol. Sem., Pittsburgh, Pa., 1896; m. Le Nettie Algelena Gowdy, July 5, 1888; children—G. Millage, Walter B., Donnell G., Dorothy L. (Mrs. Harry T. Richardson). Licensed, evangelist Presbyn. Ch., 1883, ordained to ministry, 1889; home missionary, Pa., and W.Va., 1891—; successively pastor First Cumberland Presbyn. Ch., Pittsburgh, First Ch., Cameron, W.Va., Upper Buffalo Presbyn. Ch. of Pa. until 1903, Third Presbyn. Ch., Los Angeles, 1903-07, First Presbyn. Ch., Alhambra,

Calif., 1908-12; supt. Anti-Saloon League for Southern Calif., 1913-33; exec. sec. Bd. of Strategy for Southern Calif. (20 Dry Groups), 1932 campaign. Police commr., Los Angeles, 1927. Dir. Anti-Saloon League of America, 1916—. Home: Eagle Rock, Calif. Died June 23, 1938.

MONTGOMERY, Thomas Harrison, Jr., zoölogist; b. New York, Mar. 5, 1873; s. Thomas Harrison and Anna (Morton) M.; student U. of Pa., 1889-91; Ph.D., U. of Berlin, 1894; m. Priscilla Braislin, 1901. Asst. prof. zoölogy, U. of Pa., 1898-1903; prof. biology, 1898-1903, dir. mus., 1899-1903, Wagner Free Inst. of Science, Phila.; prof. zoölogy, U. of Tex., 1903-08, U. of Pa., 1908—. Trustee Marine Biol. Lab., Woods Hole, Mass. Contributed about 80 scientific monographs on biol. subjects. Author: Analysis of Racial Descent in Animals, 1906. Home: Philadelphia, Pa. Died Mar. 19, 1912.

MONTGOMERY, Thomas Lynch, librarian; b. Phila., Mar. 4, 1862; s. Oswald Crathorne and Catherine Gertrude (Lynch) M.; A.B., U. of Pa., 1884; Litt.D., Muhlenberg Coll., Pa., 1913; m. Brinea Gilpin, Oct. 16, 1889; m. 2d, Susan Keim Savage, Apr. 14, 1925. Actuary and librarian, Wagner Free Inst. of Science, 1886; founder Pa. Library Club, 1890; established first br. of Phila. Free Library, 1892; trustee Free Library of Phila., and chmn. Library Com., 1894—; state librarian of Pa., 1903-21; librarian Hist. Soc. of Pa., 1921—. Sec. Pa. Free Library Commn.; commr. for preservation of hist. archives of Pa.; curator of Pa. Hist. Commission. Editor of Pa. Archives, series 5 to 7. Charter mem. Keystone Library Assn. Home: Philadelphia, Pa. Died Oct. 1, 1929.

MONTGOMERY, William Coons, banker; b. Hardin County, Ky., Nov. 24, 1866; s. Alexander Brooks and Mildred Ferguson (Coons) M.; ed. high sch., Elizabethtown, Ky.; m. Anna McAfee, 1889. Began with Bank of Elizabethtown, 1883, and continued with its successor, First Hardin Nat. Bank, of which was pres., 1922—; dir. Louisville Br. Federal Reserve Bank of Louisville, Citizens Union Nat. Bank (Louisville), Lincoln Nat. Bank (Hodgenville, Ky.). Appointed chmn. State Highway Commn., Ky., Feb. 1924, reapptd. Feb. 1926, term of 4 yrs. Democrat. Baptist. Home: Elizabethtown, Ky. Died Nov. 10, 1934.

MONTOYA, Atanasio, educator; b. Casa Colorada, N.M., Nov. 21, 1875; s. Juan M. and Anastasia (Saiz) M.; grad. U. of N.M., 1895; m. Alice Fairchild, Sept. 27, 1905; children—Annie, Katherine, Alice. Teacher, country schs., N.M., 1893-96; head of Spanish dept. U. of N.M., 1896-1902; supt. county schs., Bernalillo County, N.M., 1912-19, 1923-27; supt. pub. instrn., N.M., 1929-30. Mem. N.M. State Bd. of Edn., 1918-19. Republican. Home: Albuquerque, N.M. Died Sept. 6, 1935.

MONTOYA, Nestor, congressman; b. Old Albuquerque, N.M., Apr. 14, 1862; s. Theodosious and Chona (Cervantes) M.; A.B., St. Michael's Coll., Santa Fe, N.M., 1881; m. Florence Maes, 1899. Began newspaper work in Santa Fe, 1889; editor La Bandera Americana (The American Flag), Albuquerque, N.M. Mem. House or Senate of N.M. 20 yrs.; speaker of House, 1903; mem. Constl. Conv., 1910; mem. 67th Congress (1921-23), N.M. at large. Republican. Regent U. of N.M. Chmn. Draft Bd., Bernalillo Co., N.M., and mem. State Council of Defense, World War. Mem. N.M. Press Assn. (pres. 1906—). Moose, K.C., Rotarian. Home: Old Albuquerque, N.M. Died Jan. 13, 1923.

MOOAR, George, theologian; b. Andover, Mass., May 27, 1830; s. Benjamin and Susanna (Cummings) M.; ed. at Phillips Acad., Andover, Mass.; grad. Williams Coll., 1851; (A.M., 1854, S.T.D., 1868); Andover Theol. Sem., 1855; S.T.D., Pacific Theol. Sem., 1895; m. Sarah A. Comstock, Oct. 10, 1855. Pastor South Congl. Ch., Andover, 1855-61; 1st Congl. Ch., Oakland, Calif., 1861-72; Plymouth Av. Ch., Oakland, 1874-89. Prof. systematic theology, church history, 1870-92, and prof. apologetics and church history, Pacific Theol. Sem., 1892—. Mem. commn. of 25 who drew up statement of doctrines requested by Nat. Congl. Council, 1882. Editor of the Pacific, 1886-96. Author: Historical Manual of the South Church of Andover, 1859; Be of Good Cheer, with Other Sermons of Encouragement, 1889; The Religion of Loyalty, 1865; Prominent Characteristics of the Congregational Churches, 1866; Hand-Book of the Congl. Churches of California, 1875; The Enduring and Varying Beauty of a Good Man's Life, 1859; Abraham Mooar and His Descendants, 1901; The Cummings Memorial, 1903. Home: Oakland, Calif. Died 1904.

MOODIE, Roy Lee, anatomist, paleontologist; b. Bowling Green, Ky., July 30, 1880; s. William Lemuel and Sarah Estelle (Gregg) M.; A.B., U. of Kan., 1905; Ph.D., U. of Chicago, 1908; m. Catherine M. Wood, June 29, 1910; children—William Ross, Catherine Ann, Sarah Lee. Prof. biology, Warrensburg (Mo.) Normal Sch., 1908; instr. zoölogy, U. of Kan., 1908-09, asst. prof., 1909-13; prof. anatomy, Baylor U., Dallas, Tex., 1913-14; instr. in anatomy, 1914-15, associate, 1915-16, asst. prof., 1916-18, asso. prof., 1918-23, U. of Ill. Coll. of Medicine; sabbatical yr. in Southern Calif., in research work, 1923-24; asso. prof. anatomy and research librarian, U. of Ill., at Chicago, 1924-28; prof. paleodontology, Coll. of Dentistry, U. of Southern Calif., 1928; paleopathologist Wellcome Hist. Med. Mus., London, 1929—. Democrat. Baptist. Author: Coal Measures Amphibia of North America (Carnegie Instn.), 1916; The Antiquity of Disease, 1923; Paleopathology—an Introduction to the Study of Ancient Evidences of Disease, 1923. Editor: Studies in the Paleopathology of Egypt (by Ruffer), 1921; also author Studies in Paleopathology (Annals of Med. History); Studies in Paleodontology, I-XXV. Home: Los Angeles, Calif. Died Feb. 16, 1934.

MOODY, Dwight Lyman, evangelist; b. Northfield, Mass., Feb. 5, 1837; had limited edni. facilities; worked on farm until 1854; clerk in shoe store, Boston, 1854-56; joined Congl. Church; went to Chicago, 1856; engaged in missionary work; soon built up Sunday school of over 1,000 children; in service of Christian Commn. during war; later missionary, Chicago Y.M.C.A. The church built for his converts was destroyed in the fire of 1871, but rebuilt; he was joined by Ira D. Sankey, and together they held revival meetings all over U.S. and Great Britain; then continuously in evangelistic work; established three schools at Northfield, Mass., and one in Chicago. Died 1899.

MOODY, Frank Sims, banker; b. Tuscaloosa, Ala., Oct. 29, 1849; s. Washington and Jane Hamilton (Sims) M.; attended lectures U. of Ala., though not a matriculated student, 1864-65; Washington and Lee U., 1867-70 (Robinson prize medal and A.B.); cashier First Nat. Bank of Tuscaloosa, 1871-73; LL.B., U. of Ala., 1874; m. Mary Farley Maxwell, Jan. 5, 1876. Pres. First Nat. Bank of Tuscaloosa, 1879—; pres. Tuscaloosa Bd. of Trade and Industries; practiced law from 1875 for a number of years; engaged in farming. Mem. Ala. Senate 3½ terms, last term expiring Jan. 1915. Democrat. Baptist. Trustee Ala. Girls' Tech. Inst., 1895-1907. Co. chmn. Council of Defense and co. food administrator, 1917-18. Died Feb. 21, 1920.

MOODY, Gideon Curtis, U.S. senator, lawyer; b. Cortland, N.Y., Oct. 16, 1832; s. Stephen and Charlotte M.; academic edn.; studied law in Syracuse; removed to Indiana and admitted to bar, 1852; pros. atty. Floyd County, 1854; served in Civil War; lt. 9th Ind. vol. inf., April 1861; rose to col., Nov. 15, 1862; mustered out of vols., May 1861; apptd. capt. 19th U.S. inf., and served until 1864. Located in Dak., 1864; mem. and speaker, territorial ho. of reps.; asso. justice Supreme Court of territory 5 yrs.; del. Nat. Rep. Conv., 1868, 1888, 1892; mem. constitutional convs., S.D., 1883, 1885; chmn. of com. to draft and present memorial to Congress asking for admission as a State; elected U.S. senator for S.D. by legislature under constitution of 1885; reëlected Oct. 16, 1889, serving until 1891. Home: Deadwood, S.D. Died 1904.

MOODY, Joseph Burnley, theologian; b. Clarksville, Va., June 24, 1838; s. William A. and Emily (Royster) M.; college edn.; D.D., Bethel, 1881; m. Jennie Lee Jones, Dec. 22, 1869; 1 son, Claude D. Formerly wholesale mcht., Louisville, Ky.; entered ministry Bapt. Ch., 1876; pastor Paducah, Ky., Martin, Tenn., Central Ch., Memphis, Hot Springs, Ark., Tampa, Fla., San Antonio, Tex., etc.; gained wide recognition as debater on religious subjects; served as dean Hall-Moody Coll. (named after him), Ouachita (Ark.) Coll. and Ewing (Ill.) Coll. Long associated in editorship of Bapt. publs. Premillennialist. Home: Jacksonville, Fla. Died Sept. 6, 1931.

MOODY, Walter Dwight, managing dir. Chicago Plan Commn.; b. Detroit, Jan. 16, 1874; s. Rev. Edward Bursell and Anna Maria (Guilloz) M.; ed. pub. schs.; m. Lillian Hannah Slater, June 24, 1896. Traveling salesman with wholesale millinery firm, Detroit, 1891-98; v.p. and foreign buyer, millinery house of Mitchell-Moody-Garton Co., 1898-1904; sales mgr. of millinery house of Gage Bros. & Co., Chicago, 1904-07; vice chmn. trade extension com. Chicago Assn. of Commerce, 1906; business mgr. of the Assn., 1907-09, gen. mgr. 1910; chmn. membership com., 1907, and added 1,300 members; originator and chmn. com. Coliseum Good Fellowship Supper, Mar. 1907 (called Moody's Dinner)—2,400 persons present; chmn. Okla. trade extension delegation, 1907; com. of 100 on Deep Waterway Conv., 1908; of com. of 100 on Assn. bldg. bonds, 1909; mng. dir. Chicago Plan Commn., 1911—. Delivered 200 illustrated lectures on Plan of Chicago. Dir. Nat. Chem. Co., Ltd. Dir. Red Cross membership campaign, May 1917, which netted 418,000 members; chmn. ways and means com., Chicago Library War Council, Sept. 1917—; chmn. campaign exec. com., War Recreation Bd. of Ill., Feb. 1918—. Author: Men Who Sell Things (12 edits.); Wacker's Manual of the Plan of Chicago; What of the City. Editor-in-chief, business administration course, LaSalle Extension U. Home: Chicago, Ill. Died Nov. 21, 1920.

MOODY, Walter Sherman, electrical engr.; b. Chelsea, Mass., Sept. 20, 1864; s. Luther R. and Emily Sherman M.; B.S. in E.E., Mass. Inst. Tech., 1887; m. Florence C. Gilmore, 1891; 1 dau., Jean (Mrs. Guglilmo Camilli). Instr. physics and electricity, Mass. Inst. Tech., 1887-88; asst. engr., Thomson Electric Welding Co., 1889-92; in engring. dept. Thomson-Houston Co. (now Gen. Electric Co., of Schenectady, N.Y.), 1892-1932; was chief engr. transformer dept. of the co., later cons. engr. for the entire dept., including works at Pittsfield and Lynn, Mass., Erie, Pa., Ft. Wayne, Ind., and Oakland, Calif.; now cons. engr. Identified specially with design and mfr. of transformers, developing the "H" and air blast types of transformers. Conglist. Republican. Fellow Am. Inst. E.E. Home: Pittsfield, Mass. Died Nov. 7, 1938.

MOODY, William Henry, jurist; b. Newbury, Mass., Dec. 23, 1853; s. Henry L. and Melissa Augusta (Emerson) M.; grad. Phillips Acad., Andover, Mass., 1872; A.B., Harvard, 1876; studied law in office of Richard H. Dana, Boston; LL.D., Amherst and Tufts colls., 1904; unmarried. Admitted to bar, 1878, and began practice at Haverhill, Mass. City solicitor, 1888-90; dist. atty. for Eastern Dist. of Mass., 1890-95; elected 54th Congress, 1895, for unexpired term (1895-97) of Gen. William Cogswell, deceased; reëlected 55th to 57th Congresses (1897-1903); resigned from 57th Congress, Apr. 30, 1902; Sec. of the Navy, May 1, 1902-July 1, 1904; Atty. Gen. of U.S., July 1, 1904-Dec. 16, 1906, in cabinets of President Roosevelt; asso. justice Supreme Court of U.S., Dec. 17, 1906-Nov. 20, 1910, when retired on account of ill health. Republican. Home: Haverhill, Mass. Died July 2, 1917.

MOODY, William Revell, educator; b. Chicago, Mar. 25, 1869; s. Dwight Lyman (evangelist) and Emma C. (Revell) M.; A.B., Yale, 1891; Litt.D., Rutgers, 1921; m. Mary Whittle, Aug. 29, 1894. Since death of his father had charge of the Northfield schools founded by the latter. Author: The Life of Dwight L. Moody, 1900. Was editor Record of Christian Work. Home: East Northfield, Mass. Died Oct. 12, 1933.

MOODY, William Vaughn, author; b. Spencer, Ind., July 8, 1869; s. Francis Burdette and Henrietta Emily (Stoy) M.; A.B., Harvard, 1893, A.M., 1894, Litt.D., Yale, 1908. Asst. in English, Harvard, and Radcliffe Coll., 1894-95; instr. English and rhetoric, 1895-1901, asst. prof., 1901-07, U. of Chicago. Mem. Am. Acad. Arts and Letters. Author: The Masque of Judgment (lyrical drama), 1900; Poems, 1901; The Fire-Bringer, 1904; History of English Literature; The Great Divide, 1907; The Faith Healer (play), 1909. Editor: Cambridge Milton and other English classics. Died Oct. 17, 1910.

MOODY, Zenas Ferry, governor; b. Granby, Mass., May 27, 1832; common sch. edn., located in Ore., 1851; m. Mary Stephenson, Nov. 19, 1853. Was govt. surveyor; long engaged in transportation business in Ida. and Mont.; was mem. Ore. Ho. of Rep. (speaker 1880-82); gov. of Ore., 1883-87; del. Rep. Nat. Conv., Chicago, 1888. Died Mar. 14, 1917.

MOON, Edwin G., lawyer; b. Montrose, Ia., Nov. 12, 1870; s. Charles P. and Mira (Griswold) M.; A.B., State U. of Ia., 1897; LL.B., Kent Coll. of Law, Chicago, 1899; m. Luella Jean Mowatt, Nov. 14, 1901; children—Edwin St. Clair (dec.), John Paul. Mem. firm Gilmore, Moon & Bannister, Ottumwa, 1900—; mem. Ia. State Senate from 13th Senatorial Dist., 1908-09; asst. U.S. atty., Southern Dist. of Ia., 1914-18, U.S. atty., 1918-22, resigned; again U.S. atty., 1934—. Democrat. Episcopalian; chancellor P.E., Ch., Diocese of I. Elk. Home: Ottumwa, Ia. Died Jan. 22, 1939.

MOON, (Frederick) Franklin, forester; b. Easton, Pa., July 3, 1880; s. William White and Ophelia Frances (Nightingale) M.; g.s. Samuel Moon, the artist; A.B., Amherst, 1901; post-grad. Harvard, 1902-04; M.F., Yale U. Forest Sch., 1909; m. Marion P. B. Stutson, June 1, 1912; 1 son, (Frederick) Franklin. Forest reconnaissance, Conn., summer 1908; Ky. reconnaissances for U.S. Forest Service, 1909; forester N.Y. Forest, Fish and Game Commn., in charge Highlands of Hudson Forest Reservation, 1909-10; prof. forest engring., 1912-20, dean and prof. of silviculture, 1929—, New York State Coll. of Forestry, Syracuse, N.Y. Delegate to World's Forestry Congress, Rome, 1926, and spent yr. studying systems of forest education, etc., in 11 European countries. Joint author: Elements of Forestry; The Book of Forestry. Died Sept. 3, 1929.

MOON, John Austin, congressman; b. Albemarle County, Va., Apr. 22, 1855; ed. Acad. Bristol, Va., and King Coll., Bristol, Tenn.; m. Addie M., d. late Chief Justice James W. Deaderick, of Tenn., Oct. 8, 1884. Admitted to bar, 1874; Dem. nominee for Gen. Assembly, 1880; city atty. Chattanooga, 1881, 1882; mem. Dem. State Com., 1888; judge Circuit Ct., 1889-97; mem. 55th to 66th Congresses (1897-1921), 3d Tenn. Dist.; del.-at-large Dem. Nat. Conv., 1900. Home: Chattanooga, Tenn. Died June 26, 1921.

MOON, Parker Thomas, univ. prof.; b. N.Y. City, June 5, 1892; s. Alfred Goodrich and Mary Esther (Parker) M.; B.S., Columbia, 1913, Ph.D., 1921; m. Edith Conway, Sept. 3, 1921; 1 dau., Alice. William Mitchell fellow, Columbia, 1913-14. Gilder fellow, 1914-15; instr. history, 1915-17, 1919-21, asst. prof., 1921-25, asst. prof. internat. relations, 1925-26, asso. prof., Columbia, 1926-31, prof., 1931—. Mng. editor Polit. Science Quarterly, 1921-28, editor, 1928—. Served on Col. House Commn. of Inquiry, 1917-18; mem. staff Am. Commn. to Negotiate Peace, 1918-19; sec. (internat.) Com. on Territorial Problems, Peace Conf., 1919; mem. nat. com. Pan-Am. Inst. Geography and History, 1935. Catholic. Author: A Syllabus of Imperialism and World Politics, 1919; The Labor Problem and the Social Catholic Movement in France, 1921; A Syllabus on International Relations, 1925; Imperialism and World Politics 1926. Co-author: Modern History, 1923; Ancient and Medieval History, 1929; Ancient, 1929; The United States and the Caribbean, 1929; World History; 1932. Home: New York, N.Y. Died June 11, 1936.

MOONEY, Charles A., congressman; b. St. Marys, Ohio, Jan. 5, 1879; s. Michael J. and Catherine (Salmon) M.; grad. high sch., St. Marys; m. Isabelle MacMahon, Jan. 21, 1903; children—Charles A., Isabelle, William D. Began as clk., 1903, in office of father, general mgr. for Ohio of Mich. Mut. Life Ins. Co.; continued with same co. as district at Cleveland, O., 1909-13. State agt. National Life Ins. Co., Cleveland. Mem. Ohio State Senate, 1915-17. Mem. 66th and 68th to 71st Congresses (1919-21 and 1923-31), 20th Ohio Dist. Democrat. Roman Catholic. Home: Cleveland, O. Died May 29, 1931.

MOONEY, Charles Patrick Joseph, editor; b. Bardstown Junction, Ky., Sept. 15, 1865; s. John Francis and Hannah (Spraggins) M.; B.S. and A.B., A.M., St. Mary's Coll., Ky., 1886; LL.D., Southwestern U., 1923; m. Corinne G'Sell O'Connor, June 6, 1891. Learned telegraphy at 14; taught sch. in Ky. 2 yrs.; editor weekly newspaper, Ark., 2 yrs.; reporter, Avalanche, Memphis, 1890; city editor Scimitar, 1891-96; mng. editor Commercial Appeal, 1896-1902, New York Daily News, 1902-03; mng. editor and editorial writer, New York American, 1903-05; mng. editor Chicago Examiner, 1905-08; mng. editor Comm. Appeal, 1908—; pres. Commercial Pub. Co. V.p. Associated Press, 1924-25. Del. Dem. Nat. Conv., Baltimore, 1912. Dir. St. Louis Federal Reserve Bank. Trustee U. of Tenn., William B. Moore Sch. of Tech.; dir. Red Cross. Catholic. Home: Memphis, Tenn. Died Nov. 22, 1926.

MOONEY, Daniel Francis, diplomat; b. St. Marys, O., Jan. 16, 1865; grad. St. Marys High Sch., 1882; LL.B., Ohio State U., 1894. Received appmt. to U.S. Mil. Acad. but did not enter; city solicitor, St. Marys, 1896-1900; mem. Ohio Senate, 1908-10, 1912-13; E.E. and M.P. to Paraguay, 1914—. Died Nov. 14, 1930.

MOONEY, Edmund L., lawyer; b. June 25, 1865; LL.B., New York U., 1886. In practice in New York, 1886. Died Oct. 15, 1933.

MOONEY, James, ethnologist; b. Richmond, Ind., Feb. 10, 1861; s. James and Ellen (Devlin) M.; ed. pub. schs.; entered office daily newspaper, 1879, learning trade; had already begun Indian studies which became life work; m. Ione Lee Gaut, 1897. Removed to Washington, 1885, and became mem. of Bur. of Am. Ethnology. For yrs. conducted extended field investigations among the Southern and Western Indian tribes, particularly the Cherokee and tribes of the Great Plains; prepared govt. Indian exhibits for Chicago, Nashville, Omaha and St. Louis expositions. Author: (monographs) Funeral Customs of Ireland; Holiday Customs of Ireland; Sacred Formulas of the Cherokee; Siouan Tribes of the East; The Messiah Religion and the Ghost Dance; Calendar History of the Kiowa Indians; Myths of the Cherokee; Indian Articles, New International and Catholic encyclopedias. Died Dec. 22, 1921.

MOONEY, Joseph F., clergyman; b. Pike County, Pa., July 8, 1848; s. Patrick and Mary (Winter) M.; grad. St. John's Coll., Fordham, N.Y.; Ph.D., Mt. St. Mary's, Md.; LL.D., Fordham and Notre Dame U., Ind. Ordained R.C. priesthood, June 3, 1871; pastor St. Patrick's, Newburgh, N.Y.; prof. philosophy, St. Joseph's Sem., Troy, N.Y., vicar gen., July 8, 1892; domestic prelate of the Holy See, June 3, 1896; rector Church of the Sacred Heart, New York, Jan. 29, 1890; prothonotary apostolic, Mar. 10, 1904; pres. New Rochelle College. Home: New Rochelle, N.Y. Died May 13, 1923.

MOONEY, Robert Johnstone, advertising; b. Steubenville, O.; s. William Henry and Amanda Wiley (Crawford) M.; prep. edn., high sch. (Steubenville), Mt. Pleasant Mil. Acad. (Ossining, N.Y.), Duff's Business Coll. (Pittsburgh); studied Gymnasium, Weimar, Germany, and U. of Berlin; M.A. and Ph.D., Heidelberg U.; full course New York Law Sch.; unmarried. Formerly mem. editorial staff N.Y. Tribune; asso. pub. and part owner Chicago Inter-Ocean, 1907; v.p. Mahin Advertising Co., 1914-15, William H. Rankin Advertising Co., 1915-19; pres. Conover-Mooney Adv. Co., 1919-29; v.p. Kirtland-Engel Co. Republican. Presbyn. Author of How to be Healthy, Trim and Strong. Home: Chicago, Ill. Died July 10, 1937.

MOONEY, Urban Drening, clergyman; b. Mobile, Ala., Feb. 17, 1878; s. Rev. John Drening and Margaret (Hamilton) M.; A.B., Southwestern Coll., Clarksville (now Memphis), Tenn., 1896, grad. Clarksville Theol. Sem., 1899; D.D., Ala. Presbyn. Coll., 1911; m. Floy Cecil, Sept. 9, 1902; children—Urban D., Floy Cecil, Margaret C. Ordained ministry Presbyn. Ch. in U.S., 1899; pastor Second Ch., Birmingham, Ala., 1899-1913, Napoleon Av. Ch., New Orleans, 1913-30; dir. Christian and social welfare work among colored people, 1930—, under auspices of Presbyn. Ch. in U.S. Chmn. Home Missions Bd., Presbytery of New Orleans; mem. Presbyn. Foundation and Advisory Com. on Edn., same denom. Chmn. La. Inter-Racial Commn. Mem. Welfare Bd., New Orleans, World War. Home: New Orleans, La. Deceased.

MOONLIGHT, Thomas, governor Wyo.; b. Forfarshire, Scotland, Nov. 10, 1833; emigrated to U.S., 1856; was farmer and later worked in glass factory; served private to col. and bvt. brig. gen. through Civil war; later sec. of State of Kan.; member Kan. senate 1873-74; adj. gen. Kan., 1883-84; nominated for gov., 1886, but defeated; gov. Wyo., 1888-90; U.S. minister to Bolivia, 1894-97; Democrat. Died 1899.

MOORE, Addison Webster, college prof.; b. Plainfield, Ind., July 30, 1866; s. John Sheldon and Adaline (Hockett) M.; A.B., DePauw U., Greencastle, Ind., 1890, A.M., 1893; Cornell, 1893-94; Ph.D., U. of Chicago, 1898; m. Ella E. Adams, Sept. 1, 1891 (died 1924); 1 dau., Catherine Adams. Asst. in philosophy, 1895-97, asso., 1897-98, instr., 1898-1902, asst. prof., 1902-04, asso., prof., 1904-09, prof., 1909—, U. of Chicago. Lecturer on philosophy, Harvard, 1918. Author: Pragmatism and Its Critics, 1910; Existence, Meaning and Reality. Asso. Author: Studies in Logical Theory, 1903; Creative Intelligence, 1916. Died Aug. 25, 1930.

MOORE, Alexander Pollock, editor; b. Pittsburgh, Nov. 10, 1867; s. George K. and Ann J. (Phillips) M.; Carry U., Pittsburgh, 1877-81; m. Lillian Russell, June 12, 1912 (died 1921). Newspaper business, 1878—, as reporter, city editor, mng. editor and pub.; was part owner Pittsburgh Telegraph, and Pittsburgh Chronicle-Telegraph, mng. editor Pittsburgh Press; editor-in-chief Pittsburgh Leader, 1904—; pres. Leader Pub. Co.; purchased New York Daily Mirror and Boston Advertiser, 1928. A.E. and P. to Spain, 1923-25; A.E. and P. to Peru, 1928—. Republican. Mem. M.P. Ch. Mason. Died Feb. 17, 1930.

MOORE, Alfred Stibbs, judge; b. Beaver, Pa., Sept. 13, 1846; s. Alfred R. and Jane (Small) M.; A.B., Washington and Jefferson Coll., 1867, A.M., 1870; m. Celia J. Richardson, Oct. 18, 1883; m. 2d, Florinda M. Knox, July 21, 1902. Admitted to bar, 1871; practiced at Tidioute, Pa., 1872, Butler, Pa., 1873-75, Beaver, Pa., 1876-1902; dist. atty., Beaver County, Pa., 1881-84; U.S. dist. judge, 2d Div., Dist. of Alaska, 1902-10; resumed law practice, Beaver, Pa., Dec. 1910. Mem. M.E. Ch. Died Jan. 18, 1920.

MOORE, Alice Medora Rogers, author; b. Quincy, Ill.; d. Hon. William Timothy and Catherine Wilhelmina (Murray) Rogers; grad. Quincy High Sch., 1877; spl. studies Radcliffe Coll., 1893-97; Boston U. Law Sch., 2 yrs.; m. Dr. Fred Porter Moore, Jan. 6, 1880 (died 1889); children—Arthur William (dec.), Fred Porter, Katherine Elizabeth (dec.), Oliver Timothy (dec.). Spl. writer various mags. and newspapers; editor woman's page, Cambridge (Mass.) Press, 1898. Lecturer on radiation theory of light and color. Fellow Royal Soc. Arts, London; was pres. Boston Ruskin Club, etc. Author: Tom Blivens in Wormdom, 1890; In the Fireflies' Glow, 1901; The Radiation Theory of Light and Color, 1911; Color and Image in the Eye, 1911. Traveled extensively in America, Europe and the Orient. Home: Watertown, Mass. Deceased.

MOORE, Andrew Charles, biologist; b. Spartanburg County, S.C., Dec. 27, 1866; s. Thomas John and Mary Elizabeth (Anderson) M.; A.B., S.C. Coll. (now U. of S.C.), 1887; grad. student, U. of Chicago, 1898-99, fellow, 1899-1900; studied, Marine Biol. Lab., Woods Hole, Mass., summers, 1901-03; m. Vivian May, Sept. 20, 1900. Supt. city schs., Spartanburg, S.C., 1888, Camden, S.C., 1888-90; prin. City High Sch., Birmingham, Ala., 1890-98; asso. prof. biology, geology and mineralogy, 1900-03, prof. biology, 1903—, chmn. faculty, 1907-08, acting pres., 1908-09, and 1913-14, dean, 1909-13, U. of S.C. Mem. Bd. of Sch. Commrs., Columbia, S.C., 1902—(chmn. 1906—). Democrat. Presbyn. (elder). Home: Columbia, S.C. Deceased.

MOORE, Aubertine Woodward (Auber Forestier), musician, author; b. Montgomery County, Pa., Sept. 27, 1841; d. Joseph Janvier and Elizabeth Graham (Cox) Woodward; ed. in Phila. pvt. schs. and tutors; m. Samuel H. Moore, Dec. 22, 1887. One of the earliest in the field of Scandinavian music in America; pioneer of musical lecture recitals, having given illustrated talks on music and musicians in many cities, 1880—; writer and lecturer on origin and evolution of the Niblung story; conductor of classes in history and theory of music; musical and lit. critic, Wisconsin State Journal, 1900-11; conducted classes in history of music, musical appreciation and analysis, Madison Musical Coll., 1909-12; editor dept. music and musicians, Simmons Mag., Mar. 1910-12. Translator: The Spellbound Fiddler, by Kristofer Janson, 1880; Voice Culture, by Theo. Hauptner, 1886; (asst.) Norway Music Album, 1881; Songs From the North, 1907; etc.; also many song words. Author: Echoes From Mist-Land, 1877; For My Musical Friend, 1900; For Every Music Lover, 1902; Faustina—A Venetian Queen of Song; Grandfather's Strad. Home: Madison, Wis. Died Sept. 23, 1929.

MOORE, Bertha Pearl, author; b. Memel (then Germany), Sept. 14, 1894; d. Benjamin and Helen (Heymann) Pearl; came with parents to the U.S. at age of 3; ed pub. and high schs. of N.Y. City; student Columbia (non-grad.); m. Blaine F. Moore, Ph.D., Dec. 20, 1922. Formerly social worker with University Settlement House, N.Y. City, and teacher in pub. and pvt. schs. Mem. League of American Pen Women. Author: Sarah and Her Daughter, 1920; The Love Child, 1923. Home: Washington, D.C. Died May 1, 1925.

MOORE, Blaine Free, political scientist; b. Republic, O., Aug. 6, 1879; s. B. Franklin and Martha (Free) M.; A.B., U. of Kan., 1901; fellow in political science, U. of Ill., 1907-08, A.M., 1908; George William Curtis fellow, Columbia, 1908-09, Ph.D., 1912; m. Bertha Pearl, Dec. 22, 1923 (died May 1, 1925); m. 2d, Dr. Mary Meek Atkeson, Mar. 25, 1929. Was successively teacher, principal Provincial High Sch., supt. in charge Province of Zambales, Philippine Islands, also mem. Junta Provincial and Provincial Service Bd., 1901-06; instr. in govt., U. of Mich., 1909-10; asst. prof. polit. science, George Washington U., 1910-13; lecturer U. of Wis., 1913-14; spl. expert U.S. Commn. on Industrial Relations, 1914-15; prof. polit. science and chmn. dept. polit. science, U. of Kan., 1915-21; spl. expert U.S. War Trade Bd., 1918-19; prof. polit. science, American Univ., Washington, D.C., 1921; asst. mgr. finance dept. U.S. Chamber Commerce, 1922—. Author: Cumulative Voting in Illinois, 1909; The Supreme Court and Unconstitutional Legislation, 1913; Commerce and Industry of the Netherlands, 1919; Foreign Trade of Japan, 1922. Home: Washington, D.C. Died June 15, 1941.

MOORE, Burton Evans, physicist; b. Westerville, O., Apr. 8, 1866; s. Royal and Rachel (Evans) M.; A.B., Otterbein U., Westerville, 1888; A.M., Cornell, 1890; student, univs. of Strassburg and Berlin, 1893-94; Ph.D., U. of Göttingen, 1907; m. Harriette Clemens, Sept. 1, 1897 (died 1909); m. 2d, Hanna Eberle, Dec. 16, 1911. Instr. physics, Lehigh U., Pa., 1891-92, U. of Ill., 1895-96; instr. physics, 1896-1902, asst. prof., 1902-06, prof., 1906—, U. of Neb. Made research in excitation stages in Open Arc Spectra. Home: Lincoln, Neb. Died July 15, 1925.

MOORE, C. Ellis, lawyer; b. Middlebourne, O., Jan. 3, 1884; s. Lycurgus Passmore and Kate (Cunningham) M.; B.Sc., with honors, Muskingum Coll., 1907; LL.B., Ohio State U., 1910 (twice selected as mem. univ. debating teams); m. Nannie B. Hammond, June 30, 1910; children—Charles Lycurgus, Martha Christine. Began law practice, Cambridge, 1910; elected pros. atty. Guernsey County, 1914, reëlected, 1916; mem. 66th to 72d Congresses (1919-33), 15th Ohio Dist. Pres. Central Nat. Bank. Dir. Chamber Commerce. Republican. Elder U.P. Ch. Trustee Muskingum Coll. Home: Cambridge, O. Died Apr. 2, 1941.

MOORE, Charles Arthur; b. West Sparta, N.Y.; s. William Ropes and Caroline M. (Van Ness) M.; ed. at Rochester, N.Y., and Lynn, Mass.; m. Mary Campbell. Pres. and dir. Manning, Maxwell & Moore, Inc., ry. and machinists' tools; dir. Am. Bank Note Co., Continental Ins. Co., Nat. Mchy. Co. Chevalier Legion of Honor, France. Pres. Am. Protective Tariff League, 1900-10; v.p., trustee St. John's Guild. Home: Greenwich, Conn. Died Dec. 6, 1914.

MOORE, Charles Brainard Taylor, officer U.S.N.; b. Paris, Ill., July 29, 1853. Apptd. from Ill., and grad. U.S. Naval Acad., 1873; midshipman, May 31, 1873; ensign, July 16, 1874; promoted through grades to rear admiral, June 14, 1911. Served on Alaska and Shenandoah, 1873-74, Pensacola, 1874-75, Passaic, 1876, Alliance, Monongahela and Wyoming, 1877, Essex, 1877-79, Franklin, 1880-81, Onward, 1881-83, Galena, 1883-85; Navy Yard, Boston, 1885-86; Alert, 1887-90; Naval Acad., 1890-93; Newark, 1893-96; Naval Acad., 1896-97; naval sta., Port Royal, 1897-98; comd. Nantucket, 1898; exec. officer Alexander, 1898, Bennington, 1898-1900, Monterey, 1900-01; comd. Brutus, 1901; Navy Yard, Mare Island, 1901-04; naval gov. of Tutuila, Samoa, commandant of naval sta., and comdg. station ship, 1904-08; Navy Yard, Phila., 1908; comdg. Colorado, 1909; Naval War Coll., and Examining and Retiring bds., 1910; comdt. Naval Training Stas., San Francisco, 1911. Olongapo and Cavite, P.I., 1912, Hawaii, 1913; retired, July 29, 1915. Mem. exec. com. State Council Defense, for Macon Co., Ill., 1917-18; chmn. "Four-Minute Men," Decatur, Ill. Also mem. exec. council "Four-Minute Men" of Ill., 1917-18. Del. Ill. Constl. Conv., 1920—. Home: Decatur, Ill. Died Apr. 4, 1923.

MOORE, Charles Cadwell, engineer; b. Alpine, N.Y., July 12, 1868; s. Lewis William and Mary Beaks (Harding) M.; grad. St. Augustine Coll. (now defunct), Benicia, Calif., 1884; m. Lillian M. Breed, Nov. 15, 1893. In employ San Francisco Tool Co., 1885-95; succeeded to the business as Charles C. Moore & Co., engineers, which was inc. 1902 as Charles C. Moore & Co., Engineers, Inc., specializing in motive power and hydraulic work, of which pres.; chmn. board C. C. Moore & Co., Engineers, Inc.; pres. Sylmar Packing Corp.; dir. Anglo & London Paris Nat. Bank, Anglo Calif. Trust Co., Anglo-National Corp., North American Investment Co., Occidental Insurance Co., West Coast Life Ins. Co., Ocean Shore Ry. Co. Commr. to Europe to secure foreign warships for Portola Celebration, San Francisco, 1906 (secured 7 ships); pres. Chamber of Commerce, San Francisco, 1908-09 (elected hon. mem. 1909); chmn. exec. com. Citizens' Health Com. for eradication of bubonic plague through extermination of rats, 1908; chmn. financial com. P.P.I. Expn., 1910-11; elected pres. P.P.I. Expn., 1911; dir. foreign land div. Liberty Loan Com. 12th Federal Reserve Dist., 1918; dir. State Council of Defense, May-Nov. 1918. Decorated 2d Class Order of Chia Ho (China), 1st Class, Order of Sacred Treasure (Japan), Knight of Order of Crown (Italy), Order of St. Olaf (Norway); Grand Commander Order of George I (Greece); Commander of the Legion of Honor (France). V.p. Boy Scouts America; pres. Soc. of Calif. Pioneers. Republican. Home: San Francisco, Calif. Died Apr. 17, 1932.

MOORE, Charles Herbert, prof. of art; b. New York, Apr. 10, 1840; s. Charles and Jane Maria (Benson) M.; ed. pub. schs. of New York; hon. A.M., Harvard, 1890; m. Mary Jane Tomlinson, July 19, 1865; m. 2d, Elizabeth Fisk Hewins, Dec. 30, 1881. Instr. freehand drawing and water color, 1871-79, drawing and principles of design, 1879-91, asst. prof. design in the fine arts, 1891-96, prof. art, 1896-1909, curator William Hayes Fogg Art Mus., 1895-96, dir., 1896-1909, Harvard; resigned Sept. 1, 1909; emeritus prof. art, 1911. Hon. asso. A.I.A., Royal Inst. Brit. Architects. Author: The Development and Character of Gothic Architecture, 1899; Examples for Elementary Practice in Delineation; Character of Renaissance Architecture, 1905; Mediæval Church Architecture of England, 1912; Swedenborg: Servant of God, 1918. Died Feb. 15, 1930.

MOORE, Charles Leonard, author; b. Phila., Mar. 16, 1854; s. Joseph and Mary Elizabeth M.; ed. Phila. pub. schs.; unmarried. U.S. consular agt. at San Antonio, Brazil, 1878-79. Author: Atlas, 1881; Poems Antique and Modern, 1883; Book of Day Dreams, 1887; Banquet of Palacios, 1889; Odes, 1896; Ghost of Rosalys, 1900; The Red Branch Crests—a Trilogy, 1904; Incense and Iconoclasm, 1915; Idols and Ideals, 1919. Home: New York, N.Y. Deceased.

MOORE C(harles) Ulysses, pediatrist; b. Alden, Ia., Jan. 1, 1877; s. Henry Vrooman and Sarah Eugenia (Balcom) M.; M.Di., Ia. State Teachers' Coll., 1901; B.A., U. of Tex., 1906; student U. of Colo. Sch. of Medicine, 1906-07; M.D., U. of Minn., 1910, M.S. in Pediatrics, 1916; studied Harvard, 1915; m. Nettie B. Rosenberry, Sept. 11, 1907; children—Mary Katherine (adopted), Charles Balcom. Practiced, Carthage, S.Dak., 1910-14; located at Portland, Ore., 1916; instr. pediatrics, U. of Ore. Med. Sch., 1919-23; pediatrist Multnomah County Hosp., Crittenden-Wemme Home; lecturer on nutrition, Utah Agrl. Coll., summers, 1923, 24; dir. Nutritional Research Lab., U. of Ore. Med. Sch. Capt. Children's Bur., Am. Red Cross, World War; in Italy 6 mos., France 10 mos.; capt. M.R.C. Mem. bd. dirs. Ore. League for Conservation of Pub. Health; mem. governing com. Gorgas Memorial Inst. for Ore.; organizer Ore. Infant Welfare Soc. and started its clinics, 1920. Fellow Am. Coll. Physicians, A.M.A. Republican. Mem. bd. First M.E. Ch. Author: Nutrition of Mother and Child, 1923, 4th edit., 1935; also numerous articles on rickets, breast feeding, beriberi, pyloric obstruction and vitamin research. Mem. bd. dirs. Portland Federal Savings & Loan Assn. Home: Portland, Ore. Deceased.

MOORE, Clarence Bloomfield, archæologist; b. Phila., Jan. 14, 1852; s. Bloomfield H. and Clara S. (Jessup) M.; A.B., Harvard, 1873; unmarried. Traveled in nearly every part of Europe, in Egypt, Syria, Asia Minor, Greece, Turkey, U.S.; made journey across the Andes and down the Amazon, 1876; around the world, 1878-79; for past 20 yrs. exploring Indian mounds, S.C., Ga., Fla., Ala., Ark., Miss., and La. Author many papers published by Acad. Natural Sciences, Phila. Home: Philadelphia, Pa. Deceased.

MOORE, Clarence Lemuel Elisha, mathematician; b. nr. Bainbridge, O., May 12, 1876; s. George Taylor and Lydia Ann (Bradshaw) M.; B.Sc., Ohio State U., 1901; A.M., Cornell U., 1902, Ph.D., 1904; studied univs. of Göttingen, Turin and Bonn; m. Belle Pease Fuller, June 11, 1913; 1 dau., Hazel Fuller. Asst. in mathematics, Ohio State U., 1900-01, scholar in mathematics, 1901-02, fellow, 1902-03, asst., 1903-04, Cornell U.; instr. mathematics, 1904, asst. prof., 1909, asso. prof., 1916, prof., 1920—, Mass. Inst. Tech. Fellow Am. Acad. Arts and Sciences. Democrat. Contbr. to Am. Jour Mathematics, Annals of Mathematics, Proc. Am. Acad. Home: Newton, Mass. Died Dec. 5, 1931.

MOORE, Clifford Herschel, univ. prof.; b. Sudbury, Mass., Mar. 11, 1866; s. John Herschel and Julia Ann (McCullough) M.; A.B., Harvard, 1889; Ph.D., U. of Munich, 1897; Litt.D., Colorado Coll., 1914; m. Lorena Leadbetter, July 23, 1890. Prof. Greek, Phillips Acad., Andover, Mass., 1892-94; instr., 1894-95, asst. prof. Latin, 1895-98, U. of Chicago; asst. prof. Greek and Latin, 1898-1905, prof. Latin, 1905—, Pope professor of Latin, 1925—, dean faculty arts and sciences, 1925—, Harvard. Prof. Latin, Am. Sch. Classical Studies, Rome, 1905-06. Trustee Phillips Acad., 1902—, Charity of Edward Hopkins. Fellow Am. Acad. Arts and Sciences. Editor: Allen's Medea, 1899; Horace's Odes and Epodes, 1902. Author: Religious Thought of the Greeks, 1916, 2d edit., 1925; Pagan Ideas of Immortality, 1918. Home: Cambridge, Mass. Died Aug. 31, 1931.

MOORE, Daniel Decatur, journalist; b. Moscow, Tex., Sept. 19, 1869; s. John Washington and Martha Jane (Rowe) M.; 1st wife dec.; children—Martha Grace, Sylvia D.; m. 2d, Louise M. Séguin, May 16, 1908; children—Daniel S., Andre Brown, Lalise. Began editorial work at St. Joseph, Mo.; with Times-Picayune, New Orleans, 1895-1923 (editor and gen. mgr., 1910-23); pub. Ft. Worth Record, 1923-25; librarian New Orleans Pub. Library, 1928-32; U.S. collector internal revenue, 1933-34; retired. Vice pres. Associated Press, 1915-16; mem. bd. dirs. Associated Press and Am. Newspaper Pubs. Assn. several years. Episcopalian. Home: New Orleans, La. Died Dec. 19, 1938.

MOORE, D(aniel) McFarlan, electrical engr.; b. Northumberland, Pa., Feb. 27, 1869; s. Rev. Alexander Davis and Maria Louisa (Douglas) M.; Lehigh U., 1886-89; m. Mary Alice Elliott, June 5, 1895. With Edison Co., 1890-94; organizer and v.p. Moore Light Co., and Moore Elec. Co. and gen. mgr. both cos. for 18 yrs.; a pioneer in commercializing luminous and non-luminous gaseous conduction; sold Moore Light interests to Gen. Electric Co., 1912. Granted over 100 U.S. patents on elec. and other inventions, many of them among the earliest in radio, X-ray and tube-lighting fields. Fellow Am. Inst. Elec. Engrs. Republican. Presbyterian. Invented gaseous conduction lamps, 1924, that made facsimile photographs by radio reception; and produced lamps, 1925, that were the first to receive motion by radio; made greatly improved television, 1929, and facsimile lamps that were used exclusively for the most advanced demonstrations at expositions in large cities. Author of many published scientific papers read before univs., colls. and scientific socs. Formerly mgr. Moore Light Dept., Gen. Electric Co.; retired, but was active in writing, speaking, inventing the Pianochord, etc. Died June 15, 1936.

MOORE, David Hastings, bishop; b. Athens, O., Sept. 4, 1838; s. Hon. Eliakim Hastings and Amy (Barker) M.; A.B., Ohio U., 1860, A.M., 1863; D.D., Ohio Wesleyan, 1875; LL.D., Mt. Union Coll., 1896, U. of Denver, 1899; m. Julia Sophia Carpenter, June 21, 1860; son, Eliakim Hastings. Ordained M.E. ministry, 1860. Served in Civil War; pvt. and capt. Co. A, 87th Ohio Inf., and maj. and lt. col., 125th Ohio Inf. in Civil War. Pastor at Columbus, Cincinnati, etc.; pres. Cincinnati Wesleyan Coll., 1875-80; pres. Colo. Sem., and chancellor U. of Denver, 1880-89; prof. polit. economy, U. of Colo., 1889; editor Western Christian Advocate, 1889-1900; elected bishop, 1900. Stationed at Shanghai, China, with spl. jurisdiction over M.E. missions in China, Japan and Korea, 1900-04; stationed at Portland, Ore., 1904-08, at Cincinnati, 1908-12, retired 1912. Home: Indianapolis, Ind. Died Nov. 23, 1915.

MOORE, Dunlop, clergyman; b. Lurgan, County Armagh, Ireland, July 25, 1830; s. Dunlop and Margaret (Kerr) M.; studied at Edinburgh and Belfast; grad. 1854 (D.D.); m. Miss R. A. Louis, Hamburg, Germany, Aug. 20, 1870. Missionary of Irish Presbyn. Ch. to Gujurat, India, 1855-67; to Jews in Vienna, 1869-74; in 1875 became pastor Presbyn. Ch., New Brighton, Pa.; for some yrs. engaged in evangelistic work and in furnishing articles to religious weekly journals and quarterly reviews. Assisted in translating Bible into Gujurati tongue; in same language wrote treatises on Jainism and Mohammedanism. Edited The Gynandipaka in same language, while in India, etc. Contributed to Schaff-Lange Commentary and to Schaff-Herzog Encyclopædia. Died 1905.

MOORE, Edmond H., lawyer; b. Milton, O., Oct. 16, 1862; s. Alexander F. and Elizabeth M.; ed. high sch., Youngstown, O. Began practice at Youngstown, 1891; now mem. Moore, Barnum & Hammond; mayor of Youngstown, 1896-1900; state supt. ins. of Ohio, 1911-14; mem. Dem. Nat. Com., Ohio, 1912-20, resigned. K.P., Elk. Home: Youngstown, O. Died Dec. 6, 1925.

MOORE, Edward Bruce, U.S. commissioner of patents; b. N. Anson, Me., Dec. 25, 1851; s. William and Almeda (Wyman) M.; ed. high sch. and pvt. tutors; unmarried. Page U.S. Senate, 1866-67; admitted to bar, 1881; asst. examiner U.S. Patent Office, 1883, law clerk, 1898, prin. examiner, 1899-1901, asst. commr., 1901-07, commr. of patents, 1907-13; mem. patent law firm Moore & Clarke, Washington. U.S. spl. commr. Paris Expn., 1900; U.S. del. Internat. Patent Congress, Stockholm, 1908, and in same year successfully negotiated with the German Govt. the treaty relating to the nonworking of patents in Germany by Am. inventors and mfrs.; as spl. diplomatic rep. to arrange convs. relating to patents with Denmark, Sweden, Norway, Russia, Austria, Italy, France, Spain and Belgium, 1909; commd. as spl. expert attaché to Am. delegation to 4th Internat. Congress of Am. States, Buenos Aires, and prepared convs. relating to patents, trade-marks and copyrights which were adopted by that Congress, 1910; apptd. chmn. Am. delegation to Conf. of Internat. Union for protection of Industrial Property, Washington, 1911, 40 nations being represented. Home: Washington, D.C. Died Sept. 7, 1915.

MOORE, Edward Colman, music editor; b. Fond du Lac, Wis., Jan. 22, 1877; s. Alfred Louis and Sarah Louise (Colman) M.; prep. edn., high schs., and St. John's Mil. Acad., Delafield, Wis.; B.A., Yale, 1899; LL.B., Northwestern U., 1902; m. Hazel Humble, Oct. 28, 1911. Began newspaper work as music critic, Chicago Daily Journal, 1909, continuing until 1921; same position with Chicago Tribune, 1921—. Home: Ravinia, Ill. Died Oct. 6, 1935.

MOORE, Edward Jay, anti-saloon worker; b. near Norwich, N.Y., Sept. 6, 1861; s. Rev. Samuel and Laura M.; grad. Bloomsburg (Pa.) State Normal Sch., 1882; A.B., U. of Puget Sound, 1891, D.D., 1913; studied Allegheny (Pa.) Coll., 1891-92, A.M., Ph.D., 1893; m. Lu Crippen, Jan. 20, 1884; children—Blanche L., Minnie E., George E. (dec.), Florence R. Ordained M.E. ministry, 1886; pastor nr. Seattle, Wash., 1886-90, Tacoma, 1890-94, Cleveland, O., 1894-1901; supt. Anti-Saloon League, Cincinnati Dist., 1901-06; asst. state supt. Ohio League, 1906-08; state supt. Mo. Anti-Saloon League, 1908-13; state supt. Pa. Anti-Saloon League, 1913-16; asst. gen. supt. Anti-Saloon League of America, 1916-25; state supt. Ohio Anti-Saloon League, 1925-31, sec. Ohio Dry Federation, 1931-32; retired. Admitted to Ohio bar, 1908, Mo. bar, 1911. Mem. Commn. of Anti-Saloon League to Eng. and France, 1918, spending 3 months investigating moral conditions surrounding A.E.F. Mem. Chamber of Commerce, Columbus. Died Dec. 19, 1935.

MOORE, Edward Mott, physician and surgeon; b. Rahway, N.J., July 15, 1814; family moved to Rochester, 1830; grad. med. dept., Univ. of Pa., 1838; practiced in Rochester; held various coll. chairs, notably that of surgery, Buffalo Med. Coll., 1858-83; was pres. Med. Soc., State of N.Y., and 1st pres. State bd. health. Distinguished for researches on the heart's action, greatly increasing pathol. knowledge pertaining to heart diseases. Author numerous med. papers. Was 2d pres. Nat. Surg. Assn., pres. Nat. Med. Assn., Med. Assn. State of N.Y.; pres. bd. trustees of park system of Rochester. Home: Rochester, N.Y. Died 1902.

MOORE, Edward W., capitalist; b. Canal Dover, O., July 1, 1864; s. Philip and Abby M.; common sch. edn.; m. Louise Chamberlin, Oct. 28, 1891. Began as office boy, Everett, Weddell & Co., bankers, Cleveland, 1880; clerk cashier's office, Nickel Plate R.R., 1883-88; with East End Bank, Cleveland, 1888-90; one of organizers, 1891, sec. and treas., 1891-99, v.p., 1900-01, Dime Savings & Banking Co., resigned; one of the organizers, 1901, Western Reserve Trust Co. (v.p.); pres. Lake Shore Electric Ry. Co.; dir. in numerous electric ry. cos. in and around Cleveland, Toledo and Detroit. Republican. Presbyn. Home: Cleveland, O. Died May 8, 1928.

MOORE, Edwin King, rear admiral U.S.N.; b. Georgetown, O., July 24, 1847; s. Joseph Austin and Nancy Jane (King) M.; grad. U.S. Naval Acad., 1868; m. Eva, d. Gen. James H. Carleton, U.S.A., of San Francisco, Oct. 2, 1877 (died 1921). Promoted ensign, 1869; master, 1870; lt., 1873; lt. comdr., 1894; comdr., 1899; capt., Oct. 11, 1903; rear admiral, Sept. 7, 1908. Has served in many capacities; comd. steamer, Patterson, in Alaska, 1895-97; U.S. Naval Acad., 1898; comd. Helena, Philippines, 1899-1901; Navy Yard, Boston, 1902-04; comd. flagship Chicago, Pacific Sta., 1905; mem. Naval Examining and Retiring Bds., 1906-07; comdt. Navy Yard, Portsmouth, N.H., 1908-09; retired by operation of law, July 24, 1909. Died Sept. 1, 1931.

MOORE, Eliakim Hastings, university prof.; b. Marietta, O., Jan. 26, 1862; s. David Hastings and Julia Sophia (Carpenter) M.; A.B., Yale, 1883, Ph.D., 1885; U. of Berlin, 1885-86; hon. Ph.D., U. of Göttingen, 1899; LL.D., U. of Wis., 1904; Sc.D., Yale, 1909; Math.D., Clark University, 1909; Sc.D., Univ. of Toronto, 1921; Sc.D., Northwestern U., 1927; m. Martha Morris Young, June 21, 1892; children—David Hastings (dec.), Eliakim Hastings. Tutor mathematics, Yale, 1887-89; asst. prof. mathematics, 1889-91, asso. prof., 1891-92, Northwestern U.; prof. mathematics, 1892-1931, head of dept., 1896-1931, U. of Chicago. Editor Trans. Am. Math. Soc., 1899-1907; asso. editor Proc. Nat. Acad. Sciences, 1915. Asso. fellow Am. Acad. Arts and Sciences; fellow A.A.A.S. (v.p. sect. A, 1910, pres. 1921). Home: Chicago, Ill. Died Dec. 30, 1932.

MOORE, Ella Maude, poet; b. Warren, Me., July 22, 1849; d. Samuel Emerson and Maria (Copeland) Smith; pub. sch. edn.; m. Joseph E. Moore, June 11, 1872. When a school girl composed the poem "Rock of Ages" (not the hymn); winner, 1884, among 7,000 competitors, of $500 prize from Youth's Companion for best story for girls. Author: Songs of Sunshine and Shadow, 1880. Home: Thomaston, Me. Died May 1922.

MOORE, Eva Perry; b. Rockford, Ill., July 24, 1852; d. Seely and Elizabeth (Benedict) Perry; A.B., Vassar Coll., 1873; m. Philip North Moore, Nov. 6, 1879. Corr. sec. and treas. Gen. Fedn. of Women's Clubs, 1894-1900, v.p., 1904-08, pres., 1908-12, hon. pres. 1914—. Pres. Mo. Fed. Women's Clubs, 1901-05; pres. Assn. Collegiate Alumnæ, 1903-07; mem. Superior Jury, St. Louis Expn., 1904; exec. com. of League to Enforce Peace; dir. Nat. Civic Fed. Alumnæ trustee Vassar Coll., 1902-08; pres. Visiting Nurse Assn., St. Louis, 1910-14; v.p. St. Louis Provident Assn.; chmn. Municipal Nurses' Bd. under Dept. of Pub. Welfare; mem. Com. on St. Louis Community Trust, 1915-20; pres. Nat. Council of Women, 1916-25, then hon. pres.; v.p. Internat. Council of Women. Mem. U.S. Internat. Com., Pan-Am. Scientific Congress, meeting in Lima, Peru, 1924; mem. women's com. of Council Nat. Defense, 1917-19; exec. com. League of Nations Non-Partisan Assn. Conglist. Home: St. Louis, Mo. Died Apr. 28, 1931.

MOORE, Forris Jewett, chemist; b. Pittsfield, Mass., June 9, 1867; s. Forris Jewett and Ellen S. (Wightman) M.; B.A., Amherst, 1889; Ph.D., U. of Heidelberg, Germany, 1893; m. Emma B. Tod, of Edinburgh, Scotland, Aug. 9, 1892. Lab. asst., Amherst Coll., 1889-90; instr. in chemistry, Cornell U., 1893-94; asst. in chemistry, 1894-95, instr., 1895-1902, asst. prof., 1902-10, asso. prof., 1910-12, prof. organic chemistry, 1912—, Mass. Inst. Tech. Lecturer organic chemistry, Harvard, 1910-11, 1917-18, 1918-19. Fellow Am. Acad. Arts and Sciences. Author: Outlines of Organic Chemistry, 1910; Experiments in Organic Chemistry, 1911; A History of Chemistry, 1918. Home: Cambridge, Mass. Died Nov. 20, 1926.

MOORE, Francis, brigadier gen. U.S.A.; b. in Scotland, Apr. 6, 1841. Pvt. and sergt. Co. M, 1st Colo. Cav., 1861-63; capt., 65th U.S.C.T., Dec. 29, 1863; lt. col., Feb. 18, 1865; bvtd. lt. col., Mar. 13, 1865, "for faithful and meritorious services during the war"; hon. mustered out, June 21, 1865; maj. 65th U.S.C.T., June 21, 1865; hon. mustered out, Jan. 8, 1867; 2d lt. 9th U.S. Cav., July 28, 1866; 1st lt., July 12, 1867; capt., Aug. 24, 1872; maj. 5th Cav., July 28, 1892; lt. col. 10th Cav., May 6, 1899; col. 11th Cav., Feb. 2, 1901; brig. gen., Feb. 25, 1901; retired by operation of law, Apr. 6, 1905. Died May 2, 1928.

MOORE, Frank A., judge; b. Ellsworth, Me., Nov. 5, 1844; s. Heard L. and Bathsheba (Higgins) M.; ed. pub. schs., Ellsworth, and Normal Inst., Iowa Falls, Ia.; supt. schs., Hardin County, Ia., 1872-76; admitted to bar, 1874; m. Emma Shintaffer, Apr. 15, 1866. Practiced law, St. Helens, Ore., 1877—; county judge, Columbia County, 1882-86; mem. Ore. Senate, 1888-92; asso. justice Supreme Ct. of Ore., 1892—. Republican. Grand Master of Masons, Ore., 1892-93; Grand Comdr. K.T., 1900-01. Deceased.

MOORE, Frank Lincoln, clergyman; b. Olivet, Mich., July 18, 1866; s. Merritt and Mary A. (Wright) M.; U. of Mich., 1890-91; grad. Chicago Theol. Sem., 1897, D.D. same 1920; post-grad. U. of Minn., 1898-99; m. Coral E. Leigh, July 9, 1891; children—Alice, Austin Leigh, Roger Wright. Ordained Congl. ministry, 1892; pastor Oak Park Ch., Minneapolis, Minn., 1897-99, Edgerton, Wis., 1899-1902, New London, Wis., 1902-05, 1st Ch., Cheyenne, Wyo., 1905-13; supt. Congl. Home Missionary Soc., Colo. and Utah, 1913-18; supt. Colo. Congl. Conf., 1913-18; v.p. Home Missions Council of Colo., 1916-17; advisory head Denver Congl. City Missionary Soc., 1913-18; Nat. sec. of missions Congl. Home Missionary Soc., N.Y. City, 1918-26; sec. Congl. Ch. Extension Bds., Western Div., 1926—. Chaplain Wyo. Ho. of Rep., 1911; incorporator, 1910, and 1st pres. Wyo. Children's Home Finding Soc. Mason. Home: Chicago, Ill. Died Mar. 28, 1935.

MOORE, Franklin Benjamin, educator; b. Clinton County, O., May 17, 1874; s. Ethelbert and Minnie (Arnold) M.; grad. Indianapolis Business U., 1893; m. Alice Frazee, June 25, 1896; 2 children. Began teaching in Indianapolis, 1893; pres. Rider Coll., Trenton, N.J. Republican. Mason. Died Feb. 27, 1934.

MOORE, Frederick Wightman, univ. dean; b. East Lyme, Conn., Oct. 18, 1863; s. Ezra and Juliette (Beckwith) M.; A.B., Yale, 1886, Ph.D., 1890; unmarried. Spent 2 yrs. in travel and study in Europe, including three semesters at U. of Berlin; lecturer on sociology, Wharton Sch. of Finance (U. of Pa.), 1891-92; adj. prof., 1892-1902, prof. history and economics, 1902-08, prof. history, 1908—, dean acad. faculty, 1904—, Vanderbilt U. Translator: Outlines of Sociology, by Dr. Ludwig Gumplowicz, of Austria, 1899. Home: Nashville, Tenn. Died 1911.

MOORE, G. Bedell, lumber mfr.; b. Elizabeth, N.J., 1840; s. Richard Channing and Julia (Grant) M.; acad. edn. Dickinson Sem., Williamsport, Pa.; m. Elizabeth Blasdel, Apr. 12, 1905. Engaged in lumber business, 1871—; pres. W. Tex. Bank & Trust Co. (San Antonio), Laredo (Tex.) Electric & Ry. Co., Val Verde Irrigation Co., San Felipe Irrigation & Mfg. Co. (Del Rio, Tex.), Orange (Tex.) Rice Mills Co.; dir. Phys. and Surg. Hosp., Associated Charities, San Antonio. Home: San Antonio, Tex. Died 1908.

MOORE, George Foot, theologian; b. West Chester, Pa., Oct. 15, 1851; s. William Eves (D.D., LL.D.) and Harriet Francina (Foot) M.; A.B., Yale, 1872, A.M., 1883; grad. Union Theol. Sem., 1877; D.D., Marietta Coll., 1885, Yale, 1897, Göttingen U., 1909; LL.D., Western Reserve U., 1903, Harvard, 1906; Litt.D., Yale, 1915; D.H.L., Hebrew Union Coll., Cincinnati, 1925; m. Mary S. Hanford, April 25, 1878 (died 1924); 1 son, Albert Hanford. Ordained Presbyn. ministry, 1878; pastor Putnam Ch., Zanesville, O., 1878-83; prof. Hebrew, Andover Theol. Sem., 1883-1902; preacher, 1900-03, prof. theology, 1902-04, Frothingham prof. history of religion, 1904—, Harvard. Fellow Am. Acad. Arts and Sciences (pres. 1921-24). Author: Commentary on Judges (International Critical Commentary), 1895; The Book of Judges, Translation and Notes (Polychrome Bible), 1898; The Book of Judges in Hebrew, Critical Edition, with Notes, 1900; The Literature of the Old Testament, 1913; History of Religions, Vol. I, 1913, revised edit., 1920, Vol. II, 1919; Metempsychosis, 1914; Judaism, 2 vols., 1927. Died May 16, 1931.

MOORE, George Godfrey, life insurance; b. Phila., Pa., Nov. 28, 1872; s. Thomas C. and Emma D. (Brown) M.; ed. pub. schs.; m. Georgie Mothershead, Sept. 29, 1902. In glass mfg. business with father at Findlay, O., and Camden, N.J., 1890-99; on staffs of various newspapers, 1899-1903; in life ins. business, 1903—; pres. and gen. mgr. Nat. Reserve Life Ins. Co., Topeka, 1920—; has been official of various banks. Dist. mgr. Am. Red Cross, World War. Treas. Kan. State Chamber Commerce. Republican. Baptist. Mason, Elk. Owned one of largest western pvt. collections of Am. first editions and rare books; also collector of ancient fire arms; athletic field at Washburn Coll., Topeka, named after him, "Moore's Bowl"; large farming interests; owner Georgian Court Stables of show horses; breeder of registered Herefords and Percheron horses. Home: Topeka, Kan. Died Mar. 15, 1939.

MOORE, Harrie G., merchant; b. Brighton, Ill., July 5, 1864; s. Sebastian Clark and Deborah Kates (Butler) M.; direct descendant of Abram Clark, signer Declaration of Independence; common sch. edn.; m. Pearle D. Scales, Sept. 2, 1886; 1 dau., Meda M. In employ Roodhouse (Ill.) Bank, 5 yrs.; with John Deere Plow Co., Kansas City, Mo., 18½ yrs.; sec. Racine-Sattley Co., Racine, Wis., 1½ yrs.; mgr. Big 4 Implement Co., Kansas City, Mo., 3½ yrs.; in business as wire mcht. for self, 1911-15; v.p. and gen. sales mgr. Keystone Steel & Wire Co., Peoria, Ill., 1915-25, retired. Republican. Methodist. Rotarian. Traveler and lecturer; head H. G. Moore Travel Agency; author and pub. Moore's Around the World Travel Guide. Home: Peoria, Ill. Died June 3, 1939.

MOORE, H(arry) Humphrey, artist; b. New York, 1844; s. Capt. George H. and Eliza L. (Humphrey) M.; ed. Inst. for Deaf and Mutes, Phila.; under Prof. David Bartlett, Poughkeepsie, Inst. for Deaf and Mutes, Hartford, Conn.; studied with Prof. Bail, New Haven, Conn., for perspective; oil painting under Prof. S. Waugh, Phila., and in Paris with Gérôme, Boulanger and Yvon, at École des Beaux Arts; m. Isabel de Cistue, of Sargossa, Spain, 1872. Went to Grenada, 1870, and made a number of oil sketches of the Alhambra; later at Tangier, Tetuan, and Fez, painting Moorish scenes; in New York, 1874-81, and later in San Francisco, Japan, Paris, and 9 yrs. at Nice, France; located permanently in Paris. Order Carlos III of Spain. Roman Catholic. Died Jan. 2, 1926.

MOORE, Henrietta Greer, minister; b. Newark, O.; d. Oliver Perry and Lucinda (Parsons) M.; removed in infancy to Cincinnati; ed. in schs. in Warren Co., O., and by pvt. tutors. Became a teacher; later an active worker in the woman's crusade and a lecturer in interest of temperance and woman suffrage; removed to Springfield, O., 1887; ordained minister in Universalist Ch., June 1891; pastor Dayton, O., and pres. Ohio Woman's Universalist Missionary Alliance. Temporary chmn. Ohio Prohibition State Conv., 1895; pres. largest equal suffrage club in Ohio. Died Jan. 28, 1940.

MOORE, Henry Lynn; b. Georgetown, O., Aug. 28, 1854; s. Joseph Austin and Nancy (King) M.; A.B., Dartmouth, 1877, A.M., 1880; m. Nettie Center, Dec. 25, 1879; children—Guernsey Center (dec.), Edith, Helen (dec.). Moved to Minn., 1877; was mem. Moore Bros., Brace & Co., real estate, Minneapolis; v.p. and treas. Minn. Loan & Trust Co., 1895—. Trustee Dartmouth Coll. Republican. Conglist. Home: Minneapolis, Minn. Died Dec. 1928.

MOORE, Hugh Kelsea, chemical engr.; b. Andover, Mass., Jan. 3, 1872; s. Albert Weston and Sarah Frances (Norton) M.; grad. high sch., Lynn, Mass., 1891; student Mass. Inst. Tech., 1893-96; hon. D.Sc., Univ. of Me., 1924; m. Mary Esther Tebbetts, Jan. 1, 1902; children—Mrs. Katherine Burgess Durell, Hugh Kelsea, Jr., Dorothy Esther. Began with Electro-Chem. Co. at Rumford Falls, Me., 1897; with Moore Electro-Chem. Co. and Am. Electro-Chem. Co. until 1903; with Burgess Sulphite Fibre Co. (later Brown Co.) as chief chemist and chem. engr., 1903-34. Served as mem. Chem. Engring. Com., Council of Nat. Defense, 1917-18, also mem. Div. of Chemistry Nat. Research Council, and mem. and treas. Naval Consulting Bd. of New Hampshire; mem. N.H. legislature, 1923-24; candidate at primaries for gov. of N.H., 1930. Pres. Am. Inst. Chem. Engrs., 1925-26. Congregationalist. Mason, Elk. Author: Incomplete Hydrogenation of Cotton Seed Oil, 1917; Testing of Lubricating Oils, 1917; Chemical Engineering Aspect of Renovating a Sulphite Mill, 1918; Analysis of the Explosion Process of Recovering Soda Salts from Black Liquor, 1919; Accident Prevention in the Mill, 1919; Fundamentals of Electrolytic Diaphragm Cells, 1920; The Use and Value of Physical and Chemical Constants, 1920; Scientific Facts about Pure and Impure Milk, 1921; The Production of Hydrochloride Acid by Direct Union of Hydrogen and Chlorine, 1922; Development of Taxation, 1923; Fundamental Principles of Multiple Effect Evaporative Separation, 1923. Made investigation in evaporation and separation, and in 1929, designed, built and operated a ten-effect multiple effect evaporator; made investigations in refrigeration; investigations in electrolysis, inventing and patenting the unsubmerged diaphragm cell, 1897, which revolutionized that industry; invented and patented, 1925-27, new method of making calcium arsenate; invented and patented, 1913-15, stationary furnace for recovery of soda content from black liquor; invented and patented, 1926-27, a new acid resisting hydraulic cement; invented and patented, 1932-34, a new process of converting sodium sulphate into caustic soda and other chemicals; invented and patented, 1934, new metal filter cloth and method of making same; took out about 45 other patents in U.S. with the corresponding foreign patents, relating to pulp making, pulp bleaching, evaporation, continuous process of hydrogenating oil, mfg. of sodium sulphide, refrigeration, etc. Awarded gold medal, Am. Inst. Chem. Engrs., 1920, "for best contributions to applied science since 1913"; Perkin medalist, 1925. Retired from active business 1934. Home: New Port Ritchie, Fla. Died Dec. 18, 1939.

MOORE, James Edward, surgeon; b. Clarksville, Pa., Mar. 2, 1852; s. Rev. George W. and Margaret (Ziegler) M.; Poland Union Sem., Poland, O., U. of Mich.; M.D., Bellevue Hosp. Med. Coll. (New York U.), 1873; post-grad. study, New York, 3 yrs.; Germany, France, Eng., 1885-87; m. Louie C. Irving, Feb. 1887. Practiced medicine, Ft. Wayne, Ind., 1873-74, Emelenton, Pa., 1876-82, Minneapolis, 1882—. Specialist in surgery, 1888—; first specialist in surgery exclusively, west of New York; surgeon-in-chief of Northwestern Hosp., 1897—; prof. surgery, 1904—, chief dept. of surgery, 1908—, U. of Minn. Fellow Am. Surg. Assn. (v.p. 1905), Am. Coll. Surgeons (gov.). Author: Moore's Orthopedic Surgery, 1898; General Principles of Surgical Treatment (Am. Practice of Surgery, Bryant & Buck, 1906). Home: Minneapolis, Minn. Deceased.

MOORE, James Hobart, lawyer; b. Berkshire, N.Y., June 14, 1852; s. Nathaniel F. and Rachel A. (Beckwith) M.; acad. edn.; m. Lora Josephine Small, Apr. 26, 1883. Bank clerk, Binghamton, N.Y., 1871-73; located in Chicago, 1873; admitted to Ill. bar, 1881. With his brother, William H., formed the 4 great corps. known as the "Moore group," with a combined capital of $187,000,000, all later absorbed in the U.S. Steel Corp.; they also promoted the Nat. Biscuit Co. and other combinations of capital. Dir. Am. Can Co. Home: Santa Barbara, Calif. Died July 8, 1916.

MOORE, James Miles, soldier; b. Phila., Oct. 26, 1837; s. John W. and Catherine (Miles) M.; ed. grammar schs., Phila., and acad., Pottstown, Pa.; m. Annie L. Wertheim, May 29, 1877. Entered Union Army, Apr. 18, 1861, pvt. Co. G, 19th Pa. Inf.; discharged Aug. 8, 1861; apptd. 2d lt. 90th Pa. Vol. Inf., Feb. 21, 1862; 1st lt., Mar. 10, 1862; capt. a.q.m., March 11, 1863; transferred to regular army with same rank, July 2, 1864; maj. q.m., June 13, 1867; lt. col. and deputy q.m. gen., July 2, 1883; col. and asst. q.m. gen., Jan. 14, 1895; retired for age, Oct. 26, 1901; apptd. to the rank of brig. gen., Apr., 1904. died 1905.

MOORE, James W., physicist, educator; b. Easton, Pa., June 14, 1844; s. Samuel and Elizabeth Barnes (Wamsley) M.; grad. Lafayette, 1864, A.M., 1867; M.D., Univ. of Pa., 1869; m. Rachel Phillips, d. Rev. James Flannery, Phila., July 30, 1874. Prof. mechanics and experimental philosophy, Lafayette Coll. Conferee Internat. Congress of Electricians, Phila., 1884; Chicago, 1893. Author: The Elements of Natural Philosophy; and numerous works, lectures, addresses and papers on physics; also on med. subjects. Dean Pardee Sch. of Science. Home: Easton, Pa. Died 1909.

MOORE, John, R. C. bishop of St. Augustine,—consecrated May 13, 1877; b. Castletown, Delvin, County Westmeath, Ireland, June 27, 1835; went to Charleston, S.C., 1848; ed. in Collegiate Inst. there; studied classics and philosophy in France and theology in Rome; ordained priest, April 9, 1860; and received at Rome cap of Doctor of Theology. Was asst. and later pastor of Cathedral, Charleston, S.C., 1860-65; pastor St. Patrick's Ch., Charleston, 1865-77; also vicar-gen., diocese of Charleston, 1872-77. Died 1901.

MOORE, John, surgeon, brig. gen. U.S.A., retired, 1890; b. Ind., Aug. 16, 1826; entered U.S.A., asst. surgeon, June, 1853; served in Fla.; in Utah Expdn., 1857; in Cincinnati Marine Hosp., 1861-62. Promoted surgeon, June, 1862; med. dir. Central Grand Div., Army of Potomac, 1862-63; med. dir. dept. and army of the Tenn., 1863; was with Sherman at Atlanta and March to the Sea; bvtd. lt. col. and col.; asst. med. purveyor with rank of lt. col., 1883-86; surgeon gen. of army with rank of brig. gen., 1886-90. Died 1907.

MOORE, John D(enis Joseph), labor relations adviser; b. Springfield, Mass., May 15, 1874; s. John Joseph and Mary (McDonald) M.; B.S., Mass. Inst. Tech., 1895; m. Julia Frances Leader, Aug. 19, 1903; children—Mary Frances, John D. J., Richard Anthony. Began as draftsman, 1896, master mechanic Lewiston (Me.) Bleachery, 1896-98; engr. Westinghouse Elec. and Mfg. Co., and Fore River Shipbuilding Co. (Bethlehem Steel Co.) until 1903; cons. engr., New York, 1903-17; production mgr. U.S. Shipping Bd., Emergency Fleet Corp., World War; in machinery mfg., 1919-32; tech. advisor NRA and Nat. Labor Relations Bd., 1933-37; mem. N.Y. State Labor Relations Bd., 1937—. Conservation commr. State of N.Y., 1911-15; engr. mem. Bldg. Code Revision Commn., N.Y., 1908-09; drafted (Dix) plan, 1912, for state-owned hydro-electric development in N.Y. Democrat. Catholic. Home: Brooklyn, N.Y. Died Oct. 1, 1940.

MOORE, J(ohn) Howard, teacher, author; b. Linden, Mo., Dec. 4, 1862; s. William A. and Mary (Barger) M.; student Oskaloosa (Ia.) Coll., 1880-84; A.B., Univ. of Chicago, 1898; m. Jennie Darrow, 1899. Lectured in Mo., Kan., and Ia., 1890-93; teacher in Chicago high schs., 1898—. Author: Better-World Philosophy, 1899; Universal Kinship, 1906; The New Ethics, 1907; Ethics and Education, 1911; High School Ethics (book one), 1913; The Law of Biogenesis, 1914; Savage Survivals, 1915. Died June 17, 1916.

MOORE, John M., lawyer; b. in Pulaski County, Ark.; s. Israel M. and Nancy J. (Martin) M.; ed. acads. and by pvt. instr.; served in C.S.A., paroled Charlotte, N.C., 1865; m. Annie C. Turner, 1873 (died 1901). In gen. practice, Little Rock, Ark., 1871—; mem. firm Moore, Smith, Moore & Trieber. Reporter Supreme Court of Ark, 1875-79; chmn. Dem. State Central Com., 1882-90. Pres. Ark. State Bar Assn., 1909; Little Rock Bar Assn., 1910; mem. commn. on uniform state laws of Am. Bar Assn. Died Mar. 5, 1924.

MOORE, John Trotwood, author; b. Marion, Ala., Aug. 26, 1858; s. Judge John and Emily (Billingslea) M.; A.B., Howard Coll., Ala., 1878; m. Florence W. Allen, 1885 (died 1896); m. 2d, Mary Brown Daniel, 1900; children—Austin Merrill, Helen Lane and Mary Daniel (twins). Prin. Moore Acad., Monterey and Pine Apple, Ala.; apptd. by gov., capt. Co. H, Ala. N.G., 1884; moved to Columbia, Tenn., 1885; took up the rearing of blooded stock near Columbia, Tenn.; afterward began lit. work. Editor Trotwood's Monthly, 1905-06; with Robert Love Taylor, editor The Taylor-Trotwood Magazine, 1906-11. Dir. depts. libraries, archives and history, Tenn. State Library, 1919—. Mem. Tenn. Confederate Pension Bd. Commr. Nashville Gen. Hosp., 1921-23; pres. Tenn. Archæol. Soc.; pres. Meriwether Lewis Memorial Assn. Baptist. Democrat. Mason, K. of P. Author: Songs and Stories from Tennessee, 1897; "Ole Mistis," 1897; A Summer Hymnal—A Tennessee Romance, 1901; The Bishop of Cottontown, 1906; The Gift of the Grass; Uncle Wash—His Stories, 1910; The Old Cotton Gin, 1910; Jack Ballington, Forester, 1911; The Ghost Flower; Red Eagle and White (hist. novel), 1924; Tennessee—The Volunteer State (with A. P. Foster), 1924; The Human Mill, 1924; Hearts of Hickory (novel), 1926; Tom's Last Forage, 1926; Ballads of the Unafraid (verse), 1927. Home: Nashville, Tenn. Died May 10, 1929.

MOORE, John W., clergyman, educator; b. Cape Girardeau, Mo., 1861; grad. St. Vincent's Coll., Cape Girardeau, 1879; LL.D., DePaul U. Ordained R.C. priest, 1885; pastor Ch. of Immaculate Conception, Germantown, Phila.; pres. St. John's Coll., Brooklyn, N.Y., and rector Brooklyn Diocesan Sem., 1906—. Died June 3, 1925.

MOORE, John White, chief engr. U.S.N.; b. Plattsburg, N.Y., May 24, 1832; s. Amasa C. and Charlotte E. (Mooers) M.; ed. Plattsburgh Acad. and Williston Sem. and pvt. instrn., New York; m. Emily, d. Capt. Horace B. Sawyer, U.S.N., Nov. 19, 1863. Apptd. 3d asst. engr. U.S.N., May 21, 1853; promoted 2d asst. engr., June 27, 1855; 1st asst. engr., July 21, 1858; chief engr., Aug. 5, 1861; retired with rank of commodore, May 24, 1894; advanced to rank of rear admiral retired, June 29, 1906, for services during Civil War. Served in Navy Dept., 1853; on Saranac, Mediterranean Sta., 1853-56; Niagara, first Atlantic cable expdn., 1857-58, flagships Colorado and Roanoke, Home Squadron, 1858-60; flagship Richmond, Mediterranean Squadron, 1860-61; Richmond in West Indies, West Gulf Blockading Squadron and Lower Miss. River, 1861-63; engagements with rebel batteries and ram Manassas at head of passes and with rebel defenses at Pensacola, 1861; passage and capture of Fts. Jackson and St. Philip; capture of New Orleans; passage of Vicksburg batteries; Vicksburg batteries and ram Arkansas, 1862; batteries at Port Hudson; capture of Port Hudson, 1863; originator of chain cable protection on sides of wooden ships; also of "war paint" for making ships less visible in action and at night, and of fighting-tops, later universally used in war vessels; supt. of ironclads at New York and Boston, 1863-67; fleet engr. on staff of Admiral Farragut, European Squadron, 1867-68; Navy Yard, Portsmouth, N.H., 1868-72; fleet engr. of Asiatic sta., 1872-75; Navy Yard, Washington, 1876-79; Bd. of Inspection, 1879-82; fleet engr. Pacific sta., 1882-84; Navy Yard, New York, 1886-88; Navy Yard, Mare Island, 1888-93; insp. machinery at Union Iron Works, San Francisco, 1893-94; Navy Yard, New York, during the Spanish War, 1898. Home: Brooklyn, N.Y. Died Mar. 30, 1913.

MOORE, Joseph, lawyer; b. Leesville, La., Sept. 21, 1870; s. Joseph William and Eliza Bridget (Kavanaugh) M.; La. State U., 1890-92; LL.B., Tulane, 1894; m. Annie F. Reid, May 10, 1900. Began practice at Lake Charles, 1894; mem. firm Schwing & Moore until 1916; city atty., Lake Charles, 1896-97 (resigned); dist. atty., 15th Dist. of La., 1901-05 and 1909-13; U.S. atty., Western Dist. of La., 1917-21; resigned; mem. law firm Moore & Johnson, of Shreveport, La. Pvt. and corpl. Co. G, 1st La. Vols., Spanish-Am. War. Democrat. Baptist. Home: Shreveport, La. Died Jan. 26, 1923.

MOORE, Joseph Arthur, publisher; b. Stratford, Can., Jan. 5, 1879; s. Charles P. and Anna (Colloton) M.; ed. pub. schs.; m. Margaret Goodrich; children—Joseph Arthur, Mary Jane; m. 2d, Clarine Lewis. Came to U.S., 1899, naturalized citizen, 1917. Formerly v.p. F. M. Lupton, publisher, New York; v.p., gen. mgr. Hearst Gen. Mag. Co.; pres. Ridgway Co., also of Morning Telegraph, Inc. Home: New York, N.Y. Died June 19, 1937.

MOORE, Joseph B., judge; b. Commerce, Mich., Nov. 3, 1845; s. Jacob J. and Hapsabeth (Gillett) M.; student Hillsdale (Mich.) Coll., 1865-67, law dept. U. of Mich., 1868-69; A.M., Hillsdale, 1879, LL.D., 1903; m. Ella L. Bentley, Dec. 3, 1872. Admitted to bar, 1869; practiced at Lapeer, Mich., 1869-88; mayor of Lapeer, 1874-75; mem. Mich. Senate, 1878-80; judge 6th Jud. Circuit, 1888-96; justice Supreme Court of Mich., 1896-1926, now retired. Republican. Died Mar. 24, 1930.

MOORE, Julian H(awkes), judge; b. Denver, Colo., Feb. 24, 1882; s. David Hastings (bishop, M.E. Ch.) and Julia Sophia (Carpenter) M.; grad. Woodward High Sch., Cincinnati, O., 1900; student U. of Cincinnati, 1901; A.B., U. of Denver, 1905, LL.B., 1907; m. Ora Bowman, Dec. 9, 1909 (dec.); children—Marjory, Martha Lee. Admitted to Colo. bar, 1907, and began practice at Denver; examiner of titles, Torrens Land Act, 1908-11; dep. dist. atty., Denver, 1909-12; asst. atty., city and county of Denver, 1913-15; judge, Dist. Ct., Denver, 1916-28; justice, Supreme Ct., Colo., 1929—. Republican. Methodist. Home: Denver, Colo. Died June 25, 1933.

MOORE, Lillian Russell, actress, singer; see Lillian Russell.

MOORE, Louis Herbert, journalist; b. Brooklyn, N.Y., Nov. 1, 1860; s. Hazon Webster and Emily (Leathers) M.; B.A., St. Stephen's Coll., Annandale, N.Y., 1885; m. Alice Mace, Feb. 9, 1887. With United Press, New York, 1886, 87; London corr. same, later mgr. at London, 1889, 91; European mgr. United Associated Press, of New York, 1892-98; founded Am. Press Telegram Co., 1899; foreign editor and organizer service of Daily Express, London, 1900-02; resumed management of Am. Press Telegram Co., 1902, supplying British newspapers with Am. and Canadian spl. cable services and articles. Reported Armenian massacres from Constantinople; present at coronation of Czar Nicholas II, of Russia; also at funeral of Alexander III, coronation of Alfonso XIII, of Spain, and reported many other events of pub. interest. Episcopalian. Died 1918.

MOORE, Miles Conway, banker; b. Rix Mills, O., Apr. 17, 1845; s. Amos Lord and Mary (Monroe) M.; educated Bronson Inst., Point Bluff, Wis.; LL.D., Whitman College, Washington; m. Mary Elizabeth Baker, Mar. 1873 (dec.). Began at Blackfoot, Mont., 1865; mem. firm of H. E. Johnson & Co., Walla Walla, 1867-68; mem. Paine Bros. & Moore, gen. mdse. and farm implements, 1869-78; associated with D. S. Baker in ry. building and grain buying; v.p., 1889, pres., 1899—, Baker-Boyer Nat. Bank; pres. M. C. Moore & Sons, loans and investments. Mayor of Walla Walla, 1877; last gov. Wash. Ty., apptd., 1889, and served 7 mos. Mem. bd. of overseers Whitman Coll. (pres. bd. 1913—); exec. council Am. Bankers' Assn., 1909-12; pres. Wash. State Bankers' Assn. Republican. Home: Walla Walla, Wash. Died 1920.

MOORE, Mrs. N. Hudson, author; b. New York, N.Y.; d. Ward W. and Louisa (Howland) Hudson; m. Samuel P. Moore, Dec. 2, 1890; 1 son, Edmund W. Contbr. to mags. on antiques, art and nature topics. Author: Old China Book; Old Furniture Book, 1903; The Lace Book, 1904; Flower Fables and Fancies, 1904; The Collector's Manual, 1906; The Pewter Book; Deeds of Daring Done by Girls, 1906; Old Clock Book, 1911; Old Glass Book, 1924. Died Oct. 1, 1927.

MOORE, Nathaniel Drummond, corp. official; b. Negaunee, Mich., Oct. 5, 1880; s. Nathaniel Drummond and Ellen (Montague) M.; ed. pub. and pvt. schs.; m. Marguerite Hamilton, Feb. 26, 1908; 1 dau., Evelyn Natalie (wife of Dr. R. T. Haverstock). Assayer in Ida. and Brit. Columbia, 1898-99; chainman in engring. dept. The Pacific Coast Co., 1899-1901, asst. engr., chief engr., later v.p., 1901-31, v.p. and gen. mgr., 1931-39, pres., 1939—; also pres. Pacific Coast Coal Co., Pacific Coast Cement Co., Pacific Coast Railway Co., Pacific Coast R.R. Co., Pacific Coast Steamship Co., Pacific Coast Engring. Co. Mem. Federated Industries of Wash., Coal Operators Assn. of Wash., Seattle Chamber Commerce. Home: Seattle, Wash. Died May 18, 1940.

MOORE, Philip North, mining engr.; b. Ind., July 8, 1849; s. Col. Henry C. and Susan (North) M.; A.B., Miami U., 1870, A.M., 1873, LL.D., 1920; Columbia Sch. of Mines, 1870-72; m. Eva Perry, Nov. 6, 1879. Assistant Mich. Geol. Survey, 1872, Mo. Geol. Survey, 1873, Ky. Geol. Survey, 1873-77; mining engr. and metallurgist, Leadville, Colo., 1878-81; treas. and mng. dir. Slate Creek Iron Co., Bath County, Ky., 1882-89; in St. Louis, 1889—; mgr. Courey Placer Mining Co. and German Bar Mining Co., Virginia City, Mont., 1897-1900; pres. Rose Run Iron Co. of Bath County, Ky.; pres. Tecumseh Iron Co. of Ala., 1890-1908, Admiralty Zinc Co., Okla., 1915-17. Mem. Engring. Council, 1917-19, engring. div. of Nat. Research Council, 1918-19; mem. War Minerals Relief Commn., Dept. Interior, 1919-21. Pres. Am. Inst. Mining Engrs., 1917. Home: St. Louis, Mo. Died Jan. 19, 1930.

MOORE, Ransom Asa, agronomist; b. Kewaunee, Wis., June 5, 1861; s. Seth and Johanna (Werner) M.; ed. State Normal Sch., Oshkosh, Wis.; M.A., U. of Wis., 1932; m. Nettie M. Rogers, July 17, 1889. Lived on farm until 1882; teacher common and graded schs., 8 yrs.; county supt. schs., 6 yrs., resigned, 1895, to become asst. to Dean Henry, of Coll. of Agr., U. of Wis.; was given gen. charge of short course in agr., later took up breeding of grains and forage plants; emeritus agronomy. Congregationalist. Author of many bulls. and editor ann. reports Wis. Experiment Assn., 1902-29; also of agronomy sect. "Plant Production" (text-book). Home: Madison, Wis. Died Feb. 26, 1941.

MOORE, Richard Bishop, chemist; b. Cincinnati, May 6, 1871; s. William Thomas and Mary A. (Bishop) M.; went to Eng. with parents, 1878; student Argyle Coll., London, Eng., 1881-83, St. Edmund's Coll., London, 1883-85, Institut Keller, Paris, 1885-86, Univ. Coll., London, 1886-90, U. of Chicago, 1896-97, B.S., 1896; D.Sc., U. of Colo., 1916; m. Callie Pemberton, June 11, 1902; m. 2d, Georgie Elizabeth Dowell, June 18, 1924. Lived in Southport and London, Eng., 1878-95; instr. chemistry, Oswestry High Sch., Eng., 1890-91, Birkbeck Inst., London, 1891-93; asst. in chemistry, U. of Chicago, 1896; instr. chemistry, U. of Mo., 1897-1905; prof. chemistry, Butler Coll., Indianapolis, 1905-11; soil scientist, Lab. of Phys. and Chem. Investigations, Bur. of Soils, Washington, Aug. 20, 1911-Oct. 1912; phys. chemist in charge of the chemistry and metallurgy of rare metals, 1912-19, chief chemist and chief div. mineral technology, U.S. Bur. Mines, 1919-23; gen. mgr. The Door Co., engrs., New York, 1923-26; dean of science, head chem. dept., Purdue, 1926—. Made survey for U.S. Geol. Survey, of the thermal waters of the Yellowstone Nat. Park for radio-active properties, 1906; with Sir William Ramsey, London, Eng., 1907-08; in charge all helium work for U.S. Bur. Mines, 1918-23. Mem. U.S. Helium Bd., 1920-23. Author: A Laboratory Chemistry, 1904; also papers on radio-activity, inorganic physical chemistry, and rare gases. Died Jan. 20, 1931.

MOORE, Robert, civil engr.; b. New Castle, Pa., June 19, 1838; s. Henry C. and Amelia (Whippo) M.; A.B., Miami U., 1858, A.M., 1866; m. Alice Filley, Oct. 3, 1878. Engaged in civ. engring., 1863—, chiefly in location and constrn. of rys.; built lines which are now parts of larger ry. systems, such as I.C., Ill. Southern, C.&A. and B.&O. Southwestern rys.; was sewer commr. and mem. Bd. Pub. Improvements, St. Louis, 1877-81; acted as consulting engr. for numerous rys. and reorganization coms.; was apptd. mem. Brazos River Bd., and Southwest Pass Bd. of Engrs.; mem. Bd. of Edn. of St. Louis, 1897-1913 (pres. bd. 1905-06, 1909-10). Past pres. Am. Soc. C.E., St. Louis Engrs. Club. Republican. Home: St. Louis, Mo. Died July 24, 1922.

MOORE, Robert S., shipbuilder; b. San Francisco, Calif., Mar. 22, 1857; s. Joseph and Anne M.; Ph.B., U. of Calif., 1881; m. Florence Howe, June 1887. Engaged in mech. engring., 1873—; founder, chmn. bd., Moore Dry Dock Co. (built 65 steamships during World War); chmn. bd. The Paraffine Cos., Inc., San Francisco; pres. Pacific Securities Co.; asst. to pres. Moore Investment Co. Republican. Mason. Home: Menlo Park, Calif. Died Feb. 16, 1930.

MOORE, Robert Walton, congressman; b. Fairfax, Va., Feb. 26, 1859; s. Thomas and Hannah (Morris) M.; ed. U. of Va.; LL.D., William and Mary Coll. and National Univ., Washington, D.C.; unmarried. Admitted to Va. bar, 1880; asst. to Edmund Baxter in representing numerous ry. and steamship cos. in matters relating to interstate commerce, 1907-10, succeeding him in 1910; counsel in cases before Interstate Commerce Commn.; succeeded Judge Baxter as spl. counsel on his decease, 1910. Mem. State Senate, Va., 1887-90; Cleveland presdl. elector, 1892; mem. Va. Constl. Conv., 1901-02; asst. gen. counsel U.S. R.R. Administration, 1918-19; elected to 66th Congress (1919-21), May 27, 1919, to fill vacancy; reëlected 67th to 71st Congresses (1921-31), 8th Va. Dist.; apptd. asst. sec. of State, Sept. 1933. Apptd. counselor of the Dept. of State, 1937. Was mem. bd. of visitors U. of Va., William and Mary Coll.; mem. State Bd. of Edn., Va. Regent Smithsonian Instn. Mem. George Washington Bicentennial Commn.; chmn. Fredericksburg Battlefield Park Commn., apptd. mem. Internat. Joint Commn., Dec. 27, 1939. Democrat. Episcopalian. Known as speaker on hist. and other subjects. Home: Fairfax, Va. Died Feb. 8, 1941.

MOORE, Samuel, prof. English; b. Lancaster, Pa., Apr. 4, 1877; s. Henry Clay and Mary Ida (Caldwell) M.; grad. Central High Sch., Philadelphia, Pa., 1895; A.B., Princeton, 1899; Ph.D., Harvard, 1911; m. Margaret Rebecca Gibbs, Nov. 25, 1903; children—Samuel, Kingsley Gibbs, Henry C., Edward Cadwell. Instr. in English, U. of Kan., 1907-08; lecturer in English, Bryn Mawr Coll., 1911-12; instr. in English U. of Wis., 1912-13, asst. prof., 1913-15; asso. prof., U. of Mich., 1915-21, prof., 1921—. Apptd. editor Middle English Dictionary, 1930, production under auspices U. of Mich. and Am. Council Learned Socs. Democrat. Anglo-Catholic. Author: The Elements of Old English (with T. A. Knott), 1919; Historical Outlines of English Phonology and Morphology, 1925. Home: Ann Arbor, Mich. Died Sept. 26, 1934.

MOORE, Samuel Wallace, lawyer; b. Geauga Co., O., Jan. 24, 1862; s. Mortimer George and Eliza Cordelia (Fairbanks) M.; B.S., Adelbert Coll. (Western Reserve U.), 1884; LL.B., U. of Kan., 1887; m. Edith Gilham Marty, Aug. 9, 1921. Began practice in Kansas City, Mo., 1888; mem. firm Lathrop, Morrow, Fox & Moore, 1895-1920; gen. counsel Kansas City Terminal Ry. Co., 1906-18; gen. solicitor Kansas City Southern Ry. Co., 1903-20; gen. counsel same ry., 1920—; moved to N.Y. City, 1920; mem. firm Moore & Bell. Served as gen. solicitor of group of rys. of the Southwest, headed by K.C. Southern, under dir. gen. of railroads, during federal control, 1918-20. Republican. Episcopalian. Home: Kansas City, Mo. Died Dec. 11, 1938.

MOORE, Stephen, manufacturer; b. Sudbury, Mass., Feb. 9, 1835; s. Ephraim and Mary (Rogers) M.; ed. pub. and high schs., Saxonville, Mass.; corr. course in psychology and psychology of religion, U. of Chicago. Began as partner S. B. & Homer Rogers, as S. B. Rogers & Co., 1865; merged with S. Sudbury Mfg. Co., Mousam Mfg. Co., 1876, Nat. Fibre Board Co., 1892, treas. from beginning; dir. Leatheroid Mfg. Co.; dir. Market Trust Co. Republican. Held many offices in Bapt. denomination, deacon many yrs.; pres. Mass. Bapt. S.S. Assn., 24 yrs.; dir. North End Mission; trustee Bapt. Old People's Home; was pres. Boston Bapt. Social Union. Home: Newton, Mass. Died Feb. 22, 1920.

MOORE, Thomas Verner, clergyman, educator; b. Louisville, Ky., Oct. 22, 1877; s. John Newton and Charlotte (McIlvain) M.; Ph.D., Catholic U. of America, 1903, student of philosophy, U. of Leipzig, 1904-05; studied medicine, Georgetown U., 1911-13, Munich, Germany, 1913-14; M.D., Johns Hopkins, 1915. Ordained priest, R.C. Ch., 1901; fellow in psychology, Catholic U. of America, 1903; lecturer Inst. of Pedagogy, same univ., New York, 1903-04; fellow in psychology, U. of Calif., 1909; prof. philosophy, St. Thomas Coll., Washington, D.C., 1909-11; instr. psychology, Catholic U. of America, 1910-16, asso. prof., 1916-22, prof., 1922—. Became Benedictine Monk, Sept. 8, 1924. Served as capt. and maj. M.C., U.S.A., in France, World War, 1918-19. A founder, first pres., Benedictine Foundation, Washington, D.C.; dir. clinic for mental and nervous diseases, Providence Hosp., Washington, D.C., 1916—. Author: A Historical Introduction to Ethics, 1915;

Dynamic Psychology, 1924. Home: Brookland, D.C. Died May 22, 1926.

MOORE, Veranus Alva, M.D.; b. Houndsfield, N.Y., Apr. 13, 1859; s. Alva and Antinenette Elizabeth M.; B.S., Cornell, 1887; M.D., Columbian (now George Washington) U., 1890; V.M.D., U. of Pa., 1911; D.Sc., Syracuse, 1919; m. Mary L. Slawson, July 12, 1892; children—Erwin Veranus, Mary Eastman, Norman Slawson. Engaged in investigation of infectious diseases, Bur. of Animal Industry, U.S. Dept. of Agr., 1890-96; chief of Div. of Animal Pathology, U.S. Dept. Agr., 1895-96; prof. comparative pathology, bacteriology and meat inspn., 1896-1929, dean, 1908-29, N.Y. State Veterinary Coll., Cornell U.; supt. Ithaca Memorial Hosp., 1929—. Author: Laboratory Directions for Beginners in Bacteriology, 1900; The Pathology and Differential Diagnosis of Infectious Diseases of Animals, 1908; Principles of Microbiology, 1912; Bovine Tuberculosis and Its Control, 1913. Home: Ithaca, N.Y. Died Feb. 11, 1931.

MOORE, Vida Frank, college prof.; b. Steuben, Me.; d. Capt. Henry D. and Susan Elvira (Kingsley) M.; Ph.B., Wesleyan U., Conn., 1893, M.S., 1897; Ph.D., Cornell U., 1900; unmarried. Prof. philosophy, Mt. Holyoke Coll., 1893-97; prof. philosophy and pedagogy, Elmira Coll., 1901—. Trustee Steele Memorial Library, Elmira. Conglist. Author: Ethical Aspect of Lotze's Metaphysics, 1901. Home: Elmira, N.Y. Died June 11, 1915.

MOORE, Walter William, theologian; b. Charlotte, N.C., June 14, 1857; s. Isaac Hudson and Martha (Parks) M.; A.B., Davidson Coll., N.C., 1878; Union Theol. Sem., Va., 1878-81; D.D., Central U., 1885; LL.D., Davidson, 1892; m. Loula S. Fries, May 18, 1886; children—Lisette Fries (Mrs. A. R. Bird), Walter Vogler, Francis Hudson, Mary Louise. Ordained Presbyn. ministry, 1881; evangelist in Western N.C., 1881-82; pastor Millersburg, Ky., 1882-83; prof. Hebrew lang. and lit., 1883-1912, pres., 1904—, Union Theol. Sem., Richmond, Va. Trustee Hampden-Sidney Coll. Moderator Presbyn. Gen. Assembly, 1908. Author: A Year in Europe, 1904; The Indispensable Book, 1910; Appreciations and Historical Addresses, 1914; The Value of the Church, 1918; A Real Boy Scout, 1920. Died June 14, 1926.

MOORE, William Emmet, newspaper editor; b. La Grange, Mo.; s. William Pike and Catherine Linn (Threlkeld) M.; ed. Whipple Acad., Jacksonville, Ill., and U. of Mo., LL.D., 1941; unmarried. Reporter Quincy (Ill.) Herald and Journal, 1899-1901, Chicago American, 1901-04; city editor Chicago Inter Ocean, 1904-07; mem. staff New York Herald, 1907-08; night editor Chicago Inter Ocean, 1909-12, mng. editor, 1912-14; editorial writer, Chicago Daily News, 1914; city editor and mng. editor New York Tribune, 1915-17; with the Baltimore Sun, 1922—; mng. editor of The Sun, chief news editor of The Sun and The Evening Sun, and v.p. of the company. Private Ill. Vol. Inf., Spanish-Am. War; capt. Signal Corps, U.S. Army, Oct. 1917-Oct. 1919; served in France on General Pershing's Headquarters staff; awarded Victory medal with battle clasps for Aisne-Marne, Marne-Vesle and St. Mihiel campaigns, G. H. Q. citation, and Chateau-Thierry, (French) Medal. Author: Democratic Campaign Text Book, 1920; U.S. Official Pictures of the World War, 1920. Home: Baltimore, Md. Died Dec. 27, 1941.

MOORE, William Eves, pastor emeritus Second Presbyn. Ch., Columbus, O., 1894 (pastor, 1872-94); b. Strasburgh, Pa., April 1823; grad. Yale, 1847, A.M., 1850; D.D., Marietta, 1873; LL.D., Lake Forest, 1893; m. Hariet F., d. Rev. George Foot, Newark, Del., Sept. 19, 1850. Principal Fairfield Acad., Conn., 1847-49; studied theology privately; pastor First Presbyn. Ch., West Chester, Pa., 1850-72; moderator gen. assembly, 1890; permanent clerk gen. assembly, 1884—; stated clerk Synod of Ohio, 1882—. Author: Digest of the Acts and Deliverances of the General Assembly, 1861, 1873, 1886, 1898. Died 1899.

MOORE, William Henry, capitalist; b. Utica, N.Y., Oct. 25, 1848; s. Nathaniel F. and Rachel A. (Beckwith) M.; entered Amherst Coll., 1867; admitted to Wis. bar, 1872; settled at Chicago and made a specialty of corp. law; m. Ada W. Small, 1879. With his brother, James H., formed the four great corporations known as the "Moore group," with a combined capital of $187,000,000, all now absorbed in the U.S. Steel Corp.; also promoted other large industrial corporations, including the Diamond Match Co., Nat. Biscuit Co., Am. Tin Plate Co., Am. Steel Hoop Co., and many other corps. Chmn. bd. Nat. Biscuit Co.; dir. D.,L.&W. Ry. Co., Am. Cotton Oil Co., First Nat. Bank of New York, Am. Can Co. Home: New York, N.Y. Died Jan. 11, 1923.

MOORE, William Sturtevant, commodore U.S.N.; b. Duxbury, Mass., Feb. 23, 1846; s. Josiah and Maria Foster (Doane) M.; B.S., Lawrence Scientific Sch. (Harvard), 1867; grad. U.S. Naval Acad., 1868; m. Caro Garland Burwell, Feb. 6, 1901. Apptd. from Mass., acting 3d asst. engr. vol. navy, Oct. 10, 1866; 3d asst. engr. in regular service, June 2, 1868; promoted 2d asst. engr., June 2, 1869; passed asst. engr., June 11. 1876; chief engr., Aug. 10, 1893; comdr., Mar. 3, 1899; capt., Mar. 21, 1903; retired as commodore, June 30, 1906. At U.S. Naval Acad., 1866-67; Navy Yard, Boston, 1867; Naval Acad., 1867-68; on board Yantic, 1868-69; Bur. of Steam Engring., 1870-72; Frolic, 1872-73; Navy Yard, Washington, 1873; Bur. Steam Engring., 1873; Brooklyn, 1873-74; Bur. Steam Engring., 1875-76; coast survey steamer Blake, 1876-78; Minnesota, 1878-79; Bur. Steam Engring., 1879-82; Tallapoosa, 1882-84; Ossipee, 1884-87; Bureau of Steam Engineering, 1887-91; Vesuvius, 1891-94; Naval Examining Board, Phila., 1894-95; Dolphin, 1895-96; Texas, 1896-97; Columbia, 1897-98; receiving-ship Vermont, 1898-99; insp. machinery for the navy at Cramps' shipyard, 1899-1903; insp. of machinery for Mass. dist., 1903-05; Navy Yard, Boston, 1905-06. Mem. Mass. Ho. of Rep., 1909, 1910. Died July 12, 1914.

MOORE, Willis Luther, meteorologist; b. Scranton, Pa., Jan. 18, 1856; s. Luther T. and Lucy E. (Babcock) M.; ed. Binghamton pub. schs.; student of natural sciences under scientific staff of Weather Bur., 15 yrs.; LL.D., Norwich, 1896; D.Sc., St. Lawrence, 1906. Entered signal corps (now weather bur.), rose through successive grades to local forecast official, Milwaukee, 1891-94; won professorship meteorology, open competitive exam. against 23 contestants, 1894; chief U.S. Weather Bureau, 1895-1913; one of U.S. representatives in First Internat. Radio Congress, London, 1912; prof. applied meteorology, George Washington U. Owner and manager, 1907-19, large fruit, grain and stock farm, at Rockville, Md. Lecturer for the Royal Inst., London, 1912; lecturer in lyceum and chautauqua circuits. Author: Moore's Descriptive Meteorology, 1901; The New Air World, 1922; Spiritual Gravity of the Cosmist. Home: Pasadena, Calif. Died Dec. 18, 1927.

MOOREHEAD, Warren King, archeologist; b. Siena, Italy, of American parents, Mar. 10, 1866; ed. in high schs. and Denison U.; spent 3 yrs. in study under Dr. Thomas Wilson, the curator of prehistoric anthropology, Smithsonian Instn.; 4 yrs. in investigation of Ohio mounds at own expense; hon. M.A., Dartmouth, 1901; hon. D.Sc., Oglethorpe, 1927, Denison, 1930; m. Evelyn Ludwig, Nov. 10, 1892; children—Ludwig King, Singleton Peabody. In charge of work in the Ohio Valley, Utah, Colo. and N.Mex. for Chicago Expn.; made valuable finds in altar mounds of Scioto Valley, explorations New England, Tex., etc.; formerly curator of mus. for Ohio State U. and Hist. Soc.; now dir. dept. of archeology, Phillips Academy. Served for 26 years as mem. U.S. Bd. of Indian Commrs. investigating Indian reservations for Dept. Interior until bd. abolished, 1933; exploration of Cahokia Mounds for U. of Ill., 1920-23 and 1927, Etowah Mounds investigation, 1925-27. Pres. North Am. Civic League, Boston, Mass.; trustee Peabody Mus. Salem. Author: Hopewell Explorations, Fort Ancient; The Stone Age; The American Indian; Stone Ornaments of American Indians; Archæology of Maine; Cahokia Mounds; Archæology of the Arkansas Valley. Home: Andover, Mass. Died Jan. 5, 1939.

MOOREHEAD, William Gallogly, theologian; b. Rix Mills, O., 1836; s. David and Margaret (Henderson) M.; A.B., Muskingum Coll., 1858, later A.M.; Allegheny Theol. Sem., 1858-59, Xenia Theol. Sem., 1859-62; (D.D., U. of Wooster, 1876; LL.D., Miami U., 1898); married. Ordained United Presbyn. ministry, 1862; missionary of Am. and Foreign Christian Union in Italy, 1862-69; pastor First Ch., Xenia, O., 1870; prof. N.T. lit. and exegesis, 1873, pres. faculty, 1899—, Xenia Theol. Seminary. Author: Outline Studies in Old Testament, 1893; Studies in the Four Gospels, 1900; Outline Studies in Acts—Ephesians, 1902; Outline Studies in Philippians—Hebrews, 1905. Home: Xenia, O. Died Mar. 1, 1914.

MOORES, Charles Bruce, lawyer; b. Benton, Mo., Aug. 6, 1849; s. John Henry and Virginia La Fayette (Lamon) M.; A.B., Willamette U., Salem, Ore., 1870; LL.B., U. of Mich., 1877; m. Sarah E. Chamberlin, Nov. 1, 1881. Began practice in Salem, Ore., 1877; chief clk. Ore. Ho. of Rep., 1880; pvt. sec. to gov. of Ore., 1882-87; speaker Ore. Ho. of Rep., 1895; register U.S. Land Office, Oregon City, Oregon, 1897-1903; chmn. of Commn. Public Docks, Portland, 1910-19; chmn. Rep. State Central Com. of Ore., 1912—. Trustee Willamette U., 1878—. Methodist. Odd Fellow. Home: Portland, Ore. Deceased.

MOORES, Charles Washington, lawyer; b. Indianapolis, Feb. 15, 1862; s. Charles Washington and Julia Dumont (Merrill) M.; bro. of Merrill M.; A.B., Wabash Coll., 1882, A.M., 1885 (Litt.D., 1912); LL.B., Central Law Sch., Indianapolis, 1883; m. Elizabeth Nichols, Oct. 5, 1896. Mem. Pickens, Moores, Davidson & Pickens; U.S. commr., 1888—. Mem. Indianapolis Bd. Sch. Commrs., 1900-09 (v.p. 1903-08, pres. 1908-09); dir. Butler Coll., 1903-09, Indianapolis Art Assn., 1909, and 1918—; mem. Ind. Hist. Commn., 1915—; pres. Ind. Historical Society. Author: Caleb Mills and the Indiana School System, 1905; Life of Abraham Lincoln for Boys and Girls, 1909; Story of Christopher Columbus, 1912; Lincoln Selections, 1913; History of Indiana for Boys and Girls, 1916. Lecturer, Ind. Law Sch., 1896—, and Indiana U. Sch. of Law, 1920—. Home: Indianapolis, Ind. Died Dec. 7, 1923.

MOORES, J(ames) Henry; b. Croton, Licking Co., O., Apr. 2, 1846; s. Robert Baxter and Caroline A. (Ball) M.; ed. Mich. Agrl. Coll. (hon. M.A., 1913); m. Sarah Lois Stevens, 1873 (died 1886); m. 2d, Sarah Frances Goodman, Apr. 1887. Began dealing in pine lands, Mich., 1873; engaged in lumbering on Muskegon River, 1880-85, shipping to Chicago; founder, 1881, and first postmaster village of Moorestown; bought yellow pine lands in Miss., 1887, and moved to Miss., 1897; returned to Lansing, Mich., 1906; pres. Lansing Pure Ice Co., Lansing Foundry Co. Presented "Moores Park" (20 acres) to City of Lansing, 1908; also built Moores River Drive and opened to the public about same time. Republican. Conglist. Home: Lansing, Mich. Died Aug. 24, 1918.

MOORES, Merrill, congressman; b. Indianapolis, Ind., Apr. 21, 1856; s. Charles Washington and Julia Dumont (Merrill) M.; student Butler Coll., Ind., 1870-72, 1873-75, Willamette U., Salem, Ore., 1872-73; A.B., Yale, 1878; LL.B., Central Law Sch. of Ind., 1880; unmarried. Admitted to bar, 1880; chairman Rep. Co. Com. of Marion Co., Ind., 1892-96; asst. atty. gen. of Ind., 1894-1903. Commr. from Ind. on Nat. Conf. on Uniform State Laws, 1909-25. Mem. 64th to 68th Congresses (1915-25), 7th Ind. District. Presbyn. Home: Indianapolis, Ind. Died Oct. 21, 1929.

MOORHEAD, Louis David, surgeon; b. Chicago, Ill., Nov. 22, 1892; s. Edward Louis (M.D.) and Jeannette (Snell) M.; A.B., St. Ignatius Coll., Chicago, 1913; S.B., U. of Chicago, 1914, S.M., 1915; A.M., Loyola U., 1916; M.D., Rush Med. Coll., 1917; unmarried. Practiced in Chicago, 1917—; sr. house surgeon Cook Co. Hosp., 1917-19; dean and asso. prof. surgery, Loyola U. Sch. of Medicine, 1918—; sr. attending surgeon Mercy Hosp.; surgeon R.I. R.R. System, C.&E.I. R.R., Belt R.R. of Chicago, Chicago Elevated Lines. Chief of examining bd. Archdiocese of Chicago; mem. bd. dirs. Catholic Hosp. Assn., also of St. Mary's of the Wood, Ind. Fellow Am. Coll. Surgeons. Catholic. Home: Chicago, Ill. Died Apr. 26, 1928.

MOORMAN, Charles Harwood, judge; b. Big Spring, Ky., Apr. 24, 1876; s. William James and Margaret (Bush) M.; m. Lily Belknap, Nov. 28, 1914; children—Morris Belknap, Charles H. Admitted to bar 1900; judge Court of Appeals of Ky., 1921-23; judge U.S. Dist. Court, Western Dist. of Ky., 1924-25; judge U.S. Circuit Court of Appeals, 6th Circuit, Jan. 1925—. Served with Am. Red Cross in France, Nov. 1917-May 1918; commd. capt. J. A. Gen.'s Dept., U.S.A., May 1918; maj., Nov. 1918. Republican. Mason. Home: Louisville, Ky. Died Jan. 26, 1938.

MOOT, Adelbert, lawyer; b. Allen, N.Y., Nov. 22, 1854; s. Charles D. and Mary (Rutherford) M.; ed. State Normal schs.; Albany Law Sch., 1875-76; m. C. A. Van Ness, July 22, 1882; children—Richmond Dana, Welles Van Ness, Seward Adelbert. Practiced law Nunda and Buffalo, N.Y., 1876—. Mem. bd. Commrs. of Statutory Consolidation that consolidated all gen. statutes of N.Y. from 1777 to 1909. Regent U. State of N.Y., 1912—, also vice chancellor, 1921—. Vice pres. Am. Unitarian Conf. for many yrs.; pres. N.Y. State Conf. 4 yrs. Independent Republican. Home: Buffalo, N.Y. Died Sept. 12, 1929.

MOQUÉ, Alice Lee, writer; b. New Orleans, Oct. 20, 1865; d. Judge Charles West and Sarah Elizabeth (Smith) Hornor; ed. Washington High Sch., and Moravian Female Coll., Bethlehem, Pa.; read law 2 yrs. and medicine 3 yrs.; m. Walter C. Snelling, Oct. 20, 1882 (died 1892); m. 2d, John Oliver Moqué, June 27, 1894. Washington rep. American Press Assn., 4 yrs.; press rep. in Washington for Nat. Am. Woman Suffrage Assn.; press chmn. Washington Woman Suffrage Council; editor "Washington's Pot Bouille" news; spl. feature writer Washington Star. Adj. gen. Woman's Nat. Cuban League; original mem. Mother's Congress. Delivered, by invitation, an address on "Women in the Civil Service of the United States," in Old Town Hall, London, 1895. Author: Delightful Dalmatia, 1914; Bodymaster's Daughter, 1897. Active mem. Motor Corps, Woman's Vol. Aid of District Chapter Am. Red Cross. Home: Washington, D.C. Died July 16, 1919.

MORA, F(rancis) Luis, artist; b. Montevideo, Uruguay, S.A., July 27, 1874; s. Domingo and Laura (Gaillard) M.; ed. Manning's Sem., Perth Amboy, N.J., pub. schs., New York and Boston; art edn. Sch. of Drawing and Painting, Mus. Fine Arts, Boston, Art Students' League, New York; m. Sophia Brown Compton, Sept. 12, 1900; 1 dau., Rosemary; m. 2d, May G. Safford, July 6, 1932. Elected v.p. Art Students' League, after completing studies there. Beginning about 1892 did illustrating work for all the leading mags. and periodicals. First important commission, large decorative panel for main reading hall, Lynn (Mass.) Pub. Library, 1900; represented in all most important art exhbns. in America, 1894—; painted decorations for Mo. State Bldg., St. Louis Expn., 1904; also mural decorations for Orpheum Theatre, Los Angeles; decorative panel Red Cross

Hdqrs., Washington. While student, received Sears prize, Mus. Fine Arts, Boston, Rothschild prize, Art Students' League, New York; later gold medals, Phila. Art Club, 1901, and Am. Fine Arts Soc., Phila., 1902; bronze medal, St. Louis Expn., 1904; 1st Hallgarten prize, Nat. Acad. Design, 1905; Beal prize, New York Water Color Club, 1907; Evans prize, Salmagundi Club, 1908; Shaw prize, same, 1910; silver medal, Internat. Fine Arts Expn., Buenos Aires, 1910; 2 gold medals, San Francisco Expn., 1915; Carnegie prize, Nat. Acad., New York, 1930. Teacher in drawing and painting classes, N.Y. School of Art for 9 years. N.A., 1906; mem. Municipal Art Soc. Represented in Met. Mus., New York; Atlanta Mus.; Newark Mus.; Dallas Art Assn.; Toledo Mus. of Art; Butler Gallery of Art, Youngstown, O.; Richmond (Ind.) Art Assn.; Royal Art Gallery, Ottawa, Can.; perm. collection of Nat. Acad. Design; painting of late President Warren Harding in White House; portrait of Andrew Carnegie for Carnegie Corp. centenary gift to libraries. Murals for post offices in Clarkesville, Tenn., and Catasauqua, Pa.; painting "Our Christian Era" for Dun and Bradstreet office, New York World's Fair. Home: New York, N.Y. Died June 5, 1940.

MORALES, (Luis) Sánchez, merchant; b. San Juan, P.R., Nov. 27, 1867; s. Manuel Sánchez Appellániz and Ana (Morales); ed. Institute Civil, San Juan; m. María Ubeda, of San Juan, P.R., Dec. 14, 1902; children—Luis (dec.), María Isabel, Rafael (dec.), Aurora, Luis, Elena, Rafael. Newspaper writer, later mgr. father's business; gen. agt. New York Life Ins. Co. for a number of yrs.; organized with brothers, 1902, Sánchez Morales & Co., mchts. with mfrs.' agts.; pres. Commercial Bank of P.R., 1917-23; dir. Banco Popular, San Juan. Asst. treas. of P.R., 1898; mayor of San Juan, 1899; a founder of Republican party in P.R., 1899; v.p. Puerto Rican Atheneum, 1902; mem. House of Delegates, Puerto Rico, 1900-04; mem. Exec. Council (Senate) of P.R., 1904-17 (pres. 1912-17); mem. Bd. of Equalization and Review of Taxes, 1923-25; mem. Senate from San Juan, 1924—(v.p. and chmn. finance committee; pres. of the Senate of Puerto Rico, 1931-33). Introduced resolution asking the Pres. of the U.S. to declare free trade between the U.S. and Puerto Rico, 1901; mem. Food Commn. of P.R., 1917—, Mil. Exemption Dist. Bd. for P.R., 1917—; chief transportation service for P.R. of U.S. Food Administration, 1917—. Trustee U. of Porto Rico, 1923-30, and again, 1933. Pres. Y.M.C.A. of San Juan; pres. U.S. Civil Legion Div. of P.R., 1932. Mem. Scholar Fraternity of Puerto Rico. Catholic. Chmn. Victory Loan Com. for P.R., 1919. Home: San Juan, P.R. Died Mar. 27, 1934.

MORAN, Annette, artist; b. Louisville, Ky., Jan. 18, 1835; ed. pvt. schs.; began drawing at early age; m. Edward Moran, distinguished artist, 1865 (died 1901). Received diploma World's Columbian Expn. for original drawings; has exhibited in art galleries all over U.S.; has had many of her pictures published in magazines. Episcopalian. Deceased.

MORAN, Daniel Edward, consulting engr.; b. Orange, N.J., April 12, 1864; s. Daniel E. and Annie A. (Blake) M.; C.E., Sch. of Mines, Columbia U., 1884, M.Sc., 1911; m. Sarah V. Kelly, of Glasgow, Scotland, 1896; children—Sarah Sylvester (Mrs. George C. Fraser), Daniel E., Dorothy A. (Mrs. Carl Bricken), Archibald A., Hugh B. Became mem. Moran, Maurice & Proctor, 1917, title now Moran & Proctor; cons. engr. Phila. and Camden Bridge, Mid-Hudson Bridge (Poughkeepsie, N.Y.), Federal Reserve Bank Bldg., Port of New York Authority, Hudson River Bridge and Detroit Internat. Bridge, San Francisco-Oakland Bay Bridge, Triborough Bridge. Democrat. Home: Mendham, N.J. Died July 3, 1937.

MORAN, Francis Thomas, clergyman, sociologist; b. Valparaiso, Ind., Feb. 16, 1865; s. Peter and Catherine (Kelleher) M.; studied classics at prep. sem., Milwaukee, Wis., and St. Charles Coll., Ellicott City, Md., philosophy and theology, St. Mary's Sem., Cleveland, O.; D.D., St. Mary's U., Baltimore, Md., 1901. Ordained R.C. priest, 1888; pastor Holgate, O., 1888, Immaculate Conception Ch., Toledo, O., 1889-90, St. Mary's Ch., Clyde, O., 1890-96, St. Mary's Ch., Akron, 1896-1901; rector St. Patrick's Ch., Cleveland, 1901—; domestic prelate with title of monsignor, 1922; chmn. Diocesan Sch. Bd., 1922—; also mem. Diocesan Council and Diocesan Bd. of Administration. Treas. Catholic Ednl. Assn., 1905—. Active in civic affairs, dir. Chamber of Industry, Cleveland, 1907-11; dir. Associated Charities, 1908-12, Anti-Tuberculosis League, 1910—; chmn. Home Finding Bur. of Humane Soc., 1912-21; chmn. Federal Labor War Bd., Cleveland, 1918-19. Has traveled extensively in Mexico, Europe and the Orient. Home: Cleveland, O. Died Oct. 28, 1929.

MORAN, James Thomas, telephone executive; b. North Haven, Conn., Sept. 19, 1864; s. Thomas and Maria (Cullom) M.; grad. Hillhouse High Sch., New Haven, Conn.; LL.B., Yale, 1884, LL.M., 1885; m. Mary E. McKenzie, Apr. 27, 1898; children—Esther (dec.), Helen Elizabeth. Admitted to Conn. bar, 1884; apptd. atty. Southern N.E. Telephone Co., New Haven, 1884, later gen. atty.; dir., v.p. and gen. mgr., and pres., Feb. 6, 1917—; trustee Conn. Savings Bank, Conn. Ry. & Lighting Co. Mem. Conn. State Council of Defense, 1917-19; chmn. Sinking Fund Commn. City of New Haven, 1924-27. Mem. bd. dirs. Dept. of Pub. Welfare State of Conn., Hosp. of St. Raphael. Mem. Gen. Hosp. Soc. of Conn. (pres.), Telephone Pioneers of America (pres. 1927). Catholic. Home: New Haven, Conn. Deceased.

MORAN, (John) Léon, artist; b. Phila., Pa., Oct. 4, 1864; s. Edward and Elizabeth (McManes) M.; ed. pub. schs., Phila.; studied art under father, and at Nat. Acad. Design, New York, and in London and Paris; returned to U.S., 1879; established studio, New York, 1883; m. Helen, d. Rev. J. N. Steele, of New York, Apr. 27, 1892. Frequent exhibitor Nat. Acad. Design, New York, and elsewhere; gold medal Phila. Art Club; gold medal, Am. Art Soc., Phila., 1904. Principal works: Waylaid; An Interrupted Conspiracy; An Amateur; The Duel; An Idyl; Eel Fishing; Intercepted Dispatches; Madonna and Child; Between Two Fires; Madonna; etc. Home: Plainfield, N.J. Died Aug. 4, 1941.

MORAN, (Edward) Percy, artist; b. Phila., Pa., July 29, 1862; s. Edward and Elizabeth (McManes) M.; ed. in Paris; studied art under father and uncle, S. J. Ferris, Phila., and Nat. Acad. Design, New York; also in London and Paris; m. Virginia Bremond Crosby, Dec. 16, 1891. First Hallgarten prize, Nat. Acad. Design, 1886; 1st gold medal, Am. Art Assn., 1888. Frequent exhibitor; specialties colonial subjects and modern women. Principal works: A Corner of the Studio; The Wood-Cutter's Daughter; The Duet; Afternoon Tea; The Miller's Daughter; Divided Attention; The Dancing Lesson; The Rehearsal for the Ball; A Japanese Fantasy; A Forgotten Strain; Her Grace; Schooldays Over; Between Two Fires; The Lion of the Hour; The Right of Way; The Wish; Welcome; An April Shower. In recent years has been engaged on works of Am. hist. subjects. Died Mar. 25, 1935.

MORAN, Peter, painter, etcher; b. Bolton, Lancashire, Eng., Mar. 4, 1841; s. Thomas and Mary (Higson) M.; bro. of Thomas M.; grad. Harrison Grammar Sch., Phila., 1857; studied with his brothers, Thomas and Edward Moran; also in Eng., 1863; m. Emily Kelley, of Dublin, Ireland, July 7, 1867 (who was also a painter and etcher); m. 2d, Sarah D. C. Francis, Nov. 21, 1911. Mem. The Art Club of Phila.; pres. Soc. of Etchers. His paintings are principally of landscapes and animal subjects. Home: Philadelphia, Pa. Died Nov. 9, 1914.

MORAN, Thomas, painter; b. Bolton, Lancashire, Eng., Jan. 12, 1837; s. Thomas and Mary (Higson) M.; came to U.S., 1844; ed. pub. schools, Phila.; apprenticed to wood engraver; afterwards studied art under James Hamilton, and later in Paris and Italy; became known as an illustrator and landscape artist; m. Mary Nimmo, Apr. 1862; children—Paul Nimmo (dec.), Mrs. Wirt Tassin, Ruth B. Accompanied the U.S. Geol. Expdn. to the Yellowstone country in 1871; in 1873 went on a similar expdn., painting the pictures, entitled respectively, "Grand Cañon of the Yellowstone" and "Chasm of the Colorado," which were purchased by Congress, and are now in the Capitol at Washington. N.A., 1884. Home: Santa Barbara, Calif. Died Aug. 25, 1926.

MORAN, Thomas A., lawyer; b. Bridgeport, Conn., Oct. 7, 1839; s. Patrick and Ann M.; ed. dist. schools in Wis. and Liberty Acad., Salem, Wis., 1859-61; grad. Albany, N.Y., Law School, 1865 (hon. LL.D. from Notre Dame Univ., Jesuit Coll., Chicago, and Mt. St. Mary Coll., Emmitsburg, Md.); m. Josephine Quinn, Dec. 31, 1868. Elected judge circuit court, Cook Co., Ill., June 1879; reëlected 1885, 91; apptd. judge appellate court of 1st dist., Ill., March 1886; resigned office of judge, March 1892, and entered on practice of law as head of Moran, Kraus, Mayer & Stein. Democrat. Home: Chicago, Ill. Died 1904.

MORAN, Thomas Francis, univ. prof.; b. Columbia, Mich., Jan. 9, 1866; s. John and Mary M.; A.B., U. of Mich., 1887; Ph.D., Johns Hopkins, 1895; admitted to Mich. bar, 1887; m. Louise R. Upham, Aug. 5, 1896; children—George Upham, Thomas Francis, Alice Louise. Supt. of schs., Elk River, 1887-92; prof. history and economics, Purdue U., Sept. 1895—. Mem. faculty U. of Ill. summer session, 1914. Mem. ednl. com. Nat. Security League; asso. dir. speaking div., Com. on Pub. Information, Washington, Jan. 1-May 1, 1918; Fred Morgan Kirby lecturer on civil rights, Lafayette Coll., Pa., 1921; mem. Ind. State Hist. Commn., 1923-25. Sr. Warden and lay reader P.E. Ch. Author: Formation and Development of the Constitution, 1904; The Theory and Practice of the English Government, new edit., 1908; American Presidents, 1917. Home: Lafayette, Ind. Died Oct. 1928.

MORAWETZ, Victor, lawyer; b. Baltimore, Md., Apr. 3, 1859; s. Dr. L. F. M.; ed. pvt. schools and foreign univs.; LL.B., Harvard, 1879; hon. A.M., Columbia Univ., 1888; LL.D., Williams College, Mass., 1914; m. Violet Westcott, 1911 (dec.); m. 2d, Marjorie Nott, 1924. Admitted to bar, 1880, and engaged in practice of law, principally as counsel and atty. for ry. and other corps. Author: Law of Private Corporations, 1882; Banking and Currency Problems in the U.S., 1909; Elements of the Law of Contracts, 1927. Home: New York, N.Y. Died May 18, 1938.

MORDECAI, Alfred, brig. gen. U.S.A.; b. Phila., Pa., June 30, 1840; s. Maj. Alfred (U.S.A.) and Sara Ann (Hays) M.; grad. U.S. Mil. Acad., 1861; m. Sally S. Maynadier, Nov. 1, 1866; m. 2d, Dora Varney, Sept. 6, 1892. Bvtd. 2d lt. topog. engrs., June 24, 1861; promoted through grades to col., ordnance, Jan. 31, 1891; brig. gen. U.S.A., Jan. 19, 1904. Bvtd. maj., Sept. 7, 1863, "for gallant and meritorious services in siege of Ft. Wagner, S.C."; lt. col., Mar. 13, 1865, "for distinguished services in the field and faithful and meritorious services in ordnance dept. during the war." Served as ordnance officer, 1861-65; engaged in operations against Charleston, S.C., 1863-4; chief of ordnance, Army of the James, May-Sept. 1864, later in Army of Tenn. and Army of the Cumberland till July 4, 1865. Instr. ordnance and gunnery, U.S. Mil. Acad., 1865-69 and 1874-81; comd. Leavenworth Arsenal, Kan., 1870-74, Watervliet Arsenal, 1881-86 and 1898-99, New York Arsenal, 1887-92, Springfield Armory, 1892-98, Benecia Arsenal, Calif., 1899-1902; on duty, office chief of ordnance, U.S.A., 1902-04; retired at own request over 40 yrs.' service, Jan. 20, 1904. Died Jan. 20, 1920.

MORDECAI, Samuel Fox, prof. law; b. Richmond, Va., Dec. 12, 1852; s. Samuel Fox and Ellen M.; ed. pvt. schs., N.C., and U. of Va.; LL.D., Trinity Coll., Durham, N.C., 1911; m. Betty Grimes, Nov. 10, 1875. Admitted to bar by Supreme Court of N.C., 1875; mem. Battle & Mordecai, 1876-1904; lecturer on law, Wake Forest Coll., N.C., 1900-04; dean Law Sch., Trinity Coll. (now Duke U.), Sept. 1, 1904—. Democrat. Episcopalian. Author: Mechanics' Liens, 1897; Negotiable Instruments Law in North Carolina, 1899; Lex Scripta, 1905; Mordecai's Law Lectures, 1907, 2d edit., 1915; Case Book on Remedies (with Prof. A. C. McIntosh), 1910; Mordecai's Law Notes, 1912-13, additions to same, 1914-19; Questions and Answers on Real Property, 1922; Questions and Answers on 2d Blk., 1923. Home: Durham, N.C. Died Dec. 29, 1927.

MORE, E(noch) Anson, author; b. Dayton, O., Apr. 11, 1854; s. Enoch Anson and Katherine Hay (Elmer) M.; pub. sch. edn.; m. Caroline Augusta Bacon, Oct. 17, 1887; children—John Douglas (dec), Robert Elmer. Sec. The J. S. Brown & Bro. Mercantile Co., 1901-1908. U.S. dep. disbursing agt. in Colo., 1917-19. Col. 1st Regt. Colo. N.G., 1884-86. Conglist. Republican. Author: Let It Burn, 1892; Out of the Past, 1895; A Captain of Men, 1905; A Vision of Empire, 1915. Home: Denver, Colo. Died June 2, 1932.

MORE, Paul Elmer, editor, author; b. St. Louis, Dec. 12, 1864; s. Enoch Anson and Katherine Hay (Elmer) M.; A.B., Washington U., 1887, A.M., 1892, LL.D., 1913; A.M., Harvard, 1893; LL.D., U. of Glasgow, 1931; Litt.D., Columbia and Dartmouth, 1917, Princeton, 1919; m. Henrietta Beck, June 12, 1900; children—Mary Darrah, Alice. Asst. in Sanskrit, Harvard, 1894-95; asso. in Sanskrit and classical lit., Bryn Mawr Coll., 1895-97. Lit. editor The Independent, 1901-03, New York Evening Post, 1903-09; editor The Nation, 1909-14. Mem. Am. Acad. Arts and Letters. Author: Shelburne Essays (11 vols.), 1904—; Life of Benjamin Franklin, 1900; Platonism, 1917; The Religion of Plato, 1921; Hellenistic Philosophies, 1923; The Christ of the New Testament, 1924; Christ the Word, 1927; The Demon of the Absolute, 1928, The Catholic Faith, 1931; The Sceptical Approach to Religion, 1934. Editor (with F. L. Cross) Anglicanism, 1935. Translator: Judgment of Socrates; Prometheus Bound; Century of Indian Epigrams. Home: Princeton, N.J. Died Mar. 9, 1937.

MOREHEAD, John Alfred, head of International Ch. Agencies, Luth. Church; b. Pulaski County, Va., Feb. 4, 1867; s. James W. and Katherine Barbara (Yonce) M.; A.B., Roanoke Coll., Va., 1889; grad. Luth. Theol. Sem., Mt. Airy, Phila., 1892; studied at Berlin and Leipzig, 1901-02; D.D., Roanoke, 1902; LL.D., Pa. Coll., 1921; D.Th., University of Leipzig, 1922 and U. of Paris, France, 1935; S.T.D. from Elisabeth University, Hungary, 1929; m. Nellie Virginia Fisher, Oct. 6, 1892. Ordained Evang. Luth. ministry, 1892; incumbent Burke's Garden Pastorate, Va., 1892-94, First English Luth. Ch., Richmond, Va., 1894-98; pres. and prof. systematic theology, Southern Luth. Theol. Sem., 1898-1908; pres. Roanoke Coll., 1908-19. Pres. United Synod of the South, 1910-14. Chmn. European Commn. of Nat. Luth. Council, 1919-23; exec. dir. Nat. Luth. Council, 1923-30; chmn. editorial com. Luth. World Almanac and Ency., 1924-30; pres. Second Lutheran World Conv., Copenhagen, 1929; giving full-time service as pres. exec. com. Continuation Work of Luth. World Conv., Feb. 1930—. Awarded Knighthood and Cross of Order of Dannebrog, 1930, by King of Denmark, in recognition of services rendered in post-World War relief and in furthering unity among Lutherans; Knight Order of White Rose, 1st Class, Finland, 1932; elected hon. pres. Luth. World Conv. for life, 1935. Died June 1, 1936.

MOREHEAD, John Motley, mfr.; b. Charlotte, N.C., July 20, 1866; s. Col. John Lindsay and Sarah Smith (Phifer) M.; A.B., U. of N.C., 1886; m.

Mary Garrett, Apr. 5, 1893. Interested in mfg. and farming; v.-p. Leaksville Woolen Mills, Spray, N.C., Thrift Mfg. Co.; dir. Highland Park Mfg. Co. Mem. 61st Congress (1909-11), 5th N.C. Dist.; mem. Rep. Nat. Com., Mar. 1, 1916—. Presbyn. Home: Charlotte, N.C. Died Dec. 13, 1923.

MOREHOUSE, Daniel Walter, astronomer, coll. pres.; b. Mankato, Minn., Feb. 22, 1876; s. Aaron and Sabra Ann (Burleson) M.; N.W. Christian Coll., Excelsior, Minn., 1895-97; S.B., Drake University, 1900; S.B., U. of Chicago, 1902; S.M., Drake U., 1902; Ph.D., U. of Calif., 1914; LL.D., Butler U., 1932; m. Myrtle Slayton, June 9, 1903; children—Charles Aaron, Vega Lorraine, Frances Roberta. Prof. physics and astronomy, Drake U., 1900—. Vol. research asst., Yerkes Obs., summer 1909; instr. astronomy, U. of Calif., 1911-12; dean of men, Drake U., 1919-22, acting pres. and dean Coll. of Liberal Arts, 1922-23, pres. and dean Coll. of Liberal Arts, 1923-1930, again president, 1930—. Fellow Ia. State Acad. of Science (pres. 1921-22). Discovered Comet (c), 1908 (Morehouse), Sept. 1, 1908; awarded Donahue Comet Medal, 1908; also community award to citizen rendering most distinguished service to the city of Des Moines in 1928. Mem. Christian (Disciples) Church; pres. Internat. Conv. of Disciples of Christ, 1934-35. Home: Des Moines, Ia. Died Jan. 21, 1941.

MOREHOUSE, Frederic Cook, editor; b. Milwaukee, Wis., Mar. 19, 1868; s. Linden Husted and Lydia E. (Phelps) M.; educated pvt. sch., high sch., under pvt. instr.; Litt.D., Lawrence Coll., Wis., 1921; L.H.D., Kenyon Coll., Ohio, 1925; m. Lilias E. Macon, June 24, 1891; children—Lilias Pope (Mrs. R. L. Farrar, dec.), Howard Lord (dec.), Clifford Phelps, Editor Church Eclectic, 1896-1900; editor The Living Church, 1899—; pres. Morehouse Publishing Co. Mem. Gen. Conv. P.E. Ch., 1910—. Author: Some American Churchmen, 1892; Evolution of Parties in the Anglican Communion, 1905. Home: Milwaukee, Wis. Died June 25, 1932.

MOREHOUSE, George Read, physician; b. Mt. Holly, N.J., March 25, 1829; s. Rev. George Youngs, D.D., and Martha (Read) M.; grad. Princeton, 1848 (Ph.D., 1892); Jefferson Med. Coll., 1851; Univ. of Pa., M.D., 1875; acting asst. surgeon in charge spl. hospital for nervous diseases in Phila., 1862-65; m. Mary, d. David C. Ogden, of N. J., 1887. Collaborator on surg. subjects. Home: Philadelphia, Pa. Died 1905.

MOREHOUSE, Henry Lyman, clergyman; b. Stanford, N.Y., Oct. 2, 1834; s. Seth S. and Emma B. (Bentley) M.; A.B., U. of Rochester, 1858; grad. Rochester Theol. Sem., 1864; (D.D., Rochester, 1879, LL.D., 1908); unmarried. Ordained Bapt. ministry, 1864; pastor E. Saginaw, Mich., 1864-73, East Av. Ch., Rochester, N.Y., 1873-79; corr. sec., 1879-93, field sec., 1893-1902, corr. sec., 1902—, Am. Bapt. Home Mission Soc. Pres. Mich. Bapt. State Conv., 1870; corr. sec. N.Y. Bapt. Union for Ministerial Edn., 1877-79, Am. Bapt. Edn. Soc., 1893-1903; prominent in organizing Am. Bapt. Edn. Soc. and the Gen. Conv. of Am. Baptists; mem. Am. com. of Bapt. World Alliance, 1905—; editor missionary periodicals. Trustee Kalamazoo Coll., 1868-73, Bapt. Union Theol. Sem., Chicago, 1867-72, Rochester Theol. Sem., 1874-9, Columbian U., 1894-97. Pres. Ministers' Benefit Bd. of Northern Bapt. Conv., 1911—. Author: Baptist Home Missions in America, 1883; History First Baptist Church, Brooklyn, N.Y., 1899. Home: Brooklyn, N.Y. Died May 5, 1917.

MOREHOUSE, Linden Husted, editor, publisher; b. Lower Sandusky (now Fremont), O., Jan. 24, 1842; s. Andrew and Lavinia M.; ed. pub. schs., Fremont, O.; commercial edn., Cleveland, O.; m. Lydia E. Phelps, Aug. 31, 1864; father of Frederic Cook M. Editor and publisher, 1870—, becoming pres. The Young Churchman Co., publishers The Young Churchman, The Shepherd's Arms, The Living Church, etc. Home: Wauwatosa, Wis. Died Aug. 9, 1915.

MOREHOUSE, William Russell, banker, author; b. Bay City, Mich., Feb. 10, 1879; s. Levi and Ida May (Vaughn) M.; ed. high sch., San Jacinto, Calif.; hon. M.B.A., U. of Southern Calif., 1904; m. Helen Merryman, Feb. 7, 1904; children—Idella, Helen (Mrs. John D. Lusk), Alice, Lee. Began with Union Bank of Savings, Los Angeles, 1904; later v.p. Security First National Bank, Los Angeles. Republican. Methodist. Mason. Author: Bank Letters, 1918; Bank Business Building, 1918; Bank Window Displays, 1919; Bankers Guide Book, 1920; How to Succeed in the Bank, 1924; Bank Checks and Bank Deposits, 1928; Constructive Customer Relations. Home: Los Angeles, Calif. Died Dec. 7, 1937.

MOREY, Arthur Thornton, lawyer; b. Brooklyn, N.Y., Aug. 11, 1875; s. Franklin and Mary (Thornton) M.; grad. East Denver (Colo.) High Sch., 1895; LL.B., Columbia, N.Y., 1899; m. Mary Verona Wireback, Aug. 19, 1905; children—David Howard, Mary Verona. Admitted to N.Y. bar, 1900, and began practice in N.Y. City; removed to St. Louis, 1904; admitted to Mo. bar, 1904; apptd. gen. atty. and dir. Commonwealth Steel Co., 1904, and gen. mgr., 1916-29 (retired). Trustee and sec. bd. The Principia Sch. and Coll., St. Louis; mem. Christian Science Publication Com. for Mo. Charter mem. Nat. Safety Council (Chicago) and 2d pres., 1915-16. Republican. Christian Scientist. Mason. Home: St. Louis, Mo. Died May 15, 1936.

MOREY, Chester S., wholesale grocer; b. Medina, Dane Co., Wis., Mar. 3, 1847; s. William H. and Abagail (Baird) M.; ed. dist. and high schs.; m. Anna L. Clough, Dec. 12, 1877 (died 1890). Pvt. Co. I, 36th Wis. Vols.; promoted to corporal and bvtd. 2d lt. Became traveling salesman for Sprague, Warner & Co., Chicago, 1869, mem. firm, 1880; incorporated C. S. Morey Mercantile Co. (wholesale grocers), Denver, 1884, of which is pres.; became pres. and gen mgr. Great Western Sugar Co., 1900, now chmn. bd. Republican. Home: Denver, Colo. Deceased.

MOREY, William Carey, univ. prof.; b. N. Attleboro, Mass., May 23, 1843; s. Reuben and Abby C. (Bogman) M.; served 2d lt. to capt. and bvt. maj. and lt. col. U.S.V., 1862-65; A.B., U. of Rochester, 1868, A.M., 1871; student Rochester Theol. Sem., 1869; Ph.D., Franklin Coll., 1881; D.C.L., Denison, 1903, Rochester, 1908; m. Margaret P., d. Gen. John G. Parkhurst, of Coldwater, Mich., Aug. 4, 1896. Tutor Latin, U. of Rochester, 1869-70; prof. history and English lit., Kalamazoo Coll., 1870-72; prof. Latin and history, 1872-83, history and polit. science, 1883—, U. of Rochester. Trustee, dir. and organizer Reynolds Library, 1884-1904. Author: Outlines of Roman Law, 1884; Outlines of Roman History, 1900; Outlines of Greek History, 1903; Outlines of Ancient History, 1906; The Study of Roman Law in Liberal Education, 1911; Federalism and International Liability, 1913; Ancient Peoples, 1915; The Sale of Munitions of War, 1916; Reminiscences of the "Pundit" Club, 1923; Diplomatic Episodes, 1925. Died Jan. 21, 1925.

MORGAN, Anna, teacher; b. Auburn, N.Y.; d. Allen Denison and Mary Jane (Thornton) M.; ed. at Auburn. Began professional career as a public reader in connection with Mrs. Scott Siddons, 1883; founded the Anna Morgan School of Expression, 1887, producing plays by Ibsen, Maeterlinck and others. Author: Art of Speech and Deportment, 1909; My Chicago, 1916. Compiled "Selected Readings," 1909. Home: Chicago, Ill. Died Aug. 25, 1936.

MORGAN, Anne Eugenia Felicia, writer, lecturer; b. Oberlin, O., Oct. 3, 1845; d. Prof. John M. (of Oberlin Theol. Sem.) and Elizabeth Mary (Leonard) M.; A.B., Oberlin, 1866, A.M., '1869; unmarried. Studied psychol. interpretation of literature, music and art, wrote for press, tutor in various schs., 1866-72; studied philosophy in Germany, 1872-74; tutor in langs., Oberlin, 1875-76; instr. Greek and Latin, Vassar, 1877-78; studied in Europe, 1886-87, 1893-94; prof. philosophy, Wellesley, 1878-1900; invented and published (1897) game called "Bellecycle," scores serving in experimental psychology as records of efficient force of player. Author: The White Lady, 1886; Scripture Studies on the Origin and Destiny of Man, 1887. Home: Saratoga, Santa Clara Co., Calif. Died 1909.

MORGAN, (James) Appleton, Shakespearean scholar; b. Portland, Me., Oct. 2, 1845; s. Peyton Randolph and Joanna D. (Appleton) M.; A.B., Racine (Wis.) Coll., 1867, A.M., 1870; LL.B., Columbia, 1869; m. Olive Morse, Mar. 27, 1877. Asso. counsel Erie Ry. and N.P. R.R., 1875-85; retired from professional practice, 1886; pres. New York & Palisade R.R. Co.; pres. Shakespeare Press Publishing Co. Developed a theory that the Shakespeare plays, as printed in the 1623 folio, are not always strictly monographs but the work of many actors and stage censors, improving them constantly from their original mounting by Shakespeare, and in support of that theory published the Bankside Edition of Shakespeare, in 20 vols. Founded, 1885, and pres., 1885-1925, Shakespeare Soc. of New York (presented with gavel and box made of wood from Shakespeare precincts at Stratford-on-Avon, 1892, and loving cup, 1907, New York, on 7th and 21st anniversaries of election to presidency of this soc.); v.p. gen. Nat. Soc. War of 1812, pres. N.J. State Soc. same, 1898-1901, treas., 1908—. Rescued Poe cottage from demolition and placed 3 tablets in identification of Poe's residences in New York, 1895-1924. Author: The Shakespearean Myth, 1880; Shakespeare in Fact and Criticism, 1884; A Study in the Warwickshire Dialect, 1884; Shakespeare's Pronunciation as Deduced from the Puns in the Plays, 1884; Shakespearean Commentators, 1885; Digesta Shakespeareana, 1887; The People and the Railways, 1888; The Society and the Fad, 1890. Editor: Addison on Contracts, 1875; Best on the Principles of Evidence, 1876; Forsyth on Trial by Jury, 1876; The Bankside Shakespeare, 22 vols., 1888-92; The Bankside Restoration Shakespeare, 5 vols., 1905-08; Genealogical History of the Family of Morgan from A.D. 605 to present times, 1880; Mrs. Shakespeare's Second Marriage and the Transference of 16 non-Quarto Plays to the First Folio, 1925. Presented to Central Park, N.Y. City, 1926, a cutting from mulberry tree growing from root of tree planted at New Place, Stratford-on-Avon, by Shakespeare, in 1607. Died Aug. 15, 1928.

MORGAN, Carey E., clergyman; b. nr. Indianapolis, Aug. 21, 1860; s. Daniel Amaziah and Mary Ann (McCaslin) M.; A.B., Butler Coll., Indianapolis, 1883, A.M., 1885; m. May Dailey, Oct. 11, 1883. Ordained Christian (Disciples) ministry, 1886; pastor, Atlanta and Arcadia, Ind., 1886-87, Wabash, Ind., 1887-94, Portland Av. Ch., Minneapolis, 1894-99, 7th St. Ch., Richmond, Va., 1899-1903, Paris, Ky., 1903-11, Vine St. Ch., Nashville, Tenn., Jan. 1, 1912—. Trustee Butler Coll., 1893-95, George Peabody Coll. for Teachers, Nashville, 1915—; curator Transylvania U., 1903-12. Lecturer on pastoral theology, Vanderbilt, 1917—. Mason. Died May 10, 1925.

MORGAN, Casey Bruce, naval officer; b. Augusta, Ga., Oct. 29, 1867; grad. U.S. Naval Acad., 1888. Promoted ensign, July 1, 1890; lt. jr. grade, Feb. 16, 1898; lt., Mar. 3, 1899; lt. comdr., July 1, 1905; comdr., Sept. 15, 1909; capt., July 1, 1914. Served on Raleigh, Spanish-Am. War, 1898; insp. equipment, San Francisco, Calif., 1905-06; exec. officer, Milwaukee, 1906-08; insp. in charge 11th Light House Dist., Detroit, Mich., 1908-10; comd. Dubuque, 1910-11, Nashville, 1911-12, Missouri, 1912-13; at Naval War Coll., Newport, R.I., 1913; in charge Navy Publicity Bur. and Navy Recruiting Sta., New York, 1913-14; comd. Minnesota, 1914-16; at Naval War College, Newport, R.I., 1917; comd. Squadron Six Patrol Force Atlantic Fleet, 1917; comdr. Agamemnon, Aug. 21, 1917-18; force transport officer, staff comdr. C. and T. Force, 1918-19; comdr. Imperator, May-Aug. 1919; promoted rear admiral, Oct. 1919; comdg. Transport Force, 1919; comdt. Naval Station, Cavite, P.I., 1919-20; comdr. Special Service Squadron, 1921—. Pres. G.C.M. New York, 1922-23; retired on own request, 1923. Died Aug. 17, 1933.

MORGAN, Charles Carroll, lawyer, author; b. Meredith Bridge (now part of Laconia), N.H., July 25, 1832; s. Charles and Sarah Ann (Robinson) M.; matriculated in Brown U. but left coll. on account of trouble with eyes; (hon. M.A., Dartmouth, 1895); m. Marianna Robinson Gove, Oct. 12, 1858 (died 1873). Ednl. writer and lecturer until 1869; lawyer, patent, trade-mark and copyright cases, 1869-1900. Republican. N.H. lay del. to Internat. Congl. Council, Edinburgh, 1908. Author: Colton's American School Geography, 1863. Part author: Fitch's Physical Geography, 1864; Colton's Parlor and Library Atlas, 1864; Loyd's Battle History of the Great Rebellion, 1865. Editor: Two Centuries' Church History of Dunstable-Nashua, N.H., by Prof. J. Wesley Churchill, with Life of the Author, etc., 1918. Lifelong investigator geog. and metaphysical problems. Home: Nashua, N.H. Died Oct. 23, 1918.

MORGAN, Charles Henry, congressman; b. Allegany Co., N.Y., July 5, 1843; ed. pub. and high schs., Wis.; pvt. to capt., 1st and 21st Wis. Inf., 1861-65; LL.B., Albany Law Sch., 1866. Pros. atty. Barton Co., Mo., 4 yrs.; mem. Mo. Ho. of Rep., 1872-74; mem. 44th, 45th, 48th, 53d and 61st Congresses (1875-79, 1883-85, 1893-95, 1909-11). Presdl. elector-at-large, 1882. Lt. col. 5th Mo. Inf. in Spanish-Am. War, 1898. Home: Joplin, Mo. Died 1912.

MORGAN, Charles Herbert, clergyman; b. in Oakland Co., Mich., Nov. 13, 1852; s. Hiram and Mary (De Witt) M.; Albion (Mich.) Coll., 1873-74; A.B., Northwestern U., 1877, A.M., 1880; S.T.B., Boston U., 1879, Ph.D., 1882; m. Emma Webster, June 22, 1887 (died 1918); 1 son, Leslie Webster (dec.); m. 2d, Mrs. Victoria Wellman, Jan. 29, 1921. Ordained M.E. ministry, 1879; pastor at Marquette, Mich., 1879-81, Fowlerville, 1881-82, Romeo, 1882-84, East Saginaw, 1884-87, Adrian, 1887-89, West Bay City, 1889-91, Howell, 1891-95, Vassar, 1895-97, Saginaw, 1897-99, Cass City, 1899-1901, Rochester, 1901-02; associated with Bible study dept. Epworth League, Chicago, 1902-03; asst. editorial sec. Open Door Commn. of M.E. Ch., New York, 1903-05; asst. editorial sec. Missionary Edn. Movement, New York, 1905-18; spl. writer in Centenary Com. of M.E. Ch., New York, 1918-20; sec. Missionary Prayer League, Brooklyn, 1920-21; spl. Biblical writer and editor, with Oxford U. Press, New York, 1922-28; asso. pastor E. Grand Boul. Church, Detroit, 1928-32; pres. Brotherhood Retired Preachers, Detroit Conf. A founder Epworth League, Cleveland, O., May 1889. Author: Studies in the Old Testament, 1905; Scholar's Edition of the Bagster Bible, 1906; The Psalms as Daily Companions, 1919; John, the Interpreter of Christ, 1921; A Year's Bible Course, 1925; Young Folks' Edition of Bible, 1927; Forty Market Mushrooms of America, 1938. Home: Fenton, Mich. Died Oct. 30, 1939.

MORGAN, Charles Hill, mechanical engr., mfr.; b. Rochester, N.Y., Jan. 8, 1831; s. Hiram and Clarissa Lucina (Rich) M.; ed. Lancaster and Clinton acads. and evening schs., Clinton, Mass.; m. Harriet C. Plympton, 1852 (died 1862); m. 2d, Rebecca A. Beagary, Aug. 4, 1863. Draftsman, 1855-60; in business at Phila., 1860-64; gen. supt., 1864-87, dir., 1876-87, Washburn & Moen Co., Worcester, Mass.; consulting engr. Am. Wire Co., Cleveland, 1887—; pres. Morgan Spring Co., 1881—, Morgan Constrn. Co., 1891—; 1st v.p. and dir. Am. Wire Co. of Cleveland. Trustee Worcester Poly. Institute. Conglist. Republican. Home: Worcester, Mass. Died 1911.

MORGAN, Daniel Nash, banker; b. Newtown, Conn., Aug. 18, 1844; s. Ezra and Hannah (Nash) M.; academic edn.; m. Medora H. Judson, June 10, 1868. Mem. Bridgeport (Conn.) Common Council, 2 terms; mayor, 1880-84; mem. Conn. Ho. of Rep., 1883, Senate, 1885-86, and 1893; treas. of U.S., June 1, 1893-July 1, 1897; candidate for gov. of Conn., 1898, for U.S. Senate, 1899. Democrat. Pres. City Nat. Bank, Bridgeport, 1879-93, U.S. Trust Co., Washington, D.C., 1907; pres. Mechanics & Farmers Savings Bank, Bridgeport, 10 yrs. Pres. Bridgeport Hosp., 1891-99. Founder S.R. in State of Conn., 1893, v.p., 1893-1922, pres., 1922-23 (pres. emeritus). Home: Bridgeport, Conn. Died May 30, 1931.

MORGAN, David E., judge; b. Coalport, O., Nov. 8, 1849; s. Evan P. and Anne (Evans) M.; grad. Normal Sch., Platteville, Wis., 1873; spl. course in langs., U. of Wis.; unmarried. Admitted to bar, 1879; practiced at Devils Lake, N.D., from 1883. Dist. atty., Ramsay Co., N.D., 1885-89; judge Dist. Ct., 2d Dist., 1889-1901; justice Supreme Ct. of N.D., 1901-11 (chief justice, 1904-11); resigned, Oct. 30, 1911. Republican. Home: Devils Lake, N.D. Died May 11, 1912.

MORGAN, Dick Thompson, congressman; b. Prairie Creek, Ind., Dec. 6, 1854; s. Valentine and Frances (Thompson) M.; S.B., Union Christian Coll., Merom, Ind., 1876, M.S., 1882; LL.B., Central Law Sch., Indianapolis, 1880; (LL.D., Bethany [W.Va.] College, 1917); m. Ora Heath, May 30, 1878. Practiced at Terre Haute, Ind.; mem. Ind. Ho. of Rep. 1880-81; editor and pub. Terre Haute Courier, 1882-86; atty. A.,T.&S.F. Ry., Garden City, Kan., 1886-89; settled Guthrie, Okla., Apr. 22 1889; register, U.S. Land Office, Woodward Okla., 1904-08; mem. 61st to 66th Congresses (1909-21), 8th Okla. Dist. Republican. Author: Morgan's Manual of U.S. Homestead and Townsite Laws, 1890; Morgan's Digest of Oklahoma Statutes and Supreme Court Decisions, 1893; Morgan's School Land Manual, 1901; Land Credits—A Plea for the American Farmer, 1915. Home: Woodward, Okla. Died July 4, 1920.

MORGAN, Edward Broadbent, lawyer; b. Wethersfield, Conn., Dec. 18, 1862; s. Samuel Broadbent and Ellen Theresa (Blinn) M.; B.A., Yale, 1886; Harvard Law Sch., 2 yrs.; m. Grace Firth Welles, Apr. 12, 1909. Began practice, 1888; with Teller & Orahood; mem. firm of Teller, Orahood & Morgan, 1890-98, alone; pres. Morgan Real Estate & Investment Co. Mem. Colo. Tax Commn., 1915—, chmn., 1919—. Pres. State Hist. and Natural Hist. Soc. of Colo.; v.p. Colo. Forestry Assn.; pres. Colo. Yale Assn. Republican. Home: Denver, Colo. Died Sept. 6, 1935.

MORGAN, Edward M., postmaster; b. Marshall, Mich., Nov. 16, 1855; s. Charles H. and Mary J. M.; ed. common schs.; m. Fannie Tattersall, 1891. Began as mail carrier, New York, 1873; gen. supt. of city delivery, New York Postoffice, 1889-97; asst. postmaster, 1897-1907; postmaster, 1907-17, and 1921—. Pres. Nat. Assn. of Postmasters. Home: New York, N.Y. Died Jan. 9, 1925.

MORGAN, Edwin Vernon, diplomatist; b. Aurora, N.Y., Feb. 22, 1865; s. Henry A. and Margaret (Bogart) M.; A.B., Harvard, 1890, A.M., 1891; student U. of Berlin, 1891-92, 1894-95; unmarried. Asst. in history, Harvard, 1892-94; instr. in history, Adelbert Coll., Cleveland, 1895-98; sec. to Samoan High Commn., Apr. 1899; sec. legation, Seoul, Korea, 1900; vice and deputy consul gen. at Seoul, Korea, 1900, transferred as 2d sec. of embassy to St. Petersburg, 1901; apptd. confidential clerk to 3d asst. sec. of state, Washington, 1902; consul at Dalny, Manchuria, 1904; E.E. and M.P. to Korea, Mar.-Nov. 1905, to Cuba, 1905-10, to Uruguay and Paraguay, 1910-11, to Portugal, 1911-12; ambassador E. and P. to Brazil, Jan. 18, 1912—. Chevalier Légion d'Honneur (France). Hon. mem. Instituto Historico e Geographico Brasileiro, Rio de Janeiro. Home: Aurora, N.Y. Died Apr. 16, 1934.

MORGAN, Ezra Leonidas, coll. prof.; b. Bone Gap, Ill., Aug. 22, 1879; s. Allyn Theodore and Rosina (Smith) M.; A.B., McKendree Coll., 1904; M.A., U. of Wis., 1912; Ph.D., Mass. State Coll., 1932; m. Mary F. Flint, June 26, 1906; children—Elizabeth, Esther, Mary, Ruth. Extension prof. community organization, Mass. State Coll., Amherst, 1912-19; dir. rural service, Am. Red Cross, hdqrs. Washington, D.C., 1919-21; prof. and chmn. dept. rural sociology, in charge training for public welfare work, U. of Mo., 1921—. Mem. Governor's Social Security Survey Com., 1936, State Social Security Commission, 1937. Methodist. Mason. Kiwanian. Home: Columbia, Mo. Died Oct. 12, 1937.

MORGAN, F(isher) Corlies, univ. treas.; b. Philadelphia, Pa., May 16, 1875; s. John Buck and Sarah Fisher (Corlies) M.; prep. edn., Friends Select Sch., Germantown, Phila.; A.B., U. of Pa., 1896; LL.B., 1900; m. Mary Newbold Welsh Frazer, Sept. 5, 1908 (now dec.); m. 2d, Lilian Bartow Smith, June 4, 1917. In gen. practice of law, Phila., 1899-1917; mem. legal dept. The United Gas Improvement Co., 1900-10; treas. U. of Pa., 1910—; treas. Univ. Mus.; dir. Germantown Trust Co., San Luis Valley Land & Cattle Co. Served in various positions including asst. mgr. Pa.-Del. Div. Am. Red Cross, 1917-19. Trustee Moore Sch. of Elec. Engring.; mgr. Grad. Hosp. of U. of Pa. Republican. Presbyn. Home: Philadelphia, Pa. Died June 13, 1939.

MORGAN, (Miles) Forrest, librarian; b. Rockville, Conn., Mar. 20, 1852; s. Miles Chandler and Philura M.; ed. country sch.; (hon. A.M., Trinity, 1903); m. Frances R. Fisher, May 28, 1879. Mgr. of printing and advertising Travelers Ins. Co., and editor Travelers Record (monthly), 1882-96; engaged in lit. work. Asst. librarian Watkinson Library, Hartford, Conn. Mem. Conn. Hist. Society. Unitarian. Editor: Walter Bagehot's works, 1891. Editor: (and part writer) Reclus' Bird's-Eye View of the World, 1887; Connecticut as a Colony and a State, 1904; Ridpath's New Complete History of the United States. Home: Hartford, Conn. Died Feb. 24, 1924.

MORGAN, George, author, editor; b. Concord, Del., Oct. 10, 1854; s. James Wesley and Elizabeth M.; A.B., U. of Del., 1875, A.M., 1878 (LL.D., 1917); m. Mary R. Churchman, Dec. 25, 1879; children—Mrs. Anna Morgan Roberts. Ralph, Mary Churchman. In Phila. journalism, 1875-1929, on Times, Press and Record. Author: The True Patrick Henry, 1907; The True LaFayette, 1919; The City of Firsts—a Complete History of Philadelphia, 1920, 2d edit., 1926; The Life of James Monroe, 1921; Patrick Henry, revised, with full bibliography, 1929. Home: Philadelphia, Pa. Died Jan. 8, 1936.

MORGAN, George Hagar, secretary; b. Plattsburg, N.Y., Dec. 16, 1838; s. William Henry and Mary Louise (Hagar) M.; ed. Plattsburgh Acad.; m. Ella F. Morean, Sept. 13, 1866. Taught sch. at Hebron, Wis., 1857-58; bookkeeper and cashier, Milwaukee, 1858-59, St. Louis, 1860-64; sec. and treas. Merchants' Exchange of St. Louis, Jan. 6, 1865—(oldest sec. in point of service of any commercial assn. in U.S.). Treas. St. Louis Traffic Bur. Capt. Co. B, 7th Regt. Enrolled Mo. Militia during Civil War. Sec. St. Louis Provident Assn.; dir. Hosp. Saturday and Sunday Assn. Republican. Conglist. Home: St. Louis, Mo. Died Oct. 31, 1911.

MORGAN, George Wilson, lawyer; b. East Orange, N.J., June 28, 1875; s. William Henry and Geraldine (Woods) M.; A.B., Oberlin (O.) Coll., 1897, LL.D., 1922; LL.B., Columbia, 1900; m. Helen E. Demuth, Nov. 10, 1906; children—George Wilson, Gerald Demuth, Barbara Woods. Admitted to N.Y. bar, 1900, and began practice at N.Y. City; mem. Breed, Abbott & Morgan; chmn. bd. F. W. Dodge Corp.; dir. Underwriters Trust Co., N.J.&N.Y. R.R. Co. Dep. asst. dist. atty., N.Y. County, 1902-03; supt. of elections, N.Y., 1903-06. Trustee Oberlin Coll.; dir. Beekman Street Hospital. Republican. Home: New York, N.Y. Died Mar. 28, 1931.

MORGAN, Harry Hays, consul gen.; b. New Orleans, Dec. 24, 1860; s. Philip Hickey and Beatrice Leslie (Ford) M.; ed. pvt. tutors at Brussels, Belgium and Bonn, Germany, until 16; Exeter Academy, Exeter, N.H., 1876-78; studied law with his father, 1880-84; m. Laura, d. Gen. Judson Kilpatrick, of N.J., June 29, 1897. Sec. Am. Legation, City of Mexico, 1882-85; consul at Horgen, Switzerland, 1897-98, Aarau, Switzerland, 1898-1902, Lucerne, Switzerland, 1902-06, Stuttgart, Germany, June 22, 1906-Apr. 29, 1907, Amsterdam, Netherlands, 1907-10; consul gen. at Barcelona, Spain, May 11, 1910-13, at Hamburg, Germany, 1913-17; detailed as spl. agt. to investigate conditions in Cuba, May 15, 1917; rep. in Cuba of food and fuel administrations and war trade and shipping bds., Aug. 1917-Jan. 1, 1919; apptd. Am. consul gen. to Antwerp, Dec. 17, 1918, to Brussels, May 10, 1919; apptd. commr. of U.S. to negotiate direct with the Belgian Govt. on the reconstruction of Belgium, May 20, 1919; consul gen. at Buenos Aires, Argentina, 1923-25; retired. Died Mar. 19, 1933.

MORGAN, Henry William, dentist; b. Davidson Co., Tenn., Oct. 25, 1853; s. Dr. William Henry and Sarah Ame (Noel) M.; grad. Nashville High Sch., 1873; M.D., Vanderbilt U., 1875; D.D.S., Phila. Dental Coll., 1876; m. Matilda Alloway Evans, Nov. 3, 1880. Prof. operative dentistry, 1886—; dean Sch. of Dentistry, 1911-19, Vanderbilt Univ. Trustee Walden U. (pres. bd.), Meharry Med. Sch. (pres. bd.), Monteagle S.S. Assembly. Mem. M.E. Ch., S. Mason. Past Grand Chancellor and Past Sup. Rep. K.P. of Tenn.; Past Grand Regent and Past Sup. Rep. Royal Arcanum. Home: Nashville, Tenn. Died Jan. 17, 1920.

MORGAN, James Dudley, physician; b. Washington, July 5, 1862; s. James Ethelbert and Norah T. (Digges) M.; A.B., Georgetown U., 1881, M.D., 1885; Beaujon Hosp., Paris, France, 1885-86, Anpitheâtre d' Anatomie des Hôpitaux, Paris, 1886; m. Mary Abell, Dec. 2, 1892. Demonstrator of anatomy, 1888-89, lecturer on differential diagnosis, 1897-98, Georgetown U.; asso. and clin. prof. medicine, George Washington U., 1910-17; phys. to Garfield Hosp., 1899—; chief of medical service Emergency Hosp., 1904—. Home: Chevy Chase, Md. Died Nov. 21, 1919.

MORGAN, James Henry, coll. pres.; b. Concord, Del., Jan. 21, 1857; s. Samuel Jefferson and Julia Fooks (James) M.; A.B., Dickinson Coll., 1878, A.M., 1881; Ph.D., Bucknell U., 1892; LL.D., Pa. Coll., 1916, Franklin and Marshall Coll., 1917, U. of Pittsburgh, 1919; D.D., Wesleyan U., 1917; m. Mary Rebecca Curran, Dec. 30, 1890; children—Julia, Margaret Harris, Hugh Curran. Teacher, 1878-79, vice-prin., 1879-81, Pennington (N.J.) Sem.; teacher, Rugby Acad., Phila., 1881-82; prin. Dickinson Coll. Prep. Sch., Carlisle, Pa., 1882-84; adj. prof. Greek, 1884-90, prof. Greek, 1890-1914, dean, 1903-14, acting pres., 1914-15, pres., 1915-28, 1931-32, and 1933-34, Dickinson College. Sch. dir. Carlisle, Pa., 1898-1904. Mem. Gen. Conf. M.E. Ch., 1916. Mem. M.E. Ch. Author: History of Dickinson College, 1933. Home: Carlisle, Pa. Died Oct. 17, 1939.

MORGAN, James Norris, soldier; b. Alton, Ill., Nov. 2, 1839; s. James Madison and Elizabeth (McCrellish) M.; ed. McKendree Coll., Ill., 1854-57; m. Ella Dora Dimmick, May 4, 1875 (died 1909). Traveled across the plains on foot, Leavenworth to Denver, 1859; spent 15 mos. in the gold mines and returned to Alton, Ill.; enrolled in vol. service, Apr. 26, 1861; mustered into Ill. provisional regt., May 11, 1861, and into U.S. Vols., June 25, 1861; 2d lt., Co. B, 22d Ill. Vols., June 25, 1861; 1st lt., Mar. 1, 1862; capt., June 13, 1862; hon. mustered out, July 7, 1864; enlisted as pvt. 144th Ill. Inf., Sept. 10, 1864; commd. capt., Sept. 10, 1864; maj., Sept. 26, 1864; lt. col., Mar. 18, 1865; mustered out, July 14, 1865; commd. 2d lt. 38th U.S. Inf., July 28, 1866; 1st lt., June 12, 1867; capt., June 20, 1873; retired from active service with rank of maj., Apr. 17, 1897; advanced to rank of lt. col. retired, Apr. 23, 1904. Participated in many battles in depts. of Miss. and the South; while serving as capt. at battle of Stone River, Tenn., after several color bearers of the regt. had been wounded or killed, took the colors and rallied the regt. (about to disintegrate) and marched the regt. to Gen. Jefferson C. Davis; in action at Adairsville, Ga., May 1864, captured complete complement, as to officers and men of his co.; served in Southwest after the war; with co. built telegraph line, Separ, N.M., to Mex. boundary, 35 miles, in 24 working hours. Bvtd. 1st lt. and capt. "for gallant and meritorious service on the field at Stone River"; maj. "for gallant and meritorious service on the field at New Hope Ch., Ga." Republican. Mason. Home: Alton, Ill. Died Aug. 5, 1925.

MORGAN, John Livingston Rutgers, chemist; b. New Brunswick, N.J., June 27, 1872; s. Brockholst (D.D.) and Mary (Rutgers) M.; B.S., Rutgers Coll., 1892, Sc.D., 1916; A.M., Ph.D., U. of Leipzig, 1895; m. Luna M. Rutgers, June 2, 1914. Asst. in chemistry, Stevens Inst., 1895-96, instr. quantitative analysis, Brooklyn Poly. Inst., 1896-97; tutor chem. physics and chem. philosophy, 1897-1901, adj. prof. physical chemistry, 1901-05, prof., 1905—, Columbia. Fellow Chem. Soc. London, A.A.A.S. Author: The Principles of Mathematical Chemistry (from the German of G. Helm), 1897; The Theory of Solution and Its Results, 1897; The Elements of Physical Chemistry, 5th edit., 1914; Physical Chemistry for Electrical Engineers, 2d edit., 1909. Home: New York, N.Y. Died Apr. 13, 1935.

MORGAN, John Pierpont, financier; b. Hartford, Conn., Apr. 17, 1837; s. Junius Spencer and Juliet (Pierpont) M.; grad. English High Sch., Boston; student U. of Göttingen; (LL.D., Yale University, 1908, Harvard University, 1910); m. Amelia Sturges, 1861 (died 1862); m. 2d, Frances Louise Tracy, 1865 (has 1 son, 3 daughters, 11 grandchildren); father of John Pierpont M., Jr. Entered bank of Duncan, Sherman & Co., 1857; became agt. and atty. in U.S., 1860, for George Peabody & Co., bankers, London, in which his father was partner; mem. Dabney, Morgan & Co., investment securities, 1864-71; became mem., 1871, of firm of Drexel, Morgan & Co., now J. P. Morgan & Co., leading pvt. bankers of U.S.; also J. S. Morgan & Co., London. Largely occupied as financier in largest reorganizations of rys. and consolidation of industrial properties; floated U.S. bonds issue of $62,000,000 during Cleveland administration; organized and floated securities of U.S. Steel Corp., 1901 (capital $1,100,000,000); secured Am. subscriptions of $50,000,000 to British war loan of Apr., 1901; organized existing agreement of anthracite operators of Pa., also of soft coal interests in Ohio, Ind. and Pa.; controls over 50,000 miles of rys., large Am. and British ocean transportation lines. Gave site, bldgs. and funds amounting to about $1,500,000 to Lying-In Hosp., New York, and large donations to the New York trade Schs., the Cathedral of St. John the Divine, and many other instns.; has made valuable gifts to Am. Mus. Natural History, Met. Mus. Art and New York Pub. Library. Owns famous collections of pictures (including famous Gainsborough painting), books, MSS., curios, etc. Yachtsman, has been commodore New York Yacht Club; built "Columbia," which defeated "Shamrock" for America's Cup, 1899 and 1901. Pres. Met. Mus. of Art. Grand Cross Order of the Red Eagle, Germany, 1911. Home: New York, N.Y. Died Mar. 31, 1913.

MORGAN, John Tyler, U.S. senator from Ala., 1877-1907; b. Athens, Tenn., June 20, 1824; emigrated to Ala. when 9 yrs. old; academic edn.; admitted to bar, 1845; practiced until elected to the senate. Presidential elector, 1860; delegate to Ala. Secession Conv., 1861; joined C.S.A., May 1861, as private; promoted through all grades to col. 51st Ala. regt., which he raised; was brig. gen., 1863-65. After war resumed practice at Selma, Ala.; presdl. elector, 1876. Democrat. Apptd. by President Harrison as arbitrator on Bering Sea fisheries, 1892; apptd. by President McKinley, July 1898, one of commrs. to organize govt. in Hawaii, after passage of annexation bill. Home: Selma, Ala. Died 1907.

MORGAN, Maud, harpist; b. N.Y. City, Nov. 22, 1864; d. George Washbourne (organist, 1822-92) and Eleanor M.; studied music with her father and with the artist Alfred Toulmin, and later with the chevalier, Charles Oberthür, harpist to the Queen of Belgians. Début as harpist in 1875, in a concert with Ole Bull and has since then been heard in all leading Am. cities. Harpist in Grace Ch., New York, 1895-1920. Conductor Lenox Choral Soc., 7 yrs. V.p. Nat. Assn. Harpists, Inc., and mgr. of its first convention concert, at Carnegie Hall, New York, at which 93 harps were played together; also mgr. 2d conv., Chicago, Apr. 1922; drilled and conducted ensemble of 93 harps at both New York and Chicago convs. in Handel's "Largo." Conducts summer sch. for harp (1st harp sch. in America). Hon. pres. Central Soc. of Harpists. Home: New York, N.Y. Died Dec. 12, 1941.

MORGAN, Michael Ryan, brig. gen.; b. Nova Scotia, Jan. 18, 1833; ed. in New Orleans, up to 1850; grad. U.S. Mil. Acad., 1854; m. Judith Porter, d. Edward and Harriet Howard Adams, of Charlestown, Mass., May 30, 1860; m. 2d, Antoinette Mary, d. John S. and Emma S. Prince, of St. Paul, Jan. 9, 1879. Second lt. 3d Arty., July 1, 1854; promoted through grades to lt. col. asst. commissary gen., U.S.A., Aug. 28, 1888; col., July 14, 1890; brig. gen. commissary subsistence U.S.A., Oct. 8, 1894. Bvtd. maj., lt. col. and col., July 6, 1864, "for distinguished services"; brig. gen., Apr. 9, 1865, "for gallant and meritorious services." Served at various frontier posts until 1859; was on Harper's Ferry expdn. to suppress John Brown's raid, 1859; chief commissary of subsistence, Dept. of the South; on staff Gen. U. S. Grant, 1864; took part in siege of Petersburg, Va., June to Sept. 1864, and the engagements in that section, and up to the surrender of Lee; commissary of subsistence U.S.A., 1894-97; retired by operation of law, Jan. 18, 1897. Now v.p. Security Trust Co., St. Paul, Minn. Died 1911.

MORGAN, Morris Hicky, prof. classical philology, Harvard; b. Providence, R.I., Feb. 8, 1859; s. Morris B. and Isabelle (Manton) M.; grad. Harvard, 1881, A.M., Ph.D., Harvard, 1887; LL.D. (Hobart); m. Eleonora Semmes Gibson, Baltimore. Author: De Ignis Eliciendi Modis apud Antiquos, 1890; Dictionary to Xenophon's Anabasis, 1892; translation of Xenophon's The Art of Horsemanship, 1893; Bibliography of Persius, 1893; The Phormio of Terence, 1895; Eight Orations of Lysias, 1895; A School Latin Grammar, 1899; The Minor Works of Tacitus, 1904; The Language of Vitruvius, 1906. Home: Cambridge, Mass. Died 1910.

MORGAN, Octavius, architect; b. Canterbury, Eng., Oct. 20, 1850; s. Giles Chapman and Caroline (Adams) M.; studied architectural drawing in Eng.; came to America, 1870; m. Mrs. Margaret Weller Offenbacher, Oct. 16, 1885. Practiced, Denver, 1871-72, Los Angeles, Calif., 1873—; mem. Morgan, Walls and Morgan. Architect Childs' Opera House, Nadeau Hotel, Cordona Bldg., Odd Fellows Hall, Farmers & Merchants Bank Bldg., Morosco Theatre, I. N. Van Nuys Bldg., W. P. Story Bldg., W. I. Hollingworth Bldg., Los Angeles Stock Exchange, and many pvt. residences, Los Angeles. Pres. Allied Architects' Assns. Fellow A.I.A. (dir.). Republican. Episcopalian. Died Mar. 29, 1922.

MORGAN, Samuel Tate, manufacturer; b. Wake Co., N.C., May 15, 1857; s. Samuel Davidson and Talithia Adaline (Tate) M.; ed. Bingham's Mil. Sch. and Horner's Mil. Sch., N.C.; m. Sally F., d. Hon. George W. Thompson, of Wake Co., Sept. 15, 1875. Left sch. at 17 to assist widowed mother on plantation; removed to Durham, N.C., 1879, and engaged in grain and provision business, also handling fertilizers; organized the Durham Fertilizer Co., 1881, which grew into the Va.-Carolina Chem. Co., of which is pres.—the largest co. of the kind in the world, with paid-up capital of $46,000,000, mfg. 1,000,000 tons of fertilizer per year; also pres. Southern Cotton Oil Co., Charleston (S.C.) Mining & Mfg. Co. Democrat. Baptist. Home: Richmond, Va. Died Apr. 1920.

MORGAN, Tali Esen, musical author, conductor; b. Llangynwyd, Glamorganshire, S. Wales, Oct. 28, 1858; s. Thomas Llyfnwy (noted Welsh historian) and Gwen M.; studied music from childhood; came to Scranton, Pa., with the family in 1877; hon. Mus.D.; m. Mary J. Jones, Jan. 31, 1881 (died 1938); children—Ethel, Oscar, Edith, Kays, Paul (dec.), Marion. Manager and conductor of summer music festivals at Ocean Grove for 17 yrs., directing choruses of 1,200 voices and orchestra of 100; dir. vol. ch. choir (200) at the Central Meth. Ch., Brooklyn; dir. New York Festival Chorus; founder and pres. Internat. Corr. Sch. of Music; dir. Mt. Vernon (N.Y.) Choral Club of 1st M.E. Ch. (200 voices). Founder Nat. Assn. Organists, also Musicians Club of New York. Author of a standard course of music instrn. for teachers and pub. sch. supervisors. Home: Asbury Park, N.J. Died June 30, 1941.

MORGAN, Thomas J., Baptist minister, corr. sec. Am. Baptist Home Mission Soc., 1893—; b. Franklin, Ind., Aug. 17, 1839; s. Rev. Lewis M.; ed. Franklin Coll., leaving in senior yr. to enlist in 7th Ind. vol. inf., 1861; served 3 months and then took charge of public schools, Atlanta, Ill.; 1st lt., 70th Ind. vol. inf., 1862; served until 1865, rising to rank bvt. brig. gen.; prominent in enlistment of colored troops. Entered Rochester Theol. Sem., 1865; grad. same, 1868 (LL.D., Franklin Coll., 1894; D.D., Univ. of Chicago, 1874); m. 1870 Caroline Starr. Prof. homiletics and church history, Baptist Theol. Sem., Chicago 7 yrs.; prin. normal schools, Providence, R.I., and elsewhere. Commr. Indian affairs, 1889-93. Editor: Home Mission Monthly. Author: Educational Mosaics, 1887; Students' Hymnal, 1888; Studies in Pedagogy, 1888; Patriotic Citizenship, 1895; Praise Hymnal, 1897; Negro in America, 1900. Home: Yonkers, N.Y. Died 1902.

MORGAN, Thomas John, lawyer, socialist leader; b. Birmingham, England, October 27, 1847; s. Thomas John and Hannah (Simcox) M.; ed. Sunday and evening schools; worked at machinist's trade 38 yrs.; m. Elizabeth Chambers, Jan. 26, 1868. Active in labor movement, 1871—; Socialist Labor nominee for mayor of Chicago, 1891; one of the com. to secure the location of the World's Fair at Chicago; represented the labor orgns. of the U.S. before Congressional com. at Washington, requesting opening of World's Fair on Sunday. Grad. Chicago Law Coll., 1895; is now in practice as a lawyer. One of com. of 100 selected by Civic Fedn. to recommend reforms in Chicago pub. schs. Sec. Nat. Campaign Com., Social Dem. Party, 1900; Social Dem. candidate for state's atty., Cook Co., Ill., 1900. Lecturer Nat. Sociol. Convocation, Lake Bluff, Ill., 1900. Nominee Socialist Party for city atty., Chicago, 1903, for judge Superior Court, Cook Co., Ill., 1903, 1907, for U.S. senator, 1909; chmn. Ill. State campaign com. Socialist Party, 1904; mem. State com. and Cook Co. exec. com., 1905; chmn. Cook Co. Central and exec. com., 1906; mem. Central and exec. com., 1907. Editor and pub. The Provoker, 1909—. Home: Chicago, Ill. Died Dec. 10, 1912.

MORGAN, Thomas W., warden; b. Benton Co., Mo., Apr. 18, 1862; s. Thomas T. and Kate (Monroe) M.; grad. High Sch., Eureka, Kan., 1880; m. Jennie Stilwell, May 10, 1888 (died 1915); children—Miriam, Maurice. Was the founder and editor of Eureka Messenger (weekly newspaper), 1884-1901; owner and pub. Ottawa Daily Republic, 1902-15. Postmaster, Eureka, Kan., 1894-98; mem. bd. mgrs. State Reformatory, Kan., 1907-11; pres. State Bd. Penal Instns., 1911-13; warden U.S. Penitentiary, Leavenworth, Kan., 1913-Dec. 1918; mem. Dem. State Central Com., Kan., 24 yrs.; cashier and mgr. First Nat. Bank, Eureka, Kan. Trustee Ottawa U. Conglist. Mason. Home: Eureka, Kan. Deceased.

MORGAN, Tom P., humorist; b. East Lyme, Conn., Dec. 1, 1864; s. Joseph P. and Mary Ann M.; at school about 3 yrs. in Conn., about 7 in Kan.; unmarried. Republican. Has contributed to leading publs. using humor. Regular contbr. to Curtis publications; contributing daily humorous column to Kansas City Star. Home: Rogers, Ark. Died July 7, 1929.

MORGAN, William, artist; b. London, England, 1830; began his art education at the Nat. Acad. of Design, New York; later studied at Havre, France. His specialty is genre pictures. Asso. Nat. Acad., 1865—; mem. Artist Fund Soc., etc. Home: New York, N.Y. Died 1900.

MORGAN, William Forbes, sec. Dem. Nat. Committee; b. New York, N.Y., Sept. 22, 1879; s. William Forbes and Ellen Bond (Robinson) M.; ed. Harrow, Harrow-on-the-Hill, Eng., 1893-99; m. Edith Livingston Hall, Feb. 1904 (died 1920); 1 son, William Forbes; m. 2d, Sarah Jackson Coonley, Sept. 5, 1933. Entered stock exchange business, 1899; partner E. Rollins, Moss & Bro., Boston, 1903-06; partner Wilmerding, Morgan & Livermore, 1906-12; dep. gov., Farm Credit Adminstrn., 1933-35; then sec. Dem. Nat. Committee. Maj. 12th N.Y. Inf. during World War. Treas. for Men Blinded in Battle. Democrat. Episcopalian. Mason. Home: Washington, D.C. Died Apr. 20, 1937.

MORGAN, William Henry, dentist; b. Logan Co., Ky., Feb. 22, 1818; s. Joseph Underwood M.; grad. dentistry, Baltimore Dental Coll., 1848; grad. in medicine, Univ. Nashville, 1871; m. Sarah A. Noel, Nov. 30, 1852. Pres. Tenn. Dental Assn., 1867; pres. Am. Dental Assn., 1871; dean dept. dentistry, Vanderbilt Univ., and prof. clinical dentistry, same, 1879-1900; mem. book com., Southern Meth. Pub. House for 30 yrs.; mem. bd. trustees, Central Tenn. Coll., for 20 yrs. and 5 yrs. pres. of bd. Apptd. Indian commr. by Grover Cleveland during his 1st administration. Home: Nashville, Tenn. Died 1901.

MORGAN, William Henry, mfr.; b. Pittston, Pa., June 1, 1865; s. Thomas R. (Sr.) and Elizabeth (Nicholas) M.; student Mt. Union Coll. and spl. training in father's shop, in elec. and mech. engring.; m. Annette Sharer Morgan, Mar. 2, 1897; 1 son, William Henry. V.p. 1894-97, pres., 1897—, Morgan Engring. Co. A.d.c. on staff of Gov. George K. Nash 4 yrs., with rank of col. Trustee Mt. Union College. Republican. Home: Alliance, O. Died Mar. 29, 1928.

MORGAN, William M., congressman; b. Licking Co., O., Aug. 1, 1870; s. James M. and Mary Eleanor M.; ed. pub. schs. and pvt. study of lit. and science; m. Jennie Legge, 1903 (dec.); 1 dau., Martha Eleanor; m. 2d, Mrs. Jane Logan Crossland, 1925. Mcht. and farmer. Mem. 67th to 71st Congresses (1921-31), 17th Ohio Dist. Republican. Methodist. K.P., Elk, Woodman, Kiwanian. Home: Newark, O. Died Sept. 17, 1935.

MORGAN, William Yost, author, editor; b. Cincinnati, O., Apr. 6, 1866; s. W. A. and Minnie D. (Yost) M.; A.B., U. of Kan., 1885; m. Colie Adair, Nov. 1890. Editor and proprietor of Hutchinson (Kan.) News and Herald. State printer of Kansas, 1898-1902; member Kan. Ho. of Rep., 1905-11; lt. gov. of Kan., terms 1914-16, 1916-18. Was Y.M.C.A. sec. with A.E.F. in France. Chmn. Bd. Regents Kan. Ednl. Instns. Republican. Presbyn. Mason. Author: Journey of a Jayhawker, 1905; A Jayhawker in Europe, 1911; The Near East, 1913; Yurrup As Is, 1926. Director of Exchange Nat. Bank. Home: Hutchinson, Kan. Died Feb. 17, 1932.

MORIARTY, William Daniel, economist; b. Oil City, Pa., Dec. 15, 1877; s. William Henry and Elizabeth Cornelia (Holland) M.; A.B., U. of Mich., 1904, A.M., 1905, Ph.D., 1909; m. Dorothy Elizabeth McMahan, Dec. 27, 1905; 1 son, John Singleton. Head of English dept., Northwestern State Normal Sch., Okla., 1905-07; instr. English, 1907-13, asst. prof., 1913-17, asst. prof. English and economics, 1917-19, U. of Mich.; asso. prof. business administration, U. of Wash., 1919-23, prof., 1923-26; prof. economics, U. of Southern Calif., 1926-29, prof. economics and dir. School of Merchandising, 1929—. Ednl. dir. Los Angeles Advertising Club, 1926-29; president Calif. Commodity Exchange, 1930-33. Democrat. Conglist. Mason. Author: Economics of Marketing and Advertising, 1923; Economics for Citizenship, 1925. Died Apr. 14, 1936.

MORISON, George Shattuck, civil engineer; b. New Bedford, Mass., Dec. 19, 1842; s. Rev. Dr. John Hopkins and Emily (Rogers) M.; grad. Harvard, 1863 (A.M., LL.B., 1866); admitted to bar New York, 1866; engaged as engineer at Kansas City, 1867-71; in Mich. and Ind., 1871-73; at New York, 1873-87; first on Erie Ry., later in gen. practice; lived at Chicago, 1887-98, retaining New York office; returned to New York, 1898. Apptd. by President Cleveland, 1894, mem. bd. engrs. to determine greatest practical length of span for bridge across the North river at New York; mem. bd. to locate deep water harbor in Southern Calif., 1896-97; mem. bd. cons. engrs. dept. of docks, New York, 1895-97. Mem. Isthmian Canal Commn., 1899-1901. Was chief engr. bridge across the Ohio at Cairo, Ill., and across the Mississippi at Memphis, Tenn.; also 4 others across the Mississippi, 10 across the Missouri, etc. Died 1903.

MORITZ, Robert Edouard, university prof.; b. Christiansthal, Germany, June 2, 1868; s. Karl Robert and Martha Marie (Stahlhut) M.; B.S., Hastings (Neb.) Coll., 1892; Ph.M., U. of Chicago, 1896; Ph.D., U. of Neb., 1901; Ph.N.D., U. of Strassburg, 1902; m. Cassia L. Kennedy, Aug. 29, 1895. Instr. mathematics, 1893-94, prof., 1894-98, Hastings; instr. mathematics, 1898-1902, adj. prof., 1902-03, asst. prof., 1903-04, U. of Neb.; prof. mathematics, U. of Washington, Seattle, 1904—. Author: Plane Trigonometry, 1911; Spherical Trigonometry, 1913; Memorabilia Mathematica, 1914; also Quotientiation-process, Theory of Ratients, Cyclic-harmonic Curves. Conglist. Died Dec. 28, 1940.

MORLAN, Webster Smith, lawyer; b. Crawford Co., O., Apr. 19, 1848; s. Joseph and Mary McBride (Jackson) M.; ed. Ia. Luth. Coll., Albion, Ia.; m. Mary E. Evans, Neb., Jan. 10, 1874. Admitted to bar, 1869; dist. atty., 8th Jud. Dist., Neb., 1883-87; atty. for western div. of C.,B. & Q. R.R., 1888—, in Neb., Kan. and Colo. Republican. Home: McCook, Neb. Died Oct. 22, 1915.

MORLEY, Edward Williams, chemist; b. Newark, N.J., 1838; s. Rev. Sardis Brewster and Anna C. (Treat) M.; bro. of John Henry M.; A.B., Williams Coll., 1860, A.M., 1863; (hon. Ph.D., U. of Wooster, 1878; LL.D., Adelbert Coll., 1891, Williams Coll., 1901, Lafayette Coll., 1907, U. of Pittsburgh, 1915; ScD., Yale, 1909; m. Isabella E. Birdsall, Dec. 24, 1868. Prof. chemistry, Western Reserve Coll., Hudson, O. (afterward removed to Cleveland and named Adelbert Coll.), 1869-1906; also prof. chemistry, Cleveland Med. Coll., 1873-88. Has devised improved apparatus for gas analysis, etc. Hon. mem. Royal Inst., London; asso. fellow Am. Acad. Arts and Sciences; fellow A.A.A.S. (pres. 1895-96). Home: West Hartford, Conn. Died Feb. 24, 1923.

MORLEY, Frank, univ. prof.; b. Woodbridge, Suffolk, Eng., Sept. 9, 1860; s. Joseph R. and Elizabeth (Muskett) M.; A.B., King's Coll., Cambridge, 1883, A.M., 1886, ScD., 1898; m. Lilian Janet Bird, of Hayward's Heath, Sussex, Eng., July 11, 1889; children—Christopher D., Felix M., Frank V. Master, Bath Coll., Eng., 1884-87; instr., 1887-88, prof. pure mathematics, 1888-1900, Haverford Coll., Pa.; prof. mathematics, Johns Hopkins, 1900-28. Author: (with Prof. James Harkness) Elementary Treatise on the Theory of Functions, 1893; Introduction to the Theory of Analytic Functions, 1898; (with F. V. Morley) Inversive Geometry, 1933. Home: Baltimore, Md. Died Oct. 17, 1937.

MORLEY, George Bidwell, banker; b. Painesville, O., Oct. 16, 1857; s. John Rufus and Catharine Bidwell (McVay) M.; ed. pub. schs., Ft. Scott, Kan.; m. Lulu Avery, Apr. 27, 1881. With Second Nat. Bank (now Second Nat. Bank and Trust Co.), Saginaw, 1876—, teller until 1882, cashier, 1882-1901, pres. 1901-29, chmn. bd., 1929—; pres. Mich. Sugar Co.; v.p. Wallace & Morley Co., Wallace Stone Co.; dir. Huron Portland Cement Co., Consol. Coal Co., Bad Axe Grain Co., Brewer-Neinstedt Lumber Co.; dir. Detroit Br. Federal Reserve Bank of Chicago. Mem. board of trustees of Home for the Aged, Saginaw Welfare League. Home: Saginaw, Mich. Died Dec. 25, 1935.

MORLEY, John Henry, clergyman; b. Hartford, Conn., Jan. 3, 1840; s. Rev. Sardis Brewster and Anna C. (Treat) M.; bro. of Edward Williams M.; A.B., Williams Coll., 1863; A.M., 1866; grad. Andover Theol. Sem., 1866; (LL.D., Williams, 1900); m. Edith T. Johnson, Oct. 12, 1871. Ordained Congl. ministry, 1867; with U.S. Christian Commn., 1864-66; pastor Magnolia, Ia., 1866-69, Sioux City, Ia., 1869-76, Winona, Minn., 1876-83, St. Paul, 1883-84; supt. Am. Home Missionary Soc. for Minn., 1884-99; pres. Fargo (N.D.) Coll., 1900-06; pastor Springfield, Vt., 1906-09, Turners Falls, Mass., 1910-13; pres. Windom Coll., Montevideo, Minn., 1913-18; lecturing and lit. work, 1918—. Home: Minneapolis, Minn. Died Apr. 27, 1923.

MORLEY, Margaret Warner, author; b. Montrose, Ia., Feb. 17, 1858; d. Isaac and Sarah Robinson (Warner) M.; grad. New York City Normal Coll., 1878; unmarried. Taught in N.Y. (Oswego) State, and Milwaukee (Wis.) normal schs., and Leavenworth (Kan.) High Sch.; biology in Armour Inst., and Free Kindergarten Assn. training class, Chicago; lecturer in Boston. Author: A Song of Life, 1891; Life and Love, 1895; The Bee People, 1899; The Honey Makers, 1899; Little Mitchell, 1904; The Renewal of Life, 1906; Donkey John of the Toy Valley, 1909; The Carolina Mountains, 1913; Will-o'-the-Wasps, 1913. Home: Tryon, N.C. Died Dec. 12, 1923.

MORLING, Edgar Alfred, judge; b. Boonville, N.Y., Apr. 21, 1864; s. Alfred and Eliza (Hines) M.; LL.B., Albany (N.Y.) Law Sch., 1886; LL.D., Morningside College, 1928; m. Flora B. Tripp, Apr. 25, 1888 (died Oct. 6, 1920); children—William Edgar (dec.), Ruth (Mrs. Reuben A. Shover), Max Milton, Maynard Alfred. Admitted to N.Y. bar, 1886, and began practice at Boonville; moved to Emmetsburg, Ia., 1889; asso. justice Supreme Court of Ia., 1925—, for term ending Dec. 31, 1936. Trustee Morningside Coll. (Sioux City, Ia.). Republican. Methodist. Mason. Odd Fellow. Home: Emmetsburg, Ia. Died Oct. 15, 1932.

MORMAN, James Bale, economic expert; b. Ilfracombe, Eng., July 7, 1866; s. Thomas and Anne (Bale) M.; came to U.S., 1876; grad. Cook Acad., Montour Falls, N.Y., 1886; A.B., U. of Rochester, 1890; A.M., pro merito, 1902; spl. studies, Rochester Theol. Sem., 1890-91; m. Harriet J. Cogswell, Nov. 1, 1897. Editor and translator Report of U.S. and Am. Commns. for study of agrl. coöperation and rural credits in Europe, 1913; editor and abstractor agrl. material for Am. Economic Rev., 1913-15; with Federal Farm Loan Bur., Washington, D.C., 1916-June 30, 1925; retired. Baptist. Author: The Principles of Social Progress, 1901; The Principles of Rural Credits, 1915; The Place of Agriculture in Reconstruction, 1919; Farm Credits in the United States and Canada, 1924. Died Nov. 15, 1930.

MORRELL, Imogene Robinson, artist; b. Attleboro, Mass.; d. Otis and Sarah Dean (Raymond) Robinson; m. 1869, Col. Abram Morrell. Began art education at Newark, N.J.; later studied New York; taught at Charlestown, and Auburndale, Mass.; pupil at Düsseldorf, Germany, 1856, of Adolf Schrödter and Camphausen, and at Paris, 1864, of François Louis Français and Thomas Couture. Remained in Paris over 10 yrs. Pres. and established, 1879, Nat. Acad. of Fine Arts, Washington. Is portrait and hist. painter; has received 14 medals for her art works. Especially notable paintings are: The First Battle of the Puritans; Washington Welcoming the Provision Trains at Newburgh, N.Y., in 1778; A Historical Portrait of General John A. Dix, at the Capitol; also portraits of Howell Cobb, John C. Spencer, Mrs. Cleveland, Collis P. Huntington, President Garfield, W. W. Corcoran, etc. These

portraits, with other works, were destroyed in a fire in 1896. Died 1908.

MORRILL, Charles Henry, banker (retired); b. Concord, N.H., July 14, 1842; s. of Ephriam and Mahala M.; ed. Colby Acad., New London, N.H.; m. Harriet Currier, 1862 (died 1917); children—Charles Albert, Arthur Currier, Edgar, Lampery, Minnie Harriet. Pvt. 11th N.H. Vols., 1862-65. Pvt. sec. Gov. A. Nance, of Neb., 1879-83. Regent State U. of Neb., and pres. bd., 1891-1901; commr. St. Louis Expn., 1904; Neb. mem. Rep. Nat. Com., 1904-08. Founder Morrill Geological yearly expeditions from U. of Neb.; museum building erected by U. of Neb. at cost of $300,000 named "Morrill Hall" in his honor. Morrill County, Neb., named in his honor, also City of Morrill, Scotts Bluff Co., Neb. Awarded medal by Kiwanis Club of Lincoln, Neb., "for distinguished service to city and state." Home: Stromsburg, Neb. Died Dec. 11, 1928.

MORRILL, Edmund N., banker, gov.; b. Westbrook, Me., Feb. 12, 1834; s. Rufus and Mary (Webb) M.; ed. Westbrook Acad.; supt. schools, Westbrook, 1856; removed to Kan., 1857; elected, Oct. 1857, to first Free State legislature; reëlected to legislature, Jan. 1858, under the Lecompton constitution; served, pvt. to sergt., 7th Kan. cav., 1861-62; apptd. capt. and commissary of subsistence, Aug. 1862; bvt. maj. for meritorious service; m. Caroline J. Nash, Dec. 25, 1869. Co. clerk, Brown Co., Kan., 1866, 1868 and 1870; clerk dist. court, 1867 and 1869; State senator, 1872 and 1876; pres. pro tem., senate, 1877; mem. Congress, 1883-91; gov. Kan., 1894-96; elected by Congress, 1890, mgr. of the homes for disabled vol. soldiers; opened 1st bank in Brown Co., Kan., 1871; still conducts it; was 7 yrs. pres. 1st Nat. Bank, Leavenworth. Home: Hiawatha, Kan. Died 1909.

MORRIS, Benjamin Wistar, P.E. bishop; b. Wellsborough, Pa., May 30, 1819; s. Hon. Samuel W. Morris, and great g.s. Samuel Morris, capt. 1st City Troop of Phila., in Revolutionary war; grad. Gen. Theol. Sem., 1846 (D.D., Columbia and Univ. of Pa., 1868); m. Hannah, d. Henry F. Rodney, Lewes, Del., 1852. Ordered deacon, 1846; ordained priest, 1847; pastor St. Mathew's Ch., Sunbury, Pa.; rector St. David's Manayunk, Pa.; rector St. Luke's Germantown, Pa.; consecrated Dec. 3, 1868, missionary bishop of Ore. and Wash., divided into two sees, 1880, then became bishop of Oregon. Author: Presbyterian, Baptist and Methodist Testimony to Confirmation; etc. Died 1906.

MORRIS, Charles, author, compiler; b. Chester, Pa., Oct. 1, 1833; s. Samuel Pearson and Margaret (Burns) M.; ed. Chester, Pa.; unmarried. Taught in pub. schs.; later prof. in Acad. of Ancient and Modern Languages, Phila.; with mfg. house, 1860-78; since then devoted entirely to literature; has written much on scientific subjects; editor New Science Review, 1895. Author or Compiler: A Manual of Classical Literature; Historical Tales (11 vols.); Man and His Ancestor; Four Graded School Histories of the United States; History of the World, for Schools; New Century History of the United States, 1900; The World's Famous Orators, 1903; Hero series (4 vols.), 1906-07; Home Life in All Lands (3 vols.), 1907-09; Industrial and Commercial Geography, 1910; History of Pennsylvania (for schools), 1912; Heroes of Discovery in America, 1919; Heroes of Progress in America, 1919; Heroes of the Army in America, 1919; Heroes of the Navy in America, 1919. Editor: Half Hours With the Best American Authors; and other works in same series (18 vols.); The Ency. Dictionary (Phila. edit.); The Imperial Reference Library; Winston's Encyclopædia; Winston's graded series of dictionaries; etc. Home: Philadelphia, Pa. Died Sept. 6, 1922.

MORRIS, Charles, brig. gen.; b. Charlestown, Mass., May 3, 1844; s. Charles W. (U.S.N.) and Caroline (Devens) M.; ed. pub. schs., Charlestown, Mass.; grad. U.S. Mil. Acad., 1865, Arty. Sch., 1878; m. Gertrude Missroon, 1867. Commd. 2d and 1st lt. 19th Inf., June 23, 1865; transferred to 37th Inf., Sept. 21, 1866, to 5th Inf., May 19, 1869, to 5th Arty., Dec. 15, 1870; capt., Mar. 6, 1882; maj. 7th Arty., Mar. 8, 1898; lt. col. Arty. Corps, Feb. 2, 1901; col., Feb. 21, 1902; brig. gen. U.S.A., May 2, 1908; retired by operation of law, May 3, 1908. Home: Portland, Me. Died Oct. 27, 1912.

MORRIS, Clara, actress; b. Toronto, Ont., 1849; lived there until 3 months old, then to Cleveland and grew up there; m. Frederick C. Harriott, 1874 (he died 1914). Became a member of the ballet of the old Academy of Music, Cleveland, 1861, rapidly advancing to leading lady; in 1869 became leading lady at Wood's Theatre, Cincinnati; became mem. Daly's Fifth Av. Co., New York, 1870; soon became prominent in emotional rôles and has appeared as star in prin. Am. theatres. Leading rôles: Camille; Alixe; Miss Multon; Mercy Merrick in "The New Magdalene"; Cora, in "L'Article 47"; etc. Author: The Trouble Woman, 1904; Life of a Star, 1906; Dressing-Room Receptions, 1911. Died Nov. 20, 1925.

MORRIS, Douglas, judge; b. Knightstown, Ind., Jan. 5, 1861; s. John and Hannah (Scovell) M.; A.B., Asbury (now DePauw) U., Greencastle, Ind., 1882; m. Pamela A. Spann, Oct. 6, 1892; children—Han-

nah S., Douglas J. Admitted to bar, 1883, and practiced at Rushville. Dem. nominee for Congress, 1888; judge Circuit Court, 8th Jud. Circuit, 1898-1904. judge Supreme Court, of Ind., 1910-17. Democrat. Presbyn. Home: Rushville, Ind. Died July 8, 1928.

MORRIS, Edward, packer; b. Chicago, Oct. 1, 1866; s. late Nelson and Sarah (Vogel) M.; pub. sch. edn. Engaged in business, 1880—; pres. and treas. Morris & Co., Fairbank Canning Co.; dir. Nat. Packing Co., First Nat. Bank, Nat. Live Stock Bank, A. M. Rothschild & Co., and officer or dir. in numerous other corps. Mem. Chicago Bd. of Trade. Home: Chicago, Ill. Died Nov. 3, 1913.

MORRIS, Edward Dafydd, clergyman; b. Utica, N.Y., Oct. 31, 1825; s. David E. and Ann (Lewis) M.; A.B., Yale, 1849; A.M., 1852; grad. Auburn Theol. Sem., 1852; (D.D., Hamilton, 1863; LL.D., Maryville, 1885); m. Frances Elizabeth Parmelee, July 29, 1852 (died 1866); m. 2d, Mary Bryan Treat, Mar. 26, 1867 (died 1893); father of Edward Parmalee M. Ordained Presbyn. ministry, 1852; pastor Auburn, N.Y., 1852-55, Columbus, O., 1855-67; prof. theology, Lane Theol. Sem., Cincinnati, 1867-97; retired. Author: Ecclesiology, 1885; The Presbyterian Church, New School, 1904. Home: Columbus, O. Died Nov. 21, 1915.

MORRIS, Edward Parmelee, university prof.; b. Auburn, N.Y., Sept. 17, 1853; s. Edward Dafydd and Frances Elizabeth (Parmalee) M.; A.B., Yale, 1874; univs. of Leipzig and Jena, 1884-85; (hon. A.M., Williams, 1884, L.H.D., 1904; Litt.D., Harvard, 1909); m. Charlotte Webster Humphrey, Jan. 2, 1879. Prof. Greek, Drury Coll., 1879-84; prof. Latin, Williams Coll., 1885-91, Yale, 1891—. Author: The Mostellaria of Plautus, with notes, 1880; The Pseudolus of Plautus, with introduction and notes, 1890; The Captives and Trinummus of Plautus, with introduction and notes; On Principles and Methods in Latin Syntax, 1902; The Satires of Horace; The Epistles of Horace. Home: Saybrook, Conn. Died Nov. 16, 1938.

MORRIS, Effingham Buckley, lawyer; b. Phila., Pa., Aug. 23, 1856; s. Israel W. and Annie (Buckley) M.; A.B., U. of Pa., 1875, A.M., LL.B., 1878, LL.D. in 1928; m. Ellen' Douglas Burroughs, Nov. 5, 1879; children—Rhoda Fuller (Mrs. Trenchard Emlen Newbold), Eleanor Burroughs (Mrs. Stacy Barcroft Lloyd), Caroline Mitchell (Mrs. John Frederic Byers), Effingham B. Admitted to bar, 1878. Pres. Girard Trust Co., 1887-1928, chmn. of the bd., 1928—; dir. Pa. R.R. Co. and of its affiliated lines; dir. various corps. Treas. Council of Defense and Com. of Pub. Safety, Commonwealth of Pa., World War. Pres. Acad. Natural Sciences, Wistar Inst. Anatomy and Biology, Moore Sch. of Elec. Engring. (U. of Pa.). Republican. Home: Ardmore, Pa. Died Jan. 22, 1937.

MORRIS, Elias Camp, clergyman; b. Murray Co., Ga., May 7, 1855; s. James and Cora Cornelia (Morris) M.; ed. pub. schs., Ala.; attended lectures at Roger Williams Univ., Nashville, Tenn.; (D.D., State U. of Ky., 1892; Ph.D., State Normal Sch., Ala., 1902); m. Fannie E. Austin, Nov. 27, 1884. Ordained Bapt. ministry, 1879; pastor Centennial Baptist Ch., Helena, Ark., June 1879—. Founder Ark. Bapt. Coll., Little Rock, and trustee, 1884—; pres. Nat. Bapt. Conv., 1894—; mem. exec. com. Bapt. Gen. Conv. of N. America, Bapt. World Alliance, Federal Council Chs. of Christ in America. Mason, Odd Fellow, K.P. Home: Helena, Ark. Died Sept. 5, 1922.

MORRIS, Felix James, actor; b. England; studied medicine; removed to U.S. and was drug clerk at Albany, N.Y. Worked his way up on the stage from supernumerary to leading man in legitimate comedy rôles. First notable success as the Scotch Professor in "On 'Change"; has since appeared in numerous comedies and in vaudeville; recently as the Old Tutor in "At the White Horse Tavern," Wallack's Theatre, New York. Died 1900.

MORRIS, Frank Hubbard, auditor for the U.S. navy, 1897—; b. Pontiac, Mich., Aug. 18, 1851; academic education at Ann Arbor, Mich. Resides in Washington, D.C. Died 1900.

MORRIS, George Edward, judge; b. Utica, N.Y., July 17, 1862; s. Edward E. and Eliza (McClements) M.; Cazenovia Sem., 1873-76, Genesee Wesleyan Sem., Lima, N.Y., 1879-80; LL.B., Albany Law Sch., 1885; m. Maude E. Mylroie, Jan. 29, 1899. Practiced in N.Y. state, 1885-88; asst. city atty., Seattle, Wash., 1891; judge Superior Ct., Seattle, Nov. 11, 1902-Mar. 1909; apptd. judge Supreme Ct. of Wash., Mar. 1909, and elected for terms 1911-17, 1917-23 (chief justice 1915, 16). Republican. Methodist. Home: Olympia, Wash. Deceased.

MORRIS, George Kenneth, clergyman; b. Trenton, N.J., Aug. 18, 1837; s. George W. and Jane Van Derveer (Hankinson) M.; grad. Pennington (N.J.) Sem., 1860, Nat. Sch. Elocution and Oratory, 1876; (hon. A.M., 1868, D.D., 1881, Dickinson Coll.; LL.D., Taylor U., 1896); m. Sarah Elizabeth Smith, Dec. 10, 1862; father of George Van Derveer M. Ordained M.E. ministry, 1860; prof. practical theology, Boston U., 1894-1900; pastor Euclid Av. Ch., Cleveland, 1900-10; presiding elder Cleveland dist., E. Ohio

Conf., 1906-10; pastor Hamline Ch., Steubenville, O., Sept. 1910-15. Lectured in Eng. and Scotland, 1873, Nat. Sch. of Oratory, 1876-89. Republican. Home: Waban, Mass. Died Dec. 23, 1918.

MORRIS, George Perry, author; b. Montclair, N.J., Feb. 18, 1864; s. Charles B. and Mary (Perry) M.; A.B., Rutgers Coll., 1888 (A.M., 1910); in economics and history, Johns Hopkins; m. Martha Turner, May 5, 1892. On editorial staff Mail and Express, New York, 1888-90; asso. editor The Congregationalist, Boston, 1891-1907; on staff Boston Herald, 1907-11, of Christian Science Monitor, 1911-18; asst. editor Advocate of Peace, 1918—. Author: The Norwegian Co. System, 1894; Historic Towns of New England, 1898. Home: Washington, D.C. Died June 12, 1921.

MORRIS, George Van Derveer, clergyman; b. Bridgeton, N.J., Dec. 5, 1867; s. George Kenneth and Sarah Elizabeth (Smith) M.; A.B., Dickinson Coll., 1889, A.M., 1892; B.D., Drew Theol. Sem., 1891; D.D., Dickinson, 1907; m. Anna Young Terry, May 17, 1894; children—Anna Katharine, George William. Ordained M.E. ministry, 1892; pastor Norwood Ch., Cincinnati, 1891-94, Batavia, O., 1894-97, Franklin, O., 1897-99, Clifton and Mt. Lookout chs., Cincinnati, 1899-1903, Centenary Ch., Lexington, Ky., 1903-11, First M.E. Ch., Frankfort, Ind., 1911-13, First Ch., Laporte, Ind., 1913-17, Maple Av. Instl. and Community Ch., Terre Haute, Ind., 1917-18, First Ch., Brazil, Ind., 1919-20; enforced rest, lit. research and pulpit supply at Woods Hole, Mass., 1921-22, Federated Ch., Truro, Cape Cod, Mass., June-Oct. 1923, 24, 25. Mem. Ky. Bd. of Edn., 1903-11. Traveled and studied abroad, 1892, 1907, 11. Republican. Author: A Man for A' That, 1902; Polly, A Fairy Tale of Love, 1907. Editorial staff writer Western Christian Advocate; office mgr. W. McKee Keeley Co., 1925—. Home: St. Petersburg, Fla. Died Aug. 3, 1928.

MORRIS, Howard, lawyer; b. Madison, Wis., Oct. 6, 1856; s. W. A. P. and Harriet P. (Grannis) M.; A.B., U. of Wis., 1877, LL.B., 1879; admitted to bar, 1879; m. Julia A. Robertson, Oct. 4, 1886 (died 1913). Gen. Solicitor Wis. Central cos., 1890-93; receiver and gen. counsel, 1893-99, gen. counsel, 1899-1905, v.p., 1905-06, Wis. Central System; pres. and trustee Am. McKenna Process Co. Home: Los Angeles, Calif. Died Oct. 23, 1922.

MORRIS, Ira Nelson, diplomatist, author; b. Chicago, Ill., Mar. 8, 1875; s. Nelson and Sarah (Vogel) M.; grad. Phillips Academy, Andover, Mass., 1892; educated Sheffield Scientific School (Yale Univ.), class of 1895; m. Constance Lily Rothschild, 1898; children—Constance Irene, Ira Victor. Retired from active financial affairs, but extensively interested in many banks, rys. and corps.; commissioner gen. to Italy, 1913, in behalf of Panama, P.I. Expn. U.S. minister to Sweden (under Presidents Wilson and Harding), 1914-23, resigned. Decorated Grand Officier Legion of Honor (France); Grand Cross Royal Order of Northern Star (Sweden); Grand Cross of the White Rose (Finland); Grand Cordon (Persia); Kongelige Norske Order of St. Olav (Norway); Grand Cross and Grand Cordon (Italy); Grand Cordon Star of Rumania; Knight and Commander Order of Isham Niftquor (India). Author: With the Trade Winds, 1897; From an American Legation, 1926. Founder Internat. Radio Forum. Extensive traveler. Home: Chicago, Ill. Died Jan. 15, 1942.

MORRIS, J(ames) Cheston, physician; b. Philadelphia, Pa., May 28, 1831; s. Dr. Caspar and Anne (Cheston) M.; A.B., U. of Pa., 1851, A.M. and M.D., 1854; m. Hannah A., d. Isaac Tyson, Jr., of Baltimore, 1854 (died 1867); m. 2d, Mary E., d. Lawrence Johnson, Jan. 11, 1870 (died 1912). Specialty nervous diseases, Phila.; holds important hosp. appmts.; contract surgeon U.S.A., Oct. 1862-Aug. 1863; examiner and lecturer U. of Pa., 1855-63. Has invented and patented several devices. Curator Am. Philos. Soc., 1889-1901; dir. biol. and micros. dept. Phila. Acad. Natural Sciences, 1897-1917. Pres. Va. Mining & Improvement Co., 1874-1903, and forester, 1903-1909. Translator: (with notes and additions) Lehmann's Chemical Physiology, 1856; Ethics of Solomon, 1894; Kosmos of Solomon, 1909. Author: Milk Supply of Large Cities; Water Supply of Philadelphia. Fellow Coll. of Physicians, Phila., 1857—. Home: West Chester, Pa. Died 1923.

MORRIS, Lewis Coleman, surgeon; b. Clazemont, Va., Jan. 23, 1872; s. Edward W. and Matilda (Coleman) M.; M.D., U. of Va., 1892; m. Bessie Jemison, Dec. 13, 1907. Practiced in Birmingham, Ala., 1893—; prof. gynecology and abdominal surgery, U. of Ala. Grad. Sch. of Medicine, 1912—; gynecologist, St. Vincent's Hosp.; gynecologist and abdominal surgeon, Hillman Hosp. Fellow Am. Coll. Surgeons. Democrat. Episcopalian. Home: Birmingham, Ala. Died Mar. 23, 1923.

MORRIS, Martin Ferdinand, asso. justice Court of Appeals of D.C.; b. Washington, D.C., Dec. 3, 1834; s. John F. and Joan Lawton (Colbert) M.; grad. Georgetown Univ., D.C., 1854; (LL.D., 1877); admitted to bar; practiced Baltimore, 1863-67; after that in Washington, until the establishment of the Court of Appeals of D.C., 1893, when he was apptd. the first asso. justice of that court; retired July 1, 1905. Prof. law dept., Georgetown Univ., 1876—. Unmarried. Author: Lectures on the History of the Development of Constitutional and Civil Liberty, 1898. Home: Washington, D.C. Died 1909.

MORRIS, Nelson, packer; b. Black Forest, Germany, Jan. 21, 1839; self-educated; emigrated to U.S. at 12; went to Chicago, 1854; secured employment in stock yards; 2 yrs. later began business for himself; m. Sarah Vogel, 1863. Pres. Nelson Morris & Co.; officer or dir. several banks and other enterprises; founded the present packing firm of Morris & Co. and the Fairbank Canning Co., 1880. Home: Chicago, Ill. Died 1907.

MORRIS, Newbold; b. N.Y. City, Jan. 12, 1868; s. Augustus Newbold and Eleanor Colford (Jones) M.; LL.B., Columbia, 1891; spl. student Columbia U., Sch. Polit. Science 2 yrs.; École des Sciences Politique, Paris, 1 semester; grad. U.S. Command and Gen. Staff Sch., 1924; m. Helen Schermerhorn Kingsland, Apr. 9, 1896; children—Augustus Newbold, George Lovett Kingsland, Stephanus Van Cortlandt. Admitted to N.Y. bar, 1892; retired 1913. Capt. 12th Inf. N.Y. Vols., Spanish-Am. War, 1898; lt. col. and chief of Subsection on Enemy Resources, Gen. Staff, G.H.Q., A.E.F., World War; col. 432d F.A., O.R.C. Commr. State Training Sch., N.Y., 1908-11. Trustee Columbia U., Teachers Coll. (Columbia), Vanderbilt Clinic; v.p. Home of Incurables. Citation from Gen. Pershing "for exceptionally meritorious and conspicuous services"; Conspicuous Service Cross, N.Y. State; Spanish-Am. War Medal; Victory medal with 2 battle clasps. Trustee Diocese of Mass. P.E. Ch.; mem. Ho. of Deputies, P.E. Ch., 1922, 25; vestryman Trinity Ch., Lenox, Mass. Republican. Home: New York, N.Y., and Lenox, Mass. Died Dec. 20, 1928.

MORRIS, Page, judge; b. Lynchburg, Va., June 30, 1853; student William and Mary Coll.; grad. Va. Mil. Inst., 1872; m. Elizabeth Statham, Feb. 21, 1877. Asst. prof. mathematics at latter, 1872-73; prof. mathematics, Tex. Mil. Inst., 1873-76; prof. applied mathematics, Agrl. and Mech. Coll. of Tex., 1876-79; returned to Lynchburg, Va.; admitted to Va. bar, 1880; Rep. nominee for Congress, 6th Va. Dist., 1884; removed to Duluth, Minn., 1886; municipal judge, City of Duluth, Feb. 1889; city atty., Duluth, 1894; judge 11th Jud. Dist., Minn., Aug. 1895—resigned, Sept. 1896; mem. 55th to 57th Congresses (1897-1903), 6th Minn. Dist.; U.S. dist. judge, Dist. of Minn., Mar. 1903—. Home: Duluth, Minn. Died Dec. 16, 1924.

MORRIS, Robert Clark, lawyer; b. Bridgeport, Conn., Nov. 19, 1869; s. Dwight and Grace Josephine (Clark) M.; LL.B., Yale, 1890, M.L., 1892, D.C.L., 1893; studied Continental jurisprudence in Europe, 1890-91; m. Aline Brothier, May 30, 1931 (died 1932). Admitted to Conn. bar, 1890; located in practice, New York, 1894; lecturer on French law, 1895-1904, internat. arbitration and procedure, 1904-12, and govt. and citizenship, 1925-26—all in law dept. of Yale U.; apptd., by President Roosevelt, to represent U.S. as agent and counsel before U.S. and Venezuelan Claims Commn., 1903. Declined apptmts. as U.S. dist. judge and justice Supreme Ct. of N.Y. Counsel to supt. of banks of State of N.Y. in connection with failures of pvt. bankers, 1915; counsel to atty. gen. of New York, 1917, in case against Bolo-Pacha, the propagandist who operated in United States and France; apptd. agent and gen. counsel representing U.S. before Mixed Claims Commn. (U.S. and Germany), 1922, during this service 12,000 claims filed, aggregating $1,479,064,313, resigned, May 24, 1923; retained by State of Missouri to argue branch bank case before U.S. Supreme Ct., 1923. Pres. Rep. Co. Com., N.Y. Co., 1901-03. Author: International Arbitration and Procedure, 1911; The Sovereign Citizen (under nom de plume, An American), 1920; The Pursuit of Happiness, 1930; also pamphlet, The Spirit of Liberty, 1931; and several publs. supporting the govt. in the World War. Established the Aline Brothier Morris Fund, 1932, in memory of his wife to continue her patriotic work in support of the fundamental principles of our govt.; also established, 1934, at Morris, Conn., Aline Brothier Morris Reading Room, and James Morris Museum in memory of his grandfather for whom town was named. Home: New York, N.Y. Died Oct. 13, 1938.

MORRIS, Roger Sylvester, M.D.; b. Ann Arbor, Mich., Sept. 24, 1877; s. George Sylvester and Victoria (Celle) M.; A.B., U. of Mich., 1900, M.D., 1902; m. Mary Bledsoe Carter, Sept. 10, 1907; 1 son, Roger Sylvester. Instr. medicine, U. of Mich., 1903-06; asst. res. phys., Johns Hopkins Hosp., and asso. in medicine, Johns Hopkins U., 1906-11; asso. prof. medicine, Washington U. Med. Sch., St. Louis, 1911-13; prof. medicine, U. of Cincinnati, 1915—; dir. med. clinic, Cincinnati Gen. Hosp., 1915—. Commd. maj., Med. O.R.C., 1917; lt. col., M.C. U.S.A., 1918, with A.E.F. Author: Clinical Laboratory Methods, 1913; Clinical Laboratory Diagnosis, 1923. Home: East Cincinnati, O. Died Mar. 2, 1934.

MORRIS, Samuel Leslie, clergyman; b. Abbeville, S.C., Dec. 25, 1854; s. James Hervey and Ann E. (McCaslan) M.; A.B., Erskine Coll., 1873; grad. Columbia (S.C.) Theol. Sem., 1876; LL.D., 1919; m. Ella M. Brice, Oct. 23, 1877; children—Mrs. Margie Akers, Mrs. Hattie Gilbert, Mrs. Marion Wood, Samuel L. Ordained Presbyn. ministry, 1877; pastor Walhalla, S.C., 1876-82; pastor and evangelist, Edgefield, S.C., 1882-89; pastor Macon, Ga., 1889-1901; sec. home missions, Gen. Assembly Presbyn. Ch. U.S., 1901-33; now pastor of Morningside Church, Atlanta, Ga. Mem. Pan-Presbyn. Alliance, 1899. Trustee Columbia (S.C.) Theol. Sem., Adger Coll., Durant (Okla.) Coll. Author: The Task that Challenges, 1917; Christianizing Christendom, 1919; Presbyterianism, Its Principles and Practice, 1922; The Records of the Morris Family, 1922; The Romance of Home Missions, 1924; The Fact of Christianity, 1927; The Drama of Christianity, 1928. Died May 10, 1937.

MORRIS, Thomas Armstrong, pres. Indianapolis Water Co., 1888—; b. Nicholas Co., Ky., Dec. 26, 1811; s. Morris and Rachel (Morris) M.; learning printers' trade, 1923-26, at private school, 1926-30; grad. West Point, 1834; m. Elizabeth Rachel, d. John Irwin, 1840. Breveted 2d lt. 1st artillery, U.S.A., 1834; assigned, 1835, to asst. Maj. Ogden, of engineer corps, in constructing National road in Ind. and Ill., having charge of division between Richmond and Indianapolis; resigned from U.S. service; was resident engr. Ind. State service; had charge construction Central Canal, was chief engr. Madison & Indianapolis R.R., superintended building it from Vernon to Indianapolis, 1841-47; chief engr. Terre Haute & Richmond R.R. and of Indianapolis & Bellefontaine R.R., 1847-52; chief engr. Indianapolis & Cincinnati R.R., 1852-54; pres. same, 1854-57; pres. Indianapolis & Bellefontaine R.R., 1857-59; chief engr. Indianapolis & Cincinnati R.R., 1859-61; planned and superintended construction of Union depot, Indianapolis, 1853. Apptd. q.m. gen. of Ind. by Gov. Morton, 1861; had charge of one of 1st regts. of Ind. vols.; gen. 1st brigade of troops that went from Ind.; served in W.Va. campaign; comd. at and won battles of Philippi, Laurel Hill and Carrick's Ford; mustered out July 27, 1861; chief engr. Indianapolis & Cincinnati R.R., 1862-66; pres. and chief engr. Indianapolis & St. Louis R.R., 1865-69; receiver Indianapolis, Cincinnati & Lafayette R.R., 1869-72; one of commrs. to select plans and superintend construction new State Capitol, 1877. Life trustee Consumers' Gas Trust Co. Home: Indianapolis, Ind. Died 1904.

MORRIS, Thomas John, judge; b. Baltimore, Md., Sept. 24, 1837; s. John and Sarah (Chancellor) M.; A.B., Harvard, 1856; m. Sarah P., d. Joseph Cushing, Jr., June 11, 1868. Admitted to bar, 1861; practiced at Baltimore, 1861-78; U.S. dist. judge, Dist. of Md., 1879—. Republican. V.p. Am. Unitarian Assn.; v.p. Enoch Pratt Free Library, Baltimore; trustee Johns Hopkins U. Home: Baltimore, Md. Died June 6, 1912.

MORRIS, William, actor; b. Boston, Mass., 1861; s. Henry and Maria (Lloyd) M.; m. Etta Hawkins, Oct. 1891. Joined Boston Museum Stock Co. when 14; afterward in cos. of Augustin Daly, Mme. Modjeska and Charles Frohman; was first leading man in Charles Frohman's Empire Stock Co., opening that theatre as Lt. Hawkesworth in "The Girl I Left Behind Me"; resigned, 1894, to star in "The Lost Paradise," "Under the Red Robe," "The Adventure of Lady Ursula," and in 1901, formed a partnership with Edward E. Rice, and starred in H. V. Esmond's play, "When We Were Twenty-One." Home: New York, N.Y. Died Jan. 12, 1936.

MORRIS, William Charles, cartoonist; b. Salt Lake City, U., Mar. 6, 1874; s. William Charles and Diantha (Empey) M.; ed. grammar and high schs., Salt Lake City; self taught in drawing; m. May Pratt, June 29, 1902. Prior to cartooning was gold miner, clerk, teamster, and sign writer. Cartoonist for Spokane Spokesman Review, 1904-13; free lance at New York, 1913-15; cartoonist for Harper's Weekly, Independent, N.Y. Evening Mail, George Matthew Adams Service, now free lance work. Work reproduced widely in European and Am. mags. and newspapers. Cartoonist for Rep. Nat. Com. Presidential Campaign, 1936. Author: Spokesman Review Cartoons, 1908; The Spokane Book, 1913; One Hundred Men of Rockland County, 1929. Home: Grand View, N.Y. Died Apr. 5, 1940.

MORRISON, Albert Alexander, clergyman; b. Dublin, Ireland, Mar. 8, 1862; s. Alexander and Ann (Brue) M.; brought to U.S., 1871; studied Union Theol. Sem. 2 yrs., Gen. Theol. Sem. 1 yr.; Ph.B., Ill. Wesleyan U., 1887, M.A. and Ph.D., 1889; m. Caroline Conover, Mar. 1, 1886; children—Margaret W., Dorothy Conover, Jean, Alexander, Robert O. Deacon, 1886, priest, 1887, P.E. Ch.; rector of St. Matthew's Ch., Brooklyn, N.Y., 1889-99, Trinity Ch., Portland, Ore., 1899-Nov. 1, 1929 (emeritus). Republican. Mason. Researcher in psychology and psychical research. Home: Portland, Ore. Died June 28, 1931.

MORRISON, Alexander Francis, lawyer; b. Weymouth, Mass., Feb. 22, 1856; s. Archibald and Ellen (Hart) M.; A.B., U. of Calif., 1878; LL.B., Hastings Coll. of Law, 1881; m. May B. Treat, 1893. Practiced, San Francisco, 1881—; mem. Morrison, Dunne & Brobeck. Democrat. Home: San Francisco, Calif. Died Nov. 13, 1921.

MORRISON, Charles B., lawyer; b. Broom Co., N.Y., 1853; high sch. edn.; LL.B., Union College of Law, Chicago, 1877; m. Emma Mason, 1880. Admitted to Ill. bar, 1877, and began practice at Dixon; was state's atty., Lee Co., Ill., 1880-98; practiced law, Chicago, with late S. H. Bethea, 1898-1905; U.S. dist. atty., Northern Dist. of Ill., Mar. 1905-Sept. 1, 1906, resigned; retained by U.S. Govt. to prosecute Standard Oil Co. under Sherman "anti-trust" law; master in chancery, federal cts., Chicago, 1910—; spl. asst. atty. gen. of U.S. Republican. Home: Dixon, Ill. Died Apr. 25, 1932.

MORRISON, Charles Walthall, musician; b. Covington, Ky., July 30, 1856; s. David and Martha (Mitchell) M.; grad. Oberlin Conservatory of Music, 1880 (Mus.B., 1906, hon. A.M., 1903; Mus.D., Cornell Coll., 1909); studied music Berlin and Leipzig, 1882-85, Berlin, 1894-95; m. Kate Winship, July 17, 1889. Instr. pianoforte, 1880-82, 1885-92, prof. pianoforte, 1892—, and dir., 1902-24, Oberlin Conservatory of Music (dir. emeritus). Conglist. Republican. Home: Oberlin, O. Died May 16, 1927.

MORRISON, Clinton, capitalist; b. Livermore, Me., Jan. 21, 1842; s. Dorilus (1st mayor of Minneapolis) and Harriet P. (Whitmore) M.; ed. pub. schs. of Minneapolis; m. Julia Washburn, 1873 (died 1883). Began early in business as asst. to his father, one of the pioneer lumber mfrs. of Minneapolis; engaged with bro., George H., in general merchandising, outfitting, etc., 1863, as Morrison Brothers, succeeding to lumber, sawmill and logging interests of father, the firm name continuing until decease of George H., Jan. 1882; extensively identified in N.P. Ry. interests; was in control of the Minneapolis Harvester Works, later sold to Walter A. Woods Harvester Co.; pres. Farmers & Mechanics Savings Bank, 1876-1904. Pres. Northwestern Knitting Co.; v.p. North Star Woolen Mill Co. Republican. Universalist. Gave to City of Minneapolis 10 acres land for art museum. Home: Minneapolis, Minn. Died Mar. 11, 1913.

MORRISON, Frederick Douglas, educator; b. Hartford Co., Md., Sept. 30, 1837; s. Mansel E. and Susan Elizabeth (Morris) M.; ed. pvt. schs. and tutors; m. Mary Abbie Patrick, 1865 (dec.). From 1864 supt. Md. Sch. for the Blind. Home: Baltimore, Md. Died 1904.

MORRISON, George Austin; b. Fordown, Scotland, Nov. 30, 1832; s. Alexander and Christian (Lyall) M.; ed. at Aberdeen, Scotland; m. Lucy Anne King, May 26, 1863. Chmn. bd., now dir. N. K. Fairbank Co.; v.p. Washington Trust Co.; dir. Atlas Portland Cement Co., Terminal Warehouse Co.; trustee New York Life Ins. Co., Greenwich Savings Bank. Home: New York, N.Y. Died Feb. 26, 1916.

MORRISON, Henry Clay, bishop; b. Montgomery Co., Tenn., May 30, 1842; s. Robert R. and Mary A. (Duvall) M.; common sch. edn.; studied Latin, Greek and Hebrew pvtly. with Dr. N. H. Lee, 4 yrs.; (D.D., Ala. State Agrl. Coll.); m. Mrs. M. E. Ray, June 25, 1868. Entered M. E. Ch., S., ministry; pastor First Ch., Atlanta, Ga., 1886; missionary sec., 1890-98; bishop, 1898—. Raised $140,000 and paid off debt of Bd. of Missions; elected to office 3 times by Gen. Conference. Home: Leesburg, Fla. Died Dec. 29, 1921.

MORRISON, James Dow, bishop; b. Waddington, N.Y., Oct. 16, 1844; s. Rev. John and Mary (Dow) M.; A.B., McGill U., Montreal, 1865, A.M., 1868, LL.D., 1880; D.D., Union, 1879; m. Harriet, d. Rev. M. Townsend, canon Christ Ch. Cathedral, Montreal, June 1, 1869. Deacon, 1869, priest, 1870, P.E. Ch.; pastor Hemmingford, Can., 1869-71, Herkimer, N.Y., 1871-75, Ogdensburg, 1875-97; consecrated 1st missionary bishop of Duluth, Feb. 2, 1897; organized Diocese of Duluth, 1907, of which became diocesan bishop (resigned 1922). Archdeacon of Ogdensburg, 1881-97. Paddock lecturer to the Gen. Theol. Sem. of New York, 1898. Home: Ogdensburg, N.Y. Died Jan. 31, 1934.

MORRISON, Jasper Newton, maj. U.S.A.; b. Wayne Co., Mo., March 17, 1849; ed. in public school and at acad. in Fruitland, Mo.; m. Jane M. Pettit, July 17, 1884. Taught school, 1871; supt. schools, Wayne Co., Mo., 1872; admitted to bar, 1875; pros. atty. Wayne Co., Mo., 1876-82; practiced until 1888; chief clerk Bureau Military Justice, War Dept., 1888-96, apptd. maj. and judge advocate U.S.A., 1896. Died 1902.

MORRISON, John F., army officer; b. Charlottesville, N.Y., Dec. 20, 1857; s. John and Hannah (Lamont) M.; grad. U.S. Mil. Acad., 1881; m. Kate McCleery, Aug. 16, 1887. Commd. 2d lt., 20th Inf., June 11, 1881; promoted through grades to brig. gen., Nov. 20, 1915; maj. gen., May 15, 1917; retired, Dec. 20, 1921. Served in Cuba with 20th Inf., 1899, in Philippines, 1899-1902; mil. attaché, with Japanese Army, Russo-Japanese War, 1904; sr. instr. Army Staff Coll., 1907-12; later served in Manila, P.I.; apptd. comdr. Camp Sevier, Greenville, S.C., 1917; Europe, Sept.-Dec. 1917; dir. of training, U.S.A., Dec. 1917-Mar. 1918; comd. 8th Div., Mar. 3-June 1918; comd. Western Dept. to Aug. 17, 1919. Awarded D.S.M., 1919. Died Oct. 22, 1932.

MORRISON, Levi; b. Georgetown (now Sheakleyville), Pa., Aug. 8, 1839; s. Daniel and Julia Ann (Snyder) M.; ed. select and country schs.; m. Caroline S. Philips, May 28, 1868 (died 1910). In lumber business, Pa., and W.Va., 1869-90; now sr. mem. Advance Argus Co., publishers; farmer since boyhood. Served as pvt. Pa. Militia, 1863. Mem. Pa. House of Rep., 1884, 99, 1901 (speaker pro tem two joint sessions to elect U.S. senator, 1899). Progressive. Del. by apptmt. of gov. of Pa. to Farmers' Nat. Congress, 1894—, mem. exec. com. 12 yrs., then treas. Baptist. Home: Greenville, Pa. Died Dec. 14, 1917.

MORRISON, Lewis, actor, b. Jamaica, W.I., 1845; served as officer in U.S.A., Civil war, 3½ yrs.; entered dramatic profession, 1865, Varieties Theatre, New Orleans, under Lawrence Barrett; afterward appeared as Iago with Tommaso Salvini; supported Edwin Forrest, Edwin Booth, Charlotte Cushman before starring with his own company; leading character of recent yrs. is Mephisto in Faust; m. Miss Florence Roberts. Home: Peekskill-on-Hudson, N.Y. Died 1906.

MORRISON, Mary J. Whitney ("Jenny Wallis"), author; b. Saccarappa, Me., June 13, 1832; d. Luke and Cynthia (Smith) Whitney; ed. Lowell, Mass., High School; m. D. Wallis Morrison, Nov. 4, 1857. Contributor Youth's Companion, Harper's Young People, and other children's publs. Editor: Songs and Rhymes for the Little Ones (contains 17 of her own poems), 1884. Author: Stories True and Fancies New, 1898. Home: Waltham, Mass. Died 1904.

MORRISON, Mrs. May Treat; b. San Francisco, Calif., Sept. 8, 1858; d. George and Clarinda (Littlefield) Treat; Ph.B., U. of Calif., 1878; grad. study Germany, 1881-82, U. of Zurich, 1882-84; m. Alexander Francis Morrison, Apr. 27, 1893 (died 1921). Trustee Mills Coll., Oakland, 1916-28; trustee Calif. Acad. of Sciences, 1926—; mem. bd. mgrs. Children's Hosp., San Francisco (pres. 1919-21); pres. bd. mgrs. San Francisco Protestant Orphanage, 1909-10; del. to Internat. Fed. Univ. Women, Amsterdam, 1926. Republican. Unitarian. Donor of A. F. Morrison Memorial Library and endowment, to U. of Calif., 1928; donor of fellowship to Lick Observatory, Univ. of Calif., 1928. Home: San Francisco, Calif. Died Oct. 2, 1939.

MORRISON, Nathan Jackson, pres. Fairmount Coll., 1895—; b. Franklin N.H., Nov. 25, 1828; s. Nathan Smith and Susannah (Chase) M.; grad. Dartmouth, 1853 (D.D., 1868; LL.D., U. of Missouri, 1884); m. Miranda Capen Dimond, July 8, 1863. Worked his way through coll.; studied theology Oberlin, 1854-57, at same time tutor Greek and Latin Oberlin Coll.; ordained pastor Congl. Ch., Rochester, Mich., Feb. 11, 1858; helped reorganize Olivet Coll., 1859; prof. Greek, later mental philosophy, then pres., 1865-72; founded and started Drury Coll., Springfield, Mo., and pres., 1873-88; prof. philosophy Marietta Coll., 1888-95; in 1895 sent by Congl. Edn. Soc., Boston, to develop Fairmount Acad. into a college. Home: Wichita, Kan. Died 1907.

MORRISON, Theodore Nevin, bishop; b. Ottawa, Ill., Feb. 18, 1850; s. Rev. Theodore Nevin and Anna Eliza (Howland) M.; A.B., Ill. Coll., Jacksonville, 1870; grad. Gen. Theol. Sem., New York, 1873; D.D., Ill. Coll., 1895; S.T.D., Western Theol. Sem., 1905; LL.D., Chicago Law Sch.; m. Sarah Buck, d. of Rev. Arthur Swazey, of Chicago, Oct. 28, 1879. Deacon P.E. Ch., July 13, 1873; missionary, Pekin, Ill., 1873-76; priest, Feb. 19, 1876; rector Ch. of the Epiphany, Chicago, 1876-99; elected bishop, Nov. 30, 1898; consecrated, Feb. 22, 1899, bishop of Iowa. Home: Davenport, Ia. Died Dec. 27, 1929.

MORRISON, William Ralls, lawyer; b. Monroe Co., Ill., Sept. 14, 1825; s. John and Anne (Ralls) M.; ed. McKendree Coll.; pvt. in Mexican war and in battle of Buena Vista; went to Calif., 1849, returned to Ill., 1851; admitted to Ill. bar. Clerk Circuit Ct., Monroe Co., 1852-54; mem. Ill. legislature, 1854-60, 1871-72 (speaker, 1859-60). Organized and was col. 49th Ill. Vols., 1861-Dec., 1863; mem. Congress, 1863-65, 1873-87; chmn. Com. on Ways and Means, 1875-77, 1883-87; introduced, besides several others, the tariff bill known as the "horizontal" or "Morrison" bill; defeated for reelection, 1886; defeated for U.S. Senate in Ill. legislature, 1885, by John A. Logan; interstate commerce commr., 1887-97, and chmn. of the commn., 1891-97. Democrat. Home: Waterloo, Ill. Died 1909.

MORRISSEY, Andrew, clergyman; b. Thomastown, Co. Kilkenny, Ireland, Jan., 1860; primary studies completed in nat. schs. of Ireland; A.B., U. of Notre Dame, 1878; (LL.D., U. of Mich., 1903; Ph.D., Sacred Congregation of Studies, Rome, 1906). Prof. mathematics, Sacred Heart Coll., Watertown, Wis., 1880-85; dir. of studies, 1885-92, pres., 1893-1905, pres. bd. trustees, 1906—, U. of Notre Dame; provincial Congregation of the Holy Cross in U.S., 1906-12. Died May 28, 1921.

MORRISSEY, Andrew Marcus, judge; b. Livonia, N.Y., Dec. 27, 1871; s. Andrew and Catharine (Dowling) M.; ed. pub. schs.; unmarried. Admitted to Neb. bar, 1896, and practiced at Valentine and Lincoln, Neb. Apptd. chief justice Supreme Court of Neb., Jan. 1915, and elected for term ending Jan. 6, 1921; reëlected, Nov. 1920, for term ending Jan. 1927; mem. faculty Northwestern U. Law Coll., summer 1925. Mem. Co. H, 2d Neb. Vols., Spanish-Am. War, 1898. One of the speakers at Gray's Inn, London, on the occasion of the visit of the Am. Bar Assn. to England, 1924. Catholic. Home: Omaha, Neb. Died Sept. 9, 1933.

MORROW, Cornelius Wortendyke, clergyman, educator; b. Brooklyn, N.Y., Feb. 8, 1855; s. Cornelius Wortendyke LaFayette and Jane Eliza (Chase) M.; A.B., Columbia, 1876; grad. Union Theol. Sem., 1879; (D.D., Oskaloosa Coll., 1910); m. Rosalie Caroline Lippmann, Jan. 14, 1880. Preached as licentiate, Kensington, Conn., 1879-82; ordained Congl. ministry, 1885; pastor Bethlehem, Conn., 1882-87, Danbury, 1887-93, 2d Ch., Norwich, 1893-1902; prof. philosophy, Fisk U., Nashville, Tenn., 1902—; also coll. pastor, 1902-12, dean, 1912-13, acting pres., 1914-15, dean and prof. philosophy same university, 1915-21, dean emeritus, 1921—. Was member board of education, Danbury, and Norwich, and trustee Otis Pub. Library, Norwich; mem. exec. bd., Bethlehem House Social Settlement. Republican. Home: Nashville, Tenn. Died Mar. 29, 1923.

MORROW, Dwight Whitney, diplomat; b. Huntington, W.Va., Jan. 11, 1873; s. James E. and Clara (Johnson) M.; A.B., Amherst, 1895; LL.B., Columbia, 1899; LL.D., U. of Rochester, 1920, Princeton, 1925, Williams, 1926, Pennsylvania, 1926, Yale, 1927, Harvard, 1928, Brown, 1928; m. Elizabeth Reeve Cutter, June 16, 1903; children—Elisabeth R., Anne S. (Mrs. Charles A. Lindbergh), Dwight W., Constance C. Entered employ of law firm of Simpson, Thacher & Bartlett, New York, 1899; mem. of firm, 1905-14; mem. J. P. Morgan & Co., 1914-27; apptd. ambassador to Mexico, 1927. Del. to 6th Pan Am. Conf., 1928; del. to Naval Conference, London, England, 1930. Chmn. Prison Inquiry Commn. of N.J., 1917; chmn. N.J. State Bd. Instns. and Agencies, 1918-20. Trustee Amherst Coll., Union Theol. Sem., Russell Sage Foundation, Carnegie Endowment for Internat. Peace, Commonwealth Fund; regent Smithsonian Instn. Adviser to Allied Maritime Transport Council, Feb.-Dec., 1918; dir. War Savings Com. of N.J., 1918. Chmn. President's Aircraft Bd., 1925. Awarded D.S.M., 1919, by Gen. Pershing "for exceptionally meritorious and distinguished services" in connection with mil. shipping matters and Mil. Bd. of Allied Supply. Home: Englewood, N.J. Died Oct. 5, 1931.

MORROW, Edwin P., governor; b. Somerset, Ky., Nov. 28, 1878; s. Judge T. Z. and Jennie Crosson (Bradley) M.; ed. St. Mary's Coll. (St. Mary, Ky.), Cumberland Coll. (Williamsburg, Ky.); A.B., Centre Coll., Ky.; LL.D., U. of Ky.; LL.B., Cincinnati Law Sch., 1900; m. Katherine Hale Waddle, June 18, 1905; children—Edwina H. (wife of Dr. Joseph Horgan), Charles Robert. United States district atty., Eastern Dist. of Ky., 1911-15; Rep. caucus nominee for U.S. Senate, 1912; candidate for governor of Ky., 1915; elected governor 1919, term of 4 yrs. Mem. U.S. R.R. Labor Bd., Chicago, 1924-26; now mem. U.S. Bd. of Mediation, Washington. Second lt. 4th Ky. Vols., Spanish-Am. War. Presbyn. Mason. Home: Somerset, Ky. Died June 15, 1935.

MORROW, George Keenan, mcht.; b. Alliston, Ont., Can., Sept. 10, 1873; s. Thomas Casserly and Mary (Keenan) M.; prep. edn., high sch., Collingwood, Ont.; student St. Michael's Coll., Toronto, Ont.; m. Mary Brewster, Aug. 23, 1906. Chmn. bd. Hecker Products Corp.; dir. Remington-Rand, Inc., Ward Baking Co., McLellan Stores Co. Home: Whitestone, L.I., N.Y. Died May 17, 1941.

MORROW, George Washington, prohibitionist; b. Champaign Co., Ill., May 27, 1863; s. James and Sarah A. (Laughead) M.; ed. high sch. and acad.; grad. Christian Bibl. Inst., Stanfordville, N.Y., 1889; D.D., Defiance (O.) Coll., June 1915; m. Susie E. Whitmore, Oct. 15, 1885. Ordained "Christian" ministry, 1889; pastor Clove, N.Y., 1889, St. Johnsville, N.Y., 1889-90, Randolph Vt., 1891-99; supt. Vt. Anti-Saloon League, 1899-1905; supt. Mich. Anti-Saloon League, 1905-13 (1,955 saloons closed under his administration—1 "dry" county in 1905, 34 in 1913); sec. Anti-Saloon League of America, 1913-21, nat. lecturer, 1922-25; now lecturer World's League vs. Alcoholism. Pres. Vt. Interdenom. S.S. Assn. 4 yrs.; v.p. Vt. State Christian Endeavor Assn. 2 yrs. Republican. Home: Detroit, Mich. Died June 24, 1934.

MORROW, Mrs. Honoré (Willsie), writer; b. Ottumwa, Iowa; d. William Dunbar and Lilly Bryant (Head) McCue; B.A., U. of Wis.; m. William Morrow; children—Richard Dunbar, Felicia, Penn. Editor of Delineator, 1914-19. Author: Heart of the Desert, 1913; Still Jim, 1915; Lydia of the Pines, 1916; Benefits Forgot, 1917; The Forbidden Trail, 1919; The Enchanted Canyon, 1920; The Exile of the Lariat, 1923; The Devonshers, 1924; We Must March, 1925; On to Oregon, 1926; Forever Free, 1927; The Father of Little Women, 1927; With Malice Toward None, 1928; Mary Todd Lincoln, 1928; Splendor of God, 1929; The Last Full Measure, 1930;

Tiger! Tiger!, 1930; Black Daniel, 1931; Beyond The Blue Sierra, 1932; Argonaut, 1933; Yonder Sails the Mayflower, 1934; Let the King Beware, 1935; Demon Daughter, 1939. Died Apr. 12, 1940.

MORROW, James Binkley, newspaperman; b. New Phila., O., Sept. 29, 1855; s. John W. and Wilhelmina Hunter (Binkley) M.; ed. pub. schs. New Philadelphia and Dover, O.; m. Katharine Miller, Aug. 22, 1878. Republican. Presbyterian. Home: Washington, D.C. Died June 19, 1924.

MORROW, James E., prin. Allegheny High School; b. Brooke Co., Va., now Hancock Co., W.Va., March 28, 1837; s. Alexander M.; ed. Fairview, Va., Acad., 1850-53; grad. Jefferson Coll., Pa., 1856, A.M., 1875; Ph.D., 1889; m. Clara J. Johnson, Sept. 19, 1867. Engaged in teaching, 1856-58; admitted to bar, 1859; served in Union army, 1861-64, as pvt. and intermediate grades to capt. Co. F, 1st Va. inf. vols. Honorably disch., Dec. 10, 1864, by reason of expiration of term of service. Resumed teaching after war. Republican. Presbyn. Home: Allegheny, Pa. Died 1904.

MORROW, Jay Johnson, army officer; b. Fairview, W.Va., Feb. 20, 1870; grad. U.S. Mil. Acad., 1891, Engr. Sch. of Application, 1894; m. Harriet M. Butler, Oct. 15, 1895. Commd. add. 2d lt. engrs., June 12, 1891; promoted through grades to lt. col., Mar. 11, 1915; col. (temp.), Aug. 5, 1917; brig. gen. N.A., June 26, 1918; returned to rank of col., May 20, 1919; retired at own request, Aug. 5, 1922. Instr. dept. practical mil. engring., U.S. Mil. Acad., 1895-96, 1898-1901; in Philippines, 1901-03; mil. gov. Province of Zamboanga, 1901-02; engr. Commr. Dist. of Columbia, 1907-09; engr. of maintenance and at times acting gov. Panama Canal, 1916-17; arrived in France, May 12, 1918; chief engr. 1st Army, and dep. chief engr. A.E.F., 1918; assigned to comd. Camp A. A. Humphreys, Va., Dec. 30, 1918; again engr. of maintenance, Panama Canal, June 1919-Mar. 1921; gov. same, Mar. 1921-Oct. 1924; Am. mem. and chmn. Spl. Commn. on Boundaries, Tacna-Arica Arbitration, Mar. 1925-June 1929. Decorated Officer Legion of Honor (France), 1918. Presbyn. Home: Englewood, N.J. Died Apr. 16, 1937.

MORROW, John, congressman; b. nr. Darlington, Wis., Apr. 19, 1865; s. John and Ellen M.; ed. high sch. and normal univ.; m. Virginia F. Dale, 1891. Teacher and supt. pub. schs. until 1896; admitted to N.M. bar, 1895; mem. N.M. Ho. of Rep., 1897-98; city atty. Raton, N.M., 1900-01; pres. Bd. of Edn., Raton, 1902-23; mem. 68th to 70th Congresses (1923-29), N.M. at large. Democrat. Home: Raton, N.M. Died Feb. 25, 1935.

MORROW, Prince Albert, dermatologist; b. Mt. Vernon, Ky., Dec. 19, 1846; s. William and Mary (Cox) M.; A.B., Princeton Coll., Ky., 1864; M.D., Univ. Med. Coll. (New York U.), 1874; (hon. A.M., New York U., 1883); m. Lucy B. Slaughter, Apr. 23, 1874. Attending surgeon, City Hosp., New York, 1884-1904; clin. prof. venereal diseases, 1884—, lecturer dermatology, 1882, 1883, clin. prof. genitourinary diseases, 1886-90, emeritus prof., 1890, Univ. and Bellevue Hosp. Med. Coll.; attending physician skin and venereal dept., New York Hosp., 1890-1904; cons. dermatologist, St. Vincent's, and City hosps., N.Y. City. Author: Venereal Memoranda, 1885; Drug Eruptions, 1887; Atlas of Skin and Venereal Diseases, 1888-89; System of Genito-Urinary Diseases, Syphilology and Dermatology (3 vols.), 1892-94; Leprosy, 1899; Social Diseases and Marriage, 1904. One of the founders and editor Journal of Cutaneous and Genito-Urinary Diseases. Died Mar. 17, 1913.

MORROW, Thomas Robert, lawyer; b. Hartford, Conn., Jan. 24, 1857; s. John and Margaret (Campbell) M.; A.B., Yale, 1880, LL.B., 1882 (John A. Porter Prize); m. Flora E. Burt, July 3, 1883. Entered office of Lathrop & Smith, Kansas City, Mo., 1882; became mem. Lathrop, Morrow & Fox, Jan. 1, 1885, now Lathrop, Morrow, Fox & Moore; 1st gen. atty., Kansas City Southern Ry. Co.; solicitor for A.,T.&S.F. R.R. for Mo. and Ia., 1905—. Was the first to announce the rule that transportation of freight by railroad common carriers is interstate, notwithstanding the fact that the points of origin and destination of the shipment are both in the same state, if in the natural course of the haul the shipment has to traverse the soil of another state (decided by Supreme Court of U.S., 1902). Police commr., Kansas City, May 2, 1891-Feb. 9, 1893. Mason. Home: Kansas City, Mo. Deceased.

MORROW, W. K., pres. Standard Rice Co., Inc.; b. Lavacca Co., Tex., May 9, 1867; s. Walter H. and Martha R. (McCown) M.; ed. rural sch. and commercial coll.; m. Josephine Burton, April 17, 1900; children—Josephine V., Kyle. Clerked in a retail store at Schulenberg, Tex.; entered employ of Ed. H. Cunningham Co., 1887, as cashier and bookkeeper, advancing to v.p.; mem. of firm T. H. Thompson and Co., succeeded by Kirkland and Morrow, 1899-1902; organized Lane City Rice Milling Co., later changed to Standard Rice Co., Inc., 1902, and pres. from that time; pres. and dir. Nineteen Leonard St. Corp. (N.Y. City), Houston Rice Co., Memphis Rice Mill, Ark. Rice Co., Crowley Rice Co. Presbyterian. Mason. Home: Houston, Tex. Died Feb. 8, 1938.

MORROW, W(illiam) Carr, lawyer; b. Wilmington, Del., Nov. 7, 1876; s. Samuel and Catherine M. (Carr) M.; A.B., Stanford, 1901; LL.B., Columbia, 1906; m. Bessie Taylor, Feb. 1, 1909; children—William C., Thomas H. T. Admitted to Wash. bar, 1906; practiced at Tacoma and Seattle; mem. Grosscup & Morrow, 1908—; apptd. spl. counsel, Apr. 1924, to represent U.S., in recovery of certain school sections in Naval Oil Reserve No. 1, Calif. Mem. Co. H, 2d Ore. Vol. Inf., and served throughout Spanish-Am. War and Philippine Insurrection, 1898-1900. Republican. Protestant. Home: Tacoma, Wash. Died Jan. 25, 1935.

MORROW, William Chambers, author; s. William Chambers and Martha (McCreary) M.; student Howard Coll., Ala., and U. of Ala. Author: Ape, Idiot, and Other People; Bohemian Paris of To-day, 1899; A Man, His Mark, 1899; Lentala of the South Seas, 1908. Dir. of creative writing in Cora L. Williams Inst., Berkeley. Home: San Francisco, Calif. Died Apr. 3, 1923.

MORROW, William W., judge; b. nr. Milton, Ind., July 15, 1843; s. William and Margaret (Hood) M.; removed with parents to Adams Co., Ill., 1845; removed to Santa Rosa, Calif., 1859; ed. pub. grammar and high schools; LL.D., Wabash Coll., Ind., 1899, U. of Calif., 1913; m. Margaret Hulbert, June 18, 1865; children—William Hulbert, Maud (wife of late Rear Adm. Augustus F. Fechteler). Eleanor (Mrs. Harry L. Roosevelt). Admitted to bar, 1869; asst. U.S. atty. for Calif., 1870-74; chmn. Rep. State Central Com., 1879-82; atty. State Bd. Harbor Commrs., 1880-83; spl. counsel for U.S. before French and Am. Claims Commns., 1881-83; same before Alabama Claims Commn., 1882-85; chmn. Calif. delegation Rep. Nat. Conv., 1884; mem. 49th to 51st Congresses (1885-91); U.S. dist. judge, Northern Dist. of Calif., 1891-97; judge U.S. Circuit Ct. and U.S. Circuit Ct. of Appeals, 9th Jud. Circuit, 1897, until retired. Trustee Carnegie Instn., Washington; incorporator Am. Nat. Red Cross Soc., 1905 (mem. Central Com.). Vice pres. Am. Soc. Internat. Law; hon. v.p. San Francisco Council Boy Scouts of America; mem. Simplified Spelling Bd. Conglist. Author: Introduction to California Jurisprudence. Home: San Francisco, Calif. Died July 24, 1929.

MORSE, Alexander Porter, lawyer; b. St. Martinsville, La., Oct. 19, 1842; s. Isaac Edward and Margaretta Smith (Wederstrandt) M.; student Mt. St. Mary's Coll., Emmittsburg, Md.; A.B., Princeton, 1862 (hon. Ph.D., 1885); LL.B., Georgetown U., 1872; ed. in English, French and Spanish; m. Ellen Clarke, Apr. 18, 1883. Pvt. Scott's 1st La. Cav., 1861-62; capt., adj. and insp. gen., Majors' div., Green's cav. corps, C.S.A., 1863-64. Admitted to bar, Washington, 1872; practiced before all courts of D.C., exec. depts., and Supreme Ct. of U.S.; has been of counsel for citizens of U.S. before several mixed (internat.) commns. of claims sitting in Washington, 1880—; specialty—internat. and constl. law. Was of counsel before Electoral Commn. (Tilden and Hayes), 1878; also for State of La. in several leading cases on constl. law, in Supreme Ct. of U.S., and in "Insular Cases" before same court. Asso. counsel for French Republic before French-Am. Claims Commn., 1881-84; agt. and counsel of U.S. before commn. to arbitrate claims of Venezuela Steam Transportation Co. against Venezuela, 1894; asst. atty. of U.S. before Spanish Treaty Claims Commn., 1901-02; arbitrator under protocol between Hayti and U.S. in Van Bokkelen claim, May 24, 1888. Author: Citizenship by Birth and Naturalization, 1881. Home: Washington, D.C. Died July 2, 1921.

MORSE, Anson Daniel, college prof.; b. E. Cambridge, Lamoille Co., Vt., Aug. 13, 1846; s. Harmon and Elizabeth Murray (Buck) M.; brother of Harmon Northrop Morse; A.B., Amherst, 1871, A.M., 1874; studied U. of Heidelberg, 1876, 1883; (LL.D., Union Coll., 1895, Amherst, 1908); m. Margaret Duncan Ely, Sept. 3, 1878. Taught in Williston Sem., Easthampton, Mass., 1872-75; instr. polit. economy, 1876-77, prof., 1877-78, prof. history and polit. economy, 1878-92, Winkley prof. history, 1892—, emeritus, 1908, Amherst. Home: Amherst, Mass. Died Mar. 13, 1916.

MORSE, Benjamin Clarke, army officer; b. Macon, Mo., Oct. 15, 1859; s. Benjamin Clarke and Martha Ellsworth (Blunt) M.; grad. U.S. Mil. Acad., 1884; m. Jessie Cable (grad. Wellesley, 1889), Mar. 6, 1890. Commd. 2d lt. 23d Inf., June 15, 1884; promoted through grades to col. 13th Inf., July 1, 1916; trans. to 44th Inf., June 22, 1917; brig. gen. N.A., Aug. 5, 1917. Prof. mil. science and tactics and comdt. cadets, Agrl. and Mech. Coll. of Tex., 1890-94; participated in Spanish-Am. War, 1898, Philippine insurrection, 1899; personal aide to Maj. Gen. William R. Shafter, 1900-01; asst. adj. gen., 1901, actg. adj. gen., 1902, Dept. of Cal.; participated in Moro campaigns, P.I., 1903-04; 2d occupation of Cuba, 1906-09; prof. mil. science and tactics, and comdt. cadets, U. of Ill., 1910-13; occupation of Vera Cruz, Mexico, 1914; apttd. comdr. 169th Brigade N.A., Camp Custer, Battle Creek, Mich., Aug. 25, 1917; hon. disch. as brig. gen. N.A., Apr. 1, 1918; col. 33d Inf., Canal Zone, Oct. 1918. Presbyn. Home: Marquette, Mich. Died Apr. 16, 1933.

MORSE, Charles Henry, organist, conductor; b. Bradford, Mass., Jan. 5, 1853; s. Eben D., and Mary A. M.; grad. N.E. Conservatory of Music, 1873; Boston U. Coll. of Music, 1876, Mus. Bac., 1877; hon. M.A., Dartmouth, 1915; m. Frances S. N. Kimball, Dec. 24, 1874 (died 1917); children—Nathaniel Niles, Harold Marston; m. 2d, May C. Conant, May 1, 1918 (died 1922); m. 3d, Margaret B. Barnes, Oct. 11, 1924. Started as teacher of piano and organ N.E. Conservatory of Music, 1873-77; 1st prof. music and dir. Coll. of Music, Wellesley Coll., 1875-84; founder and dir. Northwestern Conservatory of Music, Minneapolis, 1885-91; organist and choirmaster Plymouth Ch., Brooklyn, 1891-99; previously in various chs., principally in Boston, from age of 15; also St. Paul, 1885, and Minneapolis later; first dir. of music, 1901-16, and first prof. music, 1916-18, Dartmouth Coll.; conductor of Gounod Club, Minneapolis, Minn., and of Conn. Valley Choir Union. Musical editor Plymouth Hymnal; retired on Carnegie pension, 1924. Trustee N.E. Conservatory of Music. Vice pres. Brooklyn Inst. Arts and Sciences (music dept.) from its organization. Editor: (for organ) The Church Organist, 2 vols.; The Junior Church Organist; The Contemporary Organist and March Album; (for female voices) The Wellesley Collection; Short and Easy Anthems (mixed voices), 1904; Songs for the Chapel (for male voices), 1909; Easy Anthems, 1925. Home: Riverdale, N.H. Died June 4, 1927.

MORSE, Charles Hosmer, mfr.; b. St. Johnsbury, Vt., Sept. 23, 1833; s. John and Elizabeth (Hosmer) M.; ed. St. Johnsbury Acad.; m. Martha J. Owens, June 30, 1868 (died 1903); 2d, Mrs. Helen H. Piffard, July 22, 1911. Left St. Johnsbury Acad., Dec. 11, 1850, to become clerk for E. & T. Fairbanks & Co., scale mfrs., became mem. Fairbanks, Greenleaf & Co., Chicago, 1862, and Fairbanks, Morse & Co., Jan. 1, 1872, of which is now chmn. bd. dirs. Republican. Conglist. Home: Winter Park, Fla. Died May 5, 1921.

MORSE, Edward Lind, painter, writer; b. at Poughkeepsie, N.Y., Mar. 29, 1857; s. Samuel Finley Breese and Sarah Elizabeth (Griswold) M.; B.A., Yale, 1878; Royal Acad. Art, Berlin, 1884-88; Grand Ducal Acad. of Art, Weimar, Germany, 1888-91; Julien Acad., Paris, 1891, 1892; m. Charlotte Dunning Wood, July 24, 1888 (died 1898); 2d, Clara Lounsbery (née Croxson), Oct. 16, 1899. Exhibited in Paris Salon, 1893; exhbns. Nat. Acad. Design, Soc. Am. Artists, etc.; spl. exhbns. of work in Washington, New York, Chicago, St. Louis, etc. Unitarian. Author: Samuel F. B. Morse, His Letters and Journals, 1914. Home: Pittsfield, Mass. Died June 9, 1923.

MORSE, Edward Sylvester, zoölogist; b. Portland, Me., June 18, 1838; s. Jonathan K. and Jane Seymour (Beckett) M.; ed. at Bethel, Me., Acad.; later 3 yrs. with Louis Agassiz at Lawrence Scientific Sch. (Harvard); (hon. Ph.D., Bowdoin College, 1871; A.M., Harvard Univ., 1892; D.Sc., Yale Univ., 1918; Doctor of Human Letters, Tufts Coll., 1922). Professor of comparative anatomy and zoölogy, Bowdoin, 1871-74; prof. zoölogy, Imperial U., Tokio, Japan, 1877-80; dir. Peabody Museum, Salem, Mass., 1880—. Lecturer, Harvard U., 1872-73; keeper Japanese pottery, Mus. Fine Arts, Boston, 1892—; authority on Japanese ceramics. Mem. jury of awards, Chicago Expn., 1893, Buffalo Expn., 1901, St. Louis Expn., 1904. Fellow Am. Acad. Arts and Sciences; mem. numerous scientific societies. Decorated with Order of the Rising Sun (Japan), 1898; 2d degree Order of Sacred Treasure (Japan), 1922. Author: First Book of Zoölogy, 1875; Japanese Homes and Their Surroundings, 1886; Catalogue of the Morse Collection of Japanese Pottery (Mus. of Fine Arts, Boston), 1901; Glimpses of China and Chinese Homes, 1902; Mars and Its Mystery, 1906; Japan Day by Day, 1917. Home: Salem, Mass. Died Dec. 20, 1925.

MORSE, Edwin Wilson, editor, writer; b. Natick, Mass., Mar. 29, 1855; s. Maj. Edwin C. and Mary (Wilson) M.; grad. Phillips Exeter Acad., 1874; A.B., Harvard, 1878; m. Florence L. Stone, Sept. 14, 1881. On staff New York Tribune 5 yrs.; became editorial corr. Boston Transcript and mus. editor New York Commercial Advertiser, 1883; editor The Book Buyer, 1887-94; editor book dept., Charles Scribner's Sons, New York, 1894-1904; sec. and dir., same, 1904-10. Author: Causes and Effects in American History, 1912; The Vanguard of American Volunteers, 1918; The Life and Letters of Hamilton W. Mabie, 1920. Died Oct. 5, 1924.

MORSE, Frank Lincoln, mfr.; b. Ithaca, N.Y., Sept. 14, 1864; s. Ben and Sarah (Fitchette) M.; ed. high sch., Ithaca; spl. study in tech. lines; m. Cora M. Perry, Apr. 7, 1900. In hay pressing and tow mill business, Algona, Ia., 1884-87; mfr. flax tow, Orange, Ia., 1887-90; became connected, 1890, with Morse Mfg. Co., Trumansburg, N.Y., inc., 1898, as Morse Chain Co., later moving to Ithaca, now pres. and treas. same; also pres. First Nat. Bank of

Orlando (Fla.), Morse Products, Inc., Barr-Morse Corporation. Patentee of about 50 inventions relating mostly to silent chain and power transmission. Mem. advisory com. State Ins. Fund and of finance com., same fund, for State of New York. Director of City Hospital, Ithaca, N.Y. Republican. Unitarian. Home: Ithaca, N.Y. Died Mar. 25, 1935.

MORSE, Fremont; b. Manchester, Mass., Jan. 19, 1857; s. Joseph Haskell and Mary Elizabeth (Girdler) M.; Ph.B., U. of Calif., 1879; m. Mary Walker Eastman, Apr. 4, 1888; children—Henry Eastman, Alice Fremont, Isita Girdler. With U.S. Coast and Geodetic Survey, 1879—; triangulation and topography, 1879-81; astronomer steamship Hassler, S.E. Alaska, 1882-83; triangulation and astron. work, Calif., 1884-90; astron. work in Alaska, 1891-98; gen. surveys, Pacific States and Alaska, 1898-1902; observer trans-Pacific longitude, San Francisco-Manila, 1903-04; Alaska boundary survey, 1904-13; astron. work Atlantic Coast and gen. surveys, 1914-15; dir. Coast Surveys, Manila, 1916, 17, 18; insp. San Francisco field station, 1919-Mar. 1, 1924 (retired). Republican. Conglist. Home: Berkeley, Calif. Died 1936.

MORSE, Godfrey, lawyer; b. Wachenheim, Germany, May 19, 1846; s. Jacob Maas and Charlotte (Mehlinger) M.; came to America, 1854; A.B., Harvard, 1870, LL.B., 1872; (hon. A.M., Tufts Coll., 1900); m. Mrs. Janet Conrad, Jan. 26, 1907. Admitted to bar 1873, and entered practice at Boston. Mem. Boston Sch. Com., 1876-78, Boston Common Council, 1882-83 (pres. 1883); asst. counsel for U.S., in Ct. of Commrs. of Alabama Claims, 1882-84; mem. Bd. Ct. House Commrs., Boston, 1885-92; trustee Am. Surety Co. of New York. One of founders and pres. Leopold Morse Home for Infirm Hebrews, and Orphanage; trustee Boston Dental Coll.; v.p. Home for Incurables; pres. Boston Fedn. of Jewish Charities. Chairman Dem. State Com. of Mass., and Dem. City Com., Boston, 1898. Home: Boston, Mass. Died 1911.

MORSE, Harmon Northrop, chemist; b. Cambridge, Vt., Oct. 15, 1848; s. Harmon and Elizabeth Murray (Buck) M.; A.B., Amherst (Mass.) College, 1873 (LL.D., 1915); Ph.D., U. of Göttingen, 1875; m. Caroline Augusta Brooks, Dec. 13, 1876 (died 1887); m. 2d, Elizabeth Dennis Clarke, Dec. 24, 1890. Asst. in chemistry, Amherst, 1875-76; asso. prof. chemistry, Johns Hopkins U., 1876-91, and prof. analytical chemistry and adj. dir. of the chem. lab., 1891, prof. inorganic and analytical chemistry, and dir. of chem. laboratory. Fellow Am. Acad. Arts and Sciences. Avogadro medalist. Research asso. Carnegie Instn. of Washington; prin. investigations, osmotic pressure. Author: Exercises in Quantitative Chemistry, 1905. Home: Baltimore, Md. Died Sept. 8, 1920.

MORSE, Harry Wheeler, physicist; b. San Diego, Calif., Feb. 25, 1873; s. Philip and Sarah (McDonald) M.; A.B., Leland Stanford Jr. U., 1897; Ph.D., U. of Leipzig, 1901; m. Isabel Grace Gray, Aug. 8, 1904; children—Philip Gray, Cecily, Constance, Anthony John. Instr. physics, 1902-10, asst. prof., 1910-12, Harvard; prof. chemistry, U. of Calif., 1912-13; in charge of scientific work, Western Precipitation Co., Los Angeles, 1913-18; tech. mgr. Am. Trona Corp., 1918-19; consulting chemist and metallurgist, 1920—. Fellow Am. Acad. Arts and Sciences. Translator: Ostwald, Letters to a Painter on the Theory and Practice of Painting, 1906; Ostwald, Fundamental Principles of Chemistry, 1907. Joint Author: Ostwald and Morse's Elementary Modern Chemistry, 1907. Author: Chemistry and Physics of the Lead Accumulator, 1912. Home: Stanford University, Calif. Died Mar. 12, 1936.

MORSE, Hosea Ballou, commr. Chinese Govt.; b. Brookfield, N.S., July 18, 1855; s. Albert David and Mercy Dexter (Park) M.; descendant from ancestors settled at Dedham, Mass., 1636, left for Halifax, 1775, returned to Medford, Mass., 1865; A.B., Harvard, 1874; LL.D., Western Reserve, 1913, Harvard, 1924; m. Annie Josephine Welsford, Feb. 8, 1881. Apptd. asst. in Imperial Chinese Customs Service, July 1874; promoted deputy commr., 1887, commr., 1896; statis. sec. (commr. customs) to insp. gen. of customs (chief of dept. statistics, printing and supplies), 1903-07; retired, 1909. In 1885 was sent by Imperial decree on spl. mission in connection with peace terminating the Franco-Chinese War; detached for spl. duty, 1885-87, in connection with reorgn. of the (subsidized) China Merchants' Steam Navigation Co.; apptd., 1899, by Imperial decree, spl. commr. to arrange for opening of Province of Hunan to foreign trade; adviser to Chinese Delegation, Financial Conf., Brussels, Belgium, Sept. 1920. Pres. Am. Assn. of China; mem. council Royal Asiatic Soc. of Eng. (hon. mem. of China Br.); chmn. bd. Y.M.C.A., Shanghai. Asso. mem. Colonial Soc. of Massachusetts. Decorations (by imperial rescript); Double Dragon, III div., 2d class, 1885, civ. rank of 3d class, with blue button, 1893; Double Dragon, III div., 1st class, 1903; civ. rank, 2d class, with red button, 1908; Order of Chia Ho, 3d class, 1916, 2d class, 1922 (China). Author: Currency of China, 1906; The Trade and Administration of China, 1908, revised edit., 1920; The Guilds of China, 1909; The International Relations of the Chinese Empire, Vol. I, 1910, Vols. II and III, 1918; The Chronicles of the East India Company in China (1635-1834), Vols. I-IV, 1926, Vol. V, 1929; (with H. F. MacNair) Far Eastern International Relations, 1931. Home: Camberley, Surrey, Eng. Died Feb. 13, 1934.

MORSE, James Herbert, author; b. Hubbardston, Mass., Oct. 8, 1841; s. Augustus and Lucinda (Wright) M.; A.B., Harvard, 1863, A.M., 1866; m. Lucy Gibbons, May 12, 1870. Head of the late Morse and Rogers Sch., 1868-1904. Author: Summer Haven Songs, 1886. Home: New York, N.Y., and Cotuit, Mass. Deceased.

MORSE, John Lovett, M.D.; b. Taunton, Mass., Apr. 21, 1865; s. Erastus and Sarah Seabury (Bassett) M.; A.B., Harvard, 1887, A.M., M.D., 1891; m. Adelaide M. Fairbrother, Sept. 3, 1906; 1 son, Lovett. Practicing phys. at Boston, 1892-1937, retired; asst. clin. medicine, 1896-1900, instr. pediatrics, 1903-06, asst. prof., 1906-11, asso. prof., 1911-15, prof., 1915-21, prof. emeritus, 1921—, Harvard; cons. phys. Children's Hosp., Infants' Hosp., Floating Hosp., and Beth Israel Hospital. Home: Newton, Mass. Died Apr. 3, 1940.

MORSE, John Torrey, Jr., author; b. Boston, Mass., Jan. 9, 1840; s. John Torrey and Lucy Cabot (Jackson) M.; A.B., Harvard, 1860, Litt.D., 1911; m. Fanny P. Hovey, June 10, 1865. Practiced law at Boston, 1862-80; devoted to lit., 1880—. Mem. Mass. Ho. of Rep., 1876; overseer Harvard, 1879-91; co-editor, with Henry Cabot Lodge, the Internat. Review, 4 yrs. Author: Life of Alexander Hamilton (2 vols.), 1876; Life and Letters of Oliver Wendell Holmes (2 vols.), 1896; Life and Letters of Col. Henry Lee, 1906; Memoir of Thomas Sergeant Perry; also (in American Statesmen Series, of which was editor): Abraham Lincoln (2 vols.); John Quincy Adams; Thomas Jefferson; John Adams; Benjamin Franklin. Home: Needham, Mass. Died Mar. 28, 1937.

MORSE, Lucy Gibbons, author; d. James Sloane G. (author "We Are Coming, Father Abraham") and Abby (Hopper) Gibbons; g.d. Isaac T. Hopper; m. James Herbert Morse, May 12, 1870. Author: The Chezzles, 1888; Rachel Stanwood, 1894. Home: Cotuit, Mass. Died July 13, 1936.

MORSE, Richard Cary, clergyman; b. Hudson, N.Y., Sept. 19, 1841; s. Richard C. and Sarah Louisa (Davis) M.; A.B., Yale, 1862, A.M., 1865; grad. Princeton and Union Theol. sems., 1867; LL.D., Pa. Coll., 1918; D.D., Colgate, 1920; m. Jane E., d. Joshua M. Van Cott, June 21, 1883. Asst. editor New York Observer, 1867-69; ordained Presbyn. ministry, Jan. 15, 1869; gen. sec. internat. com. Y.M.C.A., 1869-1915, and continued as consulting gen. sec. for life, also of Nat. Council of Y.M.C.A. of U.S.; identified with supervision and extension of Y.M.C.A., chiefly in North America, also in other parts of the world. Hon. Am. sec. World's Com., Y.M.C. Assns. (hdqrs. Geneva, Switzerland); advisory dir. Y.M.C.A., New York; mem. grad. com. Yale Y.M.C.A.; in the interest of the work, beginning with 1872, made many trips to Great Britain and the Continent; also in 1903 and 1907 in the same interest, tours to India, Australia, China, Korea, Japan, the Philippines and Russia. Was in France during the World War in 1918. Author: Polity of Young Men's Christian Associations, 1904; Fifty Years of Federation (Y.M.C.A.), 1905; History of the North American Y.M.C.A., 1913; My Life with Young Men, 1917. Home: Brooklyn, N.Y. Died Dec. 25, 1926.

MORSE, Robert McNeil, lawyer; b. Boston, Mass., Aug. 11, 1837; s. Robert McNeil and Sarah M. (Clark) M.; A.B., Harvard, 1857; m. Anna E. Gorham, Nov. 1863; father of Margaret Fessenden M. Admitted to Suffolk bar, 1860; practiced in Boston. Mem. Mass. Senate, 1866, 67, Ho. of Rep., 1880 (chmn. judiciary com. and leader of house). Overseer of Harvard, 1880-94. Home: Falmouth, and Jamaica Plain, Mass. Deceased.

MORSE, Roy L., lawyer; b. Racine, Wis., Mar. 8, 1870; s. James B. and Jane (Smith) M.; B.A., Ripon (Wis.) Coll., 1894; student Wis. Law Sch.; m. Beatrice Kellogg, May 12, 1897; children—Birney K., Beatrice G. Admitted to Wis. bar, 1896, and began practice at Ripon; dist. atty. Fond du Lac Co., Wis., 1901-05; U.S. atty., Eastern Dist. of Wis., July 1, 1923—. Mem. Exemption Bd., World War. Republican. Conglist. Home: Milwaukee, Wis. Died May 12, 1927.

MORSE, Sidney, educational dir.; b. Ledyard, Conn., Aug. 19, 1874; s. Richard B. and Mary Hannah (Watrous) M.; student Mass. Agrl. Coll., Amherst, Mass., 1892-93; m. Alice Louise Wattson, 1901; 1 son, Rogers Watrous; m. 2d, Jeanne Moeglin Krish, 1931. Assistant mgr. King-Richardson Co., publishers, Richmond, Va., 1896-98; asso. dir. Home Corr. Sch., Springfield, Mass., 1900-03; editor and mgr. book dept. Success Mag., 1904-08; mng. editor Craftsman Mag., 1908; ednl. dir. People's Univ., St. Louis, 1909-13; editorial dir. Success Co., Petersburg, N.Y., 1914-17. Sent to France to represent Y.M.C.A. in liaison with Am. Library Assn., in distribution of books through the Army, 1918; assigned to coördinate records of A.E.F.-Y.M.C.A. in central bureau, at Paris, 1918, and became chief of Records Bur.; sec. of War Hist. Bur. of A.E.F.-Y.M.C.A., Paris and New York, 1919-20. Lecturer on Americanization and Citizenship. Sec. Nat. Am. Council; chmn. exec. bd. Motion Picture Chamber of Commerce of America (non-theatrical), 1923-24; mem. Nat. Commn. on Enrichment of Adult Life, 1932—; mem. advisory bd. Home Library Foundation. Mason. Exec. sec. Bur. Social and Ednl. Service, Grand Lodge of N.Y., 1921-27; in charge service dept. of Bd. of Gen. Activities, Grand Lodge of N.Y., 1927-28; v.p. and gen. mgr. Educational Pub. Corp., N.Y. (pubs. The Grade Teacher and St. Nicholas mags.), 1929—. Author: Household Discoveries, 1908; Freemasonry in the American Revolution, 1924; Freemasonry and the Drums of '75, 1927. Died Jan. 26, 1939.

MORSE, Waldo Grant, lawyer; b. Rochester, N.Y., Mar. 13, 1859; s. Adolphus and Mary E. (Grant) M.; of old New England families on both sides; attended U. of Rochester 2 yrs.; spent 2 yrs. in travel and reading; studied law in office of Martindale & Oliver; m. Adelaide P., d. Albert Cook, of Seneca Falls, N.Y., June 22, 1886. Admitted to bar at Buffalo, 1884; in practice at New York, 1888—. Was apptd. a Palisades commr. by Gov. Morton; drew Palisades Nat. Reservation bills (which passed N.Y. and N.J. legislatures) and a Congressional bill. Pres. and dir. State Bank of Seneca Falls; dir. and v.p. and counsel Kinatome Patents Corp.; counsel Am. Voting Machine Corp., Co-op. G.&T. Exchange, Inc., Perley Morse & Co. Mem. Am. Scenic and Historic Preservation Soc. and of com. in charge of legislation for the preservation of the Highlands of the Hudson; was 2d pres. Morse Soc. America. Home: Yonkers, N.Y. Deceased.

MORSE, Warner Jackson, plant pathologist; b. Waterbury Center, Vt., Oct. 30, 1872; s. Daniel Jackson and Jane (McKee) M.; grad. Johnson (Vt.) Normal Sch., 1893; B.S., U. of Vt., 1898, M.S., 1903, Sc.D., 1923; Ph.D., U. of Wis., 1912; m. Mary A. Leland, July 6, 1898; 1 dau., Ruth Esther. Teacher natural sciences, Montpelier (Vt.) Sem., 1899-1901; asst. botanist, Vt. Expt. Sta., 1901-06; instr. botany, 1901-05, asst. prof. bacteriology, 1905-06, U. of Vt.; plant pathologist, 1906-23, dir., 1921—, Me. Agrl. Expt. Sta. Mason. Home: Orono, Me. Died Mar. 25, 1931.

MORSS, Charles Anthony, banker; b. Boston, Mass., July 13, 1857; s. Charles Anthony and Mary Elizabeth (Wells) M.; grad. Boston High Sch., 1875; m. Martha Houghton Reed, 1893; children—Philip Reed, Charles A., James Reed, Marian. Began in wool business with Warren D. Hobbs, 1873; admitted as partner firm Hobbs, Taft & Co., 1884; associated with father, firm of Morss and Whyte, 1887, and became treas. Simplex Wire & Cable Co., formerly part of Morss & Whyte; resigned as treas., Dec. 1917; gov. Federal Reserve Bank, Dec. 20, 1917-Dec. 31, 1922. Republican. Home: Newton, Mass. Died July 5, 1927.

MORSS, Everett, mfr.; b. Boston, Mar. 6, 1865; s. Charles Anthony and Mary Elizabeth (Wells) M.; grad. English High Sch., Boston, 1881; S.B., Mass. Inst. Tech., 1885; A.M., Tufts, 1923; m. Ethel Reed, June 8, 1891; children—Constance (Mrs. Gardiner H. Fiske), Everett, Noel. Pres. Simplex Wire & Cable Co., Franklin Foundation; trustee Morss Real Estate Trust; dir. various companies. Member priorities com. War Industries Board, Washington, D.C., 1917-18, chief of brass sect., 1918. Mem. Corp. Mass. Inst. Tech. (treas., mem. exec. com.). Pres. Boston Chamber Commerce, 1921. Fellow Am. Inst. E.E. Republican. Home: Boston, Mass. Died Dec. 28, 1933.

MORSS, Samuel E., pres. Indianapolis Sentinel Co. and editor-in-chief Sentinel, Feb. 1, 1888—; b. Ft. Wayne, Ind., Dec. 15, 1852; s. Samuel S. and Susan A. M.; grad. high school, 1871; m. Carrie J. Godfroy, June 23, 1875. Mem. editorial staff and editor-in-chief Ft. Wayne Gazette, 1871-75; editor and part propr. Ft. Wayne Sentinel, 1875-80; one of founders and editor Kansas City Star, 1880-82; traveled in Europe, 1882-83; editorial writer and Washington corr. Chicago Times, 1883-88; del. at large and chmn. Ind. delegation Nat. Dem. Conv., 1892; del. at large and mem. resolutions com., Nat. Dem. Conv., 1900; U.S. consul gen., Paris, 1893-97. Home: Indianapolis, Ind. Died 1903.

MORTENSON, Peter Alvin, supt. schs.; b. near Westfield, Wis., Dec. 10, 1869; s. Ole and Jessina M.; parents natives of Denmark; ed. U. of Wis., U. of Chicago; m. Josephine Johnson, Feb. 21, 1894. Began as teacher dist. schs., Wis., 1890; connected with pub. schs. of Chicago, 1897—; successively teacher, prin. Key Sch. 2 yrs., Washington Sch. 5 yrs., supt. Parental Sch. 9 yrs., asst. supt. schs., supt. schs., Sept. 1918-Jan. 1924; now supt. Chicago Parental School. Home: Chicago, Ill. Died Jan. 5, 1937.

MORTON, Charles, brig. gen.; b. Chagrin Falls, O., Mar. 18, 1846; s. Charles Eldridge and Huldah Atwater (Noah) M.; m. Elizabeth Lloyd, d. Maj. Gen. Langdon C. Easton, U.S.A., Apr. 8, 1873; m. 2d, Mrs. Sabina (Page) Pemberton, Sept. 25, 1904. Served as pvt. Co. I, 13th and 25th Mo. Inf., and Co. H, 1st Mo. Engrs., July 29, 1861-Sept. 14, 1864; apptd. U.S. Mil. Acad., July 1, 1865, grad. 1869;

apptd. 2d lt. 3d U.S. Cav., June 15, 1869; promoted through grades to brig. gen. U.S.A., Apr. 19, 1907; retired by operation of law, Mar. 18, 1910. Bvtd. 1st lt., Feb. 27, 1890, for action against Indians in Tonto country, Ariz., June 5, 1871. Died Dec. 20, 1914.

MORTON, Charles Gould, army officer; b. Cumberland, Me., Jan. 15, 1861; s. Allen and Mary A. (Colley) M.; grad. U.S. Mil. Acad., 1883, Army War Coll., 1905; m. Ida Hastings, Oct. 15, 1885 (died 1921); m. 2d, Eleanor M. Huff, June 14, 1922. Commd. 2d lt., June 13, 1883; promoted through grades to brig. gen., July 14, 1916; maj. gen., June 17, 1917. Served on frontier, in Philippines, in Panama, Tex. border; comdr. 10th Div., 1916-17, 29th Div., 1917-19; comdg. Hawaiian Dept., 1919-21; duty at War Dept., 1921-22; comdg. 9th Corps Area, 1922-25; retired Jan. 15, 1925. Awarded D.S.M.; Croix de Guerre with two palms; and Comdr. Legion of Honor (France). Home: Los Gatos, Calif. Died July 18, 1933.

MORTON, Eliza Happy, author; b. Westbrook (now N. Deering, suburb of Portland), Me.; d. William and Eliza Hannah (Phenix) M.; ed. Westbrook Sem. Began as teacher at 16; made specialty of geography; in charge of teaching of geography in Normal Dept., Battle Creek Coll., Mich., 1880-83; 17 yrs. sec., treas. Me. Tract Soc. and Me. branch, Review and Herald Pub. Co. of Washington (office at Portland). Author: Lessons on the Continent, 1883; Potter's Elementary Geography, 1888; Potter's Advanced Geography, 1891 (also teachers' edits. of both works); Morton's Elementary Geography, 1900; Morton's Advanced Geography, 1901; Thought—Its Origin and Power, 1905; Star Flowers, or Songs in the Night (poems), 1912. Also the words of many songs and hymns, among the most popular of which are The Songs My Mother Sang (music by D. B. Towner), My Mission, and Longing for Rest. Home: Portland, Me. Died July 31, 1916.

MORTON, Frank Roy, surgeon; b. Philadelphia, Pa., Aug. 13, 1880; s. Henry S. and Frances (Silvera) M.; M.D., Coll. of Medicine, U. of Ill., 1901; grad. study Breslau, Germany, and Vienna, 1903-04; m. Mabel W. Edwards, June 10, 1907; children—Dorothy M., Frances M. Interne, Cook County Hosp., 1901-02; began practice at Chicago, 1904; chief surgeon Standard Oil Co. (Indiana), 1915—. Fellow Am. Coll. Surgeons. Republican. Mason. Home: Chicago, Ill. Died June 16, 1934.

MORTON, George Carpenter, paint and varnish mfr.; b. Boston, Mass., Sept. 23, 1868; s. John Dwight and Maria E. (Wesson) M.; ed. English High Sch., Boston; m. Harriet L. Evans, June 6, 1893; children—Eugene Evans, John Dwight, Marjorie. In paint and varnish mfg. business from 1886; with Carpenter, Woodward & Morton, incorporated, 1892, as Carpenter-Morton Co., asst. treas., 1892-98, treas. and gen. mgr., 1898-1921, pres. and gen. mgr. from 1921; pres. Carpenter-Morton Co. of Ill.; incorporator Eliot Savings Bank; trustee Boston Penny Savings Bank (mem. bd. of investment). Republican. Christian Scientist. Home: Boston, Mass. Died Dec. 11, 1930.

MORTON, George Edwin, animal husbandman; b. Johnstown, Wis., June 17, 1879; s. of James and Janet Ann (McFarlane) M.; B.L., Milton Coll., Wis., 1899; studied U. of Wis., 1901-03; B.S., Colo. State Agrl. Coll., 1904; m. Elizabeth Maude Hyslop, July 5, 1905 (died 1930); children—William (dec.), George Edwin, Logan Douglas, Gordon (dec.), Craig, Elizabeth Maude, Stuart. Asst. and asso. prof. animal husbandry, U. of Wyo., 1904-07; prof. animal husbandry, 1907—, head of dept., 1909—, Colo. Agrl. Coll.; state dairy commr., ex-officio, of Colo., 1913-29; expert in animal husbandry, U.S. Dept. of Agr., 1906-07. Official judge for Holstein-Friesian Assn. America, Nat. Duroc Jersey Breeders Assn., Am. Spotted Poland China Breeders Assn; v.p. Nat. Western Stock Show. Mason. Home: Fort Collins, Colo. Died July 11, 1939.

MORTON, Henry, pres. Stevens Inst. of Technology, 1870—; b. New York, Dec. 11, 1837; s. Rev. Dr. Henry Jackson and Helen (McFarlan) M.; ed. Episcopal Acad., Phila.; grad. Univ. of Pa., A.M., 1857 (Sc.D., Univ. of Pa.; Ph.D., LL.D., Princeton); m. Clara Whiting Dodge, 1863. Published translation of hieroglyphic text of the Rosetta Stone, 1859; conducted expdn. to observe and make photographs of total solar eclipse in Iowa, 1868; was prof. chemistry Univ. of Pa., 1868-70; resident sec. Franklin Inst. and editor of its journal, 1864-70. Mem. U.S. Light House Bd., 1878-86; mem. Nat. Acad. of Sciences, 1873—. Has given over $80,000 toward endowment of the Stevens Inst. of Technology. Home: Hoboken, N.J. Died 1902.

MORTON, Henry H., surgeon; b. Hoboken, N.J., 1861; s. Edmond Ludlow and Josephine (Holdich) M.; ed. Dr. Chapin's Sch. and Grammar Sch. No. 35, New York; M.D., Long Island Coll. Hosp., 1882; post-grad. study, Prague, Munich, Berlin, Vienna and Paris; unmarried. Emeritus prof. genito-urinary diseases, L.I. Coll. Hosp.; attending genito-urinary surgeon St. Peters Hosp., Brooklyn. Mem. Com. on Venereal Diseases in Surg. Gen.'s Office, World War. Author: Genito-Urinary Diseases and Syphilis, 1902 (6 edits.). Home: Brooklyn, N.Y. Died May 3, 1940.

MORTON, James Ferdinand, curator; b. Littleton, Mass., Oct. 18, 1870; s. James Ferdinand and Caroline Edwards (Smith) M.; A.B., A.M., Harvard, 1892; speaker's diploma, Sch. of Expression, 1894; m. Pearl K. Merritt, Mar. 3, 1934. Field sec. New York State Single Tax League, 1916-18, for N.Y. State Farmers' Nat Single Tax League, 1917-18; sec. Common Commercial Language Co., 1918-24; curator Paterson (N.J.) Museum, 1925. Originator of intercollegiate debates; lectures on social and lit. topics; former mem. Home Colony, Wash., editor The Demonstrator. Pres. Nat. Amateur Press Assn.; v.p. Esperanto Assn. N. America; pres. Thos. Paine Nat. History Assn.; fellow Mineral. Soc. America. Author: The Curse of Race Prejudice, 1906. Home: Paterson, N.J. Died Oct. 7, 1941.

MORTON, James Madison, Jr., judge; b. Fall River, Mass., Aug. 24, 1869; s. of James M. and Emily F. (Canedy) M.; A.B., Harvard, 1891, A.M. and LL.B., 1894; m. Nancy J. B. Brayton, June 10, 1896; children—Brayton, Sarah, Hugh. Practiced at Fall River; mem. Bd. of Police, Fall River, 1903-12; apptd. U.S. dist. judge, Mass., Aug. 1912; appointed United States circuit judge, Dec. 1931. Republican. Dir. Boys' Club of Fall River; chmn. bd. Wentworth Inst., Boston; overseer Harvard Coll., Unitarian. Home: Fall River, Mass. Died June 26, 1940.

MORTON, Jennie Chinn, writer; b. Bellsgrove, Franklin Co., Ky.; d. Judge Franklin and Annie (Bell) Chinn; ed. pvt. schs., Frankfort and Shelbyville, Ky.; m. John Calhoun Morton, banker (died 1860). Editor of The Register, mag. of Ky. State Hist. Soc., also sec.-treas. and regent of this soc.; known as "lady laureate" of Kentucky. Presbyn. Author: Her Dearest Friend (story-poem), 1909. Home: Frankfort, Ky. Died Jan. 9, 1920.

MORTON, Jeremiah Rogers, lawyer; b. Clark Co., Ky., Feb. 10, 1842; s. John and Ann Elizabeth (Rogers) M.; ed. Transylvania Acad.; grad. law sch., Ky., Univ.; m. Mary C. Gratz, Nov. 19, 1879. Admitted to Ky. bar, Feb. 1868. Was in Confederate army summer of 1862 to end of war, except when a prisoner in Camp Chase and Camp Douglas. Judge 10th jud. dist., including Fayette Co. and city of Lexington, 10 yrs. Democrat. Home: Lexington, Ky. Deceased.

MORTON, Joy, merchant; b. Detroit, Sept. 27, 1855; s. J. Sterling and Caroline (Joy) Morton; desc. Richard Morton, Plymouth, Mass., 1625; on mother's side desc. Thomas Joy, who built the first town-house of Boston, 1650, a replica of which Mr. Morton now owns, at Pier No. 1, near mouth of Chicago River; ed. Talbot Hall, Nebraska City, Neb.; m. Carrie, d. Judge George B. Lake, of Omaha, Sept. 23, 1880; children—Jean (Mrs. Joseph M. Cudahy), Sterling; m. 2d, Margaret Gray, Jan. 16, 1917. Sr. mem. firm Joy Morton & Co., 1885—; chmn. bd. Morton Salt Co., pres. Standard Office Co., Morton Building Corp. Founder of the Morton Arboretum, Lisle, Ill.—a foundation for practical, scientific research work in horticulture and agriculture. Home: Lisle, Du Page Co., Ill. Died May 9, 1934.

MORTON, Julius Sterling, sec. agr. U.S.; b. Adams, N.Y., April 22, 1832; s. Julius D. and Emeline (Sterling) M.; ed. Monroe, Mich., and Univ. of Mich.; grad. Union Coll., N.Y., 1854. Moved to Nebraska City, Nebraska Ty.; engaged in farming. Originator of the annual Arbor Day, observed in Western prairie States; was sec., 1858, and soon after acting gov. Territory of Neb.; was mem. Territorial legislature; an original mem. and later pres., Neb. Territorial Bd. of Agr. and Territorial Hort. Soc.; has been pres. Am. Forestry Assn.; sec. of agr. of U.S., 1893-97. Democrat; now affiliated with gold-standard wing. Editor: The Conservative, a weekly journal. Home: Nebraska City, Neb. Died 1902.

MORTON, Levi Parsons, vice president of the U.S.; b. Shoreham, Vt., May 16, 1824; s. Rev. Daniel Oliver and Lucretia (Parsons) M.; desc. of George Morton, of Battery, Yorkshire, financial agt. in London of Mayflower Pilgrims, who arrived at Plymouth, Mass., on ship Ann, in 1623; grad. Shoreham Acad.; (LL.D., Dartmouth, 1881, Middlebury, 1882); m. Lucy Kimball (died 1871); 2d, Anna Livingston Street, Feb. 12, 1873 (five children: Edith Livingston, Lena, Helen, Alice and Mary Morton). Founded banking houses of L. P. Morton & Co. and Morton, Bliss & Co., New York; Morton, Rose & Co., Morton, Chaplin & Co., London, and Morton Trust Co., New York; pres. Morton Trust Co., Fifth Av. Trust Co. Hon. commr. Paris Expn., 1878; mem. 46th Congress (1879-81), 6th N.Y. District; U.S. minister to France, 1881-85; v.p. of the U.S., 1889-93; gov. of N.Y., 1895-96. Republican. Home: Rhinecliff-on-Hudson, N.Y. Died May 16, 1920.

MORTON, Oren Frederic, author; b. Fryeburg, Me., Jan. 27, 1857; s. Harrison G. O. and Helena T. (Gibson) M.; B.L., U. of Neb., 1879; m. Helen Louise Moody, July 21, 1915; 1 son, Harry Frederic. Teacher and gen. newspaper writer until 1907; writer of county histories, 1907—. Republican. Methodist. Author: Under the Cottonwoods, 1900; Winning or Losing, 1901; Land of the Laurel, 1903; Story of Daniel Boone, 1912; Practical History of Music, 1914; also histories of following counties: Pendleton, W.Va., 1910; Highland, Va., 1911; Preston, W.Va., 1913; Monroe, W.Va., 1916; Bath, Va., 1917; Rockbridge, Va., 1919; Alleghany, Va., 1922; Winchester, Va., 1924; also History Virginia Conference, United Brethren Church, 1922. Home: Winchester, Va. Died May 1926.

MORTON, Paul, Sec. of the navy; b. Detroit, May 22, 1857; s. J. Sterling (Sec. of Agr., 1893-97) and Caroline (Joy) M.; bro. of Joy M.; m. Charlotte Goodridge, Oct. 13, 1880. With Burlington system Dec., 1872, to Feb. 1, 1890, beginning as clerk in land office of B.&M. R.R. at Burlington, 1872, serving as asst. gen. freight agt. and gen. pass. agt. and ending as gen. freight agt. of the C.,B.&Q. R.R.; v.p. Colo. Fuel & Iron Co.; pres. Whitebreast Fuel Co., 1890-96; 3d v.p. A.,T.&S.F. Ry., 1896-98, 2d v.p. same, 1898-1904; sec. of the navy, July 1, 1904-July 1, 1905, in cabinet of President Roosevelt; pres. Equitable Life Assurance Soc. of U.S., 1905—. V.p. Pan-Am. R.R., Mar. 15, 1910—. Home: New York, N.Y. Died 1911.

MORTON, Samuel Walker, M.D.; b. Marcus Hook, Pa., Aug. 1, 1861; s. William H. and Anna (Walker) M.; M.D., U. of Pa., 1886; m. Mary Pleasants Hildeburn, June 26, 1888. Practiced in Phila., 1887—; pres. Pa. Epileptic Hosp. and Colony Farm. Progressive. Home: Philadelphia, Pa. Died Jan. 12, 1931.

MOSBY, John Singleton, lawyer, soldier; b. Powhatan Co., Va., Dec. 6, 1833; s. Alfred D. and Virginia I. (McLaurine) M.; grad. U. of Va., 1852; m. Pauline Clarke, Dec. 30, 1856. Admitted to bar, 1855; practiced at Bristol, Va., 1855-61. Pvt. and later adj. in 1st Va. Cav., C.S.A., 1861-62; was col., 1862-65, of Mosby's Partisan Rangers, an independent cav. command, which did much damage by cutting communications and destroying supply trains in the rear of U.S.A., capturing cav. outposts, etc. Practiced law in Va. after war. Became Republican; supported Grant, 1872; U.S. consul at Hongkong, 1878-85; then lawyer in San Francisco and as counsel for S.P. R.R. Co.; spl. agt. Gen. Land Office for Colo., 1901; asst. atty. in Dept. of Justice, Washington, May 1904-July 1, 1910. Author: Mosby's War Reminiscences and Stuart's Cavalry Campaign, 1887; Stuart Cavalry in the Gettysburg Campaign, 1908. Home: Warrenton, Va. Died May 30, 1916.

MOSCHCOWITZ, Alexis Victor, surgeon; b. Giralt, Hungary, Apr. 25, 1865; s. Morris and Rezi (Friedlander) M.; came to America, 1880; ed. Gymnasia, Miskolcz and Eperjes, Hungary; Ph.G., New York Coll. Pharmacy (Columbia), 1885; M.D., Coll. Phys. and Surg. (Columbia), 1891; m. Milly Loewi, Dec. 22, 1898. Prof. clin. surgery, Coll. Phys. and Surg. (Columbia), 1913—; cons. surgeon, Mt. Sinai, Beth David, and United Israel Zion hosps. Colonel Med. R.C. Fellow Am. Coll. Surgeons. Died Dec. 21, 1933.

MOSELEY, Edward Augustus, sec. Interstate Commerce Commn.; b. Newburyport, Mass., Mar. 23, 1846; s. Edward Strong and Charlotte Augusta (Chapman) M.; acad. edn.; m. Kate M. Prescott, 1870. Admitted to bar Supreme Ct. of U.S.; has been mem. Mass. Legislature, and held other offices; sec. Interstate Commerce Commn., 1887—. Leading authority in U.S. upon all measures or appliances designed to procure the safety of railroad employes and travelers upon railroads; performed signal service in Cuba in drafting a ry. law and fixing ry. classifications, tariffs, etc.; apptd. by President Roosevelt asst. recorder of Anthracite Coal Strike Commn. Received the thanks of the Commonwealth of Mass. "for disinterested services in the cause of humanity." Mason. Author: Arbitration as Applied to Railways and Their Employes; Safety Appliances on Railroads; One Hundred Years of Interstate Commerce; John Boyle O'Reilly, the Man; Railway Accidents in the United States. Home: Washington, D.C. Died 1911.

MOSELEY, Edward Buckland, brig. gen. U.S.A.; b. Phila., Oct. 1, 1846; s. Nathaniel B. and Maria (Worthington) M.; acad. edn., Phila.; grad. Auxiliary Faculty of Medicine, U. of Pa., 1866, M.D., 1868; resident phys., Phila. Hosp., 1868-69; m. Florence C. David, Dec. 9, 1875. Sergt., Pa. Militia Arty., 1862, participating in Antietam campaign; 1st lt. asst. surgeon U.S.A., Nov. 10, 1871; capt. asst. surgeon, Nov. 10, 1879; maj. surgeon, Jan. 9, 1892; lt. col. deputy surgeon gen., Feb. 14, 1902; col. asst. surgeon gen., Mar. 17, 1906; brig. gen. and retired for physical disability incurred in line of duty, May 10, 1907. Served in campaigns against Sioux, Cheyenne, and Ute Indians in Wyo., Neb., and Colo., in P.I., 1899-1900; organized and in charge Santa Monica Mil. Hosp., Manila; in charge 2d Reserve hosp. and chief surgeon Dept. Southern Luzon; later chief surgeon Dept. Colo. until retired. Home: Hollywood, Calif. Died Aug. 3, 1923.

MOSELEY, Mercer Pamplin, banker; b. Pamplin City, Va., Jan. 7, 1872; s. William Henry and Nannie Elizabeth (Pamplin) M.; ed. pub. sch.; m. Grace Agnes Russell, Dec. 6, 1899. First engaged in mercantile and brokerage business and later organized and was officially connected with lumber mfg.; entered journalistic work, 1901; was pres. and gen. mgr. Commercial Newspaper Co., pub. New York Commercial to 1917; pres. New York Securities Co.; v.p. Am. Exchange-Pacific Nat. Bank, Sept. 1, 1917—; dir. Sackett & Wilhelms Corp., Remington Typewriter Co., Chrysler Motor Corp., etc. Democrat. Baptist. Home: New York, N.Y. Died Apr. 25, 1928.

MOSER, Christopher Otto, v.p. Am. Cotton Coöp. Assn.; b. Dallas, Texas, May 29, 1885; s. Christian and Anna (Buhrer) M.; grad. high sch., Dallas; B.S., Tex. Agrl. and Mech. Coll., 1904; m. Norma K. Nagle, Jan. 4, 1911; children—Christopher Otto, Norman Nagle, Charles Frank. State feed insp., Tex. Agrl. and Mech. Coll., 1905; dairy expert, U.S. Dept. Agr., Washington, D.C., 1907; instr. in animal husbandry, Tex. Agrl. and Mech. Coll., 1908; organizer, 1908, pres. and gen. mgr. until 1912, Moser Hygienic Dairy Co., Dallas; organizer, 1910, mgr. until 1915, Coons-Moser Silo Co.; organizer, 1912, pres. and gen. mgr. until 1915, North Tex. Creamery Co.; proprietor Moser Constrn. Co., 1910-15; organizer, sec.-mgr., 1919-21, Tex. Farm Bur. Cotton Assn.; organizer, sec.-mgr., 1921-25, pres. and gen. mgr., 1925-30, Am. Cotton Growers Exchange; v.p. and sec. Am. Cotton Coöp. Assn., 1930—; v.p., sec. The Cotton Stabilization Corp. Mem. exec. com. and pres., 1929-33, Nat. Coöp. Council; chmn. Am. Inst. of Coöperation, 1929, now mem. exec. com.; also mem. exec. com. Nat. Agrl. Council. Organizer Dallas County Seed Breeders Assn., 1915, Tex. Holstein-Friesian Breeders Club (pres.), 1917, Tex. Farm Bur. Fed., 1919. Mem. Com. for the Nation to rebuild prices and purchasing power. Govt. agrl. agent, 1914-20. Mem. A. and M. Coll. Ex-Students Assn. (pres. 1914-15). Presbyn. Mason. Home: Dallas, Tex. Died July 1935.

MOSER, Jefferson Franklin, naval officer; b. Allentown, Pa., May 3, 1848; s. John B. and Henrietta (Beidelman) M.; grad. U.S. Naval Acad., 1868; m. Nancy C. McDowell, Oct. 20, 1874; children—Robert McD. (dec.), Samuel B. (dec.), Jefferson F. (dec.), Helen C. Commd., midshipman, June 2, 1868; promoted through grades to rank of rear adm. and retired after 40 yrs.' service, Sept. 29, 1904. Mem. expdns., 1869-70, 72, 73, 75, exploring and surveying ship canal routes across Nicaragua and Panama; coast survey service, 1875-80, 1884-90, 1893-96; comd. U.S. Steamer Albatross in exploring salmon streams of Alaska and on Agassiz expdn. to South Seas, etc.; comd. gunboats Albatross and Bennington during Spanish-Am. War; gen. supt. and v.p. Alaska Packers Assn., San Francisco, 1904-18. Ordered to active service in U.S.N., Apr. 6, 1917, on special duty 12th Naval Dist. until June 15, 1919. Author: Alaska Salmon and Salmon Fisheries, 1899; Alaska Salmon Investigations, 1902. Home: Alameda, Calif. Died Oct. 11, 1934.

MOSES, Alfred Joseph, mineralogist; b. Brooklyn, July 25, 1859; s. Thomas P. and Margaret M.; acad. edn., Woburn, Mass.; E.M., Columbia, 1882, Ph.D., 1890; U. of Munich, 1895-96; m. Elizabeth B. Gilbert, June 23, 1887; 2d, Margaret C. Magrath, Aug. 18, 1906. Asst. in mineralogy, 1882-85, instr. mineralogy and metallurgy, 1885-90, adj. prof. mineralogy, 1890-97, prof., 1897—, Columbia U. Fellow N.Y. Acad. Sciences, A.A.A.S. Author: Mineralogy, Crystallography and Blowpipe Analysis, 1895; Characters of Crystals, 1899. Home: New York, N.Y. Died Feb. 27, 1920.

MOSES, Bernard, univ. prof.; b. Burlington, Conn., Aug. 27, 1846; s. Richard and Rachel (Norton) M.; Ph.B., U. of Mich., 1870, LL.D., 1901; Ph.D., Heidelberg, 1873; LL.D., U. of Calif., 1918; m. Mary Edith Briggs; 1 dau., Auria (Mrs. Jean Georges Cornelius). Professor history, Albion Coll., 1875; prof. history and polit. science, U. of Calif., 1876—. Mem. U.S. Philippine Commn., 1900-02. Del. Pan-Am. Scientific Congress, Santiago de Chile, Internat. Conf. Am. States, Buenos Aires. Minister plenipotentiary on spl. mission to Chile. Author: Politics (with W. W. Crane); The Establishment of Municipal Government in San Francisco; The Government of the United States, 1906; South America on the Eve of Emancipation, 1908; The Spanish Dependencies in South America, 1914; Spain's Declining Power in South America, 1730-1806, 1919; Spanish Colonial Literature in South America, 1922; The Intellectual Background of the Revolution in South America (1810-14), 1926. Died Mar. 4, 1930.

MOSES, Montrose Jonas, author, editor; b. in New York City; s. of Montefiore J. and Rose (Jonas) M.; B.S., Coll. City of New York, 1899; m. Lucille Dorothy, d. James A. Herne, Feb. 1, 1911 (died 1921); 1 son, Montrose James; m. 2d, Leah Agnes Houghtaling, June 19, 1923. Editorial staff, Lit. Digest, 1900-02; editor series of ednl. works, 1902-03; dramatic editor The Reader Magazine, 1903-07; dramatic critic The Independent, and The Book News Monthly, 1908-18, and of The Bellman (Minneapolis), 1910-19 Editor: Everyman, a Morality Play (annotated edit. with critical intro.), 1903, 08; Memorial edit. The Plays of Clyde Fitch, 1915. American editor, The Green Room Book and Anglo-American Dramatic Register; Representative Plays by American Dramatists (3 volumes), 1918; Representative British Dramas: Victorian and Modern, 1918, 31; A Treasury of Plays for Children, 1921; Representative Continental Dramas—Revolutionary and Transitional, 1924; Clyde Fitch and His Letters (collaboration), 1924; Representative American Dramas: National and Local, 1925; Another Treasury of Plays for Children, 1926; British Plays from Restoration to 1820, 1929; Dramas of Modernism and Their Forerunners, 1931. Translator: The Passion Play of Oberammergau, 1909; On Emerson and Other Essays, by Maurice Maeterlinck, Belgian dramatist, 1912. Author: Francesca da Rimini (a critical study); Famous Actor-families in America, 1906; Children's Books and Reading, 1907; Henrik Ibsen, the Man and His Plays, 1908; Maurice Maeterlinck (intro. to spl. edit. of Pelléas and Mélisande, 1908); The Literature of the South, 1909; The Life of Heinrich Conried, 1916; The American Dramatist, 1911, 17, and a complete rewriting, 1925; Maurice Maeterlinck—A Study, 1911; Introduction to Browning's "The Ring and the Book," 1927; The Fabulous Forrest—The Record of an American Actor, 1929. Home: New York, N.Y. Died Mar. 29, 1934.

MOSES, Thomas Freeman, physician; b. Bath, Me., June 8, 1836; s. William Vaughan and Sarah (Freeman) M.; A.B., Bowdoin Coll., 1857, A.M., 1860; M.D., Jefferson Med. Coll., Phila., 1861; m. Hannah Appleton Cranch, May 7, 1867. Acting asst. surgeon U.S.A., 1862-64; mem. Pension Examining Bd., Urbana, O., 1889-92; pres. Urbana U., 1886-94. Fellow Am. Acad. Medicine, Geol. Soc. America. Translator: Unity of Natural Phenomena (from French of Emile Seigey), 1873. Home: Waltham, Mass. Died Nov. 21, 1917.

MOSESSOHN, David N., lawyer, publicist, arbiter; b. Ekaterinoslav, Russia, Jan. 1, 1883; s. Nehemiah (LL.D.) and Theresa (Nissenson) M.; brought to U.S. at age of 5; grad. high sch., Portland, Ore., 1900; LL.B., U. of Ore., 1902; m. Manya Lerner, July 9, 1905; children—Zelda (dec.), Boris Dayyan. Admitted to Ore. bar, 1902, to U.S. courts, 1904, Calif., 1909, N.Y., 1923; began practice at Portland; dept. dist. atty., Multnomah Co., Ore., 1908-10; moved to New York, 1918; pub. The Jewish Tribune, 1902—, editor, 1927—; exec. dir. Associated Dress Industries of America, 1918-23, exec. chmn. and supreme arbiter, 1923—; chmn. bd. Consol. Investors' Plan, Inc. Arbitrator Arbitration Soc. of America, Silk Assn. of America, chancellor Council on Am. Jewish Student Affairs. Mem. Am. Jewish Com. and of Palestine Chamber of Commerce in New York (dir.), Nat. Adv. Com. Leo N. Levi Memorial Hospital (Hot Springs, Ark.), Nat. Council Jewish Consumptives' Relief Soc. (Denver). Republican. Mason. Home: New York, N.Y. Died Dec. 16, 1930.

MOSESSOHN, Moses Dayyan, lawyer, economist; b. Aug. 17, 1884; s. Nehemiah (LL.D.) and Theresa (Nissenson) M.; grad. high sch., Portland, Ore., 1901; LL.B., U. of Ore., 1905; m. Blanche Lillian (pianist), d. Rabbi B. M. Kaplan, of San Francisco, Jan. 8, 1919. Admitted to Oregon bar, 1905, to U.S. Courts, 1907, U.S. Supreme Court, 1914, N.Y. State courts, 1923, Interstate Commerce Commn., 1936; acting sec. Portland Chamber Commerce, 1903-15; sec. Portland Rose Festival Assn., 1914-16; mem. Mosessohn & Mosessohn, 1905-18; moved to New York, 1918; exec. dir. United Waist League of America, 1918-23; exec. chmn., gen. counsel United Women's Wear League of America and affiliated organizations, 1923-33; exec. chmn. and gen. counsel Asso. Dress Industries of America, 1930-33; pub. The Jewish Tribune, 1903-31; editor The League Review. Chmn. and counsel Trade Organization Associates and other trade orgns.; chmn. and counsel various Code authorities under NRA. Americanization instr. public evening schs., Portland, 1916-18; sec. War Service Com. for women's garment industries, World War; councillor Jewish Fedn. of Philanthropies, New York. Mem. advisory bd. Evening Trade Sch., New York; mem. exec. com. Commercial Standards Council; N.Y. Anti-Defamation League; vice chairman of Am. Arbitration Assn. Mason. Elk. Author: Guide to American Citizenship; Trade Organizations as Effected under NRA; The Employer and the New Labor Movement; An Analysis and Explanation of the Robinson-Patman Anti-Discrimination Law, etc. Home: New York, N.Y. Died Aug. 1, 1940.

MOSESSOHN, Nehemiah, editor, theologian, lawyer; b. Crimea, Russia, Apr. 15, 1853; son. Rev. Moses and Thema (Dayyan) M.; father was chief rabbi of Odessa; grad. Szitomir Rabbinical Sch., 1873; LL.D., U. of Odessa, 1869; Dr. Oriental langs., St. Petersburg, 1876; LL.B., U. of Ore., 1902; m. Theresa Nissenson, Aug. 16, 1881; children—(first marriage) Clara (Mrs. Louis Tobler), (second marriage) David N., Moses D. Came to America, 1887; rabbi Phila., Dallas, Tex., and Portland, Ore., until 1902; editor The Jewish Tribune, Portland, Ore., 1902-18, and New York, 1918—; elected founder-editor Jewish Tribune, 1923. Asso. editor Hebrew Encyclopedia. Admitted to bar, Sup. Court of Ore., 1902, to Calif., 1903, U.S. Dist. and Circuit courts, 1902. Nat. dir. Jewish Consumptives Relief Soc., Denver. Author: Almah Again. Home: New York, N.Y. Died Dec. 10, 1926.

MOSHER, Clelia Duel, M.D., personal hygiene; b. Albany, N.Y., Dec. 16, 1863; d. Cornelius Duel, M.D., and Sarah (Burritt) M.; prep. edn., Albany Girls Acad.; stu. Wellesley, Cornell U., U. of Wis.; A.B., Stanford, 1893; A.M., 1894; M.D., Johns Hopkins, 1900; LL.D. from Mills College, Oakland, Calif., 1934; unmarried. Externe Johns Hopkins Hosp. Dispensary and gynecol. asst. Dr. Howard A. Kelly's Sanitarium, 1900-01; gen. practice, Palo Alto, Calif., 1901-10; asst. prof. personal hygiene, Stanford U., 1910-22, asso. prof., 1922-28, prof., 1928-29 (emeritus); also med. adviser to women, same univ., 1910-29. With Am. Red Cross, in France, Nov. 1917-Feb. 1919. serving as med. investigator Children's Bur., asst. med. adviser, later asso. med. dir. Bur. of Refugees and Relief. Democrat. Mem. Dutch Ref. Ch. Author: Health and the Woman Movement, 1915, 1918; Woman's Physical Freedom, 1923; Personal Hygiene for Women (Am. and British edits.), 1927. Home: Stanford University, Calif. Deceased.

MOSHER, Eliza Maria, physician; b. Cayuga Co., N.Y., 1846; d. Augustus and Maria (Sutton) M.; grad. Friends' Acad., Union Springs, N.Y., 1862; M.D., U. of Mich., 1875; unmarried. Resident phys. Mass. Reformatory for Women, 1877-79, supt. same, 1881-83; asso. prof. physiology and resident phys., Vassar Coll., 1883-86; prof. hygiene, dept. literature, science and the arts, and women's dean, U. of Mich., 1896-1902; lecturer on physiology, Chautauqua Summer Sch. of Physical Edn., 1888—; lecturer on hygiene, Adelphi Coll., Brooklyn, 1903-06. Author: Health and Happiness, 1911. Home: Brooklyn, N.Y. Died Oct. 16, 1928.

MOSHER, George Clark, M.D.; b. Mt. Blanchard, O., Aug. 8, 1858; s. George Stanford and Charlotte (Fitch) M.; Ohio State U., 1876-78; M.D., Ky. Sch. of Medicine (U. of Louisville), 1882; studied Berlin, Munich and London, 1890; Sloane Maternity Hosp., of Coll. Phys. and Surg., New York, 1893; (hon. A.M., Oberlin College, Ohio, 1912); m. Ida Beagle (A.B., Oberlin, 1880), Jan. 1, 1883; children—Mrs. Ruth Place, George Frederic, Mrs. Gladys Strong. Lecturer on obstetrics, 1891-93, prof., 1893-1907, Kansas City (Mo.) Med. Coll.; prof. obstetrics and head of dept., Sch. of Medicine, U. of Kan., 1907-12; mem. Med. Council same, 1908-09-10; obstetrician, Kansas City Gen., and Trinity hosps.; cons. obstetrician, Bethany and St. Vincent hospitals; formerly attending phys. St. Margaret's Hosp. and lecturer on obstetrics to Scarritt Training Sch. for Missionary Nurses. Fellow Am. Acad. Medicine, Am. Coll. Surgeons, Am. Assn. Obstetricians (pres.). Breeder of Holstein-Friesian dairy cattle and Hampshire swine at Hillycroft Farm, Hickmans Mills, Mo.; was treas. World's Fair Holstein Assn., St. Louis Expn., and took 1st prize and championship, both male and female entries. Conglist. Mason. Home: Kansas City, Mo. Deceased.

MOSHER, George Frank, editor; b. S. China, Me., Feb. 12, 1844; s. William and Betsy Ward (McLaughlin) M.; A.B., Bowdoin, 1869; LL.D., Findlay Coll., 1887; m. Frances M. Stewart, Sept. 25, 1871; children—Alfrieda M., Elizabeth S. Spl. agt. to field hosps. for N.H. troops, 1864; with the Morning Star, Dover, 1869-81; U.S. consul, Nice, France, and Sonneberg, Germany, 1881-85; pres. Hillsdale (Mich.) Coll., 1886-1901; editor Morning Star, Boston, 1901-11; an editor the Watchman, Oct. 1, 1911. Was pres. city council, Dover, 3 yrs.; mem. N.H. Ho. of Rep., 1877-79 (chmn. com. State Normal Sch.); trustee Hillsdale Coll. and Bates Coll. Republican. Baptist. Home: Boston, Mass. Died Aug. 16, 1929.

MOSHER, Gouverneur Frank, bishop; b. Stapleton, S.I., N.Y., Oct. 28, 1871; s. Jacob Simmons and Emma Starr (Montgomery) M.; grad. model dept. State Normal Sch., Albany, N.Y., 1886; Union Coll., 1888-92; grad. Berkeley Div. Sch., Middletown, Conn., 1896; D.D., Union Coll. (Schenectady, N.Y.) and Berkeley Div. Sch., 1920; m. Fanny Southard Stewart, Sept. 10, 1898; 1 son, John Stewart. Deacon, 1896, priest, 1898, P.E. Ch.; missionary in China, 1896-1920; bishop Missionary Dist. of P.I., Feb. 25, 1920—. Dept. to Gen. Conv., 1904, 10, 16. Central executive, Am. Red Cross, Manila. Author: Handbook of the China Missions, 1913. Died July 19, 1941.

MOSHER, Howard Townsend, lawyer; b. Albany, N.Y., July 6, 1868; s. Jacob S. (M.D.) and Emma Starr (Montgomery) M.; A.M., Union Coll., Schenectady, N.Y., 1890; m. Mary Josephine Seward, July 6, 1893. Instr. and prof. French, Union Coll., 1892-98; admitted to N.Y. bar, 1901, and began practice at Rochester; mem. Smith & Mosher; lecturer on citizenship, U. of Rochester, 1910-14. Candidate for state senator, 1904, for surrogate of Monroe Co., 1906, for mayor of Rochester, 1911, 15; chmn. Dem. Co. Com., 1908-10. Mem. Prison Reform Commn. of State of N.Y., 1913-15, State Workmen's Compensation Commn., 1914-15; dir. Municipal Govt. Assn. of N.Y. Episcopalian. Home: Rochester, N.Y. Died Feb. 15, 1919.

MOSHER, Robert Brent, consul; b. Washington, Dec. 6, 1856; s. Theodore and Mary (Brent) M.; ed. Rock Hill Coll., Ellicott City, Md.; m. Nita Byrne Moser, July 14, 1886. Apptd. clk., War Dept., Washington, 1888; transferred to State Dept., 1890; chief Bur. of Appointments, 1898-1905; consul at Collingwood, Can., 1905-06, Port Elizabeth, S. Africa, 1906-10; consul-gen. at Hankow, China, 1910-11; consul at Plauen, Germany, 1911-15, at Victoria, B.C., Mar. 2, 1915—. Editor, Executive Register of the United States, 1789-1902, 1902. Died Sept. 22, 1927.

MOSHER, Thomas Bird, publisher, editor; b. Biddeford, Me., Sept. 11, 1852; s. Benjamin and Mary Elizabeth (Merrill) M.; ed. pub. schs., Biddeford, Me., and Boston; (hon. A.M., Bowdoin Coll., 1906); m. Anna M. Littlefield, July 2, 1892. Began publishing choice and limited edits. of books in belles lettres, Oct. 1891; began editing and publishing The Bibelot, Jan. 1895, a reprint of poetry and prose, largely from scarce editions and sources not usually known; completed, with index, in 21 vols., 1915. Edited and published Am. edit. of The Germ, 1898; Swinburne's Poems and Ballads, 1899; Rossetti's Poetical Works, 1902; the first absolute facsimile reprint of Fitzgerald's Omar Khayyam of 1859, 1902; besides editing and compiling bibliography in Old World edit. of Fitzgerald's entire texts of Omar. Home: Portland, Me. Died Aug. 31, 1923.

MOSIER, Jeremiah George, prof. soil physics; b. Pike Co., O., Jan. 8, 1862; s. David and Amanda Rachel (Brill) M.; student Nat. Normal U., Lebanon, O., 1883-85; B.S., U. of Ill., 1893; m. Lydia C. Miller, June 22, 1892. Teacher in rural schs., Champaign Co., Ill., 1885-88, and village sch., Sadorus, Ill., 1893-94; asst. in geology, U. of Ill., 1894-97; engaged in farming, 1897-98; instr. in high sch., Urbana, 1899-1900, Champaign, 1900-02; instr. soil physics, 1902-05, asst. prof., 1905-11, prof., 1911—, U. of Ill., also chief of soil physics, Agrl. Expt. Sta.; in charge of detailed soil survey of State of Ill. Pres. Bd. of Edn., Urbana, 1907-09. Methodist. Author: Laboratory Manual of Soil Physics, 1911; Soil Physics and Management; Climate of Illinois; Soils and Crops. Home: Urbana, Ill. Died 1922.

MOSIMAN, Samuel K(insinger), coll. pres.; b. Middletown, O., Dec. 17, 1867; s. Christian and Anna (Kinsinger) M.; A. B. Wittenberg Coll., Springfield, O., 1897, A.M., 1905; grad. McCormick Theol. Sem., 1905. B.D., 1908; Nettie F. McCormick Hebrew scholar, U. of Halle, Germany, 1905-07; Ph.D., Halle. 1907; Litt.D., Wittenberg Coll., 1920; m. Amalia S. Krehbiel, July 10, 1902 (died 1905); m. 2d, Emilie S. Hamm, Aug. 12, 1909. Supt. Mennonite Indian Mission Sch., Cantonment, Okla., 1897-1902; teacher of Greek and philosophy, Lebanon (O.) Coll., 1908; prof. O.T. lang. and lit., 1908-09, pres., Sept. 1909—, Bluffton (O.) Coll. Pres. Middle Conf. of Mennonites, 1908-10; mem. Federal Council of Chs. of Christ in America, and mem. commn. on ch. and social service same; chmn. Mennonite Bd. of Education. Democrat. Rotarian. Home: Bluffton, O. Died Jan. 24, 1940.

MOSKOWITZ, Belle Israels, social service; b. N.Y. City, Oct. 5, 1877; d. Isidor and Esther (Freyer) Lindner; ed. Horace Mann Sch., and Teachers Coll., New York; m. Charles Henry Israels, Nov. 11, 1903 (died 1911); children—Carlos Lindner Israels, Miriam Israels (Mrs. Cyril M. E. Franklin), Josef Israels; m. 2d, Dr. Henry Moskowitz, Nov. 22, 1914. Dir. amusements and exhbns., Ednl. Alliance, 1900-03; mem. staff of The Survey, 1908-10; field sec., Playground and Recreation Assn. of America, 1912; clk. of grievance bd., Dress and Waist Mfrs.' Assn., 1913; mgr. labor dept., 1914-16; pub. relations counsellor, 1917—; sec. Governor's Labor Bd., 1920-21; sec. Ednl. Council, Port of New York Authority, 1921—; sec. Mayor's Com. of Women on Nat. Defense, 1916-17; dir. Council Jewish Women; sec. N.Y. State Reconstruction Commn., 1919-21; v.p. Assn. to Promote Proper Housing for Girls; vice chmn. Dem. Nat. Com. Jewish religion. Home: New York, N.Y. Died Jan. 2, 1933.

MOSLER, Henry, artist; b. New York, June 6, 1841; removed with family to Cincinnati, 1851, and to Nashville, Tenn., 1854; studied wood-engraving and painting without much outside aid; draftsman on The Omnibus, a Cincinnati comic weekly, 1855; pupil of James H. Beard, 1859-61; art corr., with Western army, for Harper's Weekly, 1862-63; apptd. on staff Gen. R. W. Johnson. Studied in Dusseldorf and Paris, 1863-66. Returned to Europe, 1874. Honors: Medal, Royal Acad., Munich, 1874; Salon, hon. mention, 1879; "Le Retour," purchased by the French govt. for the Musée de Luxembourg, 1879; gold medal, Internat. Exhbn., Nice, France, 1884; Prize Fund Exhbn., New York, prize, $2,500, 1885; Salon, gold medal, 1888; Expn. Universelle, Paris, silver medal, 1889; Hors Concours, 1890; Chevalier de la Légion d'Honneur, France, 1892; Officier d'Académie, France, 1892; Archduke Carl Ludwig of Austria, gold medal, 1893; grand gold medal and diploma of honor, Atlanta Expn., 1895; Thos. B. Clarke prize, Nat. Acad. Design, 1896; gold medal, "The Art Club," Philadelphia, 1897; gold medal, Charleston, S.C., 1902. Pictures in many public art museums, as: Luxembourg, New York Art Mus., Sidney Art Mus., Cincinnati, Springfield, Corcoran Art Gallery, Washington, etc. A.N.A., 1895. Mem. Loyal Legion. Home: New York, N.Y. Died Apr. 21, 1920.

MOSS, Albert Bartlett, banker; b. Belvidere, Ill., Nov. 29, 1849; s. Edward and Mary (Carter) M.; ed. high sch. and pvt. sch., Belvidere; m. Celia A. Moss, Mar. 10, 1880. Extensively engaged in various lines of business more than 40 yrs.; pres. Moss Mercantile Co. (Payette, Ida.), 1st Nat. Bank, Payette Valley Bank, Malheur Irrigation Co.; treas. Payette Valley R.R. Co. Mem. Ida. State Constl. Conv., 1890; Rep. nominee for gov. of Ida., 1898; many yrs. mem. exec. com. Rep. State Central Com.; several times elected mayor of Payette. Chmn. bd. trustees Ida. State Insane Asylum. Episcopalian. Mason. Home: Payette, Ida. Died Mar. 14, 1914.

MOSS, Frank, lawyer; b. Cold Spring, N.Y., Mar. 16, 1860; s. John R. and Eliza (Wood) M.; student Coll. of City of New York; (LL.D., Taylor U.); m. Eva E. Bruce, Jan. 24, 1883. Was pres. bd. of police, New York, 1897; asso. counsel to "Lexow Investigating Com.," and, 1899, leading counsel to "Mazet and Thompson Investigating Coms."; sr. asst. dist. atty. of N.Y. City, 1909-14; mem. Moss, Marcus & Wels. Prof. med. jurisprudence, New York Coll. and Hosp. for Women; pres. New York Ophthalmic Hospital. Republican. Author: The American Metropolis (history of New York), 1897; America's Mission, 1918. Home: New York, N.Y. Died June 5, 1920.

MOSS, Hunter Holmes, Jr., congressman; b. Parkersburg, W.Va., May 26, 1874; s. of Hunter Holmes and Harriett Wilson (Blair) M.; LL.B., W.Va. U., 1896; m. Anna Baker Ambler, Apr. 30, 1902. Began practice, Parkersburg, 1896; mem. Moss, Marshall & Forrer. Pros. atty. Wood Co., W.Va., 1900-04; judge Circuit Ct., 4th Circuit, 1904-12; mem. 63d and 64th Congresses (1913-17), 4th W.Va. District. Mason, Elk. Republican. Episcopalian. Home: Parkersburg, W.Va. Died July 15, 1916.

MOSS, James Alfred, author, army officer; b. Lafayette, La., May 12, 1872; grad. U.S. Mil Acad., 1894. Commd. 2d lt. 25th Inf., June 12, 1894, promoted through grades to lt. col., Nov. 2, 1918; col. N.A., Aug. 5, 1917-Aug. 31, 1919; col. regular army, Dec. 15, 1920; retired, Oct. 31, 1922. Served in Cuba with 24th Inf., Spanish-Am. War; recommended for two brevets "for gallant and meritorious conduct" at Battle of El Caney, July 1, 1898; in Philippine Insurrection, July 1899-July 1902; awarded silver star "for gallantry in action," in the Cuban campaign; with American Expeditionary Force in France, June 19, 1918-Aug. 31, 1919; organized and commanded 367th Infantry, "The Buffaloes," comdt. 1st Corps Schools, chief of staff Provost Marshal Generals Department, deputy provost marshal general, A.E.F.; a.d.c. to Maj. Gen. Henry C. Corbin, 3 years; instr. School of the Line and Army Staff Coll., Ft. Leavenworth, Kan., 4 yrs.; spl. duty Office of Chief of Staff, U.S.A. (Gen. Leonard Wood), 1911-12, in connection with reduction and simplification of army administration; originator of present system of army correspondence and designer simplified muster and pay rolls and various other forms. Founder and pres. gen. U.S. Flag Assn. Author: Manual of Military Training, 1914; Questions on Manual of Military Training, 1917; Army Orders, 1914; Trench Warfare, 1917; Questions on Infantry Drill Regulations, 1917; Spanish for Soldiers (collaborator), 1916; Junior Military Manual (collaborator), 1917; Our Flag and Its Message (collaborator), 1917; Manual for Medical Officers (collaborator), 1917; Military Students' Textbook, Vols. I, II, III and IV (collaborator), 1919; Practical Topography (collaborator), 1919; America in Battle (collaborator), 1920; Château-Thierry—An American Shrine (collaborator), 1920; The Flag of the United States and the Story of "The Star Spangled Banner," 1923; The American Flag—Its Glory and Grandeur, 1929; The Flag of the United States—Its History and Symbolism, 1930; The Spirit of the American Flag, 1933; Your Rights Under the Constitution, 1935; The Constitution of the United States (People's Edition), 1935; The Fellow-American Service (a patriotic industrial service), 1937; Our Country's Flag, 1937; Your Flag and Mine—Its Message, 1938; Patriotic Revival Manual, 1939; US—A Presentation of Americanism, 1939. Editor: The Quartermaster Review and sec. The Quartermaster Assn., 1921-23. Originator of Flag Week, June 8 to 14 of each year. Died Apr. 23, 1941.

MOSS, Lemuel; b. Boone Co., Ky., Dec. 27, 1829; s. Rev. Demas and Esther (Lewis) M.; grad. Univ. of Rochester, 1858 (D.D., 1868; LL.D., 1883); Rochester Theol. Sem., 1860; m. Harriet Bingham, Dec. 24, 1851. Printer by trade; pastor 1st Bapt. Ch., Worcester, Mass., 1860-64; Woodbury, N.J., 1894-96; sec. U.S. Christian Commn., 1864-65; prof. theology Univ. at Lewisburg, Pa. (now Bucknell), 1865-68; N.T. interpretation, Crozer Theol. Sem., Upland, Pa., 1872-74; pres. Univ. of Chicago, 1874-75; Ind. Univ., 1875-84; pres. American Baptist Historical Soc., 1895-1900; v.p. 1900-02; v.p. Am. Bapt. Missionary Union, 1883-84. Lecturer on Christian Sociology, Bucknell Univ., 1898—; mem. Nat. Council Edn., 1880-84; pres. dept. higher edn. in Nat. Edn. Assn., 1883-84. Chmn. com. of 15 apptd. by the Bapt. Nat. Socs. in 1902 to consider better adjustment of agencies and methods. Editor of National Baptist, 1868-72; The Ensign, Minneapolis, 1889-93; The Commonwealth, Phila., 1897. Author: Annals of United States Christian Commission, 1866; Baptists and the National Centenary, 1876; What Baptists Stand For, 1893; A Day with Paul, 1895; etc. Home: New York, N.Y. Died 1904.

MOSS, Mary, author; b. Chestnut Hill, Phila., 1864; d. William and Mary (Noronha) M.; ed. pvt. sch. at Chestnut Hill; unmarried. Began writing, 1900 (newspaper spls.), also short stories in McClure's, Ainslie's, Scribner's, Everybody's, etc.; critical articles in Bookman; essays in Atlantic Monthly, critical essays The Outlook, unsigned articles in The Nation, and novelettes, Fruit Out of Season, 1902, and Julian Meldohla, 1903, in Lippincott's Magazine. Author: A Sequence in Hearts, 1903; The Poet and the Parish, 1906. Died Apr. 2, 1914.

MOSS, Woodson, university prof.; b. Columbia, Mo., Sept. 28, 1852; s. James Hugh and Susan A. (Woodson) M.; student U. of Mo., M.D., U. of Mo., 1874 (LL.D., 1901); studied in Europe, 1890; m. Sarah Anderson, May 19, 1881 (died 1905); 2d, Mrs. Luella Wilcox, Nov. 22, 1911. Instr. medicine, demonstrator anatomy, 1875-78, prof. anatomy and demonstrator, 1878-83, prof. anatomy and physiology, 1883-91, anatomy and practice of medicine, 1891-1900, practice of medicine and therapeutics, 1900-17, tutor, 1906-17, U. of Missouri. Died Oct. 6, 1920.

MOTON, Robert Russa, educator; b. Amelia County, Va., Aug. 26, 1867; s. Booker and Emily (Brown) M.; grad. Hampton Institute, Va., 1890; LL.D., Va. Union U., Richmond, 1916, Wilberforce, 1916, Oberlin, 1916, Williams, 1920, Howard, 1930; Litt.D., Lincoln U., 1920; hon. M.A., Harvard University, 1929; m. Elizabeth Hunt Harris, June 7, 1905 (died 1906); m. 2d, Jennie Dee Booth, July 1, 1908; children—Katherine, Charlotte, Robert, Allen, Jennie. Comdt., Hampton Inst., 1890-1916; succeeded Booker T. Washington as prin. Tuskegee Inst., 1915; dir. Dunbar Nat. Bank, New York; retired as president emeritus Tuskegee Inst. Savings Bank, 1935, now director. Chairman U.S. Commn. on Edn. in Haiti, 1930; mem. National Advisory Com. on Edn., Advisory Com. on Education in Liberia. Trustee People's Village Sch. (Mt. Meigs, Ala.), Industrial Home Sch. for Colored Girls (Peak, Va.), Lincoln U., Penn Sch. (Frogmore, S.C.), Fisk U. (Nashville, Tenn.), Hampton Institute, Bethune-Cookman Coll. (Daytona Beach, Fla.), Calhoun (Ala.) Colored Sch., Voorhees N. & I. Sch. (Denmark, S.C.), Phelps Stokes Fund; dir. Provident Hosp. (Chicago), Nat. Health Circle; chmn. com. on colored work and mem. home div. Y.M.C.A. (nat. council 1924); chmn. Tuskegee Inst. Chapter Am. Red Cross; mem. com. on ch. and race relations, Federal Council Chs. of Christ in America; mem. com. on awards in edn., Harmon Foundation; mem. advisory bd. Am. Inter-racial Peace Com. Mem. Nat. Negro Business League (pres., 1919—). Independent Republican. Baptist. Mason. Author: Racial Good Will, 1916; Finding a Way Out (autobiography), 1920; What the Negro Thinks, 1929. Recipient of Harmon Award in Race Relations, 1930, Spingarn medal, 1932. Home: Capahosic, Va. Died May 31, 1940.

MOTT, George Scudder, clergyman, author; b. New York, N.Y., Nov. 25, 1829; grad. New York Univ., 1850; Princeton Theol. Sem., 1853 (A.M., D.D., Princeton, 1874); pastor Presbyn. Chs., Rahway, N.J., 1853-58; Newton, N.J., 1859-69; Flemington, N.J., 1869-95; pres. Am. Sabbath Union. Author: Prodigal Son; Resurrection of the Dead; Perfect Law; etc. Home: East Orange, N.J. Died 1901.

MOTT, Jordan Lawrence, president J. L. Mott Iron Works; b. New York, N.Y., Nov. 10, 1829; s. Jordan and Mary W. M.; grad. U. City of New York, 1849. Entered office of his father, of same name; became partner, 1853, and succeeded to management, 1866; J. L. Mott Iron Works, large mfrs. of plumbing fixtures; pres. J. L. Mott Co. (Trenton, N.J.). Alderman 23d and 24th wards, pres. bd. of aldermen and acting mayor, New York, 1879; was mem. Rapid Transit Commn., under whose conditions present elevated railroads in New York were chartered. Presdl. elector, 1876, 1888. Democrat. Died July 26, 1915.

MOTT, Lewis Freeman, educator; b. N.Y. City, Sept. 29, 1863; s. John W. and Mary I. (Edgar) M.; B.S., Coll. City of New York, 1883, M.S., 1886; Ph.D., Columbia, 1896; m. Alice Garrigue, Dec. 29, 1897. Tutor, 1884-97, prof. English, 1897-1934, Coll. City of N.Y., retired. Treas., 1892-98, pres., 1899-1900, Am. Dialect Soc.; 1st v.p., 1905, mem. exec. council, 1908-10, pres., 1911, Modern Lang. Assn. America. Chevalier Legion of Honor (France), 1932. Author: The System of Courtly Love, 1894; The Provençal Lyric, 1901; Ernest Renan, 1921; Sainte-Beuve, 1925. Editor of City College Quarterly, 1906-28. Home: New York, N.Y. Died Nov. 20, 1941.

MOTT, Luther Wright, congressman; b. Oswego, N.Y., Nov. 30, 1874; s. John T. and Alice J. (Wright) M.; A.B., Harvard Univ., 1896; (LL.D., St. Lawrence Univ., 1919); m. Ruth W. Johnson, Dec. 10, 1902. In banking business, Oswego, 1897—; v.p. First National Bank of Oswego. Mem. 62d Congress (1911-13), 28th N.Y. District and 63d to 67th Congresses (1913-23), 32d Dist. Pres. Oswego Chamber Commerce, 5 yrs., N.Y. State Bankers' Assn., 1910-11; trustee Y.M.C.A., Oswego Orphan Asylum. Presbyn. Home: Oswego, N.Y. Died July 10, 1923.

MOTT, Valentine, surgeon; b. New York, N.Y., Nov. 17, 1852; s. Alexander B. and Arabella (Phelps) M.; A.B., Columbia, 1872, A.M., 1875; A.B., Trinity Coll. (Cambridge U.), Eng., 1876; M.D., Bellevue Hosp. Med. Coll. (New York U.), 1878; m. Emily Langdon Erving, Apr. 21, 1892. In practice at New York, 1878—; attending surgeon outdoor dept., Bellevue Hosp., 1879; went to Paris, 1887, as representative Am. Pasteur Inst.; studied under Louis Pasteur the prophylactic treatment for hydrophobia; brought away the 1st inoculated rabbit which Pasteur permitted to leave his laboratory. Fellow N.Y. State Med. Assn. Home: New York, N.Y. Died June 19, 1918.

MOTTET, Henry, clergyman; b. May 20, 1845; s. Joseph and Philippine M.; A.B., Coll. City of New York, 1869; S.T.B., Gen. Theol. Sem., 1873; S.T.B., Hobart, 1892; m. Jeanie Gallup, May 14, 1895. Deacon, 1873, priest, 1874, P.E. Ch.; curate, 1873-79, rector, 1879—, Ch. of the Holy Communion, New York. Trustee St. Luke's Hosp., Soc. of St. Johnland. Home: New York, N.Y. Died June 10, 1929.

MOTTIER, David Myers, botanist; b. Patriot, Ind., Sept. 4, 1864; s. John David and Lydia (Myers) M.; A.B., Ind. U., 1891, A.M., 1892; Ph.D., U. of Bonn, 1897; U. of Leipzig, 1898; Biol. Sta., Naples, 1898; m. Antoinette J. Snyder, Aug. 31, 1893. Instr. botany, 1891-93, asso. prof., 1893-98, prof., 1898-1937 (emeritus), Indiana University. Life mem. Bot. Soc. America; fellow A.A.A.S. Author: Practical Laboratory Guide, for First Year in Botany, 1902; Fecundation in Plants, 1904; College Textbook of Botany, 1932. Home: Bloomington, Ind. Died Mar. 25, 1940.

MOULTON, Charles Wells, publisher, editor; b. Alexander, N.Y., Sept. 22, 1859; s. Byram and Corinna (Wells) M.; ed. pub. schs. Alexander, Warsaw and Batavia, N.Y.; m. Carrie J. Hurd, Nov. 28, 1882. Taught sch. 4 yrs.; founded pub. library, Attica, N.Y., 1880; founder and editor Literature, 1881, and in active editorial service from that time; editor Queries, ednl. monthly, 1884-89, The Magazine of Poetry, 1889-96, and editor several minor works. As pub. and editor has issued about 150 vols., notably, A Woman of the Century (in assn. with Frances E. Willard and Mary A. Livermore); Library of Literary Criticism of English and American Authors (a lit. cyclo. in 8 vols.), 1901-05. Editor: The Doctor's Recreation Series, 12 vols., 1904-05; In My Lady's Name. Republican. Home: Buffalo, N.Y. Died Mar. 17, 1913.

MOULTON, Charles William, chemist; b. Elmira, N.Y., May 6, 1859; s. William J. and Alice (Lyon) M.; A.B., U. of Minn., 1885; Ph.D., Johns Hopkins, 1889; m. Emma Selden, Sept. 20, 1887. Instr. physics and chemistry, Shattuck School, Faribault, Minn., 1885-87, 1889-92; asso. prof. chemistry, 1892-94, prof., 1894—, Vassar College. Home: Poughkeepsie, N.Y. Died Sept. 13, 1924.

MOULTON, Edwin F., educator; b. Moulton Hill, Ascott, P.Q., Apr. 7, 1835; s. Calvin and Adaline (Hudson) M.; A.B., Oberlin, 1865, A.M., 1868; (Ped.Ph., Antioch Coll., 1911); m. Ellen Margaret Reed, Mar. 24, 1863 (died 1892); m. 2d, Alice Davis Burton, Apr. 7, 1894. Pvt. in Union Army short time during Civil War; prin. N.E. Christian Inst., Wolfboro, N.H., 1866-68; supt. pub. schs., Glendale, O., 1868-69, Oberlin, 1869-76, Warren, 1876-88; supervisor pub. schs., Cleveland, O., 1888-90, asst. supt., 1890-92, supt., 1902-06. Mem. bd. trustees, Grand River Inst., Austinburg, O., 1882— (pres. 10 yrs.); pres. bd. trustees Kent (O.) State Normal Coll., 1910—. Republican. Conglist. Mason; mem. Royal Arcanum (Supreme Chaplain nat. order). Home: Warren, O. Died Mar. 1919.

MOULTON, George Mayhew, insurance; b. Readsboro, Vt., Mar. 15, 1851; s. Joseph Tilton and Jane Maria (Babcock) M.; went to Chicago with parents, 1853; grad. Central High Sch., Chicago, 1868; m. Anna Florence Garland, Mar. 12, 1873. Builder of grain elevators and other bldgs., 1870-1905; pres. Pioneer Fire Proof Construction Co., 1877-1902, and other interests; president Western Life Indemnity Co., 1890—. Major Second Regt. Ill. N.G., 1886, col., 1894, comdg. regt., during Spanish-Am. War, 1898; organized local police force, Havana, 1898-99; insp. gen. Ill. N.G., 1901-03; brig. gen., Apr. 8, 1903; maj. gen., July 1, 1907; retired, Nov. 1, 1907; comd. 1st div. Ill. N.G. Republican. Mason, held nearly every office in Masonry; Grand Master of Grand Encampment, K.T. of U.S.A., 1904-07; Most Worshipful Grand Master, Grand Lodge A.F. & A.M., 1901-02; Most Excellent Grand High Priest, Grand Chapter R.A.M., 1895; Most Illustrious Grand Master, Grand Council R. and S.M., 1889, etc.; pres. Ill. Masonic Homes. Comdr.-in-chief Spanish War Veterans. Home: Chicago, Ill. Died July 24, 1927.

MOULTON, Louise Chandler, novelist and poet; b. Pomfret, Conn., April 10, 1835; d. Lucius L. and Louisa R. (Clark) Chandler; m. William U. Moulton, 1855 (died 1898). Author: Bed-Time Stories, 1873; More Bed-Time Stories, 1874; New Bed-Time Stories, 1880, and many others. Edited: (with biographies) Garden Secrets, 1887; A Last Harvest, by Philip Bourke Marston, 1891; Collected Poems of Philip Bourke Marston, 1893, Selections from Poems of Arthur O'Shaughnessy, 1894. Wrote reviews or literary letters for New York Tribune, 1870-76; for Boston Herald, Jan. 1886-1892. Died 1908.

MOULTON, Richard Green, university prof.; b. Preston, Eng., May 5, 1849; s. James Egan and Catherine (Fiddian) M.; A.B., London U., 1869; A.B., University of Cambridge, England, 1874, A.M., 1877, hon. LL.D., 1923; Ph.D., Univ. of Pa., 1891; m. Alice Maud Cole, of Sheffield, Eng., Aug. 13, 1896. Cambridge U. extension lecturer in lit., 1874-90; lecturer Am. Soc. Extension Univ. Teaching, 1891, London Soc. same, 1891-92; prof. literature in English, 1892-1901, lit. theory and interpretation and head dept. general literature, 1901-19, emeritus prof., 1920—, U. of Chicago. Fellow Royal Society of Literature, 1923. Author: Shakespeare as a Dramatic Artist, a Study of Inductive Literary Criticism, 1885; The Ancient Classical Drama, a Study of Literary Evolution, 1890; Four Years of Novel Reading—Account of an Experiment in the Study of Fiction, 1895; The Literary Study of the Bible, 1896; A Short Introduction to the Literature of the Bible, 1901; The Moral System of Shakespeare, 1903, republished under the title, Shakespeare as a Dramatic Thinker, 1907; World Literature and Its Place in General Education, 1911; The Modern Study of Literature, 1915; The Whole Bible at a Single View, 1918. Editor: The Modern Reader's Bible, in 25 vols., 1895-1923, as single volume, 1907; same for schools, New Testament, 1920, Old Testament, 1922. Home: Hallamleigh, Tunbridge Wells, England. Died Aug. 15, 1924.

MOULTON, Willis Bryant ophthalmologist; b. Cornish, Me., July 3, 1862; s. David O. and Mehitable P. M.; ed. pub. and high schs., S. Portland, Me.; M.D., Med. Sch. of Me. (Bowdoin), 1883; (hon. A.M., Colby, 1898); m. Estelle M. Cole, Apr. 14, 1886. Formerly clin. prof. ophthalmology and otology, Med. Sch. of Me. (Bowdoin Coll.), mem. exec. faculty, 1900-21 (when med. sch. was discontinued); ophthalmic and aural surgeon, Me. Gen. Hosp., 1893-1927, consulting ophthalmic and aural surgeon, 1927—, pres. of staff 1924-27; consulting surgeon, Central Me. Gen. Hosp. (Lewiston), and Webber Hosp. (Biddeford, Me.) until 1932. Home: Portland, Me. Died Oct. 8, 1938.

MOUNT, Finley Pogue, mfr. agrl. implements; b. Montgomery Co., Ind., Nov. 26, 1866; s. Elijah C. and Elizabeth Sophia (Pogue) M.; B.S., Wabash Coll., 1890, A.M., 1898; m. Henrietta Wedding Allen, June 9, 1896 (dec.). Admitted to Ind. bar 1892, and practiced at Crawfordsville, 1892-1912, Indianapolis, 1912-16; apptd. receiver M. Rumely Co. and Rumely Products Co., Jan. 19, 1915; organizer, 1916, becoming pres. Advance-Rumely Co. and its successor, Advance-Rumely Corp.; pres. Advance-Rumely Thresher Co., Inc. Trustee Wabash Coll., 1902—. Republican. Presbyn. Home: Chicago, Ill. Died Aug. 7, 1938.

MOUNT, James Atwell, governor of Indiana; b. on farm in Montgomery Co., Ind., March 23, 1843; attended country schools in winter; served through Civil war in the Wilder brigade. After war attended the Presbyn. Acad., Lebanon, Ind., for a year; then engaged in farming in his native county; now has farm of 500 acres; was State senator 4 years; elected, 1896, gov. of Ind. for term Jan. 1897, to Jan. 1901. Republican. Home: Indianapolis, Ind. Died 1901.

MOUNT, Wallace, judge; b. Oregon City, Ore., Jan. 16, 1859; s. Henry Duckwall and Rebecca (Stevens) M.; B.S., U. of Ore., 1883, law student, 1883-85; m. Ida Hosler, Jan. 4, 1899. Admitted to bar, 1885, and practiced at Sprague, Wash. Pros. atty. 3d Dist., Wash., 1888; judge Superior Ct., 3d Dist., 1889-96; mem. Wash. Ho. of Rep., 1899; asso. justice Supreme Ct. of Wash., Jan. 15, 1901— (chief justice, 1904-06). Republican. Grand Master, I.O.O.F., Washington, 1896-97. Home: Spokane, Wash. Died Sept. 4, 1921.

MOUNTCASTLE, Robert Edward Lee, lawyer; b. Jefferson City, Tenn., Feb. 21, 1865; s. A. J. and Cornelia Frances (Williams) M.; A.B., Carson and Newman Coll., Tenn., 1880; A.B., Washington and Lee U., Va., 1882; m. Eliza Bird Salmon, Mar. 20, 1889. Admitted to bar, 1885; practiced at Lynchburg, Tenn., 1885-92, Morristown, Tenn., 1892-1903, Knoxville, Tenn., 1903—, in firm of Shields, Cates & Mountcastle. Mem. Tenn. State Exec. Com., 1900-04; Tenn. mem. Dem. Nat. Com., 1904—. Apptd. adj. gen. on staff of gov. of Tenn., Jan. 1903. Presbyn. Home: Knoxville, Tenn. Died Aug. 8, 1913.

MOUZON, Edwin DuBose, bishop; b. Spartanburg, S.C., May 19, 1869; s. Samuel Cogswell and Harriet (Peurifoy) M.; A.B., Wofford College, South Carolina, 1889; D.D., Southwestern U., 1905, LL.D., 1911; LL.D., Duke Univ., 1930; also from Southern Methodist U., 1935; m. Mary Elizabeth Mike, May 19, 1890 (died Nov. 19, 1917); children—Hattie Peurifoy (Mrs. C. H. Thomas), Julia Elizabeth (Mrs. J. Richard Spann, dec.), Edwin D., Mary Josephine (Mrs. J. G. Peurifoy), J. Carlisle, Olin T.; m. 2d, Mrs. Mary Pearl Langdon, Aug. 21, 1919. Entered Tex. Conf. M.E. Ch., S., 1889; pastor in Tex. at Bryan, 1889, Austin, 1890, Caldwell, 1891-93, Galveston, 1894, Flatonio, 1895, Abilene, 1896-97, Ft. Worth, 1898-1901, Central Ch., Kansas City, Mo., 1901-04, Travis Park Ch., San Antonio, Tex., 1904-08; prof. theology, Southwestern U., Georgetown, Tex., 1908-10; elected bishop, May 1910. Made official visits to missions in Mex., 1911, and to S.A., 1915. Took part in founding Southern Meth. U., Dallas, Tex.; mem. bd. trustees Scarritt Coll. Christian Workers, Nashville, Tenn.; chmn. Commn. on Interdenom. Relations and Church Union; in charge 1st Episcopal Dist., including Md., W.Va., Va. and Dist. of Columbia; del. Ecumenical Conf., Toronto, 1911, London, 1921, Atlanta, 1931; pres. Bd. of Christian Edn., M.E. Ch.; chmn. Commn. sent to South America, 1930, to set up the Autonomous Methodist Ch. of Brazil. Democrat. Mason. Author: Does God Care?; Fundamentals of Methodism; The Program of Jesus (Cole lectures), 1925; The Missionary Evangel (Fondren lectures), 1925; Preaching with Authority (Yale lectures on preaching), 1929. Died Feb. 10, 1937.

MOWBRAY, H(arry) Siddons, painter; b. Alexandria, Egypt, Aug. 5, 1858; brought to U.S., 1859; ed. Drury Acad., N. Adams, Mass., and U.S. Mil. Acad., 1875; studied painting under Bonnât, Paris, 1878; in New York, 1878—; m. Helen A. Millard, 1888. Prin. works, Aladin, Evening Breeze, Le Destin, etc.; mural decorations in residences of F. W. Vanderbilt, C. P. Huntington, J. Pierpont Morgan, Appellate Court House and University Club Library, New York; residence of Larz Anderson, Washington; Federal Court Room, Cleveland; council room, University Club, New York; art gallery of Hon. Breckinridge Long, St. Louis; church and library at Washington, Conn. Clark prize, Nat. Acad. Design, 1888. Dir. Am. Acad. in Rome, 1903. N.A., 1891; mem. Nat. Com. of Fine Arts, A.I.A. Home: Washington, Conn. Died Jan. 13, 1928.

MOWER, Charles Drown, naval architect; b. Lynn, Mass., Oct. 5, 1875; s. Charles F. and Juliet (Drown) M.; ed. Lynn public schools; m. Frances Hollingsworth Petrikin, Dec. 7, 1915; 1 son, Charles Petrikin. In office of Arthur Binney, naval architect in Boston, as draftsman, 1895-98; with B. B. Crowninshield, naval architect, 1898-99; left in 1899 to become designing editor of The Rudder, New York yachting mag.; official measurer New York Yacht Club. seasons of 1903, 04; measured yachts Shamrock III and Reliance for Am. cup races, 1903. With Navy Dept., 1917-19; pvt. practice, 1919—. Republican. Author: How to Build a Motor Launch, 1900; How to Build a Knockabout, 1901; How to Build a Racing Sloop, 1901; How to Build a Cruiser, 1903. Home: Pelham Manor, N.Y. Died Jan. 17, 1942.

MOWRY, William Augustus, educator; b. Uxbridge, Mass., Aug. 13, 1829; s. Jonathan and Hannah (Brayton) M.; student Brown U., 1854-57; (hon. A.M., Brown, 1866; Ph.D., Bates Coll., Me., 1882; LL.D., Whitman Coll., Wash., 1906); m. Caroline E. Aldrich, Apr. 29, 1858. Prin. Providence English High Sch., 1859-64; capt. 11th R.I. Inf., 1862-63; supt. schs., Cranston, R.I., 1864-66; prin. English and Classical Sch., Providence (private acad.), 1864-84; editor Jour. of Education, 1884-86, Education (mag.), 1886-91; supt. schs., Salem, Mass., 1891-94; mem. Sch. Bd., Providence, 1869-74, Boston, 1888-91; pres. Martha's Vineyard Summer Inst., 1887-1905. Pres. R.I. Inst. of Instrn., Am. Inst. of Instrn., and of Dept. of Higher Edn. of N.E.A. Conglist. Republican. Has lectured before univs., colls., normal schs. and teachers' insts. in 25 states. Author: A History of the United States, 1896; The Uxbridge Academy, a Brief History, 1897; First Steps in the History of Our Country, 1898, revised edit., 1907; American Inventions and Inventors, 1900; Marcus Whitman and Early Oregon, 1901; The Territorial Growth of the United States, 1902; American Heroes, 1903; American Pioneers (with Blanche S. Mowry), 1905; Essentials of United States History (with same), 1906; Recollections of a New England Educator, 1908; Descendants of John Mowry of Rhode Island, 1909; Camp Life, 1914. Home: Hyde Park, Mass. Died May 22, 1917.

MOXOM, Philip Stafford, clergyman; b. Markham, Can., Aug. 10, 1848; s. Rev. Job Hibbard and Anne (Turner) M.; served with Army of the Cumberland at Ft. Donelson as "capt.'s boy," 1862; enlisted in 17th Ill. Cav., Oct. 3, 1863, serving until Nov. 30, 1865; student Kalamazoo (Mich.) Coll., 1866-68, Shurtleff Coll., Ill., 1868-70; A.B., U. of Rochester, 1879, A.M., 1882; studied Rochester Theol. Sem., 1875-88; (D.D., Brown U., 1892); m. Isabel Elliott, Sept. 6, 1871 (died 1919); m. 2d, Mrs. Jessie Braman Daggett, June 1920. Ordained to ministry, Sept. 19, 1871. Pastor First Bapt. Ch., Cleveland, O., 1879-85, First Bapt. Ch., Boston, 1885-93, South Congl. Ch., Springfield, Massachusetts, 1894-1917, and pastor emeritus, June 30, 1917—. University preacher, Harvard, 1894-97; preacher at Yale, Cornell, Vassar, Wellesley, Amherst, Williams, Dartmouth, Bowdoin, Chicago, etc.; Lowell lecturer, 1895, presented paper on Immortality, before World's Parliament of Religions and sermon before World's Peace Congress; del to various Internat. Peace congresses. Internat. Congl. Council, Boston, 1899. Author: The Aim of Life, 1894; From Jerusalem to Nicæa—The Church in the First Three Centuries, 1895; The Religion of Hope, 1896; Two Masters: Browning and Turgenief, 1912. Mem. Ecumenical Council, Constance, Baden, Aug. 2, 1914, which was broken up by Germany's declaration of war. Died Aug. 13, 1923.

MOYER, Gabriel Hocker, lawyer; b. Palmyra, Pa., Nov. 9, 1873; LL.B., Dickinson Sch. of Law, Carlisle, Pa., 1898; m. Bertha Elizabeth Smith, Nov. 28, 1901. Admitted to Pa. bar. 1902, and began practice at Lebanon; mem. Pa. Ho. of Rep., 1905-09; formerly gen. mgr. State Workmen's Ins. Fund. Republican. Lutheran. Mem. Patriotic Order Sons of America (nat. treas.). Odd Fellows, Elks. Home: Lebanon, Pa. Died May 8, 1939.

MOYER, Harold Nicholas, physician; b. Canajoharie, N.Y., Aug. 14, 1858; s. Waldstein and Ellen (Young) M.; early edn. pub. schs.; M.D., Rush Med. Coll., Chicago, 1879; attended univs. and hosps. in Vienna and Heidelberg for post-grad. study, 1882-83; married. Asst. phys. Ill. Eastern Hosp. for Insane, Kankakee, 1879-82; in pvt. practice in Chicago, 1884—. Formerly maj. surgeon 2d Regt., Ill. N.G.; Cook Co. physician, 1887-88. Republican. Home: Chicago, Ill. Died Dec. 7, 1923.

MOYER, William Henry, prison warden; b. nr. Williamsport, Pa., Apr. 23, 1860; s. Moses and Susan A. (McGill) M.; ed. Muncy (Pa.) Normal Sch.; business coll., Williamsport, Pa.; Nat. U. Law Dept., Washington, D.C.; m. Katrine Hill, Nov. 25, 1885. Teacher dist. schs., Lycoming Co., Pa., 1877-80, high sch., Williamsport, 1881-90; clk. War Dept., Washington, 1890-95; clk. Dept. of Justice, 1895-96; examiner and spl. examiner, same, 1896-1903; warden U.S. Penitentiary, Atlanta, Ga., 1903-15; agt. and warden Sing Sing Prison, Ossining, N.Y., 1916-19; asst. dir. dept. of delinquency, Bd. of Temperance and Moral Welfare, Presbyn. Ch. in U.S., Mar. 1, 1920-July 20, 1921; reorganized Ky. State Reformatory, Aug. 1920-Mar. 1921; gen. supt. District of Columbia penal instns., July 1921—. Mem. 12th Regt. N.G. Pa., 1883-90, advancing to insp. rifle practice; also served as commissary sergt., sergt. maj., capt. and adj., 2d Regt. D.C. Militia, 1890-95. Republican. Mason, Elk, Moose. Home: Lorton, Va. Died Oct. 25, 1923.

MRAK, Ignatius, R.C. bishop; b. Hotoula, parish of Poljane, Carniola, Austria, Oct. 10, 1816; ordained priest, 1837; parish priest in Carniola until 1845, when he came to U.S. as missionary to Indians in Northern Mich.; established many mission stations; vicar-gen. Sault Ste. Marie, 1860-69; bishop of Marquette and Sault Ste. Marie, 1869-78; resigned because of infirmities; from 1881 titular bishop of Antinœ. Died 1901.

MUCKENFUSS, Anthony Moultrie, chemistry; b. Charleston, S.C., Aug. 5, 1869; s. Benjamin Anthony and Martha Louisa (Stewart) M.; A.B., Wofford (S.C.) Coll., 1889, A.M., 1890; Ph.D., Johns Hopkins, 1895; studied univs. of Berlin, Va., Columbia, Karlsruhe and Chicago; m. Margaret Katherine Galloway, 1897; children—Ralph Stewart, Elizabeth Willis, Charles Galloway (dec.). Prof. chemistry and physics, Millsaps Coll., Miss., 1893-1902; prof. chemistry, U. of Ark., and state chemist, 1902-05; prof. chemistry, U. of Miss., 1905-15; prof. chemistry, Emory U., Atlanta, Ga., 1915-20; research chemist, Roessler and Hasslacher Chemical Co., Perth Amboy, N.J., 1920-32; acting prof. chemistry, U. of Fla., 1932-35. Methodist. Home: Melrose, Fla. Died Apr. 17, 1941.

MUCKEY, Floyd Summer, nose and throat specialist; b. Medford, Minn., Feb. 5, 1858; s. Lorenzo and Rachel Hosmer (Wilkins) M.; student U. of Minn., 1877-79; M.D., C.M., McGill U., Montreal, Can., 1883; m. Hilma C. Olson, Dec. 27, 1905. Practiced at St. Paul, 1884, Minneapolis, 1885-93; collaborated with late Prof. William Hallock of Columbia U., in investigation of voice production, 1893-1913; pres. Muckey Patents Corp. First to give a working analysis of tone, to photograph manometric flame, to make a demonstrating photograph of vocal cords in action, etc. Author: The Natural Method of Voice Production, 1916. Lecturer on voice production at N.Y. Post-Grad. Med. School. Home: New York, N.Y. Died Feb. 22, 1930.

MUCKLE, John Seiser, engineer; b. Phila., Pa., Dec. 12, 1862; s. Mark Richards and Caroline (Seiser) M.; ed. pvt. schs.; m. Katharine Craig Wright, Dec. 28, 1901; 1 son, Craig Wright. Mem. engring. firm Muckle & Co., Phila., 22 yrs.; now retired. Inventor of high pressure fire pumping system, also of elevator door safety lock. Was 3d Comdr. Pa. Naval Force (Naval Militia); lt. U.S.N., Spanish-Am. War, 1898; naval aide staffs of Govs. Stone and Stuart of Pa., rank of capt. (naval); hon. mem. Canadian Soc. of Phila.; mem. Brit. and Canadian Recruiting Mission, World War. Pres. Pa. Seamen's Home: v.p. (br.) English-Speaking Union. Cavalier Order of the Crown (Italian), 1920, cavalier officer, 1925. Chmn. Citizens' Reception Com., Phila., Jan.-Oct. 1924. Republican. Episcopalian. Mason. Home: Haverford, Pa. Died Mar. 20, 1929.

MUCKLÉ, M(ark) Richards, journalist; b. Phila., Sept. 10, 1825; s. Michael and Mary M.; ed. pub. schs. and a commercial coll.; m. Caroline Seiser, Nov. 7, 1850. Connected with Phila. Public Ledger from 1842 in various capacities; errand boy, counter clerk, cashier, and for 40 yrs. business mgr.; tendered commission as 2d lt. U.S. Marine Corps by President Polk, 1842; col. on staff of Gov. Bigler, Pa., 1852. Mem. Pa. German Soc., 1853— (v.p. 13 yrs.); one of founders, 1860, and 1st v.p. German Hosp., Phila.; treas. of relief com. which sent about $50,000 for relief of German widows and orphans of Franco-Prussian War; commd. by Count Bismarck to receive contributions of books for Imperial U. and Nat. Library, Strassburg, destroyed during war, and sent 13,000 vols.; decorated by German Emperor for services with Order of Crown, 1874, and Order of Red Eagle, 1883; was first to propose the Centennial celebration, 7 yrs. before it took place, 1876; one of incorporators Am. Dist. Telegraph Co. (sec. and treas.), German-Am. Title & Trust Co. (pres.). One of founders Franklin Reformatory Home; pres. Pa. Soc. for Prevention of Cruelty to Animals; hon. mem. Soc. Prevention of Cruelty to Animals. Mason. Mem. Pa. Grand Lodge and Grand Encampment I.O.O.F., 1846— (grand treas., 1856—), grand treas. Sovereign Grand Lodge I.O.O.F., 1895—. Home: Philadelphia, Pa. Died Mar. 30, 1915.

MUDD, Harvey Gilmer, surgeon; b. St. Louis, Aug. 29, 1857; s. Henry Thomas and Sarah Elizabeth (Hodgen) M.; student Washington U., 1876-78; M.D., St. Louis Med. Coll. (Washington U.), 1881; studied in Berlin, Vienna, Paris, London, Edinburgh, 1885-87; m. Margaret De La Plaux Clark, Jan. 20, 1892; 1 son, Stuart. Emeritus prof. surgery, med. dept. Washington U., 1899—; chief surgeon and dir., St. Luke's Hosp., 1899—. Fellow Am. College of Surgeons, Am. Surgical Assn. Republican. Home: St. Louis, Mo. Died Aug. 16, 1933.

MUDD, Seeley Wintersmith, mining engr.; b. Kirkwood, Mo., Aug. 16, 1861; s. Henry Thomas and Sarah Eliz. (Hodgen) M.; E.M., Washington U., St. Louis, 1883; m. Della Mulock, Feb. 24, 1887; children—Harvey S., Elizabeth (dec.), Seeley G., Henry T. (dec.). Assayer and supt. copper dept., St. Louis Smelting & Refining Co., 1883-85; went to Leadville, Colo., 1885; mgr. Small Hopes Consolidated Mining Co. and Borel Mining Co., 1887-1912; mgr. Ibex Mining Co (Little Johnnie Mine), 1899-1902; consulting engr. in the West for N.J. Zinc Co., 1902-04; moved to Los Angeles, Calif., 1903; consulting engr. on Pacific Coast for Guggenheim Exploration Co. and Am. Smelting & Refining Co., 1904-05; pres. and mgr. Queen Esther Mining and Milling Co., Kern Co., Calif., 1904-09; pres. Cyprus Mines Corp., Coeur d'Alene Syndicate Mining Co. Commd. maj., Engr. O.R.C., Feb. 12, 1917; active duty, Jan. 14, 1918; asst. dir. U.S. explosives plants, Washington; promoted col. U.S.A., May 24, 1918; hon. disch., Jan. 20, 1919. V.p. Y.M.C.A., Los Angeles; trustee Pomona Coll., Southwest Museum. Republican. Conglist. Home: Los Angeles, Calif. Died May 24, 1926.

MUDD, Sydney E., congressman; b. Gallant Green, Md., June 20, 1885; s. Hon. Sydney E. M.; A.B., Georgetown University, Washington, D.C., 1906, LL.B., 1909. Admitted to bar, Maryland and D.C., 1910; served as instr. criminal law, Georgetown U. Sch. of Law; Rep. candidate for Md. legislature, 1909; asst. dist. atty., D.C., 1911-12, 1912-14; mem. 64th to 68th Congresses (1915-25), 5th Md. Dist. Home: La Plata, Md. Died Oct. 11, 1924.

MUDD, Sydney Emanuel, congressman; b. Charles Co., Md., Feb. 12, 1858; A.B., St. John's Coll., Md., 1878; studied law privately and in law dept. U. of Va. Admitted to bar, 1880; in practice at La Plata, Md. Mem. Md. Ho. of Delegates, 1879, 1881, 1896 (speaker, 1896); mem. 51st Congress (1889-91) and 55th to 61st Congresses (1897-1911), 5th Md. Dist. Del. Rep. Nat. Conv., 1896, del.-at-large, 1900 (chmn. Md. delegation at both). Home: La Plata, Md. Died 1911.

MUDGE, Henry U., railway pres.; b. Minden, Sanilac Co., Mich., June 9, 1856; s. John and Sarah Ann (Getty) M.; ed. pub. schs. of Mich. and Kan.; m. Arwilda Morris, July 11, 1878. Began ry. service with A.,T.&S.F. Ry. Co., in Kan., Aug. 1872, in track dept.; from then filled positions with same co. in track, sta., telegraph, train service, road master, train master, div. supt., gen. supt., 1896-1900, and gen. mgr., 1900-05; 2d v.p., 1905-09, pres., 1909-15, and chief executive officer, C.,R.I.&P. Ry. Co.; also pres. C.,R.I. & Gulf R.R., 1910-15; pres. D.&R.G. Ry. Co. and Rio Grande Southern R.R. Co., Nov. 11, 1915. Pres. Am. Ry. Assn. Home: Denver, Colo. Died Jan. 30, 1920.

MUDGE, James, clergyman; b. W. Springfield, Mass., Apr. 5, 1844; s. Rev. James and Harriet W. (Goodridge) M.; A.B., Wesleyan U., 1865, A.M., 1868; S.T.B., Boston U., 1870; (S.T.D., Wesleyan, 1891); m. Martha M. Wiswell, Apr. 29, 1873. Ordained M.E. ministry, 1868; pastor in Mass., 1868-73 and 1883-1908; missionary in India, 1873-83. Lecturer on missions, Boston U. Sch. of Theology, 1888-1913. Sec. N.E. Conf. M.E. Ch., 1889—; sec. and treas. Conf. Missionary Soc., 1886—; dir. Meth. Ministers' Relief Assn., etc.; mem. Gen. Conf., 1900 (a sec.); sec. Boston Itinerants' Club, 1906—, Sterling Camp Meeting Assn., 1897-1914, Malden Ch. Federation. Editor: Lucknow Witness (9 vols.); Good Stories and Best Poems (3 vols.); Poems with Power to Strengthen the Soul; Sunday School Missionary Speaker; Heart Religion; also 30 vols. N.E. Conf. Minutes. Author: Handbook of Methodism; History of Methodism; Faber; Memorial of Rev. Z. A. Mudge; Pastor's Missionary Manual; China; Growth in Holiness; Best of Browning; Honey from Many Hives; The Life of Love; The Land of Faith, The Saintly Calling; The Life Ecstatic; Fenelon the Mystic; The Riches of His Grace; History of the New England Conference; The Perfect Life; Christian Experience; Hymns of Trust. Now S.S. editor same. Supt. largest S.S. home dept. in the world. Home: Malden, Mass. Died May 7, 1918.

MUELLER, Hermann, prof. of German, Providence High schools, 1894—; b. Meningen, Germany, Oct. 24, 1860; s. Wilhelm M., violoncello artist; grad. Falkenburg Victoria Acad., 1879; (Ph.D., R.I. School of Languages); m. Emily A. Wagner. Aug. 25, 1889; was prin. Breslau Union School, 1888; instr. German, Providence, 1889—; lecturer; Providence editor New York Figaro; has been connected with other German journals; pres. and prin. R.I. Sch. of Languages; prof. German, La Salle Acad. Author: Deutsche Gedichte, a Collection of Poems for High Schools, 1898. Home: Providence, R.I. Died 1909.

MUELLER, Paul Ferdinand, newspaperman; b. Crimmitschau, Saxony, Germany, July 7, 1857; s. Hellmuth and Augusta (Leonhardt) M.; ed. high sch., Germany, and Cooper Inst., N.Y. City; m. Mrs. Julia M. Weifenbach Lucke, of Hamburg, Germany, Mar. 26, 1898; 1 son, Paul Hellmuth, and 3 step-children—Emma (Mrs. E. A. Julius), William B. Lucke, Bertha (Mrs. Matenaers). Came to U.S., 1871, naturalized citizen, 1878. Began as errand boy in importing house, later salesman and then free lance writer for daily and weekly newspapers, English and German; first salaried newspaper position, Phila. Gazette, 1891; came to Chicago Expn., 1893, as corr. eastern papers; editorial writer and mng. editor Abendpost, Chicago, 1894-1914, then pres. The Abendpost Co. and editor-in-chief Abendpost and Sonntagpost; mem. bd. dirs. Baldwin Co. (Ala.) Colonization Co. Home: Chicago, Ill. Died Jan. 9, 1931.

MUHLEMAN, Maurice Louis, deputy asst. treas. of U.S.; b. nr. Alton, Ill., Nov. 27, 1852; s. John Godfrey and Marguerite (Bischoff) M.; common and high sch. edn., St. Louis; LL.B., Columbian (now George Washington) U., 1879, LL.M., 1884; m. Harriet F. Pettes, 1879; m. 2d, Carolyn J. Barrow, Feb. 1, 1893. Entered U.S. Treasury service, 1872, one of the first appmts. after competitive civil service exams.; deputy asst. treas. of U.S. at New York, 1888-1901. Municipal research work, New York, 1910-11. Mem. finance and currency com. New York Chamber of Commerce. Author: The Money of the United States, 1894; Monetary Systems of the World, 1896; Treasury System of the U.S., 1907; Banking Systems of the World, 1908; Monetary and Banking Systems, 1908; A Plan for a Central Bank, 1910; Governmental Supervision of Banks, 1911. Home: Bronxville, N.Y. Died June 12, 1913.

MUIR, Charles Henry, army officer; b. Erie, Mich., July 18, 1860; s. James H. and Lydia (Gould) M.; grad. U.S. Mil. Acad., 1885, Inf. and Cav. Sch., Ft. Leavenworth, Kan., 1895 (head of class); m. May, d. Col. C. E. Bennett, Oct. 14, 1887. Commd. 2d lt. 17th Inf., June 14, 1885; promoted through grades to brig. gen. N.A., Aug. 5, 1917—; maj. gen., N.A., Nov. 28, 1917; brig. gen. U.S.A., Jan. 27, 1919; maj. gen. U.S.A., Mar. 8, 1921; retired July 18, 1924. Gained first place in Army Rifle Team, 1890; with 10 companions attacked Rosario, P.I., Jan. 1900, drove out Gen. Malvar's hdqrs., captured $25,000 from his treasury and released 300 Spanish prisoners; mem. Ga. Staff, Washington, 1903-07; comd. 28th Div., A.E.F., Dec. 12, 1917; comd. Camp Hancock, Ga., Jan. 1918; 4th Corps, Oct. 13, 1919. Campaign badges Indian Wars, Spanish-Am. War, Cuban Occupation, Philippine Insurrection, China Relief Expdn.; Victory badge with 6 stars; Croix de Guerre with palms; Knight Comdr. Order St. Michael and St. George; Comdr. Légion d'Honneur; D.S.C. and D.S.M.; rifle medals 2d Class Dept., 1st and 2d Class Div., 1st Class Army. Died Dec. 8, 1933.

MUIR, Downie Davidson, Jr., mining engr.; b. Lincoln, Neb., Jan. 1, 1884; s. Downie Davidson and Armista (Wilson) M.; E.M., Columbia, 1906; m. Jewel Balfour, Sept. 24, 1908; children—Milene Balfour, Downie Davidson 3d. Began as mucker, 1906; supt. Combination Fraction Mine, Goldfield, Nev.,

1908-09; with U.S. Smelting, Refining & Mining Co., Salt Lake City, Utah, 1910—, in exploration dept., 1910-16, mgr. zinc smelters and mines, Mo., 1917-18, mgr. mines, Salt Lake City, 1919-22, gen. mgr. Utah dist., 1922-24, v.p. and gen. mgr. in charge western operations, 1924—; v.p. in charge of western operations U.S. Smelting, Refining and Mining Co., Mar. 1934—; v.p. and gen. mgr. U.S. Fuel Co., 1924-35, pres., 1935—. Mem. President's Economic Com., 1932. Home: Boston, Mass. Died Oct. 23, 1937.

MUIR, John, geologist, explorer, naturalist; b. Dunbar, Scotland, Apr. 21, 1838; s. Daniel and Anne (Gilrye) M.; ed. in Scotland and at U. of Wisconsin; (hon. A.M., Harvard U., 1896; LL.D., U. of Wis., 1897, U. of California, 1913; Litt.D., Yale U., 1911); m. Louise Strentzel, 1880. Discoverer of the Muir Glacier, Alaska; visited the Arctic regions on the U.S. steamer Corwin in search of the DeLong expdn.; has labored many yrs. in cause of forest preservation and establishment of nat. reservations and parks. Mem. Am. Acad. Arts and Letters; fellow A.A.A.S. Author: The Mountains of California, 1894; Our National Parks, 1901; Stickeen, the Story of a Dog, 1909; My First Summer in the Sierra, 1911; The Yosemite, 1912; Story of My Boyhood and Youth, 1913. Editor: Picturesque California. Traveled and studied in Russia, Siberia, Manchuria, India, Australia and New Zealand, 1903-04, in S. America, 1911, in Africa, 1911-12. Home: Martinez, Calif. Died Dec. 24, 1914.

MUIR, John, investments; b. Scarborough, Toronto, Can., June 10, 1847; s. Alexander and Adah (Bell) M.; ed. pub. and night schs.; m. Mary Elizabeth Newbanks, Oct. 5, 1868; children—George Allan, Ella (dec.), Mary Olive, John, Abby Oakes, Elizabeth, Margaret, Jessie, Edwin Hawley. Began with Kan. Pacific Ry. and advanced to gen. frt. agt.; traffic mgr. N.P. Ry., 1883-86, C.&O. Ry. and Pacific Mail S.S. Co., 1886-98; founder, 1898, and head of John Muir & Co., N.Y.; originator of partial payment plan for standard bonds for small investors; handled New York real estate on a large scale; chmn. "baby bond com." of Liberty Loan orgn., 2d Federal Reserve Dist., New York, World War. Republican. Presbyn. Home: New York, N.Y. Died Jan. 23, 1935.

MUIR, Joseph Johnstone, clergyman; b. Parsonstown, Ireland; s. A. J. and Mary F. (Stothard) M.; ed. pub. and pvt. schs. in Ireland and Scotland; D.D., Columbian (now George Washington) U., 1895; m. Lizzie Glover, June 13, 1868. Came to U.S., 1865; ordained Bapt. ministry, 1869; pastor Montana, N.J., 1869-71, East Marion, N.Y., 1871-73, Ticonderoga, N.Y., 1873-75, Macdougal St. Ch., N.Y. City, 1875-79, Park Ch., Port Richmond, N.Y., 1880-83, North Ch., Phila., 1883-89, E St. Temple Bapt. Ch., Washington, D.C., 1889-Aug. 31, 1924 (retired); chaplain U.S. Senate, Jan. 1921—. Mason. Home: Washington, D.C. Died Nov. 17, 1927.

MUIRHEAD, James Fullarton, editor; b. Glasgow, Scotland, Dec. 25, 1853; s. John James and Isabella R. (Fullarton) M.; M.A., U. of Edinburgh, 1874; attended lectures in history, U. of Leipzig, 1884-85; (L.H.D., Hobart, 1907); m. Helen, d. J. P. Quincy, of Boston, Feb. 14, 1894. Assisted in editing Chambers Encyclopedia, 1874-77; asso. with Karl Baedeker, pub. guide books, Leipzig, 1877-1914, removing 1st to London, in 1903 to U.S., and in 1911 returning to London; now asso. with Muirhead Guidebooks, Ltd. ("The Blue Guides"). Author: America, the Land of Contracts, 3d edit., 1902. Joint editor, with Col. S. R. Honey, of Sixty American Opinions on the War, 1915. Home: London, Eng. Died Apr. 7, 1934.

MUKERJI, Dhan Gopal, author; b. Calcutta, India, July 6, 1890; s. Kissori and Bhuban (Goswami) M.; prep. edn., India; Ph.B., Leland Stanford, 1914; m. Ethel Ray Dugan, 1918; 1 son, Dhan Gopal II. Came to U.S., 1910. Mem. Am. Oriental Soc. Brahman. Author: Kari the Elephant, 1923; Caste and Outcast, 1923; M. Brother's Face, 1924; Face of Silence, 1926; Gay Neck (A.L.A. medal, 1927), 1927; A Son of Mother India Answers, 1928; Chief of the Herd, 1929; Visit India With Me, 1929; The Song of God, 1931; Daily Meditation, 1933; Path of Prayer, 1934. Home: New Milford, Conn. Died July 14, 1936.

MULDOON, Peter J., bishop; b. Columbia, Calif., 1863; s. John and Catherine (Coughlin) M.; early edn. pub. schs., Stockton, Calif.; later studied at St. Mary's, Ky., and St. Mary's, Baltimore. Ordained R.C. priest, 1886; asst. pastor St. Pius' Ch., Chicago, 1887-89; chancellor of the Archdiocese of Chicago and sec. to the archbishop, 1889-95; pastor St. Charles Borromeo's Ch., Chicago, 1895-1908; consecrated auxiliary bishop of Chicago, July 25, 1901, bishop of Rockford, Ill., Dec. 15, 1908. Died Oct. 8, 1927.

MULFINGER, George Abraham, prof. English; b. Chicago, Ill., Mar. 31, 1865; s. Rev. George Leonard and Anna M. (Schlothauer) M.; A.B., Baldwin-Wallace Coll., Ohio, 1884; A.B., Northwestern U., 1885; B.D., Garrett Bibl. Inst., 1887; Ph.D., U. of Chicago, 1902; univs. Tübingen, Berlin, 1889-91, and Munich, 1911-12; m. Ida Rohn, June 16, 1891; children—Carl Leonard, M.D., George Leonidas, Rudolph Mark, Wilhelmina Anne. Pres. German-Wesleyan Coll., Mt. Pleasant, Ia., 1890-92; reader U. of Chicago, 1892-94; head dept. of German, South Div. High Sch., Chicago, 1894-1905; prof. German lit. and philology, Allegheny Coll., Pa., 1905-18; research work, U. of Chicago, 1918-20; act. prof. German and philosophy, Carleton Coll., Minn., 1920-21; prof. English Nebraska Wesleyan Univ., 1921-22; prof. English Heidelberg U., 1922-33; retired. Republican. Methodist. Author: Lenau Studies (German-Am. Annals), 1897. Home: Oak Park, Ill. Died May 12, 1935.

MULHAUPT, Frederick J(ohn), artist; b. Rock Port, Mo., Mar. 28, 1871; s. Jacob and Margaret (Liebig) M.; ed. common schs.; student in art schs. of Kansas City, Chicago, New York and Paris; m. Agnes Leone Kingsley, Feb. 22, 1921; 1 son, Frederick Kingsley. Exhibited in Paris Salon and major exhbns. in U.S.; represented in John Herron Art Inst. (Indianapolis); Reading (Pa.) Mus. Awarded Evans prize (figure), Salmagundi Club, 1907; Porter prize, same, 1921; bronze medal Phila. Art Week, 1925; popular vote, Minneapolis, 1924, Allied Artists, 1925; Gedney Bunce prize, Conn. Acad. Fine Arts, Hartford, 1927; hon. mention, Allied Artists, 1929, Nat. Arts Club, 1929, A.N.A., 1926; mem. Allied Artists America, North Shore Arts Assn. of Gloucester, Mass. (trustee), Artists' Fund Soc., Am. Art Assn. (Paris). Republican. Mason. Hon. mention Ogunquit Art Centre, 1931; first prizes landscape and marines, Rochester, N.H., 1933. Home: Gloucester, Mass. Died Jan. 10, 1938.

MULHOLLAND, William, hydraulic engr.; b. Belfast, Ireland, Sept. 11, 1855; s. Hugh and Ellen (Deakers) M.; ed. Christian Bros. Sch., Dublin; LL.D., U. of Calif., 1914; m. Lillie Ferguson, July 3, 1890. Supt. and chief engr. water works of Los Angeles, 1886—; devised plans and estimates and superintended the construction of Los Angeles aqueduct for conveying a supplementary water supply from Sierra Nevada Mts., 250 miles distant, at a cost of $24,500,000; consulting engineer numerous irrigation and water supply projects. Chief engr. Dept. of Pub. Service, Los Angeles. Died July 22, 1935.

MULKEY, Frederick William, lawyer; b. Portland, Ore., Jan. 6, 1874; s. Marion Francis and Mary Elizabeth (Porter) M.; A.B., U. of Ore., 1896; LL.B., New York Law Sch., 1899; unmarried. Admitted to bar, 1898. Mem. Portland City Council, 1900-02 (pres. 1902); mem. and chmn. Ore. State Tax Commission, 1905-06; elected U.S. senator from Ore., Jan. 23, 1907, for short term expiring Mar. 3, 1907; again elected U.S. senator, Nov. 5, 1918, for term ending Mar. 3, 1919, but resigned, Dec. 17, 1918. Chmn. Pub. Docks Commn., Portland, Ore., 1911-16. Baptist. Home: Portland, Ore. Died May 4, 1924.

MULL, George Fulmer, coll. prof.; b. Reading, Pa., Oct. 7, 1851; s. Aaron and Sarah (Fulmer) M.; A.B., Mercersburg (Pa.) Coll., 1872, A.M., 1875; course in theology same, 1873-76; U. of Leipzig, 1876-77; Litt.D., Franklin and Marshall Coll., 1910; m. Anna Frances, d. Elnathan Elisha Higbee, D.D., LL.D., Mercersburg, Oct. 11, 1877; children—Lucy Frances, Sarah Katharine, Elnathan Higbee. Instr. Latin and Greek, 1872-76, prof. Latin, 1877-80, Mercersburg; recording clerk state dept. Pub. Instrn., Harrisburg, Pa., 1881-84; rector Franklin and Marshall Acad., 1884-86; adj. prof. English lit. and Latin, 1886-91, prof. English lit., 1891-92, prof. Latin lang. and lit., 1892-1927 (emeritus), sec. faculty, 1894-1927, and sec. trustees, 1910-27, Franklin and Marshall Coll. Republican. Mem. Ref. Ch. in U.S. Home: Lancaster, Pa. Died Dec. 22, 1935.

MULL, J. Harry, shipbuilder; b. Philadelphia, Pa., 1864. Formerly pres. and gen. mgr. William Cramp & Son Ship and Engine Building Co. (retired). Mem. Soc. Naval Architects and Marine Engrs. Home: Philadelphia, Pa. Died July 27, 1936.

MULLALY, John, journalist; b. Belfast, Ireland, 1835; (LL.D., St. John's Coll., Fordham, N.Y.; Litt.D., Christian Bros. Coll., St. Louis). Began newspaper work as reporter New York Tribune, under Horace Greeley; later reporter Evening Post, under William Cullen Bryant; on staff New York Herald, 6 yrs., and was spl. corr. on expdn. to lay a submarine cable across Gulf of St. Lawrence, and 1st three Atlantic telegraph expdns., 1857-58; during expdns. was sec. to Prof. Morse, and Cyrus W. Field; pub. and editor Met. Record (R.C. official organ), New York, 14 yrs.; editor The Seminary (monthly), 1892-96. Discovered peculiar properties of aluminum in application to surface printing; inventor aluminography; pres. U.S. Aluminum Printing Plate Co. Was commr. of health, New York, and mem. bd. assessors. Originated new system of parks north of Harlem River; agitated investigation of milk supply, etc. Author: The Laying of the Cable; A Trip to Newfoundland to Lay the Gulf of St. Lawrence Cable; The Milk Trade of New York; More Public Parks; etc. Home: New York, N.Y. Deceased.

MULLAN, George Vincent, judge; b. N.Y. City, Aug. 7, 1872; s. John and Jane (Jebb) M.; Ph.B., Coll. of St. Francis Xavier, New York, 1894; LL.B., New York U., 1895; m. Helen St. Clair, June 28, 1899; children—Georgia St. Clair, Janet St. Clair. Admitted to N.Y. bar, 1896; employed by Philbin, Beekman & Menken, 1897-1901; asso. with John Purroy Mitchel and W. Bruce Cobb as Mullan, Cobb & Mitchel, 1902-11, Mitchel & Mullan, 1911-13; mem. Tax Bd., N.Y. City, 1914-15, Court House Bd., 1915-16; apptd. justice Supreme Court of N.Y., Feb. 1916, elected as Rep. and Progressive candidate, term 1916-30. Home: New York, N.Y. Died Dec. 30, 1931.

MULLAN, James McElwane, denominational sec.; b. Ft. Loudon, Franklin Co., Pa., Jan. 19, 1869; s. William Neal and Mary Ann (Williams) M.; grad. 1st Pa. State Normal Sch., Millersville, Pa., 1891; grad. Theol. Sem. Ref. Church in U.S., 1897; B.D., Franklin and Marshall Coll., 1901, D.D. from same college in 1929; m. Annie Elizabeth Ault, of Ft. Loudon, Sept. 23, 1897; children—Isabel (Mrs. Charles O. Gunther, Jr.), James Kenneth, Anna Mary. Teacher pub. schs. 6 yrs.; ordained ministry Ref. Ch. in U.S., 1897; pastor Ch. of Incarnation, Newport, Pa., 1897-1900, St. Mark's Ch., Baltimore, Md., 1900-16; supt. Home Missions of Ref. Ch. in U.S., 1916—; exec. secretary Commission on Social Service. Member Joint Com. on War Industrial Communities during World War and later had charge of orgn. of Baltimore Federation of Chs.; mem. Commn. on the Ch. and Social Service of Federal Council of Chs. of Christ in America; chmn. Commn. on Comity and Missions, Pa. Council of Chs. Mem. bd. of visitors Theol. Sem. Ref. Ch. in U.S., 1913-16. Mason, Woodman. Home: Upper Darby, Pa. Died Aug. 24, 1933.

MULLAN, W. G. Read, educator; b. Baltimore, Jan. 28, 1860; student of Loyola Coll., 1874-77; entered Soc. of Jesus, 1877; studied philosophy, Woodstock Coll., Md., 1880-83; prof. Fordham Coll., 1883-87; Georgetown Coll., 1887-88; studied divinity Woodstock Coll., 1888-92; v.p. Fordham Coll., 1892-97; prof. junior yr., Holy Cross Coll., 1897-98; became pres. Boston Coll., 1898; v.p. Georgetown Univ., 1903-05; prof. in Fordham Coll., 1905-06; v.p. Fordham Univ., 1906-07; pres. Loyola Coll., Baltimore, Md., 1907—. Died 1910.

MULLANY, John Francis, clergyman; b. Utica, N.Y., July 19, 1853; s. Thomas and Margaret M.; grad. Manhattan Coll. (A.M., LL.D.); studied philosophy and theology, Troy Sem. Ordained R.C. priesthood, 1880; active in establishing winter schs.; in inaugurating summer sch. at Cliff Haven, N.Y.; pastor St. John the Baptist Ch., Syracuse, N.Y. Editor: The Pioneer Church, 1889; Old and New Spain, 1890; Literature and the Church, 1892; Catholic Education and American Institutions, 1893; Culture of Spiritual Sense, 1900; Mirror of True Manhood, 1901; Dante and His Times, 1901; Dante and the Divina Commedia, 1902; Bible Studies, 1903; Old World Seen Through American Eyes, 1903. Died 1916.

MULLEN, Arthur Francis, lawyer; b. Kingston, Ont., Can., May 31, 1873; s. James and Emily (Clancy) M.; ed. Fremont (Neb.) Normal Sch. and Neb. Normal Sch. (Wayne); LL.B., U. of Mich., 1900; m. Mary T. Dolan, June 18, 1903; children—Arthur J., Margaret E. (dec.). Practiced in Neb., 1900—, at Omaha, 1911—; practicing under own name at Omaha, Neb.; and mem. Mullen & Shea, Washington, D.C.; county atty. of Holt Co., 1901-07; atty. gen. of Neb., 1910-11; mem. and sec. Neb. Tornado Com., 1913; mem. Dem. Nat. Com., 1916-20 and 1924-35; mem. exec. com. same, 1918-20; vice chmn. Nat. Democratic Campaign Com., 1932-34; floor leader of Roosevelt force in Chicago Conv., 1932. K.C. Elk. Home: Omaha, Neb. Died July 14, 1938.

MULLEN, James William, editor; b. Homestead Twp., Iowa County, Ia., Mar. 1, 1875; s. Thomas and Joanna (O'Shea) M.; ed. pub. schs.; unmarried. Learned printer's trade, Cedar Rapids, Ia.; moved to San Francisco, Calif., 1902; editor and mgr. Labor Clarion, 1911—. Mem. San Francisco Bd. of Health, 1909-10; mem. Draft Bd., Fair Trade Bd., World War. Pres. Labor Council Hall Assn.; trustee Typographical Union; mem. Pub. Edn. Soc., Vocational Guidance Soc. Democrat. K.C., Moose. Home: San Francisco, Calif. Died July 25, 1931.

MULLEN, Tobias, R.C. bishop; b. County Tyrone, Ireland, 1818; ed. at Castlefin School and Maynooth Coll., Ireland, receiving minor orders there; came to Pittsburgh, Pa., 1843; finished theological studies. Ordained priest Sept. 1, 1844; held various pastoral charges in Diocese of Pittsburgh; rector St. Peter's, Allegheny, Pa., 1854; vicar gen. diocese, 1864-68. Consecrated, Aug. 2, 1868, bishop of Erie, Pa. He was given a coadjutor, 1898. Died 1900.

MULLENBACH, James, labor arbitrator; b. Houghton, Mich., Oct. 10, 1870; s. Philip and Margaret (Wilson) M.; grad. Fargo (N.D.) Coll., 1896, Chicago Theol. Sem., 1899; grad. work univs. of Halle and Berlin, Germany, 1899-1901; m. Annie L. Towns, June 18, 1902; children—Katherine, Margaret (Mrs. R. B. Robertson), Jane, Philip, Anna. Minister Tabernacle Congl. Ch. and resident Chicago Commons, 1901-03; supt. Municipal Lodging House, Chicago, 1904-09; asst. supt. United Charities, Chicago, 1909-12; supt. Oak Forest Instns. of Cook County, Ill., 1912-14; labor arbitrator for clothing trades, particularly with Hart, Schaffner & Marx and Amalgamated Clothing Workers of America, 1912—; spl. rep. Nat. Labor Bd. in Chicago; mem. Nat. Oil Labor Bd., Washington, D.C. Mem. Bd. of Edn., City of Chicago, 1924-31; mem. Commn. on Ch. and

Industry of Chicago Ch. Federation. Conglist. Home: Chicago, Ill. Died Apr. 3, 1935.

MULLER, Carl Christian, musician, composer; b. Saxe-Meiningen, Germany, July 3, 1831; s. Johann Georg and Elisabeth M.; studied music there; came to U.S., 1854; was employed in piano factory; became leader of orchestra, Barnum's Museum; later teacher in harmony; unmarried. Composer of vocal and instrumental music; published songs, male-quartettes, piano music, violin music, one-string-quartette, one sonata for violin and piano, 3 sonatas for organ; symphonies, overtures, instrumental solos, anthems, etc., in manuscript. Translator of Sechter's Fundamental Harmonies, and author of complementary tables (4 sets). Home: New York, N.Y. Died June 4, 1914.

MULLER, W. Max., orientalist; b. Gleissenberg, Germany, May 15, 1862; s. Frederic and Pauline (Barthel) M.; studied at univs. of Erlangen, Leipzig, Berlin, Munich, Ph.D., Leipzig; resident of U.S. from 1888; m. Bettie Caspar, Apr. 13, 1889. Has worked repeatedly in archeol. research in Egypt; sent there in 1904, 06, 10, by Carnegie Instn.; prof. in R.E. Sem., Phila., 1890—. Asst. prof. Egyptology, U. of Pa. Lutheran. Author: Asia and Europe After the Egyptian Monuments, 1893; The Love Poetry of the Ancient Egyptians, 1899 (both in German); Egyptological Researches, 1906, 1910; Mythology of the Ancient Egyptians (in The Mythology of all Races), 1918; also smaller books. Joint editor: Gesenius Hebrew Dictionary, 1905. Home: Philadelphia, Pa. Died July 12, 1919.

MULLETT, Mary B., writer, editor; b. Vevay, Ind.; d. Eugene R. and Valeria (Harding) M.; ed. pub. schs. of Clinton, Ia. Formerly spl. feature writer for New York Sun, New York Times and newspaper syndicates; mem. editorial staff American Magazine, Nov. 1917— (mng. editor, 1917-24). Died Nov. 22, 1932.

MULLIGAN, Charles J., sculptor; b. Armagh, Ireland, 1867; pupil of Lorado Taft, Chicago. Mem. Soc. Western Artists. Home: Chicago, Ill. Died Mar. 25, 1916.

MULLIGAN, James Hilary, lawyer; b. Lexington, Ky., Nov. 21, 1844; s. Dennis and Ellen Alice (McCoy) M.; A.B., St. Mary's Coll., Montreal, Can., 1864; LL.B., Coll. of Law, Ky. U., 1869; m. Genevieve Morgan Williams, Oct. 5, 1881. Practiced at Lexington, Huston & Mulligan, and Mulligan & Blanchamp, 1869-1904; editor and propr. Lexington Daily Transcript, 1893-94. Judge Recorder's Ct., Lexington, 1870-76; mem. Ky. Ho. of Rep., 1881-88, Senate, 1890-94; consul-gen. at Samoa, under joint protectorate, 1894-95; resigned Jan. 1, 1896; Independent Democrat. Catholic. Author: Samoa, Government, Commerce and People (U.S. Govt. publ.), 1896. Collaborated with Lloyd Osborne, in booklet announcing death of Robert Louis Stevenson, 1894; writer of miscellaneous prose and verse, including "In Kentucky." Home: Lexington, Ky. Died July 2, 1916.

MULLIGAN, Richard Thomas, naval officer; b. N.Y. City, May 14, 1856; grad. U.S. Naval Acad., 1876. Ensign, Jan. 2, 1880; lt., jr. grade, May 23, 1886; lt., Dec. 16, 1891; lt. comdr., Oct. 10, 1899; comdr., June 28, 1905; capt., Mar. 11, 1909. Served on New York during Spanish-Am. war; Office of Naval Intelligence, Navy Dept., 1904-05; comd. Marblehead, 1905-06, Yorktown, 1906-07; with Bur. of Navigation, Navy Dept., 1907-10; comd. North Dakota, 1910; transferred to retired list, upon own application, with rank of commodore, June 30, 1910. Home: Elizabeth, N.J. Died Feb. 23, 1917.

MULLIKEN, Alfred Henry, railway supplies; b. Augusta, Me. Began as office boy, Crerar, Adams & Co., Chicago, Nov. 1, 1868; organized firm of Pettibone & Mulliken, 1880; incorporated Pettibone, Mulliken & Co., 1885, serving as sec.-treas.; reorganized company under title of Pettibone, Mulliken Co., July 1912 (capital $10,000,000) and from then served as pres.; also chmn. bd. and pres. Mulliken & Roberts, Inc., investment bankers, New York; dir. Continental & Commercial Nat. Bank, Chicago. Life mem. Art. Inst. Chicago, Am. Mus. Natural History (New York). Home: Chicago, Ill., and New Canaan, Conn. Died Sept. 1, 1931.

MULLIKEN, Samuel Parsons, chemist; b. Newburyport, Mass., Dec. 19, 1864; s. Moses J. and Sarah D. (Gibbs) M.; S.B., Mass. Inst. Tech., 1887; Ph.D., U. of Leipzig, 1890; post-grad. study Clark U., Mass., 1891; m. Katherine W. Mulliken, June 27, 1893; children—Robert S., Samuel G. P., Katherine F. Asst. in chemistry, U. of Cincinnati, 1887-88; asso. in chemistry, Bryn Mawr Coll., 1892; instr. and acting head of chem. dept., Clark U., 1892-94; instr. organic chemistry and organic analysis, 1895-1904, asst. prof., 1905-13, asso. prof. organic chem. research, 1913-26, professor of organic chemistry, 1926—, Mass. Inst. Technology. Major Chemical Warfare Service, U.S.A., 1918. Author: Laboratory Experiments on the Class Reactions and Identification of Organic Substances, 1896; The Compounds of Carbon with Hydrogen and Oxygen, 1904; The Commercial Dye-stuffs, 1909; The Compounds of Carbon with Nitrogen, Hydrogen, and Oxygen, 1916; The Compounds of the Higher Orders, 1922. Home: Newburyport, Mass. Died Oct. 24, 1934.

MULLIKIN, Sidney Albert, publisher, philanthropist; b. Mt. Olivet, Ky., Jan. 4, 1871; s. James S. and Elizabeth (Rankin) M.; ed. pub. schs.; m. Nellie Sprague, Aug. 8, 1898. Founder, 1906, and pres. The S. A. Mullikin Co., pubs. personal help books; originator of co-operative personal help methods of salesmanship, assisting students in colleges and univs. in securing edn. and launching into vocational careers; treas. Wakefield Hotel Co. Treas. World's Purity Federation, 1917-20. Ind. Democrat. Methodist. Mason. Home: Cincinnati, O. Died Dec. 14, 1923.

MULLIN, William Valentine, surgeon; b. Iowa City, Ia., Feb. 14, 1884; s. William and Catherine (Whalen) M.; student U. of Ia., 1902-04; M.D., U. of Denver, 1908; post-grad. in oto-laryngology, Killian and Halle Clinics, Germany, 1914; m. Louie M. Nichols, June 7, 1913; 1 dau., Harriet C. House surgeon St. Joseph's Hosp., Denver, 1908-09; gen. practice Holly, Colo., 1909, in practice Colorado Springs, 1909-26; became specialist in oto-laryngology, 1910; head oto-laryngol. dept., Cleveland (O.) Clinic, 1926—. Lt. M.C., U.S.A., Gen. Hosp. No. 19, Oteen, N.C., World War. Examiner Am. Bd. Oto-laryngology. Fellow Am. Coll. Surgeons. Republican. Home: Cleveland, O. Died Apr. 25, 1935.

MULLINS, Edgar Young, theologian; b. Franklin Co., Miss., Jan. 5, 1860; s. Seth G. and Cornelia B. M.; student Agrl. and Mech. Coll. of Tex., 1876-79; grad. Southern Bapt. Theol. Seminary, 1885; student Johns Hopkins U., 1891-92; D.D., Carson and Newman Coll., Tenn., 1896, also McMaster U., Toronto, Can., 1925; LL.D., Richmond Coll., Va., and Baylor U.; m. Isla May Hawley, June 2, 1886; children—Edgar Wheeler (dec.), Roy Granberry (dec.). Ordained Bapt. ministry, 1885; pastor Harrodsburg, Ky., 1885-88, Lee St. Ch., Baltimore, 1888-95, First Ch., Newton, Mass., 1896-99; pres. Southern Bapt. Theol. Sem., 1899—. Editor The Evangel, Baltimore, 1890-95; sec. Foreign Mission Bd., Southern Bapt. Conv., 1895-96; pres. Southern Bapt. Conv., May 1921-24; pres. Baptist World Alliance, 1923—. Author: Why Is Christianity True?, 1905; The Axioms of Religion, 1908; Baptist Beliefs, 1912; Freedom and Authority in Religion, 1913; Commentary on Ephesians and Colossians, 1913; The Life in Christ; The Christian Religion in its Doctrinal Expression; Talks on Soul Winning, 1920; Spiritualism a Delusion, 1920; Christianity at The Cross-Roads, 1924. Home: Louisville, Ky. Died Nov. 23, 1928.

MULLINS, Isla May, author; b. Summerfield, Ala., Apr. 30, 1859; d. Anson Wheeler and Lydia Maria (Cobb) Hawley; educated at Judson College, Marion, Ala., later work in music, drawing, painting, etc., under pvt. tutelage; m. Edgar Young Mullins, June 2, 1886; children—Edgar Wheeler (dec.), Roy Granberry (dec.). Author: Side by Side, A Child Study, 1898; An Upward Look for Mothers, 1900; The Boy from Hollow Hut, 1911; The Blossom Shop, 1913; Anne of the Blossom Shop, 1914; Anne's Wedding, 1916; The Mt. Blossom Girls, 1918; Tweedie, 1919; Uncle Mary, 1922; Timothy's Second Wife, 1922; Captain Pluck, 1923; When Yesterday was Young, 1926; Edgar Young Mullins, 1929; House Beautiful, 1934. Home: Louisville, Ky. Died Feb. 6, 1936.

MULRY, Joseph Aloysius, university pres.; b. N.Y. City, Feb. 8, 1874; s. Thomas and Parthenia (Crolius) M.; classical studies St. Francis Xavier's Coll., New York; philosophy and theology, Woodstock (Md.) Coll. Joined Soc. of Jesus (Jesuits), 1890; ordained R.C. priest, 1905; v.p. Loyola Coll., Baltimore, Md., 1907; lecture tours, 1908-11; pres. St. Peter's Coll., Jersey City, N.J., 1911-15; pres. Fordham U. N.Y. City, 1915—. Died Aug. 31, 1921.

MULVANE, David Winfield, lawyer; b. Princeton, Ill., Jan. 4, 1863; s. Joab and Sarah Ann (Ross) M.; A.B., Yale, 1885; m. Mrs. Helen McKenna, of N.Y. City, May 5, 1906 (died 1929). Admitted to bar, 1890; mem. Rep. State Central Com. of Kan., 1898; mem. Republican Nat. Com., 1900-12 and 1920—. Mason, Elk. Methodist. Home: Topeka, Kan. Died Nov. 9, 1932.

MULVIHILL, Michael Joseph; b. La Salle, Ill., July 17, 1855; s. Michael and Mary (Cregan) M.; ed. parochial sch. and commercial coll.; m. Margaret A. Finnegan, Jan. 6, 1880 (died 1914). Clk. Natchez Cotton Seed Oil Co., 1869-71; learned machinist's trade and worked in Chicago Rolling Mills until 1876; gen. mercantile business, Vicksburg, 1876-98; a founder, 1896, and incorporator City Savings & Trust Co. Obtained franchise and promoted Vicksburg Electric Street R.R., serving as its sec. 6 yrs.; postmaster of Vicksburg, 1902-14; mgr. The Valley Dry Goods Co. (dept. store), 1914-24. Mem. Rep. Nat. Com., 1917-24. Mem. Catholic Knight of America (1st state pres., 1882), Knights of Columbus (1st grand admiral of Miss., 1914). Elected hon. mem. Vicksburg Camp No. 32, U.C.V., 1898; elected hon. col. for life of 155th U.S. Inf., 1931. Pronounced by President Roosevelt, 1907, as "the most capable and efficient postmaster in the United States." Patented a levee building machine, 1884; made definite recommendations, 1927, in paper read before Miss. River Commn., for control of Miss. River, which was received with general commendation. Del. from Miss. to Patent Centennial Celebration, Washington, 1891. Author of "Vicksburg, Fort St. Peter and Fort Snyder" (a brief history of the early settlement and of battles of the Civil War), also a history of the "First Mississippi Regiment," 1931. Awarded Hirsch cup for outstanding civic service, Vicksburg, Miss., 1931. Home: Vicksburg, Miss. Died Nov. 21, 1935.

MUMFORD, Charles Carney, lawyer; b. Medford, Mass., Nov. 11, 1860; s. Benjamin G. and Jane (Dean) M.; A.B., Brown U., 1881, A.M., 1884; m. Emma M. Van Slyck, Apr. 27, 1887. Admitted to bar, 1883; practiced at Providence (except 15 mos. at Buffalo, N.Y.), 1883-1905; was clk. Municipal Ct. and asst. atty. gen. R.I.; mem. R.I. Ho. of Rep., 1893-94 and 1903; justice Superior Court, 1905-09; since in gen. practice; apptd. by U.S. Court in separation of N.Y.,N.H.&H. R.R. from its trolley lines; trustee R.I. Trolley Lines. Republican. Episcopalian. Mason. Home: Providence, R.I. Died Oct. 22, 1918.

MUMFORD, Ethel Watts, author; b. New York City; d. Dickson Given and Mary Atwater (Hughes) Watts; studied art at Julian Acad., Paris, and with Merie Guise, New York; began writing in connection with illustration and travel; m. George Dana Mumford, 1894; 1 son, George; m. 2d, Peter Geddes Grant, of Scotland, 1906. Author: The Wedding Song; The Pageant of the Seven Seas, 1925; Hand-Reading Today, 1925; (plays) The Young Idea; Good Night Nurse; The Scenario; Sick-a-bed; His Majesty the Queen; Easy Money; It Pays to Smile (dramatization of story by Nina Wilcox Putnam). Home: Sands Point, L.I., N.Y. Died May 2, 1940.

MUMFORD, Herbert Windsor, univ. prof.; b. Moscow, Mich., Feb. 26, 1871; s. Elisha Charles Lindsley and Julia Ann (Camburn) M.; student Albion Coll., Mich., 2 yrs.; B.S., Mich. State Coll., 1891, D.Agr., 1927; m. Lena Crosby, July 5, 1898; children—Dwight Curtis, Mary, James Satterlee (dec.), Herbert Windsor, Jr., Virginia (Mrs. Robert R. Kimbell). Instr. Mich. State Coll. and asst. Agrl. Expt. Sta., 1895-96; asst. prof. agr. and animal husbandry investigator, 1896-99, prof. agr., 1899-1901, Mich. State Coll.; prof. animal husbandry, and chief in animal husbandry, Expt. Sta., U. of Ill., 1901—, also dean Coll. of Agr. and dir. Agrl. Expt. Sta. and Extension Service, 1922—; dist. director Farm Credit Administration, 1933—. Investigated live stock conditions in Great Britain, France, Belgium and Holland, 1897, Argentine Republic, 1908. Sec. Farm Home Reading Circle, Mich., 1895-99; expert in breeding and feeding of live stock; chmn. cattle jurors, St. Louis Expn., 1904; mem. Am. Study Commn. for German Agriculture, 1928; mem. Mexican Agrl. Commn., 1930; mem. Spl. Com. of the Assn. of Land-Grant Colleges and Universities on the Agrl. Situation in 1932. Republican. Methodist. Author: Beef Production, 1907; also many bulls. Mich. and Ill. expt. stas. Joint author: Practical Farming and Gardening, 1902. Died May 31, 1938.

MUMFORD, James Gregory, physician; b. Rochester, N.Y., Dec. 2, 1863; s. George Elihu and Julia Emma (Hills) M.; A.B., Harvard, 1885, M.D., 1890; m. Helen Sherwood Ford, Jan. 6, 1892. In practice of medicine and surgery at Boston, 1890-12. Apptd. surgeon to Carney Hosp., 1892, to out-patients Mass. Gen. Hosp., 1894; asst. in surgery, 1895, instr., 1902, Harvard Med. Sch.; visiting surgeon Mass. Gen. Hosp., 1905-12; phys.-in-chief to Clifton Springs (N.Y.) Sanatorium and Hospital, 1912—. Served as surgeon Naval Brigade, Mass. Vol. Militia, 1892-93; surgeon U.S.A. Med. Reserve Corps. Fellow Am. Surg. Assn., Am. College Surgeons, Mass. Med. Society. Episcopalian. Republican. Trustee Hobart College. Author: Narrative of Medicine in America, 1903; Clinical Talks on Minor Surgery, 1903; Surgical Aspects of Digestive Disorders, 1905; Surgical Memoirs and Other Essays, 1908; Practice of Surgery, 1910- 2d edit., 1913; One Hundred Surgical Problems, 1911; A Doctor's Table Talk, 1912. Editor the Harvard Medical School, a History (3 vols.) by Thomas F. Harrington, M.D., 1905. Home: Clifton Springs, N.Y. Died 1914.

MUMFORD, John Kimberly, writer; b. Watkins, N.Y., Nov. 15, 1863; s. Prosper D. and Harriet (Tanner) M.; student Princeton U.; m. Corolyn C. Bailey, Mar. 19, 1895. Staff writer for New York newspapers. Had charge of New York Journal force in Cuba during latter part of Spanish-Am. War. Expert dealer in Oriental carpets. Author: Oriental Rugs, 1900. Home: Athens, N.Y. Died Apr. 17, 1926.

MUMFORD, Samuel Cranage; b. Detroit, Mich., Oct. 4, 1872; s. Benjamin Pardon and Rosalie Sarah (Cranage) M.; grad. Central High Sch., Detroit, 1889; post-grad. work in langs., 1889-91; m. Lillian Gove, 1909; 1 dau., Mary Mayo. With Detroit Edison Co., 1889-1932, comptroller, 1905-21, treas., 1921-32; sec. and treas. Huron Farms Co.; treas. Nat. Heliofloor Co.; v.p. Industrial Morris Plan Bank of Detroit; pres. House Financing Corp. of Detroit; retired, 1932. Member Detroit Bd. of Edn., 1907-29 (pres. 3 yrs.); vice-pres. Better Business Bureau of Detroit; chairman exec. com. Detroit Industrial Safety Council; pres. Detroit Council, Boy Scouts America. Republican. Episcopalian. A leader in development of pub. schs. of Detroit. Home: Detroit, Mich. Died Nov. 20, 1939.

MUNDÉ, Paul Fortunatus, physician; b. Dresden, Saxony, Sept. 7, 1846; s. Charles and Bertha (von Hornemann) M.; his father, Charles Mundé, a political refugee, brought him to U.S., 1849; ed. Boston Latin School; grad. Harvard Med. School, 1866 (master in obstetrics, Vienna, 1871; LL.D., Dartmouth, 1897); m. Eleanor Claire Hughes, Nov. 11, 1873. Acting med. cadet, U.S.A., 1864; vol. asst. surgeon in war between Prussia and South Germany, 1866; battalion surgeon, Bavarian army, with rank 1st lt., Franco-German war, 1870-71; studied at European univs., 1871-73; resident physician to the Maternity, Würzburg, 1867-70; settled in practice in New York, 1873. Specialist in gynecology and consulting obstetrics. Editor Am. Jour. of Obstetrics, 1874-92; pres. N.Y. Obstet. Soc., 1886-88; pres. Am. Gynecol. Soc., 1897-98; mem. many other socs.; prof. gynecology New York Polyclinic, 1882 (emeritus), and at Dartmouth Med. Coll., 1880—. Hon. fellow Edinburgh Obstet. Soc.; hon. pres. Internat. Congress of Obstetricians and Gynecologists, 1897, 1899. Author: Obstetric Palpation, 1880; Minor Surgical Gynecology, 1880; Appendix to Midwifery of Cazeaux and Tamier, 1884; Pregnancy and the Puerperal State, 1887; Diseases of Women, 1891. Died 1902.

MUNDELEIN, George William, cardinal; b. N.Y. City, July 2, 1872; s. Francis and Mary (Goetz) M.; A.B., Manhattan Coll., 1889; theol. studies St. Vincent Sem., Beatty, Pa.; D.D., Urban Coll. of Propaganda, Rome; S.T.D., Propaganda, 1908. Ordained priest R.C. Ch., 1895; sec. to Bishop McDonnell, Brooklyn, N.Y., and pastor Lithuanian Ch., 1895-97; chancellor of diocese, 1897-1909; apptd. censor, Liturg. Acad., Nov. 14, 1903; apptd. domestic prelate, Nov. 21, 1906; titular bishop of Loryma and auxiliary bishop of Brooklyn, Sept. 21, 1909-Nov. 1915; archbishop of Chicago, Nov. 30, 1915—; elevated to cardinalate, Mar. 24, 1924. Founder and pres. Seminary of St. Mary's of the Lake, at Mundelein, Ill., 1913. Mem. Ancient Acad. of the Arcadia, 1907. Died Oct. 2, 1939.

MUNDHEIM, Samuel, merchant; b. Washington, D.C., Nov. 26, 1871; s. Lewis and Fanny (Forster) M.; ed. pub. schs.; m. Stella W. Kaufmann, Feb. 21, 1905; children—Marshall, Louise. Chmn. bd. Am. Safety Razor Co.; dir. Compo Shoe Machinery Corp., U.S. Vitamine Corp.; pres. Safety Stemming Plug Co. Republican. Home: New York, N.Y. Died Mar. 16, 1940.

MUNDIE, William Bryce, architect; b. Hamilton, Ont., Apr. 30, 1863; s. William and Margaret (Bryce) M.; ed. pub. schs. and Hamilton Collegiate Inst.; m. Bessie Russel Jenney, 1892; children—Elizabeth Jenney, Margaret Bryce, Jean Fraser (Mrs. Luther Bowden De Forest). Draftsman in office of W. L. B. Jenney, Chicago, 1884-91; mem. Jenney & Mundie, 1891-1905, later Jenney, Mundie & Jensen, now of Mundie, Jensen, Bourke & Havens. Architect Chicago Bd. of Edn., 1898-1905. Fellow A.I.A. Republican. Home: Chicago, Ill. Died Mar. 27, 1939.

MUNDY, Ezekiel Wilson, librarian; b. Metuchen, N.J., June 16, 1833; s. Luther Bloomfield and Frances Eliza (Martin) M.; A.B., U. of Rochester, 1860, A.M., 1863; Rochester Theol. Seminary, B.T., 1860-63; (Litt.D., Syracuse, 1904, Rochester, 1910); m. Emily Kendall, Jan. 15, 1873. Ordained Bapt. ministry, 1863; pastor First Bapt. Ch., 1863-66, Independent Ch., 1866-79, St. Mark's P.E. Ch., 1883-94, Syracuse, N.Y.; librarian Syracuse Pub. Library, 1880-1915, librarian emeritus, 1915—. Died June 8, 1916.

MUNDY, Talbot, author; b. London, Eng., Apr. 23, 1879; ed. Rugby. In British Govt. service in India and East Africa, 1900-09; came to U.S., 1911; regular contbr. to Ridgway publs., 1911—. Author: Rung Ho!, 1914; Winds of the World, 1915; King of the Khyber Rifles, 1916; Hira Singh—When India Came to Fight in Flanders, 1918; The Ivory Trail, 1919; The Eye of Zeitoon, 1920; Told in the East, 1920; Guns of the Gods, 1921; The Nine Unknown, 1922; Om, 1923; The Devil's Guard, 1925; Queen Cleopatra, 1929; Cock of the North, 1929; Black Light, 1930; Jimgrim, 1931; Jungle Jest, 1932; The Lion of Petra, 1933; Tros of Samothrace, 1934; Purple Pirate, 1935; Full Moon, 1936; The Thunder Dragon Gate, 1936; East and West, 1937; Old Ugly-face, 1939. Home: Anna Maria, Fla. Died Aug. 5, 1940.

MUNFORD, Mary Cooke Branch; b. Richmond, Va.; d. James Read and Martha Louise (Patteson) Branch; ed. George F. Merrill's Sch., Richmond, and Misses Peebles and Thompson Sch., New York; m. Beverley Bland Munford, Nov. 22, 1893 (died 1910); children—Mary Safford (wife of Hiester Hoogewerff, U.S.N.), Beverley Bland. Closely identified with ednl. movement in Va. and South, 1900—; a founder Richmond Edn. Assn., 1900; chmn. Coördinate Coll. League, for opening U. of Va. to women; pres. Coöperative Edn. Assn. of Va., 1910-25; v.p. Nat. Consumers' League; mem. bd. visitors U. of Va.; trustee Nat. League on Urban Conditions among Negroes. Mem. War Work Council Y.W.C.A. Chmn. Woman's Com. Council National Defense (Va. Div.); mem. Va. War History Commn.; mem. Woman's Inter-Racial Com. (Va.), Committee on Colored Work. Organized first child study groups in Virginia. Episcopalian. Home: Richmond, Va. Died July 3, 1938.

MUNGER, Theodore Thornton, Congl. clergyman; b. Bainbridge, N.Y., Mar. 5, 1830; s. Dr. Eben. and Cynthia (Selden) M.; grad. Yale, 1851; Yale Theol. Sem., 1855 (D.D., Ill. Coll., 1883, S.T.D., Harvard, 1904). Pastor Congl. chs., Dorchester, Mass., 1856-60; Haverhill, Mass., 1862-70; Lawrence, Mass., 1870-75; San Jose, Calif., 1875-76; N. Adams, Mass., 1876-85; United Ch., New Haven, from 1885, now pastor emeritus; fellow Yale Univ. Author: On the Threshold; The Appeal to Life; Horace Bushnell, Preacher and Theologian; Character Through Inspiration; Essays for the Day. Home: New Haven, Conn. Died 1910.

MUNGER, Thomas Charles, judge; b. Fletcher, O., July 7, 1861; s. Samuel C. and Margaret M. (Ervin) M.; student Ia. (now Grinnell) Coll., 1881-83; Union Coll. of Law, Chicago, 1883-84; admitted to bar, 1885; m. Carrie A. Case, June 5, 1888; children—Mrs. Ruth James, Alfred C., Margaret. Mem. Neb. legislature, 1895-97; county atty., Lancaster County, 1897-1901; U.S. dist. judge, Dist. of Neb., Mar. 1, 1907. Republican. Home: Lincoln, Neb. Died Nov. 29, 1941.

MUNGER, William Henry, judge; b. Bergen, N.Y., Oct. 12, 1845; s. Elbert and Anna M.; brought up on farm; ed. in pub. schs.; went to Cleveland, O., 1865; m. Jennie M. Fowler, Mar. 30, 1871. Worked in dry goods store; read law; admitted to bar, 1868; same yr. located in Fremont, Neb.; mem. Constl. Conv., 1875; U.S. dist. judge, Dist. of Neb., Feb. 1897—. Home: Omaha, Neb. Died Aug. 11, 1915.

MUNHALL, Leander Whitcomb, evangelist; b. Zanesville, O., June 7, 1843; s. David and Abigail Rice (Moore) M.; mostly self-educated; M.A., Chattanooga U.; D.D., Taylor U., and U. of New Orleans; m. Mary E. Thomas, Sept. 21, 1871; children—Elizabeth Hamlin, LeRoy (dec.), Earl (dec.), Mrs. Adelaid Smyth, Mrs. Ruth Manning. Enlisted in Co. C, 79th Ind. Vol. Inf., Aug. 1862; promoted corporal, sergt., color bearer, sergt. maj. and adj. of regt. and took part in 33 battles. Began as evangelist M.E. Ch., 1874, and has preached for more than 50 years; became editor The Methodist (weekly), Phila. Represented Phila. Ann. Conf. in Gen. Conf. of M.E. Ch. 6 times, 1904-28. Author: Breakers! Methodism Adrift, 1913. Home: Germantown, Phila., Pa. Died Jan. 7, 1934.

MUNK, Joseph Amasa, coll. dean; b. Columbiana Co., O., Nov. 9, 1847; s. Jacob and Maria (Rosenberry) M.; Mt. Union Coll., Ohio; M.D., Eclectic Med. Coll. of Ohio, Cincinnati, 1869; m. Emma Sarah Beazell, Jan. 9, 1873. Practiced at Lindsay, O., 1870-71, Chillicothe, Mo., 1871-81, Topeka, Kan., 1881-92, Los Angeles, Calif., 1892—; dean and prof. climatology, Calif. Eclectic Med. Coll., 1907—. Pres. Nat. Eclectic Med. Assn., 1910-11; trustee Southwest Mus.; mem. Archæol. Inst. America. Pvt. Co. I, 178th Regt., Ohio Vol. Inf., 1864-65; mem. G.A.R. Partner Munk Bros.' cattle ranch, Cochise Co., Ariz.; founder Munk Bot. Garden and Arboretum, Compton, Calif., for testing foreign trees and plants. Author: Arizona Bibliography, 1900, 3d edit., 1914; Arizona Sketches, 1905; Musical Compositions, 1916; Album of 2,000 Arizona kodak pictures, 1918; Southwest Sketches, 1920; Activities of a Lifetime, 1924. History of Arizona Literature, 1925; Features of an Arizona Library, 1926. Began making collection of books on Ariz. in 1884 and in 1908 made gift of his library of Arizoniana, now numbering 16,000 vols., to Southwest Museum. Home: Los Angeles, Calif. Died Dec. 4, 1927.

MUNKITTRICK, Richard Kendall, author; b. Manchester, Eng., Mar. 5, 1853; s. Richard and Augusta (Thorburn) M.; ed. pub. and pvt. schs.; m. Jeannette Agnes Turner, July 5, 1883. On staff of Puck, 1881-89; editor Judge from 1901-05. Author: Farming, 1891; The Moon Prince and Other Nabobs, 1893; New Jersey Arabian Nights, 1893; The Acrobatic Muse, 1896; The Siambangaree, 1898. Home: Summit, N.J. Died 1911.

MUNN, Charles Allen, editor; b. New York; s. Orson Desaix and Julia Augusta (Allen) M.; A.B., Princeton, 1881. Pres. and dir. Munn & Co.; editor The Scientific American. Mem. exec. com. Am. Federation Arts. Home: New York, N.Y. Died Apr. 3, 1924.

MUNN, Charles Clark, author; b. Southington, Conn., May 11, 1848; s. Charles E. and Eliza (Clark) M.; reared on farm; ed. country sch.; left farm at 17; commercial traveler for 30 yrs.; m. Mary E. Hill, Sept. 28, 1882. Author: Pocket Island (4th edit.), 1900; Uncle Terry—a Story of the Maine Coast, 1900; Rockhaven, 1902; The Hermit, 1904; Boyhood Days on the Farm, 1907; Myrtle Baldwin, 1908; The Castle Builders, 1910; The Heart of Uncle Terry, 1915; Camp Castaway, 1916. Home: Springfield, Mass. Died July 8, 1917.

MUNN, John Pixley, life insurance; b. Gates, nr. Rochester, N.Y., Dec. 11, 1847; A.B., U. of Rochester, 1870; M.D., Bellevue Hosp. Med. Coll. (New York U.), 1876. Asst. med. dir. U.S. Life Ins. Co., 1877-83, became med. dir., 1883, pres., 1902, now chmn. bd.; visiting surgeon Randall's Island Hosp., 1879; curator St. Luke's Hosp., 1879-82; pres. Arlington Refrigerator Co.; v.p. New Netherland Bank of New York; dir. Crex Carpet Co., Railway Steel-Spring Co.; trustee U.S. Savings Bank of City of New York. Trustee U. of Rochester, 1886; mem. Council New York U. Died Aug. 15, 1931.

MUNN, Orson Desaix, publisher; b. Monson, Hampden Co., Mass., June 11, 1824; grad. Monson Acad.; clerked 2 yrs. in a Springfield book-store, then in a country store in Monson until 1846, when, with Alfred E. Beach (died 1896), he bought the Scientific American, then 6 months old, of which he is still at the head. Established Scientific American Supplement, 1876, and a monthly Architects' and Builders' Edition, 1885. For over 50 yrs. also at head of Munn & Co., patent solicitors; m. Julia Augusta Allen, 1849 (died 1894). Has summer residence at Llewellyn Park, on Orange Mountain, N.J., with a large farm near by, stocked with Dutch belted cattle. Died 1907.

MUNN, William Phipps, physician, surgeon, and, 1895—, Health Commr. of Denver; b. Pittsburgh, Pa., Dec. 10, 1864; s. Dougald and Isabella (McCall) M.; grad. Univ. of Mich., M.D., 1886; practiced in Allegheny, Pa., 1886-90; removed to Colo., 1890; prof. histology and pathology Gross Med. Coll., 1890-92; prof. genito-urinary diseases and clinical surgery, Univ. of Denver, 1892-97; mem. State Bd. of Health, Colo., 1893—; pres. Colo. State Med. Society, 1900-01. Home: Denver, Colo. Died 1903.

MUNOZ, Jorge, E.E. and M.P. of Guatemala to U.S.; b. City of Guatemala, Mar. 4, 1857; s. Don Narciso and Doña Jesus (Aqueche) de Muñoz; grad. Colegio Seminario de Guatemala, 1872, Academia de Derecho (law sch.), Guatemala, as Doctor of Law, 1878; unmarried. Engaged in general practice of law in Guatemala from 1878, also on several occasions consulting solicitor of govt. of Guatemala; apptd. by President Reyna Barrios, Sept. 1894, minister of foreign affairs, serving until 1897; several times judge Court of Appeals at Guatemala and representative to Nat. Assembly; on spl. mission as E.E. and M.P. to U.S., Oct. 1901, and in Aug. 1904, regularly apptd. as E.E. and M.P. of Guatemala to U.S. Corr. mem. Royal Acad. of Law and Jurisprudence, Madrid. Received from the Queen Regent of Spain decoration of Order of Isabel the Catholic, as active member comendador. Died 1906.

MUNRO, Dana Carleton, univ. prof.; b. Bristol, R.I., June 7, 1866; s. John B. and Abby Howland (Batt) M.; A.B., Brown U., 1887, A.M., 1890, L.H.D., 1912; m. Alice Gardner Beecher, July 16, 1891; children—Dana Gardner, Jeannette, Caroline Walker, Alice Beecher, Winthrop Marshall. Instr. and asst. prof. Roman and medieval history, U. of Pa., 1893-1902; prof. European history, 1902-15, and director summer session, 1904-06, U. of Wis.; prof. medieval history, Princeton U., 1915—. Research asst. to Com. on Pub. Information, 1917-18; chmn. Nat. Bd. for Hist. Service, 1918-19. Fellow Royal Hist. Soc. Commandeur de l'Ordre de la Couronne. Editor, 1894-1902, and contributor of 8 numbers, 1894-99, Translations and Reprints from Original Sources of History; mng. editor Am. Hist. Review, 1928-29. Author: Medieval History, 1902; Essays on the Crusades (joint author), 1902; A Source Book of Roman History, 1904; Medieval Civilization (joint author), 1904, Part II, 1906; Syllabus of Medieval History, 8th edit., 1919; German War Practices, 1917; German Treatment of Conquered Territory, 1918; The Middle Ages, 1921, 28. Editor: Paetow's Guide to Study of Mediæval History (revised edit.), 1931. Died Jan. 13, 1933.

MUNRO, David Alexander, asst. editor North American Review; b. Maryburgh, Ross-shire, Scotland; grad. at Edinburgh Univ., A.M., 1872; for a number of yrs. connected with literary dept., Harper & Bros.; published Garden and Forest, 1887-89; gen. mgr. North American Review, 1889-96, and editor, 1896-99, and from then asst. editor under Mr. G. B. M. Harvey; has contributed articles to New York Times, Evening Post, The Hour, Harper's Weekly, Garden and Forest, etc. Supervised collation and transmission of American contributions to last edition Liddell & Scott's Greek Lexicon; arranged the comparative Greek-English New Testament (Harper & Bros.). Collaborated with Dr. Philip Schaff in preparation of his Companion to the Study of the Greek New Testament; etc. Home: New York, N.Y. Died 1910.

MUNRO, Emily Gardner, educator; b. Bristol, R.I.; d. Otis and Hannah Billings (Waldron) M.; Ph.B., Brown U., 1898, A.M., 1907; unmarried. Instr. English, St. Mary's Sch., Burlington, N.J., 1899-1900; in charge Christadora House (social settlement), New York, 1900-01; instr. English, Albany (N.Y.) Academy for Girls, 1901-09; principal St. Margaret's Sch. for Girls, Waterbury, Conn., 1909—. Episcopalian. Home: Waterbury, Conn. Died Jan. 1924.

MUNRO, John Cummings, surgeon; b. Lexington, Mass., Mar. 26, 1858; s. James Smith and Alice (Phinney) M.; A.B., Harvard, 1881, M.D., 1885; m. Mary Squibb, Nov. 17, 1887. In practice at Boston, 1886—; asst. in anatomy, 1889-93, asst. demonstrator, 1893-95, asst. in clin. surgery, 1894-96, instr., 1896-98, instr. surgery, 1898-1903, lecturer, 1903-05, Harvard; asst. visiting surgeon Boston City Hosp., 1893-1903; surgeon-in-chief Carney Hosp., 1903—. First lt. U.S.A. Med. Reserve Corps, July 1908—. Fellow Am. Surg. Assn., Am. Academy Medicine, A.A.A.S., Phila. Acad. Surgery. Home: Boston, Mass. Died 1910.

MUNRO, Walter Lee, surgeon; b. Bristol R.I., Sept. 4, 1857; s. John B. and Abby H. (Batt) M.; A.B., Brown U., 1879, A.M., 1882; M.D., Harvard, 1885; interne Boston City Hosp., 1884-85, Boston Lying-in Hosp., 1885; m. Sarah Frances Rose, Dec. 7, 1887. Practiced in Meriden, Conn., 1885-86; settled at Providence, 1886; surgeon to out-patients, R.I. Hosp., 1886-95; visiting surgeon R.I. Hosp., 1895-1914, consulting surgeon same hospital, 1914—; consulting surgeon St. Joseph's Hosp., 1897—; cons. surgeon Memorial Hosp., Pawtucket; visiting surgeon State Hosp. for Mental Diseases, 1912-21. F.A.C.S. Home: Providence, R.I. Died Oct. 23, 1939.

MUNRO, Wilfred Harold, univ. prof.; b. Bristol, R.I., Aug. 20, 1849; s. John B. and Abby Howland (Batt) M.; A.B., Brown, 1870, A.M., 1873; post-grad. course, Brown, 1889-90, univs. of Freiburg and Heidelberg, 1890-91; L.H.D., Hobart, 1910; m. Susan Wilkinson Goodwin, Dec. 28, 1875. Master in De Veaux Coll., Niagara Falls, N.Y., 1870-71; asso. prin. St. Mark's Sch., Salt Lake City, 1871; in South and Central America, 1873; prin. Le Roy (N.Y.) Acad. Inst., 1875-79; pres. De Deaux Coll., 1881-89; asso. prof. history and director of university extension, 1891-99, prof. European history, 1899-1911, emeritus prof., 1911, Brown U. Pres. R.I. Alpha of Phi Beta Kappa, R.I. Hist. Soc., 1906—, R.I. Soc. S.A.R., Barnard Club, Churchmen's Club, A.E. Club, 1907—; gov. R.I. Soc. Colonial Wars, R.I. Soc. Mayflower Descendants (dept. gov. gen.). Mem. Providences Sch. Com., 1910—. Fellow Am. Geog. Soc. World wide traveler. Episcopalian. Author: Tales of an Old Seaport, 1917; Among the Mormons in the Days of Brigham Young, 1927. Editor new edit. of Works of W. H. Prescott (22 vols.), 1905-06; Record Book of R.I. Soc. Mayflower Descendants, 1911. Home: Providence, R.I. Died Aug. 9, 1934.

MUNROE, Charles Edward, chemist; b. Cambridge, Mass., May 24, 1849; s. Enoch and Emeline Elizabeth (Russell) M.; S.B., summa cum laude, Harvard U., 1871; Ph.D., George Washington U., 1894, LL.D., from same univ., 1912; m. Mary Louise, d. Prof. George Frederick Barker, June 20, 1883; children—Mrs. Winifred M. Mathews, Russell Barker, (George) Treadway Barker, Mrs. Dorothy Rouzer, Mrs. Charlotte Dolph. Assistant in chemistry, Harvard, 1871-74; professor chemistry, U.S. Naval Acad., 1874-86; chemist to torpedo corps, U.S. Naval Torpedo Sta. and War College, 1886-92; head prof. chemistry, 1892-1918, dean Corcoran Scientific School, 1892-98, and dean faculty of graduate studies, 1893-1918 (emeritus), George Washington U. Mem. U.S. Assay Commn. 1885, 90, 93; visitor U.S. Naval Acad., 1898; organized and directed on Analostan Island a vol. torpedo corps, 1898; consulting expert of Engr. Bd. on defense of Washington, 1898; expert spl. agt. in charge chem. industries of the U.S. for censuses of 1900, 05, 10; consulting expert U.S. Geol. Survey, U.S. Bur. of Mines and Civil Service Commn.; chmn. advisory com. Am. Ry. Assn. for drafting of regulations governing transportation of explosives, 1905; supt. denatured alcohol exhibit, Jamestown Expn., 1907, and mem. jury on chemicals. Apptd. by Swedish Acad. Sciences, 1900, to nominate candidate for Nobel prizes in chemistry. Inventor of smokeless powder and authority on explosives; author of over 100 books and papers on chemistry and explosives. Chmn. com. on explosives investigations, Nat. Research Council, 1918-28; chief explosives chemist, U.S. Bur. Mines, 1919-33. Cons. specialist on explosives, U.S. Forest Service, 1934—. Comdt. Order of Medjidieh, Turkey, 1901; Officer Order of Leopold of Belgium, 1920. Hon. fellow Am. Inst. Chemists; fellow Chem. Soc., London, Am. Acad. Arts and Sciences, Soc. Chem. Industry, Eng., A.A.A.S.; pres. Am. Chem. Soc., 1898-99, Washington Chem., Soc., 1895-96; chmn. com. on explosives Am. Soc. Testing Materials. Fellow Am. Inst. Chemistry. Home: Forest Glen, Md. Died Dec. 7, 1938.

MUNROE, Henry Smith, mining engr.; b. Brooklyn, Mar. 25, 1850; E.M., Columbia, 1869, Ph.D., 1877 (hon. Sc.D., 1904); m. Alice M. Brown, Sept. 12, 1882; children—Mrs. Eleanor M. Green, Robert K. Munroe. Asst. geologist Ohio State Geol. Survey, 1870-71; asst. chemist U.S. Dept. Agr., 1870-72; asst. geologist and mining engr. Geol. Survey of Yesso, Japan, 1872-75; prof. geology and mining, U. of Tokio, 1875-76; adj. prof. surveying and practical mining, 1877-91, prof. mining, 1891-1915 (emeritus), dean faculty applied sciences, 1897-99, mem. univ. council, 1895-1915, Columbia U. Consulting engr. U.S. Bureau Mines, 1917. Home: Litchfield, Conn. Died May 4, 1933.

MUNROE, Hersey, topographic engr.; b. Lake City, Fla., Jan. 30, 1868; s. Benjamin Hersey and Jennie Lucy (Bowen) M.; ed. common schs. and Corcoran Scientific Sch., Washington; received certificate from Columbian U. for topog. drafting, 1889; m. Alice Lindsay Brandon, Dec. 3, 1890; 1 son, Thomas Brandon; m. 2d, Daisy W. Cushman, Dec. 21, 1912. Appointed topographer U.S. Geol. Survey, 1894; surveyed and mapped large areas of phosphate land in Fla., iron in N.C. and Ohio, and coal in W. Va.; in charge topographic work on Colorado River, Ariz. and Calif., for irrigation of arid lands, 1902-03; in charge of topographic field work in Me., N.H., Vt., N.J., 1903-05; made surveys vicinity of Lewiston, Me., 1906, topograhic surveys in Me., 1907, Pa., 1908, Me. and N.H., 1909; in charge topographic surveys in Me., 1910-11, in Me. and Pa., 1912-13, Me. and Vt., 1914-15, Me. and N.H., 1916-17; apptd. geographer, U.S. Geol. Survey, July 1, 1917. Mil. mapping for War Dept., Hampton Roads and vicinity, Va., 1918; topographic work in Vt., 1919; in charge topographic work in Miss., 1920-21; topographic survey in Vt., 1922-23, Vt. and N.H., 1924-25; in charge topographic mapping in N.E. states, 1925-26; instr. topographic mapping, Atlantic Div., U.S. Geol. Survey, 1927; in charge mapping Shenandoah Nat. Park, Va., 1928-30; mapping vicinity of Healing Springs, Va., 1931, vicinity of Catskill, N.Y., 1931-32. Served 2d and 1st lt. Co. A, 2d Battalion, D.C.N.G., 1889-94 (resigned). Home: Washington, D.C. Died Feb. 17, 1935.

MUNROE, James Phinney, mfr.; b. Lexington, Mass., June 3, 1862; s. James S. and Alice B. (Phinney) M.; B.S., Mass. Inst. Technology, 1882; Litt.D., George Washington U., 1918; Phi Beta Kappa, William and Mary Coll., Va., 1919; m. Katharine Winthrop Langdon, July 2, 1885; children—Alice Langdon (dec.), Katharine Langdon (Mrs. Frederic L. Day), Elizabeth Winthrop. Sec. of faculty, Mass. Inst. Tech., 1882-89; mem. firm James S. Munroe & Co., 1889—; treas. Munroe Felt & Paper Co., Boston, 1897—, pres., 1910—. Pres. Alumni Assn. Mass. Inst. Tech., 1894-97; life mem. corp. Mass. Inst. Tech., 1897—, sec., 1909—; mng. editor Technology Review, 1899-1908; chmn. Lexington Sch. Com., 1907-09; chmn. Mass. Commn. for the Blind, 1908-18; exec. dir. "Boston 1915," 1910-11; dir. Nat. Com. Prevention Blindness; v.p. N. Bennet St. Industrial School; treas. Garland School; treas. Residuary Estate of George O. Smith. Mem. Lexington Hist. Soc. (pres. 1898), Nat. Soc. Vocational Edn. (pres. 1910-11), Boston Chamber Commerce (chmn. com. on edn., 1909-12), Bostonian Soc., Unitarian Laymen's League (dir.), Mas. Civic League (chmn. civil service com.); vice chmn. Federal Bd. for Vocational Edn., 1917-21; chmn. M.I.T. Com. for Nat. Service, 1917; pres. Benev. Fraternity of Chs., 1927—. Author: The New England Conscience, 1915; The Human Factor in Education, 1920; A Life of Francis Amasa Walker, 1923. Editor: Discussions in Education, by Francis A. Walker, 1899; History of Lexington, revised by Lexington Hist. Soc., 1913. Home: Boston, Mass. Died Feb. 2, 1929.

MUNROE, Kirk, author; b. nr. Prairie du Chien, Wis., Sept. 15, 1850; s. Charles and Susan (Hall) M.; ed. common schs., Appleton, Wis., Cambridge, Mass., and Harvard Univ. Engineering School; m. Mary, d. Mrs. Amelia Barr, Sept. 15, 1883; m. 2d, Mabel, d. William F. Stearns, 1924. Assisted in explorations of routes for Santa Fe and Northern Pacific rys., on western plains, 1867-68; was a friend of both "Kit" Carson and "Buffalo Bill." First editor Harper's Round Table, 1879-82. Founded League of Am. Wheelmen at Newport, R.I., May 31, 1880. Author: Wakulla; The Flamingo Feather; Derrick Sterling; Crystal Jack & Co., and Delta Bixby; The Golden Days of '49; Dorymates; Campmates; Canoemates; Raftmates; The Fur Seal's Tooth; Snow Shoes and Sledges; Rick Dale; The Painted Desert; The White Conquerors; At War with Pontiac; Through Swamp and Glade; With Crockett and Bowie; Under Orders; Prince Dusty; Cab and Caboose; The Coral Ship; Big Cypress; The Ready Rangers; The Copper Princess; In Pirate Waters; Forward March; Shine Terrill; Midshipman Stuart; A Son of Satsuma; The Blue Dragon; Under the Great Bear; Brethren of the Coast; The Belt of Seven Totems; The Outcast Warrior, 1905; For the Mikado, 1906 (all books for boys). Editor: Eminent Men of Our Time. Home: Coconut Grove, Fla. Died June 16, 1930.

MUNROE, William Adams, lawyer; b. Cambridge, Mass., Nov. 9, 1843; s. William Watson and Hannah (Foster) M.; grad. Cambridge High Sch., 1860, Harvard Coll., A.B., 1864, A.M., 1867; Harvard Law Sch.; m. Sarah Danforth Whiting, Nov. 22, 1871. Admitted to bar, Aug. 1868; began practice, Sept. 1869; partner with George O. Shattuck (Shattuck & Munroe), 1870-97, until Mr. Shattuck's death; firm was Shattuck, Holmes & Munroe, 1872-82, Oliver Wendell Holmes (now of U.S. Supreme bench) being partner until apptd. judge Supreme Jud. Court of Mass., 1882. Was commr. to revise Cambridge city charter, and for 13 yrs. on Cambridge Sch. Com. Pres. Perry Mason Co., publishers of Youth's Companion. Republican. Baptist; pres. Am. Bapt. Missionary Soc., Boston Bapt. Bethel; pres. bd. trustees Newton Theol. Instn.; pres. Am. Congo Reform Assn.; chmn. bd. trustees 1st Bapt. Ch., Cambridge; dir. Gen. Theol. Library, Boston; trustee Cambridge Hosp. Mem. Boston Bapt. Social Union. Home: Cambridge, Mass. Died 1905.

MUNSELL, Albert Henry, portrait painter; b. Boston, Jan. 6, 1858; s. Luke and Margaret (Johnston) M.; ed. Boston pub. schs., 1866-74; A.M., Mass. Normal Art Sch., 1881; student École des Beaux Arts, Paris, 1885-88, awarded 5 medals; m. Juliet, d. Alexander Ector Orr, 1894. Exhibited at Paris Salon, 1886, 1887, 1888, also at Boston, New York, Chicago, Pittsburgh. Instr. Mass. Normal Art Sch., 1881—; lecturer on artistic anatomy and color composition. Patented new instruments for color measurement, and invented a system of pigment colors, which has been introduced in schs. of Boston, New York, Baltimore, Mexico City, etc. Pres. Mass. Industrial Art Teachers' Assn. Author: Color Notation, 1905; Atlas of the Color System, 1910; Color Balance, 1913. Home: Chestnut Hill, Mass. Died June 28, 1918.

MUNSELL, Charles Edward, chemist; b. New York, N.Y., Apr. 22, 1858; s. Jabez E. M.; Ph.B., Columbia Sch. of Mines, 1878, Ph.D., 1884. Employed as chemist, 1878-79; milk insp., New York City Health Dept., 1880-85; state milk insp., N.Y. State Bd. of Health, 1881-83; analyst and asst. chemist, Devoe & Raynolds Co., 1886-1917; chemist Standard Oil Co., Nov. 1917—. Home: Portchester, New York. Died Mar. 16, 1918.

MUNSEY, Frank Andrew, publisher; b. Mercer, Me., Aug. 21, 1854; s. Andrew Chauncey and Mary Jane (Hopkins) M.; ed. pub. schs. in Me.; unmarried. Started business career in country store; became mgr. Western Union Telegraph office, Augusta, Me.; went to New York, 1882, and started The Golden Argosy, juvenile weekly; in Feb. 1889, launched Munsey's Weekly, converted Oct. 1891, into Munsey's Magazine; also owns The Argosy, All-Story Weekly, New York Mail, Sun and Globe, and Evening Telegram. Author: Afloat in a Great City, 1887; The Boy Broker, 1888; A Tragedy of Errors, 1889; Under Fire, 1890; Derringforth, 1894. Home: N.Y. City; Manhasset, L.I.; Elizabethtown, N.Y. Died Dec. 22, 1925.

MUNSON, C(yrus) La Rue, lawyer; b. Bradford, N.Y., July 2, 1854; s. Edgar and Lucy Maria (Curtis) M.; prep. edn. Episcopal Acad. of Conn., Cheshire, 1868-71; LL.B., Yale 1875 (hon. M.A., 1894); m. Josephine Anthony White, Nov. 7, 1877; m. 2d, Minnie Wright Tuller, Oct. 20, 1891. Practiced at Williamsport, Pa.; mem. Candor & Munson; lecturer Yale Law Sch. Pres. Savings Instn., E. Keeler Co., Williamsport Passenger Ry. Co., Eagles Mere Light Co., Scootac Ry. Co., Munson Lbr. Co., Ltd.; v.p. Williamsport Wire Rope Co. Trustee James V. Brown Pub. Library; pres. Lycoming Hist. Soc.; pres. Pa. State Bar Assn., 1902-03. Home: Williamsport, Pa. Died Dec. 8, 1922.

MUNSON, Frank C., ocean transportation; b. Havana, Cuba, Jan. 13, 1876; s. Walter D. and Emily M. (Wood) M.; grad. Adelphi Acad., Brooklyn, N.Y., 1895; m. Belle L. Maze, June 27, 1900 (died 1908); m. 2d, Cora P. Mallory, Dec. 9, 1909. Began as office boy, Munson Steamship Line, 1896; was made mgr. Cuban dept. same line, 1903, treas. Munson Steamship Line, 1907, v.p., 1908, pres. Munson Line, 1916—; also pres. following s.s. cos.—Maritima Cubana, Munamar, Mundelta, Munisla, Munplacé, Munsomo, Munwood, Sudbury, Mundale; pres. Munson Bldg. Corp., Munson Inland Water Lines, Pub. Warehouses of Matanzas, Ltd., 67 Wall St. Restaurant Corp., Beaverson Corp., Caibarien Transport Co., Hill St. Hotel Co.; trustee Atlantic Mut. Ins. Co., Bank of N.Y. & Trust Co. Mem. Port and Terminal Com., N.Y. City, 1914-16; mem. Shipping Com. of Nat. Council of Defense, Apr.-Sept. 1917; apptd., Sept. 17, 1917, mem. War Trade Bd., representing U.S. Shipping Bd., and served 12 mos.; mem. N.Y. Bd. of Trade and Transportation, Brooklyn Chamber of Commerce, Mchts.' Assn. Port of New York, Pan Am. Soc. (council), Am.-Brazilian Assn., Argentina-Am. Soc. (dir.). Pres. Brooklyn Y.M.C.A.; mem. bd. Brooklyn Bur. Charities, Brooklyn Parks and Playgrounds Assn. (pres.). Republican. Conglist. Home: New York, N.Y. Died Sept. 24, 1936.

MUNSON, James Decker, M.D.; b. Independence, Mich., June 8, 1848; s. Saron Beach and Harriet (Decker) M.; ed. Pontiac (Mich.) High Sch., 1868-69; M.D., U. of Mich., 1873 (hon. A.M., 1904); m. Marion M. Ward, Mar. 23, 1904. Began practice of medicine, Detroit, May 1873; physician St. Luke's Hosp., 1876-78; asst. phys. Eastern Mich. Asylum, 1878-85; med. supt. Northern Michigan Asylum, Sept. 1885-1924 (emeritus). Home: Traverse City, Mich. Died June 24, 1929.

MUNSON, James Eugene, stenographer, inventor; b. Paris, N.Y., May 12, 1835; studied at Amherst, but was not grad.; studied shorthand and became an expert stenographer. Settled in New York, 1857, and was court stenographer over 30 yrs.; reported Beecher-Tilton case for New York Sun. Expended much labor in simplifying existing systems of shorthand, the result being the "Munson System." Invented process of setting and justifying type automatically, and machines for doing same; also assisted in inventing a machine for operating typewriting machines by telegraph. Author: The Complete Phonographer, 1866; Dictionary of Practical Phonography, 1875, 1906; Phrase Book of Practical Phonography; The Art of Phonography, 1898; A Shorter Course in Munson Phonography, 1900; First Phonographic Reader, 1904; Phonographic Dictation Book, 1904; Munson's Pocket Dictionary of Phonography, 1906. Home: New York, N.Y. Deceased.

MUNSON, John P., biologist; b. Jolster Sunfjord, Norway, Feb. 21, 1860; s. Peter and Elizabeth (Dvergsdal) M.; came to U.S., 1864; B.S., U. of Wis., 1887, M.S., 1892; Ph.B., Yale, 1891; Ph.D., U. of Chicago, 1897; m. Sophie Josephine, d. Rev. A. Mikkelsen, of Chicago, Dec. 30, 1897; 1 dau., Esther Ingeborg (dec.). Master in English, Augustana Coll., Sioux Falls, S.D., 1889-91; fellow in zoölogy, U. of Chicago, 1893-97; investigator in biology, Woods Hole, Mass., 1894; hon. fellow in biology, Clark U., 1897; head Dept. of Biology, Wash. State Teachers' Coll., 1899—; dir. zoölogy, Seaside Lab., Port Renfrew, B.C., 1903. Lecturer 7th Internat. Zoöl. Congress, Boston, 1907, 8th Internat. Zoöl. Congress, Graz, Austria, 1910; research Christiana, Berlin, Naples, 1910. Awarded Walker 1st prize, Boston Soc. Natural History, 1911. Fellow A.A.A.S., Western Soc. Naturalists, Royal Soc. (London). Author: Education through Nature, 1903; Supermatogenesis of the Butterfly, 1906. Collaborator on Am. Jour. Anatomy, etc. Spent many yrs. in comparative cell studies, 25 plates completed. Home: Ellensburg, Wash. Died Feb. 27, 1928.

MUNSON, Loveland, judge; b. Manchester, Vt., July 21, 1843; s. Cyrus and Lucy (Loveland) M.; grad. Burr and Burton Sem. there, 1862; m. Mary, d. Rev. A. B. Campbell, of Mendon, Ill., May 4, 1882. Editor Manchester Journal, 1863-66; admitted to bar, 1866, and practiced at Manchester. Town clerk, 1866-73; register of probate, 1866-76; mem. Constl. Conv., 1870; mem. Vt. Ho. of Rep., 1872, 74, 82, Senate, 1878 (pres. pro tem); judge of probate, 1883-89; justice Supreme Court of Vt., 1889-1917 (chief justice 1915-17); declined reëlection. Republican. Home: Manchester, Vt. Died Mar. 24, 1921.

MUNSON, Myron Andrews, author; b. Chester, Mass., May 5, 1835; s. Garry and Harriet (Lyman) M.; A.B., Harvard, 1860, A.M., 1865; grad. Andover Theol. Sem., 1864; studied geology, Yale, 1885-86; m. Jessie Dewey Chidsey, Oct. 26, 1887. Pvt. 60th Mass. Vols., July 28-Nov. 30, 1864; ordained Congl. ministry, 1866; pastor, Pittsford, Vt., 1865-69, Northfield, Minn., 1870-71, Dorchester, Mass., 1874-76, Fairhaven, Vt., 1878-79; supt. of schs., 1882; instr. in Rollins Coll., 1889-90. Organized a Munson reunion, 1887, convening 500 kinsfolk; another, 1896. Republican. Author: Iron More Golden Than Gold, 1873; Duty Contemplated as Due-ty, 1874; Water as a Mirror of the Wisdom and Goodness of God, 1877; The Handwriting of God Upon Slate, 1881; Eulogy Upon Col. Samuel Lyman, 1877; The Munson Record (2 vols.), 1896; Traditions Concerning the Origin of the American Munsons, 1897; The Portsmouth Race of Monsons-Munsons-Mansons, 1910. Home: New Haven, Conn. Died Oct. 3, 1922.

MUNSON, Samuel Lyman, mfr.; b. Norwich (now Huntington), Mass., June 14, 1844; s. Garry and Harriet (Lyman) M.; ed. Williston Sem., Easthampton, Mass., and commercial coll., Albany, N.Y.; m. Susan Babcock Hopkins, May 21, 1868; children—Harriet Lyman, Anne Hopkins, Edward Garry, Paul Babcock, Samuel Lyman, Amy Treadwell, Robert. Became mem. Munson, Richardson & Co., 1867, later Munson & Dwight, mfrs. collars; conducted business alone, Jan. 1, 1869-Mar. 1, 1911, then pres. and treas. S. L. Munson Co. Rep. presdl. elector, 1900. Pres. trustees Madison Av. Dutch Ref. Ch.; v.p. Memorial Hospital, Albany. Pres. Weekapaug (R.I.) Chapel Soc.; mgr. State Soc. of S.R. and regent Phillip Livingston Chapter S.R.; pres. Masonic Veterans' Assn.; mem. nat. council Soc. of Founders and Patriots. Dir. Albany Chamber Commerce. Fellow Am. Geog. Soc. Life mem. Sulgrave Institution. Home: Albany, N.Y. Died May 19, 1930.

MUNSON, Thomas Volney, nurseryman, viticulturist; b. Astoria, Ill., Sept. 26, 1843; s. William and Maria (Linley) M.; bro. of William Benjamin M.; B.S., Ky. U., Lexington, 1870; M.Sc., State Agrl. and Mech. Coll., Ky., 1883, on thesis "Forests and Trees of Texas"; (D.Sc., Ky. State U., 1906); m. Ellen Scott Bell, 1870. Taught common sch. 3 yrs. in Ill.; prof. science, Ky. U., 1870-71; 3 yrs. at Lexington, Ky., in nursery business with wife's father; 3 yrs. at Lincoln, Neb.; then in business at Denison, Tex., as nurseryman and originator of new fruits. Mem. Texas World's Fair Commn., 1903-04; chmn. exec. com. Texas Farmers' Insts., 1902-03; mem. Internat. Jury of Awards, St. Louis Expn., 1904. Chevalier du Mérite Agricole, 1888, for aid to France in viticultural matters. Author: Foundations of American Grape Culture, 1909. Home: Denison, Texas. Died Jan. 21, 1913.

MUNSON, Welton Marks, horticulturist; b. Howell, Mich., Apr. 8, 1866; s. Ferdinand Walker and Frances (Lake) M.; B.S., Mich. Agrl. Coll., 1888, M.S., 1892; Ph.D., Cornell U., 1901; m. Mattie Allen, Dec. 26, 1901. Asst. in horticulture, Cornell, 1889-91; prof. horticulture and horticulturist, Me. Agrl. Expt. Sta., U. of Maine, 1891—. Deceased.

MUNSON, William Benjamin, capitalist; b. nr. Astoria, Ill., Jan. 7, 1846; s. William and Maria (Linley) M.; student Abington (Ill.) Coll., 1 yr.; B.S., Agrl. and Mech. Coll. (Ky. U.), 1869; m. Mary Ellen Newton, Sept. 3, 1876; children—Linley, Maud, Theda, William B., Eloise. Civ. engr. and contractor on constrn. of Rockford, Rock Island & St. Louis R.R., 1870-71; admitted to bar, Sherman, Tex., 1872; mem. Gunter & Munson, 1873-83, operating in land and investing largely in cattle, 1880-83; became owner of large cattle ranch in Randle Co., Tex.; bought First Nat. Bank, Denison, Tex., 1886, and became its pres.; organized, 1888, and pres. Denison & Washita R.R. Co., Southwestern Coal & Improvement Co., and operated coal mines at Coal Gate, Ind. Ty.; became pres. Sherman, Shreveport & Southern R.R. Co.; v.p. Denison, Bonham & New Orleans R.R., 1900-12; an organizer and v.p. Southern Surety Co., 1904-05; pres. Denison Light & Power Co., Denison Cotton Mill Co. Democrat. Home: Denison, Tex. Died Feb. 6, 1930.

MÜNSTERBERG, Hugo, psychologist; b. Danzig, Germany, June 1, 1863; s. Moritz M.; grad. Danzig Gymnasium, 1882; post-grad. studies in philosophy, natural sciences and medicine in Leipzig and Heidelberg, 1882-87, Ph.D., Leipzig, 1885, M.D., Heidelberg, 1887; (A.M., Harvard, 1901; LL.D., Washington U., 1904; Litt.D., Lafayette Coll., 1907); m. Selma Oppler, 1887. Instr. and asst. prof., U. of Freiburg, 1887-91; prof. psychology, 1892—, and dir. Pyschol. Lab., Harvard. Harvard exchange prof. at U. of Berlin, 1910-11. Organizer and 1st dir. of Amerika-Institut of the German Govt., 1910-11. V.p. Internat. Congress Arts and Sciences, St. Louis, 1904, Internat. Psychol. Congress, Paris, Internat. Philos. Congress, Heidelberg, 1908. Fellow Am. Acad. Arts and Sciences; v.p. Boston Authors Club; mem. Washington Acad. Sciences; pres. Boston German Assn. Author: Psychology and Life, 1899, Grundzüge der Psychologie, 1900; American Traits, 1902; The Americans, 1904; Eternal Life, 1905; Science and Idealism, 1906; Philosophie der Werte, 1908; The Eternal Values, 1909; Psychology and the Teacher, 1909; American Problems, 1910; Psychology and Industrial Efficiency, 1912; American Patriotism, 1913; Grundzüge der Psychotechnik, 1914; Psychology and Social Sanity, 1914; The War and America, 1914; The Peace and America, 1915. Editor of Harvard Psychological Studies, 1903—. Home: Cambridge, Mass. Died Dec. 16, 1916.

MUNZ, Friedrich, editor; b. Stuttgart, Germany, Mar. 24, 1865; s. Jacob and Katharine M.; student State Seminary, Esslingen, Germany; German College, Mount Pleasant, Iowa, 1886-89; (A.M., Central Wesleyan Coll., 1893; D.D., German Wallace Coll., Berea, O., 1897); m. Margaret Keller, 1886. Pres. German Coll., 1892-96. Editor Haus und Herd (family mag. in German), also German S.S. publs. issued by Jennings & Graham. Nat. pres. German Epworth League, 1900-12; dean theol. dept., Central Wesleyan Coll., Warrenton, Mo. Author: Homiletik, 1897; Verborgene Klippen, 1899; Der Krüppel von Nürnberg, 1902; Lobe den Herrn, 1905; Pilger Klänge, 1907; Der Jesuit; Die Bücher der Bibel, 1911. Mem. Gen. Conf. M.E. Ch., 1900, 04, 08, 12. Home: Warrenton, Mo. Died Sept. 14, 1916.

MUNZIG, George Chickering, portrait painter; b. Boston, 1859; s. Carl Ernest and Anna Marie (Kuhn) M.; ed. Brimmer Sch., Boston, and Acad. Julian and Lefebvre, Paris; unmarried. Engaged from 1872 as portrait painter in Boston; has painted portraits of Alfred Gwynne Vanderbilt and many other members of the Vanderbilt family, Mme. Melba, Mme. Theresa Tietjens, Mme. Theresa Carreno, Mrs. Agnes Booth, Mrs. James Brown Potter, Mrs. Stuyvesant Fish and many others prominent in society, gov. George Boutwell of Mass., etc. Home: New York, N.Y. Died 1908.

MURCH, Chauncey, clergyman, Egyptologist; b. W. Alexander, Pa., Jan. 1, 1856; s. Rev. James C. and Mary Ann (Strain) M.; ed. pub. schs. New Concord, O., Muskingum Coll., A.B., 1876, A.M., 1879; attended Xenia (Ohio) and Allegheny (Pa.) theological seminaries; (D.D., Western Univ. of Pennsylvania, 1899); m. Amelia S. Canfield, Aug. 4, 1880. Licensed by Allegheny Presbytery, Apr. 18, 1882; ordained by Northern Ind. Presbytery. Sent to Egypt by United Presbyn. Bd. of Foreign Missions, Oct. 1883. Home: Luxor, Egypt. Died 1907.

MURCHISON, Kenneth Mackenzie, architect and writer; b. New York City, Sept. 29, 1872; s. Kenneth M. and Katherine (Williams) M.; Ph.B., Columbia, 1894; studied École des Beaux Arts, Paris, 1897-1900; Litt.D. from Columbia U., 1929; m. Aurélie de Mauriac, Apr. 5, 1903; children—Katherine, Aurélie. Began practice at N.Y. City, 1902; architect of D.,L.& W. terminals, Hoboken, N.J., and Buffalo, N.Y.; Baltimore Union Sta.; Havana Union Sta.; Jacksonville Union Terminal; Munson S.S. Line Bldg., N.Y. City; Beaux-Arts Apts., N.Y. City; U.S. Marine Hosp., Staten Island; First Nat. Bank Bldg., Hoboken; New Colonial Hotel, Nassau; Dunes Club, Narragansett, R.I.; Sands Point (L.I.) Bath Club; also many co-operative apartment houses; former v.p. Central Savings Bank, New York; mem. bd. govs. Real Estate Bd. of New York. Served as capt., engrs., U.S.A., 1918-19. Decorated Officier d'Académie and Legion of Honor (France). Fellow Am. Inst. Architects. Home: New York, N.Y. Died Dec. 16, 1938.

MURDOCH, John, librarian; b. New Orleans, July 9, 1852; s. John and Elizabeth (Smith) M.; A.B., Harvard, 1873, A.M., 1876; m. Abby De Forest Stuart, July 23, 1884. Naturalist and observer U.S. Internat. Polar Expdn. to Point Barrow Arctic Alaska, 1881-83; librarian Smithsonian Instn., 1887-92; farmer, Middleboro, Mass., 1892-96; asst. in catalogue dept., 1896-1906, 1st asst., 1906-23, Boston Public Library. Trained in zoölogy at Mus. of Comparative Zoölogy, Harvard; has made spl. study of the Eskimos. Fellow A.A.A.S. Author: Natural History (in Report of Point Barrow Expedition), 1885; Ethnological Results of the Point Barrow Expedition, 1892. Home: Allston, Mass. Died Sept. 22, 1925.

MURDOCH, John Gormley, prof. of English; b. Pittsburgh, Oct. 11, 1861; s. William Anderson and Catharine (Fry) M.; A.B., Princeton, 1883, A.M., 1885; unmarried. Fellow in mental science, Princeton, 1883-84; teacher, Troy (N.Y.) Acad., 1885-1913; instr. English, 1887-1902, prof., Sept. 1902—, Rensselaer Poly. Inst. Socialist. Hon. mem. Rensselaer Soc. of Engrs. Author: Economics as the Basis of Living Ethics, 1913. Home: Troy, N.Y. Died Mar. 15, 1917.

MURDOCH, Thomas; b. Forres, Morayshire, Scotland, Oct. 26, 1829; s. John and Jane (Nicol) M.; ed. in Scotland; unmarried. Established as wholesale grocer, 1856; now pres. Reid, Murdoch & Co., Chicago. Home: Chicago, Ill. Died 1909.

MURDOCK, Charles Albert, printer, pub.; b. Leominster, Mass., Jan. 26, 1841; s. Albert H. and Charlotte Dorothy (Hills) M.; ed. Leominster High Sch.; widower. Moved to Calif., 1855; entered the printing business, 1867, retired in 1915. Editor of the Pacific Unitarian (monthly magazine), 1891—. Appointed register, land office, Humboldt, Calif., 1863; mem. Calif. Ho. of Rep., 1883; mem. Bd. of Edn., San Francisco, 1894-96; civ. service commr., 1902-03; mem. Bd. of Supervisors, San Francisco, 1907-16. Mem. bd. dirs. Calif. Sch. Mech. Arts, Associated Charities (San Francisco); Babies Aid Soc.; pres. Boys Aid Soc. Sec. William and Alice Hinckley Fund; trustee Henry Pierce Library; trustee Hathaway Fund. Treas. Pacific Coast Conf. Unitarian Ch. Republican. Author: Horatio Stebbins—His Ministry and Personality, 1921; A Backward Glance at Eighty, 1921. Home: Piedmont, Calif. Deceased.

MURDOCK, Harold, banker; b. Boston, Mass., 1862; s. Rev. John Nelson and Martha (Ballard) M.; hon. A.M., Harvard, 1916; m. Mary Lawson, 1890; 1 son, Kenneth Ballard. Pres. Nat. Exchange Bank, Boston, 1899-1907; v.p. Nat. Shawmut Bank, Boston, 1907-20. Dir. Harvard Univ. Press, 1920—. Fellow Am. Acad. Arts and Sciences. Author: The Reconstruction of Europe, 1889; Sir William Kircaldy of Grange, 1906; Earl Percy's Dinner Table, 1907; The Great Boston Fire, 1909; The Nineteenth of Apr. 1775, 1923; Earl Percy Dines Abroad, 1924; Bunker Hill, 1927. Home: Chestnut Hill, Mass. Died Apr. 5, 1934.

MURDOCK, Joseph Ballard, naval officer; b. Hartford, Conn., Feb. 13, 1851; s. Rev. John Nelson and Martha (Ballard) M.; grad. U.S. Naval Acad., 1870; m. Anne Dillingham, June 26, 1879. On N. and S. Atlantic stas., 1870-74; coast survey duty, 1875-79; instr. in physics, Naval Acad., 1880-83; elec. duty, Phila., 1884; torpedo sta., 1886-88; Asiatic sta., 1888-91; elec. duty, Navy Yard, New York, 1891-94; home and European stas., 1894-97; Naval War Coll., 1897-99; exec. officer U.S.S. Panther during Spanish-Am. War; exec. officer New York, 1899-1901; War Coll., Nov. 1900; comdr., June 16, 1901; capt., Jan. 22, 1906; rear admiral, Nov. 20, 1909. Comd. Alliance, Jan.-Oct. 1903, Denver, May 1904-Oct. 1905; duty at Navy Dept., 1906; comd. Rhode Island in cruise of fleet around the world, 1907-09; comdt. Navy Yard, New York, May 15, 1909-10; comdr. 2d Div. Atlantic Fleet, 1910-11; comdr.-in-chief U.S. Asiatic Fleet, 1911-12; retired on attaining age limit, Feb. 13, 1913. Ordered to duty at Navy Yard, Portsmouth, N.H., 1918, 19. Mem. N.H. Ho. of Rep., 1921, 23. Author: Notes on Electricity and Magnetism, 1884. Home: Hill, N.H. Died Mar. 23, 1931.

MURFEE, James Thomas, educator; b. Southampton Co., Va., Sept. 13, 1833; s. James Wilson and Anne (Parker) M.; C.E., Va. Mil. Inst., Lexington, 1853; m. Laura Owen, July 11, 1861; father of Hopson Owen M. Prof. natural science, Madison Coll., Uniontown, Pa., 1853-54, Lynchburg Coll., Va., 1856-58; prof. mathematics, U. of Ala., 1860-62; comdt. cadets (with rank of col. Ala. troops), U. of Ala., 1862-65; lt. col. 41st Ala. Regt., C.S.A., 1863; comd. cadets in engagement with Federal troops, Tuscaloosa, Ala., Apr. 3, 1865; architect and rebuilder U. of Ala., 1867-69; pres. Howard Coll., Ala., 1871-87;

founder, 1887, and supt., 1887-1906, Marion (Ala.) Inst.; retired on Carnegie Foundation, 1906. Mem. bd. visitors and chmn. com. instrn. and govt., U.S. Mil. Acad., 1893-96. Home: Tuscaloosa, Ala. Died Apr. 23, 1912.

MURFIN, James Orin, lawyer; b. Portsmouth, O., Jan. 7, 1875; s. James Orin and Josephine Hurd (Smith) M.; Litt.B., U. of Mich., 1895, LL.B., 1896, LL.D., 1938; m. 2d, Mabelle Chapin Jennings, Feb. 15, 1930. Began practice in Detroit, 1896; mem. Bowen, Douglas, Whiting & Murfin, 1897-1908. Mem. Mich. Senate, 1901-03; judge Circuit Court, 1908-12. Regent U. of Mich., 1918-26 and 1926-38. Chmn. Dist. Bd. 1, Eastern Dist. of Mich., World War. Republican. Home: Detroit, Mich. Died 1940.

MURFREE, Mary Noailles ("Charles Egbert Craddock"), author; b. Murfreesboro, Tenn., Jan. 24, 1850; d. William L. and F. Priscilla Dickinson M.; great g.d. Col. Hardy Murfree, of Revolutionary fame. For yrs. concealed her identity and sex under her pen-name. Author: In the Tennessee Mountains, 1884; Where the Battle Was Fought, 1884; Down the Ravine, 1885; The Prophet of the Great Smoky Mountain, 1885; In the Clouds, 1886; The Mystery of Witchface Mountain, 1895; The Young Mountaineers, 1897; The Champion, 1902; The Frontiersman, 1905; The Fair Mississippian, 1908. Home: Murfreesboro, Tenn. Died Aug. 1, 1922.

MURKLAND, Charles Sumner, educator; b. Lowell, Mass., May 20, 1856; s. John and Jean (Lambert) M.; A.B., Middlebury Coll., 1881, A.M., 1884 (D.D., 1900); S.T.B., Harvard, 1883; Ph.D., Dartmouth, 1893; m. Helen Mary Tupper, July 30, 1884. Ordained Congl. ministry, 1884; pastor Chicopee, Mass., 1884-86, Franklin St. Ch., Manchester, N.H., 1886-93; pres. N.H. Coll. Agr. and Mechanic Arts, 1893-1903; prin. Brewster Free Acad., Wolfboro, N.H., 1907—. Republican. Home: Wolfboro, N.H. Died Nov. 11, 1926.

MURLIN, Lemuel Herbert, univ. pres.; b. Mercer Co., O., Nov. 16, 1861; s. Orlando and Esther (Hankins) M.; A.B., De Pauw U., 1891, S.T.B., 1892; studied U. of Pa., 1896, Clark U., 1897; in Europe, 1898; B.D., Garrett Bibl. Inst., 1899; S.T.D., U. of Denver, 1897; D.D., Cornell Coll., 1897; LL.D., De Pauw, 1909, U. of Vt., 1911, Wesleyan, 1912, U. of Me., 1915, Harvard, 1921; m. Ermina Fallass (Ph.D., prof. modern langs., Cornell Coll.), Oct. 12, 1893. Teacher, pub. schools and in Ft. Wayne Coll., 1877-86; pastor Trinity Ch., Ft. Wayne, Knightsville and Vincennes, Ind., 1886-94; instr. De Pauw U., 1891-92; pres. Baker U., Baldwin, Kan., 1894-1911; pres. Boston (Mass.) U., 1911-25; pres. De Pauw Univ., 1925-28. Actg. pastor Am. Ch., Berlin, 1909-10, pastor, 1928-29. Mem. Gen. Conf. M.E. Ch. 5 times between 1900-24; chmn. Gov.'s Commn. on Higher Edn. in Kansas and Massachusetts. Home: Wayland, Mich. Died June 20, 1935.

MURPHREE, Albert Alexander, univ. pres.; b. Walnut Grove, Ala., Apr. 29, 1870; s. Capt. Jesse Ellis and Helen (Cornelius) M.; student Walnut Grove (Ala.) Coll., 1880-87, Peabody Coll., Nashville, Tenn., 1890-92; A.B., U. of Nashville, Tenn., 1894, A.M., 1902; LL.D., Rollins Coll., Fla., 1909; LL.D., U. of Ala., May 1919; m. Jennie, d. Col. John A. Henderson, of Tallahassee, July 27, 1897; children—Alberta, Mary (dec.), Martha, John A. H., Albert A. Began teaching in rural schs. in Tenn., 1887; was supt. Cullman (Ala.) city schs.; prin. Summit (Ala.) Inst.; prin. city high sch., Cleburne, Tex., 2 yrs.; prof. mathematics, 1895, pres., 1897-1905, Fla. State Coll.; pres. State Coll. for Women, 1905-09, U. of Fla., July 1, 1909—. V.p. Nat. Assn. of State Univs., 1921; pres. Fla. Bapt. Conv., 1922-24; v.p. Southern Baptist Conv., 1924-25. Editor Fla. School Exponent, 1907-09. Lt. col. gov.'s staff, Fla. Democrat. Baptist. Mason. Home: Gainesville, Fla. Died Dec. 20, 1927.

MURPHY, Alfred J., judge; b. Detroit, Mich., Jan. 1, 1868; s. James and Mary (Sexton) M.; B.A., Detroit U., 1887, M.A., 1889; LL.B., Detroit Coll. of Law, 1893; m. Margaret Wallburga Ducey, June 29, 1903; 1 dau., Margot. Began practice at Detroit, 1893; circuit judge, 3d Jud. Circuit of Mich., 1899-Feb. 1919; resigned to resume practice; candidate for justice Supreme Court of Mich., 1913; of counsel for Henry Ford in Ford libel case against the Chicago Tribune, 1919; elected judge Circuit Court, 1923, re-elected, 1929. Republican. Home: Detroit, Mich. Died Aug. 5, 1931.

MURPHY, Arthur Phillips, congressman; b. Hancock, Mo., Dec. 10, 1870; s. William H. and Sallie A. (Kanada) M.; C.E., Sch. of Mines and Metallurgy, Rolla, Mo., 1887; m. Jessie Boren, Mar. 12, 1904. Telegraph operator, 1888-93; admitted to bar, 1894; local atty. St.L.&S.F. Ry., 1889-1905; atty. for Creek Nation of Indians in Ind. Ty., 1903-05. Sec. Rep. Congressional Com., 1902-03; mem. 59th (1905-07) and 61st (1909-11) Congresses, 16th Mo. Dist. Republican. Episcopalian. Mason. Home: Rolla, Mo. Died Feb. 1, 1914.

MURPHY, Charles F., politician; b. New York, N.Y., June 20, 1858; s. John M.; ed. pub. and parochial schs.; married. Began work in wire works; later street car driver. Became leader 18th Assembly Dist., New York, 1892; was commr. of docks and ferries, New York, and treas. of the board; chmn. Tammany Democracy, 1902, and sachem, 1902—. Catholic. Home: New York, N.Y. Died Apr. 25, 1924.

MURPHY, Daniel D., lawyer; b. New Diggings, Wis., Aug. 22, 1862; s. John G. and Ellen (McCarthy) M.; grad. State Normal Sch., Platteville, Wis., 1883; LL.B., U. of Iowa, 1887; LL.D., Grinnell (Ia.) Coll., 1917; m. Henrietta Johnsen, June 16, 1888; 1 son, Clarence Francis. In practice at Elkader, Ia., Aug. 1, 1888—; v.p. Elkader State Bank; dir. St. Olaf Savings Bank, Elkport Savings Bank, Clayton Co. State Bank, Moresby Island Lumber Co., Ltd. Co. atty. Clayton Co., Ia., 1891-95. Mem. Ia. State Bd. Edn. from its orgn., 1909-July 1, 1925, pres. 1914-25; regent Columbia Coll., Dubuque; mem. State Board of Vocational Education; trustee Elkader pub. schs. Catholic. Candidate for Congress, 4th Ia. Dist., 1910. Home: Elkader, Ia. Died May 30, 1931.

MURPHY, Dominic I., consul gen.; b. Phila., Pa., May 31, 1847; A.B., Central High Sch., 1865; studied law; m. Mrs. Bessie T. Atkinson, Oct. 24, 1904. Clerk, supervising examiner, and chief clerk U.S. Pension Office, 1871-89; 1st deputy commr. of pensions, 1893-96, commr. of pensions, 1896-97; practiced patent law, 1902-04; editor and pub. The New Century (weekly jour.), 1903-05; sec. Isthmian Canal Commn., Apr. 20, 1904-May 31, 1905; consul at Bordeaux, France, 1905-09, at St. Gall, Switzerland, Apr. 10, 1909-14; consul at Amsterdam, Holland, Feb. 11, 1914-15; consul gen. at Sofia, Bulgaria, Feb. 22, 1915, at Stockholm, Sweden, July 8, 1919—. Detailed to London Consulate Gen. for spl. duty, as chief war claims dept. in charge of claims against British Govt., May 20-Oct. 15, 1915; in charge Brit. interest in Bulgaria, Aug. 1916-Dec. 1918. Received from British Government silver fruit bowl with "Thanks of British Nation for very special services" rendered British subjects, especially to prisoners of war and interned men in Bulgaria. Hon. commr. to International Maritime Expn., Bordeaux, 1907. Home: Washington, D.C. Died Apr. 13, 1930.

MURPHY, Edgar Gardner, author; b. Ft. Smith, Ark., Aug. 31, 1869; s. S. W. and Janie (Gardner) M.; alumnus U. of the South, 1889; (hon. A.M., Yale U., 1904; D.C.L., U. of the South, 1911); m. Maud, d. George A. and Martha Brigham King, of Concord, Mass., Aug. 31, 1891. Minister P.E. Ch., 12 yrs., withdrawing from ministry, 1903, to engage exclusively in ednl. and civic work. Was exec. sec. Southern Edn. Bd. and v.p. Conf. for Edn. in South; retired, by reason of ill health, 1908. Was organizer and sec. Southern Soc. for Consideration of Race Problems and Conditions of the South, holding nat. conf. at Montgomery, Ala., 1900; was also chmn. Ala. Child Labor Com.; organizer and 1st sec. Nat. Child Labor Com.; resigned, 1908. Editor Official Reports of Conf. on Race Problems of South, and of 6th, 7th and 8th sessions of Conf. for Edn. in South. Author: Words for the Church, 1896; The Larger Life, 1896; Problems of the Present South, 1904; The Basis of Ascendancy, 1909. Home: New York; and Montgomery, Ala. Died June 23, 1913.

MURPHY, Edmund Albert; b. Cincinnati, O., Mar. 4, 1861; s. Thomas F. and Catharine (Nolan) M.; ed. parochial high sch., and night sch., Cleveland; m. Anna B. L'Estrange, July 5, 1887; 11 children. Was gen. mgr. Cleveland Union Stockyards Co. 20 yrs.; pres. and gen. mgr. same, 15 yrs. (resigned, 1925), now chmn. bd. Pres. Chamber of Industry, Cleveland, 1913; chmn. War Bd. No. 1, World War. Republican. Catholic. Home: Cleveland, Ohio. Died Oct. 5, 1932.

MURPHY, Edward Jr., senator; b. Troy, N.Y., Dec. 15, 1834; s. Edward and Mary M.; ed. St. John's Coll., Fordham; m. Julia Delehanty, Sept. 27, 1866. Pres. Troy Gas Co.; v.p. Mfrs. Nat. Bank; treas. Kennedy & Murphy Brewing & Malting Co. Mayor of Troy, 1875-83; chmn. Dem. State Com. of New York, 1887-95; U.S. senator, 1893-99. Home: Troy, N.Y. Died 1911.

MURPHY, Evert James, dir. Federal Reserve Bank; b. Sewellsville, Belmont Co., O., Aug. 18, 1860; s. George Washington and Talitha (Taylor) M.; student Hopedale (O.) Coll. and Valparaiso (Ind.) U.; m. Rosella D. Hill, May 6, 1886; children—Grace G. (Mrs. D. N. Hunt), Geo. Curtis, James E. Teacher, pub. schs., Ill., 1881-95; traveling salesman, 1895-98; milling business, Ill. and Okla., 1898-1900; farmer and stock raiser, 1900—; owner of "Valley View Farm" —3500 acres; v.p. Security Nat. Bank, Clinton, Okla.; dir. Oklahoma City Br. of Federal Reserve Bank of Kansas City, 1924—, chmn. bd., 1926—. An organizer, 1904; and former mem. Okla. Territorial Bd. of Agr.; mem. Okla. Territorial Ho. of Rep., 1903, Senate, 1905. Mem. Bd. of Regents, Okla. Agrl. and Mech. Coll., 1905-07. Mem. Christian (Disciples) Ch. Home: Cinlton, Okla. Died June 1, 1929.

MURPHY, Francis, gospel temperance evangelist; b. Wexford, Ireland, April 24, 1836; common school edn.; m. Elizabeth J. Ginn, April 10, 1856. Served in Union army; delivered 1st public address in Portland, Me., April 3, 1870; organized temperance reform clubs of Me., and was 1st pres.; delivered 1st address in Pittsburgh, Nov. 26, 1876; there 45,000 people signed the pledge in what was called the "Old Home Church" in 5th Av.; the work spread until through the country over 10,000,000 had signed the pledge; afterward did successful work in England; served as chaplain in the war against Spain. Home: Pittsburgh, Pa. Died 1907.

MURPHY, Frank Morrill, financier; b. Jefferson, Me., Sept. 4, 1854; s. B. F. and Lucy (Oakes) M.; ed. pub. schs., Manitowoc, Wis.; m. Ethel M. Meany, Aug. 1, 1892. At age of 14 entered employ of Thomas Windiate, Manitowoc, Wis., who controlled several large commercial enterprises; later worked in lumber camps of Wis.; interested in stage transportation line in Calif., 1872-77, when moved to Ariz., and has been associated with development of that state from that time. Was associated with "Diamond Joe" Reynolds in operation of Congress Mine; sec. and promoter Santa Fé, Prescott & Phoenix R.R., 1891-92, pres., 1894—; pres. Prescott Nat. Bank, from its origin until 1910; became pres. Prescott & Eastern R.R., Bradshaw Mountain R.R., Ariz. & Calif. R.R. Republican. Home: Prescott, Ariz. Died June 23, 1917.

MURPHY, Franklin, governor; b. Jersey City, N.J., Jan. 3, 1846; s. William H. and Abby Elizabeth (Hagar) M.; acad. edn. Newark, N.J.; (LL.D., Lafayette Coll., 1901, Princeton U., 1902); pvt. to 1st lt. 13th N.J. Vols., 1862-65; m. Janet Colwell, June 24, 1868 (dec.). Established, 1865, and from then pres. Murphy Varnish Co. Mem. Newark Common Council, 1883-86; mem. N.J. Assembly, 1885; chmn. Rep. State. Com., 1892—; mem. Rep. Nat. Exec. Com., 1900-08; gov. of N.J., 1902-05; received 77 votes for vice-presidential nomination, Rep. Nat. Conv., Chicago, 1908; member Rep. Nat. Com., 1900—; U.S. commr. Paris Expn., 1900. Mem. bd. mgrs. Nat. Home for Disabled Vol. Soldiers, 1905-12. Pres. gen. Nat. Soc. S.A.R., 1898-1900. Pres. Essex Co. (N.J.) Park Commission. Home: Newark, N.J. Died Feb. 24, 1920.

MURPHY, Franklin William, lawyer; b. Pleasant Valley, Wis., Aug. 24, 1869; s. Edward Joseph and Mary Ann (McCue) M.; LL.B., U. of Minn., 1893; m. Estelle M. McGray, Dec. 11, 1895; 1 son, Franklin Mac. Admitted Minn. bar, 1893, practiced continuously at Wheaton, now also at Minneapolis; mem. Murphy, Johanson & Winter; engaged extensively in farming, banking and other business from 1899; pres. First Nat. Bank of Wheaton, 1932—; organizer West Central Minn. Development Assn., pres., 1912-16; member governing bd. Minn. State Fair, 1909-21, pres., 1919-20; chmn. Minn. Century of Progress Commn., 1932, 33; regional dir. Pub. Works Adminstrn., 4th Dist., 1933-34; mem. State Planning Bd. for Minn., 1934-35. Mem. bd. regents U. of Minn., term 1933-39; mem. Wheaton Bd. Edn. for 21 years; chmn. Legislative Com. of Nat. Corn Belt and other farm orgns. Independent. Presbyn. Mason. Has made extensive study of economics; also known as farm leader. Home: Wheaton, Minn. Died Nov. 22, 1940.

MURPHY, Frederick E., newspaper pub.; b. Troy, Wis., Dec. 5, 1872; s. James M. and Mary Ellen (McGraw) M.; student U. of Notre Dame, 1889-93; m. Katherine Connolly, Jan. 16, 1901. With Minneapolis Tribune from 1893, successively head of mech., circulation and adv. depts., pres. same paper, 1921—; also pres. Manistique Pulp & Paper Co., Manistique Light & Power Co., Mutual Holding Co., W. J. Murphy Co., Red River Farm & Land Co., Frederick E. Murphy Co.; owner and operator Femco Farms, 6,000 acres, Breckenridge, Minn.; breeder of pure-blooded Holsteins and Percherons. Del. to World Wheat Conf., Geneva, and London, 1933; mem. staff of tech. advisers to U.S. delegation to World Economic Conf., London, 1933; Am. rep. Internat. Wheat Advisory Com. of Internat. Monetary and Economic Conf., Rome, 1934. Republican. K.C. Home: Minneapolis, Minn. Died Feb. 14, 1940.

MURPHY, George H., U.S. consular service; b. Scuppernong, N.C., Sept. 28, 1860; s. Rev. Joseph W. and Sarah Mary Mathews (Vaughan) M.; m. Margarethe Schmidt, of Dundee, Scotland, Jan. 16, 1888. Apptd. Am. consular clerk, June 22, 1886; vice and deputy consul at Chemnitz, 1886-89; deputy consul gen., 1889-90, vice and deputy consul gen., Apr.-Dec. 1890, at Berlin; consular agt. at Hanover, 1890-93; vice commercial agt. at Luxemburg, 1893-96; apptd. vice consul at Colon, Jan. 17, 1898; designated to inspect consulates on west coast of Colombia, Central America and Mexico, 1898, designated to inspect certain consulates in Mex., Nov. 19, 1898; vice and deputy consul at Bremen, 1899-1900, at Magdeburg, Feb.-Dec. 1900; vice and deputy consul gen. at Frankfort, 1900-04; designated to inspect certain consulates in Germany, Nov. 18, 1904; consular agt. at St. Catharines, Ont., Mar. 1905-July 1906; consul-gen.-at-large, July 1, 1906-Apr. 1914; consul gen. at Cape Town, S. Africa, Apr. 27, 1914-Oct. 1920, at Zurich, Switzerland, Oct. 20, 1920—. Died Oct. 16, 1924.

MURPHY, Grayson M(allet)-P(revost); b. Phila., Pa., Dec. 19, 1878; s. Howard and Anita (Mallet-Prevost) M.; student Haverford (Pa.) Coll., 1896-98; grad. U.S. Mil. Acad., 1903; m. Maud Donaldson,

Apr. 19, 1906; children—Grayson M.-P., Robert Donaldson. Second lt. 17th Inf. U.S.A., 1903-07; mem. G.M.P. Murphy & Co.; pres. Fifth Av. Bus. Securities Company; dir. various companies. Mem. War Council and commr. for Europe of Am. Red Cross in France, 1917. Served in Spanish-Am. War as pvt. 1st Pa. Inf., and capt. Provisional N.G. of Pa.; World War as maj. and lt. col. Gen. Staff, 42d Div. in charge of operations; aviation officer A.E.F. in Great Britain, Nov. 1918-Feb. 1919. D.S.M.; Officer Legion of Honor (France); Commendatore Order of Crown of Italy; Comdr. Order of Leopold II. Home: New York, N.Y. Died Oct. 18, 1937.

MURPHY, J. Harvey, clergyman; b. Paterson, N.J., Apr. 28, 1882; s. John Francis and Anne (Van Emburgh) M.; student Rutgers Prep. Sch., 1900-02; A.B., Rutgers Coll., 1906; A.M., New Brunswick Theol. Sem., 1909; D.D., Central Coll., Pella, Ia., 1924; m. Sara Frances Harder, Nov. 24, 1909; children—Charles Harder (dec.), John Edward, Frances Harder. Ordained to ministry of Reformed Ch. in America, 1909; pastor First Reformed Ch., Phila., 1909-11, Trinity Ch., Amsterdam, N.Y., 1911-16, Central Av. Ch., Jersey City, N.J., 1916-21, First Reformed Ch., Hudson, N.Y., 1921—. Vice pres. Gen. Synod, Reformed Ch. in America, 1928, 1930, pres., 1938-39. English preacher at The Hague, 1931. Mem. bd. supts. New Brunswick Sem., 1924-29, Western Theol. Sem., 1934-39. Mason. Home: Hudson, N.Y. Died Sept. 19, 1941.

MURPHY, James Cornelius, architect; b. Louisville, Ky., Feb. 8, 1864; s. Cornelius and Honora (McNamara) M.; LL.B., U. of Louisville, 1890; m. Mary Sue Strain, June 18, 1890; children—Honor, Benita (Mrs. J. Merlin Guthrie), Mary Denis. Began as architect with brother, D. X. Murphy, at Louisville, 1881, partner D. X. Murphy & Bro., 1891—; firm architects for Louisville City Hosp., Federal Land Bank, Federal Reserve Bank, St. Agnes Ch., St. Joseph Infirmary, Waverly Hills Sanitarium, U.S. Marine Hospital (all of Louisville); also hospitals in 5 other states. Pres. Louisville Garage Corp.; v.p. Louisville Electric Mfg. Co. Member National Conf. City Planning; chmn. City Planning Commission, Louisville; member exec. com. Community Chest and American Red Cross, Louisville. Trustee U. of Louisville. Fellow Am. Inst. Architects. Republican. Mem. Knights of Columbus. Home: Louisville, Ky. Died Apr. 14, 1935.

MURPHY, John Benjamin, surgeon; b. Appleton, Wis., Dec. 21, 1857; s. Michael and Ann (Grimes) M.; M.D., Rush Med. Coll., Chicago, 1879 (LL.D., U. of Ill.), 1905, Catholic U. of America, Washington, 1915); M.Sc., Univ. of Sheffield, Eng., 1908; m. Jeanette C. Plamondon, Nov. 25, 1885. Practiced at Chicago, 1879-82; studied in Germany, 1882-84; resumed practice in Chicago; head of dept. of surgery and clin. surgery, Northwestern U. Med. Sch.; chief surgeon to Mercy Hosp.; 1st lt. U.S.A. Medical Reserve Corps, 1908. Received Lætare medal from Notre Dame U., 1902. Fellow Am. College Surgeons, Am. Surg. Assn., Royal Coll. Surgeons of England, 1913. Home: Chicago, Ill. Died Aug. 11, 1916.

MURPHY, J(ohn) Francis, landscape artist; b. Oswego, N.Y., Dec. 11, 1853; moved to New York, 1875; self-taught in art. First exhibited at Nat. Acad. of Design, 1876; received 2d Hallgarten prize, 1885, for his painting "Tints of a Vanished Past"; also, 1887, Webb prize of Soc. of Am. Artists. A.N.A., 1885, N.A., 1887. Home: New York, N.Y. Died Jan. 30, 1921.

MURPHY, John T., editor, pub.; b. Deerfield, Mass., Sept. 7, 1860; s. Daniel and Abigail (Guiness) M.; ed. Drury Acad., North Adams, Mass.; m. Elizabeth M. Flynn, Apr. 9, 1901; 1 son, Morgan. Formerly with Boston Globe, Springfield Republican, Troy (N.Y.) Times, North Adams Transcript, Pittsfield Jour., The Globe, St. Paul, Minn.; founder, 1890, and now pres. Evening Telegram, Superior, Wis.; owner Ft. Myers (Fla.) Press, 1914-18; large land owner in Fla.; treas. dir. Cayuna Iron Ore Co.; chmn. Rep. presdl. electors, Wis., 1921; chmn. gen. arrangements com., President Coolidge summer vacation, 1928. Home: Superior, Wis. Died Dec. 14, 1932.

MURPHY, Joseph Aloysius Charles, bishop; b. Dundalk, Co. Louth, Ireland, Dec. 24, 1857; s. Joseph and Mary (Haughey) M.; brought to U.S., 1866; ed. St. Ignatius Coll. (Loyola U.), Chicago; normal and higher lit. classes, St. Stanislaus Sem., Florissant, Mo.; philosophy and theology, Woodstock Coll., Md. Joined Soc. of Jesus (Jesuits), 1875; ordained priest R.C. Ch., 1888; mem. faculty various periods, St. Louis U., U. of Detroit, St. Mary's (Kan.) Coll.; teacher of classics, St. Xavier Coll., Cincinnati; professional and pastoral work, St. John's Coll., British Honduras, 1905-10; on staff Marquette U., 1910-19; named by Pope Pius XI, bishop of Birta, Mesopotamia, and vicar apostolic of British Honduras, Dec. 23, 1924. Established college mags.; Dial. at St. Mary's, Kan., 1890; Tamarack, U. of Detroit, 1896; Fleur de Lis, St. Louis U., 1900. Died Nov. 25, 1939.

MURPHY, Nathan Oakes, gov. Ariz.; b. Jefferson, Me., Oct. 14, 1849; s. B. F. and Lucy A. M.; pub.

sch. edn.; taught sch. in Wis., 1866-69; removed to Calif., 1870, Prescott, Ariz., 1883; m. Sarah E. Banghart, Aug. 6, 1884. Apptd. sec. Ariz. Ty., 1889; gov. Ariz. Ty., 1892-94, 1898-1902; del. to Congress, 1895-97. Home: Prescott, Ariz. Died 1908.

MURPHY, Richard Louis, senator; b. Dubuque, Ia., Nov. 6, 1875; s. John Stanford and Ann (White) M.; ed. high sch., Dubuque; m. Ellen Emma McGuire, June 16, 1917; children—Charles Joseph, Mary Louise, Aileen (dec.), Elinor Ann, Imelda, Ellen. Began as reporter for Telegraph Herald, 1892, city editor, 1892-1902, editor, 1902-14; collector internal revenue, Ia., 1913-20; income tax counselor, 1920-30; U.S. senator from Ia., 1933—, term 1933-39. Dir. Pub. Library, Dubuque. Democrat. Catholic. Elk. Home: Dubuque, Ia. Died July 16, 1936.

MURPHY, Samuel Silenus, supt. schs.; b. Greene Co., Ala., Oct. 8, 1867; s. Dr. Samuel Silenus and E. M. (Steele) M.; A.B., U. of Ala., 1890, A.M., LL.D., 1925; m. Marie Marechal, Dec. 1898; m. 2d, Edith Marechal, June 1909. Teacher from 1890; supt. pub. schs., city and county of Mobile, Ala., Sept. 1900—. Formerly mem. Ala. State Text-Book Commn. Rotarian. Presbyn. Home: Mobile, Ala. Died Nov. 4, 1926.

MURPHY, Starr Jocelyn, lawyer; b. Avon, Conn., June 17, 1860; s. Rev. Elijah Douglas and Harriette Luceannah (Jocelyn) M.; A.B., Amherst, 1881; LL.B., Columbia, 1883; m. Julia Brush Doubleday, June 9, 1887. Personal counsel and representative of John D. Rockefeller in his benevolences, 1904—; mem. Gen. Edn. Bd., Rockefeller Foundation; trustee and sec. Rockefeller Inst. for Med. Research; member China Med. Bd. (Rockefeller Foundation); sec.-treas. Bur. Social Hygiene. V.p., dir. Am. Linseed Co. and Colo. Fuel & Iron Co., and officer and dir. in other corps. Home: Montclair, N.J. Died Apr. 4, 1921.

MURPHY, Thomas, Presbyn. clergyman; b. County Antrim, Ireland, Feb. 6, 1823; came to U.S. 1834; grad. Princeton (with 2d honor), 1845; (D.D., 1872; LL.D., Washington Coll., Tenn., 1891); m. Ann Sortor, June 15, 1848. Pastor Frankford Presbyn. Ch., Philadelphia, 1849-94 (emeritus); 10 times delegate to gen. assembly Presbyn. church; commr., 1873, to gen. assemblies of Scotland and Ireland; in Irish assembly offered the resolution which was the first step toward the holding of the great Pan-Presbyn. Council; took the lead as chairman in organizing 22 new churches in Presbytery of Philadelphia; presided at "Log-College" anniversary, Sept. 5, 1889. Author: Cradle of the Presbyterian Church in America; Pastoral Theology; Pastor and People; Duties of Church Members to the Church. Home: Blawenburgh, N.J. Died 1900.

MURPHY, Thomas Dowler, art publisher, author; b. Monroe, Ia., July 4, 1866; s. Hugh M. and Caroline (Dowler) M.; A.M., Simpson Coll., Indianola, Ia., 1888; m. Ina Culbertson, Mar. 28, 1894; 1 son, Thomas C. Editor Red Oak Express, 1888-98; pres. Thomas D. Murphy Co., art pubs., 1901—; v.p. Red Oak Nat. Bank. Republican. Author: British Highways and Byways, 1908, 3d edit., 1909; In Unfamiliar England, 1910; Seven Wonderlands of the American West, 1912, 25; On Old-World Highways, 1914; On Sunset Highways, 1915; Oregon the Picturesque, 1917; New England Highways, 1924. Home: Red Oak, Ia. Died Sept. 15, 1928.

MURPHY, Thomas Edward, clergyman; b. New York, N.Y., Jan. 27, 1856; s. Myles and Bridget (Nolan) M.; acad. edn. at Coll. St. Francis Xavier, New York; later studied at Sault-au-Récollet, Can., 1875-76; West-Park-on-Hudson, N.Y., 1876-79; Woodstock Coll. Md., philos., 1879-82, theol., 1887-90. Ordained R.C. priest, Aug. 24, 1890; mem. Soc. of Jesus; prof. Latin and Greek, Georgetown U., D.C., 1882-87; v.p. same, 1891-93; pres. Coll. St. Francis Xavier, 1894-1900; prefect of studies, 1900-06, pres., Feb. 5, 1906-Oct. 1911, Holy Cross Coll., Worcester, Mass.; treas. Brooklyn (N.Y.) Coll., 1912-16; pastor St. Ignatius' Ch., Brooklyn, 1912—. Died Dec. 15, 1933.

MURPHY, William Robert, journalist; b. Wilmington, Del., 1885; Central High Sch., Phila., 1902; B.A., B.S., U. of Pa., 1906; M.A. from Board of Public Education, Phila. for "A School Survey"; postgrad. studies in English and philology, 1905-08. Staff, Evening Telegraph, Phila., 1904-13, as music, dramatic and lit. editor, later chief editorial writer; editorial writer, foreign editor, dramatic editor, etc., Evening Public Ledger, Phila., 1914-24; asso. editor Lit. Rev., Pub. Ledger, Phila., and Evening Post, New York, 1924-26; editorial staff, Pub. Ledger and Evening Ledger, 1927—. Phila. editor, Musical America, 1919—; editor Art Alliance Bull., 1933—. At different times asso. editor Musical Leader, Chicago, Young Americans (New York), The Editor, American Suburbs; editorial writer, Evening Times (Phila.). During war mem. field div. Council Nat. Defense, at Washington. Mem. War Savings Orgn., Treas. Dept.; mng. editor National Defense (official mag.). Charter mem. Phila. Operatic Soc. Author: Story of Philadelphia (pub. in celebration of "Founders' Week"),

1908; The Literary School; also "Stories of Operas" (syndicated). Home: Philadelphia, Pa. Died Apr. 1, 1936.

MURRAH, William Belton, bishop; b. Pickensville, Ala., May 1851; s. William (D.D.) and Mary S. M.; grad. Southern U., Greensboro, Ala., 1874; (D.D., Centenary Coll., La., 1887; LL.D., Wofford Coll., S.C., 1897); m. Beulah Fitzhugh, Feb. 1881. Joined North Miss. Conf., M.E. Ch., S., 1876; stationed at Oxford, Miss., 1877-81, Winona, Miss., 1881-85, Aberdeen, Miss., 1885-86; v.p. Whitworth Coll., Brookhaven, Miss., 1886-90; pres. Millsaps Coll., Jackson, Miss., 1892-1910; elected bishop M.E. Ch., S., 1910. Has been a representative of his ch. in all the important councils from 1890; mem. Ecumenical Conf., Washington, 1891, London, 1901, and fraternal messenger to Gen. Conf., Can., 1902. Publs. include popular addresses, lectures, sermons and contbns. to religious periodicals. Home: Memphis, Tenn. Died Mar. 5, 1925.

MURRAY, Arthur, major general U.S.A.; b. Bowling Green, Mo., Apr. 29, 1851; s. Samuel Fenton and Mary Frances M.; grad. U.S. Mil. Acad. (No. 2 in class), 1874; admitted to bar, U.S. Circuit Ct., St. Louis, 1895; honor grad. No. 1, Arty. Sch., Ft. Monroe, Va., 1880; m. Sara Wetmore De Russy, Apr. 29, 1880. Apptd. 2d lt. 1st U.S. Arty., June 15, 1874; instr. philosophy, U.S. Mil. Acad., 1881-86; acting judge advocate, Dept. of the Mo., 1887-91; acting adj. gen., Dept. of Dakota, 1891; apptd. capt. and q.m., 1896 (declined); prof. mil. science and tactics, Yale, 1896-98; capt. 1st Arty., 1898; acting judge advocate 1st Army Corps, and of depts. of Matanzas and Santa Clara, Jan.-May 1899; on duty in judge advocate gen.'s office, June-Aug. 1899; apptd. col. 43d U.S. Vol. Inf., Aug. 1899; comdg. sub-dist. Samar and Leyte, P.I., 1900; dist. comdr., 1st dist., Dept. of the Visayas, 1900-01; apptd. maj. and judge advocate, 1901 (declined); maj. artillery corps, Aug. 1, 1901; lt. col., Apr. 14, 1905; col., Oct. 1, 1906; brig. gen. chief of arty. U.S.A., Oct. 1, 1906; maj. gen., Mar. 14, 1911; retired, Dec. 4, 1915. Comdt. Sch. of Submarine Defense, 1901; comdr. Western Dept. and 3d Div., San Francisco, 1915; returned to active service as comdr. Western Department, 1917-18. Awarded Distinguished Service Medal. V. chmn. Am. Red Cross, 1915-16. Hon. mem. Berzelius Soc., Yale U. Author: A Manual for Courts-Martial, 1893; Mathematics for Artillery Gunners, 1893; Manual of Arms, Adapted to the Springfield Rifle (Caliber 45), 1898. Home: Washington, D.C. Died May 12, 1925.

MURRAY, Augustus Taber, univ. prof.; b. N.Y. City, Oct. 29, 1866; s. Robert Lindley and Ruth (Shearman) M.; A.B., Haverford Coll., 1885, LL.D., 1931; Ph.D., Johns Hopkins, 1890; studied univs. of Leipzig and Berlin, 1890-91; m. Nella H. Gifford, Sept. 2, 1891; children—Robert Lindley, Frederic Seymour, Francis King, Minerva, Lydia. Prof. Greek, Earlham Coll., 1888-90, Colo. Coll., 1891-92; with Stanford U., 1892-1932, formerly prof. Greek, then prof. classical lit.; annual prof. Am. Sch. of Classical Studies, Athens, Greece, 1922-23. Federal food administrator for Northern Unit of Santa Clara County, Calif., 1918. Mem. mng. com. Am. Sch. Classical Studies at Athens. President of College Park Assn. Friends; minister of Friends Meeting, Washington, 1929-34. Author: College Greek Compositions, 1902; transl. of The Antigone of Sophocles (with H. R. Fairclough), 1902; The Anabasis of Xenophon (edited with notes and vocabulary), 1914; transl. of The Odyssey of Homer (Loeb Classical Library), 1919; The Iliad (same series), 1925; Four Plays of Euripides, 1931; The Religious Poems of Whittier, with an Interpretative Essay, 1934; Private Orations of Demosthenes (Loeb Classical Library), Vol. I, 1936, Vols. II and III, 1939. Home: Palo Alto, Calif. Died Mar. 8, 1940.

MURRAY, Charles Bernard, chemist, metallurgist; b. Worcester, Mass., Apr. 6, 1866; s. Peleg Freeman and Mary (Prince) M.; grad. Worcester High School, 1883; B.S., Worcester Poly. Inst., 1887, Dr. Engring., 1937; m. Ellen Lincoln Robinson, Jan. 29, 1890; children—Philip Freeman, Mildred Alice (Mrs. Grover C. Burrows). Employed by Joliet (Ill.) Steel Works, 1887; chemist Buena Vista Furnace Co., at Buena Vista, Va., 1891-92, Minn. Iron Co., Two Harbors, Minn., 1892; chemist and metallurgist Carnegie Steel Co., Pittsburgh, 1892-1905; partner Crowell & Murray, 1907—, pres., 1927—. Registered professional engr., state of Ohio. Republican. Episcopalian. Mason. Author: Iron Ores of Lake Superior (with Benedict Crowell), 1911 (7 edits.). Home: Cleveland, O. Died Mar. 25, 1939.

MURRAY, Charles Burleigh, journalist; b. Brandon, Vt., June 10, 1837; s. Orson S. and Catherine Maria (Higgins) M.; acad. edn.; m. Sarah M. Powell, 1865 (died 1878); 2d, Anna Cora Thomas, 1884. Farmer along special lines, 1857-62; Cincinnati commission merchant, 1862-72. Established the Cincinnati Commercial Review (weekly), Mar. 1872; purchased Cincinnati Price Current, Aug. 1872, consolidating the two publications, sold the Price Current at close of 1912. Leading statistician of the pork-packing industry of the U.S., 1872-1912, and prominent authority on grain interests, crop information, etc.; supt., statistician and exec. sec., Cincinnati Chamber of Commerce, 1891-May 1911. Author and compiler: Life Notes of Charles Burleigh Murray. Home: Cincinnati, Ohio. Died Mar. 5, 1918.

MURRAY, Charles H., judge; b. San Francisco, Jan. 2, 1855; s. Henry Kennedy and Abbie Sheldon (Billings) M.; grad. Mt. Pleasant Acad., 1872; admitted to bar, 1876; m. Grace Peckham, Feb. 11, 1893. Rep. leader 8th Assembly Dist.; pres. Lincoln League; exec. mem. Republican Com.; chmn. 9th Congressional Com.; mem. Rep. State Com., 1894-96, 1902-08, 1908-12; mem. exec. com., 1904-06; was Rep. candidate for assembly, for dist. atty., Co. of New York, 1893; counsel to U.S. marshal, 1877; supervisor of census, 1890; spl. asst. U.S. dist. atty., 1892; police commr., New York, 1894; aqueduct commr., New York, 1897; quarantine commr. N.Y. state, 1901-05; pres. Rep. Co. Com., New York, 1904; judge N.Y. state Court of Claims, 1905-17. Home: New York, N.Y. Died Sept. 6, 1916.

MURRAY, David, educator, author; b. Bovina, N.Y., Oct. 15, 1830; grad. Union Coll., N.Y., 1852, (Ph.D., Univ. of State of N.Y., 1863; LL.D., 1874, Union Coll.; 1873, Rutgers Coll.); m. Martha Neilson, Dec. 1867. Prin. Albany Acad., 1857-63; prof. in Rutgers Coll., 1863-73; adviser to Imperial Minister of Education, Japan, 1873-79; received, 1878, decoration Rising Sun in recognition of services; sec. Regents of the Univ. of the State of N.Y., 1880-89; lecturer on history of edn. in Japan, Johns Hopkins, 1897. Author: Story of Japan; History of the Regents for the work on "Public Service of State of New York"; History of Education in New Jersey. Home: New Brunswick, N.J. Died 1905.

MURRAY, John Gardner, bishop; b. Lonaconing, Md., Aug. 31, 1857; s. James and Ann (Kirkwood) M.; ed. Wyoming Sem., Kingston, Pa., 1876-79; Drew Theol. Sem., N.J., 1879-81; m. Clara A. Hunsicker, of Osage City, Kan., Dec. 4, 1889; children—John Gardner, Clara H., Barbara (dec.), Ann K., Ruth, Esther. Engaged in business, 1881-92; deacon, 1893, priest, 1894, P.E. Ch.; in charge of missionary work in Southern Ala., 1893-96; rector Ch. of the Advent, Birmingham, Ala., 1896-1903, Ch. of St. Michael and All Angels, Baltimore, 1903-09; elected bishop of Miss., 1903, Ky., 1904 (declined both); consecrated bishop coadjutor of Md., Sept. 29, 1909, bishop of Md., Jan. 18, 1911; elected presiding bishop P.E. Ch., Oct. 1925, for term 1926-31 inclusive. Address: 409 N. Charles St., Baltimore, Md. Died Oct. 3, 1929.

MURRAY, John Scott, univ. prof.; b. Anderson, S.C., Sept. 23, 1857; s. Rev. John Scott and Claudia Rebecca (Edwards) M.; M.A., Furman U., Greenville, S.C., 1878; studied Johns Hopkins, Göttingen, Leipzig and Berlin univs.; LL.D., Furman, 1917, Mercer, 1917, U. of S.C., 1918; unmarried. Practiced law at Anderson, S.C., 1880-82; prof. Latin lang. and lit., U. of S.C., 1888-91, also Sanskrit, 1889-91; prof. Greek lang. and lit., 1892-1917, German, 1892-94, French, 1903-11, modern langs., 1917-18, Mercer U.; prof. ancient langs., Furman U., 1918-28 (emeritus); prof. Latin, Winthrop Summer Sch., Rock Hill, S.C., 1919, 20. Mem. Rhodes Com. of Selection for Ga., 1907-16; mem. Am. Philol. Assn., Classical Assn. Atlantic States, Johns Hopkins and Furman alumni assns. Democrat. Baptist. His valuable library was destroyed by fire when Furman Science Hall was burned in 1922. Home: Greenville, S.C. Died Jan. 12, 1930.

MURRAY, Lawrence O., government official; b. Addison Hill, Steuben Co., N.Y., Feb. 18, 1864; s. Thomas and Ellen M.; student Niagara U., 2 yrs.; LL.B., Metropolis Law Sch., New York, 1893; LL.B., New York U., 1893; LL.B., from law dept. of Regents of U. of State of N.Y., 1893; LL.M., Georgetown (D.C.) Coll., 1895; LL.M., George Washington U., 1894; D.C.L., Catholic U. of America, 1897; (LL.D., Niagara U., 1902); unmarried. Admitted to bar, 1893; pvt. sec. to asst. sec. of the treasury, 1893-96; chief of organization div., Treasury Dept., 1896-98; deputy comptroller of the currency, 1898-99; trust officer Trust Co. of America, New York, 1899-1902; sec. and trust officer Central Trust Co., Chicago, 1902-04; asst. sec. Dept. Commerce and Labor, 1904-08; comptroller of the currency, Apr. 1908-Apr. 1913. Address: Elkland, Pa. Died June 10, 1926.

MURRAY, Oscar G., railway pres.; b. Bridgeport, Conn., May 20, 1847; s. Alexander and Catherine (Nichols) M.; ed. at Bridgeport. Entered ry. service, 1872, as ticket agt. Galveston, Houston & Henderson Ry. at Galveston; with same road until 1880 in various positions to gen. freight and pass. agt.; gen. freight and pass. agt. Gulf, Colo. & Santa Fé Ry., 1880-85; traffic mgr. Mo. Pacific Lines in Tex., and Tex. & Pacific Ry., 1885-86; freight traffic mgr. Mo. Pacific Ry. at St. Louis, 1886-88; same, Cincinnati, Indianapolis, St. Louis & Chicago and its successors, the C.,C.,C.&St.L. Ry. and C.&O. R.R., 1888-92; 2d v.p., same, 1892-96; 1st v.p. in charge of traffic B.&O., Feb. 15-Feb. 29, 1896; receiver B.& O. R.R. jointly with John K. Cowen, Feb. 29, 1896-Apr. 1899; again 1st v.p., 1900-Jan. 1, 1904, pres. 1904-10, chmn. bd. dirs., Jan. 1910—, B.&O. R.R. Co. Address: B.&O. R.R. Co., 2 Wall St., New York. Died Mar. 14, 1917.

MURRAY, Peter, army officer; b. in Calif., Apr. 21, 1867; grad. U.S. Mil. Acad., 1890. Commd. 2d lt. 3d Inf., June 12, 1890; 1st lt. 5th Inf., Mar. 18, 1897; trans. to 21st Inf., July 21, 1897; capt. 18th Inf., Nov. 26, 1899; q.m., Aug. 24, 1907; maj. 22d Inf., May 10, 1911; assigned to 3d Inf., Sept. 1, 1914; trans. to 29th Inf., Mar. 1, 1915; lt. col., July 1, 1916; col. of inf. (temporary), Aug. 5, 1917; brig. gen. N.A., Feb. 8, 1918; col. of inf., Apr. 2, 1918. With 21st Inf., 5th Army Corps, Santiago, Cuba, 1898; with 21st and 18th Inf. in Philippine Insurrection, 1899-1901; with A.E.F., France, Dec. 1, 1917-May 12, 1918; comd. 3d Brig., 2d Div., Feb. 15-Mar. 15, 1918, in training area; on Verdun-St. Mihiel front, Mar. 15-May 8, 1918, when returned to U.S. on account of physical disability; col., Insp. Gen.'s Dept., May 25-June 12, 1918; col., Gen. Staff Corps, June 12, 1918—. Address: War Dept., Washington, D.C. Died Dec. 26, 1941.

MURRAY, Robert, brigadier gen. U.S.A.; b. Elk Ridge, Anne Arundel Co., Md., Aug. 6, 1822; s. Daniel and Mary (Dorsey) M.; ed. by tutors at home, pub. sch. in Howard Co., Md., and U. of Pa.; m. at Benecia, Calif., Adelaide S. Atwood, of Me., Jan. 10, 1861. Apptd. from Md., asst. surgeon U.S.A., June 29, 1846; capt. asst. surgeon, June 29, 1851; maj. surgeon, June 23, 1860; lt. col. asst. med. purveyor, July 28, 1866; col. surgeon, June 26, 1876; col. asst. surgeon gen., Dec. 14, 1882; brig. gen. surgeon gen. U.S.A., Nov. 23, 1883; retired by operation of law, Aug. 6, 1886. Bvtd. lt. col. and col., Mar. 13, 1865, for services during the war. Home: Elk Ridge, Howard Co., Md. Died Jan. 1, 1913.

MURRAY, Robert Drake, senior surgeon U.S. Marine Hosp. Service; b. Oblton, O., Apr. 21, 1845; s. Joseph Arbor and Nancy (Drake) M.; ed. common schools, Bluffton, O.; grad. Cleveland Med. Coll., 1868; Jefferson Med. Coll., Phila., 1871; m. Lillie, d. Rev. C. A. Fulwood, D.D., Key West, Apr. 18, 1875 (died 1887). Was 1st vol. from Niles, O., in Civil war; served in 7th Ohio vol. inf. and 12th Ohio Vol. cav. Was wounded 4 times and war prisoner. Prominent in quarantine and epidemic service; comd. 1st epidemic cordon in U.S., 1882, at Brownsville, Tex.; served during yellow fever epidemic at Key West, 1875; Fernandina, 1877; New Orleans, 1878; Florida, 1888; Brunswick, 1893; Mississippi, 1897, 1898; New Orleans and Key West, 1899. Mem. Am. Med. Assn., Am. Public Health Assn., Fla. Med. Assn., Tenn. State Med. Soc., Am. Pomol. Soc., N.Y. Medico-Legal Soc., Am. Assn. Polit. and Social Science, Am. Hist. Assn., A.A.A.S., S.A.R. Writer of yellow fever and quarantine articles published in Treasury Dept. Reports and med. jours. Address: U.S. Marine Hosp., Key West, Fla. Died 1903.

MURRAY, Samuel, sculptor; b. Phila., Pa., June 1870; s. William Murray and Margaretta (Hannigan) M.; pupil of Thomas Eakins; married. Awarded gold medal, 1894; hon. mention, Art Club of Phila., 1897. Exhibited at Paris Expn., 1900; hon. mention, Buffalo Expn., 1901; silver medal, St. Louis Expn., 1904; decorated Witherspoon Bldg., Phila., with prophets; represented in Fairmount Park, Phila.; statues of Commodore Barry, U.S.N. and Dr. Joseph Leidy, Phila.; Bishop Shanahan memorial, St. Patrick's Cathedral, Harrisburg, Pa.; Father Corby memorial, Notre Dame U., Ind.; statue of Admiral George W. Melville, League Island Park, Phila.; represented in the Met. Mus., New York; busts of Admiral George W. Melville, Archbishop Ryan; Pa. State Battlefield Monument at Gettysburg, Pa.; Father Corby statue, erected on the Gettysburg Battlefield; Deshong Memorial, Chester, Pa., statue of Senator Boles Penrose, Capitol Park, Harrisburg, Pa.; etc. Address: 3324 Lancaster Av., Phila., Pa. Died Nov. 3, 1941.

MURRAY, William D., lawyer; b. N.Y. City, July 17, 1858; s. John W. and Mary S. (Davidson) M.; A.B., Yale, 1880; LL.B., Columbia, 1882; m. Mary E. Mosher, Dec. 28, 1893; 1 son, George M. Practiced in N.Y. City, 1882-1938; member of International Committee Y.M.C.A., 1891—; trustee National Board of Y.W.C.A. Mem. of board of trustees of Eastern Association School; mem. National Council Y.M.C.A.; a founder and mem. exec. com. Boy Scouts America; trustee com. on work, John R. Mott, Inc.; trustee Committee on Promotion of Friendship between America and Far East; trustee, treasurer Trustees of World Student Christian Fed. Awarded Silver Buffalo by Boy Scouts America. Mem. Psi Upsilon Fraternity. Presbyn. Author: Life and Works of Jesus; Bible Stories to Tell Children, 1910; My Three Keys, 1920; Fun with Paper Folding, 1928; As He Journeyed (biography), 1929; What Manner of Man Is This?; The Message of the Prophets; History of Boy Scouts of America. Home: Plainfield, N.J. Office: 68 William St., New York, N.Y. Died Nov. 20, 1939.

MURRAY, William Francis, postmaster; b. Boston, Sept. 7, 1881; s. William Francis and Josephine (Madden) M.; grad. Boston Latin Sch., 1900; A.B., Harvard, 1904, LL.B., 1906; m. Mary A. Lappen, Aug. 11, 1912. In law practice at Boston, 1906—; mem. firm Brown, Field & Murray. Mem. Boston Common Council, 1904, 05; mem. Mass. Ho. of Rep., 1907, 08; mem. Gov.'s Council, 1910; mem. 62d Congress (1911-13), 9th Mass. Dist., and 63d Congress (1913-15), 10th Dist.; resigned, Sept. 1914; postmaster of Boston, Oct. 1, 1914—. Democrat. Catholic. Pvt. and corpl. Co. 10, U.S. Vol. Signal Corps, during Spanish-Am. War. Mem. Kappa Gamma Chi. Home: Charlestown, Mass. Office: 141 Milk St., Boston, Mass. Deceased.

MURRAY, William Henry Harrison, clergyman, author; b. Guilford, Conn., Apr. 26, 1840; grad. Yale, 1862; licensed to preach, 1863; pastor chs. in Greenwich and Meriden, Conn., 1864-68; Park St. Congl. Ch., 1868-73; also gave Sunday evening talks in Boston Music Hall, 1869-73; resigned pastorate in 1874; engaged in business pursuits; and preaching to independent congregations. Author: Camp Life in the Adirondacks, 1868; Music Hall Sermons, 1870-73; Words Fitly Spoken, 1873 L3; Sermons Delivered from Park Street Pulpit, 1874; Adirondack Tales, 1877; How Deacon Tubman and Parson Whitney Kept New Year, 1887; Adirondack Adventures; Adventures in the Wilderness; Busted ex-Texan; Cones for the Campfire; Daylight Land; Deacons; How J. Norton, trapper, Kept Christmas; John Norton's Thanksgiving; Lake Champlain; Mamelons and Ungava; Mystery of the Woods; Story the Keg Told Me. Address: Guilford, Conn. Died 1904.

MURRAY, William Spencer, cons. engr.; b. Annapolis, Md., Aug. 4, 1873; s. of James Daniel and Elizabeth (Spencer) M.; E.E., Lehigh U., South Bethlehem, Pa., 1895, Dr. Engr., 1923; m. Ella Day Rush, Sept. 23, 1907; children—Richard Rush, John Maynadier, William Spencer. In charge of electrification New York div. of N.Y.,N.H.&H. R.R., 1905-17; mem. McHenry & Murray, gen. ry. engring. and electrification, 1913-17; pres. Housatonic Power Co., 1917-19; chmn. U.S. Superpower Survey, 1912-21; chmn. bd. dirs. Murray & Flood, Inc. Fellow Am. Inst. Elec. Engrs. (v.p. 1913-14); mem. Chi Phi. Clubs: Engineers, Bankers (N.Y. City); Graduate (New Haven); Cosmos (Washington, D.C.). Home: Catskill, N.Y. Office: 7 Dey St., New York, N.Y. Died Jan. 9, 1942.

MUSE, William Foster, newspaper pub.; b. Milan, Ill., July 14, 1860; s. John Watters and Elizabeth (Millikin) M.; B.S., Cornell Coll., Ia., 1883; LL.D., 1927; A.B., Ill. Wesleyan; m. Lillian Duncan, of Cedar Rapids, Ia., July 16, 1889 (dec.); 1 dau., Elizabeth. Began as reporter Rock Island (Ill.) Union, 1883; mgr. and basso Ottumwa Male Quartet, 1896-99; editor Mason City (Ia.) Globe-Gazette, 1898—. Postmaster of Mason City, 1910-15. Trustee Cornell Coll. Mem. Sons of Vets., Phi Delta Theta. Republican. Methodist. Mason (K.T.), K.P., Elk. Clubs: Rotary, Mason City Country, Clear Lake Country. Author of book of travels around the world, 1927. Home: 22 River Heights. Office: Globe Gazette, Mason City, Ia. Died May 10, 1931.

MUSE, William Sulivane, brig. gen. U.S. Marine Corps; b. Dorchester Co., Md., Apr. 8, 1842; s. William H. (M.D.) and Elizabeth Richardson (Sulivane) M.; ed. pvt. sch. and Cambridge Acad.; unmarried. Entered U.S. vol. navy, May 11, 1862; commd. 2d lt. U.S. Marine Corps, Mar. 18, 1864; 1st lt., Apr. 24, 1867; capt., Dec. 18, 1880; maj., June 2, 1898; lt. col., Mar. 3, 1899; col., Jan. 31, 1900; brig. gen., June 29, 1906; retired, Aug. 14, 1900. Episcopalian. Republican. Home: Cambridge, Md. Died 1911.

MUSGRAVE, George Clarke, soldier, author; b. Folkstone, Eng., May 1, 1873; s. Rev. J. J. M.; A.B., City of London Coll.; Royal Arty. Coll., Woolwich, Eng. Exploration in Africa; capt. Cuban Army, 1896; attaché intelligence dept. U.S. Army, Santiago Campaign, 1898; scout Boer War, S. Africa, 1899-1900; spl. medal "for valor in the field." Author: The Cuban Insurrection, 1898; Under Three Flags in Cuba, 1899; In South Africa with Buller, 1900; Under Four Flags for France, 1918. Home: New York, N.Y. Deceased.

MUSGRAVE, Harrison, lawyer; b. Charlotte, Mich., Oct. 28, 1860; s. Joseph and Miranda S. (Pancoast) M.; student Olivet (Mich.) Coll., 1876-77, U. of Mich., 1878-80; LL.B., Columbian (now George Washington) U., 1884; m. Meta D. Kimberly, Nov. 7, 1899. Practiced in Chicago, 1885—; now mem. Musgrave, Oppenheim & Lee; specializes in corp. and commercial law. Republican. Home: Chicago, Ill. Died July 18, 1921.

MUSGRAVE, William Everett, M.D., editor; b. Farmington, Tenn., Sept. 12, 1869; s. William Everett and Susan Casander (Thomas) M.; M.D., George Washington U., 1901; m. 2d, Florence Moore, Oct. 31, 1921. Pathologist, Bur. Science, Manila, P.I., 1902-09; prof. medicine and dean Coll. Medicine, also dir. Philippine Gen. Hosp.; dir. of hosps., U. of Calif. for several yrs. from 1918; editor Calif. and Western Medicine, and of Better Health Magazine. Acting asst. U.S. Army, 1901-03; capt. M.C., World War. Home: Ben Lomond, Calif. Died Mar. 9, 1927.

MUSICK, John Roy, author; b. St. Louis Co., Mo., Feb. 28, 1849; grad. N. Mo. State Normal School, B.S., 1874; read law; admitted to Mo. bar, 1877 practiced until 1882; from then devoted to journalism and authorship; m. Augusta P. Roszelle, June 13, 1876. Author: Columbian Historical Novels (12 vols., comprising the History of the United States in 12 stories); Hawaii; Our New Possessions; History Stories of Missouri. Home: Kirksville, Mo. Died 1901.

MUSIN, Ovide, violinist, teacher; b. Nandrin, suburb of Liege, Belgium, Sept. 22, 1854; s. Jaques and Louise (de Mille) M.; grad. with highest distinction, Royal Conservatory, Liege, 1868; pupil of Henri Leonard; m. Annie Louise Hodges-Tanner (soprano), Oct. 7, 1891. Toured widely as soloist in Europe, also with leading singers and pianists; first came to U.S., 1884, and later appeared with own concert co. in the leading cities of U.S., Can. and Mexico, and made 2 tours of the world; spl. virtuoso prof. of violin, by appmt. of King Leopold, Royal Conservatory, Liege, 1899-1908; resigned to establish Belgian Violin Sch. in N.Y. City. Decorated Comdr. Order of the Crown and Officer Order of Leopold (Belgian); Comdr. Order of the Nisham Uftikar (French); also Officer Pub. Instrn. of France, Holland, etc. Catholic. Author: (with Henri Leonard) Belgian School for Violin (4 vols.). Composer: (violin solos) Caprice de Concert, No. 1 and No. 2, with Orchestra; Mazurka Romantique; Mazurka de Bravoure No. 2; Valse de Concert; Lullaby and Prayer. Wrote life story, "My Memories," and pub. of own works. Home: New York, N.Y. Died Nov. 24, 1929.

MUSSER, George Washington, judge; b. in Sacramento Valley, Calif., May 15, 1862; s. Christian and Mary (O'Reilley) M.; B.S., Northern Ind. Normal Sch. (now Valparaiso U.), 1886; m. Belle McCoy, Apr. 2, 1891. Admitted to bar, Nov. 1891; practiced at Colorado Springs, Colo., 1893-1909; justice Supreme Ct., Colo., term 1909-15; resumed law practice. Democrat. Mason (Grand Master of Colo., 1909-10), Odd Fellow. Home: Denver, Colo. Died Aug. 7, 1921.

MUSSER, John Herr, physician; b. Strasburg, Pa., June 22, 1856; s. Benjamin (M.D.) and Naomi (Herr) M.; ed. Pa. State Normal Sch.; M.D., U. of Pa., 1877; m. Agnes Harper, Sept. 16, 1880. In practice at Phila. from 1877, confining practice to internal medicine; instr., 1881-84, asst. prof., 1884, later prof. clin. medicine, U. of Pa.; pathologist to Presbyn. Hosp., 1884-88; phys. to Phila., Univ., and Presbyn. hosps.; consulting phys. Jewish Hosp., W. Phila. Hosp. for Women, Germantown, Chestnut Hill hosps. and Mercy Hosp. (Springfield, Mass.). Fellow Coll. Physicians. Author Medical Diagnosis (5 edits.). Editor: Nothnagel's Practice, Vol. IV—Diseases of the Lungs, Pleura; A Handbook of Practical Treatment (Musser and Kelly). Died Apr. 3, 1912.

MUSSEY, Ellen Spencer, lawyer; b. Geneva, O., 1850; d. Platt R. (author Spencerian System of Penmanship) and Persis Duty Spencer; acad. education; read law in office of Gen. Mussey, and at Cornell; LL.M., Washington Coll. of Law, 1899; LL.D. from the same institution in 1927; m. Gen. Reuben Delavan Mussey, June 14, 1871 (died 1892). Admitted to bar, 1893, to bar of Supreme Court of U.S., 1896. Was attorney for several foreign legations; counsel for several national patriotic and labor organizations; founder and hon. dean Washington Coll. Law; secured from Congress bill giving mothers in D.C. same right to their children as the fathers; also giving married women the right to do business and to control their own earnings; and secured 1st appropriation for public kindergarten in D.C. One of founders Am. Nat. Red Cross; past pres. Legion of Loyal Women; chmn. women's citizens' com. for 36th Nat. G.A.R. Encampment, Washington, 1902; v.p.-gen. D.A.R.; v.p. bd. of edn., Washington. Chairman Com. on Legal Status of Women, Nat. Council of Women. First woman to hold position as dean of a law sch., afterwards hon. dean. Home: Washington, D.C. Died Apr. 21, 1936.

MUSTARD, Wilfred Pirt, univ. prof.; b. Uxbridge, Ont., Can., Feb. 18, 1864; s. John and Mary (Pirt) M.; scholar, U. of Toronto, 1882-86, A.B., with gold medal in classics, 1886, fellow, 1886-89, examiner, 1889-91, A.M., 1890; fellow Johns Hopkins, 1890-91, Ph.D., 1891; D.Litt., U. of Toronto, 1921; m. Charlotte Rogers Smith, Aug. 5, 1921; prof. of Latin, Colorado Coll., 1891-93; instr. Latin, 1893-94, prof., 1894-1907, Haverford (Pa.) Coll.; collegiate prof. Latin, Johns Hopkins, 1907-19, prof., 1919—. Corr. fellow Royal Virgilian Acad. of Mantua, 1922; corr. mem. Classical Assn. of England, 1924; asso. editor Am. Jour. of Philology, etc. Presbyn. Author: Selections from Ovid's Metamorphoses, 1893; Classical Echoes in Tennyson, 1904; The Eclogues of Baptista Mantuanus, 1911; The Piscatory Eclogues of Jacopo Sannazaro, 1914; The Eclogues of Faustus Andrelinus and Ioannes Arnoletus, 1918; The Sacred Eclogues of Antonio Geraldini, 1924; Aeneas Silvius, De Curialium Miseriis, 1928; The Eclogues of Henrique Caiado, 1932. Home: Baltimore, Md. Died July 30, 1932.

MUZIO, Claudia, soprano; b. Pavia, Italy, 1892; pupil, piano and voice, of Mme. Casaloni, of Turin. Début as Manon, at Arezzo, Feb. 7, 1912; sang in Italian cities and in S. America, Paris and London; New York début with Met. Opera Co. as Tosca, Dec. 4, 1916; repertoire includes Carmen, Norma, Gilda, Mimi, Desdemona, etc. Died May 24, 1936.

MUZZARELLI, Antoine (Jules César Venceslas Ermanigilde), educator; b. Angoulême, France, Sept. 20, 1847; A.M., Univ. of Lyons; studied civ. and mil. engring.; grad. École Centrale des Arts et Manufactures, Paris; m. Mary Prescott Brandow, Nov. 5, 1898. Entered French army in corps of engrs., 1867; served through Franco-German war (wounded at Coulmiers, nr. Orléans), and in Paris against communards, 1871; twice imprisoned by communists; sent to Chile and Peru by French Sec. of War as war corr.; became active politician with Gambetta, and pres. Democratic com. in Paris under McMahon; arrested and sent to prison for pub. political manifestation in Paris, 1876; came to U.S., 1877; became teacher of modern lang. and lit. Made Officier d'Académie by decree of French govt. Aug. 8, 1896, for distinguished services in the cause of education. Mason. Author: The Academic French Course (2 vols. and 2 vols. of keys), 1892; A Brief French Course, 1901; Le Pays de France, 1902. Editor: Le Barbier de Séville (with notes and full vocabulary), 1902. Lt. Grand Comdr., deputy for U.S. and Canada. Home: New York, N.Y. Deceased.

MYER, Albert Lee, brig. gen. U.S.A.; b. Troy, N.Y., Nov. 14, 1846; s. Col. Aaron B. and Julia A. M.; ed. pub. schs. of Troy; m. Minnie B. Henderson, June 15, 1870. Served as pvt. Co. F, 3d Battalion, 11th U.S. Inf., and sergt. and q.m.-sergt. Co. F, 29th Inf., Oct. 26, 1865-June 11, 1868; apptd. from army, 2d lt. 29th Inf., Dec. 6, 1867; transferred to 11th Inf., Apr. 25, 1869; 1st lt., June 28, 1878; capt., Dec. 8, 1886; maj., Mar. 2, 1899; lt. col. 27th Inf., Apr. 22, 1901; transferred to 11th Inf., Aug. 1, 1901; col. 17th Inf., Feb. 23, 1903; transferred to 11th Inf., Mar. 24, 1903; brig. gen. U.S.A., Mar. 23, 1907; retired. Mason. Died July 16, 1914.

MYER, Isaac, lawyer, author; b. Phila., March 5, 1836; academic edn.; grad. Univ. of Pa., law dept., 1857; admitted to Pa. bar, and, 1889, to N.Y. bar; m. Mrs. Mary H. (Abbott) Sharpsteen, June 1889. At one time U.S. Commr. Western Pa.; contributor to periodicals; now contributing to Monumental Records (New York) on Ancient Egyptian subjects. Author: Presidential Power Over Personal Liberty, 1862; The Waterloo Medal, 1885; The Qabbalah; The Philosophy of Ibn Gebirol, or Avicebron, 1888; On Dreams, by Synesius, 1888; Scarabs, 1894; The Oldest Books in the World: Taken from Papyri and Monuments, 1900. Home: New York, N.Y. Died 1902.

MYER, Jesse Shire, physician; b. Salisbury, Mo., Dec. 17, 1873; s. Jacob and Mary (Shire) M.; A.B., and Pe.B., U. of Mo., 1893; M.D., Marion Sims Coll. Medicine (Med. Dept. St. Louis U.), 1896; post-grad. work, Berlin, Strassburg and Vienna, 1896-98, 1906; m. Helen Rosenberg, Nov. 4, 1907. Instr. clin. chemistry and microscopy, Marion Sims Coll. Medicine, St. Louis, 1898-1902; similar position, Med. Dept. Washington U., 1902-12, asso. in medicine, 1912—; specialist in internal medicine; phys. to Jewish Hosp.; formerly visiting phys. St. Louis City Hospital. Author: Life and Letters of Dr. William Beaumont, 1912. Home: St. Louis, Mo. Died Oct. 29, 1913.

MYER, Joseph Charles, coll. dean; b. Newark, N.J., May 15, 1893; s. John H. and Susan (Ebert) M.; B.S., Dartmouth, 1917; C.P.A., N.J., 1925, N.Y., 1930; LL.D., St. John's Coll., Brooklyn, N.Y., 1931; m. Eleanor K. Schilling, Apr. 27, 1920. Clerk, Pace & Pace, accountants, N.Y. City, 1919-21; accountant and instr., Pace Inst., 1921-27; organizer, 1927, then dean of St. John's Coll. Sch. of Accounting, Commerce and Finance; proprietor of Standard Text Press. Served as 2d lt. inf., U.S.A., 1917-19. K.C., Elk. Author: Standard Accounting Text (21 vols.), 1927; Audit Procedure Reminder, 1931. Home: Lakewood, N.J. Died Apr. 5, 1934.

MYERS, Barton, capitalist; b. Norfolk, Va., Mar. 29, 1853; s. Moses and Julia Grammer (Barton) M.; ed. pvt. schs.; m. Katherine Macky Baldwin, Dec. 27, 1882; children—Robert Baldwin, Katherine Barton, Louisa Barton (wife of Rev. J. Hubard Lloyd), Francis Stuart, Barton. Apptd. vice consul at Norfolk, for British Govt., 1877, consul 1918-24 (retired). Mayor of Norfolk, 1886-88; chmn. Port Commn., Norfolk. Mem. Nat. Foreign Trade Council; mem. Chamber of Commerce, Norfolk (pres. 1914-20). Active as agt. War Dept. during World War. Democrat. Episcopalian. Home: Norfolk, Va. Died Dec. 23, 1927.

MYERS, Clifford R., archivist; b. Mason, W.Va., Oct. 16, 1886; s. Edward Brindsley and Anna Elizabeth (Braudy) M.; A.B., W.Va. U., 1907, A.M., 1909; studied U. of Chicago, summers 1914, 15; m. Emelyn Dowell Morton, June 21, 1924. Asst. supt. pub. schs., Ravenswood, W.Va., 1909-10; instr. high sch., Clarksburg, 1910-13, Concord State Normal Sch., 1913-14, high sch., Hibbing, Minn., 1914-16; state historian and archivist, W.Va., July 17, 1919—. Mem. Co. E, 131st Inf., 33d Div., U.S.A., World War; lost leg in action at Hamel, Somme, France, July 4, 1918. Methodist. Mason, Odd Fellow, Elk, Kiwanian. Home: Charleston, W.Va. Died Feb. 27, 1936.

MYERS, Cortland (Roosa), clergyman; b. Kingston, N.Y., June 3, 1864; s. Abram and Martha (Osterhoudt) M.; A.B., Univ. of Rochester, 1887; grad. Rochester Theol. Sem., 1890; D.D., Temple Univ., 1899, LL.D., 1920; m. Jennie Estelle Williams, July 8, 1890; 1 son, Cortland. Ordained Bapt. ministry, 1890; pastor First Ch., Syracuse, 1890-93, 1st Ch., Brooklyn, from 1893, Tremont Temple, Boston, until 1921. Author: Making a Life, 1899; The New Evangelism; The Attractive Church; The Boy Jesus, 1908; The Real Holy Spirit, 1909; Real Prayer, 1912; The Man Inside, 1916; Money Mad, 1917; Dangers of Crooked Thinking, 1924; How Do We Know?, 1927; The Fact of a Future Life, 1931. Home: Los Angeles, Calif. Died Dec. 26, 1941.

MYERS, Frank Kerchner, judge; b. Wilmington, N.C., Mar. 7, 1874; s. Charles D. and Lossie (de Rosset) M.; grad. Cape Fear Acad., Wilmington, 1889; m. Roberta Atkinson Smith, Apr. 20, 1897; children—Josephine Macon (Mrs. John A. Vincent), Elizabeth de Rosset (Mrs. Burnet R. Maybank), Frank K. With audit and maintenance dept. A.C.L. R.R., 1890-94; admitted to S.C. bar, 1896, law clk. and ct. reporter, 1894-1908; master in equity, Charleston Co., S.C., 1908-34; U.S. dist. judge, 1934—. Democrat. Episcopalian. Mason, K.P. (Supreme Rep.). Home: Charleston, S.C. Died Aug. 2, 1940.

MYERS, George Sylvester, judge; b. Risingsun, O., April 21, 1881; s. Albert Schweitzer and Hannah (Neukom) M.; student Ohio Northern U., 1898-99, Wooster Coll., 1903-07; LL.B., Western Reserve U., 1910; m. Louise Birch Myers, Oct. 14, 1915; children—John Albert (dec.), Jane Carson (dec.). Admitted to Ohio bar, 1910, and began practice of law at Cleveland; mem. of Ohio Gen. Assembly from Cuyahoga Co., 1917-20; sec. of state of Ohio, 1933-37; elected asso. justice Ohio Supreme Court for term, 1937-42. Democrat. Episcopalian. Home: East Cleveland, O. Died May 9, 1940.

MYERS, George William; b. Champaign Co., Ill., Apr. 30, 1864; s. Robert Henry and Mary Helen (Shawhan) M.; B.L., Univ. of Ill., 1888, M.L., 1891; studied engring., Univ. of Ill., and science, U. of Munich, Ph.D., 1896; m. Mary Eva Sin, June 27, 1889; children—Sarah Helen, Joseph William, Margaret Elizabeth, Eleanor (dec.). Instr., asst. prof. and asso. prof. mathematics, 1888-96, asso. prof. astronomy and mathematics and dir. of obs., 1896-97, prof. astronomy and applied mathematics and dir. of obs., 1897-1900, U. of Ill.; head of astronomy and mathematics, Chicago Inst., 1900-01; prof. teaching of mathematics and astronomy, College of Education, Univ. of Chicago, 1901-29. Author: Rational Elementary and Grammar School Arithmetics; Myers-Brooks Elementary and Grammar School Arithmetics, 1907; Myers Arithmetics (three). Joint author: First Year Mathematics for Secondary Schools, 1907; Geometric Exercises for Algebraic Solution, 1907; Second-Year Mathematics for Secondary Schools, 1909; Teachers' Manual for First-Year Mathematics, 1911; Myers and Atwood, Algebra; Myers' Elementary Algebraic Geometry, 1921; editor and joint author of Standard Mathematical service; etc. Home: Chicago, Ill. Died Nov. 23, 1931.

MYERS, James Jefferson, lawyer; b. Frewsburg, N.Y., Nov. 20, 1842; s. Robert and Sabra (Tracy) M.; A.B., Harvard, 1869, A.M., LL.B., 1872. In practice at Boston, 1874—; pres. and dir. Conrey Placer Mining Co., Poor Farm Placer Mining Co., Shaler Water Power Co.; v.p., dir. Cambridge Trust Co.; dir. Walworth Mfg. Co. Mem. Mass. Legislature, 1893-1903 (speaker of House, 1900-03). Republican. Home: Cambridge, Mass. Died Apr. 13, 1915.

MYERS, Jerome, artist; b. Petersburg, Va., Mar. 20, 1867; s. Abram and Julia (Hillman) M.; art edn., Cooper Union, New York, Art Students' League; m. Ethel Klinck, Oct. 25, 1905; 1 dau., Virginia. Awarded bronze medal, St. Louis Expn., 1903; Clarke prize, Nat. Acad. Design, 1919; 2d, Altman prize, National Academy of Design, 1931; Carnegie prize, 1936; Altman prize, 1937. Represented in Met. Mus. of Art, Brooklyn Mus. Art, Art Inst. Chicago, Phillips Memorial Gallery, Corcoran Gallery (Washington), Rochester Art Mus., Milwaukee Art Inst., Newark Mus., Los Angeles Mus., Del Gado Mus. (New Orleans), Whitney Am. Museum of Art, John Gellatly Collection owned by Smithsonian Instn. Awarded Isador gold medal, Nat. Acad. Design, 1938. Nat. Academician. Home: New York, N.Y. Died June 19, 1940.

MYERS, Johnston, clergyman; b. Kingston, N.Y., Dec. 14, 1859; s. Abram and Martha (Osterhoudt) M.; A.B., U. of Rochester, 1882; B.D., Rochester Theol. Sem., 1885, D.D.; D.D., Georgetown, 1895, Ewing Coll., 1897, U. of Rochester, 1912; m. Mary Rachel Bonsall, Dec. 1891; children—Martha (Mrs. Malcolm Hart), Robert B., Dorothy (Mrs. Jerome Keith). Ordained Bapt. ministry, 1885; pastor Ninth St. Ch., Cincinnati, 1885-95, Immanuel Ch., Chicago, 1895-1926. Trustee Chicago Theol. Sem., 1896-1910; pres. Bapt. Ministers' Conf. of Chicago many yrs.; 1st v.p. Northern Bapt. Conv. Mason. Home: Chicago, Ill. Died Oct. 29, 1935.

MYERS, Paul Noxon, mfr. paper products; b. Larchmont, N.Y., May 1, 1878; s. Walter Frederick and Mary Frances (Hovey) M.; student high sch., St. Paul, Minn., and St. John's Mil. Acad., Delafield, Wis.; m. Reine Humbird, May 17, 1906; children—Paul N., John Humbird, Elizabeth. With Wright, Barrett & Stilwell, wholesale paper, St. Paul, 1895-1914; now pres. Waldorf Paper Products Co.; v.p. Motor Power Equipment Co.; dir. many companies. Pres. St. Paul Community Chest, 1923-24. Trustee Carlton Coll., Northfield, Minn., St. Paul Inst., Summit Sch., St. Paul, Shattuck Sch., Faribault, Minn. Republican. Episcopalian. Home: St. Paul, Minn. Died Dec. 3, 1929.

MYERS, Philip Van Ness, author; b. Tribes' Hill, N.Y., Aug. 10, 1846; s. Jacob and Catherine L. (Morris) M.; A.B., Williams, 1871, A.M., 1874; Yale Law Sch., 1873-74, LL.B., 1890; (LL.D., Belmont Coll., 1891, U. of Cincinnati, 1913; L.H.D., Miami, 1891); m. Ida C. Miller, July 20, 1876. Pres. Farmers' Coll., Ohio, 1879-90; prof. history and polit. economy, 1890-1900, dean acad. faculty, 1895-97, U. of Cincinnati; hon. lecturer in history, same, 1919—. Lecturer at various home camps under Y.M. C.A., 1917-18. Author: Ancient History, 1882; Mediæval and Modern History, 1889; General History, 1889 (trans. into Chinese and Arabic); Eastern Nations and Greece, 1890; History of Rome, 1890; History of Greece, 1897; Rome, Its Rise and Fall, 1900; The Middle Ages, 1902; The Modern Age, 1903; History as Past Ethics, 1913. Died Sept. 20, 1937.

MYERS, Quincy Alden, judge; b. Logansport, Ind., Sept. 1, 1853; s. Isaac N. and Rosanna (Justice) M.; B.A., Dartmouth, 1875, M.A., 1880; LL.B., Albany Law Sch. (Union Coll.), 1877; m. Jessie D. Cornelius, Mar. 3, 1886. Practiced at Logansport; in partnership with Hon. M. Winfield, 1877-82, with Hon. John C. Nelson, 1882-1906. City atty., Logansport, 1885-87; co. atty., Cass Co., 1895-97, 1903-09; Rep. presdl. elector, 1900; judge Supreme Ct. of Ind., 1909-15. Trustee City Schs., Logansport, Home of Friendless, DePauw U. Pres. Am. Inst. Criminal Law and Criminology. Methodist. Home: Indianapolis, Ind. Died Dec. 27, 1921.

MYERS, Theodore Walter, banker and broker; b. New York, Jan. 11, 1844; s. Lawrence M.; ed. in pvt. schs. Capt. 3d Regt., Sickles' brigade, in Civil War; later capt. 9th Regt., N.G.S.N.Y.; connected with City Guard for yrs. Became clerk in Wall St. house, 1864, mem. N.Y. Stock Exchange; later mem. of several firms; organized, 1884, bank of Theodore W. Myers & Co. Negotiated a loan of $14,000,000 for the city at 2½ per cent, the lowest rate ever obtained by any municipal govt.; 1898, head of banking firm of Theodore W. Myers & Son, N.Y. City; retired from active business, 1902. Was park commr., 1887, and treas. of dept.; city comptroller, 1888-91; renominated and reëlected by both Republicans and Democrats for term 1891-93. Democrat. Died Mar. 19, 1918.

MYHRMAN, Othelia; b. Finspong, Sweden, July 9, 1859; d. Peter and Maria (Mork) M.; grad. high sch., Finspong, 1875; came to U.S., 1875. Corr. sec. and mgr. free employment bur., Swedish Nat. Assn. of Chicago, 1894-1914 (over 200,000 men and women given employment); organizer, 1926, and pres. Am. Daughters of Sweden. Decorated with Gustav V gold medal, 1919; Order of Vasa, 1923 (Sweden). Republican. Lutheran. Home: Chicago, Ill. Died May 22, 1936.

MYNDERSE, Wilhelmus, lawyer; b. Seneca Falls, N.Y., Nov. 25, 1849; ed. Mt. Pleasant Mil. Acad., Sing Sing, N.Y.; grad. Williams Coll., 1871, Columbia Univ. Law Sch., 1875; married. Practices law in New York; specialty marine law. Dir. Am. & Foreign Marine Ins. Co., Nat. Surety Co., Nat. Exchange Bank (Seneca Falls); trustee Franklin Trust Co., etc. Dir. L. I. Hist. Soc., Brooklyn Hosp., Church Charity Foundation of L.I. Home: New York, N.Y. Died 1906.

MYRICK, Harry Pierce, editor; b. Pontiac, Mich., Aug. 27, 1857; A.B., U. of Mich., 1878, law student, 1878-79. Mng. editor Milwaukee Sentinel, 1884-1900; editor Milwaukee Free Press, 1901-15; editor state printing and mem. State Printing Bd., 1915—. Home: Madison, Wis. Died July 1, 1916.

MYRICK, Herbert, publisher, editor; b. Arlington, Mass., Aug. 20, 1860; s. Henry L. and Lucy Caroline (Whittemore) M.; B.S., Mass. Agricultural College, and Boston U., 1882; m. Elvira Lawrence Kenson; children—Cristine, Helen L., Donald. For many yrs. pres. Phelps Pub. Co. and editor-in-chief of its weekly, New England Homestead, Springfield, Mass.; pres. Am. Education Press, pub. Current Events; chmn. The Bushnell Co., pub. Dakota Farmer. Pub. Good Housekeeping Mag., 1900-11; founder Good Housekeeping Inst. Pub. and editor Am. Agriculturist (New York), Orange Judd Farmer (Chicago), 1888-1920, Southern Farming (Atlanta), 1912-17, Farm and Home, Chicago and Springfield, 1880-1925; founded, 1910, Sch. of Agr., Domestic Science and Manual Training; founded, 1901, Farmers' Polit. League (beginning of farm bloc). Developed metallic system for drawing fibre of cotton, and pres. Metallic Drawing Roll Co., 1891-1923. An original advocate of coöp. dairying, tariff on farm products, fed. system agrl. expt. stas., rural free delivery, coöp. buying and selling by farmers, federal farm loan act, and various other movements in behalf of edn. and agriculture. Erected Myrick Bldg., Springfield, Mass., 1907-08, and presented Broadway to that city; lectured throughout U.S. to establish Federal Land Bank system; dir. at large Fed. Land Bank of Springfield; dir. Fed. Intermediate Credit Bank of Springfield. Chmn. The Americas Commn. for The Riff, leading the internat. organization, Friends of The Riff, 1926. Author: Coöperative Finance, 1912; The Federal Farm Loan System, 1916; Financing Second Mortgages (as a means whereby tenants may own their farms), 1920; Rural Credits System of United States, 1922; How to Use the Agricultural Credits Act of March 4, 1923; Poems by Mother and Son, 1926; Making the Boy into a Citizen (autobiography of first 21 yrs.), 1926. His periodical, Farm and Home, was the first in the world to provide (coöperating with Westinghouse) a universal radiophone service to its subscribers throughout U.S., 1921. Owner of Wisset Farms, 600 acres. Home: Wilbraham, Mass. Died July 6, 1927.

MYRICK, John Rencklin, soldier; b. Westfield, N.J., Nov. 9, 1841; s. James and Rebecca Aiken (Miller) M.; ed. village schs., Westfield and Cranford, N.J., to 1854; pub. sch., Brooklyn, to Apr. 1855; clerk in stores, 1855-61; m. Harriet Augusta Moore, Jan. 22, 1867. Pvt. Co. B, 13th N.Y. State Militia, Apr. 23-Aug. 6, 1861; 2d lt. and 1st lt. 3d U.S. Arty., Nov. 18, 1861; capt. 38th U.S. Inf. (declined), July 28, 1866; capt. 3d U.S. Arty., Dec. 1, 1872; maj., Feb. 12, 1895; lt. col. 2d U.S. Arty., Oct. 16, 1899; col. Arty. Corps, U.S.A., Aug. 1, 1901; brig. gen. U.S.A., Apr. 17, 1903, retired Apr. 18, 1903. Bvtd. capt. Feb. 20, 1864, maj., Oct. 7, 1864, for gallantry in action. Republican. Died 1909.

MYRON, Paul, see Paul Myron Wentworth Linebarger.

N

NABUCO, Joaquim, Brazilian diplomatist; b. Recife, Brazil, Aug. 19, 1849; s. Senator Nabuco; m. Evelina, d. Baron d' Inohan. Mem. Brazilian Parliament during the Empire; took active part in abolition of slavery, 1879-88; envoy extraordinary in England, 1900-05; sent on a spl. mission to Italy to advocate rights of Brazil in question between Brazil and England with regard to British Guiana boundaries, the King of Italy being the arbitrator; work in that Arbitration, comprising documents and atlas, forms series of 18 vols.; apptd. ambassador to Washington, 1905, when Brazil created in U.S. her first embassy. Pres. 3d Pan-Am. Conf. (LL.D., Columbia). Author: (In Portuguese): Um Estradista do Imperio, or the life of his father, Senator Nabuco, which is a constl. history of the reign of Dom Pedro II; Minha Formacão, polit. and lit. autobiography); (in French) Pensées Détachées et Souvenirs, Paris, 1906. Died 1910.

NADAL, Charles Coleman, lawyer; b. Greencastle, Ind., Dec. 8, 1855; s. Bernard Harrison (D.D.) and Sarah Jane (Mayse) N.; ed. by father; student Law Sch., Columbia, 1878; m. Mary Taylor Warrin, Oct. 15, 1890. Admitted to N.Y. bar, 1878, and began practice at N.Y. City; gen. counsel Fidelity & Casualty Co. of New York, 1887—, v.p., 1910—; counsel and dir. The Macmillan Co.; mem. firm Nadal, Jones & Mowton. Episcopalian. Home: New York, N.Y. Died July 19, 1931.

NADAL, Ehrman Syme, author; b. Greenbrier Co., Va., 1843; s. Rev. Dr. Bernard H. and Jane (Mays) N.; undergraduate, Columbia, 1860-62; A.B., Yale, 1864, A.M., 1874. One of the secretaries of U.S. Legation, London, 1870-71, 1877-84. Lecturer in English composition, Columbia, 1892-93. Author: Impressions of London Social Life, 1875; Essays at Home and Elsewhere, 1882; Zwiebak—Notes of a Professional Exile, 1895; A Virginian Village, 1917. Address: New York, N.Y. Died July 26, 1922.

NAGEL, Charles, sec. Commerce and Labor; b. Colorado County, Texas., Aug. 9, 1849; s. Dr. Hermann and Friedericke (Litzmann) N.; LL.B., St. Louis Law Sch., 1872; studied Roman law, polit. economy, etc., U. of Berlin, 1873, hon. Doctor of Political Science, 1928; LL.D., Brown U., 1911, also Villanova U., Pa., and Washington U., St. Louis; m. Fannie Brandeis, Aug. 4, 1876; m. 2d, Anne Shepley, May 1, 1895. Admitted to bar, 1873, and practiced at St. Louis; mem. firm Finkelnburg, Nagel & Kirby, 1903-05, Nagel & Kirby, 1905-09, and after 1913, later Nagel, Kirby, Orrick & Shepley; lecturer, St. Louis Law Sch., 1885-1909; dir. St. Louis Union Trust Co., South Western Bell Telephone Co., Anheuser Busch, Inc., Busch Sulzer Bros. Diesel Engine Co. Mem. Mo. Ho. of Rep., 1881-83; pres. St. Louis City Council, 1893-97; mem. Rep. Nat. Com., 1908-12; Sec. of Commerce and Labor in cabinet of President Taft, Mar. 1909-Mar. 1913. Trustee Central Inst. for Deaf St. Louis, Washington U.; councillor Nat. Industrial Conf. Board, Inc., New York City. Home: St. Louis, Mo. Died Jan. 5, 1940.

NAGLE, Charles Francis, naval officer; b. in Ireland, Sept. 4, 1841; s. William and Ellen (Cotter) N.; arrived in America, Dec. 4, 1850; ed. pub. schs. and Commercial and Math. Acad., Brooklyn; m. Alice W., d. William Holt, Aug. 11, 1880. Apptd. 3d asst. engr. U.S.N., rank of midshipman, Aug. 3, 1863; promoted master, July 26, 1866; lt., Apr. 15, 1874; chief engr. with rank of lt. comdr., June 29, 1906; retired July 26, 1892, account of physical disability due to exposure on Arctic expdn. With Admiral Farragut in West Gulf Blockading Squadron, 1863 to close of Civ. War; saved U.S. steamer Chicopee from sinking, Jan. 1867, received thanks of admiral comdg. the station. Total sea service 16 yrs., 2 mos., including cruises in N. Atlantic and S. Pacific, Asiatic and European stas., and shore duty at Boston, New York and Portsmouth, N.H., navy yards. Mem. gen. court-martial at Brooklyn Navy Yard 3 yrs. after retirement. Medal for creditable service in Civ. War; medal from King of Siam, Bangkok, 1874, permitted to accept by spl. act of Congress; medal Mil. Order of Loyal Legion of U.S. Home: Brooklyn, N.Y. Died May 26, 1914.

NAGLE, James C., civil engr.; b. Richmond, Va., Oct. 9, 1865; s. John and Ellen Mary (Smith) N.; B.Sc., U. of Tex. (engring. course), 1889, M.A., 1892; C.E., Western U. of Pa. (now U. of Pittsburgh), 1892; M.C.E., Cornell U., 1893; m. Emily St. P. Davis, July 1, 1903. Asst. engr. Austin & Northwestern Ry., 1888; topographer Tex. Geol. Survey, 1889-90; prof. civ. engring., 1890-1913, dean engring. faculty, 1911-13, Agrl. and Mech. Coll. of Tex.; chmn. Bd. of Water Engrs., State of Tex., Sept. 1, 1913-Aug. 31, 1917; prof. civ. engring., dean of engring. and dir. Tex. Engring. Experiment Station, Agrl. and Mech. Coll. of Tex., 1917-22. Was chief engineer Brazos & Burleson Ry., 1894; asst. chief engr. Houston, East & West Tex. Ry., 1899; agt. and expert in irrigation investigation, U.S. Dept. Agr., 1899-1902, and spl. agt., 1908; engr. Burleson Co. Improvement Dist. No. 1, 1908-10, 1914-16; consulting engineer, gen. practice; mem. Nagle, Witt, Rollins Engineering Co., Dallas, Tex., 1919—; also mem. Nagle & Thompson, hydraulic engrs., 1923—. Author: Field Manual for Railroad Engineers, 1897. Home: Dallas, Tex. Died Apr. 6, 1927.

NAGLE, Patrick Sarsfield; b. Decatur County, Ind., Nov. 23, 1858; s. George and Mary (Burke) N.; ed. St. Mary's Coll., St. Marys, Kan.; m. Angie McCartney, 1894. Settled in Okla., 1889; began law practice, 1884; U.S. marshal, by apptmt. of President Cleveland, 1896-97; actively identified with the Farmer-Labor movement in Okla. Home: Kingfisher, Okla. Deceased.

NAGLER, Floyd August, hydraulic engring.; b. Howard City, Mich., Jan. 11, 1892; s. August Frederick and Carrie (Fox) N.; B.S., Mich. State Coll., 1914; M.S., U. of Mich., 1915, Ph.D., 1917; m. Marion Dell Truax, Sept. 1, 1921; children—Robert Carlton, Phyllis Jane, Donald Floyd. Asst. engr. Fargo Engring. Co., 1914-17; same with Robert E. Horton, 1917-20; with State U. of Ia., 1920—; asst. prof. mechanics and hydraulics until 1922, asso. prof., 1922-26, prof. hydraulic engring., 1926—; dir. Ia. Inst. Hydraulic Research, 1931—; part time sr. engr. in charge hydraulic investigations, U.S. Engr. Dept., Rock Island Dist., 1927-29; cons. practice. Was 2d lt. science and research div., meteorol. sect. U.S. Signal Corps, 1918-19. Awarded Collingwood prize, Am. Soc. C.E., 1919, 20; Norman medal, same soc., 1930. Republican. Methodist. Home: Iowa City, Ia. Deceased.

NAIL, James H., lands and cattle; b. Fannin Co., Tex., Mar. 26, 1856; s. William N.; ed. pub. sch.; m. Chloe A. Black, Sept. 13, 1893. Rancher and cattle raiser, Fannin County, Tex., 1873—; owner of 100,000 acres of land; dir. Federal Reserve Bank of Dallas, Tex. Home: Fort Worth, Tex. Died Aug. 2, 1928.

NAISMITH, James, prof. physical edn.; b. Almonte, Ont., Can., Nov. 6, 1861; s. John and Margaret (Young) N.; A.B., McGill U., 1887; grad. Presbyn. Coll., Montreal, Can., 1890; grad. Y.M.C.A. Coll., Springfield, Mass., 1891, M.P.E., 1910; M.D., U. of Colo., 1898; m. Maude E. Sherman, June 20, 1894; children—Margaret Mason, Hellen Carolyn, John Edwin, Maude Annie, James Sherman. Dir. physical edn., McGill, 1887-90, Y.M.C.A. Coll., Springfield, 1890-95; physical dir. Y.M.C.A., Denver, Colo., 1895-98, U. of Kan., 1898—. Mil. service with 1st Kan. Regt., 4 mos., 1916; with Y.M.C.A. in France 19 mos., in U.S., 3 mos., 1917-19. Originated the game of basket ball, 1891. Republican. Presbyn. Mason. Author: Basket Ball Rules, 1891; The Modern High School (sect. on athletics), 1911; The Basis of Clean Living, 1918. Home: Lawrence, Kan. Died Nov. 28, 1939.

NALDER, Frank Fielding, dir. coll. extension; b. Penshurst, Prov. of Victoria, Australia, Nov. 5, 1876; s. Frank and Annie Elizabeth (Scott) N.; brought to U.S., 1884; B.A., State Coll. of Wash., 1901; M.A., Columbia, 1902; Ph.D., U. of Calif., 1916; m. Alma Blankenship, June 25, 1905 (died 1926); children—Lila Craig, Philip Richard, Frances Janet; m. 2d, Mabel Luella Mark, Aug. 21, 1928. Registrar and instructor in history, State College of Washington, 1903-08; supt. schools, Tekoa, Wash., 1908-09; dept. state pub. instrn., Wash., 1909-11; dir. edn., Wash. State Reformatory, 1912-13; with extension div., U. of Calif., 1914-19; prof. social science and dir. college extension, State Coll. of Wash., 1919—. Republican. Presbyn. Author: Washington State High School Manual, 1910. Home: Pullman, Wash. Died Jan. 17, 1937.

NAMMACK, Charles Edward, M.D.; b. New York, June 24, 1856; s. William and Eliza (Williams) N.; Ph.B., St. Francis Xavier's Coll., New York, 1895; M.D., Bellevue Hosp. Med. Coll. (New York U.), 1881; LL.D., Fordham U., 1908; m. Mary Halpin, June 2, 1887 (dec.). Attending phys. out-patients, New York Hosp., 1881-1904; lecturer on anatomy and physiology, New York Board of Edn., 1886-90; U.S. examining surgeon for pensions, 1886-88; surgeon of New York police, 1887—; visiting phys. Gouverneur Hosp., 1893-98, Bellevue Hosp., 1896—, St. Lawrence Hosp., 1906-16, St. Vincent's Hosp., 1909-22; prof. clin. medicine, Cornell U. Med. Coll., New York, 1898—. Consulting phys. to St. Joseph's Hosp., Yonkers. Address: New York, N.Y. Died Oct. 4, 1926.

NANCE, Albinus, governor; b. La Fayette, Ill., Mar. 30, 1848; s. Hiram and Sarah R. (Smith) N.; studied Knox Coll., Galesburg, Ill.; m. Sarah White, Sept. 30, 1875. Pvt. Co. H, 9th Ill. Cav., Apr. 4, 1864-Oct. 31, 1865; admitted to bar, 1870; practiced at Osceola, Neb., 1870-78; pres. Osceola Bank and Stromsburg Bank, 1879-83; mem. Neb. Ho. of Rep., 1875-79 (speaker 1877-79); chmn. Neb. delegation Rep. Nat. Conv., Cincinnati, 1876; gov. of Neb., 1879-83. Congregationalist. Home: Lincoln, Neb. Died 1911.

NANCRÈDE, C(harles) B(eylard) Guérard de, surgeon; b. Phila., Dec. 30, 1847; s. Thomas Dixie and Mary Elizabeth (Bull) N.; student U. of Pa., 1864-66, M.D., 1869, hon. A.B., 1893, as of class of 1868, hon. A.M., 1895; M.D., Jefferson Med. Coll., 1883; LL.D., 1898, hon. A.M., Univ. of Michigan, 1893; m. Alice Dunnington, June 3, 1872. Practiced Phila. and held various surg. chairs and hosp. appointments there; prof. surgery and clin. surgery, and surgeon Univ. Hosp., U. of Mich., 1889—, Dartmouth Med. Coll., 1900-13; emeritus, 1913. Maj. and chief surgeon, U.S. Volunteers, 1898; chief surgeon 3d Div., 2d Army Corps; served with 5th Army Corps, Cuba, in Santiago campaign. Pres. Am. Surg. Assn., 1908-09. Author: Principles of Surgery, 1899. Contbr. to med. encys. and text books. Address: Ann Arbor, Mich. Died Apr. 13, 1921.

NAPHEN, Henry Francis, congressman, lawyer; b. in Ireland, Aug. 14, 1847; brought to Mass. when a child; ed. public schools and by private tutors; LL.B., Harvard U., 1878; post-graduate course, same; attended Boston Univ. Law School; admitted to bar, 1880. Mem. sch. com., Boston, 1882-85; State senator, 1885-86; mem. Congress, 1899-1903, 10th Mass. dist. Democrat. Address: Boston, Mass. Died 1905.

NAPIER, George Moultrie, lawyer; b. Walker County, Ga., Mar. 28, 1863; s. Nathan Campbell and Julia Louise (Sharpe) N.; A.B., North Ga. College, 1882; A.M., U. of Ga., 1898; m. Frances Nunnally, Dec. 14, 1905. Began practice at Monroe, Ga., 1885; moved to Atlanta, 1900; mem. firm Napier, Wright & Wood. Solicitor gen., Stone Mountain Jud. Circuit, 1913-20; atty. gen. of Ga., 1921-29. Col., judge adv. gen., Ga. N.G., 1899-1908. Democrat. Methodist. Mason; Grand Master of Masons of Ga., 1910-12; Potentate Yoarab Shrine Temple, 1917-18; Comdr. Old Guard Battalion; dir. George Washington Nat. Masonic Memorial Assn., Alexandria, Va. Home: Decatur, Ga. Died May 4, 1932.

NASH, Arthur; b. Tipton County, Ind., June 26, 1870; s. Evermont and Rachel (Mitchel) N.; ed. high sch., Greentown, Ind., and Theol. Sch., 7th Day Adventists, Battle Creek, Mich.; m. Maud Lena Southwell, Apr. 9, 1899. Educated for ministry but abandoned the pulpit (Disciples of Christ) after short experience; entered clothing mfg. business, Columbus, O., 1909; founder, 1916, and pres. A. Nash Co., wholesale tailors, Cincinnati; developed the "Nash Plan" of co-ownership of industry by the workers. Universalist. Mason. Author: The Golden Rule in Business, 1923. Home: Cincinnati, O. Died Oct. 30, 1927.

NASH, Charles Ellwood, clergyman; b. Allamuchy, N.J., Mar. 31, 1855; s. Rev. Charles P. and Sarah Ann (Wade) N.; A.B., Lombard U., 1875, A.M., 1878; B.D., Tufts Coll., 1878, S.T.D., 1891; m. Carrie M. Sawtelle, Dec. 31, 1878; children—Carrie Ruth, Faith Tenney, Beth Hazel, Joy Pendleton, Hope. Universalist pastor, Stamford, Conn., 1878-81, Newtonville, Mass., 1881-84, Akron, O., 1884-91, First Ch., Brooklyn, 1891-95; pres. Lombard Coll., Galesburg, Ill., 1895-1904; field sec. Universalist Ch., 1904-07; pastor Los Angeles, 1907-29; supt. Calif. churches, 1907-22. Home: Los Angeles, Calif. Died Apr. 4, 1932.

NASH, Edgar Smiley, editor, writer; b. Phila., Pa., July 6, 1872; s. Joseph D. (M.D.) and Florence (Smiley) N.; A.B., Brown U., 1894; m. Florence de Lacy Beck, Oct. 30, 1895; children—Charles Edgar, Mary Elizabeth. Editorial writer Philadelphia Record, 1895-98; asso. editor Saturday Evening Post, 1898-1901. Mason; Dist. Dep. G.M. of Pa., 1913-18. Home: Wyncote, Pa. Died Aug. 17, 1935.

NASH, Edwin A., judge; b. Bedford, Can., Oct. 26, 1836; s. Adolphus and Harriet (Smith) N.; ed. Genesee Wesleyan Sem., Lima, N.Y.; admitted to bar, 1861; m. Frances A. Morgan, Sept. 22, 1863. Dist. atty., 1869-73, county judge, 1878-96, Livingston County, N.Y.; justice Supreme Court of N.Y., 7th Dist., and justice Appellate Div., 4th Dept., 1896-1906. Address: Avon, N.Y. Died 1911.

NASH, Francis Philip, college prof.; A.B., Harvard, 1856, A.M., 1866, LL.B., 1859; hon. L.H.D., Trinity, 1895; LL.D., Union, 1895; married. Prof. Latin, Hobart Coll., 1871-76 and from 1882, later emeritus prof. Latin lang. and lit. Address: Geneva, N.Y. Died 1911.

NASH, George Kilbon, gov. of Ohio; b. York Twp., Medina County, O., Aug. 14, 1842; ed. Western Reserve U. and Oberlin Coll.; left without graduating; taught school; studied law; admitted to bar; edited Ohio State Journal, 13 months; became chief clerk in office of Sec. of State of Ohio; pros. atty., Franklin Co., 1879-82; judge Supreme Court, 1883-85; practiced law at Columbus; long active in Rep. State politics; sec. Franklin County Com., 1868; chmn. State Com. several yrs.; elected gov. of Ohio for terms, 1900-02, and 1902-04. Address: Columbus, O. Died 1904.

NASH, Harriet A. (Miss), short story writer; b. Gardiner, Me., Oct. 2, 1864; d. Samuel and Ellen (Millikin) N.; ed. pub. sch., Skowhegan, Me., grad. high sch., 1882. First occupation stenographer, bookkeeper, etc., later in banking business and elec. work; treas. Skowhegan Elec. Light Co. Congregationalist. Author: Polly's Secret, 1902. Address: Skowhegan, Me. Died 1907.

NASH, Henry Sylvester, theologian; b. Ohio, 1854; A.B., Harvard, 1878; S.T.B., Episcopal Theol. Sch., Cambridge, Mass., 1881; hon. D.D., Trinity Coll., Conn., 1893; S.T.D., Harvard, 1907; m. Bessie Curtis, June 26, 1883. Deacon, 1881, priest, 1882, P.E. Ch.; prof. lit. and interpretation of N.T., Episcopal Theol. Sch., 1884—. Author: The Genesis of the Social Conscience, 1896; Ethics and Revelation, 1898; History of the Higher Criticism of the New Testament, 1900; The Atoning Life, 1907. Address: Cambridge, Mass. Died Nov. 6, 1912.

NASH, Herbert Charles, librarian Stanford U.; b. Nice, France, 1857; academic edn. France and England; vice-consul of U.S., Nice, France, 1877-81. Address: Stanford University, Calif. Died 1902.

NASH, Leonidas Lydwell, clergyman; b. in Mecklenburg County, Va., Aug. 2, 1846; s. Hugh W. and Martha Jane (Mullen) N.; pub. sch. and military edn.; read law and medicine in Va.; studied theology, passed Conf. Course in N.C.; D.D., Rutherford Coll., N.C., 1889; m. Louise Taylor, Dec. 2, 1873. Licensed M.E. ministry, 1872; ordained deacon, 1876, elder, 1878; mem. N.C. Conf. M.E. Ch., S., and 15 yrs. on circuits as follows: Bath Circuit, 3 yrs., Williamston Circuit, 2 yrs., Greenville Circuit, 4 yrs., Rolesville Circuit, 2 yrs., Leasburg Circuit, 4 yrs. Stationed Central Ch., Raleigh, 4 yrs., Fifth St. Ch., Wilmington, 3 yrs., Centenary Ch., Newbern, 1 yr., Hay St. Ch., Fayetteville, 3 yrs., Washington, N.C., 3 yrs., Rocky Mount, 2 yrs., Henderson, 3 yrs., St. John and Gibson, 2 yrs., Hamlet, N.C., Feb. 1, 1911—. Now conf. evangelist, for N.C., M.E. Ch., S. Served a short time in Confederate Army, Civil War. Democrat. Author: Spiritual Life, 1898; Early Morning Scenes in the Bible, 1910; The Christian Family, 1915. Address: Hamlet, N.C. Died July 11, 1917.

NASH, Lyman Junius, lawyer; b. Shelby, Orleans County, N.Y., Jan. 18, 1845; s. Francis and Catherine Van Bergen (Curtis) N.; A.B., Lawrence Coll., Appleton, Wis., 1870, A.M., 1872; m. Emma Arathusa Guyles, Sept. 2, 1873; children—Archie Lyman, Alice May, Francis John. Principal Manitowoc High Sch., 1870-72; admitted to Wis. bar, 1872; practiced law 37 yrs. Mem. Wis. State Bd. Bar Examiners, 1901-08 (pres. 1906-08). Mem. Wis. State Bar Assn. (pres. 1906-07). Trustee Lawrence Coll., 1886—. Reviser of Wis. statutes, 1910-20; annotator of Wis. statutes, 1920-25. Home: Manitowoc, Wis. Died Mar. 23, 1930.

NASH, Paul Cleveland Bennett, consul; b. Geneva, N.Y., Apr. 28, 1877; s. Francis Philip and Katherine Cleveland (Coxe) N.; ed. Hobart Coll., Mass. Inst. Tech., Boston, and at Paris, and Rome; m. Baroness Margherita Mayneri, Oct. 2, 1905. Sec. Am. Legation and consul gen., Bangkok, Siam, 1903-04; consul at Venice, 1904-07, at Vladivostok, Russia, 1907-08, Rheims, France, Mar.-May, 1908; consul gen. at Budapest, Hungary, 1908—. Died Jan. 7, 1913.

NASH, William Alexander, banker; b. Hudson, N.Y., Jan. 18, 1840; s. Thomas P. and Sarah J. N.; widower. Pres., later chmn. bd. Corn Exchange Bank; pres. New York Clearing House Bldg. Co., Corn Exchange Safe Deposit Co.; v.p., dir. Audit Co. of New York; 2d v.p., trustee Bowery Savings Bank; mem. Am. com. management Royal Ins. Co. of Eng.; dir. Pittsburgh Steel Co., Home Life Ins. Co., Lloyds Plate Glass Ins. Co. (v.p.), Queen Ins. Co. of America, Internat. Elevating Co.; trustee Am. Surety Co.; pres. N.Y. Produce Exchange Safe Deposit & Storage Co.; trustee Title Guarantee & Trust Co. Home: New York, N.Y. Died Aug. 30, 1922.

NASH, William Hoit, brig. gen. U.S.A.; b. Gallipolis, O., June 22, 1834; s. Hon. Simeon N.; ed. Gallia Acad., Gallipolis, O., and Marietta Coll., 1849-51; was in large wholesale and retail house in Cincinnati, 1853-56; in business for self, 1857-60; m. 2d, Mrs. Mary Maxon Wilson, Feb. 22, 1892. Entered mil. service as telegraph operator, June 1, 1861, dept. W.Va.; apptd. capt. commissary subsistence vols., Nov. 26, 1862; transferred to same corps, regular army, Nov. 17, 1865; promoted maj. commissary subsistence, July 14, 1890; lt. col. asst. commissary-gen., June 10, 1896; col. asst. commissary-gen., Feb. 4, 1898; apptd. commissary-gen. subsistence, U.S.A., with rank of brig. gen., April 21, 1898; retired from active service, May 2, 1898. Address: Columbus, O. Died 1902.

NASMYTH, George (William), sociologist, internationalist; b. Cleveland, O., July 9, 1882; s. William Henry and Emma Isabel (Beeman) N.; A.B., Cornell, 1906, A.M., 1908, M.E., Ph.D., 1909; studied successively univs. of Berlin, Goettingen, Heidelberg and Zurich, 1910-13, Harvard, 1914; m. Florence Gross, June 22, 1909. Traveled extensively through universities of all the European nations in the interest of the international student movement; instr. physics, Cornell U., 1906-10. Del. 7th Internat. Congress of Students, Rome, 1911; pres. "Corda Fratres," Internat. Federation of Students, 1911-13; sec. of Com. on Price of 1917 Wheat Crop, Aug. 1917; head, administrative div. U.S. Fuel Administration, Washington, 1917-19. A founder, mem. administrative com. and lecturer economics, Trade Union Coll., under auspices Boston Central Labor Union, 1919; press rep. at Paris Peace Conf., 1919; del. Inter-allied and Neutral Conf. of Coöperative Socs., Paris, 1919; del. Internat. Meeting of World Alliance for Promoting Internat. Friendship Through the Churches, at The Hague, 1919; internat. organizer, World Alliance. Democrat. Society of Friends (Quakers). Author: Social Progress and the Darwinian Theory, 1916. Home: Ithaca, N.Y. Died Sept. 20, 1920.

NASON, Albert John, coal operator; b. East Smithfield, Pa., June 1, 1878; s. John Hesler and Louisa Levantia (Hathaway) N.; B.S., Carleton Coll., Northfield, Minn., 1901; m. Mary Ethel Eaton, Oct. 23, 1902; children—Margaret (Mrs. Horace Fishback, Jr.), John William, Robert Eaton (dec.), Philip Hathaway, Albert John. President Manhattan Investment Co.; v.p. The Wabasha Corp.; treas. Hathaway Farms, Inc. Chmn. for Minn. of United War Fund Campaign, 1918. Trustee Carleton Coll. Republican. Conglist. Mason. Home: Angus, Wis. Died Aug. 29, 1934.

NASON, Frank Lewis, mining engr.; b. New London, Wis., May 12, 1856; s. Lewis Clark and Maria Julia (Stickles) N.; A.B., Amherst, 1882, A.M., 1885; one term Yale Div. Sch.; m. Thalia Abigail Painter, July 26, 1885 (died 1906); children—Stanley Lewis, Alexis Painter (dec.); m. 2d, Madeleine Reynolds, December 1909. Instr. mathematics, Rensselaer Polytec. Inst., 1882-88, taking special course in chemistry and metallurgy; asst. state geologist of N.J., 1888-90, of Mo., 1890-92; mining engr. and consulting engr. for the Ringwood Co., Ringwood, N.J., Basic Iron Ore Co., Oxford, N.J., 1892—, mining geologist, N.J. Zinc Co., 1903-15, Standard Oil Co., Witherbee, Sherman & Co.; mining engineer U.S. Steel Corp., Va.-Carolina Chem. Co. Author: Iron Ores of Missouri, 1892; To the End of the Trail, 1902; The Blue Goose, 1903; The Vision of Elijah Berl, 1905. Home: W. Haven, Conn. Died Sept. 12, 1928.

NASSAU, Robert Hamill, missionary; b. at Montgomery Square, nr. Phila., Oct. 11, 1835; s. Charles William (D.D.) and Hannah McClintock (Hamill) N.; A.B., Princeton, 1854, A.M., 1857; grad. Princeton Theol. Sem., 1859; M.D., U. of Pa., 1861, hon. S.T.D., 1891; ordained to Presbyn. ministry, and started as missionary to Africa, July 2, 1861; m. Mary Cloyd Latta, Sept. 1862 (died 1870); m. 2d, Mary Brunette Foster, Oct. 10, 1881 (died 1884). Resigned as missionary, Dec. 1906, after 45 yrs.' service; pioneer, explorer, translator, contbr. to science; sent large ethnol. collections to U. of Pa., and Princeton; sent first entire carcass of gorilla to U.S. and the only perfect gorilla brains examined by anatomists, up to 1891. Author: Crowned in Palmland, 1874; Mawedo, 1881; Fetichism in West Africa, 1904; The Path She Trod, 1909; Tales Out of School, 1911; Corisco Days, 1910; The Youngest King, 1911; Where Animals Talk, 1912; In an Elephant Corral, 1912; My Ogowe, 1913; History of the West Africa

Mission, 1919; also grammar and Bible transl. in Benga lang. of W. Equatorial Africa. Address: Ambler, Pa. Deceased.

NAST, Albert Julius, editor; b. Cincinnati, Apr. 4, 1846; s. William (D.D.) and Margaret Eliza (McDowell) N.; A.B., Wesleyan U., Conn., 1868, A.M., 1871; hon. D.D., Ohio U., Athens, 1892, Wesleyan, 1907; m. Sarah McDermott, Sept. 7, 1876 (died 1883); children—William Gamble (dec.), Marie Eleanor (wife of Dr. William B. Wherry); m. 2d, Alice G. Kendall, July 29, 1896 (died 1921). In editorial office The Methodist, New York, 1865-66; ordained M.E. ministry, 1869; pastor Cincinnati, 1869-70, Pittsburgh, 1870-72, Cleveland, 1872-74, Pomeroy, O., 1874-76, Columbus, O., 1876-77, Malta, O., 1877-78; prof. Latin and German, Wesleyan Coll. for Women, Cincinnati, 1878-80, Ill. Wesleyan U., 1880-83; asst. editor, 1884-92, editor 1892-1918, Der Christliche Apologete, Cincinnati, O. Chmn. bd. mgrs. Bethesda Hosp., Cincinnati, 1919-30. Delegate Gen. Conferences of Meth. Episcopal Church, 1896, 1900, 04, 08, 12, 16; to Ecumenical Confs., London, 1901, Toronto, 1911; fraternal del. Evang. Assn., 1907. Pres. bd. trustees German Wallace Coll., Berea, O., 1903-13, Baldwin-Wallace Coll., Berea, O., 1914-18, William Nast College, Kin Kiang, China, 1904-23. Visited China, Japan and Philippine Islands, 1920-21. Republican. Home: Cincinnati, O. Died Mar. 27, 1936.

NAST, Thomas, artist; b. Landau, Bavaria, Sept. 27, 1840; came with parents to U.S., 1846; ed. in public schools; when very young employed in office of Frank Leslie's Illustrated Newspaper; soon began to furnish sketches and drawings for the engravers. Traveling artist for British and Am. newspapers with Garibaldi in Italy, 1860-61; after that with Harper's Weekly as political cartoonist; has illustrated several books. Also known as lecturer, with a splty. of illustrating his address by rapid work in caricatures, drawn on the platform, and by paintings in oil on canvas, executed in presence of his auditors. Address: Morristown, N.J. Died 1902.

NATE, Joseph Cookman; b. Evanston, Ill., Mar. 26, 1868; s. John and Mary Jane (Leonard) N.; B.S., Ill. Wesleyan U., Bloomington, 1890, M.S. and M.A., 1893; LL.B., Northwestern U., 1892; grad. study U. of Berlin, 1892-93; D.D., Miami U., Oxford, O., 1909; m. Ruth Eleanor Evans, Nov. 12, 1892; children—Mildred Evans (Mrs. Ronald V. Rike), Ruth Elizabeth (Mrs. George W. Liljestrom), Joseph. Admitted to Ill. bar, 1893, and practiced at Chicago until 1899; ordained ministry M.E. Ch., 1899; pastor Atlanta, Ill., 1899-1903, Beardstown, 1903-07, Jacksonville, 1907-11, Champaign, 1911-12; exec. sec. Ednl. Forward Movement, instns. of M.E. Ch., Ill., 1912-14; dist. supt. Champaign-Danville Dist., Ill., Conf. M.E. Ch., 1914-20; asst. sec. Bd. of Edn. M.E. Ch., N.Y. City, 1920-22; dir. Am. Foundation for the Blind, N.Y. City, 1922-24; ednl. and lit. work, 1924-27; nat. visitation officer, colls. and univs., Sigma Chi Fraternity, 1927—. Trustee Wesley Foundation (U. of Ill.), Ill. Woman's Coll. (Jacksonville, Ill.), Chaddock Sch. for Boys (Quincy, Ill.). Del. to Gen. Conf. M.E. Ch., 1916, 1920. Mem. Sigma Chi (nat. pres., 1899-1901). Republican. Mason. Author: History of Sigma Chi, Vol. 1, 1925, Vol. 3, 1931. Home: Denver, Colo. Died July 30, 1933.

NATHAN, Edgar Joshua, lawyer; b. N.Y. City, Jan. 25, 1860; s. Gershom and Rosalie (Gomez) N.; LL.B., Columbia, 1881; m. Sara N. Solis, June 4, 1890; children—Edgar J., Rosalie N. (Mrs. Henry S. Hendricks), Emily S. Practiced at N.Y. City, 1881—; mem. firm Cardozo & Nathan; mem. advisory bd. Am. Exchange-Irving Trust Co. Vice pres. and trustee Jewish Social Service Assn., Inc. Republican. Home: New York, N.Y. Died June 18, 1929.

NAVE, Frederick Solomon, lawyer; b. at Lewis Center, O., Jan. 7, 1873; s. Orville James and Anna Eliza (Semans) N.; A.B., Ohio Wesleyan U., 1895; LL.B., Northwestern U., 1897; m. Elise W. Jones, Mar. 26, 1901. Instr. Greek and Latin, Northwestern U. Acad., 1895-96; clerk Ariz. Code Revision Commn., 1899-1901; dist. atty. Santa Cruz Co., Ariz., 1900; U.S. atty. for Ariz., 1902-05; asso. justice Supreme Ct., Ariz., 1905-09; retired Apr. 1, 1909, and later in law practice. Mem. exec. com. Nat. Irrigation Congress, 1908-09. Pres. Ariz. Bar Assn., 1911-12 (v.p., 1910-11). Republican. Address: Globe, Ariz. Died Sept. 27, 1912.

NAVE, Orville James, army chaplain; b. at Galion, O., Apr. 30, 1841; s. Solomon P. and Jane Ann (Johnson) N.; pvt. Co. A, 111th Ill. Inf., Aug. 14, 1862-June 6, 1865; A.B., Ohio Wesleyan U., 1870, A.M., 1873, hon. D.D., 1895; LL.D., Neb. Wesleyan, 1897; m. Anna Eliza Semans, Sept. 6, 1870; 1 son, Frederick Solomon N. Entered Ohio Conf. M.E. Ch., 1870; post chaplain U.S.A., July 27, 1882; chaplain 3d Inf., 1901-05; chaplain maj. and retired, Apr. 30, 1905; pres. Nave's Topical Bible Home Sch., 1904—. Corr. sec. for Corps of Army Chaplains, 1888-94. Republican. Author: Nave's Topical Bible, 1897; Student's Bible, 1907; also various text-books for use in connection with his Bible sch. Pres. Meth. Hosp. Assn., Los Angeles, 1908-13; pres. and field sec. Assn. of Chaplains of Mil. and Naval forces U.S., 1912-13; pres. Juvenile Protective League of Los Angeles and Los Angeles Co. Chaplain-in-chief G.A.R., 1914-15; chaplain city and county jails; pres. Prisoner's Friend Soc. of City and County of Los Angeles. Address: Los Angeles, Calif. Died June 24, 1917.

NAYLOR, Emmett Hay, trade Assn. exec.; b. St. Paul, Minn., Sept. 13, 1885; s. William Alexander and Genevieve Charlotte (Hay) N.; A.B., Dartmouth, 1909; LL.B., N.Y. Law Sch., 1911; M.A., Harvard, 1912; m. Ruth H. Caldwell, Jan. 17, 1914; children—Genevieve Hay, Winford C., Cynthia Morgan. Sec. Springfield Chamber Commerce, 1912-14; hon. sec.-treas. Nat. Assn. Commercial Organization Secretaries, 1913; exec. sec. Writing and Cover Paper Mfrs. Assns., 1914—; pres. Am. Trade Assn. Executives, 1920, dir. 1937; pres. Trade Assn. Executives in N.Y. City, 1921, dir., 1937; pres. Child Edn. Foundation. Vice pres. Psi Upsilon (exec. council). Maj. Ordnance Officers' Res. Corps. Republican. Presbyterian. Author: The Value of Trade Associations, 1918; Trade Associations—Their Organization and Management, 1921; History of Trade Associations in America, 1923. Home: Cummington, Mass. Died July 1938.

NEAD, Benjamin Matthias, lawyer; b. Antrim, Pa., July 14, 1847; s. Benjamin Franklin and Ellen (Wunderlich) N.; A.B., Yale, 1870; hon. Litt.D., Franklin and Marshall Coll., 1917; admitted to bar, 1872; m. Libbie J. Hayes, Oct. 10, 1875 (died 1882); m. 2d, Annie E. Zollinger, Jan. 12, 1892 (died 1906). Practiced in Franklin County, Pa., until 1875; in office of auditor-gen. of Pa., 1875-81, since then in practice at Harrisburg. Served on Cooper Tax Commn., 1881, and on com. of expert accountants apptd. by Gov. Pattison, 1883, to devise new system of keeping accounts of state; receiver Nat. Bank of Middletown, Pa., 1894; Dem. candidate for Congress, in 1894. Pres. Harrisburg Bd. of Trade, 1904-05. Mem. Alumni Advisory Bd. of Yale Corp., 1913—. Author: Sketches of Early Chambersburg Guide to County Officers; Early Government of Pennsylvania; Brief Review of the Financial History of Pennsylvania; History of Waynesboro, 1901; Some Hidden Sources of Fiction, 1909. Address: Harrisburg, Pa. Died Mar. 31, 1923.

NEAL, Alva Otis; b. Franklin, Ind., Sept. 23, 1870; s. William M. and Harriet E. (Mozingo) N.; B.S., Franklin (Ind.) Coll., 1892, M.S., 1895; post-grad. work, U. of Chicago, and Columbia U.; Pd.D., Franklin Coll., 1923; m. Elsie C. Holman, Nov. 8, 1893. Successively prin. high schs., Franklin and Madison, Ind., and supt. schs., Madison, Franklin and Kokomo, 1892-1912; state high sch. insp., Ind., 1912-14; prof. sch. administration and registrar, U. of Ariz., 1914-17, also state high sch. insp.; specialist in rural administration, U.S. Bureau of Education, 1917-20; dir. gen. univ. extension and high sch. visitor, registrar, U. of Arizona, 1920—. Pres. Ariz. State Teachers' Assn., 1921-22. Lecturer U. of Calif., 1922. Mem. com. on engring. and edn. for secondary schs. of Council Nat. Defense. Pres. Ind. State Teachers' Assn., 1912-13. Democrat. Presbyn. Mason. Editor Geography of Arizona. Address: Tucson, Ariz. Died Nov. 2, 1925.

NEAL, David (Dalhoff), artist; b. Lowell, Mass., Oct. 20, 1838; s. Stephen B. and Mary (Dalhoff) N.; ed. high school, Lawrence, Mass.; Munich Royal Acad. (great medal); went to Europe, 1862; studied in Paris and Munich; m. Marie, d. the Chevalier Ainmiller, Dec. 9, 1862 (died 1897). Painted numerous hist.-romantic works, including Mary Stuart and Riccio, Oliver Cromwell Visits John Milton, Nuns at Prayer, James Watt, In the Crypt, Retour du Chasse, etc. Later work is portraiture, including Adolph Sutro, Rev. Mark Hopkins, Judge Hoffman of Calif., D. O. Mills, Teackle Wallis, Misses Gladys and Beatrice Mills (daughters of Ogden Mills), Prof. Henry Green, Whitelaw Reid; also "The Rialto," Venice. Died May 2, 1915.

NEAL, Herbert Vincent, biologist; b. Lewiston, Me., Apr. 3, 1869; s. John and Caroline (Noyes) N.; A.B., Bates Coll., 1890, also Sc.D.; A.B., Harvard, 1893, A.M., 1894, Ph.D., 1896; U. of Munich, 1896-97; m. Helen Phillips Howell, June 8, 1899; children—Margaret, Helen, John Howell. Prof. biology, Knox Coll., Galesburg, Ill., 1897-1913; prof. zoölogy, Tufts Coll., 1913—, also dean Grad. Sch. Researches on the morphology of the vertebrate head; associate director Harpswell Lab., South Harpswell, Me., 1908-15; director Mt. Desert Island Biol. Laboratory, 1926-32. Trustee of Bradford and Bates Colleges. Alderman, 6th Ward, Galesburg, 1906-09. Republican. Episcopalian. Fellow A.A.A.S. (sec. sect. F, 1910-20), Am. Acad. Arts and Sciences; member American Society Zoölogists (sec., treas. Central br., 1910-11, pres. 1930). Author: Comparative Anatomy of Vertebrates, 1936; Chordate Anatomy, 1939. Home: Salisbury Cove, Me. Died Feb. 21, 1940.

NEAL, James Arthur; b. Bedford, Ind., May 7, 1866; s. John and Mahala E. (Mitchell) N.; ed. pub. schs., Frankfort, Kan.; m. Mary Palmer Metcalf, Dec. 3, 1903. Began as clk. in grocery store at 13; cashier of bank at 19; resigned at 22 to become practitioner of Christian Science; Doctor of Christian Science. Dir. First Ch. of Christ, Scientist; trustee under will of Mary Baker Eddy. Republican. Address: Brookline, Mass. Died May 3, 1930.

NEAL, James Henry, banker; b. Boston, Mass., July 22, 1872; s. Henry V. and Priscilla (Boston) N.; ed. pub. schs. and under pvt. tutors; m. Lillian Frances Lansing, 1892. Began in employ of Hinckley Locomotive Works, Boston; later with West End Street Ry. Co., of which became v.p. and gen. auditor; pres. Boston Elevated Ry. Co., 1918-Dec. 1919 (resigned); pres. First Peoples Trust of Boston. Inventor of the addendagraph (adding typewriter) and various ry. appliances. Republican. Home: Cambridge, Mass. Died Apr. 4, 1935.

NEAL, Robert Wilson, educator, author; b. Murrayville, Ill., Apr. 2, 1871; s. Robert David and Sarah Jane (Wilson) N.; A.B., U. of Kan., 1898, A.M., 1899; A.M., Harvard, 1903, Yale, 1908; m. Stella May Miller, 1895; 1 son, Robert Miller. Country teacher, stenographer, law clk., newspaper writer, 1888-93; admitted to bar; teacher U. of Kan., high sch., U. of Cincinnati, Rutgers Coll., until 1904; World's Work staff, 1904-06; successively asst. prof. English and German, asso. prof. English, dir. major journalism, Mass. State College, 1906-20; head of dept. of journalism and writing, Home Corr. Sch., Springfield, Mass., 1920—; instr. short story, Columbia, summer 1921; mem. bd. dirs. and vice-pres. Home Corr. Sch. Editor Sunday feature page, Springfield Union, 1911-17, Boston American, 1912-13; New Bedford Standard, 1915-18. Mem. com. on O. Henry Memorial Award, 1919, 1926. Author: Thought-Building in Composition, 1912; Short Stories in the Making, 1914; Today's Short Stories Analyzed, 1918; Editorials and Editorial Writing, 1921; News and Newswriting, 1925. Home: Springfield, Mass. Died May 6, 1939.

NEAL, Thomas, mfr.; b. Corunna, Ont., Sept. 27, 1858; s. Henry N. and Mary (Proctor) N.; ed. pub. schs., Detroit; m. Elizabeth M. Davies, May 14, 1884. An organizer, 1884, and sec. and gen. mgr. Acme White Lead & Color Works, until 1911, chmn. finance com., 1911-24; pres. Gen. Motors Co., 1910-12, chairman board, 1913-15; chairman Equitable Trust Co. of Detroit; dir. Crowley Milner Co. Republican. Episcopalian. K.T. Home: Detroit, Mich. Died Oct. 6, 1940.

NEALE, Walter, publisher, author; b. Eastville, Va., Jan. 21, 1873; s. Judge Hamilton Smith and Elizabeth Bowdoin (Smith) N.; direct desc. in 11th generation of Sir George Yeardley, Colonial gov. of Va., and in 8th generation of Capt. Charles Neale of Va.; ed. under pvt. tutors and at Coll. William and Mary; m. Margaret Ellen Stuart, June 9, 1897; children—Walter, Emma (Mrs. George Slover), John, Charles Smith, Robert E. Lee. Founder, 1894, and pres. Neale Pub. Co.; founder the Conservative Review, 1898; founder, 1911, and mgr. Cosmopolitan Press; founder, 1912, Neale's Monthly; founder, 1919, and pres. Authors & Publishers Corp.; founder, 1921, and pres. Scenario Supply Corp. Episcopalian. Author: The Betrayal (novel), 1910; The Sovereignty of the States (polit. treatise), 1910; Life of Ambrose Bierce, 1927. Compiler: Masterpieces of Southern Poets (anthology), 1912. Address: New York, N.Y. Died Sept. 28, 1933.

NEEDHAM, Charles Austin, landscape artist; b. Buffalo, N.Y., Oct. 30, 1844; s. Elias Parkman and Lorana (Newberry) N.; pupil of Art Students' League and of August Will, New York; m. Fannie Montross, 1868. Hon. mention and medal, Atlanta Internat. Expn., 1895; 1st hon. mention N.Y. State Agrl. Expn., Syracuse, 1898; bronze medal, Paris Expn., 1900; silver medal, Charleston Expn., 1902; bronze medal, St. Louis Expn., 1904. Represented in St. Louis Mus. of Fine Arts, and Annual Exhbn. of Am. Water Colors, 1906-07-08. Home: New York, N.Y. Died 1923.

NEEDHAM, Henry Beach, writer; b. Castile, N.Y., Aug. 10, 1871; s. Charles W. and Caroline M. (Beach) N.; student Brown U., 3 yrs.; LL.B., Columbian (now George Washington) U., 1894; m. Mary M. Master, Dec. 28, 1910. Admitted to D.C. bar and practiced law, 1894-96; reporter New York Evening Post, 1896-97, real estate editor, 1897-1900; asst. managing editor McClure's Mag., 1900-01; staff writer World's Work, 1905-06; gen. mag. writer, 1904—. Apptd. by President Roosevelt spl. commr. to investigate labor and housing conditions in Canal Zone, 1908; spl. corr. Collier's Weekly, Roosevelt foreign tour, 1910. Home: Wyncote, Pa. Died June 17, 1915.

NEEDLES, Arthur Chase, ry. pres.; b. Baltimore, Md., Jan. 10, 1867; s. John Amos and Augusta (Strattan) N.; ed. pub. schs. and Swarthmore (Pa.) Coll.; m. Bessie Parker Williams, Nov. 14, 1899 (died 1923); 1 son, John Oliver; m. 2d, Hortense Edith Clarke, Dec. 18, 1928. Began as rodman, Washington, Ohio & Southern Ry., 1882; with N.&W. Ry., 1883—, as rodman, yard clk. and brakeman, 1883, night and day yardmaster, 1884, later yardmaster at Pulaski and Bluefield until 1890, asst. trainmaster and trainmaster, 1890-1901, asst. supt. Pocahontas div., May-June 1901, successively supt. Shenandoah, Norfolk and Pocahontas divs. until 1904, gen. supt., 1904-12, gen.

mgr., N.&W. Ry., 1912-18, v.p. in charge operation, Jan.-June 1918, federal mgr., 1918-20, again v.p. in charge operation, 1920-21, v.p. in charge operation and traffic, 1921-24, pres., 1924—. Quaker. Home: Roanoke, Va. Died Oct. 25, 1936.

NEELEY, George A., congressman; b. Detroit, Pike County, Ill., Aug. 1, 1879; s. George M. and Elizabeth (Stephens) N.; ed. Southwestern Baptist U.; grad. Law Dept. U. of Kan., 1904; m. Eva M. Hostetler, Oct. 31, 1904. Practiced law at Wellston, Okla., 1904-05, Chandler, 1905-08, Hutchinson, Kan., 1908—. Pres. Hutchinson Mut. Fire Ins. Co., Farmers Hall Ins. Co. Candidate for Congress, 1910; elected to Congress, Jan. 11, 1912, to succeed E. H. Madison, dec.; reëlected, Nov. 1912, 63d Congress (1913-15), 7th Kan. Dist. Mem. Christian (Disciples) Ch. Mem. of com. apptd. to investigate "money trust," 1913. Home: Hutchinson, Kan. Died Jan. 1, 1919.

NEELY, Henry Adams, second P.E. bishop of Me., consecrated Jan. 25, 1867; b. Fayetteville, N.Y., May 14, 1830; grad. Hobart Coll., Geneva, N.Y., 1849, hon. D.D., 1866; tutor Hobart, 2 years; ordered deacon, 1852; ordained priest, 1854; rector Calvary Ch., Utica, N.Y., 1853-55; first rector Christ Ch., Rochester, N.Y., 1855-62; chaplain Hobart Coll., 1862-64; asst. minister Trinity Ch., New York, 1864-67. Chairman House of Bishops, 1889-95. Address: Portland, Me. Died 1899.

NEELY, Thomas Benjamin, bishop; b. Philadelphia, Pa., June 12, 1841; s. Thomas and Frances (Armstrong) N.; ed. mainly in Phila.; hon. A.M., Dickinson, 1875; S.T.D., Simpson Coll., Indianola, Ia., 1884; Ph.D., Chattanooga U., 1886; LL.D., Mt. Union Coll., 1890; m. Elizabeth Cheney Hickman, Mar. 1882 (died 1912). Entered ministry M.E. Ch. in Phila. Ann. Conf., 1865; pastor in Phila. and vicinity 29 yrs., presiding elder 6 yrs.; elected to 6 consecutive Quad. Gen. Confs. M.E. Ch., and always leader of the delegation; editor ch. S.S. and tract literature, books, etc., and corr. sec. S.S. Union and Tract Soc. M.E. Ch., 1900-04; elected bishop, 1904; in Buenos Aires, Argentina, and in charge of work of M.E. Ch. in S.A., 1904-08; opened new missions in Panama and Bolivia, with service also in U.S.; returned to U.S., 1908, then with episcopal duty in U.S., also in Mexico; retired, 1912. Author: Sunday School books, 1900-04; Juan Wesley, El Gran Reformador Religioso, 1905; South America, a Mission Field, 1906; La Predicasion Tradato Practico de Homiletica, 1907; South America, Its Missionary Problems, 1909; The Bishop and the Supervisional System of the Methodist Episcopal Church, 1912; The Minister in the Itinerant System, 1914; Neely's Parliamentary Practice, 1914; American Methodism, Its Divisions and Unification, 1915; Doctrinal Standards of Methodism, including the Methodist Episcopal Churches, 1918; The League the Nation's Danger, 1919; Present Perils of Methodism, 1920; The Revised Ritual of 1916, 1920; The Only Condition, 1920; Methodist Episcopal Church and Foreign Missions, 1923; also many other religious books. Home: Philadelphia, Pa. Died Sept. 4, 1925.

NEF, John Ulric, chemist; b. Herisau, Canton Appenzell, Switzerland, June 14, 1862; s. John Ulric and Anna Katharine (Mock) N.; A.B., Harvard, 1884; Kirkland fellow, Harvard, 1884-87; Ph.D., U. of Munich, 1886; m. Louise Bates Comstock, May 17, 1898 (died 1909). Prof. chemistry and dir. chem. lab., Purdue, 1887-89; asst. prof. chemistry and acting head chem. lab., Clark U., 1889-92; prof. chemistry, 1892-96; head of dept., 1896—, U. of Chicago. Fellow Am. Acad. Arts and Sciences. Home: Chicago, Ill. Died Aug. 13, 1915.

NEFF, Frank Howard, educator; b. Cleveland, O., July 30, 1865; s. William Alfred and Eliza (Mong) N.; grad. Case Sch. Applied Science, 1887; instr. civ. engring., Case Sch. Applied Science, 1887-89; student École des Ponts et Chaussées and the Sorbonne, Paris, 1889-90; m. Ida Crawford Brown, Dec. 23, 1903 (died 1914); children—Frank Howard, Edward Brown. Asst. prof. and prof. civ. engring, Case Sch. Applied Science, 1907—; pres. Electric Ry. Improvement Co.; pres. Forest City Electric Co. Republican. Conglist. Home: South Euclid, O. Died 1936.

NEFF, George N(orth), publisher; b. Winchester, Ind., June 6, 1861; s. Andrew J. and Ann H. (Chaffee) N.; ed. DePauw U., Greencastle, Ind.; m. Willie E. Witty-Alderson, Jan. 2, 1915. Began as reporter and solicitor Corn Belt Farm Dailies, Inc., pubs. Daily Drovers Journal (Chicago), Daily Drovers Telegram (Kansas City, Mo.), Daily Journal Stockman (Omaha), Daily Nat. Live Stock Reporter (St. Louis), later becoming pres.; v.p. Anchor Loan & Trust Co.; dir. Inter-State Nat. Bank. Republican. Methodist. Mason. Home: Kansas City, Mo. Deceased.

NEFF, John Henry, urologist; b. Harrisonburg, Va., Sept. 12, 1887; s. John Henry and Brownie (Morrison) N.; A.B., U. of Va., 1907, M.D., 1910; m. Harriet Louise Fitzgerald, June 1, 1916; children—Mary Elizabeth, John Henry, George Fitzgerald. Interne and house surgeon U. of Va. Hosp., 1910-16; acting asso. prof. surgery, U. of Va., 1917-19, successively adj. prof., asso. prof. and prof. urology, 1916—. Democrat. Episcopalian. Home: University, Va. Died Nov. 1938.

NEFF, Joseph Seal, M.D.; b. Phila., Pa., Feb. 27, 1854; s. Charles and Mary (Seal) N.; A.B., U. of Pa., 1873, A.M., 1876; M.D., Jefferson Med. Coll., 1875; LL.D., Ursinus, 1912; D.P.H., Jefferson Med. Coll. and U. of Pa., 1912; m. Harriet Ludlow June 4, 1879; m. 2d, Clara L. Gibbons, June 2, 1894; m. 3d, Lena Keyes Holder, Dec. 23, 1922. Began practice at Philadelphia, 1875; attending physician, Phila. General Hospital, 1882-89, Jefferson Medical College Hospital, 1883-89; mem. auxiliary faculty, Jefferson Med. Coll., 1880-89 (retired from active work, account of ill health). Dir. Jefferson Med. Coll. Hosp., 1893-1907; dir. pub. health and charities, Phila., 1907-14; mem. Bd. Charities and Correction (about) 1895-99. Mem. Pa. State Council of Defense, World War. Republican. Episcopalian. Home: Narberth, Pa. Deceased.

NEFF, Silas S., teacher; b. W. Overton, Pa., Sept. 16, 1853; s. Israel and Sarah N.; grad. State Normal Sch., Millersville, Pa., 1870-75; Luth. Theol. Sem., Mt. Airy, Pa., 1878; Yale Div. Sch., 1879-80; m. Hannah May Hood, 1880. Began teaching, 1870; lecturer on edn., 1884-93; originated system of mind development; founded, 1893, and later became pres. Neff Coll. of Oratory, Phila. Baptist. Author: Talks on Education and Oratory, 1900; Power Through Perfected Ideas, 1911. Address: Philadelphia, Pa. Died Oct. 26, 1937.

NEGLEY, James Scott, soldier, financier; b. E. Liberty, Pa. (now East End of Pittsburgh), Dec. 22, 1826; ed. public schools and Western U. of Pa.; enlisted in Duquesne Grays at 17, when it became part of 1st Pa. regt., and served through Mexican war; after war engaged in mfg.; elected brig. gen. 18th div. Pa. militia; offered his div. to State authorities in Dec. 1860; in 10 days in April 1861, organized, clothed and equipped brigade for 3 months' service; re-commissioned brig. gen.; served through war, taking part in many battles; took a leading part in battle of Stone River, Dec. 31, 1862, and was promoted maj. gen. of vols.; led forward movement upon Tallahoma and took prominent part at Chickamauga; m. Kate De Losey (died); m. 2d, Grace Ashton. Mem. Congress, 1869-73, 1875-77, 1885-87; actively engaged in promotion and construction of rys.; acted as pres. and v.p. of several ry. cos.; 15 yrs. one of mgrs. Nat. Home for Volunteers; pres. Nat. Union League of America; mem. G.A.R. and other mil. orgns. Home: Plainfield, N.J. Died 1901.

NEHER, Fred, chemist; b. Troy, N.Y., Apr. 30, 1867; s. John Henry and Harriet Vandenberg (Price) N.; A.B., Princeton, 1889, A.M., 1891; fellow, U. of Chicago, 1896-98; m. Harriet Hutchins, Sept. 7, 1898; children—John Hutchins, Sara Wadsworth. Chemist, U.S. Fish Commn., 1890; asst. in chemistry, 1891-92, instr., 1892-98, asst. prof. organic chemistry, 1898-1903, prof., 1903—, head of dept., 1903-14, Princeton U. Coöperating with Bur. of Mines in war gases investigation, 1917-18. Home: Princeton, N.J. Died Dec. 10, 1929.

NEHLIG, Victor, artist; b. at Paris, France, 1830; studied under Leon Cogniet and Abel de Pujol; came to U.S., 1856; later resided in Havana, Cuba; then opened studio in New York; returned to France, 1872. A.N.A., 1863, N.A., 1870. Address: Paris, France. Deceased.

NEHRLING, Henry, ornithologist, botanist; b. Howard's Grove, Sheboygan County, Wis., May 9, 1853; s. Carl and Elizabeth (Ruge) N.; grad. Teachers' Sem., Addison, Ill., 1873; m. Sophia Schoff, July 20, 1874 (died 1911); children—Lydia, Walter, Bruno, Hildegard (dec.), Hulda, Arno, Werner, Hedwig Else (dec.), Berthold; m. 2d, Mrs. Betty P. Mitchell, June 7, 1916. Deputy collector and insp. customs, Milwaukee, 1887-90; sec. and custodian Pub. Mus., Milwaukee, 1890-1901. Investigator in ornithology, botany, horticulture; specialist in ecology of N.Am. birds; collaborator Bur. Plant Industry, U.S. Dept. Agr.; specialist in ecology of N. Am. birds, also in palms, tropical shade trees, etc. Fellow Am. Ornithologists' Union; mem. Am. Forestry Assn. Author: Die Nordamerikanische Vogelwelt, 1891; Our Native Birds of Song and Beauty (2 vols.), 1893, 1896; Die Amaryllis, 1908. Home: Gotha, Fla. Died Nov. 22, 1929.

NEIDLINGER, William Harold, composer; b. Brooklyn, N.Y., July 20, 1863; studied composition and orchestration with Dudley Buck and C.C. Müller, New York, 1880-90, and with Danreuther, London, 1896-98. Composer (books): Small Songs for Small Singers, 1896; Earth, Sky and Air in Song (books 1 and 2), 1900; Owl and the Woodchuck; Squirrel and the Crow; Primer on Voice and Singing; Little Folks' Song Book. Also comic operas, Ulysses, prod. by the Bostonians, 1901, and Sweet Anne Page, 1903. In charge for many yrs. of Neidlinger Sch. for the Unusual Child, East Orange. Home: East Orange, N.J. Died Dec. 1924.

NEIL, Edward Wallace, P.E. clergyman; b. Newark, N.J.; ordained deacon, 1880, priest, 1882; asst. rector St. Philip's, Garrison, N.Y., 1881-83; founder, 1883, then rector Ch. St. Edward the Martyr, New York. Author: Faithful Woman; Sermons, etc. Address: New York, N.Y. Died 1908.

NEIL, Matt Marshall, judge; b. Fayetteville, Tenn., Jan. 26, 1849; s. Newton F. and Virginia E. N.; ed. Washington and Lee U., 1867-69; taught sch., 1869-72; student Lebanon (Tenn.) Law Sch., 1872; admitted to bar, 1873; m. Eliza C. Green, Feb. 17, 1874. Practiced at Trenton, Tenn., 1873-95; judge of Court of Chancery Appeals, 1895-1902; asso. justice Supreme Ct. of Tenn., 1902-18 (chief justice, Feb. 17, 1913-Sept. 1, 1918); mem. law firm Jackson, Neil & McRee, Memphis, 1918—. Democrat. Presbyn. Pres. Tenn. State Bar Assn., 1892. Author: The Growth of Legal Principles, 1894. Home: Memphis, Tenn. Died June 23, 1925.

NEILL, John Selby Martin; b. St. Paul; s. Edward Duffield and Nancy (Hall) N.; A.B., Delaware Coll., Newark, 1881; studied Columbian Law U., 1881-83; m. Margaret G. Evans, Nov. 7, 1883. Removed to Helena, Mont., 1883; surveyor gen. of Mont., 1894-97; bought, 1897, the Helena Independent, which he conducted until Aug. 1903, when he sold paper; long active in polit. affairs. Mem. Dem. Nat. Com., 1900-04, Congressional Campaign Com., 1904-06. Repurchased Helena Independent, Oct. 1904. Address: Helena, Mont. Died Mar. 22, 1912.

NEILSON, Thomas Rundle, surgeon; b. Philadelphia, Pa., Oct. 29, 1857; s. Thomas and Sarah Claypoole (Lewis) N.; A.B., U. of Pa., 1877, A.M., M.D., 1880; m. Louise Fotterall, Jan. 12, 1898. Became prof. genito-urinary surgery, U. of Pa. Sch. of Medicine, 1903, later emeritus; surgeon emeritus Hosp. of P.E. Ch.; cons. surgeon St. Christopher's Hosp. for Children. Republican. Episcopalian. Home: Philadelphia, Pa. Died Oct. 25, 1939.

NEILSON, William George, metallurgical engr.; b. Phila., Aug. 12, 1842; grad. Polytechnic Coll. of Pa., 1862; connected with Elizabethtown forges, 1869-70; Pa. Steel Co., 1870-71; gen. mgr. Logan Iron & Steel Co., 1871-76; mgr. Standard Steel Works, 1877-90; v.p. Wellman Iron and Steel Co., 1890-92; mgr. Taylor Iron and Steel Co., 1893-95; pres. Republic M. and M. Co., 1892-1905, Adirondack Mountain Reserve, 1887-1904; treas. Keystone Drop Forge Wks., 1899-1905. Mem., 1872— (sec. centennial com., 1876, and mem. bd. mgrs., 1886-88), Am. Inst. Mining Engrs. Address: Philadelphia, Pa. Died 1907.

NELAN, Charles, cartoonist; b. Akron, O., Apr. 10, 1859; s. Daniel and Catherine (Madden) N.; ed. Buchtel Coll.; studied art Nat. Acad. Design, New York; m. Margaret A. Kennedy, artist, 1897. Began cartoon work Cleveland Press, 1888; then with Scripps-McRae League of Western newspapers; and subsequently cartoonist for New York Herald, Phila. North American, etc. Published "Cartoons of Our War with Spain," 1898. Address: Philadelphia, Pa. Died 1904.

NELSON, Adolphus P., congressman; b. nr. Holmes City, Douglas County, Minn., Mar. 28, 1872; s. Nels A. and Christine (Kron) N.; A.B., Hamline U., 1897 (pres. of class); LL.D., Upper Ia. U., 1919; m. Lulu E. Strang, Aug. 4, 1897; 1 dau., Dolores Elizabeth. Began in banking business, 1895; pres. First Bank of Grantsburg, Wis., 1896—; pres. Burnett County State Bank; asso. dir. Old Line Life Ins. Co.; sec. and treas. Hickerson Roller Mill Co., Grantsburg Loan, Title & Realty Co.; mem. 3d session, 65th Congress, and mem. 66th and 67th Congresses (1919-23), 11th Wis. Dist. Republican. V.p. bd. trustees Hamline U.; regent U. of Wis. 14 yrs., pres. bd. 2 yrs. Pres. General Laymen's Assn. M.E. Ch. Mason. Home: Grantsburg, Wis. Died Aug. 22, 1927.

NELSON, Alexander Lockhart, educator; b. Augusta Co., Va., Aug. 21, 1827; s. Alexander Franklin and Eliza (Guy) N.; A.B., Washington Coll. (now Washington and Lee U.), 1849; M.A., U. of Va., 1853; hon. LL.D., Washington and Lee, 1906; m. Elizabeth Harvey, d. Capt. David E. Moore, g.d. Gen. Andrew Moore, July 5, 1855. Acting professor mathematics, U. of Va., 1853-54; prof. mathematics, 1854-1906, emeritus prof., 1906, Washington and Lee U. Wrote: Chapter on Surfaces of the Second Order, Nichols' Analytic Geometry, 1893. Address: Lexington, Va. Died 1910.

NELSON, Benjamin F., mfr., financier; b. Greenup Co., Ky., May 4, 1843; s. William and Emeline (Benson) N.; attended common schools of Ky.; m. Martha Ross, 1869 (died 1874); m. 2d, Mary Fredenburg, 1875. Pres. Hennepin Paper Co.; chmn. bd. B. F. Nelson Mfg. Co.; dir. Northwestern Nat. Bank of Minneapolis, Northwestern Nat. Life Ins. Co. Served in 2d Ky. Cav. under Generals Joseph Wheeler, W. Forrest and John H. Morgan, during Civil War. Democrat. Methodist. Mem. bd. of mgrs. Minn. State Prison; regent U. of Minn.; trustee Hamline U. Home: Minneapolis, Minn. Died Jan. 11, 1928.

NELSON, Bertram Griffith, lecturer, prof. public speaking; b. Paoli, Wis., Oct. 7, 1876; s. Charles Brown and Julia Amanda (Grover) N.; student U. of Mich., 1898-99; A.B., U. of Chicago, 1902; m. Lillian Dorothea Block, 1905; children—Margaret Dorothea, Frances, Bertram Griffith. Mem. faculty,

U. of Chicago, Dept. Pub. Speaking, 1902—, asst., 1902-04, asso., 1904-07, instr., 1907-13, asst. prof., 1913-20, asso. prof., 1922—; dir. Reynolds Student Clubhouse 1923, dean 1927. Asso. dir. Nat. Hdqrs., Four-Minute Men, Com. on Pub. Information, 1917-18; mem. Nat. Advisory Council, same com., 1918; mem. Pub. Speaking Com. 2d Liberty Loan, 7th Fed. Reserve Dist. Republican. Baptist. Home: Chicago, Ill. Died Dec. 28, 1938.

NELSON, Charles Alexander, librarian; b. Calais, Me., Apr. 14, 1839; s. Israel Potter and Jane (Capen) N.; A.B., Harvard U., 1860, A.M., 1863; student Lawrence Scientific Sch., 1861-62; m. at Newbern, N.C., Emma, d. Benson and Eliza (Quick) Norris, July 25, 1872 (died 1926); children—Gertrude Jane, Ruth Augusta, Benson Israel (dec.). Began library work at Gorham (Me.) Male Acad., 1855; assistant Harvard College Library, 1857-60, 1863-64; teacher, 1860-61 and 1863-64; civ. engr. q.m.'s dept., U.S.A., 1864-65; supt. of schs., justice of the peace, and other civ. offices at Newbern, N.C., 1865-73; in book business, literary and library work, at Boston, until 1879; prof. Greek, Drury Coll., Mo., 1879-80; catalogue librarian Astor Library, New York, 1881-88; librarian Howard Memorial Library, New Orleans, 1888-91; asst. librarian Newberry Library, Chicago, 1891-93; dep. and reference librarian, Columbia U., 1893-1909 (retired). On staff Mercantile Assn. of New York, 1913-26. Dean of Am. Librarians. Home: Mt. Vernon, N.Y. Died Jan. 12, 1933.

NELSON, Cleland Kinloch, bishop; b. nr. Cobham, Va., May 23, 1852; s. Keating L. S. and Julia (Rogers) N.; A.B., St. John's Coll., Md., 1872; hon. D.D., 1891, and U. of the South, 1892; attended lectures Berkeley Div. Sch.; m. M. Bruce Matthews, June 12, 1877. Deacon, 1875, priest, 1876, P.E. Ch.; rector St. John the Baptist, Germantown, Pa., 1876-82, Ch. of the Nativity, S. Bethlehem, Pa., 1882-92. consecrated bishop of Ga., Feb. 24, 1892; became bishop of Atlanta, Dec. 1907. First pres. Synod of Sewanee. Address: Atlanta, Ga. Died Feb. 13, 1917.

NELSON, Daniel Thurber, physician; b. Milford, Mass., Sept. 16, 1839; s. Drake and Lydia Thurber (Pond) N.; A.B., Amherst, 1861, A.M., 1864; M.D., Harvard, 1865; m. Sarah Helen Travis, Nov. 24, 1862. Med. cadet Mason U.S. Gen. Hosp., 1862-65; acting asst. surgeon in armies of James and Potomac, 1865; surgeon Flying Hosp. of 24th Army Corps at surrender of Gen. Lee; practiced, Chicago, 1865—; prof. physiology and histology, Chicago Med. Coll., 1866-79; prof. clin. gynecology, Rush Med. Coll., 1880-98; inventor of several surgical instruments. Del. Internat. Med. Congress, London, 1881, Washington, 1887, Berlin, 1890. Address: Chicago, Ill. Died July 19, 1923.

NELSON, Edward William, naturalist; b. Manchester, N.H., May 8, 1855; s. William and Nancy M. (Wells) N.; grad. Cook County Normal School, Chicago, 1875; hon. A.M., Yale, 1920; hon. Sc.D., George Washington U., 1920; unmarried. Scientific explorations in Alaska, 1877-81; naturalist of the U.S. revenue steamer Corwin during her cruise on the Arctic search expdn. for the Jeannette in 1881; with Bur. Biol. Survey, Dept. of Agr., 1890-1929, chief field naturalist, 1907-12, in charge of biol. investigations, 1913-14, asst. chief, 1914-16, chief, 1916-27, prin. biologist, 1927-29; engaged in research, 1929-31; research asso., Smithsonian Institution, 1930—. Mem. Death Valley expdn. (Dept. of Agriculture), 1890-91; a large part of time from 1892-1906 was passed in zoöl. and bot. explorations in Mexico. Fellow Am. Ornithologists' Union (pres. 1908-09); pres. Biol. Soc. Washington, 1912-13; mem. Washington Acad. Sciences; corr. mem. Soc. Natural History of Mex.; v.p. Am. Soc. Mammalogy, 1918-19, pres. 1920-23; hon. mem. Calif. Acad. Sciences, Cooper Ornithological Club. Author: Report on Natural History Collections Made in Alaska, 1887. Also numerous monographs. Home: Orosi, Calif. Died May 19, 1934.

NELSON, Elnathan Kemper, chemist; b. Cincinnati, Nov. 25, 1870; s. Henry Francis and Maria Louisa (Davis) N.; B.S. in chemistry, U. of Illinois, 1894; m. Tuley C. Wetzel, Apr. 29, 1903; children—Elnathan Kemper, Berkeley Everett; m. 2d, Blanche Kennon Parker, Nov. 17, 1931. Served as chief chemist, Swift & Co., Chicago, 1895-1902; with Joslin, Schmidt & Co., chem. engrs., Cincinnati, 1902-03; chemist, Nelson Morris & Co., Chicago, 1903-04; in business on own account, 1904-07; asst. chemist, 1908-12, chief essential oils lab., drug div., 1912-27, sr. chemist div. of food research, 1927—, United States Bureau of Chemistry and Soils. Researches on composition of essential oils and chem. constitution of their constituents, also analytical work on oils and pharm. preparations containing them, and their derivatives, etc. Presbyn. Home: Silver Spring, Md. Died Nov. 9, 1940.

NELSON, Frank Howard, clergyman; b. Hartford, Conn., Sept. 6, 1869; s. Henry Wells and Hortense Chew (Lewis) N.; B.A., Hobart College, 1890; grad. Gen. Theol. Sem., 1894, D.D., 1906, LL.D., 1924, S.T.D., 1935; m. Mary Adams Eaton, June 6, 1907; 1 dau., Ruth. Deacon, 1894, priest, 1899, P.E. Ch.; asst. minister St. George's Ch., N.Y. City, 1894-99; asst. minister Christ Ch., Cincinnati, 1899-1900, rector, 1900—. Mem. bd. dirs. U. of Cincinnati, Cincinnati Community Chest; mem. Council of Social Agencies, Juvenile Protective Assn., Anti-Tuberculosis League. Mason. Home: Cincinnati, O. Died Oct. 31, 1939.

NELSON, George Francis, clergyman; b. Granville, O., Dec. 11, 1842; s. Franklin Nelson and Elizabeth Jane (Asher) N.; LL.B., Chicago U., 1871; D.D., Trinity, 1896, St. Stephen's, 1896. Deacon, 1877, priest, 1879, P.E. Ch.; asst. St. Andrew's Ch., Phila., Pa., 1877-79, Grace Ch., New York, 1879-83; rector Ch. of the Nativity, New York, 1881-83; vicar Grace Chapel, New York, 1883-95; sec. to bishop of New York, 1883-1908; asst. sec. House of Bishops, 1883-1916; canon Cathedral of St. John the Divine, 1911-19, hon. canon, 1919—; registrar Diocese of New York, 1886—; supt. New York City Mission, 1894-1902; archdeacon of New York, 1902-12; registrar Gen. Conv. and sec. House of Bishops, 1917-22; chaplain Mil. Order of Loyal Legion. Address: New York, N.Y. Died Mar. 16, 1932.

NELSON, Henry Addison, Presbyterian clergyman; b. Amherst, Mass., Oct. 31, 1820; s. Seth and Sophia (Aspenwell) N.; grad. Hamilton, 1840 (A.M., D.D.); taught select school, Eaton, N.Y., 1840-41; taught classical dept., Cortland Acad., Homer, N.Y., 1841-43; studied Auburn Theol. Sem., 1843-46; m. Margaret, d. Rev. Henry Mills, D.D., prof. Auburn Theol. Sem., Feb. 23, 1847 (died 1878). Pastor Presbyn. Ch., Auburn, N.Y., 1846-56; 1st Presbyn. Ch., St. Louis, 1856-68; prof. systematic and pastoral theology, Lane Theol. Sem., Cincinnati, 1868-74; pastor 1st Presbyn. Ch., Geneva, N.Y., 1874-85; acting pastor, Independence, Mo., 1885-86; editor The Church at Home and Abroad, 1887-97. Author: Seeing Jesus; Sin and Salvation, 1885; Home Whispers. Address: Wooster, O. Died 1906.

NELSON, Henry Loomis, author, editor; b. New York, Jan. 5, 1846; s. Theophilus and Catherine (Lyons) N.; ed. Williams Coll.; A.M., LL.B., Columbia; hon. L.H.D., Williams; m. Ida Frances Wyman, Oct. 14, 1874. Admitted to bar, 1869; Washington corr. Boston Post, 1878-85, editor, 1885-86; editor-in-chief Harper's Weekly, 1894-98; prof. political science, Williams Coll., 1902—. Mem. Am. Inst. Arts and Letters. Author: Our Unjust Tariff Law, 1884; John Rantoul (novel), 1884; The Money We Need, 1896. Address: Williamstown, Mass. Died 1908.

NELSON, Julia Bullard, educator, lecturer; b. High Ridge, Conn., May 13, 1842; d. Edward and Angeline (Raymond) Bullard; ed. Denmark (Ia.) Acad. and Hamline U., then at Red Wing, Minn.; m. Ole Nelson, Sept. 25, 1866 (died 1869). Taught school 6 years in Minn. and Conn. before marriage; taught Freedmen's Sch. in Tex., 1869-73; prin. pub. free sch., Columbus, Tex., 1871-73; went to Europe; taught colored sch., Athens, Tenn., 1875-77; prin. Warner Institute, Jonesboro, Tenn., 1877-81, and 1883-88; preached; organized Congl. Ch. at Jonesboro and did Prohibition work in E. Tenn. V.p. and lecturer, Minn. W.C.T.U., 1888-90; v.p. 1881-83, pres. 1890-97, Minn. Woman Suffrage Assn.; lecturer for Nat. Woman Suffrage Assn., 1890-96; editor White Ribbon, W.C.T.U. paper, 1902-06; supt. franchise Minn. W.C.T.U.; exec. mem. Minn. E.F.L., 1912—. Writer of prose and poetry. Address: Red Wing, Minn. Died Dec. 24, 1914.

NELSON, Julius, biologist; b. Copenhagen, Denmark, Mar. 6, 1858; s. Christian and Julie Marie Pauline (Jorgensen) N.; B.S., U. of Wis., 1881, M.S., 1883; Ph.D., Johns Hopkins, 1888; m. Nellie Cynthia Chase, Aug. 9, 1888. Prof. biology, Rutgers Coll., and biologist, N.J. Agrl. Coll. Expt. Sta., 1888—. Biologist, N.J. Expt. Sta., investigating oyster culture, 1888-92, bovine tuberculosis, 1893-1901; biologist, N.J. State Tuberculosis Commn., 1894-95; biologist under spl. act of N.J. Legislature, 1901, renewed 1907; coöperating with chief, Bur. of Shell Fisheries, N.J., 1911—; v.p. and consulting adviser, Lederle Labs., New York, 1910-11. Mem. Highland Park (N.J.) Bd. Edn. 3 terms (resigned). Pres. N.J. State Micros. Soc. Contbr. to Chandler's Cyclo., Bailey's Encyclo. of Agr. Address: New Brunswick, N.J. Died Feb. 16, 1916.

NELSON, Knute, senator; b. in Norway, Feb. 2, 1843; came to U.S., 1849; ed. Albion Coll.; pvt. and non-commd. officer 4th Wis. Inf., 1861-64; wounded and captured at Port Hudson. Admitted to bar, 1867; mem. Wis. Ho. of Reps., 1868-69; went to Alexandria, Minn., 1871; county atty., Douglas County, 1872-74; Minn. Senate, 1875-78; presdl. elector, 1880; regent U. of Minn., 1882-93; mem. 48th to 50th Congresses (1883-89), 5th Minn. Dist.; elected gov. of Minn., 1892, reëlected 1894; resigned, 1895; U.S. senator, 5 terms, 1895-1925. Republican. Address: Alexandria, Minn. Died Apr. 28, 1923.

NELSON, Rensselaer Russell, jurist; b. Cooperstown, N.Y., May 12, 1826; s. Samuel and Catharine Ann (Russell) N.; grad. Yale, 1846; admitted to bar, 1849; began practice in Buffalo, but in 1850 went to St. Paul. Apptd., 1857, asso. justice Territorial Supreme Court, and upon admission of Minn. to the Union, 1858, was apptd. dist. judge for the dist. of Minn., serving until 1896; resigned. Democrat. Address: St. Paul, Minn. Died 1904.

NELSON, Richard Henry, bishop; b. New York, N.Y., Nov. 10, 1859; s. Edward Delavan and Susan Blanchard (Macdonald) N.; A.B., Trinity Coll., Conn., 1880, A.M., 1883; U. of Leipzig, 1880-81; Berkeley Div. Sch., Conn., 1881-83; hon. D.D., Trinity, and Berkeley, 1904; S.T.D., U. of Pa., 1904; m. Harriet Schuyler Anderson, Jan. 20, 1885; children—Richard McD., John L. Deacon, 1883, priest, 1884, P.E. Ch.; asst. St. John's Ch., Stamford, Conn., 1883-84; rector Grace Ch., Waterville, N.Y., 1884-87, Christ Ch., Norwich, Conn., 1887-97, St. Peter's Ch., Phila., 1897-1904; consecrated bishop coadjutor of Albany, N.Y., May 19, 1904; became bishop of Albany, May 17, 1913; resigned, July 1, 1929. Home: Albany, N.Y. Died Apr. 25, 1931.

NELSON, Robert W., type founder; b. Granville, N.Y.; common sch. edn. Began in printing office at Joliet, Ill.; became part owner Joliet Daily News and later in printing business, Chicago; with others organized Am. Press Assn., of which was v.p.; became interested in Thorne typesetting machine, 1886, of which was pres.; dir. and gen. mgr., 1894—, pres., 1901—, Am. Type Founders Co.; also pres. Nat. Paper & Type Co. Home: Westfield, N.J. Died July 28, 1926.

NELSON, Sofus Bertelson; b. Veile, Denmark, Dec. 21, 1867; came to U.S., 1877; D.V.M., Ia. State Coll., 1889; post-grad. work, Royal Vet. College, Copenhagen, Denmark, 1893; m. Jettchen Uhden-Nelson, Nov. 28, 1895. House surgeon Vet. Dept. Ia. State Coll., 1889-90; practicing veterinarian, 1890-95; prof. vet. science and head of dept., 1895-1917, dean, 1917—, Coll. Vet. Science, State Coll. of Wash.; state veterinarian of Wash., 1895-1913; mem. Wash. State Bd. of Health, 1895-1913; veterinarian Wash. State Expt. Sta., 1895-1915; dir. extension service, 1919—; sec. Spokane Vet. Coll. Republican. Conglist. Mason. Home: Pullman, Wash. Died June 4, 1931.

NELSON, Thomas Kinloch, clergyman; b. Alexandria, Va., Apr. 11, 1879; s. Kinloch and Grace Fenton (McGuire) N.; student Episcopal High Sch., Alexandria, 1896, McGuire's Sch., Richmond, 1897; B.A., M.A., U. of Va., 1907; B.D., Va. Theol. Sem., 1911, D.D., 1920; spl. student Yale Div. Sch., 1920; unmarried. Head of classical dept., Episcopal High Sch., 1901-06; deacon, 1910, priest, 1911, P.E. Ch.; prof. Greek, St. John's U., Shanghai, China, 1910-13; rector Christ Ch., Salem, Va., 1914-16; vice rector Va. Episcopal Sch., Lynchburg, Va., 1916-19; prof. O.T., Va. Theol. Sem., 1920—; chaplain Episcopal High Sch., 1923—. Democrat. Home: Alexandria, Va. Died Jan. 28, 1940.

NELSON, William, editor; b. Rutherglen, Scotland, July 1, 1839; s. John and Margaret (Correns) N.; ed. in common schs. and printing offices; m. Mary E. Fretwell, Aug. 22, 1866. Began apprenticeship in Monroe (Wis.) Sentinel office, 1852, and worked in Richland Center, Lancaster, Platteville, Mineral Point, Wis., and in the Galena (Ill.) Gazette office before Civ. War. Served in Co. I, 10th Wis. Inf., Oct. 14, 1861-June 7, 1865; was sergt. and 1st sergt. After war became joint propr. with Gen. Rusk and D. B. Priest, of Viroqua (Wis.) Censor; later editor La Crosse Republican and Leader; moved to Utah, 1876; U.S. marshal for Utah, 1876-78; then in Salt Lake City; in various positions on the Salt Lake Tribune, 1881—, editor-in-chief, 1907—. Mem. Wis. Senate, 1872-73; mem. Bd. of Edn., Salt Lake City, 1891-95 (pres. 1894-95). Home: Salt Lake City, Utah. Died Oct. 26, 1913.

NELSON, William, lawyer, author; b. Newark, N.J., Feb. 10, 1847; s. William and Susan (Cherry) N.; pub. sch. edn.; hon. A.M., Princeton, 1896; m. Salome W. Doremus, 1889. Engaged in journalism in Newark and Paterson several yrs.; admitted to N.J. and U.S. bars; practiced at Paterson, 1875—; U.S. commr.; chmn. Pub. Records Commn. N.J.; corr. sec. N.J. Hist. Soc., 1880—; mem. Am. Hist. Assn., Am. Anthrop. Assn., Am. Antiq. Soc., N.Y., Pa., Ala. and Minn. hist. socs.; corr. mem. N.E. Hist.-Geneal. Soc., N.Y. Geneal. and Biog. Soc. Editor: New Jersey Archives. Author: The Indians of New Jersey; The Doremus Family in America; History of the City of Paterson; Personal Names of Indians of New Jersey; Early Will-making in New Jersey; The Law of Marriage and Divorce in New Jersey. Home: Paterson, N.J. Died Aug. 10, 1914.

NELSON, William Rockhill, journalist; b. Ft. Wayne, Ind., Mar. 7, 1841; s. Isaac De Groff and Elizabeth (Rockhill) N.; ed. at Notre Dame U., Ind., hon. LL.D., 1911; m. Ida, d. Robert Houston, Nov. 29, 1881. Founder Western Gallery of Art, Kansas City. Founder, 1880, and later owner and editor-in-chief Kansas City Star. Dir. Associated Press. Home: Kansas City, Mo. Died Apr. 13, 1915.

NELSON, Wolfred, physician, author; b. Montreal, P.Q., Can., Apr. 9, 1846; s. Dr. Horace and Cornelia B. (MacNeil) N.; g.s. late Dr. Wolfred N., the Canadian rebel of 1837; ed. McGill U. in faculties of science, arts, and medicine, M.D., 1872; C.M., M.D., Bishop's Coll., Lennoxville, Que., 1872; mem. Coll. Phys. and Surg. P.Q., 1876; m. Frederika W., d. James de Long, Apr. 27, 1875. Practiced at Panama, Colombia, 1880-85; traveled in Central and S. America, Mexico and W.I., collecting data in climatology and tropical diseases, 1885-88; in practice at New York, 1890—; sanitary commr. to Cuba for New York Herald, 1904, 05. Non-resident representative fellow McGill U. for U.S.; a founder of Canadian Soc. of New York, 1897, an incorporator, 1910, 2d pres., 1898-99; dir. Calvary Chapter No. 283, Brotherhood of St. Andrew, New York; a founder and pres. New York Graduates' Soc. of McGill U., 1895. Apptd. by Queen Regent of Spain, a commr. in ordinary Royal Order of Isabella the Catholic. Author: Apercu de Quelques Difficultés à vaincre dans le Construction du Canal de Panama, 1887; Five Years at Panama, 1888, 1891; Cinq Ans. à Panama, Paris, 1890. Address: New York, N.Y. Died Jan. 1913.

NESBIT, Charles Francis, insurance; b. Akron, O., June 23, 1867; s. Frank C. and Ellen M. (Wright) N.; student Westminster Coll., Fulton, Mo.; m. Clara Ford, Jan. 10, 1893; 1 son, Frank Ford. Engaged in insurance business at Washington, D.C., 1893—; pres. Masonic Mut. Life Assn., 1912-13; apptd. supt. of ins., D.C., Jan. 1914; commr. div. of mil. and naval ins., War Risk Bureau, Washington, Oct. 23, 1917-Mar. 1919; one of original dirs. Nat. Budget Com., 1919; v.p. Bliss Electrical School, 1900—; ins. adviser to Internat. Brotherhood of Electrical Workers, and Union Coöperative Ins. Assn., Washington, D.C. (the 1st legal reserve life ins. co. to be owned and operated by a labor organization); also actively identified with organization of the Union Labor Life Ins. Co., owned by several labor brotherhoods. Mem. Ch. of the Covenant (Presbyn.). Home: Washington, D.C. Died 1934.

NESBIT, Harrison, banker; b. Osceola, Mo., Sept. 15, 1875; s. Scott and Annetta (Johnson) N.; prep. edn., Episcopal High Sch. of Virginia and Berkeley Sch., Washington, D.C.; student Mass. Inst. Tech.; LL.B., Nat. Univ. Law Sch., Washington, 1900, LL.M., 1901; m. Edith Herron, Nov. 25, 1896; children—Scott Herron, Edith Caroline, Nancy Elizabeth. Admitted to bar, and practiced law 9 yrs.; pres. Bank of Pittsburgh Nat. Assn., 1910—; pres. Highland Nat. Bank, Pittsburgh; dir. and mem. exec. com. Westinghouse Electric and Mfg. Co.; dir. Weirton Steel Co., Kaufmann Dept. Stores, Four States Coal Co., H. R. Mallinson and Co. Trustee Mercy Hospital. Democrat. Presbyn. Home: Warrenton, Va. Died 1931.

NESBIT, Valentine Jordan, lawyer; b. Camden, S.C., Jan. 20, 1883; s. Ralph and Cora (Jordan) N.; A.B., U. of the South, Sewanee, Tenn., 1904; A.M., Princeton, 1905; student law dept. U. of Pittsburgh, 1905-08; m. Virginia Preston Means, Dec. 12, 1911; children—Ralph 3d, Sarah Palmer. Admitted to Ala. bar, 1908, and later practiced at Birmingham; v.p. and dir. Montevallo Coal Mining Co., Straven Coal Mining Co.; dir. Continental Securities Co.; hon. consul of Belgium, 1918—. Democrat. Episcopalian. Home: Birmingham, Ala. Died Feb. 8, 1938.

NESBIT, Wilbur D(ick), author; b. Xenia, O., Sept. 16, 1871; s. John Harvey and Isabel (Fichthorne) N.; ed. pub. sch., Cedarville, O.; m. Mary Lee Jenkins, 1899; children—Richard Harvey, John Robert, Wilbur Daniel. Feature writer on Baltimore American, Chicago Tribune, Chicago Evening Post, 1899-1912. V.p., dir. copy staff, Wm. H. Rankin Co., Chicago. Author: The Trail to Boyland, 1904; The Gentleman Ragman, 1906; The Land of Make-Believe and Other Christmas Poems, 1907; A Friend or Two, 1908; Your Flag and My Flag; etc. Home: Evanston, Ill. Died Aug. 20, 1927.

NETTLETON, Alvred Bayard, soldier, journalist, writer; b. Berlin, Delaware Co., O., Nov. 14, 1838; s. Hiram and Lavinia (Janes) N.; reared on farm; A.B., Oberlin Coll., 1863, A.M., 1866; m. Melissa Tenney, Jan. 8, 1863; 1 dau., Caroline Nettleton Thurber. Enlisted in U.S. vols. while at Oberlin Coll., 1861; served in the field through the Civ. War; promoted 1st lt. 2d Ohio Cav., Oct. 8, 1861; capt., Mar. 10, 1862; maj., July 18, 1863; lt. col. comdg. regt., Nov. 5, 1864; col., Apr. 22, 1865; bvtd. brig. gen. vols., Mar. 13, 1865, "for gallant and meritorious service"; resigned after close of war, June 13, 1865; fought in 72 battles and minor engagements, including capture of Knoxville, Grant's campaign of the Wilderness, Sheridan's campaigns of the Shenandoah Valley, the siege of Richmond and service against Confed. Indians in Ind. Ter.; had 3 horses shot in action; after war studied law; editor and part propr. Sandusky (O.) Daily Register, 1867-68; del. Rep. Nat. Conv., 1868; pub. Chicago Advance, 1868-69; associated with Jay Cooke in projection and constrn. of N.P. R.R., 1870-75; mng. editor Philadelphia Inquirer, 1875-76; in mining and mfg., 1877-80; founder, editor and propr. Minneapolis Daily Tribune, 1880-85; mem. Anti-Saloon Rep. Nat. Com., 1884-89; asst. sec. U.S. Treasury, 1890-93, acting sec. several months after death of Sec. Windom. Mem. World's Columbian Commn., 1890-93; trustee of Oberlin Coll., 22 yrs. Retired from business to do lit. work, 1909. Republican. Congregationalist. Author: Trusts or Competition, 1900. Address: Chicago, Ill. Died 1911.

NETTLETON, Walter, artist; b. New Haven, Conn., June 19, 1861; s. William Alfred and Eliza Lyman (Thomson) N.; B.A., Yale, 1883, hon. B.F.A., 1902; began study of art at Yale Sch. of the Fine Arts, 1878, Art Students' League, New York, 1883; began painting in Paris, 1884; worked under Boulanger, Lefèbvre, Carolus Duran and Alexander Harrison; continued study in Paris, with occasional intermission, until 1890; unmarried. Painted in Brittany until 1894; first picture exhibited at Paris Salon, 1889; constant exhibitor at Salon, world's fairs, and at prin. Am. exhbns., 1889—. Mem. advisory com. on art, Panama P.I., Expn., San Francisco, 1915; chmn. Stockbridge exhbn. of painting and sculpture. Hon. mention, Salon, 1892; voted exempt from jury exam., Paris, 1900; silver medal, St. Louis Expn., 1904; bronze medal, Buenos Aires, 1910. Pictures are in pub. collection of The Players, New York, Boston Art Club, Museum of Fine Arts, New Britain, Conn., Jackson Library, Stockbridge, Mass., and Vassar College. Specially well known for Breton subjects and more recently for N.E. winter scenes. A.N.A., 1905. Republican. Home: Stockbridge, Mass. Died July 28, 1936.

NEUMANN, F(erdinand) Wight, impresario; b. Hamburg, Germany, Nov. 3, 1851; s. Neumann and Berta (Heckscher) N.; ed. gymnasium and coll., Hamburg; m. Lillian Denny Mallory, May 6, 1897. Came to U.S., 1877; at Chicago, 1884—; originally appeared under his auspices, at Chicago, Boston Symphony Orchestra, Met. Opera Co., N.Y., Boston Grand Opera Co., also Paderewski, Josef Hofmann, Schumann-Heink, Sembrich, Kubelik, Eames, Ysaye, Elman, Calvé, Melba, Nordica, Caruso and many others. U.S. consul at Cologne, Germany, 1897. Republican. Presbyn. Home: Chicago, Ill. Died Oct. 22, 1924.

NEUMARK, David, prof. Hebrew; b. Szczerzec, nr. Lwow, Galicia, Poland, Aug. 3, 1866; s. Solomon and Schifrah (Schuetz) N.; ed. various schs. in Poland; Ph.D., U. of Berlin, 1896; Rabbi, 1897; m. Dora Turnheim, June 7, 1898. Rabbi, at Rakonitz, nr. Prague, 1897-1903; editor in chief Hebrew Encyclopedia, Berlin, 1904-07; prof. philosophy, Hebrew Union Coll., Cincinnati, O., 1907—. Editor Journal of Jewish Lore and Philosophy, Cincinnati, 1919—. Mem. B'nai B'rith. Author: Die Freiheitslehre bei Kant und Schopenhauer, 1896; Geschichte der juedischen Philosophie, Vol. I, 1907, II, 1910; History and Dogmas in Judaism (Hebrew), Vol. I, 1913, II, 1919; The Philosophy of the Bible, 1918; History of Jewish Philosophy (Hebrew), Vol. I, 1921. Home: Cincinnati, O. Died Dec. 15, 1924.

NEVILLE, Wendell Cushing, officer U.S.M.C.; b. Portsmouth, Va., May 12, 1870; s. Willis H. and Mary Elizabeth (Cushing) N.; ed. Galt's Acad. (Norfolk, Va.), U.S. Naval Acad.; m. Frances Adelphia Howell, Jan. 4, 1898; 1 dau., Frances Howell (Mrs. J. P. W. Vest). Apptd. naval cadet, Sept. 13, 1886; commd. 2d lt. U.S. Marine Corps, July 1, 1892; promoted through grades to maj. gen., Dec. 9, 1920. With 1st Batt. at taking of Guantanamo Bay, Spanish-Am. War, 1898; comdr. co. in Boxer Campaign, China; participated in capture of Peking; in Philippine Campaign; mil. gov. Province of Basilan, 1901-02; comdr. marines at taking of Havana, 1906; comd. 2d Regt. Marines at taking of Vera Cruz, Mexico, Apr. 1914; comdr. Am. Legation Guard, Peking, 1915-17; comd. 5th Regt., 4th Brigade Marines, 2d Div., A.E.F., Jan.-July 1918, participating in occupation Toulon sector and in Aisne-Marne offensive (Bois de Belleau); comd. 4th Brigade, July 1918-Aug. 1919, participating in battles of Soissons, St. Mihiel, Blanc Mont, Meuse-Argonne, march to the Rhine, occupation of Coblentz bridgehead, etc. Bvtd. capt., Aug. 10, 1898, "for conspicuous conduct" in Battle of Guantanamo Bay, Cuba; awarded Congressional Medal of Honor, "for distinguished conduct" during engagement at Vera Cruz, Apr. 21 and 22, 1914; D.S.M., "for exceptionally meritorious and distinguished services," in World War; D.S.M. (Navy); Croix de Guerre with palm (French) "for gallantry in action," also Croix de Guerre with palm "for Battle of Blanc Mont," and 3 other croix de guerre, 2 bronze stars and 2 palms (all French); Officer Legion of Honor (French). Episcopalian. Apptd. comdt. Marine Corps, Mar. 5, 1929. Address: Washington, D.C. Died July 8, 1930.

NEVILLE, William, lawyer; b. Washington County, Ill., Dec. 29, 1843; s. Capt. Harvey and Aly (Harriman) N.; ed. McKendree Coll., Lebanon, Ill.; sergt. Co. H, 142d Ill. inf., in Civil war; mem. Ill. legislature, 1872; removed to Neb., 1874; mem. Neb. legislature, 1876; Dem. and anti-monopoly candidate for Congress, 1884; register U.S. Land Office, N. Platte, Neb., 1885-90; m. Mary Ann Keith, 1882 (died 1884); m. 2d, Irene Morrison Rector, 1886. Mem. G.A.R.; judge 13th Neb. jud. dist., 1891-95, elected judge Supreme Court, 1896. Mem. Congress, 1899-1903, 6th Neb. dist. Democrat. Removed to Ariz., Apr. 1903; elected to Ariz. legislature, 1904, and made chmn. judiciary com. V.p. Trans-Mississippi and Internat. Expn., Omaha, Neb., and pres. Neb. State Bd., 1898. Address: Douglas, Ariz. Died 1909.

NEVIN, Ethelbert, musician; b. Edgeworth, Pa., Nov. 25, 1862; m. 1888, Anne Paul. Composer of a large amount of music, notably songs, including "Bed-time Song," "Cradle Song," "I Once Had a Sweet, Little Doll," "Milkmaid's Song," etc. Address: Edgeworth, Pa. Died 1901.

NEVIN, George Balch, composer; b. Shippensburg, Pa., Mar. 15, 1859; s. Samuel Williamson and Harriet Macomb (Balch) N.; ed. Cumberland Valley State Normal Sch. and 2 yrs. at Fafayette Coll.; hon. M.A., Lafayette, 1915, Mus.Dr., 1925; m. at Easton Pa., Lillias Clara Dean, Apr. 25, 1888; children—Kenneth Shadwell (dec.), Gordon Balch, Shirley Dean. Writer of sacred songs, duets, anthems and cantatas; among his compositions may be named: Arise! Shine! for Thy Light Is Come (anthem for Christmas); four-part songs, My Bonnie Lass She Smileth, It Was a Lover and His Lass, O Mistress Mine, Smile Again, My Bonnie Lassie, O Little Mother of Mine. Songs, When the Kye Come Hame, Sigh No More, Ladies, The Heavenly Voice, Turn Ye, Even Unto Me, Jesus Word of God Incarnate (Ave Verum), O Taste and See, O Lord God, to Whom Vengeance Belongeth (war anthem), Sing and Rejoice, Rest in Peace, Ye Flanders Dead, In That Day Shall This Song Be Sung, There Were Shepherds, Once More the Twilight Glow, Ring Out, Wild Bells, Last Night (song), Hail Gladdening Light (anthem), The Vesper Hour at Sea (organ), At the Sepulchre (Easter anthem), God Will Make All Things Right (mixed voices, men's voices and solo), Into the Woods My Master Went (solo, mixed men's and women's voices), The Shepherd's Evening Prayer (organ), The Day of the Lord Cometh (anthem), The Infant Light (Christmas duet), Beloved, Let Us Love One Another (anthem), The Words on the Cross, Jesus, Do Roses Grow So Red?, The White Comrade (anthem), The Saving Victim (anthem for Lent, mixed voices), George Washington Processional (words by Lillias C. Nevin, mixed voices), The Master's Garden (anthem for mixed voices); cantatas—The Crown of Life (for general use, mixed and men's voices), The Gift of God, The Angel of the Dawn (Easter cantata, mixed voices, words by Lillias C. Nevin), The Incarnation (Christmas cantata, mixed and men's voices), also The Adoration (Christmas cantata, mixed and men's voices), and The Crucified, (Easter cantata, words of both by Lillias C. Nevin). Organized "The Victory Drummers," 1918, 40 in all, averaging about 60 yrs. of age, for patriotic rallies, World War. Presbyn. elder. Home: Easton, Pa. Died Apr. 17, 1933.

NEVIN, James Banks, editor; b. Rome, Ga., Sept. 9, 1873; s. Mitchel Albert and Helen (Underwood) N.; A.B., U. of Ga., 1892; m. Mary Bryan, Nov. 23, 1902. Mem. Ga. Ho. of Rep., 1896-98; city editor and mng. editor Rome Tribune, 1900-06; asso. editor Washington (D.C.) Herald, 1906-10; mng. editor Atlanta Georgian and Sunday American, 1910-12; later editor-in-chief Atlanta Georgian and v.p. Atlanta Georgian Pub. Co. Capt. Ga. Inf. Vols., 2d Regt., Spanish-Am. War. Trustee at large, U. of Ga. Democrat. Episcopalian. Mason, Elk. Home: Atlanta, Ga. Died Nov. 18, 1931.

NEVIN, Robert Jenkins, clergyman; b. Allegheny, Pa., Nov. 24, 1839; s. Rev. Dr. John W. N.; grad. Franklin and Marshall Coll., Lancaster, Pa., 1859, hon. D.D., Union; LL.D., Hobart; unmarried. Served in Civil war as lt. 122d Pa. vols., 1862; later capt., Battery I, Pa. vol. arty., and bvt. maj. U.S. vols. Grad. Gen. Theol. Sem., New York, 1867; rector Ch. of the Nativity, Bethlehem, Pa., 1868; rector St. Paul's Ch., Rome, Italy, 1869—; pres. conv., and of standing com., Am. Chs. in Europe; del. Am. Chs. in Europe to Gen. Conv. P.E. Ch. in U.S., 1889—. Built St. Paul's Am. Ch., Rome, 1870-76. Author: St. Paul's Within the Walls, 1878; Reunion Conf. at Bonn, 1875. Address: Rome, Italy. Died 1906.

NEVIN, Robert Peebles, journalist; b. Shippensburg, Pa., 1820; s. John and Martha (McCracken) N.; graduate Jefferson (now Washington and Jefferson) Coll., 1842, A.M.; m. Elizabeth Duncan Oliphant (died 1898). Established Pittsburgh Daily Leader, 1870, Pittsburgh Times, 1880. Author: Black Robes, Sketches of Mission and Ministers on the Border and in the Wilderness; Les Trois Rois; Beautiful River and Other Poems; Tracks of a Traveler, 1877-78, and About a Dog, 1902. Address: Edgeworth, Pa. Died 1908.

NEVIN, Theodore Williamson, editor; b. Sewickley, Pa., July 24, 1854; s. Daniel E. and Margaret I. N.; ed. Western U. of Pa. (now U. of Pittsburgh), studied law and took special courses at Dresden and Leipzig, 1876; m. Mary Elizabeth Appel, Nov. 12, 1890. Consecutively reporter, proofreader, telegraph editor, editorial writer, mng. editor and editor-in-chief Pittsburgh Leader, 1876-1906; pres. Leader Publishing Co., 1877-1906. Author: Pittsburgh and the Men Who Made It; Ralph Ranscomb, Banker, 1908. Home: Sewickley, Pa. Died Nov. 2, 1918.

NEVIUS, Henry M., lawyer; b. Monmouth Co., N.J., Jan. 30, 1841; s. James S. and Hannah (Bowe) N.; descendant of Joanus Nefus, Newburgh, N.Y., 1636; acad. and high sch. edn., Freehold, N.J., and Grand Rapids, Mich.; m. Matilda H. Herbert, Dec. 27, 1871. Pvt. Co. K, 1st N.Y. Lincoln Cav., Aug. 12, 1861 (co. recruited in Grand Rapids and joined

N.Y. regt. in field); discharged as regimental q.m. sergt., Dec. 31, 1862, to become 2d lt. Co. D, 7th Mich. Cav.; later joined 25th N.Y. Cav.; while serving as 1st lt. in comd. of co. in front of Washington, lost left arm, July 11, 1864; hon. discharged, July 1865. Engaged in ins. business; apptd. U.S. assessor internal revenue, Monmouth County, N.J., 1866; admitted to practice as atty., 1873, counsellor, 1876; practiced at Freehold, 1873-75, then at Red Bank, N.J.; mem. N.J. Senate, 1888, 1889, 1890 (pres. 1890); judge Circuit Ct., Hudson County Dist., 1896-1903; pros. atty. Monmouth County, 1904-08, resigned. Republican. Comdr. Dept. of N.J. G.A.R., 1884-86; comdr.-in-chief G.A.R., 1908-09. Address: Red Bank, N.J. Died 1911.

NEW, Clarence Herbert, author, editor; b. N.Y. City, Nov. 14, 1862; s. Tobias and Lizzie A. (Parmelee) N.; ed. Adelphi Acad., Brooklyn, 1868-72, Betts Mil. Acad., Stamford, Conn., 1876, Brooklyn Poly. Inst., 1877-80; m. Rachel Tatum, Nov. 10, 1891. Traveled twice around the world, 1880-81, and 1891, visiting nearly every country; through S. America, 1884; shipwrecked on clipper ship "Eric the Red," Sept. 5, 1880, on coast of Victoria, Australia; foreign corr., 1884, 1891. Constructing engr., 1886-92; editor, writer and pub., 1893—; editor Truth, 1895; mgr. N.Y. and London Literary Press, 1897-1910; editor Reel Life, 1913-14. Author: Adventures of a Diplomatic Free Lance (series), 1909-31—the longest continuous series with same leading characters ever published—nearly 3 million words—also prod. in motion pictures, and some of the stories republished in Cassell's New Mag., London; Mysteries of the Sea (republished in Premier Mag., London, series over the pen-name "Culpeper Zandtt"), 1911-12, 1914-18; The Unseen Hand (war novel), 1918; Deep Water Men and the Glowing Ember (series in Blue Book Mag. and Premier Mag., London), 1920-21; The Peculiar Resources of Pennington White (series), 1924; The Grigsbys (series in mags.), 1925; "Galt, M.D." (East Indian series, by Culpeper Zandtt), 1926-27; Buccaneers Limited (series, by "Stephen Hopkins Orcutt"), 1927-28; Mysteries of Today (series), by Culpeper Zandtt, 1928-29; Deep Water Life (series), by Stephen Hopkins Orcutt, 1929. Address: New York, N.Y. Died Jan. 8, 1933.

NEW, Harry Stewart, postmaster gen.; b. Indianapolis, Ind., Dec. 31, 1858; s. John C. and Melissa B. N.; ed. Indianapolis pub. schs. and Butler University; hon. LL.D. from Butler University, 1927. With Indianapolis Journal for twenty-five years, as reporter, editor, and pub., 1878-1903; later pres. Bedford Stone and Construction Co. Mem. Ind. State Senate, 1896-1900; mem. Rep. Nat. Com., 1900-12 (chmn. 1907-08); U.S. Senator, 1917-23; postmaster general, Mar. 5, 1923-Mar. 5, 1929; capt. and a.a.g. 3d Brigade, 2d Div., 7th Army Corps, Spanish-Am. War, 1898. U.S. Commr. Century of Progress Expn., Chicago, 1933-34. Home: Indianapolis, Ind. Died May 9, 1937.

NEW, John Chalfant, publisher, treasurer of U.S.; b. Vernon, Ind., July 6, 1831; grad. Bethany Coll., Va., 1851; admitted to bar, Indianapolis, 1852; clerk of courts, Marion Co., Ind., 1856; q.m. gen. of Ind., 1861; State senator, 1862; after war was banker for many yrs. Apptd. Treas. of U.S. by President Grant, 1875; Asst. Sec. of Treasury by President Arthur, 1882; consul gen. at London, England, by President Harrison, 1889. Republican. Address: Indianapolis, Ind. Died 1906.

NEWBERNE, Robert Edward Lee, M.D.; b. nr. Wallaceton, Norfolk Co., Va., Sept. 9, 1872; s. William N. and Mary (Creekmore) N.; M.D., Georgetown U., D.C., 1893; D.D.S., N. Pacific Coll. Dental Surgery, Portland, 1896; B.S., George Washington U., 1900, M.S., 1901; unmarried. Was in Indian Service, Ida., Ariz., and Wash.; went to Manila, P.I., 1902, and later active in pub. health work; pres., Bd. Med. Examiners, P.I.; chief Free Dispensary div., Philippine Gen. Hosp.; lecturer on psychiatry, neurology, dermatology, med. ethics and legal medicine, U. of Philippines, also lecturer on med. jurisprudence, Coll. of Law, U. of Philippines. Mem. Vol. Med. Service Corps; chief med. supervisor U.S. Indian Service, 1918—. Mem. P.I. Med. Assn. (pres. 1911-12). Address: Washington, D.C. Died Feb. 15, 1926.

NEWBERRY, Perry, writer; b. Union City, Mich., Oct. 16, 1870; s. Capt. Frank D. and Fannie E. (Stone) N.; ed. pub. high sch.; m. Bertha Bair, Oct. 18, 1892; m. 2d, Ida L. Brooks, Sept. 12, 1936. In fire ins. business, Chicago, 1887-97; on art dept. San Francisco Examiner, reporter and editor of various papers, 1897-1905; bought San Francisco Wave in 1901 and was its editor until it went out of existence; writer of boys' serials, short stories, novelettes, etc. Republican. Presbyn. Sec. San Francisco League that opposed Abe Ruef machine in 1905; sec. regular Rep. League anti-machine orgn., 1907, and associated with Spreckels, Honey, and others in campaign of 1908; mem. Rep. County Com. of San Francisco County, 1905-09. Pres. Forest Theatre Soc. of Carmel, 1913-14. Y.M.C.A. sec. with 77th Div., A.E.F., 1918-19. Author: Bob Westlake's Golden Luck; Castaway Island; Black Boulder Claim; Forward Ho!; The Last Mayor of Las Pasturas; The Houseboat Mystery; also (with Alice MacGowan) The Million Dollar Suitcase, Shaken Down, The Seventh Passenger, The Mystery Woman, Who Is This Man? Home: Carmel-by-the-Sea, Calif. Died Dec. 6, 1938.

NEWBERRY, Walter Cass, capitalist; b. Waterville, N.Y., Dec. 23, 1835; s. Col. Amasa S. N. (U.S. loan commr. under President Polk); acad. edn.; entered commercial house of uncle, Oliver Newberry, Detroit, 1858; was one of executors of his estate. Enlisted in Civil War, pvt. 81st N.Y. Inf.; lt., 1861; capt., 1862; maj. (promoted in 24th N.Y. Cav.), 1863; col., 1864; bvt. brig. gen., Mar. 31, 1865, for services at Dinwiddie C.H., where he was severely wounded. Settled in Petersburg, Va., Sept. 1865; mayor, 1869; supt. pub. property, Va., 4 yrs.; built reservoir water works, Richmond. Removed to Chicago, 1876; engaged in mercantile business and as executor and trustee estates of his family; postmaster, 1888-89; mem. 52d Congress, 1891-93. Home: Chicago, Ill. Died July 20, 1912.

NEWBOLD, W(illiam) Romaine, univ. prof.; b. Wilmington, Del., Nov. 20, 1865; s. William Allibone and Martha Smith (Baily) N.; A.B., U. of Pa., 1887, Ph.D., 1891, LL.D., 1921; m. Ethel Sprague Kent Packard, Apr. 9, 1896. Teacher Latin, Cheltenham Mil. Acad., 1887-89; instr. Latin and lecturer in philosophy, 1889-91, lecturer in philosophy, 1891-94, asst. prof. philosophy, 1894-1903, prof., 1903-07, Adam Seybert prof., 1907—, U. of Pa.; dean Grad. Sch. same, 1896-1904. Editor psychol. dept. American Naturalist (with Prof. E. D. Cope), 1895-96. Lecturer, Bohlen Foundation, Phila., 1920; at Gen. Theol. Sem., 1923, 1925. Episcopalian. Home: Philadelphia, Pa. Died Sept. 26, 1926.

NEWBURGER, Joseph, cotton merchant; b. Coffeeville, Miss., June 12, 1858; s. Leopold and Esther (Lichtenstadter) N.; B.A., Spring Hill (Ala.) Coll., 1875; m. Rose Cohen, Mar. 6, 1922; children—Joy, Mary. In cotton business, 1880; pres. Newburger Cotton Co., 1916; chmn. bd. Southland Cotton Co., A.B.C. Trailer Truck Co.; pres. Compress Land Co., Merchants & Cotton Press & Storage Co.; owner Newburger Linter Co.; half owner Newburger Co., Coffeeville, Miss.; partner Federal Compress Co., Silvan, Newburger & Co. (New Orleans), Samuel Newburger & Co. (New York). Built Packing Corp. for City of Memphis; one of the founders of Jewish Temple, Memphis; chmn. drive to build Bishop Gailor Memorial Cathedral; pres. Memphis Santa Claus Good Fellows Club. Pres. Congregation Children of Israel; trustee or dir. Methodist Hosp., Porter Leath Orphanage. Lt. Coffeeville Guards, 1880. Mason. Home: Memphis, Tenn. Died Dec. 17, 1926.

NEWBURGER, Joseph Emanuel, judge; b. New York, 1853; s. Emanuel and Lottie N.; LL.B., Columbia, 1874; unmarried. Admitted to bar, 1874, and practiced at New York, 1874-90. Justice City Court, 1890-95, Court of Gen. Sessions, 1896-1905; justice Supreme Court of N.Y., 1st Dist., 1906-23. Democrat (nominated by Dem., Rep. and Independence League parties); retired, 1923; official referee of Supreme Court of N.Y., 1924—. Home: New York, N.Y. Died July 19, 1931.

NEWCOMB, Arthur Thurston, M.D.; b. Killawog, N.Y., Dec. 8, 1871; s. Franklin T. and Elizabeth (Thurston) N.; grad. Homer (N.Y.) Acad.; studied Cortland (N.Y.) Normal Sch.; M.D., U. of Md., 1893; post grad. study, Johns Hopkins, 1893-94, U. of Chicago, 1899, Johns Hopkins, 1903; research, Vienna, 1912-13; m. Mary Marcella Lerch, Jan. 1, 1924; 1 son, Arthur T. U.S. phys. and surg., Ft. Mojave, Ariz., 1894-98; practiced at Pasadena, 1900—, with increasing limitation to internal medicine; attending physician many years Pasadena Hospital; senior mem. Newcomb, Snyder & Busby Clinic; officer med. staff; chief of med. service Base Hosp., Camp Kearny, San Diego, Calif. Pioneer on Pacific Coast in electro-cardiography and fluoroscopy. Fellow Am. Coll. Physician, 1920. Republican. Presbyn. Home: Pasadena, Calif. Died July 18, 1938.

NEWCOMB, Charles Benjamin, writer, metaphysician; b. Boston, Mass., June 22, 1845; s. John J. and Mary S. N.; ed. Boston pub. schs.; m. Ida M. Thomas, Sept. 17, 1868 (died 1882); m. 2d, Katharine Hinchman, July 27, 1887. Author: All's Right With the World; Discovery of a Lost Trail; Principles of Psychic Philosophy, 1911. Address: Brookline, Mass. Died Mar. 18, 1922.

NEWCOMB, Charles Leonard; b. W. Willington, Conn., Aug. 7, 1854; s. Charles Leonard and Martha Jane (Hudson) N.; B.S. and M.E., Worcester Poly. Inst., 1880; m. Inez Louise Kendall, Jan. 20, 1874; children—Charles Leonard, Lucy Bradford (Mrs. F. O. Bushnell), Robert Everett, Alice Lavinia (Mrs. A. R. Wright), Benjamin Rudolph, Austin Hudson. Began as apprentice Murless Foundry, then machinist apprentice Senior Machine Shop; millwright and stationary engr., Florence Mills; millwright and machinist, Rock Mill Mfg. Co., Rockville, Conn.; machinist Pratt and Whitney Co., Hartford, Conn.; machinist American Clutch Co., Middletown, Conn.; became supt. Am. Elec. Lighting Co., New Britain, Conn., out of which grew Thomson-Houston Electric Co. of Lynn, Mass., and which was merged into the General Electric Co.; supt. Deane Steam Pump Co., Holyoke, Mass., 1881; gen. mgr. Internat. Steam Pump Co., Deane Plant, Holyoke, Mass., 1899, and continued in the same position from 1914, when company was merged into the Worthington Pump and Machinery Corp.; gen. mgr. Deane Works, Holyoke, Mass., and Blake-Knowles Works, East Cambridge, Mass., of Internat. Steam Pump Co., 1907-11; pres. Holyoke Co-operative Bank. Inventor of the rotary deluge nozzle adapted for use on top of aerial ladder, converting the aerial ladder into a water tower; specialized in steam and hydraulic engring. and acted in a consulting capacity as expert in various lines of engring. Councilman and alderman, Holyoke, Mass., 1886-88; mem. Holyoke Fire Commn. (chmn., 1893-1910). Mason, Elk. Republican. Baptist. Wrote: Fire Hydrants (trans. Am. Soc. Mech. Engrs.); Experiments on Various Types of Fire-Hydrants (Jour. N.E. Water Works Assn.). Trustee Worcester Poly. Inst. Home: Holyoke, Mass. Died Mar. 13, 1930.

NEWCOMB, Ezra Butler, clergyman; b. Indianapolis, Ind., Dec. 18, 1852; s. Horatio Cooley and Eliza (Pabody) N.; U. of Minn., 1871-73; newspaper work, Indianapolis, 1874-76; studied law, 1876-79; practiced Indianapolis and Minneapolis, 1879-83; student McCormick Theol. Sem., 1883-86; D.D., Parsons, 1897; m. Minnie A. Beardsley, May 31, 1876; children—Philip B. (dec.), Horatio M. (dec.), Theodore A. Ordained ministry Presbyn. Ch. U.S.A., 1886; pastor First Ch., Ft. Dodge, Ia., 1886-89, 1st Ch., LaPorte, Ind., 1889-96, Westminster Church, Keokuk, Iowa, 1896-1922, Lindsay, California, 1922-30. Commissioner General Assembly of Presbyterian Ch., U.S.A., various times; del. Pan-Presbyn. Council, New York, 1909, Aberdeen, Scotland, 1913; mem. Permanent Jud. Commn. Presbyn. Ch., 1908-11, 1918-21; mem. Advisory Council on Ch. Extension, 1908-12; moderator Synod of Ia., 1908, mem. exec. com., 1915-18; pres. Bd. Iowa Presbyn. Home Missions, 1907-15, Inter-Ch. Federation of Iowa, 1912-17; mem. field council Synod of Calif., 1924-27. Dir. McCormick Theol. Sem., 1892-1922; trustee Parsons Coll., 1898-1911. Republican. Mem. Soc. Mayflower Descendants, S.A.R. (chaplain Ia. State Soc. 1899, 1909, pres. 1912). Home: Pasadena, Calif. Deceased.

NEWCOMB, Horatio Victor, capitalist; b. Louisville, Ky., July 26, 1844; ed. there and in England and France; entered counting-room of H. D. Newcomb & Co., commn. mchts., Louisville; later became partner in Warren, Newcomb & Co., New York. After death of his father, who had been pres. of Louisville & Nashville R.R. Co., became dir., soon after v.p. and later pres. of that co.; retired 1880. Organized, 1880, and was for several yrs. pres. U.S. Nat. Bank, New York. Home: New York, N.Y. Died 1911.

NEWCOMB, Katharine Hinchman, teacher, healer; b. Brooklyn, N.Y., Dec. 16, 1852; d. James A. and Elizabeth (Norton) Hinchman; ed. Young Ladies' Sem., Detroit; m. Charles Benjamin Newcomb, July 27, 1887. Author: Helps to Right Living; Steps Along the Path, 1911. Address: Brookline, Mass. Died July 25, 1920.

NEWCOMB, Simon, astronomer; b. Wallace, N.S., Mar. 12, 1835; s. John Burton and Emily (Prince) N.; ed. by his father; came to U.S., 1853; teacher in Md., 1854-56; computor on Nautical Almanac, 1857; grad. Lawrence Scientific Sch., Harvard, B.S., 1858; hon. LL.D., Columbian, 1874, Yale, 1875, Harvard, 1884, Columbia, 1887, Edinburgh, 1891, Glasgow, 1896, Princeton, 1896, Cracow, 1900, Johns Hopkins, 1902, Toronto, 1904; Sc.D., Heidelberg, 1886, Padua, 1892, Dublin, 1892, Cambridge, 1896; Doctor of Mathematics, Christiania, 1902; D.C.L., Oxford, 1899; Master of Mathematics and Doctor of Natural Philosophy, Leyden, 1875; m. Mary Caroline, d. Dr. Charles A. Hassler, U.S.N., and g.d. of the founder of the Coast Survey, Aug. 4, 1863. Apptd., 1861, prof. mathematics, U.S.N.; assigned to duty at U.S. Naval Observatory; negotiated contract for and supervised construction of 26-inch equatorial telescope; sec. U.S. Transit of Venus Commn., 1871-74; observed transit of Venus at Cape of Good Hope, 1882. Dir. Nautical Almanac Office, 1877-97; retired 1897. Made many astron. researches, given to the world in over 300 papers; prof. mathematics and astronomy, Johns Hopkins, 1884-94, and editor Am. Jour. Mathematics. 1874—, correspondent, and 1893—, one of the 8 foreign associates, Institute of France (first native American since Franklin to be so honored); made Officer of Legion of Honor of France, 1893, Comdr., 1907; Knight of the Prussian Order of Merit for Science and Art, 1906 (receiving spl. authority from U.S. Congress to accept these honors); mem., 1869—, v.p., 1883-89, later foreign sec. Nat. Acad. Sciences; pres. Soc. for Psychical Research, 1885-86; pres. A.A.A.S., 1877, of Am. Math. Soc., 1897-98, of Astron. and Astrophys. Soc. of America, 1899, 1905; pres. Internat. Congress of Arts and Sciences at La. Purchase Expn., 1904; honorary or corr. mem. of every scientific, astron. or math. soc. of 1st rank in the world. Received Royal Astron. Soc. gold medal, 1874, Huygens gold medal, Dutch Soc. of Sciences, 1878, Royal Soc. gold medal, 1890; Bruce medal, Astron. Soc. of Pacific, 1898, Schubert prize (Russia), and Sylvester prize (Johns Hopkins Univ.). Author: The Stars, 1901; Astronomy for Everybody, 1903; Reminiscences of an Astronomer, 1903; Spherical Astronomy, 1906; Side Lights on Astronomy, 1906; also various other books on astron.

and econ. topics, mag. articles, etc. Published the tables of the motions of the stars, the planets and the moon now used by astronomers in their computations and as the basis of the navigation of the vessels of the world. Address: Washington, D.C. Died 1909.

NEWCOMBE, Frederick Charles, botanist; b. Flint, Mich., May 11, 1858; s. Thomas and Eliza (Gayton) N.; B.S., U. of Mich., 1890; Ph.D., U. of Leipzig, 1893; m. Susan Eastman, June 25, 1884. Teacher Mich. Sch. for Deaf, 1880-87; instr. botany, 1890-92, asst. prof., 1893-97, jr. prof., 1897-1905, prof., 1905-23, U. of Mich., later emeritus. Fellow A.A.A.S. (v.p. Sect. G, 1910); mem. Bot. Soc. America (pres. 1917), Botanists of Central States (pres.), Mich. Acad. Science (pres.), Hawaiian Bot. Soc. (pres. 1924), Hawaiian Acad. Science (pres. 1925). Del. Internat. Congress Arts and Sciences, St. Louis, 1904 (sec. sect. plant physiology). Author of many articles describing original researches on plants. Editor-in-chief Am. Jour. of Botany, 1914-18. Home: Honolulu, T.H. Died Oct. 4, 1927.

NEWCOMER, Alphonso Gerald, university prof.; b. Mt. Morris, Ill., Sept. 13, 1864; s. Henry F. and Elizabeth Ann (Knodle) N.; A.B., U. of Mich., 1887; A.M., Cornell U., 1888; held classical fellowship, Cornell, 1887-88; m. Carrie M. Jackson, Sept. 23, 1887. Instr. Latin and French, Knox Coll., 1889-91; asst. prof. English, 1891-95, asso. prof., 1895-1906, prof. English, 1906—, Leland Stanford Jr. U. Author: Practical Course in English Composition, 1893; Elements of Rhetoric, 1898; Selections from Landor (edited), 1899; American Literature, 1901; Rhetoric in Practice (with S. S. Seward, Jr.), 1905; English Literature, 1905; Twelve Centuries of English Poetry and Prose (with Alice E. Andrews), 1910. Address: Palo Alto, Calif. Died Sept. 16, 1913.

NEWCOMER, Waldo, capitalist; b. Baltimore, Md., Sept. 14, 1867; s. Benjamin Franklin and Amelia Louisa (Ehlen) N.; A.B., Johns Hopkins, 1889; m. Margaret Vanderpoel, Oct. 7, 1897 (died 1920); children—Benjamin Franklin, Adelaide Vanderpoel, Margaret Waldo. Pres. Nat. Exchange Bank; chmn. exec. com. Baltimore Trust Co., Mar. 1929-Jan. 1932; v.p. Atlantic Coast Line Co., Northern Central Ry. Home: Baltimore, Md. Died July 29, 1934.

NEWEL, Stanford, E.E. and M.P. of U.S. to Netherlands, 1897-1905; b. Providence, R.I., June 7, 1839; s. Stanford and Abby Lee (Penniman) N.; grad. Yale, 1861, hon. A.M., 1864; grad. Harvard Law School, 1864. Removed to St. Anthony's Falls, Minn., May 1855; practicing lawyer, St. Paul, 1864—; m. Helen F., d. Ernest and Helen M. Fiedler, June 24, 1880. Delegate to Nat. Rep. Convs., 1884 and 1892. One of Am. delegation to Peace Conf. at The Hague, 1899; apptd. E.E. and M.P. to Netherlands and Luxemburg, June 5, 1903; resigned June 30, 1905. Address: St. Paul, Minn. Died 1907.

NEWELL, Charles Herbert, banker, mfr.; b. Pawtucket, R.I., July 11, 1865; s. George Washington and Ellen Frances (Read) N.; ed. high sch., Pawtucket; m. Etta Louise Matteson, Dec. 10, 1889; children—Herbert M., Richmond M. Became connected in boyhood with Slater Nat. Bank, of which his father was cashier, and succeeded him as cashier; treas. Slater Trust Co., 1900-03; trustee Estate of Frederic Clark Sayles, 1903-30. Republican. Conglist. Home: Providence, R.I. Died May 14, 1935.

NEWELL, Cicero, soldier; b. Ypsilanti, Mich., Aug. 12, 1840; s. Josiah and Priscilla (Chamberlain) N.; ed. dist. sch.; m. Nellie Lerch, Apr. 2, 1863. Enlisted Co. H, 1st Mich. Vol. Inf., Apr. 16, 1861, 3 mos. service; reënlisted and elected 1st lt. Troop D, 3d Mich. Cav., Aug. 1861; capt., Troop K, Mar. 31, 1862; maj. 10th Mich. Cav., Aug. 19, 1863; hon. discharged, 1865; participated in more than 30 battles and many skirmishes; had command of 10th Mich. Cav. at Battle of Greenville, Tenn., when Gen. John A. Morgan was killed. U.S. Indian agt. for the Brule Sioux, of Dak., 1879-80. Founder Parental Sch., Seattle, Wash., 1891. Republican. Mason. Author: Indian Stories, 1912. Home: Portland, Ore. Deceased.

NEWELL, Edward Theodore, numismatist; b. Kenosha, Wis., Jan. 15, 1886; s. Frederick Seth and Frances Cecilia (Bain) N.; B.A., Yale, 1907, A.M., 1909; m. Adra Nelson Marshall, Apr. 22, 1909. Researcher in numismatics and kindred subjects (coins, intaglios, seal cylinders and scarabs), 1907—. Fellow Royal Numismatic Soc., British Numismatic Soc.; mem. Am. Numismatic Soc. (pres., 1916—). Trustee of American Schools of Oriental Research. Awarded medal of Royal Numismatic Soc. (Eng.) "for distinguished services in numismatic research," 1925. Served as 1st lt. Mil. Intelligence Division, U.S.A., 1917-18. Republican. Author: (books and pamphlets), Reattribution of Certain Tetradrachms of Alexander the Great, 1912; The Dated Alexander Coinage of Sidon and Ake, 1916; The Seleucid Mint of Antioch, 1918; Tarsos Under Alexander, 1919; Myriandros, 1920; The Octobols of Histiæa, 1921; The Kyparissia Hoard, 1921; The Coinages of Demetrius Poliorcetes, 1927; The Coinage of the Eastern Seleucid Mints, 1938. Awarded Prix Allier de Hauteroche, Académie Française, 1929. Awarded medal of the Societe Française de Numismatique, 1936. Home: Huntington, L.I., N.Y. Died Feb. 18, 1941.

NEWELL, Frederick Haynes, engineer; b. Bradford, Pa., Mar. 5, 1862; s. Augustus William and Anna M. (Haynes) N.; grad. Mass. Inst. Tech. (mining engr.), 1885; m. Effie Josephine Mackintosh, Apr. 3, 1890; children—Josephine (wife of Prof. James M. O'Gorman), Constance, Roger Sherman (dec.), John Mackintosh. Mining in Colo.; asst. Ohio Geol. Survey; miscellaneous engring. in Pa., Va., etc.; asst. hydraulic engr. U.S. Geol. Survey, 1888-90, hydrographer, 1890-1902; chief engr., 1902-07, dir., 1907-14, consulting engr., U.S. Reclamation Service, 1914; prof. civil engineering, U. of Ill., 1915-19; pres. Research Service, 1919. Member of U.S. Land Commission, U.S. Inland Waterways Commn., Nat. Advisory Bd. for Fuels and Structural Materials, Giant Power Survey of State of Pa.; engr. mem. Pa. Water and Power Resources Bd. Sec. Nat. Geog. Soc., 1903; mem. Am. Engineers (pres. 1919), Washington Soc. Engrs. (pres. 1907), Washington Acad. Sciences (v.p. 1907). Awarded Cullum gold medal by Am. Geog. Soc. Author: Agriculture by Irrigation, 1894; Hydrography of the Arid Regions, 1891; The Public Lands of the United States, 1895; Irrigation in the United States, 1902; Hawaii, Its Natural Resources, 1909; Principles of Irrigation Engineering, 1913; Irrigation Management, 1916; Engineering as a Career, 1916; Water Resources, Present and Future Uses, 1919; Water Powers of Virginia; Natural Resources of Puerto Rico. Home: Washington, D.C. Died 1932.

NEWELL, George Edwards, clergyman; b. Chester, Pa., Mar. 22, 1877; s. William and Katherine (Edwards) N.; A.B., Park Coll., Parkville, Mo., 1904, D.D., 1915; student Princeton Theol. Sem., 1905-06; grad. Auburn Theol. Sem., 1907; m. Agnes Lasley, Aug. 22, 1906; children—Mary Virginia, Pauline Edwards, Catherine Agnes. Ordained Presbyn. ministry, 1907; pastor successively King City, Mo., Third Ch., Kansas City, Mo., First Church, Hastings, Neb. and, 1929—. First Church, Wichita, Kan. Member General Assembly Presbyterian, Church of U.S. (apportionment com.), Presbyn. Synod of Neb., Hastings Presbytery, Neb. Christian Endeavor (pres.). Spl. religious work, Camp Funston, Kan., World War. Pres. Neb. State Hygiene and Welfare Assn.; trustee Hastings Coll., Omaha Theol. Sem. Republican. Mason. Home: Wichita, Kan. Died July 24, 1933.

NEWELL, Lyman Churchill, college prof.; b. Pawtucket, R.I., Sept. 18, 1867; s. George W. and Ellen F. (Read) N.; Ph.B., Brown U., 1890, A.M., 1891; Ph.D., Johns Hopkins, 1895; m. Carolyn E. Strong, Sept. 7, 1898. Teacher chemistry, Pawtucket High Sch., 1890-92, Somerville (Mass.) High Sch., 1895-98, Normal Sch., Lowell, Mass., 1898-1904; prof. chemistry, Boston U., 1904—. Fellow Am. Academy of Arts and Sciences. Conglist. Republican. Author: General Chemistry, 1914; Laboratory Manual of Inorganic Chemistry for Colleges, 1916; Practical Chemistry, 1922; Experiments in Practical Chemistry, 1923; College Chemistry, 1925; Experiments in College Chemistry, 1925; Laboratory Exercises for a Brief Course in Chemistry, 1927; Brief Course in Chemistry, 1929; (pamphlets) Teachers' Problem, 1900, and Chemistry and Physics in Normal School (written for Paris Expn.). Contbr. to Jour. Chem. Edn. (dept. editor), and Dictionary of Am. Biography. Home: Brookline, Mass. Died Dec. 13, 1933.

NEWELL, Peter (Sheaf Hersey), author, illustrator; b. McDonough County, Ill., Mar. 5, 1862; s. George Frederick and Louisa N.; ed. Bushnell, Ill., until 16 or 17 yrs. of age; m. Leona Dow Ashcraft, Feb. 5, 1884. Author: Topsys and Turveys, 1893; Topsys and Turvys (No. 2), 1894; A Shadow Show, 1896; Peter Newell's Pictures and Rhythms, 1899; The Hole Book, 1908; Jungle Jangle, 1909; The Slant Book, 1910; The Rocket Book, 1912. Contbr. to mags. Illustrator of several books. Address: Leonia, N.J. Died Jan. 15, 1924.

NEWELL, Quitman Underwood, physician; b. Whistler, Ala., June 14, 1886; s. William Henry and Minerva Amita (Thompson) N.; prep. edn. Barton Acad., Mobile, Ala., 1902-04; M.D., U. of Ala., 1911; m. Katie Lou Kelley, June 30, 1920 (died 1924); children—Quitman Underwood, Doris Louise. Interne Washington U. Hosp., 1911-12, resident obstetrics and gynecology, 1912-14; asst. in clin. obstetrics and gynecology, Washington U. Med. Sch., 1914-21, instr., 1921-25, asst. prof., 1925-33, asso. prof., 1933-36, prof., 1936; mem. staff of Barnes, St. Louis Children's, St. Louis Maternity, St. Lukes, Mo. Baptist, Mo. Pacific hosps. Served as capt. Evacuation Hosp., 18, U.S. Army, 1917-19. Diplomate Am. Bd. Obstetrics and Gynecology; fellow Am. Coll. Surgeons. Democrat. Baptist. Mason. Author of numerous med. articles and of monograph, "Human Tubal Ova," 1930. Home: St. Louis, Mo. Died Nov. 5, 1940.

NEWELL, Robert Henry ("Orpheus C. Kerr"); author; b. New York, Dec. 13, 1836; s. Robert and Ann (Lawrence) N.; academic edn.; literary editor New York Mercury, 1858-62; on staff New York World, 1869-74 (edited column social studies); then editor Hearth and Home, a weekly journal. Author: Orpheus C. Kerr Papers (4 vols. of humorous letters on the Civil war), 1862-68; The Palace Beautiful, and Other Poems, 1865; Avery Glibun, an American Romance, 1867; The Cloven Foot, 1870; Versatilities (poems), 1871; The Walking Doll (a novel), 1872; Studies in Stanzas, 1882; There Was Once a Man, 1884. Address: Brooklyn, N.Y. Died 1901.

NEWELL, William Augustus, physician, governor, congressman; b. Franklin, O., Sept. 5, 1817; s. James H. and Eliza D. N.; grad. Rutgers Coll., 1836, A.M., 1839; LL.D., 1871; M.D., U. of Pa., 1839; established practice in N.J.; mem. Congress, 1847-49, 1849-51 and 1865-67; originated U.S. Life Saving Service, 1848; originated Delaware breakwater; originated U.S. Agrl. Bureau, and purchase of the Mount Vernon estate for agrl. purposes; gov. N.J., 1857-59; supt. Life Saving Service, 1860-64; candidate for gov., N.J., 1876—defeated by Gen. George B. McClellan; gov. Washington Ty., 1880-84; U.S. Indian insp., 1884; resident surgeon to Soldiers' and Sailors' Home, State of Washington, 1894-98; resigned. Practiced profession when not in public life. Address: Allentown, N.J. Died 1901.

NEWELL, William Henry, lawyer, banker; b. Durham, Me., Apr. 16, 1854; s. William R. and Susannah K. (Weeks) N.; grad. Farmington (Me.) State Normal Sch.; m. Ida F. Plummer, Sept. 20, 1883; children—Gladys E. (Mrs. Daniel T. Drummond), Dorothy (Mrs. Roscoe E. Halliday). Admitted to Me. bar, 1878, and began practice at Lewiston; city solicitor, Lewiston, 1890; mayor of Lewiston 4 terms to 1902; county atty. Androscoggin County, 1892-94; judge of Probate Court, 1905-13, and 1919—; pres. Mfrs. Nat. Bank of Lewiston; v.p. Androscoggin & Kennebec Ry. Co. Democrat. Conglist. Mason. Home: Lewiston, Me. Died May 3, 1934.

NEWELL, William Wells, author; b. Cambridge, Mass., Jan. 24, 1839; s. William and Frances B. (Wells) N.; grad. Harvard, 1859, Harvard Divinity Sch., 1863; was minister (Unitarian), but left ministry and became teacher and writer; permanent sec. Am. Folk-Lore Soc.; editor Jour. of Am. Folk-Lore, 1888-1900. Author: Games and Songs of American Children, 2d edit., 1903; Words for Music (verse), 2d edit., 1904; King Arthur and the Table Round, 1897; Sonnets and Madrigals of Michelangelo Buonarotti, 1900; Legend of the Holy Grail, 1902. Address: Cambridge, Mass. Died 1907.

NEWELL, William Whiting, church financial specialist; b. Wappingers Falls, N.Y., Aug. 29, 1868; s. William Whiting and Helen (Pert) N.; theol. edn. at Oratoire, Geneva, Switzerland; hon. D.D., Drury, 1906; m. Nellie Bennett, Nov. 7, 1892. Ordained Congl. ministry, 1891; pastor Winthrop, Minn., 1891-92, Morley Memorial Ch., Duluth, 1892-96, Bethany Ch., St. Paul, 1896-98, Compton Hill Ch., St. Louis, 1898-1905; sec. Congl. Ch. Bldg. Soc., Chicago, 1905-17. Mason. Home: River Forest, Ill. Deceased.

NEWHALL, Alfred Augustus, missionary; b. Cambridgeport, Mass., Jan. 4, 1844; s. Alfred Augustus and Margery Fowle (Thompeson) N.; pvt. 5th Mass. Vols., 1864; A.B., U. of Rochester, 1872, A.M., 1894; grad. Rochester Theol. Sem., 1875; m. Mary A. Wood, 1876; m. 2d, Marie Menke, 1884. Ordained Bapt. ministry, 1875; missionary of Am. Bapt. Missionary Union at Ramapatam, India, 1875-79; in U.S. on health furlough, 1879-83; student Bapt. Union Theol. Sem., Ill., 1880-81; missionary at Hanamaconda, Zizams Dominions, India, 1883-90; prof. Greek and Bible studies, Leland U., 1894-1908. Address: Woburn, Mass. Died 1910.

NEWKIRK, Garrett, physician, dentist; b. Calhoun County, Mich., May 3, 1847; s. Cornelius L. and Anna (Hammond) N.; M.D., Rush Med. Coll., 1868; attended Chicago Coll. Dental Surgery later; m. Martha E. Martin, Dec. 1872. Practiced dentistry Chicago, 1883-1900; later in Los Angeles and Pasadena, Calif.; dean Coll. Dentistry, U. of Southern Calif., 1901-06; pres. State Bd. Dental Examiners, 1907-08. Pres. Central Illinois Dental Assn., 1884, Ill. State Dental Soc., 1893-94, Chicago Dental Soc., 1899-1900. Author: Rhymes of the States (a geography for boys and girls), 1896; Æsop's Fables Retold, 1916. Address: Pasadena, Calif. Died Apr. 7, 1921.

NEWKIRK, Newton, editor, writer; b. Bentleyville, Washington County, Pa., Aug. 29, 1870; s. Joseph Alexander and Nancy (Hopkins) N.; Ph.B., Mt. Union Coll., Alliance, O., 1893; m. Queen Josephine Craft, June 9, 1897. Editor "All Sorts," a humorous column each week-day in The Boston Post, 1901-34; creator of "The Bingville Bugle," a full-page humorous Sunday feature in The Boston Sunday Post, and syndicated to other newspapers. Mason. Author: Stealthy Steve, the Six-Eyed Sleuth, 1904; The Stork Book, 1907; Recollections of a Gold Cure Graduate, 1906; The Tale of a Check Book, 1906; Back to Nature, 1911; Doc & Jim & Me, 1906; One Injun and 3 to Carry, 1907; Humorous Tales of the Woods, 1913. Home: Brookline, Mass. Died May 15, 1938.

NEWLANDS, Francis Griffith, senator; b. Natchez, Miss., Aug. 28, 1848; s. James Birney and Jessie

(Barland) N.; entered class, 1867 at Yale Coll., remained until middle junior yr.; studied Columbia Law Sch.; hon. A.M., Yale, 1901; m. Clara Adelaide Sharon, 1874; m. 2d, Edith McAllister, 1888. Admitted to D.C. bar, 1870; went to San Francisco, and practiced law there until 1886, when he became a trustee of the estate of William Sharon, formerly U.S. senator from Nev.; removed to Nev., 1889; was active as advocate of bimetallism; for yrs. v.chmn. Nat. Silver Com.; active in irrigation development and other matters of western interest; mem. 53d to 57th Congresses (1893-1903); framed the Newlands Reclamation Act and was mem. com. on Ways and Means, Foreign Affairs, etc.; was elected by the Dem. party U.S. senator, terms, 1903-09, 1909-15, 1915-21; chmn. com. on Interstate Commerce; prominent in rate legislation; author of bill for river regulation, trade commn. Address: Reno, Nev. Died Dec. 24, 1917.

NEWLEAN, John Walter, corp. official; b. Chicago, Ill., Oct. 28, 1875; s. John and Charlotte (Sellergren) N.; common sch. edn.; m. Mae McMaster, June 27, 1905. With C.,B.&Q. R.R., 1892-93, U.P. R.R., 1893-1901, Harriman Lines, U.P. R.R., S.P. R.R., 1901-09; gen. auditor for receivers of C.,G.W. R.R., 1909-10; gen. auditor for reorg. com. C.,G.W. R.R., 1910-11; gen. auditor I.C. R.R., Indiana Southern R.R., 1911-12; controller Wells Fargo & Co., 1912-18; v.p. Am. Ry. Express Co., 1918-19; v.p., then pres. Nat. Aniline and Chem. Co., 1920-23; v.p. and treas. Am. Ry. Express Co., 1923—; dir. Wells Fargo & Co., Wells Fargo & Co. of Cuba, Wells Fargo Latin-Am. Corp.; mem. consulting bd. Wells Fargo & Co., S.A., Mexico. Home: Bronxville, N.Y. Died Nov. 4, 1928.

NEWLON, Jesse H(omer), prof. education; b. Salem, Ind., July 16, 1882; s. Richard Rosecrans and Arra Belle (Cauble) N.; A.B., Ind. U., 1907; A.M., Columbia, 1914; LL.D., U. of Denver, 1922; m. Letha Hiestand, Dec. 29, 1909. Prin. high sch., Charlestown, Ind., 1905-06; teacher history and mathematics, high sch., New Albany, Ind., 1907-08; teacher history and civics, high sch., Decatur, Ill., 1908-12, prin., 1912-16; prin. high sch., Lincoln, Neb., 1916-17; supt. schs. Lincoln, 1917-20, Denver, 1920-27; prof. education, Teachers Coll., Columbia, 1927—; dir. Lincoln Experimental Sch. of Teachers Coll., 1927-37, chmn. div. of instrn., 1934-38, dir. div. of foundations of edn., 1938—. Mem. Neb. Children's Code Commn., 1919-20, Commn. on Social Studies, 1929-33, Commn. Relation Sch. and Coll., 1932—. Mem. N.E.A. (pres. 1924-25), Prog. Edn. Assn. (exec. bd.), Am. Assn. Adult Edn. (exec. bd. 1930-34). Mason. Author: (with C. H. Johnston and F. G. Pickell) Administration of Junior and Senior High Schools, 1922; The Newlon-Hanna Speller (with Paul R. Hanna), 1933; Educational Administration as Social Policy, 1934; Education for Democracy in Our Time, 1939. Asso. editor School Executive, 1927—. Awarded Butler medal by Columbia, 1925. Home: New York, N.Y. Died Sept. 1, 1941.

NEWMAN, Albert Henry, theologian; b. Edgefield County, S.C., Aug. 25, 1852; s. John B. and Harriett (Whitaker) N.; A.B., Mercer U., Macon, Ga., 1871; grad. Rochester Theol. Sem., 1875; grad. student Hebrew, Armaic, Arabic, Southern Bapt. Theol. Sem., 1875-76; LL.D., Southwestern Bapt. U., 1883, McMaster U., 1914, Mercer U., 1921; D.D., Mercer U., 1885; m. Mary Augusta Ware, July 15, 1873; children—Horatio Hackett, Elizabeth Nuckolls (Mrs. Frederick Eby), Henry Ware, Albert Broadus. Acting prof., 1877-80, Pettingill prof. ch. history, 1880-81, Rochester Theol. Sem.; prof. ch. history, McMaster U., Toronto, Ont., 1881-1901, Baylor U., Tex., 1901-08; prof. ch. history and dean, Southwestern Bapt. Theol. Sem., Fort Worth, 1908-13; prof. church history, Baylor U., 1913-21; prof. church history, Mercer U., 1921-29 (prof. emeritus). Professorial lecturer ch. history, U. Chicago, 1906 and 1926; prof. ch. history and comparative religion, Vanderbilt U., 1917-18; visiting prof. of ch. history, McMaster U., autumn 1927 and 1928-29. Author: The Baptist Churches in the United States, 1894; History of Anti-Pædobaptism to A.D. 1609, 1897; Manual of Church History (2 vols.), 1900, 1903; A Century of Baptist Achievement, 1901. Translator and editor Immer's Hermeneutics of the New Testament, 1877; Anti-Manichean Works of Augustine, Nicene and Post Nicene Fathers. Dept. editor for church history of the new Schaff-Herzog Ency. of Religious Knowledge, 1905—. Address: Austin, Tex. Died June 4, 1933.

NEWMAN, Allen George, sculptor; b. N.Y. City, Aug. 28, 1875; s. Allen George and Ada Evelyn (Hinde) N.; ed. Coll. City of New York; pupil Nat. Acad. Design, New York; m. Florence Allan, Mar. 28, 1900. Prin. works: bronze group, "Triumph of Peace," Atlanta, Ga.; "The Hiker," Spanish-Am. War soldier, Providence, Rhode Island (duplicates erected in various cities by United Spanish War Vets.); marble figures, "Night and Day," Harriman Bank, New York; Henry Hudson Monument, erected by Colonial Dames of America, 72d St. and Riverside Drive, New York; Gen. Philip Sheridan Monument, Scranton, Pa.; Joel Chandler Harris Monument, Atlanta, Ga.; monument to the women of the South, Jacksonville, Fla.; statue of General Oates gov. of Ala., Montgomery; statue of General Stirling Price, Keytesville, Missouri; Doughboy Monument, and World War Monument, Pittsburgh; portrait statue of Daniel S. Dickinson, Binghamton, N.Y.; Koehler memorial, U.S. Mil. Acad., West Point; sculptured marble frieze, entrance lobby, Jersey City Med. Center. Awarded Competitive Prize for design for valor medal, Nat. Arts Club, 1917. Methodist. A.N.A., 1926. Home: New York, N.Y. Died Feb. 2, 1940.

NEWMAN, Angelia French Thurston, lecturer; b. Montpelier, Vt., 1837, d. Daniel Sylvester and Matilda (Benjamin) Thurston; student Lawrence U., Appleton, Wis.; m. Frank Kilgore, 1856 (died a few months after marriage); m. 2d, David Newman, 1859 (died 1893). Taught sch., Montpelier, Vt., and later in Madison, Wis.; removed to Lincoln, Neb., Aug. 1871; Western sec. Women's Foreign Missionary Soc. M.E. Ch., 1871-79; later became active in work for the protection of Mormon women and children, and became Western sec. Nat. Home Missionary Soc.; unsalaried representative of Utah Gentiles at Washington, before com. of 49th, 50th and 51st Congresses, secured an appropriation of $80,000, as result of which a home was established in Salt Lake City for Mormon women and children escaped from polygamy. Has been state supt. of prison and flower mission work for W.C.T.U. in Neb. 25 yrs.; supt. Mormon work for Nat. W.C.T.U., 1886; 1st woman to Quadrennial Gen. Conf. M.E. Ch., 1888. Hospital insp. H.I., during Philippine War, 8 mos.; nat. organizer Cassiday Flower Mission, 20 yrs. Author: Heathen at Home, 1888; McKinley Carnations of Memory, 1904; Italian Winter; Sacrifice of Iphigenia; Adam's First Wife, Lilith, Adam's Second Wife, Eve; The Tragedy of Christianity. Address: Lincoln, Neb. Died 1910.

NEWMAN, Bernard J., sanitarian; b. Hoosick Falls, N.Y., Mar. 15, 1877; s. Richard and Elizabeth (McClosky) N.; Meadville (Pa.) Theol. Sch., 1897-1901; spl. study New York Sch. of Philanthropy, 1908; spl. study municipal engring., Harvard, 1914; Certified Sanitarian, U. of Pa., 1915; m. Kate Kincaid, Oct. 5, 1905; 1 son, William Kincaid. Exec. sec. Philadelphia Housing Commission, 1911-16; dir. Pa. Sch. for Social Service and Public Health, 1916-18; sanitary expert, Ordnance Dept., U.S.A., 1918; sanitarian, Reserve Corps U.S. Pub. Health Service, 1919-23; Chief of Research Branch, Office of Industrial Hygiene and Sanitation, 1918-20, acting sanitarian-in-charge, 1920; managing dir., Philadelphia Housing Assn., 1921—. Mem. sub-com. on housing, White House Conf. on Child Health and Protection; chmn. com. on legislation and administration, President's Conf. on Home Bldg. and Home Ownership (mem. correlating coms. on research, com. on objectives and standards, com. on housing and the community, com. on orgn. programs); mem. commn., to codify health laws of Phila.; mem. and sec. Phila. Zoning Commn., 1916-18, mem., 1924-27. President Pa. Housing and Town Planning Assn., 1935-38; pres. Better Housing Bldg. and Loan Assn., 1925-38; v.p. Regional Planning Fed. of Phila. Tri-State Dist., 1929-38; housing consultant National Housing Com., 1937-38. Fellow American Pub. Health Assn.; mem. Am. Acad. Polit. and Social Science, Internat. Fed. Housing and Town Planning (mem. council; mem. tech. com.), Wayne (Pa.) and Phila. Advisory Com. on Housing (both of Pub. Works Adminstrn.), 1935-37; chmn. advisory site com., Phila. Housing Authority; treas. Social Service Directory Com.; mem. Pa. advisory bd. Federal Writer's Project, Works Project Adminstrn.; mem. Sectional Com. on Bldg. Code Requirements for Light and Ventilation, Federal Housing Adminstrn. Independent Republican. Unitarian. Joint Author: Lead Poisoning in the Pottery Trades, 1921. Editor and Compiler: Housing in Philadelphia, ann., 1921—. Co-editor: Housing Quarterly. Home: Philadelphia, Pa. Died Oct. 6, 1941.

NEWMAN, Carol Montgomery, educator; b. Wytheville, Va., Oct. 29, 1879; s. Thomas J. and Alda (Roper) N.; A.B., King Coll., Bristol, Tenn., 1897; M.A., U. of Virginia, 1901, Ph.D., 1903; LL.D., King College, 1927; m. Caroline Amelia Fain, Jan. 2, 1902; children—Thomas Fain, Virginia Fain, Carol Montgomery, James Preston. Instr. in English, U. of Va., 1899-1901, 1902-03; asso. prof. English, 1903-07, prof. rhetoric, 1907-16, prof. English, 1916—, dean of Academic Dept., 1915-20, Va. Poly. Inst. Democrat. Presbyterian. Mason. Editor: De Quincey's Essays, 1905; Shakespeare's Julius Cæsar, 1914. Address: Blacksburg, Virginia. Died Sept. 8, 1941.

NEWMAN, Edgar Douglas, lawyer, banker; b. Woodstock, Va., Mar. 26, 1854; s. Benjamin P. and Elizabeth (Hickman) N.; Randolph-Macon Coll., Ashland, Va.; grad. Va. Mil. Inst., Lexington, Va., July 4, 1876 (first in class); m. Mary O. Walton, Dec. 20, 1877; children—Wilbur Lauck, Edgar Walton, Helen, Harold Hastings, Houston Hickman, Douglas Cook. Practiced, Woodstock, 1878—; pres. Shenandoah Nat. Bank, and Shenandoah Valley Loan & Trust Co. (Woodstock), Massanutten Nat. Bank (Strasburg), 1st Nat. Bank (Luray); v.p. Citizens' Bank (New Market); pres. People's Bank (Mt. Jackson, Va.). Captain Va. Vol. Co., 2d Regt., 1880-85; chmn. Dem. County Com., Shenandoah County, Va., 1883-86; mem. Dem. State Exec. Com., 1900-04; judge County Ct., Shenandoah County, 1886-98. Chmn. dist. draft bd. Western Dist. of Va., 1917-18. Home: Woodstock, Va. Died Sept. 21, 1927.

NEWMAN, Frances, author. librarian; b. Atlanta, Ga., d. William Truslow and Frances Percy (Alexander) N.; ed. Washington Seminary (Atlanta), Mrs. Semple's (New York), Agnes Scott Coll., Decatur, Ga.; grad. Library Sch., Carnegie Library of Atlanta, 1912. Librarian Fla. State Coll. for Women, 1913; head of lending dept. Carnegie Library, Atlanta, 1914-22; librarian Ga. Sch. of Tech., 1924—. Author: The Short Story's Mutations, 1924; The Hard-Boiled Virgin, 1926; also Rachel and Her Children, winner of O. Henry prize for best very short story, 1924. Contbr. to Am. Mercury, Bookman, Saturday Rev. Home: Atlanta, Ga. Died Oct. 22, 1928.

NEWMAN, Henry Parker, M.D., surgeon; b. Washington, N.H., Dec. 2, 1853; s. James Madison and Abby (Everett) N.; ed. New London (N.H.) Lit. and Scientific Instn. and Dartmouth Coll.; M.D., Detroit Med. Coll., 1878; studied 2 yrs., Bonn, Leipzig and Strassburg; hon. A.M., Dartmouth, 1894; m. Fanny Louise Hodges, 1882; children—Eugene Bush (dec.), Helen Everett (Mrs. Hubert A. Shaw), Willard H. (M.D.), Isabel Fairbanks (dec.). Began at Chicago, 1880; prof. gynecology and clin. gynecology, dir. and treas., Coll. Phys. and Surg., Chicago; pres. and prof. diseases of women, Chicago Post-Grad. Med. Sch. and Chicago Policlinic; pres. and surgeon-in-chief Marion Sims Hosp. Exam. surgeon-in-chief for U.S.A., Recruiting Force, Dist. No. 1, 1917-18. U.S. sec. (sect. abdominal surgery and gynecology) Pan-Am. Congress, Cuba, 1901, Panama Canal Zone, 1904, Guatemala City, 1908, San Francisco, 1915 (sec.-treas.). Contbr. largely to med. literature. Home: San Diego, Calif. Died Sept. 21, 1936.

NEWMAN, Jacob, lawyer; b. Nov. 12, 1854; s. Salmon and Pauline (Lewis) N.; A.B., U. of Chicago, 1873; m. Minnie Goodman, May 30, 1888; children—John H., Mrs. Elysabeth Trounstine, George I. Admitted to Ill. bar, 1875; mem. firm of Newman, Poppenhusen, Stern & Johnston. Republican. Home: Chicago, Ill. Died Sept. 29, 1928.

NEWMAN, Jared Treman, lawyer; b. Enfield, Tompkins County, N.Y., Nov. 4, 1855; s. Isaac Harmon and Cornelia Ann (Treman) N.; Ph.B., Cornell U., 1875; LL.B., Union, 1879; teacher, Enfield, N.Y., 1875-76, Blossburg, Pa., 1876-77; m. Jane Edwards Williams, Oct. 7, 1886; children—Mary Louise (Mrs. Walter Johnston), Robert Williams (dec.), Henry Otis, Charles Hardy. Admitted to bar, 1880; spl. county judge, Tompkins County, N.Y., 1882-86; city atty., Ithaca, 1895-99; mayor of Ithaca, 1907-08; law lecturer, Cornell Law Sch., 1897-99; mem. law firm of Newman & Newman; developer of residential real estate in Ithaca. Mem. bd. of dirs. First Nat. Bank; trustee Ithaca Savings Bank. Trustee Cornell U., 1895-1903, and 1907-33, Auburn Theol. Sem., 1898-1906. Presbyn. Republican. Home: Ithaca, N.Y. Died May 11, 1937.

NEWMAN, John Philip, M.E. bishop; b. New York, Sept. 1, 1826; ed. Cazenovia Sem., N.Y.; hon. D.D., U. of Rochester; LL.D., Otterbein U., and Grant Memorial U.; studied theology; entered M.E. ministry, 1849; traveled in Europe, Palestine and Egypt, 1860-61; held pastorates at Hamilton, N.Y., Albany and New York; in New Orleans, 1864-69, organizing in South 3 annual conferences, 2 colleges and a church paper; in 1869 organized and became pastor Metropolitan M.E. Ch., Washington; chaplain U.S. Senate, 1869-74; inspector U.S. consuls in Asia, 1874-76; pastor Metropolitan Ch., Washington, 1876-79; Central Ch., New York, 1879-82; Madison Av., Ch., New York, 1882-84; attended Gen. Grant in last illness; pastor Metropolitan Ch., Washington, 1885-88; elected bishop, 1888. Noted as pulpit orator and lecturer. Author: From Dan to Beersheba; Thrones and Palaces of Babylon and Nineveh; Christianity Triumphant; America for Americans; The Supremacy of Law. Address: San Francisco, Calif. Died 1899.

NEWMAN, Robert, physician; b. Königsberg, Prussia; s. Gustav Lebrecht and Rosalie Jacobine (Molkentin) N.; ed. at gymnasium; engaged in war for liberty, 1849, fighting in barricades; later adj. Batallion Homburg, in the Palatinate. After Liberalists were defeated went to Switzerland; later came to U.S.; grad. Long Island Coll. Hosp., 1863; Bellevue Hosp. Med. Coll., 1869; m. Ada B. K. Blackwell, Oct. 1877. Commissioned 1863, State's vol. surgeon, going to front several times on gov.'s order; has held many dispensary and hosp. apptmts. Mem. Am. Electro-Therapeutic Assn. (pres., 1896, later chmn. exec. council); pres. faculty and prof. N.Y. School of Physical Therapeutics; one of the founders, 1878, and first v.p. Medico-Legal Society. Author: Electricity in Genito-Urinary Diseases; also monographs and papers on electrolysis and electro-therapeutics. Inventor of electrodes for treatment of stricture by electrolysis, and of devices for use in electrotherapy. Address: New York, N.Y. Deceased.

NEWMAN, Stephen Morrell, clergyman, college president; b. West Falmouth, Me., Nov. 21, 1845;

s. Joseph and Helen Mar (Morrell) N.; A.B., Bowdoin Coll., 1867, A.M., 1870; B.D., Andover Theol. Sem., 1871; hon. D.D., Bowdoin, 1887; m. M. Louie McManus, Aug. 15, 1871. Pastor Trinitarian Congl. Ch., Taunton, Mass., 1871-78, First Ch., Ripon, Wis., 1878-85, First Ch., Washington, D.C., 1885-1906; pres. Eastern Coll., Front Royal, Va., 1908-09, Kee Mar Coll. for Women, Hagerstown, Md., 1909-11, Howard U., Washington, 1912-18. Prof. mathematics and biology, Ripon College, Wis., 1880-82; prof. ch. history, Theol. Dept. Howard U., Washington, D.C., 1887-91. Mem. Colonial Soc. America (pres.). Republican. Home: Washington, D.C. Died Nov. 21, 1924.

NEWMAN, William H., railway pres.; b. in Prince William County, Va., Sept. 6, 1847; s. Albert and Adelaide (Fewell) N.; ed. pvt. schs. in Ky.; m. Bessie Carter, Feb. 18, 1874. Station agt. Tex. & Pacific Ry., Shreveport, La., 1869-72, gen. freight agt., 1872-83; traffic mgr. Southwestern System lines, comprising Tex. & Pacific, Internat. & Great Northern, Galveston, Houston & Henderson and M., K. & T. rys., 1883-85; traffic mgr. Mo. P. Ry., 1885-87, v.p. Mo. P., 1887-89; 3d v.p. C.&N.-W. Ry., 1889-96; 2d v.p. G.N. Ry., 1896-98; pres. L.S.&M.S. Ry. Co., 1898-1909, N.Y.C.&H.R. R.R. Co., 1901-09, M.C. R.R. Co., 1905-09, C.,C.,C.&St.L. Ry. Co., 1905-09; dir. N.Y. Central Lines. Address: New York, N.Y. Died Aug. 10, 1918.

NEWMAN, William Truslow, judge; b. Knoxville, Tenn., June 23, 1843; s. Henry B. and Martha A. N.; m. Fanny Alexander, Sept. 1871. Entered 2d Tenn. Cav., C.S.A., in the ranks, when 17 yrs. of age; promoted lt., 1862; wounded and captured in Ky., 1863; exchanged Aug. 1863; wounded, losing right arm, nr. Jonesboro, Ga., July, 1864. Located at Atlanta, Ga., at close of war and studied law; admitted to bar, 1866; city atty., Atlanta, 1871-83; U.S. dist. judge, Northern Dist. of Ga., 1886—. Address: Atlanta, Ga. Died Feb. 14, 1920.

NEWMARK, Harris, retired mcht.; b. Neumark, Loebau, West Prussia, July 5, 1834; s. Philipp and Eshter (Meyer) Neumark; ed. pub. schs., West Prussia; came to U.S., 1853; m. Sarah Newmark, Mar. 24, 1858 (died 1910); wife was d. Joseph Newmark, who founded Elm St. (Jewish) Congregation, New York, about 1824. Entered business in Los Angeles, with brother, J. P. Newmark, 1853; later partner Rich, Newmark & Co. and Newmark, Kremer & Co.; established wholesale grocery, as H. Newmark, later H. Newmark & Co., succeeded, 1885, by M. A. Newmark & Co.; mem. K. Cohn & Co., hides and wool; pres. The Harris Newmark Co., real estate holdings. Active for many yrs. in development of Los Angeles; an organizer of Los Angeles Bd. of Trade, Los Angeles Pub. Library and of Southwest Museum; founder town of Newmark, Calif.; endowed part of Jewish Orphans' Home in memory of his wife. Republican. Jewish religion. Mem. B'nai B'rith. Mason. Author: Sixty Years in Southern California, 1915. Home: Los Angeles, Calif. Died Apr. 4, 1916.

NEWMARK, Maurice Harris, merchant; b. Los Angeles, Calif., Mar. 3, 1859; s. Harris and Sarah (Newmark) N.; ed. pvt. acads., Los Angeles, N.Y. City and Paris, France; m. Rose, d. Joseph P. Newmark, July 3, 1888; 1 dau., Florence (Mrs. S. S. Kauffman). Began, 1876, with H. Newmark & Co., wholesale grocers, Los Angeles (v.p.); pres. Los Angeles Brick Co.; pres. Harris Newmark Co. (real estate, etc.); dir. Farmers & Merchants Nat. Bank; mem. commn. that consolidated harbor towns with Los Angeles; harbor commr., 1909. Pres. Associated Jobbers, 1899-1912; pres. Southern Calif. Wholesale Grocers' Assn., 1905-17; dir. Bd. of Trade; former dir. and v.p. Mchts.' and Mfrs.' Assn.; former dir. Chamber Commerce. Trustee Southwest Mus., Los Angeles. Mem. B'nai B'rith. Republican. Jewish. Scottish Rite Mason. An editor of Harris Newmark's Sixty Years in Southern California, 1925. Home: Los Angeles, Calif. Died July 5, 1929.

NEWSOM, John Flesher, mining geologist; b. Elizabethtown, Ind., Sept. 6, 1869; s. Nathan and Mary (Flesher) N.; A.B., Ind. U., 1891; A.M., Leland Stanford Jr. U., 1892; post-grad. student and teacher, Stanford U., 1899-1901, Ph.D., 1901; m. Adelaide Frances Perry, Mar. 17, 1896; 1 son, John Branner. Asst. geologist, Geol. Survey of Ark., 1891-93; structural and stratigraphic work on carboniferous strata of Northern Arkansas, 1891-93; instructor geology, 1895-96, assistant professor 1896-98, Indiana Univ.; in charge geol. field work in Southern Ind., 1896-97; examined phosphate deposits of Ark., 1897-99; studied prin. mining regions of central and western U.S., 1898; asst. prof., 1898, asso. prof. mining, 1901-09, prof., 1909, Leland Stanford Junior U. Engaged in work on geology of Santa Cruz Mountains, Calif., during summers 1901-04; also various professional exams. of mining properties, 1900-09; professional exams. of mining properties in South America, North America and the Orient, 1910-24. Republican. Author: Syllabus of Lectures on Economic Geology, 1895. Home: Palo Alto, Calif. Died Oct. 24, 1928.

NEWSOM, William Monypeny, stock broker; b. Columbus O., July 7, 1887; s. Logan Conway and Sally (Monypeny) N.; grad. Hill Sch., Pottstown, Pa., 1906; Ph.B., Yale, 1909; m. Frances Billings, May 15, 1915; 1 dau., Sally. Mgr. N.E. div. Breakwater Co., builders of govt. breakwaters, 1909-13; with Parkinson & Burr, stock brokers, New York, 1913-14; asst. to mgr. military and promotion depts. Remington Arms Co., 1915; sec. and treas. Sundstrand Adding Machine Sales Co., 1916-25; with Watson & White, brokers, 1927; mem. Berg, Eyre & Kerr, 1928-38, Hubbard Bros. & Co., 1938-39, Lawrence Turnure & Co., members N.Y. Stock Exchange, 1939—. Served as 1st lt. Mil. Intelligence Div., U.S. Army, 1917-18. Protestant. Author: White-tailed Deer, 1926. Contbr. to Forest and Stream, Outdoor Life, Field and Stream. Home: New York, N.Y. Died Feb. 1, 1942.

NEWSON, Henry Byron, educator; b. Mt. Gilead, O., July 10, 1860; s. Samuel P. and Nancy (Kingman) N.; Ohio Wesleyan U., A.B., 1883, A.M., Ph.D., 1891; student in physics and mathematics, Johns Hopkins, 1883-84, U. of Heidelberg, 1886-87, Leipzig, 1887-88; m. Mary Frances Winston, July 21, 1900. Prof. science and mathematics, Western Normal Coll., Bushnell, Ill., 1889-90; instr. mathematics, 1890-92, asso. prof., 1892-1905, prof. mathematics. 1905—, U. of Kan. Mng. editor Kan. U. Science Bull.; author of numerous research articles in pure mathematics. Unitarian. Address: Lawrence, Kan. Died 1910.

NEWTON, Alfred Edward; b. Phila., Pa., Aug. 26, 1863; s. Alfred Wharton and Louisa (Swift) N.; ed. pvt. schs.; hon. degrees, Temple U., 1919. Haverford, 1925, U. of Pa., 1935; m. Babette Edelheim, 1890; children—Caroline, Edward Swift. Sold stationery in book shop at the age of 15; entered electrical business in Philadelphia, 1890, continuing until 1931. Pres. Edwin Forest Home; pres. Friends of Library U. of Pa.; trustee Free Library, Phila. Founder Trollope Soc.; pres. Johnson Soc. (Eng.). Collector of 1st editions of important English books, with library of about 10,000 vols. Author: The Amenities of Book-Collecting and Kindred Affections, 1918; A Magnificent Farce and Other Diversions of a Book-Collector, 1921; Doctor Johnson (a play), 1923; The Greatest Book in the World and Other Papers, 1925; This Book-Collecting Game, 1928; A Tourist in Spite of Himself, 1930; End Papers, 1933; Derby Day and Other Adventures, 1934; also various brochures. Frequent contbr. to Atlantic Monthly and other publs. Home: Berwyn, Pa. Died Sept. 29, 1940.

NEWTON, Byron R(ufus), tax commissioner City of New York; b. Wirt, Allegheny County, N.Y., Aug. 4, 1861; s. Laurens C. and Irene (Scott) N.; Oberlin Coll., 1882-84; m. Winifred Cattle, Oct. 3, 1900; children—Irene (dec.), John C., Margaret C. Began newspaper work in Buffalo, N.Y., 1887; legislative corr. Washington, D.C., and Albany, N.Y., 1892-1900; war corr. for Associated Press in Spanish-Am. War, 1898; rep. Am. newspapers at British-Am. Joint High Commn. session in Quebec, 1898; apptd. sec. Pan-Am. Expn., 1901; on staff New York Herald, 1902-10, organized and conducted first newspaper aeronautic dept. in U.S., and aided Wright Brothers and Glenn H. Curtiss in early efforts; apptd. mem. Nat. Advisory Com. for Aeronautics, 1913; later asso. editor U.S. Air Services, Washington, D.C. Directed publicity in Woodrow Wilson's presidential campaign, 1912; apptd. asst. sec. of Treasury, Oct. 1, 1913; apptd. collector of customs, Port of New York, Oct. 1, 1917; retained by chambers of commerce, state of New York, 1922, to oppose St. Lawrence ship canal project; retained by anthracite coal operators in pub. relations capacity, 1923-26; apptd. mem. Bd. of Taxes and Assessments, New York City, as commr. for Queens Borough, Jan. 1934. Home: Bayside, L.I., N.Y. Died Mar. 20, 1938.

NEWTON, Charles Damon, lawyer; b. Birdsall, Allegheny County, N.Y., May 25, 1861; s. Daniel and Polly A. (Brundage) N.; student Geneseo (N.Y.) State Normal Sch., 1882-86, law dept. U. of Mich., 1888-89; m. Nellie E. Durfee, Aug. 10, 1887; children—Mrs. Mary Youngs, Mrs. Elizabeth Gilmore (dec.), Mrs. Dorothy Campbell, George D., Josephine. Began practice at Geneseo, N.Y., 1890; mem. Newton, O'Connor & Newton; dir. Livingston County (N.Y.) Trust Co.; mem. N.Y. Senate, 1914-18; atty. gen. of N.Y., 1919-22. Republican. Presbyn. Mason, Odd Fellow. Home: Geneseo, N.Y. Died Oct. 30, 1930.

NEWTON, Isaac Burkett, banker; b. Norwich, N.Y., Sept. 7, 1861; s. Isaac Sprague and Jane Campbell (Dunlap) N.; grad. Norwich Acad., 1878; Hopkins Grammar Sch. (New Haven, Conn.), 1879; A.B., Yale, 1883; m. Mary Mitchell, Jan. 21, 1885 (died 1900); children—Rowena Mitchell (Mrs. Robert L. Leonard), Burkett Dunlap; m. 2d, Winifred Randolph, Dec. 31, 1910. Sec., treas. Harper & Reynolds Co., Los Angeles, Calif., 1884-1919; dir. Farmers & Merchants Nat. Bank, 1907-26; chmn. bd. Los Angeles Br. Federal Reserve Bank of San Francisco, 1920-26; chmn. bd. and federal reserve agt. Federal Reserve Bank of San Francisco, 1926—. Republican. Conglist. Home: San Francisco, Calif. Died June 22, 1934.

NEWTON, James Thornwell, U.S. commr. patents; b. Morgan Co., Ga., July 17, 1861; s. William H. and Miriam K. (Walker) N.; B.S., U. of Ga., 1880; LL.B., Georgetown U., D.C., 1896; m. Helen Bennett, Sept. 18, 1901; children—William F., Margaret L., Helen K. With U.S. Patent Office, examiner, 1891, law clk., 1893-95, chief clk., 1895-96, prin. examiner, 1896-1914, 1st asst. commr., Mar. 19, 1914, and commr. of patents, 1917-21; now mem. firm Marks & Clerk, patent attys. Democrat. Presbyn. Compiler: Digest of Patent Office Trade-mark Decisions, 1896. Home: Washington, D.C. Died Mar. 14, 1935.

NEWTON, McGuire, physician; b. Norfolk, Va., May 25, 1876; s. John Brockenbrough and Roberta Page (Williamson) N.; McGuire's Univ. Sch., Richmond, Va.; M.D., Univ. of Coll. of Medicine, Richmond, 1897; unmarried. Began practice, Richmond, 1897; specialist in diseases of children; prof. pediatrics, Univ. Coll. of Medicine, 1907-12; prof. pediatrics, Med. Coll. of Va., July 1, 1912—; pediatrist to Memorial and Richmond City hosps. Mem. State Board of Health, 1922—. Democrat. Episcopalian. Home: Richmond, Va. Died May 18, 1923.

NEWTON, Oscar, banking; b. Crystal Springs, Miss., Mar. 4, 1877; s. James Marius and Martha (Willing) N.; ed. Newton Inst., Crystal Springs, and Southwestern Presbyn. U., Clarksville, Tenn.; m. Loraine Johnson, July 12, 1896; children—Oscar, Louise (Mrs. Louise Newton McDaniel), Jere. Began as clerk and assistant cashier, Mutual Bank, Crystal Springs, 1895; cashier Brookhaven (Miss.) Bank & Trust Co., 1899-1909; pres. Jackson (Miss.) State Nat. Bank, 1910-25; dir. Federal Reserve Bank of Atlanta, 1920-35, chmn. bd., federal reserve agt., 1925-35; gov. Federal Reserve Bank Atlanta, 1935-36, pres., 1936—. Chmn. Liberty Loan campaigns, Jackson, World War. Chmn. Bd. of Edn., Jackson, 5 yrs.; pres. Jackson Chamber Commerce 2 terms; pres. Miss. Bankers Assn. Trustee Y.M.C.A., Atlanta. Democrat. Presbyn. (ruling elder North Av. Ch.). Mason. Home: Atlanta, Ga. Died Feb. 10, 1939.

NEWTON, R(ichard) Heber, clergyman; b. Phila., Pa., Oct. 31, 1840; s. Rev. Richard and Lydia (Greatorex) N.; brother of William Wilberforce N.; A.B., U. of Pa., 1862; studied Episcopal Divinity School, Philadelphia, 1862-63; hon. D.D., Union U., 1875; m. Mary E., d. Charles S. Lewis, Apr. 14, 1864 (died 1913). Deacon, 1862, priest, 1866, P.E. Ch.; asst. St. Paul's, Phila., 1862-63, Ch. of Epiphany, Phila., 1863-64; in charge Trinity Ch., Sharon Springs, N.Y., 1864-66; rector St. Paul's, Phila., 1866-69, All Souls, New York, 1869-1902; select preacher to Leland Stanford Jr. U., 1903. V.p. Congress of Religion; noted for radical liberality of religious views frequently expressed in sermons. Author: Right and Wrong Uses of the Bible, 1883; The Book of the Beginnings, 1884; Philistinism, 1885; Social Studies, 1886; Church and Creed, 1891; Christian Science, 1898; Parsifal, 1904. Address: East Hampton, N.Y. Died Dec. 19, 1914.

NEWTON, Walter Hughes, lawyer; b. Minneapolis, Minn., Oct. 10, 1880; s. Thomas Rogers and Mary (Hughes) N.; LL.B., U. of Minn., 1905; m. Cora M. Noracon, June 14, 1905; children—Grace Laura (Mrs. Philip G. Murray), Walter Hughes (U.S.N.), John Marshall. First asst. county atty., Hennepin County, Minn., 1914-18; member 66th to 71st Congresses (1919-31), 5th Minn. Dist., resigned, July 1, 1929, to become sec. and administrative asst. to President Hoover. Served in Ho. of Rep. as mem. Com. on Foreign Affairs and Com. on Interstate and Foreign Commerce, also as mem. Rep. Steering Com. of House and sec. to Rep. Com. on Committees; mem. bd. regents Smithsonian Instn.; asst. dir. Speakers' Bur. of Rep. Nat. Com., 1924, dir. in senatorial and congressional campaigns of 1926 and in nat. campaign of 1928; mem. Federal Home Loan Bank Bd., 1933-34; resumed practice of law. Baptist. Mason. Author: The Hoover Administration, 1936. Home: Minneapolis, Minn. Died Aug. 10, 1941.

NEWTON, Watson J., lawyer; b. in Eng., 1848; ed. in Eng.; LL.B., Nat. U., Washington, 1877, hon. LL.D.; m. Ellen J. Black. In practice at Washington, 1877—; pres. Realty Appraisal & Title Co. Prof. med. jursiprudence, Nat. U.; prof. law of evidence, Washington Coll. of Law, 1896—. Author: Brambleton Fair (musical comedy), 1891; Cupid and Creeds (novel), 1901. Wrote words of The Columbian Anthen; words and music of The Flag of Washington. Home: Washington, D.C. Died Jan. 16, 1913.

NEWTON, William Wilberforce, clergyman; b. Phila., Nov. 4, 1843; s. Rev. Richard and Lydia (Greatorex) N.; brother of Richard Heber N.; A.B., U. of Pa., 1865, hon. D.D.; m. Emily Stevenson Cooke, Nov. 16, 1870. Deacon, 1868, priest, 1869, P.E. Ch.; asst. Ch. of Epiphany, Phila., 1869-70; rector St. Paul's Brookline, Mass., 1870-75, Trinity, Newark, N.J., 1875-77, St. Paul's, Boston, 1877-82, St. Stephen's, Pittsfield, 1881-1900. Organized Am. Congress of Chs., which met at Hartford, Conn., 1885, and Cleveland, O., 1886. Author: A Run Through Russia; Philip McGregor; The Voice of St. John; Summer Sermons from a Berkshire Pulpit; Life of Dr. W. A. Muhlenberg; The Child and the Bishop; New Tracts for New Times; The Abiding Value of First Principles; Thekla's Journal; The Gate of the Temple. Address: Brookline, Mass. Died June 25, 1914.

NIBLACK, Albert Parker, naval officer; b. Vincennes, Ind., July 25, 1859; s. Hon. William E. and

Eliza (Sherman) N.; grad. U.S. Naval Acad., 1880; grad. Naval War Coll., 1916; m. Mary A. Harrington, Nov. 24, 1903. Promoted through grades to rear adm., Aug. 1917; retired July 25, 1923. Served on Pacific Sta., 1880-82; survey and exploration, Alaska, 1884-88; Squadron of Evolution, 1889-92; flag lt. N. Atlantic Squadron, 1893-94; insp. naval militia, 1895-96; writer and lecturer, Naval War Coll., on signaling and naval tactics, 1893-96; prize essayist, Naval Inst., 1890 and 1896; naval attaché at Berlin, Rome and Vienna, till breaking out of war with Spain, in which he served on blockade of Cuban ports, participating in battle of Nipe Bay; transferred to Flagship Olympia at Manila, Nov. 1898; participated in suppression of the Filipino insurrection, Feb. 1899-July 1, 1901; in campaigns about Manila, Ilo Ilo, Subig Bay and Lyngayen Gulf; China, Feb.-Oct. 1900, during "Boxer" campaign; sec. naval commn. in P.I., 1901; insp. target practice, 1902; Naval Station, Hawaii, 1903; comdg. U.S.S. Iroquois, 1904-06; Pacific Squadron, 1906-07; comdg. ships at Naval Acad., 1907-09; comdg. U.S.S. Tacoma, June 1909-May 1910; naval attaché, Am. Legation, Buenos Aires, June 1, 1910-Nov. 1911; naval attaché, Am. Embassy, Berlin, Dec. 30, 1911-July 1913; Atlantic Fleet, 1913-16, comdg. U.S.S. Michigan; comd. 3d seaman regt. in occupation of Vera Cruz, Mex., Apr. 1914; mem. Gen. Bd.; on outbreak of war ordered to command Div. 1 and later Squadron 1, battleship force, Atlantic Fleet; comdg. Squadron 2, patrol force and of U.S. naval forces based on Gibraltar, Nov. 1917; comd. of U.S. naval forces in Western Mediterranean until after armistice; in Eastern Mediterranean, in Adriatic, Jan.-Mar. 1919; dir. Naval Intelligence, Navy Dept., Apr. 1, 1919-Sept. 15, 1920; naval attaché Am. Embassy, London, Oct. 1, 1920-Jan. 1921; vice admiral comdg. U.S. Naval Forces in European waters, Jan. 15, 1921. Elected dir. Internat. Hydrographic Bur. of Monaco, Feb. 1924, and elected pres. Mar. 1, 1927, for term of 5 yrs.; v.p. Soc. Naval Architects and Marine Engrs. 12 yrs., later hon. v.p. for life. Commended for rescue of crew of Am. ship, "Ocean King," which foundered in May 1887. Awarded D.S.M. (U.S.) for services in World War; Comdr. Royal Victorian Order, Companion St. Michael and St. George, and Kt. Comdr. St. Michael and St. George (Gt. Britain); Comdr. Legion of Honor (France); Grand Officer Avis (Portugal); Comdr. St. Maurice and St. Lazarus (Italy); White Eagle, 2d Class (military) and White Eagle, 1st Class (civil) by Serbia; Order of the Sacred Treasure (Japan); Grand Officer Ouissam Alonite, by the Sultan of Morocco; Grand Officer of Niftar Ichitar, by the Bey of Tunis; Grand Officer St. Charles of Monaco; Grand Officer of Striped Tiger (China). Author: The Coast Indians of Alaska and Northern British Columbia, 1889. Address: Washington, D.C. Died Aug. 20, 1929.

NIBLEY, Charles Wilson, bishop; b. Hunterfield, Midlothian County, Scotland, Feb. 5, 1849; s. James and Jean (Wilson) N.; self-ed.; m. Rebeca Neibaur, Mar. 30, 1869. Brought to U.S., 1855; presiding bishop Mormon Ch., 1907—; v.p. Brigham Young Coll.; pres. San Vincente Lumber Co., Nibley-Channel Lumber Co.; v.p. F. S. Murphy Lumber Co., Utah Lumber Co., Utah State Nat. Bank, Utah-Idaho Sugar Co.; dir. Z.C.M.I., Zion's Savings Bank & Trust Co., Western Pacific R.R. Republican. Home: Salt Lake City, Utah. Died Dec. 11, 1931.

NICCOLLS, Samuel Jack, clergyman; b. Greenfield Farm, Westmoreland County, Pa., Aug. 3, 1838; s. William Todd (an officer in War of 1812) and Elizabeth (Jack) N.; grad. Jefferson (now Washington and Jefferson) Coll., 1857; student Western Theol. Sem., Pa., 1857-60; hon. D.D., Centre Coll., 1865, Princeton, 1896; LL.D., Hanover, 1885, Washington and Jefferson, 1898; m. Margaret A. Sherrick, Aug. 17, 1860. Licensed to preach, 1859; ordained Presbyn. ministry, 1860; pastor Chambersburg, Pa.; 1860-65; chaplain 126th Pa. Vols., 1863; pastor Second Presbyn. Ch., St. Louis, 1865—. Moderator Presbyn. Gen. Assembly, 1872; mem. revision com. of confession of faith, 1890, 1900; moderator Synod of Mo., 1905; pres. bd. McCormick Theol. Sem. Author: Eastern Question in Prophecy, 1872. Contbr. to religious press. Address: St. Louis, Mo. Died Aug. 19, 1915.

NICE, Harry (Whinna), gov.; b. Washington, D.C., Dec. 5, 1877; s. Henry and Drucilla (Arnold) N.; student Baltimore City Coll., 1889-93, Dickinson Coll., Carlisle, Pa., 1893-93, U. of Md., 1896-99; m. Edna Viola Amos, June 5, 1906; children—William Stone (dec.), Harry Whinna, Jr. Admitted to Md. bar, 1899, practicing in Baltimore, 1899—; mem. firm Dickerson & Nice, 1920—; judge of Appeal Tax Court, Baltimore, 1920-24; states atty. and asst. states atty., Baltimore, 1912-19; mem. Baltimore City Council, 1903-05; sec. to mayor of Baltimore, 1905-08; supervisor elections, Baltimore, 1908-12; elected gov. of Md., Nov. 1934 for term, 1935-39; later in practice of law. Republican. Methodist. Mason, K.P., Odd Fellow, Elk, Moose. Home: Baltimore, Md. Died Feb. 25, 1941.

NICHOLAS, Anna, newspaper writer; b. Meadville, Pa.; d. Dr. John and Rachel (Gardiner) N.; ed. pub. and pvt. schs., Meadville, Pa. On editorial staff Indianapolis Journal, 1881-1904; editorial writer Indianapolis Star, 1904—. Occasional contributor to other newspapers and periodicals. Author: An Idyl of the Wabash (short stories), 1898; The Making of Thomas Barton (short stories), 1913; A History of Crown Hill, 1926. Home: Indianapolis, Ind. Died Jan. 29, 1929.

NICHOLAS, William Gardiner, newspaper writer; b. Meadville, Pa., Mar. 6, 1853; s. Dr. John and Rachel (Gardiner) N.; brother of Anna N.; ed. pub. schs., Meadville, Pa., and vicinity; m. Ella Jean Lemon, Sept. 21, 1897. Connected with Indianapolis Journal, 1872-79; spent yr. in Colo.; with Chicago Times (staff writer), 1880-83; with National Republican, Washington, 1883-84; on Chicago Bd. of Trade, 1885-92; in newspaper business, 1893—; Washington corr. Chicago Evening Post, Indianapolis Journal and other papers, 1894-99; financial and spl. writer for chain of leading papers and for corps., with residence in New York, 1900—. Home: New York, N.Y. Died May 2, 1915.

NICHOLL, Horace Wadham, composer; b. nr. Birmingham, Eng., Mar. 17, 1848; s. John and Ann (Wadham) N. (descendant of founder Wadham Coll., Oxford, Eng.); gen. edn. schs. of Birmingham; studied music and composition under father, and studied piano and organ under various professors; m. Cornelia Mather (lineal descendant of Rev. Increase Mather), July 27, 1889. Organist of various chs. in Eng. and America, 1866-90, and gave numerous classical organ recitals; also instr. in counterpoint, single and double fugue, and composition. Composer: Mass in E flat, 1872; Eight Characteristic Pieces (piano duet), 1885; Twelve Sentiments Poétiques (piano), 1888; Sonata for Piano ('cello), 1889; "Hamlet"—Psychic Sketch, for orchestra, 1889; Cloister Scene, solo and chorus, 1889; Twelve Melodic Studies (piano), 1891; Three Melodic Pieces (piano), 1899; Twelve Grand Preludes and Fugues for Organ, 1900; Six Short Preludes and Fugues; Six Symphonic Preludes and Fugues; Fantasies on Psalms CXXX and XXIII, 1900; Three Offertories, 1901; Symphonic Sonata (A.), 1902; Symphonic Poem "Life," and Six Symphonic Studies, 1903; various organ movements, and other works; also four "connected" Oratorios; Symphonies; Symphonic Poem "Tartarus"; orchestral suite in A Major (five movements); etc.; chamber music (quartet and trio); 12 concert preludes and fugues in all the different counterpoints, for pianoforte, 1915; six preludes and fugues, pianoforte, 1918; etc. Home: New York, N.Y. Died Mar. 10, 1922.

NICHOLLS, C(harles) W(ilbur) deLyon, author; b. Nichols, Conn., Dec. 17, 1854 (of the Sir Richard Nicolls branch); s. George Kneeland and Armina de Lyon (Seeley) N.; grad. Williston Sem., Easthampton, Mass., 1874; entered Yale, 1874, but withdrew because of ill health; pupil in singing, Bristol's Conservatoire, 1874-76, student Johns Hopkins, 1877-80, Concord Sch. of Philosophy, summers, 1879-82, in philosophy at Seabury Div. Sch., 1882-84; grad. Gen. Theol. Seminary, New York, 1887; unmarried. Ordained priest, P.E. Ch., 1888; vicar St. Thomas', New Haven, 1887-88; rector St. Stephen's, Staten Island, 1888-92; chaplain Dept. Pub. Charities and Corrections, New York, 1893-97; vicar St. Luke's, New York, 1897-99. Became Roman Catholic, 1899; took lectures in moral theology and dogma, Gregorian U., Rome, 1899-1900. Originator of the Sunday Kindergarten Assn. and the Free Sch. of Italian singing. Gov.-gen. Scions of Colonial Cavaliers. Author: The Greek Madonna, 1894; The Decadents, 1899; The Sunday Kindergarten Art History Catechism, 1903; The Ultra-Fashionable Peerage of America, 1904; The Sunday Kindergarten Primer of American Philosophy, 1907; Annals of a Remarkable Salon, 1910; The Art-History Primer, 1911; The 469 Ultra-Fashionables of America, 1912; Miss Detrimental—A Social Career. Democrat. Address: New York, N.Y. Deceased.

NICHOLLS, Francis Tillon, judge; b. Donaldsonville, Ascension Parish, La., Aug. 20, 1834; grad. U.S. Mil. Acad., 1855; assigned to 3d Arty.; served against Seminole Indians; was on frontier duty, 1856; resigned, Oct. 1, 1856; practiced law, Napoleonville, La., 1857-61; in C.S.A., 1861-65; capt. and lt. col. 8th La., 1861-62; col. 15th La. and brig. gen., 1862; lost an arm at battle of Winchester, Va., and a foot at Chancellorsville; supt. conscript bur., trans-Miss. dept., 1864-65; practiced law in Ascension Parish, La., 1865-76, and in New Orleans, 1880-88; gov. of La., 1877-80 and 1888-92; chief justice Supreme Ct. of La., 1893-1904, asso. justice, 1904—. Democrat. Address: New Orleans, La. Died 1912.

NICHOLLS, Rhoda Holmes, artist; b. Coventry, Eng.; d. Rev. William Groome and Marion (Cooke) Holmes; ed. by governesses and finishing sch., London; student Bloomsbury Sch. of Art, London; won Queen's scholarship; m. Burr H. Nicholls, 1884; children—Rhoda Olive, Arundel Holmes. Exhibited in Rome, Turin, Munich, Royal Acad., London, and all Am. exhbns. Awarded medals in Prize Fund, New York, Boston, Atlanta, Nashville and Charleston, and the W. Indies and Interstate expns., Chicago, Buffalo and St. Louis expns., New York Water Color Club. On staff of Art Interchange, and Art Amateur; co-editor Palette and Brush. Home: Stamford, Conn. Died Aug. 1930.

NICHOLLS, Samuel Jones, lawyer; b. Spartanburg, S.C., May 7, 1885; s. Judge George W. and Minnie L. N.; educated Bingham Sch., Wofford Coll., and Va. Poly. Inst.; student U. of Chicago Law Sch.; m. Eloise M. Clark, Mar. 7, 1915. Began law practice Spartanburg, S.C., 1906, as mem. firm of Nicholls & Nicholls; also county atty. Spartanburg County, 1907—; mem. S.C. Ho. of Rep., 1906-09; served by spl. appmt. as asso. justice Supreme Ct. of S.C.; mem. 64th to 66th Congresses (1915-21), 4th S.C. Dist.; later in law practice as mem. Nicholls, Wyche & Byrnes. Democrat. Organizer and 3 yrs. capt. Co. I, 1st Inf., N.G.S.C. Past Exalted Ruler Spartanburg Lodge 637 B.P.O.E.; Past Sachem I.O.R.M. Methodist. Home: Spartanburg, S.C. Deceased.

NICHOLS, Charles A., congressman; ed. pub. schs. Sec. Detroit Police Dept., 1905-08; city clk., 1908-12; mem. 64th to 66th Congresses (1915-21), 13th Mich. Dist. Republican. Home: Detroit, Mich. Died Apr. 25, 1920.

NICHOLS, Charles Henry, civil engineer; b. Braintree, Vt., July 12, 1864; s. Norman and Hannah Tracy (Brigham) N.; B.S., Norwich U., Vt., 1886, M.C.E., 1893; C.E., Thayer Sch. Civ. Engring. (Dartmouth), 1888; m. Isa Dyer, Feb. 9, 1889. Draftsman Boston Bridge Works, 1888-89; asst. bridge engr., N.Y., Providence & Boston R.R., 1889-91; asst. engr. Keystone Bridge Works, Pittsburgh, 1891-93; engr. for Milliken Bros., New York, 1893-94; asst. engr. for Post & McCord, 1894-1902; engr. for Snare & Triest, 1902-03, Kirby, Petit & Green, architects, 1903-08, McKim, Mead & White, 1908-10; chief engr. Trowbridge & Livingston, architects, 1910-12; entered in pvt. practice, Feb. 1912; mem. firm Bigelow & Nichols, 1913—. Trustee Norwich U. Republican. Home: Bogota, N.J. Died Oct. 30, 1927.

NICHOLS, Charles Lemuel, M.D.; b. Worcester, Mass., May 29, 1851; s. Lemuel B. and Lydia C. (Anthony) N.; A.B., Brown U., 1872, A.M., 1875, Litt.D., 1918; M.D., Harvard Med. Sch., 1875; m. Caroline C. Dewey, 1877; m. 2d, Mary J. Brayton, 1884. Practiced in Worcester, 1878—. Mem. bd. of fellows, Brown U.; trustee Westboro State Hosp. Mem. Am. Antiq. Soc. (sec. for foreign corr.). Republican. Episcopalian. Author: A Bibliography of Worcester; A List of Massachusetts Almanacs; Isaiah Thomas, Printer (with bibliography). Home: Worcester, Mass. Died Feb. 19, 1929.

NICHOLS, Edward Hall, surgeon; b. Reading, Mass., Jan. 6, 1864; s. Edward Childs and Abbie Susan (Hall) N.; A.B., Harvard, 1886, A.M., 1892, M.D., 1892; m. Edith Walker Judd, Oct. 3, 1894. Exec. asst. and asst. supt., Boston City Hosp., 1892-94; asst. pathologist, 1896-99, demonstrator surg. pathology, 1897-1901, instr., 1901-04, asst. prof. in surg. pathology and surgery, 1904-13, asso. prof., 1914-16, clin. prof. surgery, 1916—, Harvard Med. Sch. Dir. Cancer Lab., Research Croft Fund, Boston, 1899-1905; in med. charge of Harvard football team, 1904—; surgeon-in-chief to 1st Harvard surg. unit with British Army in France, 1915; maj. Med. O.R.C., 1917; chief surgeon U.S. Base Hosp. 7; in France, July 1918-Jan. 1919; lt. col. M.C. Unitarian. Fellow Am. Acad. Arts and Sciences, Am. Coll. Surgeons. Author of numerous articles pertaining to surgery. Address: Boston, Mass. Died June 12, 1922.

NICHOLS, Edward Leamington, physicist; b. of American parentage, at Leamington, Eng., Sept. 14, 1854; s. Edward Willard and Maria (Watkinson) N.; B.S., Cornell, 1875; univs. of Leipzig, Berlin, 1875-78; Ph.D., U. of Göttingen, 1879; fellow Johns Hopkins U., 1879-80; LL.D., U. of Pa., 1906; D.Sc., Dartmouth Coll., 1910; m. Ida Preston, May 25, 1881 (died 1928); children—Elizabeth (Mrs. Montgomery Hunt Throop), Robert Preston. With Edison at Menlo Park, N.J., 1880-81; prof. physics and chemistry, Central U. of Ky., 1881-83; prof. physics and astronomy, U. of Kan., 1883-87; prof. physics, Cornell, 1887-1919, prof. emeritus, 1919—. Founder of the Physical Review and editor, 1893-1912. Fellow Am. Acad. Arts and Sciences. Pres. A.A.A.S., 1907, Am. Physical Soc., 1908-09, Kan. Acad. Science, 1884-86. Author: The Galvanometer, 1894; A Laboratory Manual of Physics and Applied Electricity, 2 vols. (with Profs. Merritt, Bedell and others), 1895; The Elements of Physics, 3 vols. (with Prof. W. S. Franklin), 1896; Outlines of Physics, 1897; Studies in Luminescence (with Prof. Merritt), 1910; Fluorescence of the Uranyl Salts (with Prof. Howes), 1919; Cathodo-Luminescence and the Luminescence of Incandescent Solids (with Howes and Wilber), 1928; and numerous papers in scientific jours. on experimental physics. Home: Ithaca, N.Y. Died Nov. 10, 1937.

NICHOLS, Edward Tattnall, ry. official; b. Pensacola, Fla., Aug. 12, 1852; s. Edward Tattnall (rear-adm. U.S.N.) and Caroline Elizabeth (Bowers) N.; ed. Poly. Inst., Brooklyn; St. Paul's Sch., Concord, N.H.; m. Mary E. Hall, June 10, 1880. Clk. to the chief of staff of U.S. Fleet in Asiatic waters, Apr. 1870-July 1872; Korean expdn., 1871. Entered ry. service, 1876; served as asst. sec. 1st div., St. Paul

& Pacific R.R. and its successors, St. Paul, Minneapolis & Man. Ry. and G.N. Ry.; v.p. G.N. Ry.; pres., Northern Securities Co.; dir. C.&S. Ry. Co.; trustee G.N. Iron Ore Properties. Republican. Episcopalian. Home: New York, N.Y. Died Mar. 20, 1934.

NICHOLS, Edward West, educator; b. Petersburg, Va., June 27, 1858; s. James Nathaniel and Anne (Wynn) N.; ed. McCabe's U. Sch., Va. Mil. Inst., U. of Va. (summer courses); m. Evelyn Junkin Rust, Nov. 14, 1905. Prof. engring., 1882-90, mathematics, 1890-1907, supt. with rank of maj. gen. of engrs., Va. Mil. Inst. Chmn. Va. Council of Defense, 1917-18; maj. engrs., U.S.A., 1918-19. Engaged for several yrs. in collaboration with Dr. P. H. Dudley in scientific work connected with rys., especially in matter of correlation of rolling stock and permanent way. Democrat. Episcopalian. Author: Nichols's Analytic Geometry, 1891; Nichols's Differential and Integral Calculus, 1901. Home: Lexington, Va. Died July 1, 1927.

NICHOLS, Ernest Fox, physicist; b. Leavenworth, Kan., June 1, 1869; s. Alonzo Curtis and Sophronia (Fox) N.; B.Sc., Kan. Agrl. Coll., 1888; M.Sc., Cornell U., 1893, D.Sc., 1897; student physics, Cornell, 1889-92, U. of Berlin, 1894-96, Cambridge U., 1904-05; hon. D.Sc., Dartmouth, 1903; LL.D., Colgate, Clark, Wesleyan, 1909, Vt., 1911, Pittsburgh, 1912, Dennison, 1914, Dartmouth, 1916; m. Katharine Williams West, June 16, 1894. Prof. physics, Colgate U., 1892-98, Dartmouth Coll., 1898-1903; prof. exptl. physics, Columbia, 1903-09; pres. Dartmouth Coll., 1909-16; professor physics, Yale, 1916-20; dir. pure science, Nela Research Labs., Nat. Lamp Works, Cleveland, O., 1920-21; pres. Mass. Inst. of Technology, June-Nov. 1921 (resigned because of poor health); dir. Nela Research Lab., 1929—. Research associate Carnegie Institution Washington, 1907-09, Bur. of Ordnance, Navy Dept., 1917-19. Rumford medal of Am. Acad. Arts and Sciences, 1905. Mem. Nat. Acad. Sciences (chmn. physics and engring. sect., 1917-20); fellow Am. Acad. Arts and Sciences, A.A.A.S. (v.p. 1903). Collaborator Astrophysical Journal; contbr. of many papers to scientific jours. in U.S. and abroad, on radiation and other physical subjects. Address: Cleveland, O. Died Apr. 29, 1924.

NICHOLS, Francis Henry, newspaper corr., author; b. Brooklyn, Oct. 31, 1868; s. William C. and Isabella G. N.; grad. West Division High Sch., Chicago; unmarried. During Spanish-Am. War, was corr. for New York newspapers in Cuba, Puerto Rico, Haiti and Jamaica. In May 1898, carried to Gen. Maximo Gomez in Cuba the news of the declaration of war with Spain, and obtained an interview with him on the subject for New York World. One of two war correspondents who were first two Americans to enter Havana after signing of peace protocol. In 1901, as corr. of the Christian Herald, went to China; rode 750 miles from Pekin to Sian in the province of Shensi, thence 700 miles in canoes on the Han River to Hankow. Author: Through Hidden Shensi, 1902. Address: New York, N.Y. Died 1904.

NICHOLS, George Elwood, botanist; b. Southington, Conn., Apr. 12, 1882; s. George Edward and Mary Sampson (Smith) N.; grad. Hillhouse High Sch., New Haven, 1900; B.A., Yale, 1904, Ph.D., 1909; studied U. of Chicago, 1910; m. Grace Elizabeth Walker, June 23, 1909; children—Marion Louise, Grace Evelyn, George Emory, Mary Martha. Asst. in botany, Yale, 1904-09, instr. same, 1909-15, asst. prof., 1915-23, asso. prof., 1923-26, prof., 1926—; asso. prof. University of Michigan Biol. Sta., 1920-26, professor, 1926—; director Yale Botanical Gardens. Bot. adviser on sphagnum (for surg. dressings) to A.R.C. during World War. Mem. Botanical Society America (treas. 1925-32; vice pres. 1933), Ecological Soc. America (pres. 1932). Republican. Baptist. Home: New Haven, Conn. Died June 20, 1939.

NICHOLS, Harry Peirce, clergyman; b. Salem, Mass., Sept. 3, 1850; s. Charles Saunders and Amelia Ann (Ainsworth) N.; A.B., Harvard, 1871; B.D., Andover Theol. Sem., 1875; grad. Phila. Div. Sch., 1876; D.D., New York U., 1904; m. Alice M. Shepley, June 8, 1881; children—Mrs. Margaret Nichols Hardenbergh, John Donaldson. Deacon, 1876, priest, 1877, P.E. Ch.; rector St. Paul's, Brunswick, Me., 1877-83; asst. Trinity, New Haven, Conn., 1883-92; rector St. Mark's, Minneapolis, Minn., 1892-99, Holy Trinity Ch., New York, 1899-1922 (retired). Dep. Gen. Conv., Minn., 1895, 98, N.Y., 1904, 22, 25. Republican. Author: Bohlen Lectures on the Temporary and the Permanent in New Testament Revelation, 1905. Home: North Conway, N.H. Died Nov. 15, 1940.

NICHOLS, Henry Sargent Prentiss, lawyer; b. Columbia, Pa., Nov. 2, 1858; s. Joseph Darwin and Emily (Darrah) N.; ed. pub. schs., Pa., and private tutor; A.B., U. of Pa., 1879; m. Isabel McIlhenny, June 4, 1895. Admitted to bar, 1881; formerly asst. gen. counsel Pa. R.R. Co., retired. Trustee Presbyterian Hosp. Del. Universal Congress Lawyers and Jurists, St. Louis, 1904. Republican. Presbyn. Died June 7, 1936.

NICHOLS, Herbert, author; b. Walpole, N.H., Feb. 7, 1852; s. Amos and Lydia N.; B.S. in architecture, Worcester (Mass.) Poly. Inst., 1871; Ph.D., Clark U., 1891; m. Jenny L. Clark, Oct. 1, 1900. Civ. engr. Pa. R.R., 1871-85; instr. psychology, Harvard, 1890-93; lecturer Johns Hopkins, 1896. Author: The Psychology of Time, 1891; Our Notions of Number and Space, 1894; A Treatise on Cosmology, 1904; also monographs and articles and stories in mags. Home: Brookline, Mass. Died Dec. 6, 1936.

NICHOLS, James, insurance; b. Fairfield County, Conn., Dec. 24, 1830; s. Isaac and Betsy (Platt) N.; widower. Admitted to bar, 1854; asst. clerk Superior Ct., 1854-56; judge of probate for Hartford Dist., 1861-64; in ins. business, 1867-1915; pres., 1887-1915, chmn. bd. dirs., 1915—; Nat. Fire Ins. Co.; pres. Mechanics & Traders Ins. Co., 1900-15; dir. Phœnix Mut. Life Ins. Co., Soc. for Savings. Republican. Conglist. Home: Hartford, Conn. Died Apr. 29, 1916.

NICHOLS, John Richard, clergyman; b. Watkins, N.Y., Dec. 16, 1854; s. John and Esther (Townsend) N.; prep. edn., Starkey Acad.; A.B., Oberlin Coll., 1879, B.D., 1883; D.D., Marietta Coll., 1898, Oberlin, 1923; m. Nellie E. Hawley, July 6, 1881; children—Ruth G., Helen Hawley (wife of Eugene L. Porter, M.D.), John Herbert, Florence May (Mrs. C. C. Adams), Marian T. (dec.). Ordained Congl. ministry, 1883; pastor Garrettsville, O., 1883-87; engaged in work for foreign population, Cleveland, 1887-91; pastor successively Medina, O., Marietta, O., and Rogers Park Ch., Chicago, until 1922; supt. Chicago Congl. Missionary and Extension Soc., 1922-26; pres. Chicago Ch. Federation, 1927-29. Trustee Marietta Coll., Union Theol. Coll. (Chicago). Home: Evanston, Ill. Died Dec. 1932.

NICHOLS, Othniel Foster, civ. engr.; b. Newport, R.I., July 29, 1845; s. Thomas Pitman and Lydia Foster N.; C.E., Rensselaer Poly. Inst., 1868; m. Jennie Swasey, Nov. 21, 1876. Chief engr., 1888-95, gen. mgr., 1892-95, Brooklyn Elevated R.R.; 1896-1903, prin. asst. engr. in charge Williamsburg (East River) bridge; chief engr., 1904-06, now consulting engr. Dept. of Bridges, New York; pres. dept. engring., Brooklyn Inst. Arts and Sciences. Residence: Brooklyn, N.Y. Died 1908.

NICHOLS, Walter Hammond, author, educator; b. Chicago, Ill., Feb. 19, 1866; s. Joshua Rufus and Charlotte Elizabeth (Hammond) N.; prep. edn., Salt Lake Acad. and Salt Lake Collegiate Inst.; B.S. in chemistry, U. of Mich., 1891; studied U. of Chicago, U. of Colorado; M.A., Teachers Coll., Columbia, 1901; m. Esther Blanche Connor, Sept. 27, 1892; children—Helen Blanche (dec.), Alan Hammond (killed in U.S. Aviation Service, 1918), John Ralph, Dorothy Esther. Asst. in edn. and history, U. of Colo., 1896-98; sec. Teachers Coll. (Columbia), 1898-1900; prof. history and economics, U. of Colo., 1901-03; v.p. Mercantile Bank & Trust Co., Boulder, Colo., 1903-07; teacher, later supt. schs., Palo Alto, Calif., prin. Palo Alto Union High Sch., 1915—. Republican. Conglist. Author: Trust A Boy!, 1923; The Measure of a Boy, 1925; Cowboy Hugh, 1927; A Morgan Rifleman, 1928. Contbr. to Modern School Readers, Book VI, 1927. Home: Palo Alto, Calif. Died Oct. 10, 1935.

NICHOLS, William Ford, bishop; b. Lloyd, N.Y., June 9, 1849; s. Charles Hubert and Margaret Emilia (Grant) N.; A.B., Trinity Coll., Conn., 1870, A.M., 1873; grad. Berkeley Div. Sch., 1873; D.D., Trinity, 1888, Kenyon Coll., 1888; m. Clara Quintard, May 18, 1876. Deacon, 1873, priest, 1874, P.E. Ch.; pvt. sec. to Bishop Williams of Conn., 1871-76; asst. Holy Trinity, Middletown, Conn., 1873-75; rector St. James', W. Hartford, Conn., and Grace Ch., Newington, Conn., 1875-77, Christ Ch., Hartford, 1877-87, St. James', Phila., 1887-90; prof. ch. history, Berkeley Div. Sch., 1885-87; consecrated assistant bishop of Calif., June 24, 1890, bishop of Calif., Apr. 6, 1893. Founded, 1893, and dean Ch. Div. Sch. of the Pacific until 1923. Delegate to Seabury Centenary, Aberdeen, Scotland, 1884; asst. sec. house of bishops, 1886; declined election as bishop coadjutor of Ohio, 1888; deputy to Gen. Conv. P.E. Ch., 1889; pres. Province of Pacific, 1915-21. Author: On the Trial of Your Faith (an Episcopal charge), 1895; A Father's Story of the Earthquake and Fire of 1906; Apt and Meet, Counsels to Candidates for Holy Orders, 1909; Some World-Circuit Saunterings, 1913, etc. Home: San Francisco, Calif. Died June 5, 1924.

NICHOLS, William Henry, mfg. chemist; b. Brooklyn, N.Y., Jan. 9, 1852; s. George Henry and Sarah Elizabeth (Harris) N.; student, Poly. Inst., Brooklyn, 1865-68; B.S., New York U., 1870, M.S., 1873; LL.D., Lafayette, 1904, New York U., 1920; Sc.D., Columbia, 1904, U. of Pittsburgh, 1920, Tufts, 1921; m. Hannah W. Bensel, Feb. 14, 1873. Engaged as mfg. chemist, copper refiner and smelter, 1870—; pres. Nichols Copper Co., 1890-1918, later dir.; chmn. bd. Allied Chem. & Dye Corp.; pres. Gen. Chem. Co., 1899-1907, chmn. bd., 1907-20, later dir.; dir. Corn Exchange Bank, Title Guarantee & Trust Co. Vice chmn. bd. of Poly. Inst. of Brooklyn. Apptd. chmn. com. on chemicals, Council Nat. Defense, Apr. 1917. Incorporator Am. Chem. Soc. (pres. 1918-19); mem. Soc. Chem. Industry (pres. 1904-05); past pres. Soc. Chem. Industry, 8th International Congress Applied Chemistry, 1912. Commendatore of Crown of Italy, 1912; Knight Order of SS. Maurizio e Lazzaro, 1920. Conglist. Republican. Home: New York, N.Y. Died Feb. 21, 1930.

NICHOLS, William Theophilus, author; b. Cincinnati, Mar. 31, 1863; s. William N. and Isabella M. (Blackman) N.; A.B., Yale, 1884; m. Helen F. Hull, Nov. 18, 1896; children—Florence Hull, Leverett Hull. Mem. editorial staff New Haven (Conn.) Morning News, 1884-87, New York Times, 1887-93, Cincinnati Tribune, 1894; mng. editor Manchester (N.H.) Union, also engaged in lit. work, 1910—. Trustee U. of N.H., 1918-24. Democrat. Conglist. Author: The War for the Island, 1915; Making Good, 1915; Safety First Club, 1916; Safety First Club and the Flood, 1917; Safety First Club Fights Fire, 1923. Home: Manchester, N.H. Died Jan. 26, 1931.

NICHOLSON, George Edward, mfr., natural gas producer; b. N.Y. City, Jan. 13, 1861; s. Thomas and Hanna (Gowland) N.; ed. pub. schs.; m. Florence Belle Foster, Oct. 12, 1881 (died 1903); m. 2d, Ida H. Anderson, June 30, 1910; children—George Albert, Ralph Edward. Zinc mfr., Nevada, Mo., and Iola, Kan., 1896-1903; cement mfr., Iola and Independence, Kan., 1904-12; pres. Hawkeye Portland Cement Co., 1906-12, Dixie Portland Cement Co., 1906-12; pres. Iola Portland Cement Co., 1907-11; pres. La Harpe (Kan.) Spelter Co. and Tulsa (Okla.) Spelter Co., 1913-15; pres. Kusa (Okla.) Spelter Co. and Nicholson Corp., 1915—; pres. Nat. Cement Co., 1920—; pres. Kansas City (Mo.) Gas Co., 1922-33. Trustee Baker U. Republican. Methodist. Endowed chair of philosophy, Baker U.; Florence B. Nicholson Sch. of Theology, Baroda, India; Union Theol. Sem., Manila, P.I. Home: Kansas City, Mo. Deceased.

NICHOLSON, George T., railway official; b. Belvidere, N.C., July 1, 1856; s. William and Sarah N.; student U. of Kan.; m. Julia M. Watson, Sept. 9, 1885. Clerk in U.S. Indian Service at various Indian agencies, 1876-1881; clerk in gen. pass. and ticket office A.,T.&S.F. R.R., 1882, promoted successively to rate clerk, chief rate clerk, chief clerk, asst. gen. pass. and ticket agt. and gen. pass. agt. to 1897; gen. pass. agt. St.L.&S.F. Ry., 1897-98; pass. traffic mgr., 1898-1905, 3d v.p., 1905—. A.,T.&S.F. Ry. System. Home: Chicago, Ill. Died Mar. 30, 1913.

NICHOLSON, Henry Hudson, engr.; b. Rushford, Wis., May 25, 1850; s. Henry Williams and Sarah D. (Howe) N.; ed. Antioch Coll., O., Harvard, and Heidelberg, Germany; A.M., hon. causa, Lawrence U., Wis., 1872; m. Jennie S. Higgins, Mar. 1872; children—Edward Everett, Winifred Christine, Rachel Lloyd. Served pvt. 49th Wis. Inf., 1864-65; prof. science, State Normal Sch., Peru, Neb., 1874-82; prof. chemistry and dir. chem. labs., U. of Neb., 1882-1905; consulting engr. Hamilton Mines Co., 1898-1903, Ingold Placer Mining Co., Black Jack Gold Mines Co., Ore.; mgr. and engr. Standard Consolidated Mines Co.; directing engr. Killen-Warner-Stewart Co., Chicago; consulting engr. Killen-McLaughlin-Reese Co., Cuba, 1907; also for Alpine Gold Mining Co., Red Cliff, Colo., Plumas-Lincoln Copper Co., Doyle, Calif. Author several papers on scientific subjects. Home: Lincoln, Neb. Died Aug. 17, 1940.

NICHOLSON, Isaac Lea, P.E. bishop of Milwaukee; b. Baltimore, Jan. 18, 1844; s. Johns J. and Jane (Ricketts) N.; grad. Dartmouth, 1869; D.D., Nashotah Theol. Sem., Wis.; m. Adele Everett Ellicott, 1880 (died 1897). Ordered deacon, 1871; ordained priest, 1872; asst. at St. Thomas' Ch., Hanover, N.H., 1871-72; St. Paul's Ch., Baltimore, 1872-75; rector Ch. of the Ascension, Westminster, Md., 1875-79; St. Mark's, Phila., 1879-91; elected bishop of Ind., 1883, but declined; bishop of Milwaukee, 1891—. Address: Milwaukee, Wis. Died 1906.

NICHOLSON, James William, educator; b. Tuskegee, Ala., June 16, 1844; s. Washington Biddle and Martha William (Wafer) N.; removed to La. with parents in infancy; A.M., Homer Coll., 1870; LL.D., Poly. Inst. of Ala., 1893, Tulane U., 1904; m. Sallie D. Baker, July 30, 1876. Entered C.S.A. in 17th yr., 1861; served throughout the war in 12th La. Inf.; 2d sergt. for 3 yrs.; twice promoted to lieutenancy but declined. At close of war began teaching; prof. mathematics, Homer Coll., 1870-72; founded and conducted seminary in Claiborne Parish, La., 1868-77; prof. mathematics, 1877—, pres. 1882-84, 1887-96 (resigned both times), La. State U. Twice elected state lecturer of Patrons of Husbandry, and led in movement which resulted in establishment of the state Bur. of Agr. and Immigration, 1879; one of the founders, 1883, pres. 1892 and for many yrs. chmn. exec. com., La. Ednl. Assn.; pres. Southern Ednl. Assn., 1903. Author of a series of arithmetics, an elementary algebra, a trigonometry, a differential and integral calculus; also many monographs on math. subjects. Address: Baton Rouge, La. Deceased.

NICHOLSON, John Page, soldier, editor; b. Phila., July 4, 1842; s. James B. and Adelaide B. N.; hon. A.M., Marietta College, 1882; Litt.D., Pennsylvania

Coll., 1888; married. Enlisted 28th Pennsylvania Infantry, July 23, 1861; regimental commissary sergt., Aug. 2, 1861; 1st lt., July 21, 1862; 1st lt. q.-m., Sept. 10, 1862; hon. mustered out, Oct. 10, 1865; bvts. for meritorious services and gallantry; capt., maj. and lt. col., Mar. 13, 1865; served in and with Army of Western Va., Banks' corps; Armies of Va., the Potomac, the Cumberland and Ga., in many battles from Bolivar, Va., Sherman's march to the sea and through the Carolinas, to the final surrender of the Confederate forces. Recorder-in-chief Mil. Order Loyal Legion, 1885—; chmn. U.S. Gettysburg Nat. Park Commn.; mem. G.A.R., Mil. Service Instn. U.S., and other mil. socs.; v.p., trustee Soldiers' and Sailors' Home, Erie, Pa. Translator and Editor: The History of the Civil War in America (Comte de Paris). Editor and Compiler: Pennsylvania at Gettysburg, 2 vols. Home: Philadelphia, Pa. Died Mar. 8, 1922.

NICHOLSON, John Reed, lawyer; b. Dover, Del., May 19, 1849; A.B., Yale, 1870; LL.B., Columbia, 1873; m. Isabella Hayes Hager, June 3, 1884 (died 1924); children—Ellen Hayes, John Reed. In 1870 accompanied late Prof. O. C. Marsh on a paleontol. expdn. through Rocky Mountains and great plains; practiced law, New York, 1873-76; afterward practiced at Dover, Del., later at Wilmington; solicitor for town of Dover, 1880-85; atty. for Kent County, 1885-92; atty. gen. of Del., 1892-95; chancellor, 1895-1909; chmn. Wilmington Com. on Nat. Defense. Editor: Delaware Chancery Reports, Vol. VIII. Home: Wilmington, Del. Deceased.

NICHOLSON, Reginald Fairfax, naval officer; b. Washington, D.C., Dec. 15, 1852; grad. U.S. Naval Acad., 1873; served during Civil War as captain's clk., U.S.S. State of Georgia, Aug. 1 to 31, 1864; promoted ensign, July 16, 1874; lt., jr. grade, Jan. 22, 1880; lt., Jan. 17, 1886; lt. comdr., Mar. 3, 1899; comdr., Sept. 17, 1902; capt., July 1, 1907; rear admiral, May 19, 1911. Served on Oregon during Spanish-Am. War; Bur. of Navigation, Navy Dept., 1901-04; comd. Tacoma, 1904-05; Bur. of Equipment, Navy Dept., 1906; Bur. of Navigation, 1906-07; comd. Nebraska, 1907-09; Bd. of Inspn. and Survey, Navy Dept., 1909; chief Bur. of Navigation, 1909-12; comd. Asiatic Fleet, 1912-14; mem. Gen. Bd., Navy Dept., 1914; retired on account of age, Dec. 15, 1914; recalled to active duty, Sept. 1917, as naval attaché, Chile, Peru and Ecuador. Address: Washington, D.C. Died Dec. 19, 1939.

NICHOLSON, Samuel D., senator; b. Prince Edward Island, Can.; s. Donald M. and Catherine (McKenzie) N.; ed. pub. schs. P.E. Island and Bay City, Mich.; m. Annie Nerey, Nov. 28, 1887 (died 1915). Settled at Leadville, Colo., 1881; prominently identified for many yrs. with mining interests of Colo.; pres. and gen. mgr. Western Mining Co.; dir. Denver Nat. Bank, Denver Tramway Co., Am. Nat. Bank (Leadville), First Nat. Bank (Monte Vista, Colo.). Mayor of Leadville 2 terms, 1893-97; U.S. senator from Colo., 1921-27. Republican. Presbyn. Mason, Elk. Home: Leadville, Colo. Died Mar. 24, 1923.

NICHOLSON, Samuel Edgar, sec. Nat. Anti-Saloon League; b. near Elizabethtown, Ind., June 29, 1862; s. Samuel and Rhoda (Holliday) N.; A.B., Earlham College, Richmond, Ind., 1885; LL.D., Friends U., Wichita, Kan., 1916; m. Rhoda Elma Parker, May 28, 1889. Recording clerk of Western Yearly Meeting of Friends, 1890-99; editor and pub. Russiaville (Ind.) Observer, 1891-93, Kokomo Times, 1893-94; mem. Ind. Ho. of Rep., 1895-99 (chmn. ednl. com., com. on rules, and of Rep. steering com., 1897); author of Ind. "Nicholson Law" (temperance measure), 1895; pres. Ind. Good Citizens' League, 1895-98; field sec. Ind. Anti-Saloon League, 1898, 1899; supt. Md. Anti-Saloon League, 1900-03, Pa. Anti-Saloon League, 1904-10; sec. Nat. Anti-Saloon League, 1898—; nat. legislative supt. Anti-Saloon League, 1910-12. Editor and mgr. The American Friend, nat. organ of Friends in America, Richmond, Ind., 1913-17; nat. organizer of Anti-Saloon League, 1918-22. Mem. exec. com. of Friends Five Years Meeting (nat.); chmn. Nat. Friends Prohibition Bd., 1912—; presiding clerk Indiana Yearly Meeting of Friends, 1919-25; mem. Friends Pub. Board, 1922-27. Asso. sec. Nat. Council for Prevention of War, 1922-23; head Quaker Relief Mission in Russia, 1923-24; asso. sec. World Alliance Internat. Friendship through Chs., 1925; asso. supt. New York Anti-Saloon League, 1926-31; mem. executive com. Federal Council Chs. of Christ in America, 1928—. Minister Friends (Quakers), 1891—. Republican. Home: Media, Pa. Deceased.

NICHOLSON, Samuel M., mfr.; b. Providence, R.I., February 25, 1861; s. William Thomas and Elizabeth Dexter (Gardiner) N.; m. Mary Jewett Coe, 1885. Entered mech. dept. Nicholson File Co., Providence, R.I., 1879, pres. and gen. mgr., 1893—; pres. Am. Screw Co., 1903—; chmn. bd. Industrial Trust Co.; dir. Am. Enterprise Mfrs.', Mechanics and State mutual fire ins. cos., Narragansett Electric Co., Title Guarantee Co., Rhode Island Ins. Co., Industrial Safe Deposit Co., Union Trust Co., Rhode Island Electric Protective Co. Vice pres. Rhode Island Soc. Prevention of Cruelty to Animals. Served as a.d.c., title of col., staff of Gov. Elisha Dyer. Republican. Home: Providence, R.I. Died Apr. 7, 1939.

NICHOLSON, Somerville, commodore U.S.N.; b. New York, Jan. 1, 1822; s. Maj. A. A. and Helen Bache (Lispinard) N.; apptd. midshipman, June 21, 1839; passed midshipman, July 2, 1845; master, Sept. 9, 1853; lt., May 5, 1854; lt. comdr., July 16, 1862; comdr., Jan. 2, 1863; capt., June 1870; commodore, Jan. 1880; retired, Apr. 1881. During Civil War comd. steam gunboat "Marblehead" and steamer "State of Georgia" in blockading service. Address: Washington, D.C. Died 1905.

NICHOLSON, William Jones, army officer; b. Washington, D.C., Jan. 16, 1856; s. Commodore Somerville (U.S.N.) and Hannah (Jones) N.; grad. Inf. and Cav. Sch., 1883; LL.D., Georgetown U., 1919; m. Harriette Fenlon, Feb. 6, 1833; children—William Fenlon, Mrs. Helen Lispenard Crean. Commd. 2d lt. cav., U.S.A., Aug. 15, 1876; advanced through grades to col., Aug. 24, 1912; brig. gen. N.A., Aug. 5, 1917. Served in Spanish-Am. War, Mexican Punitive Expdn., and as comdr. Camp Meade, 1917, Camp Upton, 1918; in France, 1918, participating in Avocourt sector, Meuse-Argonne offensive, Bois Belleu-Côte 360 sector, Nov. 8-11, 1918; retired Jan. 16, 1920. Awarded D.S.M., 1919, "for exceptionally meritorious and distinguished services"; D.S.C. for "distinguished and exceptional gallantry at Bois de Bouge on Sept. 29, 1918"; officer, Legion of Honor (France); promoted brig. gen. regular army, Feb. 28, 1927, by spl. act of Congress. Catholic. Home: Washington, D.C. Died Dec. 20, 1931.

NICHOLSON, William Rufus, Reformed Episcopal bishop; b. Greene County, Miss., Jan. 8, 1822; grad. La Grange Coll., Ala., 1857; D.D., Kenyon Coll., O.; m. Jane, dau. Dr. Franklin Shaw, Nov. 27, 1845; m. 2d, Katharine Stanley, dau. Charles Hamilton Parker, Oct. 18, 1866. Was successively rector in P.E. church in New Orleans, Cincinnati, Boston and Newark, N.J. In 1874 became a member of the Reformed Episcopal church; rector Second R.E. church, Philadelphia; consecrated bishop, 1876; subsequently chosen dean of the R.E. Theol. Sem., Philadelphia. Author: The Blessedness of Heaven; Bearing of Prophecy on Inspiration; Why I Became a Reformed Episcopalian; The Real Presence; The Call to the Ministry; etc. Address: Philadelphia, Pa. Died 1901.

NICKELS, John Augustine Heard, commodore U.S.N.; b. Boston, Jan. 12, 1849; s. Capt. Edward C. and Sarah (Colburn) N.; grad. U.S. Naval Acad., 1869; m. Cornelia A. Parker, Nov. 13, 1879. Promoted ensign, July 12, 1870; master, Nov. 20, 1872; lt., June 10, 1876; lt. comdr., Feb. 1, 1898; comdr., Nov. 29, 1900; capt., June 28, 1905; commodore and retired, June 30, 1906. Served on Sabine and Richmond, 1869-71; Iroquois and Lackawanna, Asiatic station, 1872-75; Navy Yard, Boston, 1875; Montauk, 1875-76; Adams, 1876-79, Navy Yard, Boston, 1879-80; coast survey duty, 1880-81; Navy Yard, Norfolk, 1881-82; Hartford, 1882-85; Navy Yard, New York, 1885-87; Chicago, 1887-91; Navy Yard, New York, 1891-94; Newark, Chicago and San Francisco, 1894-95; Navy Yard, New York, 1896-97; exec. officer of Marblehead, 1897-99; Navy Yard, New York, 1899-1901; comd. Topeka, 1901-03; insp. 7th light house dist., 1903-05; commandant naval stas. Charleston and Port Royal, S.C., 1905-06. Address: Washington, D.C. Died 1910.

NICKERSON, Hiram Robert, railway pres.; b. N. Wayne, Me., Dec. 13, 1853; s. Hiram Snow and Mary Jane (Smith) N.; ed. Westbrook (Me.) Sem. and Kent's Hill (Me.) Coll.; m. Margaret A. Mahan, Dec. 28, 1876. Served messenger to gen. supt. A.,T. &S.F. R.R., 1872-94; asst. gen. mgr., June-Dec. 1894, gen. mgr., 1894-99, v.p. and gen. mgr., 1899-1903, v.p., 1903-07, Mexican Central Ry. Co.; pres. Rio Grande, Sierra Madre & Pacific R.R., Sierra Madre & Pacific Ry., 1907-09; pres. Mexican Am. Steamship Co., Mexican & Northern Steamship Co.; v.p. and gen. mgr. Tampico Harbor Co.; pres. El Paso Southern Ry., May 1907—; pres. S. Atlantic Trans-Continental R.R. Co., Aug. 12, 1911—; v.p. Mexican Nat. Constrn. Co., U.S. Banking Co. of Mex.; dir. Mexican Central Ry., Merchants' Nat. Bank, Topeka, Kan.; pres. Turner Fink Co., New York. Mason. Home: Orange, N.J. Died Mar. 8, 1915.

NICKEUS, Johnson, lawyer; b. Dist. of Columbia, July 24, 1850; ed. common schools and by private tutors; admitted to bar, 1874; served 2 terms in upper house Dak. legislature, later dist. atty. and then atty.-gen. for Dak. Ty.; consul in S. America, 2 yrs. under Harrison administration; removed to Wash., 1891; mayor of Tacoma, 1896-1900. Address: Tacoma, Wash. Died 1901.

NICOL, Charles Edgar, lawyer; b. Brentsville, Prince William County, Va., Feb. 22, 1854; s. Aylett and Mary Jane (Williams) N.; grad. Latin, Greek and French, Richmond (Va.) Coll., 1874; U. of Va., 1874-75; m. Marie Louise Bauder, Nov. 17, 1880; m. 2d, Florence Nash, 1908. Admitted to Va. bar, 1875; identified with important litigation in state and federal cts., Va., and in Washington, D.C., and Europe; pres. Alexandria (Va.) Nat. Bank. Mem. Va. Ho. of Rep., 6 yrs.; judge Circuit Ct. of Va., 1895-1907. Trustee Richmond Coll., Eastern Coll. Va. Democrat. Baptist. Mason. Address: Alexandria, Va. Died Oct. 21, 1924.

NICOLAY, John George, author; b. Essingen, Bavaria, Feb. 26, 1832; s. Jacob and Helena N.; ed. in common schools; learned printer's trade in office of Free Press, Pittsfield, Ill.; later became its publisher, editor and propr.; m. Therena Bates, June 15, 1865 (died, 1885). Private sec. to President Abraham Lincoln, 1860-65; U.S. consul at Paris, France, 1865-69; marshal U.S. Supreme Court, 1872-87. Author: The Outbreak of Rebellion, 1881; (with Col. John Hay) Abraham Lincoln, A History (10 vols.), 1890. With same edited Abraham Lincoln: Complete Works. Contributed biog. sketch of Abraham Lincoln to English edition Encyclopædia Britannica; writer of many mag. articles. Address: Washington, D.C. Died 1901.

NICOLL, De Lancey, lawyer; b. Shelter Island, L.I., N.Y., June 24, 1854; s. Solomon Townsend and Charlotte Ann N.; St. Paul's Sch.; A.B., Princeton, 1874; LL.B., Columbia, 1876; m. Maud Churchill (died 1924); children—Josephine Cuyler (dec.), De Lancey. In practice at New York, 1876—; sr. mem. Nicoll, Anable & Nicoll. Asst. dist. atty., N.Y. Co., 1885-88, dist. atty., 1891-94; del. Constl. Conv., 1894, 1915. Democrat. Home: New York, N.Y. Died Mar. 31, 1931.

NICOLL, James Craig, artist; b. New York, Nov. 22, 1847; s. John Williams and Elizabeth Phillips (Craig) N.; ed. at Quackenbos' Sch., New York; studied painting under M. F. H. de Haas; widower. Has exhibited at prin. expns.; received medals at Paris Expn., Am. Prize Fund, Boston, New Orleans, etc. Sec. Internat. Jury Awards on Paintings, Chicago Expn., 1893. N.A., 1885; sec. Nat. Acad. Design; founder, and 10 yrs. sec., later pres., Am. Water Color Soc. Address: New York, N.Y. Died July 25, 1918.

NICOLL, Matthias, Jr., state health commr., N.Y.; b. N.Y. City, Feb. 12, 1868; s. Matthias and Alice Mary (Large) N.; B.A., Williams Coll., 1889; M.D., Coll. Phys. and Surg. (Columbia), 1892; m. Alice Maude Wing, Dec. 14, 1899; children—Alice Mary, Lilian Wing, Nancy Fay. Resident phys. Chambers Street Hosp., New York, 1893-95, New York Foundling Hosp., 1896-97; pathologist and attending phys. New York Foundling Hosp. 10 yrs., New York Infant Asylum 3 yrs.; attending phys. Seton Hosp. (for tuberculosis) 3 yrs., Willard Parker Hosp. 13 yrs. (for some time cons. phys.); asst. dir. and chief div. of diagnosis, N.Y. City Dept. of Health, 6 yrs., 1908-14; clin. prof. infectious diseases Univ. and Bellevue Hosp. Med. Sch.; dir. pub. health edn. and sec. N.Y. State Dept. Health, 1915-17; dep. commr. of health, N.Y., 1917-23, commr. of health, 1923-30; county commr. health, Westchester County, N.Y., 1930-38. Mem. bd. visitors State Hosp. for Incipient Tuberculosis; pres. State and Provincial Health Authorities of North America. Fellow Am. Pub. Health Assn. (Governing council, exec. board), Acad. of Medicine. Episcopalian. First demonstrated (with Dr. William H. Park) the value of intraspinal use of tetanus antitoxin in treatment of lockjaw, 1914-15. Author of many articles on med. and other subjects. Retired from public service, Apr. 1938. Home: Rye, N.Y. Died May 13, 1941.

NICOLLS, William Jasper, civil and mining engr.; b. Camden, N.J., Apr. 23, 1854; grandnephew Lt. Gen. Sir Jasper Nicolls, K.C.B. (English comdr.-in-chief in India, 1839), g.s. Lt. Col. William Dann Nicolls, Royal Arty., Jamaica; s. Jasper William N. (C.E.) and Ellen Baillie, d. of Rev. William Baillie; ed. Hill Sch., Pottstown, Pa.; m. Clara Valentine Lyon, 1882. Asst. engr. Reading Ry., 1873; chief engr. Pa. Steel Co., 1875; chief engr. L.I. Ry., 1880; mining engr., 1882—. Author: The Railway Builder; Story of American Coals, 1898; Coal Catechism, 1900; Greystone, 1901; A Dreamer in Paris, 1904; Brunhilda of Orrs Island, 1908; Daughters of Suffolk, 1910; Wild Mustard, 1914. Home: Malvern, Pa. Died Feb. 14, 1916.

NICUM, John, pres. and prof. mental and moral science and Hebrew, Wagner Memorial Luth. Coll., 1894-1902; b. Winnenden, Würtemberg, Germany, Jan. 6, 1851; s. John and Anna Margaret (Schaefer) N.; ed. Muhlenberg Coll., Allentown, Pa., and Theol. Sem., Phila., D.D., 1893; m. Jos. J. Sanner, Apr. 30, 1878. Pastor Frackville, Pa., 1876-78; Phila., 1878-80; Syracuse, N.Y., 1880-87; 1887—, pastor St. John's Evang. Luth. Ch., Rochester, N.Y.; sec. gen. council Evang. Luth. Ch. in N. America, 1886-97; sec. and pres. German Home Mission Bd., same, 1887-97. Author: History of the New York Ministerium; Gleichniss-Reden Jesu, 1884; Laws of the State of New York Relating to Churches, 1886; Confessional History of the Lutheran Church in the United States, 1891. Translated, with additions, Wolf's The Lutherans in America. Contbr. to Meusel Kirchliche's Handlexikon, Leipzig, and Lutheran Cyclopædia. Address: Rochester, N.Y. Died 1909.

NIEDRINGHAUS, Frederick G., capitalist; b. Province of Westphalia, Germany, Oct. 21, 1837; s. Frederick W. and Mary N.; ed. in schs. in Germany; came to U.S., 1855; m. Dena Key, 1860; 1 son, Thomas Key. Pres. Nat. Enameling & Stamping Co., Granite Realty & Investment Co.; dir. Blanke-Wenneker Co., St. Louis Pressed Brick Co.; v.p. Granite City Gas Co. Mem. 51st Congress (1889-91), 8th Mo. Dist. Republican. Methodist. Home: St. Louis, Mo. Died Nov. 25, 1922.

NIEDRINGHAUS, George W., mfr.; b. St. Louis, Mo., May 28, 1864; s. William F. and Mary (Bittner) N.; ed. Smith Acad., St. Louis, and Williston Sem., Mass.; m. Fanita Hayward, Nov. 14, 1889. Treas., 1884-99, St. Louis Stamping Co., which was absorbed, 1899, by Nat. Enameling and Stamping Co., of which was factory mgr., Granite City, Ill., 1900-08, manager steel mills, Granite City, 1908-19, pres., 1919—; also chmn. bd. Granite City National Bank; pres. Granite City Gas & Fuel Co.; dir. M.P. Ry. Republican. Methodist. Home: St. Louis, Mo. Died Apr. 19, 1928.

NIEDRINGHAUS, Henry Frederick, congressman; b. St. Louis, Dec. 15, 1864; ed. pub. schools and Smith Acad., St. Louis; m. Ariel L. Cargo, 1930. Member 70th to 72d Congresses (1927-33), 10th Mo. Dist. Chmn. bd. govs. Shriners' Hosp. for Crippled Children. Republican. Mason. Home: St. Louis, Mo. Died Aug. 3, 1941.

NIEDRINGHAUS, Thomas Key, mfr.; b. St. Louis, Oct. 21, 1860; s. of F. G. and Dena (Key) N.; ed. Washington U., St. Louis, and Wesleyan U., Conn.; m. Hennie B. Johnson, Apr. 18, 1888. Became sec. St. Louis Stamping Co., 1880, continuing until co. was merged into the National Enameling and Stamping Co., of which became v.p.; v.p. Commonwealth Steel Co.; sec. Granite Realty and Investment Co. Rep. caucus nominee for U.S. senator, Jan. 5, 1905. Mem. exec. com. Rep. Nat. Com., 1912-16. Methodist. Home: St. Louis, Mo. Died Oct. 26, 1924.

NIEHAUS, Charles Henry, scuptor; b. Cincinnati, O., Jan. 24, 1855; s. John Conrad and Sophia (Block) N.; ed. Cincinnati schs.; art edn. Royal Acad., Munich, Germany; took degree and won 1st medal ever given to Am., and prizes at different times; m. Letetia Gorman, 1888; 1 dau., Marie J.; m. 2d, Regina Armstrong, 1900. Won award, Columbian Expn., Chicago, Ill., 1893; gold medals, Buffalo Expn., 1901, Charleston Expn., 1902, St. Louis Expn., 1904. Executed: Garfield statue, Cincinnati; Ingalls, Allen, Garfield, and Morton, in rotunda of Capitol, Washington; statues of Gibbon and Moses, Congressional Library, Hahnemann at Scott Circle, Washington; Astor historical doors, Trinity Ch., New York; pediment to Appellate Court House, New York; statues of Hooker and Davenport, Conn. State House; statue to Drake, erected by Standard Oil Co., at Titusville, Pa.; two large groups, "Mineral Wealth," Buffalo Expn., 1901; statues of Lincoln, Farragut and McKinley, Muskegon, Mich.; Lincoln, Buffalo; Apotheosis of St. Louis for St. Louis Expn.; equestrian statue Gen. Forrest, Memphis, Tenn.; statue of McKinley and lunette for tomb at Canton, O.; Benjamin Harrison monument, Indianapolis; pediment, State Capitol, Frankfort, Ky.; Beardsley monument, Bridgeport, Conn.; two statues of Gov. Goebel, Frankfort, Ky.; John Paul Jones monument, Washington; monument Senator Chandler of Mich., Francis Scott Key, Baltimore, Md.; Hoboken Soldiers' and Sailors' Memorial; Newark Soldiers' and Sailors' Memorial; Soldiers' and Sailors' Memorial, Hackensack, N.J.; Gold Star memorial, Des Moines, Ia. Henry Clay and Ephraim McDowell, in Statuary Hall, Washington. A.N.A., 1902, N.A., 1906. Home: Grantwood, N.J. Died June 19, 1935.

NIEMAN, Lucius W., newspaperman; b. Bear Creek, Sauk County, Wis., Dec. 13, 1857; learned printer's trade; studied Carroll Coll.; m. Agnes Elisabeth Guenther Wahl, Nov. 28, 1900. Was reporter, city editor, and mng. editor Milwaukee Sentinel; establisher Milwaukee Journal, 1882, and later propr. and editor; this paper awarded the Pulitzer Medal, 1919, "for the most disinterested and meritorious service rendered by any American newspaper" in 1918. Home: Milwaukee, Wis. Died Oct. 1, 1935.

NIEMEYER, John Henry, artist; b. Bremen, Germany, June 25, 1839; s. Charles Henry and Margareta Dorettea (Otto) N.; came to U.S., 1843; studied at Paris under L. Jacquesson de la Chevreuse, Jean Léon Gerome, and at École des Beaux Arts; hon. A.M., Yale, 1874; m. Anna, d. Rev. Goyn Talmage, July 10, 1888. Painter of portraits and landscapes. Street prof. drawing, Yale Sch. of the Fine Arts, 1871-1908, emeritus, 1908. A.N.A., 1905. Address: New Haven, Conn. Died Dec. 7, 1932.

NIES, James Buchanan, clergyman; b. Newark, N.J., Nov. 22, 1856; s. Simon and Antoinette Fredrika (Landano) N.; B.A., Columbia, 1882, M.A., 1887, Ph.D., 1888; grad. Gen. Theol. Sem., 1885; m. Jeanie Dows Orr, Sept. 3, 1891. Deacon, 1885, priest, 1886, P.E. Ch.; asst. Holy Trinity Chapel, N.Y. City, 1885-86; rector St. John's Ch., Tuckahoe, N.Y., and St. John's, Upper New Rochelle, 1886-87, Christ Chapel, Brooklyn, 1887-93, Ch. of the Epiphany, Brooklyn, 1893-98, Christ Ch., Sharon, Conn., 1905-07; mainly engaged in Oriental travel and research, 1898—. Author: Ur Dynasty Tablets, 1920. Joint author: Historical Religions and Economic Texts and Antiquities in the Babylonian Collection of James B. Nies, 1919. Address: Brooklyn Heights, N.Y. Died June 19, 1922.

NIESZ, Homer E., electrical engr.; b. Canton, O., Jan. 22, 1868; s. John K. and Margaret (Billings) N.; Ph.B., Mt. Union Coll., Alliance, O., 1886; m. Ollie Mae Wasson, Aug. 5, 1901; m. 2d, Ruth Crawley Patterson, Dec. 25, 1928. With the Commonwealth Edison Co. and its predecessors, 1887—; successively asst. supt. construction, asst. to supt., asst. to v.p., mgr. Cosmopolitan Electric Co., later mgr. industrial relations; pres. Commonwealth Edison Bldg., Loan & Savings Assn. Mem. Nat. Safety Council (pres. 1927-28), Western Soc. Engrs. (pres. 1925-26). Republican. Home: Chicago, Ill. Died Aug. 7, 1931.

NIEUWLAND, Julius Arthur, clergyman, educator; b. Hansbeke, Belgium, Feb. 14, 1878; s. John Baptist and Philomena (Van Hoeck) N.; A.B., Notre Dame U., 1899, Sc.D., 1901; Ph.D., Catholic U., 1904. Ordained priest R.C. Church, 1903; member faculty U. of Notre Dame, 1904—; dean Coll. of Science, 1920-23, prof. organic chemistry, 1923—; curator Bot. Herbarium and E. L. Greene Herbarium; bot. librarian. Founder Nieuwland Herbarium, Am. Midland Naturalist. Morehead medalist, 1932; Am. Institute medalist, 1935; Wm. H. Nichols medalist, 1935. Fellow Ind. Acad. Science (v.p. 1929; pres. 50th jubilee year, 1934). Author: Some Reactions of Acetylene, 1904. Editor of a de luxe edition of Le Conte's unpublished plates, 1917. Contbr. on bot., acetylene, boron chemistry and intermediates for synthetic rubber. Died June 11, 1936.

NIEZER, Charles M., lawyer, and capital investments; b. Monroeville, Ind., Mar. 31, 1877; s. J. Bernard and Sarah T. (Evanson) N.; student Notre Dame U., 1895-98; A.B., Ind. U., 1899, LL.B., 1900; A.M., Columbia, 1901; m. Rose M. Fox, Oct. 18, 1906 (died 1927); children—Louis Fox, Rosemary Lau, Margaret Sarah. Admitted to Ind. bar, 1901, and began practice at Fort Wayne; pres. General Refunding Corporation, Tokheim Oil Tank & Pump Co.; chmn. bd. directors Hartford City Paper Company; director Home Telephone & Telegraph Co.; dir., Farnsworth Television & Radio Corporation. Member Allen County Council of Defense, World War, also chmn. Ft. Wayne Home Service Sect. Am. Red Cross, and dir. Ft. Wayne Liberty Loan and War Savings Stamps Campaigns. Trustee Ind. U., 1919-35; trustee Gilbault Sch. for Boys, Cathedral Fund; sec. treas. and trustee Our Sunday Visitor. Mem. Board of Governors and Bd. of Auditors, Cath. Ch. Extension Soc. of America. Mem. Ind. Bar Assn., Allen County Bar Assn. (pres. 1920), Am. Bankers Assn. (v.p.), Anti-Tuberculosis League (dir.), Ft. Wayne Chamber Commerce (pres.), S.A.R. Democrat. Home: Ft. Wayne, Ind. Died May 18, 1941.

NIGHTINGALE, Augustus Frederick, educator; b. Quincy, Mass., Nov. 11, 1843; s. Thomas J. and Alice (Brackett) N.; A.B., Wesleyan U., 1866, A.M., 1869; Ph.D., Upper Ia. U., 1891; LL.D., Simpson Coll., 1901; m. Fanny Orena, d. Rev. C. H. Chase, Aug. 24, 1866. Prof. Latin and Greek, Upper Ia. U., 1866-68; pres. Northwestern Female Coll., Evanston, Ill., 1868-71; prof. Latin and Greek, Simpson Coll., Ia., 1871-72; supt. pub. schs., Omaha, Neb., 1872-74; prin. Lake View High Sch., Ill., 1874-90; asst. supt. Chicago pub. schs., 1890-92; supt. Chicago high schs., 1892-1901; supt. of schs., Cook Co., Ill., 1902-10. Elected, 1898, trustee U. of Ill., pres. bd., 1902-03; pres. Neb. State Teachers' Assn., 1873, Neb. State Sabbath Sch. Assn., 1873, Ill. State Teachers' Assn., 1887, secondary dept. N.E.A., 1888; pres. North Central Assn. of Colls. and Secondary Schs., 1898; chmn. com. N.E.A. on coll. entrance requirements, 1895-99; mem. Ednl. Commn. of Ill., 1906-10. Author: Requirements for Admission to American Colleges. Editor: Twentieth Century Text Books (100 Vols.). Writer and lecturer on ednl. subjects. Home: Evanston, Ill. Died Dec. 4, 1925.

NIKANDER, John Kustaa, college pres.; b. Lammi, Finland, Sept. 3, 1855; s. John Kustaa and Hedvig Maria (Metsmaa) N.; ed. Lyceum, and Theol. Dept. of Univ., Helsingfors, Finland; D.D., Augustana Coll., 1906; m. Sanna Kristina Rajala, July 29, 1902. Ordained Finnish Evang. Luth. ministry, 1879; pastorates in Finland; came to U.S., 1884; pastor chs. at Hancock, Calumet and Allouez, Mich., 1885-97; pres. Suomi Coll. and Sem., Hancock, also prof. same and minister to various chs.; pres. Suomi Synod. Author: Bible History (in Finnish), 1906; Martti Luther, 1917. Editor of the official ch. calendar. Home: Hancock, Mich. Died Jan. 13, 1919.

NILAN, John Joseph, bishop; b. Newburyport, Mass., Aug. 1, 1855; ed. Nicolet (Can.) Coll. and St. Joseph's Sem., Troy, N.Y. Ordained priest R.C. Ch., 1878; served at Framingham and Abington, Mass., and St. James Ch., Boston, until 1892; pastor St. Joseph's Ch., Amesbury, Mass., 1892-1910; consecrated bishop of Hartford, Apr. 28, 1910. Address: Hartford. Conn. Died Apr. 13, 1934.

NILES, Alfred Salem, judge; b. St. Louis, Oct. 28, 1860; s. Rev. Henry Edward and Jeannie Eliza (Marsh) N.; A.B., Princeton, 1879, A.M., 1882; LL.B., U. of Md., 1881; m. Mary Hamilton Waters, Oct. 28, 1889; children—Mrs. Josephine McClellan, Emory Hamilton, Alfred Salem, Henry Edward. Admitted to bar, 1881; mem. firm Niles & Wolff, 1882-1906 and 1912-15, Niles, Wolff, Barton & Morrow, Jan. 1915—. Associate judge Supreme Bench of Baltimore, 1906-12, resigned. Democrat. Dean Baltimore Law Sch. from 1904 until its merger with U. of Md. Law Sch., Sept. 1913; lecturer constl. law, same, 1913—. Counsel for Hopkins Place Savings Bank, Baltimore Life Ins. Co., etc.; counsel to Liquor License Board, Baltimore, 1904-06; mem. Bd. Charities and Corrections, 1904-06; chmn. mayor's advisory com. for fire relief work, 1904; mem. State Board of Law Examiners, 1906; pres. City Club, of Baltimore, Jan. 1-May 1, 1912; mem. Bd. Police Commrs. of Baltimore, 1912-16. Trustee McDonough Sch. for Boys, 1909-15; regent U. of Md., 1913-20. Pres. Baltimore City Bar Assn., 1916-17. Mem. "New Charter" Bd. of Baltimore City, 1917-18. Home: Baltimore, Md. Died Nov. 2, 1926.

NILES, George McCallum, M.D.; b. Marshallville, Ga., Oct. 25, 1864; s. Lewis Oscar and Margaret Ophelia (Sperry) N.; Mercer U., Macon, Ga.; U. of Louisville, Ky.; M.D., Univ. and Bellevue Hosp. Med. Coll. (New York U.), 1886; m. Annie Holleman, Sept. 24, 1903. Began practice, Marshallville, 1886; removed to Atlanta, 1908; specialist in gastro-intestinal diseases; prof. gastro-enterology and clin. medicine, Atlanta Med. Coll. Democrat. Mason. Author: Pellagra, an American Problem, 1912; Diagnosis and Treatment of Digestive Diseases, 1914; also numerous articles in med. jours. Home: Atlanta, Ga. Died June 5, 1932.

NILES, Henry Clay, judge; b. Kosciusko, Miss., Oct. 21, 1850; s. Hon. Jason and Harriet N.; common sch. edn.; read law in his father's office; m. Mrs. V. C. Allen, 1885. Admitted to bar, 1872. Mem. Miss. Legislature, 1878 and 1886; del. Rep. Nat. Conv., 1880; U.S. Dist. atty., Northern Dist. Miss., 1890-91; U.S. dist. judge, Northern and Southern Dists. of Miss., 1892—. Republican. Address: Jackson, Miss. Died Sept. 26, 1918.

NILES, Kossuth, rear admiral U.S.N.; b. Belleville, Ill., June 14, 1849; s. Nathaniel and Maria Louisa (Thoma) N.; served in Civil War, 142 Ill. Vols., 1864; grad. U.S. Naval Acad., 1869; m. Elizabeth Challenor, Dec. 31, 1873. Promoted through the various grades and retired by statutory age limit, June 14, 1911, in the grade of rear admiral. Lighthouse insp., 8th dist., 1901-03; comdg. Bennington, Pacific sta., 1903-04, Boston, Pacific sta., 1904-05; gen. insp. ordnance, New York, 1905-08; comdg. Battleship Louisiana on cruise around the world, 1908-09; mem. Lighthouse Bd., 1909-10; mem. and pres. Naval Exam. and Retiring Bds., Washington, 1910-11. Mem. Mil. Order Loyal Legion, U.S. Naval Inst. Home: Winsted, Conn. Died Dec. 6, 1913.

NILES, Nathan Erie, rear admiral U.S.N.; b. Wellsboro, Pa., Dec. 27, 1847; s. Alanson E. and Angeline N.; apptd. from Pa. and grad. U.S. Naval Acad., 1868; m. Blanche Rousseau, Oct. 12, 1876. Promoted ensign, Apr. 19, 1869; master, July 12, 1870; lt., July 7, 1874; lt. comdr., Jan. 5, 1896; comdr., Mar. 25, 1899; capt., Sept. 13, 1904; rear admiral, Nov. 12, 1908. Served in Nipsic, N. Atlantic sta. and Darien surveying expdn., 1868-70; in Saranac, Resaca, and St. Marys, Pacific Fleet, 1870-73; Manhattan, and Ossipee, N. Atlantic sta., 1873-75; Marion, European sta., 1875-78; Navy Yard, Portsmouth, 1879-82; Iroquois, 1882-85; Hydrographic Office, 1885-88; Atlanta, 1888-91; Navy Yard, Norfolk, Va., 1891-95; Lancaster, 1895-97; Bureau of Equipment, 1898; comd. Piscataqua during Spanish-Am. War, 1898; Navy Yard, Norfolk, Va., 1898-1900; comd. Nashville, 1900-03; Naval Home, Phila., 1903-05; comd. Maine, 1905-07; comdg. receiving-ship Hancock, July 1907-Dec. 1908; gov. Naval Home, Phila., 1908-09; retired by operation of law, Dec. 27, 1909. Address: Washington, D.C. Died Nov. 28, 1930.

NILES, Nathaniel, lawyer; b. S. Kingston, R.I., Sept. 15, 1835; s. Rev. William Watson and Mary (Wilson) N.; ed. Phillips Andover Acad.; m. Anna Eliza Thompson, Oct. 27, 1859 (died 1905); m. 2d, Ella Capers Jones, Dec. 2, 1910. Admitted to bar, 1857. Speaker N.J. Assembly, 1872; govt. dir. U.P. R.R., 1879; pres. Tradesmen's Nat. Bank, New York, 1884-89. Visitor, U.S. Naval Acad. Author of several important laws passed in N.J. Legislature, among which is one that established 1,200 free sch. libraries in the state, and another giving all riparian lands of the state to the free sch. fund. Home: New York. Died June 29, 1917.

NILES, William Harmon, geologist; b. Northampton, Mass., May 18 1838; s. Rev. Asa and Mary A. (Marcy) N.; student in comparative anatomy with Prof. Louis Agassiz, 1862-66; S.B., Lawrence Scientific Sch. (Harvard), 1866; Ph.B., Sheffield Scientific Sch. (Yale), 1867; hon. A.M., Wesleyan U., 1870; LL.D., Temple U., Phila., 1903; m. Helen M. Plympton, 1869. Prof. geology and geography,

1871-1902, emeritus prof. geology, 1902, head dept. geology, 1878-1902, Mass. Inst. Tech.; stated lecturer, 1882-88, prof. and head dept. geology, 1888—, Wellesley Coll. Lecturer on Natural Science, Mass. State Teachers' Inst., 10 yrs.; gave pub. lectures upon geol. and geog. subjects, speaking from 50 to 100 times each session, 1867-90. Pres. Boston Soc. Natural History, 1892-97 (councillor, 1870); pres. Appalachian Mountain Club three terms; fellow Am. Acad. Arts and Sciences. Address: Boston, Mass. Died 1910.

NILES, William White, lawyer; b. Waterford, N.Y., July 22, 1860; s. William Watson and Isabel (White) N.; prep. edn., Seileck Sch., Norwalk, Conn., and Kimball Union Acad., Meriden, N.H.; A.B., Dartmouth, 1883, A.M., 1886; LL.B., Albany (N.Y.) Law Sch., 1886; m. Florence M. Brown, Jan. 23, 1912; children—Charlotte, Roma, William W. Admitted to N.Y. bar, 1886, and began practice at N.Y. City; mem. Niles & Johnson, 1891—; dir. Cohoes Co., Interborough Rapid Transit Co. Mem. N.Y. Assembly, 1895; counsel for sub-com. on borough govt., N.Y. City Charter Revision Commn., 1900 (drafted chapter on borough govt. giving local self-govt.); mem. Ivins N.Y. City Charter Commission (drafted chapters on edn., charities and correction), 1908-09; conceived Bronx River Parkway and drafted law creating Bronx River Parkway Commn., of which was v.p., 1907-25; mem. Taconic State Park Commn., 1927—, chmn., 1930—. Mem. bd. govs., and exec. com. New York Zoöl. Soc., 1905—, sec., 1926—. Pres. Bronx Soc. of Arts and Sciences; mem. Character Com. of New York Bar; mem. City Plan Com. of City of N.Y. Recipient of gold medal from N.Y. Soc. of Arts and Sciences for Bronx Parkway work. Mem. pres. Bronx Bd. of Trade; v.p. Tree Planting Assn., Citizens Union. Republican. Episcopalian. Home: Riverdale, N.Y. Died Jan. 12, 1935.

NILES, William Woodruff, bishop; b. Hatley, P.Q., Can., May 24, 1832; s. Daniel Swit and Delia (Woodruff) N.; A.B., Trinity Coll., 1857, A.M., 1860; grad. Berkley Div. Sch., 1861; S.T.D., Trinity, Conn., 1870, LL.D., 1896; D.D., Dartmouth, 1879; D.C.L., Bishop's Coll., Que., 1898; m. Bertha Olmsted, June 5, 1862. Deacon, 1861, priest, 1862, P.E. Ch.; rector Wiscasset, Me., 1861-64; prof. Latin lang. and lit., Trinity Coll., 1864-70; rector Warehouse Point, Conn., 1868-70; consecrated bishop of N.H., 1870. Joint editor the Churchman, 1867. Pres. corp. St. Paul's Sch., Concord, Holderness Sch. for Boys, Plymouth, N.H., St. Mary's Sch., Concord; pres. trustees P.E. Ch. in N.H.; trustee Trinity Coll., 1870—. Mem. commn. for revising prayer-book and revising marginal readings in Bible, and for revising the Lectionary of the Church. Address: Concord, N.H. Died Mar. 31, 1914.

NILSSON, Hjalmar; b. Nora, Sweden, Sept. 24, 1860; s. Anders and Marie (Anderson) N.; came to U.S., 1881, naturalized citizen, 1893; C.E., Sch. of Technology, Orebro, Sweden, 1878; m. Christine Neuman, 1882 (died 1923); children—Maria Christine (Mrs. Carl R. Chindblom), Verner Hjalmar; m. 2d, Brita Larson, Apr. 19, 1924. Learned coppersmith's trade in father's shop in Sweden; worked at the trade in Boston; journalist, 1895—, in Worcester, Mass., and St. Paul and Minneapolis, Minn.; dep. oil insp. Hennepin Co., by appt. of gov., 1909-19; chief oil insp. State of Minn., terms 1919-31. Mem. U.S. Oil Insprs.' Assn. (v.p.), Tech. Soc. of Orebro, Sweden (life), Am. Scandinavian Foundation, Swedish-Am. Hist. Soc., Vasa Order America (pres. Minn. dist. 1910); a founder United Scandinavian Singers America, 1886; dir. choruses, Boston, Worcester, St. Paul, Minneapolis, 1885-1931; pres. Am. Union Swedish Singers, 1910-14, 1920-24, hon. pres., 1924— (dir. in chief, 1914, dir. in chief N.W. dist. 1916-27); editor and pub. Musiktidning (official organ Am. Union Swedish Singers), 1913-24. Presented with Honor Emblem by Asso. Swedish Singers, Stockholm, 1918, "for success in promoting Swedish song in America"; Knight of Royal Swedish Order of Vasa, 1st class, by King Gustaf V, 1919; Knight of Royal Swedish Order of North Star, 1928. Democrat. Lutheran. Author: Svenskarne i Worcester, 1898; Ett triumftåg genom Svenska bygder, 1910; I Dur och Moll, 1935 (memoirs of 60 yrs. promoting Swedish music in U.S.); also many tech. bulletins. Home: St. Paul, Minn. Died Dec. 24, 1936.

NINDE, Edward Summerfield, clergyman; b. Cincinnati, O., Jan. 1, 1866; s. Bishop William Xavier and Sophronia E. (Falley) N.; B.A., Wesleyan U., Conn., 1887, M.A., 1890, D.D., 1905; B.D., Garrett Bibl. Inst., Evanston, Ill., 1889, D.D., 1903; traveled and studied in Europe, 1889-91. Ordained M.E. ministry, 1891; pastor Bay Port, Mich., 1891-92, Wyandotte, 1892-95, Birmingham, 1895-96, Detroit, 1896-1900, Ann Arbor, 1900-05; travel and study, 1905-07; pastor Mathewson St. Ch., Providence, R.I., 1907-17, 1st Ch., Germantown, Phila., 1917-22, West Chester, Pa., 1922-29. Chaplain of Pennsylvania State Senate, 1923-27. Author: The Story of the American Hymn; George Whitefield, Prophet-Preacher, 1924. Republican. Home: Philadelphia, Pa. Died Aug. 15, 1935.

NINDE, William Xavier, M.E. bishop, 1884—; b. Cortland, N.Y., June 21, 1832; grad. Wesleyan U., Conn., 1855, A.M., 1858; D.D., 1874; LL.D., Northwestern, 1892. Prof. practical theology Garrett Biblical Inst., Evanston, Ill., 1873-79, pres., 1879-84. Address: Detroit, Mich. Died 1901.

NIPHER, Francis Eugene, physicist; b. Port Byron, N.Y., Dec. 10, 1847; s. Peter and Roxalana P. (Tilden) N.; Ph.B., State U. of Ia., 1870, A.M., 1873; LL.D., Washington U., 1905; m. Matilda Aikins, July 1, 1873; children—Mary E. (Mrs. E. N. Birge), Edith C. (Mrs. H. M. Pollord), Elma F. (Mrs. J. C. Dawson), Clara Ellen, Edwin Tilden. Instr. in phys. lab., State U. of Ia., 1870-74; prof. physics, 1874-1914, and prof. emeritus, 1914—, Washington U., St. Louis. In 1889 showed that positive or reversed photographic pictures could be best produced by development in the light instead of in the dark-room; developed perfect pictures on the most sensitive plates with the developing bath fully exposed to direct sunlight. Made an extensive study of the nature of elec. discharge. Mem. and addressed Internat. Congress Arts and Sciences, St. Louis, 1904, also chmn. sect. cosmical physics. Research asso. Carnegie Instn., Washington. Author: Theory of Magnetic Measurements, 1886; Electricity and Magnetism, 1895; Introduction to Graphical Algebra, 1898; Experimental Studies in Electricity and Magnetism, 1914. Home: St. Louis, Mo. Died Oct. 6, 1927.

NISBET, James Douglas, M.D.; b. Waxhaw, S.C., July 30, 1861; s. John Newton and Mary Jane (Phifer) N.; A.B., Davidson Coll., N.C., 1881; studied Charleston Med. Coll., 1882; M.D., Louisville Med. Coll., 1886; m. Emma Beulah Hayes, Oct. 22, 1908. Practiced gen. med. in Lancaster County, S.C., 1886-89; post-grad. study New York Polyclinic, 1889-90; passed Bd. Regents, 1890; practiced as specialist diseases of the digestive system, New York, 1900-02; post-grad. study, U. of Paris, 1892, Tübingen, 1893, Berlin, 1894; resumed spl. practice, New York, 1895; past prof. diseases of digestive system, N.Y. Polyclinic; retired from practice, Sept. 1923. Fellow New York Acad. Medicine; mem. Soc. Med. Jurisprudence. Author: Diseases of the Stomach, 1898. Home: Van Wyck, S.C. Died July 27, 1933.

NISSEN, Ludwig, merchant; b. Schleswig-Holstein, Germany, Dec. 2, 1855; s. Hans Friedrich and Lucie (Dawartz) N.; ed. pub. schs.; m. Katharine Quick, Dec. 27, 1882. Came to U.S., 1872, naturalized citizen, 1879. Began as bootblack in N.Y. City; entered jewelry business, 1881; pres. Ludwig Nissen Co., importers pearls and precious stones; v.p. N.Y. & Hanseatic Corp.; dir. Dime Savings Bank of Brooklyn, New Maiden Lane Safe Deposit Co., Selkirk Gold Mining Co., N.Y. Bd. of Trade and Transportation. Organizer and pres. Am. Jewelers Protective Assn.; pres. Mfrs. Assn. of N.Y., Nat. Jewelers Bd. of Trade; chmn. Citizens Union, Brooklyn League; commr. for State of N.Y. to Paris Expn., 1900; dir. Nat. Assn. Mfrs. many yrs. Republican. Lutheran. Mason. Home: Brooklyn, N.Y. Died Oct. 26, 1924.

NIVEN, William, mineralogist; b. Bellshill, Lanarkshire, Scotland, Oct. 6, 1850; s. William and Sarah (Brown) N.; ed. common schs.; came to U.S. 1879; m. Nellie Blanch Purcell, Jan. 26, 1886 (dec.); children—William Albert, David Sumner (dec.), Norman Sumner, Kingsley Burns, Harold Andrew, Mrs. Elna Blanche Harrison, Francis Joseph, Malcolm, Robert Nelson. Engaged in mineral investigations. Discovered 3 new minerals, yttrialite, thorogummite and nivenite, in Llano Co., Tex., 1889, and the new mineral aguilarite, at Guanajuato, Mex., 1891; discovered remains of prehistoric city or nation, hundreds of square miles in extent, in State of Guerrero, Mex., 1891; also discovered buried prehistoric cities beneath the Valley of Mexico, 1911. Was asst. commr. of Arizona to New Orleans Expn. Hon. life mem. Am. Mus. Natural History; titled mem. Scientific Society Antonio Alzate, Mexico; fellow Am. Geog. Soc. (New York), Royal Soc. of Arts (London). Address: Houston, Tex. Died June 2, 1937.

NIXON, Brevard, lawyer; b. Catawba Springs, Lincoln County, N.C., Oct. 8, 1866; s. James and Mary (Proctor) N.; ed. Catawba Coll., Newton, N.C., Rock Springs Sem., Denver, N.C., U. of N.C.; m. Fanny Shell, Jan. 1902; 1 dau., Cornelia. Clk., store of Proctor Bros., 1884; teacher, Pine Grove and Broadway Sch., 1884, River Bend Acad. and Hoyles Bridge Acad., 1886, Lowesville Acad., 1887-89, high sch., Stanley Creek and Mount Holby, 1894, Pine Grove Acad., 1895; editor and mgr. Mount Holby News, 1894; admitted to N.C. bar, 1895, and began practice at Charlotte; mem. firm McCall & Nixon, 1895-1905; alone, 1905—. Prin. clk. of N.C. Ho. of Rep., 1899-1901. House sec. Y.M.C.A., Camp Greene, World War. Democrat. Democratic leader in N.C. Author: Country Couplets; also hist. and polit. articles. Home: Charlotte, N.C. Died Aug. 14, 1937.

NIXON, George Stuart, senator; b. Newcastle, Calif., Apr. 2, 1860; s. John H. and Mary Ann (Estill) N.; ed. pub. sch., Newcastle, Calif., and Oakland (Calif.) Business Coll.; m. Kate Imogene Bacon, Jan. 30, 1887. Was telegraph operator at Newcastle, Calif., Brown's, Nev., Candalaria, Nev.; clerk First Nat. Bank, Reno, Nev.; then organized and became cashier and later pres. First Nat. Bank of Winnemucca, Nev.; also pres. Nixon Nat. Bank, Reno, and Tonopah (Nev.) Banking Corp. Leader in the development of irrigation enterprises in Nev. Was state chmn. Silver Party in Nev.; mem. Nev. Legislature, 1890; U.S. senator from Nev., terms 1905-11, 1911-17. Republican. Address: Reno, Nev. Died June 5, 1912.

NIXON, Lewis, shipbuilder; b. Leesburg, Va., Apr. 7, 1861; s. Joel Lewis and Mary Jane (Turner) N.; early edn. Leesburg; grad. U.S. Naval Acad., 1882, at head of class, and sent to Royal Naval Coll., Greenwich, Eng., by Navy Department; m. Sally Lewis Wood, Jan. 29, 1891 (died 1937); 1 son, Stanhope Wood; m. 2d, Mary Doran Martin, June 28, 1938. Transferred to construction corps of navy, 1884; in 1890 designed battleships Oregon, Indiana and Massachusetts, and then resigned from Navy to become superintending constructor of Cramp Shipyard, Phila.; resigned, 1895, and started Crescent Shipyard, Elizabeth, N.J., on own account, where he built 100 vessels in 6 yrs., among others the submarine torpedo-boat Holland and seven other submarines, the monitor Florida, torpedo-boat O'Brien and cruiser Chattanooga; organized Standard Motor Constrn. Co.; propr. Lewis Nixon's Shipyard; started, 1895, and president until 1904, International Smokeless Powder Company; pres. Nixon Nitration Works, Raritan River Sand Co. Apptd. by Mayor Van Wyck, pres. East River Bridge Commn., 1898; trustee and pres. Webb Inst. of Naval Architecture. Democrat; succeeded Richard Croker as leader of Tammany Hall, Nov. 1901-May 1902; chmn. finance com. Dem. Congressional Campaign Com., 1902. Mem. N.Y. State Commn. to St. Louis Expn. Commr. pub. wks. Borough of Richmond, 1914-15; supt. pub. works of State of N.Y., 1919; pub. service commr. State of N.Y., 1919-20. Mem. bd. of visitors to U.S. Naval Acad., 1902, by appmt. of President Roosevelt. Received in spl. audiences by the King of England, Popes Pius X and XI, Emperor Nicholas of Russia, King of Belgians, Premier Mussolini and presidents of Argentine, Chile, Colombia, Panama, Costa Rica and Guatemala. Del. Dem. Nat. convs., 1900, 04, 08, 12, 20, 24, 32; chmn. Dem. State Conv., Buffalo, 1906; apptd. by President Taft, del. 4th Pan-Am. Conf., Buenos Aires, 1910, and E.E. and M.P. on special mission to represent U.S. at Chilean Centenary, 1910. Home: New York, N.Y. Died Sept. 23, 1940.

NIXON, Oliver Woodson, literary editor The Inter Ocean; b. Guilford County, N.C., Oct. 25, 1825; s. Samuel N. His father was first man in State to free his slaves, removing to Ind., 1830. B.S., Farmers' Coll., O., 1848; Jefferson Med. Coll., Phila., 1854; LL.D., Whitman Coll., Wash., 1897; m. Louise Elstun, Batavia, O., 1855. Went to Calif., overland, 1850; raised 39th O. vols., 1861; was med. dir. Army of Mo.; on Gen. Pope's staff; served 2 terms treas. Hamilton Co., O., at Cincinnati. Established Evening Chronicle, Cincinnati, 1870, and with brother, William Penn N., consolidated it with Cincinnati Times; joined him, 1878, in purchase of The Inter Ocean, later disposing of it. Author: How Marcus Whitman Saved Oregon for the Union, 1895; Memories of a Forty-Niner, 1903. Residence: Chicago, Ill. Died 1905.

NIXON, William C., railway official; b. Earlville, Ill., Feb. 15, 1858; s. William and Sarah C. (Musselman) N.; pub. sch. edn. Began ry. service with A.,T.&S.F. Ry., 1879; supt. terminals, Chicago, to 1896, gen. agt. freight dept., 1896-97, supt. Chicago div., 1897-1900, A.,T.&S.F. Ry.; gen. supt., 1900-02, gen. mgr., 1902-04, 2d v.p. and gen. mgr., 1904-06, Gulf, Colo. & Santa Fé Ry.; v.p. and gen. mgr. S.L.&S.F. R.R. Co. (Frisco Lines), 1906-11, v.p., 1911, receiver, 1913—. Address: St. Louis, Mo. Died Dec. 15, 1916.

NIXON, William Penn, journalist; b. Fountain City, Wayne County, Ind., Mar. 19, 1833; s. Samuel and Rhoda (Hubbard) Butler N.; A.B., Farmers' Coll., O., 1854; LL.B., U. of Pa., 1859; m. Mary Stites, Sept. 1861 (died 1862); m. 2d, Elizabeth, d. Charles Duffield, June 15, 1869. Practiced law Cincinnati until 1868; mem. Ohio Legislature, 1865-68; business mgr. Cincinnati Chronicle, 1868-72; 1872—, connected with the Chicago Inter Ocean as business mgr., publisher, gen. mgr. and editor. Apptd. Lincoln Park commr., 1896, pres., 1897; del.-at-large Rep. Nat. Conv., 1896; apptd. collector of port of Chicago, 1897, reapptd. 1901. Home: Chicago, Ill. Died 1912.

NOBLE, Alfred, civil engr.; b. Livonia, Mich., Aug. 7, 1844; s. Charles and Lovina D. N.; served in Army of the Potomac, 3 yrs.; C.E., U. of Mich., 1870, LL.D., 1895, U. of Wis., 1904; m. Georgia Speechly, May 31, 1871. In charge improvements of St. Mary's Falls Canal and St. Mary's River, 1870-82; gen. asst. engr. N.P. R.R., 1883-86; supervised constrn. of various important ry. and other bridges across the Miss. River and elsewhere, 1886-1904; mem. Nicaragua Canal Bd., 1895, U.S. Bd. Engrs. on Deep Waterways, 1897-1900, Isthmian Canal Commn., 1899-1903; mem. bd. consulting engrs. Panama Canal,

1905; chief engr. East River div., P.,N.Y.&L.I. R.R. Co., 1902-09. Awarded John Fritz medal, for "notable achievements as a civil engr.," 1910; Elliott Cresson medal, Franklin Inst. for "distinguished achievement in field of civ. engring.," 1912. Home: New York, N.Y. Died Apr. 19, 1914.

NOBLE, Annette Lucile, author; b. Albion, Orleans County, N.Y., July 12, 1844; d. Dr. William and Emelia (Stiles) N.; grad. Phipps Union Sem., 1863; unmarried. Wrote constantly, 1870—. Traveled extensively in Europe, Egypt, Palestine, Syria, etc. Author: Uncle Jack's Executors; Eunice Lathrop, Spinster; Love and Shawl-Straps; After the Failure; The Silent Man's Legacy; The Crazy Angel, 1901. Address: Albion, Orleans County, N.Y. Died Nov. 27, 1932.

NOBLE, Charles Franklin, oil producer; b. Ill., Dec. 1, 1872; s. Scott Orange and Rhoda Kinder (Jones) N.; student Park Coll., Parkville, Mo., 1889-91; m. Alta Duncan, 1896. Mercantile and mining business, 1891-1902; partner John M. Cooper & Co., Baxter Springs, Kan., 1898-1902; oil producer and refiner, 1903—; a pioneer in mid-continent field, Kan. and Okla.; pres. Creek Oil Corp., San Juan Oil Syndicate. Republican. Christian Scientist. Mason, Elk. Home: Tulsa, Okla. Died Dec. 22, 1931.

NOBLE, Charles Henry, brigadier gen. U.S.A.; b. Dayton, O., May 10, 1843; s. Daniel Winthrop and Harriet Maria (Blood) N.; ed. at Indianapolis; m. Mary E. Palmer, Aug. 21, 1890. Served pvt. and corporal, Co. K, 1st Ind. Cav., June 20, 1861-June 19, 1864; capt., Aug. 1864-Feb. 1866; 2d lt. 16th U.S. Inf., Feb. 23, 1866; transferred to 34th Inf., Sept. 21, 1866; 1st lt., Feb. 10, 1867; transferred to 16th Inf., Apr. 14, 1869; capt., Nov. 26, 1884; maj. 25th Inf., Oct. 4, 1898; lt. col. 16th Inf., Feb. 2, 1901; col. 10th Inf., June 9, 1902; brig. gen. U.S.A. and retired, Oct. 20, 1906. In Civil War served in W.Va. under Gens. Reynolds and Milroy; escort to Gens. Fremont, Sigel and Howard in Va. campaigns; taken prisoner at 2d Bull Run; after exchange joined Army of Potomac, and attached to hdqrs. Army and engaged in Richmond campaign; after appmt. in regular service was with regt. in South and at frontier and other posts; in Spanish-Am. War, 1898, comd. battalion, 16th Inf., in Cuba, and regt. at battle of San Juan Hill; maj. 25th Inf., lt. col. 16th Inf., and col. 10th Inf., in P.I. Home: Indianapolis, Ind. Died Mar. 4, 1916.

NOBLE, Charles P., M.D.; b. Federalsburg, Md., Nov. 15, 1863; s. William D. and Mary A. (Houston) N.; studied at Ia. Agrl. Coll., 1880-82; M.D., U. of Md., 1884, Sc.D., 1907; m. Mira Rose, Sept. 15, 1885; m. 2d, Elizabeth M. Scanlan, Oct. 7, 1915. Began practice at Phila., 1884; connected with Phila. Lying-in Charity, 1884-89; surgeon-in-chief Kensington Hosp. for Women, 1889-1910; gynecologist, Stetson Hosp., 1889-1908; consulting surgeon, Phila. Lying-in Charity, Woman's Hospital, Chester County Hosp., later resumed private practice. Specialist in diseases of women and abdominal surgery, also medical consultant. Co-editor with Howard A. Kelly, and one of the authors of the Kelly-Noble Gynecology and Abdominal Surgery. Address: Radnor, Pa. Died Nov. 21, 1935.

NOBLE, Edmund, author, journalist; b. Glasgow, Scotland, Jan. 8, 1853, of English parents; s. John and Eliza (Nevatt) N.; ed. in Lancashire, Eng. Began newspaper work on St. Helen's Newspaper and Advertiser; reporter and editor of St. Helen's Standard, 1872-73; reporter, 1873-80, editorial writer, 1880-82, Liverpool Courier; editor and propr. Liverpool City News, 1882; in Russia as correspondent London Daily News, London Daily Globe, Manchester Guardian, Glasgow Herald, 1882-84; foreign editorial writer, New York Herald, 1887; editor Am. edit. on Free Russia, 1892-94; sec. Soc. Am. Friends of Russian Freedom, 1892-1904; on the staff of the Boston Herald for 46 yrs. Engaged in philos. studies and formulation of an interpretation of nature. Author: The Russian Revolt, 1885; Russia and the Russians, 1900; Before the Dawn (part author), 1901; The White Cross, a Story of the World's Last War, Boston Herald, 1900; Purposive Evolution—The Link Between Science and Religion, 1926; Our Slumbering World—a Plea for the Awakened Mind, 1928. Home: Malden, Mass. Died Jan. 8, 1937.

NOBLE, Frederick Alphonso, clergyman; b. Baldwin, Me., Mar. 17, 1832; s. James and Jane (Cram) N.; A.B., Yale, 1858; Andover Theol. Sem., 1858-60; Lane Theol. Sem., 1861; D.D., Western Reserve Coll., 1872; LL.D., Oberlin, 1899; m. Lucy A. Perry, Sept. 15, 1861 (died 1895); m. 2d, Leila M. Crandon, July 1, 1897. Ordained to the ministry, 1862; pastor House of Hope Ch., St. Paul, 1861-67, Third Ch., Pittsburgh, 1868-75, Center Ch., New Haven, 1875-79, Union Park Ch., Chicago, 1879-1901. Moderator Nat. Council Congl. Chs., 1898; pres. Am. Missionary Assn., 1898-1900; 1st pres. New West Edn. Commn., 1879-98; edited The Advance, 1886-88. Del. Missionary Conf., London, 1888, Internat. Conf. Congl. Chs., London, 1891, 2d Council, Boston, 1899. Author: Divine Life in Man, 1896; Discourses on Philippians, 1897; Our Redemption, 1898; Typical New Testament Conversions, 1901; The Pilgrims, 1907; Spiritual Culture, 1914. Address: Evanston, Ill. Died Dec. 31, 1917.

NOBLE, G. Kingsley, curator, explorer; b. Yonkers, N.Y., Sept. 20, 1894; s. G. Clifford and Elizabeth (Adams) N.; high sch., Yonkers, 1913; A.B., Harvard, 1917, A.M., 1918; Ph.D., Columbia, 1922; m. Ruth Crosby, Aug. 13, 1921; children—G. Kingsley, Alan Crosby. Leader of Harvard expdn. to Guadeloupe, 1914, to Newfoundland, 1915; zoölogist Harvard expdn. to Peru, 1916; leader Am. Mus. expdn. to Santo Domingo, 1922; lecturer on vertebrate palæontology, Columbia; curator of herpetology, Am. Mus. Natural History, 1919—, also curator exptl. biology, 1928—. Visiting prof. zoölogy, U. of Chicago, 1931; visiting prof. in biology, New York U., 1939. Member Advisory Bd. New York Aquarium. Ensign U.S.N.R.F. Republican. Unitarian. Author: The Biology of the Amphibia, 1931. Asso. editor Jour. of Morphology. Home: Englewood, N.J. Died Dec. 9, 1940.

NOBLE, Henry Smith, physician; b. Hinesburgh, Vt., Oct. 8, 1845; s. A. Smith and Susan (Patrick) N.; A.B., Tufts Coll., 1869; LL.D., 1905; M.D., Coll. Phys. and Surg. (Columbia), 1871; m. Edna J. Chaffee, Mar. 14, 1871. House phys. Hartford City Hosp., 1871-72; practiced at Chester, Vt., 7½ yrs.; asst. phys. Hartford (Conn.) Retreat for 1 yr.; asst. phys. Conn. Hosp. for the Insane, 1 yr., and Mich. Asylum for the Insane, Kalamazoo, Mich., 2 yrs.; asst. phys., 1884-97, asst. supt., 1897-1901, supt., 1901, Conn. Hosp. for the Insane. Republican. Universalist. Address: Middletown, Conn. Mar. 16, 1915.

NOBLE, John, artist; b. Wichita, Kan., Mar. 15, 1874; s. John and Elizabeth (Turner) N.; ed. Cincinnati Acad. Fine Arts; pupil of Jean Paul Laurens, Acad. Julian and Acad. Beaux Arts, Paris; also studied in Brussels and in Eng.; m. Amelia Peiche, 1909; children—John, Towanda. Winner $1,000 prize, Salmagundi Club, 1922; William A. Clark prize, Corcoran Gallery of Art, Washington, D.C., 1923; Carnegie prize, Nat. Acad. Design, 1928; Wadsworth Athenæum prize of Hartford, Conn.; also hon. mention. Painted portrait of Gov. Ferguson for State Capitol of Okla.; represented in Delgado Mus., New Orleans; Nat. Gallery, Washington, D.C.; R.I. Sch. of Design; John Gellatly Collection, Smithsonian Inst.; Corcoran Gallery permanent collection; Brooklyn Mus.; Singer Mus., Hagerstown, Md.; also in pub. collections, Dallas (Tex.), Wichita (Kan.), Salmagundi Club, and many others. A.N.A., 1924, N.A., 1927. Episcopalian. Home: New York, N.Y. Died 1934.

NOBLE, John Willock, Sec. of the Interior; b. Lancaster, O., Oct. 26, 1831; s. Col. John and Catherine (McDill) N.; A.B., Yale, 1851; LL.B., Cincinnati Law Sch., 1852; LL.D., Miami U., 1890, Yale, 1892; m. Lizabeth Halsted, Feb. 8, 1864 (died 1894). Admitted to bar, Columbus, O., 1853, St. Louis, 1855, Keokuk, Ia., 1856; city atty., Keokuk, 1859-60; enlisted in Union Army, serving through war in 3d Ia. Cav. as lt., adj., maj., lt. col. and col.; bvtd. brig. gen. by act of Congress for service in the field, Mar. 13, 1865. After war returned to St. Louis and engaged in practice there; U.S. dist. atty., 1867-70, prosecuting whisky and tobacco frauds of that period; was offered portfolio of solicitor-gen. by Gen. Grant, but declined. Sec. of the Interior, in cabinet of President Harrison, 1889-93. Republican. Mem. G.A.R., Mo. Commandery Loyal Legion, Sons of Veterans. Home: St. Louis, Mo. Died Mar. 22, 1912.

NOBLE, Robert Houston, army officer; b. Federalsburg, Md., Nov. 3, 1861; s. Dr. William D. and Mary A. (Houston) N.; grad. U.S. Mil. Acad., 1884; LL.B., U. of Md., 1892; A.M., St. John's Coll., Md., 1894; admitted to bar, Md., 1892, Calif., 1910; graduate of The Army War College, 1912; m. Mrs. Ethel E. Sherwood, May 14, 1921. Commd. 2d lt. 1st Inf., June 15, 1884; 1st lt. 15th Inf., June 15, 1891; trans. to 1st Inf., July 20, 1891; maj. a.-a.-g. vols., June 20, 1898; hon. discharged vols., Mar. 19, 1899; maj. a.-a.-g. vols., Sept. 5, 1899; hon. discharged vols., June 30, 1901; capt. inf., U.S.A., Oct. 12, 1898; assigned to 3d Inf., Jan. 1, 1899; maj. 9th Inf., Oct. 4, 1907; trans. to 1st Inf., Nov. 11, 1907, to 12th Inf., May 8, 1911; lt. col. inf., Feb. 1, 1913; assigned to 22d Infantry, July 22, 1914; colonel, July 1, 1916; brigadier general N.A., April 16-Nov. 12, 1918. Participated in Geronimo campaign, 1885-86; a.-d.-c. to Gen. Shafter, 1897-99; Santiago campaign; Philippine Insurrection; adj. gen. to Gens. Grant, Hughes, Snyder and Baldwin, and adj. gen. Dept. Visayas, 1900-02; a.-d.-c. to Govs. Gen. Taft, Wright, Ide and Smith, P.I., 1902-08; in charge militia affairs, Western Dept., 1913-14; comdg. 22d Inf., Mexican border, Sept. 1914-Sept. 1916; punitive expdn. in Mex., Nov. 1916-Feb. 1917; at El Paso, Tex., and Chickamauga Park, Ga., to Apr. 6, 1918, and in 5th Div. A.E.F., France, to May 2, 1918; attached to 30th and 77th divs. A.E.F. to Aug. 11, 1918; comd. 158th Brig. and attached to 79th Div., Aug. 14-Oct. 11, 1918; returned to U.S., Mar. 24, 1919; in charge nat. guard affairs, Western Dept., Apr. 21, 1919—. Recommended for bvt. lt. col., Spanish-Am. War. Address: Washington, D.C. Died Oct. 26, 1939.

NOBLE, William Brown, clergyman; b. Bedford, Pa., Apr. 13, 1841; s. Joseph Brown and Charlotte (Davis) N.; A.B., Jefferson (now Washington and Jefferson) Coll., 1863; grad. Duff's Mercantile Coll., 1863, Western Theol. Seminary, 1866; D.D., Parsons Coll., Iowa, 1881; LL.D., Occidental Coll., Calif., 1910; m. Margaret F. Murphy. Ordained Presbyn. ministry, 1866; home missionary Glenwood, Ia., 1866; pastor Ft. Madison, Ia., 1867-71, Mattoon, Ill., 1871-72, Faggs Manor, Pa., 1872-81, Norristown, Pa., 1881-86, San Diego, Calif., 1886-92, San Rafael, Calif., 1892-98, Redlands, Calif., 1898-1901; synodical supt., Synod of Calif., 1901-12; permanent clerk Gen. Assembly of Presbyn. Ch. in U.S.A., 1900—. Home: Coronado, Calif. Died Aug. 5, 1915.

NOBLE, W(illiam) Clark, sculptor, painter; b. Gardiner, Me., Feb. 10, 1858; s. Clark and Emma (Freeman) N.; ed. pub. and pvt. schs.; apprenticeship in sculpture, Boston, later studied under Grenough, Hunt, and Peter Toft, painter, of London; m. 2d, Emilie Bleecker, 1912; 1 son, William Clark (by 1st marriage). Prin. works: Bust of John McCullough, Phila. Actors' Soc., 1887; Soldiers' and Sailors' monument, Newport, R.I., 1890; statue of Robert Burns, Providence, R.I.; design and working model of the Mothers' Memorial, Washington, D.C.; William E. Channing statue, Newport, Rhode Island; statue of Governor Curtin, Bellefont, Pa.; statue of Msgr. Doane, Newark, N.J.; Brooks Memorial, in Ch. of the Incarnation, New York; statue of Gen. Porter, Van Courtland Park, N.Y. City; large model, for bronze and marble, of Maj. Pierre Charles L'Enfant, for Washington, D.C., and N.Y. City; designed models for gold and silver money, Guatamala, 1925, Panama, 1930, 31, 35, also for National John Philip Sousa Memorial; painting (heroic size) Crucifixion of Christ. Mem. Com. on Parks, Highways and River and Harbor, Arts Com., Police and Fire Com., Washington. Home: Washington, D.C. Died May 10, 1938.

NOBLE, William Lincoln, M.D.; b. Russell, St. Lawrence County, N.Y., Dec. 23, 1860; s. William and Phoebe (Grant) N.; M.S., St. Lawrence U., Canton, N.Y., 1885; M.D., Rush Med. Coll., Chicago, 1888; m. Marion Holden, Nov. 1, 1899; children—William Holden, Henry Holden, Jane Holden. Practiced at Chicago, 1888—; supt. Cook Co. Insane Asylum, 1890; county phys. Cook Co., 1891-92; member staff Illinois Charitable Eye and Ear Infirmary, 1893-1905, surgeon and chief of eye dept., 1896-1905; prof. ophthalmology, Ill. Post-Grad. Med. Sch.; clin. opthalmologist, dir. and sec. West Side Hosp.; chief of staff, Ill. Charitable Eye & Ear Infirmary. Pres. bd. trustees U. of Ill., 1923-25; mem. Ill. State Med. Soc. (pres., 1916-17). Republican. Conglist. Home: Evanston, Ill. Died Oct. 14, 1937.

NOBLES, Milton, actor, playwright; b. at Almont, Lapeer County, Mich., Sept. 28, 1847; ed. Madison, Wis.; m. Dolly Woolwine, June 29, 1881. Made first stage appearance in the West, 1867; played in support of Joseph Jefferson, Edwin Forrest, Edwin Booth, Lawrence Barrett and others until he began starring in plays written by himself in 1875. Author: Under Martial Law; A Man of the People; Love and Law; The Whirlwind's Harvest, The Phœnix; Interviews; A Son of Thespis; For Revenue Only; Love Goes on Forever; The Unwritten Law; From Sire to Son; Bilgeville Junction; A Blue Grass Widow; Why Walker Reformed; Belinda Bailey's Borders; The Days of '49. Address: Brooklyn, N.Y. Died June 14, 1924.

NOÉ, Adolf Carl, paleobotanist; b. Gratz, Austria, Oct. 28, 1873; s. Adolf Gustav and Marie (Krauss) von Noé; student U. of Gratz, 1894-97, U. of Göttingen, 1897-99; A.B., U. of Chicago, 1900, Ph.D., 1905; hon. mem. University of Innsbruck, 1922; hon. Ph.D., Gratz, 1923; Golden Medal from University of Vienna, 1923; m. Mary Evelyn Cullaton, July 3, 1901; children—Mary Helen, Valerie. Demonstrator in paleobotany, U. of Gratz, 1895-97; came to U.S., 1899, naturalized citizen, 1904; instr. science and modern langs., Burlington Inst., 1901-02; instr. German, Stanford, 1901-03; instr., asst. prof. German lit., U. of Chicago, 1903-23; asst. prof. paleobotany, same, 1923-24, asso. prof., 1924—. Geologist Ill. State Geol. Survey, 1921—, Ia. Geol. Survey, 1923-25, Ky. Geol. Survey, 1922; mem. Allen & Garcia Coal Commn. to Soviet Russia, 1927. Treas. Am. Com. for Vienna Relief, 1921. Author: Fossil Flora of Northern Illinois, 1926; Golden Days of Soviet Russia, 1931; Ferns, Fossils and Fuels, 1931. Home: Chicago, Ill. Died Apr. 10, 1939.

NOEL, Edmund Favor, governor; b. nr. Lexington, Miss., Mar. 4, 1856; s. Leland and Margaret A. (Sanders) N.; ed. Louisville (Ky.) High Sch., 3 yrs.; read law under uncle, Maj. D. W. Sanders, Louisville, 1875-76; m. Loula Hoskins, June 4, 1890 (died 1891); m. 2d, Mrs. Alice Tye Neilson, Sept. 12, 1905. Admitted to bar, 1877, in practice at Lexington, 1877—; mem. law firm Noel & Neilson. Mem. Miss. Ho. of Rep., 1881-82; dist. atty., 1887-91; mem. Senate, 1895-1903 and 1920-28; capt. Co. K, 2d Miss. Inf., Spanish-Am. War; gov. of Miss.,

1908-12. Democrat. First chmn. of 1st Conf. of Govs. held in U.S., at Washington, May 1908. Bapt. Mason. Home: Lexington, Miss. Died July 30, 1927.

NOEL, Joseph Roberts, corp. official; b. Waco, Tex., Mar. 3, 1872; s. Theophilus and Harriet Sarah (Harris) N.; grad. high sch., Chicago, 1891; Rush Med. Coll. 2 yrs.; M.D., Jefferson Med. Coll., Phila., 1894; m. Alice Mabel Warner, July 3, 1895; children—Harriett Warner (Mrs. Lyman T. Burgess), Virginia Warner (Mrs. Elmer E. Long), Theophilus, II. Practiced at Chicago, 1895-97; mgr. for father, Theo. Noel, proprietary medicines, 1897-1901; gen. organizer Nat. Assn. Retail Druggists, 1901-05; founded North West Savings Bank, 1905, which later became Noel State Bank, chmn. bd. until suspension, 1931; pres. Theo. Noel Co., mfrs. proprietary medicines. Chmn. citizens com. in charge allocation of Cook Co. Jail and Criminal Court Bldg. Pres. Chicago Assn. Commerce, 1921. Republican. Conglist. Home: Oak Park, Ill. Died Mar. 10, 1940.

NOGUCHI, Hideyo, medical research; b. Inawashiro, Yama, Fukushima, Japan, Nov. 24, 1876; s. Sayoske Kobiyama and Shika N.; pub. schs., Japan, and spl. instrn. under pvt. tutors in German, French and English, and in Chinese lit.; M.D., Tokyo Med. Coll., 1897; U. of Pa., 1901-03; Statens Serum Institut, Copenhagen, 1903-04; hon. M.Sc., U. of Pa., 1906; titular professorship, Imperial Govt. of Japan, 1911; Ph.D., Japanese Govt., 1914; hon. M.D., Sch. of Med. and Pharm. of Yucatan; D.Sc., Brown, 1921, Yale, 1921; M.D., honoris causa, U. of Paris, 1925. Asst. Gen. Hosp., Tokyo, 1897-98; asst. Govt. Inst. for Infectious Diseases, 1898-1900; quarantine officer, Yokohama Harbor Sta., 1899; phys. in charge of Central Hosp. under Internat. Sanitary Bd. of New Chwang, China, 1899-1900; lecturer on pathol. anatomy, Tokyo Dental Coll., 1898-99; asst. in pathology, U. of Pa., 1901-03; research asst., Carnegie Instn., 1903-04; asst., asso., asso. mem., 1903-14, mem., 1914—, Rockefeller Inst. for Med. Research. Contributions: Pure cultivation of syphilitic organism (Treponema pallidum); demonstration of presence of Treponema pallidum in the brain of general paresis and in the spinal cord of locomotor ataxia (connection between syphilis and general paresis and tabes dorsalis); cultivation of causative micro-organisms of infantile paralysis and rabies (hydrophobia); introduction of skin test for syphilis (luetin reaction); introduction of a method for obtaining a bacteria-free vaccine for smallpox; isolation and cultivation of the micro-organisms causing yellow fever (Leptospira icteroides), and development of preventive vaccine and curative serum for yellow fever, 1918-21. Awarded Order of Merit by Emperor of Japan, 1915; John Scott Medal, City of Phila., 1921; etc. Author: Snake Venoms, 1909; Serum Diagnosis of Syphilis and Luetin Reaction, 1910; Laboratory Diagnosis of Syphilis, 1923. Home: New York, N.Y. Died May 21, 1928.

NOLAN, John I., congressman; b. San Francisco, Jan. 14, 1874; s. James and Sarah N.; pub. sch. edn.; m. Mae E. Hunt, Mar. 23, 1913. Iron moulder by trade; officer Internat. Moulders' Union of N. America, 1906—. Mem. Bd. of Supervisors, city and county of San Francisco, 1911; sec. San Francisco Labor Council, 1912; mem. 63d to 67th Congresses (1913-23), 5th District Calif. Republican. Home: San Francisco, Calif. Died Nov. 18, 1922.

NOLAN, Preston M(eredith), financial counsel; b. Uhrichsville, O., Jan. 14, 1875; s. James J. and Amanda (Creal) N.; ed. pub. schs.; studied manual training, also studied under univ. extension and pvt. tutor; m. Grace Gordon, June 5, 1897. Began in mech. dept. Wabash R.R.; auditor Ind. banks, 1901-02; chief appraiser, Peabody, Houghteling & Co., bankers, Chicago, 1903-07; operated independently as Preston M. Nolan & Co., appraisers for banks and life ins. cos., 1907—; first in America to use Bank of England system of real property valuation. Mem. Nat. Assn. Real Estate Bds. (dir. 1908). Republican. Mason. Author: Nolanisms, 1917; Scientific Appraisal of Real Property, 1919; Pertinent and Impertinent, 1923; Appraising for Banks, 1924; The Great Tomorrow, 1924; Collected Verse, 1928; Business First, 1928; From Chaos to Safety, 1929. Home: Chicago, Ill. Died Jan. 9, 1931.

NOLAN, Thomas, prof. architectural constrn.; b. Williamsport, Pa., Aug. 4, 1857; s. Patrick Edmund and Cornelia Augusta (Beardsley) N.; B.S., U. of Rochester, 1879, M.S., 1882, Stoddard gold medal for mathematics and for a dissertation, hon. A.M., 1911; Sch. of Mines, Columbia, 1882-84, Ph.B., 1884; spl. grad. work, Columbia, 1897-98, A.M., 1904; traveled and studied in Europe under Daumet atelier, École des Beaux Arts, 1888-89, again traveled in Southern Europe, pursuing archtl. and archæol. studies, 1896. Practiced at Rochester, 1884-87, 1889-95, designing many pvt. and pub. bldgs. in N.Y. State and architect Chamber of Commerce bldg., Rochester, the first steel skeleton constrn. high bldg. in Western N.Y.; instr. architecture, 1898, in charge of courses in archtl. constrn., 1900-04, asst. prof. architecture, 1904-11, prof. archtl. constrn., 1911—, U. of Pa.; prof. architecture, U. of Mo., 1899. Del. World's Congress of Architects, London, 1906; chmn. com. on uniform specifications and contracts, Phila. Chapter A.I.A.; mem. commn. apptd. to revise bldg. laws of Phila.; expert adviser, U.S. Civ. Service Commn., 1913. Fellow A.I.A. (com. on basic building codes for U.S., 1914-15; official rep. of A.I.A. in Am. Soc. for Testing Materials, 1915—; chmn. A.I.A. com. on materials and methods, 1916-18). Editor-in-chief of Building Construction and Superintendence and of Kidder-Nolan Architects' and Builders' Handbook. Episcopalian. Home: Moylan, Pa. Died Sept. 6, 1926.

NOLAN, Val, lawyer; b. Evansville, Ind., Feb. 21, 1892; s. John J. and Valentine F. (Fitz-William) N.; student Ind. U., 1912-15, U. of Chicago, 1917; m. Jeannette Covert, Oct. 4, 1917; children—Val, Alan Tucker, Kathleen Covert. Admitted to Indiana bar, 1915; dep. pros. atty. 1st Jud. Circuit, Ind., 1916-17; in practice at Evansville, 1919-30; city atty., Evansville, 1930-33; U.S. dist. atty. Southern Dist. of Ind., 1933—. V.p. and cons. counsel Hearthstone Life Insurance Co., Indianapolis, 1938. Declined position of chief counsel to U.S. High Commr. to Philippines, 1937. Pvt. U.S.A., 1917; 1st lt. F.A., 1918; lt. F.A., U.S.R., 1919. Mem. Social Service Commn., Venezuela, 1939. Trustee Evansville Coll., Ind. U., James Whitcomb Riley Hosp. for Crippled Children, Indianapolis. Mem. Evansville Bar Assn. (pres. 1930). Democrat. Catholic. Home: Evansville, Ind. Died Oct. 11, 1940.

NOLEN, John, city planner, landscape architect; b. Phila., Pa., June 14, 1869; s. John C. and Matilda (Thomas) N.; Ph.B., U. of Pa., 1893; post-grad. work, U. of Munich, 1900; A.M., Harvard, 1905; hon. Sc.D., Hobart, 1913; m. Barbara Schatte, Apr. 22, 1896; children—John, Barbara (Mrs. David Strong), Edward, Humphrey. Connected with American Soc. for Extension of Univ. Teaching, 1893-1903. Engaged in practice at Cambridge, Mass., 1905—. Among his more important works are: Gen. plans for Babson Inst. (Wellesley Hills, Mass.), Smith Coll. (Northampton, Mass.), Bates Coll. (Lewiston, Me.); park systems for Madison (Wis.), Chattanooga (Tenn.), La. Crosse (Wis.), New London (Conn.), Sacramento (Calif.); plans and repts. for improvement of Roanoke (Va.), San Diego and Sacramento (Calif.), Montclair and Glen Ridge (N.J.), Reading, Erie and Lancaster (Pa.), Madison and La Crosse (Wis.), North Adams, Cohasset and Walpole (Mass.), Schenectady and Niagara Falls (N.Y.), Bridgeport (Conn.), Akron (O.), Flint (Mich.), Elkhart (Ind.), Asheville (N.C.), Dubuque (Ia.); gen. plans for new towns and suburbs, Kingsport (Tenn.), Venice and Clewiston (Fla.), Mariemont (Cincinnati) and Loveland Farms (Youngstown, O.), Overlook Colony (Claymont, Del.); regional plans for Wyomissing (Pa.), New York and environs (with others), Phila. Tri-State Dist., San Diego (Calif.), and Happy Valley (nr. Johnson City, Tenn.); plans for Francis William Memorial Pk. (East Walpole, Mass.). Adjudicator competitive designs for city plan of Dublin, Ireland. Member advisory housing com. of Emergency Fleet Corp.; chief bur. of housing and town planning, Army Ednl. Commn.; town planner, Union Park Gardens, U.S. Shipping Bd., and Niagara Falls project, U.S. Housing Corp.; consultant city planning and park bds., Flint, Mich. Mem. bd. dirs. Am. Planning and Civic Assn., Soc. Planning Officials; past pres. Nat. Conf. on City Planning, Am. City Planning Inst.; past pres. and mem. exec. com. Internat. Federation for Housing and Town Planning (London, Eng.); consultant for Nat. Resources Bd. (Vt.), Nat. Park Service, Housing Div. P.W.A., and Resettlement Adminstrn. Editor: Repton's Art of Landscape Gardening, 1907; City Planning, 1929. Author: Madison, a Model City, 1910; Replanning Small Cities, 1911; New Ideals in the Planning of Cities, Towns and Villages, 1919; New Towns for Old, 1927. Lecturer on city planning, Harvard University. Recipient of award by Oberlaender Trust for promotion of closer relation in field of city planning between Germany and U.S., 1931. Home: Cambridge, Mass. Died Feb. 19, 1937.

NOLEN, William Whiting, teacher; b. at Phila., July 16, 1860; s. Charles Willard and Abigail Williams (Whiting) N.; A.B., Central High Sch., Phila., 1878; A.B., summa cum laude, Harvard, 1884, A.M., 1886; attended Harvard Law Sch. 2 yrs.; unmarried. Asst. in biology, Harvard, 1884-86; from 1886 engaged in pvt. teaching in connection with Harvard U. work, which has developed until it occupies the time, whole or part, of over 50 teachers, and gives instrn., in any year, to upward of 450 university students. Protestant Episcopalian. Formed one of leading collections of early Am. lithographs in New England and largest pvt. collection of Lincolniana in Mass. Address: Cambridge, Mass. Died June 5, 1923.

NOLL, Arthur Howard, clergyman; b. Caldwell, N.J., Feb. 4, 1855; s. Arthur B. and Mary (Hamilton) N.; studied in his father's schs., and read law; admitted to N.J. bar as atty., 1876, as counselor, 1879; practiced in Newark, N.J., until 1882; engaged in railroading in Mexico, and was cashier of the Mexican Central Ry. in City of Mexico; resigned 1885 and prepared for ministry of P.E. Ch. at U. of the South; LL.D., St. John's Coll., Md., 1908; m. Florence, d. Dr. Thomas Dunn English, Oct. 26, 1887 (died 1926); 1 son, Maxwell Hamilton. Deacon, 1887, priest, 1888, P.E. Ch.; held parishes in Texas, Miss., New Orleans and Tenn.; sec. and historiographer of the Diocese of Tenn., 1899-1929; registrar, U. of the South, Sewanee, Tenn., 1902-15; engaged in settlement and ednl. work, St. Raphael's House, Monterey, Tenn., 1916-17; sr. canon, St. Mary's Cathedral, Memphis, 1918-29; pres. Noll Studio, Inc.; teacher and lecturer Jas. Lee Mem. Acad. of Arts. Past pres. Am. Soc. Bookplate Collectors and Designers (life). Author: A Short History of Mexico, 1890; From Empire to Republic, 1903; History of the Church of the Diocese of Tennessee, 1900; The Peruvians, 1905; General Kirby-Smith, 1907; The Life and Times of Miguel Hidalgo y Costilla, 1910; In Quest of Aztec Treasure, 1910. Editor: The Little Giant and Other Wonder Tales, by Thomas Dunn English, 1904; Dr. Quintard, Chaplain C.S.A., and Second Bishop of Tennessee, 1905; Alexander Gregg, First Bishop of Texas, 1912. Designer of bookplates. Home: Memphis, Tenn. Died July 17, 1930.

NOLTING, William Greaner, architect; b. Baltimore, Md., Nov. 11, 1866; s. Adolphus William and Virginia Temperance (Higgins) N.; grad. high sch., Richmond, Va.; m. Fannie Amanda Bonn, Sept. 21, 1893; children—Wm. Wyatt, Frances. Began as mem. firm Wyatt & Nolting, Baltimore, 1887; firm architects for Baltimore City Court House; Veterans' Bureau, Washington, D.C., and many other pub. and pvt. bldgs.; pres. St. Paul Building Co., Green Spring Land Co. Democrat. Episcopalian. Home: Glencoe, Baltimore County, Md. Died Nov. 14, 1940.

NONES, Robert Hodgson, dentist; b. Wilmington, Del., Jan. 28, 1864; s. Dr. Samuel Smith and Harriet (Alexander) N.; ed. Northwest Grammar Sch., Phila.; grad. Phila. Dental Sch., 1885; m. Susie Cooper Wilkins, Feb. 19, 1884; children—George Wilkins (dec.), Robert Hodgson. Dean dental dept. and prof. prosthetic dentistry, crown and bridge work, dental metallurgy and clin. dentistry, Medico-Chirurg. Coll.; dental surgeon to Phila. Hosp. Mem. Bd. Edn., Phila. Pres. Pa. State Dental Soc. Mason. Home: Philadelphia, Pa. Died Dec. 28, 1936.

NORBECK, Peter, senator; b. Vermilion, S.D., Aug. 27, 1870; s. George and Karen (Kongsvig) N.; student U. of S.D.; m. Lydia Anderson, June 1900. Pres. Norbeck Co., well drillers. Mem. S.D. Senate, 3 terms; served as lt. gov. S.D.; gov., 1917-19 and 1919-21; U.S. senator 3 terms, 1921-39. Republican. Lutheran. Home: Redfield, S.D. Died Dec. 20, 1936.

NORBURY, Frank Parson, M.D.; b. Beardstown, Ill., Aug. 5, 1863; s. Charles Joseph and Elizabeth Peters (Spence) N.; attended Ill. Coll., Jacksonville, hon. A.M., 1903; Medico-Chirurg. Coll., Phila., 1886-87; M.D., L.I., Coll. Hosp., Brooklyn, 1888; post-grad. studies in Phila. and New York; m. Mary E. Garm, Oct. 2, 1890; children—Frank Garm, Elizabeth. Office and field asst. U.S. Engr. Corps, U.S.A., civ. asst., 1881-85; resident phys., Pa. Instn. for Edn. Feeble-Minded Children, Elwyn, Pa., 1888; asst. phys. Ill. Central Hosp. for the Insane, 1888-93; prof. mental and nervous diseases, Keokuk (Ia.) Med. Coll.—Coll. Phys. and Surg.; lecturer on psychophysics, Ill. Coll., 1894-1902; alienist Bd. of Administration of Ill. and supt. Kankakee (Ill.) State Hosp.; pres. and med. dir. Norbury Sanatorium, Jacksonville, Ill. Asso. editor, 1890-95, editor, 1896-1906, Medical Fortnightly, St. Louis. Pres. Miss. Valley Med. Assn.; pres. Ill. State Conf. of Charities and Corrections, 1906-07. Mem. Nat. Com. for Mental Hygiene (acting medical director World War); Ill. State Bd. Welfare Commrs. Republican. Consultant in neuropsychiatry, Wabash Railroad Employees Hosp. Assn. Home: Springfield, Ill. Died Mar. 14, 1939.

NORCROSS, George, clergyman; b. Erie, Pa., Apr. 8, 1838; s. Hiram and Elizabeth (McClelland) N.; A.B., Monmouth Coll., Ill., 1861, A.M., 1864; studied McCormick Theol. Sem., Chicago, 1861-62, Monmouth Theol. Sem., 1862-63, Princeton Theol. Sem., 1864-65; D.D., Princeton, 1879; m. Mary S. Tracy, Oct. 1, 1863 (died 1866); m. 2d, Mrs. Louise (Jackson) Gale, Apr. 22, 1867. Stated supply N. Henderson, Ill., 1863-65; ordained Presbyn. ministry, June 6, 1865; pastor N. Henderson, 1865-66, Galesburg, Ill., 1866-68, Second Ch., Carlisle, Pa., 1869-1909, pastor emeritus, 1909; stated supply Rockledge, Fla., Nov. 1, 1909-May 1, 1910. Editor: (and part author) The Centennial Memorial, Presbytery of Carlisle, 1890; The Story of a Thirtieth Anniversary, 1899. Address: Carlisle, Pa. Died Mar. 8, 1915.

NORCROSS, Grenville Howland, lawyer; b. Boston, Mass., Feb. 2, 1854; s. Otis and Lucy Ann (Lane) N.; grad. Pub. Latin Sch., Boston, 1871; A.B., Harvard, 1875, LL.B., 1877; unmarried. Admitted to Mass. bar, 1879, practiced in Boston, 1879—. Mem. Bostonian Society (pres. emeritus). Unitarian. Home: Boston, Mass. Died Feb. 12, 1937.

NORCROSS, Orlando Whitney, builder and contractor; b. Clinton, Me., Oct. 25, 1839; s. Jesse S. and Margaret Ann (Whitney) N.; moved to Salem,

Mass., 1843; ed. pub. schs.; m. Ellen P. Sibley, May 17, 1870. Worked in leather business; served in Union Army, 1861-64; associated with his brother, James A., in firm of Norcross Bros., Salem, 1866; moved to Worcester, 1868; bought brother's interest, 1897; sole owner, 1897-1902; later pres. The Norcross Brothers Co. Firm built important structures in all leading Am. cities. Was mem. of commn. to investigate and report on the condition of Chicago Custom House and Postoffice, apptd. by Sec. of Treasury Bristow, 1875; remodeled White House, 1902-03; built New York Pub. Library, Astor, Lenox and Tilden Foundations, 1903-07, Harvard Med. Schs., Boston, 1903-06; removed by submarine excavation Henderson's Point at Kittery Navy Yard, providing 15 feet of water in channel where there was 10 feet of ledge above water; constructed pneumatic caisson foundations of new Boston Custom House, 1910-11. Furnished 500,000 cubic ft. of granite for Pa. Sta., N.Y. City. Dir. State Mut. Life Assurance Co. Trustee Clark Coll. Address: Worcester, Mass. Died Feb. 27, 1920.

NORCROSS, Wilbur Harrington, coll. prof.; b. Ralston, Pa., June 28, 1882; s. William Harrington and Martha Jane (Rees) N.; A.B., Dickinson Sem., 1902; A.B., Dickinson Coll., 1907, A.M., 1913; Ph.D., Johns Hopkins U., 1920; m. Agnes Frysinger, Dec. 23, 1911 (died 1917); m. 2d, Helen Burns, Aug. 9, 1918; 1 dau., Isabel Mullin. Ordained to ministry M.E. Ch., 1907; pastor, Viva, Pa., 1904-07, Duncannon, Pa., 1907-08; mem. Central Pa. Conf., 1907; teacher Greek and Latin, Dickinson Sem., 1908-14, dean, 1912-14; instr. of psychology, Dickinson Coll., Carlisle, Pa., 1916-17, asso. prof., 1917-23, prof., 1923—, dean jr. class, 1929-39; prof. psychology and head of dept. Summer Sch., Johns Hopkins U., 1928—. Served as 1st lt. San. Corps, U.S.A., attached to Med. Research Lab., 1918-19; maj. Res. Corps, 1924—. Dir. Carlisle Y.M.C.A. Trustee Todd Memorial Home, M.E. Home for Children. Democrat. Mason. Home: Carlisle, Pa. Died June 11, 1941.

NORDBERG, Bruno Victor, mechanical engr., inventor; b. Helsingfors, Finland, Apr. 11, 1857; s. Carl Victor and Dores (Hinze) N.; grad. Poly. Institute, Helsingfors, 1878; Dr. Engring., U. of Mich., 1923; m. Helena Hinze, Sept. 24, 1882. Came to U.S., 1879, naturalized citizen, 1897; mfr. steam engine regulators, Milwaukee, 1891; latter built motive power engines and machinery for mines, complete power plants, etc.; pres. and chief engr. Nordberg Mfg. Co. Inventor of many machines and devices used throughout the world; built complete system of air compressors and hoists, operated with compressed air, covering the principal shafts in the Butte, Mont., mining camp; built the first modern steam engines with equilibrium poppet valves in America. Republican. Lutheran. Home: Milwaukee, Wis. Died Oct. 30, 1925.

NORDELL, Philip Augustus, clergyman, writer; b. Stockholm, Sweden, Jan. 19, 1846; s. Per and Carin (Palmquist) N.; brought to America, 1853; ed. Phila. Coll. of Pharmacy, 1864-66; U. of Lewisburg, Pa., 1866-69; A.B., U. of Rochester, 1870, D.D., 1886; grad. Rochester Theological Seminary, 1873; m. Lizzie V. Turner, July 14, 1870; m. 2d, Florence E. Gallup, Apr. 29, 1890. Hosp. steward, 197th Regt., Pa. Vols., July 13-Nov. 11, 1864; ordained Bapt. ministry, 1873; pastor Chili, N.Y., 1873-74, Lee, Mass., 1874-77, Weymouth, Mass., 1877-82, New London, Conn., 1882-92; asst. prof. N.T. lit. and exegesis, U. of Chicago, 1892-93; asso. editor Bible study, Union S.S. publs., 1893-1908, editor, 1908-11; later writer for Charles Scribner's Sons and Am. Bapt. Publn. Soc., and lecturer on O.T. subjects. Progressive. Author: Biblical Studies for Adult Classes, 1902; Preparations for Christianity, 1911; Keystone Senior Studies, Vol. I, 1912, Vol. II, 1913; The Modern Church, 1913. Home: Brookline, Mass. Died Mar. 11, 1930.

NORDHOFF, Charles, author, journalist; b. Westphalia, Prussia, 1830; came with parents to America, 1835; ed. Woodward Coll., Cincinnati; was 9 yrs. at sea, in employ of Harper & Bros., 1857-61; New York Evening Post, 1861-71; New York Herald, 1874—. Author: Man of War Life; The Merchant Vessel; Whaling and Fishing; Stories of the Island World; Secession Is Rebellion; Freedmen of the South Carolina Sea Islands; Slavery Injurious to Free Laborers; Cape Cod Stories; California for Health, Pleasure and Residence; Northern California, Oregon and Sandwich Islands; Communistic Societies of the United States; Politics for Young Americans; The Cotton States Under Reconstruction; God and the Future Life. Address: Coronado, Calif. Died 1901.

NORDICA, Lillian, prima donna; b. (Lillian Norton) Farmington, Me., 1859; musical edn. N.E. Conservatory, by John O'Neill, and with San Giovanni, Milan, Italy; m. Mr. Gower; m. 2d, Herr Döme; m. 3d, George Washington Young, July 29, 1909. Operatic début, Brescia, Italy, in "La Traviata"; appeared in London, 1887, and in Paris, St. Petersburg and other European capitals. Repertoire embracing 40 operas and all the standard oratorios; best known in Wagnerian parts; appeared in grand

opera in U.S. several seasons. Address: New York, N.Y. Died May 10, 1914.

NORMAN, Robert Claude, tax commr.; b. Washington, Ga., Sept. 23, 1875; s. Robert R. and Mary (Neeson) N.; grad. high sch., Washington, 1891; m. Louise Johnson, Apr. 9, 1912; children—Claudia Louise, Robert Claude. Admitted to Ga. bar, 1899; solicitor City Court, Washington, 1903-11, solicitor gen. Toombs Circuit, 1913-21; mem. Industrial Commission of Ga., 1925-27; state tax commr., Ga., 1927-31. Lt. col. governor's staff, 1923-27. Pres. Ga. Bapt. Young People's Union, 1905-09, Ga. Bapt. S.S. Assn., 1922-24. Trustee Mercer U. Democrat. Mason, K.P. (Grand Master of Exchequer, 1903—.) Home: Washington, Ga. Died 1932.

NORRIS, Charles, M.D.; b. Hoboken, N.J., Dec. 4, 1867; s. Joseph Parker and Frances Ann (Stevens) N.; Ph.B., Sheffield Scientific Sch. (Yale), 1888; M.D., Coll. of Phys. and Surg., Columbia, 1892; post-grad. work, Kiel, Gottingen, Berlin and Vienna, 1894-96; m. Eugenie Gebhart, Sept. 3, 1908. Instr. pathology, Coll. of Phys. and Surg., 1896-1904; dir. labs. Bellevue Hosp., 1904-18; chief med. examiner City of N.Y., 1918—; prof. forensic medicine, New York U., 1933. Decorated Chevalier de la Couronne (Belgium). Episcopalian. Home: New York, N.Y. Died Sept. 11, 1935.

NORRIS, Charles E., pub. utilities; b. Port Leyden, N.Y., Oct. 30, 1876; s. Michael and Mary A. (Gillespie) N.; student St. James' Sch., 1884-93, Albany Law Sch., 1900-01; hon. M.A., Villanova Coll., 1909; m. Anna M. Holland, Oct. 15, 1905; 1 son, John Holland; m. 2d, Nora Clark Ahearn, June 7, 1920; m. 3d, Marie Blanchfield, Apr. 30, 1934. Admitted to N.Y. bar, 1901; practiced at Carthage until 1926; mem. law firm of Cullen, Norris & Reynolds, Watertown, N.Y.; gen. counsel to Westchester Lighting Co. (Mount Vernon, N.Y.). The Yonkers Electric Light & Power Co. (Mount Vernon, N.Y.). Mem. Dem. State Com., N.Y., 1910-27. Supervisor town of Wilna, N.Y., 1907-08; dep. state commr. of excise, 1912-17. Elk, K.C. Home: Irvington-on-Hudson, N.Y. Died Nov. 1, 1941.

NORRIS, Edwin Lee, governor; b. Cumberland County, Ky., Aug. 15, 1865; grad. Southern Normal Sch., Ky. Engaged in law practice in Mont.; mem. Mont. Senate; lt.-gov. of Mont., 1905-09, gov., 1909-13; later mem. law firm Norris, Hurd & Rhoades. Democrat. Home: Great Falls, Mont. Died Apr. 25, 1924.

NORRIS, Frank, novelist; b. Chicago, 1870; s. B. F. N.; ed. San Francisco High School, U. of Calif., Harvard; studied art in Paris, 1887-89; m. Jeanette Black, 1900. War corr. San Francisco Chronicle, in S. Africa during Uitlander insurrection, 1895-96; editor San Francisco Wave, 1896-97; war corr. McClure's Magazine, in Cuba, 1898. Author: McTague, The Octopus; etc. Died 1902.

NORRIS, Henry, surgeon; b. Phila., Pa., May 27, 1875; s. Joseph Parker and Isabel Nevins (Fry) N.; M.D., U. of Pa., 1896; m Ethel B. Wheeler, Aug. 3, 1898; children—Susan W., Henry. Ethel Stuart, Charles. Began practice at Phila., 1896; moved to Rutherfordton, N.C., 1906; founded Rutherford Hosp. (surgical), 1906; retired from active practice. Mem N.G. Pa., 1903-06, North Carolina N.G., 1913-17; commd. maj. Med. Corps. U.S.A., Aug. 5, 1917, div. surgeon 30th Div., A.E.F., 1918; hon. discharged, Mar. 23, 1919. Republican. Episcopalian. Home: Bryn Mawr, Pa. Died Oct. 6, 1941.

NORRIS, Henry Hutchinson, electrical engr.; b. Phila., Apr. 26, 1873; s. Samuel Wilson and Mary Rachel N.; ed. Phila. Manual Training High Sch.; took course in applied electricity, Johns Hopkins, 1894; M.E., Cornell, 1896; B.Engring. Johns Hopkins, 1927; m. Annie T. Reese, Dec. 23, 1899 (died 1922); children—Elinor Rachel (Mrs. P. C. Roundy). Rachel Hutchinson (Mrs. H. C. Haydn II); m. 2d, Helena R. Walley, June 5, 1926. Was designer and draughtsman for elec. firms; assistant instr. Johns Hopkins, 1892-94; asst. prof., 1900-05, prof. elec. engring., 1905-13, head dept., 1909-13, Cornell; asso. editor, 1913-21, mng. editor, 1921-22, engring. editor, 1922-23, Electric Railway Journal; supervisor of personnel and special instruction, Boston Elevated Railway. Supt. tests, Electric Ry. Test Commn., and mem. Internat. Jury of Awards, sec. group on elec. machinery. St. Louis Expn., 1904; spl. expert in connection with reorganization of Am. St. Ry. Assn., 1905. Sec. Soc. Promotion of Engring. Edn., 1909-14; fellow American Institute Electrical Engrs. (manager 1909-12). Author: Electrical Machinery (with H. J. Ryan and George L. Hoxie); Introduction to the Study of Electrical Engineering. Editor: (with B. V. Swenson) Report of Electric Railway Test Commission; editor for Am. Electric Ry. Assn., of annual vol. entitled "Electric Railway Practices," 1923-28. Home: Winchester, Mass. Died Apr. 14, 1940.

NORRIS, Henry McCoy, mech. engr.; b. Trenton, N.J., Jan. 21, 1868; s. John Hurd and Cora McCoy (Bunnell) N.; State Normal and Model schs., Trenton; Trenton Acad.; Lawrenceville (N.J.) Sch.; Sibley Coll. (Cornell U.), 1890-91; m. Sarah Boyd

Nixon, Nov. 24, 1892. Served apprenticeship, Bement, Miles & Co., Phila.; designer, Ferracute Machine Co., Bridgeton, N.J., Brown & Sharpe Mfg. Co., Providence, R.I., Pond Machine Tool Co., Plainville, N.J., to 1892; insp. Garvin Machine Co., New York, 1893; supt. Appleton Mfg. Co., Phila., 1894, Riehle Bros. Testing Machine Co., 1895; gen. mgr. Campbell & Zell Co., Baltimore, 1896; supt., engr. and works mgr. Bickford Drill & Tool Co., Cincinnati, 1897-09; sec., dir. Cincinnati Bickford Tool Co., 1909—. Republican. Presbyterian. Mem. Am. Soc. M.E. (chmn. Cincinnati Sect., 1919, mgr. nat. society, 1920-23), Ohio Soc. S.R. (pres. 1919), Ohio Soc. Colonial Wars (gov. 1916). Editor: Digest of Physical Tests. Author: Fifty-six Points of Vantage; Ancestry and Descendants of Lieutenant Jonathan and Tamesin (Barker) Norris, 1906; History of the Drilling Machine. Inventor first speed-box used on a machine tool; designed 1st high-speed lathe and high-speed, high-power radial drill; devised current formula for ascertaining the power required to drive drills in metals at various speeds and feeds. One of 8 efficiency engrs. selected for service in ordnance dept., Watertown Arsenal, 1917; mech. expert, Council Nat. Defence, 1917; mech. engr., Ordnance Dept. at-large, 1918. Mem. U.S. War Industries Board. Address: Cincinnati, O. Died Dec. 27, 1925.

NORRIS, Homer Albert, musician; b. Wayne, Kennebec County, Me., 1860; s. Mary H. N.; gen. edn. Auburn, Me.; grad. in music, N.E. Conservatory of Music, Boston, in organ, piano, harmony, counterpoint and composition; studied 4 years in Paris under Theodore Dubois, Guilmant, Gigout and Godard; unmarried. Teacher musical composition along lines pursued in Paris Conservatory of Music; lecturer on musical æsthetics; organist and choirmaster, St. George's Episcopal Ch., New York. Author: Practical Harmony on a French Basis, 1896; The Art of Counterpoint, 1899; The Flight of the Eagle, 1905. Contbr. to Chicago Music, Philadelphia Etude, Musical Courier, New York, on the theory of music, 1890—. Address: New York, N.Y. Died Aug. 14, 1920.

NORRIS, James Flack, chemist; b. Baltimore, Jan. 20, 1871; s. Rev. Richard and Sarah Amanda (Baker) N.; A.B., Johns Hopkins, 1892, fellow in chemistry, 1894-95, Ph.D., 1895; honorary Sc.D., Bowdoin Coll., 1929; m. Anne Bent Chamberlin, Feb. 4, 1902. Asst., 1895-96, instr., 1896-1900, asst. prof. organic chemistry, 1900-04. Mass. Inst. Tech.; prof. chemistry, Simmons Coll., Boston, 1904-15, Vanderbilt U., 1915-16; prof. organic chemistry, in charge grad. students in chemistry, dir. research lab. organic chemistry, Mass. Inst. Tech., 1916—. In charge offense chem. research, war gas investigations, U.S. Bur. Mines, 1917-18; asso. mem. Naval Consulting Bd., 1916; lt. col., U.S.A., in charge U.S. Chem. Warfare Service, Eng., 1918; in charge investigation mfr. war gases in German chem. plants, 1919. Chmn. div. chemistry and chem. tech. Nat. Research Council, 1924-25, mem. exec. bd., 1925-33. Lecturer on organic chemistry, Harvard, 1912-14, Clark U., 1913-14, Bowdoin, 1929. Medalist American Institute of Chemists, 1937; Secretary Soc. of Arts of Boston, Mass., 1902-04; president Am. Chem. Soc., 1925-26 (pres. Northeastern sect., 1905-06); pres. Chem. Teachers' Assn. of N.E., 1906-08, Technology Club, 1906-09; v.p. Internat. Union of Pure and Applied Chemistry, 1925-28. Fellow Am. Acad. Arts and Sciences (v.p., 1934—), A.A.A.S. (chmn. Sect. C, 1930). Author: The Principles of Organic Chemistry; Experimental Organic Chemistry; Text-book of Inorganic Chemistry for Colleges (with R. C. Young); Laboratory Exercises in Inorganic Chemistry (with K L. Mark). Home: Boston, Mass. Died Aug. 4, 1940.

NORRIS, James Lawson, patent atty.; b. Washington, Oct. 15, 1845; s. John Edmund and Eliza Tidings (Phillips) N.; student Dickinson Coll., Pa., 1864-66; m. Annie Virginia Robinson, Sept. 26, 1867 (died 1895). Examiner in U.S. Patent Office for a few yrs.; in practice as patent atty.; 1869—. Apptd., 1891, one of commrs. to appraise lands condemned by govt. for Nat. Rock Creek Park. Pres. Oak Hill Cemetery Co., Mut. Protection and Franklin Ins. cos.; dir. Children's, and mem. bd. visitors, Providence hosps. Pres. Jackson Dem. Assn. of D.C., 1887—; mem. Gen. Inaugural Com., 1884, 1888, 1892 (chmn.), 1896, 1900, 1904, 1908; treas. Dem. Congressional Com. 1888-1904; del. Dem Nat. convs., 1892, 1900, 1904; mem. Dem. Nat. Com., 1892-96, 1900 and 1904 (asst. treas. 1896-98, treas. 1898-1900). Gathered extensive library relating to Andrew Jackson. Home: Washington, D.C. Died 1910.

NORRIS, Mary Harriott, author; b. Boonton, N.J., Mar. 16, 1848; d. Charles Bryan and Mary L. (Kerr) N.; A.B., Vassar, 1870. Founder and prin. of pvt. sch., New York, 1880-96; dean of women, Northwestern U., 1898-99. Author: The Grapes of Wrath, 1901; The Story of Christina, 1907; The Veil, 1907; The Golden Age of Vassar, 1915. Editor: Silas Marner, 1890; Marmion, 1891; Evangeline, 1897; Kenilworth, 1898; Quentin Durward, 1899. Trustee Equal Franchise Soc. of N.J. Address: Morristown, N.J. Died Sept. 14, 1919.

NORRIS, True Livingston, editor; b. Manchester, N.H., May 4, 1848; s. Arthur F. L. and Olive W. (Wallace) N.; acad. edn.; pvt. 5th Mass. Vols., 1864-65; m. Lillian G. Hurst, May 20, 1890. Admitted to bar, 1868; practiced at Boston, 1868-75, Washington, 1872-76, Concord, N.H., 1876-80; on staff New York Herald, 1883-85, Boston Globe, 1885-88; editor, 1888—, propr., 1893—, Portsmouth (N.H.) Times (daily) and the States and Union (weekly). Mem. Governor's Council, 1892-93; collector customs, Dist. of N.H., 1893-98; mem. Dem. Nat. Com., 1896-1908; del. Dem. Nat. convs., 1900, 1904. Address: Portsmouth, N.H. Died Dec. 4, 1920.

NORRIS, William, actor; b. N.Y. City, June 15, 1872; s. Elias M. and Harriet (Maye) Block; ed. at North Cosmopolitan Sch. and Boys' High Sch., San Francisco; m. Mabel Mordaunt, June 1, 1910. First professional appearance with George Lederer's Stock Company, 1892; played part of the German lunatic in original "Belle of New York" Company, 1897; appeared in "His Excellency, the Governor," "Children of the Ghetto," "Francesca da Rimini," etc.; leading comedian in "Land of Nod," "Tom Jones," "A Modern Eve," "Around the Map," "Maytime," and numerous others; joined Cosmopolitan Productions Co., to play in motion pictures, 1922. Home: New York, N.Y. Died Mar. 3, 1929.

NORRIS, William Fisher, prof. ophthalmology, U. of Pa.; b. Phila., Jan. 6, 1839; s. Dr. George W. and Mary P. (Fisher) N.; grad. U. of Pa., 1857, A.M., 1860; grad. med. dept., 1861; asst. surgeon U.S.A., 1863-65; in charge Douglas Gen. Hosp., Washington, 1864; pres. Am. Ophthalmol. Soc., 1885-89. Fellow Coll. Physicians of Phila. (pres. ophthalmic sect., 1894); one of surgeons to Wills Eye Hosp. Author: Medical Ophthalmology (with Prof. S. Stricker; Versuche über Hornhaut Entzündung, Vienna, 1869); A Contribution to the Anatomy of the Human Retina (with Dr. James Wallace); A Contribution to the Anatomy of the Human Retina (with Dr. C. A. Oliver); A Text Book of Ophthalmology. Address: Philadelphia, Pa. Died 1901.

NORSWORTHY, Naomi, univ. prof.; b. New York, Sept. 29, 1877; d. Samuel B. and Eva A. (Modridge) N.; state diploma, N.J. State Normal Sch., 1896; B.S., and higher diploma, Teachers Coll. (Columbia), 1901; Ph.D., Columbia, 1904. Teacher Morristown (N.J.) public schs., 1896-99; asst. in psychology, 1901-02, tutor, 1902-04, instr., 1904-09, Teachers Coll.; adj. prof. psychology, Columbia, 1909—. Author: The Psychology of Mentally Deficient Children, 1906. Address: New York, N.Y. Died Dec. 25, 1916.

NORTH, Charles H., physician; b. Palmyra, N.Y., Oct. 27, 1868; s. Henry M. and Sarah J. (Grover) N.; ed. pub. and pvt. schs.; M.D., U. of Buffalo, 1898; m. Luella Barber Robinson, Nov. 15, 1905. Entered service Matteawan Hosp. for Insane Criminals, 1898; transferred as asst. phys. to Dannemora State Hosp. for Insane Felons upon its opening, 1900, supt., 1904—. Address: Dannemora, N.Y. Died Dec. 12, 1917.

NORTH, Edward, prof. Greek language and literature, Hamilton; b. Berlin, Conn., March 9, 1820; grad. Hamilton, 1841; L.H.D., 1869, N.Y. U. Regents; LL.D., 1887, Madison, now Colgate, U.; m. Mary Frances, d. Hon. S. Newton Dexter, July 31, 1844. 1848—, prof. Greek, 1881—, a trustee, and 1890—, mem. exec. com. Hamilton Coll.; 1855—, necrologist Hamilton alumni; 1856—, editor Alumniana, in Hamilton Monthly. Address: Clinton, N.Y. Died 1903.

NORTH, Emmett Pipkin, ophthalmologist; b. Labaddie, Mo., Aug. 13, 1877; s. Eugene B. and Mary Sale (Pipkin) N.; student Central Coll., Fayette, Mo., 1893-97; M.D., Beaumont Med. Coll., St. Louis, 1900; m. 2d, Carolyn Tweedie, May 19, 1927. Asst. phys. St. Louis City Hosp., 1900-01; house surgeon M.P. Ry. Hosp., 1901-03; phys. in charge St. Louis South Side Dispensary, 1903-04; asso. ophthalmologist St. John's Hosp.; asst. prof. ophthalmology, St. Louis U. Med. Dept., 1933; ophthalmologist M.P. Ry. Co. Hosp., Masonic Hosp. and St. Louis Pub. Service; cons. ophthalmologist B.&O. R.R. and other rys.; pres. Mo. State Bd. of Health, 1917-25 and, 1933—. Lt. comdr. U.S.N.R.F. Mem. Mo. State Med. Soc. (pres. 1925), St. Louis Med. Soc. (pres. 1921), Mo. Pacific Ry. Surgeons Assn. (pres. 1931-32). Democrat. Presbyn. Mason. Home: St. Louis, Mo. Died Dec. 27, 1935.

NORTH, Frank Mason, clergyman; b. New York, N.Y., Dec. 3, 1850; s. Charles Carter and Elizabeth (Mason) N.; A.B., Wesleyan U., 1872, A.M., 1875, D.D., 1894, LL.D., 1918; m. Fannie L. Stewart, May 27, 1874 (dec.); children—Adolphus Stewart (dec.), Mason Longacre (dec.); m. 2d, Louise J. McCoy, Dec. 23, 1885; 1 son, Eric McCoy. Ordained M.E. ministry, 1873; pastor Florida, N.Y., 1873-74, Amenia, 1874-76, Cold Spring-on-Hudson, N.Y., 1876-78, New York City (chapel in East 109th St. erected), 1879-81, White Plains, N.Y., 1882-84, New York (Calvary M.E. Ch. erected), 1884-87, Middletown, Conn., 1887-92; corr. sec. N.Y. City Ch. Extension and Missionary Soc., 1892-1912; corr. sec. Nat. City Evang. Union of M.E. Ch., 1896-1912; editor The Christian City, New York, 1892-1912; corr. sec. Bd. of Foreign Missions of M.E. Ch., 1912-24, sec. council, 1924—. Chmn. exec. com., 1912-16, pres., 1916-20, Federal Council Chs. of Christ in America. Chevalier Legion of Honor, 1919; Officier de l'Instruction Publique, France, 1920; Officer of the Royal Order of George I, Greece, 1920. Wrote: "Where Cross the Crowded Ways of Life" (hymn), 1903; also other hymns. Home: Madison, N.J. Died Dec. 17, 1935.

NORTH, Simon Newton Dexter, statistician; b. Clinton, N.Y., Nov. 29, 1849; s. Dr. Edward and Mary F. (Dexter) N.; grad. Hamilton Coll., 1869; LL.D., Bowdoin, 1902, U. of Ill., 1904; m. Lillian Sill Comstock, July 8, 1875. Mng. editor Utica Morning Herald, 1869-86; editor and joint propr. Albany Express, 1886-88; sec. Nat. Assn. of Wool Mfrs., Boston, and editor Quarterly Bulletin, 1888-1903; mem. U.S. Industrial Commn., 1898-99; chief statistician for mfrs., 12th Census; dir. U.S. Census, 1903-09. Chmn. Am. Sariff Commn. to Germany, 1906. Asst. sec. and statistician, Carnegie Endowment for Internat. Peace, 1910-21. Pres. N.Y. State Associated Press, 1885-86; mem. Am. Statis. Assn. (pres. 1910). Author: An American Textile Glossary, 1895; A History of the American Wool Manufacture, 1903; "Old Greek," An Old Time Professor in an Old-Fashioned College (memoir of Dr. Edward North), 1905; Simeon North —First Official Pistol Maker of the United States (a memoir), 1913. Address: Washington, D.C. Died Aug. 3, 1924.

NORTHCOTT, William Allen, lawyer, ins. expert; b. Murfreesboro, Tenn., Jan. 28, 1854; s. Gen. R. S. and Mary (Cunningham) N.; moved to Clarksburg, W.Va., 1861; student U.S. Naval Acad., 1869-73; m. Ada R. Stoutzenberg, Sept. 11, 1882. Admitted to W.Va. bar, 1887; settled in Greenville, Ill., 1879; state's atty., Bond Co., Ill., 1882-92; head consul, Modern Woodmen of America, 1890-1903; specialist on adequate fraternal ins. rates; lt. gov. of Ill., 1897-1905; moved to Springfield, Ill., 1905; U.S. dist. atty. Southern Dist. of Ill., 1905-14; pres. Inter-Ocean Casualty Co. Mason, Odd Fellow, K.P., Modern Woodman, Court of Honor, Elk. Republican. Episcopalian. Address: Springfield, Ill. Died Jan. 25, 1917.

NORTHEN, William Jonathan, governor; b. Jones Co., Ga., July 9, 1835; s. Peter and Louisa N.; A.B., Mercer U., 1853; LL.D., Mercer, 1892, Richmond, Va., Coll., 1894, Baylor U., Tex., 1900; m. Mattie M. Neel, Dec. 19, 1860. Began teaching, 1854; asst., 1876-77, prin. 1857-61, Mt. Zion High Sch., Hancock County, Ga.; pvt., 1861-65, in co. comd. by his father, in C.S.A.; again prin. Mt. Zion High School, 1865-74; farmer nr. Sparta, Hancock County, 1874-90. Pres. Hancock Co. Farmers' Club from its origin; pres., 1886-88, State Agrl. Soc.; mem. Ga. Ho. of Rep., 1877-78 and 1880-81, Senate, 1884-85; gov. of Ga., 1890-94; later mgr. Ga. Immigration and Investment Bureau. Democrat. President Southern Baptist Convention, 1899-1902, National Bapt. Congress, 1893, Ga. Bapt. Conv., 1902—; v.p. Am. Tract Soc., 1903—, S.S. Union, 1904—, Am. Bible Soc., 1907—. Home: Atlanta, Ga. Died Mar. 25, 1913.

NORTHEND, Mary Harrod, author; b. Salem, Mass., May 10, 1850; d. William Dummer and Susan Steadman (Harrod) N.; ed. pub. schs., Salem; unmarried. Began writing in 1904; 1st article pub. in Good Housekeeping; specialist in Colonial architecture, gardens and interior decorating; contbr. to Century, Outlook, Country Life in America, Country Gentleman, Ladies' Home Journal, House and Garden, McCall's, Good Housekeeping, etc.; collected over 30,000 negatives and photographs of views pertaining to Colonial and modern houses, interiors, gardens and antiques. Conglist. Author: Colonial Homes and Their Furnishings, 1912; The Party Book (with Winifred Fales), 1912; Historic Homes of New England, 1914; Remodeled Farmhouses, 1915; Colonial Architecture (with Harold Donalson Eberlein), 1915; Garden Ornaments, 1916; Memories of Old Salem, 1917; The Art of Home Decoration, 1921; Possibilities of a Small House, 1923; We Visit Old Inns, 1925; American Glass, 1926. Home: Salem, Mass. Deceased.

NORTHEND, William Dummer, lawyer; b. Byfield, Mass., Feb. 26, 1823; s. John N.; grad. Bowdoin Coll., 1843, A.M., LL.D.; also A.M., Dartmouth. Admitted to bar, Oct. 1845; mem. Mass. senate, 1861-62. Author: The Bay Colony; Speeches and Essays on Political Subjects. Address: Salem, Mass. Died 1903.

NORTHROP, Cyrus, univ. pres.; b. Ridgefield, Conn., Sept. 30, 1834; s. Cyrus and Polly (Fancher) N.; A.B., Yale, 1857, LL.B., 1859; LL.D., Yale, 1886, U. of Wis., 1904, Ill. College, 1904, South Carolina College, 1905, and Carleton College, 1917; m. Anna E., d. J. D. Warren, Sept. 30, 1862. Admitted to Conn. bar, 1860; clerk Conn. Ho. of Rep., 1861, Senate, 1862; editor New Haven Palladium, 1863; prof. rhetoric and English lit., Yale, 1863-84; pres. U. of Minn., 1884-1911, pres. emeritus, Apr. 1, 1911. Home: Minneapolis, Minn. Died Apr. 3, 1922.

NORTHROP, David Ward, lawyer; b. Sherman, Conn., Feb. 19, 1844; s. David and Clarissa L. (Ward) N.; A.B., Wesleyan U., Conn., 1868; LL.B., Albany Law Sch. (Union U.), 1870; m. Mary A. Stewart, Sept. 14, 1870. Began practice at Middletown, Conn., 1871; pres. Middletown Electric Light Co., 1885-1912. Mem. Conn. Ho. of Rep., 1871, 1881-82; judge of probate for Dist. of Middletown, 1873-80; sec. state of Conn., 1883-84; mayor of Middletown, 1884-85; postmaster, Middletown, 1886-89; state auditor of Conn., 1891-92, 1897-98; del. Conn. Constl. Conv., 1902. Democrat. Trustee Wesleyan Univ., 1880-1910. Address: Middletown, Conn. Died Dec. 1918.

NORTHROP, Harry Pinckney, bishop; b. Charleston, S.C., May 5, 1842; s. C. B. and Hannah E. (Anderson) N.; student Georgetown Coll.; A.B., Mount St. Mary's Coll., Emmitsburg, Md., 1860; studied 4 yrs. in theol. sem. there; then at Am. Coll., Rome. Ordained R.C. priest, 1865; asst. Ch. of the Nativity, New York, 1865-66; asst. pastor St. Joseph's Ch., Charleston, S.C., 1866-68; missionary priest in N.C., at New Berne, 1868-72; asst. pastor pro-cathedral, 1872-78; pastor Sullivan's Island; pastor St. Patrick's, Charleston, 4 yrs.; consecrated bishop, Jan. 8, 1882, as vicar-apostolic of N.C. and titular bishop of Rosalia; transferred by papal brief to See of Charleston, S.C., Jan. 27, 1883. Address: Charleston, S.C. Deceased.

NORTHROP, Henry Davenport, author; b. Poultney, N.Y., Mar. 10, 1836; s. Daniel and Sophia (Williams) N.; A.B., Amherst, 1857; Union Theol. Sem., 1858-59; Yale Div. Sch., 1860; m. Josephine L. Merrick, May 25, 1862. Ordained Presbyn. ministry, 1860; pastor Brooklyn, 1860-62, London, Eng., 1863-67, New York, 1868-74, Hartford, Conn., 1874-79, N. Tenth St. Ch., Phila., 1881-86, Ridley Park, Pa., 1887-91. Author: Grandest Century in World's History, 1900; John Winslow, 1901; World Renowned Authors, 1902; Standard History of the U.S., 1905; Young People's History of the World, 1905. Compiler and editor Sunday School Speaker and Entertainer, 1905. Home: Philadelphia, Pa. Deceased.

NORTHROP, Herbert L., surgeon; b. 1866; M.D., Hahnemann Med. Coll., Phila., 1889. Practiced in Phila., 1889—; prof. and head dept. of surgery, Hahnemann Med. Coll. Address: Philadelphia, Pa. Died May 3, 1936.

NORTHROP, Stephen Abbott, clergyman; b. Granville, O., Apr. 7, 1852; s. Rev. William Ray and Laura (Abbott) N.; Denison U., Granville, 1872-75; A.B., Colgate U., 1876, A.M., 1879; grad. Rochester Theol. Sem., 1877; D.D., Franklin (Ind.) Coll., 1895; m. Celestia Amelia Joslin, Aug. 16, 1877. Ordained Baptist ministry, Oct. 4, 1877; pastor, Fenton, Mich., 1877-82, 1st Ch., Ft. Wayne, Ind., 1882-95, 1st Ch., Kansas City, Mo., 1896-1906, 1st Ch., Los Angeles, 1906-09, 1st Ch., Kansas City, Kansas, 1909-18; again of 1st Ch., Fenton, Mich., 1918—. Pres. mgrs. Bapt. Ministers' Home, Fenton; pres. Ind. Bapt. State Conv., 3 yrs., Ottawa Chautauqua Assembly, 1898, Carthage Chautauqua, 1909; pres. trustees Kansas City Theol. Sem., 1902-06; pres. Humane Soc., Kansas City, Baptist Ministers' Alliance, Kansas City, Kan. Chaplain 2 Rep. Nat. Convs.; invited to open World's Columbian Commn., Chicago, 1892; del. World's Temperance Centennial, Saratoga Springs, N.Y., 1908; del. Nat. Conf. on Interstate Liquor Question; some time chaplain Actor's Alliance U.S.; del. World Court Congress, Cleveland, 1915. First to introduce boy's brigade movement from Scotland; also Christian organization of traveling men and railroad men in U.S. Author: A Cloud of Witnesses, 1893. Home: Fenton, Mich. Died Mar. 25, 1918.

NORTHRUP, Ansel Judd, lawyer; b. Madison County, N.Y., June 30, 1833; s. Rensselaer and Clarissa (Judd) N.; brother of William Perry N.; A.B. (salutatorian), Hamilton Coll., 1858, A.M., 1861, LL.D., 1895; law student, Columbia, 1858-59; m. Eliza Sophia Fitch, Nov. 24, 1863 (died 1914). Admitted to N.Y. bar, 1859, and in practice at Syracuse, 1859—, except while judge. U.S. Circuit Ct. commr., 1870-97; U.S. commr., 1897—; judge Onondaga Co., 1882-94; commr. to revise the statutes and code of N.Y., 1895-1901. V.p. and pres. Loyal League during and after Civil War; lay commr. to General Assembly Presbyn. Ch., Saratoga, 1890, Buffalo, 1904, Atlantic City, 1910. Trustee Syracuse Savings Bank, Oakwood Cemetery. President Onondaga Hist. Assn. Author: The Powers and Duties of Elders in the Presbyterian Church; Northrup Genealogy, 1908; "The Judiciary," in Polit. History of N.Y. from Cleveland to Hughes, 1911. Editor: History of the Class of 1858, Hamilton College, 1898; 75th Anniversary, First Presbyterian Church, Syracuse, 1899; Early Records of the First Presbyterian Church, Syracuse, 1902. Republican. Presbyterian. Home: Syracuse, N.Y. Deceased.

NORTHRUP, Edwin Fitch, electrothermic engr.; b. Syracuse, N.Y., Feb. 23, 1866; s. Ansel Judd and Eliza Sophia (Fitch) N.; A.B., Amherst, 1891; Cornell U. last half of 1891; fellow and Ph.D. in physics, Johns Hopkins, 1895; hon. D.Sc., Lehigh U., 1932; m. Margaret Jane Stewart, Oct. 9, 1900. In practical elec. work in the West, 1895-96; prof. physics, U. of Tex., 1896-97; became asst. to Prof. H. A. Rowland, Baltimore, 1898, in development of his multiplex printing telegraph system, and later chief constructing engr. Rowland Printing Telegraph Co. until 1902; sec. Leeds & Northrup Co., mfrs. of elec. instruments, Phila., 1903-10; mem. physics faculty, Princeton U., 1910-20; v.p. and tech. adviser Ajax Electrothermic Corp., Trenton, N.J. Has been granted a number of U.S. patents for new instruments and methods of producing and measuring high temperatures. Author: Methods of Measuring Electrical Resistance, 1912; Laws of Physical Science, 1917; Zero to Eighty, 1937. Extended research upon elec. conductivity and properties of matter at elevated temperatures. Inventor of Ajax-Northrup high frequency induction furnace; patentee of methods and numerous devices for inductive heating used throughout the world; developed means for producing high speed linear motions with polyphase currents. Médaille de bronze, Paris Expn., 1900; Edward Longstreth medal, 1912; Elliott Cresson medal, 1916; Edward Goodrich Acheson gold medal and $1,000, 1931. Home: Princeton, N.J. Died Apr. 29, 1940.

NORTHRUP, George Washington, prof. systematic theology U. of Chicago, 1892—; b. Antwerp, N.Y., Oct. 15, 1826; grad. Williams, 1854, Rochester Theol. Sem., 1857; D.D., Rochester, 1864; LL.D., Kalamazoo, 1879. Ordained Baptist minister, Rochester, N.Y., 1857; prof. ch. history Rochester Theol. Sem., 1856-57; pres. and prof. systematic theology Baptist Union Theol. Sem., Morgan Park, Ill., 1867-92. Address: Chicago, Ill. Died 1900.

NORTHRUP, William Perry, M.D.; b. Peterboro, N.Y., Jan. 11, 1851; s. Rensselaer and Clarissa (Judd) N.; A.B., Hamilton Coll., 1872, A.M., 1875; M.D., Coll. Physicians and Surgeons (Columbia), 1878; LL.D., Knox Coll., Galesburg, Ill., 1920; m. Antoinette Stebbins, Sept. 1, 1886 (dec.); m. 2d, Julia Radcliffe Cowing, Feb. 1914 (died 1922). Instr. Greek, Knox Coll., 1872-76; adj. prof. pediatrics, 1893-96, prof., 1896-1919, emeritus prof., 1919—; Univ. and Bellevue Hosp. Med. Coll. (New York U.). Attending phys. to Presbyn. Hosp., cons. prof. pediatric service, 1919—; cons. phys. New York Foundling Hosp.; cons. phys. to Willard Parker Hosp. and the hospitals of Health Dept. of New York, N.Y. Infant Asylum, Washington Heights Hosp., Open Air Hosp. for tuberculosis in children, Seabreeze, Coney Island, N.Y. (under care of Assn. for Improvement Condition of the Poor), Babies' Hosp., Newark, N.J., State Orthopedic Hosp., Haverstraw, N.Y. American editor: Ashley and Wright's Diseases of Children, 1900; Nothnagel's Encyclopædia of Practical Medicine, Am. edit., vol. 4, 1902; wrote original article on diphtheria in latter. Contbr. to med. jours. on open air treatment of pneumonia, open air roof gardens on city houses, open air roof wards, city hosp., etc. Address: New York, N.Y. Died Nov. 20, 1935.

NORTHUP, John Eldridge, lawyer; b. Marshall County, Ia., Aug. 28, 1868; s. James Eldridge and Ippoletta (Eastman) N.; A.B., Drake U., Des Moines, Ia., 1891; grad. student U. of Chicago, 1893-95; m. Mary Elizabeth Chisholm, Dec. 26, 1894; 1 dau., Dorothy. Admitted to Ill. bar, 1899, and practiced at Chicago, 1899—; mem. Pringle, Northup & Terwilliger, 1902-04, Northup, Arnold & Fairbank, 1912-16, Northup & Klein, 1917-22; with Mayer, Meyer, Austrian & Platt, 1922-26; asst. state's atty., Cook Co., 1906-12; spl. state's atty. Cook Co., 1913-14; spl. asst. to atty. gen. of U.S., 1921-22; 1st asst. U.S. dist. atty., 1926-29; apptd. 1st asst. states atty., Ill., 1929, and led in securing Chicago Sanitary Dist. fraud convictions, 1932. Mem. firm Kane, Northup & Rathbun. Presbyn. Mason, Odd Fellow; mem. Royal League. Home: Chicago, Ill. Died Oct. 10, 1940.

NORTHUP, William Guile, banker, mfr.; b. Salisbury Centre, N.Y., July 21, 1851; s. Daniel A. and Louisa (Guile) N.; ed. pub. schs.; m. Leila Tucker, Nov. 12, 1874; children—Marjorie, William Guile. Connected with mfr. of woolens, at Minneapolis, 1874—; pres. North Star Woolen Mill, 1898—; chmn. bd. Farmers' & Mechanics' Savings Bank; v.p. Minneapolis Trust Co., Real Estate Title Ins. Co.; dir. First Nat. Bank, Minneapolis-Trust Joint Stock Land Bank. Trustee Washburn Memorial Home. Republican. Universalist. Home: Wayzata, Minn. Died July 31, 1929.

NORTON, Alice Peloubet (Mrs. Lewis Mills Norton), writer lecturer; b. Gloucester, Mass., Feb. 25, 1860; d. Francis N. (D.D.) and Mary Abby (Thaxter) Peloubet; A.B., Smith Coll., 1882, A.M., 1897; Boston Normal Sch. of Household Arts, 1896; Mass. Inst. Tech., 1896-97; grad. work U. of Chicago; m. Lewis Mills Norton, June 6, 1883 (died 1893); children—Margaret, John Foote, Grace Peloubet (Mrs. E. H. Lorenz), Louise Chabrier (Mrs. G. W. Swain), Lewis Mills. Teacher high sch., Brookline, Mass., 1896-1900; teacher Chicago Inst., 1900-01; asst. prof. teaching of home economics, Sch. of Edn. U. of Chicago, 1901-04; asst. prof. household administration, U. of Chicago, 1904-13; dietitian of Cook Co. (Ill.) Instns., 1913-14; sec. Am. Home Economics Assn., 1915-18; editor Jour. Home Economics, Baltimore, 1915-20; prof. home economics, Constantinople Woman's Coll., 1920-23; acting head of Home Economics Dept. Ind. U., 1924-25. Lecturer Hartford Sch. of Sociology, 1894, Lasell Sem., 1893-99, Y.W.C.A. Sch. of Domestic Science, Boston, 1895-1900, Boston Cooking Sch., 1898-1900. Dir. Chautauqua (N.Y.) Sch. Domestic Science, 1909-05, 1915-17; editor for home economics, U.S. Food Administration, July 1917-Dec. 1918; with war savings div., Treasury Dept., 1919. Alumnæ trustee Smith Coll., 1905-08. Author: Food and Dietetics; Food for Children; The Cooked Food Supply. Address: Northampton, Mass. Died Feb. 23, 1928.

NORTON, Arthur Brigham, oculist; b. New Marlborough, Mass., Sept. 15, 1856; s. Salmon K. and Sarah Jane (Brigham) N.; ed. New Marlborough Acad., Great Barrington High Sch.; M.D., New York Homœ. Med. Coll. and Hosp., 1881; College of New York Ophthalmic Hosp., 1882, (degree Oculi et Auris Chirurgus); m. Leah Louise Pixley, Nov. 25, 1885. Prof. ophthalmology, New York Homœ. Med. Coll. and Hosp., 1902-07, Coll. New York Ophthal. Hospital, 1882—; oculist to the Hahnemann and Laura Franklin Free hosps.; surgeon New York Ophthal. Hosp. Pres. N.Y. County Homœ. Med. Soc. Author: Ophthalmic Diseases and Therapeutics; Essentials of Diseases of the Eye, 1904. Address: New York, N.Y. Died June 18, 1919.

NORTON, Arthur Henry, college pres.; b. Hartford, N.Y., Dec. 9, 1870; s. Lyman and Cynthia (Gates) N.; B.S., Syracuse U., 1899, Pd.D., 1916; A.M., Colgate, 1913; m. Susen Perlet Hurd, July 23, 1902; children—Ruth Norton, Mary Norton; (stepchildren) Dr. Charles D. Hurd, Mrs. Gertrude Hurd Benedict. Began teaching dist. sch., 1891; prin. Mexico (N.Y.) Acad., 1900-04, Cook Acad., Montour Falls, 1904-11; prof. mathematics and astronomy, Elmira Coll., 1911-19, v.p. 1916-19; pres. (first) Keuka Coll. for Women, 1919-35 (later emeritus); dir. Elmira Sch. Religious Edn., 1916-19; chmn. Yates County Consumers Council. Made survey of 76 schs. and colls. for Interch. World Movement, 1919-20; Y.M.C.A. sec. in France, with 26th Div., 1 yr.; div. dir. Neufchâteau Area; personally commended by Gen. Pershing, for service at the front. Pres. Bapt. Missionary Conv. of N.Y., 1926-27; mem. exec. com. N.Y. State S. S. Assn.; mem. examining com. New York State Regents, 1927. Trustee Keuka Coll.; v.p. Bapt. Missionary Conv. of N.Y., 1925-26; mem. finance com. Bapt. Missionary Conv., 1932-34. Mason. Address: Keuka Park, N.Y. Died Apr. 30, 1939.

NORTON, Charles Dyer, banker; b. Oshkosh, Wis., Mar. 12, 1871; s. Rev. Franklin B. and Harriet (Dyer) N.; A.B., Amherst, 1893; m. Katherine McKim Garrison, Oct. 23, 1897. Employed by Scribner's Mag., New York, 1893; with Northwestern Mut. Life Ins. Co., Chicago, 1895-1909; asst. sec. of the Treasury, 1909-10; sec. to the President (Taft) 1910-11; v.p. First Nat. Bank of N.Y., 1911-18; pres. First Security Co., N.Y., 1918—. Also pres. Coal & Coke Ry. Co., New Gauley Coal Corp.; v.p. W.Va. Coal & Coke Co.; trustee Adams Express Co.; dir. Am. Ry. Express Co., First Nat. Bank, Equitable Life Assurance Soc., Montgomery Ward & Co., Del., Lackawanna & Western Coal Co., Am. Telephone & Telegraph Co., First Security Co., W.P. Railway Co., Tide Water Oil Co., Tide Water Pipe Line Co., Southwestern Constrn. Co., Mont. Farming Corp. Trustee Am. Red Cross, Metropolitan Museum of Art, Am. Acad. in Rome; trustee, treas. Am. Fedn. of Arts, Russell Sage Foundation, Sage Foundation Homes Co. Home: New York, N.Y. Died Mar. 6, 1922.

NORTON, Charles Eliot, prof. history of art, Harvard, 1874-98, prof. emeritus, 1898—; b. Cambridge, Mass., Nov. 16, 1827; s. Prof. Andrews and Catherine (Eliot) N.; grad. Harvard, 1846; Litt.D., Cambridge, Eng., 1884; L.H.D., Columbia, 1885; LL.D., Harvard, 1887, Yale, 1901; hon. D.C.L., Oxford U., Eng., 1900; m. Susan, d. Theodore Sedgwick, 1862. Entered commercial office in Boston, 1846; went as supercargo on East Indian voyage, 1849; later made several trips to Europe. Known as a Dante scholar and an authority on art; 1st pres. Archæol. Inst. America, 1879-90; pres. Dante Soc. Author: Considerations on Some Recent Social Theories; Historical Studies of Church Building in the Middle Ages; Notes of Travel and Study in Italy. Editor: North American Review, 1862-68; Letters of James Russell Lowell; Writings of George William Curtis; Correspondence of Carlyle and Emerson, and of Gœthe and Carlyle; Reminiscences and Letters of Thomas Carlyle; Letters of John Ruskin. Translator of Dante's Vita Nuova and Divina Commedia. Address: Cambridge, Mass. Died 1908.

NORTON, Charles Ladd, engr.; b. Springfield, Mass., Dec. 11, 1870; s. Francis and Jennie Maria (Atwater) N.; B.S., Mass. Inst. Tech., 1893; m. Frances Torrey, Sept. 24, 1895. Prof. Industrial physics and dir. Div. Industrial Coöperation and Research, Mass. Inst. Tech.; officer and dir. of a number of indusl. corps., interested in the manufacture of asbestos products; cons. engr. on matters relating to heat and fire protection. Fellow Am. Acad. Arts and Sciences. Episcopalian. Home: Boston, Mass. Died Sept. 8, 1939.

NORTON, Charles Ledyard, author; b. Farmington, Conn., June 11, 1837; s. John Treadwell and Elizabeth (Cogswell) N.; grad. Yale, 1859; studied in Yale Scientific Sch. until outbreak of Civil war; private 7th N.Y.N.G., 1861-62; capt. 25th Conn. vols., 1862-63; col. 78th U.S. colored troops, 1863-66; served mainly in Dept. of Gulf; mustered out, Jan. 1866; m. E. Mélanie Richards, Sept. 1, 1863 (died 1900); m. 2d, A. E. Phillips, 1904. Editor Christian Union, 1868-78; editor Domestic Monthly, American Canoeist, Outing, etc. Author: Canoeing in Kanuckia (with John Habberton); A Handbook of Florida; Political Americanisms; Jack Benson's Log; A Medal of Honor Man; Midshipman Jack; A Soldier of the Legion; The Queen's Rangers. Home: Sandwich, Mass. Died 1909.

NORTON, Charles Phelps, lawyer, educator; b. Buffalo, N.Y., May 15, 1858; s. Charles Davis and Mary Jeanette (Phelps) N.; A.B., Harvard, 1880; unmarried. Practiced in Buffalo, 1885—; organized Buffalo Law Sch., 1887; registrar, lecturer, instr. and prof. elementary law, contracts, practice, and bills and notes, for 21 yrs.; elected v. chancellor U. of Buffalo, 1905, chancellor, 1909-20, both offices unsalaried; created under-grad. depts., uniting them with local professional schs. and organizing a municipal univ. to continue work of pub. schs. which, in 1920, was endowed by popular subscription. Republican. Presbyn. Author: Norton on Bills and Notes (Horn Book Series), 1893. Home: Buffalo, N.Y. Died July 11, 1922.

NORTON, Charles Stuart, rear adm. U.S.N.; b. Albany, N.Y., Aug. 10, 1836; grad. U.S. Naval Acad., 1855; m. Mary E. Pentz, Mar. 29, 1872; m. 2d, Elisabeth Killough, July 25, 1906. Passed midshipman, 1858; master, 1858; lt., 1860; lt. comdr., 1862; comdr., 1870; capt., 1881; commodore, 1894; rear adm., Feb. 1, 1898. Served during Civil War on Charleston, S.C., blockade, Potomac Flotilla and at Hampton Roads, Va., 1861-62, participating in several engagements; at battle of Port Royal, S.C.; in N. Atlantic Blockading Squadron, 1862-64; W. Gulf Blockading Squadron, 1864-65; after war comd. several vessels and served on Bd. of Inspection and Survey; rear adm. comdg. S. Atlantic Sta., 1894-96; comd. Washington Navy Yard and Sta., 1896-98; retired by operation of law, Aug. 10, 1898. Home: Westfield, N.J. Died 1911.

NORTON, David Z., banker; hon. A.M.; LL.D.; m. Mary, d. William B. and Mary (Newell) Castle, Oct. 11, 1876; children—Miriam (Mrs. F. R. White), Robert Castle, Laurence Harper. Became messenger Commercial Nat. Bank, Cleveland, Apr. 1, 1868, later cashier until 1890, when resigned to enter firm of Oglebay, Norton & Co., iron ore; pres. Citizens Savings & Loan Assn. until it was merged with the Citizens Savings & Trust Co., of which was 1st v.p., and pres., 1910-19; v.p. Baker R. & L. Co.; dir. Am. Shipbuilding Co., Nat. Refining Co., Columbia Steamship Co., Union Trust Co.; trustee Soc. for Savings, Lake View Cemetery Assn. Trustee Western Reserve U., Adelbert Coll., Kenyon Coll., Cleveland Mus. of Art, Art Sch., University Sch., Western Reserve Hist. Soc. Home: Cleveland, O. Died Jan. 6, 1928.

NORTON, Edith Eliza Ames ("Eliza Dunn"), author; b. Lockport, N.Y., Dec. 6, 1864; d. Col. James D. and Helen Exena (Allen) Ames; m. Thomas Herbert Norton, Dec. 27, 1883; 1 son, Robert Ames. Mem. Nat. Inst. Social Sciences, D.A.R., Soc. Colonial Dames. Extensive travels in Africa, Asia and Europe. Author: Rugs in Their Native Land, 1910. Oriental rug expert. Home: White Plains, N.Y. Died Oct. 30, 1929.

NORTON, Edwin, manufacturer, inventor; b. Rockton, Ill., Mar. 27, 1845; s. Oliver W. and Henrietta W. N.; ed. common schs.; served in Union Army in Civil War; m. Lucy E. Akin, Oct. 9, 1876. Inventor and mfr. sheet metal working machinery, rolling mills; v.p. Norton Bros., Chicago, many yrs.; 1st pres. Am. Can Co. Among his notable inventions are: Automatic furnace and rolling mill for making tin plate and thin sheet steel; machine for automatic manufacture of hermetically sealed cans; machines and processes for preserving food products in vacuum. Address: New York, N.Y. Died Jan. 1, 1916.

NORTON, Eliot, lawyer; b. Cambridge, Mass., July 1, 1863; s. Charles Eliot (prof. history of fine arts, Harvard, 25 yrs.) and Susan Ridley (Sedgwick) N.; cousin of Charles William Eliot; A.B., Harvard, 1885, A.M., LL.B., 1888; m. Margaret Palmer Meyer, Sept. 2, 1890. Admitted to bar, 1889, in practice at New York, 1889—; counsel for a number of prominent individuals and large corporations. Decorated by King of Italy as Chevalier Order of Sts. Maurico and Lazare. Author: Lincoln, Lover of Men. Home: New York, N.Y. Died Oct. 18, 1932.

NORTON, Frederick Owen, educator; b. Brudenell, P.E.I., Can., Feb. 3, 1868; s. Frederick Peter and Ann Rosina (Davis) N.; student Prince of Wales Coll., P.E.I., 2 yrs.; A.B., (highest honors and valedictorian), Transylvania Coll., 1893, A.M., 1895; classical grad. Coll. of the Bible, Lexington, Ky., 1895; fellow U. of Chicago, 1903-06, Ph.D., 1906; m. Frances L. Minter, Nov. 9, 1904. Prin. grammar sch., Hamilton, P.E.I., 1888-89; prin. high sch., New Glasgow, 1889-91; asso. prin., 1895-98, prin., 1899-1900, Western Coll., LaBelle, Mo.; regent and prof. Latin and philosophy, Culver-Stockton Coll., 1898-99; instr.

Univ. High Sch., Chicago, 1903-05; prof. N.T., 1906-18, dean Coll. of Liberal Arts, 1907-22, v.p. and prof. ednl. psychology, 1918-22, Drake U., prof. and head dept. N.T. Lit., 1922—, Crozer Theol. Seminary. In Army Ednl. Corps, A.E.F., as dean Am. soldiers in U. of Paris, France, 1918-19. Author: A Lexicographical and Historical Study of Diatheke, 1908; Christian Bible School Commentary (co-author), 1912; The Rise of Christianity, 1924. Home: Chester, Pa. Died Feb. 29, 1924.

NORTON, George Lowell, editor, pub.; b. Castine, Me., Mar. 1, 1837; s. George Dunham and Eunice (Shepardson) N.; ed. pub. schs., Castine; m. Mary Jane Wainwright, Oct. 12, 1911. Went to sea in boyhood and served on sailing vessels until 1861; officer on steamships in U.S. q.m.'s dept., 1861-65; master on steamships running between New York and Southern ports, 1865-71; harbor master, New Orleans, 1871-76; supervising insp. of steam vessels for Gulf States, by appmt. of Pres. Hayes, 1876-84 (resigned); editor and pub. Marine Journal, New York, 1885—; pres. Marine Journal Co. Commr. of pilots; mem. bd. govs. N.Y. State Nautical Sch.; mem. Nat. Bd. of Steam Navigation. Home: New York, N.Y. Died Mar. 24, 1923.

NORTON, George W., newspaper man; b. Strong, Me., Aug. 25, 1855; s. Jeremiah Rice and Amanda F. (Stevens) N.; grad. State Normal Sch., Farmington, Me., 1876; hon. A.M., Colby Coll., 1908; m. Hattie L. Conant, Dec. 22, 1894. Taught sch. several yrs.; prin. Bridgton, Me., 1878-83, Westbrook, Me., 1883-88; reporter, 1888-92, editor, 1892—, Portland Evening Express. Del.-at-large Rep. Nat. Conv., 1900; treas. Rep. State Com.; mem. Me. Exec. Council, 1917-20. Sec. state com. of the No-License Movement, in Me., 1911. Home: Portland, Me. Died Oct. 22, 1920.

NORTON, George Washington, trustee; b. Russellville, Ky., Sept. 12, 1865; s. George W. and Martha (Henry) N.; Ph.B., Yale, 1885; m. Margaret Macdonald Muldoon, June 8, 1897. Mgr., executor or trustee of estates, 1889—; dir. Louisville br. Federal Reserve Bank of St. Louis, B. F. Avery & Sons, Inc., Price Chem. Co., Louisville Ry. Co. Chmn. financial bd. Southern Bapt. Theol. Sem. Republican. Address: Louisville, Ky. Died Dec. 10, 1924.

NORTON, Grace, author; b. Cambridge, Mass., Apr. 7, 1834; d. Andrews and Catherine (Eliot) N.; pvt. edn. Author: Studies in Montaigne, 1904; Early Writings of Montaigne and Other Papers, 1904. Compiler and Editor: Le Plutarque de Montaigne, 1906; The Influence of Montaigne; The Spirit of Montaigne, 1908. Address: Cambridge, Mass. Died May 5, 1926.

NORTON, Harold Percival, naval officer; b. New York, N.Y., Nov. 4, 1855; s. Charles E., and Emily A. (Norton) N.; grad. U.S. Naval Acad., 1879; m. Mrs. D. P. McCartney, née Mary V. Barbour, Dec. 27, 1911. Promoted asst. engr., June 10, 1881; passed asst. engr., Oct. 12, 1891; chief engr., Feb. 10, 1899; transferred to the line as lt., Mar. 3, 1899; lt. commander, Oct. 26, 1901; commander, Oct. 10, 1906; captain, Sept. 16, 1910; rear admiral, July 1, 1918. Served at Elswick, England, as insp. machinery for the Albany, 1898-1900; on Albany, 1900-04; at Navy Yard, N.Y. City, 1904-06; with Bur. Steam Engring., Navy Dept., 1906-10; insp. engring., Navy Dept., 1910-11; with Bur. Steam Engring., 1911-12; mem. Bd. Inspection Shore Stations, Navy Dept., 1912-13; apptd. mem. Naval Examining Bd., Washington, D.C., July 28, 1913. Episcopalian. Home: Washington, D.C. Died Feb. 11, 1933.

NORTON, John Warner, painter; b. Lockport, Ill., Mar. 7, 1876; s. John Lyman and Ada (Gooding) N.; Harvard, 1895-97; Art Inst. Chicago, 1900-02, M.F.A., 1927; m. Margaret Francis, Sept. 2, 1903; children—Margaret Francis (Mrs. Henry Garrett), John Francis, Nan. Specialist in mural decorations. Prin. bldgs. decorated: Sioux City (Ia.) Court House; Tavern Club, Daily News Bldg., Loyola U. Library, Board of Trade Bldg., Chicago Motor Club (all Chicago); Beloit (Wis.) Coll. Mus. of Ethnology. Rep. at Art Inst. Chicago. Awarded gold medal, Am. Inst. Architects. Served with 1st U.S. Vol. Cav., Spanish-Am. War. Home: Chicago, Ill. Died Jan. 7, 1934.

NORTON, Porter, lawyer; b. Buffalo, N.Y., July 9, 1853; s. Charles Davis and Jeanette (Phelp) N.; m. Jeanie W. Norton, July 9, 1879. Admitted to N.Y. bar, 1874, practiced at Buffalo, 1874—; sr. mem. firm of Norton, Penney, Spring & Moore; dir. Western N.Y. & Pa. Ry. Co., Internat. Ry. Co. Trustee DeVeaux Coll., Niagara Falls, N.Y. Republican. Episcopalian. Home: Buffalo, N.Y. Died Feb. 2, 1918.

NORTON, Richard, educator; b. Dresden, Germany, Feb. 9, 1872; s. Charles Eliot and Susan (Sedgwick) N.; A.B., Harvard, 1892; studied afterwards in Germany and at Am. Sch. of Classical Studies, Athens. Dir. Am. Sch. of Classical Studies, Rome, 1899-1907; visited Central Asia for purpose of archæol. investigation, 1903, and the Cyrenaïca, 1904 and 1909. Dir. of Archæol. Inst. of America and Boston Mus. Fine Arts expn. to excavate ruins of Cyrene, 1910-11. Organizer and head of Am. Vol. Motor Ambulance Corps, serving with the French army, 1914-18. Died Aug. 2, 1918.

NORTON, Sidney Augustus, chemist; b. Bloomfield, Trumbull County, O., Jan. 11, 1835; s. Charles H. and Caroline Brayton (Cornell) N.; A.B., Union Coll., N.Y., 1856, A.M., 1859; M.D., Miami Med. Coll., Cincinnati, 1869; univs. of Bonn, Leipzig and Heidelberg, 1870-71; hon. M.D., Western Reserve, 1869; Ph.D., Kenyon, 1878; LL.D., U. of Wooster, 1881, Union U., 1899; m. Sarah J. Chamberlain, June 20, 1864 (died 1868); m. 2d, Jessie Carter, June 20, 1876 (died 1911). Instr. natural science, Cleveland High Sch., 1858-66; prof. chemistry, Miami Med. Coll., 1867-72; acting prof. physics, Union Coll., 1873; prof. chemistry, Starling Med. Coll., 1878-79; prof. chemistry, 1873-95, prof. emeritus, 1899, Ohio State U. Author: Elements of Natural Philosophy, 1870; Essays and Notes, 1874; Elements of Physics, 1875; Elements of Inorganic Chemistry, 1878; Organic Chemistry, 1884. Editor revised edition of Weld's English Grammar, 1863. Address: Columbus, O. Died Aug. 30, 1918.

NORTON, Stephen Alison, clergyman; b. Bradford, Pa., June 9, 1854; s. William W. and Frances (McCoy) N.; Carleton College, Minn., 1872-76, D.D., 1895; A.B., Amherst, 1878; Hartford (Conn.) Theol. Sem., 1879; B.D., Chicago Theol. Sem., 1881; m. Therina L. Hunt, 1881 (died 1897); children—Paul Willard, Ruth (dec.); m. 2d, Mary F. Penfield, May 20, 1899; 1 dau., Dorothy Penfield. Ordained Congl. ministry, 1881; pastor, Amboy, Ill., 1881-84, Princeton, Ill., 1884-91, Highland, Calif., 1892-93, First Ch., San Diego, Calif., 1894-1902, 1st Ch., Woburn, Mass., 1902-22, Manhattan Beach, Calif., 1922-25, retired; pastor emeritus Woburn (Mass.), 1st Congl. Ch., 1925—. Dir. Congl. Publ., Edn., and Home Missionary socs. Author: The Old Puritanism and the New Age, 1903; The Call of the Heights, 1910. Home: Claremont, Calif. Died Jan. 1, 1930.

NORTON, William Bernard, religious editor; b. Freeport, Ill., Oct. 19, 1857; s. Galen G. and Julia Frances (Ford) N.; A.B., Northwestern U., 1880, A.M., 1883; B.D., Garrett Bibl. Inst., 1882; Ph.D., Syracuse U., 1896; m. Marie Therese Werneburg, Dec. 23, 1881; children—Mrs. Louise N. French, Lowrey Ford (dec.), Mrs. Julia N. Clemes, Frederic Wm. Pastor chs. in Ia. and Ill. until 1908; writer City News Bur. of Chicago, 1906-08; religious editor Chicago Tribune, 1908-29; editor Methodist Episcopal Advocate (monthly), 1910-19. Research sec. Methodist Hist. Soc., Rock River Conf., 1910-29; corr. sec. and annalist, Garrett Biblical Inst. Alumni, 1905-26. Spent 2 yrs. in tour of the Orient, Egypt, Palestine and Europe. Republican. Mason. Author: Church and Newspaper, 1930; Facing the Golden West (poems), 1931. Lecturer on India and newspapers. Founder, 1936, of lectureship on ch. and newspaper in Garrett Biblical Inst., Evanston, Ill. Home: Portland, Ore. Died Aug. 31, 1936.

NORTON, William Edward, artist; b. Boston, Mass., June 28, 1843; s. Daniel and Mary (Carr) N.; pupil Lowell Inst., Boston, of George Inness, of Jacquesson, de la Chevreuse, and A. Vollon, Paris; m. Sarah D. Ryan, Sept. 23, 1868 (died 1904). Awarded 3 gold medals in America; hon. mention, Paris Salon, 1895. Exhibited at Paris Expn., 1900; regular exhibitor at the Royal Acad., London, and exhibited Phila., Chicago, St. Louis expns.; awarded Osborne prize for marine painting, 1905, and again, 1906. Address: New York, N.Y. Died Feb. 25, 1916.

NORTONI, Albert Dexter, lawyer; b. New Cambria, Macon County, Mo., Jan. 26, 1867; s. Dr. Edward Warren and Hannah T. (Howell) N.; ed. in common schs. and by pvt. instrn.; m. Maggie L. Francis, Dec. 22, 1892 (died 1894); m. 2d, Emma T. Belcher, July 3, 1906. Practiced in Macon, Linn and Chariton cos., Mo., and at St. Louis; city atty., New Cambria, 2 terms; pvt. sec. to Congressman C. N. Clark, 1 term; Rep. nominee for probate judge of Macon Co., 1894 (declined); apptd., Jan. 1, 1903, asst. U.S. dist. atty., and moved to St. Louis; judge St. Louis Court of Appeals, 1905-16; resigned and resumed practice; apptd. judge Circuit Court, City of St. Louis, May 20, 1931, presiding in Div. No. 2 in equity; member Mo. Public Service Commission, 1936-41; v.p. Continental Life Ins. Co., Continental Securities & Holding Co. Curator U. of Mo., 1913-19, also of Forest Park Coll., St. Louis; mem. Mo. Code Commn., 1914-15; served as mem. mng. com. Sch. of Mines and Metallurgy, Rolla, Mo., 1913-19. Progressive candidate for gov. of Mo., 1912, and mem. exec. com. Progressive Nat. Com.; del. at large Progressive Nat. Conv., 1912 (platform com.) and chmn. Mo. nat. delegation, 1916; dir. Progressive Bur. Dem. Nat. Com., 1916; dir. Non-Partisan Assn. for League of Nations of World Court. Mem. S.R. (pres. St. Louis Chapter, 1928; v.p. State Soc. and mem. state bd. mgrs.), N.E. Soc. of St. Louis (pres. 1922-23, also 1931-32). Presbyn. Home: St. Louis, Mo. Deceased.

NORWOOD, C(harles) Augustus, lawyer; b. Hamilton, Mass., Aug. 21, 1880; s. Caleb J. and Martha A. (Dane) N.; A.B., Harvard, 1902, LL.B., 1905; m. Elisabeth F. Gragg, Mar. 25, 1916. Admitted to Mass. bar, 1905, practiced at Boston, 1905—; gen. counsel First Ch. of Christ, Scientist, 1917-29; now mgr. coms. on publication of the church. Mem. Mass. legislature, 1911, 12, Senate, 1913-15. Republican. Mason. Home: Brookline, Mass. Died May 25, 1940.

NORWOOD, Charles Joseph, geologist, mining engr.; b. New Harmony, Ind., Sept. 17, 1853; s. Joseph Granville and Mary Frances (Pugh) N.; ed. U. of Mo. and under pvt. teachers, M.S., Ky. Agrl. and Mech. Coll., 1906; m. Sarah E. White, Oct. 5, 1876. Asst. geologist, Mo. Geol. Survey, 1872-74, Ky. Geol. Survey, 1874-80; prof. natural science, Bethel Coll., Russellville, Ky., 1877-81; editorial writer Russellville Herald-Enterprise, 1879-82; mining engr., gold, silver and coal companies, 7 yrs.; chief insp. mines, Ky., 1884-97; curator Ky. State Geol. Dept., 1893-97; dean and prof. mining and metallurgy, Coll. Mines and Metallurgy of State U. of Ky., Jan. 1902-June 1918; chief State Dept. of Mines, 1902-20; dir. State Geol. Survey, 1904-12; prof. mining and head dept. mines and metallurgy, Coll. of Engring., U. of Ky., Jan. 1920—. Supt. and designer Ky. mineral exhibit, St. Louis Expn., 1904; represented Ky. at Nat. Conf. Weights and Measures, 1906-07; mem. Ky. Commn., Jamestown Expn., 1907. Episcopalian. Mason (32°). Home: Lexington, Ky. Died Jan. 20, 1927.

NORWOOD, Edwin P., author; b. Cucamonga, San Bernardino County, Calif., Apr. 20, 1881; s. Edwin P. and Mary Emma (Craig) Norwood; grad. high school, San Bernardino, 1900; m. Ann Bussert (concert and opera singer), 1923. Newspaper reporter until 1905, later publicity dir. amusement enterprises on Pacific Coast and handling nat. concert tours; spl. rep. Maude Adams, 1915-16; in charge publicity for Ringling Bros., 1917-27; institutional writing, Ford Motor Co., 1930-32; publicity dir. Lyme Art Assn., 1934-35, mng. dir., 1936—. Author: The Adventures of Diggeldy Dan, 1922; In the Land of Diggeldy Dan, 1923; The Friends of Diggeldy Dan, 1924; Davy Winkle in Circusland, 1926; The Other Side of the Circus, 1926; The Circus Menagerie, 1929; Ford Men and Methods, 1931. Contbr. to Ency. Britannica, article, "American Circus," 1929. Home: Old Lyme, Conn. Died Oct. 13, 1940.

NORWOOD, Robert, clergyman; b. New Ross, N.S., Mar. 27, 1874; s. Joseph William and Edith Matilda (Harding) N.; B.A., U. of King's Coll., Windsor, N.S., 1897, M.A., 1902, D.C.L., 1921; post-grad. work in philosophy, Columbia, 1908-10; D.Litt., Acadia U., Wolfville, N.S., 1924; S.T.D., U. of Pa., 1926; D.D., Rollins Coll., 1929; m. Ethel McKeen, Sept. 12, 1899; children—Aileen, Jean, Robert Edmund (dec.). Deacon, 1897, priest, 1898, P.E. Ch.; missionary, St. Andrew's Ch., Neil's Harbor, Cape Breton, 1898-99; curate St. Luke's Ch., Hubbards, N.S., 1899-1901; rector Trinity Ch., Bridgewater, N.S., 1901-07, All Saints Ch., Spring Hill, 1908-10; asst. rector Trinity Ch., Montreal, Can., 1910-12; rector Memorial Ch., London, Ont., 1912-17, St. Paul's Ch., Overbrook, Phila., 1917-25, St. Bartholomew's Ch., New York, 1925—. Naturalized citizen of U.S., 1923. Author: His Lady of the Sonnets, 1915; The Witch of Endor, 1916; The Piper and the Reed, 1917; The Modernists, 1918; The Man of Kerioth, 1919; Bill Boram, 1921; Mother and Son, 1925; The Heresy of Antioch, 1928; The Steep Ascent, 1928; The Man Who Dared to Be God, 1929; His Glorious Body, 1930; Issa, 1931. Home: New York, N.Y. Died Sept. 28, 1932.

NORWOOD, Thomas Manson, senator; b. Talbot County, Ga., Apr. 26, 1830; s. Caleb Merriman and Jeannette (Manson) N.; A.B., Emory Coll., Ga., 1850; m. Anna M. Hendree, June 2, 1853 (dec.). Taught sch., 1851, Monroe County, Ga.; admitted to Ga. bar, Mar. 1852; established practice at Savannah; pvt. in C.S.A.; U.S. senator, 1871-77; candidate of one of the two factions of Dem. party for gov. of Ga., 1880; mem. Ga. Ho. of Rep., 1885-89; resumed practice of law at Savannah, 1889-96; judge City Ct. of Savannah, 1896-1908; retired, Jan. 1, 1908. Author: Plutocracy, or American White Slavery (politico-social novel), 1888; Mother Goose Carved by a Commentator, 1900; Patriotism, Democracy or Empire—A Satire, 1900. Home: Savannah, Ga. Died June 19, 1913.

NOSS, Theodore Bland, educator; b. Waterloo, Juniata County, Pa., May 10, 1852; s. Rev. George and Isabella (Coulter) N.; ed. pub. schs., Nossville, Pa.; grad. State Normal Sch., Shippensburg, Pa., 1874, Syracuse U., 1880, Ph.D., 1883; m. Mary Blanche Graham, May 17, 1883. Traveled and studied in Europe, 1879, 1889 and 1893; prin. State Normal Sch., California, Pa., 1883—. Republican. Local preacher M.E. Ch.; lay del. Gen. Conf. M.E. Ch., Cleveland, 1896; active mem. Nat. Ednl. Assn., pres. normal dept., 1899. Author: (publ. State Normal Sch.): Outlines of Psychology and Pedagogy, 1890; The Child Study Record, 1900; The Chapel Hymnal, 1900. Address: California, Pa. Died 1909.

NOTESTEIN, Jonas O., coll. prof.; b. Canaan, O., July 11, 1849; s. I. N. and Elizabeth (Frank) N.; A.B., U. of Wooster, O., 1873, A.M., 1876; Litt.D., Western U. of Pa., now U. of Pittsburgh, 1897; L.H.D., Wabash Coll., Ind., 1921; LL.D., Coll. of Wooster, 1923; m. Margaret J. Wallace, Aug. 9, 1876;

children—Wallace, Mary B. (dec.), Frank B., Lucy Lilian, Margaret W. Instr. Latin, 1873-74, adj. prof., 1874-80, prof. Latin lang. and lit., 1880—, Coll. of Wooster. Editor Wooster Quarterly, 1889-1920. Commissioner Gen. Assembly Presbyn. Ch., 1892, 1926. Home: Wooster, Ohio. Died June 15, 1928.

NOTT, Charles Cooper, judge; b. Schenectady, N.Y., Sept. 16, 1827; s. Joel Benedict and Margaret Tayler (Cooper) N.; A.B., Union College, 1848; LL.D., Williams, 1874; m. Alice Effingham Hopkins, Oct. 22, 1867. Practiced law at New York until outbreak of Civil War; served as captain 5th Iowa Cavalry and colonel 176th New York Volunteers; captured at fall of Brashear, La., June 1863; prisoner in Tex. for 13 months. Apptd. by President Lincoln, Feb. 22, 1865, judge of Court of Claims; apptd. chief justice same, Nov. 23, 1896, by President Cleveland; retired, Dec. 31, 1905. Author: Mechanics' Lien Laws; Sketches of the War; Sketches of Prison Camps; The Seven Great Hymns of the Mediæval Church; Court of Claims Reports (48 vols.); The Mystery of the Pinckney Draught, New York, 1909. Home: Princeton, New Jersey. Died Mar. 6, 1916.

NOTTINGHAM, William, lawyer; b. Town of De Witt, Onondaga County, N.Y., Nov. 2, 1853; s. Van Vleck and Abigail Maria (Williams) N.; A.B., Syracuse U., 1876, A.M., 1877, Ph.D., 1878, LL.D., 1903; m. Eloise Holden, Oct. 26, 1881. Admitted to bar, 1879, in practice at Syracuse, 1879—; mem. firm Goodelle & Nottingham, 1881-1900, Goodelle, Nottingham Bros. & Andrews, 1900-07, Nottingham & Nottingham, 1907-10, Nottingham, Nottingham & Edgcomb, 1910—. Organized Syracuse Trust Co. (atty.); dir. and atty. Empire State R.R. Corp., N.Y. Telephone Co., Dyneto Electric Co. Regent U. State of N.Y., 1902-15; trustee Syracuse U., 1892-1902. Republican. Methodist. Mem. N.Y. State Bar Assn. (pres. 1912). Home: Syracuse, N.Y. Died Jan. 23, 1921.

NOTZ, Frederick William Augustus, univ. prof.; b. Lehren-Steinsfeld, Württemberg, Germany, Feb. 2, 1841; s. Rev. Gottlieb and Louisa (Burger) N.; grad. Maulbronn Sem., 1859; Ph.D., U. of Tübingen, 1863, Ph.D. renewed "honoris causa" on 50th anniversary of Tübingen, 1913; m. Julia Schulz, June 20, 1875. Pvt. tutor in Germany to 1866; came to America, and tutor in Ga., 1866-68; prof. Pa. Coll., Gettysburg, 1868, Muhlenberg Coll., Allentown, Pa., 1869-72; prof. Greek and Hebrew, Northwestern U., Watertown, Wis., 1872—. Sec. German Am. Press Assn., 1870; pres. German Sch. Assn. of Pa., 1871; editor Lutherische Schulzeitung, 1876-94; mem., sec. regents, Martin Luther Coll., New Ulm, Minn.; mem. bd. official visitors, U. of Wis., 1902-06, regent, 1914-18. Author: (Latin monograph) Character and Qualifications of Lutheran Colleges, 1873. Translator: Conrad Dieterici Institutiones Catecheticæ, 1875. Home: Milwaukee, Wis. Died Dec. 1922.

NOTZ, William Frederick, economist; b. Watertown, Wis., Aug. 10, 1879; s. Frederick William Augustus and Julia (Schulz) N.; B.A., Northwestern Coll., Watertown, Wis., 1897; studied economics and philology, univs. of Pa., Leipzig and Wisconsin; M.A., U. of Wis., 1907, Ph.D., 1909; LL.D., Georgetown U., 1929; m. Rebecca Laurens Love, August 20, 1918; children—Ellen Cornelia, William Alan, Nataly Faith. Prof., Northwestern Coll., 1904-13; spl. agt., U.S. Bur. Corps., 1913-15; spl. agt. Fed. Trade Commn., 1915. Research in European countries, 1914, covering cartels and industrial combines, unfair competition and trust legislation, for U.S. Bur. Corps.; chief of export trade div. of Fed. Trade Commn., 1919-27; investigated co-operative movement in Europe for Fed. Trade Commn., 1923; prof. of economics, Sch. of Foreign Service, Georgetown U., 1919—, also mem. exec. com. of faculty, 1920—, and dean, 1923—; sr. economic analyst, Bur. Foreign and Domestic Commerce, U.S. Dept. Commerce, 1927-29; lecturer Univs. of Berlin, 1925, Cologne, Leipzig, Prague and Kiel, 1930, George Washington U., summer 1931. Chmn. bd. of dirs. Acad. of World Economics, Washington, D.C., 1932—. Officer Order of Star (Roumania), 1927. Author: The Masoretic Text of Nahum, critically compared with the ancient versions, 1909; Monopolies in the Ancient Orient, 1917; American Foreign Trade as Promoted by the Webb-Pomerene and Edge Acts (with Richard S. Harvey), 1921; Friedrich List in America, 1925; Representative International Cartels, Combines and Trusts, 1929; Friedrich List's Werke, 1931. Home: Washington, D.C. Died June 4, 1935.

NOURSE, Edward Everett, theologian; b. Bayfield, Wis., Dec. 24, 1863; s. Joseph Harvey and Isobel Laurie (Rittenhouse) N.; student Lake Forest Acad. and U., 1883-86, Macalester Coll., St. Paul, 1886-87; A.B., Lake Forest U., 1888, D.D., 1907; grad. Hartford Theol. Sem., 1891, S.T.B., 1893; post-grad. Hartford Sem., 1893-94, U. of Jena, 1891-95; m. Ettie Fay Silvernail, May 16, 1891; children—Helen Isobel, Edward Fenn, Harvey Zenos, Ralph Carver. Licensed to preach by Chicago Presbytery, 1890; ordained Presbyn. ministry, 1893; pastor Second Congl. Ch., Berlin, Conn., 1895-98; instr., 1898-1900, asso. prof., 1900-05, prof. Bibl. theology 1905—, Hartford Theol. Sem. Lecturer, Mt. Holyoke Coll., 1903-16. Conglist. Republican. Author: Brief Commentary on The Epistles of Paul, 1911. Contbd. many articles on Bibl. subjects to New International Ency. and Ency. of Religion and Ethics and 3d edit. of Ency. Americana; one of the editors of the Standard Dictionary of the Bible (1909), and New Standard Dictionary of the Bible (1926). Home: Hartford, Conn. Died Apr. 29, 1929.

NOURSE, Elizabeth, artist; b. Cincinnati; d. Caleb E. and Elizabeth Le Breton (Rogers) N.; first studied in Cincinnati, later under Boulanger and Lefebvre, Julian Acad., then pupil of Carolus Duran and Henner, Paris. Medals: Chicago Expn., 1893; Nashville, Tenn., 1897; Carthage Inst., Tunis, 1897; silver medal, Paris Expn., 1900; silver medal, St. Louis Expn., 1904. Elected Associée, 1895, Sociétaire des Beaux Arts, 1901. Represented in Cincinnati Arts Mus., Chicago Art Inst., Detroit Art Museum, Grand Rapids Mus., Lincoln (Neb.) Mus., Nat. Mus., Adelaide, Australia, Luxembourg Mus., Paris, Nat. Gallery (Washington), art gallery of St. Xavier's Coll. (Cincinnati, O.), Wightman Memorial Art Gallery (Notre Dame, Ind.); Art Mus. (Newark, N.J.). Gold medal, San Francisco Expn., 1915; Laetre medal, U. of Notre Dame, 1921. Address: Paris, France. Died Oct. 8, 1938.

NOURSE, Henry Stedman, civil engr.; b. Lancaster, Mass., April 9, 1831; s. Stedman N.; grad. Harvard, 1853, A.M.; m. Mary B. Thurston, Sept. 12, 1870. Prof. ancient languages, Phillips Exeter Acad., 1853-55; adj. and capt. 55th Ill. vol. inf. and commissary of musters, 17th army corps, 1861-65; constructional engr. and supt. Bessemer Steel Works, Steelton, Pa., 1866-74; mem. Mass. Ho. Reps., 1883; mem. Massachusetts senate, 1885-86; trustee Worcester Insane Hosp., 1888-98; mem. Mass. Free Public Library Commn., 1890-1903, Mass. Bd. Charity, 1898-1903. Republican. Author: Early Records of Lancaster, 1643-1725, 1884; The Story of the 55th Regiment of Illinois Infantry, 1887; The Military Annals of Lancaster, 1740-1865, 1889; The Birth, Marriage and Death Register, etc., of Lancaster, Mass., 1643-1850, 1890; History of the Town of Harvard, Mass., 1891; The Ninth Report of the Free Public Library Commission, 1899; Narrative of the Captivity and Restoration of Mrs. Mary Rowlandson, 1903. Address: South Lancaster, Mass. Died 1903.

NOYES, Arthur Amos, chemist; b. Newburyport, Mass., Sept. 13, 1866; s. Amos and Anna Page (Andrews) N.; S.B., Mass. Inst. Tech., 1886, S.M., 1887; Ph.D., U. of Leipzig, 1890; LL.D., U. of Me., 1908, Clark U., 1909, U. of Pittsburgh, 1915; Sc.D., Harvard, 1909, Yale, 1913; unmarried. Assistant in analytical chemistry, 1887-88, instr., 1890-92, instr. organic chemistry, 1892-94, asst. and asso. prof., 1894-99, prof. theoretical chemistry, 1899-1919, dir. Research Lab. Physical Chemistry, 1903-07 and 1909-19, acting pres., 1907-09, Mass. Inst. Tech.; dir. Gates Chem. Lab., Calif. Inst. Tech., 1915—. Editor Review of Am. Chem. Research, 1895-1901. Mem. Nat. Acad. Sciences (editor of its Proc., 1915-16), National Research Council (chmn. 1918), American Chemical Society (pres. 1904); fellow American Academy of Arts and Sciences, A.A.A.S. (pres. 1927). Awarded Willard Gibbs medal of Am. Chem. Society, 1915; Davy medal of Royal Society of London, 1927; Richards medal of American Chemical Soc., 1932. Author: Qualitative Chemical Analysis of Inorganic Substances, 1895; Laboratory Experiments on the Class Reactions and Identification of Organic Substances (with S. P. Mulliken), 1899; The General Principles of Physical Science, 1902; Electrical Conductivity of Aqueous Solutions, 1907; Chemical Principles (with M. S. Sherrill), 1921; Qualitative Analysis for the Rare Elements (with W. C. Bray), 1927; Chemistry of Solutions, 1932. Home: Pasadena, Calif. Died June 3, 1936.

NOYES, Charles Lothrop, clergyman; b. Ceylon, India, Sept. 11, 1851; s. Joseph Thomas and Elizabeth A. (Smith) N.; came to U.S., 1864; B.A., Yale, 1875; studied Union Theol. Sem., 1877-78, Andover Theol. Sem., 1878-80; D.D., Harvard, 1909; unmarried. Ordained Congl. ministry, 1881; pastor Third Ch., Jersey City, N.J., 1881-82, Winter Hill Ch., Somerville, Mass., 1883—. Pres. Somerville Associated Charities; trustee Somerville Pub. Library, Andover Theol. Sem. Pres. Boston Browning Soc. Editor: Pilgrim Songs, 1902; The Pilgrim Hymnal, 1904; New Pilgrim Hymnal, 1912. Address: Winter Hill, Mass. Died Aug. 8, 1923.

NOYES, Charles Phelps, wholesale druggist; b. Lyme, New London County, Conn., Apr. 24, 1842; s. Daniel Rogers and Phoebe Griffin (Lord) N.; ed. Lyme (Conn.) Acad., and Williston Sem., Easthampton, Mass.; m. Emily H. Gilman, Sept. 1, 1874. Began as clk. in banking house of Gilman & Son, New York, 1860; gen. mcht., Port Huron, Mich., 1864-68; removed to St. Paul, Minn., 1868, and became partner in Noyes, Pett & Co., wholesale druggists, later Noyes Bros., and since 1871, Noyes Bros. & Cutler, inc. 1915, of which became pres.; also pres. State Savings Bank; v.p. West Pub. Co.; dir. Mchts. Nat. Bank, St. Paul Fire & Marine Ins. Co.; pres. Oakland Cemetery Assn. Republican. Presbyn. Author: Noyes-Gilman Ancestry, 1907. Home: St. Paul, Minn. Died Apr. 30, 1921.

NOYES, Clara D.; b. Port Deposit, Md.; d. Enoch and Laura Lay (Banning) N.; ed. pvt. schs.; grad. Sch. of Nursing, Johns Hopkins Hosp., Baltimore, 1896. Supt. Training Sch. for Nurses, N.E. Hosp. for Women and Children, 1897-1901; supt. Hosp. and Tr. Sch. for Nurses, St. Luke's Hosp., New Bedford, Mass., 1901-10; gen. supt. Tr. Sch. for Nurses, Bellevue and Allied Hosps., New York, 1910-16; dir. Bur. Nursing Service, Am. Red Cross, 1916-18; dir. Dept. of Nursing Service, A.R.C., 1918—; spl. lecturer on hosp. adminstrn., Teachers Coll. (Columbia). Pres. Nat. League of Nursing Edn., 1912-15; chmn. Nat. Com. on Rank for Army Nurses, 1918, 19, 20; chmn. Nat. Com. Red Cross Nursing Service; pres. Am. Nurses Assn. and chmn. com. nat. hdqrs.; 1st v.p. Internat. Council of Nurses. Awarded medal, Nat. Inst. Social Sciences, "for service of high and inestimable value to her country and its wounded"; Florence Nightingale medal by Internat. Com. Red Cross, 1923; Bulgarian Red Cross, 1927; Medal of Honor (France), 1929; Saunders medal and Medaille d' Argent Reconnaissance de la Français, 1933. Unitarian. Editor Red Cross Dept. Am. Jour. of Nursing; editor Johns Hopkins Nurses Alumnæ Mag., 1927. Chmn. editorial com. "History American Red Cross Nursing Service." Home: Washington, D.C. Died June 3, 1936.

NOYES, Crosby Stuart, editor Washington Evening Star; b. Minot, Me., Feb. 16, 1825; A.M., Bowdoin Coll.; when a young man became Washington corr. of Eastern papers; reporter on Washington Star, 1855; later asst. editor; in 1867 acquired an interest; editor-in-chief, 1867—; m. Elizabeth S., d. Rev. Thomas Williams, 1856. Address, Washington, D.C. Died 1908.

NOYES, Daniel Rogers, mcht.; b. Lyme, Conn., Nov. 10, 1836; s. Col. Daniel Rogers and Phoebe Griffin N.; ed. pub. and pvt. schs.; m. Helen A. Gilman, Dec. 4, 1866. Served in U.S.V. in Civil War. Founded, 1869, and later became head of Noyes Bros. & Cutler, St. Paul; dir. Merchants' Nat. Bank. Pres. Minn. State Soc. for Prevention of Cruelty, St. Paul Relief Soc. (founder); organizer Minn. Red Cross Soc. (an incorporator of nat. soc.). Republican. Presbyn. Vice moderator Presbyn. Gen. Assembly, 1902, mem. Com. for Revision of the Creed, Presbyn. Ch.; v.p. Am. S. S. Union.; pres. Minn. Soc. S.A.R. Home: St. Paul, Minn. Died 1908.

NOYES, Edward MacArthur, clergyman; b. New Haven, Conn., Oct. 12, 1858; s. Rev. Gurdon Wheeler and Agnes (MacArthur) N.; A.B., Yale, 1879, B.D., 1882; D.D. from Middlebury (Vt.) Coll., 1926; Post-Grad. Sch., Yale, 1883; m. Mary Caroline Simpson, July 3, 1884 (died 1892); children—Margaret Elizabeth (Mrs. Ross Hunt Skinner), Alice Louise (dec.), Edward Simpson; m. 2d, Grace Brewster Alvord, July 6, 1904; children—MacArthur, Elizabeth Brewster, Catherine Alvord. Ordained Congl. ministry, 1883; pastor Pilgrim Ch., Duluth, Minn., 1883-94, 1st Ch. in Newton, Newton Center, Mass., 1894-1929, Tourist Ch., Daytona Beach, Fla., 1929-37. Pres. Am. Congregational Assn., Boston, 1918-37. Republican. Home: Newton Center, Mass. Died Dec. 17, 1939.

NOYES, Frank Eugene, publisher; b. Appleton, Wis., Apr. 21, 1856; s. Luther B. and Belle (Woodward) N.; student Lawrence Coll., Appleton, 1873-77, U. of Wis., 1878; m. Belle Carter, Sept. 11, 1890; children—Eugene Carter, Linwood Irving, Fama Isabella (Mrs. Walter P. Keith). Learned typesetting, 1868; studied law, 1879; associated with father in publishing the Marinette (Wis.) Eagle, 1884; pub. Marinette Eagle-Star, 1893—; established Ironwood (Mich.) Daily Globe, 1919, Marshfield (Wis.) News-Herald, 1927. Mem. Wis. Press Assn. (past pres.), Wis. Daily Newspaper League (past pres.). Republican. Episcopalian. Kiwanian. Mason (33°); Grand Master Grand Council R. and S.M., 1909; Grand High Priest Grand Chapter R.A.M., 1914. Erected many hist. and geog. markers and monuments. Home: Marinette, Wis. Died Nov. 28, 1941.

NOYES, George Henry, lawyer; b. McLean, Tompkins County, N.Y., Apr. 18, 1849; s. John and Mary Stanton (Millard) N.; removed to Delafield, Waukesha County, Wis., 1855; A.B., U. of Wis., 1873, LL.B., 1874, LL.D., 1904; m. Agnes A. Haskell, Nov. 1876. Asst. state librarian of Wis., 1873-74; practiced law in Milwaukee, 1874—, except while serving as judge Superior Ct., Milwaukee Co., Jan. 1, 1888-Mar. 1, 1890; mem. firm of Miller, Noyes & Miller, 1890-1906; gen. counsel Northwestern Mut. Life Ins. Co., Milwaukee, 1906—. Mem. bd. of regents U. of Wis., 1890-1902 (v.p. 1897-08, pres. 1899-1901); mem. bd. commrs. for erection of State Hist. Library Bldg., Wis. Pres. Wis. State Bar Assn., 1904-05. Prepared notes for Vol. III, Wis. Reports, published as "Dixon's Notes." Home: Milwaukee, Wis. Died Jan. 1916.

NOYES, Guy Lincoln, M.D., educator; b. Boston, Mass., Aug. 6, 1872; s. Emerson Aldrich and Sobrina (Robinson) N.; M.D., U. of Vt., 1894, U. of Mich., 1901; grad. work, Harvard Med. Sch., 1907; m. Lucia M. Wiegand, Aug. 27, 1902; 1 son, Guy Emerson. Began practice at Burlington, Vt., 1894; demonstrator ophthalmic and aural surgery, U. of Mich., 1902; prof. diseases eye and ear, U. of Mo., 1902-10; chief of ophthalmic service, Univ. Hosps., 1903—; dean Sch. of Medicine, U. of Mo., 1913—. 1st lt. Med. Reserve, U.S.A., 1911; capt. Med. Sect. O.R.C., 1917-18. Fellow Am. Coll. Surgeons; certificate, Am. Bd. Otolaryngology, 1925; mem. Am. Acad. Ophthalmology. Episcopalian. Mason. Home: Columbia, Mo. Died Feb. 4, 1930.

NOYES, Henry Drury, M.D.; b. New York, N.Y., 1832; grad. New York U., 1851, A.M., 1854; grad. Coll. Phys. and Surg., 1859; m. Isabella Beveridge, 1859; m. 2d, Anna M. Grant, 1870. On surgical staff New York Hospital nearly 3 years; specialist eye and ear diseases; prof. ophthalmology and otology Bellevue Hosp. Med. Coll., 1866—, (also prof. ophthalmology Univ. Bellevue Hospital Med. Coll.). First to make known in U.S. use of cocaine as local anæsthetic in ophthalmic surgery. Member Am. Med. Assn.; a founder (sec. 10 years, pres. 5 years) Am. Ophthalmol. Soc. Author: Text Book on Diseases of the Eye. Address: New York, N.Y. Died 1900.

NOYES, Henry Erastus, brigadier gen. U.S.A.; b. Belfast, Me., Aug. 23, 1839; s. Henry and Rebecca (Tyler) N.; grad. U.S. Mil. Acad., 1861; m. Louise W. Walker, July 2, 1864. Apptd. 2d lt. 2d Dragoons, June 24, 1861; assigned to duty with Light Battery E, 3d Arty.; participated in battles of Bull Run, on defenses of Washington and expdn. to Port Royal, S.C.; 1st lt, 2d Cav., Feb. 15, 1862; served in battles of South Mountain, Antietam, Fredericksburg, Beverly Ford, Brandy Sta. (bvtd. capt., Aug. 1, 1863, "for gallant and meritorious services"), later in Shenandoah Valley campaign, battles of Winchester, Opequan, and Nashville; capt. 2d Cav., Jan. 25, 1865; bvtd. maj., Apr. 2, 1865 "for gallant and meritorious services at capture of Selma, Ala." After Civil War participated in Indian campaigns against the Sioux in Wyo., etc.; maj. 4th Cav., June 14, 1879; served in campaign against Warm Spring Apaches, 1880; lt. col. 5th Cav., July 1, 1891; transferred to 2d Cav., Aug. 1892; col. 2d Cav., May 31, 1898; served at Chickamauga, Mobile and Tampa, in Aug. 1898, and afterward in Cuba; retired, Nov. 16, 1901; advanced to rank of brig. gen. retired, by act of Apr. 23, 1904. Author: Noyes' Genealogy. Address: Berkeley, Calif. Died July 10, 1919.

NOYES, La Verne W., mfr.; b. Genoa, N.Y., Jan. 7, 1849; s. Leonard R. and Jane (Jessup) N.; B.Sc., Ia. State Coll., 1872, D.E., 1915; m. Ida E. Smith, May 24, 1879 (died 1912). Removed to Batavia, Ill., 1876, and engaged in mfg.; invented the Noyes dictionary holder, 1879, and invented and patented more than 100 mech. devices; began mfr. of agrl. implements and organized the Aermotor Co., of which became pres. Pres. trustees Chicago Acad. Sciences; governing life mem. Art Inst. Chicago; trustee Lewis Inst.; mem. Civic Federation Chicago; v.p. gen. Nat. Soc. S.A.R.; pres. Ill. Mfrs. Assn., Nat. Business League of N. America. Gave Ida Noyes Hall to U. of Chicago, as memorial; many scholarships for boys of Lewis Inst. Home: Chicago, Ill. Died July 24, 1919.

NOYES, Theodore Richards, president Oneida Community, Ltd.; b. Putney, Vt., July 25, 1841; s. John Humphrey N., founder of Oneida Community (died 1886); ed. in Oneida Community; grad. Yale Med. School, 1867; mem. Oneida Community all his life until age of 40; one of those instrumental in its conversion to an ordinary joint stock co., in 1880, pres., 1895—. Address: Kenwood, Madison County, N.Y. Died 1903.

NOYES, Walter Chadwick, lawyer; b. Lyme, Conn., Aug. 8, 1865; s. Richard and Catherine (Chadwick) N.; ed. Cornell; m. Luella Shapley Armstrong, Oct. 22, 1895; children—Marian Armstrong, Catherine Chadwick, Ruth Brewster. Admitted to bar, 1886; judge Court of Common Pleas, New London County, Conn., 1895-1907; U.S. circuit judge, 2d Circuit, 1907-13; resigned and resumed practice at New York; later gen. counsel Delaware & Hudson Co. and in gen. practice at New York. U.S. del. Internat. Conf. on Maritime Law, Brussels, 1909, 1910. Author: The Law of Inter-Corporate Relations, 1902; American Railroad Rates, 1905. Home: New York, N.Y. Died June 12, 1926.

NUGENT, John F., senator; b. LaGrande, Ore., June 28, 1868; s. Edward and Agnes P. (Frost) N.; ed. pub. schs., Silver City, Ida.; m. Adelma Ainslie, May 15, 1895; 1 son, George Ainslie. Began practice at Silver City, Ida., 1898; pros. atty. Owyhee County, Ida., 4 terms; chmn. Dem. County Central Com., Owyhee County, 2 terms; chmn. Dem. State Central Com., Ida., 2 terms; apptd. mem. U.S. Senate by Gov. Moses Alexander, Jan. 22, 1918, to fill vacancy caused by death of Hon. James H. Brady, elected Nov. 1918, term 1919-21, resigned Jan. 1921; mem. Fed. Trade Commn., 1921-27; senior mem. law firm Nugent & O'Hara (Washington, D.C.), 1927—. K.P., Elk, Woodman of World. Home: Boise, Ida. Died Sept. 18, 1931.

NUGENT, Paul Cook, civil engr., educator; b. New Orleans, La., Jan. 4, 1871; s. Perry and Amanda (Cook) N.; A.B., Roanoke Coll., 1889; A.M., 1894; C.E., Rensselaer Poly. Inst., 1892; m. Mary Louise Logan, Sept. 12, 1899. Teacher of civ. engring., 1896—; prof. civ. engring., Syracuse U., 1902-19; prof. civ. engring., U. of Ariz., 1920—. Methodist. Author: Plane Surveying. Address: Tucson, Ariz. Died July 15, 1924.

NUNN, Paul N., engr.; b. Medina, O., July 31, 1860; s. Charles Robert and Miriam (Kendall) N.; ed. science, pedagogy and engring.; m. Agnes Aird Geddes, June 24, 1886. Prin. high sch., 1885-88; chief engr. Telluride (Colo.) Power Co., 1890-1911, builder and operator of first hydro-electric power industry in U.S. and later (in Utah) of the highest-voltage and longest-distance transmission, including experimental research and educational work; chief engr. Ontario Power Co., Niagara Falls, 1902-10, during design and constrn. of that plant; pres. Telluride Power Co. Mason. Home: San Diego, Calif. Died Oct. 27, 1939.

NUSSBAUM, Paul Joseph, bishop; b. Phila., Pa., Sept. 7, 1869. Joined congregation of Passionist Fathers; ordained R.C. priest; served as 2d consultor of Eastern Province of Passionist Fathers; became 1st bishop Diocese of Corpus Christi, Mar. 2, 1917; later bishop of Marquette, Mich. Home: Marquette, Mich. Died June 24, 1935.

NUTTALL, George Henry Falkiner, biologist; b. San Francisco, July 5, 1862; s. Robert Kennedy (M.D.) and Magdalena (Parrott) N.; ed. U.S., Germany, England, France, Switzerland; M.D., U. of Calif., 1884; Ph.D., U. of Göttingen, 1890: hon. M.A., Cambridge, 1900, Sc.D., 1906; m. Paula von Oertzen, Apr. 26, 1894. Asst. and later asso. in hygiene, Johns Hopkins, 1891-94; hon. asst. Hygienic Inst., Berlin, 1894-99; univ. lecturer in bacteriology and preventive medicine, later reader in hygiene, 1900-06, Quick prof. of biology, 1906—, U. of Cambridge. Fellow Christ's College, later fellow Magdalene Coll., Cambridge; hon. sec. British Nat. Com. for Internat. Hygienic Congresses, 1906—; Harben lecturer, Royal Institute Public Health, 1908; Herter lecturer, Johns Hopkins, 1912; Harvey lecturer, New York Acad. Medicine, 1912; Weir Mitchell lecturer, Coll. Phys. and Surg., Phila., 1912; examiner for diplomas in pub. health and tropical medicine and hygiene, Cambridge; same for diplomas in tropical medicine, U. of Liverpool, and for Royal Army Med. Corps; dir. Molteno Inst., U. of Cambridge; founder and editor jours. of Hygiene and Parasitology. Mem. Advisory Com. for Plague Investigations in India (Indian Govt.), Imperial Bur. Entomology (Colonial Office, London); Fish Preserv. Com. (Dept. Agr. and Fish, London); Pathol. Advisory Com. (War Office); Tropical Diseases Com. Royal Soc.; fgn. hon. mem. Am. Acad. Arts and Sciences. Author: Hygienic Measures in Relation to Infectious Diseases (published in both English and German), 1893; Blood Immunity and Blood Relationship, 1904; The Bacteriology of Diphtheria (with Graham Smith and others), 1908, 1913; Ticks (with C. Warburton and others). Address: Cambridge, Eng. Died Dec. 16, 1937.

NUTTALL, Zelia, archeologist; b. San Francisco, Calif.; d. Robert Kennedy and Madeline (Parrott) N.; ed. in Eng., France, Germany and Italy; m. the late Alphonse L. Pinart, 1880 (divorced 1887); 1 dau., Mrs. Arthur C. Laughton. An extensive traveler; has made spl. study of antiquities and Colonial history of Mexico. Hon. spl. asst. Peabody Mus. of Am. Archæology and Ethnology, Cambridge, Mass.; hon. prof. archeology, Nat. Mus., Mexico, 1908—. Mem. Internat. Jury of Awards, Chicago Expn., 1893, St. Louis Expn., 1904; mem. advisory council dept. of anthropology, U. of Calif. Fellow Am. Anthropol. Assn., Am. Ethnol. Soc., Am. Geog. Soc., Met. Mus. Art, A.A.A.S., Hispanic Soc. America, Royal Anthropol. Institute. Awarded gold medal Hist. Expn., Madrid, 1892, Chicago Expn., 1893, Buffalo Expn., 1901. Wrote: Codex Nuttall (facsimile of the ancient Mexican Codex), also New Light on Drake, 1914; New Light an Ancient American Calendars, 1926. Died Apr. 12, 1933.

NUTTER, George Read, lawyer; b. Boston, Mass., Aug. 9, 1863; s. Thomas Franklin and Julia Adelaide (Read) N.; grad. Boston Latin Sch., 1881; A.B., Harvard, 1885, A.M. and LL.B., 1889; grad. study U. of Munich, Germany; unmarried. Admitted to Mass. bar, 1889, and began practice at Boston with Warren & Brandeis; mem. Brandeis, Dunbar & Nutter, 1896-1916, Dunbar, Nutter & McClennen, 1916-29, Nutter, McClennen & Fish, 1929—. Chmn. Legal Advisory Bd., Boston, and four-minute man, World War. Mem. Judicature Commn., 1919-21; member Charter Commn., Boston, 1923; mem. exec. com. Good Govt. Assn., City of Boston, 1904-34; pres. Social Law Library; trustee Harvard Law Review (mem. 1st bd. editors 1887); mem. advisory bd. Mass. Law Review. Independent in politics. Home: Boston, Mass. Died Feb. 21, 1937.

NUTTING, Charles Cleveland, zoölogist; b. Jacksonville, Ill., May 25, 1858; s. Rev. Rufus and Margaretta Leib (Hunt) N.; A.B., Blackburn U., Ill., 1880, A.M., 1882; m. Lizzie B. Hersman, Aug. 10, 1886; 1 dau., Elizabeth H.; m. 2d, M. Eloise Willis, June 16, 1897; children—Willis D., Carl B. Engaged in explorations for Smithsonian Instn. in Central America, 1881-82; prof. zoölogy and curator Mus. of Natural History, 1886—, prof. and head dept. of zoölogy, 1890—, State U. of Ia. Engaged in spl. scientific researches in Costa Rica, 1882; Nicaragua, 1883; Florida, 1885; Saskatchewan River, 1891, West Indies, 1888, 1893, Plymouth, Eng., and Naples, Italy, 1895; Calif., 1905 and 1909; Barbados, 1917-18; member of civilian scientific staff of U.S.S. "Albatross" during Hawaiian cruise, 1902; collaborator, Reports of the Siboga Expdn., 1909-11; dir. Barbados-Antiqua Expdn. from State Univ. of Ia., 1918, and Fiji-New Zealand Expdn., 1922. Author: Narrative of Bahama Expedition from University of Iowa, 1893; American Hydroids, Parts 1, 2, 3, 1900, 1904; Report on Gorgoniacea of the Siboga Expedition, 1910; Narrative Barbados-Antigua Expedition, 1918; Narrative of the Fiji-New Zealand Expedition, 1924. Home: Iowa City, Iowa. Died Jan. 23, 1927.

NUTTING, Herbert Chester, philologist; b. N.Y. City, Jan. 14, 1872; s. Nathan and Caroline Augusta (Jelliff) N.; B.A., Yale, 1895, Ph.D., 1897; m. Jessie May Le Roy, July 14, 1897; children—Elizabeth May, Marcus, Lee. Instr. Greek and Sanskrit, 1897, instr. Latin, 1898, asst. prof., 1904, asso. prof., 1919, prof., 1924—, U. of Calif. Joint editor U. of Calif. publs. in Classical Philology; joint editor Classical Jour., 1916-30. Mem. advisory com. Am. Acad. at Rome, 1926-27. Conglist. Author: A Latin Primer, 1911; A First Latin Reader, 1912, same, with Exercises, 1913; Advanced Latin Composition, 1904; Supplementary Latin Composition, 1905; Junior Latin Plays, 1922; Teachers' Course in Latin Composition, 1922; Ad Alpes—A Story of Roman Life, 1923; The Latin Conditional Sentence, 1925; Latin Songs (Splendor Noctis, etc.), 1927. Editor: Plautus's Trinummus, 1903; Cicero's Tusculan Disputations, 1909. Home: Berkeley, Calif. Died Sept. 23, 1934.

NUTTING, Mary Olivia, author; b. Randolph Center, Vt., July 1, 1831; d. William and Mary Barrett (Hubbard) N.; grad. Mt. Holyoke Sem. (now Coll.), 1852. Teacher, 1853-70, librarian, 1870-1901, librarian emeritus, Mt. Holyoke Coll. Author: Steps in the Upward Way, 1867; Our Summer at Hillside Farm, 1867; The Story of William the Silent and the Netherland War, 1869; The Days of Prince Maurice, 1894. Wrote 4 chapters of History of Mt. Holyoke Seminary (Stow), 1887. Wrote under pen name "Mary Barrett" until 1894. Died 1910.

NUTTING, Wallace, clergyman, antiquarian; b. Marlboro, Mass., Nov. 17, 1861; s. Albion and Elizabeth Sanborn (Fifield) N.; Harvard, 1883-86, Hartford Theol. Sem., 1886-87, Union Theol. Sem., 1887-88; D.D., Whitman Coll., Wash., 1893; D.Humanities, Washington and Jefferson, 1935; m. Mariet Griswold, May 5, 1888. Ordained Congl. ministry, 1888; pastorates at Newark (N.J.), St. Paul (Minn.), Seattle (Wash.), and Providence (R.I.); retired from ministry, 1905, on account of ill health and thereafter devoted attention to pictorial representation of landscapes and early Am. life, also European life, especially English. Republican. Author: (also illustrator) Old New England Pictures, 1913; Vermont Beautiful, 1922; The Windsor Handbook, 1917; Furniture of the Pilgrim Century, 1921-23; revised edit., 1924; Massachusetts Beautiful, 1923; Connecticut Beautiful, 1923; New Hampshire Beautiful, 1923; Maine Beautiful, 1924; Pennsylvania Beautiful, 1924; Ireland Beautiful, 1925; Photographic Art Secrets, 1927; New York Beautiful, 1927; England Beautiful, 1928; Furniture Treasury (3 vols.), 1928 and 1933; The Clock Book, 1924; Virginia Beautiful, 1930; Wallace Nutting's Biography, 1936. Home: Framingham Centre, Mass. Died July 19, 1941.

NYDEGGER, James Archibald, M.D.; b. Ft. Pendleton, nr. Oakland, Md., June 26, 1864; s. Louis Napoleon and Mary (Chisholm) N.; B.L., St. John's Coll., Annapolis, Md., 1890, A.M., D.Sc., 1912; M.D., Univ. of Md., 1892; certificate, London School Tropical Medicine, 1915; unmarried. Appointed assistant surgeon U.S.P.H.S., July 1, 1892; passed assistant surgeon, July 7, 1896, surgeon, Feb. 4, 1909. Served at Baltimore, Gulf Quarantine (Miss.), Charleston, S.C., Reedy Island Quarantine (Del.), S. Atlantic Quarantine (Ga.), New Orleans, Cape Charles (Va.) Quarantine, Cincinnati, New York, Liverpool, London, Paris, Madrid, etc. In charge yellow fever post-epidemic areation, New Orleans and vicinity, 1898-99; served as exec. officer through epidemic of yellow fever, New Orleans, 1899; etc. Originated hygienic survey in schs. by U.S.P.H.S., 1912; prof. tropical medicine, U. of Md., 1913-16. Mem. bd. visitors and govs. St. John's Coll., Annapolis, Md. Republican. Presbyn. Mason. Author: The Chisholms; The MacQueens; Chronicles, 1930; Fate of the White Bird, 1931. Home: Baltimore, Md. Died Feb. 18, 1934.

NYDEN, John Augustus, architect; b. Sweden, Mar. 25, 1878; s. Carl Gustaf Johansson and Marie Christina (Humble) N.; came to U.S., 1895; student Valparaiso U., with George A. Fuller of N.Y. City, and at Art Inst. Chicago until 1901; passed examination U. of Ill. for practice of architecture, 1904; made 4 trips to Europe to study architecture; m. Alma Ottilia Hemmings, Apr. 9, 1902; children—Mrs. Adelaide N. Hill and Valborg (daughter). Began practice in Chicago, 1907, now pres. John A. Nyden Co.; prin. works: Admiral Hotel, Commonwealth Hotel, Fairfax Hotel.

Builders and Merchants Bank Bldg., Bethany Old People's Home (Chicago); Minnehaha Acad. (Minneapolis); John Morton Memorial Bldg. (Phila.); new Stadium for State of Ill. (Springfield); etc.; state architect of Ill., 1926-27; pres. Admiral Hotel Co. Commd. maj. Q.M. Corps, U.S.A., May 23, 1918; lt. col. Res., July 12, 1923; certificate of capacity for colonel, June 29, 1926; served in supervising construction Gen. and Debarkation hosps. in U.S. and as liaison officer between Construction Div. and Surg. Gen.'s office, Washington, D.C. Mem. A.I.A. Republican. A founder Edgewater Swedish Mission Ch., Chicago. Home: Evanston, Ill. Died Sept. 4, 1932.

NYE, Frank E., soldier; b. in Maine; grad. U.S. Mil. Acad., 1869. Apptd. 2d lt. 2d Cav., June 15, 1869, serving principally on frontier until Apr. 10, 1873, when resigned. Engaged in ins. business, Augusta, Me., 1873-84. Reëntered army as capt. commissary of subsistence, Nov. 20, 1884, and continued in commissary dept.; promoted maj., June 1, 1896, lt. col. commissary gen., Sept. 9, 1898, col. asst. commissary gen., Apr. 1, 1901—. Lt. col., July 1898, and col., Oct. to Dec. 1898, in commissary service, U.S.V. Deceased.

NYSWANDER, Reuben Edson, Jr., prof. physics; b. Antwerp, O., Jan. 4, 1878; s. Reuben Edson and Henrietta W. (Youche) N.; A.B., Indiana U., 1901, A.M., 1904; Ph.D., Cornell U., 1908; m. Ada M. DeBell, Aug. 17, 1909; children—Virginia Ruth, Reuben Edson. Asst. in physics, Ind. U., 1899-1902, Purdue U., 1903; magnetic observer, U.S. Coast and Geodetic Survey, 1903-06; instr. in physics, Ind. U., 1908-09; prof. physics, 1909, prof. physics and electrical engring., 1919-20, prof. physics, dir. Sch. Elec. Engring., 1919-30, asso. dean Sch. of Science and Engineering, 1931-37, dean Sch. of Elec. Engineering, 1929-31, dean School of Science and Engineering, 1937—, U. of Denver. Prof. physics, Ind. U. Summer Sch., 1915. Methodist. Inventor polarization photometer. Home: Denver, Colo. Died Apr. 8, 1941.

O

OAKES, George Washington Ochs, journalist; b. Cincinnati, O., Oct. 27, 1861; s. Julius and Bertha (Levy) Ochs (name Americanized from George Washington Ochs to George Washington Ochs-Oakes, by decree of Pa. Courts, 1917); B.A., U. of Tenn., 1880; Grad. Sch. Columbia U., Ph.D., 1924; m. Miss Gans, Jan. 30, 1907 (died 1913); children—George Washington, John Bertram. Mayor of Chattanooga, Tenn., 1894-95, 1896-97; pres. Bd. Edn., 1897-1900; pub. Paris edit. of New York Times, at Paris Expn., 1900; gen. mgr. Phila. Times, 1901-02; editor in chief The Public Ledger, Phila., 1902-15; editor Current History Magazine (pub. by New York Times Co.), 1915—. Pres. Chattanooga Chamber Commerce, 1899-1900; mem. exec. com. Nat. Municipal League, 1893-99. Mem. Com. of 1000 for Suppression of Vice (New York); hon. pres. Civitan Club of New York, 1926—; pres. Chattanooga Soc. of New York, 1924—. Decorated by French Govt. Chevalier Legion of Honor, 1900. Home: New York, N.Y. Died Oct. 26, 1931.

OAKES, James, soldier; b. nr. Limestoneville, Pa., Apr. 4, 1826; s. Samuel and Sarah (Montgomery) O.; grad. U.S. Mil. Acad., 1846; m. Anna Maria de Beelen, Nov. 11, 1854. Served in Mexican War; bvtd. 1st lt. and capt. for gallantry; afterward on frontier service; wounded by Indians, Aug. 12, 1850; 1st lt., June 30, 1851; capt. 2d Cav., Mar. 3, 1855; maj. 5th Cav., Apr. 6, 1861; lt. col. 4th Cav., Nov. 12, 1861; col. 6th Cav., July 31, 1866. Declined commn. of brig. gen. vols., May 17, 1861; led regt. in Tenn. and Miss. campaign, 1862; in mustering and recruiting service, 1863; comd. dist. of Ill., 1863-66; bvtd. brig. gen. U.S.A., Mar. 30, 1865. In charge, Freedman's Bur. and comd. dist. of Austin, Tex., 1867-69; afterward on northern frontier of Tex. and in Kan. and Ariz.; retired at own request, over 30 yrs.' service, Apr. 29, 1879. Home: Washington, D.C. Died 1910.

OAKLEAF, Joseph Benjamin, collector of Lincolniana, lawyer; b. Moline, Ill., Oct. 1, 1858; s. Benjam Peter and Mary (Ekelof) O.; ed. country pub. sch.; LL.D., Lincoln Memorial U., 1928; m. Josephine Anderson, Jan. 27, 1880; 1 son, Josephus LeRoy. Admitted to Ill. Bar, 1886, and entered practice at Moline; city atty. Moline, 1890-96; dir. State Sav. Bank & Trust Co., 1908-18; senior mem. J. B. & J. L. Oakleaf. Dir. Ill. State Hist. Soc.; mem. Lincoln Memorial Commn. Pres. John Ericsson Republican League of Ill., 1929-30. Lutheran. Known as collector of Lincolniana and credited with having one of the largest collections in existence pertaining to Abraham Lincoln. Compiler: Bibliography of Lincoln Literature, 1925. Lecturer and writer on Lincoln. Died June 2, 1930.

OAKLEY, Horace Sweeney, lawyer; b. Prescott, Wis., June 2, 1861; s. George M. and Jane S. (Sweeney) O.; prep. edn., pub. schs.; LL.B., National U., Washington, 1881; student U. of Mich., 1881-83; unmarried. Admitted to Ill. bar, 1883, and later to bar of U.S. Supreme Court; mem. Wood and Oakley. Deputy Commr. Am. Red Cross to Greece, 1918-19. Trustee Orchestral Assn., Civic Music Assn., Newberry Library, Am. Sch. Classical Studies at Athens. Democrat. Home: Chicago, Ill. Died Dec. 16, 1929.

OAKLEY, Imogen Brashear, writer, lecturer; b. Dover, O., Oct. 14, 1854; d. Basil Brown and Mary Catherine (Whitacre) Brashear; grad. Collegiate Sch. (defunct), Pittsburgh, Pa., 1871; traveled in Europe and Asia; m. John M. Oakley, 1880 (died 1897); 1 son, Thornton. Chmn. civil service dept. Gen. Fedn. of Women's Clubs for 10 yrs., now advisory chairman. Mem. Phila. Art Alliance. Unitarian. Author: History of Civil Service Reform in England, India and the United States, 1904. Address: Philadelphia, Pa. Died Sept. 14, 1933.

OAKLEY, Seymour Adams, newspaper editor; b. Shandaken, N.Y., Dec. 18, 1869; s. John Hoyt and Armeda Helen (Hood) O.; grad. high sch., Wyoming, Ill., 1888; m. Grace Mary Sanasace, Apr. 2, 1902; children—Frederic Russell, Philip Seymour, John Edward. Began as reporter on Peoria Herald-Transcript, Jan. 1900; city editor Peoria Journal, 1904-05; city editor Peoria Star until 1914, editor in chief, 1914—. Mem. Ill. Chamber of Commerce (mem. publicity com.). Republican. Home: Peoria, Ill. Died Apr. 3, 1933.

OAKMAN, Walter G., financier; A.B., U. of Pennsylvania, 1864, A.M., 1867; m. Eliza Conkling. President, director Hudson Cos., Greeley Sq. Realty Co.; formerly chmn. board Guaranty Trust Co. of N.Y.; v.p., dir. Jefferson & Clearfield Coal & Iron Co.; dir. Am. Car & Foundry Co., Brooklyn Heights R.R. Co., Brooklyn Rapid Transit Co., Buffalo, Rochester & Pittsburgh Ry. Co., etc. Home: New York, N.Y. Died Mar. 18, 1922.

OATES, William Calvin, governor; b. in Pike (now Bullock) Co., Ala., Dec. 1, 1835; s. William O. and Sarah (Sellers) O.; ed. at Lawrenceville Acad., Ala.; m. Sallie Toney, Mar. 1882. Served capt. to col., C.S.A.; was in 27 battles; wounded 6 times and lost his right arm. Practiced law after war; mem. Ala. Ho. of Rep., 1870-72; mem. Constl. convs., 1875, 1901; elected 47th to 53d Congresses (1881-95); resigned from 53d Congress, 1894; gov. of Ala., 1895, 1896. Democrat. Defeated for U.S. senator because not an advocate of free coinage of silver at the 16 to 1 ratio. Brig. gen. vols., May 28, 1898-Mar. 10, 1899. Author: The War Between the Union and the Confederacy and Its Lost Opportunities. Home: Montgomery, Ala. Died 1910.

OBENCHAIN, William Alexander, college prof.; b. Buchanan, Va., Apr. 27, 1841; s. Thomas Jefferson and Elizabeth Ann (Sweetland) O.; grad. (1st honor) Va. Mil. Inst., 1861; (hon. A.M., Centre Coll., Ky.); m. Eliza Calvert, July 8, 1885. In engr. corps C.S.A., 1861-65; promoted to capt. for "skill and meritorious conduct"; staff engr., Army of Northern Va. Prof. mathematics and engring., Hillsboro (N.C.) Mil. Acad., 1866-67; prof. mathematics and commandant cadets, Western Mil. Acad., New Castle, Ky., 1868-70; prof. mathematics, French and German, and commandant of cadets, U. of Nashville, 1870-73; prof. mathematics, 1878—, pres., 1883-1906, Ogden Coll. Hon. v.p. Dept. Congress of Higher Edn., Chicago Expn., 1893; mem. nat. council Nat. Econ. League, exec. com. Ky. State Tax League. Episcopalian (sr. warden). Home: Bowling Green, Ky. Died Aug. 1916.

OBER, Frederick Albion, author; b. Beverly, Mass., Feb. 13, 1849; s. Andrew Kimbal and Sarah (Hadlock) O.; bro. of Sarah Endicott O.; ed. public schs. and pvt. study; married. Hunted birds in Florida and explored Lake Okeechobee region, 1872-74; made ornithol. investigation of Lesser Antilles, W. Indies, 1876-78, and 1880, discovering 22 new species of birds, and adding many types to collections of Smithsonian Instn. in Proceedings of which his results were published; traveled in Mexico, 1881, 1883 and 1885; later in Spain, N. Africa, S. America and again in W. Indies, to which islands he was commr. for Chicago Expn., 1891-92. In real estate business, 1908—. Author: In the Wake of Columbus, 1893; Josephine, Empress of the French, 1895; Under the Cuban Flag, 1896; Crusoe's Island, 1898; Puerto Rico and Its Resources, 1892; A Brief History of Spain, 1899; The Storied West Indies, 1900; A Boy Among the Pueblos, 1902; The Boy Buccaneers, 1902; Two Boys with Columbus, 1903; Our West Indian Neighbors, 1904; History of Mexico, Central America and Cuba, 1904; With Osceola the Seminole, 1905; A Friend of King Philip, 1906; A Guide to the West Indies, 1907; In King Philip's War, 1907; The Heroes of American History Series (12 vols.), 1907. Died June 1, 1913.

OBER, Henry Kulp, clergyman, educator; b. nr. Mastersonville, Pa., Jan. 2, 1878; s. Michael Ruhl and Susan Baker (Kulp) O.; grad. Millersville (Pa.) State Normal Sch., 1898, B.Pd., 1910, M.Pd., 1911; B.S., Franklin and Marshall Coll., 1918, M.S., 1921; M.A., Columbia, 1922; grad. student U. of Pa., 1922-24; D.D. from Franklin and Marshall College in 1927; m. Cora Brinser Hess, May 25, 1899; children—Stanley Hess (dec.), Grace Hess, Ruth Hess, Henry K. (dec.). Teacher rural schs., Pa., 1897-1902; with Elizabethtown Coll., 1902—, pres. 1916-27; boro engr. Elizabethtown Boro, 1904—; sec.-treas. Buch Mfg. Co.; etc. Licensed as minister Ch. of the Brethren, 1904, bishop, 1915; pres. Lancaster S.S. Assn.; mem. Gen. Bd. Religious Edn., Edn. Com. of Pa.; v.p. Pa. State S.S. Assn.; pres. bd. trustees Elizabethtown Coll. Republican. Author: (with others), Training the Sunday School Teacher, 1913; Principles of Education, 1923; The Plain People of Lancaster County; Child Rights, 1934. Home: Elizabethtown, Pa. Died Mar. 12, 1939.

OBERHOFFER, Emil, conductor; b. Munich, Bavaria, Aug. 10, 1867; ed. under Father Cyrill Kistler, and at lit. coll., studied in Paris under I. Philipp. Settled at St. Paul, Minn., as condr. Schubert Club Chorus and Orchestra, Minneapolis Appolo Club, 1897; condr. Minneapolis Symphony Orchestra for 19 yrs., giving 170 concerts each yr. at home and in other cities; prof. music, U. of Minn., many yrs.; condr. Symphony Orchestra, Hollywood, Calif., summers, 1923, 26; guest conductor Los Angeles Philharmonic, San Francisco Symphony, St. Louis Symphony, Detroit Symphony orchestras. Home: Savage, Minn. Died May 22, 1933.

OBERHOLTZER, Ellis Paxson, author; b. Phila., Pa., 1868; s. John and Sara Louisa (Vickers) O.; ed. Univ. of Pa. and Berlin, Heidelberg, Freiburg, Paris and Vienna; Ph.D., U. of Pa., 1893; Litt.D., U. of Pittsburgh, 1921; m. Winona McBride. Engaged in newspaper work for a number of yrs. and magazine writer; editor of American Crisis Biographies. Director of historical pageants, Philadelphia, 1908 and 1912; Valley Forge, 1928. Sec. Pa. State Bd. Motion Picture Censors, 1915-21; sec. Transatlantic Soc. America, 1922-26; sec. Phila. Br. English-Speaking Union, 1926—; dir. English-Speaking Union of the U.S.; corr. sec. Hist. Society of Pennsylvania; sec. Scottish Memorial Assn., 1925—, also of Valley Forge Park Commn., 1925—. Author: Jay Cooke, the Financier of the Civil War, 2 vols., 1907; Henry Clay, 1909; Philadelphia, the City and Its People, 2 vols., 1911; A History of the United States since the Civil War. Vol. I, 1917, Vol. II, 1921, Vol. III, 1925, Vol. IV, 1931, Vol. V, 1936; The Morals of the Movies, 1922; Memoir of John Bach McMaster, 1933. Home: Philadelphia, Pa. Died Dec. 8, 1936.

OBERLAENDER, Gustav, mfr.; b. Germany, June 2, 1867; s. Wilhelm and Ida (Bergerhoff) O.; grad. high sch., Dusseldorf, Germany, 1885; hon. Ph.D., Heidelberg (Germany) Univ., 1933; m. Alice Penny, June 29, 1895; 1 dau., Dorothy Alice (Mrs. Harold M. Leinbach). Came to U.S., 1888, naturalized citizen, 1900. Clk. in bookstore, bank and piano business, 1888-96; in mineral water business, Indianapolis, Ind., 1896-1906; founder, 1906, treas., sec. and gen. mgr. until 1929, Berkshire Knitting Mills; pres. Oberaldo Finance Corp.; trustee New York & Hanseatic Corp. Founder and pres. Oberlaender Trust, for better understanding between citizens of U.S. and Germany. Trustee Carl Schurz Memorial Assn.; pres. bd. Reading Hosp.; patron University Mus. of Phila.; founder G. Oberlaender Foundation for Edn. and Charity. Awarded Leibnitz gold medal, Berlin Acad. Art and Science; decorated Comdr. Order of Crown of Italy; Goethe Medal (Germany). Home: Reading, Pa. Died Nov. 30, 1936.

O'BRIEN, Charles F., congressman; b. Jersey City, N.J., Mar. 7, 1879; A.B., A.M., Fordham U.; student New York Law Sch. Admitted to N.J. bar and began practice at Jersey City; has been judge 2d Criminal Court and dir. pub. safety, Jersey City; mem. 67th and 68th Congresses (1921-25), 12th N.J. Dist. Presented name of Gov. Edward I. Edwards of N.J., as nominee for Pres. of U.S., Dem. Nat. Conv., San Francisco, 1920. Home: Jersey City, N.J. Died Nov. 14, 1940.

O'BRIEN, Denis, judge Court of Appeals, N.Y., 1889—; b. Ogdensburg, N.Y., March 1837; academic edn. there; admitted to bar, May 1861; removed to Watertown; mayor Watertown, 1878-79; mem. Dem. State Com., 1880-83; atty. gen. N.Y., 1884-88. Present term expires, 1917. Home: Watertown, N.Y. Died 1909.

O'BRIEN, Edward Charles, diplomat; b. Ft. Edward, N.Y., Apr. 20, 1860; s. James and Mary (Walsh) O.; ed. Granville (N.Y.) Mil. Acad.; (LL.D., Georgetown U., 1897). In flour commn. business, Plattsburg, N.Y., several yrs.; disbursing officer, Ho. of Rep., Washington, D.C., 1889-91; U.S. commr. of navigation, 1892, 93; mem. staff of Gov. Levi P. Morton, of N.Y., 1895, rank of brig. gen.; pres. Bd. of Docks, City of New York, 1895-98; chmn. Internat. Deep Waterways Conv., Cleveland, O., 1896; E.E. and M.P. to Paraguay and Uruguay, 1905-09 (resigned); negotiated and signed extradition, naturalization and arbitration treaties with Paraguay, and treaty of naturalization with Uruguay; as dean of diplomatic corps in Paraguay, effected a cessation of civil war in Paraguay; engaged in many important enterprises for maritime ports and extension of business in S.A. Home: New York, N.Y. Died June 21, 1927.

O'BRIEN, Edward Joseph Harrington, author, editor; b. Boston, Dec. 10, 1890; s. Michael F. and Minna G. O'B.; Boston College, 1906-08, Harvard, 1908-09; m. Romer Wilson, of Sheffield, England,

July 26, 1923 (died 1930); 1 son, John Bernard; m. 2d, Ruth Gorgel, of Harburg, Germany, Oct. 26, 1932; children—Ruth Ingeborg, Dorothy Erika. Asso. editor The Poetry Jour., 1912-15, Poet Lore, 1914-15; editor New Stories, 1933-35 (founder). Author: (verse) White Fountains, 1917; (verse) Distant Music, 1921; The Advance of the American Short Story, 1923; Hard Sayings, 1927; The Dance of the Machines, 1929; Son of the Morning, 1932. Editor: The World's History at a Glance, 1913; Walks and Talks About Boston, 1916; Poems of the Irish Revolutionary Brotherhood, 1917; The Best Short Stories (ann.), 1915-40; Best British Short Stories (ann., first four vols. with John Cournos), 1921-40; The Masque of Poets, 1918; The Great Modern English Stories, 1919; Selected Short Stories (by FitzJames O'Brien), 1925; Modern English Short Stories, 1930; The Twenty-five Finest Short Stories, 1931; Modern American Short Stories, 1932; New English Short Stories, 1935; The Guest Book, 1935; Elizabethan Tales, 1937; The Fifty Best American Short Stories; 1914-1939, 1939. Edited volumes by Synge, Arnold Thompson, Davidson, Lowell and Swinburne. Translator: The Inferno (by Henri Barbusse); Three War Poems (by Paul Claudel); Job le Pauvre (by Jean de Bosschère); plays by August Stramm and O. W. Milosz; etc. European story editor Metro-Goldwyn-Mayer, 1937-39. Home: London, England. Died Feb. 25, 1941.

O'BRIEN, Frank A., priest; b. Monroe, Mich., June 7, 1851; s. Michael and Margaret O.; brother of M. Raphael O.; ed. Davis Sch., Monroe, Assumption Coll, Sandwich, Ont., Mt. St. Mary's Sem., Cincinnati; (hon. A.M., U. of Mich., 1894; LL.D., U. of Notre Dame). Ordained R.C. priest, 1877; pvt. sec. Bishop Borgess, of Detroit; asst. in chancellor's office; prof. at Assumption Coll.; pastor pro tem, St. John's Ch., Monroe, Mich.; asst. at St. Vincent's, Detroit; rector St. Augustine's Ch., Kalamazoo, Mich., 1883—, and later dean of Kalamazoo Dist. Founded St. Anthony's Sch. for Feeble Minded Children, St. Agnes Foundling Home, Barbour Hall (seminary for little boys), and Nazareth Acad. for education of young ladies. Was mem. bd. examiners at West Point under President Harrison's administration; mem. State Bd. Charities and Correction; editor Kalamazoo Augustinean, 1893-1914. Author: Memorials on Mackinac Island; Monsignor De Beaver; John Nicolet. Pres. Mich. Hist. Commn. Apptd. domestic prelate to Pope Pius X, Feb. 14, 1913. Died Dec. 19, 1921.

O'BRIEN, Frederick, author; b. Baltimore, Md., 1869; s. William J. and Catherine (McCarthy) O'B.; m. Gertrude Frye, 1897. Sailor, 1887-88; hobo, casual worker, 1891-94; newspaper work, beginning 1894, in Ohio, New York, Calif., Hawaii, the Orient and Europe; pub. Manila Cablenews, 1902-09; corr. New York Herald, 1903-09, including Japanese-Russian War; traveled around the world, 1906-07; in South Seas several yrs. and in the Orient, Europe, Africa, West Indies, S. and Central America until 1927. Fellow Am. Geog. Soc. Author: White Shadows in the South Seas, 1919; Mystic Isles of the South Seas, 1921; Atolls of the Sun, 1922. Home: Sausalito, Calif. Died Jan. 9, 1932.

O'BRIEN, James Putnam, clergyman, educator; b. Walton, N.S., Can., Sept. 19, 1861; s. James Putnam and Sarah (Densmore) O'B.; A.B., Oberlin Coll., 1884; B.D., Oberlin Theol. Sem., 1887, grad. study, 1890-91; D.D., Drury Coll., Springfield, Mo., 1914, Kansas City (Kan.) U., 1910; m. Lizzie Rust Coffin, Sept. 28, 1887; children—Esther Lucilla (dec.), Henry Rust, George Putnam, Carlton (dec.). Came to U.S., 1880; naturalized citizen, 1891. Ordained ministry Presbyn. Ch., 1887; pastor Olena and Peru, O., 1887-90, St. Louis, Mo., 1891-98, Kansas City, Mo., 1898-1901; entered Congl. ministry, 1891; supt. and dist. edn. sec. Congl. S.S. and Pub. Soc., 1901-18; dean Talledega (Ala.) Theol. Sem., 1918-22; pres. Straight Coll., New Orleans, 1922—. Died Apr. 16, 1931.

O'BRIEN, John, editor; b. Garrenjames, Parish of Imogeela, Co. Cork, Ireland, Apr. 2, 1838; s. James and Margaret (Foley) O.; came to U.S., 1850; ed. St. Charles' Coll., Md., and St. Joseph's Sem., Troy, N.Y. Ordained R.C. priest, June 6, 1868; asst. pastor, Charlestown, Mass., 1868-71; pastor, Concord and Lexington, Mass., 1871-73, Ch. of the Sacred Heart, E. Cambridge, Mass., 1873—. Founded, 1888, and from then editor, Sacred Heart Review. Made Domestic Prelate with title of monsignor by Pope Pius X, 1909. Deceased.

O'BRIEN, John F., judge; A.B., Georgetown U., 1896; m. Hilda Le G. Lockwood. Apptd. by Gov. Alfred E. Smith asso. justice of N.Y. State Supreme Court of Appeals for term 1927-41. Home: New York, N.Y. Died Dec. 25, 1939.

O'BRIEN, John Joseph, investment banking, pub. utilities; b. Chicago, Ill., Apr. 2, 1869; s. James and Bridget (Long) O'B.; ed. parochial and pub. schs. and business coll.; m. Julia Hoy, 1890 (died 1895); 1 dau., Katharine J. (Mrs. H. F. Carbaugh). Began at 18 in employ of the Pullman Co.; became connected, 1889, with the Chicago office of the United Edison Mfg. Co., which was merged into the Gen. Electric Co. in 1892, and continued in charge of accounting with latter co. until 1902; asso. with H. M. Byllesby in forming the Byllesby organization, of which was treas. and gen. auditor, and upon the death of Col. Byllesby in 1924, was elected pres. of H. M. Byllesby and Co.; officer or dir. numerous corporations. Trustee Edison Electric Institute. The operated utility cos. serve approximately 1600 cities and towns in 20 states. Catholic. Home: Chicago, Ill. Died Aug. 7, 1936.

O'BRIEN, Morgan Joseph, lawyer; b. New York, Apr. 28, 1852; A.B., St. John's Coll., New York, 1872; A.M., St. Francis Xavier Coll., New York, 1873; LL.B., Columbia, 1875; (LL.D., St. John's, 1888, Columbia, 1904, Notre Dame, 1920; Ph.D., Villanova, 1902); m. Rose M. Crimmins; children—Genevieve (Mrs. Lyttleton Fox), Rosalie (Mrs. Henry James), Madeleine (Mrs. Stuart D. Preston), Morgan J., Esmond P., Justin C., Estelle (Mrs. William F. Cogswell), Maude (Mrs. Gerald Dempsey), Kenneth. Corp. counsel of New York; elected judge Supreme Court of N.Y., for terms, 1887-1901, 1901-15; served in Trial Div., 1887-96, Appellate Div., 1896-1906 (resigned); counsel to law firm Conboy, Hewitt, O'Brien & Boardman; trustee Provident Loan Society of New York. Chevalier Legion of Honor (France). Home: New York, N.Y. Died June 16, 1937.

O'BRIEN, Thomas Dillon, lawyer; b. La Pointe, Wis., Feb. 14, 1859; s. Dillon and Elizabeth (Kelly) O'B.; ed. pub. schs.; studied law in office of Young & Newell, St. Paul; m. Mary C. Cruice, Apr. 24, 1888. Admitted to Minn. bar, 1880, and began practice at St. Paul. Was asst. city attorney of St. Paul; co. atty., Ramsey Co., Minn., 1891-93; state ins. commr., from 1905; apptd. asso. justice Minn. Supreme Ct., Oct. 1909, for unexpired term (1909-11) of C. B. Elliott, resigned. Formerly mem. Dem. Nat. Com. Capt. Battery A, Minn. N.G. 2 yrs. Home: St. Paul, Minn. Died Sept. 3, 1935.

O'BRIEN, Thomas James, ambassador; b. Jackson, Mich., July 30, 1842; s. Timothy and Elizabeth (Lander) O.; LL.B., U. of Mich., 1865, LL.D., 1908; m. Delia Howard, Sept. 4, 1873 (died 1926). Engaged in law practice at Marshall, Mich., 1865-71, and at Grand Rapids from 1871; asst. and gen. counsel Grand Rapids & Ind. Ry., 1871-1905; E.E. and M.P. to Denmark, 1905-07; A.E. and P. to Japan, 1907-11, to Italy, Aug. 11, 1911-Sept. 17, 1913. Candidate for justice Supreme Court of Mich., 1883. Home: Grand Rapids, Mich. Died May 19, 1933.

O'CALLAGHAN, Peter Joseph, clergyman; b. Milford, Mass., Aug. 6, 1866; s. Peter and Margaret (O'Sullivan) O'C.; A.B., Harvard, 1888; theol. studies St. Thomas Coll., Catholic U. of America; D.D., St. Mary's Sem., 1919. Ordained R.C. priest, 1893; asst. at Ch. of St. Paul the Apostle, New York, 1893-95; preacher of missions, 8 yrs., 1895-1903 (except 1 yr. as novice master of Paulist Community, St. Thomas Coll., Catholic U., 1898-99); treas. St. Mary's Ch., 1903-04; pastor St. Mary's Ch., and superior of the Paulist Fathers, Chicago, July 1904-Aug. 1915; rector Apostolic Mission House, Catholic U., Washington, and editor The Missionary Mag., 1915-21; founder and pres. Catholic Home Mission Soc. Founder of Community of Dominican Sisters of Sick Poor. Dir. United Com. on War Temperance Activities in the Army and Navy. Pres. Catholic Total Abstinence Union of America, 1909-16, reëlected Aug. 1924; vice chmn. Citizens Com. of 1,000; vice pres. William Jennings Bryan Memorial Assn.; vice pres. Nat. Temperance Council; U.S. del. to Internat. Anti-Alcohol Congress at The Hague, 1911, Milan, 1913, Copenhagen, 1923; mem. Permanent Com. of Internat. Congress Against Alcoholism. Home: Temperance, Mich. Died Aug. 11, 1931.

OCHS, Adolph S., newspaper pub.; b. Cincinnati, O., Mar. 12, 1858; s. Julius and Bertha (Levy) O., common sch. edn., Knoxville, Tenn.; hon. M.A., Yale Univ., 1922; LL.D., Columbia, 1924, Univ. of Chattanooga, 1925, New York U., 1926, Dartmouth College, 1932; L.H.D., Lincoln Memorial Univ., 1928; m. Effie Miriam, d. Rev. Isaac M. Wise, Feb. 28, 1883, 1 dau., Iphigene Bertha (Mrs. Arthur Hays Sulzberger). Carrier newsboy and printer's apprentice at Knoxville, Tenn., 1869-73; newspaper compositor, 1873-77; became owner and publisher (1878), Chattanooga Times, of which remained propr.; became pub. and controlling owner New York Times, 1896; purchased Philadelphia Times, 1901, Phila. Pub. Ledger, 1902, and consolidated Times with the Ledger, which sold to Cyrus H. K. Curtis, 1912. Dir. and mem. exec. com. Associated Press, 1900—. Comdr. Legion of Honor (France), 1919. Awarded gold medal, Nat. Inst. Social Sciences, 1927. Made possible the publ. of Dictionary of Am. Biography by making $500,000 available to Am. Council Learned Socs. for preparation of the manuscript; provided subvention for revival and continued publ. of Am. Year Book; initiated and organized $5,000,000 Endowment Fund, Hebrew Union Coll., Cincinnati. Originator and founder Chattanooga-Lookout Mountain Park. Citizen emeritus of Chattanooga. Died Apr. 8, 1935.

OCHSNER, Albert John, surgeon; b. Baraboo, Wis., Apr. 3, 1858; s. Henry and Judith (Hottinger) O.; B.Sc., U. of Wis., 1884; M.D., Rush Med. Coll., Chicago, 1886; studied medicine univs. of Vienna and Berlin, 1887-88; (LL.D., U. of Wis., 1909); m. Marion H. Mitchell, Apr. 3, 1888. Has practiced in Chicago, 1889—; chief surgeon Augustana and St. Mary's hosps., 1896—; prof. clin. surgery, Med. Dept. U. of Ill., Chicago, 1900—; maj., Med. R.C. U.S.A., 1916. Fellow Am. Surg. Assn., Am. Coll. Surgeons, Royal Coll. Surgeons (Ireland), Royal Microscopical Society (London). Author: Handbook on Appendicitis, 2d edit., 1906; Clinical Surgery for the Instruction of Practitioners and Students, 6th edit., 1905; Organization, Management and Construction of Hospitals, 1907; Surgery of Thyroid and Parathyroid Glands, 1910; Yearbook of Surgery, 1917-23. Treatise on Surgical Diagnosis and Treatment, 1918. Died July 25, 1925.

OCHTMAN, Leonard, artist; b. Zonnemaire, Zeeland, Holland, Oct. 21, 1854; s. John and Hendricka (Fonteine) O.; settled in Albany, N.Y., with family, 1866; was draftsman in engraving office; had studio at Albany, 2 yrs.; took winter course at Art Students' League, New York, but in his splty. of landscapes is entirely self-taught; m. Mina Fonda, June 23, 1891; children—Dorothy, Leonard, Arthur Fonda. Traveled in Eng., France and Holland, 1885; regular exhibitor at Nat. Acad. Design, 1882—, and at art socs. throughout the country, and received many medals and awards. N.A., 1904. Home: Cos Cob, Conn. Died Oct. 27, 1934.

O'CONNELL, David Joseph, congressman; b. N.Y. City, Dec. 25, 1868; s. James and Mary O'C.; ed. pub. schs.; m. Mary Agnes Green, 1893. In pub. business, New York, many yrs.; an organizer and first sec. Allied Bds. of Trade, Brooklyn; mem. 66th and 68th to 71st Congresses (1919-21, 1923-31), 9th N.Y. Dist.; mem. Booksellers' League of New York. Democrat. Catholic. Home: Brooklyn, N.Y. Died Dec. 29, 1930.

O'CONNELL, Dennis Joseph, bishop; b. Charleston, S.C.; ed. St. Charles' Sem. and St. Mary's Coll., Charleston; S.T.D., Propaganda, Rome, 1877. Ordained R.C. priest; sec. to Cardinal Gibbons; head of Am. Coll. in Rome; rector Catholic U. of America till 1909; consecrated auxiliary bishop of San Francisco, 1909; apptd. bishop of Richmond, Va., Jan. 16, 1912. Died Jan. 1, 1927.

O'CONNELL, James, labor advocate; b. Minersville, Pa., Aug. 22, 1858; s. James and Margaret (Donough) O.; pub. sch. edn.; m. Ellen Gallagher, June 12, 1886; children—Martin J., Marion M., James Jr., Thomas E. Machinist by trade; pres. Internat. Assn. Machinists, 1891-1910; 2d v.p. Am. Fed. Labor, 1895-1935; pres. metal trades dept. A.F. of L., 1911-35; retired; rep. Am. labor movement to British Trades Union Congress, Plymouth, Eng., 1899; apptd. mem. Commn. on Industrial Relations, Apr. 1913. Mem. exec. com. on labor of Council Nat. Defense, 1917. Mem. Washington Bd. of Trade. Democrat. Catholic. Home: Washington, D.C. Died Oct. 30, 1936.

O'CONNELL, John Joseph, army officer; b. Co. Kerry, Ireland, Dec. 16, 1840; s. John and Nan (Cahill) O'C.; came to U.S. in youth; acad. edn. in Can.; m. Margaret Le Boutillier, 1870. Prof. mathematics and literature, Seton Hall Coll., N.J., at outbreak of Civil War; served as Private Co. A, U.S. engrs., Feb. 3, 1865-Nov. 11, 1867; 2d lt. 1st Inf., Oct. 28, 1867; promoted through grades in regular army to col. 30th Inf., Apr. 20, 1903; brig. gen. and retired by operation of law, Dec. 16, 1904. Served in Black Hills campaign, against Sioux Indians, 1875; in Geronimo campaign against Apaches, 1882; in Pine Ridge (Dak.) Indian campaign, 1894; was the first Am. officer in command of troops to land in Cuba after declaration of war, 1898, swam ashore from boat; also served in P.I. Catholic. Home: Washington, D.C. Died Jan. 4, 1927.

O'CONNELL, John Matthew, congressman; b. Westerly, R.I., Aug. 10, 1872; s. Michael Berkeley and Ellen (Hurley) O'C.; D.D.S., Phila. Dental Coll., Temple U., 1905; m. Marie Galli, Nov. 28, 1907; 1 son, John Matthew. Began as dentist, Westerly, 1905; mem. R.I. Ho. of Rep., 1928-31; member 73d to 75th Congresses (1933-39), 2d R.I. Dist. Served as 1st lt. Headquarters San. Train, U.S.A., 16 mos., World War; now maj. Dental Reserve. Democrat. K.C., Elk. Home: Westerly, R.I. Died Dec. 6, 1941.

O'CONNELL, William Henry, banker; b. Egremont, Mass., July 29, 1843; s. William and Welthea Ann (Karner) O'C.; ed. common sch.; m. Caroline Bushnell Brown (of the Penfields of Portland, Conn.), of S. Egremont, Mass., Apr. 13, 1868. With Citizens Nat. Bank as runner, Apr. 1, 1865, pres. Jan. 15, 1908-Jan. 1918, then chmn. bd. same; dir. Kohler Mfg. Co. Democrat. Conglist. Home: Baltimore, Md. Died Oct. 1928.

O'CONNOR, Andrew, sculptor; b. Worcester, Mass., June 7, 1874; s. Andrew and Mary (McFadden) O.; pupil of father from childhood. Prin. works: Central porch, St. Bartholomew's Ch., New York; 11 marble statues, Essex Co. Ct. House, Newark, N.J.; basrelief, Library of J. P. Morgan, New York; Gen. Liscum monument, Arlington; Gen. Thomas monument, Tarrytown; bronze statue, Gen. Lawton, Indianapolis; marble statue, Gen. Lew Wallace, Capitol, Washington, and bronze statue, same, Crawfordsville, Ind.; monument to Gov. John A. Johnson, St. Paul; original model statue of Commodore Barry, Luxembourg Mus.; original design bronze St. Bartholomew's doors and marble portrait of Edward Tuck, Luxembourg Museum; statue of Lincoln, Springfield, Ill.; Roosevelt Memorial, Glen View, Ill.; bronze statue of Lafayette, Baltimore; statue of Lincoln, Royal Exchange, London; Lincoln, Providence, R.I.; Daniel O'Connell, Dublin; Mourning Woman, Nat. Gallery, London. Awarded 2d medal, Paris Salon, 1906, 1st medal, 1928. Chevalier Légion d'Honneur. Died June 9, 1941.

O'CONNOR, James, congressman; b. Apr. 4, 1870; LL.B., Tulane U., 1900; m. Florence Bland, 1903. Practiced at New Orleans, 1900—; asst. city atty., 1912-18; judge Criminal Court, Parish of New Orleans, 1918-19 (resigned); mem. 66th to 71st Congresses (1919-31), 1st La. Dist.; now 2d asst. atty. gen. of La. Democrat. Home: New Orleans, La. Died Jan. 7, 1941.

O'CONNOR, John Joseph, bishop; b. Newark, N.J., June 11, 1855; s. Thomas and Catherine (Farrell) O.; A.B., Seton Hall Coll., 1873, A.M., 1875; div. at Am. Coll., Rome, and U. of Louvain, Belgium. Ordained R.C. priest, 1877; prof. philosophy and theology, Seton Hall Coll. and Sem., 1878-95; pastor St. Joseph's, Newark, 1895-1901; consecrated bishop of Newark, N.J., July 25, 1901. Home: South Orange, N.J. Died May 20, 1927.

O'CONNOR, Joseph, journalist; b. Tribes Hill, N.Y., Dec. 17, 1841; s. Joseph and Mary (Finlay) O'C.; grad. Univ. of Rochester, 1863; admitted to bar, 1869, but never practiced; m. Miss E. M. Johnson, Nov. 20, 1877. Teacher of languages, Rochester Free Acad.; reporter and later editor Democrat and Chronicle, Rochester, 1870-73; editor Indianapolis Sentinel, 1873-75; editorial writer New York World, 1875-78; editor Buffalo Courier, 1879-85, Rochester Post-Express, 1886-96; writer of "The Rochesterian" in Rochester Post-Express, 1898—. Author: Poems, 1895. Intro. to "Don Quixote" and "Great English Plays" in World's Great Books (1898, 1900). Wrote: Through Dry Places Seeking Rest, Blackwood, Jan. 1901. Home: Rochester, N.Y. Died 1908.

O'CONNOR, T. V., chmn. U.S. Shipping Bd.; b. 1870. Moved with parents to Buffalo, N.Y., 1872; LL.D., Lincoln Memorial U. Marine engr. and master; pres. Licensed Tugmen's Assn. of Great Lakes, 1906-08; pres. Internat. Longshoremen's Assn., 1908-21; mem. N.Y. State Industrial Bd., 1921; apptd. vice chmn. U.S. Shipping Bd., 1921, apptd. chmn. bd., 1924, reapptd. chmn., 1926. Mem. advisory council Lincoln Memorial U. Died Oct. 17, 1935.

O'DAY, Daniel, capitalist; b. in Ireland, Feb. 6, 1844; came to U.S. in infancy; ed. in Buffalo, N.Y., public schools; went to Pa. oil regions, 1865; became connected with oil transportation business; constructed, 1873-76, pipe lines which were afterward consolidated with United Pipe Line system; this was later united with other interests in Nat. Transit Co., of which he is v.p.; also pres. Northwestern Ohio Natural Gas Co., etc. Home: New York, N.Y. Died 1906.

O'DEA, Edward John, bishop; b. Boston, Mass., Nov. 23, 1856; s. Edward and Ellen (Kelly) O.; grad. St. Michael's Coll., at Portland, Ore., 1876, Grand Sem., Montreal, 1882. Ordained R.C. priest, 1882; asst., Cathedral, Portland, Ore., and sec. to the archbishop, Archdiocese of Oregon, 1882-92; rector St. Patrick's Ch., Portland, 1893-96; consecrated 3d bishop Diocese of Nesqually, Sept. 8, 1896; apptd. asst. to Pontifical Throne, Oct. 8, 1925. Knight Comdr. Crown of Italy, 1927. Died Dec. 25, 1932.

O'DEA, James, stage-author; b. Hamilton, Can., Dec. 25, 1871; s. P. and B. (Collins) O.; ed. Hamilton pub. schs.; married. Has written about 500 sets of song words, popular, semi-classical and classical, principally for stage uses. Author: Daddy Longlegs (book of songs for children), 1900; Jingleman Jack (verse for children), 1901; Uncle Sam, a comedy. Also lyrics for Wizard of Oz, The Top o' the World, The Moon Prince, The Golden Horn, and Lady of the Slipper, to Victor Herbert's music; also other musical comedies. Home: Rockville Centre, N.Y. Died Apr. 12, 1914.

ODELL, Benjamin Barker, governor; b. Newburgh, N.Y., January 14, 1854; s. Hon. Benjamin Barker and Ophelia (Bookstaver) O.; student Bethany Coll., W.Va., 1873, Columbia Univ., 1873-5 (LL.D., 1903); m. Estelle Crist, Apr. 25, 1877 (died 1888); m. 2d, Mrs. Linda (Crist) Traphagen (1st wife's sister), 1891. Engaged in banking and commercial enterprises at Newburgh and N.Y. City; pres., dir. Central-Hudson Steamboat Co., etc. Member Rep. State Com., 1884-96; chmn. Rep. State Exec. Com., 1898-1900; mem. 54th and 55th Congresses (1895-99), 17th N.Y. Dist.; declined renomination; gov. of N.Y., 2 terms, 1901-05. Home: Newburgh, N.Y. Died May 9, 1926.

ODELL, Joseph Henry, clergyman; b. London, Eng., May 20, 1871; s. Rev. Joseph and Henrietta (Baker) O.; student Mason Coll., Birmingham, Eng.; grad. East Keswick (Eng.) Theol. Sem., 1894; D.D., Lafayette Coll., 1908; LL.D., U. of Del.; m. Winifred Kendall, of London, Eng., July 4, 1895; children—Mrs. Marjorie Rosamond Bradford, Helen Winifred. Ordained Presbyn. ministry, 1894; came to U.S., 1894; editor in chief Scranton (Pa.) Tribune-Republican and Scranton Truth, 1913-14; formerly polit. editorial writer Phila. Pub. Ledger and Evening Ledger; pastor Fulton, N.Y., 1894-1902, Scranton, Pa., 1902-14, 1st Ch., Troy, N.Y., 1915-18. Pres. Del. Sch. Auxiliary Assn.; v.p. U. of Del. Press; pres. Del. Sch. Foundation. War corr. for the Outlook on Western Front, 1918; chaplain 13th Pa. Inf. 10 yrs. Republican. Author: The New Spirit of the New Army, 1918; Unmailed Letters, 1924. Home: Wilmington, Del. Died Aug. 29, 1929.

ODELL, William Robert, cotton mfr.; b. Randolph Co., N.C., Mar. 3, 1855; s. John Milton and Rebecca (Kirkman) O.; student Trinity Coll., Durham, N.C., 1871-75; m. Elizabeth Sergeant, 1880 (died 1907); children—Fred Chambers, Ralph Milton, Arthur Gould; m. 2d, Mrs. Clara Branson, Apr. 5, 1912. In cotton mfg. business, 1877—; treas. and dir. Kerr Bleaching and Finishing Works, Concord, N.C.; pres. J. M. Odell Mfg. Co. (Pittsboro, N.C.); mem. N.C. Senate 2 terms, 1905-07. Trustee Duke U. (formerly Trinity Coll.); chmn. County Bd. of Edn., Cabarrus Co., N.C. Democrat. Mem. M.E. Ch., S. Rotarian. Home: Concord, N.C. Died Mar. 25, 1938.

ODELL, Willis Patterson, clergyman; b. Laconia, N.H., Dec. 14, 1855; s. Joseph L. and Abbie (Swain) O.; A.B., Boston U., 1880, A.M., 1890, Ph.D., 1896; D.D., Allegheny Coll., 1895; m. Mary F. French, June 30, 1881 (died 1904); m. 2d, Eva J. Beede (M.A.), Nov. 21, 1906 (died 1928). Entered Methodist Episcopal ministry, 1880; ordained deacon, 1883, elder, 1886; pastor Cliftondale, Mass., 1880-83, Wesley Ch., Salem, Mass., 1883-86, Center Ch., Malden, Mass., 1886-90, Delaware Av. Ch., Buffalo, 1890-95, Richmond Av. Ch., Buffalo, 1895-98, Calvary Ch., New York, 1898-1904, First Ch., Germantown, Phila., 1904-07, St. Mark's Ch., Brookline, Mass., 1911-17; supt. Meth. Chs. in Boston Dist., 1917-20, Calvary Ch., New York, 1920-26; mem. N.H. legislature, 1926-28, chaplain, 1920-30. Mason. V.p. Nat. Bank, Lakeport, N.H. Trustee Boston U., Tilton Sch. Died June 22, 1931.

ODELL, Willmot Mitchell, lawyer; b. Cleburne, Tex., Mar. 16, 1878; s. James Mitchell and Arabella (Murchison) O.; LL.B., U. of Tex., 1899; LL.M., Georgetown U., 1900; m. Rita Harris. Mem. Ramsey & Odell, Cleburne, 1901-17; U.S. dist. attorney, Northern District of Tex., 1917-19; mem. Goree, Odell & Allen, 1919—. Mem. Bd. of Regents U. of Tex. Democrat. Baptist. Mason. Home: Fort Worth, Tex. Died Nov. 14, 1932.

ODENBACH, Frederick Louis, meteorologist; b. Rochester, N.Y., Oct. 21, 1857; s. John and Elizabeth (Minges) O.; A.B., Canisius Coll., Buffalo, N.Y., 1881; studied in univs. of Europe. Joined Soc. of Jesus, 1881; prof. physics and chemistry, 1893-1903, then prof. astronomy and meteorology, St. Ignatius Coll., Cleveland, also founder, 1895, and dir. Meteorol. Obs.; now prof. astronomy, John Carroll U., Cleveland. Inventor of ceraunograph and an elec. seismograph; the 6th observer of the Helvetian halo, Dec. 6, 1901. Died Mar. 15, 1933.

ODLIN, Arthur Fuller, lawyer; b. Concord, N.H., Apr. 25, 1860; s. Woodbridge and Abby Pratt (Comstock) O.; student Dartmouth, 1877-79; LL.D. cum laude, Boston U. Sch. of Law, 1885; m. Mary Emma Allen, Oct. 5, 1886; children—Lawrence Allen, Mrs. Evelyn Attwood. Admitted to bar, 1885, and practiced in Mass., Ohio and Fla.; atty. gen. Puerto Rico, 1899-1901; judge Court of First Instance, Manila, P.I., 1901-04; served as judge U.S. Dist. Court of Puerto Rico, 1921-25; later in practice at Jacksonville, Fla. Opened with Judge William A. Kincaid, the first nisi prius court in P.I., under the U.S. Govt. Republican. Unitarian. Died June 7, 1926.

ODOM, William (MacDougall); b. Columbus, Ga., May 30, 1884; s. John David and Maria (Carughi) O.; grad. N.Y. Sch. Fine and Applied Art, 1909; studied in Italy, France and England; unmarried. Pres. New York Sch. Fine and Applied Art and founder of Paris br. Has lectured in Italy, France and England. Republican. Episcopalian. Author: The History of Italian Furniture, Vol. I, 1918, Vol. II, 1919. Chevalier Legion of Honor (France). Died Jan. 29, 1942.

O'DONAGHUE, Denis, bishop; b. Daviess Co., Ind., Nov. 30, 1848; early edn. Meinrad's Coll. and St. Thomas' Sem., Bardstown, Ky.; studied theology Grand Sem., Montreal. Ordained R.C. priest, Sept. 6, 1874, and apptd. asst. priest St. John's Ch., Indianapolis; was chancellor Vincennes Diocese 21 yrs.; permanent rector St. Patrick's Church, Indianapolis, 1885-1910; consecrated auxiliary, and titular bishop of Pomario, Apr. 25, 1900; apptd. bishop of Louisville, Ky., Feb. 1910. Died Nov. 7, 1925.

O'DONNELL, Charles Leo, clergyman; b. Greenfield, Ind., Nov. 15, 1884; s. Neil and Mary (O'Donnell) O'D.; A.B., U. of Notre Dame, 1906; studied theology, Holy Cross Coll., Washington, 1906-10; studied Harvard; Ph.D., Catholic U. of America, 1910. Ordained priest R.C. Ch., in the Congregation of Holy Cross, June 24, 1910; prof. English lit., U. of Notre Dame, 1910-28, pres., 1928—. Asso. editor Ave Maria. Chaplain, A.E.F., Feb. 1918-May 1919. Elected provincial of Congregation of Holy Cross in United States, Aug. 1920, and asst. superior general, 1926. Chevalier Order of Crown of Italy, 1931. Author: Newman's Gentleman, 1916; The Dead Musician and Other Poems, 1916; Cloister and Other Poems, 1922; A Rime of the Rood and Other Poems, 1928. Editor: Notre Dame Verse, 1917. Home: Notre Dame, Ind. Died June 4, 1934.

O'DONNELL, Mary Eleanor, editor; b. Council Bluffs, Ia., July 28, 1882; d. John P. and Ellen (Sheedy) O.; grad. St. Francis Acad., Council Bluffs; studied univs. of Iowa and Pa.; connected with various papers as spl. sociol. writer; went abroad on spl. investigation work for a syndicate of papers, and as contbr. to mags.; editor Woman's Page, Philadelphia Press, 1904-06, Woman's Syndicate section, Philadelphia North American, 1906-07; editor Designer, New York, 1907-09; asso. editor Delineator from 1909; also editor of woman's section Chicago Tribune, and writes working girls' page in Chicago Sunday Tribune, under name of Alice Mason. Lecturer upon sociol. subjects. Died Aug. 11, 1913.

O'DONNELL, Thomas Jefferson, lawyer; b. Mendham Tp., Morris Co., N.J., June 2, 1856; s. Michael and Amy (O'Connell) O.; ed. pub. and pvt. schs., N.J.; engaged in newspaper work in N.J. and New York, 1873-79; removed to Denver, 1879; m. Katharyn Dwyer, Oct. 24, 1881. Admitted to bar, 1880, and entered practice at Denver. Dem. candidate for Congress from Colo. at-large, 1890; candidate for U.S. senator before Colo. Gen. Assembly, 1911; contest resulted in deadlock; received large note in primaries, 1912, for Democratic nomination for senator. Chmn. Colo. delegation, Dem. Nat. Conv., 1904, and seconded nomination of Parker for President. V.p. Colo. Commn. to St. Louis, Expn., 1904 (one of original organizers and mem. original exec. com.). Commr. Nat. Conf. Commrs. on Uniform State Laws. Home: Denver, Colo. Died June 11, 1925.

O'DONOVAN, Charles, pediatrician; b. Baltimore, Md., Feb. 7, 1860; s. Charles and Henrietta H. (Jenkins) O'D.; A.B., Georgetown Coll., D.C., 1878, A.M., 1888; M.D., U. of Md., 1881; LL.D., Loyola, 1910; m. M. Rosa Shriver, June 2, 1896; children—Eleanor M. (Mrs. Henry C. Evans), M. Edith, Charles, M. Rosalie. Practiced at Baltimore, 1881—; prof. pediatrics and clin. medicine, U. of Md., 1899—; visiting phys. Md. Gen., St. Joseph's and Bon Secours hosps. Mem. Charter Bd. of Baltimore, 1918. Democrat. Mem. Knights of Columbus. Home: Baltimore, Md. Died Jan. 23, 1930.

O'DONOVAN, William Rudolf, sculptor; b. Preston Co., Va., Mar. 28, 1844; s. Col. James Hayes and Mary (Bright) O.; self taught in art; served in Staunton Arty. C.S.A., Apr. 17, 1861, to surrender at Appomattox; m. Mary Corcoran, 1893. Established studio in New York after war; has executed many important portrait busts and bas-reliefs, including: Wm. Page, N.A., which was presented to the Nat. Acad. Design; Arthur Quartly, N.A., R. Swain Gifford, N.A., Winslow Homer, N.A., Thomas Elkins, N.A., Edmund Clarence Stedman; busts of Walt Whitman and Gen. Joseph Wheeler; relief of Mme. Blavatskey from life, and recently, after 10 yrs. devoted to painting, busts of Generals Daniel E. Sickles and James Grant Wilson; statues of Washington for Caracas, Venezuela, for monument commemorating the Peace at Newburgh, N.Y., for Trenton battle monument; equestrian statues of Lincoln and Grant for Soldiers' and Sailors' Arch, Prospect Park, Brooklyn; reliefs for Oriskany battle monument; statue of Archbishop Hughes, St. John's Coll., Fordham; memorial tablet to Bayard Taylor, Cornell U., bust of late Charles P. Daly; statues for soldiers' monuments in various parts of the country. One of the 4 founders of the famous Tile Club; mem. Hudson-Fulton Commn., Nat. Com. for the Celebration of Peace Among the English-Speaking Peoples; advisory mem. Maine Monument Com. A.N.A., 1878. Home: New York, N.Y. Died Apr. 20, 1920.

OEHMLER, Leo, music teacher, composer; b. Pittsburgh, Pa., Aug. 15, 1867; s. Rudolf Christian and Elizabeth (Foerster) O.; certificate, Western U. of Pa., 1885; grad. Royal Conservatory of Music, Schwarzburg-Sondershausen, and Sterns Conservatory, Berlin, Germany; pupil of Sauret, Radecke, Nolte, Gruenberg, Kayser and others; m. Lillian Katherine Heche, Dec. 25, 1911. Teacher piano, violin, harmony and composition in Pittsburgh and neighboring cities for many yrs.; moved to Pasadena, Calif., 1907. Republican. Lutheran. Composer of 325 works, including piano solos, pieces for violin and piano, songs, etc.; best known work is Cleopatra Suite in 4 parts, for piano, also for orchestra. Home: Pasadena, Calif. Died Nov. 3, 1930.

OELRICHS, Hermann, shipping mcht.; b. Baltimore, Md., June 8, 1850; s. Henry and Julia (May) O.; received thorough edn. in U.S. and Germany; entered office, 1871, became partner, 1875, and senior mem., 1887, Oelrichs & Co., Am. agts. North-German Lloyd Steamship Co. Also prominent in amateur athletics; has been mem. Nat. Dem. Com. Home: New York, N.Y. Died 1906.

OEMLER, Marie Conway, author; b. Savannah, Ga., May 29, 1879; d. Richard Hoban and Helena (Browne) Conway; ed. convent, pub. schs., but mainly at home; m. John Norton Oemler, July 31, 1901; children—Elizabeth Heyward, Alan Norton. Mem. Poetry Soc. of S.C., Poetry Soc. of Ga. Author: Slippy McGee, 1917; A Woman Named Smith, 1919; The Purple Heights, 1920; Where The Young Child Was, and Other Christmas Stories, 1921; Two Shall Be Born, 1922; His Wife in Law, 1925; The Holy Lover, 1927; Sheaves, 1928; Johnny Reb, 1929; Flower of Thorn, 1931. Died June 6, 1932.

OERTEL, Johannes Adam, artist, clergyman; b. Fürth, Bavaria, Nov. 3, 1823; s. Thomas Friedrich and Maria Magdalena O.; studied art in Nüremberg and Munich (D.D., Univ. of the South). Worked at engraving until 1848; came to U.S., 1848; had studio, 1857-61, Madison, N.J., and Brooklyn, N.Y.; after 1861 in Westerly, R.I.; painted many scriptural and other pieces, and animals; m. Julia Adelaide Torrey. Deacon, 1867, priest, 1871, P.E. Ch.; rector Lenoir, N.C., 1869-80; Morgantown, N.C., 1880; later prof. Christian art, Univ. of the South. Painter of "Rock of Ages" and series of 4 large pictures, embracing the entire "Plan of Redemption," presented to Univ. of the South, Suwanee, Tenn. Besides paintings he has executed much wood carving for ecclesiastical use. Has done ch. work in Lenoir, N.C., Washington, New York, Glen Cove, L.I., Jackson, Tenn. Home: Vienna, Va. Died 1909.

O'FARRELL, Patrick, lawyer; b. Ireland, 1832; s. James O'F.; ed. in Ireland; came to U.S., 1862, to enlist in Union army; served in 69th N.Y. (Corcoran's Irish Legion), pvt. to capt., ending at Appomattox; wounded 5 times in battle; bvtd. capt. "for gallant and distinguished conduct at battle of Reams' Station, nr. Petersburg, Va.," Aug. 25, 1864; grad. Nat. Univ., Washington (LL.B., LL.M.); admitted to bar, Supreme Court, D.C., June 1885, Supreme Court, U.S., April 1889. Active Republican until campaign of 1900; changed to Democrat on issue of imperialism. Wrote: O'Farrell's Financial Dialogue, 1896 (in favor of gold standard). Home: Washington, D.C. Died 1902.

O'FERRALL, Charles Triplett, lawyer, governor; b. Frederick Co., Va., Oct. 21, 1840; s. John and Jane (Green) O'F.; grad. law dept., Washington Coll., Va., 1869; m. Feb., 1865, d. Col. Robert McLain, Miss.; m. 2d, Jan. 1881, d. Col. Wm. C. Knight. At age of 17 was elected clerk co. court, Morgan Co., Va. (now W.Va.), for term of 6 yrs. Served, pvt. to col., in Confederate cav., 1861-65; wounded several times, once through the lungs. Served 2 yrs. in Va. house of dels.; 6 yrs. as judge; 12 yrs. mem. Congress; gov. Va., 1894-98. Located in Richmond, 1898; gen. counsel for many corporations. Is a gold Dem. and declined to support Bryan in 1896 and 1900. Pres. life ins. co. and dir. various corporations. Mem. United Confed. Vets. Home: Richmond, Va. Died 1905.

OFFENHAUER, Roy Ernest, univ. pres.; b. Montezuma, O., Aug. 10, 1881; s. Julius and Elizabeth (Yaney) O.; B.S., Marion (Ind.) Normal Coll., 1903; A.B., Otterbein, 1905; student Miami U., 1906, Harvard, 1909; A.M., Columbia, 1917; hon. D.Ped., O. Northern U., 1934; m. Ella May Smith, Aug. 4, 1907; children—Ruth Ernestine (dec.), Wendell Dean (dec.), Helen Geraldine (Mrs. Lehman Otis), Wayne Berrey, Robert Dwight. Teacher, supt. schs., prin. high schs., 1899-1918; prin. high sch., Lima, O., 1918-24; supt. schs., 1924-37; pres. Bowling Green (O.) State U., 1937—. Dir., treas., mem. exec. com. N.E.A. Chamber of Commerce. Mem. M.E. Ch. Mason. Home: Bowling Green, O. Died Dec. 29, 1938.

OFFIELD, Charles Kirkpatrick, lawyer; b. Lewiston, Ill., July 12, 1845; s. Franklin Pike and Martha K. O.; matriculated in Northwestern U., but in freshmen yr., 1864, served for 9 mos. in Ky. and Mo. as sergt. of the 134th Ill. Vols.; LL.B., U. of Mich., 1869; m. May R. Munson, 1875. Admitted to Ill. bar, 1870; became mem. of Goodwin, Offield & Towle, making a spl ty. of soliciting patents and patent litigation; firm now Offield, Towle, Graves & Offield. Dir. Dental Protective Supply Co. of the U.S., Chicago Postal Pneumatic Service Co. Republican. Home: Chicago, Ill. Died Aug. 22, 1918.

OFFLEY, Cleland Nelson, naval officer; b. Georgetown, D.C., June 8, 1869; s. Holmes E. and Mary (Nelson) O.; grad. U.S. Naval Acad., 1889; m. Margaret A. Greenlees, July 14, 1891. Promoted asst. engr., July 1, 1891; passed asst. engr., Dec. 14, 1896; transferred to the line as lt., Mar. 3, 1899; lt. comdr., July 1, 1905; comdr., July 1, 1910; capt., Aug. 10, 1916. Served on Oregon, Spanish-Am. War, 1898, Solace, 1903-05; engr. officer Colorado, 1905-06; with Bur. Steam Engring., Navy Dept., 1906-08; fleet engr. Pacific Fleet, 1908-09; at U.S. Naval Acad., 1909-10; engr. officer Navy Yard, Puget Sound, 1910-13; exec. officer New Hampshire, 1913-14; comdr. Prometheus, 1914-15; engr. officer Navy Yard, Mare Island, Calif., 1915-19; insp. engring. material, Pittsburgh, 1919-21; insp. engineering material, Hartford, Conn., 1921—. Advanced 4 numbers in rank "for eminent and conspicuous conduct in battle" during Spanish-Am. War. Home: Hamilton, Va. Died 1935.

OGDEN, Charles Franklin, congressman; b. Charleston, Ind.; s. Floyd and Mary (Pounds) O.; grad. high sch.; LL.B., U. of Louisville, Ky., 1896; m. Lula Whiteside, 1898. Began practice at Louisville, 1897; mem. Ky. Ho. of Rep., 1898, 99; mem. 66th and 67th Congresses (1919-23), 5th Ky. Dist. Republican. Mem. Christian (Disciples) Ch. Was commissioned officer old Louisville Legion; capt. 8th U.S. Inf., Spanish-Am. War, 1938. Home: Anchorage, Ky. Died Apr. 10, 1933.

OGDEN, George Dickie, ry. official; b. Homer City, Pa., May 16, 1868; s. George Hill and Nancy H. (Dickie) O.; student Washington and Jefferson Coll., class of 1890; m. Mary B. McCandless, June 21, 1893. Entered service of Pa. R.R. Co. as agt. at Homer City, June 1, 1887; promoted through various positions to asst. gen. freight agt. same rd., at Phila., Mar. 1, 1906, gen. freight agt., 1912-16, traffic mgr. Central Region, at Pittsburgh, Pa., 1920-23, traffic mgr. Eastern Region, Phila., 1923-29, asst. v.p. in charge traffic, New York, 1929-31, v.p., New England, 1931-33, asst. v.p. in charge traffic, New York, 1933—. Organized Traffic Emergency Com., Pittsburgh, 1917, for movement of war materials; organized Export Div. General Operating Com. of Eastern Railroads, Dec. 1917, hdqrs. N.Y. City; title changed to Freight Traffic Com., North Atlantic Ports, of which was chmn. until June 11, 1918, then chmn. The Exports Control Com., representing the R.R. Administration, having charge of transportation of all freight going overseas, for War and Navy depts., allied govts. and others. Republican. Presbyn. Mason. Died Oct. 4, 1936.

OGDEN, Henry (Harry) Alexander, artist; b. Philadelphia, Pa., July 17, 1856; s. Henry S. and Anna A. (Bulkley) O.; ed. high sch., Brooklyn, N.Y., art study Brooklyn Inst., Brooklyn Acad. Design, Nat. Acad. Design and Art Students League of New York; m. Louise E. Wilmot, Nov. 29, 1882 (died 1923); 1 son, Harry Wilmot (dec.). Staff artist with Frank Leslie, publishers, 1873-81; New York artist, Strobridge Lithograph Co., Cincinnati, O., 1881-1932. Republican. Episcopalian. Illustrator: Our Army For Our Boys, 1906. Co-author: Boys' Book of Famous Regiments, 1914. Compiler: Our Flag and Our Songs, 1917, George Washington—for Young People, 1932. Has specialized on historical, uniform and costume painting; made 71 color plates for U.S. Govt. showing U.S. army uniforms, 1888-1906, mil. plates for Pageant of America (Yale Univ. Press) and costume and uniform plates for Chronicles of America Picture Corp. Died June 15, 1936.

OGDEN, Henry Warren, congressman; b. Abingdon, Va., Oct. 21, 1842; s. Elias and Louisa (Gordon) O.; removed to Warrensburg, Mo., 1851; worked on father's farm summers and attended common schools winters; served in C.S.A., lt., 16th Mo. inf.; later on staff Brig. Gen. Lewis; paroled, Shreveport, June 8, 1865; then engaged in farming in La.; mem. State Constl. Conv., 1879; mem. La. ho. reps., 1880-88, and speaker, 1884-88; elected to 53d Congress to fill vacancy caused by apptmt. of N. C. Blanchard to be U.S. senator; reëlected to 54th and 55th Congresses. Home: Benton, La. Died 1905.

OGDEN, Herbert Gouverneur, asst. U.S. Coast and Geodetic Survey, 1869—; and insp. of hydrography and topography, 1898; b. New York, April 4, 1846; s. Morgan Lewis and Eliza Glendy (McLaughlin) O.; ed. private schools and tutors; apptd. aid, April 22, 1863, promoted to asst., 1869, U.S. Coast and Geodetic Survey; m. Mary A. Greene, May 28, 1872. Served, 1863, with army on defenses of Washington; 1864, with navy in sounds of N.C.; 1865, with Nicaragua expdn.; 1870, as topographer with 1st naval exploring expdn. to Isthmus of Darien; 1893, in charge of party locating internat. boundary between British Columbia and Alaska; etc. Mem. U.S. Bd. on Geographic Names; expert in topography and chartography. Deceased.

OGDEN, Robert Curtis; b. Philadelphia, Pa., June 20, 1836; s. Jonathan and Abigail (Murphey) O.; ed. in select sch., Phila.; (M.A., Yale, 1902; LL.D., Tulane, 1903; L.H.D., Union College, N.Y., 1909); m. Ellen Elizabeth Lewis, Mar. 1, 1860 (died 1909). Mem. firm of John Wanamaker, 1885-1907, retired Apr. 1, 1907. Mem. State Johnstown Flood Relief Commn., Pa., 1889; pres. trustees Hampton Inst., Hampton, Va.; pres. directors Union Theol. Sem., New York; trustee Tuskegee Inst., Ala.; pres. Southern Edn. Bd., Conf. for Edn. in the South; trustee Gen. Edn. Bd.; apptd. mem. Taft's Commn. to Liberia, 1909, but declined. Hon. mem. Clio Soc., Princeton. Home: New York, N.Y. Died Aug. 6, 1913.

OGDEN, Rollo, newspaperman; b. Sand Lake, N.Y., Jan. 19, 1856; s. Rev. Isaac Gray and Emma (Huntington) O.; A.B., Williams, 1877, L.H.D., 1903; Andover Theol. Sem., 1877-79; Union Theol. Seminary, 1879-80; m. Susan M. Mitchell, Nov. 30, 1881. Ordained Presbyn. ministry, 1881; asso. pastor First Ch., Cleveland, 1880-81; missionary City of Mexico, 1881-83; pastor Case Av. Ch., Cleveland, 1883-87; in lit. work, New York, 1887-1903; on staff, 1891-1920, editor, 1903-20, New York Evening Post; editor New York Times, 1922—. Home: Summit, N.J. Died Feb. 22, 1937.

OGILVIE, Clinton, artist; b. New York, N.Y., Dec. 28, 1838; studied painting under James M. Hart and, 1866-67, in Paris. Has spent several seasons abroad at Paris, Nice and Mentone. Asso. Nat. Acad., 1864—; makes exhibitions of landscapes; notably of Swiss and French scenery. Home: New York, N.Y. Died 1900.

O'GORMAN, Thomas, bishop; b. Boston, Mass., May 1, 1843; s. John and Margaret (O'Keefe) O.; ed. in Chicago and St. Paul, 1850-53; studied in France, 1853-65—grad. 1863; (D.D., from Pope Leo XIII, 1893). Pastor Rochester, Minn., 1867-78; mem. Paulist community, N.Y., 1878-82; pastor Faribault, Minn., 1882-85; first pres. Coll. of St. Thomas, Merriam Park, St. Paul, and prof. of dogmatic theology, 1886-90; prof. modern ch. history, Catholic U., Washington, 1890-95; consecrated bishop of Sioux Falls, S.D., Apr. 19, 1896. Author: A History of the Roman Catholic Church in the United States; etc. Died Sept. 8, 1921.

O'HAGAN, Thomas, author, lecturer; b. Toronto, Can., Mar. 6, 1855; s. John and Bridget (O'Reilly) O'H.; St. Michael's Coll., Toronto; A.B., Ottawa U., Ont., 1882, A.M., 1885; Ph.D., Syracuse U., 1889; grad. student Cornell U., 1893-94, U. of Wis. and U. of Chicago, 1901, 02, Grenoble U., France, U. of Louvain, Belgium, U. of Bonn, Germany, and U. of Fribourg, Switzerland, 1903, 04; Litt.D., Laval U., Quebec, 1914, Ottawa U., 1924; LL.D., Notre Dame U., 1917. Began on Daily Tribune, Duluth, Minn., 1891; editor New World, Chicago, 1910-13. Author: Essays on Catholic Life, 1916; Songs of Heroic Days, 1916; Complete Poetical Works, 1922; With Staff and Scrip, 1924; Dean Harris in Makers of Canadian Literature series, 1924; The Genesis of Christian Art, 1926; Intimacies in Canadian Life and Letters, 1927; Father Morice (in Ryerson History Readers), 1927; Spain and Her Daughters, 1930; Dudheen Dreams, 1930; What Shakespeare Is Not, 1936. Home: Toronto, Ont., Can. Died Mar. 2, 1939.

O'HAIR, Frank Trimble, congressman; b. Edgar Co., nr. Paris, Ill., Mar. 12, 1870; s. John H. and Nancy Evalyn O'H.; A.B., DePauw U., 1893; m. Ruth Harding Huston, May 10, 1905. Began practice of law, Paris, Ill., 1893; mem. 63d Congress (1913-15), 18th Ill. Dist. Democrat. Mason, Red Man, K.P., Elk. Home: Paris, Ill. Died Aug. 3, 1932.

O'HANLON, Thomas, educator, and clergyman; b. New York, N.Y., Mar. 23, 1832; s. John and Catharine (Landers) O.; A.B., Rutgers Coll., and Princeton U., 1863, A.M., 1865; (D.D., Dickinson Coll., 1869; LL.D., Washington Coll., Tenn., 1893); m. Hannah M. Mapes, Mar. 4, 1856. Pres. Pennington (N.J.) Sem., 1870-1903 (resigned). Ordained M.E. ministry, 1855. Died Sept. 1912.

O'HARA, Edward H., publisher; b. Skaneateles, N.Y., Dec. 27, 1853; s. John and Catherine (Healey) O'H.; ed. pub. schs., under tutors and 1 yr. Syracuse U.; m. Anna Hogan, Aug. 20, 1883. Worked at printing trade till 1877; in editorial dept. Syracuse Herald, 1879-1903, pub., 1903—, also part owner; director Salt Springs Nat. Bank. Pres. Municipal Service Bd., Syracuse, 1885-87; trustee State Coll. of Forestry. Representative, by apptmt. of Governor Roosevelt, with former state engr., and two senators and two assemblymen, elected by their different bodies, on Bridge Authority Commn., to recapture Bear Mountain Bridge across the Hudson, Peace Bridge at Buffalo, the bridge at Poughkeepsie and to build two other bridges on the Hudson and one or more internat. bridges across the St. Lawrence River (this commission being still in existence). Mem. com. of 12 American publishers and editors selected by British Govt., 1918, to inspect British operations on the battle lines in Europe; also one of eighty Am. newspaper pubs., guests of Edwin Denby, sec. of navy, to witness maneuvering of U.S. Navy at Culebra Cut, Caribbean Sea, 1924. Author: World War at Its Climax, 1922. Home: Syracuse, N.Y. Died Feb. 10, 1936.

O'HARA, Frank, prof. economics; b. Lanesboro, Minn., Mar. 24, 1876; s. Owen and Margaret (Nugent) O'H.; B.A., U. of Minn., 1900; M.A., U. of Notre Dame, 1901; Ph.D., U. of Berlin, 1904; m. Linda Helen Maley, Aug. 25, 1908. Editor Catholic Progress, Seattle, Wash., 1904-05; prof. economics, U. of Notre Dame, 1905-07; dir. Interlaken Sch., LaPorte, Ind., 1907-08; prof. economics, Catholic U., 1909—, dean Sch. of Philosophy, same, 1920-24; organizer and dean Knights of Columbus Evening Sch., 1919-28; dir. Merchants Bank & Trust Co. Chmn. edni. com. of Knights of Columbus, 1920-27, also past grand knight Washington Council K.C., and past dist. dep.; chairman Parish Credit Union National Committee, 1930—. Author: Unemployment in Oregon, 1914; Introduction to Economics, 1915; The Non-Partisan League, 1917; Outlines of Economics, 1933. Editor of Catholic Rural Life Magazine, 1927-30. Home: Washington, D.C. Died July 30, 1938.

O'HARRA, Cleophas Cisney, geologist; b. Bentley, Ill., Nov. 4, 1866; s. Jefferson Wood and Paulina (Robertson) O.; A.B., Carthage (Ill.) Coll., 1891, LL.D., 1920; Ph.D., Johns Hopkins, 1898 (Phi Beta Kappa); m. Mary Phebe Marvel, June 15, 1893; children—Berry Marvel, Paul Wyatt, Wayne Gilder, Mariam. Instr. Latin and physics, 1891-92, prof. natural and phys. sciences, 1892-95, v.p., 1894-95, Carthage Coll.; prof. mineralogy and geology, 1898-1911, pres. and prof. geology, July 1, 1911—, S.D. State Sch. of Mines. Chmn. S.Dak. State Coal Commn., 1917-18; mem. State Advisory Bd. Federal Fuel Administration, 1917-19; ednl. dir. Soldier Training, S.Dak. State Sch. of Mines, World War. Fellow Geol. Soc. America, A.A.A.S. Conglist. Author: The White River Badlands; The Mineral Wealth of the Black Hills, 1929; joint author The Geology, Mineralogy, and Scenic Features of Custer State Park, S.D. Editor in chief, Black Hills Engineer. Home: Rapid City, S.D. Died Feb. 21, 1935.

O'HERN, Charles A., clergyman; b. Lawrence, Kan., Dec. 31, 1881; s. Patrick and Mary (Starr) O.; ed. St. Ignatius' Coll., Chicago; Am. Coll., Rome, Italy; Ph.D., Roman Acad. of St. Thomas Aquinas, 1905; (D.D., Univ. of the Propaganda, Rome, 1907). Ordained priest R.C. Ch., July 15, 1906; apptd. v.rector Am. Coll., Rome, June 25, 1907; coadjutor rector, with right of succession, May 16, 1916; succeeded to rectorship, Aug. 28, 1917, after death of the rector, Archbishop Kennedy. Named pvt. chamberlain to Pope Pius X, Nov. 11, 1911, to Pope Benedict XV, Sept. 1914; domestic prelate of Papal Household, Nov. 14, 1917. Died May 13, 1925.

O'HERN, Lewis Jerome, clergyman; b. Olean, N.Y., June 12, 1878; s. Patrick and Ellen (Casey) O.; Baccalaureate in Sacred Theology, Catholic U. of America, 1903; S.T.D., U. of St. Apolinare, Rome, 1911, D.C.L., 1912; LL.D., Little Rock Coll., Ark., 1928. Ordained priest R.C. Ch., 1903; prof. dogmatic theology and canon law, Paulist House of Studies, Catholic U. of America, 1912-21; exec. sec. to Cardinal Hayes, 1917—; apptd. rector Apostolic Mission House and editor of The Missionary, 1921. Mem. bd. dirs. Catholic Missionary Union. K.C. (4th degree). Died Dec. 12, 1930.

O'HIGGINS, Harvey, author; b. London, Ont., Can., Nov. 14, 1876; s. Joseph P. and Isabella (Stephenson) O.; student U. of Toronto, 1893-97; m. Anna G. Williams, of Toronto, July 1901. Asso. chmn. Com. on Pub. Information, Washington, D.C., 1917-18. Author: The Smoke Eaters, 1905; Don-a-Dreams, 1906; A Grand Army Man, 1908; Old Clinkers, 1909; The Beast and the Jungle (with Judge Ben B. Lindsey), 1910; Under the Prophet in Utah (with Frank J. Cannon), 1911; The Argyle Case (with Harriet Ford), 1912; The Dummy (with Harriet Ford), 1913; Polygamy, 1914; Silent Sam, 1914; Adventures of Detective Barney, 1915; Mr. Lazarus (with Harriet Ford), 1916; From the Life, 1919; On the Hiring Line (with Harriet Ford), 1919; The Doughboy's Religion (with Judge Ben B. Lindsey), 1919; The Secret Springs, 1920; Some Distinguished Americans, 1922; The American Mind in Action (with Dr. Edward H. Reede), 1924; Julie Cane, 1924; Clara Barron, 1925. Home: Martinsville, N.J. Died Feb. 28, 1929.

OHL, Henry, Jr., labor official; b. Milwaukee, Wis., Mar. 16, 1873; s. Henry and Mary Elizabeth (Dietrich) O.; ed. pub. and evening schs. of Milwaukee; m. Anna W. E. Fleischmann, Apr. 7, 1894; children—Harry David, Veronica Elizabeth (Mrs. Charles Kunde), Cora Agnes (Mrs. Alfred E. Boppel). Began as printer, 1886; sec. Allied Printing Trades Council, Milwaukee, 1903-05; del. Milwaukee Federated Trades Council, 1908—; field rep. Internat. Typog. Union, 1906-08; editor The Typo, 1906-09; incorporator Commonwealth Mut. Savings Bank, Milwaukee, 1912; dep. clk. City of Milwaukee, 1910-12; organizer Am. Fed. of Labor and Wis. State Fed. of Labor, 1914—; pres. Wis. Fed. of Labor, 1917—. Mem. Wis. Ho. of Rep., 1917-18; editor Wis. Federation Bulletin, 1921—; editor Wisconsin Labor, 1924—; mem. President's Advisory Council on Economic Security, 1934-35; mem. Federal Board for Vocational Edn., 1935—. Mem. bd. trustees Milwaukee Labor Coll., 1921-35; mem. Wis. Univ.-Labor Joint Com. on Edn. for Workers in Industry, 1927-40; sec. Wis. Unemployment Relief Commn., 1931-32; mem. Wis. Advisory Bd. on Unemployment Compensation, 1931-35; mem. Wis. Council NRA Employment Service, 1934-40. Mem. Farmer-Labor Fed. K.P., Eagles. Home: Okauchee, Wis. Died Oct. 16, 1940.

OHL, Jeremiah Franklin, clergyman; b. Cherryville, Pa., June 26, 1850; s. Milton and Mary Elizabeth (Schick) O.; Mercersburg (Pa.) Coll., 1866-67; A.B., Muhlenberg Coll., Pa., 1871, A.M., 1874, Mus.D., 1893; grad. Luth. Theol. Sem., Phila., 1874; D.D., Wittenberg Coll., Springfield, O., 1921; m. Olivia Elizabeth Kessler, Mar. 10, 1873 (died Jan. 16, 1919); children—Hermine Elizabeth (wife of Prof. C. Theodore Benze), Else Rebecca, Frederick William. Ordained Luth. ministry, June 3, 1874; pastor, Quakertown (Pa.) Parish, 1874-93; organizer and rector Luth. Deaconess Motherhouse, Milwaukee, and instr. Theol. Sem. Luth. Ch., Chicago, 1893-98; city missionary, Phila., 1899-1930; supt. Phila. City Mission of Evang. Luth. Ch., 1903-30. Lecturer, Luth. Theol. Sem., Phila., 1910-11; mus. editor The Helper, 1882-91; lecturer at summer schs. Frequent delegate General Council Evang. Luth. Church in North America (now United Luth. Ch. in America), and mem. com. on liturgy and hymn books, 1885—; mem. Inner Mission Bd. and other bds. many yrs.; long active in prison reform work, and frequent del. to Nat. Prison Congress; del. to Internat. Prison Congress, 1910. Trustee Muhlenberg Coll., 1877-93; dir. Theol. Sem. Evang. Luth. Ch., Chicago, 1894-99; hon. pres. Inner Mission Soc. of Phila. Editor: Little Children's Book (mus.), 1885; revised and enlarged edit. Church Song (with Rev. Dr. Joseph A. Seiss), 1892. Chief mus. editor and contbr. to Common Service Book of the Lutheran Church, 1917, and the Parish School Hymnal, 1926. Author: School and Parish Hymnal (with tunes), 1892; School and Parish Service Book (with music), 1892; The Responsories of Matins and Vespers Set to Music, 1909; The Inner Mission, A Handbook for Christian Workers, 1911; also festival anthem, "I Will Extol Thee," for Quadri-Centennial of the Reformation (2d prize), 1917; "The Living Hope," Easter cantata, 1923; "The Christ Child," Christmas cantata, 1925; "The Good Shepherd," cantata for gen. use, 1927. Home: Philadelphia, Pa. Died Jan. 21, 1941.

OHL, Josiah Kingsley, journalist; b. Brownsville, Pa.; s. Rev. Dr. John Franklin and Louisa West (Ray) O.; ed. Kenyon Coll. (hon. A.M., 1901, LL.D., 1917, same); m. Maude Annulet Andrews. Staff of Atlanta Constitution, 1887-96; Washington corr. same and London Daily Telegraph, and attached to Washington bureau of New York Herald, 1896-1906; corr. New York Herald in China, Japan, Korea, P.I., India, 1907-13; editorial staff New York Herald, 1913-18; editor-in-chief and mng. editor New York Herald, 1918—, and dir. New York Herald Co. and chmn. its exec. com. Trustee James Gordon Bennett Memorial Home for Journalists. Lt. col. on staff Gov. of Ga., 1902-06. Chevalier Order of Leopold (Belgium); Comdr. Order of the Crown (Italy); Comdr. Order of King George the First (Greece); Chevalier de la Legion d'Honneur (France). Died June 27, 1920.

OHLMACHER, Albert Philip, physician; b. Sandusky, O., Aug. 19, 1865; s. Christian John and Anna (Scherer) O.; ed. high sch., Sycamore, Ill.; M.D., Northwestern U., 1890; m. Grace M. Peck, June 14, 1890. Prof. comparative anatomy and embryology, Coll. Phys. and Surg., Chicago, 1891-94; prof. pathology, Chicago Policlinic, 1892-94; prof. pathology and bacteriology, med. dept. Ohio Wesleyan U., Cleveland, 1894-97; dir. pathol. lab., Ohio Hosp. for Epileptics, Gallipolis, 1897-1901; prof. pathology, med. dept. Northwestern U., 1901-02; supt., Ohio Hosp. for Epileptics, 1902-05; dir. biol. lab., Frederick Stearns & Co., Detroit, 1905-07; in pvt. practice splty. epilepsy and treatment of infections by bacterial or vaccine therapy, Detroit, 1907—. Home: Detroit, Mich. Died Nov. 10, 1916.

OKAKURA, Kakuzo, curator, author; b. Fukui, Japan, 1862; grad. Imperial U., Tokyo, 1880; (hon. A.M., Harvard, 1911). Sec. to minister of edn., Japan, and in charge of musical affairs, 1886; sent abroad to make observations as to art, 1886-87; mgr. and dir. Imperial Art Sch., Tokyo, 1887-98, resigned; assisted in organizing the Nippon Bijitsuin (art acad., 1898), advisor, 1906-10, curator, 1910—, Chinese and Japanese dept. Mus. Fine Arts, Boston; lecturer on æsthetics, Imperial U., Tokyo, 1909—; mem. Imperial Archæol. Commn. (Japan). Author: The Book of Tea, 1906; The Ideals of the East, 1904; The Awakening of Japan, 1904. Died Sept. 2, 1913.

O'KELLEY, Thomas Washington, clergyman; b. Hall County, Ga., Dec. 16, 1861; s. Edward Washington and Elizabeth (Barnes) O.; A.B., Mercer U., Macon, Ga., 1889, A.M., 1891 (D.D., 1899); m. Mary Lee Alexander, 1891 (died 1893); m. 2d, Rosa Burt Meriwether, 1900; children—Thomas Washington, Mary, William Meriwether. Ordained ministry Bapt. Ch., 1888; prin. Hiawassee (Ga.) High Sch., 1889-90; prof. Latin, Mercer U., 1890-92; pastor 1st Ch., Hawkinsville, Ga., 1892-93, 1st Ch., Griffin, 1893-99, West End Ch., Atlanta, 1899-1902, 2d Ch., Little Rock, Ark., 1902-04, 1st Ch., St. Joseph, Mo., 1904-11, 1st Church, Raleigh, N.C., 1911—. Mem. Foreign Missionary Bd. of Southern Bapt. Conv. Democrat. Home: Raleigh, N.C. Died July 12, 1927.

OLAYA, Enrique, diplomat; b. Guateque, Colombia, S.A., Nov. 11, 1882; s. Justiniano and Emperatriz (Herrera) O.; ed. Univ. of Bogotá; Dr. Law and Social Science, Brussels, Belgium; m. Teresa Londoño of Bogotá, 1911. Began, 1905, as chief Div. of Diplomatic History, Ministry of Foreign Affairs, Colombia; sec. Legation of Colombia, at Caracas, Venezuela; minister of Foreign Affairs; E.E. and M.P. to Argentine Republic and to Chile; senator Colombia, 1921; E.E. and M.P. from Colombia to U.S., 1922—. Decorated Orden del Mérito (Chilean); Busto del Libertador (Venezuelan). Died Feb. 18, 1937.

OLBRICH, Michael B., lawyer; b. Chemung, Ill., Sept. 29, 1881; s. Jacob and Maria (Weitzel) O.; B.L., U. of Wis., 1902 (Phi Beta Kappa), LL.B., 1904; m. Isabel Wilson, July 10, 1907; children—Isabel M., Wilson, Stuart, Marshall, Michael, John J. Practiced at Madison, 1905—; mem. Olbrich & Siebecker; joint counsel in proceedings which enjoined Gov. Francis E. McGovern from forcibly ousting Ins. Commr. H. L. Ekern from office in 1913; joint atty. for late U.S. Senator Paul O. Husting in proceeding to compel issuance of certificate of election, 1914; dir., sec. and treas. Bond & Mortgage Corp. (Madison), Judith Basin Land Co., Fair Oaks Land Co., Linden Hill Land Co., Home Ranch Co. Del. Rep. Nat. Conv., 1912, 1916; made speech nominating Senator R. M. LaFollette as candidate for President of U.S., in Rep. Nat. Conv., 1912 and 1916; treas. Rep. State Central Com., Wis., 1912; commr. on Uniform State Laws; chmn. nonpartisan Progressive campaign for gov. of Wis., 1914. Dep. atty. gen. of Wis., Jan. 1919-Jan. 1921; exec. counsel to gov. of Wis., 1921-26; spl. counsel for State of Wis. in litigation before U.S. Supreme Court in case of C.,B.&Q. R.R. Co. vs. U.S. R.R. Commn. to test power of I.C.C. to fix intra-state passenger fares; etc. Sec. Madison Parks Foundation. Regent U. of Wis., 1925—. Home: Madison, Wis. Died Oct. 10, 1929.

OLCOTT, Charles Sumner, publisher, author; b. Terre Haute, Ind., Feb. 20, 1864; s. John Milton and Merrium (Brown) O.; A.B., DePauw U., 1883, A.M., 1886; m. Allie Gage, June 23, 1886; children—Gage (dec.), Charles Milton, Lyman Howard. Gen. mgr. private library dept. of Houghton, Mifflin Co., publishers, 1891-1933. Mem. Prudential Com. Am. Bd. Commrs. Foreign Missions and chairman finance committee of same. Republican. Conglist. Author: George Eliot—Scenes and People in Her Novels, 1910; The Country of Sir Walter Scott, 1913; The Lure of the Camera, 1914; The Life of William McKinley, 1916. Home: Cambridge, Mass. Died May 3, 1935.

OLCOTT, Chauncey (Chancellor John Olcott), actor; b. Buffalo, N.Y., July 21, 1860; ed. Buffalo common schs.; brought out as singer by the late R. M. Hooley, 1880; m. Margaret O'Donovan, Sept. 28, 1897. With Hooley's co. 2 yrs., then consecutively with Haverly's co., Carncross Minstrels, Denman Thompson, Duff's Opera Co. for several seasons; sang 2 yrs. in England in comic opera, then succeeded W. J. Scanlan as star in Irish musical dramas; has since appeared in various leading rôles in U.S. and England. Home: New York, N.Y. Died Mar. 18, 1932.

OLCOTT, Eben Erskine, mining and metall. engr., transportation official; b. N.Y. City, Mar. 11, 1854; s. John N. and Euphemia Helen (Knox) O.; student Coll. City of New York; E.M., Columbia, 1874; m. Kate, d. Commodore Alfred Van Santvoord, of New York, 1884. Mining and metall. engr. formerly in practice in Western States, Mexico and S. America; pres. Hudson River Day Line; v.p. Lincoln Safe Deposit Co. Inaugurated movement for Tri-centennial celebration, 1909, of entrance of Hendrick Hudson into Harbor of New York, Sept. 11, 1609. Pres. Am. Inst. Mining Engrs., 1901-02. Home: New York, N.Y. Died June 5, 1929.

OLCOTT, Frederic P., pres. Central Trust Co., 1884—; b. Albany, N.Y., 1841; ed. Albany Acad.; entered his father's bank; afterward in lumber business; later connected with Blake Bros. & Co., bankers and brokers, New York, and with Phelps, Stokes & Co. One term comptroller of State of N.Y. Died 1909.

OLCOTT, George N., university prof.; b. Brooklyn, N.Y., Sept. 19, 1869; s. George M. and Jennie (Arnold) O.; A.B., Columbia, 1893, fellow 1894-96, 1896-97, Ph.D., 1899; fellow Am. Sch. Classical Studies, Rome, 1897-98; m. Zita Ledderucci, of Rome, July 19, 1902. Lecturer Roman archæology, 1898-1904, asst. in Latin, 1901-04, prof., 1905—, Columbia. Editorial contbr. on numismatics, Am. Jour. Archæology, 1898-1905. Author: Studies in the Word-formation of the Latin Inscriptions—Substantives and Adjectives with special reference to the Latin Sermo Vulgaris, Leipzig, 1898; Thesaurus Linguæ Latinæ Epigraphicæ, A Dictionary of the Latin Inscriptions, Rome, 1904. Deceased.

OLCOTT, Henry Steel, theosophist, author; b. Orange, N.J., Aug. 2, 1832; s. Henry Wyckoff and Emily (Steel) O.; ed. pvt. schs. and Univ. City of New York, class of 1847-51; m. Mary E. Morgan, 1860; divorced. Agrl. editor, New York Tribune, 1858-60; spl. commr. War and Navy depts., U.S., with rank of col., 1863-66; admitted N.Y. bar, 1866; commissioned by the President, 1878, to report on trade relations between U.S. and India. In 1875 helped to found, at New York, the Theosophical Soc. (hdqrs. in India; operates in 42 countries) and is its pres. Editor Theosophist (mag.), 1879—; hon. member Société d'Ethnographie, Royal Asiatic Soc. (Japan and China branches), Bengal Acad. Music, Institut Psychologique International, etc. In recognition of his services toward revival of Hindu philosophy in India the late Taranath Tarka Vachaspati, one of the most learned pandits of India (author of the Sanskrit Dictionary), conferred on him the sacred thread of the

Brahmin caste, and adopted him into his gotra—a unique honor to a white man. Author: Sorgho and Imphee (the new sugar canes), 1857; Yale Agricultural Lectures, 1858; The Olcott Family, 1874; People from the Other World, 1875; Posthumous Humanity (translated and edited), 1887; Old Diary Leaves (3 vols.), 1895, 1899, 1903; The Buddhist Catechism, 1882 and since (41 edits. in 23 langs.); Theosophy, Religion and Occult Science, 1885. Began an ednl. movement in Ceylon, 1880, for the benefit of the Buddhists and their religion, which in 1905 had 250 schs. and 3 colls. with nearly 30,000 pupils. Died 1907.

OLCOTT, Jacob Van Vechten, congressman; b. New York, May 17, 1856; s. John N. and Euphemia Helen (Knox) O.; student Coll. City of New York, 1870-75; LL.B., Columbia, 1877; LL.D., St. Stephen's Coll., N.Y., 1892, Kenyon Coll., 1905; m. Laura I. Hoffman, 1882 (died 1924). In practice of law from 1881; dir. Marconi Wireless Telegraph Co. of America. Municipal civ. service commr., New York, under Mayor Strong, 1895-98; mem. 59th to 61st Congresses (1905-11), 15th N.Y. Dist. Republican. Episcopalian. Trustee and v.p. St. Luke's Hosp.; pres. New York P.E. Pub. Sch.; trustee Ch. Mission to Deaf Mutes, Clergymen's Retiring Bd. Home: New York, N.Y. Died June 1, 1940.

OLCOTT, William Morrow Knox, lawyer; b. New York, Aug. 27, 1862; s. John N. and Euphemia Helen (Knox) O.; brother of Eben Erskine and Jacob Van Vechten O.; A.B., Coll. City of New York, 1881, A.M., 1883; LL.B., Columbia, 1883; m. Jessica A. Baldwin, Dec. 6, 1888; 1 son, Neilson; m. 2d, Florence A. Cobbett, June 30, 1931. In practice at New York, 1883—; sr. mem. Olcott, Gruber, Bonynge & McManus, 1897; mem. Olcott, Olcott & Glass until 1930; sr. mem. Olcott, Holmes, Glass, Paul & Havens; vice pres. Lawyers Engring. and Surveying Co., James Everard's Breweries; dir. James Everard's Companies, Inc., Hudson River Day Line, Hudson River Steamboat Co., Inc.; treas. Suffolk Co. Alderman 21st Dist., 1895-96; dist. atty., N.Y. Co., 1896-98; judge City Court, 1898-99. Republican. Home: New York, N.Y. Died May 10, 1933.

OLCOTT, William Tyler, author; b. Chicago, Jan. 11, 1873; s. William Marvin and E. Olivia (Tyler) O.; B.S., Trinity Coll., Hartford, 1896 (M.A., 1912); grad. N.Y. Law Sch., 1900; m. Clara Eunice Hyde, June 16, 1902. Admitted to N.Y. and Conn. bars. Republican. Episcopalian. Author: A Field Book of the Stars, 1907; In Star Land with a Three-inch Telescope, 1909; Star Lore of All Ages, 1911; Sun Lore of All Ages, 1914; The Book of Stars for Young People; Field Book of the Skies, 1929. Home: Norwich, Conn. Died July 1936.

OLDBERG, Oscar, pharmacist; b. Alfta, Sweden, Jan. 22, 1846; s. Anders and Frederika Katrina (Ohrstromer) O.; ed. Swedish pub. schs., pvt. teachers and, 1857-60, at Gymnasium, Gefle, Sweden; (Pharm. D. honoris causa, Nat. Coll. Pharmacy, Washington, 1881; LL.D., Northwestern U., 1911); came to U.S., 1864; m. Emma Parritt, May 19, 1873; father of Arne O. Engaged in ednl. and lit. work; vice-consul of Sweden and Norway at Memphis, Tenn., 1872; chief clerk and acting med. purveyor, U.S. Marine Hosp. Service 7 yrs., and at same time mem. faculty of Nat. Coll. Pharmacy; dean Sch. of Pharmacy, Northwestern U., 1886-1911. Mem. Com. Revision U.S. Pharmacopœia, 1880—. Author: Companion to the United States Pharmacopœia (Oldberg and Wall), 1884; Weights and Measures, 1885; Laboratory Manual of Chemistry (with John H. Long), 1894; Home Study in Pharmacy, 1890; Fifteen Hundred Examples of Prescriptions and Formulas, 1892; Inorganic Chemistry, General, Medical and Pharmaceutical, 1900; Pharmaceutical Problems and Exercises. Home: Chicago, Ill. Died Feb. 27, 1913.

OLDER, Fremont, newspaperman; b. Appleton, Wis., Aug. 30, 1856; s. Emory and Celia M. (Augur) O.; ed. prep. dept. Ripon (Wis.) Coll., 1 yr.; m. Cora Miranda Baggerly, Aug. 22, 1893. Began newspaper work, 1884; was city editor The Call; mng. editor The Bulletin 24 yrs.; now editor The Call-Bulletin. Died Mar. 3, 1935.

OLDFIELD, William Allan, congressman; b. Franklin, Ark., Feb. 4, 1874; s. Milton T. and Anne (Matheny) O.; A.B., Ark. Coll., 1896; m. Fannie Pearl Peden, June 1, 1901. Sergt. and 1st lt. Co. M, 2d Ark. Vols., Spanish-Am. War, 1898. Admitted to bar, 1899; pros. atty. 3d Jud. Circuit of Ark., 1902-06; mem. 61st to 70th Congresses (1909-29), 2d Ark. Dist. Democrat. Methodist. Home: Batesville, Ark. Died Nov. 19, 1928.

OLDHAM, William Fitzjames, bishop; b. Bangalore, India, Dec. 15, 1854; s. James and Mary Elizabeth (Burling) O.; ed. Bishop Cotton's Grammar Sch. (Madras, India), Madras Christian Coll., Allegheny Coll. (Meadville, Pa.); A.B., Boston U., 1883, D.D., 1890; m. Marie Augusta Mulligan, Sept. 13, 1875. Began in M.E. Ministry, 1883; founded Malaysia Mission of M.E. Ch., Singapore, Straits Settlements, 1884; founded Anglo-Chinese Sch., Singapore, 1885; founded chair, and was prof. missions and comparative religions, Ohio Wesleyan U., 1895-1900; asst. sec. Missionary Soc. M.E. Ch., 1900-04; missionary bishop M.E. Church for Southern Asia, 1904-12; corr. sec. Bd. of Foreign Missions M.E. Ch., 1912-16; elected bishop M.E. Ch., May 20, 1916. Lecturer, Nathan Grades Foundation, Syracuse U., 1913; lecturer on missions, Boston Theol. Sch., 1930. Author: Thoburn—Called of God, 1918; India, Malaysia, The Philippines; Malaysia—Nature's Wonderland. Died Mar. 27, 1937.

OLDHAM, William K., planter; b. Richmond, Ky., May 29, 1865; s. William K. and Kate (Brown) O.; Central U., Richmond, Ky., 1882-85; m. Lillian Munroe, Feb. 1, 1894; children—William K., Lillian. Moved to Ark., 1885; now owner farm of 2,100 acres. Mem. Ark. Ho. of Rep., 1907, Senate, 1911-13; pres. of Senate, 1913, and acting gov. of Ark. Trustee Ouachita Coll., Oldham High Sch.; mem. bd. Ark. Tuberculosis Sanatorium, Ark. Cotton Growers Coöp. Marketing Assn.; chmn. Cotton Reduction Com.; mem. State Planning Bd. Democrat. Baptist. Home: England, Ark. Died May 6, 1938.

OLDS, George Daniel, mathematician; b. Middleport, N.Y., Oct. 14, 1853; s. Eli D. and Mary (Shurtleff) O.; A.B., U. of Rochester, 1873, A.M., 1876; grad. work Heidelberg and Berlin, 1879-83; LL.D., Rochester, 1907, Amherst College, 1921, Wesleyan U., Conn., 1927; m. Marion E. Leland, June 16, 1886; children—Leland, George Daniel, Clara Leland (Mrs. I. J. Bissell), Marion (Mrs. George E. Keeler). Teacher Albany (N.Y.) Acad., 1873-79; prof. mathematics, U. of Rochester, 1884-91, Amherst Coll., 1891-1927, dean, 1909-22, acting pres. and pres.-elect, 1923-24, pres. 1924-27, pres. emeritus. Home: Amherst, Mass. Died May 10, 1931.

OLDS, Robert Edwin, lawyer; b. Duluth, Minn., Oct. 22, 1875; s. James Edwin and Lillian May (Goodrich) O.; A.B., summa cum laude, Harvard, 1897, LL.B., 1900; m. Rose Wilhelmina Nabersberg, Sept. 16, 1902. Practiced in St. Paul, 1900-17, inclusive; mem. Davis, Kellogg and Severance, afterwards Davis, Severance and Olds; counselor Am. Red Cross Commn. to France, Jan. 1918-Jan. 1919; European commr. in charge of Am. Red Cross operations abroad, Jan. 1919-July 1921; mem. for North America, of commn. apptd. by 12th Internat. Conf. at Geneva to report plan of world organization for Red Cross, 1923; Am. mem. Arbitration Tribunal apptd. to adjust pecuniary claims between the U.S. and Great Britain under the Treaty of 1910, 1923-25; pres. bd. trustees Am. Library in Paris, 1924-25; mem. commn. appointed by League of Nations to report plan in internat. coöperation for disaster relief, 1924, 25; apptd. asst. sec. of state Oct. 1, 1925; undersecretary of state, July 1, 1927-28; mem. Sullivan & Cromwell, 1928—. Mem. Permanent Court of Arbitration, The Hague, Dec. 1931—; mem. Reparation Commission under Treaty of Versailles, Oct. 20, 1929—; Am. member Permanent Internat. Commission provided by Treaty of Conciliation between U.S. and Finland; mem. Econ. Consultative Com., League of Nations, 1920—; also of following orgns. at Paris: Council of Internat. Chamber Commerce; bd. of govs. Am. Hosp.; bd. dirs. Am. Library; v.p. Am. Memorial Day Assn.; etc. Mem. Central Com. and Exec. Com. Am. Nat. Red Cross, 1927-28. Trustee Carnegie Endowment for Internat. Peace. Republican. Home: New York, N.Y. Died Nov. 14, 1932.

OLDS, Walter, lawyer; b. Morrow Co., O., Aug. 11, 1846; s. Rev. Benjamin and Abigail (Washburn) O.; ed. pub. schs., and Capital U., Columbus, O.; m. Marie J. Merritt, July 1, 1873. Pvt. Co. A., 174th Ohio Volunteer Infantry in Civil War; admitted to bar, Supreme Court of Ohio, 1869, and began practice at Columbia City, Ind., 1869; mem. Indiana Senate, 1877-79; judge of Circuit Court, 1884-88, resigned; justice Supreme Ct., Ind., Jan. 7, 1889-June 15, 1893, resigned; practiced law, Chicago, 1893-1901, Ft. Wayne, Ind., Mar. 1901—. Ind. atty. for N.Y.,C.&St.L. R.R. Co., dist. atty. N.Y. Central Ry. Co.; local atty. L.E.&W. R.R. Co., Ohio Electric Ry. Co., etc. Mem. Olds, Townsend & Thomas. Republican. Methodist. Home: Fort Wayne, Ind. Died July 30, 1925.

O'LEARY, Cornelius M., M.D., educator; b. Ireland, 1840; came to U.S. in boyhood; ed. in Montreal, Can., Fordham, N.Y., and Notre Dame (Ind.) Univ.; grad. med. dept., Univ. City of New York, 1864; (LL.D., Univ. State of N.Y.). Was mem. N.Y. Bd. of Health and State Commr. of Pharmacy; prof. logic and metaphysics, and later of Latin and Greek, Manhattan Coll. Home: New York, N.Y. Deceased.

O'LEARY, Wesley A(lvah), ednl. administration; b. Southboro, Mass., Sept. 12, 1873; s. James Otis and Amy Amelia (Corkum) O'L.; B.S., Dartmouth, 1895; grad. study, summer schs., Harvard, Clark U. and Mass. Inst. Tech.; Sc.D. in Industrial Edn., Stout Institute, 1932; m. Iris Prouty, June 6, 1914. Teacher pub. schs., Southboro, Mass., 1896-97, St. Mark's Sch., Southboro, 1897-98, pub. schs., Portsmouth, N.H., 1899-1904; teacher and prin. pub. schs., New Bedford, Mass., 1904-13; mem. faculty Pratt Inst., Brooklyn, 1913-15; dir. Essex Co. (N.J.) Vocational Schs., 1914-17; asst. commr. of edn., N.J. Dept. Pub. Instrn., 1917—. Organizer and dir. sch. for training equipment officers, Ordnance Dept., U.S.A., World War. Home: Elizabeth, N.J. Died Jan. 1937.

OLER, Wesley Marion; b. Baltimore, Md., Apr. 3, 1856; s. William H. and Catherine (Horn) O.; ed. City Coll., Baltimore; m. Elizabeth Kimberly, Nov. 12, 1890. For many yrs. largely engaged in publishing, banking, and other lines of business in Baltimore; moved to N.Y. City, 1904; now chmn. bd. Knickerbocker Ice Co.; pres. American Ice Co.; trustee Larchmont Park Assn.; formerly trustee and chmn. finance com. Woman's Coll. of Baltimore. Methodist. Mason. Home: Larchmont, N.Y. Deceased.

OLIN, Arvin Solomon, educator; b. Low Moor, Ia., Oct. 19, 1855; s. Nelson and Harriet (Holly) O.; A.B., Ottawa (Kan.) U., 1892, LL.D., 1915; A.M., U. of Kan., 1894; studied Clark U., U. of Chicago; m. Martha Davis, Sept. 6, 1882. Began as teacher pub. schs., 1873, later prin. and supt. at Peabody, Lawrence, Iola, Ottawa and Kansas City, Kan.; instr. or condr. about 40 normal insts.; instr. in edn., 1893-94, asso. prof., 1894-99, prof., 1899—, U. of Kan.; mem. Kan. State Bd. Edn., 1893-95. Democrat. Mason. Author: Syllabus in History of Education, 1894; Outlines in History of Education, 1900. Homes: Palo Alto, Calif., and Lawrence, Kan. Died Mar. 26, 1935.

OLIN, John Myers, lawyer; b. Lexington, O., July 10, 1851; s. Nathaniel G. and Phoebe (Roberts) O.; A.B., Williams Coll., 1873, A.M., 1876; LL.B., Univ. of Wis., 1879, and entered practice at Madison, Wis.; m. Helen Remington, June 14, 1880. Instructor rhetoric and oratory, 1874-78, professor federal jurisprudence, sales and juries, 1885-87, real property, wills and torts, 1894-1905, property, 1905-10, U. of Wisconsin; sr. member Olin, Butler, Stebbins & Stroud. Trustee Northwestern Mut. Life Ins. Co., 1907-19. Pres. Madison Bd. Park Commrs., 1894-1909, Wis. State Forest Commn., 1903-05. Home: Madison, Wis. Died Dec. 7, 1924.

OLIN, Richard M., dir. of health service; b. Perry, N.Y., May 23, 1875; s. Milo H. and Mary A. (Chapin) O.; student U. of Buffalo; M.D., Bellevue Hosp. Med. Coll. (New York U.), 1899; m. Nellie B. Jenks, Nov. 22, 1898; children—Richard, Philip, Chapin. Began practice at Caro, Mich., 1899; state commr. of health, Mich., 1917-27; dir. of health service, Mich. State Coll., 1927—. Republican. Presbyn. Mason, Odd Fellow, Elk. Home: East Lansing, Mich. Died Oct. 5, 1938.

OLIN, Stephen Henry, lawyer; b. Middletown, Conn., Apr. 22, 1847; s. Stephen (D.D., LL.D.) and Julia (Lynch) O.; A.B., Wesleyan U., 1866, A.M., 1869, LL.D., 1894; Litt.D., Columbia U., 1923; m. Alice, d. S. L. M. Barlow, Oct. 23, 1879 died 1882); m. 2d, Emeline Dodge, d. Oliver Harriman, Mar. 21, 1903. Acting pres. Wesleyan U., 1922-23. Trustee Astor Library, 1888-95, New York Pub. Library, 1895—, and Wesleyan U., 1880—; v.p. N.Y. Bar Assn., 1898-99; pres. Univ. Settlement Soc., 1902-06. Maj. and judge advocate 1st and 2d brigades, N.G.S.N.Y., 1882-89; lt. col. and a.-a.-g. 1st Brigade, 1889-98; col. and chief of staff N.G.S. N.Y., 1898-1903. Mem. exec. com. Internat. Conciliation. Homes: Rhinebeck, N.Y., and New York, N.Y. Died Aug. 6, 1925.

OLIN, Walter Herbert, scientific agriculturist; b. Walnut Grove, Calif., Aug. 7, 1862; s. Nelson and Harriet M. (Holly) O.; grad. Kan. Agrl. Coll., Manhattan, 1889, M.Sc., 1893; spl. history student, U. of Chicago, 1898; m. Winnifred Estella Cotton, Nov. 27, 1890 (died 1910); children—Winnifred Helen (Mrs. W. H. Roberts), Estella G. (dec.), Walter Eugene; m. 2d, Eleanor Lee, June 7, 1915. Teacher of rural schs., 1880-86; prin. and supt. schs., Waverly, Osborne and Ottawa, Kan., 1890-1901; instr. farm crops, Ia. State Coll., 1902-04; prof. agronomy, 1904-06, vice dean of agr., 1906-08, Colo. Agrl. Coll.; dir. agrl. extension, U. of Ida., 1911-14; organized agrl. dept. and commr. of agr., D.& R.G.W. R.R., Denver, 1914-16; supervisor farm marketing, Frisco Lines, St. Louis, Mar. 1, 1916-Oct. 1918; supervisor of agr., D.&R.G. R.R., Oct. 15, 1918—. Baptist. Mason. Author: Olin's Commercial Geography, 1900; American Irrigation Farming, 1913. Home: Denver, Colo. Died June 21, 1933.

OLIN, William Milo, sec. Commonwealth of Mass., 1890—; b. Warrenton, Ga., Sept. 18, 1845; s. William Milo and Mary Augusta (Bowen) O.; ed. common schs. Worcester and Grafton, Mass., and high sch., Leicester, Mass.; m. Lizzie Wadsworth Read, Nov. 3, 1869. Pvt. 36th Mass. Vols., 1862-65; reporter and editor Boston Daily Advertiser, 1865-79; pvt. and mil. sec. to Govs. Talbot and Long, 1879-82; pvt. sec. to Collector Worthington, 1882-85, to U.S. Senator Dawes, 1885-90, to Collector Beard, 1890. Adj. gen., G.A.R., 1882, insp. general, 1896, sr. v.-comdr.-in-chief, 1903; lt. col. and asst. adj. gen., 1st Brigade, Mass. Vol. Militia, 1882-89. Republican. Home: (Roxbury) Boston, Mass. Died 1911.

OLIPHANT, Herman, lawyer; b. Forest, Ind., Aug. 31, 1884; s. Albert G. and Martha Jane (Richardson) O.; A.B., Marion (Ind.) Coll., 1907; A.B.,

Ind. U., 1909; J.D., U. of Chicago, 1914; m. Julia Sims, Sept. 10, 1905; children—Thalia Levon, Charles Albert, Malcolm William. Instr. English lang., Marion College, 1907-11; instr. law, 1914-15, asst. prof., 1915-16, asso. prof., 1916-19, prof., 1919-21, U. of Chicago Law Sch.; prof. law, Columbia U., 1921-29; prof. law, Inst. of Law, Johns Hopkins, 1929-Mar. 1933; gen. counsel Farm Credit Administration until Nov. 1933; gen. counsel to sec. of the Treasury, 1933-34; gen. counsel, Dept. of Treasury, 1934—. Asst. dir. of War Trade Intelligence, 1917-18; asst. dir. industrial relations div. of Emergency Fleet Corp., 1918-19. Democrat. Home: Bay Ridge, Annapolis, Md. Died Jan. 11, 1939.

OLIVER, Arthur L., lawyer; b. Leemon, Mo., Jan. 5, 1879; s. Henry Clay and Mary Louise (Alexander) O.; ed. State Normal Sch., Cape Girardeau, Mo.; LL.B., U. of Tex., 1900; m. Mary Esther Roberts, Nov. 27, 1907; children—John Roberts, James Arthur. Began practice at Caruthersville, 1900; served as mem. Mo. Ho. of Rep. and Mo. Senate; U.S. atty., Eastern Dist. of Mo., Aug. 4, 1914—. Elected 1st lt. N.G. Mo., Dec. 1901, later capt.; maj. 6th Unattached Batt., 1904; organized 6th Regt. N.G. Mo., 1908, and elected col. Democrat. Presbyn. Mason, K.P., Elk. Home: St. Louis, Mo. Died July 3, 1928.

OLIVER, Charles Augustus, ophthalmologist; b. Cincinnati, Dec. 14, 1853; s. George Powell and Maria Louisa O.; A.B., U. of Pa., 1873, M.D., 1876, A.M., 1878; (hon. A.M., Lafayette, 1900); m. Mary Schermerhorn Henry, June 6, 1888. Surgeon to Wills Eye, and Philadelphia hosps. Author: Correlation Theory of Color Perception; Ophthalmic Methods in Recognition of Nerve Diseases, 1895; (co-author) Text Book of Ophthalmology. Home: Philadelphia, Pa. Died 1911.

OLIVER, Daniel Charles, congressman; b. N.Y. City; s. Henry and Ann (Rogers) O.; student Coll. City of New York. In dry goods importing business, 1894—; mem. Bd. of Edn., N.Y. City, 20 yrs.; mem. N.Y. Assembly 2 terms, 1915, 16; mem. 65th Congress (1917-19), 23d N.Y. Dist. Democrat. Home: New York, N.Y. Deceased.

OLIVER, Edwin Austin, author; b. New York, N.Y., May 1, 1855; s. John W. and Ellen (Woods) O.; ed. pub. schs. New York, and Yonkers; unmarried. Became connected with Yonkers Statesman, 1877, becoming successively reporter, business mgr., asso. editor, and editor in chief, 1908-21; was sec., treas. Yonkers Pub. Co. Republican. Mason. Author: Tattles of a Traveler, 1896; Holiday Tales, 1907; Remnant Rhymes, 1911. Home: Yonkers, N.Y. Died Apr. 22, 1924.

OLIVER, George Tener, senator; b. in Ireland, Jan. 26, 1848; of Am. parents who were visiting there; s. Henry and Margaret (Brown) O.; A.B., Bethany Coll., W.Va., 1868, A.M., 1873; (LL.D., Lafayette Coll., Pa., 1912); m. Mary Kountze, Dec. 19, 1871. Admitted to bar, 1871, and practiced at Pittsburgh, 1871-81; in iron and steel mfg., 1881-1901; purchased Pittsburgh Gazette and Pittsburgh Chronicle Telegraph, 1900, of which became publisher. Pres. Central Bd. Edn., Pittsburgh, 1881-84; presdl. elector, 1884; elected U.S. senator, Mar. 17, 1909, for unexpired term (1909-11) of Philander Chase Knox, resigned; reëlected for term 1911-17. Home: Pittsburgh, Pa. Died Jan. 22, 1919.

OLIVER, Grace Atkinson, author; b. Boston, Sept. 24, 1844; ed. there; lived in Boston until 1890; m. John Harvard Ellis, 1869 (died 1871); m. 2d, Dr. Joseph Pearson Oliver, 1879. State trustee Danvers Lunatic Asylum; mem. Salem school bd.; pres. Salem Soc. for Higher Edn. of Women; pres. Visiting Nurse Assn. of Marblehead. Author: Lives of Mrs. Barbauld, Maria Edgeworth and Dean Stanley; Sketches; etc. Edited: Tales of Maria Edgeworth; Essays of Mrs. Barbauld; Poems of Ann and Jane Taylor; etc. Home: Salem, Mass. Died 1899.

OLIVER, Henry W., capitalist; b. Dungannon, Ireland, Feb. 1840; s. Henry W. and Margaret (Brown) O.; emigrated to Pittsburgh, 1842; ed. Newell's Acad. there; m. Edith A. Cassidy, 1862. Served 12th Pa. vols., Civil war. Pres. Pittsburgh common council, 1879-82; del. Rep. Nat. convs., 1872-76-88-92; presdl. elector, 1880; apptd. mem. commn. to draw up and submit to Congress a new tariff bill, 1882; Rep. candidate for U.S. senator, 1881. Pres. Oliver Iron Mining Co.; chmn. bd. dirs. Pittsburgh & Western Ry. (pres. 1889-94), Oliver & Snyder Steel Co., Oliver Iron & Steel Co.; and other concerns. Home: Pittsburgh, Pa. Died 1904.

OLIVER, James, inventor; b. Whitehaugh, Roxburghshire, Scotland, Aug. 28, 1823; came with family to U.S., 1835; lived on farm, nr. Geneva, N.Y., 1835-36; at Mishawaka, Ind., 1836-55. Learned foundry trade; began to manufacture plows, 1855; invented the "chilled plow" and acquired wealth. Home: South Bend, Ind. Died 1908.

OLIVER, James Harrison, naval officer; b. Houston Co., Ga., Jan. 15, 1857; s. Thaddeus and Sarah Penelope (Lawson) O.; Washington and Lee U., 1872; grad. U.S. Naval Acad., 1877; m. Marion Carter Oliver, Dec. 7, 1893. Ensign, 1881; promoted through grades to rear adm., Jan. 5, 1917. Made 9 cruises at sea, averaging a little over 2½ yrs. each; station duty at Ft. Monroe, Providence, Newport, R.I., Cincinnati; dir. Naval Intelligence Office, Jan. 20, 1914; gov. Virgin Islands and comdt. Naval Sta., 1917-19; duty Navy Dept., Apr. 1919-Jan. 1921 (retired.). Home: Shirley, Va. Died Apr. 6, 1928.

OLIVER, Joseph Doty, mfr.; b. Mishawaka, Ind., Aug. 2, 1850; s. James and Susan (Doty) O.; student U. of Notre Dame, Ind., to 1865, De Pauw U. to 1866; m. Anna Gertrude Wells, Dec. 10, 1884; children—James Oliver, Mrs. Gertrude Cunningham, Joseph D., Susan Catherine. With Oliver Chilled Plow Works (founded by father), from 1866, pres., 1908; chmn. bd. Oliver Farm Equipment Co.; dir. P.,C.,C.&St.L. R.R. Co., First Nat. Bank (Chicago), Chase Nat. Bank (New York). Pres. bd. dirs. Purdue U., 1906-24. State chmn. W.S.S., World War. Republican. Presbyn. Home: South Bend, Ind. Died Aug. 6, 1933.

OLIVER, Martha Capps, author; b. Jacksonville, Ill.; d. of Joseph and Sarah (Reid) Capps; grad. Ill. Conf. Female Coll. (Ill. Woman's Coll.), 1862; m. William A. Oliver, Dec. 28, 1865. Compiler: A Year of Sacred Song, 1895; A Year of Good Wishes, 1895; 'Round the Year with the Poets, 1900. Author: The Story of Columbus Told in Rhyme (with Ida Scott Taylor McKinney), 1893; Lift Me Higher, 1901; Heather Bells, 1901; Lift Up Your Heads, 1901; An Easter Legend, 1902; Resurgam, 1902. Home: Jacksonville, Ill. Deceased.

OLIVER, Paul Ambrose, manufacturer; b. at sea, July 18, 1831, on his father's ship, "Louisiana," flying the U.S. flag; s. of Capt. Paul A. and Mary (Van Dusen) O.; ed. at Hamburg and Altona, Germany; unmarried. Second lt. 12th N.Y. Inf., Oct. 29, 1861; 1st lt., May 17, 1862; capt., Apr. 22, 1864; transferred to 5th N.Y. Inf., June 1, 1864; bvtd. brig. gen. vols., Mar. 8, 1865; awarded Congressional Medal of Honor, Oct. 12, 1892, "for while being in charge of a brigade assisted in preventing Union troops firing into each other at Resaca, Ga., May 15, 1864." Powder mfr., Luzerne County, Pa., 1870—. Died May 18, 1912.

OLIVER, Robert Shaw, assistant sec. of war; b. Boston, Sept. 13, 1847; ed. at Milton, Mass., Concord, N.H., and Churchill's Mil. Sch., Sing Sing, N.Y.; married; children—John Rathbone, Mrs. Elizabeth Stevens, Mrs. Cora Choate, Marion L. Apptd. 2dt lt. 5th Mass. Cav., Sept. 27, 1864 (at 17 yrs. of age); a.-d.-c., Cav. Brigade, 3d Div., 25th Army Corps, Feb. 3, 1865; asst. adj.-gen. 3d Div., 25th Army Corps, Sept. 3, 1865; entered regular army as 2d lt. 17th Inf., Feb. 25, 1866; 1st lt. 8th Cav., Mar. 7, 1867; resigned, Oct. 31, 1869; with Rathbone, Sard & Co., stove mfrs., Albany, N.Y., 1871-1903; asst. sec. of war, Sept. 1, 1903-Apr. 30, 1913. Served in N.Y.N.G. as col. 10th Inf., Aug. 25, 1873; lt. col. and asst. adj. gen. 9th Brigade, July 11, 1878; brig. gen., insp. gen. State of N.Y., Jan. 1, 1880; brig. gen. 5th Brigade, Jan. 10, 1883, 3d Brigade, Dec. 30, 1890; hon. retired at own request, Aug. 30, 1903. Civ. service commr. of Albany, May 28, 1894-Jan. 1, 1895; police commr., Jan. 1, 1895-June 1898. Home: Washington, D.C. Died Mar. 16, 1935.

OLLESHEIMER, Henry, banker; b. Fuerth, Bavaria, Feb. 11, 1856; s. Lipman and Friedericka O.; m. Sarah S. Scheuer, May 25, 1882. Came to U.S., 1873; pres. Met. Bank, New York, 1905—; dir. Met. Life Ins. Co., William Bradley & Son, Gen. Am. Tank Corp. of New York, Broadway Safe Deposit Co. Home: New York, N.Y. Died Nov. 6, 1933.

OLMSTED, Charles Sanford, bishop; b. Olmstedville, N.Y., Feb. 8, 1853; s. Levi and Maria M. (Beach) O.; brother of James Frederic and William Beach O.; student St. Stephen's Coll., N.Y., 1869-73; grad. General Theol. Sem., 1876; (S.T.D., Hobart, 1895; D.D., Gen. Theol. Sem., 1902); m. Mary M. Deuel, May 24, 1877. Deacon, 1876, priest, 1877, P.E. Ch.; rector, Morley, N.Y., 1876-84, Cooperstown, N.Y., 1884-96, Bala, Pa., 1896-1902; consecrated bishop of Colo., May 1, 1902. Author: December Musings (poems), 1898; Discipline of Perfection (Reinecker Lectures), 1902. Lecturer on The Creeds, in Church Club Lectures, 1895; Essay on Mediæval Poets, 1904. Home: Denver, Colo. Died Oct. 21, 1918.

OLMSTED, Charles Tyler, bishop; b. Cohoes, N.Y., Apr. 28, 1842; s. Charles A. and Ardelia (Wilkinson) O.; A.B., Trinity Coll., Conn., 1865, A.M., 1868; studied divinity at St. Stephen's Coll., Annandale, N.Y.; (S.T.D. Hobart Coll., 1893; D.C.L., Syracuse U. 1903; LL.D., Hamilton Coll., 1909); m. Catharine, d. Joseph Lawrence, Apr. 25, 1876. Prof. mathematics, St. Stephen's Coll., 1866-68; deacon, 1867, priest, 1868, P.E. Ch.; asst. Trinity Parish, New York, 1868-84; rector Grace Ch., Utica, N.Y., 1884-99; vicar St. Agnes' Chapel, Trinity Parish, New York, 1899-1902; consecrated bishop coadjutor of Central N.Y., Oct. 2, 1902; became bishop of Central N.Y., July 11, 1904. Home: Utica, N.Y. Died Mar. 26, 1924.

OLMSTED, Frederick Law, landscape architect; b. Hartford, Conn., Apr. 26, 1822; studied Yale, 1843; A.M., Amherst; LL.D., Harvard and Yale; m. Mary Perkins Olmsted, June 13, 1859. Farmer 7 years; landscape architect and supt. Central Park, New York, 1857; sec. U.S. Sanitary Commn., 1861-63; with his partners designed public parks of New York, Brooklyn, Boston, Bridgeport, Trenton, Montreal, Buffalo, Chicago (south side), Milwaukee, Louisville, U.S. Capitol grounds and terrace; World's Fair, Chicago, and a great number of private places. Author: Walks and Talks of an American Farmer; Our Seaboard Slave States; A Journey Through Texas; A Journey to the Back Country. Home: Brookline, Mass. Died 1903.

OLMSTED, George Welch, public utilities exec.; b. Ridgway, Pa., May 18, 1874; s. Samuel Ashbel and Fannie Frances (Welch) O.; ed. Brockway (Pa.) Grammar Sch.; m. Iva Catherine Groves, June 17, 1904; children—Robert Groves, Elizabeth. Pres. Delaware Olmsted Co., Olmsted Securities Corp., United Gas & Electric Corp.; v.p. Eastern Seaboard Securities Corp., Empire Power Corp., Kings County Lighting Co., Long Island Lighting Co.; sec. J. G. Curtis Leather Co.; treas. B. V. Harrison Co. Trustee Allegheny Coll., Tanners Research Lab., Cincinnati; dir. Utilities Mutual Ins. Co. Mem. nat. exec. bd. of Boy Scouts America. Republican. Methodist. Mason. Home: Ludlow, Pa. Died Jan. 16, 1940.

OLMSTED, James Frederic, clergyman; b. New York, Mar. 3, 1859; s. Levi and Maria M. (Beach) O.; bro. of Charles Sanford and William Beach Olmsted; B.A., Trinity Coll., 1884, M.A., 1887; B.D., Gen. Theol. Sem., 1892; m. Julia Campbell Smith, Aug. 17, 1892, Master St. Mark's Sch., Southboro, Mass., 1884-88; deacon and priest P.E. Ch., 1891; asst. St. George's, Newburgh, N.Y., 1891-92; rector St. John's Ch., Champlain, N.Y., 1892-93, Christ Ch., Schenectady, N.Y., 1893-97, St. Mary's, Burlington, N.J., 1897—. Examining chaplain to the bishop of N.J.; mem. Standing Com. Diocese of N.J.; deputy General Conv., 1901. Home: Burlington, N.J. Died Feb. 4, 1914.

OLMSTED, James Greeley, mfr.; b. LeRoy, N.Y., June 25, 1857; s. Hamden Aubry and Frances (Sprague) O.; ed. LeRoy Acad.; m. Edith Bentley, Sept. 18, 1884. On farm until 17; moved to Des Moines, Ia., 1875, and began by wheeling freight for C.,R.I.&P. Ry. later pass. agent at sta.; became mem. Bentley & Olmsted, shoe mfrs., 1884; retired. Home: Pasadena, Calif. Died Jan. 27, 1937.

OLMSTED, John Charles, landscape architect; b. Geneva, Switzerland, Sept. 14, 1852, of Am. parents; s. Dr. John Hull and Mary Cleveland Bryant (Perkins) O.; Ph.B., Yale, 1875; studied landscape architecture under Frederick Law Olmsted and later became his partner; m. Sophia Buckland White, Jan. 18, 1899. With partners, designed park systems of Boston; Essex Co., N.J.; Chicago (South Parks); Buffalo and Rochester, N.Y.; Hartford, Conn.; Louisville, Ky.; Milwaukee, Wis.; Seattle and Spokane, Wash.; and scores of parks in other cities and towns, and grounds of univs., colls., sanitariums, pub. libraries, state capitols, town halls, exhbns., including grounds of Chicago Expn., 1893, Seattle Expn., 1909, Lewis and Clark Expn. (prel. sketch plan), Portland, Oregon, 1906, Canadian Industrial Expn., Winnipeg, Man., and hundreds of pvt. places. In partnership with Frederick Law Olmsted (Jr.), 1898—. Home: Brookline, Mass. Died Feb. 24, 1920.

OLMSTED, Marlin Edgar, congressman; b. Ulysses Tp., Potter Co., Pa.; s. of Henry J. and Evalena (Cushing) O.; acad. edn.; (LL.D., Lebanon Valley Coll., 1903, Dickinson, 1905); m. Gertrude Howard, Oct. 26, 1899. Admitted to bar, 1878, and entered practice at Harrisburg. Mem. 55th to 57th Congresses (1897-1903), 14th Pa. Dist. and 58th to 62d Congresses (1903-13), 18th Dist.; chmn. com. on insular affairs, etc. Republican. Home: Harrisburg, Pa. Died July 10, 1913.

OLMSTED, Millicent, author; b. Cleveland, O.; d. Henry Sanford and Helen (Bishop) O.; ed. Miss Mittleberger's Sch. for Girls; 2 yrs. study and travel in Eng., France and Italy, and travel in U.S. With Cleveland Plain Dealer, 1899-1901, as society editor, editor woman's page, etc.; with Cleveland Leader, 1902-05; editor children's dept. monthly mags. In advertising and publicity work, 1908—; writer of financial advertising; secretary William Ganson Rose, Incorporated, Cleveland. Episcopalian. Author: (children's stories) Daffy-Down-Dilly; The Land of Never Was, 1908; The Land of Really True, 1909; Harmony Wins, 1913. Home: Cleveland, O. Died June 3, 1939.

OLMSTED, William Beach, educator; b. N.Y. City, Feb. 26, 1864; s. Levi and Maria M. (Beach) O.; A.B., Trinity Coll., 1887; hon. A.M., Yale, 1908; L.H.D., Trinity Coll., Conn., 1910; m. Anne Nelson Starkweather, July 22, 1891; children—Wm. Beach, Frederick Nelson, Anne Nelson. Master in St. Mark's Sch., Southboro, Mass., 1887-97; headmaster Pomfret Sch., 1897—. Ordained deacon by Bishop Charles Sanford Olmsted, 1908, priest, 1909, P.E. Ch. Home: Pomfret, Conn. Died Dec. 11, 1929.

OLNEY, George W., editor, statistician; b. Charleston, S.C., June 5, 1835; s. George W. and Olive (Bartlett) O.; prep. edn. Charleston, S.C., and

Univ. Grammar Sch., Providence, R.I.; LL.B., Harvard, 1855. Entered journalism as one of pubs. New York Daily Day Book, 1858; war corr. Richmond Enquirer and Charleston Courier, 1861-63; dramatic writer New York Herald, 1866; editorial writer New York World, 1868-76; editor of the Spectator (ins. paper), New York, 1873-76; mng. editor, 1878-99, editor, 1899—, The Weekly Underwriter, New York. Editor The World Almanac, pub. by New York World, 1870—. V.p. Underwriter Printing & Pub. Co. V.p. Soc. of The Cincinnati in R.I. Home: New York, N.Y. Died June 20, 1916.

OLNEY, Peter Butler, lawyer; b. Oxford, Mass., July 21, 1843; s. Wilson and Eliza L. (Butler) O.; bro. of Richard O.; A.B., Harvard, 1864, LL.B., 1866, A.M., 1872; m. Mary Sigourney Butler, Nov. 12, 1879. In practice at New York, 1866—; sr. mem. Olney & Comstock, 1897—. Dist. atty., New York Co., 1883-85; U.S. referee in bankruptcy, 1898—. Apptd. commr. with William C. Whitney and George Bliss, under act of N.Y. Legislature, 1879-80, to compile, and afterwards to revise, laws of the state affecting pub. interests of City of New York, which work was adopted by the legislature as the Consolidation Act of 1882; trustee Teachers Coll. New York. Died Feb. 9, 1922.

OLNEY, Richard, secretary of state; b. Oxford, Mass., Sept. 15, 1835; s. Wilson and Eliza L. (Butler) O.; bro. of Peter Butler O.; A.M., Brown Univ., 1856; LL.B., Harvard, 1858; (LL.D., Harvard, 1893, Brown, 1893, Yale, 1901); m. Agnes P. Thomas, Mar. 6, 1861. Admitted to bar, 1859, and entered practice at Boston. Mem. Mass. Ho. of Rep., 1874; Atty. Gen. of U.S., Mar. 6, 1893-June 9, 1895; Sec. of State, June 10, 1895-Mar. 4, 1897, in cabinet of President Cleveland. Tendered ambassadorship to England, Mar. 1913, but declined; tendered governorship Federal Reserve Bd., Apr. 1914, but declined; Am. mem. Internat. Commn., under treaty bet. U.S. and France, June 1915—. Democrat. Fellow Brown U., 1894-97; regent Smithsonian Instn., 1900-08. Home: Boston, Mass. Died Apr. 9, 1917.

OLNEY, Richard, congressman; b. Milton, N.H., Jan. 5, 1871; A.B., Brown U., 1892; married; children—Richard, Nancy, Catharine. Wool mcht. Mem. Mass. Ho. of Rep., 1902; mem. Mass. Minimum Wage Commn., 1911; mem. 64th to 66th Congresses (1915-21), 14th Mass. Dist. Democrat. Apptd. mem. World War Foreign Dept. Commn., Feb. 1923. Home: Boston, Mass. Died Jan. 15, 1939.

OLNEY, Warren, lawyer; b. Davis Co., Ia., March 11, 1841; s. William and Eliza Ann (Green) O.; student Central U. of Ia., U. of Mich., 1 year; LL.B., Univ. of Mich., 1868; m. Mary Jane Craven, Sept. 11, 1865; father of Warren O., Jr. Pvt. to capt. in Civil War, May 21, 1861-Aug. 15, 1865; served in West and Southwest; admitted to bar, San Francisco, 1869; nominated as mayor of Oakland, Calif., by both Rep. and Dem. convs., 1903; elected. Dir. Calif. Title Ins. & Trust Co.; pres. S. San Francisco Dock Co. Trustee Mills College. Home: Oakland, Calif. Died June 2, 1921.

OLNEY, Warren, Jr., lawyer; b. San Francisco, Oct. 15, 1870; s. Warren and Mary Jane (Craven) O.; A.B., U. of Calif., 1891, LL.D., 1919; A.B., Harvard, 1892; LL.B., Hastings Coll. of Law, 1894; m. Mary M. McLean, Oct. 24, 1899; children—John McLean, Warren, Constance Sarah. Practiced in San Francisco, formerly as Olney & Olney (father and son), firm of Olney, Pringle & Mannon, 1907-10, Page, McCutchen, Knight & Olney, 1910-12, McCutchen, Olney & Willard, 1913-19; atty. for regents of U. of Calif., 1911-19; gen. atty., 1907-13, gen. counsel, 1913-15, receiver, 1915-16, again gen. counsel, 1916-19, W. P. Ry. Co.; asso. justice Supreme Court of Calif., 1919-21; mem. McCutchen, Olney, Mannon & Greene, 1921—. Asst. prof. law, Hastings Coll. of Law, 1895-1904; lecturer Sch. of Jurisprudence, U. of Calif., 1904-07. Mem. State Registration Bur. having charge of registration for the draft in Calif.; chmn. Dist. Exemption Bd. for Div. 1, 1917-18; chmn. State Mil. Welfare Commn., 1917-18. Home: Berkeley, Calif. Died Mar. 25, 1939.

OLP, Ernest Everett; b. La Plata, Mo., July 18, 1874; s. Rev. Minard F. and Mary (Fairbrother) O.; A.B., Northwestern U., 1900; m. Louise Etta Ernst, June 24, 1908. Sec. and div. mgr. Standard Oil Co., Chicago, 1901-04; sec. Edn. Adv. Agency, Chicago, 1904-05; mgr. Fisk Teachers Agency, Chicago, 1905—, also pres.; gen. mgr. Nat. Teachers Agency, Washington, D.C., 1918—, also pres.; pres. Education Service; organizer and dir. Am. Coll. Bur., Chicago and New York. Mem. bd. dirs. Baxter (Tenn.) Sem. Republican. Methodist. Home: Evanston, Ill. Died Mar. 23, 1928.

OLSEN, Nils Andreas, agrl. economist; b. Herscher, Ill., Aug. 31, 1886; s. Andreas Christian and Anna (Risetter) O.; A.B., Luther Coll., Decorah, Ia., 1907; A.M., U. of Wis., 1909, Harvard, 1912; unmarried. Instr. in history and economics, Muhlenberg Coll., Allentown, Pa., 1909-10; asst. in history, Harvard, 1910-12; farm mgr., 1912-19; with U.S. Dept. Agr., 1919—, chief of Bur. Agrl. Economics, July 1928—. Del. from U.S. Govt. to World Wheat Conf., London, and Internat. Dairy Congress, Copenhagen, 1931. Home: Washington, D.C. Died July 28, 1940.

OLSON, Floyd Bjerstjerne, governor; b. Minneapolis, Minn., Nov. 13, 1891; s. Paul A. and Ida Marie (Nelson) O.; LL.B., U. of Minn., 1915; grad. Northwestern Coll. of Law, Minneapolis, 1915; m. Ada Krejci, June 14, 1917; 1 dau., Patricia. Admitted to Minn. bar, 1915, and began practice at Minneapolis; mem. Larrabee & Olson, 1915-19; asst. county atty., Hennepin Co., Minn., 1919-20, county atty., 1920-30; elected governor of Minn. on Farmer-Labor ticket, 1930, for term 1930-32; reëlected for terms, 1933-36. Lutheran. Elk. Home: Minneapolis, Minn. Died Aug. 22, 1936.

OLSON, Harry, lawyer; b. Chicago, Aug. 4, 1867; s. Olof and Clara C. (Oberg) O.; student Washburn Coll., Kansas, 1887, 1888 (LL.D., 1915); LL.B., Union Coll., Law, Chicago, 1891; LL.D., Lake Forest (Ill.) Univ., 1923; m. Bernice Miller June 1, 1902; children—Harry, Sanford, Jane. Admitted to Illinois bar, 1891; assistant state's attorney for Cook Co., 8 yrs. under C. S. Deneen and 2 yrs. under John J. Healy; chief justice Municipal Court of Chicago, 1906-30. Trustee Northwestern Univ., 1908-27, Lake Forest Univ., 1923—. Republican. Lutheran. Mason. Home: Chicago, Ill. Died Aug. 1, 1935.

OLSSON, Olof, pres. Augustana Coll. and Sem., 1891—; b. in Vermland, Sweden, March 31, 1841; ed. Upsala (D.D., Rock Island, 1892; Ph.D., Upsala, 1893); m. Anna Johnson, 1864 (died 1887). Ordained Lutheran minister, 1863; came to U.S., 1869; was pastor in McPherson Co., Kan., and member Kan. legislature; prof. theology, Augustana Sem., 1876-88; pastor Woodhull, Ill., 1890; then prof. and pres. Augustana Coll. Author: At the Cross; Greetings from Afar; The Christian Hope; To Rome and Home Again. Died 1900.

OLYPHANT, Robert; b. N.Y. City, Aug. 26, 1853; s. Robert Morrison and M. Sophia (Vernon) O.; ed. pvt. schs. and 1 yr. in Paris; m. Caroline Wetmore Muller, May 1880 (died 1910); children—Mrs. Amy Gordon Anderson, Robert Morrison, Sophie Vernon (dec.), Donald; m. 2d, Marie Viele, Aug. 1912. Began with Union Car Spring Co., 1872; mem. Ward, Talbot & Olyphant, coal mchts., N.Y. City, 1874-1910. Enlisted in 7th Regt., N.G.N.Y., 1871; successively a.d.c. staff of Gov. Robinson, acting gen. insp. and gen. insp. rifle practice, insp. 1st Brigade, asst. adj. gen. 1st Brigade, bvt. brig. gen. (retired 1914). Hon. pres. U.S. Hosp. Fund of N.Y. Fellow Nat. Acad. Design. Republican. Presbyn. Home: New York, N.Y. Died Nov. 30, 1928.

OLYPHANT, Robert Morrison; b. New York, Sept. 9, 1824; A.B., Columbia Univ., 1842 (now oldest living alumnus). Chmn. exec. com. and mem. bd. mgrs. The Del. & Hudson Co. Mem. Am. Acad. Polit. and Social Science, Am. Mus. Natural History. Home: New York, N.Y. Died May 1917.

O'MALLEY, Austin, oculist; b. Pittston, Pa., Oct. 1, 1858; s. William and Catherine (Ward) O.; A.B., Fordham U., 1878; studied philosophy Gregorian U., Rome, Italy, 1878-81; Ph.D., Georgetown U., 1888, M.D., 1893; studied medicine univs. of Berlin and Vienna, 2 yrs.; LL.D., Notre Dame U., 1895. Instr. bacteriology, Georgetown U., 1893-95; prof. English lit., Notre Dame U., 1895-1903. Author: Thoughts of a Recluse, 1898; Essays in Pastoral Medicine, 1906, 1907; Cure of Alcoholism, 1913; Keystones of Thought, 1914, 1915; Ethics of Medical Homicide and Mutilation, 1919. Extensive contbr. of med. lit. and ednl. articles to mags. Mem. Am. Acad. of Polit. and Social Science, British Med. Guild of St. Luke. Address: Philadelphia, Pa. Died Feb. 25, 1932.

O'MALLEY, Frank Ward, author; b. Pittston, Luzerne County, Pa., Nov. 30, 1875; s. William and Catherine (Ward) O.; studied architecture, 1893-94, drawing and painting, Art Students' League, Washington, 1894-95; spl. courses U. of Notre Dame, Ind., 1895-98; studied drawing, painting and sculpture, Pa. Acad. Fine Arts, Phila., 1898-1902; m. Grace Edsall Dalrymple, Sept. 1, 1917; children—Ward, Kathleen Edsall. Illustrator and contbr. light verse, 1902-06; reporter and humorous and spl. writer New York (morning) Sun, 1906-19. Author: (plays, with Edward Waterman Townsend) The Head of the House, produced 1909; A Certain Party, produced 1910; (books) The War Whirl in Washington, 1918; The Swiss Family O'Malley, 1928. Home: Brielle, N.J. Died Oct. 19, 1932.

O'MALLEY, Henry, commr. fisheries; b. St. Johnsbury, Vt., Mar. 22, 1876; s. P. F. and Julia Ellen (Canty) O'M.; grad. St. Johnsbury Acad., 1895; m. Annie Thompson, July 15, 1903. Entered service of U.S. Bur. of Fisheries, 1897, at the station at St. Johnsbury, Vt.; apptd. field asst. for Pacific Coast, 1918; commr. of fisheries, by appmt. of President Harding, May 13, 1922-1933; supt. fisheries, Baird, Calif., 1933-34; retired. Mem. Am. Fisheries Soc. (pres. 1918), Pacific Fisheries Soc. (pres. 1917). Republican. Episcopalian. Mason, Odd Fellow, Elk. Made extensive investigations of fisheries conditions in Alaska; discovered a salt solution process for separating dead from live fish eggs. Home: Seattle, Wash. Died Apr. 24, 1936.

OMAN, Joseph Wallace, naval officer; b. Columbia County, Penn., Aug. 15, 1864; s. Henry Freas and Mary Jane O.; grad. U.S. Naval Acad., 1886; m. Virginia Center Morse, Nov. 22, 1907; children—Joseph Wallace, William Morse, Virginia Morse. Ensign, July 1, 1888; lt. jr. grade, Oct. 11, 1896; lt., Mar 3, 1899; lt. comdr., Jan. 1, 1905; comdr., Mar. 2, 1909; capt., Feb. 13, 1912; promoted rear admiral, July 1, 1918. Served on Helena, Spanish-Am. War, 1898; comdg. Mariveles, in Philippine insurrection, 1899; at Naval War Coll., Newport, R.I., 1905; exec. officer, Lancaster, 1905-06; navigator, Rhode Island, 1906; exec. officer same, 1906-09; at Naval War Coll., 1909; insp. equipment, Navy Yard, N.Y. City, 1909-11; comd. Tacoma, 1911, Des Moines, 1911, Maine, 1911-12; capt. of yard, Navy Yard, Boston, 1912-14; comd. North Carolina, 1914-15, Georgia, 1915-16; supervisor New York Harbor, 1916-17; comdr. Squadron Five, Patrol Force, Atlantic Fleet, 1917; comdr. Leviathan, July 1917-Mar. 1918; comdt. 2d Naval Dist., Mar. 1918-Mar. 1919; gov. Virgin Islands (U.S.), 1919-21; retired. Address: New York, N.Y. Died July 1, 1941.

O'MEARA, Mark, surgeon; b. Clinton, N.Y., Dec. 25, 1874; s. Patrick and Bridget (McCabe) O'M.; grad. high sch., Plattsburg, N.Y.; student Plattsburg Normal Sch.; M.D., Albany Med. Coll., 1903; post-grad. work, Post-grad. Med. Sch. and Hosp., and New York Polyclinic, New York; m. Nora Margaret Lahey, Oct. 1, 1910. Practiced at Kingston, N.Y., 1906—; chief of staff, Benedictine Hosp.; mem. bd. mgrs. N.Y. Training Sch. for Girls, Hudson, N.Y.; v.p. bd. mgrs. Ulster Co. Tuberculosis Hosp., 1909—; chmn. clinics, Ulster County Com. for Prevention Tuberculosis; chmn. Ulster County Pub. Health Com. of Catholic Charities of Archdiocese of N.Y. Republican. K.C., Elk. Home: Kingston, N.Y. Died 1937.

O'MEARA, Stephen, journalist; b. Charlottetown, P.E.I., July 26, 1854; s. Stephen and Maria (Meade) O.; came with parents to Charlestown, Mass., when 10 years of age; grad. Harvard Grammar Sch., 1868, Charlestown High Sch., 1872; hon. A.M., Dartmouth, 1888; LL.D., Boston Coll., 1908; m. Isabella M. Squire, Aug. 5, 1878. Reporter on Boston Globe, 1872-74; joined staff of Boston Journal, 1874, as reporter, later becoming, successively, city editor, news editor, gen. mgr., and editor-in-chief and publisher; sold Journal, Oct. 1902, and retired. Later police commr., City of Boston. Home: Boston, Mass. Died Dec. 14, 1918.

O'MELVENY, Henry William, lawyer; b. Central City, Marion County, Ill., Aug. 10, 1859; s. Harvey Kilpatrick Stuart and Anna Wilhelmina (Rose) O'M.; A.B., U. of California, 1879, LL.D., 1931; LL.D., Occidental Coll., 1928; m. Marie Antoinette Schilling, May 28, 1887; children—Stuart, Donald, John. Admitted to bar, 1881, in practice at Los Angeles, 1881—; mem. firm O'Melveny, Tuller & Myers. Director Farmers & Merchants Nat. Bank. Dept. dist. atty., Los Angeles County, 1883-85; president, Los Angeles Civ. Service Commn., 1903-04; mem. Pub. Library Bd., Los Angeles, 1908-10; park commr., 1910—; mem. State Parks Commn. Democrat. Episcopalian. Trustee Calif. Inst. Tech. (v.p.). Home: Los Angeles, Calif. Died Apr. 14, 1941.

OMWAKE, George L(eslie), coll. pres.; b. Greencastle, Pa., July 13, 1871; s. Henry and Eveline (Beaver) O.; grad. State Normal Sch., Shippensburg (Pa.), 1893, Mercersburg (Pa.) Acad., 1895; A.B., Ursinus Coll., Collegeville, Pa., 1898, A.M., 1901; B.D., Yale, 1901; Ped.D., Franklin and Marshall Coll., Pa., 1910, LL.D., 1923; LL.D., Lafayette Coll., 1923; m. Sophie Hendricks Casselberry, Aug. 28, 1906; children—Stanley, Eveline Beaver. Lecturer on edn., 1901-03, dean and prof. history and philosophy of edn., 1903, v.p., 1909, pres., 1912-36, pres. emeritus, 1936—, Ursinus College. Sec. Assn. Coll. Presidents of Pa. (pres. 1918); mem. Pa. State Edn. Assn. (trustee). Asst. dir. Com. on Pub. Safety of Pa., 1917. Mem. Council Ref. Chs. of America Holding Presbyn. System (pres. 1920-21), Am. sect. World Alliance of Ref. and Presbyn. Chs. (chmn. 1926-27), Bd. Christian Edn., Ref. Ch. in U.S., Ref. Churchmen's League (exec. com.); chmn. scholarship dept. The Presser Foundation, Phila.; mem. Nat. Commn. on Church Related Colleges, Pa. Chapter S.R., Huguenot Soc. of Pa. (pres., 1932—). Editor and co-author: J. H. A. Bomberger, Centenary Volume, 1917; Forward Movement Handbook of the Reformed Church in the U.S., 1920; The Great Advance, 1926. Home: Collegeville, Pa. Died Feb. 3, 1937.

OMWAKE, John, mfr. playing cards; s. Henry and Eveline (Beaver) O.; m. Teressa Iredell. Elected pres. U.S. Playing Card Co., 1902, chmn. bd., 1929—; elected pres. U.S. Printing Co., 1906, name changed to U.S. Printing & Lithographing Co., of which pres. until 1932, chmn. bd., 1932—; dir. Cincinnati Br. Federal Reserve Bank of Cleveland; dir. 2d Nat. Bank (Cincinnati), Norwood-Hyde Park Bank & Trust Co., Firemen's Mutual Ins. Co. of

Providence, R.I. Mem. bd. dirs. Community Chest of Cincinnati, Cincinnati C.C., Widows' and Old Men's Home, and Home for the Friendless (Cincinnati). Home: Cincinnati, O. Died Apr. 23, 1939.

ONAHAN, William James; b. Leighlin-Bridge, County Carlow, Ireland; s. John and Johanna O.; ed. at Liverpool; LL.D., and Lætare medal, U. of Notre Dame; moved to Chicago, 1854; m. Margaret Gertrude Duffy, 1860 (died 1902). Pres. Home Savings Bank, Chicago. City collector, 1869-71, 1879-87; city comptroller, 1887-91; also mem. bd. edn., and pres. library board. Organized 1st gen. Catholic Congress, Baltimore, 1889, Columbia Catholic Congress, Chicago, 1893; decorated, 1895, by Pope Leo XIII and apptd. hon. pvt. chamberlain to Pope, hence spoken of as "premier Catholic layman of U.S." Home: Chicago, Ill. Died Jan. 12, 1919.

ONDERDONK, Frank Scovill, clergyman; b. Mission Valley, Tex., May 31, 1871; s. Gilbert and Martha Jane (Benham) O.; student Southwestern U. (D.D.), Georgetown, Tex., 4 years (elective course); m. Rowena Tyson, Oct. 12, 1892; children—Mrs. Martha Kuykendall, Mrs. Rowena Horlyk, Mrs. Ruth Mitchell, Mrs. Mary Elizabeth Manchester. Minister M.E. Ch., S., 1892; in W. Tex. Conf., 1892-97; missionary at San Luis Potosi, Mexico, 1897-1901 (built church and mgr. Trinity Hosp.); presiding elder 1 year and pastor 2 yrs. in Mexico City, 1901-03; presiding elder Guadalajara, 1903-07; pres. Colegio Wesleyano, San Luis Potosi, Mex., 1907-14; supt. Mex., Italian and Bohemian missions in Tex., Nov. 1914—. Del. Congress on Christian Work in Latin America, Panama, 1916; del. Latin Am. Congress, Havana, Cuba, June 1929; del. gen. Conf. M.E. Ch., S., 5 times between 1906 and 1926; del. Ecumenical Meth. Conf., Atlanta, Ga., 1931. Address: San Antonio, Tex. Died June 7, 1936.

O'NEAL, Emmet, governor; b. Florence, Ala., Sept. 23, 1853; s. Gov. Edward A. and Olivia (Moore) O.; studied U. of Miss., 1870-71; A.B., U. of Ala., 1873; m. Lizzie Kirkman, July 21, 1881. Admitted to bar, 1875; presdl. elector, 8th Ala. Dist., 1888, Ala.-at-large, 1892, 1908; U.S. atty. Northern Dist. of Ala., 1893-97; mem. Dem. State Exec. Com. for state-at-large; mem. of Constl. Conv. for state-at-large, 1901; del. Dem. Nat. Conv., 1904; gov. of Ala., term 1911-15. Mem. exec. com. Conf. of Governors, 1911-12. Pres. Ala. State Bar Assn., 1909-10; mem. gen. council Am. Bar Assn., 1911. Chmn. Ala. delegation Dem. Nat. Conv., 1912; dir. Navy League; referee in bankruptcy, 1917-18; chmn. Dist. Exemption Bd., Div. 1. Author: The State Constitution. Home: Birmingham, Ala. Died Sept. 7, 1922.

O'NEIL, Charles, rear admiral U.S.N.; b. Manchester, Eng., Mar. 15, 1842; s. John and Mary Anne (Francis) O.; m. Mary C. Frothingham, Apr. 6, 1869. Entered U.S.N. as master's mate, July 1861, on sloop "Cumberland," and with it at capture of Forts Hatteras and Clarke, Aug. 1861, and in engagement with Confederate iron-clad "Merrimac," Mar. 8, 1862; rescued Lt. Morris from drowning; was favorably mentioned in dispatches and promoted acting master, May 1, 1862; was in both attacks on Fort Fisher; promoted acting vol. lt., May 30, 1865. Commd. lt., Mar. 11, 1868; lt. comdr., Dec. 18, 1868; comdr., July 1884; capt., July 21, 1897; rear admiral, Apr. 22, 1901. Chief Naval Bur. of Ordnance, 1897-1904; retired, Mar. 15, 1904; detailed for spl. ordnance duty abroad for 1 yr., Mar. 27, 1904. Address: Washington, D.C. Died Feb. 28, 1927.

O'NEIL, Frank R., journalist; b. Belleville, Ill., Apr. 24, 1851; Irish parentage; ed. pub. schs. of Belleville to 1866; m. Hettie J. Peters, July 2, 1872. Began newspaper work in 1870; published papers at New Athens, DuQuoin, and Belleville, Illinois, until 1874; Springfield (Ill.) legislative corr., St. Louis Republican, 1874; later served Republican and Post-Dispatch in nearly all writing capacities; editor-in-chief Republican, 1885-88; best known through work as reporter and corr.; also v.p. Post-Dispatch. Address: St. Louis, Mo. Died 1908.

O'NEIL, James, actor; b. in Ireland, 1847; s. Edmond O.; came to U.S. in boyhood. Made 1st stage appearance at National Theatre, Cincinnati, 1867; joined Bob Miles co., 1869; successive seasons leading man with Ford co., Baltimore; John Ellsler co., Cleveland; McVicker Stock Co., Chicago, 1872; Hooley's, Chicago, 1874; toured California, 1874; Union Square co., New York, 1875-77; in San Francisco, 1877-80, where he appeared in rôle of Christ in the "Passion Play"; starred in "A Celebrated Case"; then for 15 yrs. as Edmond Dantes, in "Monte Cristo"; later as D'Artagnan in Grundy's version of "The Three Musketeers." Home: New London, Conn. Died Aug. 10, 1920.

O'NEIL, John Francis, mfr.; b. Brockport, N.Y., Apr. 23, 1857; s. Daniel and Ellen (McMahon) O.; ed. pub. schs., Corry, Pa.; m. Jessie Bird Winall, May 5, 1885; children—Laurence Winall, Sara Francis (Mrs. J. H. Wallis), Ellen Doris. Learned machinist's trade at Corry, and worked at same in Dubuque, Ia., 1879-88, becoming supt. of Dubuque Iron Works; moved to St. Louis 1888, as gen. supt. Fulton Iron Works, of which became pres. and chmn. bd.; retired. Mem. Interstate High. Commn. (Pan-Am.). Home: St. Louis, Mo. Died Dec. 3, 1926.

O'NEIL, Joseph Henry, banker; b. Fall River, Mass., Mar. 23, 1853; s. Patrick Henry and Mary (Harrington) O'N.; grad. Quincy Grammar Sch., Boston; m. Mary Anastasia Ingoldsby, July 1, 1884; 1 son, Joseph Henry. Pres. Federal Trust Co., 1899-1922; chmn. bd. Federal Nat. Bank, 1922—; dir. Mass. Bonding & Ins. Co. Mem. Boston Sch. Com., 1874-77; mem. Mass. Ho. of Rep., 1879-84; mem. bd. dirs. Pub. Instns., Boston, 1881-87 (chmn. bd.); city clk., Boston, 1887-89; mem. Congress, 1889-95; asst. treas. of U.S. at Boston, 1895-99; mem. bd. commrs. Sinking Funds of Boston, 1899-1908. Trustee Mass. Gen. Hosp., 1912—. Home: Roxbury, Mass. Died Feb. 19, 1935.

O'NEIL, Ralph Thomas, lawyer; b. Osage City, Kan., Aug. 8, 1888; s. Thomas J. and Margaret (Hughes) O'N.; grad. high sch., Osage City, 1905, Baker U., Baldwin, Kan., 1909; LL.B., Harvard, 1913; m. Margaret Heizer, Aug. 15, 1919; children—Robert Heizer, Ralph Thomas. Admitted to Kan. bar, 1913, and began practice at Osage City; moved to Topeka, Kan., 1919; mem. firm O'Neil & Hamilton, 1924—; dir. and gen. counsel Victory Life Ins. Co.; gen. counsel Preferred Risk Fire Ins. Company; pres., O'Neil Hardware Company, Osage City, Kan.; dir. Citizens State Bank, Pyramid Life Ins. Co. Nat. comdr. American Legion, 1930-31 (dept. comdr. of Kan. 1925; nat. vice comdr., 1927; chmn. nat. citizens mil. training camps com., 1929; mem. nat. defense com., 1930). County atty., Osage County, Kan., 1914-17; city atty., Topeka, 1921-27. Mem. Kan. State Bd. of Regents, 1932-40, chmn., 1938-39. Served with 11th U.S. Inf., advancing to capt., 1917-19; divisional citation. Decorated silver star, Order of Comdr. of the Crown of Italy. Mem. Kan. State Bar Assn. (pres.). Democrat. Presbyn. Mason, Elk. Home: Topeka, Kan. Died May 25, 1940.

O'NEILL, Edmond, chemist; b. Nashville, Tenn., Dec. 13, 1859; s. Eugene and Bertha (Strachauer) O'N.; Ph.B., U. of Calif., 1879; post-grad. studies Coll. of Chemistry, U. of Calif. and univs. of Berlin and Strassburg; m. Edith Vernon Ward, June 1904. Instr. chemistry, 1879-86, asst. prof., 1888-90, asso. prof., 1890-1906, prof., 1906—, and dir. labs., U. of Calif. Consulting chemist Union Oil Co., Calif. Del. from Calif., and v.p. Congress Applied Chemistry, Berlin, 1903, Rome, 1906. Chmn. chemists com. Calif. State Council Defense, 1917-18; mem. exec. com. engring. div., Nat. Research Council. Mem. Am. Chem. Soc. (organizer and 1st pres. Calif. sect.). Home: Berkeley, Calif. Died Oct. 4, 1933.

O'NEILL, Eugene M., newspaperman; b. Wexford, Ireland, 1850; ed. in univs. of Ireland; married. Admitted to the bar; editor and pub. Pittsburgh Dispatch, 1877-1902. Address: New York, N.Y. Died Nov. 26, 1926.

O'NEILL, Hugh, lawyer; b. Bodie, Calif., June 25, 1882; s. John and Margaret (Russell) O'N.; LL.B., Hastings Coll. of Law, U. of Calif., 1903; m. Lily Theoline Ingwaldson, Apr. 22, 1913. Admitted to Calif. bar, 1903, and began practice at San Francisco; removed to Alaska in 1910; in law practice at Nome, 1911—; editor and mgr. Nome Democrat, 1912 and 1914; U.S. commr. for Cape Nome Precinct, 1917-20; apptd. spl. assistant to U.S. atty., 1920; asst. U.S. atty., 1921-22; city atty. of Nome, 1922-33; U.S. atty. 2d Div., Territory of Alaska, 1933—. Mem. Dem. Territorial Com. for Alaska, 1914—. Address: Nome, Alaska. Deceased.

OPDYCKE, Leonard Eckstein, lawyer; b. Warren, O., Sept. 26, 1858; s. of Emerson and Lucy Wells (Stevens) O.; A.B., Harvard, 1880, A.M., LL.B., 1883; m. Edith Bell, Oct. 12, 1893. Practiced law, 1884-97. Mgr. and v.p. New York Assn. for Improving the Condition of the Poor; trustee United Charities. Chevalier of the Italian Order of St. Morris and St. Lazarus. Translator: Tales from the Ægean, 1894; The Book of the Courtier, 1901, 1903. Home: New York, N.Y. Died Sept. 3, 1915.

OPDYKE, William Stryker, lawyer; b. New York, Oct. 6, 1836; s. George and Elizabeth Hall (Stryker) O.; A.B., New York U., 1856; LL.B., Albany Law School, 1861; admitted to bar, 1861; m. Margaret E. Post, Oct. 20, 1863. Mem. N.Y. Assembly, 1873. Dir. Del. & Hudson Co. Mem. Council New Univ. Home: Alpine, N.J. Died Oct. 20, 1922.

OPERTI, Albert (Jasper Ludwig Roccabigliera), artist; b. Turin, Italy, Mar. 17, 1852; s. of Giuseppi and Amelia Operti; ed. Dublin, Ireland, and at Glasgow (Scotland) High Sch.; grad. Portsmouth Naval Sch., entered British naval marine service; resigned, 1868; studied art and sculpture; m. Martha M. Green, Sept. 7, 1881. Became artist, caricaturist, and scenic artist in New York theatres; studied Arctic history; made 2 voyages to Arctic regions with Comdr. R. E. Peary, U.S.N.; spl. corr. New York Herald on Peary expdns., 1896-97; made 1st casts of N. Greenland Eskimos ever made, for Am. Mus. Natural History, New York. Painted hist. pictures "Rescue of the Greeley Party" and "Farthest North" for army and navy depts., Washington; also "The Schwatka Search"; "Finding DeLong in the Lena Delta (Jeanette)"; "Dr. Kane"; portrait of Comdr. Peary; Ziegler polar ship "America"; mural paintings in Am. Mus. Natural History, New York, and Pittsfield (Mass.), Mus. Illustrated books: Nearest the Pole; Northward Over the Great Ice; The White World; Through the First Antarctic Night; Snow Land Folk. Selected as artist by U.S. Govt. to Chicago Expn. Decorated by Grand Duke Alexis of Russia. Address: New York, N.Y. Died Oct. 29, 1927.

OPHÜLS, William, pathologist; b. Brooklyn, Oct. 23, 1871; s. Carl Julius and Clara (Wilhelms) O.; grad. gymnasium, Crefeld, Germany, 1890; U. of Würzburg, 1890-93; U. of Berlin, 1894; med. staatsexamen, Göttingen, 1895; M.D., U. of Göttingen, 1895; m. Emmy Feldmann, May 6, 1903; children—Clara Louise, Ernst Carl, Elinor Helen, Gertrud. Asst. at Pathol. Inst., Göttingen, 1896-97; prof. pathology and bacteriology, U. of Mo., 1897-98, Cooper Med. Coll., San Francisco, 1898-1912; prof. pathology, Stanford, 1919—; pathologist, Lane Hosp., San Francisco, 1898—. Pres. Bd. Health, San Francisco, 1907-10. Republican. Writer on tuberculosis, coccidioidal granloma, arteriosclerosis, nephritis, etc. Home: San Francisco, Calif. Died Apr. 27, 1933.

OPP, Julie (Mrs. William Faversham), actress; b. New York, Jan. 28, 1871; d. John and Mary (Dwyer) O.; ed. convent, New York; m. 2d, William Faversham, Dec. 29, 1902. First appearance as "Hymen" in "As You Like It," St. James Theatre, London, Dec. 2, 1896; leading lady with Sir George Alexander for 5 yrs.; later engaged by the Frohmans to support William Faversham; starred with husband, 1902—, in "The Squaw Man," "The World and His Wife," "The Barber of Orleans," "The Faun," etc. Author: The Squaw Man (made from the play by Edwin Milton Royle). Home: New York, N.Y. Died Apr. 8, 1921.

OPPENHEIM, Ansel, railway official; b. New York, Jan. 5, 1847; s. Isaac and Henrietta O.; ed. pub. schools and Free Acad., New York; m. Josie Greve, July 21, 1869. Admitted to Minn. bar, 1878; v.p. and dir. C.G.W. Ry.; dir. Minn.&N.W. Ry., Chicago, St. Paul & Kansas City Ry., St. Paul Union Stock Yards Co.; v.p. and dir. Interstate Investment Trust Co., Ltd. Home: St. Paul, Minn. Died Dec. 9, 1916.

OPPENHEIM, James, author; b. St. Paul, Minn., May 24, 1882; s. Joseph and Matilda (Schloss) O.; student, Columbia, 1901-03; m. 3d, Linda Gray; children by first marriage—Ralph, James J. Assistant head worker of the Hudson Guild Settlement, New York, 1901-03. Teacher and acting superintendent, Hebrew Tech. Sch. for Girls, New York, 1905-07. Author: Pay-Envelopes (short stories), 1911; The Nine-Tenths (novel), 1911; The Olympian, 1912; Idle Wives, 1914; Songs for the New Age, 1914; The Beloved, 1915; War and Laughter (poems), 1916; The Book of Self (poems), 1917; The Solitary (poems), 1919; The Mystic Warrior, 1921; Golden Bird, 1923; The Sea (collected poetry), 1924; American Types—A Preface to Analytic Psychology, 1931. Contbr. short stories, articles and poems to American, Hearst's, Harpers, New Republic, Freeman, Century, The Thinker, Am. Mercury, Collier's mags. Editor The Seven Arts Magazine, 1916-17. Home: New York, N.Y. Died Aug. 4, 1932.

OPPENHEIM, Nathan, physician; b. Albany, N.Y., Oct. 17, 1865; s. Gerson and Theresa (Stein) O.; A.B., Harvard, 1888; M.D., Coll. Phys. and Surg. (Columbia), 1891; m. Bertha Elsberg, June 15, 1897. Attending phys., children's dept., New York Red Cross Hosp., and N.Y. City Children's Hosp. and Schs.; specialist in diseases of children. Author: The Development of the Child, 1899; The Medical Diseases of Childhood, 1900; The Care of the Child in Health, 1901; Mental Growth and Control, 1902. Home: New York, N.Y. Died Apr. 5, 1916.

OPPENHEIM, Samuel, author; b. N.Y. City, Dec. 2, 1859; s. Isaac and Melia (Oppenheim) O.; ed. Coll. City of New York, Evening High Sch., Cooper Union; attended Prof. Dwight's law lectures, Columbia; studied law in office of, and was asso., 1892-1901, in practice with Simon Sterne; unmarried. Admitted to N.Y. bar, 1885; sec. exec. com. bd. dirs. M.,K.&T. Ry. Co., 1889-91, and asst. gen. counsel same co., 1896-1901; sec. to commn. apptd. by Gov. Levi P. Morton to recommend changes in methods of legislation in N.Y., 1895; sec. Central Park Improvement Co., 1887-1901; treas. Leavenworth Bridge Co., 1901. Mem. Am. Jewish Hist. Soc. (rec. sec., 1914—). Democrat. Author: The Early Congressional Debates and Reporters, 1889; An Early Jewish Colony in Western Guiana (1658-66), 1907, 08; The Early History of the Jews in New York (1654-1664), 1909; The Jews and Masonry in the United States Before 1810, 1910; The Dutch Records of Kingston, Ulster County, N.Y., Part I (1658-64), 1912; The Chapters of Isaac the Scribe (1772), 1914; More About Jacob Barsimson, the First Jewish Settler in New York, 1925. Home: Bronx, New York, N.Y. Died Aug. 11, 1928.

OPPER, Frederick Burr, artist; b. Madison, Lake County, O., Jan. 2, 1857; s. Lewis and Aurelia

(Burr) O.; left school at 14; worked a yr. or more in the village newspaper office; moved to New York and worked in a store for a short time and then, having sold some humorous sketches to "Wild Oats" and other comic papers, went to drawing as a profession; m. Nellie Barnett, 1882; children—Lawrence, Sophia. On art staff Frank Leslie's 3 yrs.; artist of Puck, 18 yrs.; severed connection with Puck to accept offer from Hearst's New York Journal, May 1899. Illustrator for Bill Nye, Mark Twain, Hobart (Dinkelspiel), Dunne (Dooley), etc. Author: The Folks in Funnyville (with his own verses and pictures); Our Antediluvian Ancestors, 1902; Happy Hooligan, 1902; Alphonse and Gaston, 1902; John Bull, 1903. Home: New Rochelle, N.Y. Died Aug. 29, 1937.

ORAHOOD, Harper M., lawyer; b. Columbus, O., June 3, 1841; s. William J. and Ann (Messenger) O.; pub. and high sch. edn.; m. Mary Esther Hurlbut, Oct. 1, 1863. Joined emigrant train for Colo. in 1860; spent 10 yrs. in mercantile pursuits at Black Hawk and Central City; admitted to bar, 1873; practiced for many yrs. in partnership with Henry M. Teller and his bro., Willard; mem. firm of Orahood & Orahood; pres. Riverside Cemetery Assn., Fairmount Cemetery Assn. Was 1st lt. and commissary of subsistence, and later capt., Co. D, 3d Regt. Colo. Vol. Cav., Civil War; col. on staff of Gov. McIntire, 1895; served as city atty., Blackhawk, Central City and Denver; postmaster Blackhawk, 1862-71; county clerk Gilpin Co., Colo., 1866, 1867; dist. atty. 1st Jud. Dist., Colo., 1877-80; mem. sch. bd. Dist. No. 1, Denver, 7 yrs. (pres. 1 yr.). Republican. Presbyn. Mason (33°); Past Grand Master of Masons of Colo.; Past Grand Comdr. K.T. Comdr. Dept. of Colo. and Wyo., G.A.R., 1901. Home: Denver, Colo. Died Sept. 15, 1914.

ORBISON, Thomas James, M.D., neuro-psychiatrist; b. India (parents U.S. citizens), Nov. 13, 1866; s. James and Nancy Dunlop (Harris) O.; student Haverford Coll., 1884-88; M.D., U. of Pa., 1898, also Doctor of Medical Jurisprudence; m. 2d, Paula Poedder, Nov. 6, 1923; children—(by former marriage) Virginia Thomas, Joan Winsor. Began practice, Phila., 1899; served as asst. instr. mental and nervous diseases, U. of Pa., also on faculty Polyclinic Hosp. and Orthopedic Hosp.; removed to Los Angeles, Calif., 1907; practice limited to mental and nervous diseases; served on faculty Los Angeles County Gen. Hosp., Whittier State Sch., Children's Hosp., Santa Rita Clinic, etc. Mem. N.G. Pa., 1885-86; served in Spanish-Am. War, 1898; mem. 1st Troop, Phila. City Cav., 1899-1907; capt. Med. Corps, World War, with A.E.F., 1917-19; chief of Latvian Sect., Baltic Mission. Mem. Los Angeles Soc. Mental and Nervous Diseases (pres.), Southern Calif. Acad. Criminology (pres.). Awarded Baltic Cross; Latvian Jubilee medal; Order of St. Vladimir, 4th Class. Republican. Presbyn. Mason. Author: Children, Inc. Home: Los Angeles, Calif. Died Mar. 26, 1938.

ORCUTT, Calvin B., manufacturer, financier; b. Wyoming, N.Y., Sept. 5, 1847; ed. Middlebury Acad.; m. Harriet M. Willett, 1872. Began business as asst. in wholesale drug house in New York, then with Fisk & Hatch, Wall St., bankers; took charge of the business of marketing coal produce of Chesapeake & Ohio Ry. Co.; later in charge of Collis P. Huntington's interests at Newport News, Va.; pres. Newport News Shipbuilding & Dry Dock Co., Chesapeake & Ohio Coal Agency Co., Newport News Light and Water Co., Old Dominion Land Co.; dir. First Nat. Bank of Newport News. Home: Elizabeth, N.J. Died 1911.

ORDAL, Ola Johannessen, clergyman, educator; b. nr. Bergen, Norway, Aug. 2, 1870; s. Johannes J. and Martha (Sandal) O.; brought to U.S., 1880; A.B., Luther Coll., Decorah, Ia., 1898; grad. Lutheran Seminary, St. Paul, Minn., 1901; post-grad. work, U. of Washington, 1922-23; m. Anna Christina Leque, June 18, 1902; children—Nils Johan, Martha Marie, Erling Leque (dec.), Olaf Gerhard Leque, Gertrude Dorothy, Gordon Monroe. Ordained Luth. ministry, 1901; pastor New Whatcom (now Bellingham), Wash., 1901-09, also missionary work; pastor Red Wing, Minn., 1909-13, Tacoma, Wash., 1913-21; pres. Pacific Luth. Coll., 1921-28; pastor at Bellingham, Washington, 1928—. Editor Pacific Herold, 1906-08, 1913-17. Pres. Nat. Young People's Socs. America, 1912-15; mem. bd. inspection Luther Theol. Sem., St. Paul, Minn., 1910-13; mem. Bd. Ch. Extension, 1910-13. Republican. Home: Bellingham, Wash. Died Dec. 27, 1936.

ORDEAN, Albert Le Grand, banker; b. New Brighton, Pa., Aug. 22, 1856; s. D. Ribot and Martha (Shovier) O.; ed. pub. schs.; m. Louise Harter, July 19, 1883. Began as clk. in bank, Canton, 1875; moved to Colo., 1879, to Duluth, Minn., 1882; became pres. Merchants Nat. Bank, consolidated, 1889, with Duluth Nat. Bank under title of First Nat. Bank, of which became pres.; pres. Stone-Ordean-Wells Co.; dir. Gt. Northern Ry. Co., Consolidated Abstract Co., First Nat. Bank (St. Paul, Minn.). Mem. bd. dirs. Nat. Budget Com. (N.Y.). Republican. Episcopalian. Home: Duluth, Minn. Died Sept. 21, 1928.

ORDONEZ, Castor, biologist; b. Palencia, Spain, Mar. 28, 1880; s. Nicanor and Rufina (Cabiedes) O.; A.B., Central House of Padres Paules, Madrid, 1901, A.M., 1902; Ph.D., St. Mary's Sem., Perryville, Mo., 1915; Sc.D., De Paul U., 1917. Mem. faculty St. Vincent's Sem., Philippine Islands, 1904-10; editor weekly mag., "Eco de Leyte y Samar," 1911-12. Sec. Spanish section Eucharistic Congress, Chicago. Teacher, De Paul U., 1914—, dir. dept. of biology and mem. bd. of trustees. Known for experimental work in crossing turkey and hen, experiments on cancer in rats, and discoveries in uses of electricity. Naturalized citizen, 1926. Catholic; mem. Congregation of the Mission. Author: Primer Sinodo Diocesano (Culbayog, Samar, P.I.), 1911; Educational Biology, Genetics and Eugenics, 1932; also various laboratory manuals. Compiler: Abridged Calculus, 1908; Compendium of Universal History, 1908. Home: Chicago, Ill. Died June 28, 1938.

ORDRONAUX, John, lawyer; b. in New York, Aug. 3, 1830; grad. Dartmouth Coll., 1850, LL.D., 1895; Harvard Law Sch., 1852, Nat. Med. Coll., Columbian Univ., 1859; LL.D., Trinity Coll., 1870. Served as surgeon in Union Army in Civil war; lecturer on med. jurisprudence, Columbia Coll. Law Sch., 1861-97; same in Dartmouth Coll., U. of Vt. and Boston U., 1865-73; N.Y. State commr. in lunacy, 1872-82. Practiced law in New York, 1882—. Author: Jurisprudence of Medicine, 1869; Metrical Translation of the Regimen Sanitatis Salerne, 1870; Judicial Aspects of Insanity, 1878; Constitutional Legislation in the U.S., 1890. Residence: Glen Head, L.I. Died 1908.

ORDWAY, John Morse, educator, chemist; b. Amesbury, Mass., Apr. 23, 1823; s. Samuel and Sally (Morse) O.; A.M., Dartmouth, 1844; m. Virginia C. Moore, 1854 (died, 1860); m. 2d, Mrs. Charlotte H. Manross, 1864 (died, 1874); m. 3d, Evelyn M. Walton, 1882. Worked in apothecary shop, Lowell, Mass., 1836-38; mgr. chem. works, Lowell, 1 yr.; supt. Roxbury Color and Chem. Co., Roxbury, Mass., 6 yrs.; chemist Drybrook Chem. Works, Johnston, R.I., 2 yrs.; chemist, then mgr., then supt., Manchester Print Works, Manchester, N.H., 5 yrs.; supt. Bayside Alkali Works, Boston, 9 yrs.; prof. industrial chemistry and metallurgy, Mass. Inst. of Tech., 15 yrs., and part of same time instr. in Boston U.; 13 yrs. prof. Tulane U., and prof. biology in H. Sophie Newcomb Coll. (dept. of Tulane U.). Address: New Orleans, La. Died 1909.

ORDWAY, Samuel Hanson, lawyer; b. N.Y. City, June 8, 1860; s. Aaron Lucius and Frances Ellen (Hanson) O.; A.B., Brown U., 1880 (valedictorian), LL.D., 1917; A.M., LL.B., Harvard, 1883; m. Frances Hunt Throop, May 30, 1894; children—Frances Hanson (dec.), Samuel Hanson. Practiced in N.Y. City, 1884—; mem. Spencer, Ordway & Wierum. Asst. dist. atty., New York Co., 1901; mem. Commn. to Revise Tax Laws of N.Y. State, 1906; mem. commn. apptd. by Gov. Hughes to investigate speculation in securities and commodities, 1909. Active in civil service reform work and for many yrs. chmn. exec. com. Civil Service Reform Assn.; pres. N.Y. State Civil Service Commn., 1915-17; justice Supreme Court of N.Y., 1917. Mem. U.S. dist. Board for New York City (selective service bd.), 1918; pub. service commr. for 1st Dist. of N.Y., 1918. Republican. Trustee and fellow of Brown U. Pres. Civil Service Reform Assn. Episcopalian. Home: New York, N.Y. Died Apr. 19, 1934.

O'REAR, John Davis, diplomatic service; b. Audrain County, Mo., Mar. 21, 1870; s. Benjamin Franklin and Margaret (Colton) O.; grad. Mexico (Mo.) High Sch., 1890; taught sch. and studied law, 3 yrs.; m. Eugenie Violet Bragg, 1905. Practiced in Mexico, Mo., 1893-1913; elected city atty., 1898; pros. atty., Audrain Co., 2 terms, 1904-08; mem. Dem. State Com.; apptd. E.E. and M.P. to Bolivia, June 26, 1913. Address: La Paz, Bolivia. Died July 14, 1918.

O'REILLY, Bernard Patrick, college pres.; b. Rochester, N.Y., June 3, 1874; s. James and Bridget (O'Farrell) O'R.; B.A., U. of Besançon, France, 1895. Ordained priest R.C. Ch., 1903; pres. St. Mary's College, Dayton, O., 1908-18; later pres. U. of Dayton. Author: Vocations to Teaching Orders, 1907; Catholic College Prayer Book, 1912. Address: Dayton, O. Died 1932.

O'REILLY, Charles J., bishop; b. St. John, N.B., Can., Jan. 4, 1860; ed. St. Joseph's Coll., Memramcook, and Grand Sem., Montreal. Ordained priest, R.C. Ch., at Portland, Ore., 1890; in charge missions at Oswego and Tegardville, 1890-94; rector Ch. of Immaculate Heart of Mary, Portland, 1894-1903; consecrated 1st bishop of Baker City, Aug. 25, 1903; trans. to Lincoln, Neb., 1918. Was editor Catholic Sentinel, Portland, several yrs. Home: Lincoln, Neb. Died Feb. 4, 1923.

O'REILLY, James, bishop; b. in Ireland, 1856; ed. at All Hallows Coll., nr. Dublin. Ordained priest R.C. Ch.; served as asst. at Stillwater and Lake City, Minn.; pastor Ch. of St. Anthony of Padua, Minneapolis, 1886-1910; consecrated bishop of Fargo, May 10, 1909. Home: Fargo, N.D. Died Dec. 18, 1934.

O'REILLY, Mary Boyle, humanitarian; b. Boston, May 18, 1873; d. John Boyle and Mary (Smiley) O'R.; ed. Convent Sacré Cœur, 1880-90; spl. coll. courses; unmarried. Editorial writer; lecturer on sociology; social worker; investigator in N.H. baby farms investigation, 1910. Trustee Children's Institutions Dept., Mass., 1905-11; prison commr., Mass., 1907-11. Foreign corr. and war relief worker in France, Russia, Eng., 1913-17; lecturer for war relief funds, 1918. Catholic. Home: Auburndale, Mass. Died Oct. 21, 1939.

O'REILLY, Robert Maitland, surgeon gen. U.S.A.; b. Phila., Jan. 14, 1845; s. John and Ellen (Maitland) O.; M.D., U. of Pa., 1866; m. Miss Pardee, Aug. 16, 1877. Apptd. from Pa., med. cadet, U.S.A., Jan. 7, 1864; apptd. asst. surgeon, May 14, 1867; capt. asst. surgeon, May 14, 1870; maj. surgeon, Nov. 1, 1886; lt. col. deputy surgeon gen., Feb. 21, 1900; col. asst. surgeon gen., Feb. 14, 1902; brig. gen. surgeon gen. U.S.A., Sept. 7, 1902; retired with rank of major gen., Jan. 14, 1909. During Spanish-Am. War was in vol. service May 9, 1898, to May 12, 1899, as lt. col. chief surgeon. Address: Washington, D.C. Died Nov. 3, 1912.

O'REILLY, Thomas Charles, bishop; b. Cleveland, O., Feb. 22, 1873; s. Patrick and Delia (Readdy) O'R.; grad. St. Ignatius High Sch., John Carroll U., Spencerian Business Coll., all of Cleveland; grad. North Am. Coll., Rome, 1899; S.T.D., U. of Propaganda, Rome, 1899; LL.D., U. of Notre Dame, 1909. Ordained priest R.C. Ch., 1898; asst. pastor St. John the Evangelist Cathedral, Cleveland, 1899-1901; prof. philosophy and theology, St. Mary's Sem., Cleveland, 1901-10; chancellor Diocese of Cleveland, 1910-16, vicar gen., 1916-21; pastor St. John the Evangelist Cathedral, 1911-28; vicar gen. for religious, 1922-28; judge Matrimonial Court, Cleveland, 1910-28; bishop of Scranton, Pa., 1928—. Address: Scranton, Pa. Died Mar. 25, 1938.

ORENDORFF, Alfred, lawyer; b. Logan County, Ill., July 29, 1845; s. Joseph and Elizabeth (Stevens) O.; ed. Wesleyan U., Bloomington, Ill.; LL.B., Albany Law Sch., 1866; m. Julia Jayne Williams, June 22, 1870. Admitted to bar, 1867; mem. law firm Orendorff & Patton. Capt. Co. I, 133d Ill. Inf.; adj. gen., Ill., 1892-96. Mem. Ill. Gen. Assembly, 1873-74; chmn. Dem. State Central Com.; candidate State treas., Ill.; del. Dem. Nat. convs. Pres. Internat. Bank (Vinita, I. T.), Sterling Life Ins. Co. (Springfield, Ill.). Pres. Ill. State Hist. Soc.; pres. Ill. State Bar Assn.; pres. Sangamon Co. Bar Assn.; del. Universal Congress Lawyers and Jurists, St. Louis, 1904. Address: Springfield, Ill. Died 1909.

ORLADY, George Boal; b. Petersburg, Huntingdon County, Pa., Feb. 22, 1850; s. Henry (M.D.) and Martha C. (Boal) O.; student Pa. State Coll., 1864-65, M.A., 1911, M.S., 1918; student Bellwood Acad., 1866; S.B., Washington and Jefferson Coll., 1870; M.D., Jefferson Med. Coll., 1871; studied law with Hon. Samuel Steel Blair, Holidaysburg, Pa., 1873-75; LL.D., Washington and Jefferson, 1898, Temple U., 1918, Juniata Coll., 1919, U. of Pa., 1920; m. Mary Irvin Thompson, Feb. 21, 1877. Practiced medicine at Petersburg, 1871-73; admitted to Pa. bar, 1875; dist. atty. Huntingdon County, 1878-87; apptd. judge Superior Court of Pa., 1895; elected for terms 1895-1906, 1906-16, 1916-26. Mem. Pa. State Bar Assn. (pres. 1913). Grand Master of Masons, Pa., 1908-09. Home: Huntingdon, Pa. Died Sept. 9, 1926.

ORME, John Pinckney, farmer, stockraiser; b. Poolesville, Md., Nov. 28, 1852; s. Charles Henry and Deborah (Pleasants) O.; civ. engring. course, U. of Mo., 1869-70; m. Ella Eugenia Tompkins, Mar. 5, 1880 (died 1898); children—Mrs. Clara Kyle, Ora, Mrs. Doris Leeds, Charles Henry. Engaged as civ. engr. until 1877; settled on homestead in Ariz., 1878, later took up timber claim and 320 acres under desert act; surveyed and built second canal in Salt River Valley, 1879, and dir. same until 1918; retired from active business, 1918. Mem. Bd. of Supervisors of Maricopa County, 1900-12; mem. Constl. Conv. of Ariz., 1910; pres. Salt River Valley Water Users' Assn., 1909-17; regent U. of Ariz., 1916-17; mem. exam. bd. of artillery applicants, Ariz., World War; state appraiser Fed. Farm and Loan Bank of Berkeley, Calif., 1917-19. President Pioneers' Assn. of Ariz. Mem. 6th, 7th and 8th Ariz. legislatures. Democrat. Episcopalian. Mason, Odd Fellow. Home: Phoenix, Ariz. Died Nov. 11, 1936.

ORMOND, Alexander Thomas, college pres.; b. Punxsutawney, Pa., Apr. 26, 1847; student Miami U., 1869-70; A.B., Princeton, 1877, A.M., 1878, Ph.D., 1880; LL.D., Miami, 1900; m. Mary Huston, 1884. Prof. philosophy and history, U. of Minn., 1880-83; prof. mental science and logic, 1883-98, McCosh prof. philosophy, 1898-1913, Princeton; pres. Grove City (Pa.) Coll., Aug. 1913—. Author: Basal Concepts in Philosophy; Foundations of Knowledge, 1900; Concepts of Philosophy, 1906; also a number of papers on philos. subjects. Address: Grove City, Pa. Died Dec. 18, 1915.

ORMSBEE, Ebenezer Jolls, governor; b. Shoreham, Vt., June 8, 1834; s. of John Mason and Polly (Willson) O.; ed. pub. schs., Vt. Scientific and Lit. Instn. (Brandon) and Green Mountain Acad., Woodstock, Vt.; hon. A.M., Middlebury, 1875, Dartmouth, 1884; LL.D., Norwich U., 1893; m. Jennie L. Briggs, Aug. 27, 1862; m. 2d, Mrs. Frances (Wadhams) Davenport, Sept. 26, 1867. Admitted to bar, 1861; 2d lt. Co. G, 1st Vt. Inf., and capt. Co. G, 12th Vt. Inf., 1861-63. Asst. U.S. internal revenue collector, Dist. of Vt., 1868-72; state's atty., Rutland Co., Vt., 1870-74; mem. Gen. Assembly, 1872, Senate, 1878; trustee Vt. Reform Sch., 1880-84; lt. gov. of Vt., 1884-88; gov., 1886-88; commr. to Pi-Ute Indians, 1891; U.S. land commr. of Samoa, 1891-93. Republican. Episcopalian. Pres. Brandon Nat. Bank. Trustee Vt. Soldiers' Home. Address: Brandon, Vt. Died Apr. 3, 1924.

ORNDORFF, William Ridgely, chemist; b. Baltimore, Sept. 9, 1862; s. William Wellmore and Mary J. (Ridgely) O.; student Baltimore City Coll., 1876-81; A.B., Johns Hopkins, 1884, Ph.D., 1887; studied at univs. of Greifswald, Berlin, Heidelberg, 1897-98, U. of Munich, 1906-07; m. Charlotte Heinrich, 1912; children—Mary Ridgely, William Ridgely. Instr. chemistry, 1887-90, asst. prof. organic chemistry, 1890-1908, organic and physiol. chemistry, 1898, Cornell U.; prof. organic and physiol. chemistry, 1902—, and mem. faculty Arts and Sciences, the faculty of the Grad. Sch. and Univ. faculty, and of med. faculty (at Ithaca), Cornell. Mem. Internat. Jury of Awards, Paris Expn., 1889, St. Louis Expn., 1904 (sec. Group Jury No. 23, Dept. of Liberal Arts), Panama P.I. Exposition, San Francisco, 1915; special agent U.S. Census, 1890. Contbr. of results of original chem. research to Am. Chem. Jour., Berichte der Deutschen Chemischen Gesellschaft, Jour. Am. Chem. Soc. and Jour. of Physical Chemistry. Author: Laboratory Manual of Organic Chemistry, 1922. Translator: Dr. E. Salkowski's Laboratory Manual of Physiological and Pathological Chemistry, 1904. Co-author in revision of Remsen's Organic Chemistry, 1922. Home: Ithaca, N.Y. Died Nov. 1, 1927.

ORNE, Caroline Frances, author; b. Cambridge, Mass., Sept. 5, 1818; d. John Gerry and Ann (Stone) O.; ed. in schools and acad. at Cambridgeport, and at Mr. Ebenezer Bailey's High Sch. for Young Ladies, Boston, 1832-36; was 1st librarian (17 yrs.) Cambridge Public Library. Author: Lucy's Party and Other Tales, 1842; Sweet Auburn and Mount Auburn (poems), 1876; Morning Songs of American Freedom (poems), 1876. Address: Cambridge, Mass. Died 1905.

ORNE, John, Orientalist; b. Newburyport, Mass., April 29, 1834; s. of John and Sarah Ingalls (Morse) O.; A.B., Amherst, 1855, Ph.D., 1896, "for eminent attainments in Arabic lang. and lit."; m. Louisa F. Lindsay, Nov. 1867. Has taught in Newburyport, Salem and Cambridge high schools; curator Arabic MSS., Semitic Mus., Harvard, 1899—. Published numerous papers on Oriental subjects; deciphered and translated sundry Arabic inscriptions on mortuary tablets in Semitic Mus. Address: Cambridge, Mass. Died 1911.

ORR, Alexander Ector, merchant; b. Strabane, County Tyrone, Ireland, Mar. 2, 1831; came to U.S. on a visit, 1850, and in 1851 settled permanently in New York; m. Juliet Buckingham Dows, 1857 (died 1872); m. 2d, Margaret S. Luquer, 1873. Was employed in shipping and commn. houses; in 1858 became clerk, and 1861 partner, David Dows & Co.; mem. Produce Exchange, 1859—; has several times been its pres.; also pres. New York Chamber of Commerce and of the Bd. of Rapid Transit Commrs. of N.Y.; and a dir. of many of New York's financial and philanthropic instns. Pres. N.Y. Life Ins. Co., 1905-07; v.p. Mechanics & Metals Nat. Bank; trustee U.S. Trust Co. Died June 3, 1914.

ORR, Charles Prentiss, judge; b. Allegheny (now Pittsburgh), Pa., Feb. 22, 1858; s. Robert and Margaret A. (Fake) O.; A.B., Hamilton Coll., 1879, LL.D., 1910; m. Anna Lyon Lazear, May 27, 1886. Studied law with Thomas C. Lazear, Pittsburgh; admitted to bar, 1881; mem. firm of Lazear & Orr, 1886-1909; U.S. dist. judge, Western Dist. of Pa., Apr. 10, 1909—. Republican. Presbyn. Mem. Pa. State Bar Assn. (twice v.p.). Home: Pittsburgh, Pa. Died May 16, 1922.

ORR, George, consular service; b. Phila., Pa., Sept. 29, 1886; s. William and Annie (Millikin) O.; grad. Northeast High Sch., Phila., 1903; student Temple Coll., 1906-07; m. Clara H. Rose, Aug. 11, 1920. Ry. and municipal engr. until 1920; consul at Panama, 1920-25, at Paris, 1925-29, Stavanger, Norway, 1929-32, Caracas, Venezuela, 1932—. Served as 1st lt. and capt. 32d Engrs., U.S.A., 1917-19. Home: Atlantic City, N.J. Died Apr. 3, 1937.

ORR, James Lawrence, cotton mfr.; b. Abbeville, S.C., Aug. 29, 1852; s. James L. and Mary J. (Marshall) O.; ed. King's Mountain Mil. Acad., 1868-70; grad. U. of Va., 1872; studied law school, U. of Va.; m. Bettie Bates Hammett, Nov. 12, 1873. Asst. sec. U.S. legation, St. Petersburg, Russia, 1873; mem. legislature, S.C., 1874-78; solicitor 8th circuit, S.C., 1880-88; pres. and treas. Piedmont Mfg. Co., 1891—; pres. and treas. Orr Mills, 1899—; trustee Clemson Agrl. Coll. 4 yrs.; trustee S.C. Med. Coll., Converse Coll., v.p. Am. Spring Co. and Mills Mfg. Co., Greenville; dir. Nat. Bank, Am. Bank, People's Bank, Greenville. Democrat. Episcopalian. Address: Greenville, S.C. Died 1905.

ORR, James Washington, lawyer; b. Reading, Hillsdale County, Mich., Sept. 14, 1855; s. James and Mary Elizabeth (Underhill) O.; ed. at home under mother; student law dept. U. of Mich., 1873-75; m. Jennie, d. Gov. George W. Glick, June 21, 1883. Admitted to Mich. bar, 1877; practiced in Atchison, 1881—; successively mem. Martin & Orr, Waggener, Martin & Orr, Waggener, Horton & Orr, and Waggener, Doster & Orr, until 1910; practiced alone, 1910—; specialist in ry. and corp. law; mem. Dem. State Central Com., 1884-1908; del. to 9 Dem. nat. convs., and 7 times mem. com. to notify presdl. nominee of his nomination; mayor of Atchison 3 terms, 1901-07; mem. Kan. Ho. of Rep. 2 terms, 1911-13; majority leader and chmn. judiciary com. of House, 1913; author of pub. utilities law, Orr viaduct law, drainage laws; spl. asst. atty. gen. of U.S., 1915, in charge of Govt. suit against S.P. Co. and others, including Central Pacific Ry., to dissolve relations existing between those companies. Christian Scientist. Mason. Home: Atchison, Kan. Died Feb. 6, 1927.

ORR, Joseph Kyle, Masonic official; b. N.Y. City, Feb. 21, 1857; s. Joseph Kyle and Elezabeth (Kyle) O.; Coll. City of New York, 1870-71; m. Frances Bradley, Oct. 17, 1883. Began with H. J. Libby & Co., dry goods commn. bus., New York, 1872; moved to Columbus, Ga., and was connected with J. Kyle & Co., 1873-83; founded, 1883, J. K. Orr Shoe mfrs., of which was pres., located at Atlanta, 1897-1937. Pres. Atlanta Chamber of Commerce. Trustee Agnes Scott Coll. (Atlanta), George Peabody Coll. for Teachers (Nashville, Tenn.), Martha Berry Sch. (Rome, Ga.). Democrat. Presbyn. Grand Comdr. of K.T. of Ga., 1895; Grand Sword Bearer, Grand Encampment, 1904, and regularly advanced to Grand Master, Grand Encampment K.T., U.S.A., 1919. Founder Knights Templar Foundation, a loan fund, that reached in 7th yr. over $3,000,000, helping 14,000 college students in the U.S. Home: Atlanta, Ga. Died Sept. 18, 1938.

ORR, William, teacher; b. Phila., Pa., Nov. 16, 1860; s. William and Catharine (Reid) O.; B.A., Amherst College, 1883, M.A., 1892, L.H.D., 1937; m. Charlotte Evelyn Pettis, Aug. 7, 1889 (died 1931); children—Alan Gardner, Helen Theresa, Philip Gardner (dec.), Charlotte Reid (dec.); m. 2d, M. C. M. Benson, Sept. 10, 1936. Principal Hopkins Acad., Hadley, Mass., 1883-85, Smith Acad., Hatfield, 1885-88; science master, 1888-94, v.prin., 1894-1900, prin., 1900-10, high sch., Springfield; curator, Mus. Natural History, Springfield, 1895-1910; deputy commr. of edn. for Mass., 1910-16; sr. ednl. sec., Internat. Com. Y.M.C.A., 1916-20; spl. mission Y.M.C.A. in Europe, 1920-27. Dir. ednl. bur. War Work Council Y.M.C.A., 1917-18; chmn. com. on edn. of Commn. on Training Camp Activities, War Dept., 1917-18. Trustee Internat. Y.M.C.A. Coll., Springfield, Mass.; exec. sec., trustee Albanian Am. Agrl. Sch.; ednl. adviser Thessalonica Agrl. and Industrial Inst.; exec. sec. Am. com. of Y.M.C.A. Sch., Geneva, Switzerland. Decorated Order Polonia Restituta (Poland), 1923; awarded Pyncheon medal, Springfield, Mass., 1937. Episcopalian. Mason. Author: Eight Geological Excursions in Springfield and Vicinity; Pageants and Pageantry (with Esther W. Bates); History of Classical High School, Springfield, Mass., 1936. Home: Fairhaven, Mass. Died July 21, 1939.

ORRIS, S. Stanhope, educator; b. Pa., Feb. 19, 1838; grad. Princeton, 1862; Princeton Theol. Sem., 1865, Ph.D., L.H.D. Instr. Latin, Princeton, 1865-66; pastor of Spruce Creek Presbyn. Ch. (Central Pa.), 3½ yrs.; studied 1 yr. in Germany, supplied a chapel of Collegiate Dutch Ch., New York, 1 yr.; prof. Greek language and literature, Marietta Coll., 3½ yrs.; prof. Greek lang. and lit. and instr. Greek philosophy, 1877-1902, later prof. emeritus; spent 1 yr. as dir. Am. School of Classical Studies, Athens, Greece; 1 yr. in study of modern Greek and topography of Greece. Author: Greek Text of "The Teaching of the Twelve Apostles," with translations of the same; numerous articles on Biblical research and classical philology. Address: Harrisburg, Pa. Died 1905.

ORT, Samuel Alfred, theologian; b. Lewistown, Pa., Nov. 11, 1843; s. Samuel and Christina O.; A.B., Wittenberg Coll., 1863, D.D., 1877, LL.D., 1893; LL.D., Wooster, 1893; m. Ann Eliza Senteny, Sept. 23, 1875. Ordained Luth. ministry, 1865; pastor Louisville, 1874-78, New York, 1878-80; prof. christian theology, Wittenberg Theol. Sem., 1880-1910; pres. Wittenberg Coll., 1882-1900. Del. Gen. Synod Luth. Ch., 1873—; pres. Gen. Synod, 1887. Address: Springfield, O. Died 1911.

ORTEIG, Raymond; born at Louvie-Juzon, France; s. Jean and Jeanne (Davancens) O.; ed. night sch., N.Y. City; m. Marie Ruisques, Oct. 26, 1892; children—Raymond, Evariste, Jean B. Mgr. Hotel Martin, 1892-1902; dir. Raymond Orteig, Inc. Donor of $25,000 prize to Col. Charles A. Lindbergh for transatlantic flight, 1927. Decorated Legion of Honor (France). Home: New York, N.Y. Died June 6, 1939.

ORTH, Charles J., composer; b. Milwaukee, Wis.; pupil of Hugo Kaun and Frank Neumann. At 16 composed "In the Clock Store," played by Sousa in transcontinental concert tour; also composed Romance (performed by Chicago, Boston and St. Louis symphony orchestras); Nocturne in E-flat, for violin and piano; concerto, for 2 clarinets; scherzo, 2 sonatas, piano pieces, etc. Address: Milwaukee, Wis. Died Feb. 1, 1921.

ORTH, John, musician; b. nr. Annweiler, Germany, Dec. 2, 1850; brought to U.S. when 1 yr. old, parents settling at Taunton, Mass.; began learning piano at 8; played the organ in one of the Taunton chs. at 12; studied in Boston, 1866-70, teaching in the Conservatory and in the city, and playing in ch. to earn means to continue studies in Germany, 1870-75, under Kullak, Lebert, Pruckner, Deppe, Liszt on piano, and composition with Faiszt, Weitzmann, Kiel and P. Scharwenka; m. Lizette Emma Blood, May 28, 1883 (died 1913). 1875—, pianist and teacher in Boston; composed numerous piano pieces. Home: Boston, Mass. Died May 3, 1932.

ORTH, Lizette Emma, composer; b. Milford, N.H., July 6, 1858; d. of James and Emeline (Wheeler) Blood; m. John Orth, May 28, 1883. Composer: Mother Goose Songs Without Words (70 easy piano compositions), 1897; A Dozen Miniatures for the Piano, 1899; Ten Pictures from Tone Land for the Piano, 1899; On the White Keys, an introduction to the piano, 1900; Sixty Songs from Mother Goose's Jubilee, an opera for children, 1900; A Dozen and Three, piano pieces; Song of the Sea Shell (opera); Four and Twenty Songs for Sleepy Time; also over 150 published piano pieces, besides various songs. Address: Brookline, Mass. Died Sept. 14, 1913.

ORTH, Samuel Peter, coll. prof.; b. Capac, Mich., Aug. 1, 1873; s. Rev. John and Katharine (Troeller) O.; B.S., Oberlin Coll., 1896; studied law and polit. science U. of Mich., 1896-97; grad. student (fellow) polit. science and pub. law, 1902-03, Ph.D., 1903, Columbia; m. Jane Davis, Aug. 17, 1899. Prof. polit. and social science, Buchtel Coll., Akron, O., 1897-1902; practiced law Cleveland, O., 1903-12; prof. polit. science, Cornell U., 1912—. Lecturer on internat. law, economics and polit. science, Western Reserve U., Case Sch. of Applied Science and Oberlin Coll., 1904-10; pres. Bd. of Edn., Cleveland, 1904-05; asst. U.S. atty., 1905-08. Accompanied Cook Arctic expdn. to Greenland, 1894. Author: Centralization of Administration in Ohio, 1903; Five American Politicians, 1903; A History of Cleveland, 1909; Socialism and Democracy in Europe, 1913; Readings on the Relation of Government to Industry, 1915; The Imperial Impulse, 1916; The Boss and the Machine, 1918. Address: Ithaca, N.Y. Died Feb. 26, 1922.

ORTMANN, Arnold Edward, naturalist; b. Magdeburg, Prussia, Apr. 8, 1863; s. Prof. Edward Franz and Bertha (Lorenz) O.; gymnasium edn., Magdeburg and (grad.) Schleusingen (Thuringia); studied at univs. of Jena, Kiel and Strassburg; Ph.D., Jena, 1885; Sc.D., U. of Pittsburgh, 1911; m. Anna Zaiss, Dec. 5, 1894. Served as 1-yr. vol. in 5th Thuringia Inf., German Army, 1882-83; qualified as lt. reserves, Mar. 1883; zoölogist and palæontologist; on collecting expdn. to Zanzibar, Africa, 1890-91; came to U.S., 1894; curator invertebrate palæontology, Princeton, 1894-1903; curator invertebrate zoölogy, Carnegie Mus., Pittsburgh, 1903—; instr. geol. geography, 1909-10, prof. phys. geography, 1910-25, prof. zoölogy, 1925—, U. of Pittsburgh. Mem. Princeton Arctic (Peary relief) expdn., 1899. Author: Flora Hennebergica, 1887; Grundzüge der Marinen Tiergeographie, 1896; Continuation of Die Decapodon in Bronn's Klassen und Ordnungen des Tierreiches, 1898-1900; Tertiary Invertebrates of the Princeton Expdn. to Patagonia, 1902. Home: Pittsburgh, Pa. Died Jan. 3, 1927.

ORTON, Edward, geologist; b. Deposit, Delaware County, N.Y., Mar. 9, 1829; A.M., Hamilton Coll., 1848, Ph.D., LL.D., Ohio State U.; m. Mary M. Jennings, 1855; m. 2d, Anna D. Torrey, 1875. State geologist of Ohio, 1869—; pres. Antioch Coll., O., 1872-73; pres. Ohio State U., 1873-81, prof. of geology, 1873—. Author of "Petroleum," etc., in U.S. Geol. reports, Kentucky geol. survey. Joint author Vols. 1, 2 and 3 and author Vols. 5, 6 and 7, "Geology of Ohio;" also many geological papers. Pres. Geol. Soc. of America in 1897; pres. Am. Assn. Adv. Science, 1898-99. Address: Columbus, O. Died 1899.

ORTON, Edward, Jr., engineer, mfr.; b. Chester, N.Y., Oct. 8, 1863; s. Dr. Edward and Mary (Jennings) O.; E.M., Ohio State U., 1884; D.Sc. from Rutgers Coll., N.J., 1922; m. Mary Princess Anderson, Oct. 30, 1888 (died 1927); m. 2d, Mina Althea Orton, Oct. 6, 1928. Chemist and supt. blast furnaces, 1884-88; 1st to regularly mfr. "ferro-silicon," or high silicon alloy of iron in U.S., Bessie Furnace New Straitsville, O., 1887-88; entered clay industries, 1888; managed several plants, 1888-93. Began agitation, 1893, which resulted in establishing, 1894, of 1st school in U.S. for instr. in tech. of clay, glass and cement industries, of which was dir. until 1916; dean Coll. Engring. Ohio State U., 1902-06 and 1910-16; retired from univ. work, 1917. State geologist of Ohio, 1899-1906. Commd. maj., O.R.C., Jan. 5, 1917; called into active service in motors div. Q.M. Corps, May 9, 1917; lt. col. Motor Transport Corps, Sept. 6, 1918. Awarded D.S.M., June 2, 1919. Col. Q.M., O.R.C., Sept. 25, 1919; brig. gen. Q.M., O.R.C., Sept. 27, 1923. Pres. Reserve Officers' Assn. of Ohio, 1922-23. Began manufacture, 1896, of pyrometric cones, for regulating firing process of ceramic products and other wares burned in kilns; developed lab. and testing sta. for study of clay and ceramic products, 1900. Wrote: Clays of Ohio and the Industries Established Upon Them, Rep. Ohio Geol. Survey, Vol. V, 1884; The Clay-Working Industries of Ohio, Vol. VII, same, 1893. Also numerous tech. articles and reports. Home: Columbus, O. Died Feb. 10, 1932.

ORTON, William Allen, plant pathologist; b. N. Fairfax, Vt., Feb. 28, 1877; s. Gardner Gregory and Electa Wilcox (Allen) O.; B.S., U. of Vt., 1897. M.S., 1898, Sc.D., 1915; m. Helen A. Davis, Apr. 20, 1903; children—Helen Alberta, Alice Louise, William Allen (dec.). Asst. botanist, Vt. Agrl. Expt. Sta. and instr., U. of Vt., 1897-99; plant pathologist, U.S. Dept. of Agr., June 1, 1899-Oct. 31, 1924, in charge investigation cotton, truck and forage crop diseases, Bureau Plant Industry, and v. chmn. Federal Hort. Bd., 1912-24; sci. dir. and gen. mgr. Tropical Plant Research Foundation, 1924—. Conglist. Writer bulletins U.S. Dept. Agr. on sea island cotton, cotton and potato diseases, plant breeding and related subjects, and tropical agr. Home: Takoma Park, D.C. Died Jan. 7, 1930.

OSBON, Bradley Sillick, naval officer; b. Rye, Westchester County, N.Y., Aug. 16, 1828; s. Rev. Abiathar Mann and Elizabeth E. (Sillick) O.; ed. common schools, New York, and Conn., until went to sea at 10 yrs. of age; self-taught; m. Eliza Balfour, Feb. 14, 1868. Served in Chinese Navy (as comdr.), Argentine Navy (as comdr.), U.S. Navy (signal officer) and Mexican Navy (admiral). During Civil War served under Du Pont, Farragut and Worden (specially mentioned by Farragut); during Spanish-Am. War was vol. naval scout and was 1st to discover Cervera's fleet off Island of Curaçoa, May 14, 1898, and reported to State Dept.; received letter of thanks for service; twice in Arctic Ocean and once in Antarctic Ocean. One term capt., one commodore, and two rear adm., Nat. Assn. Naval Veterans, U.S. of A.; was flag officer comdg. U.S. Veteran Navy, with rank of commodore. Decorated by Venezuelan Govt. with Order of "Busto del Liberatador." Founder and editor The Nautical Gazette, 1871, 1st maritime newspaper published in the U.S. Author: Osbon's Hand Book United States Navy, 1863; United States Veteran Navy List, 1900; A Sailor of Fortune, 1906. Lecturer on travels and adventures; asso. editor of the American Shipbuilder, and of Tourist Magazine, 1910. Address: New York, N.Y. Died May 6, 1912.

OSBORN, Abraham Coles, college pres.; b. Scotch Plains, N.J., February 20, 1831; s. Jonathan and Amelia (Van Deursen) O.; A.B., Colgate U., Hamilton, N.Y., 1855, A.M., 1858; grad. Hamilton Theol. Sem., 1858; D.D., Shurtleff College, Ill., 1867; LL.D., Colgate, 1905; m. Emma J. Hatfield, (dec.). Ordained Bapt. ministry, 1858; pastor Jefferson St. Ch., Louisville, Ky., 1858-62, Fourth Ch., St. Louis, 1862-69, Tabernacle Ch., Brooklyn, 1869-73, South Ch., New York, 1873-77, First Ch., N. Adams, Mass., 1877-84, First Ch., Albion, N.Y., 1884-95; pres. and prof. theology, Benedict Coll., Columbia, S.C., 1895-1910. Mem. corp. Colgate U. Mason, K.T. Author: The Mormon Doctrine of God and Heaven. Address: North Adams, Mass. Died Jan. 16, 1916.

OSBORN, Edwin Faxon, clergyman, author, lecturer; b. Climax, Mich., Sept. 7, 1859; s. David and Eliza Maria (Faxon) O.; A.B., Kalamazoo (Mich.) Coll., 1889; Newton Theological Instn., 1891-92; grad. Rochester Theol. Sem., 1894; hon. A.M., Ewing (Ill.) Coll., 1901, D.D., 1902; m. Laura Bertha Judson, July 31, 1884; children—Judson Pierre (dec.), Lurene (Mrs. Robt. S. Tubbs), Harold Gray, Paul Romaine. Student-pastor, 1881-84; ordained Bapt. ministry, 1885; pastor Watertown, N.Y., 1894-96; lit. work, Kalamazoo, 1896-99; prof. history and lit., Ewing Coll., 1899-1900; pastor First Bapt. Ch., Evansville, Ind., 1900-02; lit. work, bible evangelism and lecturing, 1902—. Author: Some Essentials of Christian Growth, 1896; The Vanishing of the Prince, 1898; Some Foundation Stones of Christian Character, 1906; The Teaching of the Parables, 1906; Onar, 1909; The Words and Deeds of Jesus (the adult life of Jesus, in the language of the four gospels combined, without comment or the repetition of the same matter; used also as a textbook in pub. schs.; dramatized for use in Christian orgns.), 1927. Founded Narcotics Abstinence League, 1920; called meeting of rep. tobacco reformers at Aurora, Ill., 1921, seeking union of forces; reorganized Narcotics Abstinence League, 1922, taking name of Life Conservation League (pres. 1932—). Home: Kalamazoo, Mich. Died July 29, 1937.

OSBORN, Erastus William, newspaperman; b. Winthrop, Me., Oct. 24, 1860; s. Thomas Alden and Maria Frances O.; ed. acads. Winthrop, Me., Ashland, Mass., Auburn, N.Y.; m. Ida Birdsall, June 12, 1889. Began newspaper work at Auburn, 1880-87; joined staff New York Evening World, Jan. 1888, dramatic editor, 1896-98, editorial writer and lit. editor The World, Jan.-Dec. 1923, dramatic critic Evening World, 1923-29 (retired). Home: Auburn, N.Y. Died May 4, 1930.

OSBORN, Eugene Ernest, railway official; b. Norwalk, Conn., May 1, 1854; s. John and Lydia A. (Duncomb) O.; Ph.B., Yale, 1874; LL.B., Columbian (now George Washington) U., 1876; m. Ada M. Gibbs, Aug. 27, 1879. Practiced law in Marquette County, Mich., 1876-94; gen. atty. C.&N.W. Ry. Co., 1894-1901; v.p. C.&N.W. Ry. Co., and C.,St.P.,M.&O. Ry. Co., 1901-Oct. 20, 1910; resigned. Address: New York, N.Y. Died July 21, 1914.

OSBORN, Frank Chittenden, civil engr.; b. Greenland, Ontonagon County, Mich., Dec. 18, 1857; s. Reuben Howard and Livonia (Chittenden) O.; C.E., Rensselaer Poly. Inst., 1880; m. Annie Paull, Oct. 27, 1880. Asst. engr. Louisville Bridge & Iron Co., 1880-85; prin. asst. engr. Keystone Bridge Co., 1885-87; mem. firm G. W. G. Ferris & Co., Pittsburgh, inspectors and designers of structural steel works, 1887-89; asst. to M. J. Becker, chief engr., Ohio Connecting Ry. about 4 months in 1889; chief engr. King Bridge Co., Cleveland, 1889-92; later in private practice as consulting and designing engr. for structural steel work; president Osborn Engring. Co., Cleveland, O., 1900-10, and 1917-19; pres. Osborn Realty Co. Dir. Lake Shore Banking & Trust Co. Mem. Cuyahoga County Bldg. Commn., 1908-15. Mason. Author: Tables of Moments of Inertia and Squares of Radii of Gyration, 1894. Home: Cleveland, O. Died Jan. 31, 1922.

OSBORN, H(enry) Fairfield, paleontologist; b. Fairfield, Conn., Aug. 8, 1857; s. William Henry and Virginia Reed (Sturges) O.; A.B., Princeton, 1877, Sc.D., 1880; LL.D., Trinity, 1901, Princeton, 1902, Columbia, 1907, Union Univ., Schenectady, N.Y., 1928; D.Sc., Cambridge U., 1904, Yale, 1923, Oxford, 1926, New York, 1927, Ph.D. from Christiana, 1911; honorary Doctorate from U. of Paris, 1931; m. Lucretia Thatcher, d. Gen. Alexander J. and Josephine Adams Perry (died 1930); children—Virginia Sturges (Mrs. Robt. Gordon McKay), Alexander Perry, Henry Fairfield, Josephine Adams (Mrs. Jay Coogan), Gurdon Saltonstall (dec.). Asst. prof. natural science, 1881-83, prof. comparative anatomy, 1883-90, Princeton Da Costa professor biology, 1891-96, zoölogy, 1896-1910, research professor zoölogy, 1910—, dean faculty of pure science, 1892-95, Columbia; curator department vertebrate paleontology, 1891-1910, hon. curator, 1910—, asst. to pres., 1899-1901, v.p. and trustee, 1901-08, pres. trustees, 1908-33, honorary president, 1933—, American Museum Natural History; vertebrate paleontologist, 1900-24, sr. geologist, 1924—, U.S. Geol. Survey; with Canadian Geol. Survey, 1900-04; as chmn. exec. com. N.Y. Zoöl. Soc., 1896-1903, was active in founding N.Y. Zoöl. Park; chmn. zoöl. and paleontol. advisory coms. Carnegie Instn., Washington, 1902; elected sec. Smithsonian Instn., Dec. 4, 1906, but declined. Pres. Am. Soc. Naturalists, 1892, Am. Morphol. Soc., 1898, N.Y. Acad. Sciences, 1898-1900, Marine Biol. Assn., 1896-1901, New York Zoöl. Soc., 1909-23 (later hon. life pres.), Am. Soc. Paleontologists, 1903, Audubon Soc. N.Y. State, 1910, Am. Bison Soc., 1914-15, Second Internat. Congress of Eugenics, 1921, A.A.A.S., 1928; v.p., N.Y. Zoöl. Soc., 1897-98, Washington Acad. Sci., 1911, Am. Philos. Soc., 1922-28, Hispanic Soc. America, 1919-24 (later hon. v.p.); trustee Brearley School for Girls, 1894-1919 (president 1901-16), Marine Biological Lab., 1890-1901, Hispanic Society America, 1909-24, Kahn Foundation for Foreign Travel of Am. Teachers, 1911-26, N.Y. Pub. Library, 1911-19. Councilor, Nat. Acad. Sciences, 1906-13, Am. Philos. Soc., 1907-19, Institut de Paléontologie Humaine, 1919—. Mem. award com., Hayden Geol. Memorial medal of Phila. Acad. Natural Sciences, Nat. Inst. Social Sciences, Daniel Giraud Elliot fund of Nat. Acad. Sciences and Popular Science Inst. Elector N.Y. U. Hall of Fame, 1910—. Chmn. N.Y. State Roosevelt Memorial Commn., 1920—. Fellow New York Acad. Sciences, American Geog. Soc. (life), American Acad. Arts and Sciences. Medals: Nat. Inst. Soc. Sciences, 1913; Hayden Memorial Geol. Award, 1914; Gaudry (Geol. Soc. of France), 1918; Darwin (Royal Soc.), 1918; Cullom (Am. Geog. Soc.), 1919; Pasteur Inst., 1921; Société Nationale d'Acclimatation de France, 1923; Roosevelt Memorial Association, 1923; Holland Society, 1925; Wollaston (Geol. Soc. of London), 1926; Daniel Giraud Elliot Medal, 1929. Comdr. de l'Ordre de la Couronne de Belgique, 1919. Author: From the Greeks to Darwin, 1894; Evolution of Mammalian Molar Teeth, 1907; The Age of Mammals, 1910; Huxley and Education, 1910; Men of the Old Stone Age, 1915; Origin and Evolution of Life, 1917; Impressions of Great Naturalists, 1924; The Earth Speaks to Bryan, 1925; Evolution and Religion in Education, 1926; Creative Education, 1927; Man Rises to Parnassus, 1927; Fifty-two Years of Research, 1930; Cope, Master Naturalist, 1931; also 8 memoirs; over 860 scientific and educational papers. Editor: A Naturalist in the Bahamas (John I. Northrup Memorial), 1910; Fifty Years of Princeton '77, 1927. Home: Garrison, N.Y. Died Nov. 6, 1935.

OSBORN, Henry Leslie, zoölogist; b. Newark, N.J., July 5, 1857; s. Moses Morris and Susan Amelia (Hedenberg) O.; student prep. dept. Drew Theol. Sem., 1872-75; A.B., Wesleyan U., Conn., 1878; Ph.D., Johns Hopkins, 1884; traveled and studied in Europe, 1889, 1926, studied at Zoöl. Sta., Naples, 1907, 10; LL.D., Hamline U., St. Paul, Minn., 1927; m. Effie Miller Loag, July 7, 1887. Assistant in zoölogy, Wesleyan U., 1878-81; fellow Johns Hopkins, 1881-84; agt. U.S. Fish Commn., 1879-80; prof. zoölogy, Purdue U., Lafayette, Ind., 1884-87; prof. biology, 1887—, dean of faculty, 1918-31, acting president, 1923 and 1923-35, Hamline U., dean emeritus, 1931—. In charge of summer school courses in zoölogy, Cold Spring Harbor, New York, 1891-92, Chautauqua, N.Y., 1895-1904, Dept. Animal Biology, U. of Minn., 1913, 14. Wrote: Report on Newfoundland Cod-fishing Industry (U.S. Census), 1880; Hamline University in the World War, 1920; Alumni Record of Hamline University, 1924; articles on morphology of Trematodes in scientific publs. Home: St. Paul, Minn. Died Jan. 3, 1940.

OSBORN, Luther W., consul gen. of U.S. to Samoa and Tonga, 1897—; b. Ithaca, N.Y.; served in Union army in Civil war; afterward settled in Neb.; mem. Neb. bar 25 yrs.; delegate Nat. Rep. Conv., 1876; mem. Nat. Rep. Com., 1876-80; senior vice comdr. G.A.R., Dept. of Neb. In Samoa, dean of all consular or diplomatic bds., 1899, and to March 1, 1900; dean of representatives acting as and for King and Council, May 1899 to March 1, 1900; chief justice of Samoa, May 1899 to March 1900. Died 1901.

OSBORN, Norris Galpin, newspaperman; b. New Haven, Conn., Apr. 17, 1858; s. Minott A. and Catherine Sophia (Gilbert) O.; A.B., Yale, 1880, A.M., 1886; m. Kate Gardner, Dec. 27, 1881; children—Innis G., Minott A., Mrs. Dorothy Bristol, Gardner, Mrs. Katherine Bennitt. Reporter, 1880-84, editor, 1884—, New Haven Register; controlling editor of New Haven Journal-Courier, 1907—. Wrote on many topics over name "Trumbull" in New York Herald, 1895—. Staff officer Conn. Nat. Guard, with rank of col.; v.p. Conn. Sound Money League, 1896; mem. several state commns. Del. Conn. Constl. Conv., 1892. Democrat. Episcopalian. Pres. bd. dirs. and chmn. bd. parole Conn. State Prison, Wethersfield. Active in many wars; recruiting officer 102d Inf., 26th Div.; alien property custodian. Editor and contbr. to The Monographic Study of Connecticut, 1925; also editor Men of Mark in Connecticut. Home: New Haven, Conn. Died May 6, 1932.

OSBORN, Thomas Ogden, soldier, lawyer, diplomat; b. Jersey, O., 1832; s. Samuel and Hannah (Meeker) O.; ed. Delaware Coll., O.; grad. Ohio State U., 1854; unmarried. Read law with Gen. Lewis Wallace, began practice Chicago, 1859. Recruited 39th regt., Ill. inf., at beginning of Civil war, serving as col. (regt. selected to represent Ill. in the Army of the Potomac), and fought in Shenandoah Valley. Apptd. to command 39th Ill., 13th Ind., 62d and 67th Ohio regts., which were actively engaged in siege and capture of Fort Sumter and Fort Drury; received commn. of maj. gen. "for promptly and efficiently placing his command in position and attacking and driving off the enemy." After war resumed practice; elected treas. Cook County, Ill. Apptd. one of mgrs. Nat. Soldiers Home. Mem. Internat. Commn. to settle disputed claims between U.S. and Mexico; apptd. minister to Argentine Republic, 1873, served until 1885. Address: Chicago, Ill. Died 1904.

OSBORNE, Arthur Dimon, lawyer; b. Fairfield, Conn., Apr. 17, 1828; s. Hon. Thomas B. O. (grad. Yale, 1817, M.C., judge County Court, prof. of law, Yale) and Elizabeth Huntington (Dimon) O.; A.B., Yale, 1848; admitted to bar, 1850; m. Frances Louisa Blake, Aug. 2, 1858 (died 1893). Practiced at Fairfield, 1850-54, and at New Haven, 1882—; clk. Supreme and Superior courts, New Haven, 1860-81; pres. Second Nat. Bank, New Haven, 1881-99, since v.p. and dir.; dir. N.Y.,N.H.&H. R.R. Co., 1895-1906 (resigned); also Consol. Ry. Co., N.E. Navigation Co. Mem. Conn. Ho. of Rep., 1854; mem. Bd. of Edn., New Haven, 1879-81. Republican. Wrote and published several hist. papers; also History of Dolbeare Family, and Memorials of Ancestry, and Kindred. Address: New Haven, Conn. Died Apr. 14, 1920.

OSBORNE, (Samuel) Duffield, author; b. Brooklyn, N.Y., June 20, 1858; s. Samuel S. and Rosalie Willoughby (Duffield) O.; grad. Poly. Inst. of Brooklyn, 1875; A.B., Columbia, 1879, LL.B., 1881, A.M., 1882; unmarried. Practiced law, New York, 1881-92; asst. sec. and acting sec. dept. city works, Brooklyn, 1892-94. Author: The Spell of Ashtaroth, 1888; The Robe of Nessus, 1890; The Secret of the Crater, 1900; The Lion's Brood, 1902; The Angels of Messer Ercole,

1907; Engraved Gems, 1912; The Authors' Club—An Historical Sketch, 1913; Xanthippe on Woman Suffrage, 1915. Editor of Livy's Roman History, 1898, in "The Appletons' Library of the World's Great Books," 1898; Macaulay's Lays of Ancient Rome, 1901. Address: New York, N.Y. Died Nov. 20, 1917.

OSBORNE, Edward William, bishop; b. Calcutta, India, Jan. 5, 1845; s. John Francis and Louisa (White) O.; ed. Gloucester, Eng. Ordained in the Ch. of England, 1869; parish clergyman, 1869-75; mission priest of St. John Evangelist, 1875, Oxford, Eng., 1875-77, Boston, 1877-89; superior of the Mission at Capetown, South Africa, 1890-97; was provincial superior in Africa; consecrated coadjutor bishop, Oct. 23, 1904, bishop, 1906; retired, Oct. 1916. Author: The Children's Saviour, 1879; The Children's Faith, 1882; The Saviour King, 1890; Story of Daniel, 1913; Our Wonderful Faith, 1913; Wonderful Things in the Catechism, 1913. Home: San Diego, Calif. Died July 5, 1926.

OSBORNE, Edwin Sylvanus, soldier, lawyer; b. Bethany, Pa., Aug. 7, 1839; grad. U. of Northern Pa. and Nat. Law School, Poughkeepsie, N.Y.; admitted to Pa. bar, Feb. 26, 1861; served, private to maj., U.S. vols., 1861-65; led notable charge at the battle of the Wilderness, May 6, 1864; took part in many battles; apptd. judge advocate in regular army, with rank of maj., 1865, but resigned and practised law at Wilkesbarre; maj. gen. 3d div. Pa. Nat. Guard, 1870-80; dept. commander G.A.R., Pa., 1883; member Congress, 1885-91. Address: Wilkesbarre, Pa. Died 1900.

OSBORNE, George Abbott, coll. prof.; b. Danvers, Mass., Dec. 21, 1839; s. George A. and Elvina (Smith) O.; B.S., Lawrence Scientific Sch. (Harvard), 1860; unmarried. Instr. mathematics, Lawrence Scientific Sch., 1860-61; asst. prof. mathematics, U.S. Naval Acad., 1861-65; prof. navigation and nautical astronomy, 1866-70, prof. mathematics, 1870-1902, Walker prof., 1902-10, Walker prof. emeritus, 1910—, Mass. Inst. Tech. Episcopalian. Author: Examples of Differential Equations, 1886; Differential and Integral Calculus, 1891, revised, 1906. Home: Boston, Mass. Died 1927.

OSBORNE, Henry Zenas, printer, editor, congressman; b. New Lebanon, N.Y., Oct. 4, 1848; s. Rev. Zenas and Juliaette (Bristol) O.; pub. sch. edn.; enlisted at 16, Feb. 23, 1865, as pvt. Co. E, 192d N.Y. Inf.; hon. discharged Aug. 28, 1865; m. Helen Annas, Dec. 11, 1872. Printer, reporter and newspaper corr., New Orleans, 1873-78; editor and pub. Bodie, Calif., 1878-84, Los Angeles Evening Express, 1884-97; gold mining, 1897-1907. Captain California N.G., 1889-95, retired; U.S. receiver pub. moneys, Bodie Land Dist., 1878-84; U.S. collector customs, Los Angeles Dist., 1890-94; U.S. marshal, Southern Dist. of Calif., 1898-1906; del. Rep. Nat. Conv., Chicago, 1888; mem. exec. com. Rep. State Central Com., Calif., 1890-1900, except 2 yrs.; rep. nominee for Congress, 10th Dist. Calif., 1914; commr. Bd. of Pub. Works, Los Angeles, 1914-15; mem. 65th to 67th Congresses (1917-23), 10th Calif. Dist. Pres. New Orleans Typog. Union, 1873; 1st v.p. Internat. Typog. Union, 1876; pres. Los Angeles Chamber of Commerce, 1912; mem. Southern Calif. Editorial Assn. (pres.), Calif. Press Assn. (v.p.). Mason. Sr. vice comdr.-in-chief G.A.R., 1912-13. Home: Los Angeles, Calif. Died Feb. 8, 1923.

OSBORNE, James van Wyck, lawyer; b. New York, N.Y., May 28, 1897; s. James W. and Leila Grey (van Wyck) O.; student Hackley Sch., Tarrytown, N.Y., 1912-15, Yale, 1915-17; A.B., Columbia, 1921, LL.B., 1922; m. Calvert Cabell, Sept. 25, 1917. Reporter N.Y. Times, 1917-18; admitted to N.Y. bar, 1923; partner Osborne and Shrewsbury, N.Y. City, 1923-35; later practiced in own name as of counsel with Cabell and Cabell. Served with United States Naval Reserve, in active service in Office of Naval Intelligence, 1918-19. Independent Democrat. Episcopalian. Author: The Greatest Norman Conquest, 1937. Home: New York, N.Y. Died July 23, 1940.

OSBORNE, Oliver Thomas, M.D.; b. New Haven, Conn., Nov. 14, 1862; s. Oliver S. and Ellen (Sturges) O.; M.D., Yale, 1884, A.M., 1900; post-grad. work, Leipzig, 1885; m. Mary W. Tyler, 1888. Practiced at New Haven, 1886; prof. therapeutics, Yale Med. Sch., 1911-25, prof. therapeutics emeritus, 1925—; prof. materia medica, therapeutics and clin. medicine, chief med. clinic, New Haven Dispensary; chmn. med. bd. Gaylord Farm Tuberculosis Sanatorium, 1903-40. Mem. Am. Therapeutic Soc. (pres. 1905), New Haven County Med. Assn. (pres. 1899); mem. Revision Com. U.S. Pharmacopeia; mem. council pharmacy and chemistry A.M.A. Republican. Episcopalian. Home: New Haven, Conn. Died Nov. 11, 1940.

OSBORNE, Thomas Burr, chemist; b. New Haven, Conn., Aug. 5, 1859; s. Arthur D. and Frances Louisa (Blake) O.; A.B., Yale, 1881, spl. studies chemistry, Ph.D., 1885, hon. Sc.D., 1910; m. Elizabeth Annah Johnson, 1886; children—Arthur Dimon, Francis Blake (dec.). Research chemist, Conn. Agrl. Expt. Sta., 1886—; also research asso. Carnegie Instn., Washington, and Yale. Asso. editor Journal of Biological Chemistry. Dir. Second Nat. Bank of New Haven. Fellow Am. Acad. Arts and Sciences; mem. Am. Soc. Biol. Chemists (pres. 1910). Gold medal, Paris, 1900; John Scott medal, 1922. Author: Proteins of the Wheat Kernel, 1907; The Vegetable Proteins, 1909, rev. edit., 1924; also numerous papers on the chemistry and nutritive value of the vegetable proteins. Home: New Haven, Conn. Died Jan. 29, 1929.

OSBORNE, Thomas Mott, penologist; b. Auburn, N.Y., Sept. 23, 1859; s. David Munson and Eliza (Wright) O.; A.B., Harvard, 1884; L.H.D., Hobart, 1905; m. Agnes Devens, Oct. 27, 1886 (died 1896); children—David Munson, Charles Devens, Lithgow, Robert Klipfel. Pres. Auburn Pub. Co. (Auburn Citizen); connected other mfg. cos. Mem. Auburn Bd. Edn., 1885-91, 1893-95; candidate for lt. gov. of N.Y. on Independent ticket, 1898; mayor of Auburn, 1903-05; mem. Pub. Service Commn., 2d Dist., N.Y., 1907-09; forest, fish and game commr., N.Y., Jan.-May 1911 (resigned). Del. Dem. Nat. Conv., 1896, Nat. (gold standard) Conv., 1896, Monetary Convs., 1897, 98, Trust Conf., Chicago, 1899, Dem. State Convs., 1904, 06, 12, Dem. Nat. Com., 1924. Chmn. N.Y. Commn. on Prison Reform, 1913. Spent a week in Auburn, New York, Prison under conditions of convict, 1913, to study prison conditions; apptd. warden Sing Sing Prison and assumed charge Dec. 1, 1914; indicted by Westchester County Grand Jury for alleged "perjury and neglect of duty," 1915; upon trial case was dismissed by judge without hearing defendant's testimony; reinstated as warden, July 1916; resigned Oct. 1916; lt. comdr. naval reserve, Aug. 1, 1917; comd. naval prison, Portsmouth, N.H., Aug. 1, 1917-Mar. 17, 1920, relieved at own request. Chmn. Nat. Soc. Penal Information. Traveled extensively, 1872-78, 1894-1901. Author: Within Prison Walls, 1914; Society and Prisons, 1916; Prisons and Common Sense, 1924. Home: Auburn, N.Y. Died Oct. 20, 1926.

OSBORNE, William McKinley, U.S. consul gen. at London, 1897—; b. Girard, O., Apr. 26, 1842; ed. Poland Sem., O., and Allegheny Coll., Pa.; attended law school, U. of Mich., 1863-64; admitted to Mich. bar, June 1864; practiced Youngstown, O.; mayor Youngstown, 1874-75; later in Boston, Mass.; mem. Boston bd. of police, 1885-93; sec. Nat. Rep. Com., 1896. A cousin of President McKinley. Died 1902.

OSENBAUGH, Charles Merril, coll. pres.; b. Lancaster, O., July 10, 1870; s. James and Emily (Dean) O.; grad. Northeast Mo. State Teachers Coll., Kirksville, 1889; A.B., U. of Denver, 1907, A.M., 1913; m. Bess Drives Anderson, June 17, 1896; children—Merril Anderson, Hattie Drives (Mrs. Walter Pillsbury). Prin. pub. sch., Kirksville, 1889-91, high sch., Rich Hill, Mo., 1891-93, high and elementary schs., Denver, from 1893, high sch., San Jose, Calif., 1913-17; pres. Calif. State Teachers Coll., Chico, 1917—. Mem. Home Guard, World War. Republican. Methodist. Mason; mem. Woodmen of World, Royal Arcanum. Originator of the Study Plan Institute for teachers; established Mt. Shasta Summer School ("open air"). Home: Chico, Calif. Died Nov. 1930.

OSGOOD, Farley, electrical engr.; b. Boston, Mass., Apr. 5, 1874; s. George Laurie and Jeannette Callotte (Farley) O.; student Mass. Inst. Tech., class of 1897; m. Clare Stratford Hoe, Nov. 12, 1902; 1 son, Richard Hoe. Began with Am. Telephone & Telegraph Co., 1897, advancing to tech. div. mgr.; gen. mgr. and chief engr., New Milford (Conn.) Power Co., 1903-07; with Pub. Service Electric Co., Newark, N.J., 1907—, v.p. and gen. mgr., Apr. 1, 1917-Oct. 1, 1924, later cons. engr. Fellow Am. Inst. Elec. Engrs. (pres. 1924-25). Episcopalian. Home: South Orange, N.J. Died Oct. 6, 1933.

OSGOOD, Henry Brown, army officer; b. in Me., Oct. 13, 1843. Apptd. 2d lt. 27th Me. Inf., Sept. 30, 1862; 1st lt., Dec. 15, 1862; hon. mustered out of vols., July 17, 1863; apptd. U.S. Mil. Acad. from Me., 1863, grad. 1867; apptd. 2d lt. 3d Arty., June 17, 1867; 1st lt., Apr. 20, 1870; capt. commissary of subsistence, Oct. 5, 1889; maj. same, Jan. 26, 1897; lt. col. commissary of subsistence vols., Aug. 5-Oct. 24, 1898, and Dec. 20, 1898-Mar. 2, 1899; lt. col. deputy commissary gen., Feb. 2, 1901; col. asst. commissary gen., Jan. 19, 1905; brig. gen. and retired, Oct. 13, 1907. Awarded medal of honor, Jan. 24, 1865, for voluntarily remaining in the service during the invasion of Pa., July 1863, his term of service having expired. Address: Washington, D.C. Died 1909.

OSGOOD, Henry Osborne, author, editor; b. Peabody, Mass., Mar. 12, 1879; s. Joseph Henry and Alice Wheeler (Osborne) O.; ed. pub. schs.; student music with Clayton Johns, Everett Truette and others, of Boston, and abroad under pvt. tutors; m. Therese Karl, Mar. 9, 1909; 1 son, Peter. Asst. sec. Boston Fruit and Produce Exchange, 1896; editor Boston Music Co., 1902; studied in Europe; spent 5 yrs. in Munich, asst. conductor at Royal Opera House, 1908-11; joined foreign staff Musical Courier, 1910, trans. to Paris, 1913, joined editorial staff in New York, 1915, later asso. editor. Author: Mildred, Tom and Old Salt, 1922; So This Is Jazz, 1926. Translator of Mozart's Marriage of Figaro, Donizetti's Don Pasquale and Elixir of Love. Composer of numerous songs and piano pieces. Home: New York, N.Y. Died May 9, 1927.

OSGOOD, Herbert Levi, prof. history; b. at Canton, Me., Apr. 9, 1855; s. Stephen and Joan (Staples) O.; A.B., Amherst, 1877, A.M., 1880; studied Yale and U. of Berlin, 1879-82; Ph.D., Columbia, 1889; m. Caroline Augusta Symonds, July 22, 1885. Instr. English, Worcester (Mass.) Acad., 1877-79; teacher history, Brooklyn High Sch., 1883-89; adj. prof. history, 1890-96, prof., 1896—, Columbia. Author: The American Colonies in the Seventeenth Century, 1904. Editor in chief of Minutes of the Common Council of the City of New York, 1675-1776 (8 vols.), 1906. Contbr. of hist. and econ. articles to Polit. Science Quarterly. Home: New York, N.Y. Died Sept. 11, 1918.

OSGOOD, Howard, clergyman; b. Plaquemine Parish, La., Jan. 4, 1831; s. Isaac and Jane Rebecca (Hall) O.; student Harvard, 1846-49, A.B., 1858, A.M., 1861; D.D., Brown U., 1868; LL.D., Princeton, 1894; m. Caroline Townsend Lawrence, Apr. 14, 1853 (died 1898). Ordained Baptist ministry, 1856; pastor at Flushing, L.I., 1856-58, at New York, 1860-66; prof. Hebrew, Crozer Theol. Sem., Pa., 1868-74, Rochester Theol. Seminary, 1875-1900, resigned. Was member Am. com. for revision of O.T. Address: Rochester, N.Y. Died 1911.

OSGOOD, Irene, author; see Mrs. Robert Harborough-Sherard.

OSGOOD, John Cleveland, coal operator; b. Brooklyn, Mar. 6, 1851; s. Samuel Warburton and Mary Hill (Cleveland) O.; ed. pub. schs., Davenport, Ia., and Brooklyn, and Friends' Boarding Sch., Providence, 1862-64. Began as office boy in a Providence cotton mfr.'s office, later clerk for a commission firm in New York; cashier First Nat. Bank of Burlington, 1874-77; coal mining, 1877-82; in 1882 reported on coal resources of Colo. and became more extensively identified with coal and iron interests; organized Colo. Fuel Co., 1887, later consol. with the Colo. Coal & Iron Co., forming the Colo. Fuel & Iron Co., which he organized, 1892, and of which he was pres. or chmn. of bd. till June 24, 1903 (resigned). Patron Am. Mus. Natural History, New York. Home: Redstone, Colo. Died Jan. 4, 1926.

OSGOOD, Samuel Walter, mining engr.; b. Chicago, Sept. 20, 1876; s. Samuel and Elizabeth (Olds) O.; B.Sc. and M.E., Mich. Coll. of Mines, 1900; m. Mary Isalene Kenner, Sept. 1, 1909. Served as consulting engr., superintendent or mgr. for many well known mining men or cos.; mgr. old Clark mine, Keweenaw Co., Mich.; discoverer, 1907, of Tenn. zinc fields and mgr. Am. Zinc, Lead & Smelting Co.'s mines, mills and exploration work, also mgr. for American Metal Co., same dist.; pres. Samuel W. Osgood & Co., and successor, Osgood, Carter and Co., consulting mine and mill engrs.; pres. Am. Graphite Co., Chemical Carbon Refining Co. Mem. Joint Com. on Mil. Engring., Chicago, 1917. Home: Chicago, Ill. Died Oct. 4, 1921.

O'SHAUGHNESSY, Edith Coues (Mrs. Nelson O'Shaughnessy), author; b. Columbia, S.C.; d. Elliott and Jeanie Augusta (McKinney) Coues; ed. Convent of Notre Dame, Md., and under pvt. tutors; m. Nelson O'Shaughnessy (diplomat), Apr. 22, 1901; 1 son, Elim. Catholic. Author: A Diplomat's Wife in Mexico, 1916; Diplomatic Days in Mexico, 1917; My Lorraine Journal, 1918; Alsace in Rust and Gold, 1919; Intimate Pages of Mexican History, 1920; Viennese Medley, 1924; Married Life, 1925; Other Ways and Other Flesh, 1929; Marie Adelaide, 1929. Address: New York, N.Y. Died Feb. 18, 1939.

O'SHAUGHNESSY, M. M., hydraulic engr.; b. Limerick, Ireland, May 28, 1864; s. Patrick and Margaret (O'Donnell) O'S.; Queen's Coll., Cork; Queen's Coll., Galway; B.Engring., with honors, Royal U., Dublin, 1884; m. Mary Spottiswood, Oct. 21, 1890. Came to America, 1885; asst. engr. S.P. Co., 1886-87; civ. engr., townsites and water, 1890, 1892-93; chief engr. Calif. Midwinter Internat. Expn., San Francisco, 1893-94; chief engr. Mountain Copper Co., etc., 1895-96; practiced at San Francisco, 1897-98; consulting and constrn. hydraulic engr., 20 sugar plantations, Hawaii, 1899-1906; in practice in Calif., 1907; chief engr. Southern Calif. Mountain Water Co.; city engr. of San Francisco, 1912-32; consulting engr. Public Utilities Commission, 1932—; builder Hetch Hetchy Water and Power Supply, Eleanor Dam, O'Shaughnessy Dam, Priest Dam and Aqueduct, Twin Peaks Tunnel, Stockton St. Tunnel, Sunset Tunnel, San Francisco Municipal Rys.; cons. engr. for Detroit, Seattle, Portland, San Diego. Republican. Roman Catholic. Author of articles on irrigation in Hawaii and other tech. subjects. Awarded James Laurie prize, Am. Soc. C.E., 1913. Home: San Francisco, Calif. Died Oct. 12, 1934.

O'SHAUGHNESSY, Nelson, diplomat; b. New York, N.Y., Feb. 12, 1876; s. James Francis and Lucy (Waterbury) O'S.; Georgetown Coll., 1892; A.B., U. of Oxford, England, 1899; studied internat. law at Inner Temple, London, 1899-1901, and foreign langs. in various countries of Europe; LL.D., Fordham U., 1922; m. Edith Louise Coues, Apr. 22, 1901; 1 son, Elim. Apptd. sec. Legation, Copenhagen, 1904; 3d sec. embassy, Berlin, 1905, St. Petersburg, 1906, Vienna, 1907; sec. legation Bucharest, Roumania, 1909; 2d sec. embassy, Mexico, 1911, sec., 1912, chargé d'affaires, July 17, 1913, continuing during non-recognition by U.S. of govt. of Gen. Huerta; given passports by Huerta govt., Apr. 22, 1914; spl. diplomatic agent attached to Vienna, Aug. 3, 1914; retired from diplomatic service, 1916, as sec. of embassy of first class. Rep. in S. America of Western Union Telegraph Co., 1918-19, to procure cable concessions between North and South America; rep. of Am. bondholders on Bd. of the Autonomous Monopolies of Kingdom of the Serbs, Croats and Slovenes, Belgrade. First Plattsburg Training Camp, Aug. 1, 1915. Roman Catholic. Republican. Address: New York, N.Y. Died July 26, 1932.

O'SHAUNESSY, George Francis, congressman; b. Galway, Ireland, May 1, 1868; s. Stephen and Margaret (Flynn) O'S.; brought to U.S. at 4; ed. De LaSalle Inst. New York, 1881-84; LL.B., Columbia Law Sch., 1889; m. Julien M. Keily, June 24, 1902. In law practice at New York, 1889-1907, Providence, 1907—; sr. mem. firm O'Shaunessy & Cannon. Secretary of exec. com. Shepard Democracy, Brooklyn, 1894-95; mem. Tammany Hall Gen. Com., 1898-1902; deputy atty. gen. N.Y., 1904-05; asst. corp. counsel, New York, 1906-07; mem. R.I. Legislature, 1910; mem. 62d to 65th Congresses (1911-19), 1st R.I. Dist.; Dem. candidate for U.S. Senate, 1918; collector internal revenue for R.I., 1919-1921. Home: Providence, R.I. Died Nov. 27, 1934.

O'SHEA, John Augustine, music teacher; b. Milford, Mass., Oct. 15, 1864; s. John Augustine and Ellen (Morris) O'S.; grad. N.E. Conservatory of Music, Boston, 1885; music dept. Boston U., 1887, Mus.D., 1935; m. Ella E. O'Brien, June 30, 1891; children—John Augustine, William Aloysius, George Gabriel, Eleanor Blanche (dec.), Arthur Ambrose, Norman Francis, Walter Benedict, Joseph Bernard, Dorothy Marie. Teacher of voice, organ, piano, harmony and theory of music; asst. dir. music Boston pub. sch., 1901-15, dir., 1915-35, dir. emeritus, 1935—; organist St. Joseph's R.C. Ch., 1883-1901, St. Cecilia's R.C. Ch., 1901—, celebrating golden jubilee as organist Feb. 1, 1933; mem. Music Commn. City of Boston, under 3 mayors; mem. Mass. State Tercentenary Music Com.; chmn. Boston Tercentenary Music Com.; gave organ recitals at Pan-Am. Expn., Buffalo, St. Louis Fair. Mem. advisory bd. Nat. Broadcasting Co.'s Music Appreciation Hour. Awarded gold medal by Boston U., 1887, for original composition of best piece of chamber music in sonata form. K.C. Composer and arranger numerous published compositions, sacred and popular, for voice, also piano and organ pieces. Home: Brookline, Mass. Died Sept. 16, 1939.

O'SHEA, John J., editor; b. Cork, Ireland, 1841. Began as reporter and became sub-editor Freeman's Journal (Dublin), and later editor Weekly Freeman and Evening Telegraph; on editorial staff United Ireland, 1883-93; asso. editor The Catholic World (monthly) to 1897, also editor The Young Catholic; removed to Phila., 1897; editor Catholic Standard and Times, 1897—; asso. editor The American Catholic Quarterly Review. Founder and editor The China Gazette and war corr. at various times, English and Am. papers in China and Japan. Author: The Two Archbishops Hendrick, 1904; That Scamp, 1905; (with late Monsignor Bernard O'Reilly) Life of Pope Leo XIII. Address: Philadelphia, Pa. Died Mar. 2, 1920.

O'SHEA, Michael Vincent, univ. prof.; b. Le Roy, N.Y., Sept. 17, 1866; s. Michael and Margaret (Fitzgerald) O'S.; B.L., Cornell, 1892; m. Harriet Frisbie Eastabrooks, June 1894; children—Harriet Eastabrooks, M. Vincent, Stanley Daniel, Katharine Gaylord. Prof. psychology and edn. State Normal Sch., Mankato, Minn., 1892-95; prof. Teachers Coll., Buffalo, 1895-97; prof. edn. U. of Wis., 1897—. Lecturer on edn. and related matters in America, Eng., and Scotland, studied European edn., 1906. Chmn. Am. Com. Internat. Congress of Edn., Liège, Belgium, 1905, and of Internat. Congress of Home Edn., at Brussels, 1910; dir. survey of all-year schs., Newark, N.J., 1925; dir. survey of Mississippi ednl. system, 1925-26; dir. survey of Va. ednl. system, 1927. Pres. Soc. College Teachers of Education, 1911-12; chmn. ednl. bd. The Children's Book Club. Author: Education as Adjustment, 1903; Dynamic Factors in Education, 1906; Linguistic Development and Education, 1907; Social Development and Education, 1909; Every-day Problems in Teaching, 1912; Mental Development and Education, 1920; First Steps in Child Training, 1920; The Trend of the Teens, 1920; Faults of Childhood and Youth, 1920; Every-day Problems in Child Training, 1920; Tobacco and Mental Efficiency, 1923; Reacting With a Purpose—Our Children (American Library Association series), 1925; The Child: His Nature and His Needs, 1925; Newer Ways With Children, 1929; (with others) The Great White Plague, 1913; Consolidation of Schools in Wisconsin, 1913; The Child and His Spelling, 1914; Every-day Spelling Series, 1915; How Much English Grammar, 1925. Edited several vols. of the School and Home Classics; editor-in-chief World Book Encyclopædia; also Experimental Education Series; the Childhood and Youth Series; the Parents Library. Editor The Junior Home Mag., and The Nation's Schools. Home: Madison, Wis. Died Jan. 14, 1932.

O'SHEA, William James, educator; b. N.Y. City, Oct. 10, 1863; s. William J. and Mary (Crimmins) O'S.; B.S., Coll. City of New York, 1887; M.S., Manhattan Coll., 1889; LL.D., Fordham U., 1913; grad. work at St. Francis Xavier Coll., New York U., Columbia and studied at Bellevue Med. Coll.; m. Anna Walsh, 1897; children—William J., Vincent J., Maurice C. Began as teacher pub. schs. of N.Y. City, 1887; made a principal, 1896; organized Pub. Sch. No. 171, and prin., 1901-06; apptd. dist. supt., 1906, asso. supt. schs., 1918, supt., 1924-34. Decorated Chevalier Legion of Honor (France); Chevalier Order of the Crown (Belgium); N.Y. Acad. Pub. Edn. award for distinguished service in public edn. Democrat. Catholic. Home: New York, N.Y. Died Jan. 16, 1939.

OSLER, William, physician; b. Tecumseh, Ont., July 12, 1849; s. Rev. F. L. and Ellen Frere (Pickton) O.; Trinity Coll., Toronto, 1868; M.D., McGill U., 1872; Univ. Coll., London, and univs. of Berlin and Vienna, 1872-74; LL.D., McGill, 1895, Aberdeen, 1898, Toronto, 1899, Yale, 1901, Harvard, 1904, Johns Hopkins, 1905, Edinburgh, 1898; D.C.L., Trinity U., Toronto, 1902, Durham, 1913; Sc.D., Oxford, 1904, Liverpool, 1910, Dublin, 1912; F.R.C.P., 1883; F.R.S., 1898; created a Baronet of the United Kingdom, 1911; m. Grace Linzee (Revere) Gross, May 1892. Prof. insts. of medicine, McGill, 1874-84; prof. clin. medicine, U. of Pa., 1884-89; prof. principles and practice of medicine, 1889-1905, hon. prof. medicine, 1905—, Johns Hopkins; physician-in-chief Johns Hopkins Hosp., 1889-1905; Regius prof. medicine, Oxford U., 1905—. Student (fellow) of Christ Church Coll., Oxford. Author: The Cerebral Palsies of Children, 1889; Chorea and Choreiform Affections, 1894; Lectures on Abdominal Tumors, 1895; Angina Pectoris and Allied States, 1897; The Principles and Practice of Medicine, 1912: Cancer of the Stomach, 1900; Science and Immortality (Ingersoll lecture Harvard U.), 1904; Æquanimitas, and Other Addresses, 1900; Counsels and Ideals, 1906; An Alabama Student and Other Essays, 1908. Editor of System of Medicine. Address: Oxford, England. Died Dec. 29, 1919.

OSMOND, I(saac) Thornton, physicist; b. nr. Phila., Pa.; s. William Ramsey and Ann (Samms) O.; A.B., Mt. Union Coll., 1871, A.M., 1874; M.S., Cornell, 1881; married. Asst. prof. Mt. Union Coll., 3 yrs.; adj. prof. Poly. Coll., Phila., 2 yrs., Clinton (N.Y.) Liberal Inst., 2 yrs.; prof. physics, Pa. State Coll., 1879—. Mem. bd. examiners Internat. Elec. Exhbn., Phila., 1884; meteorologist State Bd. of Agr., Pa., several yrs. physicist for construction of respiration calorimeter for U.S. Bur. of Animal Industry and Pa. Agrl. Expt. Sta. Died Sept. 7, 1939.

OSMUN, Thomas Embley ("Alfred Ayres"), rhetorician, author, critic; b. Montrose, Summit County, O., Feb. 26, 1834; s. George and Mildred Washington (Ayres) O.; ed. Cleveland, O., Acad., Oberlin Coll., studied 6 yrs. in Paris and Berlin; unmarried. Returned to U.S., 1859; one of editors Standard Dictionary. Author: The Orthœpist, 1880; The Verbalist, 1881; Acting and Actors, 1894; The Mentor, 1897; The Essentials of Elocution, 1897; Some Ill-Used Words, 1901. Address: New York, N.Y. Died 1902.

OSTERBERG, Max, consulting engr.; b. Frankfort-on-Main, Germany, June 12, 1869; s. Henry and Toni O.; ed. realschule, Germany, 1876-85; E.E., Columbia Coll. Sch. of Mines, 1894; A.M., Columbia Coll. Sch. of Pure Science, 1896; apptd. hon. univ. fellow, 1895, in mathematical physics; unmarried. Past v.p. New York Elec. Soc. Editor Electric Power, 1894-96. Editor Proceedings of the International Electrical Congress, Chicago, 1894 (Am. Inst. Elec. Engrs.). Author: Thermo-dynamics of Reversible Cycles in Gases and Saturated Vapors, 1894; Synopsis of Current Electrical Literature, 1896. Home: Staten Island, N.Y. Died 1904.

OSTERHAUS, Hugo, rear admiral; b. Belleville, Ill., June 15, 1851; apptd. from Mo., and grad. U.S. Naval Acad., 1870; promoted ensign, July 13, 1871; master, Feb. 12, 1874; lt., Mar. 13, 1880; lt. comdr., Mar. 3, 1899; comdr., July 2, 1901; capt., Feb. 19, 1906; rear admiral, 1909. Served on Plymouth, 1870-73; N. Atlantic Sta., 1873-76; Powhatan, 1876-77; Hydrographic Office, 1877-78; Navy Yard, Norfolk, 1878-79; coast duty, 1879-82; Enterprise, 1882-86; Navy Yard, Norfolk, 1886-89; Enterprise, 1889-90; Franklin and Pensacola, 1890; Baltimore, 1890-91; Atlanta, 1891-92; Naval Acad., 1892-95; staff N. Atlantic Fleet, 1895-97; Naval Acad., 1897-99; Monongahela, 1899-1900; exec. officer Kentucky, 1900-01; comd. Culgoa, 1901; Naval Acad., 1901-03; comd. Monterey, 1903-04; Cincinnati, 1904-05; mem. Bd. Inspection and Survey, Washington, 1905-07; comd. Connecticut, 1907; comdr. 2d div. Atlantic Fleet, 1910; comdr.-in-chief Atlantic Fleet, 1911; retired June 15, 1913. Address: Washington, D.C. Died June 11, 1927.

OSTERHAUS, Peter Joseph, brigadier gen. U.S.A.; b. Coblentz, Germany, Jan. 4, 1823; came to U.S., 1849; LL.D., Northwestern, 1904. Commd. maj. 2d Mo. Rifle Battalion, Apr. 27, 1861; hon. mustered out, Aug. 27, 1861; col. 12th Mo. Inf., Dec. 19, 1861; brig. gen. vols., June 9, 1862; maj. gen. vols., July 23, 1864; hon. mustered out, Jan. 15, 1866; apptd. brig. gen. U.S.A., by spl. act of Congress, Mar. 3, 1905, and retired, Mar. 17, 1905. Comd. a div. under Gen. Curtis, at Pea Ridge, Ark., March 6-8, 1862, and a div. Army of the Southwest, May 1862; comd. 9th Div., 13th Army Corps during Vicksburg campaign, May-July 1863; comd. 1st Div., 15th Army Corps, under Gen. Grant, at Chattanooga, Nov. 23-25, 1863; comd. same div. during Atlanta campaign, May-Sept. 1863; comd. 15th Army Corps, Army of the Tenn., Sept. 1864-Jan. 1865; chief of staff to Gen. Canby during Mobile campaign; later comd. mil. dist. of Miss. until Jan. 15, 1866. U.S. consul at Lyons, France, 1866-77. Died Jan. 2, 1917.

OSTERHOLM, Martin, univ. prof.; b. Warburg, Halland, Sweden, Aug. 13, 1863; s. Peter E. and Anna B. (Schubert) O.; student State Coll. of Jönköping, 1878-82; came to America, 1882; A.B., Augustana Coll., Ill., 1885; grad. student, U. of Neb., 1889-91, A.M., 1890; student Yale, 1892, U. of Chicago, 1893, under Prof. Hjalmar Edgren, 1893-96; Ph.D., Cotner U., Neb., 1896; m. Emma Lindwall, Nov. 15, 1892; children—Lenore, Marie Louise (Mrs. Paul Wertz), Robert William. Prof. German and history, Bethany Coll., Kan., 1885-87; organized Neb. Pub. Co., Lincoln, Neb., 1887; organized and conducted the first evening sch. for workmen and foreigners at Lincoln, Neb., 1887-88, and at Omaha, 1891-92; took active part in Neb. politics, especially, 1891-92, as temperance speaker; founded, with C. A. Elmén, Svenska Journalen, 1891; organized Swedish Am. Book Co., Omaha, 1891; prof. modern langs., Cotner U., 1893-96; prof. German and English, 1896-1901, modern langs., 1901-03, Carthage Coll., Ill.; prof. modern langs., Heidelberg U., 1903—. Lutheran. Wrote part of Edgren-Burnet French Dictionary, 1898; assisted in revising Edgren's Spanish Grammar. Home: Tiffin, Ohio. Died Dec. 10, 1927.

OSTHAUS, Edmund, painter; b. Hildesheim, Germany, Aug. 5, 1858; s. Henry O., ed. Gymnasium Josephinum, Hildesheim, Germany, Royal Acad. of Arts, Düsseldorf, Germany, 1874-82; pupil of Andreas Müller, Peter Jansen, E. V. Gebhardt, E. Deger and C. Kröner; m. 2d, Isabel Carleton, Feb. 17, 1903; 1 son, Franz. Came to U.S., 1883, to Toledo, O., as prin. Toledo Acad. Fine Arts, 1886; later abandoned sch. to devote entire time to painting; principally pictures of shooting and fishing, hunters, dogs and horses. Address: Toledo, O. Died Jan. 30, 1928.

OSTRAND, James Adolph, judge; b. Tromsoe, Norway, Jan. 20, 1871; s. Johan Bróndlund and Anna (Peterson) O.; LL.B., U. of Minn., 1898; m. Emma S. Wettstein, Dec. 16, 1903; children—Margaret, James Adolph, Helen Elizabeth. Came to U.S., 1892, naturalized citizen, 1898. Practiced law in Philippines, 1900-09; judge Court of Land Registration, P.I., 1909-11; chief judge, same court, 1911-14; judge Dist. Court, Manila, 1914-20; chief justice, Appellate Land Court, Santo Domingo, 1920-21; apptd. asso. justice Supreme Court P.I., 1921, resigned, June 1933. Mem. 3d U.S. Inf., Spanish-Am. War, 6 mos. Republican. Lutheran. Home: Manila, P.I. Died Apr. 15, 1937.

OSTRANDER, Dempster, lawyer; b. Clay, N.Y., Nov. 20, 1834; s. James H. and Asenath (Sheffield) O.; ed. pub. schs., N.Y. and Wis., and U. of Wis., partial course; m. Sarah E. Manville, Dec. 24, 1856. In law practice and ins. business, 1855—. Author: The Insurance Contract, 1887; Law of Fire Insurance, 1897; Social Growth and Stability, 1892; The Social Crisis, 1896; Half Hours, 1898; Problems of Life, 1899; Brief on Immortality, 1902. Home: Chicago, Ill. Died 1907.

OSTRANDER, Fannie Eliza, author; b. North Haven, Conn.; d. John Milton and Mary A. (Ladd) O.; grad. Wis. State Normal Sch.; also studied under pvt. teachers; teacher 4½ yrs.; unmarried. Critic, editor and writer for Chicago publishing house, 1899. Contbr. verse and prose to mags. Author: When Hearts Are True, 1897; Beautiful Bible Stories, 1899; Baby Goose, His Adventures, 1900; Frolics of the A B C, 1901; The Gift of the Magic Staff, 1902; Little Pixies Abroad, 1905; Goose Family Tales, 1905; Little White Indians, 1907; The Boy Who Won, 1910. Address: New Haven, Conn. Died May 4, 1921.

OSTRANDER, Isabel (Isabel Ostrander Lamb), author; b. N.Y. City, Sept. 14, 1885; d. Thomas Egenton and Harriet Elizabeth (Bradbrook) O.; ed. St. Mary's Episcopal Convent, Miss Veltin's Sch., Misses Graham's Sch. (all of N.Y. City); grad. Am. Acad. Dramatic Arts, N.Y. City, 1903; m. Arthur John Lamb, June 6, 1907 (divorced 1910). Began writing, 1911; specialized in mystery and detective stories. Episcopalian. Author: The Primal Law, 1915; (with William J. Burns) The Crevice, 1915; At 1:30, 1915; The Heritage of Cain, 1916; The Clue in the Air, 1917; Suspense, 1918; The Island of Intrigue, 1918; The Twenty-Six Clues, 1918; Ashes to Ashes, 1919; How Many Cards?, 1920; The Crimson Blotter, 1921; McCarty, Incog., 1922; Dust to Dust, 1923; Annihilation, 1923. Home: Long Beach, L.I., N.Y. Died Apr. 23, 1924.

OSTRANDER, John Edwin, mathematician; b. Slingerlands, N.Y., Mar. 20, 1865; s. John and Catharine (Van Den Bergh) O.; A.B. and C.E., Union Coll., N.Y., 1886, A.M., 1889; m. Sarah C. Cowan, Sept. 26, 1888; children—Katharine, John Edwin. Engr. sewer constrn., West Troy, N.Y., 1886; asst. engr. C.G.W. Ry., 1887; engr. in state engring. dept. of N.Y., 1888-91; instr. civ. engring., Lehigh U., 1891-92; prof. civ. engring. and mechanic arts and irrigation engr., Expt. Sta., U. of Ida., 1892-97; prof. mathematics and civ. engring. Mass. State Coll., 1897-1935, prof. emeritus, 1935—; meteorologist, Mass. Agrl. Expt. Sta., 1897-1928; acting prof. astronomy, Amherst, 1900, 01, 07. Mem. Com. No. 6 on Mathematics in Tech. Secondary Schs. of U.S. for Internat. Commn. on Teaching of Mathematics; mem. Pub. Safety Com., 1917. Democrat. Episcopalian. Mason. Contbr. Johnson's Ency., 1893, Webster's New Internat. Dictionary, 1907. Home: Amherst, Mass. Died Oct. 19, 1938.

OSTRANDER, Russell Cowles, judge; b. Ypsilanti, Mich., Sept. 1, 1851; s. Simon and Ellen Gardner (Cowles) O.; LL.B., U. of Mich., 1876; m. Dora Porter, May 8, 1878 (died); m. 2d, Lou S. Davis, Oct. 12, 1892. In law practice, 1877—; Circuit Court commr., Ingham County, Mich., 1877-80, pros. atty., 1881-82; mayor of Lansing, 1896-97; mem. State Bd. Law Examiners, 1895-1904; pres. Mich. State Bar Assn., 1903-04; asso. justice Supreme Ct. of Mich., Jan. 1, 1905—. Republican. Episcopalian. Address: Lansing, Mich. Died Sept. 12, 1919.

OSTROM, Henry, evangelist; b. Sept. 19, 1862; s. Henry and Harriet O. Conducts meetings in chs. under federated denominations and in factories, mines, theatres, colls., etc. Author: Out of the Cain Life; Replete Religion; The Dearest Psalm; Greatness; Dulari; Crisis in Church Work, 1908; Rich in Yesterdays, 1909. Address: Chicago, Ill. Died Dec. 20, 1941.

OSWALD, Felix Leopold, author, naturalist; b. Namur, Belgium, Dec. 6, 1845; grad. Brussels U., 1865; also studied at Göttingen and Heidelberg, A.M., M.D. Went to Mexico with the corps of Belgian vols., 1866; corr. of various French and English periodicals, 1878-97. Author: Physical Education, 1882; Household Remedies, 1885; Summerland Sketches, 1880; The Poison Problem, 1886; Zoölogical Sketches, 1883; Days and Nights in the Tropics, 1888; The Bible of Nature; Body and Mind, 1901; also many essays and papers in mags. and reviews. Address: Grand Rapids, Mich. Died 1906.

OSWALD, John Clyde, editor, publisher; b. Ft. Recovery, O., July 11, 1872; s. John and Elizabeth (Beardsley) O.; high school edn.; married; children—Elizabeth, John Clyde. Began in printing business at Ft. Recovery, 1885; moved to New York, 1894; editor The American Printer, 1897-1925; managing editor of The Gregg Writer. Instr. Columbia Sch. of Bus. President of American Inst. Graphic Arts, Typothetæ of City of N.Y., Nat. Editorial Assn., Federation of Trade Press Assn., N.Y. Trade Press Assn. (1909-10), Internat. Benjamin Franklin Soc., Art Alliance America; treas. Nat. Alliance of Arts and Industry; sec.-treas. Graphic Arts Research Bur.; sec. Nat. Graphic Arts Expns., Inc.; chmn. American Committee Internat. Press Exhbn., Cologne, 1928. Republican. Conglist. Mason. Author: Benjamin Franklin, Printer; Benjamin Franklin in Oil and Bronze; A History of Printing; Printing in the Americas. Home: Pelham Manor, N.Y. Died June 22, 1938.

OTEY, Peter Johnston, congressman, 6th Va. dist., 1895-1903; b. Lynchburg, Va., Dec. 22, 1840; grad. Va. Mil. Inst., July 1, 1860; participated as cadet in defense of Va. in John Brown raid; engr. on Va. & Ky. R.R., 1860-61; joined C.S. Army, Apr. 1861; took part in Western campaign culminating at Donelson and Shiloh; in inf. Army Northern Va. until close of war; wounded at battle of New Market; after 4 months returned; comd. brigade under Early, for some months as senior field officer. In railroad, banking and ins. business in Va., 1860—. Democrat. Address: Lynchburg, Va. Died 1902.

OTIS, Edward Osgood, M.D.; b. Rye, N.H., Oct. 29, 1848; s. Rev. Israel T. and Olive Morgan (Osgood) O.; A.B., Harvard, 1871, M.D., 1877; hon. Sc.D., Tufts Coll., 1924, U. of N.H., 1924; m. Marion Faxon, June 6, 1894; children—Olive, John Faxon, Edward O., William Faxon, Brooks. Settled in practice of medicine in Boston, 1880; specialty pulmonary diseases, particularly tuberculosis, and writer and speaker on its prevention; connected with various med. instns.; cons. phys. to tuberculosis dept., Boston Dispensary; visiting phys. to Home for Consumptives; apptd. prof. pulmonary diseases and climatology in Tufts Coll. Med. Sch., 1901; visiting and cons. phys. to Mass. State Sanatorium, Rutland. Del. Congress of Tuberculosis, London, 1901. Mem. med. bd. Loomis Sanatorium; trustee Montgomery Colored Indusl. Sch. Maj., U.S. Med. R.C. Conglist. Republican. Fellow Am. Coll. Phys. (gov.); mem. Am. Climatol. Assn. (pres. 1898); pres. Boston Assn. for Relief and Control of Tuberculosis; hon. dir. Nat. Tuberculosis Assn.; U.S. del. Internat. Congress of Tuberculosis, Rome, 1912. Author: Tuberculosis, Its Cause, Cure and Prevention, 1909; Pulmonary Tuberculosis, 1917; also series of articles on Climatic Reports for Wood's Reference Handbook of the Med. Sciences, 1917. Awarded Pray prize, by New Hampshire Med. Soc., 1897, for essay, "Causes and Conditions of Pulmonary Tuberculosis and How to Avoid Them," and again in 1930, for essay, "The Prevention of Disease and Some Applications of Preventive Medicine." Address: Exeter, N.H. Died May 28, 1933.

OTIS, Elwell Stephen, army officer; b. Frederick City, Md., Mar. 25, 1838; s. William and Mary A. C. (Late) O.; grad. U. of Rochester, 1858; LL.B., Harvard Law Sch., 1861. Commd. capt. 140th N.Y. Inf., Sept. 13, 1862; lt. col., Dec. 23, 1863, later promoted to col.; hon. mustered out, Jan. 14, 1865, because incapacitated by wound; bvtd. brig. gen., Mar. 13, 1865; apptd. from N.Y., lt. col. 22d U.S. Inf., Mar. 2, 1869; col. 20th Inf., Feb. 8, 1880; brig. gen., Nov. 28, 1893; maj. gen. vols., May 4, 1898; maj. gen. U.S.A., June 16, 1900; retired by operation of law, Mar. 25, 1902. Bvtd. col., Mar. 2, 1867, for battle of Spottsylvania, Va.; maj. gen., Feb. 4, 1899, for mil. skill and most distinguished service in P.I. Assigned to duty in San Francisco, May 19, 1898, mobilizing and shipping troops to P.I.; departed for Philippines, July 15, 1898, and relieved Maj. Gen. Merritt as comdg. gen. U.S. Philippine forces and gov. of islands, Aug. 29, 1898; conducted operations against insurgents and performed duties of mil. gov. until May 5, 1900. Mem. of U.S. Philippine Commn., 1899. Assigned to command Dept. of the Lakes, headquarters Chicago, on Oct. 29, 1900. Residence: Rochester, N.Y. Died 1909.

OTIS, Harrison Gray, journalist, soldier; b. nr. Marietta, O., Feb. 10, 1837; s. Stephen and Sarah (Dyar) O.; (paternal grandfather a Revolutionary soldier); m. Eliza A. Wetherby, Sept. 11, 1859 (died 1904). Enlisted as pvt. 12th Ohio Inf., June 25, 1861; 2d lt., Nov. 12, 1862; 1st lt., May 20, 1863; transferred to 23d Ohio Inf., July 1, 1864; capt., July 15, 1864; bvtd. maj. and lt. col. vols., Mar. 13, 1865, "for gallant and meritorious services during the war"; hon. mustered out, July 26, 1865; twice wounded. Official Reporter Ohio Ho. of Rep., 1866-67; foreman Govt. Printing Office, 1868-69; chief of div. U.S. Patent Office, 1870-76; spl. agt. U.S. Treasury in charge of Seal Islands of Alaska, 1879-81. In Calif. journalism, 1876—; editor and gen. mgr. Los Angeles Times. Apptd. brig. gen. U.S.V., May 27, 1898; comd. 1st Brigade, 2d Div., 8th Army Corps in the P.I.; led brigade at capture of Caloocan, Feb. 10, 1899; bvtd. maj. gen. vols., Mar. 25, 1899, "for meritorious conduct at battle of Caloocan"; hon. discharged, July 2, 1899. U.S. commr. to Centennial of Mexican Independence, 1910. Address: Los Angeles, Calif. Died July 30, 1917.

OTIS, Norton P., congressman, mfr.; b. Halifax, Vt., Mar. 18, 1840; ed. pub. schs. Albany and Yonkers, N.Y. Entered father's elevator works at age of 18, connected with the business in various capacities, 1858—, and as treas., v.p., pres. and chmn. bd. dirs. Otis Elevator Co. Mayor Yonkers, N.Y., 1880; mem. N.Y. State Assembly, 1883; pres. N.Y. Commn. to the Paris Expn., 1900; pres. St. John's Riverside Hosp., Yonkers. Rep. candidate for Congress, 1900; mem. Congress, 19th N.Y. dist., 1903-05. Republican. Residence: Yonkers, N.Y. Died 1905.

OTIS, Philo Adams, real estate; b. Berlin Heights, O., Nov. 24, 1846; s. James and Margaretta Graves (Adams) O.; removed to Chicago, with parents, 1857; grad. Western Reserve Coll., Hudson, O., 1868; m. Alice J. Sanford, June 20, 1890; 1 son, James Sanford. Associated with his father in real estate business until his death, 1895; in business alone, 1895—. Long and actively identified with musical enterprises; one of founders of Apollo Musical Club, 1872 (bd. mgrs. many yrs. and pres. 1890-93); sec. trustees Thomas Orchestra (now Chicago Symphony Orchestra), 1894—; chmn. music com. First Presbyn. Ch. Republican. Author: History of the First Presbyterian Church, Chicago, 1912; Chicago Symphony Orchestra, 1924; Impressions of Europe; The Hymns You Ought to Know, 1928. Home: Chicago, Ill. Died Sept. 23, 1930.

OTIS, William Augustus, architect; b. Almond, Allegany County, N.Y., Aug. 14, 1855; s. Maj. Seth T. and Frances L. (Kellogg) O.; C.E., U. of Mich., 1878; studied École des Beaux Arts, Paris, 3 yrs.; m. Elizabeth Lincoln Shackford, Sept. 11, 1888; children—Samuel S., Louise. Head draftsman W. L. B. Jenney, architect, Chicago, later partner, Jenney & Otis, Chicago, till 1889; co-partner Otis & Fuller, 1922—. Lecturer on history of architecture at Chicago Art Inst. Republican. Home: Winnetka, Ill. Died June 9, 1929.

OTIS, William Kelly, physician, surgeon; b. Catskill, N.Y., Sept. 9, 1860; s. Fessenden Nott and Frances H. (Cooke) O.; grad. Columbia Coll., 1882; Coll. Phys. and Surg., New York, 1885; m. Florence Cecilia Hoyt, Apr. 27, 1887. Consulting surgeon City Hosp.; attending surgeon St. Mark's Hosp. Prof. genito-urinary surgery, New York Sch. Clinical Medicine. Contbr. to med. mags.; to Foster's Practical Therapeutics, Wood's Reference Handbook of the Med. Sciences, Morrow's System Genito-urinary Diseases, Chandler's Ency. Address: New York, N.Y. Died 1906.

O'TOOLE, William Joseph, diplomat; b. Monarch, Pa., Mar. 25, 1894; s. Edward and Sarah (Goodwin) O'T.; B.A., Catholic U. of America, 1915; m. Deborah Kinney, Feb. 26, 1919. With U.S. Coal & Coke Co., Gary, W.Va., summers, 1906-15, auditor, 1915-16, sec.-treas., 1916-19; v.p. and mgr. sales, 1919-22, Central Pocohontas Coal Co., Crystal Block Coal & Coke Co. and Crystal Block Mining Co., all of Welch, W.Va.; dir. Gary Nat. Bank, 1921-22; E.E. and M.P. to Paraguay, Jan. 18, 1922—. Grad. 1st lt. inf., 2d O.T.C., Ft. Benjamin Harrison, Ind., Nov. 25, 1917; attached to 86th Div., Camp Grant, Ill.; student Small Arms Firing Sch., Camp Perry, O.; trans. to infantry, Central O.T.S., Camp Grant, Ill., and acted as instr. till close of war. Republican. Catholic. Died Aug. 27, 1928.

OTT, George, clergyman, editor; b. Württemberg, Germany, Nov. 9, 1852; s. Jacob and Maria (Seitzinger) O.; ed. common schs., night schs. and under pvt. tutors; m. 3d, Mary M. Graf, Apr. 11, 1911; children—(by first marriage) Eleonora Aurora, Thusnelda Olga; (by second marriage) Viola (dec.), Ralph John, Aaron J., Walter Emanuel (dec.). Came to U.S., 1876; deacon, 1878, elder, 1880, Evangelical Ch.; pastor, successively, New Castle, Pa., Dunkirk, N.Y., Pittsburgh, Pa., Cleveland, O., Rochester, Pa., North East, Pa., and Akron, Ebenezer and Geneva, N.Y., until 1914; editor Evangelische Zeitschrift, 1914-18; retired. Served in German army 2 yrs.; naturalized citizen of U.S., 1884. Home: Dunkirk, N.Y. Died Dec. 14, 1926.

OTT, Isaac, physician; b. Northampton County, Pa., Nov. 30, 1847; s. Jacob and Sarah Ann (La Barre) O.; student Lafayette Coll., 1864-67, hon. A.M., 1876; M.D., U. of Pa., 1869; univs. of Leipzig and Berlin, 1869; fellow in biology, Johns Hopkins, 1879; m. Katherine K. Wykoff, Oct. 14, 1886. In practice of medicine at Easton, Pa., 1869—; resident phys. St. Mary's Hosp., Phila., 1871; lecturer physiology, U. of Pa., 1878; prof. physiology, 1894—, dean, 1895-96, Medico-Chirurg. Coll., Phila.; consulting neurologist, Norristown (Pa.) Asylum. Presbyn. Democrat. Author: Action of Medicines, 1878; Modern Antipyretics, 1892; Contributions to Physiology and Pathology of Nervous System; Cocaine, Veratria and Gelsemium, 1872; Text-Book of Physiology, 1904; Internal Secretions, 1910. Home: Easton, Pa. Died Jan. 1, 1916.

OTTAWAY, Elmer James, newspaper pub.; b. Flushing, Mich., June 18, 1871; s. William Jay and Helen (Brown) O.; B.L., U. of Mich., 1894; m. Blanche Owen Whiting, June 22, 1899 (died 1907); children—William Whiting, John Palmer; m. 2d, Ruth Louise Haller, Aug. 31, 1910; 1 son, James Haller. Reporter, night city editor and asst. mng. editor, Detroit Free Press, 1895-99, Washington corr., 1899-1900; established Port Huron Daily Herald, 1900, merged, 1910, with Daily Times as Times-Herald, of which became pres.; part owner St. Petersburg (Fla.) Times, 1930—. Pres. U. of Mich. Alumni Assn., 1921-24. Pres. Mich. Press Club (University Press Club), 1920-23; district gov., 23d dist. Rotary Internat., 1931-32, and mem. Vienna Press Com., 1931-32, and R.I. Convention Com., 1934. Republican. Methodist. Mason, Elk, K.P. Home: Port Huron, Mich. Died Sept. 7, 1934.

OTTENDORFER, Oswald, proprietor New York Staats-Zeitung; b. Zwittau, Moravia, Feb. 26, 1826; studied in U. of Vienna; went to U. of Prague, learned Czech language and studied law. Was active in the revolutions in Vienna against the Metternich govt., 1848, and later volunteer in the Schleswig-Holstein war against Denmark, and in the revolutions in Saxony and Baden. Upon their supression he fled to Switzerland, 1849; came to U.S., 1850; secured employment in counting-room of the Staats-Zeitung. When Jacob Uhl, the propr., died, 1852, he aided the widow of latter, Mrs. Anna Uhl, in the management, and, in 1859, married her (she died, 1884). Was alderman, 1872-74; candidate for mayor, 1874; reform Democrat; active in anti-Tammany movements. Gave $300,000 to build and endow an ednl. instn. in his native town; founded a home for aged and indigent men on Long Island; also the Ottendorfer Free Library, New York. Address: New York, N.Y. Died 1900.

OTTINGER, Albert, lawyer; b. N.Y. City, Sept. 10, 1878; LL.B., New York U., 1898. Began practice in N.Y. City, with brother, Nathan, 1900, later with Delafield, Gould Longfellow, and Kurtzman & Frankenheimer; mem. N.Y. Senate, 1917-21; became asst. atty. gen. of U.S., 1921; atty. gen. of N.Y., term 1925-26. Republican. Candidate for gov. of N.Y., 1928. Died Jan. 13, 1938.

OTTLEY, Passie Fenton (Mrs. John King Ottley); b. Columbus, Miss.; d. Fenton Mercer (M.D.) and Passie (Butler) McCabe; ed. Mary Baldwin Sem., U. of Chicago and Woman's Coll. of Miss.; D.Litt., U. of Ga., 1926; m. John King Ottley, Mar. 21, 1890; children—Passie May (Mrs. George W. McCarty), John King. A founder of federated movement of organized women in Ga.; active in social work; chmn. State Library Commn. of Ga.; pres. bd. trustees Tallulah Falls Indusl. Sch. First Dem. Nat. Com. woman from Ga. Presbyn. Home: Atlanta, Ga. Died Aug. 18, 1940.

OTTMAN, Ford Cyrinde, clergyman; b. Seward, N.Y., Aug. 15, 1859; s. Abraham and Ellen (Boyce) O.; A.B., Lafayette Coll., Easton, Pa., 1883, D.D., 1905; student Princeton Theol. Sem., 1883-84, Free Ch. Coll., Edinburgh, Scotland, and U. of Leipzig, 1884-85; grad. Princeton Theol. Sem., 1886; m. Louise Steele, Sept. 17, 1888. Ordained Presbyn. ministry, 1886; pastor Memorial Ch., Newark, N.J., 1886-1903, 1st Ch., Stamford, Conn., 1903-09; apptd. Gen. Assembly's Commn. to Far East, 1909; exec. sec. Nat. Service Commn. of Presbyn. Ch., U.S.A., 1917—; pres. Bd. Church Erection. Republican. Author: The Unfolding of the Ages in the Revelation of St. John, 1905; God's Oath, 1911; Imperialism and Christ, 1912; Biography of J. Wilbur Chapman, 1919; The Coming Day, 1921; Biography of Herbert Booth. Dean Stony Brook Sch. for Boys, Stony Brook, N.Y., 1922. Home: Stamford, Conn. Died Dec. 15, 1929.

OTTS, John Martin Philip, Presbyterian clergyman; b. Union, S.C., June 7, 1838; grad. Davidson Coll., N.C., 1860, Theol. Sem., Columbia, S.C., 1862, D.D., LL.D.; m. Lelia J. McCrary, 1864. Ordained to Presbyn. ministry, 1863; pastor Greensborough, Ala., 1863-67; Columbia, Tenn., 1867-73; Wilmington, Del., 1873-78; Chambers Memorial Ch., Philadelphia, 1878-85; then at Talladega, Ala.; later at Knoxville, Tenn. Was in Egypt and Palestine, 1890-91; lecturer on "Explorations in Bible Lands." Author: Nicodemus With Jesus; Light and Life for a Dead World; The Southern Pen and Pulpit; Interdenominational Literature; The Gospel of Honesty; Laconisms; The Fifth Gospel; Unsettled Questions; At Mother's Knee; Christ and the Cherubim. Address: Knoxville, Tenn. Died 1901.

OUCHTERLONY, John Arvid, physician; b. in Sweden, June 24, 1838; s. Capt. August F. O.; ed. in Sweden; grad. med. dept., U. of New York, 1861; served as med. officer in Union army, 1861-65; removed to Louisville. Prof. principles and practice of medicine and clinical medicine, U. of Louisville; holder of several hosp. apptmts. Knight Pontifical Order of St. Gregory and Royal Swedish Order of the Polar Star. Address: Louisville, Ky. Died 1905.

OUDIN, Maurice Agnus, electrical mfg.; b. New York, Mar. 31, 1866; s. Lucien and Sophie Josephine (Agnus) O.; A.B., Coll. City of New York, 1885; E.E. and M.S., Princeton, 1891; m. Susan Worth Folger, Dec. 31, 1895. Engr. with Gen. Electric Co., 1891—, later v.p. Internat. Gen. Electric Co. Republican. Episcopalian. Specially interested in Far Eastern affairs; decorated by Emperor of Japan with Order of Rising Sun, 1911. Author: Standard Polyphase Apparatus and Systems. Home: Schenectady, N.Y. Died Nov. 5, 1929.

OULAHAN, Richard Victor, newspaper man; b. Washington, D.C., May 23, 1867; s. Richard and Mary (Proud) O.; ed. pub. and pvt. schs. in District of Columbia; m. Anne McGowan, Nov. 3, 1892; m. 2d, Sue Courts, Oct. 8, 1919. Began with Washington Critic, 1886; news editor and asso. editor of Roanoke (Va.) Daily Telegram (subsequently Roanoke Times), 1888-89; with Washington bur. The United Press, 1889-97; assistant in Washington bur. and chief Washington corr., later publisher and chief European corr. The Sun, New York, 1897-1912; chief Washington corr. New York Times, 1912—. Chief of New York Sun staff at Russian-Japanese Peace Conf., Portsmouth, N.H., 1905; chief New York Times staff "ABC" (American-Mexican) Peace Conf., Niagara Falls, Ont., Can., 1914, also World War Peace Conf., Paris, 1918-19, Conf. on Limitation of Armament, Washington, D.C., 1921. Chmn. Standing Com. of Congressional Correspondents, 1913-17. Mem. first Am. Editorial Mission to visit Western battlefronts at invitation of British Govt., in 1918; staff corr. N.Y. Times in Far East, 1923-24. Home: Washington, D.C. Died Dec. 30, 1931.

OUTCAULT, Richard Felton, comic artist; b. Lancaster, O., Jan. 14, 1863; s. J. P. and Catherine (Davis) O.; grad. McMicken U., Cincinnati; m. Mary Jane Martin, Dec. 25, 1890. Started as a comic artist, 1895. Creator of Hogan's Alley, New York World, 1895; Yellow Kid, New York Journal, 1896-97; Pore li'l Mose, 1901, and Buster Brown, 1902, N.Y. Herald; on staff N.Y. Journal several yrs.; later pres. Outcault Advertising Co., Chicago, Ill. Author: Buster, Mary Jane and Tige, 1908; Buster Brown, the Busy Body, 1909; Real Buster and the Only Mary Jane, 1909; Buster Brown in Foreign Lands, 1912; Buster Brown—the Fun Maker, 1912; Buster Brown and His Pets, 1913. Home: Flushing, L.I., N.Y. Died Sept. 25, 1928.

OUTERBRIDGE, Albert Albouy, lawyer; b. Bermuda, Apr. 20, 1841; s. Alexander E. and Laura C. (Harvey) O.; LL.B., U. of Pa., 1862; unmarried. Admitted to bar, 1862; editor-in-chief of Weekly Notes of Cases, 1874-1899; reporter Supreme Ct. of Pa., 1881-85, and edited several vols. of "Reports"; trust officer, Land Title & Trust Co., of Phila., 1885-1913, v.p., Oct. 1, 1913—. Address: Philadelphia, Pa. Died Jan. 23, 1917.

OUTERBRIDGE, Alexander Ewing, Jr., metallurgist; b. Phila., July 31, 1850; s. Alexander Ewing and Laura C. (Harvey) O.; ed. Episcopal Acad., Phila., and pvt. tutor in analyt. chemistry; attended lectures on physics and chemistry as asst. to Prof. Henry Morton, U. of Pa.; m. Mary Ely Whitney, 1880 (died 1881); 1 son, George Whitney; m. 2d, Margaret Hall Dunn, Jan. 29, 1905. Apptd. asst. in assay lab., U.S. Mint., Phila., 1868; sent to New Orleans to establish assay dept. of branch mint, 1879-80; metallurgist for A. Whitney & Sons Car Wheel Works, Phila., 1880-88; metallurgist William Sellers & Co., Inc., Phila., 1888—. Lecturer on indusl. economics, Wharton Sch. of Finance, U. of Pa.; apptd. prof. metallurgy, Franklin Inst., 1901. Republican. Episcopalian. Mem. Franklin Inst. of Phila. Awarded Elliott Cresson gold medal and John Scott legacy medal and premium from Franklin Inst. and City of Phila. for original discoveries in "molecular physics of iron." Extensive contbr. to newspapers and tech. mags. Home: Philadelphia, Pa. Died Jan. 15, 1928.

OUTERBRIDGE, Eugene Harvey, merchant; b. Phila., Mar. 8, 1860; s. Alexander Ewing and Laura C. (Harvey) O.; ed. pvt. sch., Phila.; m. Ethel Boyd, Oct. 27, 1891; children—Ethel Harvey, Kenneth Boyd. Agent at New York of Harvey & Co., of Newfoundland, 1878-81; sole resident partner of Harvey & Outerbridge, 1881-1923; pres. Harvey & Outerbridge, Inc., 1923—; pres., treas. The Pantasote Leather Co., N.J., The Pantasote Co., N.Y.; pres. The Agasote Millboard Co.; dir. D. & H. Co., Chase Nat. Bank of N.Y., Equitable Life Assurance Soc. Pres. Chamber Commerce State of N.Y., 1916-17. Home: New York, N.Y. Died Oct. 10, 1932.

OUTHWAITE, Joseph H., lawyer; b. Cleveland, O., Dec. 5, 1841; s. George and Harriet (Hodgson) O.; grad. Zanesville High Sch., 1861; read law while teaching grammar sch., Columbus, O., 1864-67; m. Ellen R. Peabody, June 8, 1870. Admitted to bar, 1867; practiced in Mo., 1867-71; returned to Columbus, O., 1871; pros. atty. Franklin Co., O., 1874-79; trustee Children's Home, 1880-84; mem. Columbus Sinking Fund Commn., 1883-85; mem. Congress, 1885-95; civilian mem. U.S. Bd. Ordnance and Fortification, 1895-1900; trustee Ohio State U., 1897; pres. Columbus Bd. Trade, 1900. Democrat. Helped organize gold Democratic movement, 1896; elector-at-large on Palmer and Buckner ticket, 1896. Pres. Asso. Charities of Columbus; pres. Ohio Soc. for Prevention of Tuberculosis; pres. State Tuberculosis Commn., apptd. by gov., Sept. 1902. Dean Coll. of Law, Ohio State U., Jan. 1905—. Home: Columbus, O. Died 1907.

OVENSHINE, Samuel, brigadier gen. U.S.A.; b. in Pa., Apr. 2, 1843. Apptd. from Md., 2d lt. 5th U.S. Inf., Aug. 5, 1861; 1st lt., Sept. 25, 1861; capt., March 30, 1864; maj. 23d Inf., July 10, 1885; lt. col. 15th Inf., Jan. 31, 1891; col. 23d Inf., April 26, 1895; brig. gen. U.S.A., Oct. 19, 1899; retired at own request, over 30 yrs.' service, Oct. 20, 1899; brig. gen. U.S.V., Aug. 13, 1898; hon. discharged, Apr. 17, 1899; brig. gen. U.S.V., Apr. 17, 1899; hon. discharged, Oct. 20, 1899. Home: Washington, D.C. Died July 5, 1932.

OVERALL, John Wesley, farmer, mcht.; b. Liberty, DeKalb County, Tenn., Feb. 7, 1855; s. Wesley and Arena (White) O.; A.B., Cumberland U., Tenn., 1877, LL.B., 1881; m. Mary Oliver, Dec. 4, 1894. Began as farmer and mcht. at Liberty, Tenn., 1886; organizer, 1902, and pres. Bank of Liberty; organizer, 1904, and dir. Bank of Auburn; organizer, 1908, and pres. Overall Hawes Hat Co., Nashville; pres. Lebanon & Sparta Turnpike Co.; dir. Tenn. Bank & Trust Co. Supt. pub. schs., DeKalb County, Tenn., 1881-85; U.S. marshal for Middle Dist. of Tenn., 1898-14; mem. Rep. State Com., Tenn., 1890-1900; del. Rep. Nat. Conv., Minneapolis, 1892, St. Louis, 1896 (credentials com.), Chicago, 1904 and 1908; declined nomination on Rep. ticket for gov. of Tenn., 1910, on account of ill health; received entire Rep. vote in legislature for U.S. senator, 1913; Rep. nominee for gov., 1916. Methodist. Odd Fellow. Home: Nashville, Tenn. Died Mar. 13, 1923.

OVERHOLSER, Edward; b. Sullivan, Ind., June 20, 1869; s. Henry and Emma (Hanna) O.; prep. edn., St. Francis Instn. for Boys at Osage Mission, Kan.; student Lawrence Coll., Appleton, Wis.; m. Allie Garrison, May 26, 1903; 1 son, Edward Herbert. Builder and mgr. of theatre, Oklahoma City, 1890-1918; associated with father in costrn. r.rs., hotels, telephone lines, etc.; pres. Oklahoma City Chamber Commerce, 1922—; v.p. Prudential Fire Ins. Co. (Oklahoma City). Mgr. first Okla. State Fair, first water works in Oklahoma City; mem. Sch. Bd., Oklahoma city, also chmn. Bd. County Commrs.; mayor of Oklahoma City, 1915-19. Mem. Okla. N.G., 1893-1903. Republican. English Lutheran. Mason. Home: Oklahoma City, Okla. Died Apr. 21, 1931.

OVERMAN, Lee Slater, senator; b. Salisbury, N.C., Jan. 3, 1854; s. William and Mary E. O.; A.B., Trinity Coll., N.C., 1874, A.M., 1876; LL.D., Trinity Coll. and Davidson Coll.; m. Mary, d. Senator A. S. Merrimon, Oct. 31, 1878; children—Margie (Mrs. Edwin C. Gregory), Kathryn (Mrs. Gilbert Hambley), Grace (Mrs. Edgar N. Snow). Taught sch., 1875-76; pvt. sec. to Gov. Vance, 1877-78, to Gov. Jarvis, 1879; admitted to bar, 1878; began practice of law at Salisbury, 1880. Mem. N.C. Ho. of Rep., 1883, 87, 93, 1900 (speaker 1893); Dem. caucus candidate for U.S. Senate, 1895; pres. Dem. State Conv., 1900; presdl. elector at large, 1900; U.S. senator 5 terms, 1903-33. Trustee U. of N.C., and Trinity Coll. Home: Salisbury, N.C. Died Dec. 12, 1930.

OVERS, Walter Henry, bishop; b. Harbury, Eng., Mar. 26, 1870; s. John and Sarah (Culley) O.; ed. Wolverhampton Tech. Sch., Rochdale Bible Sch., Eng.; B.Ph., Taylor U., Upland, Ind., 1899, M.A., 1900; Ph.D., Grove City (Pa.) Coll., 1908; S.T.D., Hobart Coll., 1925; m. Mary Davis Sweet, Sept. 20, 1900; children—Helen May, Irene Elizabeth, Robert Perry. Sent from Eng. as missionary of United M.E. Ch. to West Central Africa, 1893; discovered 250,000 natives who practiced human sacrifice, slavery and polygamy; established 35 schs. and chs.; came to U.S. on account of ill health, 1898, naturalized citizen, 1904; pastor various chs. in N.Y. State; joined P.E. Ch., 1910; rector St. Luke's Ch., Mechanicsburg, N.Y., 1910, St. Paul's Ch., Wellsboro, 1910-12, Ch. of the Ascension, Bradford, Pa., 1912-19; bishop of Liberia, Dec. 18, 1919-Nov. 30, 1925; a gen. sec. field dept. of Nat. Council P.E. Ch., 1925-28; later rector Grace Ch., Hastings-on-Hudson, N.Y.; retired. Mem. bd. dirs. Nat. Bd. of Edn., Liberia. Republican. Mason, Odd Fellow, Elk. Author: The Ljebus, 1903; Stories of African Life, 1924; Sketches in Ebony and Ivory, 1928. Home: Jamestown, N.Y. Died June 17, 1934.

OVERSTREET, Jesse, congressman; b. Johnson County, Ind., Dec. 14, 1859; s. Gabriel M. and Sarah L. O.; A.B., Franklin (Ind.) Coll., 1882, A.M., 1885; m. Katharyne C. Crump, June 7, 1898. Admitted to bar, 1886; practiced at Franklin, 1886-96, Indianapolis, 1896—. Mem. 54th to 60th Congresses (1895-1909), 7th Ind. District. Mem. Rep. State Central Com., 1892; mem. Rep. Nat. Congressional Com., 1896-1904. Mem. Nat. Monetary Commn. Address: Indianapolis, Ind. Died 1910.

OVERTON, Daniel Hawkins, clergyman; b. West Yaphank, L.I., N.Y., July 28, 1862; s. Daniel Terry and Charry A. (Hawkins) O.; A.B., Lafayette Coll., 1888, A.M., 1891, D.D., 1916; grad. Union Theol. Sem., 1891; m. Carrie Corey Terry, Sept. 1, 1892 (died 1911); m. 2d, Ethel Elane Edwards, June 22, 1912. Ordained Presbyterian ministry, 1891; in charge Goodwill Chapel, Madison Av. Ch., New York, 1888-91; pastor Immanuel Chapel, University Pl. Ch., 1891-95, Greene Av. Ch., Brooklyn, 1895-1907; supt. ch. extension, Brooklyn Presbytery, 1907-08; pastor Islip, 1908—; chaplain N.Y. State Hosp. for Insane, Central Islip. Del. Gen. Assembly Presbyn. Ch., Los Angeles, Calif., 1903. Dir. Bushwick Hosp., Brooklyn, 10 yrs., v.p. 4 yrs. Mason. Wrote: (booklets) The Old Tide Mill, 1905; Church Membership, 1906. Home: Islip, Suffolk County, N.Y. Died Aug. 22, 1920.

OVERTON, Grant (Martin), author, editor; b. Patchogue, N.Y., Sept. 19, 1887; s. Floyd Alward and Ardelia Jarvis (Skidmore) O.; Princeton U., 1904-06; m. Clara Wallace, June 1, 1921. With New York Sun, 1906-08; connected with Denver Post and San Francisco Examiner until July 1909; sailed before the mast on British ship Wayfarer, San Francisco to Leith, Scotland, July-Dec. 1909; again with New York Sun, 1910, editorial writer, 1916, lit. editor, 1918-19; with George H. Doran Co., book pubs., 1922-24; fiction editor Collier's, 1924-27. Author: The Women Who Make Our Novels, 1918; When Winter Comes to Main Street, 1922; American Nights Entertainment, 1923; Cargoes for Crusoes, 1924; The Philosophy of Fiction, 1928; The American Novel, 1929; The Answerer (novel from the life of Walt Whitman), 1921; The Thousand-and-First Night, 1924. Editor: The World's 100 Best Short Stories, 1927; The World's 50 Best Short Novels, 1929. Home: Patchogue, N.Y. Died July 4, 1930.

OVERTON, James Bertram, plant physiologist; b. Richmond, Mich., Dec. 23, 1868; s. John M. and Charlotte Stuart (Mills) O.; Ph.B., U. of Mich., 1894; Ph.D., U. of Chicago, 1901; honorary Sc.D., Illinois Coll., 1930; m. Mary E. Cochran, December 26, 1901; children—James Bertram, Mary Katherine, Jane Cochran (Mrs. T. W. Vieaux). Assistant principal, high school, Black River Falls, Wisconsin, 1894-95; sr. master in mathematics, St. John's Mil. Acad., Delafield, Wis., 1895-98; asst. in botany, U. of Chicago, 1901; research asst. Carnegie Instn., Washington (at Bonn, Germany), 1903-04; prof. biology, Ill. Coll., Jacksonville, 1901-04; instr. botany, 1904-07, asst. prof., 1907-12, asso. prof. plant physiology, 1912-15, prof., 1915—, U. of Wis. Research asso., part time, Carnegie Instn., 1925-29. Republican. Episcopalian. Author: A Textbook of General Botany (with G. M. Smith and others), 1924. Contbr. to scientific jours. of Europe and America. Address: Madison, Wis. Died Mar. 18, 1937.

OVERTON, Winston, judge; b. Marksville, La., Oct. 4, 1870; s. Judge Thomas and Laura (Waddill) O.; B.S., La. State U., 1890; m. Cecil Maude Legare, Apr. 14, 1909; children—Margaret Cecil, Laura Winston. Admitted to La. bar, 1892, and began practice at Lake Charles, 1893; city atty., Lake Charles, 1899-1906; judge Dist. Court, 15th La. Dist., 1908-20; justice Supreme Court of La., 1921—. Chmn. judiciary com. Constl. Conv. of La., 1921. Democrat. Home: Lake Charles, La. Died Sept. 9, 1934.

OVINGTON, Earle, aeronautical engr.; b. Chicago, Ill., Dec. 20, 1879; s. Edward J. and Mary Wickes (Barnes) O.; E.E., Mass. Inst. Tech., 1904; grad. Bleriot Sch. of Aeronautics, Pau, France, 1911; m. Adelaide Alexander, Apr. 19, 1911; children—Audrey, Kester. Began as asst. in X-ray lab. of Thomas A. Edison, 1898, later with expt. lab. Edison Electric Illuminating Co.; with New York Telephone Co., 1899-1900; founder, 1905, pres., 1905-08, Ovington Mfg. Co.; founder, 1908, pres., 1908-10, Ovington Motor Co.; pres. Vitalait Lab., Inc., Vitalait Lab. of N.E., and Vitalait Lab. of Pacific Coast, preparing bacteriol. cultures for med. use, 1912-19; founder, 1918, pres. 1918-20, Sandy Point (Me.) Shipbuilding Co.; pres. Curtiss Flying Sta., Atlantic City, N.J., 1918-20; cons. elec. and aeronautical engr., Santa Barbara, Calif., 1920—; Pacific Coast factory rep. Curtiss Aerocars. Lieutenant comdr. U.S.N. Res. Winner Boston Globe Tri-State Air Race and $10,000 prize, also John R. McLean trophy ($2,500), 1911. First U.S. Air Mail pilot, 1911. Founder, mem. and pres., Early Birds (aviation assn.). Republican. Presbyn. Inventor Ovington High Frequency Apparatus and other elec. appliances; owner Ovington Air Terminal, Santa Barbara. Address: Santa Barbara, Calif. Died July 21, 1936.

OVINGTON, Irene Helen, pres. Training School for Nurses, Brooklyn, N.Y.; b. New York, N.Y., Dec. 21, 1836; academic edn. Compiled "Comforting Thoughts" (from Henry Ward Beecher), 1884, F2; inventor conveniences for sick room; trustee Memorial Hosp. Author: Helps to Home Nursing, 1890. Home: Brooklyn, N.Y. Died 1905.

OWEN, Emmett Marshall, congressman; b. Hollonville, Ga., 1877; grad. Gordon Inst., Barnesville, Ga.; B.L., U. of Ga., 1900; m. Alma Jones, 1904 (died 1928); children—Mrs. H. B. Floyd, Emmett Marshall. Mem. Ga. Legislature, 1902-06; solicitor City Court, Zebulon, 1908-12; solicitor gen. Flint Judicial Circuit, 1913-23, Griffin Judicial Circuit, 1923-33; mem. 73d to 76th Congresses (1933-41), 4th Ga. Dist. Democrat. Home: Griffin, Ga. Deceased.

OWEN, Fred K., editor; b. Milo, Me., Oct. 10, 1865; s. William H. and Clara M. (Johnson) O.; prep. edn., Coburn Classical Inst.; A.B., Colby Coll., 1887, hon. A.M., 1931; m. Alice Gertrude Smith, Sept. 16, 1896; children—Raymond S., Dorothy L. (Mrs. Leo F. Heal). In newspaper profession, 1889—; with Auburn (Me.) Gazette, 1889-93; city editor Lewiston Sun, 1893-94; editor Taunton (Mass.) News, 1894-96; night editor Portland Press, 1896-1910, asso. editor, 1910-21; editorial writer Evening Express, 1921-24, editor, 1924—. Dir. Port of Portland Authority, 1922—; del. Rep. Conv. Cleveland, 1924. Mason. Elk. Home: Portland, Me. Died Mar. 19, 1940.

OWEN, John S., lumberman; b. Clarkston, Mich., May 1, 1849; s. John G. and Maria Ann (Sabine) O.; grad. high sch. and Eastman's Business Coll., Poughkeepsie, N.Y.; m. Cora M. Rust, Jan. 10, 1872 (died 1895); children—Aloney Rust, John G., Katharine (dec.), Ralph Woodland, Frank Gilchrist (dec.); m. 2d, Mrs. Josephine M. Shaw, May 23, 1899. Began in lumbering business at Eau Claire, 1873; pres. John S. Owen Co., John S. Owen Lumber Co., Chippewa Farm Land Co.; sec. O. & D. Realty Co., Park Assn., Frawley Land Co., dir. Barber Land Co., Rust-Owen Lumber Co. Mem. Wis. State Highway Commn. 6 yrs. Republican. Episcopalian. Home: Eau Claire, Wis. Died June 20, 1939.

OWEN, Mary Alicia, author; b. St. Joseph, Mo., Jan. 29, 1858; d. Hon. James Alfred and Agnes Jeannette (Cargill) O.; ed. pvt. schs. and Vassar Coll. Made important discoveries in Voodoo magic, 1888, which she announced in folk-lore socs.; admitted to tribal membership with the Indians, 1892, joined their secret socs. and wrote of their beliefs and customs; turned her attention to gypsies, 1898. Pres. Mo. Folk-Lore Soc. Author: Ole Rabbit's Plantation Stories; Voodoo Tales; The Daughter of Alouette and an Ozark Gypsy; Folk Lore of the Musquakie Indians; Oracles and Witches; The Sacred Council Hills; Rain Gods of the American Indians; Messiah Beliefs of the American Indians; Home Life of Squaws. Address: St. Joseph, Mo. Died Jan. 5, 1935.

OWEN, Stephen Walker, clergyman; b. Franklin County, Pa., Sept. 13, 1837; s. John Walker and Elizabeth O.; early edn. by father who was teacher; grad. in theology, Missionary Inst. (now Susquehanna U.), Selinsgrove, Pa., 1863; D.D., Newberry Coll., S.C., 1892; LL.D., Susquehanna U., 1908; m. Cordelia A. Levers, July 10, 1862. Ordained Evang. Luth. ministry; pastor St. John's Ch., Hagerstown, Md., 1869—. Pres. Gen. Synod of Evang. Luth. Ch. in U.S., 1907-09; member bd. dirs. Home for the Aged, Washington; pres. bd. dirs. Susquehanna U. Address: Hagerstown, Md. Died Apr. 16, 1916.

OWEN, Thomas Henry, judge; b. nr. Jasper, Ark., Feb. 24, 1873; s. James P. and Anna Eliza (Horner) O.; ed. Valley Springs Acad., Ark.; m. Beulah Davis, Sept. 14, 1898 (died 1907); m. 2d, Louise Hall Parker, Mar. 11, 1916. Began practice at Jasper, Ark., 1894; removed to Muskogee, Okla., 1896; city atty. and councilor, Muskogee, 1901-03; county atty., Muskogee County, 1910-12; justice Criminal Court of Appeals, Okla., 1909-11; asso. justice Supreme Court of Okla., from Apr. 16, 1917, for term expiring Jan. 15, 1923; elected chief justice, Apr. 30, 1919; resigned May 1, 1920; served as trust officer Am. Nat. Bank of Oklahoma City; resigned Sept. 1, 1926, to enter gen. law practice. Del. at large to Dem. Nat. Conv., Baltimore, 1912, San Francisco, 1920. Presbyn. Elk, Woodman. Home: Oklahoma City, Okla. Died Sept. 19, 1938.

OWEN, Thomas McAdory, lawyer, author; b. Jonesboro, Ala., Dec. 15, 1866; s. Dr. William Marmaduke and Nancy L. (McAdory) O.; A.B. and LL.B., U. of Ala., 1887, A.M., 1893, LL.D., 1904; m. Marie Susan, d. John Hollis Bankhead, Apr. 12, 1893. Practiced law Bessemer, Carrollton and Birmingham, Ala., 1887-1901; led in agitation resulting in establishment of Ala. State Dept. of Archives and History, 1901, later, dir. Has rare collection of Ala. and Southern Americana. Founder, and pres. Ala. Library Assn., 1904—; sec. Ala. Soc. S.R., 1894—; comdr.-in-chief of United Sons of Confed. Veterans, 1905-07 (historian-general 1907-17); founder and 1st pres. Ala. Anthrop. Soc., 1909; founder Confederate History Club, Feb. 4, 1911. Author: City Code of Bessemer, Ala., 1888; Bibliography of Alabama, 1897; Bibliography of Mississippi, 1899; Annals of Alabama, 1819-1900 (addendum to 3d edit., Pickett's History of Ala.), 1900; separate genealogies of Lester, Strother, Eaton, Stansel, Lacey, Kelly, Fisher and Ross families; History of Montgomery, Ala., 1907; title "Alabama" in Catholic Cyclopedia; History of Alabama; Dictionary of Alabama Biography, 1920. Editor Trans. Ala. Hist. Soc., vols. 1 to 5, 1898-1905; Report Ala. Hist. Commn., 1901; editor Gulf States Hist. Mag., 1902-03; editor publs. Ala. State Dept. Archives and History. Address: Montgomery, Ala. Died Mar. 25, 1920.

OWEN, Walter Cecil, judge; b. nr. Trenton, Pierce County, Wis., Sept. 26, 1868; s. Bradley and Ellen (Johnston) O.; LL.B., U. of Wis., 1891; m. Alta L. Otis, Oct. 30, 1891. Practiced, Superior, Wis., as mem. firm of Crownhart, Owen & Foley, 1891-98; moved to Maiden Rock, Pierce County, Wis.; elected mem. State Senate, Nov. 1906, to fill vacancy; reëlected for full term of 4 yrs., 1908; atty. gen. of Wis., terms 1913-15, 1915-17; justice Supreme Court of Wis., term 1918-28; reëlected without opposition for term, 1928-38. Republican. Mason, K.P., Elk, Woodman. Home: Madison, Wis. Died Apr. 15, 1934.

OWEN, Wesley M., judge; b. Covell, Ill., Aug. 17, 1869; s. Martin Jefferson and Sarah (Hopkins) O.; LL.B., Ill. Wesleyan Law Sch., 1894; m. Ora May Augustine, Jan. 7, 1894. Practiced at LeRoy, Ill.; mem. firm of Wesley M. and Leslie J. Owen (twin brothers); organized a company and commd. capt., Spanish-Am. War, but was not called into active service; city atty., LeRoy, several terms; mem. Ill. Ho. of Rep., 1903; asso. justice Supreme Ct., 2d Jud. Dist., Canal Zone, 1908-11; resumed practice at Bloomington, Ill., 1911. Republican. Methodist. Address: Bloomington, Ill. Died Oct. 16, 1917.

OWEN, William Baxter, college prof.; b. Wysox, Pa., Sept. 13, 1843; s. Samuel and Mary Flower (Patrick) O.; A.B., Lafayette Coll., Pa., 1871, A.M., 1874; Ph.D., Princeton, 1887; Litt.D., Franklin and Marshall, 1911; m. Eva F. C. Peters, June 30, 1898. Tutor, Greek, 1871-74, adj. prof., 1874-82, prof. Latin and Greek, 1882-86, prof. Latin lang. and lit., 1886—, Lafayette Coll. Mem. Simplified Spelling Bd. (advisory council). Presbyn. Author: Explanatory Notes on Eusebius, 1874; Explanatory Notes on Athenagoras, 1875; Historical Sketches of Lafayette College, 1876; The Advancement of Science in Its Relations to Education, 1888; The Humanities in the Education of the Future, 1912. Editor: Cicero's De Oratore, 1895. Address: Easton, Pa. Died Dec. 4, 1917.

OWEN, William Bishop, educator; b. Union Sta., Licking County, O., Apr. 30, 1866; s. Thomas Walter and Elizabeth (Bishop) O.; A.B., Denison U., 1887; studied U. of Berlin, 1897; U. of Halle, 1900-01; Ph.D., U. of Chicago, 1901; m. Lucy Caroline Anderson, Oct. 3, 1890; children—Roberts Bishop, William Bishop, Anderson Ashley. Instr. Western Pa. Classical and Scientific Instr., 1887-88; pvt. instr., 1888-92; fellow, 1892-94, tutor, instr., asst. prof. and asso. prof. Greek, 1894-1905, asso. prof. edn., 1905-09, U. of Chicago; prin. and dean, U. of Chicago Secondary Schs., 1901-09; pres. Chicago Normal Sch., 1909—. Pres. N.E.A., 1922-23; pres. Ill. Secondary Teachers Assn., 1923. Address: Chicago, Ill. Died Feb. 17, 1928.

OWEN, William Otway, army officer; b. Nollichucky River, Tenn., July 6, 1854; s. Robert Latham and Narcissa Clarke (Chisholm) O.; ed. Va. Mil. Inst., 1873-75; M.D., U. of Va., 1878; m. Anna Rives Chalmers, July 14, 1884. Apptd. asst. surgeon, U.S. Army, May 23, 1882; capt. asst. surgeon, May 23, 1887; maj. brigade surgeon, U.S. Vols., June 4, 1898; hon. discharged June 30, 1899; retired on account of disability in line of duty, Nov. 23, 1905; re-commissioned as col. Med. Corps, by act of Congress, May 27, 1916; curator Army and Med. Mus. and Library, Washington, to July 6, 1918, when retired. Prof. anatomy, Georgetown U. Mem. bd. dirs. Garfield Memorial Hosp., Washington. Mason, K.P. Home: Washington, D.C. Died Dec. 25, 1924.

OWEN, William Russell, clergyman; b. Portsmouth, Va., Dec. 25, 1879; s. Austin Everett and Mary Henrietta (Hall) O.; B.A., U. of Richmond, Va., 1901, D.D., 1916; B.D., Crozer Theol. Sem., 1904; m. Nellie Arthur Plummer. Ordained Bapt. ministry, 1904; pastor Huntingdon Ch., Baltimore, Md., 1904-09, Capitol Av. Ch., Atlanta, Ga., 1909-14, Hanson Pl. Ch., Brooklyn, N.Y., 1914-17, Memorial Ch., Phila., 1917-19, 1st Ch., Macon, Ga., 1920-27, University Church, Coral Gables, Fla., 1927-28, First Church, Columbus, Ga., 1928-30, First Church, Asheville, N.C., 1930-32. Special preacher Y.M.C.A. with 28th Division, 1st F.A., in France, 1919; temporary chaplain, Chaumont. Pres. Bapt. Y.P.U., Ga., 1920-23. Democrat. Author: If the Child Were Not Born, 1906; The Wise Man's Camel, 1921; The Song at Sunrise, 1923; Play Fair, Professor, 1925; Love Letters of an Athlete, 1926; Couriers of Courage, 1929. Speaker Winona Lake Bible Conf.; lecturer. Home: Asheville, N.C. Died Mar. 29, 1938.

OWENS, John Edwin, surgeon; b. Charlestown, Md., Oct. 14, 1836; s. John and Martha J. (Black) O.; prep. edn. acads. in Md.; M.D., Jefferson Med. Coll., Phila., 1862; spl. course in surg. anatomy and operative surgery under Dr. D. Hayes Agnew, Phila.; m. Alethea S. Jamar, Dec. 30, 1869. Res. phys. Blockley Hosp., Phila., 1 yr.; entered med. service Union Army, 1863, and assigned to duty in mil. hosp., Chicago; consulting surgeon St. Luke's Hosp.; chief surgeon I.C. Ry., 1869-1911, C. and N.W. Ry., 1888—; med. dir. Chicago Expn., 1893. Lecturer on surg. diseases urinary organs, 1867-71, on principles and practice of surgery, 1871-82, prof. orthopedic surgery, 1879-82, Rush Med. Coll.; prof. principles and practice of surgery, Woman's Med. Coll., 1877-83; prof. operative and surg. anatomy, 1882-91, of principles and practice of surgery and clin. surgery, Chicago Med. Coll. Episcopalian. Home: Chicago, Ill. Died Dec. 20, 1922.

OWENS, Madison Townsend; b. Apollo, Pa., Apr. 13, 1852; s. Samuel and Elizabeth (Townsend) O.; matriculated in State U. of Ia., 1872, LL.B., 1878; unmarried. Admitted to Ia. bar, 1878, and began practice at Waterloo; county atty. Black Hawk Co., Ia., 5 yrs.; moved to Los Angeles, Calif., 1888; police judge, Los Angeles, 1889-99; settled in Whittier, Calif., 1900, and served as city atty.; mem. firm Owens & Wingert; 1st v.p. United Bond & Mortgage Co., Los Angeles. Served as lt. col. staffs of Govs. Sherman and Larabee, Ia.; joined Calif. N.G., 1889; served as maj. and signal officer, col. and judge adv. gen.; retired with rank of brig. gen., Feb. 1916. Mem. bd. trustees Whittier Library, 1906—; chief of Whittier Div., Am. Protective League, World War. Mem. Rep. State Central Com.; presdl. elector, 1924. Mason. Home: Whittier, Calif. Died Jan. 29, 1929.

OWENS, Michael Joseph, inventor, mfr.; b. in Mason County, Va. (now W.Va.), Jan. 1, 1859; s. John and Mary (Chapman) O.; ed. pub. schs.; m. Mary E. McKelvey, 1889. Learned glass blower's trade at Wheeling, Va.; founder Union Flint Glass Co., Martins Ferry, O., 1882; entered employ of Libbey Glass Co., Toledo, O., 1888, made mgr. of works same yr.; in charge of model glass factory of the company, at Chicago Expn., 1893; an organizer, 1895, of Toledo Glass Co., for mfr. of glass tumblers by means of a machine, which he invented, which gathers from furnace the glass required for each bottle, revolutionizing the bottle-making industry; inventor machine for mfr. cut glass; perfected sheet-glass drawing apparatus, by means of which a sheet of glass 6 feet wide is continuously drawn from molten glass at a speed of 108 feet per hour; v.p. and gen. mgr. Owens Bottle Co., Libbey-Owens Sheet Glass Co. Awarded Elliott Cresson medal, by Franklin Inst., for bottle-making machine, 1916. Home: Toledo, O. Died Dec. 27, 1923.

OWENS, Robert Bowie, electrical engr.; b. Anne Arundel County, Md., Oct. 29, 1870; s. James and Maria Louise (Bowie) O.; grad. Charlotte Hall Mil. Sch., Md., 1886; Johns Hopkins, 1887-89; E.E., Columbia, 1891, A.M., 1899; B.Sc., ad eundem, McGill U., Montreal, 1900, M.Sc., 1900, D.Sc., 1903; research student Cambridge U., Eng., 1899; unmarried. Supt. Greenwich Gas & Elec. Co., 1889-91; prof. elec. and steam engring., U. of Neb., 1891-98; Tyndall fellow in physics, Columbia, 1898-1901; Macdonald prof. elec. engring., McGill U., 1898-1909; elec. engr. Southern Power Co., 1909-10; sec. Franklin Inst., Phila., 1910-24, also editor Jour. Franklin Inst., and dir. Bartol Research Foundation, 1921-24; pres. Fox Hall Farm, Harwood, Md., 1927—; dir. Md. Acad. Scis., 1930-31, and editor its jour. Commd. capt. Signal Corps, U.S.A., May 1917, and served in office of chief signal officer, Washington, D.C.; liaison officer French and British scientific commns., and with Personnel Div. of Aviation Sect. Signal Corps; capt. and maj. Signal Corps, A.E.F.; chief of Signal Corps Intelligence Div. in charge of organization; chief signal officer A.E.F., H.Q., London; in charge of and operated all telephone and telegraph communications between A.E.F., France and Eng., and all Am. owned cables (Western Union and Commercial) between Eng. and U.S., June-Dec. 1918. Mem. Internat. Elec. Congress and Internat. Jury of Awards, World's Fair, Chicago, 1893; dir. Electricity and Machinery Bldg., Trans-Miss. Expn., 1898 (gold medal); mem. Internat. Elec. Congress and Internat. Jury Awards, La. Purchase Expn., 1904 (commemorative medal). Mem. Am. Inst. E.E. (v.p.), Canadian Soc. of Civil Engineers (pres. elec. sect.). Hon. Companion D.S.O. (British); fellow Royal Soc. Can. Discoverer of the Alpha ray; inventor of radio direction finding, electromagnetic system for guiding ships and aeroplanes, differentiating machine, electric accelerometer. Address: Washington, D.C. Died Nov. 1, 1940.

OWRE, Alfred, dental educator; b. Norway, Dec. 16, 1870; s. Lewis and Laura Cecelie O.; Kristiania Borger og Real Skole; D.M.D., U. of Minn., 1894, B.A., 1910; M.D., C.M., Coll. Phys. and Surg. (Hamline U.), 1895; Sc.D., Columbia, 1929; m. Franc Charlotte Hockenberger, Sept. 1, 1915; children—Alice Cecelie, Alfred. Student asst. in operative dentistry, 1893-94, instr. in dental metallurgy, 1895-96, instr. in operative dentistry and dental metallurgy, 1896-97, clin. prof. operative dentistry, 1899, dean and prof. of theory and practice, 1905-27, Coll. of Dentistry, U. of Minn.; dean prof. theory and practice of dentistry, Sch. of Dental and Oral Surgery, Columbia, 1927—. Member various Internat. Dental Congresses; Minn. State Dental Assn. (pres. 1902), mem. Am. Dental Assn. (v.p. 1907). Lt. col. Dental O.R.C., 1924—. Contbr. to text books and dental and medical jours. Address: Pine Plains, Dutchess County, N.Y. Died Jan. 2, 1935.

OWST, Wilberfoss George, musician; b. London, England, June 13, 1861; s. Wilberfoss and Isabel O.; ed. King's College, London, and in music at Stuttgart 7 yrs.; studied law 3 yrs. before studying music in Germany; student of Doctors Immanual Faisst, Percy Goetschius, Paul Glengel and Herren Carl Doppler and Hermann Zumpe; unmarried. Composer of numerous anthems and church works, secular vocal quartets and choruses, cantata for chorus and orchestra The Message of the Winds; the authorized official hymn for the opening of the Jamestown Expn., 1907; a melodrama (Rossetti's), White Ship; also several songs. Mem. Guild of Organists, Eng. Address: Baltimore, Md. Died Jan. 17, 1928.

OXNARD, Benjamin Alexander, sugar refiner; b. New Orleans, La., Dec. 10, 1855; s. of Thomas and Louise Adeline (Brown) O.; S.B., Mass. Inst. Tech., 1875; m. Robbie Giffen, Apr. 27, 1899. Engaged in sugar refining at Brooklyn, N.Y., until 1889; became largely identified with production of cane and beet sugar; pres. Adeline Sugar Co., New Orleans, 1892-1921; pres. Savannah Sugar Refining Co., 1916—. Republican. Catholic. Home: Savannah, Ga. Died Aug. 19, 1924.

OXNARD, Henry Thomas, beet sugar mfr.; b. Marseilles, France, June 22, 1860; s. Thomas and Louise Adeline (Brown) O.; A.B., Harvard, 1882; m. Marie Pichon, Nov. 15, 1900. Devoted himself to establishing beet-sugar industry of U.S.; v.p. Am. Beet Sugar Co.; dir. Central Sugar Corp., Savannah Sugar Refining Corp. Republican. Home: Upperville, Va. Died June 8, 1922.

OXNARD, Robert, sugar refiner; b. La., Oct. 9, 1853; s. Thomas and Louise Adeline (Brown) O.; ed. pub. schs.; m. Nellie Stetson, Apr. 28, 1891. Began as corr. clk. with Zaldo & Co., sugar exporters, Havana, Cuba, 1872; sugar refiner, Brooklyn, N.Y., 1876-87; pres. Am. Sugar Refinery Co., 1888-1904, also sec. Western Sugar Refinery Co., both of San Francisco; pres., later v.p. Am. Beet Sugar Co., 1905-22; later chmn. bd. Calif. Sea Products Co.; dir. Savannah Sugar Refining Corp. Republican. Catholic. Home: San Francisco, Calif. Died Feb. 1930.

OXTOBY, Frederic Breading, Bible teacher; b. Saginaw, Mich., Oct. 20, 1881; s. John Thomas and Mary Ewing (Veech) O.; B.A., U. of Mich., 1905; B.D., McCormick Theol. Sem., 1908; studied Univs. of Berlin and Marburg, 1908-10; M.A., U. of Chicago, 1914; D.D., Alma (Mich.) Coll., 1918; m. Frieda Farrand Boynton, Dec. 20, 1913; children—John Boynton (dec.), Frederic Breading, Robert Boynton, Bayard Ewing. Nettie F. McCormick fellow in O.T., in Europe, 1908-10; instr. in O.T., Chicago Theol. Sem., 1910-14; head of Bible dept. and of religious edn., Huron Coll., 1915-26; head of dept. of religion and of philosophy, Illinois Coll., 1927—; instr. summer conferences, among them—Internat. Council of Religious Edn., Lake Winnepesaukee, N.H., 1925; Presbyn. Nat. Young People's Training Sch., Wooster, O., 1925, 29; Tex. Presbyn.-Congl. Conference, Waxahachie, 1926; Internat. Council of Religious Edn., Geneva Glen, Colorado, 1930. Republican. Kiwanian. Author: Making the Bible Real, 1921; Israel's Religious Development, 1927; The Life Story of the Bible, 1929. Home: Jacksonville, Ill. Died Oct. 19, 1941.

OXTOBY, Walter Ewing, lawyer; b. Erie County, Pa., Oct. 19, 1876; s. John T. (D.D.) and Mary (Veech) O.; LL.B., U. of Mich., 1898; m. Emma W. Schmidt, June 12, 1906 (died 1923); children—Carl S. (dec.), Alice Mary, Dorothy Anne. Admitted to Mich. bar, 1898, and began practice at Detroit; mem. firm Lightner, Oxtoby, Hanley & Crawford, 1905-31; in practice alone, 1932—; v.p. Carl E. Schmidt & Co., tanners, Leather Patents Corp. Republican. Presbyn. Home: Detroit, Mich. Died Oct. 30, 1934.

OXTOBY, William Henry, theologian; b. North East, Erie County, Pa., Jan. 1, 1871; s. Rev. John T. and Mary Ewing (Veech) O.; U. of Mich., 1890-92; grad. McCormick Theol. Sem., 1895, receiving Bernadine Orme Smith Fellowship; univs. of Jena and Berlin, Germany, 1895-96; LL.D., Occidental Coll., Los Angeles, Calif., 1931; m. Ida J. Corning, Sept. 7, 1898; children—Gurdon Corning, Florence Corning, John Corning. Ordained Presbyn. ministry, 1897; pastor 1st Ch., Muncie, Ind., 1897-1903, Tabernacle Ch., Phila., 1903-13; prof. Hebrew exegesis and O.T. lit., San Francisco Theol. Sem., 1913-30, pres. and prof. apologetics and missions, 1930-37, prof. Biblical poetry, 1937—. Moderator Synod of Calif., 1927. Dir. Am. Waldensian Soc. Home: San Anselmo, Calif. Died Sept. 5, 1938.

OYEN, (Olaf) Henry, author; b. Christiania, Norway, Nov. 29, 1883; s. Ole K. and Henrietta (Johansen) O.; brought to America, 1884; pub. sch. edn.; m. Mar. 28, 1916, Sara, d. David and Mattie Goldsmith. Reporter and editorial writer Chicago Tribune, 1904-10; engaged in lit. work, 1910—. Author: Joey The Dreamer, 1911; The Man Trail, 1915; The Snow Burner, 1916; Gaston Olaf, 1917. Home: Forest Hills, L.I., N.Y. Died Oct. 23, 1921.

OYSTER, James F., business man; b. Washington, Feb. 14, 1851; s. George M. and Rosa A. O.; ed. pub. schs. and Rittenhouse Acad., Washington; m. Emma A. Detweiler, Nov. 9, 1886. Engaged in butter, cheese and egg business, 1870—. President of Charles Schneider Baking Company. Pres. Bd. of Edn., Washington, 1907—, Chamber of Commerce, 1910; dir. Bd. Trade. Mason. Dir. Federal Reserve Bank, Dist. No. 5, Richmond, Va., 1914—; chmn. Rent Commn., 1919, 20; commr. Dist. of Columbia—both presdl. apptmts. Home: Washington, D.C. Died May 19, 1925.

OZMUN, Edward Henry, consul gen.; b. Rochester, Minn., Aug. 6, 1857; s. Abraham and Maria (Schenck) O.; student lit. dept. U. of Wis., 1875-78; lit. dept. U. of Mich., 1878-79, LL.B., 1881; m. Clara B. Goodman, Nov. 21, 1894. Admitted to bar, 1881; practiced at St. Paul, 1881-97; counsel, N.P. R.R. Co., 1882-86. Member Minn. Senate, 1893-97; consul at Stuttgart, 1897-1906; consul gen. at Constantinople, 1906—. Mem. bd. to reorganize the consular service, 1906; made journeys far into the interior of Asia Minor, and in Syria, Palestine and Egypt, collecting data upon which governmental reports were published, 1907-08; made addresses before chambers of commerce of leading cities of U.S., on econ. subjects and foreign trade, also lectures at the larger univs. on diplomatic and consular services, winter of 1908-09. Republican. Pres. St. Paul Bar Assn., 1890-97; sec. Minn. State Bar Assn., 1893-97; mem. State Bd. of Examiners in Law, examiner on internat. law, torts, frauds and damages, 1890-97. Author of Minn. Corrupt Practices Act of 1895. Deceased.

P

PABST, Frederick, brewer; b. Nicholausreith, Saxony, Mar. 28, 1836; Gottlieb and Fredericka P.; emigrated to U.S., 1848; self ed.; m. Marie, d. Philip Best. Was captain steamer Comet on Great Lakes. Became a brewer in 1862. Now pres. Pabst Brewing Co., Wis. Nat. Bank; v.p. Second Ward Savings Bank; dir. Milwaukee Mechanics' Ins. Co., Milwaukee Fire Ins. Co., etc. Home: Milwaukee, Wis. Died 1904.

PACE, Edward Aloysius, psychologist; b. Starke, Fla., July 3, 1861; s. George E. and Margaret (Kelly) P.; A.B., St. Charles Coll., Catonsville, Md., 1880; S.T.B., Propaganda, Rome, 1883, S.T.D., 1886; Ph.D., U. of Leipzig, 1891. Prof. philosophy, Catholic U. of America, Washington, D.C., 1891—. Editor Catholic Ency. and of The New Scholasticism. Died Apr. 26, 1938.

PACE, Jerome Grant, physician; b. Wyoming Co., Pa., Mar. 18, 1867; s. Hiram C. and Frances (Beers) P.; M.D., Medico-Chirurg. College of Phila., 1888; m. Isabel Shippey-James, 1894. Began practice at Phila., 1888; med. dir. and supt. Mod. Woodmen of America Sanatorium, Woodmen, Colo., 1920; now supt. and med. dir. District Tuberculosis Hosp., Lima, O., cons. physician Glockner and Beth-el hosps.; v.p. Colo. Sch. of Tuberculosis. Democrat. Episcopalian. Mason. Rotarian. Home: Lima, O. Deceased.

PACE, Julian Harrison, clergyman; b. Liberty Hill, Tex., Mar. 30, 1878; s. Henry T. and Lou Elizabeth (Mayhall) P.; B.L., Baylor U., Waco, Tex., 1908; student Southern Bapt. Theol. Sem., Louisville, 1911-12; D.D., Howard Payne Coll., Brownwood, Tex., 1919; m. Ella S. Douglass, Dec. 7, 1904; children—Loura Dale (Mrs. Vernon Sherwood), Julian Henry, Ray Stinson, Sarah Frances (Mrs. Roland Nystrom). Ordained to the ministry of the Baptist Church, 1899; teacher and minister, various schools and churches, 1899-1908; pastor Anson, Texas, 1908-13, Dublin, 1913-18, Galveston, 1918-20, Waxahachie, 1920-24, Beaumont, 1924—. Mem. exec. bd. Bapt. Gen. Conv. of Tex., 1917—, becoming pres. Mason. Traveled in Europe, Syria, Palestine and Egypt, 1923. Home: Beaumont, Tex. Deceased.

PACE, Mary Anna, editor, critic; b. Temple, Tex., July 29, 1880; d. William J. and Olive (Wilder) P.; A.B., Baylor U., Waco, Tex., 1899; M.A., U. of Chicago, 1902; grad. scholar, Yale, 1904-05. Asst. in editorial dept. Current Literature, 1906-11; reader and editor, G. W. Dillingham Pub. Co., 1912-16; now on editorial staff New York American (Sunday). Mem. Intercollegiate Socialist Soc., U.D.C. Baptist. Home: New York, N.Y. Died Apr. 22, 1922.

PACHMANN, Vladimir de, pianist; b. Odessa, Russia, July 27, 1848; ed. in music by father (prof. Vienna U.), and by Dachs, at the Conservatory of Music, Vienna; m. Maggie Oakey, his former pupil, 1884 (divorced). First concert tour in Russia, 1869; played in Germany, 1877; first visit to U.S., 1891; has frequently toured Europe and U.S.; celebrated for remarkable technique and for refinement of tone. Decorated Knight Order of Dannebrog (Denmark), 1885; Beethoven medal, London Philharmonic Soc., 1916. Died Jan. 7, 1933.

PACK, Charles Lathrop, forester, economist; b. Lexington, Mich., May 7, 1857; s. George Willis and Frances (Farman) P.; ed. pub. schs. and Brooks Sch., Cleveland; studied forestry in Black Forest, Germany; spent several yrs. exploring forests of Canada, the Northwest, La. and Miss.; LL.D., Trinity Coll., 1918; Dr. Business Administration, Syracuse U., 1925; LL.D., Oberlin (Ohio) College, 1926; Sc.D., Rutgers Univ., New Brunswick, N.J., 1930; m. Alice Gertrude Hatch, April 28, 1886. Founder Cleveland Trust Co. Pres. Nat. War Garden Commn., 1917-19, Am. Forestry Assn., 1916-20, Nat. Conservation Congress, 1913; mem. N.J. Conservation and Development Commn.; pres. of World Court League; chmn. French Agrl. Com. of Am. Com. for Devastated France. Awarded Great Medal, Nat. War Garden Commn., 1919; Grand Medal of Honor, Société Nationale d'Acclimatation de France; French decoration Le Mérite Agricole, 1919; Liberty service medal, 1919, from Nat. Inst. Social Sciences; awarded the Crawford medal (England), 1923; Collectors' Club medal, New York, 1924; Lindenburg medal (Berlin, Germany), 1926. Commander Order of the Crown (Italian), 1924. Upon invitation of President Roosevelt, attended as expert the White House Conf. of Governors, May 1907; apptd. mem. Conservation Commn.; aided in reforestations of France, Eng. and Italy after World War. Elected pres. Am. Nature Assn. (Washington), 1922, and of Am. Treas. Assn., 1923. Trustee Walter Hines Page Memorial Sch. of Internat. Relations; mem. bd. Institute of International Education. Was member 1st City Troop of Cleveland, Cleveland Chamber of Commerce (pres.). Was mem. Indianapolis Sound Money Conv., also of Monetary Commn. Trustee Western Reserve U.; business trustee of The Tropical Plant Research Foundation. Republican. Presbyn. Author: War Garden Victorious Memorial Trees; Roads of Remembrance; School Book of Forestry, 1922; Trees as Good Citizens, 1923; Forestry Primer, 1926; Victoria—the Half-Length Portraits and the Two Pence Queen Enthroned, 1923; Thomas Hatch of Barnstable and Some of His Descendants; Forests and Mankind, 1929; Forest Facts for Schools, 1931; etc. Home: Lakewood, N.J. Died June 14, 1937.

PACK, Frederick James, geologist; b. Bountiful, Utah, Feb. 2, 1875; s. John and Mary Jane (Walker) P.; B.S. in M.E., U. of Utah, 1904; M.A., Columbia, 1905, Ph.D., 1906; m. Sadie Grant, Nov. 25, 1896; children—Eugene Grant, Alvin Grabau, Marion, Eleanor. Deseret prof. geology, U. of Utah, 1907—; pres. and mgr. Utah-Wyo. Consolidated Oil Co. Acquired title to large tracts of land in Wyo., 1908, and developed region into one of most important oil and natural gas dists. of Wyoming. Mormon. Author: New Discoveries Relating to the Wasatch Fault, 1926; Structure of Thermal Springs on the Wasatch Fault, 1927; Dinosaurs in Western America, Ten Lessons in Geology, 1931; Breadth of Mormonism, 1932; Origin and Meaning of Six Hundred Place Names in Utah, 1935; Origin and Nature of the Barmeville Salt Flats, 1937; Lake Barmeville, 1938. Home: Salt Lake City, Utah. Died Dec. 2, 1938.

PACKARD, Alpheus Spring, prof. zoölogy and geology, Brown Univ., 1878—; b. Brunswick, Me., Feb. 19, 1839; s. Prof. Alpheus Spring and Frances Elizabeth (Appleton) P.; (mother a sister of Mrs. President Pierce); grad. Bowdoin, 1861; LL.D., 1901; Me. Med. School, 1864; studied under Agassiz, Lawrence Scientific School, 3 yrs.; S.B., Harvard Univ. (out of course), 1864; m. Elizabeth Derby, d. Samuel Baker Walcott, Oct. 1867. Asst. surgeon Me. Vet. Vols., 1864-65; librarian and custodian Boston Soc. Natural History, 1865-66; curator Essex Inst., 1866; curator, afterward dir., Peabody Acad. Science, 1867-78; State entomologist Mass., 1871-73; mem. U.S. Entom. Commn., 1877-82; an honorary pres. Zoöl. Congress, Paris, 1889; a founder and 20 yrs. editor-in-chief,

Am. Naturalist. Author: Observations on the Glacial Phenomena of Labrador and Maine, 1891; A Text Book of Entomology, 1898; Lamarck, the Founder of Evolution, His Life and Work, 1901, also (in French), 1903; A Naturalist on the Labrador Coast, 1891. Home: Providence, R.I. Died 1905.

PACKARD, Alton, artist, cartoonist, lecturer; b. Taunton, Mass., May 9, 1870; s. Leonard Franklin and Ellen Maria (Eaton) P.; U. of Minn.; studied music under late George W. Sumner, drawing, Minneapolis Art Sch.; m. Carrie V. Pettit, Oct. 24, 1894. Cartoonist, Minneapolis Journal, 1889, later Chicago Times, Chicago Saturday Blade, Dayton (O.) Herald; dir. art advertising dept. Nat. Cash Register Co., Dayton, 1894-95; lyceum lecturer and entertainer, Redpath Lyceum Bur., 1895—. On Faculty Federal Schs., Minneapolis, Minn. Democrat. Presbyn. Charter mem. Internat. Lyceum Assn. (treas. 1909). Home: Oklahoma City, Okla. Died Aug. 29, 1929.

PACKARD, Burdett Aden, miner, cattleman; b. Portville, N.Y., Nov. 1, 1847; s. Ashley G. and Virtue V. (Crandall) P.; ed. Alfred (N.Y.) Acad.; m. Ella L. Lewis, Dec. 27, 1879 (died 1893); m. 2d, Carlota W. Holbrook, May 1903. At 16 went into lumber business with his father, at 18 began merchandising; in oil business in Pa., 1870-82; then in mining and cattle business in Ariz.; owned, developed and sold several mines at Tombstone; in cattle business from 1884, operating in Sonora, Mex., and Ariz.; became pres. First Nat. Bank, Douglas, Ariz., 1907 (chmn. bd. and pres.). Mem. Ariz. Legislature 2 terms. Democrat. Mason. Home: Douglas, Ariz. Died Mar. 12, 1935.

PACKARD, Charles Stuart Wood, capitalist; b. Phila., Pa., June 2, 1860; s. John H. (M.D.) and Elisabeth (Wood) P.; ed. Rugby Acad. and U. of Pa.; m. Eliza Gilpin McLean, Apr. 1882; 1 son, John Hooker. Sec. and treas. Phila. Warehouse Co., 1882-86; treas. Washington Mfg. Co., 1886-92; from 1892 with The Pennsylvania Co. for Insurances on Lives and Granting Annuities, as auditor, 1892-93, treas., 1893-99, pres. and dir., 1899—; dir. many corps. Episcopalian. Home: Philadelphia, Pa. Died July 9, 1937.

PACKARD, George Byron, orthopedist; b. Jericho, Vt., May 9, 1852; s. Cyrus and Melissa (Mead) P.; prep. edn. Underhill (Vt.) Acad.; M.D., U. of Vt., 1874; post-grad. work, Univ. Med. Coll. (New York U.); m. Carrie Sanborn, June 6, 1883. Practiced at Hartford, Conn., 1880-89, Denver, Colo., 1889—; president of staff, Children's Hosp.; prof. orthopedic surgery, U. of Colo., 1895-1915. Fellow Am. Coll. Surgeons. Republican. Conglist. Home: Denver, Colo. Died Feb. 1927.

PACKARD, George Randolph, ins. exec.; b. Phila., Pa., Sept. 25, 1872; s. John Hooker and Elisabeth (Wood) P.; ed. pvt. schs., Phila.; m. Elizabeth Waln Wistar Brown, Oct. 30, 1895; children—Mary Farnum (wife of Dr. Arthur E. Billings), Elisabeth Wood (Mrs. Herbert Church), Ruth (Mrs. Frederick R. Drayton), George Randolph. Began in ins. business at Phila., 1889; chmn. bd. Stokes, Packard, Haughton & Smith, Inc.; v.p. United Firemen's Ins. Co.; dir. Lumbermen's Ins. Co., Phila. Nat. Ins. Co., Provident Trust Co., Provident Mutual Life Ins. Co. Mgr. Pa. Hosp., Phila. Dispensary, Phila. Lying-In Charity Hosp.; trustee Bryn Mawr Hosp., Phila. Lying-In Charity Hosp. Episcopalian. Home: Villa Nova, Pa. Died Jan. 10, 1936.

PACKARD, Horace, surgeon; b. West Bridgewater, Mass., Aug. 9, 1855; s. John H. and Phebe M. (Hayward) P.; ed. State Normal Sch., Bridgewater, Mass.; M.D., Boston U. Sch. of Medicine, 1880; m. Mary A. Hooper, 1883 (died 1923). Practiced in Boston, 1885-1925 (retired); emeritus prof. surgery, Boston Univ.; consulting surgeon Mass. Homœ. Hosp. Fellow Am. Coll. Surgeons. Unitarian. Home: Boston, Mass. Died Jan. 24, 1936.

PACKARD, James Ward, mfr.; b. Warren, O., Nov. 5, 1863; s. Warren and Mary E. (Doud) P.; M.E., Lehigh U., 1884; m. Elizabeth A. Gillmer, Aug. 1904. Engr., 1884, with Sawyer-Man Elec. Co., later absorbed by Westinghouse Elec. Co.; organizer, 1890, and pres. Packard Elec. Co.; organizer, 1897, and pres. Packard Motor Car Co.; invented and developed the Packard Car, also inventor of many processes and devices in incandescent elec. lighting. Republican. Episcopalian. Home: Warren, O., and Lakewood, N.Y. Died Mar. 20, 1928.

PACKARD, Jasper, journalist; b. Mahoning Co., Ohio, Feb. 1, 1832; grad. Univ. of Mich., 1855; m. Harriet S. Tibbits, Oct. 4, 1855. In Union army, 1861-66; all grades, private to bvt. brig. gen. Auditor La Porte Co., Ind., 1866-68; member Congress, 1869-75; internal revenue agt., 1876-84. Lived at La Porte, Ind., 1856-88. In New Albany, 1888—; propr. and editor New Albany Evening Tribune. Member Ind. legislature, 1896-98. Republican. Home: New Albany, Ind. Died 1899.

PACKARD, John Hooker, physician; b. Philadelphia, Aug. 15, 1832; grad. Univ. of Pa., 1850; (A.M., M.D., 1853); m. Elisabeth Wood, June 3, 1858 (died 1897). Demonstrator anatomy, Univ. of Pa., 1862-63; acting asst. surgeon, U.S.A., 1861-65; surgeon to Episcopal Hosp., 1863-84; Pa. Hosp., 1884-96; Woman's Hosp., 1876-77. Author: Minor Surgery; Lectures on Inflammation; Operative Surgery. Translator of Malgaigne on Fractures; editor Medical Directory of Philadelphia, 1868-71; etc. Home: Philadelphia, Pa. Died 1907.

PACKARD, Joseph, P.E. clergyman; b. Wiscasset, Me., Dec. 23, 1812; s. Rev. Hezekiah and Mary (Spring) P.; ed. at his father's private school and Phillips' Acad., Andover, Mass.; grad. Bowdoin, 1831; (D.D., Kenyon Coll., O., 1847); m. Rosina, d. Gen. Walter Jones, of Washington, Jan. 1838. Deacon, 1836; priest, 1837; prof. Bristol Coll., Pa., 1834-36; prof. sacred literature, P.E. Theol. Sem. of Va., 1836-90 (15 yrs. dean); from 1890 emeritus prof. Mem. Am. Com. for Revision of the Bible, 1872-85; prepared commentary on Malachi for Lange's Commentary, 1874. Died 1902.

PACKARD, Joseph, lawyer; b. Fairfax Co., Va., Apr. 10, 1842; s. Joseph (D.D.) and Rosina (Jones) P.; A.B., Kenyon Coll., Ohio, 1860, A.M., 1867; studied in Law School, U. of Virginia; (hon. D.C.L., U. of the South, 1901; LL.D., Kenyon, 1911); m. Mrs. Laura Dillon, Apr. 13, 1868; m. 2d, Meta Hanewinckel, Dec. 27, 1882. Instr. history and lit., Kenyon Coll., 1860-61; served as pvt. and corporal of arty., Stonewall Brigade, and lt. of arty. on ordnance duty with reserve train, Army of N.Va., 1861-65; began practice at Leesburg, Va., 1868; removed to Baltimore, 1868; mem. Venable & Packard, 1871-92, since alone. Pres. Baltimore Reform League, 1894-1900, Baltimore Sch. Bd., 1900-98; chmn. Charter Revision Commn. of Baltimore, 1909. Democrat. Episcopalian; deputy Gen. Conv. P.E. Ch., 1886-1919. Home: Baltimore. Died Nov. 24, 1923.

PACKARD, William Alfred, educator; b. Brunswick, Maine, Aug. 26, 1830; s. Rev. Prof. Alpheus Spring and Frances E. (Appleton) P.; A.B., 1851, A.M., 1854, Bowdoin; teacher, Phillips Acad., Andover, Mass., 1852-53; tutor Bowdoin, 1853-54; grad. Andover Theol. Sem., 1857; studied Univ. of Göttingen, 1857-58; (hon. A.M., Dartmouth, 1864, Princeton, 1896; Ph.D., Hamilton, 1868; D.D., Bowdoin, 1894); m. Susan Breese Gallagher, 1861 (died 1886). Instr. modern languages, Bowdoin, 1859; prof. modern languages, 1859-63, prof. Greek lang. and lit., 1863-70, Dartmouth; prof. Latin lang. and lit., Princeton, 1870—. Revised, with translations from later edit., Curtius' History of Greece; wrote memorial sketches of lives of earlier Princeton presidents and professors. Died 1909.

PADDOCK, Buckley B.; b. Cleveland, Jan. 22, 1844; s. Boardman and Margaret (Buckley) P.; spent boyhood among trappers and in logging camps of Northwest; no sch. advantages; m. Emmie M. Harper, Dec. 10, 1867. Entered C.S.A. at 16, becoming capt.; reputed to be youngest commd. officer in the army. Admitted to bar in Miss. and practiced until 1873; entered newspaper business with Ft. Worth Democrat; later went into banking, and promoted and built Ft. Worth & Rio Grande R.R., from Ft. Worth to Brownwood, Tex., 142 miles, and was pres. of rd. 5 yrs.; sold ry. to St.L.&S.F. R.R. Co. and engaged in investment securities; retired Dec. 31, 1909; dir. St.L.&S.F. R.R. Mayor of Ft. Worth, 1892-1900; hon. pres. for life Ft. Worth Chamber Commerce, which he organized, 1891. Democrat. Presbyn. Home: Ft. Worth, Tex. Died Jan. 9, 1922.

PADDOCK, Lucius Carver, editor, publisher; b. Grand Rapids, Mich., Aug. 10, 1859; s. Augustus and Esther Eliza (Gload) P.; ed. high sch., Grand Rapids; Master of Journalism, U. of Colo., 1927; m. Lena Butsch, Oct. 13, 1880; children—Edna (Mrs. Charles A. Monroe), Percy Butsch, Alva Adams. Began as reporter, Boulder, Colo., 1880, on Leadville Dispatch, 1887, Aspen (Colo.) Chronicle, 1889; editor Boulder (Colo.) Daily Camera, 1891—; pres. Boulder Pub., Inc., Register Colo. State Land Bd.; commr. of immigration, Colo.; mem. State Bd. of Corrections. Del. to Dem. Nat. Conv., 1928; Dem. elector, 1932, leading the ticket; mem. State Recovery Board. Democrat, Elk, Woodman of the World; mem. Royal Arcanum. Home: Boulder, Colo. Died July 31, 1940.

PADDOCK, Robert Lewis, bishop; b. New York, Dec. 24, 1869; s. Bishop John Adams and Frances Chester (Fanning) P.; A.B., Trinity, 1894, A.M., 1897; grad. Berkeley Div. Sch., 1897; (D.D., Berkeley, 1908; S.T.D., Hobart, 1908, Trinity Coll., Conn., 1910); m. Miss H. J. Aitken, Jan. 9, 1923. Deacon, 1897, priest, 1898, P.E. Ch.; in charge of mission, Southington, Conn., 1897; gen. sec. Ch. Students' Missionary Assn. and asst. St. Paul's Ch., Cleveland, 1897-98; vicar Pro-Cathedral, and canon Cathedral of St. John the Divine, New York, 1898-1902; rector Ch. of the Holy Apostles, New York, 1902-07; consecrated bishop of Eastern Ore., Dec. 18, 1907 (resigned Sept. 1922). Asso. field sec. Y.M.C.A. hdqrs., Paris, France, 1 yr. Died May 17, 1939.

PADEREWSKI, Ignace Jan, pianist, composer; b. Province of Podolia, Russian Poland, Nov. 6, 1860; began to learn piano at 3 and at 7 was placed under teacher; studied at Conservatory of Warsaw under Jonatha and Rogueski, later studied composition under Friedrich Kiel, at Berlin and piano under Theodore Leschetizky, at Vienna; hon. Ph.Doc., University of Lemberg, 1911; hon. Mus. Doc., Yale, 1917; Ph.Doc., U. of Cracow, 1919; C.L.D., Oxford University, 1920; m. Baroness de Rosen, 1899 (died 1934). First concert tour in Poland and Russia; prof. piano and counterpoint, conservatory of Strasbourg, in 1885-86; teacher Conservatory of Warsaw at 18; début Vienna, 1887, Paris, 1888, London, 1890, New York, 1891; made 11 tours in U.S., and played in leading cities of Europe, N. and S. America, Australia, New Zealand and S. Africa; established "Paderewski Fund," prizes for Am. composers, 1900. Devoted time mainly during the World War to concertizing for benefit of Polish war sufferers and to pub. speaking in behalf of Poland; organized in U.S., 1917, Polish Vols., known as the Polish Army in France; officially recognized as rep. of Polish people at Washington, D.C., 1917-18; led in organizing Polish Republic, 1918-19; premier of Poland, 1919; mem. Peace Conf., Paris, 1918-19, and first del. of Poland to Council of Ambassadors, and to League of Nations, 1920. Comdr. Order of the Crown (Italian), 1898; Comdr. Order of Carlos III (Spanish), 1902; Officer Legion of Honor (French), 1909, and Grand Cross, same order, 1922. Composer: (opera) Manru, prod. in Europe, 1901, U.S., 1902; also Symphony, Concerto for Piano and Orchestra, sonatas, variations, and many pieces and songs. Mem. Am. Acad. of Arts and Letters. Author: The Paderewski Memoirs (with Mary Lawton), 1938. Home: Morges, Switzerland. Died June 29, 1941.

PADGETT, Lemuel Phillips, congressman; b. Columbia, Tenn., Nov. 28, 1855; s. John B. and Rebecca Ophelia (Phillips) P.; A.B., Erskine Coll., S.C., 1876 (LL.D., 1916); m. Ida B. Latta, Nov. 11, 1880. Admitted to bar, 1877; in practice at Columbia, 1879—. Presdl. elector, 1884; mem. Tenn. Senate, 1898-1900; mem. 57th to 67th Congresses (1901-23), 7th Tenn. District. Democrat. Chmn. Com. Naval Affairs, 62d to 65th Congresses; mem. Nat. Monetary Commn.; regent Smithsonian Instn., Dec. 1917—. Home: Columbia, Tenn. Died Aug. 2, 1922.

PAETOW, Louis John, univ. prof.; b. Milwaukee, Wis., Jan. 9, 1880; s. Christian and Dorothea (Garling) P.; B.L., U. of Wis., 1902, M.L., 1903; Ph.D., U. of Pa., 1906; studied U. of Paris, 1905; Harrison fellow in history, U. of Pa., 1904-06; m. Lily Gavit Kollock (Ph.D., U. of Pa.), June 6, 1911; children—Charles Kollock, Dorothea Garling. Teacher of history, high sch., Grand Rapids, Wis., 1903-04; acting prof. history, U. of Colo., 1904-05; instr. history, U. of Wis., 1906-07; asso. in history, U. of Ill., 1907-11; asst. prof. medieval history, 1911, asso. prof., 1917, prof., 1919—, U. of Calif. Research work in Paris, 1925-26 (sabbatical leave). A rep. of Am. Hist. Assn. on com. on medieval Latin Studies of Am. Council of Learned Socs. Fellow and mem. council of Mediæval Acad. of America. Author: Arts Course at Medieval Universities, 1910; Guide to the Study of Medieval History, 1917. Editor and translator: Battle of the Seven Arts (by Henri d'Andeli), 1914; Morale Scolarium of John of Garland, 1927. Editor of The Crusades and other historical essays presented to Dana C. Munro, 1927. Home: Berkeley, Calif. Died Dec. 22, 1928.

PAGAN, Oliver Elwood, lawyer; b. Toledo, O., Sept. 2, 1858; s. Lewis and Maria (Stover) P.; prep. edn. high sch., South Bend, Ind.; student law dept. U. of Mich., 1879-81; m. Alice Josephine Schram, May 1, 1883; children—Albert Elwood, Robert Schram, Mrs. Laura Miller. Asst. U.S. atty., Chicago, 1888-1903; spl. asst. atty. gen., Washington, D.C., 1903—; active in prosecuting violations of anti-trust, interstate commerce, sedition, income-tax, nat. bank, election, land, internal revenue, postal and customs laws; cases against India revolutionists, I.W.W.'s and Socialists, at Chicago, war frauds at Washington, and Volstead Act violations at Savannah, Cincinnati, Cleveland, Phila., Pittsburgh, South Bend, Chicago, San Francisco, Los Angeles and Puerto Rico. Episcopalian. Author: Federal Precedents, Civil and Criminal, 1894. Home: Washington, D.C. Died Apr. 2, 1932.

PAGE, Alfred Rider, judge; b. Carlinville, Ill., Oct. 7, 1859; s. Charles and Angeline (Rider) P.; freshman yr., Williams Coll.; LL.B., New York U., 1880; hon. A.M., Williams, 1907; LL.D., New York U., 1916; m. Elizabeth M. Roe, Apr. 27, 1886; children—Helen W. (dec.), Elizabeth M., Mrs. Marjorie Schauffer. In law practice at New York from 1880; atty. Bd. of Excise, 1895; atty., State Dept. Excise, 1896-1900; mem. N.Y. Senate, 1905-08; justice Supreme Ct. N.Y., term Jan. 1, 1910-Dec. 31, 1923; justice Appellate Div., 1st Dept. 1916-23 (resigned). Mem. Kings Co. Rep. Com., 1887-90, N.Y. Co. Com., 1894-1910; placed Charles E. Hughes in nomination for gov., 1908. Mem. Dutch Ref. Ch. Mason. Died Feb. 3, 1931.

PAGE, Bertrand A., insurance official; b. Yalesville, Conn., May 11, 1873; s. George Washington and Mary Jane (Smith) P.; student Hartford (Conn.) High Sch. and Wethersfield (Conn.) Acad.; m. Cecile Somerset Whitney, of Hamilton, Bermuda, Oct. 27, 1898; children—Nelson Whitney, Janet Hotchkiss. Asst. sec., Travelers Ins. Co., Hartford, Conn., 1901-04, sec., 1904-12, v.p., 1912—, also dir. Fellow Casualty Actuarial Soc. of America. Republican. Conglist. Home: Hartford, Conn. Died July 30. 1941.

PAGE, Calvin, banker; b. North Hampton, N.H., Aug. 22, 1845; s. Simon D. and Judith (Rollins) P.; grad. Phillips Exeter Acad., 1863; Harvard, 1864-65; studied law; (hon. A.M., Dartmouth, 1892); m. Arabella J. Moran, Jan. 6, 1870. Practiced law, Portsmouth, 1868-1910, retiring as mem. Page, Bartlett & Mitchell; identified with many important cases; pres. N.H. Nat. Bank, Portsmouth Trust & Guarantee Co., Granite State Fire Ins. Co., Portsmouth Fire Assn., Piscataqua Fire Ins. Co., Manchester & Lawrence R.R., Concord & Portsmouth Railroad, and dir. Upper Coos R.R. Chmn. High Sch. Com., Portsmouth, 1883—; mayor of Portsmouth, 1883-84, 99; mem. State Constl. Conv., 1889; mem. N.H. Senate, 1893-94, 1903-04, 1917-18; U.S. collector internal revenue, Dist. of N.H., including Me. and Vt., 8 yrs., under President Cleveland. Trustee Portsmouth Hosp. Democrat. Unitarian. Mason. Home: Portsmouth, N.H. Died Dec. 1919.

PAGE, Carroll Smalley, senator; b. Westfield, Vt., Jan. 10, 1843; s. Russel Smith and Martha Malvina (Smalley) P.; ed. People's Acad., Morrisville, Vt.; Lamoille Central Acad., Hyde Park, Vt.; (LL.D., Norwich U., 1893); m. Ellen Frances Patch, Apr. 11, 1865 (died 1914). Dealer in raw calfskins; pres. Lamoille County Savings Bank & Trust Co., Lamoille County Nat. Bank; dir. Swanton (Vt.) Savings Bank & Trust Co., St. Johnsbury & Lake Champlain R.R. Mem. Vt. Ho. of Rep., 1869-72, Senate, 1874-76; mem. Rep. State Com., 1872-90 (sec.-treas. 1878-84, chmn. 1886-90); register of probate, 1880-91; savings bank examiner, 1884-88; gov. of Vt., 1890-92; elected U.S. senator, Oct. 21, 1908, for unexpired term (1908-11) of Redfield Proctor, deceased; reëlected for terms 1911-17, 1917-23. Home: Hyde Park, Vt. Died Dec. 3, 1925.

PAGE, Charles, soldier; b. in Va., 1829. Apptd. asst. surgeon, U.S.A., Dec. 2, 1851; capt. asst. surgeon, Dec. 2, 1856; maj. surgeon, Apr. 16, 1862. Bvtd. lt. col., U.S.A., for faithful and meritorious services during war; promoted lt. col., surgeon, June 30, 1882; col., asst. surgeon-gen., Nov. 17, 1887; retired Dec. 4, 1893; advanced to brig. gen., U.S.A., retired, Apr. 23, 1904. Served during Civil War in various hosps. and with Army of the Potomac, of which was asst. med. dir., 1864-65, and med. dir., 2d corps, Mar.-Aug. 1865. Home: Baltimore, Md. Died 1906.

PAGE, Charles, oil producer, philanthropist; b. Stevens Point, Wis., June 2, 1861; s. James W. and Mary Elizabeth (Gottrey) P.; ed. pub. schs.; m. Lucille Rayburn, July 22, 1908; 1 dau., Mary. Began as railroad telegraph operator; engaged in mining, timber and land development, Ida., Colo., Wash., Ore., Wyo. and B.C.; settled in Okla., 1902, and is largely identified with oil interests, pub. utilities, farming and mfg.; founder of Sand Springs, Okla.; built Shell Creek Dam (cost of $1,500,000) to supply water to Sand Springs and Tulsa; pres. Sand Springs R.R. Co., San Springs Power, Light & Water Co., Sand Springs Gas Co., Sand Springs State Bank; built Sand Springs Cotton Mill (cost $2,000,000), 2d largest cotton textile mill west of Miss. River. Founder, 1908, Sand Springs Home for 100 orphans with incorporated endowment sufficient for permanent maintenance; founder "Widows' Colony," to assist widows to become self-supporting. Home: Sand Springs, Okla. Died Dec. 27, 1926.

PAGE, Charles, lawyer; B.A., Yale, 1868; law student univs. of Brussels and Berlin, 1868-69; m. Sallie Hette Myers, Sept. 12, 1877. Admitted to Calif. bar, 1870, and since in practice in San Francisco; specializes in admiralty practice. Home: San Francisco, Calif. Deceased.

PAGE, Edward Day, capitalist; b. Haverhill, Mass., May 10, 1856; s. Henry A. and Maria (Clarke) P.; Ph.B., Sheffield Scientific School (Yale), 1875; m. Cornelia Lee, May 1, 1883. Entered employ of Faulkner, Page & Co., dry goods commn. mchts., 1875; successively mgr., 1880-84, partner, 1884-98, sr. partner, 1898-11, retired and liquidated. Spl. partner Holbrook, Corey & Co., commercial paper, 1912—; pres. South Orange & Maplewood Traction Co.; treas. Montrose Realty & Improvement Co., Vygeberg Co. Councilman Borough of Oakland, N.J., 1902-06, mayor, 1909-11, recorder, 1912—; mem. Bergen Co. (N.J.) Dem. Com., 1914—; mem. exec. com., Citizens' Union, New York, 1896-98; mem. Com. of Seventy, New York, 1894; pres. Good Govt. Club, 14th Assembly Dist., 1894-97; mem. Gov. Hughes' Commn. on Speculation in Commodities and Securities, 1909; mem. N.J. Commn. on the Care of Mental Defectives, 1913; trustee People's Inst. (New York). Chairman N.Y. advisory committee on army supplies of the Chamber of Commerce U.S.A., 1917. Democrat. Pres. Mchts'. Protective Assn.; dir., chmn. com. on coml. law, Mchts'. Assn. of New York; mem. Chamber Commerce State of N.Y. Author: Morals in Modern Business, 1908; Trade Morals, 1914. Editor Sussex Register, Newton, N.J., 1917—. Home: Oakland, N.J. Died Dec. 25, 1919.

PAGE, George T., judge; b. Spring Bay, Ill., Sept. 22, 1859; s. Thaddeus Constantine Sobieska and Cordelia Ellen (Shope) P.; ed. dist. schs., Tazewell Co., Ill., and pub. and high schs., Metamora, Ill., 6 mos. at U. of Ill.; studied law in office of Page & Ellwood, Metamora, Ill.; m. Jessie S. Stevens, Sept. 7, 1887; 1 son, Gerald H. Taught sch. in country dists. while studying law; admitted to bar, 1882; went to Colo. for health, 1882, and practiced law at Denver, 1882-84, at Peoria, Ill., to 1919; judge U.S. Circuit Court of Appeals, 7th Circuit, 1919-30; retired Oct. 1, 1930; became chmn. Commercial Merchants Nat. Bank & Trust Co. Presbyn. Home: Peoria, Ill. Died Nov. 4, 1941.

PAGE, Henry, judge; b. Somerset Co., Md., June 28, 1841; ed. U. of Va., 1857-61. Admitted to bar, 1864, and practiced at Princess Anne, Md.; mem. Md. Constl. Conv., 1867, which framed present constitution; state's atty. Somerset Co., 1870-84; presdl. elector-at-large, 1888; mem. 52d Congress, 1891-93; resigned to become judge 1st Jud. Dist. of Md.; later became asso. judge Ct. of Appeals of Md. until 1909. Democrat. Home: Princess Anne, Md. Died Jan. 7, 1913.

PAGE, James Morris, educator; b. Sylvania, Va., Mar. 4, 1864; s. Thomas Walker and Nancy Watson (Morris) P.; A.M., Randolph-Macon Coll., Va., 1885; Ph.D., U. of Leipzig, 1887, with mathematics as major subject; fellow Johns Hopkins, 1895-96; LL.D., Randolph-Macon, 1909; m. Elinore Mildred McGlone, July 26, 1900; children—James Morris, Elinore Louise, Anne, Constance Morris, William Fontaine (dec.), Mann, John Cary. Taught own pvt. sch., 1887-96, Cobham, Va.; adj. prof., 1896-1900, prof. mathematics, 1900—, U. of Virginia. Was chmn. faculty (then chief exec. officer), U. of Va., June 1903-Sept. 1904; now dean same. Author: Ordinary Differential Equations, 1896. Died Mar. 18, 1936.

PAGE, John Henry, brig. gen.; b. New Castle, Del., Mar. 26, 1842; s. Capt. John (U.S.A.) and Mary Elizabeth (Blaney) P.; early edn. in Italy and France; returned to U.S., 1857; student at Northwestern U. when war broke out; m. Eliza Tracy Shaw, May 1, 1871. Served pvt. Chicago Light Arty., May-Aug. 1861; apptd. 2d lt. 3d U.S. Inf., Aug. 5, 1861; promoted through grades to col. 3d Inf., May 30, 1895; brig. gen. vols., Sept. 21-Nov. 30, 1898; brig. gen. U.S.A., July 26, 1903. Bvtd. capt., Dec. 13, 1862, "for gallant and meritorious services" in battle of Fredericksburg, Va.; maj., July 2, 1863, for same in battle of Gettysburg. Served with regt. 1st Brigade 2d Div. 5th Corps Army of the Potomac; participated in the sieges of Yorktown, Richmond, battles of Gaines' Mill, White Oak Swamp, Malvern Hill, 2d Bull Run, Antietam, Fredericksburg, Chancellorsville, Gettysburg, Siege of Petersburg, and Appomatox, after war in frontier service in Kan.; had command of inf. column on Sully Expdn. against Indians in Ind. Ty. and established, in 1868, Camp Supply; after that in various camps and stas.; comd. regt. during Coeur d'Alene mining troubles, 1893, and Coxeyite troubles on Northern Pacific; comd. regt. at Battle of El Caney and Siege of Santiago; comd. regt. 3 yrs. in Philippines, returning, 1902; retired at own request after 40 yrs.' service, July 27, 1903. Mem. Loyal Legion, G.A.R., Army and Navy Union, Soc. of Santiago. Died Oct. 9, 1916.

PAGE, Logan Waller, engineer; b. Richmond, Va., Jan. 10, 1870; s. Legh R. and Page (Waller) P.; ed. Powder Point Sch., Bear Island Acad., Va. Poly. Inst. and Harvard; m. Anne P. Shaler, Oct. 17, 1903. Geologist Mass. Highway Commn. and dir. testing lab., Lawrence Scientific Sch. (Harvard), 1893-1900; chief Div. of Tests, Dept. Agr., 1900-05; dir. U.S. Office of Pub. Roads, 1905—. Author: The Testing of Road Materials, 1901; Roads, Paths and Bridges. Home: Washington, D.C. Died Dec. 9, 1918.

PAGE, Marie Danforth, painter; b. Boston; d. John Nourse and Hannah Maria (Rhodes) Danforth; ed. Gannett Inst. and Sch. of Mus. of Fine Arts; hon. M.A., Tufts Coll., 1933; m. Dr. Calvin Gates Page, June 10, 1896; children—Margaret Davenport, Susan Davenport. Was awarded bronze medal, Panama P.I. Expn., 1915; Julia A. Shaw prize, National Acad. of Design, 1916; Philadelphia prize, 1916; Richard S. Greenough Memorial prize, Newport Art Assn., 1919; Isador medal, Nat. Acad. Design, 1923; bronze medal, Phila. Sesquicentennial; Harold Swift prize, Grand Central Galleries; prize, Springfield Art Assn., Duxbury Art Assn. Awarded Thomas A. Proctor prize, Nat. Acad. Design, 1928. A.N.A., 1927. Episcopalian. Home: Boston, Mass. Died Mar. 3, 1940.

PAGE, Richard Lucian, naval officer; b. Fairfield, Va., Dec. 20, 1807; s. William Byrd and Anne (Lee) P.; ed. Clarke Co. and Alexandria, Va.; m. Alexina, d. Richard and Elizabeth (Calvert) Taylor. Entered U.S.N., 1824; served until outbreak of Civil war; resigned; became brig. gen. C.S.A. Took part in fight at Port Royal; was in command Ft. Morgan in Mobile Bay, when, after gallant defense, it finally fell. At close of war retired to civil life. Vestryman and senior warden Christ P.E. Ch. Home: Norfolk, Va. Died 1901.

PAGE, Robert Newton congressman; b. Cary, N.C., Oct. 26, 1859; s. Allison Francis and Kate (Raboteau) P.; ed. Cary High Sch. and Bingham Sch., N.C.; m. Flora Shaw, June 20, 1888. Lumber mfr., 1880-1900; treas. Aberdeen & Asheboro R.R. Co., 1890-1902; pres. Citizens Bank and Trust Co. (Southern Pines); pres. Page Trust Co., Jan. 1927—; mem. 58th to 64th Congresses (1903-17), 7th N.C. Dist. Democrat. Home: Aberdeen, N.C. Died Oct. 3, 1933.

PAGE, S(amuel) Davis, lawyer; b. Phila., Pa., Sept. 22, 1840; s. William Byrd (M.D.) and Celestine Anna (Davis) P.; A.B., with honor, Yale, 1859, studied law at U. of Pa. and Harvard; m. Isabella Wurts, Sept. 25, 1861. Practiced in Phila., 1864—; mem. Page & Page. Mem. City Council, Phila., 1877-81, 1882-83 (resigned); Dem. candidate for city treas., 1879, 82; city controller, 1883-84; asst. treas. of U.S. at Phila., 1886-90; mem. commn. apptd. by Gov. Pattison to investigate accounts of John Bardsley, city treas., with Keystone Nat. Bank. Episcopalian. Home: Philadelphia, Pa. Died Oct. 11, 1921.

PAGE, Thomas Nelson, former Am. ambassador to Italy, author; b. Oakland Plantation, Hanover County, Va., Apr. 23, 1853; s. of Maj. John and Elizabeth Burwell (Nelson) P.; ed. Washington and Lee U., 3 sessions; LL.B., U. of Va., 1874; (Litt.D., Washington and Lee, 1887, Yale Univ., 1901, and Harvard Univ., 1913; LL.D., Tulane Univ., 1899, William and Mary College, 1906; Washington and Lee, 1907); m. Anne Seddon Bruce, 1886 (died 1888); m. 2d, Florence Lathrop Field, widow of Henry Field, of Chicago, 1893 (died 1921). Practiced law, Richmond, Va., 1875-93; lecturer. Member Am. Acad. Arts and Letters. Author: In Ole Virginia, 1887; Two Little Confederates, 1888; On Newfound River, 1891, 1906; The Old South, 1891; Among the Camps, 1891; Elsket and Other Stories, 1892; Befo' de War (with Armistead C. Gordon); Pastime Stories, 1894; The Burial of the Guns, 1894; Unc' Edinburg; Meh Lady; Marse Chan; Polly; Social Life in Old Virginia; The Old Gentleman of the Black Stock, 1896 (revised edit., 1901); Two Prisoners, 1897; Red Rock, 1898; Santa Claus's Partner, 1899; A Captured Santa Claus, 1902; Gordon Keith, 1903; The Negro—The Southerner's Problem, 1904; Bred in the Bone, 1905; The Coast of Bohemia (poems), 1906; Under the Crust, 1907; The Old Dominion—Her Making and Her Manners, 1908; Robert E. Lee, The Southerner, 1908; Tommy Trot's Visit to Santa Claus, 1908; John Marvel, Assistant, 1909; Robert E. Lee, Man and Soldier, 1912; The Land of the Spirit, 1913; Life of Thomas Jefferson (in Italian), 1918; Italy and the World War, 1920. Ambassador extraordinary and plenipotentiary to Italy, June 21, 1913-Aug. 1919. Grand Cordone SS. Maurizio and Lazzaro (Italy), 1921. Home: Washington, D.C. Died Nov. 1, 1922.

PAGE, Thomas Walker, economist; b. Cobham, Va., Dec. 4, 1866; s. Thomas Walker and Nancy Watson (Morris) P.; Randolph-Macon College, 1884-86; U. of Va., 1889; U. of Leipzig, 1893-96, Ph.D., 1896; univs. of Oxford and Paris, 1896-97; m. Celeste Alspaugh, Aug. 8, 1900; children—Thomas Walker, Celeste Walker, Rose Walker. Dean, Coll. of Commerce, U. of Calif., 1900-02; head of dept. economics, U. of Tex., 1903-04; prof. history and economics, U. of Calif., 1904-06; prof. economics, U. of Virginia, 1906-11; mem. U.S. Tariff Board, 1911-12; spl. tax commr. Va., 1914-15; mem. U.S. Tariff Commn., 1918-22, chmn. 1920-22, vice chmn., 1930—. Mem. Dist. Electoral Bd., 1914-18; mem. several war coms., 1917-18; mem. exec. com. Am. Econ. Assn. (v.p. 1922); pres. Nat. Tax Assn., 1924-25; mem. Inst. Economics, Am. Hist. Assn. Episcopalian. Democrat. Mem. editorial bd. Am. Economic Review, 1918-20. Died Jan. 13, 1937.

PAGE, Walter Gilman, artist; b. Boston, Mass., Oct. 13, 1862; s. Charles Jewett and Kate Chase (Norcross) P.; ed. pvt. schs. and Boston Latin Sch.; studied art at Mus. Fine Arts, Boston, and Paris, 1885-89; m. Harriette L. Wolever, Jan. 1, 1904. Exhibited Paris Salon, 1887, 88, 89; also prin. exhbns. in U.S.; portraits in Mass. and Vt. capitols, City Hall, Portland, Me., Colby Coll., Tufts Coll., etc. Mass. commr. to Buffalo Expn., 1901; an organizer Pub. Sch. Art League; mem. Boston School Bd., 1894-97; chmn. Mass. State Art Commn.; charter mem. Soc. Preservation N.E. Antiquities; sec. Mass. Soc. Founders and Patriots, 1921; chmn. Boston Commn. on Hist. Sites; pres. Alumni Sch. Museum of Fine Arts, Boston, 1924-25. Author: Interior Decoration of School-houses. Republican. Unitarian. Studio: Nantucket, Mass. Died Mar. 24, 1934.

PAGE, Walter Hines, ambassador, editor; b. Cary, N.C., Aug. 15, 1855; s. Allison F. and Catherine (Raboteau) P.; student Randolph-Macon Coll., Va., 1872-76; fellow Johns Hopkins, 1876-78; (LL.D., Randolph-Macon, and univs. of Cambridge and Aberdeen; D.C.L., Oxon, and Edinburgh); m. Alice, d. Dr. William Wilson, of Mich., 1880. Editor St. Joseph (Mo.) Daily Gazette, 1880-81; on staff New York World, 1882; founder, and editor State Chronicle, Raleigh, N.C., 1882-83; on staff New York Evening Post, 1883-87; mgr. The Forum, 1887-90 and editor, 1890-95; lit. adviser Houghton, Mifflin & Co., 1895-99; editor of The Atlantic Monthly, 1896-99.

The World's Work, 1900-13; ambassador extraordinary and plenipotentiary to Great Britain, 1913—. Mem. Doubleday, Page & Co., publishers, 1899—. Mem. Gen. Fund. Bd., Internat. Health Bd. Author: The Rebuilding of Old Commonwealths, 1902. Home: Garden City, L.I., N.Y. Died Dec. 22, 1918.

PAGE, William Nelson, civil and mining engr.; b. Campbell Co., Va., Jan. 6, 1854; s. Edwin Randolph and Olivia (Alexander) P.; prep. edn., Leesburg (Va.) Acad.; spl. course in engring., U. of Va.; m. Emma Hayden Gilham, Feb. 9, 1882; children—Delia Hayden, Edwin Randolph, Mary Josephine, Randolph Gilham. Rodman on location and constrn. C.&O. Ry., New River Cañon, 1871-72; located and built Mill Creek Cañon br. ry., 1874; in charge of party locating double track ry., ordered by Congress, from the Ohio River to Hampton Roads, Va., 1875-76; gen. manager Hawk's Nest Coal Co., 1877-80; built and operated Victoria Blast Furnace, Goshen, Va., 1880-85; located and built Powellton br. of C.&O. Ry., 1885-89, and developed Mt. Carbon Collieries; organized and developed the Gauley Mountain Coal Co., 1889-1917, and now consulting engr. same; built the Deepwater, Tidewater, and Virginian rys.; was consulting coal engr. for Amalgamated Copper Co. and many other cos. Mem. W.Va. N.G. 20 yrs., advancing to brig. insp. gen. Mayor of Ansted, W.Va., 10 yrs. An incorporator and dir. Sheltering Arms Hosp. Chief of Internat. Jury of Awards, Mines and Metallurgy, St. Louis Expn., 1904. Episcopalian. Mason. Home: Washington, D.C. Died Mar. 7, 1932.

PAHLOW, Gertrude Curtis Brown, author; b. Reading, Mass.; d. Charles Freeman and Elizabeth Anna (Harrison) Brown; ed. in Reading, Boston and abroad; m. Edwin William Pahlow, June 14, 1905; children—Hugh, Gertrude. Author: The Gilded Chrysalis, 1914; The Cross of Heart's Desire, 1916; The Glory of Going On, 1919; Murder in the Morning, 1931; Honeymoon Trail, 1931; The Bright Torch, 1933; Hermitage Island, 1934; Cabin in the Pines, 1935. Home: Columbus, O. Died Jan. 29, 1937.

PAIGE, Calvin D., congressman; b. Southbridge, Mass., May 20, 1848; s. Calvin A. and Mercy (Dresser) P.; ed. pub. schs. and Southbridge High Sch.; m. Ida Francis Edwards, Oct. 1873. Pres. Central Mills Co. (cotton), Southbridge Savings Bank. Served as selectman, Southbridge; mem. Mass. Ho. of Rep. and mem. Gov.'s Council; Rep. presdl. elector, 1904; was mem. Rep. State Com.; mem. 63d to 68th Congresses (1913-25), 3rd Mass. Dist. Pres. Quinabaug Hist. Society. Mem. Joint Commn. on Postal Service. Home: Southbridge, Mass. Died Apr. 25, 1930.

PAIGE, Hildegard Brooks, author; b. Dresden, Germany, Feb. 8, 1875; d. Maj. Thomas Benton and Hannah (Hulse) Brooks; sister of Alfred Hulse Brooks; B.S., Swarthmore Coll., 1895; m. Sidney Paige, Mar. 20, 1909. Author: Without a Warrant, 1901; The Master of Caxton, 1902; Daughters of Desperation, 1903; The Larky Furnace, 1906. Died June 15, 1920.

PAINE, Albert Bigelow, author, editor; b. New Bedford, Mass., July 10, 1861; s. Samuel E. and Mercy C. P.; ed. pub. schs., Xenia, Ill. Editor League dept. St. Nicholas Magazine, 1899-1909. Lit. executor of Mark Twain. Mem. National Inst. of Arts and Letters. Author: Rhymes by Two Friends (with William Allen White), 1893; The Hollow Tree, 1898; The Arkansaw Bear, 1898; The Little Lady, Her Book, 1901; The Hollow Tree and Deep Woods Book, 1901; The Wanderings of Joe and Little Em, 1903; The Commuters, 1904; Thomas Nast—His Period and His Pictures, 1904; A Little Garden Calendar, 1905; The Tent Dwellers, 1908; Captain Bill McDonald, Texas Ranger, 1909; Elsie and the Arkansaw Bear, 1909; The Hollow Tree Snowed-In Book, 1910; Mark Twain, A Biography, 1912; Hollow Tree Nights and Days, 1916; The Boy's Life of Mark Twain, 1916; Mark Twain's Letters, 1917; Dwellers in Arcady, 1919; A Short Life of Mark Twain, 1920; The Car That Went Abroad, 1921; In One Man's Life, 1921; Single Reels, 1923; Joan of Arc—Maid of France, 1925; The Girl in White Armor, 1927; Jan, the Romantic, 1929; Life and Lillian Gish, 1932; Golden Cat, 1934; Mark Twain's Notebook, 1935. Decorated Chevalier Legion of Honor (France), 1928. Home: West Redding. Died Apr. 9, 1937.

PAINE, Albert Ware, lawyer; b. Winslow, Me., Aug. 16, 1812; s. Frederic and Abiel (Ware) P.; A.B., Waterville (now Colby) Coll., 1832; studied law 3 yrs. and admitted to bar, at Bangor, Me., 1835, where has ever since practiced; m. Mary Jones Hale, July 9, 1840 (died 1901). Was the only press corr. in the Aroostook war, 1830, his letters having been widely copied; originated depts. of banking and ins. and was ins. commr. of Me., 1868-73, bank commr., 1873; tax commr., 1874; mem. Gen. Ins. Conv. of U.S., 1871. Pres. Me. Telegraph Co., 25 yrs.; treas. Mt. Hope Cemetery Corp., 50 yrs.; dir. Bangor Savings Bank, since its organization, 1852. Republican. Author: Paine Genealogy, Ipswich Branch, 1881; The New Philosophy, 1884; The Territorial History of Bangor and Vicinity, 1887; History of Mt. Hope Cemetery, Bangor, 1907. Home: Bangor, Me. Died 1907.

PAINE, Charles, gen. mgr. Panama R.R., May 1899—; b. Haverhill, N.H., Apr. 25, 1830; s. George and Martha O. (Porter) P.; ed. at various schools until 14 yrs. old; after that self-taught; m. Olivia B. Hebard, May 1851. On Vt. Central R.R., 1845; Vt. & Canada R.R., 1850; surveys in Wis., 1856; supt. Mich. Southern and Northern Ind., 1858; chief engr., 1864-72; gen. supt., 1872-81, Lake Shore & Mich. Southern R.R.; gen. mgr. West Shore R.R., 1881-84; gen. supt. N.Y.,Pa.&O. R.R., and v.p. N.Y., Lake Erie & Western R.R., 1885; in charge of several Pittsburgh industries, 1886; from 1891 consulting engr. New York. Author: Elements of Railroading. Home: Tenafly, N.J. Died 1906.

PAINE, Charles Jackson, soldier; b. Boston, Aug. 26, 1833; s. Charles Cushing and Fannie Cabot (Jackson) P.; brother of Robert Treat P.; g.g.s. Robert Treat P. (signer Declaration of Independence); A.B., Harvard, 1853, A.M., 1858; admitted to Mass. bar, 1856; m. Julia, d. John Bryant, of Boston, 1867. Capt. 22d Mass. Inf., Oct. 5, 1861; maj. 30th Mass. Inf., Jan. 16, 1862; col. 2d La. Inf., Oct. 23, 1862; brig. gen. vols., July 4, 1864; bvtd. maj. gen. vols., Jan. 15, 1865, "for meritorious and valuable services"; hon. mustered out, Jan. 15, 1866; comd. brigade during siege of Pt. Hudson, 1863; served under Gen. B. F. Butler, 1864; led div. colored troops in attack on Newmarket, Va., Sept. 29, 1864; after Lee's surrender comd. dist. of Newbern. For many yrs. dir. C.,B.&Q. R.R., A.,T.&S.F. R.R. and Mexican Central R.R. Was one of the three spl. envoys accredited to the govts. of France, Great Britain, and Germany in the interests of internat. bimetallism, 1897. Mem. Corp., Mass. Inst. Tech. Prominent yachtsman; owned Puritan, Mayflower and Volunteer, all successful defenders of America's cup. Home: Weston, Mass., and Boston. Died Aug. 12, 1916.

PAINE, Francis Brinley Hebard, electrical engr.; b. Chicago, Apr. 12, 1869; s. Charles and Olivia B. (Hebard) P.; m. Julia Wood Miller, May 2, 1900. Labs. of Westinghouse Electric & Mfg. Co., Pittsburgh, 1889-91; mem. Charles Paine & Sons, cons. engrs., New York, 1891-93; mgr. and engr. Westinghouse Electric & Mfg. Co., Boston, New York, and for 2 yrs. in the Orient, 1893-1906; gen. mgr. constrn. Ontario Power Co., 1906-13, Niagara, Lockport & Ontario Power Co., 1906-13; cons. engr., 1913—. Episcopalian. Fellow Am. Inst. E.E. Home: New York, N.Y. Died Sept. 16, 1917.

PAINE, Francis Ward, mining engr.; b. Boston, Mass., Aug. 1, 1888; s. William Alfred and Ruth Felton (Ward) P.; grad. Hill Sch., Pottstown, Pa., 1906; B.A., Yale, 1910; M.A., U. of Wis., 1911; m. Frances Joyce Hatch, Jan. 5, 1929. Prof. mining geology, Mich. Coll. of Mines, 1911-12; mem. Paine, Webber & Co., brokers and investment bankers, Boston, 1919—; treas. Copper Range Co.; dir. New River Co., Midland Steel Products Co., Maine Gas Co. President Free Hosp. for Women. Conglist. Home: Chestnut Hill, Mass. Died Aug. 22, 1940.

PAINE, Halbert Eleazer, lawyer; b. Chardon, O., Feb. 4, 1826; grad. Western Reserve Coll., 1845 (A.M.; LL.D.). Served in Union army through Civil war, becoming brig. gen. and bvt. maj. gen. U.S. vols. Mem. Congress from Milwaukee dist., 1865-71. Practiced law in Milwaukee. Apptd. commr. of patents, 1888, to succeed Ellis Spear. Author: Paine on Elections, 1888. Home: Washington, D.C. Died 1905.

PAINE, Harriet Eliza ("Eliza Chester"), author; b. Rehoboth, Mass., May 5, 1845; d. Rev. John Chester and Eliza (Folger) P.; grad. Wheaton Sem., Norton, Mass., 1862; studied German and French abroad; unmarried. Taught in Wheaton Sem., and in pvt. schs., Boston; prin. Robinson Sem., Exeter, N.H., 1875-78. Author: Bird Songs of New England, 1882; Girls and Women, 1890; Chats with Girls on Self-Culture, 1891; The Unmarried Woman, 1892. Editor: Life of Eliza Baylies Wheaton, 1907. Home: Groveland, Mass. Died 1910.

PAINE, Henry Gallup, agent for authors; b. Albany, New York, Apr. 24, 1859; s. Henry Delavan and Lucy (Gallup) Paine; A.B. from Columbia University, 1880; m. Frances B. Martin, June 4, 1889; children—Ethel, Mrs. Frances P. Park; m. 2d, Ann Miller, June 28, 1913. Founder Columbia Spectator, 1877; editorial asst. St. Nicholas, 1882-87; associate editor Puck, 1887-93; mng. editor Harper's Weekly, 1893-1900; editorial staff New York Daily News, 1901-03; asso. editor Associated Sunday Magazines, 1903; editor New York Tribune Lit. Review, 1904-07; editor Nat. Sunday Magazine, 1911-13; sec. Simplified Spelling Board, 1915-21, treas. 1921—; editor Authors' League Bulletin, 1923-27. Author: Handbook of Simplified Spelling, 1920; The Little Minute Man, 1924. Home: New York, N.Y. Died May 30, 1929.

PAINE, Horace Marshfield, physician; b. Paris, N.Y., Nov. 19, 1827; academic edn. (A.M., Hamilton Coll., 1859); grad. med. dept. Univ. of City of New York, 1849 (hon. M.D., Univ. of State of N.Y., 1882); m. Charlotte, d. Salmon Mann, of Norfolk, Mass., 1852. Mem. eight yrs. bd. mgrs. Middletown, N.Y., and Gowanda, N.Y., State Homœ. Hosp. for the Insane; mem., 1850—, and sec., 1861-73, N.Y. State Homœ. Med. Soc.; mem., 1850—, Am. Inst. Homœopathy; 21 yrs. mem. N.Y. State Bd. Homœ. Med. Examiners. Has devoted yrs. of effort to promote legislation extending equal civil rights and privileges to representatives of all recognized med. schools, and to elevate and unify med. ednl. standards through State control of med. licensure. Author: Laws of the State of New York Regulating the Practice of Medicine, 1860. Home: Atlanta, Ga. Died 1903.

PAINE, John Alsop, Oriental and classical archeologist; b. Newark, N.J., Jan. 14, 1840; s. Dr. John Alsop and Amanda (Kellogg) P.; A.B., Hamilton, 1859, A.M., 1862, Ph.D., 1874; grad. Andover Theol. Sem., 1862; Sheffield Scientific Sch. (Yale), and Sch. Mines, Columbia, 1866-67; univs. of Leipzig, and Halle, 1869, 1870. Ordained, 1867; engaged by bd. of regents to enlarge flora of State of N.Y., 1862-67; prof. natural science, Robert Coll., Constantinople, 1867-69; prof. natural history and German, Lake Forest (Ill.) U., 1870-71; Coll. Phys. and Surgeons, and asso. editor The Independent, 1871-72; archeologist for 1st expdn. of Palestine Exploration Soc. east of the Jordan and Dead Sea, 1872-74; edited and published Journal of Christian Philosophy, 1882-84; staff of the Century Dictionary, 1887, 1888; curator Met. Mus. of Art, New York, 1889-1906. Author: Catalogue of Plants Found in Oneida County and Vicinity, 1865; Fifth Statement, Containing "Identification of Mount Pisgah," 1875 (Palestine Exploration Soc.); Handbook of Sculptural Plaster Casts and Bronze Reproductions in the Metropolitan Museum of Art. Researches in the archeology of Chaldea, Asia Minor, Syria, Palestine, and Egypt, in the history and antiquities of unsuccessful attempts made in the Sixteenth Century to colonize the eastern coast of N. America, in the chemistry and radio-activity of rare elements. Home: Tarrytown, N.Y. Died July 24, 1912.

PAINE, John Knowles, prof. of music, Harvard, 1875—; b. Portland, Me., Jan. 9, 1839; s. Jacob S. and Rebecca Beebe (Downes) P.; studied music under Hermann Kotzschmar there; made 1st appearance as organist, 1857; studied in Germany under Haupt and others, 1858-61; made artistic tour there, 1866-67; instr. of music, Harvard, 1862-73; (A.M., Mus.D.). Composer of music to "Œdipus Tyrannus" of Sophocles as performed in Greek at Cambridge, 1881; Spring symphony; symphony in C minor; symphonic poems; Shakespeare's Tempest; Island Fantasy, Overture to As You Like It; cantatas, Nativity and Song of Promise, choruses to Birds of Aristophanes; etc.; opera of Azara; "Centennial Hymn" to Whittier's words, sung at opening Phila. Expn., 1876; Columbus march and hymn for World's Columbian Expn., 1892; Hymn of the West, words by Stedman, sung at the opening of the St. Louis Expn., 1904; also mass, oratorio of St. Peter; cantatas, Realm of Fancy and Phoebus Arise; etc. Home: Cambridge, Mass. Died 1906.

PAINE, Nathaniel, banker; b. Worcester, Mass., Aug. 6, 1832; s. Gardiner and Emily (Baker) P.; ed. pub. schs., Worcester; (hon. A.M., Harvard, 1898); m. Susan M. Barnes, June 14, 1865. First teller Mechanics Bank of Worcester, 1848; teller City Bank, 1854, cashier, 1857, pres., 1898—; v.p. Worcester Trust Co., Worcester Five Cent Savings Bank. Mem. City Council 2 yrs.; dir. Free Pub. Library 18 yrs. Mem. council Mass. Hist. Soc.; treas. Worcester Co. Hort. Soc. 26 yrs., Am. Antiq. Soc. 44 yrs. Republican. Unitarian. Author: Early Paper Currency of Massachusetts; Early American Imprints; Random Recollections of Worcester; Early American Broadsides. Editor: Christopher Columbus Diary, etc. Home: Worcester, Mass. Died Jan. 14, 1917.

PAINE, Ralph Delahaye, author; b. Lemont, Ill., Aug. 28, 1871; s. Samuel Delahaye and Elizabeth Brown (Philbrook) P.; A.B., Yale, 1894; M.A., U. of New Hampshire, 1920; m. Katharine Lansing Morse, Apr. 5, 1903. Joined staff Philadelphia Press, 1894, and was war corr. during Cuban Rebellion, Spanish-Am. War and Boxer uprising in China, and spl. corr. in Eng., 1901 and 1903; with New York Herald in charge of crusade against beef trust, 1902; asso. editor Outing Magazine, 1906. With Allied Naval Forces in war zone, 1917-18. Federal fuel administrator, 1918; mem. N.H. Legislature, 1919, N.H. State Bd. Edn., 1919-21. Democrat. Author: The Stroke Oar, 1908; College Years, 1909; The Ships and Sailors of Old Salem, 1909; The Head Coach, 1910; The Fugitive Freshman, 1910; A Cadet of the Black Star Line, 1910; Sandy Sawyer, Sophomore, 1911; The Wrecking Master, 1911; The Book of Buried Treasure, 1911; The Careless Sophomore (play), 1911; Campus Days, 1912; The Dragon and the Cross, 1912; The Judgments of the Sea, 1912; The Steam Shovel Man, 1913; The Adventures of Captain O'Shea, 1913; The Wall Between, 1914; The Twisted Skein, 1915; The Long Road Home, 1916; Sons of Eli, 1917; The Fighting Fleets, 1918; The Call of the Offshore Wind, 1918; The Old Merchant Marine, 1919; The Corsair in the War Zone, 1920; The Fight for a Free Sea, 1920; Ships Across the Sea, 1920; Lost Ships and Lonely Seas, 1921; First Down, Kentucky!, 1921; Comrades of the Rolling Ocean, 1923; Roads of Adventure, 1922; Blackbeard-Buccaneer, 1922; Privateers of '76, 1923. Home: Durham, N.H. Died Apr. 29, 1925.

PAINE, Robert Findlay, newspaperman; b. Cleveland, O., Mar. 8, 1856; common sch. edn.; m. Wanda Pole; children—Harriet Eva, Edith Lily, Robert Findlay. Reporter, 1879-82, editor, 1882-1902, Cleveland Press; gen. mgr. Scripps-McRae Press Assn., 1897-1905; editorial sec. Scripps papers; chief editorial writer Newspaper Enterprise Assn.; formerly mgr. Pacific Coast Service, later mgr. Paine Service; retired, Oct. 31, 1929. Home: San Francisco, Calif. Died Aug. 29, 1940.

PAINE, Robert Treat, philanthropist; b. Boston, Mass., Oct. 28, 1835; g.g.s. Robert Treat P. (signer Declaration of Independence); s. Charles Cushing and Fannie Cabot (Jackson) P.; bro. of Charles Jackson P.; A.B., Harvard, 1855, A.M., 1856; m. Lydia Williams Lyman, Apr. 24, 1862 (died 1897). Admitted to bar, 1859; practiced until 1870; then retired. Mem. Mass. Ho. of Rep., 1884; Dem. and Independent nominee for 49th Congress, 1884. Organized, 1879, and pres., 1879—, Wells Memorial Workingmen's Inst.; pres. Workingmen's Coöperative Bank, 1886-1903; pres., 1878-1907, hon. v.p., 1907—, Associated Charities of Boston; pres. Workingmen's Bldg. Assn., Workingmen's Loan Assn., bd. trustees Episcopal Theol. Sch., People's Inst., Am. Peace Soc., 1891—; v.p. Boston Children's Aid Soc., Industrial Aid Soc., N.E. Watch and Ward Soc.; with his wife, created and endowed with $200,000 a trust for charitable purposes, 1890, named The Robert Treat Paine Assn. Died 1910.

PAINE, William Alfred, banker; b. Merrimacport, Mass., Jan. 29, 1855; s. Rev. Albert and Sarah (Sargent) P.; ed. grammar and high schs., Mass., Wis. and Ill.; m. Ruth F. Ward, Apr. 18, 1887; children—Francis Ward, Ruth Sargent (Mrs. John H. Blodgett), Esther Humphrey (Mrs. Morris F. LaCroix), Stephen, Dorothy Bowen (Mrs. David A. Brayton). Clerk in Blackstone Nat. Bank, Boston, 1873-80; founder, 1880, becoming head, Paine, Webber & Co., Boston; organized, 1898, and pres., Copper Range Co. Republican. Home: Boston, Mass. Died Sept. 24, 1929.

PAINE, Willis Seaver, banker; b. Rochester, N.Y., Jan. 1, 1848; s. Col. Nicholas E. and Abby M. (Sprague) P.; grad. Rochester Collegiate Inst. (valedictorian), 1864; student, Williams Coll.; A.B. (with honors), U. of Rochester, 1868; LL.D., Manhattan Coll., 1886, George Washington U., 1908; m. Ruby S., d. Henry A. Tilden, Apr. 6, 1888 (died 1896); m. 2d, Virginia C., d. Eliphalet S. Brown, July 18, 1900. Studied law in office of Sanford E. Church and admitted to bar 1869; apptd., 1874, one of trust company examiners of State of N.Y. with result of closing three cos. in N.Y. City whose debts to depositors aggregated over $6,000,000; reapptd., 1875, receiver of Bond St. (formerly Atlantic) Savings Bank, 1876, whose failure was, with three exceptions, largest of its kind in the U.S. (succeeded in paying gen. creditors 86 per cent and the preferred creditors in full); at the end of the trust, received the thanks of Court and also was presented with engrossed complimentary resolutions by permanent com. of depositors. Apptd. by Gov. Cornell, with William Dowd, 1880, commr. to compile and revise banking laws of N.Y., which revision was enacted 1882, and received for same in 1883 thanks by N.Y. legislature (commrs. serving without pay); supt. Banking Dept. State of N.Y., 1885-89, resigning to become pres. The State Trust Co.; resigned to travel around the world; declined position of subtreasurer at New York, tendered by President Cleveland, 1885; was pres. The Trust Co. of New York and Merchants Safe Deposit Co.; was chmn. finance com. Tradesmen's Nat. Bank and pres. Consolidated Nat. Bank of N.Y. City; resigned and made second tour around the world; now v.p. U.S. Fire Ins. Co.; trustee Met. Savings Bank, etc. An organizer trust co. sect. Am. Bankers Assn., also of savings bank sect. and mem. exec. com.; apptd. by Gov. Whitman mem. Mohansic Lake Reservation Com. (pres.) and reapptd. by Govs. Smith and Miller and continued as pres. Col. on staff of Gov. Flower. Elected alumnus Williams Coll., 1922; hon. mem. Rochester Union Grays. Author: Paine's New York Banking Laws (7 edits.); Paine's National Banking Laws (7 edits.); Paine's Building and Loan Association; Summary of Failed Savings Banks (2 edits.); Paine's Analysis of the Federal Reserve Act. Home: New York, N.Y. Died Apr. 13, 1927.

PAINTER, Franklin Verzelius Newton, coll. prof.; b. Hampshire Co., Va., Apr. 12, 1852; s. Israel and Juliana (Wilson) P.; A.B., Roanoke Coll. (with 1st honor of class and a gold medal for proficiency in metaphysics), 1874, A.M., 1877; grad. Theol. Sem., Salem, Va., 1878; studied at Paris and Bonn, 1882; D.D., Pa. Coll., 1895; Litt.D., Susquehanna U., 1908; m. Laura Trimble Shickel, Aug. 9, 1875; children—Julia Elizabeth (Mrs. A. H. Throckmorton), Margaret Verzelia (Mrs. Thomas E. King), Elizabeth Trimble (Mrs. H. W. A. Hanson), Theophilus Shickel, Laura Holland (Mrs. Harold C. George), Ruth Elaine (Mrs. J. G. Randall). Ordained Gospel ministry, 1878; instr., 1878-82, prof. modern langs., 1882-1906, prof. education, 1906—, Roanoke Coll. Established Va. Teachers' Reading Assn., 1885. First pres. Greater Salem Club, 1919. Retired from ministry and teaching, 1921. Author: A History of Education, 1886; History of Christian Worship (with Prof. J. W. Richard), 1891; Introduction to English Literature, 1894; Introduction to American Literature, 1897; A History of English Literature, 1900; The Reformation Dawn, 1901; Poets of the South, 1903; Elementary Guide to Literary Criticism, 1903; Poets of Virginia, 1907; Introduction to Bible Study, 1911. Home: Marion, Va. Died Jan. 18, 1931.

PAINTER, Henry McMahon, M.D.; b. West Haven, Conn., July 12, 1863; s. Henry Wheeler and Abigail (Kitching) P.; A.B., Yale, 1884, B.S., 1885; M.D., Coll. Phys. and Surg. (Columbia), 1888; m. Carrie Stevens, June 30, 1891; children—Sidney, Thomas; m. 2d, Loraine Wyman, July 14, 1926. In practice, New York, 1888—; prof. clin. obstetrics, Coll. Phys. and Surg., 1905—; consulting obstetrician, Sloane Hosp. for Women. Republican. Conglist. Home: New York, N.Y. Died Mar. 11, 1934.

PALEN, Frederick Pomeroy, ship building; b. Jenningsville, Pa., Apr. 20, 1872; s. Peter E. and Rachel J. (Young) P.; desc. Gylbert Palen, from Holland about 1680 and settled near Kingston on Hudson; M.E., Cornell U., 1894; m. Lina Livingston Mayo, Oct. 18, 1906; 1 son, Frederick Pomeroy. Began as draftsman Newport News Shipbuilding & Dry Dock Co., 1894, chief draftsman, 1899-1904, asst. chief engr., 1906-12, assistant gen. mgr., 1912-15, v.p., 1915-29; retired. Republican. Episcopalian. Home: New York, N.Y. Died Dec. 2, 1933.

PALEN, Rufus James, banker; b. Hudson, N.Y., Jan. 13, 1843; s. Joseph Gilbert and Caroline Anne (Little) P.; U. of Mich., 1861-62 (left sch. to enter Union Army); 2d lt. Co. G, 128th N.Y. Vols., Aug. 1862-Aug. 1863; maj. 78th U.S.C.T., Aug. 1862-Jan. 1866; m. Ellen Seager Webbe, Sept. 17, 1878. Began as asst. cashier, 1878, later cashier, pres., 1894, 1st Nat. Bank, Santa Fé, N.M.; clk. Sup. and 1st Jud. Dist. cts., Ty. of N.M., 1873-77; treas. Ty. of N.M., 1891-95 and Oct. 1911-Jan. 15, 1912; mem. Capitol Bldg. Bd., Capitol Rebldg. Bd. and Capitol Extension Bd.; mem. Bd. of Equalization, Ty. of N.M., 2 yrs.; trustee N.M. Asylum for Deaf and Dumb 11 yrs. Republican. Episcopalian. Home: Santa Fé, N.M. Died Mar. 14, 1916.

PALLEN, Condé Benoist, editor, author; b. St. Louis, Mo., Dec. 5, 1858; s. Montrose A. and Anne E. (Benoist) P.; A.B., Georgetown U., 1880, A.M., 1883, LL.D., 1896; Ph.D., St. Louis U., 1885; m. Georgiana McDougal Adams, Feb. 18, 1886; children—Charles McDougal, Condé DeSales, Esther Janet, Georgiana A., Louis B., Anne E., Emma Mary, Frances Josephine, Louise B., Thomas A., Montrose B. (dec.). Editor Church Progress and Catholic World, 1887-97; lecturer on lit. subjects, 1885—. Read papers on Am. Catholic literature at Catholic Congress, Baltimore, 1889; delivered Ode on Centenary of Georgetown U., 1889. Contbr. on philos. and lit. subjects to Catholic publs. Catholic revisory editor New Internat. Encyclopædia, Ency. Americana; mng. editor Catholic Encyclopedia, 1904-20. Pres. Encyclopædia Press, Inc., pubs. Catholic Ency., 1912-20; pres. Associate Arts Corp. Author: The Philosophy of Literature, 1897; Epochs of Literature, 1898; What Is Liberalism?, 1899; New Rubaiyat (poems), 1899; The Feast of Thalarchus (dramatic poem), 1901; The Death of Sir Launcelot, and Other Poems, 1902; The Meaning of the Idylls of the King, 1904; Collected Poems, 1915; Education of Boys, 1916; Crucible Island, 1919; As Man to Man, 1927. Editor of Universal Knowledge Foundation. Died May 26, 1929.

PALLISER, Melvin G., lawyer; b. Newark, N.J., July 2, 1873; s. George and Letitia (Bird) P.; prep. edn., pvt. schs.; student New York Law Sch., 1893-96; m. Frances Jeannette Dorland, July 28, 1897; 1 dau., Margaret (Mrs. Miner Worthington Tuttle). Admitted to N.Y. bar, 1896, and began practice at N.Y. City; pres. Franjean Realty Co., Midhampton Realty Co.; dir. Dayton Malleable Iron Co., Pratt & Letchworth, Triest Contracting Corp., etc. Mem. Dem. State Com., N.Y., 1916-20. Episcopalian. Home: New York, N.Y. Died July 5, 1940.

PALMA, Tomas Estrada, Cuban patriot; b. Bayamo, Cuba; studied law at Univ. of Seville, but never practiced. Took part in the Cuban revolution of 1868-78, in the early part of which his mother had been captured and starved to death by the Spaniards. Her death made him heir to a vast estate, which the Spaniards confiscated. He became pres. Cuban Republic, but was captured, 1877, and imprisoned until hostilities ceased, 1878; then went to Honduras; became teacher and later postmaster-gen.; married a d. of Pres. Guardiola. Came to the U.S.; settled in Central Valley, Orange Co., N.Y. During last revolution delegate-at-large and minister plenipotentiary for Cuban Republic. President of Cuba, May 20, 1902—. Home: Havana, Cuba. Died 1908.

PALMER, Abraham John, clergyman; b. Frenchtown, N.J., Jan. 18, 1847; s. Rev. Abraham M. and Mary E. (Baldwin) P.; pvt. Co. D, 48th N.Y. Vols., 1861-64; prisoner 9 months; A.B., Wesleyan U., Conn., 1870, A.M., 1873; (D.D., Syracuse, 1885, Allegheny Coll., 1885); m. Emma T. Lacy, Oct. 13, 1874. Ordained M.E. ministry, 1871; pastor Jersey City, N.J., 1871-74, New York, 1874-79, Kingston, N.Y., 1879-82, New York, 1882-85, Brooklyn, 1885-86, Yonkers, N.Y., 1886; presiding elder New York Dist., 1887-92; pastor St. Paul's Ch., New York, 1892-96; missionary sec. M.E. Ch., 1896-1900; presiding elder Newburgh Dist., 1901-05; presiding elder Poughkeepsie Dist., 1905-08; corr. sec. New York Conf. Commn. on Annuities and Vested Funds, 1909—. Mem. N.Y. Senate, 27th Dist., 1913-14. Editor World Wide Missions, 1896-1900. Chmn. Andersonville Monument Dedication Commn., State of N.Y., 1914. Sec. Ocean Grove (N.J.) Assn., 1915-17; sec. Annuities Bd. of Foreign Missions M.E. Ch., 1918—. Home: Milton-on-Hudson, N.Y. Died Apr. 18, 1922.

PALMER, Albert de Forest, physicist; b. Tewksbury, Mass., July 26, 1869; s. Albert deForest and Mary Jane (Spear) P.; Ph.B., Brown U., 1891, Ph.D., 1895; grad. study Johns Hopkins, 1891-93; m. Charlotte Morrill, July 5, 1899; children—Edward Standish, Albert deForest. Instr. in physics, Brown U., 1893-96, asso. prof. physics, 1896-1934, asso. prof. emeritus, 1934—, chmn. of dept. of physics, 1926-34; works in his private laboratory, Pasadena, 1935—; visiting research fellow, Calif. Inst. Tech., 1927-28. Fellow Am. Physical Soc., Optical Soc. of Am., A.A.A.S. Baptist. Author: Theory of Measurements, 1912. Home: Pasadena, Calif. Died Jan. 12, 1940.

PALMER, Albert Marshman, theatre mgr.; b. North Stonington, Conn., July 27, 1838; s. Rev. A. G. P. (D.D.); ed. private schools and Suffield Inst.; grad. law school, Univ. of N.Y., 1860, but never practiced; librarian Mercantile Library, New York, 1869-72; mgr. Union Sq. Theatre, 1872-82; afterwards of Madison Sq. Theatre and Palmer's Theatre, Broadway and 30th St.; has always maintained a co. of selected players to present best modern plays at the home theatre and in prin. Am. cities. Founder, and 14 yrs. pres., Actors' Fund of America; one of founders, now v.p., Players Club, New York; now mgr. Richard Mansfield. Married. Home: New York, N.Y. Died 1905.

PALMER, A(lexander) Mitchell, attorney gen. of U.S.; b. Moosehead, Pa., May 4, 1872; s. Samuel B. and Caroline (Albert) P.; A.B. (highest honors), Swarthmore Coll., 1891; LL.D., Swarthmore, 1919, Lafayette, 1919, George Washington, 1920; m. Roberta Bartlett Dixon, Nov. 23, 1898 (died 1922); 1 dau., Mary Dixon; m. 2d, Margaret Fallon Burrall, Aug. 29, 1923. Admitted to bar, 1893; practiced with Hon. John B. Storm until his death, 1901, then alone; dir. Stroudsburg National Bank, Stroudsburg Water Co., International Boiler Co.; now mem. Palmer, Davis & Scott, Washington. Mem. 61st to 63d Congresses (1909-15), 26th Pa. Dist.; apptd. judge U.S. Court of Claims, Apr. 1915, resigned Sept. 1, 1915; alien property custodian under "Trading with the Enemy Act," Oct. 22, 1917-Mar. 1919; atty. gen. of U.S., in Cabinet of President Wilson, 1919-21. Mem. exec. com. Dem. Nat. Com., 1912-20; received 267 votes for nomination for president at Dem. Nat. Conv., San Francisco, 1920. Mem. Soc. of Friends. Home: Stroudsburg, Pa. Died May 11, 1936.

PALMER, Alice Freeman, educator; b. Colesville, N.Y., Feb. 21, 1855; d. James Warren and Elizabeth (Higley) Freeman; grad. Univ. of Mich., 1876 (Ph.D., 1881; L.H.D., Columbia, 1887; LL.D., Union Coll., 1895). Taught Lake Geneva, Wis., 1876-77; Saginaw, Mich., 1877-79; prof. history, Wellesley Coll., 1879-81; pres. Wellesley Coll., 1881-87; dean woman's dept., Univ. of Chicago, 1892-95; m. George Herbert Palmer, prof. philosophy, Harvard, 1887. Mass. commr. to World's Columbian Expn.; mem. Mass. State Bd. of Edn.; pres. Woman's Edn. Assn., Boston; trustee Wellesley Coll.; pres. corporation Inst. for Girls in Spain; etc. Home: Cambridge, Mass. Died 1902.

PALMER, Anna Campbell ("Mrs. George Archibald"), author; b. Elmira, N.Y., Feb. 3, 1854; d. James Barbour and Sally Peck (Carpenter) Campbell; orphaned at 14; became teacher in pub. schs.; m. George Archibald Palmer, Sept. 28, 1880 (died 1912); children—Georgianna, Sally (Mrs. Carl A. Waterbury). Was on the editorial staff Elmira Evening Star 3½ yrs.; later corr. Buffalo Illustrated Express; later editorial staff Elmira Daily Advertiser. Author: Lady Gay and Her Sister, 1891; Lady Gay, 1898; A Dozen Good Times, 1898; and many others. Was editor Key Note, musical mag. and has written librettos for several cantatas. Spl. writer Elmira Telegram. Home: Elmira, N.Y. Died June 18, 1928.

PALMER, A(rchie) Emerson; b. Winterton, N.Y., Jan. 13, 1853; s. Daniel Wilson and Miriam (Buchanan) P.; A.B., Wesleyan U., Conn., 1874, A.M., 1877; married. On staff New York Tribune as reporter and editor, 1874-98; on staff North American Review, 1889-92; sec. New York City Board Edn., 1898-1923, retired. Author: What America Owes to the Old World (in Factors in American Civilization), 1893; Solar Energy (in Life and the Conditions of Survival), 1895; The New York Public School, 1905; The Riddle of Life, 1923. Home: Winterton, N.Y. Deceased.

PALMER, Arthur Hubbell, university prof.; b. Cleveland, O., June 30, 1859; s. Charles Winslow and Lucy Williams (Hubbell) P.; A.B., Western Reserve, 1879, A.M., 1881; in Europe, 1881-83; (hon. A.M., Yale, 1891); m. Fredrikke Marie Schjöth, of Christiania, Norway, July 8, 1884. Teacher West High Sch., Cleveland, 1879-80; tutor Western Reserve Coll., 1880-81; prof. German lang. and lit., 1883-91, librarian, 1886-91, Adelbert Coll.; prof. German lang. and lit., Yale, 1891—. Trustee Am. Scandinavian Foundation, New York; mem. advisory council Simplified Spelling Bd. Edited: Riehl's Burg Neideck, 1893; Schiller's Wilhelm Tell, with Introduction, Notes and Vocabulary, 1898, 1915; Schiller's Thirty Years' War, 1899; Goethe's Hermann und Dorothea, 1903; Translated Poems and Songs by Björnstjerne Björnson, 1915. Home: New Haven, Conn. Died Nov. 6, 1918.

PALMER, Arthur William, prof. chemistry, U. of Illinois, 1889—; b. London, England, Feb. 17, 1861; public school edn. in Ill.; grad. Univ. of Ill., B.S., 1883; (Sc.D., Harvard, 1886); m. Anna Fletcher Shattuck, Aug. 9, 1893. Studied in Berlin and Göttingen, 1888-89; from 1895 in charge of State chem. water survey of Ill. Published preliminary report, Jan. 1897. Home: Champaign, Ill. Died 1904.

PALMER, Benjamin Morgan, Presbyn. clergyman; b. Charleston, S.C., Jan. 25, 1818; s. Rev. Edward P.; ed. Univ. of Ga., and Theol. Sem., Columbia, S.C. (D.D., LL.D.). Pastor 1st Presbyn. Ch., Savannah, Ga., 1841-43; 1st Presbyn. Ch., Columbia, S.C., 1843-56; 1st Presbyn. Ch., South, New Orleans, 1856—. Prof. ch. history and polity, Theol. Sem., Columbia, S.C., 1853-56; moderator 1st Southern assembly, Augusta, Ga., 1861. One of founders, 1847, of Southern Presbyn. Review. Author: Sermons (2 vols.), 1876; The Family in Its Civil and Churchly Aspects, 1876; Formation of Character, 1889; The Broken Home, 1890; Theology of Prayer, 1894; etc. Home: New Orleans, La. Died 1902.

PALMER, Bertha Honoré, see Mrs. Potter Palmer.

PALMER, Charles Ray, clergyman; b. New Haven, Conn., May 2, 1834; s. Ray and Ann Maria (Waud) P.; A.B., Yale, 1855, A.M., 1858 (D.D., 1889); grad. Andover Theol. Sem., 1859; m. Mary C., d. Alfred S. Barnes, of Brooklyn, Feb. 10, 1869 (died 1888). Ordained Congl. ministry, 1860; pastor Tabernacle Ch., Salem, Mass., 1860-72; pastor, 1872-95, emeritus, 1895, First Congl. Ch., Bridgeport, Conn. Corporate mem. A.B.C.F.M., 1871-1901; fellow Yale, 1880-1910; sec. Burroughs Home, Bridgeport, 1885-95; dir. Gen. Hosp. Soc. of Conn., 1896—. Home: New Haven, Conn. Died Apr. 22, 1914.

PALMER, Charles Skeele, chemist; b. Danville, Ill., Aug. 4, 1858; s. Rev. William Randall and Clara E. (Skeele) P.; A.B., Amherst, 1879, A.M., 1882; Ph.D., Johns Hopkins Univ., 1886; University of Leipzig, Germany, 1892-93; m. Harriet B. Warner, Sept. 30, 1886 (died 1932); children—Mrs. Helen W. P. Bissell, Leigh W., Mrs. Winifred W. P. Bennett. Prof. chemistry, U. of Colo., 1887-1902; pres. Colo. Sch. of Mines, 1902-03; chief chemist Washoe Smelter, Anaconda, Mont., 1903-04; asso. editor Engineering and Mining Journal, 1904-06; chem. engr. for large textile mills; fellow, Mellon Inst. of Industrial Research, U. of Pittsburgh, Nov. 1915-17. Consulting chemist United Fuel Gas Co., Charleston, W.Va., 1920. Episcopalian. Mason. Defined chemical terms in Webster's Internat. Dictionary, 1890 edition. Translated 1st edition Nernst's "Theoretical Chemistry," 1895. Invented, 1900, and patented, 1907, basic process for cracking oils to gasoline, sold to Standard Oil Co. of Ind., 1916. Author: Chemical Oxidation Tables, 1897; A Possible Approach to the Shakespeare Question (paper in Johns Hopkins Alumni Mag.), June 1937. Home: Pittsburgh, Pa. Died Nov. 30, 1939.

PALMER, Chase, chemist; b. Saco, Me., Sept. 19, 1856; s. Bartlett and Elizabeth (Chase) P.; student Princeton, 1874-76; A.B., Johns Hopkins, 1879, grad. prize scholar, fellow, 1879-82, Ph.D., 1882; m. Olive Edwards, Nov. 26, 1895. Instr. Mass. Inst. Tech., State Normal Sch. (Salem, Mass.), and Tufts Coll., 1882-88; state assayer, Mass., 1885-88; prof. chemistry, Wabash Coll., 1888-90; mgr. lead and zinc mines, Joplin, Mo., 1890-94; prof. chemistry, Du Pont Manual Training High Sch., Central U., and Ky. State Coll., 1895-1906; spl. chemist for water, 1906-07, chemist, 1907-19, U.S. Geol. Survey; chief chemist for Southern Pacific Co., 1919-21; consulting chemist, San Francisco. Episcopalian. Home: San Francisco, Calif. Died Nov. 18, 1927.

PALMER, Chauncey D., physician and surgeon; b. Zanesville, O., Sept. 18, 1839; s. Micah and Harriet (Sherman) P.; grad. Woodward High Sch., Cincinnati, 1857; M.D., Med. Coll. of Ohio, 1862; interne Good Samaritan Hosp., Cincinnati, 1862-63; m. M. Adelaide White, May 5, 1868. Asst. surgeon Camp Dennison, O., 1862-65; prof. obstetrics and gynecology, 1869-75, gynecology and clin. gynecology, 1875-1906, emeritus prof. obstetrics, gynecology and clin. gynecology, 1906—, Med. Coll. of Ohio (U. of Cincinnati); clinician in obstetrics and gynecology, Cincinnati Hosp., 1883-1906; med. examiner Mut. Benefit Life Ins. Co., 1875-1909. Conglist. Author: American System of Gynecology, 1888; Clinical Gynecology, 1895; American Text of Obstetrics, 1904; Jewett's System of Obstetrics, 1905. Home: Avondale, Cincinnati, O. Died Jan. 10, 1917.

PALMER, Claude Irwin, college prof.; b. in Barry Co., Mich., May 31, 1871; s. Clark Hubbard and Martha Thompson (Kellogg) P.; A.B., U. of Mich., 1903; post-grad. work, U. of Chicago; m. May Belle Hill, Aug. 31, 1897; children—Ethel May, Clark Francis. Teacher in dist. and high schs., Mich., 8 yrs.; mem. faculty Armour Inst. Tech., Chicago, 1903—, becoming prof. mathematics and dean of students. Presbyn. Author: Arithmetic with Applications, 1912; Geometry with Applications, 1912; Algebra with Applications, 1912; Trigonometry and Logarithms, 1913; Plane Trigonometry with Tables, 1914; Plane Geometry, 1915; Solid Geometry, 1918; Analytic Geometry, 1921; Practical Calculus, 1923; College Algebra, 1928. Home: Chicago, Ill. Died Apr. 8, 1931.

PALMER, Cornelius Solomon, lawyer; b. Underhill, Vt., Nov. 2, 1844; s. Jonah Ferris and Chloe (Mead) P.; ed. com. schs. and Underhill Acad.; m. Annis R. Fassett, Oct. 20, 1872. Pvt. Co. F, 13th Vt. Inf., Civil War; admitted to Vt. bar, 1874; began practice at Jericho; mem. Vt. Ho. of Rep., 1880; apptd. by Pres. Arthur asst. U.S. atty. for Dak. Ty., 1882; asso. justice Supreme Ct. of Dak., 1884-88; resumed practice in Sioux Falls, S.D., 1888; mem. S.D. Senate, 1896-97; returned to Burlington, 1903, where he engaged in practice. Republican. Conglist. Mason. Home: Burlington, Vt. Died June 13, 1932.

PALMER, Erastus Dow, sculptor; b. Pompey, Onondaga Co., N.Y., Apr. 2, 1817; ed. there; (A.M., Union Coll.). Early turned his attention to sculpture. Among his best known works are: "The Infant Ceres," "Morning and Evening," "Peace in Bondage," "The Angel of the Sepulchre," "The White Captive" (in Metropolitan Museum); statue of Robert R. Livingston (in Capitol at Washington); also portraits and ideal works. Home: Albany, N.Y. Died 1904.

PALMER, Frank Herbert, clergyman, editor; b. Cambridge, Mass., Mar. 6, 1853; s. Asher Causin and Ann Rowland (Folsom) P.; A.B., Amherst, 1875, A.M., 1878; grad. Andover Theol. Sem., 1880; m. Lucy Sophia White, of Honolulu, July 6, 1880 (died 1891); children—Herbert Hall, Allison Cleveland (dec.), Helen (Mrs. Percy Rideout), Gladys (Mrs. William Thyng); m. 2d, Jessie Maud Davies, of Sackville, Nova Scotia, May 12, 1892; children—Raymond Percival, Allison Wesselhoeft. Instructor in Latin and Greek, Oahu College, Honolulu, 1876-78; ordained Congregational ministry, 1880; pastor in N.E., 1880-95; asso. editor and editor, Education, 1891-1931. Organizer, 1901, and pres. The Palmer Co., ednl. publishers. Hon. mem. A.B.C.F.M. Progressive. Collaborator: (with Mrs. Rosa Sawin) Right-at-Hand Stories, 1906; (with Maud E. Kingsley) English Texts (series), 1905—; Outline Studies in Community Civics, 1917. Home: Braintree, Mass. Died Oct. 8, 1936.

PALMER, Frank Wayland, U.S. public printer; b. Manchester, Ind., Oct. 11, 1827; s. Zacheus M. and Selima S. P.; ed. Jamestown, N.Y.; m. Mrs. Joie B. Goodwin, Oct. 22, 1862. Served apprenticeship as printer on Jamestown Journal; its editor and joint publisher, 1848-58; editor and joint publisher Dubuque, Ia., Times, 1858-61; State printer, Ia., 1861-68; Congressman, 1869-73; editor-in-chief Chicago Inter Ocean, 1873-76; postmaster Chicago, 1877-85; public printer, 1889-94, and 1897-Sept. 1905. Home: Washington, D.C. Died 1907.

PALMER, Frederic, clergyman; b. Boston, Aug. 6, 1848; s. Julius Auboyneau and Lucy Manning (Peabody) P.; A.B., Harvard, 1869, A.M., 1872; S.T.B., Andover Theol. Sem., 1872; D.D., Episcopal Theol. Sch., Cambridge, 1910; m. Mary Towle, May 22, 1877. Pastor Congl. Ch., Revere, Mass., 1874-78; deacon, 1878, priest, 1879, P.E. Ch.; asst. Emmanuel Ch., Boston, 1878-79; acting rector Lonsdale, R.I., 1879-80; rector Jenkintown, Pa., 1880-88, Christ Ch., Andover, Mass., 1888-1913; lecturer on homiletics, Harvard Div. Sch., Sept. 1913-16. Asso. editor The Episcopal Register, and The Church, Phila., 1882-86; asso. editor The Church, Boston, 1896-99; editor and sec. Harvard Theol. Rev., 1913—. Author: Studies in Theologic Definition, 1895; The Drama of the Apocalypse, 1903; The Ring and the Book, 1908; The Winning of Immortality, 1910; with wife, Poems by Frederic and Mary Palmer, 1912; Heretics, Saints and Martyrs, 1925; The Virgin Birth, 1924. Home: Cambridge, Mass. Died July 4, 1932.

PALMER, George Herbert, univ. prof.; b. Boston, Mass., Mar. 19, 1842; s. Julius Auboyneau and Lucy Manning (Peabody) P.; A.B., Harvard, 1864, A.M., 1867; U. of Tübingen, 1867-69; grad. Andover Theol. Sem., 1870; LL.D., U. of Mich., 1894, Union, 1895, Harvard, 1906, Dartmouth, 1909, U. of Calif., 1917; Litt.D., Western Reserve U., 1897, Princeton, 1912; m. Ellen Margaret Wellman, 1871 (died 1879); m. 2d, Alice Freeman (pres. Wellesley Coll.), 1887 (died 1902). Tutor Greek, 1870-72, curator Gray collection of engravings, 1872-76, instr. philosophy, 1872-73, asst. prof., 1873-83, prof., 1883-89, Alford prof. natural religion, moral philosophy and civil polity, 1889-1913 (emeritus), Harvard. Overseer Harvard U., 1913-19; trustee Wellesley Coll. Fellow Am. Acad. Arts and Sciences. Author: The Glory of the Imperfect, 1898; Self Cultivation in English, 1897; The Field of Ethics, 1901; The Nature of Goodness, 1904; The Life and Works of George Herbert (3 vols.), 1905; The Life of Alice Freeman Palmer, 1908; The Teacher, 1909. Intimations of Immortality in the Sonnets of Shakespeare, 1912; The Problem of Freedom, 1911; Trades and Professions, 1915; Formative Types of English Poetry, 1918; Altruism—Its Nature and Varieties, 1919; The Autobiography of a Philosopher, 1930; Trades and Professions, 1932. Translator: The Odyssey, 1884; The Antigone of Sophocles, 1899. Home: Cambridge, Mass. Died May 7, 1933.

PALMER, Henrietta Lee, author; b. (Lee) Md., 1834; m. John Williamson Palmer, M.D., 1855. Writer for New York Tribune and Graphic; contributor to various periodicals. Author: The Stratford Gallery, 1859; Home Life in the Bible, 1881. Home: Baltimore, Md. Deceased.

PALMER, Henry E., insurance; b. Centerville, O., July 31, 1841; s. Levi S. and Elizabeth (Cowles) P.; ed. country schs., Wis., few months; chiefly self ed.; enlisted Union Army, July 31, 1861; 2d lt., Co. A, 11th Kan. Inf., Aug. 20, 1862; 1st lt., Dec. 31, 1862; capt., Feb. 24, 1863; regt. changed to cav., May 1863; acting asst. adj. gen., Dist. of the Plains, chief of staff of Gen. P. E. Connor's command, Powder River Indian expdn., June-Nov. 1865; pioneer in Wis., 1853, Neb., 1860, Colo., 1860, Kan., 1861, Wyo., 1865-66 (1st settler on Big Horn River, 1866), Mont., 1866, Ida., 1867; m. Laura Z. Case, June 25, 1870. Sr. mem. H. E. Palmer, Son & Co., gen. insurance, 1869—; sec. Sheridan (Wyo.) Land Co.; mem. fire and police commn., Omaha, 1897-98; postmaster, Omaha, 1904-08; pres. Omaha Bd. of Trade; 2d v.p. bd. mgrs. Nat. Home for Disabled Vol. Soldiers, 1903-10. Comdr. Neb. dept. G.A.R., 1884-85; Grand High Priest R.A.M., Neb., 1884-85. Republican. Episcopalian. Home: Omaha, Neb. Died Apr. 2, 1911.

PALMER, Henry L., life ins. president; b. Mt. Pleasant, Pa., Oct. 18, 1819; com. sch. edn. Admitted to bar; practiced at West Troy, N.Y., until 1849, when he removed to Wis.; practiced law in Milwaukee; was also active leader in State politics as Democrat. Candidate for gov. Wis., 1863; mem. Wis. Assembly, 1853, 1860, 1862, 1873 (speaker 1853 and at spl. session, 1862); State senator, 1867, 1868; co. judge Milwaukee Co., 1873-74; resigned to become pres. Northwestern Mutual Life Ins. Co., which position he still holds. Prominent in Masonry, now in 8th term as Grand Comdr. Supreme Council Northern Jurisdiction of U.S., Scottish Rite Masons; oldest living Past Grand Master, Grand Encampment, Knights Templar of U.S. Home: Milwaukee, Wis. Died 1909.

PALMER, Henry Wilber, congressman; b. Clifford, Pa., July 10, 1839; s. Gideon W. and Elizabeth P.; ed. Wyoming (Pa.) Sem., 1850-57, Ft. Edward (N.Y.) Inst., 1859; LL.B., Nat. Law Sch., Poughkeepsie, N.Y., 1860; admitted to bar, 1861; m. Ellen M. Webster Sept. 12, 1861. In practice at Wilkes-Barre, Pa., 1861—. Mem. Pa. Constl. Conv., 1872-73; atty. gen. of Pa., 1879-83; mem. 57th to 59th Congresses (1901-07) and 61st Congress (1909-11), 11th Pa. Dist. Home: Wilkes-Barre, Pa. Died Feb. 15, 1913.

PALMER, Horatio Richmond, author, composer, lecturer, publisher; b. Sherburne, N.Y., Apr. 26, 1834; s. Anson B. and Abbey (Knapp) P.; ed. Rushford Acad. and in chief musical centres of Europe; (Mus. Doc., U. of Chicago, 1881, Alfred Univ., 1882); m. Lucia A. Chapman, 1855. In charge of Church Choral Union, New York, 7 yrs.; dean Chautauqua Summer Music Sch. and dir. Chautauqua Choir, 14 yrs. Author and composer of hymns: Yield Not to Temptation; Galilee, Blue Galilee; Come, Sinner, Come; By and By We Shall Meet Him; The Rose of Sharon; Shall I Let Him In?; etc.; also Theory of Music; Piano Primer; Dictionary of Musical Terms; Biographical Dict. of Musicians, etc. Home: Park Hill-on-Hudson, N.Y. Died 1907.

PALMER, Irving Allston, metallurgist; b. New Waverly, Ind., May 20, 1866; s. Lawson and Margaret (Stottlemeyer) P.; B.S. in chemistry, Lafayette Coll., 1887, M.S., 1890; m. Mary A. Maxwell, Sept. 12, 1895. Assayer, chemist, asst. supt., supt. and consulting metallurgist, various smelting and refining companies in U.S. and Mexico, 1887-1916; prof. metallurgy Colo. Sch. of Mines, 1917—. Republican. Joint author: (with A. J. Weinig) The Trend of Flotation. Home: Golden, Colo. Died Apr. 29, 1936.

PALMER, John McAuley, lawyer, senator; b. Eagle Creek, Ky., Sept. 13, 1817; removed to Ill., 1831, settling in Carlinville, 1839; admitted to bar, 1839; delegate to State constl. convention, 1847; State senator, 1852-56; Presdl. elector on Rep. ticket, 1860; del. to Peace Convention, Washington, Feb. 4, 1861. Col. 14th Ill. vols., May 1861; brig. gen. vols., Dec. 20, 1861; with Gen. Pope at capture of New Madrid and Island No. 10; commanded 1st brigade,

1st div., army of the Mississippi; afterward comd. a division; promoted maj. gen. vols., Nov. 29, 1862; participated in battle of Stone River, Chickamauga; led 14th corps in Atlanta campaign. Gov. Ill., 1869-73, as Republican; rejoined Democratic party; U.S. senator, 1891-97; presdl. candidate of National ("gold standard") Democrats, 1896. Home: Springfield, Ill. Died 1900.

PALMER, John Williamson, author, editor; b. Baltimore, April 4, 1825; grad. Univ. of Md., M.D., 1847; m. Henrietta Lee, 1855. Was 1st city physician San Francisco, 1849-50; traveled in Hawaii, China, Malacca, Burmah, Arracan and Hindostan; was surgeon of war steamer in Hon. East India Co.'s service, 2d Burmese war, 1851-52; returned to U.S., 1853, becoming contributor to Putnam's, Harper's, the Atlantic, and later The Century mags.; Confederate war corr. New York Tribune in Civil war; editor Century and Standard Dictionaries. Author: A Portfolio of Autograph Etchings, 1882; After His Kind, 1886; For Charlie's Sake, and Other Lyrics and Ballads, 1901. Translator: L'Amour (Michelet), 1859; La Femme (same), 1859; Histoire Morale des Femmes (Legouvé), 1860. Home: Baltimore, Md. Died 1906.

PALMER, Julius Auboineau, sea-captain-journalist; b. Boston, March 1, 1840; ed. Mayhew Public School, Topsfield and Andover academies; went to sea at 17; commanded ships "Nightingale" and "Island Home," and steamship "Kalorama." Special corr. Boston Transcript and New York Evening Post at Honolulu; private sec. ex-Queen Liliuokalani at Washington, 1896-97; of Puritan ancestry; became Roman Catholic and received, 1877, special benediction from Pope Leo XIII. Author: Mushrooms of America; About Mushrooms; One Voyage (fiction); Memories of Hawaii; Again in Hawaii; etc. Deceased.

PALMER, Leslie Richard, banker, lawyer; b. Thompson Ridge, N.Y., Feb. 20, 1877; s. Richard H. and Anna (Dickinson) P.; grad. Ithaca High Sch., 1893; Ph.B. and LL.B., Cornell, 1897; m. Edith Suplee, Jan. 29, 1916; children—Richard, Wayne. Began practice at N.Y. City, 1897; admitted to firm of Olney & Comstock, 1899; specialized in corp. and real estate law until 1914; pres. First Nat. Bank of Yonkers, Yonkers Securities Co., Croton Docks Co., First Nat. Bank of Hastings, Yonkers Safe Deposit Co., 75 Maiden Lane Corp.; chmn. board Ossining Trust Co.; v.p. Brunswick Site Co. Has erected some of largest bldgs. in N.Y. City, including the Brunswick Bldg., Waldorf Bldg., Murray Hill Bldg., etc. Trustee 5th Av. Assn., 1915-19. Republican. Presbyn. Mason. Home: Irvington-on-Hudson, N.Y. Died Aug. 31, 1930.

PALMER, Loren, editor; b. Chateaugay, N.Y., Mar. 15, 1881; s. Rev. Lucius Loren and Maria Wray (Leech) P.; B.S., Wesleyan U., Conn., 1903; m. Beatrice de Pau Fox, Jan. 1, 1907; children—Barbara Lorraine, Patricia de Pau, Agnes L'Hommedieu, Lucius Loren. Began as reporter New York Sun, 1903; asst. city editor same, 1914-15, Sunday editor, 1915-17; mng. editor Every Week, 1917-18, Popular Science Monthly, 1918-20; asso. editor Collier's Weekly, 1920-21, mng. editor, 1921-24, editor 1924-25; advisory and fiction editor Everybody's, Delineator and Designer mags., 1925-26; editor Delineator, 1927-28; fiction editor Liberty Mag., 1928—. Home: Bayside, L.I., N.Y. Died June 23, 1930.

PALMER, Lynde, see Mary Louise Peebles.

PALMER, Pauline, artist; b. McHenry, Ill.; d. Nicholas and Franciska (Spangemacher) Lennards; studied Art Inst. Chicago and in Paris, with Collin, Prinet, Courtois and Simon; m. Dr. Albert E. Palmer, May 21, 1891. Exhibited Paris Salon, 1903, 04, 05, 06, 11; Naples Esposizione de Belle Arti, 1911; expns. of Omaha, Neb., 1898, Buffalo, 1901, St. Louis, 1904, and San Francisco, 1915; also in the principal cities of U.S. Represented in permanent collection Art Inst. Chicago, Muncie (Ind.) Art Assn., and in museums of Rockford and Aurora, Ill., San Diego, Calif., etc. Silver medal, Colarossi's, Paris; bronge medal, Acad. de la Grande Chaumiere, Paris; bronze medal, St. Louis Expn., 1904; Young Fortnightly prize, Art Inst. Chicago, 1907; Marshall Field prize, Chicago, 1907; William O. Thompson portrait prize, Art Inst. Chicago, 1914; Fine Arts Bldg. prize, Chicago, 1914; Julius Rosenwald purchase prize, Art Inst. Chicago, 1915; hon. mention, Am. Painters Exhbn., Art Inst., Chicago, 1916; also Clyde Carr prize, 1917, Edward Butler Purchase prize, 1920 (both Art Inst. Chicago); silver medal, Chicago Soc. Artists, for painting, "In the Open," 1920; silver medal, Peoria Soc. Allied Arts, Peoria, for painting "The Blizzard," 1921; Fine Arts Building prize, Art Inst. Chicago, 1924; Morris Rosenwald prize for painting, 1926; prize of $500, Chicago Galleries Assn., 1928, also prize of $400 from same association in 1931; bronze medal award Salon Chicago Artists, 1935; gold medal, Assn. of Chicago Painters and Sculptors, 1936, Mr. & Mrs. Jule F. Brower prize of $300 for painting "Provincetown" from Art Inst. Chicago; "The Gingham Girl," purchased by The City of Chicago, 1925; paintings in pvt. collections of Frank Logan, Edward B. Butler, Homer Stillwell, Mme. Schumann-Heink, Paul Schulze, S. Valentine, all of Chicago. Represented in Nat. Acad. Design, New York, 1932; Century of Progress Exhbn., Art Inst. Chicago, 1933. Pres. Art Inst. Alumni Assn., 1927; dir. Drama League, Arts Club and MacDowell Soc.—all of Chicago; mem. jury Ann. Exhbn. of Am. Paintings and Sculpture, Art Inst. Chicago, 1928. Member of jury and jury of awards, Winter Exhibition, Art Institute Chicago, 1933, Chicago Galleries Assn., 1935, Chicago Painters and Sculptors, Feb. 1936. Studio: Chicago, Ill. Died Aug. 15, 1938.

PALMER, Potter, capitalist; b. Rensselaerville, N.Y., 1826; son of a farmer; became clerk in store and later in bank, Dunham, N.Y.; engaged in business in Oneida Co., N.Y., later in Lockport, N.Y.; removed to Chicago; established leading dry goods store there, which later became Field, Palmer & Leiter. Retired, 1867, and invested his fortune in real estate and its improvement; m. Bertha Honoré, Chicago, 1871. Fire of 1871 wiped out his estate, but he rebuilt the Palmer House (hotel) and other buildings and accumulated large fortune. Gave $200,000 to Woman's Building, World's Columbian Expn., in which his wife was pres. board lady managers. Home: Chicago, Ill. Died 1902.

PALMER, Mrs. Potter (Bertha Honoré Palmer); b. Louisville, Ky.; d. Henry H. and Eliza Dorsey (Carr) Honoré; grad. convent sch., Georgetown; m. Potter Palmer, 1871 (died 1902). Became social leader; elected, 1891, pres. bd. of lady mgrs. Chicago Expn.; visited Europe and interested foreign govts. there in the Fair; apptd. by President only woman mem. of Nat. Commn. for Paris Expn., 1900; awarded decoration Legion of Honor by French Government. Home: Chicago, Ill. Died May 5, 1918.

PALMER, Samuel Sterling, clergyman; b. Columbus Grove, O., Mar. 5, 1861; s. Thomas and Mary (Sterling) P.; grad. Ohio Normal U., 1882; A.B., U. of Wooster, 1887, A.M., 1890; grad. McCormick Theol. Sem., 1890; D.D., Wooster, 1899; m. Della McCortle, Aug. 6, 1890; children—Arthur Thomas, Paul Whitney, Robert Sterling, Mary Anita. Ordained Presbyn. ministry, 1890; pastor Sterling, Ill., 1890-93, Brooklyn Ch., Oakland, Calif., 1893-98, Broad St. Ch., Columbus, O., Oct. 1898—. Trustee U. of Wooster. Moderator Presbyn. Gen. Assembly, 1920; mem. Nat. Bd. of Home Missions. Home: Columbus, O. Died Nov. 15, 1930.

PALMER, Stephen S., manufacturer; b. New York, Dec. 7, 1853. Pres. N.J. Zinc Co. and dir. various mfg., ry., ins., banking, gas and electric cos. Mem. Met. Mus. of Art, Am. Mus. Natural History, New York Bot. Garden. Home: Princeton, N.J. Died Jan. 29, 1913.

PALMER, Thomas Waverly, coll. pres.; b. Snow Hill (now Furman), Ala., May 19, 1860; s. Dabney and Martha A. (Simpson) P.; prep. edn. Howard Coll., Marion, Ala., 1877-78; A.M., U. of Ala., 1881, grad. in engring., 1882, LL.D., 1906; m. Lulu Rainer, Dec. 22, 1886; children—Stella (Mrs. Henry Gustave Hotz), Thomas Waverly, Lulu Rainer. Instr. mathematics, 1881-82; asst. prof., 1882-83, prof., 1883-1907, dean of acad. faculty, 1905-07, U. of Ala.; pres. Alabama Coll., 1907—. Mem. Ala. State Text-Book Commn., 1913-18; chmn. State Bd. for Vocational Edn., 1917-19; pres. Ala. Edn. Assn., 1921-22; mem. State Council of Edn. V.p. Merchants and Farmers Bank, Union Springs, Ala., 1921—; dir. Protective Life Ins. Co., Birmingham, 1922—. Home: Montevallo, Ala. Deceased.

PALMER, Thomas Witherell, senator; b. Detroit, Jan. 25, 1830; s. Thomas and Mary (Witherell) P.; student U. of Mich., class of 1849, A.B., 1876; m. Lizzie Pitts Merrill, Oct. 16, 1855. Made pedestrian tour in Spain and traveled in S. America; later a mcht. Appleton, Wis.; in real estate business, Detroit, 1853-55; later lumber mcht. and mill-owner in Mich. Mem. Mich. Bd. of Estimates, Detroit, 1873; mem. Mich. Senate, 1878, defeated for nomination for Congress, 1876; defeated for nomination for gov., 1880; U.S. senator, 1883-89; E.E. and M.P. to Spain, 1889-90; pres. World's Columbian Commn., 1892-93. Republican. Pres. Waterways Conv., Sault Ste. Marie, Aug. 1887. Home: Detroit, Mich. Died June 1, 1913.

PALMER, Truman Garrett, statistician; b. West Walworth, N.Y., Mar. 27, 1858; s. Nathaniel L. and Margaret Lavinia (De Nise) P.; ed. pub. and high schs., Rochester, N.Y.; m. Virginia Elizabeth Lincoln, June 13, 1884. Western mgr. for a number of yrs. of Frank Leslie's Illustrated Weekly, New York Daily Graphic, and other eastern illustrated papers; became interested in Calif. land operations and began study of agrl. economics, especially in its relation to culture of sugar beets; exec. sec. Am. Beet Sugar Assn., U.S. Beet Sugar Industry, U.S. Sugar Mfrs.' Assn., 1902—. Republican. Methodist. Author: Sugar at a Glance; Beet Sugar Industry of the U.S.; Concerning Sugar; Sugar Beet Seed; Production of Sugar from Beet Roots. Home: Washington, D.C. Died May 29, 1925.

PALMER, Walter Launt, artist; b. Albany, N.Y., Aug. 1, 1854; s. Erastus Dow and Mary (Seaman) P.; studied art with F. E. Church, Hudson, N.Y., 1870-72, and in Paris, 1873-74, 1876-77, under Carolus Duran; m. Zoe de V. Wyndnam, Dec. 26, 1895; 1 dau., Beatrice W. Specialist as painter of winter scenes. Awarded 2d Hallgarten prize, Nat. Acad. Design, 1887; medal, Chicago Expn., 1893; gold medal, Art Club, Phila., 1894; Evans prize, Am. Water Color Soc., 1895; 1st prize, Boston Art Club, 1895; 2d prize, Nashville Expn., 1897; hon. mention, Paris Expn., 1900; silver medal for water colors, Buffalo Expn., 1901, and Charleston Expn., 1902; silver medal for water colors and bronze medal for oil, St. Louis Expn., 1904; silver medal Phila., 1907; bronze medal, Buenos Aires, 1910; Butler prize, Chicago, 1919; Du Pont prize, Wilmington, 1926. A.N.A., 1887, N.A., 1897. Home: Albany, N.Y. Died Apr. 16, 1932.

PALMER, William Jackson, ry. official; b. Kent Co., Del., Sept. 18, 1836; s. John and Matilda (Jackson) P.; ed. pub. and pvt. schs., Phila.; m. Queen M. Palmer, Oct. 30, 1870. Commissioned capt. 15th Pa. Cav., Sept. 28, 1861; col., Sept. 8, 1862; bvt. brig. gen. vols., Nov. 6, 1864, for valuable services during the war; hon. mustered out, June 21, 1865; awarded congressional medal of honor, Feb. 24, 1894, for having with 150 men attacked and defeated a superior force of the enemy, capturing their field piece and about 100 prisoners, without the loss of a man, at Red Hill, Ala., Jan. 14, 1865. Entered ry. service, 1853, as rodman; employed 4 yrs. Pa. R.R.; treas., dir. surveys and mgr. construction Kan. Pacific Ry., 1861-70; pres. Denver & Rio Grande Ry., 1870-83; pres. Mexican Nat. Ry., 7 yrs.; pres. Rio Grande Western Ry., 1883-1901. Home: Colorado Springs, Colo. Died 1909.

PALMER, William Pendleton, mfr.; b. Pittsburgh, Pa., June 17, 1861; s. James Stewart and Eleanor Pendleton (Mason) P.; grad. Pittsburgh Central High Sch., 1878; m. Mary Boleyn Adams, July 24, 1898. Sec. Carnegie, Phipps & Co., 1887; gen. sales agent, 1888-94, asst. to pres., 1895-96, Carnegie Steel Co.; 2d v.p. Illinois Steel Co., 1896-98; gen. mgr. and pres. Am. Steel & Wire Co., 1899—; also pres. American Mining Co. Trustee Lakeside Hosp., Case Library and Oberlin Coll.; pres. Western Reserve Hist. Soc. Republican. Episcopalian. Home: Euclid Heights, Cleveland, O. Died Dec. 17, 1927.

PALMORE, William Beverly, clergyman; b. Fayette Co., Tenn., Feb. 24, 1844; s. William Pledge and Elizabeth Ann (Hobson) P.; ed. pvt. schs. and Vanderbilt U.; (D.D., Central Coll., Fayette, Mo.). Served under Gen. John S. Marmaduke, C.S.A., and surrendered his div. flag at close of Civil War; ordained to M.E. Ch., S. ministry and began preaching in Kansas City, Mo., 1877; entered editorial work in St. Louis, 1890; editor and pub. St. Louis Christian Advocate. Has lectured and preached in nearly every country of the world, 1880—; assisted in establishing Collegio Palmore in Mexico and Palmore Inst. in Japan. Mem. 2d Ecumenical Meth. Conf., Washington, 1891, 3d, London, 1901, and 4 Gen. Confs. of the ch. Founder of Order of New Century Knighthood (boys). Pres. bd. of curators of Central Coll. for Women; chaplain Mo. Senate, Mo. state penitentiary. Chosen Prohibition nominee for Vice President of U.S., 1908, but declined. Prohibitionist. Home: St. Louis, Mo. Died July 5, 1914.

PAM, Max, lawyer, b. in Bohemia, July 16, 1865; s. Alexander and Cecilie (Oesterreicher) P.; came to United States with family, 1868, and settled at Chicago; high school education, Chicago; studied law in offices of Adolph Moses; admitted to bar, 1886. Mem. Moses, Newman & Pam, 1889-91, Moses, Pam & Kennedy, 1891-97, Pam & Donnelly, 1897-98, Pam, Donnelly & Glennon, 1898, later Pam, Calhoun & Glennon, Pam & Hurd, 1903—. Associated as counsel with John W. Gates and others in organization of Am. Steel & Wire Co., 1899; conducted legal part of consolidation U.S. Steel Corp., 1901; one of counsel in organization of Internat. Harvester Co., 1902, Nat. Packing Co., 1902; associated with E. H. Harriman in re-organization Kansas City, Pittsburgh & Gulf and allied cos. into Kansas City Southern R.R., of which was gen. counsel and dir. until 1905; counsel and in charge organization Allis-Chalmers Co., 1900 (counsel and dir.); organized, 1901-02, Am. Steel Foundries; was counsel in organization Chicago Title & Trust Co.; with Charles G. Dawes, organized Central Trust Co. of Ill., 1902 (was gen. counsel); counsel with others in reorganization B.&O. Southwestern R.R.; organized with others, U.S. Nat. Gas Co., 1905. Founder sch. of Journalism, U. of Notre Dame. Home: Chicago, Ill. Died Sept. 14, 1925.

PAMMEL, Louis Hermann, botanist; b. La Crosse, Wis., Apr. 19, 1862; s. Louis and Sophie (Freise) P.; B.Agr., U. of Wis., 1885, M.S., 1889; Ph.D., Washington U., 1898; D.Sc., U. of Wis., 1925; m. Augusta Emmel, June 29, 1888; children—Edna Caroline (Mrs. R. A. Needham), Harriet Mathilda (Mrs. J. L. Seal), Doris Marie, Lois Hermina (Mrs. L. L. Blundell), Violet Emmeline, Harold Emmel. Pvt. sec. Dr. W. G. Farlow, of Harvard, 1885-86; asst. to Dr. Trelease, Shaw Sch. of Botany, St. Louis, 1886-89; spl. work U.S. Dept. Agr., and Div.

Forestry, 1889; prof. botany, Ia. State Coll. Agr. and Mechanic Arts, 1889—, and botanist of the Expt. Station. Pres. Ia. Acad. Sciences, 1893 and 1923, Ia. Park and Forestry Assn., 1905-07. V.p. Sect. G, A.A.A.S., 1919. Author: Weeds of the Farm and Garden, 1910; Manual of Poisonous Plants, 1910. Home: Ames, Ia. Deceased.

PANBOURNE, Oliver. See Howard Rockey.

PANCOAST, Henry Khunrath, M.D.; b. Philadelphia, Feb. 26, 1875; s. Seth and Susan George (Osborn) P.; grad. Friends' Central Sch., Phila., 1892; M.D., U. of Pa., 1898; m. Clara Louise Boggs, Apr. 7, 1903. Resident physician, U. of Pa. Hosp., 1898-1900; asst. instr. in clin. surgery and asst. demonstrator in surgery, U. of Pa., 1901-04; lecturer on skiagraphy, U. of Pa., and skiagrapher to Univ. Hosp., 1905-11; prof. Röntgenology, U. of Pa., and Röntgenologist to Univ. Hosp., 1912—; cons. Röntgenologist, Bryn Mawr Hosp., 1923; cons. physiologist U.S. Bur. Mines, 1923-28; consultant radiol. clinic, Phila. Gen. Hosp.; radiologist Chestnut Hill Hospital, Phila., 1931-35. Pres. First Am. Congress of Radiologists, 1933. Trustee treas. Tabernacle Presbyn. Ch., Phila., 1911-19. Med. Corps U.S. N.R.F., 1918, grade of asst. surgeon, rank lt. (j.g.); inactive list 1919, grade of passed asst. surgeon, rank lt. Republican. Died May 20, 1939.

PANCOAST, Henry Spackman, author; b. Germantown, Pa., Aug. 24, 1858; s. Charles Stacey and Mary Anne (Shelmerdine) P.; ed. Germantown Academy and by pvt. tutor; L.H.D., Trinity, 1912; A.M., U. of Pa., 1913; m. Dorothea Napier, June 2, 1897; children—Charles Edward, Henry Stacey, Margaret Lindsay. Admitted to bar, 1882; retired from practice, 1887, to engage in teaching and in lit. work. Author: Introduction to English Literature, 1895, 4th edit., 1917; Introduction to American Literature, 1898, revised edit., 1911; A First Book of English Literature (with P. V. D. Shelly), 1911, 1923; Frank Norris, intro. to McTeague, in The Modern Library, 1918. Editor: Standard English Poems, 1900; Standard English Prose, Bacon to Stevenson, 1902; Early English Poems (with J. D. E. Spaeth), 1911; A Vista of English Verse, 1911; English Prose and Verse from Beowulf to Stevenson, 1915. Home: Chestnut Hill, Phila., Pa. Died Mar. 25, 1928.

PANCOAST, Thomas Jessup, realtor; b. Moorestown, N.J., July 13, 1865; s. Josiah Dunn and Sarah Middleton (Thorn) P.; ed. Friend's High Sch., Moorestown; m. Katharine Rogers Collins, Jan. 17, 1889; children—Josiah Arthur, Norwood Henry (dec.), Thomas Lesley (dec.), Maurice (dec.), Russell Thorn, Norman Lester. With Edward T. Steele & Co., wholesale cloth, Phila., Pa., 1880-88; mem. Collins & Pancoast, builders' and farmers' supplies Merchantville, N.J., 1888-1912; pres. First Nat. Bank, Merchantville, 1911-12; moved to Miami Beach, Fla., 1912, engaged in land development; pres. Miami Beach Improvement Co.; pres. Miami Beach Bay Shore Co., Miami Beach First Nat. Bank, Pancoast Hotel Co. Mayor of Miami Beach, 1918-20. Pres. Miami Beach Chamber Commerce; treas. Miami Beach Realty Bd., Miami Beach Welfare Bd.; mem. exec. bd. Com. of One Hundred. Republican. Quaker. Home: Miami Beach, Fla. Died Sept. 16, 1941.

"PANSY," author. See Isabella M. Alden.

PAPE, Eric, painter; b. San Francisco, Oct. 17, 1870; s. F. L. M. and Maria (Meier) P.; pub. sch. edn., San Francisco; art edn. in Paris under Boulanger, Lefebvre, Constant, Doucet, Blanc and Delance and at École des Beaux Arts under Gérôme and Laurens; has lived in Eng., France, Germany, Mexico and Egypt; m. Alice, d. Prof. Lewis B. Monroe, Aug. 16, 1894 (died 1911); m. 2d, Alice Byrne, Sept. 17, 1920. Instructor Cowles Art Sch., Boston, 1897; founded, 1898, and dir. and head instr. Eric Pape School of Art until 1913. Exhibited 22 pictures at the Paris Salon, Chicago Expn., 1893, Munich Kunst Austellung, 1897; 120 paintings Omaha Expn., 1899, Paris Expn., 1900; 100 paintings and drawings Buffalo Expn., 1901, St. Louis Expn., 1904; etc. Home: Manchester, Mass. Died Nov. 7, 1938.

PAPI, Gennaro, conductor; b. Naples, Italy, Dec. 1886; s. Salvatore and Margherita (Bonhomme) G.; grad. in piano and harmony, Naples Conservatorio of Music, 1904; studied di Pietro a Maiella, Naples; m. Amalia Russo, Nov. 1907; children—Carolina, Federico. Came to U.S., 1913, naturalized, 1927. Began as asst. condr. San Carlo, Naples, 1905; with condrs. Mugnone, Mancinelli, Richard Strauss, 1905-08; chorus maestro Imperial Theater, Varsavia, 1909-10; at Regio Torino Theater and at Covent Garden with Campanini, 1911-12; assistant to Toscanini at N.Y. Metropolitan Opera, 1913-16; condr. N.Y. Metropolitan Opera, 1916-25 and from 1935; conducted in Buenos Aires, Mexico City, Milano, Bavaria and Chicago, 1925-35; leading conductor of Chicago Civic Opera, St. Louis Grand Opera and Metropolitan Opera House, 1935—. First to broadcast Puccini's music (operas), 1928, over NBC network. Cavaliere della Corona d'Italia. Home: Naples, Italy. Died Nov. 29, 1941.

PAQUIN, Paul, physician; b. in Canada, June 23, 1860; student Bourget Coll., Rigaud, Can., McGill U., Pasteur Inst., Paris, and other European med. instns.; M.D., U. of Mo., 1887; m. Hannah Belle Lyons. Prof. bacteriology, pathology and comparative medicine, U. of Mo. several yrs.; med. investigator, experimenter, hygienist; sec. Mo. Bd. Health, 1896-99; dir. and exec. of Hospital and Health Bd., Kansas City, Mo. Died June 23, 1916.

PARADISE, Frank Ilsley, clergyman; b. Boston, Dec. 5, 1859; s. William T. and Mary J. (Carnes) P.; A.B., Yale, 1888; B.D., Berkeley Div. Sch., 1890; m. Caroline Wilder Fellowes, June 30, 1890; children—Scott Hurtt, Dorothea Chester, Robert Campbell, Nathaniel Burton; m. 2d, Dorothy Pyman, of England, Oct. 15, 1915; children—Jean Isley, Diana Gray. Deacon, 1890, priest, 1891, Episcopal Ch.; rector St. Peter's Ch., Milford, Conn., 1890-93, St. Luke's Ch., E. Greenwich, R.I., 1893-94; dean New Orleans, La., 1894-98; Grace Ch., Medford, Mass., 1898-1915; acting rector Am. Ch. of Holy Trinity, Paris, 1919-20. Author: Abraham Lincoln, Democrat, 1921; Jesus Christ and the Spirit of Youth, 1923; Mazzini, the Prophet of Democracy, 1926. Lecturing upon Am. history and the new relationship with England. Died Feb. 24, 1926.

PARAMANANDA, Swami, lecturer, author; b. Bengal, India; s. Ananda Guha-Thakurta; ed. in India. Came to U.S., 1906; lectured widely in United States and Europe. Author: Book of Daily Thoughts and Prayers; The Path of Devotion; Vedanta in Practice; The Way of Peace and Blessedness; Reincarnation and Immortality; Plato and Vedic Idealism; Christ and Oriental Ideals; Emerson and Vedanta; Self-Mastery; Faith as a Constructive Force; Concentration and Meditation; Creative Power of Silence; Spiritual Healing; The Secret of Right Activity; (verse) The Rhythm of Life; The Soul's Secret Door; The Vigil. Translator: The Bhagavad-Gita; The Upanishads, Vol. I. Founder, 1912, and editor Message of the East (monthly mag.). Home: La Crescenta, Calif. Died June 21, 1940.

PARDEE, Don Albert, judge; b. Wadsworth, Medina Co., O., Mar. 29, 1837; s. Aaron and Eveline (Eyles) P.; acting midshipman U.S. Naval Acad., 1854-57; m. Julia E. Hard, Feb. 3, 1861. Admitted to bar, 1859; practiced at Medina, O., 1859-61; maj. 42d Ohio Inf., Oct. 27, 1861; lt. col., Mar. 14, 1862; bvtd. col. vols. and brig. gen. vols., Mar. 13, 1865, "for gallant and meritorious services during the war." Resumed practice at New Orleans, 1865; register in bankruptcy, 1867; judge 2d Jud. Dist. of La., 1868-80; del. La. Constl. Conv., 1879; Rep. candidate for atty.-gen., 1880; U.S. circuit judge, 5th Jud. Circuit, May 1881—. Removed to Atlanta, June 1898. Home: Atlanta, Ga. Died Sept. 26, 1919.

PARDEE, George Cooper, governor; b. San Francisco, Calif., July 25, 1857; s. Enoch Homer and Mary Elizabeth (Pardee) P.; Ph.B., U. of Calif., 1879, A.M., 1882; M.D., U. of Leipzig, 1885; LL.D., U. of Calif., 1932; m. Helen N. Penniman, Jan. 25, 1887; children—Florence Mary (dec.), Madeline Anna, Carol Marietta (dec.), Helen Penniman. Practice confined to diseases of the eye and ear. Mem. Bd. of Health, 1889-91, City Council, 1891-93, mayor, 1893-95, Oakland, Calif.; regent State U., 1899-1903; gov. of Calif., 1903-07. Republican. Mem. Nat. Conservation Commn., 1907-09; chmn. Conservation Commn. State of Calif., 1911-15; chmn. State Forestry Commn., 1919-23, 1928-30; pres. bd. dirs. East Bay Municipal Utility Dist., 1924—; mem. Oakland Port Commn., 1927—; chmn. Calif. Joint Federal-State Water Resources Commn., 1930. Mason. Home: Oakland, Calif. Died Sept. 1, 1941.

PARDEE, Israel Platt, banker; b. Hazleton, Pa., May 12, 1852; s. Ario and Anna M. (Robison) P.; E.M., Lafayette Coll., Pa., 1874, M.S., 1877; m. Alice Lee, Feb. 28, 1889. Chemist Port Oram (N.J.) Iron Works, 1875-76; asst. supt. Musconetcong Iron Wks., 1876-79; supt. Secaucus Iron Wks. (N.J.), 1879-82; supt. Musconetcong Iron Wks. and Mines, and gen. mgr., treas. Secaucus Iron Co., 1882-94; pres. Hazleton (Pa.) Nat. Bank, 1894-1929, chmn. bd., 1929—; pres. Hazleton Iron Works, 1898—. Hon. president board of trustees Lafayette Coll. Republican. Home: Hazleton, Pa. Died Oct. 14, 1934.

PARDOW, William O'Brien, S.J., priest, educator; b. New York, June 13, 1847; s. Robert and Augusta Garnett (O'Brien) P.; grad. Coll. of St. Francis Xavier, New York, 1864; 3 yrs.' post-graduate course of philosophy, Woodstock Coll., Md.; 4 yrs. in divinity, Bible exegesis and Hebrew, Univ. of Laval, France (no degrees—being a Jesuit). Pres. St. Francis Xavier Coll., 1891; provincial superior of N.Y. and Md., 1893; under his administration, spiritual care of the Catholics in the Island of Jamaica, West Indies, was transferred from England to U.S.; curate Ch. of St. Ignatius Loyola, New York, 1901-03; lecturer new Jesuit Instn., St. Andrew-on-Hudson, N.Y., 1903-06; curate Ch. of Gesu, Philadelphia, 1906—. Died 1908.

PARET, William, bishop; b. New York, Sept. 23, 1826; s. John and Hester P.; A.B., Hobart, 1849, A.M., 1852 (S.T.D., 1867, LL.D., 1886); m. Maria G. Peck, Aug. 22, 1849; 2d, Mrs. Sarah Haskell, Apr. 21, 1900. Deacon, 1852, priest, 1853, P.E. Ch.; pastor Clyde, N.Y., 1852-54, Pierrepont Manor, N.Y., 1854-65, East Saginaw, Mich., 1865-67, Elmira, N.Y., 1867-69, Williamsport, Pa., 1869-76, Washington, D.C., 1876-85; consecrated bishop of Maryland, Jan. 8, 1885. Died 1911.

PARHAM, Frederick William, M.D.; b. New Orleans, Mar. 20, 1856; s. John Greenway and Mary E. (Blunt) P.; student Randolph-Macon Coll., Va., 1873-75; M.D., U. of La., 1879; m. Mary K. Duncan, Dec. 15, 1892; children—Frederick D., Duncan, Mildred, Mary L., Lister (dec.), Landfried (dec.). Practiced in New Orleans, 1879—. Fellow Internat. Soc. of Surgery, Am. Surg. Assn. (v.p. 1917), Am. Coll. of Surgeons (bd. regents, 1920-26). Democrat. Protestant. Maj. (inactive list) M.C., U.S.A., 1917-20. Home: New Orleans, La. Died May 7, 1927.

PARISH, John Carl, prof. history; b. Des Moines, Ia., July 25, 1881; s. Leonard Woods and Emma White (Stuart) P.; M.Di., Ia. State Normal Sch., 1902; Ph.B., State U. of Ia., 1905, A.M., 1906, Ph.D., 1908; m. Ruth Leavitt Davison, Oct. 6, 1908; 1 son, David Stuart. Teacher high sch., Winterset, Ia., 1902-04; asst. editor State Hist. Soc. of Ia., 1907-10; student of archives in France and Spain, 1908-09; engaged in writing, 1910-14; asst. prof. history, 1914-15, prof., 1915-17, Colorado Coll.; asso. editor State Hist. Soc. of Ia., 1919-22; editor of The Palimpsest (hist. monthly), 1920-22. Sec. Conf. of Hist. Socs., 1919-22; lecturer on Ia. history, State U. of Ia., 1920-22; asst. prof. history, 1922-24, asso. prof., 1924-27, prof., 1927—, U. of Calif. at Los Angeles. Commd. 1st lt. Inf., U.S.A., 1917, capt., 1919; served with Intelligence Sect., 1st Am. Army, A.E.F., 1918. Conglist. Author: Robert Lucas (biography), 1907; John Chambers, 1909; George Wallace Jones, 1912; The Man with the Iron Hand, 1913. Editor Robert Lucas Journal of the War of 1812; Autobiography of John Chambers. Mng. editor Pacific Historical Review, 1932-36. Died Jan. 13, 1939.

PARK, Charles Caldwell, author; b. Allegheny City, Pa., Aug. 19, 1860; s. James and Sarah (Gray) P.; student Cornell U., 1879-80; M.D., Bellevue Hosp. Med. Coll., 1888; studied univs. of Vienna and Heidelberg, 1889-90; m. Helen Kittredge, Mar. 10, 1886. Began practice in N.Y. City, 1888; removed to Calif., 1893; raised money in Pittsburgh, Pa., to establish and maintain the "Fort Duquesne Cafe," of which was in charge, 1917-18, under auspices of Y.M.C.A., with A.E.F., in France. Dir. Santa Barbara County Nat. Bank. Formerly hon. pres. Associated Charities, Santa Barbara, Calif. Republican. Unitarian. Author: The Plaything of the Gods, 1912; Tales of Old California. Home: Santa Barbara, Calif. Died Aug. 14, 1931.

PARK, Edward Amasa, theologian; b. Providence, R.I., Dec. 29, 1808; grad. Brown, 1826; Andover Theol. Sem., 1831; (D.D., Harvard, 1844; LL.D., Brown, 1846; m. Anne Maria, dau. William Edwards of Hunter, N.Y. (great-granddau. Rev. Jonathan Edwards), Sept. 1836. Pastor Congregational Church, Braintree, Mass., 1833-35; prof. moral philosophy, Amherst, 1835-36; prof. sacred rhetoric, 1836-47, Christian theology, 1847-81, emeritus prof., 1881—, Andover Theol. Sem. Founded, 1844, editor-in-chief, 1851-84, and for 40 years one of principal editors, Bibliotheca Sacra. Author: Discourses and Treatises on the Atonement; Discourses on Some Theological Doctrines as Related to the Religious Character. Died 1900.

PARK, Franklin Atwood, vice-pres. Singer Mfg. Co.; b. Taunton, Mass., Jan. 22, 1868; s. John Francis and Catherine Amelia (Parlow) P.; B.S., Mass. Inst. Tech., 1895; m. Mary Fairbanks Bosworth, Aug. 26, 1896; children—Malcolm Sewell, Marjorie Lincoln (Mrs. Gerard Swope, Jr.), Franklin Atwood. Supt. Baxter D. Whitney & Son, Winchendon, Mass., 1896-1901, Singer Mfg. Co., South Bend, Ind., 1901-03; mgr. Singer Mfg. Co. Ltd., Clydebank, Scotland, 1904-12; v.p. Singer Mfg. Co. of N.J., mfrs. sewing machines, 1912—; pres. Safe Deposit Co. of New York; v.p. Poinsett Lumber & Mfg. Co., Diehl Mfg. Co., Bourne & Co., Ltd. Life mem. Corp. of Mass. Inst. of Technology. Conglist. Home: New York, N.Y. Died June 17, 1938.

PARK, Lawrence, architect; b. Worcester, Mass., Dec. 16, 1873; s. John Gray and Elizabeth Bigelow (Lawrence) P.; student Harvard, 1892-96; m. Maria Davis Motley, Nov. 16, 1905. Practiced at Boston, 1901—. Non resident curator Dept. of Colonial Art, Cleveland (O.) Mus. of Art. Republican. Unitarian. Author: Major Thomas Savage of Boston and His Descendants, 1915; Joseph Badger, 1708-1765, 1918. Home: Groton, Mass. Deceased.

PARK, Milton, newspaperman; b. Augusta, Ga., Jan. 1, 1846; s. Rev. John Thompson Sankey and Tabitha Ann (Skinner) P.; served in C.S.A., 1862-65; participated in prin. battles of Army of Tenn. student Mercer U., Ga., 1865-67; m. Alice V. Wimberly, Feb. 15, 1875. Pres. Southern Ala. Coll., Greenville, 1883-85, Kyle (Tex.) Sem., 1890-91; editor Southern Mercury, Dallas, Tex., 1891—; pres.

Southern Mercury Pub. Co., 1892—; also interested in copper mining in Tex. and N.M., and banking. Chmn. Populist Nat. Exec. Com., 1896-1900; presdl. elector-at-large on Populist ticket ("Middle of the Road"), 1900, 1904. Adj. gen. U.C.V., Trans-Miss. dept., 1898-1910. Mason. Home: Dallas, Tex. Died May 8, 1914.

PARK, Roswell, surgeon; b. Pomfret, Conn., May 4, 1852; s. Rev. Roswell and Mary (Baldwin) P.; A.B., Racine (Wis.) Coll., 1872, A.M., 1875; M.D., Northwestern, 1876; (hon. M.D., Lake Forest, 1892; A.M., Harvard, 1895; LL.D., Yale, 1902); m. Martha P. Durkee, 1880. Demonstrator anatomy, Woman's Med. Coll., Chicago, 1877-79; adj. prof. anatomy, Northwestern U., 1879-82; lecturer on surgery, Rush Med. Coll., Chicago, 1882; prof. surgery, U. of Buffalo, and surgeon to Buffalo Gen. Hosp., 1883—. Attended President McKinley after he was shot, Sept. 1901. Author: Lectures on Surgical Pathology, 1891; History of Medicine, 1897; Text-Book of Surgery (2 vols.), 1896; The Principles and Practice of Modern Surgery, 1907. Home: Buffalo, N.Y. Died Feb. 15, 1914.

PARK, Royal Wheeler, headmaster; b. Kaufman, Tex., June 20, 1897; s. James Walter and Lyda Matilda (Thompson) P.; student Southern Meth. U., 1915-16, Army and Navy Sch., 1916-17; B.S., U.S. Mil. Acad., 1919; grad. Inf. Sch., 1920; M.A., Stanford U., 1931; m. Katherine Alice Blake, May 8, 1925. Commd. 2d lt. U.S.A., Nov. 1, 1918; 1st lt. inf., 1920; comdg. company, and battalion adj., 4th Inf., 1920-22; with 7th Inf., June 30-Sept. 28, 1922 (resigned); comdt. of cadets, Palo Alto Mil. Acad. and Urban Mil. Acad., 1923-25; founder and headmaster of Pacific Coast Mil. Acad., Menlo Park, Calif., 1925-35; founder and headmaster Park Mil. Acad., Menlo Park, Calif., 1935—. Maj. of inf., Calif. N.G., Sept. 1924—. Methodist. Mason. Home: Menlo Park, Calif. Died Mar. 1, 1941.

PARK, Sam, consular service; b. Bedford, Ia., July 3, 1857; s. Joseph and Sarah J. (Parker) P.; ed. pub. schs., Bedford; m. Mary M. Lintner, June 1904; children—Elizabeth, Samuel, Suzanne. Engaged in lumber and oil business, 1882—; organizer and later pres. Industrial Lumber Co. of Beaumont, Tex. (now of Elizabeth, La.); organizer and v.p. Beaumont Nat. Bank; organizer, prin. owner and pres. 3 yrs. Am. Lumber Co., Merryville, La.; now retired; U.S. vice consul, Biarritz, France, 1920—. Col. on staff of Gov. Tom Campbell of Tex. Decorated Medaille de la Reconnaissance Française. Mason. Died May 6, 1937.

PARK, Samuel Culver, mayor; b. Cheyenne, Wyo., Nov. 16, 1869; s. Boyd and Jane (Culver) P.; A.B., U. of Mich., 1911, as of 1891; m. Ella Thomas, Jan. 17, 1894. Entered employ Bank of Commerce, Salt Lake City, 1894, and became cashier; pres. and mgr. Boyd Park, Inc., mfg. wholesale and retail jewelers. Served in Utah N.G. as pvt. to brig. gen., retiring Dec. 31, 1908; mem. Utah State Senate, 1903-07; mem. Bd. of Edn., Salt Lake City, 1909-12 (resigned); mayor of Salt Lake City, Utah, 1912-16. Republican. Episcopalian. Mason. Home: Salt Lake City, Utah. Died Feb. 18, 1920.

PARK, William Hallock, M.D.; b. New York, Dec. 30, 1863; s. Rufus and Harriet (Hallock) P.; A.B., Coll. City of New York, 1883; M.D., Coll. Phys. and Surg. (Columbia), 1886; U. of Vienna, 1 yr., 1889-90; LL.D., Queen's U., 1910; D.Sc., New York U., 1926, Yale U., 1929, Columbia U., 1929; unmarried. Prof. bacteriology and hygiene, Univ. and Bellevue Hosp. Med. Coll. (New York U.), 1897-1937, and dir. New York Health Dept. Bur. of Labs., 1894-1937 (emeritus); consulting bacteriologist, State Dept. of Health, 1914—, and med. examiner in bacteriology, 1917—; cons. bacteriologist, U.S. Quarantine Service, 1921—. Pres. Am. Public Health Assn., 1923. Author: Pathogenic Microörganisms, 10th edit., 1933; Public Health and Hygiene, 2d edit., 1927; Who's Who Among the Microbes, 1929. Home: New York, N.Y. Died Apr. 6, 1939.

PARKE, John Grubb, engineer-soldier; b. Chester Co., Pa., Sept. 22, 1827; grad. West Point, 1849; assigned to topographical engrs.; engaged in boundary surveys for Govt. until 1861. Promoted capt. topographical engrs., Sept. 9, 1861; apptd. brig. gen. vols., Nov. 23, 1861; served in Burnside's expedition to N.C.; bvtd. lt. col. U.S. army; promoted maj. gen. vols.; chief of staff under Burnside; reached bvt. rank maj. gen., U.S. army; commd. maj. engrs., June 17, 1864; lt. col., Mar. 4, 1879; col., Mar. 7, 1884; retired, 1889; supt. Mil. Acad., West Point, 1887-89. Author: Explorations and Surveys for a Railroad Route from the Mississippi River to the Pacific Ocean. Died 1900.

PARKER, A. Warner, lawyer; b. Prince William Co., Va., Dec. 24, 1872; s. Joseph and Jane Randolph (Peticolas) P.; ed. grammar and high schs., Lynchburg, Va.; m. Rae B. Smith, Sept. 4, 1894. Began in mercantile business, Washington, D.C., 1888; clk. in War Dept., 1897-1903; Immigration Service, 1903; law officer Bur. of Immigration, 1906-19; spl. asst. to atty. gen. U.S., 1908-19; admitted to bar of Supreme Court of U.S., 1912; became mem. Parker & Parker. Collaborated with Hon. William Williams, 1908-10, in preparing immigration bill which was passed by Congress, Feb. 5, 1917. Democrat. Presbyn. Home: Chevy Chase, Md. Died Mar. 30, 1939.

PARKER, Alexis du Pont, capitalist; b. Wilmington, Del., July 26, 1859; s. Stevens and Mary Griffiths (Lewis) P.; B.A., Racine Coll., 1879, M.A., 1882; S.T.B., Gen. Theol. Sem., New York, 1883 (studied to understand theology but never intended to join ministry); D.C.L., U. of the South, 1926; m. Eliza Bowley Bryan, Sept. 14, 1887 (died 1913); children—Anne (Mrs. George C. Cunningham), Helen (wife of Dr. H. B. Wilmer), Emily (Mrs. Reginald H. Morris). Cowboy in Wyo., 1883, then as day laborer on section, D.&R.G. R.R., Colo., 1884; then went to round house as engine wiper, to machine shops, store house and to auditor's office where became chief clerk, same ry.; apptd. auditor for receiver of Union Pacific, Denver & Gulf Ry., 1893; and for receiver Denver, Leadville & Gunnison Ry., 1894; gen. aud., 1899-1905, v.p. in charge of all depts., 1905-16, C.&S.Ry. Co.; pres. Colo. Midland Ry., 1909-11; pres. Denver & Interurban Ry., Colo. R.R., Colorado Springs & Cripple Creek Ry. Co. to 1916; pres. Florence Goldfield Mining Co., 1904-19; pres. Am. Briquet Co., 1919-29. Died Mar. 2, 1932.

PARKER, Alton Brooks, jurist; b. Cortland, N.Y., May 14, 1852; s. John Brooks and Harriet F. (Stratton) P.; student Cortland Acad. and Cortland Normal Sch.; LL.B., Albany Law Sch., 1873; (LL.D., Union, 1902, McGill Univ., 1913, and U. of Toronto, 1915, College of William and Mary, 1921); m. Mary L., d. M. I. Schoonmaker, of Accord, N.Y., Oct. 16, 1873; m. 2d, Amelia Day Campbell, Jan. 16, 1923. Admitted to bar; practiced in Kingston; surrogate Ulster Co., 1877-85; tendered office of first asst. postmaster-gen., 1885; chmn. Dem. State Com., 1885; apptd. justice Supreme Ct. of N.Y., 1885, elected, 1886; mem. Ct. of Appeals, 2d Div., 1889-92; mem. gen. term, 1893-96, of Appellate Div., 1896-97; chief justice of Ct. of Appeals of N.Y., Jan. 1, 1898-Aug. 5, 1904; resigned to accept Dem. nomination for the Presidency made on first ballot, July 9, 1904; del.-at-large and N.Y. mem. platform committee Dem. Nat. Conv., 1908; permanent chmn. Dem. State Conv., N.Y., 1908, temporary chmn., 1910, permanent chmn., 1912. Again practicing law as mem. Parker, Marshall, Miller and Auchincloss; was chief counsel for managers impeachment trial of Gov. Sulzer, 1913. Vice-pres. League to Enforce Peace; pres. Nat. Civic Federation, 1919—. Home: Esopus, N.Y. Died May 10, 1926.

PARKER, Benjamin Franklin, secretary; b. Conneaughtville, Pa., July 27, 1839; s. Ledyard and Hannah (Thompson) P.; ed. Meadville (Pa.) pub. schs. and Acad.; pvt. to 1st lt. U.S.V., 1861-65, participating in battles of 2d Bull Run, Missionary Ridge, etc.; m. Lucille W. Penniman, Feb. 3, 1868. Served lt. to lt. col. Wis. N.G., 28 yrs.; lt. col. 3d Wis. Inf., Spanish-Am. War, serving in Puerto Rico. Past Grand Master Ancient Order United Workmen of Wis.; Internat. Sec. Internat. Order of Good Templars, 1885-1908. Grand Sec. of Wis., 1873-1900, and from 1909. Home: Milwaukee, Wis. Died Jan. 24, 1912.

PARKER, Charles Edward, judge; s. John Mason P.; A.B., Hobart Coll., Geneva, N.Y., 1857, A.M., 1879. Del. N.Y. Constl. Conv., 1867-68; justice Supreme Ct. of N.Y., 6th Dist., 1892-1906; was judge Appellate Div., 3d Dept. Republican. Home: Owego, N.Y. Died 1909.

PARKER, Charles Edward, missionary; b. Robeson Co., N.C., Feb. 13, 1872; s. Edward Burch and Eliza Jane (Smith) B.; student Trinity Coll., Randolph Co., N.C.; diploma, Drew Sem., 1901, B.D., 1928; m. Sarah Binney Turner, Nov. 23, 1904; children—Eleanor (Mrs. Philip M. Umstead), Virginia, Rebecca F. (dec.). Missionary, M.E. Ch., in India, 1901—, in charge Vikarabad Nizam's Dominions until 1910, and from 1911, successively supt. in charge, Hyderabad Dist., Hyderabad-Vikarabad Dist., Vikarabad Dist., now Hyderabad-Telugu Dist. Has gained 60,000 Indian converts to Christianity. Mem. Bd. Foreign Missions, M.E. Ch. Republican. Mason. Home: Hyderabad, Deccan, India. Died Aug. 17, 1933.

PARKER, Charles Morton, pres. Am. Radiator Co.; b. Charleston, Ill., June 1, 1868; s. George W. and Nellie (Ferguson) P.; C.E. Rensselaer Poly. Inst., 1889. Began in employ of Rio Grande Western R.R., 1890; became connected with Am. Radiator Co. as foundryman, 1899, then sec. to exec. com., European dir., 1901-08, treas., 1908-13, later pres. Served as maj. Air Service, with A.E.F., World War. Home: New York, N.Y. Died Sept. 27, 1934.

PARKER, Cortlandt, lawyer; b. Perth Amboy, N.J., June 27, 1818; s. James and Penelope (Butler) P.; ed. Perth Amboy Mil. Acad. and other schools; grad. 1st Rutgers Coll., 1836 (LL.D., Rutgers and Princeton); m. Elizabeth Wolcott, d. Richard W. Stites, of Morristown, N.J., Sept. 1847. Studied law in office of Hon. Theodore Frelinghuysen, of Newark, 3 yrs.; admitted atty., Sept. 1839, counsellor, Sept. 1842, in N.J.; still practices law; oldest practitioner in N.J. Prosecutor of pleas, Essex Co., 1857-67; has declined several tendered apptmts. and nominations (judge Supreme Court, 1867; judgeship Court Ala. Claims, 1874; minister to Russia, 1877; minister to Vienna, 1882; nomination by conv. to Congress), etc. Sent to Louisiana, 1876, by President Grant, to witness count of electoral votes; was one of the law revisers, 1875-76. Was Whig, 1839-56, then became Republican; several times candidate for U.S. senate. Home: Newark, N.J. Died 1907.

PARKER, Daingerfield, brig. gen.; b. New Rochelle, N.Y., May 23, 1832; s. Foxhall Alexander, Sr. (commodore U.S.N.) and Sara Jay Bogardus P.; of old Va. Parker family; ed. various leading schs. and acads.; m. Amelia Nisbet, 1861. Served as subaltern and capt., 3d U.S. Inf., Apr. 26, 1861-Apr. 14, 1884; maj. 9th Inf. to May 15, 1889; lt. col. 20th and 13th Inf. to Nov. 26, 1894; col. 18th Inf. to May 23, 1896, when retired for age; promoted brig. gen. U.S.A. retired, by act of Apr. 23, 1904. Participated in battles of 1st and 2d Bull Run, Antietam, Fredericksburg, Chancellorsville, Gettysburg (where won bvt.), and comd. Fort Slocum in Early's attack on Washington; comd. 3d Inf., at times, during Civ. War; afterward comd. Mil. Prison, St. Louis. Comd. troops at opening of Cherokee strip. Episcopalian. Home: Washington, D.C. Died Feb. 25, 1925.

PARKER, Edmund Southard, banker; b. Mifflintown, Pa.; s. Andrew (lawyer, member Congress) and Ann Eliza (Doty) P. (descendants of early settlers of the state); ed. at Tuscarora Acad. As a boy entered Mifflin Co. Nat. Bank, Lewistown, Pa.; returned to Mifflintown, 1865, and established banking house of Doty, Parker & Co. (later Parker & Co.), the first bank to be organized in the county; in 1887 helped organize Columbia Nat. Bank, Washington; elected first cashier, and later pres.; later pres. Nat. Met. Bank, Washington, till Jan. 1908, when resigned. Home: Washington, D.C. Died Oct. 21, 1921.

PARKER, Edward Cary, in charge federal grain supervision; b. St. Paul, Minn., Aug. 4, 1881; s. Charles Delavan and Frances Abigail (Comings) P.; student Minn. Agr. Sch., 1899-1901; B.S., U. of Minn., 1905; m. Edith Carter, Feb. 11, 1908; 1 son, Ward Follett. Asst. agriculturalist, Minn. Agrl. Expt. Station, 1905-08; agrl. adviser to Manchurian Govt., 1908-12; ranching and land development, Mont., 1913-23; marketing specialist U.S. Dept. Agr., 1923-33, in charge federal grain supervision, Bur. Agrl. Economics, U.S., 1933—. Sec. Mont. Ranches Co., 1915-19; pres. Treasure State Ranches Co., 1919-23. Unitarian. Author: Field Management and Crop Rotation, 1915; also U.S. Dept. Agr. bulls. on grain, 1932-34. Home: Chevy Chase, Md. Died July 21, 1939.

PARKER, Edward Frost, M.D.; b. Charleston, S.C., Dec. 16, 1867; s. Francis Le Jau and Elizabeth (Frost) Parker; U. of Virginia, 1886; M.D., Med. Coll. State of S.C., 1889; certified by Am. Examining Bds. for Ophthalmology and Otolaryngology; m. Harriet Horry Frost, Nov. 5, 1907. Prof. eye and ear diseases, Medical College, State of S.C.; specialist in eye, ear, nose and throat. Hon. fellow Am. Laryngol., Rhinol. and Otol. Soc. Wrote The History of Surgery in South Carolina (Trans. of S.C. Med. Assn.), 1893. Home: Charleston, S.C. Died Mar. 28, 1938.

PARKER, Edward Melville, bishop; b. Cambridge, Mass., July 11, 1855; s. Henry Melville and Fanny Cushing (Stone) P.; prep. edn., St. Paul's Sch., Concord, N.H., 1868-74; B.A., Keble Coll., Oxford, Eng., 1878, M.A., 1881; grad. course, Oxford, 1878-79; (D.D., Berkeley Div. Sch., 1906; D.C.L., Bishop's Coll., Lennoxville, Can., 1907; D.D., Dartmouth, 1914); m. Grace Elmendorf, 1885 (died 1888); m. 2d, Isabella Goodrich, Oct. 1, 1914. Deacon, 1879, priest, 1881, P.E. Ch.; a master St. Paul's Sch., 1879-1906; consecrated bishop coadjutor of N.H., Feb. 9, 1906; succeeded as bishop of New Hampshire, Apr. 1, 1914. Died Oct. 22, 1925.

PARKER, Edward Sanders, Jr., lawyer; b. Graham, N.C., Mar. 1, 1872; s. Edward Sanders and Ellen Caroline (Northam) P.; prep. edn. Oak Ridge (N.C.) Inst.; student law dept. U. of N.C.; m. Mary Eliza Mebane, June 3, 1897; 1 dau., Caroline N. Admitted to N.C. bar, 1893; practiced with father, firm Parker & Parker, until 1914; now mem. Brooks, Parker, Smith & Wharton, Greensboro. Gen. counsel Dixie Fire Insurance Co., Jefferson Standard Life Insurance Co., N.C., and many cotton mfg. cos. Mem. N.C. Ho. of Rep., 1923. Trustee Oak Ridge Inst., U. of N.C. Democrat. Presbyn. Home: Greensboro, N.C. Died Sept. 23, 1933.

PARKER, Edwin B., lawyer; b. Shelby Co., Mo., Sept. 7, 1868; student Central Coll., Fayette, Mo.; LL.B., U. of Tex., 1889; m. Katherine Putnam, d. Gen. James G. Blunt, of Leavenworth, Kan., Dec. 1894. With M.,K.&T. Ry., 1889-93; practiced at Houston, Tex., with Baker, Botts, Baker & Lovett, of which became partner, firm name later changed to Baker, Botts, Parker & Garwood; assisted as a "dollar a year man" at Washington, D.C., in orgn. of War Industries Bd. of which was made a member, and priorities commr.; after signing of Armistice served as chmn. U.S. Liquidation Commn.; gen. counsel, mem. bd. dirs. and exec. com. Texas Co., 1920-22; umpire, Mixed Claims Commns., U.S. and Germany, 1923—; sole commr. Tripartite Claims Commn., U.S., Austria and Hungary, 1926—. Trustee Carnegie Endowment for Internat. Peace, George Washington U. Chmn. exec. com. Am. Soc. Internat. Law; chmn. bd., Chamber Commerce, U.S.A., 1927—. Awarded D.S.M. (U.S.); Officer Legion of Honor (France); Commendatore dell'Ordine della Corona d'Italia; Commandeur de l'Ordre de la Couronne (Belgium); Order of Polonia Restituta, grade of Comdr. with the Star (Poland). Died Oct. 30, 1929.

PARKER, Edwin Pond, clergyman; b. Castine, Me., Jan. 13, 1836; s. Rev. Wooster and W. A. (Pond) P.; A.B., Bowdoin, 1856; grad. Bangor Divinity School, 1859; (D.D., Yale University, 1875; LL.D., Trinity College, 1913); m. Lucy M. Harris; m. 2d, Laura A. Gilbert. Ordained Congl. ministry; pastor Second Ch., Hartford, Conn., 1860-1912, pastor emeritus, 1912. Fellow, Yale, 1895—. Writer and composer of several hymns and tunes; compiler of several hymnals. Author: History of Second Church of Christ, in Hartford, 1892. Home: Hartford, Conn. Died May 28, 1920.

PARKER, Emmett Newton, judge; b. York County, Pa., May 12, 1859; s. John and Mary R. (Phillips) P.; ed. pub. schs., Ia.; LL.B., Cincinnati Law School, 1882; LL.D. from College of Puget Sound, 1932; m. Emma Garretson, 1884; children—Mrs. Anna T. Butler, Theodore, Mrs. Helen J. Hart, Mrs. Evangeline Middleton. Settled at Tacoma, Wash., 1888; judge Municipal Ct., 1890-92; judge Superior Court for Pierce Co., Wash., 1893-97; city atty., Tacoma, 1900-01; judge Supreme Court of Wash., 1909-33, retired, chief justice, 1921-22. Republican. Home: Tacoma, Wash. Died Dec. 8, 1939.

PARKER, Fitzgerald Sale, clergyman, author and editor; b. Parish of Caddo, La., Mar. 16, 1863; s. Rev. Dr. Linus (a bishop of M.E. Ch., S.) and Ellen Katherine (Burruss) P.; U. of La., 1879; N.E. Conservatory Music, 1883; Tulane U., 1886-87; (D.D., Centenary Coll. of La., 1894); m. Lucy Irwin Paxton, April 17, 1901; children—William Paxton, Fitzgerald Sale. Entered ministry M.E. Ch., S., 1885; pastor chs. New Orleans, Santa Ana, Calif., New Iberia, Lake Providence, Jackson, La., and El Paso; asst. sec. Epworth League and asst. editor Epworth Era, M.E. Ch., S., 1904-10; gen. sec., editor Epworth Era, 1910-30; with editorial dept., General Bd. Christian Edn., 1930-35. Mem. Gen. Conf., 1906, 1914; mem. Centenary and Ednl. commns. of M.E. Ch., S.; mem. Commn. on Nationalism, Bd. Temperance and Social Service, Ednl. Commn., M.E. Church, S., 1926; v.p. Meth. Benevolent Assn. Author: The Missionary Appeal, 1904; The Devotional Study of the Bible, 1905; Personal Work, 1906; Provincetown, 1924; The Spiritual Life, 1925; The Practice and Experience of Christian Worship, 1929; also reviews. Collaborator on Methodist Hymnal, 1902, 1931-35. Home: Nashville, Tenn. Deceased.

PARKER, Francis Hubert, lawyer; b. East Haddam, Conn., Sept. 23, 1850; s. Hon. Ozias H. and Maria M. (Ayer) P.; A.B., Wesleyan U., 1874; LL.B., Yale, 1876; admitted to Conn. bar and began practice, 1876; m. Mrs. Adelaide Fowler, née Leeds, Dec. 9, 1891. Mem. Conn. Gen. Assembly, 1878, 1880, 1909; Rep. candidate for Conn. Senate, 1894; pros. atty. City of Hartford, 1887-91, 1894-95; chmn. Rep. City Com., 1896-1900; referee in bankruptcy Hartford Co., 1898-1900; U.S. atty. Dist. of Conn., 1900-08; corp. counsel City of Hartford, 1908-10, and pros. atty. (3d time), 1915-17; pres. East Haddam, Conn. Pres. bd. trustees Conn. Sch. for Boys, 1899-1909. Chmn. library com. Conn. Hist. Soc.; pres. Hartford Bar Library Assn. Died Feb. 9, 1927.

PARKER, Francis Warner, lawyer; b. Alton, Ill., Apr. 1, 1858; s. Washington and M. H. (Sallee) P.; A.B., Shurtleff Coll., 1878, A.M., 1884 (LL.D., 1903); removed to Chicago, 1879; m. Alma Chapman, 1883; 2d, Margaret, d. Hon. John H. Kedzie, Chicago, 1913. Admitted to bar, 1880; connected with U.S. Patent Office, 1880-83; in practice in Chicago, 1883—. Mem. Ill. Ho. of Rep., 1st Senatorial Dist., 1885-87; mem. of the "One Hundred and Three" who elected Gen. John A. Logan U.S. senator; state senator from 5th (Hyde Park) Dist., 1902-05. Trustee U. of Chicago, Bapt. Theol. Union, and Shurtleff Coll. Mason. Mem. exec. com. Nat. War Work Council Y.M.C.A.; dir. Y.M.C.A. Divisional Area, in France, 1917-18. Home: Evanston, Ill. Died Oct. 1922.

PARKER, Francis Wayland, pres. Chicago Inst., 1899—; b. Bedford, N.H., Oct. 9, 1837; s. Robert and Mille (Rand) P.; reared on farm; ed. village school and acads.; had charge of schools in N.H. and Ill. until 1861. Served through Civil War, pvt. to col. 4th N.H. vols.; severely wounded at Deep Bottom, James River; mustered out, Aug. 1865. Prin. grammar school, Manchester, N.H., 1865-68; Normal School, Dayton, O., 1868-72; supt. schools, Quincy, Mass., 1875-80; a supervisor of schools, Boston, 1880-83; prin. Cook Co. Normal School (Ill.), 1883-96. Principal Chicago Normal School, 1896-99. Studied psychology, philosophy, history and pedagogy, King William's Univ., Berlin, 1872-75 (A.M., Dartmouth; LL.D., Lawrence Univ.). Author: How to Study Geography, 1889; Uncle Robert's Geographies. Home: Chicago, Ill. Died 1902.

PARKER, Frank Wilson, judge; b. Sturgis, Mich., Oct. 16, 1860; s. James Wilson and Maria Antoinette P.; ed. pub. schs., Sturgis, Mich., until 1878, followed by limited course in acad. dept., U. of Mich.; LL.B., U. of Mich., 1880; m. Lillian L. Kinney, Sept. 28, 1892 (died 1893); 1 dau., Lillian Rosamond (Mrs. Rufus A. Palm, Jr.); m. 2d, Anna Davis, Oct. 26, 1904; 1 son, Frank Wilson. Removed to N.M., 1881, and practiced law until 1898; asso. justice Supreme Court of N.M. Ty., Jan. 10, 1898-Jan. 1912; justice Supreme Court State of N.M., 1912— (chief justice, 1919-20, and Jan. 1, 1923-Jan. 1, 1929). Republican. Home: Las Cruces, N.M. Died Aug. 3, 1932.

PARKER, Franklin Eddy, lumber mfr.; b. Bangor, Me., Jan. 28, 1867; s. Edward Everett and Laura Matilda (Eddy) P.; A.B., Harvard, 1889; student Harvard Law Sch., fall of 1889; m. Mary Beecher Bishop, Mar. 23, 1892. With Mont. Union Ry., Butte, 1890; chief clk. gen. agt.'s office, U.P. Ry., Butte, 1891; coml. agt. P.M. Ry., Bay City, Mich., 1891-93, supt. water lines, same, Ludington, Mich., 1893-94; sec.-treas. Eddy, Sheldon Co., lumber mfrs., Bay City, Mich., 1894-1901, Mershon, Eddy, Parker Co., Saginaw, 1901-08, pres., Oct. 1908—; v.p., dir. W. C. Edwards & Co., Ltd., Ottawa, Ont., 1915—. Pres. Saginaw Valley Lumber Dealers' Assn., 1902-03, Nat. Wholesale Lumber Dealers' Assn., 1912-13. Episcopalian. Home: Bay City, Mich. Deceased.

PARKER, George Albert, teacher of music; b. Kewanee, Ill., Sept. 21, 1856; s. Henry C. and Mary F. P.; grad. Kewanee High Sch., Royal Conservatory of Music, Stuttgart, 1881; post-grad. student of Die Neue Academie der Tonkunst, Berlin, 1881-82; (hon. Mus. Doc., Syracuse U., 1893); m. Mary D. Sims, Sept. 5, 1883. Instr. piano, 1882-83, prof. piano and organ, 1883—, dir. dept. of music, 1888—, acting dean Coll. Fine Arts, 1896-98, dean, 1906-23, dean emeritus and prof. organ, 1923—, Syracuse U. First founder Am. Guild of Organists; v.p. and mem. exec. com., N.Y. State Music Teachers' Assn. Home: Syracuse, N.Y. Died July 3, 1939.

PARKER, George Amos, supt. parks; b. Fitzwilliam, N.H., Apr. 28, 1853; s. George Washington and Julia Ann (Deeth) P.; grad. Mass. Agrl. Coll., 1876; diploma Boston U.; m. Jannie Waterman Richmond, Dec. 6, 1876; children—Arthur Vassar, Andrew Richmond, Robert Lyman, Priscilla. Head gardener, Vassar Coll., 1876-79; successively, supt. Cliffdale (Judge Boardman's Estate), Ophir Farm (John Roach's Estate), supervisor station grounds and approaches, N.Y.,N.H.&H. R.R.; supt. of pub. parks, Hartford, Conn. Republican. Conglist. Mason. Home: Hartford, Conn. Died Sept. 13, 1926.

PARKER, George Frederick, journalist; b. Lafayette, Ind., Dec. 30, 1847; s. Thomas W. and Eliza Ann (Kirk) P.; ed. pub. schs. of Ia., 1854-68; U. of Ia., 1868-70; (LL.D., Simpson, 1908, Washington and Lee, 1909; A.M., Ia. State U., 1909); m. Eloise Florence Dibble, Apr. 27, 1890 (died 1922); children—Charles Harris, John Frederick. Entered journalism, Oct. 1873; edited papers in Ia., Ind., Washington, D.C., N.H., Pa. and N.Y. City; was 1st mng. editor New York Press, 1887-88; contbr. to London Times for 10 years after 1895, and to many mags. in England and U.S. Connected with Dem. Nat. Com., 1880, 84, 88, 92 and 1904; asst. postmaster of Phila., 1885-87; U.S. consul at Birmingham, Eng., 1893-98; commr. in United Kingdom for La. Purchase Expn., 1901-04; sec. trustees of Equitable Life Assurance Soc., 1905-10; sole partner Parker & Bridge. Sec. press and publicity com. of Gen. Conv. P.E. Ch., 1913-19. Independent Democrat. Episcopalian. Author: Recollections of Grover Cleveland, 1909. Home: New York, N.Y. Died May 31, 1928.

PARKER, George Proctor, lawyer; b. American Fork, Utah, Mar. 27, 1885; s. Thomas B. and Elizabeth (Proctor) P.; A.B., Brigham Young U., 1906; LL.B., U. of Mich., 1911; m. Nellie Oliver, June 11, 1907; children—G. Alton, Dorothy, Thomas O., Edward. Admitted to Utah bar, 1911, and began practice at Provo; dir. Farmers & Merchants Bank of Provo. County atty. Utah Co., 1916-17; dist. judge 4th Jud. Dist., Utah, 1925-28; atty. gen. of Utah for term 1929-33. Republican. Morman. Home: Salt Lake City, Utah. Deceased.

PARKER, Henry Taylor, critic; b. Boston, Mass., Apr. 29, 1867; s. William Fisk and Susan Sophia (Taylor) P.; student Harvard, 1886-89; studied in Europe, 1889-91; unmarried. New York corr. Boston Transcript, 1892-98, 1901-03; London corr. Boston Transcript and New York Commercial Advertiser, 1898-1900; dramatic critic, 1903-04, dramatic and mus. critic, 1904-05, New York Globe; dramatic and mus. critic Boston Transcript, 1905—. Has made study of European theatres, opera houses, etc. Author: Eighth Notes (essays on music), 1921. Home: Boston, Mass. Died Mar. 30, 1934.

PARKER, Herbert, lawyer; b. Charlestown, Mass., Mar. 2, 1856; s. George A. and Harriet Newell (Felton) P.; student Harvard, class of '78, A.B., 1896; (LL.D., Tufts, 1905); m. Mary Carney Vose, Sept. 22, 1886. Admitted to bar, 1884; principally engaged as trial lawyer. Asso. justice 2d Dist. Ct. of Eastern Worcester, 1886-87; asst. dist. atty. and dist. atty., Middle (Mass.) Dist., 1887-99; atty. gen. of Mass., 1901-05; dir. State Mut. Life Ins. Co. of Worcester; pres. bd. trustees Pub. Reservations of Mass. (standing com.). Mem. Mass. Constl. Conv., 1917-19; chmn. Mass. Bay Colony Tercentenary Commn., 1930. Pres. bd. trustees Clark Coll. and Clark U. Fellow Am. Acad. Arts and Sciences. Unitarian. Republican. Home: South Lancaster, Mass. Died Feb. 11, 1939.

PARKER, Hilon Adelbert, engineer; b. Plessis, N.Y., Dec. 30, 1841; s. Alpheus and Lucinda P., of Revolutionary stock; acad. edn.; m. Mary E. Cunningham, May 25, 1871 (dec.); 2d, Grace Rowley, Nov. 1894. Served pvt. to 1st lt., 1861-65; fought at Cold Harbor, Petersburg, Shenandoah Valley, Richmond, etc. Entered ry. service, 1866; held various positions, 1866-85; v.p. and chief engr. Chicago, Kansas & Neb. Ry., 1885-89, also gen. mgr., 1888; asst. to the pres. C.,R.I.&P. Ry., 1889-90, and 1893-98, 3d v.p. 1890-93, 2d v.p. 1898-99, 1st v.p. and gen. mgr. Mar. 1899-Apr. 1903; resigned; cons. engr. Grand Trunk Pacific Ry., 1909. Home: Chicago, Ill. Died 1911.

PARKER, Horatio William, composer; b. Auburndale, Mass., Sept. 15, 1863; s. Charles Edward and Isabella Graham (Jennings) P.; ed. at Auburndale and in Europe; grad. Royal Conservatoire, Munich, 1885; (hon. A.M., Yale, 1892; Mus. Doc., Cambridge U., Eng., 1902); m. Anna Ploessl, of Munich, Bavaria, Aug. 9, 1886. Prof. music, Cathedral Sch. of St. Paul, Garden City, L.I., 1885-87; organist Holy Trinity Ch., New York, 1888-93, Trinity Ch., Boston, 1893-1901; prof. theory of music, Yale, 1894—. His Hora Novissima was performed Chester (Eng.) Festival, July 1899, at Festival of the Three Choirs, Worcester, Eng., Sept. 1899 (first Am. composition ever on one of these Festival Programs); awarded Met. Opera prize ($10,000), Apr. 1911, for opera "Mona"; also the prize ($10,000) offered by Nat. Federation of Women's Clubs for Am. Opera was awarded to the opera "Faryland," Oct. 1914. Member Am. Acad. Arts and Letters. Author: Cantatas—King Trojan, The Kobolds; oratorios—Hora Novissima, 1898; St. Christopher, 1898; A Wanderer's Psalm (given under composer's direction, Hereford Festival, Eng., 1900). Home: New Haven, Conn. Died Dec. 18, 1919.

PARKER, Hosea Washington, lawyer; b. Lempster, N.H., May 30, 1833; s. Benjamin and Olive (Nichols) P.; Washington Acad. and Green Mountain Liberal Inst.; Tufts Coll., 1885-86 (hon. M.A., 1883, LL.D., 1913); studied law under Edmund Burke, Newport, N.H.; admitted to bar, 1859; m. Lovisa Southgate, May 30, 1861 (died 1904). Began practice at Lempster, but soon removed to Claremont; mem. N.H. Ho. of Rep., 1859, 1860; mem. 42d and 43d Congresses (1871-75); pres. bd. trustees Tufts Coll. Supt. Universalist S.S., Claremont, for nearly 60 yrs., and pres. of 3 nat. gen. convs. of the ch. Mason. Pres. People's National Bank. Home: Claremont, N.H. Died Aug. 21, 1922.

PARKER, James, officer U.S.A.; b. Newark, N.J., Feb. 20, 1854; s. Hon. Cortlandt and Elisabeth Wolcott (Stites) P.; student Phillips Acad., Andover, and Rutgers Coll.; grad. U.S. Mil. Acad., 1876; A.M., Rutgers, 1878; m. Charlotte M. Condit, 1879. Second lt. 4th Cav., June 15, 1876; promoted through grades to brig. gen., Mar. 3, 1913; maj. gen. N.A., Aug. 5, 1917. Served in Indian Ty., 1876-77, Mexican border disturbances (Tex.), 1878-79, Ute campaign, Colo., 1879-81, Geronimo Apache campaign, Ariz., 1885-86; instr. cav., West Point, 1894-98; served in Spanish-Am. War and Philippine insurrection, 1898-1901; a.-a.-g., Washington, 1901-03; adj. gen. Northern Div. U.S.A., 1904-05; dir. Cav. Sch., Ft. Riley, Kan., 1905-06; with Cuban army of pacification, 1906-09; comdg. 11th Cav., Ft. Oglethorpe, Ga., 1909-12; in Europe on cav. reorganization bd., Sept. to Dec. 1912; assigned as comdr. 1st Cav. Brigade, San Antonio, Tex., Mar. 25, 1913; comd. mobilization troops, Brownsville Dist., Tex., 1916; comdr. 1st Provisional Inf. Div., Camp Wilson, Tex., 1917; comd. and trained all troops in Dept. of Tex., May-Aug. 1917; comd. 32d Div. (Mich. and Wis. troops) to Dec. 1917, 85th Div. (Mich. and Wis. troops), to Feb. 20, 1918; on observation duty in France, Oct., Nov. 1917; in action nr. Armentières, nr. St. Quentin and at Chemin des Dames, Oct. 1917; retired by operation of law, Feb. 20, 1918. Pres. bd. charged with revision small arms firing regulations, 1904; bd. which revised cav. drill regulations, 1902; in charge Militia Div., War Dept., 1903-04; recommended for bvts. for gallantry in action at San Mateo, Manaoag, and Vigan, P.I., 1899; awarded Congressional Medal of Honor "for distinguished gallantry" at Vigan, P.I., Dec. 4, 1899, and silver stars for gallantry in 3 actions; D.S.M. for services in World War. Author: The Mounted

Rifleman, 1916; The Old Army, Memories, 1929. Home: Newport, R.I. Died June 2, 1934.

PARKER, James Cutler Dunn, musician; b. Boston, June 2, 1828; s. Samuel Hale and Sarah P.; A.B., Harvard, 1848, A.M., 1856; (Mus. Doc., Alfred U.); studied law, Boston, 1848-51; studied music, Leipzig, 1851-54; m. Maria Derby, Sept. 6, 1859. Organist Trinity Ch., Boston, 1864-91; examiner N.E. Conservatory of Music, Boston, 1893—. His principal works are: Redemption Hymn; Blind King; St. John; Life of Man (oratorio), composed for solo, chorus and orchestra; also several ch. services. Home: Brookline, Mass. Died 1916.

PARKER, James Henry, banker; b. Johnston Co., N.C., Jan. 4, 1843; s. Mathew and Martha P.; served C.S.A., 1861-64, lt. of cav.; took course in medicine, practiced in N.C. 2 yrs.; m. Julia A. Jones, 1877. In cotton and naval store business, Charleston, S.C., 1870-82; in New York, 1882—; pres. U.S. Nat. Bank many yrs.; chmn. bd. dirs. Mut. Alliance Trust Co.; dir. Nat. Bank of Commerce, Nat. Reserve Bank, Coal & Iron Nat. Bank. Pres. New York Cotton Exchange 2 years. Ex-comdr. Confed. Vet. Corps of N.Y. Died Jan. 27, 1915.

PARKER, James Southworth, congressman; b. Great Barrington, Mass., June 3, 1867; ed. Cornell U., 1885-87; m. Marion Williams, June 21, 1899. Formerly teacher, St. Paul's Sch., Concord, N.H.; farmer, Salem, N.Y., 1898—; mem. N.Y. Assembly, 1904-05 and 1908-12; mem. 63d to 72d Congresses (1913-33), 29th N.Y. Dist. Republican. Home: Salem, N.Y. Died Dec. 19, 1933.

PARKER, John Milliken, governor; b. Bethel Church, Miss., Mar. 16, 1863; s. John Milliken and Roberta (Buckner) P.; ed. pub. schs.; m. Cecile Airey, Jan. 11, 1888; children—John M., Thos. A., Virginia. Engaged in cotton business, New Orleans, La., 1880—; pres. Jno. M. Parker Co. Mem. New Orleans Bd. of Trade (pres. 1893), New Orleans Cotton Exchange (pres. 1897-98), Southern Commercial Congress (pres., 1910, 11). Progressive Party nominee for vice-pres. of U.S., 1916, but nat. orgn. came to an end before election of 1916; arbitrator in settlement of metal trade workers' strike, New Orleans, 1918. Gov. of La., term 1920-24; in charge of flood relief in La., 1927. Democrat. President Mississippi Valley Assn., 1919. Presbyn. Home: New Orleans, La. Died May 20, 1939.

PARKER, Joseph Benson, rear admiral U.S.N.; b. Carlisle, Pa., June 20, 1841; s. Rev. Joseph and Mary (Sheerer) P.; A.B., Dickinson Coll., 1860, A.M., 1863; M.D., Bellevue Hosp. Med. Coll., 1862; m. Margaret J. Yorke, Oct. 1868. Appt. asst. surgeon U.S.N., Mar., 1863; advanced through various grades to med. dir., and retired, June 20, 1903, with rank of rear-admiral. Served on Asiatic Pacific, West India stas. and at various navy yards and hosps. Home: Philadelphia, Pa. Died Oct. 21, 1915.

PARKER, Leonard Fletcher, college prof.; b. Arcade, N.Y., Aug. 3, 1825; s. Elias and Dorothy F. (Fletcher) P.; A.B., Oberlin, 1851, A.M., 1860 (D.D., 1895); Oberlin Theol. Sem., 1851-53; m. Sarah C. Pearse, Aug. 21, 1853; m. 2d, Mrs. Nellie Greene Clarke, Aug. 19, 1903. Supt. schs., Brownsville, Pa., 1853-56, Grinnell, Ia., 1856-60; ordained Congl. ministry, 1862; prof. Greek, Iowa (now Grinnell) Coll., 1860-70; prof. history, State U. of Ia., 1870-87; Parker prof. history, 1888-98 (emeritus), Iowa Coll. First lt. Co. B, 46th Ia. Inf., May-Sept. 1864; mem. Ia. Ho. of Rep., 1868-70. Republican. Author: History of Education in Iowa, No. 17 of state monographs for U.S. Bur. of Edn., 1890; History of Poweshiek County, Iowa, 1911. Home: Grinnell, Ia. Died 19—.

PARKER, Lottie Blair, author, playwright; b. Oswego, N.Y.; d. George and Emily (Hitchcock) Blair; grad. Oswego Normal Sch.; studied for stage under Wyzeman Marshall, Boston; m. Harry Doel Parker, theatrical mgr. Began with stock co., Boston Theatre; later with traveling companies, among them Mme. Janauschek's and Lawrence Barrett's; last important engagement was in title rôle of "Hazel Kirke." Entered New York Herald Prize contest for one-act play, submitting 2 plays, one of them, "White Roses," receiving hon. mention; this play was later successfully prod. at Lyceum Theatre, and in London, under title of "Red Roses." Author: Homespun (novel), 1909; (plays) Way Down East, 1897; Under Southern Skies, 1901; A War Correspondent; Lights of Home; The Redemption of David Corson (dramatization of novel by Charles Frederick Goss). Home: Great Neck, N.Y. Died Jan. 5, 1937.

PARKER, Moses Greeley, physician; b. Dracut, Mass., Oct. 12, 1842; s. Theodore and Hannah (Greeley) P.; desc. through father from Deacon Thomas P., and through mother from Andrew Greeley; prep. edn. Phillips Acad., Andover, Mass., to 18; studied, L.I. Coll. Hosp. Med. Sch., Brooklyn; M.D., Harvard Med. Sch., 1864; U. of Vienna, 1873-74, Paris, 1874-75; unmarried. Asst. surgeon 2d U.S.C. Cav., 1864-65; located in Lowell, Mass., 1866; specializes as oculist and aurist; phys. to St. John's Hosp., Lowell, 30 yrs., Lowell Gen. Hosp. (trustee, 1898—), Dispensary and Ministry at Large, 10 yrs. Dir. and mem. exec. com. since orgn., 1883, N.E. Telephone and Telegraph Co. (also interested in Bell Telephone Co. since its orgn.). Pres. Ayer Home, Lowell Day Nursery Assn.; trustee Howe Sch., Billerica, Mass., 1877—. Del. Nat. Arbitration and Peace Congress, New York, 1907. Republican. Unitarian. Mem. various med. societies. Mason. Has made a spl. study of electricity and was the first to photograph the elec. current and show that it takes the form of spirals. Home: Lowell, Mass. Died Oct. 1, 1917.

PARKER, R(ichard) Wayne, congressman; b. Morristown, N.J., Aug. 6, 1848; s. Hon. Cortlandt and Elizabeth Wolcott (Stites) P.; bro. of James and Charles Wolcott P.; A.B., Princeton, 1867, A.M., 1870; LL.B., Columbia, 1869; m. Eleanor K. Gordon, Jan. 2, 1884. Admitted to bar, 1870, and began practice at Newark. Mem. N.J. Assembly, 1885, 1886; candidate for Congress, 1892; mem. 54th to 61st Congresses (1895-1911), 7th N.J. Dist., and 63d Congress (for unexpired term, Dec. 1914-Mar. 1915) and 64th, 65th and 67th Congresses (1915-19) and (1921-23), 9th N.J. Dist. Republican. Home: Newark, N.J. Died Nov. 28, 1923.

PARKER, Samuel Chester, college prof.; b. Cincinnati, May 31, 1880; s. Samuel B. and Elizabeth Helen (Chappell) P.; B.A., U. of Cincinnati, 1901; A.M., Teachers Coll. (Columbia), 1903; fellow in education, Columbia, 1906-07; m. Lucile R. Jones, June 4, 1904. Prof. edn., Miami U., Oxford, O., 1903-09; asso. prof. edn., 1909-13, prof., 1913—, dean Coll. of Edn., 1911-16, U. of Chicago. Author: History of Modern Elementary Education; Methods of Teaching in High Schools; Methods of Teaching in Elementary Schools; Types of Elementary Teaching and Learning. Home: Chicago, Ill. Died July 21, 1924.

PARKER, William Belmont, editor, writer; b. Hasbury, Eng., Sept. 19, 1871; s. Rev. Joseph J. and Elizabeth (Sadler) P.; grad. Phillips Acad., Andover, Mass., 1893; A.B., magna cum laude, Harvard, 1897; m. Helen Louise Newton, May 29, 1906; children—Newton B., Barrett, William James, Elizabeth Lee. Asst. editor Atlantic Monthly, 1898-1902; lt. advisor Houghton, Mifflin & Co., 1902-04; instr. English, Harvard, 1904-05; lecturer in English, Columbia, 1905-08; advisory editor of Associated Sunday Magazines, 1906-08; lit. editor World's Work, 1908; editor and lit. advisor The Baker & Taylor Co., 1909-12; lit. advisor Century Co., 1912; business manager The Churchman, 1912-14; on staff of S. Pearson & Son, 1914-18; commd., 1918, by Hispanic Soc. of America to prepare series of biographical handbooks on republics of Hispanic America; secretary for resources, Harvard Dental School, 1931—. Author: Life of Edward Rowland Sill, 1915; Life of Justin S. Morrill, 1924; Great University Memorials, etc. Editor: Lowell's Anti-Slavery Papers, 1903; Sir Philip Sidney's Certaine Sonets, 1904; Complete Poems of Edward Rowland Sill, 1906; Psychotherapy, 1908-09; The Wisdom of Emerson, 1909; Cubans of To-Day, 1919; Peruvians of To-Day, 1919; Bolivians of To-Day, 1920; Chileans of To-Day, 1920; Argentines of To-Day, 1920; Paraguayans of To-Day, 1920; Uruguayans of To-Day, 1921. Joint editor: Letters and Addresses of Thomas Jefferson, 1905. Home: South Orange, N.J. Died Oct. 6, 1934.

PARKER, William H., congressman; b. May 5, 1847; served in Union Army, 1861-66; LL.B., Columbian (now George Washington) Univ., 1868; admitted to bar, 1868; m. Clara E. Thomas, Jan. 27, 1867. Collector Internal revenue, Colo. Ty., 1874-76; asst. U.S. atty., Colo. Ty., 1876, and later U.S. atty.; removed to Deadwood, Dak. Ty., 1877; mem. Constl. Conv., 1885; was mem. senate; elected mem. S.D. Ho. of Rep., 1889; state's atty., Lawrence Co., S.D., 2 terms, 1902-06; mem. 60th Congress, at-large, S.D., 1907-09. Republican. Home: Deadwood, S.D. Died 1908.

PARKHILL, Charles Breckinridge, lawyer; b. Leon Co., Fla., June 23, 1859; s. George W. and Elizabeth (Bellamy) P.; student Randolph-Macon Coll., Va., 1876-78, U. of Va., 1880-82; m. Genevieve Perry, 1884 (died 1885); 1 dau., Genevieve (Mrs. J. M. Lykes); m. 2d, Helen Wall, Nov. 30, 1891; children—Barbara (Mrs. Beman Beckwith), Elizabeth (Mrs. S. L. Lowry, Jr.), Joseph F., Charles B., Richard C. (dec.), Helen (Mrs. C. A. Rudisill), Emala (Mrs. A. Pickens Coles), John. Admitted to Florida bar, 1882; member Florida Senate, 1888-90; solicitor of Criminal Court of Record of Escambia County, Fla., 1897-1904; judge Circuit Court, 1st Judicial Circuit, Florida, 1904-05; asso. justice Supreme Court of Fla., 1905-12 (resigned); in law practice at Tampa, 1912—; city atty. of Tampa, 1913-16. Commd. maj., judge advocate U.S.A., Nov. 15, 1917; served with A.E.F.; state's atty. 13th Jud. Circuit, Fla., 1920—, present term ending 1933. Democrat. Methodist. Past Grand Chancellor K.P.; Elk. Home: Tampa, Fla. Died May 13, 1933.

PARKHURST, Charles, editor, b. at Sharon, Vt., Oct. 29, 1845; s. Chester and Sarah A. P.; A.B., Dartmouth, 1878, A.M., 1881; studied, Andover Theol. Sem.; (D.D., U. of Vermont, 1888, Allegheny Coll., 1888); LL.D., from De Pauw U., 1914; m. Lucia A. Tyler, 1878. Ordained deacon, April 29, 1876, elder, May 4, 1879, M.E. Ch.; pastor, Hyde Park, Vt., 1875-76, Bradford, Vt., 1876-77, Fairlee and N. Thetford, Vt., 1877-78, Montpelier, Vt., 1878-80, Auburndale, Mass., 1880-81, Baker Memorial Ch., Concord, N.H., 1881-83, Garden St. Church, Lawrence, Mass., 1883-86, Dover, N.H., 1886-88; editor Zion's Herald, Boston, 1888-Apr. 1919, resigned. Home: Somerville, Mass. Died Feb. 1921.

PARKHURST, Charles Henry, clergyman; b. Framingham, Mass., Apr. 17, 1842; s. Charles F. W. and Mary (Goodale) P.; A.B., Amherst, 1866, A.M., 1869, D.D., 1880, LL.D., 1892; prin. Amherst High Sch., 1867-69; studied theology at Halle, 1869-70, Leipzig, 1872-73; taught in Williston Sem., Easthampton, Mass., 1870-71; m. Ellen Bodman, Nov. 23, 1870; m. 2d, Mrs. Eleanor Marx, Apr. 19, 1927. Ordained Presbyn. ministry, 1872; pastor Congl. Ch., Lenox, Mass., 1874-80, Madison Sq. Presbyn. Ch., New York, 1880-1918. Became pres., 1891, Soc. for Prevention of Crime, and his assertion of partnership of police with criminals led to an investigation of the New York police by the N.Y. Legislature. Trustee Amherst, 1892-1902. Author: Forms of the Latin Verb Illustrated by the Sanskrit, 1870; The Blind Man's Creed, and Other Sermons, 1883; The Pattern on the Mount, 1885; Three Gates on a Side, 1887; What Would the World Be Without Religion?, 1888; The Swiss Guide, 1889; Our Fight with Tammany, 1895; The Sunny Side of Christianity, 1901; A Little Lower Than the Angels, 1909; My Forty Years in New York, 1923. Address: Ventnor, N.J. Died Sept. 8, 1933.

PARKHURST, C(hristopher) Francis, judge; b. Providence, R.I., Sept. 17, 1854; s. William H. and Sarah (Tanner) P.; A.B., Brown U., 1876; admitted to bar, 1879; m. E. Louise Eliot, June 6, 1882. Mem. Providence Common Council, 1892-95, R.I. Senate, 1900-02; asso. justice Supreme Ct. of R.I., 1905-17, chief justice, Mar. 8, 1917-Feb. 1, 1920. Republican. Episcopalian. Home: Providence, R.I. Died July 1, 1925.

PARKHURST, Frederic Hale, lawyer; b. Unity, Me., Nov. 5, 1864; s. Jonathan Fuller and Susan (Haskell) P.; ed. pub. schs., Bangor; LL.B. and LL.M., Columbian (now George Washington) U., 1887; m. Marie J. Reid, Sept. 21, 1887; 2d, Dorothy Woodman, June 1, 1911. Admitted to Me. bar, 1887; practiced in Bangor, 1887—; mem. Common Council, 1893-94 (pres. 1894); mem. Me. Ho. of Rep., 1895-96, 1899, 1900, 01, 02, Senate, 1907-08; commissary gen. of Me. on staff of Gov. Hill, 1901-04; chmn. Rep. State Com., 1912-15; mem. State of Me. Com. on Pub. Safety and chmn. Penobscot Co. Br., 1917. Home: Bangor, Me. Died Jan. 31, 1921.

PARKHURST, Howard Elmore, composer; b. Ashland, Mass., Sept. 13, 1848; s. Charles F. W. and Mary (Goodale) P.; brother of Charles Henry P.; A.B., Amherst, 1873; m. Marie S. Huss, Nov. 17, 1885. Author: A Complete System of Harmony, 1908; A Complete Method for the Modern Organ, 1911; The Church Organist, 1913; The Beginnings of the World's Music, 1914; Rambles in Music Land, 1914. Home: Englewood, N.J. Died Aug. 18, 1916.

PARKHURST, John Adelbert, astronomer; b. Dixon, Ill., Sept. 24, 1861; s. Sanford Britton and Clarissa (Hubbard) P.; A.B., Wheaton (Ill.) Coll., 1897; S.B., Rose Poly. Inst., Terre Haute, Ind., 1886, S.M., 1897; m. Anna Greenleaf, Nov. 21, 1888. With pvt. astron. obs., Marengo, Ill., 1892-97; with Yerkes Obs., 1898—, successively as vol. research asst., asst. Carnegie investigator in stellar photometry, instr., asst. prof. and as asso. prof. astronomy, 1919—. Conglist. Author: Spectra of Stars of Secchi's Fourth Type (with Hale and Ellerman), 1903; Researches in Stellar Photometry, 1906. Home: Williams Bay, Wis. Died Mar. 1, 1925.

PARKHURST, John Foster, jurist; b. Wellsboro, Pa., Feb. 17, 1843; s. Dr. Curtis and Jane (Kasson) P.; ed. pub. schs., Lawrenceville, Pa.; studied law in office of Judge Guy H. McMaster, Bath, N.Y.; m. Alice, d. Judge Guy H. McMaster, July 22, 1886. Admitted to bar, Rochester, N.Y., 1865; partner with Judge McMaster, 1872-87; del.-at-large State Constl. Conv., 1894 (mem. judiciary and suffrage coms.; chmn. com. on county, town and village offices); judge State Court of Claims, 1887-1901; justice Supreme Court, by appmt., 1901-02, elected, 1902, for term expiring Dec. 31, 1916. Home: Bath, N.Y. Died 1906.

PARKHURST, John Gibson, lawyer; b. Oneida Castle, N.Y., Apr. 17, 1824; s. Stephen and Sally (Gibson) P.; grad. Oneida Acad., 1843. Read law in office of Graves & Dodge, 1843-47; admitted to N.Y. bar, 1847; practiced Oneida Co., N.Y., 1847-49; practiced in Mich., 1849-61; m. Amelia C. Noyes, Nov. 10, 1852 (died 1861); 2d, Josy B. Reeves, Aug. 10, 1863 (died 1870); 3d, Frances J. Fiske, Apr. 23, 1874 (died 1900). Sec. Nat. Dem. Conv., Charleston, 1860; enlisted Union army, Sept. 10, 1861; served lt. col. and col. 9th Mich. Inf.; provost marshal 14th

Army corps, provost marshal-gen. Dept. of the Cumberland; provost marshal-gen. Mil. Div. of the Tenn.; brig. gen. vols. on staff Gen. George H. Thomas, 1862-65; U.S. marshal, dist. of Mich., 1866-69; resumed practice; E.E. and M.P. of U.S. to Belgium, 1888-89. Democrat. Home: Coldwater, Mich. Died 1906.

PARKINS, Almon Ernest, geographer; b. Marysville, Mich., Jan. 10, 1879; s. John H. and Mariah (Cooley) P.; B.Pd., Mich. State Normal Coll., Ypsilanti, 1906, A.B., 1911, hon. M.Edn., 1922; B.S., U. of Chicago, 1912, Ph.D., 1914; m. Eleanor Grace Stone, June 29, 1905. Instr. agrl. geology and geography, U. of Mo., 1914-16; prof. geography, George Peabody Coll., 1916—. Field rep. division of cotton, Agrl. Adjustment Administration, 1935. Distinguished service award, Nat. Council of Geography Teachers, 1934. Unitarian. Mason. Author: Historical Geography of Detroit; Development of Transportation in Pennsylvania; The South, Its Economic-Geographic Development, 1937; author of the department of "Junior High School Geography" in the Class Room Teacher. Co-author: McMurry and Parkins Geographies, 1921; Maddox and Parkins, Forestry and Forest Industries; Miller and Parkins, Geography of North America. Co-editor and co-author: Our Natural Resources and Their Conservation, 1937. Editor: Annals of Assn. Am. Geographies; of series of sch. and coll. maps. Mem. publn. bd. Peabody Jour. of Edn.; chmn. com. 1933 Yearbook, Nat. Soc. Study of Edn. Home: Nashville, Tenn. Died Jan. 3, 1940.

PARKINSON, Daniel Baldwin, normal sch. pres.; b. nr. Highland, Ill., Sept. 6, 1845; s. Alfred Jackson and Mary Eugenia (Baldwin) P.; B.S., McKendree Coll., 1868, A.M., 1874, Ph.D., 1898; spl. student Northwestern U., 1873-74; m. Julia F. Mason, Dec. 28, 1876 (dec.); 2d, Mary Alice Raymond, July 30, 1884. Prof. physical and chem. sciences, 1874-97, pres., 1897-1913, now pres. emeritus, Southern Ill. Normal U. Pres. Ill. State Teachers' Assn., 1906; pres. Southern Ill. Teachers' Assn. Republican. Methodist; active S.S. worker. Home: Carbondale, Ill. Died Oct. 8, 1923.

PARKINSON, John Barber, univ. prof.; b. Edwardsville, Ill., Apr. 11, 1834; s. Peter and Valinda (Barber) P.; A.B., U. of Wis., 1860, A.M., 1863, LL.D., 1920; m. Frances Jane Gray, Dec. 19, 1861; children—Marshall Monroe, Mary (Mrs. A. T. Schroeder) dec., John Monroe, Ben Carroll, Henry Gray, Stanley Barber (dec.), Harriet, Myra. Instr. U. of Wis., 1861-62; county supt. schs., Lafayette Co., Wis., 1862-64; regent, 1866-67, prof. mathematics, 1867-72, civ. polity and constl. law, 1872-74, civ. polity and polit. economy, 1876-93, constl. and internat. law, 1893-1910, active v.p., 1885-1910, v.p. and prof. constl. and internat. law emeritus, 1910, U. of Wis. in journalism, and pres. Wis. Bd. Centennial Mgrs., 1874-76. Unitarian. Home: Madison, Wis. Died Apr. 2, 1927.

PARKINSON, Robert Henry, lawyer; b. Cape Elizabeth, Me., Aug. 10, 1849; s. of Royal and Juanna (Griffin) P.; A.B., Dartmouth, 1870; m. Helen B. McGuffey, 1878 (died 1925); children—Elizabeth D., June G., Stirling B., Kelso S. (dec.). Admitted to bar, St. Louis, 1872; practiced in Cincinnati; removed to Chicago, 1893; specialty in patent and trade-mark law; has conducted many important causes before federal cts. and U.S. Supreme Ct. Republican. Conglist. Home: Chicago, Ill. Died Dec. 26, 1927.

PARKMAN, Henry, banker; b. Boston, May 23, 1850; s. Samuel and Mary Eliot (Dwight) P.; A.B., Harvard, 1870, A.M., 1874, LL.B., 1873; admitted to bar, 1874; m. Mary Frances Parker, Aug. 21, 1890. Practiced law, Boston, 1874-95; treas. Provident Instn. for Savings, Boston, 1895—. Mem. Boston Common Council, 6 yrs., Mass. Ho. of Rep., 3 yrs., Senate, 2 yrs., Mass. Prison Commn., 1894-1915, Mass. Constl. Conv., 1917. Republican. Home: Boston, Mass. Died June 1924.

PARKS, Charles Wellman, naval officer; b. Woburn, Mass., Mar. 22, 1863; s. Granville and Elizabeth A. P.; C.E., Rensselaer Poly. Inst., 1884; LL.B., Columbia Law Sch., 1899; LL.D., George Washington U., 1921; m. Miss M. B. Frear, Apr. 14, 1887. Served as chief engr. Denver, Memphis & Atlantic Ry., and elec. engr. Elec. Mfg. Co., Troy, N.Y.; head dept. of physics, Rensselaer Poly. Inst., 9 yrs. Commd. civ. engr. U.S.N., rank of ensign, July 19, 1897; promoted through grades to rear adm., Jan. 11, 1918; retired Dec. 1, 1921. Served with Bur. Yards and Docks, Navy Dept., Spanish-Am. War, 1898; pub. works officer, Navy Yard, Phila., 1912-14, Naval Sta., Hawaii, 1908-09 and 1915-17; apptd. chief Bur. Yards and Docks, Navy Dept., Jan. 11, 1918. Supt. liberal arts, Paris Expn., 1889; special agent Bur. of Education, at Chicago Expn., 1893, exhibiting model town library of 5,000 vols.; visited and reported on expns. at Antwerp, Lyon and Zürich; reported on forestry systems of Europe. Officier de l'Instruction Publique (France), 1889; D.S.M. (U.S.), 1919, for distinguished services in World War; Comdr. Legion of Honor (France), 1920. Home: Woburn, Mass. Died June 25, 1930.

PARKS, Clifford C., banker; b. Neponset, Ill., Apr. 18, 1860; son of Granville C. and Nancy (McKee) P.; ed. pub. schs.; m. Harriet R. Elrick, Nov. 4, 1914 (dec.); children—Nancy, Charlotte. With First Nat. Bank, Glenwood Springs, Colo., 1887-1916; with First Nat. Bank, Denver, Colo., 1916—, dir. and v.p., 1916—; pres. First Nat. Securities Corp. Receiver U.S. Land Office, Glenwood Springs, 1890-94; auditor, State of Colo., 1895-96. Regent of U. of Colo., 1914-20. Republican. Mason. Home: Denver, Colo. Died June 21, 1937.

PARKS, Edward Lamay, univ. prof.; b. Dundee, N.Y., Jan. 26, 1851; s. George Hamlin and Julia (Hollister) P.; A.B., Northwestern U., 1873, A.M., 1876; B.D., Garrett Bibl. Inst., 1878, D.D., 1887; m. Isabella B. Webb, July 30, 1879; children—Julia H. (Mrs. A. Marcus), Sarah R., George E., Emma W., Charles W., Frances W. (dec.), Isabelle M. Instr. in Northwestern U., 1872-79; ordained M.E. ministry, 1878; pastor Ingleside Av. Ch., Chicago, 1879-80; pres. Simpson Coll., Indianola, Ia., 1880-86; prof. systematic theology, with ethics and sociology, Gammon Theol. Sem., 1886-1904; pastor Siloam Springs, Ark., 1905-07; prof. economics, 1907-28, treas. and registrar, 1909-19, dean of men, 1919-26, Howard U. Dir. Bible schs. and lecturer in Chautauqua, 1891—. Author of various studies in systematic theology, the Christian life, and books of the Bible. Home: Washington, D.C. Died May 24, 1930.

PARKS, James Lewis, clergyman; b. New York, June 12, 1848; s. Rev. Martin Phillips and Georgiana Clough (Mabry) P.; bro. of Rev. Leighton P.; grad. Gen. Theol. Sem., 1871; (S.T.D., Hobart Coll., 1886); m. Julia Brydges Waring, Jan. 27, 1853. Deacon, 1871, priest, 1872, P.E. Ch.; rector St. Paul's, Oakland, Calif., Holy Trinity, Middletown, Conn., St. Peter's, Phila., Calvary Ch., New York, 1896—. Died Feb. 18, 1912.

PARKS, James Lewis, prof. law; b. Middletown, Conn., Mar. 2, 1886; s. James Lewis and Julia (Waring) P.; A.B., Columbia, 1907, LL.B., 1910; m. Louise Bentley, June 18, 1910; children—Mrs. Carolyn Mosher Oldham, Louise Bentley, Jacqueline Lewis, James Lewis. Admitted to N.Y. bar, 1909, and began practice at N.Y. City; prof. law, George Washington U., 1914-17, Law Sch., Ind. U., 1917-19; prof. law, Law Sch., U. of Mo., 1919—, dean, 1928—; visiting prof. law, summers, U. of Chicago, 1920, 24, Columbia, 1922, 23, U. of Tex., 1925, U. of Mich., 1926, 27, U. of N.C., 1928, U. of Minn., 1929, U. of Iowa, 1932; in cons. practice. Democrat. Episcopalian. Author: Cases on Mortgages, 1926. Chmn. of com. of Mo. Bar Assn. for preparation of Mo. annotations to Am. Law Inst. Restatement of Law. Home: Columbia, Mo. Died Mar. 6, 1934.

PARKS, Leighton, clergyman; b. N.Y. City, Feb. 10, 1852; s. Rev. Martin Phillips and Georgiana Clough (Mabry) P.; B.D., Gen. Theol. Sem., 1876; hon. A.M., St. John's, Md., 1890, D.D., 1892; S.T.D., Harvard, 1900; m Margarita Alden Haven, of Geneva, Switzerland, Aug. 12, 1878; children—Alice (wife of Sir. John Barran), Ellen Stanley, Georgette (Mrs. Albert L. Roper, dec.). Deacon, 1876, priest, 1877, P.E. Ch.; rector Emmanuel Ch., Boston, 1878-1904, St. Bartholomew's Ch., New York, 1904-25. Author: His Star in the East; The Winning of the Soul and Other Sermons, 1893; Moral Leadership, 1914; The Crisis of the Churches, 1922; What Is Modernism? 1924; Turnpikes and Dirt Roads. Died Mar. 21, 1938.

PARKS, Marvin McTyeire, educator; b. Marietta, Ga., Nov. 29, 1872; s. William Asbury and Ann D. (Moore) P.; A.B., Emory Coll., Ga., 1892; student U. of Chicago, 1894-95, Harvard, 1896; LL.D., U. of Ga., 1915; m. Ruth Vaden, Sept. 8, 1896; children—Ruth Vaden (Mrs. L. G. Callahan), William Vaden, Marvin M., Catherine Carroll, Dorothy Virginia. Prof. Latin, Andrew Coll. (Ga.), 1892-94; same, Wesleyan Coll. (Ga.), 1896-97; instr. high sch., Savannah, 1897-1903; prof. pedagogy, 1903-04, acting pres., 1904-05, pres., 1905, Ga. State Coll. for Women; mem. State Bd. of Edn., state supt. of schs., Ga., 1922-23. Methodist. Author of letters, "Around the World," pub. in Atlanta Journal, 1909-10. Home: Milledgeville, Ga. Died Dec. 29, 1926.

PARKS, Rufus, rear admiral U.S.N.; b. Bangor, Me., Apr. 9, 1837. Apptd. asst. p.m. U.S.N., Sept. 12, 1861; p.m., Apr. 14, 1862; pay insp., Feb. 23, 1877; pay dir., Aug. 10, 1886; retired, Apr. 9, 1899, with rank of rear admiral for services during Civil War. Home: Norfolk, Va. Died Aug. 9, 1913.

PARKS, Wythe Marchant, naval officer; b. Norfolk, Va., Sept. 8, 1856; s. of John W. and Victoria P.; ed. at Norwood, Va., and at Norfolk Academy; m. Lilian Baird, Aug. 17, 1882; children—Lilian Baird, Victoria Marchant, Marshall. Appointed assistant engineer U.S. Navy, May 8, 1877; promoted through grades to rear admiral, Feb. 13, 1913. Made Arctic cruise on U.S.S. Alliance, 1881, search of the Jeannette; served in Miantonomoh during Spanish-Am. War; was fleet engr. Pacific Squadron on Flagship Iowa; Bur. of Steam Engring., Navy Dept., 1901-08; head Dept. of Steam Engring., Navy Yard, New York, 1908-10; mem. Naval Examining Bd., Washington, 1910-13; gen. insp. of machinery for Navy, July 11, 1913-Sept. 8, 1920; retired Sept. 8, 1920. Home: Philadelphia, Pa. Died Sept. 17, 1938.

PARLANGE, Charles, U.S. judge eastern dist. La., Jan. 15, 1894—; b. New Orleans, July 23, 1851; ed. by private tutors and in Centenary Coll., Jackson, La.; hon. U.S. commr. for La. to Paris Expn., 1878; delegate to constl. conv., 1879; mem. State senate, 1880-85; U.S. atty. eastern dist. La., 1885-89; lt. gov. La., 1892-93; asso. justice La. Supreme Court, 1893-94. Home: New Orleans, La. Died 1907.

PARLETTE, Ralph, author, lecturer, editor; b. nr. Delaware, O., Aug. 30, 1870; s. Rev. John and Elizabeth (Phillips) P.; grad. high sch., La Rue, O., 1887; grad. Ohio Northern U., Ada, O., 1891; A.M., 1899, Litt.D., 1918; m. Gay MacLaren, Jan. 6, 1928. Editor University Herald, Ada., 1890-97. Business, educational, inspirational lecturer, 1897—; editor The Lyceum Magazine, 1909-28; mem. Parlette & Snyder, publishers, Ada Herald; v.p. Parlette-Padget Co., Chicago; mem. Padget, Parlette & Padget, Chicago. Charter mem. International Lyceum and Chautauqua Assn. Author: The University of Hard Knocks, 1914; The Big Business of Life, 1917; It's Up to You, 1918; The Salvation of a Sucker, 1919; The Best Is Yet to Come, 1919; Pockets and Paradises, 1922; Make Sure of Your Home, 1924; Dollars and Destiny, 1924; Go-Getters and Go-Givers, 1925; Swat the Snake and Coöperate, 1925; The Thrift Series; The Trust Series; The Building and Loan Series; Pointers from Parlette; A Globegadder's Diary—How We Went Round the World, 1927. Home: Chicago, Ill. Died Nov. 19, 1930.

PARLIN, Frank Edson, educator; b. Leeds, Me., June 3, 1860; s. William O. and Emily (Dodge) P.; A.B., Bates Coll., 1886, A.M., 1889, Ped.D., 1912; m. Etta May Baker, Aug. 12, 1884 (died 1888); children—Raymond Washington, Emily May; m. 2d, Hattie Emroy Start, Nov. 21, 1889 (died 1909); m. 3d, Marguerite L. McKeever, Dec. 3, 1910; children—Frank Edson, John Oliver, Marguerite Emily. Prin. Greeley Inst., Cumberland, Me., 1883-85, Brigham Acad., Bakersfield, Vt., 1886-90; supt. schs., Stockbridge, Mass., and prin. Williams Acad., 1891-93; supt. schs., Natick and Needham, 1893-96, Natick, 1896-1900, Quincy, 1900-09, of Woodward Inst., Quincy, 1901-09; supt. schs., Cambridge, 1909-12, Chelsea, 1913-27; retired Oct. 1, 1927; mem. editorial dept. Ginn & Co., 1927-30. Mason. Author: The Quincy Word List, 1902; The Parlin Genealogy, 1913; English Phonetics, 1923. Home: Hampstead, N.H. Died Mar. 28, 1939.

PARLIN, William Henry, mfr.; b. Canton, Ill., Dec. 24, 1847; s. William and Caroline (Orendorff) P.; ed. pub. schs., Canton; m. Susan Gale Cooke, 1901. Has been connected from 1869, with Parlin & Orendorff Co., mfrs. agrl. implements, of which has been pres., 1897—; pres. Canton Gas & Electric Co. Republican. Home: Canton, Ill. Died Mar. 5, 1920.

PARLOA, Maria, author, domestic economist; b. in Mass., 1843; lecturer; contributor to mags. on food preparation and household management. Author: First Principles of Household Management and Cookery; Kitchen Companion; The Young Housekeeper; New Cook Book and Marketing Guide; Home Economics. Home: Bethel, Conn. Died 1909.

PARMELE, Mary Platt, author; b. Albany, N.Y., July 14, 1843; d. Judge Zephaniah and Cornelia (Jenkins) Platt; ed. at acad. conducted by the Abbott brothers, New York; m. S. J. Agnew; m. 2d, Theodore W. Parmele. Extensive contbr. of philos. articles and stories to revs. and mags., 1892—. Also Chart of Civilization, 1250-1850, "Who, When and What." Author: Series of Short Histories—France, England, United States, Germany, Spain, Russia, Rome and Italy, 1892-1902; The Kingdom of the Invisible; Answered in the Negative; Ariel. Home: New York, N.Y. Died 1911.

PARMELEE, Henry Francis, lawyer; b. New Haven, Conn., June 22, 1875; s. Henry Spencer and Mary Frances (Parmele) P.; grad. Hopkins Grammar Sch., New Haven, 1891; Ph.B., Sheffield Scientific Sch. (Yale), 1894; LL.B., Harvard, 1897; m. Charlotte Stanley Land, Mar. 9, 1914. Admitted to Conn. bar, 1898, and began practice at New Haven; in gen. practice at New Haven, also in N.Y. City, 1912-16; served as spl. asst. to atty. gen. of U.S. in litigation arising out of govt.'s war activities, 1923-29. Mem. Conn. State Commn. on Rivers and Harbors, 1909-11; mem. Commn. on City Plan, of New Haven. Republican. Conglist. Home: New Haven, Conn. Died Dec. 28, 1934.

PARMENTER, Charles Sylvester, professor biology; b. Chariton, Ia., Oct. 15, 1860; s. Irving and Salena (Durall) P.; A.B., Ill. Wesleyan U., 1883, A.M., 1886; Ph.D., Allegheny Coll., Pa., 1895; m. Mabel Perry, Dec. 22, 1902. Prof. natural sciences, 1883-92, prof. biology, 1892—, v.p., 1900—, Baker Univ. Mem. State Bd. Edn., Kan., 1894-96 inclusive. Progressive Republican. Methodist. Home: Baldwin, Kan. Died Oct. 4, 1922.

PARMLEY, Joseph William, dealer western lands; b. Mifflin, Wis., Jan. 12, 1861; s. Joseph and Jane (Ashton) P.; student State Normal Sch., Platteville, Wis., 1879-80, Lawrence U., Appleton, Wis., 1880-83; m. Lissie Baker, Oct. 13, 1887. Pres. Scranton Clay Products Corp., Edmunds Co. Abstract Co., McPherson Co. Abstract Co.; breeder of Shetland ponies. Former mem. legislature of S.D., and state highway commr., S.D. Mem. S.D. State Coal Mine Commn. Pres. Canada to Canal Highway (sponsor of road from Bowsman, Manitoba, Can., to Panama Canal); active in promoting better farming, good roads, hydro-electric power in Mo. River; known as "Father of the Yellowstone Trail," the first 100 miles having been named the "Parmley Highway"; promoter of the Canada to Canal Highway and of International Peace Garden, Turtle Mountains, North Dakota and Manitoba. Republican. Methodist. Mason. Home: Ipswich, S.D. Died Dec. 15, 1940.

PARMLEY, Walter Camp, civil engr.; b. Rock Co., Wis., Dec. 8, 1862; s. Russell and Lucy Esther (Dean) P.; B.Met. Engring., U. of Wis., 1887, M.S., 1893; m. Rose Webster, Mar. 13, 1889; children—Marjorie (Mrs. Wm. Lentz), Florence (Mrs. Roy W. Chesnut). Mem. Parmley & Finkle, engrs., San Bernardino, Calif., 1887-89; engr. on Bear River Canal, Ogden City Water Works, and city engr., Ogden, 1889-93; asst. city engr., Peoria, Ill., 1893-96, also pvt. practice; engr. spl. sanitation, Cleveland, O., 1896-1903; cons. practice, N.Y. City, 1904—; has specialized in reinforced concrete constrn. for sewers and pipe lines; inventor of reinforced concrete designs widely in use. Pres. Essex County Mosquito Extermination Commn. Republican. Congregationalist. Home: Upper Montclair, N.J. Died Feb. 19, 1934.

PARNELL, Harvey, governor; b. Cleveland Co., Ark., Feb. 28, 1880; s. William and Mary (Martin) P.; ed. high sch., Warren, Ark.; m. Mabel Winston, June 2, 1903; children—Martha Dell, Mary Frances. Clk. in hardware store, Warren, 1898-99; clk. with E. P. Remley & Co., Dermott, 1900-02; gen. mercantile business, Dermott, 1902-10; engaged in farming, 1910—. Mem. Ark. Ho. of Rep., 1919-21, Ark. Senate, 1921-25; lt. gov. of Ark., 1927-Mar. 14, 1928; gov. of Ark., 1928-33. Democrat. Methodist. Mason. Home: Dermott, Ark. Died Jan. 16, 1936.

PARR, Samuel Wilson, univ. prof.; b. Granville, Ill., Jan. 21, 1857; s. James and Elizabeth Fidelia (Moore) P.; B.S., U. of Ill., 1884; M.S., Cornell U., 1885; studied U. of Berlin, 1900, Polytechnikum, Zürich, 1901; hon. Sc.D., Lehigh U., 1925, Illinois Coll., Jacksonville, Ill., 1929; m. Lucie A. Hall, Dec. 27, 1887; children—Elisabeth, Harold Lucien. Instr. gen. science, 1885-86, prof., 1886-91, Ill. Coll.; prof. applied chemistry, U. of Ill., Jan. 1891—; dir., 1904-05, Ill. State Water Survey; consulting chemist on coal investigation, Ill. State Geol. Survey, 1905—. Devised the Parr calorimeter for determining the heat value of coal and other hydrocarbons, widely used in America and Europe; also a new type of calorimeter for determining and recording the heat value of combustible gases; alloys with acid resisting properties, and a new calorimeter bomb with effective platinum substitution in its construction. Author: The Chemical Examination of Water, Fuel, Fluegases and Lubricants. Wrote reports on Composition and Analysis of Ill. Coals, also bulls. of U. of Ill. Engring. Expt. Sta., Ill. Geol. Survey, etc. Awarded Chandler medal, 1926. Home: Urbana, Ill. Died May 16, 1931.

PARR, William David, clergyman, capitalist; b. Big Springs, Ind., Nov. 10, 1855; s. Alfred D. and Margaret (Jones) P.; A.B., De Pauw U., 1875, A.M., 1883; B.D., Drew Theol. Sem., 1878; (D.D., Clark U., Atlanta, Ga., 1891; S.T.D., De Pauw, 1899); m. Cora Walton, Jan. 11, 1883. Entered ministry M.E. Ch., 1878; pastor Sac City, Ia., 1878, Buena Vista (Ind.) Mission, 1878, Westfield, 1879-82, Cambridge City, 1882-85, Waterloo, 1885-88, Elkhart, 1888-93, Kokomo, 1893-98, Wayne St. Ch., Kokomo, 1898-1901; presiding elder Kokomo Dist., 9 mos., 1901; asst. sec. Bd. of Ch. Extension, 1901-05; chaplain 3d Regt., I.N.G., 9 yrs. Mem. Gen. Conf. M.E. Ch. 4 times; del. Ecumenical Conf., London, Eng., 1901; pres. bd. trustees Wesleyan Foundation, Purdue U.; trustee De Pauw U., Taylor U.; a founder and dir. M.E. Hosp., Indianapolis; dir. Winona (Ind.) Assembly. V.p. and sec. Globe Stove & Range Co., etc. Republican. Mason. Home: Kokomo, Ind. Died Aug. 12, 1918.

PARRINGTON, Vernon Louis, prof. English; b. Aurora, Ill., Aug. 3, 1871; s. John William and Louise (McClellan) P.; A.B., Harvard, 1893; M.A., Coll. of Emporia, 1895; studied British Mus., London, and Bibliothèque Nationale, Paris, 1903-04; m. Julia Rochester Williams, July 31, 1901; children—Elizabeth (Mrs. Donald Partridge Thomas), Louise Wrathal, Vernon Louis. Instr. in English and French, Coll. of Emporia, 1893-97; instr. in English and modern langs., U. of Okla., 1897-98, prof. English, 1898-1908; asst. prof. English, U. of Wash., 1908-12, prof., 1912—; mem. faculties of summer sessions U. of Calif., 1922, Columbia, 1923, U. of Mich., 1927. Democrat. Episcopalian. Author: Main Currents in American Thought (vols. I, II), 1927; Sinclair Lewis—Our Own Diogenes, 1927. Editor: The Connecticut Wits, 1926. Home: Seattle, Wash. Died June 16, 1929.

PARRISH, Celestia Susannah, educator; b. Swansonville, Va., Sept. 12, 1853; d. Perkins and Jane (Walker) P.; student Roanoke Female Inst., Danville, Va., 1874-76; grad. State Normal Sch., of Va., 1886; U. of Mich., 1890-91; Ph.B., Cornell U., 1896; studied U. of Chicago, summers, 1897, 98, 99; unmarried. Teacher pub. and pvt. schs., 1869-74, city schs., Danville, Va., 1874-83; Roanoke Female Inst., 1883-84; State Normal Sch. of Va., 1884-92; prof. philosophy and edn., Randolph-Macon Woman's Coll., 1892-1902; prof. edn., State Normal Sch. of Ga., 1902-11; state supervisor schs., Ga., 1911-18. Pres. Ga. Congress of Mothers; v.p. Assn. Collegiate Alumnae (organizer 1st Southern br.; pres. Va. br.); 1st pres. Southern Assn. College Women; organizer Coll. Y.W.C.A.'s in the Virginias and Carolinas. Baptist. Home: Atlanta, Ga. Died Sept. 7, 1918.

PARRISH, Clara Weaver, artist; b. Selma, Ala.; d. William M. and Lucia Frances (Minter) Weaver; art edn., Art Students' League, New York, Académie Colarossi, Gustav Courtois, Raphael Collin, Paris; m. William Peck Parrish. Has exhibited Paris Expn., Paris Salon, Royal Acad., London and Liverpool, and current ann. exhbns. in America. Water color prize, Woman's Art Club, 1902; Watrous figure prize, 1913; silver medal Appalachian Expn., 1911; silver medal, Panama, P.I. Expn., 1915; Saltus prize, 1916; Nat. Arts Club prize, 1924. Home: New York, N.Y. Died Nov. 13, 1925.

PARRISH, Karl Calvin, mining engr.; b. Leon, Ia., Dec. 12, 1877; s. Robert Leal and Himena (Hoffman) P.; Parsons Coll., Fairfield, Ia.; M.E., Colo. Sch. of Mines, 1901; m. Blanche Emmons, Nov. 5, 1908; children—Karl Calvin, Jane Emmons. Assayer, Blue Grass Mining Co., Nederland, Colo., 1901; mining expert for Western Venture Co., examining properties in N.M., Ariz. and Calif., 1903-04; supt. Andes Mining Co., Guamoco, Colombia, S.A., 1904-09; prospecting for mines in Colombia, 1909-10; discovered and located Chicago and Las Ramas group of mines in Guamoco Dist., Colombia, and general mgr. same; in charge Bar Principal Mining Co., Guamoco, 1913-19; consulting engr., Barranquilla, Colombia; mgr. Parrish & Co., Compañia Urbanizadora de "El Prado," Parrish Investment Co., Compañia Minera de los Valles, Barranquilla, 1919—, Cia. Minera del Nare; built residential addition to Barranquilla and modern water works system; also various municipal elec. power plants in Colombia; with others, building railroad over Andes Mountains, to cost approximately $10,000,000; etc. Home: Des Moines, Ia. Died Nov. 3, 1933.

PARRISH, Lucian Walton, congressman; b. Van Alstyne, Tex., Jan. 10, 1878; s. Jefferson C. and Mattie J. (Hannah) P.; A.B., U. of Tex., 1906, A.M., LL.B., 1909; m. Gladys Edwards, Sept. 4, 1912. Began as cowboy and earned money to pay expenses of edn.; mem. Wantland & Parrish, Henrietta, 1909-19; chmn. Dem. Exec. Com. of Clay Co., Tex., 1917-18; mem. 66th Congress (1919-21), 13th Tex. Dist. Chmn. Sch. Bd., Henrietta Independent Sch. Dist.; pres. Chamber of Commerce, Henrietta. Mason. Missionary Baptist. At college was capt. of track team and champion hammer thrower of the South; was elected pres. Students' Assn. U. of Tex. (highest honor). Home: Henrietta, Tex. Died Mar. 27, 1922.

PARRISH, Randall, author; b. Henry Co., Ill., June 10, 1858; s. Rufus P. and Frances A. (Hollis) P.; student U. of Ia. (L.H.D., 1911); m. Rose Tyrrell, Aug. 6, 1902. Admitted to bar in Ia.; practiced at Wichita, Kan., 1879-83; prospected in Ariz. and N.M., 1883-85; later in newspaper work on daily papers in Denver, Omaha, Sioux City and Chicago, and as mgr. country papers in Neb. and Ill.; more recently in spl. commercial journalism in Chicago. Author: When Wilderness Was King, 1904; My Lady of the North, 1904; Historic Illinois, 1905; Beth Norvell, 1907; My Lady of the South, 1909; Keith of the Border, 1910; Gordon Craig, 1912; Beyond the Frontier, 1915; The Strange Case of Cavendish, 1919; Comrades of Peril, 1919; Mystery of the Silver Dagger, 1920; Gift of the Desert, 1921. Home: Kewanee, Ill. Died Aug. 9, 1923.

PARRISH, Robert Lewis, lawyer, mfr.; b. Covington, Va., Oct. 29, 1876; s. Robert L. and Margaret (Care) P.; McCabe's U. Sch., Petersburg, Va., 1889-96; Univ. of Va., 1896-99; m. Gray Morehead, Jan. 16, 1907. Admitted to Va. bar, 1899, and began practice at Covington; counsel C.&O. Ry. Co.; pres. Covington Nat. Bank, Covington Grocery Co., Oriskany Ore & Iron Co. Democrat. Episcopalian. Home: Covington, Va. Died July 23, 1915.

PARRISH, Stephen, painter; b. Phila., July 9, 1846; s. Dillwyn and Susanna (Maxfield) P.; ed. pvt. schs., Phila.; m. Elizabeth Bancroft, Apr. 21, 1869; 1 son, Maxfield. Mercantile pursuits till age of 31; then applied himself to art, studying a yr. under local teacher; took up etching and produced his 1st plate, 1879; has exhibited at New York, Boston, Phila., London, Liverpool, Munich, Paris, Vienna and Dresden. Home: Cornish, N.H. Died May 15, 1938.

PARROTT, James Marion; born 1874; M.D., Tulane U., 1895. Surgeon Parrott Memorial Hosp. Formerly pres. N.C. State Med. Soc.; fellow Am. Coll. Surgeons. Home: Kinston, N.C. Died 1934.

PARRY, David Maclean, manufacturer; b. on farm nr. Pittsburgh, Mar. 26, 1852; s. Thomas J. and Lydia (Maclean) P.; worked on farm until 17 yrs. old, attending sch. winters, and also receiving instrn. from his mother; m. Cora Harbottle, 1875 (died 1882); 2d, Hessie Maxwell, 1883. Clerked at Lawrenceburg, Ind., Columbus City, Ia., and New York, 1869-73; in hardware business, Connersville, Ind., 1873-76; traveling salesman, 1876-78; in hardware business, Rushville, Ind., 1878-82; established mfg. business, Rushville, 1882; removed it to Indianapolis, 1886; was pres. Parry Auto Co.; retired from mfg. business, 1911; became pres. Indianapolis, Newcastle & Toledo Electric Ry.; v.p. S.D. Central Ry., Farmers Trust Co. Republican. Mason. Pres. Carriage Builders' Nat. Assn., Ind. Mfrs. Assn.; pres. Nat. Assn. of Mfrs. of U.S.A., 4 yrs., Citizens' Industrial Assn. America, 2 yrs. Author: The Scarlet Empire. Home: Indianapolis, Ind. Died May 12, 1915.

PARRY, Will H.; b. N.Y. City, June 29, 1864; s. William M. and Elizabeth (Gillette) P.; studied Coll. City of New York, and Columbia; m. Harriet Phelps, Jan. 15, 1891. Editor and pub. newspapers in Ore., 1884-88; city editor and mng. editor, Post-Intelligencer, Seattle, 1888-94; city comptroller, Seattle, 1894-1900; alderman at large, 1900-02; pres. City Council, 1902-06; treas. and mgr. Moran Shipbuilding Co., 1900-15; mem. Federal Trade Commn., 1915—. Chmn. ways and means com. and exec. com., Alaska-Yukon-Pacific Expn., 1906-09; treas. and dir. Seattle Chamber of Commerce, 1896-1916. Progressive Republican. Episcopalian. Home: Seattle, Wash. Died Apr. 21, 1917.

PARSELL, Charles Victor, educator; b. Akron, N.Y., Nov. 14, 1851; s. Isaac and Sophronia (Kendrick) P.; student Cornell U., 1868-71; A.M., St. Lawrence U., 1881; m. Genevieve C. Carroll. Consecutively teacher, vice-prin. and prin. Fairfield (N.Y.) Sem., 1872-79; pres. Clinton Liberal Inst., 1879-93; prin. Cascadilla Sch., Ithaca, N.Y., 1893-July 1915. Home: Ithaca, N.Y. Died Apr. 16, 1920.

PARSON, Hubert Templeton; b. Toronto, Sept. 18, 1872; s. Henry Edwin and Eliza S. (McGibben) P.; ed. high sch., Brooklyn, N.Y.; m. Maysie Adelaide Gasque, Oct. 1893. Began, 1892, as accountant with F. W. Woolworth Co., five and ten cent stores; advanced through various positions to sec., treas., gen. mgr., and was pres., 1919-32; retired under age limit of 60 yrs. Republican. Baptist. Home: West End, N.J. Died July 9, 1940.

PARSONS, Albert Ross, musician, archeologist, genealogist; b. Sandusky, O., Sept. 16, 1847; s. Bvt. Lt. Col. John Jehiel and Sarah (Averill) P.; received pvt. instruction Buffalo and New York; studied in Germany, 1867-72; Royal Conservatory, Leipzig, Carl Tausig's High Sch. of Pianoforte, Berlin, and Prof. Theodore Kullak's New Acad. of Music, Berlin; m. Alice Eva Van Ness, Apr. 23, 1874. Specialist in musical pedagogy, technics and æsthetics; also prominent in archeology. Prof. Georg. Ebers, Egyptologist and novelist, sent autograph and photograph with thanks for "Profoundly suggestive work, New Light from the Great Pyramid." Democrat. Composer pianoforte pieces, songs. Designed the symbolic pyramid mausoleum, Greenwood cemetery, New York. Dante lecturer and readings; Bacon-Shakespeare. Author: Wagner's Beethoven, 1870; Science of Pianoforte Practice; New Light from the Great Pyramid, 1893; The Virtuoso Handling of the Piano, Advanced Exercises, 1917. Died June 14, 1933.

PARSONS, Albert Stevens, reformer, publisher; b. Northfield, Mass., Nov. 16, 1841; s. Hon. Albert C. and Hannah (Stevens) P.; ed. pub. schs.; m. Louise H. Ilsley, Sept. 4, 1871. Went to Boston, 1861, and entered publishing business; was with publishing house of Charles Scribner & Co., New York, 1868-71; treas. Standard Diary Co., 1871-1918. Chairman exec. com. Anti-Imperialist League, Am. Free Trade League; treas. N.E. Cremation Society; dir. Cambridge Civil Service Reform Assn., Free Religious Assn. of America. A founder and 1st sec. League of Am. Wheelmen. Independent in politics. Home: Lexington, Mass. Died Dec. 1922.

PARSONS, Azariah Worthington, M.D.; b. Worthington, Mass., Mar. 31, 1857; s. Cyrus Morton and Sarah Celina (Cole) P.; ed. under pvt. tutors; M.D., Harvard, 1880; M.D., Nat. Sch. of Medicine, Mexico, 1898; post-grad. work, Vienna, Paris and London, Cairo, Tokyo, Calcutta; m. Elizabeth Creelman Graham, Nov. 2, 1915. Chief surgeon Mexican Nat. R.R., 1885-90; med. dir. Am. Hosp., City of Mexico, 1886-90; served as U.S. examining surgeon for pensions, in Mexico. Mason. Home: Oakwood, Tex. Died Sept. 4, 1931.

PARSONS, Charles, artist; b. Hampshire, Eng., May 8, 1821; ed. New York; art student, Nat. Acad., New York. Lithographic artist, 1838-61; dir. Harper & Bros. art dept., 1861-89. A.N.A. Home: Boonton, N.J. Died 1910.

PARSONS, Charles, pres. Rome, Watertown & Ogdensburg R.R., 1883—; b. Alfred, Me., Feb. 6, 1829; ed. dist. schools and Yarmouth, Me., Acad.; engaged in business in New Orleans, 1853-54; Savannah, Ga., 1854-61; 1862—, in New York; pres. Midland R.R. of New Jersey, 1880-81; pres. New York & New England R.R. Co., 1892-93. In 1894 purchased and reorganized South Carolina & Georgia R.R.; was its pres. until he sold it to the Southern Ry. Co. in 1899; apptd., 1897, receiver Ogdensburg & Lake Champlain R.R., and chmn. com. to reorganize it: sold it to Rutland R.R. Co., 1899; on com. that reorganized the Brooklyn, the Union and Seaside Elevated R.R.s of Brooklyn, N.Y., which were sold under foreclosure, 1898; chmn. exec. com. Continental Trust Co. Mem. N.Y. Stock Exchange, 1870—. Home: New York, N.Y. Died 1904.

PARSONS, Charles Baldwin, ship broker; b. Middletown, N.J., July 3, 1835; s. Walter Chamberlain and Mary (Morford) P.; acad. edn.; m. Elizabeth M. Bergen, Jan. 20, 1868. Served in Civil War, 1861-65; rank, capt. engrs., and bvt. maj.; was chief engr., 25th Army Corps; sea capt., 1865-90. Treas. Shrewsbury Twp., 1890-99; trustee Am. Seaman's Friend Soc., 1904—; sec. N.J. Bd. Pilot Commrs.; chmn. bldg. com. Seaman's Home and Inst., 1907-09. Pres. New York Maritime Exchange, 1902-06, N.J. S.S. Assn., 1898-1901, Mission Yacht Assn., 1904—. Comdr. Arrowsmith Post G.A.R., 1892-93 and 1902-05; mem. N.Y. Commandery Loyal Legion; high priest, Hiram Chapter, R.A.M. Author: Genealogical Record of Morford Family of Middletown, 1910. Home: Red Bank, N.J. Deceased.

PARSONS, Claude Van, congressman; b. McCormick, Ill., Oct. 7, 1895; s. Charles Moses and Sarah Tennessee (Reid) P.; grad. Southern Ill. State Normal U., 1923; unmarried. Teacher, schs. of Pope County, 1914-22; county supt. schs., Pope Co., Ill., 1922-30; editor and pub. newspapers, 1924-30. Mem. 71st Congress (elected to fill vacancy, 1929-31), and 72d to 76th Congresses (1931-41), 24th Ill. Dist. Pres. Southern Ill. Teachers Assn., 1926, County Supts. Assn. of Ill., 1930. Democrat. Mason. Rotarian. Home: Golconda, Ill. Died May 24, 1941.

PARSONS, Eben Burt, clergyman; b. Pittsfield, Mass., Mar. 3, 1835; s. Orenzo and Roxana (Burt) P.; A.B., Williams Coll., 1859, A.M., 1862; prin. high sch., Greenfield, Mass., 1859-62; science course, Harvard, 1862, theol. course, Union and Auburn Theol. sems., 1862-65; teacher mathematics, Cooper Inst., New York, 1863; (D.D., Maryville Coll., Tenn., 1881); m. Clara Bigelow, June 15, 1869. Ordained chaplain 116th U.S. Colored Inf., Apr. 11, 1865, by Presbytery of New York, but saw no active service; pastor Presbyn. Ch., Baldwinsville, N.Y., 1868-88; sec. of faculty, Williams Coll., 1888-1909. Mem. Phi Beta Kappa (sec. Gamma Chapter, Mass., 1890—; senator United Chapters, 1889, sec., 1889-91, and v.p., 1894). Author: Obituary Record, 5 vols., 1880-1905 (Williams Coll.); Phi Beta Kappa Handbook and General Catalogue, 1900; History of the Class of 1859, Williams College; Catalogue and History, Gamma Chapter, Phi Beta Kappa, 1903. Died Jan. 23, 1913.

PARSONS, Edmund Byrd, surgeon; b. Moscow, Tex., Nov. 21, 1864; s. Edmund Cantrell Bethell and Marjanna Caroline (Byrd) P.; prep. edn., Moscow Masonic High Sch. and Masonic Inst. (both defunct); M.D., Tulane, 1885; m. Bessie Morris, Jan. 1894; children—Edith Byrd (Mrs. Joseph Franklin Myers), Alfred Morris. Practiced in eastern Tex. 10 yrs., at Palestine, Tex., 1900—; chief surgeon Internat.-Gt. Northern R.R. Hosp., at Palestine, 1917—; chief surgeon Mo.-Pacific Lines, Tex. and Louisiana. Former mem. Tex. State Bd. of Health, and health officer Palestine and Anderson Co. Fellow Am. Coll. Surgeons. Mason. Democrat. Home: Palestine, Tex. Died Mar. 13, 1938.

PARSONS, Eugene, editor; b. Henderson, N.Y., June 14, 1855; s. Rev. Reuben and Abigail (Mack) P.; A.B., U. of Chicago, 1883, grad. courses in English and philosophy, 1894, 99, 1900; unmarried. Teacher Latin and French, Des Moines (Ia.) Coll., 1883-84. Editor Progress, 1899-1900; asso. editor Current Encyclopædia, 1901-02, The World To-Day, 1902-03. Author: Tennyson's Life and Poetry, and Mistakes Concerning Tennyson, 1892; George Washington, a Character Sketch, 1898; History of Colorado, 1917. Edited: Tennyson's Works (Farringford edit., 10 vols.), 1902. Lecturer on Colo. history, Denver pub. schs., 1915. Home: Denver, Colo. Died June 22, 1933.

PARSONS, Fannie Griscom, ednl. philanthropist; b. New York, N.Y., Sept. 23, 1850; d. John Hoskins (M.D.) and Henrietta (Peale) Griscom; ed. pvt. and pub. schs.; Moravian Sem., Bethlehem, Pa.; m. Henry Parsons, lawyer, Mar. 5, 1873. Founder, 1902, and dir. Bur. of Children's Sch. Farms, Dept. of Parks, New York; pres. Internat. Children's Sch. Farm League. Presbyn. Author of various articles on children's gardens, etc. Decorations: Silver medal, St. Louis Expn., 1904; gold medal, Jamestown Expn., 1907; gold medal and hon. mention, Internat. Tuberculosis Congress, Washington, 1908; diplomas, Am. Inst., 1902-12. Spl. collaborator U.S. Bur. Edn., div. sch. garden army. Home: New York, N.Y. Died Sept. 29, 1923.

PARSONS, Floyd William, editor, engr.; b. Keyser, W.Va., Jan. 23, 1880; s. Marshall J. and Mary C. (Long) P.; ed. U. of W.Va.; E.M., Lehigh U., 1902; m. Maud A. Freystedt, Oct. 28, 1903; children—Doris L., Jean M. Chief engr. Stonewall (W.Va.) Coal & Coke Co., 1902; dist. engr. Lehigh Valley Coal Co., Wilkes-Barre, Pa., 1903; res. engr. Consolidation Coal Co., Frostburg, Md., 1904; chief engr. New River Consolidated Coal & Coke Co., Rush Run, W.Va., 1905; asst. prof. mining, Mich. Coll. of Mines, Houghton, Mich., 1905-06; chief engr. Victor Am. Fuel Co., and C.&S.E. Ry. Co., Denver, Colo., 1906; asso. editor Engineering and Mining Journal, 1907-10; founder, and editor Coal Age, 1910-18; regular contbr. to World's Work, 1918-22; mem. board of dirs., editorial dir. and vice-pres. Robbins Publishing Co.; editor Gas Age-Record, and Industrial Gas (both of New York); contbg. editor Advertising and Selling; dir. Richmond Radiator Co., Dresser Mfg. Co., Vitaglass Corp. of America. Asst. to Harry A. Garfield, U.S. Fuel Administrator, World War; mem. commn. of journalists invited by British and French govts. to visit England and France, 1918. Presbyn. Author: American Business Methods, 1921; Everybody's Business, 1923. Home: New York, N.Y. Died Aug. 7, 1941.

PARSONS, Francis, banking; b. Hartford, Conn., Jan. 13, 1871; s. John Caldwell and Mary (McClellan) P.; B.A., Yale U., 1893, LL.B., 1897, M.A., 1925; m. Elizabeth Alden Hutchins, June 22, 1897; children—Mary (Mrs. Barclay Robinson), John Caldwell, Francis (dec.), Elizabeth Hutchins (Mrs. William S. Warner). Member staff Hartford Courant, 1893-95; in practice of law at Hartford, 1897-1904; secretary, v.p. and office atty. Security Co., Hartford, 1904-23, vice chmn. bd. and dir. of successor, Hartford Nat. Bank & Trust Co. until 1934, retiring as exec. officer, now dir.; trustee Soc. for Savings. Mem. Hartford Bd. of Edn., 1907-08, 1921-24; mem. Bd. Park Commrs., Hartford, 1908-18; v.p. and dir. Hartford Pub. Library; pres. bd. trustees Watkinson Library (Hartford). Asst. q.m. gen., State of Conn., 1899-1900; sergt. 5th Militia Cav., Conn. N.G., 1911-14; capt. Conn. State Guard, 1917-18; overseas service, Am. Red Cross, 1918-19. Chmn. bd. trustees Hartford Grammer Sch.; fellow of corp. Yale Univ.; dir. Am. Sch. at Hartford for Deaf, Wadsworth Atheneum. Republican. Conglist. Author: The Friendly Club and Other Portraits, 1922; A Time of Preservation, 1935. Home: Hartford, Conn. Died Dec. 30, 1937.

PARSONS, Frank, lawyer, educator, author; b. Mt. Holly, N.J., Nov. 14, 1854; s. Edward and Alice B. (Rhees) P.; grad in math. and engring. course, Cornell, 1873; unmarried. Was on ry. engring. staff; later taught sch.; admitted to Boston bar; chief clerk for law firm for a time; then opened offices of his own; text writer for Little, Brown & Co., publishers; public lecturer on economics and sociology; prof. history and political science Kan. Agrl. Coll., 1897-1900; lecturer on law, Boston Univ., 1892—; prof. polit. science and dean Coll. of Liberal Arts, Ruskin Univ.; dir. dept. history, Bureau Econ. Research, Washington, Testified before U.S. Industrial Commn. on public ownership of railroads, telegraphs and telephones, 1901-02; traveled throughout Europe and America studying ry. systems, co-operative instns., etc. Lectured in leading cities of Pacific Slope for Univ. Extension Assn. of Chicago; also given courses, Cooper Union, New York, etc. Author: The Story of New Zealand, 1904; The Heart of the Railroad Problem, 1906; The Railways, the Trusts and the People, 1906. Home: Mt. Holly, N.J. Died 1908.

PARSONS, Frank Alvah, lecturer on art; b. Chesterfield, Mass., Apr. 1, 1868; s. Alvah and Sarah (Sanderson) P.; ed. Wesleyan Sem.; studied art in Italy, France, Eng. and Austria, 4 times; grad. dept. of Fine Arts, Teachers Coll. (Columbia), 1905; B.S., dept. edn. Teachers Coll.; unmarried. Lecturer Boston (Mass.) and vicinity, 1890-98; instr. Columbia U., 1899-1905; pres. and dir. New York Sch. of Fine and Applied Art, New York, Paris and Italy, 1905—. Prof. advertising display, New York U., 1915. Lecturer dept. art, Brooklyn Inst. Arts and Sciences, on interior decoration for New York decorators and architects, 1903-14; on art before women's clubs, civic associations and teachers' convs. in 38 states; delivered course lectures yearly at Met. Museum Art. Author: Principles of Advertising Arrangement, 1912; Interior Decoration, Its Principles and Practice, 1915; The Psychology of Dress, 1920; The Art Appeal in Advertising Display. Co-Author: Advertising, Its Principles and Practice; Art, Its Principles and Practice Applied to Modern Life, 1916. Chevalier Legion of Honor (France). Lived in New York City. Died May 26, 1930.

PARSONS, Frank Nesmith, judge; b. Dover, N.H., Sept. 3, 1854; s. Rev. Benjamin F. and Mary A. (Nesmith) P.; A.B., Dartmouth, 1874 (LL.D., 1904); m. Helen F. Pike, Oct. 26, 1880. Admitted to bar, 1879; practiced at Franklin, 1879-95; mem. N.H. Constl. Conv., 1889; state law reporter, 1891-95; mem. exec. council of Gov. John B. Smith, 1893-94; mayor of Franklin, 1895; asso. justice, 1895-1902, chief justice, 1902-24, Supreme Court of N.H.; mem. N.H. legislature, 1925-28; mem. and pres. N.H. Constl. Conv., 1930; pres. and trustee Franklin Savings Bank; v.p. Franklin Nat. Bank. Republican. Home: Franklin, N.H. Deceased.

PARSONS, Harry deBerkeley, engineer; b. N.Y. City, Jan. 6, 1862; s. William Barclay and Eliza Glass (Livingston) P.; B.S., Columbia, 1882; M.E., Stevens Inst. Tech., 1884; hon. D.E. from same institution in 1926; m. Frances Walker, Dec. 16, 1890. Consulting engr. in New York, 1885—; prof. steam engring., 1891-1907, emeritus prof. practical engring., 1907—, Rensselaer Poly. Inst.; cons. engineer Nicaragua Canal constrn., 1893. Mem. N.Y. State Voting Machine Commn., 1898-1915, and Met. Sewerage Commn., 1908-14; consulting engr. for New York Zoöl. Soc., reports and appraisals Cramp Ship & Engine Building Co., Pressed Steel Car Co., Consol. Gas Co.'s plants, numerous paper cos., Seaboard Air Line, New Hampshire Traction Co., and many water powers, etc. Designed dams at Spier Falls, and Sherman Island, and cons. engr. for Palmer Falls and Glens Falls dams; chmn. Commn. on Street Cleaning and Waste Disposal, N.Y. City, 1906-07, and cons. engr. Bd. of Estimate, City of N.Y., for work connected with Catskill water supply, 1909-11; dist. appraisal officer, Detroit, Bur. Aircraft Production, U.S.A., 1918-19. Awarded Rowland prize, 1925, Croes medal, 1930, Am. Soc. Civil Engineers. Episcopalian. Author: Steam Boilers, Their Theory and Design, 5th edit., 1917; Disposal of Municipal Refuse, 1906; Tidal Phenomena of the Harbor of New York. Home: New York, N.Y. Died Jan. 26, 1935.

PARSONS, Mrs. Henry, ednl. philanthropist. See Fannie Griscom Parsons.

PARSONS, Herbert, congressman; b. New York, Oct. 28, 1869; s. John Edward (q.v.) and Mary Dumesnil (McIlvaine) P.; A.B., Yale, 1890; U. of Berlin, 1890-91, Harvard Law Sch., 1891-93, Metropolis Law Sch., 1893-94; m. Elsie Worthington Clews, Sept. 1, 1900. Admitted to bar, 1895; sr. mem. Parsons, Closson & McIlvaine. Alderman of New York, 1900-03; candidate for Congress, 1900, 12th N.Y. Dist.; mem. 59th to 61st Congresses (1905-11), 13th N.Y. Dist. Chmn. Rep. Co. Com., 1905-10; mem. Rep. Nat. Com. and of exec. com., 1916-20; del.-at-large N.Y. State Constl. Conv., 1915. Vet. 7th Regt., Co. K, and formerly maj. and judge advocate on staff of 1st Brigade N.G.N.Y.; commd. maj., Aviation Sect. Signal O.R.C., July 1917, and detailed to Mil. Intelligence; lt. col. on Gen. Staff A.E.F., Sept. 1918; served during last half 1918 as asst. chief of staff, G2, 5th Div.; asst. to mil. attaché, Berne, Switzerland, Jan., Feb. 1919. Pres. Greenwich House Settlement, Memorial Hosp. for Treatment of Cancer and Allied Diseases; pres. trustees Canton Christian College. Presbyn. Home: Rye, N.Y. Died Sept. 16, 1925.

PARSONS, James Russell, Jr., educator; b. Hoosick Falls, N.Y., Feb. 20, 1861; s. James Russell P.; grad. Trinity Coll. (valedictorian), 1881, A.M., 1883; LL.D., 1902; m. Mrs. William Starr Dana (née Frances Theodora Smith), Feb. 8, 1896. Private sec. to Rt. Rev. John Williams, bishop of Conn., 1882-83; school commr., 1st dist., Rensselaer Co., 1884-87; U.S. consul, Aix-la-Chapelle, Germany, 1888-90; insp. of secondary schools for Univ. of State of N.Y., 1891; insp. of teachers' training classes under N.Y. State dept. public instruction, 1891; dir. of exams., Univ. of State of N.Y., 1892-97; dir. of coll. and high school depts., same, from 1898; also sec. of the univ., 1900—; dir. and sec. consul gen., City of Mexico, Apr. 1904—. Author: Prussian Schools Through American Eyes, 1891; French Schools Through American Eyes, 1892. Wrote: Regents' Academic Syllabus, 1891. Died 1905.

PARSONS, John Edward, lawyer; b. New York, Oct. 24, 1829; s. Edward Lamb and Matilda (Clark) P.; A.B., New York U., 1848, A.M., 1851; (hon. A.M., Yale, 1851); m. Mary Dumesnil McIlvaine, Nov. 5, 1856; m. 2d, Florence Van Cortlandt Bishop, d. Benjamin N. Field, Mar. 12, 1901; father of Herbert P. Admitted to bar, 1852; dir. Met. Trust Co.; trustee Bank for Savings. Pres. Woman's Hosp., Cooper Union, Gen. Memorial Hosp. Home: New York, N.Y. Died Jan. 16, 1915.

PARSONS, Lewis Baldwin, soldier, lawyer; b. Genesee Co., N.Y., April 5, 1818; s. Lewis Baldwin and Lucina (Hoar) P.; grad. Yale, 1840, A.M., in course, 1843, LL.B., Harvard Univ. Law School, 1844; city atty., Alton, Ill., 1846-49; atty., treas., pres. Ohio & Mississippi R.R., 1854-78; capt. vols., Oct. 31, 1861; col., April 4, 1862; brig. gen., May 11, 1865, on autographic order of Pres. Lincoln for spl. services; was chief of rail and river transportation of the armies of U.S. during the Civil war; bvt. maj. gen. for meritorious services and mustered out April 30, 1866; m. Sarah Green Edwards, Sept. 21, 1847 (died 1850); m. 2d, Julia Maria Edwards, July 5,

1852 (died 1857); m. 3d, Elizabeth Darrah, Dec. 28, 1869 (died 1887). Dem. candidate for lt. gov. Ill., 1880, with U.S. Senator Lyman Trumbull, candidate for gov.; pres. Ill. Soldiers' and Sailors' Home, 1895-98. Retired. Home: Flora, Ill. Died 1907.

PARSONS, Payn Bigelow, sanitary expert; b. Baldwinsville, N.Y., Feb. 12, 1872; s. Eben Burt and Clara (Bigelow) P.; A.B., Williams Coll., 1892; M.D., Albany Med. Coll., 1897; Cornell Med. Coll., 1904-05; m. Ella Mae Emerson, June 30, 1900. Bacteriologist, New York Subway air investigations, 1905, New York Bay investigation, 1906, Pollution Commn. and Met. Sewerage Commn., 1907, Lederle labs., 1908; dir. labs. of Met. Sewerage Commn., New York, 1909-13; chief bacteriologist, New York lab. of U.S. Bur. Chemistry, Nov. 1, 1913-25; bacteriologist N.Y. State Conservation Commn., 1925—. Home: New York, N.Y. Died Sept. 1931.

PARSONS, Richard, univ. prof.; b. Moate, Ireland, June 25, 1847; s. Richard and Margaret (Payne) P.; A.B., Ohio Wesleyan Univ., 1868, A.M., 1871, Litt.D., 1921; student Am. Sch. of Classical Studies, Athens, Greece, 1893-94; m. Eusebia M. Larason, Oct. 3, 1871; children—Helen Maria, Harry Edward, Margaret Rosse, Grace Ethel, Arthur John, Robert Lawrence. Prof. Greek, Ohio Wesleyan, 1875—. Author: Cebes' Tabula, 1888; Did Paul Preach on Mars Hill? Iphigenia Among the Taurians, 1913. Home: Delaware, O. Died Feb. 11, 1926.

PARSONS, Robert Stevens, civil engr.; b. Hohokus, N.J., May 26, 1873; s. Solomon and Louise (Towt) P.; B.S., Rutgers Coll., 1895, C.E., 1900; m. Eleanor Howse, 1897; children—Eleanor, Roberta. Connected with various depts. of engring., Erie R.R., leading to gen. supt., 1912-15; chief engr. same rd., 1915-20, gen. mgr., 1920-22, v.p., 1922—. Mem. N.J. Highway Commn., 1917-20. Trustee Rutgers Coll. Republican. Methodist. Mason. Rotarian. Home: Youngstown, Ohio. Died May 18, 1928.

PARSONS, Samuel, landscape architect; b. New Bedford, Mass., Feb. 8, 1844; s. Samuel B. and Susan (Howland) P.; student Haverford Coll., 1857-60; B.S., Yale, 1863; m. Martha E. Francis, Oct. 25, 1865. Landscape architect, 1876—; mem. Vaux & Co. until 1895, Samuel Parsons, Inc., 1916—. Late landscape architect of Greater New York City; park commr. and pres. park bd., Manhattan and Richmond, N.Y., short terms, 1905, 1907; has designed and executed landscape gardening in many parts of U.S.; designed park of 1,400 acres at San Diego, Calif. Republican. Quaker. Author: Landscape Gardening, 1891; How to Plan Home Grounds, 1905; Art of Landscape Architecture, 1915. Editor: Hints on Landscape Gardening (by Prince Pückler Muskau), 1917. Home: New York, N.Y. Died Feb. 3, 1923.

PARSONS, Thomas Smith, agronomist; b. Ivinghoe, Eng., Aug. 5, 1873; s. Henry and Emily (Williams) P.; brought to America, 1880; B.S., S.Dak. Agrl. Coll., Brookings, S.D., 1897, M.S., 1899; post-grad. work Mich. Agrl. Coll.; m. Mabel Doughty, June 25, 1902. Science teacher and prin. high schs., S.D., and Durango, Colo., to 1909; prof. agronomy, U. of Wyo., and agronomist U.S. Expt. Sta., Laramie, Wyo., 1910—. Crops and soils specialist for Wyo., 1918—; editor Wyoming Stockman-Farmer, Cheyenne; state seed analyst. Republican. Methodist. Author: Manual of Agriculture and Nature Study, 1908. Home: Laramie, Wyo. Died Feb. 27, 1923.

PARSONS, William Barclay, civil engr.; b. N.Y. City, Apr. 15, 1859; s. William Barclay and Eliza Glass (Livingston) P.; A.B., Columbia, 1879, C.E., 1882; LL.D., St. John's, Md., 1909; Sc.D., Princeton, 1920, Trinity, 1921; D.Eng., Stevens, 1921; m. Anna DeWitt Reed, May 20, 1884; children—Mrs. Sylvia Weld, Wm. Barclay. Consulting engr., N.Y. City, 1885; dep. chief engr., 1891-94, chief engr., Rapid Transit Commn. New York, 1894-1904; survey Chinese railways, 1898-99; mem. Isthmian Canal Commn., 1904; bd. of consulting engrs., Panama Canal, 1905; advisory engr. Royal Commn. London Traffic, 1904; chief engr. Cape Cod Canal, 1905-14; chmn. Chicago Transit Com., 1916; also many other engring. wks. Lecturer Cambridge U., 1929. Chief of engrs. (brig. gen. N.G.N.Y.), Spanish-Am. War; maj., lt. col., col. 11th U.S. Engrs., World War; now brig. gen. engr. R.C., U.S.A. Awarded D.S.M. (U.S.), also citation for conspicuous distinguished service and victory medal and 5 clasps; D.S.O. (British); Officer Legion of Honor (French); Order of Crown (Belgian). Fellow Am. Acad. Arts and Sciences; etc. Trustee Columbia U., 1897— (chmn. bd. from 1917), N.Y. Pub. Library, Carnegie Instn. (Washington). Vestryman Trinity Ch., New York. Author: Turnouts, 1883; Track, 1885; Rapid Transit in Foreign Cities, 1895; American Engineer in China, 1900; The American Engineers in France, 1920; Robert Fulton and the Submarine, 1923; etc. Home: New York, N.Y. Died May 9, 1932.

PARSONS, William Edward, architect; b. Akron, O., June 19, 1872; s. William Cheney and Sarah Day (Seymour) P.; B.A., Yale U., 1895; B.S., Columbia, 1898; awarded McKim fellowship, 1899; studied École des Beaux Arts, Paris; m. Myra Louise Matthews, 1911; children—Louise Kellogg, Seymour. Began in office of John Galen Howard, New York, 1901; apptd. consulting architect, U.S. Govt., in Philippines, 1905; directed execution of the Burnham plans for Manila and Baguio; designed many pub. bldgs., including Philippine Gen. Hosp., U. of Philippines, Manila Hotel; planned the restoration of the old city walls and moats of Manila as public parks, and established standards of pub. architecture which have been generally followed; resigned, 1914, and associated in practice with E. H. Bennett; firm under the name of E. H. Bennett & Wm. E. Parsons; mem. Bennett, Parsons & Frost, 1922—; designers of civic improvements at Chicago, St. Paul, Buffalo, Phoenix, Pasadena, Palm Beach, San Juan, P.R., and Washington, D.C.; adviser George Rogers Clark Sesquicentennial Commn. for Memorial at Vincennes, Ind.; cons. architect Resettlement Adminstrn., 1935; asso. prof. architecture, Yale, 1938—. Mem. Am. Inst. Architects. Republican. Episcopalian. Died Dec. 17, 1939.

PARSONS, William Wood, educator; b. Terre Haute, Ind., May 18, 1850; s. Thomas and Elizabeth (Ryman) P.; grad. Ind. State Normal Sch., Terre Haute, 1872; A.M., Ind. U., 1886; LL.D., De Pauw U.; m. Harriet Emily Wilkes, Dec. 23, 1880. Asst. prof. English, 1876-79, head of dept., 1879, v.p. 1882, pres. 1885-1921, Ind. State Normal Sch., pres. emeritus, 1921—. Chmn. bd. First Nat. Bank; treas. Wabash Bldg., Loan & Savings Assn. Pres. bd. of mgrs. Rose Orphan Home; mem. bd. of mgrs. Rose Poly. Inst. Methodist. Republican. Home: Terre Haute, Ind. Died Sept. 28, 1925.

PARTINGTON, Frederick Eugene, educator; b. Portland, Me.; s. Joseph and Lura C. (Smiley) P.; A.B., Brown U., 1879, A.M., 1885; studied and lived abroad, France and Germany, 4 yrs.; m. Elizabeth Hamilton Bateman, June 12, 1890. Newspaper corr., Germany, 1880-81; headmaster, New Paltz (N.Y.) Acad., 1882-84, Staten Island (N.Y.) Acad., 1884-1907; dir. National Park Sem., Forest Glen, Md., 1907-18; staff writer Washington Cathedral, 1918-19. Lecturer on history and travel; writer of short stories. Episcopalian. Home: Portland, Me. Died Sept. 21, 1924.

PARTON, Arthur, landscape artist; b. Hudson, N.Y., Mar. 26, 1842; s. George and Elizabeth (Woodbridge) P.; bro. of Ernest P.; studied in Pa. Acad. Fine Arts, Phila. Exhibited 1st pictures there, 1862; located in New York, 1865; regular exhibitor at Nat. Acad. Design; received gold medal, Am. Art Assn., 1886; Temple medal, Phila.; hon. mention, Paris Expn., 1900. Represented at Met. Mus. Art and other leading collections. A.N.A., 1871, N.A., 1884. Home: Yonkers, N.Y. Died Mar. 7, 1914.

PARTON, Ernest, landscape artist; b. Hudson, N.Y., Mar. 17, 1845; s. George and Elizabeth (Woodbridge) P.; bro. of Arthur P.; ed. Hudson Acad. and private tutors; studied art with brother, Arthur; went to England, 1873; has since resided there; m. 2d, d. of William Gough, of Birmingham, Eng. Medals and diplomas Salon and Internat. Expn., Paris, Chicago Expn., etc. Among his larger pictures are "Waning of the Year," "Woodland Home," etc. Died Sept. 15, 1933.

PARTON, Henry Woodbridge, portrait and landscape painter; b. Hudson, N.Y.; s. George and Elizabeth (Woodbridge) P.; ed. pub. schs.; unmarried. Exhibited at Nat. Acad. Design, Royal Acad., London. Mem. Painters and Sculptors Galleries, New York. N.A., 1929. Home-Studio: New York, N.Y. Died Mar. 1, 1933.

PARTRIDGE, Edward Lasell, M.D.; b. Newton, Mass., Sept. 27, 1853; s. Joseph Lyman and Zibiah Nelson (Willson) P.; M.D., Coll. Phys. and Surg. (Columbia), 1875; hon. A.M., Williams, 1880; m. Gertrude E., d. Prof. Theodore W. Dwight, LL.D. (founder Columbia U. Law Sch., 1859). Served as visiting phys. New York Maternity, Nursery and Child's, Sloane Maternity and New York hosps.; now consulting phys. New York Hosp.; prof. obstetrics, New York Post-Grad. Med. Coll., 1886-87; lecturer obstetrics, 1888, adj. prof., 1889-93, Med. Dept. Columbia. Pres. New York Nursery and Child's Hosp., 1917-21; pres. Washington Sq. Home for Friendless Girls; trustee New York Instn. for Edn. of Blind, Washington Sq. Assn. (pres.), New York Dispensary, Northern Dispensary. Hudson-Fulton commr., 1909; pioneer in movement which led to creation of the Highlands of the Hudson River Reservation; commr. Palisades Interstate Park. Hon. mem. New York Med. and Surg. Soc.; pres. Gen. Knox Headquarters Assn.; pres. Huguenot Soc.; trustee Am. Scenic and Hist. Preservation Soc.; gov. Soc. Colonial Wars; mem. various socs. Author: Manual of Obstetrics, 1908. Editor: Verrier's Manual of Obstetrics, 1884. Home: New York, N.Y., and Cornwall, N.Y. Died May 2, 1930.

PARTRIDGE, John Slater, judge; b. Susanville, Calif., June 22, 1870; s. John C. and Helen E. (Slater) P.; A.B., U. of Calif., 1892, A.M., 1894; unmarried. Admitted to Calif. bar, 1897, and began practice at San Francisco; U.S. dist. judge, Northern Dist. of Calif., Mar. 3, 1923—. Republican. Episcopalian. Elk. Home: Berkeley, Calif. Died May 20, 1926.

PARTRIDGE, Sidney Catlin, bishop; b. New York, Sept. 1, 1857; s. George Sidney, Jr. and Helen Derby (Catlin) P.; A.B., Yale, 1880; B.D., Berkeley Div. Sch., 1884, D.D., 1900; m. Charlotte Irene Mills, June 10, 1884 (died 1886); 1 dau., Helen Louise (Mrs. Geo. E. Chapin); m. 2d, Agnes Simpson, Nov. 27, 1900; 1 dau., Amalia Ortwed Lucy. Deacon, 1884, priest, 1885, P.E. Ch.; went to Shanghai, China, as missionary; taught at St. John's Coll. and chaplain St. Mary's Hall, Shanghai, 1884-87; rector Boone Sch. and missionary, Wu-chang, China, 1887-99; consecrated missionary bishop of Kyoto, Japan, Feb. 2, 1900; elected bishop Diocese of West Mo., Mar. 8, 1911, and enthroned in Grace Ch., Kansas City, June 27, 1911. Home: Kansas City, Mo. Died June 22, 1930.

PARTRIDGE, William Ordway, sculptor, author; b. Paris, France, Apr. 11, 1861; s. George Sidney and Helen Derby (Catlin) P.; student Columbia, 1885; art edn. Rome, Florence, Paris; hon. A.M., Adelphi Coll., 1904; m. Margaret Ridgely Schott, 1905. Lecturer on fine arts, Columbian (now George Washington) U., 1897-1903; served as lecturer before Nat. Social Science Assn., Concord Sch. Philosophy, Brooklyn Inst., etc. Works include statue of Samuel Tilden, Riverside Drive, New York; Shakespeare, Lincoln Park, Chicago; bronze statue of Alexander Hamilton, Brooklyn; bronze statue of Thomas Jefferson, Columbia U.; Pieta, St. Patrick's Cathedral, New York; Pocahontas Jamestown, Va. Exhibited Salon, Paris; Royal Acad., London and Berlin. Author: Art for America; The Song Life of a Sculptor; The Technique of Sculpture; The Angel of Clay (novel), 1900; Nathan Hale, the Ideal Patriot, 1902; The Czar's Gift (novel), 1906. Died May 22, 1930.

PARVIN, Theodore Sutton, high Freemason and librarian; b. Cedarville, N.J., Jan. 15, 1817; grad. Woodward Coll., Cincinnati, 1836; removed to Iowa, 1838, and was private sec. to first gov. (Lucas); first librarian of Iowa Ty.; purchased nucleus of Territorial (now State) library; dist. atty., 1839; co. judge 2 or 3 terms; State register of lands; prof. natural science and librarian State U. of Iowa; librarian Iowa Hist. Soc. Founded, 1844, and built Iowa Masonic Library, occupying the only masonic library building in the world; has been librarian from its founding. Is a 33d-degree Mason and Knight Templar; has served as grand recorder, grand encampment K.T. of U.S., and has been 55 years grand sec. and librarian Grand Lodge of Iowa; m. Agnes McCully, May 17, 1843. Home: Cedar Rapids, Ia. Died 1901.

PASCO, Samuel, senator; b. London, Eng., June 28, 1834; s. John and Amelia (Nash) P.; removed to Prince Edward Island, and later to Mass. with his father's family when quite young; A.B., Harvard, 1858, A.M., 1872; prin. Waukeenah Acad., Fla., 1859-61; private and non-commd. officer C.S.A., 1861-65; m. Jessie, d. William Denham, Oct. 28, 1869. Clerk Circuit Ct., Jefferson Co., Fla., 1866-68; admitted to bar, 1868; in practice at Monticello, Fla., 1868-87. Mem. Dem. State Com., 1872-88 (chmn. 1876-88), Dem. Nat. Com., 1880-1900; presdl. elector-at-large, 1880 and 1908; pres. Fla. Constl. Conv., 1885; mem. Fla. Ho. of Rep., 1886-87 (speaker 1887); U.S. senator, 2 terms, 1887-99; mem. Isthmian Canal Commn., 1899-1904. Grand master of Masons, Fla., 1870-72; grand master I.O.O.F., 1885; grand high priest R.A.M., 1909; maj. gen. Fla. div. U.C.V., 1910-11; chmn. Fla. Chickamauga Monument Commn., 1910-12. Home: Monticello, Fla. Died Mar. 13, 1917.

PASSMORE, Ellis Pusey, banker; b. Rising Sun, Md., Feb. 1, 1869; s. Ellis Pusey and Mary E. (Lincoln) P.; Friends Sch., Swarthmore Coll., 1893; hon. M.A., Swarthmore Coll., 1918; m. Emily Pusey Shelmire, June 16, 1898; children—Mary L., Elizabeth P. Served as cashier Nat. Bank of Avondale, Pa.; cashier Traders' Nat. Bank, Scranton, Pa.; v.p. Franklin Nat. Bank, Phila.; also gov. Federal Reserve Bank of Phila. and pres. Bank of North America; pres. Bank of North America and Trust Co., 1923—. Chmn. com. in charge of Liberty Loans, World War. Pres. Union League of Phila.; treas. and mem. bd. Swarthmore College. Republican. Mem. Soc. of Friends. Mason. Home: Chestnut Hill, Phila., Pa. Died Jan. 22, 1928.

PASSMORE, Lincoln K., insurance; b. Rising Sun, Md., Sept. 2, 1850; s. Ellis Pusey and Mary (Lincoln) P.; ed. pub. schs.; m. Ellen F. Faxon, Apr. 22, 1891; children—John Faxon (dec.), Lincoln Alan, Frances Heppe. Teacher pub. schs. 4 yrs.; with Peter Wright & Sons, export grain, Phila., 1874-82; later in same business with others; became trustee Penn Mut. Life Ins. Co., 1889, 2d v.p., 1903, v.p., 1906—; dir. Bank of North America; apptd. by A. Mitchell Palmer mem. Advisory Com. on Alien Life Insurance Companies, Sept. 1918. Quaker. Republican. Home: Philadelphia, Pa. Died Mar. 4, 1935.

PATCH, Frank Wallace, physician; b. Wayland, Mass., Mar. 22, 1862; s. Samuel and Elizabeth J. (Noyes) P.; M.D., Boston U. Sch. of Medicine, 1888; Rotunda Hosp., Dublin, Ireland, 1893; m. Kate Whiting, Oct. 19, 1893; m. 2d, Virginia Allen, Aug. 19, 1913. Settled in Framingham in gen. practice, 1888; established Woodside Cottages, as pvt. sanitarium, 1900; pres. Framingham Improvement Assn.; mem. consulting bd. Westboro State Hospital. Pres. Internat. Hahnemannian Assn., 1907, Mass. Homœ. Med Soc., 1911. Died Sept. 7, 1923.

PATCH, Kate Whiting, author; b. Elizabeth, N.J., Aug. 22, 1870; d. Frederic A. and Catherine (Allen) Whiting; ed. pub. and pvt. schs.; Wellesley Hills, Mass.; m. Frank Wallace Patch, M.D., Oct. 19, 1893. Author: Middleway, 1897; Rainy Days and Sunny Days (juvenile), 1899; Old Lady and Young Laddie, 1900; Prince Yellowtop (juvenile), 1903. Home: Framingham, Mass. Died 1909.

PATCH, Nathaniel Jordan Knight, commodore U.S.N.; b. Otisfield, Me.; s. Benjamin and Harriet E. F. P.; apptd. to U.S. Naval Acad. from Mass., Sept. 20, 1865, grad. 1869; unmarried. Served in sea service 22 yrs. and shore or other duty 14 yrs.; retired with rank of commodore, June 30, 1905. Home: Buffalo, N.Y. Died Jan. 12, 1913.

PATCHIN, Frank Glines, author; b. Wayland, N.Y. Dec. 19, 1861; s. Cameron and Harriet (Glines) P.; A.B., Cornell, 1882; LL.B., Albany Law Sch., 1883; m. Elizabeth Calisher, Sept. 1895. Reporter and asst. night editor New York Press, 1889-92; city editor New York Journal, 1893-95; asst. city editor Washington Post, 1895-96; again on New York Journal, 1897; later night editor New York Recorder; news editor, 1901-07, gen. mgr., 1907-09, Rochester Post Express. Republican. Mason. Author: The Pony Rider Boys Series (10 vols.); The Circus Boys (6 vols.); The Battleship Boys (8 vols.); The Range and Grange Series (6 vols.); The Boys of Steel Series (12 vols.); The Meadow-Brook Girls (6 vols.); The Automobile Girls (3 vols.); Grace Harlowe Overseas Series (8 vols.); Grace Harlowe Overland Rider Series (10 vols.); Little Soldiers of France; Little Boy Heroes of France; Little Daughters of France; Uncle Jim's Bible Stories (3 vols.), 1923. Now night editor Democrat & Chronicle, Rochester. Home: Rochester, N.Y. Died Mar. 22, 1925.

PATERSON, Van Rensselaer, jurist; b. Ogdensburg, N.Y., about 1850; grad. Albany Normal Coll., 1872; Union Coll., LL.B., 1875; began practice of law Stockton, Calif.; m. Amy Kelsey, 1880. Elected city atty., 1878, 79, resigned; superior judge, 1879; re-elected, 1884; elected justice Supreme Court, 1886, for 12-year term, but resigned, 1894, and resumed practice at San Francisco. Prominent candidate for U.S. senator, 1899, legislature adjourning without election. Home: San Francisco, Calif. Died 1902.

PATON, Lewis Bayles, educator; b. N.Y. City, June 27, 1864; s. Robert Leighton Stuart and Henrietta (Bayles) P.; A.B., New York U., 1884, A.M., 1893; grad. Princeton Theol. Sem., 1890; studied U. of Berlin, 1890-92; Ph.D., U. of Marburg 1897; D.D., New York U., 1906; m. Suvia Davison, Dec. 30, 1896 (died 1904); 1 dau., Suvia Lanice (Mrs. Arthur E. Whittemore); m. 2d, Mrs. Loraine Seymour (Brown) Calhoun, June 30, 1915 (died 1924); m. 3d, Katharine Hazeltine, July 14, 1925. Ordained Presbyn. ministry, 1890; transferred to Congl. Ch., 1892; instr. O.T. exegesis and criticism, 1892-93, asso. prof., 1893-1900, Nettleton prof., 1900—, Hartford Theol. Sem. Dir. Am. Sch. Oriental Study and Research in Palestine, Jerusalem, 1903-04. Author: Early History of Syria and Palestine (Semitic Series); Jerusalem in Bible Times, 1908; Esther (Internat. Critical Commentary); Early Religion of Israel, 1910; Spiritism and Cult of the Dead in Antiquity, 1921. Editor: Recent Christian Progress, 1909. Asso. editor Am. Jour. Archæology. Home: West Hartford, Conn. Died Jan. 24, 1932.

PATON, Thomas Bugard, lawyer; b. N.Y. City, May 7, 1861; s. Thomas and Theresa Francesca (Bugard) P.; ed. pub. schs.; spl. course Columbia U.; m. Adele Coutant Holden, 1885. Admitted to N.Y. bar, 1883, and began practice at N.Y. City; editor law dept. of Journal of Banking 6 yrs.; founder Banking Law Journal, 1889, and sold out 1908; gen. counsel Am. Bankers Assn., 1908— Author of many statutes relating to banking which have been adopted by various states. Republican. Episcopalian. Home: Forest Hills, L.I. Died Mar. 28, 1933.

PATON, William Agnew, author; b. New York, N.Y., Apr. 20, 1848; s. William and Anne S. (Agnew) P.; ed. pvt. schs.; m. Margaret Atlee Jackson, Jan. 23, 1911. Pub. New York World, 1877-81; trustee Nat. Republican, 1881-85; U.S. commr., 1883; 1st business mgr. Scribner's Magazine, 1885-87. Independent Republican. Hon. mem. Royal Acad. Sciences, Letters and Arts, Palermo. Author: Down the Islands, a Voyage to the Caribbees, 1887; Picturesque Sicily, 1897; The First Landfall of Columbus, 1907; Home Rule Ballads, 1907. Home: Princeton, N.J. Died Dec. 11, 1918.

PATRICK, Fred Albert, merchant, mfr.; b. Marengo, Ill., Nov. 8, 1857; s. Richard Montgomery and Emma (Page) P.; grad. high sch., Ann Arbor, Mich., 1876; student U. of Mich., 1876-77; m. Louise Cook, 1880 (died 1901); children—Rosamond (Mrs. Mitchell F. Jamar, Jr.), Isabelle (Mrs. John J. McDonald, Jr.), Marjorie (dec.), Barbara (dec.); m. 2d, Katherine Beneteau, May 14, 1906. Sr. partner F. A. Patrick & Co., drygoods, Marengo, 1881-91; pres. McHenry County Butter Co., 1885-91; treas. and mgr. Stone-Ordean-Wells Co., wholesale grocers, Duluth, Minn., 1891-1901; pres. F. A. Patrick & Co., drygoods (mfr. and wholesale), 1901-28; chmn. bd.

Duluth Glass Block Store Co.; pres. Patrick Duluth Corp., F. A. Patrick Bldg. Co. Mem. Charter Commn. and Park Bd., Duluth. Mem. Gen. Com. 9th Federal Res. Dist., in charge Liberty Loan campaigns, northeastern Minn., World War. Republican. Presbyn. Mason, Elk. Home: Duluth, Minn. Died Dec. 16, 1931.

PATRICK, George Edward, chemist; b. Hopedale, Mass., Oct. 22, 1851; s. Delano and Mary (Maynard) P.; B.S., Cornell, 1873, M.S., 1874; m. Hattie E. Lewis, June 19, 1879. Instr. chemistry, Cornell, 1873-74; asst. prof. and prof. chemistry, U. of Kan. 1874-83; chemist Ia. Agrl. Expt. Sta., 1888-95; prof. agrl. chemistry, Ia. State Coll., 1890-95; asst. chemist U.S. Dept. Agr., 1896—; in charge dairy lab. Bureau Chemistry, 1901—. Died Mar. 22, 1916.

PATRICK, Hugh Talbot, neurologist; b. New Philadelphia, O., May 11, 1860; s. Abraham W. and Mary (Talbot) P.; student U. of Wooster, 1878-80; M.D., Bellevue Hosp. Med. Coll. (New York U.), 1884; studied nervous and mental diseases abroad, 1891-94; m. Fannie E., d. Judge Joseph E. Gary, of Chicago, Apr. 28, 1896; children—Talbot, Catherine, Elizabeth (dec.). Prof. nervous and mental diseases, Chicago Policlinic, 1896—; emeritus prof. nervous and mental diseases, Northwestern U.; President American Neurol. Assn., 1907, Miss. Valley Medical Assn., 1905, and twice of Chicago Neurol. Soc. Home: Chicago, Ill. Died Jan. 15, 1939.

PATRICK, Mary Mills, coll. pres.; b. Canterbury, N.H., Mar. 10, 1850; d. John and Harriet (White) P.; student Lyons Coll., Ia., 1866-69; A.M., State U. of Ia., 1890; univs. of Heidelberg, Zürich, Leipzig, 1892-95; Ph.D., U. of Berne, 1897; spl. studies in Near East langs.; LL.D., Smith Coll., 1914; Litt.D., Columbia Univ. 1922. President Istanbul Woman's College, 1890-1924 (emeritus). Member Psychol. Congresses, Munich, 1896, Paris, 1900; Philos. Congresses, Paris, 1900, Bologna, 1911, Harvard. 1926. Author: Armenian Translation of Text-Book of Physiology, Constantinople, 1876; Sextus Empiricus and Greek Skepticism, 1899; Sappho and the Island of Lesbos, 1912, 24; The Greek Sceptics, 1929; Under Five Sultans, 1929; A Bosporus Adventure, 1934. Decorated by Sultan Hamid of Turkey and King Boris of Bulgaria. Home: Palo Alto, Calif. Died Feb. 25, 1940.

PATRICK, Mason Mathews, army officer; b. Lewisburg, W.Va., Dec. 13, 1863; s. Alfred Spicer (M.D.) and Virginia (Matthews) P.; B.S., U.S. Mil. Acad., 1886; grad. Engring. Sch. of Application, 1889; m. Grace W. Cooley, Nov. 11, 1902; 1 son, Bream Cooley. Commd. add. 2d lt. engrs., U.S. Army, 1886; promoted through grades to col., 1916; brig. gen. N.A., 1917, and maj. gen. Nat. Army, 1918; maj. gen. U.S. Army, 1921. Asst. instr., practical mil. engring., U.S. Mil. Acad., 1892-95; in charge 1st and 2d dists., improvement Miss. River, 1897-98; sec. Miss. River Commn., St. Louis, Mo., 1898-1901; duty Office, Chief of Engrs., Washington, D.C., 1901-03; instr. U.S. Mil. Acad., 1903-06; comdg. U.S. Mil. Acad. detachment of engrs., 1904-06; chief engr. Army Cuban Pacification, 1907-09; river and harbor work, Norfolk, Va., 1909-12; mem. bd. raising U.S.S. Maine, 1910-12; improvement Great Lakes, Detroit, Mich., 1912-16; comdg. 1st Regt. Engrs., 1916-17; comdt. Engr. Sch., Washington Barracks, D.C., 1916-17; chief engr. lines of communication. and dir. constrn. and forestry operations, A.E.F. in France, Sept. 1917-May 1918; chief of Air Service, A.E.F., May 1918-July 1919; div. engr., Gulf Div., New Orleans, La., 1919-20; asst. chief of engrs., 1920-21; comdt. Engr. Sch., Camp Humphreys, Va., July-Oct. 1921; apptd. chief of Air Service, Oct. 1921, reapptd. Oct. 1925; retired Dec. 13, 1927; apptd. Pub. Utilities Commr. of D.C., June 1929, resigned as chmn. Sept. 1933. Awarded D.S.M.; Comdr. Legion of Honor, Order Sts. Maurice and Lazarus; Knight Comdr. Order of the British Empire; Comdr. Crown of Belgium; Grand Officer Crown of Italy. Died Jan. 29, 1942.

PATRICK, Robert Goodlett, coll. pres.; b. Greenville, S.C., Jan. 15, 1866; s. John Bellinger (prin. Patrick Mil. Inst., Anderson, S.C.) and Maria Louisa (Goodlett) P.; grad. Patrick Mil. Inst., 1882; B.A., Furman U., S.C., 1885; Th.M., Southern Bapt. Theol. Sem., Ky., 1883—; (D.D., Howard College, Ala., 1896); m. Hellen Manly, June 27, 1888. Ordained Bapt. ministry, 1888; pastor Yorkville, S.C., 1888-92, First Ch., Maysville, Ky., 1892-95, Siloam Ch., Marion, Ala., 1896; pres. Judson Coll., Marion, Ala., 1896-1913. Pres. Southern Bapt. Ednl. Assn., 1907-12; sec. Ala. Bapt. Edn. Common., 1912-13. Democrat. Home: Chicago, Ill. Died Jan. 1, 1920.

PATTEE, William Sullivan, univ. dean; b. Jackson, Me., Sept. 19, 1846; s. Daniel and Mary Ann (Bixby) P.; A.B., Bowdoin, 1871, A.M., 1874; (LL.D., Ia. Coll., 1894); m. Julia E. Tuttle, Nov. 30, 1871. Admitted to bar, 1878; prof. equity and dean Coll. of Law, U. of Minn., 1888—. Mem. Minn. Ho. of Rep., 1884-85. Republican. Author: Illustrative Cases in Contracts; Illustrative Cases in Equity; Illustrative Cases in Personality; Illustrative Cases in Realty; Elements of Contracts; Elements of Equity. Home: Minneapolis, Minn. Died 1911.

PATTEN, Amos Williams, theologian; b. Baltimore, Feb. 11, 1848; s. William and Harriet (Edwards) P.; A.B., Northwestern U., 1870, A.M., 1873; B.D., Garrett Bibl. Inst., 1871 (D.D., 1888); studied univs. of Berlin and Leipzig; m. Belle R. Harrison, Dec. 5, 1871 (died 1875); m. 2d, Ella S. Prindle, Oct. 25, 1883. Entered Rock River Conf. M.E. Ch., 1871; pastor in Ill. at Crete, Lockport, Chicago, Dixon, Evanston, Aurora, Joliet and Chicago, until 1899; prof. Bibl. lit., Northwestern U., 1899-1923, emeritus. Traveled in Europe, Palestine and Egypt, and has lectured on Bibl. and archeol. subjects. Trustee Northwestern U., 1887-99, Wesley Hosp., Chicago. Republican. Editor: Bennett's Christian Archæology, 1898. Home: Evanston, Ill. Died June 13, 1924.

PATTEN, James A., grain commn. mcht.; b. Freeland Corners, Ill., May 8, 1852; s. Alexander R. and Agnes (Beveridge) P.; ed. country schs.; m. Louise Buchanan, Apr. 9, 1885; children—Agnes, Thomas Beveridge (dec.), John Lowrie. Clerk in country store, 1869-71; on grandfather's farm, 1871-74; employe state grain inspection dept., Chicago, 1874-78; with G. P. Comstock & Co., 1878-80, and with brother George W., in grain commn. business, as Patten Bros., 1880-1903; mem. firm of Bartlett, Frazier & Carrington, 1903-10; retired. Director Continental & Commercial Nat. Bank, City Nat. Bank of Evanston, Peoples Gas Light & Coke Co., Commonwealth Edison Co., Chicago Title & Trust Co., C.,R.I.&P. Ry. Co. Mayor of Evanston, Ill., 1901-05. Presbyn. Home: Evanston, Ill. Died Dec. 8, 1928.

PATTEN, James Horace, lawyer, publicist; b. nr. Spring Hill, Kan., Dec. 23, 1877; s. Harrison Henry and Gertrude (Pratt) P.; A.B., U. of Kan., 1896; A.B., Harvard, 1897; student Grad. Sch. same, 1897-1902, A.M., 1899; LL.B., Harvard, 1905; m. Olive Young Latimer, d. of late Senator A. C. Latimer, of S.C., Oct. 12, 1909. Instr. in economics, Harvard, 1900-02; apptd. prof. polit. science, U. of New Brunswick, 1902; admitted to Mass. bar, 1905; practiced in D.C.; gen. counsel Farmers' Edn. and Cooperative Union of America, 1909-14; asst. sec. Farmers' Nat. Congress, 1911-17, sec., 1917-19; attorney Ry. Executives Advisory Com., 1916-20. First sergeant provisional Co. C, Mass. N.G., Spanish-Am. War, 1898-99. Sec. Immigration Restriction League; chmn. nat. legislative com. World's Purity Fedn., 1909-13, asst. legislative supt. same, 1913-26, and mem. exec. bd., 1927—; chmn. nat. legislative com. Immigration Restriction League; legislative rep. of State Council of Jr. Order United Am. Mechanics, State of New York. Commd., by Sec. of Labor, 1923, to investigate certain conditions in Hawaii, Guam, Japan, China and the Philippines. Editor: Graduate Hand-book, 1900. Home: Washington, D.C. Died Apr. 25, 1940.

PATTEN, John A., manufacturer; b. Delavan, Ill., Sept. 27, 1867; s. Maj. George W. and Charlotte (Holmes) P.; pub. sch. edn.; (LL.D., Baker U.); m. Edith Manker, Oct. 2, 1890. Pres. Patten Mfg. Co., Chattanooga Packet Co., Tennessee River Navigation Co., Hamilton Realty Co., Bee Dee Stock Medicine Co., Chattanooga Trust Co.; mng. partner Chattanooga Medicine Co.; was partner in Stone Fort Land Co., 1903-06, which removed stone hill, covering 6 blocks in centre of Chattanooga, and improved same. Especially active for many yrs. in improvement of waterways; pres. Tenn. River Improvement Assn.; treas. bd. trustees U. of Chattanooga; trustee Goucher Coll. of Baltimore; v.p. Conf. for Edn. and Industry in the South. Home: North Chattanooga, Tenn. Died Apr. 26, 1916.

PATTEN, Simon Nelson, university prof.; b. Sandwich, Ill., May 1, 1852; s. William and Elizabeth (Pratt) P.; Northwestern U., 1874-76; Ph.D., A.M., Halle, Germany, 1878; (LL.D., U. of Ill., 1905). Principal public schools of Ill. and Ia., 1882-88; prof. polit. economy, U. of Pa., 1888-1917. Author: Premises of Political Economy, 1885; Economic Basis of Protection, 1890; Theory of Dynamic Economics, 1892; Theory of Social Forces, 1896; Development of English Thought, 1899; Theory of Prosperity, 1902; Heredity and Social Progress, 1903; The New Basis of Civilization, 1907; Product and Climax, 1909; The Social Basis of Religion, 1911; Reconstruction of Economic Theory, 1912; Culture and War, 1916. Died July 24, 1922.

PATTEN, Thomas Gedney, postmaster; b. New York, Sept. 12, 1861; s. Thomas and Maria L. (Gedney) P.; ed. Mt. Pleasant Acad., Ossining, and Columbia Coll. and Law Sch.; m. Henrietta Floyd, Oct. 31, 1890. Mem. 62d Congress (1911-13), 15th N.Y. Dist., and 63d and 64th Congresses (1913-17), 18th Dist.; postmaster of N.Y. City, 1917-21. Democrat. Home: New York, N.Y. Died Feb. 23, 1939.

PATTEN, William, zoölogist; b. Watertown, Mass. Mar. 15, 1861; s. Thomas and Mary Low (Bradley) P.; B.S., Lawrence Scientific Sch. (Harvard), 1883; A.M., Ph.D., Leipzig, Germany, 1884; m. Mary Elizabeth Merrill, June 28, 1883; 1 son, Bradley Merrill. Asst. in Lake Lab., Milwaukee, Wis., 1886-89; prof. biology, U. of N.D., 1889-93; prof. zoölogy, Dartmouth, 1893—. Trustee Marine Biol. Lab., Woods

Hole. Mem. Nat. Research Council for Biology and Agr. Author: The Evolution of the Vertebrates and Their Kin, 1912; The Grand Strategy of Evolution, 1920. Pres. Sect. F (zoölogy) A.A.A.S., 1918. Home: Hanover, N.H. Died Oct. 27, 1932.

PATTERSON, Adoniram Judson, clergyman; b. Spring Township, Pa., Apr. 3, 1827; s. James and Nancy (Holt) P.; ed. pub. schs. and pvt. instrn. (D.D., W. Springfield Acad., 1869, Tufts, 1905); m. Jane Lippitt, Aug. 26, 1851. Pastor of Universalist chs., Girard, Pa., 1853-55, Portsmouth, N.H., 1855-66, Roxbury, Mass., 1866—, pastor emeritus, 1888—. Pres. Mass. Conv. Universalists, 1873-78; mem. N.H. legislature, 1866. Mason, Odd Fellow, hon. mem. G.A.R. Author: Semi-Centennial Memorial, 1871. Home: Roxbury, Mass. Died 1909.

PATTERSON, Alvah Worrell, lawyer; b. Hendricks Co., Ind., Jan. 15, 1870; s. William and Juan Fernandes (Worrell) P.; Central Normal Coll., Danville, Ind.; LL.B., George Washington U., 1899, LL.M., 1900, D.C.L., 1901; m. Anna M. Brown, Sept. 18, 1901. Newspaper work Heppner, Ore., 1891-97; with Dept. of Interior, Washington, 1901, asst. atty. until 1914, 1st asst., 1914-21; became mem. Bd. of Appeals, 1921, chmn. Oct. 1931; now review counsel Federal Emergency Adminstrn. of Pub. Works. Episcopalian. Mason. Home: Washington, D.C. Died Apr. 22, 1938.

PATTERSON, Andrew Henry, coll. dean; b. Winston-Salem, N.C., Sept. 28, 1870; s. Rufus Lenoir and Mary Elizabeth (Fries) P.; Ph.B., B.E., U. of N.C., 1891; A.B., Harvard, 1892, A.M., 1893; hon. D.Sc., U. of Georgia, 1927; m. Eleanor Spurrier, d. Eben Alexander, Sept. 8, 1897; children—Mary Fries (Mrs. Samuel J. Fisher, Jr.), Howard Alexander. Instr. physics, 1894-97, adj. prof., 1897-98, prof. physics and astronomy, 1898-1908, U. of Ga.; prof. physics, 1908—, dean Sch. Applied Science, 1911—, U. of N.C. Fellow Am. Physical Soc., A.A.A.S. Democrat. Episcopalian. Home: Chapel Hill, N.C. Died Sept. 9, 1928.

PATTERSON, Antoinette De Courcey, author; b. Phila., Pa., Sept. 17, 1866; d. Samuel Gerald and Lizzie Otto (Barclay) De Courcey; ed. Miss Sanford's Sch., Phila.; m. Thomas Hamilton Hoge Patterson. Mem. Phila. Art Alliance. Author: Sonnets and Quatrains, 1913; Undine (poem), 1914; The Son of Merope, 1916; The Enchanted Bird, 1917. Translator: Old Swedish Fairy Tales, 1925. Home: Philadelphia, Pa. Died Apr. 30, 1925.

PATTERSON, Burd Shippen; b. Pottsville, Pa., June 21, 1857; s. Joseph S. and Sarah Elizabeth (Weaver) P.; grad. Pottsville High Sch., 1873; m. Anna Marie McLeod, June 11, 1884 (died 1898). Admitted to Schuylkill Co. bar, 1878; editor The Sentinel, 1881-82; secretary Pottsville, Pa., Board of Trade, 1889-91; pres. Schuylkill Electric Ry., 1890-91; editor and chief propr. Miners Journal, Pottsville, 1890-91; sec. Pa. Anti-Quay Assn., 1892-93; editor Pittsburgh Times, 1893-1904, Pittsburgh Post, 1904-08; sec. statistics com. of Provisional Lake Erie and Ohio River Ship Canal Commn. of Chamber of Commerce of Pittsburgh, 1895, and of Lake Erie and Ohio River Ship Canal Co., 1905-16; sec. Lake Erie & Ohio River Ship Canal Assn., Dec. 1910—; sec. Lake Erie and Ohio River Canal Bd., Oct. 26, 1915—; sec. Civ. Service Commn. of Pittsburgh, May 12, 1909-14. Sec. Garfield Rep. Com. Schuylkill Co., 1881-82; sec. Independent Rep. State Conv. of Pa., 1882; pres. Central Rep. Club, Pottsville, 1890-91; del. Union Party State convs., 1901, 02, and Lincoln Party State Conv., 1906; sec. Union Party Com., Allegheny Co., 1901-03, Lincoln Party Com., Allegheny Co., 1905-06; suggested and was sec. Sesqui-Centennial Celebration of Pittsburgh, 1908; mem. Pittsburgh Civic Commn., 1908-11; sec. Hist. Soc. of Western Pa., May 1909—; sec. Com. on Celebration of the Beginning of Steam Navigation on the Western Rivers, Pittsburgh, Oct. 30-Nov. 1, 1911. Author of first playground law, passed by Pa. legislature, 1895; sec. business men's advisory com. of Pittsburgh Playground Assn., 1909—. Asst. sec. Allegheny Co. Com. Pub. Safety, 1917-18. Pres. Ohio Valley Hist. Assn., 1916-17 (v.p. 1914-16); sec. Miss. to Atlantic Internal Waterways Com., 1919—. Mem. Pittsburgh Civil Service Commn., 1923—. Episcopalian. Author: The Head of Iron, a Romance of Colonial Pennsylvania, 1908. Home: Pittsburgh, Pa. Died June 19, 1924.

PATTERSON, Charles Brodie, author; b. Nova Scotia, Canada, Mar. 19, 1854; s. Purdie P.; ed. in Nova Scotia; m. Louise Lippincott, of London, Eng. Lecturer on comparative religion, "New Thought" and metaphysical lines. Formerly editor mags., Mind and Arena; edited vols. 1, 2, 3, Library of Health, 1898-1900. Fellow Soc. Sciences, Letters and Art, London; hon. mem. Contemporary Authors' Soc. of Europe, from which received cross of 3d class. Author: Dominion and Power, 1902; The Will to Be Well, 1902; The Measure of a Man, 1904; Living Waters, 1912; In the Sunlight of Health, 1913. Died June 23, 1917.

PATTERSON, Charles Edward, lawyer; b. Corinth, Vt., May 3, 1842; s. James H. and Fidelia (Howes) P.; A.B., Union Coll., 1860; m. Fanny Maria Seymour, Apr. 25, 1871. Speaker N.Y. Assembly, 1882. Democrat. Home: Bennington, Vt. Died Feb. 21, 1913.

PATTERSON, Charles Loeser; b. Pottsville, Pa., Dec. 25, 1855; s. Frederick G. and Elizabeth (Burlew) P.; grad. high sch., Pottsville, 1872; studied under pvt. tutors; m. Cornelia McCune, Oct. 10, 1888; 1 dau., Elizabeth McCune. Civ. and mining engr., Lehigh Valley R.R., 1875-82; became salesman, 1883, Repauno Chem. Co. (merged in 1903 with E. I. du Pont de Nemours & Co.); in charge Southern office of the co. at Atlanta, Ga., 1886-92; gen. western agt. same co., at Chicago, 1892-96, gen. sales agt., at Wilmington, Del., 1896-1903; dir. of sales E. I. du Pont de Nemours & Co., 1903-07, v.p. in charge sales and mem. bd. dirs., 1907—; dir. Union Nat. Bank, E. I. du Pont de Nemours & Co. of Pa. Pres. Associated Charities, Wilmington. Republican. Episcopalian. Home: Wilmington, Del. Died Aug. 19, 1930.

PATTERSON, C(hristopher) Stuart, banker; b. Phila., Pa., June 24, 1842; s. Joseph and Jane (Cuyler) P.; ed. U. of Pa.; m. Ellen Stuart, Oct. 16, 1867. Admitted to bar, 1865; in practice at Phila., to 1893; v.p., 1893-1901, pres., 1901—, Western Savings Fund Soc. of Phila.; dir. Pa. R.R. Co., 1895—. Formerly prof. constl. law, U. of Pa. Author: Railway Accident Law; Federal Restraints on State Action. Home: Chestnut Hill, Philadelphia, Pa. Died Nov. 9, 1924.

PATTERSON, Edward, jurist; b. New York, N.Y., 1839; s. Edward and Martina Halmage P.; (LL.D., Williams, Hobart, Columbia and Univ. of N.Y.); admitted to bar, 1860; m. Isabel Liddon Cox. Justice N.Y. Supreme Court, 1887-96—appellate div., 1896—; presiding justice 1st Dept.; present term expires 1914. Home: New York, N.Y. Died 1910.

PATTERSON, Edward White, congressman; b. Pittsburg, Kan., Oct. 4, 1895; s. William L. and Ida (White) P.; LL.B., U. of Kan., 1922; student U. of Chicago, 1920; m. Leah Kennedy, Aug. 31, 1921; children—Patricia, James K. Admitted to Kan. bar, 1922; pros. atty. Crawford Co., 1927-28; mem. 74th and 75th Congresses (1935-39), 3d Kan. Dist. Served as sergt., U.S.A., with A.E.F. in France, World War. Democrat. Presbyn. Home: Pittsburg, Kan. Died Mar. 7, 1940.

PATTERSON, Flora Wambaugh, mycologist; b. Columbus, O., Sept. 15, 1847; d. Rev. A. B. and Sarah Sells Wambaugh; student Antioch Coll., O.; A.B., Wesleyan Coll., Cincinnati, 1865, A.M., 1882; A.M., State U. of Ia., 1895; 3 yrs. at Radcliffe Coll., Harvard U., and asst. at Gray Herbarium, Harvard; m. Capt. Edwin Patterson, Aug. 12, 1869 (dec.). Apptd. asst. pathologist, 1896, mycologist in charge pathol. and mycol. collections and taxonomy of fungi, Bur. Plant Industry, U.S. Dept. Agr., until 1923. Home: Brooklyn, N.Y. Died Feb. 6, 1928.

PATTERSON, Francis F., Jr., congressman; b. Newark, N.J., July 30, 1867; s. Francis F. and Abigail Derrickson (Null) P.; ed. pub. and pvt. schs.; m. Isabel Fowler Leyburn, Sept. 23, 1896. Began in newspaper office at 13; with Camden Courier, 1883-90; N.J. ed. Phila. Record, 1890-94; owner and publisher of the Camden Post Telegram, 1894-1923; chmn. West Jersey Trust Co.; dir. West Jersey Title Co. Served as private 6th Regiment N.J.N.G. 6 yrs.; mem. N.J. Ho. of Rep., 1900; county clk. Camden Co., 1900-20; mem. 66th Congress (1919-21), for unexpired term of W. J. Browning; mem. 67th to 69th Congresses (1921-27), 1st N.J. Dist. Republican. Presbyn. Mason, Elk. Home: Merchantville, N.J. Died Nov. 30, 1935.

PATTERSON, Frank Miner, lawyer; b. Albany, N.Y., June 29, 1873; s. P. John and Julia (Corcoran) P.; A.B., Yale, 1896; LL.B., Albany Law Sch. (Union U.), 1899; hon. LL.M., Union U., 1904; unmarried. Admitted to N.Y. bar, 1899, and began practice at N.Y. City; served as atty. and counsel Guaranty Trust Co., Mechanics & Metals Nat. Bank (now Chase Nat. Bank), Société General (Paris), Deutsche Bank (Germany), Banca Crissavelonei (Roumania), Bank of Chosen (Japan), Banco di Roma (Italy), Bank of Hongkong, Union News Co., etc.; served as counsel for Portugal and Switzerland; commr. for claims, N.Y. City, 1911-13; counsel N.Y. State Dept. of Banks, 1911-15; chmn. commn. which revised banking laws state of N.Y., 1912-13. Identified with Dem. Nat. Com. and Dem. State Com., N.Y., 1900—, and chmn. exec. com. of latter, campaign of 1910, resulting in election of John A. Dix as gov. of N.Y. Master of Richmond County Fox Hounds, 1911-15. Home: New York, N.Y. Died Apr. 9, 1939.

PATTERSON, Gaylard Hawkins, coll. prof.; b. Slippery Rock, Pa., Aug. 18, 1866; s. Asa M. (M.D.) and Sara (Patterson) P.; Allegheny Coll., Pa.; A.B., Ohio Wesleyan, 1888; Ph.D., Yale, 1890; S.T.B., Boston U., 1892; A.M., Harvard, 1893; m. Helen McKellar, of Toronto, Can., 1893 (died 1896); m. 2d, Millicent Louise Webber, of Toronto, Dec. 19, 1900; 1 dau., Eunice Louise. In M.E. ministry, 1893-1907; prof. history and economics, 1907-10, dean and prof. social science, 1910-14, Coll. Liberal Arts, Willamette U.; fellow in sociology, U. of Wis., 1914-15; prof. economics and sociology, Dickinson Coll., 1915—. Author: The Social Significance of the Heaven and Hell of Islam (Old and New Testament Student); The Chief Aim of High School Education; The High School Course of Study in Relation to the Elementary Course from a Social Point of View (Proc. Ore. State Teachers' Assn., 1909). Home: Carlisle, Pa. Died June 5, 1940.

PATTERSON, George Robert, congressman; b. Lewistown, Pa., Nov. 9, 1863; s. Joseph Alexander and Anna Granville P.; ed. pub. schs. and Lewistown Acad.; m. Mary Cleaver, Mar. 1886. Was salesman in the hardware business; for past 10 yrs. has been in flour and feed business; now agt. Minneapolis mills in Central Pa. Active in politics; mem. Congress, 12th Pa. dist., 1901-07. Republican. Home: Ashland, Pa. Died 1906.

PATTERSON, George Washington, coll. prof.; b. Corning, N.Y., Feb. 1, 1864; s. George Washington P., Jr., and Frances De Etta (Todd) P.; g.s. Lt. Gov. George Washington Patterson (N.Y., 1848); B.A., Yale, 1884, M.A., 1891; S.B., Mass. Inst. Tech., 1887; Harvard Law Sch., 1888-89; Ph.D., U. of Munich, 1899; m. Merib Susan Rowley, July 2, 1890; children—Gertrude (Mrs. C. B. Haff), George Washington (dec.), Robert Rowley. Instr., asst. prof. and jr. prof. physics, 1889-1901, junior prof. elec. engring., 1901-05, prof. 1905-15, prof. engineering mechanics, 1915—, asst. dean Coll. of Engineering, 1922—, U. of Michigan. Pres. First Nat. Bank, Ann Arbor, Mich. Pres. Patterson Library, Westfield, N.Y. Author: Industrial Photometry, 1891; Electrical Measurements (with Henry Smith Carhart), 1895; Revolving Vectors, 1911. Dir. Erie & Kalamazoo R.R. Co. (N.Y. Central System). Home: Ann Arbor, Mich. Died May 22, 1930.

PATTERSON, Isaac Lee, governor; b. Benton Co., Ore., Sept. 17, 1859; s. Francis Austin and Caroline (Tatom) P.; ed. Christian Coll., Monmouth, Ore. (now Monmouth State Normal Sch.); m. Mary Elizabeth Woodworth, May 12, 1886; children—Isaac Lee, Phillip Woodworth. Chmn. Rep. Central Com., Marion Co., Ore., 1892; mem. State Senate, from Marion Co., 1894-98; collector of customs, Portland, 1898-1907; mem. State Senate from Polk and Benton counties, 1919, 21; chmn. Rep. State Central Com., Ore., 1924-26; gov. of Ore., term 1927-30 inclusive; farmer. Mason, Elk, Moose, Woodman; mem. A.O.U.W. Rotarian. Home: Salem, Ore. Died Dec. 21, 1929.

PATTERSON, James Kennedy, university pres.; b. Glasgow, Scotland, Mar. 26, 1833; s. Andrew and Janet (Kennedy) P.; A.B., Hanover Coll., Ind., 1856, A.M., 1859 (hon. Ph.D., Hanover Coll., 1875; LL.D., Lafayette Coll., 1896, U. of Vt., 1910, U. of Ky., 1916); m. Lucelia, d. Capt. Charles F. Wing, of Greenville, Ky., Dec. 27, 1859. Prin. Greenville (Ky.) Presbyn. Acad., 1856-59; prof. Latin and Greek, Stewart Coll., Tenn., 1860-61; prin. Transylvania High Sch., 1861-65; prof. history and metaphysics, 1865-1910, pres., 1869-1910, pres. emeritus, 1910, State U. of Ky. Pres. Assn. of Land Grant Colls., 1903; made memorable and successful fight, 1881-82, to sustain constitutionality of act levying tax for support of State Coll. (now univ.) Del. Internat. Geog. Congress, Paris, 1875, British Assn. at Bristol, 1875, and Leeds, Eng., 1890. Wrote leading editorials in Courier-Journal, Louisville, 1871-74; occasional contbr. to Scottish-American, New York. Fellow Royal Hist. Soc. of Great Britain, Soc. of Antiquaries, Scotland. Trustee Hanover Coll., Ind., and State U. of Ky. Democrat. Presbyn. Home: Lexington, Ky. Died Aug. 15, 1922.

PATTERSON, James Lawson, educator; b. Savannah, O.; s. John and Christian P.; Ph.B., Lafayette Coll., Pa., 1877; hon. D.Sc., Princeton, 1886; m. Katharine R. Shewell, June 26, 1879. Instr. mathematics, The Hill Sch., Pa., 1876-82; mathematical master, Lawrenceville (N.J.) Sch., 1883-94; prof. mathematics, Union Coll., 1894-97; head master Chestnut Hill (Pa.) Acad., 1897-1923. Home: Chestnut Hill, Pa. Died May 31, 1937.

PATTERSON, James O'Hanlon, congressman; b. Barnwell, S.C., June 25, 1857; s. Edward L. and Sarah Louise (Myers) P.; ed. Barnwell High Sch. and Houghton Inst., Augusta, Ga.; m. Hattie A. Holman, Nov. 30, 1876. Admitted to bar, 1886, and since in practice at Barnwell. Probate judge, 2 terms; mem. S.C. Ho. of Rep., 1898-1904; mem. 59th to 61st Congresses (1905-11), 2d S.C. Dist. Democrat. Methodist. Home: Barnwell, S.C. Died 1911.

PATTERSON, John Fulton, clergyman; b. nr. Wellsville, O., Nov. 13, 1856; s. Thomas M. and Catharine (Smith) P.; A.B., Mt. Union Coll., 1878, A.M., 1882; grad. Western Theol. Sem., 1882; (D.D., Miami, 1898, Lafayette, 1899); m. Ida O. Brown, Sept. 13, 1882 (died 1914). Ordained Presbyn. ministry, 1882; pastor Mingo Ch., Finleyville, Pa., 1882-87, 6th Ch., Pittsburgh, 1887-94, Central Church, Orange, N.J., 1894—; dir. Bd. of Foreign Missions Presbyn. Ch., 1898—, and of the Princeton Theol. Sem., 1899—. Stated clk. Presbytery of Morris and Orange, 1910—, and of Synod of N.J., 1913—. Republican. Home: Orange, N.J. Died Oct. 21, 1924.

PATTERSON, John Henry, brig. gen.; b. New York, Feb. 10, 1843; s. Edward and Martena G. (Talmage) P.; brother of Edward P.; ed. pub. schs. and acad., Brooklyn; m. Mary E. Forbes, Dec. 27, 1871.

m. 2d, Grace L. Learned, Jan. 3, 1900. Apptd. from N.Y., 1st lt. 11th Inf., May 14, 1861; transferred to 20th Inf., Sept. 21, 1866; capt., July 28, 1866; maj. 3d Inf., May 19, 1891; lt. col. 1st Inf., Jan. 21, 1895; transferred to 22d Inf., Nov. 4, 1895; col. 20th Inf., Sept. 28, 1898; brig. gen. vols., Sept. 21-Nov. 30, 1898; brig. gen. U.S.A., Jan. 18, 1899; retired Feb. 6, 1899, on account of wounds received July 1, 1898, El Caney, Cuba. Bvtd. capt., Oct. 1, 1864, "for gallant services at Chapel House, Va."; Congressional Medal of Honor, July 23, 1897, "for most distinguished gallantry in action at the Wilderness, May 5, 1864." Home: Albany, N.Y. Died Oct. 5, 1920.

PATTERSON, John Henry, manufacturer; b. on farm nr. Dayton, O., Dec. 13, 1844; s. Col. Jefferson P. (grandson Col. Robert P., one of original proprs. of Cincinnati) and Julia (Johnston) P.; worked as boy in father's saw and grist mill; studied at Miami College, Oxford, O.; A.B., Dartmouth, 1867; m. Katherine Beck. Collector of tolls, Miami canal, 1867-70; in retail coal business Dayton, and later interested in coal mining, Jackson Co., O.; mgr. Southern Ohio Coal & Iron Co. several yrs. Has made the perfection and introduction of cash registers his life work; identified with National Mfg. Co., Dayton, 1882, dir., 1883; organized Nat. Cash Register Co., 1884; became pres. and mgr. Advocate of coöperation between employer and employe; lecturer and writer on labor questions and municipal and legislative reform. After an exhibit at the Paris Expn. of 1900 of his company's industrial enterprise, and especially of his efforts for the benefit of his employes, received the decoration of Legion of Honor from French Government. Home: Dayton, O. Died May 7, 1922.

PATTERSON, John Letcher, univ. chancellor; b. Lexington, Ky., June 10, 1861; s. John Wallace and Margaret Lightner (Scott) P.; A.B., U. of Ky., 1882, A.M., 1886, Litt.D., 1916; A.B., Harvard, 1883; LL.D., U. of Louisville, 1909, Transylvania Coll., 1930; m. Ellen Harris, Feb. 8, 1893. Prin. high Sch., Versailles, Ky., about 1889-92; prof. Greek, Louisville Boys' High Sch., 1894-1901; asso. prin. Patterson-Davenport Prep. Sch., 1901-10; dean (full exec. authority) Coll. Arts and Sciences, 1908-22, chancellor, 1922-26, chancellor emeritus and prof. ancient languages, 1926, acting pres., 1928-29, prof. ancient languages, grad. school, 1929—, U. of Louisville, also dir. grad. sch. Life mem. Internat. Longfellow Soc., Am. Philol. Assn.; pres. Alumni Assn. U. of Kentucky, 1912-13; pres. Assn. Ky. Colleges, 1915-16; v.p. Assn. Colls. and Secondary Schs. of Southern States, 1919-20; mem. Commn. on Instns. of Higher Edn. in the Southern States, 1920-25; hon. v.p. Permanent Blind Relief War Fund, 1916—; speaker for U.S. Food Administration, etc., during the war. Counsellor Federal Bd. for Vocational Edn., Dist. 7, 1920-23. Author: Lyric Touches, 1893; A Plan for Organization of Colleges and Universities During the War, 1918. Editor and translator: Medea of Euripides, 1894; Cyclops of Euripides, 1900; Bion's Lament for Adonis, 1909; translation of Lament of Adonis, 1931; Some Lyrics of Pseudo-Anacreon, 1933. Home: Louisville, Ky. Deceased.

PATTERSON, Joseph McDowell, ophthalmologist; b. Cynthiana, Ky., June 15, 1865; s. John L. and Amanda (Queen) P.; prep. edn. Smith's Classical Sch. (Cynthiana) and Georgetown (Ky.) Coll.; M.D., Pulte Med. Coll., Cincinnati, 1887, New York Ophthalmic Coll., 1898; m. Blanche Bowman, Dec. 14, 1887. Began practice, Augusta, Ky., 1887; moved to Kansas City, Mo., 1900; prof. ophthalmology, otology and laryngology, Kansas City U., and eye, ear and throat surgeon to St. Mary's Hosp., 1900-12. Fellow Am. Coll. Surgeons; pres. Am. Ophthal., Otol. and Laryngol. Soc., 1908. Mason. Democrat. Mem. Christian Ch. Home: Kansas City, Mo. Deceased.

PATTERSON, Lemuel B., packer; b. Roodhouse, Ill., Jan. 24, 1869; s. James L. and Mary (Willmington) P.; ed. pub. schs.; m. Harriet B. McAdoo, May 12, 1908. Began in employ of Swift & Co., 1886, and became mgr. Omaha plant, 1903; v.p. Nat. Packing Co., 1904-12; pres. People's Ice & Cold Storage Co., Omaha; pres. Hygienic, and Empire State ice cos. Baptist. Home: Chicago, Ill. Died May 30, 1927.

PATTERSON, Malcolm Rice, governor; b. Somerville, Ala., June 7, 1861; s. Josiah and Josephine (Rice) P.; A.M., Christian Brothers' Coll., Memphis; also studied at Vanderbilt Univ. Admitted to bar, 1883, and practiced at Memphis. Dist. atty. Shelby Co., Tenn., 1894-1900; elected 57th to 59th Congresses (1901-07), 10th Tenn. Dist.; gov. of Tenn., 2 terms, 1907-11; now judge first Circuit Court, Shelby Co., Tenn. Democrat. Home: Memphis, Tenn. Died Mar. 8, 1935.

PATTERSON, Raymond Albert, Washington corr. Chicago Tribune, 1894—; b. Chicago, Aug. 21, 1856; s. Robert W. P. (D.D.); Yale, class 1878; m. Mary Young Hogan, Oct. 11, 1892. On staff Chicago Tribune from 1878, as reporter, telegraph editor, night editor, corr., Sunday editor, acting mng. editor; located in Washington, 1894—; writes daily letters for Tribune from Washington and elsewhere under pen name of "Raymond." Died 1909.

PATTERSON, Robert Franklin, consular official; b. Belfast, Me., Mar. 9, 1836; s. John T. and Mary F. P.; academic edn., Belfast, Me.; m. Marion B. Hudson, Aug. 3, 1878. Enlisted June 1861, 2d lt. and regimental q. m. 5th Iowa inf.; in Mo. campaign under Gen. Fremont; took part in capture New Madrid and Island No. 10; siege and capture Corinth, Miss., battle of Iuka (wounded), battle of Corinth; promoted lt. col. 29th Iowa inf., took part in siege of Vicksburg, battle of Helena, Ark., capture Little Rock, siege Spanish Fort, Ala., capture Mobile; promoted bvt. col. and brig. gen. "for gallant and meritorious service at Spanish Fort and Mobile." Settled at Memphis, Tenn., after war; 13 yrs. collector internal revenue at Memphis; postmaster Memphis, 1889-93; consul gen. at Calcutta, India, May, 1897—. Republican. Deceased.

PATTERSON, Robert Mayne, clergyman; b. Phila., July 17, 1832; s. John and Margaret (Mayne) P.; grad. Phila. High Sch., 1849; official reporter U.S. Senate, 1850-55; grad. Princeton Theol. Sem., 1859; (D.D., Princeton, 1879; LL.D., Lafayette, 1887); m. Margaret Baxter McClay, d. Rev. James Nourse, of Washington, 1861 (died 1863); m. 2d, Rebecca Thomas, d. Joseph Malin, of Chester Valley, Pa., 1867. Ordained Presbyn. ministry, 1859; pastor Great Valley, Pa., 1859-67, South Ch., Phila., 1867-80, Great Valley, 1881, pastor emeritus, 1906—. asso. editor The Presbyterian, 1870-80; editor Presbyterian Journal, 1880-93. Moderator, Synod of Pa., 1890; mem. 13 Gen. Assemblies Presbyn. Ch. and 7 of their spl. commns.; author of measures consolidating synods and enlarging their power, 1880, and of the Inerrancy Deliverance of 1892; mem. Pan-Presbyn. councils, London, 1875, Phila., 1880, Belfast, 1884. Author: Skeptic Reclaimed, 1888; Isaiah and the Higher Critics, 1889; William Blackwood, 1894; American Presbyterianism, 1896; The Angels and Their Ministrations, 1900; Short Method with Skeptics, 1900. Editor: The Second General Council of the Presbyterian Alliance; Witherow's Which Is the Apostolic Church? Address: Malvern, Pa. Died 1912.

PATTERSON, Robert Wilson, editor of Chicago Tribune; b. Chicago, Nov. 30, 1850; s. Rev. R. W. P.; ed. Chicago public school, prep. dept. Chicago Univ., and Lake Forest Univ.; grad. Williams Coll., 1871; began to study law in Chicago, but gave it up after great fire and became reporter on Chicago Times; later 1½ yrs. on The Interior (religious weekly); since 1873 with Chicago Tribune, beginning as asst. night editor, later becoming Wash. corr., editorial writer, mng. editor, and, on death of Joseph Medill, editor-in-chief; m. Elinor, d. late Joseph Medill. Home: Chicago, Ill. Died 1910.

PATTERSON, Ross Vernet, M.D.; b. New Orleans, La., Oct. 5, 1877; s. John Harrison and Marguerite Jeanne (Vernet) P.; Washington U., St. Louis, 2 yrs.; M.D., Jefferson Medical College, 1904; Sc.D., La Salle Coll., 1931, Colgate U., 1932; LL.D., Ursinus Coll., Pa., 1935, Wake Forest College, 1937; unmarried. Sub-dean, Jefferson Med. Coll., 1906-16, dean, 1916—; Sutherland M. Prevost prof. therapeutics, 1934—. Capt. Med. R.C., U.S.A., 1917, lt. col., 1922. Home: Philadelphia, Pa. Died 1938.

PATTERSON, Shirley Gale, prof. Romance langs.; b. N.Y. City, July 24, 1884; s. Samuel W. and Ella J. (MacLean) P.; A.B., Amherst, 1906; M.A., Cornell Univ., 1908, Ph.D., 1911; grad. study, Columbia Univ., 1906-08, New York Law School (nights), 1907-08; LL.B., Hamilton Coll. Law., 1917; hon. A.M., Dartmouth, 1925; m. Olive May Bode, Oct. 1, 1923; 1 son, Roger Francis. Resident fellow Cornell, 1908-09; foreign fellow from Cornell to the Sorbonne, École des Hauntes Études, Spain, Italy, 1909-10; instructor in Romance langs., U. of Chicago, 1910-11; instr. U. of Chicago Law School, 1910-11; prof. and head dept. Romance langs., U. of Idaho, 1911-15; spl. lecturer in Law Sch., same univ., 1913-15; asst. prof. Romance langs., Dartmouth, 1915-24, prof., 1924—. Teacher summer sessions, Columbia, 9 summers; lecturer by invitation to French univs., 1924, on France-Am. intellectual relations; lecturer at the Sorbonne, March to April, 1930. Decorated Officier d'Academie and Officier de l'Instruction Publique (both by France). Trustee Hartford Conservatory of Music; mem. bd. of visitors Amherst College, 1929—. Republican. Author: The Puy, a Pre-Renaissance Literary Influence, 1911; l'État de Guerre et Projet de Paix Perpetuelle, 1921; Intermediate French Prose Composition, 1924. Died May 28, 1938.

PATTERSON, Thomas, lawyer; b. Harlem, Pa., Nov. 14, 1856; s. Robert and Eliza (Baird) P.; A.B., Western U. of Pa., (now U. of Pittsburgh), 1876, A.M., 1879, also LL.B.; m. Harriet Wilson, June 2, 1892. Admitted to bar, 1881, and entered practice at Pittsburgh; sr. mem. Patterson, Crawford, Miller and Arensberg. Government del. to Universal Congress Lawyers and Jurists, St. Louis, 1904. Pres. Pa. Bar Assn., 1907; chmn. Pa. State Bd. of Law Examiners, 1915. Home: Shields, Pa. Died Mar. 1929.

PATTERSON, Thomas Macdonald, senator; b. Co. of Carlow, Ireland, Nov. 4, 1839; s. James and Margaret (Mountjoy) P.; came to U.S. in childhood; 1 yr. at Asbury (now De Pauw) U., and 1 yr. Wabash Coll.; m. Katherine Grafton, 1863 (died 1902). Admitted to bar, and since in practice at Denver; editor and propr. Rocky Mountain News, 1890—. City atty., Denver, 1874; last territorial del. from Colo. to 44th Congress (1875-77); mem. 45th Congress (1877-79); mem. Dem. Nat. Com., 1874-80; Dem. nominee for gov. of Colo., 1888; U.S. senator, 1901-07; Dem. nominee for gov., 1914. Home: Denver, Colo. Died July 23, 1916.

PATTERSON, (Anne) Virginia Sharpe, author; b. Delaware, O.; d. Hon. George Washington and Caroline Rebecca (Snider) Sharpe; sister of Alfred Clarence Sharpe; ed. pvt. schs. and Delaware Female Coll.; m. Robert E. Patterson, Jan. 4, 1866. Resided here until 1892, when removed to Indiana. Was editor of first children's page in America. Active in nat. conservation movement; leader in widespread bird-house campaign among sch. children; del. Conservation convs., St. Paul and Kansas City. Apptd. del. Rivers and Harbors Congress, 1910; first woman to have place on program of Ind. Municipal League Conv. Author: Dickey Downy (bird story). Home: Kokomo, Ind. Died May 30, 1913.

PATTERSON, Walter Kennedy, educator, bank officer; b. Bartholomew Co., Ind., Aug. 18, 1844; s. Andrew and Janet (Kennedy) P., who came from Scotland in 1842; ed. pub. schs. and under tutelage of his brother, James Kennedy Patterson; hon. A.M., U. of Kentucky, 1896; unmarried. Assistant in Transylvania High School, 1863-65; principal Bethel Acad., Nicholasville, Ky., 1869-72, McAfee Inst., Mercer Co., Ky., 1873-76, Central Acad., Fayette Co., Ky., 1876-79; prin. acad. of U. of Kentucky, 1880 until its close, 1911. V.p. Second Nat. Bank of Lexington, Ky., 1915— (dir.). Democrat. Presbyn. Died July 14, 1932.

PATTERSON, William Brown, sociologist; b. Brownsville, Pa., May 4, 1873; s. John Radcliffe and Anna Sparks (Brown) P.; ed. Western U., Ph.D., 1918; m. Louise Jenkins, Jan. 30, 1907. Newspaper work, Pittsburgh and N.Y., 1894-1906; gen. sec. Methodist Brotherhood, and editor Methodist Men, 1906-12; sec. Commn. on Social Service, and gen. sec. Interch. Fedn. of Phila., 1912-14; gen. sec. Am. Inst. Social Service, 1915-16; gen. auditor cinema dept. Y.M.C.A., A.E.F., 1917-19. V.p. Old Colony Corp., 1920—. Republican. Author: Modern Church Brotherhoods, 1911; Religion in Social Action, 1914. Home: Scarsdale, N.Y. Deceased.

PATTERSON, William R., denominational sec.; b. Cedar Falls, Ia., Sept. 14, 1868; s. Samuel and Jennie (Hearst) P.; B.S., Ia. State Teachers Coll., 1889; Ph.B., State U. of Ia., 1895; studied Halle and Berlin, Germany; Ph.D., U. of Pa., 1898; m. Lizzie Wallace, June 11, 1902; 1 dau., Margaret Wallace. Asst. prof. commerce and statistics, State U. of Ia., 1898-1902; also state statistician; registrar, Tenement House Dept., N.Y. City, 1902-04; prof. commerce and statistics, State U. of Ia., 1904-06; professional accountant and business reorganization until 1910; asst. commr. pub. works, N.Y. City, 1910-14; financial sec. Presbyn. Bd. Home Missions, 1916-23; comptroller Gen. Council of Presbyn. Ch. in U.S.A., 1923; auditor United Soc. of Christian Endeavor. Mason. Home: Jackson Heights, L.I., N.Y. Died June 30, 1929.

PATTESON, Seargent Smith Prentiss, lawyer; b. Amherst Co., Va., Dec. 15, 1856; s. Dr. David and Elizabeth (Camm) P.; ed. pvt. sch. and pvt. teachers and Randolph-Macon Coll., 1872-73; unmarried. Admitted to Va. bar, 1877; served pvt., non-commd. and commd. officer in Va. vols. in Richmond 7 yrs.; chmn. City Dem. Com., 1892; mem. Va. Legislature, 1899-1901; practicing at Richmond; elected member Virginia legislature, Nov. 1927. Episcopalian. Democrat. Home: Richmond, Va. Died Jan. 26, 1931.

PATTI, Adelina (Baroness Cederstrom), prima donna; b. Madrid, Feb. 19, 1843; d. Salvatori Patti; m. Marquis de Caux, 1868; m. 2d, Signor Ernesto Nicolini, 1886 (died 1898); m. 3d, Maron Rolf Cederstrom, Jan. 25, 1899. Studied under Ettore Barili. Childhood in U.S.; début, New York, Nov. 1859; London, May 1861; retired, 1907. Died Sept. 27, 1919.

PATTILLO, Nathan Allen, coll. dean; b. Loachapoka, Ala., Nov. 7, 1867; s. Rev. Nathan Winfield and Rebecca Garland (Allen) P.; B.S., Southern U., 1887, A.M., 1890; Ph.D., Johns Hopkins, 1897; m. Grace Peale Hank, June 8, 1898 (died 1915); children—Nathan Allen, Grace Keener. Instr. mathematics, Southern U., 1888-90; prof. same, Millsaps Coll., Miss., 1892-94, Ala. Normal Coll., 1897-99; prof. mathematics, 1899—, dean, 1907—, actg. pres., 1912-13, 1919-20, 1931-33, Randolph-Macon Woman's Coll. Mem. M.E. Ch., S. Student Univ. of Paris, 1920-21. Home: Lynchburg, Va. Died Sept. 8, 1936.

PATTISON, Everett Wilson, lawyer; b. Waterville, Me., Feb. 22, 1839; s. Robert Everett (D.D.) and Frances (Wilson) P.; brother of James William P. (q.v.); A.B., Waterville (now Colby) Coll., 1858 (LL.D., 1906); A.M., Shurtleff Coll., Ill., 1867; m. Marcia Scott Whitehouse, June 15, 1861 (died 1884); m. 2d, Alice M. Gould, Sept. 24, 1892. Prin. West

Gardiner (Me.) Acad., 1859; prof. Oread Inst., Worcester, Mass., 1859-61; entered U.S. Vols. at Boston, May 28, 1861, as pvt. Co. I, 2d Mass. Inf.; became 1st sergt., 2d lt., 1st lt. and capt. Co. F, same regt. Practicing law, St. Louis, 1865—; was atty. St. Louis Sch. Bd. 2 terms. Author: Digest of Missouri Reports (9 vols.); a work on Missouri Code Pleading; and one on Criminal Instructions. Home: St. Louis, Mo. Died Nov. 14, 1919.

PATTISON, James William, artist; b. Boston, Mass., July 14, 1844; s. Robert Everett (D.D.) and Frances (Wilson) P.; bro. of Everett Wilson P.; ed. pub. schs., Worcester, Mass.; pvt. to sergt. Co. G, 57th Mass. Inf. in Army of the Potomac, 1863-65; art edn. under James M. Hart, R. S. Gifford, George Inness, New York, 1866-67, Albert Flamm, Düsseldorf, and Luigi Chialivia, Paris, 1873-79; m. Elizabeth Abbott Pennell, 1871 (dec.); m. 2d, Helen Searle, 1876 (dec.); m. 3d, Hortense Roberts, 1905. Painter of figures, domestic animals, landscapes, marines, etc.; exhibitor at Paris Salon, 1879-81, at National Academy, New York, many yrs., at Am. Water Color Soc., New York, 15 yrs., at Pa. Acad. Fine Arts, Art Inst. of Chicago, many times, Chicago Expn., 1893, St. Louis Expn., 1904 (medal); also medal at Boston, 1882; constant exhibitor at art galleries all over the country. Dir. Sch. of Fine Arts, Jacksonville, Ill., 1884-96; faculty lecturer on the collections, Art Inst. of Chicago, 1896—; editor Fine Arts Journal, Chicago, Aug. 1910—. Pres. Chicago Soc. Artists; mem. Municipal Art League of Chicago, Soc. Western Artists. Author: Painting in the Seventeenth and Eighteenth Centuries, 1901; Painters Since Leonardo, 1904. Home: Park Ridge, Ill. Died May 30, 1915.

PATTISON, John M., gov.; b. Clermont Co., O., June 13, 1847; enlisted in Union Army at 16, 1864; grad. Ohio Wesleyan Univ., 1869; admitted to Ohio bar, 1872. Mem. Ohio State legislature, 1873; atty. for com. of safety, Cincinnati, 1874-76; mem. State senate, 1890; mem. 52d Congress; gov. Ohio, 1906-08. Democrat. V.p. and mgr., 1881-91, pres., 1891—, Union Mut. Life Ins. Co. Home: Cincinnati, O. Died 1906.

PATTISON, John R., lawyer; b. nr. Cambridge, Md., Jan. 6, 1860; s. John R. and Mary A. (Burroughs) P.; pub. schs. and Cambridge Acad.; m. Lillian S. Stapleford, Sept. 18, 1888. Admitted to bar, July 1882, and practiced at Cambridge; became chief judge 1st Jud. Circuit of Md., 1909, and asso. judge Ct. of Appeals; resumed practice of law. Democrat. Home: Cambridge, Md. Died Feb. 12, 1940.

PATTISON, Martin, mining; b. Niagara Co., Ont., Can., Jan. 17, 1841; s. Simeon Thayer and Emmarella (Pattison) P.; ed. common schs., Can. and Mich.; m. Grace E. Frink, May 1879. In lumber business until 1881; bought iron lands in Minn. and associated with others in purchase of lands in Ariz.; organizer and pres. Denn-Ariz. Copper Co.; organizer and dir. Shattuck-Ariz. Copper Co.; pres. Juanita Mining Co. (Mexico), Pattison Coal & Iron Co. (Wyo.); pres. U.S. Nat. Bank (Superior, Wis.). Member Mich. Ho. of Rep., 1871-72; sheriff of Douglas Co., Wis., 1884-85; mayor of Superior, 3 terms. Progressive. Christian Scientist. Mason, Odd Fellow, K.P., Elk. Home: Superior, Wis. Died Dec. 20, 1918.

PATTISON, Robert Emory, gov. Pa.; b. Quantico, Md., Dec. 8, 1850; went to Phila., 1857; A.B., Central High School, 1870; admitted to bar, 1872; comptroller city of Phila., 1877-82; gov. Pa., 1882-86; mem. U.S. Pacific Ry. Commn., 1887-90; again gov. Pa., 1891-95; Dem. candidate for gov. Pa., 1902—defeated. Home: Philadelphia, Pa. Died 1904.

PATTISON, Thomas Harwood, prof. of homiletics and pastoral theology, Rochester Theol. Sem.; b. Cornwall, England, Dec. 14, 1838; s. S. R. P. (F.G.S.) and Marina (Ching) P., both of London, England; grad. Regent's Park Coll., England, 1862 (D.D., Colgate, Brown, Williams); m. Emily A., d. R. W. Bainbridge, Middleton House, Durham, England, 1868. Author: The Making of William Carey, 1892; The History of the English Bible, 1894; The Making of the Sermon, 1898; Public Worship, 1900; The Ministry of the Sunday School, 1902. Died 1904.

PATTISON, William J., publisher; b. New York, N.Y., Feb. 11, 1870; s. Robert John and Catharine (Bremner) P.; ed. pub. schs. and under pvt. tuition; m. Ada Louise Watson, Apr. 22, 1896. Was with New York Evening Post, 1886-1914, and pub., sec. and treas., 1902-14; treas. and gen. mgr. Scranton (Pa.) Republican, 1915-25; became treas. and gen. mgr. The Scranton (Pa.) Sun. Home: Scranton, Pa. Died Dec. 27, 1939.

PATTON, Carl Safford, clergyman; b. Greenville, Mich., May 14, 1866; s. James Lawrence and Sarah (Allen) P.; A.B., Oberlin, 1888; grad. Andover Theol. Seminary, 1892; D.D., Oberlin Coll., 1908; D.D., Williams College, 1933; Ph.D., U. of Mich., 1913; m. Harriet V. Harrison, Dec. 29, 1892. Ordained Congl. ministry, 1892; pastor Auburn, Me., 1892-1901, Ann Arbor, Mich., 1901-11, 1st Ch., Columbus, O., 1911-17; pastor 1st Ch., Los Angeles, Calif., 1917-26 and 1929-33; prof. homiletics and practical theology, Chicago Theol. Seminary, 1926-29; prof. homiletics, Pacific Sch. of Religion, 1933—. Moderator Nat. Council Congl. Chs., 1931-33, Gen. Council Congl. and Christian Chs., 1931-34. Author: Truth in Small Packages, 1909; Sources of the Synoptic Gospels, 1913; Religion in the Thought of Today, 1924; The Use of the Bible in Preaching, 1936; The Preparation and Delivery of Sermons, 1938; Two Minute Stories. Died Oct. 16, 1939.

PATTON, Cornelius Howard, clergyman; b. Chicago, Ill., Dec. 25, 1860; s. William Weston (D.D., LL.D.) and Mary Boardman (Smith) P.; A.B., Amherst, 1883; B.D., Yale, 1886; D.D., Amherst, 1899, Williams, 1921; m. Pauline Whittlesey, June 5, 1889; children—Augusta, Catharine. Ordained Congl. ministry, 1887; pastor Westfield, N.J., 1887-95, Duluth, Minn., 1895-98, First Ch., St. Louis, 1898-1904; home sec. A.B.C.F.M., 1904-29, emeritus. Trustee Amherst Coll. Author: The Lure of Africa; World Facts and America's Responsibility; The Business of Missions; Eight O'Clock Chapel (with W. T. Field); The Rosary; Foreign Missions Under Fire; God's World; The Rediscovery of Wordsworth; The Amherst Wordsworth Collection—A Descriptive Bibliography. Donor of large collection of Wordsworthiana to Amherst Coll. Home: West Hartford, Conn. Deceased.

PATTON, Francis Landey, theologian; b. Warwick, Bermuda, Jan. 22, 1843; s. George John Bascombe and Mary Jane (Steele) P.; ed. Warwick Acad., Knox Coll., Toronto, U. of Toronto; grad. Princeton Theol. Sem., 1865; D.D., Hanover Coll., 1872, Yale, 1888; LL.D., U. of Wooster, 1878, Harvard, 1889, Toronto, 1894, Yale, 1901, Johns Hopkins, 1902, U. of Maryland, 1907, Princeton U., 1913; hon. A.M., Princeton, 1896; m. Rosa Antoinette, d. Rev. J. M. Stevenson, D.D., Oct. 10, 1865; children—George Stevenson, Francis Landey, Robert Hunter, John MacMillan Stevenson (dec.), Rosa Cecilia (dec.), Paul Richard (dec.), Alexander Hodge (dec.). Ordained Presbyn. ministry, 1865; pastor, 84th St. Ch., New York, 1865-67, Nyack, 1867-70, South Ch., Brooklyn, 1871; Cyrus H. McCormick prof., Theol. Sem. of the Northwest (now McCormick Sem.), Chicago, 1872-81; also pastor Jefferson Park Ch., Chicago, 1874-81; prof. relations of philosophy and science to the Christian religion, Princeton Theol. Sem., 1881-88, this chair being founded and endowed for Dr. Patton by late Robert L. Stewart; prof. ethics, Princeton U., 1886-1913, pres. 1888-1902, Princeton U.; pres. and prof. philosophy of religion, Princeton Theol. Sem., 1902-13. Moderator Presbyn. Gen. Assembly, 1878. Author: The Inspiration of the Scriptures; Summary of Christian Doctrine; Fundamental Christianity, 1926. Died Nov. 25, 1932.

PATTON, G(eorge) Farrar, M.D.; b. Rankin Co., Miss., Feb. 27, 1853; s. William Lee and Sarah Holloway (Mayson) P.; acad. edn., Masonic Acad., Gilmer, Tex.; M.D., Friedrich Wilhelm U., Bonn, Prussia, 1876; m. Ruth Lindsay Simmons, June 4, 1892; 1 son, Ralph Clifton. Asst. resident phys. Miss. River Quarantine Sta., 1877-80; insp. Nat. Bd. of Health, summers, 1881-83; now emeritus prof. practice of medicine, Grad. Dept., Tulane U.; visiting phys. Charity Hosp., 1893—(registrar from 1906); mem. La. State Bd. of Health, 1892-96 (sec. 1896-1906). Home: New Orleans, La. Died Apr. 2, 1934.

PATTON, Henry William, editor; b. Palmyra, Mo., July 14, 1856; s. Alfred and Priscilla (Thomas) P.; ed. pub. schs.; law student, U. of Mo., 1879-80; m. Mrs. Sarah S. McMillan, Oct. 1, 1914. Reporter and city editor, Los Angeles Times and Herald, 1884-87; editor and owner successively Los Angeles Capital, Everett (Wash.) Independent, Aberdeen (Wash.) Bulletin, Eureka (Calif.) Standard, and mgr. American-Reveille, Bellingham, Wash. Discoverer and first explorer Salton Sea, 1891 (trip made for San Francisco Examiner); exploration trip to Tiburon Island, Gulf of Calif., 1896. Maj. and ordnance officer, N.G. Calif., 1888. Register U.S. Land Office, Los Angeles, 1886-91; spl. agt. Interior Dept. Indian Service, 1893-98; chmn. Exemption Bd., Hoquiam, 1917; sec. to congressional party visiting battle front in France, 1917. Made cruise of 7 months to South Sea Islands, 1918; sailed to west coast of South and Central America and Mexico, 1919, New Zealand and The Fiji Islands, 1921. Now special writer for Seattle, Portland and Los Angeles papers. Mason, Elk. Home: Hoquiam, Wash. Deceased.

PATTON, Horace Bushnell, geologist; b. Chicago, Sept. 18, 1858; s. William Weston (D.D., LL.D.) and Mary Boardman (Smith) P.; bro. of Normand Smith and Cornelius Howard P.; A.B., Amherst, 1881; studied geology, mineralogy and petrography, U. of Leipzig, 1883-85, U. of Heidelberg, 1885-87, Ph.D., 1887; m. Louise Alice Torrey, June 10, 1904. Instr. natural science and mathematics, Howard U., 1881-83; instr. petrography and mineralogy, U. of Heidelberg, 1887-88; prof. geology, Rutgers, 1888-90; mem. Mich. State Geol. Survey and instr. mineralogy, Mich. Sch. Mines, 1891-92; prof. geology and mineralogy, Colo. Sch. Mines, Golden, Sept. 1893—. Author: Lecture Notes on Crystallography, 1896. Died 1929.

PATTON, Jacob Harris, author; b. Fayette Co., Pa., May 20, 1812; grad. Jefferson Coll., Pa., 1839 (A.M., 1842; Ph.D., 1885); grad. Union Theol. Sem., 1846; m. Caroline Obear, 1854 (died 1880). Tutor Nashville Univ., 1840-43; Union Sem., 1843-46; classical school, New York, N.Y., 1846-87; engaged in literary work. Author: Four Hundred Years of American History; Natural Resources of the United States; Political Economy for American Youth; Political Parties in the United States; Which Religion Satisfies the Wants of the Soul?; A Popular History of the Presbyterian Church in the United States; etc. Died 1903.

PATTON, James McDowell, M.D., ophthalmologist; b. Mercersburg, Pa., Sept. 24, 1876; s. John Samuel and Mary Holmes (McDowell) P.; B.S., Bellevue (Neb.) Coll., 1901, A.M., 1904; M.D., U. of Neb., 1904; m. Agnes Deborah Hatfield, Aug. 16, 1904; 1 son, John Hatfield. Began practice at Omaha, 1904; mem. firm Gifford, Patton, Callfas, Potts, Cassidy and Fairchild, oculists and aurists; prof. ophthalmology, Coll. of Medicine, U. of Neb., 1925—; ophthalmologist M.E. Hosp., Clarkson Memorial Hosp., University Hosp. Served as maj. Med. Corps, U.S.A., overseas, 1918-19. Fellow Am. Coll. Surgeons. Republican. Presbyn. Home: Omaha, Neb. Died June 20, 1930.

PATTON, John, lawyer; b. Curwensville, Pa., Oct. 30, 1850; grad. Yale, 1875; Columbia Coll. Law School, 1877; engaged in law practice at Grand Rapids, Mich.; m. Frances Stevens Foster, Oct. 1, 1885. Apptd. U.S. senator from Mich., May 5, 1894, on death of Senator Stockbridge, and served until the meeting of the legislature, Jan. 1895. Pres. Grand Rapids Library Commn. Home: Grand Rapids, Mich. Died 1907.

PATTON, John Shelton, librarian; b. nr. Staunton, Va., Jan. 10, 1857; s. Alfred Taylor and Virginia (Harris) P.; prep. edn. at acads., Waynesboro and Charlottesville, Va.; student U. of Va., 1877-80; m. Beatrice Faber, June 14, 1881; children—Kenneth Stuart, Leicester, Evelyn Virginia (Mrs. John Callan Brooks). Served as councilman, alderman, mayor and supt. schs., Charlottesville; librarian U. of Va., 1903-27. Chmn. Charlottesville Library Bd.; mem. Sch. Bd.; mem. Bd. of Apptmt. Miller Manual Labor Sch.; trustee Home for the Aged. Democrat. Presbyterian. Author: Monticello and Its Master, 1925; Verses, 1927. Editor: Book of the Poe Centenary, 1909; Poems of John R. Thompson, 1920. Home: Charlottesville, Va. Died Oct. 1, 1932.

PATTON, Joseph McIntyre, physician; b. Ralston, Pa., Dec. 8, 1860; s. Joseph R. and Janet (Vevers) P.; ed. Hasbrouck's Inst., N.J.; M.D., Univ. Med. Coll. (New York U.), 1882; m. Grace Klumb, Aug. 5, 1886. Practicing medicine in Chicago, 1882—; chief asst. med. clinic, 1883-90, prof. physical diagnosis, 1890-91, prof. clin. medicine, 1891—, Coll. of Medicine U. of Ill., Chicago; prof. diseases of the chest, Chicago Policlinic, 1891—; prof. gen. anæsthesia and physical diagnosis, dental dept., U. of Ill., 1892-1907; attending phys., Cook County Hosp. Republican. Author: Clinical Lectures on Diseases of the Heart, Lungs and Pleura; Anæsthesia and Anæsthetics. Home: Chicago, Ill. Died Apr. 16, 1930.

PATTON, Normand Smith, architect; b. Hartford, Conn., July 10, 1852; s. William Weston (D.D., LL.D.) and Mary Boardman (Smith) P.; bro. of Horace Bushnell and Cornelius Howard P.; A.B., Amherst, 1873, A.M., 1876; student Mass. Inst. Tech., 1874; m. Frances M. Keep, Jan. 1, 1885 (died 1895); m. 2d, Emma Louise Ilett, Apr. 9, 1907. Has made a specialty of public bldgs.; architect for bd. of edn., Chicago, 1897-98; designed many schs. and coll. bldgs. and pub. libraries in that city and elsewhere; mem. Normand S. Patton, Holmes & Flinn, architects. Director Am. Inst. Architects, S.A.R.; pres. Chicago Congl. Club, 1896. Home: Oak Park, Ill. Died Mar. 16, 1915.

PATTON, Raymond Stanton, hydrographic engr.; b. Degraff, O., Dec. 29, 1882; s. Oliver and Ida M. (Cloninger) P.; Ph.B., Western Reserve U., 1904; m. Virginia Mitchell, Nov. 7, 1912; children—Raymond Stanton, Virginia Mitchell, Helen Mitchell. With Coast and Geodetic Survey, 1904—; engaged in field surveys, Atlantic and Pacific coasts of U.S., Alaska and Philippine Islands, and was made chief of party and comdg. officer survey vessels, in charge surveys in Western Alaska, among them, of approaches to Kuskokwim River, 1912-13, 1914-15; chief of Coast Pilot Sect., 1915-17; lt. and lt. comdr. U.S. Navy, 1917-19; in charge chart production and correction to 1929; dir. Coast and Geodetic Survey, Apr. 29, 1929—. Life trustee Nat. Geog. Soc. Mem. engineering advisory com. on coast erosion, N.J. State Bd. of Commerce and Navigation; mem. National Research Council. Dir. Am. Shore and Beach Preservation Assn.; trustee Woods Hole Oceanographic Institute. Author: U.S. Coast Pilot, Alaska—Yakutat Bay to Arctic Ocean (Govt. Printing Office), 1916; U.S. Coast Pilot, Pacific Coast—California, Oregon and Washington (same), 1917; Report of Engring. Advisory Com. of N.J. Bd. of Commerce and Navigation on Coast Erosion, 1922-24. Died Nov. 25, 1937.

PATTON, Robert Howard, lawyer; b. Auburn, Ill., Jan. 18, 1860; s. Mathew and Margaret J.P.; B.S., Ill. Wesleyan U., 1883, M.S., 1885; studied law Ill. Wesleyan Law Sch. and law office Patton & Hamilton, Springfield, Ill.; m. Mary Etta Gordon, Sept.

23, 1886. Admitted to Ill. bar, 1885; practices at Springfield. Prohibitionist; del. Nat. Conv. 6 times; temporary chmn. Prohibition Nat. Conv., Columbus, O., 1908, and declined presdl. nomination; permanent chmn. Nat. Conv., St. Paul, 1916; prepared the original draft of the Ill. "local option" law. Author and mover of "Single Issue" platform adopted at Pittsburgh Conv., 1896; declined vice-presidential nomination at same conv. Mem. exec. com. Ill. State Prohibition Com. (chmn. 1912-18); candidate for gov. of Ill. on Prohibition ticket, 1904; elected Nat. chmn. Prohibition Party, 1904, and declined; spl. asst. U.S. dist. atty., 1920. K.P. Home: Springfield, Ill. Died Mar. 12, 1939.

PATTON, Walter Melville, coll. prof.; b. Montreal, Can., Nov. 12, 1863; s. James and Margaret (Mathewson) P.; McGill U., Montreal, 1887-90; B.D., Wesleyan Theol. Coll., Montreal, 1891; U. of Chicago, 1893-94; Heidelberg, Germany, 1894-95, 1897, Ph.D., 1897; Leyden, Holland, 1895-97; M.A., Yale, 1904; D.D., Baker, 1908; m. Harriet Webster Royan, of Manchester, Eng., June 22, 1893. Ordained M.E. ministry, 1891; prof. Wesleyan Theol. Coll., 1891-99; instr. semitics, Yale, 1899-1904; prof. Bibl. lit., Baker U., 1904-08; prof. O.T., Wesleyan Theol. Coll., 1908-13; lecturer in semitics, McGill U., 1911-13; prof. history of religion, Carleton Coll., Northfield, Minn., 1913—; dir. of the library, same, 1916—. Author: Ahmed ibn Hanbal and the Mihna, 1897; Israel's Account of the Beginnings, 1915. Home: Northfield, Minn. Died Aug. 5, 1928.

PATTON, Willard, composer, teacher; b. Milford, Me., May 26, 1853; s. Daniel Hall and Elizabeth (Jones) Patton; grad. high school, Bangor, Me., 1870; studied under pvt. tutors 3 yrs.; studied music with Solon Wilder, Frederick Davenport, James Whitney, Dudley Buck, etc.; m. Alesta V. Hebberd, Mar. 21, 1875. Organized Handel Assn., Bangor, 1874; prod. first operetta, The Gallant Garroter, 1881; dir. music, Hamline U., 1886-89; prod. "La Fianza" (light opera), Minneapolis, 1890, "Isaiah" (oratorio), 1897; organized Philharmonic Club and conducted same, 1897-1901; founder, 1912, and dir. Sch. of Vocal Art, Minneapolis. Composer: Studio Fancies (song album); Wabunheim Blossoms (song album); Usona (festival cantata); summer (chaminade); part song, The Call of Spring. Home: Minneapolis, Minn. Died Dec. 12, 1924.

PATTON, William Augustus, ry. official; b. Union Furnace, Pa., Oct. 21, 1849; s. George Washington and Mary (Burket) P.; pub. and high sch. edn.; m. Katharine J. Linn, Dec. 13, 1876. With Pa. R.R., from Jan. 11, 1865, beginning as clerk in office of gen. supt. at Altoona, Pa., gen. asst., 1884-97, asst. to pres., Feb. 10, 1897-Dec. 31, 1918, v.p., 1884-99, pres., June 14, 1899-Dec. 31, 1918, New York, Phila. & Norfolk R.R.; retired. Commr. Valley Forge Park; pres. John Edgar Thomson Sch. for Girls; trustee Presbyn. Hosp., Phila.; dir. Phila. Y.M.C.A. and mem. Internat. Com. Y.M.C.A.; mem. Pa. Soc. S.R., Franklin Inst. Republican. Presbyn. Home: Radnor, Pa. Died Dec. 6, 1927.

PATTON, William Macfarland, civ. engr.; b. Richmond, Va., Aug. 22, 1845; s. John M. and Margaret F. P.; ed. pvt. schs.; grad. E. M., and C. E., Va. Mil. Inst., 1869; m. Annie G. Jordan. Was chief engr. Mobile & Birmingham R.R. and of Louisville, St. Louis & Texas R.R.; engr. in charge of bridges across Susquehanna, Schuylkill, Ohio, Warrior, Tombigbee and Mobile rivers; engr. sewers for cities and other important works. Was prof. engring., Va. Mil. Inst.; later prof. civ. engring., Va. Poly. Inst. Author: Practical Treatise on Foundations, 1893 W9; General Treatise on Civil Engineering, 1894. Home: Blacksburg, Va. Died 1905.

PAUL, Amasa Copp, lawyer; b. at Wakefield, N.H., Sept. 12, 1857; s. Hiram and Mary Porter (Copp) P.; ed. pub. schs.; student Dartmouth Coll.; LL.B., National Law Sch., Washington, D.C., 1880; LL.M., Columbian (now George Washington) U., 1882; m. Ella M. Williams, May 11, 1881 (died 1908); m. 2d, Mrs. Martha A. Turner, Nov. 25, 1930. Teacher, Franklin Sch., Washington, 1877-80; asst. examiner U.S. Patent Office, 1881-84; engaged in practice at Minneapolis, Minn., 1884—; mem. Paul & Paul, 1884-1922, Paul, Paul & Moore, 1922—. Republican. Conglist. Author: The Law of Trademarks, 1902. Home: Minneapolis, Minn. Died Nov. 13. 1936.

PAUL, Charles Howard, civil engr.; b. Rockport, Mass., Mar. 10, 1875; s. Howard H. and Lucy D. (Dousett) P.; High Sch., Malden, Mass.; Mass. Inst. Tech., 1892-95; m. Camilla M. Wheeler, June 19, 1907. With Mass. State Bd. of Health, 1895; Met. Water Works, Boston, 1896-1900; Bur. of Filtration, Phila., 1901-04; engr. U.S. Reclamation Service, 1904-15. Was constrn. engr. Lower Yellowstone project engr. Minidoka project, irrigation investigations eastern Ore.; in charge of constrn. Arrowrock Dam, Boise, Ida., Jan. 1911-Dec. 1915 (then world's highest dam); with Miami Conservancy Dist., Dayton, O., Dec. 1915—, on design and constrn. of flood control works for Miami Valley, including five large hydraulic fill dams, constrn. engr., 1915-16, later asst. chief engr., chief engr., also cons. engr. and in gen. cons. practice; consultant to various govt. depts. on dams, river control, etc. Mgr. Internat. Air Races, 1924; mng. dir. Dalton Industrial Assn., 1925-31; member Dayton City Commission, 1926-29; dir. Dayton Community Chest. Trustee Y.M.C.A. (pres. 1933-34). Home: Dayton, O. Died Oct. 6, 1941.

PAUL, Charles Thomas, clergyman, educator; b. Bowmanville, Ont., Can., Aug. 15, 1869; s. Harvey and Eliza (Mitchell) P.; studied foreign languages under teachers in America and Europe; B.A., Hiram (Ohio) College, 1901, M.A., 1902; post-grad. work in Romance langs., Western Reserve U., 1902-03; D.D. College of Missions, 1933; m. Jessie May Williams, 1891. Founder, and prin. Toronto (Can.) Sch. of Langs., 1894-97; ordained ministry Disciples of Christ, 1898; pastor Cecil St. Ch. of Christ, Toronto, 1897-1900; founder, 1897, and editor Christian Messenger (official organ Disciples of Christ in Ont.) and The Tibetan (devoted to ethnology of Central Asia and Christian missions in Tibet); prof. modern langs., Hiram Coll., 1900-05; missionary in China and prof. English, U. of Nanking, 1905-06; prof. comparative religion and missionary linguistics Hiram Coll., 1907-10; founder, 1910, and pres. Coll. of Missions, Indianapolis. Mem. Bd. of Missionary Preparation, New York, also chmn. com. on Buddhism; mem. lit. sect. Com. on Cooperation in Latin America, New York. Mem. Panama Congress on Christian work in Latin America, 1916; wrote hist. introd. to Report on Message and Method; visited capitals of S. America and delivered addresses in Spanish; in Orient, studying Buddhism of China and Japan, 1922-23; prof. comparative religion, Sch. of Religion, U. of Mich., 1925-26; pres. Coll. of Missions (removed 1928 to Hartford, Conn.) and head of Latin Am. dept., Hartford Sem. Foundation, 1929—. Author: Missionary Mountain Peaks, 1912; Presentation of the Christian Message to Pagan Africa, 1914; The Call of China, 1919; The Presentation of the Christian Message to Buddhists, 1919. Home: Hartford, Conn. Died Nov. 25, 1940.

PAUL, Henry Martyn, astronomer; b. Dedham, Mass., June 25, 1851; s. Ebenezer and Susan (Dresser) P.; A.B., Dartmouth, 1873, C.E., 1875, A.M., 1876; m. Augusta Anna Gray, Aug. 27, 1878. Asst. astronomer, U.S. Naval Obs., 1875-80; prof. astronomy, Imperial U., Tokyo, Japan, 1880-83; again asst. astronomer, Naval Obs., 1883-97; prof. mathematics, U.S.N., 1897—; astronomer Naval Obs., 1897-99; engr. Bur. Yards and Docks, Navy Dept. 1899-1905; teaching mathematics, U.S. Naval Acad., 1905-12; on retired list of Navy, 1913. Choir-singer and precentor in Washington chs.; pres. 1896-98, financial sec. 1898-1903, Choral Soc. of Washington. Home: Washington, D.C. Died Mar. 15, 1931.

PAUL, John. See Charles Henry Webb.

PAUL John, U.S. judge western dist. Va., 1883—; b. Rockingham Co., Va., 1839; s. Peter and Maria P.; ed. Roanoke Coll.; lt. Co. F, 1st Va. cav., in Civil war; grad. law dept. Univ. of Va., 1867; atty. for commonwealth, 1870-77; mem. State senate, 1877-81; mem. Congress, 7th Va. dist., 1880-83; m. 1874, Katherine S. Green. Home: Harrisonburg, Va. Died 1901.

PAUL, John Rodman, lawyer; b. Phila., Pa., Aug. 6, 1852; s. John Rodman (M.D.) and Elizabeth Duffield (Neill) P.; A.B., U. of Pa., 1872, A.M., 1875; unmarried. Admitted to bar, 1875; senior mem. Biddle, Paul, Dawson & Yocum, Phila.; dir. Phila. Savings Fund, Athenæum of Phila. Trustee Drexel Inst., Drexel estate; v.p. Fairmount Park Art Association. Author: Digest of Acts and Decisions Relating to Passenger Railways, 1884. Home: Chestnut Hill, Pa. Died Jan. 27, 1941.

PAUL, Joshua Hughes, prof. natural science; b. Salt Lake City, Utah, Jan. 20, 1863; s. James Patton and Elizabeth (Evans) P.; student U. of Utah, 1880-85 (no degrees issued at that time); student Ill. Wesleyan U., 1897-1905, Ph.B., M.A., Ph.D., from same university; m. Annie M. Pettegrew, 1883 (died 1931); children—Stella Maud (dec.), Lucile Annie Paul (dec.), Leslie Joshua, James Pettegrew, Jean Hamilton (dec.), George William. Instr. in lit. and science, later prof., U. of Utah, 1882-89; asso. editor Salt Lake Herald, 1890; pres. Brigham Young Coll., 1891-94; pres. Agrl. Coll. of Utah, 1895-97; asso. editor Deseret News, 1900; pres. Latter Day Saints Coll., 1899-1906; then prof. natural science, U. of Utah, asso. prof. of English emeritus, 1926—. Democratic nominee for Congress, 1928 and 1930; dir. old-age pensions, Salt Lake County, 1929-32. Camp naturalist for Utah Boy Scouts, 1924-32. Mormon. Author: Out of Doors in the West, 1911; Farm Friends and Spring Flowers, 1913; Farm Foes and Bird Helpers, 1913; Forest Groves and Canyon Streams, 1913; Western Natural Resources, 1914; Floods in Utah, 1926. Co-author: Natural Science in Public Schools, 1928. Died Mar. 6, 1939.

PAUL, Nanette Baker, lecturer; b. Delaware Co., O.; d. William Baker, of Leicestershire, England; LL.B., Washington (D.C.) Coll. of Law, 1900; m. Daniel Paul, Apr. 11, 1888. Admitted to D.C. bar, 1900. Lecturer and teacher on "The Human Side of the Bible." V.p. Susan B. Anthony Foundation. Author: Paul's Parliamentary Law, 1908; Parliamentary Chart, 1908; The Heart of Blackstone, 1911; The Great Woman Statesman (Susan B. Anthony), 1925. Owner of the Madam Mountford collection of costumes from the Holy Land. Home: Washington, D.C. Died Apr. 10, 1928.

PAUL, Willard Augustus, M.D.; b. Parkman, Me., July 19, 1855; s. Daniel and Mary (Hobart) P.; ed. Bloomfield Acad., Me., 1871-73, and Me. Wesleyan Sem., 1874-78, teaching pub. schs., winters, 1872-78; M.D., Hahnemann Med. Coll. and Hosp., 1881; m. Jenny C. Stevens, Sept. 22, 1881. House surgeon, Hahnemann Hosp., Chicago, 1881-82; practiced at Rock Island, Ill., 1882-94, mem. bd. health and library board and dir. Free Med. Dispensary; at Boston, 1895—; asst. in gynecology, Boston U. Sch. of Medicine, 1898—. Asst. phys. Examining Bd., Selective Service, World War. Pres. Harvard Improvement Assn., 1901-03, Harvard Congl. Soc., 1897-1905. Trustee Me. Wesleyan Sem. and Woman's Coll., Sch. of Expression of Boston. Unitarian; mem. Laymen's League of Unitarian Ch. Author: My Symphony; A Morning and Evening Prayer; Autobiography of Don, a series of nature studies; Toast to the American Flag: Wartime Prayer of Peace and Happiness. Home: Weston, Mass. Died Dec. 2, 1926.

PAULDING, Charles Cook, lawyer; b. N.Y. City, Dec. 10, 1868; s. William H. and Anne Mitchell (Depew) P.; A.B., Yale, 1889; unmarried. Mng. clerk, Alexander & Green, New York, 1891-93; asst. gen. attorney, 1893-1907, solicitor, 1908-21, N.Y. Central R.R. Co.; asst. v.p. N.Y. Central Lines, 1921-27, vice pres., 1927-33, then advisory counsel. Home: New York, N.Y. Died Sept. 26, 1938.

PAULHAMUS, W. H., fruit grower. Pres. Puyallup and Sumner Fruit Growers' Assn., Puyallup Fruit Canning Co., Western Wash. State Fair; has served as mem. State Senate. Home: Sumner, Wash. Died Apr. 14, 1925.

PAULUS, Francis Petrus, painter, etcher; b. Detroit, Mar. 13, 1862; s. Charles and Catherine (Miller) P.; pupil Pa. Acad. Fine Arts; Royal Acad. Fine Arts, Munich, under Loefftz, 1886-88, 1890-93; École des Beaux Arts, Paris, Léon Bonnât; m. Adele Frutig, June 3, 1903. Instr. drawing and painting, Detroit Mus. of Art, 1889-90; asso. dir. Detroit Art Acad., 1895-1903; dir. Ann Arbor Art Sch., 1896-98, Sch. of Art, Bruges, 1905—. Trustee Detroit Art Mus., Founders Society. Mason. Home: Detroit, Mich. Died Feb. 3, 1933.

PAXON, Frederic John, merchant; b. Phila., July 22, 1865; s. Philip Henry and Eliza Hinton (Hatt) P.; grad. Camden (N.J.) High Sch.; m. Mrs. Hazeltine Martha (Peddy) Speir, Apr. 23, 1913 (died 1934); m. 2d, Mrs. Pearl Agan Hartley, 1935. Entered employ Am. Baptist Publ. Society, 1880, gen. mgr. for Southern States, Atlanta, Ga., 1887-1900 (resigned); president Davison-Paxon Co., dept. store, 1901—; founder and director Atlanta Retail Merchants' Assn. Jury commr., Fulton Co., Ga. Pres. Atlanta Convention Bur.; chmn. Ways and Means Committee, Southeastern Fair Assn. (pres.); president The Presidents' Club; chmn. advisory board Uncle Remus Memorial Assn., Florence Crittendon Home. Served as pvt. Atlanta Grays and Atlanta Arty.; lt. col. staff of Gov. Joseph M. Terrell 6 yrs.; chief of staff with rank of col. under Govs. Joseph M. Brown and John M. Slaton; retired with rank of col., June 13, 1913. Baptist. Mason. Elk. Awarded silver cup, 1925, by City of Atlanta, for public services in 1924. Home: Atlanta, Ga. Died June 30, 1939.

"PAWNEE BILL." See Gordon W. Lillie.

PAXSON, Edgar Samuel, artist; b. E. Hamburg, N.Y., Apr. 25, 1852; s. William Hambleton and Christian (Hambleton) P.; ed. log sch. house and 1 yr. at Friends' Inst., E. Hamburg, N.Y.; m. Laura Milicent Johnson, June 5, 1874. Began art work as a scenic painter at Deed Lodge, Mont., 1878, with splty. in painting of the Am. Indian and hist. incidents connected with him and the Am. pioneer. Took part in Nez Percé War, 1877-78; served 10 yrs. pvt. to 2d lt., 1st Regt. Nat. Guard, Mont.; 1st lt. 1st Mont. Inf., U.S.V., for Spanish-Am. War; served 8 mos. in Philippines but resigned because of failing health; award silver medal as Mont. soldier. Engrossed memorial of appreciation by Mont. Legislature, 1905, for work and display at La. Purchase Expn.; exhibited at Portland Expn., 1905. Represented in collections in U.S., London, Paris, etc. Prin. works: Custer's Last Fight; 6 hist. murals in Mont. Capitol; 8 murals in new County Court House, Missoula, Mont.; Reception and bronze tablet "Sacaye-wea," and "From the High Places They Watched the Tide of Emigration," etc. Republican. Home: Missoula, Mont. Died Nov. 9, 1919.

PAXSON, Edward M., jurist; b. Buckingham, Pa., Sept. 3, 1824; ed. in Quaker schools; edited Newtown Journal, 1843; later Daily News, Phila.; admitted to bar, Bucks Co., 1850, later removing to Phila.; judge court of common pleas, Phila., 1869-74; judge Supreme Court of Pa., 1874-95; chief justice, 1889-95; retired. Home: Philadelphia, Pa. Died 1905.

PAXTON, John Gallatin, lawyer; b. Lexington, Va., Sept. 17, 1859; s. Elisha Franklin and Elizabeth Hannah (White) P.; father was brig. gen. C.S.A. and was killed in command Stonewall Brigade, at Chancellorsville, May 3, 1863; Va. Mil. Inst.; LL.B., Washington and Lee U., 1880; m. Mary Neill, d. Richard Harrison and Mary (Wyatt) Gentry, of Columbia, Mo., 1885 (died 1903); m. 2d, Anne Dandridge, d. William F. and Anna Aylett (Anderson) Junkin, of Lexington, Va., 1906. Began practice at Independence, Missouri, 1880; v.p. First Nat. Bank, Independence. Democrat. Author: Elisha Franklin Paxton Memoirs and Memorials, 1905. Home: Independence, Mo. Died Sept. 24, 1928.

PAXTON, John Randolph, clergyman; b. Canonsburg, Pa., Sept. 18, 1843; s. John and Elizabeth Dill (Wilson) P.; A.B., Jefferson Coll., Pa., 1866; grad. Western Theol. Seminary, Allegheny, Pa., 1869; (D.D., Union Coll., 1883). Served pvt. and 2d lt., 140th Pa. Regt., Union Army, 1862 until end of Civil War; then reëntered coll.; ordained Presbyn. ministry, 1871; pastor Churchville, Md., 1871-74, Pine St. Ch., Harrisburg, Pa., 1874-78, New York Av. Ch., Washington, D.C., 1878-82, West Ch., New York, 1882-93, New York Ch., New York, 1897-98; retired. Home: New York, N.Y. Died Apr. 11, 1923.

PAXTON, Joseph Francis, university prof.; b. Louisville, Mo., Nov. 14, 1864; s. Luke Huff and Mary Ann (Prewitt) P.; A.B., summa cum laude, U. of Mo., 1891; A.M., Harvard, 1895; studied and traveled in Europe and Asia, 1900-01; student Am. Sch. Classical Studies, Rome; m. Fantine Samuels (A.B., U. Okla.), Dec. 23, 1902; children—Adelaide Frances (Mrs. H. P. McCrimmon), Josephine (Mrs. Neill Sanborn). High school instr. Latin and Greek, 1888-90; instr. Latin, U. of Mo., 1891-94; univ. scholar, Harvard, 1894-95; prof. Latin and Greek, U. of Oklahoma, 1896-1906, prof. Greek and classical archæology, 1906—, then prof. Greek; mem. faculty U. of Calif., 1915-16; prof. Latin, U. of Okla., summers 1930, 31. Mem. Christian Ch. Editor University (Okla.) Anthology. Home: Norman, Okla. Deceased.

PAXTON, Thomas B., lawyer; b. Clermont Co., O., June 4, 1835; s. Thomas and Rebecca (Barber) P.; studied law in offices of Tilden, Rairden & Curwen, Cincinnati, O.; student Ohio Wesleyan U., Delaware, O., 1856-58; LL.B., Cincinnati Law Sch., 1860; m. Mary Adelaide Wharton, Nov. 4, 1863. Practiced in Cincinnati, 1860—; was associated in practice with George H. Pendleton; county solicitor, Hamilton Co., 1873; partner John W. Warrington, 1875 until latter's appmt. as judge U.S. Court of Appeals, 1909. Chmn. bd. trustees, City Workhouse, 1874-79; trustee Ohio Soldiers' and Sailors' Home, 1886-94 (chmn. bd., 1890-94); mem. Ohio State Game and Fish Commn., 12 yrs.; mem. bd. trustees in charge constrn. new City Hall, Cincinnati, 1888-93; mem. commn. for proposed new State Capitol Bldg. at Columbus, O. Trustee Cincinnati Coll. Democrat. Mason. Home: Cincinnati, O. Died Apr. 26, 1922.

PAXTON, William McGregor, artist; b. Baltimore, Md., June 22, 1869; s. James and Rose (Daugherty) P.; art edn., École des Beaux Arts, Paris; m. Elizabeth Vaughan Okie, Jan. 3, 1899. Began painting under Dennis Bunker at Cowles Art Sch. Painted portrait of President Cleveland and of many prominent persons. Represented in permanent collections of Met. Mus. of Art, Pa. Acad. Fine Arts, Boston Mus. Fine Arts, Corcoran Gallery of Art, Cincinnati Mus. of Art, Detroit Mus. of Art, Wadsworth Athenæum (Hartford, Conn.), Butler Inst. (Youngstown, Ohio), N.A., 1928. Home: Newton Center, Mass. Died May 13, 1941.

PAXTON, William Miller, prof. ecclesiastical, homiletical and pastoral theology, 1883—, and pres. faculty, 1900—, Princeton Theol. Sem.; b. Adams Co., Pa., June 7, 1824; grad. Pa. Coll., 1843, Princeton Theol. Sem., 1848 (D.D., LL.D., Jefferson Coll.); pastor Presbyn. Ch., Greencastle, Pa., 1849-51; 1st Presbyn. Ch., Pittsburgh, Pa., 1851-66; prof. sacred rhetoric Western Theol. Sem., 1860-65; pastor 1st Presbyn. Ch., New York, 1866-83; for several yrs. teacher Union Theol. Sem. Mem. from 1866 (pres., 1880-84), Presbyn. Bd. Foreign Missions; mem. 1867-83 (pres., 1876-78), Presbyn. Bd. Home Missions. Moderator gen. assembly Presbyn. Ch. of U.S., 1880; trustee Princeton Coll., 1867—; trustee Leake & Watts Orphan Asylum, New York, 1866-83; trustee Sailors' Snug Harbor, New York, 1866-83. Died 1904.

PAYNE, Bruce Ryburn, coll. pres.; b. nr. Morganton, N.C., Feb. 18, 1874; s. Jordan Nathaniel and Anne E. (Warlick) P.; B.A., Trinity (now Duke U.), N.C., 1896, M.A., 1902, LL.D., 1917; M.A., Columbia, 1903, Ph.D., 1904, Litt.D., 1929; Ed.D., Miami Univ., Oxford, O.; m. Lula Carr, Dec. 7, 1897; 1 son, Carr. Principal Morganton (N.C.) Acad., 1896-99; supt. county schs., 1898-99; instr. Durham High Sch., 1899-1902; prof. philosophy and edn., William and Mary Coll., Va., 1904-05; prof. secondary edn., 1905-06, dir. summer session, 1906-11, prof. psychology, 1906-11, U. of Va.; pres. George Peabody Coll. for Teachers, Nashville, Jan. 1, 1911—. Author: Elementary Curricula of Germany, France, England and America, 1905. Died Apr. 21, 1937.

PAYNE, Charles Henry, corr. sec. of bd. of edn. M.E. Church, 1888—; b. Taunton, Mass., Oct. 24, 1830; grad. Wesleyan Univ., 1856; studied theology Concord, N.H., Biblical Inst. (D.D., Dickinson Coll., 1871; LL.D., Ohio State Univ., 1875); m. Mary Eleanor Gardiner, March 24, 1887. Pastor, 1857-76, Sandwich, E. Bridgewater and Fall River, Mass.; Providence, R.I.; Brooklyn, N.Y.; Philadelphia and Cincinnati; pres. Ohio Wesleyan Univ., 1876-88. Delegate to Meth. Ecumenical Conf., London, 1881; to Gen. Conf. M.E. Church, 1880, 84, 88, 92, 96. Has traveled extensively in Europe, Egypt, Greece, Syria and the Holy Land. Author: Methodism, Its History and Results; Temperance; Women and Their Work in Methodism. Home: New York, N.Y. Died 1899.

PAYNE, Charles Rockwell, M.D.; b. Wadhams, N.Y., June 22, 1880; s. Daniel French and Alice H. (Steele) P.; A.B., Cornell, 1902; M.D., Cornell U. Med. Coll., 1906; m. Marion L. Bowman, June 27, 1906; children—John Daniel, Roger Barton, Robert Lincoln. Practiced at Wadhams, 1906—; cons. phys. and lecturer on neuropsychiatry, Champlain Valley Hosp., Plattsburg, N.Y.; asst. phys., Utica State Hosp., 1925—. Associated with father in hydro-electric development in Adirondacks until his death, Jan. 6, 1916; pres. Essex Horse Nail Co.; dir. Lake Champlain Nat. Bank. Contract surgeon U.S.A., Gen. Hosp. 30, Plattsburg Barracks, Aug. 22, 1918-Mar. 1, 1919. Pres. of Wadhams Free Library. Republican. Translator: Freud's Theories of Neuroses (by Eduard Hitschmann), 1912; Significance of Psychoanalysis for the Mental Sciences (by Otto Rank and Hans Sachs), 1916; The Psychoanalytic Method (by Oskar Pfister), 1916. Home: Wadhams, N.Y. Died July 30, 1926.

PAYNE, Edward Waldron; b. Cincinnati, O., Mar. 19, 1857; s. Francis E. and Mariette (Waldron) P.; ed. pub. schs.; m. Ida Keys, April 23, 1885. Was pres. State Bank of Springfield many years, retiring 1921. Established Payne collection of prehistoric implements of the stone age. Home: Springfield, Ill. Deceased.

PAYNE, Eugene Beauharnais, lawyer; govt. official; b. Seneca Falls, N.Y., Apr. 15, 1835; s. Thomas H. and Susannah N. S. P.; (nephew late U.S. Senator Henry B. Payne); ed. Waukegan, Ill., Acad.; grad. law dept. Northwestern Univ., 1860; admitted to bar, 1860; m. Adelia T. Wright, Jan. 26, 1862. Organized 1st co. of Union troops at Waukegan, Ill., Apr. 16, 1861; served through Civil war as 2d lt., capt., maj. and lt. col., 37th Ill. vols.; bvtd. brig. gen. U.S. vols. Mem. Ill. legislature, 1866-69; practiced law, 1869-87; from 1887 officer of Pension Bureau. Author: Payne's Annotated Digest of the Decisions of Dept. of Interior in Pension Claims, 1897 to 1905. Home: Washington, D.C. Died 1910.

PAYNE, George Frederick, pharmacist; b. Macon, Ga., Apr. 7, 1853; s. George and Emily Hebsibah (Sims) P.; prep. edn. pvt. schs., Ga.; Ph.G., New York Coll. Pharmacy, 1876; student Columbia Sch. Mines, 1873-74; M.D., Atlanta Coll. Phys. and Surgeons, 1892; Phar. D., Atlanta Coll. of Pharmacy, 1910; m. Anna Ruby Nichols, Nov. 11, 1884. State chemist of Ga., 1890-98; chemist Ga. State Bd. of Pharmacy, 1891-1906 (sec. and treas. 1899-1906); one of founders, 1891, prof. pharmacy, 1891—, pres., 1910—, Atlanta Coll. Pharmacy; prof. chem. analysis, Southern Dental Coll., 1899-1910. Chmn. com. of Am. Pharm. Assn. on advancement of status of pharmacists in U.S. Army, Navy and Pub. Health Service, 1894-1905 and 1909-10; mem. com. of revision of U.S. Pharmacopœia, 1900-10; pres. Am. Pharm. Assn., 1902-03; 1st v.p. Nat. Assn. Bds. of Pharmacy, 1904-05. Mason. Author: Payne's Dictionary of Pharmacy. Home: Atlanta, Ga. Died Apr. 19, 1923.

PAYNE, Henry C., postmaster gen. U.S., Jan. 8, 1902—; ry. mgr.; b. Ashfield, Mass., Nov. 23, 1843; s. Orrin P. and Eliza (Ames) P.; grad. Shelburne Falls, Mass., Acad., 1859; removed to Milwaukee, 1863; cashier dry goods store, 1863-67; m. Lydia W. Van Dyke, Oct. 15, 1867. Served consecutively as sec. and chmn. Young Men's Rep. Club, 1872—; sec. and chmn. Rep. Co. Com.; sec. and chmn. Rep. State Central Com., retiring 1892; mem. Rep. Nat. Com., 1880—; postmaster Milwaukee, 1876-86; pres. Milwaukee Electric Ry. and Light Co., 1889—; pres. Wis. Telephone Co., 1886—; pres. Am. Street Railway Assn., 1893-94; receiver Northern Pacific R.R., 1893-95. Home: Milwaukee, Wis. Died 1904.

PAYNE, John Barton, lawyer; b. Pruntytown, Va. (now W.Va.), Jan. 26, 1855; s. Dr. Amos and Elizabeth Barton (Smith) P.; pvt. schs., Orleans, Fauquier Co., Va., 1860-70; LL.D., George Washington U., 1919, U. of Cincinnati, 1920, Coll. of William and Mary, Washington and Lee Univ. (Lexington, Va.), 1926; m. Jennie Byrd, d. Thomas B. Bryan, May 1, 1913 (died 1919). Admitted to bar, 1876; practiced at Kingwood, Preston Co., W.Va., 1877-82; chmn. of Dem. Com., Preston Co., 1877-82; special judge Circuit Court, Tucker Co., W.Va., 1880; mayor of Kingwood, 1882; practiced law at Chicago, 1883-93; judge Superior Court, Cook Co., Ill., 1893-98 (resigned); sr. mem. Winston, Payne, Strawn & Shaw, Chicago, to Jan. 1, 1918; gen. counsel U.S. Shipping Bd. Emergency Fleet Corp., Washington, 1917-18; gen. counsel U.S. Railroad Administration, 1917-19; chmn. U.S. Shipping Bd., 1919-20; sec. of interior in cabinet of President Wilson, Feb. 1920-Mar. 4, 1921; also dir. gen. of railroads, May 18, 1920-Apr. 1921; chmn. Am. Red Cross, Oct. 1, 1921—; United States commr. to negotiate recognition of Mexico, 1923. Chmn. bd. govs. League of Red Cross Societies of Paris (with membership of Red Cross socs. of 58 nations). President Board of South Park Commrs., Chicago, 1911-24. Democrat. Decorated Comdr. Legion of Honor (French), also French Red Cross, Medaille du Cinquantenaire; Grand Order of Leopold II (Belgium); Grand Cross of Order of King Geo. I of Greece; Order of Rising Sun of Japan, with Grand Cordon; first Class Chiabo, with Grand Cordon (China); Costa Rican Red Cross, Medal of Merit; Chilian Red Cross, Grand Cross of Honor; Swedish Red Cross medal; Greek Red Cross medal; Commanders' Cross with Star of the Order of Polonia Restituta (Poland), Belgian Red Cross, Medal of 1st Class; Austrian Red Cross, First Class Medal of Honor. Home: Washington, D.C. Died Jan. 24, 1935.

PAYNE, John Bayly, ry. official; b. Bowling Green, Ky.; s. George Bayly and Emma Fox (Fleenor) P.; ed. Ogden Coll., Bowling Green; m. Annie Glover Gibson; children—John Bayly, Robert Gibson, Mary Dietrich (Mrs. G. Gannon), William Gibson. Began in mech. dept. A.,T.&S.F. R.R., Topeka, Kan.; in transportation dept. Mexican Central R.R., Juarez, Mexico; in traffic dept. Tex. & Pacific Ry., 1893—, successively stenographer, rate clk., commercial agt., asst. gen. freight agt., gen. freight agt., asst. freight traffic mgr., traffic mgr. and v.p.; v.p. Cisco North Eastern Ry., Tex.-Pacific Motor Transport Co.; Abilene & Southern Ry. Co., Tex.-N.M. Ry. Co., Pecos Valley Southern Ry. Co., Weatherford, Mineral Wells & Northwestern Ry. Co., Tex. Short Line Ry.; v.p. Denison & Suburban Pacific Ry.; traffic mgr. group 5 rys. in Southwest, and chmn. Dallas dist. com., U.S.R.R. Administration, World War. Home: Dallas, Tex. Died Nov. 9, 1938.

PAYNE, Oliver Hazard, capitalist; b. Cleveland; s. U.S. Senator Henry B. and Mary (Perry) P.; grad. Yale, 1863, A.B., 1878, as of class of 1863. First 1t., capt., maj., and lt. col. 124th Ohio Inf., Sept. 11, 1862; col., Jan. 1, 1863; bvtd. brig. gen. vols., Mar. 13, 1865, "for faithful and meritorious services." Iron mfr. and oil refiner, Cleveland, 1866-84, New York, 1884—. Dir. Coal Creek Mining and Mfg. Co., Va. & Southeastern Ry. Co. Gave $500,000 to aid in establishing and maintaining Cornell U. Med. Coll., New York. Home: New York, N.Y. Died June 27, 1917.

PAYNE, Robert Lee, physician, surgeon; b. Lexington, N.C., Mar. 28, 1857; s. Robert L. (M.D.) and Winifred Tunstall (Wilson) P.; ed. U. of N.C.; M.D., Jefferson Med. Coll., Phila., 1881; m. Mary Emma Hankins, Feb. 14, 1882. Practiced at Lexington, 1879-96, at Norfolk, 1896—; supt. of health, Davidson Co., 10 yrs.; surgeon Southern Ry. and Chesapeake and Clyde S.S. cos.; gynecologist St. Vincent's Hosp., Norfolk; mem. and examiner in physiology, N.C. Bd. of Med. Examiners; dir. and med. dir. Jamestown Expn. Co.; chief surgeon, Norfolk Southern R.R. Co. Pres. Seaboard Med. Society. Democrat. Presbyn. Home: Norfolk, Va. Died Feb. 8, 1918.

PAYNE, Sereno Elisha, congressman; b. Hamilton, N.Y., June 26, 1843; s. William Wallace and Betsy (Sears) P.; A.B., U. of Rochester, 1864; (LL.D., Colgate, 1902, U. of Rochester, 1903); m. Gertrude Knapp, Apr. 23, 1873 (died 1911). In practice at Auburn, 1866—; sr. member Payne, Payne & Clark, 1908—. City clerk, 1868-71; supervisor, 1871-72; dist. atty. Cayuga Co., 1873-79; pres. bd. of edn. Auburn, N.Y., 1879-82; mem. 48th Congress (1883-85), 26th N.Y. Dist., 49th Congress (1885-87), 27th Dist., 51st to 62d Congresses (1889-1913), 31st Dist., and 63d Congress (1913-15), 36th Dist. Chmn. Com. on Ways and Means, 1899-1910; was active in framing McKinley and Dingley Tariff laws; author of the Payne Tariff Bill, 1909. Member High Joint Commn. to negotiate treaty with Canada, 1898. Home: Auburn, N.Y. Died Dec. 10, 1914.

PAYNE, William Henry, lawyer, soldier; b. Clifton, Va., June 15, 1830; ed. Univ. of Mo., Va. Mil. Inst. and Univ. of Va. Organized and was 1st capt. Black Horse cav., comdg. it at Bull Run; promoted maj. 2 weeks after that battle; lt. col. 4th Va. cav., June 1862, col. Sept., 1863, brig. gen., C.S.A., Nov. 1864, comdg. brigade in Gen. Fitzhugh Lee's div.; 3 times seriously wounded in battle. Practiced law in Washington, D.C., after war, becoming counsel for the Southern R.R. Died 1904.

PAYNE, William Morton, educator, literary critic; b. Newburyport, Mass., Feb. 14, 1858; s. Henry Morton and Emma Merrill (Tilton) P.; has lived in Chicago, 1868—; ed. pub. schs., Newburyport, and Chicago, after that self educated; (LL.D., U. of Wis., 1903); unmarried. Asst. librarian Chicago Pub. Library, 1874-76; teacher in Chicago high schs., 1876—; lit. editor Chicago Morning News, 1884-88; Chicago Evening Journal, 1888-92; asso. editor The Dial, 1892-1915; editorial writer Chicago Journal, 1917-18. As literary critic, chiefly concerned with modern literature (especially poetry) in English, French, German, Italian and Scandinavian. Chmn. com. on Philol. Congress, Chicago, 1893; pres. Chicago French Club, 1887-90; sec.-treas. 20th Century Club, 1889-1915; pres. Chicago Lit. Club, 1911-12. Lecturer English lit., U. of Wis., 1900, U. of Kan., 1904, U. of Chicago, 1904. Author: The New Education, 1884; Little Leaders, 1895; Editorial Echoes, 1902; Various Views, 1902; The Greater English Poets of the Nineteenth Century, 1907; Leading American Essayists, 1909; Björnstjerne Björnson, 1910. Translator: Björnson's "Sigurd Slembe," 1888; Jaeger's "Henrik Ibsen," 1890, Björnson's Arnljot Gelline, 1917, from the Norwegian. Editor: English in American Universities, 1895; American Literary Criticism, 1904; Select Poems of Swinburne, 1905; Swinburne's Mary Stuart, 1906. Home: Chicago, Ill. Died July 11, 1919.

PAYNE, William Wallace, astronomer; b. Somerset, Mich., May 19, 1837; s. Jesse D. and Rebecca Ann (Palmer) P.; A.B., Hillsdale (Mich.) Coll., 1863, M.A., 1864; LL.B., Chicago Law Sch., 1866; hon. Ph.D., Hillsdale, 1894; D.Sc., Carleton Coll., 1916; m. Josephine Vinecore, June 8, 1870; 1 dau., Jessie Vinecore. Prof. mathematics and astronomy and dir. Goodsell Obs., 1871-1908, acting dean, 1896-99, Carleton Coll.; dir. of obs. of Nat. Watch Co., Elgin, Ill., May 15, 1909—. Editor Sidereal Messenger, 1882-92, Astronomy and Astro-Physics, 1892-95, Popular Astronomy, 1893-1909. Home: Elgin, Ill. Died Jan. 29, 1928.

PAYNTER, Thomas H., senator; b. Lewis Co., Ky., Dec. 9, 1851; s. Elisha and Sarah P.; student Centre Coll., Ky., 1870-71; m. Elizabeth K. Pollock, May 25, 1876. Admitted to bar, 1872, and began practice at Frankfort, Ky. Co. atty. Greenup Co., 1876-82; mem. 51st to 53d Congresses (1889-95); resigned from 53d Congress, 1894; judge Ky. Ct. of Appeals, 1894-1906; U.S. senator, 1907-13. Democrat. Home: Frankfort, Ky. Died Mar. 8, 1921.

PAYSON, Franklin Conant, lawyer; b. Portland, Me., Sept. 4, 1856; s. Henry M. and Emma (Conant) Payson; g.s. Rev. Edward Payson, D.D.; A.B., Bowdoin Coll., 1876, A.M., 1879, LL.D., 1911; m. Grace Wheaton Merrill, Oct. 4, 1883; children—Robert, Donald Merrill. Admitted to bar, 1878, and entered practice at Portland; also pres. The Portland Co.; trustee Me. Savings Bank; dir. Fidelity Trust Company. Overseer, Bowdoin Coll., 1897-1910, trustee, 1910—; chmn. bd. mgrs. Children's Hosp.; chmn. Portland Chapter Am. Red Cross. Home: Portland, Me. Died Feb. 17, 1930.

PAYSON, George Shipman, clergyman; b. Harpersfield, N.Y., Sept. 11, 1845; s. Phillips and Elizabeth (Boutelle) P.; A.B., Yale, 1866; grad. Union Theol. Seminary, 1871; (D.D., New York U., 1898); m. Sara, d. William Armour, of Chester, Eng., June 26, 1883. Ordained Presbyn. ministry, 1874; pastor Mt. Washington Ch., N.Y.C., 1874-1920. Dir. Thessalonica Agrl. and Industrial Inst. Republican. Sec. Philothean Soc. (clergymen), 1882—. Author: All for Christ, 1877; The Vital and Victorious Faith of Christ, 1913; Forty Years in the Wilderness, 1914. Home: New York, N.Y. Died Feb. 20, 1923.

PAYSON, William Farquhar, author and publisher; b. N.Y. City, Feb. 18, 1876; s. Francis and Mary Farquhar (Dabney) P.; student Columbia, class of 1896; m. Mary Farquhar King, Oct. 27, 1897; m. 2d, Clara Moores, Aug. 1927. On staff New York Times, 1893-95; mng. editor Vogue about 2 yrs.; editor Clips, 2 yrs.; v.p. and lit. adviser Sturgis & Walton Co., pubs. New York, 1909-13; pres. Payson & Clarke, Ltd., pubs., 1924-28; American editor The Connoisseur; pres. Connoisseur Pubs. of America, Ltd., 1926; editor The Field and treas. Field and Country Press, 1928-29; pres. William Farquhar Payson, Inc., pubs., N.Y. City, 1931. Author: (with Arthur Goodrich) The Joker (four-act play, prod. 1925); Mahogany, Antique and Modern—A Study of Its History and Use in the Decorative Arts (editor), 1926; Candles in the Sky (four-act play, prod. 1931); Give Me Tomorrow (novel), 1935. Home: New York, N.Y. Died Apr. 15, 1939.

PEABODY, Augustus Stephen, investment banker; b. Chicago, Ill., Dec. 3, 1873; s. Francis Bolles and Harriet Cutter (Ten Broeck) P.; A.B., Yale, 1895; LL.B., Northwestern U., 1897; m. Grace Van Alstyne, 1906 (died 1929). Entered Peabody, Houghteling & Co., investment bankers, 1897, later becoming mem. of same, which was succeeded, 1929, by Peabody & Co. (inc.). Hon. pres. Citizen's Assn. Chicago, Civic Music Assn. of Chicago, Chicago Chamber Music Society; 2d v.p. Chicago Symphony Orchestra. Republican. Episcopalian. Home: Chicago, Ill. Died Apr. 27, 1934.

PEABODY, Cecil Hobart, engineer; b. Burlington, Vt., Aug. 9, 1855; s. Selim H. and Mary Elizabeth (Pangborn) P.; S.B., Mass. Inst. Tech., 1877; m. Sarah Angeline Knight, 1885. Prof. mathematics, Imperial Agrl. Coll., Sapporo, Japan, 1878; asst. prof. mech. engring., U. of Ill., 1881; asst. prof. steam engring., 1883, prof. naval architecture and marine engring., 1893-1920 (emeritus), Mass. Inst. Tech. Author: Thermodynamics of the Steam Engine, 1889; Tables of the Properties of Saturated Steam, 1888; Valve Gear for Steam Engines, 1892; Steam Boilers (with Prof. E. F. Miller), 1897; Manual of Steam Engine Indicator, 1900; Naval Architecture, 1904; Thermodynamics of the Steam Turbine; Propellers, 1912; Computations for Marine Engines, 1913. Imperial Order of the Rising Sun (Japanese), 3d class. Died 1934.

PEABODY, Charles, archeologist; b. Rutland, Vt., Nov. 9, 1867; s. Robert Singleton and Margaret Augusta (Goddard) P.; A.B., U. of Pa., 1889; A.M., Harvard, 1890, Ph.D., 1893; m. Jeannette Ennis Belo, Jan. 8, 1895; children—Jeannette Felicie, Margaret (dec.), Caryl, Alfred Horatio, Belo. Engaged in archeol. investigations from 1893, and has written monographs on the so-called "plummets," mound explorations in Mississippi and exploration of Jacobs Cavern, Mo. Dir. dept. archeology, Phillips Acad., Andover, Mass.; curator European archeology, Peabody Museum, Harvard. Corr. mem. de l'Assn. pour l'Enseignement des Sciences Anthropologiques (France), etc.; Officier de l'Académie (French Govt.). Episcopalian. Republican. Chmn. bd. for Am. School in France of Prehistoric Studies, Archæol. Inst. America. Died Aug. 16, 1939.

PEABODY, Charles Augustus, lawyer; b. Sandwich, N.H., July 10, 1814; private edn.; studied law in Baltimore and at Harvard Law School; established practice in New York, 1839; m. Julia Caroline Livingston, 1846; m. 2d, Mary E. Hamilton, 1881; m. 3d, Athenia L. Bowen, 1890. Mem. conv. that organized Rep. party in N.Y., 1855; justice Supreme Court, N.Y., 1855-57; commr. of quarantine, 1858; apptd., 1862, by President Lincoln, judge U.S. Provisional Court of La.; chief justice Supreme Court of La., 1863-65; declined apptmt. as U.S. atty., eastern dist. of La., 1865. Has been v.p. Assn. for Reform and Codification of the Law of Nations; delegate of U.S. Govt. to Internat. Congress of Commercial Law, 1885. Retired. Home: New York, N.Y. Died 1901.

PEABODY, Charles Augustus, officer corps.; b. New York, Apr. 11, 1849; s. Judge Charles Augustus and Julia Caroline (Livingston) P.; A.B., Columbia, 1869, LL.B., 1871. Pres. Mutual Life Ins. Co. of New York, Jan. 1906-Sept. 1927; mem. bd. mgrs. D. & H. Co.; chmn. exec. com. and dir. I.C. R.R. Co.; trustee Atlantic Mut. Ins. Co.; dir. U.P. R.R. Co., Central of Ga. Ry. Co., P.,F.W.&C. R.R. Co., City Bank Farmers Trust Co., Nat. City Bank. Home: New York, N.Y. Died Apr. 26, 1931.

PEABODY, Francis, lawyer; b. Salem, Mass., Sept. 1, 1854; s. S. Endicott and Marianne Cabot (Lee) P.; desc. Francis Peabody, Essex Co., Mass., 1635; student Cheltenham Coll., Eng.; B.L., Trinity Coll., 1877; student law in chambers, Lincoln's Inn, 1 yr.; admitted to bar, Middle Temple, 1877; returned to Boston, entered law office of Morse, Stone & Greenough, and spent 1 yr. at Harvard Law Sch.; m. Rosamond Lawrence, Jan. 13, 1881; children—Rosamond (Mrs. B. Nason Hamlin), Martha (Mrs. M. W. W. Prowse), Sylvia (Mrs. Clarence V. S. Mitchell). Admitted to Mass. bar, 1879, and began practice at Boston. Episcopalian. Home: Milton, Mass. Died Feb. 9, 1938.

PEABODY, Francis Greenwood, theologian; b. Boston, Dec. 4, 1847; s. Ephraim (D.D.) and Mary Jane (Derby) P.; A.B., Harvard, 1869, A.M., 1872; S.T.B., 1872; D.D., Yale, 1887, Harvard, 1909; LL.D., Western Reserve, 1907; m. Cora Weld, June 11, 1872; children—William Rodman, Gertrude Weld, Francis Weld (dec.), John Derby (dec.). Ordained 1874; pastor First Parish Ch., Cambridge, 1874-80; Parkman prof. theology, Harvard, 1881-86, Plummer prof. Christian morals, 1886-1913, prof. emeritus, 1913—, acting dean Divinity Sch., 1885-86, 1893-94, dean 1901-05, overseer, 1877-82. Author: Mornings in the College Chapel, Short Addresses to Young Men on Personal Religion, 1896; Afternoons in the College Chapel, 1898; Jesus Christ and the Social Question, 1900; Religion of an Educated Man, 1903; Jesus Christ and the Christian Character, 1904; Mornings in the College Chapel, 2d series, 1907; The Approach to the Social Question, 1909; Sunday Evenings in the College Chapel, 1911; The Christian Life in the Modern World, 1914; Religious Education of an American Citizen, 1917; Education for Life, the Story of Hampton Institute, 1918; A New England Romance, 1920; The Apostle Paul and the Modern World, 1923; The Church of the Spirit, 1925; Reminiscences of Present Day Saints, 1927; Prayers for Various Occasions and Needs, 1930; Privileges of Old Age, 1931; The Rhythm of Life, 1932. Died Dec. 28, 1936.

PEABODY, Francis Stuyvesant, capitalist; b. Chicago, Ill., July 24, 1859; s. late Francis Bolles and Harriet Cutter (Ten Broeck) P.; Ph.B., Yale, 1881; m. May Henderson, Nov. 1887; m. 2d, Mary Gertrude Sullivan, Feb. 12, 1909. Entered the coal trade, 1881, building up the Peabody Coal Co., of which is pres. apptd. chmn. Coal Production Com. of Council Nat. Defense, 1917. Democrat. Home: Chicago, Ill. Died Aug. 27, 1922.

PEABODY, Francis Weld, M.D.; b. Cambridge, Mass., Nov. 24, 1881; s. Francis Greenwood and Cora (Weld) P.; A.B., Harvard, 1903, M.D., 1907; m. Virginia Grigsby Chandler, 1919; 1 son, Francis Weld. Assistant resident phys., Johns Hopkins Hosp., 1908-09; fellow in pathology, Johns Hopkins U., 1909-10; asst. resident phys., Rockefeller Hosp., 1911-12; resident phys., 1912-15, phys., 1915-21, Peter Bent Brigham Hosp., Boston; visiting phys. and dir. Thorndike Memorial Lab., Boston City Hosp.; prof. medicine, Harvard Med. Sch., 1921. Mem. bd. trustee China Med. Bd. of Rockefeller Foundation. Commd. 1st lt. Med. R.C., maj. M.C. U.S.A., 1918; mem. Red Cross Commn. to Roumania, 1917. Home: Boston, Mass. Died Oct. 13, 1927.

PEABODY, Frederick Forrest, mfr.; b. Northfield, Vt., July 6, 1859; s. Levi C. and Sarah (Brown) P.; pub. sch. edn.; m. Sarah Blanche Griffith, Jan. 10, 1882; m. 2d, Kathleen Burke, Apr. 5, 1920. Began as clerk, 1876, pres., 1907-17, chmn. bd. 2 yrs., Cluett, Peabody & Co., Inc.; retired. Republican. Presbyn. Home: Santa Barbara, Calif. Died Feb. 23, 1927.

PEABODY, Frederick William, author, lawyer; b. Brooklyn, N.Y., June 6, 1862; s. of Enoch Wood and Cornelia (Marshall) P.; student Poly. and Collegiate Inst., Brooklyn, and Columbia; LL.B., cum laude, Columbia Law Sch., 1888; m. Anna G. May, Sept. 21, 1893; children—Mary May (Mrs. J. Leslie Hotson), Helen Peabody; m. 2d, Frances R. Bliss, of Halifax, N.S., Mar. 17, 1910; children—Richard, Alexander. Admitted to N.Y. bar, 1888, and began practice as mem. Peabody, Baker & Peabody, N.Y. City; retired 1912. Served as counsel for sons of Mary Baker Eddy in suit against Mrs. Eddy. Founder, 1927, and mng. director Am. Assn. Favoring Reconsideration of the War Debts. Author: The Religio-Medical Masquerade, 1912. Co-author: (with Prof. Woodbridge Riley and Charles E. Humiston, M.D.) The Faith, the Falsity and the Failure of Christian Science, 1926. Home: Ashburnham, Mass. Deceased.

PEABODY, George Foster, banker; b. Columbus, Ga., July 27, 1852; s. George H. and Elvira (Canfield) P.; ed. pvt. schs., Columbus, Ga.; hon. A.M., Harvard, 1903; LL.D., Washington and Lee, 1903, U. of Ga., 1906; m. Mrs. Katrina (Nichols) Trask, Feb. 5, 1921 (died 1922). In banking business many yrs., now retired. Treas. Dem. Nat. Com., 1904-05; dep. chmn. govt. dir. Federal Reserve Bank, New York, 1914-21. Chmn. State of N.Y. Reservation Commn. at Saratoga Springs, 1910-15 and 1930; trustee Am. Ch. Inst. for Negroes, Hampton Normal and Agrl. Inst., Penn Normal and Industrial Sch., Fort Valley High and Industrial Sch., Colo. College Skidmore Coll., Ga. Warm Springs Health Foundation. Home: Saratoga Springs, N.Y. Died Mar. 4, 1938.

PEABODY, George Livingston, physician; b. New York, Aug. 27, 1850; s. Judge Charles Augustus and Julia Caroline (Livingston) P.; bro. of Charles Augustus P.; A.B., Columbia, 1870, A.M., M.D., 1873; post-grad. studies Vienna, Strassburg, Paris, London; m. Jane de Peyster Huggins, Apr. 18, 1883. Clin. lecturer medicine, 1884-87; prof. materia medica and therapeutics, 1887-1903, trustee, 1884-90, mem. Univ. Council, 1891-95, Columbia; was phys. to New York, Roosevelt, Bellevue, and St. Luke's hosps.; retired. Home: Newport, R.I. Died Oct. 30, 1914.

PEABODY, Henry Clay, judge; b. Gilead, Me., Apr. 14, 1838; s. John Tarbell and Mercy Ingalls (Burbank) P.; A.B., Dartmouth, 1859; m. Ellen Adams, July 26, 1867. Admitted to bar, 1862; practiced at Portland, 1862-80; judge of probate, Cumberland Co., Me., 1880-1900; justice Supreme Jud. Ct. of Me., 1900—. Republican. Home: Portland, Me. Died 1911.

PEABODY, James Hamilton, governor; b. Topsham, Vt., Aug. 21, 1852; s. Calvin and Susan L. P.; ed. pub. schs., Topsham, Vt.; m. Frances L. Clelland, Mar. 19, 1878. Settled in Colo.; was bookkeeper, then mcht.; banker, 1885—; gov. of Colo., elected 1902 for 2-yr. term, expired Jan. 10, 1905; candidate for re-election, 1904, but Dem. candidate was seated for short time, 1905; the legislature declaring him elected, served as gov. for 1 day when he resigned in favor of the lt. gov. Republican. Mason. Home: Cañon City, Colo. Died Nov. 23, 1917.

PEABODY, Josephine Preston, author; b. New York; d. Charles Kilham and Josephine (Morrill) P.; ed. Girls' Latin Sch., Boston, and at Radcliffe Coll., 1894-96; m. Lionel Simeon Marks, June 21, 1906. Instr. English lit. Wellesley Coll., 1901-03. Author: Old Greek Folf-Stories (Riverside Literature Series), 1897; The Wayfarers—A Book of Verse, 1898; Fortune and Men's Eyes—New Poems with a play, 1900; Marlowe, a drama, 1901; The Singing Leaves, 1903; Pan—A Choric Idyl (for music), 1904; The Wings, drama, 1905; The Book of the Little Past, 1908; The Piper, drama, 1909 (obtained the Stratford-on-Avon prize, 1910, and was then produced in England; prod. in America, 1911); The Singing Man (poems), 1911; The Wolf of Gubbio (drama), 1913; Harvest Moon (war poems), 1916. Home: Cambridge, Mass. Died Dec. 4, 1922.

PEABODY, Robert Swain, architect; b. New Bedford, Mass., Feb. 22, 1845; s. Ephraim (D.D.) and

Mary Jane (Derby) L.; bro. of **Francis Greenwood** P.; A.B., Harvard, 1866, A.M., 1870; pupil École des Beaux Arts, Paris, 1868; married, 1871. Practicing architecture at Boston, 1870—; chmn. Boston Park Commission, 1909. Overseer, Harvard, 1888-99 and 1907-12. Home: Boston, Mass. Died Sept. 23, 1917.

PEABODY, Selim Hobart, educator, author; b. Rockingham, Vt., Aug. 20, 1829; s. Rev. Charles Hobart and Grace Stone (Ide) P.; grad. Univ. of Vt., 1852 (Ph.D., 1877; LL.D., Univ. of Iowa, 1881); m. Mary Elizabeth Pangborn, 1852. Prin. Burlington, Vt., High School, 1852; prof. mathematics, Fairfax, Vt., 1853; prof. mathematics and civ. engring., Polytechnic Coll. of Pa., Phila., 1854; prin. high school, Fond du Lac, Wis., 1859; supt. schools, Racine, Wis., 1862; prof. physics, Chicago High School, 1865; prof. mathematics and civ. engring. Mass. Agrl. Coll., 1871; prof. mech. engring., Ill. Industrial Univ., 1878; pres. U. of Illinois, 1880-91; chief dept. Liberal Arts, World's Columbian Expn., 1893. Editor and statistician, U.S. Commn. to Paris Expn., 1899-1900; supt. div. Liberal Arts, Pan-Am. Expn., Buffalo, Aug. 31, 1900—. First editor-in-chief, later asso. editor Internat. Cyclopædia; sec. Chicago Acad. of Sciences, 1874-88; pres., 1892-95; pres. Nat. Council of Edn., 1889-91. Author: Astronomy, 1869; Juvenile Natural History, 3 vols., 1869; New Practical Arithmetic, 1872; American Patriotism, 1880; Charts of Arithmetic, 1900; etc. Home: Chicago, Ill. Died 1903.

PEABODY, William Rodman, lawyer; b. Boston, Mass., Mar. 3, 1874; s. Francis Greenwood and Cora (Weld) P.; A.B., Harvard, 1895, LL.B., 1898; m. Katharine Peabody, Oct. 8, 1908; children—Gertrude, Anne Putnam, Katharine, Cora Weld. Admitted to Mass. bar, 1898, and began practice at Boston; mem. Peabody, Brown, Rowley & Storey; chmn. bd. Western Mass. Cos.; v.p. United Electric Light Co. of Springfield, Pittsfield Electric Co.; dir. various companies. Pres. Am. Sch. of Classical Studies at Athens. Unitarian. Home: Milton, Mass. Died Jan. 12, 1941.

PEACE, Bony Hampton, newspaper pub.; b. Greenville Co., S.C., Aug. 16, 1873; s. Jackson Patrick and Judieth Ballenger (Tinsley) P.; ed. pub. and pvt. schs.; m. Laura Estelle Chandler, Nov. 27, 1894; children—Jones Jackson (dec.), Martha Gertrude (Mrs. Geo. G. Leake), Roger Craft, Charlie, Laura Estelle (Mrs. C. T. Echols), Bony Hampton, Joe Earle (dec.), Mary Ann (dec.), Frances Lucile. Began in printing trade, Greenville, at age of 12; pub. Greenville News, 1917—; pub. Greenville Piedmont, 1927—; pres. and treas. Greenville News Co., Piedmont Pub. Co. Mem. advisory bd. Emma Moss Booth Memorial Hosp. Democrat. Baptist. Mason. Kiwanian. Home: Greenville, S.C. Died Jan. 24, 1934.

PEACH, Robert Westly, bishop; b. Oak Hill, Ill., Nov. 27, 1863; s. Samuel Westly and Anna Robertson (Wiggins) P.; student South Ky. Coll. and U. of Mo., U.S. Mil. Acad., 1883-85; grad. Ref. Episcopal Theol. Sem., Phila., 1890, D.D., 1915; Ph.B., Boston U., 1896; grad. student in philosophy, same univ., 1897-98; m. Harriet Elizabeth Burrows, Sept. 24, 1890; children—Ruth Eggleston (dec.), Anna Harriet (Mrs. DeWitt A. Bandeen), Eggleston Westly, Dorothy Sarah (Mrs. Ernest F. Hobbins). Rector Trinity Ref. Episcopal Church, Ashtabula, O., 1890-93; acting pastor First Ch., Boston, 1893-94; pastor First Presbyn. Ch., Quincy, Mass., 1894-1900, Second Presbyn. Ch., Camden, N.J., 1900-07; rector Emmanuel R.E. Ch., Newark, N.J., 1907-24; bishop coadjutor R.E. Synod of New York and Phila., 1924, and bishop, 1930; presiding bishop R.E. Ch., 1931; prof. ecclesiastical history and Christian evidences, Theol. Sem., Sept. 1924—, also trustee, 1919—, and dean, 1930—. Pres. R. E. Publication Soc. and Bd. of Home Missions; editor 5th R. E. revision Book of Common Prayer, Phila., 1930; editor in chief Episcopal Recorder, 1932; mem. exec. com. of Federal Council of Chs. Republican. Has specialized in hymnology for many yrs. and formed a collection of over 6,000 hymnal books. Home: Upper Darby, Pa. Died Dec. 23, 1936.

PEACOCK, Dred, lawyer; b. Stantonsburg, N.C., Apr. 12, 1864; s. C. C. (M.D.) and Eva (Heath) P.; A.B., Trinity Coll., N.C., 1887, A.M., 1888, Litt.D., 1899; m. Ella Carr, June 9, 1887; children—John R., Mrs. Odelle Marsh. Prin. Lexington (N.C.) Sem., 1887-88; prof. Latin, Greensboro (N.C.) Coll., 1888-94, pres. 1894-1902; gen. agt. Provident Life Ins. Co., 1902-04; furniture mfg. business, High Point, N.C., 1904-11; practicing law, 1912—; city atty. High Point, 1920-27; v.p. High Point Savings and Trust Co.; dir. Commercial Nat. Bank. Trustee Duke U., Greensboro Coll. Mem. Am. and N.C. bar assns., Phi Beta Kappa. Democrat. Mem. M.E. Ch., S. Elk. Home: High Point, N.C. Died Mar. 10, 1934.

PEACOCK, Thomas Brower, author, lecturer; b. Cambridge, O., Apr. 16, 1856; s. Thomas William and Naomi (Carson) P.; ed. Zanesville, O. Has invented and patented a fire escape, railroad switch and other articles; m. April 27, 1904. Democrat. Author: Poems of the Plains and Songs of the Solitudes, 1887. Wrote Columbian Ode, read by him at opening of World's Columbian Expn.; also plays: The Mystery of the New Moon Murders (tragedy), 1902; Nil Desperandum (5-act drama), 1902. Home: Kansas City, Kan. Died Mar. 1, 1919.

PEACOCK, Wesley, Sr., educator; b. Thomasville, Ga., Dec. 24, 1865; s. Delamar Clayton and Mary Ann (McKinnon) P.; grad. S. Ga. Coll., Thomasville, 1884; Ph.B., U. of Ga., 1887; A.M., Emory U., 1928; grad. study Columbia, 1922, Ga. Sch. of Tech., 1923, Emory U., 1925, U. of Tex., 1927, Southern Methodist U., 1930; m. Seline Egg, Dec. 28, 1893 (dec.); 1 son—Wesley; m. 2d, Edith Wing, July 4, 1903; children—Donald W., Margaret, Dorothy. Supt. schs., Uvalde, Tex., 1891-94; founder, 1894, and now pres. emeritus, Peacock Mil. Acad.; founder, 1928, Radio Sch. of Psychology; founder, Sch. for Stutterers, 1935. Democrat. Methodist. Wrote: Your Nerves and You, Your Dreams and You, Your Emotions and You, Sense of Humor Test, Psychoanalyst. Clinical psychologist; mental therapist in nervous diseases. Home: San Antonio, Tex. Died Aug. 19, 1941.

PEAIRS, Hervey B., educator; b. Muskingum Co., O., May 11, 1866; s. John B. and Jerusha H. (Davis) P.; high school, Vinland, Kan.; studied U. of Kan.; m. Carrie E. Reece, July 30, 1890. With Haskell Inst., Indian sch., Lawrence, Kan., for many years from 1887, becoming supt.; became gen. supt. Office of Indian Affairs, Washington, D.C. Methodist. Mason. Died Sept. 2, 1940.

PEAK, John Lee, lawyer; b. Scott Co., Ky., 1839; s. J. J. and E. A. P.; A.B., Georgetown (Ky.) Coll., 1858 (LL.D., 1906); LL.B., Louisville Law Sch., 1860; m. Mattie H., d. James H. Daviess, of Georgetown, Dec. 4, 1862. Admitted to bar, 1861; in practice at Kansas City, Mo., 1870—; now sr. mem. Peak & Strother. Pros. atty. Jackson Co., Mo., 1887-91; E.E. and M.P. to Switzerland, 1895-97. Democrat. Home: Kansas City, Mo. Died 1910.

PEAKS, Archibald Garfield, educator; b. Greene, Ia., Nov. 12, 1880; s. Justin Hamlin and Margaret (Greer) P.; grad. Upper Ia. Normal Sch., Fayette, Ia., 1905; Ph.B., Upper Ia. U., 1906; Pd.M., N.Y. U., 1907, Pd.D., 1911; m. Emilie H. Staudermann, Sept. 1, 1909. Teacher and prin. high schs. in Ia., 1898-1904; asst. prin. Manual Training High Sch., St. Louis, 1909-12; prin. State Normal Sch., Johnson, Vt., 1913—. Conglist. Mason. Home: Johnson, Vt. Died Nov. 7, 1918.

PEALE, Albert Charles, geologist, paleobotanist; b. Heckscherville, Pa., Apr. 1, 1849; s. Charles W. and Harriet (Friel) P.; A.B., Central High Sch., Phila., 1868, A.M., 1873; M.D., U. of Pa., 1871; m. Emily W., d. Rev. George F. Wiswell, Dec. 23, 1875. Mineralogist and geologist, U.S. Geol. and Geog. Survey of the Territories, 1871-79; geologist U.S. Geol. Survey, 1883-98; aid, sect. paleobotany, U.S. Nat. Mus., 1898—. Author: Yellowstone National Park and Thermal Springs, 1882; The Classification of American Mineral Waters, 1887; Mineral Springs of the United States, 1886; The Natural Mineral Waters of the United States, 1895; Classification of Mineral Waters, 1902; Biographical Sketches of Charles Willson Peale and of Titian R. Peale, 1905; The Stratigraphic Position and Age of the Judith River Formation. Home: Washington, D.C. Died 1913.

PEALE, Rembrandt, coal operator; b. Lock Haven, Pa.; s. Samuel Richard and Harriet Frances (Alter) P. Pres. Peale, Peacock & Kerr, miners and shippers of coal; apptd. adviser to U.S. Fuel Administrator, Sept. 1917; apptd. Dec. 1919 by the President to U.S. Bituminous Coal Commission. Home: New York, N.Y. Died Nov. 1934.

PEARCE, Charles Edward, lawyer, cogressman; b. Whitesboro, N.Y., May 29, 1842; grad. Union Coll., 1863; served in U.S.V., 1863-65 as capt. and maj. 16th N.Y. H. Arty.; participated in battles before Petersburg and Richmond, and in capture of Ft. Fisher and Wilmington, N.C.; later served on staff Maj. Gen. A. H. Terry, and as provost marshal gen., E. Dist., N.C.; received thanks of legislature of N.Y. for meritorious conduct at siege of Ft. Fisher. Settled in St. Louis, 1866; admitted to bar, 1867; comd. St. Louis Nat. Guard, 1875; organized 1st regt., 1877, and was its 1st col.; chmn. Sioux Treaty Commn., 1891; went to India, China and Japan, 1895, to investigate industries of the Orient. Mem. Congress, 12th Mo. dist., 1897-1901. Republican. Home: St. Louis, Mo. Died 1902.

PEARCE, Charles Sprague, artist; b. Boston, Mass., Oct. 13, 1851; s. Shadrach Houghton and Mary Ann (Sprague) P.; studied under Bonnât, Paris; m. Louise C. Bonjean, of Paris, June 9, 1888. Awards: silver medals, Boston, 1878, 81, gold medal, 1884; prize $300, for best figure picture, Pa. Acad. Fine Arts, 1881, Temple gold medal, 1885; hon. mention, Paris Salon, 1881, 3d class gold medal, 1883; gold medal of honor, Ghent, Belgium, 1886; 2d class gold medal, Munich, 1888; grand diploma of honor, Berlin, 1891; gold medals, San Francisco, 1894, Atlanta, 1895; hors concours, Paris Salon, 1891; gold staats medal, Vienna, 1898; silver medal, Buffalo Expn., 1901. Member jury of awards, Paris Expn., 1889; Antwerp Expn., 1894; chmn. Paris advisory com. and jury of reception, Chicago Expn., 1893; Paris advisory com. and jury of reception, St. Louis Expn., 1904. Chevalier Legion of Honor, France, 1894; Order of Leopold, Belgium, 1895; Order of the Red Eagle, Prussia, 1897; Order of Danebrog, Denmark, 1898. A.N.A. Died May 1914.

PEARCE, Eugene Hamer, clergyman, educator; b. Brown Co., O., Sept. 16, 1843; A.M., Nat. Normal U., Ohio, 1866; A.M., Ky. Wesleyan Coll., 1867; studied law at Cincinnati; admitted to Ky. bar, 1868; student Drew Theol. Sem., 1875-76; (D.D., Center Coll., Ky.); m. Annie E., d. Charles Q. Armstrong, of Louisville, Oct. 15, 1874. Entered Ky. Conf. M.E. Ch., S., 1876; pastor in Kentucky at Covington, 1876-77, Paris, 1877-78, Versailles, 1879-83, Nicholas, 1883-84, Danville, 1884-93; pres. Ky. Wesleyan Coll., 1895-1900; pastor Paris, 1900-01, Lancaster, 1902-04, Danville, 1904-05; Pres. Ky. Chautauqua Assembly, Lexington, 1886-91; mem. Univ. and Coll. Commn. M.E. Ch., S., 1898—. State commr. Vienna Expn., 1873; del. Ecumenical Conf., London, 1901, Nat. Inter-Ch. Fedn., New York, 1905; mem. Nat. Com. of 40 of Am. Ch. Federation, 1908—; chmn. Fedn. Com. M.E. Ch., S., 1908-12. Home: Danville, Ky. Died 1914.

PEARCE, James Alfred, judge; b. Chestertown, Md., Apr. 2, 1840; s. James Alfred and Martha J. (Laird) P.; A.B., Princeton, 1860, A.M., 1863; (LL.D., St. John's College, Md., 1903, and Princeton U., 1915); m. Eunice Rasin, Nov. 1, 1866. Admitted to bar, 1864; practiced at Chestertown, 1864-97; state's atty., Kent Co., 1867-75; asso. judge Ct. of Appeals of Md., term 1897-1912. Democrat. Home: Chestertown, Md. Deceased.

PEARCE, J(ames) Newton, chemist; b. Oswego, Ill., Dec. 21, 1873; s. James Titsworth and Mary Catherine (Gannon) P.; Ph.B., Northwestern U., 1896, Ph.M., 1897; studied U. of Chicago, 1900-02; Ph.D., Johns Hopkins, 1907; m. Martha Anne Slater (Ph.B., U. of Mich., 1899), Aug. 25, 1904. Chemist with James S. Kirk & Co., soap mfrs., Chicago, 1897-99; instr. chemistry, Township High Sch., La Salle, Ill., 1900-02; instr. chemistry, Northwestern U., 1902-05; asst. prof. chemistry, 1907-19, asso. prof. phys. chemistry, 1919-20, prof., 1920—, State U. of Iowa. Methodist. Mason. Mem. com. on contact catalysis of colloid div., Nat. Research Council, 1927—. Mem. bd. editors Jour. Physical Chemistry, 1932. Home: Iowa City, Ia. Died Nov. 14, 1936.

PEARCE, John Elias, mayor; b. Big Clifty, Ky., Mar. 8, 1876; s. James C. and Florence L. (Pearce) P.; ed. pub. schs.; m. Katherine Pope, 1909. Formerly telegraph operator; resident of Galveston, Tex., 1896—; in stevedore business; lessee Hotel Galvez; mayor-pres. Galveston City Commn., 1925—. Republican. Mason, Elk. Home: Galveston, Tex. Died July 8, 1935.

PEARCE, Liston Houston, clergyman, editor; b. nr. Springfield, O., May 27, 1838; s. Harvey B. and Vilator L. (Houston) P.; student Fort Wayne Coll., Ind.; B.P., Northwestern U., 1865, A.B., 1866, A.M., 1870; B.D., Garrett Bibl. Inst., Ill., 1866; (D.D., Chattanooga U., 1888); m. Jennie M. Wheeler, Oct. 15, 1867 (died 1886); m. 2d, Mrs. Katherine A. Oler, Dec. 16, 1889. Chaplain 132d Ill. Inf. in Civil War; entered M.E. ministry, 1866; pastor (Mich. Conf.) Otesgo, 1866, Kalamazoo, 1867-68, Niles, 1869, Centerville, 1870-71, Grand Rapids, 1872-74, Battle Creek, 1875-76, Lansing, 1877, (Va. Conf.) Alexandria, 1878-80, (Baltimore Conf.) Monroe St. Ch., Baltimore, 1881-82, Exeter, 1883-85, Frederick City, 1886, St. Johns, 1887-88, (Central N.Y. Conf.) Elmira, Hedding, 1889-92, First Ch., Cortland, 1893-96; presiding elder Geneva Dist., Central N.Y. Conf., 1897-1903; editor Baltimore Methodist, 1904-06, Daily Christian Advocate (Baltimore) 1908, Northern Christian Advocate, 1907-14. Home: Clifton Springs, N.Y. Died Feb. 24, 1924.

PEARCE, Richard Mills, Jr., pathologist; b. Montreal, Can., Mar. 3, 1874; s. Richard Mills and Sarah (Smith) P.; ed. Boston Latin Sch.; M.D., Harvard, 1897; spl. study at U. of Leipzig, Germany, 1902. D.Sc., Lafayette Coll., Pa., 1915; m. May Harper Musser, Nov. 6, 1902; children—Agnes M., John M. Resident pathologist, Boston City Hosp., 1896-99; instr. pathology, Harvard, 1899-1900; demonstrator and later asst. prof. pathology, U. of Pa., 1900-03; dir. Bender Hygienic Lab., Albany, N.Y., 1903-08; prof. pathology and bacteriology, Albany Med. Sch., 1903-08; dir. Bur. of Pathology and Bacteriology, N.Y. State Dept. of Health, 1903-08; prof. pathology, Univ. and Bellevue Hosp. Med. Coll. (New York U.), 1908-10; prof. pathology, 1910-11, prof. research medicine, 1910-20, U. of Pa.; gen. dir. Div. of Med. Edn., Rockefeller Foundation, 1920—. Chmn. med. div. Nat. Research Council, 1918; maj., M.C. U.S.A., 1918. Author: Medical Research and Education, 1913; The Spleen and Anemia, 1917. Home: New York, N.Y. Died Feb. 16, 1930.

PEARCE, Webster Houston, college president; b. Whitmore Lake, Mich., May 12, 1876; s. Francis Edwin and Adella Elizabeth (Glenn) P.; grad. Mich. State Normal Coll., Ypsilanti, 1901; A.B., Albion (Mich.) Coll., 1904; A.M., U. of Michigan; m. Ada Juliette Wellington, June 23, 1899; children—Dariel

Wellington, Ella Louise, Gertrude Marjorie, Jean Etta, John Webster. Supt. schs., Springport, Mich., 1897-1902; prin. high sch., Albion, 1902-04, Adrian, Mich., 1905-08; asso. prof. mathematics, Mich. State Normal Coll., 1909-16; prof. mathematics, Central State Teachers Coll., Mount Pleasant, Mich., 1917-27; supt. pub. instrn., Mich., 1927-33; pres. Northern State Teachers Coll., 1933—. Mayor of Mount Pleasant, 1920-27. Methodist. Mason. Home: Marquette, Mich. Died Oct. 10, 1940.

PEARL, Raymond, biologist; b. Farmington, N.H., June 3, 1879; s. Frank and Ida May (McDuffee) P.; A.B., Dartmouth, 1899, Sc.D., 1919; Ph.D., U. of Mich., 1902; U. of Leipzig, 1905, Univ. Coll., London, 1905-06, Carnegie Instn. Table, Naples Zoöl. Station, 1906; LL.D., University of Maine, 1919; Litt.D., from St. John's College, 1935; m. Maud M. DeWitt, June 29, 1903; children—Ruth DeWitt, Penelope Mackey. Asst. in zoölogy, 1899-1902, instr., 1902-06, U. of Mich.; instr. U. of Pa., 1906-07; biologist and head of dept. biology, Maine Agrl. Expt. Sta., 1907-18; prof. biometry and vital statistics, Sch. of Hygiene and Pub. Health, Johns Hopkins, 1918-25, research professor, 1925-30, prof. biology, Medical School, Johns Hopkins, 1923—; statistician, Johns Hopkins Hospital, 1919-35; director Inst. for Biol. Research, Johns Hopkins, 1925-30, professor of biology, School of Hygiene, 1930—. Engaged in biol. researches on variation in fishes, with Biol. Survey Great Lakes (U.S. Fish Commn.), 1901-02; awarded grants for research on variation in organisms from Carnegie Inst., 1904, 05, 06; expert, poultry breeding, U.S. Dept. Agr.; non-resident lecturer Grad. Sch. of Agr., Ames, Iowa, 1910, Lansing, Mich., 1912, Washington, 1939; Lowell lecturer, Boston, Mass., 1920; special lecturer, U. of London, 1927; Harrington lecturer U. of Buffalo, 1928; Heath Clark lecturer U. of London, 1937; Patten Foundation lecturer, Indiana University, 1938. Member exec. com. and chmn. agrl. com. Nat. Research Council, 1916-18, and mem. exec. board, 1919-35; chief of statis. division U.S. Food Administration, 1917-19; pres. Internat. Union for Scientific Investigation of Population Problems, 1928-30. Mem. bd. visitors and govs. St. John's Coll., 1928-34; trustee Science Service, 1929-35. Editor Quarterly Review of Biology, Human Biology; asso. editor Biometrika, 1906-10, Journal Agrl. Research, 1914-18, Genetics, 1915—, Journal Exptl. Zoölogy, 1915—, Metron, 1920—, Biologia Generalis, 1923-27, Acta Biotheoretica, 1937—. Decorated Knight of the Crown of Italy, 1920, Officer, 1929. Author: Variation and Differentiation in Ceratophyllum, 1907; Variation and Correlation in the Crayfish (with A. B. Clawson), 1907; Poultry Diseases and Their Treatment (with F. M. Surface and M. R. Curtis), 1911; Modes of Research in Genetics, 1915; Diseases of Poultry (with F. M. Surface and M. R. Curtis), 1915; The Nation's Food, 1919; The Biology of Death, 1922; Introduction to Medical Biometry and Statistics, 1923; Studies in Human Biology, 1924; The Biology of Population Growth, 1925; Alcohol and Longevity, 1926; To Begin With, 1927; The Rate of Living, 1928; Constitution and Health, 1933; The Ancestry of the Long-lived (with Ruth D. Pearl), 1934; The Natural History of Population, 1939. Home: Roland Park, Baltimore, Md. Died Nov. 17, 1940.

PEARNE, Wesley Ulysses, lawyer; b. New York, Apr. 1, 1851; s. Benjamin Marshall and Emily Ann (Swathel) P.; grad. State Normal Sch., Cortland, N.Y., 1870; B.A., Wesleyan U., Conn., 1874; m. Harriette Cornelia Arnold, Apr. 25, 1883. Admitted to bar, 1879. Trustee Wesleyan U., 1902—; dir., sec. Masonic Bldg. Assn. Mem. and sec. Bd. of Edn., Middletown, 1878-1907; mem. Common Council, 1880-82; mem. Conn. Ho. of Rep., 1901, 1905; clerk City Ct., 1879-95; judge same, 1895—. Mem. 2d Regt. Inf., Conn. N.G., 1875-98, capt. Co. H, last 13 yrs. Del. Conf. on Uniform Legislation, Washington. Trustee and sec. Kent Literary Club. Mason. Home: Middletown, Conn. Died July 5, 1917.

PEARRE, George Alexander, congressman; b. Cumberland, Md., July 16, 1860; s. Hon. George A. and Mary (Worthington) P.; A.B., Princeton U., 1880; A.B., W.Va. U.; LL.B., U. of Md., 1882; m. Elizabeth G. Shoupe, Nov. 22, 1898. In practice at Cumberland, 1882—. Lt. col. Md. N.G., 1889-92; mem. Md. Senate, 1890-92; pros. atty., 1895-99; mem. 56th to 61st Congresses (1899-1911), 6th Md. Dist.; declined renomination, 1910, and resumed practice of law. Republican. Home: Cumberland, Md. Died Sept. 19, 1923.

PEARSALL, Benjamin Simon, mfr.; b. Otsego Co., N.Y., July 29, 1866; s. Edwin and Helen (Smith) P.; ed. common schs.; m. Leah Calkins, Dec. 20, 1893; children—Richard Dana, Alice Manville, Raymond Marvin, Mary Harriett, Claire Lucille. Butter and oleomargarine mfg., 1907—; pres. B. S. Pearsall Butter Co., Ill. Mfrs.' Mut. Casualty Co., Ill. Mfg. Casualty Co., Elgin Finance Corp.; mem. City Council, Elgin, 6 yrs. (brought about a complete clean-up of city affairs). Pres. Old Peoples Home, Elgin; v.p., later pres. Elgin Jr. Coll.; chmn. exec. com. Laymen's Missionary Movement; supt. 1st Bapt. S.S.; dir. World's S.S. Assn. until 1924. Pres. Inst. Margarin Mfg., Washington, D.C., June 1923—; mem. Elgin Chamber Commerce (pres. 1916-19), Nat. Chamber Commerce. Mason. Home: Elgin, Ill. Died Mar. 1, 1935.

PEARSALL, James Welch; b. N.Y. City, Oct. 17, 1839; s. Silas and Ellen (Parker) P.; ed. pub. schs.; m. Hannah W. Myers, Jan. 4, 1860 (died 1899); m. 2d, Sara Crary Rhodes, Sept. 14, 1901. Wholesale butter mcht. 20 yrs.; supt. Domestic Sewing Machine Co. 18 yrs.; mfr. paper patterns 7 yrs.; retired, 1901. Mem. Gen. Conf. M.E. Ch., 1904, 08, 12, 16; mem. Book Com., 1904—. Pres. bd. trustees John St. Ch., N.Y. City; trustee Drew Theol. Sem., Centenary Coll. Inst., Am. Bible Soc., Centenary Fund and Preachers' Aid Soc., Brooklyn Meth. Hosp. Home: Ridgewood, N.J. Died June 24, 1918.

PEARSON, Alfred John, educator; b. Landskrona, Sweden, Sept. 29, 1869; s. Hans and Johanna (Nilson) P.; brought to U.S. in infancy; A.B., Bethany Coll., Lindsborg, Kan., 1893, A.M., 1896; Ph.D., Yale, 1896; LL.D., Drake U., Des Moines, Ia., 1926; m. Thea Pauline Swenson, 1901; children—Paul Harold, Thea Elaine. Began teaching at Upsala Coll., Brooklyn, N.Y., 1896; apptd. prof. German lang. and lit., Drake U., 1907; E.E. and M.P. to Poland, Mar. 28, 1924, to Finland, 1925-30; dean of Coll. Liberal Arts, Drake U., 1930—. Apptd. by Gov. B. F. Carroll of Ia. to study pub. schs. in Germany, 1911; engaged in Liberty Loan drive, 1918; dir. in Y.M.C.A. overseas service, France and Germany, 1918-19. Nat. sec. Luth. Brotherhood America, 1923-24; chmn. Municipal Housing Commission of Des Moines; pres. Swedish-Am. Tercentenary Commn. of Ia. Republican. Decorated Order Polonia Restituta (Poland), 1925; Order White Rose (Finland), 1930. Author: Helps in the Study of English Classics, 1901; The Oden Review, 1917; The Rhine and Its Legends, 1919; The Moselle in History and Legend, 1919; The Land of a Thousand Lakes, 1932. Translations: The Baltic; The Viking. Died Aug. 10, 1939.

PEARSON, Alfred L., lawyer; b. Pittsburgh, Pa., Dec. 28, 1838; s. Joseph and May P.; ed. Jefferson Coll., Pa. Entered Union army, Aug. 1862 as capt. Co. A 155th Pa. vols.; promoted to maj., lt. col. and col.; bvtd. brig. gen. and maj. gen. of vols.; received congressional medal of honor for gallant conduct. Maj. gen. Nat. Guard of Pa. for 7 yrs. Admitted to bar, 1861; dist. atty. Allegheny Co., Pa., 3 yrs.; has served in select councils, Pittsburgh; now in third term as mem. bd. of mgrs., Nat. Home for Disabled Soldiers. Home: Shields, Pa. Died 1903.

PEARSON, Andrew C., publisher; b. Coffeyville, Kan., Nov. 17, 1873; s. Samuel Martin and Ella Anne (Cameron) P.; A.B., Baker U., 1895, hon. A.M., 1920; LL.B., Northwestern U., 1896; m. Lelia Campbell, Aug. 24, 1897; children—Josephine Rae (Mrs. Theodore Hughes Arnold), Dorothy Louise, Andrew Cameron, Forrest C., John R. Claim adjuster, Liability Indemnity Ins. Co., Chicago, 1896-97; mgr. Pearson Bros. Dept. Store, Osawatomie, Kan., 1897-98; advertising salesman Dry Goods Reporter, Chicago, 1898-1904; dept. mgr. Dry Goods Economist, New York, 1904-06, advertising mgr., 1906-10, v.p. and gen. mgr., 1910-20; sec. United Publishers Corp., 1913, then treas., later, v.p., and chmn. bd., 1926—; pres. Economist Group Publs., 1924—; chmn. bd. United Business Publishers, Inc., 1928—; v.p. Newton Falls Paper Co. Trustee Baker U. Pres. Nat. Publishers Assn.; nat. chmn. Am. Pubs. Conf.; dir. Merchants Assn. (New York), U.S. Chamber Commerce, 1922-24. Republican. Conglist. Mason. Home: Montclair, N.J. Died Mar. 31, 1933.

PEARSON, Arthur Emmons, paper mfr.; b. Boston, Mass., Jan. 9, 1869; s. William Henry and Nancy Delia (Benjamin) P.; descendant of John Pearson, of Reading, Mass., 1637; ed. pub. schs.; m. Mildred Eloise James, Oct. 2, 1920. Connected with Hollingsworth & Whitney Co., 1889—, mgr. of traffic. Life mem. Mass. Soc. Colonial Wars, Soc. for Preservation of N.E. Antiquities, Bostonian Soc.; mem. Mass. Soc. War of 1812, Mass. Soc. S.A.R., Valley Forge Hist. Society (first v.p.), N.H. Hist. Soc., Unitarian Laymen's League. N.H. State Govt. voted appreciation be extended to him for erection of memorial in Cloister of Colonies, Washington Memorial Chapel, Valley Forge, Pa., in honor of men of N.H.; established foundation and effected agreement with Am. Unitarian Assn. for Unification Addresses (perpetual) the first of which was delivered by Dr. Charles W. Eliot, 1919; the second by Dr. Joseph Fort Newton, of N.Y. City, 1923; the third by Dr. Samuel A. Eliot of Boston, in Chicago, 1929. Unitarian. Compiler: geneal. record of four thousand descendants of John Pearson and John Benjamin (Colonial Families of U.S. of America, Vols. II and VII). Home: West Newton, Mass. Deceased.

PEARSON, Charles William, educator, clergyman; b. Selby, Yorkshire, Eng., Aug. 7, 1846; s. Rev. John Mowbray and Ann (Bentley) P.; ed. in Yorkshire schs. to 1860; grad. Northwestern Univ., 1871, A.M., 1872; m. Sarah Helen French, June 15, 1875. Apprentice to Liverpool firm of ship owners, 1860-61; sailed from Liverpool to Calcutta; clerk in wholesale cloth house, Leeds, Eng., 1861-64; with London firm of accountants, 1865; with a firm in Buenos Aires, S.A., 1865; teacher in M.E. Mission Sch., Buenos Aires, 1866; student Northwestern Univ., 1867-71; tutor German and history, Northwestern Univ., 1871-76; pastor M.E. chs., Bangor and Breedsville, Mich., 1876-77; tutor in German and history, 1877-81, prof. English literature, 1881-1902, Northwestern Univ. An article entitled "Open Inspiration versus a Closed Canon and Infallible Bible," published in the Evanston Index and the Evanston Press, Jan. 18, 1901, and reprinted in many other papers started a controversy which led him to resign from his chair at Northwestern, and from the M.E. Ch.; pastor Unitarian Ch., Quincy, Ill., 1902—. Author: Methodism, a Retrospect and an Outlook, 1891; The Carpenter Prophet, 1902. Home: Quincy, Ill. Died 1905.

PEARSON, Edmund Lester, author; b. Newburyport, Mass., Feb. 11, 1880; s. Edmund Carlton and Tamzen Maria (Richardson) P.; A.B., Harvard, 1902; m. Mary S. Sellers, Oct. 15, 1908. Author: The Old Librarian's Almanack, 1909; The Library and the Librarian, 1910; The Believing Years, 1911; Voyage of the Hoppergrass, 1913; Theodore Roosevelt, 1920; Books in Black or Red, 1923; Studies in Murder, 1924; Murder at Smutty Nose, 1926; Five Murders, 1928; Queer Books, 1928; Dime Novels, 1929; Instigation of the Devil, 1930; More Studies in Murder, 1936. Editor: Life of Henry Tufts (autobiography of a criminal), 1930. Died Aug. 8, 1937.

PEARSON, Edward Jones, ry. official; b. Rockville, Ind., Oct. 4, 1863; s. Leonard and Lucy (Jones) P.; B.S. in C.E., Cornell U., 1883; M.A., Trinity Coll., Conn., 1926; m. Gertrude S. Simmons, June 7, 1899. Began in engineering dept., Mo. Pacific Ry., 1881, on the extension from Atchison to Omaha; ry. constrn. in Ind. Ty. and Tex., 1882; terminal constrn. at Portland, Ore., 1883-84; supervisor St. Paul and Minn. div., N.P. Ry., 1884; in charge of constrn. train service until 1890; div. engr. same rd. on lines east of Livingston, 1890-92; prin. asst. engr. Wis. Central Ry., Chicago & Calumet Transfer Co., and Chicago Terminals (leased by N.P. Ry.), 1892-94; with N.P. Ry., 1894, as supt. Yellowstone, Rocky Mountain and Pacific divs., and asst. gen. supt. in charge transportation, later chief engr., same rd., to 1905; chief engr. Chicago, Milwaukee & St. Paul Ry. (Pacific extension), 1905-11; 1st v.p. Mo.U.-Iron Mountain Ry., June 1, 1911-Mar. 26, 1915; 1st v.p. Tex. & Pacific Ry. Co., 1915-16; v.p. N.Y.,N.H.&H. R.R. Co., 1916-17, pres. May 1, 1917, federal mgr., June 10, 1918-Feb. 1920, pres., Feb. 1920—. Home: New Haven, Conn. Died Dec. 7, 1928.

PEARSON, Fred Stark, engineer; b. Lowell, Mass., July 3, 1861; s. Ambrose and Hannah P.; A.M.B., Tufts Coll., 1883, A.M.M., 1884 (Sc.D., 1900, LL.D., 1905); m. Mabel Ward, Jan. 5, 1887. Instr. chemistry, Mass. Inst. Tech., 1879-80; instr. mathematics and applied mechanics, Tufts, 1883-86; mining engr. U.S. and Brazil, 1886-88; mgr. Somerville (Mass.) Electric Light Co., 1888-89; chief engr. West End St. Ry., Boston, 1889-93, Dominion Coal Co., 1893-94, Met. St. Ry. Co., New York, 1894-99; consulting engr., 1899—. Pres., dir. Barcelona Traction, Light & Power Co., Limited, Mexico Tramways Co., Rio de Janeiro Tramway, Light & Power Co., Mexican Light & Power Co., Ltd., Mexico North Western Ry. Co. Home: Great Barrington, Mass. Died May 7, 1915.

PEARSON, Henry Clemens, editor, author; b. Le Roy, Minn., Feb. 13, 1858; s. Charles Henry and Emily Catharine (Clemens) P.; ed. pub. schs.; m. Adelaide Ella French, Oct. 24, 1885. With Tyer Rubber Co., Andover, Mass., 1875-81; mgr., Hayward Rubber Co., Bozrahville, Conn., 1881-83; gen. newspaper work and fgn. corr., 1885-89; founded, 1889, and editor The India Rubber World. Expert on India rubber, Paris Expn., 1900, St. Louis Expn., 1904; v.p. Internat. Rubber Expn., New York, 1911. Fellow Royal Geog. Soc., Am. Geog. Society. Republican. Episcopalian. Mason. Author: Crude Rubber and Compounding Ingredients, 1899; What I Saw in the Tropics, 1906; Rubber Country of the Amazon, 1911; Pneumatic Tires, 1921; Rubber Machinery, 1920. Inventor of "Shuffle-Ball," "Cue-Ball Bowls" and other lawn games. Donor pvt. library of 1,000 volumes on India rubber to Los Angeles Pub. Library, 1935. Home: Altadena, Calif. Died June 10, 1936.

PEARSON, Henry Greenleaf, prof. English; b. Portland, Me., Dec. 26, 1870; s. George Henry and Mary Frances (Hitchcock) P.; A.B., Harvard, 1893; m. Elizabeth Ware Winsor, Sept. 6, 1898; children—Anne Winsor (dec.), Theodore, Mary (dec.), Robert Winsor, Henry Greenleaf. Instr. in English, Mass. Inst. Tech., 1893-98, asst. prof., 1898-1907, asso. prof., 1907-15, prof. and head of dept., 1915-19, head of dept. of English and history, 1919—. Independent in politics. Unitarian. Author: Principles of Composition, 1897; Life of John A. Andrew, Governor of Mass., 2 vols., 1905; An American Railroad Builder, 1911; James S. Wadsworth of Geneseo, 1913; Life of William Howe McElwain, 1917; A Business Man in Uniform, 1923; An American Soldier and Diplomat (with Elsie Porter Mende), 1927; Son of New England (life of J. J. Storrow), 1932; Richard Cockburn Maclaurin, President of the Massachusetts

Institute of Technology, 1937. Home: Newton Center, Mass. Died Dec. 28, 1939.

PEARSON, James John, engineer; b. Thornhill, Dumfriesshire, Scotland, Sept. 22, 1858; s. Rev. James and Frances P., of Newcastle-on-Tyne, Eng.; prep. edn. Elmfield Coll., St. Peter's, York, Eng.; grad. Elswick Sch. Tech., Newcastle, 1878; studied engring. under Lord (then Sir W. G.) Armstrong; medallist with honors in all physics; m. Mabel Hattersley, of Harrowgate, Eng., July 22, 1912. Tech. and traveling corr. for Textile Manufacturing, Mechanical World, Sanitary Engineering; Chemical News, 1879-81; chief engr. for Palmer's Ship & Iron Co., Jarrow-on-Tyne, 1881-84; asst. mgr. afloat and guarantee engr. for Hawthorne, Leslie & Co., St. Peter's-on-Tyne, 1884-86; charge of machinery construction in Austrian torpedo chasers, Leopard and Panther; the fighting equipment of the Chilean cruisers, Blanco Encalada and Almirante Cochrane; the steam trials of the Italian cruiser, Giovanni Bausan; the machinery constrn., at Yokosuka Sta. (Japan), of the Japanese cruisers, Naniwa and Takachiho-Kan, 1886-88; cons. and contracting engr., Yokohama, Japan; constructing and installing textile mills, ice plants, bridges, steam vessels, arsenal equipment, etc., 1888-91; mgr. Nassau Elec. Co., New York, 1892-95; cons. engr. at New York, 1895—. Volunteered for war service to Brit. Govt. and served in Eng. through 1916-17, as examining and investigating engr. for Ministry of Munitions, War Office and Naval Bd.; also chief dilution officer for Bedford Area, and acting chief for London. Made inspection and report of the principal shipyards throughout all Europe for clients, 1918-19. Home: New York; Bridgewater, Conn.; and San Francisco, Calif. Died Sept. 25, 1926.

PEARSON, Leonard, editor of Veterinary Mag.; b. Evansville, Ind., Aug. 17, 1868; s. Leonard and Lucy (Jones) P.; grad. Cornell, B.S., 1888; grad. Univ. of Pa., V.M.D., 1890; unmarried. Prof. veterinary medicine, dept. of veterinary medicine, Univ. of Pa., 1891—, and dean, 1897—; state veterinarian of Pa., 1895—; sec. State Live Stock Sanitary Bd., 1896—; pres. Am. Veterinary Med. Assn., 1899-1900; pres. Pa. State Veterinary Assn., 1895-96; mem. Phila. Bd. of Health, 1904—, Pa. Bd. of Health, 1905—. Republican. Home: Philadelphia, Pa. Died 1909.

PEARSON, Paul Martin, governor; b. nr. Litchfield, Ill., Oct. 22, 1871; s. Samuel Martin and Ellen (Cameron) P.; A.B., Baker U., 1891, A.M., 1895, Litt.D., 1909; grad. study, Northwestern, and Harvard; m. Edna Wolfe, June 11, 1896; children—Andrew Russell, Leon Morris, Barbara Wolfe, Ellen Cameron. Teacher high sch., Cherryvale, Kan., 1891-94; teacher, Northwestern U., 1896-1901; prof. of public speaking, Swarthmore (Pa.) Coll., 1902-19. Editor The Speaker; of Lyceum Mag., 1903-08; founder and pres. Swarthmore Chautauqua Assn., 1912-30; gov. of Virgin Islands, 1931-35; asst. dir. Housing div. Pub. Works Administration. Member Society of Friends. Member advisory com. speaking div., Com. on Pub. Information, Washington; mem. exec. com. speakers' bur., Am. Red Cross; dir. sect. on entertainment, Nat. War Work Council Y.M.C.A., 1917-19. Pres. Lyceum and Chautauqua Mgrs. of America, 1921-23, The Internat. Lyceum and Chautauqua Assn., 1921-23. Author: Intercollegiate Debates, 1909; Extemporaneous Speaking, 1912. Home: Washington, D.C. Died Mar. 26, 1938.

PEARSON, Peter Henry, coll. prof.; b. Landskrona, Sweden, Mar. 1864; s. Hans and Johanna (Nilson) P.; came to U.S. at age of 5; A.B., Roanoke Coll., Va., 1890; A.M., U. of Berlin, 1893; fellow, U. of Neb.; traveled in Eng., France and Switzerland, studying ednl. methods there; L.H.D., 1906; m. Esther Lincoln, 1898; children—Agnes, Karl G. Asst., 1887, prof. English and German, 1892, prof. and head dept. English lang. and lit., 1895, and v.p. 1917, Bethany Coll.; now professor edn., Upsala Coll., East Orange, N.J., v.p. of the college, 1928-30. Represented Bethany Coll. at Jubileum of U. of Upsala, Sweden, Sept. 1893. Lutheran. Lecturer on Shakespeare, the Elizabethan Drama, U. of Kan., 1911. Pres. Kan. State Assn. Teachers of English, 1914-15. Mem. fgn. div. U.S. Bur. Edn., 1918. Rep. U.S. Bur. of Edn. in Europe, studying schools of Scandinavia, 1920-21. Hon. mem. of Chartered Inst. of Am. Inventors. Author: Prairie Vikings, 1927; Methods of Learning, 1931; Shakespeare—Plots and Studies of Chief Plays, 1935; Subjects and Story Plots, 1940. Edited editions of Macaulay's "Essay on Milton," 1904, Longfellow's "Evangeline," 1904, and "Courtship of Miles Standish," 1905. Home: East Orange, N.J. Died 1940.

PEARSON, Raymond Allen, educator; b. at Evansville, Ind., Apr. 9, 1873; s. Leonard and Lucy S. (Jones) P.; grad. Cornell U., 1894, M.S., 1899; spl. studies in agrl. science; LL.D., Alfred U., 1910; D.Agr., U. of Neb., 1917; m. Fanny Alice Dunsford; children—Ruth Markham, Raymond Allen (dec.). Assistant chief of dairy div., U.S. Dept. Agr., 1895-1902; gen. mgr. Walker-Gordon Lab. Co., New York and Phila., 1902-03; prof. dairy industry, Coll. of Agr., Cornell U., 1903-08; commr. of agr. of N.Y. State, Apr. 1908-Feb. 1912; pres. Ia. State Coll. of Agr. and Mech. Arts, 1912-26; pres. U. of Md., 1926-35; spl. asst. to adminstr. U.S. Farm Security Adminstrn., U.S. Dept. Agriculture, 1935—. Asst. sec. of agriculture during war emergency, Aug. 1917-18. Received gold medal, Paris Expn., 1900, as collaborator. Home: Hyattsville, Md. Died Feb. 13, 1939.

PEARSON, Richmond, diplomatist; b. Richmond Hill, N.C., Jan. 26, 1852; s. Judge Richmond Mumford and Margaret (Williams) P.; A.B., Princeton, 1872, A.M., 1875; m. Gabrielle Thomas, 1882. Admitted to N.C. bar, 1874; U.S. consul, Verviers and Liége, Belgium, 1874-77; mem. N.C. Legislature, 1885-89; mem. 54th, 55th, 56th Congresses (1895-1901), 9th N.C. Dist.; U.S. consul at Genoa, Italy, Dec. 1901-Dec. 1902; E.E. and M.P. to Persia, 1902-07, to Greece and Montenegro, 1907-09. Republican. Home: Asheville, N.C. Died Sept. 12, 1923.

PEARSONS, Daniel Kimball, philanthropist; b. Bradford, Vt., Apr. 14, 1820; s. John and Hannah (Putnam) P.; ed. pub. sch., 1826-36; taught sch., 1836-41; M.D., coll. in Woodstock, Vt., 1842; practiced in Chicopee, Mass., until 1857; m. Marietta Chapin, Aug. 1847. Farmer, Ogle Co., Ill., 1857-60; in real estate business in Chicago, 1860-87; retired from business but remained dir. in Chicago City Ry. Co. and other corps. Alderman, Chicago, 1873-76. Made donations aggregating over $4,000,000 to colls. and charities, including $280,000 to Chicago Theol. Sem., and $600,000 to Beloit Coll., to which he has added others during past 2 yrs.; $150,000 to Mt. Holyoke Coll.; $100,000 to Lake Forest U. and other donations to 30 colls. in 20 different states, coupling each gift with the requirement that a larger sum be raised from other sources before his gift becomes available; final gift, his home at Hinsdale, Ill., to that village for pub. library and museum. Died Apr. 27, 1912.

PEARY, Robert Edwin, arctic explorer, discoverer of North Pole; rear admiral U.S.N. (retired); b. Cresson, Pa., May 6, 1856; s. Charles N. and Mary (Wiley) P.; C.E., Bowdoin Coll., 1877 (Sc.D., 1894, LL.D.; LL.D., Edinburgh and Tufts); m. Josephine Diebitsch, 1888. Entered U.S. Navy as civil engr., Oct. 26, 1881; asst. engr. Nicaragua Ship Canal under Govt. orders, 1884-85; engr. in charge of Nicaragua Canal Surveys, 1887-88; invented rolling-lock gates for canal. Made reconnaissance, 1886, of the Greenland inland ice-cap, east of Disco Bay, 70° N. lat.; chief of Arctic expdn. of Acad. National Sciences of Phila., June 1891-Sept. 1892, to N.E. angle of Greenland (Independence Bay, 81°37′ N. lat.); discovered and named Melville Land and Heilprin Land, lying beyond Greenland; determined insularity of Greenland, for which he received the Cullom medal of Am. Geog. Soc., Patron's medal of Royal Geog. Soc., London, and medal of Royal Scottish Geog. Soc., Edinburgh. Made another arctic voyage, 1893-95; made thorough study of little tribe of Arctic Highlanders; discovered, 1894, famous Iron Mountain (first heard of by Ross, 1818), which proved to be meteorites, one of them weighing 90 tons (the largest known to exist); made summer voyages, 1896-1897, bringing the Cape York meteorites to U.S.; comdr. Arctic expdn. under auspices of Peary Arctic Club of New York, 1898-1902; rounded northern extremity of Greenland Archipelago, the last of the great Arctic land groups; named the northern cape, the most northerly land in the world (83°39′ N. lat.), Cape Morris K. Jesup; attained highest north in Western Hemisphere (84° 17′ N. lat.). Sailed north again, July 1905, in S.S. Roosevelt, specially built by Peary Arctic Club; returned Oct. 1906, having reached "highest north" (87°6′ N. lat.). Started on 8th Arctic expdn., July 1908, on the Roosevelt, proceeding northward to Kane Basin, through Robeson channel, establishing winter base at Cape Sheridan, Sept. 5, 1908; left Cape Sheridan for Cape Columbia, Feb. 15, 1909, in 5 detachments; the detachments were sent back one after another, the 4th, in command of Capt. Bartlett, leaving Peary nr. the 88th parallel; from here, with 1 member of his crew and 4 Eskimos, made final dash of 130 miles to the pole in 5 days, which they reached Apr. 6, 1909; spent 30 hours at and beyond the pole; the journey from Cape Columbia to the pole was made in 27 marches, the return trip to Cape Columbia was made in 16 marches. Promoted to rank of rear admiral, and given thanks of Congress by special act of Congress, Mar. 3, 1911. Spl. gold medals of Nat. Geog. Soc. (Washington); Royal Geog. Soc. (London); Phila. Geog. Soc., Peary Arctic Club and Explorers Club; awarded the Hubbard gold medal by the Nat. Geog. Society, Culver gold medal, Chicago Geog. Soc.; Kane gold medal, Phila. Geog. Soc.; Daly and Cullom gold medals, Am. Geog. Soc.; gold medal of Imperial German, Austrian, and Hungarian socs.; Royal, Royal Scottish, Italian, and Belgian socs.; Swiss, Paris, Marseilles, Normandy, and City of Paris. Pres. Am. Geog. Soc., 1903; pres. 8th Internat. Geog. Congress, Washington, 1904; hon. v.p. 9th Internat. Geog. Congress, Geneva, 1908, and 10th, at Rome, 1913; pres. Explorers Club, and Aerial League America, U.S. Govt. del. Internat. Polar Commn., Rome, 1913; sec. Internat. Polar Commn.; chmn. Nat. Aerial Coast Patrol Commn. Made Grand Officier d'Honneur, France, 1913; hon. mem. Philadelphia Geog. Soc., Am. Alpine Club, Nat. Geog. Soc., Am. Mus. Natural Hist., N.Y. Chamber of Commerce, and all prin. home and foreign geog. socs. Author: Northward Over the Great Ice, 1898; Nearest the Pole, 1907; The North Pole, 1910; Secrets of Polar Travel, 1917. Died Feb. 20, 1920.

PEASE, Charles Giffin, reformer; b. N.Y. City, Dec. 4, 1854; s. Joseph Mott and Eliza Ann (Giffin) P.; ed. Friends' Sem., New York; Shaw & Sanford Sch.; New York Dental Coll., 1888-89; D.D.S., Phila. Dental Coll., 1890; Medico-Chirurg. Coll. and Hosp., Phila., 1889-90; M.D., New York Homeo. Med. Coll. and Flower Hospital, 1891; m. Clara Estelle Egan, 1881 (died 1883); m. 2d, Mary Leonora Spear, June 1, 1901 (died 1904); practiced as dentist, 1890, and as med. consultant, 1891—; prof. oral surgery Metropolitan Post-Grad. Sch. of Medicine, 1894-97; prof. materia medica, therapeutics and pathology, New York Dental Sch., 1895-97. Veteran 7th Regt. N.Y.N.G. (hon. disch. 1884). Organizer and pres. Non-Smokers' Protective League of America; treas. Am. Philharmonic Acad.; mem. Pub. Good Soc. (exec. com.), Auxiliary League of Salvation Army. Author: Divine Power, or Spiritual Interpretation of the Scriptures, 1904; Exposé of Christian Science Methods and Teaching Prevailing in the First Church, C.S., New York City, 1905; The Smoking Rector, 1936. Home: New York, N.Y. Died Oct. 7, 1941.

PEASE, Charles Henry; b. Mundy Twp., Genesee Co., Mich., Mar. 18, 1873; s. Benjamin Fish and Charlotte Elizabeth (Odell) P.; ed. Fremont (Neb.) Normal Sch.; LL.B., U. of Mich., 1904; m. Mabel McGlinchey, Aug. 22, 1900; 1 son, Lester Floyd. Bookkeeper and teller First State & Savings Bank, Flushing, Mich., 1896-1902; partner law firm Gaffney & Pease, Cadillac, Mich., 1904-06; organizer and cashier Raymondville (Tex.) State Bank, 1907-14, pres., 1914-21; organizer, 1921, and sec.-treas. Lower Rio Grande Valley Water Users Assn.; founder and pub. Gravity Irrigation News. Represented group of water users before Congress and Govt. depts. at Washington, D.C., 1926-29; active in promoting movement which resulted in negotiation between U.S. and Mexico to divide internat. waters for irrigation and power development; editor and business mgr. Hidalgo County Independent, Edinburgh, Tex.; through this paper waged a successful fight, 1929-31, against official graft that ended in the indictment of 21 county officers and public contractors. Free lance writer. Home: McAllen, Tex. Died Sept. 27, 1933.

PEASE, Ernest Mondell, author; b. West Union, Ia., Dec. 24, 1859; s. Charles Franklin and Abigail (Foster) P.; A.B., U. of Colo., 1882, A.M., 1885, LL.D., 1902; fellow Johns Hopkins, 1884-86; student Bonn, 1885, 1891; m. Minnie, d. Ira A. Adams, of West Derby, Vt., 1886; m. 2d, Mary Ball, d. Mahlon V. Johnson, of Denver, 1898. Instr. Latin, Smith Coll., 1886; prof. Latin, Bowdoin College, 1886-91, Stanford U., 1891-1902. Editor Students' Series of Latin Classics, 36 vols. (with H. R. Fairclough). Author: Relative Value of MSS. of Terence; The Development of Latin Satire; The Greeting in the Letters of Cicero. Home: Upper Montclair, N.J. Died Dec. 21, 1936.

PEASE, Francis Gladheim, astronomer; b. Cambridge, Mass., Jan. 14, 1881; s. Daniel and Katharine Bangs (James) P.; high sch., Highland Park, Ill.; B.S., Armour Inst. Tech., 1901, M.S., 1924, D.Sc., 1927; D.Sc., Oglethorpe U., Atlanta, Ga., 1934; m. Caroline T. Furness, Apr. 20, 1905. Optician and observer, Yerkes Obs., Williams Bay, Wis., 1901-04; instrument designer, Mt. Wilson Obs., Pasadena, Calif., 1904-07, 1908-13, astronomer, 1911—; supt. "Scientific Shop" Works, Evanston, Ill., 1907-08. Chief draftsman for the Nat. Research Council, Washington, D.C., World War, 1918. Protestant. Has made direct photographs and spectograms of nebulæ and star clusters and of the moon and planets; also interferometer measures of star diameters, measurement of the velocity of light. In charge of the design of 100-inch telescope, 50-foot interferometer telescope; asso. in optics and instrument design, 200-inch reflector, Calif. Inst. Tech., etc. Home: Pasadena, Calif. Died Feb. 7, 1938.

PEASE, Frederick Henry, musical dir., composer; b. Farmington, O., Aug. 24, 1839; s. Peter Pindar and Ruth (Crocker) P.; ed. Oberlin Coll. and Mich. State Normal Coll.; studied music in Boston with B. J. Lang and B. F. Baker, in Italy with San Giovanni, in Dresden with Gustav Scharfe and Jahnssen; m. Josephine Dolsen, Nov. 7, 1859 (dec.); 2d, Abby Hunter, Mar. 10, 1887. Prof., Oct. 1863—, now head dept. of music and dir., Conservatory of Music, Mich. State Normal Coll.; organist chs., Jackson, Mich., 7 yrs., Detroit, 15 yrs., Ypsilanti, Mich., 5 yrs. Episcopalian. Author: The Old Clock on the Stairs; Pease's Singing Book; Choral Instruction Course; Choral Song Book. Composer: Remember Thy Creator; Pilgrim and Stranger; Reaper and Flowers; A Psalm of Life; When the Heart Is

Young; He Is There; Life's Story; Te Deum Laudamus; Charge Them That Are Rich; etc. Died 1909.

PEASE, Zephaniah W., newspaper editor; b. New Bedford, Mass., Aug. 21, 1861; s. Peleg and Joanna (Morton) P.; grad. high sch., New Bedford, 1877; m. Anna F. Bryden, Oct. 24, 1888; 1 son, Bryden; m. 2d, Mrs. Eliza C. White, Oct. 14, 1922. Began as reporter New Bedford Mercury, 1880, editor, 1895—. Collector of customs, Port of New Bedford, 1895-1900. One group of 25 newspaper editors sent by Carnegie Foundation to study conditions in Europe, 1927. Democrat. Author: The Catalpa Expedition, 1897. Editor: History of New Bedford (3 vols.), 1918; Life in New Bedford One Hundred Years Ago (from diary of J. R. Anthony), 1923; The Diary of Samuel Rodman, 1928; Fifty Years, 1930. Home: Fairhaven, Mass. Died June 24, 1933.

PEASLEE, John Bradley, educator; b. Plaistow, N.H., Sept. 3, 1842; s. Reuben and Harriet Atwood (Willets) P.; A.B., Dartmouth, 1863, A.M., 1866; LL.B., Cincinnati Coll., 1866; (hon. Ph.D., Ohio State Univ., 1878); m. Lou Wright, Apr. 25, 1878. Prin. North Grammar Sch., Columbus, O., 1863-64; 1st asst. and prin. dist. and intermediate schs. Cincinnati, 1864-74; supt. Cincinnati pub. schs., 1874-86; clerk of courts, Hamilton Co., O., 1888-95. Dem. nominee for lt. gov. of Ohio, 1895; pres. Ohio Forestry Bur., 1889-95; dir. Univ. of Cincinnati; pres. Ohio State Bd. Examiners for Teachers; trustee Miami U., 1871-79. During superintendency introduced systematic course in "memory gems," and inaugurated "author-day" and "arbor-day" celebrations in the schs.; awarded, 1879, diploma of life membership in U. of Turin in recognition of excellence of Cincinnati sch. exhibit at Paris Expn., 1878; in 1889 the Am. Forestry Congress planted and dedicated oak-tree in Fairmount Park, Phila., as recognition of his services in promoting cause of popular forestry. Author: Trees and Tree Planting, with Exercises and Directions for the Celebration of "Arbor-Day"; Occasional Verses and Sacred Poems, 1905. Compiler: Graded Selections for Memorizing at Home and in School. Home: Cincinnati, O. Died 1912.

PEASLEE, Robert James, judge; b. Weare, N.H., Sept. 23, 1864; s. Robert and Persis Boardman (Dodge) P.; ed. Cushing Acad., Ashburnham, Mass. and (grad.) Arms Acad., Shelburne Falls, Mass.; LL.B., Boston U., 1886; hon. A.M., Dartmouth, 1898; LL.D., Dartmouth Coll., 1926, Boston U., 1927; m. Nellie Dorcas, Sept. 12, 1893 (died 1915); m. 2d, Sarah Congdon Hazard, 1917. Admitted to New Hampshire bar, 1886, practiced in Manchester until 1898; justice Supreme Court of N.H., 1898-1901; asso. justice Superior Court, 1901-07; asso. justice Supreme Court, 1907-24, chief justice, 1924-34; resumed practice with Demond, Woodworth, Sulloway, Piper & Jones, Concord, New Hampshire. Democrat. Lecturer on municipal and constl. law, Dartmouth Coll., 1887-89, on domestic relations, Boston U. Law Sch., 1911—; revised city laws and ordinances of Manchester, 1892. Chmn. Commn. to Revise N.H. Public Laws, 1923. Home: Manchester, N.H. Died Aug. 23, 1936.

PEATE, John, M.E. clergyman; b. in Ireland, May 6, 1820; self-educated (A.M., D.D., Allegheny Coll., Pa.); m. Mary Tilden, Nov. 20, 1845. Worked on farm in boyhood; 12 yrs. bricklayer, Buffalo, N.Y.; 50 yrs. in pastorates as regular ordained minister, M.E. Ch.; has traveled extensively in four quarters of globe. Makes telescope mirrors for pleasure; made 61-inch mirror for Am. Univ., Washington, D.C., and others. Home: Greenville, Pa. Died 1903.

PEATTIE, Elia Wilkinson, journalist; author; b. Kalamazoo, Mich., Jan. 15, 1862; d. Frederick and Amanda (Cahill) Wilkinson; moved to Chicago in early girlhood; m. Robert Burns Peattie, May 10, 1883 (died 1930); children—Edward Cahill, Barbara (dec.), Roderick, Donald Culross. Wrote short stories; reporter on Chicago dailies until 1888; then became editorial writer Omaha World-Herald; afterward in Chicago; lit. critic Chicago Tribune, 1901-17. Author: Lotta Embury's Career, 1915; The Newcomers, 1916; Sarah Brewster's Relatives, 1916; Memory's Painted Windows, 1919; The Wander Weed, 1923; Songs From a Southern Garden. Home: Tryon, N.C. Died July 12, 1935.

PEATTIE, Robert (Burns), newspaperman; b. Waushara Co., Wis., Oct. 5, 1857; s. John and Elizabeth (Culross) P.; ed. pub. schs., Chicago; m. Elia A. Wilkinson, May 10, 1883. Began on staff Chicago Times, 1880; with Chicago Daily Herald, 1883-84, Chicago Daily News, 1884-87; mng. editor World-Herald, Omaha, 1888-96; became editorial writer for Chicago Tribune, 1901, now New York corr. for same; was Chicago corr. New York Times, 10 yrs. Democrat. Episcopalian. Home: New York, N.Y. Died Dec. 15, 1930.

PEAVEY, Leroy Deering, pres. Babson's Reports, Inc.; b. Exeter, N.H., Mar. 11, 1876; s. Sam Roswell and Mary Augusta (Smith) P.; grad. Phillips Exeter Acad., 1894; B.S., Mass. Inst. Tech., 1898; m. Fannie R. Nottage, Oct. 31, 1901; children—Ethelyn Bartlett, Dorothy Nottage, Marion Frances, Grace

Augusta, Roswell Charles, Edith Gilman. Engaged in structural steel work, N.Y. City and Boston, 1898-1900; asst. engr. Am. Bridge Co. and Boston Bridge Works, 1900-03; chief engr. H. P. Converse Co., bridge and building contractors, Boston, 1903-10; with Babson's Statis. Orgn., 1910—, dir. and v.p., 1912-25, pres., 1925-34. Mem. Ch. of the Nazarene. Lecturer. Home: Watertown, Mass. Died Mar. 25, 1937.

PEAY, Austin, governor; b. Christian Co., Ky., June 1, 1876; s. Austin and Cornelia Frances (Leavell) P.; student Centre Coll., Danville, Ky.; m. Sallie Hurst, Sept. 19, 1895. Admitted to Ky. bar, 1895; settled at Clarksville, Tenn., 1896; mem. Tenn. Ho. of Rep., 1901-03; chmn. Dem. State Com., Tenn., 1905; gov. of Tenn., term Jan. 1923-Jan. 1925; reëlected term Jan. 1925-Jan. 1927. Baptist. Died Oct. 2, 1927.

PECHIN, Edmund Cash, mining engr.; b. Philadelphia, Dec. 9, 1834; s. John C. and Margaret (Cash) P.; B.A., U. of Pa., 1856, A.M., 1859; m. Mary L. Shelley, June 1863. Practiced law until 1867; afterward mining engr. A founder of Am. Inst. Mining Engrs.; mem. various societies. Designed cooling plates for blast furnace boshes. Has written many tech. papers on mining iron ores and coals and mfg. iron; retired to farm. Home: Buchanan, Va. Died Feb. 5, 1928.

PECK, Annie Smith, mountain climber; b. Providence, R.I., Oct. 19, 1850; d. George Bacheler and Ann Power (Smith) P.; A.B., U. of Michigan, 1878, A.M., 1881; studied German and music in Germany, 1884-85, 1st woman to study in Am. Sch. of Classical Studies, Athens, 1885-86; specialized in Greek and archeology; unmarried. Taught two terms in Providence schs.; later preceptress in Saginaw (Mich.) High Sch.; teacher mathematics in Bartholomew's Sch. for Girls, Cincinnati; preceptress Montclair (N.J.) High Sch.; prof. Latin, Purdue U.; prof. Latin, Smith Coll. Gave parlor lectures on Greek and Roman archeology, 1887-89; pub. lecturer, 1890—, on Greek archeology mountain climbing and South America from tourist and commercial standpoint. Distinguished mountain climber: Matterhorn, 1895, Popocatepetl and Orizaba, Mexico, 1897; Fünffingerspitze (Tyrol), 1900, also other Alpine summits; Mt. Sorata (Bolivia), to 20,500 feet, 1904; exploration in Peru at source of Amazon (Marañon), ascent 18,000 feet on highest peak of Raura Range, first ascent nameless rock mountain, 16,300 feet, 1906; Mt. Huascarán, Peru, partial ascents without guides, 1904, 1906; with two Swiss guides reached summit north peak, Sept. 2, 1908, first ascent, 21,812 ft., which is 1,500 ft. higher than Mt. McKinley and highest point in America yet attained by any American; July 10, 1911, 1st ascent of two peaks of Mt. Coropuna, Peru, 21,250 feet. Official del. of U.S. to Internat. Congress of Alpinism, Paris, 1900; del. 2d Pan-Am. Conf. of Women in connection with 3d Pan-Am. Scientific Congress, Lima, Peru (only U.S. del. to read paper in Spanish); lectured in S. America, in Spanish and Portuguese, on U.S. industries and ednl. instns., 1915, 16; visited Brazil Centennial Expn., 1922; 9th visit to S. America, 1925; 10th visit to S. America (in airplane), 1929-30. Presented by Govt. of Peru with gold medal; silver slipper (stirrup) presented by Lima Geog. Soc.; decoration of Order Al Merito (Chile) at dinner in honor of 80th birthday, Nov. 24, 1930. Fellow Royal Geog. Soc. Baptist. Author: A Search for the Apex of America, 1911; The South American Tour, 1914, 24; Commercial and Industrial South America, 1922, 27; Flying Over South America—2,000 Miles by Air, 1932. A recognized authority on S. America; north peak of the twin mountain Huascarán, named "Cumbre Ana Peck," in her honor, by Lima Geog. Soc. Home: New York, N.Y. Died July 18, 1935.

PECK, Bayard Livingston, lawyer; b. Hudson, N.Y., Aug. 16, 1869; s. Horace Robinson and Anna (Van Deusen) P.; A.B., Hamilton Coll., Clinton, N.Y., 1891, A.M., 1893; law study New York U., 1892-93; m. Elizabeth Stuart Butler, Nov. 2, 1907; children—Betty Stuart, Barbara Livingston. Admitted to N.Y. bar, 1895; clk. Surrogate Court, Columbia County, 1893-96; began practice at N.Y. City, 1896; counsel for ednl. and charitable instns., and for a number of estates and pvt. trusts; pres. Alloy Steel Forging Co., 1919-25. Police justice of Village of Belle Terre, L.I. Mem. Real Estate Board, N.Y. City, and Chamber of Commerce, Brooklyn; alumni trustee Hamilton Coll., 1916-19. Ind. Democrat. Sec. Bd. of Trustees First Presbyn. Ch., Brooklyn. Home: Brooklyn, N.Y., and Belle Terre, L.I., N.Y. Died Oct. 29, 1931.

PECK, Charles Howard, surgeon; b. Newtown, Conn., June 18, 1870; s. Albert W. and Louise W. (Booth) P.; prep. edn., Newtown Acad.; M.D., Coll. Phys. and Surg. (Columbia), 1892; LL.D., Fordham U., 1924; m. Betsy F. Chaffee, of Montreal, Can., Sept. 2, 1896; children—Charles Howard (dec.), Nelson Chaffee, Dexter Belknap. Surg. practice in N.Y. City, 1895—; asst. instr. operative surgery, 1900, instr. surgery, 1904, asso. in clin. surgery, 1908, asst. prof., 1909, prof., 1910—, Coll. Phys.

and Surg.; surgeon to Roosevelt Hosp.; cons. surgeon to French, Memorial, Rupture and Crippled, Stamford (Conn.), White Plains (N.Y.), Greenwich (Conn.), and Vassar Brothers (Poughkeepsie, N.Y.) hosps. Commd. maj. Med. O.R.C., May 9, 1917; lt. col. Med. Corps, N.A., June 6, 1918; col. M.C., Aug. 24, 1918; col. Med. O.R.C., May 9, 1919. Served as mem. Gen. Med. Bd. Council Nat. Defense and as chmn. N.Y. State Nat. Defense Assn.; organizer and dir. Base Hosp. No. 15, U.S.A., at Chaumont as a 3,000 bed hosp.; apptd. sr. consultant in gen. surgery, A.E.F., Apr. 1918; served in France until July 7, 1918; chief Dept. of Gen. Surgery (in rotation with Drs. W. J. and C. H. Mayo), Surgeon Gen.'s Office, Washington, D.C., Aug. 1, 1918-Feb. 4, 1919. Awarded D.S.M., Mar. 26, 1919; made hon. mem. 68th Batt., Alpine Chasseurs, "for services rendered to French Army" during Battle of Chemin des Dames, Oct. 1917; Officier de l'Instruction Publique (French). Home: New York, N.Y. Died Mar. 28, 1927.

PECK, Edward Porter, grain mcht.; b. Akron, O., Oct. 22, 1855; s. James Porter and Elizabeth Huntington (Ames) P.; ed. high sch., Omaha, Neb.; m. Mary Bishop, Sept. 19, 1876 (dec.); children—Elizabeth Ames (Mrs. Joseph Barker), Helen Bishop (Mrs. R. B. H. Bell), Lyman, Louise (Mrs. Denise Barkalow). Began in wholesale grain and grain elevator business at Omaha, 1877; with Omaha Elevator Co., 1877—, v.p. and gen. mgr., 1903—; mem. Omaha Grain Exchange (dir.; pres., 1912, 27). Pres. The Terminal Elevator Grain Mchts. Assn.; dir. Chamber Commerce of U.S. Republican. Episcopalian. Home: Omaha, Neb. Died Nov. 25, 1937.

PECK, Epaphroditus, lawyer; b. Bristol, Conn., May 20, 1860; s. Josiah Tracy and Ellen Lewis (Barnard) P.; grad. Hartford (Conn.) High Sch., 1877; LL.B., Yale, 1881; m. Grace Brownell, Aug. 21, 1886 (died 1931); children—Mrs. Margaret P. McEwan, Grace B. (dec.), Dorothy A. (dec.), Eleanor L. (dec.), Mildred A. Began practice at Bristol, 1882; asso. judge Hartford Co. Court of Common Pleas, 1897-1912. Instr., Yale Law Sch., 1903-13. Representative in Conn. Legislature, 1925-35, mem. Com. to Revise Conn. Statutes, 1930. Dir. Bristol Savings Bank. Pres. Pub. Library; dir. and sec. Bristol Hosp.; v.p. Corp. for Congl. Nat. Council. Author: Law of Persons and Domestic Relations, 1913, 3d edit., 1930; History of Bristol, Conn., 1932. Home: Bristol, Conn. Died Oct. 29, 1938.

PECK, Ferdinand Wythe, capitalist; b. Chicago, July 15, 1848; s. Philip F. W. and Mary (Kent) P.; A.B., U. of Chicago, 1868; LL.B., Union Coll. of Law, Chicago, 1869; m. Tilla C. Spalding, Nov. 17, 1870. Admitted to bar, 1869; pres. Chicago Auditorium Assn., 1886-1900; 1st v.p. Columbian Expn., 1893 (chmn. finance com.); pres. Chicago Athenæum 15 yrs.; v.p. Chicago Bd. Edn., 4 yrs.; a founder, Ill. Humane Soc.; U.S. commr. gen., Paris Expn., 1900. Home: Chicago, Ill. Died Nov. 4, 1924.

PECK, Frederick Burritt, geologist; b. Seneca Castle, N.Y., Aug. 19, 1860; s. Henry Jones and Mary Diantha (Gray) P.; A.B., Amherst, 1886; Ph.D., U. of Munich, Germany, 1896; m. Cora Burr Horton, June 12, 1901. Teacher mathematics and natural sciences, Trinidad, Colo., 1886-91; asst. in geology, Amherst and Smith colls., 1891-94; asso. prof. geology, 1897-1901, prof. mineralogy and geology, 1901—, Lafayette Coll., Easton, Pa. Asst. geologist U.S. Geol. Survey, 1898-1909. Presbyn. Died Nov. 2, 1925.

PECK, George Bacheler, M.D.; b. Providence, R.I., Aug. 12, 1843; s. George Bacheler and Ann Power (Smith) P.; A.B., Brown, 1864 (also same yr., diploma for course in civ. engring.), A.M., 1867; Hahnemann Med. Coll., Phila., 1869-70; M.D., Yale, 1871; post-grad. Sheffield Scientific Sch. (Yale), 1871-72; unmarried. Practiced medicine, Providence, 1875-1928; admitting phys. R.I. Homœ. Hosp., 1886-1901, also trustee. Mem. Providence Sch. Com., 1881-96; mem. bd. mgrs. R.I. Bapt. State Conv., 1876-1910; clk. Narragansett Bapt. Assn., 1877-87, 1892-1915 (moderator 1889). Major Providence Marine Corps of Arty., 1869-71; lt. 2d Regt., R.I. Vols., Dec. 13, 1864-July 5, 1865; wounded at Sailor's Creek, Apr. 6, 1865; surgeon Battalion Light Arty. Div. R.I. Militia, 1876-79; lt. comdg. Battery A, R.I. Militia, during the Spanish-Am. War. Asst. chemist U.S. Naval Torpedo Sta., 1872-74; in charge chem. dept. U. of Vt., fall of 1874. Republican. Hon. pres. Am. Inst. Homœopathy, 1912 (and chmn. of International Bur., 1902-18); pres. R.I. Homœ. Med. Soc., 1885, 86, R.I. Soldiers and Sailors Hist. Soc., 1892-96. Mason. Editor (largely author): Seventh Regiment R.I. Vols. in Civil War, 1862-65, 1903. Home: Woodville, R.I. Died Nov. 20, 1934.

PECK, George Clarke, clergyman; b. Lowell, Mass., Sept. 13, 1865; s. J. Oramel and Susan (Robinson) P.; A.B., Yale, 1889; student Union Theol. Sem., 1890; B.D., Drew Theol. Sem., 1892; D.D., Syracuse, 1905; m. Kate Hamilton Marshall, Oct. 8, 1889; 1 son, James O. (adopted). Ordained M.E. ministry, 1892; pastor Westport, Conn., 1892-94, Bay Shore,

L.I., 1894-97, 1st Ch. Mt. Vernon, N.Y., 1897-1905, Elm Park Ch., Scranton, Pa., 1905-07, St. Andrews Ch., New York, 1907-12; exec. sec. N.Y. City Soc. M.E. Ch., 1912-13; pastor 1st Ch., Baltimore, 1913-19; supt. Md. Gen. Hospital, 1919—. Trustee Drew Sem. for Young Women. Author: Ringing Questions, 1902; Old Sins in New Clothes, 1904; Method of the Master, 1912; Desert, Pinnacle and Mountain, 1914; Men Who Missed the Trail, 1917; Side-Stepping Saints, 1918; Forgotten Faces, 1919; Cross-Lots and Other Essays, 1921; The Pot of Gold, 1922; Flashes of Silence, 1924. Editor: The Christian City. Home: Baltimore, Md. Died Jan. 21, 1927.

PECK, George Lyman, ry. official; b. Sandusky, O., July 10, 1858; s. Otis Lyman and Martha Jane P.; common sch. edn.; widower. Entered ry. service, 1873, as messenger boy, Toledo div., Pa. Co.; consecutively telegraph operator, 1874-76, train dispatcher, 1876-81, same co.; train dispatcher, Columbus, Hocking Valley & Toledo Ry., 1881-82; train master, Toledo div., Pa. Co., 1882-94; supt., Richmond div., P.,C.,C.&St.L. Ry., 1894-96; supt. Pittsburgh div., same., 1896-1901; gen. supt., Southwest system, Pa. Lines West of Pittsburgh, Jan.-June 1901; gen. mgr. Pa. Lines West of Pittsburgh, 1901-12, 5th v.p., Jan. 1, 1913; federal mgr. same under U.S. R.R. Administration, 1918-20, v.p. in charge personnel Pa. System, 1920-28 (retired). Home: St. Davids, Pa. Died Mar. 18, 1932.

PECK, George Record, lawyer; b. Steuben Co., N.Y., May 15, 1843; s. Joel M. and Amanda (Purdy) P.; ed. common schs.; (LL.D., U. of Kan., 1887, Union Coll., N.Y., 1896, and Bethany Coll., W.Va.; A.M., Milton Coll., 1902); m. Arabella Burdick, Oct. 24, 1866 (died 1896). Pvt. to capt. 1st Wis. Heavy Arty. and 31st Wis. Inf., 1861-65; admitted to bar, 1866; practiced at Independence, Kan., 1871-74, Topeka, Kan., 1874-93, Chicago, 1893—; sr. mem. Peck, Miller (John S.) & Starr (Merritt), 1894-1912. Gen. solicitor A.,T.&S.F. R.R. Co., 1881-95; gen. counsel C.,M.&St.P. Ry., Sept. 15, 1895-Jan. 1910, from then consulting counsel. U.S. atty. Dist. of Kan., 1874-79; declined appmt. to U.S. Senate for unexpired term, from Kan., 1892. Republican. Home: Oconomowoc, Wis. Died Feb. 22, 1923.

PECK, George Wilbur, governor, author; b. Henderson, N.Y., Sept. 28, 1840; s. David B. and Alzina P.; ed. pub. schs. until 1855; went to Wis., 1843, and learned printer's trade; m. Francena Rowley, 1860. In 1860 bought half interest in Jefferson Co. Republican, Jefferson, Wis. Served 2½ yrs., pvt. and lt., 4th Wis. Cav., in Civil War. In 1866 started at Ripon, Wis., a newspaper called The Representative; later owned the La Cross Democrat until 1874; founded The Sun, La Crosse, 1874, removed it to Milwaukee, 1878, and called it Peck's Sun; became noted for humorous sketches, and particularly the Peck's Bad Boy series. Mayor of Milwaukee, 1890-91; gov. of Wis., 1891-95. Democrat. Author: Peck's Bad Boy and His Pa, 1882; The Groceryman and Peck's Bad Boy, 1883; Peck's Boss Book, 1898; Peck's Uncle Ike and the Red Headed Boy, 1899; Sunbeams—Humor, Sarcasm and Sense, 1900; Peck's Bad Boy with the Circus, 1906; Peck's Bad Boy with the Cowboys, 1907. Died Apr. 16, 1916.

PECK, Harry Thurston, editor, author; b. Stamford, Conn., Nov. 24, 1856; s. Harry and Harriet Elizabeth (Thurston) P.; A.B., Columbia, 1881, A.M., 1882, L.H.D., 1884; Ph.D., Cumberland, 1883; studied Berlin, Paris, Rome: (LL.D., Alfred, 1903, Columbia, 1904); m. Elizabeth H. DuBois, Aug. 26, 1909. Tutor in Latin, 1882-86, Latin and Semitic langs., 1886-88, prof. Latin lang. and lit., 1888-1904, Anthon prof., 1904-10, Columbia U. Classical lecturer in Barnard Coll., 1893; editor The Bookman, 1895-1907; lit. editor New York Commercial Advertiser, 1897-1901. Author: The Adventures of Mabel, 1896; Twenty Years of the Republic, 1906; Studies in Several Literatures, 1909; Literature, 1909; The New Baedeker, 1910; A History of Classical Philology, 1911. Editor: Harper's Classical Dictionary; The Internat. Cyclopædia (15 vols.); The New Internat. Encyclopedia (20 vols.); American Atlas of the World; The Library of the World's Literature; Masterpieces of Literature; Classical Studies; Columbia Univ. Bulletin; Columbia Univ. Studies in Classical Philology; Students' Series of Latin Classics, 32 vols. (with Ernest M. Pease). Translator of Petronius. Home: New York, N.Y. Died Mar. 23, 1914.

PECK, Henry Allen, astronomer; b. Mexico, N.Y., May 4, 1863; s. Henry Carter and Margaret Augusta (Allen) P.; A.B., Syracuse U., 1885, A.M., 1888; Ph.D., U. of Strassburg, 1896; m. Kittie V. Becker, Aug. 3, 1887; 2d, Jessie Rankin Tyler, Dec. 22, 1898. Teacher common schs., 1879-81; teacher mathematics, Williamsport-Dickinson Sem., Williamsport, Pa., 1885-87; instr. astronomy, 1887-93, prof., 1893—, dean Coll. Liberal Arts, 1917—, Syracuse U. Methodist. Republican. Home: Syracuse, N.Y. Died Nov. 17, 1921.

PECK, Hiram David, lawyer; b. Harrison Co., Ky., Mar. 23, 1844; s. John W. and Nancy Jane (Veach) P.; pvt. Co. A, 86th Ohio Inf., May-Sept., 1862; A.B., Miami U., 1862; LL.B., Harvard, 1865; (LL.D., U. of Cincinnati, and Miami, 1891); m. Harriet Emily Weld, Nov. 18, 1868. Asst. city solicitor, Cincinnati, 1873-76; city solicitor, 1876; judge Superior Court of Cincinnati, 1883-89; sr. mem. Peck, Shaffer & Peck, 1890—. Home: Cincinnati, O. Died Oct. 11, 1914.

PECK, John Hudson, lawyer; b. Hudson, N.Y., Feb. 7, 1838; s. Hon. Darius and Harriet M. (Hudson) P.; A.B., Hamilton Coll., 1859, A.M., 1862 (LL.D., 1889); m. Mercy P. Mann, Aug. 7, 1883 (died 1914). Admitted to bar, 1861, and practices at Troy, N.Y. Mem. N.Y. Constl. Conv., 1894; chmn. Rensselaer Co. New Court House Commn., 1894-97; a trustee for erection of Hart Memorial Library Bldg., 1894-97. Pres. Rensselaer Poly. Inst., 1888-1900; trustee Troy Female Sem., 1883—; treas. trustees Diocese of Albany. An original incorporator Scenic and Historic Preservation Soc. State of N.Y. Home: Troy, N.Y. Died May 4, 1919.

PECK, John Weld, lawyer; b. Wyoming, Cincinnati, O., Feb. 5, 1874; s. Hiram David and Harriet Emily (Weld) P.; Miami U., Oxford, O., 1891-92, LL.D., 1915; A.B., Harvard, 1896; LL.B., Cincinnati Law Sch., 1898; m. Nelle Wright, Jan. 7, 1899 (died 1931); children—Jane Wright, Emily Nelle; m. 2d, Alma Helm, Aug. 5, 1933. Practiced, Cincinnati, 1898-1919, mem. Peck, Shaffer & Peck; U.S. dist. judge, Southern Dist. Ohio, 1919-23, resigned; mem. Peck, Shaffer & Williams; gen. counsel Union Gas & Electric Co.; gen. solicitor C.N.O.&T.P. Ry. (Southern R.R.); prof. law (part time) Law Sch. U. of Cincinnati; mem. State Banking Adv. Bd. of Ohio, 1933—. Trustee Miami U. (pres. bd.), Cincinnati Southern Ry., 1914-19. Mem. City Council, 1912, 13 (majority leader). Episcopalian. Homes: Wyoming, Cincinnati, Ohio. Died Aug. 10, 1937.

PECK, Paul Frederick, prof. history; b. Grinnell, Ia., July 15, 1873; s. Ira Stafford and Martha Jane (Carney) P.; A.B., Ia. (Grinnell) Coll., 1897; Law Sch. State U. of Ia., 1897-98; U. of Chicago, 1898-1901, fellow, 1899-1901, Ph.D. (in history), 1901; m. Grace Parsons, Aug. 15, 1907. Prof. history, Pa. State Normal Sch., Bloomsburg, Pa., 1901-05, Grinnell Coll., Sept. 1, 1905—. Exchange lecturer in Am. history, Harvard U., 2d semester, 1913. Republican. Conglist. Author: The Government of Pennsylvania, 1905. War work, Mar. 1918-Sept. 1919, under Am. Red Cross; home service rep., Camp Shelby, Mar.-Nov. 1918; in Paris, Nov. 1918-Sept. 1919, with rank of capt., as asst. chief and chief of home service in France, and later as dir. home service work of Am. Red Cross throughout Europe. Home: Grinnell, Ia. Died Nov. 20, 1925.

PECK, Samuel Minturn, author; b. Tuscaloosa, Ala., Nov. 4, 1854; s. E. Wolsey Peck (chief justice) and Lucy Lam (Randall) P.; A.M., U. of Alabama, 1876; Litt.D. from same, 1927; unmarried. Extensive writer of verse, essays, fiction, short stories and novels. Author of many popular songs and lyrics, of which his "Grape Vine Swing" and the Yale College song, "The Knot of Blue," are best known. Author: (poems) Cap and Bells, 1886; Rings and Love Knots, 1892; Rhymes and Roses, 1895; Fair Women of To-Day, 1896; The Golf Girl, 1899; (fiction) Alabama Sketches, 1900; Maybloom and Myrtle (poems), 1910; Swamp Tales, 1912; The Autumn Trail (poems), 1925. Elected by Ala. State Legislature and commd. by gov. first poet laureate of Ala., Mar. 7, 1931. Episcopalian. Home: Tuscaloosa, Ala. Died May 3, 1938.

PECK, Theodore Safford, soldier; b. Burlington, Vt., Mar. 22, 1843; s. Theodore Augustus and Delia Horton (Safford) P.; prepared for coll. and then enlisted in Civil War; (hon. A.M., Norwich U., Vt., 1896); m. Agnes Louisa Leslie, Oct. 29, 1879; father of Theodora Agnes P. Served in 1st Vt. Cav. and 9th Vt. Inf., pvt. to capt. and on staff in Army of the Potomac almost 4 yrs.; awarded Congressional Medal of Honor "for distinguished gallantry in action at Newport Barracks, N.C., Feb. 2, 1864"; later comd. 1st Brigade Vt. N.G. and adj. gen. of Vt., 1881-1900. In ins. business, 1868—. Mem. Bd. of Visitors U.S. Mil. Acad., 1891. Republican. Conglist. Past. comdr. Vt. Commandery Loyal Legion, Medal of Honor Legion of the U.S., Dept. Vt. G.A.R.; 1st gov. Vt. Soc. Colonial Wars; deputy gov. gen. for Vt. of Gen. Soc. of Colonial Wars; S.A.R. Mason (grand marshal Grand Lodge of Vt., 10 yrs.). Home: Burlington, Vt. Died Mar. 15, 1918.

PECK, Tracy, university prof.; b. Bristol, Conn., May 24, 1838; s. Tracy and Sally (Adams) P.; A.B., Yale, 1861, A.M., 1864; univs. of Berlin and Bonn, 1861-63; (LL.D., Rutgers, 1902); m. Elizabeth Harriet Hall, of Hadleigh, Eng., Dec. 22, 1870. Tutor, Yale, 1864-67, 1869-70; prof. Latin, Cornell, 1871-80, Yale, 1880-1908, emeritus prof., 1908. Dir. Am. Sch. Classical Studies in Rome, 1898-99. Pres. Am. Philol. Assn., 1885-86. Trustee Williston Sem., Easthampton, Mass., 1883-1908. With Prof. Clement L. Smith, of Harvard, editor-in-chief of series of Latin authors annotated for coll. use (15 vols. issued); with Prof. J. B. Greenough, of Harvard, editor coll. edition of Livy, Books XXI, XXII, 1893. From 1909 lived in Rome, Italy. Died Nov. 25, 1921.

PECKHAM, Frank Edwin, surgeon; b. Hopkinton, R.I., May 13, 1862; s. Peleg E. P.; Ph.B., Brown U., 1885; M.D., Harvard, 1890; m. Alice E. Fancher, 1892. Practiced in Providence, 1890—; visiting orthopedic surgeon to St. Joseph's Hosp., Jan. 1, 1904—. Fellow Am. Coll. Surgeons. Republican. Conglist. Home: Providence, R.I. Died Mar. 9, 1924.

PECKHAM, George Williams, librarian; b. Albany, N.Y., Mar. 23, 1845; s. George W. and Mary (Perry) P.; student Milwaukee Acad., 1860-63; pvt. to 1st lt., Wis. Arty., 1863-65; Antioch Coll., 1866; Albany Law Sch., 1866-67; M.D., U. of Mich., 1881; (LL.D., U. of Wis., 1894); m. Elizabeth Gifford, Sept. 16, 1880. Prin. high sch., Milwaukee, 1885-92; supt. schs., Milwaukee, 1892-96; librarian Milwaukee Pub. Library, 1896-1910. Pres. Wis. Acad. of Sciences, Arts and Letters, 1891-93; pres. bd. of trustees of Milwaukee Pub. Mus., 1892-96. Author: (with wife) Observations on Sexual Selection in Spiders, 1890; Habits and Instincts of Solitary Wasps, 1898; Wasps, Social and Solitary, 1905. Home: Milwaukee, Wis. Died Jan. 11, 1914.

PECKHAM, John J(udah), lawyer; b. Indianapolis, Ind., June 5, 1878; s. Orville and Anne M. (Jameson) P.; A.B., Harvard, 1900; LL.B., Northwestern U., 1903; unmarried. Began practice in Chicago, 1903, with Peckham, Brown & Packard (estab. 1872), which became Miller, Starr, Packard & Peckham, 1911, and Brown, Packard, Peckham & Barnes, 1922; temporarily resigned, Sept. 1, 1927. Mem. Law Club. Democrat. Home: Chicago, Ill. Died May 22, 1937.

PECKHAM, Orville, lawyer; b. Newport, R.I., Oct. 30, 1846; s. Francis B. and Elizabeth Bentley (Oman) P.; Ph.B., Brown U., 1867; admitted to R.I. bar, 1869; m. Anne Jameson, Mar. 8, 1876. Practiced at Providence, R.I., 1869-72, then at Chicago; spl. atty. First Nat. Bank of Chicago from 1879; retired. Democrat. Home: Indianapolis, Ind. Died Nov. 8, 1927.

PECKHAM, Rufus Wheeler, jurist; b. Albany, N.Y., Nov. 8, 1838; s. Judge Rufus Wheeler and Isabella (Lacey) P.; ed. at Albany Acad. and in Phila.; studied law; admitted to bar, Dec. 1859; (LL.D., Union Coll., 1894, Yale, 1896, Columbia, 1901); m. Harriette Arnold, Nov. 14, 1866. Dist. atty. Albany Co., 1868; corp. counsel, City of Albany, 1880-81; justice Sup. Ct. of N.Y., 1883-86; asso. justice Ct. of Appeals, N.Y., 1886-95; asso. justice U.S. Supreme Court, Dec. 3, 1895—. Home: Washington, D.C. Died 1909.

PECKHAM, Stephen Farnum, chemist; b. Fruit Hill, Providence, R.I., Mar. 26, 1839; s. Charles and Hannah Lapham (Farnum) P.; student chemistry, Brown U., 1859-61 (hon. A.M., 1870); m. Mary Chace Peck, June 13, 1865 (died 1892); m. 2d, Dr. Hattie C. W. Van Buren, Aug. 1, 1902. Hosp. steward U.S.A., 1862-65; chemist to Calif. Petroleum Co., 1866, Calif. Geol. Survey, 1867; instr. chemistry, Brown, 1867-68; prof. chemistry, Washington and Jefferson Coll., 1868-69, Me. Agrl. Coll., 1869-71, Buchtel Coll., 1871-72, U. of Minn., 1872-80; spl. agt. U.S. Census, 1880-85; chemist, Union Oil Co. of Calif., 1893-94; chemist to Commrs. of Accts., New York, 1898-1908, Dept. of Finance, New York, 1908-11; cons. chemist, New York, 1911—. State assayer, Me., 1869-71, Minn., 1873-80, R.I., 1887. Author: Elementary Chemistry, 1873; Report on Production, Technology and Uses of Petroleum, 1885; Solid Bitumens, 1909. Home: Brooklyn, N.Y. Died July 12, 1916.

PECKHAM, Wheeler Hazard, lawyer; b. Albany, N.Y., Jan. 1, 1833; s. Hon. Rufus Wheeler P.; ed. Albany Acad. and Union Coll.; admitted to bar; has been connected with many important cases; apptd., 1884, dist. atty. of New York, resigned same year. Home: New York, N.Y. Died 1905.

PECKHAM, William Clark, physicist; b. S. Royalston, Mass., Aug. 13, 1841; s. Rev. Samuel Howland and Sarah (Clark) P.; pvt. 23d Mass. Vols., 1861-62; A.B., Amherst, 1867, A.M., 1873; student Union Theol. Sem., 1871-72; m. Katalena Whittier, Jan. 1, 1868. Prof. mathematics and physics, Adelphi Acad., 1875-96; prof. physics, Adelphi Coll., 1896—. On editorial staff of Scientific American, 1897—, contributing editor, 1921—; science lecturer in Free Lectures for the People, Bd. of Edn., New York. Fellow Am. Physical Soc., Am. Acad. Arts and Sciences, Brooklyn Inst. Arts and Sciences. Home: Brooklyn, N.Y. Died Oct. 3, 1922.

PECKHAM, William Gibbs, lawyer; b. Newport, R.I., Feb. 7, 1849; s. William G. and Mary Hull (Perry) P.; A.B., Harvard, 1867; U. of Heidelberg, 1868-69; LL.B., New York U., 1870; m. Laura Thurston, June 1, 1875. Admitted to bar, 1870, and began practice at New York. Represented Northampton bank in suits growing out of the famous robbery, in which $2,000,000 was stolen, bringing suit against brokers and others who had received stolen securities and defending suits against bank with unvarying success; was employed in all the large railroad cases against Gould and Sage in New York, and more lately against Mr. Yerkes' railroads in Chicago. Associated with late George W. Curtis and Carl Schurz in managing independent part of Cleveland campaign, 1884, and at same time chmn. N.J. "mugwumps." Home: Westfield, N.J. Died Apr. 13, 1924.

PEDDLE, John B(ailey), educator; b. Terre Haute, Ind., Feb. 27, 1868; s. Charles R. and Mary Elizabeth (Ball) P.; B.S., Rose Poly. Inst., 1888, M.S., 1895, M.E., 1900; m. Alice E. Oney, June 21, 1897; children—John Elliott (dec.), Juliet Alice, Elinor Mary. With Thomson-Houston Electric Co., Lynn, Mass., 1888-90, Dodge Coal Storage Co., Nicetown, Pa., 1890-91, Worthington Hydraulic Co., Brooklyn, N.Y., 1891-94; instr. in drawing, Rose Poly. Inst., 1894-96, asso. prof. machine design, 1896-1904, prof., 1904—, acting president, 1928-30. Conglist. Author: Construction of Graphical Charts, 1910. Home: Terre Haute, Ind. Died Apr. 6, 1933.

PEDEN, Edward Andrew, merchant; b. Calhoun Co., Ga., Mar. 5, 1868; s. David Dantzler and Fannie (Dickey) P.; ed. Sam Baily Inst., Griffin, Ga.; m. Ione Allen, 1894 (died 1902); children—Allen V., Edward D., Ione H.; m. 2d, Cora Root, 1904; 1 dau., Stella A. Began in office of Inman & Co., cotton dealers, Houston, 1883; entered hardware and mill supply business, 1890; founder, 1902, and pres. Peden Iron & Steel Co., now chmn. bd. of successor, Peden Co., also chmn. bd. Deepwater Refineries, Houston Lighting & Power Co.; pres. Ship Channel Land Co., Goose Creek Oil Co.; treas. and dir. Ashbel Smith Land Co.; dir. First Nat. Bank, etc. Trustee William M. Rice Inst., Glenwood Cemetery Assn. Federal food adminstr. of Tex., World War; at request of Herbert Hoover went to Paris and organized European Child Relief Bur. of Am. Relief Assn.; chmn. com. that raised $800,000 for Home of Y.W.C.A. in Houston, 1919. Democrat. Presbyn. Awarded Houston Rotary Club gold medal as citizen who had performed greatest disinterested service to fellow citizens, 1923. Home: Houston, Tex. Deceased.

PEDRINI, Armando, banker; b. Bologna, Italy, Nov. 30, 1870; s. Innocenzo and Assunta (Righi) P.; grad. Royal Tech. Inst., Bologna, 1890; m. Inez Siccardi, June 15, 1912. Came to U.S., 1901, naturalized citizen, 1910. A founder Bank of Italy, San Francisco, 1904; past exec. v.p., dir. and mem. exec. and advisory coms. Bank of America, Nat. Trust & Savings Assn.; past pres. National Bankitaly Co., Bankitaly Co. America, Corp. of America; past v.p., mem. exec. com. and bd. dirs. Transamerica Corp.; retired. Acting consul gen. of Italy at San Francisco Jan.-Apr. 1921 and Jan.-Feb. 1923; pres. of Com. for Endowment of Chair of Italian Culture, U. of Calif.; pres. com. First Italian Book Exhbn., San Francisco; v.p. San Francisco br. Italy-America Soc. Decorated Grand Officer Crown of Italy, 1929; gold medal for service to Italian culture. Republican. Catholic. Home: San Francisco, Calif. Died Jan. 20, 1940.

PEEBLES, Alvin Roy, physician; b. Battle Creek, Mich., Aug. 9, 1884; s. Alvin Russell and Lillian S. (Skinner) P.; Grand Rapids (Mich.) High Sch.; M.D., U. of Mich., 1906; m. Elizabeth Barrett, Apr. 28, 1910. First asst. in medicine, U. of Mich., 1907; instr. medicine, 1908-09, asst. prof., 1909-10, prof. theory and practice of medicine, 1910-12, prof. preventive and exptl. medicine, 1912—, U. of Colo. Dir. Henry S. Denison Research Lab. in Medicine and Allied Science of U. of Colorado. Home: Boulder, Colo. Died Oct. 22, 1917.

PEEBLES, James Martin, physician; b. Whitingham, Vt., Mar. 23, 1822; s. James and Nancy (Brown) P.; grad. Oxford Acad., N.Y., 1841; M.D., Pa. U. of Medicine and Surgery (M.A., Phila. U.; med. diplomas Univ. Hosp. Phila., and Phila. Polyclinic); m. Mary M. Conkey. Pres. Calif. Coll. of Science, 4 yrs.; prof. Eclectic Med. Coll., Cincinnati, O., 3 yrs.; was the owner and editor several newspapers. Mem. Indian Peace Commn., 1868; U.S. consul Trebizonde, Turkey, 1869; represented U.S. Arbitration League at Internat. Peace Commn. of Europe, Paris. Fellow Anthrop. Soc., and Psychol. Assn., London, Acad. Arts and Sciences, Naples; pres. Psychic Research Soc., Calcutta, India; etc. Spiritualist: Theosophist; world's missionary-at-large for N.S.A. Author: Five Journeys Around the World, 1907; Buddhism and Christianity Face to Face, 1909; Spirit Mates—Marriage and Divorce, 1909. Pres.-founder Peebles Coll. of Science and Philosophy, 1914. Founder Calif. Centenarian Clubs, 1915; pres. Calif. Humanitarian League. Home: Los Angeles, Calif. Died Feb. 15, 1922.

PEEBLES, Mary Louise ("Lynde Palmer"), author; b. (Parmlee) Lansingburgh (a part of Troy), N.Y.; m. A. A. Peebles. Author: The Little Captain, 1861; Helps Over Hard Places, 1862; The Good Fight, 1866; The Honorable Club, 1867; Drifting and Steering, 1867; One Day's Weaving, 1868; Archie's Shadow, 1868; John-Jack, 1869; Jeannette's Cisterns, 1881; Twinkle and Wrinkle, 1889; Two Blizzards, 1889; A Question of Honor, 1893; Where Honor Leads, 1894. Home: Troy, N.Y. Died Apr. 25, 1915.

PEEK, Frank William, Jr., electrical engr.; b. Mokelumne Hill, Calif., Aug. 20, 1881; s. Frank W. and May (Stedman) P.; A.B., Stanford, 1905; M.E.E., Union U., Schenectady, N.Y., 1911; m. Merle Bell, Aug. 9, 1913. With Gen. Electric Co., 1905, cons. and research engr., 1910—; engr. in charge gen. transformer engring. dept., 1927-31, chief engr. Gen. Electric Co., Pittsfield, 1931—. Specialized in development laws of corona, research in high voltage phenomena, in lightning, high voltage transmission, measurements of natural lightning and production of 5,000,000 volts artificial lightning. Rep. of Am. Inst. E.E. on Nat. Research Council. Fellow Am. Inst. E.E. (dir.), Am. Physical Soc., Franklin Inst. Awarded Thomas Fitch Rowland prize, Am. Soc. C.E., 1924; Levy medal, Franklin Inst., 1926. Episcopalian. Author: Dielectric Phenomena in High Voltage Engineering, 1915, 29 (in French, 1924). Home: Pittsfield, Mass. Died July 26, 1933.

PEEKE, George Hewson, clergyman; b. Rotterdam, N.Y., Mar. 18, 1833; s. Christopher Yates and Hester (Mabie) P.; A.B., Rutgers, 1857; grad. Ref. Dutch Theol. Sem., 1860; m. Margaret Bloodgood Peck, author, May 17, 1860 (died 1908). Ordained Presbyn. ministry, 1860; pastor South Bend, Ind., 1860-61, Brooklyn, N.Y., 1863-65, Jersey City, N.J., 1865-70, Davenport, Ia., 1870-73, Owasco, Ia., 1873-76, Chicago, 1876-82, Sandusky, O., 1883-90, Cleveland, 1890-94; preacher-at-large, 1898—. Prohibitionist. Author: The Spiritual Body in Relation to the Divine Law of Life, 1912. Home: Sandusky, O. Died Dec. 26, 1915.

PEEKE, Margaret Bloodgood, writer, teacher; b. Mechanicsville, N.Y., Apr. 8, 1838; d. Garry Marshall and Narcissa (Benedict) Peck; ed. pub. and pvt. schs.; m. Rev. George H. Peeke, May 16, 1860. Taught pub. sch., New York, 1853-54, her own pvt. sch., Irvington, N.J., 1855-59; removed to Chicago, 1876; on staff of and part owner, the Alliance, till 1882; wrote prize story books; taught Hermetic philosophy in New York, Chicago, Boston, Washington, etc., 1893-98. Visited Hermetic socs. abroad, 1898-99; has assembly of followers in Sandusky, O. Insp. gen. in America of Martinist Order of France; mem. Behaists of Persia; mem. Rose-Cross Martinist Fraternity, Treasurer of Light of France, Hermetic Soc. of France. Author: Born of Flame, 1892; Zenia the Vestal, 1893. Home: Sandusky, O. Died 1908.

PEEL, William Lawson, banker; b. Webster Co., Ga., Nov. 29, 1849; s. James Gamble and Elizabeth (Stapleton) P.; ed. pub. sch. and business Coll.; m. Lucy Marion Cook, Apr. 22, 1874 (dec.); children—Mrs. Lucy Kiser, Mrs. Sarah Watts, Mrs. Marion Calhoun, William Lawson (dec.). Began in banking business at Americus, Ga., 1871; cashier State of Ga. Bank, Atlanta, 1876-80; organized 1880, Maddox-Rucker Banking Co., changed, 1908, to Am. Nat. Bank, of which was cashier, v.p. and pres.; retired, 1916, when bank merged into Atlanta Nat. Bank, of which is director. Mem. staff of 3 govs. of Ga., title of col. Trustee Ga. Mil. Acad., Young L. G. Harris Coll. Democrat. Methodist. Mason. Home: Atlanta, Ga. Died Feb. 2, 1927.

PEELE, Stanton Judkins, judge; b. Wayne Co., Ind., Feb. 11, 1843; s. John Cox and Ruth (Smith) P.; ed. pub. schs., and sem. in Ind.; LL.D., Valparaiso and Howard univs.; corporal, later 2d lt. Ind. Vols., in Civil War; m. Lou R. Perkins, July 16, 1866 (died 1873); m. 2d, Arabella, d. Judge Milton C. Canfield, Oct. 16, 1878 (died 1915); m. 3d, Bertha (Barnitz) Byrne, d. Col. Albert Barnitz, U.S.A., Apr. 16, 1918. Admitted to bar, 1866; practiced at Winchester, Ind., 1866-68, Indianapolis, 1869-92. Mem. Indiana House of Representatives, 1877-79; mem. 47th Congress (1881-83); judge 1892-1905; chief justice, 1906-13, U.S. Court of Claims; retired. Mem. bd. of control, Ind. Reform Sch. for Boys, 1891-92; prof. law of partnership and bailment, George Washington U., 1901-11. Pres. trustees Washington Coll. of Law, Presbyterian Home for the Aged, and Garfield Hospital, 1910-24; pres. West Nottingham (Synodical) Academy, Cecil Co., Md., 1914-25; pres. Sch. Bd., Montgomery Co., Md., 1914-18; pres. Chevy Chase com. governing village, 1914-18; advisory mem. bd. of mgr. Y.M.C.A., Washington; vice-moderator Washington Presbytery, 1916. Vice moderator Synod of Baltimore, 1920-21. Home: Washington, D.C. Died Sept. 4, 1928.

PEERY, David Henry, mining broker; b. Salt Lake City, Apr. 13, 1866; s. David Harold and Elizabeth (Higginbotham) P.; ed. pub. schs. and Univ. of Utah; unmarried. Engaged in mining in Utah. Clerk U.S. Dist. Court, Ty. of Utah, 1893-95; mem. gov's. staff, 1894; State senator, Utah, 1898-1900; Utah mem. Dem. Nat. Com., 1904—. Mason, Elk. Home: Salt Lake City, Utah. Died 1907.

PEERY, Rufus Benton, educator, clergyman; b. Burkes Garden, Va., Apr. 9, 1868; s. Thomas and Sarah Henrietta (Repass) P.; A.B., Roanoke Coll., Salem, Va., 1890, A.M., 1895; Theol. Sem., Gettysburg, Pa., 1890-92; Ph.D., Pa. Coll., 1895; U. of Chicago, 1898-1901; U. of Denver, 1906-07; D.D., Midland Coll., Kan., 1909; m. A. Letitia Rich, Aug. 21, 1895; children—Harold Rich, Thomas Benton, Rob Roy, Paul Denver, William Wallace, Donald Lee. Ordained English Luth. ministry, 1892; missionary and prof. theology in Japan, 1892-1903; lecturer on Oriental and missionary subjects, 1903-05; pastor St. Paul's Luth. Ch., Denver, 1905-12; pres. Midland Coll., Atchison, Kan., 1912-19; prof. philosophy, Lenoir Coll., Hickory, N.C., 1920-24; pastor Zion Luth. Ch., Wooster, O., 1924-31, Trinity Lutheran Ch., Raleigh, N.C., 1931—. Author: The Gist of Japan, 1897 (8 edits.); Lutherans in Japan, 1900; Lectures to Young Men (Japanese), 1902. Home: Raleigh, N.C. Died Oct. 25, 1934.

PEET, Louis Harman, author; b. Brooklyn, Aug. 16, 1863; s. John Henry and Caroline (Northrup) P.; grad. Poly. Inst., Brooklyn, 1882, Yale, 1887; m. Nellie Marvin Perkins, Oct. 14, 1897. Was 3 yrs. on staff New York Times; from 1892 connected with American Book Co. Author: Who's the Author?, a Guide to American Literature, 1901; Trees and Shrubs of Prospect Park, 1903; Trees and Shrubs of Central Park, 1905. Home: Brooklyn, N.Y. Died 1905.

PEET, William, mfr.; b. Chattries, Eng., Mar. 25, 1847; s. Robert and Sarah Jane (Stafford) P.; ed. pub. schs., Eng.; came to America, 1862; m. Nettie Zooter, Aug. 18, 1870. Located in Kansas City, Mo., 1872, and associated with 2 brothers, Robert and Jesse, in soap mfg. business, as Peet Bros.; name changed to Peet Bros. & Co., 1873, and in 1898 to Peet Bros. Mfg. Co., of which is pres.; v.p. Union Oil Co., Kansas City Cotton Mills Co. Republican. Christian Scientist. Mason. Home: Kansas City, Kan. Died Mar. 4, 1934.

PEFFER, Harry Creighton, chemistry; b. Enon Valley, Pa., Aug. 15, 1873; s. Christian Gottloeb Luther and Fannie Jane (Creighton) P.; B.S., Pa. State Coll., 1895, M.S., 1908; m. Mary Carolyne Rebhun, Dec. 29, 1897; children—Ella Louise, Jane Creighton (Mrs. Charles Wheeler Shook), Harry Creighton, David McNair. Chemist, Carnegie Steel Co., Homestead, Pa., 1895; control chemist Pa. Salt Mfg. Co., 1896-1900; supt. expt. plant and lab. dir. Pittsburgh Reduction Co., 1900-03; gen. supt. and dir. research, Aluminum Co. of America, E. St. Louis, Ill., 1903-08; consultant same at Pittsburgh, 1908-13; dir. Sch. of Chem. Engring., Purdue, 1911—; mem. bd. management Purdue Engring. Expt. Sta.; v.p. Rostone, Inc. Orgn. mgr. U.S. Explosives Plant C, World War. Mem. Ind. Gas Standards Commn., 1917-18. Republican. Episcopalian. Mason. Kiwanian. Holder patents on chem. and industrial processes, bldg. materials, mech. devices, welding. Home: West Lafayette, Ind. Died July 17, 1934.

PEFFER, William Alfred, senator; b. Cumberland Co., Pa., Sept. 10, 1831; s. John and Elizabeth (Souder) P.; m. Sarah Jane Barber, Dec. 28, 1852. Began teaching at 15, working on his father's farm summers; removed to Ind., 1853, to Mo., 1859, thence to Illinois; engaged in farming. Enlisted as pvt. 83d Ill. Inf., 1862, mustered out, June 1865—rank of lt.; acted as adj. and judge-advocate and q.m. Began law practice, Clarksville, Tenn., Aug. 1865; removed to Kan.; established Fredonia Journal, and Coffeyville Journal; mem. Kan. Senate, 1874; Rep. presdl. elector, 1880; editor Kansas Farmer, 1881; U.S. senator, 1891-97, elected by People's Party; Prohibition candidate for gov., 1898. Now engaged in lit. work. Author: Peffer's Tariff Manual, 1888; The Way Out: The Farmer's Side, 1891; Americanism and the Philippines, 1900; Rise and Fall of Populism in the United States, 1900. Home: Topeka, Kan. Died Oct. 7, 1912.

PEGRAM, George Herndon, civil engr.; b. Council Bluffs, Ia., Dec. 29, 1855; s. Capt. Benjamin Rush and Mercy Adelaide (Robbins) P.; C.E., Washington U., 1877, M.A., 1905, LL.D. from the same university in 1928; m. Jessie Mirrielees Crawford, Sept. 8, 1897; children—Jean Forsyth, Mercy Robbins, Geo. H. (dec.). Engr. on construction Utah & Northern Ry. of Ida., 1877-78; prin. asst. to C. Shaler Smith, bridge engr., 1878-80; chief engr. Edge Moor Iron Co., Wilmington, Del., 1880-86; cons. engr., New York, 1886-89; cons. engr., Mo.P. R.R., 1889-93; chief engr. U.P. System, 1893-98; was also cons. engr. Pioneer Electric Power Co. during constrn. of its plants at Ogden and Salt Lake City; chief engr. Manhattan Elevated R.R., 1898-1905, Interborough Rapid Transit Co., 1905—, also Rapid Transit Subway Constrn. Co., 1905—, and New York Rys. Co., 1912—. Was designer Kansas City Elevated R.R. and St. Louis Union Sta.; invented and patented Pegram truss for bridges, 1889; designed and built combined highway and ry. bridge across Arkansas River at Ft. Smith, Ark., 1890. Home: South Orange, N.J. Died Dec. 23, 1937.

PEGRAM, John Combe, lawyer; b. Owensborough, Ky., Aug. 26, 1842; s. William B. and Charlotte Amelie (Combe) P.; grad. U.S. Naval Acad., 1863; m. Isabel Homer, Nov. 3, 1864 (died 1892). Served with S. Atlantic Blockading Fleet off Charleston on various vessels and on staff comdr.-in-chief; resigned from navy, 1866; grad. Harvard Law Sch., 1868; admitted to R.I. bar, 1868; sr. mem. Pegram & Cooke, 1885—; mem. R.I. Ho. of Reps., 1869-70; mem. Providence City Council, 1873-75; U.S. register in bankruptcy, 1875-89; acting judge Municipal Ct.,

Providence, 1889 and 1901, master in chancery, 1900—. Trustee R.I. Hosp., R.I. State Sanatorium. Pres. R.I. br. Am. Red Cross. Home: Providence, R.I. Died 1909.

PEIRCE, Arthur Winslow, educator; b. Arlington, Mass., June 3, 1860; s. John Winslow and Anna Lydia (Pierce) P.; A.B., Tufts Coll., 1882, hon. Litt.D., 1899; m. Lydia Paine Ray, June 25, 1903. Teacher, 1882-1891, head master, 1891-97, Goddard Sem., Barre, Vt.; head master, Dean Acad., Franklin, Mass., 1897—. Trustee Tufts Coll. Pres. Franklin Library Assn.; pres. Fletcher Hosp.; mem. of council N.E. Hist.-Geneal. Soc., N.E. Assn. of Colls. and Prep. Schs., Head Masters' Assn. Author: History of Franklin (Mass.) Library, 1907. Home: Franklin, Mass. Died Dec. 20, 1934.

PEIRCE, Benjamin Osgood, physicist; b. Beverly, Mass., Feb. 11, 1854; s. Benjamin Osgood and M. (Seccomb) P.; A.B., Harvard, 1876; Ph.D., U. of Leipzig, 1879; student Berlin, 1879-80; m. Isabella Turnbull Landreth, July 27, 1882. Taught in Boston Latin Sch., 1880-81; instr. mathematics, 1881-84, asst. prof. mathematics and physics, 1884-88, Hollis prof. mathematics and natural philosophy, 1888—, Harvard. Fellow Am. Acad. Arts and Sciences, Am. Philos. Soc., A.A.A.S., etc. Author: Theory of the Newtonian Potential Function; Table of Integrals, Boston, 1899; Experiments in Magnetism. Home: Cambridge, Mass. Died Jan. 14, 1914.

PEIRCE, Charles Santiago Sanders, logician; b. Cambridge, Mass., Sept. 10, 1839; s. Prof. Benjamin P. (leading mathematician of his time); mother was d. U.S. Senator Mills, of Mass.; brother of Herbert Henry Davis P.; A.B., Harvard, 1859, Sc.B. (chemistry, summa cum laude), 1863; m. (Harriett) Melusina Fay, 1862; m. 2d, Juliette Froissy. Has always been devoted to the theory and art of reasoning; researches in branches of mathematics, hist. criticism, psychology, etc.; first formulated the philos. principle which he named "Pragmatism"; retired to Pike Co., Pa., 1887, to devote himself completely to logic. Lecturer Harvard U., 1903; Lowell Inst., winter of 1903-04. Fellow Am. Acad. Arts and Sciences. Author: Photometric Researches, 1878. Edited (with extensive additions): Studies in Logic, by mems. of Johns Hopkins U., 1883; "Linear Associative Algebra," by Benjamin Peirce, 1882. Home: Milford, Pa. Died Apr. 19, 1914.

PEIRCE, Cyrus Newlin, dentist; b. Philadelphia, Mar. 5, 1829; s. Cyrus and Ruth S. P.; grad. Phila. Coll. of Dental Surgery, 1855; m. Charlotte L. Lundy. Practiced dentistry 54 yrs. Was prof. dentistry 45 yrs. and 30 yrs. dean Pa. Coll. Dental Surgery; sec. Woman's Med. Coll. of Pa. 40 yrs. Retired. Home: Philadelphia, Pa. Died 1909.

PEIRCE, Harold, insurance; b. Bristol, Pa., Sept. 28, 1856; s. Charles W. and Mary (Vanuxem) P.; B.S., U. of Pa., 1876; m. Charlotte Converse, June 21, 1882; children—George (dec.), Edmund Converse, Margaret, Mary, Elizabeth (Mrs. Stanley A. Hunter). In mfg. business, 1875-86; gen. agt., New York Life Ins. Co., 1886—. Was sec. Commn. for Investigation and Control of Chestnut Tree Blight Disease in Pennsylvania. Home: Haverford, Pa. Died Apr. 12, 1932.

PEIRCE, Herbert Henry Davis, diplomat; b. Cambridge, Mass., Apr. 11, 1849; s. Prof. Benjamin P. (the leading mathematician of his time); mother was d. U.S. Senator Mills, of Mass.; bro. of Charles Santiago Sanders P.; ed. Cambridge, Mass., and Exeter, N.H., and Harvard class of 1871; studied geology Royal Sch. of Mines, London; m. Helen N. Jose. Apptd. sec. U.S. Legation at St. Petersburg, Russia, May 1894; attended coronation of Nicholas II, May 1896; apptd. 1st sec. of Embassy, 1898-1901; served 10 times as U.S. chargé d'affaires; apptd., Nov. 15, 1901, 3d asst. sec. of State, in which capacity had charge, under orders from the President, of the reception of the plenipotentiaries of Russia and Japan and of the arrangements for their deliberation during their negotations for peace, held at Portsmouth, N.H., 1905, receiving from them, Aug. 20 of that year, for communication to the President, the first announcement of peace; apptd. spl. counsel for the claimants and counsel for the U.S. Govt. in arbitration cases between the U.S. and Russia, which was decided in favor of the U.S. by Mr. T. M. C. Asser, the Dutch arbitrator, Nov. 29, 1902; E.E. and M.P. to Norway, June 22, 1906-May 31, 1911, when retired from diplomatic service. Counsel for U.S. in Am. and British Claims Arbitration, 1912—. Assigned to Am. Embassy as spl. agt. to assist the Am. ambassador, with rank of minister plenipotentiary, Feb. 1915. Commandeur, Légion d'Honneur of France, May 16, 1902; Order of the Double Dragon, China, 1903; Grand Cross of St. Olaf, Norway, May 31, 1911. Home: Petrograd, Russia. Died Dec. 5, 1916.

PEIRCE, James Mills, prof. mathematics, Harvard, 1869—; b. Cambridge, Mass., May 1, 1834; grad. Harvard, 1853 (A.M.). Tutor there, 1854-58 and 1860-61; asst. prof. mathematics, 1861-69, univ. prof., 1869-85, Perkins professor, 1885—, sec. academic council, 1872-90, dean of grad. school, 1890-95, dean of faculty of arts and sciences, 1895-98; unmarried. Author: Text-Book of Analytic Geometry, 1857; Three and Four-Place Tables, 1871; Elements of Logarithms, 1874; Mathematical Tables Chiefly to Four Figures, 1879. Home: Cambridge, Mass. Died 1906.

PEIRCE, Silas, merchant; b. Boston, Mass., Aug. 16, 1860; s. Silas and Almira (Hall) P.; grad. English High School, Boston, 1878; m. Annie Kendig, Apr. 7, 1885. Entered, 1878, wholesale grocery business of Silas Peirce & Co., Boston (established, 1815, by great-uncle, Silas Peirce), now pres. Silas Peirce & Co., Ltd.; asst. treas. Old Corner Book Store. Pres. Boston Wesleyan Assn.; trustee, treas. Boston U.; dir. Boston North End Mission, Boston Y.M.C.A.; mem. book com. M.E. Ch.; active in philanthropic lines. Republican. Home: Egypt (Scituate), Mass. Died Dec. 10, 1922.

PEIRCE, William S., army officer; b. Burlington, Vt., May 16, 1864; s. Albert Gallatin and Delia Juliet (Benjamin) P.; student U. of Vt., 1881-84 (hon. A.M., 1908); grad. U.S. Mil. Acad., 1888; m. Harriet Roberts, Apr. 19, 1911. Additional lt., 1st Arty., June 11, 1888; 2d lt. 2d Arty., Sept. 3, 1888; 1st lt. Ordnance Dept., Jan. 15, 1892; capt., July 7, 1898; maj., June 25, 1906; lt. col., Feb. 12, 1910; colonel, Apr. 6, 1915; brig. gen., Feb. 18, 1918. Served as assistant officer, Watervliet Arsenal, Sandy Hook Proving Ground, Rock Island Arsenal and Springfield Armory; as inspector of ordnance Midvale and Bethlehem Steel companies; as asst. in Office of Chief of Ordnance; comdr. Springfield Armory; served overseas and as asst. chief of ordnance, Washington, 1917—. Specialist in matters pertaining to mfr. of small arms. Episcopalian. Died July 10, 1923.

PEIRSON, Alden, artist; b. Baltimore, Oct. 19, 1873; s. Thomas G. and Mary E. (Russell) P.; ed. Md. Inst. Sch. of Art and Design, Baltimore; Charcoal Club, Baltimore; Art Students' League, New York; m. Katharine Gasaway, Dec. 28, 1898. Began in Baltimore, 1894; art mgr. American Magazine, Jan. 1912—; art mgr. Caxton Advertising, Inc. Home: New York, N.Y. Deceased.

PEIXOTTO, Ernest Clifford, artist, writer; b. San Francisco, Oct. 15, 1869; s. Raphael and Myrtilla J. (Davis) P.; ed. San Francisco; art at Acad. Julian, Paris, under Benjamin-Constant and Jules Lefebvre; m. Mary G. Hutchinson, Jan. 28, 1897. Exhibited Paris Salons many times and in leading Am. exhbns.; hon. mention at Salon for picture, "A Woman of Rijsoord," also awards at other exhibitions; has illustrated for Scribner's Magazine, besides many books, including Theodore Roosevelt's "Life of Cromwell" and Henry Cabot Lodge's "Story of the Revolution." Lived many years in Europe, writing and illustrating papers for Scribner's and other leading Am. periodicals. Painted large murals "Le Morte d'Arthur" for library, Cleveland, 1911, and since in many rooms in Paris, New York and Calif.; murals in Seamen's Bank for Savings, New York, 1927, Bank of New York, also Embassy Club of New York, 1928. Went to France, Mar. 1918, as official artist attached to A.E.F., with rank of captain, following entire American campaign (drawings now in New National Museum, Washington); dir. painting studios, A.E.F. Art Training Center, Bellevue, France, 1919; dir. dept. of mural painting, Beaux-Arts Inst. of Design, New York, 1919-26; consultant on murals N.Y. World's Fair, 1939; chmn. Am. com. Fontainebleau Sch. Fine Arts. A.N.A., 1909. Decorated Chevalier Legion of Honor, 1921, Officier, 1924. Pres. School Art League, 1936. Mem. National Society Mural Painters (pres.), Architectural League (vice-pres.); painter mem. Art Commn. of City of New York; corr. mem. Hispanic Soc. America (rep. in permanent collection by three paintings and many drawings); hon. mem. of Am. Institute of Architects. Author: By Italian Seas, 1906; Through the French Provinces, 1910; Romantic California, 1911; Pacific Shores from Panama, 1913; Our Hispanic Southwest, 1916; A Revolutionary Pilgrimage, 1917; The American Front, 1919; Through Spain and Portugal, 1922; A Bacchic Pilgrimage, 1932. Died Dec. 6, 1940.

PEIXOTTO, Jessica Blanche, univ. prof.; b. New York, Oct. 9, 1864; d. Raphael and Myrtilla J. (Davis) P.; Ph.B., U. of California, 1894, Ph.D. from same school, 1900; student at Sorbonne, Paris, 1896-97. Prof. social economics, U. of Calif., 1905-35, prof. emeritus. Mem. State Board of Charities and Corrections, 1912-23. Author: The French Revolution and Modern French Socialism, 1901; Getting and Spending at the Professional Standard of Living, 1927. Chief child conservation sect., Council of Nat. Defense, 1917-18. Home: Berkeley, Calif. Died Oct. 19, 1941.

PEIXOTTO, Sidney Salzado, social worker; b. N.Y. City, May 9, 1866; s. Raphael and Myrtilla Jessica P.; self-ed.; m. Phyllis Frankel, of Brisbane, Australia, May 19, 1921. Commd. maj. N.G. of Calif., 1903; founder, 1895, and pres. Columbia Park Boys' Club of San Francisco; founder, 1908, and pres. Pub. Schs. Athletic League of San Francisco; pres., 1907-09 inclusive, of Pacific Athletic Assn. of Amateur Athletic Union U.S.A.; mem. 1st Playground Commn., San Francisco, 1908; founder, 1921, City Boys Baseball League (dir.). Originator of walking vacation trips for boys; has led parties of 50 or more up and down Calif. Coast, 1895—; originator self-supporting travel tours for parties of boys; led party of 43 through Australia, 1909-10; party of 42, San Francisco to New York and return, 1910-11; party of 47 San Francisco around the world, 1913-14; party of 43, San Francisco to Portland, Me., and return, 1916-17; party of 42, San Francisco to the Far East and Australia, 1919-20. Hebrew. Awarded 30 yrs.' service medal by Federated Boys' Clubs of America, 1920. Home: San Francisco, Calif. Died Aug. 9, 1925.

PELHAM, John, judge; b. Alexandria, Ala., Aug. 23, 1865; s. Charles and Louise Margaret (Johnston) P.; Washington (D.C.) High Sch.; LL.B., Law Dept., Columbian (now George Washington) U., 1887, LL.M., 1888; m. Ellen Miles, Oct. 10, 1895. Began practice at Anniston, Ala., 1888; city atty., 1893-94; judge 7th Jud. Circuit of Ala., 1899-1911; asso. judge Ct. of Appeals of Ala., Mar. 11, 1911—, and presiding judge, Oct. 1, 1914—. Democrat. Home: Anniston, Ala. Died Mar. 5, 1917.

PELL, Ella Ferris, artist; b. St. Louis, Jan. 18, 1846; art edn. in New York, under Prof. William Rimmer, of Boston, and in Paris under Jean Paul Laurens, Ferdinand Hombert and Gaston Saint Pierre. Is painter, sculptor, illustrator; exhibited Paris Salon, 1889-90; illustrated "Through the Invisible," by Paul Tyner. Her principal works are a statue of "Andromeda" (heroic size); a large painting, "The Fall of Adam"; "Salome," now owned by the Boston Art Club. V.p. Ladies Art Assn., N.Y., 1895; pres. Liberal Art League, New York, 1896. Home: Beacon, N.Y. Died Nov. 5, 1922.

PELL, George Pierce, lawyer, author; b. Raleigh, N.C., June 19, 1870; s. Rev. William E. and Virginia C. (Ramsay) P.; ed. Trinity Coll. (now Duke U.), N.C., and Columbian (now George Washington) U.; LL.B., Georgetown U.; m. Mary V. DeShazo, May 25, 1892; children—Mrs. Mary Lea, William E., Josephus D. Editor of Twin City Sentinel, Winston-Salem, N.C., 1890, Mt. Airy (N.C.) News, 1891-93; reading clk. State Senate, sessions of 1889, 91, 93; proofreader and asst. librarian of Pub. Documents, Govt. Printing Office, Washington, 1894-97; admitted to bar, 1897; judge of Superior Court of N.C., 1910-11; corp. commr. of N.C., 1913-34; dean Raleigh Law School, 1914—. Democrat. Member M.E. Church, S. Author: Pell's Revisal of North Carolina, 1908; Pell's Banking and Negotiable Instrument Law, 1910; Pell's Forms of Pleading and Practice, 1912; Pell's Monographs on the Law, 1918. Died May 11, 1938.

PELL, Robert Paine, coll. pres.; b. Washington, N.C., June 12, 1860; s. Rev. William E. and Virginia C. (Ramsay) P.; A.B., University of N.C., 1881, Litt.D., 1904; LL.D., Austin College, 1924, University of S.C., 1928; m. Anness Huske Shepherd, 1889; children—Jesse Shepherd, William Edward. Instr. English, U. of N.C., 1881-83, U. Summer Normal Sch., 1881-82; student Union Theol. Sem., Hampden-Sidney, Va.; evangelist Presbyterian Synod of N.C., 1887-95; pastor Presbyn. Ch., Newberry, S.C., 1895-96; pres. Presbyterian Coll. for Women, Columbia, S.C., 1896-1902, Converse Coll., 1902-33, emeritus. Orlando, Fla. Died Feb. 7, 1941.

PELLEW, Henry Edward; b. Canterbury, England, April 26, 1828; s. Honorable and Rev. George (D.D., dean of Norwich) and Frances Addington (d. Viscount Sidmouth) P.; M.A., Trinity College, Cambridge, 1853; M.A., Oxford, 1870; m. Eliza, d. Judge William Jay, 1858 (died 1868); 2d, Augusta Jay (sister of 1st wife), 1873; father of Charles Ernest P. Was one of the founders of Keble Coll., Oxford, and mem. council; J.P. for Middlesex; was on exec. bds. Hanwell Lunatic Asylum, Feltham Industrial Sch., Westminster Bridewell and others and identified with various London hosps. and charities. Came to U.S., 1873; organized Bur. of Charities in New York in association with Theodore Roosevelt, Sr. A. S. Hewitt and others; active in organizing night refuges, free circulating library, coffee houses, the first tenement house reform movement and the erection of improved dwellings. Commr. of pub. schs.; pres. Soc. for Improving Condition of Poor, Sanitary Reform, St. George's and other socs. Has resided in Washington, D.C., 1888—, where he is interested in work among the Negroes, in the formation of the Washington P.E. Diocese and in aiding the building of the Washington Cathedral. Homes: Washington, D.C., and Sharon, Conn. Died Feb. 4, 1923.

PELOUBET, Francis Nathan, author; b. N.Y. City, Dec. 2, 1831; s. Chabrier and Harriet (Hanks) P.; A.B., Williams, 1853; grad. Bangor (Me.) Theol. Sem., 1857; (D.D., Univ. of Tenn., 1884, Williams College, 1913); m. Mary A. Thaxter, Apr. 28, 1859. Ordained Congl. ministry, 1857; pastor Lanesville, 1857-60, Oakham, 1861-66, Attleboro, 1867-71, Natick, 1872-83—all in Mass.; author S.S. publications, 1874—. Mem. Religious Edn. Assn. Author: Select Notes on the International Sunday School Lessons, 44 annual vols., 1875-1920 (more than 2,000,000 have been sold); three grades of Sunday School

Quarterlies for the Scholars, 1880-1919; Suggestive Illustrations on Matthew, John and Acts (3 vols.), 1898-99; Loom of Life, 1900; The Teacher's Commentary on Matthew and on Acts, 1901; Front Line of the Sunday School Movement, 1904; Studies in the Book of Job, 1906. Edited Select Songs for the Sunday School, Nos. 1, 1884, and 2, 1893; Revision of the Oxford University Bible Helps, the Cyclopedic Concordance, 1903; a second revised edition of Smith's Bible Dictionary, the International Bible Dictionary, 1912; Treasury of Biblical Information, 1913; Oriental Light, 1914, for Holman's Bible Helps. Home: Auburndale, Mass. Died Mar. 27, 1920.

PELTER, Fred Paul, ry. official; b. Augusta Springs, Va., Aug. 1, 1875; s. George W. and Effie G. (Brown) P.; ed. pub. schs., Covington, Va., and Richmond, Ky.; m. Eliza Manning, Mar. 25, 1903; children—Fred P., Edwin M. Began in ry. service, 1889, as messenger L.&N. R.R., at Richmond, Ky.; telegraph operator same rd. and in maintenance of way dept. A.,T.&S.F. Ry., and various positions Elgin, Joliet & Eastern Ry., 1890-1902; agt. Southern Ry. at Birmingham, Ala., 1902-06, and with same road as trainmaster, 1906, asst. supt., 1907, supt. Nashville, Chattanooga, Appalachia, Asheville and Memphis divs., until 1918; gen. supt. Southeastern dist. same rd., 1918-20, Southwestern dist., 1920-21; gen. mgr. Norfolk Southern R.R., 1921-25, v.p. and gen. mgr., 1925—; dir. Goldsboro Union Station Co. Methodist. Mason. Home: Norfolk, Va. Died Feb. 1928.

PELZ, Paul Johannes, architect; b. Seitendorf, County of Waldenburg, Silesia, Germany, Nov. 18, 1841; s. Eduard L. and Henriette (Helfensrieder) P.; ed. Coll. St. Elizabeth, and Coll. of the Holy Spirit, Breslau; did not graduate, but left at 16 to join father, who settled in U.S., 1851; studied architecture, 1859-66, in New York under Detlef Lienau; m. Mary Eastbourne, d. Horatio Gates Ritter, Feb. 23, 1895. In practice as architect; was connected with U.S. Lighthouse Bd. as architect and civ. engr.; and designed many light houses. Architect of Congressional Library Bldg.; Georgetown Coll. Academic Bldg.; Carnegie Library, and Music Hall Bldg., Allegheny, Pa.; U.S. Govt. Army and Navy Hosp., Hot Springs, Ark.; Chamberlain Hotel, Old Point Comfort, Va.; Clinic Hosp., U. of Va.; Aula Christi, Chautauqua, N.Y.; Machinery Hall, St. Louis Expn., and many others. Fellow Am. Inst. Architects. Home: Washington, D.C. Died Mar. 30, 1918.

PEMBERTON, Henry, chemist; b. Phila., Feb. 11, 1826; s. John and Rebecca (Clifford) P.; brother of the late Confederate lt. gen., John C. P.; ed. in Phila. and under Daniel Murray, nr. Baltimore; m. Caroline Hollingsworth, 1841; m. 2d, Agnes, d. Hon. Thomas Williams, 1867. For 17 yrs. chief chemist, mng. dir. and v.p. Pa. Salt Mfg. Co. (chemicals); retired from business. In 1865 contracted in Denmark for monopoly of kryolite for N. and S. America. Author: The Path of Evolution Through Ancient Thought and Modern Science, 1903. Address: Philadelphia, Pa. Died 1911.

PEMBERTON, William Young, lawyer; b. Nashville, Tenn., June 1, 1842; s. William and Martha (Brooks) P.; Masonic Coll., Lexington, Mo.; LL.B., Lebanon (Tenn.) Law Sch., 1861; unmarried. Practiced law at Versailles, Mo., 1861-62, at Helena, Mont., 1865—. Dist. atty., 2d Jud. Dist., Mont. Ty., 1883-87; mem. Mont. Constl. Conv., 1884; dist. judge, 2d Jud. Dist., 1891-92; chief justice Supreme Ct. of Mont., 1893-99. Democrat. Librarian, State Hist. and Miscellaneous Library, Helena, 1909-20. Mason. Address: Excelsior Springs, Mo. Died Aug. 26, 1922.

PENCE, Edward Hart, clergyman; b. Columbus, Ind., Apr. 10, 1868; s. David and Nancy (Hart) P.; B.S., Hanover (Ind.) Coll., 1889, M.A., 1889; student McCormick Theol. Sem., 1889-92; D.D., Beloit Coll., 1900; m. Jessie Archer, June 24, 1892; children—David William (dec.), Jessie Norma (wife of Rev. John H. Gardner, D.D.), Edna Louise (Mrs. W. Ernest C. Huthwaite). Ordained ministry Presbyn. Ch., U.S.A., 1892; pastorates in Colo. and Wis., 1892-1900; pastor Fort Street Ch., Detroit, 1900-17, Westminster Ch., Portland, Ore., 1917-27; recalled to Fort Street Ch., 1927. Mem. Exec. Commn. and Bd. of Edn., Presbyn. Ch., U.S.A.; moderator of Presbytery, Detroit and Synod of Mich.; dir. McCormick Theol. Sem. and Presbyn. Theol. Sem. (both of Chicago), San Anselmo Theol. Sem., San Francisco; pres. Tappan Assn., Ann Arbor, Mich.; mem. depositors' com. of 50, First Nat. Bank, Detroit; chmn. com. to investigate Detroit Welfare Bur., 1929. Y.M.C.A. morale and Liberty Loan speaker, Camp Lewis, Ore., World War. Won 2d place, Ind. State oratorical contest, 1889. Democrat. Mason. Home: Grosse Pointe Park, Mich. Deceased.

PENCE, Lafayette, hydraulic mining; b. Columbus, Ind., Dec. 23, 1857; s. David and Nancy (Hart) P.; B.S., Hanover (Ind.) Coll., 1877; m. Clara Vawter, Dec. 18, 1881. Admitted to Ind. bar, 1878; practiced at Winfield, Kan., 1879-81, Rico, Colo., 1881-85; moved to Denver, 1885; mem. Colo. Ho. of Rep., 1883-85; county atty., Arapahoe County, 1887-88; mem. 53d Congress (1893-95), as candidate of Populists and Silver Democrats; introduced the first graduated income tax; later engaged in hydraulic mining. Democrat. Home: Washington, D.C. Died Oct. 22, 1923.

PENCE, Thomas Jones, newspaperman; b. Raleigh, N.C., Mar. 28, 1873; s. Thomas and Anna Elizabeth (Jones) P.; A.B., Wake Forest (N.C.) Coll.; unmarried. Newspaper work, Raleigh, 1894-1901; Washington corr. Raleigh News and Observer, Louisville Times and other papers, 1901-11; also reported U.S. Senate for New York Sun several yrs. In charge Publicity Bur. of Dem. Nat. Com., Chicago, campaign of 1908; dir. and mgr. publicity campaign of Woodrow Wilson in campaign that resulted in his nomination at Baltimore, 1912; asst. to chmn. Dem. Nat. Com., 1912—; dir. permanent hdqrs. Dem. Nat. Com., Mar. 1913—. Home: Washington, D.C. Died Mar. 27, 1916.

PENDEXTER, Hugh, author; b. Pittsfield, Me., Jan. 15, 1875; s. George Jefferson and Clara B. (Watson) P.; grad. Nicholl's Latin Sch., Lewiston, Me., 1896; hon. M.A., Bates Coll., Lewiston, Me., 1933; m. Helen M. Faunce, 1897; children—Hugh, Faunce. On staff Rochester (N.Y.) Post Express, 1900-11; writing, 1911—. Republican. Universalist. Mason. Author: The Scarlet Years; The Fighting Years; The Border Breed; Rifle Rule; Flaming Frontier; White Dawn; The River Frontier; The Dark Road; The Trail of Pontiac; Red Man's Courage; Log Cabin Men; The Blazing West; The Woods Runners; The Long Knives; Go Ahead Davie; The Homesteaders; The Torch Bearers; Devil's Brew; Bust Fighters; Call of the Wilderness. Address: Norway, Me. Died June 11, 1940.

PENDLETON, Charles Rittenhouse, editor, publisher; b. on farm, Effingham County, Ga., June 26, 1850; s. Philip C. (editor The Magnolia) and Catharine (Tebeau) P.; brother of Louis (Beauregard) P.; common sch. edn.; studied classics under pvt. instr.; m. Sallie Patterson Peeples, Nov. 26, 1879. Engaged in journalism as a young man; editor Macon (Ga.) Daily Telegraph, 1896—. Mem. Ga. Ho. of Rep., 1882-83; del. Dem. Nat. Conv., 1896, del.-at-large, 1904 (mem. notification com.); chmn. Ga. delegation, Dem. Nat. Conv., 1912; mem. Bibb County (Ga.) Bd. Edn., 1905—. After 2d defeat of Bryan, made appeal to South to secede from Bryan Democracy of the North and West and run Southern candidates for President on sound money platform. Chmn. State Dem. Exec. Com., 1910. Address: Macon, Ga. Died 1913.

PENDLETON, Edmund, author; b. Cincinnati, 1845; s. Col. Nathaniel Greene and Anne (James) P.; ed. by pvt. tutors; m. Cornelia Marcy; m. 2d, Margaret Rivière Hetzel. Served in Civil War as 2d lt., 4th N.Y. Heavy Arty., 1863-64; pres. Cincinnati Expn. Arts and Industries, 1875-79; pres. Cincinnati Musical Festivals, 1880-82. Author: A Conventional Bohemian, 1886; A Virginia Inheritance, 1888; One Woman's Way, 1890; A Complication in Hearts, 1902. Address: Laurel, Md. Died 1910.

PENDLETON, Edwin Conway, rear admiral U.S.N.; b. Richmond, Va., May 27, 1847; s. A. G. and Selina C. P.; apptd. to U.S. Naval Acad. by the President, at-large, Oct. 10, 1863, grad. 1867; m. Mary R. Saxton, Apr. 2, 1872. Promoted ensign, Dec. 18, 1868; master, Mar. 21, 1870; lt., Mar. 21, 1871; lt. comdr., Aug. 4, 1889; comdr., Mar. 21, 1897; capt., Jan. 21, 1902; rear admiral, Aug. 28, 1907. Summer of 1864 was in active service on Marion in pursuit of Confederate steamers Florida and Tallahassee; served on Minnesota and Onward, 1867-70; Portsmouth and Wasp, 1871; Supply, 1872-73; on duty Navy Yard, Washington, 1872, 1874, 1876-78, 1888-92; on bd. Congress, 1874-76; Swatara, 1879-82; on duty Naval Obs., 1883-86; on bd. Atlanta, 1886-88; exec. officer Monterey, 1893-95; on duty Bur. of Ordnance, Navy Dept., 1895-97; supt. naval gun factory, Washington, 1897-1900, 1902-05; comd. Atlanta, 1900-02; commandant, Navy Yard, Washington, 1905; comd. Missouri, 1905-07; commandant Navy Yard, League Island, Pa., 1907-09; retired, May 27, 1909. Address: Washington, D.C. Died Sept. 27, 1919.

PENDLETON, Ellen Fitz, coll. pres.; b. Westerly, R.I., Aug. 7, 1864; d. Enoch Burrows and Mary Ette (Chapman) P.; A.B., Wellesley, 1886, A.M., 1891; student Newnham Coll., Cambridge, Eng., 1889-90; Lit.D., Brown U., 1911; LL.D., Mt. Holyoke Coll., 1912, and Smith Coll., 1925; LL.D., U. of Toronto, 1927, Williams Coll., 1931. Tutor in mathematics, 1886-88, instr., 1888-97, sec. 1897-1901, dean and asso. prof. mathematics, 1901-11, pres., June 1911-July 1936, Wellesley Coll. Mem. Coll. Entrance Exam. Board; mem. Am. Acad. Polit. and Social Science. Mem. Jury of Award for Am. Peace Prize founded by Edward Bok. Home: Wellesley, Mass. Died July 26, 1936.

PENDLETON, Elliott Hunt, lawyer; b. Cincinnati, Dec. 8, 1859; s. Elliott Hunt and Emma (Gaylord) P.; A.B., Harvard, 1882, hon. A.M., 1913; student Cincinnati Law Sch., 1883; admitted to bar, 1883; m. Isabella Eckstein, June 4, 1885; children—Harriet Holabird (dec.), Isabelle Eckstein, Elliott Hunt. Candidate for state senator, 1895; mem. exec. com. Nat. Municipal League, 1903-16; editor and propr. The Citizens' Bulletin (devoted to municipal reform), 1903-13. Mem. Ch. Divine Science, Cincinnati. Home: Cincinnati, O. Died July 10, 1926.

PENDLETON, Francis Key, lawyer; s. George H. Pendleton (U.S. senator and U.S. minister to Germany) and Alice Key Pendleton; g.s. of Francis Scott Key, author of The Star Spangled Banner; A.B., Harvard, 1870, LL.B., 1875; m. Elizabeth La Montagne, Dec. 10, 1890. Corp. counsel, City of N.Y., 1907-10; justice Supreme Court N.Y., 1st Dist., term expiring Dec. 31, 1921, resigned Apr. 1, 1920. Dir. Guardian Life Ins. Co. of America, N.Y. Coal Co., Low Volatile Coal Co., N.Y. Title & Mortgage Co. Democrat. Episcopalian. Home: New York, N.Y. Died July 26, 1930.

PENDLETON, Joseph Henry, officer U.S.M.C.; b. Rochester, Pa., June 2, 1860; s. Joseph Rhodes and Martha J. (Cross) P.; grad. U.S. Naval Acad., 1882; m. Mary Helen Fay, Aug. 20, 1884; children—Helen Fay (Mrs. Albert Rockwell) Edgar Bache. Apptd. 2d lt. U.S.M.C., July 1, 1884; promoted through grades to brig. gen., Aug. 29, 1916; maj. gen., Dec. 9, 1923. Comdr. marine barracks, Sitka, 1892-94, 1899-1904; on Yankee, Spanish-Am. War, 1898; comd. 1st Regt., 1st Brig. of Marines, 1904-06; comd. Marine Barracks, Guam, 1906; same, Puget Sound, Wash., 1906-09; comd. 1st Brig. of Marines, P.I., 1909-10; post comdr. and comdg. officer 2d Regt., Olongapo, P.I., 1910-12; comd. Marine Barracks, Portsmouth, N.H., 1912; comd. 1st Provisional Regt., Nicaragua, 1912; comd. forces at Masaya, Nicaragua, at bombardment of fortifications of Coyotepe and Barranca, Oct. 3, 1912; led assault and capture of those places, Oct. 4; comd. 2d Regt., 2d Provisional Brig., at Guantanamo Bay, Cuba, 1913; comd. Marine Barracks, Puget Sound, Wash., 1913-14; comd. 4th Regt., San Diego, Calif., and two expdns. to waters of Pacific coast of Mexico, 1914-16; comd. 4th Regt. U.S. Marines and U.S. forces on shore in Santo Domingo, from June 19, 1916; comd. column U.S. Marines on advance into Santo Domingo from Monte Cristo to Santiago; received surrender of City of Santiago, D.R., July 6, 1916; apptd. comdr. 2d Provisional Brig., Santo Domingo, Dec. 31, 1916; administered depts. of War and Navy and of Interior and Police, Nov. 1916-Oct. 1918, and for 6 months of 1917-18 was, also actg. mil. gov. of Dominican Republic; comd. Marine Barracks, Parris Island, S.C., Nov. 11, 1918-Sept. 26, 1919; comdg. 2d Advanced Base Force, U.S. Marine Corps, San Diego, Calif., Oct. 1, 1919-Oct. 4, 1921; comdg. 5th Brig. Marines, San Diego, Oct. 4, 1921-Mar. 1924; comdg. Marine Corps Base, San Diego, Mar. 1924-June 2, 1924 (retired). Mayor of Coronado, Calif., 1928-30; mem. Coronado Sch. Bd. 14 yrs. Past pres. San Diego Chapter S.A.R. Dir. Calif.-San Diego Centennial Expn., 1934-35. Episcopalian. An adopted mem. Thlingket tribe of Alaskan Indians. Home: Coronado, Calif. Died Feb. 4, 1942.

PENDLETON, Louis (Beauregard), author; b. Tebeauville, Ga., Apr. 21, 1861; s. Philip C. and Catharine (Tebeau) Pendleton; educated in private school and two years college; student at Sorbonne, Paris, 4 summers; unmarried. Contributing editorial writer Macon (Georgia) Daily Telegraph, 1899-1914; later in charge a syndicated editorial service. Author: Life of Alexander H. Stephens (Am. Crisis Biography Series), 1908; The Wedding Garment, 1894 (translated into Swedish, German, French and Braille); The Sons of Ham, 1895; In the Okefinokee, 1895; Corona of the Nantahalas, 1895; Carita, 1898; Lost Prince Almon, 1898; In the Camp of the Creeks, 1903; A Forest Drama, 1904; In Assyrian Tents, 1904; Captain Ted, 1918; Kidnapping Clarence, 1922; The Princess Lilitu, 1924; The Invisible Police, 1932 (translated into Braille—latter and Wedding Garment pub. in Eng. 1935); Grapes of Wrath, 1937. Home: Bryn Athyn, Montgomery County, Pa. Died May 13, 1939.

PENDLETON, Nathaniel Dandridge, bishop; b. Lowndes County, Ga., Feb. 19, 1865; s. Philip Coleman and Catherine (Tebeau) P.; B.Th., Theol. Sch. of Acad. of the New Church (Swedenborgian), Phila., 1889; m. Cornelia Vosburg, Apr. 8, 1890 (died 1891); 1 dau., Ora Cornelia; m. 2d, Beatrice Walton Childs, Aug. 30, 1899; children—Philip Childs, Marion Childs, Jean Lowrie, Willard Dandridge, Nancy Tebeau. Ordained 1st (ministerial) degree New Ch., 1889; minister Emanuel Ch., Chicago, 1889-91; ordained 2d (pastoral) degree, Mar. 2, 1891; pastor Emanuel Ch., 1891-1903, Pittsburgh Ch. of the New Jerusalem, 1903-14; ordained 3d (Episcopal) degree, Nov. 17, 1912; elected bishop of the General Ch. of the New Jerusalem by the Gen. Assembly, June 15, 1916; Episcopal seat Bryn Athyn, Pa., diocese, including congregations in the U.S., Can., Eng., France, Holland, Sweden, Brazil, Natal (South Africa) and Australia. Pres. Acad. of the New Ch., Bryn Athyn, Pa.; pres. Corp. of the Gen. Ch.; prof. theology Theol. Sch., Bryn Athyn. Contbr. theol. and philos. articles to New Church Life, official organ of the Gen. Ch. Home: Bryn Athyn, Pa. Died Dec. 29, 1936.

PENFIELD, Edward, artist; b. Brooklyn, June 2, 1866; ed. Art Students' League, N.Y. Art editor Harper's Magazine, Harper's Weekly and Harper's Bazar, 1891-1901; later devoted time exclusively to illustrating, designing and painting. Originator of the poster in America, and used numerous "textures" in reproducing his drawings not attempted before in relief printing from zinc or other plates. Designed all posters for Harper's Magazine, 1893-99; poster calendars, etc., for R. H. Russell, and posters and designs for various purposes; illustrated a number of mag. articles in color. Executed decorations for breakfast room of Randolph Hall, Cambridge, Mass.; also decorations for Rochester Country Club. Author: Holland Sketches, 1907; Spanish Sketches, 1911. Home: Pelham Manor, N.Y. Died Feb. 8, 1925.

PENFIELD, Frederic Courtland, diplomat, writer; b. Connecticut, April 23, 1855; s. Daniel and Sophia (Young) P.; grad. of Russell's Mil. Sch., New Haven; spl. studies in Germany and England; hon. A.M., Princeton, 1907; LL.D., Hobart Coll., 1914, New York U., 1917, and U. of Pa., 1917; L.H.D., Catholic U. of America, 1915; m. Katharine Albert McMurdo, d. of Albert Welles, 1892 (died 1905); m. 2d, Mrs. Anne Weightman Walker, 1908. Had thorough schooling in journalism; apptd. U.S. vice-consul gen. at London, 1885; diplomatic agt. and consul gen. to Egypt, rank of minister resident, 1893-97; ambassador to Austria-Hungary, July 1913, until severance of diplomatic relations, 1917; in diplomatic service until Feb. 4, 1920; resigned with thanks of President and Dept. of State. Fellow Royal Geographical Soc., London, 1886; officer of French Acad., 1898, and awarded decoration of "Palmes Académique" by French Govt.; given Grand Cross of Order of Medjidieh, by Sultan of Turkey, and Grand Comdr. Degree of Order of Osmanieh by Khedive of Egypt, 1897; Cross of the Legion of Honor, 1904, in recognition of prominence in discussing relative merits of canal routes, leading to Am. Govt. purchasing from French co. all rights at Panama; for benefactions to Catholic ednl. instns. was made a marquis by the Pope, 1909, and honored by Pope Pius X, 1911, with Grand Cross of St. Gregory, being first American to receive highest class of this order; presented Sevres vase by French Govt.; hon. knighthood and Grand Cross of Brit. Empire by King George V.; Grand Cross of Paulownia, by Emperor of Japan; Grand Cordon of Sts. Maurice and Lazarus, by Italian Govt.; Grand Cordon of Star of Roumania, by King Ferdinand; rep. of President of U.S. at funeral of Emperor Francis Joseph, and coronation of Charles as king of Hungary. Traveled extensively in Africa, India, China and Japan. Author: Present Day Egypt, 1899; East of Suez, 1907. Wrote articles on econ. and internat. subjects for leading reviews and magazines of America and Great Britain. Art collector. Recognized authority on subjects pertaining to diplomacy, modern Egypt and internat. politics. In European war was charged with diplomatic interests of Great Britain, France, Roumania, Italy and Japan in Austria-Hungary, and many times received formal thanks of these govts. Home: New York, N.Y. Died June 19, 1922.

PENFIELD, Roderic Campbell, editor; b. Monmouth County, N.J., Dec. 20, 1864; s. Homer and Martha (Campbell) P.; ed. pub. sch., Elyria, O.; m. Geraldine, d. Rev. A. J. Kynett, Phila., May 22, 1890 (died 1896); m. 2d, Georgette Armandine Giffault, Feb. 19, 1910. Editor and writer on dramatic subjects; sec. Pictorial News Co., New York; dir. Am. Planograph Co., Ultima Printing Utilities Co.; also writer for the stage, 1901—, and on editorial staff New York Evening Mail. Presbyn. Republican. Co-author: Lady Teazle; The Cheerful Giver. Author: The White Hen; The Princess Piccola; Madame Clicquot; Jones, N.Y. Founder and editor, The Opera Mag., 1914-16, The Greenwich Village Spectator, 1917-18; gen. mgr. The Japan Advertiser and The Trans-Pacific, 1918-19; Am. editor and mgr. The World Salesman, Yokohama, Japan, 1919—. Address: New York, N.Y. Died 1921.

PENFIELD, Samuel Lewis, prof. mineralogy, Sheffield Scientific School, Yale; b. Catskill, N.Y., Jan. 16, 1856; s. George H. and Ann Augusta (Cheesman) P.; ed. there and at Wilbraham, Mass.; grad. Sheffield Scientific Sch., Yale, 1877; studied at Strassburg and Heidelberg; A.M., Yale, 1896; LL.D., U. of Wis., 1904; m. Grace Chapman, Jan. 26, 1897. Author: Brush-Penfield Determinative Mineralogy and Blowpipe Analysis, 1898; Contributions to Mineralogy and Petrography from the Laboratories of the Sheffield Scientific School (with L. V. Pirsson), 1901; also many papers pertaining to mineralogy, crystallography and chemistry in Am. Jour. Science and Art. Address: New Haven, Conn. Died 1906.

PENFIELD, Walter Scott, lawyer; b. Auburn, Ind., Feb. 13, 1879; s. Judge William L. and Lunette (Walter) P.; prepared for coll. at Howe Mil. Sch.; B.A., U. of Mich., 1900; LL.B., George Washington U., 1903; atty. Dept. of State, Washington, D.C., 1901-04; asst. to U.S. counsel and Am. sec. of The Hague Court in arbitration of the Pious fund case bet. Mex. and U.S., 1902; asst. to U.S. and Venezuelan counsel and sec. of delegations to The Hague Court in arbitration of the Venezuelan preferential treatment case, 1903; in practice at Auburn, Ind., 1904; city atty., 1904-06; county atty., 1905-07; moved to Washington, D.C., 1907. Offered position asst. U.S. atty. special mission to Cuba for Spanish Treaty Claims Commn., 1908; counsel for Mexico in Sanchez Azcona case, 1911; apptd. atty. Panama Legation, Washington, and of counsel in arbitration as to boundary dispute bet. Costa Rica and Panama, 1912; same to Dominican Legation and in controversy as to boundary dispute bet. Hayti and Dominican Republic. Sometime counsel legations of Nicaragua, Salvador and Venezuela. Prof. internat. law, Washington Coll. of Law, 1909-12, U.S. del. Pan-Am. Financial Congress, Washington, 1915 (sec. of Pan-ama-U.S. group com.); U.S. del. and mem. com. for U.S. on internat. law, Pan-Am. Scientific Congress, Washington, 1915 (sec. U.S. delegation); del. Internat. Peace Congress, San Francisco, 1915; counsel for Germany in Appam case, 1916; asked to accept offer appmt. as adviser in foreign affairs to Siamese Govt., 1917; del. 2d Pan-Am. Commercial Conf., Washington, 1919; del. and tech. adviser in internat. law of Panama to Peace Conf., Paris, 1919. Apptd. by sec. of U.S. Treas., mem. Panama Group Com. of Inter-Am. High Commn., 1919; U.S. del. and mem. com. for Panama of 2d Pan-Am. Financial Congress, Washington, 1920; offered appmt. solicitor Dept. of State, 1920. Decorated Order of the Bust of the Liberator, 3d class, Venezuela, 1920. Mem. Inst. Politics, Williamstown, 1923; del. 21st Internat. Congress Americanists, The Hague, 1924; asst. sec. Inter-parliamentary Union, Berne and Geneva, 1924; atty. Pan-Am. Union "Kolb" Case establishing its legal status, 1925; spl. rep. exec. com. 1st Pan-Am. Congress of Journalists, Washington, 1926; del. Nat. Conf. Street and Highway Safety, Washington, 1926; del. 3d Pan-Am. Commercial Conference, Washington, 1927; member Acad. International Law, The Hague, 1924; mem. Internat. Congress History and Geography, Buenos Aires, 1924; apptd. del. Pan-Am. Scientific Congress, Lima, 1924; spl. lecturer internat. law and Am. diplomatic relations, U. of Ill., 1925. Dir. Washington Loan and Trust Co. Chmn. Com. on Pan.-Am. Union and mem. Am. Br.; mem. Nat. Assn. Constl. Govt. (v.p.), Am. Peace Soc. (dir.; mem. exec. com.), Am. Soc. Internat. Law, Am. Bar Assn. (v.p.). Republican. Episcopalian. Home: Washington, D.C. Died Apr. 11, 1931.

PENFIELD, William L., lawyer; b. Dover, Lenawee County, Mich., April 2, 1846; s. William and Lucinda (Felton) P.; lived on farm in boyhood; grad. U. of Mich., 1870; m. Luna Walter, June 28, 1875. Instr. German and Latin, Adrian Coll., Mich., 1870-72; admitted to bar, Adrian, 1872; located as lawyer at Auburn, Ind., 1873; city attorney; member Rep. State Com., 1884; presidential elector and electoral messenger, 1888; delegate Nat. Rep. Conv., 1892; judge 35th circuit of Ind., 1894-97; solicitor U.S. Dept. of State, 1897-1905; resigned to resume law practice. Republican. Counsel for U.S. in internat. arbitration of U.S. vs. San Domingo, Peru, Haiti, Nicaragua, Guatemala, Salvador and Mexico, securing for U.S. awards aggregating $2,250,000; counsel for U.S. in the "Pious Fund" case between Mexico and the U.S. before The Hague Tribunal; counsel for U.S. and for Venezuela in the Venezuelan arbitration before The Hague Tribunal, 1903; spl. commr. to Brazil, July 1905; agt. and counsel for U.S. Govt. in pending arbitration between U.S. and Nicaragua, 1907. Authority on internat. law. Address: Washington, D.C. Died 1909.

PENGELLEY, Arthur Lorne, bishop; b. nr. Rice Lake, Ont., Can., Nov. 1, 1879; s. Theodore Robert and Fannie (Swann) P.; grad. Ref. Episcopal Sem., Phila., 1909, D.D., 1921; m. Mabel Frances Jameson, June 19, 1912. Deacon and presbytr, Ref. Episcopal Ch., 1909; supt. Spl. Missionary Jurisdiction of the South, 1909-14; consecrated bishop, June 24, 1914; in charge Bishop Cummin's Training Sch. for Ministers, of Ref. Episcopal Ch. among the colored race. Pres. Bible Soc. of Charleston, 1919-20. Home: Summerville, S.C. Died Apr. 24, 1922.

PENHALLOW, David Pearce, botanist; b. Kittery Point, Me., May 25, 1854; s. Andrew Jackson and Ann Josepha (Pickering) P.; B.S., Mass. State Coll., 1873, Boston U., 1888; M.S., McGill U., 1896, D.Sc., 1904; m. Sarah A. Dunlap, May 4, 1876. Prof. botany and chemistry, 1876-80, acting pres., 1879-80, Imperial Coll. of Agr., Sapporo, Japan; botanist to Houghton Farm Expt. Sta., 1882-83; prof. botany, McGill U., 1883—. Editor Canadian Record of Science, 1888-90; asso. editor American Naturalist, 1897-1907; editor for paleobotany Botanisches Centralblatt, 1902-07. Mem. Brit. Assn. com. on Canadian ethnology, 1897-1904 (chmn., 1902-04); chmn. Royal Soc. of Can. com. on ethnology, 1902-04; spl. commr. World's Industl. and Cotton Centennial Expn., 1884. Trustee Marine Biol. Lab., Woods Hole, Mass.; dir. and sec. Biol. Stas. of Can.; dir. Atlantic Coast Biol. Sta., St. Andrews, N.B., 1907—; chmn. Assn. Am. Biol. Research Stas., 1908-09; Brit. Assn. com. on pleistocene fauna and flora of Can., 1897-1901; Governors Fellow on corp. of McGill U. Pres. Montreal Hort. Soc., 1888-92, Dominion Pomol. Soc., 1890, Soc. Plant Morphology and Physiology, 1899, Am. Soc. Naturalists, 1908-09, Natural History Soc. Montreal, 1904—; fellow Royal Soc. Canada (pres. Sect. IV, 1896-97), A.A.A.S. (v.p. Sect. G, 1908-09), Bot. Soc. America, Geol. Soc. America. Publications on bot. subjects, chiefly on paleobotany, about 150 titles. Address: Montreal, Quebec. Died 1910.

PENICK, Charles Clifton, bishop; b. Charlotte Co., Va., Dec. 9, 1843; s. Edwin Anderson and Mary (Hamner) P.; ed. Hampden-Sidney Coll. and Danville, Va., Mil. Inst.; served in 38th Va. Regt., C.S.A.; grad. Alexandria Sem., 1869; D.D., Kenyon Coll.; m. Mary Hoge, 1881. Deacon, 1869, priest, 1870, P.E. Ch.; rector Bristol, Tenn., 1869-70, Mt. Savage, Md., 1870-73, Baltimore, 1873-77, Louisville, 1883-93, Richmond, Va., 1894-99, Fairmount, W.Va., 1899-1904, Ascension Ch., Frankfort, Ky., 1908-12; consecrated bishop of Cape Palmas, W. Africa, Apr. 1877. Author: More Than a Prophet; Advice to the Church in Africa; Hopes, Perils and Struggles of the Negroes in America; What Can the Church Do for the Negro in the United States?; Everlasting Life; The Dead Memories—Lessons and Duties of the Confederacy; The Science of Missions; Social Side of Christ's Life; Conquest of the World by Christianity. Address: South Boston, Va. Died Apr. 13, 1914.

PENN, Arthur A., writer, composer; b. London, Eng., 1880; s. William and Elizabeth Hindley (Hewitt) P.; ed. pvt. schs., Eng.; m. Eleanor Worthington Onderdonk, 1908. Formerly musical and dramatic critic various provincial dailies in Eng. Mem. Am. Soc. Composers, Authors and Publishers. Episcopalian. Wrote: (comic operas—libretti and music) Yokohama Maid; Your Royal Highness; The Lass of Limerick Town; Captain Crossbones; Rose of the Danube; Smilin' Through; The China Shop; etc.; also (songs) Carissima; The Magic of Your Eyes; Sunrise and You; The Lamplit Hour; House on the Hillside; Across the River; etc. Writer of verse. Home: New London, Conn. Died Feb. 6, 1941.

PENN, I(rvine) Garland, educational sec.; b. New Glasgow, Amherst County, Va., Oct. 7, 1867; s. Isham and Maria L. (Irvine) P.; high sch. Lynchburg, Va., 1886; M.A., Rust Coll., Holly Springs, Miss., 1890; Litt.D., Wiley Coll., Marshall, Tex., 1908; m. Anna Belle Rhodes, Dec. 26, 1889; children—Mrs. Wilhelmina Franklin, Irvine Garland, Mrs. Georgia S. Williams (dec.), Mrs. Elizabeth H. McClellan, Mrs. Louise Sandipher, Mrs. Marie Miller, Mrs. Anna Belle Maxwell. Principal of pub. sch. of Lynchburg, 1886-95; national commr. Negro exhibits, Atlanta Exposition, 1895; asst. gen. sec. Epworth League, M.E. Ch., 1897-1912; corr. sec. Bd. of Edn. for Negroes, 1912-25; later ednl. sec. endowments and field promotion, dept. ednl. instns. for Negroes, Bd. of Edn., M.E. Ch. Trustee Wiley Coll. (Marshall, Tex.), Clark U. (Atlanta), Gammon Theol. Sem. (Atlanta), Walden Coll. (Nashville, Tenn.). Mem. Joint Commn. on Unification of M.E. Ch., 1920-28, mem. Commn. on Interdenominational Relations; mem. Gen. Conf. M.E. Ch. 10 quadrenniums, 1892-1932 (sr. mem. in point of service). Republican. Author: The Afro-American Press and Its Editors, 1892; The College of Life or Self Educator, 1896; The United Negro, 1903. Home: Walnut Hill, Cincinnati, O. Died July 22, 1930.

PENN, Julius Augustus, army officer; b. Mattoon, Ill., Feb. 19, 1865; s. Julius Augustus and Mary (Brock) P.; grad. U.S. Mil. Acad., 1886; Inf. and Cav. Sch., Ft. Leavenworth, Kan., 1891 (valedictorian); Army War Coll., 1907; unmarried. Commd. 2d lt. 13th Inf., July 1, 1886; promoted through grades to rank of col., July 5, 1916. Transferred to 49th Inf., June 1917; brig. gen. N.A., Aug. 5, 1917; served with A.E.F., 1918-19; adj. gen., Mar. 10, 1919, in charge war prison sec. and gen. prisoners sec. Methodist. Mason. Home: Batavia, Clermont County, O. Died May 13, 1934.

PENNELL, Elizabeth (Robins) (Mrs. Joseph Pennell), author; b. Phila., Pa., Feb. 21, 1855; b. Edward and Margaret (Holmes) Robins; ed. Convent of Sacred Heart, Conflans, Paris, and Eden Hall, Torresdale, Phila.; m. Joseph Pennell, artist, 1884. Spent many yrs. in Europe; contbr. British and Am. newspapers. Author: (works illustrated mostly by husband) Life of Mary Wollstonecraft, 1884; Feasts of Autolycus, 1896; Charles Godfrey Leland, 1906; French Cathedrals, Monasteries and Abbeys, 1909; Our House and the People in It, 1910; Our House and London Out of Our Windows, 1912; Our Philadelphia, 1914; Nights, 1915; The Lovers, 1917; (with husband) The Life of Whistler, 1908. Editor: (with husband) Whistler Journal, 1921. Address: New York, N.Y. Died Feb. 8, 1936.

PENNELL, Joseph, artist, illustrator, author; b. Phila., July 4, 1860; pupil Pa. Acad. Fine Arts and Pa. Sch. of Industrial Art; m. Elizabeth Robins. Medals at Paris, Phila., Chicago and Buffalo; 1st class gold medal, Paris Expn., 1900, Dresden, 1902; Grand Prix, St. Louis Expn., 1904; gold medal, Liege, 1905; Grand Prix, Milan, 1906. Barcelona, 1907, Brussells, 1910; Amsterdam, 1912; San Francisco, Calif., 1916; mem. Jury Hors Concours, Rome, 1911;

Diplome d'Monneur, Amsterdam, 1912; 2 medals, London, 1913, Florence, 1914; chmn. Jury Hors Concours, Internat. Exhbn., Leipzig, 1914; same, Panama Expn., 1915; commemorative medal same, 1915. Represented in Luxembourg, and collection City of Paris; Cabinet des Estamps (France); Uffizi Gallery (Florence); Modern Gallery (Venice); Modern Gallery (Rome); collection of H.M., the King of Italy; British Museum; Belgian Nat. Gallery; Library of Congress, Washington, D.C., Pa. Acad., Phila., Carnegie Inst., etc. Chmn. Internat. Jury Awards, St. Louis Expn., 1904, San Francisco Expn., 1915; asso. chmn. U.S. Com. on Pub. Information, 1917-19; medals and thanks of Govt. and Liberty Loan Com., 1918-19. N.A., 1909; fellow Am. Acad. Arts and Letters. Author: A Canterbury Pilgrimage, 1885; An Italian Pilgrimage, 1886; Two Pilgrims' Progress, 1887; Our Sentimental Journey Through France and Italy, 1888; Pen Drawing and Pen Droughtsmen, 1889; Our Journey to the Hebrides, 1889; The Stream of Pleasure, 1891; The Jew at Home, 1892; Play in Provence, 1892; To Gypsyland, 1893; Modern Illustration, 1895; The Illustration of Books, 1896; The Alhambra, 1896; The Work of Charles Keene, 1897; Lithography and Lithographers, 1900; The Authorized Life of J. McN. Whistler (with Mrs. Pennell), 1910; Pictures of War Work in America, 1918; Etchers and Etching, 1919. Editor: (with wife) The Whistler Journal, 1921. Illustrated a large number of books. Address: New York, N.Y. Died Apr. 23, 1926.

PENNEWILL, James, judge; b. Sussex County, Del., June 16, 1854; s. Simeon and Anna E. (Curry) P.; A.B., Princeton, 1875; read law with Hon. N. B. Smithers, 1875-78; m. Alice Hazel, Dec. 5, 1888. Admitted to bar, Oct. 1878; practiced at Dover, as partner successively with George P. Fisher, George V. Massey, and James L. Wolcott; he and latter were solicitors in Del. for Pa. R.R. Co. until 1897; justice Supreme Court of Del., 1897-1933 (chief justice 1909-33); retired on account of age limit. Republican. Was at one time chmn. Rep. State Central Com. of Del. Address: Dover, Del. Died Dec. 29, 1935.

PENNEWILL, Simeon Selby, gov.; b. Greenwood, Del., July 23, 1867; s. Simeon and Anna E. (Curry) P.; ed. pub. schs. and Wilmington Conf. Acad.; m. Elizabeth H. Halsey, Dec. 30, 1920; m. 2d, Lydia Wright Elder Feb. 27, 1929. Mem. Del. Senate, 1899-1907; gov. of Del., 1909-13. Republican. Presbyn. Home: Dover, Del. Died Sept. 9, 1935.

PENNEY, Charles George, brig. gen. U.S.A.; b. Newark, O., July 14, 1844; s. George W. and Ermina G. (Smith) P.; ed. Kenyon Coll., Ohio; m. Ida Walker. Enlisted pvt. Co. C, 76th Ohio Inf., Aug. 16, 1862; discharged, July 10, 1863; 2d lt. U.S..CT., July 10, 1863; 1st lt., Jan. 8, 1864; capt., Mar. 20, 1864; hon. mustered out, June 16, 1866; apptd. 2d lt. 38th U.S. Inf., July 28, 1866; 1st lt., Nov. 4, 1867; assigned to 6th Inf., Dec. 15, 1870; capt., June 26, 1883; maj. chief q.-m. vols., May 12, 1898; lt. col. chief q.m. vols., Aug. 11, 1898; hon. discharged from vols., Mar. 15, 1899; maj. 8th U.S. Inf., Aug. 15, 1898; transferred to 22d Inf., Oct. 24, 1898; lt. col. 23d Inf., Feb. 2, 1901; col. 29th Inf., May 9, 1902; brig. gen., Aug. 13, 1903; retired at own request after 40 yrs.' service, Aug. 14, 1903. Bvtd. 1st lt., Mar. 2, 1867, for Vicksburg; capt., Mar. 2, 1867, for Ft. Blakely, Ala. Home: Nordhoff, Calif. Died Dec. 13, 1926.

PENNEY, Mark Embury, educator; b. Western Bay, Newfoundland, Oct. 23, 1880; s. John Bishop and Sarah (Halfyard) P.; S.T.B., Boston U., 1907; A.B., Cornell U., 1910; Ph.D., 1913; m. Alma Rosa Thorne, June 14, 1916; 1 dau., Margaret Ellen. Began as actg. prof. philosophy and edn., Central Coll., Fayette, Mo., 1912; instr. philosophy, 1913, asst. prof., 1914, asso. prof., 1915, prof., 1916, actg. dean Teachers Coll., 1917-20, Syracuse U., also dir. ednl. lab. and built the psychol. lab., and introduced modern exptl. psychology; completely reorganized the curricula of all the courses in Teachers Coll.; special lecturer in Edn., Ohio U., 1921; prof. edn. Cornell U., 1922-23; prof. edn. Ohio State U., 1923-24; pres. Millikin U., 1924-30; later engaged in writing and in the development of color effects in visual sensations and in pigment, as applied to multi-color press; later state director Division of Rehabilitation. Served in Army Ednl. Corps, A.E.F., at Beaume, France, Jan.-June 1918. Republican. Mason. Author: Why Knowledge of the Laws of Human Behavior Makes for Success, 1921; The Development of Educational Psychology in Teachers Colleges; Changes in the Curriculum of Teacher Training Institutions. Home: Springfield, Ill. Died Aug. 12, 1937.

PENNEY, Thomas, lawyer; b. London, Eng., May 6, 1859; s. Thomas and Hannah (Nagle) P.; came to U.S., 1874; A.B., Yale, 1887, LL.B., 1889; m. Celia E. Patterson, Sept. 15, 1891; children—Norman, Charles P., Thomas, Mrs. Margaret Stewart. Practiced at Buffalo, 1890—; pres. Internat. Ry. Co., Buffalo, 1908-12, v.p. and gen. counsel, 1912-26; counsel for law firm of Penney & Penney, 1926—. Dist. Atty., Erie Co., 1899-1902. As dist. atty. of Erie Co. in 1901, prosecuted Leon Czolgosz, assassin of President McKinley. Republican. Presbyn. Mason (Grand Master of N.Y., 1916-17). Home: Buffalo, N.Y. Died Nov. 11, 1933.

PENNIMAN, James Hosmer, author; b. Alexandria, Va., Nov. 8, 1860; s. James Lanman and Maria Davis (Hosmer) P.; A.B., Yale, 1884; Litt.D., Franklin and Marshall, 1914, U. of Pa., 1918. Founder Maria Hosmer Penniman Memorial Library of Edn., which is the dept. library of Sch. of Edn., U. of Pa., and of Penniman Memorial Library of Edn., Yale and Brown (Yale Penniman Library now numbers 80,000 books, many rare, and some unique; it is one of the largest libraries of education in the world). Author: Common Words Difficult to Spell, 1891; Prose Dictation Exercises, 1893; The School Poetry Book, 1894; Practical Suggestions in School Government, 1899; Penniman's New Practical Speller, 1900; Books and How to Make the Most of Them, 1910; George Washington as Commander in Chief, 1917; George Washington as Man of Letters, 1918; George Washington and Mt. Vernon, 1921; Our Debt to France, 1921; What Lafayette Did for America, 1921; Philadelphia in the Early Eighteen Hundreds, 1923. Home: Philadelphia, Pa. Died Apr. 6, 1931.

PENNIMAN, Josiah Harmar, provost, U. of Pa.; b. Concord, Mass., July 20, 1868; s. James Lanman and Maria Davis (Hosmer) P.; A.B., U. of Pa., 1890, Ph.D., 1895, LL.D., 1922, D.C.L., 1939; LL.D., U. of Alabama, 1906, Washington Coll., Mo., 1907, Ursinus Coll., 1921, Juniata Coll., 1925; Litt.D., Swarthmore Coll., 1924; L.H.D., Muhlenberg Coll., 1929; LL.D., Franklin and Marshall Coll., 1929, Lafayette Coll., 1933, Lehigh U., 1934; m. Mrs. Ida Jutte Walther, 1929. Prof. English lit, 1896—; dean faculty, 1897-1909, vice-provost, 1911-20, actg. provost, 1920-23, provost, 1923-39, also pres., 1923-30, U. of Pa., retired, 1939. Trustee U. of Pa., Evans Inst. Lt. col., U.S. Army (Reserve). Made Chevalier de la Legion d'Honneur, 1934. Author: The War of the Theatres, 1897; A Book About the English Bible, 1919; and many articles on ednl. and lit. topics. Editor of Ben Jonson's Poetaster and Thomas Dekker's Satiromastix, in the Belles Lettres Series, 1905. Home: Philadelphia, Pa. Died Apr. 10, 1941.

PENNINGTON, Alexander Cummings McWhorter, brig. gen. U.S.A.; b. Newark, N.J., Jan. 8, 1838; s. Alexander C. M. and Ann Johnston (Kennedy) P.; ed. pvt. schs. and acad., 1844-55; grad. U.S. Mil. Acad., 1860; A.M., Princeton, 1864; m. Clara Miller French, Feb. 5, 1863. Bvt. 2d lt. 2d Arty., July 1, 1860; commd. 2d lt., Feb. 1, 1861; 1st lt., May 14, 1861; capt., Mar. 30, 1864; col. 3d N.J. Cav., Oct. 1, 1864; hon. mustered out of vol. service, Aug. 1, 1865; maj. 4th Arty., Nov. 8, 1882; lt. col., Nov. 28, 1892; col. 2d Arty., Oct. 29, 1896; brig. gen. vols., May 4, 1898; hon. discharged from vols., Apr. 12, 1899; brig. gen. U.S.A., Oct. 16, 1899; retired at own request after 40 yrs.' service, Oct. 17, 1899. Bvtd.: capt., June 9, 1863, for Beverly Ford, Va.; maj., July 3, 1863, for Gettysburg campaign; lt. col., Oct. 19, 1864, for Cedar Creek, Va.; col., Mar. 13, 1865, for services during the war; brig. gen. vols., July 15, 1865, "for faithful and meritorious services during the war." Served throughout Civil War in the field, at Fort Pickens, Fla., and Army of the Potomac; comd. 1st Brigade, 3d Cav. Div., Army of the Potomac; comd. Camp Black, Hempstead, L.I., May-July 1898; comd. Dept. of the Gulf, July 1898-Mar. 1899. Address: New York, N.Y. Died Nov. 30, 1917.

PENNINGTON, Edmund, ry. official; b. La Salle, Ill., Sept. 16, 1848. Entered ry. service, 1869, as warehouseman, continuing for 1 yr.; passed through various grades to asst. supt. C.,M.&St.P. Ry.; supt. Minneapolis & Pacific Ry. until June 1888; supt., 1888-98, gen. supt., 1898-99, gen. mgr., 1899-1905; elected v.p., July 31, 1905, continuing as gen. mgr., pres., 1909-22, later chmn. Minneapolis, St. Paul & Sault Ste. Marie Ry.; dir. 1st Nat. Bank, Minneapolis. Home: Minneapolis, Minn. Died May 2, 1926.

PENNINGTON, J(ohn) Rawson, surgeon; b. Corydon, Ind., Sept. 3, 1858; s. Charles Peter and Rebecca (Conrad) P.; student Ind. State Normal Sch. and Nat. Normal U., Lebanon, O.; M.D., U. of Md., 1887; hon. M.D., Ky. Sch. of Medicine, 1892; spl. courses in rectal surgery, St. Mark's Hosp., London, Eng., 1893; m. Olive Beryl Blachley, Apr. 28, 1900. Practiced at Chicago, 1893—; prof. rectal diseases, Chicago Clin. Sch., 1897-1900; prof. rectal surgery, Chicago Polyclinic, 1900-1915; prof. operative surgery and rectal diseases, Chicago Coll. Medicine and Surgery, 1908-12; later prof. proctology, Ill. Post-Grad. Med. Sch. Republican. Methodist. Mason. Author: Treatise on the Diseases and Injuries of the Rectum, Anus and Pelvic Colon, 1923. Home: Chicago, Ill. Died Feb. 3, 1927.

PENNINGTON, Leigh H., botanist; b. Macon, Mich., Oct. 26, 1877; s. Baron H. and Claribel (Pratt) P.; high sch., Tecumseh, Mich., 1897; A.B., U. of Mich., 1907, Ph.D., 1909; m. Mary Blanche Van Fleet, Aug. 27, 1902; 1 dau., Edna Phyllis (Mrs. Walter Clement Percival). Instr. in botany, Northwestern U., 1909-10; asst. prof. botany, Syracuse U., 1910-12, asso. prof., 1912-14; prof. forest pathology, N.Y. State Coll. Forestry, 1914—; expert in forest pathology, U.S. Dept. Agr., summers 1911, 12; collaborator, New York Bot. Garden, summers, 1913, 14; pathologist or collaborator U.S. Dept. Agr., 1917—. Republican. Methodist. Mason. Research in white pine blister rust. Home: Syracuse, N.Y. Deceased.

PENNINGTON, Samuel Hayes, M.D.; b. Newark, N.J., Oct. 16, 1806; Princeton, 1825, A.M., LL.D.; Rutgers Med. Coll., New York. Was pres. bd. of edn. Newark for 9 years; pres. Med. Soc. of N.J.; pres. trustees of Princeton Theol. Sem., 1877-97; trustee of Princeton, 1856—; pres. N.J. Hist. Soc. Retired from medical practice and became pres. Newark City Nat. Bank. Address: Newark, N.J. Died 1900.

PENNOYER, Sylvester, lawyer, lumberman, governor; b. Groton, N.Y., July 6, 1831; educated at home and at Homer, N.Y., Acad.; grad. Harvard Law School, 1854; married. Removed to Ore., 1855; engaged in lumbering; gov. of Ore., 1886-94; mayor of Portland, 1896. Democrat. While gov. received, from Sec. of State Gresham, suggestions made by Pres. Cleveland and replied: "I will attend to my business; let the President attend to his." Address: Portland, Ore. Died 1902.

PENNY, George Barlow, musician, educator; b. Haverstraw-on-Hudson, N.Y., June 30, 1861; s. Rev. Joshua and Sarah J. (Barlow) P.; B.S., Cornell, 1885; musical edn. Syracuse U. and pupil of G. D. Wilson, Max Pinner, New York, Dudley Buck, Dr. Percy Goetschius, Clarence Eddy, I. V. Flagler and abroad; m. Jessie Smith, Aug. 25, 1887; m. 2d, Beulah Ray White, Jan. 6, 1891; children—Carl Park, Vernon Kellogg (dec.). Taught at Girton College, Dalhousie Coll., Halifax, N.S., 2 yrs., Met. Coll. of Music, New York, 1 yr.; State Normal Sch., Emporia, Kan., 2 yrs.; organizer, dean Sch. Fine Arts, prof. mus. composition, organ and voice, lecturer upon history of fine arts, 1890-1903, U. of Kan., organizer and dean of Sch. of Fine Arts, Washburn Coll., Kan., 1903-07. Univ. organist, Cornell, 3 yrs., U. of Kan., 13 yrs.; official organist City Auditorium, Topeka, Kan., 1903-07; organist and choirmaster, Grace Episcopal Ch., Kansas City, 1905-09; dir. Fine Arts Inst., Kansas City, 1906-09. Dir. several choral socs., especially Topeka Oratorio Soc. and Rochester Oratorio Soc. Dir. Rochester Conservatory of Music; lecturer on music, U. of Rochester; choirmaster, 1st Presbyn. Ch. Composer of music for Episcopal ch. services. Lecturer upon architecture, sculpture, painting and music for 30 yrs. Made 4 Oriental trips, 3 as lecturer; also 8 European trips for archæol. and art purposes. Became prof. theory, history and lit. of music, Eastman Sch. of Music, U. of Rochester. Dean Am. Guild of Organists (Rochester Chapter). Episcopalian. Republican. Address: Rochester, N.Y. Died Nov. 15, 1934.

PENNYBACKER, Mrs. Percy V.; b. Petersburg, Va.; d. Rev. Dr. J. B. and Martha (Dews) Hardwicke; educated at Classic High Sch., Leavenworth, Kan., Sam Houston Teachers' Coll., Huntsville, Tex.; studied in New York, France, Germany and England; m. Percy V. Pennybacker, Oct. 31, 1884 (died 1899). Was teacher 14 yrs.; pres. Am. History Club, Austin, 1901; pres. State Federation Women's Clubs, Tex., 1901-03; treas. Gen. Federation Women's Clubs, 1904-06, auditor and chmn. program com., 1906-08, chmn. endowment com., 1911-12; pres. Gen. Federation of Women's Clubs, 1912-16. Trustee Chautauqua (N.Y.) Instn.; pres. Chautauqua Woman's Club of Chautauqua Instn., N.Y., 1917—; dir. Leslie Woman Suffrage Commn.; mem. Y.W.C.A. Nat. War Board of One Hundred; mem. advisory com. Food Administration of Tex.; spl. rep. in War Camp Community Service, nat. hdqrs., New York, 1918-19; chmn. Child Welfare Com. of League of Women Voters, 1920. Asso. mem. Dem. Nat. Com., 1919-20. Chmn. citizenship dept. Gen. Federation of Women's Clubs, 1920-24; chmn. Nat. Women's Com., Near East Relief, and chmn. Nat. Women's Com. for Restoration Louvain Library; mem. Jury of Award, Woodrow Wilson Foundation, term 1925-28; mem. Texas Centennial Commn., 1934—. Author: History of Texas, 1888. Home: Austin, Tex. Died Feb. 4, 1938.

PENNYPACKER, Galusha, brig. gen., bvt. maj. gen. U.S.A., retired; b. Chester County, Pa., June 1, 1844; s. Joseph J. and Tamson Amelia (Workizer) P.; ed. Phoenixville, Pa., Classical Inst.; unmarried. Entered Union Army, Apr. 1861, as non-commd. staff officer 9th Pa. Vols. for 3 months; served in the Shenandoah Valley, Va.; entered for the war, Aug. 22, 1861, as capt. Co. A, 97th Pa. Vols.; promoted maj., Oct. 7, 1861; served in 10th corps in Dept. of the South, 1862-63, including the engagements at Fts. Wagner and Gregg, James Island, siege of Charleston, capture Ft. Pulaski, and taking of Fernandina and Jacksonville, Fla.; joined Army of the James in Va., Apr. 1864; promoted lt. col., Apr. 3, 1864; col., June 23, 1864; comd. at Swift Creek, May 9, Drury's Bluff, May 16, Chester Station, May 18, and Green Plains, May 20, 1864; assigned to command 2d Brigade, 2d Div., 10th corps, Sept. 1864; was in successful assault on Ft. Fisher, N.C., Jan. 15, 1865; awarded Congressional Medal of Honor "for distinguished bravery in battle"; brig. gen. vols., Feb. 18, 1865; bvt. brig. gen. vols., Jan. 15, 1865; bvt. maj. gen. vols., Mar. 13, 1865; apptd. col. 34th (later changed to 16th)

Inf., U.S.A., July 28, 1866; bvt. brig. gen. U.S.A., Mar. 2, 1867, bvt. maj. gen. U.S.A., Mar 2, 1867; brig. gen. U.S.A., retired, Apr. 23, 1904; several times severely wounded, and was youngest general officer in War of the Rebellion; after war served as regimental and post comdr. and comd. departments at various times; placed on retired list on account of wounds, 1883. Home: Philadelphia, Pa. Died Oct. 1, 1916.

PENNYPACKER, Henry, educator; b. West Chester, Pa., Dec. 2, 1866; s. Charles Harrison and Elizabeth Ann (Pyle) P.; grad. Phillips Exeter Acad., 1884; A.B., Harvard, 1888; m. Anna H. Carpenter, June 20, 1889; 1 son, Thomas R. Asst., Adelphi Acad., Brooklyn, 1889-91; jr. master, 1891-1904, master, 1904-10, head master, 1910-20, Boston Latin Sch. Episcopalian. Chmn. Com. on Admission, Harvard Coll. Home: Cambridge, Mass. Died Nov. 19, 1933.

PENNYPACKER, Isaac Rusling, editor; b. Phoenixville, Chester County, Pa., Dec. 11, 1852; s. Dr. Isaac Anderson and Anna Maria (Whitaker) P.; ed. The Hill School, Pottstown, Pa.; Litt.D., Pa. Coll., 1916; m. Charlotte Whitaker, 1877; children—Isaac Anderson, Charlotte, Julia Elizabeth, Mary R. (Mrs. John Griffin), Maria W. (Mrs. John H. Lance), Grace Adams. Propr. and editor Wilmington (Del.) Morning News, 1880-82; on editorial staff of Philadelphia Press and Philadelphia Inquirer, 1883-99. Pres. Netherlands Soc. of Phila.; mem. Haddonfield (N.J.) Town Council, 1903-06. Dir. several mfg. cos. Mem. Meade Memorial Commn., 1915, General Pennypacker Memorial Commn., 1919; chmn. Valley Forge Park Commission, 1927-32. Author: Gettysburg and Other Poems; Life of General Meade ("Great Commanders" series), 1899; Bridle-Paths, 1911; The Valley Campaign, 1911; The Gettysburg Campaign, 1913; The Snow-Shoe Trail and Other Poems, 1913; Military Historians and History, 1929; The Valley Forge Burned by the British Troops, September 1777, 1929; also article, Philadelphia, in Johnson's Cyclo., and numerous hist. papers; Quaker Origins, 1927; Meade in Command, 1929; Valley Forge, 1930; "Fort Beversrode and Beyond," historical address, 1934, before Pa. Hist. Soc., The Netherlands Soc. and other organizations in commemoration of 300th anniversary of purchase by the Dutch from Indians of land now within City of Philadelphia. Editor: Autobiography of Governor Pennypacker. Home: Ardmore, Pa. Died Sept. 23, 1935.

PENNYPACKER, Samuel Whitaker, governor; b. Phoenixville, Pa., Apr. 9, 1843; s. Dr. Isaac Anderson and Anna Maria (Whitaker) P.; brother of Isaac Rusling P.; ed. Grovemont Sem., Phoenixville, and West Phila. Inst.; pvt. 26th "Emergency" Regt., 1863, at Gettysburg; LL.B., U. of Pa., 1866; LL.D., U. of Pa., and Franklin and Marshall Coll., and Muhlenberg Coll.; m. Virginia Earl Broomhall, Oct. 20, 1870. Pres. Law Acad. of Phila., 1867; mem. Bd. Pub. Edn., Phila., 1886-89; judge Ct. of Common Pleas No. 2, Phila., 1889-96, pres. judge, 1896-1902; gov. of Pa., 1903-07; mem. Pa. State R.R. Commn., 1912; mem. Pub. Service Commn. Pa. (chmn. 1915). Collected notable library of early Pa. imprints. Trustee U. of Pa. Past comdr. Fred Taylor Post, No. 19, G.A.R.; mem. Am. Philos. Soc. (councillor), Maatschappijder Nederlandsche Letterkunde of Leyden; pres. Hist. Soc. Pa., Philobiblon Club; sr. v.p. Pa. Soc. S.R.; president Pa. German Soc.; pres. Netherlands Soc. Phila. Author: Weekly Notes of Cases (asst.), 45 vols.; Anthony Wayne; Pennsylvania Colonial Cases; Annals of Phoenixville and Vicinity; Historical and Biographical Sketches; Index to the English Common Law Reports; The Settlement of Germantown; Congress Hall; Capture of Stony Point; General Weedon's Orderly Book at Valley Forge; Pennypacker's Supreme Court Reports (4 vols.); Pennsylvania in American History; Pennsylvania the Keystone; and other books and papers. Republican. Home: Pennypacker's Mills (Schwenkville P.O.), Pa. Died Sept. 2, 1916.

PENROSE, Boies, senator; b. Phila. Pa., Nov. 1, 1860; s. Richard Alexander Fullerton and Sarah Hannah (Boies) P.; brother of Charles Bingham, Richard A. F., Jr., and Spencer P.; A.B., Harvard, 1881. Admitted to the bar, 1883, and practiced in Philadelphia. Mem. Pa. Ho. of Rep., 1884-86, Senate, 1887-97 (pres. pro tem, 1889, 1891); U.S. senator, 4 terms, 1897-1921. Chmn. Rep. State Com., 1903-05; mem. Rep. Nat. Com., 1904--, except 1912-16; del. Rep. nat. convs., 1900, 04, 08, 16. Author: History of the City Government of Philadelphia. Home: Philadelphia, Pa. Died Dec. 31, 1921.

PENROSE, Charles Bingham, physician; b. Phila., Pa., Feb. 1, 1862; s. Richard Alexander Fullerton and Sarah Hannah (Boies) P.; A.B., Harvard, 1881, A.M., Ph.D., 1884; M.D., U. of Pa., 1884, LL.D., 1909; m. Katharine Drexel, Nov. 17, 1892. Resident phys. Pa. Hosp., 1885-86, and out-patient surgeon; surgeon to Gynecean Hosp. from its foundation, 1887; surgeon German Hosp., 1890; prof. gynecology, U. of Pa., 1893-99; retired. Author: Text-Book of Diseases of Women. Contbr. to med. publs. and to scientific jours. on math. and phys. subjects. Address: Philadelphia, Pa. Died Feb. 27, 1925.

PENROSE, Charles William, mem. 1st presidency Church of Jesus Christ of Latter Day Saints; b. Camberwell, London, Eng., Feb. 4, 1832; m. Lucetta Stratford, Jan. 21, 1855. Joined Ch. of Jesus Christ of Latter-day Saints in London, May 14, 1850; missionary in Eng. 10 yrs.; came to U.S., 1861, and settled in Utah; again missionary in Eng., 1865-68, and in 1885; took charge editorial dept. Ogden Junction (newspaper), 1870; made high priest and mem. High Council of Weber Stake; became editor in chief Deseret News, Salt Lake City, 1877; made 2d counselor to Angus M. Cannon, pres. of Salt Lake Stake, 1884; apptd. editor in chief Salt Lake Herald, 1893; asst. ch. historian; made mem. quorum of 12 apostles, July 7, 1904; 2d counselor to Joseph F. Smith, in the first presidency of the church, 1911-18, to Heber J. Grant, 1918-21, 1st counselor, 1921—; pres. European Mission, 1906-10. Mem. Ogden City Council, 1871-75; del. to Constl. Conv., Utah, 1872; mem. territorial legislature, 1880-84; del. Constl. Conv., Utah, 1887. Author: Mormon Doctrine; Rays of Living Light; Priesthood and Presidency, 1898; What Mormons Do Believe; Why I Am a Mormon. Home: Salt Lake City, Utah. Died May 16, 1925.

PENROSE, Clement Andariese, physician; b. St. Louis, Mo., Jan. 2, 1874; s. Col. Charles Bingham (U.S.A.) and Clara (Andariese) P.; B.A., Johns Hopkins, 1893, M.D., 1897; m. Helen Stowe, Dec. 14, 1905. Served on staffs of Drs. Osler, Halsted and Kelly, and later practiced alone in Baltimore; licensed also to practice in Mass., Pa. and D.C.; specialist in dietetics, general efficiency and functional disorders; surgeon in chief and v. dir. Bahama Expdn., 1903; chmn. Food Economy Commn., Baltimore, 1917; capt. Med. O.R.C., Apr. 9, 1917; maj., Sept. 4, 1917; with British and Am. armies in Europe, studying sanitation in camps and army fronts; report filed with surgeon gen. U.S.A. Mem. exec. com. Ch. Home and Infirmary. Republican. Presbyn. Author of med. part "Bahama Islands," 1905. Home: Baltimore, Md. Died July 4, 1919.

PENROSE, Clement Biddle, judge; b. Carlisle, Pa., Oct. 27, 1832; s. Charles Bingham and Valeria Fullerton (Biddle) P.; A.B., U. of Pa., 1850, A.M., 1853, LL.D., 1901; m. Mary Linnard, Sept. 30, 1857; father of Stephen Beasley Linnard P. Admitted to bar, 1853, and practiced at Phila. One of judges Orphans' Ct. of Phila., Feb. 1878 to Jan. 1, 1919. Annotator of Taylor's Medical Jurisprudence, 1866. Home: Germantown, Philadelphia, Pa. Died 1911.

PENROSE, Richard Alexander Fullerton, M.D.; b. Carlisle, Pa., Mar. 24, 1827; s. Charles Bingham and Valeria Fullerton (Biddle) P.; Dickinson Coll., 1846, LL.D., 1872; med. dept. U. of Pa., 1849; m. Sarah Hannah Boies, 1858. Father of U.S. Senator Boies Penrose. Became consulting surgeon Phila. Hosp. and gave clinical lectures on diseases of women and children there; prof. obstetrics and diseases of women and children, U. of Pa., 1863. A founder of The Children's Hosp. of Phila., the Hosp. of the U. of Pa., the Gynecean Hosp. and Am. Gynecol. Soc. Address: Philadelphia, Pa. Died 1908.

PENROSE, Richard Alexander Fullerton, Jr., geologist; b. Phila., Pa., Dec. 17, 1863; s. Richard Alexander Fullerton and Sarah Hannah (Boies) P.; A.B., Harvard, 1884, A.M., Ph.D., 1886; unmarried. Geologist in charge survey of Eastern Tex., for Tex. Geol. Survey, 1888; apptd., 1889, by Geol. Survey of Ark. to make detailed reports on the manganese and iron ore regions of Ark.; asso. prof. economic geology, 1892-95, prof., 1895-1911, U. of Chicago. Lecturer on economic geology at Stanford, 1893; spl. geologist U.S. Geol. Survey, 1894, to examine and report on gold dists. of Cripple Creek, Colo. Mem. bd. mgrs. Phila., Germantown & Norristown Ry. Co.; dir. various mining corps., also Ridge Avenue Passenger Ry. Co. of Phila. Trustee U. of Pa., 1911-27; pres. Acad. Natural Sciences of Phila., 1922-26. Asso. editor Journal of Geology. Mem. Soc. Economic Geologists (pres. 1920-21); mem. Nat. Research Council (geology com., 1917-18, div. of geology and geography, 1919-23); del. Internat. Geol. Congress, Stockholm, 1910, Toronto, 1913, Brussels, 1922, Madrid, 1927; mem. Fairmount Park Commn. (Phila.). Republican. Author: The Nature and Origin of Deposits of Phosphate of Lime; Geology of the Gulf Tertiary of Texas; Manganese: Its Uses, Ores, Deposits; The Iron Deposits of Arkansas; What a Geologist Can Do in War; The Last Stand of the Old Siberia. Home: Philadelphia, Pa. Died July 31, 1931.

PENROSE, Spencer, mining engr.; b. Phila., Nov. 2, 1865; s. Richard Alexander Fullerton and Sarah Hannah (Boies) P.; A.B., Harvard, 1886; m. Mrs. Julie Villiers (Lewis) McMillan, Apr. 26, 1906. A founder, dir. Utah Copper Co.; a pioneer in Cripple Creek (Colo.) Mining Dist. and identified with several of its mines; pres. Broadmoor Hotel Co., Cheyenne Mountain Co., Garden City Co., Manitou & Pikes Peak Ry., Pikes Peak Auto Highway Co., Pikes Peak Automobile Co., Mt. Manitou Park & Incline Ry. Co., Broadmoor Hotel Water & Power Co., The Manitou Mineral Water Co.; dir. Kennecott Copper Corp., Beaver Park Co., Braden Copper Co. Col. on staff of Gov. Peabody of Colo., 1903-04. Home: Colorado Springs, Colo. Died Dec. 7, 1939.

PENROSE, William Henry, col. U.S.A., retired Mar. 10, 1896; b. Madison Barracks, Sackett's Harbor, N.Y., Mar. 10, 1832; s. Capt. James W. P., U.S.A.; ed. Dickinson Coll.; became civ. and mech. engr.; m. Harriet E. Adams, g.d. Maj. Gen. Brown, U.S.A. Apptd., Apr. 1861, 2d lt. 3d U.S. inf., and in May, 1st lt.; served through Civil War in Army of Potomac; col. 15th N.J. vols., Apr. 1863; brig. gen. vols., 1865; won bvts. through all grades in regular army to brig. gen.; after war promoted through regular grades to col., 1893, and was in command 16th inf. when retired. Residence: Salt Lake City, Utah. Died 1903.

PENTECOST, George Frederick, clergyman; b. Albion, Ill., Sept. 23, 1842; s. Hugh L. and Emma (Flower) P.; student Georgetown U., Ky., 1860-62; hon. A.M., Hamilton Coll., 1870; D.D., Lafayette Coll., 1889; LL.D., Central U. of Ky., 1904; chaplain 8th Ky. Cav. U.S.V., 1862-64; m. Ada, d. Dr. Augusta Webber, Oct. 6, 1863. Pastor Greencastle, Ind., 1864, Evansville, Ind., 1866-67, Covington, Ky., 1867-68, Brooklyn, N.Y., 1868-71, Boston, 1871-80, Brooklyn, 1880-87; evangelical work in Scotland, 1887-88; spl. mission to English-speaking Brahmins in India, 1889-91; minister Marylebone Ch., London, 1891-97; pastor First Presbyn. Ch., Yonkers, N.Y., 1897-1902; pastor Bethany Presbyn. Ch., Phila., 1914—. Was spl. commr. of Presbyn. and A.B.C.F.M. Missionary socs. of U.S. in Japan, China and P.I. Author: The Angel in the Marble, 1876; In the Volume of the Book, 1876; A South Window, 1876; Out of Egypt, 1884; Bible Studies (10 vols.), 1880-89; Birth and Boyhood of Christ, 1896; Forgiveness of Sins, 1897; Systematic Beneficence, 1897; Precious Truths, 1898. Home: Philadelphia, Pa. Died Aug. 7, 1920.

PENTON, John Augustus, publisher; b. Paris, Ont., Can., May 12, 1862; s. Thomas and Anna Ryall; ed. pub. schs., Sarnia, Ont.; m. Adah Nell Whelan, 1916. Came to U.S., 1883, naturalized citizen. Long identified with iron foundry industry in different sections of the country; began publication of The Foundry, 1892; an organizer of The Iron & Steel Press Co., Cleveland, 1901, succeeded, 1904, by the Penton Pub. Co., which later published "Steel," formerly Iron Trade Rev., Daily Metal Trade, The Foundry, New Equipment, Digest, A.B.C. of Iron and Steel, Penton's Foundry List, Great Lakes Red Book, etc.; chmn. bd. The Penton Publishing Co. Decorated Order of Reconnaissance Française, 1st Class, 1920; Chevalier Legion of Honor, 1921, Cross Legion of Honor, 1926. Home: Santa Barbara, Calif. Died Sept. 8, 1940.

PEOPLES, Christian Joy, naval officer; b. in Iowa, Oct. 17, 1876; s. Robert A. and Lydia (Love) P.; St. Ignatius Coll., Sacred Heart Coll., Vallejo High Sch.; spl. course U. of Calif.; m. Leila Warren, Mar. 18, 1901; children—Leila, Pamela. Appointed to the Supply Corps of the Navy, with rank of ensign, Mar. 27, 1900; promoted through the grades to rear adm., July 1, 1917. Supply officer of U.S.S. Wilmington, Asiatic Sta., 1901-04; Navy Dept., 1904-11; supply officer battleship Utah, Atlantic Fleet, 1910-14; apptd. gen. insp. Supply Corps and asst. to chief of bur. of supplies and accounts, Navy Dept., 1914-20. Developed purchase system of the navy; standardized the steaming coal and fuel oil system; navy rep. of exports control com. during World War; also of clearance div. War Industries Bd., etc.; actg. paymaster gen. of the Navy, Jan.-May 1921; gen. insp. Supply Corps for Pacific Coast, 1921-30; in charge of Naval Supply Depot, Brooklyn, N.Y., 1930-33; paymaster gen. of Navy and Chief of Bur. Supplies and Accounts, Navy Dept., 1933-35; dir. Procurement Div. of Treasury, 1933-39; gen. inspector Supply Corps for Pacific Coast, 1939—. Home: Washington, D.C. Died Feb. 3, 1941.

PEOPLES, William Thaddeus, librarian; b. Wilmington, Del., Jan. 1, 1843; s. James and Catherine (Gallagher) P.; A.B., St. Mary's Coll., Wilmington, 1862; m. Kate Neimyer, Nov. 29, 1882. Librarian, Mercantile Library, New York, 1873-1916; later emeritus, Nat. (Gold) Dem. nominee for Congress, 6th N.J. Dist., 1896. Pres. New York Library Club, 1886-87, N.Y. State Library Assn., 1893-94; mem. Am. Inst. (sec. 1897-1902); sec. Clinton Hall Assn., New York, 1901-18. Office: New York, N.Y. Deceased.

PEPLE, Edward Henry, author; b. Richmond, Va., Aug. 10, 1869; s. Gustavus Adolphus and Sarah Bell (Lowndes) P.; ed. acad. John P. McGuire, Richmond, Va., high schs., etc.; Litt.D., U. of the South, 1921; unmarried. Removed to New York, 1895; worked as accountant in various instns. and until 1902 served as expert accountant, principally with Am. Bridge Co. Mem. Southern Soc., and The Virginians. Author: A Broken Rosary, 1903; The Prince Chap, 1903; Semiramis, 1907; Mallet's Masterpieces, 1908; The Spitfire, 1908; A Night Out, 1909. Plays prod.: The Prince Chap; The Love Route; The Mallet's Masterpiece; The Call of the Cricket; The Spitfire; The Littlest Rebel; The Clairvoyant; Cur and Coyote, 1913; A Pair of Sixes (prod. 1914); The Girl (prod. 1915); An Auto-Biography (pub. 1915); Friend Martha (prod. 1917); Maggie (prod. 1918); The War Dog (pub. 1918); Ladies' Day (prod. 1920); Her Birthright (prod. 1921). Address: New York, N.Y. Died July 28, 1924.

PEPPER, Charles Melville, journalist; b. Bloomfield, O., Nov. 11, 1859; s. Rev. George W. and Christine (Lindsay) P.; Ph.M., U. of Wooster, 1881; m. Kittie Rose Baldwin, May 4, 1884; 1 dau., Nora. Washington corr. Chicago Tribune, 1886-95; staff corr. New York Herald, 1896-97; from Cuba, to leading Am. papers, 1897-1901. Del. Pan-Am. Conf., City of Mexico, 1901; St. Louis Expn. commr. to Cuba, 1902; apptd. spl. Pan-Am. Ry. Commr., 1903; foreign trade commr. Dept. Commerce and Labor, 1906-09; fgn. trade adviser to State Dept., Sept. 1, 1909-Oct. 1, 1913; resigned. Canadian reciprocity commr. for State Department, 1910-11; dir. Chile Am. Assn., 1918—; chmn. Pan-Am. Ry. Com., 1924—. Author: Tomorrow in Cuba, 1899; Everyday Life in Washington, 1900; Panama to Patagonia, 1906; The West in the Orient, 1908; Life of Louis Klopsch, 1910; American Foreign Trade, 1919; The Life and Times of Henry Gassaway Davis, 1920. Address: New York, N.Y. Died Nov. 4, 1930.

PEPPER, George Dana Boardman, theologian; b. Ware, Mass., Feb. 5, 1833; s. John and Eunice (Hutchinson) P.; A.B., Amherst, 1857; grad. Newton Theol. Instn., 1860; D.D., Colby, 1867, Amherst, 1882; LL.D., Lewisburg, 1882, Colby, 1890; m. Annie Grassie, Nov. 29, 1860; father of Charles Hovey. Ordained Baptist ministry, 1860; pastor First Ch., Waterville, Me., 1860-65; prof. ecclesiastical history, Newton Theol. Instn., 1865-67; prof. systematic theology, Crozer Theol. Sem., 1868-82; pres. Colby U., 1882-89; out of health and traveling, preaching, etc., 1889-92; prof. Bibl. lit., Colby U., 1892-1900. Author: Outlines of Theology. Address: Waterville, Me. Died Jan. 30, 1913.

PEPPER, George Hubbard, anthropologist; b. Tottenville, S.I., N.Y., Feb. 2, 1873; s. David J. and Alice S. Hubbard P.; high sch. edn.; student Am. Mus. Natural History, 1892; student anthropology, Harvard, 1895-96; m. Jessie J. Crellin, Oct. 24, 1901. Engaged in archæol. work, Staten Island, 1895; exploration work, Hyde Southwestern expdn. for Am. Mus. Natural History, 1896-1909, asst. dept. anthropology, in charge div. of the Southwest, 1896-1909; exploration work in Mex., 1904, and in Ecuador, with the George G. Heye expdn., 1907; asst. curator Am. archæology, U. of Pa. Mus., Jan. 1909-10, acting curator, 1910-14; actg. curator, Heye Museum, 1914-16, Mus. of the Am. Indian (Heye Foundation), N.Y. City, 1917-23. Lecturer on American archæology and ethnology. Home: New York, N.Y. Died May 13, 1924.

PEPPER, Irvin St. Clare, congressman; b. on farm, Davis County, Ia., June 10, 1876; s. John and Mary E. (Prettyman) P.; grad. Southern Ia. Normal School, Bloomfield, 1897; LL.B., George Washington U., 1905; unmarried. In law practice at Muscatine, Ia., Jan. 1, 1906—; mem. firm Carskaddan & Pepper. County atty., Muscatine County, 2 terms, 1906-10; mem. 62d Congress (1911-13), 2d Ia. Dist. Democrat. Battalion adj. 34th Regt., Ia. N.G. Mason, Elk. Address: Muscatine, Ia. Died Dec. 22, 1913.

PEPPER, John Robertson, merchant; b. Montgomery County, Va., Apr. 6, 1850; s. Robert R. and Mary (McClaren) P.; ed. Christiansburg Commercial Coll.; grad. in Chautauqua course, 1883; m. Miss Charlie Read, Nov. 18, 1875; children—Mrs. Mary Ketchum, Samuel M. Wholesale grocer; pres. grocery cos., Greenville, Greenwood, Yazoo City and Rosedale, Miss.; pres. Memphis Machine Works. Trustee of Cossitt Library, Memphis; commr. Goodwyn Inst., Memphis. Author: Modern Sunday School Superintendent, 1885; Quiver Tips for Lovers of Sunday School Work, 1894; Tried Plans for Sunday School Work, 1895; Thirty Years at the Superintendent's Desk, 1909; Well-Nigh 50 Years at the Superintendent's Desk, 1929. Home: Memphis, Tenn. Died Mar. 31, 1931.

PERABO, (John) Ernst, pianist, composer; b. Wiesbaden, Germany, Nov. 14, 1845; s. Michael and Christine (Hübner) P.; came to America with parents, 1852; early showed unusual musical talent and through William Scharfenberg, of New York, a com. was formed to take charge of his edn.; was sent to Europe in 1858, and studied piano under Profs. Moscheles and E. F. Wenzel, of Leipzig Conservatory; harmony under Drs. Papperitz, Hauptmann and Richter, and composition under Carl Reinecke. Located at Boston; appeared at concert of Harvard Musical Assn., in 1866, and at every winter concert of same orgn., 1866—, also giving 4 matinées each season, interpreting works of leading German composers. Performed at music teachers' convs. at Ypsilanti, Mich., 1895, Wiers, N.H., 1901, Peoria, Ill., 1906, Lincoln, Ill., and Washington, Ind., 1908. Composer of many piano pieces, transcriptions, concert arrangements, etc. Studio: Boston, Mass. Died Oct. 29, 1920.

PERCIVAL, Henry Robert, P.E. clergyman; b. Phila., 1854; A.M., U. of Pa., 1872; D.D., Nashotah, Wis. Theol. Sem., 1891; deacon, 1877; priest, 1878; asst. Christ Ch., 1878-80; titular rector Ch. of the Evangelists, 1880—. Author: The Doctrine of the Episcopal Church; The Glories of the Episcopal Church; A Digest of Theology; The Invocation of Saints Treated Theologically and Historically; The Seven Ecumenical Councils, Their Canons and Dogmatic Decrees. Address: Philadelphia, Pa. Deceased.

PERCY, Frederick Bosworth, M.D.; b. Bath, Me., July 3, 1856; s. David T. and Adrianna (Bosworth) P.; A.B., Yale, 1877; M.D., Boston U. Sch. of Medicine, 1880; m. Ada Goodsell, June 15, 1881 (died 1891); m. 2d, Elinor B. Wheelock, Jan. 31, 1893. Began practice at Dorchester, Mass., 1880; Brookline, 1880—; instr., 1880, and prof. materia medica, 1881-1909, prof. clin. medicine, 1909—, Boston U. Med. Sch.; phys., Mass. Homœ. Hosp., 1892—; consulting phys., Westborough Insane Hosp., 1900—, and Emerson Hosp., 1902—. Trustee Mass. State Sanitarium, 6 yrs.; mem. Sch. Bd., Brookline, 10 yrs. Mem. Mass. Homœ. Med. Soc. (sec. 1883-86, pres. 1893) Boston Homœ. Med. Soc. (pres. 1886, sec.). Home: Brookline, Mass. Died June 15, 1928.

PERCY, LeRoy, senator; b. Washington County, Miss., Nov. 9, 1861; s. William A. and Nannie I. (Armstrong) P.; A.B., U. of the South, 1879; LL.B., U. of Va., 1881; m. Camille Bourges, Dec. 9, 1883; 1 son, William Alexander. Admitted to bar, 1881, in practice at Greenville, Miss., 1881—; also owning extensive land interests. Elected U.S. senator, Feb. 22, 1910, for unexpired term (1910-13) of A. J. McLaurin, deceased. Home: Greenville, Miss. Died Dec. 24, 1929.

PERCY, Walker, lawyer; b. Washington County, Miss., Nov. 18, 1864; s. William Alexander and Nancy I. (Armstrong) P.; bro. of LeRoy P.; A.M., U. of the South, Sewanee, Tenn., 1883; LL.B., U. of Va., 1885; m. Mary Pratt De Bardelehen, Apr. 17, 1888. In practice at Birmingham, Nov. 18, 1885—; sr. mem. Percy, Benners & Burr. Mem. Ala. Ho. of Rep., 1911; author of and secured passage of bill giving commn. form of govt. to Birmingham. Democrat. Episcopalian. Home: Birmingham, Ala. Died Feb. 8, 1917.

PERCY, William Alexander, lawyer, author; b. Greenville, Miss., May 14, 1885; s. U.S. Senator LeRoy and Camille (Bourges) P.; A.B., U. of the South, 1904, Litt.D., 1939; LL.B., Harvard, 1908; unmarried. Began practice at Greenville, 1908; retired. With Commn. for Relief in Belgium, 1916; 1st lt. infantry, 2d Officers' Training School, Leon Springs, Tex., Aug.-Oct. 1917; served with 37th Div., A.E.F., in France; hon. discharged as capt., 1919. Author: (verse) Sappho in Levkas, 1915; In April Once, 1920; Enzio's Kingdom, 1924; Selected Poems, 1930; Lanterns on the Levee (autobiography), 1941. Home: Greenville, Miss. Died Jan. 21, 1942.

PEREA, Pedro, sheep raiser, farmer; b. Bernalillo, N.M., Apr. 22, 1852; ed. St. Michael's Coll., Santa Fé, N.M.; Georgetown U., D.C., and St. Louis U., Mo.; m. Miss Montoya, 1877. Mem. Territorial council 4 times; delegate Rep. Nat. Conv., 1896; delegate in Congress from N.M., 1899-1901. Address: Bernalillo, N.M. Died 1906.

PERHAM, Sidney, gov.; b. Woodstock, Me., Mar. 27, 1819; ed. public schools; became teacher and farmer; m. Almina J. Hathaway, 1843. Mem. State Bd. Agr., Me., 1852-53; speaker Me. legislature, 1855. Presidential elector, 1856, 1892; clerk Supreme Jud. Court, Oxford Co., Me., 1859-63; congressman, 1863-69; gov. Me., 1871-74. Republican since the organization of the party. Washington, D.C. Died 1907.

PERIN, Charles Page, consulting engr.; b. West Point, N.Y., Aug. 23, 1861; s. Col. Glover (asst. surgeon gen. U.S.A.) and Elizabeth (Page) P.; A.B., Harvard, 1883; studied École des Mines, Paris; m. Keokee Munroe Henderson, July 7, 1887 (died 1913); m. 2d, Katharine Sharp Hoyt, Nov. 5, 1925. Served in various capacities with Carnegie Steel Company, later gen. mgr. and pres. blast furnaces collieries, Va. and Ky.; made study of fuel supply for Trans-Siberian Ry., for Russian Govt.; conducted surveys for iron and coal across India and developed iron resources of that country, resulting in Tata Iron & Steel Co. and Mysore Iron Works; consulting engr. Lung Yen Mining Corp., China; chief engr. appraisal commn. attached to Peace Commn., 1919; mem. firm Perin & Marshall, New York City; also dir. Stonega Coke & Coal Co. Mem. Am. Iron and Steel Inst. (past pres.), China Soc. (v.p.). Episcopalian. Author: Mission en Sibérie (pub. in France), 1901. A pioneer in development of manufacture of pure iron by electrolysis. Home: New York, N.Y. Died Feb. 16, 1937.

PERIN, George Landor, clergyman; b. Jasper Co., Ia., July 31, 1854; s. Caleb and Mary J. (Metteer) P.; Willamette U., Salem, Ore., 2 yrs.; A.B., St. Lawrence U., N.Y., 1878, D.D., 1890; m. Florence N. Hobart, Nov. 6, 1901. Ordained Universalist ministry, 1878; pastor in Ohio, 1878-82, Shawmut Ch., Boston, 1883-90; first missionary Universalist Ch. to Japan, 1890-94; again pastor Shawmut Ch., Boston, 1894-1910. Founder, 1901, and pres. Franklin Square House, a home for working girls and students; trustee Mt. Pleasant Home for Aged Men and Women; trustee N.E. Conservatory of Music, Curry Sch. of Expression (Boston), Dean Acad. (Franklin, Mass.). Mason. Wrote: The Sunny Side of Life, 1901; Why, Fadder, Why? How I Was Healed of Paralysis; Healing Affirmations. Home: Brookline, Mass. Died Dec. 1921.

PERINE, Edward Ten Broeck; b. Plainfield, N.J., Oct. 19, 1870; s. James Randolph and Maria V. (Ten Broeck) P.; grad. Plainfield High Sch., 1888; student Sch. of Arts, Columbia, class of 1892 (non-grad.); m. Nancy Tenney Mapes, Nov. 1, 1891; children—Mrs. Elsie Fullerton, Mrs. Rita Merritt. Cashier U.S. Mortgage & Trust Co., New York, 1893, treas., 1903; gen. mgr. The Audit Co. of New York, 1904-07, pres., 1907-09; dep. state comptroller of N.Y., 1909; mem. Perine & Company, C. P. As., 1911—; receiver and assignee important Wall Street bankruptcies. Author: The Story of the Trust Companies, 1916; Here's to Broadway!, 1930. Home: New York, N.Y. Died Jan. 16, 1941.

PERISHO, Elwood Chappell, geologist; b. Westfield, Ind.; s. Joshua M. and Lydia Anna (Chappell) P.; B.S., Earlham Coll., Ind., 1887, M.A., 1891, LL.D., 1913; M.S., U. of Chicago, 1895; hon. D.Sc. from State Coll. of S.Dak., 1928; m. Inez Beebe, Aug. 30, 1916. Prof. mathematics, Guilford Coll., 1887-93; fellow, U. of Chicago, 1894-95; prof. geology, State Normal Sch., Platteville, Wis., 1895-1903; prof. geology and dean Coll. Arts and Sciences, U. of S.D., and state geologist of S.D., 1903-14; pres. S.D. State Coll. Agr. and Mech. Arts, 1914-19; lecturer and prof. geology, Guilford Coll., N.C., 1921—. Mem. S.D. State Council Defense, 1917-19; lecturer patriotic work, 1917-18; work in Am. army camps, 1918-19; ednl. adminstr. and lecturer, faculty of Am. Army U., Beaune, France, 1919—, mem. U.S.A. Ednl. Corps in Europe, 1919. Pres. S.D. Ednl. Assn., 1913, S.D. Conservation Congress, 1911-13; chmn. coll. work and adminstrn. sect. Assn. Am. Agrl. Colls., 1916-17. Chautauqua lecturer, 1920. Republican. Mem. Soc. Friends. Editor The Friends Messenger, 1926-32. Author: The Erosion History of Southwest Wisconsin; The Ores of Southwestern Wisconsin; South Dakota's Artesian Basin and Its Wells; State College and the Tenth Generation. Died Aug. 14, 1935.

PERKINS, Albert Thompson, ry. official and consulting engineer; b. at Brunswick, Me., Oct. 2, 1865; s. Charles S. and Mary S. (Murray) Perkins; A.B. magna cum laude, Harvard, 1887, hon. A.M., 1919; m. Eva Spotswood Lemoine, Feb. 16, 1898; 1 dau., Katherine Lemoine (Mrs. Lloyd C. Stark). With C.,B.&Q. Ry. at Chicago, 1887, supt. terminals, St. Louis, 1897-1902, supt. St. Joseph div., 1902-06; consulting engr. and r.r. adviser to Municipal Bridge and Terminals Commn., St. Louis, 1906-08; same to St. Louis Union Trust Co., 1908—; served as exec. officer, engr. or pres. various rys., including St. Louis, Brownsville & Mexico, New Iberia & Northern, Chicago, Milwaukee & Gary and Apalachicola Northern, and as adviser on terminal matters to several cities; pres. Peoples Motorbus Co. (St. Louis); director numerous corps., including Laclede Steel Co., St. Louis Pub. Service Co., St. Louis Refrigerating & Cold Storage Company. Mil. training, Plattsburg Camp, and St. Louis; maj. Engr. R.C., June 28, 1917; lt. col. N.A., July 6, 1917; col. U.S.A., Aug. 13, 1918, and assigned to 14th Engineers. Sailed for France, July 1917; with British 3d Army and 2d Army; successively dep. mgr., mgr. and dir. Light (Combat) Rys., A.E.F.; participated at Paaschendaele Ridge, Cambrai, 1917, Marne-Aisne, Somme, St. Mihiel, Meuse-Argonne offensives; hon. discharged, Mar. 11, 1919; col. U.S., comdg. 327th (Combat) Engrs. to 1930; now col. Aux. Res. Decorated D.S.M. (U.S.); Order St. Michael and St. George (British). Mem. Bd. of Overseers, Harvard, 1925-31, pres. bd., 1930-31. Trustee Mo. Bot. Garden, Ranken Sch. of Mech. Trades; mem. nat. exec. com. Mil. Training Camps Assn.; pres. Community Fund of St. Louis; dir. St. Louis Chamber of Commerce. Mem. Nat. Aeronautic Assn. (pres. St. Louis Chapter), Soc. Am. Mil. Engrs. (pres.). Republican. Home: Clayton, Mo. Died Nov. 22, 1936.

PERKINS, Angie Villette Warren; b. at Danielson, Windham County, Conn., Nov. 6, 1858; d. Lysander and Marcia (Mason) Warren; A.B., Wesleyan U., Conn., 1876, A.M., 1879; m. Charles Albert Perkins, Sept. 19, 1883. Asst. prof. French and Latin, Wellesley Coll., 1879-80; grad. student Harvard Annex, 1880; lady prin. Lawrence U., Appleton, Wis., 1881-83; dean woman's dept., U. of Tenn., 1897-1900. Regent Knoxville chapter D.A.R., 1898-1900; pres. Union Presbytery Missionary socs.; v.p. for Tenn. Women's Foreign Missionary Soc. of Presbyn. Ch.; pres. Tenn. Federation of Women's Clubs, 1900-04; dir. Gen. Federation Women's Clubs, 1904-06; corr. sec., 1906-08. Actively interested in edn., missions and women's clubs, and Young Women's Christian Assn.; pres. Knoxville Y.W.C.A., 1907-09, Ossoli Circle, 1896-97, 1911-12; elected mem. Knoxville Sch. Bd., Dec. 7, 1915 (the 1st woman on sch. bd. S. of Ohio River) and pres., 1917—. Author: San Diego to Sitka, 1903; Our Year Abroad, 1911. Address: Knoxville, Tenn. Died Jan. 29, 1921.

PERKINS, Charles Elliott, ry. official; b. Cincinnati, Nov. 24, 1840; went to Burlington, Ia., 1859; became clerk in office of asst. treas. of Burlington & Missouri River R.R.; asst. same, 1862-65; supt., 1865; later dir. Mem. bd. directors C.,B.&Q. R.R. Co., 1875; v.p., 1876-81, pres. 1881-1901; resigned Feb. 21, 1901. Address: Burlington, Ia. Died 1907.

PERKINS, Charles Enoch, lawyer; b. Hartford, Conn., Mar. 23, 1832; s. Thomas C. and Mary (Beecher) P.; A.B., Williams, 1853; m. Lucy Adams, Aug. 25, 1855 (died 1891). Admitted to bar, 1855; began practice as partner with father, firm of Perkins & Perkins; later sr. mem. Perkins, Wells & Scott. Mem. Common Council several terms and served as city attorney, Hartford; mem. Conn. Ho. of Rep., 1871. Republican. Conglist. Home: Hartford, Conn. Died Jan. 8, 1917.

PERKINS, Charles Plummer, commodore U.S.N.; b. Great Falls, N.H., Feb. 18, 1848; s. Moses P. and Elizabeth (Nute) P.; early edn. schs. of Dover, N.H., Haverhill and Salem, Mass.; grad. U.S. Naval Acad., 1869; m. Kate Stevens, Aug. 19, 1885; m. 2d, Ellen O., d. Judge J. J. Graves, Oct. 8, 1904. Promoted ensign, 1871; master, 1872; lt., 1874; lt. comdr., 1896; comdr., 1899; captain, 1904; retired as commodore, June 30, 1908. Served on many duties and stas.; was on Amazon survey, 1878, "Jeannette" search expdn., 1881, Tampico River expdn., 1883; comdg. coast survey steamer Eagre, Hydrographic Survey, Hell Gate, 1886; supt. compasses, Navy Dept., 1892-95; Spanish-Am. War Service on board monitor Monadnock, Manila; later comd. U.S.S. Michigan, Adams, Alert, Philadelphia, Boston, Concord, and Pensacola; in Panama campaign, 1903-04; commandant Naval Training Sta., San Francisco, 1906-07; later asst. to commandant Pacific Naval Dist.; pres. Statutory Bd. Survey, and commandant Pacific Naval Dist., 1908-09. Author of monograph on cruise of "Alliance" in search of "Jeannette," and collaborator textbook for U.S. Naval Acad., in "Marine Surveying." Address: Berkeley, Calif. Died Oct. 5, 1913.

PERKINS, DeForest H.; b. Brooksville, Me., Dec. 25, 1873; s. Charles H. and Ruth (Grindle) P.; Ph.B., U. of Me., 1900, M.A., 1905; LL.B., U. of Ill., 1906; studied U. of Chicago, Ind. U.; m. Jennie C. Powers, Aug. 1, 1900. Teacher pub. schs., 1893-96; prin. Freedom (Me.) Acad., 1900-02; Skowhegan High Sch., 1902-08; supt. schs., Dist. of Madison and Skowhegan, 1908-11; supt. schs., Portland, Me., 1911-18; exec. sec. Portland Chamber of Commerce, 1918—. Republican. Methodist. Mason. Home: Portland, Me. Deceased.

PERKINS, Dwight Heald, architect; b. Memphis, Tenn., Mar. 26, 1867; s. Marland Leslie and Marion (Heald) P.; student Mass. Inst. Tech., 1885-87; m. Lucy A. Fitch, Aug. 18, 1891; children—Eleanor Ellis, Lawrence Bradford. Instr. in architecture, Mass. Inst. Tech., 1887-88; practice at Chicago, 1894—; mem. firm Perkins, Chatten & Hammond. Architect for Chicago Bd. of Edn., 1905-10; chmn. sub-com. on playgrounds, Spl. Park Commn., 1899-1909; mem. Municipal Art Commn. of Chicago; mem. plan com. of Cook Co. Forest Preserve, 1916-22; pres. Northwest Park Dist. Commn. of Evanston, 1911-16; hon. pres. Regional Planning Assn. of Chicago. Home: Evanston, Ill. Died Nov. 2, 1941.

PERKINS, Edmund Taylor, civil engr.; b. Scottsville, Va., Sept. 8, 1864; s. Edmund Taylor and Mary Sydnor (Addison) P.; C.E., A.B., Union Coll., N.Y., 1885, A.M., 1888; m. Jean Waters, June 3, 1903 (dec.); m. 2d, Louise Lamson-Scribner, Aug. 17, 1918. Topographer U.S. Geol. Survey, 1885-1902; engr. U.S. Reclamation Service, 1902-10; pres. Edmund T. Perkins Engring. Co., Chicago, Nov. 1, 1910—. Pres. Am. Reclamation Federation; pres. Nat. Drainage Congress; mem. State of Fla. Everglades Engring. Commn. Mem. Am. Assn. Engrs. (pres. 1917-18). Democrat. Episcopalian. Home: Chicago, Ill. Died May 21, 1921.

PERKINS, Elisha Henry, banker, lawyer; b. Baltimore, Nov. 16, 1850; s. Elisha Henry P. (M.D.) and Elizabeth A. (Berry) P.; A.B., Princeton, 1871, A.M., 1874; LL.B., U. of Md., 1873; m. Jean Davidson Falconer, June 6, 1878; children—Charlotte Soutter, Jean Falconer (Mrs. Walter Stevenson Finlay, Jr.). Practiced law, Baltimore, 1873-88; pres. Provident Savings Bank, 1888-1926, chmn. bd., 1926—; dir. Safe Deposit & Trust Co., Equitable Soc. Pres. Trustees of the Poor, 1896-1900; supervisor city charities, Baltimore, 1900-21; finance commr., 1904-08. Dir. Princeton Theol. Sem., 1900-28; ruling elder First Presbyn. Ch., 1881—. Republican. Home: Baltimore, Md. Died Sept. 30, 1931.

PERKINS, Emily Swan, hymnologist; b. Chicago, Ill., Oct. 19, 1866; d. George Wallbridge and Sarah Louise (Mills) P.; sister of the late George W. Perkins; ed. Central High Sch., Cleveland, 1880-85. Founder, 1922, and corr. sec. of the Hymn Society "to promote the production and use of better hymns and tunes in church worship." Composer of music appearing in Presbyn. and other hymnals. Served as chmn. Van Courtlandt Chapter Am. Red Cross, World War. Founder Women's Republican Club, Riverdale-on-Hudson. Mem. nat. bd. Y.W.C.A., 1923-28; volunteer social worker. Author: Stonehurst Hymn Tunes, 1921; Riverdale Hymn Tunes, 1938. Home: New York, N.Y. Died June 27, 1941.

PERKINS, Frank Walley, U.S. coast survey; b. Staten Island, N.Y., June 24, 1844; s. Francis and Miriam Phillips (Walley) P.; ed. Canaan (N.H.) Acad., 1855-58; Middleboro (Mass.) Acad., 1858-60; Eagleswood Inst., N.J., 1860-61; Pujol Mil. Acad., N.Y., 1861-62; unmarried. Spl. relief officer, U.S. Sanitary Commn., sanitary store keeper, Army of Potomac, 2d officer Sanitary Hosp., Washington, Oct. 1862-June 9, 1863. Entered U.S. Coast and Geod. Survey as aid and asst., June 10, 1863; retired. Home: Morristown, N.J. Died 1922.

PERKINS, Frederick, army officer; b. in Me., Aug. 21, 1857; grad. U.S. Mil. Acad., 1883. Commd. 2d lt. 5th Inf., June 13, 1883; 1st lt. 16th Inf., Feb. 24, 1891; trans. to 8th Inf., July 20, 1891; capt. inf., July 26, 1898; assigned to 8th Inf., Jan. 1, 1899; maj. 13th Inf., Aug. 7, 1906; adj. gen., Apr. 7, 1908; lt. col. 20th Inf., Mar. 2, 1912; col., Feb. 21, 1916; brig. gen. N.A., Aug. 5, 1917; hon. discharged as brig. gen. N.A., Mar. 1918. Comd. Provost Guard at Mil. Prison, Ft. Leavenworth, Kan., 1891-94, adj. of Mil. Prison, 1894-95; in Cuba, Spanish-Am. War, to July 15, 1898; apptd. comdr. 166th Inf. Brigade, Camp Sherman, Chillicothe, O., Sept. 1917. Address: Washington, D.C. Died Apr. 25, 1940.

PERKINS, George Clement, senator; b. Kennebunkport, Me., Aug. 23, 1839; s. Clement and Lucinda (Fairfield) P.; reared on farm; went to sea at 13, and was cabin boy and sailor until 1855, when he shipped before the mast on a sailing vessel bound for San Francisco, and on arrival there went to Oroville; m. Ruth A. Parker, 1864. Carried on a successful mercantile business, San Francisco; later engaged in banking, milling, mining and the steamship business; mem. Goodall, Perkins & Co., owners Pacific S.S. Co.; first to introduce steam whalers for Arctic Ocean and operated numerous ships on Pacific Ocean from Alaska to Mex. Mem. Calif. Senate, 1869-76; gov. of Calif., 1879-83; apptd. U.S. senator, July 24, 1893, to fill vacancy and elected, Aug. 8, 1893, for remainder of same term; reëlected, 1895, 1903, 1909; term expired 1915. Republican. Home: Oakland, Calif. Died Feb. 26, 1923.

PERKINS, George Douglas, newspaper editor; b. Holly, Orleans County, N.Y., Feb. 29, 1840; s. John D. and Lucy F. (Forsyth) P.; went West in boyhood; learned printer's trade, Baraboo, Wis.; m. Louise E. Julien, 1869. With brother started the Cedar Falls Gazette, 1860; pvt. 31st Ia. Regt., 1862-63; editor Sioux City Journal, 1869—. Mem. Ia. Senate, 1874-76; U.S. marshal Northern Dist. of Ia., 1882-85; mem. 52d to 55th Congresses (1891-99), 11th Ia. Dist.; del-at-large from Ia. Rep. Nat. convs., 1876, 80, 88, 1908. Address: Sioux City, Iowa. Died Feb. 3, 1914.

PERKINS, George Henry, univ. prof.; b. Cambridge, Mass., Sept. 25, 1844; s. Rev. Frederick Trenck and Harriet Thompson (Olmsted) P.; A.B., Yale, 1867, Ph.D., 1869; LL.D., U. of Vt., 1911; Litt.D., Knox, 1912; m. Mary Judd Farnham, Aug. 16, 1870; children—Hattie Olmsted (dec.), Henry Farnham. Prof. zoölogy, botany and geology, 1869-1898, geology, 1898—, v.p. and dean Coll. of Arts, 1898—, and actg. pres., 1917-19, U. of Vt. State entomologist of Vt., 1880-95; state geologist, 1898—. Author: A Flora of Vermont, 1888; Reports on Injurious Insects, 1880-91; Report on the Marble, Slate and Granite Industries of Vermont, 1898, and Reports of State Geologist, 1900—. Contbr. to Encyclopædia Britannica and other encys., and about 100 titles in scientific periodicals. Address: Burlington, Vt. Died Sept. 12, 1933.

PERKINS, George Walbridge, financier; b. Chicago, Jan. 31, 1862; s. George Walbridge and Sarah Louise (Mills) P.; ed. pub. schs., Chicago; hon. LL.D., Wooster and U. of Vt.; m. Evelyn Ball, 1889. Started business career in Chicago office N.Y. Life Ins. Co., 1877; became successively bookkeeper, cashier, insp. of agencies, supt. western dept., 3d v.p., 1892, in charge of agency force, with hdqrs. at home office, 2d v.p., 1898; chmn. of finance com., N.Y. Life, 1900, v.p., 1903. Became partner in banking firm of J. P. Morgan & Co., 1901, retired 1910; dir. Internat. Mercantile Marine Co., U.S. Steel Corp.; chmn. of finance com. and dir. Internat. Harvester Co.; dir. Fla. East Coast Ry., Great Am. Ins. Co., Am. Alliance Ins. Co. Trustee Vassar College; dir. Y.M.C.A.; pres. N.Y. Palisades Interstate Park Commn.; mem. bd. mgrs. and exec. com. New York Botanical Garden and Park Dist. Protective League; trustee N.Y. Scenic and Historic Preservation Soc. Home: Riverdale, N.Y. Died June 18, 1920.

PERKINS, Herbert Farrington, pres. Internat. Harvester Co.; b. Constantinople, Turkey, Oct. 18, 1864; s. George Augustus (prof. nat. sciences, Robert Coll.), and Sarah Elizabeth (Farrington) P.; brought to U.S., 1865; B.A., Yale, 1887; m. Margaret Dana Head, Dec. 14, 1892; children—Franklin Head, Mrs. Helen Knight, Margaret, Elizabeth. With Nat. Malleable Castings Co., Chicago, 1887-99; became connected with McCormick Harvester Co., 1899, and continued with its successor, Internat. Harvester Co., 1st v.p., 1922-29, pres., 1929-31; pres. Wis. Steel Co., Wis. Lumber Co.; v.p. Personal Loan & Savings Bank. Adviser to chmn. War Labor Policies Bd., Washington, D.C., 1918; apptd. through U.S. Chamber of Commerce as mem. Pres. Wilson's first industrial Conf., Washington, 1919, elected a vice chmn. Nat. Industrial Conf. Bd., 1928. Republican. Home: Chicago, Ill. Died Jan. 1, 1936.

PERKINS, James Breck, congressman from 32d dist., N.Y., 1901-09; b. St. Croix, Wis., Nov. 4, 1847; U. of Rochester, 1867, LL.D.; engaged in practice of law; city atty. of Rochester, 1874-78; mem. N.Y. Assembly, 1898; mem. Nat. Institute of Arts and Letters. Author: France Under Richelieu and Mazarin, 1887; France Under the Regency, 1892; France Under Louis XV, 1897; Richelieu (Heroes of the Nations Series), 1900. Address: Rochester, N.Y. Died 1910.

PERKINS, James Handasyd, banker; b. Milton, Mass., Jan. 11, 1876; s. Edward Cranch and Jane Sedgwick (Watson) P.; A.B., Harvard, 1898; m. Katrine Parkman Coolidge, Nov. 22, 1906; children—Eleanor H. (Mrs. Franklin E. Parker, Jr.), Richard S., Elizabeth Joan. With Walter Baker & Company, Ltd., 1898-1905; v.p. Am. Trust Co., Boston, 1905-08; v.p. Nat. Commercial Bank, Albany, N.Y., 1908-12, pres. 1912-14; v.p. Nat. City Bank, New York, 1914-19, exec. mgr., 1916-19; mem. banking firm Montgomery & Co., 1919; pres. Farmers Loan & Trust Co., 1921-29; chmn. City Bank Farmers Trust Co.; chmn. bd. Nat. City Bank of N.Y., 1933—; chmn. bd. Internat. Banking Corp.; dir. Anaconda Copper Mining Co., Am. & Foreign Ins. Co., Eagle Indemnity Co., Federal Union Ins. Co., Globe Indemnity Co., Liverpool & London & Globe Ins. Co., Ltd., Newark Fire Ins. Co., Queen Ins. Co. of America, Royal Indemnity Co., Star Ins. Co. of America, Consol. Edison Co. of N.Y., New York Edison Co., Sperry Realty Co., Union Pacific System, 150 William St. Corporation, and many other insurance companies. Pres. New York Clearing House, 1937—. Trustee Miriam Osborn Memorial Home Assn. Mem. 1st comm. to France, American Red Cross; commissioner to France and Europe, Am. Red Cross, June 1917-Sept. 1918; resigned to enter A.E.F.; duty at G.H.Q., asst. chief of staff 2d Army, later of 3d Army; lt. col. Q.M.C., Nov. 7, 1918; asst. chief of staff, 3d Army (Army of Occupation), Nov. 1918-Jan. 1919. D.S.M. (U.S.); Officer Legion of Honor (France); Comdr. Order of the Crown (Belgium). Treas. New York Co. Chapter Am. Red Cross, Jan. 1920-July 1921. Mem. Am. Bankers' Assn. (exec. council, finance com., 1915-18), N.Y. State Bankers' Assn. (pres. 1913-14). Home: Greenwich, Conn. Died July 12, 1940.

PERKINS, Janet Russell, botanist; b. Lafayette, Ind., May 20, 1853; d. Cyrus Grosvenor and Jane Rose (Houghteling) P.; U. of Wis., 1867-72, A.B., 1901; studying France and Germany, 1872-75; teacher in Chicago, 1875-95, except 3 yrs.' study and travel Sandwich Islands, Europe, Azores and Calif.; U. of Berlin, 1895-98; U. of Heidelberg, 1898-99, Ph.D. Apptd. by Carnegie Instn. of Washington to prepare material for flora of Philippines, 1902; collected plants in Jamaica, B.W.I., three winters, 1914-17. Wrote 3 monographs on Monimiaceæ and other higher tropical plants, in Engler's Botanische Jahrbücher; also Part IV, "Monimiaceæ," for Das Pflanzenreich, 1901; Fragmenta Floræ Philippinæ, Contributions to the Flora of the Philippine Islands, 3 Fascicles, 1904; "Styracaceæ" for Das Pflanzenreich, 1907, published by Royal Prussian Academy; "Monimiaceæ" for Das Pflanzenreich, 1911; Beiträge zur Kenntnis der Monimiaceen Papuasiens, Engler's Botanische Jahrbücher, 1915; Uebersicht ueber die Gattungen der Monimiaceæ sowie Zusammenstellung der Abbildungen und der Literatur ueber die Arten dieser Familie bis zum Jahre, 1925; Uebersicht über die Gattungen der Styracaceæ sowie Zusammenstellung der Abbildungen und der Literatur über die Arten dieser Familie bis zum Jahre, 1928. Unitarian. Address: Chicago, Ill. Died July 7, 1933.

PERKINS, John Russell, educator; b. Wells, Me., Apr. 4, 1868; s. Samuel H. and Sarah (Allen) P.; A.B., Dartmouth, 1889, A.M., 1892; Ph.G., Tufts Coll., 1890; student Harvard Summer Sch., 1892; m. Mary W. Brown, Sept. 14, 1903. Prin. State Normal Sch., Danbury, Conn., 1904—. Pres. Conn. State Teachers' Assn., 1907-08. Trustee Danbury Pub. Library. Conglist. Odd Fellow. Home: Danbury, Conn. Died May 14, 1923.

PERKINS, Lucy Fitch, author, illustrator; b. Maples, Ind.; d. Appleton Howe and Elizabeth (Bennett) Fitch; grad. Mus. Fine Arts Sch., Boston, 1886; m. Dwight Heald Perkins, Aug. 18, 1891; children—Eleanor Ellis, Lawrence Bradford. Teacher in Sch. Fine Arts, Pratt Inst., Brooklyn, 1887-91. Author: (and illustrator) A Book of Joys, 1907; The Goose Girl; Cornelia; The Dutch Twins; The Japanese Twins; The Irish Twins, and others of the series. Editor and illustrator Dandelion Classics, and illustrator of other books. Mem. League of Women Voters. Home: Evanston, Ill. Died Mar. 18, 1937.

PERKINS, Maurice, Nott prof. analytical chemistry Union Coll., 1865—; b. New London, Conn., Mar. 14, 1836; studied Göttingen, Heidelberg, Tübingen; A.M., Harvard, 1865; M.D., Albany Med. Coll., 1870; asst. prof. chemistry Coll. Phys. and Surg., New York, 1862-63; asst. Lawrence Scientific School, Harvard, 1863-65. Author: Manual of Qualitative Analysis. Address: Schenectady, N.Y. Died 1901.

PERKINS, Randolph, congressman; b. Dunellen, N.J., Nov. 30, 1871; s. James H. and Elizabeth (Kelly) P.; ed. pub. schs.; m. Louise Tuttle Morris, Jan. 29, 1909. Admitted to N.J. bar, 1893, and began practice at Jersey City; mayor, Westfield, N.J., 1904-06; mem. N.J. Ho. of Assembly, 1905-07; author Perkins railroad tax act, 1906; mem. 67th to 73d Congresses (1921-35), 6th N.J. Dist. Republican. Mason, Elk. Home: Woodcliff Lake, Bergen County, N.J. Died May 25, 1936.

PERKINS, Reece Wilmer, univ. pres.; b. Brandywine Summit, Delaware County, Pa.; s. Joseph and Margaret (Frame) P.; A.B., Bucknell U., 1872, A.M., 1875, Ph.D., 1893; B.D., Crozer Theol. Sem., 1875; m. Sallie Evans Rhoads, 1893. Taught pub. schs. and high sch. in Lock Haven, Pa., and in Normal Sch.; ordained Bapt. ministry, 1877; pastor Camden, N.J., 1877-87, Lock Haven, Pa., 1887-1901; pres. Leland U., New Orleans, 1901—. Was prominent in founding Lock Haven Hosp. and Lock Haven Chorus. Address: New Orleans, La. Died 19—.

PERKINS, Robert Patterson, carpet mfr.; b. N.Y. City, Dec. 3, 1861; s. Charles Lawrence and Elizabeth West (Nevin) P.; A.B., Harvard, 1884, A.M., 1921; unmarried. Clk. D.,L.&W. R.R., 1884-86; salesman P. Lorillard & Co., 1886-88; N.Y. agt. H. C. Thacher & Co., 1888-92; sec. E. S. Higgins Carpet Co., 1892-99, pres., 1899-1901; elected pres., 1901, Hartford Carpet Corp. which absorbed E. S. Higgins Carpet Co., and pres. of its successor, The Bigelow-Hartford Carpet Co., 1914—. Lt. col. Am. Red Cross, 1917; commr. in Italy, taking over relief work there, 1917. Clubs: Harvard (pres. 1919), Knickerbocker, Union, The Brook, Racquet and Tennis, Nat. Golf Links, Garden City Golf, Piping Rock, New York Yacht. Home: Centerport, L.I., N.Y. Office: 385 Madison Av., New York, N.Y. Died Apr. 28, 1924.

PERKINS, Roger Griswold, prof. preventive medicine; b. Schenectady, N.Y., May 17, 1874; s. Maurice and Annie Dunbar (Potts) P.; A.B., Union Coll., 1893; A.B., Harvard, 1894; M.D., Johns Hopkins, 1898; hon. M.A., Union U., 1925; m. Edna, d. Charles F. Brush, Nov. 14, 1905; children—Charles Brush, Roger Griswold, Maurice, John Morris. Resident pathologist, Lakeside Hosp., Cleveland, 1898-1901; fellow, Rockefeller Inst., 1902-03; lecturer on bacteriology, 1901-04, asst. prof. pathology and bacteriology, 1904-08, asso. prof. pathology and hygiene, 1908-11, prof. hygiene and preventive medicine, 1911-30, later prof. emeritus, Western Reserve Md. Sch. City bacteriologist, Cleveland, 1906-07, 1913-14; chief Bur. of Lab., Div. of Health, 1914-23; consultant to commr. of health and dir. labs., 1923-30; mem. Filtration Commn., Cleveland, 1913. Trustee Brush Foundation, 1931—. Presbyterian. Mem. Am. Red Cross Commn. to Roumania, 1917-18; med. asso. to scientific attaché, Am. Embassy, Paris, 1918; dir. sanitation div., Am. Red Cross Commn. to Balkan States, 1919. Home: Wakefield, R.I. Died Mar. 28, 1936.

PERKINS, Thomas Nelson, lawyer; b. Milton, Mass., 1870; s. Edward C. and Jane S. (Watson) P.; A.B., Harvard, 1891, LL.B., 1894, LL.D., 1926; LL.D., Dartmouth, 1930; admitted to bar, 1893; m. Louisa C. Adams, June 6, 1900. In practice at Boston, 1894—; mem. Ropes, Gray, Boyden & Perkins; dir. and mem. exec. com. B.&M. R.R.; dir. Merrimac Chemical Co., Sullivan Machinery Co. (chmn. bd. and mem. exec. com.), Gen. Foods Corp., Am. Telephone & Telegraph Co., Stone & Webster, Inc. (exec. com.), Southern Pacific Co., First Nat. Bank of Boston (exec. com.), Elliott Investment Co. (Santa Barbara). Fiduciary Associates (Boston), New England Pub. Service Corp. (exec. com.), Fiduciary Tr. Co., Gen. Printing Ink Corp., Loew's, Inc., Guarantee Co. of No. America, Flintkote Co.; trustee Eastern Gas and Fuel Associates. Chmn. bd. Commercial Radio Internat. Com. During World War was mem. Priorities Com., chief counsel War Industries Bd.; mem. Am. Commn. to Inter-Allied War Conf. (Paris); asst. to sec. of war and asst. dir. of munitions. U.S. citizen member Reparation Commn. (Paris), 1924-26, and mem. Com. of Experts, 1929 (alternate to chmn.); pres. Arbitral Tribunal of Interpretation, The Hague, 1926-30. Fellow, President and Fellows of Harvard Coll.; mem. Am. Acad. of Arts and Letters. Home: Westwood, Mass. Died Oct. 7, 1937.

PERKINS, (David) Walton, pianist, composer; b. Rome, N.Y., Nov. 16, 1847; s. David W. and Jane Huntington (Fitch) P.; ed. Milwaukee (Wis.) Acad., and Phillips Acad., Exeter, N.H., 1857-65; piano studies under S. B. Mills, Alfred H. Pease, Theo. Kullak and Anton Rubenstein; theory under August Mickler and Friedrich Siebmann; m. Cornelia H. Richards, June 17, 1879 (died 1892); children—William Richards, Theodore Walton; m. 2d, Gertrude Grosscup, Feb. 20, 1895. Founder, mgr. and asso. dir. Sherwood Music School, 1897-1901; pres. Chicago Conservatory of Music, 1907—. Home: Chicago, Ill. Died Feb. 8, 1929.

PERKINS, William Oscar, composer, conductor; b. Stockbridge, Vt., May 23, 1831; s. Orson Perkins; ed. Kimball Union Acad. and attended lectures, Harvard, 1854; Mus. Doc., Hamilton Coll., N.Y., 1879; unmarried. Studied music in Boston and Europe; taught music in Boston; choral conductor, normal music school instr., lecturer and writer on musical and other topics. Has published more than 60 musical works. Lived in New York, 1882-86, in London, Eng., 1886-94, teaching, lecturing and composing; spent 1895 in the South; in Boston, 1895—. Author: The War in South Africa, or Boer and Briton, 1900. Address: Boston, Mass. Died 1902.

PERKY, Kirtland Irving, lawyer; b. Smithville, Wayne County, O., Feb. 8, 1867; s. John Firestone and Esther (Martin) P.; B.S., Ohio Northern U., Ada, 1888; law dept., U. of Ia., 1889-90; m. Ella Hunter, Apr. 18, 1891 (dec.); 1 dau., Mrs. Esther Woodhouse. Began practice at Wahoo, Neb., 1890; moved to Ida., 1894; chmn. Dem. State Central Com., Ida., 1900-02; judge 4th Jud. Dist., Ida., 1901-03; U.S. senator, Dec. 1912-Feb. 6, 1913, filling vacancy occasioned by death of Weldon B. Heyburn; moved to Calif., 1923; in practice at Los Angeles. Author bill to prevent removal cases against corps. from state to federal courts on grounds of diverse citizenship when corp. defendant maintains business place within jurisdiction of state court. Home: Long Beach, Calif. Died Jan. 8, 1939.

PERLEY, Sidney, lawyer; b. Boxford, Mass., Mar. 6, 1858; s. Humphrey and Eunice (Peabody) P.; ed. pub. schs., Boxford; LL.B., Boston U., 1886; m. Harriet Hood Spofford, June 11, 1889; children—Eleanor Spofford, Richard Hood. Admitted to Suffolk bar, 1886; began practice at Salem. Editor The Essex Antiquarian, 1897-1909; mem. bd. edn., Salem, 1901-03, 1907-11. Author: History of Boxford, Mass., 1880; Historic Storms of New England, 1891; Law of Interest, 1893; Dwellings of Boxford, Mass., 1894; Adjudicated Forms, 1895; Mortuary Law, 1896; Probate Practice (Mass.), 1898; Massachusetts Practice, 1902; Indian Land Titles of Essex County, Mass., 1912; The Hovey Book, 1914; The Plumer Genealogy, 1917; Service under the Covenant, 1921; History of Salem, Mass., Vol. I, 1924, Vol. II, 1926, Vol. III, 1928; and many pamphlets and articles of an hist. character. Home: Salem, Mass. Died June 9, 1928.

PEROT, Thomas Morris, mfr.; b. Phila., May 8, 1828; s. Francis P.; grad. Phila. Coll. Pharmacy, 1849; m. Rebecca C. Siter, Nov. 3, 1858. Wholesale druggist Phila., 1850-69; from 1869 head of the oldest business house in U.S., The Francis Perot's Sons Malting Co., established in Phila., 1687; 7th generation in direct descent from founder. Pres. the Mercantile Library Co., 1861-1900; pres. Woman's Med. Coll. of Phila., 1st med. coll. for women established in the world, 1864-1900. Is 1st v.p. Phila. Bd. of Trade; pres. of the Pa. Soc. for the Prevention of Cruelty to Children. Residence: Philadelphia, Pa. Died 1902.

PERRIN, Bernadotte, univ. professor; b. Goshen, Conn., Sept. 15, 1847; s. Lavalette and Ann Eliza (Comstock) P.; A.B., Yale, 1869, Ph.D., 1873; univs. of Tübingen, Leipzig and Berlin, 1876-79; LL.D., Western Reserve, 1893; m. Luella Perrin, Aug. 17, 1881 (died 1889); m. 2d, Susan Lester, Nov. 25, 1892. Teacher Yale, and Hartford High Sch., 1869-81; prof. Greek, Western Reserve U., 1881-93; prof. Greek, 1893-1901, Lampson prof. Greek lit. and history, 1901-09, emeritus, 1909, Yale U. Pres. Am. Philol. Assn., 1897. Editor: Cæsar's Civil War, 1882; Homer's Odyssey, Books I-IV, 1889; Homer's Odyssey, Books V-VIII, 1894; School Odyssey, eight books and vocabulary (with T. D. Seymour), 1897; Six of Plutarch's Greek Lives—Themistocles and Aristides, transl. with introduction and commentary, 1901; Cimon and Pericles, 1910; Nicias and Alcibiades 1912; Plutarch's Lives (translated), Loeb Classical Library, vols. I-VIII, 1914-19. Fellow Am. Acad. Arts and Sciences. Home: New Haven, Conn. Died Aug. 31, 1920.

PERRIN, John, banker; b. Rossville, Ind., Jan. 17, 1857; s. James J. and Margaret (Cason) P.; B.A., Yale, 1879; m. Ellenor Cathcart, d. Maj. Hervey Bates, Oct. 3, 1883; children—Hervey Bates, John Bates (dec.). Mem. Perrin Bros., hardware, Lafayette, Ind., 1879-89; in Europe studying banking, 1889-90; v.p., 1890-99, Perrin Nat. Bank, Lafayette, founded, 1868, by his father, who was continuously its pres.; organized, 1900, and pres. until 1910, Am. Nat. Bank, Indianapolis which later consolidated with Fletcher Nat. Bank; chmn. board Fletcher Am. Nat. Bank, Indianapolis, 1910-12; chmn. Federal Reserve Bank of San Francisco, 1914-26. Mason. Address: South Pasadena, Calif. Died Dec. 27, 1931.

PERRIN, John William, librarian; b. Eugene, Ind.; s. William Jasper and Susan (Allen) P.; A.M., Wabash Coll., 1889; grad. student Johns Hopkins, 1890-92; grad. student and hon. fellow, U. of Chicago, 1892-93, Ph.D., 1895; m. Harriet Naylor Towle, Apr. 16, 1890 (died 1910). Prof. of history and politics, Allegheny Coll., Pa., 1894-98; prof. of history, Adelbert Coll. (Western Reserve U.), 1898-1904; Albert Shaw lecturer, Am. diplomatic history, Johns Hopkins, 1904; lecturer on Am. history, Allegheny Coll., 1905; librarian, Case Library, Cleveland, 1905—. Organized, 1899, and chmn. until 1903, Conf. of Collegiate and Secondary Sch. Instrs. of Western Reserve U.; sec. Dept. of Higher Edn. N.E.A., 1902; pres. Ohio Library Assn., 1907-08. Republican. Author: History of the Cleveland Sinking Fund of 1862; History of Compulsory Education in New England. Mem. Cleveland Heights (O.) Board of Education, Jan. 1, 1912-Jan. 1, 1916 (president 1914-16). Home: Cleveland, O. Died July 14, 1924.

PERRIN, Marshall Livingston, univ. prof.; b. Wellesley Hills (then Frantville), Mass., July 31, 1855; s. Noah and Philenia Winship (Stone) P.; A.B., Harvard, 1874, A.M., 1876; post-grad. student, Harvard, 1877-80; in German univs., 1883-88; Göttingen U., instr., 1885-88, Ph.D., 1889; m. Mary Josephine Williams, Feb. 23, 1889 (died 1890); 1 son, Harold Livingston. Sec. U.S. Fishery Expdn. on Pacific Coast and among McLeod Indians (Calif.), 1874; teacher, Stone's Sch., Boston, 1880-83; sec. sch. bd., Wellesley, Mass., 1881-83; lektor Göttingen U., 1885-88; instr., 1888-89, asst. prof., 1889-91, prof. Germanic langs., 1891—, also of Sanskrit, 1910—, Boston U. Supt. pub. schs., Wellesley, Mass., 1893-1909; lecturer ednl. topics. Trustee of Wellesley Free Library, 1898-1917. Protestant. Republican. Author: Drill Book in Algebra, 1883; Chronik von Thomas Castelford, 1889; Tables and Drill Books in German, 1900. Taught modern languages at U. of Nanking and at Ginling Coll., China, 1920-21. Student of Oriental religions at their sources. Home: Wellesley Hills, Mass. Died Dec. 2, 1935.

PERRIN, Raymond St. James, author; b. New York, Sept. 4, 1849; s. Peter Alphonse and Martha (Brecken) P.; ed. pvt. schs. in New York and N.J.; independent pvt. student all life, especially of philosophy; m. Augustine Vergens, Feb. 22, 1872. Engaged in mfg. varnishes and pres. Perrin, Payson & Co., 1878-1901; pres. Perrin Varnish Co., 1901—. Author: Student's Dream (anonymous), 1881; Religion of Philosophy, 1885; Evolution of Knowledge, 1905. Home: Chatham, New Jersey. Died August 30, 1915.

PERRIN, Willard Taylor, clergyman; b. Cambridge, Mass., June 2, 1850; s. Noah and Philenia Winship (Stone) P.; A.B., Harvard, 1870; S.T.B., Boston U., 1874, Ph.D., 1898; m. Lucy Ellen Denton, Apr. 12, 1876. Ordained M.E. ministry, 1874; pastor in Mass. at Allston, 1874-75, Wilbraham, 1876-78, Springfield, 1879-81, Charlestown, 1882-84, Worcester, 1885-87, Lowell, 1888-90, S. Boston, 1892-96, First Ch., Boston, 1897-98, Dorchester, 1899; presiding elder Boston Dist., 1900-04; pastor Bromfield St. Ch., Boston, 1905, Melrose, Mass., 1906-09. Mem. Gen. Conf., 1900, 4th Ecumenical Meth. Conf., 1911; trustee Boston U.; pres. N.E. Deaconess Assn., 1898-1919, pres. emeritus, 1919—; dir. Lord's Day League of N.E. Address: Boston, Mass. Died July 7, 1929.

PERRINE, Enoch, univ. prof.; b. Hightstown, N.J., Nov. 18, 1853; s. Joseph and Abigail (Appleget) P.; A.B., Brown U., 1874, A.M., 1882; hon. Litt.D., Pa. Coll., 1892; m. Maria A. McMurran, Dec. 25, 1879 (died 1903); m. 2d, Grace B. Roberts, 1905. Editor Trenton (N.J.) True American, 1874-75, Manasquan (N.J.) Seaside, 1876; teacher of Latin, Peddie Inst., Hightstown, N.J., 1878-86; John P. Crozer prof. rhetoric, 1886-1902, prof. English lang. and lit., 1902—, Bucknell U. Univ. extension and Chautauqua lecturer; licentiate of Bapt. Ch. Address: Lewisburg, Pa. Died Apr. 11, 1920.

PERRINE, Frederic Auten Combs, elec. engr.; b. Manalapan, N.J., Aug. 25, 1862; s. James A. and Rebecca A. (Combs) P.; ed. Freehold, N.J., Inst., 1870-79; grad. Princeton, 1883, A.M., 1886, D.Sc., 1885; spl. studies in elec. engring.; post-graduate student Princeton, 1883-85; m. Margaret J. Roebling, June 28, 1893. Asst. electrician U. S. Electric Light Co., 1885-89; mgr. insulated wire dept., John A. Roebling's Sons Co., 1889-92; treas. Germania Electric Co., 1892-93; prof. elec. engring., Leland Stanford Jr. U., 1893-1900; chief engr., Standard Electric Co., of Calif., 1898-1900, pres. Stanley Electric Mfg. Co., Pittsfield, Mass., 1900-04; later consulting engr. Editor Journal of Electricity, San Francisco, 1894-96; Elec. Engring., Chicago, 1896-98. Author: Conductors for Distribution, 1903. Residence: Plainfield, N.J. Died 1908.

PERRY, Albertus, clergyman, lecturer; b. N.Y., Nov. 5, 1873; s. William Noah and Jennie (Cornell) P.; A.B., Northwestern U., 1899; studied Garrett Bibl. Inst., U. of Chicago; non-res. student, Temple U. and U. of Wis.; Ph.D., Temple U., 1910; m.

Octavia Ackerman, July 30, 1898; 1 son, Russel A. Pastor M.E. chs. in Chicago and vicinity, 14 yrs. to 1918; in charge finances, states of Mich., Wis., Ill., Ia. and Neb., for Am. Red Cross, 1918-19, World War; conductor finance campaigns for colleges of M.E. Ch., 1919-24; v.p. Washington Coll., Chestertown, Md., 1924-26; Near East travel and study, 1927-31; pastor Erie (Ill.) M.E. Ch., 1931-35, Morrison Ch., 1935-39, Broadway Meth. Ch., Chicago, 1939—. Del. World's Sunday School Conv., Zurich, 1913, Glasgow, 1924, Durban, S. Africa, 1940. Visited Palestine 17 times in charge ednl. tours. Extensively engaged as lecturer before Rotary and other clubs. Address: Chicago, Ill. Died May 23, 1940.

PERRY, Alexander James, brigadier gen. U.S.A.; b. New London, Conn., Dec. 11, 1828. Grad. U.S. Mil. Acad., 1851; bvt. 2d lt. 2d Arty., July 1, 1851; 2d lt., July 1, 1852; 1st lt., Sept. 27, 1854; capt. asst. q.m., May 17, 1861; lt. col. q.m. vols., Aug. 20, 1862-Jan. 15, 1863; col. q.m., Aug. 2, 1864-Jan. 1, 1867; maj. q.m. U.S.A., July 29, 1866; lt. col. deputy q.m. gen., Mar. 3, 1875; col. asst. q.m. gen., Aug. 31, 1883; retired by operation of law, Dec. 11, 1892; advanced to rank of brig gen. retired, by act of Apr. 23, 1904. Bvtd. maj., lt. col., and col., Mar. 13, 1865, for services during the war; brig. gen., Mar. 13, 1865, for service in q.m. dept. during the war. Home: Washington, D.C. Died Mar. 26, 1913.

PERRY, Alfred Tyler, college pres.; b. Geneseo, Ill., Aug. 19, 1858; s. George Bulkley and Maria Louise (Tyler) P.; A.B., Williams, 1880, A.M., 1891; grad. Hartford Theol. Sem., 1885; D.D., Williams, 1901; m. Anna Morris, Apr. 13, 1887. Ordained Congl. ministry, 1886; asst. pastor Memorial Church, Springfield, Mass., 1886; pastor Ware, Mass., 1887-90; prof. bibliology and librarian, Hartford Theol. Sem., 1891-1900; pres. Marietta Coll., 1900—. Address: Marietta, O. Died Oct. 18, 1912.

PERRY, Arthur, banker; b. Westerly, R.I., Mar. 31, 1857; s. Charles and Temperance (Foster) P.; A.B., Harvard, 1880; m. Emma A. Foster, Jan. 19, 1882; children—Arthur, Henry H., Priscilla F. (wife of Dr. F. C. Hall). Asst. cashier Washington Nat. Bank, Westerly, 1881-91; mgr. bond dept. Thomson-Houston Electric Co., Boston, 1891-92; mgr. bond dept. Gen. Electric Co., Boston, 1892-93; v.p. and gen. mgr. United Electric Securities Co., 1894-98; mem. Perry, Coffin & Burr, bankers, 1898-1916, and of Arthur Perry & Co. after liquidation of Perry, Coffin & Burr, Apr. 1916; trustee Washington Trust Co. (Westerly). Trustee Northfield Schs. (E. Northfield, Mass.), Bryn Mawr Coll. Mem. Religious Soc. of Friends. Home: Boston, Mass. Died Nov. 16, 1930.

PERRY, Arthur Latham, economist, historian; b. Lyme, N.H., Feb. 27, 1830; s. Rev. Baxter and Lydia Gray P.; grad. Williams Coll., 1852; LL.D., Union Coll., 1874; D.D., Doane Coll., Neb., 1883; m. Mary Brown Smedley, Aug. 1856. Prof. history and political economy Williams Coll., 1853-91; prof. emeritus, 1891—; v.p. Williamstown Nat. Bank, 1884-86; prin. occupation, 1891—, hist. writing. Democrat. Author: Political Economy; Introduction to Political Economy; Principles of Political Economy, 1891; Origins in Williamstown, 1894; Williamstown and Williams College, 1900; many public addresses in behalf of free trade. Address: Williamstown, Mass. Died 1905.

PERRY, Carroll, clergyman; b. Williamstown, Mass., Feb. 2, 1869; s. Arthur Latham and Mary Brown (Smedley) P.; student Phillips Acad., Andover, Mass., 1884-86; B.A., Williams Coll., Williamstown, 1890, D.D., 1933; B.D., Yale, 1894; m. Grace Hawley Underwood, Oct. 11, 1898; children—Francis Underwood (dec.), Theodora, Carroll. Ordained ministry Episcopal Ch., 1896; curate Grace Ch., N.Y. City, 1896-98; rector St. Phillips Ch., Garrison, N.Y., 1898-1907, St. Peter's Ch., Boston, 1907-11, St. Paul's Ch., Brookline, Mass., 1911-16, Ch. of Ascension, Ipswich, Mass., 1920—. Trustee Gov. Dummer Acad., S. Byfield, Mass. Democrat. Author: (with J. S. Zelie) Bill Pratt, Sawbuck Philosopher, 1895; A Professor of Life (Biographical Sketch of Arthur Latham Perry of Williams College), 1923. Lecturer. Home: Ipswich, Mass. Died Oct. 2, 1937.

PERRY, Charles, banker; b. Westerly, R.I., Mar. 3, 1851; s. Charles and Temperance (Foster) P.; ed. high sch., Westerly, Friends Sch., Providence, R.I.; m. Clara V. Foster, Jan. 19, 1875. Asst. cashier, Washington Nat. Bank, Westerly, 1872-81, cashier, 1881-1904; v.p. Washington Trust Co., 1904-06, pres., 1906—; dir. Puritan Life Ins. Co., Westerly Textile Co. Pres. Memorial Library Assn. of Westerly, 1893—; pres. Westerly Hosp., 1921—; trustee Northfield (Mass.) School; mem. bd. Wheeler Sch. and Library, North Stonington, Conn. Republican. Mem. Soc. of Friends. Home: Westerly, R.I. Died Aug. 21, 1929.

PERRY, David, army officer; b. Ridgefield, Conn., June 11, 1841; s. Samuel and Sophia P.; ed. Rev. D. H. Short's prep. sch.; m. S. Louise Hoyt, Jan. 28, 1885. Apptd. from N.J., 2d lt. 1st Cav., U.S.A., Mar. 24, 1862; 1st lt., July 27, 1862; capt., Nov. 12, 1864; maj. 6th Cav., Apr. 29, 1879; lt. col. 10th Cav., Apr. 20, 1891; col. 9th Cav., Dec. 11, 1896; retired on account of disability in line of duty, July 5, 1898; advanced to rank of brig. gen. retired, by act of Apr. 23, 1904. Bvtd. maj., Apr. 1, 1865, for faithful and meritorious services during the war; lt. col., Dec. 26, 1866, for engagement with Indians on Owyhee river, Ida., Dec. 26, 1866; col., Apr. 5, 1868, for engagement with Indians on Malheur river, Ore., Apr. 5, 1868. Home: Washington, D.C. Died 1908.

PERRY, David Brainerd, college pres.; b. Worcester, Mass., Mar. 7, 1839; s. Samuel and Mary (Harrington) P.; A.B., Yale, 1863, A.M., 1866, B.D., 1867, D.D., 1898; m. Helen Doane, July 3, 1876. Tutor in Yale, 1865-67 and 1869-71; ordained Congl. ministry, 1872; tutor, 1872-73, acting pres. and prof. Latin and Greek, 1873-81, pres. and prof. psychology, 1881—, Doane Coll. Address: Crete, Nebraska. Died May 21, 1912.

PERRY, Edward Baxter, concert pianist; b. Haverhill, Mass., Feb. 14, 1855; s. Baxter E. and Charlotte (Hough) P.; studied in Boston till 20 yrs. of age, after that in Germany; piano under Theodore Kullak, Mme. Clara Schumann, and Franz Liszt; spl. course at U. of Berlin, and Poly. Inst., Stuttgart, 1875-78, and 1883-85 (non-grad.); m. Netta A. Hopkins, June 21, 1882. Lost sight by accident while playing with a knife at 2 yrs. of age; prof. of music, Oberlin Coll., 1881-83; gave over 3,000 piano recitals and appeared in every state of U.S. except Utah and Ida.; originator of the lecture-recital method, and gave over 3,100 lecture recitals. Decorated, Paris, 1898, Chevalier de Melusine. Author: Descriptive Analyses of Piano Works, 1904; Stories of Standard Teaching Pieces, 1908. Wrote several hundred articles for musical mags., principally the Etude, Phila. Instr. at Hood Coll., Frederick, Md., 1921-22, at Lebanon Valley Coll., 1922—. Home: Annville, Pa. Died June 13, 1924.

PERRY, Edward Delavan, univ. prof.; b. Troy, N.Y., Dec. 20, 1854; s. Amos Stone and Sarah (Hillhouse) P.; A.B., Columbia, 1875, LL.D., 1904; Ph.D., U. of Tübingen, 1879; m. Alice Van Schaick, 1883 (died 1924). Tutor, and instr. Greek and Sanskrit, 1880-91, prof. Sanskrit, 1891-95, Jay prof. of Greek, 1895-1931, dean faculty of philosophy, 1902-09, Columbia, professor emeritus, 1931. Corresponding sec. Am. Oriental Soc., 1894-95; pres. N.Y. Soc. Archæol. Inst. America, 1897-1900 and 1903-10; mem. mng. com. Am. Sch. Classical Studies in Athens, 1897—(actg. chmn. 1918-19). Home: New York, N.Y. Died Mar. 28, 1938.

PERRY, E(noch) Wood, artist; b. Boston, July 31, 1831; went to New Orleans, 1848; studied at Düsseldorf and Paris, 1852-53, then in Rome and Venice. U.S. consul at Venice, 1856-58; returned to U.S.; visited Sandwich Islands; settled in New York, 1865; painted portraits of many distinguished men and numerous genre pictures. Rec. sec. Nat. Acad. Design, 1871-73. A.N.A., 1868, N.A., 1869. Address: New York, N.Y. Died Dec. 15, 1915.

PERRY, Everett Robbins, librarian; b. Worcester, Mass., Oct. 5, 1876; s. Moses and Mary Jennie (Robbins) P.; A.B., Harvard, as of 1903; B.L.S., N.Y. State Library Sch., 1903; m. Lilla Gertrude Simmons, June 17, 1906; children—Richard Waldo, Edward Caswell, Norman Conrad, Beatrice Virginia. With St. Louis Pub. Library, Harvard Coll. Library, New York Pub. Library; librarian, Los Angeles Pub. Library, Sept. 11, 1911—. Mem. A.L.A. (1st v.p.). Home: Los Angeles, Calif. Died Oct. 30, 1933.

PERRY, George Dorn, newspaper editor; b. Sandusky, O., Dec. 10, 1887; s. Jay Jonas and Rosa (Hess) P.; student Stanford U., 1906-11; m. Zella Hannah Johnson, Dec. 24, 1914; 1 son, Earl Jay. Reporter Sandusky Star-Journal and Sandusky Register, 1905-06; with Flint (Mich.) Journal, 1911-28, successively as state editor, sports editor, city editor and mng. editor; mng. editor Saginaw (Mich.) News, 1928-37, editor, 1937—. Mason. Presbyterian. Home: Saginaw, Mich. Died Nov. 20, 1940.

PERRY, James Clifford, sanitarian; b. Pasquotank County, N.C., Jan. 5, 1864; s. James Decatur and Margaret Caroline (Morgan) P.; student U. of N.C., 1881-83; M.D., U. of Md., 1885; m. Nancy Nash Elliott, 1916. Apptd. asst. surgeon U.S.P.H.S., Mar. 21, 1889; passed asst. surgeon, Apr. 19, 1893; surgeon, Mar. 1, 1904; sr. surgeon, Mar. 4, 1915; asst. surgeon gen., Feb. 1, 1918; med. dir., July 10, 1930, U.S. Pub. Health Service. Organized protective quarantine at Hongkong, China, governing vessels for U.S. ports, 1899; organized quarantine service Philippine Islands and chief quarantine officer, 1900-03; on sanitary staff Isthmian Canal Commn. as chief quarantine officer, 1905-14, also health officer City of Panama, 1909-14; spl. investigations Chicago Health Dept.; spl. investigations at Richmond, Ind., to determine incidence of tuberculosis, and Health Dept., Columbia, S.C., 1915; served as chief med. officer Ellis Island, N.Y.; experience in control of cholera plague, yellow fever, also other communicable diseases and pub. health administrn. Democrat. Methodist. Address: San Francisco, Calif. Died Oct. 19, 1936.

PERRY, James De Wolf, clergyman; b. Bristol, R.I., Dec. 22, 1839; s. James De Wolf and Julia Bourn (Jones) P.; A.M., Brown U., 1860; student Berkeley Div. Sch., Conn.; grad. P.E. Div. Sch., Phila., 1864; D.D. Jefferson Med. Coll., Phila., 1886; m. Elisabeth Russell Tyson, Nov. 2, 1866; children—Robert S., Julia Bourn, James De Wolf, Elizabeth Russell, Emily Tyson; m. 2d, Marian Frazer Harris, Oct. 29, 1914. Deacon, 1861, priest, 1864, P.E. Ch.; asst. minister Grace Ch., Providence, 1861-62, St. Luke's, Phila., 1862-64; asso. rector St. Paul's, Pawtucket, R.I., 1864-66; rector Calvary Ch., Germantown (Phila.), 1866—. Pres. Convocation of Germantown, 1886-1902; warden and v.p. Ch. Training and Deaconess House, Phila., 1896—; pres. Standing Com. Diocese of Pa., 1900—; del. Gen. Conv., 1892, 98; mem. Gen. Bd. of Missions, 1898-1910. Home: Germantown, Philadelphia, Pa. Died Apr. 11, 1927.

PERRY, John Hoyt, lawyer; b. Southport, Conn., July 26, 1848; s. Oliver Henry and Harriet Eliza (Hoyt) P.; B.A., Yale, 1870, M.A., 1873; LL.B., Columbia, 1872; m. Frances Virginia Bulkley, Sept. 23, 1874. Mem. firm of Ferry, Woodward & Perry, Norwalk, Conn., 1872-86, Woodward & Perry, 1886-87, Perry & Perry, Bridgeport, 1887-89; judge Ct. of Common Pleas, 1889-93; mem. Perry, Perry & Hill, Bridgeport, 1893-1902 (retired); pres. Southport Savings Bank. Instr. evidence and contracts and lecturer on parliamentary law, Yale Law Sch. Mem. Conn. Ho. of Rep., 1877, 78, 81, 89 (speaker 1889); member Conn. Senate, 1913-15; 1st v.p. Conn. Constl. Convention, 1902. Trustee Hartford Seminary Foundation; pres. Pequot Library Assn.; dir. Fairfield Historical Soc. Republican. Conglist. Address: Southport, Conn. Died Sept. 2, 1928.

PERRY, Lilla Cabot, painter, author; b. Boston, Jan. 13, 1848; d. Samuel and Hannah Lowell (Jackson) Cabot; ed. in Boston; studied painting in Boston and in Paris at Julian's and Colarossi's studios in 1887 and later; m. Thomas Sergeant Perry, Apr. 9, 1874. Painter after leaving art schools, first pictures exhibited at Paris Salon, 1889; silver medal, Mass. Mechanics' Assn., 1892; bronze medal, St. Louis Expn., 1904; bronze medal, Panama P.I. Expn., 1915. Author: Poems in Prose (transl. from Tourguenieff), 1883; Heart of the Weed, 1886; Garden of Hellas, 1891; Impressions, 1898; The Jar of Dreams, 1923. Address: Boston, Mass. Died Feb. 28, 1933.

PERRY, Louis Clausiel, coll. pres.; b. Ridgeway, Va., Aug. 19, 1877; s. M. F. and Louisa H. (Brower) P.; A.B., Rutherford Coll., 1896, A.M., 1897; B.D., B.S., Vanderbilt U., 1904; Ph.D., U. of Oskaloosa, 1910; m. Elva Kenney, June 7, 1906; 1 dau., Elva Victoria. Pres. Hayesville Coll., N.C., 1897-99; pres. Columbia Coll., Ore., 1904-05; prof. history and social science, Hendrix Coll., Conway, Ark., 1905-09; pres. Scarritt-Morrisville Coll., Morrisville, Mo., June 20, 1909-15; founded Tex. Mil. Coll., Terrell, 1915. Commd. col., 1918. Methodist. Democrat. Mason. Chmn. bd. govs. Lion's Internat. (Tex. and N.M.), 1924. Home: Terrell, Tex. Died Nov. 2, 1926.

PERRY, Marsden Jasiel, financier; b. Rehoboth, Mass., Nov. 2, 1850; s. Horatio Nelson and Malvina (Wilson) P.; ed. dist. schs. and pvtly. Went to Providence, 1871; pres. Am. Ring Traveller Co., 1881-89; became dir. Bank of America (later Union Trust Co.), 1881, dir. latter; dir. Nicholson File Co., Gen. Electric Co., Am. Screw Co. Collected large Shakespearean library, said to be the largest pvt. collection of Shakespearena in U.S. Home: Providence, R.I. Died Apr. 15, 1935.

PERRY, R(ichard) Ross, lawyer; b. Washington, D.C., Feb. 20, 1846; s. Augustus Emory and Mary Jane P.; A.B., Georgetown U., D.C., 1864, A.M., 1865, LL.D., 1892; m. Callie Thaw, Nov. 15, 1870. Admitted to the D.C. bar, May 1868, in practice at Washington, 1868—; head of firm of R. Ross Perry & Son. Dir. Riggs Nat. Bank, Columbia Instn. for the Deaf, Corcoran Gallery of Art, Carnegie Pub. Library. Author: Perry on Common Law Pleading, 1897. Home: Washington, D.C. Died July 17, 1915.

PERRY, Roland Hinton, sculptor, portrait painter; b. New York, Jan. 25, 1870; s. George and Ione (Hinton) P.; ed. pvt. sch. in N.Y.; entered École des Beaux Arts, 1890; studied Académie Julian and Académie Delacleuse, Paris, 1890-94; m. 2d, Mrs. May Hanbury Fisher, Feb. 3, 1906; 1 son, Roland Albertus. Principal works: Bas-reliefs of Sibyls, Library of Congress, 1895; Fountain of Neptune, same, 1897; The Valkyrie, painting, 1899; The Lion in Love, sculpture, 1899; spandrels on Dewey Arch, New York, 1899; Circe, statue, 1900; Langdon doors, Buffalo Hist. Soc., 1901; frieze for New Amsterdam Theatre, New York, 1903; statue of Dr. Benjamin Rush, Washington, 1904; statue Pennsylvania, finish of dome of Capitol, Harrisburg, Pa., 1904; statue of Gen. George S. Greene, Gettysburg, Pa., 1906; group for N.Y. State monument for Lookout Mountain, Tenn., 1907; lions for Conn. Av. Bridge, Washington, 1908; memorial of N.Y. State, Andersonville, Ga., 1910; equestrian statue of Gen. John B. Castleman, of Louisville, Ky.; statue of Gen. Curtis for Ogdensburg, N.Y., and Gen. Wadsworth, Gettysburg; soldier monument to 38th Inf. ("The Rock of the Marne") for Syracuse, N.Y., 1920; "Daughter of

Pan" fountain, Estate of Mary Duke Biddle, at Irvington-on-the-Hudson. Specialized in painting portraits, 1917—. Address: Richmond, Mass. Died Oct. 27, 1941.

PERRY, Thomas, rear admiral U.S.N.; b. Elmira, N.Y., May 26, 1844; s. Guy Maxwell and Elizabeth Asia (Taylor) P. Grad. U.S. Naval Acad., 1865; promoted through successive grades until commissioned capt. During Spanish-Am. War comd. flagship Lancaster at base of supplies, Key West, Fla.; naval sec. Lighthouse Bd., 1899-1901; comd. U.S. battleship Iowa; attached to Pacific and N. Atlantic sta., 1901-03; capt. New York Navy Yard, May 1903-May 1904; commandant Pensacola Navy Yard, May 1904-May 1905; pres. Naval Examining Bd., May 1905-May 26, 1906; rear admiral, Sept. 8, 1905; retired, May 26, 1906. Address: Port Deposit, Md. Died Mar. 7, 1918.

PERRY, Thomas Sergeant, author; b. Newport, R.I., Jan. 23, 1845; s. Christopher Grant and Frances (Sergeant) P.; A.B., Harvard, 1866, A.M., 1869; m. Lilla Cabot, Apr. 9, 1874; children— Margaret, Edith (Mrs. Edward Ballantine), Alice de Vermandois (wife of Hon. Joseph Clark Grew). Author: Life and Letters of Francis Lieber, 1882; English Literature in Eighteenth Century, 1883; From Opitz to Lessing, 1884; The Evolution of the Snob, 1886; Library of Adventure (with William Dean Howells), 1886; Greek Literature, 1890; John Fiske, 1905. Address: Boston, Mass. Died May 7, 1928.

PERRY, Walter Scott, art dir.; b. Stoneham, Mass., Dec. 26, 1855; s. Benjamin M. and Elizabeth (Kittredge) P.; studied Mass. Normal Art Sch., Boston; traveled and studied in Europe, Egypt, India, China and Japan; M.A., Pratt Inst., Brooklyn, N.Y., 1899; hon. M.A., St. Lawrence U., 1905; m. Clara Fairfield, July 7, 1902; children—Fairfield Scott, Walter Merton. Dir. of drawing, pub. and evening schs., Fall River, Mass., 1875-79; dir. drawing and art edn., Worcester, Mass., 1879-87; dir. Sch. of Fine and Applied Arts, Pratt Inst., Brooklyn, 1887-1928. Trustee Madura Coll., India; dir. Art Alliance America; hon. sec. Egypt Exploration Fund. Republican. Presbyterian. Author: Egypt, the Land of the Temple Builders, 1898 and 1910; With Azir Girges in Egypt, 1913; also various sets of drawing books and mag. articles, 1882-1927. Lecturer on architecture, sculpture, painting, etc. Home: Brooklyn, N.Y. Died Aug. 22, 1934.

PERRY, William Flake, prof. English and philosophy Ogden Coll., 1883—; b. Jackson County, Ga., Mar. 12, 1823; s. Hiram and Nancy (Flake) P.; grad. Brownwood Acad., 1846; A.M., Howard Coll., Marion, Ala.; m. Ellen Douglas Brown, Jan. 1, 1851. Engaged in teaching in 1848; elected, Feb. 1854, to organize public edni. system in Ala.; held the office 3 terms; entered C.S.A., May 1862, as maj. 44th Ala. regt.; became col. and brig. gen. Comd. regt. at Antietam, Fredericksburg, Gettysburg; comd. brigade at Chickamauga, in Longstreet's E. Tenn. campaign, battle Wilderness, Spottsylvania, Cold Harbor, seige of Petersburg, Appomattox. Address: Bowling Green, Ky. Died 1901.

PERSHING, Cyrus L., lawyer; b. Youngstown, Pa., Feb. 3, 1825; s. Christopher S. and Elizabeth (Long) P.; A.M., Jefferson Coll., Cannonsburg, Pa., 1848; LL.D., Washington and Jefferson Coll.; m. Mary L. Royer, Sept. 23, 1851. Candidate for Congress, 1856, 1858; mem. Pa. legislature from Cambria County, 1862-66, inclusive; candidate for judge Supreme Court, 1869; pres. judge courts of Schuylkill County, Oct. 1872, to Aug. 1899; resigned; Democratic nominee for gov. Pa., 1875; presided over famous Mollie Maguire trials in Schuylkill County, Pa. Contributor to law journals of Pa. Address: Pottsville, Pa. Died 1903.

PERSHING, Howell Terry, M.D.; b. Johnstown, Pa., Mar. 18, 1858; s. Judge Cyrus L. and Mary L. (Royer) P.; Ph.B., Lafayette Coll., 1878, M.Sc., 1881, LL.D., 1908; M.D., U. of Pa., 1883; m. Anna M. Smith, Dec. 18, 1884; 1 son, Howell T. Teacher natural science, French and German, Wilkes-Barre Acad., 1878-80; science master, Lawrenceville (N.J.) Sch., 1884-89; located in practice at Denver; alienist and neurologist; prof. nervous and mental diseases, U. of Denver, 1892-1910; prof. neurology and psychiatry, U. of Colo., 1911-20 and 1922—. Mem. advisory council Simplified Spelling Bd. Author: The Disorders of Speech (part of Twentieth Century Practice of Medicine), 1897; The Diagnosis of Nervous and Mental Diseases, 1901; also Treatment of Diseases of Peripheral Nerves, part of Therapeusis of Internal Diseases, 1913. Home: Denver, Colo. Died Nov. 29, 1935.

PERSON, Hiram Grant, clergyman; b. Batchellerville, N.Y., Sept. 17, 1866; s. Hiram and Emily J. (Noyes) P.; A.B., Williams Coll., 1891 (class orator); student Princeton Theol. Sem., 1 yr.; B.D., Auburn (N.Y.) Theol. Sem., 1894; D.D., Williams Coll., 1916; m. Georgia Harriet Ferry, May 10, 1898. Ordained Presbyn. ministry, 1894; pastor Chittenango, N.Y., 1894-98, Seneca Falls, 1898-1907, Eliot Ch., Newton, Mass., Jan. 1, 1907—. Trustee Poultney (Vt.) Acad.; corp. mem. A.B.C.F.M. Minister in residence, Auburn Theol. Sem., 1918; lecturer religious leadership, Yale Sch. of Religion, 1917. Dir. Mass. Home Missionary Soc., Boston City Miss. Soc., Congl. Ch. Union. "Four-Minute Man" and Y.M.C.A. sec. in World War. Author: Noon-day Messages from a College Chapel, 1917-18. Home: Newton, Mass. Died Aug. 20, 1923.

PERSONS, Augustus Archilus, chemist; b. Enon, Ala., Nov. 15, 1866; s. J. W. and E. P. P.; B.S., Ala. Poly. Inst., 1886, M.S., 1888; U. of Chicago, summer sessions, 1899, 1900; m. Mabel Knox, Sept. 27, 1893. Prof. natural science, Ala. Normal Coll., Troy, 1889-92; prof. chemistry and chemist, Fla. Agrl. Coll. Expt. Sta., and consulting chemist, F.C. &P. and Plant Ry. systems, 1892-98; prof. chemistry, U. of Ala., 1898-1908; supt. city schs., Bessemer, Ala., 1908-09. Consulting chemist M.&O. Ry., 1898—; agrl. editor Fla. Citizen, Jacksonville, Fla., 1894-96. Mem. bd. of visitors U.S. Mil. Acad., 1905. Pres. dept. superintendence Ala. Ednl. Assn., 1911-12. Address: Bessemer, Ala. Died Feb. 25, 1917.

PERSONS, Warren Milton, consulting economist; b. W. De Pere, Wis., Mar. 12, 1878; s. Milton Potter and Lorette Lucinda (Case) P.; West De Pere High Sch., 1895; B.S., U. of Wis., 1899, Ph.D., 1904; m. Irmagarde Keller, Sept. 5, 1906; 1 dau., Margaret J. (Mrs. Le Baron R. Foster). Asst. in mathematics 1901-02, instr., 1902-06, U. of Wis.; asst. prof. econs., Dartmouth Coll., 1906-12; prof. economics, 1913-18, dean of Judson M. Bemis Dept. of Bus. Adminstrn. and Banking, 1914-18, Colorado Coll.; prof. economics, Harvard, 1919-28. Mem. firm Warren M. Persons and Associates, consultants in applied economics. Mem. Colo. Ho. of Rep., 1913-14. Editor Review of Economic Statistics, 1919-28. Vice-pres. Nat. Investors Corp., 1928; dir. same and 2d, 3d and 4th Nat. Investors Corps., 1928-32. Del. of U.S. Govt. to meeting of Internat. Inst. of Statistics, Cairo, Egypt, 1927-28. Fellow Am. Statis. Assn. (pres. 1923), Am. Acad. Arts and Sciences. Author of The Construction of Index Numbers, Indices of Business Conditions, Forecasting Business Conditions, Government Experimentation in Business. Home: New York, N.Y. Died Oct. 1937.

PESCHAU, Ferdinand William Elias, clergyman; b. Clausthal, Hanover, Germany, Feb. 17, 1849; s. Henry and Wilhelmina (Muehlhan) P.; came to U.S. as boy; settled in Wheeling, W.Va.; A.B., A.M., Pa. Coll. Gettysburg, 1872; theol. course there; D.D., N.C. Coll., 1891; m. Clara J. Myers, June 3, 1873. Supt. pub. schs., Evansville, Ind., 3 yrs., Nebraska City, Neb., 2 yrs.; ordained Luth. ministry, Sept. 17, 1876; pastor Nebraska City, Neb., 2 yrs., Nashville, Tenn., 5 yrs., Wilmington, N.C., 11 years, Greensburg, Pa., 7 years, Miamisburg, O., 1899—. Prof. German, Neb. Coll., Dr. W. E. Ward's Sem., and Vanderbilt U.; pres. Middle Tenn. Synod; pres. N.C. Synod 4 yrs., Southern Gen. Synod 2 yrs.; pres. Luther League of Ohio, 2 yrs., S.W. Conf. of Ohio Luth. Synod, 5 yrs.; several times del. nat. and internat. convs.; del. Luth. General councils, Easton, Erie, Norristown, Pa., Chicago, Milwaukee, Minneapolis. Mem. bd. edn. Nebraska City; trustee N.C. Coll.; sec. Southern Theol. Sem., 7 yrs.; trustee Greensburg, Pa., Sem., 7 yrs.; elected pres. N.C. Coll., 1883, but declined. Commr. State of N.C. to Centennial of Washington's Inauguration, New York, 1889. Associate Editor Lutheran Visitor 10 years. Wrote Ode to General Andrew Jackson, sung at monument unveiling, Nashville, 1880; Centennial Ode, Greensburg, Pa., 1899, and other songs. Toured through Denmark, France and Germany, 1907; first Am. Luth. minister to preach in German in historic church at Schmalkalden, where Luther had preached; became sec. Dist. Synod of Ohio for the 3d time. Lectured in 34 states of the Union, and in Ont. and N.S., Can. Chaplain Md. Assn. in Ohio, 1911. Address: Miamisburg, O. Deceased.

PETERKIN, Daniel, salt merchant; b. Scotland, July 24, 1872; s. James and Isabella (Hall) P.; ed. in Scotland; came to U.S. in May 1892; m. Jeanette Knights, Oct. 14, 1904; children—Daniel, Jeanette. Connected with Joy Morton & Co., 1896—; pres. Morton Salt Co.; treas. Standard Office Building Corp., Morton Bldg. Corp. Home: Chicago, Ill. Died Mar. 10, 1941.

PETERKIN, George William, bishop; b. Washington County, Md., Mar. 21, 1841; s. Rev. Joshua P. and Elizabeth (Hanson) P.; ed. Episcopal High Sch. of Va., 1856-58; U. of Va., 1859; served pvt. to 2d lt., 21st Va. Inf., C.S.A.; adjt. of regt., from June 3, 1862; aide to Brig. Gen. W. N. Pendleton, chief of arty., Army Northern Va.; grad. Theol. Sem. of Va., 1868; D.D., Kenyon, 1878; D.D., Washington and Lee, 1878, LL.D., 1892; m. Constance Gardner, d. Cassius F. Lee, Oct. 29, 1868 (died 1877); m. 2d, Marion McIntosh, d. John Stewart, June 12, 1884. Deacon, 1868, priest, 1869, P.E. Ch.; asst. to his father at St. James' Ch., Richmond, Va., 1868-69; rector St. Stephen's Ch., Culpeper, Va., 1869-73, Memorial Ch., Baltimore, 1873-78; consecrated 1st bishop of W.Va., May 30, 1878. In charge P.E. mission in Brazil, 1893, and visited the field; made missionary tour of P.R., 1901. Mem. bd. of mgrs. Domestic and Foreign Missionary Soc. of P.E. Ch.; v.p. Am. Ch. Missionary Soc. Edited: Records of the Protestant Episcopal Church in Virginia and West Virginia, 1902. Author: A Handbook for Members and Friends of the Protestant Episcopal Church. Address: Parkersburg, W.Va. Died Sept. 22, 1916.

PETERS, Andrew James, mayor; b. Jamaica Plain, Mass., Apr. 3, 1872; s. Andrew James and Mary Richards (Whitney) P.; A.B., Harvard, 1895, LL.B., 1898; m. Martha R. Phillips, June 23, 1910; children—Andrew J., Alanson (dec.), John P. (dec.), Bradford, Robeson, David McClure. Mem. Mass. House of Rep., 1902, Senate, 1904-05; mem. 60th, 61st, 62d and 63d Congresses (1907-15), 11th Mass. Dist. (resigned Aug. 15, 1914); asst. sec. of the Treasury, in charge of customs, 1914-17 (resigned Mar. 15, 1917); mayor of Boston, term 1918-22. Apptd. mem. U.S. Sect. Internat. High Commn., 1917. Democrat. Episcopalian. Died June 26, 1938.

PETERS, Edward Dyer, mining engr.; b. Dorchester, Mass., June 1, 1849; s. Henry Hunter and Susan Barker (Thaxter) P.; Sch. of Mines, Freiberg, 1869; M.D., Harvard, 1877; m. Anna Quincy, d. Benjamin Cushing, Sept. 28, 1881. Territorial assayer of Colo., 1872; lecturer, 1903-04, prof. metallurgy, Harvard, 1904—. Mem. Am. Inst. Mining Engrs. Author: Modern Copper Smelting, 1887; Principles of Copper Smelting, 1907; also many tech. and scientific monographs. Address: Dorchester, Mass. Died Feb. 17, 1917.

PETERS, Frederick Romer, newspaper pub.; b. Zanesville, O., July 21, 1874; s. John Wesley (D.D.) and Caroline Matilda (Romer) P.; student prep. dept. Ohio Wesleyan U.; B.Litt., U. of Cincinnati, 1896; grad. study U. of Berlin; m. Clara Adelaide Margedant, June 12, 1907; children—William Wesley, Mary Margedant. Began as reporter Cincinnati Post, 1899, later telegraph editor and city editor until 1905; mgr. for Indiana of Scripps-McRae Press Assn., 1905; editor, 1906, and later pub. Evansville Press; pub. Terre Haute Post, 1909-29; editor Indianapolis Times, 1922-23; mgr. Western Ind. group of Scripps-Howard Newspapers, 1916-29; president Evansville Press Co.; trustee Newspaper Enterprise Assn. of Ohio. Methodist. Mason. Conducted campaign which in 1914 resulted in conviction of city officials of Terre Haute, in federal courts, on charge of election corruption. Home: Evansville, Ind. Died June 16, 1935.

PETERS, George Henry, commodore U.S.N.; b. Chester County, Pa., Sept. 22, 1854; s. John and Lavinia Urner (Price) P.; grad. U.S. Naval Acad., 1874, at head of class and with highest cadet mil. rank; m. Louisa Beardsley McCarty, June 17, 1878. Promoted ensign, 1875; master, 1881; lt., 1886; lt. comdr., 1899; comdr., 1903; capt., 1907; commodore, and retired at own request, June 30, 1908. Routine and spl. naval service to 1885; had charge of Atlantic coast pilot work, Coast Survey, and instituted gen. plan still followed by the Survey in this work, 1886-88; served in Squadron of Evolution (1st "white squadron"), 1888-91; at office of Naval Intelligence and on bd. Minneapolis, 1891-97; comd. Sylvia on blockade duty N. Coast of Cuba, 1898, War with Spain; exec. officer Iowa, 1900; comd. force landed at Panama to maintain free transit of the Isthmus, during a revolution, 1901, specially commended in despatches; supt. compasses, Navy Dept., 1903, mem. bd. on wireless telegraphy (then being introduced into the service); Asiatic Sta., 1905-07, comd. Cincinnati, Raleigh, and commandant Cavite and Olongapo (P.I.). Mem. U.S. Naval Inst. Home: Washington, D.C. Died June 15, 1916.

PETERS, J.A., D.D., clergyman Reformed (German) Ch. in U.S.; pres. Heidelberg U., Ohio. Address: Tiffin, O. Died 1901.

PETERS, John Andrew, jurist; b. Ellsworth, Me., Oct. 9, 1822; grad. Yale (with first honors), 1842; studied at Harvard Law School, 1843-44; LL.D., Colby U., 1884; Bowdoin Coll., 1885; Yale, 1893; m. Fannie E. Roberts, Sept. 23, 1857. Admitted to bar, 1844; afterward resided in Bangor, becoming recognized leader of the bar. Mem. Me. senate, 1862-63; Me. Ho. of Reps., 1864; atty. gen. Me., 1865-68. Mem. Congress, 1871-77; asso. justice, 1873-83; chief justice, 1883 to Jan. 1, 1900, Supreme Judicial Court of Me.; voluntarily retired. Address: Bangor, Me. Died 1904.

PETERS, John Punnett, clergyman; b. New York, Dec. 16, 1852; s. Thomas McClure and Alice Clarissa (Richmond) P.; A.B., Yale, 1873, Ph.D., 1876; univs. of Berlin and Leipzig, 1879-83; D.D., Yale, 1895; Sc.D., U. of Pa., 1895; m. Gabriella Brooke, d. Thomas March Forman, Aug. 13, 1881. Deacon, 1876, priest, 1877, P.E. Ch.; tutor, Yale, 1876-79; in charge St. John's Ch., Dresden, Germany, 1881-83; prof. O.T. lang. and lit., P.E. Div. Sch., 1884-91; prof. Hebrew, U. of Pa., 1885-93; in charge expdn. of U. of Pa. to Babylonia, conducting excavations at Nippur, 1888-95; rector St. Michael's Ch., New York, 1893-1919. Canon residentiary, Cathedral of St. John the Divine, 1904-10. Later rector emeritus of St. Michael's Ch., and prof. N.T. lit. and langs., U. of the South, Sewanee, Tenn. Author: Scriptures, Hebrew and Christian (English title—The Bible for

Home and School), Vols. I and II, 1886, 1889; Nippur, or Explorations and Adventures on the Euphrates, 1897; The Old Testament and the New Scholarship, 1901; Early Hebrew Story, 1904; Some Tombs in the Necropolis of Marissa (with Dr. Hermann Thiersch), 1905; Annals of St. Michael's, New York, for One Hundred Years, 1807-1907, 1907; Modern Christianity, 1909; Jesus Christ and the Old Commandments, 1913; The Religion of the Hebrews, 1914; Animals' Christmas Tree, 1916. Translator and Continuator: Political History of Recent Times (with appendix covering period 1876-81), 1882. Editor: Diary of David McClure, 1899; Labor and Capital, 1902. Collaborator: The Bible as Literature, 1896; The Universal Anthology, 1899; The Historian's History of the World, 1908. Active in social problems in New York City; pres. Independent Club, 1896-1916; chmn. Com. of Fourteen, 1905-16. Address: New York, N.Y. Died Nov. 11, 1921.

PETERS, Lulu Hunt (Mrs. Louis H. Peters), M.D., author; b. Milford, Me.; d. Thomas Albert and Alice (Marsh) Hunt; grad. Me. State Normal Sch., Castine, Me.; M.D., U. of Calif., 1909, A.B., U. of Southern Calif., 1911; m. Louis H. Peters. Began practice at Los Angeles, 1911; writer of syndicated daily health features and many mag. articles on health. Decorated Order of St. Sava (Serbian), and Order of Scanderbeg (Albanian) for post-war child welfare and pub. health work in Balkans, with Am. Red Cross. Episcopalian. Author: Diet and Health, with Key to the Calories, 1918; Diet for Children, 1924. Home: Los Angeles, Calif. Died June 27, 1930.

PETERS, Madison Clinton, clergyman; b. Lehigh County, Pa., Nov. 6, 1859; s. Morgan and Maria (Kemmerer) P.; student Muhlenberg Coll., and Franklin and Marshall Coll., 1877-78; grad. Heidelberg Theol. Sem., Ohio; D.D., Heidelberg and Ursinus; m. Sarah H. Hart, June 1, 1890. Ordained Reformed Ch. ministry, 1880; pastor First Presbyn. Ch., Phila., 5 yrs., Bloomingdale Ref. Ch., New York, 11 yrs., Sumner Av. Ch., Brooklyn, Ch. of the Epiphany, New York, until 1907; People's preacher. Author: Justice to the Jew, 1899; The Wit and Wisdom of the Talmud, 1900; The Jew as a Patriot, 1901; The Great Hereafter, 1895; The Panacea for Poverty; Empty Pews, 1886; Sanctified Spice, 1895; The Birds of the Bible, 1901; The Man Who Wins, 1905; The Jews in America, 1905; Will the Coming Man Marry?, 1905; After Death—What?, Sermons that Won the Masses, 1908; Abraham Lincoln's Religion, 1909; How to Make Things Go, 1909; Haym Salomon, 1911; The Mission of Masonry, 1913; The Jews Who Stood by Washington, 1915; Seven Secrets of Success, 1916; Americans for America, 1916; The Masons as Makers of America, 1917; All for America, 1917. Address: New York, N.Y. Died Oct. 12, 1918.

PETERS, Ralph, railway pres.; b. Atlanta, Ga., Nov. 19, 1853; B.A., U. of Ga., 1872. Supt. and purchasing agt., Atlanta St. Rys., 1872-74; chief clk. Samuel M. Felton, Jr., gen. supt. P.C.&St.L. Ry., at Pittsburgh, 1874-81; supt. Logansport div. of "Pan Handle" system, few mos., 1881, then supt. Little Miami div., Cincinnati, 1881-1901, also filling a number of important offices of Pa. R.R. during various periods of this time; gen. supt. Southwest System of Pa. Lines West of Pittsburgh, hdqrs. at Columbus, O., 1901-05; pres. and gen. mgr. Long Island R.R., Apr. 5, 1905—, also New York and Rockaway Beach Ry. Co., New York, Brooklyn & Manhattan Beach Ry. Co., Montauk Steamboat Co., Ltd., and 18 other subsidiary lines of the L.I. System; federal mgr. L.I. R.R. during federal control. Chmn. Com. on Railroad Mail Pay (representing practically all rys. in U.S.). Home: Garden City, L.I., N.Y. Died Oct. 9, 1923.

PETERS, Samuel Ritter, congressman; b. Pickaway County, O., Aug. 16, 1842; s. Lewis S. and Margaret (Ritter) P.; grad. Ohio Wesleyan U., with class '64 (although left coll., 1861, to enter army); received A.B., 1894; LL.B., U. of Mich., 1867; m. Amelia C. Doan, Apr. 18, 1867. Sergt. to capt., 73d Ohio Vols., 1861-65. Admitted to bar, 1867; practiced at Newton, Kan., until 1907, when retired. Mem. Kan. Senate, 1875; judge 9th Jud. Dist. of Kan., 1875-83; mem. 48th to 51st Congresses (1883-91). Republican. Address: Newton, Kan. Died 1910.

PETERS, Thomas Pollock, lawyer; b. Hartford, Conn., May 17, 1868; grad. Poly. Inst. of Brooklyn, 1889; A.B., Columbia, 1893; LL.B., St. Lawrence U., 1909, J.D., 1911; m. Lou Augusta Darlington, Apr. 24, 1895. Editor-in-chief Brooklyn Times, 1894-1910; practiced law, 1910—. Dir. Brooklyn Public Library, 1897-1907. Presdl. elector, 1904. Dir. Home Trust Co., Manhattan Bridge Three-Cent Line. Home: Brooklyn, N.Y. Died Dec. 3, 1936.

PETERS, Thomas Willing, consul gen.; b. Phila., Pa., Nov. 4, 1855; s. Francis and Maria (Miller) P.; ed. in pvt. day sch. in Phila., mil. sch. in New Haven, prep. sch. for univ. and in Switzerland and France; m. Anne Bona Shober, Mar. 11, 1901. Engaged as stock grower in Wyo., 1878-89. Am. comml. agt. at Plauen, Germany, 1889-96, consul, 1896-1903; consul gen. at St. Gall, Switzerland, 1903-07, at Munich, Bavaria, Mar. 30, 1907; consul gen. at Kingston, Jamaica, Sept. 18, 1913—. Died Jan. 2, 1917.

PETERS, William Henry, M.D.; b. Cincinnati, O., May 15, 1881; s. William Sebald and Mary (Vascon) P.; A.B., St. Xavier Coll., 1900, M.A., 1907; M.D., U. of Cincinnati, 1909; m. Ida May Spence, June 18, 1910; children—Mary Eleanor, William John, Margaret. Asst. bacteriologist, Cincinnati Gen. Hosp., 1910-12; chief med. inspector, Dept. of Health, Cincinnati, 1912-18, commr. of health, 1918-34. Dir. Am. Red Cross, Hamilton County, O. Catholic. Editor of health articles in Cincinnati newspapers. Home: Cincinnati, O. Died Mar. 13, 1936.

PETERSON, Alfred Emanuel, clergyman; b. Litchfield, Minn., Nov. 8, 1873; s. Peter H. and Anna (Ring) P.; Pillsbury Acad., Owatonna, Minn., 1897; B.A., U. of Minn., 1902; studied U. of Chicago Div. Sch., 1908-10; D.D., Fargo (N.D.) Coll., 1914; m. Mabel Gooch, Feb. 19, 1902 (died 1912); 1 dau., Miriam Anna; m. 2d, Buena V. Beach, Dec. 15, 1914; children—Sidney Beach, Judson H. Ordained Bapt. ministry, 1902; pastor successively at Crookston, Minn., Superior, Wis., Chicago, Fargo, N.D., and Spokane, Wash., until 1919; editor Ill. Baptist News. Gen. supt. Ill. Bapt. State Conv., 1919—; dir. missionary promotion, representing Ill. in Bapt. Nat. missionary orgns. Mem. bd. dirs. Shurtleff Coll. (Alton, Ill.), Northwestern Bapt. Hosp. Assn. (St. Paul, Minn.). Republican. Home: Oak Park, Ill. Died Jan. 6, 1938.

PETERSON, Arthur, author; b. Phila., Pa., Sept. 20, 1851; s. Henry and Sarah (Webb) P.; ed. pvt. schools, Phila.; m. Georgiana, d. late Charles J. Harrah, Mar. 30, 1891. Entered pay corps of navy, Feb. 23, 1877; served in various parts of world, his last cruise being in the P.I. on U.S.S. Baltimore, in squadron comd. by Admiral Dewey; promoted to pay insp., Apr. 10, 1902; resigned Sept. 20, 1902, after 25 yrs.' service. Became editor, 1868-74, Saturday Evening Post, Phila., of which father was pub. Author: Songs of New Sweden, 1887; Penrhyn's Pilgrimage, 1894; Collected Poems, 1900; Sigurd, 1910; Collected Poems and Andvari's Ring, 1916. Episcopalian. Home: Overbrook, Pa. Died Feb. 18, 1932.

PETERSON, Frederick, M.D.; b. Faribault, Minn., Mar. 1, 1859; s. John Frederick and Hilma (Lindholm) P.; ed. high sch. and pvt. tutors; M.D., U. of Buffalo, 1879; hon. Ph.D., Niagara U., 1893; LL.D., U. of Pa., 1919; m. Antoinette Rotan, Apr. 3, 1895; children—Frederika, Virgilia. Instr. neurology, 1897-1903, clin. lecturer psychiatry, 1901-03, clin. prof., 1903—, Columbia; pres. bd. of mgrs. Craig Colony for Epileptics, 1892-1902; prof. insanity, Woman's Med. Coll. of New York Infirmary, 1890-95; pres. N.Y. State Commn. in Lunacy, 1902-06. Pres. New York Neurol. Soc., 1897-99. Author: Mental Diseases, 1899; American Text-book of Legal Medicine and Toxicology, 1903; Poems and Swedish Translations, 1883; In the Shade of Ygdrasil, 1893; A Song of the Latter Day, 1904; Chinese Lyrics, 1916; The Flutter of the Gold-Leaf, 1922; Creative Re-education, 1936. Home: Bridgewater, Conn. Died July 9, 1938.

PETERSON, Harry Claude, museum curator; b. Algona, Ia., Aug. 11, 1876; s. Julius Embret and Amy (Summers) P.; ed. pub. schs. of Algona, Ia., and Mayfield, Calif.; student Mayfield High Sch., 1890-92; m. Lillian Williams, June 24, 1902; 1 son, Harry Austin. Curator Stanford U. Museum of Fine Arts, 1899-1918; head of field research, Calif. History Dept. of Calif. State Library, 3 years; spl. feature writer of Calif. history, Oakland Tribune, 3 years; curator Sutter's Fort Hist. Museum, 1925—. Mem. Palo Alto City Council 8 years; chmn. history and landmarks com. Calif. State C. of C.; founder "Days of '49 Whiskers Club" as part of Sacramento's '49 Celebration, 1922; mem. bd. dirs. Sacramento Golden Empire Centennial, 1939. Active in marking historical places in Calif., especially in Mother Lode region, Sacramento, along Southern Pacific right of way; consultant on historical data for motion pictures, "Pony Express," "The Big Trail," "Sutters Gold"; Calif. dir. Ore. Trails Memorial Assn. Mem. Calif. Historic Landmarks Club of Los Angeles (state sec.), Calif. Historic Landmarks League (dir.). Mem. K.P., E. Clampus Vitas. Contbr. numerous historical articles to newspapers and mags.; cooperated with Julian Dana on "Sutter of California" and "The Dawn of Gold," pageant. Co-editor of Pony Express Courier; author of booklet "The Romance of California and Guide to the Mother Lode." Lecturer on Calif. history to Sacramento High Sch. Home: Palo Alto, Calif. Died Jan. 23, 1941.

PETERSON, Joseph, psychologist; b. Huntsville, Utah, Sept. 8, 1878; s. Hans Jordan and Inger Mary (Christensen) P.; student U. of Utah, summer 1900, U. of Calif., summers 1901, 03; B.Pd., Brigham Young Acad., Provo, Utah, 1902; S.B., U. of Chicago, 1905, Ph.D., 1907; m. Rhoda Richards Robinson, May 28, 1903; children—Joseph Kimbark, Wynford Richards, Ruskin Jay (dec.), Merlin Dewey. Prin. schs., Kanab, Utah, 1899-1901, Cassia Acad., Oakley, Ida., 1901-04; instr. psychology, 1907-08, prof., 1908-11, Brigham Young U.; prof. psychology, U. of Utah, 1911-15; professorial lecturer in psychology, 1915-16, asst. prof., 1916-18, chmn. dept., 1918, U. of Minn.; prof. psychology, George Peabody Coll.

for Teachers, 1918—. Instr. psychology and edn., Drake U., summer 1907; prof. psychology, U. of Chicago, summers 1914, 26, U. of Calif., summer 1931. Mem. Am. Psychol. Assn. (pres. 1933-34), Southern Soc. Philosophy and Psychology (pres. 1921-22). Mem. Nat. Research Council, 1926-29, and 1932-35; mem. Board of Nat. Research Fellowships in Biol. Sciences, 1933-36. Editor book reviews Am. Journal of Psychology, asso. editor Mental Measurement Monographs. Author: Combination Tones, etc., 1908; (with Lt. Q. J. David) The Psychology of Handling Men in the Army, 1918; Comparative Abilities of White and Negro Children, 1923; Early Conceptions and Tests of Intelligence, 1925; (with Lyle H. Lanier) Studies in the Comparative Abilities of Whites and Negroes, 1929; also Learning in Children, Chapter in A Handbook of Child Psychology, 1931. Home: Nashville, Tenn. Died Sept. 20, 1935.

PETERSON, Olof August, paleontologist; b. Hellgum och Rådom, Westernorrlands, Län, Sweden, Jan. 2, 1865; s. Pher Isaacson and Christina Brita Christopherson; ed. pub. sch. near birthplace; came with parents to U.S., 1882; m. Eda Louise Hermann, Oct. 15, 1901. Employed, 1888-91, with Prof. O. C. Marsh, then U.S. paleontologist; after that with Prof. H. F. Osborn in Am. Mus. Natural History, New York, 1891-96; with Princeton scientific expdn. to Patagonia, 1896, and continued in Princeton U. Mus. until Jan. 1, 1900; curator mammalian paleontology, Carnegie Mus., Pittsburgh. Writer of numerous papers on research topics in paleontology. Address: Pittsburgh, Pa. Died Nov. 13, 1933.

PETERSON, Peter, clergyman; b. Sweden, Nov. 21, 1866; s. Peter and Mary (Bengtson) P.; B.A., Gustavus Adolphus Coll., St. Peter, Minn., 1892; grad. Augustana Theol. Sem., Rock Island, Ill., 1894, Th.D., 1920; m. Mathilda Johnson, Oct. 17, 1894; children—Elmer T., Mildred I. (wife of Rev. Arvid P. Chindblom), Ruth (wife of Dr. Harold B. Hanson). Came to United States with parents in 1869, naturalized citizen, 1892. Ordained ministry Evang. Luth. Church, 1894; missionary in Utah, 1894-95; pastor successively at Essex, Ia., Galesburg, Ill., 1st Ch., St. Paul, Minn., 1st Ch., Stanton, Ia., Immanuel Ch., Chicago, until 1918; pres. Ill. Conf. Evang. Luth. Augustana Synod of N.A., 1919—. Mem. bd. dirs. Minnesota Coll., Minneapolis, Iowa Luth. Hosp., Des Moines, Augustana Hosp., Chicago, Immanuel Deaconess' Inst., Omaha, Chicago Luth. Bible Sch. and orphans homes at Andover, Ill., and Stanton, Ia. Bd. of Missions of the Augustana Synod; trustee Home Mission Bd. and Exec. Bd. of Ill. Conf. (both of Augustana Synod); trustee Nat. Luth. Council of North America; trustee Anti-Saloon League of Minn. and v.p. of State League; pres. Chicago Luth. Council, Luth. Home Mission Conf. for Ill. and Adjacent States. Republican. Decorated by King of Sweden with Knighthood of Royal Order of the North Star, 1926. Home: Chicago, Ill. Died June 3, 1940.

PETERSON, Reuben, obstetrician, gynecologist; b. Boston, Mass., June 29, 1862; s. Reuben and Julia Turner (Beale) P.; desc. George Soule and John Alden of the Mayflower; A.B., Harvard U., 1885, M.D., 1889; hon. Sc.D., Univ. of Mich., 1936; m. Josephine Davis, Mar. 6, 1890; children—Reuben, Marion, Ward Davis, Julia. In gen. practice at Grand Rapids, Mich., 1890-98; prof. gynecology, Post-Grad. Med. School of Chicago, 1898-1901; asst. prof. obstetrics and gynecology, Rush Med. Coll., 1898-1901; prof. obstetrics and gynecology, U. of Mich. Med. Sch., 1901-31; emeritus professor 1931—; med. dir. U. of Mich. Hosp., 1911-18; retired from practice, 1933. Maj. M.C., U.S. Army, and med. adviser to governor of Mich., 1917-19. Fellow American Coll. Surgeons (a founder), Am. Gynecol. Soc. (hon. 1931 —; pres. 1911); member Massachusetts Medical Society, hon. fellow American Medical Assn., Michigan State Med. Society (pres. 1915), Edinburgh Obstet. Society, Michigan Obstet. and Gynecol. Society, Washtenaw County Med. Society (pres. 1902). Democrat. Unitarian. Author: Demonstration Course in Obstetrics, 1930, 2d edit., 1937. Editor: Peterson's Obstetrics, 1907. Contbr. many articles on medical topics to professional publications. Home: Powder Point, Duxbury, Mass. Died Nov. 25, 1942.

PETRIE, George Laurens, clergyman; b. Cheraw, S.C., Feb. 25, 1840; s. George Holinshead Whitfield and Mary Jane P.; student Davidson (N.C.) Coll., 1856-57; A.B., Oglethorpe (Ga.) U., 1859, A.M., 1862, LL.D., 1923; Columbia Theol. Sem., 1862; D.D., Hampden-Sidney (Va.) Coll., 1887; m. Mary Cooper, Nov. 29, 1864; 1 son, George. Ordained ministry Presbyn. Ch. in U.S., 1863; chaplain 22d Ala. Vols., C.S.A., 1863 to 1865; teacher Classical Sch., Montgomery, Ala. 1865-66; prof. Latin, Oakland (Miss.) Coll., 1866-70; pastor Greenville, Ala., 1870-72. Petersburg, Va., 1872-78, Charlottesville, Va., 1878—. Author: Jacob's Sons, 1910; Israel's Prophets, 1912. Home: Charlottesville, Va. Died Mar. 1931.

PETRY, Edward Jacob, biologist, chemist; b. nr. Gnadenhutten, O., June 24, 1880; s. Jacob and Anna

Catherine (Schmitt) P.; B.S. in Agr., Ohio State U., 1907; grad. study Cornell U., 1907-11; M.S., Purdue U., 1914; grad. study U. of Mich., 1918-20; Ph.D., Mich. State Coll., 1925; m. Dora Margaret Plueddemann, Sept. 16, 1909; 1 son, Ralph Aurelius. Teacher pub. schs., Tuscarawas County, O., 1899-1901; asst. in chemistry and botany, Ohio State U., 1906-07; asst. in botany, Cornell U., 1907-10; instr. in agronomy, Purdue, 1911-16, asst. prof. agrl. botany, 1916-18, field asst. U.S. Dept. Agr., 1918; instr. in botany, U. of Mich., 1918-20; prof. botany and head of dept. of botany and plant pathology, S.D. State Coll., 1920-23; cons. botanist, 1923-24; collaborator, U.S. Dept. Agr., 1920-29; survey botanist S.D. Geol. and Biol. Survey, 1924-25; prof. biology and head of dept., Hendrix Coll., 1926-29; same, Central Coll., Fayette, Mo., 1929-31; prof. botany and asso. in physiology, Coe Coll., Cedar Rapids, Ia., 1931-33; cons. biologist Cedar Rapids Water Works, 1933-35; pres. Iowa Memorial Arboretum Assn., 1933—; consulting biochemist, 1933—; chief chemist Consumers Cooperative Assn.; chemist Ebony Paint Company, Kansas City, Mo., 1937—. Temporary agent U.S. Department of Agriculture, 1926; bot. curator, Ark. Mus. of Natural History, Little Rock, 1928-29. Moravian. Mason. Author of Experiment Sta. Bulls. Original research furnishing proof of symbiotic nitrogen fixation in non-legume flowering plants. Home: Cedar Rapids, Ia. Died Oct. 8, 1939.

PETTEE, James Horace, missionary; b. Manchester, N.H., July 16, 1851; s. Horace and Elizabeth Fairbanks (Wilson) P.; A.B., Dartmouth, 1873; grad. Andover Theol. Sem., 1877; D.D., Dartmouth, 1898, Ia. (now Grinnell) Coll., 1898; m. Bella Wilson, Aug. 1, 1878. Ordained Congl. ministry, May 8, 1878; missionary of A.B.C.F.M. in Japan, 1878—. Trustee Doshisha Schs., Kyoto, Japan, Okayama Orphanage; pres. Japan Soc. Christian Endeavor, 1915—; chmn. com. eleemosynary work Federated Missions in Japan. Japan corr. The Congregationalist and Christian World, Boston, 1880—. Author: Mr. Ishii and His Orphanage, 1891; A Chapter of Mission History in Modern Japan, 1894. Died Feb. 17, 1920.

PETTEE, William Henry, prof. mineralogy, economic geology and mining engring., U. of Mich.; b. Newton Upper Falls, Mass., Jan. 13, 1838; s. Otis and Matilda (Sherman) P.; grad. Harvard, 1861, A.M., 1864; studied and taught in Harvard, 1862-65; studied in School of Mines, Freiberg, Saxony, 1865-68; m. Sybilanna Clarke, July 8, 1874. Instr. and asst. prof. mining, Harvard, 1869-75; part of same time asst. geol. survey of Calif. At U. of Mich, 1875—. Address Ann Arbor, Mich. Died 1904.

PETTEE, William Jay, merchant; b. Kalamazoo, Mich., Apr. 3, 1867; s. Theodore and Helen (Scobie) P.; ed. pub. schs.; m. Daisy Beatty, Nov. 21, 1888; children—Margaret M. (Mrs. Howard D. Mitchell), Helen Beatty (Mrs. Carl W. Fugitt). Began in hardware business, Osage City, 1887; moved to Oklahoma City, 1889; pres. and treas. W.J. Pettee & Co., hardware, 1889—. Vice chmn. Liberty Loan Drives and Okla. State merchant rep. Food Administration, World War; col. staff of Gov. Williams, 1918-20. Chmn. United Charity Drive, Salavation Army Drive, Am. Legion Drive. Mem. State Retail Hardware Dealers Assn. (pres. 1904, 24, 25), 89'ers Assn. (pres.), Oklahoma City C. of C. (pres. 1920-21). Republican. Mason, Elk, K.P. Home: Oklahoma City, Okla. Died Dec. 24, 1928.

PETTENGILL, Heman Judson, telephone official; b. Brunswick, Me.; s. Herman and Rebecca (Hamilton) P.; ed. pub. schs.; m. Elizabeth Keene, 1875 (died 1897); children—Harrison V., Heman J., Russell A.; m. 2d, Mrs. Elizabeth Lee Murphy, Nov. 2, 1904. With Western Union Telegraph Co. until 1882; mgr. Am. Rapid Telegraph Co., and supt. Postal Telegraph Cable Co., 1882-99; identified, from 1899, with cos. affiliated with Am. Telegraph & Telephone Co.; pres. Southwestern Telegraph & Telephone Co., Dallas, Tex., 1903-11; elected pres. Southwestern Bell Telephone System, hdqrs. St. Louis, 1912—, chmn. bd., 1912-27 (retired). Mem. Old Time Telegraphers' Assn. (pres.). Republican. Episcopalian. Mason. Home: Clayton, Mo. Deceased.

PETTIBONE, Augustus Herman, lawyer; b. Bedford, O., Jan. 21, 1835; s. Augustus Norman and Nancy Leonard (Hathaway) P.; A.B., U. of Mich., 1859; read law at Milwaukee; m. Mary Clarinda Speck, July 16, 1868; m. 2d, Seraphine Deery, Nov. 22, 1899. Enlisted as pvt., 19th Wis. Inf., 1861; 2d lt. and capt. Co. A, 20th Wis. Inf., 1862; promoted maj. during siege of Vicksburg; served to end of war. Practiced law Greenville, Tenn., 1865-75, Knoxville, 1875-85; presdl. elector, 1868; atty. gen. 1st Jud. Circuit, Tenn., 4 yrs.; mem. 47th to 49th Congresses (1881-87), 1st Tenn. Dist.; asst. U.S. atty., Dist. Tenn., 6 yrs.; mem. Tenn. Ho. of Rep., 1896-98; spl. agt. U.S. Land Office, 1898-1904; apptd. agt. U.S. Dept. Agr., 1904. Republican (voted for Lincoln). Presbyterian. Comdr. Dept. Tenn., G.A.R., 1888-89. Mason. Address: Nashville, Tenn. Died Nov. 26, 1918.

PETTIGREW, George Atwood, Grand Sec. Masonic Bodies of S.D.; b. Ludlow, Vt., Apr. 6, 1858; s. Josiah Walker and Susan Ann (Atwood) P.; prep. edn., Black River Acad. (Ludlow), Colgate Acad. (New London, N.H.); M.D., Dartmouth, 1883; m. Eudora Zulette Stearns, Oct. 19, 1887; children—Mrs. Addie Stearns Fay, Madeleine A. Settled in Dak., 1883; practiced at Flandreau, S.D., 15 yrs., and govt. phys. to Sioux Indians same length of time; Grand Sec. Masonic Bodies of S.D., 1889—. Joined Dak. N.G., 1884; surgeon gen. Dak. Ty., 1885-89; pres. Bd. of Edn., Sioux Falls, S.D., 1910-18; pres. Children's Home Soc., 1908—; chmn. Minnehaha Co. Red Cross, 1918-21. Probation officer U.S. Dist. Court for S.D. Republican. Baptist. Mason (33°, Past Sovereign, Red Cross Constantine); elected Grand Sec., Grand Chapter R.A.M., 1889, Grand Sec. A.F. and A.M. of S.D., 1894, Grand Recorder Commandery K.T., 1895, Grand Recorder Council R. and S.M., 1916; Past Most Worthy Grand Patron Order Eastern Star of N. America, 1913-16; Ill. Potentate El Riad Shrine, 1908-09; Exalted Ruler 262 B.P.O.E., 1907. Home: Sioux Falls, S.D. Died Apr. 13, 1938.

PETTIGREW, Richard Franklin, senator; b. Ludlow, Vt., July 23, 1848; s. Andrew and Hannah B. (Sawtelle) P.; removed, 1854, to Evansville, Rock County, Wis.; ed. Evansville Acad., Beloit Coll., and in law dept. U. of Wis.; LL.B., U. of Wis., 1879; m. Bessie V. Pittare, Feb. 27, 1879; 1 son, Franklin Sawtelle. Went to Dakota, 1869, as surveyor in employ of U.S. dept. surveyor; settled at Sioux Falls; in law practice, 1872-80. Mem. Dakota Legislative Council, 1877-81; del. in 47th Congress (1881-83); mem. S.D. Constl. Conv., 1883; mem. Territorial Council, 1884-85; U.S. senator from S.D., 1889-1901. Republican. Left Rep. party on account of the attitude of the party on finance and trust; supported Bryan, 1896, 1900; led opposition in Senate against policy of the administration in annexing P.I. and adopting a colonial policy. Author: The Course of Empire; Imperial Washington. Home: Sioux Falls, S.D. Died Oct. 5, 1926.

PETTIJOHN, John J.; b. Flora, Ill., Oct. 17, 1875; s. Thomas and Harriet (Clark) P.; unlimited state teachers' certificate, Wis., 1905; A.B., U. of Wis., 1911; grad. work, same univ., 1911-13; m. Elizabeth S. Shenkenberg, June 17, 1903. Supt. pub. schs. in Wis., 1900-09; sec. dept. of instruction by lectures, Extension Div. U. of Wis., 1909-13; dir. extension div. U. of N.D., 1913-14, U. of Ind., 1913-18; asso. dir. Nat. Four-Minute Men, Com. on Pub. Information, 1918; dir. div. of ednl. extension Bur. of Edn., Department of Interior, 1919; asst. to pres. and dir. summer session, U. of Minn., 1921—. Democrat. Conglist. Mason. Home: Minneapolis, Minn. Died Mar. 20, 1923.

PETTINGELL, Frank Hervey, investment broker; b. Newburyport, Mass., Jan. 2, 1868; s. Nathaniel Henry and Mary Anna (Feltch) P.; ed. pub. schs. and business coll.; m. Medora Anna Wilson, Sept. 5, 1905; children—Frank Hervey, Mary Agnes. Began as investment broker, Colorado Springs, Colo., 1892; moved to Los Angeles, Calif., 1912; mem. firm Frank H. Pettingell; hon. pres. Los Angeles Stock Exchange; chmn. County and Municipal Affairs Com. of Commercial Bd. of Los Angeles; dir. Nat. Pacific Oil Co. Mem. bd. dirs. Pub. Library, Los Angeles (1st v.p.). Mem. A.L.A. (pres. trustees sect. 1920-21), Calif. Library Assn. (pres. trustees sect. 1920-25), Los Angeles Library Commn., 1916—. Mem. Soc. Colonial Wars State of Calif. (gov. 1919-20), and Gen. Soc. Colonial Wars (historian gen. 1921-26), S.R. in State of Calif. (pres. 1921-22), and Gen. Soc. same (gen. 2d v.p. 1923-26), Calif. General. Soc. (hon. pres.), Nat. Soc. Americans of Royal Descent (hon. v.p. gen.), Internat. Congress Genealogy (pres. 1915). Writer on Pettingell and Feltch pedigrees. Home: Los Angeles, Calif. Died May 8, 1926.

PETTIS, Clifford Robert, forester; b. Delancy, N.Y., Aug. 10, 1877; s. Homer R. and Margaret (Davidson) P.; Ithaca High Sch., 1896; F.E., Cornell U., 1901; m. Maude E. Otis, Nov. 2, 1904; 1 dau., Elizabeth Otis. State forester of N.Y., 1902-10; supt. state forests, N.Y., May 31, 1910—; collaborator, 1906-09, forest expert, 1909—, U.S. Forest Service; cons. forester Vt. Agrl. Expt. Sta., 1907-09; lecturer U. of Vt., 1908. Author of ann. reports Forestry Dept., N.Y., and bulls. Listing officer 10th Engrs., 20th Engrs. (forest). Home: Albany, N.Y. Died Jan. 29, 1927.

PETTIT, George Albert Joseph, clergyman; b. Dunmore, Ireland, Sept. 15, 1858; s. William and Elizabeth S. (Petty) P.; ed. pub. schs. and by pvt. tutors, New York. Entered Soc. of Jesus, July 30, 1880; after completion of the 7 yrs. of prep. training customary with Jesuits, taught English and classics, Gonzaga Coll., Washington, 1887-90, Fordham Coll., 1890-92; returned to Woodstock Theol. Sem., Md., where was ordained to priesthood, June 1895, by Archbishop Satolli; prefect of discipline and v.p., Fordham Coll., 2 yrs.; reapptd., 1899-1900, and pres., 1900-04; pres. Novitiate of St. Andrew-on-Hudson, Poughkeepsie, N.Y., Apr. 5, 1904—. Died Feb. 27, 1917.

PETTIT, Henry, civ. engr. and architect; b. Phila., Dec. 23, 1842; s. Robert (U.S.N.) and Laura (Ellmaker) P.; great g.s. Col. Charles P., mem. Continental Congress, also of Chief Justice Thomas McKean, signer of Independence; ed. U. of Pa. to jr. yr.; hon. M.S., U. of Pa., 1877; studied civil engring., architecture, music; unmarried. In engring. dept. Pa. R.R. Co., bridges and buildings constrn. dept., 1862-74; sent by U.S. Centennial Commn. as spl. agt. to Vienna Expn., 1873; engr. and architect U.S. Centennial Exposition, Phila., 1873-77, main bldg., machinery hall, etc.; chief Bur. of Installation, U.S. Centennial Expn., 1876; architect U.S. Commn., Paris Expn., 1878; mem. Advisory Art Com. for Pa. at Chicago Expn., 1893. Traveled extensively; made 2 tours round the world. Republican. Presbyn. Mem. Am. Philos. Soc. (curator 1897-1900); mem. Legion of Honor of France; Order of St. Olaf, Norway; Isabella of Spain; Iftakar of Tunis; Loyal Legion U.S. Dir. Union League, Phila., 1877-78. Author: A Twentieth Century Idealist, 1905; Symbolism in Christianity (pamphlet), 1906. Also system of "peace flags"—nat. ensigns with white border; being the evolution of ordinary flags of truce in war times, into higher significance, indicative of peaceful methods in lieu of war—originally published, Oct. 1891, and adopted, Oct. 12, 1891, at Independence Hall, Phila., by the Human Freedom League; since then used extensively in many countries, notably at The Hague Peace Temple, in connection with jud. arbitration confs.; the U.S. ensign with a white border as peace flag planted by Capt. Peary at the North Pole, 1909. Home: Philadelphia, Pa. Died Aug. 11, 1921.

PETTUS, Edmund Winston, U.S. senator from Ala., 1897-1909; b. Limestone County, Ala., July 6, 1821; ed. common schools, Ala., and Clinton Coll., Tenn.; admitted to bar, 1842; began practice at Gainesville, Ala.; m. Mary S. Chapman, June 27, 1844. Elected, 1844, solicitor for 7th circuit; served as lt. in Mexican war. Went on horseback, with party of neighbors, to Calif., 1849; returned, 1851; judge 7th circuit, 1855-58; resigned and removed to Selma, practicing law there; in C.S.A., maj. to brig. gen., 1861-65. Democrat. Residence: Selma, Ala. Died 1907.

PETTY, Alonzo McAllister, clergyman; b. Burning Springs, Wirt County, W.Va., Nov. 9, 1860; s. Henderson and Hulda C. (Wright) P.; student Berryville Acad., Bethel Coll., Russellville, Ky., and Lane U., LeCompton, Kan.; D.D. from Linfield (Ore.) Coll., 1910, Redlands (Calif.) U., 1910; m. Ida V. King, 1881 (died 1915); children—Carl Wallace (dec.), Alonzo Ray (dec.), Faunce Fern; m. 2d, Mrs. Anna Gilchrist Murdoch, Dec. 15, 1916. Ordained Bapt. ministry, 1881; pastor Meriden, Kan., 1881-82, Madison St. Ch., Topeka, 1883, Valley Falls, 1884, Santa Ana, Calif., 1884-88, Stockton, 1888-89, Dixon, 1897-1902; supt. Southern Calif. Capt. Conv., 1902-08; dist. sec. Am. Bapt. Home Mission Soc. of Pacific Coast, 1908-14; joint sec. of all Bapt. bds. of Northwest, 1914-19; field sec. New World Movement, 1919-23; field rep. Am. Bapt. Home Mission Soc., 1923-33 (retired). Mason. Home: Glendale, Calif. Died Jan. 24, 1937.

PETTY, A(lonzo) Ray, clergyman; b. Santa Ana, Calif., July 17, 1887; s. Alonzo McAllister and Ida Viola (King) P.; B.A., Occidental Coll., Los Angeles, Calif., 1915, D.D., 1921; student Rochester Theol. Sem., 1909-10, Union Theol. Sem., 1915-16; m. Nancy Louise Tedford, Nov. 8, 1911; children—Nancy Viola, Alonzo Ray. Student sec. Los Angeles Y.M.C.A., 1910-12; dir. work for men and boys, Temple Bapt. Ch., Los Angeles, 1912-14; ordained Bapt. ministry, 1917; chaplain Ione (Calif.) State Reformatory, 1914-15; pastor Judson Memorial Ch., N.Y. City, 1915-26, Bapt. Temple, Phila., 1926-29; First Ch., Kansas City, Mo., 1929—. A founder and v.p. Judson Health Center. Mem. bd. dirs. Ministers' and Missionaries' Benefit Bd. of Northern Baptist Conv.; member exec. com. Northern Baptist Conv.; dir. Deering Community Center; mem. Nat. Golden Rule Baptist Advisory Com., Baptist Union Bd. of Kansas City, Council of Chs. of Kansas City (exec. com.). Republican. Mason. Lecturer Chautauqua Lyceum student conferences, Bible conferences. Preacher Amherst, Dartmouth, Princeton and Cornell colleges. Contbr. to 1928 "Best Sermons." Author: Songs of the Tenements and Other Verse, 1925. Home: Kansas City, Mo. Died Oct. 25, 1932.

PETTY, C(arl) Wallace, clergyman; b. Topeka, Kan., Aug. 23, 1884; s. Alonzo M. (D.D.) and Ida V. (King) P.; B.L., Occidental Coll., 1906, D.D., 1920; D.D., Denison, 1923; B.D., Rochester Theol. Sem., 1909; LL.D., U. of Pittsburgh, 1926; m. Eloise Wells, May 12, 1910; children—Barbara Wells, Jessie Eloise. Ordained Bapt. ministry, 1909; pastor First Ch., New Brighton, N.Y., 1909-10, Creston Av. Ch., N.Y. City, 1910-20, Mt. Morris Ch., N.Y. City, 1920-22, First Ch., Pittsburgh, 1922—. Mem. bd. mgrs. Am. Bapt. Home Mission Soc. Univ. preacher at Cornell U., U. of Chicago, Wells, Illinois, Minnesota; lecturer on homiletics, Divinity Sch., U. of Chicago, summer 1929. Mason. Republican. Home: Pittsburgh, Pa. Died Sept. 9, 1932.

PETTY, Orlando Henderson, M.D.; b. Cadiz, O., Feb. 20, 1874; s. Asbury F. and Sarah (Kyle) P.; B.S., Franklin Coll., New Athens, O., 1890, A.M.,

1900; M.D., Jefferson Med. Coll., 1904; m. Marcia P. Mellersh, Apr. 8, 1908; children—Clara M., Orville A. II. Began practice at Phila., 1904; prof. metabolic diseases, U. of Pa. Grad. Sch. of Medicine; chief dept. of diseases of metabolism, Phila. Gen. Hosp. and Hosp. U. of Pa. Grad. Sch. of Medicine; consultant in diseases of metabolism and malnutrition, Shriners' Hosp. for Crippled Children; consultant in metabolic disorders, Rush Hosp. for Consumptives. Served as lt. Med. Corps U.S.N., with 5th U.S.M., in France, World War. Dir. pub. health, city of Philadelphia. Mem. Phila. County Med. Soc. (pres.), Med. Club of Phila. (pres.), Army and Navy Legion of Valor (past nat. comdr.). Decorated Congressional Medal of Honor and D.S.C. (both U.S.); Croix de Guerre with Palm (France); War Cross (Italy). Republican. Episcopalian. Mason. Author: Diabetes—Its Treatment by Insulin and Diet, 1924. Address: Philadelphia, Pa. Deceased.

PEW, Marlen Edwin, editor; b. Niles, O., June 3, 1878; s. Horace Samuel and Mary Elizabeth (Tucker-Edmonds) P.; educated in pub. schs.; LL.D., Washington and Lee U.; m. Margaret Susan Barr, 1910; children—Susan Margaret, Marlen E., Samuel H. Reporter, Cleveland Press, 1894-97; New York rep. Scripps-McRae Pess Assn., 1897-1900; various editorial capacities New York Evening Jour., 1900-02; eastern mgr. Newspaper Enterprise Assn., 1903-07; editor Newspaper Enterprise Assn., 1907-10, The Boston Traveler, 1910-12; news mgr. United Press Assn., of which was one of the organizers, 1912; editor Phila. News-Post, 1912-14; apptd. press rep. of the sec. of War, Washington, D.C., 1917, and organized War Dept. News Bur., originating the Am. system of pub. war casualty lists; also originated system adopted by Army and Navy of authorized statements for press publn.; editor and mgr. Internat. News Service, 1919-22; editor and v.p. The Editor and Publisher, 1922—; trustee Science Service, Inc. Mem. advisory bd. Sch. of Journalism of Columbia U.; chmn. New York Business Papers Conf. Democrat. Protestant. Home: Wading River, L.I. Died Oct. 15, 1936.

PEXTON, George Ellsworth; b. Vernon, N.Y., Sept. 23, 1863; s. George and Catherine (Rivenburgh) P.; pub. sch. edn.; m. Annie S. Saunders, June 6, 1895; children—George Ellsworth, Sidney Vernon. In hotel business, Evanston, Wyo., and Ogden, Utah, 1893-1903; interested in real estate, ranches and mercantile instns. Pres. First Nat. Bank (also chmn. bd.), Bear River Coal Co., Evanston, Wyo., Scofield (Utah) Coal Co. Rep. Nat. Com., 1902-18. V.p. State Commn. to St. Louis and Portland expns. Home: Evanston, Wyo. Died Oct. 18, 1939.

PEYSER, Theodore A., congressman; b. Charleston, W.Va., Feb. 18, 1873; ed. pub. schs. Engaged in life ins. business; mem. 73d and 74th Congresses (1933-37), 17th N.Y. Dist. Democrat. Home: New York, N.Y. Died Aug. 8, 1937.

PEYTON, John Howe, railway pres.; b. Howard County, Mo., Mar. 17, 1864; s. William Preston and Sarah Elizabeth (Munford) P.; ed. Roanoke Coll., Salem, Va., 1876-81; unmarried. Began as rodman Richmond & Louisville R.R., 1881; engring. work for various rys., 1881-92; engaged as engr. and contractor, 1892-98; U.S. Army service, 1899; mem. commn. Episcopal Ch. to P.I., 1899-1900; resident engr. C.&O. Ry., 1900-01; chief engr. Great Eastern R.R., 1901-02; mem. engring. corps, 1902-10, asst. to the pres., 1910-14, chief engr. constrn., 1912-14, L.&N. R.R.; pres. Nashville, Chattanooga & St. Louis Ry., Mar. 1914—; also v.p. Paducah & Ill. R.R. Trustee U. of the South (Sewanee, Tenn.), Peabody Coll. for Teachers (Nashville). Episcopalian. Mason. Author: American Transportation Problem, 1907. Home: Nashville, Tenn. Died Sept. 14, 1918.

PFAFF, Franz, physician; b. Grafenort, Silesia, Mar. 16, 1860; early edn. at Dresden; studied natural science, univs. of Leipzig, Munich and Zurich; Ph.D., Zurich; first asst. in chem. laboratory, U. of Geneva, and pvt. docent there; was dir. chem. laboratory, Province of Amazonas, Brazil; studied med. plants in Brazil 3 yrs.; pursued med. studies at univs. of Strassburg, Wurzburg and Basel; M.D., Strassburg; also studies in hosps. at London, L.S.A. Instr. physiology, 1894-95, instr. pharmacology, 1895-1900, instr. physiol. chemistry, 1898-1900, asst. prof. pharmacology and therapeutics, 1900-05, prof. same, 1905—, Harvard Med. Sch. Died 1926.

PFAFF, Orange Garrett, surgeon; b. Westfield, Ind., Apr. 28, 1857; s. Dr. Jacob L. and Jane (Wall) P.; pub. and high schs., Indianapolis, M.D., Ind. Med. Coll., 1882; post-grad. work in New York and at U. of Berlin; hon. A.M., Wabash Coll., 1907; m. Mary Alvey, Nov. 25, 1885. Resident phys., Marion County (Ind.) Infirmary, 1882-84; in practice at Indianapolis, 1884—; specialist in abdominal surgery, 1890—; lecturer, clin. prof. gynecology, 1890-91, prof. gynecology, 1892—, Ind. U. Med. Sch. Maj. M.R.C. U.S.A. Republican. Home: Indianapolis, Ind. Died Aug. 26, 1927.

PFAFF, William, printer; b. New Orleans, La., Nov. 24, 1871; s. William and Sidonie (Gansz) P.; ed. Seventh Street Protestant Orphans Home, New Orleans; m. Corinne H. Sievers, Oct. 21, 1891; children—William Sievers, Edna Regina (Mrs. Wm. H. Briede, Jr.), Corinne Amelia, Genevieve Pauline (Mrs. Wesling L. Hille). Began as errand boy with Bennett & Patterson, New Orleans, 1883; sec.-treas. Searcy & Pfaff, Ltd., 1901—; pres. Union Homestead Assn., Title & Mortgage Guarantee Co.; dir. Am. Bank & Trust Co. Was pres. United Typothetæ America, New Orleans Assn. Commerce. Democrat. Methodist. Mason, Elk. Home: New Orleans, La. Died Jan. 28, 1940.

PFAHLER, William H., mfr.; b. Columbia, Pa., Mar. 27, 1844; s. Henry and Mary P.; ed. in schs. of Columbia, Pa., Millersville (Pa.) State Normal Sch.; left to enter Union Army as pvt., Mar. 1862, and served 3 yrs. in 45th Pa. Vols.; discharged at end of war as 1st lt. and regimental q.m.; regt. served during entire war with Burnside, 9th Army Corps, and participated in battles of Antietam, South Mountain, Vicksburg, Knoxville, Tenn., and last of Grant's campaign from the Wilderness to the close of war; m. Anna Bilderback, 1874. Associated with Abram Cox Stove Co., 1885, of which was treas.; pres. Model Heating Co. Organized and later pres. Nat. Founders' Assn.; assisted in organizing Nat. Metal Trades Assn.; hon. mem. administrative council of two bodies. One of original com. of 7 which organized Com. of 70 which brought about overthrow of polit. ring which had ruled Phila. With Senator Marcus A. Hanna was associated in organizing Civic Federation (mem. exec. council). Republican. Mem. Loyal Legion. Home: Philadelphia, Pa. Died 1908.

PFOTENHAUER, Frederick, clergyman; b. nr. Celle, Hanover, Germany, Apr. 22, 1859; s. Rev. Hermann and Louise (Köhler) P.; Gymnasium, Celle; came to America, 1875; grad. Concordia Coll., Ind., 1877; grad. Concordia Sem., Mo., 1880, D.D., 1920; m. Helene Brauer, Oct. 10, 1882; children—Gertrud, Martha, Else, Martin, Hermann, Helen, Ernst, Dorothea, Karl, Esther, Friedrich. Ordained Luth. ministry, 1880; pastor, Odessa, Minn., and traveling missionary in Minn. and the tys. of Dakota and Montana, 1880-87; pastor at Lewiston, Minn., 1887-94, Hamburg, Minn., 1894-1911. Pres. Minn. and Dak. Dist. of the Evang. Luth. Synod of Mo., Ohio and other states, 1891-1908; 1st v.p., 1908-11, pres., 1911-35, then hon. pres. Evang. Luth. Synod of Mo., Ohio and other states. Home: Chicago, Ill. Died Oct. 19, 1939.

PHALEN, Paul Stephens, clergyman; b. Camden, N.Y., Jan. 20, 1881; s. Frank Lowe and Emma (Stephens) P.; A.B., Amherst, 1903; S.T.B., Harvard, 1908; m. Charlotte Robertson, Sept. 3, 1910; children—Elizabeth, Leslie Robertson. Ordained Unitarian ministry, 1908; minister in Mass. and Me., until 1922; minister First Unitarian Soc., Newton, Mass., 1922—. Home: West Newton, Mass. Died Mar. 13, 1938.

PHELAN, James Duval, senator; b. San Francisco, Calif., Apr. 20, 1861; s. James and Alice (Kelly) P.; A.B., St. Ignatius U., 1881; Ph.D., Santa Clara Coll., 1903; studied law, U. of Calif.; unmarried. Vice pres. Calif. Commn. to Chicago Expn., 1893; mayor of San Francisco 3 terms, 1897-1902; pres. Relief and Red Cross Funds (a corp.), after San Francisco disaster; was regent U. of Calif., park commr. and trustee Pub. Library, San Francisco; chmn. charter assn. which gave new charter to San Francisco; pres. adornment assn. which procured the Burnham plans for San Francisco; pres. Playground Commn. of San Francisco. Appointed by Dept. of State to visit Europe, 1913, to support invitation of the President to foreign countries to participate in Panama-Pacific Expn.; apptd. by Dept. of State, to investigate the fitness of the Am. minister to the Dominican Republic, 1914; U.S. senator from Calif., 1915-21. Democrat. Toured world, 1921-22, and published book "Travel and Comment." Home: Saratoga, Calif. Died Aug. 7, 1930.

PHELAN, James J., banker; b. Toronto, Ont., Can., Oct. 14, 1871; s. James W. and Catherine (Colbert) P.; brought by parents to U.S., 1878; ed. pub. schs., Boston, Mass.; LL.D., Boston Coll., 1925; m. Mary Meade, June 19, 1899 (died 1907); children—James J., Katharine (Mrs. Henry Milton Lyons), Caroline I. (Mrs. Joseph De Vore Norton); m. 2d, Mabel J. McGaffee, Apr. 23, 1913; children—M. Priscilla, Virginia M., Patricia Colbert. Began with Hornblower & Weeks, Boston, 1888, partner, 1900—; mem. Boston Stock Exchange, 1897—; dir. Mass. Bonding & Ins. Co. (chmn. finance com.), Union Mills, Inc., Bangor & Aroostook R.R. (exec. com.); mem. exec. com. N.E. Power Assn.; trustee Mass. Utilities Associates, Boston Wharf Co., U.S. Smelting, Refining & Mining Co., Suffolk Savings Bank for Seamen and Others. Mem. Mass. Naval Brigade, 1893-96. Mem. exec. com. all Liberty Loan drives, Boston, and chmn. Boston-Metropolitan Victory Loan Drive; asst. food administrator, Mass., and exec. mgr. Pub. Safety Com., World War; emergency fuel administrator, Mass., 1922-23. Mem. San Francisco Relief, Chelsea Fire, Salem Fire, Messina Earthquake and Ohio Floods, relief coms. for Mass. Mem. bd. mgrs. Children's Hosp., Boston Community Health Assn., Franklin Foundation (v.p.), Travelers Aid Soc.; trustee Notre Dame U. Decorated Knight of Malta (first in U.S.), Knight Comdr. Order of Pope Pius IX, Grand Cross Sovereign Mil. Order of Malta. Catholic. Home: Brookline, Mass., and Manchester-by-the-Sea, Mass. Died Oct. 16, 1934.

PHELAN, Michael Francis, congressman; b. Lynn, Mass., Oct. 22, 1875; s. James and Rebecca (Griffin) P.; A.B., Harvard, 1897, LL.B., 1900; m. Marie Van Depoele, June 22, 1904. Began practice of law, Lynn, Mass., 1900; mem. Mass. Ho. of Rep., 1905-06; mem. 63d to 66th Congresses (1913-21), 7th Mass. District. Democrat. Catholic. Home: Lynn, Mass. Died Oct. 12, 1941.

PHELAN, Richard, R.C. bishop; b. nr. Ballyraggatt, County Kilkenny, Ireland, Jan. 1, 1828; s. Michael and Mary (Keoghan) P.; ed. private tutors and Coll. of St. Kyran, Kilkenny; came to U.S., 1850; studied St. Mary's Theol. Sem., Baltimore; ordained priest, May 4, 1854; stationed in Indiana County, Pa., short time; 3 yrs. asst. Cathedral, Pittsburgh; pastor Freeport, Pa., 10 yrs.; St. Peter's Ch., Allegheny, Pa., 1868; was administrator and later vicar-gen. and consecrated coadjutor bishop of Pittsburgh, Pa., Aug. 2, 1885, succeeding to vacant see on death of Bishop Tuigg, Dec. 7, 1889. Died 1904.

PHELAN, Warren Waverly, educator; b. Brooklyn, N.Y., Sept. 20, 1869; s. Edward and Jennie Elizabeth (Preston) P.; A.B., Columbia, 1894, A.M., 1896; studied U. of Tenn. and U. of Chicago; Ph.D., George Washington U., 1903; LL.D., Okla. Bapt. U., 1920; m. Lila M. Laws, Aug. 9, 1900; 1 son, Kenneth L. Head master Nat. Capital Univ. School, Washington, D.C., 1896-1900; supt. schs. Miss. and Ind., 1900-04; dean Sch. of Edn., U. of Chattanooga, 1904-07, Baylor U., 1907-12, U. of Okla., 1912-26; pres. Okla. Bapt. U., 1926-31; prof. psychology and edn., Okla. Agrl. and Mech. Coll., 1931—; dir. Mid-Continent Life Ins. Co. Reorganized U. of Honan, Kaifeng, China, 1923, on basis of Am. univs. Mem. Com. of 100 of Nat. Civic Fedn.; mem. Joint Com. on the Russian Situation; mem. State Com. of Y.M.C.A. State Assn.; dir. Southwest Field Council of Y.M.C.A. Democrat. Mason. Author: Studies in Adolescence, 1924; lecturer. Home: Stillwater, Okla. Died July 31, 1935.

PHELPS, Albert Charles, prof. architecture; b. Lockport, Ill., Apr. 8, 1873; s. Albert and Harriet Laura (Sprague) P.; B.S., U. of Ill., 1894, M. Arch., 1903; studied Bavarian Tech. Sch., Munich, 1897-98; traveled and studied abroad, 1901, 1912-13, 1931; m. Carolyn Blount Lynd, Aug. 14, 1902; 1 son, George Lynd. Draftsman in Chicago offices, 1894-97; licensed architect, Illinois, 1898; practiced Joliet, 1898-99; instructor Coll. Architecture, 1899-1903, asst. prof., 1903-13, prof., 1913—, World War memorial prof. architecture, 1920—, Cornell U., in charge of history of architecture. Lecturer Met. Mus. Art, New York. Dir. architectural tours for the Inst. of Internat. Edn. of Carnegie Foundation, 1923-24; dir. architectural tours for The Bur. of Univ. Travel, Inc., 1925-31. Fellow A.I.A. Mason. Democrat. Home: Ithaca, N.Y. Died July 4, 1937.

PHELPS, Ashton, journalist; b. New Orleans, July 14, 1853; s. John and Clara Marean (Clark) P.; ed. pub. schs., New Orleans, and pvt. sch. at Bellevue, Va.; m. Blanche Moulton, May 21, 1885. Engaged in journalism in New Orleans, 1879—; pres. Times-Picayune Pub. Co., owners of the Times-Picayune newspaper, also one of the editorial writers on polit. and econ. questions and all matters relating to cotton. Mem. Bd. Liquidation City Debt of New Orleans; dir. Kingsley House Industrial Sch. Episcopalian. Democrat. Home: New Orleans, La. Died Dec. 11, 1919.

PHELPS, Charles, surgeon; b. Milford, Mass., Dec. 12, 1834; s. Dr. Thaddeus and Mary (Gould) P.; A.M., Brown U., 1855; M.D., Coll. Phys. and Surg. (Columbia), 1858; m. Isabel M. James, 1863. In practice at New York, 1858—; specialist in surgery; surgeon to Bellevue and St. Vincent's hosps. Author: Traumatic Injuries of the Brain, 1890; also various monographs on surgical subjects. Died Dec. 30, 1913.

PHELPS, Charles Edward, soldier, jurist, author; b. Guilford, Vt., May 1, 1833; s. John and Almira Hart (Lincoln) P.; lived in Md. from 1841; A.B., Princeton, 1852; A.M., 1855, LL.D., 1906; studied law at Harvard, 1852-53; after some time spent in foreign travel began practice in Baltimore; m. Martha Woodward, 1868. Mem. city council, Baltimore, on Reform ticket, 1860 (popular revolt against local misrule of "Know Nothing" party); capt. and maj., 1859-61, Md. Guard; in Union Army as lt. col. and col. 7th Md. Vol. Inf., 1862-64; horse killed under him, was wounded and taken prisoner, May 8, 1864, while leading charge on works at Spottsylvania, having assumed command while charge was in progress, after fall of two successive commanders; recaptured by Sheridan's cav.; promoted bvt. brig. gen. U.S.V. and awarded Congressional medal of honor for "most distinguished gallantry." Elected to Congress on Union ticket, 1864; re-elected on Conservative ticket, 1866; as mem. Naval Committee was instrumental in securing retention of U.S. Naval Acad. at Annapolis; supported 14th amendment to Constitution, but opposed the radical measures and policy of reconstruction, and particularly the 15th amendment; declined exec. apptmt. as judge Md. Court of Appeals; pres. Baltimore sch. bd., 1876; served during strike riots, 1877, as col. 8th Md. regt. Elected judge, Supreme bench, Baltimore, 1882 (Independent ticket), for 15-yr. term; re-elected for like term, 1897; term unanimously extended by Md. legislature of 1902. Prof. law, Univ. of Md., 1884-1906. Author: Juridical Equity, 1894; Falstaff and Equity, 1901; One of the Missing, 1905. Home: Baltimore, Md. Died 1908.

PHELPS, Charles Edward, Jr., engineer; b. Baltimore, Jan. 31, 1871; s. Charles Edward and Martha (Woodward) P.; ed. through primary and grammar schs. of Baltimore; grad. manual training sch., 1889, tech. course, Johns Hopkins, 1891-94, receiving certificate of proficiency; m. Maude Griswold Thelin, Nov. 29, 1899. Engaged with elec. st. ry., and engring. cos., 1888-96; in pvt. practice as consulting engr. Retained, 1902, by City of Cleveland to report and estimate upon cost of elec. st. and commercial lighting project adopted by city council; retained by cities of Johnstown and Rochester, N.Y., 1903, in litigation over construction and operation of underground elec. conduit systems; and by City of Montreal, to report and estimate upon an underground conduit system, project adopted by bd. of aldermen; retained by Comptroller Grout of New York, 1905, to assist in investigation of prices charged for electric st. lighting; chief engineer of Electric Commn. of Baltimore, 1898, in charge constrn. of underground comduit; sec. Municipal Lighting Commn. of Baltimore, 1900—; chief engr. Pub. Service Commn. of Md., 1910—; engr. mem. Md. State Bd. of Health, 1915—. From 1898 devoted efforts to questions affecting relations of public service corps. to public; retained, 1906, by Nat. Civic Fedn. in investigation and appraisal of municipal electric lighting plants and their operation; and, 1907, by Cambridge, Mass., in connection with constrn. of underground conduits by the city. Episcopalian. Home: Baltimore, Md. Died Dec. 23, 1918.

PHELPS, Charles Henry, lawyer; b. Stockton, Calif., Jan. 1, 1853; s. Charles W. and Mary Wilson (Smith) P.; LL.B., Harvard, 1874; m. Mary Booth, of Oakland, Calif. Practiced in San Francisco, 1874-82, later in New York; mem. firm of Phelps & East; trustee of estates. Republican. Mem. Assn. Bar City of New York. Died 1933.

PHELPS, Delos Porter, lawyer; b. Warren County, Ill., Nov. 16, 1837; s. Porter and Mary Ellen (Rees) P.; A.M., Monmouth (Ill.) Coll., 1862, LL.D., 1906; m. Sarah Jeannette Tucker, Apr. 13, 1870. Admitted to bar, 1866; practiced at Monmouth, 1866-80; Dem. candidate for Congress, 1878; began building railroad, 1879, between Peoria and Keithburg, Ill. (later the Ill. div. of the Ia. Central Ry.), and was v.p., gen. mgr., and gen. counsel same; organized the company that bridged the Mississippi River at Keithsburg, Ill., about 1884; in 1886 purchased a two-fifth interest in the Weir Plow Co. and was v.p. and gen. mgr. until 1894; chmn. Dem. State Central Com. 4 yrs.; asst. treas. of U.S. at Chicago, 1894-98; resumed practice of law in Chicago, 1894. Died June 28, 1914.

PHELPS, Edward Bunnell, journalist, author; b. New Haven, Conn., July 26, 1863; s. Alfred William and Mary A. (Bunnell) P.; A.B., Yale, 1885, A.M., 1902; m. Blanche Louise Lewis Dey, Apr. 12, 1897. In journalism, 1885; founded, 1894, Thrift, monthly ins. jour., later changed to The American Underwriter Magazine and Insurance Review; for 15 yrs. pres. of the Thrift Pub. Co., N.Y. City, which publishes it and ins. books. Author: War Risks, 1898; Tropical Hazards, 1901; Origin and Evolution of the Modern Club, 1902; A Decade Without a Parallel in the History of American Insurance, 1905; A Statistical Study of Infant Mortality (reprinted from Quarterly Publns. of the Am. Statis. Assn.), 1908; American Mortality Statistics for the Nine Years, 1900-1908 (1910); A Statistical Survey of Infant Mortality's Urgent Call for Action (reprinted from report of 1st ann. meeting of Am. Statis. Assn.), 1911; Neurotic Books and Newspapers as Factors in the Mortality of Suicide and Crime (reprinted from Bull. of the Am. Acad. Medicine), 1911; The Mortality of Alcohol, 1911; The Relation of Women's Work and Infant Mortality (reprinted from spl. rep. of U.S. Bur. of Labor), 1911. Died July 24, 1915.

PHELPS, Edward John, lawyer, diplomat; b. Middlebury, Vt., July 11, 1822; grad. Middlebury Coll., 1840, LL.D., 1870; studied law; admitted to Vt. bar, 1843; removed to Burlington, Vt., 1845; 2d comptroller U.S. Treasury, 1851-53; delegate to Vt. Constitutional convention, 1870; presided over Centennial celebration, battle of Bennington, 1877; pres. Am. Bar Assn., 1880; Democratic candidate for gov. Vt., 1880, defeated; prof. law Yale, 1881-85; U.S. minister to Great Britain, 1885-89; candidate of Democrats in Vt. legislature for U.S. senator, 1890; apptd., 1893, and served as one of the counsel of U.S. Govt. in Court of Arbitration in Bering Sea controversy; Kent prof. law, Yale. Died 1900.

PHELPS, Edward Shethar, insurance; b. Burlington, Ia., Apr. 21, 1858; s. Charles Henry and Eunice Adams (Webb) P.; ed. pub. schs.; m. Jessie Garrett, May 29, 1883 (now dec.); children—Helen G. (dec.), Katherine W., Edward S. (dec.), Mauro G. (dec.), Frances G., Charles H.; m. 2d, Josephine N. Churchill, Aug. 2, 1930. U.S. internal revenue service, 1874-83; fire ins. business, Burlington, Ia., 1883—; proprietor Phelps Ins. Agency; pres. First Ia. State Trust & Savings Bank, 1928-32; pres. Citizens Water Co., Miss. Pearl Button Co.; v.p. Burlington Casket Co.; pres. Burlington Hotel Co. Dir. Burlington Chamber Commerce. Democrat. Episcopalian. Died Jan. 7, 1939.

PHELPS, Erskine Mason, merchant; b. Stonington, Conn., Mar. 31, 1839; s. Charles H. and Ann (Hammond) P.; ed. Williston Sem., Easthampton, Mass.; m. Anna Wilder, Oct. 26, 1865. In banking house of Allan, Copp & Nesbitt, St. Louis, 1857-61, then went to Boston, and in 1864 removed to Chicago and founded a wholesale boot and shoe house in partnership with George E. P. Dodge (Phelps, Dodge & Palmer), 1865-89; sold out to Edwards-Stanwood Shoe Co., of which was dir.; dir. Merchants Loan & Trust Co., Commonwealth Edison Co. Mem. Dem. Nat. Com., 1888; chmn. Ill. Dem. State Com., 1888. Consul for Colombia, 1884—; pres. Hahnemann Hosp.; pres. Nat. Business League. Home: Chicago, Ill. Died 1910.

PHELPS, George Turner, creative critic; b. Wyoming (Melrose), Mass., Dec. 18, 1867; s. Charles Alanson and Letitia (Frost) P.; A.B., Harvard, 1891; pvt. instrn. in music through whole period; unmarried. Pvt. teacher in music, Greek, Latin, English, logic, psychology; pvt. lab. study of teaching, and of art in architecture, sculpture, painting, language, music, the theatre. Contributor of prose and verse to various publs., gave lectures and lecture-recitals. Conglist. Author: Parsifal, an English Text for the Score, together with the German Poem [stage version], 1904 (the first published attempt to preserve in English the balance, phrase by phrase, between text, declamation, orchestra, of a Wagner drama). Field of work: Aesthetics; special research spheric vision; original contributions (theatr'-acoustic art): (a) in optics, 1. visual design (theatre and fine arts), 2. sphere-mount, 3. auto-frame; (b) in acoustics, 1. tangent bi-sphere resonance (voice), 2. sphere-segment-focus architecture. Home: Bristol, N.H. Died Feb. 26, 1920.

PHELPS, Guy Fitch, author; b. Coyville, Kan.; s. Mark Yale and Naomi (McDonald) P.; ed. pub. and pvt. schs.; course of 3 yrs. in English and composition, and 6 yrs. in metaphysical, scientific and lit. studies; m. Onneatta Ramsdell, 1897 (died 1901); m. 2d, Ethel Viola Poling, 1906. Moved with parents to Ida. early in boyhood, and grew up in mining camps, and with cowboys on cattle range; spent some yrs. trapping and hunting; engaged in publishing and newspaper work; began lecturing and traveling, 1894. Served in France, World War, stationed in Louvre Mus., Paris, as lecturer on classical exhibits. Author: Ethel Vale, 1910; Mountains of the Morning, 1916; Black Prophet, 1916; Angel o' Deadman, 1917; Moan of the Tiber, 1917; The Battle-Born (pub. in Australia); Onneatta, 1920; Red Judas, 1922; The Absurdities of Evolution, 1924; (serials) The Light of the Alleghenies; The Dreamer of Gunsight Cañon; Pals of the Death Trail; Tales of the Deadland. Home: Salem, Oregon. Died Dec. 15, 1933.

PHELPS, Harry, officer U.S.N.; b. Jersey City, N.J., Feb. 10, 1861; s. Henry E. and Julia A. (Truesdale) P.; grad. U.S. Naval Acad., 1880; m. Mary E. Thompson, Apr. 1, 1883. Served on European Sta., 1880-82; apptd. midshipman, June 22, 1882; ensign (jr.), Mar. 3, 1883; ensign, June 26, 1884; lt. (jr.), June 19, 1892; lt., May 10, 1896; lt. comdr., June 8, 1902; comdr., July 1, 1907; capt., Mar. 4, 1911; commodore, retired, June 30, 1911. Served on Coast Survey, 1882-84; on N. Pacific Survey, 1884-88; on board U.S.S. Texas, blockade and battles off Santiago, Cuba, May-July 1898; on active duty at Navy Yard, Norfolk, Va., Apr. 1918—. Author: Practical Marine Surveying, 1890. Home: Southport, N.C. Deceased.

PHELPS, Stephen, clergyman; b. Lewistown, Ill., Feb. 6, 1839; s. Myron and Adaline (Rice) P.; A.B., Jefferson (now Washington and Jefferson) Coll., Pa., 1859; grad. Western Theol. Sem., Pa., 1862; D.D., Washington and Jefferson Coll., 1881, Lenox Coll., 1881; LL.D., Coe Coll., 1915; m. Amelia McComb, June 20, 1862 (died 1881); m. 2d, Sarah Frances Miller, Dec. 25, 1882. Ordained Presbyn. ministry, 1863; pastor successively Sioux City, Ia., Waterloo, Janesville, Cedar Valley, Vinton, until 1881; 1st pres. Coe Coll., 1881-87; pastor 1st Ch., Council Bluffs, 1887-96; founder, and prof. homiletics and pastoral theology, Omaha Presbyn. Theol. Sem., 1891-1902; pastor Essex, Ia., and Bellevue, Neb., until 1916; also prof. Bible instrn., Bellevue Coll., 1904-16; hon. retired because of age. Commr. Presbyn. Gen. Assembly 6 times; moderator 5 Presbyteries and 2 Presbyn. Synods; was trustee Coe Coll., Corning Acad., Presbyn. Theol. Sem., Omaha, and Bellevue Coll. Republican. Died Mar. 4, 1930.

PHELPS, Thomas Stowell, rear admiral U.S.N., retired Nov. 2, 1884; b. Buckfield, Me., Nov. 2, 1822; apptd. to U.S. Navy Jan. 17, 1840; grad. U.S. Naval Acad.; passed midshipman, 1846; promoted through grades to rear admiral, Mar. 1, 1882. Served in Mexican war; Indian war on the Northwest coast, 1855-56; Paraguay expedition, 1858-59; also throughout Civil war. Before the war saw extensive service in U.S. Coast Survey; commander-in-chief S. Atlantic station, 1883-84. Author: Sailing Directions for the Straits of Magellan; Reminiscences of Seattle; also many historical articles. Died 1901.

PHELPS, Thomas Stowell, Jr., rear admiral U.S.N.; b. Portsmouth, Va., Nov. 7, 1848; s. Rear Admiral Thomas Stowell and Margaret Riché (Levy) P.; grad. U.S. Naval Acad., 1869; m. Elwena Dewees Martin, Oct. 18, 1877. Promoted through the various grades to rear admiral, July 24, 1909. Served at all the stations and on various vessels; on board U.S.S. Raleigh, at Manila, in Spanish-Am. War; commandant Mare Island Navy Yard and Sta., 1907-Mar. 25, 1910; retired, Nov. 7, 1910. Republican. Episcopalian. Home: Oakland, Calif. Died Nov. 3, 1915.

PHELPS, William Henry, clergyman, editor; b. Kalamazoo, Mich., Nov. 28, 1872; s. Edwin Jay and Lillie Cordelia (Perry) P.; grad. high sch., Kalamazoo, 1891; B.L., Albion (Mich.) Coll., 1894; M.L., Northwestern U., 1895; student Boston U. Sch. of Theology 2 yrs.; m. Mabel E. Smith, June 2, 1896; 1 dau., Margaret Clare Canright. Ordained M.E. Ch., 1899; pastor Martin, Mich., 1895-97, Coleman, 1898, Lansing, 1899, Grand Rapids, 1899-1902, Manistee, 1902-04, Three Rivers, 1904-07, Battle Creek, 1907-14; dist. supt., Lansing Dist., 1914-20; editor Michigan Christian Advocate, 1920—. Mem. bd. Methodist Foundation of Mich. Home: Royal Oak, Mich. Died June 23, 1939.

PHELPS, William Woodward, naval officer; b. Baltimore, Md., Nov. 26, 1869; grad. U.S. Naval Acad., 1889; married; children—Constance (dec.), Woodward (dec.), Southwick. Commissioned ensign, U.S. Navy, July 1, 1891, and promoted through grades to rear admiral, Dec. 31, 1921. Served on Bancroft, Spanish-Am. War, 1898; exec. officer Mayflower, 1905-06; navigator and exec. Kentucky, 1906-07; on Constellation, and at Naval Sta., Newport, R.I., 1907-10; exec. officer Delaware, 1910-12; comdr. Iowa, 1912, Baltimore, 1912-13, Iowa, 1913, Reina Mercedes, 1913-15; at Naval War Coll., Newport, R.I., 1915-16; comd. Louisiana, 1916-17; actg. hydrographer, 1917; comdr. transport Great Northern, Nov. 1917-Sept. 1918; comdr. Leviathan, Sept. 1918-Apr. 1919; staff Naval War Coll., Apr. 1919-May 1920; comdg. Arizona, June 1920-June 1921; chief of staff, Naval War Coll., Aug. 1921-June 1922; comdr. Yangtze Patrol, U.S. Asiatic Fleet, July 1922-Nov. 1923; mem. Gen. Bd. of the Navy, 1924-26; comdr. Fleet Base Force, U.S. Fleet, 1926-28; comdt. Navy Yard, Portsmouth, N.H., 1928-31, N.Y. Naval Dist. and Navy Yard, Brooklyn, 1931-33; retired, July 1, 1933. Awarded Navy Cross and letter of commendation from sec. of War for services in World War. Episcopalian. Died May 11, 1938.

PHENIX, George Perley; b. Portland, Me., Sept. 25, 1864; s. John Colby and Mary Jane (Elden) P.; A.B., Colby Coll., 1886, Sc.D., 1911; m. Maria Elizabeth Stevens, July 9, 1889; 1 son, Spencer. Teacher, Hebron (Me.) Acad., 1886-88, State Normal Sch., New Britain, Conn., 1888-93; prin. State Normal Sch., Willimantic, Conn., 1893-1904; dir. academic work and teacher training, Hampton (Va.) Inst., 1904-19, vice prin., 1908-30, dir. summer sch., 1906-29, pres., 1930—, also trustee; trustee Calhoun Colored Sch., Ala. Supervisor Negro training, S.A.T.C., at Washington, D.C., 1918. Conglist. Home: Hampton, Va. Died Oct. 1930.

PHIFER, Fred Wood, M.D., surgeon; b. Statesville, N.C., Dec. 28, 1876; s. William Stoughton and Mary Jane (Morrison) P.; M.D., U. of Md., 1902; m. Margaret Giffen, of Cairo, Egypt, June 24, 1903; children—Fred Wood, John Knox. Practiced at Abbeville, S.C., and Statesville, N.C.; moved to Wheatland, Wyo., 1908; founder, sr. surgeon and chief of staff Wheatland Gen. Hosp.; pres. Wheatland Hosp. Sch. for Nurses. Democrat. Presbyn. Mason, Odd Fellow. Home: Wheatland, Wyo. Died May 31, 1935.

PHILBIN, Eugene A., judge; b. New York, N.Y., July 24, 1857; s. Stephen and Eliza (McGoldrick) P.; ed. Coll. St. Francis Xavier, New York and Seton Hall Coll., S. Orange, N.J.; LL.B., Columbia, 1885; LL.D., Seton Hall Coll., 1904; m. Jessie Holladay, June 28, 1887. Admitted to bar, 1886, and practiced at New York; was sr. mem. firm Philbin, Beekman, Menken & Griscom. Commr. N.Y. State Bd. Charities, 1899-1900; dist. atty., N.Y. County, Dec. 1900-Jan. 1901. Regent of U. of State of N.Y., 1904-13; served on com. of 5 citizens apptd. by Theodore Roosevelt to investigate conditions at Ellis Island Immigrant Sta.; apptd. justice Supreme Ct. N.Y., Apr. 1913, term expiring Dec. 31, 1927. Knight Comdr. Order of St. Gregory the Great, by Pope Pius X. Trustee Catholic U. America, St. Patrick's Cathedral, New York. Pres. Parks and Playgrounds Assn. City of New York; v.p. Charity Orgn. Soc., Prison Assn.; dir. State Charities Aid Assn. Democrat. Home: New York, N.Y. Died Mar. 14, 1920.

PHILBROOK, Warren Coffin, judge; b. Sedgwick, Me., Nov. 30, 1857; s. Luther Groves and Angelia (Coffin) P.; grad. State Normal Sch., Castine, Me., 1877, Coburn Classical Inst. (then Waterville Classical Inst.), 1878; A.B., Colby Coll., 1882, LL.D., 1910; admitted to bar, 1884, to Supreme Court of U.S., 1909; m. Ada M. Foster, Aug. 1882. Practiced law at Waterville, Me., 1887-1912; twice apptd. judge of Waterville Municipal Court; mayor of Waterville, 1899-1901; mem. Me. Ho. of Rep., 1897-99; asst. atty. gen. of Me., 1905-09; atty. gen., 1909-11; asso. justice Supreme Jud. Court of Me., 1913-29; apptd. active retired justice. Republican. Unitarian. Mason (Past Master, Past High Priest, Past Commander, Past Grand Comdr. of Grand Commandery of Me.); Past Grand Chancellor K.P. of Me. Died May 31, 1933.

PHILIP, John W., commodore U.S.N.; b. New York, N.Y., Aug. 26, 1840; apptd. to Naval Acad., 1856; midshipman, Jan. 1, 1861; promoted through grades to commodore, 1898; blockading service in Civil war and while executive officer of the Pawnee was wounded in the leg in the Stone River fight; on detached service in command of Woodruff Scientific Expedition Around the World, 1877; afterward on various duties and stations; in command of battleship Texas, Oct. 18, 1897; served in Cuban waters in the Spanish war, and was in the engagement with Cervera's fleet in July 1898. Commanding North Atlantic squadron, flagship Texas. Died 1900.

PHILIPP, Emanuel Lorenz; b. Sauk County, Wis., Mar. 25, 1861; s. Luzi and Sabina (Ludwig) P.; common sch. edn.; m. Bertha Schweke, Oct. 27, 1887. Farmer, sch. teacher, telegraph operator, ry. station agt. and train dispatcher to 1893; in lumber business at Philipp, Miss., 1893-1903; elected pres. Union Refrigerator Transit Co., 1897, and its propr. and mgr., 1903—. Pres. Humane Soc., Milwaukee; regent Marquette U. Active in politics in Wis.; mem. Rep. Nat. Com., 1908; police commr. City of Milwaukee, 1909-14; governor of Wisconsin 3 terms, 1915-21. Mason. Wrote: The Truth About Wisconsin Freight Rates, 1904; Political Reform in Wisconsin, 1908. Home: Milwaukee, Wis. Died June 15, 1925.

PHILIPS, George Morris, normal sch. prin.; b. Atglen, Pa., Oct. 28, 1851; s. John Morris and Sarah (Jones) P.; A.B., Bucknell U., 1871, A.M., 1874, Ph.D., 1884; LL.D., Temple U., 1906, U. of Pa., 1913; m. Elizabeth M. Pyle, Dec. 27, 1877. Prof. mathematics, Monongahela Coll., 1871-73; prof. higher mathematics, Pa. State Normal School, 1873-78; prof. mathematics and astronomy, Bucknell U., 1878-81; prin. Pa. State Normal Sch., West Chester, 1881—. Dir. Nat. Bank of Chester County; pres. Dime Savings Bank, West Chester. Trustee Bucknell U., Chester County Hosp.; mem. Coll. and Univ. Council of Pa., 1895-1912; mem. and sec. State Commn. to codify and revise sch. laws of Pa., 1907-11; mem. State Bd. of Edn. of Pa., 1911-14. Mem. bd. Pa. Bapt. Ednl. Soc. and Am. Bapt. Publ. Soc.; trustee Crozer Sem., Am. Bapt. Hist. Soc.; pres. Chester County Hist. Soc., 1894—, Pa. State Teachers' Assn., 1891. Author: (with Isaac Sharpless) Astronomy, 1882; Natural Philosophy, 1883; Key to Philosophy (with C. C. Balderston), 1884; Civil Government of Pennsylvania, 1893; Geography of Pennsylvania, 1895; Nation and State, 1905; Pennsylvania Geography, 1907; The Silver-Burdett Arithmetics (with Dr. Robert F. Anderson), 1913. Owner large collection (about 1,700 volumes) of modern Assn. books. Died Mar. 11, 1920.

PHILIPS, John F., judge; b. Thralls Prairie, Mo., Dec. 31, 1834; s. John G. P.; student U. of Mo., 1851-53; A.B., Centre Coll., Ky., 1855; LL.D., Centre Coll., Ky., Central Coll., Mo., Univ. of Missouri, 1890, and Missouri Valley College. Admitted to bar, 1857; practiced at Georgetown, Mo.; del. Missouri Constl. Conv., 1861; col. 7th Mo. Cav. U.S.V., 1861-65; practiced law, Sedalia, Mo., 1865-82; del. Dem. Nat. Conv., 1868; elected to 44th Congress (1875-77); reëlected to 46th Congress, Jan. 10, 1880, for unexpired term (1880-81) of A. M. Lay, deceased; removed to Kansas City, 1882; Supreme Ct. commr., 1883-85; presiding judge Kansas City Court of Appeals, 1885-88; U.S. dist. judge, Western Dist. Mo., 1888-1910; retired. Del. Pan-Presbyn. Conv., Edinburgh, 1877. Home: Kansas City, Mo. Died Mar. 13, 1919.

PHILLER, George, retired banker; b. Phila., Pa.; s. George and Esther (Gaw) P.; ed. pvt. schs. Pres. First Nat. Bank, 1873-1904; dir. Fidelity Trust Co., The United Gas Improvement Co., The United Lighting & Heating Co. Home: Philadelphia, Pa. Died 1916.

PHILLIPPI, Joseph Martin, clergyman, editor; b. London Mills, Ill., Mar. 2, 1869; s. Martin and Caroline (Swartz) P.; A.B., Westfield (Ill.) Coll., 1893, A.M., 1896, D.D., 1906; B.D., Bonebrake Theol. Sem., 1896; Ph.D., Ill. Wesleyan U., 1904; m. Marie Edna DeWitte, Sept. 22, 1899; 1 son, Dale Martin. Ordained ministry U.B. Ch., 1896; prof. Latin and Greek, Westfield College, 1897-1902; editorial staff Religious Telescope, 1902—, chief editor, 1909—. Trustee and sec. bd. Otterbein Home, of Lebanon, O. (successor to Shakers). Republican. Author: (thesis) Helenic Preparation for Christ, 1904; The Sword Unsheathed, or The Bible for the Masses, 1911; Shakerism, or The Romance of a Religion, 1912. Home: Dayton, O. Died Sept. 27, 1926.

PHILLIPS, Alexander Hamilton, univ. prof.; b. Lawrenceville, N.J., May 15, 1866; s. John Feaster and Hannah (Warne) P.; B.S., Princeton, 1887, Sc.D., 1899; m. Mabel Harriett Knight, Dec. 2, 1896 (died 1934). Asst. in biology, 1888-89, demonstrator, 1889-92, instr. mineralogy, and biology, 1892-93, mineralogy, 1893-98, asst. prof., 1898-1903, prof. 1903—, Princeton U., also head dept. of geology. Discovered radium in Am. ore. Mem. City Council, Princeton, N.J., 1906-11, mayor, 1911-16; v.p. Bd. of Fish and Game Commrs., N.J., 1919—. Republican. Episcopalian. Fellow A.A.A.S., Geol. Soc. America, Mineral. Soc. America (pres.). Sr. warden Trinity Ch., Princeton. Author of a text-book and papers on mineralogy. Died Jan. 20, 1937.

PHILLIPS, Alexander Lacy, clergyman; b. Chapel Hill, N.C., Sept. 20, 1859; s. Charles and Laura Caroline (Battle) P.; A.B., U. of N.C., 1880, D.D., 1896; m. Susan Ida Moseley, Jan. 4, 1883. Ordained Presbyterian ministry, 1883; pastor in N.C. and Ala.; sec. Bd. Colored Evangelization of the South, 1889-98; pastor Nashville, Tenn., 1898-1901; supt., 1901-02, sec. of publn., 1902-03, gen. supt., 1903—, Sabbath schs. and young people's socs. of Southern Presbyn. Ch.; mem. Bd. Fgn. Missions, 1897; mem. bd. managers Missionary Education Movement. Author: Manual of Graded Instruction, 1902; Geography of Palestine, 1904; Call of the Home Land, 1906; Teacher Training Course (Vol. 1), 1909. Home: Richmond, Va. Deceased.

PHILLIPS, Alfred Edward, civil engr.; b. Rouses Point, N.Y., June 18, 1863; s. John and Jane Annie (Irwin) P.; A.B. and C.E., Union U., Schenectady, N.Y., 1887, A.M., 1890, Ph.D., 1894; m. Lizzie Langdon, June 19, 1895; children—Jane Ann Langdon, Laura Langdon. Prof. civil engring., Purdue U., Lafayette, 1887-94; pvt. practice, Indianapolis, 1894-99; also acting prof. bridge and hydraulic engring., U. of Wis., 1895-96; prof. civil engring., Armour Inst. Tech., 1899—. Republican. Episcopalian. Author: Stresses in Bridges and Roof Trusses, 1901; Plane Surveying, 1904; Highway Construction (with A. H. Byrne), 1904; Masonry Construction (with same), 1904; Irrigation, 1907. Home: Evanston, Ill. Died Apr. 19, 1931.

PHILLIPS, Andrew Wheeler, univ. dean; b. Griswold, Conn., Mar. 14, 1844; s. Denison and Wealthy (Wheeler) P.; Ph.B., Yale, 1873, Ph.D., 1877; A.M., Trinity Coll., Hartford, 1875; m. Maria S. Clarke, Apr. 23, 1867 (died 1895); m. 2d, Agnes DuBois Northrop, d. Rufus E. Hitchcock, of Waterbury, Conn., June 27, 1912. Tutor, 1877-81, asst. prof. mathematics, 1881-91, prof., 1891-1911, dean Grad. Sch., 1895-1911, emeritus, 1911, Yale U. Pres. trustees Hotchkiss Sch., Lakeville, Conn.; trustee Hopkins Grammar Sch., New Haven, Conn. Joint-author: Transcendental Curves (Newton and Phillips), 1875; Graphic Algebra (Phillips & Beebe), 1882; The Elements of Geometry (Phillips and Fisher), 1896 (transl. into Japanese); Trigonometry and Tables (Phillips and Strong), 1898; The Orbit of Swift's Comet, 1880V (Beebe and Phillips), 1891. Editor: The Connecticut Almanac, 12 numbers, 1882-93. Home: New Haven, Conn. Died Jan. 20, 1915.

PHILLIPS, Arthur L., banker; b. Boonton, N.J., June 18, 1872; s. Thomas and Martha (Lewis) P.; ed. pub. schs.; m. Harriet Otto, 1893; 1 dau., Mrs. Hazel P. Balch. Began as messenger Merchants and Mfg. Nat. Bank, Newark, N.J., Nov. 1899, and promoted through various offices to pres., May 1, 1921, later title Merchants & Newark Trust Co. School commr. Twp. of South Orange 4 yrs. Mem. Liberty Loan Com., World War. Republican. Presbyn. Mason. Home: Maplewood, N.J. Died Mar. 22, 1937.

PHILLIPS, Asa Emory, consulting engr.; b. Sept. 8, 1869; s. Robert A. and Anne (d'Boyer) P.; C.E., Lehigh U., 1890; m. Myra Estelle Randall, Mar. 7, 1891; children—Donald Boyer, Mrs. Dorothy Randall Moyer, Mrs. Ruth Sutherland Martinez, Charles Emory; m. 2d, Virginia Nalle Boyd, Nov. 6, 1909; children—Asa Emory, James Boyd. Began practice at New York, 1890; engr. on flood prevention and sewer disposal, Dist. of Columbia, 1899—; designed and built largest pump station (at that time) in the world, 1907. Episcopalian. Home: Washington, D.C. Died Jan. 1, 1936.

PHILLIPS, Barnet, journalist; b. Phila., Pa., Nov. 9, 1828; grad. Univ. of Pa., 1847; studied in Europe and engaged in journalism; on staff of New York Times, 1872—. Author: The Struggle; Burning Their Ships. Died 1905.

PHILLIPS, Charles, poet, educator; b. New Richmond, Wis., Nov. 20, 1880; s. Patrick and Martha (MacConaghy) P.; De La Salle Coll., Toronto, Can.; M.A., St. Mary's Coll., Oakland, Calif., 1914. Mng. editor Northwestern Chronicle, St. Paul, 1901-03, The New Century, Washington, 1903-06; editor Republican Voice, New Richmond, 1906-07; editor, mgr. The Monitor, San Francisco, 1907-15; prof. English lit., U. of Notre Dame, 1924—. Co-founder and co-editor Pan, Poetry and Youth, 1925; asso. lit. editor Catholic World Mag. Overseas war work, with K.C., France, Germany, Oct. 1918-July 1919; with Am. Red Cross, Poland, 1919-22, rank of capt. Am. del. Internat. Congress Young Men's Soc., Rome, 1921; spl. commr. Nat. Catholic Welfare Conf. to Mexico, 1925. Mem. nat. council Polish Am. Scholarship (Kosciuszko Foundation). Author: Back Home—An Old-fashioned Poem, 1913; The Divine Friend (poetic drama prod. Oct. 1915, by Margaret Anglin); Tarcisius (drama), 1917; The Shepherd of the Valley (drama, prod. 1918); A Buccaneer of Christ, 1918; A Saint for Soldiers, 1918; The New Poland, 1923 (London), 1923 (New York); The Teacher's Year, 1924; The Doctor's Wooing (novel), 1926; High in Her Tower (verse), 1927; also several plays. Died Dec. 29, 1933.

PHILLIPS, David Graham, author; b. Madison, Ind., Oct. 31, 1867; s. David G. and Margaret (Lee) P.; A.B., Princeton, 1887. Author: The Great God Success, 1901; Her Serene Highness, 1902; A Woman Ventures, 1902; Golden Fleece, 1903; The Master Rogue, 1903; The Cost, 1904; The Plum Tree, 1905; The Social Secretary, 1905. The Deluge, 1905; The Reign of Gilt, 1905; The Fortune Hunter, 1906; The Second Generation, 1907; Light-Fingered Gentry, 1907; Old Wives for New, 1908; The Worth of a Woman, 1908; The Fashionable Adventures of Joshua Craig, 1909; The Hungry Heart, 1909. Unmarried. Home: New York, N.Y. Died 1911.

PHILLIPS, Duane Seneca, clergyman; b. Stamford, Vt., Sept. 8, 1834; s. Seneca and Lydia D. (Millard) P.; B.A., Williams, 1860; D.D., Racine Coll., Wis., 1892; m. Sophia C. Manser, Dec. 27, 1860. Deacon, 1862, priest, 1863, P.E. Ch.; rector St. Peter's Ch., Bennington, Vt., 1862-67, St. Paul's Ch., Kankakee, Ill., 1867-1904, emeritus. Dean Diocese of Chicago, 1879—; mem. Standing Com. same, and pres., 1889—. Republican. Author: Word and Works, 1875; Talks for the Times, 1877; Reminiscenes of a Long Pastorate, 1910. Home: Kankakee, Ill. Died May 23, 1917.

PHILLIPS, Francis Clifford, chemist; b. Phila., Apr. 2, 1850; s. William Smith and Frederica (Ingersoll) P.; student, U. of Pa., M.A., 1878, Ph.D., 1894; D.Sc., U. of Pittsburgh, 1919; m. Sarah O. Phillips, 1881. Prof. chemistry, Western U. of Pa. (now U. of Pittsburgh) 1875—. Home: Ben Avon, Pa. Died Feb. 16, 1920.

PHILLIPS, Henry Wallace, author; b. New York, Jan. 11, 1869; s. Charles Jeter and Adelaide Augusta (Smith) P.; ed. pub. schs. and Drisler Sch.; m. Louise Moore Millspaugh, Aug. 17, 1898. Author: Red Saunders, 1902; Plain Mary Smith, 1905; Mr. Scraggs, 1906; Red Saunders' Pets, and Other Critters, 1906; The Mascot of Sweetbriar Gulch, 1908; Trolley Folly, 1909. Home: New York, N.Y. Died May 24, 1930.

PHILLIPS, Jesse J., justice supreme court of Ill., 1893—; b. Montgomery County, Ill., 1837; grad. Hillsboro (Ill.) Acad., 1857; admitted to bar, 1861; served, capt., maj. and lt. col. 9th Ill. regt.; bvt. col. and brig. gen.; twice nominated for State treasurer, but defeated; practiced law at Hillsboro until elected judge 5th circuit, Ill., 1879-93. Democrat. Died 1901.

PHILLIPS, John, physician; b. Welland, Ont., Can., Feb. 19, 1879; s. Robert and Ann Jane (McCullough) P.; grad. high sch., Welland; M.B., U. of Toronto, 1903, honor grad., silver medallist; m. Cordelia Sudderth, Sept. 18, 1907; 1 son, John Edward. Came to U.S., 1903, naturalized citizen, 1918. Instr. in medicine, Western Reserve U., Cleveland, O., 1906-10, demonstrator of anatomy, 1906-07, asst. prof. medicine, 1910-19, asst. prof. therapeutics, 1919—; asst. visiting physician, Lakeside Hosp., 1910-19; cons. phys. St. Johns Hosp., 1919—; Capt. Med. Corps, U.S.A., 1918. A founder and trustee Cleveland Clinic Foundation, dir. of medicine, 1921—; trustee Cleveland Med. Library Assn. Fellow A.M.A., Am. Coll. Physicians (mem. bd. regents). Republican. Presbyn. Contbr. abt. 60 articles to Jour. Am. Med. Assn., Am. Jour. Med. Sciences, etc.; wrote sect. on Diseases of Pleura, Mediastinum and Diaphragm, in Cecil's Textbook on Internal Medicine, 1927. Home: Cleveland, O. Died May 15, 1929.

PHILLIPS, John Bakewell, orange grower; b. Pittsburgh, 1854; s. Ormsby and Anne (Bakewell) P.; ed. pvt. sch., Pittsburgh, langs. in Germany, France, and Italy; m. Eliza Shallcross, Nov. 5, 1883. For some yrs. from 1880, treas. and mgr. Pittsburgh Dispatch, until poor health made resignation necessary; dir. Dispatch Pub. Co.; an orange grower in Riverside, Calif., 1890—. Was active in affairs of Diocese of Los Angeles; deputy to 6 triennial Gen. Convs. of P.E. Ch. Independent Republican. Died Dec. 23, 1911.

PHILLIPS, John Burton, educator; b. Holt, Mich., Oct. 8, 1866; s. Silas H. and Adelphia Caroline (Ferguson) P.; A.B., Ind. U., 1889, A.M., 1891; Ph.D., Cornell, 1897; studied U. of Göttingen, 1908, The Sorbonne, and College de France, Paris, 1909; m. Mrs. Honora Elder Sherman, July 2, 1903. Asst. sociology librarian, N.Y. State Library, 1900-02; prof. economics and sociology, U. of Colo., 1902-12;

acting prof. administrative law, U. of Mich., 1908; mem. Colo. Tax Commn., 1912-17 (chmn. 1915-17); prof. economics and sociology, Ind. U., 1917—. Author: Methods of Keeping the Public Money of the United States, 1900; Comparative Summary and Index of State Legislation in 1901 (with Robert H. Whitten), 1902; Freight Rates and Manufactures in Colorado, 1909. Died Oct. 9, 1923.

PHILLIPS, John Charles, naturalist; b. Boston, Mass., Nov. 5, 1876; s. John Charles and Anna (Tucker) P.; S.B., Lawrence Scientific Sch. (Harvard), 1899; M.D., Harvard, 1904; grad. Boston City Hosp., 1906; m. Eleanor Hyde, Jan. 11, 1908; children—John C., Jr., Madelyn, Eleanor, Arthur. Not in practice. Trustee Peabody Mus., Cambridge; pres. bd. trustees Peabody Mus., Salem. Joined second Harvard Surgical Unit, November 1915, and assigned to British Gen. Hosp. No. 22, in France; served with Med. Corps, Sept. 20, 1917-July 22, 1919; maj. in comd. Field Hosp. No. 33, 4th Div. regular army. Asso. curator of birds, Mus. Comparative Zoölogy, Harvard. Trustee Boston Soc. Natural History; chmn. Mass. Conservation Council. Author of papers on birds, genetics, experimental animal breeding, sport, travel and conservation. Home: Wenham, Mass. Died Nov. 14, 1938.

PHILLIPS, John Herbert, superintendent pub. schs.; b. Covington, Ky., Dec. 12, 1853; s. Evan and Elizabeth (Herbert) P.; A.B., Marietta Coll., 1880; post-grad. course, U. of Edinburgh and U. of Chicago; LL.D., Marietta, 1905; U. of Ala., 1906; m. Nellie T. Cobbs, Dec. 27, 1886; m. 2d, Minnie Holman, Aug. 17, 1898. Supt. pub. schs., Birmingham, Ala., 1883—. Pres. Southern Ednl. Assn., 1895; pres. council education N.E.A., 1902. Author: History and Literature in Grammar Schools, 1892; The Negro and Education, 1894; Old Tales and Modern Ideals, 1905. Home: Birmingham, Ala. Died July 21, 1921.

PHILLIPS, Lee Allen, corp. official; b. Ashton, Ill., Aug. 24, 1871; s. Milton Eaves and Magdalena (Wetzel) P.; A.B., Southwestern Coll., 1892; A.M., 1894; grad. work U. of Kan., 1894; LL.B., De Pauw U., 1895; m. Catherine Coffin, Dec. 19, 1895; children—Lucile Gertrude (wife of Dr. Wayland A. Morrison), Katharine Louise (Mrs. Herbert Godfrey Day). Admitted to Calif. bar, 1895, and became mem. firm Cochran, Williams & Phillips; asso. counsel Pacific Mut. Life Ins. Co., 1907-14, exec. v.p., 1914-33; organizer and pres. Pacific Finance Co., 1920-33 and Pacific Indemnity Co., 1926-33, chmn. bd., 1933—; also chmn. bd. Consol. Steel Corp. Republican. Conglist. Home: Los Angeles, Calif. Died Jan. 7, 1938.

PHILLIPS, Llewellyn, college prof.; b. in Wales, Apr. 15, 1869; s. Lemuel and Margaret (Davis) P.; B.A., Bucknell U., 1892; student Rochester Theol. Sem., 1899; studied univs. of Chicago and Berlin; D.D., John B. Stetson U., 1909; m. Jennie Davis, July 29, 1902. Instr. Bucknell Acad., 1892-99; fellow in N.T., U. of Chicago, 1901; prof. education and Bibl. lit., 1902—, dean of the coll., 1918—, Bucknell U. Baptist. Mem. Soc. Bibl. Lit. and Exegesis. Home: Lewisburg, Pa. Died Jan. 9, 1923.

PHILLIPS, Milton Eves, educational dir.; b. Millville, Pa., Aug. 17, 1844; s. Allen H. and Sarah E. P.; ed. Greenwood Sem., Pa.; Ph.M., Simpson Coll., Ia.; D.D., Baker U., Kan.; m. Magdalena E. Wetzel, Jan. 27, 1867. Teacher in pub. schs., as prin. high schs., city supt., etc., 1860-85; prof. mathematics, Simpson Coll., 1885-91; pres. Southwest Kan. Coll., Winfield, 1891-95; dean U. of Southern Calif., Los Angeles, 1895-1900; chancellor Kan. Wesleyan U., Salina, 1900-02; ednl. dir. Rutherford Inst., New Haven, Conn., 1902—. Mem. Kan. State Bd. Edn., 1892-95; pastor Whitneyville (Conn.) Congl. Ch., 1902—. Died 1909.

PHILLIPS, Morris, journalist, mag. writer; b. London, England, May 9, 1834; s. Philip Phillips; elementary edn. in Cleveland, O., finished under pvt. tutors, New York, studied law Buffalo and New York; m. Elizabeth Rode, July 5, 1865 (died 1877). Was associated with the poet, N. P. Willis, as asso. editor New York Home Journal from Sept. 1854, until his death, Jan. 1867, then became chief editor and sole proprietor. Wrote for many publications; traveled widely in this hemisphere and visited Europe many times; spl. corr. daily newspapers, and writer of travel sketches for leading mags. Author: Abroad and at Home, 1893. Home: New York, N.Y. Died 1904.

PHILLIPS, Nelson, judge; b. Jefferson, Tex., May 3, 1873; s. C. E. and Jennie L. (Arrington) P.; ed. pub. schs. and 2 yrs. at Bingham Sch., Mebane, N.C. Admitted to Tex. bar, 1895; practiced at Hillsboro, Tex.; apptd. by gov. judge 18th Jud. Dist. of Tex., Jan. 1904; practiced at Dallas, 1905-12; apptd. asso. justice Supreme Court of Tex., Mar. 1912, elected same, Nov. 1912; apptd. chief justice, May 27, 1915, elected chief justice, Nov. 1916; reëlected, Nov. 1918; resigned to resume practice of law at Dallas, 1921; sr. mem. Phillips & Phillips. Home: Dallas, Tex. Died Mar. 31, 1939.

PHILLIPS, Percival, newspaper corr.; b. Brownsville, Pa., July 2, 1877; s. Hibbard S. Phillips (M.D.); ed. pub. schs. and pvtly.; unmarried. On staff Pittsburgh morning newspapers, 1895-1901; in Græco-Turkish campaign for syndicate Am. newspapers, 1897; special and war corr. on staff London Daily Express, 1901—. In charge war news service during Russo-Japanese War, first from Tokio, afterwards with 1st Siberian Army corps, Imperial Russian army, in Manchuria; traveled extensively Japan and China, etc.; with Sir Alfred Jones' party in Kingston, Jamaica, earthquake, 1907; in Balkans during Near Eastern crisis, 1909; Barcelona riots and other missions in Spain, 1909; with President Roosevelt during European tour, 1910; in Portugal during revolution, 1910; represented Daily Express during earlier part of Turco-Italian war in Tripoli, 1911, and subsequently was special corr. for same newspaper at the Coronation Durbar and Indian tour of King George V, 1911; with Bulgarian Army during first Balkan war, 1912-13; present at the siege of Adrianople; with Belgian army from outbreak of European war until fall of Antwerp; afterwards with British army in the field, one of first 5 war correspondents accredited with British armies in France, 1915, for London Daily Express, Morning Post, Daily Graphic; served throughout war and until signing of peace treaty with the British forces (detached in Easter week, 1916, for rising in Dublin). Accompanied Prince of Wales throughout Canadian tour, 1919, in Italy for socialist riots, and afterwards in Egypt, 1919-20, during native crisis. Chevalier Legion of Honor, 1919. Fellow British Inst. Journalists. Died Jan. 29, 1937.

PHILLIPS, Philip Lee, librarian, cartographer; b. Washington, D.C.; s. Philip and Eugenia (Levy) P.; ed. pub. schs.; m. Imogen D. Hutchins, 1899. With Library of Congress, 1876—, chief dir. of maps, 1897—. Did important work in solving boundary questions, such as Alaska, and Venezuela. Fellow Royal Geog. Soc. London. Decorated Order of Bolivar (Venezuela). Author or Editor: Virginia Cartography, 1896; Alaska and the Northwestern Part of North America (1588-1898), 1898; List of Maps and Views of Washington and District of Columbia, 1900; List of Books, Magazine Articles and Maps Relating to Brazil (1800-1900), 1901, to Central America (1800-1900), 1902, to Chile, 1903; List of Maps of America in Library of Congress, 1901; Check List of Large Scale Maps Published by Foreign Governments (Great Britain excepted) in Library of Congress, 1904; The Kohl Collection of Maps Relating to America (now in Library of Congress), 1904; First Map of Kentucky, 1908; List of Geographical Atlases in Library of Congress, 4 vols., 1909-20; Rare Map of Virginia and Maryland, 1911; The Lowery Collection, 1912; Notes on Cataloging, Care and Classification of Maps and Atlases, 1915; Rare Map of the Northwest, 1916; The Beginnings of Washington, 1917; First Map and Description of Ohio, 1918; List of Atlases and Maps Applicable to the World War, 1918. Home: Washington, D.C. Deceased.

PHILLIPS, Richard Jones, M.D.; b. Chester County, Pa., May 30, 1861; s. Harvey and Ann (Baily) P.; ed. Kennett Square, Pa., and acad. at West Chester, Pa., to 1880; M.D., Jefferson Med. Coll., Phila., 1883; m. Lydia Meredith, 1888; 1 dau., Mrs. Helen P. Scott. Late adj. prof. diseases of eye, Phila. Polyclinic and Coll. for Graduates in Medicine; retired from practice, 1925. Author: Spectacles and Eyeglasses, 1892. Wrote chapter on Spectacles and Their Adjustment in American Text-Book on Diseases of the Eye, Ear, Nose and Throat, 1899. Home: Upper Darby, Pa. Deceased.

PHILLIPS, Thomas W., producer of petroleum and natural gas, banker; b. Mt. Jackson, Pa., Feb. 23, 1835; s. Ephraim and Ann P.; married. Engaged in petroleum industry, 1861—; one of the largest individual producers in U.S.; pres. Citizens' Nat. Bank, New Castle, Pa.; interested in philanthropic work; mem. of various coll., benevolent and religious bds.; interest in both state and nat. politics; originator of Campaign Text-Book, first used during the Garfield campaign of 1880 (since then textbooks have been prominent features of nat. campaigns). Mem. 53d and 54th Congresses (1893-97); introduced bill creating Industrial Commn., which afterwards became a law; apptd. mem. commn., elected its v.p.; at conclusion of its work, Feb. 1902, made supplementary report which attracted wide attention and from which was evolved the law creating the Bur. of Corps. Republican. Died July 21, 1912.

PHILLIPS, Ulrich Bonnell, univ. prof.; b. LaGrange, Ga., Nov. 4, 1877; s. Alonzo Rabun and Jessie Elizabeth (Young) P.; A.B., U. of Georgia, 1897, A.M., 1899; Ph.D., Columbia U., 1902, hon. Litt.D., 1929; hon. A.M., Yale, 1929; m. Lucie Mayo-Smith, Feb. 22, 1911; children—Ulric Bonnell, Richmond Mayo (dec.), Mabel Elizabeth, Worthington Webster. Fellow and tutor in history, U. of Georgia, 1897-1900; fellow Columbia, 1900-02; instr. history, 1902-07, asst. prof., 1907-08, U. of Wis.; prof. history and polit. science, Tulane U., 1908-11; prof. Am. history, U. of Mich., 1911-29; same, Yale, 1929—. Albert Kahn fellow, tour around world and to central Africa, 1929-30. Lecturer in Am. history, U. of Calif., 1924. Ednl. dir. Y.M.C.A., Camp Gordon, Ga., 1917-18; capt. U.S.A., Mil. Intelligence, 1918-19. Author: Georgia and State Rights (awarded Justin Winsor prize, Am. Hist. Assn. 1901), 1902; History of Transportation in the Eastern Cotton Belt, 1908; Life of Robert Toombs, 1913; American Negro Slavery, 1918; Life and Labor in the Old South (awarded Little, Brown & Co. prize for best unpublished work on Am. history), 1929. Editor: Plantation and Frontier Documents, 1909; The Correspondence of Robert Toombs, Alexander H. Stephens and Howell Cobb, 1913; Florida Plantation Records (with James David Glunt), 1927. Home: New Haven, Conn. Died Jan. 21, 1934.

PHILLIPS, Wendell Christopher, surgeon; b. Hammond, N.Y., June 9, 1857; s. Samuel and Mary (Merrill) P.; ed. Potsdam (N.Y.) Normal Sch., 1876-79; M.D., Univ. Med. Coll. (New York U.), 1882; m. Lucia M. Taggart, of New York and Newport, R.I. Consulting aural surgeon to New York Post-Grad. and Flushing hosps., aural surgeon, Manhattan Eye and Ear Hosp. Fellow Am. Coll. Surgeons and mem. or officer many other assns. Founder of Am. Federation of Organizations for the Hard of Hearing, 1919 (1st pres. 1920). Home: New York, N.Y. Died Nov. 16, 1934.

PHILLIPS, William Battle, mining engr.; b. Chapel Hill, N.C., July 4, 1857; s. Charles and Laura Caroline (Battle) P.; A.B., U. of N.C., 1877, Ph.D., 1883; studied Sch. of Mines, Freiberg, Germany; m. Minerva Ruffin McNeil, Oct. 8, 1879; m. 2d, Angie Isabel Miller, Jan. 21, 1908. Chemist, N.C. Expt. Sta., 1877-82, Navassa Guano Co., 1882-85; prof. agrl. chemistry and mineralogy, U. of N.C., 1886-88; mining engr., Birmingham, Ala., 1888-92; prof. chemistry and metallurgy, U. of Ala., 1891-93; chemist, Tenn. Coal, Iron & Ry. Co., Birmingham, 1894-98; with Engineering and Mining Journal, and American Manufacturer, and Iron World, 1893 and 1897-98; dir. U. of Tex. Mining Survey, 1901-05, Bur. Economic Geology and Technology, U. of Tex., 1909-14; pres. Colo. Sch. of Mines, 1914-16; removed to Houston, Tex. Democrat. Presbyn. Mason. Contbr. nearly 300 articles to scientific and tech. publs. Died June 8, 1918.

PHILLIPS, William Fowke Ravenel, M.D.; b. Bedford County, Va., July 13, 1863; s. Dinwiddie B. and Nannie F. (Walden) P.; ed. Chatham, Va., 1875-78; M.D., Columbian (now George Washington) U., 1890; unmarried. Med. climatologist, U.S. Weather Bur., 1895-1904, also in charge library same, 1898-1904; prof. hygiene, 1891-92 and 1895-1909, dean, Dept. of Medicine, 1904-09, prof. practical anatomy, 1905-09, George Washington U.; sec. Anatom. Bd. of D.C., 1902-11; prof. anatomy, U. of Ala., Sch. of Medicine, Mobile, 1911-15, Med. Coll. of S.C., Charleston, 1915-33; visiting prof. anatomy, Georgetown U. Sch. of Medicine, Washington, D.C., 1934—. Fellow Fedn. of State Medical Bds. of U.S., S.C. Academy of Science, A.A.A.S. Editor: Climate and Health, 1896-97, and author of numerous articles on med. climatology. Died 1935.

PHILPUTT, Allan Bearden, clergyman; b. Bedford County, Tenn., May 6, 1856; s. Barton and Elizabeth (Bearden) P.; removed to Ind. with parents, 1867; A.B., Ind. U., 1880, A.M., 1886; grad. student classical philology, Harvard, 1888; spl. student in Hebrew, N.T. and liturgics, Episcopal Sem., Phila., 1895-96; D.D., Temple U., Phila., 1896; LL.D., Drake U., Ia., 1900; m. Anna Maxwell, Sept. 23, 1880. Ordained ministry Disciples of Christ, 1879; pastor, Bloomington, Ind., 1879-86; asst. prof. Latin and Greek, Ind. U., 1887-88; pastor First Ch., Phila., 1890-98, Central Christian Ch., Indianapolis, 1898—. Dir. Butler Coll., Indianapolis; trustee United Soc. Christian Endeavor; mem. exec. com. United Christian Missionary Soc. Republican. Died Apr. 19, 1925.

PHILPUTT, James M(cBride), clergyman; b. Bedford County, Tenn., Sept. 17, 1860; s. Barton and Elizabeth (Bearden) P.; removed with parents to Ind., 1868; A.B., Ind. U., 1885, A.M., 1887; grad. Union Theol. Sem., 1888; post-grad. work same seminary, 1890; D.D., New York U., 1896; spl. studies, Berlin, 1910-11; m. Nellie Pettit, Oct. 18, 1888 (died 1897); m. 2d, Lillian Reynolds, Mich., Apr. 2, 1902. Ordained ministry Disciples of Christ, 1888; pastor 2d Ch., N.Y. City, 1885-89; organizer, and pastor Lenox Av. Union Ch., N.Y. City, 1889-1902; pastor Richmond Av. Ch., Buffalo, 1902-03; 1st pastor Union Av. Ch., St. Louis, 1904-10; pastor Central Ch., N.Y. City, 1912-16, Charlesville, Va., 1917-18, Eureka, Ill., 1919-22. With Am. Red Cross, 1918-19. Del. Ecumenical Missionary Conf., Edinburgh, Scotland, 1910. Traveled in interest of missions, 1910-11, 1922-24. Home: Riverside, Calif. Deceased.

PHIN, John, publisher; b. nr. Melrose, Scotland, Sept. 9, 1830; s. Philip and Mary (Haig) P.; ed. Melrose Parish Sch., Musselburgh Acad., and spl. classes in Edinburgh in studies for civ. engring.; came to U.S., 1851; m. Martha Jane Burnet, Sept. 12, 1855. Prof. chemistry and technology, People's Coll., Havana, N.Y., 1864-66; prof. agr., Pa. Agrl. Coll. (now State Coll.), 1866-67; went to New York, 1869, as editor of Manufacturer and Builder; later editor of The Technologist, American Journal of

Microscopy, and The Young Scientist. Life mem. Am. Inst., New York; charter mem. New York Micros. Soc. Presbyn. Author: Open Air Grape Culture, 1862; Chemical History of the Creation, 1872; Practical Treatise on Lightning Rods, 1872; Workshop Companion, 1879; How to Use the Microscope (6 edits.), 1876-90; Cements and Glue, 1881; Trichina Spirals, How to Detect and How to Prevent, 1881; How to Become a Good Mechanic, 1883; Practical Dictionary of Apiculture, 1884; Trade Secrets and Private Receipts, 1887; Common Sense Currency (Gold Standard), 1894; Useful and Precious Minerals, 1898; Shakespearean Notes and New Readings, 1901; The Shakespeare Cyclopædia and New Glossary, 1902; Seven Follies of Science, 1906; The Atmosphere as Evidence of Creative Design, 1907; Nature Study Under the Microscope, 1909. Home: Paterson, N.J. Died Dec. 29, 1913.

PHINIZY, Bowdre, newspaper pub.; b. Augusta, Ga., Dec. 27, 1871; s. Bowdre and Mary Lou (Yancey) P.; A.B., Princeton, 1892, A.M., 1894; Johns Hopkins, 1893-94; U. of Va., summer, law, 1894; Harvard Law School, 1895; married. Admitted to Ga. bar, and practiced, Augusta, 1894-96; owner and pub. Augusta Herald, 1894—, Banner-Herald, Athens, Ga., 1921; v.p. Union Savings Bank. Mem. Ga. Ho. of Rep., 1894-96; mem. Dem. State Com., 1906-07, 1910-12. Trustee U. of Ga., 1907-23, Med. Coll. of Ga. Home: Augusta, Ga. Died Feb. 8, 1931.

PHINIZY, Hamilton, lawyer; b. Augusta, Ga., June 27, 1864; s. Thomas Burdell and Frances Emily (Hamilton) P.; grad. Acad. of Richmond County, Ga., 1880; A.B., U. of Ga., 1883 (1st honors); studied law, U. of Va., 1885-86; unmarried. Admitted to Ga. bar, 1886 and practiced at Augusta; owner and operator of large plantations; pres. Herald Publishing Co.; v.p. Ga.-Carolina Warehouse & Compress Co.; dir. Ga. R.R. & Banking Co. Democrat. Unitarian. Home: Augusta, Ga. Died Apr. 16, 1938.

PHIPPS, Frank Huntington, brigadier gen. U.S.A.; b. Northampton, Mass., Aug. 9, 1843; s. George W. and Sophia Ann (Lyman) P.; ed. in various pub. and pvt. schs.; entered U.S. Mil. Acad., 1859, grad., 1863; m. Louisa De Hart Patterson, June 11, 1867 (died 1881); m. 2d, Anna Lally, Nov. 13, 1894. Commd. 1st lt. ordnance, June 11, 1863; capt., June 23, 1874; maj., Dec. 4, 1882; lt. col., July 7, 1898; col., Feb. 17, 1903; retired by operation of law, Aug. 9, 1907; advanced to rank of brig. gen. retired, Aug. 9, 1907. Bvtd. capt., Mar. 13, 1865, "for faithful and meritorious services in ordnance dept." In ordnance dept., served at various arsenals and dept. headqrs.; mem. Bd. Ordnance and Fortification, 1894-99; comd. Springfield Armory, Mass., until 1907. Home: Washington, D.C. Died Mar. 28, 1925.

PHIPPS, Henry, mfr., capitalist; b. Phila., Pa., Sept. 27, 1839; s. Henry and Hannah P.; ed. pub. sch., Allegheny City, Pa.; LL.D., U. of Pa., 1913; m. Anne C. Shaffer, Feb. 6, 1872; children—John S., Henry C., Howard, Amy, Helen. Office boy, bookkeeper for Dillworth & Bidwell, spike mfrs., 1856-61; partner in Bidwell & Phipps, agts. DuPont Powder Company, 1861; also partner in small iron mill, Kloman & Phipps; later associated with Thomas M. and Andrew Carnegie in iron and steel manufacture, building up fortune. Presented large conservatories, and was interested in the tuberculosis movement in Phila., and other cities; gave Phipps Inst. to U. of Pa.; built a psychiatric clinic in connection with Johns Hopkins Hosp., Baltimore; gave $1,000,000 to New York for sanitary tenement houses, etc. Home: Great Neck, L.I., N.Y. Died Sept. 22, 1930.

PHLEGAR, Archer A., lawyer; b. Christiansburg, Va., Feb. 22, 1846; s. Eli and Ann C. (Trigg) P.; ed. Montgomery Male Acad., Christiansburg, Va.; m. Sue S. Shanks, June 5, 1872. Began practicing law, 1867; commonwealth's atty., Montgomery County, Va., 1870-77; mem. Va. Senate, 1877-79, 1904-08. Judge Supreme Ct. of Appeals of Va., Oct. 8, 1900-Feb. 22, 1901, to fill a vacancy. Democrat. One of receivers Va. Iron, Coal and Coke Co., 1901-03; was v.p. Va. & Southwestern Ry.; gen. counsel, V.&S.W. Ry. Co. Home: Bristol, Va. Died Dec. 1912.

PHOENIX, Lloyd, yachtsman; b. N.Y. City, Oct. 7, 1841; s. J. Phillips and Mary (Whitney) P.; grad. U.S. Naval Acad., 1861; unmarried. Served as midshipman, master and lt. through the Civil War; resigned commn., 1865; prominent as yachtsman after leaving the navy. Episcopalian. Mem. Loyal Legion. Home: New York, N.Y. Died Mar. 31, 1926.

PHYFE, William Henry Pinkney, author; b. New York, N.Y., June 13, 1855; s. James Duncan and Julia Matilda P.; ed. by pvt. tutors, and Columbia Coll.; did not grad. because of weak eyes; m. Edith Toms Bell, Feb. 17, 1909. Author: The School Pronouncer; How Should I Pronounce?; Seven Thousand Words Often Mispronounced; The Test Pronouncer; Five Thousand Words Often Misspelled; Five Thousand Facts and Fancies, a small encyclopædia; Ten Thousand Words Often Mispronounced; Twelve Thousand Words Often Mispronounced; Napoleon—The Return from St. Helena, 1907; Eighteen Thousand Words Often Mispronounced, 1913. Died Mar. 7, 1915.

PHYTHIAN, Robert Lees, commodore U.S.N.; b. Johnstown, Pa., July 31, 1835. Grad. U.S. Naval Acad., 1856; served in navy during Civil War, 1861-65, as exec. officer of large ships, and in command of a small vessel; was supt. N.Y. Nautical School; 3 times supt. U.S. Naval Obs.; served in U.S. Naval Acad. 5 yrs. as head Dept. of Navigation, and 4 yrs. supt.; retired, July 29, 1897. Home: Annapolis, Md. Died Jan. 20, 1917.

PIATT, John James, author; b. James' Mills, Ind., Mar. 1, 1835; s. John Bear and Emily (Scott) P.; ed. Capital U., Columbus, O., and Kenyon Coll., Ohio; m. Sarah Morgan Bryan, June 18, 1861. Clerk U.S. Treas. Dept., 1861-67; librarian U.S. Ho. of Rep., 1871-75; U.S. consul at Cork, Ireland, 1882-93; at Dublin, Apr.-Sept. 1893. Contributed verse and prose (editorial) to Louisville Journal, 1857-60; editorially connected with Cincinnati Chronicle, 1868-69; with Cincinnati Commercial as lit. editor and corr., 1869-78. Author: (poems) Poems of Two Friends (with W. D. Howells), 1860; The Nests at Washington and Other Poems (with Mrs. Piatt), 1864; Poems in Sunshine and Firelight, 1866; Western Windows, 1869; Landmarks, 1871; Poems of House and Home, 1879; Idyls and Lyrics of the Ohio Valley, 1884; The Children Out of Doors (with Mrs. Piatt), 1885; At the Holy Well, 1887; A Book of Gold, 1889; Little New-World Idyls, 1893; The Ghost's Entry and Other Poems, 1895; also, in prose, Pencilled Fly-Leaves, 1880; A Return to Paradise. Editor: The Union of American Poetry and Art, 1880; The Hesperian Tree, 1900, 1903. Home: North Bend, Hamilton Co., O. Died Feb. 16, 1917.

PICARD, George Henry, author; b. Berea, O., Aug. 3, 1850; s. Jonathan Newman and Mary (Fairchild) P.; B.S., Baldwin U., 1869; M.D., Cincinnati Med. Coll., 1877; m. Mary S. Kellogg, 1878. Author: A Matter of Taste, 1887; A Mission Flower, 1887; Old Boniface, 1888; Madame Noel, 1900; The Bishop's Niece, 1905. Home: New York, N.Y. Died Oct. 7, 1916.

PICK, Bernhard, clergyman; b. Kempen, Prussia, Dec. 19, 1842; s. Anselm and Fannie P.; ed. at Breslau and Berlin; grad. Union Theol. Sem., 1868; hon. Ph.D., New York U., 1877; D.D., Pa. Coll., 1893; m. Kate Spindler, June 16, 1868. Ordained Presbyn. ministry, 1868; pastor New York, 1868-69, N. Buffalo, N.Y., 1869-70, Syracuse, 1870-74, Rochester, 1874-81; pastor Luth. chs., Allegheny, Pa., 1881-95, Albany, N.Y., 1895-1903; occasional supply, New York, 1903-05; pastor Newark, N.J., 1905—. Author: Luther as a Hymnist, 1875; Jewish Life in the Time of Jesus (in German), 1880; Index to Lange's Commentary on the Old Testament, 1882; Life of Jesus According to Extra-Cannonical Sources, 1887; The Jews Since the Destruction of Jerusalem, 1887; The Talmud, 1890; General Index to the Ante-Nicene Fathers, 1887; Historical Sketch of the Jews Since Their Return from Babylon, 1892; Vade Mecum Homileticum, vol. 1—The Old Testament, 1899; The Extra Canonical Life of Christ, 1903; Hymns and Poetry of the Eastern Church, 1908; Remains of Gospels and Sayings of Christ, 1908; Apocryphal Acts of Paul, Peter, John, Andrew, and Thomas, 1909; Translations of the Bible, 1913; The Cabala, 1913; Jesus in the Talmud, 1913. Editor: Luther's Eine Feste Burg, in 21 languages, 1883; Luther's Hymn of the Reformation, in English, 1892; Lyra Gerhardti, 1906; The Devotional Songs of Novalis (German and English), 1910. Translator: Jewish Artisan Life in the Time of Christ (from the German of Prof. Delitzsch), 1883; Essence of Christianity (from German of Prof. Cremer), 1903; also 12 vols. comprising the Foreign Religions Series, 1908. Died Apr. 10, 1917.

PICKARD, Florence Willingham, author, artist; b. Smyrna, S.C., Mar. 7, 1862; d. Thomas Henry and Cecilia Matilda (Baynard) Willingham; ed. Wesleyan Female Coll., Macon, Ga., 1874-77; Miss Sallie Reynold's Sch., Albany, Ga., 1877-79; Woman's Coll., Richmond, Va., fall term, 1879; Mary Baldwin's Sem., Staunton, Va., 1879-81 (gold medal in art under Madame Garcia, Paris); studied art abroad, under Lucke, Dresden, 1905, 13; m. William Lowndes Pickard, D.D., LL.D., June 15, 1886; children—Julia Baynard (Mrs. Ralph E. Bailey), Florence Martha (Mrs. L. Roland Harrison), William Lowndes (dec.), Elizabeth Belle (Mrs. Paul Daggett Karsten). Artist; paintings exhibited in Va., Ga. and Tenn. Awarded silver cup, Georgia State Fair, 1918, 19, for paintings, "Choosing the Crown" and "The Chosen Crown." Author: The Ides of March, 1901; Between Scarlet Thrones (collateral Bible study), 1919; In the Palace of Amuhiah, 1926. Painted "Christchild and Mother" (exhibited in Tenn. and Ga.). Lecturer on art and lit. Home: Tifton, Ga. Died Dec. 2, 1930.

PICKARD, John, archeologist; b. Concord, N.H., Oct. 12, 1858; s. Samuel C. and Clara H. (Moore) P.; A.B., Dartmouth, 1883, A.M., 1886; studied univs. of Leipzig, Berlin, Munich, and Am. schs. classical studies, at Athens and Rome; Ph.D., Munich, 1892; many trips to Europe for study; Dr. Fine Arts, Washington U., 1925; m. Jeanie Austin Gerrish, July 15, 1889; 1 daughter, Mrs. Caroline Gerrish Culbert. Professor emeritus of classical archeology and history of art, U. of Missouri. Pres. Mo. State Capitol Decorations Commn. Presbyn. Scottish Rite Mason; Past Venerable Master of Kadosh, Consistory of Kansas City, Mo.; Past Grand Master of Royal and Select Masters of Mo.; Past Grand High Priest Royal Arch Masons of Mo.; Past Commander Knights Templar; Past Grand Master Grand Lodge of Mo.; Past Grand Patron O.E.S. of Mo.; Past Pres. Order of High Priesthood R.A.M. of Mo.; Past Pres. Past Commanders Assn. of Mo.; Past Grand Sovereign K.G.C.; Grand Imperial Council, Red Cross of Constantine; pres. Mo. Masonic Research Council. Lecturer on art and Masonry. Home: Columbia, Mo. Died Nov. 25, 1937.

PICKARD, Josiah Little, educator; b. Rowley Mass., Mar. 17, 1824; s. Samuel and Sarah (Coffin) P.; A.B., Bowdoin, 1844, A.M., 1847; LL.D., Beloit, 1870, U. of Chicago, 1870, Bowdoin, 1894; m. Cornelia Van Cleve Woodhull, Aug. 24, 1847. Prin. of acad., Platteville, Wis., 1846-60; supt. pub. instrn. of Wis., 1860-64; supt. pub. schs. of Chicago, 1864-77; pres. U. of Ia., 1878-87; retired, 1889. Pres. Ia. Hist. Soc., 1871-1900, N.E.A., 1871, Nat. Council Edn., 1877-78. Author: School Supervision; also several ednl. works. Home: Cupertino, Calif. Died Mar. 27, 1914.

PICKARD, Samuel Thomas, journalist; b. Rowley, Mass., Mar. 1, 1828; s. Samuel and Sarah (Coffin) P.; ed. Lewiston Falls Acad., Me.; hon. A.M., Bowdoin, 1894; m. Elizabeth Hussey Whittier, Apr. 19, 1876; father of Greenleaf Whittier P. Editor and propr. Portland (Me.) Transcript, 1852-94. Lit. executor of John Greenleaf Whittier; trustee Whittier Homestead and Birthplace, Haverhill, Mass., Amesbury Pub. Library. Editor: Whittier's Life and Letters (2 vols.), 1894. Author: Hawthorne's First Diary, 1897; Whittier as a Politician, 1901; Whittier Land, 1904; Life and Letters of John Greenleaf Whittier, 1907. Home: Amesbury, Mass. Died Feb. 11, 1915.

PICKARD, William Lowndes, clergyman; b. Upson County, Ga., Oct. 19, 1861; s. James LaFayette and Ann Haseltine (Ross) P.; A.B., Mercer U., Macon, Ga., 1884, A.M., 1885; grad. Southern Bapt. Theol. Sem., Louisville, Ky., 1887; traveled and studied in Europe; D.D., U. of Ala., 1887 (at age of 27); LL.D., Mercer, 1910; m. Florence Martha Willingham, June 15, 1886; children—Julia Baynard (Mrs. Ralph E. Bailey), Florence Martha (Mrs. L. Roland Harrison), Wm. Lowndes (dec.), Elizabeth Belle (Mrs. Paul Daggett Karsten). Ordained to Bapt. ministry, 1883; pastor First Ch. Eufaula, Ala., 1887, 88, First Ch., Birmingham, Ala., 1889-93, Broadway Ch., Louisville, Ky., 1894-98, First Ch., Cleveland, O., 1899-1902, First Ch., Lynchburg, Va., 1903-07, First Ch., Savannah, Ga., 1907-14; pres. Mercer U., 1914-18; pastor Central Bapt. Ch., Chattanooga, 1919-26. Pres. bd. edn. Ga. Bapt. Conv., 1913-18; trustee Southern Theol. Bapt. Sem., 1902-14; mem. Foreign Mission Bd., Richmond, Va., 1919—; mem. Tenn. Bd. of Missions, 1919—; trustee Mercer U., Bessie Tift Coll. (for women), Forsyth, Ga.; mem. Southern Bapt. Conv. (bd. of edn. 1915—; v.p. 1923-24), Ga. Bapt. Conv. (bd. edn.). Mason. Author: Under the War Flags of 1861; also contbr. prose and poetry to mags. and reviews. Lectured in 35 states. Made emeritus pastor for life by First Bapt. Ch. of Savannah, "for distinguished services." Home: Tifton, Ga. Died Sept. 4, 1935.

PICKEL, Frank Welborn, biologist; b. Williamston, S.C., Jan. 17, 1864; s. James Elbert and Mary (Welborn) P.; A.B., Furman U., Greenville, S.C., 1886; M.S., U. of S.C., 1890; studied Johns Hopkins, 1891-94; M.Sc., U. of Chicago, 1899; m. Allie Bush Deupree, Aug. 8, 1901. Prin. high sch., Williamston, S.C., 1886-88; instr. bacteriology and hygiene, U. of S.C., 1889-91; prof. natural science, Agrl. and Mech. Coll. of Fla., 1891-92; prof. Greek and German, Mississippi Coll., Clinton, Miss., 1895-97; prof. biology, U. of Ark., 1899—. Democrat. Baptist. K.P. Home: Fayetteville, Ark. Died Oct. 18, 1922.

PICKELL, Frank Gerald, supt. schools; b. Bicknell, Ind., Aug. 31, 1885; s. Hamilton Harvey and Sarah Catherine (Nixon) P.; student Vincennes (Ind.) U., 1902-05; A.B., Ind. U., 1909; A.M., Teachers Coll. (Columbia), 1919; Litt.D., Rutgers U., 1935; m. Edith Piety, Nov. 28, 1905; children—Marjorie Kathleen, Frank Gerald. Teacher rural schs., 1905-06; supt. twp. schs., 1906-08; asst. prin. high sch., Evansville, Ind., 1909-13; prin. high sch., Richmond, Ind., 1913-17, Lincoln, Neb., 1917-20; asst. supt. schs. Cleveland, 1920-23; supt. schs. Montclair, N.J., 1923—; served various periods as visiting prof. of edn., Earlham Coll., Western Reserve U., Colo. State Teachers Coll., U. of Mich., Teachers Coll. (Columbia), N.Y. Univ., Pa. State Coll., 1920-32. Dir. Nishuane Bldg. & Loan Assn., Montclair Y.M.C.A.; mem. Nat. Council Boy Scouts of America (v. chmn. nat. com. Scout edn.), Montclair Chamber Commerce. Mem. Gov.'s Commn. to Survey N.J. Schs., 1932-33. Republican. Presbyn. Mason. Author: (with Chas. H. Johnson and Jesse H. Newlon) Junior-Senior High School Education, 1922; (with F. G. Bonser and James H. Smith) Practical Mathematics for Junior High School, 1925. Mem. editorial bd. The American School and University; cons. editor The Nation's Schools. Chmn. 1937 Yearbook of Dept. of Superintendence, N.E.A. Home: Montclair, N.J. Died Nov. 27, 1936.

PICKENS, William Augustus, judge; b. Owen County, Ind.; s. Samuel and Eliza (Baldon) P.; student Indiana U., 1879-81; studied law, Columbian (now George Washington) U., 1881-82; m. Anne Jennings Wiles, Sept. 29, 1886; children—Virginia Anne (Mrs. Don E. Brewer), Eliza (Mrs. Clifford W. Foote). Admitted to bar, 1881, and began practice at Spencer; mem. firm Pickens & Pickens, 1883-86, Fowler & Pickens, 1886-93; moved to Indianapolis, Ind., 1893; mem. firm Pickens, Cox, Conder & Bain, 1895-1931; corp. counsel, Indianapolis, 1914-17; judge Superior Court of Marion County, Ind., term 1931-34. Democrat. Mason, K.P. Mem. com. of two which drew up the secret ballot law of Indiana, passed in 1889, the first secret ballot law adopted in U.S. Home: Indianapolis, Ind. Deceased.

PICKERING, Edward Charles, astronomer; b. Boston, July 19, 1846; s. Edward and Charlotte (Hammond) P.; ed. Boston Latin School; S.B., Lawrence Scientific Sch. (Harvard), 1865, hon. A.M., 1880; LL.D., univs. of Calif., 1886, Mich., 1887, Chicago, 1901, Harvard, 1903, Pa., 1906; Ph.D., Heidelberg Univ., 1903; D.Sc., Victoria Univ., England, 1900; L.H.D., Allegheny Coll., 1912; m. Lizzie Wadsworth, d. Jared Sparks, Mar. 9, 1874. Instr. mathematics, Lawrence Scientific Sch., 1865-67; Thayer prof. physics, Mass. Inst. Tech., 1867-76; prof. astronomy and dir. Harvard Coll. Obs., 1876—. Established 1st physical lab. in U.S.; under his direction, invested capital and income of the observatory increased fourfold. Study of light and spectra of the stars spl. features of his work; devised meridian photometer and made 1,400,000 measures of the light of the stars with it. By establishing an auxiliary sta. in Arequipa, Peru, Southern stars also observed, extending the work from pole to pole, in which 240,000 photographs included. Accompanied Nautical Almanac expdn. to observe total eclipse of sun, Aug. 7, 1869; mem. U.S. Coast Survey expdn. to Xeres, Spain, Dec. 22, 1870. Awarded Henry Draper medal for work on astron. physics; gold medals, Rumford, 1891, Bruce, 1908, Royal Astron. Soc., 1886, 1901. Knight German Order pour le mérite, 1911. Mem. Nat. Acad. Sciences; hon. mem. socs. at Mexico, Cherbourg, Liverpool, Toronto, Cristiania, Upsala, Lund and mem. numerous Am. and European socs.; fellow Am. Acad. Arts and Sciences; founder and 1st pres. Appalachian Mountain Club. Author: Elements of Physical Manipulation, and edited 70 vols. of annals and other publs. of Harvard Coll. Observatory. Died Feb. 3, 1919.

PICKERING, William Alfred, lumberman; b. Buffalo, Mo., Dec. 26, 1870; s. William R. and Jane (Coggburn) P.; student Drury Coll., Springfield, Mo., 1887-90; m. Zoe Louise Cravens, Dec. 11, 1901; children—Russell Cravens, Zoe Louise, Cynthia Ann. In lumber business at Springfield, 1890, Kansas City, 1898—; pres. Pickering Lumber Co.; director Commerce Trust Co. Republican. Mason. Home: Kansas City, Mo., and Santa Monica, Calif. Died April 15, 1930.

PICKERING, William Henry, astronomer; b. Boston, Feb. 15, 1858; s. Edward and Charlotte (Hammond) P.; grad. Mass. Institute Tech., 1879; instr. there, and asst. prof. Harvard Observatory; m. Anne Atwood, d. Isaac Butts, of Boston, June 11, 1884; children—William T., Esther. Led expedition to observe total solar eclipses in Colo., 1878, Grenada, West Indies, 1886, Calif., 1889, Chile, 1893, Ga., 1900, New Hampshire, 1932; expdn. to Southern California to make observations of the moon, 1904; in 1899 discovered Phœbe, the ninth satellite of Saturn, and showed later why it revolved in a direction opposite to others; predicted existence and gave location, 1919, of 9th planet, Pluto; visited Hawaii, 1905, the Azores in 1907, in order to compare their crater formations with those in the moon. Established temporary observatory in Southern Calif., 1889, and Arequipa Sta. of Harvard Obs., 1891. Also erected obs. and telescope for Dr. Lowell at Flagstaff, Ariz., 1894; established an astron. station for Harvard Obs., in Mandeville, Jamaica, W.I., 1900, reestablished it in 1911 and converted it into a private obs., 1925, with the substitution of a new telescope for the older one, which was returned to Harvard. Interested in mountain climbing. Ascended Half Dome in Yosemite Valley, 1878, and El Misti in Peru (altitude, 19,400 feet), besides over 100 other peaks. Mem. Internat. Astronomical Union and other astron. socs.; fellow American Acad. Arts and Sciences. Author: Walking Guide to Mt. Washington Range, 1882; Investigations in Astronomical Photography (Vol. XXXII, Part I, Annals), 1895; Visual Observations of the Moon and Planets (Vol. XXXII, Part II, Annals), 1900; An Atlas of the Moon (Vol. LI, Annals), 1903; The Moon, 1903; Miscellaneous papers (Vol. LIII, Annals), 1905; Lunar and Hawaiian Physical Features Compared, 1906; Researches of the Boyden Department (Vol. LXI, Part I, Annals), 1908; A Search for a Planet Beyond Neptune (Vol. LXI, Part II, Annals), 1909; A Statistical Investigation of Cometary Orbits (Vol. LXI, Part III, Annals), 1911; Mars, 1921. Began a series of "Reports on Mars," in Popular Astronomy, 1914 (Rept. No. 44 issued in 1930). Home: Jamaica, West Indies. Died Jan. 16, 1938.

PICKETT, Charles E., congressman; b. Van Buren County, Ia., Jan. 14, 1866; s. Edgar and Glorvina E. (Ballard) P.; A.B., State U. of Ia., 1888, LL.B., 1890; m. India Parmley Ryan, June 17, 1902. Mem. law firm of Pickett & Swisher, Waterloo, Ia.; v.p. Leavitt & Johnson Nat. Bank; dir. Farmers' Loan & Trust Co., Leavitt & Johnson Trust Co. Mem. 61st and 62 Congresses (1909-13), 3d Ia. Dist. Mem. Bd. of Regents, State U. of Ia., 1896-1909. Republican, K.P., Elk. Conglist. Died July 20, 1930.

PICKETT, Fermen Layton, prof. botany; b. Bakers Corner, Ind., Jan. 10, 1881; s. (James) Harvey and Clara (Drake) P.; A.B., Indiana U., 1910, A.M., 1912, Ph.D., 1915; m. Emma Wilson, Jan. 22, 1901; children—Mary Carol (Mrs. Wathen Louis Kincheloe), Bessie Violet (Mrs. W. W. Sloan), Ruth Pauline (Mrs. Robert Loyal Garvin), Emma Maude, Mildred Aseneth (Mrs. Louis A. Dillon), Fermen Layton, Jr., Esther Melissa (Mrs. Paul Lee Dillon). Prin. high school, Cicero, Ind., 1904-05; prin. high school, Williamsville, Ill., 1905-06; critic teacher of botany, Ind. U., 1909-13; with State Coll. of Washington, 1914—, asso. prof. of botany, 1914-18, head of department, 1918-39, also dean of Graduate School, 1930-39. Trustee Wesley Foundation (State College of Washington). Methodist; lay del. Quadrennial Conf., Kansas City, 1928, Atlantic City, 1932. Home: Pullman, Wash. Died June 26, 1940.

PICKETT, La Salle Corbell (Mrs.), author; b. Nansemond County, Va., May 16, 1848; d. John D. and Elizabeth Mary (Phillips) Corbell; ed. Lynchburg Coll.; m. Gen. George Edward Pickett, C.S.A., Sept. 15, 1863 (died 1875). Began contbg. to Illustrated News, 1863; wrote editorials, short stories, poems and spl. articles. Lecturer on hist. subjects and folk lore of the South. Episcopalian. Author: Pickett and His Men (hist.), 1899; Kunno Sperits, 1900; Yule Log, 1900; Ebil Eye, 1900; Jinny, 1900; Digging Through to Manila, (poem), 1905; Sketches of Abraham Lincoln, Jefferson Davis, Gens. Lee, Jackson and Beauregard; Literary Hearthstones of Dixie, 1912; Pickett and His Men (revised and illus. edit.), 1913; Bugles of Gettysburg, 1913; Heart of a Soldier, 1913; Across My Path, 1916; What Happened to Me, 1917; Some Letters of General Pickett. Address: The Ontario, Washington, D.C. Died Mar. 22, 1931.

PICKETT, Thomas Edward, physician; b. Mill Glen, Ky., Jan. 11, 1841; s. Thomas Jefferson and Margaret Madison (Campbell) P.; A.B., Centre Coll. (Central U.), Ky., 1860, LL.D., 1900; M.D., U. of Pa., 1865; m. Abby Gray, June 18, 1873 (died 1878). Surgeon asst. in Peninsular campaign of Gen. Grant, summer of 1864; in hosp. and dispensary practice, Phila., 1865-66; began practice at Maysville, Ky., 1866; state med. examiner 14th Jud. Dist., 1874-82; mem. U.S. Bd. Pension Examiners, Maysville, 1884— (chmn.); dir. Hayswood Hosp., Maysville Pub. Library. The first to introduce massage and mobilization in treatment of fractures in U.S. Fellow Am. Acad. Medicine. Author: The Testimony of the Mounds; A Soldier of the Civil War, Gen. George E. Pickett, 1900; The Quest for a Lost Race, 1907. Died Sept. 3, 1913.

PICKETT, William Clendenin, physician; b. Meadville, Pa., 1870; s. B. B. and Mary A. (Clendenin) P.; grad. Allegheny Coll., A.B., 1892, A.M., 1895; M.D., Jefferson Med. Coll., Phila., 1895; m. Elizabeth Lovelace. Prof. nervous and mental diseases, Medico-Chirurg. Coll.; neurologist Philadelphia (Pa.) Hospital. Died 1907.

PICKHARDT, William Paul, corp. executive; b. New York, N.Y., Jan. 8, 1881; s. Carl and Paula (von Scheven) P.; B.S., Gymnase Cantonale de Neuchatel, Switzerland, 1898; B.S. in chemistry, Columbia, 1901; unmarried. With Kuttroff, Pickhardt & Co., chemicals, 1901-30, beginning as office boy, became sec. and dir. and was pres. 1925-30 (company then segregated into several new companies); chmn. bd. and dir. Synthetic Nitrogen Products Corp. (air nitrogen fertilizers), 1930-38; chmn. bd. and dir. Agfa Ansco Corp., Binghamton, N.Y., 1933—; pres. Chemnyco, Inc., chem. engring., 1935-38; pres. and dir. Unyte Corp., resin plastics, New York, 1932-36; dir. Plaskon Co., Inc., Toledo, O. (successor to Unyte Corp.), 1936—; v.p. General Aniline & Film Corp. Lutheran. Home: New York, N.Y. Died Jan. 22, 1941.

PICKING, Henry F., commodore U.S.N.; b. Somerset Co., Pa., Jan. 1840; apptd. to navy, Sept. 28, 1857; Naval Acad., 1857-61; apptd. acting master, June 4, 1861; lt., July 1862; lt. comdr., July 25, 1866; comdr., Jan. 25, 1875; capt., Aug. 4, 1889; commodore, Nov. 22, 1898; rear admiral, Mar. 3, 1899; m. Laura Sherwood, May 2, 1879. In Civil war on blockading service, at sinking of privateer Petrel, engagement with Confederate ram Merrimac, and Sewell's Point batteries (monitor engagement), 1862; in several skirmishes with batteries on Sullivan's Island, etc. Since Civil war on various duties and stations. Ordered to command navy-yard at Boston, Mar. 25, 1899. Died 1899.

PICOT, Louis Julien, physician; b. Murfreesboro, N.C., Jan. 9, 1853; s. Julien Henri and Antoinette (Vann) P.; ed. Buckhorn Acad., N.C.; M.D., Jefferson Med. Coll., Phila., 1873; following with a post-grad. course there; m. Nellie Green, Oct. 25, 1876. Sec., 1877-85, orator, 1886, and pres., 1898, N.C. State Med. Soc.; sec. and mem. State Bd. Med. Examiners, 1891-96; surgeon Seaboard Air Line R.R. Co. Dir. State Hosp. for Insane, Raleigh, N.C., 1901-07, 1907-13, 1st asst. supt. same, Apr. 22, 1909—, med. supt. same, 1911—. Trustee State Univ. of N.C., 1900-09. Home: Raleigh, N.C. Died Aug. 15, 1924.

PIDDOCK, Charles Albert, clergyman, publisher; b. Lorraine, N.Y., July 25, 1849; left public schools at 15 to enlist in 186th N.Y. vols., but was not sent to front because of his youth. Studied at Hamilton Coll. 1 yr.; grad. Colgate Univ., 1872; studied 2 yrs. at Hamilton Theol. Sem.; m. Gertrude P. Farnsworth. Pastor Baptist Ch., Claremont, N.H., 1874-78; 1st Baptist Ch., W. Springfield, Mass., 1878-81; Middleton, Conn., 1881-87; supt. Missions of Conn., 1887—; editor Christian Secretary, 1888-96; with Dr. William R. Harper, partner in Student Publishing Co. Home: Hartford, Conn. Died 1907.

PIDGIN, Charles Felton, author; b. Roxbury, Mass., Nov. 11, 1844; s. Benjamin Gorham and Mary Elizabeth (Felton) P.; grad. English High Sch., Boston, 1863; m. Lizzie Abbott Dane, July 3, 1867 (died 1868); m. 2d, Lucy Sturtevant Gardner, M.D., Nov. 25, 1873 (died 1896); m. 3d, Frances Fern, d. Edward Foster Douglas, of Madrid, N.Y., July 21, 1897. In mercantile business, 1863-73. Chief clerk, 1873-1903, chief, 1903-07, Mass. Bur. Statistics of Labor. Author: Practical Statistics, 1888; Quincy Adams Sawyer (novel), 1900; Blennerhassett (romance), 1901; Stephen Holton, 1902; The Climax, 1902; The Letter H, 1904; A Nation's Idol, 1904; Little Burr, 1905; Sarah Bernhardt Brown, 1905; The Corsican Lovers, 1905; The Hidden Man, 1906; The Toymakers, 1907; Theodosia, The First Gentlewoman of Her Time, 1907; Labor, or, The Money-God, 1908; The Further Adventures of Quincy Adams Sawyer, 1909; Chronicles of Quincy Adams Sawyer, Detective (with J. M. Taylor), 1912; The House of Shame, 1912; The Courtin', comic opera, 1913; libretto grand opera Venusia and Cupidon, 1919. Invented "visible speech system" for motion pictures, 1917. Home: Melrose, Mass. Died June 3, 1923.

PIEPER, Emil G.; b. Hoboken, N.J., Sept. 15, 1872; ed. pvt. schs., Brooklyn and N.Y. City; widower; 1 son, Clifford E. Began in ins. business with New York Bowery, 1888; with R. C. Rathbone & Co., 1895-1903; sec. Nat. Standard Ins. Co., asst. sec. Assurance Co. of America and spl. agt. Am. Ins. Co. of Boston, 1903-06; sec. R.I. Ins. Co., 1906-24; became pres., 1924; also pres. Mchts. Ins. Co. of Providence, 1924; retired. Mem. Providence Bd. of Trade. Republican. Mason. Home: Providence, R.I. Died Sept. 11, 1938.

PIEPER, Franz August Otto, theologian; b. Carwitz, Pomerania, Germany, June 27, 1852; s. Augustus and Bertha P.; came to U.S., 1870; A.B., Northwestern U., Wis., 1872; grad. Concordia Sem., 1875; D.D., Northwestern U., 1903, Decorah Coll., 1903; m. Minnie Koehn, Jan. 2, 1877. Ordained Luth. ministry, 1875; pastor Manitowoc, Wis., 1875-78; prof. theology, 1878-87, pres., 1887—, Concordia Luth. Theol. Sem. Pres.-gen. Luth. Synod of Mo., Ohio and Other States, 1899-1911. Editor Lehre and Wehre, 1878—. Author: Unsere Stellung in Lahre und Praxis, 1896; Christ's Work, 1898; Die Grunddifferenz, 1904; Conversion and Election, 1913; Die Luth. Kirche die Wahre siehtbare Kirche, 1916; Die Luth. Lehre v.d. Rechtfertigung, 1916; Christliche Dogmatik, 1917; Das Fundament des Christliche Glaubens, 1925; Die Kraft des Evangeliums, 1927. Home: St. Louis. Mo. Died June 3, 1931.

PIEPER, John Jacob, prof. crop production; b. Granite City, Ill., Jan. 24, 1886; s. John and Mary Bell (Rief) P.; B.S., U. of Illinois, 1916, M.S., 1917; Ph.D., U. of Wis., 1927; m. Nelle Grooms Dawson, Aug. 29, 1918; 1 dau., Jacqueline Marie. Asst. in crop production, coll. agr., U. of Ill., 1918-19, instr, 1919-20, asso., 1920-22, asst. prof., 1923-30, asso. prof., 1930-36, prof. and chief Agr. Exptl. Sta., 1936—; supt. Internat. Crop Contest, 1930—. Democrat. Methodist. Mason. Home: Urbana, Ill. Died Nov. 26, 1939.

PIERCE, Arthur Henry, psychologist; b. Westboro, Mass., July 30, 1867; s. Samuel and Caroline (Tufts) P.; A.B., Amherst, 1888; A.M., Harvard, 1892, Ph.D., 1899; student psychology, Harvard, 1892-93; Berlin, Strassburg and Paris, 1894-97. Unmarried. Prof. psychology, Smith Coll., 1900—. Holder Kellogg univ. fellowship, Amherst, 1894-1900. Editor Psychol. Bulletin. Author: Studies in Space Perception, 1901. Home: Northampton, Mass. Died Feb. 20, 1914.

PIERCE, Byron Root, soldier; b. E. Bloomfield, N.Y., Sept. 20, 1829; s. Silas and Mary (Root) P.; acad. edn. Rochester, N.Y.; began business life in his father's woolen factory; later became dentist, removed to Grand Rapids, Mich., 1856; also had branch office at Joliet, Ill.; m. Abbie L. Evans, Oct. 12, 1881. Entered Union Army as capt. Co. K, 3d Mich. Regt., May 13, 1861; rapidly promoted for bravery and meritorious conduct; maj. 3d Mich.

Inf., Oct. 21, 1861; lt. col., July 25, 1862; col., Jan. 1, 1863; brig. gen. vols., June 7, 1864; bvtd. maj. gen., Apr. 5, 1865, "for gallant service at battle of Sailor's Creek." Commandant Mich. Soldiers' Home from its opening, 1887, until 1891. Employed in P.O. Dept. Home: Grand Rapids, Mich. Died July 13, 1924.

PIERCE, Charles Franklin, artist; b. in New Hampshire, Apr. 1844; s. John A. and Phila A. P.; m. Luena R. Wilder, 1876 (died 1906); m. 2d, Katherine Plimpton, 1912. Home: Brookline, Mass. Died Mar. 5, 1920.

PIERCE, Edward Peter, judge; b. Templeton, Mass., Dec. 28, 1852; s. Peter and Mary (Burney) P.; A.B., LL.B., Harvard, 1877; m. Adele Duteau, Oct. 11, 1884; children— John Burney, Marie Aurelie, Edward Peter, Mrs. Lucile Louise, Wellington. Admitted to Mass. bar, 1878, and practiced in Fitchburg; mem. Pierce & Stiles till 1900; judge Superior Court of Mass., 1900-14; became justice Supreme Jud. Court of Mass., Dec. 9, 1914, resigned Nov. 1, 1937. Mem. State Bd. Bar Examiners, 1897-1900. Republican. Unitarian. Home: Brookline, Mass. Died June 22, 1938.

PIERCE, Frederick Clifton, genealogist; b. Worcester Co., Mass., July 30, 1859; s. Silas Austin and Maria N. (Smith) P.; ed. Groton Acad.; took up newspaper work, Worcester, Mass., 1879; removed to Ill., 1880; served on newspaper as city editor 10 yrs.; 10 yrs. business mgr. Chicago Journal; advertising and bus. mgr., Chicago Inter Ocean, 1900-02. Organized City Grays (co. of 3d regt., Ill. Nat. Guard); comd. it until promoted to staff Gov. Richard Oglesby; later on staff Joseph W. Fifer and Gov. John P. Altgeld; 6 yrs. sec. Ill. Nat. Guard Assn. Author: History of Grafton, Mass., 1879; Life and Services of Congressman R. M. A. Hawk, of the Sixth Illinois District; History of Rockford, Ill.; History of Barre, Mass. Also genealogies of the Field, Foster, Harwood, Whitney, Fiske, Fisk, Pierce, Peirce, Pearce, Forbes, Forbush, Gibson, Batcheller, Batchelder and Sherman families; History of Conway, Mass., and the Gibson memorial. Deceased.

PIERCE, Frederick Louis, mfr.; b. Milwaukee, Wis., July 8, 1860; s. Amos J. W. and Annie (Curry) P.; ed. pub. schs., Milwaukee; m. Frances Bosworth Hopkins, Jan. 23, 1896; 1 dau., Janet (Mrs. George Pettit Blakney). Partner A. J. W. Pierce & Co., commn. mchts., Milwaukee, 1888-1900; treas. The Cutler-Hammer Mfg. Co., mfrs. elec. apparatus, Milwaukee and New York, 1900-29; became pres. A. J. W. Pierce Realty Co., Hopkins Estate Co.; trustee and mem. finance and exec. coms. Northwestern Mut. Life Ins. Co. Dir. Columbia Hosp. Republican. Episcopalian. Home: Chenequa, Wis. Died Apr. 16, 1935.

PIERCE, Gilbert Ashville, U.S. senator-journalist; b. E. Otto, N.Y., Jan. 1841; ed. public schools; grad. law school, Univ. of Chicago; m. Maria Bartholomew, 1860. Served as lt., capt., lt. col. and col. in Union army in Civil war; member lower house, Ind. legislature, 1868-69; asso. and mng. editor, Chicago Inter Ocean, 1872-82; gov. Dakota, 1884-86; U.S. senator from N.Dak., 1889-91; editor Minneapolis Tribune, 1891-94; U.S. minister to Portugal, 1892-93. Author: Dickens Dictionary. Home: Minneapolis, Minn. Died 1901.

PIERCE, Grace Adele, author; b. Randolph, N.Y.; d. John Crowley and Marrion A. (Pingrey) P.; ed. Chamberlain Inst., Randolph N.Y., Boston, and under Wellesley and other pvt. instrs.; unmarried. Contbr. of poems, stories, prose articles, etc., to foremost mags. and newspapers; engaged on Chautauqua publs., 1901. Los Angeles publs., 1904-06. Lecturer on applied lit., short story writing, versification, editorial and gen. newspaper writing. Author: Come Unto Me (poems), 1920; The Red Cross Knight and Others (children's stories), 1921. Also opera, One Night In Venice (sung by Constantino), 1916. Orignator of the "author's rights" movement, and framed copyright law amendment for protection of scenario writers. Honored for scholarship by Société des Gens de Lettres, France; portrait with poetic work given honorable place in woman's corner of Bibliotheque National Paris, 1906; Book of child stories, The Faerie Queen, republished from John Martin's Mag., New York, 1922-23. Home: Santa Monica, Calif. Died Dec. 8, 1923.

PIERCE, H(enry) Clay, financier; b. St. Lawrence, N.Y.; s. Dr. Dyer, Ensworth and Mary Jane (Ackert) P.; Jefferson Co. high schs.; m. Minnie Finlay; children—Clay Arthur, Roy Ensworth, Theron Finlay, Perle (Mrs. Eben Richards), Violet (Mrs. James R. Dering); m. 2d, Mrs. Virginia (Prickett) Burrowes, Aug. 2, 1909. Chmn. New York bd. Nat. Rys. of Mexico; chmn. bd. Pierce Oil Corp. (St. Louis), Pierce Fordyce Oil Assn., Tenn. Central R.R. Co.; pres. Pierce Investment Trust Co. (St. Louis). Home: St. Louis, Prides Crossing, Mass., Brule River, Wis., and New York, N.Y. Died June 27, 1927.

PIERCE, Henry Hill, lawyer; b. Portland, Me., Nov. 7, 1875; s. Lewis and Mary Bellows (Hill) P.; A.B., Bowdoin, 1896, LL.D., 1926; LL.B., New York Law Sch., 1898; m. Katharine R. Curtis, May 29, 1905. Admitted to N.Y. bar, 1898; mem. Sullivan & Cromwell, 1909-29 (retired). Dir. Magor Car Corp., Canal Nat. Bank of Portland, Me., Bonneville, Ltd. Trustee of Bowdoin Coll. Democrat. Episcopalian. Home: West Baldwin, Me., and New York, N.Y. Died Mar. 1, 1940.

PIERCE, Henry Niles, P.E. bishop of Ark., 1870—; b. Pawtucket, R.I., Oct. 19, 1820; grad. Brown, 1842 (D.D., Univ. of Ala., 1862; LL.D., William and Mary, 1867; D.D., U. of the South, 1869); ordered deacon, 1848; ordained priest, 1849; missionary in Washington Co., Tex., 1849-52; rector Christ Ch., Matagorda, Tex., 1852-54; Trinity Ch., New Orleans, 1854; St. Paul's, Rahway, N.J., 1855-57; St. John's Mobile, Ala., 1857-68; St. Paul's, Springfield, Ill., 1868-70; m. Nannie Hayward Sheppard, April 18, 1854. Author: The Agnostic, and Other Poems. Home: Little Rock, Ark. Died 1899.

PIERCE, Joseph Hart, architect; b. Dundee, N.Y., Sept. 2, 1855; s. Herschel Wright and Mariette P.; ed. Dundee Acad.; Starkey Sem., Lakemont, N.Y.; archtl. training in office of W. H. Hayes, Elmira, N.Y., later of Minneapolis; m. Carrie Decker, Sept. 29, 1886. Conducted eastern office of W. H. Hayes, 1881-84; mem. Pierce & Dockstader, 1884-90, Pierce & Bickford, 1891—. Firm designed many pub. and pvt. bldgs. in Elmira, also many school and other buildings in N.Y., Pa. and N.J. Police commr. of Elmira, 1914-17. Pvt. and sergt. 30th Separate Co., N.Y.N.G., 1881-87. Republican. Methodist. Mason. Home: Elmira, N.Y. Died Aug. 28, 1932.

PIERCE, Josiah, Jr., engr., maj. and engr. officer, U.S.V.; b. Alexandrofsky, Russia, Jan. 30, 1861; ed. in Russia, England and U.S.; asso. King's Coll., London, 1879; grad. Emmanuel Coll., Cambridge, Eng., B.A., 1882 (M.A., 1886); student Mass. Inst. Tech., 1883; later at Johns Hopkins, Baltimore. Lecturer and prof. Columbian Univ.; instr. and asst. prof. Catholic Univ., Washington; asso. mem. (Telford medal and premium) Instn. Civil Engrs., London; topographer and engr., Northern Transcontinental Survey, 1883; U.S. Coast and Geodetic Survey, 1885; U.S. Geol. Survey, 1886; Ordnance Survey of Great Britain, 1888; U.S. Irrigation Surveys, 1888-91; Sinipuxent Beach Co., 1893; C.,B.&Q. R.R. and B.&O. R.R. Prin. asst. engr., topog. survey, city of Baltimore, 1893; chief engr., Va. Electric Co., 1897; chief engr., 1st div., 2d army corps, Camp Alger, 1898; chief engr., San Juan dist., Puerto Rico, 1898-99. Consulting engr. Great Falls Power Co., Washington, D.C. Home: Boonsboro, Md. Died 1902.

PIERCE, Lawrence Blunt, capitalist; b. Greenville Co., Va., Mar. 30, 1859; s. Rice B. and Martha (Blunt) P.; m. Lucie Alexander, Apr. 14, 1886. Removed to St. Louis, 1879; began as entry clk., Crow, Hargadine & Co., wholesale dry goods; sec. St. Louis Expn. and Music Hall Assn., 1883-86; became connected with Charles H. Turner & Co., real estate, admitted to firm, 1889; an organizer, 1901, and v.p., 1901-05, Commonwealth Trust Co.; one of 5 syndicate mgrs. in merger of C.,H.&D. Ry. and the Pere Marquette R.R. into one system, 1905; pres. Income Leasehold Co. (owners of the Pierce Bldg., St. Louis), Monward Realty Co. (owners Boatmen's Bank Bldg., St. Louis); chmn. bd. Am. Automobile Ins. Co. Methodist. Home: St. Louis, Mo. Died 1919.

PIERCE, Lyman L., institutional finance; b. Stockton, N.Y., May 14, 1868; s. Christopher C. and Salina (Todd) P.; grad. Chamberlin Inst., Randolph, N.Y., 1887; B.S., U. of Minn., 1892; m. Blanche A. Wright, June 19, 1895; children—Martha Foster, Virginia. With Y.M.C.A., 1893-1919; gen. sec., Cedar Rapids, Ia., 1893-94, state sec., Ohio, 1895-96; gen. sec., Trenton, N.J., 1896-99, Washington, D.C., 1900-05; nat. sec., Australia and New Zealand, 1905-07; spl. lecturer, India, 1907; lecture tour, Eng. and Wales, 1908, gen. sec., Pittsburgh, Pa., 1909-15, San Francisco, Calif., 1916-19; pres., Lyman L. Pierce Financial Orgn., 1919-30; pres. Pierce & Hedrick, financial campaigns for instns., colleges, charities, etc. Layman mem., Pacific Coast, National Bd. Y.M.C.A.; chmn. Nat. Com. on Pioneer Fields; mem. Nat. Council of Y.M.C.A.; mem. Nat. Council, Boy Scouts of America; dir. of Western Area, World Alliance, for Internat. Friendship; National dir. war campaigns Am. Red Cross, 1916-18 (author Nat. Campaign Plan Book; exec. dir. welfare campaigns, Western Mil. Dept.); mem. Nat. War Work Council and Nat. Personnel Bd., Y.M.C.A., World War. Awarded distinguished service gold medal for service to young men, Calif. State Y.M.C.A., 1931; chmn. Area Bd., Calif., Ariz., N.M., Nev., Utah and Hawaii Y.M.C.A., 1935, 36, 37, 38, 39. Trustee Coll. of the Pacific, Pacific Sch. of Religion; mem. com. of 100, Hall of Religion, Golden Gate Expn. Methodist. Mason. Author: How to Raise Money, 1931. Home: Burlingame, Calif. Died July 20, 1940.

PIERCE, Newton Barris, vegetable pathologist; b. Brockport, N.Y., Sept. 26, 1856; s. Franklin B. and Melissa (Hinman) P.; ed. common and high schs. of N.Y., Wis. and Mich., Mus. of Comparative Zoölogy, Cambridge, Mass., 1882-83; U. of Mich., 1887-89; pvt. biol. lab., 1876-89; study of plant diseases, France, Italy, and Algeria, 1890; m. Maude B. Lacy, Mar. 11, 1897. Lumber insp., 1874, chief insp., 1876, and established office of Pierce Bros., lumber inspectors, 1876-95; established pvt. lab. for biol. study, 1876-89; conducted geol. work in connection with early sinking of salt wells in Western Mich.; apptd., 1889, from U. of Mich., to take charge of vegetable pathol. investigations in Calif.; established, 1889, in charge until 1906, Pacific Coast Lab. of Vegetable Pathology for U.S. Dept. Agr.; established Wild Plant Improvement Gardens for U.S. Dept. Agr., 1902; propr. same, July 1, 1906—. Life fellow A.A.A.S. Author: California Vine Disease, 1892; Peach Leaf Curl, etc. Home: Santa Ana, Calif. Died 1917.

PIERCE, Palmer Eddy, army officer; b. Savanna, Ill., Oct. 23, 1865; s. Henry Clay and Laura (Shepherd) P.; student Grinnell (Ia.) Coll.; grad. U.S. Mil. Acad., 1891; honor grad. Army Service Sch., 1910; Army Staff Coll., 1911; m. Agnes Young, Dec. 3, 1891. Commd. 2d lt., June 12, 1891; 1st lt. 13th Inf., Mar. 23, 1898; capt. 8th Inf., Oct. 9, 1900; maj. 15th Inf., Mar. 28, 1912; lt. col., May 15, 1917; col. (temp.), Aug. 5, 1917; brig. gen. N.A., Dec. 17, 1917. Instr. chemistry, U.S. Mil. Acad., 1895-99; served in Puerto Rico, Spanish-Am. War, 1898; in Philippine Islands, 1899-1901; instr. and asst. prof. philosophy, U.S. Mil. Acad., 1901-07; instr. Army Service and Staff Sch., 1911-12; in China, 1912-14, Philippine Islands, 1914-15; apptd. mem. Gen. Staff, Feb. 16, 1916; was mem. Gen. Munitions Bd., War Industries Bd., Training Camps Athletic Commn., The War Council; arrived in France as comdr. 54th Inf. Brigade, May 1918; participated Ypres-Lys defense, Ypres-Lys offensive, Somme offensive, battles of Hindenburg line, La Selle River; returned to U.S., Mar. 1919; comdr. 151st Depot Brigade, Camp Devens, Mass., Apr.-June 1919. Awarded D.S.M. "for exceptionally meritorious and distinguished service"; Companion of the Bath (British). Conglist. Home: New York, N.Y. Died Jan. 17, 1940.

PIERCE, Wallace Lincoln, merchant; b. Boston, Mass., Mar. 15, 1853; s. Samuel Stillman and Ellen Maria Teresa (Wallis) P.; ed. Boston pub. schs.; m. Lulie Walworth, June 7, 1876 (died 1914); m. 2d, Mary Agatha Greeley, May 1, 1916. Entered employ of S. S. Pierce & Co., importers and dealers in groceries, 1871, admitted to firm, 1874, and president of corp., 1894—; dir. 2d Nat. Bank, Boston Safe Deposit & Trust Co., N.E. Life Ins. Co., Equitable Life Assurance Soc.; trustee Home Savings Bank. Trustee Boston Children's Hosp., Boston Lying-in Hospital and of the Mass. Society for the Prevention of Cruelty to Animals. Episcopalian. Mason. Home: Boston, Mass. Died Mar. 5, 1920.

PIERCE, Winslow Shelby, lawyer; b. Shelbyville, Ind., Oct. 23, 1857; s. Winslow S. and Jane Thomson (Hendricks) P.; student Pa. Coll. and U. of Va.; LL.B., U. of Mich., 1879; also studied at Columbia; m. Grace Douglass Williams, Oct. 14, 1891; children—Allison P. Moore, Winslow S., Lady Grace D. Torphichen, Helen B. Lefferts. Counsel to bd. D.&R.G.W. Ry. Co. Home: Bayville, L.I. Died July 23, 1938.

PIERPONT, James, mathematician; B.S., Worcester Poly. Inst., 1886; Ph.D., U. of Vienna, 1894; hon. A.M., Yale, 1899; LL.D., Clark U., 1909. Lecturer in mathematics, 1894-95, instr., 1895-96, asst. prof., 1896-98, prof., 1898—, Yale. Home: New Haven, Conn. Died Dec. 9, 1938.

PIERSEL, Alba Chambers, univ. prof.; b. Ky., Nov. 25, 1867; s. Rev. Levi B. and Isabella (Houghton) P.; A.B., Ohio Wesleyan U., 1890, A.M., 1895, D.D., 1917; student U. of Chicago, 1897-98; m. Blanche Smith, Jan. 1, 1896; 1 son, Wm. Guthrie. Ordained ministry M.E. Ch.; was prof. Greek lang. and lit., and dean and registrar, Ia. Wesleyan U. (now coll.); pastor First Ch., Springfield, Ill., 1909-14, Urbana, 1915-16, Grace Ch., Bloomington, 1917-19; prof. English Bible, Ill. Wesleyan U., 1919—. Author: Gospel in Miniature, 1903. Home: Bloomington, Ill. Died Mar. 27, 1934.

PIERSOL, George Arthur, physician; b. Phila., Pa., May 17, 1856; s. Jeremiah M. and Minna (Elliger) P.; C.E., Poly. Coll. of Pa., 1874; M.D., U. of Pa., 1877; m. Florence Lukens Reeder, 1898. Prof. anatomy, med. dept., Univ. of Pa., 1891-1921 (emeritus). Fellow Coll. Physicians of Phila. Editor: Human Anatomy, 1907. Home: Philadelphia, Pa. Died Aug. 7, 1924.

PIERSON, Arthur Tappan, editor; b. New York, N.Y., Mar. 6, 1837; s. Stephen H. and Sally Ann (Wheeler) P.; A.B., Hamilton Coll., 1857, A.M., 1860; grad. Union Theol. Sem., 1860, (D.D., Knox Coll., 1874); m. Sarah Frances Benedict, July 12, 1860; father of Delavan Leonard P. Ordained Presbyn. ministry, 1860; pastor W. Winsted, Conn., 1860, Binghamton, N.Y., 1860-63; stated supply Norwalk, Conn., and Troy, N.Y., 1863; pastor Waterford, N.Y., 1863-69, Second Ch., Detroit, 1869-82, Second Ch., Indianapolis, 1882-83, Bethany Ch., Phila., 1883-91, Met. Tabernacle, London, 1891-93; editor Missionary Review of the World, 1888—. Lecturer on missions, Rutgers Coll., 1891; Duff lectureship in Scotland, 1892; pastor pro tem Christ Ch., London, 1902-03 and 1907-08; lectures on Bible, Exeter Hall, London, 1904-07. Author: Crises of Missions; Miracles of Missions (4 series); Many Infallible Proofs; In Christ Jesus; Catharine of Siena; George Müller of Bristol; Keys to the Word, 1888; Seven Years in the Sierra Leone, 1899; Forward Movements of the Last Half Century, 1900; Seed Thoughts for Public Speakers, 1901; The Gordian Knot, 1902; The Keswick Convention, 1903; The Bible and Spiritual Criticism, 1906; The Bible and Spiritual Life, 1908. Homes: Brooklyn, and East Northfield, Mass. Died 1911.

PIERSON, Charles Wheeler, lawyer; b. Florida, N.Y., May 3, 1864; s. George Wilson and Sarah (Wheeler) P.; B.A., Yale, 1886, M.A., 1888; m. Elizabeth G. Groesbeck, 1903; children—George Wilson, John H. G. Admitted to N.Y. bar, 1889, and began practice in N.Y. City; with Alexander & Green, 1900—, as mem. of firm and later as counsel. Republican. Presbyn. Author: Our Changing Constitution, 1922; Introduction to The Federalist, 1923. Home: New York, N.Y. Died May 4, 1934.

PIERSON, Delavan Leonard, editor; b. Waterford, N.Y., Oct. 27, 1867; s. Arthur Tappan and Sarah Frances (Benedict) P.; A.B., Princeton, 1890, A.M., 1894; grad. Princeton Theol. Sem., 1894; m. Emma Belle Dougherty, Feb. 13, 1895 (died 1937). Engaged in editorial work, 1884—, mng. editor Missionary Review of the World, 1891-1911, editor-in-chief, 1911—; editor Northfield Echoes, 1894-1904; regular editorial writer for Record of Christian Work, 1905-25, Bible To-Day, Sunday School Times, 1907-35; pres. Christian Stewardship Fund, Inc. Author: For Each New Day, 1896; Pacific Islanders, 1906; A Spiritual Warrior—Life of Arthur T. Pierson, 1912; Why Believe It?, 1928. Home: Montclair, N.J. Died July 11, 1938.

PIERSON, Isaac, clergyman; b. Orange, N.J., Aug. 11, 1843; s. Aaron and Mary Caroline (Ogden) P.; B.A., Yale, 1866; student Yale Div. Sch., 1866-67; grad. Andover Theol. Sem., 1869; m. Sarah E. Dyer, July 10, 1877 (dec.); m. 2d, Flora J. Hale, Aug. 1, 1884. Ordained Congl. ministry, 1870; pastor Harwich Port, Mass., 1869-70; missionary, A.B.C.F.M., North China Mission, located at Yü-cho and Paoting fu, Chih-li Province, 1870-90; pastor Hamilton, N.Y., 1893-95, Union Ch., Medford, Mass., 1895-1903; field sec. Am. Tract Soc., Nov. 1904—. Clerk of Woburn Conf. Congl. Chs., 1896-1904. Home: Wellesley Hills, Mass. Died July 16, 1919.

PIERSON, Israel Coriell, actuary; b. Westfield, N.J., Aug. 22, 1843; prep. edn. Ft. Edward Inst., New York; A.B., Univ. City of New York, 1865, A.M., 1868, Ph.D., 1890. Consulting actuary and ins. journalist. Fellow New York Math. Society. Home: Plainfield, N.J. Died 1908.

PIERSON, J(ohn) Fred, soldier; b. N.Y. City, Feb. 25, 1839; s. Henry L. and Helen Maria P.; seventh in descent from Abraham Pierson, 1st pres. of Yale; acad. edn.; m. S. Augusta Rhodes, Dec. 16, 1869. Enlisted, 1857, pvt. Co. K, 7th Regt. N.Y.N.G.; attached to staff Brig. Gen. William Hall; promoted through grades 1st N.Y. Vol. Inf. to col., Oct. 9, 1862; bvtd. brig. gen., Mar. 13, 1865, "for gallant and meritorious services"; was attached to Army of Potomac; fought in most battles of that army; wounded and horse killed at Glendale; shot through chest at Chancellorsville; taken prisoner at Bristol Sta.; confined in Libby Prison. Was pres. Ramapo Foundry & Wheel Works, Ramapo Mfg. Co., New York Stamping Co., Pierson & Co., Inc. Republican. Home: New York, N.Y. Died Dec. 20, 1932.

PIERSON, Romaine, editor, pub.; b. Union Springs, N.Y., Dec. 2, 1868; s. Jesse B. and Delia (Mandeville) P.; desc. Abraham Pierson, 1st pres. Yale U.; ed. pub. sch., Union Springs, and Friends Sem. (Quaker) to 1888; m. Caroline Robinson, Sept. 11, 1918. Began in retail drug business, 1888; bought an interest in Am. Druggist, 1896, also New York Med. Jour., serving as sec. of latter 16 yrs.; propr. mng. editor and pub. The Practical Druggist, 1910—; pres. The Med. Times Co. and pub. Med. Times Mag., 1911—; mgr. Romaine Pierson, advertising. Mason. Republican. Presbyn.; elder Central Ch., New York. Home: New York, N.Y. Deceased.

PIERSON, William, surgeon; b. Orange, N.J., Nov. 20, 1830; private edn.; grad. (med. dept.) Univ. of New York, 1852 (A.M., Princeton); practices at Orange; specialist in surgery; m. Isabel F., d. B. F. Adams, of Chicago, May 14, 1856. Sec. N.J. State Med. Soc., 1856—; has held several hospital appointments; surgeon bd. of enrollment, 4th congressional dist., N.J., during Civil war; also volunteer surgeon on governor's staff, filling several assignments on battlefields. Home: Orange, N.J. Died 1900.

PIERSON, William, judge; b. Gilmer, Tex., Mar. 12, 1871; s. Marshall Samuel and Roxana (Ryan) P.; B.Litt. and B.O., Baylor U., 1896; LL.B., U. of Tex., 1898; m. Lena Haskell, July 9, 1901; children—William Haskell, Alice Lenore, Howard Meritt. Admitted to Tex. bar, 1898, and began practice at Greenville; practiced with T. D. Montrose 2 yrs. and with T. D. Starnes 4 yrs.; mem. Tex. Ho. of Rep., 1901, 03; judge Dist. Court, 8th Jud. Dist. of Tex., 1913-21; asso. justice Supreme Court of Texas, 1921—. Introduced and secured the passage of bill in Tex. legislature establishing Coll. of Industrial Arts at Denton, Tex.; a leader in fight to secure passage of bill remitting state taxes of Galveston County to City of Galveston for building the sea wall; as judge 8th Jud. Dist. tried 7 brewery cases brought by State of Tex., which had distinct influence in Tex. and U.S. on the prohibition issue. Democrat. Baptist; formerly mem. exec. bd. Bapt. Gen. Conv. of Tex. and trustee Burlson Coll. Mason, Odd Fellow, K.P., Woodman, etc. Home: Austin, Tex. Died Apr. 24, 1935.

PIETERS, Adrian John, agronomist; b. Alto, Wis., Nov. 18, 1866; s. Roelof and Hendrika (Van Zwaluwenburg) P.; B.S., U. of Mich., 1894, Ph.D., 1915; traveled and studied in Germany, 1910-12; m. Hattie May Bailey, June 30, 1896 (died 1935); m. 2d, Mary R. Burr, 1936. Botanist in charge of seed and plant introduction and distribution, U.S. Dept. Agr., 1900-06; seed grower, 1906-10; instr. botany, U. of Mich., 1912-15; agronomist with U.S. Dept. Agr., 1915-38, principal agronomist to 1938, retired. Fellow Am. Soc. Agronomy, A.A.A.S. Home: Takoma Park, D.C. Died Apr. 25, 1940.

PIETERS, Aleida Johanna, teacher; b. Holland, Mich., Oct. 31, 1876; d. Roelof and Hendrika (Van Zwaluwenburg) P.; prep. edn., Hope Coll., Holland, Mich.; student Milwaukee-Downer Coll., 1895-97; grad. State Normal Sch., Ypsilanti, Mich., 1903; A.B., U. of Mich., 1908; A.M., Ph.D., Columbia, 1923. Began teaching in rural sch., Drenthe, Mich., 1894; dean Milwaukee-Downer Coll., Milwaukee, Wis., 1921—. Presbyn. Author: A Dutch Settlement in Michigan, 1923. Died Apr. 6, 1936.

PIETRO, Cartaino di Sciarrino (C. S. Pietro), sculptor; b. Palmero, Italy, Dec. 25, 1886; s. Salvatore and Marianna (Sciarrino) Cartaino; studied in Rome; won scholarship in Palermo; mainly self-taught; m. Stella Cartaino, of Palermo, Italy, 1916. Came to U.S., 1911. Hon. mention Panama P.I. Expn., 1915. Prin. works: "The Mother of the Dead"; "Inspiration" (group); Audubon statue, Scranton, Pa.; marble fountain, Court House, Hackensack, N.J.; (busts) John Burroughs, for Am. Mus. Natural Hisory; Elihu Root, Hamilton Coll., N.Y., also for Pan-Am. Union, Washington, D.C.; John Muir, U. of Wis.; Prof. Charles S. Sergeant, Am. Mus. Natural History; Hon. William H. Taft, Peace Palace, The Hague; J. Pierpont Morgan; Alfred Gwynn Vanderbilt, Mrs. Vanderbilt and family of 2 children; (group) Mrs. Finley J. Shepard and the Misses Dorothy and Helen Gould; Gen. William Booth. Memorial Coll., Phila.; etc. Represented in Toledo Art Mus., Albright Art Galleries (Buffalo, N.Y.), Boston Art Mus. Chmn. "Friends of the Young Artist" (soc.); mem. Soc. des Beaux Arts et des Lettres, Boston Art Club. Home: Pelham, N.Y. Died Oct. 9, 1918.

PIETSCH, Karl, philologist; b. Stettin, Germany, Jan. 4, 1860; s. Carl and Marie (Neumann) P.; U. of Berlin, 1879-82, Florence, Italy, 1882-84, U. of Halle, 1886-87, Ph.D., 1887; m. Elisabeth Jäntsch, of Berlin, Germany, May 1890. Asst. librarian, Newberry Library, Chicago, 1890-96; instr. Romance philology, 1896-1900, asst. prof., 1900-01, asso. prof., 1901-10, prof. 1910—, U. of Chicago. Author: Two Old Spanish Versions of the Disticha Catonis, 1902. Died Apr. 1, 1930.

PIETSCH, Theodore Wells, architect; b. Chicago, Ill., Oct. 2, 1868; s. Charles Francis and Florence Augusta (Wells) P.; student Mass. Inst. Tech., 1885-89, École des Beaux Arts (Paris), 1892-98; m. Gertrude Zell, Nov. 7, 1911; children—Theodore Wells, John Oliver Carroll, Robert Brooke. Diploma from French govt., 1897; hon. mention in Salon (Paris), 1898. In practice at Baltimore, 1904—. Prin. works: Eastern High Sch., Zion Ch., U.S. Fidelity and Guaranty Co. Bldg., Assn. of Commerce Bldg., Jackson Place Sch., all in Baltimore; Md. House of Correction, Jessup; residence of Dr. E. G. Marr, Blythewood, Baltimore. Instr. in French to officers of 316th Regt., Camp Meade, Md., 1917-18. Awarded 2 medals in architecture, École des Beaux Arts. Asso. Am. Inst. Architects. Democrat. Catholic. Home: Baltimore, Md. Died Jan. 1930.

PIEZ, Charles, engineer; b. (of naturalized Am. parents) Mayence, Germany, Sept. 24, 1866; s. P. Jacob and Catherine (Liebig) P.; E.M., School of Mines (Columbia), 1889; hon. Dr. Commercial Science, U. of New York, 1920; m. Mrs. Laura Sadler Cocke, 1922. Entered engring. dept. of Link Belt Co., mfrs. elevating and conveying machinery, at Phila., 1889, and became successively chief engr., gen. supt., gen. mgr., and pres., chmn. bd.; dir. Drexel State Bank. V.p. and gen. mgr. Emergency Fleet Corp., 1917-18, dir. gen., Dec. 1918-May 1919. Chmn. Ill. Workmen's Compensation Commn., 1911; pres. Ill. Mfrs.' Assn., 1911-13, 1924-25. Republican. Home: Chicago, Ill. Died Oct. 2, 1933.

PIFFARD, Henry Granger, physician; b. Piffard, N.Y., Sept. 10, 1842; s. David and Ann Matilda (Haight) P.; A.B., New York U., 1862, A.M., 1865; M.D., Coll. Phys. and Surg. (Columbia), 1864; LL.D., New York U., 1899; m. Helen Hart Strong, June 17, 1868. Interne, Bellevue and City hosps., 1864-65; surgeon bvt. maj. 71st Regt. N.G.S.N.Y., 1867-68; lecturer urinary analysis, 1873-74, prof. dermatology, 1875-99, emeritus prof., 1899. New York U.; surgeon, 1871-96, consulting surgeon, 1896—, City Hosp., New York, N.Y. Author: A Guide to Urinary Analysis, 1873; Elementary Treatise on Diseases of the Skin, 1871; Cutaneous Memoranda, 1877; Materia Medica, and Therapeutics of the Skin, 1881; Modern Treatment of Eczema, 1886; Practical Treatise on Diseases of the Skin, 1891. Died 1910.

PIGMAN, George Wood, rear admiral U.S.N.; b. Delphi, Ind., Dec. 19, 1843; s. George W. and Caroline (Swarmstead) P.; apptd. to U.S.N., Sept. 28, 1861, Naval Acad., 1861-64; m. Lillie C. Howard, Nov. 7, 1871. Served on steam sloop Brooklyn, flagship Brazil Squadron, 1866-67; promoted master, Dec. 1, 1866; lt., Mar. 12, 1868; lt. comdr., Oct. 28, 1869; comdr., Oct. 12, 1886; capt., Mar. 3, 1899; rear admiral, Oct. 4, 1904. Served on various duties; comd. Alliance, 1888-89, Bennington, 1895-97, Wabash, 1901-04; retired, Jan. 11, 1905. Home: Takoma Park, Md. Died June 30, 1920.

PIKE, Clayton Warren, consulting elec. engr.; b. Fryeburg, Me., July 11, 1866; s. Cassius W. and Abbie J. (Barker) P.; ed. Fryeburg Acad.; Mass. Inst. Tech., 1886-89; m. Margaret E. Rattoo, June 30, 1909; children—Helen Margaret, John Clayton (dec.). Elec. engr., Merrimack Mfg. Co., Lowell, Mass., 1889-90; instr. elec. engring., U. of Pa., 1890-92; elec. engr., Queen Co., Inc., Phila., 1893-94, Falkenau Engring. Co., 1894-1900; v.p. and gen. mgr. Keller-Pike Co., Phila., 1900-11; chief of Elec. Bur., Phila., 1912—; cons. engr. City of Pittsburgh, 1919, Pub. Improvement Commn., Baltimore, 1922, Phila. Rapid Transit Co., 1923—, Ambassador Bridge (Detroit to Can.), 1929, Public Service Commission of New Hampshire, 1930, State Tax Commn. of N.H., 1931, Power Authority of State of N.Y., 1931. Mem. Park Commn., Fryeburg, Me., 1933. Trustee Fryeburg Acad. Republican. Author: Roper's Engineers' Handbook (joint author), 1899; Questions and Answers for Engineers, 1901. Commd. maj. Ordnance Dept. U.S.A., 1918; chief statis. sect., 1919. Home: Fryeburg, Me. Died Dec. 30, 1938.

PIKE, Robert Gordon, judge; b. Rollinsford, N.H., July 28, 1851; s. Amos W. and Elizabeth M. (Chadbourne) P.; B.S., Dartmouth, 1872, hon. A.M., 1908. Admitted to bar, 1881; city solicitor Dover, N.H., 1887-89; judge of probate Strafford Co., N.H., 1893-96; asso. justice Supreme Ct. of N.H., 1896-1901; asso. justice Superior Ct. of N.H., 1901-13, chief justice, 1913—. Republican. Trustee Berwick Acad., 1900-14; visitor Chandler Foundation of Dartmouth Coll., 1902. Died Jan. 19, 1917.

PIKE, William John, consul; b. Scranton, Pa., Mar. 24, 1864; s. John and Mary J. (Clark) P.; grad. Del. Lit. Inst., 1884; Law Sch., Columbian (now George Washington) U., 2 yrs.; unmarried. Publisher and editor weekly paper in northern Pa. until 1889; law clk. U.S. Census Bur., Washington, 1889-93; clk. Com. on Edn., U.S. Ho. of Rep., 1893-1902, also pvt. sec. former Speaker Galusha A. Grow, of Pa.; entered Am. consular service, Apr. 1903; consul at Zittau, Germany, 1903-06; v.consul at Reichenberg, Bohemia, July 4-Dec. 1, 1906; consul at Kehl, 1906-10, Reichenberg, 1910-14; consul gen. at Coburg, Germany, 1914-16; consul at St. Gall, Switzerland, 1916-20, Strassburg, France, 1920—. Mason. Home: Hallstead, Pa. Died Apr. 23, 1923.

PILCHER, James Evelyn, surgeon; b. Adrian, Mich., Mar. 18, 1857; s. Elijah Holmes (D.D., LL.D.) and Phebe Maria (Fisk) P.; A.B., U. of Mich., 1879; M.D., L.I. Coll. Hosp., 1880; A.M., Ph.D., Ill. Wesleyan U., 1887; L.H.D., Allegheny Coll., 1902; m. Mina Adela Parker, June 5, 1883. Asst. surgeon U.S.A., Dec. 3, 1883; capt. asst. surgeon, Dec. 3, 1888; maj. brigade surgeon U.S.V., June 4, 1898; retired, Oct. 31, 1900. Prof. mil. surgery, Ohio Med. U., 1896-98; lecturer on mil. hygiene, Starling Med. Coll., 1896; prof. mil. surgery, Creighton U., 1898-99; prof. anatomy and embryology, 1899-1900, sociology and economics, 1900-03, Dickinson Coll.; prof. med. jurisprudence, Dickinson Sch. of Law, 1899-1909. Mng. editor Annals Anatomy and Surgery, 1881-83, office editor Annals of Surgery, 1887-89; editor health dept. New York Christian Advocate, 1887-95; asso. editor Columbus Medical Journal, 1896-99; editor publs. Assn. Mil. Surgeons U.S., 1897-99 and 1901—. Enno Sander prize essayist, 1906; editor The Military Surgeon, 1901-09. Hon. mem. Am. Med. Editors' Assn. (pres. 1906); fellow Am. Acad. Medicine. Author: First Aid in Illness and Injury, 1892; Life and Labors of Elijah Holmes Pilcher, 1893; Columbus Book of the Military Surgeons, 1897; The Arms and Seals of the State of Pennsylvania (State Doc.), 1902; The Surgeon Generals of the Army, 1905. Died 1911.

PILCHER, Lewis Frederick, architect; b. Brooklyn, N.Y.; s. Lewis Stephen and Martha S. (Phillips) P.; Ph.B., Sch. of Architecture (Columbia), 1895; LL.D., U. of Colo., 1910. In practice in New York, N.J., Pa.; state architect, N.Y., 1913-23; commr. of sites, N.Y., 1913-23, commr. new prisons, 1916-23, mil. hosps., 1920-21, Hosp. Development Commn., 1917-23; cons. architect U.S. Veterans' Bur., 1923-25; prof. art, Vassar Coll., 1900-11; vice dean Sch. of Fine Arts, and asso. prof. architecture, U. of Pa., 1926-29; prof. architecture, Pa. State Coll., 1929-37;

institutional consultant Pa. State Authority, 1937-38; administrator P.W.A. school program, Depts. Pub. Instruction, Pa., 1935. Architect Squadron C Armory, Brooklyn; First Baptist Church, Montclair, N.J.; Gratz Coll., Phila.; Mikveh Israel Synagogue, Phila.; Terminal Dormitory, Vassar College; Realty Underwriters Building, Louisville, Ky.; Haviland Bldg., New York; Dropsie Coll., Phila.; 1st Ch. of Christ, Scientist, Glens Falls, N.Y.; armory for 8th Regt. and for 1st Cavalry, New York; architect to War Dept. in charge installations at 9th, 13th and 8th coast arty. districts, etc.; also architect for Sing Sing Prison, Wingdale (N.Y.) Prison, Cornell U. Drill Hall; armories Squadron A, Manhattan, at Buffalo, Rochester, Albany, Orleans and Troy—all of N.Y.; cons. architect to New York City for the County Court House; advisory architect to Capital Issues Commn., 1918, and Holland Tunnel. Cons. architect on hosps. of N.J. and Insular Prison, Puerto Rico; city planner, Camden, N.J., and cons. architect on Court House, City Hall and Bus Terminal. Mem. A.I.A. Author: Historic Types of Architecture. Am. editor in architecture for Allgemeines Lexikon Bildenden Kunstler; editor in architecture, Encyclopædia Americana. Died June 14, 1941.

PILCHER, Lewis Stephen, surgeon and editor; b. Adrian, Mich., July 28, 1845; s. of Elijah Holmes (D.D., LL.D.) and Phebe Maria (Fisk) P.; A.B., U. of Mich., 1862, A.M., 1863, M.D., 1866, LL.D., 1900; LL.D., Dickinson Coll., Carlisle, Pa., 1900; m. Martha S. Phillips, June 22, 1870. Hosp. steward U.S.A., 1864-65; asst. surgeon U.S.N., 1867-72; adj. prof. anatomy, L.I. Coll. Hosp., 1879-83; prof. surgery, New York Post-Grad. Med. Sch., 1885-95; surgeon M.E. Hosp., 1887-1907, German Hosp. Brooklyn, 1900-08, Pilcher Pvt. Hosp., 1910-18. Mem. Bd. Med. Examiners State of N.Y., 1913-28. Fellow Am. Surg. Assn.; asso. fellow Coll. Physicians Phila.; hon. fellow Am. Coll. Surgeons. Surgeon gen. G.A.R., 1915; comdr. in chief G.A.R., 1921-22. Editor Annals of Surgery, 1885—. Author: Treatment of Wounds, 1883. Part Author: American Text-Book of Surgery, 1890; Dennis' System of Surgery, 1895; International Text-Book of Surgery, 1900; Ochsner Surgical Diagnosis and Treatment, 1921; A Surgical Pilgrim's Progress. Died Dec. 24, 1934.

PILES, Samuel Henry, diplomat; b. Livingston County, Ky., Dec. 28, 1858; s. S. H. and Gabriella (Lilliard) P.; ed. pvt. schs., Smithland, Ky.; m. Mary E. Barnard, Sept. 15, 1891 (died 1913); children—Ross Barnard, Ruth Lilliard (Mrs. William McCausland, Jr.), Samuel H., Jr. Began practice of law at Snohomish City, Washington Ty., 1883; moved to Seattle, 1886; gen. counsel The Pacific Coast Co., 1895-1905; city atty., Seattle, 1887-89; asst. dist. atty. for counties of King, Kitsap and Snohomish, Wash. Ty., in '80s; active in politics for 20 yrs. before his election to Senate; U.S. senator, 1905-11; apptd. E.E. and M.P. to Colombia, 1922, resigned Sept. 1928; spl. ambassador for Colombian presdl. inauguration, Aug. 7, 1926. Republican. Died Mar. 11, 1940.

PILLARS, Charles Adrian, sculptor; b. Rantoul, Ill., July 4, 1870; s. John Adrian and Ella Lee (More) P.; student U. of Illinois; served as pupil and assistant of Lorado Taft 9 yrs.; student life classes of Art Inst. Chicago; m. Ruth Elizabeth Zaring; children—Charles Adrian II, Ruth Elizabeth, Ella Antoinette. Engaged upon colossal sculpture, "The Republic," and equestrian group of Columbus Quadrigæ, Chicago Expn., 18 mos., 1891-92, under Daniel French and E. C. Potter. Winner in open competition for $10,000 each, heroic statue in Greek marble, of Dr. John Gorrie, and heroic bronze statue of Edmund Kirby Smith, C.S.A. for State of Fla., both in Hall of Fame, Washington, D.C.; executed memorial flagstaff standard (bronze), St. Augustine, 1920; Bronze Group, "Citizens Memorial" for Jacksonville, 1924; heroic statue of W. B. Barnett, Jacksonville, 1929; Spivey Memorial, Lakeland, Fla. Mason. Instr. in sculpture, Ringling Sch. of Art, Sarasota, Fla. Home: Sarasota, Fla. Died June 21, 1937.

PILLSBURY, Albert Enoch, lawyer; b. Milford, N.H., Aug. 19, 1849; s. Josiah Webster and Elizabeth (Dinsmoor) P.; grad. Lawrence Acad., Groton, Mass., 1867; student Harvard U., 1867-69, hon. A.M., 1891; LL.D., Howard U., 1913, Boston U., 1929; married; 2 children. Admitted to Mass. bar, 1870; practiced at Boston, 1871—. Mem. Mass. Ho. of Rep., 1876, 77, 78, Senate, 1884, 85, 86 (pres. 1885, 86); atty. gen. of Mass., 1891-94; lecturer on constl. law, Boston U. Law Sch., 1896—. Vice chmn. United States Trust Co.; v.p. Franklin Savings Bank; trustee Lawrence Acad. (pres. bd.). Author: Daniel Webster the Orator, 1903; Lincoln and Slavery, 1913. Chmn. com. on jud. procedure, Mass. Constl. Conv., 1917; received, 1921, thanks of N.H. legislature for donation of forest lands to the State. Home: West Newton, Mass. Died Dec. 23, 1930.

PILLSBURY, Arthur Judson; b. Londonderry, N.H., Jan. 31, 1854; s. Josiah Hobart and Frances Alnora (Pervier) P.; student Kan. State Agrl. Coll. 1 yr., 1871-72; m. De Etta Warren, Sept. 15, 1881; 1 son, Warren Hobart. Admitted to Kan. bar, but took up newspaper work and pub. Tulare Register, 1883-1903; editorial writer, Oakland (Calif.) Herald, 1903-04; sec. State Bd. Examiners, Calif., 1904-07; editor Sacramento Union, 1907-08; founder The California Weekly, organ of Progressive Republicans, and editor same until it was merged with Los Angeles Outlook into California Outlook, 1911; mem. Industrial Commn. of Calif., 1911-23. Unitarian. Home: Berkeley, Calif. Died Apr. 1, 1937.

PILLSBURY, Charles Alfred, flour miller; b. Warner, N.H., Oct. 3, 1842; grad. Dartmouth, 1863; clerk and partner in commercial house, Montreal, P.Q., 1863-69; at Minneapolis, 1869—; became clerk, and later partner, with his uncle, John S. Pillsbury in flour mill; introduced roller process and enlarged the business. Founded, 1872, firm of Charles A. Pillsbury & Co., which built largest mills in the world, selling them, 1889, to an English syndicate, which also bought other mills, organizing The Pillsbury-Washburn Flour Mills Co., of which he was pres.; also pres. Minneapolis and Northern Elevator Co., owning elevators through the Northwestern grain region. Was State senator, 1877-87. Republican. Died 1899.

PILLSBURY, Charles Stinson; b. Minneapolis, Minn., Dec. 6, 1878; s. Charles Alfred and Mary Ann (Stinson) P.; B.S., U. of Minn., 1900; m. Nellie Pendleton Winston, Dec. 7, 1901; children—Philip Winston, Mary Stinson, Katharine Stevens, Helen Winston. Started in flour business, 1900; later traveled extensively; returned to business, 1908; dir. Pillsbury Flour Mills Co. (operating 12 mills with total capacity of 40,000 barrels daily), 1909—; pres. Sargent Land Co., Keewatin Mining Co.; v.p. Sutton Land Co., Meriden Iron Co.; dir. Kearsarge Land Co., Munsingwear Corp., Vassar Co.; dir. Wayne Knitting Co., Ft. Wayne, Ind.; sec.-treas. Pillsbury Lumber Co.; dir. M.,St.P.&S.S.M. R.R. Conglist. Republican. Trustee of Pillsbury Social Settlement Assn.; dir. Minneapolis Symphony Orchestral Assn. Home: Wayzata, Minn. Died May 21, 1939.

PILLSBURY, Harry N., chess player; b. Boston, Dec. 5, 1872; s. L. D. P.; early evinced a taste for mathematics; learned chess at 16 and soon developed genius in the game; played Champion Steinitz in Boston, Apr. 1892, and won 2 games out of 3, with odds of pawn and move in his favor; defeated all leading Am. experts; won world's championship at Hastings Internat. Chess Congress, Eng., Sept. 1795; 1st Am. champion since Paul Morphy, in 1858, then played in leading tournaments in U.S. and Europe; m. M. E., d. Judge Albert J. Bush, Chicago, Feb. 17, 1901. Died 1906.

PILLSBURY, Horace Davis, lawyer; b. Stockton, Calif., Oct. 9, 1873; s. Evans Searle and Estelle (Davis) P.; A.B., Harvard, 1895; m. Elizabeth Taylor, May 4, 1898; children—Olivia (Mrs. W. E. Graham), Evans S., Taylor, Margaret (Mrs. Frederick W. Coleman, III). Admitted to Calif. bar, 1898; with legal dept. Pacific Telephone & Telegraph Co., until 1925, pres. of company, 1925-35, chmn. bd., 1935—; also chmn. Southern Calif. Telephone Co.; dir. Equitable Life Assurance Soc. of U.S., Bank of California, North America, Fireman's Fund Indemnity Co., Crown Willamette Paper Co. Mem. law firm of Pillsbury, Madison & Sutro. Republican. Episcopalian. Home: San Francisco, Calif. Died Jan. 18, 1940.

PILLSBURY, John Elliott, rear admiral U.S.N.; b. Lowell, Mass., Dec. 15, 1846; s. John Gilman and Elizabeth (Wimble) P.; grad. U.S. Naval Acad., 1867; m. Florence Greenwood Aitchison, 1873. Promoted through grades to rear admiral, July 4, 1908. Served on various duties and stas., including 1 yr. in Hydrographic Office and 10 yrs. in coast survey service; comd. Coast Survey Steamer Blake, 1884-91, investigating Gulf Stream currents by anchoring the Blake in the Stream and observing the current (by means of an instrument of his invention) at various depths below surface; established position of axis of the stream in Straits of Florida and off Cape Hatteras and determined many of the laws by which its flow is governed; comd. dynamite cruiser Vesuvius off Santiago during Spanish-Am. War; afterward stationed at Boston Navy Yard, in charge of the equipment dept.; comd. U.S.S. Prairie, 1901-02; afterward on duty in Washington as mem. Gen. Bd. and asst. to chief of Bur. of Navigation, and in 1905 chief of staff North Atlantic Fleet; chief Bur. Navigation, 1908-09; retired, Dec. 15, 1908; relieved from active duty, July 1909. Died Dec. 30, 1919.

PILLSBURY, John Henry, educator; b. 77 Limington, Me., Dec. 20, 1846; s. William Cobb and Nancy (Frost) P.; grad. Wesleyan U., 1874, A.M., 1877; m. Sarah Ellen, d. Prof. Francis Asbury and Sarah (Nickerson) Robinson, of Kent's Hill, Me., Aug. 7, 1878. Ordained M.E. ministry, in Me. Conf., 1870; pastor Raymond, Me., 1868-69, Kennebunk, Me., 1869-70; taught Wilbraham Acad., 1874-75; asst. in natural history, Wesleyan U., 1875-77; instr. natural science, Springfield (Mass.) High Sch., 1877-84; prof. biology, Smith Coll., 1884-92; lecturer univ. extension, 1893-94; pastor Malden, Stoneham, and Dedham, Mass., 1894-99; prin. Waban (Mass.) Sch., 1899. Fellow Am. Acad. Arts and Sciences, A.A.A.S.; original mem. Am. Soc. Naturalists. Author: Elementary Manual of Biology, 1893; Descriptive Botanical Blanks and Synopsis of Botanical Terms, 1885. Died 1910.

PILLSBURY, John Sargent, flour miller, gov.; b. Sutton, N.H., July 29, 1828; followed several pursuits in New England until 1855; established, 1855, at Falls of St. Anthony, a hardware store, which burned, 1857; m. Mahala Fisk, Nov. 3, 1856. Engaged in flour milling, becoming, 1872, partner in Charles A. Pillsbury & Co. Built and presented the Town Hall, 1893, to Sutton, N.H., his native town; built and presented a Girls' Home to the City of Minneapolis, 1901; presented library bldg. to E. Minneapolis, 1900. Regent Univ. of Minn., 1863; State senator, 1864-76; gov. Minn., 1876-82; prevented repudiation by adjustment of State Railroad bonds. Built Science Hall and presented it to Univ. of Minn., 1889; by legislative act made life regent, Univ. of Minn., 1897. Died 1901.

PILLSBURY, Rosecrans W., lawyer, pub., mfr.; b. Londonderry, N.H., Sept. 18, 1863; s. Col. William S. and Sarah A. (Crowell) P.; Pinkerton Acad. and Manchester High Sch.; B.S., Dartmouth Coll., class of 1885; studied law, Boston Law Sch., and in office of Judge Robert J. Peaslee, Manchester, N.H.; m. Annie E. Watts, Dec. 10, 1885 (died 1911); children—Mrs. Maria Hawkes, Horace Watts, Mrs. Dorothy Bartlett; m. 2d, Harriet Ferguson Valentine, 1913. Admitted to N.H. bar, 1890, also to Fla. bar, but devoted time to business rather than law; mgr. W. S. & R. W. Pillsbury, oldest shoe factory in N.H.; owner and mgr. 300-acre farm; treas. Union Pub. Co., props. Manchester Union; pres. First Nat. Bank of Derry; dir. Greene Consolidated Copper Co., Manchester Nat. Bank, Shoe and Leather Assn., Boston; treas. Nutfield Savings Bank; pres. Manchester Mirror Co., pub. morning and evening Mirror and American, 1918—. Trustee N.H. Coll. Agr. and Mechanic Arts. Del. State Constl. convs., 1887, 1902, 11, 18; mem. N.H. Ho. of Rep., 1897-1899, 1905, 11; del. Rep. Nat. Conv., Chicago, 1904, and mem. com. to notify Mr. Roosevelt of his nomination as President; mem. bd. visitory U.S. Naval Acad., 1912. Dem. candidate for Congress, 1920. Mason. Elk. Home: Londonderry, N.H. Deceased.

PINCHBACK, Pinckney Benton Stewart, lawyer; b. Macon, Ga., May 10, 1837; of African descent; s. William and Eliza (Stewart) P.; common sch. edn., Cincinnati; m. Nina Hethorn, 1860. In Union Army, 1862-63, as capt. Co. A, 2d La. Native Guards; delegate to Reconstruction Conv., La., 1867; mem. La. senate, 1868-71; pres. pro tem. of State Senate and lt. gov., 1871-72; acting gov., 1872. Elected to Congress, Nov. 1872, from La.; 2 legislatures sat in following Jan., and he was named by one for U.S. senator for term beginning Mar. 4, 1873; the seat was contested and decided against him, Mar. 8, 1876; del. La. Constl. Conv., 1879; surveyor of customs, New Orleans, 1882. Then engaged in law practice. Del. to all Rep. Nat. Convs., 1868—. Died Dec. 21, 1921.

PINCHOT, James W., merchant; b. Milford, Pa., 1831; s. Cyril C. D. and Eliza Cross P.; ed. pvt. schs.; hon. A.M., Yale, 1905; m. Mary Eno, 1864. Went to New York in 1850. Established in business many yrs., retiring in 1875. Was 1st treas. and mem. of exec. com. for Bartholdi Statue of Liberty. Mem. Chamber Commerce. Interested in art, and one of early subscribers to Met. Mus. Art; later interested in forestry; one of founders Yale Forest Sch., New Haven, Conn.; founder Yale Summer Sch. of Forestry, Milford, Pa., and of Milford Forest Expt. Sta. Vice pres. Am. Forestry Assn. Died 1908.

PINCKNEY, Charles Cotesworth, P.E. clergyman; b. Charleston, S.C., July 31, 1812; grad. Coll. Charleston, 1831, D.D., 1870, LL.D., 1895; studied at Alexandria, Va., Theol. Sem.; rector St. James, Santee, Ga., 1835-38; Christ Ch., Greenville, Ga., 1838-50; rector Grace Ch., Charlestown, S.C., 1850—; was pres. bd. trustees Charleston Coll.; delegate to P.E. general convs., 1859-91. Author: Life of Gen. Thomas Pinckney (his grandfather). Died 1899.

PINCKNEY, Merritt Willis, judge; b. Mt. Morris, Ill., Dec. 12, 1859; s. Daniel J. and Margaret C. (Hitt) P.; B.S., Knox Coll., 1881, LL.D., 1913; LL.B., Union Coll. of Law, 1883 (valedictorian); m. Mary Van Vechten, July 24, 1885. Admitted to Ill. bar, 1883; partner with William H. Tatge, 1884-93; associated with Gustavus J. Tatge, firm of Pinckney & Tatge, subsequently Pinckney, Tatge & Abbott, until 1905; judge Circuit Court of Cook County, 1905— (judge of Juvenile Court, 1908-16). Republican. Home: Chicago, Ill. Died 1920.

PINDALL, Xenophon Overton, lawyer; b. Monroe Co., Mo., Aug. 21, 1873; s. L. A. and Nora (Snell) P.; student Central Coll., Mo.; B.L., U. of Ark., 1896; m. Mae Ruth Quelling, Sept. 15, 1902. Began practice at Arkansas City, Ark.; mem. Ark. Ho. of Rep., 1902-06; received largest popular vote of any candidate for atty. gen. of Ark., 1906, but was defeated in delegated conv.; elected to State Senate from 17th Dist., 1907; elected pres. of Senate, May 1907, and on account of inability of Gov. John S.

Little to serve, eleced as gov., May 1907-Jan. 1909; engaged in practice at Little Rock and Arkansas City. Democrat. Mem. Christian (Disciples) Ch. Mason. Home: Arkansas City, Ark. Died Jan. 2, 1935.

PINDELL, Henry Means, editor; b. St. Joseph, Mo., Dec. 23, 1860; s. James Morrison and Elizabeth (Means) P.; desc. of early Colonial ancestry; A.B., De Pauw U., 1884; m. Elizabeth Adelia Smith, Oct. 29, 1890. Owner and editor Peoria Evening Journal and Morning Transcript, and has founded several other western newspapers; city treasurer Springfield, Ill., 1887-89; twice nominated by President Wilson as ambassador to Russia, 1913; nomination confirmed by Senate, but declined. Dir. Peoria Public Library. Home: Peoria, Ill. Died Aug. 8, 1924.

PINE, Frank Woodworth, educator; b. Detroit, Oct. 11, 1869; s. Jonathan Parker and Frances Allen (Agnew) P.; A.B., U. of Mich., 1894; A.M., New York U., 1897; studied U. of Chicago, 1905; m. Mabel Edna Durand, July 9, 1901. Teacher, English and history, Manistee (Mich.) High Sch., 1894-95; instr. English, New York U., 1895-97; head of English dept., Hill Sch., Pottstown, Pa., 1898-1912; headmaster Gilman Country School, Roland Park, Md., 1912—. Del. Nat. Conf. on Uniform Entrance Requirements in English, 1916; mem. com. of examiners in English of Coll. Entrance Exam. Bd., 1917, 18. Progressive. Presbyn. Editor: Washington's Farewell Address and Webster's First Bunker Hill Oration (Gateway Series of English Classics), 1911; Franklin's Autobiography, 1912, and 1916; Dickens' Oliver Twist (Macmillan's Pocket Classics), 1917. Home: Roland Park, Md. Died Feb. 3, 1919.

PINE, John B., lawyer; b. Dubuque, Ia., Feb. 2, 1857; s. George W. and Martha A. (Sands) P.; A.B., Columbia Univ., 1877; student Columbia Law School; (L.H.D., Princeton Univ., 1915); m. Caroline Pryor, June 12, 1900. Admitted to bar, and practiced at New York from 1879. Trustee Columbia U., 1890—, and sec. bd. of trustees; mem. Art Commn. City of New York, 1907-09; chmn. Com. on Character, apptd. by Supreme Ct., 1908-09. Trustee and founder Univ. Settlement Society of New York; mgr. St. Luke's Hosp.; trustee Am. Acad. in Rome. Episcopalian. A founder, and editor Columbia University Quarterly, 1897—. Home: New York, N.Y. Died Oct. 28, 1922.

PINGREE, Hazen S., mfr., governor of Mich.; b. Denmark, Me., Aug. 30, 1840; lived on father's farm until 14 years old; then worked in cotton factory, Saco, Me.; afterward in shoe factory, Hopkinton, Mass., where he learned trade of a shoe-cutter. Private in Union army, 1st Mass. heavy art., Aug. 1, 1862, to Aug. 1865, and for about 5 months, in 1864, was a prisoner of war; after war went to Detroit; worked in shoe-factory until 1866, then with C. H. Smith established a very small shoe-factory which they later developed to the largest shoe mfg. business in the West. Was mayor of Detroit, 1889-96, elected 4 times; attained prominence by his successful project of securing vacant lots for the cultivation of potato patches by the poor. Elected gov. of Mich., 1896; re-elected, 1898. Home: Detroit, Mich. Died 1901.

PINGREE, Samuel Everett, governor; b. Salisbury, N.H., Aug. 2, 1832; s. Stephen and Judith (True) P.; A.B., Dartmouth Coll., 1857, A.M., 1867 (LL.D., Norwich University); m. Lydia M. Steele, of Stanstead, Que., Sept. 15, 1869. Pvt. Co. F, 3d Vt. Vols., 1861; 1st lt., 1861; capt., Aug. 1861; maj., Sept. 27, 1862; lt. col., Jan. 15, 1863; awarded Congressional Medal of Honor, "for gallantry at Lee's Mills, Va." (wounded). Admitted to bar, 1859, and began practice at Hartford, Vt. State's atty. Windsor Co., 1868-69; lt. gov. of Vt., 1882-84, gov., 1884-86; chmn. State Ry. Commn., 1886-94. Home: Hartford, Vt. Died June 1, 1922.

PINKERTON, William Allan, principal of Pinkerton's Nat. Detective Agency; b. Dundee, Ill., Apr. 7, 1846; s. Allan P. (noted detective) and Joan (Carfrae) P.; ed. pub. and pvt. schs., and Notre Dame Coll.; entered secret service div. U.S. Army, 1861; m. Margaret S. Ashling, Dec. 14, 1866 (died 1895). Served through Civil War, chiefly in Army of Potomac; became clerk in his father's office; later with his brother, chief asst. in the agency, succeeding to the business on death of Allan Pinkerton, July 1, 1884; operations extended to all parts of the world. Home: Chicago, Ill. Died Dec. 11, 1923.

PINKHAM, Lucius Eugene, governor; b. Chicopee Falls, Mass., Sept. 19, 1850; s. Lucius Moulton and Caroline Smith (Fiske) P.; prepared for Yale, severe injury prevented entering; studied under pvt. tutors; unmarried. Engaged in various lines of business chiefly mfg. and mercantile, in N.E., Chicago, the West, Hawaiian Islands and the Orient. Resident of Honolulu, 1891-94 and from 1898; traveled in Far East, Europe, Siberia, Asia, Japan, Philippines, etc., 1909-13. Pres. Territorial Bd. of Health 2 terms; apptd. gov. H.Ty., in 1913. Democrat. Elk. Died Nov. 2, 1922.

PINNEO, Dotha Stone, librarian; b. Cincinnati; d. of Dr. Timothy Stone and Jeannette (Lindsley) P.; father was author of Pinneo's Grammars and complier of McGuffey's Readers; ed. Greenwich (Conn.) Acad., Dr. Van Norman's Sch. and Rutgers Female College, New York. Librarian, Carnegie Library, Norwalk, Conn., 1896—; originator of entertainment entitled The Story Teller's Hour; lecturer on history, for New York Bd. of Edn., 10 yrs.; sec. Conn. State Fedn. of Women's Clubs, 12 yrs. Originated, 1914, and managed "The Children's Market," the only enterprise of its kind in the country. Name added to honor roll in Gen. Fedn. Women's Clubs, Washington, D.C. Home: Norwalk, Conn. Died Feb. 9, 1924.

PINSON, William Washington, religious work; b. Cheatham Co., Tenn., Apr. 4, 1854; s. William Carroll and Katharine (Nicholson) P.; ed. Charlotte (Tenn.) Acad. and Webb's Sch. for Boys, then at Culleoka, Tenn.; D.D., U. of Georgia, 1899; LL.D., Southern Methodist Univ., 1925; m. Belle B. Murrell, Nov. 30, 1882. Ordained ministry M.E. Church, S., 1878; pastor in Tenn. at Bell Buckle, Winchester, McMinnville, Tracy City and Franklin, in Tex. at Austin, San Antonio and Gonzales, Macon, Ga., Columbus, Ga., Louisville, Ky.; asst. sec. Bd. of Missions, M.E. Ch., S., 1906-10, general sec., 1910-22; engaged in writing. Visited mission fields of the Orient, 1912-13 and 1922. Launched centenary movement, 1916, and was chmn. Joint Centenary Commn. of M.E. Ch. and M.E. Ch., S. Author: In White and Black, 1900; Biography of Bishop W. R. Lambuth; Biography of Rev. George R. Stuart, D.D., 1927; Missions in a Changing World, 1928; China in Action, 1929. Died Oct. 7, 1930.

PIPER, Charles Vancouver, botanist; b. Victoria, B.C., June 16, 1867; s. Andrew William and Minna (Hausman) P.; B.S., U. of Wash., 1885, M.S., 1892; M.S., Harvard, 1900; (D.Sc., Kan. State U.); m. Laura Maude Hungate, Sept. 15, 1897. Prof. botany and zoölogy, Wash. Agrl. Coll., 1892-1903; agrostologist in charge of forage crop investigation, U.S. Dept. of Agr., 1903—. Fellow Am. Acad. Arts and Sciences. Author: Flora of the Palouse Region, 1901; Flora of Washington, 1906; Flora of Southeast Washington, 1914; Forage Plants and Their Culture, 1914; Flora of Northwest Coast, 1915; Turf for Golf Courses, 1917 (sr. author); The Soybean (sr. author), 1923. Home: Washington, D.C. Died Feb. 11, 1926.

PIPER, Edgar Bramwell, newspaperman; b. Warsaw, Ind., Feb. 25, 1865; s. William Gerard and Henrietta P.; removed to Ore., 1876; began work as printer in office of States' Rights Democrat, 1878; A.B., Willamette U., Salem, 1886, LL.D., 1909; m. Leona Willis, June 17, 1891; children—Edgar Eugene, Constance, John, David. Employed in various capacities in newspaper offices in Portland, San Francisco, and Seattle, 1888—; mng. editor, 1904-09, editor, 1910—, Portland Morning Oregonian. V.p. Am. Soc. Newspaper Editors; dir. North Bur. Newspaper Alliance; mem. Nat. Commn. for Celebration of Second Centenary of George Washington's Birth. Home: Portland, Ore. Died May 3, 1928.

PIPER, Edwin Ford, prof. English, author; b. Auburn, Neb., Feb. 8, 1871; s. Joseph Benson and Lucinda (Ford) P.; A.B., U. of Nebraska, 1897, A.M., 1900; studied Harvard, 1903-04; m. Janet Pressley, 1927. Instructor in English, U. of Neb., 1899-1903, 1904-05; with State U. of Iowa, 1905—, asso. prof. English, 1917-23, prof. English, 1923—. Author: Barbed Wire and Other Poems, 1917; Barbed Wire and Wayfarers, 1923; Paintrock Road, 1927; Canterbury Pilgrims, 1935. Home: Iowa City, Ia. Died May 17, 1939.

PIPES, Martin Luther, lawyer; b. Ascension Parish, La., Sept. 21, 1850; s. John and Harriet Postell (Shaffer) P.; A.B., La. State U., 1871; m. Mary Curtis Skipworth, Nov. 1, 1874; children—John Monroe, Wade Hampton, Nellie Bowden, George Alfred, Mrs. Harriet Beckett. Settled in Ore., 1875; mem. Ore. Ho. of Rep., 1880; began practice at Independence, Ore., 1881; judge Circuit Court, 2d Jud. Dist. of Ore., 1890-92; asso. justice Supreme Court of Ore., by apptmt. of Gov. Walter M. Pierce, for yr. 1924, to fill vacancy. Served as atty. for the State in cases involving State Agrl. Coll.; on construction of will endowing Reed Inst., Portland; for State in Celilo Canal Case, involving power of the State to exercise eminent domain for Federal Canal; asso. in practice at Portland, Ore., with sons John M. and George A. Republican. Elk; mem. A.O.U.W. Home: Portland, Ore. Died July 15, 1932.

PIPKIN, Charles Wooten, prof. government; b. Little Rock, Ark., Nov. 4, 1899; s. Edgar Malone and Ella (Jewell) P.; B.A., Henderson-Brown Coll., Ark., 1918, LL.D., 1929; M.A., Vanderbilt, 1919; Harvard, 1919-22; Rhodes scholar, Oxford U., 1922-25, Ph.D., 1925; Carnegie fellow in internat. law, Sorbonne, Paris, 1929-30; LL.D., Hendrix College, Conway, Ark., 1934. Instructor in English and history, Mass. Inst. Tech., 1920-22; prof. govt., La. State U., 1925—, dean of Grad. Sch., 1931—; mem. faculty, Summer Sch., U. of Tex., 1926, U. of Va., 1926, 29; visiting prof. social legislation, Columbia, 1931-32. Pres. La. State Conf. for Social Betterment, 1928; mem. Am. Com., Geneva, 1928-30; mem. Research Council on Effects of 18th Amendment, U.S. Dept. Justice, 1931; mem. com. on edn. and service and com. on legislation and administration, President's Conf. on Home Bldg. and Home Ownership, 1931; mem. Southern Regional Com. of Social Science Research Council, 1932-34; mem. White House Conf. on Social Legislation, 1935; pres. Conf. of Deans of Southern Grad. Schs., 1936-37; mem. pub. relations council Nat. Student Fedn. of America, 1936—. Mem. Gulf Dist. Rhodes Scholar Selection Com.; mem. Commn. on Interracial cooperation; mem. Am. Council, Inst. of Pacific Relations; mem. exec. com., bd. of dirs., Southern Council on Internat. Relations; mem. Nat. Com., Council on Southern Regional Development; mem. Southern Univ. Conf. on Improvement in Grad. Instrn.; mem. President's Nat. Emergency Council Com. on Southern Econ. Conditions; mem. Nat. Conf. on Grad. Study and Research (U.S. Dept. of Edn.); mem. com. on internat. relations, Am. Inst. of Cinematography; mem. Industry Com. Number 2, U.S. Dept. of Labor, Wage and Hour Div.; mem. social science advisory com. Twelve, U.S. Dept. of Agr., 1939. Democrat. Methodist. Author: The Idea of Social Justice, 1927; World Peace Is Not a Luxury, 1927; Social Politics and Modern Democracies (2 vols.), 1931; Social Legislation in the South, 1934; The Duty of the Educated Mind, 1936; A Survey of Graduate and Research Work in the South, 1937. Asso. editor Candid Opinion, 1925-28; editor La. State U. Studies, 1926—, Southwest Review, 1933-35, Southern Review, 1935—; mem. editorial bd. Am. Oxonian, 1936—; contbg. editor Rural Sociology, 1936—. Home: Baton Rouge, La. Died Aug. 4, 1941.

PIRAZZINI, Agide, theol. prof.; b. Cotignola, North Italy, Feb. 22, 1875; s. John B. and Maria (Emiliani) P.; grad. Royal Gym. and Lyceum, Rome; student Protestant Faculty of Theology, Paris, 1893; grad. Y.M.C.A. Coll., Springfield, Mass., 1896; student Drew Theol. Sem., 1899-1900; A.B., Brown U., 1903, M.A., 1905; B.D., Temple U., 1904, S.T.D., 1906; Ph.D., Columbia, 1915; m. Esther Coletti, of Rome, Sept. 1, 1900; children—Mabelle Esther, Lillian Grace, Edward Hodge, Hellen Gladys, Wilbert Wesley, Arthur Pierson, Robert David, Miriam Amata. Came to U.S., 1894, naturalized citizen, 1907. Served as asst. sec. Y.M.C.A., Paris, and gen. sec. and organizer Y.M.C.A., Rome; founder Italian M.E. Ch., Providence, R.I., 1902, First Italian Presbyn. Ch., Phila., Pa., 1906; prof. Romance langs., Temple U., 1907-08; dir. Italian dept. and prof. Hebrew exegesis and Semitic philology, Bibl. Sem. in New York, 1908—. Republican. Author: Influence of Italy on the Literary Career of Lamartine, 1917; The Psalms of David in Italian Meter. Home: New York, N.Y. Deceased.

PIRIE, John Taylor, dry goods mcht.; b. Brooklyn, N.Y., Sept. 11, 1871; s. John Thomas and Sarah (Carson) P.; B.A., Poly. Inst. of Brooklyn, 1892; m. Sophie Skirving Hunter, Oct. 20, 1897; children—Margaret Hunter (Mrs. Harold Beacom), John T., Jr., Robert S. After graduation became connected with the dry goods house of Carson, Pirie, Scott & Co., Chicago, with which continued, becoming president; director Northern Trust Co., Pub. Service Co. of Northern Ill. V.p. Chicago Zoöl. Park, Brookfield, Ill. Republican. Home: Lake Forest, Ill. Died Feb. 25, 1940.

PIRIE, Samuel Carson, dry goods; b. Amboy, Ill., Mar. 11, 1864; s. John Thomas and Sarah (Carson) P.; ed. Poly. Inst. of Brooklyn, class of 1884; m. Harriet Masters Lockwood, Jan. 17, 1899 (died 1907); children—John T. II, Isobel, Lockwood M., Samuel C., Jr. Began with Carson, Pirie, Scott & Co., Jan. 2, 1885, mem. of firm from Jan. 1, 1892, chmn. bd. from Jan. 1, 1930. Republican. Protestant. Home: Sea Cliff, N.Y. Died Aug. 11, 1938.

PIRSSON, Louis Valentine, geologist; b. New York, N.Y., Nov. 3, 1860; s. Francis M. and Louise (Butt) P.; Ph.B., Sheffield Scientific Sch. (Yale), 1882, A.M., 1902; also studied at Heidelberg and Paris; m. Eliza Trumbull, d. late George Jarvis Brush, May 17, 1902. Asst. in analyt. chemistry, 1882-83, 1884-88, instr. geology and lithology, 1892-94, asst. prof. inorganic geology, 1894-97, prof. physical geology, 1897—, Sheffield Scientific Sch. Asso. editor Am. Jour. of Science, 1897—; asst. and spl. expert, 1893-1904, and geologist U.S. Geol. Survey, 1904—. Fellow Am. Acad. Arts and Sciences. Home: New Haven, Conn. Died Dec. 8, 1919.

PIRTLE, James Speed, lawyer; b. Louisville, Ky., Nov. 8, 1840; s. Henry and Jane Anne (Rogers) P.; pvt. and high schs.; LL.B., U. of Louisville, 1861; m. Emily Bartley, May 22, 1878. Practiced, Louisville, 1863—; prof. equity, commercial and constl. law, U. of Louisville, 1873-81; pres. U. of Louisville, 1887-1905; judge of Law and Equity Ct., Louisville, 1882. Actively identified for many yrs. with banks, trust cos. and rys.; chmn. trustees of Jefferson Monument Fund; pres. Am. Printing House for the Blind; pres. Ky. Inst. for Edn. of the Blind. Democrat. Episcopalian. Royal Arch Mason. Home: Louisville, Ky. Deceased.

PITAVAL, John Baptist, archbishop; b. in France, Feb. 10, 1858; ed. Seminary of Lyons, France, and St. Mary's Sem., Baltimore, Md. Came to U.S., 1881; ordained priest R.C. Ch., Dec. 24, 1881; missionary to Colo., 1881-92; consecrated titular bishop of Sora and auxiliary to Archbishop Bourgade of Santa Fe., N.M., July 25, 1902; adminstr. of the diocese, May 2, 1908; archbishop of Santa Fe, N.M., Jan. 3, 1909. Died May 23, 1928.

PITCAIRN, Robert, railroad mgr.; b. Johnstone, nr. Paisley, Scotland, May 6, 1836; s. John and Agnes P.; removed to Pittsburgh, 1846. His friend and companion, Andrew Carnegie, when a telegraph messenger boy, secured him a similar position. From that he rose to operator in Pittsburgh office Atlantic & Ohio Telegraph Co.; became, 1853, telegraph operator in service of Pa. R.R. Co.; rose step by step, becoming supt. middle div., then supt. transportation, 1865, supt. Pittsburgh div., and in 1875 gen. agt. Pa. R.R., Pittsburgh, and supt. Pittsburgh div., and Jan. 1, 1902, resident asst. to pres. located at Pittsburgh. Is also v.p. Westinghouse Air Brake Co. and has other large interests. Home: Pittsburgh, Pa. Died 1909.

PITCHFORD, John H., judge; b. Wallhalla, S.C., Mar. 8, 1857; s. Wesley and Margaret (Nevill) P.; student Newberry (S.C.) Coll. Admitted to S.C. bar, 1878, and practiced at Clayton and Gainesville, Ga.; moved to Ft. Smith, Ark., 1890, and to Tahlequah, Okla., 1896; became mayor of Tahlequah, 1900; judge 1st Jud. Cir. Ct. of Okla., 3 terms 1907-19; asso. justice Supreme Court of Okla., Nov. 1919, term ending Jan. 1925; became vice chief justice. Democrat. Mason, Odd Fellow. Home: Oklahoma City, Okla. Died Mar. 2, 1923.

PITMAN, Benn, author of phonographic works; b. Trowbridge, Wilts, Eng., July 24, 1822; s. Samuel and Mariah P.; ed. (afterward asst.) in acad. of his brother, the late Sir Isaac Pitman, original inventor of phonography; promulgated the art in Great Britain, by lectures and teaching, for 10 yrs.; m. 1849; m. 2d, 1883. Settled in U.S., 1853; founded Phonographic Inst., Cincinnati, of which he is still pres. Original inventor of the electro-process of relief engraving, 1856; mil. recorder of state trials during Civil War; lecturer on art and teacher of artistic wood-carving, etc., in Cincinnati Art Acad., 1873-92. Author: The Reporter's Companion, 1854; Manual of Phonography, 1854; Phonographic Teacher, 1857; History of Shorthand, 1858; A Plea for American Decorative Art, 1895; Phonographic Dictionary (with Jerome B. Howard), 1899; Life of Sir Isaac Pitman, 1902; A Plea for Alphabetic Reform, 1905. Home: Cincinnati, O. Died 1910.

PITMAN, John, brig. gen. U.S.A.; b. Providence, R.I., Nov. 12, 1842; s. John T. and Caroline (Richmond) P.; grad. U.S. Mil. Acad., 1867; m. Miss L. E. Plympton, Sept. 15, 1868; m. 2d, Anne C. de Mille, Aug. 14, 1903. Enlisted as pvt. Co. G, 1st R.I. Inf., July 18, 1861; discharged, Aug. 2, 1861; pvt. Co. D, 10th R.I. Inf., May 26, 1862; disch. Aug. 30, 1862; sergt. maj. 11th R.I. Inf., Sept. 22, 1862; discharged and commd. 2d lt. 11th R.I. Inf., Apr. 14, 1863; hon. mustered out, July 13, 1863; apptd. U.S. Mil. Acad., Sept. 29, 1863; commd. 2d lt. ordnance, June 17, 1867; 1st lt., June 23, 1874; capt., May 27, 1878; maj., Sept. 2, 1894; lt. col., Feb. 17, 1903; col., Jan. 21, 1904; retired and advanced to rank of brig. gen., Nov. 12, 1906, under act of Apr. 23, 1904. Served at various arsenals, ordnance depots, foundry duty, Cold Spring, N.Y., and instr. chemistry, U.S. Mil. Acad. Home: Orange, N.J. Died Aug. 29, 1933.

PITMAN, Norman Hinsdale, author, educator; b. Lamont, Mich., June 12, 1876; s. Charles and Adeline M. (Hinsdale) P.; M.A., U. of Tenn., 1897 (Phi Gamma Delta, Phi Kappa Phi); m. Lucy Ayers, Sept. 24, 1906. Formerly teacher in U. of Tenn.; teacher Chihli (China) Prov. Coll., 1909-12; studied and traveled in Europe 12 mos.; prof. English, Peking (China) Teachers Coll., 1912-21; prof. English, Peiyang U., Tientsin, China, 1922—. Chia Ho decoration by Pres. of China, 1915, again decorated, 1919. Author: Chinese Fairy Stories, 1910; Chinese Playmates, 1911; The Lady Elect (a Chinese romance), 1913; Chinese Christmas Tree, 1914; A Chinese Wonder Book, 1919; chapt. on education, China Year Book, 1924. Died Mar. 6, 1925.

PITNER, Thomas Jefferson, physician; b. Cass Co., Ill., Nov. 17, 1842; s. William and Catherine (Price) P.; B.S., Ill. Coll., Jacksonville, 1862; M.D., Coll. Phys. and Surg. (Columbia), 1869; U. of Vienna, 1875-76; m. Eloise A. Griffith, May 28, 1889. Engaged in practice of medicine at Jacksonville, Ill., 1869—. Pres. Ill. State Med. Soc., 1900. Mem. M.E. Ch. Republican. Trustee Ill. Coll., and of Ill. Woman's Coll. Mem. Med. Advisory Bd. of Examiners during late war. Home: Jacksonville, Ill. Died Dec. 2, 1920.

PITNEY, John Oliver Halsted, lawyer; b. Morristown, N.J., Apr. 14, 1860; s. Henry C. and Sarah Louise (Halsted) P.; A.B., Princeton, 1881, A.M., 1884; m. Roberta A. Ballantine, Jan. 15, 1890; children—John Ballantine, Robert Henry. Admitted to N.J. bar, 1884, and began gen. practice, Newark; sr. mem. Pitney, Hardin & Skinner; dir. Mut. Benefit Life Ins. Co., Am. Ins. Co. Chmn. Dist. Draft Exemption Bd., Div. No. 2, N.J. Republican. Presbyn. Home: Morristown, N.J. Died Oct. 5, 1928.

PITNEY, Mahlon, jurist; b. Morristown, N.J., Feb. 5, 1858; s. Henry C. (formerly vice-chancellor of New Jersey) and Sarah Louisa (Halsted) P.; A.B., Princeton, 1879, A.M., 1882; (LL.D., Princeton and Rutgers); m. Florence T. Shelton, Nov. 14, 1891. Admitted to bar, 1882, and practiced at Morristown. Elected to 54th and 55th Congresses (1895-99); mem. N.J. Senate, 1899-1901 (pres. 1901); asso. justice Supreme Ct. of N.J., 1901-08; chancellor of N.J., term 1908-15, resigned, Mar. 1912; apptd. asso. justice Supreme Ct. of U.S., Mar. 13, 1912, to succeed John M. Harlan, deceased; resigned, Dec. 31, 1922. Republican. Home: Washington, D.C. Died Dec. 9, 1924.

PITOU, Augustus, theatrical mgr. First professional appearance in Edwin Booth's co., Winter Garden Theatre, New York, as priest in Hamlet; became leading man; began as mgr. with The Danisheffs; later leased and managed Grand Opera House, Toronto, Can.; mgr. Fifth Av. Theatre and Booth's Theatre, New York, for John Stetson; mgr. W. J. Scanlan, Robert Mantell, Joseph Murphy, Rose Coghlan, Chauncey Olcott, Kathryn Kidder and others; more recently mgr. Grand Opera House, New York, and various traveling cos.; collaborator on several successful plays, and sole author of others. Home: New York, N.Y. Died Dec. 4, 1915.

PITT, Robert Healy, clergyman, editor; b. Middlesex Co., Va., June 26, 1853; s. Douglas and Anne Catharine (Wortham) P.; Richmond (Va.) Coll., 1878, LL.D., 1902; D.D., Mercer U., 1892; m. Annie Clare Robertson, Virginia, Oct. 21, 1879 (died 1933); 8 children, 4 living. Ordained Bapt. ministry, 1879; pastor various chs. in and about Richmond, 1878-88; editor The Religious Herald, 1888 (now also owner). Trustee U. of Richmond; pres. Bapt. Edn. Commn. of Va. Democrat. Home: Richmond, Va. Died Feb. 1937.

PITTENGER, William, M.E. clergyman, author; b. Jefferson Co., O., Jan. 31, 1840; s. Thomas and Mary (Mills) P.; common school edn.; courses in Scientific School, Princeton, N.J., and School of Elocution and Oratory, Phila.; m. Winnie C. Osborne, May 1864. During Civil war was mem. Andrews Railroad Raid; received medal of honor and wrote a history of the raid. In active pastorate of M.E. Ch., 1864—; mem. Pittsburgh Conf. 6 yrs.; of N.J. Conf., 19 yrs.; from then of Southern Calif. Conf. Author: Oratory, Sacred and Secular, 1867; The Extempore Speaker, 1886; The Great Locomotive Chase, 1889; The Debater's Treasury, 1891; Toasts, 1894; etc. Home: Burbank, Los Angeles Co., Calif. Died 1905.

PITTMAN, Key, senator; b. Vicksburg, Miss., Sept. 19, 1872; s. William Buckner and Catherine (Key) P.; ed. pvt. tutors and Southwestern Presbyn. U., Clarksville, Tenn., to 1890; LL.D., Southwestern Presbyn. U., 1919, George Washington U., 1921, U. of Nev., 1937; m. Mimosa June Gates, July 7, 1900. Began practice of law in Seattle, Wash., 1892; joined movement to the Klondyke, 1897; worked as a common miner 2 yrs.; served as counsel for Australians who attacked corruption of govt. officials at Dawson; went to Nome, 1899, and participated in orgn. of a "consent" form of govt., 1st dist. atty. same; one of leading counsel for miners in their fight against a conspiracy to rob them of their mines, 1901; removed to Tonopah, Nev., 1901. Dem. candidate for U.S. senator, 1910; elected U.S. senator by popular vote, Nov. 1912, and unanimously confirmed by legislature, Jan. 1913, to fill unexpired term (ending Mar. 4, 1917) of George S. Nixon, dec.; reëlected for 4 terms, to 1941; pres. pro tempore, U.S. Senate, 73d to 76th Congresses; apptd. chmn. Senate Com. on Fgn. Relations, Mar. 5, 1933. Sec. Senate Dem. caucus, 1913-17; Dem. caucus candidate for pres. pro tem. of Senate for 4 Congresses; sec. com. on platform and resolutions of Dem. Nat. Conv., 1924; chmn. com. on platform and resolutions of Dem. Nat. Conv., 1928; selected by conv. to notify Gov. Alfred E. Smith of his nomination as candidate of the Dem. Party for President of U.S. Del. to World Economic Conf., London, June-July, 1933. Mason. Home: Tonopah, Nev. Died Nov. 10, 1940.

PITTMAN, Nathan Rowland, editor; b. in Robeson Co., N.C., Jan. 26, 1856; s. Alfred R. and Mary Catherine (McArthur) P.; B.L., Wake Forest (N.C.) Coll., 1881; Southern Bapt. Theol. Sem., Louisville, 1881; m. Annie Smith, Jan. 22, 1884. Ordained Bapt. ministry, 1881; pastor, Wadesboro, N.C., 1881-83, Macon, Mo., 1883-85, Patee Park Ch., St. Joseph, Mo., 1885-95, Mexico, Mo., 1895-99, also pastor in Clinton, Mo., Ft. Smith, Ark., and Kansas City; asso. editor Central Baptist, 1886-95, Word and Way, 1904-14; was editor Baptist Advance, Little Rock, Ark., and South Carolina Baptist. Contbr. for more than 30 yrs. of "Fragments," a dept. in several Bapt. publs. Home: Kansas City, Mo. Died June 25, 1919.

PITTMAN, William Buckner, lawyer; b. Vicksburg, Miss., Oct. 26, 1876; s. William Buckner and Katie (Key) P.; student Hunt Acad., Port Gibson, Miss., and Southwestern U., Clarksville, Tenn.; m. Bertha Gray, Nov. 27, 1924; 1 son, William Buckner. Began practice of law, 1908; dist. atty. Nye County, Nev., 1904-07; supervisor City and County of Honolulu, 1932-34; atty. gen. of Hawaii, Apr. 1934—. Home: Honolulu, T.H. Died Dec. 20, 1936.

PITTOCK, Henry Lewis, newspaper pub.; b. of Am. parents in London, Eng., Mar. 1, 1835; s. Frederick and Susannah (Bonner) P.; ed. prep. sch., Western Pa.; m. Georgiana Martin Burton, June 20, 1860. Continuously with The Oregonian, 1853—(then a weekly); founder daily Oregonian, 1861; instrumental in establishing paper mfg. industry at Oregon City, and Camas, Wash.; prominently identified with constructive enterprises in the Northwest; state printer of Ore., 1864; pres. Oregonian Pub. Co., Northwestern Nat. Bank, Northwestern Nat. Bank Bldg. Co., etc. Republican. Unitarian. Mason. Home: Portland, Ore. Died Jan. 28, 1919.

PITTS, Alexander Davidson, lawyer; b. Uniontown, Ala., Feb. 4, 1851; s. Philip Henry and Margaret Mary (Davidson) P.; A.B., Davidson (N.C.) Coll.; m. Juliet Meriwether, Feb. 26, 1886. Admitted to Ala. bar, 1879; mem. Pitts & Leva; asst. circuit solicitor 4th Jud. Circuit of Ala., 1880-88; mem. Ala. Ho. of Rep., 1888, 89, 90, and 1907-13; del. to every Dem. State Conv. in Ala., 1878—; served as U.S. atty. for Southern Dist. of Ala., by apptmt. of Pres. Wilson, Dec. 20, 1913. Democrat. Presbyn. Mason. Home: Selma, Ala. Died June 4, 1928.

PITZER, Alexander White, clergyman; b. Salem, Va., Sept. 14, 1834; s. Bernard and Frances L. (White) P.; studied Va. Collegiate Inst.; grad. Hampden-Sidney Coll., 1854; D.D., Ark. Coll., 1876; LL.D., Howard U., 1902; 1 yr. Union Theol. Sem., Va., 2 yrs. Danville, Ky.; m. Laura McClanahan, Aug. 20, 1860. Licensed to preach, Sept. 5, 1856; pastor First Ch., Leavenworth, Kan., 1858-61; returned to Va.; preached Sparta and Mount Zion, Ga., and Cave Spring and Liberty, Va., until 1867; organized, and pastor Central Presbyn. Ch., Washington, from 1868; retired. Prof. Bibl. theology, Howard U., D.C., 1876-90; pres. Washington City Bible Soc., 1873—; stated clerk Presbytery of Chesapeake, 1872—; pres. Evang. Alliance, Washington, 1886—; mem. legislative com. Am. Sabbath Union; trustee Hampden-Sidney Coll., 1865; was mem. Toronto Council of Gen. Presbyn. Alliance; mem. permanent commn. of Western Sect. of same, and com. on foreign missions and Sabbath schs.; commr. to 6 Gen. Assemblies; introduced resolution Atlanta Assembly, 1882, to establish fraternity with Northern Presbyn. Ch.; aided in preparing "declaration of principles," New York Pre-Millennarian Conf., 1878. Author: Ecce Deus Homo, 1868; Christ, the Teacher of Men, 1877; The New Life, 1884; Confidence in Christ, 1890; Manifold Ministry of the Holy Spirit, 1894; Predestination, 1899. Home: Salem Va. Died July 22, 1927.

PIXLEY, Frank, dramatist; b. Richfield, O., Nov. 21, 1867; s. Stephen and Maria Louise (Foster) P.; Ph.B., Ohio State Univ., 1886; Litt.D., Buchtel Coll., Akron, O., 1909; m. Isabel MacRoy, of Windsor, Ont., June 14, 1893. Prof. history and English, Buchtel Coll., 1887-90; mng. editor Chicago Mail, 1892-99; editor-in-chief Chicago Times-Herald, 1899-1902. Decorated Order of Christ, Portugal. Author (plays): The Carpetbagger, 1900; Thoughts and Things, 1912; The Return of Eve, 1914; Taming a Tartar, 1914; Doctor Doolittle, 1914; A Social Call, 1915; Apollo, 1915. Musical comedies: The Prince of Pilsen; King Dodo; The Burgomaster; The Enchanted Isle; Woodland; The Grand Mogul; Marcelle, The Gypsy. Home: Pebble Beach, Calif. Died Dec. 30, 1919.

PLACE, Ira Adelbert lawyer; b. New York, May 8, 1854; A.B., Cornell, 1881; hon. LL.D., Alfred U., 1924; m. Katharine B. Gauntlett, Jan. 10, 1893. Admitted to bar, 1883; entered law dept. N.Y., West Shore & Buffalo R.R. Co., 1883; in law dept. N.Y.C.&H.R. R.R., 1886—; asst. to gen. counsel until 1902, gen. atty., 1902-05, gen. counsel of all N.Y. Central Lines East of Buffalo, 1905—; v.p. same, Dec. 5, 1906—; general solicitor same road under U.S. R.R. Administration, 1919-20; v.p. N.Y. Central Lines (east and west of Buffalo), March 1920—; v.p. N.Y. State Realty and Terminal Co. Mem. Cornelian Council (pres. 1909-15). Trustee Cornell Univ., Alfred U., Hackley Sch., Memorial Hosp. Democrat. Unitarian. Died Jan. 24, 1928.

PLANT, Henry Bradley, pres. Plant system of railways and steamship lines; b. Branford, Conn., Oct. 27, 1819; ed. common schools and private instruction. Entered service of New Haven Steamboat Co., 1837; soon after became mgr. express business on New York & New Haven R.R. Later went South for Adams Express Co., becoming supt. Southern div., located at Augusta, until 1861, when he organized the Southern Express Co., of which he became president. Died 1899.

PLANT, Morton F., financier; b. New Haven, Conn., Aug. 18, 1852; ed. Russell's Mil. Sch., New Haven. Began business career 1868, in service of Southern Express Co., Memphis, Tenn.; from 1884 with Plant System of railroads, of which became v.p. until 1902, when system became part of Atlantic Coast Line R.R. Co., in which is dir. V.p. C.,I.&L. Ry. Co.; chmn. bd. dirs. Southern Express Co.; dir. Nat. Bank of Commerce; trustee Conn. Trust & Safe Deposit Co. Home: New York, N.Y. Died Nov. 4, 1918.

PLANT, Oscar Henry, univ. prof.; b. Lawrence, Kan., Sept. 30, 1875; s. Thomas Henry and Anne Marie (Stewart) P.; M.D., U. of Tex., 1902; m. Ella Mary Beissner, Dec. 26, 1904; 1 son, William Henry. Mem. faculty U. of Tex., 1902-10, U. of Pa., 1911-20, advancing to prof. in 1918; professor and head department of pharmacology, Ia. State University, 1920—. Democrat. Episcopalian. Home: Iowa City, Ia. Died Oct. 1, 1939.

PLANTZ, Myra Goodwin, author; b. Brookville, Ind., July 22, 1856; d. Thomas A. (D.D.) and Content L. (Craft) Goodwin; ed. Indianapolis High Sch., Mt. Vernon Sem., Washington, and under pvt. teachers; spent 1 yr. abroad; taught 2 yrs. in De Pauw U.; m. Samuel Plantz, Sept. 16, 1885. Pres. Conf. Missionary Soc.; mem. State Bd. Y.M.C.A., Iota Chapter Kappa Kappa Gamma. Author (books for young people): Corner Work, 1892; A Great Appointment, 1895; Why Not?, 1900. Home: Appleton, Wis. Died 1914.

PLANTZ, Samuel, university pres.; b. Johnstown, N.Y., June 13, 1859; s. James and Elsie P.; A.B., Lawrence U., Wis., 1880; S.T.B., Boston U., 1883, Ph.D., 1886; U. of Berlin, 1890-91; (D.D., Albion Coll., 1894; LL.D., Baker U., 1905; LL.D., U. of Wis., 1919, Northwestern, 1922); m. Myra A. Goodwin, Sept. 16, 1885 (died 1914). Ordained M.E. ministry, 1885; pastor Detroit, 1885-92; pres. Lawrence U., 1894—. Trustee Carnegie Foundation for the Advancement of Teaching. Author: The Church and the Social Problem, 1906. Contbr. to Hastings' Dictionary of Christ and Apostles. Home: Appleton, Wis. Died Nov. 13, 1924.

PLATNER, John Winthrop, educator; b. Lee, Mass., May 15, 1865; s. William and Emily Childs (Ball) P.; bro. of Samuel Ball P.; A.B., Yale, 1885, A.M., 1901; Union Theol. Sem., 1890-93; U. of Berlin, 1903-05; (D.D., Western Reserve, 1901); m. Clara Avery Burnham, Sept. 16, 1915. Instr. history of religion and apologetics, Union Theol. Sem., 1895-96; asst. prof. ecclesiastical history, Harvard, 1896-1901; prof. ecclesiastical history, Andover Theol. Sem., 1901—, and pres. of the faculty, 1919—. Andover professor same, Harvard U., 1908—. Ordained Congl. ministry, 1901. Fellow Am. Acad. Arts and Sciences. Author of various articles in hist. and theol. reviews, and of the sect. "The Congregationalists," in The Religious History of New England, 1917. Home: Cambridge, Mass. Died Mar. 18, 1921.

PLATNER, Samuel Ball, university prof.; b. Unionville, Conn., Dec. 4, 1863; s. William and Emily Childs (Ball) P.; bro. of John Winthrop P.; A.B., Yale, 1883, Ph.D., 1885; m. Leonora Sayre, June 29, 1892. Instr. Latin and French, 1885-90, asst. prof. Latin, 1890-92, prof., 1892—, Western Reserve U. Sec. mng. com., 1897-1911, prof. 1899-1900, Am. Sch. Classical Studies in Rome. Editor: Greek and Roman Versification (from German of Lucian Müller), 1892; Selected Letters of the Younger Pliny, 1894. Author: Topography and Monuments of Ancient Rome, 1904, 2d edit., 1911. Home: Cleveland, O. Died Aug. 20, 1921.

PLATT, Charles, M.D., author; b. Montclair, N.J., Mar. 16, 1869; s. Jesse and Amelia Adelaide (Chazotte) P.; B.S., Lehigh U., 1890; Ph.D., Ohio U., 1892; Johns Hopkins, 1893-94; studied at U. of Edinburgh, École de Medicine, Paris, Homœ. Hosp., London, at various times, 1894-1900; M.D., Hahnemann Med. College, Phila., 1900; m. Mildred Sellers Almy, Sept. 3, 1916. Chief chemist for Thomas A. Edison at his pvt. labs., Llewellyn Park, N.J., 1890-91; prof. chemistry and toxicology, Hahnemann Med. Coll., Phila., 1894-1909 (emeritus). Practicing physician, 1900-19. Asso. editor Science (New York), 1892-93. Author: Qualitative Analysis and Medical Chemistry, 1895, 5th edit., 1906; (in collaboration) Practical Medical Chemistry, 1911; The Psychology of Thought and Feeling, 1921; The Psychology of Social Life, 1922; The Riddle of Society, 1926. Edited Chazotte's The Black Rebellion in Haiti, 1927. Home: Ardmore, Pa. Deceased.

PLATT, Charles Adams, architect, landscape architect, painter; b. New York, N.Y., Oct. 16, 1861; s. John H. and Mary (Cheney) P.; studied in art schs. of New York and Paris. Awarded Webb prize, Soc. of Am. Artists, 1894. N.A.; mem. Am. Acad. Arts and Letters; fellow A.I.A. Author: Italian Gardens, 1892. Home: New York, N.Y. Died Sept. 12, 1933.

PLATT, Edmund; b. Poughkeepsie, N.Y., Feb. 2, 1865; s. John I. and Susan Frances (Sherwood) P.; A.B., Harvard, 1888; also grad. Eastman Business Coll., Poughkeepsie; studied law; m. Adele Innis, June 23, 1892; 1 dau., Catherine (Mrs. Joseph C. Lingle). Was teacher of history and English at Riverview Academy, 1888-90; served as editorial writer Superior (Wis.) Evening Telegram, 1890-91; connected with Poughkeepsie Eagle, 1891-1931, half owner, with brother, Francis W. Platt, and editor same, 1907-20. Served as water commr. and trustee City Library, Poughkeepsie; elected mem. 63d to 66th Congresses (1913-21), 26th N.Y. Dist.; chmn. Com. on Banking and Currency, 66th Congress; resigned June 7, 1920, to become mem. Federal Reserve Bd. of which was vice gov., 1920-30; v.p. Marine Midland Corp., 1930—. Republican. Mem. Dutch Ref. Ch. Author: History of Poughkeepsie, 1905. Home: Garden City, L.I., N.Y. Died Aug. 27, 1939.

PLATT, Franklin, geologist; b. Philadelphia, Pa., Nov. 19, 1844; ed. Univ. of Pa.; left before graduation; served in 32d Pa. Gray Reserve Regt., 1863. In 1864 on U.S. Coast Survey, doing surveying work with North Atlantic squadron; then on staff Gen. Orlando M. Poe, chief engr. Mil. Div. of the Mississippi until April 1865. Asst. geologist of Pa., 1874-81; then pres. Rochester & Pittsburgh Coal and Iron Co. Author: Waste in Mining Anthracite; Coke Manufacturing. Home: Philadelphia, Pa. Died 1900.

PLATT, Henry Clay, lawyer; b. New York, N.Y., Oct. 22, 1840; s. David and Sarah (Gould) P.; grad. Princeton, 1858; studied law; admitted to New York bar, 1862; has practiced, New York; m. Jennie Dusenberry, g.d. late Judge Munson, of Conn., 1864. Mem. N.Y. State Assembly, 1864-66; asst. U.S. atty., 1886-94; U.S. atty., 1894; asst. U.S. atty., 1895—, Southern dist. N.Y. Author: Old Times in Huntington, 1876. Home: Huntington, L.I., N.Y.; and New York, N.Y. Died 1904.

PLATT, Henry Russell, lawyer; b. Plattsburg, N.Y., Mar. 4, 1866; s. Theodorus and Marietta S. (Nichols) P.; A.B., Williams Coll., Mass., 1887; m. Helen Sherwood Kyle, Aug. 27, 1895; children—Theodora, Henry Russell, Jr., Sherwood Kellogg. Admitted to Vt. bar, 1890, Ill. bar, 1891, and entered practice at Chicago; now mem. Mayer, Meyer, Austrian & Platt; counsel for the Leiter Estate; counsel, dir. Nat. Life Ins. Co. of Vt.; counsel in Armour-Morris merger, 1923. Independent. Episcopalian. Home: Evanston, Ill. Died May 22, 1931.

PLATT, Isaac Hull, physician; b. Brooklyn, N.Y., May 18, 1853; s. Frederick A. and Augusta (Hull) P.; ed. Poly. Inst., Brooklyn; admitted to Ala. bar, 1875; student Columbia, 1877; admitted to N.Y. bar, 1877; M.D., L.I. Coll. Hosp., 1883; m. Emma Haviland, Sept. 2, 1886. Practiced medicine Lakewood, N.J., 1886-97; has traveled extensively in Europe; for last few years spending much time in New York. Author: Bacon Cryptograms in Shakespeare, and Other Studies, 1905; Walt Whitman, in Beacon Biographies Series. Home: Wallingford, Pa. Died Aug. 16, 1912.

PLATT, James Perry, judge; b. Towanda, Pa., Mar. 31, 1851; s. Orville Hitchcock (U.S. senator) and Annie (Bull) P.; A.B., Yale, 1873, LL.B., 1875; m. Harriet White Ives, Dec. 2, 1885. Practiced at Meriden, Conn., in firm O. H. and J. P. Platt, 1875-1902. Mem. Conn. Ho. of Rep., 1878-79; city atty. Meriden, 1879-93; judge City Ct., 1893-1902; U.S. dist. judge, Dist. of Conn., Mar. 22, 1902—. Republican. Home: Meriden, Conn. Died Jan. 26, 1913.

PLATT, Orville Hitchcock, U.S. senator, Conn., 1879-1909; b. Washington, Con., July 19, 1827; academic edn.; studied law; admitted to bar, 1849; entered practice at Meriden. Clerk State senate, Conn., 1857; State senator, 1861-62; mem. Conn. Ho. of Reps., 1864, 1869, serving last yr. as speaker. Republican. Home: Meriden, Conn. Died 1905.

PLATT, Thomas Collier, U.S. senator; b. Owego, N.Y., July 15, 1833; s. William and Lesbia (Hinchman) P.; ed. Owego Acad.; mem. class of 1853, Yale, but compelled to give up course because of ill health (A.M., 1876); m. Ellen Lucy Barstow, Dec. 12, 1852 (died 1901). Entered mercantile life; was pres. Tioga Nat. Bank at its organization; became interested in lumbering in Mich.; clerk Tioga Co., 1859-61; mem. Congress, 1873-77; elected U.S. senator, Jan. 18, 1881, and resigned, May 16, same yr., with Roscoe Conkling. Sec. and dir. U.S. Express Co., 1879, and its pres., 1880—. Pres. bd. of quarantine commrs. N.Y., 1880-88; has been pres. Southern Central R.R. and of Addison & Northern Pa. R.R. Has been recognized leader in N.Y. Rep. politics for yrs.; U.S. senator, 1897—; present term expires 1909. Mem. Rep. State Com. and exec. com. Rep. Nat. Com. Home: Owego, N.Y. Died 1910.

PLATT, William Popham, judge; b. White Plains, N.Y., May 16, 1858; s. Lewis Canfield and Laura Sherbrook (Popham) P.; ed. pub. schs., White Plains; m. Sara Stuart Dean, Oct. 1, 1890; children—Stuart Dean, William Popham (dec.). Began practice at White Plains, 1879, but permitted by courtesy to try important causes in the County Court of Westchester Co. before attaining majority; dist. atty. Westchester Co., N.Y., 1890-1906, inclusive; county judge, same county, 1901-15; justice Supreme Court of N.Y., 9th Jud. Dist., 1915—. Democrat. Episcopalian. Mason, Elk. Home: White Plains, N.Y. Died Nov. 2, 1926.

PLATZEK, M(arx) Warley, judge; b. in North Carolina, Aug. 27, 1854; ed. pvtly.; LL.B., New York U., 1876; (LL.D., Rutherford Coll., N.C., 1899, New York U., 1920). Mem. N.Y. Consti. Conv., 1894; trustee Coll. City of New York, 1904-07, Justice Supreme Court of N.Y., 1st District, 1907-20; reëlected for term ending 1934. Democrat. Home: New York, N.Y. Died July 21, 1932.

PLEASANT, Ruffin Golson, governor; b. Shiloh, La., June 2, 1871; s. Benjamin Franklin and Martha Washington (Duty) P.; Ruston Coll., 1885; Mt. Lebanon Coll., La., 1887-88 and 1888-89; La. State U., 1890-94; studied law Harvard and Yale; m. Anne Ector, Feb. 14, 1906. Lt. col. 1st La. Regt. Inf., U.S. Vols., Spanish-Am. War, 1898; began practice, Shreveport, La., 1899; city atty., Shreveport, 1902-08; asst. atty. gen., La., 1911-12; atty. gen., June 1, 1912-16; gov. of La., term 1916-20. Democrat. Baptist. Home: Shreveport, La. Died Sept. 12, 1937.

PLIMPTON, George Arthur, publisher; b. Walpole, Mass., July 13, 1855; s. Calvin Gay and Priscilla Guild (Lewis) P.; A.B., Amherst, 1876; law student Harvard, 1877; LL.D., U. of Rochester, 1912, U. of Richmond, 1913, Amherst, 1931, St. Lawrence U., 1934; L.H.D., New York U., 1923, Columbia, 1929; m. Frances Taylor Pearsons, Oct. 2, 1892 (died 1900); m. 2d, Fanny Hastings, Nov. 10, 1917. Mem. Ginn & Co., publishers, 1882—. Trustee Amherst Coll. (pres.), Barnard Coll. (treas.), Ch. Peace Union, Constantinople Coll., Union Theol. Sem.; mem. exec. com. Near East Relief. Has the largest collection of text-books from the earliest date of printing and medieval manuscripts of an ednl. character in the world; donated to Wellesley Coll., a library of 1st edits. of nearly every Italian writer, also manuscripts of the same, in memory of his wife. Trustee World Peace Foundation. Republican. Presbyterian. Lectures on education of Dante, Chaucer, and Shakespeare, illustrated by manuscripts and text-books that they studied; collector of material relating to French and Indian Wars, and author of "The Education of Shakespeare," "The Education of Chaucer" and of chapter on Mass. in the French and Indian Wars. Home: New York, N.Y. Died July 1, 1936.

PLOWMAN, George Taylor, etcher; b. Le Sueur, Minn., Oct. 19, 1869; s. George and S. E. (Taylor) P.; B.Arch., U. of Minn., 1892; studied in Paris and at Royal Coll. Arts, South Kensington, London; m. Maude H. Bell, of Mardin, Turkey, Dec. 25, 1895; children—George Taylor, Edward Grosvenor, Lawrence Carrington. Has exhibited at Royal Acad. (London), Paris Salon, and in many cities of Eng. and U.S.; etchings in permanent collections of Congressional Library, Washington; Pub. Library, New York; Mus. of Fine Arts, Boston; Met. Mus., New York; Pub. Library, Newark, N.J.; Calif. State Library, Sacramento, Calif.; British Museum and South Kensington Mus., London; Luxembourg Mus., Paris; etc. Bronze medal, Panama Pacific Expn., 1915. Divisional sec. Y.M.C.A., in France, 1918—; organized and conducted art dept. Y.M.C.A. Univ., Coblenz, Germany, 1919. Author: Etching and Other Graphic Arts, 1914; Manual of Etching, 1924. Home: Cambridge, Mass. Died Mar. 26, 1932.

PLUM, Harry Clarke, clergyman, teacher; b. Poughkeepsie, N.Y., Aug. 25, 1871; s. William Henry and Rachel Sallas (Enoch) P.; A.B., Harvard, 1897; m. Edith Greeley (A.B., Vassar Coll.), June 15, 1897. Asst., high sch., Poughkeepsie, N.Y., 1897-98; prin. high sch., Cheney Valley, N.Y., 1898-1901; deacon, 1901, priest, 1902, P.E. Ch.; rector Trinity Ch., Granville, N.Y., 1901-03, Christ Ch., Kingman, Kan., 1902-06, St. Peter's Ch., Minneapolis, Kan., 1906-09, St. Luke's Ch., Mechanicsville, N.Y., 1909-12; prin. St. Faith's Sch., Saratoga Springs, N.Y., 1912—. Home: Saratoga Springs, N.Y. Deceased.

PLUMB, Albert Hale, clergyman; b. Gowanda, N.Y., Aug. 23, 1829; s. Joseph and Caroline Robbins (Hale) P.; grad. Brown Univ., 1855, Andover Theol. Sem., 1858; (D.D., Brown); m. Harriet Eliza Dart, Oct. 27, 1858. Pastor First Congl. Ch., Chelsea, Mass., 1858-72, Walnut Av. Congl. Ch., Roxbury, Mass., 1872—. Mem. prudential com. A.B.C.F.M., 1882-1903. Home: Roxbury, Mass. Died 1907.

PLUMB, Charles Sumner, univ. prof.; b. Westfield, Mass., Apr. 21, 1860; s. David Henry and Helen Mar (Wallace) P.; B.Sc., D.Sc., Mass. Agrl. Coll.; D.Sc., Purdue, 1935; LL.D., Ohio State U., 1937; m. Helen P. Gladwin, Oct. 14, 1886; children—Helen Gladwin, Winthrop Gladwin. Asso. editor Rural New Yorker, 1883-84; 1st asst., State Agrl. Expt. Sta., Geneva, N.Y., 1884-87; prof. agr., U. of Tenn., and asst. dir. Tenn. Agrl. Expt. Sta., 1887-90; v.dir. Ind. Agrl. Expt. Sta., 1890-91, dir. same, 1891-1902; prof. agrl. science, 1890-93, animal husbandry and dairying, 1893-1902, Purdue U.; prof. animal husbandry, Ohio State U., 1902-31, emeritus. Founded, pub. and edited until 1891, "Agricultural Science," monthly mag. Sec. and treas. Soc. for Promotion Agrl. Science, 1895-99, Am. Kerry and Dexter Cattle Club, 1911-22; pres. Indiana State Dairy Assn., 1891-96 and 1902. Am. Cheviot Sheep Soc., 1901-07. Fellow Philalethes Soc.; hon. mem. English Southdown Soc., English Oxford Down Soc. Decorated Chevalier du Mérite Agricole (France), 1929. Emeritus pres. bd. trustees Gladden Community House. Mason; pres. Ohio Masonic Hist. Soc.; fellow Grand College of Rites of U.S. Author: Types and Breeds of Farm Animals, 1906, complete revision, 1919 (translated into Russian 1914 by representatives Russian Govt.; used as text in Russian colls.); A Partial Index to Animal Husbandry Literature, 1911; Beginnings in Animal Husbandry, 1913; Judging Farm Animals.

1916; American Kerry and Dexter Cattle Herd Book, Vol. I, 1920; A Study of Farm Animals, 1922; Marketing Farm Animals, 1927; Registry Books on Farm Animals, 1930; History of American Union Lodge No. 1, F.&A.M. of Ohio, 1934. Home: Columbus, O. Deceased.

PLUMB, Glenn Edward, lawyer; b. Clay, Ia., Sept. 30, 1866; s. Edward and Isabel (Mills) P.; Ph.B., Oberlin Coll., 1891; student Harvard Law Sch., 1891, 92; LL.B., Northwestern U., 1893; m. Grace E. Clarke, Jan. 1, 1895 (died 1899); m. 2d, Marie Coyle, June 27, 1907. Was of counsel for city in Blair vs. City of Chicago, known as the "99 year case." Devised Plumb Plan, adopted by the organized ry. employes assns. in U.S., for reorganization of rys., and placing com. of 15 in control, 5 members of the com. being ry. employes and a certain portion of the profits each yr. to be distributed among the ry. employes. Democrat. Conglist. Mason. Died Aug. 1, 1922.

PLUMBE, George Edward, statistician; b. Pawlet, Vt., Oct. 29, 1837; s. Rev. Elijah Whiton and Sarah (Woodman) P.; A.B., Middlebury (Vt.) Coll., 1861 (LL.D., 1908); LL.B., Albany (N.Y.) Law Sch., 1863; m. Clara P. Russel, Oct. 7, 1863 (died 1906). Practiced law at Potsdam, N.Y., 1863-68; on staff Chicago Republican, 1869-71, Inter Ocean, 1871-77; with postal service, 1877-80; on staff Chicago Daily News, and Record, 1880-1901; lit. and statis. work, 1901-06; statistician and librarian Chicago Assn. of Commerce, 1906—. Editor 16 vols. Daily News Almanac and Political Register, 1885-1900. Author: Our Curiosity Shop, 1875; Chicago, Its Natural Advantages as an Industrial and Commercial Center and Market, 1908. Home: Chicago, Ill. Died Apr. 24, 1912.

PLUME, Joseph Williams, financier, soldier; b. Troy, N.Y., Aug. 23, 1839; pvt. sch. edn.; engaged in banking business; rose to be pres.; served in Civil War as adj. 2d N.J.; a.d.c. to Brig. Gen. French; acting adj. gen. 3d Brigade, Sumner's division; acting adj. gen. 3d Div. 2d Corps; 42 yrs.' continuous service in N.J.N.G., holding every rank from pvt. to maj. gen. During Spanish-Am. War was made brig. gen. of vols. and served with 2d Corps under Gen. Graham; mustered out, Sept. 1898. Pres. Mfrs.' Nat. Bank. Now treas.-in-chief Commandery-in-Chief Loyal Legion. Died Jan. 12, 1918.

PLUMLEY, Frank, congressman; b. Eden, Vt., Dec. 17, 1844; s. William and Eliza P.; acad. edn.; law student U. of Mich., 1867-68; (hon. A.M., Norwich U., 1892, LL.D., 1905; LL.D., U. of Vt., 1909); m. Lavinia L. Fletcher, Aug. 9, 1871. Admitted to bar, 1869, and entered practice at Northfield, Vt. State's atty., Washington Co., 1876-80; mem. Vt. Ho. of Rep., 1882, Senate, 1894 (pres. pro tem.); U.S. dist. atty., 1889-94; judge Ct. of Claims of Vt., 1902-08 (chief judge 1904-08); mem. 61st to 63d Congresses (1909-15), 2d Vt. Dist. Umpire of mixed commns. Great Britain and Venezuela and Holland and Venezuela, Caracas, 1903; umpire French-Venezuela mixed commn., Northfield, 1905; del. Interparliamentary Conv., Geneva, Switzerland, 1912. Lecturer internat. law, Norwich U. (trustee, v.p.). Chmn. Rep. State Conv., 1886. Pres. Northfield Savings Bank. Home: Northfield, Vt. Died Apr. 30, 1924.

PLUMMER, Charles Griffin, M.D., surgeon; b. Chicago, Ill., Jan. 1, 1859; s. Sanford Alexander and Martha Cordelia (Cooley) P.; B.S., Teachers' Inst. and Classical Sem., Paw Paw, Ill., 1879; B.L., Northwestern U., 1884; M.D., Chicago Med. Coll., 1886; post-grad. work in N.Y. City; m. Anna Laura Colburn, Apr. 30, 1890. Practiced at Salt Lake City, Utah, 1891—; col. 1st Inf., U.N.G., 3 yrs.; mem. Utah State Commn. for Feeble-Minded, 4 yrs.; formerly regent U. of Utah and speaker extension service; mem. exec. com., chmn. Court of Honor Salt Lake Council Boy Scouts America. Republican. Episcopalian. Mason. Author: Gun Grabbing Johnny, 1923. Explorer of the Southwest; photographer of wild life. Awarded testimonial by citizens for great service to community and work with youth; award of merit on 50th anniversary of graduation by Northwestern U. Alumni Assn.; awarded 25-year vet. silver badge by Nat. Council Boy Scouts of America, Aug. 1935. Home: Salt Lake City, Utah. Died Nov. 1936.

PLUMMER, Edward Clarence, mem. U.S. Shipping Bd.; b. Freeport, Me., Nov. 23, 1863; s. Solomon Hayford and Ruth Bucknell (Harding) P.; A.B., Bowdoin, 1887, A.M., 1890; m. Lillian Gertrude Fiske, Sept. 3, 1888. Newspaper work, Bath, 1888-96; asst. p.m. U.S.N., Spanish-Am. War; began practice of law, Bath, 1898; corp. counsel, Bath, 7 yrs.; sec. Bath Chamber of Commerce 17 yrs.; atty. Atlantic Carriers' Assn. 21 yrs.; mem. U.S. Shipping Board, June 1921—, v.chmn., 1923—; trustee U.S.S.B. Emergency Fleet Corp. Republican. Conglist. Supreme Rep. K.P. Author: Tercentennial of City of Bath, 1907; Shipping Sense, 1926; Reminiscences, 1926. Home: Bath, Me. Died Mar. 20, 1932.

PLUMMER, Edward Hinkley, army officer; b. Esperanza, Elkridge, Md., Sept. 24, 1855; s. William Walker and Harriett Leoj (French) P.; grad. U.S. Mil. Acad., 1877; m. Georgia Alice Moody, Oct. 13, 1880; children—Bessie Moody, Edward Hinkley (dec.), Harriet French (dec.), Dwight Kelton (dec.), Thorington Preston, Georgia Moody. Commd. 2d lt. 10th Inf., June 15, 1877; promoted through grades to col. 35th Vol. Inf., Dec. 16, 1899 (organized the regt. and commanded it during its entire service); col. regular army, Mar. 11, 1911; brig. gen., July 1, 1916; maj. gen. N.A., Aug. 5, 1917. Q.m. in field, and regimental q.m., 1885-91; agt. Navajo and Moqui Indians, 1893-94; a.-q.m. hdqrs. 5th Army Corps, Santiago, Cuba, in charge all land transportation, wagon and pack trains, July 3-Aug. 17, 1898; aide to Maj. Gen. W. R. Shafter, Aug. 18, 1898-July 4, 1899, and May-July 1901; comdr. Ft. Egbert, Eagle, Alaska, 1904-06; at Zamboanga, P.I., 1909-10; comdg. 28th Inf. Maneuver Div., San Antonio, Tex., 1911; provost marshal gen. and acting mayor of Vera Cruz, Mexico, Apr.-Nov. 1914; comdg. regt. at Dallas State Fair, and mil. tournament, Oct. 1915; various commands in Tex. and on Mexican border; organized Dept. of Panama Canal, first comdr. of new dept., comprising canal and appurtenances, and troops, Apr.-Aug. 1917; organized and comd. 88th Div., Camp Dodge, Ia., Aug.-Nov. 1917; visited battle fronts in France, Dec. 1917-Feb. 1918, with 46th British Div., Woevre trench sector, 62d French Div., La Fere sector, 1st U.S. Div., Mars la tour; comdg. 88th Div., Feb.-Mar. 1918; discharged as maj. gen. N.A., March 14, 1918; comd. Ft. Sill, Okla., Mar.-Oct. 1918, Camp Grant, Ill., Oct.-Dec. 1918; retired as brig. gen., Nov. 30, 1918. Episcopalian. Home: Pacific Grove, Calif. Died Feb. 11, 1927.

PLUMMER, Mary Wright, librarian; b. Richmond, Ind.; d. Jonathan W. and Hannah A. P.; spl. student Wellesley, 1881-82; student of library science, Columbia, 1887-88. Librarian of Pratt Inst. Free Library, 1896-1904; dir. Pratt Inst. Library Sch., Brooklyn, 1896-1911; prin. Library Sch. of New York Public Library, 1911—. U.S. del. Internat. Congress of Libraries, Paris, 1900; pres. A.L.A., 1915-16 (v.p. 1900, 1911), N.Y. State Library Assn., 1906, N.Y. Library Club, 1896-97, 1913-14, L.I. Library Club, 1897. Author: Hints to Small Libraries, 4th edit., 1911; Verses, 1896; Contemporary Spain, 1899; Roy and Ray in Mexico, 1907; Roy and Ray in Canada, 1908; Stories from the Chronicle of the Cid, 1910. Home: New York, N.Y. Died Sept. 21, 1916.

PLUMMER, Walter Percy, newspaperman; b. Boston, Mass., Mar. 27, 1883; s. Thaddeus Pulaski and Mary Agnes (Mahlmann) P.; ed. pub. schs.; m. Helen Louise Laycock, May 15, 1909; children—Frances, Walter Elmer. Began as reporter Boston American, 1907; mng. editor Syracuse (N.Y.) Herald, 1922-23; mng. editor Albany Evening News, 1923-25; editorial dir. same and Knickerbocker Press, 1926—. Home: Albany, N.Y. Died Mar. 2, 1933.

PLUMMER, William Alberto, judge; b. Gilmanton, N.H., Dec. 2, 1865; s. Charles Edwin and Mary Hoyt (Moody) P.; Dartmouth Coll., 1884-85 (obliged to leave on account ill health); LL.B., Boston U., 1889; m. Ellen Frances Murray, Jan. 1, 1890. Admitted to N.H. bar, 1889; practiced, Laconia, with Col. Stephen S. Jewett, 1889-1907; mem. N.H. Ho. of Rep., 1893 and 1907 (floor leader Dem. party, session 1907); judge Superior Ct., N.H., 1907-13; asso. justice Supreme Ct., N.H., Dec. 13, 1913—. Dir. Laconia Nat. Bank, Laconia Bldg. and Loan Assn.; pres., trustee City Savings Bank of Laconia. Mem. Sch. Bd., Laconia, 19 yrs., pres. of bd. 16 yrs. Mason. Home: Laconia, N.H. Died Nov. 29, 1925.

PLUNKETT, Charles Peshall, naval officer; b. Washington, D.C., Feb. 15, 1864; grad. U.S. Naval Acad., 1884. Promoted ensign, July 1, 1886; lt. jr. grade, Nov. 5, 1895; lt., Nov. 15, 1898; lt. comdr., June 1, 1904; comdr., July 1, 1908; captain, Apr. 27, 1912; rear admiral (temporary), July 1, 1918, permanent rank, Apr. 7, 1919. In office of Naval Intelligence, Navy Department, 1904-05; executive officer Texas, 1905-06, Georgia, 1906-07; duty at Navy Yard, Boston, 1907-08; insp. equipment, Fore River Shipbuilding Co., Quincy, Mass., 1908-10; exec. officer North Dakota, 1910; comd. Missouri, 1910-11, Culgoa, 1911, Wabash, 1911-12; in charge navy recruiting sta., Boston, Mass., 1912, comd. South Dakota, 1913, North Dakota, 1913-15; at Naval War Coll., Newport, R.I., 1915-16; dir. gunnery training and engring., also comdg. 14-inch Naval Ry. Batteries, Jan. 3, 1916-July 7, 1918; comdg. 14-inch Naval Ry. Batteries operating with French and Am. armies in France, July 7, 1918-Jan. 1919; comdg. destroyer force U.S. Fleet, Jan.-July 1919; in charge all operations Navy transatlantic flight, May-June 1919; comdg. destroyer squadrons Atlantic Fleet, July 1, 1919-Nov. 30, 1920; chief of staff, Naval War Coll., Dec. 1, 1920-Aug. 1, 1921; pres. Bd. Insp. and Survey, Aug. 1, 1921-Dec. 1, 1922; comdt. 3d Naval Dist. and Navy Yard, New York, 1922-28, retired. Navy D.S.M. and Army D.S.M. (U.S.); Comdr. Legion of Honor (France); Portuguese Decoration, Tower and Sword. Died Mar. 24, 1931.

PLUNKETT, Charles T., cotton mfr.; b. Adams, Mass., Feb. 20, 1855; s. William C. and Lovisa (Brown) P.; ed. Adams High Sch.; m. Leila Taylor, Feb. 20, 1879 (died 1908); 1 son, Charles Taylor. Has been identified with cotton mfg. at Adams, 1877—; pres. of W. C. Plunkett & Sons Co., spinners and converters of cotton yarns; pres. Berkshire Cotton Mfg. Co., Greylock Mills; pres. Industrial Mut. Ins. Co. of Boston; dir. Berkshire Life Ins. Co., Pittsfield, Mass., Liberty Mut. Ins. Co., Boston. Pres. trustees Plunkett Memorial Hosp., Adams, Deerfield Acad., Deerfield, Mass.; treas. Adams Free Library; chmn. Sch. Com., 1918. Republican. Conglist. Home: Adams, Mass. Died July 8, 1927.

PLUNKETT, William Brown, mfr.; b. Adams, Mass., Apr. 2, 1850; s. late Gen. William C. P.; collegiate edn. Mgr. Greylock Cotton Mills at North Adams; treas. Berkshire Cotton Mfg. Co.; pres. Greylock Nat. Bank, Adams, Mass.; trustee N.Y. Life Ins. Co.; dir. Berkshire Life Ins. Co. Was mem. Governor's Council, Mass., 1897; mem. advisory bd. Rep. Nat. Com., 1896, 1900; advocate of protectionist policy. Republican. Pres. Home Market Club of Boston. Home: Adams, Mass. Died Oct. 23, 1917.

PLYM, Francis John, manufacturer; b. Bäckaby, Sweden, Sept. 16, 1869; s. Osley Johnson and Johana (Peterson) P.; brought to U.S., 1870, naturalized through father's papers; B.S., U. of Ill., 1897; LL.D., Augustana Coll., 1938; m. Jennie Barber, Mar. 10, 1903; children—Florence Barber (dec.), Lawrence John and (adopted) Marian (Mrs. Jack E. Troup), Helen. Architect, Lincoln, Neb., and Kansas City, Mo., 1897-1907; mfr. of metal products, Niles, Mich., 1907—; pres. The Kawneer Co.; pres. Niles Hotel Co.; pres. Star Pub. Co. (daily newspaper); dir. Associate Investment Co., South Bend, Ind. Pres. Am. Swedish Hist. Museum Foundation; Nat. pres. Swedish Tercentenary, Inc., 1938; dir. U. of Ill. Foundation; trustee Mich. Children's Aid Soc. Decorated Comd. Royal Order of Vasa; commemorative medal of Colony of New Sweden, Del., 1638 (both from King of Sweden). Republican. Presbyterian. Elk. Home: Niles, Mich. Died Jan. 12, 1940.

PLYMPTON, Eben, actor; b. Boston, Mass., Feb. 7, 1853; s. John Bradlee and Elizabeth Priscilla (Williams) P.; ed. pub. schs., Boston; unmarried. Actor from Sept. 11, 1871; first appearance in Stockton, Calif.; has been leading man in several companies and star. Home: Plympton, Mass. Died Apr. 12, 1915.

PLYMPTON, George Washington, engr., educator; b. Waltham, Mass., Nov. 18, 1827; s. Thomas R. and Elizabeth (Holden) P.; grad. Rensselaer Poly. Inst., C.E., 1847 (A.M., Hamilton Coll.; M.D., Long Island Coll. Hosp); m. Delia M., d. Col. Thomas Bussey of Troy, N.Y., 1855 (died 1858); m. 2d, 1861, Helen M. Bussey, sister of 1st wife. Learned machinist trade, 1844-47; practiced engring., 1847-52; prof. architecture and engring., Cleveland Univ., 1852-53; prof. mathematics, N.Y. State Normal School, Albany, 1853-56; prof. physics and engring., State Normal School, Trenton, N.J., 1857-63; prof. physics and engring., Cooper Union, New York, 1869—(dir. 1879—); same chair, Brooklyn Polytechnic Inst., 1863—; prof. chemistry and toxicology, Long Island Coll. Hosp., 1864-86; editor Van Nostrand's Engring. Mag., 1870-86; commr. elec. subways, Brooklyn, 1885-89 and 1892-96. Author: The Blowpipe; How to Become an Engineer, 1892; The Starfinder; The Aneroid. Home: Brooklyn, N.Y. Died 1907.

POCKMAN, Philetus Theodore, clergyman; b. E. Greenbush, N.Y., Feb. 26, 1853; s. John Niver and Almira (Snook) P.; A.B., Rutgers, 1875, A.M., 1878 (D.D., 1894); grad. New Brunswick Theol. Sem., 1878; m. Annie Latourette Boice, Dec. 6, 1881. Ordained Reformed Ch. ministry, 1878; pastor, Fairfield, N.J., 1878-80, Greenville Ch., Jersey City, N.J., 1881-86, First Ch., New Brunswick, Jan. 1, 1887-Jan. 1, 1912, First Presbyn. Ch., Alden, N.Y., 1912-16, 1st Ref. Ch., Hasbrouck Heights, N.J., May 1916—. Pres. Gen. Synod Reformed Ch. in America, 1911-12; pres. Bd. of Edn. Reformed Church, 1908-12; stated clk. Bd. of Supts., New Brunswick Theol. Sem., 16 yrs. Republican. Author: History of the Reformed Church, East Greenbush, N.Y., 1891. Home: Hasbrouck Heights, N.J. Died Nov. 17, 1919.

POE, John Prentiss, lawyer; mem. law firm of John P. Poe & Sons. Made speech seconding nomination of Davis for v.p., Dem. Nat. Conv., St. Louis, 1904. Codified Public General Laws of Maryland (2 vols.), 1905. Home: Baltimore, Md. Died 1909.

POE, John William, banker; b. Mason Co., Ky., Oct. 17, 1850; s. Nathan and Louisa (Harber) P.; m. Sophie M. Alberding, May 3, 1883. Left home at 18; worked at farming and ry. constr. in Mo. and Kan., later working on U.S. Govt. contracts at Fort Griffin, Tex. City marshal Fort Griffin, 1878-79; later deputy sheriff and deputy U.S. marshal in northwest Tex. and eastern N.M.; elected sheriff of Lincoln Co., N.M., 1882, 84; mem. Territorial Bd. of Equalization by appt. of Governor Otero, 1889-90; mem. and pres. State Tax Commn., 1915-17 (resigned). Identified with banking business, 1890—; pres. Citizens Nat. Bank of Roswell and First Nat. Bank of Artesia, also dir. several other banks in the Pecos Valley. Federal fuel adminstr. for N.M., during part of World War. Mem. bd. of regents N.M. Military Inst. many years. Was ranchman and agriculturist during part of earlier life. Democrat. Mason. Home: Roswell, N.M. Died July 17, 1923.

POFFENBARGER, Livia (Nye) Simpson, author, genealogist; b. Pomeroy, O., Mar. 1, 1862; d. George Perry and Phebe Almeda (Kennedy) Simpson; ed. pub. schs. and under pvt. tutor; LL.D., W.Va. U., 1919; studied law 2 yrs. in offices of Simpson & Howard, Point Pleasant, W.Va.; m. Hon. George Poffenbarger, May 10, 1894; children—Nathan Simpson, Perry Simpson. Owner and mgr. State Gazette, Point Pleasant, 1888-1913; largely instrumental in securing funds for erection of Battle Monument, at Point Pleasant, 1909, and for purchase of grounds for Tu-Endie-Wei Park (delivered dedicatory address at the park before 10,000 people); pres. Pt. Pleasant Battle Monument Commn. (speaker at monument unveiling before 30,000 people). Polit. adviser during Rep. Nat. Conv., Chicago, 1912; mem. Governors' Congress, Washington, 1908; mem. Nat. Rep. Women's Advisory Council of One Hundred, 1920-24; asso. member Nat. Rep. Executive Com., 1920, and mem. Nat. Rep. Advisory Council of Forty (men and women) to Nat. Rep. Exec. Com., 1920-24; mem. Nat. Rep. Speakers' Bur.; mem. W.Va. Rep. State Speakers Bur.; W.Va. Republican elector at large, 1924. Delivered dedicatory address at unveiling monument to World War Vets. at Charleston, W.Va., Nov. 11, 1925. Mem. bd. govs. Morris Memorial Hosp.; advisory chmn. and pub. speaker W.Va. First Good Roads Bond Issue for $50,000,000; Rep. dir. W.Va. Suffrage Campaign. State chmn. woman's com. for 3d, 4th and 5th Liberty Loans; mem. Four Minute Men, State Bd. War Savings and Thrift Stamps; organized and chmn. Red Cross and chmn. food conservation, Mason County. Presbyn. Author: Industrial and Biographical Point Pleasant, 1905; Fort Randolph, 1907; Battle of Point Pleasant, First Battle of American Revolution, 1909; Pioneer History of Mason County, W.V., 1910; Romantic and Historic West Virginia, 1932. State vice chmn. for Repeal 18th Amendment, 1932. Home: Charleston, W.Va. Died Oct. 27, 1937.

POHLMANN, Julius, physician; b. Hamburg, Germany, Jan. 26, 1848; s. Christian Herrman and Marie Louise P.; ed. at Hamburg; M.D., U. of Buffalo, 1883; m. Lily Bulloch, of Glasgow, Scotland, June 27, 1898. Dir. Mus. of Buffalo Soc. Natural Sciences, 1882-90; in med. practice, 1891—; prof. physiology, U. of Buffalo. Home: Buffalo, N.Y. Died 1910.

POLACHEK, Victor Henry, newspaperman; b. Chicago, Aug. 24, 1876; s. Henry and Lina (Green) P.; ed. pub. and high schs., Chicago; m. Evelyn Bernson, Apr. 28, 1904; children—Frank B., Victor H., Jane. Began newspaper work with Chicago Times, 1893; telegraph editor Chicago Inter Ocean, 1897, New York World, 1898; entered service Hearst newspapers, 1899; city editor New York American, 1903-04; mng. editor Chicago Examiner, 1904-14; gen. exec. officer Hearst publs., 1914-18; pub. New York American, 1918-19; resigned from Hearst orgn., 1919; pub. The Sun and The Evening Sun, New York, 1919-20; v.p. Agar-Bernson Corp., paper, 1920-22; editor Hearst newspapers, and mem. exec. council Hearst newspapers, 1922-28; mgr. Hearst Sunday newspapers, 1928-30, mem. gen. management Hearst Newspapers, 1931—, and business mgr. The American Weekly, 1937-38; retired 1939. Home: Great Neck, L.I., N.Y. Died June 11, 1940.

POLAK, John Osborn, obstetrician, gynecologist; b. at Brooklyn, N.Y., Mar. 12, 1871; s. of Karl T. and Mary E. (Osborn) P.; M.D., U. of Vt., 1891, Long Island Coll. Hosp., 1891, received Dudley medal of surgery; M.Sc., Rutgers Coll., 1889; m. Bertha L. Pitkin, June 12, 1895; 1 daughter, Mary Osborn. Was prof. of obstetrics and gynecology, Long Island College Hospital, 1910-31, also pres. of faculty and pres. bd. regents, 1931—; prof. obstetrics, Dartmouth Med. Sch., 1901-12; consulting gynecologist Deaconess, Bushwick, Coney Island, People's and Williamsburgh hospitals. Chmn. sub. com. on prenatal, maternal, and early infant care, White House Conf. on Child Health and Protection, 1931. Fellow Am. Coll. Surgeons (a founder and life mem.; mem. bd. govs., 1913, 16, 26; mem. bd. regents 1927-31). Democrat. Episcopalian. Author: Students' Manual of Obstetrics, 1914; Students' Manual of Gynecology, 1915. Died June 29, 1931.

POLAND, William Carey, coll. prof.; b. Goffstown, N.H., Jan. 25, 1846; s. Rev. James Willey and Sarah Jane (Ayer) P.; A.B., Brown U., 1868, A.M., 1871, Litt.D., 1904; univs. Berlin, Leipzig, 1875-76, Mus. at Berlin, 1878; in France, and Italy, 1878-79; m. Clara Frances, d. Prof. Albert Harkness, of Providence, R.I., Mar. 25, 1882; children—William, Albert Harkness, Reginald. Prin. Worcester (Mass.) Acad., 1868-70; instr. Greek and Latin, 1870-75, asst. prof., 1876-89, asso. prof. Greek, 1889-92, prof. history of art, 1892-1915, curator Mus. Classical Archæology, 1889-93, dir. Mus. Fine Arts, 1893-1915, prof. history of art emeritus, Sept., 1915—, Brown U. Pres. R.I. Sch. of Design, 1896-1907; lecturer on history of art, Boston U., 1901-02; formerly lecturer R.I. Sch. of Design; annual dir., 1891-92, then mem. mng. com., Am. Sch. of Classical Studies at Athens; sec. Commission of Colls. in N.E. on Admission Examinations, 1886-1905. Councilor Archæol. Inst. of America, 1907-1915 (also pres. Rhode Island Society, 1907-1915). Baptist. Author: Necrology of Brown University, 1888-1904; Syllabus of Ten Lectures on Classical Archæology, 1893; Notes on Art in the Nineteenth Century; Notes and Questions on the History of Art in the Seventeenth and Eighteenth Centuries, 1900; Notes and Questions on the History of Art During the Period of the Renaissance, 1901; Lecture Outlines on the History of Roman and Mediæval Art, 1906; Robert Feke, the Early Newport Portrait Painter, 1907. Home: Providence, R.I. Died Mar. 19, 1929.

POLK, Ralph Lane, publisher; b. Bellefontaine, O., Sept. 12, 1849; s. Rev. David and Mary Charlotte (Warner) P.; ed. Pennington (N.J.) Sem.; m. Amelia Francis Hopkins, of Greenwich, Eng., Sept. 17, 1877. Enlisted as musician in Co. G, 40th N.Y. Vols., at age of 15, remaining in service 8 mos.; hon. mustered out, Aug. 1865; entered directory business at Indianapolis, Ind., 1869; removed to Detroit, 1870, and organized R. L. Polk & Co., now the largest pubs. of directories in the world, of which he is the dominant head. Republican. Presbyn. Mason. Home: Detroit, Mich. Died Aug. 21, 1923.

POLK, Rufus King, congressman, steel mfr.; b. Columbia, Tenn., Aug. 23, 1866; s. Gen. L. E. (C.S.A.) and Sally (Moore) P.; grad. Lehigh Univ., B.S., 1887 (E.M.); m. Isabella Grier. Mem. Congress, 17th Pa. dist., 1899-1903. Democrat. In Spanish-Am. war, 1st lt. Co. F 12th regt., Pa. vols. Home: Danville, Pa. Died 1902.

POLK, William Mecklenburg, physician; b. Ashwood, Tenn., Aug. 15, 1844; s. Bishop and Lt. Gen. Leonidas P.; grad. Va. Mil. Inst., 1861; entered C.S.A. as cadet from Va. Mil. Inst., 1861; became 1st lt. arty. and asst. chief of arty., Polk's Corps, Army of the Tenn.; later capt. in adj. and insp. gen.'s dept.; M.D., Coll. Phys. and Surg. (Columbia), 1869; (LL.D., U. of the South, 1894, Columbia, 1904, U. of Ga., 1913); m. Ida A. Lyon, Nov. 14, 1866. In practice at New York, 1869—; prof. therapeutics, Bellevue Hosp. Med. Coll., 1876-79; prof. obstetrics and gynecology, Med. Dept., U. of New York, 1879-98; dean and prof. gynecology, Cornell U. Med. Coll., 1898—; gynecologist to Bellevue Hosp.; 1st lt. U.S.A. Med. Reserve Corps. Vestryman, Trinity Corp., New York. Died June 24, 1918.

POLLAK, Gustav, editor; b. Vienna, Austria, May 4, 1849; s. Lazar and Magdalena (Klein) P.; ed. in Vienna; m. Celia Heilprin, May 23, 1875. Contbr. to New York Nation, 1874—, and to New York Evening Post, chiefly on foreign politics and lit. subjects, 1881—; upon consolidation of The Nation and Evening Post, 1881, was cashier Evening Post Pub. Co., 1881-93, continuing lit. connection with The Nation and Evening Post both before and after resigning position as cashier; editor Babyhood, 1884-1909. Lectured on Austrian Dramatists, Johns Hopkins, 1905. Was candidate of Gold Democrats for state senator from Union Co., N.J., 1896. One of founders of the German-Am. Reform Union during presdl. campaign, 1892. Author: The Century Book for Mothers (with Dr. L. M. Yale), 1901; Franz Grillparzer and the Austrian Drama, 1907; The Hygiene of the Soul, 1910; Michael Heilprin and His Sons, 1913; International Perspective in Literary Criticism, 1914; Fifty Years of American Idealism, 1915; The House of Hohenzollern and the Hapsburg Monarchy, 1917. Home: New York, N.Y. Died Nov. 1, 1919.

POLLAK, Walter Heilprin, lawyer; b. Summit, N.J., June 4, 1887; s. Gustav and Celia (Heilprin) P.; prep. edn., Summit (N.J.) Acad.; A.B., Harvard, 1907, LL.B., 1910; m. Marion Heilprin, Apr. 4, 1914; children—Minna H., Ann, Louis H. Admitted to N.Y. bar, 1911, practicing at N.Y. City; formerly mem. Engelhard, Pollak, Pitcher, Stern & Clark; now counsel Cohen, Cole, Weiss & Wharton. Mem. legal staff War Industries Bd., 1917-18. Spl. asst. to U.S. atty. gen. in Arnstein bond theft case, 1923-24; counsel State Park commissions and spl. asst. atty. gen. in Long Island and Palisades Park litigations, 1925-39; consultant to Nat. Commn. on Law Observance and Enforcement, 1929-31; counsel in U.S. Supreme Court in successful appeals of Scottsboro defendants, 1932 and 1935; mem. Law Revision Commn. State of N.Y., 1934—; chmn. Railroad Investigation Commn., 1935; special asst. to U.S. atty. gen. in railway pension litigation and special counsel Railroad Retirement Bd., 1936-37; special master Interborough Receiverships, 1936; trustee Associated Gas & Electric Co., 1940. Home: New York, N.Y. Died Oct. 2, 1940.

POLLARD, Arthur Gayton, merchant; b. Plaistow, N.H., Jan. 5, 1843; s. Col. Joseph S. and Luella J. (Tucker) P.; ed. pub. schs.; m. Martha M. Fuller, Oct. 14, 1869. Mercantile business, Lowell, Mass., Jan. 1, 1864—; formerly pres. Union Nat. Bank, now chmn. bd.; pres. A. G. Pollard Co., Stony Brook R.R., Lowell Hosiery Co. Trustee Lowell Textile Sch. (chmn. bd.), Ayer Home for Children, Old Ladies' Home, Y.M.C.A., Lowell Cemetery Corp.; pres. Lowell Gen. Hospital. Baptist. Mason. Home: Lowell, Mass. Died June 5, 1930.

POLLARD, Edward Bagby, educator; b. Stevensville, Va., Oct. 9, 1864; s. Rev. John and Virginia (Bagby) P.; B.A., Richmond Coll., 1884. M.A., 1886, D.D., 1901; grad. Southern Bapt. Theol. Sem., Louisville, 1890; Ph.D., Yale, 1890-93. U. of Berlin, 1896; m. Emily Tufton Mason, June 4, 1895; children—Emily Louise, Otis Mason (dec.), Edward Bagby. Ordained Bapt. ministry, 1890; pastor, New Haven, Conn., 1890-93, Roanoke, Va., 1893-96; prof. Bibl. lit., Columbian (now George Washington) U., 1896-1902; pastor and prof. Bibl. lit., Georgetown (Ky.) Coll., 1902-06; prof. homiletics, Crozer Theol. Sem., Chester, Pa., 1906—. Editor, Service, 1910-12. Author: Paul Judson, 1905; Semitic and Oriental Women, 1907; editor Crozer Quarterly, 1924—. Home: Chester, Pa. Died July 12, 1927.

POLLARD, Isaac, pomologist; b. Plymouth, Vt., July 11, 1830; s. Isaac and Sallie (Conant) P.; ed. Black River Acad., Ludlow, Vt.; m. Viola Welch, Mar. 11, 1861 (died 1914). Went to Calif. gold fields by way of Panama, 1849; settled in Neb., 1856, and has spent many yrs. in selecting apples that can be made productive in Central Mo. Valley; owns bearing orchard of 165 acres— the largest in Neb.; imported seedless apples from Hawaiian Islands and experimenting in growing same; also extensive experiments in growing shrubs and trees adapted for prairie country. County clk., Cass Co., Neb., 1 term; county commr. 3 years. Republican. Home: Nehawka, Neb. Died Nov. 25, 1916.

POLLARD, John Garland, lawyer, gov.; b. King and Queen Co., Va., Aug. 4, 1871; s. Rev. John and Virginia (Bagby) P.; Richmond Coll., 1891; LL.B., Columbian (now George Washington) U., 1893, LL.D., George Washington U., 1921, also from Coll. of William and Mary, Washington and Lee U., U. of Richmond, Furman U.; m. Grace Phillips, Aug. 10, 1898 (died 1932); children—John Garland, Chas. P., Susie Virginia (Mrs. Herbert Lee Boatwright); m. 2d, Violet Elizabeth McDougall, July 31, 1933. Practiced, Richmond, 25 yrs. Mem. Va. Constl. Conv., 1901-02; chmn. Va. Commn. on Uniform State Laws, 1902-07; Dem. presdl. elector, 1904; atty. gen. of Va., and mem. State Bd. of Edn., 1913-17; governor of Virginia, term 1930-34. Engaged in war welfare work in France and Germany, 1918-19, subsequently engaged in adjustment of disputed war claims for War Dept.; mem. Federal Trade Commn., 1920-21. Past dean Marshall-Wythe Sch. of Govt. and Citizenship, Coll. of William and Mary, 1922-29. Pres. Children's Home Soc. of Va. for 20 yrs.; pres. Gen. Soc. Alumni Univ. of Richmond; pres. Va. Mus. of Fine Arts; chmn. Bd. of Veterans' Appeals. Democrat. Baptist. Edited Virginia Code, Annotated, 1904, and A Connotary, 1935. Home: Washington, D.C. Died Apr. 28, 1937.

POLLARD, Percival, literary reviewer Town Topics, 1897—; b. Greifswald, Pomerania, of English-German parentage, Jan. 29, 1869; s. Joseph and Marie P.; came to U.S., 1885; ed. Eastbourne Coll., Sussex; m. Charlotte T. Rénea, Jan. 22, 1899. Entered journalism on St. Joseph (Mo.) News, 1891; from then in editorial and lit. work, Chicago and New York. Author: Figaro Fiction, 1892; Cape of Storms, 1895, 1900; Posters in Miniature, 1896; Dreams of Today, 1897; The Kiss that Killed, 1898; The Imitator, 1902; Lingo Dan, 1903; Recollections of Oscar Wilde, 1906; Their Day in Court, 1909. Plays: (with Leo Ditrichstein), Nocturno (prod. 1906); The Ambitious Mrs. Alcott, in four acts (prod. Astor Theatre, New York, 1907). Home: Baltimore, Md. Died 1911.

POLLARD, William Jefferson, lawyer; b. Kingston, Mo., May 1, 1860; s. William S. and Mary Ann (Parks) P.; ed. at home and pvt. instrn. in law, and admitted to bar; unmarried. Justice of the peace, St. Louis, 2 terms; judge 2d dist. police court, 1903—. Originated the Pollard "pledge plan" for reforming drunkards—releasing the accused on signing a total abstinence pledge for 1 yr.—which has been widely copied and also enacted into the statute law of Great Britain by the British Parliament; visited Great Britain, 1906, where addressed meetings and explained the "Pollard plan"; Vt. Legislature passed a law authorizing judges to liberate men convicted of drunkenness on the "Pollard plan," a pledge to abstain from liquor for one year; plan also adopted by Legislature of State of Victoria, Australia. Was appointed by President Taft a delegate to represent the U.S. Govt. at the Internat. Congress on Alcoholism at London, Eng., July, 1909, and again to the Internat. Congress on Alcoholism at The Hague, Holland, 1911; 550 dels. and mems. to the Hague Congress signed the following declaration: "We, the undersigned members and delegates attending the 13th Internat. Congress on Alcoholism assembled in The Hague, Holland, Sept. 11-16, 1911, desire to record our gratification at the recognition in statute law by Great Britain, Vermont, U.S.A., and Victoria, Australia, of the principle of reforming drunkards by the probation on pledge method, commonly known as the Pollard plan. The possibilities of this wise and beneficent policy are so great that we desire to commend its adoption throughout the world." More than 400 dels. and mems. of the London Congress signed a similar declaration. A guest of Nat. German Abstinence Conv., in Augsburg, Germany, 1910. Mem. Soc. for Study of Inebriety (London). Mason. Home: St. Louis. Died Dec. 12, 1913.

POLLITZER, Sigmund, dermatologist; b. Richmond Co., N.Y., June 12, 1859; s. Morris and Anna (Kuh) P.; A.B. Coll. City of New York, 1879 (Phi Beta Kappa), A.M., 1882; M.D., Coll. Phys. and Surg. (Columbia), 1884; post-grad. work, 4 yrs., in Heidelberg, Berlin, Vienna, Hamburg, London and Paris; surgeon Servian army in Servian-Bulgarian war of 1885-86; m. Alice Kohn, June 8, 1893; children—Margaret (Mrs. Lindsey Hoben), Aline (Mrs. Louis S. Weiss). Began practice in New York, 1886; prof. dermatology, New York Post-Grad. Med. Sch., 1906-15, 1st lt., Med. Reserve Corps U.S.A. Major Medical R.C., 1917, and served on advisory bd. in office surgeon gen. U.S.A., Washington, and in U.S.A. Gen. Hosp. 1, N.Y. Editor Darier's Dermatology, 1920. Home: New York, N.Y. Died Nov. 1, 1937.

POLLMAN, William, banker; b. Quincy, Ill., Aug. 24, 1867; s. Frederic W. and Amelia (Brookmann) P.; ed. pub. schs., La Cygne, Kan., and Gem City Business Coll., Quincy, Ill.; m. Emma Geiser, Feb. 5, 1896; children—Louise Elizabeth (Mrs. George Prescott Lilley), Edna Geiser. Settled at Baker, 1889, and engaged in banking, cattle and sheep raising and farming; pres. First Nat. Bank; pres. Baker Loan & Trust Co., Northwest Granite Co. (Haines, Ore.), Douglas County Light & Water Co. (Roseburg, Ore.), Seaside (Ore.) Light & Power Co.; v.p. Portland Cattle Loan Co., Ore. Life Ins. Co. (Portland); treas. Eastern Ore. Building & Loan Assn. (Baker). Donated two parks to City of Baker; mayor of Baker. Republican. Presbyn. Mason. Odd Fellow, K.P. Home: Baker, Ore. Died Oct. 23, 1930.

POLLOCK, Charles Andrew, lawyer; b. Elizabethtown, N.Y., Sept. 27, 1853; s. John and Eunice Elvira (Ellis) P.; A.B., Cornell Coll., 1878, A.M., 1881, LL.D., 1908; LL.B., State U. of Ia., 1881; m. Martha Clinton, Sept. 27, 1882; children—Clara A., Mrs. Lorine Bingman, Chas. M. Began practice at Fargo, Dak. Ty., 1881; dist. atty. Cass Co., Dak. Ty., 1885-89; judge Dist. Court, 3d Jud. Dist. of N.D., 1897-1917; sr. mem. Chas. A. and Chas. M. Pollock; instr. law dept. U. of N.D. 4 yrs. Served as a v.p. Nat. Anti-Saloon League since its orgn., 1897; has spoken widely on prohibition in U.S. and Can., also in various European Countries, 1921-22. Mem. Gen. Conf. M.E. Ch., 1908, 12, 16, 20, 24, serving as chmn. temperance com. and mem. judiciary com.; a commr. on question of unification of M.E. Chs., North and South. Republican. Mason. Author of Prohibition Law of N.Dak., 1889, and of Manual of Prohibition Law of North Dakota, 1910. Home: Fargo, N.D. Deceased.

POLLOCK, John C., judge; b. Belmont Co., O., Nov. 5, 1857; s. Samuel and Jane B. (Scott) P.; A.B., Franklin Coll., 1882; m. Louise Lafferty, of Lafferty, O., Sept. 24. 1886 (died 1912); 1 dau. Lucille (Mrs. Frank H. Jennings); m. 2d, Beulah B. McColm Haas, July 11, 1924. Studied law, St. Clairsville, O., 1882-84; admitted to bar, Newton, Ia., 1884; practiced at Winfield, Kan., 1888-1901; justice Supreme Court of Kan., Jan. 1901-Dec. 1903; U.S. dist. judge, Dist. of Kan., 1903—. United Presbyterian. Republican. Home: Kansas City, Kan. Died Jan. 24, 1937.

POLLOCK, Pinckney Daniel, educator; b. Houston Co., Ga., Nov. 22, 1859; s. of James G. and Nancy P.; ed. country schs., Floyd Co., Ga.; Armurchee Acad.; B.L., Univ. of Ga.; studied univs. of Paris and Berlin, 3 yrs.; m. Eva Selman, Nov. 24, 1895. Prof. English, Mercer Univ., 1893-96; pres. same, 1896—. Chmn. exec. com. Ga. Bapt. Conv., 1899— Chmn. Ga. Bapt. Edn. Commn. from its organization, 1901; declined office State supt. of edn., 1894. Home: Macon, Ga. Deceased.

POLLOCK, Walter Briesler; b. Milton, Mass. Dec. 8, 1856; s. Andrews Fletcher and Mary (Briesler) P.; ed. pub. and night schs.; m. Helen B. Hutchinson, June 22, 1882. Identified with railroad business, 1868—; now mgr. marine dept. N.Y.C. R.R. Co.; dir. Am. & Foreign Ins. Co., Mfrs. Liability Ins. Co., Oswegatchie Light & Power Co., Internat. Pulp Co. Pres. N.Y. Produce Exchange, 1920, now treasurer. Marine dir. N.Y. Harbor for U.S. R.R. Administration, World War. Republican. Episcopalian. Mason. Home: Bayport, N.Y. Died Nov. 20, 1928.

POMERENE, Atlee, senator; b. Berlin, O., Dec. 6, 1863; s. Dr. Peter P. and Elizabeth (Wise) P.; A.B., Princeton, 1884, A.M., 1887; LL.B., Cincinnati Law Sch., 1886; LL.D., Mount Union-Scio Coll., O., 1913, also College of Wooster, O., Miami U., and Kenyon College, Gambier, O.; m. Mary H. Bockius, June 29, 1892. Admitted to bar, 1886, and began practice at Canton. City solicitor, 1887-91; pros. atty., Stark Co., O., 1897-1900; apptd. mem. Hon. Tax Commn. of Ohio, 1906; chmn. Dem. State Conv., 1910; elected lt. gov. of Ohio, Nov. 8, 1910, and U.S. senator, Jan. 10, 1911, for term 1911-17; reëlected for term 1917-23; now in practice of law, Cleveland, O., as mem. Squire, Sanders & Dempsey. Apptd. one of two attys. to prosecute Naval Petroleum Reserve "oil cases," Feb. 1924; chmn. bd. R.F.C., 1932-33. Democrat. Organized Commercial

& Savings Bank, Canton, 1909. Home: Cleveland, O. Died Nov. 12, 1937.

POMEROY, Eltweed; b. Newark, N.J., Sept. 7, 1860; s. Isaac and Mary Jane (Taylor) P.; grad. Newark Pub. High Sch., 1878; (A.M.); m. Ella Levin, Dec. 10. 1898. Was pres. corp. of Pomeroy Bros. Co., mfrs. ink, mucilage, sealing wax, etc., in whose factory profit-sharing has been several yrs. in operation; retired on account of ill-health and is now farming in Tex. Sec. 1st (Buffalo, 1899) and chmn. 2d (Detroit, 1901) Nat. Social and Polit. Conf.; sec. Direct Legislation League of N.J., from 1892; pres. Nat. Direct Legislation League from 1896; mem. various socs. standing for Fabian Socialism; prominent advocate of direct legislation by the initiative and referendum, upon which he has written extensively for mags. and reviews. Author: By the People, 1900. Editor of the Direct Legislation Record until 1904. Asso. editor The Arena. Pres. Tex. Hort. Soc.; hon. v.p. Rio Grande Hort. Soc.; v.p. Am. Pomol. Soc. Home: Donna, Tex. Deceased.

POMEROY, John Larrabee, M.D.; b. Louisville, Ky., Dec. 19, 1883; s. Danforth Wetherby and Martha Buchanan (Norris) P.; A.B., Louisville Male High Sch., 1899; M.D., Hosp. Coll. Medicine, Louisville, 1903, Bellevue Med. Coll. N.Y. City, 1909; m. Alice Lillian Brennan, Feb. 10, 1907; 1 son, Stanley Norris; m. 2d, Lecile Jones, July 6, 1930; 1 dau., Joan Lee. Interne City Hosp., N.Y. City, 1903-05; resident phys. Ward's Island Hosp., N.Y., 1905-07; asst. surgeon, U.S.A., 1907-09; asst. supt. North Brother Island Hosp., 1909-10; asst. supt. Pottenger Sanatorium, Monrovia, Calif., 1910-11; in pvt. practice at Monrovia, 1911-15; health officer Los Angeles County (comprising 36 cities, 600 employes), 1915—: prof. of public health, Coll. Medical Evangelists Medical School, Los Angeles, 1935. Served as captain Medical Corps, U.S.A., 1917-19. Dir. Los Angeles Co. Tuberculosis Assn. Fellow Am. Pub. Health Assn. (pres. Western branch). Republican. Mason. Author: Manual of Food Laws, 1928; Information for Physicians Concerning County Health, 1928; Public Health Report, 1928-29; Los Angeles County Health News (2 vols.), 1929, 30. Home: Los Angeles, Calif. Died Mar. 24, 1941.

POMEROY, John Norton, lawyer; b. S. Orange, N.J., May 7, 1866; s. John Norton (LL.D.) and Annie R. (Carter) P.; A.B., Yale, 1887, A.M., 1889; LL.B., U. of Calif., 1891; studies in law at Columbia U. and U. of Calif.; polit. science, Yale and Columbia; m. Annie Creyot Barrington, Aug. 17, 1899. Admitted to Calif. bar, 1891; instr. law dept., Stanford U., 1895-96; in 1900 filled temporary vacancies in law schs. of Washington and Lee U., and Yale U.; asst. prof. law, 1910-11, prof., 1911—, U. of Illinois. Edited editions of his father's legal treatises; Pomeroy's Equity Jurisprudence (3d edition), 1905; Pomeroy's Code Remedies (3d edit.), 1894; Pomeroy's Specific Performance (2d edit.), 1897. Also chief editor Pomeroy's Annotated Codes of California (4 vols.), 1901. Author: Pomeroy's Equitable Remedies (2 vols.), 1905; also lives of Stephen Johnson Field, and of John Norton Pomeroy in vols. 7 and 8 of Lewis's Great American Lawyers, 1909. Home: Urbana, Ill. Died June 1, 1924.

POMEROY, Ralph Brouwer, theologian; b. Nyack, N.Y., Nov. 18, 1876; s. John B. and Augusta (Leonard) P.; B.A., Columbia, 1898 (M.A., 1915); M.A., Princeton, 1913; B.D., Gen. Theol. Sem., 1901; m. Florence Louise Walton, Dec. 27, 1924. Deacon, 1901, priest, 1902, P.E. Ch.; curate Emmanuel Ch., Newport, R.I., 1902-06; asst. Trinity Ch., Princeton, N.J., 1906-13, rector, 1914-17; instr., 1917-19, prof. ecclesiastical polity and canon law, 1919-25, Gen. Theol. Sem. Lecturer on religion, Princeton, 1914-17; asso. in religion, Columbia, 1920-23; priest in charge, Holy Innocents Ch., W. Orange, N.J., 1918—; warden. New York Training Sch. for Deaconesses, 1922-24. Home: West Orange, N.J. Died Aug. 14, 1935.

POMEROY, Theodore Medad, lawyer, banker; b. Cayuga, N.Y., Dec. 31, 1824; s. Rev. Medad and Lilly (Maxwell) P.; grad. Hamilton Coll., 1842 (LL.D., 1894); m. Elizabeth Leitch, d. Robert Watson, Auburn, N.Y., Sept. 4, 1855 (died 1892). Admitted to bar, 1846; practiced law, Auburn, N.Y., until 1870; dist. atty. Cayuga Co., N.Y., 1851-56; mem. N.Y. assembly, 1857; mem. Congress, 1861-69; speaker Ho. of Reps. at close of 40th Congress; mayor of Auburn, 1875-76; State senator, N.Y., 1878-79; banker and 1st v.p. Am. Express Co. Republican. Home: Auburn, N.Y. Died 1905.

POND, Allen Bartlit, architect; b. Ann Arbor, Mich., Nov. 21, 1858; s. Elihu Bartlit and Mary Barlow (Allen) P.; A.B., U. of Mich., 1880; (hon. A.M., 1911); taught Latin, 3 yrs.; studied architecture; unmarried. In practice at Chicago, 1886—. Devotes considerable time to polit. and social movements; trustee Hull House Assn., and Gads Hill Center (social settlements), Bur. Pub. Efficiency; dir. Nat Housing Assn.; mem. Joint Com. on School Affairs; mem. City Club Com. on Edn., Union League Club Com. on Edn.; mem. Illinois Soc. of Architects Com. on Municipal Arts; mem. bd. dirs. Soc. for Prevention of Blindness; mem. Commercial Club Edn.

Com.; pres. Pub. Edn. Assn., Chicago; mem. gen. com. Nat. Conf. City Planning; mem. exec. com. Municipal Voters' League, Chicago, 1896-1923; mem. advisory bd. to fuel administrator of Ill., and dir. state orgn., World War; sec. war com. of Union League Club of Chicago (extensive propaganda), and spl. distribution agt. of U.S. Com. on Pub. Information; first chmn. Bd. of Appeals under Zoning Law, Chicago, 1923-27. Fellow A.I.A. Home: Chicago, Ill. Died Mar. 17, 1929.

POND, Ashley, lawyer; b. Wilmington, N.Y., Nov. 23, 1827; s. Jared and Statira (Bartlitt) P.; removed with parents to Mich., 1836; ed. dist. sch., Wesleyan Sem. (Albion Coll.); A.B., Univ. of Mich., 1854; studied law at Detroit, and admitted to the bar, 1856. In active practice about 45 years (retired); at one time gen. counsel L.S.&M.S. and M.C. rys. Home: Detroit, Mich. Died 1910.

POND, Charles Fremont, naval officer; b. Brooklyn, Conn., Oct. 26, 1856; s. Enoch and Sarah Ann (Utley) P.; grad. U.S. Naval Acad., 1876; m. Emma McHenry, Aug. 10, 1880; children—Charles McHenry, John Enoch, Elizabeth Keith. Ensign U.S.N., July 26, 1878; lt. (jr. grade), Oct. 2, 1885; lt., May 19, 1891; lt. comdr., July 1, 1899; comdr. Mar. 31, 1905; capt., Nov. 12, 1908; rear admiral, Feb. 13, 1914. Served at sea 24 yrs., 2 mos., on shore duty 17 yrs., 11 mos.; U.S.S. Pensacola, Lackawanna, Tuscarora and Jamestown, 1877-78; U.S. Coast and Geodetic Survey Office, Wash., 1879; engaged in survey, Pacific coast, U.S. Coast and Geodetic Survey Ship Hassler, 1879-83, 1886, U.S.S. Ranger, 1887-90, inaugurating coast and geodetic survey in Alaskan waters, 1881-83; Hydrographic Office, Wash., 1883-84, br. Hydrographic Office, S.F., 1884; U.S.S. Hartford and Wachusett, 1884-85; Naval Obs., Mare Island, Calif., 1885-87; in charge same, 1890-94; U.S.S. Alert, 1894-97; asst. insp. ordnance, Navy Yard, N.Y., 1897-98; U.S.S. Panther, Spanish-Am. War, 1898; comd. U.S.S. Iroquois, 1898-1902, and comd. Naval Sta., Hawaii, during absence of commandant, 1900-01; surveyed Midway Islands, 1900; selected site for Naval Sta., Pearl Harbor, Hawaii, and inaugurated condemnation proceedings in U.S. Courts, 1901; Naval Training Sta., San Francisco, 1902-04; superintended landing Trans-Pacific cable, Midway Islands, 1903; comd. U.S.S. Supply, Guam, 1904-05; ins. ord., comd. Naval Magazine, Mare Island, 1905-07; comd. U.S.S. Lawton, 1906, Buffalo, 1907-08; insp. 13th lighthouse dist., 1908-09; comd. Pennsylvania, 1909-11, U.S.S. Oregon and Pacific Reserve Squadron, 1911-12; comd. 12th Naval Dist., 1912-15; comdr.-in-chief Pacific Reserve Fleet, Apr.-Oct. 1915; comdr. Train, Atlantic Fleet, Dec. 1915-July 1916; comdr. Cruiser Force, Atlantic Fleet, July-Nov. 1916; retired Dec. 30, 1918. Home: Berkeley, Calif. Died Aug. 4, 1929.

POND, Frederick Eugene, editor; b. Packwaukee, Wis., Apr. 8, 1856; s. Simeon and Flora (Hotchkiss) P.; ed. Montello, Wis.; m. Frances Harriet Fox, g.d. Solomon Juneau, founder of Milwaukee, June 22, 1892. Early turned attention to sporting matters; field editor of Turf, Field and Farm, New York, 1881-86; edited Wildwood's Magazine, 1888-89, but merged it in Turf, Field and Farm, of which he became corr. editor; editor Sportsmen's Review, 1897-1917; asso. editor, Apr.-Nov. 1917, editor Nov. 1917-18, Am. Angler; Rod and Gun editor N.Y. Herald, Feb. 1923—. Author: (pen-name "Will Wildwood") Handbook for Young Sportsmen, 1876; Memoirs of Eminent Sportsmen, 1878; Gun Trial and Field Trial Records of America, 1883; Life and Adventures of Ned Buntline, 1888; Fishcraft, 1922; Sea Fishing, 1923. American Game Preserves (serial). Editor: Fugitive Sporting Sketches, 1879; Sportsmen's Directory, 1892; A Strike, 1897. Edited 3 vols. of Frank Forester's works, 1879-80, and Isaac McLellan's Poems of Rod and Gun, 1883; Charles Hallock's An Angler's Reminiscences, 1913. Home: Brooklyn, N.Y. Died Nov. 1, 1925.

POND, George Edward, journalist-author; b. Boston, Mass., March 11, 1837; grad. Harvard, 1858 (LL.B., 1860); m. Emilie Guerber, May 29, 1866 (died 1880). Served in Union army as 1st lt. in Civil war. Was asso. editor Army and Navy Journal in 1864, and subsequent years; later on editorial staff New York Times until 1870; editor Philadelphia Record, 1870-77; later on New York Sun editorial staff. Author: The Shenandoah Valley in 1864; also Driftwood Essays in Galaxy Magazine under signature "Philip Quilibet." Home: New York, N.Y. Died 1899.

POND, George Gilbert, chemist; b. Holliston, Mass., Mar. 29, 1861; s. Abel and Amelia H. (Robinson) P.; A.B., Amherst, 1881, A.M., 1884, Ph.D., 1889; U. of Göttingen, 1881-82, 85; univs. of Berlin and Munich, 1894-95; m. Helen Palmer, Aug. 1, 1888. Instr. chemistry, Amherst, 1883-88; prof. chemistry, 1888—, dean Sch. of Natural Science, 1896—, Pa. State Coll. Mem. Jury of Awards, Buffalo Expn., 1901. Episcopalian. Died May 20, 1920.

POND, Irving Kane, architect; b. Ann Arbor, Mich., May 1, 1857; s. Elihu Bartlit and Mary Barlow (Allen) P.; C.E., U. of Mich., 1879, hon. A.M., 1911, Dr. Architecture, 1930; went to Chicago, 1879;

traveled and studied abroad, 1883-84; m. Katharine L. deNancrede, June 9, 1929 (died 1935). Partner with bro. Allen B., Pond & Pond, architects, Chicago, 1886 (Pond & Pond and Edgar Martin, 1931-34); firm architects for Hull House and Chicago Commons, Chicago, Federal Bldg., Kankakee, Ill., Mich. Union and U. of Michigan League buildings, at Ann Arbor, Memorial Union bldgs. at LaFayette, Ind. (Purdue U.), East Lansing, Mich. (M.S.C.), Lawrence, Kan. (U. of Kan.), Public Hospital, St. John, N.B., Can., and numerous other important buildings in Chicago and elsewhere. Independent Democrat; interested in measures and organizations for civic and social betterment and for the advancement of fine arts. Fellow A.I.A. (pres. 1910-11; gold medal Ill. Chapter, 1909). Represented Am. Inst. Architects and U.S. Govt. at Internat. Congress of Architects, Rome and Venice, 1911; mem. Bd. of Art Advisers of Ill., 1917-25; asst. examiner U.S. Shipbuilding Labor Adjustment Bd., Great Lakes Dist., 1918. Author: The Meaning of Architecture, 1918; A Day Under the Big Top, 1924; Big Top Rhythms, 1937. Home: Chicago, Ill. Died Sept. 29, 1939.

POND, James Burton, lecture mgr.; b. Cuba, N.Y., June 11, 1838; s. Willard Elmer and Clarissa (Woodford) P.; went to Ill., 1844; to Wis., 1847; brought up on farm; learned printing trade; m. Ann Frances Lynch, Jan. 21, 1859 (died 1871); m. 2d, Martha Marion Glass, March 10, 1888. Published Markesan, Wis., Journal, 1860-61. Lt. to maj. in 3d Wis. cav., 1861-65; one of 17 survivors of band of 118 in Baxter Springs massacre by guerrilla chief Quantrell, Oct. 1863; engaged in mercantile business in West, 1865-74; bought Lyceum Lecture Bureau, Boston, 1874; removed office to New York, 1879. Author: Eccentricities of Genius, 1900, D1; A Summer in England with Henry Ward Beecher, etc. Home: Jersey City, N.J. Died 1903.

POND, Theodore Hanford, art educator, lecturer; b. of Am. parents at Beirut, Syria, Sept. 27, 1873; s. Theodore Strong (D.D.) and Julia Ida (Hanford) P.; prep. edn. under father and mother and pvt. tutors; grad. Pratt Inst., Brooklyn, N.Y., 1892; m. Marion Ruth Goff, June 30, 1903. Designer for textiles, interior decorations, wall papers, stained glass, silverware, jewelry, book covers and decorations, N.Y. City, Boston, Providence, Rochester and Baltimore, 1893-1914, also worked as wood carver, potter, silversmith and jeweler; teacher of design and drawing, Assn. Business Inst., N.Y. City, 1895-96; teacher of design, composition, wood carving, modeling and metal work, also lecturer on history of art, Rhode Island Sch. of Design, Providence, R.I., 1896-1902, dir. dept. design and applied art, 1900-02; teacher design, etc., and lecturer on history of art and theory of design, Mechanics Inst., Rochester, 1902-08, supt. dept. of fine and applied arts, 1903-08; head of dept. of design, teacher and lecturer, Md. Inst., Baltimore, 1908-11; pres. and dir. The Pond Applied Art Studios, Baltimore, 1911-14; supt. plantation, Puerto Rico, 1914-15; dir. Guild of Applied Arts, Buffalo, also instr., Chautauqua Summer Sch. Arts and Crafts, 1915-16; organizer and instr. dept. of silversmithing and jewelry, Ohio Mechanics Inst., Cincinnati, 1916-17; dir. dept. of design and applied art, Md. Inst., 1917-22; also instr. in industrial arts, Md. State Normal Sch., 1921-22, and teacher in summer schs., Johns Hopkins, Md. Inst., Baltimore City Summer Sch. for Teachers; dir. Dayton (O.) Mus. of Art, 1922-29; editor Dayton Inst. News, 1928-29; dir. Akron Art Inst., 1929-31. Home: Akron, O. Died Nov. 3, 1933.

POND, Wilf Pocklington, editor; b. at sea; s. Cabourn Pocklington and Elizabeth (Sewell) P.; ed. public sch. in England; married. Traveled through the West and South, 1886-88; editor "Tobacco," 1888-98, also spl. tech. writer for New York Sun, 1893-99; editor Spirit of the Times, 1899-1904, Sports of the Times, 1904-09; compiled Canadian edit. Century Book of Facts, 1910; editor Bit and Spur, now The Spur, 1911—; rep. and corr. English Sporting Chronicle, 1900—. Fought against the Boers in defense of Pretoria, 1880-81. Home: New York, N.Y. Died Feb. 5, 1936.

PONTIUS, Albert William, consul; b. St. Paul, Minn., Aug. 29, 1879; s. Jacob and Katherine (Christophel) P.; high sch. edn.; m. Irene G. Malzard, of St. Peter's, Jersey, Eng., Nov. 20, 1912. Apptd. after examination, student interpreter in China, Feb. 12, 1903; vice and deputy consul gen. at Tientsin, 1905-06, Newchwang, 1906-08 (also interpreter), Hankow, 1908; asst. to chief of Div. of Far Eastern Affairs, Washington, 1908-09; consul at Swatow, 1909-10; vice consul, in charge, Nanking, Jan.-May, 1910; spl. duty Hankow, 1910-11; consul, Dalny, Manchuria, Aug. 19, 1911-13; at Nanking, Nov.-May 1914; at Newchwang, June-Dec., 1914; at Foochow, 1915-18; at Canton, Apr. 1918—. Home: Canton, China. Died Feb. 25, 1923.

POOK, Samuel Hartt, naval constructor U.S.N., retired Jan. 17, 1889; b. Brooklyn, N.Y., Jan. 17, 1827; s. Samuel Moore and Martha Crum (Dickinson) P.; grad. Portsmouth Acad., N.H., 1843; apprenticed as shipwright with his father, serving 7 yrs.; m. Ellen M., d. James K. Frothingham, Charlestown, Mass., 1850. Established as naval architect Boston, designed many merchant vessels, including the clippers Red Jacket, Ocean Telegraph, Northern Light, and others, several iron ships, war frigates for Spanish govt., etc. Entered Govt. service at beginning of war, superintended construction of iron-clad Galena; placed in charge of shipyard at New Haven where 16 steamships were built during war. At close of war entered navy, asst. naval constructor Portsmouth, Boston; promoted naval constructor, 1871, served at Mare Island (San Francisco), Boston, Washington and New York until retired. Home: Washington, D.C. Died 1901.

POOL, Leonidas Moore, banker; b. New Bern, N.C., Dec. 1, 1871; s. Henry Clay and Cecelia (Moore) P.; ed. grammar schs.; m. Eugenie M. Guillemet, June 6, 1895. Resident of New Orleans, 1886—; clk. with J. O. Bigelow, stocks and bonds, until 1891; with Hibernia Nat. Bank (now Hibernia Bank & Trust Co.) until 1918, advancing to v.p.; organizer, 1918, and pres. Marine Bank & Trust Co.; v.p. Union Indemnity Co., Security Sales Co. of La., Great Union Fire & Marine Ins. Co., Guaranty Development Co., Union Title Guarantee Co.; pres. New Orleans Clearing House Assn. V. chmn. Safe River Com. of 100. Chmn. Liberty Loan campaigns, World War, 1st for La., later for Southern La.; king of Mardi Gras Carnival, 1925. Democrat. Episcopalian. Mason, Elk, Hoo Hoo. Home: New Orleans, La. Died July 18, 1929.

POOLE, Cecil Percy, engineer; b. Elizabeth City, N.C., Oct. 16, 1865; s. James Madison and Matilda (Bamford) P.; ed. pvt. schs., Elizabeth City; m. Florence D. Bockover, June 16, 1886. Asso. editor Electrical World, 1895-97, Power, 1897-99; editor Am. Electrician, 1900-05, Power and the Engineer, 1905-12; mech. engr., City of Atlanta, 1913—. Fellow Am. Inst. Elec. Engrs. Episcopalian. Author: Wiring Handbook, 1900; Designs for Small Dynamos and Motors, 1903; Diagrams of Electrical Connections, 1907; The Gas Engine, 1908. Edited dynamo and motor sect. and part of electromagnet sect. of Foster's Electrical Engineer's Pocket Book, 1909. Died Feb. 23, 1921.

POOLE, Charles Hubbard, clergyman; b. Bay Ridge, Brooklyn, N.Y., Feb. 11, 1840; s. George and Elizabeth S. (Chumar) P.; grad. Rutgers Coll., 1863, Theol. Sem. Reformed Ch., New Brunswick, N.J., 1866 (A.M., D.D., Rutgers); m. Mary S. Pohlman, June 12, 1866. Ordained to ministry Ref. Ch. in America, July 1866; corr. sec. Bd. Domestic Missions Ref. Ch. in America, 1888—. Home: Somerville, N.J. Died 1906.

POOLE, Eugene Alonzo, portrait and landscape painter; b. Poolesville, Md., Feb. 16, 1841; s. John and Anna Rebecca (Cost) P.; ed. Rockville Acad., Md., art edn. Pa. Acad. Fine Arts, Phila., and in Paris, France, with Léon Bonnât; m. Ella Towles, Jan. 7, 1880. For years had studio in Washington, D.C. Died Sept. 27, 1912.

POOLE, Frederic, lecturer; b. Great Grimsby, Yorkshire, Eng., May 15, 1863; s. Jesse and Helen P.; ed. Harley Coll., London, Cliff Coll., Derbyshire, Barnardos Children's Hosp., E. London Hosp.; m. Anna E. Jackson, of Leeds, Eng., Aug. 1888; m. 2d, Mary Dungan, May 5, 1896. Came to U.S., 1893; traveled extensively in China, investigating Chinese modern development, 1897-98, as guest of Chinese viceroys. Has lectured widely in U.S. and Europe, on China, also gives Oriental dramatic recitals. Field officer U.S.A. Ednl. Corps, A.E.F., in Eng. and France, 1917-18. Methodist. Mason. Home: Phila., Pa. Died Oct. 7, 1936.

POOLE, Murray, Edward, genealogist; b. Center Moreland, Pa., July 17, 1857; s. Edward V. and Susan (Carey) P.; A.B., Cornell U., 1880; LL.D., Nashville Coll., 1900; D.C.L., Am. Univ., 1901; m. Eva Zeliffe, Nov. 4, 1891. Admitted to N.Y. bar, 1889, and began practice at Ithaca; served as spl. county judge and surrogate, spl. dep. atty. gen., etc. Mem. Dem. State Com., 1906-10. Episcopalian. Mason. Author: Poole Genealogy, 1893; Five Colonial Families, 1902; History of Cornell University, 1916. Home: Ithaca, N.Y. Died Apr. 10, 1925.

POOLEY, Charles A., judge; b. Buffalo, N.Y., Nov. 17, 1854; s. William and Mary A. (Menary) P.; high sch., Buffalo; m. Carrie Adams, June 4. 1884; children—Harriet Adams, Charles William, Margaret Helen (Mrs. M. P. Browne). Admitted to bar, 1879, and practiced at Buffalo, principally corp. and ry. law; atty. for N.Y.C.&H.R. R.R. many yrs.; justice Supreme Court N.Y., term Jan. 1, 1911-Dec. 31, 1924; official referee Supreme Court, 1925—. Republican. Methodist. Trustee Law Library, 8th Jud. Dist., N.Y. Mason. Home: Buffalo, N.Y. Died Nov. 18, 1932.

POOR, Agnes Blake ("Dorothy Prescott"), author; d. Henry Varnum P. (banker and editor Poor's Railway Manual) and Mary Wild (Pierce) P.; ed. pvt. schs. New York. Regent Warren and Prescott Chapter, D.A.R., 1907-12; registrar Mass. Soc. Colonial Dames, 1907. Author: Brothers and Strangers, 1894; Boston Neighbors, 1898; Under Guiding Stars, 1905; Pan-American Poems, an Anthology, 1918. Home: Brookline, Mass. Died Feb. 28, 1922.

POOR, Henry William, banker; b. Bangor, Me., June 16, 1844; A.B., Harvard, 1865. Pres. Poor's Railroad Manual Co.; sr. partner of banking house of H. W. Poor & Co., of New York and Boston; dir. U.S. Casualty Co. Home: New York, N.Y. Died Apr. 13, 1915.

POOR, John Merrill, astronomer; b. West Newbury, Mass., Jan. 28, 1871; s. John Merrill and Mary Alice (Merrill) P.; A.B., 1897, Dartmouth; post-grad. work, Princeton U., 1900-03; Thaw fellow in astronomy, same, 1900-02, grad. student in astronomy, 1902-03, Ph.D., 1904; spl. study, U. of Chicago, summer of 1902; Lund (Sweden) U., 1911; m. Sarah Helen Noyes, Dec. 26, 1905; children—Dorothy Noyes, Elizabeth Merrill. Prin. Hanover High Sch., 1897-98; instr. in astronomy and mathematics, 1898-1900, instr. in astronomy, 1903-06, asst. prof., 1906-15, asso. prof., 1915-17, prof., 1917—, Dartmouth. Died Dec. 11, 1933.

POOR, Ruel Whitcomb, banker; b. New London, N.H., Sept. 29, 1860; s. William Gay and Delina A. (Freeto) P.; ed. pub. schs. and Wilton (Me.) Acad.; m. Ida M. Sawyer, Oct. 18, 1884; children—Helen Hills, Ruella (dec.). With Page Belting Co., Concord, N.H., 1877-81; with Littleton (N.H.) Savings Bank, and Littleton Nat. Bank, 1881-88, cashier of latter, Jan.-Nov. 1888 (resigned); with Garfield Nat. Bank, New York, Nov. 1888, asst. cashier, 1891, cashier, 1892, pres., 1902-25, chmn. bd., 1925-28; chmn. advisory com. Garfield Branch of Chase Nat. Bank. Republican. Mason. Home: New York, N.Y. Died Aug. 8, 1941.

POORE, Benjamin Andrew, army officer; b. Centre, Ala., June 22, 1863; s. Andrew and Keziah (Brooks) P.; grad. United States Military Academy, 1886, Infantry and Cavalry Sch., 1893; Army War Coll., 1909; m. Miss Carleton, June 20, 1888 (died 1929); children—Katharine Hale, Priscilla Carleton, Adelaide Carleton; m. 2d, Mrs. Flora B. Bullock, Oct. 22, 1930. Commd. 2d lt. 12th Infantry, July 1, 1886; promoted through grades to col. 8th Inf., July 1, 1916; brig. gen., N.A., Aug. 5, 1917; brig. general regular army, Dec. 21, 1921; maj. gen., Oct. 11, 1925. Instructor, U.S. Mil. Acad., 1893-95; engaged at Guanica, P.R., July 25, 1898, and at Hormigueros, Aug. 10, 1898; q.m. of regt. and regimental adj., 1899-1903; in Philippines, 1899-1902; comd. detachment of 6th Inf. in fight at Guin-Tabuan, Negros, Oct. 1, 1899, also various expdns.; served in field in Samar, 1905; in Alaska, 1909-10; duty Gen. Staff, Washington, D.C., 1912-14, 1914-16; dir. Army War Coll., 1912-16; in Philippine Islands and China, 1916; comdr. 162d Depot Brigade, Camp Pike, Little Rock, Ark., Sept.-Dec. 1917; comdr. 14th Inf. Brig., El Paso, Tex., Dec. 1917; comd. 7th Inf. Brig., 4th Div., Apr. 3, 1918-Aug. 1, 1919; arrived in France, May 23, 1918; engaged in Aisne-Marne offensive and defensive, St. Mihiel offensive, Meuse-Argonne offensive, July 18-Nov. 11, 1918, in Army of Occupation, Germany, Dec. 1918-July 1919; returned to U.S., Aug. 1919, and assigned to comd. Ft. D. A. Russell, Wyo.; comd. Camp Lewis and Vancouver barracks, Wash., Feb.-Sept. 1920; comd. 1st Inf. and 4th Inf. Brig. 2d Div., Ft. Sam Houston, Tex., Oct. 1920-Nov. 1924; comd. Ft. Sheridan, Ill., and 12th Inf. Brig., Nov. 1924-Oct. 1925; comd. 7th Corps Area, Omaha, Neb., 1925-27; retired June 22, 1927. Awarded D.S.M. and D.S.C. and 2 War Dept. citations (U.S.); Officer Legion of Honor and Croix de Guerre with palm (French); Croce di Guerra al Merito (Italian). Unitarian. Home: Fitchburg, Mass. Died Aug. 27, 1940.

POORE, Henry Rankin, artist; b. Newark, N.J., Mar. 21, 1859; grad. U. of Pa., 1883. Studied art at Pa. Acad. and Nat. Acad. of Design, New York; pupil of Peter Moran, Lumenais and Bouguereau; m. Katharine Stevens, June 1896. His specialty is a combination of figures with animals; has received prizes at Nat. Acad. and Am. Art Assn.; medals, Buffalo and St. Louis expns.; gold medal, Internat. Expn., Buenos Aires; silver medal, Panama P.I. Expn., 1915; purchase prize Nat. Gallery of New Zealand, A.N.A. Author: Pictorial Composition and the Critical Judgment of Pictures, 1903; The Conception of Art, 1913; The New Tendency in Art, 1915; Art Principles in Practice, 1929; Modern Art—Why, What and How, 1931; Thinking Straight on Modern Art, 1934; Art's Place in Education, 1937. Home: Orange, N.J. Died Aug. 15, 1940.

POPE, Albert Augustus, mfr. bicycles and automobiles; b. Boston, Mass., May 20, 1843; pub. sch. edn., Brookline, Mass.; because of family reverses left sch.; was clerk in shoe findings store in Boston at \$4 a week; capt. in Home Guards, 1861-62; Aug. 1862, lt. 35th Mass. inf.; served until end of war, becoming lt. col.; bvtd. for gallant conduct battles of Fredericksburg and Knoxville, Poplar Springs Church, and Petersburg; m. Abby, d. George and Matilda Linder, Newton, Mass., Sept. 20, 1871. In wholesale shoe findings business, 1865-76. Established, 1877, the Pope Mfg. Co. to manufacture and sell small patented articles; same yr. began selling imported bicycles; in 1878 introduced the bicycle mfg. industry in U.S.; became a leading manufacturer. Founded The Wheelman (absorbed in Outing) in the interests of cycling; leader in good-roads movement; has large interests in banks and other corps. Home: Boston, Mass. Died 1909.

POPE, Alexander, artist; b. Dorchester, Mass., Mar. 25, 1849; s. Alexander and Charlotte Caldwell (Cushing) P.; ed. pvt. schs., Dorchester, and Eagleswood, N.J.; self taught in art; m. Alice De Wolf Downer, Sept. 16, 1873. Devoted spare time to art and originated painted game birds carved out of pine wood, two of them being purchased by Emperor of Russia; splty. animal and also still life painting; recently devoted part time to portraits and modeling animals. "Our Vanishing Wild Life," exhibited at San Francisco Expn., selected by com. of sculpture as among the best examples of Am. sculpture. Unitarian. entitled, Upland Game Birds and Water Fowl of the United States, 1880; Celebrated Dogs of America, 1882. Home: Brookline, Mass. Died Sept. 9, 1924.

POPE, Alfred Atmore, manufacturer; b. N. Vassalboro, Me., July 4, 1842; s. Alton and Theodate (Stackpole) P.; ed. pvt. schs., Oak Grove Sem., Vassalboro, Salem (O.) High Sch., Cleveland (O.) High Sch.; m. Ada L. Brooks, May 3, 1866. Jr. mem. Alton Pope & Sons, woolen mfrs., 1865-69; sec. and treas., 1869-77, became pres., 1877, Cleveland Malleable Iron Co.; elected pres. Eberhard Mfg. Co., Cleveland, 1880, Indianapolis Malleable Iron Co., and Ewart Mfg. Co., Chicago, 1882, Toledo Malleable Iron Co., 1890 (in 1891 the Cleveland, Chicago, Indianapolis, and Toledo Malleable Iron cos. were consolidated under title of Nat. Malleable Castings Co.), of which became president. Home: Farmington, Conn. Died Aug. 5, 1913.

POPE, Carey Joseph, clergyman; b. Brownhelm, O., Jan. 23, 1858; s. Josiah and Phebe Ann (Barnes) P.; grad. Colgate Acad., Hamilton, N.Y., 1879; A.B., Colgate U., 1883, D.D., 1920; B.D., Morgan Park Div. Sch. (now in Chicago), 1886; m. Margaret L. Lyndon, Sept. 2, 1884; children—Lawrence Clement (dec.), Walter Lyndon, Mildred Rebecca (Mrs. Carrell Henry Whitnah), Ruth Margaret (Mrs. Roy Wm. True), Faith (dec.). Ordained Bapt. ministry, 1886; pastor successively Valparaiso, Ind., Osage, Ia., Ottawa, Kan., Downers Grove, Ill., Grand Island, Neb., until 1906; supt. Neb. Bapt. Conv., 1906-09; univ. pastor U. of Neb., 1913—. Trustee Grand Island Coll. Republican. Home: Lincoln, Neb. Died Nov. 29, 1932.

POPE, Curran, M.D.; b. Louisville, Ky., Nov. 12, 1866; s. Alfred Thruston and Mary Tyler (Pope) P.; desc. of Col. Nathanial Pope I, from England to Westmoreland County, Pa., 1634; prep. edn., high sch. and Rugby Sch. (pvt.); M.D., U. of Louisville, 1889; post-grad. courses, New York Post Grad. Polyclinic, and at London, Paris, Vienna, Berlin and Frankfort-on-Main; unmarried. Began practice at Louisville, 1889; resident physician Central State Hosp., 1890; lecturer on pathology, bacteriology and microscopy, Hosp. Coll. of Medicine, 1891-94; prof. neurology and psychiatry, Louisville Coll. of Medicine, 1895-99, adj. prof. neurology, psychiatry and physical therapy, Ky. Sch. of Medicine, 1902-08; prof. physical therapy, Med. Dept. U. of Louisville, 1909-10; cons. neurologist, and psychiatrist and lecturer to nurses on neurology and psychiatry, St. Anthony's Hosp.; cons. neurologist and lecturer on neurology and physical therapy, Louisville Pub. Hosp., for 25 yrs. Pres., treas. and med. dir. Pope Hosp.; pres.-treas. Pope Mining Co., pres. Princeton Oil & Gas Co., Ky. Casualty Ins. Co. Mem. Ky. Bd. Charities and Corrections, 1924-31. Member Ky. National Guard 6 yrs.; four-minute man, World War. Republican. Episcopalian. Author: Practical Hydrotherapy, 1910. Home: Louisville, Ky. Died Sept. 21, 1934.

POPE, George, mfr.; b. Boston, Mass., Jan. 9, 1844; s. William and Mary (Bogman) P.; ed. pub. schs., Brookline, Mass.; served as pvt. 44th, capt., maj. and lt. col. 54th Mass. Vols., in Civil War; m. Annie Atwood Rich, Nov. 18, 1873. In employ wholesale lumber, Boston, 1865-68, and mgr. Montreal br. for same, until 1890; pres. Hartford Cycle Co., 1890-95; treas. Pope Mfg. Co., 1895-99; v.p. Am. Bicycle Co., 1899-1901. Was street commr., Hartford, 1896-99; presdl. elector-at-large for Conn., 1896. Pres. Nat. Assn. Mfrs., 1913-17. Republican. Home: Hartford, Conn. Died Apr. 20, 1918.

POPE, James Worden, army officer; b. Louisville, Ky., June 6, 1846; s. Edmund Pendleton and Nancy (Johnson) P.; student Indiana U., Bloomington, Ind., 2 yrs.; grad. U.S. Mil. Acad., 1868; m. Mary E. Lynch, Oct. 27, 1880. Commd. 2d lt. 5th Inf., June 15, 1868; 1st lt., Mar. 20, 1879; capt. asst. q.m., Feb. 20, 1885; maj. q.m., June 11, 1897; lt. col. chief q.m. U.S. Vols., May 9, 1898; hon. disch. from vol. service, Sept. 2, 1899; lt. col. dep. q.m. gen., July 5, 1902; col. asst. q.m. gen., Feb. 16, 1907; retired, by operation of law, June 6, 1910; brig. gen. retired, Aug. 29, 1916. Participated in numerous campaigns against Indians during first 10 yrs. of service, including expdn. under Gen. Eugene A. Carr, 1868-69, campaign of Gen. Miles in I.Ty., 1874-75, operations following the Custer Massacre, 1876-77, Bannock War, 1878, etc.; in comd. U.S. Mil. Prison, 1887-95; in charge improvements in Yellowstone Park, 1897; chief q.m. Philippine Expdn., under Gen. Merritt, 1898-99; later chief q.m. depts. of Colo. and the Gulf. under Gens. Merriam, MacArthur, Funston, Baldwin, Duvall, Davis and Thomas. Recommended for bvt. of capt. "for distinguished and valuable service" in campaign against Kiowa and other Indian tribes, 1874-75. Home: Denver, Colo. Died Aug. 23, 1919.

POPE, John Russell, architect; b. New York, N.Y., Apr. 24, 1874; s. John and Mary Avery (Loomis) P.; desc. of John Pope, Dorchester, Mass., 1630; ed. College City of New York; Ph.B., Sch. of Mines (Columbia), 1894; fellow Am. Acad. in Rome, 1895; Schermerhorn traveling fellow, 1896-97; École des Beaux Arts, Paris, 1900; hon. M.A., Yale; Litt. D., Columbia; Dr. of Fine Arts, Syracuse U.; m. Sadie Jones, Oct. 31, 1912; 1 dau., Jane London. Practiced alone from 1900. Architect: Scottish Rite Temple, Washington, D.C.; Plattsburg City Hall; MacDonough Memorials; Lincoln Memorial, Hodgenville, Ky.; Richmond (Va.) Terminal Sta.; addition to Met. Museum, New York; Constitution Hall, D.A.R., and Archives Bldg., Washington; Am. Battle Monument, Montfaucon, France; memorial tomb of William B. Leeds, New York; Congregational Ch., Columbus, O.; Nassau County (L.I.) Hosp.; residence of Ogden Mills, of Mrs. Graham Fair Vanderbilt, Irwin P. Laughlin, and others; architect selected for Roosevelt Memorial, New York City and Washington, D.C., also architect for Baltimore Mus. of Art, Syracuse Memorial Hosp., University Bapt. Ch., Baltimore; additions to Brit. Mus. and Tate Gallery; London, Frick Mus., New York City, Nat. Gallery, Washington, U.S. Government Offices, London. Awarded Architectural League Medal of Honor, 1916; Gold Medal of Honor, N.Y. Chapter A.I.A.; medal Jean Leclaire Inst. of France; Chevalier Legion of Honor (French), 1922. Fellow A.I.A. Home: New York, N.Y. Died Aug. 27, 1937.

POPE, Percival Clarence, officer U.S.M.C.; b. Charlestown, Mass., Feb. 28, 1841; s. Commodore John and Sarah W. P.; ed. pub. schs.; m. Sarah W. Hartwell. Apptd. captain's clk., July 9, 1861, and served on Richmond until Nov. 4, 1861 (resigned); commd. 2d and 1st lt., U.S. Marine Corps, Nov. 25, 1861; promoted through the grades to rank of brig. gen. U.S.M.C., and retired Feb. 28, 1905. Bvtd. capt., Sept. 8, 1863, "for gallant and meritorious service in night attack upon Ft. Sumter"; also received medal for distinguished services in civil war. Home: Milton, Mass. Died Jan. 23, 1922.

POPE, Ralph Wainwright, hon. secretary Am. Inst. Elec. Engrs. (asso.); b. Great Barrington, Mass., Aug. 16, 1844; s. Ebenezer and Electa Leonard (Wainright) P.; ed. Great Barrington and Amherst, Mass.; entered service Housatonic R.R. Co., 1859; Am. Telegraph Co., as operator, 1862, continuing at New York, New Haven and Providence till 1865; q.m. Collins Overland Telegraph expdn., British Columbia, 1866; asso. editor Telegrapher, 1868; deputy supt. Gold and Stock Telegraph Co., New York, 1882; asso. editor Electrical Engineer, 1884; sec., May 17, 1885-July 31, 1911, from then hon. sec., Am. Inst. Elec. Engrs., New York. Founder and editor Electric Power, 1890; chmn. on telegraphs and signaling, committee of judges, elec. exhibits, Chicago Expn., 1893. Hon. mem. Franklin Inst., Assn. Ry. Tel. Supts. Mem. Bd. of Edn., Union, Union Co., N.J., 1918; v.p. Union Co. Bd. of Agr., 1917. Home: Elizabeth, N.J. Died Nov. 1, 1929.

POPE, William Hayes, judge; b. Beaufort, S.C., June 14, 1870; s. Joseph James and Emily Hayes (Mikell) P.; A.M., U. of Ga., 1889, LL.B., 1890; m. May Hull, Nov. 29, 1905. Adj. prof. ancient langs., U. of Georgia, 1889-90; admitted to bar, 1890; located in practice of law in New Mexico; mem. Capital Rebuilding Commn., 1895-1900; commr. from N.M. to Atlanta Expn., 1895; asst. atty. gen. N.M., 1895-97; asst. U.S. atty. for Ct. of Private Land Claims, 1896-1902; spl. U.S. atty. for Pueblo Indians of N.M., 1901-02; judge of Ct. of First Instance, P.I., 1902-03; asso. justice Supreme Ct. of N.M., 1903-09, chief justice, 1909-12; U.S. dist. judge, Dist. of N.M., 1912—. Presbyn. Home: Santa Fé, N.M. Died Sept. 13, 1916.

POPE, Young John, judge; b. Newberry, S.C., Apr. 10, 1841; s. Thomas H. and Harriet Neville (Harrington) P.; A.B., Furman U., S.C., 1860; (LL.D., U. of S.C., 1906); m. Mrs. Sallie H. F. Rutherford, d. Col. Simeon Fair, Dec. 3, 1874. Pvt. to adj. and a.a.g. Conner's brigade of Inf., C.S.A. Admitted to bar and practiced at Newberry; dist. judge, 1865-68; mayor of Newberry, 5 yrs.; was mem. S.C. Ho. of Rep., and Senate; atty. gen. of S.C., 1890-91; asso. justice, 1891-1903, chief justice, 1903-09, Supreme Ct. of South Carolina. Home: Newberry, S.C. Died 1911.

POPOFF, Stephen, prof. chemistry; b. Samocov, Bulgaria, Sept. 10, 1885; s. John Stephen and Velika (Petrova) P.; student State Normal and Training Sch., Fredonia, N.Y., 1905-08; B. Chemistry, Cornell U., 1912, grad. study, 1912-13; grad. study U. of Chicago, summers 1914-17, Lowenthal fellow, 1917-18, Ph.D., 1918; m. Elda Best Williams, June 12, 1915. Came to U.S., 1904, naturalized citizen, 1916. Head of dept. of chemistry and physics, U. of Dubuque, 1913-17; research chemist Air Nitrate Corp., 1918; instr. in chemistry, U. of Ia., 1921-23, asso. 1923-26, asst. prof., 1926-29, asso. prof., 1929, and head of div. of analytical chemistry, 1926—. Republican. Presbyn. Mason. Author: Quantitative Analysis, 1924, 27. Home: Iowa City, Ia. Died Oct. 29, 1931.

POPPENHEIM, Mary Barnett; b. Charleston, S.C., Sept. 4, 1866; d. Christopher Pritchard and Mary Elinor (Bouknight) P.; A.B., Vassar, 1888. Pres.-Gen. United Daughters of Confederacy, 1917-19, and a leader in its hist. and ednl. work; supt. Ladies Benevolent Society, Charleston, S.C.; founder Inter-Collegiate Club of S.C., and its pres. 20 yrs.; organized The Maj. Gen. de Polignac Chapter U.D.C., Paris, France, 1921. Episcopalian. Author: Heroes in Grey, 1909. An editor of South Carolina Women in the Confederacy, Vol. I, 1903, Vol. II, 1907; edited The Keystone, a monthly magazine devoted to southern women's orgn., 1899-1913. Home: Charleston, S.C. Died Feb. 12, 1936.

PORRITT, Edward, journalist; b. Bury, Lancashire, Eng., Dec. 8, 1860; s. John and Elizabeth (Longshaw) P.; ed. People's Coll., Warrington, Eng.; m. Darwen, Eng., Annie Gertrude Webb, Sept. 3, 1891. Entered journalism on Warrington Guardian; reporter Liverpool Daily Mail, 1881; chief reporter, London Echo, 1882-84; reporter and spl. corr. Globe-Democrat, St. Louis, 1884-85; in gallery of House of Commons, London, 1886-92; London editor Manchester Examiner, 1888-92; settled at Farmington, Conn., as hist. writer and contbr. to various publications, also corr. newspapers, writing on polit. subjects and giving personal attention and investigation to industrial developments in U.S. and Canada; in 1902 visited S. Africa to investigate trade and econ. conditions after the war. Corr. with Canadian Tariff Revision Commn., 1905-06. Lecturer at Harvard, 1908-09, 1909-10, U. of Calif., summer session, 1910, Johns Hopkins U., 1916. Author: Barriers Against Democracy in the British Electoral System, 1911; The Evolution of the Dominion of Canada—Its Government and Its Politics, 1918; and others. Editor: Sell's Dictionary of World's Press (London), 1889-1912. Home: Hartford, Conn. Died Sept. 8, 1921.

PORTER, Albert, lexicographer, editor; b. Eng.; s. Rev. J. Porter, D.D.; ed. at Somerset Coll., Bath, Univ. Coll., London; D.Litt., Oriental U., 1921; m. Katherine, d. Walter Edmondbury Godfrey, J.P.; Fairmont, Hampshire, 1895; 1 son, Godfrey Deverell. Came to U.S., 1893; asst. editor Forum magazine, 1896-1900, and at various times connected with Funk & Wagnalls Co. (Standard Dictionary), Merck & Co. (Med. and Surg. Bull.), Collier & Son, G. & C. Merriam Co. (Webster's Collegiate Dictionary), Doubleday, Page & Co. Editorially associated with Jewish Ency., New University Cyclo., New Schaff-Herzog Ency. of Religious Knowledge, Rev. of Revs., Ency. Farm Knowledge, Ency. Britannica, 11th edition; office editor Standard Ency. of the Alcohol Problem, 1918-21, mng. editor, 1921—. Author of article "Chess," in Jewish Ency.; "Wet" Slanders of Abraham Lincoln Refuted; editor Birds of America (Nature Lovers' Library), 1912. Home: Westerville, O. Died Mar. 3, 1930.

PORTER, A(rthur) Kingsley, archeologist; b. Stamford, Conn., Feb. 6, 1883; s. Timothy Hopkins and Marie Louise (Hoyt) P.; B.A., Yale, 1904, B.F.A., 1917; student Sch. of Architecture, Columbia, 1904-06; traveled and studied in Europe, chiefly in Italy and France, 5 yrs.; Dr. honoris causa, U. of Marburg, Germany, 1927; m. Lucy Bryant Wallace, June 1, 1912. Lecturer on history of art, 1915, asst. prof., 1917-19, Yale U.; prof. history of art, 1920-24, William Dorr Boardman prof. fine art, 1924—, Harvard Univ. In service of French Ministry of Pub. Instruction and Fine Arts, 1918-19; exchange prof. in France, 1923; exchange prof. in Spain and to the French provincial univs., 1924. Fellow Mediæval Acad. of America, Am. Acad. of Arts and Sciences, Royal Irish Soc. of Antiquaries; mem. Archæol. Inst. America; hon. mem. A.I.A. Author: Mediæval Architecture (2 vols.), 1908; Construction of Gothic and Lombard Vaults, 1912; Lombard Architecture (4 vols.. work awarded the Grande Médaille de Vermeil by Société Française d'Archéologie), 1915-17; Beyond Architecture, 1918; The Seven Who Slept, 1919; Romanesque Sculpture of the Pilgrimage Roads, 10 vols., 1923; Spanish Romanesque Sculpture, 2 vols. (translated in German and Spanish), 1928; The Virgin and the Clerk, 1929; The Crosses and Culture of Ireland, 1931. Co-editor Art Studies, 1925—. Home: Cambridge, Mass. Died July 1933.

PORTER, Benjamin Curtis, portrait painter; b. Melrose, Mass.; s. Charles P.; studied in America and in Europe; asso. 1878, academician, 1880, Nat. Acad. of Design; m. Mary Louise Clark, 1887. Medal Paris Expn., 1900; medal Buffalo Expn., 1901, St. Louis Expn., 1904. Mem. Soc. Am. Artists. Home: New York, N.Y. Died 1908.

PORTER, Charles Allen, surgeon; b. Cambridge, Mass., Sept. 9, 1866; s. Charles Burnham and Harriet Ann (Allen) P.; A.B., Harvard, 1888, A.M., M.D., 1892; m. Margaret Cochran Dewar, of Glasgow, Scotland, Apr. 13, 1898; children—Isabel De Courcy, Margaret Dewar, Charles Burnham. Practiced at Boston, 1892—; instr. surgery, 1899-1909, asst. prof., 1909-12, asso. prof., 1912-15, clin. prof., 1915, prof. clin. surgery, 1918-22, John Homans prof. surgery, 1922-27, Harvard Med. Sch., now emeritus; surgeon in chief Mass. Gen. Hosp. until 1927, now cons. surgeon. Fellow Am. Coll. Surg., Am. Surg. Assn., Soc. Clin. Surgery. Home: Boston, Mass. Died July 3, 1931.

PORTER, Charles Burnham, surgeon; b. Rutland, Vt., Jan. 19, 1840; s. James Burnham and Harriet (Griggs) P.; A.B., 1862, A.M., 1863, M.D., 1865, Harvard; m. Harriet A. Allen, June 14, 1865. Acting asst. surgeon U.S.V., Apr.-Sept. 1865; surgeon to out patients, 1866-75, visiting surgeon, 1875-1903, Mass. Gen. Hosp.; asst. demonstrator anatomy, 1867-68, demonstrator, 1868-75, instr. surgery, 1875-82, asst. prof. surgery, 1882-87, prof. clin. surgery, 1887-1903, Harvard. Sr. fellow Am. Surg. Assn. (v.p. 1892). Home: Boston, Mass. Died 1909.

PORTER, Delia Lyman, author; b. New Haven, Conn.; d. Prof. Chester S. and Delia Williams (Wood) Lyman; ed. Wellesley Coll.; m. Frank Chamberlin Porter, June 10, 1891; children—Lyman Edwards, Wm. Quincy. Organized 1900, and pres. Mothers' Club of Lowell House Settlement; organized New Haven People's Choral Union, 1901, etc.; secured first Conn. woman's factory inspectn. law, 1909; pres. New Haven Women's Church Union, 1922—; chmn. Spiritual Training Com. of Conn. P.T.A., 1923-29; chmn. Conn. Women's Law Enforcement Com., 1926-30. Conglist. Author: An Anti-Worry Recipe and Other Stories, 1905; Yearbook of Good Cheer, 1906; Year-book of Ideals for Every Day Living, 1909; Christian Discussion Club Outlines, 1914-19. Also community betterment booklets, 35,000 used, 1919. Home: New Haven, Conn. Died Jan. 16, 1933.

PORTER, Dwight, teacher; b. Hartford, Conn., Aug. 28, 1855; s. James Timothy and Elizabeth Ann P.; Ph.B., Sheffield Scientific Sch. (Yale), 1880; m. Alice Case Marsh, Sept. 21, 1881. Spl. agt. 10th Census, U.S., 1880-83; instr., 1883-85, prof. hydraulic engring., 1896—, Mass. Inst. Technology. Died 1935.

PORTER, Eleanor Hodgman, author; b. at Littleton, N.H., Dec. 19, 1868; d. Francis Fletcher and Llewella (Woolson) Hodgman; direct desc. from Gov. William Bradford of the Mayflower; ed. pub. schs., N.E. Conservatory of Music and pvt. teachers; m. John Lyman Porter, May 3, 1892. Choir and concert singer, and teacher; devoted attention to writing, 1901—. Conglist. Author: Cross Currents, 1907; The Turn of the Tide, 1908; The Story of Marco, 1911; Miss Billy, 1911; Miss Billy's Decision, 1912; Pollyanna, 1913; Miss Billy Married, 1914; Pollyanna Grows Up, 1915; Just David, 1916; The Road to Understanding, 1917; Oh, Money! Money! 1918; Dawn, 1919; Across the Years, 1919; The Tie That Binds, 1919; The Tangled Threads. Home: Cambridge, Mass. Died May 21, 1920.

PORTER, Eugene Hoffman, M.D., sanitarian; b. Ghent, N.Y., Aug. 7, 1856; s. Curtis H. and Julia (Hoffman) P.; ed. Claverack Coll., Cortland State Normal Sch., Cornell U.; M.D., New York Homœ. Med. Coll., 1885; hon. A.M., Rutgers Coll., 1889; Dr. P. H., Syracuse U., 1912; m. Alice A. Day, June 12, 1889; 1 son, George Curtis. Engaged in practice at New York, 1885; editor-in-chief of North Am. Journal of Homœopathy, 1892-1917; prof. physiol. materia medica, New York Homœ. Med. Coll. and Hosp., to 1902; N.Y. state commr. of health, 1905 to Jan. 1914; mgr. State Insane Hosp., 1897-1911. Univ. lecturer, Cornell, 1908-09. Mason, Elk. Mem. Rep. State Committee. Commr. of foods and markets for State of N.Y., Dec. 17, 1917-Jan. 1, 1923. Pres. Nat. Assn. Marketing officials. Home: Upper Lisle, N.Y. Died Aug. 11, 1929.

PORTER, F. Addison, teacher and composer; b. E. Dixmont, Me., Sept. 3, 1859; s. Albert O. and Susan (Farnham) P.; grad. N.E. Conservatory of Music, 1884; post-grad. study at Leipzig, Germany; m. Lillian Mead, Aug. 27, 1890 (dec.); children—Albert Ogden, Allegra Lucille (dec.); m. 2d, Laura Huxtable, Nov. 29, 1907. Teacher of pianoforte, 1884—; organizer and supt. normal dept., N.E. Conservatory of Music, 1892-1922. Author of N.E. Conservatory Course for Piano; composer of preludes, waltzes, nocturnes, sonatinas, etc., for pianoforte. Home: Belmont, Mass. Died Jan. 3, 1941.

PORTER, Fitz-John, maj. gen. vols. and col. U.S.A.; b. Portsmouth, N.H., Aug. 31, 1822; son of Capt. John Porter, U.S.N.; grad. West Point, 1845; instr. West Point, 1849-55; m. Harriet Pierson, dau. John Cooke, New York. Served in Mexican war, 1846-48, in principal battles; wounded at Belen Gate, City of Mexico; bvtd. capt. and maj. for gallantry; asst. adjt. gen. at Ft. Leavenworth during Kansas troubles; later asst. adjt. gen. and chief of staff on Utah expedition, when he detected and defeated scheme of Mormon authorities to make and pass $2,000,000 in counterfeit checks on U.S. Treasury, and secured conviction of the engraver. On special duty in Gulf of Mexico, Feb., 1861, saved companies of art. and inf. from surrender to Texas. Commissioned col., May 14, 1861; brig. gen. vols., May 17, 1861; maj. gen. vols., July 4, 1862; and commanded 5th army corps; bvtd. brig. gen. U.S.A. for gallant conduct battle of Chickahominy, Va. Participated in the battles of the Peninsula campaign until cashiered, Jan. 21, 1863, and "forever disqualified from holding any office of profit or trust under the Govt. of the U.S." for alleged violation of Articles of War. Charges were re-examined and new testimony (inaccessible during trial) taken by bd. apptd. by Pres. Hayes, and he was found not guilty. It was also found that he had saved the army of Northern Va. from disaster. He was reinstated as col., 1886, and retired at his own request. Was supt. mining operations in Colo., 1864-65; merchant, New York, 1865-71; supt. in erection of N.J. State Asylum for the Insane, Morristown, 1872-75; commr. public works, New York, 1875-76; asst. receiver Central R.R. of N.J., 1877-82; police commr. New York, 1884-88; fire commr., 1888-89; merchant, 1889-93; cashier postoffice, New York, 1893-97. Home: Morristown, N.J. Died 1901.

PORTER, Florence Collins; b. Caribou, Me., Aug. 14, 1853; d. Samuel Wilson and Doras (Hardison) Collins; ed. pub. schs.; m. Rev. Charles W. Porter, Nov. 3, 1873 (died 1894); children—Helen Louise, Florence Spaulding, Charles Winthrop. Assisted Mrs. J. Ellen Foster in forming Nat. Woman's Rep. Club, New York, 1888; supt. schs., Caribou, 4 yrs.; owner and editor Aroostook Republican, 1 yr.; removed to Los Angeles, Calif., 1900, as mem. staff Los Angeles Herald. Prominently identified with equal suffrage movement in Calif.; pres. Los Angeles County Equal Suffrage League, 1909; presdl. elector, 1912; del. Rep. Nat. Conv., 1924, and made seconding speech, nominating Calvin Coolidge; mem. Rep. Women's Nat. Exec. Committee, 1918; pres. Rep. Women's Fedn. of Calif. (Southern div.). Conglist. Author: Maine Men and Women in Southern California, 1913; Our Folks and Your Folks (genealogy), 1919. Home: South Pasadena, Calif. Died Dec. 31, 1930.

PORTER, Frank Monroe, law teacher; b. Richford, Wis., Aug. 15, 1857; s. Clinton Hiram and Mary (Monroe) P.; A.B., U. of Wis., 1881, LL.B., 1883; LL.M., U. of Southern Calif., 1908, LL.D., 1922; m. Suella Billmeyer, Aug. 10, 1893; 1 dau., Margaret Annette. Began practice at Madison, Wis., 1883; moved to Los Angeles, Calif., 1887; dean faculty Coll. of Law, U. of Southern Calif., 1904-27 (emeritus). Republican. Methodist. Home: Los Angeles, Calif. Died Mar. 1936.

PORTER, Gene Stratton (Mrs.), author, illustrator; b. on farm, Wabash Co., Ind., 1868; d. Mark and Mary (Shellenbarger) Stratton; pvt. edn.; m. Charles Darwin Porter, 1886. Was 2 yrs. editor camera dept. Recreation; 2 yrs. on natural history staff of Outing; 4 yrs. specialist in natural history photography on Photographic Times Annual Almanac. Author and illustrator: The Song of the Cardinal, 1902; Freckles, 1904; What I Have Done With Birds, 1907; At the Foot of the Rainbow, 1908; A Girl of the Limberlost, 1909; Birds of the Bible, 1909; Music of the Wild, 1910; The Harvester, 1911; Moths of the Limberlost, 1912; Laddie, 1913; Michael O'Halloran, 1915; Morning Face, 1916; Friends in Feathers, 1917; A Daughter of the Land, 1918; Homing with the Birds, 1919; Her Father's Daughter, 1921; The Fire Bird (poetry), 1922; The White Flag, 1923; Jesus of the Emerald, 1923. Home: Los Angeles, Calif. Died Dec. 6, 1924.

PORTER, George French; b. Chicago, Ill., July 26, 1881; s. Henry Holmes and Eliza French P.; B.A., Yale, 1903; married. Dir. Chicago Daily News, Chicago Transfer & Clearing Co., Nevada Land Co. Trustee, Art Inst. Chicago. Western treas. Prog. Nat. Com., 1912; chmn. conv. com. Prog. Nat. Com., 1916; asst. to chmn. Rep. Nat. Conv., 1920. Asst. to dir. and chief State Councils Sect. of Council Nat. Defense, Washington, Apr. 1917-Mar. 1918; capt. C.W.S.; hon. discharged, Dec. 1918. Home: Chicago, Ill. Died Feb. 23, 1927.

PORTER, Harold Everett ("Holworthy Hall"), author; b. Boston, Sept. 19, 1887; s. Albert de Lance and Louella (Root) P.; A.B., cum laude, Harvard, 1909; Litt.D., Wake Forest Coll., 1921; m. Marian, d. John L. Heffron, M.D., Sc.D., of Syracuse, N.Y., Oct. 25, 1911; children—Jean, John Heffron, Richard Montgomery Sears. With A. D. Porter Co., pubs., New York, 1910-16, pres., 1915-16. Commd. 1st lt., A.S., Sig. R. C., Feb. 27, 1918; capt. Air Service, U.S.A., July 20, 1918; maj. Air Service, O.R.C., Apr. 9, 1920. Author: Pepper, 1915; Paprika, 1915; What He Least Expected, 1917; Dormie One, 1917; The Man Nobody Knew, 1919; The Six Best Cellars (with Hugh M. Kahler), 1919; Egan, 1920; Aerial Observation, 1921; Rope, 1921; (with Robert Middlemass) The Valiant (1-act play), 1921; Colossus, 1930. Died June 20, 1936.

PORTER, Henry Dwight, missionary; b. Green Bay, Wis., Aug. 19, 1845; s. Rev. Jeremiah and Eliza (Chappell) P.; B.A., Beloit (Wis.) Coll., 1867, M.A., 1870; grad. Andover Theol. Sem., 1870; Coll. Phys. and Surg. (Columbia), 1870-71; M.D., Northwestern U. Med. Coll., 1872; (D.D., Beloit, 1890); m. Elizabeth C. Chapin, Apr. 2, 1879. Missionary A.B.C.F.M., Tientsin, China, with med. work as subsidiary, 1872-82, at Pangchuang, China, 1882-1901; developed med. dispensary and hosp. work at Pangchuang; founded Williams Hosp., 1882-85; driven out by Boxers, 1900; furlough in U.S., 1901; retired, 1906. Trustee North China Coll., Tungchou. Republican. Author: Elementary Physiology (in Chinese), 1886; Electricity (in Chinese), 1895; Henry Dickinson Smith, a Biography and Memorial, 1909; William Scott Ament, Missionary to China, 1911; Biography of Mary H. Porter, First Missionary of the W.B.M.I., 1914. Home: La Mesa, Calif. Died Oct. 23, 1916.

PORTER, Henry H., chmn. Chicago & Eastern Ill. R.R.; b. Machias, Me., Dec., 1835; entered ry. service as Chicago sta. agt. Galena & Chicago Union R.R., of which he was later paymaster and gen. ticket agt.; gen. freight agt. and gen. supt. Mich. & Northern Ind. R.R. at Chicago; dir. Chicago, Rock Island and Pacific Ry., 1869—; dir. Chicago & Northwestern, 1870-78, and for a time its gen. mgr.; dir. Union Pacific Ry., 1873-77; engaged in consolidating, 1874-77, various rys. into what is now the Chicago, St. Paul, Minneapolis & Omaha Ry., of which he was several yrs. pres.; was pres. and chmn. C.&E.I. Home: Chicago, Ill. Died 1910.

PORTER, Henry Kirke, congressman; b. Concord, N.H., Nov. 24, 1840; s. George and Clara (Ayer) P.; A.M., Brown U., 1860; (LL.D., Bucknell U., 1893); studied Newton Theol. Instn., 1861-62, Rochester Theol. Sem., 1865-66; m. Mrs. Annie (de Camp) Hegeman, Nov. 23, 1875. Enlisted 45th Mass. Vols., 1862; mustered out of service July 1863; served in U.S. Christian Commn. winter of 1864. Began business life May 1866, firm of Smith & Porter, and built up exclusive specialty as mfrs. light locomotives; firm was Porter, Bell & Co., 1871-78, H.K. Porter & Co., 1879-99; incorporated, 1899, as H. K. Porter Co., of which became pres. Mem. 58th Congress (1903-05), 31st Pa. Dist. Republican. Pres. Y.M.C.A., Pittsburgh, 1868-87, Am. Bapt. Missionary Union, 1901-04, Am. Bapt. Home Missionary Soc., 1895-97; mem. Internat. Com. Y.M.C.A., 1875—; trustee Carnegie Inst., Pittsburgh, 1890—; trustee Crozer Theol. Sem., 1871—; mem. bd. fellows Brown U., 1899—; trustee Western Pa. Inst. for Blind, 1887—, pres. bd., 1904—. Home: Pittsburgh, Pa. Died Apr. 11, 1921.

PORTER, H(enry) M(iller), banker; b. Lancaster, Pa., Nov. 2, 1838; s. John B. and Harriet H. (Kurtz) P.; ed. country schs., Cole and Adair counties, Mo.; m. Laura W. Smith, Feb. 23, 1874; children—Dora P. (widow of John T. Mason), John H. (dec.), William E., Laurene (Mrs. Harold S. Walker, dec.), Ruth (wife of Dr. James J. Waring). Successively farmer, builder of telegraph lines in Mo., Ark., Kan., Neb. and Colo., mcht. in Denver and N.M., freighter from Mo. River to Salt Lake City, Utah, and Santa Fe, N.M., stockraiser; engaged in banking, 1876—; v.p. Denver Nat. Bank. Republican. Author: A Busy Man's Theory of the Operations of Nature, 1928; Pencilings of an Early Western Pioneer, 1928; Christianity and Science vs. Paganism and Idolatry, 1930. Donor with dau., Mrs. Dora P. Mason, of 150 room sanitarium and hosp., Denver, 1930. Home: Denver, Colo. Died July 25, 1937.

PORTER, Holbrook Fitz-John, engineer; b. New York, Feb. 28, 1858; s. Gen. Fitz-John and Harriet Pierson (Cook) P.; M.E., Lehigh U., Pa., 1878; m. Rose Smith, Aug. 27, 1888; children—Fitz John, Holbrook Smith (dec.). Apprentice and draftsman, Delamater Iron Works, New York, 1878-82; asst. engr. N.J. Steel & Iron Co. (Cooper, Hewitt & Co.), Trenton, N.J., 1882-84; college engineer, 1884-86, supt. buildings and grounds, Columbia College, 1886-90; supt. Cary & Moen Steel Spring & Wire Mills, New York, 1890; supt. Braddock Wire Co., Pittsburgh, Pa., 1891; asst. mech. engr., 1891-93, asst. chief machinery dept., 1893-94, Chicago Expn.; Western representative Bethlehem Steel Co., Chicago, 1894-1901, Eastern representative, New York, 1901; v.p. and gen. mgr. Westinghouse, Nernst Lamp Co., Pittsburgh, 1902-05; cons. industrial engr., New York, 1905-12. Founder and 1st sec. Efficiency Soc., 1911; sec. Organizing Com. for Congress of Internat. Assn. for Testing Materials, 1912; expert on industrial hygiene, Pittsburgh Survey, Russell Sage Foundation, 1912; expert on "fire hazard to life," N.Y. State Factory Investigating Commn., 1912-14; installed first means of escape from fire, for bedridden hospital patients in city hospitals, N.Y. City, 1912-14; cons. engineer on employment management, Hercules Powder Co., Wilmington, Del., 1915-18; sec. Nat. Mus. of Engring. and Industry, 1918—; dir. Nat. Com. for Prevention of Blindness. Episcopalian. Home: New York, N.Y. Died Jan. 25, 1933.

PORTER, Horace, diplomatist, soldier; b. Huntingdon, Pa., Apr. 15, 1837; s. late David Rittenhouse P. (gov. Pa.) and Josephine (McDermett) P.; ed. Lawrence Scientific Sch. (Harvard); grad. U.S. Mil. Acad., 1860; (LL.D., Union Univ., 1894, Princeton Univ., 1906, Williams Coll., 1907, Harvard Univ., 1910); m. Sophie K. McHarg, Dec. 23, 1863 (died 1903). Second lt. U.S.A., Apr. 22, 1861; 1st lt., June 7, 1861; capt., Mar. 3, 1863; lt. col. and a.-d.-c. to Gen. Grant, Apr. 4, 1864; col. of staff and a.-d.-c. to the gen.-in-chief U.S.A., July 25,

1866; bvtd. capt., Apr. 11, 1862, for seige of Pulaski; Congressional Medal of Honor for Chickamauga, Sept. 20, 1863; bvtd. maj., May 6, 1864, for Wilderness; lt. col., Aug. 16, 1864, for Newmarket Heights, Va.; col. U.S.V., Feb. 24, 1865; col. U.S.A., Mar. 13, 1865, for services during war, and brig. gen., Mar. 13, 1865, "for gallant services in the field." Asst. sec. of war, 1866; exec. sec. to President Grant, 1869-73. Became v.p. Pullman Palace Car Co., 1873; was pres. N.Y., West Shore & Buffalo R.R., St.L.& S.F Ry. Co. U.S. ambassador to France, 1897-1905. Orator at inauguration of Washington Arch, New York, May 4, 1895, and dedication of Grant's Tomb, New York, Apr. 27, 1897 (for the building of which he collected the necessary funds by private subscription); at inauguration Rochambeau Statue, Washington, May 24, 1902; at Centennial of foundation of West Point Mil. Acad., June 11, 1902; interment of Paul Jones' body at Annapolis, Apr. 23, 1906, etc. Decorated with Grand Cross of Legion of Honor by French Govt., 1904; gold medal for patriotism by Sultan of Turkey, 1901. Recovered body of Paul Jones at personal expense in Paris, Apr. 7, 1905. Received by unanimous vote the thanks of Congress and privilege of the floor of both houses for life. Author: West Point Life, 1860; Campaigning with Grant, 1897. Home: New York, N.Y. Died May 29, 1921.

PORTER, James Davis, governor; b. Paris, Tenn., Dec. 7, 1828; A.B., U. of Nashville, 1846, A.M., 1849 (LL.D., 1884); law student Cumberland U., Tenn.; m. Susanna, d. Gen. John H. Dunlop, 1851. Began practice, 1850; mem. Tenn. Legislature, 1859-61; adj. gen. on staff Maj. Gen. Cheatham, C.S.A.; del. Tenn. Constl. Conv., 1870; judge 12th Jud. Circuit, 1870-74; gov. of Tenn., 1874-78; pres. Nashville & Chattanooga R.R. Co., 1879-83; asst. sec. of state, U.S., 1885-89; E.E. and M.P. to Chile, 1893-97. Chancellor U. of Nashville, 1901—; trustee Peabody Edn. Fund from 1883. Pres. Tenn. Hist. Soc. Author: Confederate Military History of Tennessee. Home: Nashville, Tenn. Died May 18, 1912.

PORTER, James Temple, univ. prof.; b. Bath Co., Va., Sept. 29, 1873; s. James Samson and Ann Virginia (Burke) P.; A.B., Randolph-Macon Coll., Ashland, Va., 1895; A.M., 1898; Ph.D., in Physics, Johns Hopkins, 1905; m. Margaret Smith Davidson, June 23, 1915. Instr. Martha Washington Coll., Abingdon, Va., 1895-96, Randolph-Macon Acad., Front Royal, Va., 1898-1901; fellow in physics, Johns Hopkins, 1904-05; instr. in physics, Williams Coll., Mass., 1905-06; adj. prof. physics, Randolph-Macon Woman's Coll., 1906-08; with U. of Tenn., 1908—, asso. prof. physics until 1910, prof., 1910—; also asst. dean Coll. Liberal Arts, 1919-25, dean, 1925—. Democrat. Mem. M.E. Ch., S. Wrote Selective Reflection in the Infra-Red Spectrum. Died Aug. 27, 1931.

PORTER, Jermain Gildersleeve, astronomer; b. Buffalo, N.Y., Jan. 8, 1852; s. John Jermain and Mary (Hall) P.; A.B., Hamilton Coll., 1873, A.M., 1876, Ph.D., 1888; U. of Berlin and Royal Obs., 1873-74; Sc.D. from the U. of Cincinnati, 1930; m. Emily Snowden, July 3, 1879; children—John Jermain, Ruth May (dec.), Harold Mitchel. Asst. prof. astronomy, Hamilton Coll., 1875-78; mem. U.S. Coast and Geod. Survey, 1878-84; dir. Cincinnati Obs. and prof. astronomy, U. of Cincinnati, 1884-1931. Observer Internat. Latitude Service, 1899-1905. Received Astron. Journal Comet prize, 1894. Author: The Stars in Song and Legend, 1901; Catalogue of 4,280 Stars, 1905; Variation of Latitude, 1908; Catalogue of Nebulæ, 1910; Catalogue of 3,164 Proper Motion Stars, 1918; All-American Time, 1918; How to Find the Stars and Planets, 1920; Catalogue of 5,000 Stars, 1925; Catalogue of Proper Motion Stars, 1930. Died Apr. 14, 1933.

PORTER, John Addison, sec. to the President of U.S.; b. New Haven, Conn., Apr. 17, 1856; grad. Yale, 1878; for 10 years editor and proprietor Hartford, Conn., Post; has been member of Conn. general assembly. Was candidate for gov. of Conn. in several Republican conventions, receiving a large number of votes. Author: Sketches of Yale Life. Died 1900.

PORTER, John Henry, capitalist; b. Cimarron, N.M., Aug. 17, 1876; s. Henry M. and Laura W. (Smith) P.; Ph.B., Yale, 1897; unmarried. Mem. Boettcher, Porter & Co., brokers, Denver, Oct. 1, 1911—. Dir. Trust Co., Denver Gas & Electric Co., Great Western Sugar Co., Moffat Coal Co. Trustee Agnes Memorial Sanatorium. Republican. Home: Denver, Colo. Died Dec. 17, 1922.

PORTER, John Lincoln, surgeon; b. Alstead, N.H., July 2, 1864; s. Samuel H. and Harriet (Emerson) P.; M.D., Northwestern U., 1894; m. Ethel, d. David Quigg, of Chicago, Feb. 9, 1899. Interne, St. Luke's Hosp., 1894-95; prof. orthopedic surgery, U. of Ill. Med. Sch., 1900-17; prof. same, Northwestern U. Med. Sch., 1917—; attending orthopedic surgeon, St. Luke's Hosp. Apptd. mem. Advisory Bd. on Orthopedics, U.S.A., Aug. 1917. Maj. M.C., U.S.A., 1918-19. Republican. Home: Evanston, Ill. Died Aug. 11, 1938.

PORTER, John Lupher, corp. officer; b. Meadville, Pa., July 1, 1868; s. James Amberson and Elizabeth Dorothy (Weber) P.; A.B., Allegheny Coll., 1890, A.M. from the same college, 1932; m. Augusta M. Fisher, Jan. 18, 1893. Began in employ of Miller Pipe Line Co., Oil City, Pa., 1891; with Nat. Transit Co., 1891-93, Anglo-Am. Oil Co., London, 1893-95; chmn. bd. Union Storage Co.; dir. sec. and treas. Hazelton Land Co.; chmn. Bondholders' Protective Com., Boise & Interurban Ry. Co., Ltd. Vice pres. and mem. fine arts com. Carnegie Inst.; vice chmn. bd. trustees and chmn. trustees com. Carnegie Inst. Tech. Founder One Hundred Friends of Pittsburgh Art. Hon. mem. Alumni Fedn. of Carnegie Inst. Tech., Associated Artists of Pittsburgh, Hindustan Assn. America; mem. various societies. Republican. Methodist. Home: Pittsburgh, Pa. Died Aug. 11, 1937.

PORTER, John William, clergyman, editor; b. Fayette Co., Tenn., Aug. 8, 1863; s. John Freeman and Martha Carolina (Tharp) P.; LL.B., Cumberland U., Tenn., 1882; Th.G., Southern Bapt. Theol. Sem., 1893; D.D., Keiche Coll., La., 1900; LL.D., Union U., Tenn., 1913; m. Lillian E. Thomas, July 19, 1892; children—Martha Frances, Mary, Blanche Bettie, John William, Russell Thomas. Practiced law in Tenn., 1882-85; ordained Bapt. ministry, 1890; pastor Germantown, Tenn., Collierville, Tenn., Pewee Valley, Ky., Maysville, Ky., Newport News, Va., and Lexington, Ky., 1st Ch., Lexington, Ky., Apr. 1908-22 (erected new bldg., said to cover more ground than any other Bapt. ch. in world); now pastor Immanuel Bapt. Ch., Lexington, Ky. Former editor and pub. The Recorder, oldest denominational paper south of Ohio River; former editor American Baptist. Mem. Anti-Evolution League; widely known as evangelist and lecturer. Trustee Georgetown (Ky.) Coll.; pres. Gen. Assn. Ky. Baptist. Democrat. Author: Baptist Debt to the World; World's Debt to the Baptist, 1914; Evangelistic Sermons, 1920; Menace of Evolution, 1921; Dangers of the Dance, 1922; Feminism, 1923. Home: Lexington, Ky. Died Sept. 7, 1937.

PORTER, Joseph Yates, physician; b. Key West, Fla., Oct. 21, 1847; s. Joseph Yates and Mary (Randolph) P.; ed. in N.J.; M.D., Jefferson Med. Coll., Phila., 1870; m. Louisa Curry, 1870. Entered army, July 1870, as acting asst. surgeon; asst. surgeon U.S.A., June 26, 1875; capt. asst. surgeon, June 26, 1880; apptd. deputy surgeon-gen. with rank of lt. col., and placed on retired list, Mar. 8, 1907, by Act of Congress, Mar. 2, 1907. Went through yellow fever epidemic at Dry Tortugas, 1873, Key West and Tampa, Fla., 1887, Key West, 1899, Miami, 1899, Pensacola, 1905; in charge govt. relief measures at Jacksonville, Fla., during epidemic in 1888; made 1st demonstrations of mosquito law of yellow fever transmission in U.S. in Tampa, 1905, in an imported case of yellow fever from New Orleans. State health officer of Fla., 1889-1917; recalled to active duty as lt. col., Med. Corps U.S.A., June 6, 1917; camp surgeon, Camp Joseph E. Johnston, Jacksonville, Fla., Oct. 1, 1917-Jan. 31, 1919; now quarantine insp. U.S. Pub. Health Service. Home: Jacksonville, Fla. Died Mar. 16, 1927.

PORTER, Linn Boyd ("Albert Ross"), author; b. Westfield, Mass., Dec. 20, 1851; s. Elijah and Mary (Loomis) P.; ed. Leicester (Mass.) Acad.; m. Mary E. Moore, Sept. 10, 1874. Author: A Black Adonis; The Garston Bigamy; Her Husband's Friend; His Foster Sister; His Private Character; In Stella's Shadow; Speaking of Ellen; That Gay Deceiver; Their Marriage Bond; Young Fawcett's Mabel; Young Miss Giddy; A Sugar Princess; Stranger Than Fiction; Riverfall. Home: Brookline, Mass. Died June 29, 1916.

PORTER, Miles Fuller, surgeon; b. Decatur, Ind., Sept. 27, 1856; s. John Pomeroy and Elizabeth (Dorwin) P.; ed. pub. schs. and pvt. tutor; M.D., Med. Coll. of Ohio, Cincinnati, 1878; hon. M.A., Franklin Coll., 1882; m. Lillie A. Wilding, June 19, 1878. Surgeon St. Joseph's Hospital; prof. of surgery, Ind. Univ. Sch. Medicine. Home: Fort Wayne, Ind. Died Dec. 6, 1933.

PORTER, Robert Percival, journalist; b. Norwich, Eng., June 30, 1852; s. late James Winearls and Jane (Harvey) P.; ed. King Edward VI Sch., Norwich, and pvtly. in America; m. Alice Russell, d. Dr. Joseph Hobbins, of Madison, Wis., 1884. Engaged in journalism on Chicago Inter Ocean, 1872; expert U.S. census, 1880-81, reporting on wealth, debt, taxation and transportation; U.S. tariff commr., 1882; editorial staff New York Tribune, and Phila. Press, 1884-87; founded the New York Press (with Frank Hatton), 1887; dir. 11th U.S. Census, 1890-94; spl. fiscal and tariff commr. of President McKinley, 1898, to Cuba and P.R., negotiating the arrangement with the late Gen. Maximo Gomez for disbanding the Cuban Army, 1899; mem. staff of The Times (London), 1904—. Has traveled extensively in U.S., Mex., S. America, Japan, Russia, the Balkans, Roumania, Turkey, and other countries, for the purpose of making industrial investigations and reports. Author: Free Trade Folly, 1886; Commerce and Industry of Japan, 1896; Life of William McKinley, 1896; Industrial Cuba, 1899; Dangers of Municipal Ownership, 1907; The Full Recognition of Japan; The Ten Republics; Japan, the Rise of a Modern Power, 1918. Home. Shropham, Norfolk, Eng. Died Feb. 28, 1917.

PORTER, Rose (Miss), author; b. N.Y., 1845; ed. pvt. sch., New York; spent some time in England; has lived in New Haven for many yrs. Author: Summer Driftwood for the Winter Fire; The Winter Fire (sequel to Summer Driftwood); Driftings from Mid-Ocean; Honoria, or the Gospel of a Life; Our Saints; A Modern St. Christopher; St. Martin's Summer; My Son's Wife; In Quietness and Confidence; Rest Awhile; A Daughter of Israel. Home: New Haven, Conn. Died 1906.

PORTER, Samuel, prof. mental science and English philology, Gallaudet Coll. (formerly Nat. Deaf Mute Coll.), 1866-84 (emeritus); b. Farmington, Conn., Jan. 12, 1810; s. Rev. Noah P. (D.D.) and M. (Meigs) P.; grad. Yale, 1829; instr. of deaf and dumb in Hartford Instn., 1832-36 and 1846-66; same in New York Instn., 1843-46; editor Am. Annals of the Deaf and Dumb, 1854-60. Unmarried. Author: Guide to Pronunciation (prefixed to Webster's International Dictionary). Died 1901.

PORTER, Silas Wright, judge; b. Warren Co., Ill., Jan. 1, 1857; s. Judge John and Mary Ellen (Robb) P.; A.B., Monmouth Coll., 1879, A.M., 1882, LL.D., 1906; admitted to bar, 1881; m. Jessie K. Babcock, Apr. 6, 1887; children—Eliot, Mrs. Dorothy Thompson, Richard Babcock, John McGill, Garrett. City atty., Monmouth, 1882-84; removed to Kan., 1886; co. atty., Ness Co., Kan., 1887-88; asso. with William J. Buchan and Winfield Freeman, Kansas City, Kan., 1891-98; justice Supreme Court of Kan., 3 terms, 1905-23; resumed general practice. Lecturer, Law Sch., U. of Kan., 1891-1893, Washburn Law Sch., 1912-17, Kansas City Law School, 1927—. Presbyn. Mason. Home: Topeka, Kan. Died May 17, 1937.

PORTER, Stephen Geyer, congressman; b. nr. Salem, O., May 18, 1869; s. David and Maria P.; ed. high sch., Allegheny, Pa.; studied medicine 2 yrs., read law with brother L.K.P.; m. Elizabeth F. Ramaley, Apr. 11, 1895 (dec.); 1 dau., Lucy Foster. Admitted to bar, 1893, and entered practice at Pittsburgh; mem. firm L. K. & S. G. Porter. City solicitor, Allegheny, 1903-06; mem. 62d to 71st Congresses (1911-31), 32d Pa. Dist.; chmn. Com. on Fgn. Affairs, 66th and 71st Congresses. Republican. Apptd. by President mem. advisory com. Limitation of Armament Conference. Home: Pittsburgh, Pa. Died June 27, 1930.

PORTER, Sydney ("O Henry"), author; b. Greensboro, N.C., 1867; acad. edn. in Tex. Was on staff Houston Post; later became publisher and editor the Iconoclast, later the Rolling Stone, Houston; went to New York, and from then engaged in lit. work, contbg. to mags. and newspapers. Author: Cabbages and Kings, 1905; The Four Million, 1906; The Trimmed Lamp, 1907; The Heart of the West, 1907; The Gentle Grafter, 1908; The Voice of the City, 1908; Options, 1909; Roads of Destiny, 1909. Home: New York, N.Y. Died 1910.

PORTER, Theodoric, commodore; b. in D.C., Dec. 14, 1849; s. late Admiral David D. P. (U.S.N.); g.s. Commodore David P.; descendant of fighting stock on both sides; grad. U.S. Naval Acad., 1869; m. Bettie, d. Judge J. Thompson Mason, of Annapolis, Md., Feb. 12, 1873 (died 1909); m. 2d, Henrietta McCulloch Cheston, d. late Michael McCulloch, of Montreal, 1910. Promoted through the various grades to capt., June 19, 1905; commodore, June 30, 1908, and retired at own request. Served 43 yrs. in U.S. Navy, 20 yrs. at sea and 23 yrs. on shore or other duty; last comd. U.S. cruiser Washington. Home: Annapolis, Md. Died June 18, 1920.

PORTER, Thomas Conrad, educator; b. Alexandria, Pa., Jan. 22, 1822; grad. Lafayette Coll., 1840; D.D., Rutgers Coll.; LL.D., F. & M. Coll.; grad. Princeton Theol. Sem., 1843; m. Susan Kunkel, Dec 24, 1850. Prof. natural sciences, Marshall Coll., 1848, until it united with Franklin Coll., then held same chair in Franklin & Marshall Coll. until 1866, when he became a prof. botany, zoölogy and general geology in Lafayette Coll.; retired from active duties, Jan. 1, 1897, but remaining with the college as curator of the botanical collections, emeritus professor and dean of the Pardee Scientific School. Has given much attention to lit. subjects, notably as the earliest American champion of Finnish literature, and in 1854 drew attention to the similarity in form and spirit between Longfellow's poem, Hiawatha, and the Finnish national epic, Kalevala, the controversy which followed arousing great interest in Europe as well as America. Author: Synopsis of the Flora of Colorado; Botany of Pennsylvania; etc. Home: Easton, Pa. Died 1901.

PORTER, Valentine Mott, lawyer; b. Mt. Vernon, Ill., Apr. 4, 1870; s. Samuel Smith (M.D.) and Helen (Van Zandt) P.; A.B., Harvard, 1892; LL.B., Washington U., 1894; m. Susan Creighton Williams, Sept. 21, 1907. Served in Spanish-Am. War, 1898, with Light Battery A, Mo. Vols., participating in the Puerto Rico expdn. Admitted to bar, St. Louis, 1894; sec. Bar Assn. of St. Louis, 1901-04; sec. Universal Congress Lawyers and Jurists, St. Louis, 1904, and editor Report of same (pub. 1905); chmn. Civic League's com. on municipal discussions, 1907-08, which projected the present City Club of St. Louis; v.p. Associated Harvard Clubs, 1907; mem. advisory bd. Mo. Hist. Soc., 1905— (v.p. 1907-13); dir. Hist. Soc. Southern Calif., 1913—. Served 15 yrs. in N.G. of Mo., chiefly in field arty., retiring, 1913, with rank of major. Has edited hist. publs. for Mo. Hist. Society. Died Jan. 23, 1915.

PORTER, Washington Tullis, lawyer; b. Cincinnati, O., Feb. 22, 1850; s. James and Margaret (Tullis) P.; grad. Chickering Inst., 1868; LL.B., Law Sch. of Cincinnati Coll., 1871; m. Flora Robinson, Dec. 20, 1871 (died 1915); children—Edward A. F. (dec.), Howard R., Forrest B., Mrs. Lilian Mirick, Fletcher D. (dec.), Washington T. (dec.). Practiced, 1871—; admitted to bar Supreme Court of U.S., 1918; atty., 1873-1908, of trustees of Cincinnati Southern Ry., and apptd. trustee of same railway for life, 1908; elected pres. bd. trustees same ry., 1929; mem. bd. of Law Examiners, Ohio, 1886-91, 1903-08. Mem. Bd. of Aldermen, Cincinnati, 1880-84; trustee Pub. Library, Cincinnati, 1891—, except for 3 yrs. Mason. Republican. Methodist. Compiler and editor: Cincinnati Southern Railway Legislation-Litigation, 1901, 3d edit., 1930. Home: Cincinnati, O. Died June 19, 1933.

PORTER, William David, lawyer; b. Hancock Co., W.Va., Jan. 3, 1850; s. James S. and Elizabeth (McCandless) P.; ed. Beaver Acad., Pa., Mantua Acad., Phila.; law dept., U. of Pa.; unmarried. Admitted to Pa. bar, 1872; practiced Pittsburgh; dist. atty. Allegheny Co., Pa., 1884-90; judge Ct. of Common Pleas, 1891-98, judge Superior Ct. of Pa., 1898—. Republican. Home: Pittsburgh, Pa. Died Feb. 9, 1930.

PORTER, William Gove, lawyer; b. Thetford Center, Vt., Sept. 4, 1858; s. Amos Phelps and Mercy Eastman (Gove) P.; A.B., Dartmouth, 1882, A.M., 1888; LL.B., Drake U., Des Moines, Ia., 1884; m. Jessie M. Yost, June 27, 1888. Admitted to bar S.D., later to U.S. Court of Appeals, 8th Circuit, and Supreme Court of U.S.; practiced in Sioux Falls, S.D., 1898—; state's atty., Custer Co., S.D., 1890-95; asst. U.S. atty., Dist. of S.D., 1898-1906, U.S. atty., 1906, again asst. U.S. atty., 1907-10; gen. solicitor for states of N. and S. Dakota, of C.,M.& St.P. Ry. Co., 1911-19. Treas. Nat. Rep. League, 1904, 06. Mason. Odd Fellow. Home: Sioux Falls, S.D. Died Aug. 11, 1927.

PORTER, William Henry, M.D.; b. N.Y. City, Sept. 4, 1853; s. Frederick E. and Elisabeth Bradley (Akin) P.; student Yale, 1873-74; M.D., Coll. Phys. and Surg. (Columbia), 1877; m. Margaret Josephine Carroll, May 21, 1880; children—Frederick Phelps, William Carroll. Practiced at N.Y. City, 1877—; prof. medicine, New York Post-Grad. Med. Sch., 1887-1912 (emeritus prof.); president of the Gamma Sugar Corporation. Republican. Conglist. Author: Eating to Live Long, 1920. Home: Norfolk, Conn. Died Mar. 27, 1933.

PORTER, William Henry, banker; b. Middlebury, Vt., Jan. 3, 1861; s. William Trowbridge and Martha Elizabeth (Samson) P.; ed. high sch. and Saratoga Acad.; LL.D., Middlebury Coll., 1911; m. Esther Jackson, 1887. Engaged in banking at New York, 1878—; now mem. J. P. Morgan & Co.; pres. Chem. Nat. Bank; dir. 5th Av. Bank, Title Guarantee & Trust Co., Fidelity & Casualty Co., Bankers Trust Co., Royal Exch. Assurance of London; trustee Mut. Life Ins. Co. of N.Y., Franklin Savings Bank. Pres. New York Clearing House Assn.; treas. Chamber of Commerce. Trustee N.Y. Univ., Middlebury Coll.; commr. Palisades Interstate Park. Home: Glen Cove, L.I. Died Nov. 30, 1926.

PORTER, William Wagener, judge; b. Philadelphia, May 5, 1856; s. Judge William A. and Emma (Wagener) P.; A.B., U. of Pa., 1875, A.M., 1878; m. Mary Augusta Hobart, Apr. 27, 1882. Admitted to bar, 1877, and practiced at Phila.; judge Superior Ct. of Pa., 1897-1903; practicing law, Phila. Republican. Author: The Law Relating to Bills of Lading, 1891; also brochure on Legal Responsibility of Clergymen Solemnizing Marriages in Pennsylvania. Died Nov. 16, 1928.

POSEY, William Campbell, ophthalmologist; b. Philadelphia, July 5, 1866; s. David Root and Emily Jewell (Campbell) P.; A.B., U. of Pa., 1886, M.D., 1889; m. Hadassah Hamilton Felton, Dec. 1910. Emeritus surgeon Wills Eye Hosp.; cons. surgeon Howard Hosp., Phila.; dir. Nat. Com. for Prevention of Blindness. Author: Treatise on Diseases of the Eye, Nose, Throat and Ear (with Dr. Jonathan Wright), 1903. Edited 6th Am. edit. Nettleship's Diseases of the Eye, 1900; The Eye and the Nervous System (with Dr. William G. Spiller), 1906; Hygiene of the Eye, 1917; The Wills Hospital (with Dr. Samuel H. Brown), 1931. Chmn. Draft Exemption Bd., 1917. Home: Radnor, Pa. Died Sept. 5, 1934.

POST, Charles William, manufacturer; b. Springfield, Ill., Oct. 26, 1854; s. Charles Rollin and Caroline (Lathrop) P.; student U. of Illinois but was not grad.; m. Leila D. Young. Partner hardware business, commercial traveler, mgr. plow factory, Springfield, Ill.; broke down from overwork, 1884; invalid and traveled for health until 1891; studied medicine, hygiene, dietetics, psychology, experiment and practice in America and Europe; led into food business; originator of prepared food industry, and Postum Coffee. Now chmn. Postum Cereal Co., Ltd., Battle Creek Paper Co., Home and Fireside Co., Ltd.; pres. Double U Co., Post Land Co. Republican. Home: Washington, D.C. Died May 9, 1914.

POST, Edwin, univ. prof.; b. Woodbury, N.J., Nov. 7, 1851; s. Rev. Samuel E. and Maria (Cutter) P.; A.B., Dickinson, 1872, A.M., 1875 (hon. Ph.D., 1884); LL.D. from Dickinson College, 1927; univs. of Berlin and Bonn, 1886-88; m. Minnie J. Thurrell, July 22, 1880 (died 1921); children—Arthur Edwin, Ruth Baker. Instr. Greek, 1872-75, v.p. and instr. Latin, 1875-77, Pennington (N.J.) Sem.; ordained M.E. ministry, 1875; pastor Hammonton, N.J., 1877-79; prof. Latin, 1879—, dean Coll. of Liberal Arts, 1904-29, DePauw (v.p. 1895-1903). Editor: Selected Epigrams of Martial, 1908. Author: Latin at Sight, 1894. Home: Greencastle, Ind. Died Oct. 9, 1932.

POST, Frank Truman, lawyer; b. West Potsdam, N.Y., Apr. 16, 1862; s. John Fobes and Harriet (Lillie) P.; A.B., St. Lawrence U., 1883, A.M., 1886, LL.D., 1924; post-grad. study, Harvard Law Sch., 1885-86; m. Mary C. Phillips, Aug. 17, 1893; children—John Phillips, Harriet C. (wife of Lt. William E. Donegan). Admitted to N.Y. bar, 1885, and began practice at Lowville, 1886; partnership with W. Worth Dewey, 1886-89; moved to Spokane, Wash., 1889; now mem. Post, Russell, Davis & Paine; pres. Washington Water Power Co. Corporation counsel, Spokane, 1893. Universalist. Home: Spokane, Wash. Died Mar. 5, 1941.

POST, George Adams, manufacturer; b. Cuba, N.Y., Sept. 1, 1854; s. Ira Allen and Harriet Newell (Curtis) P.; ed. pub. schs., acad. and normal sch., Oswego, N.Y.; m. Minnie C. Munson, June 22, 1881. With freight dept. Erie R.R., later asst. to supt. motive power, 1872; studied law at night and admitted to Pa. bar; editor and part owner Montrose (Pa.) Democrat, 1883-89; with New York World, 1889-91; v.p., 1892-94, pres. 1894, Standard Coupler Co.; pres. Geo. A. Post Co., Hudson River Bridge & Terminal Assn.; dir. Computing-Tabulating-Recording Co., Merchants Assn. of N.Y. Chairman exec. com. Ry. Supply Mfrs., 1904; chmn. Am. Ry. Appliance Exhbn., held in connection with Internat. Ry. Congress, Washington, 1905; pres. Ry. Business Assn. of U.S., 1909-18. Known as the "apostle of good humor." Mayor of Susquehanna, Pa., 1877; Dem. nominee presdl. elector, Pa., 1880; mem. 48th Congress (1883-85), 15th Dist. of Pa.; sec. Dem. Congressional Com., 1884; chmn. Pa. Dem. State Conv., 1885. Trustee N.J. State Chamber Commerce; chmn. ry. com. Chamber Commerce U.S.A. Home: Somerville, N.J. Died Oct. 31, 1925.

POST, George Browne, architect; b. New York, Dec. 15, 1837; s. Joel B. and Abby M. P.; C.E., New York U., 1858 (LL.D., Columbia, 1908); studied architecture with Richard M. Hunt; m. Alice M., d. William W. Stone, of New York, Oct. 14, 1863. Capt., maj., lt. col., and col. 22d N.Y. Vols. in Civil War. Engaged as architect at New York since the war; now head of Geo. B. Post & Sons, architects. Mem. expert com. to appoint a sculptor and select design for the LaFayette Monument erected in the Louvre, Paris; apptd. collaborator U.S. Forest Service, 1906; mem. Nat. Advisory Bd. on Fuels and Structural Materials, 1906—; mem. Bur. Fine Arts, 1909—; mem. bd. commrs. to St. Louis Expn., 1904; dir. Municipal Art Soc., 1906—; mem. council Nat. Sculpture Soc.; pres. Fine Arts Fedn. of New York, 1898. Chevalier de la Legion d'Honneur, France, 1901; A.N.A., 1907, N.A., 1908; hon. corr. mem. Royal Inst. Brit. Architects, 1907; pres. Am. Inst. Architects, 1896-99, N.Y. Chapter same, 1904, Architectural League of New York, 1893-97. Home: Bernardsville, N.J. Died Nov. 28, 1913.

POST, George Edward, Presbyn. clergyman, physician; b. New York, Dec. 17, 1838; s. Alfred C. (M.D.) and Harriet B. P.; grad. New York Free Acad. (now Coll. City of New York), 1854, A.M., 1857; grad. med. dept. Univ. of New York, 1860, Union Theol. Sem., 1861; m. Sarah Read, Sept. 17, 1863. Prof. surgery, Syrian Protestant Coll.; surgeon to Johanniter Hosp., Beirut, Syria. Author: (in Arabic) Flora of Syria, Palestine and Egypt; Text Book of Botany; Text Book of Mammalia; Text Book of Birds; Translation of Butler's Physiology; Concordance to the Bible; Text Book of Surgery; Text Book of Materia Medica; Dictionary of the Bible (in English): Flora of Syria, Palestine and Sinai, all published by Am. Mission Press, Beirut, Syria. Died 1909.

POST, James D., congressman; b. nr. Washington C.H., Ohio, Nov. 25, 1863; s. Abraham and Eliza J. (McCoy) P.; B.S., Nat. Normal U., Lebanon, O., 1882; m. May J. Snyder, May 17, 1885. Admitted to bar, 1887, and began practice at Washington C.H.; mem. Post & Reid. Mem. 62d and 63d Congresses (1911-15), 7th Ohio Dist. Democrat. Presbyn. Elk. Home: Washington Court House, O. Died Apr 1, 1921.

POST, James Howell, sugar refiner; b. New Rochelle, N.Y., Oct. 13, 1859; s. William and Eleanor (Sachett) P.; pub. sch. edn.; m. Louisa H. Wells, Oct. 26, 1887. Began as clk., 1874, and became partner, 1889, B. H. Howell, Son & Co.; pres. Nat. Sugar Refining Co. of N.J. and its subsidiary corps.; chmn. bd. Cuban-Am. Sugar Co.; trustee Title Guarantee & Trust Co., Atlantic Mut. Ins. Co., Williamsburgh Savings Bank. Pres. trustees Adelphi Coll., Brooklyn; trustee Princeton Theol. Seminary, Brooklyn Home for Children, Y.M.C.A. of Brooklyn, Bur. of Charities, Brooklyn Eye and Ear Hosp., Welfare Council of N.Y. City, etc.; dir. Brooklyn Acad. Music. Presbyn. Home: Brooklyn, N.Y. Died Mar. 5, 1938.

POST, Louis Freeland, writer; b. Vienna, N.J., Nov. 15, 1849; s. Eugene J. and Elizabeth (Freeland) P.; pub. sch. edn.; m. Anna Johnson of Hackettstown, N.J., July 6, 1871 (died 1891); children—Edna (dec.), Charles Johnson; m. 2d, Alice Thacher, Dec. 2, 1893. Learned printer's trade, Hackettstown, 1864-65; admitted to New York bar, 1870, U.S. Supreme Court, 1878, Dist. of Columbia, 1921; asst. U.S. atty., New York, 1874-75; editorial writer on New York Daily Truth, 1879-82; returned to law practice, 1883, and abandoned it, 1890. Became interested in Henry George's teachings in 1881, and thereafter advocated them; ran for Congress in New York on labor ticket, 1882, for atty. gen. of N.Y. on Greenback ticket, 1883, and for dist. atty. of N.Y. on labor ticket, 1887; edited the Daily Leader (George campaign paper), 1886; editor The Standard, 1891-92; editor Cleveland Recorder, 1896-97; founded, 1898, and, with Alice Thacher Post, editor The Public, Chicago (later pub. in New York), until 1913; asst. sec. of labor, U.S., 1913-21. Chmn. State Conv. N.Y. Labor Party, 1887, Single Tax Nat. Conf., New York, 1890, Chicago, 1893. Mem. Chicago Bd. Edn., 1906-09; mem. Chicago Charter Conv., 1906-08. Swedenborgian. Author: The George-Hewitt Campaign, 1887; Ethics of Democracy, 1905, 2d edit., 1916; The Prophet of San Francisco, 1905; Ethical Principles of Marriage and Divorce, 1906; Social Service, 1909; Land Value Taxation, 5th edit., 1915; The Deportations Delirium of 1920. Home: Chicago, Ill. Died Jan. 10, 1928.

POST, Martin Hayward, physician; b. St. Louis, Mar. 31, 1851; s. Truman Marcellus and Frances Alsop (Henshaw) P.; A.B., Washington U., 1872; prin. in St. Louis pub. schs.; M.D., St. Louis Med. Coll., 1877; in hosp. service, St. Louis City and Female hosps., 18 months; post-grad. study, London and Utrecht; m. Mary Lawrence Tyler, May 6, 1885 (dec.); 2d, Mary Brown Tanner, Jan. 6, 1906. Practicing at St. Louis since graduation. Mem. bd. mgrs. Mo. Sch. for the Blind; mem. med. staff St. Luke's Hospital. Conglist. Home: St. Louis, Mo. Died Sept. 1, 1914.

POST, Melville Davisson, author; b. Harrison Co., W.Va., Apr. 19, 1871; s. Ira Carper and Florence May (Davisson) P.; A.B., W.Va. U., 1891, LL.B., 1892; m. Ann Bloomfield Gamble, June 29, 1903 (died 1919). Admitted to bar Supreme Court of W.Va., U.S. Circuit Court of Appeals, Supreme Court of U.S. Presdl. elector and sec. Electoral Coll., 1892; mem. bd. regents of State Normal Schs.; chmn. Dem. Congl. Com. for W.Va., 1898. Author: Uncle Abner, 1918; The Mystery at the Blue Villa, 1919; The Sleuth of St. James's Square, 1920; The Mountain School Teacher, 1922; Monsieur Jonquelle, 1923; Walker of the Secret Service, 1925; The Man Hunters, 1926; The Revolt of the Birds, 1927, The Bradmoor Murder, 1929; The Garden in Asia. Mem. advisory com. Nat. Econ. League on question of efficiency in administration of justice, 1914-15; chmn. com. Am. authors supporting John W. Davis for Pres., 1924. Home: Lost Creek, W.Va. Died June 23, 1930.

POST, Wiley, aviator; b. Grand Plain, Tex., 1900; s. William Frank and May P.; m. May Lane, 1927. Farmer in Tex., later oil driller in Okla.; lost one eye in an accident, and was awarded $2,000; invested the award in a 2d hand airplane and began as flyer, 1924; made nearly 100 parachute jumps; winner of Chicago-Los Angeles Air Derby, in 9 hrs., 9 minutes and 4 seconds, 1930; made trip around the world with Harold Gatty, in 8 days, 15 hrs. and 51 minutes, in 1931; 2d round-the-world trip alone (the 1st to fly alone around the world), in 7 days, 18 hrs. and 49 minutes, in 1933. Served as aerial navigation instr. and adviser, U.S. Army. Home: Oklahoma City, Okla. Died Aug. 15, 1935.

POST, W(illiam) Merritt, painter; b. Brooklyn, Dec. 11, 1856; s. William Winfield and Annie Louise (Paine) P.; pupil Art Students' League, New York; m. Katharina Elizabeth Van Nest, June 28, 1905; 1 dau., Katharine Van Nest. Landscape painter, 1882. Hon. mention Buffalo Expn., 1901. A.N.A., 1910. Episcopalian. Home: Bantam, Conn. Died 1935.

POST, William Stone, architect; b. New York, May 10, 1866; s. George Browne and Alice Matilda

(Stone) P.; grad. St. Mark's School, Southboro, Mass., 1884; acad. course, Columbia, 2 yrs., and course in architecture 4 yrs., Ph.B., 1890; m. Lillian M., d. Gen. John B. Hood, C.S.A., June 14, 1894; children—Marion Hood (Mrs. Thos. McC. Peters), Lilian (Mrs. Catesby L. Jones), Eleanora Robertson. Practiced with father until 1904, partner George B. Post & Sons until 1930. Works: N.Y. Stock Exchange Bldg., Coll. City of New York, and Hotel Roosevelt, New York; Wis. State Capitol; Prudential and Mutual Benefit Life Ins. bldgs. of Newark, N.J.; Mt. Sinai Hosp., Cleveland; hotels Statler at Cleveland, Detroit, St. Louis, Buffalo, and Boston; Wade Park Manor and Fenway Hall, Cleveland; Olympic Hotel, Seattle; etc. Republican. Presbyn. Fellow A.I.A. Home: Bernardsville, N.J. Died July 8, 1940.

POSTLE, Wilbur Everett, M.D., surgeon; b. Franklin Co., O., Nov. 20, 1860; s. Franklin and Catherine (Smith) P.; prep. edn. Reynoldsburg (O.) Acad.; M.D., Eclectic Med. Inst., Cincinnati, O., 1890; m. Roberta Dodds, June 17, 1890. Gen. practice, 1890-1903, treatment of chronic and nervous diseases, 1903—; owner and supt. Shepard Sanitarium. Mem. Nat. and Ohio State Eclectic med. assns. Republican. Methodist. Mason. Home: London, O. Deceased.

POSTON, Elias McClellan, corp. officer; b. Nelsonville, O., Oct. 26, 1862; s. Samuel N. and Mary A. (Brodt) P.; ed. public schools, Nelsonville; m. Helena Rannells, Dec. 13, 1883; m. 2d, Therese Erb, Jan. 12, 1907; children—Donald R., Anna R. (Mrs. A. E. Renner), John B., Charlene, Carl M., Mary, Elias McC. Establishing, 1890—, electric power and light, coal, and clay mfg. cos.; now connected with ownership of Southern Ohio Power Co., United Ohio Utilities Co., Ohio Fire-Proofing Co., Hocking Valley Brick Co.; also pres. New York Coal Co., Manhattan Oil Co., Cincinnati Mining Co., Low Volatile Coal Co., Poston Securities Co., etc.; vice chmn. mining div. President's Conference on Unemployment, Sept. 1921. Republican. Mason. Home: Columbus, O. Died Oct. 9, 1931.

POTEAT, Edwin McNeill, clergyman; b. Caswell Co., N.C., Feb. 6, 1861; s. James and Julia A. (McNeill) P.; B.A., Wake Forest (N.C.) Coll., 1881, D.D., 1894; grad. Southern Bapt. Theol. Sem., 1885; student psychology and philosophy, Johns Hopkins, 1886-88; lecture courses, Yale, 1888-98; U. of Berlin, summer of 1888; LL.D., U. of S.C., 1906, Baylor U., 1907; m. Harriet Hale, d. Rev. A. J. Gordon, D.D., of Boston, Oct. 24, 1889 (died 1919); children—Gordon, Edwin McNeill, John Robinson, Priscilla, Isabella Graves, James Douglass, Clarissa Hale, Arthur Barron (dec.); m. 2d, Harriet Helen Brittingham, June 1925. Ordained Bapt. ministry, 1884; pastor, Chapel Hill, N.C., 1885; asst. prof. ancient langs., Wake Forest Coll., 1886; acting pastor Lee St. Ch., Baltimore, 1886-88; pastor Calvary Ch., New Haven, Conn., 1888-1898, Memorial Ch., Phila., 1898-1903; pres. Furman Univ., Greenville, S.C., 1903-18; platform rep. of Laymen's Missionary Movement, and Interch. World Movement, 1918-19; departmental exec. sec. Gen. Bd. of Promotion of Northern Bapt. Conv., 1919-21; prof. philosophy and ethics, Shanghai (China) Bapt. Coll., 1921-27; supply pastor First Bapt. Ch., Richmond, Va., Oct. 1927-29; pastor Second Bapt. Ch., Atlanta, Ga., 1929-31; prof. ethics and comparative religion, Mercer U., Macon, Ga., 1931-34; prof. of ethics Furman U. and Greenville Woman's Coll., 1934—. Mem. bd. mgrs., Am. Bapt. Missionary Union, 1888-1903, Bapt. Publ. Soc., 1898-1903; rec. sec. Am. Bapt. Edn. Soc., 1890-97; trustee Southern Bapt. Theol. Sem.; life mem. Am. Bible Soc.; pres. Southern Bapt. Ednl. Assn., 1912-14. Democrat. Author: The Scandal of the Cross, 1928. Died June 26, 1937.

POTEAT, William Louis, coll. pres.; b. Caswell Co., N.C., Oct. 20, 1856; s. James and Julia A. (McNeill) P.; A.B., Wake Forest Coll., 1877, A.M., 1889; post-grad. studies Marine Biol. Lab. and short time in Zoöl. Inst., U. of Berlin; LL.D., Baylor U., 1905, University of N.C., 1906, Brown U., 1927, Duke Univ., 1933; Litt.D., Mercer Univ., 1933; m. Emma J. Purefoy, June 24, 1881; children—Hubert McNeill, Louie (Mrs. Wheeler Martin), Helen Purefoy (Mrs. Laurence Stallings). Teacher in Wake Forest Coll., 1878—, prof. biology, 1883—, pres., 1905-27 (emeritus). Lecturer on Gay Foundation, Southern Bapt. Theol. Sem., 1900; Brooks lecturer on science and religion, Hamilton Theol. Sem., 1904-05, also Crozer, Rochester, Newton sems. and Univ. of Chicago; lecturer on Lewis Holland Foundation, Southwestern Bapt. Theol. Sem., 1915; McNair lecturer, U. of N.C., 1925; lecturer to Chapel Hill School of Religion, 1928. Mem. N.C. State Board of Examiners, 1897-99, State Spl. Freight Rate Commn., 1914. Pres. N.C. Acad. Science, 1902, N.C. State Conv. Anti-Saloon League, 1918-23, N.C. Conf. for Social Service, 1918-19, Southern Bapt. Edn. Assn., 1921-23; first pres. Council of Ch. Schools of the South, 1923; mem. N.C. Reconstruction Commn., 1919. Author: Laboratory and Pulpit, 1901; The New Peace, 1915; Can a Man Be a Christian Today?, 1925; The Way of Victory, 1929; Stop-Light, 1935. Home: Wake Forest, N.C. Died Mar. 12, 1938.

POTHIER, Aram J., governor; b. in P.Q., July 26, 1854; s. Jules and Domitilde (Dallaire) P.; ed. Nicolet Coll. until 1871; LL.D., Manhattan Coll., New York, 1911, Coll. Holy Cross, Worcester, Mass., 1912, Niagara U., 1912; m. Françoise de Charmigny, of France, 1902. Arrived in Woonsocket, R.I., at 18; began, 1875, as clk., Woonsocket Instn. for Savings, with which has ever since been identified, and is now pres.; also pres. Union Trust Co., Providence. Mem. R.I. Ho. of Rep., 1887-88; commr. to Paris expns., 1889, 1900; city auditor, Woonsocket, 1889-94, mayor, 1894, 95; lt. gov. of R.I., 1898; gov., 1909-15 and 1925-27 (longer in office than any other gov. since adoption of state constn.). Republican. Treas. Woonsocket Hosp., Woonsocket Anti-Tuberculosis Soc.; v.p. Am. Bankers Assn. Catholic. Home: Woonsocket, R.I. Died Feb. 3, 1928.

POTTER, Alfred Claghorn, librarian; b. New Bedford, Mass., Apr. 4, 1867; s. William James and Elizabeth Claghorn (Babcock) P.; prep. edn., Friends Acad., New Bedford; A.B., Harvard, 1889; m. Edith Van Du Zee, Dec. 21, 1893; children—Elizabeth Claghorn (Mrs. Stedman B. Hoar), William Delano. Asst., Harvard Coll. Library, 1889-1904, asst. librarian, 1904-28, librarian, 1928-36, now librarian emeritus; asso. Huntington Library, San Marino. Home: Pasadena, Calif. Died Nov. 1, 1940.

POTTER, Alfred Knight, mfr. silverware; b. Providence, R.I., July 27, 1880; s. Edward Anthony and Helen (Knight) P.; A.B., Brown U., 1902; m. Alice Marjorie Ray, May 16, 1911; children—Helen Ray, Edward Sheldon, William Ray. Vice-pres. and treas. Gorham Mfg. Co., mfrs. of silverware, etc., Providence, 1918—; dir. various companies. Unitarian. Home: Providence, R.I. Died Feb. 19, 1936.

POTTER, Charles Lewis, army engr.; b. Lisbon Falls, Me., Jan. 24, 1864; s. Benjamin R. and Susan E. (Smullen) P.; grad. U.S. Mil. Acad., 1886; grad. Engr. Sch. of Application, 1889; m. Mrs. Sophie H. Nichols, Feb. 15, 1905. Commd. 2d lt. 5th Cav., July 1, 1886; transferred to engrs., Feb. 2, 1887; promoted through grades to col., Nov. 27, 1916. Spanish War and Philippine Insurrection, 1898-1900; with river and harbor works, Memphis, 1900-03, Duluth, 1903-06, Puerto Rico, 1907-10, St. Louis, 1910-12, St. Paul, 1912-15, Portland, Ore., 1915-16, Boston, 1916-17; dir. gas service, Washington, 1917-18; in charge 2d San Francisco Engr. Dist., 1918-20; pres. Miss. River Commn., Mar. 19, 1920—. Mason. Died Aug. 6, 1928.

POTTER, Charles Nelson, judge; b. Cooperstown, N.Y., Oct. 31, 1852; s. George W. and Mary Jane (Marcellus) P.; ed. pub. schs., Grand Rapids, Mich.; LL.B., U. of Mich., 1873; admitted to Mich. bar, 1873; located at Cheyenne, Wyo., 1876; m. Bessie C. Ireland, Aug. 22, 1877; 1 dau., Mrs. Ada Armina Larwill. City atty., 1878-81, 1888-91; pros. atty. of co., 1881-83; mem. and sec. Wyo. Capitol Bldg. Commn., 1886-88; mem. Wyo. Constl. Conv., 1889; atty. gen. of Wyo., 1891-95; mem. Bd. of Edn., Cheyenne, 1888-97; justice Supreme Court of Wyo., 1895—; reëlected 1902, 1910, 1918 (chief justice, Dec. 7, 1897-1903, 1905-11, 1915-19, and 1921—). Reported for publication Wyo. Supreme Court Reports, vols. 4-22, 1898-1915. Home: Cheyenne, Wyo. Died Dec. 20, 1927.

POTTER, Cora Urquhart (Mrs. James Brown Potter), actress; b. New Orleans; d. Col. David Urquhart; m. J. B. Potter (divorced 1900). Gained fame as an amateur in New York; professional début, Haymarket Theatre, London, as Anne Sylvester in "Man and Wife," Mar. 1887; appeared Fifth Av. Theatre, New York, in "Mlle. de Bremier," Oct. 1887; from then has appeared in varied repertoire and played during three tours around the world. Was instrumental in obtaining many thousands of pounds for the various funds in aid of the troops at the front in S. Africa; also one of prominent ladies on com. of the "Maine" hosp. ship presented by America to British Govt. For past 5 yrs. has appeared continually in London in various theatres; recited the "Antigone" at Bristol (Eng.) Musical Festival, Oct. 1902. Author: My Recitations. Died Feb. 12, 1936.

POTTER, Edward Clark, sculptor; b. New London, Conn., Nov. 26, 1857; s. Nathan Day and Mary (Clark) P.; ed. Amherst Coll., class of 1882; (hon. M.A., 1907); studied sculpture under Mercei and Fremo, Paris, 1888-89; m. May Dumont, Dec. 31, 1890. Collaborated with D. C. French in sculpture for Chicago Expn., 1892-93; executed equestrian statues of Grant at Phila., 1894; Washington at Paris, 1898; Hooker at Boston, 1904; Derens at Worcester, Mass., 1905; Slocum at Gettysburg; De Soto at St. Louis Expn., 1904; also statues in Fulton Library, Washington; Zoroaster, Appellate Ct., New York; Gov. Blair, in Mich. State House; four groups at Buffalo Expn., 1901; two animal groups in J. P. Morgan's library, New York; Inadriga in Minn. State House, 1906, in collaboration D. C. French. N.A., 1906. Home: Greenwich, Conn. Died June 22, 1923.

POTTER, Edward Eels, commodore U.S.N., retired, May 9, 1895; b. Medina, N.Y., May 9, 1833; ed. Rockford, Ill., public schs.; apptd. to navy from Ill., Feb. 5, 1850; grad. U. S. Naval Acad., 1856; lt., July 9, 1858; convoyed 1st Japanese embassy to their home with steam-frigate Niagara, 1860; arrived home, Apr. 1861; ordered to Wissahickon and in her passed forts Jackson, St. Philip, etc. After war served on various duties and on many stas.; promoted capt., July 11, 1880; commodore, Jan. 1893; gov. U.S. Naval Home, Phila., 1893-95. Home: Washington, D.C. Died 1902.

POTTER, Edwin Augustus, banker; b. Bath, Me., Sept. 18, 1842; s. William and Pamelia (Gilmore) P.; ed. in schs. of Bath; m. Harriet A., d. Col. Alfred Berry, Oct. 15, 1873. Engaged in connection with his father's lumber and shipbuilding business at Bath; went to Chicago, May 1872, and established branch of Boston crockery house of Abram French & Co., which later became French & Potter Co.; mem., 1889, of the firm of Lyon, Potter & Co., pianos; one of original stockholders, 1889, and pres., 1898-1912, Am. Trust and Savings Bank. Home: Lake Geneva, Wis. Died Jan. 14, 1936.

POTTER, Eliphalet Nott, educator; b. in Union Coll. (Schenectady, N.Y.), Sept. 20, 1836; son of late Dr. Alonzo Potter, P.E. bishop of Pa.; grad. Union Coll. (D.D.; LL.D., Williams, and Trinity Coll., Toronto; D.C.L., Univ. of the South; L.H.D., St. Stephen's Coll., Annandale, N.Y.). Entered P.E. ministry, 1862; became prof. Lehigh Univ.; later pres. Union Coll., and after that chancellor of Union Univ., which he founded. Afterward pres. Hobart Coll., Geneva, N.Y., until 1897; later pres. Cosmopolitan Univ., designed to give university instruction by means of correspondence courses. Died 1901.

POTTER, Henry Codman, P.E. bishop of New York, 1887—; b. Schenectady, N.Y., May 25, 1834; s. Bishop Alonzo P., of Pa.; ed. Episcopal Acad., Phila.; Theol. Sem., Va., 1857 (A.M., 1863, D.D., 1865, LL.D., 1878, Union; LL.D., Yale, 1901; D.D., Harvard and Trinity; also Oxford and Cambridge, Eng.). Ordered deacon, 1857; ordained priest, 1858; pastorates: Christ Ch., Greensburg, Pa., 1857-58; St. John's, Troy, 1859-66; asst. Trinity Ch., Boston; rector Grace Ch., New York; sec. House of Bishops, 1863-83; coadjutor to his uncle, Horatio Potter, bishop of New York, 1883-87. Author: Thirty Years Reviewed; Young Men's Christian Associations and Their Work; The Church and Her Children; Sisterhood and Deaconesses, 1873; The Religion for Today; The Scholar and the State, 1897; The East of To-day and To-morrow, 1902; The Industrial Situation, 1902; Law and Loyalty, 1903. Died 1908.

POTTER, Henry Staples, mfr.; b. Cambridge, Mass., May 31, 1848; s. Henry and Abby Livermore Williams (Giles) P.; grad. high sch., Cambridge; m. Grace Robbins, Sept. 21, 1869 (died 1890); m. 2d, Sibyl T. Gilman, Aug. 9, 1894. Mfr. health specialties, 1872—; pres. Potter & Wrightington, proprs. Old Grist Mill, Charlestown; dir. Commonwealth Trust Co. Mem. Boston Chamber of Commerce. Republican. Mem. Bostonian Society. Home: Boston, also Magnolia, Mass. Deceased.

POTTER, Homer Dexter; b. Johnstown, N.Y., Feb. 14, 1878; s. Thomas Candé and Lydia Arletta (Churchill) P.; ed. Rollins Coll., Winter Park, Fla., and night sch., Chicago; m. Evelyn May Eastland, Sept. 11, 1913. With Gilbert & Bennett Mfg. Co., Blue Island and Chicago, 1898-1903; with Dow Wire & Iron Works, Louisville, Ky., except 2 yrs., 1903-18, advancing to supt. agencies; with Plywood Mfrs.' Assn., 1919—. Mem. Co. C, 1st Regt., Ky. State Guard, 1904-07. Presbyn. Author: Costing Principles and Practices for the Plywood Industry, 1921; Costing Principles for Furniture Factories, 1923. Home: Louisville, Ky. Died Nov. 24, 1924.

POTTER, Mrs. James Brown, see Cora Urquhart Potter.

POTTER, John Fox, farmer and lawyer; b. Augusta, Me., May 11, 1817; ed. Phillips Acad., Exeter, N.H.; studied law; went West, 1836; pre-empted land; admitted to Wis. bar, 1838; m. Frances Elizabeth Lewis Fox, 1839 (died 1863). Probate judge, 1839-51; mem. legislature, 1852-56; mem. Congress, 1857-62; U.S. consul gen. in British North America, 1862-64. Declined appointments as gov. of Dak., minister to Denmark, etc. Was mem. of the Clay battalion. Was anti-slavery Free Soiler; from 1856 a Republican. Resides on the land he pre-empted in Walworth Co., East Troy, Wis., in 1838. Home: East Troy, Wis. Died 1899.

POTTER, Louis, sculptor; b. Troy, N.Y., Nov. 14, 1873; s. Louis and Mary Elizabeth (McClellan) P.; A.B., Trinity Coll., 1896 (hon. A.M., 1909); studied painting under Charles N. Flagg and Montague Flagg; studied art 4 yrs. in Paris in ateliers of Luc-Olivier Merson and Jean Dampt; unmarried. Has made specialty of Am. and Alaska Indian groups; made several symbolic and poetic groups and several busts of eminent persons; memorial to Horace Wells, Hartford, Conn., 1909; etc. Exhibited at Paris Salon, 1899, Paris Expn., 1900, and in prin. socs. of U.S.; had spl. sculpture exhbn. in New York,

May 1909; group "Earth-Bound" in heroic size symbolized the purpose of the 1st Child's Welfare Exhibit, New York, 1911; exhibited in Roman Expn., 1911. Decorated Officier of Nichan Iftikar, by Bey of Tunis, 1900. Home: New York, N.Y. Died Aug. 29, 1912.

POTTER, Margaret Horton, author; b. Chicago, May 20, 1881; d. Orrin W. and Ellen (Owen) P.; ed. prep. sch., Chicago; post-grad. studies in Latin, Greek, English, history and philosophy under pvt. tutor; m. John Donald Black, Jan. 1, 1902. Author: A Social Lion, 1899; Uncanonized, 1900; The House of De Mailly, 1901; Istar of Babylon, 1902; The Castle of Twilight, 1903; The Flame-Gatherers, 1904; The Fire of Spring, 1905; The Genius, 1906; The Princess, 1907; The Golden Ladder, 1908. Home: Chicago, Ill. Died 1911.

POTTER, Mary Knight, author, artist; b. Boston; d. George Sabine and Mary Gill (Powell) P.; sister of Nathaniel Bowditch P.; ed. pub. schs., New York; Harvard Coll. Summer Sch., 1894-95; Met. Mus. Art, and Art Students' League, New York; Cowles Art Sch., Boston; Julien Acad., Paris; studied French and German with pvt. tutors, music, literature, etc.; unmarried. Engaged as painter several yrs., but except occasional work has given up painting for literature. Author: Art of the Vatican, 1902; The Art of the Louvre, 1904; Art of the Venice Academy 1905. Asst. editor Masters of Art, 1906. Home: Boston, Mass. Died Oct. 5, 1915.

POTTER, Orrin W., mfr.; b. Rochester, N.Y., Dec. 25, 1836; pub. sch. edn.; self-taught in higher mathematics and civ. engring.; m. Ellen Owen, 1858. Removed to Wyandotte, Mich., 1856, and clerked in rolling mill; sec. and gen. supt. Chicago Rolling Mill Co., 1864; pres. North Chicago Rolling Mill Co., 1871, for over 25 yrs. till its consolidation with the Ill. Steel Co., 1889. Retired. Home: Chicago, Ill. Died 1907.

POTTER, Paul Meredith, dramatist; b. Brighton, Eng., June 3, 1853 (his father being head master of King Edward's Sch., Bath, and editor "Bibliotheca Classica"). Foreign editor of New York Herald, 1876-83, London corr. same, 1883-84; dramatic critic, 1885-87; joined editorial staff of Chicago Tribune, 1888; began writing plays with "The City Directory," prod. by Russell's Comedians, May 1889; wrote The Ugly Duckling, 1890; The World's Fair, 1891; The American Minister, comedy, for W. H. Crane, 1892; Sheridan, or the Maid of Bath, for E. H. Sothern, 1893; Our Country Cousins, for Daniel Frohman, 1893; The Pacific Mail, for Crane, 1894; The Victoria Cross, for Sothern, 1894; Trilby (dramatization of Du Maurier's novel), 1st prod. Park Theatre, Boston, Mar. 13, 1895, then by H. Beerbohm Tree at Haymarket Theatre, London, Oct. 1895; The Stag Party, burlesque (with late E. W. Nye), 1896; The Conquerors, prod. Charles Frohman at Empire Theatre, New York, Jan. 4, 1898, and by George Alexander at St. James Theatre, London, Apr. 1898; Under Two Flags, Garden Theatre, 1901; The Red Kloof, Savoy Theatre, 1902; Notre Dame, Daly's Theatre, 1903; The School-Girl, Daly's Theatre, 1904; Nancy Stair, 1905; Barbara's Millions, 1906; The Honor of the Family, 1907; The Queen of the Moulin Rouge, 1908; The Girl from Rectors, 1909; Arsène Lupin, 1909; Israel, 1909. Resident dramatist, Palmer's Theatre, 1894-97; Am. representative at Congress of Dramatic Art, Paris Expn., 1900. Died Mar. 7, 1921.

POTTER, William, lawyer; pres. Jefferson Medical Coll., Phila.; s. of Thomas and Adaline (Coleman) P.; educated private schools and Univ. of Pa. Former pres. Thomas Potter, Sons & Co., incorporated. Apptd. by President Harrison spl. commr. to visit London, Paris, and Berlin in behalf of U.S. State and Postoffice depts., and to negotiate system of sea postoffices, 1890; del. to 4th Congress of Universal Postal Union, Vienna, 1891; U.S. minister to Italy, 1892-94; chmn. Mayor Weaver's (Phila.) advisory bd., 1905-06; nat. relief commr., 1898, went to P.R. during war with Spain; City party and Dem. party nominee for mayor of Phila., 1907. Councilor Hist. Soc. Pa.; hon. mem. Soc. Cincinnati, N.J.; mem. Permanent Relief Com., Phila.; mgr. Pa. Instn. for Deaf and Dumb. Federal fuel adminstr. for Pa., Oct. 1917-Mar. 1, 1919. Apptd. by federal court one of trustees in dissolution case against Lehigh Valley R.R. Co., Jan. 1924. Home: Chestnut Hill, Phila., Pa. Died Apr. 29, 1926.

POTTER, William Bancroft, engineer; b. at Thomaston, Conn., Feb. 19, 1863; s. of Horace A. and Charlotte S. P.; ed. Thomaston High Sch.; m. Loretta Harward, July 3, 1890; m. 2d, Rose Hubbard, Sept. 23, 1912. Training for engr. in machine shop at Hartford, which included gen. steam engring.; with Thomson-Houston Co., Lynn, Mass., on arc lighting, afterward specializing on apparatus for electric rys.; with this co. when consolidated into the Gen. Electric Co., and has resided at Schenectady, 1894—; became chief engr. ry. engring. dept., Gen. Electric Co., 1895; cons. engr. transportation dept. same co., 1929; retired 1930. Home: Schenectady, N.Y. Died Jan. 15, 1934.

POTTER, William Bleecker, mining engr.; b. Schenectady, N.Y., Mar. 23, 1846; s. Bishop Horatio and Mary Jane (Tomlinson) P.; A.B., Columbia, 1866, A.M., E.M., 1869 (Sc.D., 1904); m. Agnes Kennett Farrar, Nov. 14, 1888. Asst. in geology, Columbia, 1869-71; prof. mining and metallurgy, Washington U., 1871-93; founder, manager St. Louis Sampling & Testing Works. Asst. Mo. Geol. Survey, 1872-74; engr. Pilot Knob Iron Co., 1874-78; metallurgist Vulcan Iron & Steel Works, 1876-78; engr. Iron Mountain Co., 1882-93; mem. bd. mgrs. Mo. Geol. Survey, 1889-93. Home: St. Louis, Mo. Died July 14, 1914.

POTTER, William Henry, dentist; b. Boston, June 20, 1856; s. Silas and Caroline Daniels (Allen) P.; grad. Roxbury Latin Sch., 1874; A.B., Harvard, 1878; D.M.D., Harvard Dental Sch., 1885; hon. M.A., Harvard, 1927; m. Mary Louise Allen, June 21, 1893; children—Allen, Caroline, Mary, William, Roger. Practiced, Boston, 1885—; lecturer on operative dentistry, 1890-96, asst. prof., 1900-04, prof. 1904-27, Harvard Dental Sch. (emeritus). Fellow Am. Coll. Dentists. Dental surgeon, Am. Ambulance Hosp., Neuilly, France, 3 mos., 1914-15; commd. 1st lt. Dental Corps, U.S.A., May 7, 1917; sailed for France, May 11, 1917; mem. U.S.A. Base Hosp. No. 5; served in British hosps., later as instr. Army Sanitary Sch., Langres, France, returned to U.S., Apr. 1919; promoted maj. and lt. col. Decorated Chevalier Legion of Honor (France), 1927. Republican. Conglist. Home: Boston, Mass. Died July 27, 1928.

POTTER, William Parker, rear admiral U.S.N.; b. Whitehall, N.Y., May 10, 1850. Apptd. from N.Y., and grad. U.S. Naval Acad., 1869; promoted ensign, July 12, 1870; master, July 12, 1871; lt., Aug. 9, 1874; lt. comdr., June 12, 1896; comdr., Sept. 9, 1899; capt., Sept. 13, 1904; rear admiral, Oct. 30, 1908. Served successively on the Sabine, Franklin, Constellation, Hartford, Iroquois, 1869-74; Naval Acad., 1874-78; flag secretary N. Atlantic Fleet on board Powhatan, Marion, and Tennessee, 1878-81; Naval Acad., 1881-84; Lancaster, 1884-87; flag sec. European Squadron, 1885-86; Naval Acad., 1887-91; Baltimore, 1892; flag sec. European Squadron on board Philadelphia and Chicago, 1893-94; Naval Acad., 1895-97; exec. officer New York, 1897-99; took part in destruction of Cervera's squadron off Santiago, Cuba, July 3, 1898, and was advanced five numbers for "eminent and conspicuous conduct" in that battle; Navy Yard League Island, 1899-1901; comd. Ranger, 1901-03; Navy Dept., 1903-05; asst. to Bur. of Navigation, Navy Dept., 1905-07; comdg. Vermont, 1907; later comd. 4th div. Atlantic Fleet; chief Bur. Navigation, 1909; aid for personnel, Navy Dept., 1910-11; retired May 10, 1912. Died June 21, 1917.

POTTER, William Plumer, judge; b. Jackson Co., Ia., Apr. 27, 1857; s. Rev. James H. and Nancy (Naylor) P.; student Lafayette Coll., Easton, Pa., class of 1879; (LL.D., Lafayette, 1907, Swarthmore Coll., Pa., 1911); admitted to Iowa bar, 1880; m. Jessie L. Bacon, Mar. 13, 1884. Removed to Pittsburgh, 1881; pursued further legal studies; admitted to the Pittsburgh bar, 1883; practiced until apptd., Sept. 25, 1900, justice Supreme Ct. of Pa., and elected, Nov. 5, 1901, to same position for term of 21 yrs., beginning Jan. 1, 1902. Home: Swarthmore, and Pittsburgh, Pa. Died Apr. 14, 1918.

POTTER, William Warren, physician, editor; b. Strykersville, N.Y., Dec. 31, 1838; s. Dr. Lindorf and Mary G. P.; ed. Arcade (N.Y.) Sem. and Genesee Sem. and Coll., Lima, N.Y.; M.D., Buffalo U., 1859; m. Emily A. Bostwick, Mar. 23, 1859 (dec.). Practised medicine, Cowlesville, N.Y., 1859-61; commd., 1861, asst. surgeon 49th N.Y. Vols., served with Army of Potomac; in Libby prison 3 weeks, June 1862, but exchanged; promoted surgeon, Dec. 1862, and served with 57th N.Y. Vols. during Chancellorsville and Gettysburg campaigns; in charge 1st Div. Hosp., 2d Army Corps, 1863-65; bvtd. lt. col. N.Y. Vols. and lt. col. U.S. Vols. "for faithful and meritorious services." In practice at Buffalo, 1866—; editor Buffalo Med. Jour., July 1888—; also edits annual volume of Transactions of Am. Assn. Obstetricians and Gynecologists. Examiner obstetrics and gynecology and pres. N.Y. State Med. Examining and Licensing Bd., 1895-1909. Chmn. Sect. Obstetrics and Diseases of Women of A.M.A., 1890. Home: Buffalo, N.Y. Died 1911.

POTTERTON, Thomas Edward, clergyman, lecturer; b. Clarksburg, Mass., May 15, 1868; s. Abraham and Mary M. (Miller) P.; grad. St. Lawrence U. Theol. Sch., 1891; D.D. from same, 1905; m. Anna T. Nye, 1893. Ordained ministry Universalist Ch., 1891; pastor successively, Brookline, Somerville and Taunton, Mass., and of Ch. of Our Father, Brooklyn, N.Y., Mar. 1903—. Chmn. Bd. Fgn. Missions, 1917-21; v.p. Gen. Conv. Universalist Ch., 1923-27; pres. New York Conv. Universalists, 1926-27, trustee, term 1933-36; pres. bd. Theol. School, St. Lawrence University. Extensive traveler and widely known as lecturer. Republican. Mason. Author: The Comforter, 1903; Nineteen Hundred and Now, 1920. Home: Brooklyn, N.Y. Died Dec. 8, 1933.

POTTHAST, Edward Henry, artist; b. Cincinnati, June 10, 1857; s. Henry and Bernardina (Scheifers) P.; common sch. edn.; art edn. at Cincinnati, Munich and Paris. Represented in Cincinnati Art Mus., Art Inst. Chicago, Brooklyn Inst. Arts and Sciences, Albright Gallery (Buffalo, N.Y.), etc. N.A., 1906. Studio: New York, N.Y. Died Mar. 9, 1927.

POTTS, Alfred Fremont, lawyer; b. Richmond, Ind., Oct. 28, 1856; s. Dr. Alfred and Mary A. (Pope) P.; ed. pub. schs. to 12; law dept., U. of Mich., 1875-76; m. May Barney, Aug. 28, 1879; children—Stella Marjorie, Deborah Starr. Practiced, Indianapolis, 1877—; partner with John L. Griffiths for 25 yrs.; v.p. Citizens' Gas Co. Originator of substitute for municipal ownership of pub. utilities, adopted by Consumers' Natural Gas Co., 1887, resisting all attacks for 15 yrs. until natural gas was exhausted, saving the city $1,000,000 a yr.; same plan applied to supply artificial gas through Citizens' Gas Co., 1905—, reducing price to 55c per 1,000 cubic feet, and as low as 45c to large consumers; plan provides for self-perpetuating bd. of trustees to vote stock, and eliminates politics and stock manipulation. Republican. Contemporary (pres.), Indianapolis Literary, Marion. Home: Indianapolis, Ind. Died Apr. 25, 1927.

POTTS, Charles Sower, M.D.; b. Philadelphia, Jan. 30, 1864; s. Francis C. and Emma (Bilger) P.; A.B., Central High Sch., Phila., 1882; M.D., U. of Pa., 1885; unmarried. Resident phys. Phila. Hosp., 1885-86; practiced nr. Hazleton, Pa., 1886-87; asst. phys. State Hosp. for Insane, Norristown, Pa., 1887-88; resident phys. Univ. Hosp., Phila., 1889; instr. nervous diseases, 1893-1903, asso. in neurology, 1903-07, U. of Pa.; consulting phys., Hosp. for Insane, Atlantic Co., N.J., 1897—; neurologist to Phila. Hosp., 1901—; prof. neurology, Medico-Chirurg. Coll., 1907-16; prof. neurology, Grad. School of Medicine, University of Pa., 1917—; consulting neurologist, Lankenau Hosp., Phila. Fellow Coll. Physicians Phila. Author: Nervous and Mental Diseases, 1900, 3d edit., 1913; Electricity, Its Medical and Surgical Uses, 1911. Died Feb. 17, 1930.

POTTS, James Henry, editor; b. Troy, N.Y., Aug. 27, 1855; s. John and Jean (Findlay) P.; ed. Troy High Sch.; m. Emma Jane Wilson, Aug. 31, 1881; children—Abbie Findlay, Henry Wilson, Jean Findlay (dec.), Mrs. Katherine Saunders. Connected with the Troy Times, 1879—, asst. city editor, 1881-83, city editor, 1883-96, asso. editor, 1896-1900, editor, 1900—. V.p. Troy Soc. for Spoken English; v.p. Rensselaer County Soc. in City of New York; dir. East Side Assn., Troy. Republican. Home: Troy, N.Y. Died Sept. 29, 1926.

POTTS, Louis Moses, clergyman; b. Ekaterinoslav, Russia, Feb. 2, 1877; s. Rev. Joseph and Martha Potashinsky; name legally changed to Potts; brought to U.S. as a child; B.A., U. of Denver, 1902, M.A., 1907; D.D., Okla. City U., 1922; m. Lena Shultis, Feb. 1, 1898 (died 1911); children—Merrill Saper, Edward Wilcox, Kathryn Lucinda, Jennie Louise (Mrs. Harry R. McPhail); m. 2d, Frances Coker, Nov. 25, 1914. Ordained M.E. ministry, 1897; occupied pulpits various chs. in Colo. and Kan., 1897-1918; supt. Guthrie dist., Okla. Conf., M.E. Ch., 1918-20, supt. Okla. City dist., 1921-25; mem. Gen. Conf. M.E. Ch., Springfield, Mass., 1924; exec. sec. Okla. City U., 1920-21, during successful campaign for $1,500,-000; v.p. Central Wesleyan Coll., Warrenton, Mo., 1925-27; v.p. Ozark Wesleyan Coll., Carthage, Mo., 1927-31, pres., 1931-33; pastor M.E. Ch., Chillicothe, Mo., 1933—; liquidating agt. Ozark Wesleyan Coll.; chmn. Chillicothe Federal Housing Administrn., 1935-36, Livingston County (Mo.) Centennial Celebration, 1937. Dir. Chamber of Commerce. Republican. Mason. Rotarian. Home: Chillicothe, Mo. Deceased.

POTTS, Robert, officer U.S.N.; b. Dublin, Ireland, May 8, 1835; s. Robert and Mary (Thompson) P.; ed. pub. schs. of New York; m. Fannie Griffiss, Jan. 25, 1876 (died 1909). Apptd. 3d asst. engr. U.S.N., Feb. 17, 1860; 2d asst. engr., June 27, 1862; 1st asst. engr., Mar. 1, 1864; chief engr., Jan. 22, 1873; retired May 8, 1897; advanced to rank of rear admiral retired, June 29, 1906, for services during Civil War. Home: Baltimore, Md. Died June 24, 1913.

POTTS, Templin Morris, captain U.S.N.; b. Washington, Nov. 1, 1855; s. John and Louisa (Rose) P.; ed. Emerson Inst., Washington, and pvt. sch.; grad. U.S. Naval Acad., 1876; m. Marie Alden-Brown, May 10, 1902. Promoted midshipman, June 20, 1876; ensign, Nov. 25, 1877; lt. jr. grade, Feb. 9, 1884; lt., Feb. 28, 1890; lt. comdr., Mar. 3, 1899; comdr., Nov. 8, 1904; capt., July 19, 1908. Served on Plymouth, 1876-77; Powhatan, 1877; Constitution, and Portsmouth, 1878; Powhatan, 1879; Swatara, 1880-82; spl. duty Navy Dept., 1883-85; on Pensacola, 1885-87; Naval Acad., 1888-90; on San Francisco, 1890-93; Navy Yard, Washington, 1894-96; on Massachusetts, 1896-99; Navy Yard, New York, 1900, League Island, 1900; in charge branch Hydrographic Office, Phila., 1900-01; exec. officer Richmond, 1901-02; naval attaché, Berlin, Vienna, and Rome, 1902-04; exec. officer Brooklyn, 1904; mem. Bd. Inspection and Survey, 1904-05; naval gov. of Guam, P.I., 1905; Navy Yard at Washington, 1908-09; comdg.

Georgia, 1909; chief intelligence officer, Navy Dept., 1910; also mem. Gen. Bd. and Joint Bd.; retired June 30, 1913. Died Mar. 22, 1927.

POTTS, William, author; b. Phila., May 5, 1838; s. Joseph Kirkbride and Sidney (Bonsall) P.; academic edn.; studied conveyancing and some law in Phila.; later engaged in ins. and banking; former sec. Pen-Carbon Manifold Co.; gen. sec. Orange Bureau Asso. Charities; sec. Brooklyn Civ. Service Reform Assn., 1880; N.Y. Civ. Service Reform Assn., 1881; Nat. Civ. Service Reform League, 1881; remaining sec. of the 3 orgns. until 1894, except about 6 months in 1887 when he was chief examiner, Civ. Service Commn., N.Y. State; later v.p., etc., Nat. Civ. Service Reform League; v.p. of Outdoor Recreation League. Also greatly interested in guild and settlement work and municipal govt. Author: Evolution and Social Reform—The Socialistic Method, 1890; The Monetary Problem, 1892; From a New England Hillside, 1895; More Notes from Underledge, 1904. Compiler: Statistics of Societies, 1899; etc. Orange, N.J. Died 1908.

POU, Edward William, congressman; b. Tuskegee, Ala., Sept. 9, 1863; s. Edward William and Anna Maria P.; ed. U. of N.C.; m. Carrie Ihrie, Oct. 18, 1887; children—Mrs. Thos. A. Wadden, Geo. Ross, Mrs. Carleton E. Moran. Admitted to bar, 1885; in practice at Smithfield, N.C.; presdl. elector, 1888; solicitor 4th Jud. Dist., 1890-1901; mem. 57th to 72d Congresses (1901-33), 4th N.C. District. Democrat. Home: Smithfield, N.C. Died Apr. 1, 1934.

POU, James Hinton, lawyer; b. Tuskegee, Ala., July 21, 1861; s. Edward William and Anna Maria (Smith) P.; ed. at home and pub. sch., Smithfield, N.C.; m. Annie Elizabeth Walker, Oct. 9, 1889; children—Edith Walker (Mrs. Josiah W. Bailey), James H. Admitted to N.C. bar, 1885, and began practice at Smithfield, N.C.; moved to Raleigh, N.C., 1898, mem. Pou & Pou, 1924—. Mem. N.C. Ho. of Rep., 1885, State Senate, 1887-95 (chmn. finance com. 1893); chmn. Dem. State Exec. Com., 1894. Dir. Moses H. Cone Memorial Hosp. Co-author: North Carolina Corporation Code, 1922. Home: Raleigh, N.C. Died July 29, 1935.

POULSSON, Anne Emilie, author; b. Cedar Grove, N.J., Sept. 8, 1853; d. Halvor and Ruth Ann (Mitchell) P.; grad. Kindergarten Normal Class of Misses Garland and Weston, Boston, 1881; schooling interrupted on account of defective vision; School for Blind, South Boston, studying and teaching, 1879-82; later pvt. teaching, lecturing and literary work; unmarried. Joint editor Kindergarten Review, 1897-1904. Author: In the Child's World, 1893; Through the Farmyard Gate, 1896; Child Stories and Rhymes, 1898; Love and Law in Child Training, 1899; Holiday Songs, 1901; The Runaway Donkey, 1905; Father and Baby Plays, 1907; Songs of a Little Child's Day, 1910; The Joyous Travelers (with Maud Lindsay), 1919; The Joyous Guests (with same), 1921; Rhyme-Time for Children, 1929. Translator: Johnny Blossom, 1912; Top-of-the-World Stories, 1916; What Happened to Inger Johanne, 1919; Four Cousins, 1923; Inger Johanne's Lively Doings, 1926; The Friendly Playmate, 1931; Little Kari, 1938. Editor: The Children's Year in a Happy Home (by Mary Howitt), 1927. Home: Brookline, Mass. Died Mar. 18, 1939.

POUND, Cuthbert Winfred, judge; b. Lockport, N.Y., June 20, 1864; s. Alexander and Almina (Whipple) P.; ed. Lockport pub. schs. and Cornell; LL.D., Columbia Univ., 1926, Colgate Univ., 1926, Hobart College, 1932, New York Univ., 1932; studied law with John E. Pound, Lockport; admitted to bar, 1886; m. Emma Frances White, June 22, 1887 (died 1925); children—Alexander White, Mary (Mrs. Ralph C. Taylor). City atty., Lockport, 1889-91; mem. N.Y. Senate, 29th Dist., 1894-95; prof. law, Coll. of Law, Cornell, 1895-1904; mem. N.Y. State Civ. Service Commn., 1900-05 (pres. 1902-05); apptd. counsel to gov. N.Y., Jan. 3, 1905; apptd. justice Supreme Court, 8th Dist., May 1906, elected Nov. 1906, for term 1907-20; designated asso. judge Court of Appeals, 1915, elected Nov. 1916, for term 1917-30, reëlected Nov. 1930, for term 1931-34, chief judge for term 1932-34. Chmn. Conv. to Revise Judiciary Article N.Y. State Constitution, 1921. Republican. Episcopalian. Mason. Trustee Cornell U., 1913—. Home: Lockport, N.Y. Died Feb. 3, 1935.

POUND, Jere M., college pres.; b. Liberty Hill, Ga., Mar. 23, 1864; s. Edwin T. and Elizabeth T. (Bloodworth) P.; A.B., U. of Ga., 1884 (LL.D.); m. Ada Murphey, July 17, 1889. Teacher in Boys' High Sch., Atlanta, Ga., 1884-85; prin. Ft. Valley Inst., 1885-87; pres. Gordon Inst., Barnesville, Ga., 1887-96, 1897-1901, 1910-12; dir. Normal Dept., Ga. Normal and Industrial Coll., Milledgeville, 1896-97, 1905-08; supt. pub. schs., Macon, and Bibb Co., Ga., 1901-04; supt. East Fla. Sem., 1904-05; state supt. schs., Ga., 1910-12; pres. Georgia State Teachers' College, 1912-23; pres. Georgia State Woman's Coll., 1933—. Trustee Emory Coll. Democrat. Methodist. Mason. Twice mem. Gen. Conf. M.E. Ch., S.; lay leader N. Ga. Conf.; mem. edn. com. Laymen's Missionary Movement; mem. Minute Men M.E. Ch., S., and chmn. Minute Men. N. Ga. Conf.; etc. Home: Valdosta, Ga. Died 1935.

POWDERLY, Terence Vincent, lawyer; b. Carbondale, Pa., Jan. 22, 1849; s. Terence and Margery P.; attended pub. schs. from 7 to 13 yrs. of age; worked as switch-tender, car repairer, and machinist until 1877. Elected mayor of Scranton, 1878, on Labor ticket; reëlected, 1880, 1882. Gen. master workman, Knights of Labor, 1879-93; apptd. mem. World's Fair Commn. for Pa., 1891, by Gov. Pattison, but declined; hon. mem. G.A.R. posts in 17 states. Studied law; admitted to bar, Lackawanna Co., Pa., Sept. 24, 1894. Stumped Pa. for Hastings for gov., 1894, and N.Y., N.J., Ohio, Ill., Kan., Minn., and Ia. for McKinley and Hobart, 1896; U.S. commr. gen. of immigration, 1897-1902. In 1900 stumped Ill., Ind., Ky. and Md. for McKinley and Roosevelt. Admitted to bar, Supreme Court of U.S., 1901. In 1906 appointed spl. representative of Dept. of Commerce and Labor to study causes of emigration from Europe; chief Div. of Information in Bur. of Immigration to distribute immigrants throughout the U.S., 1907—. Author: Thirty Years of Labor; History of Labor Day. Home: Washington, D.C. Died June 24, 1924.

POWELL, Aaron Macy, editor The Philanthropist; b. Clinton, N.Y., Mar. 26, 1832; ed. public schools and State Normal School, Albany. Formerly editor National Anti-Slavery Standard and sec. Am. Anti-Slavery Soc., 1866-70; asst. sec. Nat. Temperance Soc., 1873-94, and editor Nat. Temperance Advocate; became pres. Am. Purity Alliance; m. Judith Anna Rice, 1861. Author: State Regulation of Vice. Home: Plainfield, N J. Died 1899.

POWELL, Charles Francis, officer of engr. corps, U.S.A.; b. Jacksonville, Ill., Aug. 13, 1843; ed. pub. high schs., Milwaukee; m. Margaret, d. James H. Foster, Albany, Ore., May 17, 1883. Served pvt. to sergt. maj. 5th Wis. vols., May 1861, to Sept. 1863; apptd. cadet at West Point by President Lincoln for gallantry on the field of battle; grad., 1867, as 2d lt., corps engrs.; promoted successively, 1st lt., capt., maj., lt. col. Has served with U.S. battalion of engrs.; on geodetic and topographic surveys, etc.; engr. in charge Cascades Canal, Ore., and at commencement of great jetty, mouth of Columbia River; sec. Mississippi River Commn.; engr. in charge Missouri River survey and improvement; engr. commr. D.C.; engr. Monongahela River Slack-Water System; engr. defenses and certain harbors, Long Island Sound. Home: New London, Conn. Died 1907.

POWELL, Charles L., lawyer; b. Panora, Ia., Aug. 22, 1861; s. James R. and Clarinda (Hill) P.; A.B., State U. of Ia., 1885, A.M., 1888, LL.B., 1889; m. Blanche Hay Powell, Dec. 29, 1897; 1 son, Harold Hay. Admitted to Ia. bar, 1889, and practiced in Panora until 1894; pros. atty. Guthrie Co., 1892-94; engaged in gen. practice, Des Moines, 17 yrs.; settled in Chicago, 1911; mem. Mayer, Meyer, Austrian & Platt; gen. counsel Federal Reserve Bank of Chicago, 1914—. Republican. Presbyn. K.P. Home: Chicago, Ill. Died Mar. 15, 1929.

POWELL, David, clergyman; b. Harrison Co. (now Taylor Co.), W.Va., July 18, 1831; s. Elijah and Sarah (Cather) P.; ed. common schs. in W.Va.; studied divinity partly under Rev. Benj. Bailey, but mainly by self culture; ordained to Free Bapt. ministry; m. Ellen E. Hughes, Apr. 20, 1858. Entered Union army, serving 3 yrs. 7 mos.; was on staff Gen. D. Hunter, and became 1st lt. Co. H, 12th W.Va. vols.; was in 13 regular battles and about 40 days' fighting. Supt. pub. schs., 1868-69; mem. W.Va. legislature, 1882-86. Republican. In active ministry, 1886-98; retired because of failing health. Home: Flemington, W.Va. Deceased.

POWELL, Edward Alexander, nurseryman; b. Shadeland, Pa., Jan. 27, 1838; s. Hon. Howell and Sarah (Beatty) P.; ed. pub. and private schools; L.H.D., Syracuse University, 1921; m. Lucy Caroline Smith, June 25, 1868. Taught in Western Pa., and Ohio, 1856-62; in nursery business as Powell Bros., Shadeland, 1863, removed to Syracuse, 1868; as Smith & Powell Co. added importation of blooded live stock; known as Syracuse Nurseries and Lakeside Stock Farm; added real estate branch and conducted business alone from 1904. Pres. Syracuse, Lakeside & Baldwinsville R.R.; mem. and pres. Chamber of Commerce; v.p. Onondaga County Savings Bank; pres. bd. councilors, Syracuse Home Assn.; pres. bd. trustees 1st Presbyn. Ch.; dir. Onondaga Hist. Soc. Pres. Holstein-Friesian Breeders' Club N.Y. State, Farm Bur. Onondaga Co.; was pres. Onondaga Co. Agrl. Soc. 9 yrs., Holstein Assn. America 5 yrs., Bur. of Labor and Charities 5 yrs.; also pres. Children's Aid Soc.; mem. bd. of councilors Agrl. Coll. of Syracuse U. Home: Syracuse, N.Y. Died Nov. 19, 1925.

POWELL, Edward Lindsay, clergyman; b. King William Co., Va., May 8, 1860; s. Edward Turner and Mary Anville (Cave) P.; B.L., Christian U., Canton, Mo., 1881; LL.D., Transylvania U., Ky.; m. Lida Smoot, May 11, 1887 (died 1907); m. 2d, Dr. Anna M. D. Gordon, of Mungell, C.P., India, Jan. 12, 1909. Ordained Christian (Disciples) ministry, 1881; pastor in Va. at Charlottesville, Gordonsville, Norfolk, and Lynchburg, in Ky. at Hopkinsville, Maysville, and First Ch., Louisville, 1887—. Trustee Louisville Free Pub. Library. Democrat. Author: Savonarola; Victory of Faith; Prophet's Vision and President's Dream. Home: Louisville, Ky. Died Apr. 19, 1933.

POWELL, Edward Payson, journalist, author; b. Clinton, N.Y., May 9, 1833; s. John and Mary (Johnson) P.; A.B., Hamilton Coll., 1853, A.M., 1856; grad. Union Theol. Sem., 1858; m. Lucy J. Maltbie, Aug. 4, 1874. Ordained Congl. ministry, 1861; stated supply Deansville, N.Y., 1858-61; pastor Adrian, Mich., 1861-71, Third Ch., St. Louis, 1871-73, Third Unitarian Ch., Chicago, 1874-77, Utica, N.Y., 1880-86. Editorial writer St. Louis Globe Democrat, 1871-74, The Independent, New York, 1900—, Christian Register, Boston, 1890—; asso. editor Unity, Chicago, 1894—, Arena, Boston, 1898—. Mem. Am. Arbitration Congress, Washington, 1896; one of v.p.s Congress of Religion, etc. Author: Windbreaks, Hedges and Shelters, 1900; The Country Home, 1904; In the Orchard and Fruit Garden, 1905; How to Live in the Country, 1910. Home: Sorento, Fla. Died May 14, 1915.

POWELL, G(eorge) Harold; b. Ghent, N.Y., Feb. 8, 1872; s. George T. and Marcia R. (Chase) P.; B.Agr., Cornell U., 1895, M.Agr., 1896; m. Gertrude E. Clark, July 1, 1896. Horticulturist, Delaware Coll. Agrl. Expt. Sta., Newark, 1896-1901; asst. pomologist, 1901-04, pomologist, in charge fruit transportation and storage investigations, 1904-09, asst. chief Bur. Plant Industry, 1910, U.S. Dept. Agr.; sec. and mgr. Citrus Protective League of Calif., Los Angeles, 1911; gen. mgr. Calif. Fruit Growers' Exchange, Sept. 1, 1912— (corp. markets fruit for 10,000 orange and lemon growers, representing 72% of citrus industry of Calif.). Republican. Unitarian. Mem. various hort. and agrl. socs. Author: Coöperation in Agriculture, 1913. In charge of perishable foods div., U.S. Food Administration, Washington, 1917-19. Home: South Pasadena, Calif. Died Feb. 19, 1922.

POWELL, George May; b. Fowlerville, N.Y., Aug. 16, 1835; s. Rev. Oliver Stanley and Judith Shaler (May) P.; sch. attendance restricted by delicate health; active in ednl. religious and agrl. soc. work in St. Croix Valley, Wis., 1855-61; inaugurated system of "collective exhibits" in expn., at Milwaukee, 1859; statistician Treasury Dept. during war; delivered speech, "Facts and Figures for the Hour" (minutely showing that our citizens in war time were taxed less than Europeans in time of peace), which was largely used as Lincoln campaign document, 1864; sec. Y.M.C.A., Washington, 1863-64, inaugurated movement for such assns. to own their own buildings. Founder, 1868, and from then sec. and mgr. Evangelical Press Assn.; originated numbered envelope weekly-payment plan for ch. subscriptions. Had charge, 1873, of geog. and archeol. expdn. to Egypt and Syria; publisher scientific works, relief maps, geog. indexes, etc. Organized Am. Inst. Forest Com., 1874, becoming chmn.; extensive writer on tree-planting; organized Forest Congress and Beet Sugar Congress at Centennial Expn., 1876; active in measures for promotion of peace between nations, suggesting "Supreme Court Plan" of arbitration embodied in his memorial, presented by U.S. Senator Frye, 1896, which became basis of Permanent International Peace Court adopted at The Hague. Home: Newfield, N.J. Died 1905.

POWELL, Hunter Holmes, physician; b. Middleburg, Va., Dec. 16, 1843; s. Humphrey Brooke and Ann Holmes (Boyd) P.; ed. pvt. sch. and Winchester Acad. (sch. training interrupted by Civil War); M.D., Va. Med. Coll., Richmond, 1867; (A.M., Western Reserve U., 1894); m. Emma Baker, June 4, 1874 (died 1890). Enlisted Co. K, 2d Va. Cav., C.S.A., May 1862, and served as pvt. until close of war; captured in cav. fight at High Bridge, Amelia Co., Va., Apr. 7, 1865, and held as prisoner until June 20th, following. Began practice at Winchester, Va., 1867; removed to Cleveland, 1872; prof. diseases of children, 1875-78, prof. obstetrics and pediatrics, 1878-1907, dean med. dept., 1895-1900, emeritus prof. obstetrics, 1907-11, sr. prof. obstetrics and pediatrics, 1911—, Western Reserve U. Visiting phys. Lakeside Hosp., 1879—; dir. St. Ann's Maternity and Orphan Asylum, 1881—; trustee Babies' Dispensary and Hosp., Cleveland Med. Library. Democrat. Presbyn. Home: Cleveland, O. Deceased.

POWELL, John H., M.D.; b. Lenoir, N.C., Sept. 23, 1869; s. Jones E. and Anna (Settlemyre) P.; M.D., Ga. Coll. Eclectic Medicine and Surgery, Atlanta, Ga., 1893; post-grad. work, New York Eye and Ear Infirmary, Chicago Eye, Ear, Nose and Throat Coll., Moreland Eye and Ear Hosp., London, Eng.; m. Kathlene Kelly, 1893. Began practice at Fitzgerald, Ga., 1893; removed to Atlanta, 1903; prof. eye, ear, nose and throat, Ga. Eclectic Med. and Surg. Coll., 1903-13; specialist in treatment of eye, ear, nose and throat; dir. Am. Savings Bank. Democrat. Home: Atlanta, Ga. Deceased.

POWELL, John Wesley, naturalist; b. Mt. Morris, N.Y., Mar. 24, 1834; s. of Methodist minister; attended schools in Ohio, Wis., and Ill., 2 yrs. each at Oberlin and Wheaton (Ill.) colls.; grad. Ill. Wesleyan, A.M., Ph.D. (LL.D., Columbian, 1882, Harvard, 1886, Ill. Coll., 1889; Ph.D., Heidelberg, 1886); m. Emma Dean, 1861. Served through Civil war in 2d Ill. arty., reaching rank of maj., losing right arm at Shiloh. Explored Grand Cañon of the Colorado River, 1869. Apptd. dir. U.S. Bureau of Ethnology, 1879, and of U.S. Geol. Survey, 1880; resigned latter, 1894, retaining former. Author: Explorations of the Colorado River; Report on Geology of the Uinta Mountains; Report on Arid Regions of United States; Introduction to the Study of Indian Languages; Studies in Sociology; Cañons of the Colorado; etc. Home: Washington, D.C. Died 1902.

POWELL, Lucien Whiting, artist; b. Levinworth Manor, Va., Dec. 13, 1846; s. John Levin and Maria Louise (Grady) P.; studied art in Phila. and N.Y. City, London, Sch. of Art, under Fitz, and in Rome, Venice and Paris; m. Nan Fitzhugh, Oct. 20, 1880; children—Elaine Fitzhugh (Mrs. Jesse L. Heiskell), John Levin (dec.), Mabel Lee (Mrs. Francis A. Millott), Maria Louise (dec.), Lucien Fitzhugh. Painter of Venice, and of canyons and mountains. Awarded Parsons' prize, Corcoran Gallery of Art, Washington, D.C., 1903. "The Afterglow," picture of Grand Canyon of the Colorado, now in Corcoran Gallery; picture, "Grand Canyon of the Yellowstone River," in Nat. Gallery, Washington, D.C.; pictures on perm. exhbn. in Carnegie Library and Congressional Club, Washington, D.C.; American Univ., Washington, D.C.; Holy Land collection, Georgetown Univ.; Atlanta Mus. of Art; also in many pvt. collections, including that of the late President Roosevelt. Home: Washington, D.C., and Purcellville, Va. Died Sept. 27, 1930.

POWELL, Maud, violinist; b. Peru, Ill., Aug. 22, 1868; d. William Bramwell and Minnie (Paul) Powell; common school education, Aurora, Ill.; musical edn. Chicago, Leipzig, Paris, Berlin, 1881-85; pupil of William Lewis, Henri Schradieck, Dancla, Joachim; m. H. Godfrew Turner, of London, 1904. Début at Berlin, 1885; has been soloist with Thomas, Siedl, Gericke, Nikisch, Damrosch and other orchestras; toured Germany and Austria, with New York Arion Soc., 1892; tour of British Isles and European Continent, 1899-1901; again, including Russia, 1903-04-05; toured S. Africa, 1905; from 1903 every musical season was spent in this country. Died Jan. 8, 1920.

POWELL, Robert, lawyer; b. Bertie Co., N.C., Sept. 6, 1851; s. Jesse Robert and Frances Ann (Smith) P.; B.S., U. of Miss., 1870; LL.B., Lebanon (Tenn.) Law Sch., 1871; m. Annie M. Tupper, Jan. 1, 1874 (dec.); 4 children. Began practice, Canton, 1871; mayor of Canton, 1874-79; chmn. Dem. State Conv., 1882; presdl. elector from state at-large, 1884; mem. Miss. Ho. of Rep., 1890-92; judge 7th Jud. Dist., Miss., 1896-1903; reporter Supreme Ct., Miss., 1911-23; mem. Dem. Nat. Com., 1912-16; mem. Dem. State Com., 1915—, chmn., 1920-25. Trustee Higher Ednl. Instns. of Miss. Episcopalian. Editor of Mississippi State Reports, 1911-24. Home: Jackson, Miss. Died Nov. 11, 1930.

POWELL, Talcott Williams, author and newspaperman; b. Lansdowne, Pa., Apr. 27, 1900; s. Dr. Lyman Pierson and Gertrude (Wilson) P.; student Wesleyan U., Middletown, Conn., 1918-20; m. Ysabel Allen Loney, Sept. 15, 1923 (divorced 1928); 1 son, David Talcott; m. 2d, Helen Ann Ranney, Aug. 4, 1928; 1 dau., Edes Lawrence. Began as reporter Paper Trade Jour., New York, 1920; with New York Sun, 1921-22; reporter and asst. city editor New York Tribune and New York Herald-Tribune, 1922-25; gen. mgr. and treas. Orange County Independent Corp., pub. Middletown (N.Y.) Times-Herald, 1925-27; reporter N.Y. Telegram, 1927-31; asst. exec. editor N.Y. World-Telegram, 1931-32; editor Indianapolis Times, 1933-35; exploration and writing for Cosmopolitan Mag. and Harcourt, Brace and Co. in Venezuela and West Indies, 1936; discovered and excavated site of town of Caparra, established in Puerto Rico by Ponce de Leon in 1510 and abandoned in 1521. Pulitzer Prize Committee cited articles on veteran relief in awarding N.Y. World-Telegram, 1932 gold medal, for "most meritorious public service." Served as pvt. of infantry, U.S.A., 1918, now 1st lt. Mil. Intelligence Reserve, U.S.A. Episcopalian. Author: Tattered Banners, 1933. Home: Mountain Lakes, N.J. Died Apr. 4, 1937.

POWELL, Thomas, physician; b. Montgomery Co., Tenn., Sept. 21, 1837; s. William Solomon and Sallie (Holloway) P.; ed. pub. and pvt. schs.; M.D., New York Med. Coll., 1858; post-grad. study U. of Neb.; m. Margaret Ianthe Rife, Dec. 18, 1859 (died 1889); 2d, Clara Jeannette Pond, June 25, 1893. Practiced in Ky., later in Danville, Ind., many yrs.; founder, 1904, pres. and med. dir., Powell Sanatorium, Inc., Los Angeles, Calif. Republican. Mem. Disciples of Christ. Mason. Author: Fundamentals and Requirements of Health and Disease, 1909. Home: Los Angeles, Calif. Died Aug. 17, 1916.

POWELL, William Bramwell, educator; b. Castyle, N.Y., Dec. 22, 1836; ed. pub. schs. of Ill.; academic edn. at Wheaton, Ill., Coll. (A.M., Lombard Univ., Ill.); m. Minnie Paul, May 1865. Prin. of schs., 2 yrs., Hennepin, Ill.; supt. schs., 8 yrs., Peru, Ill.; 16 yrs., Aurora, Ill.; Washington, 1885-1900; in Philippines, 1901, investigating sch. and text-book needs. Author: How to See, 1880; How to Talk, 1880; How to Write, 1880; History of United States for Beginners, 1900; joint author Series of Normal Readers, 1887; Rational Grammar of the English Language, 1900. Home: Mt. Vernon, N.Y. Died 1904.

POWELL, William David, denominational sec.; b. Madison, Miss., July 1, 1854; s. William Madison and Nancy Bumpass (Rankin) P.; A.B., Union U., Tenn., 1871, later A.M., D.D., 1886; grad. Southern Bapt. Theol. Sem., 1874; m. Mary Florence Maberry, Oct. 5, 1875; children—William E., Mrs. Anita P. Smith, Mrs. Nell Colvin, Bydie (dec.), Charles B., Mary T. (Mrs. W. P. Wilks), Paul, Florence (Mrs. H. M. Harris), Henry T., Ethel (Mrs. Wm. Val Yates), Ernest, Katharine (dec.). Ordained Baptist ministry, 1874; pres. Oak Dale Academy, Tenn., 1875, Mineola High Sch., 1876-77; S.S. evangelist in Tex., 1877-82; missionary Foreign Missionary Bd. Southern Bapt. Conv. in Mex., 1882-98, home board in Cuba, 1898-99; corr. sec. and treas., Bapt. State Bd. of Missions, in charge state, home and foreign missions, in Ky., 1906-16; sec. Am. Bapt. Home Mission Soc., 6 mos., 1916; field sec. Fgn. Mission Bd., Southern Bapt. Conv., 1917—. Democrat. Mason. Author: The Primacy of State Missions, 1912. Home: Louisville, Ky. Deceased.

POWELL, William Frank, diplomat; b. Troy, N.Y., June 26, 1848; student Sch. of Pharmacy, New York, Lincoln U., Pa., and grad. N.J. Collegiate Inst., 1865; married. Apptd. by Presbyn. Bd. of Home Missions to sch. at Leesburg for Freedmen; afterward opened first state sch. for children of freedmen, Alexandria, Va. Bookkeeper in U.S. Treasury Dept., 1881-82; elected prin. schs., 4th Dist., Camden, N.J.; prepared and carried to success the plans for introducing manual training into public schs., now in successful operation in Camden; refused consular appmts., 1881 and 1891; E.E. and M.P. to Haiti, 1897-1905. Also Am. chargé d'affaires to Santo Domingo, June 29, 1897-June 20, 1905. Home: Camden, N.J. Died Jan. 23, 1920.

POWELL, William Henry, iron mfr.; b. Monmouthshire, S. Wales, May 10, 1825; in U.S., Mar. 30, 1830; settled in Nashville, Tenn., 1833; removed to Wheeling, Va., Mar. 1843; m. Sarah Gilchrist, Dec. 24, 1847; 2d, Mrs. E. P. (West) Weaver, Apr. 29, 1879. Removed, remodeled and erected Va. Iron and Nail Works, Benwood, 1852-53; organizer and mgr. Star Nail Co., Ironton, O., 1853; gen. mgr. Lawrence Iron Works, Ironton, 1857-61. Entered Union service Aug. 1, 1861, recruited co. mustered in Petersburg, Va.; capt. Co. B, 2d regt. Va. cav. vols., Oct. 1861; served through all intermediate grades to brig. gen., and bvt. maj. gen. U.S.V., under Gens. Crook, Averill and Phil. Sheridan; comd. 2d cav. div., Sheridan's cav. corps, Shenandoah Valley campaign, 1864-65; was seriously wounded while leading charge, Wytheville, Va., July 16, 1863; left on battlefield and captured; exchanged for Gen. R. H. Lee, March 1864. Mgr. Ironton, O., Rolling Mill Co., 1865-67; gen. mgr. Clifton Nail Works, Mason Co., W.Va., 1867-76; Rep. presdl. elector 3d Va. dist., 1868; offered and declined nominations to Congress in Ohio, 1866, W.Va., 1868; gen. mgr. Belleville (Ill.) Nail Co., 1876-82; organized 1882, becoming pres. and gen. mgr. Western Nail Co.; dept. comdr. Ill. G.A.R., 1895; internal revenue collector 13th revenue dist., Ill., Mar. 1898—. Home: Belleville, Ill. Died 1904.

POWELL, Wilson Marcy, lawyer; b. N.Y. City, May 7, 1872; s. Wilson Marcy and Sarah Hopper (Brown) Powell; A.B., Harvard U., 1896, LL.B., 1898; LL.D., Swarthmore College, 1933; m. Elsie Knapp, Oct. 23, 1902; children—Wilson Marcy, Sarah Hopper, Elsie Knapp. Began practice of law in N.Y. City, 1899; trustee Franklin Savings Bank, U.S. Trust Co., N.Y. Pub. Library, Rubel Family Foundation; pres. Corp. of Swarthmore College, 1920-33, pres. emeritus of corporation, 1933—; trustee of Bennington Coll., 1925-27. Mem. Com. on Character and Fitness of Applicants for Admission to N.Y. Bar, 1st Jud. Dept., 1926; mem. Harvard Law Sch. Visiting Com. and chmn. Harvard Law Sch. Endowment Fund Com.; mem. visiting com. Arnold Arboretum and Bussey Instn., Harvard; mem. Taconic State Park Commn. of N.Y. Treas. N.Y. Yearly Meeting, and trustee and treas. Monthly Meeting of Society of Friends; treas., member board managers Schofield Normal and Industrial Sch., Aiken, S.C.; mem. exec. com. Prison Assn. of N.Y., Colored Orphan Asylum Assn. for Benefit of Colored Children in City of New York, New York Diet Kitchen Assn.; gov. and pres. Soc. of New York Hosp., Soc. of Lying-In Hosp. (New York); v.p. Manhattan Maternity and Dispensary; chmn. joint administrative bd. New York Hosp.-Cornell Med. Coll. Assn.; trustee Roosevelt Hosp., Astor, Lenox and Tilden Foundations. Republican. Home: New York, N.Y. Died Aug. 17, 1935.

POWER, Frederick Belding, chemist; b. Hudson, N.Y., Mar. 4, 1853; s. Thomas and Caroline P. (Belding) P.; grad. Phila. Coll. Pharmacy, 1874; Ph.D., U. of Strassburg, 1880; asst. to prof. of materia medica there, 1879-80; LL.D., U. of Wis., 1908; m. Mary Van Loan Meigs, Dec. 27, 1883 (died 1894); children—Mrs. Annie Louise Heimké, Donald Meigs. Prof. analytical chemistry, Phila. Coll. Pharmacy, 1881-83; prof. pharmacy and materia medica, U. of Wis., 1883-92; dir. labs. of Fritsche Bros., 1892-96, Wellcome Chem. Research Laboratories, London, Eng., 1896-1914; in charge Phytochem. Lab., Bur. of Chemistry, Washington, 1916—. Awarded Ebert prize, Am. Pharm. Assn., 1877, 1902, 06; gold medal, St. Louis Expn., 1904; silver medal, Liège, 1905; gold medal and diploma of honor, Milan, 1906; gold medal, Franco-British Exhbn., 1908; grand prize, Brussels, 1910; gold medal and diploma of honor, Turin, 1911; Hanbury gold medal, 1913. Gold medal presented by Henry S. Wellcome, London, in 1914, for chemical research; awarded the Flueckiger gold medal, 1922. Member com. of revision U.S. Pharmacopœia, 1890; U.S. del. Internat. Congress for Unification of the Formulæ of Potent Medicaments, Brussels, 1902. Editor: (with Dr. Fred Hoffman) Manual of Chemical Analysis, 1883. Died Mar. 26, 1927.

POWER, Frederick Dunglison, clergyman; b. Yorktown, Va., Jan. 23, 1851; s. Dr. Robert and Abigail M. (Jencks) P.; A.B., Bethany Coll., W.Va., 1871, A.M., 1874 (LL.D., 1890); m. Emily B. Alsop, Mar. 17, 1874. Ordained ministry Disciples of Christ; was pastor to Pres. Garfield; pastor Garfield Memorial Ch., 1875—; chaplain 47th Congress, 1881-83. Pres. Gen. Christian Missionary Soc.; trustee U.S. Christian Endeavor. Author: Bible Doctrine for Young Disciples, 1899; Sketches of Our Pioneers, 1898; Life of W. K. Pendleton, LL.D., President of Bethany College, 1902; History and Doctrine of Disciples, 1904. Asso. editor Christian Evangelist, St. Louis. Home: Washington, D.C. Died 1911.

POWER, Thomas Charles, senator; b. Dubuque, Ia., May 22, 1839; studied civ. engineering; taught sch. winters and was surveyor summers, 1858-62; also dealt in land warrants. Began forwarding merchandise to Mont., 1865-66, by wagon train from Omaha and by steamboats from Sioux City and St. Louis; opened store at Ft. Benton, 1867, as well as forwarding merchandise throughout the territory; began, 1873, to own and operate steamboat line; removed to Helena, 1878; still head of T. C. Power & Bro. and associate interests, Ft. Benton and Helena, and Am. Nat. Bank, Helena. Prominent in movement for admission of Mont. as state; U.S. senator, 1889-96. Republican. Home: Helena, Mont. Died Feb. 16, 1923.

POWERS, Caleb, congressman; b. Whitley Co., Ky., Feb. 1, 1869; s. Amos and Elizabeth (Perkins) P.; Union Coll., Ky., and State U. of Ky., Lexington; LL.B., Valparaiso (Ind.) U., 1894; post-grad. law studies, Center Coll., Danville, Ky.; m. Laura Rawlings, Jan. 26, 1896 (died 1896); m. 2d, Anna Dorothy Kaufman, Nov. 27, 1912; 1 dau., Elsie Eleanor. Admitted to Kentucky bar, 1894; supt. schs., Knox Co., Ky., 1894-98; elected sec. of state, Ky., 1899, but was unseated after a contest. On account of the assassination of William Goebel, Dem. contestant for gov. of Ky., served 8 yrs., 3 mos. and 3 days in Ky. jails; upon release, was nominated and elected to 62d Congress (1911-13), 11th Ky. Dist.; reëlected 63d to 65th Congresses, (1913-1919); asst. counsel U.S. Shipping Bd. Republican. Baptist. Author: My Own Story, 1905. Home: Washington, D.C. Died July 25, 1932.

POWERS, Carol Hoyt, educator; b. Boston, Mass.; d. William G. and Juliette M. (Merrill) Hoyt; widow of Leland Powers, public reader; children—Leland Hoyt (dec.), Haven M. Prin. Leland Powers Sch. of the Theatre. Home: Boston, Mass. Died June 1940.

POWERS, Charles Andrew, surgeon; b. Lawrence, Mass., Feb. 2, 1858; s. George Eliot and Jennie (Stone) P.; 9th in descent from Walter Powers, Concord, Mass., 1642; M.D., Coll. Phys. and Surg. (Columbia), 1883; attending surgeon New York Cancer and St. Luke's hosps., 1892; (hon. A.M., U. of Denver, 1901). Settled at Denver, 1894; emeritus prof. surgery, U. of Colorado; surgeon to various hosps.; 1st lt. Med. R.C., 1908-17; attending surgeon Am. Ambulance Hosp. of Paris (for French wounded), May 5, 1916-July 22, 1917; maj., M.C. U.S.A., assigned duty Am. Mil. Hosp. No. 1, Neuilly, sur Seine, July 22, 1917; discharged, Dec. 5, 1918; commd. lt. col. Med. R.C., July 1919. Pres. Am. Surg. Assn., 1912; fellow Am. Coll. Surgeons. Received letter of thanks (Apr. 21, 1919) and citation (Mar. 15, 1920) from Gen. John J. Pershing; officer of Order of Leopold II (Belgian), Médaille de la Reconnaissance Française, Chevalier Legion of Honor (French). Home: Denver, Colo. Died Dec. 23, 1922.

POWERS, Frederick Alton, judge; b. Pittsfield, Me., June 19, 1855; s. Arba and Naomi (Matthews)

P.; A.B., Bowdoin, 1875 (LL.D., 1906); m. May Hussey, Jan. 7, 1879; m. 2d, Virginia P. Hewes, Nov. 3, 1903. Admitted to bar, 1876, and practiced at Houlton, Me. Mem. Me. Ho. of Rep., 1885-88, Senate, 1891-92; atty. gen. of Me., 1893-96; justice Supreme Jud. Ct. of Me., 1900-07; resigned. Rep. nominee for U.S. senator, 1911, 12. Pres. Farmers' Nat. Bank, of Houlton. Overseer Bowdoin Coll., 1907-20, trustee, 1920—; trustee Me. Central Inst., North Yarmouth Acad. Home: Houlton, Me. Died Feb. 13, 1923.

POWERS, George McClellan, judge; b. Hyde Park, Vt., Dec. 19, 1861; s. H(orace) Henry and Caroline E. (Waterman) P.; A.B., University of Vermont, 1883, LL.D., 1909; Middlebury (Vermont) Coll., 1929; m. Gertrude F. Woodbury, Apr. 19, 1893; children—Horace Henry, Mildred Dorothy, Elizabeth Lillian, Roberta Frances. Admitted to bar, 1886; state's atty., 1886-88; asst. clerk Vt. Ho. of Rep., 1884-90; sec. Vt. Senate, 1890-96; mem. Ho. of Rep., 1896-98; reporter of decisions, Supreme Court of Vt., 1902-04; judge Supreme Court of Vt., 1904-06; superior judge and chancellor, 1906-Jan. 1909; asso. justice Supreme Court, Jan. 1909—, chief justice, 1913-15, asso. justice, 1915-29, again chief justice from Dec. 14, 1929. Republican. Universalist. Life trustee U. of Vt. Died June 24, 1938.

POWERS, Harry Joseph, theatrical mgr.; b. Nenagh, Tipperary Co., Ireland, Sept. 15, 1859; s. Henry Joseph and Jane (Darcey) P.; brought to Chicago, Ill., with parents in childhood; ed. St. Patrick's Acad.; m. Marie F. Deegan, May 11, 1885. Began as usher, Hooley's Theatre, Chicago, 1877, and became business mgr.; remodeled the theatre, 1898, changing name to Powers Theatre (building sold, 1923, and now occupied by annex to Hotel Sherman); pres. Amusement Co. of Ill., operating Illinois Theatre, Chicago. Catholic. Home: Chicago, Ill. Died Feb. 21, 1941.

POWERS, H(orace) Henry, judge; b. Morristown, Vt., May 29, 1835; s. Dr. Horace and Love E. (Gilman) P.; A.B., U. of Vt., 1855, A.M., 1858 (LL.D.); m. Caroline E. Waterman, Oct. 11, 1858; father of George McClellan P. Admitted to bar, 1858; mem. Vt. Ho. of Rep., 1858; pros. atty. Lamoille Co., 1861-62; mem. council of censors of Vt., 1869; mem. Vt. Constl. Conv., 1870; mem. Senate, 1872-73; speaker Ho. of Rep., 1874; judge Supreme Ct. of Vt., 1875-90; mem. 52d to 56th Congresses (1891-1901), 1st Vt. Dist. Trustee U. of Vt. from 1883. Home: Morrisville, Vt. Died Dec. 8, 1913.

POWERS, Hugh Winfield, merchant, banker; b. Dungannon, Va., Oct. 15, 1860; s. Isaac Hartsock and Darinda Jane (Quillen) P.; ed. grammar sch., and high sch. for short time; m. Lona Reeder, Sept. 14, 1887; children—Mrs. Wanda Tauber, James Cecil, Edwin Reeder, Lila Katherine (now Mrs. Faw), Mrs. Mary Richards, Margaret Ruth, Mrs. Martha Morphew. Began in hardware business, at Bristol, Tenn., 1890, became pres. Mitchell-Powers Hardware Co.; pres. Bank of Bristol, 1915—; dir. Intermountain Telephone Co.; mem. bd. aldermen, Bristol, about 10 yrs. Pres. bd. trustees Va. Intermont Coll.; trustee Bapt. Orphanage of Va.; v.p. Bristol Chamber of Commerce. Republican. Baptist. Mason. Home: Bristol, Va. Died Mar. 1938.

POWERS, James Knox, univ. pres.; b. Lauderdale Co., Ala., Aug. 15, 1851; s. William and Rosanna (Reeder) P.; A.M., U. of Alabama, 1873, after spending 2 yrs. there, with the highest grade ever made in the history of the univ., his average in the senior yr. being 99 1-5 per cent. (LL.D., 1897); m. Lou A. Reynolds, Jan. 31, 1879. Prof. mathematics, 1873, pres., 1888-97, State Normal Coll., Florence, Ala.; pres. Univ. of Ala., 1897-1901; Southern representative B. F. Johnson Pub. Co., of Richmond, Va., 1901-11; again pres. State Normal Coll., Florence, Ala., 1911—. Editor Southern Education, 1892. Grand Dictator of Knights of Honor of Ala., 1886-88; pres. Assn. of Southern Colls. and Prep. Schs., 1900-01. Home: Florence, Ala. Died Aug. 15, 1913.

POWERS, Joseph Neely, univ. chancellor; b. Havana, Ala., Mar. 15, 1869; s. William Ira and Julia (Towler) P.; ed. Southern U., Greensboro, Ala., George Robinson Coll., Henderson, Tenn., 3 summer sessions; U. of Miss.; U. of Chicago, summer; Louisville Med. Coll. 1 yr.; M.A., Georgia Coll., 1903; M.Pd., George Robinson Coll., 1903; LL.D., Mississippi Coll., 1914; B.A., Birmingham-Southern Coll., 1923; m. Ada Gavin, Dec. 24, 1888. Teacher rural schs., 8 yrs.; prin. high sch., 4 yrs.; city supt. schs., 1899-1908; state supt. edn., Miss., 1907-14; chancellor Univ. of Miss., 1914-24 and 1930-33. Democrat. Methodist. Mason. Home: Jackson, Miss. Died Oct. 4, 1939.

POWERS, Leland Todd, public reader; b. Pultneyville, N.Y., Jan. 28, 1857; s. Jacob Haven and Mary Elizabeth (Todd) P.; grad. Phillips Acad., Andover, Mass., 1875; grad. Boston U. Sch. of Oratory, 1880; m. Carol Hoyt, Dec. 25, 1895. Widely known as a pub. reader, 1890—; especially noted as interperter of Dickens; founded, 1904, The Leland Powers School of the Spoken Word, of which became head. Author: Fundamentals of Expression (with Carol Hoyt Powers), 1909; Talks on Expression, 1917. Home: Brookline, Mass. Died Nov. 27, 1920.

POWERS, Levi Moore, clergyman; b. Newry, Me., Mar. 21, 1864; s. C. H. L. and Sarahette (Moore) P.; Me. Wesleyan Sem., Kent's Hill, Me., 1881-83; Tufts Coll. and Theol. Sch., 1884-90, B.D., 1890; summer terms, Harvard, and U. of Mich.; (D.D., Tufts, 1905); m. Emma Florence Tufts, June 5, 1901. Ordained Universalist ministry, 1890; pastor Foxboro, Mass., 1890-91, Somerville, 1891-98, Buffalo, 1898-1905, Haverhill, Mass., 1905-13, Gloucester, Mass., 1913-19, Ch. of Our Father, Washington, D.C., 1919—. Trustee Universalist Pub. House, Mass. Mason. Died Dec. 27, 1920.

POWERS, Llewellyn, congressman, governor; b. Pittsfield, Me., 1838; reared on farm; grad. Colby Univ., Univ. of Albany, N.Y. Studied law; admitted to bar; practiced in Houlton, Me.; atty. Aroostook Co. 6 or 7 terms; 5 times elected to Me. legislature; speaker Me. Ho. of Reps., 1895; mem. Congress, 1877-79 and 1901-09, 4th Me. dist., succeeding C. A. Boutelle, resigned; gov. Me., 1897-1901. Republican. One of the largest lumber land owners in New England. Married. Home: Houlton, Me. Died 1908.

POWERS, Luther Milton, health commr.; b. New Hanover Co., N.C., Apr. 5, 1853; s. William and Lucy Jane (Murray) P.; student Wake Forest (N.C.) Coll., 1871-74; M.D., Washington Univ. Sch. of Medicine, Baltimore, 1877; post-grad. work, 1881, 84, 85, and 1906, various med. colls., New York; m. Mary Ella Stimson, Nov. 28, 1881. Began practice in N.C.; removed to Norfolk, Neb., 1886; U.S. pension surgeon, 1886-87; at Los Angeles, Calif., 1887—; health officer, Los Angeles, 1893-94, 1897-1911, then health commr.; formerly prof. state medicine, Los Angeles br. U. of Calif. Coll. of Medicine. Del. Internat. Congress of Hygiene of Am. Republics, Washington, 1902. Democrat. Presbyn. Mason. Home: Los Angeles, Calif. Deceased.

POWERS, Orlando Woodworth, lawyer; b. Pultneyville, N.Y., June 16, 1851; s. Josiah Woodworth and Julia (Wilson) P.; ed. Marion (N.Y.) Collegiate Inst., and Sodus (N.Y.) Acad.; LL.B., U. of Mich., 1871; m. Anna W. Whipple, Oct. 26, 1887. Dem. candidate for N.Y. legislature, 1872; admitted to bar May 30, 1873; city atty., 1876; Dem. candidate for Congress, 4th Mich. Dist., 1880; elected city atty. Kalamazoo, Apr. 1885; apptd. by President Cleveland asso. justice Supreme Ct. of Utah, May 1885, resigned Aug. 1886; in law practice at Salt Lake City, 1887—. Chmn. Gentile party of Utah in campaign against Mormons, 1888; elected to Utah Legislature, 1893; reelected chmn. Dem. State Com., Utah, 1895-96 (originated plan of organization of silver dels., and placed John W. Daniel of Va. in nomination for v.p. U.S.); candidate before Utah Legislature for U.S. senator, 1897, 1899; no election by Legislature; apptd. U.S. senator to fill vacancy from Utah by Acting Gov. Nebeker, 1900, but declined; Dem. nominee for presdl. elector, 1900, for Congress, Utah, 1904, 1906; chmn. Utah delegation Dem. Nat. Conv., Denver, 1908, and seconded nomination of W. J. Bryan for President; Dem. nominee for U.S. senator, 1911. Author: Chancery Pleadings and Practice, 1882; Practice in Supreme Court of Michigan, 1884. Home: Salt Lake City, Utah. Died Jan. 2, 1914.

POWERS, Ridgely Ceylon, governor; b. Mecca, O., Dec. 24, 1836; s. Milo and Lucy Ann (Dickinson) P.; student, U. of Mich., 1859-62 (A.B., 1910) A.B., Union Coll., N.Y., 1862, A.M., 1865; m. Louisa Born, May 5, 1875 (died 1882); 2d, Mary J. Wilson, Oct. 27, 1892. Enlisted as pvt., Co. C, 125th Ohio Vol. Inf., 1862; promoted 2d lt., 1st lt., capt., maj.; bvtd. lt. col. "for gallant conduct in Atlanta campaign"; served in 2d Div., 4th Army Corps, Army of the Cumberland; participated in battles of Murfreesboro, Chattanooga, Chickamauga, Missionary Ridge, Dandridge, Knoxville, Franklin, Nashville, etc.; was a.-a.-g. 1st Brigade and a.-a.-g. 2d Div., 4th Army Corps; mustered out, New Orleans, 1865. Bought 2,000 acre plantation in Noxubee Co., Miss., 1865, and engaged in cotton raising. Sheriff, Noxubee Co., 1868-69; elected lt. gov., Miss., 1869, becoming gov. for unexpired term (Nov. 30, 1871-Jan. 4, 1874) of Gov. J. L. Alcorn elected to U.S. Senate. Practiced civ. engring. in Ariz., 1879-1905; retired. Home: Los Angeles, Calif. Died Nov. 11, 1912.

POWERS, Samuel Leland, congressman; b. Cornish, N.H., Oct. 26, 1848; s. Larned and Ruby M. P.; A.B., Dartmouth, 1874 (A.M., 1908); law student New York U.; m. Eva Crowell, June 1898; 1 son, Leland. Admitted to the bar, 1875; in practice at Boston from 1876; now mem. Powers & Hall. Has held various local offices, Newton, Mass.; mem. 57th and 58th Congresses (1901-05); del. from Mass. to Internat. Treaty Conv., Paris, 1878. Trustee Dartmouth Coll., 1905-15; trustee N.E. Conservatory of Music, 1916—; mem. Mass. Bd. of Edn., 1915-19; mem. Mass. Constl. Conv., 1918-19; state trustee for operation Boston Elevated Ry. Co., 1918—. Republican. Author: Portraits of a Half Century, 1925. Home: Newton, Mass. Died Dec. 1, 1929.

POWERS, Sidney, geologist; b. Troy, N.Y., Sept. 10, 1890; s. Albert W. and Tillie (Page) P.; A.B., Williams Coll., 1911; M.S., Mass. Inst. Tech., 1913; Sheldon traveling fellow to Hawaiian Island, Harvard, 1915, A.M., Ph.D., 1915, research fellow, 1915-16; m. Dorothy Edwards Powers, Sept. 8, 1917; children—Deborah, Eleanor. Div. geologist Tex. Co., 1916-17; asst. geologist U.S. Geol. Survey, 1917-18; geol. officer, A.E.F., U.S.A., 1918-19; chief geologist Amerada Petroleum Corp., 1919-26, consulting geologist, 1926—. Fellow Geol. Soc. America (councilor 1931-33). Home: Tulsa, Okla. Died 1932.

POWERS, William L., educator; b. Brownville, Me., Jan. 20, 1863; s. Phineas H. and Cornelia C. (Wilder) P.; A.B., Bates Coll., 1888, Ped.D., 1917; m. Marion E. Turner, June 28, 1893; children—John Howard, Elizabeth Turner. Began as prin. high sch., Ft. Fairfield, Me., 1888; prin. high sch., Gardiner, 1892-1908, supt. schs. Ft. Fairfield-Easton Dist., 1908-09; prin. Washington State Normal Sch., Machias, Me., 1910—. Lecturer on nature topics at summer schs. and teachers' institutes. Republican. Conglist. Mason. Home: Machias, Me. Died Aug. 8, 1927.

POYNTER, Clara Martin, educator; b. nr. Paris, Ky., Dec. 17, 1846; d. Hezekiah Davis and Juliet Elmina (Jameson) Martin; B.A., Wesleyan College, Wilmington, Del., 1863; Litt.D., Centre College, Danville, Ky., 1930; m. Rev. Wiley Taul Poynter, D.D., Sept. 13, 1877 (died 1896); children—Horace Martin, Juliet Jameson, Harriet Rockwell. Lady prin. Science Hill Sch. for Girls, 1879-96, prin., 1896—. Mem. M.E. Ch., South. Home: Shelbyville, Ky. Died Mar. 7, 1937.

POYNTER, William A., gov. of Neb., 1899-1901; b. Eureka, Ill., May 29, 1848; s. Rev. W. C. P.; grad. Eureka Coll., 1867; m. Marie McCorkle, 1869. Mem. Neb. legislature, 1885; State senator, 1891, and pres. pro tem.; candidate for Congress, 1893; mem. State commn., Trans-Mississippi Expn., 1898; supreme comdr. Am. Order of Protection, Jan. 1, 1901—. Fusionist. Home: Lincoln, Neb. Died 1909.

POYNTON, John Albert; b. Longford, Ireland; s. John and Margaret (Small) P.; educated in public schools and under pvt. tutors; hon. A.M., Wesleyan U., Conn., 1933; unmarried. Came to U.S., 1893; in office of pres. of N.Y.,O.&W. Ry. Co., 1901-08; with George Foster Peabody, 1908-10; sec. to pres. Gen. Ednl. Bd., 1910-12; sec. to Andrew Carnegie, 1912-19. Trustee Carnegie Corp. of New York; v.p., dir. Empire Title & Guarantee Co.; mem. advisory bd. Central Hanover Bank & Trust Co. Mem. Council on Foreign Relations; dir. N.Y. State Colonization Society. Died Oct. 22, 1934.

POYNTZ, James M., physician; b. Scott Co., Ky., Mar. 22, 1838; s. John P.; grad. Forest Acad., 1858, med. dept. Univ. of Louisville, 1873; m. Clara Lilly, Nov. 15, 1870; 2d, Mrs. Bettie Gatewood, Feb. 9, 1886. Served in C.S.A., 1861-65; at close maj. and surgeon. Mem. State Med. Soc. of Ky., 1876—; mem. State bd. health of Ky., 9 yrs.; maj. gen. Ky. div. United Confederate Vets, 1899—. Democrat. Home: Richmond, Ky. Died 1904.

PRALL, Anning S., chmn. Federal Communications Commn.; b. Staten Island, N.Y., Sept. 17, 1870. Formerly pres. Bd. of Edn., N.Y. City; apptd. a commr. of taxes and assessments, N.Y. City, Jan. 1, 1922; mem. 68th to 73d Congresses (1923-35), 11th N.Y. Dist.; chmn. Federal Communications Commn. Democrat. Home: West New Brighton, N.Y. Died July 23, 1937.

PRALL, David Wight, educator; b. Saginaw, Mich., Oct. 5, 1886; s. Delbert Elwin and Cynthia Jane Sophia (Wight) P.; student Saginaw (Mich.) High Sch., 1900-04; A.B., U. of Mich., 1909, A.M., 1910; Ph.D., U. of Calif., 1918. Instr. Cornell U., 1910-12, U. of Tex., 1912-15; lecturer and instr. Amherst, 1918-19; instr. philosophy, Harvard U., 1920-21; instr., asst. prof., prof. philosophy, U. of Calif., 1921-30; lecturer philosophy Harvard U., 1930-31, asso. prof. philosophy, 1931-38, prof. philosophy, 1938—, acting chmn. of dept., 1938-39. Home: Cambridge, Mass. Died Oct. 21, 1940.

PRALL, William, clergyman; b. Paterson, N.J., Apr. 6, 1853; s. Edwin T. and Rachel More (Thomson) P.; student Edwards Place Sch., Stockbridge, Mass.; A.M., Ph.D., Heidelberg, 1873; LL.B., Columbia, 1875; S.T.D., Hobart Coll., 1892; m. Lilian Porter Clapp, Oct. 26, 1881 (died 1884); 1 dau., Lilian Clapp (dec.); m. 2d, Helen Ames Lothrop, Feb. 12, 1897; Admitted to bar, 1876; practiced at Paterson, N.J., 1876-86; mem. N.J. Assembly, 1883-84; drafted and secured enactment Free Pub. Library Law; 1st pres. Paterson Free Library, 1885. Deacon, 1887, priest, 1888, P.E. Ch.; rector Ch. of the Holy Communion, S. Orange, N.J., 1887-91, St. John's, Detroit, 1891-1900, St. Paul's, Albany, N.Y., 1900-06. Mem. Gen. Conv. P.E. Ch., 3 times, and as rep. of Ch. to Synod of the Ch. of Eng. in Canada. Author: The Edict of Nantes, 1925; The Revocation of the Edict of Nantes, 1926; Huguenot Settlements in America, 1928. Translator: Memories of Youth (by Giovanni Visconti Venosta), 1913. His home was at New York, N.Y. Died Mar. 22, 1933.

PRANG, Louis, engraver, lithographer, color printer, publisher; b. Breslau, Germany, Mar. 12, 1824; s.

Jonas Louis and Rosina (Scherman) P.; ed. pub. schs., 1829-38, followed by business edn. especially directed to fit him to superintend print cloth factory, studying also chemistry, color-mixing, designing, engraving, bleaching, printing dyeing, etc.; took part in revolutionary movement of 1848 and had to leave Germany; came to U.S., 1850, settling in Boston; established as wood engraver, 1851; as lithographer, 1856; as publisher, 1861; made specialty of color-printing and became publisher of reproductions of oil paintings under his trademark of "Chromos," of water color facsimiles and other art publs.; also, later, publisher of the Prang method of art instruction in pub. schs., including drawing books and material for art instruction in pub. schs.; now pres. The Prang Ednl. Co., New York; m. Rosa Gerber, Nov. 1, 1851 (died 1898); m. 2d, Mrs. Mary Dana Hicks, Apr. 15, 1900. Author: The Prang Standard of Color, illustrated with colored plates showing 1,176 colors, 1898. Joint author: (with John S. Clark and Mary Dana Hicks) Suggestions for Color Instruction, 1893. Home: Roxbury, Mass. Died 1909.

PRANG, Mary Dana Hicks, art educator; b. Syracuse, N.Y., Oct. 7, 1836; d. Major and Agnes Amelia Livingston (Johnson) Dana; grad. Allen Sem., Rochester, with post-grad. courses at Harvard; Harvard-Lowell extension course; art studies, Sch. Mus. Fine Arts, Boston; hon. A.M., Radcliffe, 1916; Ed.M., Harvard, 1921; m. Charles S. Hicks, Oct. 7, 1856 (died 1858); m. 2d, Louis Prang, Apr. 15, 1900 (died 1909). Pres. Social Art Club, Syracuse, 1875-80; dir. Prang Normal Art classes, 1884-1900; pres. Mass. Floral Emblem Soc., 1898-1901. Pres. Civic Club of Ward 19, Boston, 1909-13, Roxbury Woman's Suffrage Club, 1911-13. Author: (with John S. Clark and Walter S. Perry) The Use of Models, 1886; The Prang Complete Course in Form Study and Drawing (12 drawing books and manuals), 1889-94; The Prang Shorter Course in Form Study and Drawing (6 drawing books and manuals), 1888; Form Study Without Clay, 1887; The Prang Elementary Course in Art Instruction (12 drawing books and manuals), 1897-1900; Suggestions for Color Instruction (with John S. Clark and Louis Prang), 1893; Art Instruction for Children in Primary Schools (2 vols.), 1900. Home: Cambridge, Mass. Died Nov. 7, 1927.

PRATT, Bela Lyon, sculptor; b. Norwich, Conn., Dec. 11, 1867; s. George and Sarah Victoria (Whittlesey) P.; early edn. in pub. schs.; modeled and drew at home when a child; entered Yale Sch. of Fine Arts at 16, studying under Professors Niemeyer and Wier; (B.F.A., Yale Univ., 1899; M.A., Harvard U., 1915); entered Art Students League of New York, 1887, studying there under Augustus St. Gaudens, F. Edwin Elwell, William Chase, Kenyon Cox; worked for St. Gaudens in his studio; student at Paris, 1890, of Chapu and Falquière, entered École des Beaux Arts at head of class, same yr.; received 2 medals and 2 prizes while in Paris; returned to U.S., 1892; m. Helen Lugada Pray, Aug. 11, 1897. Instr. of modeling, Boston Mus. Fine Arts, 1893—. Has produced many works in sculpture, statues (portrait and ideal), memorials, groups, tablets, busts, medallions, etc.; two colossal groups on Water Gate of Peristyle, Chicago Expn.; Eliot medal for Harvard U., and Yale Bicentennial Medal; six 7-ft. spandrel figures for main entrance, 12-ft. figure, "Philosophy," and series of four medallions, "The Seasons," in pavilion of Library of Congress; groups and tablets (bronze) for battleships Massachusetts, Kearsarge and Alabama; recumbent figure Dr. Coit, St. Paul's Ch., Concord, N.H. (hon. mention Paris Salon, 1897); Study of Young Girl (2d medal Buffalo Expn., 1901); various groups for Buffalo Expn.; statues Bishop Brooks, Brooks House, Cambridge, Butler Monument, Lowell, Mass., Gov. John Winthrop, Jr., New London, Conn.; cenotaph for Bishop Neely, Portland, Me.; figure (marble) Rev. John Cotton, First Ch., Boston; Gen. Stevenson (bronze), State House, Boston; "Hope" (bronze figure, life size), Battleship Rhode Island; Andersonville monument for State of Conn., Andersonville, Ga.; busts of Gen. C. J. Paine, Bishop Huntington, Rev. Dr. Herrick, Dr. Homans, Dr. Richard Hodgson, Longfellow medal; Malden Soldiers' and Sailors' Monument; Harvard Spanish War Memorial; army nurses monument, State House, Boston; "Science" and "Art," front of Pub. Library, Boston; Y.M.C.A. tablet, Newport, R.I.; statue of Nathan Hale, Yale Campus; Whaleman's memorial, New Bedford, Mass.; gold medal, Panama P.I. Expn., 1915. Mem. Mass. State Art Commn. A.N.A., 1910; mem. Am. Acad. Arts and Sciences. Episcopalian. Home: Jamaica Plain, Mass. Died May 18, 1917.

PRATT, Charles Millard, merchant; b. Brooklyn, Nov. 2, 1855; s. Charles and Lydia A. (Richardson) P.; A.B., Amherst, 1879; (hon. A.M., Yale, 1903); m. Mary Seymour, d. Gov. Luzon B. Morris, of Conn., May 8, 1884. For many yrs. mem. Charles Pratt & Co.; was sec. and dir., 1899-1911, treas., 1908-11, Standard Oil Co.; was dir. Pratt & Lambert, Union Mortgage Co., Self-Winding Clock Co., Chelsea Fibre Mills, and pres. Pratt Inst., Brooklyn; trustee Amherst, 1897-1921, Vassar Coll., 1908-21; retired. Died Nov. 26, 1935.

PRATT, Dwight Mallory, clergyman; b. West Cornwall, Conn., Apr. 18, 1852; s. Ezra Dwight and Anna Aurelia (Rood) P.; grad. Williston Sem., Easthampton, Mass., 1870; A.B., Amherst, 1876, M.A., 1888; grad. Hartford Theol. Sem., 1880; (D.D., Marietta, 1901); m. Martha Augusta Rood, Oct. 11, 1882. Ordained Congregational ministry, 1880; pastor Higganum (Conn.) Ch., 1880-88, Pilgrim Ch., Pueblo, Colo., 1888-89, Williston Ch., Portland, Me., 1890-97; minister in charge, Eliot Ch., Roxbury, Boston, winter of 1897-98; pastor Walnut Hills Ch., Cincinnati, 1900-14, Housatonic Ch., Great Barrington, Mass., 1914-19; field rep. at Cleveland, O., of Pilgrim Memorial Fund (Congl.) in Ohio and Mich., 1919-20; field rep. Piedmont Coll., Demorest, Ga., 1920—. Corporate mem. A.B.C.F.M.; trustee Miami Congl. Assn.; moderator Congl. Conf. of Ohio, 1904, and dir., 1902-13; state sec. Congl. Ch. Bldg. Soc. for Ohio, 1900-14; dir. Western Tract Soc., Cincinnati, 1909-12, Lincoln Memorial Univ., Tenn., 1907-09; moderator S. Berkshire Assn., 1915-18. Author: A Decade of Christian Endeavor, 1891. Compiler and editor Scripture Readings for responsive services, 1915. Editorial writer for religious weeklies. Home: Cleveland, O. Died Apr. 12, 1922.

PRATT, Edwin Hartley, surgeon; b. Towanda, Pa., Nov. 6, 1849; s. Leonard and Betsey (Belding) P.; A.B., U. of Chicago, 1871, A.M., 1873 (LL.D., 1886); M.D., Hahnemann Med. Coll., Chicago, 1874; m. Charlotte Eva Kelly, Feb. 26, 1900. Homœ. phys. and surgeon; prof. anatomy, 1873-83, surgery, 1884-90, orificial surgery, 1890-1904, surgery, 1909—, Chicago Homœ. Med. Coll.; prof. anatomy, Hahnemannn Med. Coll., 1873-76. Editor Jour. Orificial Surgery, 1889-98. Hon. mem. numerous state socs. Author: Orificial Surgery, 1892; Composite Man, 1902. Home: Chicago, Ill. Died Mar. 6, 1930.

PRATT, Ella Farman, editor, author; b. N.Y.; d. Rev. T. T. and Hannah (Burleson) Farman; m. Charles Stuart Pratt. Was formerly edior (with Mr. Pratt) of Wide Awake, etc.; now, with Mr. Pratt, editor Little Folks. Author: Good-for-Nothing Polly; How Two Girls Tried Farming; A Girl's Money; A Little Woman; Grandma Crosby's Household; Mrs. Hurd's Niece; Anna Maylie; A White Hand; Sugar Plums. Also Happy Childern, 1896; The Play Lady, 1900; The Little Cave-Dwellers, 1901. Home: Warner, N.H. Died 1907.

PRATT, Florence Gibb; b. Brooklyn, N.Y.; d. John and Harriet (Balsdon) Gibb; ed. Packer Collegiate Inst., Brooklyn; m. Herbert Lee Pratt, Apr. 27, 1897; children—Edith Gibb (Mrs. Allan McLane, Jr.), Herbert Lee, Harriet Balsdon (Mrs. Lawrence van Ingen), Florence Gibb (Mrs. Francis E. Powell, Jr.), Frederic Richardson. Mem. Bd. of Regents of Univ. State of N.Y., term, 1927-39. Served overseas Y.W.C.A., World War. Was mem. Bd. of Edn., Glen Cove, Hughes Commn. for reorganization N.Y. govt.; pres. Bd. Nassau Hosp., Mineola, N.Y. Republican. Episcopalian. Home: New York, N.Y. Died Jan. 2, 1935.

PRATT, George Dupont; b. Brooklyn, N.Y., Aug. 16, 1869; s. Charles and Mary Helen (Richardson) P.; A.B., Amherst, 1893; m. Helen D. Sherman, Feb. 2, 1897 (died 1923); children—George D., Sherman, Eliot D., Dorothy D. (Mrs. S. C. Register); m. 2d, Vera A. Hale, Jan. 16, 1926. Was employed by Long Island Railroad as a shop hand, later assistant to the pres. and supt. of ferries to 1900; conservation commr. of State of N.Y., 1915-21; now mem. Charles Pratt & Co.; v.p., trustee Pratt Inst. (Brooklyn); dir. The Thrift. Promoter Boy Scout movement; treas. Nat. Council Boy Scouts America; trustee Amherst Coll., Metropolitan Museum, Am. Mus. Natural History. Pres. Am. Forestry Assn., 1924—. Republican. Presbyn. Home: Glen Cove, L.I., N.Y. Died Jan. 20, 1935.

PRATT, Harold Irving, capitalist; b. Brooklyn, N.Y., Feb. 1, 1877; s. Charles and Mary Helen (Richardson) P.; B.S., Amherst, 1900; m. Harriet L. Barnes, Aug. 29, 1901. Financial adviser Estate of Charles Pratt; treas., trustee Pratt Inst.; pres. The Thrift; pres., trustee Selfwinding Clock; treas. and trustee Morris Building Co.; chmn. bd. North Am. Reassurance Co., trustee Brooklyn Savings Bk. Trustee Brooklyn Hosp., and prime mover in development of its new plant; active in war work Y.M.C.A. Republican. Baptist. Home: New York, N.Y.; also Glen Cove, L.I., N.Y. Died May 21, 1939.

PRATT, Harry Hayt, congressman; b. Corning, N.Y., Nov. 11, 1864; s. George Wollage and Helen Melvina (Hayt) P.; grad. Corning Free Acad., 1882; m. Clarissa Chapman Spencer, Sept. 14, 1892; children—George Wollage, Sophie, Hugh Spencer, Harriet Stacey, Ransom, II, Helen Hayt. Asso. editor Corning Daily Journal, 1882-1906; ed. same and gen. mgr. Corning Jour. Pub. Co., 1906-19. Postmaster Corning, 1906-14; mem. 64th and 65th Congresses (1915-19), 37th N.Y. Dist.; for several yrs. with Erie R.R. in pub. relations work. Republican. Mason, Elk. Home: Corning, N.Y. Died Nov. 13, 1932.

PRATT, John Teele, financier; b. Brooklyn, N.Y., Dec. 25, 1873; s. Charles and Mary Helen (Richardson) P.; A.B., Amherst, 1896; LL.B., Harvard, 1900; m. Ruth Sears Baker, Jan. 6, 1903; children—John Teele, Virginia, Sally Sears, Phyllis, Edwin H. B. Practiced law with Carter, Ledyard & Milburn, 1900-06, Campbell, Harding & Pratt, 1906-18; formed partnership of Fosburgh, Pratt & Osborn, Jan. 1920; mem. Charles Pratt & Co.; spl. partner of G. M.-P. Murphy & Co.; dir. many companies; mgr. D.&H. RR. Co. With Am. Red Cross in Paris, Oct.-Dec. 1918, rank of maj. Chmn. Nat. Budget Com. N.Y. Trustee Pratt Inst., Bur. Municipal Research, New York. Republican. Episcopalian. Home: New York, N.Y. Died June 17, 1927.

PRATT, Le Gage, congressman; b. Sterling, Mass., Dec. 14, 1853; s. Maj. James A. and Caroline E. P.; pub. sch. edn.; m. Olive Howard Lyman Nichols, Mar. 27, 1889. In commercial business, Boston and Chicago, 1869-84; entered life ins., 1886; state agt., 1895, gen. supt. agencies, 1896, Life Ins. Clearing Co., St. Paul; southern supt. agencies, 1897, 2d v.p., 1903, v.p., 1904, Mut. Benefit Life Ins. Co. of N.J. Mem. 60th Congress (1907-09), 80th N.J. Dist. Democrat. Home: East Orange, N.J. Died 1911.

PRATT, Lewellyn, clergyman; b. Essex, Conn., Aug. 8, 1832; s. Selden M. and Rebecca C. (Nott) P.; A.B., William Coll., 1852, A.M., 1855 (D.D., 1877); studied theology under Rev. Albert Barnes, Phila.; m. Sarah Putnam Gulliver, Oct. 17, 1855; father of Waldo Selden P. Ordained Presbyn. ministry, 1864; prof. natural science, Gallaudet Coll., 1866-70; prof. Latin, Knox Coll., 1870-71; prof. rhetoric, Williams Coll., 1876-80; prof. homiletics, Hartford Theol. Sem., 1880-88; pastor Congl. Ch., N. Adams, Mass., 1871-76, Broadway Ch., Norwich, Conn., 1888—; pres. Norwich Free Acad., 1893—. Trustee Williams Coll., Hartford Theol. Seminary. Home: Norwich, Conn. Died June 14, 1913.

PRATT, Pascal Paoli, mcht., banker; b. Buffalo, Sept. 15, 1819; s. of Samuel and Sophia (Fletcher) P.; ed. Buffalo, 1825-33, acads. Hamilton, N.Y., and Amherst, Mass., 1833-35; m. Phebe, d. Frederick Lorenz, Pittsburgh, Sept. 1845 (died 1887). Became clerk in hardware business, 1836, for his brother, Samuel F., and his partner, 1840; mem. hardware firm Pratt & Co., 1840-87, and 1867-87 of Pratt & Letchword, saddlery hardware; v.p., 1856-87, pres., 1887-1900, Mfrs. & Traders' Bank, Buffalo; helped organize and became stockholder in Buffalo Iron & Nail Co., Fletcher Furnace Co., Tonawanda Furnace Co. Cast 1st vote for Harrison and Tyler, 1840; Whig and Republican. Home: Buffalo, N.Y. Died 1905.

PRATT, Richard Henry, brig. gen. U.S.A.; b. Rushford, N.Y., Dec. 6, 1840; s. Richard S. and Mary (Herrick) P.; ed. Logansport, Ind.; (LL.D., Dickinson, 1898); m. Anna L. Mason, Apr. 12, 1864. Corporal Co. A, 9th Ind. Inf., sergt. Co. A, 2d Ind. Cav., and 1st lt. and capt. 11th Ind. Cav., 1861-65; 2d lt. 10th U.S. Cav., Mar. 7, 1867; promoted through grades to col. 13th Cav., Jan. 24, 1903; retired, Feb. 17, 1903; advanced to rank of brig. gen. retired, by act of Apr. 23, 1904. Was provost marshal, Dist. of N. Ala., summer and fall 1864, and insp. and judge advocate 5th Div. Cav. Mil. Div. of Miss., Dec. 1864 to close of vol. service. Suggested and organized the Industrial Sch. for Indians at Carlisle, Pa., in 1879, and was its only supt. to July 1, 1904. Home: Rochester, N.Y. Died Mar. 15, 1924.

PRATT, Samuel Wheeler, clergyman; b. Livonia, N.Y., Sept. 9, 1838; s. George F. and Sarah A. (Wilcox) P.; A.B., Williams, 1860; grad. Auburn Theol. Sem., 1863; (D.D., Williams, 1902); m. Lucilla B. Field, Aug. 12, 1863; m. 2d, Sarah M. McKay, of Campbell, N.Y., Feb. 22, 1880. Ordained Presbyterian ministry, 1863; pastor Brasher Falls, N.Y., 1863-67, Hammonton, N.J., 1867-71, Prattsburgh, N.Y., 1872-77, Campbell, N.Y., 1877-83, Monroe, Mich., 1883-89, Campbell, N.Y., 1889—. Commr. Auburn Theol. Sem.; synodical examiner, Elmira Coll.; charter trustee Alma Coll.; moderator Synod of Geneva; vice moderator Synod of Mich.; moderator of Synod of New York, 1908; 5 times commr. to Gen. Assembly of the Presbyn. Ch. Author: A Summer at Peace; Life and Epistles of St. Paul Harmonized and Arranged in Chronological Order, 1895, 1901; The Deity of Jesus Christ According to John. Home: Campbell, N.Y. Died 1910.

PRATT, Sedgwick, brig. gen. U.S.A.; b. Georgetown, D.C., May 20, 1845; s. Henry C. and Mary Clarissa (Clitz) P.; grad. U.S. Mil. Acad., 1867; m. Martha W. Keith, Nov. 19, 1869. Served as 2d lt., 4th N.Y. Arty. and as a.-d.-c. to Brig. Gen. G. A. De Russy, U.S.V., May 26-Sept. 9, 1863; commd. 2d lt. 3d U.S. Arty., June 17, 1867; promoted through grades to col. Arty Corps, Feb. 9, 1906; brig. gen. and retired, June 22, 1906, at own request, over 40 yrs.' service. Served as arty. insp. Dept. of Calif., chief mustering officer for State of Calif., 1898; mem. Bd. of Engrs. U.S.A., 1901-03, Bd. of Ordnance and Fortifications, 1902-03; detailed to gen. staff, May 1903, and on spl. duty at hdqrs. Dept. of the Columbia, 1903-04; insp. gen. and arty. insp. Div. of the Pacific, 1904-06; in command arty. dist. of the Potomac, June 1906. Home: Washington, D.C. Died Mar. 25, 1920.

PRATT, Sereno S., secretary; b. Westmoreland, N.Y., Mar. 12, 1858; s. Enfield Loring and Mary E.

(Jessup) P.; student U. of Vt. (hon. A.M., 1913); m. Ada S. Bryden, Oct. 19, 1882. Entered newspaper work with St. Albans Advertiser, 1876; later with various met. papers; financial editor New York Times, 1903; editor Wall Street Journal, 1904-08; sec. Chamber of Commerce State of N.Y., Dec. 1908—. Episcopalian. Mason. Author: The Work of Wall Street, 1903. Home: Brooklyn, N.Y. Died Sept. 14, 1915.

PRATT, Silas Gamaliel, composer; b. Addison, Vt., Aug. 4, 1846; s. Jeremiah and Esther M. (Derby) P.; ed. common schs., Plainfield, Ill.; m. Flora Spencer Colby, 1886. Was in music business with H. M. Higgins, and Lyon and Healy, Chicago; studied in Berlin, with Kullak, Bendel and Kiel, 1868-71, with Liszt and Heinrich Dorn, 1875-76; his 1st symphony performed, 1871; organized Apollo Club, Chicago, 1872; gave several successful concerts in London and Berlin, including London concerts of original works; projected and was dir. gen. Chicago Grand Opera Festival, 1884; organized and dir. Omaha Festival; organized chorus for Music Teachers' Nat. Conv.; removed to New York; directed Fourth of July music "Chicago Day" celebration, and "Reunion of the Cities" (last great day), Chicago Expn.; gave grand Am. concert, July 4, 1895, at Antwerp Expn., etc. Pres. Pratt Inst. of Music and Art, Pittsburgh, 1906—. Composer: Zenobia, The Triumph of Columbus, and Lucille, grand operas; The Soul of a Song, concert-lecture; orchestral works, Reverie, A Serenade, Paul Revere's Ride, and The Revolution of '76; The Battle Fantasia; three grand symphonies; Centennial Overture with Ode to Peace; grotesque dances; suite for orchestra; Sandalphon, symphonic poem; grand festival overture, Voyage of Columbus; about 50 piano pieces, and many songs; also new music to America, first publicly performed at Lotos Club, New York, Jan. 15, 1903; Tell Me Ye Winged Winds, for chorus of mixed voices, performed by Mozart Soc., Pittsburgh; Lincoln Grand Symphony, for orchestra in 4 parts, for the Lincoln Centennial, etc. Author: Lincoln in Story, 1901; Pianists' Mental Velocity, 1903; Valse Lente grotesque, Reverie, and The Revolution, performed by Winderstein Orchestra; Lincoln Symphony, in 4 parts; A Tragedy of the Deep, symphonic poem; wrote libretto and composed grand opera Ollanta, 6 acts. Organized Pittsburgh Centre of Am. Music Society (chmn. 1910). Home: Pittsburgh, Pa. Died Oct. 31, 1916.

PRATT, Waldo Selden, educator, musician; b. Phila., Pa., Nov. 10, 1857; s. late Rev. Lewellyn and Sarah Putnam (Gulliver) P.; A.B., Williams College, 1878, A.M., 1881, L.H.D., 1929; Johns Hopkins, 1878-80; Mus.D., Syracuse Univ., 1898; m. Mary E. Smyly, July 5, 1887 (died 1935). Assistant dir. Metropolitan Museum of Art, 1880-82; prof. music and hymnology, 1882-1917, prof. pub. worship, 1917-25 (emeritus), Hartford Theol. Sem. Instr. elocution, Trinity Coll., Hartford, 1891-1905; lecturer musical history and science, Smith Coll., 1895-1908, Mt. Holyoke Coll., 1896-99, Inst. of Musical Art, New York, 1905-20; lecturer music and hymnology, Y.W.C.A. Training School, New York, 1908-12; organist Asylum Hill Congl. Ch., Hartford, 1882-90; condr. Hosmer Hall Choral Union, Hartford, 1882-90, St. Cecilia Club, 1884-88. Editor: St. Nicholas Songs, 1885; Songs of Worship, 1887; Musical editor: Aids to Common Worship, 1887; Century Dictionary, 1892-1909. Author: Musical Ministries in the Church, 1901; History of Music, 1907; Am. Supplement to Grove's Dictionary of Music and Musicians, 1920; Music of the Pilgrims, 1921; New Encyclopedia of Music and Musicians, 1924; A Forgotten American Portrait Painter—Peter Baumgras, 1827-1903, 1937. Home: Hartford, Conn. Died July 29, 1939.

PRATT, Wallace, lawyer; b. Georgia, Vt., Oct. 16, 1831; s. Nathan and Charlotte (Hotchkiss) P.; grad. Union Coll., N.Y., 1849; m. Adaline A. Russell, Nov. 27, 1855 (died 1874); m. 2d, Mrs. Caroline Dudley, Dec. 11, 1884 (died 1902). Studied law; practiced, Milwaukee, 1857-69; from 1869 in Kansas City; general practice; for over 25 yrs. gen. counsel, Kansas City, Fort Scott & Memphis R.R. system; senior mem. Pratt, Dana & Black. Fellow Am. Geog. Soc. Home: Kansas City, Mo. Died 1907.

PRAY, James Sturgis, landscape architect; b. Boston, Mass., Feb. 26, 1871; s. Benjamin Sweetser and Frances Motley (Gavett) P.; A.B., Harvard, "as of '95"; m. Florence M. Nichols, Oct. 30, 1901. With Olmsted Bros., Brookline, 1898-1903; in independent practice, 1903—; sr. mem. Pray & Gallagher, 1904-06, Pray, Hubbard & White, 1906-18. Asst. prof. landscape architecture, 1905-14, Charles Eliot prof., 1914—, and chmn. Sch. of Landscape Architecture, 1908-28, Harvard U. Fellow Am. Soc. Landscape Architects (v.p., pres. 1915-19, trustee 1919-21); trustee and mem. exec. com. Am. Acad. in Rome, 1915-20; founder and chmn. Nat. Conf. on Instruction in Landscape Architecture, 1920, 21; Harvard adviser to Cambridge Planning Board, 1915—; city planning expert in laying out various army cantonments, 1917, and U.S. Govt. towns for munition workers, 1918; mem. numerous professional societies; mem. Nat. Conf. on City Planning; overseer, 1916-21, Coöp. Open-Air School; mem. visiting com. on bldgs. and grounds, Radcliffe Coll.; hon. mem. Topiarian Club. Author: City Planning (with Kimball), 1913. Home: Cambridge, Mass. Died Feb. 22, 1929.

PREBLE, Fred Myron, clergyman; b. Chesterville, Me., Oct. 15, 1855; s. Otis M. and Emiline A. (Hall) P.; ed. Me. Wesleyan Sem.; grad. Waterville Classical Inst., 1877; A.B., Colby Coll., 1881, A.M., 1906; B.D., Newton Theol. Instn., 1884; D.D., Colby, 1901, Bates, 1909; m. Effie J. Pettigrew, June 6, 1889. Ordained Bapt. ministry, 1885; pastor Windsor, Vt., 1885-87, Camden, Maine, 1889-98, Auburn, Maine, 1898-1916; retired, 1916. Chaplain Vermont State Prison, 1885-87; prof. of ch. history, Cobb Div. Sch., 1907-09; pres. Me. Bapt. Conv., 1907-09. Pres. Lewiston and Auburn Children's Home; trustee Colby Coll., Newton Theol. Instn., Coburn Classical Inst. Republican. Author: Flowers in Footsteps (sermons), 1916. Home: Ludlow, Vt. Died Feb. 12, 1928.

PREETORIUS, Emil, editor of St. Louis Westliche Post; b. Alzey, Germany, March 15, 1827; grad. Giessen Univ., 1848 (LL.D.); renewal of diploma on fiftieth anniversary was made through the consul of German Empire, St. Louis, 1898; m. Feb. 1854, Magdalena Schmidt, Frankfort, Germany. Came to U.S., 1854, and has been actively identified with the German newspapers from that time. Home: St. Louis, Mo. Died 1905.

PRELLWITZ, Henry, artist; b. N.Y. City, Nov. 13, 1865; s. Rudolph and Margaretha (Mauer) P.; student Coll. City of New York, 1879-82, Art Students' League, New York, 1882-87, Académie Julian, Paris, France, 1887-90; m. Edith Mitchill, Oct. 6, 1894; 1 son, Edwin Mitchill. Opened studio, New York, 1890; exhibited paintings at Nat. Acad. Design (where received 3d Hallgarten prize, 1893), at Soc. Am. Artists, and at Pa. Acad. Fine Arts, Phila. Dir. Art Students' League, 1894-98; instr. of drawing, life classes, Pratt Inst., Brooklyn. Silver medal, St. Louis Expn., 1904; Clarke prize, Nat. Acad. Design, 1907. N.A. Home: Peconic, L.I., N.Y. Died Mar. 13, 1940.

PRENDERGAST, Albert Collins, judge; b. Limestone Co., Tex., Feb. 19, 1853; s. Davis McGee and Mary E. (Collins) P.; ed. pvt. schs., Tex.; LL.B., Law Dept., Trinity Univ., Tex. (LL.D., 1911); m. Lillian L. Conoly, Nov. 2, 1876. Began practice in Limestone Co., Tex., 1874; mem. Tex. Ho. of Rep., 1887-88; pres. Sch. Bd., Waco, Tex., 9 successive terms, 1893-1911; served as dist. judge (spl.) by election of bar and apptmt. of gov. of Tex. many times; apptd. judge of Ct. of Criminal Appeals, Tex., Jan. 1911; elected to same office, 1912, for term of 6 yrs.; presiding judge from June 1911. Democrat. Presbyn. Home: Waco, Tex. Died Jan. 6, 1922.

PRENDERGAST, Edmond Francis, archbishop; b. Clonmel, Ireland, May 5, 1843; came to U.S., 1859; studied, Ecclesiastical Sem., St. Charles Borromeo, Phila.; ordained R.C. priest, Nov. 17, 1865. Asst. at St. Paul's, Phila., 1865-66, Susquehanna Depot, Pa., 1866-67; pastor of St. Mark's, Bristol, Pa., 1868-72, Allentown, Pa., 1872-74, St. Malachy's, Phila., 1874-1911; consecrated auxiliary bishop of Phila., Feb. 1897; apptd. archbishop, May 1911. Vicar-gen. of archdiocese, 1895-97. Died Feb. 26, 1918.

PRENDERGAST, James M., broker; b. Boston, Mass., Oct. 29, 1851; s. Jeffrey and Catherine P. Entered brokerage business at Boston, 1868; dir., mem. exec. and finance coms. Boston Elevated Ry. Co.; v.p. Second Nat. Bank; dir. B.&M. R.R., Hamilton Mfg. Co., Hamilton Woolen Co. Republican. Catholic. Home: Boston, Mass. Died Nov. 29, 1920.

PRENDERGAST, Maurice Brazil, artist; b. Boston, Mass., Oct. 1861; s. Maurice and Malvina (Germaine) P.; Julien and Colorossi acads., and École des Beaux Arts, Paris, under Profs. Joseph Blanc, Courtois, Jean Paul Laurens and Jerome. Mem. various art societies. Home: New York, N.Y. Died Feb. 1. 1923.

PRENTICE, George Gordon, mfr.; b. Oberlin, O., Oct. 23, 1865; s. Harvey Monroe and Jennie Elizabeth (Hillyer) P.; ed. pub. and night schs., N.Y. City; m. Janet Eleanor Stirling, Dec. 3, 1890; children—George Gordon, Stirling Garvin (dec.), Helen Sheldon (wife of Capt. John C. Glithero), Janet Elizabeth (wife of Rev. Heinrich W. Falk), Hillyer. With Francis H. Richards Engring. Co., Cleveland, O. (assisted in bldg. 1st automatic machine for gumming, printing and folding envelopes, 1883; with Pratt & Whitney Co., Hartford, Conn., 1884-85; supt. and mgr. Yost Writing Machine Co., Bridgeport, Conn., 1886-90; with Garvin Machine Co., N.Y. City, 1891-95; organizer, 1896, owner and pres. until retirement, 1911, George G. Prentice & Co., automatic turret machinery; mem. reorgn. com. C.,R.I.&P. R.R., 1915; owner 2000-acre Prentice Ranch. Mem. Sch. Bd., New Haven, Conn., 1912-15. Rep. State of Conn. at Panama Pacific Expn., San Francisco, Calif., 1915. Inventor and patentee typewriter improvements, 1886-90; designed and built typewriter for printing on bound ledgers, 1892; improved and built Doremus automatic stamp cancelling machines, 1893; designed, built Prentice automatic multiple spindle turret (toolroom machine), 1898; designed and built steam turbine engine, 1899. Awarded gold medal by Belgium, 1905. Republican. Episcopalian. Mason. Home: San Diego, Calif. Died Dec. 5, 1941.

PRENTICE, Samuel Oscar, judge; b. N. Stonington, Conn., Aug. 8, 1850; s. Chester Smith and Lucy (Crary) P.; A.B., Yale, 1873, LL.B., 1875, M.A., 1903; (LL.D., Yale Univ., and Trinity College, 1913); m. Anne Combe Post, Apr. 24, 1901. Admitted to bar, June 1875, and began practice at Hartford, Conn., Sept. 1875; admitted to law partnership of Johnson and Prentice, 1876, which ended July 1889; corp. atty. for City of Hartford, 1882-89; apptd. exec. sec. to Gov. M. G. Bulkeley, 1889; judge Superior Ct. of Conn., 1889-1901; judge Supreme Court of Errors, 1901-20; chief justice, Feb. 20, 1913-20; retired. Mem. State Bar Examining Com., 1890-13 (chmn. 1898-13). Instr. pleading, 1896-99, prof. pleading, 1901-15, Yale Law Sch.; pres. Hartford Public Library, 1895—, and Watkinson Library, Dec. 1906—, Conn. Humane Soc., 1920—, Hartford Park Board, 1920—. Republican. Home: Hartford, Conn. Died Nov. 2, 1924.

PRENTICE, Sartell, clergyman; b. Albany, N.Y., Sept. 30, 1867; s. Sartell and Mary Adeline (Isham) P.; A.B., Amherst, 1891; student McCormick Theol. Sem., Chicago, 1891-93; grad. Union Theol. Sem., New York, 1894; D.D., Olivet Coll., Mich., 1911; m. Lydia Beekman Vanderpoel, Sept. 30, 1896; children—Pierrepont Isham, Sartell, Lydia Vanderpoel (dec.). Ordained ministry Ref. Ch. in America, 1894; pastor Pottersville, N.J., 1894-97, 5th Av. Presbyn. Ch., Newark, 1897-1905, 1st Ref. Ch., Nyack, N.Y., 1905-23 (resigned). Speaker for Am. Nat. Red Cross, Nat. Security League, Liberty Loan, etc. Chaplain with Base Hosp. 101 and Evacuation Hosp. 13, U.S.A., in France, June 1918-Feb. 1919. Author: The Cloud; Padre, a Red Cross Chaplain in France; The Heritage of the Cathedral. Home: New York, N.Y. Died Oct. 28, 1937.

PRENTICE, William Packer, lawyer; b. Albany, N.Y., August 26, 1834; s. Ezra P. and Philena C. P.; A.B., Williams Coll., 1855 (LL.D., 1905); A.M., Ph.D., U. of Göttingen, 1858; m. Florence Kelly, Jan. 29, 1863. Commissioned capt. a.a.g. vols., Nov. 26, 1861; maj., Sept. 2, 1862; lt. col. adj. gen. 10th Army Corps and chief of staff of Maj. Gen. O. M. Mitchel, Oct. 1862; resigned, Dec. 23, 1862; LL.B., Albany Law Sch., 1861; practiced in New York City, 1863-1913. Counsel, Health Bd. New York, 1873-92, State Bd. Health, 1875. Author: Police Powers, 1894. Home: New York, N.Y. Died Dec. 22, 1915.

PRENTIS, Robert Riddick, judge; b. University of Va., Albemarle Co., May 24, 1855; s. Robert Riddick and Margaret Ann (Whitehead) P.; grad. Eastman Business Coll., Poughkeepsie, N.Y., 1874; LL.B., U. of Va., 1876; LL.D., William and Mary, 1925; m. Mary Allen Darden, Jan. 6, 1887 (died 1904). Practiced at Charlottesville, Va., 1876-79, Norfolk, Jan.-Nov. 1879, Suffolk, 1879-95. Mayor of Suffolk, 1883-85; judge of Va. Circuit Ct., Norfolk Circuit, 1895-1907 (resigned); chmn. State Corp. Commn., 1907-16 (resigned); justice of Supreme Court of Appeals of Va., Nov. 16, 1916—, chief justice, Mar. 10, 1925—. Mem. Dem. State Com., 1887-92; presdl. elector, 1892; mem. Va. Tax Commn., 1910; mem. State Advisory Bd. on Taxation, 1916; pres. Nat. Assn. Ry. Commrs., 1915-16. Chmn. Commn. on Revision and Amendment of Va. Constitution, 1927; chmn. Va. Judicial Council, 1929. Dir. Lee Camp Soldiers' Home (state instn. for disabled Confederate vets.), 1907-16. Episcopalian. Mem. Va. War History Commn., 1919—. Home: Suffolk, Va. Died Nov. 25, 1931.

PRENTISS, Benjamin Mayburv, soldier; m. Belleville, Va. (now W.Va.), Nov. 23, 1819; ed. dist. schools Mo.; left home, 1841, settling at Quincy, Ill.; learned trade of rope-making, afterward engaged in the commn. business; 1st lt. in a co. formed to march against Mormons, 1844-45; capt. co. vols., Mexican war; gained distinction at Buena Vista and fought in prin. battles of war. Organized and offered co. to govt., 1861; apptd. col. 7th Ill. regt.; brig. gen., May 17, 1861; placed in command of Cairo; directed attack on large Confederate force Mt. Zion, Dec. 28, 1861, completely routing the enemy. Joined Gen. Grant at Pittsburgh Landing and arrived 3 days before battle of Shiloh; comd. new div. (6th), which had but 2 regular brigades; compelled to surrender 1st day of battle, April 6, 1862; released Oct. 1862. Apptd. maj. gen. vols., Nov. 29, 1862; served on court martial convened to try case of Fitz John Porter, Nov. 27, 1862; in command post at Helena, Ark., 1863, and on July 3, 1863, was attacked by Gens. Holmes and Price, whom he defeated. Resigned command in army, Oct. 28, 1863, and engaged in civil pursuits. Home: Quincy, Ill. Died 1901.

PRENTISS, Daniel Webster, M.D.; b. Washington, D.C., May 21, 1843; grad. Columbian Coll., Ph.B., 1861 (A.M., 1865); Univ. of Pa., M.D., 1864; resident student, quartermaster's hospital, Washington, 1861-63, and acting asst. surgeon, U.S.A., 1864-65; prof. materia medica and therapeutics, med. dept., Columbian Univ., 1879—; mem. city bd. of health,

D.C., 1864; dean med. faculty, Nurses' Training School, 1878-83; etc. Died 1899.

PRENTISS, Francis Fleury, twist drill mfr.; b. Montpelier, Vt., Aug. 22, 1858; s. Joseph Addison and Rebecca (Loomis) P.; ed. pub. schs., Winona, Minn.; m. Elisabeth S. Allen, Sept. 19, 1917. Bank clk., 1876-79; mem. Davies & Prentiss, lock mfrs., Cleveland, O., 1879-80; with J. D. Cox, organizer, 1880, Cox & Prentiss, now The Cleveland Twist Drill Co. (chmn. bd.). Pres. The Hiram House; pres. and dir. St. Luke's Hosp.; v.p. Cleveland Sch. of Art; trustee Western Reserve U., Case Sch. of Applied Science, Cleveland Art Museum, Western Reserve Hist. Soc.; pres. Cleveland Chamber Commerce. Republican. Home: Cleveland Heights, O. Deceased.

PRENTISS, George Lewis, prof. pastoral theology, church polity and mission work, 1873-96, emeritus, Union Theol. Sem.; b. Gorham, Me., May 12, 1816; grad. Bowdoin Coll., 1835 (D.D., 1854); asst. Gorham Acad., 1835-36; studied univs. of Halle and Berlin 2 yrs.; spent some time in England; pastor South Trinitarian Ch., New Bedford, Mass., 1845-50; Mercer St. Presbyn. Ch., New York, 1851-58; Ch. of the Covenant, New York, 1862-73. Author: The Agreement Between Union Seminary and the General Assembly; Fifty Years of Union Seminary; Another Decade of Union Theological Seminary, 1899; also memoirs of Sargent S. Prentiss, Thomas Harvey Skinner, D.D., and Elizabeth Prentiss, author of Stepping Heavenward (his wife, who died 1878). Died 1903.

PRENTISS, Henry James, anatomist; b. Flushing, N.Y., July 22, 1867; s. Andrew Morgan and Henrietta (Driggs) P.; M.E., Stevens Inst. Tech., 1889; M.D., Bellevue Hosp. Med. Coll., 1898; m. Lué Bradley, Apr. 18, 1895. Prosector, demonstrator and prof. of practical anatomy, Univ. and Bellevue Hosp. Med. Coll., 1898-1904; prof. anatomy, histology and embryology, State U. of Iowa, 1904—, also head of dept. and dir. labs. histology and embryology. Warden of Trinity Ch. Republican. Episcopalian. Mason. Home: Iowa City, Ia. Died May 17, 1931.

PRENTISS, John Wing, banker; b. Bangor, Me., Aug. 15, 1875; s. Samuel Rawson and Maria (Wing) P.; prep. edn., Phillips Acad., Andover, Mass.; A.B., Harvard, 1898; m. Marie Gordon Kay, Apr. 19, 1904. Began as security salesman, Hornblower & Weeks, investment bankers, 1904, partner, 1905—. Served as col. on gen. staff, U.S.A., World War. Mason. Home: New York, N.Y. Died Mar. 18, 1938.

PRESBREY, Eugene W., dramatist; b. Williamsburg, Mass., Mar. 13, 1853. Began as actor, Boston Theatre, 1874; Madison Square Theatre, New York, 1880-84; gen. stage dir. for A. M. Palmer, Madison Sq. and Palmer's theatres, 1884-96; independent producer, 1896-1906. Won recognition as water color and portrait painter, Boston, 1873-79; lecturer on dramatic subjects, Am. Acad. Dramatic Arts, New York, 1886-94; author of "Life Study," a new system of study for dramatic art and acting. Amateur designer and builder of yachts, 1886-96. Is said to have made most complete pvt. collection of marine and land shells in U.S. Mason. Author: (plays) Squirrel Inn, 1893; Giles Corey, 1893; Courtship of Miles Standish, 1894; A Ward of France, 1898; Marcelle, 1900; A Virginia Courtship, 1901; Personal, 1903; New England Folks (novel and play), 1904; Terrence, 1904; The Adventures of Gerard, 1904; Raffles, 1904; A Scrap of Paper (adapted), 1905; Susan in Search of a Husband, 1906; A Fool's Wisdom, 1906; The Right of Way, 1907; The Barrier, 1908; The Coast of Chance, 1910; The High Hand, 1912; The Other Man, 1913. Consulting expert for feature films, 1919—. Founder of Writers Club, Hollywood, 1921. Died Sept. 9, 1931.

PRESBREY, Frank; b. Buffalo, N.Y., May 22, 1855; s. Otis F. and Sarah A. (Johnson) P.; Princeton U., 1879 (hon. A.M., 1890); m. Stella Spalding, June 13, 1881; children—Charles, Marguerite and Alice. Editor and publisher Daily News-Register, Youngstown, Ohio, 1881-85; founder, and editor Public Opinion, Washington, D.C., 1886-94; publisher The Forum, New York, 1894-96; founded, Frank Presbrey Company (advertising agency); mem. advisory com. Park Av. and 46th St. br., Chase Nat. Bank. Pres. Soc. of the Genesee, 1910; v.p. Nat. Orgn., Boy Scouts America; mem. S.A.R.; chmn. advertising com. Nat. Red Cross, 1917-18. Author: Memories of Vacation Days, 1896; In Far-Away Vacation Lands, 1898; Motoring Abroad, 1906; The History and Development of Advertising, 1929. Republican. Presbyn. Home: New York, N.Y., and Greenwich, Conn. Died Oct. 10, 1936.

PRESCOTT, Albert Benjamin, chemist; b. Hastings, N.Y., Dec. 12, 1832; s. Benjamin and Experience (Huntley) P.; ed. Univ. of Mich.; grad., M.D., 1864 (Ph.D., 1886, LL.D., 1896, Univ. of Mich.; LL.D., Northwestern, 1903); m. Abigail Freeburn, Dec. 25, 1866. Asst. surgeon, U.S.V., 1864-65; in Univ. of Mich., asst. prof. chemistry, 1865; prof. organic and applied chemistry, 1870; dean school of pharmacy, 1876—; dir. chem. laboratory, 1884—. Pres. A.A.A.S., 1891; fellow Chem. Soc., London, 1876. Author: Qualitative Chemical Analysis, 1874; First Book of Qualitative Chemistry, 1879. Home: Ann Arbor, Mich. Died 1905.

PRESCOTT, Charles Henry, editor, banker; b. Barnstead, N.H., Aug. 3, 1857; s. James Lewis and Harriet Morrill (Tripp) P.; Berwick Acad.; Boston U.; admitted to bar, 1880; m. Ellen S. Hobbs, Jan. 17, 1882. Founder, 1884, and sole propr. Biddeford Daily Journal until 1921, when incorporated as Journal Pub. Corp., of which became pres.; also pres. York County Savings Bank, Biddeford & Saco R.R. Co., First Nat. Bank; v.p. Portland R.R. Co.; pres. Biddeford Improvement Co. Mem. Me. Ho. of Rep., 1883-84, Senate, 1895-96; mem. gov.'s staff, 1893-97, Gov.'s Council, 1901-06 (chmn. bd.); treas. York County, Me., 1887-90; received 291 votes in conv. for nomination for gov., 1904. Pres. Sweetser Orphan Asylum. Home: Saco, Me. Died Dec. 19, 1923.

PRESCOTT, Dorothy, author. See Agnes Blake Poor.

PRESCOTT, Frank Clarke, lawyer; b. Ottawa, Ill., Nov. 15, 1859; s. Fernando Cortes and Juliette Estelle (Clarke) P.; ed. pub. and pvt. schs. and under pvt. tutors in law, English, Spanish and French; m. Maria de los Reyes Tebbetts, Jan. 1879; 1 son, Frank C. (dec.); m. 2d, Henrietta May Pierce Barrett, Mar. 1898 (died 1929). Was telegrapher, 1876-88; then practiced law in Los Angeles, Calif., 1888-91, Redlands, 1891-1903, San Bernardino, 1903-06, Los Angeles, 1906—; sr. mem. Prescott & Prescott. City atty., Redlands, 1899; mem. Calif. Assembly, 1903-06 (speaker 1905); regent Univ. of Calif., 1905; register U.S. Land Office, Los Angeles, 1906-10. Enlisted as pvt. Oakland Light Cav., N.G.C., 1880; retired as brig. gen., 1903; served as maj., 1st Battalion, 7th Inf., U.S. Vols., Spanish-Am. War; capt. 43d Inf., Philippine Insurrection; provost judge, Island Samar, 1900; brigade staff, Iloilo, 1900-01; recommended for bvt. maj. vols., "for meritorious conduct." Republican. Episcopalian. Mason. Home: Los Angeles, Calif. Died Jan. 6, 1934.

PRESCOTT, Oliver, lawyer; b. New Bedford, Mass., July 30, 1868; s. Oliver and Helen Augusta (Howland) P.; grad. Friends Acad., New Bedford, 1885; A.B., cum laude, Harvard, 1889, A.M., 1892, LL.B., cum laude, 1892; m. Helen Maria Bryant, Dec. 31, 1895; children—Oliver, Bryant, William Crapo, Helen Luce, Lydia Coffin. Practiced, New Bedford, 1892—; mem. Crapo, Clifford, Prescott and Bullard; pres. New Bedford Gas & Edison Light Co., 1912-32; pres., New Bedford Institution for Savings, 1924-32; dir. First Nat. Bank, Wamsutta Mills, Morse Twist Drill & Machine Co. Mem. New Bedford City Council, 1894-95 (pres. 1895). Pres. of the board of trustees of the James Arnold Fund; trustee Howland Fund for Aged Women. Pres. New Bedford Bd. Commerce, 1917-19, New Bedford War Fund Assn., 1918-19. Republican. Unitarian. Home: North Dartmouth, Mass. Died Dec. 8, 1938.

PRESSER, Theodore, music pub.; b. Pittsburgh, Pa., July 3, 1848; s. Christian and Caroline (Dietz) P.; student Mt. Union (O.) Coll.; studied music, N.E. Conservatory of Music (Boston, Mass.), 1873-74, Leipzig Conservatory, 1878-80; m. Helen Louise Curran, 1890 (died 1905); m. 2d, Elise Houston, 1908. Entered retail music business, Pittsburgh, Pa., 1864; teacher of piano, Ohio Northern U., Ada, O., 1869-71, Smith Coll. and Conservatory, Xenia, O., 1872-75, Ohio Wesleyan U., 1876-78; prof. music, Hollins (Va.) Coll., 1880-83; founded The Étude, monthly music jour., at Lynchburg, Va., 1883; removed to Phila., 1884, and continued as editor The Étude until 1891; head of Theodore Presser Co., music pubs. Erected and endowed, 1914, the Presser Home for Retired Music Teachers; founded, 1916, Presser Foundation. Author: School for Pianoforte Playing; School for Four Hand Playing; Polophony Playing. Presbyn. Home: Philadelphia, Pa. Died Oct. 28, 1925.

PRESTON, Andrew W., financier; b. Beverly, Mass., June 29, 1846; s. Benjamin and Sarah P.; ed. Beverly grammar sch.; m. Frances E. Gutterson, Aug. 5, 1869. Pres., chmn. exec. com. and dir. United Fruit Co. from its organization, 1899; pres. Fruit Dispatch Co., Revere Sugar Refinery, Simmons Sugar, Ltd., Tela R.R. Co., Truxillo R.R. Co., Tropical Radio Tel. Co., United Fruit Steamship Corp., Banana Specialty Co.; v.p. Northern Ry. (Costa Rica), Abangarez Gold Fields (Costa Rica); chmn. bd. Elders & Fyffes, Ltd. (London); treas. M.D. Cressy Co. Republican. Home: Swampscott, Mass., and Fenway, Boston. Died Sept. 26, 1924.

PRESTON, Byron Webster, lawyer; b. Newton, Ia., Feb. 13, 1858; s. Sylvester S. and Amelia M. (Wild) P.; educated Eastman National Business Coll., and Iowa Coll., Grinnell; LL.D., Grinnell (Iowa) College; read law in office of Judge L. C. Blanchard, Oskaloosa, Ia.; m. Nellie Blanchard, Oct. 6, 1880. Practiced law, Oskaloosa, 1884—; pros. atty. Mahaska Co., Ia., 1892-96; city atty., Oskaloosa, 1897-98; dist. judge 6th Jud. Dist., Ia., 1903-13; judge Supreme Court of Ia., 1913-25. Republican. Episcopalian. Mason. Home: Oskaloosa, Ia. Died Jan. 18, 1939.

PRESTON, Cecil Anthony, valuation engr.; b. Phila., Sept. 16, 1852; s. Edward Hall and Margaret (McIntyre) P.; C.E., Poly. College, Phila., 1872; m. Leila Coffin Rogers, Nov. 6, 1883. Engaged in ry. survey and constrn., 1872-77; with Madeira and Mamore Ry. in Brazil, 1877-79; in service Pa. R.R., 1879-80, Nat. Rys. of Mexico, 1880-82; returned to U.S., 1882, and from then in employ Pa. R.R., successively as asst. supervisor, supervisor, asst. engr., prin. asst. engr., supt. Elmira Div., Williamsport Div., Middle Div.; valuation engr. same road, June 1, 1913—. Mason. Episcopalian. Home: Philadelphia, Pa. Died Oct. 9, 1922.

PRESTON, Douglas A., lawyer; b. Olney, Ill., Dec. 19, 1858; s. Finney D. and Phoebe (Mundy) P.; ed. pub. schs.; married. Studied law under father; admitted to Ill. bar, 1878; pros. atty. Richland Co., Ill., 1880-84; removed to Cheyenne, Wyo., 1887; practiced at Rawlins, Lander and Rock Springs; mem. Wyo. Constl. Conv., 1889; mem. Wyo. Ho. of Rep., 1903-05; apptd. atty. gen. of Wyo. by Gov. Joseph M. Carey, 1911, reapptd. by Gov. John B. Kendrick, 1915, term of 4 yrs. Democrat. Elk. Home: Rock Springs, Wyo. Died Oct. 20, 1929.

PRESTON, Erasmus Darwin, editor of Publications U.S. Coast and Geodetic Survey, Apr. 19, 1899—; b. Lancaster Co., Pa., Mar. 28, 1851; s. Simpson and Phebe D. P.; ed. State Normal School, Millersville, Pa., 1872; grad. Cornell, C.E., 1875; instr. same, 1876; fellow Johns Hopkins, 1877; studied univs. Paris and Vienna; attached to French Transit of Venus Commn., 1882; to U.S. Solar Eclipse Party, S. Pacific Ocean, 1883; astronomer Nat. Observatory, Cordoba, Argentine Republic, 1884; astron. work Hawaiian govt., 1886; U.S. scientific expdn. to Africa, 1889; transit of Mercury and internat. latitude observations, Honolulu, 1891; U.S. delegate Internat. Geodetic Assn., Stuttgart, 1898. Exec. officer Coast and Geodetic Survey, Mar. 1895-Apr. 1899. Home: Washington, D.C. Died 1906.

PRESTON, George Junkin, physician; b. Lexington, Va., 1858; s. Col. J. T. L. and Margaret J. P.; grad. Washington and Lee Univ., 1879; Univ. of Pa., M.D., 1883; m. Emma Heinrichs of Leipzig, Germany, 1882. Prof. of neurology, Coll. of Phys. and Surg., Baltimore; sec. Md. State Lunacy Commn. Author: Hysteria, 1897. Home: Baltimore, Md. Died 1908.

PRESTON, Harold, lawyer; b. Rockford, Ill., Sept. 29, 1858; s. Simon M. and Martha H. (Sargent) P.; ed. Iowa Coll. and Cornell U.; studied law Newton, Ia. Admitted to Ia. bar, 1883; moved to Wash.; m. Augusta Morgenstern, Feb. 8, 1888. Mem. Wash. Senate, 1897-1901; was second in balloting for U.S. senator in legislature of 1903. Republican. Engaged in practice of law. Home: Seattle, Wash. Died Jan. 1, 1938.

PRESTON, Harriet Waters, author; b. Danvers, Mass., 1843; ed. privately; traveled in France and England. Well known as essayist on Provençal poets, Latin literature, etc. Author: The Guardians (with Miss L. Dodge), 1888; The Private Life of the Romans (with same), 1893; also wrote series of papers on Mistral's "Calendau," Theodore Aubanet, Jacques Jasmin, Songs of the Troubadours, Arthuriad. Translator: Writings of Madame Swetchine, edited by Count de Falloux, 1869; Memoirs of Madame Desbordes Valmore, by C. A. Sainte-Beauve, 1872; Mistral's Miréio (Provençal poem), 1873; Biography of Alfred de Musset, by Paul de Musset, 1877; Georgics of Virgil, 1881. Home: Keene, N.H. Died 1911.

PRESTON, Herbert R(ush), lawyer; b. Lexington, Va., Jan. 24, 1861; s. John T. L. and Margaret (Junkin) P.; A.B. and LL.B., Washington and Lee U., 1884; m. Helen S. Cross, Dec. 8, 1898; children—Janet C., Herbert R. Admitted to Md. bar, 1886, and began practice at Baltimore; gen. solicitor B.&O. R.R. Co., gen. office, Baltimore, 1906—. Democrat. Presbyn. Home: Catonsville, Md. Died Oct. 15, 1937.

PRESTON, Howard Willis, author; b. Providence, July 29, 1859; s. Augustus H. and Abby (Howard) P.; A.B., Brown Univ., 1883, A.M., 1887; m. Florence M. Spencer, Feb. 14, 1884; children—Dorothy, Margaret (dec.), Ruth Howard, Robert Spencer. Author: Documents Illustrative of American History (2 editions), 1886, 1891; Key to New England Trees (with Prof. J. Franklin Collins), 1909. Illustrated, Key to the Trees of the Northeastern United States, 1912; Rochambeau and the French Troops in Providence, 1924; Know Rhode Island, 1927; Battle of Rhode Island, 1928; Rhode Island's Historic Background, 1930. Home: Providence, R.I. Died Feb. 1, 1936.

PRESTON, James Harry, lawyer; b. Harford Co., Md., Mar. 1860; s. James B. and Amelia (Wilks) P.; St. John's Coll., Annapolis, Md.; LL.B., Md. U. Sch. of Law, 1880; m. Helen, d. late Wilbur F. Jackson, of Baltimore, 1894; children—Alice Wilks (wife of Col. Edward C. Carrington), James H., Mary Bond (Mrs. Harry P. Galligher), Wilbur Jackson, Helen Jackson. Admitted to bar, State of Md., 1880, and practiced at Baltimore; also v.p. Calvert Bank. Mem. Md. Ho. of Dels., 1890, speaker, 1894; mem. Md. Bd. Police Commrs., 1904-08; mayor of Baltimore, terms 1911-15, 1915-19. Democrat. Chmn. Port Development Commn. of Baltimore. Pres. Centennial Commn. in commemoration of the writing of Star Spangled Banner, 1914. On staff Gov. Brown, Md., with rank of col., 1892-96. Pres. Nat. and Md. Socs. S.A.R. Chmn. Baltimore City George Washington Bi-Centennial Commn. and vice chmn. Md. State George Washington Bi-Centennial Commn. Home: Baltimore, Md. Died July 14, 1938.

PRESTON, Keith, journalist, author; b. Chicago, Ill., Sept. 29, 1884; s. William David and Jessie (Roberts) P.; Ph.B., U. of Chicago, 1905, Ph.D., 1914; M.A., Ind. U., 1907; m. Etta Sheild, June 12, 1915. Inst. Latin, 1913, asst. prof., 1915, asso. prof., 1919-23, Northwestern U. Author: Studies in the Diction of the Sermo Amatorius of the Latin Comedy, 1916; Types of Pan, 1919; Splinters, 1921; Top O'The Column, 1925. Conductor of weekly column of lit. criticism under title of "The Periscope," and daily column of humor "Hit or Miss," in Chicago Daily News. Home: Evanston, Ill. Died July 7, 1927.

PRESTRIDGE, John Newton, editor; b. Selma, Ala., Feb. 5, 1853; s. John Elijah and Sarah F. (McCraw) P.; student Howard Coll., Ala., 1869-71; Southern Bapt. Theol. Sem., 1879-83; (D.D., Furman U., S.C., 1900, Georgetown Coll., Ky., 1900, Bethel Coll., Ky., 1900); m. Fannie Clardy, May 17, 1887. Ordained Bapt. ministry; pastor New Castle and Burk's Branch, Ky., 1882-84, Hopkinsville, Ky., 1884-89, First Ch., San Antonio, Tex., 1889, Winchester, Ky., 1891-94, Williamsburg, Ky., and pres. Williamsburg Inst., 1894-98; founder, 1898, and editor, 1898-1908, Baptist Argus; aided in organizing The Baptist World Pub. Co., which bought The Baptist Argus and began The Baptist World, May 1, 1908. Suggested and promoted to success Bapt. World Congress, London, July 1905, and was chosen sec. for America. Home: Louisville, Ky. Died Oct. 29, 1913.

PREUSS, Arthur, author, editor, pub.; b. St. Louis, Mo., Mar. 22, 1871; s. Edward and Concordia (Schuricht) P.; student Canisius Coll., Buffalo, N.Y.; A.B., Quincy (Ill.) Coll., 1888, A.M., 1890; m. Marie Dohle, May 1893; 1 dau., Isabelle; m. 2d, Pauline Beuckman, Oct. 23, 1900; children—Alma (Mrs. Ray M. Dilschneider), Edward, Eleanor (Mrs. John Edw. Looney), Alfred, Wilfrid, Charles Arthur, Austin, Arline (Mrs. Raymond Aubuchon), Francis. Assistant to father, editor St. Louis Daily America, 1890-92; established the Chicago Review, 1893, changed to The Review, weekly, 1894, The Catholic Fortnightly Review, 1905, The Fortnightly Review, 1912—, appearing as monthly, 1930—, pub. at St. Louis, 1896—; literary editor B. Herder Book Co., 1896—; lit. adviser Soc. of the Divine Word Press, Techny, Ill. One of founders Soc. St. Louis Authors. Author: The Fundamental Fallacy of Socialism, 1907; A Study in American Freemasonry, 1908, 5th edit., 1924; Dictionary of Secret and Other Societies, 1924; Pohle-Preuss Dogmatic Theology (12 vols.), 1911-17; Moral Theology, by Dr. Antony Koch (5 vols.), 1918-21; Handbook of Fundamenta' Theology (Lehrbuch der Apologetik, by Rev. John Brunsmann, (4 vols.), 1928-32. Editor many important works. Home: St. Louis, Mo. Died Dec. 16, 1934.

PRIBRAM, Ernest August, physician, educator; b. Prague, Bohemia, Feb. 2, 1879; s. Otto (LL.D.) and Leonora (Popper) P.; grad. U. of Prague, 1903; post grad. work, U. of Strasbourg, Alsace; m. Mrs. Maria H. Salmonson, Mar. 21, 1918; 1 son, Karl Harry. With U. of Vienna in various capacities and as asso. prof. pathology until 1925, also served as asst. and dir. State Serum Inst., 1907-25; came to U.S., 1925; mem. faculty of Rush Med. Coll., Chicago, 1926-28; prof. bacteriology and preventive medicine, Loyola U., Oct. 1, 1928—, dir. lab., 1938—; pathologist St. Elizabeth's Hosp. (Chicago), St. Therese's Hosp. (Waukegan, Ill.). Owner and dir. microbiological collection in Vienna from 1911. Served as surgeon maj. Austrian Army and as councilor of Austrian govt. Awarded Order of Red Cross, 2d class; Knight of Austrian Franz Joseph Order; Order of Civil Merits. Mem. numerous professional Societies. Author: Culture Media for Bacteria and for Fungi, 1925; Classification of Bacteria, 1933. Home: Chicago, Ill. Died Sept. 14, 1940.

PRICE, Abel Fitzwater, naval officer; b. Lawrenceville, Pa., Dec. 13, 1847; s. William Harley and Hannah (Detwiler) P.; ed. high sch., Phila.; M.D., U. of Pa., 1868; m. Clara L. Wollaston, Dec. 27, 1883. Commd. asst. surgeon U.S.N., Nov. 10, 1868; passed asst. surgeon, Nov. 10, 1871; surgeon, Aug. 14, 1878; rank of capt., Apr. 9, 1899. Served on U.S. Flag Ship Olympia as fleet surgeon to Admiral Dewey's fleet in Philippine campaign, 1898, 1899; pres. Naval Examining Bd., 1904-09; retired, Dec. 13, 1909. Episcopalian. Home: Sandwich, Mass. Died Mar. 22, 1919.

PRICE, Bruce, architect; b. Cumberland, Md., Dec. 12, 1845; studied architecture in Baltimore and abroad; practiced, Baltimore, 1869-72; Wilkesbarre, Pa., 1872-77; then in New York; among his works are the Cathedral, Savannah, Ga.; Lee Memorial Ch., Lexington, Va.; cottages and clubhouse, Tuxedo Park, N.Y.; West End Hotel, Bar Harbor, Me.; Long Beach, N.Y., Hotel; Am. Surety Co.'s Bldg. and St. James Bldg., New York; Hotchkiss Prep. School, Lakeville, Conn.; Georgian Court, Lakewood, N.J.; Chauteau Frontenac, Quebec; Windsor St. and East End Stations, Montreal; Royal Victoria Acad., Montreal; Osborn Memorial, Yale Coll.; Welch Dormitory, Yale Coll.; Colonial Hist. Soc. Bldg., New Haven, Conn. Invented, patented and built parlor bay-window cars for Pa. and Boston & Albany railroads. Author: A Large Country House. Died 1903.

PRICE, Butler Delaplaine, brig. gen. U.S.A.; b. Phila., May 27, 1845; s. Richard Butler and Elizabeth Senter (Huntt) P.; ed. Short's Acad., Phila.; m. Clara Agnes Gilmore, Oct. 10, 1866. Apptd. 2d lt. 2d Pa. Cav., Dec. 6, 1861; 1st lt., Feb. 2, 1863; capt., Feb. 23, 1864; hon. mustered out of vol. service, Jan. 5, 1865; commissioned 2d lt. 4th U.S. Inf., May 11, 1866; promoted through grades to col. 16th Inf., Oct. 18, 1902; brig. gen. and retired at own request, after 42 yrs.' service, Dec. 26, 1905. Participated in campaigns of Army of the Potomac (except Wilderness), 1862-65; served on plains, 1867-82 and 1886-96, participating in Indian campaigns, 1867-79; served in Cuban campaign of 1898 and in Philippines, 1899-1901 and 1905. Episcopalian. Home: Washington, D.C. Died Aug. 29, 1919.

PRICE, Charles Browne, corp. official; b. Salem, Mass., Oct. 22, 1869; s. Charles H. and Fannie S. (Pettingell) P.; ed. high sch., Salem, and Bryant & Stratton Commercial Sch., Boston, Mass.; m. Agnes Grosvenor, June 5, 1895; children—Virginia (Mrs. Carleton Davenport), Charles G. In elec. supply business, 1889-1925; chmn. bd. Pettingell-Andrews Co., 1900-25; dir. numerous companies. Republican. Episcopalian. Home: Swampscott, Mass. Died May 31, 1939.

PRICE, Charles Wilson, editor; b. Barnesville, O., Dec. 22, 1857; s. Rev. Samuel and Charlotte (Alder) P.; ed. Barnesville (O.) High Sch.; m. Minnie E. Gray, Mar. 16, 1882; children—Corinne Gray (Mrs. Frederick B. Merrels), Leonice Elizabeth. Learned the printing trade and became the editor of the Barnesville (O.) Enterprise; went to Topeka, and was one of founders, 1879, and several yrs. one of editors Topeka Daily Capital. Became interested in elec. science and in 1885 joined staff of Electrical Review, New York, of which was for 37 yrs. asso. editor, and editor-in-chief, and pres. Elec. Rev. Pub. Co.; purchased the Western Electrician, 1908, and Electrocraft, 1912, consolidated with Electrical Rev.; interested in Am. Fruit Grower. Several yrs. sec. and treas. Internat. League Press Clubs. Republican. Home: New York, N.Y. Deceased.

PRICE, Eldridge Cowman, M.D.; b. Baltimore Co., Md., Feb. 21, 1854; s. Elias Cooper (M.D.) and Martha Ann (Cowman) P.; Friends High Sch., Baltimore, 1872; M.D., U. of Med., 1874, M.D., Hahnemann Med. Coll., Phila., 1875; m. Mary Haworth Ferris, Oct. 10, 1877; children—Marriott, Reginald Cooper. Practiced, Baltimore, 1875—; prof. materia medica, Southern Homœ. Med. Coll. (later Atlantic Med. Coll.), 1891-99; prof. therapeutic philosophy and materia medica, Atlantic Med. Coll. (now defunct), 1904-10, and dean, 1906-10. Editor-in-chief Homœ. Advocate and Health Journal, 1891-92; editor Southern Jour. Homœopathy, 1892-96, Am. Medical Monthly .1897-98; asso. editor North Am. Jour. of Homœopathy, 1911-13. Mem. Bd. Med. Examiners, Md., 1902-06; mem. Vol. Med. Service Corps. Pres. Md. Inst. Homœopathy; pres. Southern Homœ. Med. Assn., 1893-95, Md. State Homœ. Med. Soc., 1903-05; mem. bd. censors, Am. Inst. Homœopathy, 1898-1903, 1904-09 (necrologist, 1916-17); pres. Baltimore Homœ. Med. Soc., 1916-19; companion Order of Washington. Author: A Philosophy of Therapeutics, 1904. Co-author: A Pathogenic Materia Medica, 1895. Home: Baltimore, Md. Deceased.

PRICE, Frank, structural engr.; b. Dos Oris, Glen Cove, L.I., N.Y., May 4, 1852; s. George James and Susan Louise (Thompson) P.; ed. pub. and pvt. schs. and under tutors; mech. training in iron works of Bailey & Debevoise, New York. Apptd. supt. of building of U.S. Lighthouses, at Phoenix Iron Works, Trenton, N.J., 1879; designed and supervised machinery and apparatus for moving 220-ton obelisk, accompanied ship to Egypt and directed erection of obelisk in Central Park, New York, 1881; in charge structural dept. Phoenix Iron Co., 1881-83; asst. supt. Am. Shipbuilding Co., Phila., 1883-85; supt. reconstruction of New York Stock Exchange Bldg. without interrupting business, 1885; supt. composite Iron Works, New York, 1888; Pres. Price & Co., 1889-94; chief mill and shop inspr., L.I. R.R. Co., 1902-08; chief shop inspr. N.Y. State Barge Canal, 1909-10; chief shop inspr. for U.S. Govt. of 60-ton steel lock gates for Panama Canal, 1911-12, of Panama Canal fender chains, 1913-14; retained by Govt. in Panama Canal lock gate litigation, 1915. Home: Dos Oris, L.I., N.Y. Died Feb. 5, 1927.

PRICE, Frank J., editor; b. Neosho, Mo., Mar. 8, 1860; s. Thomas Potts and Martha A. (Sevier) P.; desc. Gen. John Sevier, of Revolutionary Army; ed. Neosho Collegiate Inst.; m. Anna Winifred Gorden, Apr. 3, 1881; children—Thomas Albert, Laura Caroline, Sidney Gorden (dec.), Martha Sevier, Frank John. Newspaper reporter, 1885-90; Washington corr. St. Louis Republic, 1891, 92, 93; on editorial staff St. Louis Globe Democrat, 1894-95; in magazine work, 1896-97; mng. editor Washington (D.C.) Times, 1897-98; on staff New York Times, 1898-1911; editorial writer News and Commercial, New York, 1901; editorial writer and Sunday editor New York Telegraph, 1902-08; on staff Phila. Telegraph, 1909-10, and chief editorial writer, 1910-12; asso. mng. editor Phila. Public Ledger, 1912-13; editorial and special writer New York Morning Telegraph, 1914-24; syndicates editorials and weekly political review. Editorial dir. Van Ree Pub. Co., Queensboro, N.Y. City. Dem. candidate for Congress from 15th Pa. Dist., 1930; prothonotary of Court of Common Pleas and recorder of deeds, Pike County, Pa. Nov. 4, 1931-Jan. 6, 1936; not a candidate for reëlection. Traveled on foot before reaching majority, over the entire Southwest, working as journeyman printer, and has written extensively upon Ozark Mountains. Presbyterian. Mason. Author: The Major's Daughter, 1891; Ruth, 1892; Industrial Defense, 1916; Diplomacy and Business, 1917; Money—Basic Values at Home and Abroad, 1920; Farmers and the Federal Reserve, 1922; Economic Reflections, 1929; also more than 200 short stories, some under nom de plume of "Faulkner Conway." Home: Lackawaxen, Pa. Died Oct. 6, 1939.

PRICE, George Edmund, lawyer; b. Moorefield, Va. (now W.Va.), Nov. 9, 1848; s. George Richard Coale and Catharine (Cunningham) P.; ed. Georgetown Coll., D.C.; read law under pvt. tutelage; m. Sallie A. Dorsey, June 12, 1878; children—John Edmund, Richard McSherry, Thomas Brooke, George Dorsey. Admitted to bar, 1871; practiced, Frederick, Md., 1871-75, Keyser, W.Va., 1875-1890, Charleston, 1890—; now mem. Price, Smith & Spilman; counsel for W.Va. in suit of Md. vs. W.Va. in U.S. Sup. Ct. for settlement of boundary line, 1892-1912; v.p. Kanawha Banking & Trust Co. Mem. W.Va. Senate, 1883-90 (pres. 1885-89). Democrat. Trustee Children's Home. Soc. of W.Va. Presbyn. Home: Charleston, W.Va. Died Feb. 6, 1938.

PRICE, George Hunter, M.D.; b. Tuskegee, Ala., Dec. 31, 1858; s. George W. F. and Elizabeth M. (Pooser) P.; B.E., Ala. Polytechnic, Auburn, Ala., 1878, M.S., 1879; M.D., Vanderbilt U., 1888; studied Vienna, Austria, 1889; m. Mattie Barr Sperry, Dec. 15, 1897. Prof. natural sciences, Ala. State Normal Sch., Florence, Ala., 1879-81; prof. same, Nashville Coll. for Young Ladies, 1881-83; house surgeon New York Polyclinic, 1888-89; asst. to chair diseases eye, ear, nose and throat, 1889-94, lecturer diseases eye, ear, nose and throat, 1894-95, prof. physiology, 1895-1905, clin. prof., and prof. diseases eye, ear, nose and throat, 1905-25, emeritus, Vanderbilt U.; sec. Sch. of Medicine, Vanderbilt U., 1900-03. Fellow Am. Coll. Surgeons. Democrat. Methodist. Past Grand Chancellor K.P. of Tenn. Home: Nashville, Tenn. Died Aug. 1, 1927.

PRICE Hickman, agriculturist; b. Jefferson City, Mo., June 9, 1886; s. John Ewing and Mary D. (Hickman) P.; B.S., Columbia, 1909; m. Mary Washington Frazer, Nov. 16, 1910; 1 son, Hickman. Reporter New York Sun, 1909-10; pub. Nashville Democrat, 1911-12; editor-pub. El Commercio, 1912-15; v.p. Am. Press Assn., 1915-20; exec. staff Motion Picture Producers and Distributors, Inc., 1920-25, Fox Film Corp., 1925-29. Grain producer in Tex., 30,000 acres; developed engineering and agronomy practices in industrialized growing of wheat which established new low cost production methods; perfected equipment to plow, plant and harvest 1,000 acres a day for each operation. In charge activities of U.S. Com. on Pub. Information in several fgn. countries, World War. Lecturer and writer on agro-industrial exploration and development, Anglo-Saxon relations and the fulfilling of Am. destiny. Home: Southport, Conn. Died Dec. 14, 1939.

PRICE, Hiram, banker; b. Washington Co., Pa., Jan. 10, 1814; common school edn.; was a merchant's clerk, then a farmer, then a small merchant. Went to Davenport, Ia., 1844; was elected pres. State Bank of Iowa, 1859, holding until 1866, when the 13 branches of that bank were changed to National banks without loss of a dollar. When the war broke out and the State had no funds he quartered and subsisted about 5,000 infantry and cavalry for several months from his individual means, and was apptd. paymaster gen. Member Congress, 1863-69, 1877-81; U.S. Commr. Indian Affairs, 1881-85. Died 1901.

PRICE, Ira Maurice, orientalist; b. Welsh Hills, nr. Newark, O., Apr. 29, 1856; s. Thomas Davis and Sarah Jane (Jones) P.; B.A., Denison U., 1879, M.A., 1882; B.D., Bapt. Union Theol. Sem., Morgan Park, Ill., 1882; Ph.D., M.A., U. of Leipzig, 1886-87; LL.D., Denison, 1903; m. Jennie Rhoads, June 13, 1882 (died 1905); children—Charles Royal, Grace Marie, Maurice Thomas, Mary Irene (dec.), Dudley Jones (dec.), Genevieve (wife of Prof. L. L. Hanawalt, Ph.D.); m. 2d, Elizabeth Mellor McDowell, Aug. 21, 1919. Prof. Greek and modern langs., U. of Des Moines, 1879-80; instr. German and French, Morgan Park (Ill.) Mil. Acad., 1881-83; instr. Hebrew, Wheaton (Ill.) Theol. Sem., 1882-83; instr. Harper's Hebrew Corr. and Summer Schs., 1882-84; instr., 1886-88, prof. Hebrew and cognate langs., 1888-92, Bapt. Union Theol. Sem.; asso. prof., 1892-1900, prof. Semitic langs. and lits., 1900-25, prof. emeritus, 1925—, U. of Chicago. Asso. editor Biblical World, 1892-1920, Am. Jour. of Semitic Langs. and Lits., 1892—, Am. Jour. Theology, 1897-1920, Jour. of Religion, 1921—. Gay lecturer, Southern Bapt. Theol. Sem., 1906; condr. Fourth U. of Chicago Travel Study Class through Bible Lands, 1909; conductor Bible reading course, Bapt. Young People's Union of America, 1892-1917. Co-founder, Mar. 1, 1889, and since secretary Theol. Faculties Union of Chicago and Vicinity. Author: Introduction into the Inscriptions Discovered by Mons. E. de Sarzec, 1887; A Syllabus of Old Testament History, 1890, 14th edit., 1925 (Spanish edit., 1915); Introduction to Old Testament, 1891; Gesenius' Hebrew Grammar, 2d Am. edit. (with Edw. C. Mitchell), 1893; The Great Cylinder Inscriptions A and B of Gudea, Part I, text, 1899, Part II, transl. 1927 (Assyriologische Bibliothek, Vols. XV and XXVI): The Monuments and the Old Testament, 1899, new re-written (18th edit.), 1925; Some Literary Remains of Rim-Sin (Arioch) of Larsa, about 2285 B.C., 1905; The Ancestry of Our English Bible, 1907, 9th revised edit., 1934, 10th edit., 1935, 11th edit., 1937; Training the Teacher (with A. F. Schauffler), 1908, Bengali, Tamil and Burmese editions, 1916; Airplane View of Old Testament History (teachers text-book), 1920; The Dramatic Story of Old Testament History, 1929, 2d edit., 1935; The Story of the Uniform Lessons (with John R. Sampey), 1930; Synchronous History of the Nations in Standard Indexed Bible (with others), 1936. Baptist. On staff Assyrian Dictionary of Oriental Inst. of U. of Chicago, Feb.-June 1932, to inaugurate a bibliography of word-studies. Home: Chicago, Ill. Died Sept. 18, 1939.

PRICE, Jacob Embury, clergyman; b. Cape May, N.J., Oct. 25, 1853; s. Rev. Jacob T. and Margaret McInnes (Miller) P.; A.B., Dickinson Coll., 1876, A.M., 1879; Ph.D., Syracuse U., 1888; D.D., Dickinson, 1891; m. Annie Bacon Ware, Dec. 26, 1876 (died 1909); children—Eugene Manning (dec.), Florence Ware (dec.), Carl Fowler, Elizabeth Singer. Prof. mathematics, and v.p. Pennington (N.J.) Sem., 1876-78; ordained M.E. ministry, 1876; pastor Merchantville, N.J., 1878-80, New Brunswick, N.J., 1880-83, Elizabeth, N.J., 1883-86, Scranton, Pa., 1886-89, St. James', New York, 1889-94, Ossining, N.Y., 1894-99, First Ch., Yonkers, N.Y., 1899-1903; dir. of charities of St. Luke's Guild, New York, 1903-07; with aid of Lady Somerset, inaugurated the work at London, 1903; pastor Bedford St. Ch., New York, 1907-08, Washington Heights Ch., New York, 1908—. Dean Ocean Grove Summer Sch., 1893-1900; one of founders Epworth League, 1889, and active in its promotion. Lyceum lecturer. Republican. Author: The Book Divine, 1890; Epworth League Workers, 1891; Manhood and the Republic, 1883. Home: New York, N.Y. Died Sept. 21, 1935.

PRICE, James L., judge; b. New Hagerstown, O., Mar. 27, 1840; s. Benjamin and Nancy P.; ed. pub. and high schs., New Hagerstown; m. Elizabeth Marshall, Mar. 10, 1868. Admitted to bar, 1862; practiced at Carrollton, O., 1862-65, Lima, O., 1883-95; judge Circuit Ct. of Ohio, 1895-1901; asso. justice Supreme Ct. of Ohio, 1901— (chief justice 1908-09), Republican. Home: Lima, O. Died 1912.

PRICE, Jesse Dashiell, congressman; b. White Haven, Md., Aug. 15, 1863; ed. pub. schs.; m. Sallie B. Amiss, Nov. 27, 1889. In mercantile and mfg. business; treas. Wicomico County 4 yrs.; mem. Md. Senate 2 terms, 1908-16 (pres. 1912-16 and lt. gov. of Md. ex-officio); mem. 63d Congress, unexpired term of J. Harry Covington, and 64th and 65th Congresses (1915-19), 1st Md. Dist.; state tax commr. of Md., Apr. 1923—, designated chmn., 1928. Democrat. Home: Salisbury, Md. Died May 15, 1939.

PRICE, John G., lawyer; b. Canton, O., Aug. 10, 1871; s. Edward P. and Katherine A. (Kielly) P.; grad. Canton High Sch.; LL.B., Georgetown U., 1905; m. Salome C. Royer, June 7, 1904; 3 children. Began practice at Columbus, 1906; mem. Ballard, Jones & Price. Asst. pros. atty., Franklin Co., 1911-15; atty. gen. of Ohio, 1919-23; mem. of Bd. of State Charities by apptmt. of gov. of Ohio, 1917-19. Maj. Columbus Reserve Guard. Republican. Grand Exalted Ruler B.P.O.E., 1924-25. K.C. Home: Columbus, O. Died Nov. 23, 1930.

PRICE, Marshall Langton, sanitarian; b. Fort Gaston, Calif.; Apr. 28, 1878; s. Maj. Curtis Ethelbert (U.S.A.) and Frances (Shaw) P.; ed. mainly by pvt. tutelage; S.I. Acad., N.Y., 1891-93; M.D., U. of Md., 1902; m. Henrietta Cowman George, June 14, 1907. Sr. resident phys., Univ. Hosp., Baltimore, 1902-03; med. officer Tuberculosis Commn. of Md., 1903-05; sec. State Bd. of Health, Md., 1907-13; mem. Md.-D.C. Sewerage Commn., 1912; commd. 1st lt. Med. Reserve Corps U.S.A., Apr. 26, 1911. Independent Democrat. Episcopalian. Delegate 6th Internat. Congress on Tuberculosis, 1908 (v.p. Sect. 6), 15th Internat. Congress on Hygiene and Demography, 1912 (sec. Sect. 6). Author of first law for state control of tuberculosis, now in effect in over 21 states in U.S. and known as the "Maryland System." Home: Baltimore, Md. Died Apr. 16, 1915.

PRICE, Milo B., educator; b. Newark, O., Sept. 10, 1867; s. Thomas Davis and Sarah Jane (Jones) P.; A.B., Denison U., 1892; student U. of Chicago, 1892-93, U. of Leipzig, 1893-96; A.M. and Ph.D., Leipzig, 1896; studied philology and history, Yale, 1896; LL.D., Denison, 1924; m. Laura May Tuttle, June 13, 1897; children—Laura, Thomas Davis. Instr. St. Mark's Sch., Southboro, Mass., 1896-97; instr. in history, Worcester (Mass.) Acad., 1897-1901; master in history, William Penn Charter Sch., Phila., Pa., 1901-04; principal Pillsbury Acad., Owatonna, Minn., 1904-31; emeritus principal, 1931-35, resumed principalship, 1935, by unanimous vote and request of trustees. Member Bd. of Edn. of the Northern Bapt. Conv., 1925-36, Minn. Bapt. State Conv., 1904-31, Minn. Bapt. Edn. Soc.; Minn. commr. to Perry Victory Centennial Celebration. Trustee Carleton Coll., 1916-31; chmn. Steele County Red Cross, 1917-19, also chmn. United War Work Campaign, 1918. Republican. Mason. Home: Owatonna, Minn. Died Feb. 19, 1940.

PRICE, Oscar Jay, M.D., surgeon; b. Adrian, Mich., Apr. 4, 1845; s. Phineas and Hannah P.; studied Adrian Coll.; M.D., U. of Mich., 1866; vol. Army of the Tenn., 1865, hosp. steward; practiced Toledo, O., 1866-68; took clin. course in New York hosps., 1867; m. Anna Wilder, Apr. 2, 1874 (died 1907); m. 2d, Mrs. Lucy House Strong, Dec. 30, 1908. In practice at Chicago, 1869—; surgeon Chicago, Alton & St. Louis R.R. over 30 yrs.; was surgeon to Cook Co. Hosp., 6 yrs. Home: Chicago, Ill. Died July 5, 1929.

PRICE, Overton Westfeldt, forester; b. Liverpool, Eng., Jan. 27, 1873; s. Overton Mosbey and Marie Christine (Westfeldt) P.; ed. in Eng., Episcopal High Sch., Alexandria, Va., and spl. course U. of Va.; in forestry 1 yr.; U. of Munich, 2 yrs.; practical work in woods in Europe, 1 yr.; Biltmore Estate, N.C., and lumber camps in North Woods; m. Alice Virginia Lindsey, Jan. 28, 1903. Entered Bur. of Forestry, U.S. Dept. Agr., as agt., June 1899; promoted supt. working plans, July, 1900; asso. forester of Bur., now Forest Service, 1901-10. Mem. and sec. sect. of forests, Nat. Conservation Commn. V.p. Nat. Conservation Assn., Mar. 1911—. Author: The Land We Live In, 1911; Boys' Book of Conservation. Home: Alexandria, Va. Died June 11, 1914.

PRICE, Richard Nye, clergyman; b. Elk Garden, Va., July 30, 1830; s. John Wesley and Mary (Miller) P.; A.B., Emory and Henry Coll., Va., 1854, later A.M.; (D.D., Weaverville Coll., Trinity Coll., and Emory and Henry, 1913); m. Ann, sister of U.S. Senator Z. B. Vance, of N. Carolina, May 8, 1855. Ordained ministry M.E. Ch., S., 1852; served in various pastorates, on circuits, in schs. and colls. and as editor ch. publs.; prof. mathematics and ancient langs., Holston Conf. Female Coll., 3 yrs.; pres. People's Coll., Pikesville, Tenn., 4 yrs.; prof. mathematics, Emory and Henry Coll., 4 yrs., Harriman U., 3 yrs. Served as pvt. Rough and Ready Guards, May-Oct., 1861; chaplain 26th N.C. Vols., 1861-62; chaplain 4th Tenn. Vols. Spanish-Am. War, Dec. 1898-Apr. 1899. Democrat. Author: Cofractions, 1898; Holston Methodism (5 vols.), 1903. Home: Morristown, Tenn. Deceased.

PRICE, Robert Martin, lawyer; b. Barton, Wis., Jan. 22, 1867; s. Robert Ralph and Harriet (Wightman) P.; Ph.B., U. of Calif., 1893; LL.B., Hastings Coll. of Law, 1896; m. Jennie Ellsworth, May 12, 1896; 1 dau., Harriet (Mrs. Theodore Hiram Fairchild). In practice at San Francisco, 1896-1900, Nome and Teller, Alaska, 1900-03, Reno, Nev., 1903—; senior mem. Price & Merrill; mem. Bd. of Edn., Oakland, Calif., 1899-1900; pres. and trustee Bd. of Edn., Reno, 1914-30; spl. master in chancery in case of U.S.A. vs. Walker River Irrigation District, 1931-36. Served as chmn. for Nev. of United War Work Campaign, 1918. Mem. bd. of visitors U. of Nev., 1911-14. Republican. Conglist. Mason, Elk. Home: Reno, Nev. Died Jan. 19, 1940.

PRICE, Sadie F., botanist; b. Bowling Green, Ky.; grad. St. Agnes Hall; unmarried. Received award medal and diploma, World's Columbian Expn., 1893, for bot. work; teacher of botany; from 1887 has been engaged in studying the flora of southern Ky., traveling through counties that are without railroads, by stage, farm-wagon, skiff, etc. Has discovered many rare plants; has made an herbarium, also sketches in water colors of the plants (1,000 or more in the higher orders alone); also water color sketches of Ky. birds. Author: Fern-Collector's Handbook and Herbarium, illustrated, 1897; Flora of Warren County, Ky., 1893; Trees and Shrubs of Kentucky, 1898. Home: Bowling Green, Ky. Died 1903.

PRICE, Samuel D., Sunday Sch. official; b. Newark, N.J., July 27, 1869; s. William and Mary Louise (Dobbins) P.; A.B., New York U., 1893, D.D., 1917; B.D., Princeton Theol. Sem., 1896; A.M., Princeton U., 1896; m. Elinor Spear De Vausney, Apr. 29, 1897; children—Adelaide Elizabeth, Elinor Gertrude. Ordained Presbyn. ministry, 1896; pastor Shrewsbury, N.J., 1898-1906, Calvary Ch., Camden, N.J., 1906-17; recording sec. N.J. S.S. Assn., 1901—; asst. sec. World's S.S. Assn., 1917-27; business secretary of same, 1927—; treasurer Lord's Day Alliance of N.J.; mem. exec. com. N.J. Christian Endeavor Union. Originator and supt. Surplus Material Dept. of World's S.S. Assn. Republican. K.P. Contbr. weekly S.S. lesson to Christian Herald, also syndicated lesson study to newspapers. Home: Montclair, N.J. Died May 17, 1932.

PRICE, Silas Eber, clergyman, educator; b. Welsh Hills, nr. Newark, O., Feb. 28, 1860; s. Thomas Davis and Sarah Jane (Jones) P.; A.B., Denison U., 1884, D.D., 1907; B.D., Morgan Park Theol. Sem., Chicago, 1887; LL.D., Ottawa U., 1924; m. Nettie May Sandon, Sept. 8, 1887; children—Clair, Hattie May. Ordained Bapt. ministry, 1887; pastor Bapt. Tabernacle, La Crosse, Wis., 1887-89, Baptist Tabernacle, Minneapolis, Minn., 1889-98, Bapt. Tabernacle, Milwaukee, Wis., 1898-1904, First Ch., Ottawa, Kan., 1904-06; pres. Ottawa U., 1906-24 (emeritus). Mem. Bd. of Edn., Northern Bapt. Convention. Republican. Home: Pasadena, Calif. Died Oct. 27, 1934.

PRICE, Theodore Hazeltine, editor; b. N.Y. City, Feb. 9, 1861; s. William Henry and Eliza Tabb (Dyer) P.; ed. pub. schs. and under tutor; m. Harriet Eugenia, d. Gen. Alexander B. Dyer, U.S.A., May 26, 1900; children—Harriet Dyer (Mrs. Howard Phipps), Betty Winston (Mrs. Archibald McM. Richards), Theodore H. Member Harris, Burrows & Hicks (stock exchange firm), New York, 1884-1900; engaged in business in his own name, 1900-10; president Price-Campbell Cotton Picker Corp., 1910—; editor and propr. Commerce and Finance (weekly). Apptd. actuary U.S. R.R. Administration, June 1, 1918. Home: New York, N.Y. Died May 4, 1935.

PRICE, Thomas Randolph, prof. English language and literature, Columbia, 1882—; b. in Va., 1839; s. Thomas Randolph P.; collegiate edn.; A.M., LL.D. Author: The Teaching of the Mother Tongue; Shakespeare's Verse Construction. Home: New York, N.Y. Died 1903.

PRICE, Warwick James, writer, lecturer; b. Cleveland, O., Nov. 25, 1870; s. Warrick and Beulah Rosalie (Farmer) P.; B.A., Yale, 1894; m. Anne Rhodelia Glover, Oct. 11, 1899 (died 1929). Master of English, St. Paul's Sch., Concord, N.H., 1894-98; spl. corr. and asst. mng. editor, The Press, Phila., 1901-05; independent mag. and newspaper writing, 1905—, along lines of internat. politics and lit. criticism, also lecturer on those subjects; asso. editor Inquirer, Phila., 1929—. Fellow Pa. Mus. Art. Republican. Author: The Right Side (verse), 1905; Nearest Things (verse), 1919; The One Book, 1927. Editor of Pope's Iliad of Homer, 1896. Home: Philadelphia, Pa. Deceased.

PRICE, William Pierce, congressman; b. Dahlonega, Ga., Jan. 29, 1835; s. William P. P.; ed. county schools; learned printing trade; foreman printing office, 1850-54; editor, 1854, at Greenville, S.C.; studied law; admitted to S.C. bar, 1856; m. Martha Ann Martin, 1856. Practiced law, Greenville, S.C.; entered Kershaw's 2d S.C. regt.; took part in battles of Bull Run and Manassas; severely wounded at Lewinsville, Va., Sept. 11, 1861; discharged from service; mem. S.C. legislature, 1864-66; resigned and returned to Dahlonega; mem. and speaker pro tem Ga. legislature during reconstruction period; twice arrested as ineligible and tried by mil. courts, which acquitted him; mem. Congress, 1871-74; pres. bd. trustees North Ga. Agrl. Coll., 34 yrs.; mayor of Dahlonega for 6 yrs. (1901). Home: Dahlonega, Ga. Died 1908.

PRICE, William Raleigh, educator; b. Belington, W.Va., Aug. 7, 1875; s. Albert and Sophia (Bonner) P.; A.B., Cornell U., 1898; Ph.D., Columbia, 1911; post-grad. work, Cornell, Berlin and Paris; m. Frances Paget, Aug. 7, 1922; children (by former marriage)—Irma Ingeborg, Frederick Wm. Instr. Male High School, Louisville, Ky., 1900-02, high schools and U. of Rochester, N.Y., 1902-06, High Sch. of Commerce, N.Y. City, 1906-11; state supervisor modern foreign langs., U. of State of N.Y., 1911—. A founder, life mem. Modern Lang. Assn. Middle States and Md., Modern Lang. Sect. N.E.A. Teachers, also a founder Modern Lang. Journal and asso. editor same 6 yrs.; a founder Am. Assn. Teachers of French, 1926, and Am. Assn. Teachers of German, 1926. Chief exponent in N.Y. State of oral method of teaching modern foreign langs. Member of Com. of Direction and Control of Modern Foreign Lang. Survey, under auspices of Am. Council on Edn., Washington, D.C. Republican. Baptist. Author: Symbolism of Voltaire's Novel, 1911; Reformlesebuch, 1913; First German Book (with F. Betz), 1915; Beginners' French (with C. H. Holzwarth), 1924; Intermediate French (with same), 1927. Editor: Le Monde où l'on s'ennuie, 1906; Irrfahrten, 1914; Selections from Maupassant, 1928; Short Selections for Oral French, 1929; Second Year French (with C. H. Holzwarth), 1933. Home: New York, N.Y. Died Mar. 17, 1936.

PRICE, William Thompson; b. Jefferson Co., Ky., Dec. 17, 1846; s. Joseph Crocket and Susan (Meade) T.; ed. pvt. schs., Ky.; univs. of Leipzig and Berlin, 1867-70. Ran away and joined Confederate Army, in youth, serving under Col. E. P. Clay, John Morgan, Forrest and Wheeler; was captured, imprisoned at Rock Island, Ill., and escaped. Dramatic critic Courier-Journal, Louisville, Ky., 1875-80; editorial writer on various newspapers; dramatic critic New York Star, 1885-86; play reader for A. M. Palmer, 1886-1906, and for Harrison Grey Fiske, 1901—; founder, 1901, and dir. Am. Sch. of Playwriting; founder and editor of The American Playwright (monthly mag.). Democrat. Episcopalian. Author: The Technique of the Drama, 1892; The Analysis of Play Construction and Dramatic Principle, 1908. Home: New York, N.Y. Died May 3, 1920.

PRICHARD, Frank Perley, lawyer; b. Charlestown, Mass., May 30, 1853; s. Abraham P. and Frances A. (Sawyer) P.; A.B., Central High Sch., 1870, later A.M.; LL.B., U. of Pa., 1874; m. Florence Newell Tilton, Apr. 14, 1898. Admitted to bar, 1874. One of editors Weekly Notes of Cases, Phila., 1875-78, American Law Register, 1882-87. Dir. Land Title & Trust Co. and Phila. Co. for Guaranteeing Mortgages. Chmn. Commn. to Revise Pa. Election Laws, 1910-13; chancellor Law Assn. of Phila., 1915—. Republican. Home: Philadelphia, Pa. Died Aug. 29, 1918.

PRICHARD, Sarah Johnson, author; b. Waterbury, Conn., Jan. 11, 1830; d. Elizur E. and Betsey J. (Cooper) P.; ed. Waterbury Acad., Dwight Place Sem., New Haven, Conn., 1846-47; grad. Mrs. Willard's Sem., Troy, N.Y., 1849. Author: Hugh's Fire on the Mountain, 1866; Kate Morgan and Her Soldiers, 1862; The Old Stone Chimney, 1865; Faye Mar of Storm Cliff, 1868; Rose Marbury, 1870; Shawny and the Lighthouse, 1871; History of Waterbury, Conn. (1674-1784), 1896; The Only Woman in the Town, and Other Stories of the American Revolution, 1898. Home: Waterbury, Conn. Died 1909.

PRICKITT, William Augustus, consul; b. Monmouth Co., N.J., Mar. 20, 1839; pub. sch. edn. Served as pvt., corporal and sergt. 14th N.J. Vols., Army of Potomac, 1862-64; capt. 25th U.S. Colored Inf., 1864; mustered out, 1865; m. Elizabeth Gilman Warner, July 6, 1865; children—Mrs. Jennie Warner Patterson, William Augustus (dec.), Elizabeth Alice (dec.), Mrs. Annie Gilman Linson, Louise Eugénie. In banking and ins., 1868-72; on N.Y. Stock Exchange, 1872-76; became farmer nr. Lakewood, N.J., 1876. Am. consul at Rheims, 1897-1905; consul gen. at Auckland, N.Z., 1905-June 9, 1914; resigned. Pres. Reunion Assn. of Survivors of 14th N.J. Vols., 1916—. Mem. G.A.R. Home: Farmingdale, N.J. Died Jan. 6, 1929.

PRIDGEON, Charles Hamilton, clergyman; b. Baltimore, Md., June 7, 1863; s. Johnson and Rebecca (McCreight) P.; A.B., Lafayette Coll., Easton, Pa., 1886, A.M., 1889; student Princeton Theol. Sem., 1886-87, 1888-89, grad. 1889; studied Free Ch. Coll. and United Presbyn. Sem., Edinburgh, Scotland, and U. of Leipzig, 1887-88, Worcester U., 1891-92; m. F. Louise Shepard, Dec. 4, 1900 (died 1928); 1 dau., Louise Hamilton (dec.); m. 2d, Emma Louise Hogg, Apr. 2, 1930. Ordained Presbyn. ministry, 1890; pastor Canonsburg, 1890-1901; withdrew from Presbyn. Ch., 1901; organizer and pastor Wylie Av. Ch. of The Evangelization Soc., 1901—, also founder and pres. Pittsburgh Bible Inst.; gen. dir. Evangelization Soc. (made trip around world to determine location for foreign missions); founder and dir. an orphanage near Gibsonia, Pa.; founder and dir. missions in China, Africa, India, and chs. and missions in U.S. Editor: Record of Faith. Home: Pittsburgh, Pa. Died July 21, 1932.

PRIDMORE, John Edmund Oldaker, architect; b. Edgbaston, Eng., July 18, 1867; s. William H. and Avice (Oldaker) P.; ed. Soho Park Sch. and Greenhill Coll., Birmingham, Eng.; m. Clara G. Lee, 1891; m. 2d, Blossom Hull, June 10, 1916; children—John E. O., Robert Hales. Came to U.S., 1880, to Chicago, 1883. Prin. works: Chapel of St. John the Divine, U. of Ill., Austin Hosp., Chicago, Am. Forestry Bldg., Paris, and many theatres and chs. in Chicago and middle west. Episcopalian. Home: Chicago, Ill. Died Feb. 1, 1940.

PRIEST, Henry Samuel, lawyer; b. Ralls Co., Mo., Feb. 7, 1853; s. Thomas J. and Amelia Elliott (Brown) P.; A.B., Westminster Coll., Mo., 1872, LL.D.; m. Henrietta K. Parsell, Nov. 9, 1876 (died 1910); children—George T., Mrs. Grace Grayson, Mrs. Jeannette Bond, Wells Blodgett; m. 2d, Mabel C. Watrous, Aug. 19, 1912. Admitted to bar, 1873; apptd. U.S. dist. judge, 1894, resigning about one year later; now sole member Boyle & Priest; has been identified with much important litigation in Mo. Democrat. Presbyn. Home: St. Louis, Mo. Died July 9, 1930.

PRIEST, Irwin G., physicist; b. nr. Londonville, Ohio, Jan. 27, 1886; s. Morgan A. and Julia A. (Schauweker) P.; B.A. from Ohio State U., 1907; m. Edna Ryan, June 26, 1917. With Bur. of Standards, Washington, D.C., 1907—, successively as lab. asst. until 1908, asst. physicist, 1908-15, asso. physicist, 1915-19, physicist, 1919—; also chief of colorimetry sect., Bur. of Standards, 1913—; research asso. of Munsell Color Co. and Munsell Research Lab., at Bur. of Standards for several periods, 1922-25, while on leave from bureau duty. Fellow A.A.A.S., Am. Phys. Society. Home: Washington, D.C. Died 1932.

PRIEST, Walter Scott, clergyman; b. New Martinsville, Va. (now W.Va.), Jan. 2, 1860; s. John Brown and Hannah (Yocum) P.; B.L., Bethany (W.Va.) Coll., 1880; D.D., Fairmount Coll., Wichita, Kan., 1922; m. Anna Evelyn Schaeffer, Sept. 24, 1884; children—Hartzell John (dec.), Mary Frances (Mrs. Byron G. Hays), Walter Scott. Pastor Atchison, Kan., 1883-85; ordained ministry Disciples of Christ, 1885; pastor Denver, Colo., 1893-97, again at Atchison, 1898-1903, Columbus, O., 1903-09, Central Ch., Wichita, 1909—. Led in organizing 5 new chs. in Wichita, recruited mostly from Central Ch. Mason. Rotarian. Visited China and Japan, 1921, and delivers (in costume) illustrated lecture, pictures taken by himself; now in evangelistic work. Home: Columbus, O. Died Apr. 21, 1929.

PRIESTLEY, George Colin, financier; b. Houlton, Me., June 10, 1862; s. George C. and Mattie (Pollock) P.; common sch. edn.; m. Lulu R. Ruland, of Enterprise, Pa., Dec. 25, 1885 (died 1924). Began as clk. in store, Pleasantville, Pa.; engaged in oil production and in 1909 was largest individual oil operator in Okla.; sold many holdings to English syndicate, but is still largely interested in oil properties and electric rys., Okla. and Tex. Elected mem. Rep. Nat. Com., 1911 (resigned Aug. 1, 1912); mem. Prog. Nat. Com., 1912-16. Home: Valley Forge, Pa. Died Apr. 5, 1938.

PRIME, Ebenezer Scudder, rear admiral U.S.N.; b. New York, Jan. 16, 1847; s. Edward Youngs and Emma (Cotrel) P.; apptd. to U.S. Naval Acad. from N.Y., Sept. 21, 1863; m. Eva Prime, Nov. 21, 1883. Promoted through the various grades to rear admiral, June 25, 1905, and retired on own request. Home: Huntington, N.Y. Died Apr. 27, 1912.

PRIME, Frederick, college prof.; b. Phila., Mar. 1, 1846; s. Frederick and Lydia (Hare) P.; served in U.S.V., 1862-63; A.B., Columbia, 1865, A.M., 1868; Ph.D., Lafayette, 1881; Royal Sch. of Mines, Freiberg, 1865-68; m. Laurette de T. Coxe, June 22, 1871. Asst. in assaying, Columbia, 1869-70; prof. geology and metallurgy, Lafayette Coll., 1870-79; mgr. and pres. of several iron cos., Pa., and Ala., 1880-92; pres. Edison Electric Light Co., of Phila., 1891-92; prof. natural history, Girard Coll., Phila., Pa., 1895—. Asst. state geologist of Pa., 1874-79. One of secs. Am. Philos. Soc., 1897-1900; a mgr. Acad. Natural Sciences Phila., 1905—; lt. gov. Pa. Soc. Colonial Wars. Edited, in English, Von Cotta's Treatise on Ore Deposits, 1870. Died July 14, 1915.

PRIME, Frederick Edward, maj. U.S.A.; retired, Sept. 5, 1871; b. Florence, Italy, Sept. 24, 1829 (son of Rufus Prime, New York merchant); grad. West Point, 1850; employed on fortifications; taken prisoner at Pensacola, Fla., 1861; later, as capt. engrs., served in Manassas campaign; successively chief engr. depts. Ky., the Cumberland and the Ohio; wounded and again prisoner; then chief engr. in Grant's Mississippi campaign, 1862-63; maj., June 1, 1863; took part in siege of Vicksburg; bvtd. col.; retired through disability from wounds received in line of duty. Home: Litchfield, Conn. Died 1900.

PRIME, Ralph Earl, lawyer; b. Matteawan, N.Y., Mar. 29, 1840; s. Alanson Jermain (M.D.) and Ruth Havens (Higbie) P.; ed. schs. and acad. White Plains, N.Y., and pvt. tutors; studied medicine with father; studied law in offices at White Plains, admitted to bar, 1861; (D.C.L., Bellevue Coll.; LL.D., U. of Wooster, 1897); enlisted pvt. 5th N.Y. Inf., Apr. 21, 1861; held four regimental commissions, participated in 13 battles, severely wounded at battle of Gaines' Mill; twice promoted "for signal bravery on field of battle," as promulgated in general orders of Army Corps Headquarters; nominated, Mar. 4, 1863, by President Lincoln to be brig. gen.; m. Annie Richards-Wolcott, Aug. 9, 1866. Began law practice late in 1863; has been city atty. of Yonkers and deputy atty. gen. N.Y.; has crossed ocean 36 times, traveled in Europe, Asia and Africa. For over 30 yrs. Presbyn. elder and represented Presbyterian Ch. in the U.S.A. at Pan-Presbyn. councils, Belfast, 1884, London, 1886, Glasgow, 1894, Washington, 1899, Liverpool, 1904, New York, 1909, Aberdeen, 1913; moderator, Presbytery of Westchester, 1894, Synod of N.Y., 1896; permanent clerk Presbytery of Westchester, 1895-1917. Chmn. Western Sect. Pan-Presbyn. Alliance. Mason. Democrat. Author: Descendants of James Prime. Home: Yonkers, N.Y. Died Sept. 27, 1920.

PRIME, Samuel Thornton Kemeys, compiler of crop statistics; b. in Weston, Conn., July 31, 1834; s. Samuel Irenaeus P.; academic edn., Rahway, N.J. Has been for 25 yrs. corr. and contributor to daily press of U.S.; splty. of crop statistics, domestic and foreign. Widower. Author: Prime's Crop Reports; Model Farmers and Their Methods. Home: Chicago, Ill. Died 1907.

PRIME, William Cowper, journalist, author; b. Cambridge, N.Y., Oct. 31, 1825; grad. Princeton, 1843 (LL.D., 1875); admitted to bar, 1846; practiced law, New York, 1846-61; part owner, 1861—, editor-in-chief, 1861-69, New York Journal of Commerce; prof. history of art, Princeton, 1884—; 1st v.p., 1874—, Metropolitan Museum of Art. Author: Tent Life in the Holy Land; Pottery and Porcelain; The Owl Creek Letters; The Old House by the River; Coins, Medals and Seals; I Go A-Fishing; Holy Cross; Along New England Roads; Among the Northern Hills. Home: New York, N.Y. Died 1905.

PRIMER, Sylvester, university prof.; b. Geneva, Wis., Dec. 14, 1842; s. Archibald and Eleanor (Jacoby) P.; removed to N.Y. at 8 yrs. of age; A.B., Harvard, 1874; studied univs. Leipzig, Göttingen and Strassburg; Ph.D., Strassburg, 1880; m. Miss L. M. Muckenfuss, Sept. 17, 1895. Served in 108th N.Y. Inf. 1 yr., and in 15th N.Y. Cav. 2 yrs. in Civil War, under Gens. Custer and Sheridan; participated in 23 battles; wounded at battle of Antietam, but afterwards reëntered service and continued until close of war; teacher, Coll. of Charleston, S.C., 1881-89, Friends' Sch., Providence, R.I., 1889-90, Colorado Coll., Colorado Springs, 1890-91; prof. Germanic langs., U. of Tex., 1891—. Democrat. Methodist. Editor: Lessing's Minna von Barnhelm; Lessing's Nathan der Weise; Goethe's Egmont; Chamisso's Peter Schlemihl; Don Antonio Gil y Zárate's Guzmán El Bueno. Home: Austin, Tex. Died Aug. 12, 1913.

PRINCE, Benjamin F., college prof.; b. Westville, O., Dec. 12, 1840; s. William and Sarah (Nauman) P.; A.B., Wittenberg Coll., Springfield, O., 1865, A.M., 1868, Ph.D., 1891; studied theology 1 yr.; m. Ellen Sanderson, Aug. 3, 1869 (died 1911). Prof. in Wittenberg Coll., 1866—. Republican. Lutheran. Editor: Centennial of Springfield, 1901. Home: Springfield, O. Died Sept. 11, 1933.

PRINCE, Frank Moody, banker; b. Amherst, Mass., July 23, 1854; s. George H. and Sarah (Nash) P.; ed. high sch., Amherst. Began as clk. First Nat. Bank, Stillwater, Minn., 1876; clk. First Nat. Bank Minneapolis, 1878-82; cashier First Nat. Bank, Stillwater, 1882-92; sec.-treas. Minn. Loan & Trust Co., 1892-94; v.p. First Nat. Bank (now First Nat. Bank & Trust Co.), Minneapolis, 1894-1903, becoming pres., 1904, later chmn. bd. dirs. Home: Minneapolis, Minn. Died Sept. 10, 1941.

PRINCE, George Harrison, banker; b. Amherst, Mass., July 18, 1861; s. George H. and Sarah E. (Nash) P.; ed. Amherst, Mass.; m. Jessie B. Robertson, Sept. 20, 1883. Entered employ of First Nat. Bank, Stillwater, Minn., May 19, 1879; elected cashier Capital Bank, St. Paul, Minn., Jan. 1891; became cashier Merchants Nat. Bank, St. Paul, Feb. 1, 1897, v.p. Jan. 1905, chmn. Nov. 27, 1912—; chmn. First Nat. Bank of St. Paul, 1929—, and First Trust Co.; v.p. First Nat. Bank (Cloquet, Minn.); dir. Consolidated Elevator Co. (Duluth), St. Paul Fire and Marine Ins. Co., First Nat. Bank of Minneapolis, Archer-Daniels Midland Co., C.G.W. Ry. Republican. Episcopalian. Home: St. Paul, Minn. Died Oct. 3, 1933.

PRINCE, George W., congressman; b. Tazewell Co., Ill., Mar. 4, 1854; s. Myron and Barbara P.; A.B., Knox Coll., 1878; m. Lillie C. Ferris, Apr. 20, 1882. Admitted to bar, 1880, and entered practice at Galesburg. City atty., 1881; chmn. Rep. Co. Com., Knox Co., Ill., 1884; mem. Ill. Ho. of Rep., 1888-91; Rep. candidate for atty. gen. of Ill., 1892; mem. 54th to 57th Congresses (1895-1903), 10th Ill. Dist., and 58th to 62d Congresses (1903-13), 15th Dist.; defeated for reëlection, 1913. Republican. Home: Los Angeles, Calif. Died Sept. 27, 1939.

PRINCE, John Tilden, author, lecturer; b. Kingston, Mass., Dec. 30, 1844; s. Noah and Olive W. (Faunce) P.; ed. Pierce Acad., Middleboro, Bridgewater Normal Sch., and Harvard Coll., 1 yr.; Ph.D., U. of Leipzig, 1889; studied Waltham (Mass.) Theol. Sch., 3 yrs.; m. Lucinda W. Smith, June 28, 1888. Taught in Washington U., 1865-70; prin. Waltham schs., 1870-78; supt. schs., Waltham, and Watertown, Mass., 1879-83; agt. Mass. Bd. Edn., 1883-1911. Lecturer at Wellesley Coll., 1897-98; teacher of pedagogy, Salem (Mass.) Normal Sch., 1904. Author: Courses of Studies and Methods of Teaching, 1886; The Schools of Germany, 1891; Series of Arithmetics (8 vols.), 1896; Manual for Teachers, 1896; School Administration, 1906; A Practical English Grammar, 1910. Home: West Newton, Mass. Died Aug. 5, 1916.

PRINCE, L. Bradford, lawyer, author; b. Flushing, New York; s. William R. and Charlotte G. (Collins) P.; LL.B., Columbia, 1866, with first honors in polit. science, alumni orator, 1868 and 1876; (LL.D., Kenyon Coll., and Colo. Coll.); m. Mary Catherine, d. Col. S. R. Beardsley, of Oswego, Nov. 17, 1881. Mem. N.Y. Assembly, 1871-75, chmn. judiciary com., having charge of impeachment of judges, New York, 1872; father of constl. amendments of 1874; mem. N.Y. Senate, 1876-77; declined governorship of Ida., 1878; chief justice of N.M., 1879-82, resigned; gov. of N.M., 1889-93; mem. Legislative Council of N.M., 1909; chmn. First State Conv. in N.M., 1911; founder Flushing Pub. Library, 1858, St. George's Brotherhood, 1870, Flushing Assn. (civic), 1886; pres. Spanish-Am. Normal Sch., 1909-12. Commr. Chicago Expn., 1893, Omaha Expn., 1899; juror of anthropology and history, St. Louis Expn., 1904. In 1880 was originator of Am. Ch. Building Fund, and devoted several yrs. to it till thoroughly established, trustee 1880—; chancellor, P.E. Dist. of N.M., 1880—; president Assn. Church Chancellors, 1919—. 1st pres. Laymen's League P.E. Ch., 1916—. Made Tercentenary Mayflower address at Plymouth, Mass., Nov. 20, 1920. Has the largest collection of Am. stone idols in existence. Prominent in Masonry, D.D.G.M. 5 terms in N.Y. Pres. Am. Apple Congress, 1910-11; v.p. Nat. Hist. Soc., 1915—; organized Soc. Preservation of Spanish Antiquities, 1913 (first pres.

1913—); hon. mem. Am. Numismatic Soc.; mem. council of governors National Highways Assn. Author: Concise History of New Mexico, 1912; Students' History of New Mexico, 1913; Spanish Mission Churches of New Mexico, 1915; Abraham Lincoln, the Man, 1917. Home: Santa Fé, N.M. Died Dec. 7, 1922.

PRINCE, Leon Cushing, coll. prof.; b. Concord, N.H.; s. Morris Watson and Katherine Buck (Farnham) P.; student New York U.; A.B., Dickinson Coll., Pa., 1898, A.M., 1900; LL.B., Dickinson Sch. of Law, 1900; attended art schs. of N.Y. City; Litt.D., Albright Coll., Pa., 1917; m. Julia C. Delavan, May 31, 1910; 1 dau., Mary DeIavan. Admitted to Pa. bar; admitted N.Y. East Conf. Methodist Church as mem, active ministry, 1900; prof. history, Dickinson Coll., 1909—; elected to State Senate of Pa., 1928, reëlected, 1932. Mem. Com. Public Safety Cumberland Co., Pa., World War; official war historian for Cumberland Co. Awarded Distinguished Service Certificate, Am. Legion. Republican. Kiwanian. Author: A Bird's Eye View of Am. History, 1907; The Sense and Nonsense of Christian Science, 1911; World Federation—A Myth or a Menace? 1912; America's Holy War, 1918; The American Soldier, 1919; The Man Who Dares, 1920; Pharaoh's Question, 1927. Editor: (with Prof. Lewis H. Chrisman) Selections from Speeches of Abraham Lincoln, 1912. Lecturer on popular subjects and occasional orator. Lincoln's Birthday orator on joint invitation of House and Senate of Pa. legislature. Home: Carlisle, Pa. Died Jan. 31, 1937.

PRINCE, Morton, M.D.; b. Boston, Mass., Dec. 21, 1854; s. Frederick Octavus and Helen Susan (Henry) P.; A.B., Harvard, 1875, M.D., 1879; LL.D., Tufts Coll., Mass., 1910; m. Fanny Lithgow Payson, Feb. 14, 1885; children—Mrs. Clara Morton Walcott, Morton Peabody. Practiced in Boston, 1880—; phys. for nervous diseases, Boston City Hosp., 1885-1913, consulting phys., 1914—; prof. nervous diseases, 1902-12, prof. emeritus, 1912, Tufts Coll. Med. Sch. Lecturer abnormal psychology, University of Calif., 1910; asso. prof. abnormal and dynamic psychology, Harvard University, 1926—. Editor Jour. Abnormal and Social Psychology, 1906—. Chmn. Boston Charter Assn. Commd. by the gov. as mgr. of Mass. Soldiers and Sailors Information Bur. in Paris, representing State of Mass. in France, 1918-19; instigated and organized the "Address [of the 500 Americans] to the Peoples of the Allied Nations," 1916; chmn. Serbian Distress Fund, 1915—; chmn. reception com. of Boston for Japanese Mission, Dec. 1917, and Serbian Mission, Jan. 1918; chmn. State and Boston reception committees for Marshal Foch, 1921, and of State Com. for General Diaz, 1921. Decorated Order Chevalier of St. Sava (Serbia), 1916; Order Rising Sun (Japan), 1918; Cross Legion of Honor (France), 1919; Royal Order of Red Cross and Order of the White Eagle (Serbia), 1920. Author: Nature of Mind and Human Automatism, 1885; Dissociation of a Personality, 1906; The Unconscious, 1913; The Psychology of the Kaiser, 1915; The Creed of Deutschtum, 1918. Collaborator: Nervous Diseases by American Authors; Am. System of Practical Medicine; Internat. System of Electro-Therapeutics. Home: Boston, Mass. Died Aug. 31, 1929.

PRINCE, Walter Franklin, psychical researcher; b. Detroit, Me., Apr. 22, 1863; s. Walter Marshall and Elmira Jane (Pray) P.; grad. Me. Wesleyan Sem., 1881; A.B., Yale, 1896, Ph.D., 1899; B.D., Drew Theol. Sem., 1896; m. Lelia M. Colman, Apr. 9, 1885 (died 1925); foster dau., Theodosia B. Pastor of M.E. churches and afterwards in P.E. chs.; latterly, asst. St. Ann's Ch., Brooklyn, N.Y., 1904; rector All Saints' Ch., Pittsburgh, 1907, St. John's Ch., San Bernardino, Calif., 1912; apptd. dir. dept. of psychotherapeutics St. Mark's Ch., New York, 1916. Investigator for Am. Soc. for Psychical Research, 1917-20; principal research officer same, 1920-25; exec. research officer Boston Soc. for Psychic Research, Mar. 1925—. Editor and secretary of advisory scientific council Am. Soc. for Psychical Research, 1921-23. Field sec. Conn. Temperance Union, 1899; asst. sec. Conn. Law and Order League, 1899; supt. Brooklyn Soc. Prevention Cruelty to Children, 1903. Author: The Doris Case of Multiple Personality (2 vols.), 1915; The Psychic in the House, 1925; The Case of Patience Worth, 1927; Noted Witnesses for Psychic Research, 1928; Leonard and Soule Experiments in Psychical Research (with Lydia W. Allison), 1929; The Enchanted Boundary, 1930; Census Report, 1931. Home: Hingham, Mass. Died Aug. 7, 1934.

PRINDLE, Franklin Cogswell, officer U.S.N.; b. Sandgate, Vt., July 8, 1841; s. Hawley and Olive (Andrew) P.; ed. pub. schs. and Rensselaer Poly. Inst., Troy, N.Y.; thrice married; m. 3d, Mrs. Fidelia E. (White) Mead, Apr. 8, 1896. Apptd. 3d asst. engr., Aug. 3, 1861; 2d asst. engr., Apr. 21, 1863; civ. engr. U.S.N., Apr. 17, 1869; retired with rank of rear adm., Feb. 27, 1901, on account of disability incurred in line of duty. Served in S. Atlantic Blockading Squadron and participated in many engagements under Commodores Dupont and Dahlgren during Civil War; served as civ. engr. of navy yards and stations, and in constrn. of naval training sta., Yerba Buena Island, San Francisco Bay, 1898-1900. Engr. and sec. Am. Dredging Co., Phila., 1876-77; engr. and supt., also sec. and treas., Carolina Oil & Creosote Co., Wilmington, N.C., 1888-90; dir., v.p., pres. Aztec Oil Co., Bakersfield, Calif., 1900-04. Republican. Baptist. Mason. Author: The Prindle Genealogy, 1906. Home: Washington, D.C. Died Mar. 7, 1923.

PRINGLE, Coleman Roberson, planter; b. Monroe Co., Ga., in the '30s; s. Coleman S. and K. P.; brought up on farm; m. Leonora G. Brantley, 1861. Moved to Sandersville, Ga., 1862; mayor Sandersville, Ga., 1871; mem. Ga. Ho. of Reps., 1882-83, 1883-95; Ga. senate, 1886-87; railroad pres. 18 yrs.; pres. Southern Forestry Congress, 1886-87; pres. U.S. Forestry Congress, 1888; pres. Ga. Prohibition Assn., 1883—. Home: Sandersville, Ga. Died 1905.

PRINGLE, Cyrus Guernsey, botanist; b. Charlotte, Vt., May 6, 1838; s. George and Louisa (Harris) P.; classical edn. in various schs. of Vt. and Canada; (hon. A.M., Middlebury Coll., 1876; Sc.D., U. of Vt., 1906). Collected extensively in forestry and gen. botany in Ariz., Sonora, Calif., Ore., and Wash., as collector for Am. Mus. Natural History, New York, 1881-84; bot. collector to Harvard U., 1885—; also keeper herbarium to U. of Vt. Has been engaged upon the thorough exploration of the flora of Old Mexico, placing large collections (about one in five of the plants new species) in 50 or more of the most important herbaria of the world. From 1888-94 contributed to Garden and Forest, Notes on the Forest Vegetation of Mexico, and Notes on Botanical Travel in Mexico. Asso. fellow Am. Acad. Arts and Sciences. Home: Burlington, Vt. Died 1911.

PRINGLE, Joel Roberts Poinsett, rear adm.; b. Georgetown, S.C., Feb. 4, 1873; s. Dominick Lynch and Caroline (Lowndes) P.; grad. U.S. Naval Acad., 1892; m. Cordelia Phythian, Jan. 25, 1899; 1 dau., Cordelia Phythian (wife of Lieut. J. D. H. Kane, U.S.N.). Commd. ensign U.S.N., July 1, 1894; advanced through grades to rear adm., Dec. 6, 1926. Became pres. Naval War Coll., Newport, R.I., 1927; now comdr. Battleship Div. 3. Died Sept. 25, 1932.

PRINGLE, Ralph, lawyer; b. Pana, Ill., Oct. 15, 1872; s. James V. and Ida (Hoopes) P.; B.A., Monmouth (Ill.) Coll., 1893; B.A., Yale, 1894; studied law State U. of Ia., 1894; m. Luella Houghton, Sept. 26, 1905. Began practice at Red Oak, 1896; mem. Rep. State Central Com., 1910-14; Rep. elector at large from Ia., 1916; U.S. atty. Southern Dist. of Ia., by apptmt. of President Harding, June 19, 1922—. Mem. Ia. State Bd. Law Examiners 15 yrs.; mem. bd. trustees Pub. Library, Red Oak. United Presbyn. K.P. Home: Red Oak, Iowa. Died Apr. 7, 1924.

PRINGLE, Robert Smith, architect; b. Summerville, S.C., Nov. 11, 1883; s. Robert Smith and Maria H. (White) P.; ed. pub. schs., Charleston and Columbia, S.C., and Verners Acad., Columbia; m. Sibylla Walker, Oct. 10, 1910; children—Robert Smith, St. Julienne Walker, Sibylla Walker, Mary Alston. Began practice at Columbia, 1902; moved to Atlanta, Ga., 1907; former partner Pringle & Smith; dir. Fulton Nat. Bank. Prin. works: First Nat. Bank, William-Oliver Bldg., W. W. Orr Doctors Bldg., Rhodes-Haverty Office Bldg., Norris Bldg., Cox-Carlton Hotel, Fulton Nat. Bank (Atlanta); Lynch Office Bldg., Jacksonville, Fla.; Venetian Hotel, Miami, Fla.; Forest Hills Ricker Hotel, Augusta, Ga. Mem. Am. Inst. Architects (pres. Ga. chapter). Democrat. Episcopalian. Mason. Home: Atlanta, Ga. Died Dec. 9, 1937.

PRINGLE, William James, lawyer; b. Madrid, N.Y., June 10, 1862; s. William and Mary Belle Pringle; Ph.B., Grinnell (Ia.) Coll., 1885, A.M., 1888; principal pub. schs., Elmwood, Ill., supt. schs., Northfield, Minn., and prin. high sch., Aurora, Ill.; student law dept. Cornell U.; LL.B., Lake Forest U., 1896; D.C.L. Chicago Law Sch., 1897; m. Dorothy Sisson Gorham, June 26, 1899; children—William J., Margaret M. In practice at Chicago, 1898—. Mem. City Council, Chicago, 4 terms, 1904-12; chmn. Com. on Gas, Oil and Electric Light 4 yrs., making reports on telephone and gas rates; mem. arbitration bd. to fix gas rates for City of Galesburg, Ill.; lecturer on law of torts and law of agency, Chicago-Kent Coll. of Law, 1898-1928. Mason. Home: Chicago, Ill. Died June 11, 1938.

PRISK, Charles Henry, editor, pub.; b. Grass Valley, Calif., Dec. 24, 1875; s. William and Mary (Hosking) P.; ed. Stanford 2 yrs.; m. Mabel P. Peterson, June 3, 1903; 1 dau., Neva Jorstad (Mrs. Charles W. Paddock). Began with The Morning Union, Grass Valley, Calif., later editor Register, Watsonville, Calif.; with others, in 1904, purchased Pasadena Star, which was merged, 1916, with Pasadena News, of which is editor and mgr.; also editor and mgr. Pasadena Post, 1932—; pres. Star-News Pub. Co., Star-News Bldg. Co. Awarded Arthur Noble gold medal for outstanding civic service. Mem. California Inst. of Associates. Republican. Presbyn. Mason. Elk. Home: Pasadena, Calif. Died Mar. 4, 1940.

PRITCHARD, Arthur John, officer U.S.N.; b. Dorchester Co., Md., Feb. 12, 1836; s. Nicholas B. and Elizabeth A. P.; pub. sch. edn.; m. Sarah E. Harrington, Oct. 19, 1871. Entered U.S.N. as asst. p.-m., Oct. 7, 1861; promoted p.-m., 1864; pay insp., Dec. 24, 1883; pay dir., 1895; retired, Feb. 12, 1898; advanced to rank of rear adm. retired, June 29, 1906. Served in Itaska, in Rear Admiral Farragut's Squadron, 1861-63, participating in engagements on Miss. River; wounded, 1862, and incapacitated 7 months; served in Wyalusing, 1863-64; Ticonderoga, European Sta., 1864-69; Benicia, 1869-71; sick leave, 1871-72; in Saranac, N. Pacific Squadron, 1872-75; Powhatan, 1875-77; trainingship Minnesota, 1878-81; served at navy pay office, Baltimore, 1882-85, 1888-92, 1896-98, 1902-05; in Pensacola, 1885-88; served navy pay office, Norfolk, Va., 1893-96. Mason. Republican. Home: Baltimore, Md. Died Sept. 5, 1916.

PRITCHARD, Arthur Thomas, M.D., surgeon; b. Marshall, N.C., Jan. 28, 1882; s. Judge Jeter C. and Augusta Lilian (Ray) P.; ed. Horner Mil. Sch., Oxford, N.C., and U. of N.C.; M.D., Jefferson Med. Coll., Phila., 1905; m. Robin Gertrude Kennett, June 6, 1910; 1 son, Arthur Thomas. Practiced at Asheville, 1906—; a founder and pres. French Brood Hosp. Commd. capt., later maj., Med. Corps, U.S.A., World War; served at Base Hosp. No. 65, Evacuation Hosp. No. 11; duty at Argonne; hon. disch., Apr. 6, 1919. Fellow Am. Coll. Surgeons. Republican. Baptist. Mason. Home: Asheville, N.C. Died May 26, 1927.

PRITCHARD, Harry Otis, educator; b. Johnson Co., Ind., July 10, 1876; s. Edgar Daily and Julia Ann (Mitchell) P.; A.B., Butler Coll., 1902; A.M., U. of Indianapolis, 1903; B.D., Yale, 1906; LL.D., Cotner Coll., Lincoln, Neb., 1916, Tex. Christian U., Fort Worth, Tex., 1922; m. Hattie Macauley Byers, Aug. 28, 1901; children—Helen Louise (Mrs. Wilson D. Criswell), Grace Jayne (Mrs. Walter E. Houck), Harmon Otis, Paul Byers, Robert Claire. Pastor Cotner Coll., 1907-13; pres. Eureka (Ill.) Coll., 1913-19; Bondurant lecturer, U. of Ill., 1916; alumnus lecturer, Yale, 1917; gen. sec. nat. bd. of edn. of Disciples of Christ, Indianapolis, 1919—, also mem. exec. com. Pres. Council of Ch. Bds. of Edn. in America, 1923-24; advisory mem. Am. Council on Edn.; mem. ednl. com. Near East Relief; mem. Commn. on Internat. Good Will, Federal Council of Chs. of Christ in America; official rep. Boy Scouts of America. Mason, K.P. Home: Indianapolis, Ind. Died Oct. 24, 1936.

PRITCHARD, Jeter Connelly, judge; b. Jonesboro, Tenn., July 12, 1857; s. W. H. and Elizabeth P.; common sch. edn. Joint editor and owner Roan Mountain Republican, 1875-87; admitted to bar, 1887; practiced at Marshall, N.C.; presdl. elector, 1880; mem. N.C. Ho. of Rep., 1884, 86, 90; Rep. candidate for lt. gov., 1888, for U.S. senator, 1891, for Congress, 1892; U.S. senator, 1894-1903; asso. justice Supreme Ct. of D.C., 1903; U.S. circuit judge, 4th Circuit, 1904-11; judge U.S. Circuit Ct. of Appeals, Jan. 1, 1912—. Pres. N.C. Protective Tariff League, 1891. Home: Asheville, N.C. Died Apr. 10, 1921.

PRITCHARD, John Wagner, editor; b. Pittsburgh, Pa., Aug. 4, 1851; s. Arthur and Ann (Pickett) P.; ed. Cooper Union, New York, Schoomaker's Sch. of Oratory, Phila., and under pvt. tutors; m. Harriet Small, May 18, 1872. Began as editor and mgr. The Daily Paragon, McKeesport, Pa., 1870; later on staff Pittsburgh Dispatch; was contbr. Pittsburgh Chronicle-Telegraph, Leader and Gazette-Times; editor and mgr. The Christian Nation (weekly), and pres. Christian Nation Pub. Co., 1884—. Author: Soldiers of the Church, 1919. Creator of Ref. Presbyn. Ch. Service Flag (War of 1914-18), accepted by U.S. Govt. for permanent exhibition in Nat. Mus., Washington; also author of presentation address to Govt., printed together with lithographed copy of the original service flag and replicas on permanent exhibition in Nat. Mus., Legislative Library in Capitol, Albany, Presbyn. Hist. Soc., Phila., etc. Home: Montclair, N.J. Died Mar. 1, 1924.

PRITCHARD, Myron Thomas, educator, writer; b. North Adams, Mass., July 27, 1853; s. Thomas and Elizabeth R. P.; A.B., Boston Univ., 1878; hon. Litt.D., Rollins College, Winter Park, Fla., 1928. Principal Comins School, Boston, 1878-94; principal Everett School, Boston, 1894-1922 (emeritus). Former v.p. and lit. editor Lothrop Pub. Co.; former editor-in-chief of Goldthwaites Geographical Magazine, also of Minerals, Teachers' World, and Public School Education. Pres. Young People's Loyal League, New England Conf. of Ednl. Workers. Pres. Seabreeze-Daytona Beach Sch. Bd. and of Halix Bird Study Club; chmn. exec. committee Florida Audubon Soc.; hon. pres. Daytona Beach Rollins Coll. Alumni Assn. Author: Poetry of Niagara, 1901. Joint author: Howe Readers; Gate to English; Heart of America Readers: Stories of Thrift for Young Americans; The Upward Path; Lessons in Citizenship. Home: Daytona Beach, Fla. Died Jan. 23, 1935.

PRITCHARD, Samuel Reynolds, prof. elec. engring.; b. Bascomville, S.C., Oct. 30, 1863; s. Claudius Hornby and Mary Blount (Reynolds) P.; student Wofford Coll., Spartanburg, S.C.; A.B., S.C. Coll., 1885; M.A., U. of S.C., 1889, Sc.D., 1932; m. Mary,

d. Hon. David Wyatt Aiken, of Cokesbury, S.C., June 20, 1895; children—Claudius Hornby, Virginia Aiken, Samuel Reynolds. Tutor and instr. mathematics, S.C. Coll., 1886-90; asst. prof. mathematics, Wofford Coll., 1890-93; prof. elec. engring. Va. Poly. Inst., 1893—; also dean of engring., 1918-28. Democrat. Methodist. Home: Blacksburg, Va. Died Sept. 30, 1935.

PRITCHARD, Stuart, M.D.; b. Auburn, Ont., Can., Mar. 31, 1882; s. Rev. James and Christina (McCrostie) P.; ed. Forest High Sch. and Goderich Collegiate Inst.; M.D., U. of Toronto, 1905; spent 10 yrs. in hosps. studying diseases of the lungs and bronchi; m. Myra Bradwell, d. Frank A. and Bessie Bradwell Helmer; g.d. Judge James and Myra Bradwell, 1915. In charge chest dept., Battle creek Sanitarium, 1913-30; pres. and gen. dir. W. K. Kellogg Foundation, Battle Creek, Mich., 1930—. U.S. del. Internat. Conf. on Tuberculosis, Rome, Italy, 1928; U.S. del. to 8th Conf. of Internat. Union Against Tuberculosis, Amsterdam and The Hague, 1932. Fellow Am. Coll. Physicians, A.M.A. Mem. numerous professional societies. Died Aug. 4, 1940.

PRITCHARD, William Hobbs, hosp. administrator; b. nr. Clarksville, O., Nov. 14, 1866; s. Calvin W. and Anna M. (Pyle) P.; M.D., Miami Med. Coll. (U. of Cincinnati), 1900; m. Helen Landacre Fishinger, Sept. 10, 1903; children—William Landacre, Marianna (Mrs. Robin Sharp). Interne, Cincinnati Gen. Hosp., 1900-01); phys. Columbus State Hosp., 1901-03, supt., 1916—; phys. Ohio Hosp. for Epileptics, Gallipolis, O., 1903-05, supt., 1905-11; spl. pvt. practice at Gallipolis, 1911-16; teacher of psychiatry, Ohio State U., 1918—. Served in Med. Corps, U.S.A., Camp Sherman, World War. Republican. Methodist. Mason. Home: Columbus, O. Died Nov. 11, 1936.

PRITCHETT, Carr Waller, clergyman, educator; b. Henry Co., Va., Sept. 4, 1823; self educated, with 8 months at St. Charles Coll., Mo., at 21 yrs. of age; spl. student astronomy and mathematics at Cambridge, Mass., 1858-59; (hon. A.M., St. Charles Coll., Mo., 1852, LL.D., Central Coll., Fayette, Mo., 1884); m. 1849, Betty Susan Smith (died 1872). M.E. clergyman; teacher 30 yrs.; helped organize Central Coll. and acted as pres. on 2 different occasions; organized Pritchett Coll., Glasgow, Mo., 1866, and was pres. 7 yrs. Astronomer, 1875—; fellow Royal Astron. Soc., 1879. Author: Publications of the Morrison Observatory, No. 1, 1885. Home: Glasgow, Mo. Died 1910.

PRITCHETT, Henry Smith, educator; b. Fayette, Mo., Apr. 16, 1857; s. Carr Waller and Betty Susan (Smith) P.; A.B., Pritchett Coll., Glasgow, Mo., 1875; Ph.D., Munich, 1894; LL.D., Hamilton Coll., 1900, U. of Pa., 1901, Harvard, Yale, 1901, Johns Hopkins, 1902, Williams Coll., U. of Mich., 1905, U. of Toronto, 1906, Brown, 1908, Miami, 1910, U. of Vt., 1911. Washington, 1915, McGill, 1917, Western Reserve, 1918, Dalhousie, 1919, U. of Colo., 1923, Union, 1924; Sc.D., Tufts Coll., 1905, Stevens Inst. Tech., 1908; Litt.D., Whitman Coll., 1919; m. Eva, d. Hall McAllister, of San Francisco, June 1900. Student with Asaph Hall in U.S. Naval Obs., 1876; asst. astronomer same, 1878; astronomer Morrison Obs., Glasgow, Mo., 1880; astronomer Transit of Venus expdn. to New Zealand, 1882; prof. astronomy and dir. obs., Washington U., St. Louis, 1883-97; supt. U.S. Coast and Geod. Survey, 1897-1900; pres. Mass. Inst. of Tech., 1900-06; pres. Carnegie Foundation for Advancement of Teaching, 1906-30 (emeritus). Dir. A.T.&S.F. Ry. Co., Nat. Broadcasting Co. (adv. council). Trustee Carnegie Instn. of Washington, Carnegie Endowment for Internat. Peace, etc. Chevalier Legion of Honor, 1922; Gold Cross Comdr., Order of George I (Greece), 1923. Home: Santa Barbara, Calif., and New York, N.Y. Died Aug. 28, 1939.

PRIZER, Edward, chmn. Vacuum Oil Co.; b. Doylestown, Pa., Mar. 3, 1856; s. Enos and Sarah (Levis) P.; ed. pub. schs. and sem.; m. Mary Crowther, Nov. 10, 1882. Began as reporter country newspaper and became business mgr.; connected with Vacuum Oil Co., 1882—, became pres., 1917, chmn. bd., 1924; dir. Savings, Investment & Trust Co., East Orange, N.J. Mem. petroleum war service com., World War. Dir. Am. Petroleum Inst. Trustee Orange Memorial Hosp. Republican. Presbyterian. Home: East Orange, N.J. Died Aug. 11, 1929.

PROBASCO, Henry, merchant; formerly in the hardware trade in Cincinnati; retired with a fortune; gave the city the Tyler-Davidson fountain on 5th St.; has been identified with much public-spirited work. Home: Clifton, Cincinnati, O. Died 1902.

PROBERT, Frank Holman, mining engr.; b. London, Eng., June 13, 1876; s. Isaac and Mary J. (Holman) P.; nat. biol. scholar, Royal Coll. Science, London, 1893; associate Royal Sch. of Mines, London, 1897; m. Jessie Agnes McGaw, May 25, 1907; 1 son, Aylwin. Engaged in investigation of mineral resources N.W. Ont., Can., 1897-98; gen. mgr. of Llanfair lead mines, N. Wales, 1898-99; mgr. Anhaltische Blei und Silberwerke, Anhalt, Germany, 1899-1900; engring. research in Ariz., for Phelps, Dodge & Co., New York, 1901-02; consulting engr., Los Angeles, Calif., 1902-09; Weed & Probert, Los Angeles and New York, 1910-12, etc.; prof. mining, 1916, dean Coll. of Mining, 1917—, U. of Calif.; consulting

engr. U.S. Bur. Mines, 1918—. Mem. spl. com. on war minerals investigation, U.S. Bur. of Mines, 1917-18; mem. Am. mining mission to Europe for investigation of mineral industry, and reparation in Northern France, 1919. Episcopalian. Died May 7, 1940.

PROBERT, Lionel Charles, ry. official; b. Batavia, N.Y., Nov. 18, 1883; ed. pub. schs.; m. Adelaide R. Taber, Oct. 22, 1909. Successively a day laborer, locomotive fireman, then engaged in engring. in railway construction, and newspaper reporter; successively vice-pres. Erie R.R., Pere Marquette Ry.; vice-pres. Chesapeake & Ohio Lines. Home: Olney, Md. Died Feb. 2, 1937.

PROBST, Charles Oliver, M.D.; b. Middleport, O., Dec. 4, 1857; s. William B. and Martha (Grant) P.; M.D., Miami Med. Coll., Cincinnati, 1882; m. Eva Lee Knight, Sept. 28, 1881. Engaged in practice, 1882—; sec. State Bd. Health 25 years from 1886. Pres. Am. Pub. Health Assn., Ohio Soc. Prevention Tuberculosis; pres. and sec. State and Provincial Bds. of Health. Mem. State Health Council. Republican. Home: Columbus, O. Died Apr. 2, 1933.

PROCTER, Addison Gilbert; b. Gloucester, Mass., July 29, 1838; s. Joseph J. and Eliza A. (Gilbert) P.; grad. high sch., Gloucester; m. Eliza B. Calef, July 10, 1860 (died 1918). A pioneer of Kan., 1857; active in free state movement; elected del. to Rep. Nat. Conv., 1860, at age of 21; the youngest and last surviving mem. of the conv. that nominated Abraham Lincoln for the presidency. In mercantile business 35 yrs. Conglist. Lecturer on personal reminiscences of Abraham Lincoln and his times. Home: St. Joseph, Mich. Died Feb. 17, 1925.

PROCTER, William Cooper mfr.; b. Glendale, O., Aug. 25, 1862; s. William A. and Charlotte Elizabeth (Jackson) P.; B.S., Princeton, 1883; LL.D., U. of Cincinnati, 1922; m. Jane Eliza Johnston, 1889. With the Procter & Gamble Co., soap mfrs., 1883—, pres., 1907-30, chmn. bd., Oct. 14, 1930—; dir. N.Y.C. R.R., 1927. Trustee Princeton U.; pres. Cincinnati Inst. of Fine Arts, Cincinnati Children's Hosp. Republican. Episcopalian. Home: Glendale, O. Died May 2, 1934.

PROCTOR, Edna Dean, author; b. Henniker, N.H., Sept. 18, 1829; d. John and Lucinda (Gould) P. Has traveled much abroad; lived some yrs. in Brooklyn. Author: Poems, 1866; A Russion Journey, 1872; Poems, 1890; The Song of the Ancient People, 1892; Mountain Maid and Other Poems of New Hampshire, 1900; Songs of America, 1906; The Glory of Toil, 1916. On Columbus Day, Oct. 12, 1892, her poem "Columbia's Banner" was part of the official program for the schools throughout the country; her song "Columbia's Emblem," celebrating the maize as nat. floral symbol, is well known. Contbr. "Letters from Abroad," 1867, and "From the Narrows to the Golden Gate," 1869, to New York Independent. Has been a life-long friend of the Indian. Home: Framingham, Mass. Died Dec. 18, 1923.

PROCTOR, Fletcher Dutton, governor; b. Cavendish, Vt., Nov. 7, 1860; s. Senator Redfield and Emily J. (Dutton) P.; student Amherst, class of 1882, A.B., 1891; (LL.D., Middlebury, 1908); m. Minnie E. Robinson, May 26, 1886. Pres. Vt. Marble Co., 1889—, Proctor Trust Co., Barney Marble Co. Mem. Vt. Ho. of Rep., 1890, Senate, 1892, Ho. of Rep., 1900, 1904 (speaker 1900) gov. of Vt., 1906-08. Republican. Home: Proctor, Vt. Died 1911.

PROCTOR, Frederick Cocke, lawyer; b. Indianola, Tex., Feb. 19, 1866; s. David Cogswell and Ann Augusta (Cocke) P.; student U. of Tex., 1883-87; m. Lucy Wofford, Dec. 10, 1889; children—David C., Josephine (Mrs. Walter Weber), Lucy (Mrs. G. Jerenee Kenyon). Practiced at Victoria, Tex., 1887-1905; removed to Beaumont, 1905, to Houston, 1916; gen. counsel Gulf Oil Cos., 1905-19. Democrat. Home: Houston, Tex. Died May 1935.

PROCTOR, Henry Hugh, clergyman; b. Fayetteville, Tenn., Dec. 8, 1868; s. Richard and Hannah (Proctor) P.; A.B., Fisk U., Tenn., 1891; B.D., Yale Div. Sch., 1894; D.D., Clark U., Ga., 1904; m. Adeline Davis, Aug. 16, 1893; children—Henry Hugh, Richard Davis (dec.), Muriel Morgan, Lillian Steele, Roy Cravath, Vashti Adeline. Ordained Congl. ministry, 1894; pastor First Ch., Atlanta, Ga., 1894-1920, Nazarene Ch., Brooklyn, 1920—. Corporate mem. A.B.C.F.M. Republican. Author: Sermons in Melody, 1916; Between Black and White, 1925. Home: Brooklyn, N.Y. Died May 12, 1933.

PROCTOR, John Robert, pres. U.S. Civil Service Commn., Dec. 1893—; b. Mason Co., Ky., March 16, 1844; took scientific course, Univ. of Pa., but left to serve, 1864-65, in confederate army; farmed, 1865-73; asst. Ky. geol. survey, 1873-80; State geologist, Ky., 1880-93; mem. U.S. Civil Service Commn., 1893—; mem. jury of awards on mines and mining, World's Columbian Expn. Home: Washington, D.C. Died 1903.

PROCTOR, John Thomas, missionary; b. Palmyra, Mo., Mar. 11, 1869; s. David M. and Emma (Redd) P.; A.B., William Jewell Coll., Mo., 1891 (D.D., 1911); B.D., U. of Chicago Div. Sch., 1897; m.

Nellie M. Burt, Dec. 16, 1896. Ordained Bapt. ministry, 1891; pastor Rosedale, Kan., 1891-92, Windsor Park, Chicago, 1893-95, Belton, Mo., 1896-97; missionary in China, 1897—. Pres. Shanghai Bapt. Coll., 1906-11; exec. sec. East China Bapt. Conference. Died Dec. 8, 1927.

PROCTOR, Redfield, U.S. senator; b. Proctorsville, Vt., June 1, 1831; s. Jabez and Betsey (Parker) P.; A.B., 1851, A.M., 1854, Dartmouth Coll.; LL.B., Albany Law Sch., 1860; m. Emily J. Dutton, May 26, 1858. Practiced law, Boston, 1860-61; enlisted as q.m. 3d Vt. regt., 1861; promoted maj. 5th Vt. regt., Sept. 1861, col. 15th Vt. vols., 1862; served as brigade and div. q.m. on staff Gen. William F. Smith; mustered out, 1863. Long head of largest mable producing co. in the world; retired. Mem. Vt. legislature, 1867, 1868, 1888; mem. and pres. pro tem. Vt. Senate, 1874-75; lt. gov. Vt., 1876-78; gov., 1878-80; sec. of war, U.S., 1889-91; U.S. senator, Vt., 1891-1911. Republican. Visited Cuba, Mar. 1898, and his speech on Cuban reconcentrados in senate after his return attracted wide attention. Home: Proctor, Vt. Died 1908.

PROCTOR, Thomas Redfield, banker; b. Proctorsville, Vt., May 25, 1844; s. Moody S. and Betsey N. (Redfield) P.; ed. English High Sch., Boston, but left just before graduation to enter U.S.N., in Civil War; (M.A., Hamilton Coll.); m. Maria W. Williams, Apr. 9, 1891. Pres. Second Nat. Bank, Utica, N.Y., Am. Hard Wall Plaster Co.; v.p. Utica Daily Press Co.; trustee Utica Savings Bank, Utica Trust Co., Utica Steam Cotton Mills, Utica Cemetery Assn. Mem. bd. visitors U.S. Naval Acad., 1910; del. 3d Nat. Peace Congress, Baltimore, 1911. Decorated by Emperor of Japan. Pres. bd. trustees House of the Good Shepherd. Mem. numerous societies. Trustee Hamilton Coll. Mason. Warden Grace Ch., Utica. Home: Utica, N.Y. Died July 4, 1920.

PROCTOR, Thomas William, lawyer; b. Hollis, N.H., Nov. 20, 1858; s. Thomas and Susan R. (Pool) P.; prep. edn., Lawrence Acad., Groton, Mass., 1873-75; A.B., Dartmouth, 1879; LL.B., Boston U. Law Sch., 1912 as of 1884; m. Anne Louise White, Mar. 20, 1895; children—Thomas White, Robert, Mary. Admitted to Mass. bar, 1883, and began practice at Boston; mem. Hardy, Elder & Proctor, 1884-85, Elder & Proctor, 1885-86, Nason & Proctor, 1894—; prof. law, Boston U. Law Sch., 1919—; trustee Hamilton Assn. (Boston), Newton (Mass.) Savings Bank. Asst. dist. atty., Boston, 1886-91; asst. city solicitor, Boston, 1891-94. Democrat. Home: Boston, Mass. Died June 30, 1931.

PROCTOR, William Martin, prof. secondary edn.; b. Denver, Colo., Jan. 26, 1875; s. Alexander and Tirzah (Smith) P.; U. of Wash., 1896-97; A.B., Whitman Coll., 1901; B.D., Chicago Theol. Sem., 1904; M.A., Stanford U., 1916, Ph.D., 1919; m. Agnes Adams, June 15, 1901; children—Stephen Alexander (died in infancy), Ruth Agnes, William Adams. Court reporter, Snohomish, Wash., 1893-96; minister Congl. Ch., 1904-09; teacher State Normal Sch., Cheney, Wash., 1909-11; prof. education and dean of faculty, Pacific U., Forest Grove, Ore., 1911-15; teaching asst. and instr., Stanford, 1916-19, asst. prof. secondary edn., 1919-23, associate prof., 1923-26, prof., 1926—, now also faculty sec. School of Education; teacher summer sessions, Harvard, 1922, Columbia, 1924, U. of Minn., 1925, U. of Wash., 1927, U. of Southern Calif., 1929, Claremont Colls., 1932. Ednl. dir. Camp Fremont, Calif., 1917-18; coördinator U.S. Vets. Bur., Stanford U., 1919-23. Mem. Bd. of Edn., Los Altos, Calif., 1918-19; dir. curriculum revision, San Francisco, 1925-30, Sacramento, 1928-31; dir. research studies, Pasadena, 1931-32. Dir. Menlo Jr. Coll., Menlo Park, Calif. (chmn. exec. com.). Pres. Nat. Vocational Guidance Assn., 1933-34; mem. Nat. Occupations Conf., 1933-34. Republican. Conglist. Author: Psychological Tests and Guidance of High School Pupils, 1921; Educational and Vocational Guidance, 1925; Vocations, 1929; The Junior High School (with Nicholas Ricciardi), 1930; Workbook in Vocations (with C. W. Wrenn and G. R. Benefield), 1931. Editor: The Junior College, 1927; The Six-Four-Four Plan of Pasadena, 1933; also (with Fred Englehardt) Monograph No. 8, District Organization (U.S. Bureau of Edn., Bull. No. 17), 1932; Annotated Bibliography on Adult Education, 1935. Home: Stanford Univ., Calif. Died Oct. 28, 1937.

PROKOSCH, Eduard, univ. prof.; b. Eger, Austria, May 15, 1876; s. Wenzel and Marie (Fischer) P.; grad. Gymnasium, Eger, 1894; state examination, U. of Vienna, 1897; came to America, 1898; grad. Nat. German-Am. Teachers' Sem., Milwaukee, Wis., 1900; A.M., U. of Chicago, 1901; Ph.D., U. of Leipzig, 1905; m. Mathilde Dapprich, June 17, 1901; children—Gertrude, Frederic, Walther. Instr. in German, U. of Chicago, 1901-04; instr. in German, U. of Wis. 1905-09, asst. prof., 1909-13; prof. Germanic philology, U. of Tex., 1913; lecturer in German, Bryn Mawr Coll., 1919-20, asso. prof., 1920-26, prof., 1926-28; Sterling research fellow, Yale, 1927-28, prof. Germanic langs., 1929, Sterling prof., 1930—; head of German dept., New York U., 1927-29, visiting prof., 1929-31 and 1933-34. Author: Introduction to

German, 1911, 24, also other German textbooks; Teaching of German in Secondary Schools, 1915; Sounds and History of the German Language, 1916; Elementary Russian Grammar, 1919; College Teaching of German, 1920; Rhythmus and Persönlichkeit in Goethe's Faust, 1925; Sprachgeschichte und Sprachunterricht, 1930; Outline of German Historical Grammar, 1933; Comparative Grammar of the Germanic Languages, 1937. Died Aug. 11, 1938.

PROSSER, Charles Smith, educator, geologist; b. Columbus, N.Y., Mar. 24, 1860; s. Smith and Emeline A. (Tuttle) P.; B.S., Cornell, 1883, M.S., 1886; (D.Sc., Union U., 1906); Ph.D., Cornell, 1907; m. Mary F. Wilson, Aug. 28, 1893. Instr. paleontology, Cornell, 1885-88; asst. paleontologist U.S. Geol. Survey, 1888-92; prof. natural history, Washburn Coll., Topeka, Kan., 1892-94; prof. geology, Union Coll., 1894-99; asso. prof. hist. geology, 1899-1901, prof. geology and head of dept., 1901—, Ohio State U. Asst. geologist U.S. Geol. Survey and on state geol. surveys of Kan., N.Y., and Ohio; geologist Md. Geol. Survey. Fellow Geol. Soc. of America, A.A.A.S. (v.p. Section E, 1915—), Am. Paleontological Society. Author: The Devonian System of Eastern Pennsylvania and New York, 1895; The Classification of the Upper Palæozoic Rocks of Central Kansas, 1895, 1902; The Upper Permian and Lower Cretaceous of Kansas, 1897; The Classification of the Hamilton and Chemung Series of New York, Part I, 1898, II, 1900; Cottonwood Falls (Kansas) Folio (with J. W. Beede), 1904; Revised Nomenclature of the Ohio Geological Formations, 1905; Anthracolithic or Upper Paleozoic Rocks of Kansas, 1910; Devonian and Mississippian Formations of Northeastern Ohio, 1912; Middle Devonian Deposits and Paleontology of Maryland (with Edward M. Kindle), 1913; Upper Devonian Deposits of Maryland (with Charles K. Swartz), 1913. Home: Columbus, O. Deceased.

PROSSER, Paul Pittman, lawyer; b. Fayette, Mo., Nov. 7, 1880; s. Lewis Smith and Mary Catherine (Dines) P.; A.B., Central Coll., Fayette, Mo., 1900; LL.B., Washington U., 1903; unmarried. In practice of law, St. Louis, Mo., 1903-07, Fayette, Mo., 1907-20; pros. atty., Howard Co., Mo., 1909-12, 1916-19; removed to Denver, Colo., 1920; atty. gen. of Colo., terms 1933-37. Maj., judge adv., U.S.A., Washington, D.C., 1918-19. Mem. advisory bd. Bur. of Charities, Denver and Denver County, 1928—; chmn. Colo. George Washington Bicentennial Commn., 1931-32. Democrat. Methodist. Home: Denver, Colo. Died June 26, 1936.

PROTHERO, James Harrison, prof. prosthetic dentistry (emeritus); b. Albany, Ill., Mar. 1, 1862; s. William P. and Angeline (Wilson) P.; ed. State Agrl. Coll., Kan.; D.D.S., Washington U., Dental Sch., 1890; m. Catherine Dooley, Oct. 1890. Practiced various places and in St. Louis until 1892; demonstrator in Mo. Dental Coll., 1890-92; identified with Northwestern U. Dental Sch., 1893—; oral radiographer; lecturer on Radiology, Northwestern U. Dental Sch. Republican. Mason. Home: Chicago, Ill. Died Apr. 8, 1929.

PROTHEROE, Daniel, conductor, composer; b. Ystradgynlais, Swansea Valley, S. Wales, Nov. 24, 1866; s. Daniel and Eleanor (Parents) P.; ed. Swansea Normal Coll.; studied music; hon. Mus. Bac., Trinity Coll., Toronto; Mus.Doc., Grand Conservatory, New York; Mus.D., Coe Coll., Cedar Rapids, Ia., 1931; won prize in local Eisteddfod when 5 yrs. of age; became leader of Ystradgynlais Choral Soc. at 18; m. Hannah Harris, Apr. 26, 1892 (died 1926). Came to U.S., 1886, naturalized citizen, 1891. Conductor Scranton Cymrodorion, 1886-94; in Milwaukee, 1894-1909; conductor Arion Musical Club (Milwaukee), Central Ch. Choir (Chicago); conductor choruses of Ill. Bell Telephone Co. (Chicago), Sherwood Junior Chorus, Daily News Choral Soc., Armour Inst. Glee Club, Chicago Welsh Male Chorus, Municipal Choral Soc. (Gary, Ind.); teacher of singing and composition, Sherwood Music Sch. Composer of cantatas, choruses, songs, etc. Home: Chicago, Ill. Died Feb. 25, 1934.

PROUT, William Christopher, lawyer; b. Boston, Mass., Dec. 24, 1886; s. William J. and Margaret A. (Ryan) P.; prep. edn., Boston English High Sch.; student Brown U., 1905-07; LL.B., Boston U., 1910; m. Mary Lidwin, June 12, 1912; children—Virginia, William. Admitted to Mass. bar, 1910, and began practice at Boston. Capt. Hdqrs. Inf., 94th Div., O.R.C., U.S.A. Pres. Am. Amateur Athletic Union of U.S., 1921-24; v.p. Am. Olympic Assn.; mem. advisory bd. Mass. Gen. Hosp. Supreme dir. Knights of Columbus, 1922—. Decorated Knight Order of St. Gregory the Great, by Pope Pius XI, 1924. Democrat. Home: Boston, Mass. Died Aug. 5, 1927.

PROUTY, Charles Azro, public, official, lawyer; b. Newport, Vt., Oct. 9, 1853; s. John Azro and Hannah B. (Lamb) P.; A.B., Dartmouth, 1875; m. Abbie Davis, Mar. 26, 1879. Asst. to Prof. S. P. Langley at Allegheny Obs., 1875-76; taught several yrs.; admitted to Vt. bar, 1882; practiced at Newport, Vt., 1882-96; mem. Vt. Ho. of Rep., 1888; reporter decisions Supreme Ct. of Vt., 1888-96; mem. U.S. Interstate Commerce Commn., Dec. 1896-Feb. 3, 1914, and chmn. same, Jan. 1912-13; apptd. dir. of valuation Interstate Commerce Commn., Feb. 3, 1914; apptd. dir. of Div. of Pub. Service and Accounting, staff of Railroad Administration, Washington, D.C., Feb. 1918. LL.D., Dartmouth, 1915. Home: Newport, Vt. Died July 8, 1921.

PROUTY, George Herbert, governor; b. Newport, Vt., Mar. 4, 1862; s. John A. and Hannah B. (Lamb) P.; ed. Newport High Sch., St. Johnsbury Acad. and Bryant & Stratton Business College, Boston; (LL.D., Middlebury College, and Norwich U., 1909, and U. of Vermont, 1910); m. Henrietta Allen, Dec. 1, 1890. Early became connected with lumber business established by his father, and became mgr. Mem. Vt. Ho. of Rep., 1896, 97; water commr., 1897-1908; mem. Vt. Senate, 1904 (pres. pro tem); lt. gov. of Vt., 1907, 08; gov. of Vt., 1908-10. Republican. Conglist. Home: Newport, Vt. Died Aug. 19, 1918.

PROVOSTY, Olivier O., judge; b. Parish of Pointe Coupée, La., Aug. 2, 1852; s. Auguste and Eliska (Labry) P.; ed. by pvt. tutor until 1865; Georgetown Coll., D.C., until grad., 1869; m. Euphemie Labatut, Dec. 26, 1876. Admitted to bar, Jan. 27, 1873; dist. atty., 1873-76; mem. La. Senate, 1888-92; mem. Constl. Conv., 1898; referee in bankruptcy for Baton Rouge div., Eastern Dist. of La., 1898-1901; asso. justice Supreme Ct. of La., 1901-22 (chief justice 1922). Catholic. Democrat. Home: New Orleans, La. Died Aug. 2, 1924.

PROWELL, George R., curator; b. nr. York, Pa., Dec. 12, 1849; s. Samuel N. and Sarah (Reeser) P.; ed. pub. schs., Pa. State Normal Sch. and U. of Wooster, O.; m. Virginia Dean; children—Nellie Brooks, Edna D., Dean. Teacher and superintendent schs.; was asso. editor Nat. Cyclo. Am. Biography, Lamb's Biog. Dictionary of U.S.; curator and librarian Hist. Soc. of York Co., Pa., 1904—. Author: History of York County, Pa.; Reading, Pa.; Camden, N.J.; The State of Delaware; The Continental Congress at York, Pa.; also the true story of Lincoln's visit to Gettysburg in 1863. Was corr. 2 daily jours. at Washington, D.C., for 12 yrs. Home: York, Pa. Died Feb. 23, 1928.

PRUDDEN, T(heophil) Mitchell, pathologist; b. Middlebury, Conn., July 7, 1849; s. Rev. George P. and Eliza A. Johnson (Prudden) P.; B.S., Sheffield Scientific Sch. (Yale), 1872, M.D., 1875 (LL.D., 1896); unmarried. Instr. chemistry, Yale, 1872-74; hosp. interne and studies in Heidelberg, Vienna, Berlin, 1875-78; asst. in pathology and histology, 1878-82, dir. pathol. and bacteriol. lab., 1882-91, prof. pathology, 1892-1909, emeritus prof., 1909, Coll. Phys. and Surgeons (Columbia U.). Lecturer normal histology, Yale, 1880-86. Dir. Rockefeller Inst. for Med. Research, 1901—. Fellow Am. Acad. Arts and Sciences. Author: Manual of Normal Histology; Text-book of Pathology, 1885, 11th edit., 1919; Story of the Bacteria; Dust and Its Dangers; Water and Ice Supplies; On the Great American Plateau, 1907. Home: New York, N.Y. Died Apr. 10, 1924.

PRUDEN, Oscar L., asst. sec. to the President; has held the office under several administrations. Home: Washington, D.C. Died 1902.

PRUGH, Byron Edgar Peart, prohibition worker; b. Rural Valley, Pa., Apr. 21, 1859; s. James Henry and Esther Emily (Peart) P.; A.B., Park Coll., Parkville, Mo., 1884, A.M., 1887; D.D., Westminster Coll., New Wilmington, Pa., 1901; m. Maude Lillie Christian, July 28, 1886 (died 1887); 1 dau., Lillie Maude; m. 2d, Sarah Markle Boyd, Mar. 6, 1889 (died 1897); children—Marie Jeannette (Mrs. Samuel Hunter Davis), Sadie Blanche Estelle (Mrs. M. J. Deichert), William Boyd; m. 3d, Mrs. Emma P. Dick, Dec. 20, 1900 (died 1922); m. 4th, Ada Marshall, June 24, 1926. Teacher pub. schs. at age of 14 and for 10 yrs. thereafter; ordained Presbyn. ministry, 1887; home missionary and pastor in Wis., Neb., Kan., Ind., S.D., Ohio and Pa. until 1906, last pastorate at Glenfield, Pa.; evangelistic work, 1906-13; state chmn. Prohibition Party of Pa., 1913-30; nat. chmn. Prohibition Party, 1924-26 (resigned); chmn. Prohibition Nat. Conv., Chicago, Aug. 1928; candidate of Prohibition Party for Congress at large from Pa., 1921. Editor The Index, monthly Prohibition paper, 1929—. Home: Harrisburg, Pa. Died Apr. 28, 1941.

PRUSSING, Eugene Ernst, lawyer, author; b. Chicago, July 12, 1855; s. Ernst and Louise (Peltzer) P.; prep. edn., high sch. and Bryant and Stratton's Business Coll., Chicago; LL.B., U. of Mich., 1878; m. Louise Schenck, July 12, 1880 (died 1900); children—Ella, Rudolph, Harry, Margaret, George, Louise; m. 2d, Lillian Edgerton Barrett, Dec. 10, 1902. Admitted to Ill. and Mich. bars, 1878, and practiced at Chicago until 1918; war work, Chicago and Washington, D.C., 1917-19; settled in Hollywood, Calif., 1921. Pres. Citizens' Assn. Chicago, 1903-04 (dir. 25 yrs.). Mem. Ethical Society, Chicago. Republican. Author: George Washington, In Love and Otherwise, 1925; The Estate of George Washington, Deceased, 1927. Home: Hollywood, Calif. Deceased.

PRYOR, Edward Bailey, banker; b. Fayetteville, W.Va., Mar. 8, 1854; s. Joseph William and Frances Frazier (Bailey) P.; ed. pub. schs., Palmyra, Mo.; married. Entered ry. service as clerk, Wabash, St. Louis & Pacific Ry., Dec. 1879, now the Wabash R.R., with which was identified, as clerk, gen. bookkeeper, and chief clerk, 1880-87, asst. auditor, 1887-1903, also asst. sec., and asst. to the v.p., 1900-03, asst. to the pres., Jan. 1, 1903-Oct. 18, 1905, v.p., Oct. 18, 1905-Dec. 1911, receiver same, 1911-Nov. 1, 1915; pres. State Nat. Bank, St. Louis, 1914-29; chmn. bd. Mississippi Valley Merchants State Trust Co., July 1, 1929—. Conglist. Home: St. Louis, Mo. Deceased.

PRYOR, Ike T., cattle raiser, banker; b. Tampa, Fla., June 22, 1852; s. David Christopher and Emma Elmira (McKissack) P.; at age of 6 had lost both parents, and at 9 became self-supporting; ed. country schs., Tenn. and Ala., 3 yrs.; m. Sarah H. Rapp, Oct. 1, 1878 (dec.); m. 2d, Mrs. Myra Stafford Early, June 7, 1893. Followed Union Army, selling newspapers, 1861-64, and was at battles of Murfreesboro, Chickamauga, Lookout Mountain and Chattanooga; removed to Texas in 1870, and became a cowboy, rancher, and large land and cattle owner; delivered first shipload of cattle at Havana, Cuba, at close of Spanish-Am. War and continued in business there until had disposed of 7,000 head at high prices. Pres. Mascott Land & Cattle Co., Zavala Land & Water Co., Stafford Land & Cattle Co., Texas and Colo. Land & Cattle Co., Texas Surety & Ins. Co.; v.p. Evans-Snyder-Buel Co., livestock commn. mchts.; v.p. R. E. Stafford & Co., bankers, Columbus, Tex. Mem. Tex. Cattle Raisers' Assn. (pres. 3 yrs.), Trans-Miss. Commercial Congress (pres. 1 yr., chmn. exec. com. 1 yr.); was chmn. Live Stock Transportation Assn.; pres. Nat. Live Stock Shippers' Protective League, 1915, Am. Nat. Live Stock Assn., 1917-19. Home: San Antonio, Tex. Died Sept. 24, 1937.

PRYOR, Roger Atkinson, judge; b. Dinwiddie Co., Va., July 19, 1828; s. Rev. Theodorick Bland and Lucy (Atkinson) P.; grad. Hampden-Sidney Coll., 1845 (LL.D.), U. of Va., 1848; m. Sara Agnes Rice, Nov. 8, 1848. Admitted to bar, 1849; editor South Side Democrat, Petersburg, Va., Enquirer and The South, Richmond, several yrs.; U.S. spl. minister to Greece, 1855; elected mem. 36th Congress (1859-61), reëlected to 37th Congress, but did not serve; del. to provisional Confederate Congress and mem. 1st Confederate States Congress, 1862; entered C.S.A. as col., 1861; brig. gen., Apr. 16, 1862; resigned commn. and reëntered service as pvt.; prisoner at Ft. Lafayette, N.Y., 1864-65. Admitted to N.Y. bar, 1866; practiced N.Y., 1866-90; judge Ct. of Common Pleas, 1890-94; justice Supreme Ct., 1894-99; resumed law practice. Home: New York, N.Y. Died Mar. 14, 1919.

PRYOR, Samuel F., corp. official; s. Joseph William and Frances Frazier (Bailey) P. Dir. Remington Arms Co., Am. Brake Shoe & Foundry Co., Am. Ship & Commerce Corp., Holland Am. Trading Corp., Nat. Carbide Corp., Remington Cash Register Co., Shell Oil Co., Union Banking Corp., W. A. Harriman & Co., William Cramp & Sons Ship & Engine Co. Died Nov. 17, 1934.

PRYOR, Sara Agnes, author; b. Halifax Co., Va., Feb. 19, 1830; d. Rev. Samuel Blair and Lucinda Walton (Leftwich) Rice; ed. pvtly.; m. Roger Atkinson Pryor, Nov. 8, 1848. Charter mem. Colonial Dames of America in State of Va.; hon. v.p. gen. D.A.R.; v.p. Mary Washington Assn.; hon. v.p. and incorporator Assn. for Preservation of Va. Antiquities. Author: The Mother of Washington and Her Times, 1903; Reminiscences of Peace and War, 1904; The Birth of the Nation, 1907; My Day, 1909. Home: New York, N.Y. Died 1912.

PRYOR, William Rice, physician; s. Roger Atkinson and Sara (Rice) P.; grad. Coll. Phys. and Surg., New York, 1881; m. Louise Allan, June 5, 1888. Prof. gynecology, New York Polyclinic, 1884—; visiting gynecologist, St. Elizabeth's Hosp.; consulting gynecologist, St. Vincent's Hosp. Author: Text Book of American Gynecology, 1896; Pelvic Inflammations, 1900; Text-Book of Gynecology, 1903. Home: New York, N.Y. Died 1904.

PUCKNER, William August, chemist; b. New Holstein, Wis., Feb. 24, 1864; s. Rudolph and Marie (Heins) P.; Ph.G., Chicago Coll. Pharmacy (now U. of Ill. Sch. of Pharmacy), 1885; attended summer course in chemistry, Harvard, and took lectures and lab. work in chemistry at U. of Heidelberg; (hon. Phar.D., U. of Pittsburgh, 1912; hon. Phar.M., Phila Coll. Pharmacy, 1919); unmarried. In retail drug business, at Chicago, 1880-90; prof. chemistry, U. of Ill. Sch. of Pharmacy, 1890-1910; chemist for Searle & Hereth Co., mfg. pharmacists, Chicago, 1896-1907; sec. council on pharmacy and chemistry, A.M.A., 1906—; mem. Com. on Revision of U.S. Pharmacopœia IX and X; mem. com. on synthetic drugs, Nat. Research Council. Home: Chicago, Ill. Died Oct. 1, 1932.

PUDDEFOOT, William George, clergyman, author; b. Westerham, Kent, Eng., May 31, 1842; s. George and Anne (Lewer) P.; ed. Westbourne Schs., London; (A.M., Bates Coll.); m. Mary Jane Dobson, of Toronto, Ont., Apr. 5, 1866. Field sec. Congl. Home Missionary Soc., 1888-1908; supt. Congl. Home Missions in Ind., 1903-15; field secretary for same, Boston, Apr. 1, 1915—. Served, corpl., in 10th Royals of Toronto, and went to La Prairie at time of 1st Fenian raid; later went to Ft. Erie as pvt. in Oakville Co., when Fenians went over last time; received silver medal for service. Author: The Minute Man on the Frontier, 1895; Hewers of Wood, 1903; Leaves from a Sky Pilot's Log. Home: Brighton, Mass. Died Dec. 8, 1925.

PUELICHER, John Huegin, banker; b. Milwaukee, Wis., Dec. 26, 1869; s. John and Mary (Huegin) P.; educated public schools; LL.D. from Beloit College, 1922; m. Matilda Siefert, Aug. 29, 1892. With Wisconsin Marine & Fire Ins. Co. Bank, 1885-93; with Marshall & Ilsley Bank, 1893—, pres., 1920—. Apptd. state dir. for Wis. of War Savings Stamps, Nov. 1917; apptd. chmn. State Annuity and Investment Bd. of Wis., 1929. Mem. Sch. Bd., Milwaukee, 1907-11; trustee Milwaukee-Downer Coll., Marquette U. Med. Sch. Mason. Home: Milwaukee, Wis. Died Jan. 28, 1935.

PUGH, Arthur Benton, lawyer; b. Hampshire Co., Va. (now W.Va.), Mar. 26, 1854; s. Lemuel and Elizabeth A. (Twiford) P.; ed. pub. schs. and U. of Va.; m. Louise Boggs Anderson, Nov. 25, 1885 (died 1896). Admitted to bar, 1878; practiced in W.Va. and Va., until 1897, then at Washington; spl. asst. to Atty. Gen. of U.S., 1906-10. As spl. counsel for U.S. in land fraud prosecutions, conducted the pioneer case (U.S. vs. Hyde, Schneider et al.) from its inception, 1903, to its conclusion and conviction of the parties in D.C., 1908. Attorney for Interstate Commerce Commn., 1910—. Democrat. Mem. Federal Council Chs. of Christ in America, 1906-16 (exec. com. 1908-12). Died Dec. 30, 1916.

PUGH, Charles E., ry. official; b. Unionville, Pa., Feb. 25, 1841; s. Elijah and Eliza P.; ed. Millersville (Pa.) Normal Sch.; m. Clara Jaggard, June 1884. Entered ry. service with Pa. R.R.; beginning Oct. 1, 1859, sta. agt., Newport; pass. conductor, 1862; train dispatcher, Phila. div., 1862-70; gen. agt., Phila., 1870-79; gen. supt. main line, at Altoona, 1879-82; gen. mgr. Pa. R.R. system East of Erie and Pittsburgh, 1882-93; 3d v.p., 1893-97; 2d v.p., 1897-Mar. 24, 1909, 1st v.p., Mar. 24, 1909-Mar. 1912. Home: Overbrook, Pa. Deceased.

PUGH, George Bernard, lawyer; b. Bradley Co., Ark., Jan. 2, 1872; s. John D. and Charlotte (Hampton) P.; ed. U. of Ark. and Vanderbilt U.; m. Elizabeth White, 1897. Admitted to Ark. bar, 1896, and began practice at Hamburg; moved to Little Rock, 1899; mem. Pugh & Wiley, 1900-06; apptd. asst. atty. C.,R.I.&P. Ry. Co., 1906; associated in practice with Thomas S. Busbee and Harvey T. Harison, 1916—. Democrat. Presbyn. Mason, Elk. Home: Little Rock, Ark. Died Mar. 18, 1933.

PUGH, James Lawrence, U.S. senator from Ala., 1880-97; b. Burke Co., Ga., Dec. 12, 1820; to Ala. in boyhood; common school edn.; studied law; admitted to bar; practiced at Eufaula; m. Miss Hunter, 1846. Presidential elector, 1848, 1856 and 1876; mem. Congress, 1859-61; mem. Confederate Congress, 1862-65; pvt. in C.S.A.; pres., Dem. State Conv., 1874; mem. Constitutional Conv., 1875. Home: Eufaula, Ala. Died 1907.

PUGH, Robert Chalfant, prof. law; b. Cincinnati, O., Sept. 10, 1857; s. George Ellis and Therese (Chalfant) P.; student St. Xavier Coll., Cincinnati; LL.B., Cincinnati Law Sch., 1879; LL.D., U. of Cincinnati, 1921; m. Ada M. Hampton, of Ilfracombe, Devonshire, Eng., Dec. 21, 1895; 1 son, Robert Hampton. Admitted to Ohio bar, 1878, and practiced at Cincinnati until 1912; judge Superior Court of Cincinnati, 1912-18; prof. law, Coll. of Law, U. of Cincinnati, 1918—, G. H. Wald prof. law of contracts, formerly asst. dean and acting dean. Democrat. Home: Cincinnati, O. Died Nov. 1935.

PUGSLEY, Charles William, college pres.; b. Woodbine, Ia., Aug. 12, 1878; s. George and Ida Alice (Kennedy) P.; grad. Woodbine Normal Sch., 1898; B.S. in Agr., U. of Neb., 1906, D.Agr., 1922; m. Lillian Florence Gibson, Feb. 22, 1906; 1 son, Albert LeRoy. Prof. Woodbine Normal Sch., 1899-1902; on farm, 1906-08; asst. prof. animal husbandry, 1908-09, head prof. agronomy and farm management, 1909-11, head prof. farm management, 1911-14, dir. agrl. extension, 1911-18, U. of Neb. State statis. agt., 1910-14, state leader in demonstration and boys' and girls' work, 1912-18, U.S. Dept. Agr.; editor The Nebraska Farmer, 1918-22; asst. sec. U.S. Dept. of Agr., 1921-23; pres. S.D. State Coll. of Agr. and Mechanic Arts, Sept. 15, 1923—. U.S. del. Internat. Inst. Agr., Rome, Italy, May 1913; Neb. mem. Am. Commn. for Investigation Agrl. Credits and Marketing Systems in Europe, 1913; mem. Nebraska Constl. Conv., 1919-20, Neb. State Board Agr., 1918-21. Gov. 19th Dist. Rotary Internat., 1928-29. Consultant of Nat. Resources Bd. to S.D. State Planning Bd., 1934-39. Home: Brookings, S.D. Died Dec. 17, 1940.

PUGSLEY, Cornelius Amory, congressman; b. Peekskill, N.Y., July 17, 1850; s. Gilbert T. and Julia Butler (Meeker) P.; ed. pub. schs. and pvtly.; m. Emma C. Gregory, Apr. 7, 1886. Clerk and asst. postmaster Peekskill P.O., 1867-70; clerk, 1870-79, cashier, 1870-97, v.p., 1897, pres., 1897—, Westchester Co. Nat. Bank. Mem. 57th Congress (1901-03), 16th N.Y. Dist. Democrat. Home: Peekskill, N.Y. Died Sept. 10, 1936.

PUJO, Arsène Paulin, congressman; b. nr. Lake Charles, Calcasieu Parish, La., Dec. 16, 1861; s. Paul and Eloise M. (Le Bleu) P.; ed. pub. and pvt. schs., Lake Charles. Admitted to bar, 1886, and began practice at Lake Charles. Mem. La. Constl. Conv., 1898; mem. 58th to 62d Congresses (1903-13), 7th La. Dist.; chmn. Com. on Banking and Currency, 62d Congress; chmn. of sub-committee making "money trust" investigation, 1912. Democrat. Chmn. Dist. Board for Western Dist. La., under Selective Service Act, 1917. Home: Lake Charles, La. Died Dec. 31, 1939.

PULITZER, Albert, editor, author; b. Mako, Hungary, July 10, 1851; s. Philip P.; ed. pvtly. Came to United States, 1867, and first began as a teacher of German, teaching a class of young ladies at the Leavenworth (Kan.) High Sch. Entered journalism at Chicago, 1869, on Ill. Staats Zeitung; removed to New York, 1871, working on New York Sun and Herald, until 1882, when founded the Morning Journal of New York (now called The American), which conducted until 1895, when, owing to ill health from overwork, sold the paper and retired to Europe. Author: Le Roman de Prince Eugène, 1904; also English translation of same, 1904. Died 1909.

PULITZER, Joseph, propr. of New York World, 1883—; b. Buda-Pesth, Hungary, Apr. 10, 1847; ed. by pvt. tutor; came to U.S., 1864; served until end of Civil War in cav. regt.; went to St. Louis; became reporter on Westliche Post (German newspaper), 1868; later its mng. editor and part propr. In 1878 bought the St. Louis Dispatch and united it with The Evening Post as the Post-Dispatch, which he still owns; mem. Mo. Legislature, 1869; Mo. Constl. Conv., 1874; was elected to 49th Congress in New York for term, 1885-87, but resigned after a few months' service; del. Cincinnati Liberal Rep. Conv., which nominated Horace Greeley for President; after that a Democrat; advocated the "National" (gold-standard) Dem. ticket, 1896. In 1903 endowed with $1,000,000 Columbia Coll. Sch. of Journalism, with agreement to give an additional $1,000,000 when school should be in successful operation. In 1887 broke down from overwork and has since been an invalid, totally blind. Died 1911.

PULITZER, Ralph, journalist; b. St. Louis, June 11, 1879; s. Joseph and Kate (Davis) P.; ed. pvt. tutelage and traveled abroad, 12 to 16; St. Marks Sch., Southboro, Mass., 2 terms; A.B., Harvard, 1900; m. Frederica Vanderbilt Webb, Oct. 14, 1905 (divorced); m. 2d, Margaret K. Leech, Aug. 1, 1928. Began newspaper work on New York World in 1900; vice pres. of Press Publishing Co., which published New York World, 1906-08, pres., 1911-30; v.p. Pulitzer Publishing Co., publishers St. Louis Post-Dispatch, 1906—. Chief work has been news supervision and editorial writing. Commd. lieutenant junior grade, U.S. Naval Reserve Force, 1917. Democrat. Author: New York Society on Parade, 1909; Over the Front in an Aeroplane, 1915. Home: Manhasset, L.I., and New York, N.Y. Died June 14, 1939.

PULITZER, Walter, publisher, author; b. New York, April 4, 1878; s. Albert and Fanny (Barnard) P.; nephew Joseph P.; ed. by pvt. tutors; m. Lillian W. Hearne, 1909 (divorced 1918); m. 2d, Caroline P. Englehart, 1919. Began chess composition, 1892; one of promoters of American Chess Magazine; editor American Tit Bits, 1902; pres. Pulitzer Pub. Co., 1911-15; founder and editor Satire, 1911-12; publisher The Welcome Guest, Pulitzer's Magazine, 1912-13, Pulitzer's Review, 1916-17; pres. Pulitzer Co., Inc.; founded weekly syndicate, Pulitzer's Pertinent Paragraphs, 1917. Author: A Cynic's Meditations, 1904; Cozy Corner Confidences, 1906; Cupid's Pack of Cards; My Auto Book, 1907; Memoirs of Albert Pulitzer, 1911; Meditations of a Mean Man, 1911. Died Sept. 5, 1926.

PULLEN, Herbert Armitage, orthodontist; b. Nashotah, Wis., Feb. 23, 1874; s. Charles Melvin and Mary R. P.; student U. of Buffalo 1 yr.; grad. U. of Minn. Coll. of Dentistry, 1897; grad. Angle Sch. of Orthodontia, 1900; m. Clare Smith, June 29, 1895. Practiced in Buffalo, 1900—; mem. teaching staff Forsyth Dental Infirmary, Boston, Mass. Episcopalian. Home: Buffalo, N.Y. Died 1935.

PULLMAN, James Minton, Universalist clergyman; b. Portland, N.Y., Aug. 21, 1836; s. James Lewis and Emily Caroline (Minton) P.; ed. Albion Acad., Orleans Co., N.Y.; grad. St. Lawrence Univ. Divinity School, Canton, N.Y., 1861 (D.D., 1879); m. Jennie S. Tracy, Jan. 26, 1862. Pastor Troy, N.Y., 1861-68; New York, 1868-85; from 1885, 1st Universalist Ch., Lynn, Mass. Was sec. Universalist Gen. Conv., 1870-78; pres. Associated Charities of Lynn, 1886—; pres. Dean Acad., Franklin, Mass.; dir. Mass. Prison Assn.; mem. Mass. State Bd. of Charities; mem. Nat. Civ. Service Reform League from its inception; mem. Mass. Soc. for Promoting Good Citizenship; counsellor Am. Inst. of Civics; mem. Nat. Conf. Charities and Correction. Home: Lynn, Mass. Died 1903.

PULSIFER, Nathan Trowbridge, mfr. varnish and colors; b. Newton, Mass., Oct. 27, 1851; s. Charles S. and Eliza (Trowbridge) P.; ed. pub. schs.; m. Almira Houghton Valentine, Oct. 13, 1880; children—Lawson Valentine, Harold Trowbridge. Pres. Valentine & Co., 1915-22, chmn. bd., 1922—; dir. Bon Ami Co., Houghton, Mifflin Co., Outlook Co., Technicolor, Inc., New York Bd. of Trade & Transportation. Mem. New York Chamber Commerce. Republican. Conglist. Home: Beachwood, N.J. Deceased.

PULSIFER, William E., publisher; b. West Sumner, Me., Apr. 16, 1852; s. Moses G. and Nancy A. (Hamilton) P.; ed. Westbrook and Kents Hill sems., Me., and Bates Coll., hon. A.M., 1908, hon. Litt.D., 1926; m. Julia M. Martin, Aug. 9, 1906. N.E. mgr. for Ginn & Co., pubs., Boston, 1884-89; treas., 1896-1909, pres., 1910-27, hon. chairman bd, 1927—, D. C. Heath & Co., ednl. pubs., New York. Lecturer, pub. sch. lecture dept., City of New York; author papers on hist. characters. Mem. City Council, Somerville, Mass., 1886-87. Republican. Mason. Home: New York, N.Y. Died Jan. 1931.

PULVER, Arthur Wadworth, lawyer; b. New York, Aug. 7, 1859; s. Myron and Mary E. P.; grad. Univ. of Rochester, 1882, A.B.; m. Lulu F. Marsh, Oct. 14, 1885. Admitted to Ill. bar, 1884. Formerly asst. atty. and atty., then gen. atty. Chicago & Northwestern Ry. Co. at Chicago. Republican. Home: Chicago, Ill. Died 1904.

PUMPELLY, Josiah Collins, lawyer; b. Owego, N.Y., Aug. 16, 1839; s. George James and Mary Susan (Pumpelly) P.; A.B., Rutgers Coll., 1860, A.M., 1863; LL.B., Columbia, 1863; m. Mrs. Margaret Lanier Winslow (died 1890); 2d, Mary Amelia Harmer, May 20, 1896. Assisted in raising and drilling men for duty in Civil War; admitted to bar, 1863. One of founders Huguenot Soc. America, Nat. Soc. S.A.R. (historian Empire State Soc. 8 yrs.); member nat. council Ch. Assn. Advancement of Interests of Labor; mem. Actor's Ch. Alliance (v.p.). Author: Our French Allies and Other Addresses, 1889. Asso. editor American Magazine. Home: New York, N.Y. Died Jan. 5, 1920.

PUMPELLY, Raphael, author, geologist; b. Owego, N.Y., Sept. 8, 1837; s. William and Mary H. (Welles) P.; ed. Owego Acad. and pvt. schs.; studied sciences and mining engring., 1854-60, in Paris, France, and at Freiberg, Saxony; LL.D., Princeton U., 1920; m. Eliza Frances Shepard, Oct. 20, 1869. Made geol. explorations in Corsica; had charge of mines in Ariz., 1860-61; made scientific explorations for Japanese Govt., 1861-63; pvt. geol. expdn. through Central, Western, and Northern China and Mongolia, 1863-64; explored Northern coal fields for Imperial Chinese Govt., 1864; journey of exploration across the Gobi desert, returned to Europe through Siberia, 1864-65; prof. mining, Harvard, 1866-73; state geologist, Mich., 1869-71; dir. Mo. Geol. Survey, 1871-73; chief of div., U.S. Geol. Survey, and in charge of mineral industries the Tenth Census, 1879-81; organized and directed Northern Transcontinental Survey, 1881-84; made the explorations of discovery inaugurating the development of the iron-ore industry of most of the iron-ore ranges of Mich. and Western Ont., 1867-1901; initiated and directed a physical-geographical and archeol. exploration of Central Asia, 1903-04, under auspices of Carnegie Instn. of Washington. Author: Explorations in Turkestan, Expedition of 1903; Explorations in Turkestan, Prehistoric Civilizations of Anau, 1908; Reminiscences, 1918; Adventures of Raphael Pumpelly, 1920. Homes: Newport, R.I., and Dublin, N.H. Died Aug. 10, 1923.

PUNDERFORD, John Keeler, pres. The Connecticut Co.; b. New Haven, Conn., July 15, 1870; s. John Courtney and Elizabeth (Rundle) P.; Ph.B., Yale, 1892; m. Clara Kimball, Dec. 10, 1919. Engaged in electric traction development, 1892—; in charge track, line and shop depts., Fair Haven & Westville R.R. (now part of The Conn. Co.), 1901-03, gen. mgr., 1903—, also v.p., 1914-25, pres., 1925—; pres. Springfield Street Ry. Co., Berkshire Street Ry. Co.; corporator New Haven Savings Bank. Mem. City Plan Commn., City Hall Bldg. Commn. Home: New Haven, Conn. Died June 11, 1936.

PUPIN, Michael Idvorsky, univ. prof.; b. Idvor, Banat, Yugoslavia, Oct. 4, 1858; s. Constantine and Olympiada P.; A.B., Columbia, 1883; Sc.D., 1904; Ph.D., U. of Berlin, 1889; LL.D., Johns Hopkins U.; m. Sarah Katharine Jackson, of New York, at London, Eng., 1888 (dec.). Asst. teacher elec. engring., 1889-90, instr. math. physics, 1890-92, adj. prof. mechanics, 1892-1901, prof. electro-mechanics, 1901-31, Columbia, prof. emeritus. Mem. various societies. Awarded Washington medal (engring.), 1928. Home: New York, N.Y. Died Mar. 12, 1935.

PURCE, Charles Lee, educator; b. Charleston, S.C., July 4, 1856; s. William and Ellen P.; attended Benedict Coll., S.C., 1878; D.D., Richmond Theol. Sem., 1883; A.B., Shaw Univ.; ordained to Bapt. ministry, 1883; m. Charlotte C. Sinkler, Jan. 2, 1885. Prof. Greek and Latin, Selma Univ., 2 yrs.; pres. same, 8 yrs.; filled pastorates, S.C., Ala., Ky.; has been missionary Am. Bapt. Home Mission

Soc. for Ala.; pres. State Univ., Louisville, Ky., 1894—. Home: Louisville, Ky. Died 1905.

PURCELL, Henry, judge; b. Wilna, N.Y., Oct. 13, 1848; s. Michael and Susan (Keon) P.; grad. Antwerp (N.Y.) Acad.; m. Cecelia R. Neary, Jan. 10, 1878. Began practice at Watertown, 1876; local counsel for N.Y.C.&H.R. R.R., 1897-1914, except 1911, when on bench; trustee Jefferson County Savings Bank; sec. and dir. Harmon Machine Co. Sch. commr., Jefferson Co., N.Y., 1873-75 inclusive; recorder, Watertown, 1882-85, city atty., 1887-88; mem. Watertown Bd. of Edn., 1887-97; county judge, Jefferson County, by appmt. of Gov. Flower, 1892; justice Supreme Ct. of N.Y., 1911; justice Supreme Ct., Feb. 24, 1914—. Democrat. Catholic. Home: Watertown, N.Y. Died Jan. 20, 1931.

PURCELL, William, editor-in-chief and pres. Rochester Union and Advertiser; b. Ft. Covington, Franklin Co., N.Y., Aug. 15, 1830; lived in Rochester from 1834; ed. common schools and 1 yr. in acad.; began delivering a route of Daily Advertiser to subscribers in morning while attending school; later entered office and learned printing business; asso. editor, 1854, and editor-in-chief, 1864, Union and Advertiser (the oldest daily in U.S. west of Hudson River; 1st number issued Oct. 25, 1856). Mem. Rochester Bd. of Edn., 1852-53; bd. of public works, 1872-73; nominated elector-at-large on N.Y. presdl. ticket, 1884, but declined; chmn. N.Y. Dem. State Com., 1877-88; Dem. candidate for sec. of state N.Y., 1881, ticket defeated; mem. N.Y. State Bd. of Mediation and Arbitration, 1886—; mem., 1870-93, and pres., 1881-93, bd. of mgrs., N.Y. State Industrial School for Juvenile Delinquents. Home: Rochester, N.Y. Died 1905.

PURCELL, William E., senator; b. Flemington, N.J., Aug. 3, 1856; s. Joseph and Johanna (Duggan) P.; pub. sch. edn.; m. Myra E. Stevens, Apr. 3, 1889. Admitted to N.J. bar, 1880; moved to Dak., 1881; now sr. mem. Purcell & Divet. State's atty., Richland Co., N.D., 1889-91; U.S. atty., Ty. of N.D., 1887-89; resigned to become mem. N.D. Constl. Conv.; apptd. by that conv. a mem. joint commn. created by enabling act between states of N. and S.D. to divide the property, apportion the indebtedness and settle all questions of dispute arising on account of division of the territory; 1st mem. Dem. Nat. Com. from N.D.; mem. N.D. Senate, 1906-10; apptd. U.S. senator from N.D., Feb. 1, 1910, for unexpired term (1910-15), succeeding F. L. Thompson, resigned. Catholic. Chmn. co. chapter Am. Red Cross; chmn. Food Conservation Com. 1917. Home: Wahpeton, N.D. Died Nov. 23, 1928.

PURDUE, Albert Homer, geologist; b. Warrick Co., Ind., Mar. 29, 1861; s. Samuel Leroy and Phoebe (Priest) P.; grad. Indiana State Normal Sch., 1886; A.B., Leland Stanford Jr. U., 1893; grad. work there, 1894; senior fellow, dept. of geology, U. of Chicago, 1895-96; (LL.D., U. of Arkansas, 1912); m. Bertha Lee Burdick, Sept. 1, 1887 (died 1888); m. 2d, Ida Pace, Dec. 22, 1898. Supt. pub. schs., West Plains, Mo., 1887-88; asst. supt. U.S. Indian Sch., Albuquerque, N.M., 1889-91; asst. geologist, Ark., 1892-93; prof. geology, 1896-1902, head prof. geology and mining, 1902-12, U. of Ark.; state geologist of Tenn., 1912—. Field asst., U.S. Geol. Survey, 1895, 1901-03, spl. field asst., 1903—; supt. mines and metallurgy for Ark., St. Louis Exposition; ex-officio state geologist of Ark., 1907-12. Editor: Resources of Tennessee. Home: Nashville, Tenn. Died Dec. 12, 1917.

PURDY, Milton Dwight, judge; b. Mogadore, O., Nov. 3, 1866; s. Milton C. and Sarah Jane (Hall) P.; A.B., U. of Minn., 1891, LL.B., 1892; admitted to bar, 1892; m. Belle M. Morin, Jan. 28, 1893; 1 dau., Florence. Asst. city atty., Minneapolis, 1893-97; asst. co. atty., Hennepin Co., Minn., 1897-98; asst. U.S. atty., 1898-1901; U.S. atty., 1901-02; asst. atty. gen. of U.S., Apr. 1, 1903-July 27, 1905; asst. to atty. gen. of U.S., July 28, 1905-July 9, 1908; U.S. dist. judge, Dist. of Minn., 1908-09; resigned May 1909; spl. asst. to the atty. gen. of U.S., 1922-24; apptd. judge U.S. Court in China, Shanghai, 1924. Mem. Prog. Nat. Com., 1912-16. Home: Minneapolis, Minn. Died Feb. 11, 1937.

PURDY, Richard Augustus, writer, playwright; b. New York, Jan. 31, 1863; s. Richard Fisher and Susan Amelia (Fairbanks) P.; ed. pub. sch. No. 35, New York; m. Clara Tillou, Oct. 31, 1896. Sec. Hudson Trust Co., Aug. 1908—, and now also v.p. "Four-minute man," 1917. Adapter of Galba, the Gladiator, from English transls. of Salvini's play, The Gladiator; also of William Tell, from the plays of same name by Schiller and James Sheridan Knowles; both plays produced and owned by Frederick Warde. Author of Chautauqua, 1923, prize play, a comedy-drama, "Crossed Wires," afterward renamed "Across the Street." Home: New York, N.Y. Died Apr. 18, 1925.

PURDY, Warren Grafton, railway pres.; b. Baltimore, Md., May 20, 1843; s. John H. and Louisa A. (Powers) P.; grad. Baltimore High Sch., 1859; m. Acca L. Colby, Mar. 13, 1865. Clerk I.C. R.R., 1859-63, Ohio & Miss. Ry., Feb.-Dec. 1863; chief clerk q.m.'s dept., U.S.A., 1864-66; with C.,R.I.&P. R.R., Jan. 1867—, as bookkeeper, 1867, cashier, 1867-77, local treas., 1877-85, sec. and treas., 1885-98, 2d v.p., 1887-97, 1st v.p., 1897-98, pres., June 1, 1898-Dec. 31, 1901; resigned. Home: Chicago, Ill. Died 1910.

PURINGTON, George Colby, educator; b. Embden, Me., June 27, 1848; s. Elisha and Delia Frances (Colby) P.; A.B., Bowdoin Coll., 1878, A.M., 1881; m. Sarah Cummings Bailey, Nov. 26, 1878. Taught dist. schs., 1866-70; asst. in Yarmouth Acad., 1870-71, in Hebron Acad., 1872-74; prin. Topsham High Sch., 1876-78, Brunswick High Sch., 1878-81, Edward Little High Sch., Auburn, Me., 1881-83; State Normal Sch., Farmington, 1883—. Overseer Bowdoin Coll.; pres. Christian Civic League of Me.; mem. N.E.A., Me. Pedagogical Soc. Mason; Past Grand Comdr. Grand Commandery of Maine. Republican. Congist. Author: Decennial History, Class of 1878, Bowdoin College, 1888; History of Farmington State Normal School, 1889. Home: Farmington, Me. Died 1909.

PURINTON, Daniel Boardman, university pres.; b. Preston Co., Va., Feb. 15, 1850; s. Rev. Jesse M. and Nancy (Alden) P.; A.B., W.Va. U., 1873, A.M., 1876; (LLD., Denison, 1889; Ph.D., U. of Nashville, 1892); m. Florence A., d. Prof. F. S. Lyon, pres. of Broaddus Coll., July 6, 1876; children—Edward Earle, Mary Lyon, John Alden, Jessie (dec.), Helen Elizabeth. Taught in prep. dept., 1873-78, prof. logic, 1878-80, mathematics, 1880-84, metaphysics, 1885-89, v.p. and acting pres., 1881-82, W.Va. U.; pres. Denison U., 1890-1901, W.Va. Univ., 1901-12, pres. emeritus. Trustee Broaddus Coll., Philippi, W.Va. Author: Christian Theism, 1889, 99. Home: Morgantown, W.Va. Died Nov. 27, 1933.

PURINTON, Herbert Ronelle, coll. prof.; b. Bowdoinham, Me., Oct. 15, 1867; s. Amos Edwin and Sarah (Moore) P.; A.B., Colby Coll. Waterville, Me., 1891, A.M., 1894; studied Newton Theol. Instn.; B.D., Cobb Div. Sch., 1894; studied Div. Sch., U. of Chicago; D.D., Hillsdale (Mich.) Coll., 1907; m. Carrie Jane Knowlton, June 29, 1894; children—Arthur Leonard, Edwin Moore, Carl Everett, Francis Knowles. Ordained Free Bapt. ministry, 1894; prof. Bibl. lit. and religion, Cobb Div. Sch., 1894-1908, Bates Coll., 1908-32. Trustee Newton Theol. Instn., Maine Central Inst. Republican. Author: Biblical Literature, 1923; Literature of the Old Testament, 1924; Literature of the New Testament (with C. E. Purinton), 1925; Achievement of the Master (with Sadie Brackett Costello), 1926; Achievement of Israel, 1927. Home: Lewiston, Me. Died Nov. 5, 1934.

PURNELL, Fred Sampson, congressman; b. Fountain Co., Ind., Oct. 25, 1882; s. Samuel J. and Odessa (Furr) P.; high school, Veedersburg, Ind.; LL.B., Ind. U., 1904; m. Elizabeth Shoaf, June 27, 1907. Admitted to Ind. bar, 1904, and since practiced in Attica; city atty. 4 yrs.; Rep. candidate for Congress, 1914 (defeated); mem. 65th to 72d Congresses (1917-33), 9th Ind. Dist. Mem. Christian (Disciples) Ch. Mason, Elk, K.P. Home: Attica, Ind. Died Oct. 21, 1939.

PURNELL, Thomas Richard, U.S. judge, Eastern dist. N.C., May 5, 1897—; b. Wilmington, N.C., 1847; s. Thomas R. and Eliza A. (Dudley) P.; entered C.S.A. at 16 yrs. of age; surrendered and paroled, Greensboro, 1865; grad. Trinity Coll., June 1869; on coming of age engaged in practice of law; m. Adelia E. Zevely, Nov. 16, 1870. Republican. Has served in both branches State legislature; has been State librarian; candidate for atty. gen. of N.C., 1892. Home: Raleigh, N.C. Died 1908.

PURPLE, Samuel Smith, M.D.; b. Lebanon, N.Y., June 24, 1822; common school edn.; grad. med. dept., Univ. City of New York, 1844; physician, New York City Dispensary, 1846-48; ward physician, bd. of health in cholera epidemic, 1849; was pres. New York Acad. Medicine, 1876-80. Author: The Corpus Luteum; Menstruation; Contributions to the Practice of Midwifery; Observations on Wounds of the Heart; etc. Died 1900.

PURRINGTON, William Archer, lawyer; b. Washington, D.C., Dec. 22, 1852; s. Tobias and Amelia Josephine (Archer) P.; B.A., Harvard, 1873; LL.B., LL.M., Columbian (now George Washington) U., 1878; LL.B., New York U., 1880; m. Anna C. (Russell) Wheatley, Dec. 31, 1895. Consular clerk, Rome, Italy, 1875-76; sec. of legation and chargé d'affaires ad interim, in Brazil, 1876-77. Began practice in New York about 1881; lecturer on relation of law to med. practice, Univ. of Bellevue Hosp. Med. Coll. Author: Christian Science, an Exposition of Mrs. Eddy's Wonderful Discovery. Collaborator in Allan McLane Hamilton's A System of Legal Medicine, 1894. Home: New York, N.Y. Died Oct. 26, 1926.

PURVES, George T., pastor Fifth Av. Presbyn. Ch., New York, 1900—; b. Phila., Sept. 27, 1852; s. William and Anna P.; grad. Univ. of Pa., 1872 (D.D., 1894); Princeton Theol. Sem., 1876 (D.D., Washington and Jefferson, 1888; LL.D., Lafayette, 1895); pastor Presbyn. Ch., Wayne, Pa., 1877-80; Boundary Av. Presbyn. Ch., Baltimore, 1880-86; 1st Presbyn. Ch., Pittsburgh, 1886-92; prof. N. T. literature and exegesis, Princeton Theol. Sem., 1892-1900. Author: The Testimony of Justin Martyr to Early Christianity; The Apostolic Age. Died 1901.

PURVIS, William Edmond, clergyman; b. Allegheny, Pa., Sept. 3, 1865; s. Samuel Anderson and Martha Ann (Pinkerton) P.; A.B., Westminster Coll., New Wilmington, Pa., 1888; grad. Pittsburgh Theol. Sem., 1891; D.D., Grove City (Pa.) Coll., 1909; m. Florence Clarkson Mealy, Apr. 2, 1891 (died 1921); children—Rev. S. J., George M., William E., Mrs. G. H. Bray, Francis P., Julian F. Ordained ministry U.P. Ch., 1891; pastor successively at Kearney, Neb., Freeport, Pa., Grove City, Pa., until 1924, Grove City Coll., 1924—. Hon. dir. Pittsburgh-Xenia Theol. Sem. Republican. Rotarian. Author: Immigrant Problems and Hopes, 1912. Home: Grove City, Pa. Died May 28, 1940.

PUSEY, William Allen, dermatologist; b. Elizabethtown, Ky., Dec. 1, 1865; s. Robert B. and Bell (Brown) P.; A.B., Vanderbilt U., 1885, A.M., 1886 (Phi Beta Kappa); M.D., University Medical Coll. (New York U.), 1888; LL.D., U. of N.M., 1925; m. Sallie Warfield Cunningham. Engaged in practice, 1889—; prof. dermatology, Coll. Phys. and Surg. (U. of Ill.), Chicago, 1894-1915, prof. emeritus. Mem. Commn. on Med. Edn., 1925-32; mem. exec. com. Nat. Research Council, 1925-31; mem. exec. com. "Century of Progress Expn. Chicago 1933." Editor Archives of Dermatology and Syphilology, 1920 to 1937 (editor emeritus). Mem. numerous professional societies. Chmn. com. on venereal diseases of Surg. General's Office U.S.A., 1917-18. Author: The Röentgen Rays in Therapeutics and Diagnosis (with E. W. Caldwell), 1903; The Principles and Practice of Dermatology, 1907; Syphilis as a Modern Problem, 1915; The Wilderness Road to Kentucky, 1921; A Doctor of the 1870's and 80's, 1931; The History of Dermatology, 1932; History of Syphilis, 1933. Home: Chicago, Ill. Died Aug. 29, 1940.

PUTERBAUGH, Leslie D., lawyer; b. Pekin, Ill., Aug. 9, 1858; s. Sabin D. and Anna E. (Rye) P.; ed. pub. schs.; unmarried. Began practice, Peoria, Ill., 1879; master in chancery, U.S. Circuit Ct., Northern Dist., Ill., 1885-90; probate judge, Peoria Co., Ill., 1890-97; judge 10th Circuit, Ill., 1897-1913 (resigned); justice Appellate Ct., 3d Dist., Ill., 1903-12; candidate for justice Supreme Court of Ill., 1913. Republican. V.p. Dime Savings & Trust Co., Peoria. Pres. bd. trustees Bradley Poly. Inst., Peoria. Mason. Editor: Puterbaugh's Pleading and Practice. Home: Peoria, Ill. Died Jan. 4, 1918.

PUTNAM, Alfred Porter, Unitarian clergyman; b. Danvers, Mass., Jan. 10, 1827; s. Hon. Elias and Eunice (Ross) P.; descendant John Putnam, Gov. John Endicott, John Porter, Maj. William Hathorne and other early settlers of Salem Colony. Was clerk in Danvers Bank; later bookkeeper in mercantile house, Boston; attended various academies, taught school; entered Dartmouth Coll., 1849; grad. Brown Univ., 1852 (D.D., Brown, 1871); Divinity School, Cambridge, Mass., 1855; m. Louise Proctor Preston, 1856 (died 1860); m. 2d, Eliza King Buttrick, 1865. Pastor Mt. Pleasant Unitarian Ch., Roxbury, Mass., 1855-64; pres. Unitarian Sunday School Soc.; traveled in Europe, Egypt and Palestine, 1862-63; minister Ch. of the Saviour (1st Unitarian), Brooklyn, 1864-86; retired to Concord, Mass., 1886, but soon began to preach and lecture again. Has been pres. Danvers Historical Society from its founding, 1889. Author: Singers' Songs of the Liberal Faith, with sketches of seventy-two Unitarian hymn writers, with selections from each, 1874; A Unitarian Oberlin, or the Life and Labors of Rev. Jasper L. Douthit of Shelbyville, Ill., 1888; General Israel Putnam and the Battle of Bunker Hill, 1901. Editor: Brooklyn Channing Celebration Volume, 1880; Old Anti-Slavery Days, 1893. Home: Salem, Mass. Died 1906.

PUTNAM, Arthur, sculptor; b. at Waveland, Miss., Sept. 6, 1873; s. Oramel Hinckley and Mary (Gibson) P.; ed. Kemper Hall, Davenport, Ia.; m. Marion Pearson, Feb. 20, 1917. Gold medal, San Francisco Expn., 1915. Prin. works: Snarling Jaguar, Metropolitan Mus., New York; Sloat monument, Monterey, Calif.; etc. Episcopalian. Lived in Paris, France, until death, May 27, 1930. Died May 27, 1930.

PUTNAM, Eben; b. Salem, Mass., 1868; s. Prof. Frederic Ward and Adelaide Martha (Edmands) P.; ed. Cambridge (Mass.) schools; m. Florence Tucker, 1890; children—Eben Fiske-Appleton, Frederic Lawrence, Margaret Adelaide. Clerk in banker's office, Boston, 1885-90; mgr. Salem Press, 1890-94, pub., 1894-1907; mng. editor Internat. Monthly, 1899-1902; dir. and treas. F. L. Putnam & Co., Inc., investments, of Boston, also of F. L. Putnam Securities Co., until 1931. Capt. Q.M. Corps, June 25, 1917-Aug. 22, 1919; served in France; lt. col. Q.M. R.C. Official historian of Mass., World War, 1923—; dept. historian, Mass. Dept. Am. Legion, 1919-20, nat. historian, 1920—. Has carried on extensive geneal. and hist. research, America and abroad. Unitarian. Mason. Author: History of Putnam Family in England and America; Putnam Lineage; Military and Naval Annals of Danvers; Gold Star Record of Mass.; History of Massachusetts in World War; Holden Genealogy; Lt. Joshua Hewes, a New England Pioneer; and other family histories. Part-author and editor of Osgood Genealogy, Converse and Allied Families, Bixby Genealogy. Editor Genealogical Magazine, 1890-1917, Genealogical Bulletin, Vt. Antiquarian, 1900-1903. Home: Wellesley Farms, Mass. Died Jan. 22, 1933.

PUTNAM, Edward Kirby, museum dir.; b. Davenport, Ia., Nov. 17, 1868; s. Charles E. and Mary L. (Duncan) P.; A.B., Ill. Coll., Jacksonville, Ill., 1891; A.M., Harvard, 1899; m. Hilma, d. C.P. Sandberg, of London and Sweden, June 17, 1906; 1 son, Edward Sandberg. Newspaper work, 1891-96; instr. Stanford, 1901-06; acting dir. Davenport Acad. Sciences (now Davenport Public Museum), 1906-28, director, 1928—. Civilian relief work in France, Am. Red Cross, 1918-19. Home: Davenport, Ia. Died May 22, 1939.

PUTNAM, Edwin, officer U.S.N.; b. Bath, Me., Sept. 28, 1840; s. Israel and Sarah Emory (Frost) P.; m. Annie M. Salter, Dec. 1870. Entered U.S.N., Sept. 1862, as asst. p.m.; served during Civil War, on Monitor Nahant in naval attacks on Charleston, S.C., and capture of the Confederate ironclad Atlanta, in Wassaw Sound, Georgia, and during latter part of war on U.S.S. Portsmouth, Adm. Farragut's W. Gulf Fleet; in charge of U.S. naval depot, St. Paul da Loanda, Africa, 1868-69; on duty on various ships and at various stas., as pay officer and gen. storekeeper, 1870-1902; advanced to rank of rear admiral and retired for age limit, Sept. 28, 1902. Home: Portsmouth, N.H. Died Dec. 31, 1925.

PUTNAM, Frederic Ward, anthropologist, zoölogist; b. Salem, Mass., Apr. 16, 1839; s. Eben and Elizabeth (Appleton) P.; B.S., Harvard, 1862; (hon. A.M., Williams, 1868; Sc.D., U. of Pa., 1894); m. Adelaide Martha Edmands, 1864 (died 1879); 2d, Esther Orne Clarke, 1882. Curator ornithology, 1856-64, curator vertebrata, 1864-66, supt. of mus., 1866-73, v.p., 1871-94, Essex Inst., and of East India Marine Soc., 1867-69, dir. of mus. Peabody Acad. Sciences, Salem, 1869-73; asst. in ichthyology, Mus. of Comparative Zoölogy, 1857-64 and 1876-78; asst. Geol. Survey of Ky., 1874, survey West of 100th meridian, U.S. engrs., 1876-79; prof. Am. archæology and ethnology, Harvard, 1886-1909, prof. emeritus, 1910; curator Peabody Museum of Harvard Univ., 1874-1909, honorary curator, 1909-13, hon. director in charge, 1913; prof. anthropology and dir. Anthrop. Mus. U. of Calif., 1903-09, prof. emeritus, 1909; state commr. inland fisheries, 1882-89; chief dept. ethnology, Chicago Expn., 1891-94; curator anthropology, Am. Mus. Natural History, 1894-1903. Decorated by French Govt. with Cross of Legion of Honor; awarded Drexel gold medal for archeol. research. Fellow Am. Acad. Arts and Sciences; mem. numerous Am. and foreign Societies. Was originator and editor of Naturalists' Directory, 1865. One of founders of The American Naturalist, 1868. Has published over 400 papers on zoölogy and anthropology; from 1870 engaged in researches and explorations in Am. archeology. Died Aug. 14, 1915.

PUTNAM, George Ellsworth, economist; b. Richmond, Kan., July 9, 1887; s. Charles Ellsworth and Ida (McGee) P.; student Ottawa (Kan.) U., 1903-05; A.B., U. of Kan., 1907; M.A., Yale, 1908; Rhodes scholar from Kan., at Oxford U., Eng., 1908-11; diploma in economics "with distinction," 1909, B.Litt., 1911; m. Clare Elise Edwards, July 6, 1911; 1 dau., Pauline Elizabeth. Asst. prof. economics, 1911-14, asso. prof., 1915-16, U. of Kan.; prof. economics Washington U., 1917-19; spl. expert U.S. Tariff Commn., summer 1918; consulting economist, Swift & Co., Chicago, July 1920—; dir. Security Mut. Casualty Co. Author: Practice Problems in Economics, 1915; The Land Credit Problem, 1916; Supplying Britain's Meat, 1923. Co-author of Tariff Information Series (U.S. Govt. publn.), 1921. Home: Hinsdale, Ill. Died June 24, 1939.

PUTNAM, George Haven, publisher; b. London, Eng., Apr. 2, 1844; s. George Palmer and Victorine (Haven) P.; ed. Columbia Grammar Sch., New York, The Sorbonne, Paris, and U. of Göttingen; hon. A.M., Bowdoin, 1894; Litt.D., U. of Pittsburgh, 1899, Columbia, 1912; served as pvt. advancing to maj. 176th N.Y. Vols., 1862-65; prisoner at Libby and Danville, Va., winter of 1864-65; m. Rebecca Kettell Shepard, July 7, 1869 (died 1895); m. 2d, Emily James Smith, Apr. 27, 1899. Pres. G. P. Putnam's Sons, publishers, New York; dir. Knickerbocker Press. Led in organizing, 1887, The Am. Copyright League, originally organized by late G. P. Putnam, 1851; became its sec. during contest for internat. copyright, resulting in copyright bill of Mar. 1891. Decorated with Cross of the Legion of Honor, France, 1891. Founder of English-Speaking Union in U.S. Author: Authors and Publishers, 1883; Question of Copyright, 1891; Authors and Their Public in Ancient Times, 1893; The Artificial Mother, 1894; Books and Their Makers in the Middle Ages, 1896; The Censorship of the Church of Rome and Its Influence upon the Production and the Distribution of Literature (2 vols.), 1907; Abraham Lincoln—the People's Leader in the Struggle for National Existence, 1909; George Palmer Putnam, 1912; Memories of My Youth, 1914; Memories of a Publisher, 1915; Some Memories of the Civil War, 1924. Pres. Am. Rights League, 1915-16, Free Trade League, 1916. Died Feb. 27, 1930.

PUTNAM, Harrington, judge; b. Shrewsbury, Mass., June 29, 1851; s. Charles Adams Varnum and Ellen (Harrington) P.; A.B., Colby Coll., Waterville, Me., 1870; studied Heidelberg, Germany, 1873; LL.B., Columbia, 1876; LL.D., Colby, 1906, Middlebury, 1911; m. Mildred Smythe, June 8, 1904; 1 son, Harrington. Admitted to bar, 1876, and practiced New York; examiner N.Y. State Civ. Service Commn., 1884-89, Brooklyn Civ. Service Commn., 1890-94; apptd., Nov. 1909, elected, Nov. 1910, justice Supreme Court of N.Y., term Jan. 1, 1911-Dec. 31, 1921; official referee, by apptmt. of Supreme Court. Lecturer on admiralty law, Cornell U. Pres. Am. Br. Internat. Law Assn. (of London), 1924. President New England Society of Brooklyn, 1926. Democrat. Home: Brooklyn, N.Y. Died Apr. 7, 1937.

PUTNAM, H(enry) St. Clair, consulting engr.; b. Davenport, Ia., July 8, 1861; s. Charles Edwin and Mary Louisa (Duncan) P.; grad. Davenport High Sch., 1880; LL.B., State U. of Ia., 1882; B.S., Rose Poly. Inst., Terre Haute, Ind., 1886, M.S., 1905, E.E., 1907; m. Dorothy van Patten Torrey, Feb. 19, 1918. In practice of law, 1882-84; in engineering dept. Thomson-Houston Electric Co., 1886-87; in mfr. of arc light carbons, 1887-96, Thomson-Houston Carbon Co., Brush Carbon Co., Am. Carbon Co.; consulting elec. engr., Chicago, 1896-1900. Phila., 1900-02, New York, 1902—; dir. Continuous Transit Co. Fellow Am. Inst. Elec. Engrs. Republican. Presbyn. Home: New York, N.Y. Died Jan. 30, 1924.

PUTNAM, James Jackson, neurologist; b. Boston, Oct. 3, 1846; s. Charles Gideon and Elizabeth Cabot (Jackson) P.; A.B., Harvard, 1866, M.D., 1870; m. Marian Cabot, Feb. 15, 1886. Lecturer, 1872-75, clin. instr. diseases of nervous system, 1875-85, instr., 1885-93, prof., 1893-1912, prof. emeritus, 1912, Harvard U. Neurologist Mass. Gen. Hosp., 1874-1909, then consulting phys. same. Author: Memoirs of Dr. James Jackson, His Father and His Brothers, 1905; Human Motives, 1915. Home: Boston, Mass. Died Nov. 8, 1918.

PUTNAM, James Osborne, chancellor Univ. of Buffalo (N.Y.); b. Attica, N.Y., July 4, 1918; s. Harvey and Myra (Osborne) P.; grad. Yale, 1839; settled as a lawyer, 1842, at Buffalo; State senator, 1854-55; Am. party candidate for sec. of State, N.Y., 1857; Lincoln elector, State-at-large, 1860; consul to Havre; U.S. minister to Belgium, 1880-82; U.S. del. to Internat. Industrial Property Congress, Paris, 1881. Author: Addresses and Orations, 1880. Died 1903.

PUTNAM, James William, educator; b. Hersman, Ill., Jan. 18, 1865; s. Daniel and Harriet (Harper) P.; Ph.B., Illinois College, 1894, A.M., 1898, LL.D., 1935; studied Univ. of Chicago; A.M., Cornell U., 1903; Ph.D., U. of Wis., 1909; LL.D., Hanover College, 1935; m. Eleanore Boston, June 24, 1896; 1 son, Russell Caldwell. Instr. and asst. prof. history and economics, Ill. Coll., 1894-1902, in charge dept., 1898-1902; asst. in history, U. of Wis., 1903-04; instr. economics, Northwestern U., 1904-06, U. of Mo., 1906-09; prof. economics, Butler Univ., 1909—, dean and v.p., 1919-34, acting pres., 1920-21, and 1933-34, pres., 1934—. Mem. Disciples of Christ. Mason. Author: The Illinois and Michigan Canal—A Study in Economic History, 1918. Home: Indianapolis, Ind. Died Jan. 23, 1940.

PUTNAM, James Wright, neurologist; b. Fredonia, N.Y., June 16, 1860; s. James Osborn and Kate (Wright) P.; prep. edn. Central High Sch., Buffalo, N.Y.; M.D., U. of Buffalo, 1882; studied in Germany, Paris, France, and Eng., 1887-89; m. Caroline Moore Graves, Apr. 25, 1889; children—James Osborne, John Graves, Roger Wright. Began practice at Buffalo, 1882; prof. nervous diseases, U. of Buffalo, 1890—; neurologist City Hosp., Gen. Hosp.; contract surgeon U.S. Gen. Hosp. No. 1, Williamsbridge, N.Y., 1918; psychiatric service, U.S. Gen. Hosp. No. 30, Plattsburg, N.Y.; neurologist to U.S. Marine Hosp., Buffalo, 1914—; consulting neuropsychiatrist U.S.P.H.S.; consultant Providence Retreat. Trustee Buffalo Seminary. Republican. Presbyterian. Home: Buffalo, N.Y. Died Mar. 23, 1938.

PUTNAM, John Bishop, publisher; b. Staten Island, N.Y., July 17, 1848; s. George Palmer and Victorine (Haven) P.; brother of George Haven, Herbert and Ruth P.; ed. Clark and Fanning's Collegiate Inst., New York, and Pa. Agrl. Coll.; m. Fannie Faulkner, Apr. 18, 1882. Entered, 1868, publishing house of G. P. Putnam's Sons, of which is now treas.; also pres. Knickerbocker Press. Author: Authors and Publishers, 1890; A Norwegian Ramble, 1902. Home: Rye, N.Y. Died Oct. 7, 1915.

PUTNAM, John Pickering, architect; b. Boston, Apr. 3, 1847; s. John Pickering and Harriet (Upham) P.; A.B., Harvard, 1868; École des Beaux Arts, Paris, 1869; Royal Acad. of Architecture, Berlin, 1870, 1871; m. Grace Cornelia Stevens, June 30, 1885. Practicing architecture at Boston from 1871. Invented the "Sanitas," "Securitas," and other plumbing, steam heating, and water purification appliances. Author: The Open Fire-Place in All Ages, 1882; The Principles of House Drainage, 1885; Improved Plumbing Appliances, 1887; The Outlook for the Artisan and His Art, 1892; Plumbing and Household Sanitation, 1911. Died Feb. 23, 1917.

PUTNAM, Ruth, author; b. Yonkers, N.Y.; d. George Palmer and Victorine (Haven) P.; A.B., Cornell U., 1878. Alumni trustee Cornell University, 1899-1909. Author: Annetje Jan's Farm, 1897; William the Silent (2 volumes), 1894; A Mediæval Princess, 1904; Charles the Bold, 1908; William the Silent (Hero Series), 1911; Alsace and Lorraine, 1915; The Name of California, 1916; Luxemburg and her Neighbors, 1918. Editor: Life and Letters of Mary Putnam Jacobi, 1925. Died Feb. 13, 1931.

PUTNAM, Warren Edward, M.D.; b. Putnam, Can., May 6, 1857; s. Thomas and Nancy (Harris) P.; descendant of John Putnam, Salem, Mass., 1634; M.D., Ohio State U., 1881; m. Anna Sherwood Hawks, Oct. 6, 1887. Practiced at Bennington, Vt., 1892—; former chmn. med. and surg. staffs Putnam Memorial Hosp., becoming consulting phys. same; U.S. examining surgeon; pres. Bennington Bd. Health; former pres. Corporation of Bennington, also of Bennington Gas Co.; corporator Bennington County Sav. Bank; pres. Cooper Industrial Sch. Surgeon Gen. of Vt., 1904-06; brig. gen. on mil. staff late Gov. Charles J. Bell; chmn. Div. Council Nat. Defense, Bennington Co., World War; pres. Bennington Bd. of Trade. Republican. Home: Bennington, Vt. Deceased.

PUTNAM, William Le Baron, judge; b. Bath, Me., May 26, 1835; A.B., Bowdoin, 1855 (LL.D., 1884, Brown, 1893); m. Octavia Bowman Robinson, May 29, 1862. Admitted to bar, 1858; practiced in Portland, 1858-92. Mayor of Portland, 1869; twice declined appmts. as judge Supreme Jud. Ct. of Me.; apptd., Sept. 1887, commr. to negotiate with Great Britain in settlement of rights of Am. fishermen in Canadian waters; also commr. under treaty between U.S. and Great Britain of Feb. 8, 1896; Dem. candidate for gov., 1888; U.S. circuit judge, 1st Circuit, 1892—. Trustee Bowdoin Coll.; pres. Me. Gen. Hosp. Home: Portland, Me. Died Feb. 5, 1918.

PUTNAM, William Lowell, lawyer; b. Roxbury, Mass., Nov. 22, 1861; s. George and Harriet (Lowell) P.; A.B., Harvard, 1882, LL.B., 1886; admitted to Suffolk bar, 1886; m. Elizabeth Lowell, June 9, 1888. Clk. in firm of Russell & Putnam, 1888-95, mem. firm, 1895-98, and since mem. Putnam & Putnam, and Putnam, Putnam & Bell; later associated as counsel with Putnam, Bell, Dutch & Santry; pres. and later chmn. bd. Package Machinery Co., of Springfield; v.p. Mass. Hosp. Life Ins. Co.; trustee Suffolk Savings Bank for Seamen and Others; pres. Gorton-Pew Fisheries Co., Ltd. (Gloucester). Mem. Corp. Mass. Inst. Tech.; trustee Boston Athenæum. Pres. First Boston Dist. Council of Boy Scouts of America. Unitarian. Home: Boston, Mass. Died July 26, 1924.

PUTNEY, Albert Hutchinson, lawyer, author; b. Boston, Sept. 28, 1872; s. Albert B. and Sarah B. (Abbott) P.; A.B., Yale, 1893; LL.B., Boston U., 1895; D.C.L., De Paul U.; Ph.D., American U.; m. Pearl L. Avery, Apr. 6, 1911. Practiced at Boston, 1895-98, Chicago, 1899-1913; prof., 1900-12, dean, 1904-12, Ill. Coll. of Law; prof. National U. Law Sch., 1914—; chief of Near Eastern Div., Dept. of State, 1913-20; dean Sch. of Diplomacy and Jurisprudence (now Sch. of the Polit. Sciences), Am. Univ., 1920—. Democrat. Mason. Author: Government in the United States, 1904; Law Library (12 vols.), 1908; United States Constitutional History and Law, 1908; Currency, Banking and Exchange, 1909; Corporations, 1909; Principles of Political Economy, 1909; Bar Examination Review, 1910; Foreign Commercial Law, 1910; Handbook of Election Laws (with James Hamilton Lewis), 1912; Historical Background of the Law of Real Property (with Charles F. Carusi), 1923. During April and May 1923, lectured in the univ. at Prague on the govt. and constn. of U.S., upon invitation of the govt. of Czechoslovakia. Officer Order of White Lion (Czechoslovakian). Hon. Persian Consul for Chicago and Washington. Home: Chicago, Ill. Died Oct. 22, 1928.

PYLE, Howard, artist, author; b. Wilmington, Del., 1853; s. William and Margaret Churchman (Painter) P.; ed. pvt. schs. and Art Students' League, New York; m. Anne Poole, Apr. 12, 1881. Author and illustrator: The Merry Adventures of Robin Hood, 1883; Pepper and Salt, 1885; Within the Capes, 1885; The Wonder Clock, 1887; The Rose of Paradise, 1887; Otto of the Silver Hand, 1888; A Modern Aladdin, 1891; Men of Iron, 1891; Jack Ballister's Fortunes, 1894; Twilight Land, 1895; The Garden Behind the Moon, 1895; Semper Idem, 1903; Rejected of Men, 1903; The Story of King Arthur and His Knights, 1903; The Story of the Champions of the Round Table, 1905; The Story of Sir Launcelot and His Companions, 1907; Stolen Treasure, 1907. Home: Wilmington, Del. Died 1911.

PYLE, Joseph Gilpin, librarian; b. Calvert, Md., May 24, 1853; s. Joseph and Milcah Churchman

(Leslie) P.; B.E., Normal Sch., Millersville, Pa., 1870; A.B., Yale, 1877; m. L. Arvilla Lewis, June 1, 1881; children—L. Lewis, Joseph Gilpin; m. 2d, Annie Walker Sanborn, Feb. 14, 1900. Teacher normal sch. and pvt. acad., 1870-73; prof. English lit. and polit. economy, Shattuck Sch., Faribault, Minn., 1877-81; asso. editor St. Paul Pioneer Press, 1881-95; editor St. Paul Globe, 1895-98, Seattle Post-Intelligencer, 1899-1903, St. Paul Globe, 1903-05; mag. and other writing, 1906-16; librarian, James Jerome Hill Reference Library, St. Paul, 1917—. Cleveland Democrat. Episcopalian. Author: The Little Cryptogram, 1886; The Godman, 1906; Should Women Vote?, 1913; Life of James J. Hill, 1916. Home: St. Paul, Minn. Died July 27, 1930.

PYLE, Katharine, author, artist; b. Wilmington, Del.; ed. at home and at pvt. schs. Author: The Rabbit Witch, 1897; The Counterpane Fairy, 1898; Stories in Prose and Verse, 1899; The Christmas Angel, 1900; As the Goose Flies, 1901; In the Green Forest, 1902; As the Wind Blows, 1902; Stories of Humble Friends, 1903; Nancy Rutledge, 1906; Theodora (with Laura Spencer Portor), 1907; Once Upon a Time in Delaware, 1911; Tales From Many Lands, 1911; Tales of Two Bunnies, 1913; Once Upon a Time in Rhode Island, 1913; Six Little Ducklings, 1915; Two Little Mice, 1917; Wonder Tales Retold, 1917; Tales of Folk and Fairies, 1919; Tales of Wonder and Magic, 1920; Lazy Matilda, 1921; Tales from Far and Near, 1922; The Black-Eyed Puppy, 1923; History of Delaware, 1924; The Katharine Pyle Fairy Tale Book, 1925. Edited and illustrated Fairy Tales from India, 1926; Tales from Greek Mythology, 1928; Tales from Norse Mythology, 1929; Charlemagne and His Knights, 1932. Home: Wilmington, Del. Died Feb. 19, 1938.

PYLE, Walter Lytle, physician; b. Phila., Dec. 20, 1871; s. William J. and Sarah Lane (Thomas) P.; A.B., U. of Pa., 1888, A.M., 1893, M.D., 1893; post-grad. study, Washington, London, Paris; m. Adelaide Besson, Apr. 11, 1898. Chief resident phys. Emergency Hosp., Washington, 1893-94; clin. asst. Polyclinic, and Wills Eye hosps., Phila., 1895; asst. surgeon Wills Eye Hosp., 1898-1905; practicing as oculist in Phila. Fellow Coll. Physicians, Phila. Mason. Author: A Manual of Personal Hygiene, 7th edit., 1918; also with Dr. George M. Gould, Diseases of the Eye, 1899; Cyclopedia of Practical Medicine and Surgery, 4th edit., 1918; Anomalies and Curiosities of Medicine, 1898. Editor Internat. Medical Magazine, 1898; sect. on ophthalmology, Am. Year Book of Medicine and Surgery, 1903-05; dept. of ophthalmology, Am. Medicine, 1902-07; International System of Ophthalmic Practice, 7 vols., 1912-19. Home: Merion, Pa. Died Oct. 12, 1921.

PYNCHON, Thomas Ruggles, P.E. clergyman, former pres. Trinity Coll.; b. New Haven, Conn., Jan. 14, 1823; s. W. H. P. and Mary (Murdoch) P.; educated Latin School, Boston; grad. Trinity, 1841, A.M., 1844 (D.D., St. Stephen's Coll., N.Y., 1865; LL.D., Columbia, 1877); classical tutor and lecturer on chemistry, Trinity, 1843-47; ordered deacon, 1848; ordained priest, 1849, P.E. Ch.; rector chs., Stockbridge and Lenox, Berkshire Co., Mass., 1849-54; Scoville prof. chemistry and natural sciences, 1854-77, moral philosophy, 1877-1902, prof. emeritus Trinity. Student Paris, 1855-56; took geol. tour through Southern France, Italy and Sicily, with spl. reference to volcanic action, and made ascent of Mt. Etna by night. Pres. Trinity, 1874-83; superintended the planning of new bldgs., erection of western side of great quadrangle and transfer of coll. to new site, 1874-78. Asso. fellow Am. Acad. Arts and Sciences, Boston; trustee Gen. Theol. Sem., New York. Author: Treatise on Chemical Physics; Life of Bishop Butler (his "Analogy" defended and his argument extended). Home: Hartford, Conn. Died 1904.

PYNE, George Rovillo, architect; b. Waterbury, Conn., Feb. 12, 1853; ed. S. Hadley, Mass.; studied architecture in offices of Putnam & Tilden and G. F. Meacham, Boston; attended Mass. Normal Art School and Lowell Inst. course of drawing and architecture, Boston; m. Sallie Sorenson, Sept. 16, 1885. Practiced Evansville, Ind., 1881-86; of firm of Gardner, Pyne & Gardner, architects, Springfield, 1888-1902; practicing alone. Home: Springfield, Mass. Died 1911.

PYNE, M. Taylor, lawyer; b. New York City, Dec. 21, 1855; s. Percy Rivington and Albertina (Taylor) P.; A.B., Princeton, 1877, A.M., 1880; LL.B., Columbia, 1879 (Litt.D., 1903); m. Margaretta Stockton, June 2, 1880. Gen. solicitor D.,L.&W. R.R., 1880-92 (mem. bd. mgrs.); Rep. presdl. elector, 1908, 16. Trustee Princeton U., Lawrenceville (N.J.) Sch.; chmn. Pub. Library Commn. State of N.J.; chmn. trustees Y.M.C.A. of N.Y.; pres. Lake Carnegie Assn.; v.p. Princeton University Press. Home: Princeton, N.J. Died Apr. 22, 1921.

PYNE, Percy Rivington, II, banker; b. N.Y. City, June 23, 1882; s. Moses Taylor and Margaretta (Stockton) P.; A.B., Princeton, 1903; unmarried. With Farmers Loan & Trust Co., New York, 1904-07; with Estate of Moses Taylor, 1907-08; founded Pyne, Kendall & Hollister, 1908; pres. Prospect Co.; dir. Cayuga & Susquehanna R.R. Co., Farmers Loan & Trust Co., United N.J. R.R. & Canal Co., Princeton Bank & Trust Co. Trustee Princeton Univ., St. Luke's Hosp., Children's Aid Soc., Y.M.C.A. of City of N.Y.; treas. Patterson Sch. (N.C.); dir. East Side br. Y.M.C.A. Republican. Episcopalian. Trustee Diocesan Com. Churches of N.Y. Home: New York, N.Y. Died Aug. 22, 1929.

PYRE, James Francis Augustin, coll. prof.; b. Porter Tp., Rock Co., Wis., Dec. 20, 1871; s. Frank and Melinda Elizabeth (Hawkins) P.; B.L., U. of Wis., 1892, Ph.D., 1897; studied in France, 1910-11; m. Marcia M. Jackman, 1908. Began teaching, U. of Wis., 1893, asso. prof. English, June 1909—. Co-author: Outlines in English Literature, 1910. Coeditor: Readings in English Literature, 1910. Died May 28, 1934.

Q

QUACKENBOS, John Duncan, M.D.; b. N.Y. City, Apr. 22, 1848; s. George Payn and Louise B. P.; A.B., Columbia, 1868, A.M., M.D., 1871; m. Laura A., d. Theodore Ward Pinckney, of N.Y. City, June 28, 1871; m. 2d, Louise D., d. late Rear Adm. White, U.S.N., June 1916. In practice at New York, 1871—, specializes mental and moral diseases. Tutor rhetoric and history, 1870-84, adj. prof. English lang. and lit., 1884-91, prof. rhetoric, 1891-94 (emeritus), Columbia U.; prof. rhetoric, Barnard Coll. for Women, 1891-93; summer headquarters at Soo-Nipi Park, Lake Sunapee, N.H.; lecturer on scientific and lit. subjects. Fellow N.Y. Acad. Medicine, N.H. Med. Society. Author: Hypnotic Therapeutics, 1908; Enemies and Evidences of Christianity, 1909; Standing Forests, 1909; Body and Spirit, 1916; Magnhild (psychic novel), 1919; Rational Mind Cure, 1925. Homes: New York, N.Y., and Lake Sunapee, N.H. Died Aug. 1, 1926.

QUAILE, George Emerson, educator; b. Omagh, Ireland, June 22, 1867; s. George and Harriet (Bailey) Q.; B.A., Dublin U., 1889, M.A., 1892; L.H.D., Trinity Coll., Hartford, Conn., 1920; m. Mary Louise Cook, 1899 (died 1929); children—Emerson Blauvelt, Reginald George. Head master St. Austin's Sch., S.I., N.Y., 1894-1901; rector St. Mary's Ch., Castleton, S.I., 1897-1901; head master Salisbury Sch., 1901—. Home: Salisbury, Conn. Died Oct. 15, 1934.

QUALTROUGH, Edward Francis, naval officer; b. Rochester, N.Y., Oct. 30, 1850; s. Joseph and Elizabeth (Gibson) Q.; apptd. from N.Y., and grad. U.S. Naval Acad., 1871; m. Leila Ray, Nov. 6, 1879. Promoted ensign, 1874; master, 1876; lt., 1883; lt. comdr., 1899; comdr., 1902; capt., July 1, 1906; commodore, 1909. Served in various capacities on board Macedonian, Savannah, Wabash, Wachusett, Despatch, Marion, Trenton, Gettysburgh, Hartford, Charleston, Mohican, Terror, Chicago, 1871-1902; comd. Atlanta, 1904-05, Yankee, 1905-06, Cleveland, 1906-07, Georgia, 1908-09; retired, July 1, 1909. Active mem. expdn. sent by U.S. to Caroline Islands, Pacific Ocean, to observe total solar eclipse, May 1883. Republican. Episcopalian. Author: Sailor's Handy Book, 1881; Boat Sailor's Manual, 1885. Home: Rochester, N.Y. Died Nov. 18, 1913.

QUARLES, Charles, lawyer; b. Kenosha, Wis., Feb. 13, 1846; s. Joseph Very and Caroline (Bullen) Q.; grad. Univ. of Mich., 1868; studied law with firm of Head & Quarles, Kenosha; m. Emma W. Thiers, Nov. 10, 1881. Admitted to bar Apr. 1875; practiced in Kenosha, 1875-88; from then in Milwaukee; mem. Quarles, Spence & Quarles, specialists in chancery and corporation law. Home: Milwaukee, Wis. Died 1908.

QUARLES, Edwin Latham, commercial orgn. specialist; b. Clarksburg, W.Va., July 4, 1880; s. Rev. Henry Lewis and Anna Gertrude (Cowherd) Q.; ed. pub. and pvt. schs. and Richmond (Va.) Coll.; m. Mrs. Kate Barbour Howard, Jan. 12, 1905. Teacher, Bowling Green (Va.) Male Acad., 1902-05; advertising dept. Richmond Times-Dispatch, 1906-07; sec. Petersburg (Va.) Chamber Commerce, 1907-10; assister in organizing, and secretary Southern Commercial Congress, 1908-11 (mem. exec. com.); dir. Greater Baltimore Com., May 1911—. Home: Baltimore, Md. Died Mar. 29, 1932.

QUARLES, James Addison, prof. philosophy, Washington and Lee Univ., from Sept. 1886; b. Cooper Co., Mo., April 30, 1837; s. Col. James and Sarah Ann (Mills) Q.; prep. edn. Kemper School, Boonville, Mo., 1844-54; grad. Westminster Coll., Mo.; studied 2 yrs. at Univ. of Va., 2 yrs. at Princeton Theol. Sem. in the class of 1860 (D.D., Westminster Coll., Mo.; LL.D., Central Univ., Ky.); m. Caroline Wallace Field, Oct. 11, 1859 (died 1901). Pastor Presbyn. chs. Glasgow, Lexington and St. Louis; pres. Elizabeth Aull Female Sem., Lexington, Mo. Author: Life of F. T. Kemper, 1884. Died 1907.

QUARLES, Joseph Very, judge; b. Kenosha, Wis., Dec. 16, 1843; s. Joseph Very and Caroline (Bullen) Q.; 1st lt. 39th Wis. Inf., 1864-65; A.B., U. of Mich., 1866; law student, 1866-67; m. Carrie A. Saunders, Sept. 25, 1868. Admitted to bar, 1868; practiced at Kenosha, 1868-82, Racine, Wis., 1882-88, Milwaukee from 1888. Dist. atty., Kenosha Co., 6 yrs., 1870-76; mayor of Kenosha, 1876; mem. Wis. Assembly, 1879, Senate, 1880-82; U.S. senator, 1899-1905; U.S. dist. judge, Eastern Dist. of Wis., 1905. Republican. Home: Milwaukee, Wis. Died 1911.

QUARLES, Ralph P., judge; b. Benton, Ky., June 10, 1855; s. James M. and Nancy J. Q.; grad. Paducah (Ky.) High Sch., 1876; m. Ida M. Strow, Nov. 23, 1881. Admitted to bar, 1877; practiced at Paducah, 1877-88, Blackfoot, Ida., 1888-89, Salmon City, Ida., 1889-96; asso. justice Supreme Ct. of Ida., 1896-1900, chief justice, 1900-02; practiced law at Boise, Ida., 1903-08, at Honolulu, 1908-11; resumed practice at Boisé, Jan. 1911; returned to Honolulu and resumed practice Jan. 1912; asso. justice Supreme Ct. of T.H., term 1914-18. Democrat. Mem. Quarles & Cherry, Salmon, Ida., 1918—. Methodist. Odd Fellow; rep. Grand Lodge I.O.O.F. at the Sovereign Grand Lodge I.O.O.F., Toronto, 1906. Home: Salmon, Ida. Died Nov. 15, 1921.

QUARLES, William Charles, lawyer; b. Kenosha, Wis., Jan. 3, 1870; s. Joseph V. and Caroline (Saunders) Q.; Ph.B., U. of Mich., 1892; m. Louise Stockton, Oct. 25, 1903. Practiced in Milwaukee, Wis., 1894—; officer and dir. many corps. Republican. Episcopalian. Home: Milwaukee, Wis. Died Apr. 17, 1939.

QUAY, Matthew Stanley, U.S. senator; b. Dillsburg, Pa., Sept. 30, 1833; grad. Jefferson Coll., 1850; admitted to bar, 1854; elected prothonotary Beaver Co., 1856 and 1859; in mil. service, 1861-65, as lt. 10th Pa. reserves, col. 134th Pa. vols.; received congressional medal of honor; lt. col. and asst. commissary gen. State mil. agt. at Washington; private sec. to gov. of Pa. Mem. legislature, 1865-67; sec. of commonwealth, 1872-78 and 1879-82; recorder of Phila., 1878-79; State treas., 1885; mem. of Rep. Nat. Com., 1885—, and its chmn. during successful presdl. campaign of 1888; mem. exec. com., 1896; U.S. senator from Pa., 1887-99; tried for misappropriation of public funds and acquitted, April 21, 1899; same day apptd. U.S. senator, ad interim, by Gov. Stone; reëlected U.S. senator Jan. 1901, to fill vacancy caused by failure of legislature to elect in Jan. 1899; term expiring 1905. Home: Beaver, Pa. Died 1904.

QUAYLE, John Francis, congressman; b. Brooklyn, N.Y., Dec. 1, 1866; s. Francis Joseph and Mary (McGarrigle) Q.; ed. pub. sch. and acad.; m. Katherine J. Sullivan, Feb. 16, 1898; children—John Francis, Kathleen J., William J. Govt. service 8 yrs.; city clk, Borough of Brooklyn, 4 yrs.; gen. contracting business, Brooklyn, 1902—; mem. 68th to 70th Congresses (1923-29), 7th N.Y. Dist. Democrat. Elk, K.C. Home: Brooklyn, N.Y. Died Nov. 27, 1930.

QUAYLE, William Alfred, bishop; b. Parkville, Mo., June 25, 1860; s. Thomas and Elizabeth (Gale) Q.; A.B., Baker U., 1885, A.M., 1888; (Ph.D., Allegheny Coll., 1892; D.D., DePauw, 1892; Litt.D., Baker Univ., 1900; LL.D., Baker, 1908, and Lawrence Coll., Wis.; Doctor of Humanities, McKendree Coll., Illinois., 1917); m. Allie Hancock Davis, Jan. 28, 1886. Ordained M.E. ministry, 1886; tutor, 1883-85, adj. prof. ancient langs., 1886-88, prof. Greek lang., 1888-91, pres., 1890-94, Baker U.; pastor Kansas City, Mo., 1894-97, Indianapolis, 1897-1900, Kansas City, 1900-04, St. James' Ch., Chicago, 1904-08; bishop M.E. Ch., 1908—. Fraternal del. to English Wesleyan Ch., 1902; mem. Joint Hymnal Revision Com. M.E. Ch. and M.E. Ch., S. Author: The Poet's Poet and Other Essays, 1897; A Hero and Some Other Folk, 1899; The Blessed Life, 1900; Books and Life, 1901; Eternity in the Heart, 1904; God's Calendar, 1907; The Song of Songs, 1910; The Pastor-Preacher, 1911; Laymen in Action, 1912; The Climb to God, 1913; Poems, 1914; Beside Lake Beautiful, 1914; Recovered Yesterdays in Literature, 1916; The Dynamite of God, 1918; The Throne of Grace, 1919; Books as a Delight, 1920; The Uncommon Common Pace, 1921; With Earth and Sky, 1922; The Healing Shadow, 1923. Home: St. Louis, Mo. Died Mar. 9, 1925.

QUEALY, Patrick J., coal mining; b. Kiltrelig, Ireland, Mar. 17, 1857; s. John and Margaret (Fennell) Q.; brought to America, 1866; grad. Gem City Business Coll., Quincy, Ill., 1874; student Johnson Coll., Quincy; m. Susie Quealey, Oct. 21, 1890. Gen. foreman Seattle Coal & Transportation Co.'s mines, New Castle, Wash., 1878-80; coal mine supt. U.P. R.R., Grass Creek, Utah, 1880-84; mem. Quealy & Hoffman, Timberline, Mont., 1884-86; state insp. coal mines, Wyo., 1886-87 (resigned); organizer, 1887, and mgr. till 1904, Rock Springs (Wyo.) Coal Co.; operating coal mines in Uinta Co., Wyo., 1904—; pres. Kemmerer Coal Co., Frontier Supply Co., San Rafael Fuel Co., Federal Coal Co., Gum-Quealy Coal Co., 1st Nat. Bank (Kemmerer), Live Stock Loan Co.; v.p. Denver Joint Stock Land Bank; and officer many other corporations. Presdl. elector, 1896; mem. Dem. Nat. Com. Founder Town of Kemmerer, 1897. Home: Kemmerer, Wyo. Died Nov. 17, 1930.

QUEENY, John Francis, mfr.; b. Chicago, Ill., Aug. 17, 1859; s. John and Sarah (Flaherty) Q.;

ed. pub. schs.; m. Olga Mendes Monsanto, of St. Thomas, Danish W.I., Feb. 5, 1896; children—Edgar, Olguita. Began in employ of Tolman & King, wholesale druggists, Chicago; with I. L. Lyons & Co., New Orleans, 1881-91; buyer, drug dept., Meyer Bros. Drug Co., St. Louis, 1892-94; mgr. sales dept. Merck & Co., chmn. mfrs., New York, 1894-97; returned to Meyer Bros. as buyer, 1897; opened local br. as mgr. for Powers-Weightman-Rosengarten Co., of Phila., 1906; organized Monsanto Chem. Works, 1901 (chmn. bd.). Mem. Am. Electrochem. Soc., Soc. Chem. Industry (Eng.). Republican. Catholic. Elk. Home: St. Louis, Mo. Died Mar. 19, 1933.

QUERBES, Andrew, banker; b. New Orleans, La., July 10, 1864; s. Antoine and Louisa Q.; ed. pvt. and pub. schs.; m. Alexandrine Ricon, Feb. 12, 1889; children—Andrew, Justin Ricon. Randolph Anthony. In wholesale grocery business, 1887-1904; mayor of Shreveport, La., 2 terms 1902-06; v.p. First Nat. Bank, until 1908, pres., 1908—; dir. Ardis Bldg. Co., Shreveport Journal Pub. Co. Democrat. Catholic. Home: Shreveport, La. Died May 24, 1939.

QUICK, (John) Herbert, author; b. near Steamboat Rock, Ia., Oct. 23, 1861; s. Martin and Margaret (Coleman) Q.; reared on farm; attended country schs.; engaged in teaching, 1882-90, becoming prin. of ward sch. in Mason City, Ia., and meantime studying law; m. Ella D. Corey, Apr. 9, 1890. Admitted to Ia. bar, 1889; engaged in practice at Sioux City, 1890-1909; asso. editor La Follette's Weekly, Madison, Wis., Dec. 1908-July 1909; editor of Farm and Fireside, Springfield, O., 1909-16; mem. Federal Farm Loan Bur., Washington, terms 1916-24 (resigned 1919). Was mem. and counsel for Citizens' Com. in Sioux City, and in that capacity prosecuted boodlers, circa 1894. Thrice nominated for mayor of Sioux City, and once elected, serving 1898-1900; nominee for supreme judge, 1902. Author: Aladdin & Co., 1904; Double Trouble, 1905; The Broken Lance, 1907; American Inland Waterways, 1909; Virginia of the Air Lanes, 1909; Yellowstone Nights, 1911; On Board the Good Ship Earth, 1913; The Brown Mouse, 1915; From War to Peace, 1919; The Fairview Idea, 1919; Vandemarks Folly, 1922; The Hawkeye, 1923. Chmn. commn. in charge of affairs in Far East, Am. Red Cross (rank of col.), 1920. Home: Berkeley Springs, W.Va. Died May 10, 1925.

QUIGGLE, Edmund Blanchard, lawyer; b. McElhattan, Pa., Feb. 8, 1886; s. James Clarence and Ella Laura Q.; student State Normal Sch., Lock Haven, Pa., 1898-1902, Pa. State Coll., 1902-04; LL.B., U. of Md., 1906; unmarried. Law clk. U.S. Forest Service, Washington, D.C., 1907, asst. dist. law officer, Missoula, Mont., 1909-10; asst. to solicitor, U.S. Dept. Agr., 1910-20; asst. solicitor internal revenue, U.S. Treasury Dept., 1920-21; mem. Williams, Myers & Quiggle, 1921—. Methodist. Mason. Home: Washington, D.C. Died Dec. 22, 1935.

QUIGLEY, Harry Nelson, lawyer; b. Galion, O., June 27, 1866; s. William C. and Emma Jane (Pague) Q.; A.B., U. of Mich., 1890, LL.B., 1891; m. Ida M. Barnhart, Oct. 16, 1895. Admitted to Ohio bar, 1894, and practiced at Marion until 1911; entered service of C.,C.,C.&St.L. Ry. Co. and Cincinnati Northern R.R. Co., Jan. 1, 1911, as asst. gen. atty., at Cincinnati, O., gen. atty. for Ohio, 1920-21, gen. atty., 1921-25, gen. counsel, 1925—; gen. counsel Peoria & Eastern Ry. Co., Louisville & Jeffersonville Bridge & R.R. Co. Republican. Methodist. Elk. Home: Cincinnati, O. Died Nov. 8, 1936.

QUIGLEY, James Edward, archbishop; b. Oshawa, Can., Oct. 15, 1854; moved with parents to Lima, N.Y., 1856; grad. St. Joseph's Coll., Christian Brothers, Buffalo, N.Y., 1872; studied Sem. of Our Lady of Angels (Niagara U.); grad. U. at Innsbrück, Austrian Tyrol., 1874; grad. Coll. Propaganda, Rome, 1879. Ordained priest, 1879; pastor St. Vincent's Ch., Attica, N.Y., 1879-84, St. Joseph's Cathedral, Buffalo, 1884-96, St. Bridget's Ch., Jan., 1896-Feb. 1897; bishop of Buffalo, 1897-1903; installed archbishop of Chicago, Mar. 10, 1903. Died July 10, 1915.

QUIMBY, Charles Elihu, physician; b. New Ipswich, N.H., June 21, 1853; s. Elihu and Nancy A. (Cutler) Q.; A.B., Dartmouth, 1874, A.M., 1877; M.D., Univ. Med. Coll. (New York U.), 1878; grad. Bellevue Hosp., 1879; m. Julia M. Cobb, Sept. 28, 1881. Practiced in N.H., 1880-82, then at New York; asst. prof. practice of medicine, 1889-90, adj. prof., 1890-95, clin. prof., 1895—, New York U.; visiting phys. City Hosp., New York, 1895—. Trustee Mary Fletcher Hitchcock Hosp., Hanover. Died Nov. 6, 1921.

QUIMBY, Harriet, dramatic critic; b. Arroyo Grande, Calif., May 1, 1884; d. William and Ursula M. (Cook) Q.; ed. pvt. tutelage, America and France; unmarried. Began as writer for San Francisco Dramatic Review, 1902, also contributing to Sunday editions of San Francisco Chronicle and San Francisco Call; joined staff Leslie's Weekly, 1906; now dramatic critic, and editor woman's page, and also conducting aviation dept., same. Traveling corr. for a year, in Egypt, Africa, Europe, S.A. and W.I. First person in the world to win license to pilot monoplane, under revised rules of Internat. Aero Club of America and France, 1910, and 1st woman in America to win aviator's license, Aug. 1, 1911. Home: New York, N.Y. Died July 1, 1912.

QUIN, Huston; b. Anchorage, Ky., Aug. 4, 1876; s. Joseph B. and Matilda B. (Huston) Q.; LL.B., U. of Louisville, 1900; m. Martha B. Rivers, June 9, 1904. Practiced with Helm & Bruce, 1900-08; 1st asst. city atty., Louisville, 1908-12; city atty., Louisville, 1917-18; judge Ky. Court of Appeals, term 1918-26; mayor, of Louisville, Nov. 1921-25; became 1st v.p. Louisville Trust Co. Mem. Law Club, Louisville. Republican. Mem. M.E. Ch., S. Mason. Home: Louisville, Ky. Died Aug. 14, 1938.

QUIN, Percy Edwards, congressman; b. Amite Co., Miss., Oct. 30, 1872; s. Rev. Henry G. and Virginia (Davis) Q.; A.B., Mississippi College, Clinton, Miss., 1893; m. Miss Aylitt Buckner Conner, Oct. 1, 1913. Began practice of law, McComb City, Miss., 1894; mem. Miss. Ho. of Rep., 1899-92; Dem. candidate for Congress, 1910 (defeated); mem. 63d to 71st Congresses (1913-31), 7th Dist. Miss. Baptist. Home: McComb City, Miss. Died Feb. 4, 1932.

QUINBY, Frank Haviland, architect; b. Armonk, N.Y., Nov. 24, 1868; s. John Jay and Hannah Griffen (Haviland) Q.; ed. Chappaqua Mountain Inst. and under pvt. tutelage; m. Elizabeth Mathews Purdy, Oct. 3, 1900 (died 1923); children—Oliver, Mrs. Margaret Cook, Elizabeth Lane, Roger, Mrs. Dorothy Landsnaes, Virginia. In gen. practice New York, 1892—; architect of many private houses at Bar Harbor, Long Branch, and Tuxedo, office bldgs., New York, mills, lofts, fire engine houses, pub. baths, etc., Kings Co. Court House in New York; grandstands at Brighton and Havre de Grace race tracks; chmn. dirs. Chappaqua Mountain Inst., 1900-07. Fellow A.I.A., 1896; pres. N.Y. State Assn. Architects, Brooklyn Chapter A.I.A. (2 yrs.); dir. L.I. Hist. Soc., Assn. for Improving Condition of the Poor, Goodwill Industries, Brooklyn Chamber Commerce; mem. N.E. Soc., Holland Soc. Democrat. Quaker. Home: Brooklyn, N.Y. Deceased.

QUINBY, Henry Brewer, governor; b. Biddeford, Me., June 10, 1846; s. Thomas and Jane E. (Brewer) Q.; A.B., Bowdoin Coll., 1869, A.M., 1872; M.D., Nat. Med. Coll., Washington, 1880; (LL.D., Bowdoin, 1909; A.M., LL.D., Dartmouth, 1909); m. Octavia M. Cole, June 22, 1870. Pres. and treas. Cole Mfg. Co., Lakeport, N.H.; pres. Laconia Nat. Bank, City Savings Bank; pres. Masonic Temple Assn. Mem. staff of Gov. Straw, 1872-73, with rank of col.; mem. N.H. Ho. of Rep., 1887-88, Senate, 1889-90; mem. Governor's Council, 1891-92 (chmn. state prison bd.); chmn. Rep. State Conv., 1896; trustee N.H. State Hosp., 1897-1909; gov. of N.H., 1909-11. Pres. Laconia City Hosp.; mem. bd. overseers Bowdoin Coll., New Hampton Instn. Mason. Unitarian. Home: Lakeport (Laconia), N.H. Died Feb. 8, 1924.

QUINBY, William Emory, editor-in-chief and chief owner Detroit Free Press, 1872-1907; b. Brewer, Me., Dec. 14, 1835; went to Detroit with family when 15 yrs. old; grad. Univ. of Mich., 1858, A.M., 1891 (LL.D., 1896); m. Adeline Frazier, Apr. 1860 (died 1905). Became connected with Free Press, 1861; U.S. minister to Netherlands, 1893-97. Home: Detroit, Mich. Died 1908.

QUINCY, Charles Frederick, mfr.; b. Newton, Mass., July 16, 1856; s. George Henry and Mary Caroline (Sweetser) Q.; ed. Newton High Sch.; m. Etta Molineux Ives, Oct. 22, 1879; children—Ada Ives (Mrs. E. W. Karcher), Polly, Edmund, Roger B. Chmn. bd. Q & C Co., Dorr Miller Differential Co., Miller Transmission Co.; pres. Kelvinator-Westchester, Inc., Quincy & Gilman Engring. Co., Q & C Packing & Lubricator Co. Home: Scarsdale, N.Y., and Center Harbor, N.H. Died 1927.

QUINCY, Josiah, mayor; b. Quincy, Mass., Oct. 15, 1859; s. Josiah Phillips and Helen F. (Huntington) Q.; A.B., Harvard, 1880; m. Ellen, widow of William R. Tyler, Feb. 17, 1900 (died 1904); m. 2d, Mary, d. Hon. Samuel R. Honey, of Newport, R.I., Nov. 1, 1905. Admitted to bar, 1884, and practiced at Boston. Mem. Mass. Ho. of Rep., 1887-88, 1890-91; chmn. Dem. State Com., 1891-92, 1906; mem. of and mgr. lit. bur. of Dem. Nat. Com. in campaign of 1892; 1st asst. sec. of state of U.S., 6 mos., 1893; mayor of Boston, 1895-99; mem. Boston Transit Commn., 1906—; mem. at-large, Mass. Constl. Conv., 1917 (chmn. com. on executives); Dem. candidate for atty. gen. of Mass., 1917. Home: Boston, Mass. Died Sept. 8, 1919.

QUINCY, Josiah Phillips, lawyer; b. Boston, Nov. 28, 1829; s. Josiah and Mary Jane (Miller) Q.; A.B., Harvard, 1850, A.M., 1853; m. Helen F. Huntington, Dec. 23, 1858; father of Josiah Q. Admitted to bar, 1854; engaged in real estate business at Boston. Removed to Quincy, 1859, where he conducted a large milk farm for many yrs.; later resident at Boston. Author: Lyteria (poem), 1854; Charicles (poem), 1856; Tax-Exemption no Excuse for Spoliation, 1874; Protection of Majorities, 1876; The Peckster Professorship, 1888; Double Taxation in Massachusetts, 1889; The Unearned Increment, 1890. Died 1910.

QUINE, William E., physician; b. Isle of Man, Feb. 9, 1847; s. William and Margaret (Kinley) Q.; ed. pub. grammar and high schs., Chicago; apprentice in pharmacy, 3 yrs.; M.D., Chicago Med. Coll., 1869; LL.D., U. of Ill., 1903; m. Lettie Mason, Nov. 14, 1876 (died 1903). Prof. materia medica and therapeutics, Chicago Med. Coll., 1870-83; prof. principles and practice of medicine, Coll. Phys. and Surg., Chicago, 1883-1913, dean same 1892-1913. Home: Chicago, Ill. Died Dec. 7, 1922.

QUINN, Daniel, Hellenist, Catholic priest; b. Yellow Springs, O., Sept. 21, 1861; s. John and Mary Elizabeth (Ryan) Q.; A.B., Mt. St. Mary's Coll., Md., 1883, A.M., 1886; studied divinity Mt. St. Mary's Sem., 1884-87; archeology at Am. Sch. Classical Studies at Athens, 1887-89, 1892-93; philology at U. of Athens, 1887-89, 1892-93, Ph.D., 1893, and Berlin U., 1891-92. Head prof. Greek, Catholic U., Washington, 1893-98; in travel and research in Greece, 1899-1902; rector of Leonine Coll., Athens, Greece, 1902-05; prof. at Antioch Coll., Yellow Springs, O., 1906-10. Author: Helladian Vistas. Widely known for researches in Grecian philology and archeology. Died Mar. 3, 1918.

QUINN, Daniel Joseph, R.C. clergyman; b. New York, May 12, 1864; s. Daniel and Mary (Spillane) Q.; A.B., Coll. of St. Francis Xavier, 1884; studied Am. Coll., Rome, Italy, 1884-88; entered Soc. of Jesus, Frederick, Md., Apr. 25, 1888; studied philosophy, sciences and mathematics, Woodstock Coll., Md., 1890-93. Teacher classics and mathematics, Boston Coll., 1893-97, Holy Cross Coll., Worcester, Mass., 1897-98; studied theology, Woodstock Coll., 1898-1902; ordained R.C. priest, June 27, 1899; prof. elocution, Holy Cross Coll., 1902-04; studied theology, The Novitiate, Poughkeepsie, N.Y., 1904-05; prof. mathematics, Boston Coll., 1905-06; pres. Fordham U., 1906-11; in mission work, 1911-15; parish work, 1915—. Died Mar. 10, 1940.

QUINN, Edmond, sculptor, painter; b. Philadelphia, Dec. 20, 1868; s. John and Rosina (McLaughlin) Q.; pupil Pa. Acad. Fine Arts and under Thomas Eakins; in Paris under Injalbert; m. Emily Bradley, Mar. 17, 1917. Executed statue of John Howard, Williamsport, Pa.; figures on Battle Monument at King's Mountain, S.C.; statue of Zoroaster, Brooklyn Inst. Arts and Sciences; decorative figures, Pittsburgh Athletic Club; bust of Edgar Allan Poe, Poe Park, New York; Swanstrom Memorial, Borough Hall, Brooklyn; statue of Edwin Booth in the character of Hamlet, Gramercy Park, N.Y. City; statue of Gen. T. C. Pemberton, at Vicksburg, Miss.; bust of Prof. Franklin W. Hooper, Brooklyn Mus.; of Chancellor Kent and Edwin Booth, Hall of Fame, New York; Victor Herbert memorial, Central Park, New York; World War Memorial, New Rochelle, N.Y.; etc. Represented in collections of Met. Mus., New York. Silver medal, Panama, P.I. Expn., 1915. Sculptor mem. Art Commn. City of New York, 1918-19. A.N.A.; mem. Nat. Inst. of Arts and Letters. Home-Studio: New York, N.Y. Died Sept. 9, 1929.

QUINN, James Baird, colonel U.S.A.; b. Cincinnati, June 9, 1843; s. David and Jane (Baird) Q.; grad. U.S. Mil. Acad., 1866; m. 3d, Estelle C. LeBlanc, June 11, 1907. Apptd. 2d lt. U.S. Engrs., June 18, 1866; 1st lt., Mar. 7, 1867; capt., Mar. 4, 1879; maj., July 22, 1888; lt. col., Jan. 29, 1903; col., May 5, 1906; retired by operation of law, June 9, 1907. Served on improvement rivers and harbors, Atlantic and Gulf coasts, and harbors of lakes Superior and Mich., construction of fortifications Atlantic and Gulf, etc. Home: New York, N.Y. Died Feb. 23, 1915.

QUINN, James H., judge; b. Kilbourn City, Wis., June 23, 1857; s. Andrew and Hannah (Mountford) Q.; ed. high sch., Minn.; studied law in office of William N. Plymat, of Mapleton, Minn.; m. Sarah M. Annis, Sept. 17, 1882; children—Cecilia L., Roswell J., Donald A. Admitted to Minn. bar, 1885; served as county attorney Martin County 5 terms, 1888-97 (resigned); appointed judge 17th Judicial Dist. of Minn., 1897; elected to same office, Nov. 1898, and reëlected, 1904 and 1910; asso. justice Supreme Court of Minn., Jan. 1917—, reëlected, 1922, for term of 6 yrs. Republican. Protestant. Died Feb. 15, 1930.

QUINN, John, lawyer; b. Tiffin, O., Apr. 24, 1870; s. James W. and Mary (Quinlan) Q.; Irish ancestry on both sides; student U. of Mich. 1 yr.; LL.B., Georgetown U., Washington, D.C., 1893; LL.B., Harvard, 1895; unmarried. Pvt. sec. to Hon. Charles Foster, Sec. of Treasury in Harrison Cabinet, 1890-93; associated in practice in N.Y. City with Gen. Benjamin F. Tracy, 1895-1900; mem. Alexander & Colby, 1900-06; head own law office, 1906—. One of organizers of Internat. Exhbn. of Modern Art, New York, 1913; hon. fellow for life Met. Mus. of Art, New York, in recognition of services in the cause of free art; an authority on modern Irish lit. and drama, and possesses valuable collection of modern art; conducted campaign which resulted in removal of all duty on modern works of art. Chevalier Legion of Honor, France, for services during the war. Tried and won in the Supreme Court U.S. case that settled constitutionality of Trading with Enemy Act and upheld validity of seizure of alien-owned property in U.S., 1920-21. Home: New York, N.Y. Died July 28, 1924.

QUINN, Ralph Hughes, publisher; b. Corydon, Ky., May 7, 1893; s. George A. and Mary (Hughes) Q.; ed. Western Ky. State Normal Sch., Bowling Green, 1908-10; m. Mary Storm, Nov. 20, 1911; 1 son, Stewart. Publisher of Monitor (weekly), Corydon, at age of 14; reporter, Henderson (Ky.) Evening Jour., 1909; circulation and advertising mgr. Henderson Morning Gleaner, 1910-14; also corr. Louisville Courier-Jour., St. Louis Post-Dispatch; advertising mgr. Cincinnati Enquirer, 1914-19; sales mgr. Cunningham-Holmes Pierce-Arrow Co., Cincinnati, 1919-20; nat. adv. mgr. Cincinnati Post, 1920-24; v.p. and business mgr. Washington (D.C.) Daily News, 1924-29, Cincinnati Post, 1929-36; pres. Post Pub. Co., 1933-36; gen. mgr. Cincinnati Enquirer, 1936—; Guardian Bank & Trust Co. Trustee Christ Hosp., Cincinnati, Clifton Meth. Ch. (pres. of bd.), Catherine Booth Hosp., Music Hall Auditorium; v.p. Press-Radio Bible Soc. Methodist. Home: Cincinnati. Died May 2, 1940.

QUINT, Wilder Dwight ("Dwight Tilton"), journalist, author; b. Salem, Mass., Nov. 15, 1863; s. Alonzo Hall and Rebecca P. (Putnam) Q.; A.B., Dartmouth, 1887, A.M., 1917; m. Alice A. Hutchings, June 19, 1902. Began newspaper work, July 1887, on Boston Advertiser, of which was night editor until 1890; night editor Boston News, 1890-92; lit. and telegraph editor, 9 yrs., and mng. editor, Dec. 1902-Nov. 1903, Boston Traveler; editorial writer and dramatic and music critic Boston Journal, 1903-07; leading editorial writer Boston Post, 1909—. Ind. Republican. Joint-author: Miss Petticoats, 1902; On Satan's Mount, 1903; My Lady Laughter, 1904; Letters of a Son to His Self-Made Father, 1903; A Self-Made Man's Wife—Her Letters to Her Son, 1905; The Golden Greyhound, 1906; Meyer & Son, 1908. Author: The Story of Dartmouth, 1914. Lecturer on journalism, Dartmouth and Boston U. Home: Cambridge, Mass. Died Jan. 4, 1936.

QUINTARD, Edward, M.D., author; b. Stamford, Conn., Jan. 21, 1867; s. Edward Augustus and Mary (Skiddy) Q.; with exception of 2 yrs. at Trinity Sch., Tivoli-on-Hudson, ed. abroad, mostly in Germany, England and France; M.D., Coll. Physicians and Surgeons (Columbia), 1887; D.C.L., University of the South, 1932; m. Estelle Hayden, June 4, 1894 (died 1926); m. 2d, Mrs. John H. Flagg, Jan. 11, 1927. Practiced, New York, 1887—; v.p., prof. medicine, and med. dir., 1900-20, emeritus, and cons. physician, Grad. Dept. Columbia U. Fellow Am. Coll. Physicians, Congress of Internal Medicine, New York Acad. Medicine, Harvey Society; mem. numerous societies. Author: Battle Hymn and Litany; Sonnets; Sea Babies and Other Babies; Extra Muros and Other Essays; From a Window; Vernal Tides and A la St. Terre. Homes: Norfolk, Conn., and New York, N.Y. Died Feb. 12, 1936.

QUINTARD, George William, iron mfr.; b. Stamford, Conn., Apr. 22, 1822, of English parentage; ed. common sch. till 15th yr.; clerk in grocery house, New York. In 1847 became mem. firm of T. F. Secor & Co., in Morgan Iron Works, New York; 3 yrs. later became co-partner same with Charles Morgan; in 1852 assumed control of works, of which he was sole mgr. till 1867 (except 2 yrs.); m. dau. of Charles Morgan. In 1867 disposed of his interest in Morgan Iron Works; became prin. propr. and pres. New York & Charleston Steamship Co. In 1869 became connected with Quintard Iron Works (steam engines and machinery). Trustee Atlantic Mut. Ins. Co., Manhattan Savings Instn. Home: New York, N.Y. Died Apr. 2, 1913.

QUINTERO, Lamar Charles, lawyer, journalist; b. Matamoros, Mex., Sept. 7, 1863; s. Jose Augustin Q. (Cuban patriot); ed. Jesuits' Coll., New Orleans, La., and under pvt. tutors; LL.B., Tulane U., 1890; m. Emma Peniston, 1895. Reporter courts, New Orleans Picayune, 1881; vice-consul to Costa Rica, 1883; consul, same, 1885; consul gen., 1890—; U.S. commr. and notary public, 1890; now dramatic and musical critic New Orleans Picayune; mem. Caffery, Quintero & Brumby. Apptd. justice of Supreme Court of Philippines by Taft Commn., 1901, but declined. U.S. del. 4th Internat. Conf. of Am. States, Buenos Aires, 1910, and E.E. and M.P. on Spl. Mission to the Chilean Centenary, 1910. Home: New Orleans, La. Died Oct. 30, 1921.

QUINTON, Cornelia Bentley Sage, art dir.; b. Buffalo, N.Y.; d. William Sparkes and Josephine (Bentley) Sage; ed. pvt. French sch. and sem., Buffalo, but principally under parents; studied Art Students' League, Buffalo and New York, under Lucius Hitchcock, George B. Bridgman, Kenyon Cox and other masters; course at École du Louvre, Paris, 1914; hon. Litt.D., Syracuse U., 1915; m. Maj. William Warren Quinton, U.S.A., retired, Oct. 31, 1917. Apptd. asst. sec. Buffalo Fine Arts Acad., 1904; served as asst. to late dir. Charles M. Kurtz, 1905-09, asst. dir., 1909-10, dir. Buffalo Fine Arts Acad., Albright Art Gallery and Albright Art Sch., 1910-24; dir. Calif. Palace Legion of Honor, 1924-30. Has organized and managed many notable exhbns. at Buffalo, San Francisco, etc. Apptd. mem. Nat. advisory com. Sesquicentennial Expn., Phila., 1926; hon. adviser Roerich Mus., New York, 1926; patron Am. Group Painters and Sculptors, Paris, 1927. Awarded bronze medal, Société des Beaux Arts, Paris, 1916; diploma, Nat. Sculpture Soc. America, 1916; Officier de l'Instruction Publique, Paris, 1917; Chevalier Legion of Honor, 1920; Sorolla medal, Hispanic Soc. America, 1924; presented with bronze medal by French representatives to commemorate French exhbn., Calif. Palace Legion of Honor, 1924. Home: San Francisco, Calif. Died May 16, 1936.

QUINTON, John Henry, civil engr.; b. Enniskillen, Ireland, Oct. 19, 1850; s. William and Anne (Thompson) Q.; B.A., Queens U., Ireland, 1871, B.E., 1872; m. Sophia Inglis Donnell, May 22, 1888. Came to U.S., 1873; leveler and transitman, S.P. Ry., until 1876; asst. engr. in charge location and contsrn. South Pacific Coast Ry., Calif., 1878-80; in charge construction 80 miles Oregonian Ry., 1880; asst. engr. and acting chief engr., Pacific Br. Mex. Central Ry., 1881-84; pvt. practice, Southern Calif., 1884-88; asst. engr. War Dept., at Portland, Ore., 1888-89; successively field engr. for Hoffman & Bates (bridge builders), asst. engr. in charge location and constrn. Santa Ana Canal, Calif., San Gabriel Power Canal, 3d St. and Broadway tunnels, Los Angeles, and in pvt. practice until 1903; consulting or supervising engr., U.S. Reclamation Service, 1903-15, also consulting engr. U.S. Indian Service. Identified with many important irrigation projects, among them the Truckee Carson Project (Nev.), Uncompahgre Project (Colo.), Strawberry Project (Utah), Minidoka Project (Ida.), Milk River Project (Mont.), Shoshone Project (Wyo.), etc., involving reclamation of 3,000,000 acres of land; mem. Quinton, Code, Hill, Leeds & Barnard, consulting engrs. (retired). Republican. Protestant. Mason. Home: Los Angeles, Calif. Died May 1939.

QUINTON, William, brigadier gen. U.S.A.; b. Dublin, Ireland, Oct. 9, 1838; s. Arthur and Letitia (Maclean) Q.; grad. Chicago (Ill.) High Sch., 1860. Enlisted as 1st sergt. Co. C, 19th Ill. Inf., June 17, 1861; disch. Nov. 2, 1861; commd. 2d lt., 19th Ill. Inf., Nov. 2, 1861; 1st lt., Mar. 1, 1863; hon. mustered out, Sept. 10, 1864; 2d lt. signal corps, Mar. 3, 1863; hon. mustered out, May 1, 1866; apptd. from Ill. 1st lt. 33d Inf., June 12, 1867; assigned to 7th Inf., May 3, 1870; capt., Apr. 18, 1884; transferred to 25th Inf., Sept. 16, 1898; maj. 14th Inf., Sept. 10, 1898; lt. col. 27th Inf., Feb. 2, 1901; transferred to 14th Inf., Apr. 22, 1901; col. 1st Inf., May 28, 1902; brig. gen., Oct. 6, 1902; retired at own request after 40 yrs.' service, Oct. 9, 1902. Home: Buffalo, N.Y. Died Sept. 16, 1916.

QUIRK, James Robert, editor, pub.; b. Boston, Mass., Sept. 4, 1884; s. Martin J. and Mary (Reddy) Q.; prep. edn., English High Sch., Boston; student Boston U. Law Sch., 1904-06; m. May Allison, Nov. 15, 1926; children—Frances Denton, Jean North. Stenographer and reporter Boston Advertiser, Boston Record, Boston Herald; later city editor Washington (D.C.) Times; mng. editor Popular Mechanics Mag., 1909-12; editor and pub. Photoplay Mag., 1914—, also of Opportunity Mag. Home: New York, N.Y. Died Aug. 1, 1932.

QUISENBERRY, Anderson Chenault, author; b. nr. Winchester, Ky., Oct. 26, 1850; s. James Francis and Emily Cameron (Chenault) Q.; desc. in 8th generation of Thomas Q. who came from County Kent, Eng., to Va., in 1622; ed. Male Acad., Winchester, and Georgetown (Ky.) Coll.; m. Corinna Broomhall, May 1, 1879. Editor Winchester Democrat, 1870-73; on editorial staff Louisville (Ky.) Ledger, 1874, Louisville Sunday Argus, 1875; founded Winchester Sun, 1878; editor Lexington Transcript, 1881-83, Lexington Press, 1883-85; deputy collector internal revenue, Lexington, 1885-89; in War Dept., Winchester Sun, 1878; editor Lexington Transcript, 1882-85. Single-Taxer. Author: Revolutionary Soldiers in Kentucky, 1896; Genealogical Memoranda of the Quisenberry Family and Other Families, 1897; Memorials of the Quisenberry Family in Germany, England and America, 1900; Lopez's Expeditions to Cuba, 1850-51, 1906; Zachary Taylor and the Mexican War, 1911; Five Hundred Kentucky Pioneers, 1912; Kentucky in the War of 1812, 1915. Home: Lexington, Ky. Died Dec. 4, 1921.

R

RABB, Kate Milner, author; b. Rockport, Ind.; M.A., Ind. U.; m. Albert Rabb, 1891; children—Albert Livingston, Martha Charlotte (Mrs. W. H. Hobbs). Author: National Epics, 1896; The Boer Boy, 1900; The Wit and Humor of America, 1907. Editor of "A Tour Through Indiana in 1840" (diary of John Parsons, of Petersburg, Va.), 1920; Indiana Coverlets and Coverlet Weavers (State Hist. Society publ.), 1928. Conductor of column in Indianapolis Star, "A Hoosier Listening Post." Appointed member Indiana Historical Commn., 1923. Member of Woman's Press Club of Indiana. Home: Indianapolis, Indiana. Died July 3, 1937.

RABENORT, William Louis, educator, author; b. Wilmington, Del., June 1, 1870; s. Carl Ludwig and Rosa Renata Florentina (Steltner) R.; grad. Normal Sch., Trenton, N.J., 1890; B.Sc., Teachers Coll. (Columbia), 1907; A.M., Columbia, 1908, Ph.D., 1911; m. Georgia Miller, July 10, 1894. Began teaching in rural sch., Bergen County, N.J., 1890; later asst. supt. schs., N.Y. City; lecturer on geography, Fordham U., 1918—. Pres. Fed. of Teachers Assn., securing legislation for edni. reforms, pensions, salary and tenure, in schs. of N.Y. Democrat. Episcopalian (trustee Broadway Temple, N.Y. City). Elk. Author: Spelling and Dictation, 1906; Spinoza As Educator, 1911; Geography of The World, 1912-18; Geography Note Books, 1925; Drill Exercises in Geography, 1929; Rainbow Readers, 1931-33. Home: Bronx, New York, N.Y. Died Oct. 1, 1938.

RABER, Oran Lee, botanist; b. Wolcottville, Ind., Jan. 14, 1893; s. Levi L. and Lida (Cowley) R.; A.B., magna cum laude, Ind. U., 1912; student Purdue U., 1913; A.M., Harvard, 1915, Ph.D., 1920; U. of Montpelier, France, 1921, U. of Paris, 1922; unmarried. Austin teacher, Harvard, 1915-17; instr. botany, U. of Wis., 1920-21; asst. prof. botany, U. of Mich., 1923-24; asst. prof. botany, U. of Ariz., 1924-26; prof. same, First Univ. Cruise Around World, 1926-27; prof. of botany, Immaculata Coll., 1929-31; editorial staff Biological Abstracts, 1927-33; asso. ecologist of the U.S. Dept. of Agriculture, 1933-34, plant physiologist, Forest Service, 1935-37; editor Southern Forest Expt. Sta., 1937—. Lt. A.S. (ballon branch), 1918-19; licensed observer and pilot spherical balloons, A.S., O.R.C.; translator with French High Commn., Washington, D.C., 1918-19; traveling fellow Am. Field Service Soc., to France, 1921-22. Unitarian. Mason. Author: Biographical Sketches of the Samuel Olin Family, 1921. Translator: The Elongated Captive Balloon (from the French), 1919; Principles of Plant Physiology, 1928; Water Utilization by Trees, 1937. Home: Wolcottville, Ind. Died Feb. 29, 1940.

RABY, James Joseph, naval officer; b. Bay City, Mich., Sept. 17, 1874; s. Cyril and Mary (Billiard) R.; grad. U.S. Naval Acad., 1895; grad. U.S. Naval Air Sta., 1926; grad. Naval War Coll., 1930; m. Jane Callaghan, Oct. 12, 1897; children—Jane McCombe (wife of Lt. Lawrence Varsy Castner, U.S.A.), John (U.S.N.), Marie Louise. Commd. ensign U.S.N., 1897; advanced through grades to capt., 1919; rear admiral, Nov. 1, 1927. Served successively on U.S.S. Constellation, Bancroft, Monongahela, Philadelphia, Oregon, Farragut, Marietta and Nero, 1895-1905; also as gun officer Monadnock, navigator of Iris, chief engr. of S. Dakota, exec. officer Maryland and in command of Ohio, and U.S.S. Supply; comdr. successively, Albany, Missouri and Georgia, World War; later comdr. Destroyer Squadron 1921, Rochester, 1922-23; comdt. Naval Air Sta., Pensacola, 1923-26; then comdr. Aircraft Squadrons of Scouting Fleet, Land service at Naval Tr. Sta., San Francisco, 1905-06; insp. machinery, Union Iron Works, San Francisco, 1907-08; later various periods at U.S. Naval Acad., as instr. in depts. of English, Marine Engring. and Seamanship, and as head of depts. of English and Seamanship; dir. personnel div. Bur. of Navigation and dir. ship movements Naval Operations Office, Navy Dept., Washington, 1918-19; capt. of Navy Yard, Washington, and asst. supt. Gun Factory, 1920-21, later comdt. 6th Naval Dist., Charleston, S.C. Took deepest known sounding nr. Guam—5269 fathoms; took out first merchant convoy under Am. escort in World War I; escorted largest number of ships to Europe; brought home first returning soldiers to be transported in battleship (U.S.S. Georgia); became naval aviator at age of 51—only admiral qualified as aviator up to 1928. Home: San Francisco, Calif. Died Jan. 15, 1934.

RACHFORD, Benjamin Knox, M.D.; b. Alexandria, Ky., Nov. 28, 1857; s. Hugh K. (M.D.) and Elizabeth Kennedy (Beall) R.; grad. Hughes High Sch., Cincinnati, 1879; M.D., Med. Coll. of Ohio, 1882; studied univs. of Germany, 1890; m. Gretchen Louise, d. Gen. William Wherry, U.S.A., Sept. 7, 1897. Resident phys. Cincinnati Hosp., 1882-83; practiced in Ky. 11 yrs., in Cincinnati, 1894—; demonstrator in bacteriology, 1894, prof. physiology, 1895-98, materia medica and therapeutics, 1898-1901, pediatrics, 1901—, Med. Coll. of Ohio. Author: Diseases of Children, 1912. Home: Cincinnati, O. Died May 4, 1929.

RADCLIFFE, Wallace, clergyman; b. Pittsburgh, Pa., Aug. 16, 1842; s. Elias and Susanna (Wallace) R.; A.B., Washington and Jefferson Coll., Pa., 1862, A.M., 1865; D.D., Lafayette, 1882; LL.D., Washington and Jefferson Coll., 1902; and George Washington U., 1910; m. Jessie R., d. Hon. E. C. Walker, May 4, 1887. Ordained Presbyn. ministry, 1866; pastor Woodland Ch., Phila., 1866-70, First Ch., Reading, Pa., 1871-85, Fort St. Ch., Detroit, 1885-95, New York Av. Church, Washington, 1895-1922, emeritus. Founder and pres. Tappan Presbyn. Assn., at U. of Mich., 1886-95; del. Pan-Presbyn. Council, London, 1888, Washington, 1899, New York, 1909,

Aberdeen, 1913, Pittsburgh, 1921, Cardiff, Wales, 1925, Boston, 1929; moderator Synod of Pa., 1876, Synod of Mich., 1889, Gen. Assembly Presbyn. Ch. in U.S.A., 1898, Synod of Baltimore, 1913; exec. commn. Presbyn. Ch. U.S.A., 1912-15. Home: Washington, D.C. Died June 6, 1930.

RADEMACHER, Joseph, R.C. bishop of Fort Wayne, 1893—; b. Westphalia, Clinton County, Mich., Dec. 3, 1840; ed. St. Vincent's Coll., Westmoreland County, Pa.; ordained priest, Aug. 2, 1863; stationed at Attica, Ind., 1863-69; pastor St. Paul's Ch., Columbia City, Ind., 1869-77; rector St. Mary's, Ft. Wayne, and chancellor of diocese, 1877-83; bishop of Nashville, 1883-93, transferred to Ft. Wayne, 1893. Home: Ft. Wayne, Ind. Died 1900.

RADER, Paul, evangelist; b. Denver, Colo., Aug. 24, 1879; s. of Rev. Daniel L. R. (M.E. Ch.); ed. U. of Denver and U. of Colo.; m. Mary Caughran; children—Pauline C., Willamine M., Harriet E. Mem. faculty U. of Puget Sound, Wash., and later athletic dir. of Hamline U., Minn.; pastor Congl. Ch., Boston; evangelist pastor Moody Memorial Ch., Chicago, 1914-21; pres. Christian and Missionary Alliance, New York, 1921-23; pres. World Wide Gospel Couriers, Chicago; dir. Chicago Gospel Tabernacle and pioneer in radio gospel broadcasting; dir. Gospel Temple, Ft. Wayne, Ind.; sponsored missionary tour of primitive tribes of Africa and Asia by motorcycle, 1937. Founder Beta Kappa (nat. fraternity). Author: Round the World, 1922; Big Bug, 1932. Home: Hollywood, Calif. Died July 19, 1938.

RADER, William, lecturer; b. Cedarville, Chester County, Pa., Dec. 17, 1862; s. William and Elizabeth (Yocum) R.; grad. Andover Theol. Sem., 1891; m. Sophie R. Wells, Oct. 21, 1885; children—Kathryn Wells, Phillip Dwight (dec.). Ordained Congl. ministry, 1891; pastor Second Ch., Biddeford, Me., 1891-92, Third Ch., San Francisco, 1895-1905, Calvary Ch., San Francisco, 1908-13; later on editorial staff Public Ledger, Phila. Lyceum and Chautauqua lecturer. Grad. Blackstone Inst. of Law, Chicago. Author: The Elegy of Faith, 1902; Truths for Today, 1902; also, Uncle Sam, or the Reign of the Common People (in Notable Speeches by Notable Speakers, of the Greater West), 1903; Liberty and Labor; Three Hundred Years of the English Bible; Shakespearean Studies. Home: San Francisco, Calif. Died Apr. 9, 1930.

RADFORD, Benjamin Johnson, theologian; b. Eureka, Ill., Dec. 23, 1838; s. Benjamin Johnson and Frances Taylor (Lawrence) R.; A.B., Eureka Coll., 1866, A.M., 1872, LL.D., 1893; m. Rhoda J. Magarity, Nov. 15, 1864. Ordained Christian (Disciples) ministry, 1867; minister and teacher in coll., Eureka, 1870-81; pastor, Des Moines, Ia., 1881-83, Cincinnati, 1885-86, Denver, 1890-92; pres. Eureka Coll., 1876-77, Drake U., Des Moines, 1882-83; dean Bible dept., Eureka Coll., 1899—. Author: Court of Destiny and Other Poems, 1883. Asso. editor of Christian Standard, Cincinnati, 1886—. Address: Eureka, Ill. Died Apr. 27, 1933.

RADFORD, Robert Somerville, professor Latin; b. Forest, Va., Jan. 31, 1869; s. Munford Washington and Laura (Somerville) R.; Ph.B., U. of Va., 1889, Ph.D., 1891, M.A., 1892; Ph.D., Johns Hopkins, 1895; studied, U. of Berlin, 1898; unmarried. Instr. Latin and Greek, U. of Va., 1888-92; instr. Latin, Acad. of Northwestern U., 1896-97; prof. Latin, Washburn Coll., 1897-99; asso. in Latin lit., Bryn Mawr Coll., 1899-1901; prof. Latin and Roman archæology, Elmira Coll., 1901-08; prof. Latin and classical archæology, U. of Tenn., 1908—. Mem. Tenn. Philol. Assn. (v.p. 1913-14). Contbr. to philol. jours. of numerous articles on the Old Latin language, versification and accent. Address: Knoxville, Tenn. Died Nov. 7, 1936.

RAE, Charles Whiteside, naval engr.; b. Hartford, Conn., June 30, 1847; s. Rev. Luzern and Martha (Whiteside) R.; prep. edn. Champlain (N.Y.) Acad.; C.E., Rensselaer Poly. Inst., 1866; grad. U.S. Naval Acad., 1868; D.Sc., U. of Pa., 1906; m. Rebecca Gilman Dodge, Jan. 9, 1890. Promoted through grades, becoming capt., Jan. 3, 1903; served at bombardment of San Juan, P.R., also in several minor actions on S. coast of Cuba and at naval battle of Santiago, July 3, 1898; advanced "for eminent and conspicuous conduct in battle" (medal). Apptd. engr.-in-chief U.S.N., with rank of rear admiral, and chief bureau of steam engring., Navy Dept., Aug. 9, 1903. Residence: Washington, D.C. Died 1908.

RAFFERTY, William Carroll, army officer; b. in Ind., Apr. 11, 1859; grad. U.S. Mil. Acad., 1880, Arty. Sch., 1884; m. Julia, d. Gen. Judson Kilpatrick, 1894. Commd. 2d lt. 1st Arty., June 12, 1880; 1st lt., Aug. 11, 1887; capt., Mar. 2, 1899; maj. Arty. Corps, Apr. 14, 1905; lt. col. Coast Arty. Corps, Jan. 20, 1908; col., Mar. 3, 1911; brig. gen. N.A., Aug. 5, 1917. Mem. Bd. on Regulation of Coast Arty. Fire, 1894-97; prof. mil. science, Seton Hall Coll., South Orange, N.J., 1897-98; comd. defenses at Galveston, Tex., 1900 at time of great cyclone and tidal wave; apptd. comd. Arty. Dist. of Baltimore, 1908; apptd. comdr. 54th Field Arty. Brigade, Camp McClellan, Anniston, Ala., Sept. 1917; comd. 29th Div., Oct.-Dec. 1917; relieved as brig. gen., May 1918; retired Dec. 31, 1919. Address: Washington, D.C. Died May 22, 1941.

RAFFETY, W(illiam) Edward, educator, editor; b. Roodhouse, Ill., May 8, 1876; s. of William Marcus and Melda Anne (Denham) R.; Shurtleff Coll., Alton, Ill., 1895-98, D.D., 1922; A.B., William Jewell Coll., Liberty, Mo., 1899, A.M., 1900; B.D., Rochester Theol. Sem., 1903; studied U. of Chicago, 1905-07; Ph.D., Kansas City U., 1908; m. Flora E. Tilton, June 3, 1903; children—Mary Virginia, Gordon Edward, Grace Richmond, Howard Tefrew. Ordained Bapt. ministry, 1898; pastor Calvary Ch., Erie, Pa., 1902-05; head-worker Association House Settlement, Chicago, 1905-07, also probation officer, Juvenile Court; pastor Edgerton Pl. Ch., Kansas City, Kan., 1908-09; prof. sociology and religious edn., Kansas City Bapt. Theol. Sem., 1908-16; editor-in-chief S.S. Publs. of Am. Bapt. Publ. Soc., Phila., Dec. 1, 1916-Mar. 31, 1924; editor-in-chief Internat. Journal of Religious Edn., Chicago, 1924-27; prof. religious edn., U. of Redlands, Calif., Sept. 1927—. Founder and first gen. supt., Daily Vacation Bible Schs. of Northern Bapt. Conv.; Y.M.C.A. war work, Camp Merritt, 1918; mem. commn. of editors sent to Western Asia by Am. Com. for Relief in Near East, 1919. Professorial lecturer religious edn., Yale U., Sept. 1922-June 1923, Bapt. Inst., Phila., 1917-24, Crozer Theol. Sem., Chester, Pa., 1924. Mem. Religious Edn. Deputation for World's Sunday School Assn. sent to Bible Lands, 1929. Pres. of Calif. Bapt. State Convention, 1931-32; acting pres. U. of Redlands, 1933; mem. bd. dirs. Spanish-Am. Seminary, U. of Calif. Religious Conf., Southern Calif. Council of Religious Edn., Calif. Ch. Council. Author: Guide to Church History, 1912; Brothering the Boy, 1913; Bible and Social Living, 1916; Church School Graded Lessons, 1924; Church School Leadership, 1925; The Smaller Sunday School Makes Good, 1927; Religious Education of Adults, 1930. Home: Redlands, Calif. Died Sept. 28, 1937.

RAFTERY, Oliver Tenry, clergyman; b. in Ireland, May 31, 1853; came to America, 1862; grad. Episcopal Acad., Cheshire, Conn., 1869; B.A., Trinity Coll., Hartford, Conn., 1873, M.A., 1876, D.D., 1908; m. Mary Edwards, d. Rev. William Henry Clarke, June 2, 1881 (died 1887); m. 2d, Adelaide Emery Brainerd, Jan. 7, 1891. Deacon, 1876, priest, 1877, Episcopal Ch.; rector St. Peter's Church, Cheshire, Conn., 1876-86; Trinity Ch., Portland, Conn., 1886—. Archdeacon of Middlesex, 1898—; examining chaplain Diocese of Connecticut, 1910—. Trustee Episcopal Acad., Cheshire, Buck Library, Portland. Home: Portland, Conn. Died May 17, 1919.

RAGON, Heartsill, judge; b. Dublin, Arkansas, Mar. 20, 1885; s. Alfred Jackson and Anna Eliza (Heartsill) R.; student Coll. of Ozarks and U. of Ark., 1905-07; LL.B., Washington and Lee U., 1908; m. Mattie Smith, Aug. 20, 1916. Began practice at Clarksville, Ark., 1908; mem. Ark. Ho. of Rep., 1911-13; dist. pros. atty., 1916-20; mem. 68th to 72d Congresses (1923-33), 5th Ark. Dist.; reëlected to 73d Congress, but resigned, May 1933, upon apptmt. as judge U.S. Dist. Court, Western Dist. of Ark. Democrat. Presbyn. Mason, K.P., Woodman. Home: Ft. Smith, Ark. Died Sept. 15, 1940.

RAGSDALE, J(ames) Willard, congressman; b. Timmonsville, S.C., Dec. 14, 1872; s. Littleton Russell and Ellen Adelaide (Byrd) R.; ed. U. of S.C.; m. Marie Louise Joynes, Nov. 15, 1900. Mem. law firm of Ragsdale & Whitney, Florence, S.C.; pres. Farmers & Mechanics Bank; dir. Citizens Bank, Peoples Bank; mem. S.C. Ho. of Rep. and State Senate; mem. 63d to 65th Congresses (1913-19), 6th S.C. Dist. Democrat. Methodist. Trustee S.C. Industrial Sch. Address: Florence, S.C. Died July 23, 1919.

RAINES, John, lawyer, congressman; b. Canandaigua, N.Y., May 6, 1840; s. John and Mary Remington R.; ed. pub. schs.; grad. Albany Law Sch., 1861; m. Kate A. Wheeler, Sept. 18, 1862. Admitted to bar, 1861, and began practice at Geneva, N.Y.; served in Civil war, 1861-63, as capt. 85th N.Y. vols.; practiced at Geneva, 1863-67; in Canandaigua, 1867—. For 17 yrs. pres. bd. edn. Canandaigua; mem. N.Y. Assembly, 1881-82, and 1885; Senate, 1886-89, mem. Congress, 1889-93; State senator again, 1895—; temporary president of the Senate, 1902—; author of the election law of N.Y., and of the N.Y. liquor tax law known as the "Raines Law." Address: Canandaigua, N.Y. Died 1909.

RAINEY, Anson, lawyer; b. Eldorado, Ark., Mar. 1, 1848; s. Christopher Columbus and Nancy B. (Baker) R.; ed. common schs.; m. Fannie I. Meriwether, Feb. 17, 1874. Pvt. Co. A, 16th Cav., C.S.A., 1863-65; admitted to La. bar, 1871; practiced at Delta for short time; moved to Waxahachie, Tex., 1873; mem. Tex. Senate, 1881-82; judge Dist. Ct., 1885-93; judge Ct. of Civil Appeals, 5th Jud. Dist. of Texas, 1893—, later chief justice. Democrat. Mem. Disciples of Christ. Chmn. dirs. Texas Masonic Orphans Home; Grand Master of Masons, Texas, 1888. Home: Dallas, Tex. Died Aug. 6, 1922.

RAINEY, Henry Thomas, congressman; b. Carrollton, Ill., Aug. 20, 1860; s. John and Kate (Thomas) R.; A.B., Amherst, 1883, A.M., 1886; LL.B., Union Coll. of Law, Chicago, 1885; LL.D., U. of Ill., 1930, Amherst, 1931, Grove City (Pa.) Coll., 1933; m. Ella McBride, June 27, 1889. In practice at Carrollton, 1885-1902; mem. 58th to 66th Congresses (1903-21), and 68th to 73d Congresses (1923-35), 20th Ill. Dist.; Dem. leader of House, 72d Congress; speaker of House, 1933—. Home: Carrollton, Ill. Died Aug. 19, 1934.

RAINEY, John W., congressman; b. Chicago, Ill., Dec. 21, 1880; s. John J. and Catherine R.; LL.B., Chicago Kent Coll. of Law, Chicago, 1909; m. Ethel F. McMahon, June 17, 1914. Asst. judge Probate Court of Cook County, Ill., 1910-12; clk. Circuit Court of Cook County, 1912-16; elected mem. 65th Congress Apr. 2, 1918, to fill vacancy, 4th Ill. Dist.; reelected from same dist. to 66th and 67th Congresses (1919-23). Democrat. Roman Catholic. Home: Chicago, Ill. Died May 4, 1923.

RAINSFORD, William Stephen, clergyman; b. Dublin, Ireland, Oct. 30, 1850; s. Marcus and Louisa (Dickson) R.; A.B., St. John's Coll., Cambridge, Eng., 1872; D.D., Trinity Coll., 1887; m. Emily Alma, d. Frederick Greene, Apr. 1878 (died 1923); children—Ralph Stewart, Lawrence, Kerr; m. 2d, Henriette Rogers, May 3, 1926. Curate St. Giles' Ch., Norwich, Eng., 1872-76; asst. rector St. James' Cathedral, Toronto, Can., 1878-82; rector St. George's Ch., N.Y. City, 1882-1906. Progressive. Author: Sermons Preached in St. George's, New York, 1890; Reasonableness of Faith, 1891; Seven Last Words on Cross, 1894; Preacher's Story of His Work, 1901; Reasonableness of the Religion of Jesus, 1908; Land of the Lion (2 yrs. in Eastern Africa), 1908; Baldwin Lectures at University of Michigan, 1911; Story of a Varied Life, 1922. Home: Ridgefield, Conn. Died Dec. 17, 1933.

RAINWATER, Clarence Elmer, sociologist; b. nr. New Canton, Ill., Oct. 1, 1884; s. Enoch John and Mary Ann (Foote) R.; A.B., Drake U., Ia., 1907, A.M., 1908; Ph.D., U. of Chicago, 1921; m. Lily Francis Williams, Sept. 5, 1907. Teacher sociology, U. of Chicago, 1913; dean Am. Coll. Physical Edn., 1917-19; asst. prof. sociology, U. of Southern Calif., 1919-21, asso. prof., 1921—. Asso. editor Jour. Applied Sociology. Democrat. Mem. Christian (Disciples) Ch. Author: Community Organization (pamphlet), 1920; The Play Movement in the U.S., 1921. Home: Los Angeles, Calif. Died July 22, 1925. Ia., July 8, 1873; s. George Pattison and Janet (McFadden) R.; grad. Newburgh (N.Y.) Acad., 1891; A.B., Union Coll., Schenectady, N.Y., 1900; grad. Pittsburgh Theol. Sem., 1903; D.D., Westminster Coll., New Wilmington, Pa., 1914; m. Martha Whyte Mahood, Nov. 22, 1904; children—Janet Mahood, Russell Watson, Sara Hammill. Ordained ministry U.P. Ch., 1904; pastor Oak Park Ch., Phila., Pa., 1904-10; asso. sec. Bd. of Home Missions, U.P. Ch. of North America, 1910-15; pastor First U.P. Ch., Wilkinsburg, Pa., 1915-17; sec. U.P. War Commn., 1917-18; asso. sec. Bd. of Home Missions, 1917-21; synodical supt. missions, Calif. Synod, 1921—; mem. gen. council of U.P. Ch.; exec. sec U.P. New World Movement, 1920-21. Home: South Pasadena, Calif. Died June 10, 1934.

RAKER, John Edward, congressman; b. nr. Knoxville, Ill., Feb. 22, 1863; s. Christian and Mary E. (Rambo) R.; ed. State Normal Sch., San Jose, Calif., 1882-84; read law with Judge E. V. Spencer, Susanville, Calif.; m. Miss Iva G., d. E. V. Spencer, Nov. 21, 1889. Admitted to bar, 1885; in practice at Alturas, Calif., 1886—; dir. First Nat. Bank, Alturas Mercantile Co., Inter-Valley Milling and Warehouse Co., Alturas Mercantile Company, Warner Valley Stock Co., Ore. District attorney Modoc County, Calif., 1895-98; judge Superior Ct., 1905-10, resigned; mem. 62d Congress (1911-13), 1st Calif. Dist. and 63d to 68th Congresses (1913-25), 2d Dist. Mem. Dem. Co. Central Com. many yrs.; chmn. Dem. State Com., 1908-10; del. Dem. Nat. Conv., Denver, 1908. Odd Fellow (Grand Master of Calif., 1908-09, Past Grand Rep. to Sovereign Grand Lodge); Mason, Grand Sachem of State Iroquois Clubs of Calif., 1906-08. Address: Alturas, Modoc County, Calif. Died Jan. 22, 1926.

RALSTON, John Chester, consulting engr.; b. Ontario, Can., May 1867; s. James G. and Mary A. (Johnston) R.; came to U.S., 1881; studied engring. under pvt. tutors; student Art Students' League, New York; m. Mary Kean Buckner, Apr. 1897; children—J. W. B., Mary Elizabeth. City engr., Spokane, Wash., 1907-09; served as chief engr. Grand Canal Irrigation Works; engr. in development of power in Sacramento Valley; asst. and dir. engr., location and constrn. 800 miles of rys.; hydraulic engr. various enterprises; supt. constrn. 5 miles of sea wall, reclaiming Potomac Flats, Potomac Park, D.C.; v.p. Pacific Coast Pipe Co. Trustee St. Luke's Hosp. Republican. Episcopalian. Mason. Home: Spokane, Wash. Died July 15, 1928.

RALSTON, Samuel Moffett, senator; b. in Tuscarawas County, O., Dec. 1, 1857; s. John and Sarah

(Scott) R.; Valparaiso (Ind.) Normal Sch., Central Ind. Normal Coll., Danville, Ind., 1884; m. Mary Josephine Backous, Dec. 26, 1881 (died 1882); m. 2d, Jennie Craven, Dec. 30, 1889. Admitted to Ind. Bar, 1886; practiced, Lebanon, Ind.; pres. Sch. Bd., 1908-11; presdl. elector, 1888, 92; gov. of Ind., 1913-17; U.S. senator, 1923-29. Democrat. Mem. law firm Ralston, Gates, Lairy, Van Nuys & Barnard, Indianapolis. Presbyn. Mason, K.P. Died Oct. 14, 1925.

RAMAGE, Carroll Johnson, judge; b. Edgefield County, S.C., May 1, 1874; s. John Constance and Mary (Pow) R.; A.B., Newberry (S.C.) Coll., 1894 (honor man), A.M., 1896, LL.D., 1929; M.S., Augustana Coll., Rock Island, Ill., 1908; Ph.D., Grove City (Pa.) Coll., 1907; m. Annie Belle Crouch, May 24, 1904. Admitted to S.C. bar, 1897, and began practice at Saluda; U.S. commr., 1907-11; served many times as spl. judge Circuit Court and as acting asso. justice Supreme Court of S.C.; mem. State Bd. of Edn., 1912-14; govt. agt. War Draft Bd., 1917-18; atty. for S.C. Canal Commn., 1923-25; pres. Planters National Bank, Saluda, 1916; mem. En Banc Court (highest appeal court in state). Trustee Newberry Coll., Newberry, S.C. Democrat. Lutheran. Mason, Odd Fellow, K.P., Woodmen of the World. Author: Digest, 61-80, South Carolina Reports, 1910, also Digest, 81-100, S.C. Reports, 1916; Peyton Randolph. Home: Saluda, S.C. Died Aug. 6, 1937.

RAMBAUT, Mary Lucinda Bonney, educator; b. Hamilton, N.Y., June 8, 1816; grad. Troy Female Sem., 1834; taught in New York, Jersey City, Beaufort and Robertville, S.C., Providence, R.I., and Philadelphia; founded, 1850, with Miss Harriett A. Dillaye, the Chestnut St. Female Sem., afterward moved to a suburb and named the Ogontz School for Young Ladies; m. Rev. Thomas Rambaut, D.D., 1888 (died 1890). Originated, 1879, the movement which resulted in forming Women's Nat. Indian Assn.; was pres.; later hon. pres.; delegate to World's Missionary Convention, London, 1888. Address: Hamilton, N.Y. Died 1900.

RAMMELKAMP, Charles Henry, coll. pres.; b. New York, Feb. 25, 1874; s. George and Meta (Krack) R.; Ph.B., Cornell, 1896, Ph.D., 1900; m. Rhoda Jeannette Capps, June 28, 1907; children—Rhoda, Charles Henry, Edith Sophie, Julian Sturtevant, Theodore. Instr. Am. history, Cornell U., 1897-1900; instr. history, Leland Stanford Jr. U., 1901-02; asst. prof., 1902-03, prof. history and polit. science, 1903-05, Ill. Coll.; prof. history, U. of Mo. Summer Sch., 1903; apptd. prof. history in Summer Sch. of U. of Ill. (resigned); pres. Ill. Coll., 1905—. Presbyn. Republican. Author: Centennial History of Illinois College. Contbr. to hist. revs. Home: Jacksonville, Ill. Died Apr. 5, 1932.

RAMSAY, Francis Munroe, rear admiral U.S.N.; b. Washington, April 5, 1835; s. Bvt. Maj. Gen. George Douglas and Frances Whetcroft (Munroe) R.; m. Anna McMahon, 1869. Apptd. midshipman from Pa., Oct. 5, 1850; served in Pacific Squadron, 1851-55; at Naval Acad., 1855-56, grad., 1856; passed midshipman, 1856; master, and lt., 1858; lt. comdr., 1862; comdr., 1866; capt., 1877; commodore, 1889-94; rear admiral, 1894-97, retired on reaching age limit, Apr. 5, 1897. Comd. U.S.S. Choctaw, and 3d div. of Mississippi Squadron, 1863-64; in engagements at Haines' Bluff, Yazoo River, Milliken's Bend, Mississippi River; commanded battery of 3 heavy guns, mounted on scows, before Vicksburg; later comd. gunboat Unadilla, N. Atlantic Squadron, 1864-65; was in engagements with Forts Fisher, Anderson, etc. After war in various services. Supt. Naval Acad., 1881-86; chief Bur. of Navigation, Navy Dept., 1889-97. Home: Washington, D.C. Died July 19, 1914.

RAMSAY, Thomas Henry, pres. Pacific Nat. Agrl. Credit Corp.; b. Cordelia, Calif., Mar. 2, 1869; s. Charles and Elizabeth (Clark) R.; ed. pub. schs.; m. Corinne Shellabarger, Aug. 14, 1907. Ranch mgr. and owner, Calif., 1900-32; pres. First Nat. Bank of Red Bluff, 1911-27; pres. Livestock Loan Co., 1925-35; pres. and gen. mgr. Pacific Nat. Agrl. Credit Corp., 1925—. Republican. Mason. Home: Red Bluff, Calif. Died May 18, 1940.

RAMSEY, Alexander, U.S. senator, gov.; b. nr. Harrisburg, Pa., Sept. 8, 1815; s. Thomas and Elizabeth (Kelker) R.; ed. common schools and partial collegiate course; studied law; began practice at Harrisburg, 1839; m. Anna E., d. Hon. Michael H. Jenks, 1845 (died 1884). Made speeches for Harrison and Tyler, 1840; chief clerk Pa. legislature, 1841; mem. Congress, 1843-47, as Whig; chmn. Whig State Central Com. of Pa., 1848; gov. Minn. Ty., 1849-53; mayor St. Paul, 1855-57; gov. Minn., 1859-63; 1st gov. to respond to Lincoln's call for troops; U.S. Senator, 1863-75; sec. of war, U.S., 1879-81; mem. Utah Commn., 1881-86; pres. Germania Bank, St. Paul, 1889. Address: St. Paul, Minn. Died 1903.

RAMSEY, George Junkin, coll. pres.; b. Rockbridge Co., Va., June 28, 1857; s. James B. (D.D.) and Sabara (Tracy) R.; A.M., Hampden-Sidney Coll., 1878; post-grad. U. of Va., 1879-80; LL.D., Southwestern Presbyterian U., 1898; m. Annie Stevens, July 1, 1884; children—Sumner Morrison, Annie Sabra, George Le Conte. Prof. Latin, Ogden Coll., Ky., 1880-84; pres. Silliman Inst., La., 1884-99; editor-in-chief B. F. Johnson Pub. Co., Richmond, Va., 1899-1902; pres. King Coll., Tenn., 1902-03, Sayre Inst., Ky., 1904-06; prof. edn., 1906-12, asst. to the pres., 1910-12, Central U. of Ky.; pres. Peace Inst., Raleigh, N.C., 1912-16; pres. South Atlantic Teachers Bur., 1916—. Federal dir. U.S. Employment Service, 1918-19. Mem. Nat. Inst. Social Sciences; mem. exec. com. Conf. for Edn. in the South (Ogden movement), 1906-13. Mason (K.T.). Address: Raleigh, N.C. Died Dec. 9, 1928.

RAMSEY, John Rathbone, congressman; b. Wyckoff, N.J., Apr. 25, 1862; s. John P. and Martha (Rathbone) R.; ed. pvt. schs.; studied law in offices of George H. Coffey, and Campbell & DeBaun, Hackensack, N.J.; m. Mary Evelyn Thompson, Jan. 26, 1898 (died 1898); m. 2d, Alice Taylor Huyler, Jan. 10, 1906; children—John Rathbone, Alice Valleau. Admitted to N.J. bar, 1883, and practiced at Hackensack, 1883—; county clk., Bergen County, 3 terms, 1895-1910; pres. Hackensack Brick Co.; dir. Peoples Trust & Guaranty Co. (Hackensack), Ridgefield Park (N.J.) Trust Co. Mem. 65th and 66th Congresses (1917-21), 6th N.J. Dist. Republican. Episcopalian. Mason, Odd Fellow, Elk. Home: Hackensack, N.J. Died Apr. 10, 1933.

RAMSEY, Joseph, Jr., railway official; b. Pittsburgh, Apr. 17, 1850; s. Joseph and Mary (Patterson) R.; ed. Western U. of Pa.; studied engring.; m. Laura Palmer, Apr. 8, 1873. In engr. corps Pittsburgh, Cincinnati & St. Louis Ry., 1869-70; asst. engr. Cincinnati & Muskingum Valley R.R., 1870-71; chief engr. on location Bell's Gap R.R., 1871; asst. engr. Lewistown div. Pa. R.R., 1871-72; engr., 1872-73, chief engr. and supt., 1873-79, Bell's Gap R.R.; chief engr. and supt. New Castle & Lake Erie R.R., 1879; chief engr. and supt. Pittsburgh Southern R.R., 1879-82; chief engr. and gen. mgr. Pittsburgh, Chartiers & Youghiogheny R.R., 1882-83; also of two other rys. and the Chartiers Block Co.; engr., 1883-86, chief engr., 1886-90, C.,H.&D. R.R.; asst. to pres. C.,C.,C.&St.L. Ry., 1890-91; pres. Peoria & Pekin Union Ry., 1890-95; v.p. Cincinnati, Wabash & Mich. Ry., 1891-92; pres. Findley Belt Ry., 1887-93; gen. mgr. C.,C.,C.&St.L. Ry., 1891-93; v.p. and gen. mgr. Dayton & Union R.R., 1892-93; v.p. Indianapolis Union Ry., 1891-93; gen. mgr. Terminal R.R. Assn. of St. Louis, 1893-95; v.p. and gen. mgr., 1895-1901, pres. 1901-05; Wabash R.R.; pres. W.&L.E. R.R. and Wabash-Pittsburgh Terminal R.R., 1901-05, Ann Arbor R.R., 1902-06, Western Md. R.R. and West Va. Central R.R., 1903-05; pres. N.Y., Pittsburgh & Chicago R.R., 1906-Nov. 1914, Lorain & Ashland, and Ashland & Western rys., 1910-Jan. 1913, Ann Arbor R.R. Co., Apr. 1910-Dec. 1912; pres. W.&L.E. R.R., June 1912—, and pres. and gen. mgr. Lorain, Ashland & Southern R.R. Co., Jan. 1913—. Republican. Home: East Orange, N.J. Died July 7, 1916.

RAMSEY, William F., lawyer, banker; b. Bell County, Tex., Oct. 25, 1855; s. John J. and Nancy (Clark) R.; A.B., Trinity U., Tehuacana, Tex., 1876, LL.B., 1877; m. Emma Johnson, d. Rev. Felix Johnson, Jan. 28, 1878 (died 1885); m. 2d, Rowena Hill, d. Malcolm Hill, Oct. 13, 1886. Began practice at Cleburne, Tex., 1877; pres. Nat. Bank of Cleburne, 1900-08, also pres. First Nat. Bank, Covington, Tex., and Farmers and Traders Bank, Rio Vista, Tex.; justice Criminal Court of Appeals, Tex., by appmt. to fill unexpired term, Jan.-Nov. 1908, and elected for term of 4 yrs.; resigned 1911, to fill appmt. as asso. justice Supreme Court of Tex., resigned, Mar. 1912, to make campaign for Dem. nomination at primaries for gov. of Tex.; resumed practice at Austin, Oct. 1912; chmn. bd. and fed. reserve agt. Federal Reserve Bank of Dallas, Jan. 15, 1916. Presdl. elector on Cleveland ticket, 1884. Presbyn. Mason, Elk. Home: Dallas, Tex. Died Oct. 1922.

RAMSEY, Willis Hinksman, mfr.; b. Alliance, O., Jan. 28, 1861; s. John N. and Mary Adella (Rockhill) R.; grad. Alliance High Sch. ,1879; m. Maggie Morgan, May 1, 1884 (died 1918); 1 dau., Margaret Henrietta; m. 2d, M. Hazel Edwards, June 1, 1922. Clk. and asst. cashier, 1st Nat. Bank, Alliance, 1879-82, and cashier of its successor, The Alliance Bank Co., 1882-93 (resigned); sec., treas., 1893-1911, v.p., sec., 1911-26, Morgan Engring. Co.; chmn. bd. City Savings Bank & Trust Co., Alliance Hardware Co.; dir. Ohio State Life Ins. Co. Mem. Sch. Bd., Alliance, 3 terms; city treas., 2 terms. Trustee, treas. Mt. Union Coll. Republican. Methodist. Home: Alliance, O. Died Nov. 25, 1936.

RANCK, George Washington, author; b. Louisville, Ky., Feb. 13, 1841; s. Solomon and Sarah (Marman) R.; attended U. of Ky.; m. Helen Carty. Author: History of Lexington, Kentucky, 1872; Girty, the White Indian; The Traveling Church, 1891; The Story of Bryan's Station, 1896; The Bivouac of the Dead and its Author, 1898; Boonesborough (Historical), 1901 (publ. Filson Club, Louisville). Address: Lexington, Ky. Died 1900.

RAND, Benjamin, author; b. Canning, N.S., July 17, 1856; s. Ebenezer and Ann Isabel (Eaton) R.; A.B., Acadia Coll., 1875, A.M., 1879, LL.D., 1925; A.B., Harvard, 1879, A.M., 1880, Ph.D., 1885; studied Heidelberg U.; unmarried. Mem. Internat. Geog. Conf., London, 1895; del. John Cabot's discovery of N. America at Halifax; guest at opening of John Cabot Tower, Bristol, Eng.; emeritus librarian of philosophy, Harvard U. Author: Abstract of Ferrier's Greek Philosophy; Life of Rev. Aaron Cleveland, Boston, 1888; Selections Illustrating Economic History since 1763, 1911; Bibliography of Economics, 1895; Life, Unpublished Letters and Philosophical Regimen of the Third Earl of Shaftesbury, 1900; Bibliography of Philosophy, 1905; Modern Classical Philosophers, 1907; The Classical Moralists, 1909; The Classical Psychologists, 1912; Shaftesbury's Second Characters, 1913; Berkeley and Percival, 1914; Locke and Clarke, 1927; Philosophical Instruction in Harvard University from 1636 to 1906, 1929; Locke's Essay, 1931; Berkeley's American Sojourn, 1932. Address: Cambridge, Mass. Died Nov. 7, 1934.

RAND, Charles Frederic, mine owner; b. Canaan, Me., Aug. 17, 1856; s. Francis Caldwell and Adeline M. (Smith) R.; m. Mary E. Burnham, Oct. 21, 1885 (died 1916). Mining iron ore in Lake Superior dist. and Cuba, 1888-1920; building rys., opening and operating mines in Cuba, 1894-1920; interested also in mines of manganese and copper ores; pres. North American Exploration Co., Exploration Investment Co., Moa Bay Iron Co.; chmn. bd. Geophysical Explorations, Ltd. Chmn. bd. Engring. Foundation, 1920-25; hon. mem. Iron and Steel Inst. of Great Britain; pres. Am. Inst. Mining Engrs., 1913-14; pres. United Engring. Soc., 1916-20. Decorated by King of Spain, 1913; Chevalier Legion of Honor, France, 1921. Republican. Unitarian. Home: West Orange, N.J. Died June 21, 1927.

RAND, Edward Augustus, P.E. clergyman, author; b. Portsmouth, N.H., April 5, 1837; s. Edward and Caroline (Paul) R.; grad. Bowdoin, 1857, A.M., 1860; m. Mary Frances Abbott, Oct. 26, 1865. Prin. high schools, Gardiner and Biddeford, Me.; grad. Bangor Theol. School, Me., 1865; in Christian Commn., Army of the Potomac, 1865; pastor Congl. chs., Amesbury, S. Boston and Franklin, Mass. Entered Episcopal ministry, 1880; missionary at Concord, Mass., where Trinity Ch. was built while he was there. Founder of Good Shepherd Parish, Watertown, Mass., and All Saints Parish, Belmont. Pres. and founder Watertown Hist. Soc. Author: When the War Broke Out, 1888; Drummer Boy of the Rappahannock, 1889; Deeds Worth Telling, 1890; Knight that Smote the Dragon: or, Young People's Gough, 1892; Down East Master's First School, 1893; Salt Water Hero, 1894; Two College Boys, 1895; Behind Manhattan Gables, 1896; Whistle in the Alley, 1899; Two Boys at a Fire, 1900; Fifer Boy of Boston Siege, 1901; Ship Ashore, 1903. Address: Watertown, N.Y. Died 1903.

RAND, Edward Lothrop, lawyer; b. Dedham, Mass., Aug. 22, 1859; s. Edward S., Jr. and Jennie A. (Lathrop) R.; A.B., Harvard, 1881, A.M., 1884, LL.B., 1884; m. Annie M. Crozier, June 29, 1893 (died 1921). In practice at Boston, 1884—. Author: Flora of Mt. Desert Island, Me., 1894; also articles on bot, subjects in various scientific publs. Botanist, La Fayette Nat. Park. Episcopalian. Home: Cambridge, Mass. Died Oct. 9, 1924.

RAND, John Prentice, physician; b. Francestown, N.H., Nov. 8, 1857; s. Thomas Prentice and Lydia (Wheeler) R.; descended from Robert R., the immigrant, Charlestown, Mass., 1635; Francestown Acad., 1880; M.D., New York Homœ. Med. Coll. and Flower Hosp., 1883; post-grad. study, New York Polyclinic, 1888; m. Harriet M. Anderson, Jan. 17, 1889 (died 1892); m. 2d, Lena M. Adams, Sept. 3, 1904. Practiced, Monson, Mass., 1883-88 and 1898-1905, Worcester, 1888-98 and 1905—; consulting physician to Westborough State Hosp., Worcester Hahnemann Hosp.; lecturer, Boston U. Sch. Medicine, 1906-16. Trustee Mass. State Sanatorium, 1903-10 (sec. 1905-10). Conglist. Mem. Am. Inst. Homœopathy, Mass. Homœ. Med. Soc. (pres. 1907), Mass. Surg. and Gynecol. Soc. (pres. 1899), Corp. of Worcester (pres.), Alumni Assn., New York Homœ. Med. Coll. and Flower Hosp. (pres. 1908). Asso. editor North American Journal of Homœopathy, 1910-12. Author: (with N. W. Rand) Random Rimes, 1897. Home: Holden, Mass. Deceased.

RAND, Stephen, naval officer; b. at Norwich, Vt., May 11, 1844. Apptd. acting 3d asst. engr. U.S.N., Dec. 17, 1864; hon. discharged, Aug. 8, 1869; apptd. asst. p.-m., Aug. 12, 1869; passed asst. p.-m., Apr. 30, 1874; p.-m., Jan. 19, 1885; pay insp., Sept. 1, 1899; pay dir., July 1, 1902; advanced to rank of rear adm. retired, May 11, 1906, for services during Civil War. Address: Washington, D.C. Died July 12, 1915.

RAND, Theodore Dehon, retired lawyer; b. Phila., Sept. 16, 1836; s. Benjamin H. and Eleanor S. R.; ed. Episcopal Acad.; attended Polytechnic Coll.; admitted to bar, 1858; practiced law; m. Elizabeth Belrose, March 10, 1864. Engaged as amateur in scientific work, chiefly in mineralogy and geology; published a number of papers on these branches, and lectured before scientific bodies. Fellow A.A.A.S.;

dir. mineralogical and geol. sect. Acad. Nat. Sciences; v.p. Franklin Inst.; treas. Am. Inst. of Mining Engrs. for 30 yrs. Address: Radnor, Delaware County, Pa. Died 1903.

RAND, William, Jr., lawyer; b. Chicago, Jan. 8, 1866; s. William H. and Harriet Husted (Robinson) R.; A.B., Harvard, 1888, A.M., 1891, LL.B., 1891; m. Rosalie Crockett, June 15, 1892. In practice in New York, 1892—; asst. corp. counsel, New York, 1895-97; asst. dist. atty., 1901-05. Home: Rye, N.Y. Died Feb. 10, 1931.

RAND, William Wilberforce, clergyman, editor, author; b. Gorham, Me., Dec. 8, 1816; s. Rev. Asa and Grata (Payson) R.; ed. Boston Latin Sch.; grad. Bowdoin Coll., 1837; Bangor Theol. Sem., 1840, D.D., U. of New York, 1883; became Reformed (Dutch) Ch. minister, 1841. Editor Am. Tract Soc., 1848; sec., 1862, editing all its books, tracts and periodicals; sec. emeritus, 1903. Author: Bible Dictionary, 1860-77. Address: New York, N.Y. Died 1909.

RANDALL, Burton Alexander, M.D.; b. Annapolis, Md., Sept. 21, 1858; s. Alexander and Elizabeth Philpot (Blanchard) R.; A.B., St. John's Coll., Annapolis, 1877, A.M., 1880; M.D., U. of Pa., 1880 (halved 1st thesis prize); Ph.D., same, in course auxiliary to medicine, 1880; m. Emma F. Leavitt, d. Charles W. and Sarah Allibone, May 30, 1893; children—Alexander B., Francenia A. (Mrs. Samuel M. Fox), John Leavitt. Asst. demonstrator of histology, med. dept. U. of Pa., 1880-82; eye and ear surgeon to Episcopal Hosp., 1882-91, to Children's Hosp., 1885; prof. of ear diseases, Phila. Polyclinic, 1888-1902; prof. ear diseases, U. of Pa., 1891-1924 (later emeritus); lecturer Grad. Sch. same univ.; eye and ear surgeon, Methodist Hosp., 1896-1901. Mem. Am. Otol. Soc. (pres.). Joint author: Photographic Illustrations of the Anatomy of the Ear, 1887; American Text-book of Diseases of the Eye, Ear, Nose and Throat, 1899. Wrote: Refraction of the Eye, American Journal of Medical Sciences, July 1885; etc. Address: Phila., Pa. Deceased.

RANDALL, Daniel Richard, lawyer; b. Annapolis, Md., Dec. 25, 1864; s. Alexander and Elizabeth P. (Blanchard) R.; A.B., with honors, St. John's Coll., Annapolis, 1883; fellow in history, Johns Hopkins U., Ph.D., 1887; studied law U. of Md.; m. Elizabeth W. Harding, Apr. 20, 1892; children—Rosamond H. (Mrs. F. F. Beirne), Richard H., William A. Elizabeth H. (Mrs. H. Stuart Stone). Admitted to Md. bar, 1890; asst. U.S. dist. atty., 1898-99; dir. Farmers' Nat. Bank. State's atty., Anne Arundel County, 1900-04; chmn. Rep. Co. Central Com., 1907-09; postmaster of Annapolis, 1909-14; mem. law firm of Randall & Leser, Baltimore, Md.; spl. asst. U.S. atty.; mem. Md. State Industrial Accident Commn. Home: Baltimore, Md. Died Apr. 13, 1936.

RANDALL, Edward Caleb, lawyer, author; b. Ripley, N.Y., July 19, 1860; s. Nelson and Priscilla (Eddy) R.; ed. Allegheny Coll.; m. Maria Louise Howard, Oct. 6, 1897; children—Virginia (dec.), Marian. Admitted to N.Y. bar, 1883; practiced at Buffalo, 1884; pres. Cataract Development Corp., Am. Super-Power Corp., Super-Power Syndicate, South Buffalo Gas Corp., South Buffalo Terminals Corp., Standard Gasoline Co. of Can., Ltd. Author: Life's Progression, 1906; Future of Man, 1908; The Dead Have Never Died, 1916; Frontiers of the After Life, 1922; The Living Dead, 1927; An Hour in the After Life; Nero's Redemption. Home: Buffalo, N.Y. Died July 3, 1935.

RANDALL, Edwin Mortimer, clergyman; b. Nepenskun Tp., Winnebago County, Wis., Jan. 14, 1862; s. Edwin Mortimer and Lucretia Caroline (Steele) R.; A.B., Baker U., Baldwin, Kan., 1886, A.M., 1890, D.D., 1902, Willamette, 1902; m. Jennie May Sweet, Nov. 15, 1888; children—May, Edwin Thomas. Admitted to M.E. ministry, 1886, deacon, 1889, elder, 1891; pastor Herington, Kan., 1887-89, Osage City, 1889-92, Washington, 1892-93, Leavenworth, 1893-96, Seattle, Wash., 1896-1903; pres. U. of Puget Sound, Wash., 1903-04; gen. sec. Epworth League M.E. Ch., May 1904-May 1912; ranching for physical recuperation, 1912-14; pastor, Seattle, 1914-17, Everett, Wash., 1917-21; exec. sec. Seattle Gen. Hosp. Assn., 1921-22; pastor, Seattle, Wash., 1922-24, Chehalis, 1924-27; retired Sept. 1927. Del. Gen. Conf. M.E. Ch., 3 times; rep. to Ecumenical Conf., Toronto, 1911; mem. Commn. on Unification of M.E. Ch. with M.E. Ch., S., 1916-20. Mason. Home: Vashon, Wash. Died June 28, 1939.

RANDALL, Emilius Oviatt, court reporter; b. Richfield, O., Oct. 28, 1850; s. D. A. Randall (D.D.) and Harriet O. R. (three great grandfathers fought in Am. Revolution); Ph.B., Cornell, 1874; LL.B., Ohio State U., 1892, LL.M., 1892; LL.D., Ohio U., 1918; m. Mary A. Coy. Pres. Columbus Bd. of Trade, 1889; admitted to bar, 1890; prof. law, Ohio State U., 1893-1909; official reporter Supreme Ct. of Ohio, 1895—. Sec. Ohio State Archæol. and Hist. Soc., 1894—; lecturer. Republican; del. Rep. Nat. Conv., 1904. Author: History of the Separatist Society of Zoar, 1899; The Mound Builders of Ohio, 1908. Joint author: History of Ohio, 5 vols., 1912. Edited 30 vols. hist. publs., Ohio State Hist. Soc.; edited 47 vols. Ohio State Reports Supreme Court Decisions; 10 vols. Reports of Ohio Appellate Court Decisions. Editor Ohio Archæological and Historical Quarterly, 1897—; asso. editor Bench and Bar of Ohio, 2 vols. Home: Columbus, Ohio. Died Dec. 18, 1919.

RANDALL, Eugene Wilson, insurance exec.; b. Winona, Minn., Jan. 1, 1859; s. Albert Davis and Maria Smith (Jayne) R.; grad. State Teachers Coll., Winona, 1879; m. Eudora A. Stone, Mar. 16, 1882; children—Clarence Brewster, Heman Ward, Frank Eugene, Martha Eudora (Mrs. Howard Tayler). Prin. high sch., Morris, Minn., 1880-82; editor and pub. Morris Tribune, 1882-88; mgr. county farm, Stevens County, Minn., 1888-91; postmaster Morris, 1891-95; sec. and gen. mgr. Minn. State Fair, 1895-1907; dean and dir. agrl. dept., U. of Minn., 1907-08; pres. Minn. Mutual Life Ins. Co., 1908-28, chairman of the board of dirs., 1928—. Chmn. 2d Red Cross drive, Minnesota, World War I. Served as pres. Minn. Pub. Health Assn., St. Paul Assn. Pub. and Business Affairs, Am. Life Conv. Trustee Hamline U. Methodist. Mason, Elk. Home: St. Paul, Minn. Died Aug. 9, 1940.

RANDALL, Frank Lange, penologist; b. Ft. Ridgely, Minnesota Territory, Sept. 30, 1856; s. Benjamin H. and Wilhelmena Helena (Lange) R.; St. John's Coll., Prairie du Chien, Wis., 1874-75; m. Winona E. Pierce, May 3, 1886. County supt. schs., Nicollet County, Minn., 1877-80; admitted to bar, 1880; county atty., Winona County, Minn., 1893-95; referee in bankruptcy, Winona, 1898-1900; gen. supt. Minn. State Reformatory, St. Cloud, Minn., 1900-13; chmn. Prison Commn. of Mass., 1913-16; dir. of prisons of Mass., July 1-Sept. 1916; retired. Mem. Am. Prison Assn., Nat. Conf. Social Work, Am. Inst. Criminal Law and Criminology. Home: Minneapolis, Minn. Died Aug. 6, 1921.

RANDALL, George Archibald; b. Oakland, Calif., Dec. 2, 1887; s. George Westcott and Helen Mar (Greive) R.; B.S., U. of Calif., 1910; m. Della E. Darden, Aug. 29, 1912; children—George Archibald, Westcott Darden, Jackson Lee. Successively constrn. engr., div. engr. and indsl. agent Southern Pacific Co., 1910-17; contract agent U.S.R.R. Adminstrn., 1917-20; dist. engr. Standard Oil Co. of Calif., 1920-23; mgr. and owner Darden & Randall Co. distributor, Buick automobiles, Ventura, Calif., 1923—; owner Darden Randall Ranch Co.; mem. advisory bd. Bank America. Mayor of Ventura, 1927-31. Trustee Memorial Hosp. Artist; illustrator of western ranch life and Indian life of the Southwest for Desert Mag., Westways and other mags. Home: Ventura, Calif. Died Oct. 6, 1941.

RANDALL, George Morton, major gen. U.S.A.; b. in Ohio, Oct. 8, 1841. Pvt. Co. A, 4th Pa. Inf., Apr. 20, 1861; discharged, July 25, 1861; apptd. from Pa., 2d lt. 4th Inf. U.S.A., Oct. 24, 1861; 1st lt., Nov. 6, 1862; maj. 14th N.Y. Arty., Aug. 16, 1864; lt. col., June 1, 1865; hon. mustered out of vol. service, Aug. 26, 1865; capt., Sept. 23, 1865; assigned to 23d Inf., Jan. 1, 1871; maj. 4th Inf., Jan. 15, 1891; lt. col. 8th Inf., Mar. 1, 1894; brig. gen. vols., May 4, 1898; col. 17th U.S. Inf., Aug. 8, 1898; transferred to 8th Inf., Sept. 16, 1898; hon. discharged from vols., Apr. 12, 1899; brig. gen. vols., Jan. 20, 1900; brig. gen. U.S.A., Feb. 6, 1901; maj. gen., June 19, 1905; retired by operation of law, Oct. 8, 1905. Bvtd. capt., Sept. 17, 1862, "for gallant and meritorious services at battle of Antietam, Md."; maj., Apr. 2, 1865, for same, Petersburg, Va.; lt. col. and col. vols., Mar. 26, 1865, "for gallantry in attack on Ft. Stedman, Va."; lt. col., Feb. 27, 1890, "for gallant service in action" against Indians at Turret Mountain, Ariz., Mar. 27, 1873, and at Diamond Butte, Ariz., Apr. 22, 1873; col., Feb. 27, 1890, "for gallant service in action" against Indians nr. Pinal, Ariz., Mar. 8, 1874, and "distinguished service" during campaign against Indians in Ariz., 1874. Home: Denver, Colo. Died June 14, 1918.

RANDALL, James Ryder, journalist; b. Baltimore, Jan. 1, 1839; s. John K. and Ruth M. R.; ed. Georgetown Coll., D.C.; LL.D., Notre Dame, Ind.; m. Katherine Hammond, 1866. Wrote the famous war song, My Maryland, and other poems. Editor the Morning Star, New Orleans, 1905-07. Guest of honor of the people of Md. on "Maryland Day" at Jamestown Expn. Address: Baltimore, Md. Died 1908.

RANDALL, Samuel Bond, teacher Calif. Coll., 1896—; b. Adams, N.Y., Feb. 26, 1860; s. Benjamin and Ellen Bond R.; ed. Northwestern Coll., Naperville, Ill., 1873-74; U. of Chicago, prep. 1875-77; grad. U. of Chicago, 1881; Bapt. Union Theol. Sem., Morgan Park, Ill., B.D., 1885; U. of Calif., M.A., 1902; m. Lottie A. Millard, June 30, 1885. Ordained to Bapt. ministry, Augusta, Wis., Sept. 30, 1885; pastor Augusta, Wis., 1885-87; at Beatrice, Neb., 1887-88; San Jacinto, Calif., 1890; Los Gatos, Calif., 1891-96. Author: Walking with God. Address: Oakland, Calif. Died 1904.

RANDALL, Wyatt William, chemist; b. Annapolis, Md., Jan. 10, 1867; s. Alexander and Elizabeth Philpot (Blanchard) R.; B.A., St. John's Coll., Md., 1884; Ph.D., Johns Hopkins, 1890; research work, Univ. Coll., London, 1895; m. Eliza P. Colston, June 23, 1898. Asst. and asso. in chemistry, 1889-98, Johns Hopkins; science master, Lawrenceville (N.J.) Sch., 1898-1900; prof. chemistry, Jacob Tome Inst., Port Deposit, Md., 1900-01; head master, Mackenzie Sch., Dobbs Ferry, N.Y., 1901-10; chemist to Md. State Dept. Health, 1911—; asso. in biochemistry, Johns Hopkins Sch. of Hygiene and Pub. Health, 1921—. Mem. Joint Com. on Definitions and Standards, 1918-26; mem. Assn. Official Agrl. Chemists (pres. 1925-26). Episcopalian. Author: Chemical Experiments (with Prof. Remsen), 1895; The Expansion of Gases by Heat, 1901; also monographs on chem. subjects and contbns. to chem. publs. Home: Guilford, Md. Deceased.

RANDOLPH, Alfred Magill, bishop; b. Winchester, Va., Aug. 31, 1836; s. Robert Lee and Mary B. T. R.; A.B., William and Mary, 1855; grad. Va. Theol. Sem., 1858; D.D., William and Mary, 1876; LL.D., Washington and Lee, 1887; D.C.L., U. of the South, 1902; m. Sallie Griffith Hoxton; father of Robert Lee R. Deacon, 1858, priest, 1860, P.E. Ch.; rector St. George, Fredericksburg, Va., 1860-62; chaplain C.S.A., 1862-65; rector Christ Ch., Alexandria, Va., 1865-67; Emmanuel Ch., Baltimore, 1867-83; consecrated coadjutor bishop of Va., 1883, bishop of Southern Va., 1892. Paddock lecturer, Gen. Theol. Sem., New York, 1902. Author: Reason, Faith and Authority in Christianity, 1902. Address: Norfolk, Va. Died Apr. 6, 1918.

RANDOLPH, Carman Fitz, lawyer; b. Jersey City, N.J., Aug. 17, 1856; s. Edgar F. and Katharine (Schanck) R.; ed. pvt. schs., Morristown, N.J., and Harvard and Columbia Law schs.; unmarried. Admitted to bar, 1879. Del. Dem. Nat. Conv., 1884, from N.J.; mem. N.J. Constl. Conv., 1894. Mem. Institut Colonial International, Brussels. Author: The Law of Eminent Domain, 1894; The Law and Policy of Annexation, 1901. Contbr. to various law revs. on legal and polit. subjects; also writer of various monographs on questions of internat. and domestic policy. Home: Morristown, N.J. Deceased.

RANDOLPH, Edward Hughes, lawyer; b. Bossier Parish, La., Mar. 12, 1858; s. Edward G. and Mary E. (Thompson) R.; Belles Lettres course, La. State U., 1874; LL.B., Tulane U., 1880, LL.D., 1907; m. Annie M. Jeffries, Oct. 14, 1884 (died 1907); m. 2d, Mary Rose Youree, July 22, 1911 (died 1919); m. 3d, Loé Mixon, Feb. 28, 1922. Engaged in practice at Shreveport, La., 1880—; mem. law firm of Wise, Randolph & Rendall; dir., gen. atty. La. Ry. & Navigation Co.; dir., v.p. div. counsel, Houston & Shreveport R.R. Co. (S.P. Lines); div. counsel Illinois Central R.R. Co.; local atty. T.P. Ry. Co.; gen counsel, Shreveport Traction Co. Mem. La. Ho. of Rep., 1884; city atty., Shreveport, 1884-94; mem. Dem. State Central Com. (resigned, 1896, after party declared in nat. platform for free silver); drafted first law in La. dealing with juveniles and delinquent children; wrote the first address to the people in the fight against the La. lottery; U.S. dist. atty. for Western Dist. of La., by appmt. of President Taft, 1911-17. Democrat. Pres. La. Bar Assn., 1909-11; pres. Shreveport Red Cross, 1917—. Home: Shreveport, La. Died Feb. 16, 1934.

RANDOLPH, Epes, railway pres.; b. Lunenburg County, Va.; s. William Eston and Sarah Lavinia (Epes) R.; m. Eleanor Taylor, Jan. 1886. Asst., locating, resident, and div. engr. for various rys., in the South and Mex., 1876-85; chief engr., Ky. Central R.R. and Cincinnati Elevated Ry., Transfer & Bridge Co., 1885-90; chief engr. and supt., Newport News & Miss. Valley Co., Ohio & Big Sandy R.R. Co., and Ky. & S. Atlantic R.R. Co., at Lexington, Ky., 1890-91, and of Chesapeake, Ohio & Southwestern and Ohio Valley ry. cos., at Louisville, 1891-94; consulting engr. in West and recuperating, 1894-95; supt. S.P. Co. in charge lines in Ariz. and N.M., at Tucson, Ariz., Aug. 1895-Aug. 1901; v.p. and gen. mgr. Los Angeles Ry. Co. and Pacific Electric Ry. Co., bldg. and operating 700 miles of electric line, 1901-04; pres., 1904-10, v.p. and gen. mgr., Feb. 1910—, Gila Valley, Globe & Northern Ry. Co., and Maricopa & Phoenix & Salt River Valley R.R. Co.; pres., 1904-09, v.p. and gen. mgr., June 1909—, Cananea, Yaqui River & Pacific R.R. Co., in Mex.; pres. S.P. R.R. Co., of Mex. and Ariz., Eastern R.R. Co., Oct. 1911—; pres. East Coast Oil Co., Albion Lbr. Co. Address: Tucson, Ariz. Died Aug. 22, 1921.

RANDOLPH, George F., railway official; b. Norwalk, O., June 29, 1856; s. John F. and Harriet (Swetland) R.; ed. Phillips Exeter Acad.; m. Annie R. Dearborn, Feb. 16, 1885; children—Katherine F. (Mrs. J. D. Lalor), Francis F. Began as clerk Cincinnati, Sandusky & Cleveland Railroad, at Sandusky, Ohio, 1873, operator and agent, 1873-75; clerk cashier's office, later paymaster, St.L.&S.F. Ry., 1875-79; sta. agt. Cincinnati, Sandusky & Cleveland and Ind., Bloomington & Western rys., 1879-81; clk. Equitable Life Assurance Soc., Paris, France, June-Oct. 1881; traveling auditor Mo.P. Ry., 1881-83; clk. gen. supt.'s office, M.,K.&T. Ry., Mar.-Aug. 1883; clk. auditor's office and chief clk. gen. freight office West Shore R.R., New York, 1883-85; gen. freight

1885-90; gen. freight agt. N.Y.&N.E. R.R., 1890-92; 1st asst. gen. freight agt., Phila. & Reading and L.V. and pass. agt. Elmira, Cortland & Northern R.R., rys., 1892-93; gen. traffic mgr., N.Y.&N.E. and Norwich & New York Transportation Co., 1893-95; gen. traffic mgr., B.&O.S.W. R.R., 1896-97; mem. bd. mgrs. Joint Traffic Assn. for B.&O. lines, 1897-99; pres. Staten Island Ry. and gen. agt. B.&O. and B.&O.S.W. rys., 1899-1903; v.p. S.I. Rapid Transit Ry. and gen. supt. N.Y. div. B.&O. R.R., 1903-04; 1st v.p. B.&O. System, also v.p., dir. B.&O.S.W. Ry. and C.,H.&D. Ry., 1904-16; chmn. of Trunk Lines Exec. Com., 1906-15; commr. Eastern Trunk Lines, Nov. 1916-Aug. 1, 1918; also traffic asst. to regional dir. U.S.R.R. Adminstrn., Jan.-July 1918; retired v.p. B.&O. R.R., Nov. 1, 1916. Dir., chmn. exec. com. Union Trust Co. of Baltimore. Q.m. gen., Gen. Staff, Md. N.G., with rank of brig. gen., 1908-12. Member French Inst. in U.S., Boston Chamber Commerce and Am. Chamber Commerce, Paris. Address: Baltimore, Md. Died Mar. 25, 1926.

RANDOLPH, Harold, pianist; b. Richmond, Va., Oct. 31, 1861; s. Innes and Anna Clare (King) R.; ed. Richmond, Va., Baltimore; studied music at Peabody Conservatory of Music; m. Emma L., d. James Albert Gary, June 4, 1896. Organist at R.C. Cathedral, 1885-90; organist and choirmaster Emmanuel P.E. Ch., 1890-1906. Dir. Peabody Conservatory of Music, 1898—. Home: Roland Park, Md. Died July 6, 1927.

RANDOLPH, Hollins Nicholas, lawyer; b. "Dunlora," Albemarle County, Va., Feb. 25, 1872; s. William Lewis and Agnes (Dillon) R.; B.L., U. of Va., 1895; m. Caroline Tison, d. George Walter, Oct. 17, 1899. Admitted to Ga. bar, 1896, and practiced at Atlanta and in the Southeast; mem. firm Randolph & Woodruff; admitted to bars U.S. and D.C. Supreme Courts, 1916. Served as gen. counsel Am. Trust & Banking Co. until consolidated with Atlanta Savings Bank, and as gen. counsel latter bank until it was acquired by the Trust Co. of Ga., 1930; counsel for receivers Seaboard Air Line Ry., 1908-10, 5th Circuit, and later counsel for the co. at Atlanta and elsewhere; organized, and was counsel St. Andrews Bay Development Co.; an organizer Fed. Res. Bank of Atlanta and later elected gen. counsel; counsel for Pres. Tinoco, of Costa Rica, to secure recognition by U.S. Govt.; served as spl. counsel Wm. Randolph Hearst in the South and as pres., dir. and counsel Atlanta Georgian; counsel Boulder Dam Development (Colorado River) and in regard to Cape Cod Canal (Mass.), also many local and nat. orgns.; atty. Reconstruction Finance Corp., Washington, D.C., 1934—; member Thomas Jefferson Memorial Commn., 1935. Represented alien property custodian in Southeast during World War and was member Capital Issues Committee 6th Fed. Res. Dist., also counsel War Finance Corp., Ga.-Fla. Agency. Del. Dem. Nat. Conv., Baltimore, St. Louis, San Francisco and New York; mem. Dem. Exec. Com., Ga. Pres. for life Stone Mountain Memorial Assn., and author of Congressional act directing five million Stone Mountain memorial coins; organizer and v.p., Good Samaritan Clinic (Atlanta) for study of ductless glands; chmn. exec. com. Am. Crime Commn. (Chicago); vice chmn. exec. com. Oglethorpe U.; presented Distinguished Service certificate by Atlanta Chamber Commerce for services rendered city of Atlanta. Mem. staff of Gov. Dorsey. Episcopalian. Mason, Odd Fellow, K.P., Elk. Mem. Am. advisory council Yenching U., Peiping, China. Home: Atlanta, Ga. Died Apr. 29, 1938.

RANDOLPH, Isham, civil engr.; b. on farm, New Market, Clarke County, Va., Mar. 25, 1848; s. Robert C. (M.D.) and Lucy Nelson (Wellford) R.; ed. chiefly by mother and 21 months in pvt. day schs. in Va.; engring. acquired by study and actual work, beginning as axman in employ of B.&O. R.R.; D.Eng., U. of Ill., 1910; D.Com.Sc., Washington and Lee U., 1917; m. Mary Henry Taylor, June 15, 1882. Chief engr. Chicago & Western Ind. R.R., and Belt Ry. of Chicago, 1880, Chicago, Madison & Northern Ry., 1886, Sanitary Dist. of Chicago, 1893-1907, consulting engr. until 1912; designed and built for the Queen Victoria Niagara Falls Park Commn. the "obelisk" dam above Horse Shoe Falls, which was built upright, on end, and tipped over into the stream, accomplishing the desired purpose; mem. Internat. Bd. of Consulting Engrs. for Panama Canal, 1905-06; mem. Advisory Bd. of Engrs. for Panama Canal, 1909; engr. Milwaukee Outer Harbor, 1909; mem. Rivers and Harbors Commn. State of Ill., 1911; chmn. Fla. Everglades Engring. Commn., 1913; chmn. Internal Improvement Commn. of Ill., Chicago Harbor Commn., etc. Was consulting engr. on track elevation, City of Baltimore, and Toronto, Can.; reviewed plans for Lake Erie and Ohio River Canal Bd., for barge canal, 1916. Awarded gold medal, Paris Expn., 1900, for work on Chicago Drainage Canal; Elliott Cresson medal, Franklin Inst., 1913, "for distinguished achievement in the field of civil engineering"; gold medal, St. Louis Expn., 1904, for useful invention (moving platform). Home: Chicago, Ill. Died Aug. 2, 1920.

RANDOLPH, John Cooper Fitz, consulting mining engr.; b. Trenton, N.J., Dec. 1846; s. Judge Joseph Fitz and Sarah Ann (Cooper) R.; brother of Joseph Fitz R.; A.B., Princeton, 1866, A.M., 1869; E.M., Columbia Sch. Mines, 1869; univs. of Göttingen, Tübingen, and Vienna, 1869-72; unmarried. In service of U.S. Govt., 1872; Japanese Govt., 1874; Chinese Govt., 1885; govt. of Republic of Colombia, S.A., 1888; took expdn. into Borneo for mining purposes, 1890; in Peru and Chile, 1899; in Nizam's State, India, 1900-01. Author of numerous tech. papers and reports. Home: Morristown, N.J. Died 1911.

RANDOLPH, Joseph Fitz, lawyer; b. New Brunswick, N.J., Dec. 4, 1843; s. Judge Joseph Fitz and Sarah A. (Cooper) R.; A.B., Yale, 1862, A.M., 1865; univs. of Berlin, Göttingen, Paris, 1862-64; m. Harriet W., d. William H. Talcott, 1872 (died 1891). Admitted to bar, 1866, and in practice in N.Y. and N.J., 1866—. Author: Randolph on Commercial Paper, 1888, 1901; Succession Law in New Jersey, 1906, 09; New Jersey Transfer Tax Laws, 1913; The Law of Faith, 1914; U.S. Inheritance and Transfer Taxes, 1917; Succession Statutes in N.J., N.Y. and Pa., 1925; Beliefs and Bible, 1929. Editor: Jarman on Wills, 1880; Williams on Executors, 1894. Home: Morristown, N.J. Died Feb. 1932.

RANDOLPH, Lewis Van Syckle Fitz, financier; b. Somerville, N.J., May 16, 1838; s. Enoch and Mary Ann (Van Syckle) Fitz R.; ed. pvt. schs., Plainfield, N.J.; (Litt.D., Carson and Newman Coll., Tenn., 1915); m. Emily Caroline, d. Matthias Price, May 16, 1867. Employed in Am. Exchange Bank, New York, 1854-63; in N.J. militia, serving, 1863, in emergency campaign and until after Gettysburg; pvt. sec. to pres. I.C. R.R. Co., 1864, later in money dept. same co., Chicago, and asst. treas. New York; dir., 1873, treas., 1874-85, I.C. R.R. Co.; sec. to executors, Samuel J. Tilden Estate, 1886, and later of Tilden Trust Corp.; succeeded late Andrew H. Green as executor and trustee under will of Samuel J. Tilden, 1903; pres. Atlantic Trust Co., 1895-1903, Atlantic Safe Deposit Co., 1900-03; dir. in many large corps., trustee several large estates, and 6 yrs. treas. New York Zoöl. Soc.; pres. Consolidated Exchange, New York, 1903-06; retired 1906. Mayor Plainfield, N.J., 1881, 82. Author: Survivals (poems), 1901; Fitz Randolph Traditions, 1907. Trustee S.A.R. Address: Plainfield, N.J. Died Jan. 1, 1921.

RANDOLPH, Lingan Strother, mech. engr.; b. Martinsburg, W.Va., May 13, 1859; s. James L. (chief engr. B.&O. R.R.) and Emily (Strother) R.; ed. Shenandoah Valley Acad., 1873-76, and Va. Mil. Inst., Lexington, 1876; M.E., Stevens Inst. Tech., 1883, D.Eng., 1921; m. Fanny Robbins, Oct. 15, 1890. Engr. of tests N.Y.,L.E.&W. R.R., 1883-85; supt. motive power F.R.&N. Co., Fernandina, Fla., 1885-87, Cumberland & Pa. R.R., Mt. Savage, Md., 1887-90; engr. of tests B.&O. R.R., 1890-92; elec. engr. Baltimore Electric Refinery, 1892-93; prof. mech. engring., 1893-1918, dean Sch. Engring., Va. Poly. Inst. Research sect. U.S. Shipping Bd. Emergency Fleet Corp., Phila., Pa. Address: Govanstown, Baltimore, Md. Died Mar. 7, 1922.

RANDOLPH, Robert Lee, ophthalmologist; b. Fredericksburg, Va., Dec. 1, 1860; s. Alfred Magill and Sallie Griffith (Hoxton) R.; ed. Episcopal High Sch. of Va., 1875-80; M.D., U. of Md., 1884; studied in Vienna, 1885-86; hon. A.M., Johns Hopkins, 1902; m. Phoebe W. Elliott, Apr. 15, 1891. Asst., 1892-99, asso., 1899, asso. prof. ophthalmology and otology, 1901—, Johns Hopkins; asso. ophthalmic and aural surgeon, Johns Hopkins Hosp. and Dispensary; ophthalmic and aural surgeon-in-chief to B.&O. R.R. Winner Alvarenga prize of Coll. of Physicians, Phila., 1901; Boylston prize of Harvard U., 1902. Address: Baltimore, Md. Died Dec. 9, 1919.

RANDOLPH, Sarah Nicholas, author; b. Edgehill, nr. Charlottesville, Va., Oct. 12, 1839; great-granddaughter Pres. Thomas Jefferson; prin. Edge Hill School, Patapsco Inst. and a school in Baltimore. Author: Domestic Life of Thomas Jefferson; The Lord Will Provide; Life of Stonewall Jackson. Address: Baltimore, Md. Deceased.

RANDOLPH, Tom, banker; b. Rome, Tenn., Nov. 13, 1854; s. John Lewis and Mary (Bradley) R.; ed. private schools; m. Fay Binkley, July 31, 1889 (dec.). Lived at Sherman, Texas, 1859-1903. Began as messenger, became cashier at 18, pres., 1886—, Merchants & Planters National Bank, Sherman; pres. Commonwealth Trust Co., St. Louis, Feb. 8, 1903; v.p. 1908-13; pres. 1913-15, and chmn. bd., June 15, 1915—, of Nat. Bank of Commerce, St. Louis. Dir. Equitable Life Assurance Soc. of U.S., St. Louis Southwestern Ry. Co., and interested in various banks, trust cos., cottonseed oil mills and other enterprises. Exec. com. Am. Bankers' Assn., 1903-06. Democrat. Home: St. Louis, Mo. Died Jan. 7, 1918.

RANDOLPH, Wallace F., brig. gen. U.S.A.; b. in Pa., June 11, 1841. Pvt. Co. F, 17th Pa. Inf., Apr. 18-June 28, 1861; apptd. 2d lt. 5th U.S. Arty., May 14, 1861; 1st lt., Mar. 1862; capt., July 1866; maj. 3d Arty., Apr. 1888; lt. col., Mar. 1898; col. 1st Arty., Oct. 19, 1899; chief of arty. U.S.A., Apr. 9, 1901; chief of arty. with rank of brig. gen., Feb. 27, 1903; maj. gen., Jan. 22, 1904; retired, Jan. 23, 1904. Served in many battles of Civil War; bvtd. capt., June 1863, "for gallantry in defense of Winchester, Va.," and maj., Mar. 1865, "for good conduct and meritorious service during the war"; commd. brig. gen. U.S.V., May 1898; mustered out of vol. service, Nov. 1898. Home: Washington, D.C. Died 1910.

RANE, Frank William, forester; b. Whitmore Lake, Mich., Dec. 11, 1868; s. William Benjamin and Ellen (Connelly) R.; B.Agr., Ohio State U., 1891; M.S., Cornell, 1892; m. Elizabeth Bailey, Sept. 6, 1893. Prof. horticulture and microscopy, W.Va. U., 1892-95; prof. agr. and horticulture, 1895-98, horticulture, 1898-1900, forestry and horticulture, 1900-06, N.H. Coll.; Mass. state forester, 1906—; lecturer on forestry Mass. Agrl. Coll.; chmn. Mass. Conservation Commn., Mass. Taxation Commn., Mass. State Forest Commn. and Mass. Soldiers' Land Commn. Home: Waban, Mass. Died May 3, 1933.

RANEY, George Pettus, lawyer; b. Apalachicola, Franklin County, Fla., Oct. 11, 1845; s. David G. and Frances H. (Jordan) R.; ed. U. of Va., 1863; served C.S.A., 1863-65; studied law U. of Va., 1866-67; m. Mary Elizabeth Lamar, Nov. 4, 1873 (dec.). Mem. Fla. Legislature, 1868-70; mem. Dem. State Exec. Com., 1876; atty. gen. of Fla., 1877-85, and reporter Supreme Ct., Fla. decisions, 1877-85; asso. justice Supreme Ct. of Fla., 1885-89, chief justice, 1889-94; resigned 1894 and resumed practice. Democrat. Presdl. elector, 1896; mem. Fla. Ho. of Rep., 1899-1902, Senate, 1902-06; mem. Dem. Nat. Com. for Fla., 1900-04; div. counsel Seaboard Air Line Ry. for Fla., 1903—. Address: Tallahassee, Fla. Died Jan. 8, 1911.

RANEY, Richard Beverly, underwriter; b. Retreat, Granville County, N.C., Feb. 7, 1860; s. Thomas Hall and Eliza Partridge (Baird) R.; academic edn., 1867-76; m. Olivia Blount Cowper, Dec. 5, 1894 (died 1896); m. 2d, Kate Whiting Denson, Apr. 28, 1903. Gen. agt. for life ins., Jan. 1, 1894—. Built, 1899, and in 1900 equipped and presented to city of Raleigh the Olivia Raney Library in memory of deceased wife. Address: Raleigh, N.C. Died 1909.

RANGER, Henry Ward, artist; b. in Western N.Y., Jan. 1858; s. Ward Valencourt and Martha Marie (Ranger) R.; ed. Syracuse U. to sophomore year; m. Helen E. Jennings, 1883. Studied art, outside of acads. and during several years' residence in France, England, and Holland. Represented by The Top of the Hill, in Corcoran Gallery. East River Idyl in Carnegie Gallery, by "High Bridge" and "Spring Woods," Met. Mus. of Art, and in some important collections here and in Europe. N.A., 1906. Address: New York, N.Y. Died Nov. 7, 1916.

RANGER, Walter Eugene, educator; b. Wilton, Me., Nov. 22, 1855; s. Peter and Eliza Minot (Smith) R.; A.B., Bates Coll., 1879, A.M., 1883; hon. A.M., U. of Vt., 1902; LL.D., Bates, 1907; Ed.D., R.I. State Coll., 1922; Sc.D., R.I. Coll. of Pharmacy and Allied Sciences, 1935; m. Mary M. Snowman, 1879 (died 1885); children—Walter Harlan (dec.), William Eugene (dec.); m. 2d, Mabel C. Bemis, July 30, 1889; children—Arthur Forest, Ruth Mabel, Robert Walter. Prin. Nichols Latin Sch., Lewiston, Me., 1879-80, Lenox (Mass.) High Sch., 1880-83, Lyndon (Vt.) Inst., 1883-96, State Normal Sch., Johnson, Vt., 1896-1900; state supt. edn., Vt., 1900-05; state commr. education R.I., 1905-35. Director or trustee various ednl. instns.; lecturer and writer on ednl., social, ethical, and fraternal subjects. Mem. Acad. Political and Social Science, N.E.A. (pres.). Mason; Past Grand Master of Masons of Vt., and Past Comdr. of Vt. Consistory. Home: Providence, R.I. Died Nov. 4, 1941.

RANKIN, B(unyan) Kirk, publisher; b. Nashville, Tenn., Mar. 27, 1874; s. David Provine and Leonora Jane (Daniel) R.; grad. Webb Sch., Bell Buckle, Tenn., 1890; student Princeton, 1890-92; m. Sue Woods Porterfield, Apr. 10, 1901; children—B. Kirk, Daniel Castleman. Reporter Nashville Banner, 1893-96, mng. editor, 1896-98; publisher of business papers, 1898-1904; pub. and owner Southern Agriculturist, 1904—; dir. American Nat. Bank. Democrat. Episcopalian. Home: Nashville, Tenn. Died Dec. 8, 1936.

RANKIN, David, farmer, capitalist; b. Sullivan County, Ind., May 28, 1825; s. William and Elizabeth (Gross) R.; ed. country sch. in Sullivan Co.; twice married, 1850 and 1878. Moved from Ind. to Ill. and later to Mo.; mem. Ill. Legislature, 3 terms. Republican. Owner and mgr. farm of 23,000 acres in Atchison County, Mo. Pres. First Nat. Bank, Tarkio; treas. Tarkio Coll., to which he gave over $150,000. Pres. Midland Plow Co. Address: Tarkio, Mo. Died 1910.

RANKIN, George Clark, clergyman, editor; b. Jefferson County, Tenn., Nov. 19, 1849; s. Creed Wilson and Martha Jane (Clark) R.; ed. Hiwassee Coll., Monroe County, Tenn.; D.D., U. of Tenn.; m. Fannie L. Denton, Sept. 30, 1875. Ordained ministry M.E. Ch., S., 1871; editor Texas Christian Advocate, 1898— (organ of M.E. Ch., S., in Tex.). Lifelong advocate of prohibition; assisted in making 150 counties "dry" in Tex.; leader in civic reform in Tex. Trustee North Tex. Female Coll., Sherman, Tex. Democrat. Mason. Author: Story of My Life, 1912. Address: Dallas, Tex. Died Feb. 2, 1915.

RANKIN, Henry Bascom; b. Sangamon (now Menard) County, Ill., Apr. 7, 1837; s. Amberry A. and Arminda (Rogers) R.; ed. North Sangamon Acad. and under pvt. tutors; student in law office of Lincoln and Herndon, Springfield, Ill., Dec. 1856-Feb. 1861; m. Alma Hurd, May 4, 1864 (died 1915); children—Fred Henry, Albert Hurd, Emma (Mrs. Clayton J. Barber). Abandoned law on account of Civil War and engaged in farming, banking and investing. Republican. Christian. Author; Personal Recollections of Abraham Lincoln, 1916; Intimate Character Sketches of Abraham Lincoln, 1924; (brochures) Our First American, Abraham Lincoln; The Lincoln Life Mask; Lincoln's Cooper Institute Speech; The Emancipation Proclamation; Barnard's Melancholy Mistake in Bronze; Walt Whitman, Poet and Patriot, (1819-1892); History Lincoln Memorial Tablets in Springfield, Ill.; Account of the Rutledge Family and Ann's Granite Monument at Petersburg, Ill.; also in Oakleaf's Lincoln Bibliography, 1925, A First Word; Sketch of a Long Life; Lincoln's Law Office, 1926. Editorial writer and press corr. Owner of album containing the following entry: "Today, Feb. 23, 1858, the owner honored me with the privilege of writing the first name in this book, A. Lincoln." Home: Springfield, Ill. Died Aug. 14, 1927.

RANKIN, Isaac Ogden, writer; b. New York, Nov. 22, 1852; s. Edward E. (D.D.) and Emily (Watkinson) R.; A.B., Princeton, 1873, A.M., 1876; B.D., Union Theol. Sem., 1877; also studied U. of Berlin; m. Martha Clark, June 23, 1880; children—Hugh, Margaret (Mrs. James M. Barker), Lawrence A. Ordained, 1878; stated supply Congl. Ch. ,Greenfield Hill, Conn., 1879; pastor Nassau and E. Nassau, N.Y., 1880, Kingsborough Av. Ch., Gloversville, N.Y., 1882-91; stated supply, Milton, N.Y., 1894; editorial writer and lit. editor, 1896-1905, asso. editor The Congregationalist, 1905-21. Author: Hewers of Wood (with Rev. W. G. Puddefoot); Closet and Altar; Prayers and Thanksgivings for a Christian Year. For 28 years contributed a weekly article "Saturday Night Thoughts" to Boston Evening Transcript. Home: Brookline, Mass. Died June 15, 1936.

RANKIN, Jeremiah Eames, pres. Howard U., 1889-1903; b. Thorton, N.H., Jan. 2, 1828; s. Rev. Andrew and Lois (Eames) R.; grad. Middlebury Coll., Vt., 1848, D.D., LL.D., Middlebury Coll.; m. Mary Howell Birge, Nov. 28, 1854. Tutor in coll., 1850; Congl. pastor, Potsdam, N.Y., St. Albans, Vt., Lowell and Boston, Mass., Washington, and Orange, N.J.; resigned presidency Howard U., Mar. 1903. Contbr. to The Independent and other religious papers; hymn writer; author of God Be With You. Author: Auld Scotch Mither, and Other Poems; Ingleside Rhymes; Subduing Kingdoms; The Hotel of God; Atheism of the Heart; Christ His Own Interpreter; Elective Affinity; Broken Cadences, Hymns Pro Patria; Word and Song (Hymns and Tunes); The Cup the Father Giveth; also articles in Biblio theca Sacra. Translator: (from German) German-English Lyrics; The Dance and the Martyr (Adolph Monod); The Aversion of Young People to Christianity. Address: Cleveland, O. Died 1904.

RANKIN, John Chambers, Presbyn. clergyman; b. Guilford County, N.C., May 18, 1816; grad. U. of N.C., 1836, D.D., Princeton. Ordained to ministry, July 18, 1839; missionary to India, 1840-48; pastor Presbyn. church, Basking Ridge, N.J., 1851-95; pastor emeritus, 1895—; m. Sarah T. Comfort, June 3, 1840; m. 2d, Mrs. N. C. Scales, Nov. 15, 1870. Author: The Coming of the Lord; also several articles in Princeton Review. Address: Basking Ridge, Somerset County, N.J. Died 1900.

RANKIN, William Bradshaw, gen. sec. The John C. Martin Ednl. Fund, June 1, 1900—; b. Greene County, Tenn., Sept. 3, 1825; s. Anthony and Margaret (Grey) R.; grad. Amherst, 1852; A.M.; D.D., Washington Coll., Tenn., 1893; m. Jane Carpenter. Reared on farm; learned blacksmith trade; prin. Rhea Acad., Greenville, Tenn., 1852-54; pres. Greeneville Coll., 1854-58; prof. mathematics Tusculum Coll., Tenn., 1859-61; unconditional Union man in Civil war; exiled from home to N.Y.; canvassed that State for Lincoln and Johnson, 1864; prin. graded sch., Wellsville, N.Y., 1864-66; ordained Presbyn. minister, 1866; served Salem and Bethel chs. and pres. Washington Coll., 1866-74; aided in establishing public school system of Tenn.; supt. public instruction Greene County, Tenn.; dist. supt. of work Am. Bible Soc., Tenn. and Tex., 1874-98; financial agt. Washington Coll., Tenn., 1898-1900. Published sermons, addresses, reports, etc. Contributor to Frank Leslie's Monthly Magazine. Home: Austin, Tex. Died 1903.

RANNEY, Ambrose Arnold, lawyer; b. Townshend, Vt., April 16, 1821; grad. Dartmouth, 1844; admitted to Vt. bar, 1847, Suffolk, Mass., bar, 1848; practiced in Boston 1848—; city solicitor, 1855-56; member Mass. legislature, 1857, 1863, 1864; member Congress, 1881-87. Republican. Address: Boston, Mass. Died 1899.

RANNEY, Ambrose Loomis, M.D.; b. Hardwick, Mass., June 10, 1848; grad. Dartmouth, 1868, A.M., 1872; med. dept. Univ. City of New York, 1870; practiced at New York, 1870—; held chairs of anatomy and of nervous diseases in various colls.; m. Marie Celle. July 25, 1876. Author: Essentials of Anatomy; Applied Anatomy of the Nervous System; Treatise on Surgical Diagnosis; Practical Medical Anatomy; Lectures on Nervous Diseases; Electricity in Medicine; also many monographs. Address: New York, N.Y. Died 1905.

RANNEY, Henry Clay, lawyer; b. Freedom, Portage County, O., June 1, 1829; s. Elijah W. and Levana (Larcomb) R.; ed. in schs. of Jefferson and Warren, O.; LL.D., Kenyon Coll.; m. Helen A. Burgess, Sept. 19, 1853. Admitted to bar, 1852; offered but declined numerous pub. offices. Democrat. Entered Army of Potomac, 1863, a.-a.-g. in battles of Fredericksburg and Chancellorsville; mentioned in orders for bravery. Dir. Cleveland & Pittsburgh R.R. Co., Cleveland & Mahoning Valley Ry. Co., Guardian Trust Co., Cleveland Stone Co., Continental Sugar Co.; trustee Soc. for Savings; v.p. local bd. Am. Surety Co.; mem. advisory bd. Citizens' Savings & Trust Co. Trustee John Huntington Benevolent Trust, Art and Poly. Trust; pres. Cleveland Mus. of Art; v.p. Case Library. Mason. Home: Cleveland, O. Died Oct. 7, 1913.

RANOUS, Dora Knowlton, editor translator; b. Ashfield, Mass.; d. Alexander Hamilton and Augusta (Knowlton) Thompson; ed. pvt. sch., Brooklyn and Sanderson Acad., Ashfield; m. William V. Ranous, May 26, 1881. Editor of ednl. text-books for Silver, Burdett & Co.; contbr. to Appleton's Annual Cyclopædia and The Criterion Magazine; editor and translator, for M. Walter Dunne, works of Guy de Maupassant (15 vols.), Gustave Flaubert (10 vols.), Benjamin Disraeli (20 vols.); for the Maison Mazarin, The Immortals—Masterpieces of French fiction (20 vols.), Crowned by the French Acad. and published under its sanction, in which series she translated René Bazin's The Ink-Stain, Anatole France's The Red Lily, André Theuriet's A Woodland Queen, and Philippe de Massa's Zibeline, A Turn of Luck. The Scar, and Mount Ida. Editor for the Nat. Alumni (with Rossiter Johnson), The Literature of Italy (16 vols.), in which series she translated Gabriele d' Annunzio's The Flame, and Matilde Serao's The Conquest of Rome; editor for The Authors' Press (with Rossiter Johnson), The Authors' Digest (20 vols.); editor and translator for the Pearson's Magazine and Pub. Co., of complete works of Guy de Maupassant (17 vols.), 1909. Author: Diary of a Daly Débutante, 1910 (first edit. published anonymously); Good English in Good Form. Mem. editorial staff Century Mag., 1913—. Address: New York, N.Y. Died Jan. 19, 1916.

RANSDELL, Daniel Moore, public official; b. nr. Indianapolis, June 15, 1842; s. John H. and Mary E. (Grubbs) R.; ed. Franklin (Ind.) Coll., 3 yrs.; served pvt. and non-commd. officer in Union Army, 1862-65; lost right arm at battle of Resaca, May 15, 1864; took course in business coll. and taught sch. 1 yr.; m. Mary Cathcart, Dec. 20, 1869. Deputy recorder Marion County, Ind., 1866-67; city clerk, Indianapolis, 1867-71; mem. City Council, 1872-73; clerk of cts., Marion County, 1878-82; mem. bd. commrs. which erected soldiers' monument at Indianapolis; mem. Rep. State Com., 1884-89; marshal, D.C., 1889-94; sergt.-at-arms, U.S. Senate, Jan. 29, 1900—. Home: Washington, D.C. Died Nov. 28, 1912.

RANSEEN, Mattis C., clergyman; b. in Sweden, Apr. 6, 1845; s. Carl M. and Carrie (Johnson) R.; came to America, 1867; grad. Augustana Coll. and Theol. Sem. (then at Paxton, Ill.), 1871; D.D., Bethany and Muhlenberg colls.; m. Anna S. Anderson, of Elgin, Ill., Oct. 3, 1872. Ordained Luth. ministry, 1871; pastor Nebo Luth. Ch., Chicago, 1910—. Pres. Iowa Conf., and Ill. Conf. (16 yrs.); v.p. Augustana Synod many yrs.; pres. Gen. Council Luth. Ch. in America 4 yrs.; one of founders Augustana Hosp., Chicago, and many yrs. its pres. Knighted by King Oscar, Sweden, 1910. Address: Chicago, Ill. Died Aug. 24, 1920.

RANSLEY, Harry C., congressman; b. Phila., Pa., Feb. 5, 1863; s. Robert H. and Mary A. (Irvin) R.; ed. pub. schs. and business coll.; m. Harrie Dilks, Mar. 31, 1902; children—Elizabeth Abigail, Harriet (dec.). Mem. Dunlap, Mellor & Co., oils and naval stores, Phila., 1899—. Mem. Ho. of Rep., Pa., 2 terms; mem. Select Council of Phila. 16 yrs. (pres. 8 yrs.); sheriff of Phila. County, 1916-20; chmn. Rep. City Com., Phila., 1916-19; elected mem. 66th Congress to fill unexpired term of J. Hampton Moore, resigned, and mem. 67th to 72d Congresses (1921-33), 3d Pa. Dist. and 73d and 74th Congresses (1933-37), 1st Pa. Dist. Republican. Episcopalian. Mason. Home: Ardmore, Pa. Died Nov. 5, 1941.

RANSOHOFF, Joseph, surgeon; b. Cincinnati, May 26, 1853; grad. Woodward High Sch., Cincinnati, 1870; M.D., Med. Coll. of Ohio, 1874; F.R.C.S., London, 1877; m. Minnie Workum Freiberg, Mar. 12, 1879. In surg. practice at Cincinnati, 1877—; demonstrator anatomy, 1877-78, prof., 1879-81, surg. anatomy and clin. surgery, 1891-1902, principles of surgery, 1902-05, surgery and clin. surgery, 1905—, Med. Coll. of Ohio (U. of Cincinnati); surgeon Cincinnati, Good Samaritan and Jewish hosps. Extensive contbr. to surg. lit. and standard compilation surg. works. Address: Cincinnati, O. Died Mar. 10, 1921.

RANSOM, Brayton Howard, zoölogist; b. Mo. Valley, Ia., Mar. 24, 1879; s. George Howard and Martha (Roach) R.; B.Sc., U. of Neb., 1899, A.M., 1900, Ph.D., 1908; fellow in zoölogy, U. of Mo., 1900-01, U. of Neb., 1901-02; student George Washington U. Med. Sch., 1902-04; m. Virginia Smith, May 4, 1904. Asst., div. of zoölogy, hygienic lab., U.S. Pub. Health and Marine Hosp. Service, 1902-03; scientific asst. in zoölogy, 1903, in charge zoölogical lab., 1904—; chief div. of zoölogy, 1906—, Bur. Animal Industry, Dept. Agr. Asst. custodian (hon.) U.S. Nat. Mus., 1905—. Author of govt. publications and articles in scientific jours. on parasitology and medical zoölogy. Mem. edit. bd. Jour. of Parasitology, Am. Jour. Tropical Medicine. Address: Washington, D.C. Died Sept. 17, 1925.

RANSOM, George Brinkerhoff, rear admiral U.S.N.; b. Chazy, N.Y., June 28, 1851; s. Harry Sawyer and Martha (Bosworth) R.; Oswego (N.Y.) Normal and Training Sch., 1869; grad. U.S. Naval Acad., 1874 (2d in class); B.C.E., U. of Wis., 1891; LL.B., Suffolk Law Sch., Boston, 1917; m. Sarah Upham, Sept. 15, 1880 (died 1912); m. 2d, Ruth Barber, Sept. 4, 1917. Commd. asst. engr. U.S.N., 1875; passed asst. engr., 1880; chief engr., 1895; comdr., 1904; capt., 1907; rear admiral, 1911; retired June 28, 1913. Chief engr. U.S.S. Concord, May 1, 1898, participating in battle of Manila Bay. Instr. in steam engring. Naval Acad., 3 yrs., and at U. of Wis., 3 yrs. Home: Plattsburg, Clinton County, N.Y. Died Feb. 25, 1924.

RANSOM, Mathew Whitaker, U.S. senator; b. Warren County, N.C., Oct. 8, 1826; atty. gen. N.C., 1852; mem. N.C. legislature, 1858-60; peace commr. from N.C. to Congress of Southern States, Montgomery, Ala., 1861; served lt. col. to maj. gen. C.S.A., 1861-65; U.S. senator, 1872-95; U.S. minister to Mexico, 1895-97. Address: Weldon, N.C. Died 1904.

RANSOM, Rastus Seneca, lawyer; b. Mt. Hawley, Peoria County, Ill., Mar. 31, 1839; s. Reuben H. and Nancy C. R.; ed. country dist. schs. and Elmira Free Acad.; m. Sarah E. Morgan, Jan. 1, 1862; m. 2d, Carol B. Edwards, Jan. 14, 1885. First lt. Co. H, 50th N.Y. Engrs.; enlisted May 1861; mustered into U.S. service, Sept. 1861; service with Army of Potomac, Peninsular Campaign; was surrogate city and county of New York, Jan. 1, 1888-Jan. 31, 1893. Democrat. Home: New York, N.Y. Died Dec. 20, 1914.

RANSOME, Frederick Leslie, geologist; b. Greenwich, Eng., Dec. 2, 1868; s. Ernest Leslie and Mary Jane (Dawson) R.; B.S., U. of Calif., 1893, Ph.D., 1896; fellow in geology, U. of Calif. (teaching mineralogy), 1893-95; m. Amy Cordova Rock, May 25, 1899; children—Janet (Mrs. H. M. Baxter), Susan Clarkson (Mrs. E. D. Fry), Violet Jane (Mrs. H. Rodney Gale, dec.), Alfred Leslie. Asst. in mineralogy and petrography, Harvard, 1896-97; asst. geologist, 1897-1900, geologist, 1900-23, United States Geol. Survey; in charge sections of western areal geology, 1912-16, and of metalliferous deposits, 1912-23; prof. econ. geology, U. of Ariz., 1923-27, and dean of Grad. College, 1926-27; prof. econ. geology, Calif. Inst. Tech., 1927—; cons. geologist U.S. Bur. Reclamation and Metropolitan Water Dist. of Southern Calif., 1928—. Lecturer on ore deposits, U. of Chicago, 1907; Silliman lecturer, Yale, 1913. Mem. Nat. Acad. Sciences (treas. 1919-24), Nat. Research Council (treas. 1919-24), Soc. Economic Geologists (pres. 1926-27), Washington Acad. Sciences (pres. 1918), Geol. Soc. Washington (pres. 1913). Author of numerous official monographs on the geology of western mining dists. and papers in scientific jours. Asso. editor Economic Geology. Address: Pasadena, Calif. Died Oct. 6, 1935.

RANTOUL, Robert Samuel, lawyer; b. Beverly, Mass., June 2, 1832; s. Hon. Robert R. R., Jr.; A.B., Harvard, 1853, A.M., 1856, LL.B., 1856; m. Harriet C. Neal. Admitted to bar, 1856; mem. Mass. Ho. of Rep., from Beverly, 1857, Salem, 1883 and 1884; collector port of Salem and Beverly, 1865-69; mayor of Salem, 1890-93; candidate for presdl. elector, Palmer and Buckner ticket, 1896. Pres. Essex Inst., 1896-1904. Address: Salem, Mass. Died 1922.

RANUM, Arthur, mathematician; b. La Crosse, Wis., Dec. 13, 1870; s. Ingebrigt and Elise (Myhren) R.; A.B., U. of Minn., 1892; grad. student and fellow Cornell U., 1893-96; grad. student and fellow, U. of Chicago, 1896-97, Ph.D., 1906; unmarried. Prof. mathematics and astronomy, U. of Wash., 1897-1904; instr. mathematics, U. of Wis., 1904-05; asst. in mathematics, Stanford, 1905-06; instr. mathematics, 1906-10, asst. prof., 1910-23, prof., 1923—, Cornell U. Contbr. articles in math. jours. of U.S. and Europe; specialist in non-Euclidean geometry and in differential geometry. Home: Ithaca, N.Y. Deceased.

RAPP, Wilhelm, editor-in-chief of The Illinois Staats-Zeitung; b. in Germany, July 14, 1827; took part in German revolutionary movement, 1848; sent for 1 yr. to fortress of Hohenasberg; afterward teacher in Switzerland; emigrated to U.S., 1852; m. at Baltimore, 1869. Editor Turnzeitung, Phila., and Cincinnati; editor Baltimore Wecker (Republican), 1857-61 (secession mob stormed this office, Apr. 19, 1861, and he had to flee for his life); edited Illinois Staats-Zeitung, 1861-66; Baltimore Wecker again, 1866-72; asso. editor, 1872-91, and chief editor Illinois Staats-Zeitung, 1891—. Author: Recollections of the German Fatherland by a German-American. Address: Chicago, Ill. Died 1907.

RASCO, Richmond Austin, lawyer, educator; b. Newton, Miss., July 5, 1871; s. James La Fayette and Mary Louise (Wilson) R.; B.S., Dickson (Tenn.) Normal Coll., 1895; LL.B., Southern Normal U., Huntington, Tenn., 1898; A.M., Ark. Normal Coll., 1904; LL.B., Stetson U., 1918; m. Annie McGhehee, June 8, 1914; children—Russell Austin, Wendell Fayette, Glynn Owen, Delphin Delmas. Prin. Chapel Inst., Thorsby, Ala., 1898-1900; founder Thorsby Normal Sch., 1902; supt. schs. Jemison, Ala., 1904-08; prof. law, Stetson U., 1909-13, dean Coll. of Law, 1913-21; prof. law, U. of Fla., 1921-23, U. of Ariz., 1923-26; prof. law, U. of Miami, 1926-27, dean Sch. of Law, 1927—. Democrat. Baptist. Mason, Odd Fellow. Home: Coral Gables, Fla. Died Nov. 16, 1931.

RASMUSSEN, Frederik, agriculturalist; b. Hals, Denmark, July 18, 1876; s. Neils and Kirstine (Jensen) R.; came to U.S., 1899, naturalized citizen, 1912; B.S. in Agr., Ia. State Coll., 1905; m. Faith Winifred Elliott, Oct. 2, 1919; children—Frederik, John Elliott, Holger and Howard (twins), Norman, David. Assistant in dairying, Purdue U., 1905-06; asst. prof. dairying, Ia. State Coll., 1906-07; prof. dairying New Hampshire State Coll., 1907-16; prof. dairy husbandry, Pa. State Coll., 1916-19; sec. of agr. of Pa., term 1919-23. Pres. Pa.-Md. Joint Stock Land Bank, Harrisburg, Pa.; exec. sec. Nat. Assn. Ice Cream Mfrs., Mar. 1, 1925—. Mem. State Council of Edn. Mem. U.S. Food Administration, World War I. Trustee Pa. State Coll. Republican. Lutheran. Mason. Traveled extensively in northern and middle Europe studying agrl. conditions. Author of various bulletins and articles relating to agr. and dairying. Home: Harrisburg, Pa. Died Feb. 21, 1932.

RASSIEUR, Leo, judge; b. Wadern, Russia, Apr. 19, 1844; s. Theodore and Margaret (Klauck) R.; came to U.S. in early childhood; grad. St. Louis Central High Sch., 1860; LL.D., McKendree Coll.; m. Mary C. Kammerer, July 9, 1872; children—Mrs. Estelle Kelsey, Leo, Mrs. Cora Parsons. Served pvt. to maj. in Mo. vols., Union Army, 1861-65; taught in pub. schs., St. Louis, 1866-67; admitted to bar, Apr. 1, 1867, at St. Louis; atty. sch. bd. by election, 1880-90; judge Probate Court, St. Louis, 1895-99, declining renomination; resumed law practice. Comdr.-in-chief G.A.R., 1900-01; pres. Mo. Vicksburg Nat. Mil. Park Commn., 1911-17. Republican. Home: St. Louis, Mo. Died June 1, 1929.

RATHBONE, Henry Riggs, lawyer; b. Washington, D.C., Feb. 12, 1870; s. Henry Reed and Clara (Harris) R.; g.s. Hon. Ira Harris, U.S. senator from N.Y.; father and mother were in the box at Ford's Theatre with Pres. Lincoln when the latter was assassinated; A.B., Yale, 1892; student Albany Law Sch., 1893; LL.B., U. of Wis., 1894; m. Laura Lucille Harney, Dec. 22, 1903. Admitted to Ill. bar, 1895, and began practice at Chicago; mem. 68th to 70th Congresses (1923-29), Ill. at-large. Republican. Mason, Odd Fellow, K.P. Home: Kenilworth, Ill. Died July 15, 1928.

RATHBONE, Jared Lawrence, capitalist, soldier; b. Albany, N.Y., Sept. 28, 1844; s. Jared Lewis and Pauline N. (Pinney) R.; stepson of U.S. Senator Ira Harris; prep. edn. Phillips Acad., Andover, Mass., and Rensselaer Poly. Inst.; grad. West Point, 1865; entered 12th inf. and was transferred 1st U.S. arty.; a.d.c. to Lt. Gen. Schofield, 1866-73; resigned from army, 1873; m. Miss M. A. Atherton, Feb. 20, 1871. Developed the noted Palo Alto ranch, on which Leland Stanford Jr. U. is now located; apptd. consul gen. of the U.S. to Paris, France, 1887-91; served in war with Spain as spl. aide at hdqrs. div. of the Pacific, on staffs Gen. Merriam, Wesley, Merritt and Otis. Decorated by French govt. as Officer Legion of Honor, for spl. and brilliant services rendered to France. Address: New York, N.Y. Died 1907.

RATHBONE, John Finley, mfr.; b. Albany, N.Y., Oct. 12, 1819; ed. Albany Acad. and Collegiate Inst., Brockport, N.Y.; built, 1845, at Albany, a stove foundry which was later the largest in the world; brig. gen. comdg. 9th brigade N.Y. Nat. Guard, 1861-67; at beginning of war was commandant Albany depot of vols.; sent 34 regts. to front; adj. gen. with rank of maj. gen. under Gov. Dix's administration; one of founders Albany Orphan Asylum; gave $40,000 to build Rathbone Library, U. of Rochester. Pres. Dudley Observatory, Mutual Fire Ins. Co. of Albany, and Albany Orphans' Asylum. Address: Albany, N.Y. Deceased.

RATHBONE, Josephine Adams, librarian; b. Jamestown, N.Y.; d. Dr. J. Henry and Elizabeth Bacon (Adams) R.; spl. student U. of Mich., 1887-91; B.L.S., N.Y. State Library Sch., 1893. Asst., Pratt Inst. Free Library, 1893-95; chief instr., 1895-1911, vice-dir., 1911-38, Pratt Inst. Sch. of Library Science. Trustee West End Free Library, Augusta, 1939—. Episcopalian. Mem. A.L.A. (pres. 1931-32; council, 1912-29), New York Library Club (sec. 1895-97, 1909-10; pres. 1918-19). Author: Viewpoints in Travel, 1919. Home: Augusta, Ga. Died May 17, 1941.

RATHBORNE, St. George Henry, author; b. Covington, Ky., Dec. 26, 1854; s. Capt. Gorges Lowther and Margaret H. (Robertson) R.; ed. high school, Cincinnati; m. Jessie Fremont Conn, May 21, 1879; children—St. George Fremont, Percy Julian, Jessie Marguerite (Mrs. Kahl Clement Bates), Paul Lewis. Editor for many yrs. in Chicago and New York; spent many winters on pineapple plantation at Eden, Indian River, Fla. Writer of fiction; author of 70 novels, and 250 juvenile books mostly under various pen names. Home: Decatur, Ga. Died Dec. 16, 1938.

RATHBUN, Richard, naturalist; b. Buffalo, N.Y., Jan. 25, 1852; s. Charles Howland R.; student Cornell, class of '75; M.S., Ind. U., 1883; hon. D.Sc., Bowdoin, 1894; m. Lena Augusta Hume, Oct. 6, 1880. Asst. in zoölogy, Boston Soc. Natural History, 1874-75; asst. geologist, Geol. Commn. of Brazil, 1875-78; asst. in zoölogy, Yale, 1879-80; curator, U.S. Nat. Mus., 1880—. Scientific asst. on U.S. Fish Commn., 1878-96, having charge of the scientific inquiry subsequent to 1887; U.S. rep. on joint commn. with Great Britain relative to preservation fisheries in waters contiguous to U.S. and Can., 1892-96; asst. sec. Smithsonian Instn., 1897—; in charge U.S. Nat. Mus., 1899—. Writer on paleontology, marine invertebrate zoölogy, fisheries and mus. adminstrn. in govt. and other publs. Address: Washington, D.C. Died July 16, 1918.

RATHMANN, Carl Gustav, educator; b. Flensburg, Germany, May 27, 1853; s. Hans Nicholas and Johanna (Lippelt) R.; student Classical Gymnasium, Flensburg, 1864-70, U. of Mo., 1872-73, U. of Chicago, summer 1900; m. Anna Elizabeth Crecelius, Aug. 18, 1879; 1 son, Walter Lincoln. Came to U.S., 1871, naturalized citizen, 1876. Teacher in country schs., Mo., 1871-75; teacher of German, grade schs., St. Louis, 1875-79; asst. dir. Ednl. Inst., St. Louis, 1879-89; dir. Ednl. Inst., Kansas City, Mo., 1889-95; prin. pub. schs., St. Louis, 1895-1903; asst. supt. schs., St. Louis, 1903—. Dir. Bd. of Children's Guardians of St. Louis, Psychiatric Clinic, St. Louis. Republican. Awarded gold medals for St. Louis sch. exhibits at St. Louis Expn., Jamestown Expn., Panama-Pacific Expn. Author: Visual Education and the St. Louis School Museum, 1914, 24; Mission of Manual Training; Physical Care and Training of Children in Europe; The Museum and the Schools in Europe; Vocational Training in Europe; Mannheim System of School Organization. Founder of Ednl. Mus. of St. Louis pub. schs.; chmn. of municipal commn. which drafted plan for care of delinquent, neglected and dependent children. Home: St. Louis, Mo. Died May 22, 1930.

RATHOM, John Revelstoke, editor, author; b. Melbourne, Australia, July 4, 1868; ed. Scotch Coll., Melbourne, and Harrow, Eng.; m. Florence Mildred Campbell. War corr. Soudan, 1886, for Melbourne Argus; Cuba, 1898, for Chicago Herald; member Bunbury expdn. to New Guinea, 1888, Schwatka's Alaska expdn., 1890; for several yrs. staff corr. Chicago Record-Herald; mng. editor, 1905-12, editor and gen. mgr., 1912—, Providence Journal. Contbr. to Scribner's and many other Am. mags., Melbourne "Australasian," London Daily Telegraph, Nineteenth Century, etc. Authority on immigration and sociol. subjects. Dir. Associated Press and mem. of exec. com., 1917—. Comdr. Crown of Italy; Chevalier Order of Leopold (Belgium). Home: Providence, R.I. Died Dec. 11, 1923.

RATHVON, William Roedel, Christian Scientist; b. Lancaster, Pa., Dec. 27, 1854; s. Horace and Louisa (Forney) R.; student Franklin and Marshall Coll., Lancaster, 1870-73; C.S.B., Mass. Metaphysical Coll., 1903; m. Lillie K. Stauffer, Dec. 27, 1877 (died 1880); 1 son, Martin Truehart; m. 2d, Ella J. Stauffer, Apr. 20, 1883 (died 1923); m. 3d, Mrs. Lora C. Woodbury, Jan. 3, 1925. Joined Christian Science Ch., Chicago, 1893; sec. to Mary Baker Eddy, 1908-10; mem. C.S. Bd. of Lectureship, 1911-18; elected dir. and treas. Mother Ch. of C.S., 1918; trustee under will of Mrs. Eddy; trustee C.S. Benevolent Assn., trustee C.S. Pleasant View Home Assn. Author of lectures and articles on Christian Science, pub. in English, French, German and Swedish. Home: Brookline, Mass. Died Mar. 2, 1939.

RAUM, Green Berry, lawyer; b. Golconda, Ill., Dec. 3, 1829; s. John and Juliet C. R.; ed. common schs.; m. Maria Field, Oct. 16, 1851. Admitted Ill. bar, 1853; later Supreme Court U.S.; mem. Nat. Dem. Conv., and supported Douglas for President, 1860. After fall of Ft. Sumter made 1st war speech in Southern Ill.; entered Union army, 1861, as maj. 56th Ill. vols.; promoted through successive grades to brig. gen.; ordered and led a successful bayonet charge at Corinth, Oct. 4, 1862; served under Grant and Sherman; severely wounded at Missionary Ridge; in Atlanta campaign held line of R.R. in rear of Sherman's army; discovered and defeated Gen. Wheeler's raid; reinforced Resaca at night and held it against Gen. Hood. In March to the Sea; had command under Gen. Hancock in Shenandoah Valley at close of war. Congressman, 1867-69; U.S. commr. internal revenue, 1876-83; commr. of pensions, 1889-93. Republican. Author: The Existing Conflict, 1884; History of Illinois Republicanism, 1900; also 7 official reports as commr. internal revenue: 1877-82, inclusive, and 4 as commr. pensions, 1889-92. Address: Chicago, Ill. Died 1909.

RAUSCH, Emil Henry, clergyman; b. Cleveland, O., Nov. 19, 1874; s. Rev. Gideon F. and Katherine (Kilmer) R.; ed. Wartburg Coll., Waverly, Ia.; grad. Wartburg Theol. Sem., Dubuque, Ia., 1897; studied U. of Mich., 1906-07; D.D., Augustana Coll., Rock Island, Ill., 1930; LL.D., Luther Coll., Decorah, Ia., 1931; m. Anna M. Hogrefe, Sept. 7, 1898; children—Laura K. (Mrs. Herman Richmann), Edmund O., Alfred G., George C., Emil H., Katherine, Hedwig, Helen (dec.). Ordained Luth. ministry, 1897; pastor successively Peoria, Ill., Marine City, Mich., and St. Paul's Ch., Waverly, Ia., 1908-32; pres. Wartburg Theol. Sem., Apr. 15, 1932—. Asso. editor Lutheran Herald, 1909-10, editor, 1910-26. Pres. Ia. Dist. Am. Luth. Ch. (successor to Evang. Luth. Synod of Ia. and Other States), 1919—; pres. Nat. Luth. Editorial Assn., 1924-26; mem. exec. com. Nat. Luth. Commn. for Soldiers' and Sailors' Welfare, World War I; mem. exec. bd. Nat. Luth. Council; pres. Luth. Home Mission Council of America, 1933-34; mem. exec. com. Nat. Luth. Ednl. Assn., 1935-36. Republican. Translator: The Life of Dr. Martin Luther for the Christian Home, 1917; Habermann's Prayers, 1918. Editor and co-translator of English edit. Wartburg Lesson Helps. Address: Dubuque, Ia. Died Aug. 19, 1938.

RAUSCHENBUSCH, Augustus, clergyman; b. Altena, Germany, Feb. 13, 1816; studied U. of Berlin; U. of Bonn, 1840; Lutheran minister, Altena, Germany, 1840-45; came to U.S., 1846; in 1850 became a Baptist; senior prof. German Baptist Theol. Sem., Rochester, N.Y., 1853-88. Author: Saturday or Sunday—Which Shall We Observe?, Biblische Trauenbilder; A History of Infant Baptism; etc. Address: Wandsbek, Germany. Deceased.

RAUSCHENBUSCH, Walter, theologian; b. Rochester, N.Y., Oct. 4, 1861; s. Augustus (D.D.) and Caroline (Rhomp) R., grad. 1st honors, classical Gymnasium, Gütersloh, Germany, 1883; A.B., U. of Rochester, 1884; D.D., U. of Rochester, 1902, and Oberlin Coll., 1916; grad. Rochester Theol. Sem., 1886; studied abroad, 1891-92, 1907-08; m. Pauline E. Rother, Apr. 12, 1893. Ordained Bapt. ministry, 1886; engaged in religious work among German immigrants, New York, 1886-97; in edn. German pastors, 1897-1902; prof. ch. history, Rochester Theol. Sem., 1902—. Earl lecturer, Berkeley, Calif., 1910; Merrick lecturer, Ohio Wesleyan U., 1911; Gates lecturer, Grinnell Coll., 1914; Taylor lecturer, Yale, 1917. Author: Christianity and the Social Crisis, 1907; Prayers of the Social Awakening, 1910; Christianizing the Social Order, 1912; Unto Me, 1912; Dare We Be Christians?, 1914; Social Principles of Jesus, 1916; A Theology for the Social Gospel, 1917. Address: Rochester, N.Y. Died July 25, 1918.

RAWL, Bernard Hazelius, dairy husbandman; b. Lexington County, S.C., May 2, 1876; s. Benjamin and Margaret (Souter) R.; B.S., Clemson Agrl. Coll., S.C., 1900; spl. course in dairy husbandry, Pa. State Coll., 1902, U. of Wis., 1904; m. Mary Dandridge Bunting, Jan. 11, 1912. Began as laborer on college farm, 1900; asst. prof. animal husbandry and dairying, Clemson Coll., 1902-05; dairy husbandman, dairy div. of Bur. of Animal Industry, Washington, 1905-09, chief of div., 1909-18; asst. chief Bureau Animal Industry, 1918-21; asst. gen. mgr. Golden State Milk Products Co., San Francisco, 1921—. K.T. Home: Berkeley, Calif. Died Sept. 24, 1924.

RAWLE, Francis, lawyer; b. Freedom Forge, Mifflin County, Pa., Aug. 7, 1846; s. Francis William and Louisa (Hall) R.; A.B., Harvard, 1869, LL.B., 1871, A.M., 1872; admitted to bar, 1871; m. Margaretta C. Aertsen, 1873 (died 1894); children—Francis, Henry. Treas. Am. Bar Assn., 1878-1902, pres., 1902-03; overseer of Harvard, 1890-1902. Mem. Am. Philos. Soc. (pres. council); dir. Phila. Library Co. Author: Revisions of Bouvier's Law Dictionary, 1883; Car Trust Securities; Life of Edward Livingston in Lives of Secretaries of State. Home: Philadelphia, Pa. Died Jan. 28, 1930.

RAWLE, James, mfr. b. Lancaster, Pa., Nov. 15, 1842; s. Francis William and Louisa (Hall) R.; brother of Francis R.; A.B., U. of Pa., 1861, A.M., 1864; m. Charlotte Collins Parker, Nov. 29, 1871. Civ. engr. in constrn. Phila. & Erie R.R., 1862-65, and 2 yrs. in its maintenance of way dept.; became connected with The J. G. Brill Co., car builders, 1872, pres., 1906—; also dir. Central Nat. Bank; mgr. Phila. Saving Fund Soc. Pvt. to 1st lt. First Troop Phila. City Cav., 1881-93. Republican. Episcopalian. Home: Bryn Mawr, Pa. Died May 1, 1912.

RAWLES, Jacob Beekman, brig. gen. U.S.A.; b. Romeo, Mich., Aug. 4, 1839; s. Aaron B. and Elizabeth (Beekman) R.; grad. U.S. Mil. Acad., 1861; m. Phoebe A. Garretson, Mar. 20, 1862. Second lt.

3d Arty., May 6, 1861; 1st lt. 5th Arty., May 14, 1861; capt., July 28, 1866; maj. 4th Arty., Aug. 10, 1877; lt. col. 1st Arty., Apr. 30, 1897; col. 3d Arty., Feb. 23, 1899; brig. gen. U.S.A., Apr. 14, 1903; retired, Apr. 15, 1903. Served first on recruiting service, then in Dept. of Gulf and on Red River Campaign from Dec. 1862, to Aug. 1864, after that in 5th Arty., Army of the Potomac, to end of war; took part in first attack on Port Hudson, La. (bvtd. capt.), and in final siege on same, in battle of Sabine Cross Roads, in operations around Mobile Bay and siege of Ft. Morgan, and in operations and battles of the 5th Corps in Va., after Aug. 1864; bvtd. maj. Apr. 9, 1865. In command Angel Island, Calif., 1899-1900, comd. Presidio of San Francisco, 1900-03. Address: San Francisco, Calif. Died July 1, 1919.

RAWLES, William A., univ. prof.; b. Remington, Ind., Dec. 4, 1863; s. Lycurgus and Catherine Baker (Oilar) R.; A.B., Ind. U., 1884, A.M., 1895; Ph.D., Columbia, 1903; fellow economics, Cornell, 1895-96; scholar in administrative law, Columbia, 1898-99; m. Harriet McClure Post, June 26, 1895; children—Katharine Robb (Mrs. Benjamin C. Nangle), Thomas Howard, Harriet Post (Mrs. Leicester Bradner), William Post. Began as principal of high school, Mitchell, Ind., 1884; asst. prep. dept. Ind. U., 1885-87; prin. high sch., Vincennes, Ind., 1887-89, Sedalia, Mo., 1889-92 and 1893-94; asst., high sch. St. Louis, 1892-93; instr. history, 1894-95, instr. history and economics, 1896-98, asst. prof., 1899-1902, asst. prof. polit. economy, 1902-04, jr. prof., 1904-08, prof. and asst. dean of liberal arts, 1908-20, dean School Commerce and Finance, 1920—, Ind. U. Republican. Author: The Government of the People of the State of Indiana, 1897; Centralizing Tendencies in the Administration of Indiana, 1903. Address: Bloomington, Ind. Died May 17, 1936.

RAWLEY, Joseph Pearson, newspaper pub.; b. Mt. Airy, N.C., May 8, 1886; s. David Albert and Susan Columbus (Fulton) R.; student King Coll. (Bristol, Tenn.); m. Minnie Gwendolyn McCoy, Aug. 9, 1907; 1 son, David Albert. With Charlotte (N.C.) Observer, 1908-12; circulation mgr. Greensboro (N.C.) News, 1912-15; purchased High Point (N.C.) Enterprise with associates, 1915, sec.-treas., later gen. mgr. and pub.; pres. Times-News Pub. Co., Terry-Smith-Rawley Co., Atlantic Bldg. & Loan Assn., v.p. Premier Silk Mills; dir. Atlantic Ins. & Realty Co., Southern Furniture Expn. Bldg. Mem. N.C. State Conservation and Development Bd. Democrat. Baptist. Mason, Elk. Home: High Point, N.C. Died Sept. 1, 1937.

RAWLINGS, Eugene Hubbard, clergyman; b. Powellton, Brunswick County, Va., Oct. 23, 1865; s. Leroy Tucker and Emily J. R.; A.M., Randolph-Macon Coll., Va., 1887, D.D., 1908; B.D., Vanderbilt, 1890; m. Fannie Bell Powell, Jan. 20, 1891. Ordained ministry M.E. Ch., S., 1890; pastor 17 yrs.; presiding elder, 1907-08; conf. missionary sec., 1908-09; ednl. sec. M.E. Ch., S., 7 yrs.; sec. Layman's Missionary Movement, 1916-18; foreign secretary for Board of Missions, Methodist Episcopal Church, South, 1917; editor of The World Outlook, M.E. Ch., S. Author of "Yet Another Day in Methodist Missions." Traveled in Japan, Korea, China, Cuba, Mexico and Brazil in supervision of foreign work of M.E. Ch., S. Home: Nashville, Tenn. Died Mar. 17, 1939.

RAWLINS, Joseph Lafayette, senator; b. Salt Lake County, Utah, Mar. 28, 1850; s. Joseph Sharp and Mary (Frost) R.; lived on farm until 18 yrs. of age; completed a classical course in Ind. U., but was not grad.; LL.D., U. of Utah, 1910; m. Julia E. Davis, Dec. 8, 1876; children—Mrs. Leda Ray, Athol, Mrs. Alta Jensen, Mrs. Lara Coffman, Boyce. Prof., U. of Deseret, Salt Lake City, 1873-75; admitted to bar, 1875, in practice at Salt Lake City, 1875—. Del. 53d Congress (1893-95); U.S. senator, 1897-1903. Democrat. Address: Salt Lake City, Utah. Died May 24, 1927.

RAWLINS, William Thomas, judge; b. Honolulu, Hawaii, Sept. 4, 1877; s. Thomas William and Marian (Evans) R.; grad. Oahu Coll., Honolulu, 1898; LL.B., Yale, 1901; m. Jane S. Somers, Mar. 19, 1902; 1 dau., Elizabeth French. Admitted to Hawaiian bar, 1901, and began practice at Honolulu; asst. U.S. dist. atty., 1907-12; apptd. judge U.S. Dist. Court, Hawaii, Jan. 15, 1924, for term ending Jan. 15, 1930. Mem. Hawaii Ho. of Rep., 1907, 15, 19; mem. Hawaiian Commn. to Washington, 1919. Republican. Episcopalian. Mason. Address: Honolulu, Hawaii. Died Dec. 18, 1928.

RAWLINSON, Frank Joseph, missionary; b. Rutlandshire, Eng., Jan. 9, 1871; s. David Joseph and Annie (Rawlinson) R.; B.A., Bucknell U., Lewisburg, Pa., 1899, hon. D.D., 1917; studied Rochester Theol. Sem., 1899-1902; A.M., Columbia, 1917; m. Carrie Mae Dietz, 1899 (died 1917); m. 2d, Florence B. Lang, July 2, 1917. Came to U.S., 1889; naturalized citizen, 1902. Ordained ministry Southern Bapt. Ch.; missionary to China, Southern Bapt. Conv., 1902-21; with Am. Bd., 1921—. With Chinese Recorder, 1912—, editor in chief, 1914—; editor in chief China Mission (Christian) Year Books, 1922-35, also report of Nat. Christian Conf., Shanghai, 1922; dir. Chinese studies for Shanghai, Municipal Council, 5 yrs. Missionary fellow, Union Theol. Sem., 1924-25, lecturer, 1925. Author: Life of Christ (in Chinese); Chinese Ideas of the Supreme Being; Naturalization of Christianity in China; Western Money and the Chinese Church; Revolution and Religion in Modern China; Chinese Ethical Ideals. Address: Shanghai, China. Died Aug. 14, 1937.

RAWN, Ira Griffith, railway pres.; b. Delaware, O., Aug. 20, 1855; pub. sch. edn. Entered ry. service, 1872; telegraph operator, train dispatcher, and train master, C.,C.,C.&I. Ry. 1887; master of transportation Ky. Central Ry., 1887-89; division supt. and supt. transportation, C.&O. Ry., 1889-90; gen. supt. B.&O.S.-W. R.R., 1890-94; gen. supt. B.&O. S.-W Ry., which was consolidation of the B.&O.S.-W. and the Ohio & Miss. Ry., 1894-1903; gen. supt., 1903-04, asst. gen. mgr., 1904-07, v. pres. in charge of operation, 1907-09, I.C. R.R.; pres. Chicago, Indianapolis & Louisville Ry. (Monon), 1909—. Home: Chicago, Ill. Died 1910.

RAWSON, Albert Leighton, artist, author; b. Chester, Vt., Oct. 15, 1828; ed. by pvt. tutor and at Black River Acad., Ludlow, Vt., D.D., LL.D., Christ Coll., Oxford, England; M.D., Sorbonne, Paris. Studied law under William H. Seward, theology under "Elder" Graves, medicine under Prof. Webster of Mass. Med. Coll.; made several visits to the Orient; made a pilgrimage from Cairo to Mecca with annual caravan, disguised as Mohammedan med. student; traveled in Yucatan and Hudson's Bay region; once alderman 15th ward, New York; painted portraits of Queen Victoria, Louis Napoleon, Empress Eugenie, etc.; illustrated Beecher's, Deem's and Crosby's Lives of Christ and many other books. Adopted as brother by Adwan Bedouins of Moab; initiated by Druses on Mt. Lebanon; one of 2 founders order Nobles of the Mystic Shrine; one of 4 founders Theosophical Soc. in the U.S.; gen. for life, Soc. Rosy Cross; 32 deg. F. & A. M., 95 deg. Royal Masonic Rite of Memphis. Author: Divine Origin of the Holy Bible, 1846; Stella, and Other Novels, 1847; Vocabularies and Dictionaries of Arabic, Persian and Turkish, 1854; Bible Handbook, 1869; Ruins and Relics of the Orient, 1870; Antiquities of the Orient, 1871; Scarlet Book of Freemasonry, 1873; History of All Religions, 1878; History of Quakers, 1878; History of Protestantism, 1878; Introduction to Holy Bible (maps and illustrations), 1879; The Archaic Library, Vols. 1 and 2, 1893; History of Mysticism, 12; also rituals for many secret socs. Home: Hillsdale Manor, N.J. Died 1902.

RAWSON, Charles A., senator, mfr.; b. Des Moines, Ia., May 29, 1867; s. A. Y. and Mary (Scott) R.; ed. high sch. and Grinnell Coll.; m. Carrie Hubbard, Feb. 1, 1900. Mfr. of clay products, 1886—; pres. Ia. Pipe & Tile Co., Eldora Pipe & Tile Company; v.p. Des Moines Brick & Tile Co.; treas. Employers Mut. Casualty Co.; mem. bd. dirs. Central Trust Co., Inter-State Business Men's Accident Co. Mgr. William S. Kenyon's campaign for U.S. Senate, 1911; chmn. Rep. State Central Com., 1912-22; appointed, Feb. 1922, mem. U.S. Senate (succeeding Hon. William S. Kenyon); resigned 1924; mem. Rep. Nat. Com., 1924-32. Dir. Roadside Settlement House Assn.; trustee Grinnell Coll.; mem. Greater Des Moines Com., Games Com. (having charge of coll. athletics in Ia.); president Home for Aged Assn. Protestant. State chmn. of War Work Council Y.M.C.A. and served in France. Home: Des Moines, Ia. Died Sept. 2, 1936.

RAWSON, Frederick Holbrook, banker; b. Chicago, May 30, 1872; s. Stephen W. and Emily (Holbrook) R.; A.B., Yale, 1895; m. Edith Kennett, Jan. 10, 1907; children—Frederick Holbrook, Kennett Longley. Began as entry clerk, 1895, with Union Trust Co., became v.p., 1901, pres. 1905, chmn. bd., 1925; co-chmn. bd. First Nat. Bank of Chicago, after merger of Union Trust Co. with First Nat. Bank, Feb. 13, 1929-Aug. 26, 1930, chmn. bd., Aug. 26, 1930-Aug. 31, 1933, when retired from active business; founded Mercantile Trust and Savings Bank and continued as chmn. bd. and dir. until 1933. Home: Chicago, Ill. Died Feb. 5, 1937.

RAY, Charles Andrew, M.D.; b. Kanawha County, W.Va., May 14, 1864; s. John E. and Deborah A. (Gay) R.; M.D., Coll. Phys. and Surg., Baltimore, 1887; m. Mamie A. Fisher, Feb. 15, 1891; children—John V., C. A., J. Seiburt. Practiced at Charleston, W.Va., 1888—; editor W.Va. Med. Jour.; mem. Kenawha County Court, 1930—; chmn. Dem. County Com. 8 yrs.; live stock farmer. Served as capt. and mem. Draft Bd., World War I. Home: Pocotaligo, W.Va. Deceased.

RAY, Charles Wayne, clergyman; b. Riley, Vigo Co., Ind., Apr. 2, 1872; s. William Riley and Hester Ann (Lee) R.; A.B., DePauw, 1900; A.M., Taylor U., 1902; D.D., Neb. Wesleyan U., 1905; m. Arethusa S. Ervin, Oct. 31, 1907; children—Helen E., Robert E. Ordained M.E. ministry in Ind., 1894; pastor Crawford, Neb., 1900-02, Valentine, 1903, Alliance, 1903-07, Norfolk, 1907-10, Columbus, 1910-13, Lyons, 1913-19, McCook, 1919-24, North Platte, 1924—. Del. to World's S.S. Conv., Rome, 1907, Zürich, 1910. Decorated by King Albert of Belgium for two poems, "No Man's Land," and "The Dead in Flandirs. Mason, deputy Grand Master I.O.O.F. Author: Bible Questions Answered, 1903; The Radiant Life, 1907; Heart Echoes, 1913; The Bright Side of Living (verse), 1916; Ray-Poems, The Tides of Fortune, 1923; also booklets. Lecturer. Home: North Platte, Neb. Died Apr. 1928.

RAY, Franklin Arnold, engr.; b. Rome, Ashtabula County, O., Apr. 13, 1862; s. Samuel and Fidelia (Hulburt) R.; E.M., Ohio State U., 1887; studied mining engring.; m. Pauline W. Hollenbeck, June 24, 1896; children—Helen Drury (Mrs. Thomas Hornsby Ferril), Frances Hurlbert (Mrs. Stuart E. Price). Chief engr. Columbus-Hocking Coal & Iron Co., 1889-92, Congo Coal Mining Co., 1892-94; asst. prof. mining engring., 1894-97, asso. prof., 1897-1900, prof., 1900-27, later prof. emeritus, dean Engring. Coll., 1904-06, Ohio State U., also consulting dir. Sch. of Mines; chief engr. Sunday Creek Coal Co., 1932, later consulting engr. In Russia, investigating coal deposits, mining conditions, coal reserves, etc., 1916—. Author of repts. and bulls. on mining investigations. Home: Granville, O. Died Aug. 9, 1938.

RAY, George Washington, judge; b. Otselic, Chenango County, N.Y., Feb. 3, 1844; reared on farm; ed. common schs. and Norwich Acad.; pvt. and brigade clerk in Union Army in Civil War; admitted to bar, 1867; practiced at Norwich, N.Y.; also largely interested in farming. Mem. 48th Congress (1883-85) and 52d to 57th Congresses (1891-1903), 26th N.Y. Dist.; resigned from 57th Congress, Sept. 17, 1902; U.S. dist. judge, Northern Dist. of N.Y., 1902—. Republican. Mem. Bd. of Edn., Norwich, 1886—, pres. over 20 yrs.; pres. trustees of Guernsey Memorial Library, Norwich; chmn. trustees of David L. Follett Memorial (Sup. Court) Law Library. Home: Norwich, N.Y. Died Jan. 10, 1925.

RAY, John Edwin, educator; b. Wake County, N.C., Jan. 22, 1852; s. James Samuel and Delitha Jane (Justice) R.; A.M., Wake Forest (N.C.) Coll., 1875; m. Finie Annis Carter, Nov. 2, 1881. Supt. Colo. State Sch. for the Deaf and Blind, 1887-94, Ky. State Sch. for the Deaf, 1894-96; prin. (supt.) N.C. State Sch. for the Blind and the Deaf, 1896—. Trustee Meredith Coll. (Raleigh, N.C.), Thomasville (N.C.) Bapt. Orphanage. Democrat. Corr. sec. Bapt. State Conv. of N.C., 1877-87. Address: Raleigh, N.C. Died June 17, 1918.

RAY, P(atrick) Henry, brig. gen. U.S.A.; b. Waukesha County, Wis., May 8, 1842; s. Adam E. and Eliza (Breasted) R.; com. sch. edn.; m. Adah Blackman, Apr. 22, 1889. Served as pvt., corpl., sergt., and 1st sergt. cos. K and A, 2d Wis. Inf., and 1st Wis. Heavy Arty., May 7, 1861-July 12, 1863; commd. 2d lt. 1st Wis. Heavy Arty., July 13, 1863; capt., Sept. 13, 1864; hon. mustered out, June 26, 1865; capt. 6th U.S. Vet. Inf., Aug. 9, 1865; hon. mustered out, Apr. 12, 1866; apptd. from Wis. 2d lt. 33d U.S. Inf., Mar. 7, 1867; transferred to 8th Inf., May 3, 1869; 1st lt., Dec. 31, 1875; capt., May 27, 1889; col. 3d U.S. Vol. Inf., May 20, 1898; maj. 8th Inf., Mar. 2, 1899; hon. mustered out of vol. service, May 2, 1899; lt. col. 7th U.S. Inf., Dec. 8, 1901; transferred to 8th Inf., May 15, 1902; col. 4th Inf., Aug. 12, 1903; brig. gen. U.S.A., and retired by operation of law, May 8, 1906. Served through Civil War in Army of the Potomac; served in Sioux and Apache Indian campaigns, 1872-76; comd. Internat. Polar expdn. to Point Barrow, Alaska, June 1881-Oct. 1883, during which traveled over 1,000 miles with dogs and sled, over unexplored region, discovered and partly explored Meade River, picked up Lieut. Schwatka and party at Ft. St. Michael and brought him to U.S.; on duty with Signal Corps, Washington, 1883-85; U.S. del. Internat. Polar Congress, Vienna, May-July, 1884; sent by President McKinley, as spl. commr. to mining dists. of Northern Alaska and British N.A., Aug. 1897; wrecked by ice nr. Ft. Yukon; seized in name of U.S. caches of food belonging to trading cos. to prevent looting by mob, and fed starving and destitute fleeing from Dawson; left Ft. Yukon, Feb. 22, 1898, and traveled by dog team up the Yukon over 1,100 miles via Chilcoot Pass to Dyea, arriving there Apr. 7, 1898. Comd. dist. of Guantanamo, Cuba, Aug. 1898-Apr. 1899; took possession of Manzanillo, Cuba, Oct. 1898, upon evacuation by Spanish Army, first occupation by U.S. of Spanish Ty. under treaty of Paris, and rules there made were precedents for all other occupations in the war; assigned by President to comd. dist. of North Alaska (all ty. N. of lat. 60° N.) and established and built the first mil. posts at Nome, Ft. Gibbon and Ft. Egbert; served in Philippines, Mar. 1902-Apr. 1903, and Sept. 1903-June 1905; comd. 3d Brigade, Dept. of Luzon, Jan.-Mar. 1904. Author of Report of International Polar Expedition, 1884. Home: Youngstown, N.Y. Died 1911.

RAY, T. Bronson, denominational sec.; b. Buckeye, Ind., Oct. 26, 1883; s. Nathan Harvey and Mary Elizabeth (Jackson) R.; A.B., U. of Kan., 1908, A.M., 1909; grad. work U. of Kan. and Harvard; m. Mary Elnetha Brownlee, June 19, 1911; children—Mary McGregor, Eleanor Elizabeth. Fellow in economics and sociology, U. of Kan., 1908-09; univ. scholar in economics, 1909-10, Henry Lee memorial fellow in economics, 1910-11, Harvard; prof. economics, Keio U., Tokyo, Japan, 1911-14; prof. economics and bus. adminstrn. Olivet (Mich.) Coll., 1915-20, also dean, 1918-19; asso. prof. economics and internat. trade, Northwestern U. Sch. of Commerce, 1920—. Conglist. Home: Lombard, Ill. Died May 16, 1936.

RAY, T. Bronson, denominational sec.; b. Buckeye, Garrard County, Ky., Aug. 14, 1868; s. William (M.D.) and Nancy Jane (Rainey) R.; A.M., Georgetown (Ky.) Coll., 1895, D.D., 1909; Th.M., Southern Bapt. Theol. Sem., 1898; m. Maude Wayts, Apr. 30, 1897 (died 1901); m. 2d, Davie Bruce Jasper, Jan. 1, 1909 (died 1923); 1 dau., Mary Nancy; m. 3d, Bettie Eula Murfee, June 14, 1926. Ordained Bapt. ministry, 1893; pastor Immanuel Ch., Nashville, Tenn., 1898-1906; ednl. sec., 1906-1914, foreign sec., 1914-29, exec. sec., 1929-32, asst. exec. sec., 1933—. Foreign Mission Bd. of So. Bapt. Conv. Independent Democrat. Author: Southern Baptist Foreign Missions, 1910; Brazilian Sketches, 1912; Only a Missionary, 1927. Editor: Highway of Mission Thought, 1907; Visited Europe, 1905, Brazil, Argentina, Chile and Spain, 1910, Mexico, 1921, Japan and China, 1921-22, Brazil and Argentina, 1930. Home: Richmond, Va. Died Jan. 15, 1934.

RAYBOLD, Walter James, paper mfr.; b. Lanesboro, Berkshire County, Mass., Aug. 10, 1864; s. Walter Richard and Harriet Sylvina (Hatch) R.; ed. pub. schs.; m. Grace Estelle, d. Harlow B. Spencer, July 11, 1893. Began as clk. Agawam Paper Co., W. Springfield, Mass., advancing to sales mgr.; an organizer, 1899, of B. D. Rising Paper Co., Housatonic, of which was v.p. and treas.; pres. Rising Paper Co., which succeeded to business of B. D. Rising Paper Co., 1928—; dir. Am. Paper Exports (New York), Berkshire Life Ins. Co., Berkshire Mut. Fire Ins. Co., Hampshire Mut. Fire Ins. Co. Trustee Sch. for Crippled Children, Home for Aged Women; mem. state exec. com. Y.M.C.A. of Mass. and R.I. (chmn., 1918-24); mem. nat. council Y.M.C.A. of N. America, 1925-27, also mem. Gen. Bd. (v.p. exec. com.); dir. Pittsfield Y.M.C.A., 1901-34, pres., 1911-17. Mem. Am. Paper and Pulp Assn. (pres. 1921-23), Writing Paper Mfrs.' Assn. (pres. 1918-21), Nat. Inst. Social Sciences. Republican. Methodist. Home: Pittsfield, Mass. Died Apr. 21, 1938.

RAYMER, Albert Reesor, ry. official; b. Markham, Ont., Can., Dec. 1, 1862; s. John N. and Christina R.; ed. Toronto U., 1881-84; m. Frances E. Hutcheson, Mar. 1887; children—Edith Alberta (Mrs. Frank T. Underhill), Paul Hutcheson, John George. Began with Northern and Pacific Junction Ry. (now part of C.N. Ry.), 1884; with Internat. Ry. of Me. (now part of C.P. Ry.), 1886-88; with Toronto, Hamilton & Buffalo Ry. (now part of Mich. Central Ry.), 1888-89; engr. on Cumberland Valley Extension, L.&N. R.R., 1889-91; asst. engr. L.S.&M.S. Ry. (now part of N.Y.C. R.R.), 1891-96; asst. chief engr. P.&L.E. R.R. (now part of N.Y.C. Lines), 1896-1920, chief engr., 1920—, also asst. v.p., 1926—. Mem. Am. Soc. C.E. (dir.), Engring. Soc. of Western Pa. (pres.), Am. Ry. Engring. Assn. Republican. Methodist. Home: Beaver, Pa. Died Aug. 10, 1931.

RAYMOND, Andrew Van Vranken, coll. pres.; b. Visscher's Ferry, Saratoga County, N.Y., Aug. 8, 1854; s. Rev. Henry A. and Catharine M. (Miller) R.; A.B., Union Coll., 1875, A.M., 1878; grad. New Brunswick Theol. Sem., 1878; D.D., Union, 1887; LL.D., Williams, 1894, S.C. Coll., 1905; m. Margaret M. Thomas, Sept. 24, 1879 (died 1907). Ordained (Dutch) Reformed Ch. ministry, 1878; pastor First Reformed Ch., Paterson, N.J., 1878-81, Trinity Reformed Ch., Plainfield, N.J., 1881-87, Fourth Presbyn. Ch., Albany, N.Y., 1887-94; pres. Union Coll., N.Y., 1894-1907; pastor First Presbyn. Ch., Buffalo, July 1, 1907—. Address: Buffalo, N.Y. Died Apr. 7, 1918.

RAYMOND, Anna Almy, teacher; b. New Bedford, Mass., Dec. 26, 1888; d. Robert Fulton and Mary (Walker) R.; A.B., Mt. Holyoke Coll., South Hadley, Mass., 1910; A.M., Boston U., 1913; grad. study Northwestern U., 1916-17; unmarried. Teacher, Greenwich (Conn.) Acad., 1910-12, Lasell Sem. for Young Women, Auburndale, Mass., 1913-15; acting prof. Latin, Cornell Coll., 1917-18; dean of women, Colby Coll., 1918-19; dean, Milwaukee-Downer Sem., 1920-21, prin., 1921—. Home: Newton Center, Mass. Died Feb. 1, 1935.

RAYMOND, Bradford Paul, educator; b. Stamford, Conn., Apr. 22, 1846; s. Lewis and Sallie A. R.; Hamline U., Minn., 1866-69; A.B., Lawrence U., Wis., 1870; B.D., Boston U., 1873; studied in Germany, 1880-81; D.D., Northwestern U., 1884, Yale, 1901; LL.D., Lawrence, 1889; m. Lulu A. Rich, Sept. 15, 1873. Ordained M.E. ministry; pastor Allen St. Ch., New Bedford, Mass., 1874-77, Chestnut St. Ch., Providence, 1877-80, Nashua, N.H., 1881-83; pres. Lawrence Univ., Appleton, Wis., 1883-89; pres., 1889-1908, prof. ethics and Bibl. lit., 1909—, Wesleyan U., Conn. Author: Christianity and the Christ. Address: Middletown, Conn. Died Feb. 27, 1916.

RAYMOND, Charles Walker, brig. gen. U.S.A.; b. Hartford, Conn., Jan. 14, 1842; s. Prof. Robert R. R.; grad. Brooklyn Poly. Inst., 1861; Ph.D., Lafayette Coll., 1875; grad. U.S. Mil. Acad., 1865; spl. studies civ. and mil. engring.; M. Clara Wise, Nov. 8, 1866. Apptd. 1st lt. engrs., June 23, 1865; capt., Mar. 21, 1867; maj., Feb. 20, 1883; lt. col., May 18, 1898; col., Jan. 23, 1904; brig. gen. and retired at own request after 40 yrs.' service, June 11, 1904. Engaged on exploration of Yukon River, Alaska, 1869; prin. asst. prof. natural and experimental philosophy, U.S. Mil. Acad., 1872-74; comd. U.S. expdn. to Northern Tasmania to observe transit of Venus, 1874; instr. mil. engring., mil. signaling and telegraphing, U.S. Mil. Acad., 1878; engr. commr., D.C., 1888-89; on engr. duty at New York and Phila.; chmn. bd. engrs. in charge of constrn. of tunnels at New York for Pa. R.R. Address: Philadelphia, Pa. Died May 3, 1913.

RAYMOND, Evelyn Hunt, author; b. Watertown, N.Y., Nov. 6, 1843; d. Alvin and Charlotte (Hatch) Hunt; ed. pvt. schs. and Mt. Holyoke Coll.; m. John Bradford Raymond, Sept. 29, 1869. Writer of juvenile fiction and short stories. Author: A Daughter of the West, 1899; Reels and Spindles, 1900; The Story of Delight, 1900; The Sun Maid, 1900; Divided Skates, 1900; A Pair of Them, 1901; Daisies and Diggleses, 1902; A Daughter of the Forest, 1902; The Mislaid Uncle, 1903; Jessica Trent Series; The Brass Bound Box, 1905; Polly the Gringo, 1905; Sunny Little Lass, 1906; The Heroine of Roseland, 1907; Little Miss Evangeline, 1908; Carlota of the Rancho, 1909; also Dorothy series, 6 vols., 1907-10. Home: Baltimore, Md. Died Apr. 18, 1910.

RAYMOND, George Lansing, educator, author; b. Chicago, Sept. 3, 1839; s. Benjamin Wright and Amelia (Porter) R.; A.B., Williams, 1862, A.M., 1865; Princeton Theol. Sem., 1865; studied art in Europe, 1865-68; Litt.D. from Rutgers Coll., 1883; L.H.D., Williams Coll., 1889; A.M., Princeton, 1896; m. Mary Elizabeth Blake, July 31, 1872; 1 dau., Maybelle (Mrs. Tyler Dennett). Ordained Presbyn. ministry, 1870; pastor Darby, Pa., 1870-74; prof. oratory, Williams Coll., 1874-80; prof. oratory and æsthetic criticism, 1880-93, æsthetics, 1893-1905, Princeton; prof. æsthetics, George Washington U., 1905-12. Lecturer. V.p. Am. Social Science Assn., Free Art League. Author: Rhythm and Harmony in Poetry and Music, 1895; Painting, Sculpture and Architecture as Representative Arts, 1895; Proportion and Harmony of Line and Color in Painting, Sculpture and Architecture, 1899; The Representative Significance of Form, 1900; The Aztec God, and Other Dramas, 1900; Ballads and Other Poems, 1901; The Essentials of Aesthetics, 1907; Psychology of Inspiration, 1908; Dante and Collected Verse, 1909; Fundamentals in Education, Art and Civics, 1911; Suggestions for the Spiritual Life, 1912; The Mountains About Williamstown, 1913; selections by M. M. Miller in A Poet's Cabinet, 1914; In An Art Philosopher's Cabinet, 1915; Ethics and Natural Law, 1920. Address: Washington, D.C. Died July 11, 1929.

RAYMOND, Harry Howard, steamship lines official; b. Yarmouth, N.S., Dec. 16, 1864; s. Samuel Flint and Margaret Hannah (Clements) R.; ed. Yarmouth Sem.; came to U.S., 1884, naturalized, 1892; m. Annie Cornell, June 18, 1890. With Mallory Steamship Co., 1885—, pres., 1914, later chmn. bd.; also chmn. bd. Clyde Steamship Co., N.Y. and Puerto Rico Steamship Co., N.Y. and Cuba Mail Steamship Co.; pres. Colombian Steamship Co.; dir. Eastern Steamship Lines. Served as lt. Naval Reserve, Spanish-Am. War; vice-chmn. Shipping Control Com., World War I. Chevalier Legion of Honor (France). Republican. Episcopalian. Mason. Died Dec. 27, 1935.

RAYMOND, Henry Warren, newspaperman; b. New York, Sept. 10, 1847; s. Henry J. and Juliette R.; A.B., Yale, 1869, A.M., 1872; LL.B., Columbia, 1771; m. Harriet White Allen, Sept. 29, 1875. On staff N.Y. Times, 1869-72, Evening Post, 1872-73, Brooklyn Union, 1873-74; lit. and mus. critic, Chicago Tribune, 1879-83; editor and propr. Germantown Telegraph, 1884-1901; pvt. sec. Gen. Tracy, Sec. of Navy, 1889-93; apptd. solicitor of state dept., by President Harrison, but Senate adjourned without confirmation; naval lecturer throughout U.S., 1893-1900. Author: The Story of Saranac, 1909. Sec., treas., mgr. Guarantee Storage Co. of Phila., 1913-19. Home: Germantown, Philadelphia, Pa. Died Feb. 18, 1925.

RAYMOND, Jerome Hall, lecturer; b. Clinton, Ia., Mar. 10, 1869; s. Henry Wilbur and Virginia (Hall) R.; A.B., Northwestern U., 1892, A.M., 1893; Ph.D., U. of Chicago, 1895; m. Nettie Josephine Hunt, Aug. 15, 1895. Stenographer to late Frances E. Willard, 1887-89; pvt. sec. late George M. Pullman, 1889-90; traveled in Europe and Asia as sec. to Bishop Thoburn, completing circuit of the globe, 1890-92; sec. and lecturer in history Chicago Soc. for Univ. Extension, 1892-93; prof. history and polit. science Lawrence U., Appleton, Wis., 1893-94; lecturer sociology and sec. class study dept., Univ. Extension Div., U. of Chicago, 1894-95; prof. sociology and sec. Univ. Extension Dept., U. of Wis., 1895-97; pres. and prof. economics and sociology, W.Va. U., 1897-1901; asso. prof. sociology, U. of Chicago, 1901-09; pres. Toledo U., and prof. economics and polit. science, 1909-10; prof. economics and polit. science, Knox Coll., 1910-12; lecturer in polit. science, U. of Calif., 1914-19. Lecturer on European social and polit. conditions. Home: Evanston, Ill. Died Feb. 22, 1928.

RAYMOND, Joseph Howard, physician; b. Brooklyn, Nov. 18, 1845; s. Israel Ward and Frances Bryant (Howard) R.; grad. Poly. Inst. of Brooklyn, 1862; A.B., Williams, 1866, A.M., 1869; M.D., L.I. Coll. Hosp., 1868; M.D., Coll. Phys. and Surg. (Columbia), 1869; m. Nannie Van Nostrand Gardiner, Sept. 2, 1875 (died 1898); m. 2d, Rachel Biddle Cravens, Apr. 9, 1901. Prof. physiology and hygiene, L.I. Coll. Hosp., 1873—; mem. Brooklyn Bd. of Edn.; health commr., Brooklyn, 1882-86; editor Brooklyn Med. Jour., 1888-1903; sec. and treas. Hoagland Lab., 1887—; sec. Polhemus Memorial Clinic, 1897—; asst. sanitary supt., Dept. of Health, New York, 1902-04. Author: Text-Book of Physiology, 1894, 1902, 05; History of the Long Island College Hospital and Its Graduates, 1899. Also various med. and sanitary articles. Died Mar. 7, 1915.

RAYMOND, Robert Fulton, judge; b. High Ridge, Stamford, Conn., June 15, 1858; s. Lewis and Sally A. (Jones) R.; Wesleyan U., 1 yr., Harvard, 1880-81; Harvard Law Sch., 1881-83, 1893-94, LL.B., 1894; admitted to bar, 1883; hon. M.A., Wesleyan, 1906; m. Mary E. Walker, Oct. 20, 1886. Practiced at New Bedford; mem. law firm of Raymond & Mitchell, 1883-1907; justice Superior Ct. of Mass., 1907—. Republican. Methodist; del. Quadrennial Gen. Conf. M.E. Ch., Chicago, 1900, Los Angeles, 1904. Mem. Am. Acad. Polit. and Social Science; dir. Mass. Peace Soc.; pres. Mass. Bible Soc.; v.p. Am. Bible Soc. Home: Newton Center, Mass. Deceased.

RAYMOND, Rossiter Worthington, mining engr.; b. Cincinnati, Apr. 27, 1840; s. Prof. Robert R. and Mary Ann (Pratt) R.; grad. Brooklyn Poly. Inst., 1858; studied univs. Munich and Heidelberg and Mining Acad., Freiberg; hon. Ph.D., Lafayette, 1869; LL.D., Lehigh U., 1906, and U. of Pittsburgh, 1915; m. Sarah M. Dwight, 1863. Capt. a.d.c. in Union Army, 1861-64; consulting engr., New York, 1864-68; U.S. commr. of mining statistics, 1868-76; lecturer on econ. geology, Lafayette Coll., 1870-82; editor Am. Jour. of Mining, 1867-68; an editor and spl. contbr. Engineering and Mining Journal, 1868—. U.S. commr. to Vienna Expn., 1873; N.Y. State commr. of electric subways for Brooklyn, 1885-88; lecturer on mining law, Columbia, 1903. One of original mems., v.p., 1871, 1876-77, pres., 1872-74, sec., 1884-1911, sec. emeritus, 1911—, Am. Inst. Mining Engrs.; Japanese Imperial Order of Rising Sun, 4th class, 1911. Author: Die Leibgarde (German), 1863; Mineral Resources of the United States in and West of the Rocky Mountains (8 vols.), 1868-75; Brave Hearts, 1873; The Man in the Moon, 1874; The Book of Job, 1878; Camp and Cabin, 1879; Glossary of Mining and Metallurgical Terms, 1881; Two Ghosts, 1879; Life of Alex L. Holley, 1883; Life of Peter Cooper, 1901; also tech. works and papers, especially on mining law. Home: Brooklyn. Died Dec. 3, 1918.

RAYMOND, Thomas Lynch, lawyer; b. East Orange, N.J., Apr. 26, 1875; s. Thomas Lynch and Eugenia A. (Launitz) R.; prep. edn. Newark Acad.; LL.B., New York U., 1896; unmarried. Began practice in Newark, 1896; judge 1st Dist. Court, Newark, 1904-08; 1st asst. pros. of pleas, Essex County, N.J., 1908-10; mayor of Newark 2 terms, 1914-17 and under commn. form, for term of 4 yrs., 1925-29; city commr. of Newark under new commn. form, terms 1917-21, 1921-25. Mem. N. Jersey Dist. Water Supply Commn., 1922-26; trustee Newark Free Pub. Library. Dir. Merchants & Mfrs. Nat. Bank, Newark. Author: Stephen Crane, 1923. Home: Newark, N.J. Died Oct. 7, 1928.

RAYMOND, William Galt, engr.; b. Princeton, Ia., Mar. 2, 1859; s. W. H. V. and Laura Guernsey (Peet) R.; ed. pub. and high schs. and U. of Kan.; C.E., Washington U., 1884, LL.D., 1905; Eng.D., U. of Mich., 1919; m. Helen Williams Bay, July 1, 1885; children—Mrs. Margaret Leonard Hammond, William Yale, Edwin Bay, Laurence Guerney (dec.). Asst. engr. in location and constrn. of rys. in Miss. Valley before graduation; instr. civ. engring., U. of Calif., 1884-90; pvt. practice (Raymond & Bay), 1890-92; town engr. Berkeley, Calif., 1892; prof. geodesy, road engring. and topog. drawing, Rensselaer Poly. Inst., 1892-1904; prof. civ. engring., 1904-22, prof. engring., 1922—, dean Coll. Applied Science, 1905—, State U. of Ia. Mem. Soc. Promotion Engring. Edn. (pres. 1911-12). Author: Plane Surveying, 1896; Elements of Roalroad Engineering, 1908; Railroad Field Geometry, 1910; Railroad Field Manual for Civil Engineers, 1915; What Is Fair?, 1917; Public and Its Utilities, 1925. Mem. Ia. State Bd. of Conciliation, 1918-19, adjusting pub. utility rates during war. Address: Iowa City, Iowa. Died June 17, 1926.

RAYNER, Emma, author; b. Cambridge, England; d. Thomas Gotobed and Mahalah (Holmes) R.; early edn. in pvt. schs.; grad. U. of Cambridge, Eng., taking math. course and obtaining honors in the math. Tripos of 1888; unmarried. On staff of Youth's Companion, 1896-1902. Author: Free to Serve, 1897; In Castle and Colony, 1899; Visiting the Sin, 1900; Doris Kingsley, Child and Colonist, 1901; Handicapped Among the Free, 1903; The Dilemma of Engeltie, 1911. Address: Goshen, N.H. Died Nov. 20, 1926.

RAYNER, Isidor, senator; b. Baltimore, Apr. 11, 1850; s. William S. and Amalie R.; student U. of

Md. and U. of Va.; m. Frances Jane Bevan, 1871. Admitted to bar, 1871, and in practice at Baltimore, 1871—. Mem. Md. Ho. of Rep., 1878-80, Senate, 1886-87, resigned; mem. 50th Congress (1887-89) and 52d and 53d Congresses (1891-95); atty. gen. of Md., 1899-1903; U.S. senator for terms 1905-11, 1911-17. Democrat. Counsel for Rear Admiral Schley before investigating commn., 1901. Home: Baltimore, Md. Died Nov. 25, 1912.

RAYNOLDS, Joshua Saxton, banker; b. Canton, O., Dec. 31, 1845; s. James Madison and Sara (Slusser) R.; ed. pub. schs., Canton; m. Sarah A. Robbins, Sept. 7, 1869; children—Ruth (Mrs. James G. McNary), Kate Saxton (Mrs. Dudley S. Dean), Herbert F., John M., Sarah M. (Mrs. Marston E. Drake). Began as clk. Stark County Bank, Canton, then with First Nat. Bank, Canton; apptd. asst. cashier Colo. Nat. Bank, Denver; successively pres. Rocky Mountain Nat. Bank (Central City, Colo.), Merchants Nat. Bank (Georgetown, Colo.); v.p. First Nat. Bank, Las Vegas, N.M., and pres. First Nat. Bank, Albuquerque; pres. First Nat. Bank, El Paso, Tex., 1924-31 (retired). Served as top sergt. U.S.A., 1864. Republican. Presbyn. Home: El Paso, Tex. Died 1932.

REA, George Bronson, diplomat; b. Brooklyn, N.Y., Aug. 28, 1869; s. Joseph B. and Charlotte A. (Bronson) R.; ed. pub. schs. and pvt. tutors; m. Harriet S. Carter, Jan. 12, 1897 (died 1927); children—William Carter, Henry Carter, Consuelo; m. 2d, Francesca Ruiz-Moron, Jan. 8, 1919; 1 dau., Gloria. War corr. N.Y. Herald, during Cuban War for Independence, 1895-97; corr. N.Y. World, Spanish-Am. War; founded Far Eastern Review, Manila, P.I., 1904; del. Philippine Govt. to Washington on tariff legislation, 1905; adviser to Dr. Sun Yat Sen, 1911-13; adviser to Chinese Ministry of Rys., 1913-14 and 1929; tech. adviser to Chinese delegation to Peace Conf., Paris, France, 1919; rep. Am. C. of C. of China at Washington, D.C., 1927-29; counsellor to Ministry of Foreign Affairs, govt. of Manchoukuo, 1932—. Captain U.S.A., World War I; asst. mil. attaché, Madrid, 1917-19. Episcopalian. Died Nov. 21, 1936.

REA, John Andrew; b. Lancaster County, Pa.; s. John and Sarah Ann (Robb) R.; Ohio Wesleyan U., 3 yrs.; A.B., Cornell U., 1869; m. Mary E. Terry, Sept. 9, 1873. Began as reporter, Phila. Press, later mng. editor Minneapolis Tribune; editor Bismarck Tribune and of Dakota edit. St. Paul Pioneer Press; register U.S. Land Office, Bismarck, under Hayes and Cleveland; sec. Constl. Conv., N.D., 1889, and organized that body; moved to Wash., 1890, and dealt extensively in timber lands; editor Daily Olympian, Olympia, Wash., 1891. Pres. emeritus bd. regents U. of Wash. Republican. Conglist. Speaker and writer on polit. topics. Home: Tacoma, Wash. Died Feb. 20, 1941.

REA, John Dougan, prof. English; b. Minneapolis, Kan., Sept. 20, 1880; s. Dr. Robert M. and Cora G. (Anderson) R.; B.A., Yale, 1903, M.A., 1905, Ph.D., 1918; m. Margaret Gentle, June 16, 1920; children—Robert St. Clair (dec.), John Alexander. Instr. in Latin, Yale, 1906-08; asst. prof. U. of Cincinnati, 1908-09; prof. English, Earlham Coll., 1909-19; prof. English, 1919-23, head dept., 1921-23, Ind. U.; head of English dept., Miami U., 1923—. Presbyn. Editor of Earlham Verse, 1914, and of Ben Jonson's Volpone, 1919. Home: Oxford, O. Died Mar. 6, 1933.

REA, John Patterson, commander-in-chief G.A.R.; b. Lower Oxford, Chester County, Pa., Oct. 13, 1840; ed. in public schools; removed to Miami County, O., 1861; enlisted in spring of 1861 as private 11th Ohio ing.; joined 1st Ohio cav., Aug. 1861; became 2d and 1st lt., capt. and bvt. maj., serving in Loring's cav. brigade, Army of the Cumberland. Grad. Ohio Wesleyan U., 1867, admitted to Pa. bar, 1868; assessor internal revenue, Pa., 1869-73; moved to Minn.; editor Minneapolis Tribune, 1874-77; established law practice, 1877; judge of probate, 1878-80; judge 4th Minn. dist., 1880-92; quartermaster gen., Minn., 1883-86, with rank of brig. gen.; commander-in-chief G.A.R., 1887. Address: Minneapolis, Minn. Died 1900.

REA, Samuel, ry. official; b. Hollidaysburg, Pa., Sept. 21, 1855; s. James D. and Ruth (Moore) R.; ed. schs. and acad.; left sch. at 15, and entered engrng. dept. Pa. R.R.; m. Mary M. Black, Sept. 11, 1879. Began as locating and constrg. engr. on various branches Pa. R.R., 1871; asst. engr. during constrn. chain suspension bridge, Pittsburgh, also on Pittsburgh & Lake Erie R.R., 1875-79; asst. engr. Pa. R.R., 1879-89; chief engr. cnstrn. belt line tunnel under Baltimore for B.&O. R.R., 1889-91; again with Pa. R.R., 1892-97, asst. to pres., and, 1897-99, as 1st asst. to pres., 4th v.p., 1899-1905, 3d v.p., 1905-09, 2d v.p., 1909-11, 1st v.p., March 1911-12, vice-pres., May 1912, pres., Jan. 1913-Oct. 1, 1925; retired under pension regulations; also pres. Pa. Co., P.,C.,C.&St.L. Ry. Co., Phila., Balto. & Wash. R.R., West Jersey & Seashore R.R. and Nor. Cen. Ry., and pres. and dir. of a large number of affiliated cos. in Pa. R.R. System. In charge constrn. New York tunnel extension and sta. of Pa. R.R. System, in recognition of successful completion of which, U. of Pa. conferred degree of Sc.D., 1910; also Sc.D., Princeton U., 1916, and LL.D., Lafayette Coll., 1916. The N.Y. Connecting R.R., including Hell Gate Bridge over East River, planned and constructed under his direction, opened for traffic, 1917. Apptd., Apr. 11, 1917, mem. exec. com. of spl. com. on nat. defense of Railroads War Bd. Awarded Franklin Medal, Franklin Inst., Phila., 1926. Author: The Railways Terminating in London. Home: Bryn Mawr, Pa. Died Mar. 24, 1929.

READ, Benjamin Stalker, telephone official; b. Carthage, Tenn., Jan. 21, 1876; s. Thomas Benton and Alice Treadway (Johnson) R.; ed. pub. schs., Tenn.; m. Sally Berry Stevens, Apr. 20, 1899; children—Joseph Charles, Benjamin Stalker. In employ Bell Telephone System at Carthage, 1890; mgr. Cumberland Telephone & Telegraph Co., at Carthage, later Owensboro, Ky., and Chattanooga, Tenn., 1895-1904; dist. mgr. same, at Louisville, 1904-08; div. supt., New Orleans, 1908-12; gen. mgr. Bell Telephone Co. of Mo., 1912, Mo. & Kan. Telephone Co., 1912-14; v.p. Southwestern Bell Telephone System at St. Louis, 1914-19; pres. Mountain States Telephone & Telegraph Co., Denver, Colo., 1919-24; pres. Southern Bell Telephone and Telegraph Co., and Cumberland Telephone and Telegraph Co. (now consolidated into Southern Bell Telephone Co.), Atlanta, Ga., 1924—; pres. Telephone Pioneers America, 1925; dir. First Nat. Bank. Mem. War Camp Survey Com., Aug.-Dec. 1918. Mem. Christian (Disciples) Ch. Mason, K.P. Home: Atlanta, Ga. Died July 23, 1935.

READ, Charles O., mfr.; b. Norton, Mass., Dec. 31, 1846; s. Charles A. and Lucy (Newman) R.; ed. pub. schs.; m. Mary E. Bliss, May 25, 1880; children—Albert Manton, Charles Newman, Frederic Bliss, Malcolm Everett, Robert Otis. Began as clk. with Sayles Finishing Plants, 1863, later gen. mgr.; pres. of Sayles Finishing Plants, Inc., from time of incorporation; also pres. Hamlet Textile Co., Ponemah Mills, Slater Trust Co., Memorial Hosp., Moshassuck Valley R.R.; trustee Estate of William F. Sayles and executor and trustee Estate of Frank A. Sayles. Hon. chmn. local chapter Am. Red Cross and chmn. Community Council of Nat. Defense, World War I. Republican. Episcopalian. Home: Pawtucket, R.I. Died July 7, 1926.

READ, George Windle, army officer; b. Indianola, Ia., Nov. 19, 1860; s. James Crisfield and Elizabeth Snell (Windle) R.; grad. U.S. Mil. Acad., 1883; grad. Army War Coll., 1914; m. Burton, d. Lt. Gen. S. B. M. Young, U.S.A., Sept. 2, 1886; children—Burton Young, Margaret Elizabeth, George W. Commd. 2d lt., 16th Inf., June 13, 1883; promoted through grades to maj. gen., March 8, 1921. Served on frontier, 1883-89; prof. mil. science, and tactics, U. of Ia., 1889-93; service in Tex., 1893-97; with Evacuation Commn., Cuba, 1898-99; in Philippine Islands, 1901-02; in Calif., Hawaii, and confidential mission abroad, 1902-04; with Gen. Staff, 1905-09; with Mil. Govt., Cuba, 1906-08; pres. Claims Commn.; gov. Province Pinar del Rio, Apr.-Oct. 1908; chief umpire, Ft. Riley, Kan., 1910; in Philippine Islands, 1910-12; insp. gen., Dept. of Mindanao; border service, Ariz., 1912-14; adj. gen., 1914-17; adj. 2d Div., Texas City, Tex., 1914-15; duty at War Dept., 1915-17; apptd. comdr. brigade, Camp Upton, L.I., N.Y., Aug. 5, 1917; apptd. comdr. cav. div., El Paso, Tex., Dec. 1917, 30th Div., Apr. 27, 1918; comdg. 2d Army Corps, June 13, 1918, until demobilization, Feb. 1, 1919; comd. Am. Embarkation Center, Le Mans, France, Feb. 1—Apr. 8, 1919; comdg. Camp Jackson, S.C., May 1, 1919-Aug. 31, 1920; comdg. 5th Corps Area, Sept. 1, 1920-Aug. 31, 1922; comdg. Philippine Dept., Oct. 4, 1922-Nov. 19, 1924; retired Nov. 19, 1924. Overseas service, May 6, 1918-Apr. 25, 1919. Gold medal Mil. Service Instn., 1889; D.S.M. (U.S.); Knight Comdr. Order Bath (British); Comdr. Legion of Honor, Croix de Guerre with palm (French). Episcopalian. Home: Washington, D.C. Died Nov. 6, 1934.

READ, John Joseph, rear admiral U.S.N.; b. Mt. Holly, N.J., June 17, 1842; s. Joseph S. and Mary (Black) R.; apptd. to U.S. Naval Acad. from N.J., 1858. Ordered into active service on Frigate Potomac, acting midshipman, 1861; promoted ensign, Nov. 25, 1862; lt., Feb. 22, 1864; lt. comdr., July 25, 1866; comdr., Dec. 11, 1877; capt., Apr. 27, 1893; rear admiral, Nov. 29, 1900. Served on Atlantic and Gulf coasts, 1861; div. officer Hartford flagship W. Gulf Blockading Squadron, 1862-63; participated in attack on Port Hudson, La., Grand Gulf, Miss., and batteries at Warrington, below Vicksburg, Miss., S. Atlantic Squadron, 1863-64; exec. officer Cuyler, participated in attack and capture of Ft. Fisher, N. Atlantic Blockading Squadron, 1864-66; De Soto, 1865-66; Rhode Island, 1866-67; exec. officer Susquehanna, 1867, Michigan, 1868-70; on Guerriere, 1870-72; exec. officer receiving-ship Vermont, and Kearsarge, 1863; exec. officer and comd. flagship Richmond, 1874-77; duty Bur. of Yards and Docks, 1878-79; light house insp., 15th dist., 1879-83, 4th dist., 1887-90, 11th dist., 1892-93; comd. Michigan, 1883-87, Iroquois, 1891-92, receiving-ship Independence, 1894-95, flagship Olympia, 1895-97, receiving-ship Richmond, 1898-1900; commandant Portsmouth Navy Yard, 1901-03, chmn. Lighthouse Bd., 1903-04; retired by reason of age, June 17, 1904. Home: Mt. Holly, N.J. Died 1910.

READ, Melbourne Stuart, univ. prof.; b. Berwick, N.S., Can., Sept. 27, 1869; s. Rev. Eliphalet O. and Margaret Catherine (Parker) R.; A.B., Acadia Coll., N.S., 1891; Sage fellow in philosophy and ethics, Cornell U., 1894-95, Ph.D., 1895; LL.D., Acadia U., Canada, 1923; m. Caroline Jane Mott, June 27, 1900. Prin. Wolfville (N.S.) High Sch., 1891-92; asso. prof. philosophy, 1895-96, prof., 1896-1900, prof. philosophy and edn., 1900-10, prof. psychology and edn., 1910—, sec. of the coll., 1910-12, v.p., 1912-21, pres. pro tem, 1921-22, Colgate U. Lecturer, Dartmouth Summer Sch., 1910, 12. Baptist. Author: English Evolutionary Ethics, 1902; An Introductory Psychology, 1911. Home: Hamilton, N.Y. Died Apr. 4, 1927.

READ, Opie, author; b. Nashville, Tenn., Dec. 22, 1852; s. Guilford and Elizabeth (Wallace) R.; ed. Gallatin, Tenn.; m. Ada Benham, June 30, 1881. Began newspaper work in Franklin, Ky., went later to Little Rock; edited Arkansas Gazette, 1878-81; on staff Cleveland Leader, 1881-83; established Arkansas Traveler, humorous paper, 1883; conducted it until 1891; then in lit. work in Chicago, 1891—. Author: Len Gansett, 1888; A Kentucky Colonel, 1889; Emmett Bonlore, 1891; A Tennessee Judge, 1893; Wives of the Prophet, 1894; The Jucklins, 1895; My Young Master, 1896; An Arkansas Planter, 1896; Bolanyo, 1897; Old Ebenezer, 1898; Waters of Caney Fork, 1899; On the Suwanee River; A Yankee from the West, 1900; In the Alamo, 1900; Judge Elbridge, 1900; The Carpetbagger (with Frank Pixley); The Starbucks, 1902; An American in New York, 1905; Son of the Swordmaker, 1905; Old Lim Jucklin, 1905; "Turkey Egg" Griffin, 1905; The Mystery of Margaret, 1907; Gold Gauze Veil, 1927. Address: Chicago, Ill. Died Nov. 2, 1939.

READ, William Augustus, banker; b. Brooklyn, N.Y., May 20, 1858; s. George W. and Rowland Augusta (Curtis) R.; grad. Brooklyn Poly. Inst., 1873; m. Caroline H. Seaman, Nov. 20, 1894. Engaged in banking in New York, 1877—; mem. banking firm of Wm. A. Read & Co.; dir. Bank of New York (N.B.A.), Central Trust Co., Interborough Rapid Transit Co. Episcopalian. Republican. Home: New York, N.Y. Died Apr. 7, 1916.

READ, William Lewis, lawyer; b. Harrison County, O., May 15, 1851; s. Ambrose and Mary Ann (Lewis) R.; student State U. of Ia.; LL.B., 1875; m. Juliet E. McMurray, Sept. 29, 1882. In practice at Des Moines, 1876—; sr. mem. firm of Read & Read; dir. Capital City State Bank, Des Moines Fire Ins. Co. Mason, 32°, Scottish Rite. Address: Des Moines, Ia. Died July 18, 1915.

READE, John Moore, prof. botany; b. Toronto, Can., Dec. 17, 1876; s. John Moore and Janet Drysdale (Bain) R.; B.S. in Agr., U. of Toronto, 1900; studied U. of Munich, 1905; Ph.D., Cornell U., 1908; m. Julia MacArthur, June 17, 1914; children—John Moore III, William Woodthorp, Janet Drysdale. Teacher and div. supt. Dept. of Pub. Instrn., Philippines, 1901-04; with U. of Ga., 1907—, prof. botany, 1908—, dir. biol. labs., 1917—. Episcopalian. Home: Athens, Ga. Died May 9, 1937.

READE, Philip, brig. gen. U.S.A.; b. Lowell, Mass., Oct. 13, 1844; s. Henry and Rowena (Hildreth) R.; cadet, U.S. Mil. Acad., July 1, 1864-Jan. 14, 1865, and June 20, 1865-Jan. 21, 1867; m. Jessie Eaton, Oct. 30, 1878. Commd. 2d lt. 3d Inf., May 13, 1867; 1st lt., Dec. 8, 1878; capt., Nov. 13, 1889; maj. insp. gen. vols., May 12, 1898; lt. col. insp. gen. vols., Jan. 18, 1899; hon. discharged from vol. service, June 30, 1901; maj. 8th U.S. Inf., Mar. 31, 1899; transferred to 5th Inf., Oct. 28, 1899; lt. col. 25th Inf., Mar. 12, 1902; transferred to 23d Inf., Apr. 6, 1903; col., Aug. 13, 1903; brig. gen. U.S.A., May 4, 1911; retired by operation of law, Oct. 13, 1908. In military service of U.S. 44 yrs., in Indian campaigns, Civil War, Spanish-Am. War in Cuba and P.I., Aguinaldo insurrection and Moro campaigns. Gov. and historian Mass., Wis. and Ill. socs. Colonial Wars; register gen. Army of Santiago-de-Cuba; founder and 1st v.p. Mil. Order Moro Campaigns; patriarch of Mass. Corral Mil. Order of the Carabao; historian Mass. Soc. S.A.R. Mason. Address: Boston, Mass. Deceased.

REAGAN, John Henninger, U.S. senator; b. Sevier County, Tenn., Oct. 8, 1818; youth on farm; ed. in country school and a yr. in coll., Maryville, Tenn.; married; went to Republic of Texas; served in Texan war against Indians; deputy surveyor public lands, 1839-44; capt. militia; capt. in active service; col. of militia; justice of the peace; began law practice, 1846; probate judge; mem. Tex. legislature, 1847; judge 9th jud. dist., Tex., 1852-57; congressman, 1857-61; mem. Tex. Secession Conv., 1861; mem. provisional Confederate Congress, 1861; postmaster-gen. Confederate States, 1861-65, sec.-treas., 1865; prisoner of war, May to October, 1865; practiced law in Palestine, Tex.; member Congress, 1875-87; author "Reagan Inter-State Commerce Bill," afterward modified by amendments of Senator Cullom into the law now in force; U.S. senator, 1887-91; chmn. Tex. State R.R. Commn. Address: Palestine, Tex. Died 1905.

REAM, Norman Bruce, capitalist; b. Somerset County, Pa., Nov. 5, 1844; ed. common and normal schs.; m. Carrie Putnam, 1876. Taught sch. 1 term;

then divided time between farm work and photography until 1861; pvt. and 1st lt. 85th Pa. Vols. until incapacitated by wounds received in battle nr. Savannah, Ga. Clerk in a Harnedsville store, 1865-66; in business, Princeton, Ill., and Osceola, Ia., 1866-71; live stock and grain commn. mcht., Chicago, 1871-88; from 1888 engaged with his large real estate, street ry. and railroad interests; dir. First Nat. Bank, Chicago, U.S. Steel Corp., B.&O. R.R. Co., Erie R.R. Co., C.,H.&D. R.R., Pere Marquette R.R., Seaboard Air Line R.R., Carolina, Clinchfield & Ohio R.R., Nat. Biscuit Co.; trustee New York Security & Trust Co., Met. Trust Co., Fidelity Phœnix Ins. Co. Home: New York, N.Y. Died Feb. 9, 1915.

REAMY, Thaddeus Asbury, physician, surgeon; b. in Frederick County, Va., Apr. 28, 1829; s. Jacob Asbury and Mary White (Bonifield) R.; ed. common schs. and pvt. teachers, Muskingum County, O.; M.D., Starling Med. Coll., Columbus, O., 1854; A.M., Ohio Wesleyan U., 1870, LL.D., Cornell Coll., Iowa, 1890; m. Sarah Amanda Chappelear, Sept. 13, 1853. Practiced Mt. Sterling, O., 1854-63, Zanesville, O., 1863-71, Cincinnati, 1871—. Post-grad. study in London and Paris, 1869. Prof. materia medica and therapeutics, Cincinnati Coll. Medicine and Surgery, 1859-61; prof. diseases of women, Starling Med. Coll., 1863-70; prof. obstetrics and diseases of women and children, 1871-88, prof. gynecology, 1888—, Med. Coll. of Ohio (now Med. Dept. U. of Cincinnati), Surgeon 122d O. V. Inf., Sept. 1862-Jan. 1863, resigned to take seat to which had been elected from Zanesville, in 55th Gen. Assembly of Ohio; surgeon 13th provost-marshall dist. of Ohio, Apr.-Sept. 1863. On gynecol. staff Good Samaritan Hosp., Cincinnati, 1871—; on staff Cincinnati Hosp., 1886-98, surgeon Reamy's Pvt. Hosp. for Women, 1878-98; cons. surg. Christ's Hosp., 1887—. Presbyn. Hosp., 1894-99. Mem. Cincinnati Acad. Medicine (pres. 1877), Ohio State Med. Soc. (pres. 1871), Am. Med. Assn. (chmn. sect. Diseases of Women, 1880), Cincinnati Obstet. Soc. (pres. 1884), Am. Gynecol. soc. (pres. 1886). Mem. M.E. Church. Republican. Extensive contbr. to med. jours. and to Trans. Ohio State Med. Soc., Am. Gynecol. Soc.; contbr. on Sub-involution of the Uterus and Vagina to Am. System of Gynecology (Mann), 1888. Address: Cincinnati, O. Died 1909.

REARICK, Allan Chamberlain, lawyer; b. Galesburg, Ill., Dec. 18, 1874; s. Francis Herman and Helen Maria (Shaw) R.; A.B., Knox Coll., Galesburg, 1897; LL.B., Columbia, 1904; m. Ethel Rawalt, June 15, 1907; children—John Shaw, Anna Maud (Mrs. Joseph W. Allen, Jr.), Allan Chamberlain. Admitted to N.Y. bar, 1904, practiced at N.Y. City, 1904—; member of the firm of Hines, Rearick, Door & Hammond; counsel M.-K.-T. R.R. Company; director C.R.I.&P. Ry. Co., Summit Trust Co. Trustee Kent Place School, Summit, N.J. Republican. Conglist. Home: Summit, N.J. Died June 4, 1940.

REAVIS, Charles Frank, congressman; b. Falls City, Neb., Sept. 5, 1870; s. Isham and Anna (Dorrington) R.; ed. high sch., Falls City; student Northwestern U., Evanston, Ill., 1898; m. Myrta Abbey, June 26, 1895. Admitted to Neb. bar, 1902, and practiced in Falls City; associated with father in practice till death of latter, 1914. Pros. atty. Richardson Co., Neb., 1904-06; mem. 64th to 67th Congresses (1915-23), 1st Neb. Dist.; resigned from 67th Congress, June 1922; apptd. spl. asst. to the attorney gen. in the prosecution of so-called war frauds, June 1922. Republican. Methodist. Mason; Elk. Home: Falls City, Neb. Died May 26, 1932.

REAVIS, James Bradly, judge; b. in Boone County, Mo., 1848; s. John N. and Elizabeth (Preston) R.; ed. pub. schs., and at Ky. U.; was not grad. because of illness; admitted to bar, Hannibal, Mo., 1872; m. Minnie A. Freeman, May 27, 1891. Edited Monroe City (Mo.) Appeal, 1872-74; removed to Pacific Coast, 1874, and to Wash. Ty., 1880, engaging in law practice. Mem. upper house Territorial Council, Wash., 1888; regent Territorial U., Wash., until statehoood; chief justice Supreme Ct., Wash., 1896-1902; retired from practice, 1909. Address: Seattle, Wash. Died Apr. 30, 1912.

REBER, Samuel, army officer; b. St. Louis, Oct. 16, 1864; s. Samuel and Margaret Messier (Reese) R.; grad. U.S. Mil. Acad., 1886; grad. course in electricity, Johns Hopkins, 1894; grad. Army War Coll., 1905; m. Cecelia Sherman Miles, Jan. 10, 1900; children— Miles, Samuel. Commd. 2d lt. 4th Cav., July 1, 1886; 1st lt. 9th Cav., July 28, 1892; 1st lt. signal corps, Jan. 27, 1894; maj. U.S.V., May 12, 1898; maj. signal officer, May 20, 1898; lt. col. chief signal officer, July 18, 1898; hon. discharged Apr. 17, 1899; capt. U.S.A., July 1, 1800; maj., Mar. 2, 1903; lt. col., Mar. 5, 1913; col. S.C., July 1, 1916; retired Nov. 30, 1919; now gen. foreign rep. Radio Corp. America. Service against hostile Indians in Arizona; in Puerto Rico campaigns; recommended for brevet capt. in action at Guanica. Served as chief signal officer of depts., divs. and army corps; extensive experiencse in ballooning and aviation; supervised nearly all internat. meets held in U.S.; in charge aviation sect. Signal Corps; with 28th and 88th divs. and with Hdqrs. 2d Army, A.E.F. in France. Sec. sect. B Internat. Elec. Congress, 1893. Mem. elec. jury Chicago and St. Louis expns.; War Dept. del. Internat. Elec. Congress, 1904; del. Internat. Telegraph Conf. Paris, 1925, Internat. Radiotelegraph Conference, Washington, 1927, World Engring. Congress on Radio (v.p.), Liege, 1930, 2d Conf. Internat. Tech. Cons. Com. on Radio, Copenhagen, 1931. Author various tech. books and papers. Home: New York, N.Y. Died Apr. 16, 1933.

RECTOR, Edward, lawyer; b. Bedford, Ind., July 7, 1863; s. Isaac and Juliet (Gardiner) R.; LL.B., U. of Cincinnati Law Sch., 1885; m. Lucy Rowland, Oct. 24, 1893. Admitted to Ill. bar, 1892, practiced at Chicago, 1892—; mem. Rector, Hibben, Davis & Macauley, 1910—. Trustee DePauw U., Greencastle, Ind. (donated Rector Hall to the univ., 1916, and established The Edward Rector Scholarship Foundation, providing free scholarships for 400 young men, 1919). Republican. Methodist. Home: Chicago, Ill. Died Aug. 1, 1925.

RECTOR, Elbridge Lee, lawyer, author; b. Seguin, Tex., Nov. 16, 1847; s. Judge Nelson S. and Harriet C. R.; ed. West Tex. Mil. Inst.; grad. U. of Va., 1871; m. Pattie E. Townes, Jan. 13, 1886; children—James Knight and Lucy Elizabeth (twins). Admitted to bar, 1877; student of polit. economy. Contbr. to Am. Magazine of Civics. Author: The Science of Money and Exchange, 1901. Mem. Texas State Senate, 1919, 20. Address: San Saba, Tex. Died July 5, 1929.

RECTOR, Frank, clergyman; b. nr. Parkersburg, Va., July 20, 1851; s. Rev. Enoch and Mindwell (Noyes) R.; A.B., Denison U., Ohio, 1878, D.D., 1903; grad. Newton Theol. Instn., Mass., 1881; m. Martha Pickering, Oct. 18, 1881 (died 1907; children—Vera (dec.), Beulah Mariam, Randolph, Gordon (dec.); m. 2d, Mary Louise Rogers, Oct. 16, 1911. Ordained Bapt. ministry, 1881; pastor 2d Ch., Newport, R.I., 1881-86, 1st Ch., Fitchburg, Mass., 1886-1900, 1st Ch., Pawtucket, R.I., 1900-30 (resigned) but continued active in ch. work. Pres. R.I. Bapt. State Conv., 6 yrs.; pres. R.I. Bapt. Edn. Soc.; trustee Newton Theol. Instn. Home: Pawtucket, R.I. Died Feb. 26, 1933.

REDDING, Joseph Deighn, lawyer; b. Sacramento, Calif., Sept. 13, 1859; s. Benjamin Barnard and Mary Prescott (Putnam) R.; grad. Calif. Mil. Acad., 1874; Harvard Law Sch., 1877-79; m. Myra Cowles, June 15, 1882. In practice at San Francisco, 1882—; counsel in Calif. for rys. and large corps. Life mem. San Francisco Art Assn. (pres. 1885-87); lecturer on art and drama; speaker and writer. Commr. from Calif. to Paris Expn., 1889. Wrote first of "grove" plays, prof. by Bohemian Club in the redwood forest, 1902, which have since revived the ancient Greek form of outdoor drama in Calif.; wrote "Natoma," the 1st successful grand opera in English lang. with Am. plot, prod. Met. Opera House, New York, 1911. Author: Book of Natoma, 1911; also numerous essays, etc. Wrote the grove play, 1912, "The Atonement of Pan" (prod. in Bohemian Grove, Aug. 1912, with David Bispham in title rôle); also essays and addresses. Composer of numerous published songs, quartets and piano pieces; wrote the music for the Bohemian grove play of 1917, "The Land of Happiness," book by Charles Templeton Crocker; conducted its initial performance, with orchestra of 70 pieces, in Bohemian Grove, Aug. 8, 1917; completed score of opera "Fay-Yen Fah," 1921 (prod. at Monte Carlo, France, Feb. and Mar. 1925); wrote the grove play, Semper Virens (prod. in Bohemian Grove, Aug. 18, 1923). Pres. Calif. Soc. of New York, 1903-08. Decorated by French Govt. Chevalier de l'ordre National de la Légion d'honneur, 1926. Home: San Francisco, Calif. Deceased.

REDDING, Leo L.; newspaper man; b. Plainview, Minn., May 5, 1867; s. George W. and Joanna (Gleed) R.; student U. of Minn., 1886; m. Jessie Fletcher, Oct. 25, 1887. Editor and pub. Evening Journal, Wichita, Kan., 1887-90; asst. editor Chicago Inter-Ocean, 1891-96; in charge war corr. in Cuba and during Spanish-Am. war for New York Herald, 1897-99; Washington corr., New York Herald, 1900, city editor and Sunday editor, until 1911; contbr. to Metropolitan, World's Work, Everybody's and Mechanics mags. Founder and pres. Leo. L. Redding & Co., for endowment work in connection with colleges and similar instns.; dir. various Red Cross, United War Work and Library Assn. campaigns, New York, 1917-19. Republican. Conglist. Home: New York, N.Y. Died June 3, 1936.

REDDING, Robert Jordan, editor, lecturer; b. Monroe County, Ga., Dec. 28, 1836; s. Anderson Westmoreland and Susan Randall (Jackson) R.; ed. in pvt. schs., and Dahlonega (Ga.) Acad. and Brownwood Inst., La Grange, Ga.; m. Mary E. Bivins, May 19, 1858; m. 2d, Sarah E. Worrill, Apr. 10, 1877; m. 3d, Sarah Elizabeth Redding, Oct. 12, 1887. Reared on farm; practiced law, 1857-59; judge inferior ct., Schley Co., Ga., 1860-61; engaged in farming, 1859-76; served capt. 46th Ga. Inf., C.S.A., 1862-65, wounded at Kenesaw Mountain, 1864. Assistant commr. of agr. of Ga., 1875-89; dir. Ga. Agrl. Expt. Sta., 1889-1906. Gen. supt. Ga. Bldg. and exhibits, Jamestown Expn., 1907. Democrat and Single Taxer. Mem. M.E. Ch., S. Author of many expt. sta. and state dept. bulls. Editor Southern World, 2 yrs., Southern Cultivator, 6 yrs.; for 20 yrs. of farm dept., Atlanta Constitution. Address: Griffin, Ga. Died June 4, 1914.

REDFIELD, Amasa Angell, lawyer, author; b. Clyde, Wayne County, N.Y., May 19, 1837; s. Luther R.; grad. U. City of New York, 1860; admitted to New York bar, 1862. Author: Handbook of United States Tax Laws, 1863; Reports of Surrogates' Courts of the State of New York, 5 vols., 1864-82; Law and Practice of Surrogates' Courts, 1875. Also (with Thomas G. Shearman) The Law of Negligence, 1869. Residence: Farmington, Conn. Died 1902.

REDFIELD, Henry Stephen, law prof.; b. Corning, Steuben County, N.Y., July 31, 1851; s. Jared A. and Mary (Hayt) R., both of N.E. descent; grad. Elmira Free Acad., 1867; in business, 1867-72; A.B., Amherst, 1877, A.M., 1887, LL.D., 1901; admitted to practice, 1879; m. Susan Woods Curtis, Oct. 19, 1880; 1 son, George Curtis (dec.). Practiced law Elmira, N.Y., as partner in Diven & Redfield, 1879-98; prof. practice and procedure, Coll. of Law, Cornell, 1898-1901; prof. law, 1901-05, Nash prof. law, 1905-16, Columbia; retired on account of illness, July 1, 1916. Author: Election of Remedies (vol. 15, Cyclopædia of Law and Procedure), 1905; The Brief on Appeal (in Brief Making), 1906. Contbr. to legal jours. Address: New York, N.Y. Died Mar. 27, 1926.

REDFIELD, William C., sec. commerce; b. Albany, N.Y., June 18, 1858; s. Charles Bailey and Mary (Wallace) R.; ed. high sch., Pittsfield, Mass.; m. Elise Mercein Fuller, Apr. 8, 1885; children—Elsie M. (Mrs. Charles K. Drury), Humphrey F. Treas. J. H. Williams & Co., Brooklyn, 1887-1901; v.p. Warp Twisting-in Machine Co., 1904; pres. J. H. Williams & Co., 1905, Sirocco Engring. Co., 1907-11; v.p. Am. Blower Co., 1909-13; dir. Equitable Life Assurance Soc., 1905-13. Commr. pub. works, Borough Brooklyn, 1902-03; Nat. Dem. party nominee for Congress, 7th N.Y. Dist., 1896; mem. 62d Congress (1911-13), 5th Dist.; Sec. of Commerce in Cabinet of President Wilson, Mar. 4, 1913-Nov. 1, 1919, retired. Democrat. Episcopalian. Pres. Nat. Inst. Social Sciences. Author: The New Industrial Day, 1912; With Congress and Cabinet, 1924; Glimpses of Our Government, 1924-25; Dependent America, 1926; We and the World, 1927. Lecturer. Home: Brooklyn, N.Y. Died June 13, 1932.

REDHEAD, Edwin Richard, paper mfr.; b. Brownville, N.Y., Jan. 6, 1851; s. Rev. Richard and Elizabeth (Barker) R.; A.B., Syracuse U., 1874; m. Sarah A. Petty, May 23, 1877 (died 1915); m. 2d, Lucille Dryer, Aug. 30, 1917. Organized, 1880, with F. G. Weeks, of Skaneateles, N.Y., the Victoria Paper Mills Co., Fulton, N.Y., and in 1885, the Oswego Falls Pulp & Paper Co., Fulton; pres. Victoria Paper Mills Co.; chmn. bd. Citizens Nat. Bank, Fulton; dir. Thousand Island Park Assn. Trustee Syracuse U., Cazenovia Sem.; pres. Fulton Pub. Library. Republican. Methodist. Address: Fulton, N.Y. Died May 30, 1924.

REDINGTON, Paul Goodwin, chief Bur. of Biol. Survey; b. Chicago, Ill., Jan. 25, 1878; s. Edward Dana and Mary Ann (Chamberlin) R.; A.B., Dartmouth, 1900; M.F., Yale, 1904; m. Ermina Elizabeth Weaver, Sept. 21, 1910; children—Edward Dana, Mary Ann, Paul Goodwin. Field work, U.S. Forest Service, 1904-Jan. 1, 1918, July 1, 1918-26, district forester, 1926-27; chief of Bur. of Biol. Survey, U.S. Dept. Agr., 1927—. City mgr. Albuquerque, N.M., Jan.-July 1918. Mem. Soc. Am. Foresters (pres. 1929). Republican. Conglist. Contbr. to Jour. of Forestry, Am. Forests and Forest Life. Home: Falls Church, Va. Died Jan. 12, 1942.

REDMOND, Daniel Walter, coll. dean; b. Oxford, N.Y., Aug. 15, 1876; s. Richard Joseph and Margaret Claire (Nowlan) R.; Ph.B., Hamilton Coll., Clinton, N.Y., 1901, Ed.D., 1931; Ph.D., Columbia, 1913; m. Bessie H. Carroll, Aug. 15, 1906; children—John Carroll, Albert Carroll, Richard Joseph. Taught Clinton (N.Y.) High Sch., 1901-04, Jenner Sch., Syracuse, N.Y., 1904-05; with Coll. City of N.Y., 1905—, dean of Coll. Liberal Arts and Science, 1926—. Attended Citizens' Training Camp, Plattsburg, N.Y., 1916, S.A.T.C., same, 1918. Catholic. Author: Leather Glove Industry in the U.S., 1913. Home: New York, N.Y. Died Nov. 13, 1934.

REDMOND, Granville, artist; b. Phila., Pa., Mar. 9, 1871; s. Charles C. and Elizabeth A. (Buck) R.; grad. State Instn. for the Deaf, Berkeley, Calif., 1890; studied art, and received hon. mention and W. E. Brown gold medal from San Francisco Art Assn.; studied under Benjamin Constant and Jean Paul Laurens, Paris; m. Carrie Annabel Jean, Nov. 1. 1899. Exhibited at Paris Salon, 1894; St. Louis Expn., 1904—picture acquired by the Jonathan Club, Los Angeles; Seattle Expn., 1909 (silver medal—the picture now in capitol at Olympia); Panama P.I. Expn., 1915. Address: Los Angeles, Calif. Died May 24, 1935.

REED, Albert Granberry, univ. prof.; b. nr. Paducah, Ky., Dec. 28, 1870; s. Dr. Pleasant G. and

Martha J. (Martin) R.; B.A., Vanderbilt, 1895; M.A., Yale, 1899; scholar, Columbia, 1897-98; fellow, U. of Chicago, 1904-05; Austin scholar, Harvard, 1906-07, Ph.D., 1907; m. Margaret McDearmon, 1898; children—Albert Granberry (dec.), Frances McDearmon (dec.), Mary Barton, John Fielding, Margaret McDearmon. Engaged in teaching, 1895—; instr. English, U. of Tex., 1901-04; instr. English, U. of Mo., 1904-08; prof. English lit., 1908—, in charge dept. comparative lit., 1914—, La. State U.; lecturer in English, U. of Tex. summer 1919; prof. English, Washington U., summers 1925-29, Duke U., summer 1930. Democrat. Methodist. Author: Rhetoric and Composition, 1905. Contbr. to ednl. and lit. jours. Editor: English Literature of the Romantic Period, 1929. Home: Baton Rouge, La. Died May 18, 1932.

REED, Alfred, judge; b. Ewing Twp., Mercer County, N.J., Dec. 23, 1839; s. George B. and Mary (Hepburn) R.; ed. Lawrenceville (N.J.) High Sch., N.J. Model Sch., Trenton, N.J.; Rutgers Coll.; left Rutgers before graduation and entered law sch., Poughkeepsie, N.Y.; LL.D., Rutgers and Princeton; m. Rosealba E. Souder, Aug. 1, 1878. Admitted to N.J. bar, 1864; mayor of Trenton, N.J., 1867; pres. judge Ct. of Common Pleas, Mercer County, 1869-74; justice Supreme Ct. of N.J., 1875-95; vice-chancellor N.J. Ct. of Chancery, 1895-1904; again justice Supreme Ct., June 16, 1904-June 16, 1911. Democrat. Presbyn. Address: Trenton, N.J. Died Dec. 6, 1918.

REED, Allen Visscher, rear admiral U.S.N.; b. Oak Hill, N.Y., July 12, 1838; s. James Warren and Adaline (Allen) R.; ed. pub. and pvt. schs.; grad. Naval Acad., 1858, No. 1 of class; m. Jane Augusta Valentine, Mar. 28, 1871. Master, Feb. 23, 1861; lt., Apr. 18, 1861; lt. comdr., Mar. 3, 1865; comdr., Apr. 1, 1872; capt., July 28, 1884; retired at own request after over 40 yrs. service, June 11, 1896; advanced to rank of rear admiral retired, June 29, 1906. Performed blockading duty in Gulf of Mexico during first 3 yrs. of Civil War, on the Water Witch, Potomac, Lackawanna and flag-ship Colorado; in N. Atlantic Blockading Squadron later, on Tuscarora and Pawtuxet, participating in both attacks on Ft. Fisher and in operations in Cape Fear and James rivers; comdg. Kansas, 1872-74; engaged in Nicaragua Canal survey; asst. hydrographer, U.S. Hydrographic Office, 1875-80; comdg. U.S.S. Alliance, 1882-84; comdg. training-ship Minnesota, 1884-86; comdg. flag-ship Richmond, S. Atlantic Sta., 1888-90; comdg. Pensacola Navy Yard, 1890-93, Navy Yard, Portsmouth, N.H., 1894-96; in June 1873, while comdg. U.S.S. Kansas at Colon, U.S. of C., convoyed the steamer Virginius out from under the guns of the Spanish steamer Bazan after the latter had officially declared the intention to strenuously oppose the Virginius from continuing her career of running arms and men into Cuba. Republican. Home: Washington, D.C. Died Jan. 14, 1917.

REED, Boardman, physician; b. Scottsville, Monroe County, N.Y., Apr. 30, 1842; s. William N. and Hylinda Lydia (Harmon) R.; ed. Beaver Dam (Wis.) Coll., 1859, Beloit (Wis.) Coll., 1865-66, arts dept. U. of Pa., 1867-68, med. dept. same, 1876-78, M.D., 1878; post-grad. courses at hosp. U. of Pa., 1880, U. of Vienna, 1885, New York Post-Grad. Med. Sch., and New York Polyclinic at various times, 1889-91, at Chicago Post-Grad. Med. Sch., 1894, Berlin, 1895; m. Gertrude Redfield Phelps, June 22, 1871. Served pvt. Co. C, 2d Wis. Inf., May 1861-Jan. 1863; capt. Co. I, 50th Wis. Inf., Apr. 1865-June 1866. In med. practice, Mar. 8, 1878—; pres. Atlantic City (N.J.) Bd. of Health, 1882-85; prof. diseases of the gastrointestinal tract, hygiene and climatology, dept. of medicine, Temple U., Phila., from shortly after dept. was instituted to 1906; attending phys. Samaritan Hosp. and Am. Oncologic Hosp., Phila., 1905-06. Editor Internat. Med. Magazine, 1898-1904. Author: Lectures to General Practitioners on Diseases of the Stomach and Intestines, 1904. Edited Am. edit. of Prof. Von Noorden's series of monographs on Diseases of Metabolism and Nutrition. Home: Alhambra, Calif. Died Oct. 31, 1917.

REED, Charles Alfred Lee, writer; b. Wolf Lake, Ind., July 9, 1856; s. Dr. Richard Cumming Stockton and Nancy (Clark) R.; M.D., Cincinnati Coll. of Medicine and Surgery, 1874; hon. A.M., Miami U., 1894; m. Irene E. Dougherty, May 27, 1880. Prof. gynecology and abdominal surgery, Cincinnati Coll. Medicine and Surgery, 1882-96; prof. clinical gynecology, Medical Coll. of Ohio (U. of Cincinnati), 1902-09, U. of Cincinnati, 1909-17, later prof. emeritus; gynecologist Cincinnati Hosp., 1898—. Maj. M.C., U.S.A., 1918. Sec. gen. 1st Pan. Am. Medical Congress, Washington, 1893; (later pres. Internat. Exec. Com.); pres. Am. Assn. Obstetricians and Gynecologists, 1898, A.M.A., 1900-01; Gynecol. Soc., Am. Coll. Surgeons, Cincinnati Coll. Surgeons; foundation member of Internat. Periodical Congress of Gynecology and Obstetrics; corr. fellow Nat. Acad. Medicine, Peru, 1894. Dir. U. of Cincinnati, 1891-1903; mem. spl. U.S. Commn. to Panama, 1905; pres. 7th Pan-Am. Medical Congress, 1915. Chevalier Legion of Honor, France, 1908. Author: Text-Book of Gynecology, 1900; Diseases of Women, 1913; Marriage and Genetics, 1913; Stomach and Intestines, 1913; Chronic Convulsive Toxemia, 1919; The First Estate (novel), 1927; also numerous monographs. Newspaper and mag. writer on medico-sociol. subjects. Home: Cincinnati, O. Died Aug. 28, 1928.

REED, Charles Bert, M.D., surgeon; b. Harvard, Ill., Mar. 1, 1866; s. Hiram V. and Elizabeth (Armstrong) R.; student U. of Mich., 1882-84; M.D., Rush Med. Coll., Chicago, 1887; m. Clare Osborne, June 21, 1892. Obstetrician to Wesley Hosp., Chicago; asso. prof. obstetrics, Northwestern U. Mem. Ill. State Med. Soc. (pres.), Chicago Med. Soc. (pres. 1929-30), Chicago Gynecol. Soc. (treas. 1904-09 and 1910-29; pres. 1909-10). Author: Quiz Manual of Histology, 1897; Masters of the Wilderness, 1909; The First Great Canadian, 1910; Albrecht v. Haller, 1915; Text Book of Obstetrics for Nurses, 1917; Clopton Havers, 1922; What Every Expectant Mother Should Know, 1923; Four Way Lodge, 1924; Curse of Cahawba, 1925; Eleanor of Aquitaine, 1927; True Tale of Lady Godiva, 1930; Operative Obstetrics for the Manikin, 1931; Sieur de St. Denis, 1934; also numerous med. and literary monographs. Home: Chicago, Ill. Died 1940.

REED, Earl Howell, artist, author; b. Geneva, Ill., July 5, 1863; s. Hiram V. and Elizabeth (Armstrong) R.; m. Carrie Collins, June 12, 1882; children—Earl Howell, Collins Bert; m. 2d, Emy Kummer, Oct. 14, 1922. Exhibited at Paris Salon and in prin. cities of U.S.; etchings in permanent collections; Congressional Library, Washington, D.C.; New York Pub. Library; Toledo Mus. Art; Detroit Mus. Art; Art Inst. Chicago; St. Louis Mus. Art; etc. Mason. Author: The Voices of the Dunes, 1912; Etching—A Practical Treatise, 1914; The Dune Country, 1916; Sketches in Duneland, 1918; Tales of a Vanishing River, 1920; The Silver Arrow, 1925. Home: Chicago, Ill. Died July 9, 1931.

REED, Edward Bliss; b. Lansingburgh, N.Y., Aug. 19, 1872; s. Rev. Edward Allen and Mary Anne (Bliss) R.; B.A., Yale, 1894, Ph.D., 1896; studied Paris and Munich, 1896-97; m. Elizabeth Burd Thompson, June 17, 1905; children—Elizabeth Burd (Mrs. Borden Helmer), William Thompson (dec.), Mary Bliss, Anne Parmelee. Mem. English Dept. Yale, 1897-1927; dir. Div. of Edn. of Commonwealth Fund, 1927—. Asst. editor Yale Rev., 1911-28. Served as regtl. sergt. maj. 10th Field Arty., Conn. N.G.; maj. Yale O.T.C.; instr. in F.A., Yale S.A.T.C.; maj. Am. Red Cross and a dep. commr. for Palestine, hdqrs. Jerusalem, Jan.-July 1919. Republican. Conglist. Author: English Lyrical Poetry, 1912; Lyra Yalensis (poems), 1913; Sea Moods (poems), 1917; Lyra Levis (poems), 1922. Editor (with David Stanley Smith) Ten Provencal Noels, by Nicholas Saboly, 1918; Publications of the Carol Society, Vols. I-XIV. Edited Christmas Carols of the Sixteenth Century, 1932. Home: New Haven, Conn. Died Feb. 15, 1940.

REED, Edwin, author; b. Phippsburg, Me., Oct. 19, 1835; s. Hon. William M. and Caroline (Drummond) R.; A.B., Bowdoin Coll., 1858, A.M.; studied in Leipzig, Germany, 2 yrs.; m. Emily Fellows, June 22, 1869. Shipbuilder, Bath, Me., 1858-80; mng. owner of freighting ships, 1860-90. Supt. pub. schs., Bath, 1868; mem. Ho. of Reps., Me., 1874-75; mayor of Bath, 1876-77. Mem. Am. Peace Soc. (v.p. 1882). Author: A New View of the Temperance Question, 1889; Brief for Plaintiff, Bacon vs. Shakespeare, 1896; Francis Bacon, Our Shakespeare, 1902; Bacon and Shakespeare—Parallelisms, 1902; Noteworthy Opinions, Pro and Con, Bacon vs. Shakespeare, 1905; Coincidences, Bacon and Shakespeare, 1906; also editor "The Bacon Nonsense"—Birmingham (Eng.) Gazette, 1906. Home: Andover, Mass. Died 1908.

REED, Elizabeth Armstrong, author; b. Winthrop, Me., May 16, 1842; d. Alvin and Sylvia Armstrong, both prominent educators; ed. largely by pvt. tutors while family lived in South; hon. A.M., Northwestern U., 1896, Ill. Wesleyan U., 1896; L.H.D., Bethany Coll., 1897; m. Hiram V. Reed, 1860. Only woman whose work has ever been accepted by Philos. Soc. of Great Britain. Mem. Internat. Congress of Orientalists, Royal Asiatic Soc., Victoria Inst. Philos. Soc. of Great Britain. Chmn. Woman's Congress of Philology, Chicago, 1893. Did editorial work on the Course of Universal Literature pub., 1896, by the Univ. Assn.; contbr. Encyclopædia Americana and Biblical Encyclopædia, 1901. Author: The Bible Triumphant, 1866; Hindu Literature: or, the Ancient Books of India, 1891; Persian Literature, Ancient and Modern, 1893; Primitive Buddhism, Its Origin and Teachings, 1896; Hinduism in Europe and America, 1914. Pres. Ill. Woman's Press Assn., 4 terms. Home: Chicago, Ill. Died June 16, 1915.

REED, Elmer Ellsworth, coll. pres.; b. Fairfield, Ia., Jan. 1, 1862; s. Dr. Charles and Ann C. (Canfield) R.; A.B., Parsons Coll., Fairfield, Ia., 1884, D.D., 1897; grad. student for M.A., Princeton; student Princeton Theol. Sem., 1886-87; grad. McCormick Theol. Sem., Chicago, 1888; LL.D., Emporia (Kan.) Coll., 1920; m. Margaret Murray, May 29, 1890; children—Ellery Francis, Elmer Dodd, Helen A., Gertrude (dec.), Margaret. Ordained Presbyn. ministry, 1888; pastor Kirksville, Ia., 1888-91, Griswold, 1891-95, Atlantic, 1895-1900; pres. Buena Vista Coll., Storm Lake, Ia., 1900-06 (advanced instn. to full college work); pres. Lenox Coll., Hopkinton, Ia., 1906-15; pres. Westminster Coll., Fulton, Mo., July 1, 1915—. Address: Fulton, Mo. Died Aug. 1926.

REED, Frank Fremont, lawyer; b. Monmouth, Ill., Aug. 18, 1857; s. Philo E. and Minerva D. R.; ed. Warren (O.) pub. schs., 1868-75; A.B., U. of Mich., 1880, LL.D., 1916; studied law, Cleveland and Warren, 1880-82; m. Hattie C. Allen, Aug. 2, 1888. Admitted to bar, 1882; specialist in law of copyrights and trade-marks; lecturer on law of copyrights and trade-marks, U. of Mich., 1893—; professorial lecturer on copyright and trade-mark law, U. of Chicago, 1903—. Home: Riverside, Ill. Died Jan. 15, 1926.

REED, Franklin Hancock; b. Geneva, Ind., Jan. 20, 1880; s. William Mundo and Hannah (Tedrick) R.; ed. pub. schs., Morris, Ill.; m. Isabelle Steep, Nov. 16, 1904; children—Edward Franklin, Margaret Louise, Mary Elizabeth. Practiced law at Morris, 1902-05, Wewoka, Indian Ty., 1905-17; devoted time to personal investments, 1917—; owner of extensive tracts of oil producing land in Okla. Republican. Mason. Donor of wading pools to children of many cities of Oklahoma, Kansas, Mo.; parks named in his honor at Tulsa, Oklahoma City, Sapulpa, Grandfield (all in Okla.). Home: Neosho, Mo. Died Oct. 9, 1931.

REED, George Edward, coll. pres.; b. Brownville, Me., Mar. 28, 1846; s. Rev. George and Ann (Hellyer) R.; A.B., Wesleyan U., Conn., 1869, A.M., 1872, S.T.D., 1886; studied Boston U.; LL.D., Lafayette, 1889; m. Ella Frances Leffingwell, June 20, 1870. Ordained M.E. ministry; pastor Willimantic, Conn., 1870-72, St. Paul's, Fall River, Mass., 1872-75, Hanson Pl. Ch., Brooklyn, 1875-78, Stamford, Conn., 1878-81, Nostrand Av. Ch., Brooklyn, 1881-84, Hanson Pl. Ch., 1884-87, Trinity Ch., New Haven, Conn., 1887-89; pres. Dickinson Coll., 1889-1911; pastor Grace Ch., Wilmington, Del., 1911-15. State librarian of Pa., 1899-1903. Contbr. to mags. and newspapers; pub. lecturer. Address: Harrisburg, Pa. Died Feb. 7, 1930.

REED, Harry Bertram, theologian; b. Independence, Ia., Feb. 2, 1872; s. Robert A. and Mary A. (Blose) R.; A.B., Thiel Coll., Pa., 1896, A.M., 1899; B.D., Chicago Lutheran Theol. Sem., 1900; D.D., Carthage (Ill.) Coll., 1919; m. Myra G. Jones, June 23, 1896; children—Edna Gertrude, Robert Bertram. Ordained Evang. Luth. ministry, 1899; pastor St. Peter's Ch., Chicago, 1899-1915; instr. O.T. exegesis, 1905-15, prof., 1915-20, Chicago Luth. Theol. Sem.; prof. O.T. exegesis and sec. Chicago Luth. Div. Sch., 1920-21; prof. O.T. exegesis and sec. of the faculty, Northwestern Luth. Theol. Sem., 1921—. Contbr. to New Testament Commentary (Second Thessalonians). Home: Minneapolis, Minn. Died June 15, 1939.

REED, Henry Albert, brig. gen. U.S.A.; b. Plattsburg, N.Y., June 23, 1844; s. Paul Adam and Charlotte Helena (Luther) R.; grad. U.S. Mil. Acad., 1870; m. Gertrudis Asenjo y del Valle, July 10, 1899; children—Henry Frederick, Paul Adam (dec.). Served pvt. to 1st lt. in command of Co. I, 24th Wis. Inf., in Civil War, 1862-65; cadet U.S. Mil. Acad., Sept. 1, 1866; apptd. 2d lt. U.S. Arty., June 15, 1870; promoted through grades to brig. gen., Feb. 17, 1906; retired, Feb. 19, 1906. Asst. prof. U.S. Mil. Acad., 1876-80, 1883-88; grad. Arty. Sch., 1874, Signal Service Sch., 1876; served in Mil. Information Div., War Dept., 1897-98; in Spanish-Am. War, Puerto Rico, Aug. 3, 1898, to close; comdg. arty. Dist. of San Juan, P.R., 1902-04; Ft. Caswell, N.C., 1904-05; comdg. arty. Dist. of Columbia, Ore., 1905. Gold medalist, Mil. Service Inst., 1891. Mason. Author: Topographical Drawing and Sketching, 1886; Photography Applied to Surveying, 1886; Spanish Legends and Traditions, 1913. Address: San Juan, P.R. Died Nov. 21, 1930.

REED, Henry Thomas, judge; b. Alburgh, Grand Island County, Vt., Oct. 1, 1846; s. George and Jane R.; m. Laura J. Webster, June 30, 1868. Admitted to bar, and practiced at Cresco, Ia. Mem. Ia. Ho. of Rep., 16th Gen. Assembly, 1876; U.S. dist. judge, Northern Dist. of Ia., Mar. 16, 1904-21. Republican. Home: Cresco, Ia. Died Feb. 22, 1924.

REED, Hugh Daniel, zoölogist; b. Hartsville, N.Y., Mar. 4, 1875; s. Charles Hart and Sarah (Acker) R.; B.S., Cornell, 1899, Ph.D., 1903; student Freiburg, 1909-10; m. Madeline Kingsley Church, Aug. 20, 1919; 1 daughter, Sarah Acker. Fellow in zoölogy, Cornell U., 1899-1900; with same univ., 1900—, as instr., asst. prof., prof., head dept. zoölogy, 1910-24. Republican. Congregationalist. Writer on sound transmitting organs in Amphibia, the poison organs and skin of fishes, the dermal rays of fishes, the fauna of Cayuga Lake Basin, melanosis in fishes, biological significance of the family, etc. Home: Ithaca, N.Y. Died Aug. 23, 1937.

REED, James Byron, congressman; b. nr. Lonoke, Ark., Jan. 2, 1881; s. G. A. Reed; LL.B., U. of Ark., 1906; m. Dora Jones, Apr. 1, 1909 (died 1926); children—James Byron, Bernard Jones. Teacher pub. schs.; member Ark. Ho. of Rep., 1907; pros. atty. 17th Jud. Dist., Ark., 2 terms, 1912-16; presdl. elector, 1920, and selected as messenger to carry returns from Ark. for President and Vice-Pres. to Washington, D.C.; mem. 68th to 70th Congresses (1923-29), 6th

Ark. Dist. Democrat. Methodist. Mason. Home: Lonoke, Ark. Died Apr. 27, 1935.

REED, James Hay, lawyer; b. Allegheny City, Pa., Sept. 10, 1853; s. Joseph A. and Eliza J. (Hay) R.; A.B., Western U. of Pa. (now U. of Pittsburgh), 1872; LL.D., Princeton, 1902, U. of Pittsburgh, 1919; m. Kate J. Aiken, June 6, 1878. Admitted to bar, 1875; in practice at Pittsburgh, 1875—; mem. firm of Knox (Philander Chase) & Reed, 1877-1902. Reed, Smith, Shaw & Beal, 1902—. U.S. dist. judge, Western Dist. Pa., Feb. 20, 1891-Jan. 15, 1892; resigned to resume practice; becoming mem. firm Reed, Smith, Shaw & McClay. Pres. Bessemer & L.E. R.R. Republican. Home: Pittsburgh, Pa. Died June 17, 1927.

REED, John, author; b. Portland, Ore., Oct. 22, 1887; s. Charles Jerome and Margaret (Green) R.; A.B., Harvard, 1910; m. Louise Bryant, author, January 1917. On editorial staff, American Magazine, 1911-13; with Metropolitan Magazine, 1913—. Corr. with Villa's army in Mexico, 4 mos., 1913, writing for Met. Mag. and New York World; war corr. in Europe for Met. Mag., Aug. 1914-Sept. 1915. Mem. bd. dirs. of The Masses and an editor same. Author: Sangar, 1912; The Day in Bohemia, 1912; Insurgent Mexico, 1914; The War in Eastern Europe, 1916; Tamburlaine and Other Poems; Red Russia. Also fiction and play writer; prod. "The Pageant of the Paterson Strike," in Madison Square Garden, New York, 1913. Home: New York, N.Y. Died Oct. 17, 1920.

REED, John Calvin, lawyer; b. Appling, Ga., Feb. 24, 1836; s. Rev. John W. and Sophia Amanda (Morgan) R.; A.B., Princeton, 1854, A.M., 1857; studied law pvtly.; admitted to bar, 1857; m. Sarah Platt, June 2, 1880 (died 1901). Served 2d and 1st lt. and capt. Co. I, 8th Ga. Vols., C.S.A., 1861-65, participating in battles of Manassas, Gettysburg, Wilderness, etc.; twice wounded. Solicitor Oglethorpe County (Ga.) Ct., 1866-67; Grand Giant, Province of Oglethorpe County, in Ku Klux Klan, 1868-71; mem. Atlanta city council, 1901-02; retired from bar, 1907, and settled at Montgomery, Ala. Author: Georgia Criminal Law, 1873; Conduct of Law Suits, 1875, 1885; American Law Studies, 1882; The Brothers' War, 1905. Home: Montgomery, Ala. Died 1910.

REED, John Oren, univ. dean; b. New Castle, Ind., Dec. 31, 1856; s. Jesse Mellette and Frances (McAllister) R.; Ph.B., U. of Mich., 1885, Ph.M., 1893; Ph.D., U. of Jena, 1897; m. May McNeal, July 8, 1886. Prin. high sch., E. Saginaw, Mich., 1885-91; grad. student, Harvard, 1891-92; instr. physics, 1892-94, asst. prof., 1894-99, jr. prof., 1899-1905, prof., 1905-09, prof. physics and dir. Phys. Lab., 1909—, dean summer session, 1899-1908, dean of Dept. of Lit., Science and the Arts, 1907—, U. of Mich. Author: Manual of Physical Measurements (with Karl E. Guthe), 1902; College Physics, 1902; College Physics (with same), 1911; High School Physics (with William D. Henderson), 1913. Address: Ann Arbor, Mich. Died Jan. 22, 1916.

REED, Joseph Rea, judge; b. Ashland County, O., Mar. 12, 1835; s. William and Rosannah (Lyle) R.; ed. Vermillion Inst., Haysville, O., 1854-57; m. Jennette E. Dinsmore, 1865; m. 2d, Edith M. Evans, Feb. 8, 1893. Admitted to bar, 1859; settled at Adel, Dallas Co., Ia., 1857; practiced law there till July 1, 1861, when became 1st lt. 2d Ia. Battery; mustered as capt. same battery, Oct. 1, 1864; mustered out, June 10, 1865. Resumed practice of law at Adel; removed to Council Bluffs, 1869; mem. Ia. Senate, 1866-68; apptd. judge Dist. Ct., Sept. 1, 1872, elected to same in same yr. and reëlected, 1876, 1880; judge Supreme Ct., Ia., 1883-89; mem. 51st Congress (1889-91); apptd. chief justice U.S. Ct. of Pvt. Land Claims, June 1, 1891, and served until that ct. terminated by limitation, June 30, 1904. Republican. Presbyn. Address: Council Bluffs, Ia. Died Apr. 2, 1925.

REED, Milton, lawyer; b. Haverhill, Mass., Oct. 1, 1848; s. William and Sophia Brown (Ladd) R.; A.B., Harvard, 1868, A.M., 1872; Harvard Law Sch.; unmarried. Practiced at Fall River, Mass.; retired; v.p. Metacomet Nat. Bank. City solicitor, 1875-80; mayor, 1883; spl. justice 2d Dist. Court, 1875-79; mem. Mass Senate, 1881; mem. State Bd. Bar Examiners, 1897-1903. Republican. Unitarian. Author: The Democratic Ideal, 1907; The Sea of Faith, 1908; A-Roving He Would Go, 1909; Golden Window of the East, 1912. Home: Fall River, Mass. Died Sept. 18, 1932.

REED, Ralph John, civil engr.; b. Port Huron, Mich., Apr. 30, 1883; s. Arthur Lucius and Anna Virginia (Kelly) R.; B.A., Pomona Coll., Claremont, Calif., 1905; B.S. in C.E., U. of Mich., 1908; m. June E. Miller, June 9, 1909 (dec.); children—John Miller, Robert Pearson; m. 2d, Alberta Mann, Sept. 23, 1929. Began with Union Oil Co. of Calif., 1908, and continued as engr. in transportation dept. until 1911, in charge engring. div., Los Angeles, 1911-14, engr. transp. dept., 1915, acting chief engr., 1916-17, chief engr., 1918-29; cons. practice, 1929—; dir. Whittier (Calif.) Nat. Trust & Savings Bank. Trustee Pomona Coll. Mem. State Bd. of Registration for Civil Engrs., Calif. Republican. Conglist. Scottish Rite Mason. Home: Los Angeles, Calif. Died July 27, 1939.

REED, Richard Clark, clergyman; b. Harrison, Hamilton County, Tenn., Jan. 24, 1851; s. James Landrum and Elizabeth Jane (McRee) R.; A.B., King Coll., Tenn., 1873; grad. Union Theol. Sem., Va., 1876; D.D., King Coll., 1891, LL.D., 1906; m. Mary Cantey Venable, Oct. 17, 1876. Ordained Presbyn. ministry, 1876; pastor Charlotte C.H., Va., 1877-85, Franklin, Tenn., 1885-89, Charlotte, N.C., 1889-92, Nashville, Tenn., 1892-98; prof. ch. history and polity, Columbia (S.C.) Theol. Sem., 1898—. Asso. editor Presbyterian Quarterly, 1902-04; co-editor, Presbyterian Standard, 1905—. Author: The Gospel as Taught by Calvin, 1896; History of the Presbyterian Churches of the World, 1905; Historical Sketch of the Presbyterian Church in U.S. (in Schaff-Herzog Encyclopedia); Religious History of the Southern Negroes. Moderator Gen. Assembly Presbyn. Ch., U.S., 1922. Address: Columbia, S.C. Died July 9, 1925.

REED, Richard Forman, judge; b. Jefferson County, Miss., Nov. 11, 1861; s. Thomas and Mary Jane (Forman) R.; matriculated in U. of Miss., but left coll. on account of ill health; law dept. Vanderbilt U., 1884-85; m. Eulalie Holden, May 18, 1893; 1 dau., Catherine Cameron (Mrs. Carl W. Rothe). Admitted to Miss. bar, 1885; practiced at Natchez; mem. firm Reed, Brandon & Brandon. Mem. Mississippi Senate, 1911-12; apptd. by Gov. Earl Brewer, justice Supreme Court, of Miss., Aug. 12, 1912, for term ending May 9, 1915; resumed practice at Natchez. Democrat. Lecturer on real property, etc., Millsaps Coll. Law Sch., Jackson, Miss., 1913-15. Methodist. Writer on local and state history. Home: Natchez, Miss. Died May 31, 1926.

REED, Robert Cameron, clergyman; b. Lucesco, Westmoreland County, Pa., Apr. 25, 1860; s. Robert and Mary (Walkinshaw) R.; A.B., Geneva Coll., Beaver Falls, Pa., 1885; D.D., 1927; grad. Ref. Presbyn. Theol. Sem., Pittsburgh, Pa., 1889; m. Margaret A. Bole, Apr. 8, 1890; children—Robert Knox Bole (dec.), Cameron Brooks, John Theron Sproull, Eleanore, Paul Lionel. Ordained ministry Ref. Presbyn. Ch., 1890; pastor successively Houston, Ill., Walton, N.Y., Cambridge, Mass., and Central Allegheny Ch., Pittsburgh, Pa., 1916—. Moderator Synod Ref. Presbyn. Ch., 1926. Trustee Ref. Presbyn. Theol. Sem., 1923—; mem. com. of three to prepare a digest of deliverances of the synod. Author: The Centenary of a Covenanter Society (1822-1922), 1923. Home: Pittsburgh, Pa. Died June 7, 1928.

REED, Roland, actor; b. Philadelphia, 1852, of a theatrical family; took children's speaking parts at Walnut St. Theatre, Philadelphia; following his sch. days, joined co. of Mrs. John Drew, Arch St. Theatre. Later was first comedian with numerous cos.; became a star in his own co., 1882, in "Cheek;" afterward produced many legitimate comedies, including "Humbug," "The Club Friend," "The Woman Hater," "Lend Me Your Wife," "Innocent as a Lamb," "The Politician," "A Man of Ideas," "Dakota," "His Father's Boy," "The Wrong Mr. Wright." Was the original Koko in "Mikado" in U.S. Home: New York, N.Y. Died 1901.

REED, Sarah A., philanthropist; b. Ashtabula, O., Mar. 16, 1838; d. William Wyndham and Elizabeth H. (Smith) R.; ed. Erie (Pa.) Acad.; unmarried. Pres. Monday Afternoon Study Class, 1879—; pres. Old Ladies' Home, Children's Home, Erie Home for the Friendless. Republican. Episcopalian. Author: Dora Bentley, 1881; The Belated Passenger, 1890; After Fifty Years, 1900; The Romance of Arlington, 3d edit., 1925; My Grandmother's Story, 1931. Home: Erie, Pa. Died Jan. 27, 1934.

REED, Stuart F., congressman; b. Barbour County, W.Va., Jan. 8, 1866; s. Milton D. and Margaret (Stuart) R.; LL.B., W.Va. U., 1889; Ph.D., Salem Coll., 1911; m. Bonnie Belle Smith, June 16, 1898. Founder and editor, Athenæum (coll. journal), 1889; editor of Telegram, Clarksburg, 1890-98; postmaster, Clarksburg, 1897-1901; mem. W.Va. Senate, 1895-99; v.p. Nat. League Rep. Clubs, 1900; a founder, 1900, v.p., 1904, Nat. Rep. Editorial Assn. of U.S.; mem. lit. bur. Rep. Nat. Exec. Com., 1904; declined appmt. as consul gen. to Buenos Aires, 1905; sec. of state of W.Va., 1909-13, 1913-17; mem. 65th to 68th Congresses (1917-25), 3d W.Va. Dist.; chmn. D.C. Com. of Congress, 1923-25. Pres. W.Va. Editorial Assn., 1893-96; mem. World's Lit. Congress, Chicago, 1893; pres. bd. trustees Broaddus Classical and Scientific Inst., 1901-08; regent and mem. exec. com. W.Va. U., 1895-98; originated Comr. Sch. of W.V.U., 1897; mem. Internat. Tax Conf., Louisville, Ky., 1909; v.p. W.Va. Semi-Centennial Commn., 1911-13. Baptist. Writer and lecturer on polit. and ednl. subjects. Eminent Comdr. K.T., 1908. Shriner. Elk. Pres. 1st State Y.M.C.A. Conv., 1910; pres. Assn. Am. Secretaries of State, 1915-17. Home: Clarksburg, W.Va. Died July 4, 1935.

REED, Sylvanus Albert, engineer; b. Albany, N.Y., Apr. 8, 1854; s. Rev. Sylvanus and Caroline (Gallup) R.; A.B., Columbia, 1874, A.M., E.M., 1877, Ph.D., 1879; univs. Würzburg and Berlin, 1878-79; m. Ella Wilshire Pomeroy, May 1895 (died 1897). Sec. to asst. commr. gen., Paris Expn., 1878; mining engr. in West till 1885; expert physical hazards, fire ins., 1886—; with Commonwealth Ins. Co., 1886-93, Official Ins. Rating, Boston, 1893; mgr. at Chicago, Western Factory Ins. Assn., 1893; with Continental Ins. Co., Chicago, 1894; mgr. Fire Ins. Tariff Assn., New York, 1895-97; consulting engr. Nat. Bd. Fire Underwriters, 1905-06; made report on San Francisco fire; sec., mgr. Suburban Fire Ins. Exchange, New York, 1908. Mem. New York Naval Battalion, 1890-92. Home: New York, N.Y. Died Oct. 1, 1935.

REED, Thomas Brackett, congressman; b. Portland, Me., Oct. 18, 1839; s. Thos. Brackett R.; grad. Bowdoin, 1860; studied law; acting asst. paymaster, U.S.N., Apr. 19, 1864, to Nov. 4, 1865; admitted to bar, 1865; began practice at Portland. Mem. Me. ho. of reps., 1868-69; state senator, 1870; atty. gen. Me., 1870-72; city solicitor, Portland, Me., 1874-77; mem. Congress, 1877-99. Speaker of 51st, 54th, 55th Congresses; re-elected to 56th Congress, resigned, 1899. Prominent candidate for President, 1896. Republican. Mem. law firm Reed, Simpson, Thacher & Carnim. Author: Reed's Rules, 1894. Editor: Modern Eloquence (10 vols.), 1901. Home: New York, N.Y. Died 1902.

REED, Thomas Milburne, judge; b. Coloma, Placer County, Calif., Jan. 29, 1857; s. Thomas Milburne and Elizabeth (Finlay) R.; ed. pub. schs. of Wash.; A.B., Princeton, 1878; m. Ida McKenney, Oct. 16, 1887 (died 1920); m. 2d, Venetia F. Pugh, Feb. 20, 1924. Admitted to bar, 1881, and began practice at Olympia; mem. Territorial Legislature, Wash. Ty., 1887-89; register U.S. Land Office, Seattle, 1889-93; mem. State Land Commn., Wash., 1893-95; judge Superior Court, Wash., 1895-97; moved to Alaska, 1900; U.S. commr., Nome, 1901-06; practiced at Nome, 1906-21; judge U.S. Court, 1st Div., Ty. of Alaska, by appmt. of President Harding, Aug. 16, 1921—. Republican. Presbyn. Mason. Elk. Home: Juneau, Alaska. Died Apr. 30, 1928.

REED, Verner Zevola, author, capitalist; b. Richland County, O., Oct. 13, 1863; s. Hugh Fulton and Elizabeth Amanda (Wolfe) R.; ed. country and village schs. and 2 terms at Eastern Ia. Normal Sch.; m. Mary Dean Johnson, July 18, 1893. In mining, banking, petroleum, mfg., ranching, land reclamation and irrigation enterprises in Colo., Wyo. and other states. Lived most of 15 yrs. abroad. Made extensive studies of Am. Indian myths and folk lore, especially among the Utes and some Pueblo tribes. Among one of first to make automobile tour to Sahara Desert. Author: Lo-To-Kah, 1897; Tales of the Sunland, 1897; Adobeland Stories, 1899; The Soul of Paris, 1913. Lecturer before clubs, colleges and societies, on peace, internat. politics and kindred subjects. Contbr. of essays, editorials, stories and ethnol. studies to various mags. and newspapers. Mem. President Wilson's mediation commn., 1917. Home: Denver, Colo. Died Apr. 21, 1919.

REED, Warren Augustus, lawyer; b. Boston, July 1, 1851; s. Augustus and Laura Ann (Leach) R., prep. edn., English High Sch. and under pvt. tutor; A.B., Harvard, 1875; spent 15 mos. in study and travel in Europe; student Harvard Law Sch., 1876-77; m. Nellie Newcomb Crocker, Dec. 3, 1878 (died 1908); children—Nellie (dec.), Laurence Bradford, Robert (dec.), Malcomb (dec.), Warren Augustus (dec.), Clarence Crocker, Mildred (dec.). Admitted to Mass. bar, 1878; practiced at Brockton, Mass., 1881—; judge Police Court of Brockton, 32 yrs.; pres. Peoples Savings Bank; dir. Brockton Nat. Bank; pres. Mass. Gen. Guaranty Fund for Savings Bank Life Insurance; chmn. Mass. Bd. of Conciliation and Arbitration; mem. Brockton Park Commn. Republican. Conglist. Home: Brockton, Mass. Died June 27, 1927.

REEDER, Frank, lawyer; b. Easton, Pa., May 22, 1845; s. Andrew H. R. (1st gov. of Kan.) and Amelia H. R.; A.B., and A.M., Princeton, 1863; LL.B., Albany Law Sch., 1868; m. Grace E. Thompson, Oct. 21, 1868. Served in Union Army, Sept., 1862-June 1866, as adj. 174th Pa. Inf., and, capt. to col., 19th Pa. Cav.; collector internal revenue, 11th Dist. Pa., 1873; brig. gen. Pa. N.G., 1874; sec. of state of Pa., 1895; commr. of banking, Pa., 1900. Home: Easton, Pa. Died Dec. 7, 1912.

REEDER, William Herron, rear admiral U.S.N.; b. Muscatine, Ia., Aug. 24, 1848; s. Dr. George and A.L. (Olds) R.; apptd. from Ia., and grad. U.S. Naval Acad., 1867; m. Ellinor Wells, Nov. 29, 1873. Ensign, Dec. 18, 1868; master, Mar. 21, 1870; lt., Jan. 31, 1872; lt. comdr., Dec. 4, 1892; comdr., Aug. 10, 1898; capt., Dec. 2, 1902; retired as rear admiral June 30, 1907. In active service during Civil War, in summer of 1863, on board the Marion, in pursuit of the Confederate steamer Tacony; served on the Piscataqua and Delaware, 1867-70; Wabash and Shenandoah, 1871-74; Navy Yard, Philadelphia, 1874-75; Alliance, 1875-77; Powhatan, 1877-80; Navy Yard, Portsmouth, 1881-83; Despatch, 1883-84; aid on expedition to Isthmus of Panama during insurrection there; Navy Department, 1885-86; Galena, 1886-89; Bureau of Equipment, Napy Department, 1889-90; Naval Acad., 1890-93; exec. officer of Charleston, 1893; comd. Naval Brigade in railroad strike, 1894, at Oakland, Calif., and opened up Southern Pacific R.R.; exec. officer Charleston in Luzon and Japan during Chinese-Japanese War; Navy Yard, Washington, 1896-97; comd. St. Mary's, 1897-98, Marcellus, 1898, St. Mary's, 1898-1901, Hartford, 1901-03; Naval War Coll., 1904; comd. Alabama, 1904-05; Navy Yard, New York, 1906-07; comd. Hancock until June 30, 1907. Address: New York, N.Y. Died 1911.

REEDY, William Marion, newspaperman; b. St. Louis, Dec. 11, 1862; s. Patrick and Ann (Marion) R.; acad. edn.; Master of Accounts, St. Louis U., 1880; m. Mrs. Margaret Chambers, July 8, 1909. On staff various St. Louis papers, 1880-93; editor, 1893—; proprietor, 1896—; Reedy's Mirror. Democrat. Home: Webster, Mo. Died July 28, 1920.

REES, Alfred Cornelius, industrial and public relations exec.; b. Grantsville, Tolle County, Utah, Feb. 9, 1876; s. Joseph Alexander and Christina Amelia (Hassell) R.; ed. Brigham Young U., Univ. of Utah and at Neuchatel, Switzerland; m. Ida May Davis, Jan. 4, 1906; children—Alfred, Lyman, Stanley, Richard, William, Elias. Began as printer's apprentice, 1890, later instr. modern languages and principal pub. schs., mgr. newspaper circulation, newspaper advertising mgr.; exec. sec. Utah Mfrs. Assn., 1916-18; founder, 1918, exec. v.p. Utah Associated Industries; founder and mgr. Utah Taxpayers Assn.; nat. chmn. Council of Am. Industry, 1925-37. Mem. State Council of Defense, Utah, World War I, and sec. Utah Div. War Resources Com. Mem. Gen. Bd. of Sunday Schs. of Church of Jesus Christ of Latter Day Saints; pres. Mormon Ch. Mission, Germany, 1937—. Republican. Author: A Brief History of the Church of Jesus Christ of Latter Day Saints (in German), 1902. Speaker and recognized authority on indsl. subjects, pub. relations and taxation. Spl. newspaper corr. on European affairs, 1937-39. Home: Salt Lake City, Utah. Died July 26, 1941.

REES, Byron Johnson, prof. English; b. Westfield, Ind., Sept. 30, 1877; s. Seth Cook and Hulda (Johnson) R.; student Brown U., 1895-98; A.B., cum laude, Harvard, 1903, A.M., with honors in English, 1904; studied Oxford U., Eng., 1910-11; m. Edith Chapin Trafford, Apr. 26, 1899. Instr. English, 1904, asst. prof., 1907, prof., 1914—, Williams Coll. Teacher S.A.T.C., Williams Coll., 1918. Editor: Walden, Thoreau, 1910; Nineteenth Century Letters, 1919; Modern American Prose Selections, 1920. Contbr. to Dialect Notes. Home: Williamstown, Mass. Died Feb. 18, 1920.

REES, Corwin Pottenger, rear admiral U.S.N.; b. Reily, O., Sept. 4, 1848; s. Thomas and Elizabeth S. (Griffin) R.; enlisted as musician, 54th O.V.I., Mar. 1864; participated in battles of Resaca, Kenesaw Mountain, Dallas, Atlanta and in march to the sea; hon. discharged, Aug. 1865; apptd. midshipman U.S.N., July 1866; grad. U.S. Naval Acad., 1870; m. Louise Merrill, Oct. 28, 1886. Promoted through various grades to rear admiral, 1909; served at all prin. ports and stas.; exec. officer U.S.S. Olympia at Battle of Manila Bay; subsequently at Torpedo Sta. 3 yrs.; comdg. U.S.S. Monongahela 2 yrs.; light house insp. 1st dist., 2 yrs.; at Navy Yard, Portsmouth, N.H., 2 yrs.; comdt. U.S. Naval Sta., Honolulu, H.I., 1908-10; retired, Sept. 4, 1910. Advanced 6 numbers "for eminent and conspicuous conduct in battle," at Manila. Republican. Home: Erie, Pennsylvania. Died Sept. 12, 1924.

REES, John Krom, prof. astronomy, Columbia, 1892—; b. New York, Oct. 27, 1851; grad. Columbia, 1872; Columbia School of Mines, E.M., 1875, A.M., 1875; Ph.D., 1895, Columbia; m. Louise E. Sands, Sept. 7, 1876. Asst. in mathematics, School of Mines, 1873-76; prof. mathematics and astronomy, Washington U., St. Louis, 1876-81. At Columbia as dir. of observatory, 1881—; instr. geodesy and practical astronomy, 1881-82; chmn. bd. of editors, School of Mines Quarterly, 1883-90; frequent contributor to astron. jours. V.p. Am. Math. Soc., 1890-91; pres. New York Acad. Sciences, 1894-96; sec. Am. Metrol. Soc., 1882-96; v.p., 1896—; sec. Univ. Council of Columbia, 1892-98. Received from French govt. decoration of Chevalier de la Legion d'Honneur, Jan. 1901. Address: New York, N.Y. Died 1907.

REES, Robert Irwin, army officer; b. Houghton, Mich., Nov. 9, 1871; s. Seth and Eugenie Malinda (Livermore) R.; B.S. and E.M., Mich. Coll. of Mines; student Harvard 1 yr., New York Law Sch., 1 yr.; distinguished grad., Army Sch. of the Line, 1913; grad. Army Staff Coll., 1914; m. Sara Isabel Gannett, Apr. 24, 1904. Corpl. Co. B, batt. engrs., May 7, 1897-Nov. 24, 1899; commd. 2d lt. 3d Inf., Oct. 1, 1899; 1st lt., Apr. 9, 1901; capt., Mar. 11, 1911; maj., Sept. 18, 1917; lt. col. (temp.), Aug. 5, 1917; col. N.A., July 27, 1918; brig. gen. (temp.), Oct. 1, 1918; col. (temp.), Aug. 6, 1918. Detailed as mem. Gen. Staff Corps, June 4, 1917; mem. war plans div., exec. div., and operations div., Gen. Staff, Washington, D.C., June 1917-Dec. 1918; chmn. Com. on Edn. and Spl. Training in charge mil. and tech. training of technicians and mechanics for the Army in ednl. institutions; later organized S.A.T.C.; arrived in France, Dec. 1918, and assigned on Gen. Pershing's staff in charge of all ednl. work in A.E.F.; returned to U.S., July 1919, and assigned as chief recreations br. of war plans div., Gen. Staff. Awarded D.S.M., Feb. 13, 1919, "for exceptionally meritorious and conspicuous service" to U.S. Govt.; Officer Legion of Honor (French), Apr. 30, 1919. Republican. Address: Washington, D.C. Died Nov. 23, 1936.

REES, Thomas, newspaper pub.; b. Pittsburgh, May 13, 1850; s. William and Mary Anne (La Forge) R.; ed. pub. schs.; m. Flora Adelia Huston, Feb. 25, 1879 (dec.); one son (dec.); m. 2d, Lou Rose Hart, July 17, 1901 (died 1930). Moved to Ia. with parents, 1853; learned printer's trade, and engaged in the trade until 1876; publisher Keokuk Constitution, 1876-81, Ill. State Register, 1881— (longest continuous service as a daily newspaper publisher in America); pres. State Register Pub. Co., 1927; dir. Ridgely Farmers State Bank, 1927. Mem. Ill. Senate, 1902-06; author law creating Ill. Good Roads Commn. Mem. Ill. Press Assn. (pres. 1901-02), Associated Press (chmn. advisory bd., 1915). Rep. publishers on Internat. Bd. of Arbitration on adjustment labor questions with unions, 1906-17, U.S. commr. to the Mediterranean and Balkan States for the Panama-Pacific Internat. Expn., 1913-14. Dem. nominee for Congress, 1916. Presented Rees Park to City of Keokuk, 1921. Mason. Author: Spain's Lost Jewels, Cuba and Mexico, 1906; Sixty Days in Europe, 1908; Egypt and the Holy Land, 1922; Our Travels in the Orient, 1923. Around the World, 1926. Home: Springfield, Ill. Died Sept. 9, 1933.

REESE, Charles Lee, chemist; b. Baltimore, Md., Nov. 4, 1862; s. John S. and Arnoldina O. (Focke) R.; grad. U. of Va., 1884; Ph.D., Heidelberg, 1886; hon. Sc.D., U. of Pa., 1919, Colgate U., 1919, U. of Delaware, 1928; hon. Sc.D., Wake Forest (N.C.) Coll., 1934, Heidelberg, 1936; m. Harriet S. Bent, April 10, 1901; children—Charles Lee, John Smith, David Meredith, Eben Bent, William Fessenden (dec.). Asst. in chemistry, Johns Hopkins, 1886-88; prof. chemistry, Wake Forest Coll., 1888, S.C. Mil. Acad., 1888-96; instr. Johns Hopkins, 1896-1900; chief chemist New Jersey Zinc Co., 1901-02, and of Eastern Dynamite Co., and dir. Eastern Lab., 1902-06; in charge chem. div. high explosive operating dept. of E. I. du Pont de Nemours Powder Co., 1902-11, chem. dir., 1911-June 1, 1924, consultant, until 1931 (retired); dir. E. I. du Pont de Nemours & Co. Member American Chem. Soc. (chmn. bd. 1930—; also pres. 1934), Am. Inst. Chem. Engrs. (pres. 1923-25), Mfg. Chemists' Assn. (pres. 1920-23). Asso. mem. Naval Consulting Bd., also chairman Delaware sect.; mem. Nat. Industrial Conf. Bd.; mem. advisory bd. to prohibition commr.; mem. visiting com. Bur. of Standards, 1930—. V.p. Internat. Union of Pure and Applied Chemistry, 1929-34; founder and chmn. Bd. Industrial Research, chmn. emeritus, 1931. Episcopalian. Contbr. to chem. jours. Home: Wilmington, Del. Died Apr. 12, 1940.

REESE, Frederick Focke, bishop; b. Baltimore, Md., Oct. 23, 1854; s. John S. and Arnoldina O. (Focke) R.; grad. U. of Va., 1875; student Berkeley Div. Sch., 1875-76; D.D., U. of Ga., 1900, U. of the South, 1908; m. Ella Parr, Nov. 11, 1879; children—Mrs. Arnoldina Freyer, Mrs. Mary Craighill, Mrs. Ella Phillips, Mrs. Louise Gibbes, Mrs. Agnes Shellman. Deacon, 1878, priest, 1879, P.E. Ch.; locum tenens St. Mark's, Baltimore, 1878; asst. Ch. of the Ascension in charge of All Saints' Ch., Baltimore, 1878-85; rector Trinity Ch., Portsmouth, Va., 1885-90, Christ Ch., Macon, Ga., 1890-1903, Christ Ch., Nashville, Tenn., 1903-08; elected bishop of Wyo., 1907, but declined; elected Feb. 13, 1908, consecrated, May 20, 1908, bishop of Ga. Rep. from province of Sewanee, Nat. Council of P.E. Ch., 1920-32. Trustee Univ. of the South. Chaplain Ga. Soc. Colonial Wars; mem. Ga. State Com. on Interracial Coöperation. Home: Savannah, Ga. Died Dec. 22, 1936.

REESE, Lizette Woodworth, author; b. Baltimore County, Md., Jan. 9, 1856; d. David and Louisa Reese; ed. private and public schools; hon. Phi Beta Kappa William and Mary Coll., 1925; Litt.D., Goucher Coll., 1931. Teacher English, Western High Sch., Baltimore, retired 1921. Author: (verse) A Branch of May, 1887; A Handful of Lavender, 1891; A Quiet Road, 1896; Wayside Lute, 1909; Spicewood, 1920; Wild Cherry, 1923; Selected Poems, 1926; Little Henrietta (verse), 1927; A Victorian Village (prose-autobiography), 1929; White April (verse), 1930; The York Road (autobiography), 1931; Pastures (verse), 1933. Bronze tablet containing "Tears," her most notable poem, was erected in Western High Sch., Baltimore, 1923. Awarded Mary P. L. Keats memorial prize ($800), 1931. Home: Baltimore, Md. Died Dec. 17, 1935.

REESE, Manoah Bostic, lawyer; b. Macoupin County, Ill., Sept. 5, 1839; s. Simon and Mary Ann (Steidley) R.; ed. schs. of Ill. and Ia. and 2 yrs. Osceola, Ia., Sem.; m. Carrie Burrows, Jan. 1, 1862 (died 1901). Removed to Neb., 1871; mem. Constl. Conv., 1875; dist. atty., 4th Jud. Dist., Neb., 1876-83; judge Supreme Ct. of Neb., 1883-90, and 1908-15 (chief justice); mem. law firm Reese, Reese & Stout, Lincoln, 1915—. Republican. Dean Coll. of Law, U. of Neb., 1893-1904. Grand Master A.F. and A.M., 1885-86; mem. Gen. Conf. M.E. Ch., New York, 1888. Home: Lincoln, Neb. Died Sept. 28, 1917.

REESE, Theodore Irving, bishop; b. N.Y. City, Mar. 10, 1873; s. Rev. George Bickham and Elizabeth Kip (Irving) R.; A.B., Columbia, 1894; Harvard Grad. Sch., 1894-95; B.D., Episcopal Theol. Sch., Cambridge, Mass., 1897; D.D., Kenyon, 1913; m. Louise Comins, June 22, 1899. Deacon, 1897, priest, 1898, P.E. Ch.; founder, and first rector St. Michael's Parish, Milton, Mass., 1897-1907; rector Trinity Ch., Columbus, O., 1907-13; elected bishop coadjutor of Diocese of Southern Ohio, Dec. 4, 1912, consecrated, Mar. 25, 1913, bishop Diocese of Southern Ohio, Oct. 3, 1929—. Chmn. Ohio State Bd. of Arbitration by appmt. of Gov. Harmon, Apr. 1900. Mem. Nat. Council P.E. Ch., 1919-25, also mem. exec. com. of Ch. Pension Fund of P.E. Ch. Democrat. Home: Cincinnati, O. Died Oct. 13, 1931.

REEVE, Arthur Benjamin, author; b. Patchogue, N.Y., Oct. 15, 1880; s. Walter F. and Jennie (Henderson) R.; B.A., Princeton, 1903; student New York Law Sch., 1903; m. Margaret A. Wilson, Jan. 31, 1906. Asst. editor Public Opinion, 1903-06; editor Our Own Times (annual, vols. IV-X), 1906-10; on staff The Survey, 1907. Author: The Silent Bullet, 1912; The Black Hand, 1912; Poisoned Pen, 1913; Adventures of Craig Kennedy, Scientific Detective (in Cosmopolitan), 1910-18; Great Cases of William J. Burns, in McClure's, 1912-13; The Dream Doctor, 1914; Guy Garrick, 1914; The War Terror, 1915; The Exploits of Elaine, 1915; The Gold of the Gods, 1915; Constance Dunlap, 1915; The Romance of Elaine, 1916; Social Gangster, 1916; Ear in the Wall, 1916; Treasure Train, 1917; The Adventuress, 1917; The Panama Plot, 1918; The Soul Scar, 1919; The Master Mystery, 1919; The Mystery Mind, 1920; The Film Mystery, 1921; Craig Kennedy Listens In, 1923; Atavar, 1924; The Fourteen Points, 1925; Craig Kennedy on the Farm, 1925; The Boy Scout's Craig Kennedy, 1925; The Radio Detective, 1926; Pandora, 1927; The Golden Age of Crime, 1931; The Clutching Hand, 1934; Enter Craig Kennedy, 1935; The Stars Scream Murder, 1936. Collaborated on writing motion picture serials, with Charles William Goddard, The Exploits of Elaine, 1914-15; with Chas. A. Logue, The Hidden Hand, The House of Hate, Tiger's Trail, the Houdini serial, The Master Mystery; with John W. Grey wrote The Carter Case, One Million Dollars Reward, and Houdini feature pictures, The Grim Game, Terror Island; serial featuring Pauline, the hypnotist in The Mystery Mind; The Return of the Riddle Rider (with Fred J. McConnell); Finger Prints; also the Radio Crime Prevention Program, on N.B.C., 1931, and other programs. Supervised Federal Writers' Projects for Works Progress Adminstrn., Trenton, N.J., 1935. Reported Lindbergh kidnapping and Hauptmann trial for Phila. Record, N.Y. Post and Syndicate. Home: Trenton, N.J. Died Aug. 9, 1936.

REEVE, Felix Alexander, asst. solicitor of the Treasury; b. Cocke County, Tenn., Sept. 4, 1836; s. Thomas J. R. and Rebecca Ann (Earnest) R. (descendant of the Oliphants of Scotland); admitted to bar at Knoxville, 1861; authorized by Pres. Lincoln to recruit and command a regt.; col. of the 8th Tenn. Inf.; m. Wilhelmina Donelson, d. of Hon. Horace Maynard. Settled first at Greenville, then at Knoxville, Tenn.; practiced law; asst. solicitor of the Treasury, 1886-93; solicitor of the Treasury, 1893-97; later again asst. solicitor of the Treasury; independent in politics. Home: Washington, D.C. Died Nov. 15, 1920.

REEVE, James Knapp, author; b. Hancock, N.Y., May 19, 1856; s. William and Agnes M.D. (Knapp) R.; ed. pub. schs.; m. Carrie S. De Nise, Dec. 15, 1880. Extensive traveler, and contbr. of travel, fiction, etc., to the press. Founder and editor of The Editor, a journal of information for writers; mgr. The Editor Pub. Co.; mgr. Outing Pub. Co., New York, 1904-09; European traveler and travel writer, 1912-13. Author: Vawder's Understudy, 1896; The Three Richard Whalens, 1897; Practical Authorship, 1900. Address: Franklin, O. Died Oct. 25, 1933.

REEVE, Sidney Armor, mech. engr.; b. Dayton, O., Mar. 27, 1866; s. John Charles (M.D.) and Emma Griswold (Barlow) R.; Ph.B., Sheffield Scientific Sch. (Yale), 1885, M.E., 1887; m. Leila A. Wellington, Dec. 7, 1892. Engaged in commercial engring. with Westinghouse, Church, Kerr & Co., 1887-94; editor Progressive Age, 1895; prof. steam and hydraulic engring., Worcester Poly. Inst., 1896-1906; lecturer on steam engring., Harvard, 1907. Lecturer, Graduate Naval Sch., Annapolis, 1911; consulting mech. engr., New York, 1908—. Author: The Entropy-temperature Analysis of Steam-engine Efficiencies, 1898; The Thermodynamics of Heat-engines, 1901; The Cost of Competition, 1906; Energy, 1909; Modern Economic Tendencies, 1921. Home: New Brighton, S.I., N.Y. Died June 12, 1941.

REEVES, Alfred Gandy, legal author; b. Millville, N.J., Dec. 3, 1859; s. Smith and Martha B. (Tucker) R.; A.B., Princeton, 1884, A.M., 1887; LL.B., Columbia, 1887; m. Josie B. Tucker, Dec. 25, 1888. Prof. law, New York Law Sch., 1891. Republican.

Presbyn. Author: Reeves' Cases on Wills, 1891; Reeves on Real Property, 1909. Home: Brooklyn, N.Y. Died Jan. 10, 1927.

REEVES, Francis Brewster, banker, mcht.; b. Bridgeton, N.J., Oct. 10, 1836; s. Johnson and Elizabeth (Riley) R.; ed. pub. schs. and Harmony Acad., Bridgeton; m. Ellen Bernard, d. Newcomb Butler Thompson, Apr. 26, 1860. Entered Girard Bank, Mar. 9, 1854, remaining until 1858, when engaged in wholesale grocery business; head of wholesale grocery firm of Reeves, Parvin & Co., 1859—; pres. Phila. Belt Line R.R. Co.; dir. Bell Tel. Co. Pa., Del. & Atlantic Telephone Co., Diamond State Telephone Co.; mem. advisory bd. Germantown Trust Co.; v.p. Germantown Savings Fund Soc.; elected dir. Girard Nat. Bank, 1881, pres., July 18, 1899. Chmn. exec. com. Municipal Reform Com. of 100, Phila., 1881-83; mem. city bd. edn., 1888-90; v.p. 1889—, Citizens Permanent Relief Com.; mem. bd. trustees General Assembly Presbyn. Ch. in U.S.A. Commd. by Phila. Relief Com. to visit Russia, 1892, to deliver steamship Conemaugh's cargo of flour to Russian authorities for relief of famine, Emperor Alexander III recognized his personal service by gift of valuable table service of gold and silver. Treas. Thomas W. Evans Mus. and Inst. Soc.; v.p. Phila. Bourse; mem. bd. mgrs. Merchants Fund, Mercantile Beneficial Assn.; mem. Am. Acad. Polit. and Social Science. Home: Germantown, Pa. Deceased.

REEVES, Ira Louis; b. Jefferson City, Mo., Mar. 8, 1872; s. Martin Rhodes and Rebecca (Zimmerman) R.; student Purdue U., 1902; C.E., U. of Vt., 1915; Litt.D., Norwich U., 1916; LL.D., Middlebury Coll., 1917; m. Carolyn Louise Smith, Dec. 28, 1898; children—Capt. Louis Paul Denslow, Dorothy Virginia Randolph. Pvt. N.G. Mo., 1891-92; pvt., corpl., sergt., Co. B, 4th U.S. Inf., 1893-97; commd. 2d lt. 17th U.S. Inf., Apr. 19, 1897; 1st lt. 17th, 4th and 16th Inf., 1899-1902; retired with rank of capt., Nov. 11, 1902, account of wounds received in action in Philippine Insurrection; recommended for brevet "for bravery and unexcelled energy," Santiago Campaign, 1898. Comdt. and prof. mil. science, Purdue U., 1902; same Miami (O.) Mil. Inst., 1910; same U. of Vt., 1912-15; pres. Norwich U., Nov. 1, 1915-Oct. 1918. Bn. q.m. Mass. Vol. Milita, 1912-14; capt. and adj., 1st Inf., Vt. N.G., 1914-15; col. same regt., 1915-17; comd. same on Mex. border, July-Sept. 1916; chmn. Vt. Com. Public Safety, 1917. Returned to active list U.S.A., Aug. 5, 1917, with grade of maj.; lt. col., Aug. 23, 1917; col., Dec. 1917. Asst. and exec. officer Militia Bur.; adj. gen. and insp. gen.'s depts., June 1917-Sept. 1918; mem. 7th, 31st and 35th divs. in France; wounded Nov. 11, 1918. Pres., comdg. officer A.E.F. Univ., Beaune, France, Feb. 9-June 15, 1919; mem. War Claims and War Credits Bd., 1919; pres. Ira L. Reeves and Associates, Chicago. Western mgr. "Crusaders," opposed to prohibition, 1931-33. Capt. Vt. Rifle Team, nat. matches, 1915. Chevalier Legion of Honor (France); D.S.M. and Purple Heart (U.S.). Republican. Methodist. Mason. Author: Bamboo Tales, 1901; Manual for Aspirants for Commissions in the United States Army, 1902; Manual for Aspirants for Commissions in the United States Military Service, 1910; ABC of Rifle, Revolver and Pistol Shooting; Military Education in United States; Ol' Rum River, 1931; Is All Well On The Potomac?. Address: Eldon, Mo. Died Oct. 23, 1939.

REEVES, Isaac Stockton Keith, commodore U.S.N.; b. Fortress Monroe, Va., Nov. 26, 1850; s. Capt. I. S. K. (U.S.A.) and Annie Dorsey (Read) R.; Lehigh U., Pa., 1872-74; Cornell U., 1874, spl. course in mech. engring.; m. Henrietta M. Young, Apr. 16, 1879. Apptd. asst. engr. U.S.N., June 30, 1875; promoted through the various grades to rank of commodore and retired, at own request, June 30, 1909. Twice consulting engr. U.S. Fish Commission; mem. Bd. Inspection and Survey, 6 yrs.; on U.S.S. Montgomery during Spanish-Am. War, and on New York in Philippine waters, 1900-03; mem. Bd. Construction, 1908-09. Home: Washington, D.C. Died July 16, 1917.

REEVES, Walter, congressman; b. near Brownsville, Pa., Sept. 25, 1848; s. Harrison and Maria (Leonard) R.; removed to Ill., 1856; lawyer by profession; m. Metta M. Cogswell, 1876. Mem. Congress, 1895-1903, 11th Ill. dist. Republican. Address: Streator, Ill. Died 1909.

REGAN, James L., printer; b. London, Eng., Aug. 10, 1850; s. James L. and Frances (Robinson) R.; ed. pub. schs., London and New York. Learned printing trade in New York; removed to Chicago, 1870, and worked for various printing offices until 1879, when established in printing business as J. L. Regan & Co.; pres. The Regan Printing House (inc., 1888). Mason. Address: Chicago, Ill. Deceased.

REGISTER, Edward Chauncey, physician; b. Rose Hill, N.C., Oct. 20, 1860; s. Dixon S. and Sarah (Wilkins) R.; ed. U. of N.C.; M.D., Univ. Med. Coll. (New York U.), 1885; post-grad. study hosps. and clinics of Europe; m. Lavinia Cotrell Montgomery, Jan. 6, 1887. Pres. and chief phys. Charlotte Sanatorium, 1906-16; editor of Charlotte Med. Jour., 1891—. Trustee Trinity Coll., Durham, N.C., 1900—; pres. Med. Exam. Bd. of N.C., 1898-1902; mem. N.C. Bd. Health, 1903—. Mem. Am. Med. Editors' Assn. (pres. 1915-16), N.C. Med. Soc. (pres. 1906), Mecklenburg County Med. Soc. (organizer 1903), Med. Councillors of N.C. (pres. 1903-06), Tri-State Med. Assn. of the Carolinas and Va. (pres. 1915). Author: Practical Fever Nursing, 1907; Typhoid Fever, 1910. Address: Charlotte, N.C. Died Feb. 1920.

REGISTER, Francis Henry, lawyer; b. Berlin, Md., Apr. 21, 1859; s. Elijah and Cornelia W. (Jarvis) R.; student Delaware Coll., Newark, Del., 2 yrs.; A.B., Lafayette Coll., Easton, Pa., 1881, A.M., 1883; LL.B., U. of Mich., 1883; m. Helen M. Donaldson, July 7, 1901; children—Francis D., Mrs. Helen Jarvis Warren, Dill B., Richard E., Lt. Paul J. (U.S.N.). Practiced in Bismarck, N.D.), 1884—; state's atty., Burleigh County, 1900-04; mayor of Bismarck, 1901-05; city atty., 1908-16; trustee State Penitentiary of N.D., 1900-02; mem. Bd. of Insanity, Burleigh County. Republican. Mason, K.P. Home: Bismarck, N.D. Died Nov. 10, 1929.

REHAN, Ada, actress; b. (Crehan) Limerick, Ireland, Apr. 22, 1860; came to U.S. in childhood. First appearance on stage at 14, Newark, N.J.; played in Phila., Baltimore, Albany and Louisville stock cos. Engaged by Augustin Daly in 1879, filling lead positions in Daly's Theatre until his death, in 1899, playing such characters in Shakespearean and old comedies as Rosalind, Katherine, Viola, Beatrice, Portia, Lady Teazle, Peggy in the "Country Girl" and many high-class modern comedy parts. Address: New York. Died Jan. 8, 1916.

REHN, Frank Knox Morton, artist; b. Phila., Apr. 12, 1848; s. Prof. Isaac and Abigail Francis (Zelly) R.; studied at Pa. Acad. Fine Arts; painter of marines, landscapes and portraits; m. Margaret Selby, d. Geo. C. Bower, 1881. Awarded 1st prize, St. Louis Expn., 1882; prize, Water Color Competitive Exhbn., New York, 1885; gold medal, Competitive Prize Fund Exhbn., New York, 1885; hon. mention, Paris Expn., 1900; bronze medal, Buffalo Expn., 1901; silver medal, Charleston Expn., 1902, St. Louis Expn., 1904; Inness prize, Salmagundi Club, 1906; Shaw purchase prize, same, 1907; gold medal, Phila. Soc. Artists, 1907. Represented in Detroit Art Mus., Boston Art Club, Buffalo Fine Arts Acad., Corcoran Gallery, Washington. N.A., 1908. Address: New York, N.Y. Died July 7, 1914.

REICH, Jacques, artist, etcher; b. Hungary, Aug. 10, 1852; studied art in Budapest; came to U.S., 1873; studied Nat. Acad. Design, New York, Pa. Acad. Fine Arts, Phila., and in Paris; m. Lina, d Emil Bellinger, Jan. 3, 1892. Located in New York in 1885. Made most of pen portraits for Scribner's Cyclopædia of Painters and Paintings, and for Appleton's Cyclopædia of American Biography; etched on copper a series of portraits of Am. and English authors; later engaged in etching and publishing a series of etched portraits of famous Americans, among them Washington, Jefferson, Alexander Hamilton, Benjamin Franklin, Daniel Webster, Abraham Lincoln, Roosevelt, Cleveland, McKinley, Paul Jones, Andrew Carnegie, George William Curtis, Andrew Jackson, U. S. Grant, James Madison, John Marshall, Wm. Howard Taft, Gen. Robert E. Lee, Dr Andrew D. White, James Abbott McNeill Whistler, Woodrow Wilson; among many pvt. plates etched are portraits of Whitelaw Reid, E. H. Harriman, H. H. Rogers, John W. Mackay, Gov. Winthrop, Mark Hanna, Charles B. Alexander, Nelson Wilmarth Aldrich, and Gen. Thomas Hamlin Hubbard. Address: New Dorp, S.I., N.Y. Died July 8, 1923.

REICHERT, Edward Tyson, univ. prof.; b. Phila., Feb. 5, 1855; s. Gabriel Adam (Jr.) and Emma Rebecca (Horn) R.; ed. pub. and pvt. schs., Phila., and U. of Pa.; post-grad. work in univs. of Berlin, Leipzig and Geneva; M.D., U. of Pa., 1879, Sc.D., 1913; m. Marion C. Welsh, June 7, 1883 (dec.); m. 2d, Jessie Adéle Ward, Nov. 11, 1919. Demonstration exptl. therapy, 1879-84, asst. in Nervous Dispensary, 1879-80, demonstrator in physiology, 1884-86, prof. 1886-1920, U. of Pa. (later emeritus prof.). Contbr. med. and other scientific articles, the results of original research, especially researches on respiration, circulation, animal heat mechanism and hemoglobins; the toxic principles of serpent venoms; on the differentiation and specificity of corresponding vital substances in relation to genera and organic evolution; and on biochemic basis for the study of problems of taxonomy, heredity, sex, species, organic evolution, etc. Assisted Edweard Muybridge in his pioneer work on animal motion and moving pictures; among the first inventors of storage battery plates; devised many forms of scientific apparatus. Research asso., Carnegie Instn., Washington. Address: Mt. Airy, Philadelphia, Pa. Deceased.

REICK, William Charles, journalist; b. Phila., Sept. 29, 1864; s. Charles William and Margaret (Turner) R.; matriculated at Harvard; m. Carrie L. Ridgway, Dec. 4, 1894. Entered newspaper work at Phila., 1883; editor London and Paris editions New York Herald, 1888-89; city editor New York Herald, 1889-1903; pres. New York Herald Co., 1903-06; pres. Public Ledger Co. of Phila., 1907-12; one of the prin. owners New York Times, 1907-12; chief owner New York Sun, Dec. 17, 1911-16; pres. Journal of Commerce, 1916-21. Episcopalian. Home: Red Bank, N.J. Died Dec. 7, 1924.

REID, Daniel Gray, financier; b. Richmond, Ind., Aug. 1, 1858; s. Daniel and Ann (Gray) R.; pub. sch. edn. Began business as clerk in Second Nat. Bank of Richmond, 1874; worked through all offices in the bank, becoming v.p., 1895. Became interested in tin plate industry at Elwood, Ind., 1892; one of organizers and pres. Am. Tin Plate Co., 1895; removed to Chicago, 1897, and to New York, 1899; one of organizers Nat. Steel Co., Am. Steel Hoop Co., and Am. Sheet Steel Co.; became dir. and mem. exec. com. U.S. Steel Corp. on its organization, 1901; dir. Am. Can Co., Bankers Trust Co., Chase Securities Corp., Lehigh Valley R.R. Co.; trustee Am. Surety Co. Address: New York, N.Y. Died Jan. 17, 1925.

REID, George Croghan, brig. gen. U.S. Marine Corps; b. Lorain, O., Dec. 15, 1840; s. Conrad and Abigail (Murdock) R.; student Oberlin Coll., 1860-63; LL.B., Columbian Law Coll., Washington, 1873; m. Ada Savage, Feb. 13, 1877. Commd. lt. U.S.M.C., July 2, 1864; served at hdqrs., 1864-66; on steam-sloop Monongahela, West Indies Squadron, 1867; a.-d.-c. to commandant, 1867; 1st lt., 1869; capt., Apr. 2, 1884; adj. and insp. with rank of maj., May 1894; promoted col., 1899; brig. gen. and retired, Dec. 15, 1904. Served in Civil War, Spanish-Am. War, and in various depts. of sea and barracks duty. Address: Washington, D.C. Died Mar. 15, 1914.

REID, George T., ry. official; b. Etna Green, Ind., Apr. 2, 1871; ed. high sch., Warsaw, Ind. Atty. for Spokane, Portland & Seattle Ry., during constrn., 1906; division counsel N.P. Ry., at Tacoma, Wash., 1908-12, and continued with same rd. as asst. to pres., and western counsel, 1912-21; also pres. North Yakima & Valley Ry., 1912-14; v.p. and western counsel N.P. Ry., Dec. 1921—; pres. Walla Walla Valley Ry. Co.; v.p. Spokane, Portland & Seattle Railway Co. Address: Seattle, Wash. Died November 30, 1927.

REID, Gilbert; b. Laurel, L.I., N.Y., Nov. 29, 1857; s. Rev. John and Ann Elizabeth (Lawrence) R.; B.A., Hamilton Coll., 1879, M.A., 1882; B.D., Union Theol. Sem., 1882; D.D., Hamilton, 1894; m. Sallie B. Reynolds, Dec. 1, 1897; children—John Gilbert, Jean Reynolds. Ordained Presbyn. ministry, 1882; missionary at Chefoo, China, 1882-85, Tsinan, 1885-92; lived at Warsaw, N.Y., 1892-94; resigned and started mission among higher classes in China, 1894, which developed into Internat. Inst. of China, under sanction of Chinese Govt., and became dir. in chief; propr. and editor Peking Post, 1917; in U.S., 1917-21; returned to Shanghai, China. Author: Glances at China, 1890; Sources of Anti-Foreign Disturbances in China, 1893; China, Captive or Free, 1921; A Christian's Appreciation of Other Faiths, 1921; also numerous books in Chinese. Address: Shanghai, China. Died Sept. 30, 1927.

REID, Philip Joseph, journalist; b. Providence, R.I., July 19, 1865; s. Patrick Henry and Katherine (Finnegan) R.; A.B., Brown U., 1887; m. Nellie J. Corcoran, Oct. 4, 1893 (died 1929); children—Mrs. Helen Reid Halla, Thomas O. (dec.), Mrs. Marian Reid Stowe, Mrs. Madeleine L'Etourneau. In U.S. postal service, Providence, R.I., 1889-90; sporting editor the Tribune, Detroit, 1890-91; reporter, 1891-94, night city editor, 1894-96, city editor, 1896-1905, news editor, 1905-06, mng. editor and editor, 1906-26, asso. editor 1926—, Detroit Free Press. Home: Detroit, Mich. Died July 21, 1930.

REID, Robert, artist; b. Stockbridge, Mass., July 29, 1862; s. Jared (Jr.) and Louisa (Dwight) R.; studied Mus. of Fine Arts, Boston, 1880 (3 yrs. asst. instr. same), Art Students' League, New York, 1885-89, Académié Julian, under Boulanger and Lefebvre; m. Elizabeth Reeves, Apr. 29, 1907. Exhibited annually in Salon, and in Paris Expn., 1889; returned to New York, 1889; one of 8 New York artists who painted frescoes of domes of Liberal Arts Bldg., Chicago Expn.; instr. painting, Art Students' League, and Cooper Inst. Awarded Clarke prize, 1897, 1st Hallgarten prize, 1898, Nat. Acad. Design; gold and silver medals, Paris Expn., 1900; W. A. Clarke prize, Corcoran Gallery, 1908; gold medal, San Francisco Expn., 1915. Painted mural decorations for many pub. and pvt. bldgs., including Library of Congress, Washington, D.C.; Appellate Court House, New York; Mass. State House, Boston; Paulist Fathers Ch., New York; Fine Arts Palace, San Francisco; windows for H. H. Rogers' Memorial Ch., Fairhaven, Mass. Represented in Met. Mus. of Art; Corcoran Gallery, and Nat. Gallery, Washington, D.C.; museums of Minneapolis, Omaha, Cincinnati, Indianapolis, Brooklyn; Albright Gallery, Buffalo; Neb. Art Assn., Lincoln; Art Assn., Richmond, Ind.; Art Assn., San Antonio, Tex.; Denver Art Assn.; Broadmoor Art Acad., Colorado Springs, Colo. Instr. figure painting, Broadmoor Art Acad. N.A., 1906; mem. Nat. Inst. Arts and Letters (life), Ten Am. Painters. Address: New York, N.Y. Died Dec. 2, 1929

REID, Whitelaw, diplomat, journalist; b. Xenia, O., Oct. 27, 1837; s. Robert Charlton and Marian (Ronalds) R.; A.B., Miami U., Oxford, O., 1856, A.M., 1859; hon. A.M., U. City of New York, 1872, Dartmouth, 1873; LL.D., Miami, 1890, Princeton, 1899, Yale, 1901, Cambridge, 1902, St. Andrew's, 1905, Manchester, 1909; D.C.L., Oxford, 1907; m. Elizabeth, d. D. O. Mills, Apr. 26, 1881. Edited Xenia (O.) News, 1858-59; legislative corr., 1860-61, war corr., 1861-62, Washington corr., 1862-68, Cincinnati Gazette. A.-d.-c. staff of Gens. Thomas A. Morris and W. S. Rosecrans in W.Va.; clerk, mil. com., 37th Congress, 1862-63; librarian Ho. of Rep., 1863-66; cotton planter, Concordia Parish, La., 1866-67. Editorial staff New York Tribune, 1868, mng. editor, 1869, editor-in-chief and chief propr., 1872-1905; began tall building movement in New York by erection new Tribune Bldg., 1873; introduced linotype and organized Linotype Co. Declined appmts. as U.S. minister to Germany, 1877 and 1881; elected to bd. of regents, 1878, vice-chancellor, 1902, and chancellor, 1904, U. State of N.Y.; U.S. minister to France, 1889-92; Rep. nominee for Vice-President U.S., 1892; spl. ambassador of the U.S. to Queen Victoria's jubilee, 1897; mem. Peace Commn. to Paris, 1898; spl. ambassador for Coronation of Edward VII, 1902; U.S. ambassador to England, 1905—. Author: After the War, a Southern Tour, 1867; Ohio in the War, 1868; Schools of Journalism, 1870; Newspaper Tendencies, 1874; Town Hall Suggestions, 1881; introduction to English edit. Talleyrand's Memoirs, 1891; Two Speeches at the Queen's Jubilee, 1897; Some Consequences of the Last Treaty of Paris, 1899; Our New Duties, 1899; Later Aspects of Our New Duties, 1899; A Continental Union, 1900; Our New Interests, 1900; Problems of Expansion, 1900; Carnegie Inst. Address, 1902; Monroe Doctrine, 1903; Greatest Fact in Modern History, 1906; How America Faced Its Educational Problem, 1906; introduction Centenary edit. Thackeray's Vanity Fair, London, 1908. Home: Purchase, N.Y. Died Dec. 15, 1912.

REID, William James, U.P. clergyman; b. S. Argyle, N.Y., Aug. 17, 1834; grad. Union Coll., 1855; D.D., Monmouth Coll., Ill.; m. Mary Bowen, Oct. 29, 1862. Pastor 1st U.P. Ch., Pittsburg, 1862—; prin. clerk U.P. Gen. Assembly, 1875—; editor The United Presbyterian, 1887—. Address: Pittsburgh, Pa. Died 1902.

REID, W(illiam) Max, merchant, author; b. Amsterdam, N.Y., June 8, 1839; s. William and Chloe (Smith) R.; ed. Amsterdam Acad.; m. Laura L. McDonald, June 8, 1860. Engaged in mer. bus., devoting leisure to local hist. research. Founder and 17 yrs. pres. Amsterdam Bd. of Trade; sec. Green Hill Cemetery; trustee Children's Home. Republican. Author: History of St. Anne's Church and Queen Anne's Chapel, 1897; The Mohawk Valley—Its Legends and Its History, 1902; The Terrible Mohawk, 1904; The Story of Old Fort Johnson, 1906; Lake George and Lake Champlain, 1910; also contbr. to jours. on hist. subjects. Address: Amsterdam, N.Y. Died Nov. 1911.

REIK, Henry Ottridge, author, medical editor, lecturer; b. Baltimore, Md., May 23, 1868; s. Henry A. and Mary A. (Neilson) R.; Ph.G., Md. Coll. of Pharmacy, 1888; M.D., U. of Md., 1891; post-grad. work, Johns Hopkins, Harvard, London and Glasgow; m. Mary Watson, June 17, 1896 (divorced Mar. 1930); m. 2d, Helen B. Calhoun, June 21, 1930. Practiced surgery (eye, ear, nose and throat), at Baltimore, 1891-1917; asso. in ophthalmology and otology, Johns Hopkins, 1896-1912; lost use of right hand through sepsis, 1916, and abandoned active practice. Exec. sec. New York Assn. for Med. Edn., 1919-20; mng. editor Internat. Med. and Surg. Survey, Mar. 1921-Apr. 1924; editor N.J. State Med. Journal, and exec. officer Med. Soc. of N.J., 1924—. Entered U.S.A. as vol., Aug. 1917; commd. capt. M.R.C., Oct 1917; maj., Apr. 1918; lt. col., Feb. 1919; served at Camp Sheridan, Ala.; sailed for France, July 8, 1918; apptd. comdg. officer of Base Hospital 67, A.E.F., Oct. 18, 1918; hon. discharged, May 13, 1919; re-commd. lt. col., M.R.C., July 12, 1919; commd. col., June 2, 1924. Author: Surgical Pathology and Treatment of Diseases of the Ear, 1906; Diseases of Ear, Nose and Throat, 1911; Safeguarding the Special Senses, 1912; Tour of America's National Parks, 1920. Lecturer on travels, with illustrations made entirely by true color photography. Address: New York, N.Y. Died June 2, 1938.

REILLEY, Mrs. J. Eugene (Laura Holmes Reilly), club woman; b. St. Louis, Mo., Nov. 28, 1861; d. Charles Francis and Mary Linn (Parry) Holmes; grad. Mary Inst. (St. Louis), Woman's Dept., Washington U., 1882; m. J. Eugene Reilley, Nov. 15, 1882. Pres. N.C. Federation of Women's Clubs 2 yrs., v.p. 3 yrs.; corr. sec. Gen. Federation Women's Clubs, 1912-16, v.p. Gen. Federation, 1916-18, hon. v.p., 1924; chmn. Club Insts. of N.C. Federation of Women's Clubs, 1926-32, later chmn. Bibl. lit.; charter mem. and mem. bd. of advisers, Soc. Mayflower Descendants in N.C., gov., 1937-38; organizer N.C. Suffrage Assn.; twice pres. Charlotte (N.C.) Sorosis; chmn. Woman's Com. Council Nat. Defense and mem. Gov.'s Council, World War I; state chmn. Better Films Com., D.A.R., 1925-26; adviser to League of Women Voters of N.C. First regent Liberty Hall Chapter D.A.R.; mem. N.C. Soc. Colonial Dames (chmn. Mecklenburg Com., 1936-38); organizer Charlotte branch Needlework Guild of America (v.p., 1930—); trustee Mint Art Mus. Mem. Advisory Com. for the Participation of Women, New York World's Fair, 1939. Home: Charlotte, N.C. Died Feb. 25, 1941.

REILLY, Frank Kennicott, publisher; b. The Grove, Cook County, Ill., Mar. 19, 1863; s. Dr. Frank W. and Alice Mary (Kennicott) R.; ed. pub. schs.; m. Cora Stone Powers, Apr. 11, 1883 (dec.); m. 2d, Carlin Muriel Walker, Feb. 28, 1912. With C.&N.W. Ry., 1878-85; various mercantile firms, 1885-94; dept. mgr. Werner Co., pubs., Chicago and Akron, O., 1894-97; mgr. Geo. M. Hill Co., pubs., Chicago, 1898-1902; mem. Madison Book Co., 1902-04; sec. and treas., The Reilly & Britton Co., 1904-13, pres., 1913—, firm name changed to The Reilly & Lee Co., 1920; v.p. Kennicott Bros. Co. Home: Chicago, Ill. Died May 25, 1932.

REILLY, James William, brig. gen. U.S.A.; b. Chambersburg, Pa., Aug. 2, 1839; s. Hon. Wilson and Elizabeth McCullough (Mills) R.; ed. Chambersburg Acad.; grad. U.S. Mil. Acad., 1863; m. Helen Julia Griffin, Nov. 4, 1875. First lt. ordnance, June 11, 1863, capt., June 23, 1874; maj., May 9, 1885; lt. col., Apr. 7, 1899; col., Feb. 18, 1903; brig. gen., Aug. 1, 1903; retired by operation of law, Aug. 2, 1903. Bvtd. capt., Mar. 13, 1865, "for faithful and meritorious services"; on staff of Gen. Schofield, in campaign of Nov.-Dec. 1864, including battles of Franklin and Nashville; also participated in Atlanta campaign on staff of Gen. McPherson; also on staff of Gen. P. H. Sheridan, 1875-80. Episcopalian. Home: Washington, D.C. Died 1910.

REINDAHL, Knute, violin maker; b. Norway, Nov. 16, 1858; s. Kittel T. and Ingred (Gulbek) R.; came with parents to U.S., 1867, naturalized citizen, 1925; ed. country schs.; returned to Norway and studied wood carving at Telemarken, 1887-88, to be better prepared for making violins; m. Anna Sofia Ellefson, May 13, 1894; children—Edna Isabell (Mrs. Arthur X. Merz), Olive Selma (Mrs. Hillis Hackedorn), Gladys Theresa (Mrs. Andreas Elviken), Margaret Ardell, Ruth Kay. In charge of wood carving dept. of Windsor Folding Bed Co., Chicago, 1890-94; same, Ebman Sima Shop, Chicago, 1894-99; self-taught as violin maker, operating in Chicago, 1894-1918; moved to Madison, Wis., 1918. Made violins for many artists, such as Emile Sauret, Franc Von Vessey, Hugo Heerman, Arthur Hartmann; maker of violin presented to Fritz Kreisler by City of Madison, 1922. Awarded diploma of Merit, Chicago Expn., 1893; diploma and medal, Paris Expn., 1900. Republican. Lutheran. Home: Madison, Wis. Deceased.

REINER, Joseph, clergyman, educator; b. Chicago, Ill., Mar. 2, 1881; s. Stephen and Frances (Leiden) R.; A.B., St. Francis (Wis.) Sem., 1900; studied U. of Innsbruck, Austria, 1900-02, St. Stanislaus Normal Sch., Cleveland, O., 1903-04, Campion Coll., Prairie du Chien, Wis., 1904-06, Woodstock (Md.) Coll., 1906-07; A.M., St. Louis U., 1914. Joined Soc. of Jesus (Jesuits), 1902; ordained priest R.C. Ch., 1913; teacher (mainly social sciences) Campion Coll., 1907-11, St. Xavier Coll., Cincinnati, 1911-12, 1915-21; Marquette U., Milwaukee, Wis., 1921-23; dean Loyola U., Chicago, 1923-31; regional secretary of sodalities, 1931—; served as regent School of Commerce and Sociology, St. Xavier College. Member Am. Red Cross com. on wounded and disabled soldiers, at Cincinnati; chaplain at Ft. Thomas, Ky., during influenza epidemic; organizing mem. Cincinnati com. on employment of ex-service men; mem. bd. dirs. Cincinnati Consumers' League, Better Housing League, Juvenile Protective Assn., Social Hygiene Soc., City Club; chmn. Joint Legislature Com. (16 orgns.). K.C. Home: Chicago, Ill. Died Oct. 14, 1934.

REINHARDT, George Frederick, physician; b. Morrisson County, Kan., June 3, 1869; s. John George and Katherine (Trusheim) R.; B.S., U. of Calif., 1897, M.D., 1900; m. Aurelia Henry, Dec. 4, 1909. Med. examiner, 1900-04; prof. hygiene and univ. phys., 1904—, U. of Calif. Bd. Med. Examiners, 1903—; organizer, 1906, of self-supporting U. of Calif. Infirmary (first of its kind in U.S.). Democrat. Address: Berkeley, Calif. Died June 7, 1914.

REINHART, Joseph W., special corp., ry. and financial expert; b. Pittsburgh, Pa., Sept. 17, 1851; s. Aaron Grantley and Katherine (McHenry) R.; ed. Western U. of Pa.; m. Lizzie Taylor Allison, Oct. 21, 1875. Entered ry. service, 1869, as clerk to div. supt. Allegheny Valley R.R., supt. rolling stock, 1875-80; auditor Richmond & Allegheny R.R., 1880-83; gen. auditor New York, West Shore & Buffalo Ry. Co., 1883-86; gen. pass. and ticket agt. L.S.& M.S. Ry., 1886-87; gen. auditor, 1888-89, v.p., 1889-93, pres., 1893-94, A.,T.&S.F. Ry.; v.p., 1891-93, pres., 1893-94, St.L.&S.F. Ry. Co.; receiver, 1893-94, A.,T.&S.F. and St.L.&S.F. ry. cos.; chief expert, U.S. Govt. (53d Congress), 1893-94. Home: Plainfield, N.J. Died 1911.

REINHOLD, Eli Spayd; b. Reinholdsville, Pa., Jan. 14, 1847; s. Jacob Brunner and Catharine (Spayd) R.; prep. edn., Classical Acad., Myerstown, Pa.; student State Normal Sch., Millersville, Pa., 1 yr.; grad. Eastman Bus. Coll., Pougkeepsie, N.Y.; studied London U., 1910; hon. A.M., Bucknell U., 1917; m. Louise Jane Compton, Apr. 10, 1866; 1 son, Milton Compton (dec.). In banking bus., Mahanoy City, Pa., 1871-1906; organizer, and exec., Union Nat. Bank, 18 yrs.; retired from active business, 1906, and became mem. faculty Crozer Theol. Sem. to organize and manage extension dept. Connected with City Council of Mahanoy City 23 yrs., as sec., treas. or member. Mem. bd. mgrs. Am. S.S. Union; charter mem. Ministers and Missionaries Benefit Bd.; former trustee Va. Union U. Republican. Baptist. Mason. Discoverer of minerals, pyrophyllite and alunogen in coal mines of Pa. Made 11 trips to Europe, Asia and Africa. Author of pamphlets on hist. subjects. Home: Chester, Pa. Died Aug. 29, 1928.

REINHOLDT, Julius William, banker; b. St. Louis, Mo., Jan. 30, 1869; s. William and Marie (Sinner) R.; grad. high sch., St. Louis, 1886; m. Frieda Barthel, Feb. 1890; children—Julius William, Roland Richard, Carl Adolphus. Began as messenger, Nat. Bank of Commerce, St. Louis, 1887, advancing to asst. cashier, 1912; v.p. and cashier Boatmens Bank (now Boatmens Nat. Bank), 1912-25, pres., 1926-29, chmn. bd., 1929-32. Republican. Presbyn. Mason. Address: Los Angeles, Calif. Deceased.

REINSCH, Paul Samuel, diplomat; b. Milwaukee, Wis., June 10, 1870; s. George J. and Clara (Witte) R.; A.B., U. of Wis., 1892, LL.B., 1894, Ph.D., 1898; studied at U. of Berlin and at Rome, and Paris; LL.D., U. of Wis., 1917, U. of Peking, 1917; m. Alma Marie Moser, Aug. 1, 1900. Asst. prof. polit. science, 1899-1901, prof., 1901-13, U. of Wis.; E.E. and M.P. to China, 1913-19; law practice, Washington, and counsellor to Chinese Govt., 1920—. Roosevelt prof., univs. of Berlin and Leipzig, 1911-12; hon. mem. faculty of U. of Chile. U.S. del. 3d Pan-Am. Conf., Rio de Janeiro, 1906, 4th Conf., Buenos Aires, 1910; U.S. del. 1st Pan-Am. Scientific Congress, Santiago, 1909; mem. Nat. Acad. of Venezuela, Pan-Am. Commn. of U.S., Am. Polit. Science Assn. (pres. 1920), Chinese Polit. Science Assn. (v.p.). Author: The Common Law in the Early American Colonies, 1899; World Politics at the End of the Nineteenth Century as Influenced by the Oriental Situation, 1900; Colonial Government, 1902; Colonial Adminstration, 1905; American Legislatures and Legislative Methods, 1907; Intellectual Currents in the Far East, 1911; International Unions, 1911; An American Diplomat in China, 1913-1919, 1922; Secret Diplomacy, 1922. Contbr. to revs. and hist. and econ. jours. Books have been translated into Japanese, Chinese, Spanish, German. Address: Washington, D.C. Died Jan. 24, 1923.

REISINGER, Hugo, art collector, merchant; b. Wiesbaden, Germany, Jan. 29, 1856; s. Dr. Franz and Apollonia (Busch) R.; grad. Royal Gym., Wiesbaden, 1875; hon. A.M., Columbia, 1910; m. Edmée, d. Adolphus Busch, Feb. 10, 1890. Importer gen. mdse., being one of largest in America, firm name of Hugo Reisinger; dir. Linde Air Products Co. (New York and Buffalo), Owens European Bottle Machine Co., Toledo, O. Lutheran. Hon. commr. to Europe for St. Louis Expn., 1904; hon. fellow for life, Met. Mus. of Art (New York), Copley Society (Boston); v.p. Germanic Mus. (Harvard), Germanistic Society (New York). Comdr. Order of the Prussian Crown; comdr. Order of Merit, with the Star of St. Michael (Bavarian); privy-councillor to the Prince Regent, Ludwig, of Bavaria. Collector of modern paintings, his collection considered by experts one of the finest in existence. Arranged for German Govt. exhbns. of German Art at Met. Mus. of Art, Copley Soc., Art Inst. of Chicago, and organized an Am. Art Exhbn. at the Royal Acad. of Berlin and the Royal Art Soc. of Munich, paying all expenses same. Interested in publication of the German classics of the 19th and 20th centuries for the purpose of making German lit. better known in the U.S., and creating a better understanding between the two nations. Home: New York, N.Y. Died Sept. 29, 1914.

REISNER, Christian Fichthorne, clergyman; b. Atchison, Kan., June 3, 1872; s. John and Rebecca Dorothy (Fichthorne) R.; A.B., Midland Coll., Fremont, Neb., 1893; S.T.B., Boston U. Sch. of Theology, 1896; D.D., Baker U., 1906; L.H.D., Kansas City Wesleyan U., 1928; LL.D., Midland Coll., Fremont, Neb., 1938; m. Charity Belle Ensworth, Apr. 30, 1902; 1 son, Ensworth Thayer. Ordained M.E. ministry, 1896; pastor London Heights, Kansas City, Kan., 1897-1903, Grace Ch., Denver, Colo., 1903-10, Grace Ch., N.Y. City, 1910-19; pastor Broadway Temple, N.Y. City; inaugurated and raised $3,500,000 to finance Broadway Temple, with which Chelsea Ch. was merged. Former asso. gen. sec. Centenary Conservation Com. of M.E. Ch., New York; chmn. N.Y. Area Retreat (Meth.); treas. Council Against Intolerance in America; chmn. N.Y. Conf. Ins. Com.; mem. of N.Y. Police Athletic League Commn.; mem. several mayor's coms. Author: Workable Plans for Wideawake Churches, 1906; Social Plans for Young

People, 1908; Weekday Prayers, 1909; The Preacher Persuader, 1910; Church Publicity, 1913; Prayers for Even-tide, 1916; Comfort and Strength from the Shepherd Psalm, 1918; Roosevelt's Religion, 1921; Prayers for the Day's Work, 1928; Disciple Winners, 1929; God's Power for Me, 1932. Home: New York, N.Y. Died July 17, 1940.

REITER, George Cook, rear admiral U.S.N.; b. Mt. Pleasant, Pa.; s. W. C. (M.D.) and Eliza Reynolds R. Grad. U.S. Naval Acad., 1865; ensign, Dec. 1, 1866; master, Mar. 12, 1868; lt., Mar. 26, 1869; lt. comdr., Nov. 1880; comdr., July 31, 1890; capt., Mar. 3, 1899; rear admiral, Mar. 31, 1905; retired, July 6, 1907. Home: Canton, O. Died May 9, 1930.

RELLSTAB, John, judge; b. Trenton, N.J., Sept. 19, 1858; s. John and Theresa (Schaidnagel) R.; ed. parish and pub. schs.; m. Mary L. Francis, Aug. 1, 1880 (died 1899); m. 2d, Mary J. Whittaker, May 4, 1905 (died 1921). Admitted to N.J. bar, 1882, and as counselor, 1889; solicitor Borough of Chambersburg, 1884-88, City of Trenton, 1889-92, 1894-96; judge Dist. Court, Trenton, 1896-1900; county judge of Mercer County, 1900-09; judge U.S. Dist. Court, N.J., May 18, 1909—. Republican. Presbyn. Home: Trenton, N.J. Died Sept. 22, 1930.

REMENSNYDER, Junius Benjamin, clergyman; b. Staunton, W.Va., Feb. 24, 1843; s. Hon. John Junius and Susan Augusta (Bryan) R.; A.M., Pa. Coll., Gettysburg, 1861; grad. Theol. Sem., same, 1865; D.D., Newberry Coll., 1880; LL.D., New York U., 1902; m. Emma L. Wagner, June 28, 1870. Served in Civil War in 131st Pa. Vols., 1862-63; ordained Luth. ministry, 1865; pastor in Phila., 1865-74, Savannah, Ga., 1874-80, in New York, 1880—; pastor St. James' Luth. Ch. Elected pres. Gen. Synod of Evang. Luth. Ch. in U.S.A., 1911; pres. Peace Commn. of the Chs. in America. Author: Heavenward, 1874; Doom Eternal, 1880; Lutheran Literature, 1882; Work and Personality of Luther, 1884; Six Days of Creation, 1886; Lutheran Manual, 1892; The Atonement and Modern Thought, 1905; Mysticism, 1908; The Post-Apostolic Age and Current Religious Problems, 1910; Eucken, and the Problem of Life, 1913; What the World Owes Luther, 1917; Lectures in University of Upsala, Sweden, 1918; Light on the Shadows of Life, 1919. Trustee Church Peace Union (founded by Andrew Carnegie). Died Jan. 2, 1927.

REMER, Helen, actress. See Helen Ware.

REMEY, George Collier, rear admiral; Burlington, Ia., Aug. 10, 1841; s. William Butler and Eliza Smith (Howland) R.; apptd. to U.S. Naval Acad. from Ia., 1855, grad. 1859; m. Mary J., d. Judge Charles Mason, July 8, 1873. Midshipman, June 9, 1859; promoted through grades to rear admiral, Nov. 22, 1898; retired Nov. 10, 1903. Served on Hartford, E. India Squadron, 1859-61; Marblehead, N. and S. Atlantic Blockading squadrons, 1862-63, Canandaigua, 1863; participated in siege of Yorktown, engagement with Confederates at White House, Pamunky River, June 29, 1862; engagements with batteries on Sullivan's Island, S.C.; engagement of Battery Wagner, Aug. 17, 1863; comd. naval battery on Morris Island, Aug. 23-Sept. 8, 1863, bombardments of Fts. Sumter and Gregg; comd. div. of boats in night attack on Ft. Sumter, Sept. 8, 1863, and was taken prisoner; exchanged as a prisoner of war, Nov. 15, 1864; served on Mohongo, 1865-67; Naval Acad., 1867-69; Sabine, 1869-70; Tehauntepec, 1870-71; Naval Obs., 1871-72; Worcester, 1872-73; Bur. of Yards and Docks, 1874-76; comd. Enterprise, 1877-78; torpedo instrn., 1878; Bur. of Yards and Docks, 1879-81; Lancaster, 1881-83; Navy Yard, Washington, 1884-86, Norfolk, 1886-89; comd. Charleston, 1889-92; Navy Yard, Portsmouth, 1892-95; mem. Naval Examining and Retiring Bds., 1895-96; comdt. Navy Yard, Portsmouth, 1896-98, 1898-1900; comdt. naval base, Key West, Fla., 1898, during war with Spain; comdr. in chief, Asiatic Fleet, 1900-02; chmn. Lighthouse Bd., 1902-03. Home: Washington, D.C. Died Feb. 10, 1928.

REMINGTON, Frederic, artist, author, sculptor; b. Canton, N.Y., Oct. 4, 1861; ed. Yale Art Sch. and Art Students' League, New York. Clerk in office, then cowboy and stockman on ranch in the West; subsequently illustrator for mags., treating mil. and western Am. subjects, and, during 1897-98, Cuban scenes. Well known as painter. Asso. mem. Nat. Acad. Design. Among his leading works in sculpture are "The Broncho Buster" and "The Wounded Bunkie." Author: Pony Tracks; Crooked Trails; Frontier Sketches; John Ermine of the Yellowstone. Home: New Rochelle, N.Y. Died 1909.

REMINGTON, Harold, lawyer; b. Quincy, Ill.; s. Frank and Mary (Webb) R.; A.B., U. of Mich., 1888; student Georgetown U. Sch. of Law, Washington, 1889-91, Columbian U. Sch. of Law, 1891-92; m. May Robertson, Nov. 1, 1893. Admitted to Ohio bar, 1892, N.Y. bar, 1911; practiced in Cleveland, 1892-1910, N.Y. City, 1911—; referee in bankruptcy, 1898-1910. An authority on bankruptcy law; rendered important assistance in framing amendments of 1910 and 1926 to federal bankruptcy law. Author: Treatise on the Bankruptcy Laws of the United States (9 volumes), 1908; Students' Treatise on Elements of Bankruptcy Law, 1911; Business Man's Manual of Bankruptcy Law, 1911; Students' Case Book on Bankruptcy Law, 1926. Home: Malba-on-the-Sound, L.I., N.Y. Died Dec. 15, 1937.

REMINGTON, Joseph Price, pharmacist; b. Phila., Mar. 26, 1847; s. Dr. Isaac and Lydia (Hart) R.; ed. Central High Sch.; Ph.G., Phila. Coll. Pharmacy, 1866, later Ph.M.; hon. Pharm.D., Northwestern U., 1899; F.C.S., F.L.S., and F.R.M.S., London; m. Elizabeth Baily Collins, June 3, 1874. Prof. pharmacy, 1874—, dir. Pharm. Lab., 1877-1915, dean, 1893—, Phila. Coll. Pharmacy. Mem. revision com. U.S. Pharmacopœia, 1880— (chmn., 1901—); pres. 1st Internat. Pharm. Congress, 1893; del. Pan-Am. Med. Congress, Washington, 1893, Mexico, 1896, 8th Internat. Pharm. Congress, Brussels, 1896; chmn. sect. 8b, 7th Internat. Congress Applied Chemistry, London, 1909, New York, 1912; del. Internat. Congress, The Hague, 1913. Author: Remington's Practice of Pharmacy, 1886. Editor: United States Dispensatory, 1883; Lippincott's Medical Dictionary, 1897; U.S. Pharmacopœia, 1890, 1906, 1913. Address: Philadelphia, Pa. Died Jan. 1, 1918.

REMLEY, Milton, lawyer; b. Lewisburg, W.Va., Oct. 12, 1844; s. Rev. James and Jane C. (Alderson) R.; B.A., State U. of Iowa, 1867, M.A., 1872; LL.D., Des Moines Coll.; m. Josephine Dennis, Sept. 8, 1869 (died 1919); children—Hubert, Mrs. Jessie A. Lovell, George E., Mrs. Alice Rutterauff; m. 2d, Mrs. Mary Doyle, Aug. 1921. Practiced, Anamosa, Ia., 1868-74; moved to Iowa City, 1874; retired from gen. practice. Del. Rep. Nat. Conv., 1888; Rep. presdl. elector at large, 1892; atty. gen. of Ia., 3 terms, 1895-1901. Lecturer on med. jurisprudence, Med. Coll. State U. of Ia., 1903-06. Trustee Des Moines Coll. many yrs.; pres. Ia. Bapt. State Convention, 1893-97. Dir. Am. Homefinding Assn., Ottumwa, Ia. Published addresses: Trial of Jesus; Higher Law; The Policy and Government of Baptist Churches; Building and Loan Association and Insurance Laws of Iowa. Home: Iowa City, Ia. Died 1929.

REMMEL, Arthur Kizer, newspaper editor; b. Winchester, Ind., June 17, 1886; s. Samuel T. and Mary Frances (Kizer) R.; ed. Voris Coll., Indianapolis, Ind., and Murat Halsted Sch. of Journalism, Cincinnati, O.; Litt.D., Fletcher Coll., University Park, Ia.; m. Nelle B. Jordan, Nov. 5, 1911; 1 dau., Emalyn Frances. Began as reporter Winchester (Ind.) Herald, 1906; mng. editor Ft. Wayne (Ind.) News-Sentinel, 1923—; v.p. News Pub. Co.; sec.-treas. Three Rivers Coal Co.; dir. Brotherhood Mutual Life Ins. Co.; pres. Sunday Evening Club (a forum); dir. Goodwill Industries, Inc.; mem. bd. Ft. Wayne Community Chest; mem. Maumee Valley Improvement Com.; mem. Ind. Tax Survey Commn., 1929-30; v.p. Ind. Taxpayers Assn. Del. to Ind. State Rep. Conv. 7 times, 1922-36, chmn. of resolutions com., 1936, del. to "Grass Roots" Conv., Springfield, Ill., 1935; lay del. to N. Ind. Conf. of M.E. Ch. Mem. Ind. Asso. Press (pres. 1937), Ind. Republican Editorial Assn. (pres. 1933-34), Ft. Wayne Chamber Commerce (dir.), Ft. Wayne Civic Council, Ft. Wayne Safety Council, Y.M.C.A. Mem. bd. trustees Ft. Wayne Rescue Home Mission. Methodist (pres. bd. of trustees, Wayne Street Meth. Ch.). Mason, K.P. Home: Fort Wayne, Ind. Died Sept. 4, 1941.

REMMEL, Harmon Liveright, mfr., underwriter, banker; b. Stratford, N.Y., Jan. 15, 1852; s. Godlove and Henrietta (Bever) R.; ed. pub schs., Fairfield Sem., N.Y.; m. Laura Lee, d. John Stafford, 1878 (died 1913); m. 2d, Elizabeth I., d. James Y. Cameron, Oct. 1915; children—Harmon L., and (adopted) Elizabeth C. Taught sch. 1 term; later, lumber business, Ft. Wayne, Ind.; mfr. lumber, Newport, Ark., 1876—; gen. agt., Ark., for Mutual Life Ins. Co. at Little Rock, 1896-1922; organizer Mercantile Trust Co. and pres. 1902-12; pres. Bankers Trust Co., 1914-23, later chmn. bd.; pres. Mercantile Fire Ins. Co. Republican candidate for Congress, 1884, for gov. of Ark., 1894, 96, 1900; mem. Ark. Ho. of Rep., 1886; sec. State Bur. of Immigration, 1888; mem. State Bd. of Charities, 1894; pres. State League Republican Clubs, 1895-96; lt. col. Ark. State Guard and Reserve Militia, 1896; collector internal revenue, Ark., 1897-1902, and May 20, 1921—. Del. at large Rep. Nat. Conv., 8 times down to 1924; del. to Monetary Conf., Indianapolis, 1897, 98 (exec. com.); committeeman from Ark. of Rep. Nat. League, 1897; chmn. Rep. State Central Com., 1900—; received vote for U.S. senator, 1903, 16; referee for federal apptmts. in Ark.; U.S. marshal Eastern Dist. of Ark., 1905-13; mem. Rep. Nat. Com., 1912—. Mem. State Capitol Commn., 1909 until building was complete; mem. Ark. State Council of Defense and chmn. four-minute men, World War I. Pres. Ark. Life Underwriters' Assn.; pres. Ark. Good Roads and Drainage Assn., 1910; elected v.p. Little Rock Chapter Nat. Aeronautic Assn., Sept. 24, 1925; pres. Little Rock Bd. of Trade, 1910-12; pres. State Bankers Assn., 1921. The first hydro-electric power dam in Ark. named in his honor, the Remmel Dam. Home: Little Rock, Ark. Died Oct. 14, 1927.

REMONDINO, Peter Charles, M.D.; b. Turin, Italy, Feb. 10, 1846; s. A.G. and Caroline (Ellena) R.; brought to U.S., 1854; ed. pub. schs., Woodstock, Ill., and Wabasha, Minn.; M.D., Jefferson Med. Coll., Phila., 1865; m. Sophia Ann Earle, Sept. 27, 1877. Acting med. cadet U.S.A., at U.S. Gen. Hosp., Annapolis, Md., and at Camp Hosp., City Point, Va., 1864; acting asst. surgeon at U.S. Gen. Hosp., Fortress Monroe, Va., and with Battery F, 3d Pa. Heavy Arty., 1865; surgeon arty. legion of Dept. of Seine Inferieure, during Franco-Prussian War, 1870-71, and surgeon Franco-Tireurs du Nord, same war; settled in San Diego, Calif., 1873; editor Nat. Popular Review, Chicago, 1892; lecturer on history of medicine and med. bibliography, Med. Dept. U. of Southern Calif. Mem. Calif. State Bd. of Health; pres: Board of Health, City of San Diego. Awarded war medal by French Govt. Mason. Author: History of Circumcision, 1891; Mediterranean Shores of America, 1892; Modern Climatic Treatment of Consumption, 1893. Home: San Diego, Calif. Died Dec. 10, 1926.

REMSBURG, John Eleazer, author, lecturer; b. Fremont, O., Jan. 7, 1848; s. George J. and Sarah A. (Willey) R.; enlisted in Union Army at 16. m. Nora M. Eiler, Oct. 9, 1870. A teacher for 15 yrs.; then became writer and lecturer in support of Free Thought and Secularism. Lectured in 52 states, tys. and provinces, delivering over 3,000 lectures in 1,250 different cities and towns. His lectures and some of his books have been translated into German, French, Dutch, Swedish, Norwegian, Bohemian, Japanese, Bengali and Singhalese langs. Supt. pub. instruction, Atchison County, Kan., 4 yrs. Author: Life of Thomas Paine, 1880; The Image Breaker, 1882; False Claims, 1883; Bible Morals, 1884; Sabbath Breaking, 1885; The Fathers of Our Republic, 1887; Was Lincoln a Christian?, 1893; Was Washington a Christian?, 1899; The Bible, 1903; Six Historic Americans, 1906; The Christ, 1909. Address: Porterville, Calif. Died Sept. 23, 1919.

REMSEN, Daniel Smith, lawyer; b. Tecumseh, Mich., July 4, 1853; U. of Mich., 1875-76, LL.B., 1878; m. Louise Bostwick Townsend, Dec. 20, 1882; children—Allen Halsey, Frances Louise (Mrs. Aric Randolph Norton), Gerard Townsend. Practiced, New York, 1878—; associated with Austin Abbott several years; mem. Remsen & Parsons, 1888-1927; mem. Remsen, Burton-Smith & Remsen, 1927-30; mem. law firm of Remsen & Remsen, 1931—; also specialist in law of wills and living trusts; dir. Westchester Trust Co. Trustee New York Kindergarten Association, The Masters School. Presbyterian. Author: Intestate Succession in the State of New York, 1886; Primary Elections, 1894; The Preparation and Contest of Wills, 1907—extended to Preparation of Wills and Trusts, 1930; Post-Mortem Use of Wealth, 1911; Charts for the Planning and Testing of Wills Before Death, 1918; also (pamphlets) The Uniform Trust for Public Uses, 1923; Wise Public Benefactions and Their Creation Under the Uniform Trust for Public Uses, 1923. Home: Bound Brook, N.J. Died Apr. 27, 1935.

REMSEN, Ira, educator, chemist; b. N.Y. City, Feb. 10, 1846; A.B., Coll. City of New York, 1865; M.D., Coll. Phys. and Surg. (Columbia), 1867; Ph.D., University of Göttingen, 1870; LL.D., Columbia, 1893, Princeton, 1896, Yale, 1901, Toronto, 1902, Harvard, 1909, Pa. Coll., 1910, U. of Pittsburgh, 1915; D.C.L., U. of the South, 1907; m. Elisabeth H. Mallory, Apr. 5, 1875; children—Ira Mallory, Charles Mallory. Prof. chemistry, Williams College, 1872-76; prof. chemistry, 1876-1913, dir. Chem. Lab., 1876-1908, sec. Academy Council, 1887-1901, president 1901-Apr. 1912, pres. and prof. emeritus, 1913, Johns Hopkins U. Founded, 1879, and became editor, Am. Chem. Jour. Medalist, 1904, pres., 1910-11, Soc. Chem. Industry; mem. Nat. Acad. Sciences (pres., 1907-13); Priestley medal, Am. Chem. Soc., 1923. Author: The Principles of Theoretical Chemistry, 1876; An Introduction to the Study of the Compounds of Carbon, or Organic Chemistry, 1885; Introduction to the Study of Chemistry, 1887; The Elements of Chemistry, 1888; Inorganic Chemistry, 1889; A Laboratory Manual, 1889; Chemical Experiments, 1895; also many scientific articles and addresses. Address: Baltimore, Md. Died Mar. 5, 1927.

REMSTER, Charles, lawyer; b. Fountain County, Ind., July 28, 1862; s. Andrew and Tamson (Smith) R.; prep. edn., high sch., Veedersburg, Ind.; student Purdue U.; m. Isabel McDaniel, Oct. 30, 1894. Admitted to Ind. bar, 1889, and began practice at Veedersburg; moved to Indianapolis, 1895; mem. firm Smith, Remster, Hornbrook & Smith. Dep. prosecutor Marion County, Ind., 1907, 08; judge Circuit Court, Marion County, 1908-14. Democrat. Mason. Home: Indianapolis, Ind. Died July 1, 1937.

REMY, Alfred, philologist, musician; b. Germany, Mar. 16, 1870; s. Jacob and Elizabeth (Wilckes) R.; ed. Johanneum, Hamburg, 1879-81; Gymnasium, Coesfeld, 1881-82; pub. sch., New York, 1882-84, Coll. St. Francis Xavier, 1884-86; A.B., Coll. City of New York, 1890; A.M., Columbia, 1905; pvt. pupil of B. O. Klein in theory of music and piano, 1890-96; m. Egbertina Wilterdink (pianiste), May 29, 1902; children—Walter (dec.), Elaine (dec.), Constance. Music critic "Vogue," 1895-97; mus. editor "The Looker-on," 1895-97; prof. harmony, counterpoint and composition, Internat. Conservatory, New York, 1895-97; lecturer on history of music, N.Y. Coll. of Music, 1896-98; prof. Greek, Seton Hall Coll., S. Orange, N.J., 1897-98; prof. modern langs., Commercial High Sch., Brooklyn, 1899-1911; instr. modern lang., High Sch. of Commerce, New York, Sept. 1911-26, chmn. dept. of modern langs., 1926-35; chmn. dept. of modern langs., Notre Dame Coll. of Staten Island, 1933—, prof. of Germanic langs., Fordham University, 1928—. Univ. extension lecturer 1906-15. In charge dept. of music, New Internat. Ency., 1901-30, Internat. Ency., 1924, 30; mus. and lit. editor T. B. Harms, 1921-26. Author: Alarcón's Novelas Cortas Escogidas, 1905; Spanish Prose Composition, 1908; First Spanish Reader, 1916; Biographical Dictionary of Musicians, 1919 (with Th. Baker). Translator of The German Classics of the 19th and 20th Centuries, 1913. Translator (into English and French) and editor of Sevcik's Intonationsschule für Violine, op. 11, 1922; Schule des Virtuosen, op. 12, 1926. Home: Bronxville, N.Y. Died Feb. 26, 1937.

REND, William Patrick, coal operator; b. in County of Leitrim, Ireland, Feb. 10, 1840; came to U.S., 1847; grad. Lowell, Mass., High School, 1857; taught school in N.J. and Md.; studied at St. John's Coll., Md.; served in 14th N.Y. vols., 1861-65; became freight clerk in Chicago; organized trucking business and later started firm of W. P. Rend & Co.; owns large mines in Ohio and Pa.; also interested in oil production; lt. col. Ill. Nat. Guard; served as arbitrator in various labor disputes. Address: Chicago. Died Nov. 30, 1915.

RENDALL, John Ballard, univ. pres.; b. Madura, Southern India, Apr. 5, 1847; s. of John and Jane (Ballard) R.; A.B., Princeton, 1870, A.M., 1873; D.D., Gale Coll., Wis., 1900; m. Harriet Elizabeth Jones, July 12, 1872; 4 sons in Presbyn. ministry. Ordained Presbyn. ministry, 1876; prof. Latin, Sept. 1870—, pres., Apr. 1906—, Lincoln U., Pa. Mem. Pa. Ho. of Rep., 1899-1900; del. Prog. National Conv., Chicago, 1912. Trustee Wilson Coll., Chambersburg, Pa.; moderator of Synod of Pa., 1908. Pres. Ministers' Social Union Phila. and Vicinity, 1914-15. Mem. Draft Exemption Bd. for Chester Co., 1917. Died Sept. 3, 1924.

RENFROW, William Cary, governor; b. Smithfield, N.C., Mar. 15, 1845; ed. common schs.; m. Jennie B. York, Oct. 17, 1875. Served in C.S.A., 1861-65; moved to Ark., 1865, thence to Okla., 1889; engaged in banking at Norman; del. 1st Territorial Conv., Okla. Ty., 1889, and suggested name of Cleveland County and Norman, as county seat, which were adopted; gov. of Okla. Ty., 1893-97. Pres. of 2 banks. Address: Oklahoma City, Okla. Died Jan. 3, 1922.

RENNERT, Hugo Albert, philologist; b. Phila., May 6, 1858; s. John and Margarethe M. (Jaeger) R.; B.S., U. of Pa., 1876, LL.B., 1881, A.M., 1890; Ph.D., U. of Freiburg-in-Baden, 1892, LL.D., 1914; m. Helen Ringgold Rasin, Nov. 17, 1897; 1 son, Hugo Rasin. Prof. Romance philology, U. of Pa., 1892—. Author: The Spanish Pastoral Romances; Lope de Vega's Comedia "Sin Secreto no ay Amor"; Der Spanische Cancionero des Brit. Mus.; Comedias of Miguel Sanchez "el Divino"; Unpublished Poems of Fernan Perez de Guzman; Poésies Inédites de Gongora; Lieder des Juan Rodriguez del Padron; Guillen de Castro's Comedia "Ingratitud por Amor," Macias, O Namorado; The Life of Lope de Vega, 1904; The Spanish Stage in the Time of Lope de Vega, 1909; Farsa a manera de Tragedia; Diego Lopez de Castro; Marco Antonio y Cleopatra. Knight Comdr. Royal Order of Isabel the Catholic. Home: Philadelphia, Pa. Died Dec. 31, 1927.

RENO, Conrad, lawyer; b. Mt. Vernon, Ala., Dec. 28, 1859; s. Maj. Gen. Jesse Lee and Mary Bradley Beanes (Cross) R.; student Lehigh U., 1878-80, Harvard Law Sch., 1880-82; LL.B., Boston U., 1883; Johns Hopkins, 1913-14; Inst. of Politics, Williams Coll., 1921; m. Susan M., d. Rev. William T. Eustis, Apr. 13, 1887. In practice at Boston, 1883-1912. Drafted the Pub. Service Tri-Partnership Bill, 1907, for regulating rates and charges, dividends and wages in pub. service corps.; also the Railroad Tri-Partnership Bill, 1908, The Gas Tri-Partnership Bill, 1909—, the Business Tri-Partnership Bill, 1911, the Interstate Railroad Capital-and-Labor Partnership Bill, for Congress, 1921, and the Coal Partnership Bill, for Congress, 1922. Author: State Regulation of Wages, 1891; Non-Residents and Foreign Corporations, 1892; Employers' Liability Acts, 1896-1903; History of the Judicial System of New England, 1900; The Partnership of Man; The Brotherhood of Nations; Tune In with God and Your Neighbors. Mem. First Corps Cadets of Boston, 1887-90, Vet. Assn., 1915-18. Inventor of the "stream" method and beam system of wireless transmission of energy, a system for transmitting energy without wires, the regenerative levitation motor, and discoverer of the spirally revolving magnetic field. Home: Daytona Beach, Fla. Died May 7, 1933.

RENOUF, Edward, chemist; b. Lowville, N.Y., Sept. 4, 1846; s. E. A. (D.D.) and Harriet L. R.; ed. Boston grammar and Latin schs., Heidelberg, Jena and Munich; Ph.D., U. of Freiburg, 1880; m. Annie V. Whelpley, Feb. 1871. Asst. in chemistry, U. of Munich, 1880-85; collegiate prof. chemistry, Johns Hopkins, 1885-1911. Author: Volhard's Experiments in General Chemistry (translation), 1887; Inorganic Preparations, 1894. Address: Monkton, Md. Deceased.

RENSHAW, Alfred Howard, mfr.; b. Staten Island, N.Y., Nov. 24, 1861; s. William and Emma (Conine) R.; Va. Mil. Inst., 1877-79; C.E., Rensselaer Poly. Inst., 1883; m. Lucy Jennings Price, Oct. 25, 1885 (now dec.); children—Howard Price (dec.), Paul, Alfred, Elizabeth Price; m. 2d, Lucy Braxton Hopkins, Apr. 20, 1899; children—Lewis Hopkins, Lucy Howard (Mrs. Guido Marchi), Palmer Chamberlaine Ricketts (dec.). Asst. engr., N.Y. Aqueduct Commns., 1884-87, U.S. Navy Yard, Charlestown, Mass., 1887-89; mem. firm Burden, Renshaw & Co., Troy, N.Y., 1889-92; treas. Trojan Car Coupler Co., 1892-93, pres., 1893-1906; pres. Standard Signal Co., 1896-1903; pres. Federal Signal Co., 1908-24; v.p. Gen. Railway Signal Company, 1923-36, chmn. of bd., Feb. 1936—; pres. General Railway Signal Products Co., 1924-28; dir. Home Bank & Trust Co., Charter Oak Title Guaranty & Fidelity Co. Engr. and maj. N.G.N.Y., 1898-1903. Chmn. Darien (Conn.) Planning and Zoning Commn., 1920-29. Trustee Rensselaer Poly. Inst. Inventor of Trojan car coupler and many other safety devices. Home: Noroton, Conn. Died June 16, 1939.

RENSHAW, Raemer Rex, univ. prof.; b. Sierraville, Calif., Aug. 31, 1880; s. Hugh Albert and Sarrah (Raine) R.; B.S., U. of Ore., 1902, M.S., 1903; Ph.D., Columbia, 1907; m. Laura Chase Birdsey, June 18, 1910; children—Birdsey, Raine; m. 2d, Mary H. Wallace, 1931. Instructor in chemistry, U. of Ore., 1902-04; fellow Columbia U., 1904-05; instr. chemistry, Wesleyan U., 1907-12, asso. prof., 1912-13; asso. prof. organic chemistry, Ia. State Coll., 1913-19; asst. prof. chem. research, Harvard Med. Sch., 1919-20; asso. prof. organic chemistry, 1920-24, prof., 1924—, New York U. Capt. Chem. W.S., U.S.A., June 6, 1918-Mar. 1, 1919. Republican. Protestant. Address: New York, N.Y. Died Sept. 23, 1938.

RENWICK, Edward Sabine, patent expert; b. New York, Jan. 3, 1823; s. James and Margaret Anne (Brevoort) R.; A.B., Columbia, 1839, A.M., 1842; widower. Became civ. and mech. engr. and supt. large iron works at Wilkes-Barre, Pa.; 1849—, in practice as expert in patent cases. In 1862, with his brother, Henry B. Renwick, repaired the Great Eastern while afloat, replating a fracture in the bilge, 82 feet long and 10 feet in greatest width, which other experts had declared an impossible feat. Invented many machines and mech. devices. Author: Practical Invention, 1893. Home: Short Hills, N.J. Died Mar. 19, 1912.

RENWICK, William Whetten, architect; b. Lenox, Mass., Oct. 30, 1864; s. Edward Sabine and Alice (Brevoort) R.; M.E., Stevens Inst. Tech., 1885; studied architecture under uncle, James Renwick, New York; sculpture, under Magnalier, of the École des Beaux Arts, Paris; painting in New York, Paris and Rome; m. Ilka Howells, Apr. 26, 1902. Entered office of the late James Renwick, 1885, jr. partner firm, 1890; engaged on many well known bldgs. in New York, among them St. Patrick's Cathedral, St. Bartholomew's Ch., All Saints' Ch., Grace Ch., etc.; later practiced alone, devoting time exclusively to ecclesiastical architecture and decoration. Architect of the Cathedral of St. Peter and St. Paul, Indianapolis; St. Aloysius' Church, New York; All Saints' Parish buildings; the chantry, south porch and open air pulpit of Grace Ch., Broadway and 10th St., New York, and many altars, monuments and decorations. Inventor of a kind of mural decoration known as "Fresco-Relief." Republican. Episcopalian. Home: Short Hills, N.J. Died Mar. 15, 1933.

REPASS, Joseph Wharton, coll. pres.; b. Bland County, Va., Nov. 8, 1861; s. Joseph and Eliza Jane R.; A.B., Hiwassee Coll., Tenn., 1884, A.M., 1887; m. Sadie A. Barbe, 1884. Began teaching in pub. schs. of Scott County, Va., 1879; prin. Greenwood (Va.) High Sch., 1884-88, Holston Inst., Tenn., 1888-91, Zollicoffer Inst., Tenn., 1891-93; founded, 1893, and pres., 1893-97, Russell Coll., Va.; prof. natural science, Martha Washington Coll., Abingdon, Va., 1897-1902; prin. Woodson Inst., Richmond, Mo., 1902-04; pres. Clarksville (Tenn.) Female Acad., 1904-05; Centenary Female Coll., Cleveland, Tenn., 1905-10, Logan Female Coll., Russellville, Ky., 1910-17, San Antonio (Tex.) Female Coll., 1917—. Address: San Antonio, Tex. Died Oct. 23, 1919.

REQUA, Mark Lawrence, mining engr.; b. Virginia City, Nev., Dec. 25, 1866; s. Isaac Lawrence Requa and Sarah J. (Mower) R.; ed. pvt. schs.; studied at Yale, 3 years; m. Florence Herrick, 1895. Developed Nev. Consol. Copper Co.; cons. engr. Bur. of Mines (resigned); built Nev. Northern Ry. Asst. to Herbert C. Hoover, U.S. food adminstr., June 1917-Jan. 1918; gen. dir. oil div., U.S. Fuel Adminstrn., Jan. 10, 1918-June 30, 1919; chmn. com. on standardization petroleum specifications, U.S. Govt., 1918-19. Mem. Am. Inst. Mining and Metall. Engrs. (v.p. 1917-20), Am. Petroleum Inst. (hon.). Chmn. valuation com. Independent Oil Producers Agency of Calif., 1915. Chmn. Calif. delegation Rep. Nat. Conv., Kansas City, Mo., 1928; mem. Rep. Nat. Com. for Calif., 1931—. Author: Relation of Government to Industry; (novel) Grubstake. Home: Santa Barbara, Calif. Died Mar. 6, 1937.

RESSLER, Edwin DeVore, coll. dean; b. Westerville, Franklin County, O., Nov. 2, 1869; s. Jacob Bruner and Emily (Shupe) R.; B.A., Otterbein U., Westerville, 1891; M.A., Ohio State U., 1897; m. May Bowden-Babbitt, Aug. 25, 1909. Taught 5 yrs. in Ohio, 4 yrs. as supt. schs., Westerville; supt. schs., Eugene, Ore., 1897-1901; asst. prof. edn., U. of Ore., 1901-02; pres. Ore. Normal Sch., Monmouth, 1902-09; prof. and head of dept. of edn., Ore. Agrl. Coll., 1909—, also dir. Summer Sch., 1909-19, dean Sch. Vocational Edn., 1918—. Republican. Mem. U.B. Ch. Mem. N.E.A. (v.p. and dir. many yrs.), sec.-treas. Ore. State Teachers Assn., 1918—. Mason. Home: Corvallis, Ore. Died Oct. 1926.

RESTARICK, Henry Bond, bishop; b. Somerset, Eng., Dec. 26, 1854; s. Edwin and Amelia Riall (Webb) R.; King James Collegiate Sch., Bridgewater, Eng.; grad. Griswold Coll., Davenport, Ia., 1882; D.D., King's Coll., Windsor, N.S., 1902; m. May L. Baker, 1882; children—Constance (Mrs. Paul Withington), Arthur Edwin, Margaret Frances (Mrs. Reynold B. McGrew). Deacon, 1881, priest, 1882, P.E. Ch.; in charge Trinity Ch., Muscatine, Ia., 1881-82; rector St. Paul's, San Diego, Calif., 1882-1902; held ch. offices of dean, examining chaplain and del. to Gen. Conv., P.E. Ch.; elected first Am. bishop of Honolulu, Apr. 17, 1902; consecrated July 2, 1902; resigned Oct. 1920. Editor Hawaiian Church Chronicle, 1907-20 and, 1930—. Author: Lay Readers, 1894; The Love of God, 1897; Addresses on the Last Seven Words; Hawaii from the Viewpoint of a Bishop, 1924; Gaetano Did Not Discover Hawaii, 1929; Sun Yat Sen, Liberator of China, 1931. Trustee Library of Hawaii, 1915—, pres. 1927-31; trustee and pres. Hawaiian Hist. Soc. Mem. Commn. for Sesquicentennial Celebration of Discovery of Hawaii, 1928. Republican. Life mem. B.P.O.E. Address: Honolulu, Hawaii. Died Dec. 8, 1933.

RETHERS, Harry Frederick, army officer; b. San Francisco, Calif., Aug. 7, 1870; A.B., U. of Calif., 1893; m. Maude H. Lee, d. Maj. Gen. J. M. Lee, Oct. 19, 1898. Served as pvt., corpl. and sergt., Co. A, 1st Inf., U.S.A., 1893-96; commd. 2d lt. Apr. 10, 1896; promoted through grades to col., July 1, 1920; apptd. brig. gen., asst. to q.m. gen., Apr. 16, 1926; retired, 1931. Participated in Santiago Campaign, Spanish-Am. War, 1898, Philippine Insurrection, 1899, Boxer Rebellion, China, 1900; col. (temp.), World War I. Awarded D.S.M. (U.S.); Order of St. Michael and St. George (British); Officer Legion of Honor (French). Home: San Francisco, Calif. Died Jan. 17, 1941.

REULING, George, ophthalmologist; b. Romrod, Germany, Nov. 11, 1839; s. Dr. Robert and Amalie (Vogler) R.; M.D., Giessen, 1865; studied ophthalmology at Berlin and Vienna; m. Elisa, d. Capt. F. Külp, Sept. 21, 1871. Surgeon Prussian Army during war with Austria; asst., Eye Hosp., Wiesbaden, 1866-67; studied, Paris, 1867-68; phys.-in-chief Md. Eye and Ear Infirmary Baltimore, 1869—; prof. eye and ear surgery, Washington U., Baltimore, 1870—; prof. ophthalmology, U. of Baltimore, 1881—; prof. eye and ear disesaes, Baltimore Med. Coll., 1886-1910, emeritus prof., 1910—; eye and ear surgeon Md. Gen. Hosp., to Med. Home of the Aged, to B.&O. R.R. Wrote papers on and invented apparatus for eye and ear surgery. Fellow Am. Acad. Arts and Sciences. Address: Baltimore, Md. Died Nov. 25, 1915.

REUTERDAHL, Arvid, educator; b. Sweden, Feb. 15, 1876; s. Jonas and Christina M. (Johanson) R.; came to U.S., 1882, Sc.B., Brown U., 1897, M.A., 1899; m. Elinor Louise Morrison, June 16, 1902; 1 son, Norman Morrison. Began teaching mathematics at Brown U., 1897; prof. physics, Colby Coll., 1904-05; engring. practice, Spokane, Wash., 1905-10; pres. Bd. of Pub. Works, Spokane, 1909-10; consulting engr., 1910-15; prof. theoretical and applied mechanics, Kansas City Poly. Inst., 1915-17; dean dept. engring. and architecture, Coll. of St. Thomas, St. Paul, Minn., 1918-22; pres. Ramsey Inst. of Tech., St. Paul, 1922—. Awarded the Doctorate in Science, 1923, by Acad. of Nations in recognition of his solution of the physical meaning of Planck's Constant and the promulgation of his theory of septad-constants. Author: Theory and Design of Reinforced Concrete Arches, 1908; Scientific Theism Versus Materialism, The Space-Time Potential, 1920; Einstein and the New Science, 1921; History of Thought, 1925; Omkara, 1925. Contbr. articles in scientific and engring. mags. One of the first in U.S. to dispute the correctness of Einstein's theories. Home: St. Paul, Minn. Died Jan. 13, 1933.

REUTERDAHL, Henry, naval artist; b. Malmö, Sweden, Aug. 12, 1871; s. Frederic and Augusta (Drake) R.; m. Pauline Stephenson, July 16, 1899.

Served as corr. during Spanish-Am. War, also during first part of European war, 1914. Lt., U.S.N.R.F., May 25, 1917; lt. comdr., Nov. 1918; retired, Dec. 27, 1921. Represented in permanent collection at U.S. Naval Academy, by 10 paintings of this cruise, presented to the navy by George von L. Meyer, Sec. of Navy; also in the Nat. Mus., Washington, Naval War Coll., Newport, and Toledo Mus.; silver medal for painting, Panama P.I. Exposition, 1915. Painted panels for steam yachts, "Noma," Vincent Astor, owner; "Viking," G. F. Baker, Jr., and for schooner "Vagrant," Harold S. Vanderbilt, owner; naval mural, Mo. State Capitol "We Are Ready Now." Formerly instr. Art Students' League. Asso. mem. U.S. Naval Inst. Address: Weehawken, N.J. Died Dec. 20, 1925.

REVEL, Bernard, coll. pres.; b. Kowno, Lithuania, Sept. 17, 1885; s. Rabbi Nahum Schrage and Leah (Gitelewitz) R.; student U. of Pa., 1908; A.M., N.Y. Univ., 1909; Ph.D., Dropsie Coll., Phila., Pa., 1911; m. Sarah Travis, June 1909; children—Norman F., Hirschel E. Came to U.S., 1906, naturalized, 1912. Pres. and prof. Rabbinical Coll. of America (now Rabbi Isaac Elchanan Theol. Sem.), 1915—; founder and pres. of Yeshiva Coll. (chartered in 1928). Fellow Jewish Acad. Arts and Sciences (v.p., 1927—); hon. pres. Union of Orthodox Rabbis of U.S. and Can. Author of "Pseudo-Jonathan on the Pentateuch"; "Karaite Halakah." Contbr. articles to Jewish Quarterly Rev., Horeb and other scientific jours. Address: New York, N.Y. Died Dec. 2, 1940.

REVELL, Alexander Hamilton, merchant, mfr.; b. Chicago, Ill., Jan. 6, 1858; s. David and Margaret (Dorgan) R.; ed. pub. schs.; m. Maude Richardson; children—Margaret (Mrs. Loring R. Hoover), Alexander H., Jr., Richardson. Furniture mfr. and mcht. Mem. Chicago Bd. of Edn.; mem. exec. com. World's Columbian Expn., 1893; trustee Northwestern U. and other instns.; prominent in reform movements. Mem. Legion of Honor, France, 1908. Home: Chicago, Ill. Died Mar. 13, 1931.

REVELL, Fleming Hewitt, publisher; b. Chicago, Ill., Dec. 11, 1849; s. Fleming H. and Emma (Manning) R.; pub. sch. edn.; m. Josephine Barbour, Sept. 12, 1872. Entered pub. and editorial profession on own account, 1869; pres. Fleming H. Revell Co., 1890—. Dir. New York Life Ins. Co. Trustee Northfield (Mass.) Sem., Wheaton (Ill.) Coll.; dir. New York Y.M.C.A.; treas. Mission to Lepers. Home: Fieldston, Riverdale, N.Y. Died Oct. 11, 1931.

REVELLE, Thomas P., lawyer; b. Fairmont, Somerset County, Md., May 16, 1868; s. George Henry and Mary Elizabeth (Ford) R.; A.B., Western Md. Coll., 1893, A.M., 1903; LL.B., U. of Wash., 1903; m. Eliza Jefferson, June 8, 1899. Practiced at Seattle, 1905—. Mem. City Council, Seattle, 1905-10; U.S. atty., Western Dist. of Wash., 1921-27 (resigned); mem. firm Revelle, Simon & Coles. Republican. Conglist. Mason, Woodman, Moose. Home: Seattle, Wash. Died July 4, 1937.

REVERMAN, Theodore Henry, bishop; b. Louisville, Ky., Aug. 9, 1877; s. Theodore and Walburga Louise (Haming) R.; St. Meinrad's Coll., St. Meinrad, Ind., 1890-91; B.A., Canisius Coll., Buffalo, N.Y., 1897, LL.D., 1933; U. of Innsbruck, Austria, 1897-1901; D.C.L., Gregorian U., Rome, 1903. Ordained priest R.C. Ch., 1901; prof. theology, Preston Park Sem., Louisville, Ky., 1903-05; pastor St. Edward Ch., Jeffersontown, Ky., 1903-21, St. Francis of Assisi, Louisville, 1921-26; bishop of Superior, Wis., Nov 20, 1926—. Home: Superior, Wis. Died July 18, 1941.

REXDALE, Robert, lecturer, author; b. Mar. 26, 1859; ed. Portland, Me., pub. schs.; learned printer's trade; took up newspaper work; asst. editor Portland Sunday Times, 1885-92; 1893, became interested in traveling lecture work, removing to Peoria, Ill.; m. Helen Therese Ilsley, June 1, 1895; children—Phyllis Evelyn (Mrs. Ernest L. Ventres), Ilsley. Telegraph editor Daily Times, Davenport, Ia., 1918-26; editor Geneseo (Ill.) Republican, 1926—. Editor "Under the Jingle Tree," in Modern Woodmen Mag., 1914-18. Author: Drifting, 1887; Rhymes, 1904; The Book of Bohemia, 1913; Quest of a Master Mason, 1915; Daughters of Mokanna, 1918. Contbr. to Life and other periodicals. Spl. contbns. are When the Mississippi Was the Great Highway, Yuletide, At Low Twelve, The Message of the Flag, To Our Absent Brothers. Home: Rock Island, Ill. Died Oct. 28, 1929.

REXFORD, Eben Eugene, author; b. Johnsburgh, N.Y., July 16, 1848; s. Jabez B. and Rebecca (Wilcox) R.; ed. Lawrence U., Appleton, Wis. (Litt.D., 1908); m. Mrs. Harriet Harsh, Dec. 1890. Writer for press ever since 14 yrs. of age. Contributed stories and poems to nearly all leading mags.; wrote a great deal about flowers and their culture, and is considered authority in this special field of work; interested in social improvement work. Wrote many songs, among which the most popular is "Silver Threads Among the Gold." Author: Brother and Lover (poem of the War), 1886; Home Floriculture, 1888-1901; Grandmother's Garden, 1890; Flowers—How to Grow Them, 1898; Four Seasons in a Garden, 1907; The Home Garden, 1908; Indoor Gardening, 1910; Amateur Gardencraft, 1912; Pansies and Rosemary (poems), 1911. Address: Shiocton, Wis. Died Oct. 18, 1916.

REXFORD, Frank A., educator; b. Smyrna, N.Y., Aug. 22, 1876; s. Frank Duane and Alice Cornelia (Forman) R.; student Oneonta (N.Y.) State Normal Sch., 1895; grad. Brockport (N.Y.) State Normal Sch., 1900; student Poly. Inst., Brooklyn, 1901-02; B.S., New York U., 1905; research in psychology and physiology, same, 1905-09; m. Gertrude Pratt, Jan. 1, 1903 (died 1906); 1 son, Pratt; m. 2d, Florence Gilliland, Dec. 23, 1910. Teacher country schs., N.Y., 1893-95; teacher science, high sch., Bay Shore, L.I., N.Y., 1900-01; teacher chemistry and biology, Erasmus Hall High Sch., N.Y. City, 1901-07; teacher of English to foreigners, 1907-09; teacher of industrial chemistry, Brooklyn Trade Sch., 1910-13; supervised agr. and civics, 1918-26, N.Y. City high schs.; dir. of civics and civic activities in high schs. of N.Y. City, 1927-32; dir. of education, Museum of City of N.Y., 1932-35. Trustee George Junior Republic; mem. Self Govt., Inc. Pvt. N.G.N.Y., 1895-97; chief zone dir. N.Y. State Boys' Working Reserve, 1917-18; dir. Emergency farm service, N.Y. City high schs., 1919; dir. N.Y. State Boys' Working Reserve and state dir. U.S. Boys' Working Reserve, 1918; "dollar a year" man, U.S. Dept. Labor, 1918-19; supervised 14,000 boys who cultivated 212,000 acres for food. Chmn. Jr. Red Cross for N.Y. City; hon. dir. Coöp. in Govt., Inc. Author: One Portion Food Table, 1913; Food Economy Charts, 1916; The Constitution of Our Country (with Clara Carson), 1925; Useful Science (with H. T. Weed), 1931; Beyond the School (with Smith, Sellin and Frabbito), 1932; also articles in mags. on civic topics. Supervised writing of "Our City—New York" (written by pupils in high schools), 1925. Fancier and breeder of ponies for children, 1935—. Home: Pinebluff, N.C. Died Jan. 3, 1941.

REYBURN, John Edgar, mayor; b. New Carlisle, O., Feb. 7, 1845; ed. pvt. tutor and Saunders Inst., W. Phila.; studied law, and admitted to bar, 1870; m. Margretta Crozier; 1 son, William S. Mem. Pa. Ho. of Rep., 1871, 74, 75, 76, Senate, 4 terms, 1876-90 (pres. pro tem., 1883); presdl. elector, 1904; mem. Congress, 4th Pa. Dist., 1890-97; reëlected to 59th Congress, 1905-07, for an unexpired term and to 60th Congress, 1907-09; elected mayor of Phila., for term 1907-11, and resigned from Congress. Republican. Home: Philadelphia, Pa. Died Jan. 4, 1914.

REYBURN, Robert, physician; b. Glasgow, Scotland, Aug. 1, 1833; s. James and Jane (Brown) R.; ed. Phila. public schools; grad. Phila. Coll. of Med., 1856; A.M., Howard U.; m. Catharine White, Feb. 5, 1854. Practiced medicine at Phila., 1856-62; entered U.S. army, 1862, as acting asst. surgeon, surgeon and bvt. lt. col. U.S. vols., 1863; asst. surgeon U.S.A., 1867. Continued practice in Washington; in 1881 was one of the surgeons in attendance upon Pres. Garfield; later dean and prof. hygiene and preventive medicine, med. dept. Howard U. Author: Clinical History of the Case of President Garfield. Frequent contbr. to med. jours. Address: Washington, D.C. Died 1909.

REYNOLDS, Alfred, naval officer; b. Hampton, Va., Sept. 7, 1853; s. Maj. Gen. Joseph J. (U.S.A.) and Mary E. (Bainbridge) R.; grad. U.S. Naval Acad., 1873; m. Louise S. Norton, April 28, 1880; m. 2d, Sarah Josephine LeCand, Oct. 4, 1921. Ensign, July 16, 1874; promoted through grades to rear adm., July 13, 1911. Served on Swatara, 1888-91, and comd. expdn. to Seoul, Corea, to protect U.S. minister and foreigners; comd. Massasoit during Spanish-Am. War; ordnance officer, Navy Yard, League Island, Pa., 1902-05; comd. Nevada, 1905-07; Naval War Coll., Newport, 1907; comd. receiving ship Franklin, 1907-08; comd. Montana, 1908-09; comd. Franklin, 1909-11; gov. of Naval Home, Phila., 1911-12; comd. Pacific Reserve Fleet, 1912-13; apptd., Aug. 15, 1912, by Pres. of U.S., to accompany Sec. of State as naval representative to funeral of Emperor of Japan; pres. Naval Examining and Retiring bds., Washington, D.C., 1913-15; retired on account of age, Sept. 7, 1915. Placed on active duty, July 20, 1917; establishing training sta., Gulfport, Miss., and in command of naval reservation there. Home: Gulfport, Miss. Died Sept. 9, 1936.

REYNOLDS, Allen Holbrook, lawyer; b. Walla Walla, Wash., Jan. 24, 1869; s. Almos Holbrook and Lettice Jane (Millican) R.; A.B., Whitman Coll., 1889, A.M., 1889; LL.B., Boston U., 1893; m. Fanny Kirkman, Nov. 7, 1894; children—William Allen, Almos Kirkman, Ruth Sarah. Practicing atty., Walla Walla, 1893-1917; pres. Farmers and Merchants Bank, 1917-23, atty. and mgr., 1923—; treas. The Kirkman Co.; dir. Walla Walla Savings and Loan Co., Northwestern Bridge Co. Pres. bd. trustees Whitman Coll.; pres. Y.M.C.A., Walla Walla, 1904-34. Republican. Conglist. Home: Walla Walla, Wash. Died Sept. 24, 1941.

REYNOLDS, Charles Bingham, author; b. Morrisania, N.Y., 1854; s. Charles O. and Lucy W. R.; A.B., Amherst, 1876; m. Miss E. Thomas, 1879. Editor Forest and Stream, 1879-1906. Author: Old St. Augustine, A Story of Three Centuries, 1885; Standard Guide to Cuba, 1905; Standard Guide to Havana, 1905; Standard Guide to St. Augustine, East Coast of Florida and Nassau, 1905; Standard Guide to Washington, 1905; Standard Guide to New York, 1906. Compiled Game Laws in Brief, 1905; Fugitives from Fate to the Port of the Havana, 1911. Home: Mountain Lakes, N.J. Died Nov. 10, 1940.

REYNOLDS, Dudley Sharpe, physician; b. Bowling Green, Ky., Aug. 31, 1842; s. Rev. Thomas and Mary (Nichols) R.; acad. edn.; M.D., U. of Louisville, 1868; A.M., Ogden Coll., Bowling Green, Ky.; m. Mary F. Keagan, May 7, 1865; m. 2d, Matilda L. Bruce, July 13, 1881; m. 3d, Lillie Bell Baldwin, June 5, 1907. Visited foreign hosps. and colls., 1872, 78, 81; prof. ophthalmology, otology and med. jurisprudence, Hosp. Coll. of Medicine (med. dept. Central U. of Ky.), Louisville, 1874-1901; pres. faculty same, 1891-93; surgeon to Louisville City Hosp., 1872-1902; surgeon C.,I.&L. Ry., 1894-99; visiting surgeon, Ky. Confed. Home, Pewee Valley; U.S. expert examining surgeon, 1882—. Chmn. sect. of ophthalmology A.M.A., 1880-81; pres. Miss. Valley Med. Assn., 1888 (treas., 1899-1901); dir. Polytechnic Soc. of Ky., 1879-94; chmn. Jud. Council Assn. of Am. Med. Colls., 1891-1901. Home: Louisville, Ky. Died Feb. 4, 1915.

REYNOLDS, Edwin, inventor; b. Mansfield, Conn., Mar. 23, 1831; ed. in schools there; entered machine shop, 1847; as apprentice. After 3 yrs. worked in various other shops; supt. shops Stedman & Co., Aurora, Ind., 1857-61; went to Corliss Steam Engine Co., Providence, R.I., 1861, gen. supt., 1871-77; gen. supt. E. P. Allis & Co. (Reliance Works), Milwaukee, 1877—; one of trustees estate of E. P. Allis after death of latter; 2d v.p. and dir. The Allis Company; pres. Milwaukee Boiler Co., the Daisy Roller Mills Co., and German-Am. Bank. Inventor of the Reynolds-Corliss engine; introduced the 1st triple-expansion pumping engine; cross-compound hoisting engines for mining work; etc. Address: Milwaukee, Wis. Died 1909.

REYNOLDS, Elmer Robert, ethnologist, botanist; b. Dansville, N.Y., July 30, 1846; s. Dr. Allen B. and Sarah W. (Van Amburg) R.; ed. New Lisbon, Wis., 1852-60; Columbian U., 1874-80; (hon. Sc.D., Albertus Magnus Univ., Wichita, Kan., 1901); in 10th Wis. vol. light arty., 1861-65; teacher U.S.N., 1866-76; in U.S. civ. service as examiner of pensions, 1877—; engaged in exploring aboriginal antiquities of Md. and Va.; knighted by King Humbert of Italy, 1887; medal from King of Portugal; bronze medal from Royal Portuguese Soc. Archæology, Lisbon, 1899. Writer of numerous monographs on the archæology of D.C., Md. and Va., scientific papers, newspaper serials, stories, etc. Address: Washington, D.C. Died 1907.

REYNOLDS, Frank Bernard, judge; b. Quincy, Mich., Jan. 20, 1874; s. Norman A. and Emoretta A. (Harding) R.; lit. dept., U. of Mich., 1891-93, law dept., 1894-95, LL.B., 1895; m. Florence M. Hilliar, Sept. 2, 1896. Admitted to Mich. bar, 1895, and practiced with father, as Reynolds & Reynolds, at Coldwater; moved to Billings, Mont., 1909; mem. firm Reynolds & Shea, 1918—. Circuit court commr. Branch County, Mich., 1897-1900; city atty., Coldwater, 1898, 99; probate judge Branch County, 1901-08; asso. justice Supreme Court of Mont., Jan. 1, 1921—. Mem. bd. Mont. Wesleyan U. Republican. Methodist. Mason. Home: Helena, Mont. Deceased.

REYNOLDS, Frederick Jesse, banker; b. Jackson, Mich., Aug. 25, 1857; s. Sheldon Clark and Martha A. (Simpson) R.; ed. pub. schs., Toledo, O., and New Haven (Conn.) Institute; m. Ida Louise Stone, Oct. 4, 1882 (died 1915); children—Harold Sheldon, Natalie (Mrs. Roland A. Spitzer), Dorothy (Mrs. Joseph W. Robinson), Kathryn (Mrs. Augustus B. Richardson). Began as clk. in office of Reynolds Bros., grain mchts., Toledo; later admitted to firm; apptd. v.p. and gen. mgr. Toledo & Mich. Belt Ry. Co., 1887, and continued until rd. was absorbed by Mich. Central R.R.; with First Nat. Bank, Toledo, 1889—, successively dir., vice pres., pres., and chmn. of board. Mason. Home: Toledo, O. Died Apr. 1, 1931.

REYNOLDS, George Delachaumette, judge; b. Gettysburg, Pa., Dec. 16, 1841; s. William M. (D.D.) and Anna (Swan) R.; A.B., Ill. State U., 1861, A.M., 1866; enlisted as pvt. in 2d Ill. Light Arty., 1861; mustered out 1866 as lt. col. 6th U.S.C. Artillery; m. Julia, d. Augustus S. and Maria Vogdes, Oct. 10, 1876. Admitted to bar at Hannibal, Mo., 1867; circuit atty., old 15th Circuit, 1868-71; removed to St. Louis, 1871, to Colo., 1874; practiced at Boulder, Colo., until 1877, when returned to St. Louis; judge St. Louis Ct. of Appeals, 1908— (later presiding judge). U.S. atty. for Eastern Dist. of Mo., 1889-93. Author of amendment to U.S. Statutes under which the La. Lottery was excluded from use of the mails, and of that part of the section of U.S. laws which excluded from naturalization persons believing in or practicing polygamy. Episcopalian. Mason. Home: St. Louis, Mo. Died Mar. 18, 1921.

REYNOLDS, George Greenwood, lawyer; b. Amenia, N.Y., Feb. 7, 1821; s. George and Abigail (Pennoyer) R.; A.B., Wesleyan U., Middletown, Connecticut, 1841, LL.D., 1871; m. Harriet Townsend, Oct. 15, 1846 (died 1903). Admitted to bar, 1844; practiced at Milton, 1845-51, Poughkeepsie, 1851-54; removed to Brooklyn, 1854; judge City Ct., Brooklyn, 1860-66, 1872-87; apptd. by gov. of N.Y. to hold Supreme Ct. in Brooklyn, 1881; apptd. by Gov. Hill, 1890, as mem. commn. to revise Judiciary Article of N.Y. State Constn.; retired from practice, 1906. Trustee Brooklyn Trust Co., Metropolitan Casualty Co., Greenwood Cemetery. Trustee Wesleyan U., 1871—, (pres. bd. 1887-1903), Methodist Episcopal Hosp.; mgr. Methodist Missionary Soc. Lay del. Gen. Conf. M.E. Ch., 1872, 76, 80, 84. Republican. Home: Brooklyn, N.Y. Died Jan. 23, 1913.

REYNOLDS, George McClelland, banker; b. Panora, Ia., Jan. 15, 1865; s. Elijah Jackson and Eliza (Anderson) R.; grad. Guthrie County High Sch., 1879; m. Elizabeth Hay, Oct. 15, 1884; 1 son, Earle Hay. Clerk Guthrie County Nat. Bank, 1879-86; in farm loan and real estate mortgage bus., Nev., 1886-88; cashier and mgr. Guthrie County Nat. Bank, 1888-93; cashier, 1893-95, pres. and dir., 1895-97, Des Moines (Ia.) Nat. Bank; cashier, 1897-1902, v.p., 1902-06, pres. and dir., Jan. 1, 1906-Aug. 1, 1910, Continental Nat. Bank, Chicago, consolidated with Commercial Nat. Bank, Aug. 1, 1910, as Continental & Commercial Nat. Bank, of which was pres. and Jan. 1921 was made chmn. of bd.; also chmn. bd. Continental & Commercial Trust & Savings Bank; the Continental & Commercial Nat. Bank consolidated, Dec. 1, 1927, with the Continental & Commercial Trust & Savings Bank as the Continental Nat. Bank and Trust Co. which was merged, Mar. 18, 1929, with Ill. Merchants Trust Co. as Continental Ill. Bank and Trust Co. of which became chmn. exec. com., later chmn. bd.; Class A dir. Fed. Res. Bank of Chicago; dir. Peoples Trust & Savings Bank (Chicago), Union Carbide & Carbon Corp., New York Life Ins. Co., Continental Ins. Co. (New York), The Pullman Company. Chmn. Chicago Clearing House Com., 1922—; pres. Am. Bankers Assn., 1908. Accompanied Am. Monetary Commn. to Europe as adviser, 1908. Pres. Citizens War Bd. of Chicago, 1917-19; became chmn. Nat. Credit Corp., Oct. 1931; apptd. head of Chicago loan agency Reconstruction Finance Corp., Feb. 1932. Republican. Home: Chicago, Ill. Died Feb. 26, 1940.

REYNOLDS, James Bronson, lawyer; b. Kiantone, N.Y., Mar. 17, 1861; s. William T. and Sarah M. (Painter) R.; A.B., Yale, 1884, B.D., 1888; post-grad. work in Paris, and Berlin; fellow sociology, Columbia; student, N.Y. Law Sch., 1900; m. Florence Blanchard Dike, July 16, 1898. As official representative of the College Y.M.C.A. of America visited Great Britain and the European continent, 1889-93, at same time studying the problems of social reform; returned to U.S., 1893, and in 1894 became headworker of the Univ. Settlement, New York; was active worker on Com. of 70, 1893; one of com. of City Club, for campaign of 1897; chmn. exec. com. of Citizens' Union in campaign of 1897; member State Tenement House Commn., apptd. by Governor Roosevelt, 1900; sec. to Mayor Low, 1902-03; spl. adviser to the President on municipal affairs of D.C.; mem. spl. presdl. commn. to investigate the Chicago Stock Yards, 1906; chmn. presdl. commn. to investigate industrial conditions at Panama; asst. dist. atty. N.Y. County, 1910-13; counsel to Am. Social Hygiene Assn., 1913-16. Home: North Haven, Conn. Died Jan. 1, 1924.

REYNOLDS, John Edwin, judge; b. Minden, La., July 3, 1863; s. Andrew Jackson and Margaret (Davidson) R.; prep. edn., Minden (La.) Male Acad.; studied law, U. of Mich.; m. Luda Jackson, Nov. 27, 1895 (died 1908); children—Hardy Jackson, Luda Elizabeth. Admitted to La. bar, 1885, and began practice at Minden, La.; became judge Court of Appeal, 2d Dist., 2d Circuit of La., Dec. 13, 1924. Pres. Reynolds Hotel, Shreveport; mem. firm of Tooke & Reynolds, operators of public utilities in various towns of La. Democrat. Mem. M.E. Ch., S. Mason, Odd Fellow, K.P. Home: Arcadia, La. Deceased.

REYNOLDS, John Hughes, banker; b. Benton, Tenn., Aug. 16, 1846; s. William Barton and Katherine Jane (Hughes) R.; student Emory and Henry Coll., Emory, Va., 1867-68; comml. schs., New York, 1864 and 1867; m. Mary Turnley, July 29, 1873. Member Cross & Reynolds, mfrs., Cleveland, Tenn., 1868-73; teller Cleveland (Tenn.) Nat. Bank, 1873, 74; cashier Cleveland Exchange & Deposit Bank, 1875-77; pres. 1st Nat. Bank, Rome, Ga., 1877-1920, chmn. bd. dir., 1920—. Dir. Chamber Commerce U.S.A., and trustee Cumberland Presbyn. Pub. House (Nashville, Tenn.), Rome Pub. Schs. Pres. Ga. Bankers' Assn., 1906-07. Home: Rome, Ga. Deceased.

REYNOLDS, John Merriman, congressman; b. Lancaster County, Pa.; s. P. H. and Ann (Barnett) R.; grad. First Pa. State Normal Sch.; A.M., Columbian (now George Washington) U.; m. Ella Hartley, June 13, 1877. Admitted to bar, 1870, and in practice at Bedford, 1870—; also interested in banking and other industries. Mem. Pa. Ho. of Rep., 1873-74; pros. atty. Bedford County, 1875-78; mem. bd. commrs. to select site and build asylum for chronic insane at Wernersville, Pa., 1892; del. Dem. Nat. convs., 1888, 92; asst. sec. of the Interior, 1893-97. Republican, 1896—; mem. 59th to 61st Congresses (1905-11), 19th Pa. Dist. Address: Bedford, Pa. Died Sept. 14, 1933.

REYNOLDS, John Parker; b. Lebanon, O., Mar. 1, 1820; s. John P. and Laura Patience (Wilson) R.; A.B., Miami U., 1838, later A.M.; LL.B., Cincinnati Coll. of Law, 1840; m. Eliza Anne Bebb, Nov. 3, 1842. Admitted to bar, 1841; practiced at Hamilton, 1841-49; engaged in stock farming in Ill., 1849-60; editor National Live Stock Journal, 1869-72. Sec. Ill. State Agrl. Soc., 1860-71; pres. State Bd. of Agr., 1873-74; pres. Ill. State Hort. Soc., 1867; sec. Inter-State Industrial Expn., Chicago, 1873-91; Ill. commr. to Paris Expn., 1867; pres. Ill. Commn. to Centennial Expn., Phila., 1876; pres. Ill. State Sanitary Commn., 1862-65; chief state insp. of grain, Ill., 1877-81; dir.-in-chief Ill. World's Columbian Fair Commn., Chicago, 1891-93. Republican. Home: Chicago, Ill. Died Mar. 27, 1912.

REYNOLDS, Joseph B., life ins. exec.; b. Saline Co., Ill., Mar. 21, 1871; s. Joseph and Rosa Anne (Lawrence) R.; ed. Hayward Coll., Fairfield, Ill., and Southern Ill. State Normal U., Carbondale; m. Pearl Gibbons, Jan. 10, 1894; 1 dau., Angeline (Mrs. W. E. Bixby). Teacher pub. schs. and dep. county clk., Butler County, Mo., 1888-94; city clk., Poplar Bluff, Mo., 1894-99; actuary, Mo. State Ins. Dept., 1900-04; pres. Kansas City Life Ins. Co., 1904—. Trustee William Jewell Coll., Liberty, Mo. Democrat. Baptist. Home: Kansas City, Mo. Died Feb. 23, 1937.

REYNOLDS, Joseph Jones, maj. gen. vols., col. U.S.A., retired June 1877; b. Flemingsburg, Ky., Jan. 4, 1822; grad. West Point, 1843; served in Texas, 1845-46; 1st lt., 1847; asst. prof. natural philosophy West Point, 1849-56; resigned from army; prof. mechanics and engring. Washington U., St. Louis, 1856-60; col. 10th Ind. vols., April, and brig. gen. vols., May 1861; served in Army of Cumberland, 1862-63; maj. gen. vols., Nov. 1862; chief of staff, Army of Cumberland; was at Chickamauga and Mission Ridge; in command Dept. of Ark., Nov. 1864 to April 1866; mustered out volunteer service, Sept. 1866; col., U.S.A., July 1866; bvtd. brig. gen. and maj. gen., 1867; commanded 5th Mil. Dist. (La. and Texas), 1867-72; elected U.S. senator from Texas, 1871, but declined; commanded 3d cav. in the Dept. of the Platte, 1872-76; m. Mary E., dau. William P. Bainbridge, 4th U.S. arty., Dec. 3, 1846. Address: Washington, D.C. Died 1899.

REYNOLDS, Joseph Smith, lawyer; b. New Lenox, Ill., Dec. 3, 1839; s. Isaac N. and Rue Ann (Holderman) R.; grad. Chicago High Sch. and Northwestern U., 1866; enlisted Co. F, 64th Ill. Inf. (Yates' Sharpshooters), Oct. 19, 1861; promoted 2d lt., Dec. 31, 1861; 1st lt., Sept. 2, 1862; capt., Aug. 14, 1863; maj., Nov. 1, 1864; lt. col., May 8, 1865; bvt. col. and brig. gen., July 11, 1865; took part in 17 battles and many skirmishes; wounded at Corinth; had sword shot from hand at Resaca; comd. regt. on Sherman's March to the Sea and through the Carolinas; led column that captured Confed. position to the left of Bentonsville, N.C., Mar. 21, 1865; took part in grand review, Washington, June 1865; m. Mattie A. Cary, Jan. 31, 1877 (died 1890). Admitted to bar, 1866; mem. Ill. Ho. of Rep., 1866-70, Senate, 1872-74; one of founders Chicago park system; mem. Chicago Bd. of Edn., 1870-74; commr. from Ill. to Vienna Expn., 1873; commr. to establish State Sch. for Feeble-Minded Children, 1875. Senior vice-comdr.-in-chief G.A.R. of U.S., 1875-76; comdr. Ill. G.A.R., 1877; 1st v.p. Soc. Army of the Tennessee, 1879. Home: Pasadena, Calif. Died 1911.

REYNOLDS, Myra, educator; b. Troupsburg, N.Y.; d. Newel Lent and Emily Knox R.; A.B., Vassar, 1880, A.M., 1892; fellow U. of Chicago, 1892-94, Ph.D., 1895. Instr. English, Wells Coll., Aurora, N.Y., 1880-82; instr. English lit., Vassar Coll., 1885-92; asst. in English, 1894-95, instr., 1895-97, asst. prof., 1897-1902, asso. prof., 1903-11, prof., 1911—, U. of Chicago. Author: The Treatment of Nature in English Poetry from Pope to Wordsworth, 1896. Compiler: Selections from the Poetry of Robert Browning, 1909; The Poetry of Lady Winchelsea, 1903. Address: Chicago, Ill. Died Aug. 19, 1936.

REYNOLDS, Myron Herbert, veterinarian; b. Wheaton, Ill., Nov. 5, 1865; s. Gardner W. and Mary A. (Budd) R.; Ia. State Coll. Agr. and Mechanic Arts, B.S., 1886, D.V.M., 1889; M.D., Ia. Coll. Phys. and Surg., 1891; Ph.G., Ia. Coll. of Pharmacy, 1891; m. Eva M. Kuhn, 1893 (dec.); m. 2d, May I. Shaw, Mar. 31, 1897; children—Gardner Shaw, Mary Janet, Robert Thomas, Margaret Shaw. Prof. vet. medicine, 1893-1917, prof. vet. medicine and in charge vet. sanitation, 1917—, Agrl. Coll. and Expt. Sta., U. of Minn. Organizer 1903, and mem. Minn. State Live Stock Sanitary Bd.; for many yrs. mem. Minn. State Vet. Examining Bd.; mem. Minn. Stallion Registration Bd., 1907—. Republican. Internat. Commission on Control of Bovine Tuberculosis. Mason. Author: Veterinary Studies for Agricultural Students, 1921. Contbr. to Microbiology (edited by C. E. Marshall), 1921; also many pamphlets, bulls. and pub. addresses on tech. subjects, especially those relating to live stock sanitation. Home: St. Paul, Minn. Died Jan. 15, 1929.

REYNOLDS, Powell Benton, univ. prof.; b. Patrick County, Va., Jan. 9, 1841; s. James B. and Roxana (Shelor) R.; Richmond Coll., 1866-70; A.M., W.Va. U., 1887; D.D., Richmond Coll., 1890; m. Virginia H. Woolwine, 1868; m. 2d, Marietta W. Love, 1874. Ordained Bapt. ministry, 1866; pres. Shelton Coll., 1872-84, Buckner Coll., 1884-85; prof. English, 1885-89, v.p. and prof. metaphysics, 1889-93, acting pres., 1893-95, prof. metaphysics and polit. science, 1895-97, prof. philosophy, 1897-1901, chaplain and prof. economics and sociology, 1901-11, W.Va. U.; retired. Home: Morgantown, W.Va. Died Dec. 29, 1914.

REYNOLDS, Robert J., gov. Del.; b. Smyrna, Kent County, Del., Mar. 17, 1838; ed. Fairfield, N.Y.; settled as farmer and fruit grower nr. Petersburg, Del.; mem. gen. assembly, 1869; State treas., 1879-83; chmn. Dem. State Com., 1883-87; gov., 1891-95. Address: Petersburg, Del. Died 1909.

REYNOLDS, Virginia Mrs., artist; b. Chicago, 1866; pupil of Carl Marr and of Heterick, Munich and Lasar, in Paris. Awards: 1st honorable mention, Miniature Exhbn., New York, 1896; exhibited at Paris Expn., 1900. Specialty, miniatures; m. W. J. Reynolds, 1893. Address: Chicago, Ill. Died 1903.

RHEA, Hortense (Mme. Rhea), actress; b. Brussels, Belgium; studied Paris Conservatoire under Beauvallet; for 10 years played in France; came to U.S., 1881, making first appearance in Boston in title rôle of "Adrienne Lecouvreur." Later took star rôles in numerous dramas and tragedies. Died 1899.

RHEAD, Louis John, artist; b. Etruria, Eng., 1857; s. George Woolliscroft and Fanny Moreton (Colley) R.; nat. scholar Art Training Sch., South Kensington, London; m. Catharine Anne Bogart Yates, 1884. Came to U.S., 1883, to be art mgr. for D. Appleton & Co. Painter in oil and water colors, exhibiting in Am. and European galleries. Gold medal, Boston, 1895, for artistic posters; gold medal, St. Louis Expn., 1904. Part time engaged in illustrating Louis Rhead series of juvenile classics (Swiss Family, Guilliver, Andersen, Grimm, etc.); other time newspaper and mag. writing on, and making, hand-made lures and flies for game fishing. Author: Book of Fish and Fishing, 1908; American Trout Stream Insects, 1916; Fisherman's Lures, 1920. Home: Amityville, N.Y. Died July 29, 1926.

RHEES, Rush, univ. pres.; b. Chicago, Ill., Feb. 8, 1860; s. John Evans and Annie (McCutchen) R.; A.B., Amherst, 1883, A.M., 1897; grad. Hartford Theological Sem., 1888; LL.D., Amherst Coll., 1900, McMaster U., Hamilton, Ont., Can., 1930, U. of Toronto, 1933; D.D., Colgate U., 1901; m. Harriet Chapin, d. L. Clark Seelye, July 6, 1899; children—Morgan John, Henrietta S., Rush, Jr. Walker instr. mathematics, Amherst, 1883-85; ordained Bapt. ministry, 1889; pastor Middle St. Ch., Portsmouth, N.H., 1889-92; asso. prof. N.T. interpretation, 1892-94, prof., 1894-1900, Newton Theol. Instn.; pres. U. of Rochester, 1900-35, pres. emeritus, 1935—. Served as trustee U. of Rochester, 1900—. Dir. Lincoln Alliance Bank of Rochester, Buffalo, Rochester and Pittsburgh Ry., Eastman Kodak Co. Trustee Mechanics Inst.; mem. bd. Bur. of Municipal Research (Rochester), Reynolds Library (Rochester); mem. exec. com., Rochester Community Chest. Author: The Life of Jesus of Nazareth, a Study, 1900; St. Paul's Experience as a Factor in His Theology, 1896. Home: Rochester, N.Y. Died Jan. 5, 1939.

RHEES, William Jones, bibliographer; b. Phila., Mar. 13, 1830; grad. Central High Sch., 1847; had charge social statistics, 7th Census, 1850-52; sec. central exec. com. in Washington of London World's Fair, 1851; became chief clerk Smithsonian Instn., 1852, and had gen. charge of the Smithsonian publications. Author: Guide to the Smithsonian Institution and National Museum; List of Publications of the Smithsonian Institution; Manual of Public Schools of Washington; The Smithsonian Institution: Documents Relative to Its Origin and History; James Smithson and His Bequest; Catalogue of Publications of the Smithsonian Institution. Editor: The Scientific Writings of James Smithson; etc. Trustee public schools 8 yrs.; one of founders and pres. Y.M.C.A.; one of founders Sons Am. Revolution. Home: Washington, D.C. Died 1907.

RHEINHARDT, Rudolph H. See George Hempl.

RHETT, Robert Goodwyn, financier; b. Columbia, S.C., Mar. 25, 1862; s. Albert Moore and Martha (Goodwyn) R.; M.A., U. of Va., 1883, LL.B., 1884; LL.D., U. of South Carolina, 1929; m. Helen Smith, Nov. 15, 1888 (died 1904); children—Mrs. Helen Simons, Mrs. Margaret Taylor, Robert Goodwyn; m. 2d, Blanche Salley, Aug. 8, 1906; children—Blanche Salley Billing, Albert Moore. Admitted to S.C. bar, 1884, and practiced at Charleston; mem. Trenholm & Rhett, later Trenholm, Rhett, Miller & Whaley; pres. S.C. Loan & Trust Co., 1896-1900; pres. Peoples Nat. Bank, 1899-1926; pres. Peoples-First Nat. Bank, 1926-28, chmn. bd., 1928-30; became chmn. bd. Peoples State Bank of S.C. (successors to former), 1930; retired. Mayor of Charleston, 1904-12. Pres. League Am. Municipalities, 1905-06; pres. Chamber of Commerce of Charleston, 1915-16; pres. Chamber of Commerce of U.S., 1916-18; chmn. State Highway Dept., 1920-26. Democrat. Home: Charleston, S.C. Died Apr. 16, 1939.

RHIND, J(ohn) Massey, sculptor; b. Edinburgh, Scotland, 1858; s. John (R.S.A., sculptor) and Catherine (Birnie) R.; ed. Scotch Acad., and Royal Acad., London, and under Dalau in Paris; m. Agnes M. Barclay, 1889. Came to U.S., 1889, and established as sculptor in New York. Presbyn. Republican. Mem. St. Andrew's Soc. Home: New York, N.Y. Died Oct. 22, 1936.

RHINE, Abraham Benedict, rabbi; b. Shavli, Lithuania, Sept. 6, 1877; s. Mayer and Bella (Appel) R.; brought to U.S., 1889; A.B., U. of Cincinnati, 1901; Rabbi, Hebrew Union Coll., Cincinnati, 1902, D.D., 1910; m. Annette Wiener, June 11, 1905 (died 1934); 1 dau., Belle Frances (Mrs. William H. Sahud). Rabbi of Congregation House of Israel, Hot Springs, Ark., 1902—. Exec. sec., trustee, and one of founders of Leo N. Levi Memorial Hosp.; mem. Bd. of Edn., 1925—, pres., 1931-33, 1938-39; chmn. Garland Co. Unemployment Com., 1932-34; trustee Ark. Sch. for Girls, 1922-32; founder and hon. pres. Ark. Jewish Assembly; founder Ark. State Assn. of Sch. Bds. (pres. 1934-39; hon. pres.; mem. Governor's Advisory Committee on Education, 1940); dir. Nat. Jewish Hosp., Denver, Colo. Mem. Central Conf. of Am. Rabbis, Am. Acad. for Jewish Research. Mason, B'nai B'rith. Translated from German "Graetz's Popular History of the Jews" (5 vols.), 1919, and from the Hebrew Old Testament "The Essence of the Bible," 1930; contbr. to Jewish Ency. Author: Leon Gordon, 1910; Tales from the Midrash, 1911. Home: Hot Springs, Ark. Died Aug. 8, 1941.

RHINELANDER, Philip Mercer, clergyman; b. Newport, R.I., 1869; s. Frederic William and Frances Davenport (Skinner) R.; A.B., Harvard, 1891; A.B., U. of Oxford, Eng., 1896, A.M., 1900; D.D., Episcopal Theol. Sch., Cambridge, Mass., 1911, Columbia, 1912; Berkeley Div. Sch., 1912; LL.D., U. Pa., 1912; D.C.L., Phila. Div. Sch., 1912; m. Helen M. Hamilton, May 9, 1905; children—Frederic William, Philip Hamilton, Laurens Hamilton. Deacon, 1896, priest, 1897, P.E. Ch.; in charge St. Mark's Ch., Chapel of Good Shepherd and St. Alban's Parish, Washington, 1896-1903; prof. ecclesiastical history, homiletics, pastoral theology and Christian evidences, Berkeley Div. Sch., Middletown, Conn., 1903-07; prof. history of religion and missions, Episcopal Theol. Sch., Cambridge, Mass., 1907-11; consecrated coadjutor bishop of Pa., Oct. 28, 1911; became bishop of the diocese, Nov. 1911, resigned on account ill health, Nov. 1923; trustee of Washington Cathedral, 1923; warden Coll. of Preachers, Washington Cathedral, 1925-37. Author: The Faith of the Cross; Think Out Your Faith; The Things Most Surely Believed; Religion in War-Time; The Gospel of the Kingdom. Address: Washington, D.C. Died Sept. 21, 1939.

RHINOCK, Joseph Lafayette, congressman; b. Owenton, Owen County, Ky., Jan. 4, 1863; s. Joseph and Eliza A. (Short) R.; ed. in pub. schs. of Covington, Ky.; m. Emma McKain, Nov. 1, 1883. Engaged in business as oil refiner from 1890. Pres. Covington Pub. Library Bd.; mem. council of Covington, 2 terms; mayor of Covington, 7 yrs.; mem. 59th to 61st Congresses (1905-11), 6th Ky. Dist. First organizer and pres. Jefferson Club, of Covington, largest political club in Ky. Democrat. V.p. Loew's Theatrical Enterprises, Joseph, Inc.; dir. Shubert Cox Theatres Co., United Theatres Co., both of Cincinnati. Address: New York, N.Y. Died Sept. 20, 1926.

RHOADES, Cornelia Harsen (Nina Rhoades), author; b. N.Y. City, Dec. 1, 1863; d. John Harsen and Annie G. (Wheelwright) R. When only a few months old had serious illness, which ultimately caused total loss of sight; never attended any school for the blind, but was educated at home; favorite occupations always reading and writing; reads all the prints in use for the blind and uses the typewriter with ease. Author: Polly's Predicament, 1906; Little Miss Rosamund, 1906; Priscilla, of the Doll Shop, 1907; Brave Little Peggy; Dorothy Brown; The Other Sylvia; Menzie's Merry Christmas; Victorine's Book; Little Queen Esther; The Girl from Arizona; Making Mary Lizzie Happy; A Real Cinderella, 1915; Independence of Nan, 1916; Plucky Little Patsy, 1917; The Adventures of Joan, 1924. Home: New York, N.Y. Died Nov. 28, 1940.

RHOADES, John Harsen, banker; b. New York, N.Y., Oct. 26, 1838; s. Lyman and Cornelia Rachel R.; private school edn.; m. Annie G. Wheelwright, Oct. 29, 1862. Pres. and trustee Greenwich Savings Bank; dir. Bank of America, Greenwich Bank, Woodbridge Co., Lincoln Trust Co., Lawyers' Title Ins. Co.; trustee U.S. Trust Co. Home: New York, N.Y. Died 1906.

RHOADES, Lewis Addison, univ. prof.; b. Skaneateles, N.Y., Dec. 19, 1860; s. Lewis H. and Rachel Parsons (Williams) R.; A.B., U. of Mich., 1884, A.M., 1886; Ph.D., U. of Göttingen, 1892; m. Anna Evans Miner, Sept. 14, 1887. Instr. Ann Arbor High Sch., 1886-88; instr. German, U. of Mich., 1888-90; prof. German, U. of Ill., 1896-1903; same, Ohio State U., 1903—. Editor (with introductions and notes): Schiller's Maria Stuart, 1893; Goethe's Iphigenie auf Tauris, 1896; Freytag's Aus dem Jahrhundert des grossen Krieges, 1898; Schiller's Jungfrau von Orleans, 1901; Biblische Geschichten (selected and annotated), 1902; Schiller's Poems and Ballads, 1908. Joint Author: Becker-Rhoades, Elements of German, 1909. Wrote: Hölty's Verhältniss zur Englischen Litteratur (doctor's thesis), 1893, Göttingen. Address: Columbus, Ohio. Died 1910.

RHOADES, Nelson Osgood, consulting engr., capitalist; b. Madison, Wis., June 2, 1869; s. Nelson Carrier and Lucy Eunice (Osgood) R.; ed. pub. schs. and under pvt. instructors. Cons. engr. in U.S., Alaska, Mexico, India and Egypt; actively interested in Mexico, 1890—, and retained by Mexican Govt. to build railroads, survey pub. lands, make municipal improvements; owner large tracts of land in Mexico; pres. Oso Sugar Co., Navito Sugar Co.; gen. mgr. Chapultepec Heights Co., mem. firm Garfield & Rhoades, Mexican counsellors and fiscal agts. Editor Colonial Families of the U.S. Mason. Died Dec. 4, 1928.

RHOADES, William Caldwell Plunkett, clergyman; b. Elbridge, N.Y., Apr. 6, 1845; s. Hon. John D. R.; A.B., valedictorian, Williams, 1866; grad. Rochester Theol. Sem., 1872; D.D., Morgan Park Theological Sem. [now U. of Chicago], 1884; D.D., Williams College, Mass., 1911; m. Anne E. Schreuder, Feb. 16, 1892. Ordained Bapt. ministry, 1874; pastor Granville, O., 1874-85, Marcy Av. Ch., Brooklyn, 1885-1916, emeritus, 1916—. Trustee Denison U., 1875-85, Brooklyn Bapt. Ch. Extension Soc., Rochester Theol. Sem., Vassar Coll. Chaplain 13th Regt. Heavy Arty. N.G.N.Y. Address: Brooklyn, N.Y. Died Nov. 5, 1923.

RHODES, Bradford, banker; b. in Beaver County, Pa., Feb. 25, 1845; s. William and Mary Maria (Baird) R.; grad. Beaver Acad.; m. Caroline A. Fuller, Feb. 27, 1878. Prin. Darlington Acad., Pa.; journalist in New York, 1872; established Rhodes' Journal of Banking, 1877, and consolidated with Bankers' Magazine (which he purchased), 1895; sold out, 1903; mem. N.Y. Legislature, 1888-90; secured passage anti-bucket-shop law and several important amendments to banking laws of the state; twice mem. exec. council Am. Bankers' Assn.; founder and first pres. 1st Nat. Bank, Mamaroneck; founder, trustee Union Savings Bank of Westchester County; pres. Quaker Ridge Estates, Mamaroneck, N.Y. Home: Mamaroneck, N.Y. Died Apr. 15, 1924.

RHODES, Eugene Manlove, author; b. Tecumseh, Neb., Jan. 19, 1869; s. Hinman and Julia (Manlove) R.; student U. of Pacific, San José, Calif., 1889-90; m. Mary Louise Davison Purple, Aug. 9, 1899; children—Alan Hinman, Barbara Antoinette (dec.). Cowboy in New Mexico for 25 yrs. Began writing for publication, 1906. Author: Good Men and True, 1911; Bransford in Arcadia, 1913; The Desire of the Moth, 1916; West Is West, 1917; Stepsons of Light, 1921; Say Now Shibboleth, 1921; Copper Streak Trail, 1922; Once in the Saddle, 1927. Home: Pacific Beach, Calif. Died June 27, 1935.

RHODES, Frederick Leland, elec. engr.; b. Boston, Mass., Oct. 25, 1870; s. John Brewer and Annie Williams (Leland) R.; S.B. in E.E., Mass. Inst. Tech., 1892; m. Effie Chandler, 1895; children—Leland Chandler, Eleanor Ann. Began with Am. Bell Telephone Co., 1892, continuing with Am. Telegraph and Telephone Co.; outside plant development engr., 1919-32; known for important work in connection with standardization of materials, apparatus and practices in underground and overhead wire systems. Fellow Am. Inst. E.E. (past chmn. bd. examiners, etc.). Republican. Unitarian. Author: Beginnings of Telephony, 1929. Contbr. to Nelson's Loose Leaf Ency., Ency. Americana and Supplement to Britannica. Home: Short Hills, N.J. Died Mar. 18, 1933.

RHODES, George Pearson, corp. official; b. New Castle, Pa., Mar. 21, 1871; s. James and Elizabeth (Peebles) R.; ed. pub. schs.; m. Ellen Bower, Nov. 26, 1895; children—John Bower, Roberta Peebles, George Pearson. With Pa. Tube Works, 1890-1900; organizer, with brother, Pa. Casting & Machine Works, 1900, v.p. and treas., 1900-24; sec. and treas. Nat. Car Wheel Co., 1905-21, pres., 1922-24; pres. Castalia Portland Cement Co., 1923—; v.p. Colonial Steel Co., 1920-27, later pres. and dir.; dir. Keystone Nat. Bank, Am. Window Glass Co., Dollar Savings Bank, Pittsburgh Steel Co., Fidelity Trust Co., Vanadium-Alloys Steel Co. Pres. St. Barnabas Free Home; trustee St. Margaret's Memorial Hosp., Calvary P.E. Ch. Republican. Mason. Home: Pittsburgh, Pa. Died Dec. 12, 1940.

RHODES, Harrison (Garfield), author; b. Cleveland, O., June 2, 1871; s. James Harrison and Adelaide Maria (Robbins) R.; A.B., Harvard, 1893; unmarried. With Stone & Kimball, pubs., Chicago (later H. S. Stone & Co.), 1894-98; bus. agt. Am. mags. and pub. houses, London, 1898-1901. Author: The Lady and the Ladder, 1906; Charles Edward, 1907; The Flight to Eden, 1907; Guide Book to Florida (with Mary Wolf Dumont); In Vacation America, 1915; American Towns and People, 1920; High Life, 1920; A Giftbook for My Mother, 1922. Plays: (with Anthony Hope) Captain Dieppe; (with Thomas A. Wise) A Gentleman from Mississippi; An Old New Yorker (with latter); Modern Marriage; The Whirl of Society; Ruggles of Red Gap, 1915; The Willow Tree (with Benrimo), prod. New York, Mar. 1917, London, Oct. 1917; Mr. Barnum (with Thomas A. Wise), prod. New York, Sept. 1918; Her Friend the King (with A. E. Thomas), 1922. Home: New York, N.Y. Died Sept. 20, 1929.

RHODES, James Ford, author; b. Cleveland, O., May 1, 1848; s. Daniel Pomeroy and Sophia (Lord) R.; ed. New York U., U. of Chicago, was not grad.; LL.D., Western Reserve U., 1893, Harvard, 1901, Yale, 1901, U. of Wis., 1904, New York U., 1908, Princeton, 1912, U. of Calif., 1916; Litt.D., Kenyon, 1903, Brown, 1914, Oxford, Eng., 1909; m. Ann Card, Jan. 4, 1872. Fellow Am. Acad. Arts and Sciences. Mem. Am. Acad. Arts and Letters. Awarded Loubat prize, Berlin Acad. of Science, 1901; gold medal, Nat. Inst. Arts and Letters, 1910; Harvard Phi Beta Kappa orator, 1915; awarded Pulitzer Prize, Columbia U., 1918. Author: History of the United States from the Compromise of 1850 (vols. I-VII, 1850-77, pub. 1893-1906); Historical Essays, 1909; Lectures on the American Civil War delivered at Oxford, 1913; History of the Civil War, 1 vol., 1917; History of the United States from Hayes to McKinley, 1877-1896, 1919; The McKinley and Roosevelt Administrations, 1897-1909, 1922. Address: Boston, Mass. Died Jan. 22, 1927.

RHODES, Jeremiah, asst. supt. Tex. schs.; b. Point Pleasant, O., Mar. 1, 1862; s. William Henry and Sarah (Schriver) R.; student Leland Stanford U., 1892-93; A.B., Indiana U., 1894; A.M., Harvard, 1898; Ph.D., Milton Coll., 1913; grad. work Columbia, 1898-99, also at U. of Chicago; m. Cora Alice Ingels, 1901; children—Elizabeth (dec.), Sarah (dec.), Jeremiah. Rural sch. teacher, high sch. prin., later supt. of city schs., 1877-1901; prof. of polit. science and European history, Kan. State Normal Sch., 1901-09; prin. N.H. State Normal Sch., 1909-11; supt. of city schs., Pasadena, Calif., 1911-19, San Antonio, Tex., 1920-25; travel, study and teaching, 1925-33; 1st asst. supt. Tex. State Dept. of Edn., 1933—. Presbyterian. Mason. Home: San Antonio, Tex. Died Jan. 6, 1938.

RHODES, Rufus Napoleon, newspaper editor; b. Pascagoula, Miss., June 5, 1856; s. Rufus Randolph and Martha (Fisher) R.; ed. in high sch., acad., Stewart Coll., and at Southwestern Presbyn. U., Clarksville, Tenn., to 1873; LL.D., U. of Ala., 1906; m. Margaret Smith, June 27, 1882. Read law under Hon. James E. Bailey, Clarksville; city atty., Clarksville, 1877-81; mem. Tenn. legislature, 1881-82; practiced in Chicago, 1883-87; founded Birmingham News, 1888, and became mgr. and editor. 2d v.p. Associated Press; del.-at-large from Ala., Nat. Dem. convs., 1892, 1904. Brig. gen. Ala. N.G. Episcopalian. Address: Birmingham, Ala. Died 1910.

RHODES, Stephen Holbrook, insurance; b. Franklin, Mass., Nov. 7, 1825; s. Stephen and Betsey (Bird) R.; pub. sch. edn.; m. Miss E. M. Godfrey, Nov. 27, 1847. Mayor, Taunton, Mass., 3 yrs.; mem. Mass. senate, 1870-71; deputy ins. commr. Mass., 1872-74; commr., 1874-79; pres. John Hancock Mut. Life Ins. Co., 1879—. Home: Brookline, Mass. Died 1909.

RIALE, Franklin Neiman, clergyman; b. Tipton, Ia., Feb. 23, 1859; s. Rev. Joshua and Lydia Jane (Boyd) R.; A.B., U. of Wooster, O., 1881, A.M., 1884, Ph.D., 1890; grad. Western Theol. Sem., Pittsburgh, 1886; Williams fellow, Harvard, 1887-88, D.D., Coe Coll., 1907; m. Alice Emma Durstine, Dec. 28, 1887; 1 dau., Margaret Alice. Ordained Presbyn. ministry, 1887; pastor Independence, Ia., 1888-94, Glenville (Cleveland, O.), 1896-1904, Tenth Ch., Chicago, 1904-08, Grace Ch., St. Louis, Mo., 1908-12, Clifton Ch., Cincinnati, O., 1913-18; mem. Presbyn. Gen. Bd. of Christian Edn., New York, 1919-24; asso. sec. Council of Ch. Bds. of Edn., New York, 1924-25; field rep. Bd. of Nat. Missions, Presbyterian Church, U.S.A., 1925-26. Republican. Author: The Sinless, Sickless, Deathless Life; The Divine Antidote to Sin, Sickness and Death; Deathless Life—The Greatest Easter Message of the World; The Creed of Jesus; The Healing Ministry of Jesus; Our Death "Complex" and Death Conqueror; The Soul's Triumphant Quest for God; Pentecost and Spiritual Healing. Lecturer. Home: Wooster, O. Died Oct. 27, 1935.

RIANO y GAYANGOS, Don Juan, diplomat; b. Madrid, Spain, Mar. 24, 1865; m. Alice F. Ward, Jan. 25, 1905. Apptd. chamberlain to King of Spain; A.E. and P. from Spain to U.S., Dec. 4, 1914—. Address: Washington, D.C. Died Nov. 18, 1939.

RICARD, Jerome Sixtus, astronomer; b. Plaisians, Drome, France, Jan. 21, 1850; s. Leger and Marianne (Eyssartel) R.; ed. high sch., Turin, Italy; came to America, 1873; student Woodstock Coll., Md.; joined Soc. of Jesus, 1872; Ph.D., U. of Santa Clara, Calif., 1887. Steadily observed and studied sunspots and faculæ, 1900-23, and discovered a method of using them in forecasting the weather long in advance. Published a daily forecast for Santa Clara County; a monthly long range weather forecast for the U.S.,

"The Sunspot"; also occasional seismographic record. Trustee U. of Santa Clara. Democrat. Contbr. to Popular Astronomy (mag.). Home: Santa Clara, Calif. Died Dec. 8, 1930.

RICE, Albert E., banker; b. in Norway, 1847; came to America, 1860; ed. pub. schs., Wis.; m. Sophia L. Brattlund, 1877. Served as pvt. 15th Wis. Inf., Civil War. Mem. Minn. Ho. of Rep., from Minneapolis, 1870, Senate, 1874-86; lt. gov. of Minn., 1886-91; mem. bd. of regents, U. of Minn., 1898—. Began in banking business at Willmar, Minn., 1882; pres. Bank of Willmar, Bank of Svea. Republican. Lutheran. Mason. Address: Willmar, Minn. Died Sept. 1921.

RICE, Alice Caldwell Hegan (Mrs. Cale Young Rice), author; b. Shelbyville, Ky., Jan. 11, 1870; d. Samuel Watson and Sallie Caldwell Hegan; ed. pvt. schs.; hon. Litt.D. from Rollins Coll., Fla., 1928; Litt.D., U. of Louisville, 1937; m. Cale Young Rice, Dec. 18, 1902. Interested in philanthropic work and was one of founders of Cabbage Patch Settlement House, Louisville. Author: Mrs. Wiggs of the Cabbage Patch, 1901; Lovely Mary, 1903; Sandy, 1905; Captain June, 1907; Mr. Opp, 1909; A Romance of Billy Goat Hill, 1912; The Honorable Percival; Cavalry Alley; Miss Mink's Soldier and Other Stories, 1918; Quinn, 1921; Turn About Tales (with husband), 1921; Winners and Losers (with husband), 1925; The Buffer, 1929; Mr. Pete & Co., 1933; The Lark Legacy, 1935; Passionate Follies (with husband), 1936; My Pillow Book, 1937; Our Ernie, 1939; The Inky Way, 1940; The Happiness Road, 1942. Home: Louisville, Ky. Died Feb. 10, 1942.

RICE, Arthur Wallace, architect; b. Roxbury, Mass., July 18, 1869; s. George Woods and Adelaide (Walker) R.; prep. edn., Roxbury (Mass.) Latin Sch.; B.S., Mass. Inst. Tech., 1891; m. Martha Davis Brewer, Oct. 3, 1911; children—Adelaide, Martha, Arthur Wallace. Began practice at Boston, 1896; mem. firm Parker, Thomas and Rice, 1907—; firm architects for R. H. Stearns Bldg., John Hancock Bldg., Boston Chamber of Commerce, Boston Consolidated Gas Co. Bldg., Boston Five Cents Savings Bank, United Shoe Machinery Bldg. Trustee Sailors' Snug Harbor. Republican. Unitarian. Home: Milton, Mass. Died Mar. 25, 1938.

RICE, Benjamin Franklin, lawyer; b. Washington, D.C., Jan. 9, 1875; s. Hon. Benjamin Franklin (U.S. senator from Ark.) and Nancy (Riddell) R.; LL.B., U. of W.Va., 1897; m. Lucile, d. James Thomas Hoblit, Oct. 1918. In service U.S. Govt., 1897-1901; began practice at Lawton, Okla., 1901; removed to Tulsa, 1904; mem. Rice & Lyons, 1907—; dir. First Nat. Bank, Title Guaranty and Trust Co. (Tulsa). Republican. Elk. Wrote: (with Thomas D. Lyons) The Law of Oil and Gas; The Oil Operator in Oklahoma; Schools and School Districts in Cities of the First Class. Home: Tulsa, Okla. Died July 27, 1924.

RICE, Calvin Winsor, engr.; b. Winchester, Mass., Nov. 4, 1868; s. Edward Hyde and Lucy J. (Staples) R.; S.B., Mass. Inst. Tech., 1890; Dr. Engineering, Tech. Hochschule, Darmstadt; m. Ellen M. Weibezahn, Aug. 6, 1904; children—Edward Winslow, Marjorie C. With Thomson-Houston Electric Co., 1889-93, and with its successor, General Electric Co., working up to the position of asst. engr. of the power and mining dept., until 1895 when he was apptd. local engr. at Cincinnati for same co.; elec. supt. Silver Lake Mines, Colo., 1895-96; later cons. engr. Anaconda Copper Mining Co.; elec. engr. Kings Co. Electric Light & Power Co., Brooklyn, 1898, and soon after elec. engr. Consolidated Telegraph & Elec. Subway Co., owning and operating the high-tension subways of New York; also chief of meter and testing dept. New York Edison Co.; 2d v.p. and sales mgr. Nernst Lamp Co., 1903; consulting engr. Gen. Electric Co., 1904-06. Mem. Jury of Awards, San Francisco Expn., 1915. Sec. Am. Soc. M.E., 1906; sec. and mem. bd. trustees New York Mus. of Science and Industry; mem. Corp. of Mass. Inst. of Tech.; mem. Am. Com., World Power Conf.; nat. counselor Purdue Research Foundation. Lt. col. O.R.C. Knight Cross Order of the White Lion (Czechoslovakia). Awarded medal of honor from Verein deutscher Ingenieure, presented at its 50th anniversary, Cologne, 1931, "in appreciation of services to technical-scientific achievement, particularly in promoting mutual internat. interests of engrs. of entire world." Home: Montclair, N.J. Died Oct. 2, 1934.

RICE, Charles Edmund, judge; b. Fairfield, Herkimer County, N.Y., Sept. 15, 1846; s. Thomas Arnold and Vienna (Carr) R.; A.B., Hamilton, 1867; LL.B., Albany Law Sch., 1869; LL.D., Lafayette Coll., 1895, U. of Pa., 1908; m. Maria Mills Fuller, Dec. 18, 1873. Admitted to bar, 1869, and practiced at Wilkes-Barré. Dist. atty. Luzerne County, Pa., 1877-79; pres. judge 11th Jud. Dist., 1879-95; pres. judge Superior Ct. of Pa., 1895-Jan. 1, 1916; retired. Republican. Address: Wilkes-Barré, Pa. Died May 16, 1919.

RICE, Charles Francis, clergyman; b. Chelsea, Mass., Apr. 14, 1851; s. William and Caroline Laura (North) R.; A.B., Wesleyan U., Conn., 1872, A.M., 1875, D.D., 1893; m. Miriam Owen Jacobs, Aug. 25, 1875 (died 1901); children—Laura Owen, William Chauncey, Horace Jacobs, Paul North, Rachel Caroline. Licensed as preacher Methodist Ch., 1873; teacher, Springfield High Sch., 1872-73; tutor Latin, Wesleyan U., 1874-77; pastor Appleton Ch., Neponset, Mass., 1878-79, Wesley Chapel, Salem, 1880-82, Webster, 1883-84, St. Paul's Ch., Lowell, 1885-87, Leominster, 1888-92, Epworth Ch., Cambridge, 1893-97, St. Luke's Ch., Springfield, 1898-99, Wesley Ch., (St. Luke's and State St. chs. united), Springfield, 1900-04; presiding elder Cambridge dist., 1905-10; pastor Winthrop St. Ch., Boston, 1911-15, South St. Church, Lynn, Mass., 1916-20, Wellington Ch., Medford, Mass., 1921-25 (retired). Del. General Conf. M.E. Church, 1904, 1908, Interch. Conf. Federation, 1905, Federal Council Chs. of Christ in America, 1912, 16, 20; mem. exec. com. Mass. Federation Chs. (pres. 1911-21); v.p. Federation Chs. and Religious Orgns. of Greater Boston. Trustee Wesleyan Acad., Wilbraham, Mass. (pres. bd. 1898-1912); pres. N.E. Conf. Trustees; chmn. bd. mgrs. N.E. Deaconess Assn. Republican. Home: Medford, Mass. Died Oct. 2, 1927.

RICE, Edmund, army officer; b. Cambridge, Mass., 1842; enlisted in Union army at beginning of Civil war; apptd., July 25, 1861, capt. 19th Mass. inf.; mustered out as col., June 30, 1865; received Congressional medal of honor for conspicuous bravery in leading his div. in a countercharge against Pickett's div., he himself falling, severely wounded, within the enemy's lines, in the battle of Gettysburg. Entered regular army, 1st lt. 40th inf., July 28, 1866; bvt. capt., maj. and col., U.S.A.; assigned to 5th inf., Dec. 31, 1870; regimental adj., July 5, 1879, to Mar. 10, 1883; on leave of absence, 1877, at time of Turko-Russian war; temporarily attached to staff of Gen. Skobeleff; promoted capt., Mar. 10, 1883; organized and comd. Columbian Guards at World's Columbian Exposition; later military attaché, Tokio, Japan; appointed col. 6th Mass. regt. by Gov. Wolcott on recommendation of Gen. Miles; apptd. insp. gen. U.S.A., May 1898; served on Gen. Miles' staff; later col. 26th vol. inf.; col. 19th U.S. inf., 1902-03; brig. gen. and retired, 1903. Invented a trowel bayonet, stacking swivel and knife-in-trenching bayonet, used in army. Address: Washington. Died 1906.

RICE, Edward Irving, business man; b. Syracuse, N.Y., July 12, 1868; s. Edward Flint and Ellen Amy (Eaton) R.; ed. St. John's Mil. Sch., Manlius, N.Y., Irving Inst., Tarrytown, N.Y.; m. Florence L. Young, Aug. 30, 1887; children—Edward Flint, Robert Irving. Pres. Edward I. Rice, Inc. (coal and ice), Syracuse Cold Storage Co.; treas. C. A. Reeve & Co., Inc., Darwin Springs Sand & Stone Co.; dir. First Trust & Deposit Co. Republican. Mason, Elk. Author: Old Jim Case of South Hollow, 1909. Home: Syracuse, N.Y. Deceased.

RICE, Edwin Wilbur, editor; b. Kingsboro, (now Gloversville), N.Y., July 24, 1831; s. Ebenezer and Eliza Ann (Port) R.; A.B., Union Coll., 1854, A.M., 1857; law student, 1854-55; Union Theol. Sem., 1855-57; D.D., Union, 1884; Litt.D., 1914; m. Margaret Eliza Williams, Jan. 1861 (died 1864); children—1 son, Edwin Wilbur; m. 2d, Mary Gardner, 1868 (died 1926); children—James G., Martin P., **Alfred B.** (dec.). Teacher, Brooklyn, 1857-58; ordained Congl. ministry, 1860; S.S. missionary, La Crosse, Wis., 1859-60, St. Louis, 1861, La Crosse, 1861-64; supt. at Milwaukee, 1864-70, asst. sec. and asst. editor at Phila., 1871-78, editor periodicals, 1878-79, editor periodicals and publs., 1879-1915, honorary editor, 1915—, Am. S.S. Union. Mem. Soc. Bibl. Lit. and Exegesis; pres. First Day or S.S. Soc. (founded 1791), 1893—. Hon. chmn. Bible Foundation Commn., 1923—. Hon. mem. A.B.C.F.M., Am. Bible Soc., and of Grad. Council Union Coll. Mem. Am. Acad. Polit. and Social Science. Author: Handbook International (Uniform) Sunday School Lessons, 1872-1917; Short Story of Origin of the Sunday School, 1913; New Movement Leaflets, 1910-11; Orientalisms in Bible Lands, 1911; History of Sunday School Movement and the American Sunday School Union, 1917; Critical Commentary on Mark, 1917; Religious Education in Early American Homes, 1917; Congregationalism 50 Years Ago in the Northwest, 1917; Life of Preparation, 1919; Literary Writings of Alfred Belden Rice, 1919; Origin and History of Uniform S.S. Lesson System (1825-1924), 1922; At Ninety, 1922; After Ninety Years, Story of a Nonagenarian, and the Educators He Has Known, 1923, 24. Contbr. to mags. and religious press. Home: Phila., Pa. Died Dec. 3, 1929.

RICE, Edwin Wilbur, Jr., engineer; b. La Crosse, Wis., May 6, 1862; s. Edwin Wilbur and Margaret Eliza (Williams) R.; A.B., Central High School, Phila., 1880, A.M., 1885; hon. A.M., Harvard, 1903; Sc.D., Union U., 1906; U. of Pa., 1924; Dr.Engring., Rensselaer Poly. Inst., 1917; began practice as elec. engr., 1880; m. Helen K. Doen, May 28, 1884; m. 2d, Alice M. Doen, Aug. 28, 1897. Supt. Thomson-Houston Electric Co., 1883-88, and tech. dir., 1884-94; v.p., 1894-1913, pres., 1913-22, hon. chmn. of board, 1922—, General Electric Co. Awarded Edison medal, 1928. Decorated Chevalier Légion d'Honneur, France; Order of Rising Sun, 3d Class with Cordon, Japan. Fellow Am. Inst. E.E. (pres. 1917). Home: Schenectady, N.Y. Died Nov. 25, 1935.

RICE, F. Willis, editor, pub.; b. Dexter, Penobscot County, Me., Oct. 9, 1848; s. John H. and Grace Elizabeth (Burleigh) R.; ed. various acads. and Alexander Inst., White Plains, N.Y.; m. Annie Rebecca Dyer, Jan. 4, 1876 (died 1912). Ry. constrn., Chicago, 1873-75; founder, 1875, and editor The National Hotel Reporter, the first publication in the interest of hotels and resorts in the U.S.; also founder Hotel Men's Mut. Benefit Assn. of U.S. (the 1st assn. of hotel men). Republican. Episcopalian. Home: Chicago, Ill. Died Dec. 17, 1931.

RICE, Frank James, mayor; b. North Adams, Mass., Feb. 5, 1869; s. Jesse H. and Caroline E. (Holbrook) R.; pub. sch. edn.; m. Charlotte A. Watrous, July 16, 1890. In real estate business, New Haven, 1893—; trustee New Haven Savings Bank. Alderman 1st Ward, 1893-1900; mayor of New Haven, 1910-18. Republican. Hon. mem. 2d Co. Governor's Foot Guard. Methodist. Mason, Odd Fellow, etc. Home: New Haven, Conn. Died Jan. 1917.

RICE, Franklin Pierce, author, editor; b. Marlborough, Mass., July 29, 1852; edn. largely private; took a partial medical course, 1873-76. Engaged 35 years in developing systematic history; published more than 150 hist., biog., or geneal. works; pioneer in record publication; trustee Systematic History Fund for the printing of original materials; a founder Worcester Soc. of Antiquity. Editor: Worcester Records (9 vols.); Vital Records of Massachusetts Towns in Course (40 vols. published); Worcester County Court and Other Records. Author: Reminiscences of Rev. George Allen; Life of Eli Thayer. Contbr. to cyclos. and newspapers. Home: Worcester, Mass. Died Jan. 4, 1919.

RICE, George Staples, engineer; b. Boston, Feb. 28, 1849; s. Reuben and Harriet Tyler (Kettell) R.; S.B., Harvard, 1870; m. Rose Breuchaud Porter, Oct. 10, 1889. Asst. engr. Lowell (Mass.) Water Works and Boston Water Works, 1869-72; div. engr. additional water supply, Boston, 1872-77; asst. engr. in direct charge main drainage works, 1877-80; mining engr. in Ariz. and Colo., 1880-87; prin. asst. engr. main drainage works, Boston, 1887, deputy chief engr. New Croton Aqueduct, New York, 1887-91; chief engr. Boston Rapid Transit Co., 1891-92; in pvt. practice and instr. in water supply and sanitary engring., Harvard, 1892-1900; deputy chief engr., 1900-04, chief engr., 1905-07, Rapid Transit Commrs., New York; div. engr. Pub. Service Commn., 1st Dist., New York, 1907-19. Home: New York, N.Y. Died Dec. 7, 1920.

RICE, Henry, merchant; b. Bamberg, Bavaria, Germany, June 28, 1835; s. Siligman and Henrietta (Newman) R.; ed. Polytechnic Sch. and Realschule, Bamberg; came to U.S. in 1850; m. Rachel Herman, Aug. 12, 1863. In New York, 1850-53; in clothing business as Henry Rice & Co., Jacksonville, Ill., 1853-61; military storekeeper, U.S. Army, 1861-62; established dry goods business, Memphis, Tenn., 1862, firm of Rice, Stix & Co., remaining there until 1879, when business was removed to St. Louis, later incorporated as Rice-Stix Dry Goods Co., of which was pres., later chmn. advisory bd. Has lived in New York, 1866—, and represents the firm in the East. Trustee Baron de Hirsch Fund; identified with many philanthropic and charitable orgns. Mem. Com. of 70 that assisted in electing Col. Strong as mayor of New York, 1894; former mem. Bd. of Edn., New York. Republican. Address: New York, N.Y. Died June 7, 1914.

RICE, Herbert Ambrose, lawyer; b. North Providence, R.I., July 25, 1866; s. Col. Randall Hopkins and Margaret (Bates) R.; A.B., Brown, 1889, A.M., 1891; LL.B., cum laude, Harvard, 1895; m. Elise D. Coe, July 27, 1910. Teacher University Grammar Sch., 1889-92; admitted to R.I. bar, 1895, later to U.S. courts, including Supreme Court; mem. Sch. Com., Pawtucket, 1890-92; coroner, Pawtucket, 1896-98; mem. R.I. Ho. of Rep., from Pawtucket, 1900-01; atty. gen. of R.I., 1912-23; gen. practice, 1923—. Represented R.I. in case of R.I. vs. Palmer—first suit by a state to test constitutionality of an amendment to Federal Constitution. Republican. Mem. Providence County Court House Commn., 1912; trustee Memorial Hosp. Episcopalian. Mem. Sons of the American Revolution (pres. R.I. Soc., 1922-23, dir. gen. Nat. Soc., 1923). Grand Master of Masons R.I., 1917. Home: Providence, R.I. Died Nov. 20, 1929.

RICE, Herbert Howard, mfr.; b. Providence, R.I., 1870; s. Leander Parker and Margaret Jane (Burnham) R.; A.B., Brown U., 1892; m. Edith Rogers Bowen, 1896; children—Carol Margaret, Katherine (Mrs. F. M. Broock), Gordon Owen, Martin Burnham. Adv. manager and sales dept., Pope Mfg. Co., mfrs. Columbia bicycles, 1892-98; mgr. Providence br. same (bicycles and automobiles), 1898-1904, Waverley automobile factory, 1904-08; v.p., later president Waverley Co., Indianapolis, 1908-16; treas., v.p., 1916-21, General Motors Corp., Detroit; pres. and gen. mgr. Cadillac Motor Car Co., 1921-25; asst. to pres. Gen. Motors Corp., 1925-30; chmn. Alaska-Pacific Highway Commn., 1930; later pres. Sweet Oil Refining Co., Petroleum Investors, Inc. Treasurer and dir. Nat. Automobile Chamber of Commerce, 1910-30; pres. Nat. Metal Trades Assn., 1914-16; chmn. on part of U.S.A. to Pan-Am. Congress of Highways,

Buenos Aires, 1925, and mem. Congress, Milan, 1926, Rio de Janeiro, 1929. Mem. Nat. War Labor Bd., 1918-19. Republican. Baptist. Home: Detroit, Mich. Died Nov. 15, 1938.

RICE, Herbert Leigh, judge; b. Wilmington, Del., Mar. 10, 1876; s. Edward Luff and Anna Louisa (Austin) R.; LL.B., Law Sch., U. of Pa., 1898; m. Helen Tyson; 1 son, Herbert Leigh. Admitted to Del. bar, 1900, and practiced at Wilmington, 1900-11; asso. justice Supreme Ct. of Del., Mar. 1, 1911—. Home: Claymont, Del. Died Dec. 1932.

RICE, Herbert Wayland, paint mfr.; b. Providence, R.I., June 22, 1869; s. Joseph William and Emily Augusta (Lamprey) R.; ed. high sch., Providence; m. Jennie Wilbur, June 22, 1893; children—Wayland Wilbur, Wilbur Lamprey, Emily Frances (Mrs. John McEntire Stewart). Began as office boy, U.S. Gutta Percha Paint Co., Providence, R.I., 1886, successively salesman, mgr., sec., 1893, pres. and treas., 1910—; pres. Morris Plan of R.I.; vice pres. Peoples' Savings Bank; dir. Rhode Island Hospital Trust Co., R.I. Hosp. Nat. Bank, Providence Gas Company, Providence Washington Ins. Co., Mortgage Guarantee & Title Co., New England Butt Co. Mem. R.I. Ho. of Rep., 1904-06; del. to Rep. Nat. Conv., 1912, 1916. Trustee Homeopathic Hosp. of R.I., Y.M.C.A.; mem. visiting com. Brown U. Mason. Home: Providence, R.I. Died Jan. 17, 1941.

RICE, Isaac Leopold, lawyer; b. Wachenheim, Rhenish Bavaria, Feb. 22, 1850; s. Mayer and Fanny R.; ed. Central High Sch., Phila.; LL.B. cum laude, Columbia, 1880; LL.D., Bates Coll., 1902; m. Julia Hyneman Barnett, 1885. Founded and was lecturer, 1882-83, Sch. of Polit. Science, Columbia; instr. Columbia Law Sch., 1884-86. Took up practice of R.R. law and engaged in R.R. service as counsel and dir. in the lines now constituting the Southern Ry.; for a time foreign rep. of the Phila. & Reading R.R.; pres. Electric Boat Co., Holland Torpedo Boat Co., Electric Launch Co., Industrial Oxygen Co., Nat. Torpedo Co., Car Lighting & Power Co., Consolidated Ry. Electric Lighting & Equipment Co., Lindstrom Brake Co., Ry. & Stationary Refrigerating Co., The Forum Pub. Co., Continental Development Co., N.J. Development Co., Quaker City Chem. Co.; pres. and treas. Casein Co. of America, Casein Mfg. Co., Nat. Milk Sugar Co., Dry Milk Co., Rosemary Creamery Co., Water Paint Co. of America; chmn. bd. dirs. Consolidated Rubber Tire Co., Buckeye Rubber Co.; dir. Société Française de Sous-Marins (Paris, France), New London Ship & Engine Co. Prominent in chess; invented the Rice-Gambit, a new chess opening. Author: What Is Music?, 1875; also many articles in North American Review, The Century and The Forum. Home: New York, N.Y. Died Nov. 2, 1915.

RICE, James Henry, Jr., naturalist; b. "Riverlands Plantation," Abbeville County, S.C., July 2, 1868; s. James Henry and Anna (Lawton) R.; ed. high sch. and S.C. Coll.; m. Jennie Maner, Apr. 30, 1892; children—James Henry, Edward Carew, Margaret (Mrs. J. L. Patterson), Samuel Maner (dec.), William Lawton, Frederic, Robert Ridgway. Various occupations, principally teaching, until 1895; editor Colonial Records of South Carolina, 1895; editor The Columbia Evening News, 1895; editorial writer on The State (Columbia, S.C.), 1896-98; editor The Field (weekly industrial), 1903-04, The Carolina Field (Georgetown, S.C.), 1905-06; sec. Audubon Soc. of S.C., 1907-10; chief game warden of S.C., 1911-13; also field agt. Nat. Assn. of Audubon Socs., 1910-13; insp. U.S. Biol. Survey, 1913-17. Democrat. Presbyn. Author: Glories of the Carolina Coast. Contbr. numerous articles and book reviews, pertaining to birds, plants, etc. Home: Wiggins, S.C. Died Mar. 23, 1935.

RICE, John Andrew, clergyman; b. Colleton County, S.C., Sept. 25, 1862; s. Richard Blake (M.D.) and Rachel Jane (Liston) R.; A.B., S.C. Coll., 1885, later A.M.; Columbia Theol. Sem., S.C., 1886-96; completed studies for Ph.D., U. of Chicago, 1903; D.D., S.C. Coll., 1894; LL.D., U. of S.C., 1905, U. of Ala., 1906; m. Anna B. Smith, Apr. 13, 1887; m. 2d, Launa Darnell, Aug. 7, 1902. Entered M.E. Ch., S., ministry, 1886; pastor Bennettsville circuit, Kingstree circuit, Darlington, Washington St. Ch., Columbia, S.C.; pres. Columbia (S.C.) Coll. for Women, 1894-1900; pastor Court St. Ch., Montgomery, Ala., 1902-07, Rayne Memorial Ch., New Orleans, 1907-11, First Ch., Ft. Worth, Tex., 1911-14, St. John's Ch., St. Louis, 1914-18, Trinity Ch., Sumter, S.C., 1918-20; prof. Old Testament, Southern Meth. U., 1920-21; pastor First Ch., Okmulgee, Okla., 1921-22, Boston Av. Ch., Tulsa, 1922-27; editor Okla. Methodist, 1927-28. Author: The Old Testament in the Life of Today; The Primacy of Religion in Education; Why I Believe in the Bible; Is Christ on Trial in Tennessee? Home: Tulsa, Okla. Deceased.

RICE, John Campbell, judge; b. Cass County, Ill., Jan. 27, 1864; s. Elbert Gallatin and Mary Ann (Camp) R.; A.B., Ill. Coll., 1885, A.M., 1888; student law dept. U. of Mich., 1888-89; LL.B., Cornell U., 1890; LL.D., Illinois Coll., 1935; m. Maude M. Beshears, Oct. 2, 1895 (died 1923); children—Elbert G., Homer B., Martha Ann, Lois Robb, Josephine E. Admitted to Ida. bar and began practice at Caldwell, 1891; an organizer Commercial Bank of Caldwell, 1894, and its pres., also pres. its successors until 1923, with exception of 3 years; an organizer, 1908, Canyon Abstract & Trust Co. Mem. Ida. House of Rep., 1897; mayor of Caldwell, 1902; asso. justice Supreme Court of Ida., 1917-23 inclusive; judge of dist. court, State of Ida., 1931—. Trustee Coll. of Ida. Democrat. Mem. Disciples of Christ. Mason. Odd Fellow. Home: Caldwell, Ida. Died Nov. 7, 1937.

RICE, John Hodgen, army officer; b. St. Louis, Mo., Jan. 6, 1870; s. Virgil and Aurelia R. R.; grad. U.S. Mil. Acad., 1893; m. Mary L. Angell, Nov. 7, 1903. Commd. 2d lt. 3d Cav., June 12, 1893; 1st lt. ordnance, Nov. 21, 1898; capt., Apr. 5, 1903; maj., Oct. 10, 1907; lt. col., July 1, 1916; col. N.A., Jan. 8, 1918; brig. gen. N.A., Feb. 18, 1918; lt. col. ordnance, Sept. 15, 1919. Served during strikes at Chicago, and at Ft. Sheridan, Ill., July-Oct. 1894; instr. mathematics, U.S. Mil. Acad., 1895-97; with regt. in Fla., Spanish-Am. War, 1898; at Manila, P.I., 1901-03; asst. to chief of ordnance, Washington, D.C., 1906-12; comdg. San Antonio Arsenal, and chief ordnance officer Southern Dept., 1912-14; chief of carriage div., Office Chief of Ordnance, 1915-17; chief of engring. div. Ordnance Dept., Washington, D.C., 1917-18; arrived in France, June 26, 1918; apptd. chief ordnance officer, A.E.F., Oct. 9, 1918; returned to U.S. Aug. 26, 1919; duty as chief of mfr. Ordnance Dept., Oct. 1919-July 1, 1921; retired from active service, July 1, 1921, on own application. Awarded D.S.M.; Comdr. Legion of Honor (French). Address: Washington, D.C. Died Jan. 7, 1940.

RICE, John Hovey, lawyer; b. Mt. Vernon, Me., Feb. 5, 1816; s. Nathaniel and Jane (Swasey) R.; common school edn.; clerk in Registry of Deeds, Augusta, Me., at 16; resided there 10 yrs.; in mercantile business; deputy sheriff; studied law; a.d.c. to Gen. Bachelor in the "Aroostook War"—i.e., Northeastern boundary dispute with Great Britain, 1838; moved to Piscataquis County, Me., 1843; m. Grace Elizabeth Burleigh, Dec. 7, 1847 (died 1898). Practiced law; pros. atty.; delegate in the 1st Rep. Nat. Conv., Phila., 1856; mem. Congress 4th Me. dist. 3 terms, 1861-67; declined 4th nomination; customs collector, Port of Bangor, Me., 1867-71; practiced law in Washington, D.C., with Edward Jordan, solicitor of the Treasury, 12 yrs.; moved to New York, 1884; in corporation and law business there, 15 yrs.; in Chicago, May 1899—. Address: Chicago, Ill. Died 1911.

RICE, Jonas Shearn, banker; b. Houston, Tex., Nov. 25, 1855; s. Frederick A. and Charlotte M. (Baldwin) R.; ed. Tex. Mil. Inst., Austin, Tex.; m. Mary J. Ross, 1887; children—Laura F., Kate Padgitt, Lottie. Began banking business at Houston; chmn. bd. Union Nat. Bank. Joined Houston Light Guards, 1874; held commn. as adj. in first regiment of militia organized in Texas after the Civil War. Home: Houston, Tex. Died Mar. 12, 1931.

RICE, Joseph J., R.C. bishop; b. Leicester, Mass., Dec. 6, 1871; ed. Holy Cross Coll., Worcester, Laval U., Montreal, Can., and at Rome, Italy; ordained priest, Sept. 29, 1894; consecrated bishop of Burlington, Apr. 14, 1910. Address: Burlington, Vt. Died Apr. 1, 1938.

RICE, Joseph Mayer, author; b. Phila., Pa., May 20, 1857; s. Mayer and Fanny R.; student Coll. City of New York; M.D., Coll. Phys. and Surg. (Columbia), 1881; m. Deborah Levinson, Oct. 10, 1900; children—Frances Violet, Lawrence Joseph Mayer. Practiced medicine at New York, 1881-88; studied psychology and pedagogics, univs. of Jena and Leipzig, 1888-90; editor The Forum, 1897-1907. Founded Soc. Ednl. Research, 1903. Author: The Public School System of the United States, 1893; The Rational Spelling Book, 1898; Scientific Management in Education, 1913; The People's Government, 1915. Contbr. of many articles in The Forum on results of tests in arithmetic, spelling, and language made in pub. schs. of a large number of cities. Home: Philadelphia, Pa. Died June 24, 1934.

RICE, Lewis Frederick, architect, civil engr.; b. Boston, Mass., May 17, 1839; s. Lewis and Susan Augusta (Brigham) R.; ed. public schools, 1845-52; West Point, 1853-54; grad. Rensselaer Poly. Inst., C.E., 1858; engr. on construction, Brooklyn water works, 1858-59; div. engr. Troy & Greenfield (Hoosac Tunnel) R.R., 1860-61; in U.S. army as lt., capt. and maj. 31st Mass. vols., 1862-65; gen. practice civ. engr., Boston, 1865-66; asst. engr. Reading & Columbia R.R., Pa., 1867; asst. engr. St. Louis, Mo., water works, 1867-71; in gen. practice architect and civ. engr., Boston, 1872-90; asst. engr. and architect Am. Bell Telephone Co., 1890—. Home: Brookline, Mass. Died 1909.

RICE, Richard Austin, coll. prof.; b. Madison, Conn., Oct. 22, 1846; s. Richard E. and Parnella (Scranton) R.; B.A., Yale, 1868; Yale Div. Sch., 1869-70; U. of Berlin and other foreign univs. and tech. schs., 1870-75; hon. M.A., Williams, 1883; m. Marion A. Foster, Nov. 28, 1876. Prof. modern langs. and lit., U. of Vt., 1875-81, prof. same, 1881-90, prof. history, 1890-1904, history of art and civilization, 1904-11; prof. emeritus, 1911—, Williams Coll.; in charge of div. of prints, Library of Congress, 1912—. Home: Washington, D.C. Died Feb. 5, 1925.

RICE, Richard Henry, mech. engr.; b. Rockland, Me., Jan. 9, 1863; s. Albert Smith and Frances Weston (Baker) R.; M.E., Stevens Inst. Tech., Hoboken, N.J., 1885; m. Alice Woodman Kimball, Mar. 26, 1898. Spl. apprentice P.,C.,C.&St.L. Ry., 1885-86; draftsman and designer, Bath Iron Works, 1886-87; designer and chief draftsman, E. D. Leavitt (engr. of Calumet & Hecla Mining Co.), 1887-91; supt. William A. Harris Steam Engine Co., 1891-95; sec.-treas., Rice & Sargent Engine Co., 1895-99, Providence Engring. Works, 1899-1903; engr. turbine dept., Gen. Electric Co., 1903—. Episcopalian. Address: Lynn, Mass. Died 1922.

RICE, Theron Hall, clergyman; b. Wetumpka, Ala., July 8, 1867; s. Theron Hall and Lydia Ann (Root) R.; Ogden Coll., Bowling Green, Ky.; A.B., Southwestern Presbyn. U., Tenn., 1889; studied U. of Va.; grad. Union Theol. Sem., Va., 1892; D.D., Davidson, 1899, Central U., 1899; LL.D., King College, Bristol, Tenn., 1918; m. Elizabeth Matthews Sherrard, May 28, 1913. Ordained Presbyn. ministry, 1892; pastor 2d Ch., Alexandria, Va., 1892-96, Central Church, Atlanta, Ga., 1896-1908; Stuart Robinson prof. English Bible and Pastoral theology, Union Theol. Sem. in Va., May 1908—. Mem. exec. com. Publ. and S.S. Work Presbyn. Ch. in U.S. Del. Pan-Presbyn. Council, Glasgow, 1896. Democrat. Home: Richmond, Va. Died Aug. 16, 1922.

RICE, Wallace (de Groot Cecil), author and lecturer; b. Hamilton, Canada, Nov. 10, 1859 (of Am. parents temporarily resident there), s. John A. (noted collector of Americana) and Margaret Van Slycke (Culver) R.; home in Chicago, July 1861—; ed. grammar sch. of Racine Coll. and Harvard College, class of 1883; hon. A.M., Lake Forest U., 1926; admitted to bar Chicago, Nov. 1884; widower; 2 children. On various newspapers and mags., 1889-1917. Author of numerous pageants including: Ft. Wayne, 1916; Pageant of the Flag, 1917; Six Little Plays for Ill. Children, Masque of Ill., Pageant of the Ill. Country, Pageant of Ill., Seven Lamps of War, 1918; Women and War, 1919; Santa Barbara, 1920; Chicago Festival Play, Birmingham, Ala., 1921; Pageant of the Dominicanesses in Ill., Springfield, Ill., 1923. Author, editor, and compiler (with sister, Frances Rice) of numerous books in poetry and prose, and of The Chicago Stock Exchange, a history, 1923; Seventy-Five Years of Gas Service in Chicago, 1925; Palmer House Old and New, 1925; Pagan Pictures, 1927; English Without a Don't, 1928; A Chicago Boy in the '60's, 1928; Infidels and Heretics (with Clarence Darrow), 1929; The Father (opera libretto from Strindberg's play), 1929. Contbr. chapter to Makers of Chicago, 1929; also ceremony for opening of Lake-to-Gulf Waterway, Chicago, June 22, 1933. Designer of Ill. centennial banner, Chicago municipal flag, 1917. Usage counsellor The English Jour. Home: Chicago, Ill. Died Dec. 15, 1939.

RICE, Willard Martin, Presbyn. clergyman; b. Lowville, Lewis County, N.Y., April 30, 1817; s. Abel Sherman and Diana (Doty) R.; grad. Wesleyan U., 1837, D.D., 1866; tutor Wesleyan U., 1837-40; m. Elizabeth Anderson McDowell, July 7, 1840. Established classical school, Phila., 1840; ordained, 1858; pastor Moyamensing Ch., 1858-63; 4th Presbyn., Phila., 1863-74; Berwyn, Pa., 1874-76, resigned; stated supply, Southwestern Presbyn. Ch., Phila., 1882-84; engaged on publications of Presbyn. bd. of publication, 1876—, of which he became mem. 1862, and recording clerk, 1862. Permanent clerk, 1858-61; stated clerk, 1861-74, and Presbytery of Phila., 1877—; stated clerk synod of Phila., 1872-81. Author: History of the Presbyterian Board of Publication and Sabbath School Work, Westminster Question Book, from years 1875-96 inclusive; Westminster Lesson Leaf, from years 1878-96 inclusive; Westminster Quarterly, from years 1880-96 inclusive; History of the Fourth Presbyterian Church of Philadelphia. Address: Philadelphia, Pa. Died 1904.

RICE, William, dentist, educator; b. Dublin, N.H., Sept. 4, 1867; s. George Matthias and Persis Fayette (Weeks) R.; D.D.S., Boston Dental Coll., 1888; D.M.D., Tufts Coll. Dental Sch., 1905; hon. Sc.D., Tufts Coll., 1929; m. Alice Mary Bates, June 25, 1889; children—Priscilla Alden, Persis Alden (Mrs. Bigelow Green). Began practice at Boston, 1888; instr. in clin. dentistry, Tufts Coll. Dental Sch., 1900-11, asst. prof., 1911-13, prof. operative dentistry, 1913—; dean Tufts Coll. Dental Sch., 1916—. Mem. Am. Acad. Dental Science (pres. 1918), N.E. Dental Soc. (pres. 1926), Mass. Dental Soc. (pres. 1922), Dental Hygiene Council of Mass. (pres. 1919-22). Mem. dental advisory bd. Dept. of Pub. Health, Commonwealth of Mass. Awarded medal "for outstanding achievement," R.I. State Dental Assn., 1927. Unitarian. Contbr. chapters in dental hygiene and oral prophylaxis to Turner's Hygiene—General and Dental, 1920. Home: Boston, Mass. Died Nov. 23, 1932.

RICE, William Ball, mfr.; b. Hudson, Mass., Apr. 1, 1840; ed. pub. schs.; worked in shoe shop until 21, then bought small fancy goods store in Boston; m. Emma L. Cunningham, Oct. 25, 1860 (died 1909).

Second lt. Co. E, 5th Mass. Vols., in Civil War, 1864; traveler for shoe factories, 1865-66; in business, 1866—, as mem. Rice & Hutchins, among the largest shoe mfrs. in U.S. Founded City Hosp., Quincy; mem. Gov.'s Council, Mass., 1894. Home: Quincy, Mass. Died 1909.

RICE, William Morton Jackson, portrait painter; b. Brooklyn, N.Y., Feb. 18, 1854; s. Edwin T. and Sylvia Augusta (Jackson) R.; B.Arch., Cornell, 1874; studied painting at Paris under Carolus Duran, 1881-84. A.N.A. Address: New York, N.Y. Died Oct. 13, 1922.

RICE, W(illia)m North, geologist; b. Marblehead, Mass., Nov. 21, 1845; s. William and Caroline Laura (North) R.; A.B., Wesleyan U., Conn., 1865; Ph.D., Sheffield Scientific Sch. (Yale), 1867; LL.D., Syracuse U., 1886, Wesleyan U., 1915; m. Elizabeth W. Crowell, Apr. 12, 1870 (died 1916); children—Edward Loranus, Charles William (dec.). Prof. geology and natural history, 1867-84, geology, 1884-1918, emeritus, 1918—, acting pres., 1907, 1908-09, 1918, Wesleyan U. Absent for study and travel in Europe, 1867-68, 1892-93, and 1911-12; asst. U.S. Fish Commn., 1873-74; asst. geologist U.S. Geol. Survey, 1891-92; supt. Conn. State Geol. and Natural History Survey, 1903-16. Mem. Geol. Soc. America (v.p., 1911), A.A.A.S. (v.p. and chmn. sect. E, 1905-06), Am. Acad. Arts and Sciences, Am. Soc. Naturalists (pres., 1891), Conn. Council Edn., 1902-08 (pres. 1902-05); became mem. N.Y. East Conference M.E. Ch., 1869 (chmn. board of examiners, 1896-1925); mem. Council of Conn. Federation of Churches, 1908—(pres. 1910-11; sec. 1913-19; pres. 1919-20; hon. pres. 1920—). Author: Geology of Bermuda, 1884; Science Teaching in the Schools, 1889; Twenty-five Years of Scientific Progress, and Other Essays, 1894; Christian Faith in an Age of Science, 1903; (with H. E. Gregory) Manual of the Geology of Connecticut, 1906 (Conn. Geol. and Natural History Survey); Return to Faith, and other Addresses, 1916; Through Darkness to Dawn, 1917; Poet of Science, and other addresses, 1919; Science and Religion—Five Supposed Conflicts, 1925. Editor 5th edit. Dana's Text-book of Geology, 1897. Address: Middletown, Conn. Died Nov. 13, 1928.

RICH, Adelbert P., lawyer; b. Cato, N.Y., May 16, 1860; s. Frank and Frances W. R.; ed. Cato Union Sch.; m. Ida Chase, 1881. Admitted to N.Y. bar, 1882; pres. bd. of edn. and bd. of health, Cato, 1882-84; spl. judge Cayuga County, N.Y., 1883-86; dist. atty., Cayuga County, N.Y., 1887-93; justice Supreme Ct. of N.Y., 1900-30; designated by gov. to Appellate Div., 2d Dept., 5 times to 1928; later practiced in N.Y. City. Home: Cato, N.Y. Died Sept. 24, 1933.

RICH, Burdett Alberto, editor; b. Cattaraugus, N.Y., Oct. 24, 1854; s. Charles J. and Lucy (Freeborn) R.; grad. Red Wing (Minn.) Collegiate Inst., 1873; A.B., Wesleyan U., Conn., 1878; m. Nellie Hagerty, July 20, 1880. Admitted to Conn. bar, 1880, N.Y. bar, 1881, Supreme Ct. of U.S., 1884; practiced in Cattaraugus, 1881-86; engaged upon legal publs. in Rochester, N.Y., 1886—, as editor Lawyers' Coöp. Pub. Co.; became editor-in-chief, 1889; also dir. and treas. Trustee and v.p. Wesleyan Sem., Lima, N.Y. Mem. Am. Acad. Polit. and Social Science. Republican. Editor: Digest of United States Supreme Court Reports, 1887; General Digest of American and English Law Reports (annually), 1888-1900; Lawyers' Reports Annotated (annually), 1899-1918; Reports of Decisions of United States Supreme Court (lawyers' edit.), 1899—; Ruling Case Law, 1914-17; District of Columbia Court of Appeals Reports, 1918, 19; American Law Reports, 1919. Editor legal monthly, Case and Comment, 1893-1909. Contbr. American Law Review and other legal publs. Home: Rochester, N.Y. Died Sept. 22, 1925.

RICH, Edward P., consulting engr.; b. Chicago, Ill., July 16, 1879; s. Marshall Byron and Mary E. (Prickett) R.; ed. Manual Training Sch., Chicago; student U. of Chicago, 1898-1900; B.S. in M.E., U. of Mich., 1903; m. Lilabel Griffiths, 1911; children—Marshall G., Kenneth G. Practiced in Chicago, 1903—; mem. firm Neiler, Rich & Co., cons. engrs. and indsl. architects, 1908—. Republican. Episcopalian. Home: Chicago, Ill. Died Apr. 19, 1937.

RICH, John Harrison, banker, mfr.; b. Lake Geneva, Wis., Dec. 30, 1856; s. Harrison and Martha (Stewart) R.; ed. pub. schs.; m. Milla Elizabeth Jones, Aug. 17, 1918. Founded pottery and sewer pipe industry, at Red Wing, Minn., of which was pres. 20 yrs., also Red Wing Malting Company; pres. Goodhue County National Bank 15 years; dir. Minneapolis Steel and Machinery Co., from orgn., 1904; mayor of Red Wing 1 term; chmn. bd. and reserve agt. Fed. Res. Bank of Minneapolis, Sept. 1914—. Trustee Shattuck Sch., Faribault, Minn.; pres. Citizens' League of Minn. 3 yrs. Democrat. Episcopalian. Mason. Home: Minneapolis, Minn. Died May 20, 1924.

RICH, John T., governor; b. Conneautville, Pa., Apr. 23, 1841; s. John W. and Jerusha (Treadway) R.; removed to Mich., 1848, locating at Elba; ed. in pub. schs.; m. Lucretia M. Winship, Mar. 12, 1863. Farmer from boyhood. Mem. Mich. Ho. of Rep., 1873-80 (speaker 1876-80), Senate, 1880-81; mem. 47th Congress (1881-83); commr. of railroads, Mich., 1887-91; gov. of Mich., 1893-96; collector of customs, port of Detroit, 1898-1906, Port Huron, Mich., 1909-13. Republican. Home: Lapeer, Mich. Died Mar. 28, 1926.

RICHARD, Charles, col. Med. Corps, U.S. Army; b. New York, Nov. 10, 1854; s. Jacob and Fredericka (Herbig) R.; B.S., Coll. City of New York, 1874; M.D., New York U., 1876; m. Laura R. Bailey, Nov. 8, 1887. Interne, Charity Hosp., New York, Apr. 1876-Sept. 30, 1877; asst. phys., Randall's Island Hosp., Oct. 1, 1877-Apr. 1, 1878; attending phys., Essex Market Dispensary, New York, 1878-79; lecturer on mil. surgery, and prof. surgery, U. of Colo., 1889-91. Apptd. from N.Y. 1st lt. asst. surgeon U.S.A., June 3, 1879; capt. asst. surgeon, June 3, 1884; maj. surgeon, Nov. 15, 1897; lt. col. Med. Corps, U.S.A., Apr. 10, 1908; col. Med. Corps, Feb. 18, 1910; brig. gen. Med. Corps N.A., Aug. 5, 1917. Dept. surgeon, Hdqrs. Eastern Dept., and asst. to Surgeon Gen. of the Army, War Dept., 1917-18. Retired from active service, Nov. 10, 1918. Address: New York, N.Y. Died Apr. 19, 1940.

RICHARD, Ernst D., lecturer; b. Bonn, Germany, July 2, 1859; s. Christolph T. K. Emmanuel and Marie (Schmuelling) R.; grad. Gymnasium, Bonn, 1879; studied univs. of Marburg and Bonn, 1879-83; Pd.D., New York U., 1894; m. Julia L. Schumacher, July 2, 1887. Began teaching, 1882; came to America 1883; prin. Hoboken (N.J.) Acad., 1890-97; lecturer history of German civilization, Columbia, 1903—. Active in world-peace movement, 1894; founded German Am. Peace Soc., 1904, New York Peace Soc., 1906; lecturer on peace topics. Author: History of German Civilization, 1911. Contbr. to Am. and German mags. Home: New York, N.Y. Died Nov. 20, 1914.

RICHARD, James William, D.D., prof. homiletics, Lutheran Theol. Sem., Gettysburg, Pa. Author: Philip Melanchthon, 1898. Address: Gettysburg, Pa. Died 1909.

RICHARDS, Alice Haliburton, regent Mt. Vernon Ladies' Assn.; b. N.Y. City, May 28, 1860; d. Cornelius Low (U.S.A.) and Julia Ellen (Lawrence) King; ed. in France and Germany and by governess; m. James G. K. Richards, Jan. 21, 1891 (dec.); 1 son, Frederick Gore (U.S.N.). Life regent Mt. Vernon Ladies' Assn. of the Union (orgn. for preservation of home of George Washington), 1927—; trustee Sulgrave Manor, England. Republican. Episcopalian. Home: Newcastle, Me. Died Oct. 1936.

RICHARDS, Charles Brinckerhoff, mech. engr.; b. Brooklyn, Dec. 23, 1833; s. Thomas Fanning and Harriet Howland (Brinckerhoff) R.; ed. pvt. schs., 1838-49; hon. A.M., Yale, 1884; m. Agnes Edwards Goodwin, Sept. 16, 1858. Was many yrs. engr. supt. Colt's Arms Co., Hartford, and, 1880-84, supt. Southwark Foundry and Machine Co., Phila.; Higgin prof. mech. engring., Yale, 1884-1909, emeritus prof., 1909. Consulting engr. for many pub. bldgs.; U.S. expert commr. to Paris Expn., 1889; inventor, 1861, of Richards' indicator for steam engine. Chevalier Legion of Honor, France. Editor Vol. III and part Vol. IV (1400 pp.) Report of U.S. Commrs. to Paris Expn. Editor engring. and tech. words and terms in Webster's International Dictionary. Home: New Haven, Conn. Died Apr. 20, 1919.

RICHARDS, Charles Herbert, clergyman; b. Meriden, N.H., Mar. 18, 1839; s. Cyrus S. and Helen D. (Whiton) R.; A.B., Yale, 1860; grad. Andover Theol. Sem., 1865; D.D., Beloit Coll., 1882; served in Christian Commn. in Civil War; m. Marie M. Miner, 1868. Pastor Congl. Ch., Kokomo, Ind., 1866-67, First Church, Madison, Wis., 1867-90, Central Ch., Phila., 1890-1903; sec. Ch. Bldg. Soc., 1903—. Condr. Monona Lake Assembly, Madison, Wis., 1881-84; pres. Wis. Home Missionary Soc., 1885-90; trustee Downer Coll., Wis., 1887-90; Yale lecturer on hymnology and ch. music, 1895; on Nat. Council Com. for Ministerial Relief, 1898-1901; trustee Nat. Council Congregational Chs., 1901-07; pres. Evang. Alliance of Pennsylvania, 1890-93; dir. Congregational Board Ministerial Relief; trustee Howard U., Washington. Author: Religious Rights of a Christian State; The Improvement of Worship; Evolution of a Redeemed Humanity; What Is Your Life? God Our Help; Spiritual Nurture of Children; The Pearl of Prayers; Evolution in Hymnology; Will Phillips; Sunday Mornings with a Pastor. Editor: Songs of Christian Praise, 1880; Scripture Selections for Responsive Reading, 1880; Songs of Praise and Prayer, 1889; Songs of the Christian Life, 1912; Book of Church Services, 1922. Editor Church Building Quarterly, 1903-09. Home: New York, N.Y. Died Feb. 16, 1925.

RICHARDS, Charles Russ, univ. pres.; b. Clarkshill, Ind., Mar. 23, 1871; s. Charles and Sarah Elizabeth (Watt) R.; B.M.E., Purdue U., 1890, M.E., 1891; M.M.E., Cornell U., 1895; D.Eng., U. of Nebraska, 1920, Purdue U., 1932; LL.D., Lafayette U., 1922, U. of Pennsylvania, 1935, Lehigh U., 1936; m. Alida Russell Beardsley, Nov. 26, 1891. Instr. mech. engring., Colo. Agrl. Coll., 1891-92; adj. prof. manual training, 1892-94, prof. practical mechanics, 1894-98, prof. mech. engring., 1898-1911, asso. dean of Industrial Coll. in charge of all engring., 1907, dean Coll. of Engring., 1909-11, U. of Neb.; prof. mech. engineering in charge of the dept., 1911-20, acting dean, Coll. of Engring. and acting dir. Engring. Expt. Sta., 1913-15, dean and dir., 1917-22, U. of Ill.; pres. Lehigh U., Bethlehem, Pa., 1922-35, later pres. emeritus; also cons. engr. Mem. of the advisory bd. Phila. Ordnance Dist. Mem. bd. visitors U.S. Naval Acad., 1934. Fellow A.A.A.S. (v.p. and chmn. sect. M. 1925, 26), Am. Soc. M.E. (mgr. 1918-21). Republican. Home: Minneapolis, Minn. Died Apr. 17, 1941.

RICHARDS, Charles Russell, educator; b. Boston, Mass., June 30, 1865; s. Charles C. and Josephine (Gleason) R.; S.B., Mass. Inst. Tech., 1885; m. Hilda Muhlhauser, 1917; m. 2d, Mildred Batchelder, 1926. Dir. dept. of science and tech., Pratt Inst., Brooklyn, 1888-98; dir. dept. manual training, Teachers Coll. (Columbia), 1898-1908; dir. Cooper Union, 1908-23; dir. Am. Assn. of Museums, 1923-26; dir. Div. Indsl. Art, Gen. Edn. Bd., 1926-30; exec. v.p., N.Y. Mus. Sci. and Industry, 1930—. Spl. investigator Dept. of Labor, State of N.Y., 1907-08. Mem. advisory com. on indsl. edn., Bd. Regents State of N.Y.; dir. various indsl. art, and museum surveys, 1914—. Chmn. commn. apptd. by sec. of commerce of U.S. to report on Internat. Expn. of Decorative Art in Paris, 1925. Vice pres. Am. Assn. of Museums, 1927—. Unitarian. Trustee Children's Aid Soc. of New York, 1904-16; mem. Corp. Mass. Inst. of Technology, 1909-14. Chevalier Légion d'Honneur (France). Author: Art in Industry; The Industrial Museum; Industrial Art and the Museum. Home: New York, N.Y. Died Feb. 21, 1936.

RICHARDS, Charles Walter, educator; b. Sumach, Ga., Oct. 10, 1877; s. William Martin and Mary Safronia (Hawkins) R.; ed. Peabody Coll., Nashville, Tenn., 1899-1901; A.B., U. of Nashville, 1903; student Harvard, 1905; LL.D., Okla. Bapt. U., 1934; m. Corinne White, Dec. 25, 1905; 1 son, Charles Walter. Began as rural sch. teacher, 1896; prin. Springfield (Tenn.) High Sch., 1903-07; supt. schs., Princeton, Ky., 1907-11, Ardmore, Okla., 1911-25; state supervisor vocational rehabilitation of Okla., 1931-32; pres. Southwestern State Teachers Coll., Weatherford, Okla., 1932-35; supt. Okla. Orphans Home, Helena, 1935—. Democrat. Baptist. Mason, K.P., Odd Fellow, Elk. Address: Helena, Okla. Deceased.

RICHARDS, De Forest, governor; b. Charlestown, N.H., Aug. 6, 1846; s. J. DeF. and Harriet B. (Jarvis) R.; grad. Kimball Union Acad., Meriden, N.H., 1863; attended Phillips Andover Acad., 1863-64; m. Elise J. Ingersoll, June 1, 1871. Mem. Ala. legislature, 1868; sheriff Wilcox County, Ala., 1868-71; county treas., 2 terms; in business, Camden, Ala., until 1885; then banking Western Neb.; pres. 1st Nat. Bank of Douglas, Wyo., 1886—. Mem. Wyo. Constitutional Conv., 1890; State senator, 1893; gov., 1898. Republican. Home: Cheyenne, Wyo. Died 1903.

RICHARDS, Ellen Henrietta, sanitary chemist; b. Dunstable, Mass., Dec. 3, 1842; d. Peter and Fanny Gould (Taylor) Swallow; A.B., Vassar, 1870, A.M., 1873; S.B., Mass. Inst. Tech., 1873; m. Robert Hallowell Richards, June 6, 1875. Instr. in Woman's Lab., 1876-84, sanitary chemistry, 1884—, Mass. Inst. Tech. As chemist of Mfrs.' Mutual Fire Ins. Co. had much to do with oils, in reference to safety from spontaneous combustion, explosion, etc.; also specialist in water analysis. Author: Air, Water and Food, 1900; First Lessons in Minerals; The Cost of Food, 1900; Cost of Shelter, 1905; First Lessons in Food and Diet; The Art of Right Living, 1905; Sanitation in Daily Life, 1907; Cost of Cleanness, 1908; Industrial Water Analysis, 1909. Home: Jamaica Plain, Mass. Died 1911.

RICHARDS, Emily S. Tanner; b. Salt Lake City, Utah, May 13, 1850; d. Nathan and Rachel Winter (Smith) Tanner; ed. grammar sch.; m. Franklin Snyder Richards, Dec. 18, 1869. Active worker in woman's societies and clubs for many yrs., and served in many offices and dir. many boards; pres. Utah Bd. of Lady Mgrs., World's Fair, Chicago, 1893; first rep. of Mormon women in organization of Nat. Council of Women of U.S., Washington, D.C., 1888; led suffrage campaign in the State Constl. Conv., 1896; pres. Dem. Women's Club; Speaker Internat. Congress of Women, Berlin, Germany, 1904. Home: Salt Lake City, Utah. Died Aug. 19, 1929.

RICHARDS, Erwin Hart, missionary; b. Orwell, O., May 4, 1851; s. Newton Samuel and Mary (Hart) R.; A.B., Oberlin Coll., 1877, A.M., 1880; S.T.B., Andover Theol. Sem., 1880; D.D., U. of New Orleans, 1903; m. Mary Jane McClelland, Oct. 25, 1903. Ordained M.E. ministry, 1880; missionary in East Africa most of time, 1880—; with Layman's Missionary Movement in U.S. and Can., 1913—; lecturer before schs. and colleges. Translator: Tonga Testament, 1890; Sheetswa Bible, 1910; also mission books in 4 langs. and all sch. books for 3 tribes. Home: Oberlin, O. Died Jan. 15, 1928.

RICHARDS, Eugene Lamb, educator; b. Brooklyn, N.Y., Dec. 27, 1838; s. Timothy P. and Agnes Treat (Lamb) R.; A.B., Yale, 1860, A.M., 1887; m. Julia L. Bacon, Nov. 27, 1861. Tutor mathematics, 1868-

71, asst. prof., 1871-91, prof. mathematics, 1891-1906, prof. emeritus 1906, Yale; director Yale Gymnasium, 1892-1902. Author: Plane and Spherical Trigonometry, with Applications, 1879; Elementary Navigation and Nautical Astronomy, 1902. Contbr. of articles on athletics, geometry and other topics to various periodicals. Address: New Haven, Conn. Died Aug. 5, 1912.

RICHARDS, Frederick Thompson, artist; b. Phila., Pa., May 27, 1864; s. Davis Bancroft and Janet (Thompson) R.; pupil of Pa. Acad. Fine Arts, Thomas Eakins, Edmund B. Bensell and Art Students' League, New York; m. Odile A. S. Hudry, Oct. 21, 1890. Exhibited at Paris Expn., 1900. On staff Life, 1889—, also Collier's Weekly; cartoonist N.Y. Herald, 1901, 02; also for N.Y. Times, N.Y. Evening Mail, Phila. Press and Phila. North American. Author: The Royal Game of Golf (series of color prints); Color Prints from Dickens (portfolio); The Blot Book. Address: New York, N.Y. Died July 8, 1921.

RICHARDS, George, capitalist; b. Pottsville, Pa., March 21, 1833; common school edn.; entered employment of Glendon Iron Co., 1851, as weighmaster at iron mine, Hurdtown, N.J.; became shift-boss and, 1853, supt.; then for over 40 years mgr. of that company's mining interests in N.J.; also pres. Dover Iron Co., Morris County Machine and Iron Co., Ogden Mine R.R. Co., Dover & Rockaway R.R. Co., Hibernia Mine R.R. Co., Hibernia Underground R.R. Co., Nat. Union Bank of Dover, Dover Printing Co., Dover Lumber Co., The George Richards Co. (controlling four stores), and dir. of railroad, mining and mfg. companies; m. Ann Elizabeth McCarty, 1860. Apptd., 1871, State dir. United Railroads of N.J., and by his position on the Pa. R.R. lease broke up monopoly of that road; member, 1891—, pres., 1894—, bd. of mgrs. N.J. State Hosp.; mem. State bd. of geol. survey. Address: Dover, N.J. Died 1900.

RICHARDS, George, lawyer; b. Boston, Mass., Mar. 23, 1849; s. George (D.D.) and Anna M. (Woodruff) R.; A.B., Yale, 1872, A.M., 1892; LL.B., Columbia, 1876; m. Harriet M. MacLaren, June 7, 1882; children—Harriet M., Mrs. Marjorie R. Reynolds, Archibald M., Mrs. Anna W. Crane, Guy H. Admitted to bar, 1876; lecturer on ins. law, Columbia, New York U. Author: Law of Insurance, 1909; Cases on Insurance, 1910, 13; Notes for Instructors, 1911. Home: New York, N.Y. Died May 24, 1930.

RICHARDS, Harry Sanger, prof. law; b. Osceola, Ia., Nov. 20, 1868; s. John Willis and Phœbe Ann (Currier) R.; Ph.B., State U. of Ia., 1892; LL.B., cum laude, Harvard, 1895; LL.D., State U. of Ia., 1904; m. Mary C. Holt, 1901. Practiced at Ottumwa, Ia., 1895-98; prof. law, State U. of Ia., 1898-1903; Jackson professor and dean Law Sch., U. of Wis., 1903—. Commissioner on Uniform State Laws for Wis. Chmn. sect. legal edn. Am. Bar Assn., 1908-09; chmn. com. legal edn. Wis. State Bar Assn., 1914-20; pres. Assn. Am. Law Schs., 1914-15. Author: Cases on Private Corporations, 1912-25; Legal Education in Great Britain, 1915. Chief of editorial div., Bur. War Trade Intelligence, War Trade Bd., 1918. Home: Madison, Wis. Died Apr. 21, 1929.

RICHARDS, Henry Melchior Muhlenberg, mfr.; b. Easton, Pa., Aug. 16, 1848; s. John William (D.D.) and Andora (Garber) R.; grad. Reading (Pa.) High Sch., 1864, U.S. Naval Academy, 1869; Litt.D., Muhlenberg Coll., Pa., 1910; m. Ella Van Leer (von Loehr), Dec. 26, 1871; children—Rev. Henry Branson, Charles Matthias, Florence, Alice. Pvt. Co. A, 26th Pa. Emergency Regt., 1863, in battle of Gettysburg, and its campaign; pvt. Co. A, 195th Pa. Regt., 1864, in W.Va., under Sheridan; midshipman U.S.N., July 21, 1865; ensign, July 12, 1870; master, July 12, 1871; lt. (sr.), Nov. 1874; resigned from service, Dec. 1874; volunteered for and served through Spanish-Am. War, 1898, also for service in war against Germany, 1917. Invented circuit-closing device for torpedoes adopted by U.S. Govt., 1872. With Phila. & Reading Ry. Co., 1875-78; served as officer during labor riots, 1877; with J. H. Sternbergh & Son, iron mfrs., Reading, Pa., 1881-99, when consolidated with Am. Iron & Steel Mfg. Co., of which was treas. and dir.; retired Aug. 1916. Treas. City of Lebanon, Pa., 1918-19. Mem. commn. apptd. by Gov. Pattison to locate frontier forts of Pa.; mem. advisory commn. for preservation of pub. records, Pa. War History Commn. Republican. Lutheran. Mason. Author: The Frontier Forts of the Blue Range, 1895; The First Discoverers of America, German, not Latin, 1898; The Descendants of Henry Melchior Muhlenberg, D.D., 1900; Pennsylvania's Emergency Volunteers at Gettysburg, 1905; Pennsylvania Germans in French and Indian War, 1905; Biography of Governor Joseph Hiester and Genealogy of Hiester Family, 1906; The Pennsylvania German in the Revolutionary War, 1775-83, 1908; Our Ancestors in the British Prisons of the Revolution, 1912; Valley Forge and the Pennsylvania Germans, 1916; The Weiser Family, 1924. Home: Lebanon, Pa. Died Sept. 28, 1935.

RICHARDS, Herbert Maule, botanist; b. Germantown, Pa., Oct. 6, 1871; s. William T. (artist) and Anna (Matlack) R. (author); S.B., Harvard, 1891, S.D., 1895; studied at Leipzig, 1895-96; visited bot. garden, Buitenzorg, Java, 1899-1900, and traveled in Japan, China, Straits Settlements and Malay Archipelago; m. Marion Elizabeth Latham, July 17, 1915. Asst. in Harvard and instr. Radcliffe Coll., 1892-95; tutor Barnard Coll. (Columbia), 1896-97; instr. Harvard U. and Radcliffe Coll., 1897-98; instr. 1898-1902; adj. prof. botany 1902-06, prof. botany, 1906—, Barnard Coll. Scientific dir. N.Y. Bot. Garden. Fellow A.A.A.S. (v.p. sect. G, 1908). Home: New York, N.Y. Died Jan. 9, 1928.

RICHARDS, John E., judge; b. San Jose, Calif., July 7, 1856; s. Richard Evan and Mary (Hamilton) R.; B.A., U. of the Pacific, 1877, M.A., 1915, LL.D., 1924; LL.B., U. of Mich., 1879; m. Mary Wallace, Nov. 23, 1881. Admitted to Calif. bar, 1879, and practiced in San Jose and San Francisco; apptd. judge Superior Court of Santa Clara Co., 1907, and served until 1913; asso. justice Dist. Court of Appeal, 1913-23; asso. justice Supreme Court of Calif., Feb. 11, 1924—, for term expiring Jan. 1, 1935. Republican. Episcopalian. Mason, Red Man. Author: Idylls of Monterey and Other Verses, 1910; The Trial of Jesus, 1915. Home: San Jose, Calif. Died June 25, 1932.

RICHARDS, John Gardiner, gov.; b. Liberty Hill, S.C., Sept. 11, 1864; s. Rev. John Gardiner and Sophie (Edwards) R.; ed. Bingham (N.C.) Mil. Inst.; m. Elizabeth Coates Workman, June 12, 1888; 11 children, 9 daughters, and 2 sons, William Henry (dec.), Stephen M. (died in mil. service, 1918). Farmer; served as magistrate, 1892-1900; mem. S.C. Ho. of Rep., 1898-1910 (mem. ways com. 10 yrs., chmn. 1 term); railroad commr. S.C., 12 yrs., chmn. 5 yrs.; defeated for governorship, 1910, 14, 18; governor term, 1927-31; became tax commr. of State of S.C. Captain Liberty Hill Rifles 14 yrs.; mem. S.C. exec. com. Council of Defense, World War; served as mem. S.C. Mil. Bd. 4 yrs.; maj. 3d Bn., 1st Regt. till retired as lt. col.; served as chmn. exec. com. Nat. Assn. Rys. and as 1st pres. Southeastern Assn. R.R. Commrs. Chmn. S.C. Natural Resources Commn.; elected to Dem. Nat. Com., Denver, Colo., and Houston, Tex. Trustee Clemson Coll., 1905-10. Democrat. Presbyn. Home: Liberty Hill, S.C. Died Oct. 9, 1941.

RICHARDS, John Kelvey, judge U.S. Circuit Court, 6th circuit; b. Ironton, O., March 15, 1856; s. Samuel and Sarah (Kelvey) R.; grad. Swarthmore Coll., Pa., A.B., 1875, LL.D., 1903; A.B., Harvard, 1877; m. Anna Willard Steece, June 12, 1890. Pros. atty. Lawrence Co., 1880-82; city solicitor Ironton, 1885-89; State senator, 1890-92; atty. gen. Ohio, 1892-96; mem. commn. to codify ins. laws of Ohio, 1895-96; counsel of coms. on taxation of 72d gen. assembly, 1896, and on drafting new excise tax laws; general counsel State Bd. of Med. Registration and Exam., 1896-98; spl. counsel State Bd. Appraisers and Assessors, 1896-98. Solicitor gen. U.S. 1897-1903, successfully arguing many grave constl. questions in Supreme court U.S., including Anti-Trust, Federal Legacy Tax, and famous Insular cases. Confirmed as judge, Feb. 23, 1903. Home: Cincinnati, O. Died 1909.

RICHARDS, Joseph Havens Cowles, clergyman; b. Columbus, O., Nov. 8, 1851; s. Henry Livingston (Episcopalian clergyman, later Catholic) and Cynthia (Cowles) R.; Boston Coll.; grad. Woodstock (Md.) Coll., 1878. Received into Soc. of Jesus, 1872; taught at Georgetown Coll., 5 yrs.; pres. Georgetown U., D.C., 1888-98; in religious work in Calif. and in novitiates of Frederick, Md., and St. Andrew-on-Hudson, Poughkeepsie, N.Y., until 1906; attached to Boston Coll. and Ch. of the Immaculate Conception, Boston, 3 yrs., and St. Ignatius' Ch., New York, 3½ yrs.; v.p. Canisius Coll., Buffalo, 1913-15; rector Loyola Sch., Regis High Sch. and Ch. of St. Ignatius Loyola, New York, 1915-19; sec.-treas. Manresa Inst., S. Norwalk, Conn., 1919—. Author: A Loyal Life, Biography of Henry Livingstone Richards, 1913. Died June 9, 1923.

RICHARDS, Joseph William, metallurgist; b. Oldbury, Eng., July 28, 1864; s. Joseph and Bridgett (Harvey) R.; A.B., Central High Sch., Phila., 1882, A.M., 1887; A.C., Lehigh U., 1886, M.S., 1891, Ph.D., 1893; Univ. of Heidelberg and Mining Acad., Freiberg, 1897-98; m. Arnamarie Gadd, of Gloucestershire, Eng., Mar. 12, 1887. Instr. metallurgy and mineralogy, 1887-97, asst. prof., 1897-1902, acting prof. metallurgy, 1902-03, prof., 1903—, Lehigh U.; prof. electro-chemistry, Franklin Inst. of Phila., 1907-10. Legal expert in chemical and metall. cases; mem. U.S. Assay Commn., 1897; rep. of Franklin Inst. to Internat. Geol. Congress, Russia, 1897; mem. jury of awards, dept. chemistry, Nat. Export Exhbn., Phila., 1899; mem. jury of awards (and chairman metall. sub-jury) Panama P.I. Expn., 1915; mem. U.S. Navy Consulting Board, 1915-18. Mem. numerous professional societies. Author: Aluminum (only treatise on that metal in English), 1887; 3d edit., 1895; Metallurgical Calculations, Part I, General Metallurgy, 1906, Part II, Iron and Steel, 1907, Part III, Non-ferrous Metals, 1908. Died Oct. 12, 1921.

RICHARDS, Lewis Loomis, pianist; b. St. Johns, Mich., Apr. 11, 1881; s. Jonathan Edwards and Hulda (Loomis) R.; ed. pub. schs.; musical edn., Royal Conservatory of Music, Brussels, Belgium; hon. A.M., Wesleyan U., Middletown, Conn., 1919; m. Berthe Emilie Smedt, of Brussels, July 11, 1908; children—Elsa Loomis, Roger Lewis. Concert tours, Europe, 1908-14; returned to U.S., 1923; head of dept. of music, Mich. State Coll. Agr. and Applied Science, 1927—. Mem. Commn. Relief in Belgium, World War; in charge distribution foodstuffs and clothing in Brussels, later at Lille, Valenciennes and Rotterdam, and asst. dir. London office; dir. Commission for Relief in Belgium Ednl. Foundation. Received medals from the cities of Brussels (Belgium) Lille and Valenciennes (France). Decorated Chevalier Order of Crown of Belgium; Reconnaissance Française; Reconnaissance de la Belgique. Republican. Episcopalian. Home: East Lansing, Mich. Died Feb. 15, 1940.

RICHARDS, T. Addison, artist-author; b. London, England, Dec. 3, 1820; came to U.S., 1831; lived in Ga., 1835-44; since then in New York; studied art at Nat. Acad. Design, in which he became associate, 1848; academician, 1851; member council and corr. sec., 1852-92; m. Mary Anthony, 1857 (died 1894). Prof. art Univ. City of New York, 1868—; first director Cooper Union Woman's Art School, 1859-60. Has traveled much in U.S. and abroad. Contbr. for many years illustrated articles, pictures and text, to Harper's Mag. Author and illustrator: The American Artist; Georgia Illustrated; Romance of American Landscape; Summer Stories of the South; Pictures and Painters; also Appleton's illustrated Handbooks of Travel. Died 1900.

RICHARDS, Theodore William, chemist; b. Germantown, Pa., Jan. 31, 1868; s. William T. (artist) and Anna (Matlack) R. (author); S.B. Haverford Coll., 1885; A.B., Harvard, 1886, A.M., Ph.D., 1888; chem. student, univs. of Göttingen, Leipzig and Tech. Sch., Dresden; Sc.D., Yale, 1905; LL.D., Haverford, 1908; Chem.D., Clark U., 1909; Ph.D., Royal Bohemian U., Prague, 1909; Sc.D., Harvard, 1910; M.D., Berlin U., 1910; D.Sc., Cambridge (Eng.), Oxford, Manchester, 1911; Ph.D., Christiania, Norway, 1911; LL.D., U. of Pittsburgh, 1915, U. of Pa., 1920; Sc.D., Princeton U., 1923; m. Miriam Stuart, d. of Prof. J. H. Thayer, of Cambridge, Mass., May 28, 1896; children—Grace Thayer (wife of Prof. James Bryant Conant), William Theodore, Greenough Thayer. Asst. prof., 1894-1901, prof. chemistry, 1901—, chmn. chem. dept., 1903-11, dir. Gibbs Memorial Lab., 1912—, Harvard. Exchange prof. from Harvard to Berlin U., 1907; Lowell lecturer, 1908; mem. Internat. Com. on Elements and Atomic Weights; adviser Carnegie Instn., 1902, research asso., 1902—, Davy medalist, Royal Soc., 1910; Faraday lecturer and medalist, Chem. Soc., 1911; Willard Gibbs medalist, Am. Chem. Soc., 1912; Nobel laureate in chemistry, 1914 (awarded 1915); Franklin medal, Franklin Inst., 1916; Lavoisier and Le Blanc medalist (Paris), 1922. Member Nat. Research Council and allied coms., 1916; consulting chemist, War Department and Bur. of Mines, 1918. With help of assistants has revised atomic weights of oxygen, copper, barium, strontium, calcium, zinc, magnesium, iron, nickel, cobalt, uranium, cæsium, sodium, chlorine, potassium, nitrogen, silver, sulphur, carbon, lithium, radioactive lead, gallium, aluminum. Investigator in physical and inorganic chemistry; recent papers concern the significance of changing atomic volume, and other effects of internal cohesive and chemical pressure; also thermochemistry and electrochemistry, etc. Fellow Am. Acad. Arts and Sciences (pres. 1919-21), A.A.A.S. (pres. 1917). Officier de la Legion d'Honneur, 1925. Home: Cambridge, Mass. Died Apr. 2, 1928.

RICHARDS, Thomas Cole, clergyman; b. Wednesbury, Eng., Feb. 24, 1866; s. George and Mary Ann (Spencer) R.; came to America, 1874; A.B., Williams Coll., 1887, A.M., 1892; grad. Hartford Theol. Sem., 1890; m. Charlotte Olive Noyes, June 10, 1890; children—Ruth, Elizabeth Warren. Ordained Congl. ministry, 1890; pastor Dudley, Mass., 1890-94, Higganum, Conn., 1894-99, Torrington, Conn., 1899-1906, Warren, Mass., 1906-11, Westboro, Mass., 1911-16, Bethany Ch., Quincy, 1916-19, Medford, 1919-28 (emeritus). Mem. John Brown Assn. (owns and cares for John Brown's birthplace). Author: Samuel J. Mills, Missionary (Pathfinder, Pioneer and Promoter, 1906; Young Men and Prayer, 1919. Home: Medford, Mass. Died Feb. 24, 1936.

RICHARDS, Mrs. Waldo (Gertrude E. Moore); b. Gardiner, Me.; d. Seth Gay and Almira Clapp (Butman) Moore; ed. pub. schs. and under pvt. tutors; m. Charles Waldo Richards, Oct. 26, 1881 (died 1902). Reader and interpreter of literature, chiefly poetry, in U.S. and Europe, appearing largely before drawing room audiences. Compiler: High Tide—Songs of Joy and Vision, from the Present-Day Poets of America and Great Britain, 1916; The Melody of Earth, 1918; Star Points, 1921; The Magic Carpet (poem); Poems for Travelers. Home: New York, N.Y. Died Jan. 7, 1927.

RICHARDS, William Alford, governor; b. Hazel Green, Wis., Mar. 9, 1849; s. Truman Perry and Eleanor (Swinerton) R.; common sch. edn. there and at Galena, Ill.; m. Harriet Alice Hunt, Dec. 28, 1874. Surveyor gen. Wyo., 1889-93; gov. Wyo., Jan. 1, 1895 to Jan. 1, 1899; asst. commr., 1899-1903, commr., 1903-07, Gen. Land Office; commr. of taxation, state of Wyo., Feb. 1909—. Home: No Wood, Wyo. Died July 26, 1912.

RICHARDS, William Rogers, clergyman; b. Boston, Mass., Dec. 20, 1853; s. George and Anna Maria (Woodruff) R.; ed. Golden Hill Inst., Bridgeport, Conn., 1866-70, Yale, A.B., 1875, Columbia Law Sch., 1875-76, Andover Theol. Sem., grad. 1879 (D.D., Univ. City of New York, 1892, Yale, 1903); m. Charlotte Barrrett Blodgett, Jan. 27, 1880. Ordained and installed pastor Central Congl. Ch., Bath, Me., Oct. 16, 1879; pastor Crescent Av. Presbyn. Ch., Plainfield, N.J., 1884-1902; pastor Brick Presbyn. Ch., New York, Oct. 1902—. Mem. Bd. Foreign Missions, Presbyn. Ch., 1890—. Dir. Union Theol. Sem., 1903—; mem. council Univ. City of New York, 1903—. Republican. Mem. S.R. Sch. commr. Plainfield, N.J., 1899-1902. Author: Ways of Wisdom, 1886; For Whom Christ Died, 1902; God's Choice of Men, 1905; The Apostles' Creed in Modern Worship, 1906. Died 1910.

RICHARDS, William Trost, artist; b. Phila., Nov. 14, 1833; s. Benjamin M. and Annie R.; ed. Phila. grammar and high schools; studied in Florence, Rome and Paris; m. Anna Matlack, 1856 (died 1900). Painter of landscapes and sea pictures; represented in permanent collections of Metropolitan Museum, New York; Pa. Acad. of Fine Arts, Phila. and Corcoran Art Gallery, Washington; Metropolitan Museum, New York; Schaube Gallery, Hamburg, Germany. Received Centennial Expn. medal, 1876; Temple medal, Pa. Acad. of Fine Arts; bronze medal, Paris Expn., 1889. Home: Newport, R.I. Died 1905.

RICHARDSON, Abby Sage, author; b. (Sage), 1837; m. Albert Deane Richardson, journalist (died 1869); lecturer. Author: Familiar Talks on English Literature; Old Love Letters; Stories from Old English Poetry; History of Our Country; Ablelard and Heloise, a Mediæval Romance. Editor: Songs from the Old Dramatists; Garnered Sheaves (collection of her husband's miscellaneous writings, with memoir). Home: New York, N.Y. Died 1900.

RICHARDSON, Anna Euretta, home economist; b. Charleston, S.C., Sept. 5, 1883; d. William Henry and Euretta Love (Miller) R.; B.S., Peabody Coll. for Teachers, Nashville, Tenn., 1903; grad. study U. of Chicago, 1904; M.A., Columbia, 1911; unmarried. Teacher pvt. and pub. schs., 1905-10; prof. home economics, Agnes Scott Coll. for Women, Decatur, Ga., 1911-12; instr. in home economics, U. of Tex., 1912-13, adj. prof., 1913-17; chief of home economics edn. service Federal Bd. for Vocational Edn., Washington, D.C., 1917-22; dean of home economics div., Ia. State Coll., 1922-26; field worker for Am. Home Economics Assn., 1926. Episcopalian. Died Feb. 3, 1931.

RICHARDSON, Basil, judge; b. Center Point, Ky., July 26, 1866; s. Robert Hildreth and Margaret (Kirkpatrick) R.; A.B., Burritt Coll., Spencer, Tenn., 1887; LL.B., U. of Louisville (Ky.), 1890; m. Mary B. Evans, 1895; children—John Evans, Margaret (Mrs. Ralph Kinnaird, dec.). Admitted to Ky. bar, 1890, practiced in Glasgow, 1890-1923; presdl. elector for Ky., 1892; became mem. state senate, 1917; circuit judge, 10th jud. dist. of Ky., 1923-30; judge of Court of Appeals of Ky., 1930-38. Mem. bd. dirs. Community Hosp., Glasgow. Democrat. Mem. Christian (Disciples) Ch. Mason. Home: Glasgow, Ky. Died Jan. 25, 1937.

RICHARDSON, Charles; b. Phila., Jan. 27, 1841; s. John and Martha (Gibbons) R.; ed. Friends' pvt. schs.; m. Hannah Perot, Nov. 19, 1874. Formerly in conveyancing and real estate business; one of founders of first title ins. co. in the world; 1st pres. The Land Title & Trust Co. of Phila., 1885-87; trustee Title Guarantee & Trust Co., New York. Mem. Nat. Municipal League (1st v.p.), Nat. Civ. Service Reform League (council), Pa. Civ. Service Reform Assn. (exec. com.); active in the Phila. Com. of 100 and subsequent reform orgns. for the last 25 years. Mem. Soc. of Friends. Home: Philadelphia, Pa. Died Nov. 19, 1922.

RICHARDSON, Charles Francis, author; b. Hallowell, Me., May 29, 1851; s. Dr. Moses Charles and Mary Savary (Wingate) R.; A.B., Dartmouth, 1871, A.M., 1874; (hon. Ph.D., Union Coll., 1895; Litt.D., Dartmouth, 1911); m. Elizabeth Miner Thomas, Apr. 12, 1878. On staff the Independent, New York, 1872-78, Sunday School Times, Phila., 1878-80; editor Good Literature, New York, 1880-82; Winkley prof. Anglo-Saxon and English lang. and lit., Dartmouth, 1882-1911. Author: A Primer of American Literature, 1878; The College Book, 1878; The Cross (poems), 1879; The Choice of Books, 1881; American Literature, 1607-1885, 2 vols., 1886-88; The End of the Beginning (romance), 1896; A Study of English Rhyme, 1909. Editor: Cooper's The Last of the Mohicans, 1897; Poe's Complete Works, 1902; Daniel Webster for Young Americans, 1903. Home: Hanover, N.H. Died Oct. 8, 1913.

RICHARDSON, Charles Freemont, coal operator; b. Waterford, Vt., Nov. 8, 1862; s. Charles Partridge and Kate (Moore) R.; ed. pub. schs., Lancaster, N.H.; m. Marcia Stevens, Sept. 2, 1885; children—Herbert Littlejohn, Ellen Lucretia (Mrs. Clyde A. Clapp). Served as gen. road foreman of engines, B.&O. R.R., and St.L.&S.F. R.R.; was also fuel agt. of latter, then ast. to general supt. of motive power, C.,R.I.&P. R.R.; asst. to pres. West Ky. Coal Co. of N.J., 1911-16, pres., 1916—, also pres. West Kentucky Coal Co. of Delaware, West Kentucky Property Co., St. Bernard Coal Co.; chmn. of traffic, West Kentucky Coal Bureau. Republican. Methodist. Mason. Kiwanian. Home: Sturgis, Ky. Died July 17, 1939.

RICHARDSON, Charles Henry, geologist; b. Topsham, Vt., Sept. 26, 1862; s. Robert Fletcher and Rosetta (Dexter) R.; Bates Coll., Me., 1887-89; A.B., Dartmouth, 1892, A.M., 1895, Ph.D., 1898; studied U. of Chicago, 1902, Johns Hopkins, 1906; m. Katharine May Davis, June 16, 1892. Prin. schs. in Vt. to 1895; fellow and instr. chemistry, etc., Dartmouth, 1895-1905; in life ins. business, Manchester, N.H., 1905-06; asst. prof. geology and mineralogy 1906, associate prof., 1907-09, prof. mineralogy, 1909—, Syracuse U. Mem. Vt. Geol. Survey, summers, 1895—. Republican. Conglist. Fellow Geol. Soc. America, A.A.A.S.; mem. advisory council Simplified Spelling Bd.; mem. council Nat. Resources Assn.; mem. 8th and del. 12th Internat. Geologic Congress; mem. gen. com. of science, arts and edn., Paris Expn., 1901. Home: Syracuse, N.Y. Died Sept. 19, 1935.

RICHARDSON, Charles Williamson, M.D.; b. Washington, Aug. 22, 1861; s. Charles F. E. and Charlotte Ann (Williamson) R.; student Columbian (now George Washington) U., 1878-80, M.D., 1884; also M.D., U. of Pa., 1884; hon. Sc.D., George Washington U., 1921, and same degree from Univ. of Pa., 1927; m. Amy Elizabeth Small, May 27, 1889. Prof. laryngology and otology, George Washington Univ., 1891-1924 (emeritus), Fellow Am. Laryngol., Rhinol. and Otol. Soc. (pres. 1902-03), Am. Otol. Soc. (pres. 1914-15), Am. Laryngol. Assn., Am. Climatol. and Clin. Soc. (pres. 1921-22); F.A.C.S. Dir. sect. of defects of hearing and speech, Office of Surgeon Gen., 1917-18; now col. Med. R.C. Pres. of the Fossils, 1927. Home: Washington, D.C. Died Aug. 25, 1929.

RICHARDSON, Clifford, chemical engr.; b. Worcester, Mass., Mar. 6, 1856; s. George W. and Lucy D. (White) R.; A.B., Harvard, 1877; m. Teresa Stoughton, Dec. 26, 1894. With U.S. Geol. Survey, 1878; asst. chemist U.S. Dept. of Agr., 1878-87; insp. asphalt and cements, engr. dept. D.C., 1887-94; supt. of tests, Barber Asphalt Paving Co., 1896-1900, and cons. chemical engr. same, 1913—; propr. New York Testing Lab., Jan. 1, 1900-10; expert in asphalt, bitumen and Portland cement. Deceased.

RICHARDSON, Ellen A., artist, writer; b. Portsmouth, N.H., Aug. 1845; d. Oren and Ann H. W. Bragdon; ed. pub. and pvt. schs.; spl. studies in art; m. A. Maynard Richardson, Apr. 28, 1870. Founder, 1st pres. (2 yrs.) and now hon. pres., George Washington Memorial Assn. (founded to promote Nat. Univ.); founder, 1894, and from then state pres. Mass. Floral Emblem Soc.; organized Home Congress; founder Mass. Business League; judge of art on bd. of awards, Chicago Expn. and Atlanta Expn.; became head of cabinet dept., art and literature, Nat. Council of Women of U.S.; speaker for U.S. at Quinquennial of Internat. Council of Women, Berlin, 1904; mem. Interparliamentary Union. Founded and edited Woman's Review; edited booklets on Home, daily, for Home Congresses, held in Boston; founded and edited, 3 yrs., The Business Folio; edited home dept., Boston Commonwealth; apptd. to write report on potteries exhibited at Chicago Expn.; contbr. and reviewer to The Arena. Home: Boston, Mass. Died 1911.

RICHARDSON, Elliott Verne, consul; b. Newburyport, Mass., Mar. 4, 1868; s. Rev. Richard Henry (D.D.) and Elizabeth Octavia (Woodbridge) R.; prep. edn., State Model Sch., Trenton, N.J.; A.B., Princeton, 1888; post-grad. work, same univ. and Johns Hopkins, 1889; m. Adelaide Palmer of S. Africa, Aug. 30, 1902; 1 son, William Allen. Newspaper work, S. Africa and Sydney, Australia, until 1909; apptd. clk. Am. Consulate, Sydney, June 1, 1909; vice and dep. consul gen., Mar. 25, 1910; consul at Moncton, Can., 1916-18, Quebec, 1918-19, Karachi, India, 1919-22, Coblenz, Germany, 1922, Berlin, 1922-23, Pernambuco, Brazil, 1923-24; spl. detail, economic survey of Republic of Haiti, 1924-25; reassigned to Karachi, 1925. Served as vol. U.S.S. Badger, 1898, Spanish-Am. War. Fellow Am. Geog. Soc. Presbyn. Died June 26, 1929.

RICHARDSON, Ernest Cushing, librarian; b. Woburn, Mass., Feb. 9, 1860; s. James Cushing and Lydia Bartlett (Taylor) R.; A.B., Amherst, 1880, A.M., 1883; Ph.D., from Washington and Jefferson, 1887; grad. Hartford Theol. Sem., 1883; (hon. A.M., Princeton, 1896); m. Grace Duncan, d. Z. Stiles Ely, of New York, June 30, 1891; 1 dau., Mary Ely (dec.). First asst. librarian, Amherst Coll., 1879-80; librarian Hartford Theol. Sem., 1884-90, asso. prof. bibliology, 1885-90; librarian Princeton U., 1890-1920, dir., 1920-23, hon. dir. and research prof. bibliography, 1923-25 (emeritus); consultant in bibliography and research, Library of Congress, 1925—. Mem. N.J. Pub. Library Commn., 1900-12; trustee Hartford Theol. Sem. Mem. A.L.A. (pres. 1904-05), Am. Library Inst. (pres. 1915-18). Author: Bibliographical Synopsis of the Ante-Nicene Fathers, 1887; Classification, Theoretical and Practical, 1901, 11, 29; Revised transls. of Eusebius' Life of Constantine, 1890; Jerome and Gennadius' Lives of Illustrious Men, 1892; critical edit. of Hieronymus u. Gennadius De Viris Illustribus, 1896; Biblical Libraries, 1914; American Books and Libraries (League of Nations Bull.), 1925; Special Collections in North American Libraries, 1927; Some Aspects of International Library Coöperation, 1928; Subject Headings in Theology, 1928; Princeton University Library Classification, 1900-20, 1929; General Library Coöperation and American Research Books, 1929; A.L.A. Plan for Research Library Service, 1930; Possibilities of Coöperative Cataloging, 1932; A World Catalog of Manuscript Books, 1933-1937, 6 parts; Aspects of Coöperative Cataloging, 1933; Jacopo da Varagine, 1935. Home: Princeton, N.J. Died June 3, 1939.

RICHARDSON, Francis Asbury, newspaper corr.; b. Baltimore, Jan. 10, 1838; s. Beale Howard and Mary (Peters) R.; student City Coll., Baltimore; m. Margaret Howard. Mng. editor Baltimore Republican at age of 23; Washington corr. Baltimore Sun, 1866-1901; has contributed to Sun several series European letters, and letters from all parts of U.S.; also reported national convs., both parties, 1872-1900; clerk U.S. Senate com. on printing, and editor Congressional Directory, 1879-81; chmn. press com. at both inaugurations of Grover Cleveland. Pub. and editor Baltimore Historical and Biographical, 1871. Retired from active work, 1901. Corr. from Washington at various periods for N.Y. Tribune, New Orleans; Picayune, Savannah News, and Atlanta Herald. Home: Washington, D.C. Died Mar. 6, 1926.

RICHARDSON, Francis Henry, artist; b. Boston, Mass., July 4, 1859; s. William Henry and Frances Stone (Coffin) R.; grad. Roxbury High Sch., Boston; pupil of William M. Hunt, Boston, Acad. Julian, Paris, under Boulanger, Lefebvre, Laurens and Benjamin Constant; m. Frances Hill, June 1, 1893; children—Beatrice (dec.), Eleonore, Jerome. Exhibited, Paris Salon, 1888-1900, also at Munich, Berlin, London, Venice, etc., and in all the principal exhbns. in America; represented in collections of Boston Art Club, Lasell Sem., Salmagundi Club, Town of Braintree, Mass., and numerous pvt. collections. Devotes attention largely to portrait work. Honorable mention, Paris Salon, 1899; medal, Am. Art Soc., Phila. Republican. Unitarian. Home: Ipswich, Mass. Died Apr. 17, 1934.

RICHARDSON, Frank Chase, neurologist; b. Boston, Mass., Aug. 11, 1859; s. George Henry and Eliza Ellen (Chase) R.; student Boston U.; M.D., Boston U. Sch. of Medicine, 1879; post-grad. work New York Post-Grad. Sch., Harvard Med. Sch. and Vienna; m. Nellie Chase, 1883. Practiced in Boston, 1879—; chief of clinic for nervous diseases, Homœ. Dispensary, and neurologist, Mass. Homœ. Hosp.; registrar and prof. neurology, Boston U. Sch. of Medicine, also clin. dir. Evans Memorial Dept. of Clin. Research and Preventive Medicine. Republican. Universalist. Mason, Odd Fellow. Home: Boston, Mass. Died June 30, 1918.

RICHARDSON, Frederick, painter; b. Chicago, Oct. 26, 1862; s. William E. and Belinda G. (Hurd) R.; ed. in St. Louis; art edn., St. Louis Sch. of Fine Arts, and Academie Julian, Paris; m. Josephine Welles, 1897; children—David Welles, Allan Barbour. Artist on staff Chicago Daily News, 15 yrs.; instr. Art Inst. Chicago, 7 yrs.; in New York, 1903—; illustrator in various mags. Painter—exhibited in Paris Salon, 1889. Published "Book of Drawings by Frederick Richardson," 1899. Died Jan. 15, 1937.

RICHARDSON, George Lynde, clergyman; b. Troy, N.Y., May 8, 1867; s. Henry and Margaret Preston (Johnston) R.; A.B., Williams, 1888, D.D., 1918; Seabury Div. Sch., 1892-93; m. Grace W. Belcher, Nov. 4, 1894 (died 1933); children—George Lynde, Elizabeth Hope (wife of Douglas J. Roberts, M.D.), Arthur Hall, Edgar Preston. Teacher of classics, high schs., Minn., 1888-92; deacon, 1891, priest, 1892, P.E. Ch.; instr. Seabury Div. Sch., Faribault, Minn., 1891-92; asst., St. John's Ch., Troy, 1892, St. Paul's Ch., Albany, N.Y., 1892-94; rector St. Peter's Ch., Bennington, Vt., 1894-98, Messiah Ch., Glens Falls, N.Y., 1898-1908, St. Mary's, Phila., Pa., 1908-18; vicar of Pro-Cathedral, Phila., 1918-22; rector St. Paul's, Burlington, Vt., 1922-28; dean of Cathedral of All Saints, Albany, N.Y., 1928-32; rector All Saints Ch., Peterborough, N.H., 1932—. Republican. Author: Arthur C. A. Hall (a biography), 1932. Mem. editorial staff The Living Ch. Home: Peterborough, N.H. Died Jan. 24, 1935.

RICHARDSON, George Tilton, journalist, author; b. Boston; s. Nathaniel and Martha A. (Moore) R.; ed. Boston Latin Sch., Boston U.; m. Cara Barnard, May 24, 1901. City editor Boston Advertiser and Record 1888-91; mng. editor Boston News, 1891-92, Providence News, 1892; dramatic critic and editorial writer of Boston Traveler, 1892-1904; editor-in-chief Boston Daily Tribune, 1907-08; mng. editor

Boston Traveler, 1908-10; editor Human Life, mag., 1910-11; editor Boston Chamber of Commerce News, 1912-14; editor Worcester (Mass.) Evening Post, 1914-37. Chmn. of Worcester Park Commission. Coauthor: Miss Petticoats, 1902; On Satan's Mount, 1903; My Lady Laughter, 1904; Letters of a Son to His Self-Made Father, 1904; A Self-Made Man's Wife, Her Letters to Her Son, 1905; The Golden Greyhound, 1906; Meyer & Son, 1908. Home: Worcester, Mass. Died Sept. 11, 1938.

RICHARDSON, Harry Alden, senator; b. Camden, Del., Jan. 1, 1853; s. Alden Bradford and Lucy (Mendall) R.; pub. sch. edn., Dover, Del., and East Greenwich, R.I.; m. Priscilla Walker, 1874; children—Alden Bradford (dec.), William Walker, Lucy Stites (dec.). Began trade as can maker at 16, in firm of Richardson & Robbins, of which father was head; upon the death of Mr. Robbins, 1876, became mem. of firm, and head of same on death of father, 1894; served as pres. Dover Gaslight Co., Del. Fire Ins. Co., Diamond State Telephone Co. Candidate for gov. of Del., 1890; elected U.S. senator, for term 1907-13. Republican. Baptist. Died June 16, 1928.

RICHARDSON, Henry Brown, mem. U.S. Miss. River Commission; b. Winthrop, Me., Aug. 23, 1837; ed. in public and private schools, Portland, Me.; 1857-59 in civil engring. offices in Portland, Milwaukee, Chicago, Boston and La.; m. Anna Howard Farrar, June 18, 1867; 1861-65, pvt. 6th La. vol. inf., lt. engrs. and capt. engrs., provisional army Confederate States army Northern Va.; prisoner of war, Johnson's Island. Mem. La. Bd. State Engrs., 1877-1904; chief State engr., 1880-1904. Home: New Orleans, La. Died 1909.

RICHARDSON, Hester Dorsey, historian, author, lecturer; b. Baltimore, Md., d. James Levin and Sarah Ann Webster (Richardson) Dorsey; ed. pvt. sch. for girls, Baltimore; m. Albert Levin Richardson, Jan. 27, 1891; 1 son, Dorsey. Contbr. poems to mags., etc., 1886-90, spl. articles under penname "Selene," Baltimore Sunday American, 1887-91; spl. corr. New York Herald, Philadelphia Press and Baltimore American, 1889-90; contbr. Harper's Weekly, N.Am. Rev., Lippincott's Mag., 1891-1902, Side Lights on Maryland History, weekly to Baltimore Sun, 1903-04. Pres. Pub. Records Commn. of Maryland (appointed by governor), May, 19, 1904; special exec. historian to represent exec. dept. of Md. in the historic work at Jamestown Expn., 1907; mem. Baltimore 200th Birthday Anniversary Com. by apptmt. of the mayor; member of the Md. Tercentenary Commission appointed by the governor; historical dir. Md. commission to the Panama P.I. Expn., 1915; historian Municipal Flag Commn. of Baltimore, 1914, by apptmt. of mayor; editor Patriotic Marylander, 1914-15. President and founder of Order of Colonial Lords of Manors in America; fellow Manorial Society Eng. Author: Feudal Customs in America, 1912; Sidelights on Maryland History (2 vols.), 1913. Home: Baltimore, Md. Died Dec. 10, 1933.

RICHARDSON, James Bailey, judge; b. Orford, N.H., Dec. 9, 1832; s. Joel and Sarah (Bailey) R.; student Yale, 1 yr.; grad. Dartmouth, 1857 (LL.D., 1896); admitted to Suffolk bar, 1859; practiced at Boston; m. Lucy Cushing Gould, Nov. 15, 1865. Mem. Mass. Ho. of Rep., 1866; mem. Boston Common Council, 1877, 1878; commr. on Revision of Boston City Charter, 1884; corp. counsel City of Boston, 1889-91; mem. Rapid Transit Commn. of Boston, 1891; asso. justice Superior Ct. of Mass., May 1892—. Trustee Franklin Savings Bank, 1876—; trustee Dartmouth Coll., 1890-1903 (Richardson Dormitory, named for him); founder of Joel Richardson scholarship at Dartmouth Coll., 1894; in honor of his father; mgr. N.E. Home for Little Wanderers, 1875—. Author: Notes on Equity Pleading and Practice in Massachusetts, 1904. Home: Boston, Mass. Died 1911.

RICHARDSON, James Daniel, congressman; b. Rutherford Co., Tenn., Mar. 10, 1843; s. John Watkins and Augusta Mary (Starnes) R.; ed. country schs. and Franklin Coll., but left before graduating to enter C.S.A. as pvt.; for 3 yrs. adj. 45th Tenn. Inf.; m. Miss Pippen, 1865. Began law practice, 1867., at Murfreesboro; member and speaker Tennessee Legislature, 1871-72; state senator, 1873-74; delegate Dem. Nat. conventions, 1876, 1896, 1900; permanent chmn. of Kansas City conv., 1900. Mem. Congress, 1885-1905; Dem. nominee for speaker of House of 56th and 57th Congresses, and received Dem. vote in the House; was chmn. Nat. Congressional Com. Grand Master of Masons in Tenn., 1873-74; Grand High Priest, Grand Chapter, R.A.M., Tenn., 1882; Insp. Gen. A.&A. Scottish Rite Masons, 33°, in Tenn.; Grand Comdr. Supreme Council of this Rite; Pro-Grand Master of Grand Lodge of Royal Order of Scotland in U.S. Editor and compiler Messages and Papers of the Presidents, and Messages and Papers of the Confederacy. Home: Murfreesboro, Tenn. Died July 24, 1914.

RICHARDSON, James Julius, physician; b. Sardis, O., Jan. 23, 1868; s. R. T. and Elizabeth R.; M.D., U. of Md., 1889; post-grad. courses New York Post-Grad. Med. Sch., U. of Edinburgh, U. of Vienna, Post-Grad. Med. Sch., London; m. Dorothy Flynn, Apr. 22, 1905. Specialist in diseases of ear, nose and throat. Home: Washington, D.C. Died June 28, 1933.

RICHARDSON, Katharine Berry, M.D.; b. Flat Rock, Ky.; d. Stephen Paine and Harriett (Benson) Berry; Ph.B., Mt. Union Coll., Alliance, O., 1882, Ph.M., 1887, LL.D. from the same college in 1931; M.D., Pennsylvania Woman's Med. Coll., Phila., 1887; m. James Ira Richardson, 1893 (died 1908). Began practice at La Crosse, Wis., 1887; moved to Kansas City, Mo., and associated in practice with sister, Dr. Alice Berry Graham, dentist, also associated with sister, 1897, in founding Mercy Hosp., for sick and crippled children who cannot pay (now 162 beds); specialized in plastic surgery of face, including hare lip and cleft palate. Protestant. Home: Kansas City, Mo. Died June 3, 1933.

RICHARDSON, Maurice Howe, surgeon; b. Athol, Mass., Dec. 31, 1851; s. Nathan Henry and Martha Ann (Barber) R.; brother of Mark Wyman R.; A.B., Harvard, 1873, M.D., 1877; m. Margaret White Peirson, July 10, 1879. In practice of surgery at Boston, 1876—; asst. anatomy, 1879-82, demonstrator, 1882-87, asst. surgery, 1883-87, asst. prof. anatomy, 1887-95, asst. prof. clin. surgery, 1895-1902, asso. prof., 1902-03, prof. clin. surgery, 1903-07, Moseley prof. surgery, 1907—, Harvard. Visiting surgeon, Mass. Gen. Hosp., 1886-1911, surgeon-in-chief, 1911—; cons. surgeon to many hosps., met. and suburban. Unitarian. Republican. Home: Boston, Mass. Died July 31, 1912.

RICHARDSON, Norval, author; b. Vicksburg, Miss., Oct. 8, 1877; s. Lee and Louise (French) R.; ed. Lawrenceville (N.J.) School, Southwestern Presbyn. U., Clarksville, Tenn.; m. Mabel McGinnis, Jan. 6, 1917; 1 dau., Anne. Second sec. Am. Legation at Havana, Cuba, 1909-11, at Copenhagen, Denmark, 1911-13 (chargé d'affaires, Apr.-June 1911); U.S. spl. envoy to funeral of King Frederick VII of Denmark, 1911; 2d sec. Am. Embassy at Rome, 1913, and sec. same, 1916-20; sec. Am. Embassy, Santiago, Chile, 1920, Lisbon, 1920-22, Tokio, 1922-23; resigned 1924. Author: The World Shut Out, 1919; Pagan Fire, 1920; Cave Woman, 1922; My Diplomatic Education, 1923; That Late Unpleasantness, 1924; Pirate's Face, 1928; Mother of Kings, 1928; Dream Boat, 1929; Third and Last, 1934; Forgotten Lady, 1937; Living Abroad, 1938. Died Oct. 22, 1940.

RICHARDSON, Oliver Huntington, univ. prof.; b. Providence, R. I., Dec. 10, 1866; s. Elias Huntington and Jane Maria (Stevens) R.; A.B., Yale, 1889; Ph.D., U. of Heidelberg, 1897; m. Eloise Wickard, June 26, 1893. Instr. history and polit. economy, Colo. Coll., 1889-90; prof. history, Drury Coll., Mo., 1892-97; asst. prof. history, Yale, 1897-1909; prof. European history, U. of Wash., 1909-30, prof. emeritus, 1930—; prof. history, U. of Southern Calif., summer 1924. Fellow Royal Hist. Society. Author: The National Movement in the Reign of Henry III and Its Culmination in the Barons' War, 1897; Syllabus of Continental European History from the Fall of Rome to 1870, 1904. Home: Seattle, Wash. Died Sept. 22, 1936.

RICHARDSON, Rufus Byam, archeologist; b. Westford, Mass., Apr. 18, 1845; s. Joseph and Lucy M. (Byam) R.; A.B., Yale, 1869, Ph.D., 1878; student Yale Div. Sch., 1869-72, Berlin, 1872-74, B.D., Yale, 1883; m. Alice Linden Bowen, Sept. 6, 1876. Prof. Greek, Ind. Univ., 1880-82, Dartmouth, 1882-93; dir. Am. Sch. Classical Studies, Athens, 1893-1903. Editor: Æschines Oration Against Ctesiphon, 1889. Author: Vacation Days in Greece, 1903; Greece Through the Stereoscope, 1907; History of Greek Sculpture, 1910. Home: Woodstock, Conn. Died Mar. 10, 1914.

RICHARDSON, Warfield Creath, educator; b. Maysville, Ky., June 23, 1823; s. Capt. Thomas Gaines and Sarah (Perry) R.; A.B., U. of Ala., 1843, A.M., 1847; (hon. Ph.D., Agrl. and Mech. Coll. of Ala., 1878; LL.D., U. of Ala., 1906); m. Catherine Cole Jones, Nov. 16, 1855; father of Belle Richardson Harrison. Prof. chemistry, mineralogy and geology, 1864-65, acting prof. Greek, 1876-77, adj. prof. English lit. and instr. mineralogy and geology, 1877, U. of Ala.; retired. Author: Gaspar (metrical romance), 1873; Fall of the Alamo (epic poem); semicentennial ode before Hist. Soc., anniversary poem before Phi Beta Kappa. Home: Tuscaloosa, Ala. Died Mar. 13, 1914.

RICHARDSON, Wilds Preston, army officer; b. in Tex., Mar. 20, 1861; grad. U.S. Mil. Acad., 1884. Commd. 2d lt. 8th Inf., June 15, 1884; 1st lt., Dec. 16, 1889; capt., Apr. 26, 1898; maj. 9th Inf., Apr. 7, 1904; trans. to 13th Inf., Apr. 7, 1908; lt. col. of inf., Mar. 11, 1911; col., Apr. 28, 1914; brig. gen. N.A., Aug. 5, 1917. A.d.c. to Brig. Gen. A. V. Kautz, Dept. of Columbia, 1891-92; instr. tactics, U.S. Mil. Acad., 1892-97; in Alaska, 1897-99; assigned as adj. Dept. of Alaska, 1900; constructing Ft. William H. Seward, 1902-04; mem. Bd. Road Commrs. for Alaska, 1905—. Died May 20, 1929.

RICHARDSON, William, congressman; b. Athens, Ala. Entered C.S.A. as pvt. when 16 yrs. old; wounded 3 times, the last wound, received at Chickamauga, totally disabling him; admitted to bar, 1867; in practice at Huntsville, Ala. Mem. Ala. Ho. of Rep.; co. judge, Madison Co., Ala., 1874-86; presdl. elector-at-large, 1888; candidate for nomination for gov. Ala., 1890; elected to 56th Congress, 1900, for unexpired term (1900-01) of Gen. Joseph E. Wheeler, resigned; reëlected to 57th to 63d Congresses (1901-15), 8th Ala. Dist. Home: Huntsville, Ala. Died Mar. 31, 1914.

RICHARDSON, William Cummings, architect; b. Concord, N.H., Mar. 12, 1854; s. David Cummings and Henrietta Goodwin (Barnard) R.; grad. high sch., Lawrence, Mass., 1872; spl. student in architecture Mass. Inst. Tech., 1873-75; asst. in architectural offices several yrs.; made 4 trips abroad for study and observation; m. Frances Shippen Webster, Oct. 5, 1882; children—Mrs. Constance Kemper, Webster (dec.), Hadwin Houghton. Practiced, Boston, 1881—; mem. Hartwell & Richardson nearly 20 yrs., then Hartwell, Richardson & Driver; later alone under firm name Hartwell & Richardson. Has designed many large bldgs. including upwards of 50 sch. bldgs. Republican. Swedenborgian. Fellow A.I.A. Mason. Home: Newtonville, Mass. Died Oct. 17, 1935.

RICHARDSON, William D., chemist; b. Jackson, Mich., Nov. 24, 1876; s. William L. and Elna (Dyer) R.; ed. high sch. and U. of Chicago, 1894-99. Chemist, 1899-1901, chief chemist, 1901—, Swift & Co., packers, Chicago. Editor, 1908-11, mem. bd. editors, 1911-16, Jour. Industrial and Engineering Chemistry. Fellow A.A.A.S. Home: Chicago, Ill. Died 1936.

RICHARDSON, William Eddy, lawyer; b. Poultney, Vt., Aug. 23, 1861; s. Francis Allan and Mary Smedley (Eddy) R.; removed with parents to Minn. at age of 8; grad. high sch., Austin, Minn., 1878; student Carleton Coll., Northfield, Minn., 2 yrs., 1879-81; m. Kay H. von Suessmilch, Dec. 27, 1882. Admitted to Minn. bar, 1882; practiced in Austin until 1885, then in Duluth; mem. Richardson & Day; largely interested in real estate, and specialized in real property; no longer in active practice; pres. Richardson, Day & Cheadle Co.; officer various land cos. Mem. Bd. of Edn., Duluth, 1891-93 (pres. 1892-93). Republican. Episcopalian. Eminent Commander Duluth Commandery K.T., 1890; Grand Comdr. K.T. of Minn., 1898; Grand Sovereign Red Cross of Constantine, 1916-17. Home: Duluth, Minn. Died Nov. 20, 1923.

RICHARDSON, William Franklin, clergyman; b. Columbus, Ill., June 30, 1852; s. Aaron and Mary (Nance) R.; A.B., Eureka (Ill.) Coll., 1876, A.M., 1879; (LL.D., Drake U., Des Moines, Ia., 1896, and Eureka Coll., 1912); m. Leora M. Emerson, May 24, 1877. Ordained Christian (Disciples) ministry, 1876; pastor Pontiac, Ill., 1875-79, Assumption, Ill., 1879-82, Grand Rapids, Mich., 1884-90, First Ch., Allegheny, Pa., 1890-92, Central Ch., Denver, 1892-94, First Ch., Kansas City, 1894-1917, Hollywood Church, Los Angeles, Calif., 1917—. Pres. State Missionary bds. in states of Mich., Colo., and Mo.; pres. Am. Christian Missionary Soc. at Jubilee Conv., Cincinnati, 1899; pres. Disciples' Congress, 1907; pres. Gen. Conv. of Chs. of Christ, 1915-16. Democrat. Home: Los Angeles, Calif. Died May 25, 1925.

RICHARDSON, William Lambert, M.D.; b. Boston, Sept. 6, 1842; s. Jeffrey and Julia Lambert (Brackett) R.; A.B., Harvard, 1864, A.M., M.D., 1867, also received hon. D.Sc. from same university; m. Olivia L. Aitchison, July 24, 1867. Instr. obstetrics, 1871-72, 1874-82, asst. prof., 1882-86, prof., 1886-1907, prof. emeritus, 1907, dean Med. Sch., 1893-99, dean faculty of medicine, 1899-1907, Harvard U.; also overseer, Harvard, 1909-15. Fellow Am. Acad. Arts and Sciences; hon. fellow Am. Gynecol. Soc. Home: Boston, Mass. Died Oct. 20, 1932.

RICHARDSON, W(illiam) Symmes, architect; b. Kingston, Mass., Feb. 1, 1873; s. Edwin Harmon and Caroline (Symmes) R.; U. of Calif., 2 yrs., class of 1894; Mass. Inst. Tech., 1½ yrs.; 1½ yrs. abroad and at École des Beaux Arts, Paris; unmarried. Mem. McKim, Mead & White for many yrs. from 1906, retired; firm architects for Bank of Montreal and Winnipeg; Girard Trust Co., Phila.; Nat. City Bank, New York; Pa. R.R. Station, New York; residence of John Innes Kane, New York, etc. Served with Am. Red Cross, in Italy, 1918. Hon. corr. mem. Am. Inst. Architects. Home: Rome, Italy. Died Apr. 5, 1931.

RICHÉ, Charles Swift, civil engr.; b. Philadelphia, Pa., July 19, 1864; s. George Inman and Elizabeth Ramsay (Wetherill) R.; grad. Friends' Central Sch., Phila., 1881; grad. U.S. Mil. Acad., 1886; grad. Engr. Sch. of Application, Willet Point, N.Y., 1889; m. Annie Weir, June 6, 1889 (died 1897); children—Swift, Weir (killed in France Dec. 19, 1918). Commd. add. 2d lt. Corps of Engrs., July 1, 1886; promoted through grades to col., July 1, 1916; served as col. 1st U.S. Vol. Inf., May 20, 1898-Oct. 28, 1898; retired Jan. 18, 1921. Engaged extensively in river and harbor work; Great Lakes harbors and connecting channels; U.S. lake survey; upper Miss. River improvement; completion Hennepin Canal, Tex. harbors, Coast Canal, Houston Ship Channel and Texas City Dike; fortifications of New Orleans, Galveston and Panama Canal; consulting engr. on grade raising of City of Galveston, Tex., 1903-04. Mem. Engring. Bd. of Rev., Sanitary Dist. of Chicago, 1924-25. Democrat. Episcopalian. Mason, Elk. Died Mar. 20, 1936.

RICHEY, Albert Sutton, electrical engr.; b. Muncie, Ind., Apr. 10, 1874; s. Webster Scott and Julia M. (Thomas) R.; B.M.E., Purdue U., 1894, E.E., 1908; m. Edith Holman Kendrick, June 14, 1907; children—Frances, Janet. Elec. engr., Union Traction Co. of Ind., until 1905; prof. electrical engring., Worcester Poly. Inst., 1905—; consulting engr., 1905—. Republican. Presbyn. Fellow Am. Inst. Elec. Engrs. Mason. Author: Electric Railway Handbook. Home: Worcester, Mass. Died June 24, 1936.

RICHMAN, Irving Berdine, lawyer; b. Muscatine, Ia., Oct. 27, 1861; s. DeWitt Clinton (jurist) and Mary (Berdine) R.; A.B. State U. of Ia., 1883, A.M., from same, 1886; Litt.D., Brown U., 1904, Grinnell Coll., 1932; m. Elizabeth Green, June 8, 1887; children—Mrs. Grace Elizabeth McMath, Clinton Berdine (dec.). Admitted to bar, 1885, and entered practice at Muscatine. Mem. Ia. Ho. of Rep., 1889, 1891; temporary chmn. Ia. Dem. Conv. that nominated Horace Boies for gov., 1889; Dem. candidate for presdl. elector, 1892; consul-gen. at St. Gall, Switzerland, 1893-98. Democrat. Hon. mem. Rhode Island Hist. Soc.; corr. mem. Hispanic Soc. America; fellow Am. Geog. Soc. Author: John Brown Among the Quakers and Other Sketches, 1894; Appenzell—Pure Democracy and Pastoral Life in Inner Rhoden, 1895; Rhode Island, Its Making and Its Meaning (intro. by James Bryce), 1902; Rhode Island—American Commonwealths Series, 1905; California under Spain and Mexico, 1911; San Francisco Bay and California in 1776 (John Carter Brown Library), 1911; Ioway to Iowa, 1930. Home: Muscatine, Ia. Died Dec. 6, 1938.

RICHMOND, Charles Alexander, univ. chancellor; b. New York, Jan. 7, 1862; s. Archibald Murray and Margaret (Law) Richmond; A.B., Princeton U., 1883, A.M., 1886; graduate Princeton Theol. Sem., 1888; D.D., Hamilton Coll., 1904; LL.D., Rutgers, 1909, New York U., 1910, Princeton U., 1915, U. of Pittsburgh, 1918, George Washington U., 1921, St. Andrews, Scotland, 1924, Union Coll., 1929; also hon. Phi Beta Kappa from Princeton, etc.; m. Sarah Cooper Locke, June 4, 1891; children—Margaret, Frances Cooper, Locke (dec.). Ordained Presbyn. ministry, 1888; pastor First Ch., E. Aurora, N.Y., 1888-94, Madison Av. Ch., Albany, N.Y., 1894-1909; pres. Union Coll. and chancellor Union U. (N.Y.), 1909-29 (emeritus). Served as major, dir. S.A.T.C., 2d Region (colleges and univs. of N.Y. and N.J.), World War. Lecturer at the Sorbonne (U. of Paris), 1923, also at Forman Coll., Lahore, India, and Kiejo Univ., Tokio, Japan. Trustee of MacKenzie Coll., Sao Paulo, Brazil. Pres. N.Y. State Coll. Presidents' Assn., 1916, Assn. Colls. and Prep. Schs. of Middle States and Md., 1915, Assn. American Colls., 1922; mem. various societies. Author: The Four Winds, 1902. Home: Washington, D.C. Died July 12, 1940.

RICHMOND, Charles Wallace, ornithologist; b. Kenosha, Wis., Dec. 31, 1868; s. Edward Leslie and Josephine E. (Henry) R.; ed. Kenosha, Wis., 1874-80, Washington, 1881-83; M.D., Georgetown (D.C.) U., 1897; student Corcoran Scientific Sch., 1886-87; m. Louise H. Seville, Aug. 31, 1897. Made natural history explorations in Central America, 1892; asst. curator div. birds, U.S. Nat. Mus., 1894-1918, asso. curator, 1918—. Fellow Am. Ornithologists' Union; mem. numerous societies. Author many papers on ornithology in Proceedings U.S. Nat. Mus., Biol. Soc. Washington, The Auk, etc. Home: Washington, D.C. Died May 19, 1932.

RICHMOND, Euphemia Johnson (Effie Johnson), author; b. nr. Mt. Upton, N.Y., 1825; d. Dr. J. and Frances Putnam (Guernsey) Johnson; m. Orson Richmond, 1846. Her early sketches, pub. in periodicals, were under the pen-name, "Effie Johnson," but her later work has been under her own name. Author: The McAllisters (a temperance story); Hope Raymond: Two Paths; The Jeweled Serpent; Harry the Prodigal; The Fatal Dower; Alice Grant; Rose Clifton; Anna Maynard, the King's Daughter; World's Women, Aunt Chloe and Her Friends; Drifting and Anchored; Scripture Primer; Adopted; Roy's Wife; How Sandy Came to His Fortune; Zoa Rodman; Dividing of the Ways; A Woman's Way; True Stories for Little People; The Prince Messiah, 1899. Home: Mount Upton, N.Y. Deceased.

RICHMOND, Frederic Courtis, humanitarian; b. New Bedford, Mass., Nov. 19, 1862; s. James Henry Crocker and Hannah Katharine (Courtis) R.; student Friends Acad., Providence, R.I., 1877-78; m. Laura Treloar Osborne, July 16, 1885; children—Frederic Courtis (dec.), Laura Gladys (wife of Edwin F. Voris, Jr.), Marguerite (wife of Walter Newton Pugh, M.D.). Began as mine supt. and mgr. at Shullsburg, Wis., July 1884; mine surveyor Compania

Del Pinas Altos, Mexico, 1893 to 1896; erecting engr. for L. C. and S. V. Trent, Salt Lake City, Utah, 1897-98; mgr. machinery dept. Salt Lake Hardware Co., 1899-1907; pres. F. C. Richmond Machinery Co., mining machinery, Salt Lake City, 1908-37, retired, 1938; pres. and dir. Tyng Trackage Co.; dir. Eureka Standard Consol. Mining Co. (former pres.); dir. Tintic Standard Mining Co., Independent Coal and Coke Co. (chmn. exec. com. 1938-39). Pres. Salt Lake City Chamber of Commerce, 1915-19, as such was ex-officio chmn. all govt. coms. in Utah during World War. Mem. State Council of Defense and chmn. Committee on State Protection, and mem. Executive Committee—all during World War; also insp. for Utah and Wyo. for Am. Protective League, auxiliary to U.S. Dept. of Justice during World War. Mem. Salt Lake City Bd. of Edn. 6 yrs.; dir. Rowland Hall, school for girls, 3 yrs.; dir. Chamber of Commerce of U.S., 1922-23. Republican. Presbyn. Mason. Home: Salt Lake City, Utah. Died Nov. 9, 1940.

RICHMOND, Mary Ellen, social worker; b. Belleville, Ill., Aug. 5, 1861; d. Henry and Lavinia (Harris) R.; grad. Baltimore High Sch.; hon. M.A. from Smith College, 1921; unmarried. Gen. sec. Baltimore Charity Organization Soc., 1891, Phila. Charity Organization Soc., 1900; dir. Charity Organization Dept. Russell Sage Foundation, 1909—. Author: Friendly Visiting Among the Poor, 1899; The Good Neighbor in the Modern City, 1907; Social Diagnosis, 1917; What Is Social Case Work?, 1922; Child Marriages (in collaboration), 1925. Editor of the Social Work Series; and other books on social work. Hon. chmn. Family Life Conf. Home: New York, N.Y. Died Sept. 12, 1928.

RICHTER, Henry Joseph, bishop; b. Neuenkirchen, Oldenburg, Germany, Apr. 9, 1838; s. John Henry and Anna Maria Elisabeth (Albers) R.; came to U.S., 1854; ed. St. Xavier's Coll. and Mt. St. Mary's Sem., Cincinnati; entered Am. Coll., Rome, 1860; grad. D.D. and ordained priest R.C. Ch., 1865. V.p. and prof. dogma, philosophy and liturgy, Mt. St. Mary's Sem., Cincinnati, 1865-70; rector St. Laurence and chaplain Acad. Mt. St. Vincent, 1870-83; consecrated 1st bishop of Grand Rapids, Mich., 1883. Died Dec. 26, 1916.

RICHTMYER, F(loyd) K(arker), physicist; b. Cobleskill, N.Y., Oct. 12, 1881; s. Robert and Elmina (Karker) R.; A.B., Cornell U., 1904, Ph.D., 1910; m. Bernice Davis, Aug. 3, 1904; children—Robert Lawson (dec.), Robert Davis, Sarah Elizabeth, Lawson Edward. Instr. physics, Drexel Inst., Phila., 1904-06; instr. physics, 1906-11, asst. prof. 1911-18, prof. 1918—, dean Grad. Sch., 1931—, Cornell U. Physicist Bur. of Standards, summer 1915; investigator Gen. Elec. Research Lab., 1919-20; lecturer Summer School, U. of California, 1923, summer quarter, Stanford, 1925, 31, summer school, Columbia U. 1929. Radio engr. Signal Corps, U.S.A., 1918; major of the Ordnance Reserve Corps, U.S.A., 1925—. Mem. Nat. Research Council (chmn. div. physical sciences 1930-35); mem. Am. Acad. Arts and Sciences, Am. Assn. Physics Teachers (v.p., 1935-36; pres., 1937—). Awarded Levy medal, Franklin Inst., 1929. Unitarian. Editor: Jour. Optical Soc. of America; Review of Scientific Instruments, International Series in Physics. Home: Ithaca, N.Y. Died Nov. 7, 1939.

RICKARDS, George Collins, first chief Militia Bur.; b. Phila., Pa., Aug. 25, 1860; s. Col. William, Jr. and Eliza A. (Tucker) R.; ed. pub. schs., Franklin, Pa.; m. Amelia Ellen Edinger, Apr. 6, 1882 (died 1927); children—Mrs. Mary E. Johnson, Mrs. Agnes F. Howe. In hardware business, Oil City, Pa., 1882-1915. Joined National Guard of Pa., 1877; promoted through grades to brig. gen., June 19, 1919; lt. col. and col. 16th Inf., U.S.A., Spanish-Am. War, 1898; served in Puerto Rico, on Mexican border, 1916-17, at head of same regt., reorganized as 112th Inf., as comdr. of which went to France and participated in battles, July-Nov., 1918, at Chateau-Thierry, Champaigne - Marne, Aisne - Marne, Fismes, Oise-Aisne, Meuse-Argonne; chief of Mil. Bur., rank of maj. gen., July 2, 1921-June 29, 1925 (retired). Served 40 yrs. in state and 8 yrs. 28 days in federal service. Awarded Long Service Medal of Pa., 1920; D.S.M. (U.S.); recommended for D.S.C. by comdg. gen. 55th Inf. Brig. and cited by Gen. Pershing. Exec. officer Polk State Sch., Polk, Pa., 1 yr. (resigned); elected register of wills, recorder of deeds and clk. of Orphans' Court, of Venango Co., Pa., Nov. 1927, reëlected, Nov. 3, 1931. Dir. ZemZem Temple Hosp. for Crippled Children, Erie, Pa. Republican. Methodist. Mason. One of ten major generals who acted as pall bearers at funeral of President Harding, also at burial of the Unknown Soldier, at Arlington Cemetery. Home: Oil City, Pa. Died Jan. 15, 1933.

RICKER, George Alfred Joy, civ. engr.; b. Portsmouth, N.H., June 30, 1863; s. Charles Clement and Sarah Mehitabel (Joy) R.; prep. edn. under father at sea, and pvt. tutor, 1881-82; spl. student in civ. engring., Mass. Inst. Tech., 1882-85; m. Bessie Turner, Nov. 24, 1887. Transit man, Erie R.R., 1881-82, asst. engr. Buffalo div., 1885-86; topog-

rapher and locating engr. N.P. Ry., 1886-87; pvt. practice civ. engring., Buffalo, 1887-1913; resident engr. Buffalo Creek R.R., 1887-97; as chief engr. built Niagara Gorge R.R., 1890-1908; chief engr. Buffalo Traction Co., 1895-99, Buffalo & Depew Electric Ry., 1900-03, Niagara Gorge Power Co., 1901-08; cons. engr. Twin Lakes (Colo.) Land & Water Co., 1898; dep. commr. highways, N.Y., 1913-15; cons. engr., Albany, N.Y., 1915-16; highway engr., Portland Cement Assn., Chicago, 1916-17; dist. engr. of same, Washington, D.C., 1918-29, and mgr. of its Gen. Educational Bur. at Chicago, 1929-30; practicing as cons. engr. Editor Motordom (official mag. N.Y. State Automobile Assn.), 1915-16. Mem. Buffalo City Civ. Service Commn., 1900-12, pres., 1910-12; mem. coördinating com. of Nat. Capital Park and Planning Commn. Democrat. Unitarian. Home: Washington, D.C. Died Nov. 2, 1933.

RICKER, Marilla M., lawyer, humanitarian; b. New Durham, N.H., Mar. 18, 1840; ed. Colby Acad., New London, to 1861; taught sch. for several yrs. and spent 2 yrs. abroad; studied law under pvt. tutor 3 yrs.; admitted to bar of Supreme Ct. of D.C., 1882, Supreme Ct. of U.S., 1891; m. John Ricker, May 19, 1863 (died 1868). Has practiced at Washington, 1882—; apptd. U.S. commr. and examiner in chancery by Dist. Supreme Ct., 1884. Has for many years been known as "the prisoner's friend," on account of practice of visiting prisons to befriend friendless prisoners; was one of asst. counselors in Star Route cases; an advocate of equal rights for woman; filed a petition which opened bar of N.H. to women, 1890; has spoken in various states in nat. campaigns of Rep. party; noted as a polit. writer and especially for articles in defense of "free thought," Thomas Paine, and Robert G. Ingersoll. Author: The Four Gospels—The Gospel of Ingersoll, Paine, John Calvin and Jonathan Edwards, 1911; I Don't Know, Do You?, 1916; I Am Not Afraid, Are You?, 1917. Home: Dover, N.H. Died Nov. 12, 1920.

RICKER, N(athan) Clifford, university prof.; b. Acton, Me., July 24, 1843; s. Gen. Ebenezer and Mary (Stacy) R.; prep. edn. pub. schs., Me.; pvt. study, Latin, French, botany, geology, architecture, etc., 3 yrs.; B.S., U. of Ill., 1872 (M. Arch., 1878, D. Arch., 1900); m. Mary Carter Steele, Aug. 25, 1875. Instr., asst. prof., and prof. architecture in charge of dept., 1873-1911, dean College of Engring., 1878-1905, U. of Ill.; prof. emeritus, Jan. 1, 1917. Mem. Ill. State Bd. Examiners of Architects, 1897-1917 (pres. 1899-1917); chmn. State Commn. on Ill. Bldg. Laws, 1911-12. Author: Trussed Roofs, 1885; Roofs, 1911; Simplified Formulas, 913. Home: Urbana, Ill. Died Mar. 19, 1924.

RICKERT, (Martha) Edith, author; b. Dover, O., July 11, 1871; d. of Francis E. and Josephine (Newburgh) R.; A.B., Vassar Coll., 1891; Ph.D., U. of Chicago, 1899; unmarried. Taught Lyons Tp. High Sch., Cook Co., Ill., 1891-94, Hyde Park High Sch., Chicago, 1894-96; studied abroad, chiefly in England, 1896-97; instructor in English, Vassar College, 1897-1900; asso. prof. English, U. of Chicago, 1924-30, prof., 1930—. Author: Early English Romances, Ancient English Christmas Carols, 1400-1700 (translated and edited for the Mediæval Library), 1908-09; The Beggar in the Heart, 1909; American Lyrics (with Jessie Paton), 1912; The Writing of English (with John Matthews Manly), 1919; Contemporary British Literature (with same), 1921; Contemporary American Literature (with same), 1922; The Writer's Index of Good Form and Good English (with same), 1923; The Bojabi Tree, 1923; New Methods for the Study of Literature, 1927; The Blacksmith and the Blackbirds, 1928; The Greedy Goroo, 1929; Severn Woods, 1929. War service with Mil. Intelligence Div., Gen. Staff, Washington, 1918-19. Home: Chicago, Ill. Died May 23, 1938.

RICKERT, Thomas A., labor leader; b. Chicago, Ill., Apr. 24, 1876; s. Charles and Hannah R.; ed. pub. schs. and business coll.; married. Actively identified with labor movement from age of 19; pres United Garment Workers of America, 1904—; 2d v.p. Am. Federation of Labor, also mem. exec. council mem. War Labor Bd. during World War; mem. Industrial Conf., called by President Wilson, Oct. 1919. Home: New York, N.Y. Died July 28, 1941.

RICKETSON, Walton, sculptor; b. New Bedford, Mass., May 27, 1839; s. of Daniel and Louisa (Sampson) R.; ed. Friends' Acad., New Bedford; unmarried. Engaged as sculptor, 1870—. Among notable works are: Portrait busts of A. B. Alcott, Louisa May Alcott, Henry D. Thoreau, George William Curtis, R. W. Emerson; also intaglios, bas-reliefs; projector and designer of Gosnold memorial tower on Island of Cuttyhunk, Mass., 1902, etc. Editor: (with Anna Ricketson) Daniel Ricketson and His Friends, 1902; New Bedford of the Past, 1903; Daniel Ricketson, Autobiographic and Miscellaneous, 1910. Home: New Bedford, Mass. Died Aug. 1923.

RICKETTS, Louis Davidson, mining engr.; b. Elkton, Md., Dec. 19, 1859; s. Palmer C. and Elizabeth (Getty) R.; B.S., in Economic Geology, Princeton, 1881; W.S. Ward fellowship same univ., 1881-83, Sc.D. (in course), D.Eng., 1925; LL.D. U. of Ariz.,

1918; m. Kate Bruce Greenway, Apr. 26, 1916. Surveyor and supt. Colo. mines, 1883-85; geologist for Wyo., 1887-90; cons. engineer Phelps, Dodge & Co., 1890-1906; chmn. bd. and dir. Valley National Bank, Phoenix, Ariz.; cons. engineer of Inspiration Consol. Copper Co., Greene Cananea Copper Co. Anaconda Copper Mining Co., etc.; dir. Phelps Dodge Corp. Trustee Calif. Inst. Technology. Author: The Ores of Leadville and Their Mode of Occurrence, 1883; Geological Reports of Wyoming, 1888-90. Home: Pasadena, Calif. Died Mar. 4, 1940.

RICKETTS, Palmer Chamberlaine, engineer, educator; b. Elkton, Md., Jan. 17, 1856; s. Palmer C. and Elizabeth (Getty) R.; C.E., Rensselaer Poly. Inst., 1875; E.D., Stevens Inst., 1905; LL.D., New York U., 1911; m. Miss Viera Conine Renshaw, Nov. 12, 1902. Instr., 1875-82, asst. prof., 1882-84, prof. tech. mechanics, 1884, dir., 1892-1901, pres. and dir., Feb. 1901—, Rensselaer Poly. Inst. Served as bridge engr., Rome, Watertown & Ogdensburg R.R. Co., 1887-91; engr. Pub. Improvement Commn., Troy, 1891-92; engr. River Commn., Corning, N.Y., 1897-98; expert in patent cases, 1886-97; dir. Nat. City Bank. Trustee and v.p. Troy Pub. Library; trustee Dudley Observatory (Albany), Albany Acad., Albany Med. Coll., N.Y. State College for Teachers; dir. Samaritan Hosp. Comdr. Order of the Crown of Italy; Comdr. Legion of Honor (France). Author: History of Rensselaer Polytechnic Institute, 2d edit., 1914. Home: Troy, N.Y. Died Dec. 10, 1934.

RICKETTS, Pierre de Peyster, chemist; E.M., Columbia, 1871, Ph.D., 1876. Asst. in mineralogy, 1871-72, assaying, 1872-77, instr., 1877-85, prof., 1885-93, prof. analytical chemistry and assaying, 1893-1900, Columbia U.; consulting chem. engr., New York, 1900—. Fellow A.A.A.S., N.Y. Acad. Sciences. Home: New York, N.Y. Died Nov. 20, 1918.

RICKS, Augustus J., U.S. judge Northern dist. O., Jan. 16, 1890—; b. nr. Massillon, O., Feb. 10, 1843; ed. Massillon public schs.; entered Kenyon Coll., Gambier, O., leaving in sophomore year to enter army, 1862 (LL.D., Kenyon Coll., 1895); m. Emma Atwater, Feb. 21, 1867. Served in Union army, June 1862, to Apr. 1865; practiced law, Cleveland, O., 1865-89. Home: Cleveland, O. Died 1906.

RICKS, James B., justice Supreme Court of Ill., 2d dist., elected May 21, 1901; b. Bear Creek Tp., Ill., Dec. 23, 1852; s. John Bond and Docia B. (Haines) R.; ed. Taylorville, Ill., public schools and 3 yrs. Ill. Wesleyan Univ.; m. Pammie L. Geltmacher, Dec. 23, 1872. Grand chancellor order of Knights of Pythias, 1885; mem. Ill. Dem. State Central Com., 1894—; nominated for justice Supreme Court of Ill., 2d dist., Apr. 12, 1901. Was chief justice, June 1904-June 1905. Home: Taylorville, Ill. Died 1906.

RIDDER, Herman, journalist; b. New York, Mar. 5, 1851; German parentage; attended New York schs.; m. 1880. Began business life at 11 as errand boy; 2 yrs. later in employ of ins. co.; ins. agt. at 20. Established Katholisches Volksblatt, 1878, Catholic News, 1886; became trustee, treas. and mgr., 1890, pres., 1907, New York Staats-Zeitung. As Independent Democrat active in Cleveland campaigns and reform movements, especially in German-Am. Reform Union; treas. Dem. Nat. Com. during campaign, 1908. Trustee Mut. Life Ins. Co., Emigrant Industrial Savings Bank; v.p. Hudson-Fulton Celebration Commn.; mgr. N.Y. State Bd. Charities; dir. Associated Press. Home: New York, N.Y. Died Nov. 1, 1915.

RIDDICK, James Edward, asso. justice Supreme Court Ark., 1894—; present term expiring 1906; b. Fayette Co., Tenn., Aug. 29, 1849; s. Edward Garrett and Harriet Ann R.; grad. Macon (Tenn.) Acad., 1868; studied law at Lebanon (Tenn.) Law School and at Univ. of Mich.; grad., LL.B., latter, 1872; m. Emma Wade Mack, May 29, 1879. Began practice at Gainesville, Ark., 1872; pros. atty. 2d circuit Ark., 1876-78; mem. legislature, 1879; judge 2d circuit Ark., 1886-94. Home: Little Rock, Ark. Died 1907.

RIDDLE, Albert Gallatin, lawyer, author; b. Monson, Mass., May 28, 1816; family removed, 1817, to Geauga Co., O.; common school edn.; admitted to bar, 1840; m. Caroline C. (dec.), d. Judge Barton F. Avery of Chardon, O., Jan. 22, 1845. Pros. atty. Geauga Co., 1840-46; mem. O. legislature, 1848-49; called 1st Free Soil conv. in Ohio; removed to Cleveland, 1850; pros. atty., 1856; defended Oberlin slave-rescuers, 1859; mem. Congress, 1861-63. Republican. Established as lawyer in Washington, 1864; retained by State Dept. to aid in prosecution of John H. Surratt for murder of President Lincoln; for several yrs. law officer Dist. of Columbia; was at head of law dept. Howard Univ. Author: Hart and His Bear; The Sugar-Makers of the West Woods; Mark Loan; Life of Benjamin F. Wade; Recollections of War Times, 1860-65; Tory's Daughter. Died 1902.

RIDDLE, George, lecturer; b. Charlestown, Mass., Sept. 22, 1851; s. Edward and Charlotte (Cutter) R.; A.B., Harvard, 1874. Made his first appearance as a reader, 1874, in Boston; was an actor, 1875-78; instr. in elocution at Harvard, 1878-81. Appeared as Œdipus Tyrannus in the original Greek at Harvard, 1881; has given Shakespearean and other readings in prin. Am. cities. Wrote: "Extracts from George Riddle's Diary," Boston Journal; etc. Editor: A Modern Reader and Speaker; George Riddle's Readings. Home: Cambridge, Mass. Died 1910.

RIDDLE, Lincoln Ware, botanist; b. Boston, Mass., Oct. 17, 1880; s. Charles W. and Mary (Ware) R.; A.B., Harvard, 1902, A.M., 1905, Ph.D., 1906; m. Gertrude Hollister Paine, June 7, 1906. Asst. in botany, 1902, Austin teaching fellow, 1905-06, Harvard; instr. in botany, 1906-09, asso. prof., 1909-18, prof., 1918-19, Wellesley; asst. prof. cryptogamic botany, and asso. curator Cryptogamic Herbarium, Harvard, 1919—. Fellow Am. Acad. Arts and Sciences, A.A.A.S. Home: Cambridge, Mass. Died Jan. 16, 1921.

RIDDLE, Matthew Brown, theologian; b. Pittsburgh, Oct. 17, 1836; s. David H. (D.D., LL.D.) and Elizabeth Blaine (Brown) R.; A.B., Jefferson (now Washington and Jefferson) College, 1852, A.M., 1855; Western Theol. Sem., 1853-55; grad. New Brunswick Theol. Sem., 1859; (D.D., Franklin and Marshall, 1870, Princeton, 1896; LL.D., Western U. of Pa., 1894); m. Anna M. Walther, of Heidelberg, Germany, Aug. 21, 1862. Adj. prof. Greek, Jefferson Coll., 1857-58; chaplain 2d N.J. Vols., 1861; ordained Reformed Ch. ministry, 1862; pastor Hoboken, N.J., 1862-65, Newark, N.J., 1865-69; prof. N.T. exegesis, Hartford Theol. Sem., 1871-87, Western Theol. Sem., 1887-1911, prof. N.T. criticism, 1911-13; retired 1913. Member Am. Com. N.T. Revision and for yrs. one of editors of Standard edit. Revised Version. Mem. Assembly's com. for revising proof-texts of Westminster Standards. Contbr. to Sunday School Series, 30 yrs. Editor: Romans (except 1st 5 chapters), Galatians, Ephesians and Colossians, in Lange's Commentary, 1869-70; Notes on the International Sunday School Lessons (N.T. portions), 1877 to 1881 inclusive; portions of the International Illustrated Commentary, vols. I-III; The International Revision Commentary, vols. II-XXXVI; Meyer's Commentary on the New Testament, vol. II; Harmony of the Four Gospels in Greek (by Dr. Edward Robinson), 1885; Harmony of the Four Gospels in English (by same), 1886; An Outline Harmony of the Gospels, 1895; also 4 vols., 7 and 8, Ante-Nicene Fathers, 6 and 10 Nicene and Post-Nicene Fathers, 1886; The Story of the Revised New Testament, 1908. Home: Edgeworth, Pa. Died Sept. 1, 1916.

RIDEING, William Henry, editor; b. Liverpool, Eng., Feb. 17, 1853; s. William Watkins and Emily (Richards) R.; ed. at pvt. schs.; went to Chicago, remaining until 1870; m. Margaret Elinor, d. C. E. Bockus, of Boston, June 14, 1887. At various times on staff Newark (N.J.) Journal, Boston Journal, Springfield Republican, New York Times, and New York Tribune; asso. editor Youth's Companion, 1881—. Asso. and mng. editor North American Review, 1888-99; editor Dramatic Notes, London, Eng., 1881-82. Author: The Boyhood of Living Authors; Thackeray's London; In the Land of Lorna Doone; The Captured Cunarder; At Hawarden with Mr. Gladstone; Many Celebrities and a Few Others (reminiscences), 1911; Young Folks Life of George Washington, 1916. Died Aug. 23, 1919.

RIDEOUT, Henry Milner, author; b. Calais, Me., Apr. 25, 1877; s. Samuel Macomber and Ellen Jane (Greely) R.; A.B., Harvard, 1899; m. Frances Cecilia Reed, June 8, 1909; children—Clara Avery, Henry Milner, Cecily Reed. Instr. English, Harvard, 1899-1904. Author: Letters of Thomas Gray, 1899; Tennyson's The Princess (edited with C. T. Copeland), 1899; Freshman English and Theme-Correcting at Harvard College (with C. T. Copeland), 1901; The Siamese Cat, 1907; Admiral's Light, 1907; Selections from Wordsworth, Byron, etc. (with C. T. Copeland), 1909; William Jones, a Memoir, 1912; White Tiger, 1915; The Far Cry, 1916; The Key of the Fields, 1917; Tin Cowrie Dass, 1918; The Foot-Path Way, 1920; Fern Seed, 1921; The Winter Bell, 1922; Barbry, 1923; Man Eater, 1924; Dulcarnon, 1925. Home: Sausalito, Calif. Died Sept. 17, 1927.

RIDGELY, Benjamin H., consul, author; b. Ridgely, Md., July 13, 1861; s. Frederick W. and Harriet (Isette-Harris) R.; ed. pvt. schs., Henry Acad., Woodford Co., Ky.; studied law but abandoned it for journalism; m. Kate Ewing Eaches, 1891. Held editorial positions on Louisville Commercial and Louisville Courier-Journal; founder, with Young E. Allison, of Louisville Truth. U.S. consul to Geneva, Switzerland, 1892-1900, to Malaga, Spain, 1900-02; consul to Nantes, France, 1902-04; consul-gen. at Barcelona, Spain, Nov. 3, 1904—. Author: The Comedies of a Consulate, 1905. Died 1908.

RIDGELY, Henry, lawyer, banker; b. Dover, Del., Jan. 19, 1869; s. Edward and Elizabeth Frazer (Comegys) R.; student Wesley Collegiate Inst., Dover, and U. of Pa.; LL.D., U. of Del., 1916; m. Mabel Lloyd Fisher, June 1, 1893; 1 dau., Philippa Elizabeth (Mrs. Harold Wolfe Horsey). Admitted to Del. bar, 1890, and began practice at Dover; pres. Farmers Bank of State of Del., 1917—. Pres. Del. State Board of Edn., 1914-16, 1935-36 and 1939-40. Trustee U. of Delaware. Chairman State Bd. of Bar Examiners, 1931—. Author: Ridgely's Digest of Delaware Judicial Reports, 1894. Home: Dover, Del. Died July 13, 1940.

RIDGELY, William Barret, banker; b. Springfield, Ill., July 19, 1858; s. Charles and Jane M. (Barret) R.; pub. sch. edn., Springfield; C.E., Rensselaer Poly. Inst., 1879; m. Ella M., d. Shelby Moore Cullom, Oct. 24, 1882 (died 1902); m. 2d, Kate A. Deering, Dec. 30, 1905. Engaged in mining, mfg. and banking in Springfield until May 1, 1899; sec. and v.p. Republic Iron & Steel Co., 1899-1901; comptroller of the currency, U.S., 1901-08. Republican. Home: Springfield, Ill. Died Apr. 30, 1920.

RIDGWAY, Robert, ornithologist; b. Mt. Carmel, Ill., July 2, 1850; s. David and Henrietta James (Reed) R.; common schs.; hon. M.S., Ind. U., 1884; m. Julia E. Perkins, Oct. 12, 1875; 1 son, Audubon Wheelock (dec.). Zoölogist, U.S. Geol. Exploration of 40th Parallel (under Clarence King), in Calif., Nev., Southern Idaho, and Utah, 1867-69; curator, div. of birds, U.S. Nat. Museum, July 1, 1880—. Mem. permanent ornithol. com. First Internat. Congress, Vienna, 1885; hon. mem. 2d Congress Ornithologique Internat., Budapest, 1891; mem. com. of patronage Internat. Congress of Zoölogy, London, 1897. Mem. various societies. Author: A History of North American Birds (5 vols., with Prof. Spencer F. Baird and Dr. Thomas M. Brewer); A Manual of North American Birds; A Nomenclature of Colors for Naturalists and Compendium of Useful Information for Ornithologists; Color Standards and Color Nomenclature; The Ornithology of Illinois (2 vols.); The Birds of North and Middle America (8 vols. published). Home: Olney, Ill. Died Mar. 25, 1929.

RIDGWAY, Robert, civil engr.; b. Brooklyn, N.Y., Oct. 19, 1862; s. Joseph Skidmore and Margaret (Stephens) R.; ed. pub. schs. and at home; hon. A.M., Harvard, 1925; hon. M.S. in C.E., New York U., 1915, and C.E., same, 1919; D.Eng., Lehigh U., 1929; D.Eng., Brooklyn Poly. Institute, 1933; m. Lillie A. Littell, May 10, 1888 (died 1927); m. 2d, Isabel L. Law, Sept. 15, 1928. Chainman, rodman and leveler, Northern Pacific Railroad, in Montana and Wisconsin, 1882-84; entered employ Aqueduct Commn., N.Y. City, 1884; asst. engr. constrn. aqueduct and various reservoirs and dams, 1886-1900; with Rapid Transit Commn., 1900-05, as asst. engr., later div. engr. in charge constrn. South Ferry Loop, tunnels under East River, from South Ferry to Joralemon St., Brooklyn, and various subways in Brooklyn; with Bd. of Water Supply for N.Y. City, 1905-12, as div. engr., later dept. engr. in charge location and constrn. of Catskill Aqueduct work including upper 60 miles of the aqueduct and Hudson River crossing at Storm King, approximate cost $30,000,000 (aqueduct drops vertically 1200 feet down shaft, crosses, under Hudson River and rises in shaft on opposite side); engr. of subway constrn. for Pub. Service Commn., 1st Dist., New York, and its successors, Transit Constrn. Commn. and Transit Commission, 1912-21; in charge of rapid transit constrn. in N.Y. City, estimated cost of work more than $300,000,000; apptd. chief engr. Transit Commn., May 1921; in charge of all engring. work of commn. in connection with new constrn. and maintenance of rapid transit lines in dual system of rapid transit for N.Y. City; apptd., July 1924, chief engr. Bd. Transportation, City of New York, in charge of all rapid transit design and construction in the city; apptd. consulting engr. same bd., 1932, retired, Dec. 16, 1933; cons. engr. Port of N.Y. Authority, Dec. 1933—; mem. Chicago Traction and Subway Commn., by apptmt. of City Council of Chicago, 1916-17, commn. reported upon and made recommendations for improvement of local transit conditions; chmn. bd. engrs. Trans-Bay Bridge, San Francisco, 1927; mem. Colorado River Bd. for Boulder Canyon Dam, 1928-32; cons. engr. Rapid Transit Subways, City of Chicago, 1930-31; cons. engr. rapid transit studies City of San Francisco, 1935. Decorated Order of the Rising Sun, 3d class (Japan), 1929. Home: New York, N.Y. Died Dec. 19, 1938.

RIDLON, John, orthopedic surgeon; b. Clarendon, Vt., Nov. 24, 1852; s. Noel P. and Nancy B. (Hulett) R.; A.B., U. of Chicago, 1875, A.M., 1878; M.D., Coll. Phys. and Surg. (Columbia), 1878; hon. A.M., Tufts College, 1899, Sc.D. from same coll., 1926; m. Emily C. Robinson, June 4, 1879. Prof. orthopedic surgery, Northwestern Univ., 1892-1908, Chicago Post-Grad. Med. Sch., 1892-93, Northwestern Woman's Med. Sch., 1898-1902, Rush Med. Coll., 1909-12; cons. sr. orthopedic surgeon, Mercy, Michael Reese and Evanston hosps., Chicago, for many yrs., and Newport (R.I.) Hosp.; cons. orthopedic surgeon, Home for Destitute Children. Capt. Med. R.C., Apr. 2, 1917; maj., Sept. 10, 1917; disch. Feb. 8, 1919; lt. col. Aux. Reserve, U.S. Army, retired, account of disabilities, 1929. Home: Newport, R.I. Died Apr. 27, 1936.

RIDPATH, John Clark, author; b. Putnam Co., Ind., Apr. 26, 1841, grad. Asbury (now De Pauw) Univ., 1863 (LL.D., Syracuse Univ., 1879); m. Hannah R. Smythe, Dec. 22,1862. Prof. De Pauw Univ.,

1869-85 (chairs of English literature, belles lettres, history and political philosophy); v.p. same, 1879-85; secured for the university the De Pauw endowment; editor The Arena, 1897-98; literary director Jones Bros. Publishing Co. Author: The Great Races of Mankind (4 vols.); The Life and Work of James G. Blaine; Bishop Taylor's Story of My Life; The Life and Times of William E. Gladstone; Epic of Life (poem); etc. Compiled The Library of Universal Literature. Home: Greencastle, Ind. Died 1900.

RIEGEL, Benjamin D.; student Lehigh U. (class of 1898); m. Leila E. Edmonston; 1 dau., Katherine E. (Mrs. G. H. H. Emory). Chmn. bd. Riegel Paper Corp. of N.J.; pres. Ware Shoals (S.C.) Mfg. Co., The Trion (Ga.) Co., Riegel Textile Corp. Home: New York, N.Y.; and Fairfield, Conn. Died Nov. 6, 1941.

RIELY, John William, asso. justice supreme court of appeals of Va.; b. Jefferson Co., Va., Feb. 26, 1839; ed. at Washington and Lee Univ., Lexington, Va.; grad., 1861; was a staff officer in Confederate army with rank of maj.; was atty. for commonwealth, Halifax Co., Va., 1871-94. Home: Richmond, Va. Died 1900.

RIES, Elias Elkan, inventor; b. Baden, Germany, Jan. 16, 1862; s. Elkan Elias and Bertha (Weil) R.; brought to U.S. at age of 3; ed. pub. schs., New York and Baltimore; tech. instrn. at Md. Inst., Baltimore; physical sciences, Johns Hopkins; m. Helen Hirshberg, Apr. 21, 1895. Elec., mech. and tech. engr.; has taken out over 250 patents. Principal pioneer inventions: The underground electric ry. conduit or "sub-trolley" system; the modern urban and long-distance alternating-current system of generation, transmission and conversion of electricity for operating electric railways, by which the earlier restrictions of the 500-volt trolley systems were successfully overcome, and which has made possible the operation of rapid-transit elevated, subway and tunnel systems now operating in N.Y. City and elsewhere, and the electrification of suburban and long distance steam rys.; also the original automatic electric motor-starters; the Ries regulating socket, the first practical device for "turning down" the light of incandescent lamps without wasteful resistance; the controller system used on electric elevators; original methods and apparatus for electric welding, riveting, soldering, metal working, etc.; methods and appliances for electric heating and cooking; telephone, phonograph and tele-phonograph systems; original processes and apparatus for mfg. iron and steel tubes from the hot billets in one continuous operation; the first practical self-starting electric motors adapted to operate on single-phase alternating current circuits; original methods and apparatus for producing talking motion pictures directly from the film; new methods and appliances for detecting the presence of unseen vessels, icebergs, etc., in fog, as well as locating and following position of hostile aircraft and submarines and also for the precise location and salvage of sunken vessels directly from the surface, by means of a novel electro-acoustic range-finder, indicating and signalling apparatus, which effectively accomplishes for the ears, in the domain of sound, what the binocular telescope has done for the eyes. Submarine detector and other inventions offered to U.S. Govt., 1917. Fellow A.A.A.S. Mason. Pres. Am. Audioscope Co. Home: New York, N.Y. Died Apr. 20, 1928.

RIESENBERG, Felix, author, engineer; b. Milwaukee, Wis., Apr. 9, 1879; s. William and Emily (Schorb) R.; ed. pub. schs. and at sea; master mariner, sail and steam; C.E., Columbia, 1911; m. Maud Conroy of Queenstown, Ireland, June 29, 1912; children—Felix Jr., William, Margaret, John. At sea, sail and steam, 1896-1907, on voyages to many parts of the world; officer U.S. Coast and Geodetic Survey, 1901-02, Wellman Polar Expdn., 1906-07; wintered at Dane's Island, Spitzbergen, in charge of camp; navigator Airship America in first attempt to reach North Pole by dirigible balloon, Sept. 1907; lt. comdr. U.S.N.R.; comdr. U.S.S. Newport, barkentime, schoolship service, 1917, 18, 19; 2d tour of duty, 1923-24. Made record passage, sail, Santa Cruze de Tenerife to New London, 26 days, Sept. 1923. Asst. dept. of buildings and grounds, Columbia U., 1911; asst. engr. Catskill Aqueduct constrn., 1912-13; chief engr. Dept. of Parks, Queens, N.Y., 1914-15; asst. engr. Bur. of Bldgs., Manhattan, 1916-17; resident engr. Columbia-Presbyn. Med. Center (constrn. work), N.Y. City, 1925-27; v.p., consulting engineer Martin Motors, Inc. Author: Under Sail, 1915; The Men on Deck, 1918; Standard Seamanship, 1922; Bob Graham at Sea, 1925; P.A.L. (novel), 1925; Vignettes of the Sea, 1926; East Side, West Side (novel), 1927; Red Horses (novel), 1928; Shipmates, 1928; Endless River, 1931; Passing Strangers, 1932; Clipper Ships, 1932; Log of the Sea, 1933; Early Steamships, 1933; Mother Sea (novel), 1933; The Left Handed Passenger (novel), 1935; Living Again (autobiography), 1936; Portrait of New York, 1938. Home: New York, N.Y. Died Nov. 19, 1939.

RIESENFELD, Hugo, conductor, violinist; b. Vienna, Austria, Jan. 26, 1885; s. Leopold and Sofie (Grunwald) R.; ed. Conservatory of Music, Vienna, and U. of Vienna; m. Mabel Gertrude Dunning, Dec. 12, 1912; 1 dau., Janet. Formerly connected with Imperial Opera House, Vienna; came to U.S., 1907; concertmeister Manhattan Opera Co., N.Y. City, 1907-11; conductor for Klaw & Erlanger 3 seasons; concertmeister and conductor, Century Opera Co., 1915; mng. dir. Rialto, Rivoli and Criterion theatres, New York, 1917-25 (resigned); mng. dir. Colony Theatre, New York, 1927; gen. musical dir. United Artists Studio, Hollywood, Calif., 1928-30. Wrote: Chopin's Dances (ballet), prod. Vienna, 1905; The Merry Martyr (comic opera), prod. Boston, 1913; Betty Be Good, musical comedy, prod. 1921; Symphonic Poem; overture, suit, songs; Children's Suite, 1928. Died Sept. 10, 1939.

RIESMAN, David, physician; b. in Saxe-Weimar, Germany, Mar. 25, 1867; s. Nathan and Sophie (Eismann) R.; ed. Ducal Gymnasium, Meningen, Germany, and pub. and high schools, Portsmouth, Ohio; M.D., U. of Pa., 1892, Sc.D.; LL.D.; m. Eleanor L. Fleisher, Jan. 20, 1908; children—David, John Penrose, Mary. Practiced at Phila., 1893—; prof. clinic medicine, Phila. Polyclinic, 1900-18; asst. prof. medicine, 1908-12, prof. clin. medicine, 1912-33 (emeritus), prof. history of medicine, 1933—, U. of Pa.; prof. clin. medicine, Grad. Sch., U. of Pa., 1933—; phys. to Phila. Gen. and University hosps.; cons. phys. to Women's, Chestnut Hill, Jewish and Kensington hosps.; pres. med. bd. Phila. Gen. Hospital. First lt. Med. O.R.C., 1917; lt. col. (retired) Med. R.C.; mem. tuberculosis and cardiovascular bd., U.S.A. Fellow Coll. of Phys. Phila., A.A.A.S.; mem. numerous societies. Editor (with Dr. Ludwig Hektoen) American Textbook of Pathology, 1901; Life of Thomas Sydenham; Medicine in the Middle Ages; Medicine in Modern Society. Home: Phila., Pa. Died June 3, 1940.

RIGBY, William Titus, soldier; b. Red Oak Grove, Ia., Nov. 3, 1841; s. Washington Augustus and Lydia (Barr) R.; A.B., Cornell Coll., Ia., 1869, A.M., 1872; m. Eva Cattron, June 18, 1870; children—William Cattron, Charles Longley, Grace Kendrick. Entered service as 2d lt. Co. B, 24th Ia. Inf., Sept. 18, 1862; capt., Oct. 2, 1863, until hon. mustered out, July 17, 1865; engaged in farming after war. Elected sec. Vicksburg Nat. Mil. Park Assn., 1895, and was one of its most active promoters before Congress; apptd. commr. same, by sec. of war, 1899, and from then in charge of work as resident commr. Prominent advocate of "sound money," 1896, 98. Mem. Miss. Hist. Soc. Democrat. Methodist. Home: Vicksburg, Miss. Deceased.

RIGDON, Jonathan, coll. pres.; b. Rigdon, Ind., Dec. 22, 1858; s. Pryor and Mary A. (Fleener) R.; Nat. Normal U., Lebanon, O., 1881; grad. Central Normal Coll., Danville, Ind., 1886; A.B., Boston U., 1891, Ph.D., 1905; Clark U., 1904-06; m. Alberta Smith, 1907. Prof. philosophy, 1887-1900, pres., 1897-1900, Central Normal Coll.; prof. ethics and philosophy, Clark Coll., Mass., 1904-06; founded, 1908, and pres. to 1916, Winona Coll., Winona Lake, Ind.; at Clark U., 1917; again pres. Central Normal Coll., 1918-29 (pres. emeritus). Lecturer and institute instr. Author: Grammar of the English Sentence, 1890; Grammar for Beginners, 1891; Outline of Psychology, 1892; College Ideals, 1915; Science and Religion, 1926; The Art of Speaking, 1932. Home: Danville, Ill. Died Dec. 30, 1933.

RIGGE, William Francis, astronomer; b. Cincinnati, Sept. 9, 1857; s. Frederick and Elizabeth (Zeppenfeld) R.; ed. St. Xavier Coll., Cincinnati, 1870-75; St. Louis U., 1881-82; Woodstock (Md.) Coll., 1882-84, and 1887-91; Ph.D., Georgetown U., D.C., 1896. Joined Soc. of Jesus, 1875; ordained priest R.C. Ch., 1890; held professorships various colleges; dir. Creighton U. Obs. and prof. astronomy and physics, 1896—. Fellow Royal Astron. Soc. A.A.A.S. Author: The Graphic Construction of Eclipses and Occultations, 1924. Specialty occultation and eclipse maps; in a notable criminal case, designated the time a photograph was taken, from a shadow in the picture. Died Mar. 31, 1927.

RIGGS, Alexander Brown, theologian; b. at Portsmouth, Ohio, June 21, 1842; s. Joseph and Rebecca G. (Baldridge) R.; A.B., Jefferson Coll., Pa., 1863; taught mathematics, Western U. of Pa., 1863-64; admitted to bar, 1865; practiced at Nashville, Tenn., 1865-66, Pittsburgh, 1866-67; student Auburn Theol. Sem., 1867-69; grad. Union Theol. Sem., 1870 (D.D., Washington and Jefferson College, 1888, LL.D., 1902; D.D., Marietta College, Ohio, 1910); m. Charlotte Bowne Richardson, Oct. 19, 1870. Ordained Reformed Dutch Church ministry, 1870; pastor Ref. ch., Fort Plain, N.Y., 1870-76, Presbyn. Ch., Waterford, N.Y., 1876-90, Seventh Presbyn. Ch., Cincinnati, 1891-1902; instr. Greek, 1894-97, prof. N.T. exegesis and instruction, May 1897-Jan. 1, 1913 (emeritus), Lane Theol. Seminary. Home: Cincinnati, O. Died Sept. 4, 1919.

RIGGS, Alfred Longley, missionary; b. Lacquiparle, Minn., Dec. 6, 1837; s. Rev. Stephen Return (D.D., LL.D.) and Mary Ann (Longley) R.; B.A., Knox Coll., Galesburg, Ill., 1858, M.A., 1861; B.D., Chicago Theol. Sem., 1862; (D.D., Yankton Coll., S.D., 1889); m. Mary Buel Hatch, June 9, 1863. Ordained Congl. ministry, 1862; pastor Lockport, Ill., 1862-67, Footville, Wis., 1867-68, Woodstock, Ill., 1868-70; missionary Dakota Indians, Santee, Neb., under A.B.C.F.M., 1870-83, and same, under Am. Missionary Assn., 1883—; also prin. Santee Normal Training Sch. and editor paper in Dakota language and in Eng. lang. Trustee Yankton College. Republican. Author and editor of various publs. in Dakota lang., 1876-1915. Died Apr. 15, 1916.

RIGGS, Austen Fox, M.D.; b. of Am. parents, in Germany, Dec. 12, 1876; s. Benjamin Clapp and Rebecca (Fox) R.; A.B., Harvard, 1898; M.D., College of Physicians and Surgeons (Columbia), 1902; post-grad. work Johns Hopkins Medical School, 1904; D.Sc., Williams Coll., 1937; m. Alice McBurney, Apr. 1904; children—Anne, Margaret W., Alice Behn, Benjamin Clapp. House surgeon Presbyn. Hosp., N.Y. City, 1902-04; settled at Stockbridge, Mass., 1907; specializes in practice of neuro-psychiatry; clinical prof. neurology, Columbia U.; consulting psychiatrist and lecturer on mental hygiene, Vassar Coll.; consulting psychiatrist, Williams Coll. Founder, pres., trustee Austen Riggs Foundation, Inc. (for free treatment of psychoneurotic patients without means). Lt. M.R.C., U.S.A.; recruited and comd. A.R.C. Ambulance Co. 13; mem. Med. Adv. Bd. dists. 1 and 2 Selective Service Draft. Fellow Am. Coll. Phys., N.Y. Acad. Medicine, A.M.A. Episcopalian. Author of "Just Nerves," "Intelligent Living," and "Play." Home: Stockbridge, Mass. Died Mar. 5, 1940.

RIGGS, Edward, missionary; b. Smyrna, Turkey, June 30, 1844; s. Elias (D.D., LL.D.) and Martha Jane (Dalzell) R.; brother of James Forsyth R.; A.B., Princeton, 1865, A.M., 1868; Union Theol. Sem., New York, 1867-69; (D.D., Princeton, 1901); m. Sarah H. Dwight, May 29, 1869. Ordained Presbyn. ministry, 1869; missionary of A.B.C.F.M. (Congl.), 1869—; at Sivas, Turkey, 1869-76, at Marsovan, 1876—; teacher Anatolia Coll., 1886—; pres. Marsovan Theol. Sem., 1901—. Wrote article on "Christian Forces in the Turkish Empire," in W. D. Grant's Christendom, 1902. Died Feb. 16, 1913.

RIGGS, Edward Gridley, ry. exec. asst.; b. New York, Mar. 24, 1856; s. James Willoughby and Mary (Gridley) R.; ed. public shcs. and pvt. tutors; m. Elizabeth S. Brown, Nov. 5, 1878. Financial and commercial writer, New York World, 1876-84; polit. writer, New York Sun, 1884-1913; now exec. asst. N.Y.,N.H.&H. R.R. Co. Independent in politics. Episcopalian. Home: Brooklyn, N.Y. Died Jan. 17, 1924.

RIGGS, Elias, missionary; b. New Providence, N.J., Nov. 19, 1810; grad. Amherst Coll., 1829 (LL.D., 1871; D.D., Hanover Coll., 1853); ordained Presbyn. missionary, 1832; ever since in service of Am. Bd. Commrs. for Foreign Missions; his wife, Martha Jane Dalzel (now deceased), sharing his labors for 55 years. Lived at Athens, 1½ years; Argos, 4½ years; Smyrna, Turkey, 14½ years; since 1853 in Constantinople. Translated the Scriptures into Armenian and Bulgarian; participated in revision of Turkish version. Author: Manual of Chaldee (or Oriental Aramean) Language; Grammar of Modern Armenian Language; Grammar of Turkish Language; Notes on Difficult Passages of the New Testament; A Harmony of the Gospels (in Bulgarian). Died 1901.

RIGGS, James Forsyth, clergyman; b. Smyrna, Turkey, Oct. 4, 1852; s. Elias (D.D., LL.D.) and Martha Jane (Dalzell) Riggs; brother of Edward Riggs; lived as a boy in Constantinople; prepared for coll. by his parents; A.B., Princeton, 1872, A.M., 1875; held Boudinot hist. fellowship of Princeton, 1872-73; took post-grad. studies under his father in Constantinople; returned to U.S., 1874; taught sch. 1 yr.; grad. Union Theol. Sem., 1878; (D.D., Rutgers, 1892); m. Belle Brittin, June 13, 1878. Pastor Presbyn. ch. Cranford, N.J., 1878-84, Reformed (Dutch) ch., Bergen Point, N.J., 1884-92; prof. N.T. Greek, Theol. Sem., New Brunswick, N.J., 1892-98; pastor Brick Presbyn. Ch., E. Orange, June 24, 1898—. Died Jan. 24, 1918.

RIGGS, James Gilbert, normal sch. prin.; b. Dexter, N.Y., May 21, 1861; s. Edwin Starr and Cynthia A. (Hardy) R.; ed. State Normal Sch., Potsdam, N.Y.; A.B., Amherst, 1888, A.M., 1893; (hon. Pd.D., State Coll. for Teachers, Albany, N.Y., 1912); m. Elizabeth Spicer, Jan. 9, 1900 (died 1915); m. 2d, E. May Jones, Dec. 23, 1918. Principal high school, Watertown, N.Y., 1891-92; supt. schs., Plattsburg, N.Y., 1893-1900; in private sch., Dobbs Ferry, 1900-05; supt. schs., Orange, N.J., 1905-11; prin. State Normal Sch., Oswego, N.Y., 1913-33. Mem. bd. mgrs. Rome State Sch.; pres. N.Y. State Hist. Assn.; pres. Central N.Y. Local Historians. Republican. Presbyn. Home: Oswego, N.Y. Died Feb. 20, 1936.

RIGGS, James Milton, lawyer; b. Scott Co., Ill., Apr. 17, 1839; s. John Adams and Orpha (Campbell) R.; partial course Eureka (Ill.) Coll.; m. Margaret Elizabeth Berry, Dec. 31, 1868. Sheriff Scott Co., Ill., 1864-66; admitted to Ill. bar, 1867; mem. Ill.

Gen. Assembly, 1870-72; state's atty., Scott Co., 1872-76; mem. 48th and 49th Congresses (1883-87). Mem. Winchester (Ill.) Sch. Bd. 19 yrs. Mem. Christian (Disciples) Ch. Democrat. Home: Winchester, Ill. Died Nov. 18, 1933.

RIGGS, John Davis Seaton, educator; b. Washington, Pa., Jan. 29, 1851; s. Edward R. and Charlotte A. (Seaton) R.; A.B., U. of Chicago, 1878, A.M., 1881; Ph.D., pro merito, U. of S.D., 1890; L.H.D., Ewing Coll., Ill., 1901; m. Mary E. Chaney, Sept. 2, 1879. In business, Rockford, 1869-75; prin. commercial dept., Salt Lake (Utah) Acad., 1878-79; prin. prep. dept. Univ. of Chicago, 1879-86; joint prin. Univ. Acad., Chicago, 1886-87; organizer and prin., 1887-96, Granville (now Doane) Acad., of Denison U.; pres. Ottawa U., Ottawa, Kan., 1896-1905, Shurtleff Coll., 1905-10; study and travel, 1910-11; dist. mgr. United Mercantile Agency, Denver, 1911-13; prin. Wolcott Sch., Denver, 1913-20. Mem. Kan. State Board of Edn., 1900-03; pres. Kan. Coll. Presidents' Assn., 1899-1905, Kan. Coll. Athletic Conf., 1903-05. Ordained ministry Bapt. Ch., 1901; life mem. Bapt. state conventions of Ohio, Kan., Ill. and Colo.; life mem. Am. Bapt. Home Mission Soc. Author: In Latinum (Cæsar), 1890; In Latinum (Cicero), 1892. Home: Denver, Colo. Deceased.

RIGGS, Kate Douglas Wiggin (Mrs. George Christopher Riggs), see Kate Douglas Wiggin.

RIGGS, Robert Baird, chemist; b. Hazelwood, Minn., May 22, 1855; s. Stephen Return and Mary A. (Longley) R.; A.B., Beloit Coll., 1876; Ph.D., Göttingen, 1883; Sc.D., Trinity, 1920; m. Maida L. Sisson, June 26, 1895. Chemist U.S. Geol. Survey, 1884-87; prof. chemistry, Nat. Coll. of Pharmacy, 1885-87, Trinity Coll., 1887-1920, retired. Home: Hartford, Conn. Died May 11, 1929.

RIGGS, Walter Merritt, college pres.; b. Orangeburg, S.C., Jan. 24, 1873; s. Harpin and Emma Julia (Gowan) R.; B.S., in electrical and mech. engring., Ala. Poly. Inst., 1893, E. and M.E., 1894; Cornell Univ., summer, 1894; (LL.D., S.C. U., 1911); m. Marie Louise Moore, Dec. 22, 1897. Instr. English, 1894-95, physics, 1894-96, Ala. Poly. Inst.; instr. elec. and mech. engring., 1896-1901, prof. and dir. engring. dept., 1901-11, acting pres., 1910-11, pres., Mar. 7, 1911—, Clemson Agrl. Coll. Chmn. S.C. Com. of Naval Consulting Bd., 1916; mem. S.C. State Council Defense, 1917-19 (chmn. com. edn. and research); Paris rep. for vocational edn., Y.M.C.A., Mar. 1919; field rep. for vocational edn., Y.M.C.A., Chaumont, France, Apr. 1919; field organizer for vocational edn., A.E.F., Army Ednl. Corps, Beaune, Cote d'Or, France, May, June 1919. Presbyn. Fellow Am. Inst. E.E.; v.p. Am. Assn. Agrl. Colls. and Expt. Stations, 1915 (exec. com. 1917—); pres. Land Grant Coll. Engring. Assn., 1918-19; exec. bd. Southern Conf. for Edn. and Industry, 1915-17; pres. Southern Intercollegiate Athletic Assn., 1913-15; pres. S.C. Intercollegiate Athletic Assn., 1900—. Lt. col. staff specialist, O.R.C., 1923—; pres. R.O.T.C. Colleges of 4th Corps Area, July 1923—. Died Jan. 22, 1924.

RIGHTOR, Henry, author; b. New Orleans, Jan. 18, 1870; s. Nicholas Henry and Louise Justine (Scudday) R.; prep. dept. Tulane U.; cadet U.S. Naval Acad., 1885-87; m. Ella B. Ernest, Apr. 8, 1896. On Times-Democrat, New Orleans, 1890-97 (founder of "By-the-Bye" column); censor of news for bd. of health during yellow fever epidemic of 1897; casualty underwriter, New Orleans, 1897—. First pres. New Orleans Press Club and Ins. Fedn. of La. Gen. chmn. Gulf Coast Naval Training Assn.; exec. com. War Camp Community Service. Democrat. Author: Harlequinade, 1900; Standard History of New Orleans, 1900; Moons and Marshes (poems), 1905. Plays: The Military Maid, 1896; The Striped Petticoat, 1898. Home: New Orleans, La. Died June 23, 1922.

RIHANI, Ameen (Fares), author; b. Freiké, Mt. Lebanon, Syria, Nov. 24, 1876; s. Fares Antoon and Anisa Jeffal (Tohmé) R.; brought to U.S., 1888; naturalized 1903; student pvt. and night schs., New York Law Sch., and Arabic sch. at Mt. Lebanon; m. Bertha Case, Oct. 1916. Mem. Poetry Soc. America, Arab Academy, Damascus. Unitarian. Author: The Quatrains of Abu'l-Ala, 1903; The Book of Khalid, 1911; The Luzumiyat of Abu'l-Ala, 1919; The Descent of Bolshevism, 1919; The Path of Vision, 1921; A Chant of Mystics and Other Poems, 1921; Maker of Modern Arabia, 1928; Around the Coasts of Arabia, 1929; Al-Yaman, or Arabia Felix, 1930; also (in Arabic) A Short History of the French Revolution, 1903; A Fable, 1903; Ar-Rihaniyat (4 vols.), 1910-11, 1923-24; The Lily of el-Ghor (novel), 1915; Out of the Harim (novel), 1917; The Kings of Arabia (2 vols.), 1924; History of Modern Najd and Ibn Sa'oud, 1928; Short History of Syria, 1928; Arabian Peak and Desert, 1930; Around the Coast of Arabia, 1930. Home: Freiké, Mt. Lebanon, Syria. Died Sept. 13, 1940.

RIIS, Jacob August, author; b. Ribe, Denmark, May 3, 1849; s. Niels Edward and Caroline B. (Lundholm) R.; educated at Latin school in Ribe; m. Elizabeth D. Nielsen, Mar. 5, 1876 (died 1905); m. 2d, Mary Phillips, July 29, 1907. Came to New York and became police reporter New York Sun; active in the small parks and playgrounds movement, and in tenement house and sch. reform; sec. New York Small Parks Commn., 1897. Author: How the Other Half Lives, 1890; The Children of the Poor, 1892; The Making of an American, 1901; The Battle with the Slum, 1902; Children of the Tenements, 1902; Is There a Santa Claus?, 1904; Theodore Roosevelt, the Citizen, 1904; The Old Town, 1909; Hero Tales of the Far North, 1910. Home: Barre, Mass. Died May 26, 1914.

RIKER, Albert Burdsall, clergyman; b. New Albany, O., Oct. 19, 1852; s. Rev. Samuel Clark and Amanda (Snider) R.; A.B., Ohio Wesleyan University, Delaware, O., 1879, A.M., 1884; D.D., Ohio Univ., 1888, Phi Beta Kappa from same, 1908; m. Mary Edith Davis (Mus. B.), Aug. 18, 1881; children—Charles Ross, Samuel Clark, Olive Marie, Albert Joyce. Licensed to preach, 1872; pastor Worthington, O., 1879-81, Columbus, 1881-84, Athens, O., 1884-87, Chattanooga, Tenn., 1887-91, Wheeling, W.Va., 1891-96, Charleston, W.Va., 1896-98; pres. Mt. Union Coll., 1898-1908; pastor Moundsville, W.Va., 1908-11, Oakland, Md., 1911-13, Parkersburg, W.Va., Oct. 1913-16, Columbus, O., 1916-23, Chillicothe, O., 1923-27, Columbus, 1927—. Mem. Gen. Conf. M.E. Ch., 1900, Chaplain Insane Hosp., Athens, O., 1884-87, W.Va. Penitentiary, 1909-11. Chmn. Columbus Vice Commn., 1918; trustee Ohio Wesleyan U., 1917—; mem. Rotary Internat., 1924. Home: Columbus, O. Died May 3, 1929.

RIKER, Andrew Lawrence, engineer, inventor; b. N.Y. City, Oct. 22, 1868; s. William J. and Charlotte L. R.; student Columbia U.; m. Edith Whiting, Apr. 9, 1890; children—Edith Whiting, Charlotte Lawrence, Andrew Lawrence. Began as elec. and mech. engr.; was pres. Riker Electric Motor Co.; was designer the Locomobile; designed and built an elec. tricycle, 1884, 4-wheeled elec. motor car, 1895, gasoline car, 1902, car which won Vanderbilt Cup race, 1908; established world's speed record on Long Island for electric cars, 1899, which was held for 10 yrs.; pres. Ventilouvre Co.; apptd. mem. Naval consulting bd., 1915 (chmn. com. on internal combustion motors). Died June 1, 1930.

RIKER, Carroll Livingston, mech. engineer; b. Staten Island, N.Y., July 31, 1854; s. Andrew Jackson and Caroline Elizabeth (Tysen) R.; ed. Sheck's Inst., New Brighton, S.I., N.Y., Leonard Inst., Coytesville, N.J., and under pvt. tutors; m. Elizabeth Chipman Carman, of St. Johns, N.B., May 10, 1877. Began in boyhood to study current and wave action in the ocean and rivers; has been granted more than 20 patents for mech. inventions; designed hull of steamboat Castleton at age of 17; designed and built refrigerating warehouse in N.Y. City, 1874 (the first ever built); designed and built, 1887, the most powerful pumping dredge constructed to that time, which was employed in filling Potomac Flats, below Long Bridge, at Washington, D.C.; established, 1882, on the Hudson River, the first factory in the U.S. for mfr. of unfermented grape juice; designed during Spanish-Am. War, 1898, and presented to U.S. Govt. a new type of torpedo that would float at any desired depth, and submitted plan by which a string of these torpedoes could be floated down upon enemy vessels or drawn around them; originator of project to control the Gulf Stream by inducing compulsory deposits of sand on the Grand Banks, by the Labrador Current (bill for appmt. of Govt. Commn. introduced in Congress, 1912); originator of plan for control of the Miss. River, so as to yield a net ann. income of $100,000,000; originator of plan for neutral control of the seas, outlined in joint resolution introduced in Congress, Feb. 1915; a founder, 1914, of Volunteers for Peace, advocating a preliminary continuous conference looking towards peace between belligerent nations in Europe. Home: New York, N.Y. Died May 7, 1931.

RIKER, John L., mcht.; v.p. and dir. Bank of New York (N.B.A.), 2d Nat. Bank, Laflin & Rand Powder Co.; v.p. and trustee 5th Av. Safe Deposit Co.; trustee Atlantic Mut. Ins. Co., Greenwich Savings Bank, Met. Trust Co.; dir. various companies. Retired. Mem. Holland Society. Home: New York, N.Y. Died 1909.

RILEY, Benjamin Franklin, clergyman; b. Pineville, Ala., July 16, 1849; s. Enoch and S. R.; A.B., Erskine Coll., 1871; studied divinity, Southern Bapt. Theol. Sem., and Crozer Theol. Sem.; D.D., U. of Ala., 1885, Erskine Coll., 1887, Baylor, 1903; F.S.Sc., from Soc. of Science, Letters and Art, London, 1898; LL.D., Simmons Coll., Tex., 1907; m. Emma Shaw, June 21, 1876; children—Oscar Ernest, Benjamin Franklin, Mary Kate (Mrs. N. C. Hoyt), Ashby Autrey, Emma Lois, Alice Grace, John Enoch, Elizabeth d'Autrey. Ordained Bapt. ministry, 1872; pastor Carlowville, Snow Hill, and Livingston, Ala., 1876; Albany, Ga., 1877-78, Opelika, Ala., 1879-82; Houston, Tex., 1900-06; pres. Howard Coll., Ala., 1888-93; prof. English lit., U. of Ga., 1893-1900; supt. Anti-Saloon League of Tex., 1907-09. Author: History of Baptists of the Southern States, East of the Mississippi, 1898. Home: Birmingham, Ala. Died Dec. 14, 1925.

RILEY, Bryan M., M.D.; b. Dawson, Neb., Feb. 7, 1874; s. Michael and Bridget M. (Ryan) R.; A.B., St. Mary's (Kan.) Coll., 1896; M.D., Creighton U., Omaha, Neb., 1900; studied Chicago Polyclinic, 1910; unmarried. Practiced at Omaha from 1900; chief of med. staff St. Joseph's Hosp.; prof. medicine, Creighton U.; dir. Dawson Bank, of Florence (Omaha), Fellow Am. Coll. Physicians. K.C. Home: Omaha, Neb. Deceased.

RILEY, Franklin Lafayette, univ. prof.; b. nr. Hebron, Miss., Aug. 24, 1868; s. Franklin Lafayette and Balsorah Indiana (Weathersby) R.; A.B., Miss. Coll., 1889, A.M., 1891; Ph.D., Johns Hopkins U., 1896; LL.D., U. of Miss., 1916; m. Fanny T. Leigh, July 15, 1891; children—John Powell, Franklin Lafayette, Walter Hillman, Herbert Adams, Charles Leigh, Frances Leigh, Edward Miles. Pres. Hillman Coll. for Young Women, 1896-97; prof. history, U. of Miss., 1897-1914; prof. history, Washington and Lee U., 1914—; prof. history U. of Southern Calif. (temporary) 1925-26. Chairman Miss. Hist. Commn., 1901-02; originator and trustee, Miss. State Dept. Archives and History, 1902-14. Reorganized Miss. Hist. Soc., 1898 (sec.-treas. 1898-1914). Lecturer Summer Sch. of South, 1908-10, summer, Johns Hopkins, 1927. Author: Colonial Origins of New England Senates, 1896; School History of Mississippi, 1900. Edited 14 vols. of publs. of the Miss. Hist. Soc., and "A Political History of the South" (South in the Building of the Nation series); lit. editor Library of Southern Literature (15 vols.); asso. editor World's Orators (10 vols.); editor General Robert E. Lee after Appomattox, 1921. Home: Lexington, Va. Died Nov. 10, 1929.

RILEY, James Whitcomb, author; b. Greenfield, Ind., 1853; s. Reubin A. and Elizabeth R.; ed. pub. schs.; (hon. A.M., Yale, 1902; Litt.D., Wabash College, 1903, and U. of Pa., 1904; LL.D., Ind. U., 1907); unmarried. Mem. Am. Acad. Arts and Letters. Began contributing poems to Ind. papers, 1873, and has long been known as "the Hoosier poet"; much of his verse is in the Middle-Western or Hoosier dialect; his earlier Hoosier dialect verse, and his first book, appeared under the pen-name, "Benj. F. Johnson, of Boone." Author: The Old Swimmin' Hole and 'Leven More Poems, 1883; The Boss Girl and Other Sketches, 1885; Afterwhile, 1887; Old-Fashioned Roses, 1888 (pub. in England); Pipes o' Pan at Zekesbury, 1888; Rhymes of Childhood, 1890; Flying Islands of the Night, 1891; Neighborly Poems, 1891; Green Fields and Running Brooks, 1892; Poems Here at Home, 1893; Armazindy, 1894; A Child-World, 1896; Rubáiyát of Doc. Sifers, 1897; Child-Rhymes, 1898; Love Lyrics, 1899; Home Folks, 1900; Farm-Rhymes, 1901; The Book of Joyous Children, 1902; An Old Sweetheart of Mine, 1902; Out to Old Aunt Mary's, 1904; A Defective Santa Claus, 1904; Songs o' Cheer, 1905; While the Heart Beats Young, 1906; The Boys of the Old Glee Club, 1907; Raggedy Man, 1907; Morning (poems), 1907; The Little Orphant Annie Book, 1908; Songs of Summer, 1908; Home Again with Me, 1908; Old Schoolday Romances, 1909; The Girl I Loved, 1910; Songs of Home, 1910; When She Was About Sixteen, 1911; The Lockerbie Book (poems), 1911; Down Around the River and Other Poems, 1911; A Summer's Day and Other Poems, 1911; When the Frost Is on the Punkin and Other Poems, 1911; All the Year Round, 1912; Knee-Deep in June and Other Poems, 1912; The Old Swimmin' Hole and Other Poems, 1912; The Prayer-Perfect and Other Poems, 1912; Good-bye Jim, 1913; A Song of Long Ago, 1913; He and I, 1913; When My Dreams Come True, 1913; The Rose, 1913; Her Beautiful Eyes, 1913; Away, 1913; Do They Miss Me?, 1913; The Riley Baby Book, 1913; Songs of Friendship, 1915. Biographical Edition of James Whitcomb Riley's Complete Works, 1916. Home: Indianapolis, Ind. Died July 22, 1916.

RILEY, John B.; b. Schuyler Falls, N.Y., Nov. 9, 1852; s. Edward S. and Catherine (Smith) R.; ed. Plattsburg (N.Y.) Acad.; m. A. Genevieve Desmond, Sept. 25, 1883. Admitted to N.Y. bar, 1879, and began practice in Plattsburg; mem. Riley & Gordon. Sch. commr. Clinton Co., N.Y., 1875-81; mayor of Plattsburg, 1883-84; supt. Indiana schs. of U.S., 1885-88; chief examiner N.Y. State Civ. Service Commn., 1888-93; Am. consul-gen., Ottawa, Can., 1893-97; corp. counsel, Plattsburg, 1902-03; co. judge, Clinton Co., 1910-12; supt. N.Y. state prisons, May 1912-Jan., 1916. Pres. bd. mgrs. Plattsburg State Normal Sch., 1900; mem. Bd. Edn., Plattsburg. Democrat. Catholic. Home: Plattsburg, N.Y. Died Nov. 1919.

RILEY, Lewis Adams, capitalist; b. Montrose, Pa., June 7, 1847; s. Rev. Henry A. and Blendina (Miller) R.; educated in academies, Montrose and Homer, New York; m. Margaret M. Drinker, Sept. 8, 1870. President Lehigh & Hudson River Ry. Co.; mem. bd. mgrs. Lehigh Coal & Navigation Co.; dir. many companies. Home: Philadelphia, Pa. Died Apr. 23, 1925.

RILEY, Melville Fuller, pub. utility exec.; b. Pittsburgh, Pa., Apr. 16, 1872; s. George N. and Hannah

H. (McCleary) R.; ed. pub. schs.; m. Carolyn Hempstead, Mar. 1, 1905; children—George H., Melville F. Jr. Began as office boy Braddock (Pa.) Gas & Light Co., 1886; with Am. Water Works & Electric Co. and subsidiaries, in various exec. positions, 1896-1922; pres. The Potomac Edison Co., 1922-32, chmn. bd., 1932-33, retired. Republican. Home: Darien, Conn. Died May 1, 1938.

RILEY, Phil Madison, editor, writer; b. Belmont, N.H., Sept. 25, 1882; s. George Williams and Emma Frances (Elkins) R.; grad. Burdett Coll., Boston, 1904; m. Caroline Maybelle Sanderson, Dec. 24, 1910; 1 dau., Slyvia Elkins. Sec. and dir. Laconia (N.H.) Lumber Works, Inc., 1899-1904; teacher, pub. schs., Waltham, Mass., 1904-05; asso. editor Photo-Era, Boston, 1905-10, 1913-16; architectural and photographic editor, Country Life in America, 1910-13; asso. editor of India Rubber World, New York, 1916—. Republican. Conglist. Co-author: The Woodcarver of Salem, 1916; The Colonial Architecture of Salem, 1919; The Colonial Architecture of Philadelphia, 1920; Pneumatic Tires, 1922. Home: Newton Center, Mass. Died Feb. 21, 1926.

RILEY, Thomas James, sociologist; b. Lenexa, Kan., Aug. 14, 1870; s. James Francis and Elizabeth Lucretia (Williams) R.; A.B., Baker U., Baldwin, Kan., 1900, A.M., 1903; Ph.D., U. of Chicago, 1904; m. Blanche Ethel Mills, Sept. 16, 1903; children—Frances E., Thomas Jas. Prof. mathematics, Baker U., 1901-02, Western State Normal Sch., Kalamazoo, Mich., 1904-06; asst. prof. sociology, U. of Mo., 1906-09; prof. sociology, Washington U., St. Louis, 1909-12. Prof. sociology, U. of Chicago, summer, 1911; dir. Sch. of Social Economy, St. Louis, 1906-12. Republican. Conglist. Pres. Board of Commrs. Charitable Instns., St. Louis, 1911-12; pres. Mo. Conf. Charities and Correction, 1910-11; sec. board examiners for probation officers Juvenile Ct., St. Louis, 1909-12; gen. sec. Bur. of Charities, Brooklyn, Aug. 1, 1912—. Author: The Higher Life of Chicago, 1904. Nat. dir. Home Service Institutes of Am. Red Cross, 1917. Spl. lecturer sociology, Barnard Coll. (Columbia U.), 1923—. Home: Brooklyn, N.Y. Died Oct. 10, 1931.

RILEY, (Isaac) Woodbridge, coll. prof.; b. New York, N.Y., May 20, 1869; s. Rev. Isaac and Katherine Antoinette Southmayd (Parker) R.; English Sch., Florence, Italy; A.B., Yale, 1892, A.M., 1898, Ph.D., 1902; m. Laura Brooks Troth, Dec. 18, 1909; children—Katharine Vaughan, Woodbridge Phelps, Edward Troth, Margaret Drinker, Annette Troth. Instr. English, New York U., 1897-98; acting prof. philosophy, U. of N.B., 1902-04; Johnston research scholar Johns Hopkins, 1904-07; prof. philosophy, Vassar College, Sept. 1908—. Asso. editor International Year Book, 1908, Psychological Bulletin, 1903-07, Logos (Italy), 1920—. Author: The Founder of Mormonism, 1902; American Philosophy, 1907; American Thought—From Puritanism to Pragmatism, 1915, enlarged edit., 1923; Le Génie Américain, 1921; The Faith, Falsity and Failure of Christian Science (joint author), 1925; From Myth to Reason, 1926; Men and Morals, 1929; The Meaning of Mysticism, 1930. Chmn. of com. of Am. Philos. Assn. to reprint works of early Am. philosophers; lecturer at the Sorbonne, 1920. Home: Poughkeepsie, N.Y. Died Sept. 2, 1933.

RINER, John Alden, judge; b. Preble Co., O., 1850; LL.B., U. of Mich., 1879. Removed to Cheyenne, Wyo., and engaged in practice; city atty., Cheyenne, 1881; U.S. dist. atty., Wyo. Ty., 1884; mem. upper house, Territorial Legislature, 1886; mem. Constl. Conv., 1889; elected to State Senate, but resigned; U.S. dist. judge, Dist. of Wyo., Sept. 23, 1890—. Home: Cheyenne, Wyo. Died Mar. 4, 1923.

RING, Welding, merchant; b. Cornwall, N.Y., Feb. 22, 1846; s. Robert E. and Rachel (Welding) R.; ed. pvt. sch.; m. Ida M. Mailler, Jan. 16, 1872; children—Julia F., Katharine M., Ida F. With grain and flour house 2 yrs.; in export and import trade, 1866—; sr. mem. Mailler & Quereau; pres. Eastern Loading Co., U.S. and Australasia Steamship Co., and U.S.&A. Lines; trustee and v.p. Williamsburg Savings Bank. Apptd. chmn. U.S. Chartering Commn., Sept. 20, 1917. Mem. Chamber of Commerce State of N.Y. (v.p.), Nat. Trade Council. Trustee Methodist and Williamsburg hosps. Democrat. Methodist. Home: New York, N.Y. Died June 19, 1929.

RINGLING, John, circus owner; b. nr. Baraboo, Wis.; first wife died June 8, 1929; m. 2d, Mrs. Emily Haag Buck, Dec. 19, 1930. Associated as a young man with four bros. in the "Classic Concert Co.," each taking part; later a member of the "Ringling Bros. Comedy Concert Co."; subsequently part owner Ringling Bros. Circus; still later became head of Ringling Bros. Barnum & Bailey Circus; sole survivor (1930) of the five brothers, and now head of American Circus Corp., including Sells-Floto Circus, Hagenbach Animal Show, John Robinson, Sparks and Al. G. Barnes shows; financially aided Tex Rickard in building Madison Square Garden, N.Y. City; built White Sulphur Springs & Yellowstone Park R.R. (Mont.), also railroad from Ardmore to Ringling, Okla.; engaged in oil production in Okla. Noted for his philanthropies. Home: Sarasota, Fla. Died Dec. 3, 1936.

RION, Hanna (H. Ver Beck), author; b. Winnsboro, S.C., July 11, 1875; d. Col. James Henry (LL.D.) and Mary Catherine (Weir) Rion; ed. Coll. for Women, Columbia, S.C., and Berlin, Germany; m. Rev. Alpheus Baker Hervey, Ph.D., June 1, 1921. Formerly writer with Northcliff's Weekly Dispatch, London, Eng.; exhibitor in water color at New York, Phila., Boston and London exhbns.; matron maternity hosp., London, 1917. Author: Verse of Ver Beck's Book of Bears, 1906; The Garden in the Wilderness, 1909; The Smiling Road, 1910; Let's Make a Flower Garden, 1912; The Truth About Twilight Sleep, 1915; Painless Childbirth in Twilight Sleep, 1915; Golden Motherhood, 1916; Verse of Ver Beck's Bears in Mother Goose Land, 1916; The Real Michael Strange, 1917; Fate and a Marionette, 1923. Home: Warwick East, Bermuda. Died May 4, 1924.

RIORDAN, Daniel J., congressman; b. New York, July 7, 1870; s. Michael and Margaret (Horrigan) R.; A.B., Manhattan Coll., 1890; m. Edith M. Caldwell, June 28, 1899. Engaged in real estate and ins. business, 1890—. Mem. N.Y. Senate, 1901-05; mem. 56th Congress (1899-1901); reëlected to 59th Congress Nov. 6, 1906, for unexpired term (1906-07) of T. D. Sullivan, resigned, and to 60th to 62d Congresses (1907-13), 8th N.Y. Dist., and 63d to 65th Congresses (1913-19), 11th Dist. Democrat. Catholic. Home: New York, N.Y. Died Apr. 28, 1923.

RIORDAN, Patrick William, archbishop; b. New Brunswick, Aug. 27, 1841; s. Mathew and Mary (Dunne) R.; boyhood spent in Chicago; studied Notre Dame, Ind.; grad. Louvain, Belgium, 1864 (D.D.). Returned to Chicago, becoming prof. theology, Sem. of St. Mary's of the Lake; pastor, Woodstock, Ill., 1868, St. Mary's Church, Joliet, Ill., 1868-71, St. James' Ch., Chicago, 1871-83; consecrated, Sept. 16, 1883, titular archbishop of Cabesa, and made coadjutor, with right of succession to See of San Francisco, to which he succeeded Dec. 28, 1884. Plaintiff in 1st case tried before Hague Tribunal, In re Pius Fund of the Californias. Home: San Francisco, Calif. Died Dec. 27, 1914.

RIORDAN, Roger, artist, author; b. in Ireland, 1848; s. Thomas and Margaret R.; ed. Dublin, Ireland; tech. edn. at Art Students League, New York; married. Has illustrated many articles in Century, Harper's, etc. Received medal and diploma for services on Internat. Jury of Awards, Paris Expn., 1900. Author: A Glance at the Literature of Japan; French Etchers. Was a collaborator on the Catalogue of the Marquand Collection. Home: Brooklyn, N.Y. Died 1904.

RIORDON, Raymond, educator; b. June 8, 1877; s. John Brown and Elisabeth (Waggart) R.; m. Ella Sanders Chambers. Teacher and school executive, 1895—; initiated sch. gardens and vacation schs. in Dist. of Columbia, also reorganized and developed night sch. and municipal playgrounds there; owner of Raymond Riordon Sch. for Boys, Highland, N.Y.; builder and designer log camps; interior decorator. Writer on adolescence and boy development. Died Apr. 21, 1940.

RIPLEY, Edward Payson, ry. pres.; b. Dorchester, Mass., Oct. 30, 1845; s. Charles P. and Anne Robinson (Payson) R.; ed. Dorchester High Sch.; m. Frances E. Harding, Oct. 4, 1871. Entered ry. service, 1868, as clerk in Boston office Pa. R.R. Co.; N.E. agt., 1872-75, gen. eastern agt., 1878-86, traffic mgr., 1886-88, and gen. mgr., 1888-90, C.,B.&Q. R.R.; 3d v.p. C.,M.&St.P. Ry., 1890-95; pres. A.,T.& S.F. Ry. Co., Jan. 1, 1896—; also pres. Gulf, Colo. & S.F. Ry. Co. Home: Riverside, Ill. Died Feb. 4, 1920.

RIPLEY, Joseph, civil engr.; b. St. Clair, Mich., Jan. 3, 1854; s. Volney Abner and Maria (Klein) R.; C.E., U. of Mich., 1876, M.E., 1911; m. Rebecca McNaughton, Feb. 5, 1881 (died 1907); children—Eva, Florence, Alice Maynard; m. 2d, Mary J. Roper, June 23, 1909; 1 son, Joseph (dec.). United States asst. engr., improvement of St. Mary's River, Mich., and St. Mary's Falls Ship Canal, Sault Ste. Marie, 1877-1906, which included building of Weitzel lock, finished 1881, Poe lock, finished in 1896; U.S. asst. engr. in charge survey and preparation of plans and estimates for canal 64 miles long, connecting Birmingham, Ala., with the Black Warrior River, 1897; general supt. St. Mary's Falls Ship Canal, Mich., 1898-1906; mem. consulting bd. internat. engrs., Panama Canal, 1905; prin. asst. engr. Panama Canal, in charge of designing the locks, dams and regulating works, and asst. chief engr. Panama Canal, 1906-07; advisory engr. N.Y. State Dept. Pub. Works, 1907-09; mem. advisory bd. of consulting engrs. N.Y. State Canals, 1909-18; chief engr. Grand Canal Improvement, China, 1918-20; consulting engr., 1920-27. Republican. Methodist. Home: Albany, N.Y. Died Sept. 28, 1940.

RIPLEY, Robert Harris, steel mfr.; b. Boston, Mass., June 6, 1876; s. Edward Payson and Frances E. (Harding) R.; prep. edn., Shattuck Sch., Faribault, Minn.; LL.B., Cornell U., 1899; m. Ada Story, Apr. 30, 1903; children— Beatrice, Robert Hampton, Wilder. Admitted to Ill. bar, 1899, and began practice at Chicago; salesman for Ry. Steel Spring Co., 1901-02, Simplex Ry. Appliance Co., 1902-05; v.p. Am. Steel Foundries Co., 1905—; pres. Am. Autoparts Co. (Detroit), Damascus Brake Beam Co. (Cleveland), Gen. Steel Castings Corp. (Eddystone, Pa.). Home: Winnetka, Ill. Died Nov. 4, 1931.

RIPLEY, William Zebina, economist; b. Medford, Mass., Oct. 13, 1867; s. Nathaniel L. and Estimate R. E. (Baldwin) R.; A.B., Mass. Inst. Tech., 1890; A.M., Columbia U., 1892, Ph.D., 1893, Litt.D. from same, 1929; LL.D., U. of Wis., 1930, Bucknell and U. of Rochester, 1931; m. Ida S. Davis, Feb. 20, 1893; children—Ruth, Davis N., William P., Bettina. Prof. economics, Mass. Inst. Tech., 1895-1901; prof. polit. economy, Harvard, 1901-33. Lecturer in sociology, Columbia, 1893-1901; expert agt. on transportation, U.S. Industrial Commn., 1900-01; Huxley memorial lecturer, Royal Anthrop. Inst., London, Eng., 1908. Author: Financial History of Virginia, 1890; The Races of Europe (Lowell Inst. Lectures), 1900; Trusts, Pools and Corporations, 1905; Railway Problems, 1907; Railroads—Rates and Regulation, 1912; Railroads—Finance and Organization, 1914; Special Report U.S. Eight Hour Commission on Trainmen's Schedules and Agreements, 1917; Main Street and Wall Street, 1927. Editor Selections and Documents in Economics, 10 vols. Dir. C.,R.I.&P. Ry., 1917-33. Administrator of labor standards, War Dept., 1918; chmn. Nat. Adjustment Commn., U.S. Shipping Bd., 1919-20; with Interstate Commerce Commn., 1920-23; spl. examiner on consolidation of rys., 1921, and filed report with Interstate Commerce Commn. Home: Newton Center, Mass. Died Aug. 16, 1941.

RIPPLE, Michael Joseph, clergyman; b. Baltimore, Md., Oct. 25, 1875; s. Leonard J. and Mary Elizabeth (Kries) R.; student Loyola Coll., Baltimore, 1894; entered Dominican Order, 1894; student St. Joseph's Priory, Somerset, O., 1897-1901. Ordained priest R.C. Ch., Oct. 10, 1901; assigned to missions and lecturing in Minneapolis, Minn., and the Northwest, 1904; co-organizer with Archbishop McNicholas of nat. movement of the Holy Name Soc., 1909; lectured throughout U.S. and Can.; organized mission work in Southern States, 1914-20; nat. dir. Holy Name Soc. and head of Dominican publs., 1920; editor Rosary Magazine, 1921. Organized great Holy Name demonstration, Washington, D.C., 1924; planned and erected imposing Dominican Priory, Jersey City, N.J., 1935. Home: Jersey City, N.J. Died Nov. 29, 1938.

RIPTON, Benjamin Henry, educator; b. Johnstown, N.Y., Mar. 21, 1858; s. Henry and Anna (Hunter) R.; A.B., Union, 1880, A.M., 1886, Ph.D., 1895, LL.D., 1909, L.H.D., 1921; LL.D., Syracuse, 1896; m. Francena Nare, June 2, 1880 (died 1915); children—Maud (Mrs. John B. Aiken, dec.), Ruth (Mrs. Thomas G. Hoffman). Prof., 1882-83, prin., 1883-85, Whitestown Sem., Whitesboro, N.Y.; prof. mathematics, 1886-94, prof. history and govt., 1894-1921, dean, 1894-1919, Union Coll., dean and prof. emeritus, 1921—. Mem. bd. edn., Schenectady, N.Y., 1903-07. Methodist; mem. Gen. Conf., 1900. Home: White Plains, N.Y. Died Nov. 6, 1936.

RISHELL, Charles Wesley, clergyman, theologian; b. nr. Williamsport, Pa., Mar. 9, 1850; s. Peter and Matilda (Robbins) R.; grad. Wittenberg Coll., Springfield, O., 1876, A.M., 1879; divinity studies, Drew Theol. Sem., Madison, N.J., and Univ. of Berlin (Ph.D., Ohio Univ.); m. Elizabeth S. Harman, Mar. 12, 1878. Entered M.E. ministry, 1876; prof. hist. theology, Boston Univ. Sch. of Theology, 1895—, asst. dean, 1904—. Mem. Soc. Bibl. Literature and Exegesis. Author: The History of Christianity, 1891; The Official Recognition of Women in the Church, 1892; The Higher Criticism, 1893; The Foundations of Christian Faith, 1899; The Child as God's Child, 1904. Home: Boston, Mass. Died 1908.

RISING, Henry, newspaper editor; b. Wyoming, Ia., Aug. 3, 1869; s. Henry Seymour and Rachel L. (James) R.; B.C.E., Cornell Coll., Mt. Vernon, Ia., 1889; m. Carrie M. Tilsley, Mar. 1, 1898. Began as reporter Spokane Daily Chronicle, Feb. 1893, mng. editor, Dec. 1894—. Republican. Mason. Home: Spokane, Wash. Died Mar. 5, 1939.

RISING, Willard Bradley, prof. chemistry, Univ. of Calif., 1872—; b. Mechlenburg, N.Y., Sept. 26, 1839; grad. Hamilton Coll., N.Y., 1864; M.E., Univ. of Mich., 1867; Ph.D., Heidelberg, Germany, 1871; instr. in chemistry, 1866-67, and prof. natural sciences, 1867-69, Coll. of Calif. State analyst of Calif., 1885—, also adviser and chemist State bd. of viticulture and State bd. of health. His spity. is thermal chemistry, and he has made a number of important discoveries. During the past 15 yrs. has been the consulting chemist of a large powder co. and has rendered important service in the field of chemistry of explosives. Mem. of jury of award, World's Columbian Expn., 1893, and at Paris Expn., 1900; mem. Assay Commn., Phila., 1903. Home: Berkeley, Calif. Died 1910.

RISLEY, Richard Voorhees, author; b. New York, Nov. 8, 1874; s. Hon. J. E. Risley, lawyer; ed. Mil School, New Rochelle, N.Y., 2 yrs.; 1 yr. Lehigh prep school, 1889-93; m. Edna F. Carlson, Aug. 5, 1896. Made several journeys abroad, 1892, including life at U.S. Legation in Denmark and visits to London, Paris, Germany, Stockholm, etc., in 1893-94-95; residence in Paris and London, visit to Calif., 1896, Europe, 1897. Author: The Sentimental Vikings, London, 1897; Men's Tragedies, 1899; The Sledge, 1900; The Anvil. Home: New Rochelle, N.Y. Died 1904.

RISLEY, Samuel Doty, ophthalmologist; b. Cincinnati, Jan. 16, 1845; s. John S. and Mary (Parker) R.; served pvt. to sergt., Union Army, 1862-65; student U. of Ia., 1865-68; M.D., U. of Pa., 1870; m. Emma D. Thompson, Mar. 11, 1871; m. 2d, M. J. Louise Robinson, Jan. 16, 1907. Lecturer and asst. surgeon in ophthalmology, U. of Pa., 1872-89; prof. diseases of the eye, Phila. Polyclinic, 1886-1900; attending surgeon Wills Eye Hosp., Phila., 1889-1917; cons. ophthalmologist Vineland, and Pa. Training Sch. for Feeble-Minded Children, and mem. bd. of mgrs. of Pa. Training School for Feeble-Minded, 1896-1914; alumni mgr. Univ. Hosp., Phila., 1906-19. Pres. Am. Acad. Medicine, 1891; fellow Coll. Physicians Phila. (pres. ophthal. sect. 1904); hon. fellow Am. Acad. Ophthalmology and Oto-Laryngology, 1912. Invented improved optometer and ophthalmoscope. Home: Media, Pa., and Philadelphia. Died Apr. 1, 1920.

RISTAD, Ditlef G(eorgsen), clergyman; b. Namdalen, Norway, Nov. 22, 1863; s. Georg Vilhelm Tetlie and Johanna (Bergitte) R.; grad. Normal Coll., Norway, 1882, Luther Theol. Sem., Minn., 1892; student U. of Chicago, 1895-96; Litt.D., St. Olaf Coll., Minn., 1935; m. Sarah Moltzau Johnson, Oct. 28, 1896; children—Alf Otto (dec.), George Rolf, Robert Nicholas. Came to U.S., 1887, naturalized citizen, 1917. Teacher, high sch., Norway, 1883-87; ordained ministry Norwegian Luth. Ch. America, 1892; pastor Edgerton, Wis., 1892-97, East Koshkonong, Wis., 1897-1901; prin. Albion (Wis.) Acad., 1901-06; pres. Park Region Coll., Fergus Falls, Minn., 1906-16, Luth. Ladies Sem., Red Wing, Minn., 1916-19; owner and editor Wis. Tobacco Reporter, 1919-23; pastor Manitowoc, Wis., 1923—. Pres. Eastern Dist. Norwegian Luth. of America, 1936-37. Pres. Norwegian Am. Hist. Assn., Tronderlaget of America; dir. Bygdelagenes Fellesraad (chmn. com. for memorial altar, Nidaros Cathedral, Norway). Knighted Order of St. Olaf, 1st class, 1930. Author: Jubelfestene paa Koshkonong, 1894; Lutheran Sunday School Hymnal, 1897; Fra det ny Normandie, Kvad (verse), 1922; The Pioneer, 1925; Fra det Norske Amerika (verse), 1930. Lecturer. Died Sept. 20, 1938.

RISTINE, George W., ry. official; b. Philadelphia, Mar. 3, 1846; pub. sch. edn., Phila.; m. Belle M. Page, 1873. Served in army and navy during Civil War. With Empire Transportation Co., clerk, agt., western supt., gen. freight agt. and mgr., June 1866-Apr. 1, 1881; asst. to pres. D.&R.G. Ry. Co., Colo. Coal & Iron Co., Mexican Nat. Ry. Co., at Colo. Springs, Colo., Apr.-Dec. 1881; asst. gen. mgr. D.& R.G. Ry. Co., Denver, Dec. 1881-Nov. 1882; gen. mgr. Tex. & St. Louis Ry., St. Louis, Jan.-Oct. 1883; commr. Trans-Continental Assn., San Francisco, Nov. 1883-Dec. 31, 1884; traffic mgr. Atlantic & Pacific R.R. and mgr. Atlantic & Pacific Fast Freight Line, San Francisco, Nov. 1, 1884-Dec. 31, 1885; gen. mgr. Erie Despatch and asst. freight traffic mgr. N.Y., L.E.&W., Chicago, 1886-91; gen. mgr. U.S. Car Co., 1892-95; receiver Colo. Midland R.R., Denver, 1895-97; pres. same, 1897-1900; arbitrator at Chicago for various roads west of Chicago and St. Louis, 1900-02; chmn. Western Pass. Agreement, Chicago, 1901-02; from June 2, pres. Rowell-Potter Safety Stop Co. and Ristine Co., Chicago. Dir. of transportation, St. Louis Expn., Jan.-Sept., 1903; pres. Tenn. Central R.R., July 1, 1908-July 1, 1909; engaged in making spl. reports on ry. properties and consulting engr. of various rys. under constrn., 1903—. Home: Evanston, Ill. Died Apr. 26, 1918.

RITCHIE, Adele, actress; b. Phila., Pa.; ed. Convent of Sacred Heart, Phila.; m. Charles Nelson Bell, July 12, 1913. Début in "Isle of Champagne," at Miner's Fifth Av. Theatre, New York, June 5, 1893; played Princess Mirane, in "The Devil's Deputy," en tour; appeared as Cleopatra, with Frank Daniels, in "The Wizard of the Nile," and later as Antoinette, in "The Cadet Girls," as Mrs. Pineapple, in "A Chinese Honeymoon," as Lady Holyrood, in "Floradora," etc.; entered vaudeville, as Mignon, in "The Girl in the Taxi." Died Apr. 24, 1930.

RITCHIE, Albert Cabell, governor; b. Richmond, Va., Aug. 29, 1876; s. Judge Albert and Elizabeth Caskie (Cabell) R.; A.B., Johns Hopkins, 1896; LL.B., U. of Md., 1898, LL.D., 1920; LL.D., St. John's, 1920, Washington Coll., 1923, Loyola Coll., Baltimore, Md., 1929; unmarried. Began practice with Steele, Semmes, Carey & Bond, Baltimore, 1898, and admitted to firm, 1900; mem. Ritchie & Janney, 1903-1920; asst. city solicitor of Baltimore, 1903-10; asst. gen. counsel to Pub. Service Commn. Maryland, 1910-13; atty. general of Md., 1916-20; gov. of Md., 4 terms, 1920-35. Prof. law, U. of Md. Law Sch., 1907-20. Gen. counsel War Industries Bd., June 1918-Dec. 31, 1918. Episcopalian. Died Feb. 24, 1936.

RITCHIE, Arthur, clergyman; b. Philadelphia, June 22, 1849; s. Arthur and Mary Rhea Barton (Hopkins) R.; B.A., U. of Pa., 1867; teacher, Episcopal Acad., Phila., 1867-68; S.T.B., Gen. Theol. Sem., 1871; (D.D.). Deacon, 1871, priest, 1873, P.E. Ch.; formerly rector Ch. of the Ascension, Chicago; of St. Ignatius' Ch., New York, 1884-1914 (pastor emeritus). Was editor of the Catholic Champion. A founder Clerical Union for Maintenance of Catholic Principles. Author: Spiritual Studies in St. John's Gospel; Six Sermons to Men. Home: Nyack, N.Y. Died July 9, 1921.

RITCHIE, John, scientist; b. Boston, Mass., 1853; s. John and Mary (White) R.; grad. English High Sch., Boston, 1869; m. Hattie M. Malcombe, 1885. Was engaged in business with father as builder; retired, 1885; pres. Alvan Clark Corp. (makers telescopes). Asst. at Harvard Coll. Obs., 1882-90. Collector of shells; largest pvt. library of conchology, and one of largest collections of shells in U.S. For 23 yrs. official in charge of collection and distribution of astron. news for U.S. Health commr. City of Boston, 1908-10. Fellow Boston Scientific Soc. (pres. 1908—). Am. Meteorol. Society, Am. Pub. Health Assn. Has done much translating of technical work of scientific and med. investigators into terms understood by the people, and has written hundreds of such articles for Boston, New York and Phila. papers. Asso. editor Am. Journal of Public Health, 1918-21. Author: (with Dr. S. C. Chandler) Science Observer Code, 1888. Home: Malden, Mass. Died July 22, 1939.

RITER, Frank Miller, lawyer; b. Phila., May 20, 1855; s. Michael Miller and Elizabeth Georgiana (Caldwell) R.; ed. Friends Central Sch., Phila.; studied law in office of E. Coppee Mitchell; LL.B., U. of Pa., 1878; (LL.D., Muhlenberg Coll., Pa., 1914); unmarried. Mem. Common Council Phila., 1883-85; asst. city solicitor, 1884-88 (resigned); mem. Pa. Ho. of Rep., 1889, 91, 93, 95; active in opposing election of M. S. Quay to U.S. Senate; dir. Dept. of Pub. Safety, Phila., 1896-99, and as dir. had restoration of Independence Hall under his supervision and control; sec. Civ. Service Bd., 1905-06; pres. Civ. Service Commn., Phila., 1906-07, and since Dec. 5, 1911. Conducted primary campaign and was chairman general committee conducting successful election of campaign of Rudolph Blankenburg for mayor of Phila., 1911. Pres. Civil Service Commn. of Phila., 1911-16. Chmn. Voters League of Phila., 1921—. Lutheran. Volunteer sec. Y.M.C.A., Camp Meade, Md., Nov., Dec., 1917; mem. commn. of Nat. Luth. Commn. for Soldiers and Sailors Welfare, in France, Sept. 1918-Jan. 1919. Chmn. Registration Commn. for City of Phila., July 17, 1923-Jan. 8, 1926, resigned; clk. of Jury Bd. for Phila., Oct. 4, 1929—. Home: Philadelphia, Pa. Died Mar. 19, 1935.

RITER, William Delamater, lawyer; b. Salt Lake City, Utah, Aug. 10, 1874; s. William Woolerton and Susan (Denton) R.; U. of Utah, 1889-94; LL.B., Columbia, 1897; m. Lennie Louise Savage, Oct. 10, 1901; children—Virginia, Denton Savage, Helen Louise. Began practice at Salt Lake City, 1897; asst. atty. Salt Lake Co., 1901-02; became mem. Sutherland, Van Cott, Allison & Riter, 1906, Van Cott, Riter & Farnsworth, 1918; apptd. asst. atty. gen. of U.S., Apr. 5, 1921-Jan. 15, 1924; resigned to resume pvt. practice. Served with Battery A, Utah Light Arty., in Philippines, Spanish-Am. War, and participated in attack on Manila, Aug. 13, 1898; returned to U.S., 1899, and resumed practice; commd. maj. O.R.C., Feb. 1919. Republican. Mason. Home: Salt Lake City, Utah. Died Jan. 19, 1927.

RITTENHOUSE, Elmer Ellsworth, conservationist; b. New York, June 9, 1861; s. Archibald S. and Susan (Sliker) R.; public school edn.; m. Adelaide B. Helper, July 31, 1886. Went to Colo., 1880; ry. telegrapher; supt. telegraph, 1888-91, asst. supt. and supt. telegraph, 1891-94, Colo. Midland Ry.; went to Korea, 1898, and engaged in ry. construction, also spl. corr. Paris and New York Herald; returned to U.S. via China and Japan, 1899; spl. corr. in Europe, 1902; editor Daily Telegraph, Colorado Springs, Colo., 1902-05; deputy supt. of ins., state of Colo., 1905-07; commr. of ins., Colo., 1907-09; pres. Provident Savings Life Assurance Society of New York, 1909-12, and established 1st health bur. for policyholders, and free health exams.; on president's staff, Equitable Life Assurance Soc., in charge health ednl. dept., 1912-14; pres. Life Extension Inst., New York, 1914-16; commr. pub. service and conservation, Equitable Life Assurance Soc. U.S., 1916—. Home: Montclair, N.J. Died Jan. 2, 1920.

RITTENHOUSE, George Brown, lawyer; b. Aurora, Neb., Dec. 25, 1878; s. Austin James and Louise Jane (Brown) R.; ed. pub. schs.; m. Mignon Ashton, June 3, 1906. Admitted to Okla. bar, 1902; practiced with A. J. & F. A. Rittenhouse, title of Rittenhouse & Rittenhouse, Chandler, Okla. Presiding judge Supreme Court Commn. Div. No. 3, Okla., term 1914-17; became mem. Rittenhouse & Rittenhouse, Oklahoma City. Democrat. Presbyn. Scottish Rite Mason. Home: Oklahoma City, Okla. Died June 13, 1925.

RITTENHOUSE, Moses Franklin, lumber mcht. and mfr.; b. Lincoln Co., Ont., Aug. 12, 1846; s. John and Elizabeth (Funk) R.; ed. Ont. pub. schs. and Eastman's Commercial Coll., Chicago; m. Emma Stover, Dec. 1871. Went to Chicago, Apr. 1864; employed in various capacities with different firms in lumber business until May 1, 1868, when entered employ of J. Biedler & Bro., lumber, becoming treas. J. Biedler & Bro. Lumber Co., 1871-83; organized Rittenhouse & Embree, lumber, May 1, 1883, incorporated as Rittenhouse & Embree Co., 1892; pres. Rittenhouse & Embree Co., Chicago, Ark. Lumber Co., J. P. Derickson Co., wholesale hardware, Minneapolis. Has done much charitable and philanthropic work. Home: Chicago, Ill. Died Nov. 7, 1915.

RITTER, Edward Frederick, clergyman, educator, administrator; b. Freemansburg, Pa., May 22, 1869; s. Louis Frederick and Mary Elizabeth (Muench) R.; A.B., Muhlenberg Coll., Allentown, Pa., 1888, A.M., 1891; Luth. Theol. Sem., Mt. Airy, Pa., 1889-91; D.D., Thiel Coll., 1921; m. Hannah Adelia Walter, 1891; children—Esther Helen, Walter Arthur, Ruth Dorothy, Minnie Irene, Frederick Luther. Ordained ministry Evang. Luth. Ch., 1892; pastor Unionville, Ont., Can., 1892-94, Hazleton, Pa., 1894-1901, Scranton, Pa., 1901-09, Lancaster, O., 1909-17, missionary supt. Dist. Synod of Ohio, 1911-15, pres., 1917-18, also exec. sec. Jubilee Fund; gen. sec. Thiel Coll., 1918-23, acting pres., 1921-23; gen. executive Federated Luth. Benevolent Soc., Toledo, O., 1923-24. Erected chs. at Unionville, Can., and Sheppton, Pa., and rebuilt chs. at Scranton and Lancaster; in charge $500,000 campaign for Thiel Coll., 1920-22, and of $250,000 Robinwood Hosp. campaign, 1924; gen. supt., mgr. Robinwood Hosp., Toledo, O., 1925—. Mem. bd. dirs. Luth. Theol. Sem., Maywood, Ill. Home: Toledo, O. Died Apr. 7, 1933.

RITTER, Louis E., civil engr.; b. Cleveland, O., Mar. 14, 1864; s. Louis and Harriet (Lambert) R.; ed. pub. schs. of Cleveland; B.S., Case Sch. of Applied Science, 1886; m. Mary Stair, 1889; children—Louis Stair, Francis Hamilton. Engaged in surveys and constrn. of Cleveland & Mahoning Valley Ry., 1886-89; U.S. asst. engr. on improvement of Miss. River, 1889-92; engr. with Jenney & Ritter & Mott, cons. civil engrs., 1899-1917; operating as L. E. Ritter, Consulting Engineer, 1917—. Identified with development of steel and reinforced concrete building design and constrn., 1892—. Died July 3, 1934.

RITTER, Paul, diplomat; b. Basel, Switzerland, Nov. 17, 1865; s. S. R. and Regula (Stahel) R.; ed. univs. of Paris, Basel, Göttingen, Jena, Leipzig; grad. Leipzig, LL.D., 1888; m. Louise Reidhaar, of Basel. Practiced law at Basel, 1888-90; attaché, Foreign Office, Berne, Switzerland, 1890-91; Swiss consul and consul gen. at Yokohama, Japan, 1892-1906; E.E. and M.P. of Switss Confederation to Japan, 1906-09, to U.S., May 1909—. Home: Washington, D.C. Died June 2, 1921.

RIVERA, Luis Muñoz, resident commr.; b. Barranquitas, P.R., July 17, 1859; s. Luis Muñoz Barrios and Monserrate Rivera Vázquez; ed. in pub. schs.; m. Amalia Marin, of Ponce, P.R., Jan. 3, 1893. Founded, 1889, and since editor and pub., La Democracia, daily; spl. rep. to Madrid, Spain, to consummate agreement for establishing home rule for P.R.; founded Liberal party in P.R., 1897; sec. of state and later pres. cabinet, 1897-99; at Washington in interests of free trade relations between U.S. and P.R., 1899-1900; organized the Federal party, 1900; established Puerto Rico Herald, New York, 1901; organized the Unionist party, 1904; mem. P.R. legislature, 3 terms; resident commr. to Washington, 1910. Home: San Juan, P.R. Died Nov. 15, 1916.

RIVERS, Moultrie Rutledge, lawyer; b. Mt. Pleasant, S.C., May 13, 1868; s. Constant Henry and Mary Elizabeth (Minott) R.; A.B., Coll. of Charleston, 1890; m. Eliza Ingraham Buist, Feb. 2, 1893; children—Mary Edwards (Mrs. Charles Webb), Moultrie Rutledge (dec.), George Lamb Buist, John Minott, Arthur Lee. Admitted to S.C. bar, 1890; mem. Hagood, Rivers & Young, 1913—; corp. counsel City of Charleston, 1918-20; atty. for various corps. Dir. S.C. Power Co., Atlantic Nat. Bank of Charleston, Citizens and Southern Bank of S.C., Port Utilities Commn. (chmn. bd. 1923). Counsel for Charleston Selective Draft Bd., World War. Pres. bd. trustees Coll. of Charleston (the oldest municipal university in the U.S.); former pres. Alumni Assn. Coll. of Charleston; chmn. Board Pub. Sch. Commrs.; pres. bd. trustees High Sch. of Charleston; mem. Soc. for Relief of Widows and Orphans of Clergy of P.E. Ch. (S.C.); former mem. State Bd. of Edn.; former mem. bd. trustees Med. Coll. of S.C.; chmn. Dem. Exec. Com. of City of Charleston. Democrat. Episcopalian. Mason. Co-author: History of the St. Andrew's Society of Charleston, S.C., 1929. Home: Charleston, S.C. Died Feb. 23, 1940.

RIVES, Alfred Landon, engr.; b. Paris, France, March 25, 1830; s. William Cabell R. (then U.S. minister to France); studied at Va. Mil. Inst. and Univ. of Va.; grad. École des Ponts et Chaussées, Paris, 1854; asst. engr. in completing U.S. Capitol Bldg., Washington; later engr. on aqueduct, Washington; then in charge U.S. Survey in improving Potomac River; later col. engrs. Confederate army; after was engr. on Chesapeake & Ohio R.R., chief engr. South

& North Ala. R.R. Offered charge of civ. engring. works of Egypt; v.p. and gen. mgr. Mobile & Ohio R.R.; v.p. and gen. mgr. Richmond & Danville R.R.; gen. supt. Panama R.R. Now chief engr. Cape Cod Canal, and gen. consulting engr. Is father of Amélie Rives (Princess Troubetzkoy) authoress. Home: Cobham, Va. Died 1903.

RIVES, George Lockhart, lawyer; b. New York, N.Y., May 1, 1849; s. Francis Robert and Matilda (Barclay) R.; A.B., Columbia, 1868, LL.B., 1873, A.M., 1872; A.B. Trinity Coll., Cambridge, Eng., 1872, A.M., 1879; (LL.D., Amherst, 1910, Princeton, 1911); m. Caroline Morris Kean, May 21, 1873 (died 1887); m. 2d, Sara Whiting Belmont, Mar. 20, 1889. Admitted to bar, 1874, and practiced at New York. Asst. sec. of state U.S., 1887-89; mem. New York Rapid Transit R.R. Commn., 1896-1902; pres. commn. to revise Greater New York Charter, 1900; corp. counsel, New York, 1902-04. Dir. Bank of New York (N.B.A.), U.S. Trust Co. Trustee Columbia Coll., 1882—(chmn. bd.), Astor Library, N.Y., 1883-88, Lenox Library, 1893-95, New York Pub. Library, Astor-Lenox and Tilden Foundations, 1895—(pres.); pres. bd. govs. N.Y. Hospital. Mem. Am. Acad. Arts and Letters. Author: The United States and Mexico, 1821-1848 (2 vols.). Home: New York, N.Y. Died Aug. 18, 1917.

RIVES-WHEELER, Hallie Ermine, author; b. Christian Co., Ky., May 2, 1878; d. Col. Stephen T. and Mary (Ragsdale) Rives; m. Post Wheeler, Tokyo, Japan, Dec. 29, 1906. Author: The Castaway, 1904; Tales from Dickens, 1905; The Magic Man (play title, Two Worlds), 1926; The Golden Barrier, 1934. Honors: Imperial Coronation Medal of the Emperor Taisho (Japanese); Commd. Grand Prix Humanitaire (Belgian); Grand Cross and Cordon Order of St. Lazarus of Jerusalem; Litt.D., Audhra Univ., Vizianagram, South India, 1939, Thirtha Pauditra (Honorary Fellow) of the University. Home: Amherst, Va. Deceased.

RIX, Charles Northrup, banker; b. Kalamazoo, Mich., May 28, 1843; s. George and Olive (Northrup) R.; grad. high sch., Dowagiac, Mich.; m. Lucy Emma Thomas, Dec. 19, 1870 (dec.); children—Fred Northrup (dec.), Lila Thankful (dec.). Served as q.m. sergt. to capt. 1st Ind. Regt. in Civil War; in pay dept. U.S.A., 1865-67; began in banking business as bookkeeper, 1867; cashier, v.p. and pres., in bank, Topeka, to 1879; removed to Ark.; pres. Ark. Nat. Bank, Hot Springs, 27 yrs.; pres., treas. City Ice Co., New Waverly Hotel Co., Hot Springs Obs. Co. Mem. Rep. State Central Com. Episcopalian. Mason; Grand Comdr. K.T. of Ark., 1891; Grand High Priest Grand Chapter Royal Arch Masons, 1890, and Grand Master Grand Council Royal and Select Masters, 1893, 94, 95; Deputy General Grand High Priest of General Grand Chapter R.A. Masons of U.S.A. Home: Hot Springs, Ark. Died Sept. 2, 1927.

RIX, Frank Reader, director of music; b. Lowell, Mass., Aug. 30, 1853; s. Benj. Franklin and Mary Elizabeth (Bryant) R.; A.B., Harvard, 1875, M.D., 1879; grad. Zuchtman Sch. of Music, Hughes Summer Sch. of Music; m. Ella M. Plumado (died 1919). Played organ and directed ch. music, 1868-99; practiced medicine, 1879-95; supervision of music, pub. schs., Lowell, 1895-98; dir. of music, N.Y. City, 1898—; instr. in music, New York Coll. of Music, also Summer Sch., New York U.; mem. music council N.Y. State Bd. of Regents. Mason. Composer: Songs of School and Flag, 1901; A Manual of School Music, 1909; The Master Singer, 1910; Voice Training for School Children, 1910; The Assembly Song Book; The Junior Assembly Song Book; The High School Assembly Song Book, 1912. Compiler: Schirmer's Academic Chorus Collection, 1916. Home: North Plainfield, N.J. Died Mar. 16, 1919.

RIXEY, John Franklin, congressman; ed. common schools, Bethel Acad. and Univ. of Va.; is lawyer and farmer; was commonwealth aty. for Culpeper Co. for 12 yrs.; mem. Congress, 1897-1905, 8th Va. dist. Democrat. Home: Brandy, Va. Died 1907.

RIXEY, Presley Marion, surgeon gen. U.S.N.; b. Culpeper, Va., July 14, 1852; s. Presley Morehead and Mary F. (Jones) R.; ed. in schs. at Culpeper and Warrenton, Va.; M.D., U. of Va., 1873; matriculated at Jefferson Med. Coll., Phila., 1873; m. Earlena I. English, Apr. 25, 1877. Asst. surgeon U.S.N., Jan. 28, 1874; passed asst. surgeon, Apr. 18, 1877; surgeon, Nov. 27, 1888; med. insp., Aug. 24, 1900; surgeon gen. with rank of rear admiral, Feb. 10, 1902-Feb. 25, 1910; med. dir. May 7, 1907. Spent 11½ yrs. on sea duty, 25½ yrs. shore duty; on shore attached successively to Naval Hosp., Phila., Navy Yard, Norfolk, and Naval Dispensary, Washington. Was the official physician to President McKinley from 1898 to time of his death, to Mrs. McKinley to time of her death, of President Roosevelt from 1901 to time of his death, and was phys. to White House 10 yrs., to Mar. 4, 1909, in addition to other duties; retired, Feb. 4, 1910; farming, 1910-17. Active service, Apr. 11, 1917, with Bur. Medicine and Surgery, Council Nat. Defense, and as insp. gen. med. activities of Navy in U.S. until Sept. 18, 1918. Decorated by Alphonso XIII, King of Spain, for services rendered officers and men on the Santa Maria following an explosion on that vessel. Home: "Rixey," Arlington Co., Va. Died June 17, 1928.

RIXFORD, Emmet, surgeon; b. Bedford, Que., Can., Feb. 14, 1865; s. Gulian P. and Caroline (Corey) R.; B.S., U. of Calif., 1887; M.D., Cooper Med. Coll., San Francisco, 1891; Eastern clinics, 1892, European clinics, 1898; m. Louise C. Campbell, July 3, 1900. Adj. prof. surgery, 1893-98, prof., 1898—, Cooper Med. Coll.; prof. surgery, Leland Stanford Jr. U., 1909-1930 (emeritus); cons. practice, 1930—. Visiting surgeon, Lane Hosp., 1895-1930, San Francisco Hosp., 1899-1930. Dir. Cooper Med. Coll. Republican. Episcopalian. Fellow Am. Surg. Assn. (pres. 1928). Home: San Francisco, Calif. Died Jan. 2, 1938.

ROACH, John Millard, street ry. pres.; b. Lowell, O., Jan. 30, 1851; s. John M. and Sarah Ann (Mackey) R.; acad. edn., Beverly, and Athens, O.; m. Katie E. Lyon. Entered employment N. Chicago St. Ry. Co. as conductor, 1872; asst. supt., 1887, supt., 1890, 2d v.p. and gen. mgr., 1893; became v.p. and gen. mgr. W. Chicago St. Ry., 1897; was also pres. Cicero & Proviso St. Ry. Co., Suburban Ry. Co., Chicago Union Traction Co.; pres. Chicago Rys. Co., 1907-Nov. 3, 1913 (resigned); dir. Chicago Surface Lines. Home: Chicago, Ill. Died Mar. 8, 1924.

ROACH, Thomas Watson, educator; b. Jefferson Co., O., Nov. 8, 1847; s. James P. and Martha (Wright) R.; ed. public schs., Ohio; taught sch.; B.S., Mt. Union Coll., Alliance, O., 1870, M.S., 1890; D.Pd., Iowa Wesleyan, 1907; Dr. Business Administration, Kan., Wesleyan U., 1924; m. Angeline Olivia Martin, Apr. 11, 1874. Supt. Marysville (Kan.) schs., 1871-72; co. supt. schs., Cloud Co., Kan., 1885-89; supt. Kan. Wesleyan Business Coll., 1892-1913; pres. Kan. Wesleyan Univ., 1903-08. V.p. of Planters' State Bank, Salina, Kan., 1900-25; mayor of Salina, 1900-01; pres. Welfare Bd., Salina, 1914-25, Salina St. R.R. Co., 1910-25. Republican. Mason. Trustee M.E. Ch., 1900—. Lay del. Gen. Conf. M.E. Ch., Los Angeles, 1904 Life mem. N.E.A. Pres. bd. trustees Kan. Wesleyan U., 1916-25. Author: Theory of Double-Entry Bookkeeping Made Easy, 1896. Home: Salina, Kan. Died Aug. 11, 1927.

ROARK, Ruric Nevel, educator; b. Greenville, Ky., May 19, 1859; s. M. Jeff. and Nancy (Davis) R.; ed. Greenville Acad. and under pvt. collegiate tutors; grad. Lebanon (O.) Univ., 1881 (Ph.D., Normal Univ.); m. Mary Creegan, 1881. Pursued spl. studies in pedagogy; taught Lebanon, O., 1881-85; prin. Normal Sch., Glasgow, Ky., 1885-89; dean dept. of pedagogy, State Coll. of Ky., 1889-1905; hon. fellow psychology, Clark Univ., 1905-06; pres. E. Ky. State Normal Sch., 1906—. Author: Psychology in Education, 1895; Method in Education, 1899; Economy in Education, 1905; General Outline of Pedagogy, 1900. Home: Richmond, Ky. Died 1909.

ROBB, Charles Henry, judge; b. Guilford, Vt., Nov. 14, 1867; s. Isaac and Clara Slater (Matthews) R.; m. Nettie M. George, 1897. Admitted to Vt. bar, 1892 and practiced at Bellows Falls, 1894-1902. Held several minor offices in Vt.; asst. atty. gen. for P.O. Dept. during investigations of 1903-04; asst. atty. gen. U.S., 1904-06; asso. justice Ct. of Appeals of D.C., 1906—. Republican. Home: Washington, D.C. Died June 10, 1939.

ROBB, Hunter, M.D.; b. Burlington, N.J., 1863; s. Thomas and Caroline (Woolman) R.; ed. Episcopal Acad., Phila., Burlington (N.J.) College; M.D., University of Pa., 1884; m. Isabel Adams Hampton, of Welland, Ont., 1894; children—Hampton, Philip, Hunter; m. 3d, Marion Wilson, May 22, 1929. Resident physician, Presbyn. and Episcopal hosps., Phila., 1884-86; asst. surgeon Kensington Hosp. for Women, 1888-89; asso. in gynecology, Johns Hopkins U. and Hosp., 1889-94; in practice at Cleveland, 1894-1914; retired from practice; was prof. gynecology, Western Reserve U. Episcopalian. Republican. Author: Aseptic Surgical Technique, 1894. Maj., M.C.U.S.A., Sept. 1918-Jan. 13, 1919; served at Camp Greenleaf, Ga., at Rockefeller Inst., New York, Camp Wheeler, Ga., and Base Hosp. Home: Burlington, N.J. Died May 15, 1940.

ROBB, James Hampden, banker; b. Phila., Pa., Oct. 27, 1846; s. James and Louisa (Werninger) R.; ed. in Europe, and mil. sch., Sing Sing, N.Y.; entered class of 1866 at Harvard, but was not grad; m. Cornelia Van Rensselaer Thayer, Nov. 24, 1868. In banking and cotton business, New York, 1868-86 (retired); mem. State Assembly, 1882; state senator, 1884-85; commr. and pres. Park Bd., New York, 1887-90; commr. and treas. original bd. commrs. Niagara State Reservation. Lt. col. and acting adj. gen. 1st Brigade N.G.S.N.Y. Declined appointment as asst. sec. state from President Cleveland, 1887. Deceased.

ROBB, Russell, engineer; b. Dubuque, Ia., Dec. 6, 1864; s. Patrick and Catharine Sedgwick (Newbury) R.; S.B., Mass. Inst. Tech., 1888; m. Edith Owen Morse, Mar. 1, 1898; children—Russell, Catharine. Engr. Thomson Electric Welding Co., 1888-91; with Stone & Webster, mgrs. pub. service corporation, 1891—, mem. firm 1905-20; sr. v.p. and treas. Stone and Webster, Inc., 1920—; dir. numerous traction, light, power and other cos. Trustee Concord Free Pub. Library. Author: Electric Wiring, 1896; Lectures on Organization, 1909. Home: Concord, Mass. Died Feb. 15, 1927.

ROBB, William Lispenard, electrical engr.; b. Saratoga, N.Y., May 9, 1861; s. Alexander J. and Esther (Lispenard) R.; B.A., Columbia, 1880; univs. of Würzburg and Berlin, 1880-83; Ph.D., U. of Berlin, 1883; Federal Poly., Zürich, Switzerland; LL.D., Trinity Coll., Conn., 1902; m. Winifred Matthews, 1893; children—Winifred Lispenard (Mrs. Wm. L. Powers), Leonard Lispenard. Submarine Mine Service, Spanish-Am. War, 1898; cons. engr., Hartford Electric Light Co., Gen. Ry. Signal Co.; head, dept. elec. engring., Rensselaer Poly. Inst., Troy, N.Y., 1902—. Democrat. Episcopalian. Home: Troy, N.Y. Died Jan. 26, 1933.

ROBB, Willis Oscar, fire ins.; b. Marysville, O., July 31, 1858; s. William H. and Amelia J. (Turner) R.; B.A., Ohio Wesleyan, 1879, LL.D., 1924; m. Juliet M. Everts, Sept. 2, 1886. Instr. Latin Farmers' Coll., College Hill, Cincinnati, 1879-83; adjuster, Ins. Adjustment Co., Cincinnati, 1884-85; spl. agt., Liverpool & London & Globe Ins. Co., Ohio & W.Va., 1885-95; gen. adjuster, Norwich Union Fire Ins. Soc., New York, 1895-1902; sec. com. on losses and adjustments, New York Bd. of Fire Underwriters, 1902-10; mgr. New York Fire Ins. Exchange, 1910-28 (now N.Y. City div. of N.Y. Fire Ins. Rating Orgn.). Home: Richmond Hill, L.I. Died July 17, 1933.

ROBBINS, Alexander Henry, lawyer; b. St. Louis, Mo., June 21, 1875; s. Alexander Henry and Annie (Robinson) R.; ed. St. Louis High Sch.; spl. scientific courses, Washington U.; LL.B., Washington U., 1898; m. Katherine F. Gundelfinger, Feb. 24, 1903. Entered law office of Judge J. G. Woerner, of St. Louis, 1898; editor Central Law Journal, 1900—. Prof. law of real property and conflict of laws, St. Louis U. Inst. of Law, 1911-15. Mo. rep. Conf. of Commrs. on Uniform State Laws; sec. Bd. of Election Commrs. of St. Louis. Democrat. Methodist. Author: American Advocacy, 1904; Conflict of Laws, 1914. Home: St. Louis, Mo. Died Jan. 4, 1922.

ROBBINS, Charles Leonidas, prof. edn.; b. Chariton, Ia., Dec. 7, 1876; s. George Thomas and Mary (Vanderbur) R.; B.A., U. of Kan., 1902, M.A., 1903; Ph.D., Columbia, 1912; m. Klara Hartman, Aug. 21, 1913; children—Jane, Charles Hartman. Teacher and prin. schs. in Kan. until 1905; prof. methods Mont. State Normal Coll., 1905-09; asst. teacher of edn., N.Y. City Training Sch. for Teachers, 1910-18; prof. edn., State U. of Iowa, 1918—. Episcopalian. Author: Teachers in Germany in the Sixteenth Century, 1912; The School as a Social Institution, 1918; The Socialized Recitation, 1920; (with Elmer Green) School History of the American People, 1925; The Will to Work, 1928. Home: Iowa City, Ia. Died Jan. 19, 1938.

ROBBINS, Edward Denmore, lawyer; b. Wethersfield, Conn., Oct. 20, 1853; s. Richard Austin and Harriet (Welles) R.; B.A., Yale, 1874 (valedictorian); studied univs. France and Jena, and at Yale, 1874-77; LL.B., Yale, 1880; m. Charlotte Swan, Feb. 12, 1908; children—Harriet W., Edward D. Engaged in law practice, 1881—; prof. jurisprudence, Yale, 1896-1902; formerly v.p. N.E. R.R. Co. and gen. counsel N.Y.,N.H.&H. R.R. Co.; mem. Conn. Ho. of Rep., 1882, 83; mem. Conn. State Bd. of Edn., 1884-1919. Republican. Home: New Haven, Conn. Died Oct. 7, 1932.

ROBBINS, Edward Everett, congressman; b. Greensburg, Pa., Sept. 27, 1861; s. Joseph and Rachel G. R.; A.B., Washington and Jefferson Coll., 1881; studied, law dept. Columbia U.; m. Luella Stauffer Moore, 1886. Admitted to Pa. bar, 1886, and began practice at Greensburg; also in coal and banking business; mem. Pa. Senate, 1888-94; mem. 55th and 65th Congresses (1897-99 and 1915-17), 22d Pa. Dist. Republican. Entered Pa. N.G., 1887; left Congress, and commd. capt. a.q.m. vols. Spanish-Am. War, May 27, 1898; maj. q.m., Aug. 27, 1898; served in Cuba and Puerto Rico; hon. disch. from vol. service, Oct. 14, 1898; apptd. q.m. gen. of Pa., rank of col., staff of Gov. Stone, 1900, and served 4 yrs. Presbyn. Elk. Home: Greensburg, Pa. Died Jan. 25, 1919.

ROBBINS, Francis LeBaron, clergyman; b. Camillus, N.Y., May 2, 1830; s. Samuel and Fanny (Osborne) R.; A.B., Williams Coll., 1854; (D.D., Union Coll.); m. Lucy M., d. Rev. Alanson Hartpence (niece Hon. Levi P. Morton), Oct. 14, 1874. Ordained Presbyn. ministry, 1860; pastor Green Hill Ch., Phila., 7 yrs.; founder and pastor 17 yrs., Oxford Presbyn. Ch., Phila.; founded Beacon Presbyn. Ch., an institutional ch., established in the midst of 100,000 working people in Kensington, Phila.; dedicated in 1888 with 3,000 persons present. Engaged of late yrs. in supplying chs. without pastors. Home: Greenfield, Mass. Died Jan. 28, 1920.

ROBBINS, Francis LeBaron, coal operator; b. Ripon, Wis., Sept. 3, 1855; s. Thomas Burr and Alice (Brockway) R.; m. Helen Gill, May 18, 1882. Is said to be the largest individual coal miner in U.S.; pres. Monongahela River Consolidated Coal & Coke Co.; dir. First Nat. Bank of Pittsburgh, Colonial Trust Co. Presbyn. Republican. Home: Allegheny, Pa. Died 1911.

ROBBINS, Hayes, author, industrial economist; b. Angelica, N.Y., Nov. 24, 1873; s. Frederick A. and Catherine (Whittlesey) R.; grad. Wilson Acad., Angelica, 1890, and Sch. of Social Economics, New York, 1896; editor its periodicals, 1896-1903; m. Anna Gillette Reed, Aug. 28, 1901; 1 son, Hayes. Sec. Civic Fedn. of N.E., 1905-09. Mem. and asst. in com. on labor, Council Nat. Defense, Washington, 1917. Asst. to pres. B.&M. R.R., 1923-26; community development and economic writing, 1926—. Republican. Unitarian. Author: (with George Gunton) Outlines of Social Economics, 1900; (with same) Outlines of Political Science, 1901; Lucius Tuttle, an Appreciation, 1915; Labor and the Common Welfare, 1919, and Labor and the Employer, 1920 (compilations, from Gompers); The Making of Tomorrow, 1920; The Labor Movement and the Farmer, 1922; Human Relations in Railroading, 1927. Home: Newton Highlands, Mass. Died Apr. 8, 1941.

ROBBINS, Henry Spencer, lawyer; b. East Stoughton, Mass., Feb. 5, 1853; s. John V. and Anastasia (Ford) R.; A.B., Yale, 1874; LL.B., U. of Wis., 1874; m. Frances F. Johnston, Dec. 12, 1883 (dec.); children—Marjorie J., Dorothy F., Isabelle M., Frances J.; m. 2d, Helen Beatrice Graham, of Toronto, Ont., 1929. Practiced law at New York, N.Y., 1874-76; moved to Chicago and associated in practice with Hempstead Washburne; firm became Trumbull (Senator Lyman Trumbull), Washburne & Robbins, 1883, and so continued until Mr. Washburne was elected mayor of Chicago; now in gen. practice alone; counsel for Chicago Bd. of Trade 26 yrs.; formerly spl. asst. to U.S. atty. gen. Democrat. Presbyn. Home: Chicago, Ill. Died Apr. 27, 1932.

ROBBINS, Horace Wolcott, lawyer, artist; b. Mobile, Ala., Oct. 21, 1842; s. H. W. and Mary E. (Hyde) R.; grad. Newton Univ., Baltimore, 1860; studied art abroad 3 yrs.; served at Harper's Ferry in 22d N.Y. regt., 1862; m. Mary A. Phelps, Sept. 27, 1865. Studied landscape painting with James M. Hart, N.A.; elected asso. Nat. Acad., 1864; academician, 1878; sec. 10 yrs. and v.p., 1894 and 1895, Nat. Acad. Design. Studied law at Columbia Law Sch., 1890; admitted to N.Y. bar, 1892. Trustee New York Sch. of Applied Design for Women; fellow in perpetuity Met. Mus. Art. Home: New York, N.Y. Died 1904.

ROBBINS, Irvin, soldier; b. Moscow, Ind., Mar. 30, 1839; s. Richard and Sarah Ann (Wood) R.; A.B., Butler Coll., Indianapolis, 1860, in law, 1860, A.M., 1863; m. Cassandra Cobb, Apr. 10, 1862. Pvt. 7th Ind. Vols., Apr. 24, 1861; adj. 76th Ind. Vols., July 1862; capt. 123d Ind. Vols., Nov. 1863; maj. same, July 1, 1864; insp. gen. and a.a.g., 1st div. 23d Army Corps in N.C., 1865; provost marshal west part N.C., summer 1865. Carriage mfr., 1871—; supt. of police, 1883. Mason. Adj. gen. of Ind. G.A.R., 1891-93; adj. gen. Nat. Encampment G.A.R., 1896; sr. v.-comdr.-in-chief G.A.R., 1899-1900. Democrat. Home: Indianapolis, Ind. Died 1911.

ROBBINS, John Williams, artist; b. Windham, Conn., Feb. 16, 1856; s. Thomas Clemmons and Harriet Louisa (Brownell) R.; ed. pub. schs., Windham; studied architecture in Boston; grad. Mass. State Sch. of Art; studied Cowles Art Sch. (Boston), Art Students' League (New York), and under pvt. masters; m. Jennie Annette Woods, Dec. 22, 1886; children—John Donald, Kenneth W. Newspaper work (cartoonist), 1888-98; exhibited oils, water colors, pastels and etchings at Conn. Acad. Fine Arts, Hartford, Conn., Nat. Acad. Design, New York; and in "one man" exhbns. Inventor of Brule print etching; exhibited Brule prints at City Club and Twentieth Century Club, Boston, proofs at Art Inst. Chicago, Congressional Library and Nat. Gallery (Washington, D.C.), Bibliothèque Nationale (Paris), etc.; also inventor of Mezzobrule, a development of Brule print. Mem. Conn. Acad. Fine Arts. Fundamentalist in religion. Home: Boston, Mass. Died June 24, 1938.

ROBBINS, Mary Caroline, author; b. Calais, Me., 1841; d. James Shepherd (author) and Charlotte Otis (Grosvenor) Pike; ed. W. Newton and Phila.; went, 1861, to Europe with her father, then U.S. minister to the Netherlands; studied water-colors with R. Swain Gifford, New York; studied art in Italy, 1874-75; m. Dr. J. H. Robbins, Apr. 30, 1881 (died 1900). Edited, with late Gail Hamilton, Wood's Household Magazine, 1871-72. Hon. regent Old Colony Chapter D.A.R. Author: The Rescue of an Old Place, 1892. Translator: (from French) Romance of an Honest Woman (Victor Cherbuliez), 1874; Old Masters of Belgium and Holland (Eugène Fromentin), 1882; Life of Fromentin (Edward Gosse), 1883; Count Xavier (Henri Gréville), 1885. Home: Hingham, Mass. Died Nov. 5, 1912.

ROBBINS, Merton Covey, publisher; b. Brattleboro, Vt., Aug. 18, 1875; s. Marcus R. and Almira L. (Covey) R.; B.S. in C.E., U. of Vt., 1898; m. Florence R. Page, Dec. 27, 1900; children—Marcus Page, Merton C., Mary Elizabeth. Western rep. Engring. News, hdqrs. in Chicago, 1899-1907; v.p. and western mgr. Am. Architect and Municipal Journal, 1907-09; adv. mgr. Class Journal Co., New York, 1909-10; gen. mgr. Iron Age and associated publs., 1910-18; became president and treas. Robbins Pub. Co., also of Robbins Publs., Inc.; pub. of Gas Age-Record, Industrial Gas, Gas Appliance Merchandising, Advertising and Selling, Am. Perfumer, Brown's Dir. of Am. Gas Cos., Gas Engring. and Appliance Catalog. Pres. New York Business Publishers Assn., 1915-16; pres. Associated Business Papers, Inc., 1920-21. Served as maj. comdg. Univ. Batt., U. of Vermont; 2d lt. and batt. adj. 1st Vt. Vols., Spanish-Am. War. Trustee U. of Vermont. Republican. Presbyn. Mason. Home: Pelham, N.Y. Died May 20, 1937.

ROBBINS, Royal; b. Boston, Dec. 12, 1865; s. Royal Elisha and Mary Elizabeth (Horton) R.; grad. Noble's Sch., Boston, 1883; A.B., magna cum laude, Harvard, 1887; m. Theresa Huntington, Nov. 14, 1888; children—Royal E. (dec.), Theresa R. Partner, Robbins & Appleton, 1887-1909; treas. Waltham Watch Co., 1902-11 (retired). Mem. Boston Common Council, 1892; mem. Mass. Ho. of Rep., 1893, 94; mem. Commn. on Relations of Employer and Employee of Mass., 1903-04; chmn. Mass. Commn. on Old Age Pensions, 1908, and mem. same, 1923-25. Republican. Home: Brookline, Mass. Died May 4, 1928.

ROBBINS, Warren Delano, diplomatic service; b. Brooklyn, N.Y., Sept. 3, 1885; s. Charles Albert and Catherine (Delano) R.; A.B., Harvard, 1908; m. Irene de Bruyn, of Buenos Aires, Sept. 3, 1910; children—Warren, Edward, Helen (Mrs. Alexander Cochrane Forbes). Served as private sec. ministers to Portugal and Argentina, 1909-10; 3d sec. Embassy, Paris, 1911-14, 2d sec. Legation, Guatemala, 1914-16; assigned to duty Div. of Latin Am. Affairs, 1916; 1st sec. to Embassy, Buenos Aires, 1917; 1st sec. to Embassy, Santiago, 1918-21; chief Div. of Near Eastern Affairs, 1921; counselor of Embassy, Berlin, 1922-24, Rome, 1925-28; E.E. and M.P. to Republic of El Salvador, 1928-30; apptd. minister plenipotentiary, White House ceremonial officer, 1931, and chief of Div. of Protocol, Dept. of State; apptd. E.E. and M.P. to Can., 1933. Unitarian. Home: Washington, D.C. Died Apr. 7, 1935.

ROBBINS, Wilford Lash, clergyman; b. Boston, Aug. 7, 1859; s. Robert Lash and Elizabeth (Falconer) R.; A.B., Amherst, 1881, A.M., 1884; B.D., Episcopal Theol. Sch., 1887; D.D., St. Stephen's, 1891, Amherst, 1903, Princeton, 1908, General Theol. Seminary, 1912; LL.D., Hobart Coll., 1905; unmarried. Deacon, 1884, priest, 1885, P.E. Church; rector Church of Our Redeemer, Lexington, Mass., 1885-87; dean of All Saints' Cathedral, Albany, N.Y., 1887-1903; dean of Gen. Theol. Sem., New York, 1903-16. Author: An Essay Toward Faith, 1900; A Christian Apologetic, 1902. Home: Bethel, Me. Died Sept. 5, 1927.

ROBE, Charles Franklin, brig. gen.; b. Canastota, N.Y., Nov. 23, 1841; s. Harvey Wayne and Parlyncia (Stevens) R.; ed. "red school houses"; m. Kate Eloise Stevens, Feb. 13, 1867. First lt. and capt., 147th N.Y. Vols. and Veteran Reserve Corps, 1862-66; 1st lt. 29th U.S. Inf., July 28, 1866; assigned to 25th Inf., Jan. 31, 1870; capt., Jan. 25, 1872; maj. 14th Inf., July 5, 1895; lt. col. 17th Inf., Sept. 16, 1898; col. 9th Inf., July 13, 1900; brig. gen. and retired, 1903. Admitted to Tex. bar. Regt. N.Y. Vol. Inf.; life mem. Nat. Rifle Assn. of America. Home: San Diego, Calif. Died 1910.

ROBERSON, Frank Remont, lecturer; b. New York, Feb. 4, 1871; s. William Henry and Eliza (Hebler) R.; ed. Albany (N.Y.) Acad., N.Y., Normal Coll.; m. Jessie Buckingham Wharton, Mar. 22, 1907. Lecturer on travel subjects, 1890—; has been 3 times around the world, 33 times in continental Europe; presented to Queen Victoria, Sultan of Turkey, Leo XIII; lectures on every country on earth. In Philippines, China War, 1893-94; S. Africa, 1900; with relief expdn. to St. Pierre, Martinique, after eruption of Mont Pelee; in Royal Italian relief expdn. to Messina, 1908, as spl. Am. rep. Home: Walden, N.Y. Died Dec. 26, 1916.

ROBERT, Henry Martyn, brig. gen. U.S.A.; b. Robertville, S.C., May 2, 1837; s. Rev. Joseph Thomas and Adeline (Lawton) R.; brother of Joseph Thomas R.; grad. U.S. Mil. Acad., 1857; m. Helen M. Thresher, Dec. 24, 1860; m. 2d, Isabel Livingstone Hoagland, May 8, 1901. Bvt. 2d lt. engrs., July 1, 1857; 2d lt., Dec. 13, 1858; promoted through grades to brig. gen. chief of engrs. U.S.A., Apr. 30, 1901; retired by operation of law, May 2, 1901. Acting asst. prof., 1856-57, in charge dept. practical mil. engring., 1865-67, U.S. Mil. Acad.; in command of exploration of a mil. route from Vancouver to Puget Sound, 1860; engr. on defenses of Washington, 1861; in charge defenses of Phila., 1861-62, New Bedford, 1862-65; chief engr. Mil. Div. of the Pacific, 1867-71; in charge various light house dists., and river and harbor improvements, 1871-95; engr. commr. D.C. and mem. Rock Creek Nat. Park Commn., 1890-91; supervising engr. 12 U.S. engr. dists., Pittsburgh to Galveston, 1897-1901; pres. U.S. Bd. of Engrs. for Fortifications, 1895-1901, New York Harbor Line Bd., 1895-1901, Phila. Harbor Line Bd., 1894-1901, etc.; mem. commn. to design sea-wall for Galveston, 1901-02 and 1915; cons. engr. to design a causeway and bridge to connect Galveston with mainland, 1907-08, 15; to design improvement of port of Frontera, Mex., 1911. Author: Robert's Rules of Order, 1876, 1893; Robert's Rules of Order Revised, 1915; Analytical and Topical Index to Reports of Chief of Engineers, U.S.A., on River and Harbor Improvements, from 1866-1887, Vol. I, 1881, Vol. II, 1889; Parliamentary Practice, 1921; Parliamentary Law, 1922. Home: Owego, N.Y. Died May 11, 1923.

ROBERTS, Arthur Jeremiah, college pres.; b. Waterboro, Me., Oct. 15, 1867; s. Albert Hall and Evaline A. (Dearborn) R.; B.A., Colby Coll., 1890; M.A., Harvard, 1900; m. Ada Louise Peabody, Aug. 27, 1895. Prof. English lit., 1895-1908, pres., July 1, 1908—, Colby Coll. Home: Waterville, Me. Died Oct. 11, 1927.

ROBERTS, Benjamin Kearney, brig. gen. U.S.A.; b. Memphis, Tenn., Nov. 28, 1846; s. Gen. Benjamin Stone and Elizabeth (Sperry) R.; ed. pvt. schs. and Norwich (Vt.) U. to 1863, A.M., 1864; m. Julia A. Roberts, Jan. 25, 1887. Second lt. 7th Ia. Cav., July 25, 1863; hon. mustered out, Dec. 22, 1864; capt. a.a.g., Nov. 12, 1864; on staff of Gen. George H. Thomas, 1865-June 1866; bvtd. maj., Mar. 13, 1865; apptd. from Conn., 2d lt. 5th U.S. Arty., Apr. 18, 1866; hon. mustered out of vol. service, July 1, 1866; 1st lt. 5th Arty., Feb. 7, 1867; capt., Apr. 25, 1888; maj. 2d Arty., Oct. 17, 1899; lt. col. Arty. Corps, Sept. 23, 1901; col., Aug. 3, 1903; brig. gen. chief of arty., June 19, 1905; retired, June 20, 1905, at own requests after 40 yrs.' service. Died July 16, 1921.

ROBERTS, Benson Howard, editor; b. Brockport, N.Y., Oct. 9, 1853; s. Rev. Benjamin Titus (33 yrs. gen. supt. Free Methodist Ch.) and Ellen L. (Stow) R.; ed. Rochester Satterlee's Inst., Chili Sem., N. Chili, N.Y.; A.B., Dartmouth Coll., 1876, A.M., 1880; partial course theol. sem., Rochester, N.Y.; D.D., Berea (Ky.) College, 1912; m. Emma J. Sellew, 1877; children—Howard (dec.), Lois E. (Mrs. H. M. Hallett), A. Sellew, Douglas (dec.), Lucy G. Principal of The A. M. Chesebrough Sem., N. Chili, N.Y., 1876-78, and 1881-1906; supt. Christian Home for Girls, Pittsburgh, Jan. 1907-May 1911; preacher to Berea (Ky.) Coll. and pastor of Union Ch., July 1911-19. Editor and pub. The Earnest Christian and Golden Rule, 1893-1906. Free Methodist. Del. to Ecumenical Missionary Conf., London, 1889, Ecumenical Conf. of Meth. Chs., London, 1901, Ecumenical Missionary Conf., New York, 1900; del. Gen. Conf. Free Meth. Ch., 1898; editor General Conf. Daily. Author: Holiness Teachings, 1893; Benjamin Titus Roberts, A Biography, 1900. One of founders Roberts-Beach Sch. for Girls, Catonsville, Md., 1920; pastor Presbyn. Ch., Relay, Md., 1922. Home: Catonsville, Md. Died Mar. 2, 1930.

ROBERTS, Brigham Henry, congressman; b. Warrington, Lancashire, Eng., Mar. 13, 1857; grad. normal dept. Deseret (now Utah) U., 1878; married. Came to U.S., 1866, settled Utah. Chiefly engaged as editor and writer; mem. Utah Constl. Conv., 1895; Dem. nominee for Congress, 1895 (defeated); elected to 56th Congress (term 1899-1901); was excluded from his seat in Congress by action of the House of Representatives, Jan. 25, 1900; the vote stood 268 to 50; not voting, 36. Has traveled extensively in U.S. and British Isles. Author: The Gospel, 1888; Life of John Taylor, 1892; Outlines of Ecclesiastical History, 1893; Succession in the Presidency of the Church, 1893; New Witnesses for God, 1895, 3 vols., 1909; Missouri Persecutions, 1900; The Rise and Fall of Nauvoo, 1900; Mormon Doctrine of Deity (controversial), 1903; Defense of the Faith and the Saints (2 vols.); Latter-Day Saints' Tour from Palmyra, N.Y., to Salt Lake City, Through the Stereoscope, 1905. Editor: Smith's Journal History of the Church (6 vols.), 1909; History of the Mormon Church (6 vols.); Seventy's Course in Theology (in 5 books). Apptd. mil. chaplain, staff of Gov. Bamberger, Apr. 1917; later chaplain 145th Field Arty., and assigned to Camp Kearny, Calif.; with regt. in France, Aug. 1918-Jan. 1919. Pres. Eastern States Mission of the Church of Jesus Christ of Latter-Day Saints (12 states), May 1922. Home: Brooklyn, N.Y. Died Sept. 27, 1933.

ROBERTS, Charlotte Fitch, chemist; b. New York, Feb. 13, 1859; d. Horace and Mary (Hart) R.; A.B., Wellesley Coll., 1880; U. of Cambridge, Eng., 1886-87; Ph.D., Yale, 1894; U. of Berlin, Germany, 1899-1900. Instr. chemistry, 1881-87, asst. prof., 1887-92, prof., 1892—, Wellesley Coll. Fellow A.A.A.S. Author: Stereochemistry, 1894. Home: Wellesley, Mass. Died Dec. 5, 1917.

ROBERTS, Clarence J., lawyer; b. Jefferson Co., Ind., Oct. 21, 1873; s. Dan A. and Perintha E. (Robinson) R.; ed. common schs. and Southern Ind. Normal Sch.; m. Eliza E. Stewart, May 2, 1897. Admitted to Ind. bar, 1894; practiced at Madison, Ind., 1894-1905, Trinidad, Colo., 1905-06, Raton, N.M., 1906-10. Dist. atty. 5th Jud. Dist., Ind., 1897-99; co. atty., Jefferson Co., Ind., 1900-05; mem. 37th Legislative Assembly, N.M., 1909; mem. N.M. Constl. Conv., 1910; apptd. asso. justice Supreme Court of N.M., Sept. 19, 1910 (chief justice, 1912-17); elected for term 1918-26; resigned to enter practice of law, Nov. 1, 1921. Republican. Home: Santa Fe, N.M. Died Jan. 27, 1931.

ROBERTS, Cyrus Swan, brig. gen.; b. Sharon, Conn., Aug. 23, 1841; s. Virgil B. and Harriott

(Swan) R.; fitted for coll. at Stratford (Conn.) Acad.; m. Nannie R., d. Judge Thomas H. Du Val, of Austin, Tex., Jan. 30, 1870. Enlisted as vol. in 22d N.Y. Militia, Civil War; served at Baltimore and Harper's Ferry, Va., until mustered out of service, Sept. 6, 1862; enlisted, same day, in 150th N.Y. Vols.; sergt. maj. of regt., Oct. 11, 1862; 2d lt., Feb. 13, 1863; 1st lt., Jan. 1, 1865; capt. and a.d.c., June 22, 1865; mustered out of vol. service, Dec. 7, 1865; second lt. 17th U.S. Inf., May 11, 1866; 1st lt., Sept. 18, 1867; capt., June 28, 1878; maj., Apr. 26, 1898; lt. col. 13th U.S. Inf., Aug. 14, 1899; col. 2d Inf., Apr. 13, 1901; brig. gen. U.S.A., Aug. 8, 1903; retired at own request after more than 40 yrs.' service, Aug. 9, 1903. During Civil War, served in campaign in western Va. and the Shenandoah, 1863-64, under Gen. Geo. Crook, to whom was aid; with Sheridan's Cav., 1865, and took part in battles of the army (wounded at Lynchburg). Served in regular army in Tex., 1866-69, in Va., 1870, Dak. and Ariz., 1870-86, Wyo. until 1894, Columbus Barracks, O., until 1899; in Tex. again until 1901; in Philippines until June 1903. Was a.d.c. to Maj. Gen. Griffin in Texas, Maj. Gen. J. J. Reynolds, Brig. Gen. George Crook in Ariz., 1882-86, during the Chiricahua, Indian troubles; adj. gen. vols. with 2d Corps during war with Spain, 1898; adj. gen., dept. Texas, 1899-1901. Home: Lakeville, Conn. Died Mar. 19, 1917.

ROBERTS, Edwin Ewing, mayor; b. Pleasant Grove, Calif., Dec. 12, 1870; s. William Ewing and Anna Maria (Johnson) R.; grad. Calif. Sch. Elocution and Oratory, San Jose, 1890, State Normal Sch., San Jose, 1891; m. Nora S. Range, Apr. 23, 1893; 1 dau., Hazel Lee (Mrs. Walter P. Johnson). Taught Sch., 1891-99; admitted to Nev. bar, 1899, and began practice at Carson City; mem. Roberts, Scanlon and Ingram. Dist. atty., Ormsby Co., 5 terms 1900-10; mem. 62d to 65th Congresses (1910-19), Nev. at large; mayor of Reno, 3 terms, 1923-35. Republican. Mason. Home: Reno, Nev. Died Dec. 11, 1933.

ROBERTS, Elizabeth Madox, author; b. nr. Springfield, Ky., 1886; d. Simpson and Mary Elizabeth (Brent) R.; Ph.B., U. of Chicago, 1921. Awards: Fisk prize, U. of Chicago, 1921; John Reed Memorial prize, Poetry (mag.), 1928; O. Henry Memorial prize for a short story, 1930; prize, Poetry Soc. of South Carolina, 1931. Author: Under the Tree (verse), 1922; The Time of Man, 1926; My Heart and My Flesh, 1927; Jingling in the Wind, 1928; The Great Meadow, 1930; A Buried Treasure, 1931; The Haunted Mirror (short stories), 1932; He Sent Forth a Raven, 1935; Black Is My Truelove's Hair, 1938; Song in the Meadow (verse), 1940. Home: Springfield, Ky. Died Mar. 13, 1941.

ROBERTS, Ellis Henry, treasurer of the U.S.; b. Utica, N.Y., Sept. 30, 1827; s. Watkin and Gwen (Williams) R.; A.B., Yale, 1850, A.M. 1853; (LL.D., Hamilton, 1869, Yale, 1884); m. Elizabeth Morris, June 20, 1851 (died 1903). Prin. Utica Free Acad., 1850-51; teacher Latin, Utica Female Sem., 1850-51; editor, 1851-80, and later, to 1889, part propr. Utica Morning Herald. Mem. N.Y. Assembly, 1866; mem. 42d and 43d Congresses (1871-75); asst. treas. U.S., 1889-93; pres. Franklin Nat. Bank, New York, 1893-97; treas. of the U.S., 1897-1905. Trustee Hamilton Coll., 1872-1900. Author: Government Revenue, Especially the American System, 1884; The Planting and the Growth of the Empire State, 1887. Home: Utica, N.Y. Died Jan. 8, 1918.

ROBERTS, Elmer, newspaper corr.; b. Lagro, Ind., Apr. 7, 1863; s. Rev. Lewis and Mary (McKim) R.; DePauw University, class of 1885 (left sr. yr. before grad.; A.M.); m. Claire Livingston, May 12, 1896 (died 1929). Reporter Terre Haute (Ind.) Express, 1885; asst. editor Peru (Ind.) Republican, 1886; advertising mgr. Ft. Wayne Gazette, 1886; reporter Chicago Daily News and City Press Assn., 1886-89; Washington corr. Chicago Times, 1890-91; polit. reporter New York Herald, 1892-93; assisted in founding Jacksonville (Fla.) Citizen, 1894-96; with Associated Press, 1897-1929, as corr. Spanish-Am. War, in London, 1899-1901, Berlin, 1902-10, Paris, 1911-29; as corr. on spl. missions to Russia, Turkey, Spain, Portugal, Holland, Denmark, Norway, Sweden, Belgium, etc. In charge Associated Press staff covering Peace Conf., Paris, 1918-20. Retired. Author: Monarchical Socialism in Germany, 1913. Officer Legion of Honor (France); Chevalier Order of Leopold (Belgium). Home: Jacksonville, Fla. Died Nov. 17, 1937.

ROBERTS, Ernest William, congressman; b. E. Madison, Me., Nov. 22, 1858; s. Orin P. and Eliza V. R.; Highland Mil. Acad., Worcester, Mass., 1877; LL.B., Boston U., 1881; m. Nella Lue Allen, Nov. 13, 1881; m. 2d, Sara M. Weeks, Feb. 2, 1898. In practice at Boston, 1881—. Mem. Chelsea (Mass.) City Council, 1887-88; mem. Mass. Ho. of Rep., 1894-96, Senate, 1897-98; mem. 56th to 62d Congresses (1899-1913), 7th Mass. Dist., and 63d and 64th Congresses (1913-17), 9th Dist.; resumed law practice. Republican. Formerly mem. board regents and of exec. com. Smithsonian Instn., Washington. Home: Washington, D.C. Died Feb. 27, 1924.

ROBERTS, Florence, actress; b. New York, N.Y., Feb. 14, 1871; d. Henry B. and Annie R.; ed. San Francisco; m. Lewis Morrison, 1890 (died 1906); m. 2d, Frederick Vogeding, actor (Holland), Apr. 19, 1920. Début at Baldwin Theatre, San Francisco, 1888, as a super doing extra work; leading woman with Lewis Morrison, in Shakespearean drama and "Faust," 1890-1901; then starred in "Zaza," "Sapho," "Marta of the Lowlands," "The Unwelcome Mrs. Hatch," "Magda," "A Doll's House," "Gioconda," "Camille," "Carmen," "Tess of the D'Urbervilles," "Maria Rosa," to 1905; starred in "Ann La Mont," 1905; "The Strength of the Weak," 1905; "The Struggle Everlasting," 1907; in "The Transformation" and "The Nigger," under Shubert management, 1908-09; all star casts in New York, "Jim the Penman," and "Diplomacy," 1910; in vaudeville and stock starring," 1912-21; then in moving pictures. Died July 17, 1927.

ROBERTS, Frank Hunt Hurd, educator; b. Mt. Vernon, O., Apr. 1, 1869; s. John Henry and Anna Dwyre (Mackey) R.; B.Ph., B.Pd., Ohio U., 1892; A.M., Kenyon Coll., 1899; Ph.D., U. of Denver, 1903, LL.D., 1915; m. Luella Hanna, Sept. 1, 1896; children—Frank Harold Hanna, Henry Buchtel. Engaged in newspaper work, Ohio, 1889-93; supt. and prin. of schs., 1889-99; prof. edn. and prin. Wyo. State Normal Sch., 1899-1903; prof. history, U. of Denver, 1903-14; also pres. N.M. Normal U., Las Vegas, 1910-21; extra-mural prof., U. of Denver, 1914-21; pres. Jr. Coll. and prin. High Sch., El Paso, 1921-26. Sent to Europe by Univ. of Denver to investigate municipal ownership, 1905. Lecturer on history and pedagogy, Colo. Chautauqua, 1901-03; lecturer Glen Park Chautauqua, 1904; inst. conductor and instr. Dir. Wyo. ednl. exhibit, Paris Expn., 1900; 1st dir. Wyo. ednl. exhibit, St. Louis Expn., 1904; sec. State Bd. Examiners, Wyo., 1901-03; sr. mem. N.M. State Bd. of Edn., 1911-17. Rep. candidate for Colo. legislature, 1908. State chmn. of Meth. "Minute Men"; "Fourminute Man"; state dir. Nat. Security League; mem. N.M. Home Guard and Vigilantes Com., World War. Pres. Y.M.C.A., 1917-19. Mem. N.M. Armory Bd., 1914-21. Del. Gen. Conf. M.E. Ch, 1916-28; mem. exec. com. of Interchurch World Movement. Author: A Comparative Study of the State and Nation, 1900; Civil Government, 1902; Civil Government of Wyoming, 1902, 3d edit., 1904; History and Civics of New Mexico, 5th edit., 1918. Offered presidency of Mo. Wesleyan Coll. twice. Rotarian. Home: Denver, Colo. Died Jan. 14, 1937.

ROBERTS, George Litch, lawyer; b. Boston, Mass., Dec. 30, 1836; s. Reuben and Jane (Litch) R.; A.B., Wesleyan U., Conn., 1859 (valedictorian), A.M., 1862; attended Harvard Law Sch., 1862; m. Hinda Barnes, Dec. 1, 1865 (died 1909); children—Odin Barnes, Harold Barnes. Admitted to Mass. bar, 1864; principally identified with patent litigation; counsel for Am. Bell Telephone Co. and Am. Tel. & Tel. Co., Nov. 1881-Jan. 1915; retired from practice; spent greater part of 7 yrs. in defending the former co. against suit of the U.S. to repeal the Bell patents. Republican. Agnostic. Mason. Wrote essay, "The Domain of Utilitarian Ethics," Internat. Journal of Ethics, 1903. Author: Objective Reality, 1925; Patentability of Inventions and the Interpretation of Patents (2 vols.), 1927. Home: Brookline, Mass. Died Apr. 29, 1929.

ROBERTS, George Lucas, univ. prof.; b. Decatur, Ind., Nov. 19, 1860; s. William and Sarah (Christie) R.; A.B., Ind. U., Bloomington, 1894; summer sch., Clark U., 1903; A.M., Columbia, 1910; Master's Diploma in Edn., Teachers Coll. (Columbia), 1910; m. Olive A. Linch, Nov. 19, 1884; children—Paul Linch (dec.), Mrs. Miriam Smiley. Teacher and prin. various schs., Ind., until 1883; prin. high sch., Greensburg, 1887-97; supt. schs., Greensburg, 1897-1901, Frankfort, 1901-03, Muncie, 1903-08; head dept. of edn., Purdue U., 1908-31 (emeritus), was also dean Purdue U. Summer Sch. for training teachers in agr.; now adviser in teachers' licensing and placement, Purdue U. Editor Educator-Journal (monthly); lecturer before teachers' insts. Mem. edn. sect. State Council Defense, 1917-19; Red Cross ednl. dir. U.S.A. Gen. Hosp. 35, 1919. Republican. Methodist. Mason. Home: West Lafayette, Ind. Died Feb. 26, 1941.

ROBERTS, George Newman, chmn. Bemis Bros. Bag Co.; b. Cambridge, Mass., Dec. 17, 1874; s. George Blagdon and Lucy (Cogswell) R.; student Cambridge Latin Sch., 1888-93; A.B., Harvard, 1897; m. May Laura Lewis, Dec. 12, 1906 (died 1934); children—George Newman, William Lewis. Newspaper reporter on N.Y. Sun, Asso. Press, 1893-99; with Bemis Bros. Bag Co., 1899—, beginning as salesman, served in various capacities, pres. in 1934, now chmn.; dir. Boott Mills, Lowell, Mass. Republican. Author of one-act plays: The Weasel, His Day off, etc. Home: Waban, Mass. Died Sept. 12, 1940.

ROBERTS, Harlan Page, lawyer; b. Wayne, O., Dec. 5, 1854; s. George and Ann Jeannette (Marvin) R.; A.B., Oberlin, 1875; studied theology, Oberlin, 1875, 76; grad. Yale Div. Sch., 1878; m. Margaret Lee Conklin, Oct. 3, 1888. Ordained Congl. ministry, 1878; pastor Silverton, Colo., 1878-81; in business in Silverton, 1881-84, and admitted to bar; co. treas. San Juan Co., Colo., 1879-82; clk. City of Silverton, 1883; located in Minneapolis, 1884. Republican. Home: Minneapolis, Minn. Died 1925.

ROBERTS, Harris Lee, army officer; b. in D.C., May 6, 1858; grad. U.S. Mil. Acad., 1880. Commd. 2d lt. 4th Inf., June 12, 1880; trans. to 19th Inf., Mar. 22, 1881; 1st lt. 21st Inf., Nov. 14, 1890; trans. to 19th Inf., July 20, 1891; capt., Apr. 26, 1898; trans. to 2d Inf., Nov. 22, 1904; maj. 26th Inf., July 28, 1905; lt. col. 22d Inf., Mar. 11, 1911; col. of Inf., Mar. 13, 1914. Served as regimental q.m., 1891-95; in charge constrn. Ft. Wayne, Mich., 1895-97; in Puerto Rico, 1898-99, Philippine Islands, 1899-1901 and 1907-08; duty Ft. Sam Houston, Tex., 1916-17. Died Dec. 27, 1918.

ROBERTS, Henry, governor; b. Brooklyn, N.Y., Jan. 22, 1853; s. George and Elvira (Evans) R.; A.B., Yale, 1877; Columbia and Yale law schs., 2 yrs.; m. Carrie E. Smith, Oct. 5, 1881. Entered service of Hartford Woven Wire Co., 1879, and on death of father succeeded him as pres.; also pres. Hartford Woven Wire Mattress Co.; dir. various companies. Alderman, Hartford, 1897; mem. Conn. Ho. of Rep., 1899-1901, Senate, 1901-03; lt. gov., 1903-05; gov. of Conn., 1905-07. Republican. Home: Hartford, Conn. Died May 1, 1929.

ROBERTS, Howard, sculptor; b. Philadelphia, Pa., April 9, 1843; studied art in Philadelphia; also in Paris at École des Beaux Arts and under Dumont and Gumery. Has produced and exhibited many ideal and portrait statues, groups and busts, including the statue of Robert Fulton in the Capitol; m. Helen Pauline Lewis, June 1, 1876. Home: Philadelphia, Pa. Died 1900.

ROBERTS, Isaac Phillips, educator; b. Seneca Co., N.Y., July 24, 1833; s. Aaron Phillips and Elizabeth (Burroughs) R.; Seneca Falls Acad.; M. Agr., Ia. State Coll., 1875; m. Margaret J. Marr, Nov. 3, 1857. Prof. agr. and dean faculty of agr., 1873-94, dir. Agrl. Expt. Sta., 1888-1903, prof. emeritus and lecturer on agr., 1903—, Cornell. Asst. editor The Country Gentleman. Author: The Fertility of the Land, 1898; The Farmstead, 1900; The Farmer's Business Handbook, 1903; The Horse, 1905; Autobiography of a Farm Boy, 1916. Home: Palo Alto, Calif. Died 1928.

ROBERTS, James Arthur, lawyer; b. York Co., Me., Mar. 8, 1847; s. Jeremiah and Alma (Roberts) R.; served in 7th Me. Battery, 1864-65; A.B., Bowdoin, 1870, A.M., 1873 (LL.D., 1898); m. Minnie Pineo, June 1, 1871; m. 2d, Martha Dresser, Dec. 11, 1884. Admitted to bar, 1875; practiced at Buffalo, 1875-94, New York, 1902—. Mem. N.Y. Assembly, 1879-80; mem. Buffalo Park Commn., 1891-93; comptroller State of N.Y., 1894-99. Pres. Greater New York Home Co., N.J. Home Co., Stuyvesant Home Co., Shoal Harbor Industries. Mason. Home: New York, N.Y. Died Nov. 19, 1922.

ROBERTS, James Cole, mining engr.; b. Warren Co., N.C., Dec. 14, 1863; s. Frederick Cox and Lavinia Ellis (Cole) R.; Bingham Sch. (military) N.C.; Ph.B., U. of N.C.; studied Columbia; m. Alice Mary Pomeroy, 1897; 1 dau., Alice Pomeroy. Chemist and mill engr. in N.C., 1885-87; chemist and metallurgist, Woodstock Iron Works, Anniston, Ala., 1887-89; examination phosphate lands in Fla., 1889-91; mgr. Enterprise Mine, Rico, Colo., 1892-95; chemist and asst. metallurgist, Globe Smelting Works, Denver, 1895-97; metallurgist, Anaconda (Mont.) Copper Co., 1897-99; prof. metallurgy, Colo. Sch. of Mines, 1899-1902; cons. engr. for Detroit Capitalists, 1902-04; engr. and metallurgist, Ampere Electro-Chem. Co. and Atmospheric Products Co., Niagara Falls, 1904-08; with U.S. Bureau Mines, in charge installations, investigations, etc., 1908-15; prof. coal mining and safety and efficiency engring., Colo. Sch. of Mines, 1915-23; now mgr. Safety Council, Denver. Democrat. Episcopalian. Mason. Home: Golden, Colo. Deceased.

ROBERTS, John Bingham, surgeon; b. Phila., Feb. 29, 1852; s. Caleb Cresson and Helen S. (Bingham) R.; A.B., U. of Pa., 1871, M.D., 1874; M.D., Jefferson Med. Coll., 1874; m. Mary Eleanor Roberts, 1897. Emeritus prof. surgery, Grad. Sch. of Medicine U. of Pa.; prof. surgery, Woman's Med. Coll. of Pa., 1890-1900. Pres. Phila. County Med. Soc., Med. Soc. State of Pa., Am. Surg. Assn.; fellow Am. Coll. Surgeons (gov. 1914, pres. 1920). Author: Paracentesis of Pericardium, 1880; Compend of Anatomy, 1881; Surgery of Human Brain, 1885; Treatise on Modern Surgery, 1885; Modern Medicine and Homœopathy, 1895; Fractures of Radius, 1897; Modern Treatment of Fractures, 1899; Deformities of the Face, 1900; Treatise on Fractures (with James A. Kelly), 1915; War Surgery of the Face, 1918. Home: Philadelphia, Pa. Died Nov. 28, 1924.

ROBERTS, Odin, lawyer; b. Boston, Mass., Jan. 22, 1867; s. George Litch and Hinda (Barnes) R.; A.B., cum laude, Harvard, 1886, L.L.B. and A.M., 1891; S.B., Mass. Inst. Tech., 1888; m. Ada Mead, Apr. 19, 1897; children—Sumner Mead, Frederick Mead, Virginia. Admitted to Mass. bar, 1891, later to practice before Supreme Court of U.S.; mem. various law firms in Boston, 1891—, Roberts, Cushman & Woodberry, 1926—; specializes in patent and trade mark law. Formerly lecturer on patent law at Mass.

Inst. Tech. and Harvard Law Sch. Mem. exec. com. Harvard Alumni Assn., Overseers' committees to visit Harvard Engring. Sch. and Harvard Astron. Observatory. Home: Boston, Mass. Died July 23, 1934.

ROBERTS, Peter, clergyman; b. Dowlais, S. Wales, July 29, 1859; grad. Brecon Memorial Coll., 1883; B.D., Yale, 1886, Ph.D., 1901; m. Rachel Evans, Apr. 1901; children—Thomas Joseph, Anna Myfanwy, Elizabeth May, Philip Warren, William Sumner, Gladys, Peter Vernon, Gertrude Charlotte, John Ruskin, Rachel Evans. Ordained Congl. ministry, 1886; pastor Scranton, Olyphant and Mahanoy City, Pa.; sec. Internat. Com. Y.M.C.A., Aug. 1907—. Mem. Senatus Academicus, London, Eng. Author: Anthracite Coal Industry, 1902; Anthracite Coal Communities, 1904; English for Coming Americans, 1908; Immigrant Races in North America, 1910; The New Immigration, 1912; The Problem of Americanization, 1921. Home: Mt. Vernon, N.Y. Died Dec. 2, 1932.

ROBERTS, Robert, lawyer; b. Manchester, Vt., 1848; s. Daniel and Caroline Diantha (Martindale) R.; A.B., U. of Vt., 1869; Columbia Law Sch., 1870-71; continued studies Paris and Geneva, 1871-72; LL.D., U. of Vt., 1912; m. Minnie Elizabeth Lyman, Oct. 20, 1886. Began practice at Burlington, 1871; mem. Vt. Ho. of Rep., 1882, Senate, 1890-91; city atty., Burlington, 1887-89, mayor, 1899-1900-01 and 1910-12. Trustee U. of Vt., State Library. Republican. Conglist. Author: Digest of Decisions of Supreme Court of Vt. from 1789-1910. Home: Burlington, Vt. Died Feb. 23, 1939.

ROBERTS, Samuel Judson, newspaperman; b. Pomeroy, O., Feb. 11, 1858; s. Rev. Edward and Caroline Matilda (Kelly) R.; acad. edn. Canton (O.) Acad.; m. Anna Trout, Nov. 10, 1888. On staff Cleveland Leader and Herald, 1878-82; circulation mgr. Canton Repository, 1882-88; founded, May 1888, and from then editor and pub., Lexington (Ky.) Leader (Rep. daily). Mem. City Council, Canton, 1885-87; Rep. nominee for mayor, 1887; chmn. Rep. State Campaign Com. of Ky. and managed campaign, 1896, in behalf of life-long friend, William McKinley, resulting in Ky. being carried for Rep. electoral ticket the first time in its history; collector of internal revenue, 7th Ky. Dist., 1897-1910. Baptist. Home: Lexington, Ky. Died Mar. 23, 1913.

ROBERTS, Seldon L., church official; b. Monroeville, Ind., Feb. 6, 1871; s. Hiram and Elizabeth Ann (Todd) R.; A.B., Franklin (Ind.) Coll., 1902, D.D., 1926; post-grad. work, U. of Chicago; m. Violet Burkhart, Oct. 13, 1898; children—Princess Clarene (dec.), Lillian Alice, Gladys Irene, Elsie Elizabeth. Ordained Bapt. ministry, 1897; pastor successively Pleasant Lake, Southport and New Bethel, Ind., Big Rock, Ill., Pleasant Lake, and Goshen, Ind., until 1910; dir. religious edn. for Bapt. chs. in State of Ind., 1910-20; dir. leadership training Am. Bapt. Publication Soc., 1920—. Mem. Professional Advisory Group for Leadership Training, and spl. com. on leadership training, Internat. Council Religious Educators. Republican. Author: Teaching in the Church School, 1927; Training Lessons for Church School Workers, 1930. Home: Philadelphia, Pa. Died June 11, 1930.

ROBERTS, Shelby Saufley, civil engr.; b. Louisville, Ky., Apr. 13, 1874; s. Bolin Emery and Margaret K. (Pickens) R.; A.B., Louisville Male High Sch., 1894; B.S., Rose Poly. Inst., Terre Haute, Ind., 1898, C.E., 1907; LL.B., Washington Coll. of Law, 1925; m. Nell Ackley Richardson, Nov. 26, 1901; children—Nell Richardson, Shelby Chilton, Sarah Pickens. Track apprentice, maintenance dept., I.C. R.R., 1898; location surveys and constrn., St. L.,P. &N. R.R., 1898-99; with L.&N. R.R., 1899, successively as asst. to engr. in charge of constrn. of terminals at Nashville; engr. in charge of improvements at Henderson, Ky., Evansville, Ind., and East St. Louis, Ill.; engr. in charge maintenance of way, Henderson and St. Louis divs.; roadmaster main stem, 1st div.; roadmaster and engr., Louisville terminals, until 1905; supt. building constrn. for F. C. Brent, Pensacola, Fla., 1905-06; asst. engr. constrn., I.C. R.R., Chicago, 1906-08; prof. ry. civ. engring., Coll. of Engring., U. of Ill., 1908-10; div. engr. on constrn., I.C. R.R., Chicago, 1911-13; pvt. practice, gen. and ry. civ. engring., 1913-18; staff officer engring. and sr. asst. engr., U.S. R.R. Administration, Southern Region, Atlanta, Ga., 1918-20; asst. dir. Bur. of Finance, Interstate Commerce Commn., in charge of the forces handling matters before the bur. in which engring. principles are involved, 1920-35, chief sect. of securities, 1935—. Admitted to bar of D.C., 1925, Supreme Court U.S., 1930. Democrat. Episcopalian. Author: Track Formulæ and Tables, 1910. Home: Washington, D.C. Died May 6, 1936.

ROBERTS, Stanley Burroughs, clergyman; b. Phelps, N.Y., Aug. 12, 1855; s. William Moon and Betsey (Burroughs) R.; prep. edn., Phelps Acad.; student Center Coll., Ky.; grad. Auburn Theol. Sem., 1882; D.D., McAllister Coll.; m. Mary Louise Hall, Dec. 27, 1882; children—Stanley Hall, Gladys Isabel, Harold Percy, Edward Carleton, Theodore McQueen (dec.). Ordained Presbyn. ministry, 1882; pastor Bethlehem Ch., Minneapolis, Minn., 1899-1929 (resigned); pastor Glen Lake, Minn., 1929—. Chaplain Camp Dodge, World War. Pres. Ministers' Casualty Union, Northwestern Bible and Missionary Training Sch., Anti-Saloon League. Prohibitionist, Republican. Mason. Home: Glen Lake, Minn. Died July 28, 1933.

ROBERTS, Stewart Ralph, prof. clin. med.; b. Oxford, Ga., Oct. 2, 1878; s. James William and Clifford Rebecca (Stewart) R.; A.B., Emory Coll., Oxford, Ga., 1902; M.D., Atlanta Coll. Phys. and Surg. (med. sch. Emory U.), 1900; B.S. and M.S., U. of Chicago, 1904; studied Harvard Medical Sch. Prof. biology, Emory Coll., 1902-06; prof. physiology, Atlanta Sch. of Medicine, 1906-09; prof. physiology, 1909-10, asso. prof. medicine, 1910-13, prof., 1913-15, prof. clin. medicine, 1919—, Atlanta Med. Coll. (Emory U.); physician to Wesley Memorial Hospital. Lt. col., Med. Corps U.S.A. and comdg. officer Base Hosp., Camp Jackson, S.C., 1918. Fellow Am. Coll. Physicians. Methodist. Author: Pellagra, 1912. Home: Atlanta, Ga. Died Apr. 14, 1941.

ROBERTS, Theodore, actor; b. San Francisco, Oct. 8, 1861; s. Martin R. and Mary E. (Newlin) R.; ed. pub. schs., San Francisco, and Calif. Mil. Acad., Oakland; m. Miss Clyde Harron, 1890. First appearance on stage, Baldwin Theatre, San Francisco, as "Barabas" in "Richelieu," May 1, 1880; went to New York with Robson and Crane, 1881; spent 2½ yrs. at sea as capt. of schooner S. E. Perry, on Pacific coast, 1885-88; returned to stage and supported Fanny Davenport, through 5 seasons; later appeared in "Ye Earlie Trouble," 1891; "The Girl I Left Behind Me," 1892; "Gismonda," 1893; "The Squaw Man"; "The Bird of Paradise"; "The Right of Way"; "The Barrier"; "The Merry Wives of Windsor," New Theatre, New York, 1910, etc. Progressive. Unitarian. Died Dec. 14, 1928.

ROBERTS, Vasco Harold, lawyer; b. St. Joseph, Mich., May 21, 1374; s. V. H. and Elizabeth (Wells) R.; Phillips (Exeter) Acad.; entered Harvard, but left to study 3 yrs. in Germany, J.U.D., insigni cum laude, U. of Heidelberg, 1900; m. Ida Bess Wagner, Sept. 3, 1902. Prof. law, Drake U., Des Moines, 1900-02; prof. law of corps. and real property, U. of Mo., 1903-08; mem. firm Boyle & Priest, St. Louis, Mo. Episcopalian. Author: Annotated Cases on the Law of Extraordinary Legal Remedies, 1905. Died 1910.

ROBERTS, Wightman Durand, editor; b. Weaverville, N.C., Aug. 25, 1873; s. Jacob Riley and Mary (Buckner) R.; ed. Weaver Coll. and Central U. of Ky.; m. 2d, Catherene Bernard, Nov. 26, 1917; children—(by 1st marriage) Ruskin (dec.); (by 2d marriage) Ruskin. Formerly country newspaper editor and railroad industrial writer; founder, 1908, Appalachian Trade Journal, Knoxville, Tenn.; editor and owner National Coal Mining News, Huntington, W.Va.; publisher of the Coal Manual (by F. R. Wadleigh). Originator of "back home" movement in Southern States; syndicate feature writer. Rep. candidate for Congress, 1924. Episcopalian. Home: Huntington, W.Va. Died Sept. 15, 1927.

ROBERTS, William Charles, pres. Central Univ., Ky.; b. Aberystwyth, Wales, Sept. 23, 1832; s. Charles Cross R.; grad. Princeton Univ., 1855; Princeton Theol. Sem., 1858; (D.D., Union, 1877; LL.D., Princeton, 1887; S.T.D., 1892); m. Mary Louise Fuller, Oct. 19, 1858. Pastor 1st Presbyn. Ch., Wilmington, Del., 1858-62; 1st Presbyn. Ch., Columbus, O., 1862-64; 2d Presbyn. and Westminster chs., Elizabeth, N.J., 1864-82. Sec. bd. home missions, 1882-86; pres. Lake Forest, Ill., Univ., 1886-92; senior sec. Presbyn. bd. home missions, 1892-98; moderator Gen. Assembly Presbyn. Ch., 1889; chmn. Gen. Assembly com. on revision of standards of Presbyn. Ch., 1890-93; was mem. Gen. Councils of the Reformed Churches at Edinburg, 1877, Belfast, 1884, Glasgow, 1896; was 20 yrs. trustee Princeton Coll. and Univ., and chmn. com. on curriculum. Author: The Great Preachers of Wales, 1865; Translation of Shorter Catechism into Welsh, 1867; New Testament Conversions, 1895; etc. Died 1903.

ROBERTS, William Henry, clergyman; b. Holyhead, Wales, Jan. 31, 1844; s. Rev. William and Katharine (Parry) R.; A.B., Coll. City of New York, 1863, A.M., 1866; grad. Princeton Theol. Sem., 1873; (D.D., Western U. of Pa., 1884, Lafayette, 1907; LL.D., Miami U., 1888); m. Sarah E. McLean, June 11, 1867. Statistician, Treasury Dept., 1863-65; asst. librarian of Congress, 1866-71; ordained Presbyn. ministry, 1873; pastor Cranford, N.J., 1873-77; librarian Princeton Theol. Sem., 1878-86; prof. practical theology, Lane Theol. Sem., Cincinnati, 1886-93; acting pastor Fourth Ch., Trenton, N.J., 1895-1900. Stated clerk Gen. Assembly Presbyn. Ch. in U.S.A., 1884—; Am. sec. The Alliance of the Reformed Chs. Throughout the World, 1888—; treas. Centenary Fund for Ministerial Relief, 1888-90, Anniversary Reunion Fund, 1895-97, and the Twentieth Century Fund, 1900-02; pres. Glasgow, Scotland, Pan-Presbyn. Council, 1896; chmn. Com. on Federation and Union, 1903—; sec. Interchurch Conf. on Marriage and Divorce, 1903-09; pres. Interchurch Conf. on Fedn., New York, 1905; moderator Presbyn. Gen. Assembly, 1907; sec. Council Reformed Chs. in U.S., 1907—; acting pres. Federal Council of Churches of Christ in America, Phila., 1908, and chmn. Exec. Com. to Dec. 1912; chmn. commn. on Evangelism, Federal Council of Chs., 1912-16; chmn. Conf. on Organic Union, 1918-19. Author: History of the Presbyterian Church, 1888; The Presbyterian System, 1895; Laws Relating to Religious Corporations, 1896; Manual for Ruling Elders, 1897, etc. Home: Wayne, Pa. Died June 26, 1920.

ROBERTSON, Abram Heaton, lawyer; b. New Haven, Conn., Sept. 25, 1850; s. Hon. John B. and Maria (Heaton) R.; A.B., Yale, 1872; LL.B., Columbia, 1874; (hon. A.M., Trinity, 1894); m. Graziella Ridgway, June 28, 1876. Mem. Conn. Ho. of Rep., 1880, 82, 83, Senate, 1885-86; judge of Probate Ct. of New Haven, 1887-95; corp. counsel City of New Haven, 1899-1901; Dem. nominee for gov. of Conn., 1904 and 1908; Dem. candidate for U.S. senator, 1905 and 1909. Dir. numerous corps. Home: New Haven, Conn. Died Aug. 5, 1924.

ROBERTSON, Alexander Mitchell, publisher; b. Province of Ont., Can., Apr. 17, 1855; s. William Davidson (Calif. pioneer of 1849) and Margaret (Mitchell) R.; ed. pub. schs., San Francisco, 1863-70; m. Jane Ellen Mayers, Feb. 8, 1882; children—Harry, Edna Ruth, Margaret Mitchell. Employed in book stores, 1870-77; organized, and partner in book firm of Billings-Harbourne & Co., San Francisco, 1877-81; went to Ariz. and engaged in various occupations; merchandising and mining, Tombstone, Ariz., 1881-84, and in Grant Co., N.M., 1884-86; returned to San Francisco and formed book firm of Pierson & Robertson, 1887; in 1889 purchased entire interest and since engaged in publishing books (under own name), notably Western authors and upon Western subjects. Democrat. Home: Redwood City, Calif. Died Feb. 12, 1934.

ROBERTSON, Alice, zoölogist; b. Phila., Pa.; d. James and Janet (Greaves) R.; B.S., U. of Calif., 1898, M.S., 1899, Ph.D., 1902. Asst. in hygiene for women, 1902-04, in zoölogy, 1904-06, U. of Calif.; instr. physiology and zoölogy, 1906-09, asso. prof. zoölogy, 1909-12, prof. zoölogy, 1912-19, Wellesley Coll. Fellow A.A.A.S. Home: Seattle, Wash. Died Sept. 22, 1922.

ROBERTSON, Alice Mary, congresswoman; b. of missionary parents, at Tullahassee Mission, Ind. Ty., Jan. 2, 1854; d. William Schenk and Ann Eliza (Worcester) R.; a descendant on maternal side of Lucy Winthrop, sister of Governor John Winthrop of Mass., and of Esther, sister of Jonathan Edwards; ed. Elmira (N.Y.) Coll.; A.M., same; LL.D., U. of Tulsa. After leaving college was clerk in Indian Office, Washington, until return to Ind. Ty. to become asst. in mission work; introduced domestic science training there; spent two years at Indian School, Carlisle, Pa.; recalled by father's death to take up his work. Established Nuyaka Mission, taught Indian school at Okmulgee, had charge of boarding school for Indian girls at Muskogee, which grew into Henry Kendall Coll., now U. of Tulsa, at Tulsa, Okla.; govt. supervisor Creek Indian schs., 1900-05; postmistress by appmt. Theodore Roosevelt, 1905-13; owned Sawokla Farm Dairy and Cafeteria, 1913-20. Mem. 67th Congress (1921-23), 2d Okla. Dist. Elected mem. Muskogee Camp of United Spanish War Vets. as recognition of work in Spanish-Am. War; had charge canteen work, Muskogee, during World War. Mem. D.A.R. Republican. Presbyn. Home: Muskogee, Okla. Died July 1, 1931.

ROBERTSON, Archibald Thomas, theologian; b. nr. Chatham, Va., Nov. 6, 1863; s. John and Ella (Martin) R.; M.A., Wake Forest (N.C.) Coll., 1885, D.D., 1894, Litt.D., 1919; Th.M., Southern Bapt. Theol. Sem., Louisville, 1888; D.D., Ouachita Coll., Ark., 1894; LL.D., Georgetown Coll., Ky., 1911; m. Ella Thomas Broadus, Nov. 27, 1894; children—John A. Broadus, Eleanor Martin, Charlotte Sinclair (dec.), Cary, Archibald Thomas. Asst. instr. N.T. interpretation, 1888, prof. Bibl. introduction, 1892, prof. interpretation N.T., 1895—, Southern Baptist Theol. Seminary. Author: The Life and Letters of John A. Broadus, 1900; Syllabus for New Testament Study, 1903; revised edit., with critical notes of Broadus' Harmony of the Gospels, 1903; The Students' Chronological New Testament, 1904; Keywords in the Teaching of Jesus, 1905; Epochs in the Life of Jesus, 1908; Short Grammar of the Greek New Testament, 1908; Epochs in the Life of Paul, 1909; Commentary on Matthew in Bible for Home and School, 1910; John the Loyal, or Studies in the Ministry of the Baptist, 1911; The Glory of the Ministry, 1911; A Grammar of the Greek New Testament in the Light of Hist. Research, 1914, 31; Studies in the Epistle of James or Practical and Social Aspects of Christianity, 1915; Studies in the New Testament, 1915; The Divinity of Christ in the Gospel of John, 1916; Paul's Joy in Christ, 1917; Making Good in the Ministry, 1918; The New Citizenship, 1918; Studies in Mark's Gospel, 1919; The Pharisees and Jesus, 1920; Luke the Historian in the Light of Research, 1920; Paul the Interpreter of Christ, 1921; Harmony of the Gospels for Students of Life of Christ, 1922; Types of Preachers in the New Testament, 1922; The Minister and His Greek New Testament, 1923; The Christ of the Logia, 1924; New Testament History (airplane view), 1923; An Introduction to the Textual Criticism of the New Testament, 1925; The Mother of Jesus (Her Problems and Her Glory), 1925; Studies in the Text of the New Testament, 1926; Minor Characters in the New Testament, 1928; Paul and the Intellectuals, 1928; Word Pictures in the New Testament (3 vols.), 1930, Vol. IV, 1931, Vol. V, 1932, Vol. VI, 1933; A New Short Grammar of the Greek Testament, 1931; Translation of Luke's Gospel (with grammatical notes), 1923; Epochs in the Life of Simon Peter, 1933; Passing on the Torch and Other Sermons, 1934. Asso. editor and author of articles on N.T. books in Cross Reference Bible, 1910; The Master Bible, 1926. Contbr. Hastings' Dictionary of Christ and the Gospels, Hastings' Dictionary of the Apostolic Age, Standard Bible Dictionary, Internat. Standard Bible Ency.; an editor "The 1911 Bible." Mem. revision com. of Am. Standard Bible, 1929—. Stone lecturer, Princeton Theol. Sem., 1916, 26; Wilkinson lecturer, Northern Bapt. Theol. Sem., 1927. Home: Louisville, Ky. Died Sept. 24, 1934.

ROBERTSON, Ashley Herman, naval officer; b. Ashmore, Ill., Dec. 14, 1867; grad. U.S. Naval Acad., 1888. Ensign, July 1, 1890; promoted through grades to rear adm., Sept. 23, 1918. Served on Castine during Spanish-Am. War, 1898; exec. officer Terror, 1905; at U.S. Naval Acad., 1905-06; engr. officer Tennessee, 1906-08; exec. officer same, 1908-09; duty Navy Yard, Puget Sound, 1909-13; comdr. Charleston, 1913, Denver, 1913-14, California, 1914-15, Colorado, 1915, San Diego, 1915-16; at Naval War Coll., Newport, R.I., 1916-17; chief of staff, 1st Naval Dist., 1917; apptd. comdr. Mount Vernon (formerly Kronprinzessin Cecile), troop transport, July 28, 1917; naval transport officer, Feb.-Apr. 1918; comdg. New Mexico (first electric drive battleship), 1918; comdg. destroyer force, Jan.-June 1919; chief of staff, Naval War Coll., 1919; comdt. 11th Naval Dist., 1923-26; vice admiral comdg. Scouting Fleet, 1926-28; apptd. comdt. 11th Naval Dist., 1928. Home: Kansas, Ill. Died July 13, 1930.

ROBERTSON, Beverly Holcombe, soldier; b. Amelia Co., Va., June 5, 1827; s. Dr. William Henry and Martha Maria (Holcombe) R.; m. Virginia Neville Johnston, Mar. 26, 1855 (died 1869). Apptd. to U.S. Mil. Acad. from Va., 1849; bvtd. 2d lt. 2d Dragoons, July 1, 1849; promoted 2d lt., July 25, 1850; 1st lt., Mar. 3, 1855; capt., Mar. 3, 1861; dismissed Aug. 8, 1861; entered C.S.A., and promoted brig. gen., June 3, 1862. Comd. brigade in Gen. Stuart's cav. div. in 2d Bull Run; participated in battle of Gettysburg; comd. coast line bet. Charleston and Savannah; subsequently took part in many engagements until close of war. Engaged in ins. business, Chicago and Washington, 1873-84; real estate business, 1884—. Died 1910.

ROBERTSON, Carl Trowbridge, editor; b. North Bloomfield, O., Jan. 31, 1876; s. George Andrew and Georgia (Trowbridge) R.; B.A., cum laude, Harvard U., 1898; m. Martha Bushea, June 12, 1912; 1 dau., Jane; m. 2d, Josephine Wuebben, July 14, 1925; 1 son, Donald Quentin. Served as reporter Cleveland (O.) Plain Dealer, 1900-04, night city editor, 1904-07, asso. editor and editorial writer, 1907—. Decorated Chevalier Order of Polonia Restituta (Poland); Order of the Redeemer (Greece); Order of Haller's Swords (Poland); hon. life member Society of Letters of U. of Torum (Poland). Democrat. Discovered "New Cave" at Mammoth Cave, Ky., 1921; with R. Kenneth Cuyler made first exploration of volcanic caves in Sao Vincente, Cape Verde Islands, 1924. Winner of nat. whist and bridge championships, 1902, 03, 07, 27, 30. Home: Cleveland, O. Died June 3, 1935.

ROBERTSON, Charles Barr, college prof.; b. Fredericksburg, O., Oct. 12, 1868; s. Wilson and Louise (Barr) R.; A.B., Westminster Coll., Pa., 1893, B.S., 1896, A.M. and M.S., 1897; grad. student, Cornell U., 1897, Clark U., 1898, Johns Hopkins, 1899; m. Jessie White McNaugher, July 14, 1898. Instr. in Westminster Coll., 1893; prin. Eau Claire Acad., Farmington, Pa., 1893-94, West Sunbury (Pa.) Acad., 1894-95; head of science dept., Indiana (Pa.) Normal Sch., 1896-1903; head of science dept., Cortland (N.Y.) State Normal Sch., 1903-07, supt. of training same sch., 1907-11; prof. extension edn., U. of Pittsburgh, 1911—, also dir. univ. extension. Republican. Presbyn. Mason. Home: Pittsburgh, Pa. Died Feb. 4, 1919.

ROBERTSON, Donald, actor; b. Edinburgh, Scotland, Dec. 12, 1860; s. John and Agnes R.; ed. George Watson's Collegiate Inst., Edinburgh, and Poly. Inst., Brooklyn. On the stage from 1879; came to America, 1873; dir. Donald Robertson Company of Players. Has appeared in leading rôles in all the prin. cities of U.S. Upon invitation of bd. of dirs. of Art Inst. of Chicago, made Fullerton Hall of the Art Inst. the producing home of his company in Oct. 1908 (the first honor of this kind ever awarded in America). List of plays includes: Ibsen's John Gabriel Borkman, Hedda Gabler, Lady from the Sea, Rosmersholm, and Ghosts; Milton's Comus; Goldoni's A Curious Mishap; Molière's Tartuffe, The Miser, and The Learned Ladies; Lamb's The Intruding Widow; Browning's A Blot on the Scutcheon; Voltaire's The Prodigal; etc. Author: Songs and Salutations, 1924. Co-author of 3-act play A Power-House. Promoter of Chicago Civic Theater. Home: Chicago, Ill. Died May 20, 1926.

ROBERTSON, Edward P., coll. pres.; b. Rock Co., Wis., Feb. 24, 1860; s. Peter and Helen (Robertson) R.; A.B., Hamline U., 1885, A.M., 1888, D.D., 1900; LL.D., U. of N.D., 1925; m. Florence E. Jackson, Nov. 18, 1885. Ordained to ministry M.E. Ch., 1885; pastor Morris, Minn., 1885-88, Marshall, 1888-91, Rochester, 1891-93; presiding elder in Minn., 1893-99; pres. Wesley Coll., U. of N.D., 1899-1931 (pres. emeritus). Mem. Gen. Conf. M.E. Ch., various times (chmn. com. on edn., 1920). Mason. Home: Grand Forks, N.D. Died Sept. 2, 1941.

ROBERTSON, Edwin Wales, banker; b. Columbia, S.C., Sept. 3, 1863; s. Thomas J. and Mary O. (Caldwell) R.; A.B., Yale, 1885; LL.B., U. of S.C., 1887; m. Evelyn Perkins Titcomb, Sept. 29, 1886. Practiced in Columbia, 1887-93; established Canal Dime Savings Bank, 1893; acquired control of Loan & Exchange Bank of Columbia, 1898, and merged the two banks under name of Loan & Exchange Bank of Columbia, also absorbing Central National Bank, Feb. 1902; nationalized the Loan & Exchange Bank, July 4, 1903, as National Loan & Exchange Bank, of which was president 1903-27, chmn. bd., 1927—, his son, Thomas J., succeeding as president; dir. Equitable Life Assurance Society of U.S.; state chmn. for S.C. of 1st, 2d, 3d and 4th Liberty Loans and chairman 5th Federal Reserve District for Victory Liberty Loan. Mem. Chamber of Commerce of U.S.A. (com. on foreign relations), Southern Settlement and Development Orgn. (exec. com.). Democrat. Episcopalian. Mason. Home: Columbia, S.C. Died Nov. 20, 1928.

ROBERTSON, Felix Huston, soldier; b. Washington, Tex., Mar. 9, 1839; s. Gen. Jerome B. and Mary E. (Cummins) R.; ed. U.S. Mil. Acad., 1857-61; resigned from West Point, Jan. 1861; spl. studies in engring. and law; m. Sarah Davis, Sept. 11, 1864; 2d, Elizabeth Dwyer, Nov. 10, 1892. Second lt. C.S.A., Mar. 8, 1861; rose successively to capt. of arty., lt. col. of arty. and in 1864, made brig. gen. of cav. and assigned to Gen. Joseph Wheeler's corps; served with him until surrender; admitted to Texas bar, 1876; farmer, 1903—. Comdr. Texas Div. U.C.V., 1911—. Home, Crawford, Tex. Died Apr. 20, 1928.

ROBERTSON, George, lawyer; b. Mahaska Co., Iowa, June 2, 1852; s. James A. and Margaret Louisa (Barkley) R.; ed. common schs., Ia., Tenn., and Mo., and Mo. State Normal Sch.; m. Laura Hiner, Sept. 3, 1879. Taught sch. 4 yrs.; admitted to Mo. bar, 1876, Supreme Ct. of U.S., 1894; city atty., Mexico, Mo., 3 terms; pub. adminstr., Audrain Co., Mo., 4 yrs.; apptd. pros. atty., Audrain Co., 1886, to fill unexpired term; atty. for Wabash R.R. Co. past 25 yrs.; trial atty. for C.&A. Ry. Co. in Mo., 1890-1900. Non-resident lecturer on pub. corps., Law Sch., U. of Mo.; counsel and dir. N. Mo. Trust Co. Mem. Christian (Disciples) Ch. K.T. Pres. North Mo. Highway Assn.; chmn. Audrain Co. Highway Bd. Author: History of Audrain Co. Home: Mexico, Mo. Died Apr. 29, 1914.

ROBERTSON, Harrison, journalist; b. Murfreesboro, Tenn., Jan. 16, 1856; s. Thomas and Elizabeth (Elliott) R.; ed. Union U. and U. of Va.; m. Marion Richardson. With Louisville Courier-Journal from 1879, as columnist, dramatic and lit. critic, chief editorial writer, asso. editor, mng. editor, gen. editorial mgr., chief of editorial staff, editor in chief, 1929—; in charge of the editorial page, 1885—. Author: How the Derby Was Won, 1889; If I Were a Man, 1899; Red Blood and Blue, 1900; The Inlander, 1901; The Opponents, 1902; The Pink Typhoon, 1906. Home: Louisville, Ky. Died Nov. 11, 1939.

ROBERTSON, James Alexander, prof. Am. history; b. Corry, Pa., Aug. 19, 1873; s. John McGregor and Elizabeth (Borrowman) R.; Ph.B., Adelbert Coll. (Western Reserve U.), 1896; L.H.D., Western Res., 1906; m. Cora Moore Halsey, Mar. 4, 1912; children—Mary Elizabeth, Richard John, James Alexander. In archives and libraries of Spain, Portugal, France, Italy, Eng., and U.S., 1902-09; with hist. research dept. Carnegie Instn. Washington, 1909; librarian Philippine Library, Manila, 1910-16; purchased, 1913, for the Govt. of P.I., the Filipiniana collection of the Compañía General de Tabacos de Filipinas, Barcelona, Spain, for $100,000; with hist. research dept. Carnegie Instn. Washington, 1916-17; with Bur. of Foreign and Domestic Commerce, Dept. of Commerce, Washington, 1917-23; research prof. Am. history, John B. Stetson U., 1923-33; archivist Hall of Records, Annapolis, Md., 1935—. Mng. editor Hispanic Am. Hist. Review, Durham, N.C.; general editor Interamerican Hist. Series; collaborator of Foreign Affairs (Washington). Has gathered the largest collection of Filipiniana in existence (over 20,000 pieces, and a large collection of MSS.). Chancellor emeritus Philippine Academy. Executive secretary Florida State Hist. Soc., 1923—; also serves as general editor of its publications. Mason. Translator and editor: Bibliography of the Philippine Islands (printed and manuscript), 1908; List of Documents in Spanish Archives Relating to the History of the United States (for Carnegie Instn., Washington), 1910; Louisiana Under the Rule of Spain, France and the United States (2 vols.), 1911; Bibliography of Early Spanish-Japanese Relations (Vol. XLIII part I, Trans. Asiatic Soc. of Japan), 1915; Relacam Verdadeira (Evora, 1557), 2 vols., 1932-33. Collaborator Stephens and Bolton, The Pacific Ocean in History, 1917; C. O. Paullin, Atlas of the Historical Geography of the United States, 1932. Editor for Fla. State Hist. Soc. of a History of Fla. (by Caroline Mays Brevard), 2 vols., 1924-25. Died Mar. 20, 1939.

ROBERTSON, J(ames) B(rooks) A(yers), governor; b. Keokuk Co., Ia., Mar. 15, 1871; s. J. B. A. and Clarissa M. (Wright) R.; ed. pub. schs.; moved to Okla., 1893; m. Olive Stubblefield, Apr. 27, 1900 (died 1914); children—Olive Frances (Mrs. David E. Hilles), James Brooks Ayers. Admitted to Oklahoma bar, 1898; county atty. Lincoln County, 1900-02; judge 10th Jud. Dist. of Okla., 1909-10; mem. State Capitol Commn., 1911; mem. Supreme Court Commn., Okla., 1911-14; candidate for Dem. nomination for gov. of Okla., 1914; gov. of Okla., 1919-23; attorney for Oklahoma Corp. Commn., 1935—. Methodist. Mason, Odd Fellow, K.P., Elk. Democratic presdl. elector at large, 1932. Home: Oklahoma City, Okla. Died Mar. 7, 1938.

ROBERTSON, James Rood, coll. prof.; b. Rockford, Ill., May 27, 1864; s. George James and Sarah (Rood) R.; A.V., Beloit (Wis.) Coll., 1886, Litt.D., 1924; A.M., U. of Mich., 1891; grad. student U. of Chicago, 1895; Ph.D., U. of Calif., 1908; m. Catherine Lansing, Dec. 24, 1896; children—Chester Lansing, Thomas Duncan, Eunice Sarah. Sec. to v.p. Iron Cliffs Mining Co., Chicago, 1886-90; prin. Tualatin Acad., Ore., 1891-93; prof. history and polit. science, Pacific U., Forest Grove., Ore., 1893-1906; asst. curator Bancroft Hist. Library and teaching fellow U. of Calif., 1906-08; prof. history and polit. science, Berea (Ky.) Coll., 1908—, acting dean, 1917-18; prof. history (leave of absence), U. of Southern Calif., 1924-25. Republican. Conglist. Author: (or editor) Petitions of the Early Inhabitants of Kentucky to the General Assembly of Virginia (1769-1792), 1915. Home: Berea, Ky. Died Apr. 15, 1932.

ROBERTSON, John Dill, surgeon; b. Indiana Co., Pa., Mar. 8, 1871; s. Thomas Sanderson and Melinda M. (McCurdy) R.; M.D., Bennett Med. Coll., Chicago, Ill., 1896; interne Cook Co. Hosp., 1896-97; m. Bessie M. Foote, June 15, 1899 (died 1930); 1 son, Thomas Sanderson, President Bennett Medical College (medical department of Loyola U.), 1905-15; prof. practice of surgery, Bennett Med. Coll., 1905—; surgeon-in-chief Jefferson Park Policlinic Hosp., 1904-15; attending surgeon Cook Co. Hosp., 1898-1913; commr. of health, Chicago, 1915-22; pres. Chicago Bd. of Edn., 1923; pres. West Park Board. Home: Chicago, Ill. Died Aug. 20, 1931.

ROBERTSON, John Stevenston, nurseryman; b. Northville, O., June 13, 1866; s. James and Janet (Kirkwood) R.; ed. pub. schs., Dodge County, Neb.; unmarried. Took homestead in Fall River County, S.D., 1892, and developed a successful orchard; lecturer at S.D. farmers' institutes, 1907-13; horticultural editor of Dakota Farmer many yrs.; mem. Dist. School Bd., 31 yrs.; pres. local telephone co. Widely regarded as an authority on horticulture; pronounced "Eminent Farmer" by S.D. State Coll., 1928; awarded gold medal, by S.D. State Hort. Soc., 1935, for 20 yrs. service as its v.p. and pres.; bronze memorial plate in his honor dedicated by same society, at Hot Springs, July 18, 1935. Republican. Presbyn. Kiwanian. Home: Hot Springs, S.D. Died July 28, 1937.

ROBERTSON, Joseph Andrew, mfr., capitalist; b. Robertson Co., Tenn., Dec. 31, 1849; s. Hugh and Martha Ann (White) R.; married twice; children—F. Ayres (by first wife), Martha Ann, Josephine Andrea, Catheryne Rose, Joseph Andrew, Charlotte, John Hugh (by second wife). Admitted to the bar at Memphis, Tenn., May 1, 1873; moved to St. Louis, 1874, and practiced law there; moved to Monterey, Mex., 1887; constructed and operated Monterey & Mexican Gulf R.R., from Monterey to Tampico, and was its gen. mgr. and pres. until 1895; resigned and engaged in mfg.; organized, and was pres. Monterey Foundry & Machine Co., Monterey Wire Nail Co., Roller Process Flour Mill Co.; established La Eugenia orange grove at Montemorlos and demonstrated that high grade citrus fruits could be produced in Mexico; established Hacienda La Carlota and erected largest sugar mill of the kind in the Republic; established and owns Monterey Brick Mfg. Co.; founder and owner Monterey News, English and Spanish editions daily; obtained concession for and constructed system of water works and drainage for city of Monterey (costing $13,000,000 gold); with other capitalists purchased and rebuilt electric street ry. system of Monterey; took part in construction of jetties at mouth of Panuca River and harbor improvements at Tampico; constructed and owned the Mineral Ry. and Terminal Co. at Monterey; engaged in building railway line into mineral regions of Sierra Madre Mountains; pres. Consumers Coal Co., Oleograph Co., Union Finance Co.; vice pres. Stallforth & Co., bankers, N.Y. City, v.p. and mng. dir. Consumers

Coal Co. Del. Republic of Mexico to Internat. Congress; diplomatic adviser to government of Mexico that succeeded Huerta. Home: San Antonio, Tex. Died Sept. 15, 1939.

ROBERTSON, Morgan, author; b. Oswego, N.Y., Sept. 30, 1861; s. Andrew and Ruth Amelia (Glassford) R.; ed. pub. schs. and Cooper Inst., New York; went to sea, 1877-86; entered jewelry business, 1886; m. Alice M. Doyle, May 27, 1894. From 1896 writer for periodicals, short sea stories. Author: A Tale of a Halo, 1894; Spun Yarn, 1898; Futility, 1898; Where Angels Fear to Tread, 1899; Masters of Men, 1901; Shipmates, 1901; Sinful Peck, 1903; Down to the Sea, 1905; Land Ho, 1908; Chivalry (play), 1913; Finnegan. Home: New York, N.Y. Died Mar. 24, 1915.

ROBERTSON, Peter, dramatic and lit. writer; b. Vale of Leven, Scotland, Apr. 5, 1847; s. John and Agnes (MacFarlane) R.; ed. Glasgow; unmarried. In mercantile business as a young man; spent several yrs. in Japan and China; located in Calif., 1875, in land and mining enterprises; began dramatic criticism in 1875; critic San Francisco Chronicle, 1881-1906. Author of plays and two libretti of comic opera: "Pyramus and Thisbe" (music by Oscar Weil); prod. Sept. 29, 1879, Bush St. Theatre, San Francisco, "His Majesty" (music by H. J. Stewart). Author: Bunders, 1875; The Seedy Gentleman, 1902; Great Actors in Old San Francisco (mag. series, Pacific Monthly). Died 1911.

ROBERTSON, Samuel Matthews, congressman; b. Plaquemine, La., Jan. 1, 1852; grad. La. State U., 1874. Admitted to bar, 1877; mem. legislature, 1879-83; prof. natural history and comdt. of cadets, La. State U., and Agrl. and Mech. Coll., Baton Rouge, 1880-87; elected to 50th Congress to fill vacancy caused by death of his father, Hon. E. W. Robertson, 1887; reëlected 51st to 59th Congresses (1889-1907), 6th La. Dist. Democrat. Home: Baton Rouge, La. Died Dec. 24, 1912.

ROBERTSON, Stuart, university prof.; b. Newark, N.J., July 9, 1892; s. William Lyall and Louise Henriette (Glorieux) R.; A.B., Princeton U., 1912, A.M., 1913, Ph.D., 1917; m. Helen Ames Farr, July 17, 1918; 1 dau., Mary Louise. Instr. in English, Temple U., 1919-24, asst. prof., 1924-29, prof., 1929—, chmn. English department, 1936—. Attended 2d O.T.C., Ft. Myer, Va., 1917; served in Air Service, U.S.A.; disch. as 1st lt., 1919. Democrat. Presbyn. Author: The Development of Modern English, 1934. Editor: Familiar Essays, 1930. Home: Philadelphia, Pa. Died May 1, 1940.

ROBERTSON, Thomas M., chief economist; b. Alamance County, N.C., Sept. 27, 1857; s. Michael S. and Lucinda E. (Euliss) R.; Pleasant Lodge Acad., N.C., 15 mos.; teacher pub. schs., later prin. acads. to 1887; LL.B., Columbian (now George Washington) U., 1896; m. Sarah Decette Albright, Dec. 24, 1884. Mem. N.C. Ho. of Rep., 1893-95; with U.S. Treasury Dept., Washington, 1895-97; with Dept. of Labor, 1897-1903, when this dept. became a bur. of Dept. Commerce and Labor; spl. examiner Bur. Corps., 1904-15; was in charge investigations of water power, cotton tare, and lumber industry; expert assisting Senate Finance Com. in tariff bill of 1913; asst. chief economist and mem. joint bd. of review Federal Trade Commn., 1915-18; mem. of bd. of review, 1919, acting chmn., 1920-22. Directed investigation of, and prepared report on, leather and shoe industries, 1918-19. Democrat. Baptist. Mason. Home: Washington, D.C. Deceased.

ROBERTSON, William Cornelius, postmaster; b. at West Elkton, O., Nov. 5, 1882; s. Dr. William Cornelius and Dr. Clara Jane (Sparks) R.; grad. high sch., West Elkton, 1898, and Mich. Mil. Acad., Orchard Lake, Mich., 1899; student Miami U., 1899-1903; m. Grace Corinne Randall, Dec. 22, 1908; children—William Cornelius, Patricia. Began as reporter Indianapolis Sentinel, 1903, asst. city editor, later news editor, 1904-05; telegraph editor Pittsburgh Post, 1906; news editor Toledo News Bee, 1907-09; mng. editor Denver Express, 1910; cable editor United Press Assn., N.Y. City, 1911; Washington corr., same assn., 1912; mng. editor Minneapolis Daily News, 1912-22, also New Orleans Times Picayune, 1922-23; editor Minneapolis Daily Star, 1923-28, mng. editor same, 1928-33; acting postmaster, Minneapolis, 1933, postmaster, Apr. 19, 1934—. Democrat. Methodist. Mason, Elk. Home: Minneapolis, Minn. Died July 18, 1935.

ROBERTSON, William Gordon, lawyer; b. Charlottesville, Va., Feb. 12, 1856; s. Judge William J. and Hannah (Gordon) R.; B.A., U. of Va., 1878, B.L., 1879; m. Nannie Anthony, Nov. 2, 1882. Admitted to bar, 1879; judge corp. ct., 1884-92; engaged in practice of law at Roanoke. Mem. Va. Constl. Conv., 1901-02. Democrat. Home: Roanoke, Va. Deceased.

ROBERTSON, Wilbur Wade, newspaper pub.; b. Blairstown, Ia., May 23, 1868; s. J. W. and Sarah J. (Cox) R.; student U. of Neb., 1885-89; m. Grace M. Barrett, Aug. 24, 1893; children—Helen (Mrs. Robert P. Wright), Wilbur H. Owner and pub. Yakima Daily Republic (evening) and Yakima Morning Herald; editor Yakima Republic, 1899—. Home: Yakima, Wash. Died Mar. 29, 1938.

ROBESON, Henry Bellows, rear admiral U.S.N.; b. New Haven, Conn., Aug. 5, 1842; s. Dr. Abel Bellows and Susan (Taylor) R.; apptd. to U.S. Naval Acad. from Conn., 1856, grad. 1860; m. Katharine Nichols Bellows, June 11, 1872. Midshipman, June 15, 1860; promoted through grades to rear adm., Mar. 28, 1899. Served on Niagara, Blockading Squadron, 1860-62; engagement at Fort McRea, Nov. 23, 1861; New Ironsides, spl. service, 1863, and S. Atlantic Blockading Squadron, 1864; participated in capture of fortifications, Morris Island, July 10, 1863; bombardments Fts. Wagner, Sumter and Moultrie; served Colorado, N. Atlantic Blockading Squadron, 1864-65; both attacks on Ft. Fisher, and comd. a landing party in attack on Ft. Fisher, Jan. 15, 1865; served Colorado, European Squadron, 1865-67; Piscataqua, Asiatic Squadron, 1867-70; aid to Vice-Admiral Rowan, 1871-73; Dictator, 1873-74; Navy Yard, New York, 1874-76; comd. Vandalia, 1876-77, 1877-79, Despatch, 1877; Naval Acad., 1877-83; Navy Yard, New York, 1883-88; mem. Advisory Bd., 1888-89; comd. Chicago, 1889-91; supervisor of New York Harbor, 1891-92; Naval War Coll., 1895; capt. of yard, Navy Yard, Portsmouth, 1895-98; retired, Mar. 28, 1899. Home: Walpole, N.H. Died July 16, 1914.

ROBIE, Edward Dunham, rear admiral U.S.N.; b. Burlington, Vt., Sept. 11, 1831; s. Jacob Carter and Louisa Willes (Dunham) R.; ed. pvt. schs. and Binghamton (N.Y.) Acad.; m. Helen Adams, June 3, 1858. Asst. engr. U.S.N., Feb. 16, 1852; promoted through various grades and retired on account of age, with rank of commodore, Sept. 11, 1893; advanced to rank of rear admiral retired, by Congress for creditable record in Civil War, May 29, 1906. Circumnavigated the globe in U.S. flagship Mississippi, of Commodore M. C. Perry's Japan expdn., 1852-55; erected and operated the first line of electric telegraph ever seen in Japan and instructed Japanese in building and operating the first steam railroad and in taking the first daguerreotypes ever seen there; on bd. U.S.S. flagship Susquehanna in expdn. to capture filibusters in Nicaragua and in laying the first ocean electric cable, Ireland to America, 1857, when cable broke; on bd. U.S. steam frigate Niagara when that vessel left Charleston, S.C., 1858, with 271 captured slaves and landed 200 of them in Monrovia, Liberia; chief engr. U.S.S. Mohican at capture of fts. at Port Royal, S.C., 1861; mem. bd. which designed the first iron floating dry dock for the U.S.N.; fleet engr. of the combined fleets at Key West, Fla., during the trouble with Spain over the Virginius, 1874, and selected and fitted out many vessels for the auxiliary naval force during Spanish-Am. War, 1898. Sr. engr. mem. of "Goldsborough Bd." to decide condition of naval vessels on Atlantic coast after Civil War; fleet engr. N. Pacific sta., 1866-69, European sta., 1871-74, Pacific Fleet, 1879-81; chief engr. Norfolk Navy Yard, 1874-77 and 1887-91, Boston Navy Yard, 1881-84, New York Navy Yard, 1884-87. Was mem. guard of honor over body of Gen. W. S. Hancock, Norristown, Pa., and body of Abraham Lincoln, City Hall, New York, Apr. 25, 1865. (Of 191 officers serving on Perry's Japan Expdn., 3 were alive Oct. 7, 1909.) Home: Washington, D.C. Died 1911.

ROBIE, Frederick, governor; b. Gorham, Me., Aug. 12, 1822; s. Hon. Toppan and Sarah T. (Lincoln) R.; desc. of Henry Robie, of Exeter, N.H., 1639, and of Samuel Lincoln, of Hingham, Mass., ancestor of Abraham Lincoln; A.B., Bowdoin, 1841; M.D., Jefferson Med. Coll., Phila., 1844; m. Olivia M. Priest, Nov. 27, 1847; m. 2d, Martha E. Cressey, Jan. 12, 1900. Practiced medicine at Biddeford, Me., 1844-55, Waldoboro, 1855-58, Gorham, 1859-60; apptd. additional p.m. vols., June 1, 1861; bvtd. lt. col. vols., Nov. 24, 1865, "for faithful and meritorious services"; hon. mustered out, July 20, 1866. Pres. First Nat. Bank, Portland, Me., 1891—; pres. Derigo Fire Ins. Co. of Me. Mem. Me. Ho. of Rep., 8 terms, during the period 1859-89 (speaker 1872, 1876), Senate, 1866-67; spl. agt. U.S. Treasury, 1866-67; mem. Gov.'s Exec. Council, under Govs. Washburn, Davis and Plaisted, 1860, 1880, 81, 82; gov. of Me., 1883-87. Master Me. State Grange, 1881-89; commr. to Paris Expn., 1878; comdr. Dept. of Me. G.A.R., 1899; pres. bd. trustees of Insane Hosps. of the State of Me., 1879-99. Home: Gorham, Me. Died 1912.

ROBIE, Walter Franklin, M.D.; b. Bradford, Vt., Oct. 22, 1866; s. Edwin Walter and Jane (Sawyer) R.; grad. Bradford Acad., 1884; A.B., Dartmouth, 1889, M.D., 1893; student U. of Mich. and Clark U.; m. Bertha Estelle Little, Feb. 17, 1890; children—Brian Walter, Nelle Bertha (Mrs. John Fisher Eaton), Everett Edwin, Carroll Herbert, Theodore Russell, Beatrice Mariam. With Hosp. Cottages for Children, Baldwinville, Mass., several yrs., propr. and supt. Pine Terrace Sanitarium, Baldwinville, 20 yrs.; lecturer on sex problems. Army surgeon C.A.C., World War; comd. Capt. Reserve Corps, Feb. 19, 1919; maj. M.O.R.C. Republican. Methodist. Author: Rational Sex Ethics, 1916, 18; Sex and Life, 1920, 3d edit., 1924; Art of Love, 1921; Sex Histories, 1922; Sex and Endocrines, 1927. Home: Baldwinville, Mass. Died Aug. 29, 1928.

ROBINETTE, Edward Burton, banker; b. Gilpentown, Md., Dec. 22, 1879; s. Hanson B. and Amanda (Shryock) R.; prep. edn., Chestnut Hill Acad., Phila., Pa.; B.S., U. of Pa., 1909; m. Mrs. S. Crozer Robinson (Meta Craig Biddle). Was asst. to provost, U. of Pa.; began banking with George S. Fox & Sons, becoming partner; partner of Stroud & Co., 1922-24, owner, 1924—; pres. Federal Bond & Share Co., U.S. Bond & Share Co. Served in U.S. Navy during the World War; attached to Admiral Sims' headquarters, London, later lt. comdr., acting as naval attaché, Stockholm, Sweden. Trustee U. of Pa., Thomas W. Evans Dental Mus. and Inst., Chestnut Hill Acad., Grad. Sch., U. of Pa., Austen Riggs Foundation; dir. Pa. Acad. Fine Arts; mem. bd. mgrs. U. of Pa. Mus., U. of Pa. Grad. Hosp. Decorated D.S. Navy Cross (U.S.); Legion of Honor (France); Order of the Crown, Médaille Commémorative du Comité National (Belgium); Order of the Sword (Sweden); Order of the White Rose (Finland). Republican. Episcopalian. Donor of $1,000,000 to U. of Pa. for establishment of a foundation for study of diseases of heart, and for development of edn. in liberal arts. Home: Philadelphia, Pa. Died Mar. 7, 1936.

ROBINS, Augustine Warner, army officer; b. Gloucester County, Va., Sept. 18, 1882; s. Col. William Todd and Sally Berkeley (Nelson) R.; grad. U.S. Mil. Acad., 1907, also Mounted Service Sch., A. C. Tactical Sch., Army Industrial Coll., Army War Coll.; m. Dorothy Gretchen Hyde, Jan. 6, 1915; children—Dorothy Gretchen, Elizabeth Warner, Helen Hyde. Served in U.S. Cav., 2d lt. to maj., 1907-17; in Air Corps, maj. to brig. gen., 1917—; apptd. chief of A. C. Matériel Div., Wright Field, Dayton, O., Apr. 4, 1935. Episcopalian. Mason. Home: Fairfield, O. Died June 16, 1940.

ROBINS, Henry Ephraim, theologian; b. Hartford, Conn., Sept. 30, 1827; s. Gurdon and Julia (Savage) R.; grad. Newton Theol. Instn., 1861; (D.D., U. of Rochester, 1868; LL.D., Colby, 1890); m. Martha J. Bird, Aug. 11, 1864 (died 1867); m. 2d, Margaret Richardson, Sept. 4, 1872 (died 1873); m. 3d, Cornelia Ewell Nott, Aug. 7, 1876 (died 1888). Ordained Bapt. ministry, 1861; pastor Central Ch., Newport, R.I., 1861-67, First Ch., Rochester, N.Y., 1867-73; pres. Colby U., 1873-82; prof. Christian ethics, Rochester Theol. Sem., 1882-1904. Pres. N.Y. State Bapt. Conv., 1873, Me. State Bapt. Conv., 3 yrs. Author: Harmony of Ethics with Theology, 1891; Christian as Distinguished from Secular Education, 1895; The Ethics of the Christian Life, or the Science of Right Living; Faith Rational. Home: Greenfield, Mass. Died Apr. 23, 1917.

ROBINS, Sally Nelson, author; b. "Timber Neck," Gloucester Co., Va.; d. William Wilmer (M.D.) and Sally Browne (Catlett) Nelson; grad. Eclectic Inst., Baltimore; m. William Todd Robins (died 1906). Asst. librarian, Va. Hist. Soc., 1896-1913; geneal. editor Richmond Times Dispatch, 1908—. Mem. Colonial Dames of America in State of Va. (2d v.p.), Descendants of Colonial Governors, Assn. for Preservation of Va. Antiquities, Equal Suffrage (Richmond, Va.); mem. exec. bd. Va. Div. of Woman's Com. of Council Nat. Defense, auxiliary to State Council of Defense; historian Nat. Soc. Colonial Dames America. Episcopalian. Author: Romances of Illustrious Virginians, 1920; Love Stories of Famous Virginians, 1923; Whisperings Celestial, 1923. Home: Richmond, Va. Died Feb. 4, 1925.

ROBINSON, Albert Alonzo, railway pres.; b. S. Reading, Vt., Oct. 21, 1844; s. Ebenezer, Jr. and Adeline (Williams) R.; brother of Stillman Williams R.; C.E., B.S., U. of Mich., 1869, M.S., 1871 (LL.D., 1900); m. Julia Caroline, d. Perez C. and Katharine C. (Bardeen) Burdick, of Edgerton, Wis., Dec. 9, 1869 (died 1881); m. 2d, Mrs. Ellen Frances Williams, sister of his first wife, Sept. 3, 1885. Asst. on U.S. lake surveys in astron. field work and on triangulation of Great Lakes about 5 months each yr., 1866-68; began ry. service, May 27, 1869, as axman in engring. corps and continued in various engring. positions on St. Joseph and Denver City R.R. up to asst. engr. until Apr. 1, 1871, when became asst. engr. in charge location and construction, A.,T.&S.F. R.R.; chief engr. same, Apr. 1, 1873, to Aug. 1890, div. supt., 1880-81, supt. bridges, bldgs. and water service, 1881-83, asst. gen. supt., 1883, gen. supt., 1883-84, gen. mgr., 1884-86, 2d v.p., 1886-88, 2d v.p. and gen. mgr., 1888-93, A.,T.&S.F. R.R.; pres. Mexican Central Ry. Co., Ltd., 1893-Dec. 1, 1906. Republican. Home: Topeka, Kan. Died Oct. 7, 1918.

ROBINSON, Albert Gardner, newspaper corr., author; b. Winchester, Mass., Feb. 21, 1855; s. Reuben Totman and Clara A. (Caldwell) R.; ed. pub. schs., Winchester, Mass. In commercial life, 1871-98; campaign corr. during Spanish-Am. War for New York Evening Post in Puerto Rico and Cuba; later in Philippines and S. Africa; editorial writer on New York Sun, 1903-12. Author: The Porto Rico of Today, 1899; The Philippines—The War and the People.

1901; Cuba and the Intervention, 1905; Cuba: Old and New, 1915; Old New England Doorways, 1919; Old New England Houses, 1920. Died Aug. 30, 1932.

ROBINSON, Benjamin Lincoln, botanist; b. Bloomington, Ill., Nov. 8, 1864; s. James Harvey and Latricia Maria (Drake) R.; A.B., Harvard, 1887; Ph.D., Strasburg, 1889; m. Margaret Louise Casson, June 29, 1887; 1 dau., Chriemhild (dec.). Asst. in herbarium, 1890-92, curator Gray Herbarium, 1892—, instr. German, 1891-94, Asa Gray prof. systematic botany, 1899—, Harvard. Fellow Am. Acad. Arts and Sciences; associate Acad. Natural Sciences of Phila.; hon. mem. Chilean Soc. Natural History; mem. numerous societies. Awarded bronze medal, St. Louis Expn., 1904; Centennial gold medal, Mass. Hort. Soc., "for eminent service to botany," 1929. Editor: Synoptical Flora of North America (by Gray, Watson, Robinson and others), 1892-97. Editor Rhodora, jour. of N.E. Bot. Club, 1899-1928; editor 7th edit. Gray's New Manual of Botany. Home: Cambridge, Mass. Died July 27, 1935.

ROBINSON, Beverley, physician; b. Philadelphia, Mar. 22, 1844; s. Moncure and Charlotte (Taylor) R.; A.B., U. of Pa., 1862; pvt. Pa. State Militia, 1863 (vol. for 90 days); M.D., Univ. of Paris, 1872; m. Anne E. Foster, Apr. 8, 1875. Practicing medicine in New York, 1873—; lecturer on clin. medicine, 1877-82, prof., 1882—, Bellevue Hosp. Med. Coll.; cons. physician St. Luke's and City hosps. Republican. Author: Nasal Catarrh and Allied Diseases; Inhalers and Inhalants; Essays on Clinical Medicine; The Treatment of Ordinary Diseases. Home: New York, N.Y. Died June 21, 1924.

ROBINSON, Byron, physician; b. Mineral Point, Wis.; s. William and Mary (Mills) R.; B.Sc., Univ. of Wis., 1878; M.D., Rush Med. Coll., Chicago, 1882; studied Heidelberg, 1884, Berlin, 1885, Vienna, 1887, London, 1890; m. Dr. Lucy Waite, 1894. Prof. anatomy and clin. surgery, Toledo (O.) Med. Coll., 1889-90; prof. gynecology and abdominal surgery, Ill. Med. Coll., 1897—; gynecologist, Woman's Hosp.; consulting gynecologist, Mary Thompson Hosp.; attending surgeon, Frances Willard Hosp. Author: Practical Intestinal Surgery (2 vols.), 1891; Landmarks of Gynecology (2 vols.), 1894; Sympathetic Chart (life size), 1894, 1904; Peritoneum, 1898; Colpo Perineorrhaphy, 1899; Mesogastrium, 1902; Utero-ovarian Artery, 1903; Abdominal and Pelvic Brain, 1905. Home: Chicago, Ill. Died 1910.

ROBINSON, Charles Dorman, landscape and marine artist; b. in Vermont, July 17, 1847; s. David G. and Mariette (Dorman) R.; ed. pub. schs., Calif., and acad., North Troy, Vt.; pupil of William Bradford, 1862, of Geo. Inness and M. F. H. De Haas, 1863, of Gignoux and Cropsey, Newport, Vt., 1866-67; studied under Boudin, also methods of Segantini, 1900, Paris; m. Kate Evelyn Wright, Sept. 24, 1874. Resided in Vt., 1861-73, Clinton, Ia., 1873-74, San Francisco, 1874— (except in Paris, France, 1899-1901); dean of Pacific Coast artists. First diploma, Mechanics' Fair, San Francisco, 1860; money award, Sacramento State Agrl. Soc., 1878; gold medal, same, 1903. Spent 19 seasons in Yosemite and high Sierras; has 84 paintings, mostly Yosemite Valley, in Great Britain. Home: San Rafael, Calif. Died May 8, 1933.

ROBINSON, Charles Henry, clergyman; b. Beulah, N.Y., Oct. 23, 1860; s. William John and Martha H. (Hamlin) R.; student Collins Inst., Pittsburgh, Pa., 1877-79; A.B., Westminster Coll., New Wilmington, Pa., 1883; D.D., 1901; grad. Pittsburgh Theol. Sem., 1886; m. Ethel Cromwell Carson, Dec. 5, 1895; children—Dorothy Hamlin (Mrs. Samuel Hyde Thompson), Charles Erskine, William John, Henrietta Cromwell, Morris Carson. Ordained ministry U.P. Ch., 1886; pastor successively Mumford, N.Y., First Ch. and North Av. Ch., Baltimore, First Ch., Wheeling, W.Va., until 1926, United Presbyn. Ch. (union of first and second chs.), 1926—. Moderator 66th Gen. Assembly U.P. Ch. of N. America, Richmond, Ind., 1924. Republican. Died Sept. 24, 1934.

ROBINSON, Charles Leonard Frost, manufacturer, yachtsman; b. Sayville, L.I.; s. Frank Tracy and Ida M. (Frost) R.; Ph.B., Sheffield Scientific Sch. (Yale), 1895; m. Elizabeth H. J. Beach, June 1896. Pres. Colt Patent Fire Arms Mfg. Co., Gatling Gun Co., Med. Coal Co.; dir. Newport (R.I.) Trust Co., Phœnix Nat. Bank (Hartford), Am. Hardware Corp. (New Britain), also Commonwealth Trust & Safe Deposit Co., Hartford Fire Ins. Co., Travelers' Life Ins. Co. Author: Thirty Thousand Miles in the Wanderer, 1903. Home: Hartford, Conn. Died July 6, 1916.

ROBINSON, Charles Mulford, author; b. Ramapo, N.Y., Apr. 30, 1869; s. Arthur and Jane H. (Porter) R.; A.B., U. of Rochester, 1891 (hon. M.A., 1905); m. Eliza Ten Eyck Pruyn, Apr. 8, 1896. An editor Rochester Post-Express, 1891-1902, with intervals of foreign travel and continuous study of civic æsthetics. Sec. Am. Park and Outdoor Art Assn., 1902-04; first sec. Am. Civic Assn., Alliance of Civic Organizations. Associate editor Philadelphia Ledger, 1904; contributing editor, The Survey, 1907-12, and Architectural Record. Specialist in municipal æsthetics and town-planning; has made plans for the improvement of Denver, Colorado Springs, Honolulu, Oakland, Los Angeles, Fort Wayne, etc.; mem. expert commn. for Columbus, O., and for Omaha, Neb.; prof. civic design (the first in U.S.), U. of Illinois, 1913—. Author: The Improvement of Towns and Cities, 12th printing, 1916; Modern Civic Art, 1903, 05, 09, 12, 17; The Call of the City, 1908; The Width and Arrangement of Streets, 1911; City Planning, 1915. Home: Rochester, N.Y. Died Dec. 30, 1917.

ROBINSON, Corinne Roosevelt; b. N.Y. City, Sept. 27, 1861; d. Theodore and Martha (Bulloch) Roosevelt; ed. principally under pvt. tutors; m. Douglas Robinson, Apr. 29, 1882 (died 1918). Active in Red Cross work, speaker in Liberty Loan campaigns, and worker in Salvation Army campaign, World War; formed N.Y. City com. for "Fatherless Children of France," of which was temp. chmn., later sec. Mem. bd. supervisors New York Orthopedic Hosp. Served as mem. exec. com. Rep. Nat. Com., also of N.Y. State Com., and during President Coolidge's campaign was mem. his advisory com.; dir. Woman's Roosevelt Memorial Assn. Mem. Poetry Soc. America (v.p.). Episcopalian. Author: The Call of Brotherhood (poems), 1912; One Woman to Another, 1914; Service and Sacrifice, 1919; Collected Poems, 1921; My Brother, Theodore Roosevelt, 1921; Out of Nymph (verse), 1930. Home: New York, N.Y. Died Feb. 17, 1933.

ROBINSON, Cyrus, mining engr.; b. Cullingworth, Yorks, Eng., Mar. 4, 1870; s. William J. and Leah (Ainsworth) R.; ed. Bradford Technical School, England; m. Harriet Newell Brooks, 1890 (she died Feb. 2, 1931); children—Leah Brooks, Eva Adelaide (dec.), Rachel Ainsworth, Richard Holt (dec.). Came to U.S., 1890; draftsman for Am. Ship Windlass Co., Providence, R.I., 1890; draftsman, later engr., Thomson-Houston Co., later General Electric Co., Lynn, Mass., 1891-93; chief engr. Jeffery Mfg. Co., Columbus, O., 1893-96; engr. and asst. to v.p. E. P. Allis Co., Milwaukee, Wis., 1896-99; chief engr. Westinghouse Machine Co., Pittsburgh, 1899; chief engr. M. Guggenheim's Sons, later Am. Smelting & Refining Co., 1900-04; consulting engr., N.Y., 1904-14 (retired). Active in design, constrn. and operation of trench digging machinery and tractors for British, French and Russian governments during World War. Home: Mt. Vernon, N.Y., and West Harwich, Mass. Died June 30, 1930.

ROBINSON, DeLorme Wilson, physician; b. Pulaski, Pa., Oct. 26, 1854; s. William Miller and Adeline (Stuart) R.; studied Allegheny Coll., 1875-79, Med. Dept. Wooster (O.) U., 1879-80; M.D., Ky. Sch. Medicine, Louisville, 1882; m. Katherine M. Blackburn, Dec. 29, 1886. Pres. 1893, 1896, supt. and ex-officio sec., 1903-07, S.D. State Bd. Health; surgeon to St. Mary's Hosp., Pierre; surgeon C.& N.-W. Ry. Pres. S.D. State Hist. Soc., 1909-10. Editor: History of Dakota Territory (in collections of S.D. Hist. Soc.), 1902. Home: Pierre, S.D. Died 1910.

ROBINSON, Douglas, capitalist; m. Corinne Roosevelt; father Theodore Douglas R. Pres. and dir. Douglas Robinson, Charles S. Brown Co., and Douglas Land Co.; dir. Bankers Trust Co.; trustee Atlantic Mut. Ins. Co. Home: New York, N.Y. Died Sept. 12, 1918.

ROBINSON, Edward, art dir.; b. Boston, Nov. 1, 1858; s. Edwin A. and Ellen (Coburn) R.; A.B., Harvard, 1879; 5 yrs. in Europe, including 15 mos. in Greece and 3 semesters in U. of Berlin; LL.D., U. of Aberdeen, Scotland, 1905; Litt.D., Columbia U., 1911, Princeton U., 1924; m. Elizabeth Gould, Feb. 21, 1881. Curator classical antiquities, 1885-1902, dir., 1902-05, Boston Mus. Fine Arts; asst. dir. Met. Mus. of Art, New York, 1906-10, and dir., 1910—. Lecturer on classical archæology, Harvard U., 1893-94, and 1898-1902; engaged selecting and arranging collections in Slater Memorial Mus., Norwich, Conn., 1887-88; selection and purchase of collection of casts for Met. Mus. of Art, New York, 1891-95; sec. Art Commn. of City of Boston, 1890-98; selection and arrangement of collection of casts in Springfield (Mass.) Art Mus. (jointly with H. W. Kent), 1898-99. Trustee Am. Acad. in Rome; mem. mng. com. Am. Sch. of Classical Studies in Athens; fellow Am. Acad. Arts and Sciences; mem. council Archæol. Inst. America (pres. New York Soc.); dir. Am. Fedn. of Arts, 1919—; corr. mem. A.I.A.; mem. German Archæol. Institute; trustee Mus. of City of N.Y., 1926—. Knight of Prussian Order of the Red Eagle, 3d class, 1909; Comdr. Royal Order of George the First (Greece), 1923; Officer of Royal Order of the Polar Star (Sweden), 1927; Officer of Royal Order of Star of Roumania, 1928. Author of catalogues of Greek and Roman Casts and Greek, Etruscan and Roman Vases in Boston Mus. of Art. Wrote: Did the Greeks Paint Their Sculptures?, Century Magazine, Apr. 1892; Annual Reports of the acquisitions in the Department of Classical Antiquities, in Annual Reports of Trustees, Mus. of Fine Arts, 1886-1903. Died Apr. 18, 1931.

ROBINSON, Edward Stevens, psychologist; b. Lebanon, O., Apr. 18, 1893; s. Clinton Cooke and Carrie Isabella (Stevens) R.; grad. high sch. Norwood, O., 1912; A.B., U. of Cincinnati, 1916; A.M., Carnegie Inst. Tech., 1917; Ph.D., U. of Chicago, 1920; m. Florence Richardson (formerly asst. prof. psychology, U. of Chicago), June 11, 1921. Instr. psychology, Yale, 1919-20; asst. prof. psychology, U. of Chicago, 1920-23, asso. prof., 1923-27; visiting asso. prof., Yale, 1926; visiting lecturer Harvard, 1927; prof. psychology, Yale, July 1, 1927—; lecturer Yale School of Law, 1932—; fellow of Trumbull Coll., 1933—, dir. gen. graduate studies, 1935—. Member trade test division, U.S. War Dept., 1918. Author: Factors Determining the Degree of Retroactive Inhibition, 1920; Practical Psychology, 1926; The Behavior of the Museum Visitor, 1928; Association Theory Today, 1931; Man As Psychology Sees Him, 1932; Law and the Lawyers, 1935. Editor The Psychological Bulletin, 1930-35, Studies in Museum Education; co-editor (with Florence Richardson Robinson) Readings in General Psychology, 1923, 29; cooperating editor The American Journal of Psychology, Journal of Social Psychology. Home: New Haven, Conn. Died Feb. 27, 1937.

ROBINSON, Edward Van Dyke, economist; b. Bloomington, Ill., Dec. 20, 1867; s. Charles Stanley and Wilhelmina (von Schwanenflügel) R.; A.B., U. of Mich., 1890, A.M., 1891; Ph.D., U. of Leipzig, 1895; m. Clare Howard, June 30, 1897. Supt. schs., Schoolcraft, Mich., 1892-93; prin. high schs., Muskegon, Rock Island, and St. Paul, 1895-1907; acting prof. economics and politics, Albion Coll., 1901; spl. lecturer on economics and polit. science, Augustana Coll., 1898; lecturer physiography and commercial geography, U. of Minn. summer sch., 1901-02; lecturer commercial geography, U. of Chicago, summer quarter, 1908; prof. of economics, U. of Minn., 1907—. Del. U. of Minn. to Darwin Centennial Celebration, Cambridge, Eng., 1909, and Five Hundredth Anniversary Celebration of U. of Leipzig, 1909. Episcopalian. Author: Nature of the Federal State, 1893; War and Economics, 1900; Division of Government Power in Ancient Greece, 1901; Text Book of Commercial Geography, 1909; Railroad Taxation in Minnesota, Analysis of the Gross Earnings Tax, 1912; The Cost of Government, National, State and Local, 1912. Home: Minneapolis, Minn. Died Dec. 10, 1915.

ROBINSON, Edwin Arlington, author; b. Head Tide, Me., Dec. 22, 1869; s. Edward and Mary E. (Palmer) R.; ed. Gardiner, Me., and Harvard U., 1891-93; Litt.D., Yale Univ., 1922, Bowdoin Coll., Brunswick, Me., 1925. Mem. National Inst. Arts and Letters, National Acad. Arts and Letters. Author: The Torrent and the Night Before, 1896; The Children of the Night, 1897, 1905; Captain Craig (poems), 1902; The Town Down the River, 1910; Van Zorn (play), 1914; The Porcupine (play), 1915; The Man Against the Sky (poems), 1916; Merlin (poem), 1917; Lancelot (poem), 1920; The Three Taverns (poems), 1920; Avon's Harvest (poem), 1921; Collected Poems, 1921 (winner of the Pulitzer prize); Roman Bartholow (poem), 1923; The Man Who Died Twice (poem), 1924 (Pulitzer prize, 1925); Dionysus in Doubt (poems), 1925; Tristram (poem), 1927 (Pulitzer prize); Collected Poems (5 vols.), 1927; Sonnets, 1928; Cavender's House (poem), 1929; The Glory of the Nightingales (verse), 1930; Matthias at the Door (verse), 1931; Nicodemus (verse), 1932; Talifer (verse), 1933. Awarded gold medal, Am. Inst. Arts and Letters, 1929. Died Apr. 6, 1935.

ROBINSON, Florence Richardson, psychologist; b. Hiawatha, Kan.; d. William John and Nellie (Moore) Richardson; A.B., U. of Neb., 1902; Ph.D., U. of Chicago, 1908; studied Univ. of Würzburg, Germany; m. Edward Stevens Robinson, June 11, 1921. Prof. psychology, Drake U., 1908-19; lecturer, 1919-20, asst. prof. psychology, 1920-21, Univ. of Chicago. Mem. nat. bd. League of Women Voters, 1933—; mem. Conn. Minimum Wage Advisory Bd., 1933—. Author: Sensory Control in the Rat, 1910. Joint editor; (with E. S. Robinson), Readings in General Psychology, 1923. Home: New Haven, Conn. Died Dec. 3, 1936.

ROBINSON, Florence Vincent, artist; b. Taunton, Mass., 1874; d. E. and L. B. R.; ed. Boston and Paris schs.; studied in Paris under Bouveret, Vignal, Harpignies. Specialties water colors and illustrations. Works bought by the State, in France, Mus. of Fine Arts, Boston, Harvard U., Cleveland Art Sch., Hispanic Mus. of New York, Brooklyn Mus., etc. Studio: New York, N.Y. Died Mar. 30, 1937.

ROBINSON, Frank Upham, brig. gen.; b. Geneseo, N.Y., Oct. 7, 1841; s. Horatio Nelson (LL.D.) and Emma Rogers (Tyler) R.; ed. Munroe Collegiate Inst., Elbridge, N.Y.; m. Nina Louise Henderson, Apr. 29, 1890. Commd. 2d lt. 41st U.S.C.T., Oct. 1, 1864; hon. mustered out, Dec. 10, 1865; 2d lt., 125th U.S.C.T., Apr. 26, 1866; hon. mustered out, Dec. 20, 1867; apptd. 2d lt. 19th U.S. Inf., Mar. 13, 1868; assigned to 2d U.S. Cav., July 14, 1869; 1st lt., Mar. 31, 1878; capt., Dec. 28, 1888; maj., Feb. 2, 1901; lt. col. 5th Cav., May 25, 1903; transferred to 13th Cav., Aug. 28, 1903; brig. gen. U.S.A.,

Apr. 8, 1905; retired, Apr. 9, 1905, at own request, over 62 yrs. of age. Episcopalian. Republican. Died Dec. 18, 1927.

ROBINSON, Franklin Clement, chemist; b. E. Orrington, Me., Apr. 24, 1852; s. Harrison and Mary (Clement) R.; A.B., Bowdoin Coll., 1873, A.M., 1876; studied chemistry during parts of 2 yrs. in Harvard; (LL.D., Bowdoin, 1903); m. Ella M. Tucker, Aug. 29, 1877. Instr. chemistry, 1874-78, prof. and Josiah Little prof. natural science, 1878-85, prof. chemistry and mineralogy, 1885—, Bowdoin, Supt. schs., Brunswick, 1877-1900; chmn. sch. com., 1901—; state assayor, 1877-1909; mem. State Bd. of Health, 1894-99. Republican. Author: The Metals (text-books), 1878; Qualitative Analysis (text-books), 1897. Home: Brunswick, Me. Died 1910.

ROBINSON, Frederick Bertrand, coll. pres.; b. Brooklyn, N.Y., Oct. 16, 1883; s. Henry Duval and Emma Louise (Ravn) R.; A.B., Coll. City of New York, 1904; A.M., New York Univ., 1906, Ph.D., 1907; LL.D., Manhattan Coll., New York, 1927, U. of Pittsburgh, 1930, Temple U., 1931; m. Julia Marie Randolph, June 30, 1909; children—Richard Randolph, Patricia Ravn. Began as teacher N.Y. City schs., 1904; with Coll. City of New York from 1906, as tutor, instr., asst. prof., asso. prof. and prof., dir. evening session, 1915-27, organizer and dir. Div. of Vocational Subjects and Civic Administration until 1927, was prof. economics and dean of School of Business and Civic Administration, acting pres. of coll., 1925-26, pres., 1927-39. Provost. Bd. Higher Edn. City of New York, 1926. Lecturer for Bd. of Edn., New York, 1907-27; lecturer on economic theory, New York U. Grad. Sch., 1908-09; mem. Mayor's Com. on Public Service Training, 1915, and first dir. of courses established for training of employes of City of New York. Business mgr. and asso. editor The City College Quarterly, 1908-18; editor Pub. Speaking Rev., 1913-14; asso. editor The English Journal, 1915-22; editor in chief of Coll. City of New York series in Commerce, Civics and Technology, 1917. Pres. Assn. Colls. and Universities of State of N.Y., 1930; mem. numerous societies and civic and philanthropic orgns. Organized and supervised emergency colleges at White Plains, Garden City and Yonkers, 1933-37. Chmn. Am. League for Human Rights, 1933; mem. Am. Soc. Legion of Honor, Chevalier Legion d'Honneur (France); Commandatore of Order of Crown of Italy. Presbyn. Mason. Author: Effective Public Speaking, 1914; Business Costs (in collaboration), 1921. Home: New York, N.Y. Died Oct. 19, 1941.

ROBINSON, Gifford Simeon; b. Tremont, Ill., May 28, 1843; s. Israel W. and Cornelia (Leonard) R.; grew up on farm; ed. dist. schs. and acad.; entered Union Army, pvt. Co. H, 115th Ill. Inf.; disabled by wound at battle of Chickamauga; attended Ill. State Normal U.; taught in Washington U., St. Louis, 2 yrs.; LL.B., Washington U., St. Louis, 1869; LL.D., State U. of Iowa, 1895; m. Janette E. Gorham, Apr. 10, 1872 (died 1893); children—Leonard Browning, Fred Hobart, Jessie, Helen; m. 2d, Clare Lunbeck, June 27, 1910. Practiced law, Storm Lake, Ia., 1870-88. Served both houses Ia. Legislature, 1876-78, 1882-86; judge Supreme Court of Ia., Jan. 1, 1888-Jan. 1, 1900; lecturer in law dept., State U. of Iowa, 1890-1900; mem. bd. control State Instns. of Iowa, 1900-13; retired. Home: Spirit Lake, Iowa. Died May 28, 1936.

ROBINSON, Harold McAfee, clergyman, educator; b. Shelbyville, Mo., Mar. 1, 1881; s. Joseph Carle and Hannah Catherine (McAfee) R.; A.B., Park Coll., 1901; B.D., Princeton Theol. Sem., 1904; grad. work same, 1909-11; studied U. of Leipzig, 1904-05; D.D., Lafayette and Park colls., 1919, University of Dubuque, Ia., 1920; LL.D., Macalester College, 1933, Trinity Univ., Texas, 1935; Dr. Relig. Edn., Waynesburg Coll., 1937; m. Mary Greer Wiley, June 29, 1915; children—Joseph Carle (deceased), Harold McA., John Greer. Ordained Presbyn. ministry, 1905; pastor Milroy, Pa., 1905-09; sec. Centennial Com., Princeton Theol. Sem., 1911-13; pastor Market Sq. Ch., Germantown, Phila., 1913-17; prof. Bible and coll. pastor, Lafayette Coll., 1917-19; sec. Presbyn. Bd. Publn. and S.S. Work, Phila., 1919-23; sec. div. of Christian Edn. in Home, Ch. and Community of Bd. of Christian Edn. Presbyn. Ch. U.S.A., 1923-27, administrative sec., 1927-34; gen. sec. Presbyn. Bd. of Christian Edn., 1934—; lecturer on Christian edn., Princeton Theol. Sem., 1927-30. Mem. Internat. Council of Religious Edn.; chmn. ednl. commn., Internat. Council, 1926-30, acting gen. sec., 1936-37, chmn. exec. com.; mem. exec. com. Council of Ch. Bds. of Edn. Mem. North Am. Administration Com. and Bd. of Mgrs. World's S.S. Assn.; mem. Nat. Council Boy Scouts of America; mem. Nat. Preaching Mission Com., Univ. Christian Mission Com.; v.p. bd. trustees Princeton Theol. Sem.; mem. bd. dirs. Presbyn. Coll. Christian Edn., Chicago; mem. Gen. Council of Presbyn. Ch. in U.S.A. Author: How to Conduct Family Worship; The Kingdom of God is at Hand. Home: Chestnut Hill, Phila., Pa. Died Mar. 4, 1939.

ROBINSON, Harriet Hanson, author; b. Boston, Feb. 8, 1825; d. William and Harriet (Browne) Hanson; ed. Boston primary and Lowell pub. schs.; became one of the intellectual group of factory girls who wrote for the Lowell Offering; m. William S. Robinson (pen-name, "Warrington"), journalist and parliamentarian, Nov. 30, 1848 (died 1876). Author: Warrington Pen-Portraits, 1877; Massachusetts in the Woman Suffrage Movement, 1883; Captain Mary Miller, a Woman Suffrage Play; The New Pandora (a classical drama), 1889; Loom and Spindle, 1898. Home: Malden, Mass. Deceased.

ROBINSON, H(arry) Perry, author; b. East Indies, Nov. 30, 1859; s. Rev. Julian and Harriett (Sharpe) R.; ed. at Westminster and Oxford; was engaged in lit. work in Eng.; came to U.S., 1883; m. Mary, d. late Thomas Lowry, of Minneapolis, Sept. 21, 1891; 2d, Florence Tester, of Surbiton, Surrey, Aug. 1, 1905. Was chief, ry. dept., Nat. Rept. campaign organization, 1896; pres. Railway Age until 1900; resided in England, 1900-10, as mng. dir. Isbiter & Co., publishers, London (1901-04), and subsequently on staff London Times, in West Indies (1909-10) and P.I., Am. corr., Oct. 1910—. Author: Men Born Equal, 1896: The Autobiography of a Black Bear, 1905; The Twentieth Century American, 1908; Animals Worth Knowing, 1910; Essence of Honeymoon, 1911. Home: London, England. Died Dec. 21, 1930.

ROBINSON, Helen Ring, writer, lecturer; b. Eastport, Me.; d. Thomas and Mary (Prescott) Ring; grad. Providence (R.I.) High Sch.; student Wellesley Coll.; m. Ewing Robinson (atty.), Feb. 13, 1902. Editorial writer Rocky Mountain News, 1906-12, also lit. critic for a number of years; active worker and speaker in political and industrial movements; mem. Colo. State Senate, 1913-17. Apptd. by Sec. Daniels mem. Navy Dept. Commn. of Tr. Camp Activities, 1917; mem. Woman's Council Defense for Colo., chmn. for Colo. of Woman's Liberty Loan Com., 1917-19. Democrat. Episcopalian. Author: Uncle Tom's Cabin for Children, 1907; Preparing Women for Citizenship, 1918. Home: Palm Springs, Colo. Died July 10, 1923.

ROBINSON, Henry Douglas, bishop; b. Lowell, Mass., Mar. 15, 1860; s. Alexander Douglas and Clara (Boate) R.; B.A., Racine Coll., 1884, M.A., 1887 (D.D., 1902); post-grad. work, U. of Chicago, 1895; m. Florence Bruce, July 12, 1885. Instr. mathematics, San Mateo (Calif.) Mil. Acad., 1885-89; headmaster, 1889-1900, warden, 1900—, Racine Coll. Grammar Sch. Deacon, 1886, priest, 1888, P.E. Ch.; missionary bishop of Nevada, 1907—. Home: Reno, Nev. Died Dec. 18, 1913.

ROBINSON, Henry Mauris, lawyer, banker; b. Ravenna, O., Sept. 12, 1868; s. George Foreman and Mary G. (Gillis) R.; student Cornell U., 1886-88; m. Laurabelle Arms, Feb. 14, 1894. Practiced law, Youngstown, 1890-1900, N.Y. City, 1900-05; moved to Calif., 1906; now chmn. bd. and vice chmn. exec. com. Security-First Nat. Bank of Los Angeles; chmn. bd. Newport News (Va.) Shipbuilding and Dry Dock Co., Security-First Nat. Co.; chmn. Pacific Southwest Realty Co.; dir. and mem. exec. com. Pacific Mutual Life Ins. Co. With Council of Nat. Defense, 1917-18; mem. Supreme Economic Council, Peace Conf., Paris, 1919; commr. U.S. Shipping Bd., 1919; rep. of U.S., First Internat. Labor Conf., 1919; mem. President's 2d Industrial Conf., 1919; chmn. Bituminous Coal Commn., 1920; mem. both committees Dawes Plan, 1924; chmn. Am. delegation to Internat. Economic Conf., 1927; mem. President Hoover's Econ. Stabilization Conf., 1929; mem. exec. com. Nat. Business Survey Conf. of U.S. Chamber Commerce, 1929-30; chmn. finance div. Nat. Drought Relief Com., 1930; mem. President's Organization on Unemployment Relief, 1930-31. Trustee Henry E. Huntington Library and Art Gallery (chmn. bd.), Calif. Inst. Technology, McKinley National Memorial Assn., Hispanic Society of America. Officer Legion of Honor (France), 1920; Comdr. of the Crown (Belgium), 1920; Officer of the Crown of Italy, 1920. Home: Pasadena, Calif. Died Nov. 3, 1937.

ROBINSON, Henry Seymour, life ins.; b. Hartford, Conn., Apr. 16, 1868; s. Henry C. and Eliza N. (Trumbull) R.; A.B., Yale, 1889; m. Sarah M. Goodwin, Nov. 9, 1898 (died 1909); children—Mrs. Sarah Blackwood, Mrs. Elizabeth Thompson; m. 2d, Marion C. Armstrong, Jan. 10, 1917; children—Henry S., William A. Admitted to Conn. bar, 1891, and practiced at Hartford until 1895; sec. Conn. Trust & Safe Deposit Co., 1895-1905, also mgr. trust dept.; v.p. Conn. Mut. Life Ins. Co., 1905-18, pres. dir., Nov. 1918—; trustee Hartford-Conn. Trust Co.; v.p. and trustee Mechanics Savings Bank. Mem. Hartford Common Council, 1903-07; mem. Hartford Bd. of Finance, 1905-08; pres. and trustee Loomis Inst. (Windsor, Conn.). Wadsworth Atheneum; trustee Watkinson Library, Watkinson Farm Sch. (all of Hartford). Republican. Episcopalian. Home: Hartford, Conn. Died Mar. 4, 1926.

ROBINSON, James E., judge; b. Maryville, O., Aug. 15, 1868; s. John W. and Sarah (Coe) R.; studied Ohio Wesleyan U., 1886-89, Ohio State U., 1892-93; m. Lula Flickinger, May 31, 1895. Began practice at Richwood, 1893; pros. atty. Union Co., O., 1900-06; judge Court of Appeals, 3d Dist. of Ohio, Jan. 1-Dec. 1, 1916; judge Supreme Court of Ohio for terms Jan. 1, 1919-Dec. 31, 1924, Jan. 1, 1925-Dec. 31, 1930. Republican. Presbyn. Home: Upper Arlington, Columbus, O. Died Jan. 27, 1932.

ROBINSON, James Harvey, historian; b. Bloomington, Ill., June 29, 1863; s. James Harvey and Latricia Maria (Drake) R.; A.B., Harvard, 1887, A.M., 1888; Ph.D., U. of Freiburg, Germany, 1890, LL.D., U. of Utah, 1922; L.H.D. from Tufts College, 1924; m. Grace Woodville Read, Sept. 1, 1887. Lecturer on European history, U. of Pa., 1891; asso. prof., 1892-95, prof. history, 1895-1919, Columbia; acting dean, Barnard Coll., 1900-01; an organizer and lecturer, New School for Social Research, New York, 1919-21. Cooperated in editing and pub. Translations and Reprints from the Original Sources of European History; an editor Annals Am. Acad. Polit. and Social Science, 1891-95. Asso. editor Am. Hist. Review, 1911-20. Author: The German Bundesrath, 1891; Petrarch, the First Modern Scholar and Man of Letters (with H. W. Rolfe), 1899, revised edit., 1914; Introduction to the History of Western Europe, 1903, enlarged edit., 2 vols., 1924-26; Readings in European History (2 vols.), 1904-05; The Development of Modern Europe, 2 vols. (with C. A. Beard), 1907, enlarged edit., 1929; Readings in Modern European History (with C. A. Beard), 2 vols., 1908-09; The New History, 1911; Mediæval and Modern Times, 1915; The Mind in the Making, 1921; The Humanizing of Knowledge, 1923; The Ordeal of Civilization, 1926. Home: New York, N.Y. Died Feb. 16, 1936.

ROBINSON, James Lee, banker, mfr.; b. Gaston Co., N.C., Apr. 30, 1872; s. William Lamertine and Mary Martha (Huffstetler) R.; grad. high sch., Gastonia, N.C., and Smith's Business Coll., Lexington, Ky.; m. Alda Smyre, Nov. 9, 1898; children—Ralph Smyre, William Lee, Alfred Smyre, James Lee, Sara Lewis, Eleanor Montgomery (dec.). Clk. in country store, 1891-95; mem. Holland and Robinson, Gastonia, 1896-99; organizer, 1899, Robinson Shoe Co., and mgr. until 1907; active v.p. First Nat. Bank, 1907-23, pres., 1923—; pres. Bank of Glover (S.C.), A. M. Smyre Mfg. Co., Arkray Mills, Inc., Arrow Mills, Inc., Parkdale Mills, Inc., Rex Spinning Co.; v.p. Bank of Belmont, Myrtle Mills, Inc., Ruby Cotton Mills, Inc.; dir. many companies. Trustee and treas. N.C. Orthopedic Hosp.; trustee Queen's Coll., Charlotte, N.C., also Davidson Coll., N.C. Democrat. Presbyn. Mason, K.P. Home: Gastonia, N.C. Died Jan. 4, 1931.

ROBINSON, Jane (Marie) Bancroft, philanthropist; b. W. Stockbridge, Mass., Dec. 24, 1847; d. Rev. George C. and Caroline M. (Orton) Bancroft; grad. Emma Willard Sch., Troy, N.Y., 1871, and N.Y. State Normal Sch. (now State Coll.), Albany, 1872; Ph.B., Syracuse U., 1877, Ph.M., 1880, Ph.D.; first woman to receive LL.D. degree from Syracuse U., 1918; first fellow in history Bryn Mawr Coll., 1886; grad. study U. of Zurich, 1886-87, U. of Paris and École des Hautes Études, Paris, 1887-88; LL.D. from U. of Southern California, 1929; m. George O. Robinson, May 7, 1891. Dean of Woman's Coll. and prof. French lang. and lit., Northwestern U., 1878-85. Founder of deaconess work of Woman's Home Missionary Soc., 1888; opened meetings, 1890, at Washington, D.C., which led to establishment of Lucy Webb Hayes Nat. Training Sch. and Sibley Hosp.; assisted at opening Training Sch., Kansas City, Mo., 1889; founder nat. tr. schs., Washington, 1888, San Francisco, 1890; founder, 1883, Western Assn. Collegiate Alumnae (now Am. Assn. Univ. Women); founder Robincroft Rest Home for Deaconesses and Women Missionaries, and Robinson Park, for retired ministers, both in Pasadena, Calif., 1923; also the Library Assembly Bldg., 1931, in Robinson Court, Pasadena, for use of students and scholars. Inst. asso. Calif. Inst. Technology, Pasadena. Del. to Ecumenical Conf. of Methodism, Toronto, Can., 1911. Author: Deaconesses in Europe and Their Lessons for America, 1889; Parliament of Paris and Other Parliaments of France, 1884; Historical Sketch of the Robinson Family, 1903. Home: Pasadena, Calif. Died May 29, 1932.

ROBINSON, John, botanist; b. Salem, Mass., July 13, 1846; s. John and Lucy Pickering (Stone) R.; ed. in schools at Salem under pvt. instr., supplemented by courses in botany at Harvard; m. Elizabeth Rollins Kemble, Oct. 17, 1869. Trustee Peabody Mus., Salem, and sec. museum com.; also trustee of Ropes Memorial (mansion house and garden), Salem Hospital, Salem Athenæum, Salem East India Marine Soc. Author: Ferns in Their Homes and Ours, 1878; Flora of Essex County, Mass. (catalogue and notes), Essex Inst., Salem, 1880; Our Trees (street trees in Salem and vicinity), Essex Inst., 1891; Bibliog. catalogue oriental coins, Essex Inst., 1913; The Marine Room of Peabody Museum, 1921. Home: Salem, Mass. Died Apr. 9, 1925.

ROBINSON, John Beverley, college prof.; b. New York, N.Y., June 10, 1853; s. Henry Barclay and Caroline (Betts) R.; Columbia, 1869-72; m. Elizabeth Devereux Umsted, July 1, 1885. Mem. Thayer & Robinson, architects, New York, 1882-97; deputy supt.

school bldgs., Bd. of Edn., New York, 1897-1910; prof. architecture, Washington U., St. Louis, 1910-16, retired. Fellow Am. Inst. Architects. Author: Principles of Architectural Composition, 1899; Architectural Composition, 1908; Economics of Liberty, 1916. Home: St. Louis, Mo. Died 1923.

ROBINSON, John Edward, bishop; b. Co. Galway, Ireland, Feb. 12, 1849; came to U.S., 1865; student Drew Theol. Sem., 1873; (D.D., Albion Coll.); m. Henrietta Lester Terry, Nov. 15, 1876. Ordained M.E. ministry, 1874; missionary in India and Burmah, Secunderabad Circuit, 1875-76, Richmondtown, Bangalore, 1877-79, Rangoon, Burmah, 1880-84; presiding elder Burmah Dist., 1885-86, Bombay Dist., 1887-96, Asanole Dist., 1896-1900, Calcutta Dist., 1900-04; elected missionary bishop of Southern Asia, May 1904. Editor of Burmah Evangelist, 1884-87, Indian Witness, 1896-1904. Mem. General Confs., 1888. 92, 1904. Author: Rise and Progress of Methodism, 1889; Apostolic Succession, 1890; Brief History of Methodism (transl. into various Indian languages), 1915. Retired, 1920. Died Feb. 15, 1922.

ROBINSON, John Marshall, commodore U.S.N.; b. Syracuse, N.Y., Nov. 12, 1851; s. John (maj. gen. U.S.A.) and Sarah Maria (Pease) R.; grad. U.S. Naval Acad., 1873; m. Anne Gertrude Harmonson, Oct. 21, 1891. Ensign, June 1874; master, Jan. 1880; jr. lt., Mar. 1883; lt., Dec. 1886; lt. comdr., Mar. 1899; comdr., Jan. 1903; capt., July 1907; retired at own request, June 30, 1908, with rank of commodore. Served on board Pensacola, Saranac, and Omaha, Pacific sta., 1873-75; Passaic, N. Atlantic sta., 1876; Yantic, Palos, and Alert, Asiatic sta., 1876-79; Michigan, on Great Lakes, 1879-82; Kearsarge, N. Atlantic, and European stas., 1882-85; Minnesota, training-ship, New York, 1886-87; inspector steel for new cruisers, 1887-88; Richmond, flagship S. Atlantic sta., 1888-90; Atlanta, White Squadron, 1890-91; Hydrographic Office, 1891-94; Navy Yard, Washington, and War Coll., 1894; Yorktown, and Monocacy, Asiatic sta., 1894-97; in charge seamen gunners, under instrn. at Navy Yard, Washington, 1897-98. During Spanish-Am. War served as navigating officer of cruiser Minneapolis and later comd. converted yacht Siren on blockade of North coast of Cuba; again in charge of seamen gunners, 1899; exec. officer Wilmington, S. Atlantic, and Asiatic stas., 1899-1902; pres. bd. examination of candidates for warrant officers in Navy and Naval Obs., Washington, and War Coll., Newport, 1902-05; comd. Cincinnati, Asiatic sta., 1905-07, War Coll., Newport, June-Aug. 1907; comd. receiving-ship Independence, 1907-08. Awarded service medals, War with Spain, Philippine Insurrection. Republican. Episcopalian. Died 1910.

ROBINSON, John Trumbull, lawyer; b. Hartford, Conn., Apr. 25, 1871; s. Henry C. and Eliza N. (Trumbull) R.; B.A., Yale, 1893; studied law in office of Henry C. Robinson, 1893-95; admitted to bar, 1896; m. Gertrude D. Coxe, Apr. 25, 1905. In practice at Hartford, Jan. 1896—; mem. Robinson, Robinson & Cole. Exec. sec. under governor, 1901, 02; U.S. atty., dist. of Conn., 1908-12. Chmn. Rep. Town Com. of Hartford, 1903-06; pres. Hartford County Bar Assn., 1929-31. Conglist. Home: Hartford, Conn. Died Nov. 27, 1937.

ROBINSON, Joseph Taylor, senator; b. Lonoke, Ark., Aug. 26, 1872; ed. pub. schs. and U. of Ark.; m. Ewilda Gertrude Miller, Dec. 15, 1896. Admitted to bar, 1895. Mem. 58th to 62d Congresses (1903-13), 6th Ark. Dist.; resigned from Congress, Jan. 14, 1913; inaugurated as gov. of Ark., Jan. 15, 1913; elected to U.S. Senate, Jan. 28, 1913; resigned as gov. and took seat as senator, Mar. 10, 1913; reelected to Senate, 1918, 1925 and 1930, present term expiring 1937. Democrat. Home: Little Rock, Ark. Died July 14, 1937.

ROBINSON, Lewis Wood, capt. U.S.A.; b. Camden Co., N.J., Mar. 7, 1840; s. William and Anna (Wood) R.; grad. Polytechnic Coll. of Pa., civil engring. course, 1861; (master mech. engring., 1864); m. Mary De'A. Rupp, Sept. 5, 1865. Entered U.S. Navy, Sept. 21, 1861, as 3d asst. engr.; served in W. Gulf blockading squadron; took part in capture Forts Jackson and St. Philip and of city of New Orleans, Apr. 1862; attack on Vicksburg by Farragut's fleet, June 28, 1862, and many other engagements, including battle of Mobile Bay, etc.; from close of Civil war on many stations and various engr. duties. Promoted 1st asst. engr., with rank of lt., Oct. 11, 1866 (title changed by law, 1874, to "passed asst. engr."); chief engr., with rank of lt. comdr., Aug. 19, 1883; grade of comdr., Mar. 21, 1895; capt., June 6, 1898. Commissioned a capt. in the line, Mar. 3, 1899. Was gen. supt. bureau of machinery, U.S. Centennial Expn., 1876; chief dept. of machinery, World's Columbian Expn., 1891-94. On duty U.S. Cruiser Atlanta, 1894, flagship Newark, Oct. 23, 1894, as fleet engr., U.S. battleship Indiana, Aug. 13, 1896, Navy Yard, Phila., 1897; inspection and recruiting duty, 1898; on duty as insp. machinery, Feb. 21, 1900. Home: Philadelphia, Pa. Died 1903.

ROBINSON, Lucien Moore, clergyman; b. Hartford, Me., Jan. 3, 1858; s. Benjamin Franklin and Adelia Fitz Alan (Moore) R.; A.B., Harvard, 1882; A.M., Haverford Coll., 1891; D.D., U. of the South, 1904; D.C.L., Phila. Div. Sch., 1917; unmarried. Deacon, 1886, priest, 1889, P.E. Ch.; asst. rector Ch. of the Epiphany, Phila., 1888-92; instr., 1891-1900, prof. liturgics and ecclesiastical polity, 1900-28, Phila. Divinity Sch.; mem. faculty, Deaconess House, Phila., 1891-1928; an examining chaplain Diocese of Pa., custodian Standard Book of Common Prayer. Mason. Editor: Murray's Manual of Mythology, 1895; Introduction to the Prayer Book, 1911. Home: East Sumner, Me. Deceased.

ROBINSON, Lucius Franklin, lawyer; b. Hartford, Conn., June 12, 1863; s. Henry Cornelius and Eliza Niles (Trumbull) R.; A.B., Yale, 1885, LL.D., 1926; m. Elinor Cooke, Dec. 5, 1894; children—Lucius F., Barclay, Henry C. Admitted to Conn. bar, 1887, and practiced since at Hartford; sr. mem. Robinson, Robinson & Cole; dir. Connecticut Mutual Life Insurance Co., Conn. Fire Insurance Co., etc. Chairman Conn. State Park and Forest Commn., 1917-37; pres. Conn. Constl. Conv., 1932. Dir. Hartford Public Library; trustee Watkinson Library. Republican. Conglist. Home: Hartford, Conn. Died June 11, 1941.

ROBINSON, Lucius W., coal bus.; s. Lucius W. and Ruth (DeMoss); student Phillips Andover Acad.; m. Harriet Virginia Overton, June 27, 1917; children—Virginia O., Ruth DeMoss, Sarah Morgan, Lucia Woodward. Began learning bus. at coal mines, 1913; pres. J. F. Massey & Co.; dir. Rochester and Pittsburgh Coal Co., Helvetia Coal Mining Co. Republican. Episcopalian. Home: Pittsburgh, Pa. Died June 6, 1941.

ROBINSON, Lucius Waterman, coal, iron mining; b. Hudson, O., Sept. 19, 1855; s. Warren and Sarah (Woodward) R.; Ph.B., Sheffield Scientific School (Yale), 1877; m. Ruth DeMoss, Sept. 9, 1900. Began mining in Tioga Co., Pa., 1877; now chmn. bd. Rochester & Pittsburgh Coal & Iron Co., Jefferson & Clearfield Coal & Iron Co., Rochester Trust & Safe Deposit Co.; pres. Pittsburgh Gas Coal Co., Brush Creek Coal Mining Co., Coal Run Mining Co., Adrian Furnace Co., Punxsutawney Fur Co.; v.p. Cowanshannock Coal & Coke Co. Republican. Home: Indiana, Pa. Died Aug. 15, 1935.

ROBINSON, Richard Lee, clergyman, educator; b. Lancaster, S.C., Oct. 31, 1872; s. Nathaniel Pressly and Agnes Elizabeth (Lathan) R.; A.B., Erskine Coll., S.C., 1892, D.D., 1912; teacher and prin. high sch. to 1896; grad. Princeton Theol. Sem., 1899; m. Anna Marshall, Dec. 22, 1904. Ordained Asso. Ref. Presbyn. ministry, 1899; pastor Camden, Ala., 1899-1909, Lancaster, 1909-10; pres. and prof. Biblical lit., Woman's Coll., Due West, S.C., July 1, 1910—; dean of Erskine Theol. Sem., Due West, 1933. Mem. Board of Foreign Missions, Asso. Ref. Presbyn. Ch. Moderator Gen. Synod Asso. Ref. Ch. Home: Due West, S.C. Died Jan. 10, 1939.

ROBINSON, Robert P., gov.; b. nr. Wilmington, Del., Mar. 28, 1869; s. Robert L. and Frances E. (Delaplaine) R.; ed. dist. sch., and Rugby Acad., Wilmington; m. Margaret H. Fouraker, June 9, 1904. Began in employ of Central National Bank, Wilmington, 1888, pres., 1916—; governor of Delaware for term 1925-29. Republican. Presbyn. Mem. The Grange. Republican. Home: Christiana Hundred, nr. Wilmington, Del. Died Mar. 4, 1939.

ROBINSON, Rowland Evans, farmer-author; b. Ferrisburgh, Vt., May 14, 1833; common school edn.; blind from 1893; m. Anna Stevens, June 24, 1870. Author: Danvis Folks; Uncle 'Lisha's Shop; In New England Fields and Woods; Uncle 'Lisha's Outing; A Hero of Ticonderoga; Sam Lovell's Camps; Vermont; A Study of Independence (in Am. Commonwealths series) 1892. Home: Ferrisburgh, Vt. Died 1900.

ROBINSON, Silas Arnold, judge; b. Pleasant Valley, N.Y., Sept. 7, 1840; s. Rev. Daniel and Ursula M. (Arnold) R.; ed. Lewis Acad., Southington, Conn., Bacon Acad., Colchester, Conn., Brookside Inst., Sand Lake, N.Y.; read law, Troy, N.Y.; admitted to bar, 1863; LL.D., Wesleyan, 1909; m. Fannie E. Norton, June 13, 1866 (died 1923); children—Charles Marcy, Lucy Norton, Fannie Imogene (dec.), Mrs. Winnifred Rymer. Practiced at Middletown, Conn.; probate judge, Middletown Dist., 1878-80; mayor, 1880-82; judge Superior Court of Conn., 1890-1910; justice Supreme Court of Errors, Feb. 5-Sept. 7, 1910; retired. Republican. Home: Middletown, Conn. Died Jan. 13, 1927.

ROBINSON, Stillman Williams, engineering expert; b. Reading, Vt., Mar. 6, 1838; s. Ebenezer, Jr. and Adeline (Williams) R.; brother of Albert Alonzo R.; C.E., U. of Mich., 1863; (Sc.D., Ohio State U., 1896); m. Mary E. Holden, Dec. 29, 1863 (died 1885); m. 2d, Mary Haines, Apr. 12, 1888. Served 4 yrs.' apprenticeship in machine shop; has taken out about 40 patents; first invention was thermometer graduating machine; invented various machines afterward, notably for shoe mfg. Asst. engr. U.S. Lake Survey, 1863-66; asst. in engineering, geodesy and mining, U. of Mich., 1866-70; prof. mech. engring. and physics, 1870-82, dean Coll. Engring., 1878, U. of Ill.; prof. mech. engring. and physics, 1882-95, prof. emeritus, 1899—. Ohio State U.; resigned to care for inventions; pres. S. W. Robinson & Son. Inspr. rys. of Ohio, 1880-84; cons. engr. Santa Fé Ry., 1888-90; also Lick telescope mountings, 1887. Received several awards and medals at expns., 1876 and 1903. Author: Teeth of Gear Wheels and the Robinson Templet Odontograph, 1876; Railroad Economics, 1882; Strength of Wrought Iron Bridge Members, 1882; Compound Steam Pumping Engines (part 2, analytical and graphical treatment), 1884; Principles of Mechanism (coll. text-book), 1896. Home: Columbus, O. Died 1910.

ROBINSON, Theodore Douglas; b. New York, Apr. 28, 1883; s. Douglas and Corinne (Roosevelt) R.; A.B., Harvard, 1904; m. Helen R. Roosevelt, June 18, 1904. Member N.Y. Assembly, 1912-13; mem. N.Y. State Senate, 1916-18, 1920-24. Asst. sec. of the navy, 1924-Mar. 5, 1929. Chmn. Progressive State Com., N.Y., 1912-14. Episcopalian. First lt., F.A. U.S.A., Aug.-Dec. 1918. Home: Mohawk, N.Y. Died Apr. 10, 1934.

ROBINSON, Thomas Linton, banker; b. Ravenna, O., June 28, 1880; s. George Foreman and Mary G. (Gillis) R.; Ph.B., U. of Mich., 1900, LL.B., 1902; m. Ysabel Bonnell, 1907; children—Laura, Henry B. Law practice, banking and mfg., Youngstown, O., 1902-17; dep. commr. for Kingdom of Italy, permanent commissioner Am. Red Cross, 1917-18; maj. U.S.A., service in France and Germany, 1918-19; officer 3d Army, Coblenz, Dec. 1918-Apr. 1919; in Berlin, Mar. 1919, on spl. mission for G.H.Q.; abroad as asst. to member of Dawes Commission, when Dawes plan became effective, 1924. Vice-pres. Am. Exchange Nat. Bank, New York, 1919-26; v.p. Guaranty Trust Co. of N.Y., 1926-29; asso. with W. C. Langley & Co., Mar. 15, 1929-Jan. 1, 1930. Vice chmn. Emergency Unemployment Relief Com., New York, 1931-33, also chmn. of mass canvass for relief, New York; appointed deputy administrator all finance codes under National Recovery Administration, resigned because of illness, Apr. 1934. Decorated Order of the Crown (Italy), Order Crown Belgium. Republican. Episcopalian. Home: E. Williston, L.I., N.Y. Died Feb. 20, 1940.

ROBINSON, William Alexander, manufacturer; b. Louisville, Ky., June 26, 1843; s. Richard Alexander, 1st, and Eliza Denne (Pettet) R.; ed. pvt. schs. and high sch., Louisville; m. Virginia Tyler, Jan. 7, 1868. Entered business in Louisville, July 1, 1859; dir. and mem. exec. com. Louisville Cotton Mill Co. (1st pres., 1887-90), Union Cement & Lime Co. (pres.); Robinson-Pettet Co., Inc., wholesale druggists (v.p.), and R. A. Robinson's Sons, Inc.; owner of large interests in Louisville real estate and in local industrial, financial and transportation orgns.; retired from active exec. positions, Jan. 1, 1907. Prominent in religious, benevolent and pub. affairs; pres. Nat. Drug Assn., 1891; v.p. Louisville Bd. Trade, 1879-84; mem. Ky. State Tax Revision Commn., 1908-10. Episcopalian; jr. warden St. Andrew's Parish; vestryman 45 yrs.; supt. S.S. 44 yrs.; deputy to Gen. Conv. from Ky. of P.E. Ch. in U.S. 8 consecutive triennial convs.; deputy to council Diocese of Ky. (annual) 39 consecutive yrs.; treas. bd. Diocesan Missions, Ky., for 38 consecutive yrs.; pres. Cook Benevolent Instn. for the Aged; pres. Louisville Bible Soc., etc. Life mem. Louisville Commercial Club; hon. life mem. Bd. of Trade. Home: Louisville, Ky. Died May 9, 1917.

ROBINSON, William Callyhan, university dean; b. Norwich, Conn., July 26, 1834; s. John A. and Mary E. (Callyhan) R.; A.B., Dartmouth, 1854; grad. Gen. Theol. Sem., 1857; (LL.D., Dartmouth, 1879; M.A., Yale, 1881); m. Anna Elizabeth Haviland, July 2, 1857; m. 2d, Ultima Marie Smith, March 31, 1891. Ordained P.E. ministry, 1857; missionary, Pittston, Pa., 1857-58; rector St. Luke's Scranton, Pa., 1859-62; admitted to bar, Luzerne Co., Pa., 1864; practiced at New Haven, 1865-95; dean Law Sch., Catholic U. of America, 1895—. Lecturer and prof. law, Yale, 1869-95; judge City Ct., New Haven, 1869-71; judge Ct. of Common Pleas, New Haven Co., 1874-76; mem. Conn. Ho. of Rep., 1874. Author: Elementary Law, 1882, revised edit., 1909; Law of Patents, 3 vols., 1890; Elements of American Jurisprudence, 1900. Died 1911.

ROBINSON, W(illiam) Courtland, clergyman; b. Delhi, N.Y., Nov. 13, 1865; s. Rev. James H. (D.D.) and Mattie A. (Stewart) R.; A.B., Princeton, 1888, A.M., 1891; grad. Princeton Theol. Sem., 1891; D.D., Syracuse U., 1905; m. F. Augusta Horner, June 24, 1891; 1 son, Rev. Stewart M. Robinson. Ordained Presbyn. ministry, 1891; pastor successively Park Street Ch., Portland, Me., Clinton, Potsdam, Park Central Ch., Syracuse, N.Y., until 1907, North Minster Ch., Phila., 1907-20, First Ch., Delhi, N.Y., 1920-30. Mem. Presbyn. Bd. of Pubn. and S.S. Work; commr. to Gen. Assembly Presbyn. Ch. 5 times and chmn. com. which introduced pension plan; moderator Phila. Presbytery, 1916-17, trustee, 1909-20. Mem. bd. dirs. Princeton Theol. Sem., 14 yrs.; trustee and v.p. bd. Lincoln U., Pa. Republican. Editor The Presbyterian, 1930-33. Home: Delhi, N.Y. Died Mar. 15, 1938.

ROBINSON, William Duffield, M.D.; b. Fulton Co., Pa., Mar. 25, 1856; s. John and Mary Ellen (Duffield) R.; grad. Chambersburg (Pa.) Acad., 1872; Ph.G., Phila. Coll. of Pharmacy, 1876; M.D., U. of Pa., 1880; m. Elizabeth T. Willian, Oct. 22, 1891. Practiced at Phila., 1880—; founder and mem. bd. dirs.

Volunteer Med. Service Corps (largest med. organization in history of the world), World War. Chairman med. board Sesquicentennial Internat. Expn., Phila., 1926. Mason. Home: Philadelphia, Pa. Died Jan. 24, 1931.

ROBINSON, William Henry, author; b. Lexington, Ill., Sept. 24, 1867; s. Henry Martyn and Anna Adelaide (Fulwiler) R.; ed. Park Coll., Parkville, Mo., and business coll., Los Angeles, Calif.; m. Grace Perley, June 27, 1894; children—Dorothy Fulwiler, Bruce Herbert. Moved to Ariz., 1886, and assisted in building the first railroad into Phoenix; actively identified with constrn. of irrigation canals and development of ranches; superintendent orange groves and orchards. Mem. Ariz. Commn. Agr. and Horticulture, 1915-19, sec., 1919-23. Formerly lt. and bn. adj., Ariz. N.G.; chmn. "Four Minute Men," World War. Republican. Unitarian. Mason. Author: The Story of Arizona, 1918; The Witchery of Rita, 1919; Yarns of the Southwest, 1921; New Guideposts for Ancient Trails, 1925; Under Turquoise Skies, 1928; When the Red Gods Made Men, 1935. Has made spl. study of aboriginal and modern native races of the Southwest. Home: Chandler, Ariz. Died Apr. 5, 1938.

ROBINSON, William J., M.D., editor, author; b. Dec. 8, 1869; Ph.G., Columbia U. Coll. of Pharmacy, 1890; M.D., Univ. Med. Coll. (New York U.), 1893; post-graduate work, univs. of Berlin and Vienna. Lecturer on chemistry, pharmacology and materia medica, Board of Pharmacy Institute, New York; pres. med. bd. and chief genito-urinary and dermatol. dept., Bronx Hosp. and Dispensary; founder and editor The Critic and Guide; editor Am. Journal Sexology and Psychoanalysis. Fellow New York Acad. Medicine, A.M.A., Royal Soc. Arts (Eng.). Author: Never Told Tales, 1908; Sexual Problems of Today, 1912; Eugenics and Marriage, 1912; Sex Morality—Past, Present and Future, 1912; Stories of Love and Life, 1913; A Clergyman's Son, 1921; Sexual Impotence, 1913; Birth Control, or The Limitation of Offspring, 1915; Treatment of Gonorrhea, 1915; Woman—Her Sex and Love Life, 1917; Sex Knowledge for Men and Boys; Prescription Incompatibilities, 1919; Sexual Truths, 1920; The Menopause, 1923; Sexaul Continence and Its Influence on the Physical and Mental Health of Men and Women, 1923; What I Believe, 1927; A Doctor's Views on Life, 1927; America's Sex and Marriage Problems, 1928; Sex, Love and Morality, 1929; The Humanitarian Calendar and Daily Maxim Book, 1929; The World's Best Books, 1929; The Oldest Profession in the World and Its Future, 1930; Dr. Robinson and Saint Peter, 1931; A Rosary of Lay Saints, 1931; Love Letters and Letters about Love, 1931; Soviet Russia As I Saw It, 1932; Happiness and How to Attain It, 1932; The Legalization of Abortion, 1933; The Maniac Hitler and His Song, 1933; Medical and Sex Dictionary, 1933. Home: New York, N.Y. Died Jan. 6, 1936.

ROBINSON, William Wallace, Jr., brig. gen. U.S.A.; b. in Ohio, Apr. 21, 1846; s. William Wallace R.; pvt. Co. E, 7th Wis., Inf., Mar. 17-June 30, 1865; apptd. from Wis., and grad. U.S. Mil. Acad., 1869. Commd. 2d lt. 3d Cav., June 15, 1869; transferred to 7th Cav., June 26, 1876; 1st lt., Aug. 14, 1876; capt. a.q.m., June 1, 1891; maj. q.m. vols., Aug. 14-Nov. 14, 1900; maj. q.m. U.S.A., Nov. 14, 1900; lt. col. deputy q.m. gen., Jan. 20, 1904! col. a.q.m. gen., Feb. 14, 1910; brig. gen. and retired by operation of law, Apr. 21, 1910. Served for many yrs. at western posts and engaged in many fights with the Indians, including Apaches, Utes, Sioux, etc.; participated in battles at Wounded Knee and Drexel Mission, S.D.; as depot q.m. commenced reconstruction of Jefferson Barracks, St. Louis, 1891; later in charge of construction of Fort Sam Houston, Tex.; had charge of shipments of supplies and troops for Alaska and Philippine Islands, during which time several millions of dollars were disbursed by him; chief q.m. Dept. of Luzon, 1902-04, Dept. of Dak., 1904-05, Dept. of the Lakes, 1905-10. Home: Seattle, Wash. Died Mar. 24, 1917.

ROBINSON, Wirt, army officer; b. Buckingham Co., Va., Oct. 16, 1864; s. William Russell and Evelyn (Cabell) R.; student Richmond (Va.) Coll., 1879-82; grad. U.S. Mil. Acad., 1887; m. Alice Phinney, Apr. 7, 1890 (died 1918); children—Alice Evelyn Rose (dec.), Wirt Russell; m. 2d, Nancy Hinman Henderson, April 22, 1920; 1 dau., Evelyn Byrd. Commd. 2d lt. 4th Arty., June 12, 1887; 1st lt., Aug. 1, 1893; capt. asst. q.m., June 20, 1898; trans. to Coast Arty. Corps, Feb. 2, 1901; maj., Jan. 25, 1907; lt. col., Apr. 1, 1911; col. and prof. U.S. Mil. Acad., 1911—. Instr. French and Spanish, U.S. Mil. Acad., 1891-92; prof. mil. science, Harvard, 1894-98; asst. prof. modern langs., U.S. Mil. Acad., 1899-1903; head Dept. of Chemistry and Explosives, School of Submarine Defense, Fort Totten, N.Y., 1904-06; asst. prof. chemistry, U.S. Mil. Acad., 1906-11, prof. and head of dept., 1911—. Author: A Flying Trip to the Tropics, 1896; Elements of Electricity, 1914. Exploring and collecting trips to various points in Colombia, Venezuela, Central America and West Indies. Home: West Point, N.Y. Died Jan. 19, 1929.

ROBSON, James A., judge; b. Gorham, N.Y., Jan. 1, 1851; s. John and Isabella (Telfer) R.; A.B., Yale, 1873; LL.B., Columbia, 1876; unmarried. Engaged in practice of law, 1876-1903; apptd. justice Supreme Ct., N.Y., 7th Dist., to succeed Hon. William H. Adams, deceased, Oct. 19, 1903; elected Nov. 1904 to same position for full term, expiring Dec. 31, 1918; apptd. asso. justice Appellate Div., 4th Dept., Jan. 8, 1907; re-designated, Jan. 1912. Republican. Home: Gorham, N.Y. Died Feb. 1, 1916.

ROBSON, May Waldron, actress; b. (Waldron) Hamilton, Ont., Nov. 1, 1868; removed with parents to Chicago; mem. choir St. Paul's Ch.; joined a Pinafore co.; from that went to Augustin Daly's Co.; then Robson and Crane's Co.; m. Stuart Robson, 1894 (died 1903), with whom she played leading female rôles of legitimate comedy. Died Dec. 22, 1925.

ROBSON, Stuart, actor; b. Annapolis, Md., March 4, 1836; 1st appeared on stage, Baltimore Museum, Jan. 5, 1852; pronounced success as Captain Crosstree in burlesque "Black-Eyed Susan," 1870; joined W. H. Crane in "Our Boarding House," and later in revivals of "A Comedy of Errors" and "Merry Wives of Windsor"; finally in "The Henrietta"; separated from Mr. Crane, 1889; starred in leading rôles of legitimate comedy; m. May Waldron Robson, 1894. Home: Highlands, N.J. Died 1903.

ROBYN, Alfred George, musician, composer; b. St. Louis, Mo., Apr. 29, 1860; s. William and Clemence Stephanie R.; father was an organist and instructed him in music; was professionally engaged as pianist while still a child; m. Isidore M., d. Anthony Schmitt, of Chicago, Oct. 18, 1909; children—Alfred G., Byron Edward. Pianist and ch. organist. Composer: Jacinta, and The Buccaneer's Bride (comic operas); Symphony in D minor, Op. 51, and symphonic poem, Pompeii (both for full orchestra); Concerto in C minor (for piano and orchestra); also many ballads, piano works, and pieces of sacred music. Operas: Yankee Consul (prod. by Castle Square Opera Co., spring, 1903); Gypsy Girl, prod. 1905; Yankee Tourist, 3-act comic opera (prod. under Henry W. Savage, 1907); Fortune Land, 3-act comic opera, 1907; The Girl from Frisco; The Boys from Home; All for the Ladies; Princess Beggar; The Girl Who Dared; Will O' the Wisp; The Bandit; Georgianna; The Garden of Perfume; The Padisha; Fountain of Youth. Oratorios: The Ascension (prod. St. Louis, May 10, 1903); Love Unending, 1907; Praise and Thanksgiving; Poppies of Old Japan, 2 acts, prod. 1925; Streets of Cairo, 1925; Fountania, 3 acts, prod. 1926; Caught Napping, 1927; Radiadayz, 1927; Venetian Love, 1928. Best known songs: Answer; You; It Was a Dream. Instrumental piece, Manzanilla. Home: New York, N.Y. Died Oct. 18, 1935.

ROCHE, Ambrose Francis, clergyman; b. S. Boston, Mass., Oct. 8, 1854; s. Nicholas Enright and Ellen Frances (Sullivan) R.; ed. St. Bonaventure's Coll., Allegheny, N.Y.; St. Joseph's Sem., Troy, N.Y. Ordained priest R.C. Ch., 1880; asst. St. John's Ch., Quincy, Mass., 1880-96; pastor St. Paul's Parish, Hingham, Mass., 1896-1900, St. Mary's Parish, West Quincy, 1900-08; St. Patrick's Parish, Watertown, 1908-28, St. Thomas Aquinas Parish, Jamaica Plain, Nov. 7, 1928—. Served as chaplain Middlesex Co. br. Am. Fedn. Catholic Socs. and Parishes; mem. Board Diocesan Consultors to Cardinal O'Connell. Made domestic prelate of Papal Court, title of Monsignor, by Pope Pius X, 1911. Was editor and pub. Quincy Monitor (monthly) for 12 yrs.; frequent contbr. to Boston Pilot. LL.D., St. Bonaventure's Coll., Allegheny, N.Y., 1919. State chaplain of Mass. Catholic Women's Guild, 1916—; chaplain gen. Daughters of Isabella, 1922—. Home: Jamaica Plain, Mass. Died Mar. 15, 1935.

ROCHE, Arthur Somers, author; b. Somerville, Mass., Apr. 27, 1883; s. James Jeffrey and Mary (Halloran) R.; student Holy Cross Coll., Worcester, Mass., 1899-1901; LL.B., Boston U., 1904; m. Ethel Kirby Rowell, Aug. 12, 1910 (died 1915); 1 son, Jeffrey; m. 2d, Ethel Pettit, Sept. 28, 1917; 1 son, Clyde. Practiced law 18 mos.; entered newspaper work, 1906. Commd. capt., Mil. Intelligence Div. U.S.A., Sept. 1918; hon. discharged, Dec. 1918. Author: Loot, 1916; Plunder, 1917; The Sport of Kings, 1917; Ransom, 1918; The Eyes of the Blind, 1919; Uneasy Street, 1920; Find the Woman, 1921; The Day of Faith (Gov. Thomas C. McRae, of Ark., declared Nov. 1, 1921, to be legal holiday in honor of book), 1921; A More Honorable Man, 1922; The Pleasure Buyers, 1925; Devil-May-Care, 1926; Come to My House, 1927; What I Know About You, 1927; The Wise Wife, 1928; The Woman Hunters, 1928; Marriage for Two, 1929; Four Blocks Apart, 1930; Rhapsody in Gold, 1931; The Wrong Wife, 1931; The Great Abduction, 1932; Slander, 1933; Conspiracy, 1934. Co-author: (play) The Scrap of Paper, 1917. Home: Palm Beach, Fla. Died Feb. 17, 1935.

ROCHE, James Jeffrey, editor-in-chief The Pilot, 1890-1905; b. Mountmellick, Queen's Co., Ireland, May 31, 1847; s. Edward and Margaret (Doyle) R.; removed to Prince Edward Island in infancy; classical course, St. Dunstan's Coll., Charlottetown; (LL.D., Notre Dame, Ind., 1891); in commercial pursuits, Boston, 1866-83; asst. editor The Pilot, under late John Boyle O'Reilly, 1883-90; mem. Metropolitan Park Commn., Boston, 1893; U.S. consul, Genoa, Italy, 1904-07; at Berne, Switzerland, Apr. 29, 1907—. Author: Songs and Satires, 1886; Life of John Boyle O'Reilly, 1891; The Story of the Filibusters, 1891; Ballads of Blue Water, 1895; Her Majesty the King, 1898; By-Ways of War; Sorrows of Sap'ed, 1904. Home: Berne, Switzerland. Died 1908.

ROCHE, John A., mayor of Chicago; b. Utica, N.Y., Aug. 12, 1844; grad. high school; learned trade of pattern-maker in New York; 1869, became dealer in machinery in Chicago and for yrs. was Northwestern representative J. A. Fay & Co., Cincinnati, mfrs. wood-working machinery; mayor of Chicago, 1887-89. Republican; v.p. Crane Elevator Co., 1889; mng. dir. Otis Elevator Co.; pres. Lake St. Elevated R.R., 1893-97. Home: Chicago, Ill. Died 1904.

ROCHE, Martin, architect. Mem. Holabird & Roche, Chicago, 1913—; firm designed Chicago Temple Bldg., Grant Park Stadium (Soldier Field), The Palmer House, Stevens Hotel (all of Chicago), etc. Apptd. mem. Bd. of Art Advisers of Ill. by Gov. Lowden, 1917. Fellow Am. Inst. Architects and Ill. chapter same. Died June 4, 1927.

ROCHE, William James, lawyer; b. Troy, N.Y., Mar. 7, 1853; s. William and Margaret (Guiry) R.; St. Mary's Acad., Troy; M.A., Manhattan Coll., New York, 1876; m. Mary L. Campion, June 15, 1880. Studied law in offices of Townsends & Browne, Troy, and admitted to bar, 1874; became mem. Townsends & Roche, 1878, and continued with its successors; now mem. Roche, Tierney & Roche. City atty., Troy, 1883-86; city comptroller, 1886-90; corp. counsel, 1890-1900; mem. State Constl. Conv., 1894. Trustee Supreme Ct. Library, Troy; trustee Troy Pub. Library. Catholic. Home: Troy, N.Y. Deceased.

ROCHESTER, William Beatty, brig. gen. U.S.A., retired Feb. 15, 1890; b. Angelica, N.Y., Feb. 15, 1826; s. Hon. William B. R.; g.s. Nathaniel R., founder of city of Rochester; academic edn.; m. Anna L. Martin, June 19, 1862. Lived in Calif., 1851-59, entered army as paymaster U.S. vols., June 1861, with rank of maj.; transferred to regular army as paymaster, Jan. 17, 1867; promoted, Feb. 17, 1882, to be paymaster gen. U.S. army, with rank of brig. gen.; retired on reaching age limit. Died 1909.

ROCKEFELLER, John Davison, capitalist, philanthropist; b. Richford, N.Y., July 8, 1839; s. William Avery and Eliza (Davison) R.; moved to Cleveland, O., 1853; pub. sch. edn.; m. Laura C. Spelman, Sept. 8, 1864 (died 1915); children—Bessie (Mrs. Charles A. Strong, dec.), Alta (Mrs. E. Parmalee Prentice), Edith (Mrs. Harold Fowler McCormick, dec.), John Davison. Was clerk in forwarding and commission house; at 19 partner in firm of Clark & Rockefeller, commission merchants; firm became Andrews, Clark & Co., and engaged in oil business; in 1867 the firm, then Rockefeller, Andrews & Flagler, operated a large oil refinery at Cleveland, and in 1870, the business was consolidated with others in the Standard Oil Co.; other interests were later acquired and the Standard Oil Trust was formed, 1882, but dissolved, 1892, after which the Standard Oil Co. operated as a New Jersey corp. until dissolved in 1911, with Mr. Rockefeller, pres. until Dec. 4, 1911, when retired. It is estimated that the total amount given by Mr. Rockefeller for philanthropic and charitable purposes up to 1921 exceeded $500,000,000. Nearly four-fifths of this sum went to the four great charitable corporations which he created: the Rockefeller Foundation, General Education Board, The Laura Spelman Rockefeller Memorial and The Rockefeller Institute for Medical Research. Republican. Baptist. Home: Pocantico Hills, N.Y. Died May 23, 1937.

ROCKEFELLER, Percy Avery; b. N.Y. City, Feb. 27, 1878; s. William and Almira (Goodsell) R.; A.B., Yale, 1900; m. Isabel Stillman, Apr. 23, 1901; children—Avery, Isabel (Mrs. Frederic W. Lincoln), Winifred (Mrs. Brooks Enemy), Faith, Gladys. Entered father's office on leaving coll.; became a dir. of numerous mining and pub. utility corporations. Mem. N.Y. Stock Exchange. Dir. The Boys' Club, Greenwich Council Boy Scouts of America; founder Am Society for Relief of French War Orphans. Mem. bd. mgrs. N.Y. Zoöl. Society; mem. Am. Mus. Natural History. Episcopalian. Home: Greenwich, Conn. Died Sept. 25, 1934.

ROCKEFELLER, William, capitalist; b. Richford, N.Y., May 31, 1841; s. William Avery and Eliza (Davidson) R.; bro. of John Davison R.; ed. Owego, N.Y., and Cleveland, O.; m. Almira Geraldine Goodsell, 1864 (died 1920); father of Wm. Goodsell and Percy Avery Rockefeller. Was bookkeeper and later partner in produce commission trade; sson after joined his brother, John D. R., in oil business; at head of the business of the Standard Oil Co. of N.J., in New York, 1865-1911; was also pres. Standard Oil Co. of New York until 1911; dir. Anaconda Copper Mining Co.; trustee Consolidated Gas Co., U.S. Trust Co.; dir. numerous railroad and utility companies. Home: New York, N.Y. Died June 24, 1922.

ROCKEFELLER, William Goodsell, capitalist; b. New York, N.Y., 1870; s. William and Almira Geraldine (Goodsell) R.; A.B., Yale, 1892; m. Elsie, d.

James Stillman, 1896. Treas. Standard Oil Co. of N.Y., until Dec. 4, 1911, when resigned; dir. Brooklyn Union Gas Co., U.P. R.R. Co., Oregon-Washington R.R. & Navigation Co., Ore. Short Line R.R. Co. Home: Greenwich, Conn. Died Nov. 30, 1922.

ROCKEY, Alpha Eugene, surgeon; b. Freeport, Ill., July 5, 1857; s. Paul Warren and Katherine (Motter) R.; A.M., Parson's Coll., 1891; M.D., Rush Med. Coll., Chicago, 1891; m. Phila Jane Watson, Oct. 10, 1880; children—Paul, Eugene Watson. Began practice at Iowa City; moved to Portland, Ore., 1891; associated in practice with sons; surgeon Multnomah Hosp. clinician in surgery U. of Oregon. Formerly lt. M.R.C., U.S.A.; served as capt. and maj. World War; lt. col. and col. M.R.C. Fellow Am. Coll. Surgeons. Republican. Home: Portland, Ore. Died Mar. 28, 1927.

ROCKEY, Howard, author; b. Philadelphia, Pa., June 3, 1886; s. Henry Chester and Mary Elizabeth (Berry) R.; ed. Drexel Inst. and Temple U.; m. Ethel Mager, 1911; 1 dau., Elizabeth Isabel. Reporter Philadelphia Inquirer, 1903-07; mgr. Service Bureau, System Magazine, 1910-12; press rep. Philharmonic Orchestra, N.Y., 1913-14; advertising agt., Phila., 1920-27; dir. publicity, Lord & Thomas and Logan, Inc., 1927-30. Served as 2d lieutenant 71st Inf., U.S. Army, 1917-19. Author: This Woman, 1924; All That I Want (pseudonym Ronald Bryce), 1925; Daughters of Luxury, 1925; Paradox, 1926; Honeymoon's End, 1926; The Varanoff Tradition (pseudonym Oliver Panbourne), 1926; The Test, 1927; Limelight, 1927; Through the Mill, 1927; The Chorus Kid, 1928; Masked Longing, 1931; The Other Woman's Way, 1932. Died May 28, 1934.

ROCKHILL, William Woodville, ambassador; b. Phila., Pa., Apr. 1854; s. Thomas Cadwallader and Dorothy Anna (Woodville) R.; ed. in Paris, France; grad. spl. mil. sch. of St. Cyr, 1873; m. Edith H. Perkins, Apr. 1900. Second sec., and sec. Am. Legation at Peking, 1884-88; chargé d'affaires ad interim, Seoul, Korea, Dec. 11, 1886-Apr. 3, 1887; two scientific missions to China and Tibet under auspices of Smithsonian Instn., 1888-92; chief clerk Dept. of State, 1893-94; 3d asst. sec. of state, 1894-95, 1st asst., 1896-97; E.E. and M.P. to Greece, Rumania and Servia, 1897-99; dir. Internat. Bur. Am. Republics, 1899-1905; E.E. and M.P. to China, 1905-09; ambassador extraordinary and plenipotentiary to Russia, June 1, 1900-April 1911, to Turkey, Apr. 1911-Nov. 1913; resigned. U.S. commr. to China, July 1900; plenipotentiary of U.S. to Congress of Peking, for settlement of Boxer troubles, Feb.-Sept. 1901, signing final protocol of Sept. 7, 1901. Author of various works on Oriental subjects. Corr. mem. Inst. de France, etc. Home: Litchfield, Conn. Died Dec. 8, 1914.

ROCKNE, Knute Kenneth, football coach; b. Voss, Norway, Mar. 4, 1888; s. Louis and Martha (Gjermo) R.; brought to U.S. at age of 5; B.S., Notre Dame U., 1914; m. Bonnie Skiles, July 15, 1914; children—William D., Knute, Mary Jean, John V. Football coach, Notre Dame U., 1914—; coached nat. coll. football champions, 1924; coach of summer schs. in football, Springfield Y.M.C.A. Coll., Ore. Agril. Coll., Utah Agrl. Coll., U. of Southern Calif., Southern Methodist U., Notre Dame U., William and Mary Coll. Elk. Home: Notre Dame, Ind. Died Mar. 31, 1931.

ROCKWELL, Alfred Perkins, mining engr., soldier; b. Norwich, Conn., Oct. 16, 1834; s. John Arnold and Mary Watkinson (Perkins) R.; grad. Yale, 1855; studied mining engring. 2 yrs. in scientific dept., Yale; 1 yr. in Mus. of Practical Geology, London, and 1 yr. at Sch. of Mines, Freiberg, Saxony (Ph.B., 1857, A.M., 1858, Yale); m. Katharine Virginia, d. Samuel E. Foote, New Haven, Conn., June 20, 1865 (died 1902). Pulled an oar in the Atlanta boat, 1852, in 1st regatta ever rowed bet. Yale and Harvard. Served 3 yrs. in army during Civil war, as capt., 1st Conn. Light Battery, Jan. 21, 1862, to June 18, 1864; col. 6th Conn. vol. inf., June 18, 1864, to Feb. 9, 1865; took part in many active engagements; bvtd. brig. gen. U.S.V., 1865, for "gallant and distinguished services in the field during campaign of 1864." On bd. of visitors U.S. Mil. Acad., 1865; prof. mining, Sheffield Scientific Sch., 1865-68, same Mass. Inst. Tech., 1868-73; chmn. bd. fire commrs., Boston, 1873-76; pres. Eastern R.R. Co., 1876-79; treas. Great Falls Mfg. Co., 1879-86; retired from active business, 1886. Represented Yale Univ. at Millenary celebration of King Alfred the Great, Winchester, Eng., Sept. 1901. Author: Roads and Pavements in France, 1896. Died 1903.

ROCKWELL, Alphonso David, physician; b. New Canaan, Conn., May 18, 1840; s. David S. and Betty R.; A.M., Kenyon Coll., 1868; M.D., Bellevue Hosp. Med. Coll. (New York U.), 1864; m. Susie Landon, Oct. 7, 1868. Asst. surgeon 6th Ohio Cav. and brigade surgeon with rank of maj., 1864-65; prof. electro-therapeutics, New York Post-Grad. Sch. Medicine, 1888-92; neurologist and electro-therapeutist, Flushing Hosp., 1904-12; retired. Member commn. to aid in establishing the method of executions by electricity. Author: Relation of Electricity to Medicine and Surgery; Treatise on the Medical and Surgical Uses of Electricity (with G. M. Beard), 9 edits.; Nervous Exhaustion, 1901; Rambling Recollections (autobiography), 1920. Home: Flushing, L.I. Died Apr. 12, 1933.

ROCKWELL, Charles H., traffic mgr. Chicago, Indianapolis & Louisville, 1897—; b. Terre Haute, Ind., Jan. 14, 1852; began his ry. experience Aug. 25, 1869, as asst. yard clerk, Cleveland, Columbus, Cincinnati & Indianapolis Ry., at Indianapolis; filled several clerical and passenger dept. positions on that and other Indianapolis roads until July 1, 1875; auditor and gen. passenger and ticket agt. Indianapolis, Peru & Chicago Ry. until Apr. 1, 1884; auditor, 1884-86, gen. passenger and ticket agt. at Cincinnati, 1886-89, Cincinnati, Hamilton & Dayton R.R.; sec. to pres. Pullman's Palace Car Co., 1889; gen. supt. Columbus, Hocking Valley & Toledo Ry., 1889-91; gen. supt. Chicago & Eastern Ill., 1891-93; asst. to pres. same, Jan. to Sept. 1893; gen. passenger agt. Cleveland, Akron & Columbus Ry., 1893-95; auditor Western Passenger Assn., 1895-97. Died 1907.

ROCKWELL, Charles Henry, naval officer; b. Chatham, Mass., Apr. 29, 1840; s. Rev. Charles and Mary (Howes) R.; ed. Sharon, Conn., and Phila.; m. Esther H. Gould, Apr. 7, 1861; m. 2d, Marianna C. Butler. Entered naval service of U.S. as acting master, July 5, 1862; acting vol. lt. Dec. 16, 1863; acting vol. lt. comdr. Mar. 27, 1865; acting master U.S.N. Nov. 19, 1866; master Mar. 12, 1868; lt. Dec. 18, 1868; lt. comdr. Feb. 26, 1878; comdr. Oct. 31, 1888; capt. Mar. 3, 1899; retired as rear admiral Apr. 29, 1902. During Civil war took part in numerous engagements and earned commendation from superiors and several promotions by good service; afterwards followed usual career of naval officer in active service. Home: Chatham, Mass. Died 1908.

ROCKWELL, Joseph H., clergyman; b. Boston, Nov. 19, 1862; s. Horace Tyler and Matilda Elizabeth (Clark) R.; Boston Coll., 1880-81; studied philosophy and theology in Jesuit Sem., Woodstock, Md. Ordained R.C. priest, 1895; prof. literature, Coll. of St. Francis Xavier, New York, 1896-98, Boston Coll., 1899-1901; v.p. Boston Coll., 1901-07; asst. to Jesuit Provincial of N.Y.-Md. Province of the Jesuit Order, 1907-11; pres. Coll. of St. Francis Xavier, New York, 1911-18; also pres. Brooklyn Coll., June 1913-18; provincial of Md.-N.Y. Province of Soc. of Jesus, July 31, 1918-22; lecturer, House of Studies, Weston, Mass., 1922—. Died Aug. 1, 1927.

ROCKWELL, Julius Ensign, editor; b. Millbury, Mass., Mar. 3, 1860; s. Henry Ensign and Sarah J. (Hathaway) R.; fitted for sophomore yr., Harvard, but instead of going to coll. took spl. lit. course; m. Mabel Rose Lewis, Aug. 14, 1882. Spl. agt. 10th Census, 1879-80; sec. U.S. Commn. to Internat. Fishery Expn., Berlin, 1880; stenographer U.S. Bur. of Edn., 1881-84, U.S. Patent Office, 1884-87; chief clerk to v.p. and gen. mgr. Mobile & Ohio R.R., Mobile, 1887-88; chief clerk Southern Ry. and Steamship Assn., Atlanta, 1889, to 1st v.p. Richmond & Danville R.R., Richmond, 1890; in charge Peirce Sch. of Shorthand, Phila., 1890-92; prin. Phonographic Inst., Cincinnati, 1893; sec. Southeastern Passenger Assn., Atlanta, 1894-97; editor Bur. of Plant Industry, Aug., 1902—. Author: The Teaching, Practice and Literature of Shorthand, 1884; Shorthand Instruction and Practice, 1891. Home: Washington, D.C. Died 1926.

ROCKWELL, William Hayden, physician; b. Brattleboro, Vt., Sept. 21, 1867; s. William Henry and Nellie Ellen R.; A.B., Yale, 1889; M.D., Coll. Phys. and Surg. (Columbia), 1892; m. Mary Jane Watson Haight, Feb. 14, 1903. Author: Pocket Text-Book of Physiology (with Dr. H. D. Collins), 1900; Pocket Text-Book of Chemistry and Physics (with Dr. Walton Martin), 1901; Pocket Text-Book of Anatomy, 1903. Revised (with Dr. Charles L. Dana) 17th Am. edit. Kirke's Handbook of Physiology, 1902. Commd. maj. Med. R.C., 1917; duty with A.E.F. in France. Died 1930.

ROCKWOOD, Charles Greene, university prof.; b. New York, Jan. 11, 1843; s. Charles Greene and Sarah (Smith) R.; A.B., Yale, 1864, Ph.D., 1866, A.M., 1867; (hon. A.M., Bowdoin, 1869, Princeton, 1896); m. Hettie H. Smith, June 13, 1867. Prof. mathematics and natural philosophy, Bowdoin, 1868-73; prof. mathematics and astronomy, Rutgers, 1873-77; prof. mathematics, 1877-1905, prof. emeritus, 1905—, Princeton. Member Princeton eclipse expdn. to Colo., 1878. Home: Princeton, N.J. Died July 2, 1913.

ROCKWOOD, Elbert William, chemist; b. Franklin, Mass., July 4, 1860; s. William and Laura Matilda (Blake) R.; B.S., Amherst, 1884, A.M., 1901; student U. of Göttingen, 1889, U. of Strassburg, 1890-91, U. of Leipzig, 1892 and 1894, U. of Chicago, 1893; M.D., State U. of Ia., 1895; Ph.D., Yale, 1904; m. Laura Clarke, Mar. 21, 1894; children—Paul Reed, Alan Clarke; m. 2d, Lillian Gertrude Smith, of Somerville, Mass., Jan. 1, 1925. Asst. in chemistry, Wesleyan, 1884-86; instr. chemistry, Cornell, 1886-87; chemist Hatch Expt. Sta. (Conn.), 1888; made prof. chemistry and toxicology, 1888, head dept. chemistry, 1904-20, prof. chemistry, 1920—, State U. of Iowa. Author: A Laboratory Manual of Physiological Chemistry, 1899, 5th edit., 1924. Introduction to Chemical Analysis for Medical Students, 1901. Home: Iowa City, Iowa. Died July 17, 1935.

ROCKWOOD, Frank Ernest, coll. prof.; b. Franklin, Mass., Dec. 20, 1852; s. Abijah Thurston and Sarah M. (Peck) R.; A.B., Brown U., 1874, A.M., 1877; U. of Leipzig, and in Rome, 1888; LL.D., Denison, 1900; D.C.L., Bucknell, 1918; m. Emma Dare Banks, May 21, 1885 (died 1904); m. 2d, Mrs. Clara L. Duncan, Sept. 20, 1917. Instr. Latin, South Jersey Inst., Bridgeton, 1874-85; prof. Latin, 1885-1917 (emeritus), dean, 1897-1917, Bucknell Univ. Republican. Baptist. Editor: Velleius Paterculus, Book II, 1893; Cicero de Senectute, 1895, revised edit., 1911; Cicero de Officiis, Book I, 1901; Cicero's Tusculan Disputations, Book I, and Dream of Scipio, 1903. Home: Overbrook, Pa. Died Jan. 2, 1935.

ROCKWOOD, George Gardner, photographer, inventor; b. Troy, N.Y., Apr. 12, 1832; acad. edn.; Ph.D., U. of Chicago; m. Araminta Bouton, 1853. Took up photography in 1855 and produced 1st carte-de-visite made in U.S.; inventor of many improvements in the art; famed for his art studies of children. Author of the scientific hoax, "Brain Pictures." Lecturer in Free Lecture Course, N.Y. Dept. Edn. Home: New York, N.Y. Died 1911.

RODDENBERY, Seaborn Anderson, congressman; b. on farm, Decatur Co., Ga., Jan. 12, 1870; s. S. A. (M.D.) and Martha A. (Braswell) R.; student Mercer U., Ga., 3 yrs.; m. Johnnie Butler, Nov. 5, 1891. Mem. Ga. Ho. of Rep., 1892, 1893; admitted to bar, 1894, and began practice at Thomasville, Ga.; also engaged in farming, 1897—; U.S. commr., 1895-96; judge Co. Ct., Thomas Co., Ga., 1897-1901; mayor of Thomasville, 1904-06; pres. Bd. Edn., Thomas Co., 4 yrs.; elected to 61st Congress, Feb. 16, 1910, for unexpired term (1910-11) of J. M. Griggs, deceased; reëlected to 62d Congress (1911-13), 2d Ga. Dist., without opposition. Democrat. Baptist. Trustee Young's Female Coll., Thomasville. Mason, K.P., Odd Fellow. Home: Thomasville, Ga. Died Sept. 25, 1913.

RODDY, Harry Justin; b. Landisburg, Pa., May 25, 1856; s. William Henry and Susan Catherine (Waggoner) R.; B.S., First Pa. State Normal Sch., Millersville, 1881, M.S., 1891; Ph.D., Kansas City (Mo.) U., 1906; m. Anna Houck Graver, Dec. 21, 1891; children—Anna Mary (Mrs. Clair G. Kinter), Henry Justin. Teacher pub. schs., 1877-87; teacher, First Pa. State Normal Sch., 1887-1904, dir. geography and geology work, 1906-08, head of science work, 1908-26; curator of museum and prof. geology, Franklin and Marshall Coll., 1926—. Sec. Lancaster City Tree Commn. Dir. Nature Study Club, Lancaster. Author: Common School Geography (2 books), 1913, 15; Industrial and Commercial Geography of Lancaster County, Pa., 1916; Origin of Concretions in Streams, 1917; The Reptiles of Lancaster County and the State of Pennsylvania, 1926; The Geology and Geography of Lancaster Co., Pa., 1920. Home: Conestoga, Pa. Deceased.

RODDY, William Franklin, financial expert; b. Larisa, Tex., June 27, 1871; s. William Christofer and Fannie E. (Stephens) R.; grad. as accountant at Omen, Tex., 1889; m. Mabel Estelle Williams, Aug. 24, 1905; 1 dau. (adopted), Mary Elizabeth. Pvt. 23d U.S. Inf., Spanish-Am. War, 1898, and Philippine Insurrection; entered Philippines Customs Service on detail from army, 1900, continuing until 1918; served as collector of customs various ports; collector of customs, Corinto, Nicaragua, 1918-27; apptd. adviser of customs, Ecuadorian Govt., Feb. 1927, dir. gen. of customs, May 1927-Feb. 1930, technical adviser of customs, 1930-Jan. 1931; mem. Kemmerer Com. for reorganization of finances, Republic of Peru, 1931; tech. adviser of customs, Republic of Colombia, May 1, 1931-Apr. 30, 1933. Presbyn. Mason. Home: Nevada City, Calif. Died Feb. 5, 1940.

RODENBERG, William A., congressman; b. Chester, Ill., Oct. 30, 1865; s. Rev. Charles and Anna (Walters) R.; A.B., Central Wesleyan Coll., Mo., 1884, A.M., 1887; m. Mary Grant Ridgway, Apr. 30, 1904; children—William Ridgway, Robert Ridgway. Admitted to bar, 1890; in practice at Washington, D.C., since retiring from Congress; chmn. bd. Washington Convention Hall Co.; v.p. Obear-Nester Glass Co. (East St. Louis). Chairman Ill. delegation, Rep. Nat. Conv., 1916; placed Frank O. Lowden in nomination for Presidency, Rep. Nat. Conv., 1920; chmn. Ill. State Conv., 1920; mem. 56th Congress (1899-1901); U.S. civ. service commr., 1901-02; mem. 58th to 62d Congresses (1903-13), and 64th to 67th Congresses (1915-23), 22d Ill. Dist. Home: East St. Louis, Ill. Died Sept. 10, 1937.

RODENBOUGH, Theophilus Francis, brig. gen. U.S.A.; b. Easton, Pa., Nov. 5, 1838; s. Charles and Emily (Cauffman) R.; ed. Lafayette Coll.; m. Elinor Frances Foster, Sept. 1, 1868. Apptd. from Pa., 2d lt. 2d Dragoons, Mar. 27, 1861; 1st lt. 2d Cav., May 14, 1861; capt., July 17, 1862; col. 18th Pa. Cav., Apr. 29, 1865; comd. brigade and Dist. of Clarksburg, W.Va.; hon. mustered out of vol. service, Oct. 31, 1865; maj. 42d U.S. Inf., July 28, 1866; retired with rank of col., Dec. 15, 1870, "loss of right arm from wound in line of duty"; advanced to rank of brig. gen. retired, by act of Apr. 23, 1904. Bvtd. maj., Sept. 19, 1864, for battle of Trevillian Sta. and Opequan, Va.; lt. col., Mar. 13, 1865, for services during war; col., Mar. 13, 1865, for battle of Todd's Tavern, Va.; brig. gen., Mar. 13, 1865, for battle of Cold Harbor, Va.; awarded Congressional Medal of Honor, Sept. 21, 1893, "for distinguished gallantry in action at Trevillian Sta., Va.," June 11, 1864, where he was severely wounded while commanding 2d U.S. Cav. Served in all campaigns of Army of the Potomac; asst. insp. gen., N.Y., 1880-83; chief bur. of elections, City of New York, 1890-1901. Sec. Mil. Service Instn., 1878—. Editor: The Army of the United States, 1896; Journal Military Service Institution, 1899. Died Dec. 19, 1912.

RODEY, Bernard Shandon, judge; b. Co. Mayo, Ireland, 1856; s. Patrick and Ellen (Macdonnell) R.; entirely self-ed.; lived in Canada, 1862-77, Boston, 1877-80, Albuquerque, N.M., 1881—; m. Minnie Codington, 1886. Admitted to bar, 1884, and practiced at Albuquerque, 1884-1906. Member N.M. Legislative Council, 1889, and author bill creating U. of N.M. and other territorial instns.; mem. N.M. Constl. Conv., 1890; del. from N.M. to 57th and 58th Congresses (1901-05), and made battle for admission of tys. to Union; U.S. dist. judge, Dist. of P.R., June 15, 1906-June 15, 1910; U.S. dist. atty., 2d Div. of Alaska, July 1911—. Republican. Author of opinions contained in, and compiler of Vols. II, III, IV and V, Puerto Rico Federal Reports. Home: Albuquerque, N.M. Died Mar. 10, 1927.

RODGERS, Cowan, banker; b. Mar. 22, 1878; s. Thomas and Lucy Graham (White) R.; student U. of Tenn.; m. Katherine C. Briscoe, Nov. 27, 1912 (dec.); children—Cowan, Earnest Briscoe. In bicycle business, Knoxville, 1898-1900; in automobile business, 1900-28; pres. City Nat. Bank, 1929-32; pres. Rodgers & Co., Highland Memorial Cemetery; v.p. Tenn. Good Roads Assn.; dist. mgr. Home Owners Loan Corp.; mem. Knox County Highway Commn., 1924-33; treas. Great Smoky Mountains Conservation Assn. Democrat. Episcopalian. Home: Knoxville, Tenn. Died Sept. 18, 1936.

RODGERS, Frederick, rear admiral U.S.N.; b. Havre de Grace, Md., Oct. 3, 1842; s. Robert Smith and Sarah (Berry) R.; bro. of John Augustus R.; apptd. to U.S. Naval Acad. from Md., 1857, grad. 1861; m. Sarah M., d. John C. Fall, of San Francisco, Feb. 2, 1882. Warranted midshipman, June 1, 1861; promoted through grades to rear adm., Mar. 3, 1899. Served on Wabash, 1861; Santee, 1861-62; exec. officer Kineo, 1862-63; participated in engagements at Donaldsonville, Port Hudson, and College Point, La., Feb.-Mar. 1862; served on Grand Gulf, Atlantic and West Gulf blockading squadrons, 1863-65; Chattanooga, 1866; Sacramento, 1866-June 6, 1867, when she was lost in the Bay of Bengal; Michigan, 1868-69; N. Pacific Squadron, 1869-72, serving on the Pensacola, St. Mary's and Saranac; insp. ordnance, Navy Yard, Washington, 1872-73; comd. Despatch, 1873-76; light house insp. 11th dist., 1876-77, 4th dist., 1881-83, 3d dist., 1887-90; comd. Adams, 1877-79, Independence, 1883-87, Philadelphia, 1890-92; supervisor New York Harbor, 1892-93; capt. of yard, Navy Yard, New York, 1893-96; comd. Massachusetts, 1896-97; mem. Naval Retiring Bd., July-Sept. 1897; mem. Bd. of Inspection and Survey, 1897, and pres. of bd., 1897-98; comd. Puritan, June-Oct. 1898, during war with Spain; pres. Bd. of Inspection and Survey, 1898-1901; sr. squadron comdr., Asiatic Fleet, 1901, and commander-in-chief, 1902; comdt., Navy Yard, New York, 1903-04; retired Oct. 3, 1904; spl. bd. duties, 1904-07. Home: St. James, R.I. died Nov. 3, 1917.

RODGERS, James Linn, consul gen.; b. Columbus, O., Sept. 10, 1861; s. Andrew Denny and Eliza (Sullivant) R.; ed. pub. and pvt. schs. and Ohio State U.; m. Frances C. Fay, Oct. 25, 1893. Editor Columbus Dispatch, 1889-95; sec. to gov. of Ohio, 1896-1900. Mem. various Ohio bds.; interested in mfg. Am. consul gen. at Shanghai, 1905-07, at Havana, 1907-18, at Montreal, Jan. 18, 1918—. Home: Columbus, O. Died Feb. 8, 1930.

RODGERS, John, naval officer; b. Washington, D.C., Jan. 15, 1881; s. John A. and Elizabeth B. (Chambers) R.; prep. edn., Lawrenceville (N.J.) Sch., 1896, 97; grad. U.S. Naval Acad., 1903; unmarried. Ensign U.S.N., Feb. 3, 1905; promoted through grades to comdr., Nov. 4, 1920; served in Spanish-Am. War; 2d naval aviator licensed (1911); in Submarine Service and on North Sea mine barrage, World War; comdr. Naval Air Sta., Pearl Harbor, T.H., 1922-25; apptd. asst. chief Bur. of Aeronautics, Sept. 1925. In charge navy sea plane in attempted non-stop flight, San Francisco to Hawaiian Islands, Sept. 1925. Home: Havre de Grace, Md. Died Aug. 27, 1926.

RODGERS, John Augustus, rear admiral U.S.N.; b. Havre de Grace, Md., July 26, 1848; s. Robert Smith and Sarah (Perry) R.; bro. of Frederick R.; apptd. to the U.S. Naval Acad. by the President, at-large, July 30, 1863, grad. June 2, 1868; m. Elizabeth B. Chambers, Mar. 30, 1880. Promoted ensign, Apr. 19, 1869; advanced through grades to rear adm., Sept. 7, 1908. Was in active service during Civil War, in the summer of 1864, on board the Marion, pursuit of the Confed. steamers Florida and Tallahassee; served successively in the Pacific squadron, on Supply and Nipsic, in the torpedo service, Hartford, Juniata, Monongahela, Trenton and Constellation, 1868-80; Navy Yard, Washington, 1880-83; Ossipee, 1884-87; mem. Steel Bd., 1887-90; Pensacola, 1890-91; Naval War Coll., 1892; Miantonomah, 1892-94; inspection duty, 1895-97; exec. officer Indiana, 1897-99; took part in the destruction of Cervera's squadron off Santiago, Cuba, July 1898, and was advanced five numbers in rank for "eminent and conspicuous conduct" in that battle; in charge 6th light house dist., 1899-1902; comd. Marietta and Albany, 1902-04; Illinois, 1904-06; insp. 3d light house dist., 1906-07; comdt. Navy Yard, Puget Sound, Wash., 1908-10. Retired July 26, 1910. Comdt. naval units, Harvard U., Mass. Inst. Tech., Boston U. and Tufts Coll., 1918. Home: Havre de Grace, Md. Died Mar. 2, 1933.

RODGERS, John Gilmour, ry. official; b. Phila., Pa., Nov. 14, 1863; s. Samuel Maurice and Isabel (Gilmour) R.; ed. Lehigh U. and under private tutors; m. Agnes P. Barney, Feb. 4, 1901. Became connected with Pennsylvania R.R. as asst. engr., 1886, supt., 1900, asst. to gen. mgr., 1909, gen. supt., 1911, asst. to pres., 1917, v.p., Mar. 1920—. Served as lt. col. engrs., U.S.A., Oct.-Dec. 1918. Republican. Presbyn. Home: Chicago, Ill. Died Apr. 12, 1923.

RODGERS, John Isaac, brig. gen. U.S.A.; b. Fayette Co., Pa., Apr. 18, 1839; s. John and Eliza R.; A.B., Waynesburg Coll., Pa., 1855; grad. U.S. Mil. Acad., 1861; m. Esther F. Rogers, Sept. 25, 1872; children—Mrs. Louisa Hall, Robert Clive. Second lt. 2d Arty., May 6, 1861; promoted through grades to brig. gen. vols., May 4, 1898; brig. gen. U.S.A., Oct. 1902, retired. Served during Civil War; comd. battery at Ft. Pickens, and light battery in La.; was in Gen. Banks' expdns. and battles in Red River campaigns, 1863-64, and siege of Port Hudson. Instr. mathematics, West Point, Oct. 1864 to June 1865; served with regt., 1865-89 (including railroad riot service in Md. and W.Va., 1877, and Mexican border trouble, 1877-81); arty. insp., 1889-98, except part of 1895-96, comdr. Fort Schuyler, N.Y.; brig. gen. vols., 1898, and chief of arty. of the army, was charged with organization and equipment of a siege train of 96 guns and mortars for service with army in the field. Has prepared Range Tables, Coast Arty. Drill Regulations and other papers on arty. pub. by War Dept. Died Aug. 2, 1931.

RODGERS, Raymond Perry, rear admiral U.S.N.; b. Washington, D.C., Dec. 20, 1849; s. Rear Admiral Raymond and Julia (Slidell) R.; grad. U.S. Naval Academy, 1868; m. Gertrude Stuyvesant. Ensign, 1869; promoted through grades to rear admiral, July 4, 1908. Served as naval attaché in France and Russia, 1893-97; exec. officer Iowa, throughout Spanish-Am. War and at Santiago, 1897-99; was advanced 5 numbers in rank for "eminent and conspicuous conduct" in battle which destroyed Cervera's Squadron off Santiago; comd. Nashville, 1899-1901, in W.I., in Philippines, and in China during Boxer troubles; capt. Kearsarge, 1904-06, in Atlantic Fleet; chief intelligence officer, Navy Dept., 1906-09; pres. Naval War Coll. and comdt. Naval Sta. in Narragansett Bay, Oct. 1909; retired by operation of law, Dec. 20, 1911. Died Dec. 28, 1925.

RODGERS, Thomas Slidell, naval officer; b. Morristown, N.J., Aug. 18, 1858; s. C. Raymond Perry and Julia (Slidell) R.; grad. U.S. Naval Acad., 1878; unmarried. Ensign, Dec. 1, 1881; promoted through grades to rear admiral, June 13, 1916. Served on Bennington and Monterey, Spanish-Am. War, 1898; exec. officer Maine, 1902-05; in charge 10th Lighthouse Dist., 1905-06; asst. comdt. 4th Naval Dist., 1906; comd. Dubuque, 1906-08; equipment officer, Navy Yard, Phila., 1908-09; comd. New Hampshire, 1909-11; supervisor, New York Harbor, 1911-12; dir. naval intelligence, 1912-13; comd. New York, 1913-15; at Naval War Coll., 1915-16; apptd. comdr. Div. Seven, Battleship Force, Atlantic Fleet, June 19, 1916; retired July 1919. Episcopalian. Died Feb. 28, 1931.

RODGERS, William Blackstock, lawyer; b. Allegheny City, Pa., July 1, 1845; s. Rev. James and Eliza (Livingston) R.; A.B., Allegheny City Coll., 1863; m. Ada M. Mevay, Jan. 21, 1891. Admitted to Pa. bar, 1866; dir. Diamond Nat. Bank, Diamond Savings Bank, Pittsburgh Gage & Supply Co. City solicitor, Allegheny City, 1870-88, Pittsburgh, 1902-09; mem. commn. to devise plan for govt. of cities, created by act of Gen. Assembly of Pa., 1876; author of act for govt. of cities of 2d class, approved, Mar. 7, 1901. United Presbyn. Home: Pittsburgh, Pa. Died May 25, 1914.

RODGERS, William Cunningham, clergyman; b. Lowestoft, Eng., Sept. 10, 1856; s. Edward and Mary Jane (Calvert) R.; B.A., Christ's Coll., Cambridge, 1878, M.A., 1882; (S.T.D., St. Stephen's, 1909); m. Laura Cooper, of London, Eng., 1880. Deacon, 1884, priest, 1885, P.E. Ch.; asst. St. Peter's Ch., Streatham, London, 1884-88, St. Paul's, Sandgate, Kent, 1888-89; rector St. Stephen's, Wilkinsburg, Pa., 1889-91; canon cathedral, Davenport, Ia., 1891-95; rector Gloversville, N.Y., 1895-96, St. Mark's, Hoosick Falls, 1896-99; headmaster St. John's School, Montreal, Can., 1899-1900; rector Grace Ch., Millbrook, N.Y., 1900-07; asst. St. Agnes' Chapel of Trinity Parish, New York, 1907-09; pres. Saint Stephen's Coll., Annandale, N.Y., 1909-19; rector Old St. David's Ch., Radnor, Pa., 1919—. Died Jan. 5, 1921.

RODGERS, William Thomas, clergyman; b. near Knoxville, Tenn., Oct. 8, 1861; s. Jacob B. and Nancy Ann (Magill) R.; A.B., Lincoln (Ill.) Coll., 1889; B.D., Cumberland Theol. Sem., Tenn., 1891; grad. Union Theol. Sem., New York, 1892; D.D., Roane Coll., 1906, Cumberland U., 1907; m. Eula, d. Capt. James Bradshaw Hunter, of Bell Buckle, Tenn., June 12, 1895; children—William Hunter, Mary E., Ruth M., Robert H., James J., Elizabeth. Licentiate Presbyn. Church, 1881; ordained Presbyn. ministry, 1884; pastor Grace Ch., Nashville, Tenn., 1892-1901, First Ch., Knoxville, 1901-06, Lucas Av. Ch., St. Louis, 1906-08, Grace Ch., Nashville, 1908-11, First Ch., Macomb, Ill., June 1911-27, First Ch., Harriman, Tenn., 1927—. Moderator Presbytery 10 terms, Synod of Tenn., 1 yr., Synod of Ill., 1925-26; mem. Synod's Council, and com. on colls. and Christian edn.; chmn. Tenn. Synod's Com. on Foreign Missions. Mason, K.P. Home: Harriman, Tenn. Died Feb. 19, 1931.

RODMAN, Hugh, naval officer; b. Frankfort, Ky., Jan. 6, 1859; s. Hugh and Susan Ann (Barbour) R.; grad. U.S. Naval Acad., 1880; Naval War Coll., 1907; m. Elizabeth Ruffin Sayre, July 3, 1889. Ensign, jr. grade, Mar. 3, 1883; promoted through grades to rear adm., May 23, 1917; admiral, July 1, 1919; retired Jan. 6, 1923. Served on Raleigh, Spanish-Am. War, 1898; exec. officer New Orleans, 1904; on Cincinnati, 1904-05, Wisconsin, 1905; comd. El Cano, 1905-07, West Virginia, 1907; insp. in charge 6th Lighthouse Dist., 1907-08; comd. Cleveland, 1909-10; inspection officer, Navy Yard, Mare Island, Calif., 1910-11; capt. same, 1911; comd. Connecticut, 1912, Delaware, 1912-13; superintendent transportation, Panama Canal and dir. Panama Railroad Co., 1914-15; comd. New York, 1915-16; mem. Gen. Bd., Navy Dept., 1916-17; comd. Div. Three, Atlantic Fleet, 1917; comd. Squadron One, Battleship Force, Atlantic Fleet, 1917; apptd. comdr. Div. Three, Battleship Force One, Atlantic Fleet, Sept. 1917; apptd. comdr. Div. 9, Battleship Force, Nov. 1917, for duty with British Grand Fleet; apptd. comdr. U.S. battleships, Apr. 1918; comd. 6th Battle Squadron in North Sea, with British Grand Fleet, 1 yr.; commd. admiral and commander-in-chief Pacific Fleet, July 1, 1919. Awarded D.S.M. and Dewey medal, Spanish War Medal and World War Medal (U.S.); Knight Comdr. Order of the Bath (British), 1918; Order of Rising Sun (Japan); Grand Cordon of Leopold II (Belgium); Comdr. Legion of Honor (France); El Sol (Peru); El Merite (Chile). Medals for Battle of Manila Bay and Spanish-Am. War. U.S. del. coronation of King George VI, London, May 1938. Presbyn. Mason. Home: Washington, D.C. Died June 7, 1940.

RODMAN, John Croom, M.D.; b. Washington, N.C., Dec. 27, 1870; s. William Blount and Camilla H. (Croom) R.; U. of N.C., 1888-89; M.D., Bellevue Hospital Medical College (New York U.), 1892; m. Olzie W. Clark, June 7, 1904; children—John C., Olzie C., Archie C., Owen G., Clark, Camillus H. Practiced Washington, N.C., 1892—; acting assistant surgeon of U.S. Pub. Health Service, 1895—; mem. N.C. State Bd. of Med. Examiners, 1908-14; chief surgeon, Washington & Vandemere (N.C.) R.R., 1905—; surgeon Norfolk Southern R.R. at Washington, D.C., 1920—. Democrat. Episcopalian. Mason. Chmn. Med. Advisory Bd., N.C. Dist. 17, 1917-18; mem. Vol. Med. Service Corps. Home: Washington, N.C. Died Jan. 24, 1941.

RODMAN, William Louis, surgeon; b. Frankfort, Ky., Sept. 7, 1858; s. John (atty. gen. Ky.) and Harriet V. (Russell) R.; M.A., Ky. Mil. Inst., 1875; M.D., Jefferson Med. Coll., Phila., 1879; m. Bettie, d. Dr. J. Q. A. Stewart, of Frankfort, Ky., Oct. 31, 1882. House surgeon Jefferson Hosp., Phila., 1879-80; army surgeon, U.S.A., 1880-82; removed to Louisville, 1882; demonstrator surgery Med. Dept., U. of Louisville, 1885-93; prof. surgery, Ky. Sch. Medicine, 1893-98; prof. surgery, Medico-Chirurg. Coll., Phila., 1898—; prof. surgery and clin. surgery, Woman's Med. Coll. of Pa., 1900—. Chmn. surg. sect. A.M.A., 1897-98; pres. Am. Med. Coll. Assn., 1902. Home: Philadelphia, Pa. Died Mar. 8, 1916.

RODNEY, George Brydges, brig. gen. U.S.A.; b. New Castle, Del., Oct. 17, 1842; s. Hon. George Brydges and Mary J. (Duval) R.; ed. at Phila.; m. Janet Warren, Jan. 27, 1870. Enlisted as pvt. independent co., Pa. arty., Apr. 24, 1861; disch., Aug. 5, 1861; apptd. from Del., 2d lt. 4th U.S. Arty., Aug. 5, 1861; 1st lt., Aug. 5, 1861; capt., Mar. 4, 1869; grad. Arty. Sch., 1869; maj., Nov. 28, 1892; lt. col., Feb. 13, 1899; col. Arty. Corps, Feb. 2, 1901; brig. gen. U.S.A., Aug. 4, 1903; retired at own request after 40 yrs.' service, Aug. 5, 1903. Bvtd. capt., Dec. 31, 1862, for battle of Stone River, Tenn.; maj., Sept. 20, 1863, for battle of Chickamauga, Ga. Died Sept. 21, 1927.

RODRIGUEZ, José Ignacio, lawyer; b. Havana, Cuba, Nov. 11, 1831; s. José Ignacio and Catalina

(Hernandez) R.; grad. Univ. of Havana, A.B., 1849; doctor of philosophy and letters, Jan. 30, 1853; licentiate of law, July 24, 1855; doctor civ. and canonical law, 1863; m. Mary A. Joyce, Apr. 14, 1884. Supernumerary prof., faculty of philosophy, Univ. of Havana, 1855; prof. natural philosophy and chemistry, Havana Prep. Tech. School, 1856; Havana Inst., 1863; mem. Superior bd. public instruction and insp. gen. public instruction, Cuba, 1866; admitted to Havana bar, 1855; judge (alcalde, mayor) pro tem. in Havana for dist. of Colon, 1864, and for dist. of Belen, 1865; one of founders and editors Revista de Jurisprudencia (law review), 1856-60; commd. to present respects of Univ. of Havana to Queen Isabella II, at Madrid, June 1860; sec. Economical Soc. of Friends of the Country, Havana, 1863, and of similar soc. at Santiago de Cuba; settled in U.S., 1869; in Washington, D.C., Jan. 1, 1870; served in various capacities for Mexico in U.S. and Mexican Claim Commn.; studied Am. law under Caleb Cushing; admitted to bar of D.C., and U.S. Supreme Court; practices in internat. law and Spanish and Spanish-Am. law; sec. Internat. Am. Conf. from Feb. 19, 1890, until its end; chief translator and head Spanish dept. Bureau Am. Republics until 1897; sec. Internat. Am. Monetary Commn., 1891; went to Paris with Am. Peace Commn. as private confidential adviser in matters of Spanish law, Sept. to Dec. 1898; sec. delegation of U.S. in Pan-Am. Conf., City of Mexico, 1902-03; became chief translator and librarian, Columbus Memorial Library in Internat. Bureau Am. Republics; counsel for claimants in the Mora, Sanguily and Delgado cases; contributor to numerous Cuban papers and to Catholic Quarterly Review, Phila., and The Forum, New York. Author: Vida de Don José, de la Luz y Caballero, 1874; Vida del Presbitero Don Felix Varela, 1878; Estudio historico sobre el origen des envolvimiento y manifestaciones prácticas de la idea la anexion de Cuba à los Estados Unidos de America, 1901. Died 1907.

ROE, Charles Francis, soldier; b. New York, May 1, 1848; s. Stephen Romer and Josephine Augusta (Foster) R.; grad. U.S. Mil. Academy, 1868; m. Katherine Bissell Bogert, July 29, 1874. Commd. 2d lt. 1st Cav., June 15, 1868; transferred to 2d Cav., Oct. 29, 1870; mustered out of service, Dec. 28, 1870; 2d lt. 2d Cav., Dec. 9, 1871; 1st lt., Dec. 20, 1880; regtl. adj., Nov. 2, 1876-Mar. 31, 1878, and Dec. 20, 1880-May 1, 1886; resigned Jan. 31, 1888; brig. gen. vols., June 10, 1898; hon. disch., Sept. 10, 1898. Served on frontier in Indian campaigns, including the Custer massacre, 21 yrs. Engaged in real estate business. Organized, 1889, Troop A, N.G.N.Y., afterwards Squadron A; apptd. maj., N.G.N.Y., Feb. 1895; maj. gen. by Gov. Black, Feb. 9, 1898; retired on account of age, May 1, 1912. Republican. Episcopalian. Home: New York, N.Y. Died Dec. 1, 1922.

ROE, Clifford Griffith, lawyer, lecturer, author; b. Rolling Prairie, Ind., June 26, 1875; s. George Washington and Marietta (Drummond) Roe; B.L., U. of Mich., 1899, LL.B., 1902; m. Elsie Martha Hercock, Mar. 7, 1910; 1 dau., Marjorie Helen. Admitted to Ill. bar, 1903; asst. state's atty., Cook Co., Ill., 1906-09; spl. prosecutor against panders ("white slave traders"), Sept. 1909-11; asst. corp. counsel, City of Chicago, 1915-18; attorney for Wilson & Co., packers, 1918—; became judge of the Illinois Court of Claims, 1931. Member faculty Ill. Coll. of Law, 1915-19. Mem. Four-Minute Men, World War; asso. mem. Legal Advisory Bd., Dist. No. 15, Chicago. Pres. Am. Bur. Moral Edn., Dec. 1909—; atty. for com. headed by John D. Rockefeller, Jr., during New York investigation, 1911-12; father of the first pandering ("white slave") law in America; former gen. counsel Am. Vigilance Assn.; v.p. Ill. Vigilance Assn.; organizer Com. of Fifteen. Mem. Disciples of Christ. Mason. Author: The Great War on White Slavery. Home: Chicago, Ill. Died June 28, 1934.

ROE, Edward Drake, Jr., mathematician; b. Elmira, N.Y., Jan. 4, 1859; s. Edward Drake and Eleanor Jane (Frost) R.; A.B., Syracuse U., 1880; student Harvard Med. Sch., 1882; A.B., Harvard, 1885; Harvard Grad. Sch., 1885-86, 1888-92, A.M., 1886; scholarship in the Med. Sch., Thayer scholarship in the Grad. Sch.; a founder and charter sec. Graduate Club of Harvard; studied U. of Erlangen, 1897-98, Ph.D., magna cum laude, 1898; m. Harriet Adelaide Bridge (Gourley), Mar. 15, 1890 (died 1898); children—Eva Gourley (Mrs. Edwin H. Gaggin), Edward Drake (dec.); m. 2d, Josephine Alberta Robinson, A.M., Feb. 1, 1911. Instr. mathematics, acad., Media, Pa., 1886-88; instr. same, pro tem., Harvard, 1890, Boston Univ., 1890-92; asso. prof. mathematics, Oberlin Coll., 1892-99, Syracuse U., 1900-01; John Raymond French prof. mathematics, Syracuse U., 1901—, and dir. of the observatory, 1919—, research prof., 1925—. Traveled in Germany, Austria and Switzerland, 1897-98, 1903, 04; tour of German univs. and 3d Internat. Congress of Mathematicians at Heidelberg, 1904. Research asso. Yerkes Obs., summer of 1915. Erected pvt. astron. obs., 1906, equipped with 6½ in. equatorial telescope, as part of residence in Syracuse. Author of some 64 publs. in math. and scientific jours., etc. Nephew of late Rear Adm. Francis Asbury Roe. Home: Syracuse, N.Y. Died Dec. 11, 1929.

ROE, Francis Asbury, rear admiral U.S.N., retired Oct. 4, 1885; b. Oct. 4, 1823; ed. Elmira Acad.; grad. U.S. Naval Acad., June 1847; m. Eliza J. Snyder, Sept. 1849. Apptd. acting midshipman U.S.N., Oct. 19, 1841; warranted midshipman, Feb. 3, 1842; promoted through grades to rear adm., Nov. 3, 1884. Served in China, Japan, Polar regions Exploring Expdn., Brazil, E. and W. Africa, West Indies, Mediterranean and Great Lakes. As exec. officer of Porpoise, 1854, had an action with 13 heavily armored pirate junks, at Koulan Bay, China, destroying 6 and dispersing the others; exec. officer of Pensacola, 1861, when it passed down the Potomac through nine miles of Confederate batteries, under constant fire; in Farragut's fleet, 1862-63, and in 6 days' battle below New Orleans and many other fights during war; suppressed 2 insurrections on great lakes during Civil war. Comd. at Vera Cruz when Maximilian was executed by Republican army of Mexico; comd. U.S.S. Saxsacus, May 5, 1864, in action with the rebel ram Albemarle, in the sounds of N.C., and defeated the ram. Author: Naval Duties and Discipline, 1864. Died 1901.

ROE, Gilbert Ernstein, lawyer; b. Oregon, Wis., Feb. 7, 1865; s. John and Jane R.; ed. U. of Wis., 1884-90, LL.B., 1890; m. Gwyneth King, Nov. 12, 1899; children—Jack E., Janet, Gwyneth. Practiced law in Wis., associated with Robert Marion LaFollette, 1890-99; at New York, 1899—, mem. Roe & McCombs, 1905-10; counsel to U.S. Senate com. on mfrs. investigating high cost of gasoline and other petroleum products, 1922-23; Eastern regional dir. La-Follette-Wheeler Progressive campaign com., 1924. Author: Our Judicial Oligarchy; Review of Selected Opinions of Chief Justices Dixon and Ryan. Died Dec. 22, 1929.

ROE, John Orlando, laryngologist; b. Patchogue, L.I., N.Y., Feb. 3, 1849; s. Stephen Smith and Huldah Sophronia (Randall) R.; Ph.C., M.D., U. of Mich., 1870; M.D., Coll. Phys. & Surg., New York, 1871; (LL.D., U. of Mich., 1913); m. Jennie E. Pomeroy, Feb. 12, 1895. Practiced Rochester, N.Y., 1872—; specializes in laryngology, rhinology and otology. Democrat. Unitarian. Wrote chapters on "Injuries and Deformities of the Nose and Throat," and on "Operations in the Upper Air Passages," in American Text Book of Diseases of the Eye, Ear, Nose and Throat, 1899; etc. Home: Rochester, N.Y. Died Dec. 24, 1915.

ROE, William Edgar, clergyman, educator; b. Cornwall, N.Y., Nov. 2, 1857; s. James Gilbert and Caroline Matilda (Clark) R.; A.B., Williams Coll., 1878, D.D., 1898; student Johns Hopkins, 1878-79; grad. Union Theol. Sem., 1886; m. Abby S. Adams, June 27, 1889; children—Samuel Adams (dec.), Caroline Clark, James Adams (dec.). Ordained ministry Presbyn. Ch., 1886; pastor successively First Ch., Jacksonville, Fla., King Ferry, N.Y., Marietta, O., and Calvary Ch., Auburn, N.Y., until 1907; prof. economics and history, Whitworth Coll., Tacoma, Wash., 1907-13; prof. Bible and history, Jamestown (N.D.) Coll., 1913—, then dean dept. religious edn. Trustee Marietta Coll., 1895-1902. Democrat. Home: Jamestown, N.D. Died Feb. 27, 1934.

ROEBER, Eugene Franz, editor; b. Torgau, Germany, Oct. 7, 1867; s. Eduard F. and Anna Emilie (Lietzo) R.; ed. univs. of Jena, Halle, Berlin; Ph.D., Berlin, 1892; m. Clara Hedwig Feier, May 6, 1900. Came to U.S., 1894; elec. engr. with Carl Hering, Phila., 1899-1903; editor Electrochemical Industry, from its foundation, 1902, and of its successors, Electrochemical and Metallurgical Industry, 1905-10. Metallurgical and Chemical Engineering, 1910—. A founder Am. Electrochem. Society, 1902, mgr. and v.p., 1902-13, pres. 1913-14. Author of Section 14 (electrochemistry) of Standard Handbook for Electrical Engineers, 1908. Home: East Orange, N.J. Died Oct. 17, 1917.

ROEBLING, Ferdinand W., capitalist; b. Saxonburg, Pa., Feb. 27, 1842; s. John A. and Johanna (Herting) R.; bro. of Washington Augustus R.; ed. Poly. Coll., Phila., specializing in chemistry; m. Margaret G. Allison, Mar. 14, 1867. Treas. John A. Roebling's Sons Co., N.J. Wirecloth Co.; pres. Union Mills Paper Mfg. Co.; v.p. Syracuse, Rochester & Eastern Ry. Co.; dir. various companies. Republican. Home: Trenton, N.J. Died Mar. 16, 1917.

ROEBLING, Ferdinand William, Jr., mfr.; b. Trenton, N.J., Sept. 29, 1878; s. Ferdinand W. and Margaret G. (Allison) R.; M.E., Lehigh, 1901; m. Ruth Metcalf, Oct. 4, 1905; children—Joseph M., Ferdinand W. 3d. Began as engr. with John A. Roebling Sons Co., mfrs. wire and wire rope, Trenton, 1901, asst. sec. and treas., 1905-17, sec. and treas., 1917-26, pres., 1926—; v.p. First Mechanics Nat. Bank, Standard Fire Ins. Co. Trustee Pomfret (Conn.) Sch. Republican. Episcopalian. Home: Trenton, N.J. Died May 29, 1936.

ROEBLING, Washington Augustus, engineer; b. Saxonburg, Pa., May 26, 1837; s. late John A. and Johanna (Herting) R.; bro. of Ferdinand W. R.; C.E., Rensselaer Poly. Inst., 1857; m. Emily Warren, Jan. 18, 1865. Joined father in constrn. of Pittsburgh suspension bridge across Allegheny River; served in Union Army, pvt. to bvtd. col., 1861-65; resigned Jan. 1865, to assist his father in building Cincinnati and Covington suspension bridge. The Brooklyn bridge was undertaken by his father, but his death, July 22, 1869, before the work had been begun, left the entire construction in his hands, and he directed it to completion. Pres. and dir. John A. Roebling's Sons Co., mfrs. iron and steel wire and wire rope, Trenton, N.J. Author: Military Suspension Bridge; etc. Home: Trenton, N.J. Died July 21, 1926.

ROEHR, Julius Edward, lawyer; b. New York, N.Y., Mar. 6, 1859; s. Edward and Sophia (Bartholdt) R.; ed. pub. schs. and business coll., Milwaukee; LL.B., U. of Wis., 1881; m. Emma Krueger, May 28, 1882. Admitted to Wis. bar, Oct. 1, 1881, and began practice at Milwaukee; splty. in ins. law; was asst. counsel to atty. gen. of Wis. in case of Equitable Life Ins. Co. vs. Host, ins. commr. of Wis., involving distribution of $15,000,000 surplus dividend in Feb. 1905, by Supreme Ct. of Wis. V.p. and gen. counsel Milwaukee Title Guaranty & Abstract Co.; gen. counsel Wis. Mutual Liability Co., Time Ins. Co., Advance Bldg. & Loan Assn.; pres. New Hope Mining Co. Circuit Ct. commr., Jan. 1, 1888—; mem. Wis. Senate, 1896-1908, 8th Dist. (Milwaukee). Republican. Home: Milwaukee, Wis. Died Jan. 31, 1930.

ROEHRIG, Frederic Louis Otto, Orientalist and philologist; b. Halle, Prussia, June 19, 1819; s. Martin Louis and Emilie (Wolter) R.; grad. Univs. of Halle, Leipzig and Paris (A.M., Ph.D., M.D.); laureate Imperial Inst. of France, receiving Volney prize for linguistics; m. Caroline Smith (died 1893). Attaché Prussian embassy, Constantinople, 1841; prof. Coll. Béziers, France, 1849; lecturer Royal Oriental Acad., Paris, 1851; asst. librarian Astor Library, New York, 1853; prof. materia medica and therapeutics, Med. Coll., Phila., 1858; acting asst. surgeon U.S.A., 1861-67; acting librarian U.S. Surgeon Gen.'s office, Washington, 1868; prof. Sanskrit and modern Oriental langs., Cornell U., 1869-85; dir. N.Y. Polyglot Bureau, 1869; instr. Sanskrit, U. of Southern Calif., 1886; univ. lecturer Semitic languages and Oriental philology, Leland Stanford Jr. Univ., 1895. Chevalier Imperial Order of the Medjidiyeh, Turkey. Home: Pasadena, Calif. Died 1908.

ROELKER, Charles Rafael, rear admiral U.S.N.; b. Osnabrück, Hanover, Germany. Apptd. from N.Y., 3d asst. engr. U.S.N., 1862; 2d asst. engineer, 1864; 1st asst. engr., 1868; chief engr., Nov. 1890; comdr., March 3, 1899; capt., March 5, 1902. Served on engring. duties at sea and on shore; mem. Bd. Inspection and Survey; rear admiral, Sept. 22, 1903, retired. Home: Washington, D.C. Died 1910.

ROEMER, John Lincoln, college pres.; b. Wheeling, W.Va., May 2, 1865; s. John and Sarah Ann (Donel) R.; A.B., W.Va. U., 1889; B.D., Western Theol. Sem., Pittsburgh, Pa., 1892; D.D., Westminster (Mo.) Coll., 1909; LL.D., Mo. Valley and Westminster, 1922; m. Lillie Pickenpaugh, June 2, 1892. Ordained Presbyn. ministry, 1892; pastor Thomas, Pa., 1892-93, South Ch., Cleveland, O., 1893-1901, First Ch., Chillicothe, O., 1901-05, Tyler Place Ch., St. Louis, Mo., 1905-14; pres. Lindenwood Coll., May 12, 1914—. Built up the college to standard 4 yr. coll., 500 students. Dir. Nat. Bank of St. Charles, Industrial Bank & Trust Co. of St. Louis. Mason. Republican. Home: St. Charles, Mo. Died Aug. 9, 1940.

ROESCH, Charles Edward, mayor; b. Buffalo, N.Y., Mar. 31, 1886; s. Jacob M. and Julia (Fuellhart) R.; ed. grammar sch., Buffalo; m. Mabel Carrie Klinck, June 10, 1914; children—Charles Jacob, William Klinck. In meat business with father, Buffalo, 1901-11; mem. Jacob M. Roesch & Sons, 1911-14; proprietor Charles E. Roesch, wholesale meats and poultry, 1916—. Mayor of Buffalo, 1930-33. Pres. N.Y. State Conf. of Mayors, 1932-33. Universalist. Republican. Mason, Elk, Oriole. Home: Buffalo, N.Y. Died Jan. 15, 1936.

ROGERS, Allen, chem. engineer; b. Hampden, Me., May 22, 1876; s. Franklin G. and Georgianna (Higgins) R.; B.S. in Chemistry, U. of Maine, 1897, M.S., 1900; Ph.D., U. of Pa., 1902; m. Maude F. Couillard, Dec. 25, 1897; 1 son, Allen Ellington. Instr. chemistry, U. of Me., 1897-1900; sr. fellow U. of Pa., 1902-03; instr. organic chemistry, same, 1903-04; research chemist Oakes Mfg. Co., L.I. City, N.Y., 1904-05; in charge industrial chemistry, Pratt Inst., Brooklyn, 1905—, also supervisor course in industrial chem. engring.; consulting practice. Maj. Chem. Warfare Service, U.S.A., in charge industrial relations, May 1917-Jan. 1918. Awarded Grasselli medal, 1920, for work done in connection with fish skins for leather. Democrat. Universalist. Mason. Author: Manual of Industrial Chemistry, 1912, 15, 20, 25. Laboratory Guide of Industrial Chemistry, 1908, 17; Elements of Industrial Chemistry, 1916, 26 (spl. overseas edition, 1919); Practical Tanning, 1922. Home: Brooklyn, N.Y. Died Nov. 4, 1938.

ROGERS, Allen Hastings, mining engr.; b. Marshfield, Mass., Feb. 19, 1871; s. Alfred and Grace Hastings (Phillips) R.; B.S. in Mining Engring., Mass. Inst. Tech., 1890; m. Sara James Damon, Sept. 14, 1897; children— Phillips Damon (dec.), Priscilla (Mrs. Maurice A. Hall), John Phillips, Elizabeth (Mrs. Jason C. Balsbaugh), Barbara Damon (Mrs. Trask H. Wilkinson). With Am. Smelting & Refining

Co. and allied cos., also with other concerns, in Western States and Mexico, until 1906; independent practice, 1906—; mem. Rogers, Mayer & Ball. "Dollar a year" man with U.S. Bur. Mines, Washington, D.C., 1917-19. Republican. Unitarian. Home: Brookline, Mass. Died Feb. 14, 1938.

ROGERS, Arthur, clergyman; b. Providence, R.I., Oct. 26, 1864; s. Horatio and Lucia (Waterman) R.; A.B., Brown U., 1886, D.D., 1909; B.D., Cambridge Theol. Sch., 1889; m. Cornelia, dau. Samuel G. Arnold, Newport, R.I., June 16, 1892; children—Samuel Greene Arnold, Arthur Waterman, Paul Curtis, Horatio Rodman. Ordained priest P.E. Ch., 1889; rector St. George's Ch., Central Falls, R.I., 1892-99, Holy Trinity Ch., West Chester, Pa., 1899-1913, St. Mark's Ch., Evanston, Ill., 1913-30 (emeritus). Bohlen lecturer, Philadelphia, 1909; lecturer St. George's Sch., Newport, R.I., 1932—. Chaplain R.I. Society of Cincinnati. Author: Men and Movements in the English Church, 1898; Prophecy and Poetry; Studies in Isaiah and Browning, 1909. Home: Newport, R.I. Died June 1938.

ROGERS, Arthur Curtis, physician; b. nr. Decorah, Ia., July 17, 1856; s. Ansel and Cynthia (Benedict) R.; B.S., Earlham Coll., Richmond, Ind., 1877 (LL.D., 1905); M.D., State U. of Iowa, 1883; m. Phoebe Coffin, July 17, 1882. Supt. Minn. Sch. for Feeble-Minded and Colony for Epileptics, Faribault, 1885—. Chairman com. on defectives Nat. Conf. Charities and Correction, 1889 and 1902. Mem. numerous med. societies. Editor-in-chief Journal of Psycho-Asthenics. Home: Faribault, Minn. Died Jan. 2, 1917.

ROGERS, Arthur Kenyon, coll. prof.; b. Dunellen, N.J., December 27, 1868; s. William Augustus and Rebecca Jane (Titsworth) R.; A.B., Colby, 1891, Litt.D., 1916; Johns Hopkins, 1891-92; Hartford Sch. of Sociology, 1894-95; Ph.D., U. of Chicago, 1898; m. Helen Worthington Rogers, Aug. 24, 1895. Instr. Chicago Acad., 1893-94; asst. supt. Charity Organization Soc., Hartford, Conn., 1895-96; instr. philosophy and pedagogy, Alfred U., 1899-1900; prof. philosophy and education, Butler Coll., Indianapolis, 1900-10; prof. philosophy, U. of Mo., 1910-14, Yale U., 1914-20. Author: A Brief Introduction to Modern Philosophy, 1899; A Student's History of Philosophy, 1901; Essays in Critical Realism (in collaboration), 1920; English and American Philosophy Since 1800, 1922; Theory of Ethics, 1922; What Is Truth?, 1923; Morals in Review, 1927; The Socratic Problem, 1933; Ethics and Moral Tolerance, 1934. Home: Rockport, Mass. Deceased.

ROGERS, Austin Leonard, seedsman; b. Cape Vincent, N.Y., Oct. 29, 1855; s. Charles and Harriet (Wilson) R.; high sch., Watertown, N.Y.; grad. Eastman Business Coll., Poughkeepsie, N.Y., 1885; m. Della M. Guile, Aug. 1882 (died 1904); children—Mabel H. (Mrs. K. D. Rose, dec.), Inez A. (Mrs. A. H. Shearer); m. 2d, Elizabeth Mulvena, July 1911. Founder, 1876, with bro. Everett E., of Rogers Bros. Seed Co.; continued business under same title after death of brother, 1890, and pres. from incorporation, 1902; has specialized as breeder and grower of garden varieties of peas and beans. Originated 2 new peas, Rogers Green Seeded Admiral and Rogers Winner; also 2 new beans, Rogers Improved Kidney Wax and Rogers Stringless Refugee. Hon. mem. Am. Seed Assn. Republican. Presbyn. Mason. Home: Alpena, Mich. Died Oct. 19, 1937.

ROGERS, B(enjamin) Talbot, clergyman; b. Rockland, Mich., Aug. 3, 1865; s. Benjamin Talbot and Sarah Louise (Johnson) R.; B.L., Lawrence U., 1886, A.M., 1889; B.D., Nashotah House, 1889, D.D., 1907; m. Nellie Lum Mead, 1889. Deacon 1889, priest, 1889, P.E. Ch.; rector St. James' Ch., Manitowoc, Wis., 1889-93; warden Grafton Hall, Fond du Lac, Wis., 1893-1916, and canon St. Paul's Cathedral; warden Racine (Wis.) Coll., 1916-19; prof. ecclesiastical history, DeLancey Divinity School, Buffalo, N.Y.; historiographer, 1929-33, and asst. minister Trinity Ch., New York; mem. staff Cathedral of St. John the Divine. Mem. commn. to arrange for a World Conf. of Christian Churches, and deputation to Europe, Egypt, and Palestine; 9 times deputy to P.E. Gen. Conv.; del. World Conf. on Faith and Order, Lausanne, Switzerland, 1927; mem. Provincial Synods of Mid-West, 1916-19, of Washington, 1926-28, of N.Y. and N.J., 1930—. Editor Cathedral edit. Works of Bishop Grafton. Home: New York, N.Y. Died Sept. 21, 1934.

ROGERS, Cephas Brainerd, mfr.; b. Saybrook, Conn., Dec. 30, 1836; s. Hervey and Elizabeth Ann (Tryon) R.; ed. common schs., acad. and select schs.; m. Margaret Clark, June 8, 1870. Associated with two brothers in firm of C. Rogers & Bros., mfrs. silverware, 1866, inc., 1899, of which was sr. mem. and pres.; united with U.S. Silver Co., 1902, and sold out to Internat. Silver Co., and retired from active business, Jan. 1, 1903; trustee City Savings Bank. Trustee Wesleyan U. (Middletown, Conn.), Meriden Hosp. Mem. City Council, Meriden, 6 yrs. Republican. Lay del. M.E. Gen. Conf., 1900, 04, 16, res. del., 1908, 12; pres. trustees First M.E. Ch., Meriden, 30 yrs. Home: Meriden, Conn. Died Mar. 16, 1919.

ROGERS, Charles Butler, banker; b. Utica, N.Y., Jan. 23, 1865; s. Publius V. and Elizabeth (Butler) R.; Hamilton Coll., N.Y., 1883-86; A.B., Harvard, 1888; U. of Berlin, 1888, 89; LL.D., Hamilton, 1928; m. Eugenie Forgy, May 3, 1900 (dec.); children—Elizabeth Butler (dec.), Annette D., Philip V., Ralph. Began as clk. First Nat. Bank, Utica, 1889, asst. cashier, 1893, v.p., 1894, pres., 1894-1927, chmn. bd., 1927-28; chmn. bd. First Bank and Trust Co., 1928-31; chmn. bd. First Citizens Bank & Trust Co. (by merger) from Oct. 1931. Trustee and treas. Hamilton Coll. Home: Clinton, N.Y. Died Dec. 22, 1937.

ROGERS, Charles Custis, naval officer; b. Smyth Co., Va., May 11, 1856; s. Charles G. and Mary W. (Campbell) R.; grad. U.S. Naval Acad., 1876; m. Alice Ashmore Walker, Jan. 3, 1888. Promoted ensign, Apr. 26, 1878; advanced through grades to capt., Oct. 25, 1908. Exec. officer of Sesolute during Spanish-Am. War; comdt. Naval Sta., Guantanamo, Cuba, 1904-06; hydrographer, Navy Dept., 1906-08; comd. Milwaukee, 1908-09; comd. Washington, 1909-10; Navy Yard, Norfolk, 1910-11; comdt., Navy Yard, Portsmouth, N.H., 1911-14; retired on account of physical disability, with rank of rear admiral, Apr. 27, 1914. Awarded medal for action off Santiago de Cuba; clasp for action off Manzanillo, Cuba; medal for Spanish-Am. War. Home: Winchester, Va. Died Dec. 4, 1917.

ROGERS, Charles Darius, physician, U.S. dist. clerk, Alaska, 1893—; b. Troy, N.Y., Feb. 4, 1866; s. John D. and Mary L. (Russell) R.; acad. edn.; grad. Albany Med. Coll., 1888; m. Jessie L., d. Col. E. Hartshorn, Dec. 19, 1888; practiced profession 2 yrs., Binghamton, N.Y.; asst. surgeon, marine hosp. service, Sitka, Alaska, 1890-93. Chmn. Dem. Territorial Conv., Chicago, 1892; was mem. Dem. Nat. Com., Alaska. Mason. Home: Juneau, Alaska. Deceased.

ROGERS, Clara Kathleen (Clara Doria), singer; b. Cheltenham, Gloucestershire, Eng., Jan. 14, 1844; d. John ("Father of English opera") and Eliza Emily (Lindley) Barnett; grad. Leipzig Conservatorium, 1860; also studied at Berlin and Milan; m. Henry Munroe Rogers, Apr. 24, 1878. Début as Isabella, in "Robert the Devil," Turin, 1863; toured Italy in operas several yrs., later at London; came to U.S., 1871, and toured several yrs.; mem. faculty, N.E. Conservatory of Music, Boston, 1902—. Author: The Voice in Speech, 1915; Memories of a Musical Career, 1919; Your Voice and You, 1924; Clear Cut Speech in Song, 1927; also composer of much music. Died Mar. 8, 1931.

ROGERS, Edmund James Armstrong, physician; b. Grafton, Ont., Mar. 27, 1852; s. James G. and Maria (Burnham) R.; ed. Trinity Coll. Sch., Port Hope, Ont.; M.D., Med. Dept., McGill Univ., Montreal, 1881; licentiate Royal Coll. Phys. and Surg., Edinburgh; spent some yrs. at civ. engring.; m. M. Georgina D. Burrell, of Brighton, Ont., 1882. Has practiced medicine in Denver, 1882—; apptd. 3 terms State Bd. of Health (last 1897-1903); prof. surgery, U. of Colo.; surgeon to several hosps. Gov. Colo. Soc. Colonial Wars, 1900; pres. Colo. State Med. Soc., 1893-94. Home: Denver, Colo. Died July 3, 1922.

ROGERS, Eustace Barron, paymaster gen. U.S.N.; b. San Francisco, May 29, 1855; s. Robert Clay and Eliza Hamilton (Ritchie) R.; ed. Lehigh (Pa.) U., U. of California; m. Anna N. Alexander, Jan. 17, 1882 (died 1908); m. 2d, Marguerite Bosch, of Spa, Belgium, May 22, 1913. Apptd. from Calif. to U.S.N., Mar. 3, 1879; p.m., May 24, 1894; pay insp., Sept. 21, 1902; pay dir., Mar. 13, 1905; p.m. gen. with rank of rear admiral, Nov. 1, 1906, and chief Bur. of Supplies and Accounts; retired, June 30, 1910. Served on U.S.S. Monterey in Spanish-Am. War; was present at taking of Manila. On duty at Navy Yard, Bremerton, Wash., and with U.S. Shipping Bd., 1917, and gen. insp., Supply Corps, on Pacific Coast, to Jan. 1918. Home: Washington, D.C. Died Mar. 5, 1929.

ROGERS, Fairman, civil engr.; b. Philadelphia, Nov. 15, 1833; grad. Univ. of Pa., 1853; prof. civil engring. there, 1855-70; also lecturer on mechanics Franklin Inst., Philadelphia, 1853-65; in Union cavalry service, 1861, and later volunteer officer U.S. engrs.; completed survey of Potomac River northward from Blakiston Island, 1862. One of original members Nat. Acad. Sciences. Author: The Magnetism of Iron Vessels. Died 1900.

ROGERS, George Alfred, industrialist; b. Plattsburg, N.Y., Mar. 26, 1876; s. Robert H. and Hattie (Schutt) R.; LL.B., Cornell U., 1897; m. Ethel S. Benson, Mar. 26, 1907; children—Helen F., George A. (dec.), James B. Admitted to N.Y. bar, 1897; gen. engring. contractor, 1898-1922; moved to Los Angeles, Calif., 1905; organizer, 1922, and developer Union Rock Co., pres., 1922—; pres. Rogers Bros. Co.; v.p. District Bond Co., Morris Plan Co. Mason. Republican. Home: Los Angeles, Calif. Died July 26, 1936.

ROGERS, Harry Lovejoy, army officer; b. Washington, D.C., Jan. 29, 1867. Commd. maj. p.m., May 2, 1898; lt. col. dep. p.m. gen., Apr. 15, 1907; col. asst. p.m. gen., Mar. 4, 1909; brig. gen. Q.M. Corps, N.A., Aug. 5, 1917-Mar. 15, 1918; brig. gen. Q.M. Corps, U.S.A., Feb. 26, 1918; q.m. gen. with rank of maj. gen., July 22, 1918, term of 4 yrs. Served under Gen. Funston, in Vera Cruz Expdn., Apr. 1914; in charge later of supply problems of expdn. under Gen. Pershing, punitive expdn., Mexico, 1916; chief q.m. with A.E.F. in France, 1917-July 1918. Died Dec. 12, 1925.

ROGERS, Henry H., capitalist; b. Fairhaven, Mass.; one of large stockholders and v.p. and dir. Standard Oil Co.; pres. and dir. Amalgamated Copper Co., Nat. Transit Co., Nat. Fuel Gas Co., N.Y. Transit Co., Richmond Light & R.R. Co.; v.p. and trustee Anaconda Copper Mining Co.; v.p. and dir. Brooklyn Union Gas Co., United Metals Selling Co.; trustee Mut. Life Ins. Co. of N.Y.; dir. U.S. Steel Corp., Atchison, Topeka & Santa Fé R.R. Co., Chicago, Milwaukee & St. Paul Ry. Co., Union Pacific R.R. Co., etc. Has made many gifts to his native town, including a library, town hall, sch., ch., etc. Home: Fairhaven, Mass. Died 1909.

ROGERS, Henry Huddleston, capitalist; b. N.Y. City, Dec. 28, 1879; s. Henry Huddleston and Abbie Palmer (Gifford) R.; prep. edn. Berkeley Sch. and Browning Sch., New York; student Columbia, 1901; grad. Sch. of Fire, Ft. Sill, Okla., 1913; m. Mary Benjamin, Nov. 7, 1900; children—Mary Millicent, Henry Huddleston; m. 2d, Mrs. Basil Miles, 1929; m. 3d, Mrs. Pauline Van Der Voort Dresser, Aug. 28, 1933. Successively vice-pres. and gen. mgr. Atlantic Coast Electric R.R., Staten Island Midland R.R.; pres. Richmond Light & R.R. Co.; v.p. Virginian Ry. Co. Was 2d and 1st lt. and capt. inf., N.Y.N.G., 1904-09; 1st lt. engrs., 1909-11, capt., 1911, advanced to colonel 1st Field Arty., 1913, and directed to reorganize regt.; maj., later lt. col. arty., U.S.A., World War; served on Mexican border, 1916, later in comd. 3d F.A., O.T. Regt., and in Aisne-Marne offensive, July 1918, and Oise offensive, action at Veste, France. Decorated D.S.M. (U.S.), Croix de Guerre with Palm (France). Home: Southampton, L.I., N.Y. Died July 25, 1935.

ROGERS, Henry Munroe, lawyer; b. Boston, Feb. 27, 1839; s. John Hicks and Lucy C. (Smith) R.; A.B., Harvard, 1862, A.M., 1866, LL.B., 1867; m. Clara Kathleen Barnett, Apr. 24, 1878 (died 1931). Admitted to bar, 1868, and began practice at Boston; mem. Rogers & North, 1901-03; Rogers, North & Johnson, 1903-07; chmn. exec. com. U.S. Employers' Liability Assurance Corp., Ltd. until June 1933, mem. executive com., 1933—. Trustee Warren Chambers Trust, Eastern Point Co. Served in U.S.N., 1862-65. Hon. comdr. in chief Mil. Order Loyal Legion, 1933—. Author: Annals of the Commandery of the State of Massachusetts, 1918; Memories of Ninety Years, 1928; Adam and Eve and Other People (verses), 1935. Home: Boston, Mass. Died Mar. 29, 1937.

ROGERS, Henry Treat, lawyer; b. East Hartford, Conn., 1846; s. Martin L. and Jane S. (Treat) R.; B.A., Yale, 1866, M.A., 1869; m. Kate Secord, Thorold, Can., Sept. 10, 1873. Admitted to Ill. bar, 1869, and practiced at Chicago; settled in Denver, 1882; mem. Rogers, Johnson and Fuller; pres. Denver Bd. of Park Commrs., 1901-04; solicitor Colo. A.,T.&S.F. Ry. Co., 1906—; chmn. board and v.p. and counsel U.S. Nat. Bank, Denver; dir. Denver Gas & Electric Light Co. Republican. Unitarian. Home: Denver, Colo. Deceased.

ROGERS, Henry Wade, judge; b. at Holland Patent, N.Y., Oct. 10, 1853; A.B., U. of Mich., 1874; A.M., 1877; law student, 1876-77; LL.D., Wesleyan U. Conn., 1890, and Northwestern U., 1915; hon. A.M., Yale U., 1907; m. Emma Ferdon Winner, June 22, 1876 (died 1922). Admitted to bar, 1877; Tappan prof. law, 1883-90, dean, 1885-1900, lecturer on domestic relations and criminal law, 1890-91, U. of Mich.; pres. Northwestern U., 1890-1900; lecturer in Law Sch., Yale U., 1900-01, prof., 1901, dean, 1903-16; U.S. circuit judge, 2d Jud. Circuit, Sept. 1913—. Chmn. World's Congress on Jurisprudence and Law Reform, Chicago Expn., 1893. Gen. chmn. Saratoga Conf. on Foreign Policy of U.S., 1898; lay del. from M.E. Ch. to Gen. Conf. of M.E. Ch., S. Memphis, 1893; temp. and gen. chmn. Dem. State Conv., Conn., 1904; chmn. Am. Bar Assn. Sect. on Legal Edn., 1893; pres. Assn. of Am. Law Schs., 1906; pres. General Laymen's Assn. of M.E. Church, 1920—. Chmn. Judiciary Com. in Gen. Conf. of M.E. Ch., Baltimore, 1908, Minneapolis, 1912, Saratoga, 1916, Des Moines, 1920; mem. of Commn. on Organic Union of M.E. Ch. with M.E. Church, South, 1916-20; chmn. Com. on Internat. Relations in Fed. Council of the Chs., Phila., 1908; pres. Laymen's Assn. of N.Y. East Conf. M.E. Ch., 1910-12, Conn. Federation of Chs., 1910-11; chmn. Am. Bar Assn. Com. on Legal Edn. and Admission to the Bar, 1906-17, also 1919, and chmn. Council on Legal Edn., 1917-19; pres. Civic Fedn. of New Haven, 1909-11; apptd. by gov. of Conn. to Nat. Conf. on Uniform Laws, Washington, D.C., 1910, to Internat. Prison Congress, Washington, 1910; pres. Peace Congress N.E. States, Hartford, 1910; pres. Nat. Council of Schs. of Religion. Author: Illinois Citations, 1881; Expert Testimony, 1883; Introduction to Constitutional History as Seen in American Law, 1889. Joint Author: Two Centuries of American Law, 1901. Contbr. to London Times edit. of Ency. Britannica, 1902, and to American Supplement to Ency. Britannica, 1897. Asso. editor of Johnsons' Universal Cyclo., 1893; editor of article on Injunctions in American Cyclo. of Law; Introduction to Zoline's Federal Criminal Law and Procedure, 1921. Contbr. to Princeton Review, North American Review, Forum, and law jours. and revs. Nominated Simeon E. Baldwin for gov. of Conn., in Dem. State Conv., 1910, and for President, at Dem. Nat. Conv., Baltimore, 1912. Trustee Ch. Peace Union (Carnegie Foundation), 1913—. Address: New York, N.Y. Died Aug. 16, 1926.

ROGERS, Horatio, jurist; b. Providence, R.I., May 18, 1836; s. Horatio and Susan (Curtis) R.; grad. Brown U., 1855; LL.D., Trinity Coll., 1896; m. Lucia Waterman, January 28, 1861; m. 2d, Emily P. Smith, Oct. 6, 1869. Studied law in office of Hon. Thomas A. Jenckes, Providence, and at Harvard Law School; admitted to R.I. bar, Jan. 1858; served in Civil war, 1st lt. to maj., 3d R.I. heavy arty.; col. 11th R.I. vols.; col. 2d R.I. vols., and bvtd. brig. gen. U.S. vols. Successively justice police court, Providence, mem. and part of time pres. common council, Providence; mem. gen. assembly of R.I., 1864-67 and 1888-89; atty. gen. of R.I.; justice Supreme Court R.I., 1891-1903. Chmn. Record Commn., city of Providence. Author: Private Libraries of Providence, 1878; Mary Dyer of Rhode Island, the Quaker martyr, 1896. Edited Hadden's Journal and Orderly Books, 1884. Address: Providence, R.I. Died 1904.

ROGERS, Howard Jason, lawyer, exposition official; b. Stephentown, Rensselaer County, N.Y., Nov. 16, 1861; s. Edwin A. and Laura (Howard) R.; A.B., Williams Coll., 1884; hon. A.M., Columbia, 1904; LL.D., Northwestern U., 1904; m. Anne North Turner, Dec. 28, 1887; children—Kathryn Howard (wife of Wolcott E. Hall, U.S.N.), Edwin J. Admitted to bar, 1887; supt. N.Y. State ednl. exhibit, Chicago Expn.; deputy state supt. pub. instrn., N.Y., 1895-99; dir. dept. edn. and social economy of U.S. Commn. to Paris Expn., 1900; chief Dept. of Edn., St. Louis Expn.; 1st asst. commr., State Dept. Edn., N.Y.; dir. N.Y. State exhibit at Seattle Exposition, 1909; dir. Investment Co., New York, 1911; asso. dir. mil. relief Am. Red Cross, 1917; mgr. Atlantic Div. Am. Red Cross, 1919-22; exec. dir. New York Co. Chapter, Am. Red Cross, 1924—. Republican. Officer Legion of Honor (France); Chevalier of SS. Maurice and Lazarus (Italy); Chevalier Order of the North Star (Sweden); Chevalier Order of Leopold (Belgium); Officer Order Red Eagle (Germany); Chevalier Order of Rising Sun (Japan), Officer Polonia Restituta (Poland). Address: New York, N.Y. Died Sept. 28, 1927.

ROGERS, J(ames) Harris, inventor; b. Franklyn, Tenn., July 13, 1850; s. James Webb and Cornelia (Harris) R.; ed. under pvt. tutors and at St. Charles Coll., London, Eng.; D.Sc., Georgetown U., 1919, U. of Md., 1919; unmarried. Settled at Hyattsville, Md., 1895; devoted life to scientific work, especially elec. research; awarded many patents relating to multiplex and rapid printing telegraphy; electric lights; the telephone and radio telegraphy. Discoverer of visual synchronism; the secret telephone and underground and underwater radio communication, the latter enabling the U.S. Govt. to carry on uninterruptedly during the World War I, communication with the allied govts., also with submarines when submerged, and with battleships, aeroplanes, etc. Hon. fellow, Med. Acad. Sciences, 1919, also Inventor's Medal; extended thanks by Md. Legislature, 1919, "for distinguished contribution to science," also by Md. Legion of Honor. Democrat. Catholic. Home: Hyattsville, Md. Died Dec. 12, 1929.

ROGERS, James Harvey, economist; b. Society Hill, S.C., Sept. 25, 1886; s. John Terrel and Florence (Coker) R.; prep. edn., St. David's Acad., Society Hill, 1900-04; A.B., U. of S.C., 1906, B.S., M.A., 1907; A.B., Yale, 1909, M.A., 1913, Ph.D., 1916; LL.D., U. of South Carolina, 1934; grad. study U. of Geneva, Switzerland, 1914-15; unmarried. Instr. in economics, U. of Mo., 1916-17, asso. prof., 1919-20; asst. prof. economics, Cornell U., 1920-23; prof. economics, U. of Mo., 1923-30; prof. of polit. economy, Yale, 1930—; Sterling prof. polit. economy, Yale, 1931—; fellow Pierson Coll. Lecturer Geneva Sch. of Internat. Studies, 5 times, 1926-35. Statistician Council of Nat. Defense, Washington, 1917-18; mem. Economic Com. League of Nations, 1933-37; spl. rep. U.S. Treasury in China, Japan and India, 1934. Served as 1st lt. U.S.A., 1918-19. Author: Stock Speculation and the Money Market, 1927; The Process of Inflation in France (1914-27), 1929; Section on Foreign Markets and Foreign Credits of the Report of the Committee on Recent Economic Changes, of the President's Conference on Unemployment, 1929; America Weighs Her Gold, 1931. Address: New Haven, Conn. Died Aug. 13, 1939.

ROGERS, James Hotchkiss, pianist, organist; b. Fair Haven, Conn., Feb. 7, 1857; s. Martin L. and Harriet (Hotchkiss) R.; ed. Lake Forest, Ill.; studied music Berlin and Paris, 1875-80; m. Alice Abigail Hall, Oct. 20, 1891. Composer of about 300 compositions, including songs. piano pieces, anthems and part-songs; three cantatas: The Man of Nazareth; The New Life; The Mystery of Bethlehem; 40 organ pieces; 3 sonatas and suites; 2 Catholic Masses; 4 complete Jewish services; also piano studies and etudes with graded compositions for students. Home: Pasadena, Calif. Died Nov. 28, 1940.

ROGERS, Jason, publisher, author; b. N.Y. City, Aug. 5, 1868; s. Thomas and Emily Louise (Cauldwell) R.; ed. grammar sch., N.Y. City (left sch. before graduation); m. Marian F. Shillaber, Nov. 12, 1894; children—Penhallow (dec.), Walter Shillaber. Began as a boy in employ Sunday Mercury, New York; successively adv. mgr. Chicago Inter-Ocean, mgr. Providence (R.I.) News, asst. pub. and pub. N.Y. Globe; editor and pub. The Advertisers Weekly, 1924-26; gen. mgr. Kansas City Journal-Post, 1926-28. Organized The Associated Newspapers, 1911; organized what became the Bur. of Advertising of Am. Newspaper Publishers' Assn., 1912; formulated plan for the Audit Bur. of Circulations, 1913; traveled widely throughout the country, 1911—, promoting cooperative plans among newspapers; active in organizing Publishers Buying Corp.—group buying of print paper by 240 newspapers to defeat high prices exacted by paper combination; dir. publicity, Atlantic div., Am. Red Cross during World War I. Presbyn. Mason. Author: Newspaper Building, 1918; Building Newspaper Advertising, 1919; Fundamentals of Newspaper Building, 1919; Newspaper Making, 1920. Home: North Falmouth, Mass. Died Apr. 26, 1932.

ROGERS, John, sculptor; b. Salem, Mass., Oct. 30, 1829; s. John and Sarah Ellen (Derby) R.; ed. Boston public schools; m. Harriet M., d. C. S. Francis, April 26, 1865. Worked at various employments until began modeling small statuette groups, 1860, mostly war subjects, while the war lasted; later social subjects, which are known as "Rogers' Groups"; numbers of these have been reproduced in composition. In larger works, made statue of Gen. Reynolds for Phila., and one of Abraham Lincoln. Address: New Canaan, Conn. Died 1904.

ROGERS, John, surgeon; b. N. Y. City, Feb. 19, 1866; s. John and Harriet Moore (Francis) R.; A.B., Yale, 1887, Ph.B., 1888; M.D., Columbia, 1891; m. Elizabeth S. White, Nov. 27, 1895; children—John, Charles (dec.), Elizabeth S. Practice, New York, 1891—; instr. clin. surgery, 1898, prof., 1909—, Cornell U. Med. Coll.; surgeon St. Francis Hosp.; cons. surgeon Bellevue and Booth Memorial hosps. Home: New York, N.Y. Died Nov. 19, 1939.

ROGERS, John Henry, judge; b. in Bertie County, N.C., Oct. 9, 1845; s. Absalom and Harriet (Rice) R.; pvt. and 1st lt., 9th Miss. Inf., C.S.A., 1862-65; A.B., U. of Miss., 1868; LL.D., Centre Coll., Danville, Ky., 1895; m. Mary Gray Dunlap, Oct. 9, 1873. Admitted to bar, 1868; practiced at Ft. Smith, Ark., 1869-70; judge Circuit Ct., 1877-82; mem. 48th to 51st Congresses (1883-91); del. Dem. State Conv., 1892; chmn. Ark. delegation Dem. Nat. Conv., 1892; U.S. dist. judge, Western Dist. of Ark., 1896—. Address: Ft. Smith, Ark. Died 1911.

ROGERS, John Jacob, congressman; b. Lowell, Mass., Aug. 18, 1881; s. Jacob and Mary Howard (Carney) R.; A.B., Harvard, 1904, A.M., 1905, LL.B., 1907; m. Edith Frances Nourse, Oct. 2, 1907. In practice at Lowell, 1908—; trustee Mechanics Savings Bank. Dir. Traders & Mechanics Ins. Co., Lowell Morris Plan Bank. Mem. Lowell city govt., 1911, Sch. Com., 1912; mem. 63d to 68th Congresses (1913-25), 5th Mass. Dist. Republican. Second lt., Co. K, 6th Mass. Inf. from orgn. to 1908; 1st lt. until 1910 (resigned). Pvt. field artillery, U.S.A., 1918. Trustee Rogers Hall Sch., Old Ladies' Home, Westford (Mass.) Acad. Conglist. Home: Lowell, Mass. Died Mar. 28, 1925.

ROGERS, John Rankin, gov. Wash.; b. Brunswick, Me., Sept. 4, 1838; common school edn.; m. Sarah L. Greene, 1861. In drug store at Boston, 1852-56; mgr. of drug store, Jackson, Miss., 1856; school teacher and farmer, Ill., 1860-66; farmer and druggist, 1866-76. Went to Kan., 1876; engaged in farming; became Farmers' Alliance organizer, 1878; later editor Kansas Commoner, Wichita; held several minor offices. Removed to Washington, 1890; mem. Wash. State legislature, 1894; 7 times elected to office; never defeated; gov., 1896-1900, 1900-04. Author: The Irrepressible Conflict; Looking Forward; The Inalienable Rights of Man; etc. Address: Olympia, Wash. Died 1901.

ROGERS, John Raphael, inventor; b. Roseville, Ill., Dec. 11, 1856; s. Rev. John A. and Elizabeth Lewis (Embree) R.; A.B., Oberlin Coll., 1875, A.M., 1898, D.Sc., 1930; LL.D., Berea (Ky.) Coll., 1919; m. Clara A. Saxton, Dec. 25, 1878. Teacher and supt. pub. schs., 1875-86; civ. engr., 1886-88; patented machine for setting type (the Rogers Typograph), 1888, and later granted between 400 and 500 patents on typesetting machines, in U.S. and foreign countries. Pres. Internat. Typograph. Co.; chief inventor in charge experimental dept., Mergenthaler Linotype Co. Trustee Berea Coll. (Ky.), Oberlin Coll. Independent Republican. Conglist. Home: Brooklyn, N.Y. Died Feb. 18, 1934.

ROGERS, Joseph Morgan, editor; b. Decatur, O., Apr. 9, 1861; s. Rev. John A. and Elizabeth Lewis (Embree) R.; brother of John Raphael R.; A.B., Berea Coll., 1879, A.M., 1897; m. Annah Teresa Sides, Apr. 25, 1889. In Indian service, 1880-81; civ. engr. and editor Shawano (Wis.) Journal, 1881-84; financial editor Philadelphia Times, 1885-86; city editor Wilmington (Del.) News, 1886-87; financial editor Philadelphia North American, 1887-88; news editor Philadelphia Times, 1888-89; mng. editor Philadelphia Inquirer, 1889-99; Sunday editor New York Herald, and part of time mng. editor Telegram, 1899-1900; on staff McClure's Magazine, 1900-01; on Phila. Inquirer, 1901—. Episcopalian. Republican. Author: History of the United States, 1899; The True Henry Clay, 1904; Life of Thomas H. Benton, 1905; Development of the North since the Civil War, 1906; A History of Grand Opera in Philadelphia; A History of the Civil War; History of the Battle of Gettysburg. Home: Germantown, Pa. Died May 16, 1922.

ROGERS, Max, comedian. Played with bro. Gus. (died 1908) as Rogers Brothers; first appeared in song and dance, at National Theatre, Bowery, New York, 1885; organized own company, 1893; entered upon series of vaudeville comedies, 1899; toured as Howard Swift, Jr., in "The Young Turk," 1909, later playing same part in New York Theatre. Home: New York, N.Y. Died Dec. 24, 1932.

ROGERS, Oscar H., M.D.; b. Green Island, N.Y., Sept. 6, 1857; s. William Clute and Susan (Harrison) R.; prep. edn. Troy (N.Y.) Acad.; C.E., Union U., 1877, Sc.D., 1932; M.D., Coll. Phys. and Surg. (Columbia), 1883; Sc.D., Columbia, 1930; m. Helen E. Carley, April 27, 1887; m. 2d, Florence Scribner Stauffer, Dec. 2, 1916. Practiced as civil engineer, 1878-80, in general practice of medicine, New York, 1883-90; med. examiner, 1890-93, asst. med. dir., 1893-1902, med. dir., 1902-12, chief med. dir., 1912-30, New York Life Ins. Co. Sec., 1894-1900, pres., 1906-08, Assn. Life Ins. Medical Directors (mem. medico-actuarial committee, 1907—). In collaboration with Actuaries Weeks, Frankland, and Hunter, originated and developed a scientific method of med. selection by means of which is offered on equitable terms to sub-standard as well as standard risks, the first successful attempt to establish med. selection upon a scientific foundation; also devised the "Dr. Rogers tycos sphygmomanometer" and the cloth bandage used with it in the taking of blood-pressure. Contbr. many papers on med. subjects. Home: Yonkers, N.Y. Died May 17, 1941.

ROGERS, Philip Fletcher, surgeon; b. Milwaukee, Aug. 14, 1870; s. George James and Mary M. (Hanson) R.; A.B., Yale, 1894; M.D., Northwestern U., 1897; interne Mercy Hosp., Chicago, 1897-99; m. Cornelia Meinhardt, Oct. 25, 1900; children—Philip M., Antoinette M., Albert Francis. Practiced, Milwaukee, 1899—. Surgeon to Emergency, Mt. Sinai, and Columbia hosps. of Milwaukee. Conglist. Commd. capt. Med. Dept. U.S.A., July 10, 1917; on surg. staff Base Hosp. No. 22, in France, June 15, 1918-Mar. 19, 1919. Maj. O.R.C., 1922. Home: Milwaukee, Wis. Died June 20, 1928.

ROGERS, Robert Cameron, author; b. Buffalo, N.Y., Jan. 7, 1862; s. Sherman S. R.; B.A., Yale, 1883; married. Editor Santa Barbara (Calif.) Morning Press. Occasional contbr. to Harper's Weekly and Buffalo Express. Author: Wind in the Clearing, and Other Poems; Will o' the Wasp; Old Dorset; Chronicles of a New York Country Side; For the King, and Other Poems, 1899; The Rosary and Other Poems, 1906. Address: Santa Barbara, Calif. Died Apr. 20, 1912.

ROGERS, Robert Emmons, prof. English; b. Haddonfield, N.J., Apr. 12, 1888; s. Charles Merrill and Mary Ellen (Pickup) R.; prep. edn., Cambridge (Mass.) Latin Sch.; A.B. and A.M., Harvard, 1909; m. Marie Baer, Jan. 23, 1918; 1 dau., Marie Desiree Baer. Instr. in English, Williams Coll., 1909-10; in theatrical business with Maude Adams Co., 1910-11; with Brooklyn (N.Y.) Eagle, 1911-12; instr. in English, Mass. Inst. Tech., 1913-17, asst. prof., 1917-23, asso. prof., 1923-34, prof., 1934—; lecturer in Massachusetts U. Extension, 1920—; columnist Boston Evening American, 1930-38. Editor Tech. Review, 1917-22; editor Creative Reading, 1927-31. Author: Behind a Watteau Picture (play), 1918; The Voice of Science in 19th Century Literature (anthology), 1920; The Fine Art of Reading, 1929; How to Be Interesting, 1931. Home: Cambridge, Mass. Died May 13, 1941.

ROGERS, Robert William, Orientalist; b. Phila., Feb. 14, 1864; s. Dr. Samuel and Mary (Osborne) R.; grad. Central High Sch., Phila., 1880; A.B., U. of Pa., 1886; A.B., Johns Hopkins, 1887; Ph.D., Haverford, 1890; Ph.D., Leipzig, 1895; D.D., Wesleyan, Conn., 1894; LL.D., Baker U., 1899, Neb. Wesleyan, 1899; Litt.D., Dickinson, 1908, U. of Dublin, Ireland, 1914, U. of Oxford, 1923, U. of Pa., 1925; m. Ida Virginia Ziegler, June 3, 1891; children—Elizabeth Frances, Robert Samuel. Instr. Greek and Hebrew, Haverford, 1887-88; prof. English Bible and Semitic history, Dickinson Coll., Pa., 1890-92; prof. Hebrew and O.T. exegesis, Drew U., 1893-1929; retired. Mem. numerous Oriental and archæol. socs., Am. and foreign. Mem. congresses of Orientalists at Stockholm and Christiania, 1889, London, 1892, Geneva, 1894, Paris, 1897, Hamburg, 1902, Copenhagen 1908. Author: Two Texts of Esarhaddon, 1889; Catalogue of Manuscripts, 1890; Inscriptions of Sennacherib, 1893; Outlines of the History of Early Babylonia, 1895; History of Babylonia and Assyria, 2 vols., 1900; The Religion of Babylonia and Assyria, 1909; Cuneiform Parallels to the Old Testament, 1912; The Recovery of the Ancient Orient, 1912; History and Literature of the Hebrew People, 1917; Great Characters of the Old Testament, 1920; Old Testament Lessons—A Lectionary, 2 vols., 1921; History of Ancient Persia, 1929. Instr. Columbia, summer sessions, 1915-21; prof. of ancient Oriental lit., Princeton, 1919-29. Life mem. St. John's Coll., Oxford. Home: Chadds Ford, Pa. Died Dec. 12, 1930.

ROGERS, Sherman S., lawyer; b. Bath, Steuben County, N.Y., Apr. 16, 1830; ed. public schools; admitted to N.Y. bar, May 1851; practiced at Bath until 1854; at Buffalo, 1854—; m. Christina Cameron Davenport, Jan. 1858 (died 1897). Twice pres. State Bar Assn.; mem. N.Y. constitutional convention, 1873; State senator, 1876; Rep. candidate for lt. gov., 1876; mem. law firm Rogers, Locke & Milburn. Address: Buffalo, N.Y. Died 1900.

ROGERS, Warren Lincoln, bishop; b. Allentown, N.J., Nov. 14, 1877; s. Samuel Hartshorne and Josephine (Lincoln) R.; B.A., U. of Mich., 1907; B.D., Union Theol. Sem., 1911; B.D., Gen. Theol. Sem., 1912; D.D., Kenyon Coll., 1925; Dr. Sacred Theology, Columbia, 1935; D.D., U. of the South, Sewanee, Tenn., 1936; m. Helen Clingen Speakman, June 29, 1911 (died 1919). Deacon and priest P.E. Ch., 1911; rector St. Thomas Ch., Detroit, Mich., 1911, 12; asso. rector Calvary Ch., Pittsburgh, Pa., 1913-16; rector St. John's Ch., Jersey City, N.J., 1916-20; dean St. Paul's Cathedral, Detroit, 1920-25; coadjutor bishop P.E. Ch., Apr. 30, 1925, bishop, Sept. 1930. Mem. Nat. Council P.E. Ch., 1929. Trustee Kenyon Coll., Western Reserve U., Lake Erie Coll. for Women, Church Pension Fund. Republican. Mason; Grand Prelate and mem. Supreme Council, K.T. of Ohio. Address: Cleveland, O. Died Nov. 6, 1938.

ROGERS, Weaver Henry, corporate financing; b. Pittsburgh, Pa., Nov. 9, 1876; s. Joseph Butcher and Margaret Thompson (Matthews) R.; desc. of Colonial ancestry; grad. U. of Pittsburgh, 1896; m. Analdean Friebertshauser, May 22, 1901; children—Dorothy Analdean (Mrs. Lloyd Hornbostel), Virginia Emily (Mrs. Nathan H. White). Became sec. and treas. of the Pittsburgh and Birmingham Traction Co., 1898; later connected with Mellon pub. utility corps. and with Gulf Refining Co.; an organizer Pittsburgh & Butler Ry. Co., Andrews Steel Co., Weaver H. Rogers & Co., etc.; served as v.p. underlying pub. utility corps. of West Penn Co. Maj. Ordnance Dept., U.S.A., World War; with Gen. staff at Tours, France, 1918; mustered out as lt. col., 1919; served as emergency adminstrn. chief, Watertown (Mass.) Arsenal. Pres. 14th Ward Bd. of Edn. Republican. Episcopalian; trustee and sec. bd. Ch. Home Assn. of W.Pa.; trustee Clergy Life Ins. Assn., Roselia Foundling Asylum and Maternity Hosp.; trustee Diocesan Council of Pittsburgh; pres. Ch. Club of Western Pa.; vestryman Ch. of the Redeemer. Mason. Home: Pittsburgh, Pa. Died Feb. 17, 1936.

ROGERS, Will, humorist; b. Oologah, I.T., Nov. 4, 1879; s. Clem Vann and Mary (Schrimpsher) R.; ed. Willie Hassell Sch., Neosho, Mo.; Kemper Mil. Acad., Boonville, short time; m. Betty Blake, Nov. 25, 1908; children—Will, Mary, Jim. Began in vaudeville at Hammerstein's Roof Garden, New York, 1905; with Ziegfeld's Follies, and Night Frolics, 1914—, except 3 yrs. in moving pictures; toured as lecturer; engaged in making talking pictures for Fox Co. Methodist. Mason, Elk. Author: Rogerisms—The Cowboy Philosopher on Prohibition, 1919; Rogerisms—The Cowboy Philosopher on the Peace Conference, 1919; Rogerisms—What We Laugh At, 1920; Illiterate Digest, 1924; Letters of a Self-Made Diplomat to His President; There's Not a Bathing Suit in Russia, 1927. Home: Beverly Hills, Calif. Died Aug. 15, 1935.

ROGERS, William Allen, cartoonist; b. Springfield, O., May 23, 1854; s. William Allen and Elizabeth (Smith) R.; ed. Worcester Poly. Inst. (non-grad.); m. Sarah Benson, Apr. 10, 1879. Illustrator and cartoonist Daily Graphic, New York, 1873-77, later for Harper's Weekly, Harper's Mag., Life, St. Nicholas, Century, etc. Mem. bd. dirs. Sch. for Disabled Soldiers. Decorated Chevalier Legion of Honor, France, on account of cartoons appearing in the Herald (New York and Paris) during World War I. Author: Hits at Politics (cartoons); America's Black and White Book (cartoons), 1917; A World Worth While, 1922; Danny's Partner, 1923; A Miracle Mine, 1925. Address: Washington, D.C. Died Oct. 20, 1931.

ROGERS, William Banks, clergyman; b. Cincinnati, Dec. 7, 1857; s. Joseph Hill and Mary Rose (McIlvain) R.; acad. and coll. course, St. Xavier's Coll., 1869-75, St. Stanislaus Sem., Normal, Florissant, Mo., 1875-79, Woodstock Coll., Md., philosophy, science, 1879-81; Louvain, Belgium, metaphysics, ethics, 1881-82; Woodstock Coll., theology, 1887-91. Taught English and classics, St. Ignatius Coll., Chicago, 1882-84, St. Xavier's Coll., Cincinnati, 1884-87; ordained R.C. priest, 1890. Prefect studies St. Xavier's Coll., Cincinnati, 1891-92, Marquette Coll., Milwaukee, 1893-95, St. Louis U., 1896-98; pres. Marquette Coll., 1898-1900, St. Louis U., 1900-08; resigned Feb. 1908, on account of ill health. In 1903 secured Marion-Sims-Beaumont Coll. of Medicine, St. Louis, as med. dept. St. Louis U. Address: Milford, O. Died July 28, 1937.

ROGERS, William Boddie, surgeon; b. Brownsville, Tenn., Nov. 22, 1856; s. William Egbert and Elizabeth (Battle) R.; common schs., Memphis; M.D., Bellevue Hosp. Med. Coll., New York, 1878; m. Kate Henderson Chalmers, Feb. 23, 1884. Demonstrator anatomy, 1878-79, prof. anatomy, 1880-81, prof. surgery and dean, 1886—, Memphis Hosp. Med. Coll.; pres. Memphis Bd. Health, 1891-92. Dir. Memphis St. Ry. Co., Atlas Mortgage & Trust Co. Democrat. Episcopalian. Mason. Home: Memphis, Tenn. Deceased.

ROGERS, William King, physician; b. Hastings, Minn., July 14, 1863; s. William King and Mary Lord (Andrews) R.; M.D., Univ. Med. Coll. (New York U.), 1889; m. Theodora Isabel Wormley, Dec. 14, 1898. Interne St. Luke's Hosp., New York, 1891-93; removed to Columbus, O., 1893; prof. otology, med. dept. Ohio State U., 1900—; attending surgeon (eye, ear, nose and throat service), Mt. Carmel and St. Francis hosps.; cons. surgeon, Children's Hosp. Pres. Ohio State Bd. for Relief and Benefit of Needy Blind. Republican. Home: Columbus, O. Died Oct. 9, 1921.

ROGERS, William Pennock, brig. gen. U.S.A.; b. Harford County, Md., Sept. 16, 1842; s. Elisha Hartshorne and Anna (Pennock) R.; ed. Aldino pub. sch.; m. Dee Browning, 1878. Corporal Co. H, 7th Md. Inf., Aug. 21, 1862; discharged, May 4, 1865; apptd. from Md., 2d lt. 44th U.S. Inf., July 28, 1866; transferred to 17th Inf., May 27, 1869; 1st lt., Oct. 3, 1872; capt., Dec. 23, 1884; maj. 20th Inf., Dec. 15, 1898; lt. col. 29th Inf., Feb. 2 1901; transferred to 22d Inf., Mar. 21, 1901; col. 30th Inf., June 28, 1902; brig. gen., Apr. 20, 1903; retired at own request, over 30 yrs.' service, Apr. 21, 1903. Served in Army of the Potomac; participated in battle of Spottsylvania C.H., May 8, 1864, where was wounded, losing left arm; served in South, 1866-70, in West, 1870-94; wounded in affair with Sioux Indians, on Heart River, Dak., Oct. 3, 1872. Address: San Antonio, Tex. Died May 12, 1916.

ROGERS, William Perry, univ. dean; b. nr. Bloomington, Ind., Mar. 3, 1857; s. William K. and Sarah (Boruff) R.; student Ind. U., 1877-80, LL.B., 1892, A.B., 1895; law student Columbia, 1895; LL.D., U. of Cincinnati, 1908; LL.D., Miami U., 1913; m. E. Belle Clark, of Bloomington, Mar. 30, 1881. Admitted to bar, 1881; practiced at Bloomington, 1881-92; prof. law, 1892-1902, dean Law Sch., 1896-1902, Ind. U.; G. H. Wald prof. law of contracts and dean, Cincinnati Law Sch. (Coll. of Law U. of Cincinnati), 1902—. City treas., Bloomington, 2 terms, 1881-85. Republican. Pres. Assn. Am. Law Schs., 1906-07. Author articles on "Guaranty" in Cyclo. of Law; on "Damages" in Modern Am. Law. Practicing law, Cincinnati, 1916—. Address: Cincinnati, O. Died Oct. 9, 1921.

ROGERSON, Charles Edward, banker; b. Boston, Sept. 29, 1855; s. Robert and Mary (Ball) R.; ed. pub. schs., Boston; m. Anne G. Johnson, June 10, 1880. Pres. Boston Safe Deposit & Trust Co., Nevins Co.; v.p. Saco-Lowell Shops; trustee Franklin Savings Bank; dir. Methuen Co., Pemberton Co., Stevens Linen Wks., Warwick Mills, Boston Storage Warehouse Co. President Com. Permanent Charity Fund, Inc.; v.p. Kitson Machine Shop; treas. Rest House, Inc.; mem. advisory bd. and custodian Frances E. Willard Settlement; dir. and trustee Permanent Funds of Mass. Soc. Prevention of Cruelty to Animals; mem. Boston Directorate, Guarantee Co. of N. America. Republican. Home: Milton, Mass. Died Feb. 3, 1932.

ROHBACH, James Alexander, prof. law; b. Northumberland County, Pa., May 23, 1864; s. Elias Philip (maj. U.S.A.) and Linda (Ryland) R.; student Susquehanna U., Selinsgrove, Pa., 1877-80; A.B., Western Reserve U., 1884, A.M., 1890; LL.B., State U. of Ia., 1893; LL.D., U. of Indianapolis, 1914; m. Louise W. Young, Jan. 4, 1893; 1 dau., Eleanor Young (dec.). Prin. high schs., Pa., 1884-90; admitted to Pa. bar, 1889, and began practice at Lewisburg; dist. atty. Union County, Pa., 1891-92; asst. prof. law, State U. of Ia., 1892-94, prof., 1894-99, also sec. of faculty, 1892-99; prof. law and sec. Ind. Law Sch., U. of Indianapolis, 1899—, dean, 1901—; lecturer on business law, Butler U., 1920—, De Pauw U., 1922—. Lt. col. and a.d.c., staffs of Govs. Jackson and Drake, Ia., 1894-98. Home: Plainfield, Ind. Died Aug. 30, 1930.

ROHE, Charles Henry, clergyman, author; b. Syracuse, N.Y., May 20, 1846; ed. Crete, Ill., public schools and Concordia Coll., Ft. Wayne, Ind.; grad. Concordia Coll., Ft. Wayne, Ind.; grad. Concordia Theol. Sem., St. Louis, 1870; m. Caroline J. Welge, 1870; m. 2d, Amelia L. Barth, 1883. Pastor Joliet, Ill., 1870-78; Detroit, Mich., 1878-82; resigned because of broken health; traveled in Europe summer of 1882; pastor Trinity Luth. Ch., Columbus, Oct. 1882—. Editor Lutherische Kirchenzeitung, Columbus, 2 yrs.; pres. Gen. Mission Bd., Ohio Synod, 15 yrs. Author of several novels, stories and 2 vols. of verse. Home: Columbus, O. Deceased.

ROHÉ, George Henry, supt. Md. State Hosp. for the Insane; b. Baltimore County, Md., Jan. 26, 1851; grad. U. of Md., M.D., 1873; A.M., Loyola Coll., Baltimore, 1895; practiced medicine in Baltimore; commr. of health, Baltimore, 1890-91; pres. Am. Public Health Assn., 1898; sec. Rush Monument Committee; m. Mary Laudermann Coffin, Jan. 18, 1890. Author: Text Book of Hygiene; Electricity in Medicine and Surgery; Handbook of Skin Diseases. Address: Sykesville, Md. Died 1899.

ROHLFS, Anna Katharine Green, author; b. Brooklyn, Nov. 11, 1846; d. James Wilson and Katherine Ann (Whitney) Green; B.A., Ripley Female Coll., Poultney, Vt., 1867; m. Charles Rohlfs, Nov. 1884; children—Rosamond (Mrs. Robert T. Palmer, deceased), Sterling (deceased), Roland. Author: The Leavenworth Case; A Strange Disappearance; The Sword of Damocles; Hand and Ring; The Mill Mystery; Marked "Personal"; Miss Hurd—an Enigma; Behind Closed Doors; Cynthia Wakeham's Money; Dr. Izard; Old Stone House, and Other Stories; 7 to 12; X, Y, Z; The Doctor, His Wife and the Clock; That Affair Next Door; Lost Man's Lane; Agatha Webb; Risifi's Daughter, a Drama; The Defense of the Bride (dramatic poem); A Difficult Problem, and Other Stories; The Circular Study; One of My Sons; The Filigree Ball; House in the Mist, 1905; The Millionaire Baby, 1905; The Amethyst Box, 1905; The Woman in the Alcove, 1906; The Chief Legatee, 1907; The Mayor's Wife, 1907; Three Thousand Dollars, 1909; The House of the Whispering Pines, 1910; Initials Only, 1911; Masterpieces of Mystery, 1912; Golden Slipper and Other Problems for Violet Strange, 1915; Mystery of the Hasty Arrow, 1917; The Step on the Stair, 1922. Dramatized The Leavenworth Case, 1892. Address: Buffalo, N.Y. Died Apr. 11, 1935.

ROHLFS, Charles, designer of furniture; b. New York, Feb. 1853; s. Peter and Fredericka Wilhelmina Dorothea (Hunte) R.; an actor for a number of yrs. with Booth and other tragedians; m. Anna Katharine Green, Nov. 1884; children—Rosamond (Mrs. R. T. Palmer, dec.), Sterling (dec.), Roland. Commenced making furniture for his own home in 1889, finally developing a new and distinctive style both as to form and ornamental design, now known as the "Rohlfs" furniture, with patronage in Europe as well as U.S. Home: Buffalo, N.Y. Died June 29, 1936.

ROHN, Oscar, mining engr.; b. Jackson, Wis., June 27, 1870; s. Frederick O. and Janette (Wilke) R.; B.S., U. of Wis., 1895; m. Mary E. Couse, May 19, 1896; m. 2d, Lou Foster Lauzier, Dec. 23, 1919. In govt. work on Alaskan exploration, 1898-99; examination of iron lands in Minn., 1900-01; mgr. Donora Mining Co., Duluth, Minn., 1902-03; cons. mining engr., 1903-06; mgr. Pittsburgh & Mont. Copper Co., 1906-09, E. Butte Copper Mining Co., 1909—. Mem. Am. Inst. Mining and Metall. Engrs., Lake Superior Mining Inst. Wrote: Report on Chittina River and Mt. Wrangell Dist., Alaska, 22d Ann. Report U.S. Geol. Survey; also articles in tech. jours. Address: Denver, Colo. Died Sept. 19, 1923.

ROHRER, Karl, commodore U.S.N.; b. Am Randen-Blumberg, Baden, Germany, Jan. 28, 1848; s. Philip and Anna Maria (Durst) R.; came to U.S., 1857; grad. U.S. Naval Acad., 1869; m. Charlotte Haight Arthur, Apr. 24, 1877. Apptd. midshipman U.S.N., 1869; promoted through various grades to commodore and retired, June 30, 1906. Home: Washington, D.C. Died May 29, 1913.

ROHWER, Henry, engineer; b. nr. Rendsburg, Holstein, Germany, Oct. 17, 1847; s. Henry and Margarete (Rohwer) R.; grad. Dr. Jessen's Poly. Inst., Hamburg, 1865; student Royal Poly. Sch., Hanover, 1865-69; came to U.S., 1869; m. Anna Sievers, Oct. 8, 1873. Topographer, chief draftsman, engr. in charge constrn., and chief engr. Burlington & Mo. River R.R., 1869-74, in Neb., and 1872, also resident engr. at Omaha of Omaha & S.W. Ry.; city engr. of Omaha, Neb., 1876-81; div. engr. locating and constructing Oregon Short Line (then branch of U.P. Ry.); engr. in charge of tunnel and later resident engr. and engr. maintenance of way, same line, 1881-85; engr. in charge location and constrn. Omaha Belt Ry. and Mo.P. extension to Omaha and Lincoln, Neb., 1885-87; assistant engineer in charge of maintenance of way M.P. Ry., Sedalia, Mo., 1887-1901; chief engr., 1901-05, cons. engr., 1905-06, same system; pvt. consulting civ. engr., 1906—. Chmn. bd. engrs. Miss. River Bridge at Thebes; mem. bd. chief engrs. for new Union Depot and terminals, Kansas City; chmn. com. engrs. for City of St. Louis, 1908, to locate municipal bridge across

Miss. River. Republican. Evang. Lutheran. Home: St. Louis, Mo. Died May 4, 1916.

ROJAS, P(edro) Ezequiel, diplomat; b. Cumana, Venezuela, Oct. 1, 1844. Identified with politics since his youth; acted as newspaperman, legislative representative, senator, pres. of Nat. Congress, and represented Venezuela in Chili, and Argentine Republic; compelled to live in exile many yrs. during oppressive govts. in his country. Minister of foreign affairs, 1893-98; E.E. and M.P. to U.S., 1900—. Decorated with Bust of Bolivar, Great Cross of St. Gregory, Prussian Crown, etc. Died June 26, 1914.

ROLAPP, Henry Hermann, lawyer; b. Flensburg, Germany, Mar. 22, 1860; s. Fritz and Anna (Thiesen) R.; ed. German grammar sch. and Realschule; LL.B., U. of Mich., 1884; m. Martha Horrocks, Dec. 9, 1885; children—Franklin H., Karl H. (dec.), Mrs. May Belle Ballif, Katherine (dec.), Walter H. Left Germany, 1877, lived in Liverpool, Eng., until 1880; settled in Salt Lake City, June 1880; admitted to bar, 1881; practiced law, Ogden, Utah, 1884-95; assessor, 1885-87, asst. county atty., 1887-91, Weber County, Utah; mem. State Bd. Corrections, 1888-95; Supreme Court jury commr., 1888-95; apptd. justice Supreme Court of Utah Ty., Nov. 1895; when Utah was admitted as a state, Jan. 1, 1896, was elected judge 2d Judicial District, Utah, serving until Jan. 1, 1905. Regent U. of Utah, 1908-14, and 1925—. Pres. Securities Corp., Los Angeles; dir. Amalgamated Sugar Co. Treas. U.S. Food Adminstrn. Sugar Distributing Com. Mormon. Address: Los Angeles, Calif. Died Jan. 8, 1936.

ROLFE, Charles Wesley, geologist; b. Arlington Heights, Ill., Apr. 17, 1850; s. Charles Wesley and Melissa Deete (Haven) R.; B.S., U. of Ill., 1872, M.S., 1878; m. Martha Kinsman Farley, Dec. 26, 1877; children—Deette, Mary A., Susan F. (Mrs. H. G. Butler), Amy L. (Mrs. A. E. Emerson). Instr. in science, U. of Ill., 1872-73; prin. schs., Sidney, Ill., 1873-74; teacher sciences, Jennings Sem., Aurora, Ill., 1874-76; prin. schs., Waterman, Ill., 1876-77; supt. schs., Kankakee, Ill., 1877-81; prep. dept., U. of Ill., 1881-85, prof. geology, 1885-1917, prof. emeritus, 1917—, U. of Ill., dir. ceramics, 1904-10. Home: Champaign, Ill. Died Apr. 5, 1934.

ROLFE, John Furman, newspaper pub.; b. Lawrenceville, Pa., May 12, 1880; s. Maro O. and Alice Estelle (Potter) R.; grad. Elmira (N.Y.) Business Coll., 1898; m. Bertha Emily Butterworth, Oct. 12, 1903. Corr. and news editor Elmira Advertiser, 1898-1901; city editor Corning (N.Y.) Leader, 1901-03, mng. editor, 1903-10, editor, 1910-12, advertising mgr., 1912-14, business mgr., 1914-28; treas. and dir. Corning Printing Co., 1910-28; gen. mgr. Hartford (Conn.) Times, 1928-29, pub., 1929—, treas. and dir., 1928—. Dir. Corning Bus. Inst., Wilbraham (Mass.) Acad., Long Meadows (Mass.) Day Sch., Hartford Hilyer Vocation Schs., Hartford Y.M.C.A., Hartford County Y.M.C.A., Travelers' Aid, Almada-Times Farm, Hartford Community Chest. Mem. U.S. Chamber Commerce, Am. Acad. Polit. Science. Episcopalian. Co-author of Men and Personality Series, 1926. Home: West Hartford, Conn. Died Mar. 20, 1937.

ROLFE, William James, Shakespearean scholar; b. Newburyport, Mass., Dec. 10, 1827; s. John and Lydia Davis (Moulton) R.; A.B., Amherst, 1849, A.M., 1865; hon. A.M., Harvard, 1859; Litt.D., Amherst, 1887; m. Eliza Jane Carew, July 30, 1856; father of John Carew R. Head master in high schs., Dorchester, Lawrence, Salem and Cambridge, Mass., 1852-68; pres. Emerson Coll. of Oratory, Boston, 1904-08. Editor: Craik's English of Shakespeare, 1867; Complete edition of Shakespeare, 40 vols., 1870-83; Tales from English History, 1888; Fairy Tales, 1889; Tales from Scottish History, 1891; Lamb's Tales from Shakespeare, 2 vols., 1892; complete edit. of Tennyson, 12 vols., 1895-98; New Edit. of Shakespeare, 40 vols., 1903-07. Author: Cambridge Course of Physics (with J. A. Gillet), 8 vols., 1868-72; Satchel Guide to Europe (revised yearly), 1872-1907; Shakespeare the Boy, 1896; Elementary Study of English, 1896; Life of Shakespeare, 1902; Shakespeare Proverbs, 1908. Address: Cambridge, Mass. Died 1910.

ROLLER, Robert Douglas, Jr., M.D.; b. Richmond, Va., May 24, 1879; s. Robert Douglas and Caroline (Booker) R.; A.B., W.Va. U., 1900; M.D., Univ. Coll. of Medicine (now Med. Coll. of Va.), Richmond, Va., 1905; unmarried. Began practice at Charleston, W.Va., 1920; chief of med. staff, Charleston Gen. Hosp.; med. dir. Hillcrest Sanatorium; consultant U.S. Vets. Bur., Charleston. Served as maj. Med. Corps, U.S.A., 1918-19; later major Medical Corps, W.Va. Nat. Guard. Democrat. Episcopalian. Home: Charleston, W.Va. Died Aug. 10, 1935.

ROLLINS, Edward Warren, investment bonds; b. Concord, N.H., Nov. 25, 1850; s. Edward H. and Ellen (West) R.; S.B. in M.E., Mass. Inst. Tech., 1871; m. Jessie Witter, 1878; children—(by 1st marriage) Ashton; (by 2d marriage) Sherwood. Engr., Colo. Central R.R., Denver, 1872-76; in banking business, Denver, 1876-99; chmn. bd. E. H. Rollins & Sons; dir. Pub. Service Co. of Colo., Cities Service Co., British Columbia Fishing & Packing Co., Ltd., Southern Calif. Edison Co. Trustee Berwick Acad. Episcopalian. Home: Dover, N.H. Died Oct. 6, 1929.

ROLLINS, Frank West, governor; b. Concord, N.H., Feb. 24, 1860; s. U.S. Senator Edward H. and Ellen (West) R.; B.S., Mass. Inst. Tech., 1881; A.M., Dartmouth, 1893; studied Harvard Law Sch.; m. Katharine W. Pecker, Dec. 6, 1882. Pres. and dir. E. H. Rollins & Sons, bankers, Boston; dir. Great Western Power Co. Asst. adj. gen. N.H., 1890-95; pres. N.H. Senate, 1895-96; gov. of N.H., 1899-1901. Republican. Originator of the "old home week," 1898. Treas., trustee St. Paul's Sch., Concord, N.H.; trustee Mass. Inst. Tech., Brantwood Camp (Greenfield, N.H.), Concord Pub. Library, Orphans' Home (Concord). Pres. N.E. Business Fed.; pres. N.H. Forestry Soc. Author: The Ring in the Cliff, 1877; The Twin Hussars, 1881; Break-o'-Day Tales, 1895; The Lady of the Violets, 1898; Old Home Week Speeches, 1900; What Can a Young Man Do?, 1907; Tourist Guide to New Hampshire. Home: Concord, N.H. Died Oct. 27, 1915.

ROLLINS, George Sherman, clergyman; b. Franklin, N.H., Apr. 28, 1864; s. Orrin J. and Hannah C. (Conner) R.; descended from James Rawlins, Ipswich, Mass., 1632; grad. Monson (Mass.) Acad., 1884; Williams Coll. (partial course); grad. Chicago Congl. Theol. Sem., 1892; post-grad. study, 2 yrs.; D.D., Fargo (N.D.) Coll., 1903, Chicago Congl. Theol. Sem., 1904; m. Helen Laurens Knowlton, Oct. 3, 1887. Ordained Congl. ministry, 1888; pastor Wilmington, N.C., 1887-90, Chicago, 1892-94, Davenport, Ia., 1894-1902, Minneapolis, 1902-07, Hope Ch., Springfield, Mass., 1907—. Trustee Chicago Congl. Sem., 1903-07. Address: Springfield, Mass. Died Apr. 13, 1916.

ROLLINS, James Wingate, civil engr.; b. Boston, Mass., Oct. 17, 1858; s. James W. and Sophia Webb (Atwill) R., S.B. in Civ. Engring., Mass. Inst. Tech., 1878; m. Clara Boyden Clark, June 17, 1892; children—Elizabeth Sargent, Wingate. Mem. Holbrook, Cabot & Daly, gen. contractors, Boston; pres. Holbrook, Cabot & Rollins Corp., 1906—; v.p., treas. Blakeslee Rollins Corporation, Boston, 1924—. Republican. Congregationalist. Home: Milton, Mass. Died Nov. 19, 1935.

ROLLINS, Montgomery, author; b. Concord, N.H., Aug. 25, 1867; s. Edward H. and Ellen Elizabeth (West) R.; student Mass. Inst. Tech., 3 yrs.; m. Grace Webster Seavey, Oct. 28, 1891. Began as clk. in banking house of E. H. Rollins & Son, Concord; later with Denver office of same firm; sec. E. H. Rollins & Sons, Boston, 1890-99; mem. Montgomery Rollins & Co., 1900-02. Financial sec. and mem. exec. com. Soc. Protection of N.H. Forests. Republican. Author: Money and Investments; Municipal and Corporation Bonds; Stocks and Their Market Places; Convertible Securities; Bond Values Tables—Interest Payable Annually; Tables of Bond Values—Semi-Annual Interest; Government Bond Values Tables; Bond, Stock and Interest Tables; Serial and Instalment Bond Values; Odd Rate Tables of Bond Values; Present Worth Tables; Double Method Interest Tables; Stock Tables; Fifth Montgomery Code; Laws Regulating the Investment of Bank Funds; etc. Home: Chestnut Hill, Mass. Died Apr. 18, 1918.

ROLLINS, Thornton, banker; b. Baltimore, Md., Oct. 7, 1840; s. William and Julia (Silvester) R.; ed. pub. schs., Baltimore. Shipowner, operating a fleet of clippers to Brazil in coffee trade; pres. Continental Nat. Bank and Md. Nat. Bank prior to their sale to the Nat. Bank of Commerce, afterward dir. of latter; dir. Merchants Nat. Bank, Continental Trust Co. Mem. Harbor Bd., Baltimore; pres. City Council; v.p., mem. bd. mgrs. West Baltimore Gen. Hosp.; mem. bd. mgrs. Spring Grove State Hosp. for the Insane, Franklin Sq. Hosp., Md. Gen. Hosp., Aged Men's and Women's Home, James Lawrence Kernan Hosp., Industrial Sch. of Md. for Crippled Children. Democrat. Episcopalian. Address: Baltimore, Md. Died July 7, 1935.

ROLLINS, Walter Huntington, clergyman; b. Newton, Mass., June 1, 1869; s. Fitzhugh S. and Augusta L. (Hanson) R.; A.B., Dartmouth, 1894; S.T.B., Andover Theol. Sem., 1898; D.D., Grinnell (Ia.) Coll., 1911; LL.D., Fargo Coll., N.D., 1920; m. Mabel B. Stone, Sept. 13, 1898; children (living)—Phyllis Huntington, Walter Huntington, Lois Stone, Helen Augusta. Ordained Congl. ministry, 1898; pastor Blackstone, Mass., 1898-1900, Wilmington, 1900-06, 1st Ch., Waterloo, Ia., 1906-14; pres. Fairmount Coll., Wichita, Kan., 1914-22; supt. N.Y. Congl. Conf., June, 1922—; exec. sec. N.Y. City Congl. Assn., Jan. 1933—. Trustee Southern Sem. Foundation, Nashville, pres. N.Y. Council of Chs. and Religious Edn., 1934-37. Mason, Grand Chaplain Ia. Grand Lodge, 1911-12. Home: White Plains, N.Y. Died Apr. 30, 1939.

ROLPH, James, Jr., governor; b. San Francisco, Calif., Aug. 23, 1869; s. James and Margaret (Nicol) R.; ed. pub. schs. and Trinity Acad., San Francisco; m. Annie Marshall Reid, June 26, 1900; children—Annette Reid (Mrs. John P. Symes), James, Georgina (Mrs. Richard C. Willets). Began as office boy in shipping firm, 1888; mem. firm James Rolph, Jr., Landis & Ellis, gen. ins., 1928—; pres. James Rolph & Co. (shipping and commn. mchts.); mayor of San Francisco, 5 terms, 1911-32; gov. of Calif., Jan. 1931-Jan. 1935. Pres. Merchants Exchange, and of Ship Owners Assn. of Pacific Coast; mem. Native Sons of the Golden West. Republican. Episcopalian. Home: San Francisco, Calif. Died June 2, 1934.

ROLSHOVEN, Julius, painter; b. Detroit, 1858; s. Frederick and Maria Theresa Hubertina (Hellings) R.; ed. Cooper Union, New York, 1877, Plassman Acad., New York; Düsseldorf Acad., 1878, Munich, 1879-82, Frank Duveneck class at Florence, 1883-84, Paris, in Atelier Toney, Robert Fleury and Bouguereau, winter of 1888; m. Anna Eliza Chickering, Mar. 10, 1887 (died 1897); m. 2d, Harriette Haynes Blazo, Dec. 1, 1915. Head of Rolshoven Life Classes at Paris, 1890-95, London, 1896-1902, with internat. attendance; received honors and medals, Munich, Paris, Brussels, Chicago, Berlin, Buffalo, St. Louis, and Florence; hors concours, Société Français of Paris. A.N.A. Home: Florence, Italy. Died Dec. 7, 1930.

ROLVAAG, Ole Edvart, educator, author; b. Rolvaag, Helgeland, Norway, Apr. 22, 1876; s. Peder Jakobsen and Ellerine Johanna (Olson) R.; ed. Augustana Coll., Canton, S. Dak., 1898-1901; B.A., St. Olaf Coll., Northfield, Minn., 1905, M.A., 1910; studied U. of Norway, 1905-06, 1923-24; m. Jennie Marie Berdahl, July 9, 1908; children—Olaf Arnljot (dec.), Ella Valborg, Karl Fritjof, Paul Gunnar (dec.). Came to U.S., 1896, naturalized citizen, 1908. Prof. Norwegian lang. and lit., St. Olaf Coll., 1906—, also head of dept. Author: Ordforklaring, 1909; Amerika-Breve, 1912; Paa Glemte Veie, 1914; Deklamationsboken, 1918; To Tullinger, 1920; Laengselens Baat, 1921; Ombring Faedrearven (essays), 1922; I De Dage, 1924; Riket Grundlaegges, 1925; (with Prof. P. J. Eikeland) Haandbok, 1916; Norsk Laesebok, I, II, III, 1919-25; Giants in the Earth, 1927; Peder Victorious, 1929. Home: Northfield, Minn. Died Nov. 5, 1931.

ROMA, Caro, composer; b. East Oakland, Calif., Sept. 10, 1866; d. Vernal Sydney and Mary Louisa (Boynton) Northey; B.M.A., N.E. Conservatory of Music; (gold medal presented by citizens of Boston). Prima donna, Tivoli Opera House, San Francisco, 8 yrs. and at Castle Square, Boston; soloist with U.S. Marine Band, Washington, D.C., and appeared with various cos. in U.S., Can. and England. Awarded Queen's medal, London, and Canadian medal, for orchestral leading. Author: Idle Moments; June the 12th and Other Idle Moments. Composer of some 300 songs. Home: Oakland, Calif. Died Sept. 23, 1937.

ROMEIKE, Henry, press clippings; b. Riga, Russia, Nov. 19, 1855; ed. in Memel, Prussia. Founded the press clipping industry in London. Came to U.S. 1887 and took charge of a press clipping bureau of which he became the head, and the growth and importance of which is very marked. "Romeiked," compiling articles or writing books from press clippings. Address: New York, N.Y. Died 1903.

ROMIG, John Samuel, clergyman; b. St. Johns, Antigua, W.I., July 29, 1869; s. Bishop Benjamin and Maria Elizabeth (Wolle) R.; brought to America, 1878; grad. Nazareth Hall Academy, 1883; A.B., Moravian Coll., Pa., 1888; B.D., Moravian Theol. Sem., 1890, D.D., 1917; m. Catharine Ulrich, Sept. 22, 1892; children—Clarence Benjamin, Helen Elizabeth. Ordained Moravian (Unitas Fratrum) ministry, 1890; pastor Coopersburg, Pa., 1890-92, Easton, 1892-96, Great Kills, N.Y., 1896-1913, 1st Ch., Phila., Nov. 30, 1913—. Editor Little Missionary, 1903-13; mem. Dist. Exec. Bd., 1st Dist. Moravian Ch., 1905-13; sec. bd. of Elders of Northern Diocese of United Brethren in U.S.A., 1913-25; del. Gen. Synod Moravian Ch., Herrnhut, Germany, 1914; mem. ad interim com. Conf. on Organic Union of the Churches, 1919; sec. Larger Life Movement, Moravian Ch., 1919-20; v.p. Pa. Bible Soc. Home: Philadelphia, Pa. Died Aug. 13, 1930.

ROMINGER, Carl Ludwig, geologist; b. Schnaitheim, Würtemberg, Dec. 31, 1820; s. Ludwig and Johanna Dorothea (Hoecklin) P.; ed. in Latin sch., then became apprentice in drug store and prepared for U. of Tübingen, where studied 1839-44, and was grad. M.D.; asst. in chem. laboratory of univ., 1844-47, and received from State annual gift of money to prosecute geol. studies, traveling over large portions of Germany, France, Austria, Switzerland, etc.; m. Frederica Mayer, Nov. 30, 1854. Came to U.S., 1848, to continue geol. studies; practiced medicine over 25 yrs., but afterward devoted attention exclusively to geology and palæontology; State geologist of Mich., 1870-84. Received medal of merit from Royal Acad., Munich, 1892. Extensive contbr. to geol. reports (wrote entire 3d and 4th vols. Mich. Reports and parts of others), 1869-83. Address: Ann Arbor, Mich. Died 1907.

RONAYNE, Maurice, educator; b. Castlemartyr, County Cork, Ireland, 1828; studied at Ecclesiastical

Coll. at Maynooth and Laval Sem.; became a Jesuit, 1853; came to U.S., 1855; taught St. John's Coll., Fordham; prof. history, St. Francis Xavier's Coll., 1888—. Author: Religion and Science; God Knowable and Known. Address: New York, N.Y. Died 1903.

RONDTHALER, Edward, bishop; b. Northampton County, Pa., July 24, 1842; s. Rev. Edward and Sarah Louisa (Rice) R. (a mem. of the Heckewelder missionary family); ed. Moravian Coll., and Theol. Sem., Bethlehem, Pa.; U. of Erlangen, 1 yr.; D.D., U. of N.C., 1880, LL.D., 1918; m. Mary E., d. Bishop Jacobson, of the Moravian Ch., N., Oct. 1, 1867; 1 son, Howard Edward, educator. Ordained Unitas Fratrum (Moravian) ministry, 1865; pastor Moravian Ch., Brooklyn, 1865-73, First Ch., Phila., 1874-77, Central Ch. of Moravians in the South, Winston-Salem, N.C., 1877-1908; ordained bishop, Apr. 12, 1891. Pres. Moravian Woman's Coll. in the South, Salem, N.C., 1834-87 (later pres. trustees); pres. Bd. Provincial Elders, and various other bds. of the Ch.; trustee Moravian Coll., and Theol. Sem.; mem. Gen. Synods, in Saxony, 1879, 89, 99, 1909, 14; deputy of Moravian Unity at Berthelsdorf, 1902, London, 1906. Author: Fifty Years of Annual Papers on World Events, 1928; also many pub. sermons, addresses and contbns. Editor official journal of the Moravians in Southern States. Home: Winston-Salem, N.C. Died Jan. 31, 1931.

ROOD, James Theron, elec. engr.; b. Worcester, Mass., Mar. 26, 1876; s. James Timothy (M.D.) and Ellen Louise (Miles) R.; B.S., in E.E., Worcester Poly. Inst., 1898; Ph.D., Clark U., 1906; m. Myrtle Merrill, July 29, 1908. Prof. mathematics and physics, Ursinus Coll., Collegeville, Pa., 1906-07; prof. physics and elec. engring., U. of Ala., 1907-09; prof. elec. engring., Lafayette Coll., 1909-18; prof. ry. elec. engring., U. of Ill., 1918-20; prof. elec. engring., U. of Wis., 1920-29; later prof. elec. engring., dean of engring., dir. engring. expt. sta. and radio sta. KOB, N.M. Coll. Agr. and Mechanic Arts; consulting practice, 1907—. Republican. Episcopalian. Contbr. articles on original investigations. Died May 23, 1934.

ROOD, Ogden Nicholas, prof. physics Columbia, 1863—; b. Danbury, Conn., Feb. 3, 1831; s. Rev. Anson and Aleida Gouverneur (Ogden) R.; grad. Princeton, 1852; studied at Univs. of Munich and Berlin, 1854-58; prof. chemistry and physics Troy U., 1858-63; m. Matilde Prunner, 1858. Was first to apply stereoscopic photography to the microscope and first to make quantitative experiments on color-contrast, to measure the duration of flashes of lightning and to make a photometer that is independent of color. Author: Modern Chromatics, 1879; also about 70 scientific papers. Mem. Nat. Acad. of Science. Address: New York, N.Y. Died 1902.

ROOKER, Frederick Zadok, R.C. bishop; b. New York, Sept. 19, 1861; s. Myron H. and Margaret (Coleman) R.; ed. in public and high schools, Albany, N.Y.; also through junior year of class of 1884, Union Coll., hon. D.D.; later at Propaganda at Rome, Ph.D., S.T.D.; ordained to priesthood, Rome, 1888; vice rector Am. Coll., 1889-94; sent from Rome to Apostolic Delegation, Washington, at end of 1894, sec., 1895-1903; apptd., 1903, bishop of Jaro, P.I. Address: Jaro, Iloilo, P.I. Died 1907.

ROONEY, John Jerome, judge, verse writer; b. Binghamton, N.Y., Mar. 19, 1866; s. John J. and Ellen T. (Shanahan) R.; moved with family to Phila.; A.B. (head of class), Mt. St. Mary's Coll., Md., 1884, A.M., 1886, LL.D., 1908; mem. staff of Phila. Record, five years; m. Marie Collins, 1903; children—John Jerome, Dunstan Collins, Roderick Shanahan, Moira Jerome. Mem. New York bar, practicing chiefly in mercantile, customs and revenue cases. Presiding judge Court of Claims, State of New York, January 1, 1913-16; spl. counsel City of N.Y., 1920. During war with Spain wrote "The Men Behind the Guns" (the first use of that phrase); "Hobson of Santiago," "Victor Blue," "McElrath, of Malate," "John Nichols of Spartanburg," "Apples Finkey, the Waterboy," "The Way in the Navy," "Reilly of F," "The Riveter," and other verse on the war, later published in book form under title, The Men Behind the Guns; also wrote "Right Makes Might," official hymn of City of New York, sung first by public school children at the 250th anniversary of the founding of the city; wrote "The Little Star in the Window," interpretation of the service flag in the World War; also "The Holy Year," poem, read at opening of exercises of the Holy Year in N.Y. City. Mem. Dem. County Com., New York County, Society of Tammany or Columbian Order. K. of C. Author: The Holy Year. Home: New York, N.Y. Died Nov. 27, 1934.

ROORBACH, George Byron, univ. prof.; b. Herkimer County, N.Y., Dec. 8, 1878; s. Emmet Howard and Angie L. (Hayes) R.; A.B., Colgate, 1903, Sc.D., 1926; grad. study, Harvard, 1908-09; A.M., U. of Pa., 1912; m. Anne Hubble, Aug. 3, 1912; children—Emmet Howard, Elizabeth Hubble, Carolyn Louise, Anne, Jean Ashley, George Brett. Prin. high sch., De Ruyter, N.Y., 1903-05; science master Peddie Sch., Hightstown, N.J., 1905-08; instructor in geography, U. of Pa., 1909-14, asst. prof., 1914-19; prof. foreign trade, Harvard Grad. Sch. of Bus. Adminstrn., 1919—. Spl. expert, U.S. Shipping Bd., 1918-19, U.S. Tariff Commn., 1921; chief of research div. U.S. Dept. Commerce (on leave of absence from Harvard), 1921-22. Made spl. investigation of financial conditions in Venezuela for Carnegie Endowment, 1915; spl. investigation of trade of Far East for Bur. Internat. Research, Harvard, 1926-27. Fellow American Academy of Arts and Sciences. Unitarian. Author: Import Purchasing, 1927; International Competetion in Trade of India, 1931; Problems in Foreign Trade, 1933. Editor: The International Trade Situation, 1921. Contbr. on trade, tariffs and internat. affairs. Home: Cambridge, Mass. Died May 23, 1934.

ROOSA, Daniel Bennett St. John, M.D.; b. Bethel, N.Y., Apr. 4, 1838; s. Charles Baker and Amelia Elmer (Foster) R.; grad., M.D., Univ. Med. Coll., New York, 1860, after academic edn. in Boston and New York, A.M., Yale; LL.D., U. of Vt.; asst. surgeon 5th N.Y. vols. among the 3 months' troops called out by President Lincoln; house surgeon N.Y. Hosp.; prof. U. City of New York, and U. of Vt.; pres. N.Y. Post-Grad. Med. School and prof. diseases of the eye. Author: The Old Hospital and Other Papers, 1886; A Pocket Medical Lexicon, 1887; Treatise on the Ear, 1891; Treatise on the Eye, 1894; A Doctor's Suggestions; On the Necessity of Wearing Glasses; Defective Eyesight, 1899. Address: New York, N.Y. Died 1908.

ROOSEVELT, George Washington, consul; b. Chester, Pa., Feb. 14, 1844; s. James S. (of New York) and Esther (Vicery) R.; ed. pub. schs., Chester, Pa., and by pvt. tutors; clerk in store until enlisted Apr. 16, 1861; served corpl. to 1st sergt., Co. K, 26th Regt., Pa. Vols.; bvtd. capt. for meritorious conduct at Gettysburg, where was severely wounded through hips and lost left leg, July 2, 1863; awarded congressional medal of honor for gallant and meritorious conduct at battles of Bull Run and Gettysburg; raised co. in Phila. upon President Lincoln's 2d call, and was elected capt., but loss of leg prevented service at front again; m. Ida Edmonston, May 1874. Apptd. U.S. consul at Auckland, New Zealand, Mar. 28, 1878; to St. Helena, Apr. 30, 1879; to Matanzas, Cuba, Sept. 1, 1880; to Bordeaux, France, May 23, 1881; consul, 1889-1905, consul-gen., Mar. 6, 1905—, at Brussels, Belgium. Republican. Presbyn. Died 1907.

ROOSEVELT, Henry Latrobe, asst. sec. of the Navy; b. Morristown, N.J., Oct. 5, 1879; s. Nicholas Latrobe and Eleanor (Dean) R.; student U.S. Naval Acad., class of 1900; m. Eleanor Morrow, Jan. 15, 1902; children—William Morrow, Henry Latrobe, Eleanor Katherine. Commd. 2d lt. U.S.M.C., 1899; promoted through grades to lt. col., 1917; during Spanish-Am. War attached to U.S.S. Mayflower, operating off coast of Cuba; asst. naval attaché, Paris, France, 1914; hdqrs. U.S. Marine Corps, Washington, 1914-16; brig. q.m. Haiti, 1916; col. in Gendarmerie d'Haiti, 1916-17; at Quantico, Va., 1917; resigned, 1920; with Radio Corp. of America, 1923, European mgr., 1925-30; pres. Radio Real Estate Corp., 1930; asst. sec. of the Navy, Mar. 17, 1933—. Episcopalian. Home: Washington, D.C. Died Feb. 22, 1936.

ROOSEVELT, Robert Barnwell, banker; b. New York, Aug. 7, 1829; s. Cornelius Van Schaick and Margaret (Barnhill) R.; admitted to bar, 1851, and practiced for 20 yrs., when retired from practice; m. d. John F. Ellis, prominent in New York before War of 1812; m. 2d, Marion T. Fortesque. Became interested in field sports and active in promotion of clubs and socs. for protection and preservation of game; pres. N.Y. Internat. Assn. for Protection of Game. Presented to N.Y. legislature bill, which was passed, for creation of a fishery commn.; mem. of the commn. for 20 yrs., and for most of that time its pres.; several yrs. editor New York Citizen; treas. War Democracy; alderman of the City of New York; commr. of Brooklyn Bridge; mem. Congress, 1873-75; chmn. exec. com. Com. of 70, in the fight against the Tweed Ring; U.S. minister to the Netherlands, 1888-90; treas. Dem. Nat. Com. at time of Cleveland's 2d election; pres. Sons of Am. Revolution; chmn. Com. for Protection of the Soldiers during the war with Spain; delegate to many Dem. convs.; on all the coms. to aid the Boers in their war with England. Author: Game Fish of North America; Game Birds; Superior Fishing; Fish Hatching and Fish Catching; Florida and the Game Water Birds; Five Acres Too Much; Progressive Petticoats; Love and Luck. Uncle of President Roosevelt. Pres. Founders and Patriots of America. Address: Sayville, N.Y. Died 1906.

ROOSEVELT, S(amuel) Montgomery, portrait painter; b. N.Y. City, 1864; s. Samuel and Mary Jane (Horton) R.; ed. St. John's Sch. (Ossining, N.Y.), Art Students' League (New York), Acad. Julien (Paris); m. Augusta E. Shoemaker, 1887. Painted portraits of Theodore Roosevelt, Bishop James H. Darlington, Oliver Belmont, Hudson Maxim, Henry F. Shoemaker, Earl of Kintore. Chevalier Legion of Honor, France, 1914. Home: Skaneateles, N.Y. Died Aug. 19, 1920.

ROOSEVELT, Theodore, twenty-sixth president of the U.S.; b. New York, Oct. 27, 1858, s. Theodore (1831-78) and Martha (Bulloch) R.; A.B., Harvard, 1880; LL.D., Columbia, 1899, Hope Coll., 1901, Yale, 1901, Harvard, 1902, Northwestern, 1893, U. of Chicago, 1903, U. of Calif., 1903, U. of Pa., 1905, Clark U., 1905, George Washington U., 1909, Cambridge U., 1910; D.C.L., Oxford U., 1910; Ph.D., U. of Berlin, 1910; m. Alice Hathaway, d. George Cabot Lee, Oct. 27, 1880 (died 1884); m. 2d, Edith Kermit, d. Charles Carow, Dec. 2, 1886. Mem. N.Y. Legislature, 1882-84; del. Rep. Nat. Conv., 1884; resided on ranch in N.D., 1884-86; candidate for mayor of New York, 1886; U.S. civil service commr., 1889-95; pres. New York Police Bd., 1895-97; asst. sec. of the navy, 1897-98; resigned to organize, with Surgeon (later Maj.-Gen.) Leonard Wood, 1st U.S. Cav. (popularly known as Roosevelt's Rough Riders); was lt. col. of regt., which distinguished itself in Cuba; promoted col. for gallantry at battle of Las Guasimas; mustered out Sept. 1898. Gov. N.Y., Jan. 1, 1899, to Dec. 31, 1900; elected Vice-President of the United States, Nov. 4, 1900, for term, 1901-05; succeeded to the presidency on death of William McKinley, Sept. 14, 1901; elected President of the U.S., Nov. 8, 1904, for term 1905-09, by largest popular majority ever accorded a candidate; Progressive Party candidate for president of U.S., 1912. Awarded the Nobel Peace Prize ($40,000), 1906. Spl. ambassador of U.S. at funeral of King Edward VII, 1910. Long a contbr. to leading mags. and reviews; known for yrs. as advocate of civil service and other reforms, nat. and municipal; contbg. editor The Outlook, 1909-14. Did much shooting of big game in the West; hunting trip in Africa, 1909-10; plaintiff in suit for libel against G. H. Newett, who had, in a newspaper article, during presdl. campaign of 1912, charged him with intoxication, but after submission of the evidence of defendant's witnesses, the charge was withdrawn in open court (Marquette, Mich., May 31, 1913) and judgment was immediately rendered in favor of plaintiff; visited S. America, 1913, and delivered addresses before univs. and learned socs.; went to Brazil, 1914, and at head of exploring party discovered and explored (Feb. 27-Apr. 26, 1914) for a distance of about 600 miles, a tributary of the Madeira River, subsequently named in his honor by Brazilian govt. "Reo Teodoro"; visited Madrid, Spain, June 1914, and lectured same month before Royal Geog. Soc., London. Defendant in suit brought by William Barnes, Jr., of Albany, N.Y., for alleged libelous utterances contained in a statement made on July 22, 1914, charging, among other things, that the "rottenness" of the N.Y. State government was due directly to the dominance in politics of Charles F. Murphy, Tammany Hall leader, and his sub-bosses aided and abetted by Mr. Barnes and the sub-bosses of Mr. Barnes; and that there was an invisible government of party bosses working through alliance between crooked business and crooked politics; the verdict of the jury, rendered at Syracuse, N.Y., May 22, 1915, was in favor of defendant. Nominated for President by Progressive Party Conv., Chicago, 1916; about 1 month later declined the nomination and supported Charles Evans Hughes, the Republican nominee. Offered to raise an army division, after declaration of war, and to go to France with same, 1917, but offer was declined by Pres. Wilson. Hon. fellow Am. Mus. Natural History, 1917. Author: Winning of the West, 1889-96; History of the Naval War of 1812, 1882; Hunting Trips of a Ranchman, 1885; Life of Thomas Hart Benton, 1886; Life of Gouverneur Morris, 1887; Ranch Life and Hunting Trail, 1888; History of New York, 1890; The Wilderness Hunter, 1893; American Ideals and Other Essays, 1897; The Rough Riders, 1899; Life of Oliver Cromwell, 1900; The Strenuous Life, 1900; Works (8 vols.), 1902; The Deer Family, 1902; Outdoor Pastimes of an American Hunter, 1906; American Ideals and Other Essays; Good Hunting, 1907; True Americanism; African and European Addresses, 1910; African Game Trails, 1910; The New Nationalism, 1910; Realizable Ideals (the Earl lectures), 1912; Conservation of Womanhood and Childhood, 1912; History as Literature, and Other Essays, 1913; Theodore Roosevelt, an Autobiography, 1913; Life Histories of African Game Animals (2 vols.), 1914; Through the Brazilian Wilderness, 1914; America and the World War, 1915; A Booklover's Holidays in the Open, 1916; Fear God, and Take Your Own Part, 1916; Foes of Our Own Household, 1917; National Strength and International Duty (Stafford Little lectures, Princeton Univ.), 1917. Home: Oyster Bay, L.I., N.Y. Died Jan. 6, 1919.

ROOSEVELT, W(illiam) Emlen, capitalist; b. New York, Apr. 30, 1857; s. James Alfred and Elizabeth Norris (Emlen) R.; m. Christine Kean. Mem. firm of Roosevelt & Son; pres. Broadway Improvement Co.; v.p. Buffalo, Rochester & Pittsburgh Ry. Co., Union Sq. Savings Bank; chmn. bd. All America Cables, Inc.; dir. Chemical Nat. Bank, Mobile & Ohio R.R., Fidelity & Casualty Co., Third Av. Ry. Co., Westchester Electric R.R. Co., Kingsbridge Ry. Co., 42d St., Manhattanville & St. Nicholas Av. Ry. Co., Belt Line Ry. Corp., Union Ry. Co., N.Y.

City Interborough Ry. Co., Terminal Warehouse Co., Dry Dock, East Broadway and Battery R.R. Co., Hastings Ry. Co., Internat. Tel. & Tel. Corp., N.Y., Westchester & Conn. Traction Co., Southern Boulevard R.R. Co., Yonkers R.R. Co. Trustee Roosevelt Hosp. Dispensary, New York Eye and Ear Infirmary. Home: New York, N.Y. Died May 15, 1930.

ROOT, Amos Ives, apiarist; b. Mogadore, O., Dec. 9, 1839; s. Samuel H. and Louisa (Hart) R.; ed. normal sch., Medina, O., until 16; m. Susan Hall, Sept. 30, 1861; father of Ernest Rob R. Pres. The A.I. Root Co., mfrs. bee-keepers' supplies, Medina, 1873—. Editor Gleanings in Bee Culture, 1872-90. Republican. Congregationalist. Author: ABC of Bee Culture (reprinted in German, French, and Spanish), 1877-88; What To Do and How To Be Happy While Doing It, 1885; ABC of Strawberry Culture, 1895; ABC of Potato Culture, 1902; Tomato Culture, 1892. Address: Medina, O. Died 1923.

ROOT, Azariah Smith, librarian; b. Middlefield, Mass., Feb. 3, 1862; s. Solomon F. and Anna (Smith) R.; A.B., Oberlin, 1884, A.M., 1887; law student Boston U., 1884-85; cataloguer, Oberlin Coll., 1885-86; student Harvard Law Sch., 1886-87; U. of Göttingen, 1898-99; m. Anna Mayo Metcalf, Apr. 30, 1887; children—Francis Metcalf, Marion Metcalf. Librarian, 1887—, professor bibliography, 1890—, Oberlin Coll. Home: Oberlin, O. Died Oct. 2, 1927.

ROOT, Edwin Park, clock mfr.; b. New Haven, Conn., June 19, 1861; s. Lafayette F. and Elizabeth (Benham) R.; ed. pub. schs.; hon. M.A., Yale, 1931; unmarried. Began in clock mfg. business with New Haven Clock Co., 1875, pres., 1923-29, chmn. bd., 1929—; v.p. and dir. First Nat. Bank & Trust Co.; v.p. and trustee National Savings Bank; dir. Morris Plan Bank, New Haven Water Co. Pres. New Haven Pub. Library, Little Theatre Co., New Haven. V.p. and mem. bd. dirs. Conn. State Prison (bd. of parole); v.p. Lowell House Assn.; trustee New Haven Hosp. Republican. Conglist. Home: New Haven, Conn. Died Feb. 7, 1938.

ROOT, Elihu, sec. of State, senator; b. Clinton, N.Y., Feb. 15, 1845; s. Prof. Oren and Nancy Whitney (Buttrick) R.; A.B., Hamilton Coll., 1864, A.M., 1867; taught at Rome Acad., 1865; LL.B., New York U., 1867; LL.D., Hamilton, 1894, Yale, 1900, Columbia, 1904, New York U., 1904, Williams, 1905, Princeton 1906, U. of Buenos Aires, 1906, Harvard, 1907, Wesleyan, 1909, McGill, 1913, Union Univ., 1914, U. of State of N.Y., 1915, U. of Toronto, 1918, Colgate, 1919, U. of Calif., 1923; Dr. Polit. Science, Univ. Leyden, 1913; D.C.L., Oxford, 1913, New York U., 1929; mem. Faculty of Political and Administrative Sciences, U. of San Marcos, Lima, 1906; Doctor, honoris causa, U. of Paris, 1921; m. Clara Wales, Jan. 8, 1878 (died 1928); children—Edith (wife of U. S. Grant, 3d, U.S.A.), Elihu, Edward Wales. Admitted to bar, 1867, and engaged in practice at New York. U.S. dist. atty., Southern Dist. of N.Y., 1883-85; del.-at-large N.Y. Constl. Conv., 1894 (chmn. judiciary com.); sec. of war in cabinet of President McKinley, Aug. 1, 1899-Feb. 1, 1904; sec. of State in cabinet of President Roosevelt, July 1, 1905-Jan. 27, 1909; U.S. senator from N.Y., 1909-15. Mem. Alaskan Boundary Tribunal, 1903; counsel for U.S. in N. Atlantic Fisheries Arbitration, 1910; mem. Permanent Court of Arbitration at the Hague, 1910—; mem. Commn. Internat. Jurists, which, on invitation of Council of League of Nations, reported plan of new Permanent Court of Internat. Justice, established 1921. President Carnegie Endowment for International Peace, 1910-25; pres. Hague Tribunal of Arbitration between Great Britain, France, Spain and Portugal, concerning church property, 1913; ambassador extraordinary at head of special diplomatic mission to Russia, during revolution, 1917; commr. plenipotentiary for U.S., Internat. Conf. on Limitation of Armament, which met at Washington, Nov. 12, 1921; mem. League of Nations com. of experts to revise World Court statute on basis of experience at court meeting at Geneva, Mar. 1929. Awarded Nobel Peace Prize for 1912; Roosevelt medal for Administration of Public Office, 1924; Woodrow Wilson Foundation medal and prize, 1926, for championship of Court of Internat. Justice. Dodge lecturer, Yale, 1907; Stafford Little lecturer, Princeton, 1913. Temporary chairman Republican National Convention, 1904, and temporary and permanent chmn., 1912; chmn. N.Y. Rep. State convs., 1908, 10, 13, 14, 16, 20, 22; pres. N.Y. College of Presdl. Electors, 1925; pres. N.Y. Constitutional Conv., 1915; chmn. trustees Carnegie Instn. of Washington, 1913—, Hamilton Coll., 1912—; trustee N.Y. Pub. Library, Met. Mus. of Art, Am. Federation of Arts, N.Y. State Charities Aid Assn. Pres. of New England Soc. in New York, 1893-95, Union League Club (New York), 1898-99, and 1915-16, Assn. Bar City of N.Y., 1904-05, Am. Soc. Internat. Law, 1906—, N.Y. State Bar Assn., 1910, Am. Bar Assn., 1915; pres. N.Y. Law Inst.; mem. Mexican Acad. of Legislation and Jurisprudence; hon. mem. Inst. of Advocates of Brazil; hon. pres. Pan-Am. Conf., Rio de Janeiro, 1906; hon. pres. Am. Inst. Internat. Law, Nat. Security League, N.Y. Assn. for the Blind, Nat. Soc. for Prevention of Blindness; pres. Century Club, New York, 1918—; corr. fellow British Acad., 1916—; hon. mem. Institut de Droit International; hon. mem. A.I.A., New York Chamber of Commerce, Soc. of the Cincinnati; mem. Am. Philos. Soc., Am. Acad. Arts and Letters; corr. fellow Mass. Hist. Soc.; fellow Am. Acad. Arts and Sciences; chmn. U.S. Govt. War Savings Investments Soc., Jan. 1918—; hon. pres. and mem. council Am. Law Inst. Del. and hon. pres. N.Y. State Convention, 1933, to act on Repeal of 18th Amendment to U.S. Constn. Grand Cordon de l'ordre de la Couronne of Belgium, 1919; grand comdr. Royal Order of George the First (Greece), 1923. Author: The Citizen's Part in Government, 1907; Experiment in Government and the Essentials of the Constitution, 1913; Addresses on International Subjects, 1916; Addresses on Government and Citizenship, 1916; Military and Colonial Policy of the United States, 1916; Latin America and the United States, 1917; Russia and the United States, 1917; Miscellaneous Addresses, 1917; Men and Policies, 1924. Home: New York, N.Y. Died Feb. 7, 1937.

ROOT, Frank Albert, publisher, author; b. Binghamton, N.Y., July 3, 1837; s. Albert B. and Marinda (Boyden) R.; ed. country schs. in N.Y. and Pa.; m. Emma Clark, Oct. 21, 1864 (died 1904). Worked on farm in '40s; was waiter boy, hodcarrier and stage driver in Pa. in early '50s; learned printing business; went to Kan., 1857; early in 1863 was express messenger on the Overland Stage Line, Atchison, Kan., to Denver, Colo.; later traveling mail agt. for 650 miles on the eastern div. of the stage line from Mo. River to Denver; made 32 trips across the plains on the "Concord" stagecoach, in 1863-65; became publisher and conducted 8 weekly and daily newspapers in Kan. and Colo., 1865-93. Republican; cast first presdl. vote for Abraham Lincoln, in 1860, going from Kan. Ter., 1,500 miles to Pa. to vote. Author: The Overland Stage to California, 1901. Address: Topeka, Kan. Died June 21, 1926.

ROOT, Frederic Woodman, teacher of singing; b. Boston, June 13, 1846; s. Dr. George Frederick R., famous composer, and Mary Olive (Woodman) R.; began music study as a child with his father; later piano instruction from Dr. B C. Blodgett, Dr. William Mason, and Dr. Robert Goldbeck; organ instruction from James Flint, New York; vocal instruction from Carlo Bassini, New York, and Vannuccini, Florence, Italy; m. Fannie Smith, Apr. 30, 1874. Trained many noted singers, conducted singing socs. and mus. festivals, and composed songs, cantatas, etc., and compiled and edited many collections of songs. His prin. ednl. work is The Technic and Art of Singing. Address: Chicago, Ill. Died Nov. 8, 1916.

ROOT, Frederick Stanley, Congl. clergyman; b. New Haven, Conn., May 7, 1853; s. Lafayette F. and Elizabeth (Benham) R.; ed. Russell Mil. Acad., New Haven; grad. Yale Law Sch., 1874, divinity sch., 1879; M.A., Bowdoin; LL.B., Yale; m. Henrietta Frances Bowditch, July 29, 1880. Resigned from ministry of Park Ch., Hartford, Conn., 1894, to enter field of gen. literature and to study social science; gen. sec. Am. Social Science Assn.; asso. mem. Nat. Inst. Arts and Letters. Author: The Tousled Hair, 1899; What Is the Matter with the Church?, 1900; also serial story, Sanguine Tommy, in Chicago Advance, 1903. Editor Social Science Journal 6 yrs. For yrs. gen. contbr. to New York Tribune, New York Evening Post, etc. Address: New Haven, Conn. Died 1906.

ROOT, Joseph Cullen, lawyer; b. Chester, Mass., Dec. 3, 1844; s. Aurelius Clark and Eliza (Abbott) R.; ed. Cornell Coll., Ia., 1 yr., Northern Ill. Coll., 1½ yrs.; grad. Eastman Bus. Coll., Poughkeepsie, N.Y., 1865; studied law with Hon. A. T. Wheeler Lyons; admitted to bar, 1883; m. Louise M. Inslee, Sept. 21, 1868. V.p. Lion Surety & Bond Co., Omaha, 1908—; dir. Corn Exchange Nat. Bank, Omaha, 1910. Founded, 1882, and head consul, 1882-90, Modern Woodmen of America; founded, 1890, and later sovereign comdr. Woodmen of the World; gov. AK-Sar-Ben. Founded Lyons (Ia.) Young Men's Assn. Library, 1859; alderman and tax collector, Lyons, 1884-85; U.S. deputy collector, 2d Ia. Dist., 1884-88; mayor Lyons, Ia., 1886-87. Pres. Associated Fraternities America, 1908. Author: Consolidation (drama), 1870; Ritual Modern Woodmen, 1882; History of Modern Woodmen, 1888; Ritual V.A.S. Fraternity, 1888; Ritual Woodmen of the World, 1890; Eminent Choppers, 1900; Ritual Columbian Circles, 1905; Ritual Boys of Woodcraft, 1909; Ritual Knights of AK-Sar-Ben, 1906, Root Family Genealogy, 1907. Home: Omaha, Neb. Died Dec. 24, 1913.

ROOT, Joseph Edward, surgeon; b. Barre, Mass., Mar. 4, 1854; s. Thomas Pitkin and Seraph (Haynes) R.; B.S., Boston U., also State Coll. of Mass.; M.D., Coll. Phys. and Surg. (Columbia), 1883; m. Ella Goodman Moseley, Mar. 4, 1885. Orthopedic surgeon St. Francis Hosp.; cons. orthopedic surgeon Manchester Memorial Hosp., Newington Home for Crippled Children, Newington Municipal Hosp. Home: Hartford, Conn. Died Dec. 18, 1933.

ROOT, Louis Carroll, banker; b. Port Byron, N.Y., Sept. 29, 1868; s. William H. and Helen (Hadger) R.; A.B., Cornell, 1892; m. Alice S. Beers, Mar. 26, 1892; children—Harold S., Helen M., Alice Carol; m. 2d, Elinor H. Fisher, Sept. 23, 1925. Fellow polit. economy and finance, Cornell, 1892-93; asst. to Indianapolis Monetary Commn., 1897-98; sec., 1901-02, 3d v.p., 1902-04, New York Security & Trust Co.; treas. Walter A. Wood Mowing & Reaping Machine Co., 1904-06; with Isidore Newman & Son, bankers, 1906-22; member of firm, 1920-22; v.p. Newman, Saunders & Co., Inc., 1922-35, retired. Author of numerous monographs on monetary questions. Secretary and later chairman executive committee (N.Y.) Reform Club Sound Currency Com., 1896-1908. Home: Spencer, N.Y. Died Feb. 20, 1939.

ROOT, Lyman C.; b. St. Lawrence County, N.Y., Dec. 19, 1840; s. Caleb Olcott and Louisa (Hildreth) R.; St. Lawrence U., 1857-60; m. Elizabeth Quinby, Dec. 15, 1869 (died 1896); children—Stella Q., Kathryn H. Long regarded as authority in bee-keeping and milk production. Prohibitionist. Universalist. Mason. Author: Quinby's New Bee-Keeping. Address: Stamford, Conn. Deceased.

ROOT, Milo Adelbert, judge; b. Bureau County, Ill., Jan. 22, 1863; s. William H. and Sarah Cordelia (Holroyd) R.; grad. high sch., Albion, N.Y., 1882; LL.B., Albany Law Sch., 1883; read law several yrs.; admitted to bar, 1884; went to Wash. Ty., 1883; m. Anna Evelyn Lansdale, Mar. 4, 1890. Judge Probate Ct., Thurston County, Wash., 1887-90; pros. atty., 1893-97; judge Supreme Ct., Wash., Jan. 23, 1905-08, resigned; reëlected for terms 1909-15; did not qualify, but resumed practice of law. Republican. Congregationalist. Mason. Home: Seattle, Wash. Died Jan. 9, 1917.

ROOT, Oren, prof. mathematics, Hamilton Coll.; b. Syracuse, N.Y., May 18, 1838; s. Oren and Nancy W. (Buttrick) R.; grad. Hamilton Coll., 1856, D.D., Rutgers Coll., 1891; L.H.D., Union Coll., 1895; m. Anna J. Higgins, Dec. 2, 1862 (died 1865); m. 2d, Ida C. Gordon, May 1867 (died 1896); m. 3d, Mrs. Anna Ray Quisenberry, Dec. 16, 1901. Admitted to Wis. bar, 1858; Presbyn. clergyman, 1874; pastor of Reformed (Dutch) Ch., Utica, N.Y., 1890, and entered that denomination. Grand high priest, Royal Arch Masons, Mo., 1868; grand comdr., Knights Templar, Mo., 1871; grand chaplain Grand Lodge F.&A.M., N.Y., 1891-92, 1905. Prof. English, State Univ., Mo., 1866-71; pres. Pritchett Coll., Glasgow, Mo., 1873-76: Co-editor Columbian Speaker, 1874; Franklin Speaker, 1875; Hamilton Declamation Quarterly, 1895. Author: Brief Elementary Trigonometry, 1899. Address: Clinton, N.Y. Died 1907.

ROOT, William Webster, M.D.; b. Niagara Falls, N.Y., Aug. 19, 1867; s. E. Volney and Amelia E. (Root) R.; B.S., Cornell U., 1890; post-grad. work in chemistry, same univ., 1892-94, also at U. of Chicago; M.D., Rush Med. Coll., Chicago, 1904; m. Anna Conant, d. late Rev. Benjamin F. Bronson, D.D., July 15, 1895; children—Manly Bronson, George Kennan (dec.), Georgiana, Hasseltine Chaplin, Anna Conant, William Webster (dec.). Instr. nat. sciences, Peddie Inst., Hightstown, N.J., 1890-92; instr. chemistry, Chicago Manual Training Sch. and U. of Chicago, 1895-1903; practicing phys., 1904—; in charge emergency hosps., and research bacteriologist, Parke, Davis & Co., Detroit, 1908-11; 1st lt. Med. Reserve Corps, 1912-17; contract surgeon at Cornell U., 1918; asst. physician, Utica (N.Y.) State Hosp., 1920-21. Founder, 1902, and sec.-treas. Alpha Omega Alpha (hon. fraternity, 39 chapters, 1931), and editor gen. catalog (1902-22), 1922; also founder, 1925, and sec.-treas. Assn. of College Honor Socs. Mason. Baptist. Contributor numerous papers on ednl. and biol. topics. Home: Slaterville Springs, N.Y. Died 1932.

ROPER, Alvin Whitehead, pianist; b. nr. Wentzville, Mo., Oct. 23, 1883; s. Rev. William Henry and Sophronia Annie (Scruggs) R.; prep. edn., Pritchett Inst., Glasgow, Mo., and Central Coll., Fayette, Mo.; A.B., Southwestern U., Georgetown, Tex., 1902; studied music, 12 yrs., Am. teachers; m. Ruth Higley, Apr. 15, 1908; children—Ruthanetta, Helen Agnes. Began study of piano at age of 7; début, 1903; made tour of the world, 1913; played in every state in the U.S. and in Can.; served as piano soloist for World's S.S. Conv., World's Congress against Alcoholism, 3 Internat. S.S. convs.; also for over 400 state and dist. convs. and abt. 100 evangelistic campaigns; appeared in nearly 500 recitals and concerts; pianist Winona Lake, Ind., 10 summer seasons; widely recognized for improvisations and as interpreter of hymns. Democrat. Methodist. Home: Winona Lake, Ind. Died Mar. 5, 1930.

ROPER, Lewis Murphree, clergyman; b. Laurens County, S.C., Mar. 21, 1870; s. Levi Hudgens and Caroline (Mahaffey) R.; A.B., Furman U., S.C., 1891, A.M., 1892, D.D., 1905; A.B., Columbian (now George Washington) U., 1892; grad. Rochester Theol. Sem., 1896; m. Leonora Mauldin, Sept. 5, 1893; children—Leonora M. (Mrs. T. L. Harris), Helen C. (Mrs. H. M. Ferguson), Ruth Mahaffey (Mrs. J. L. Woodruff), Emily Wood (Mrs. P. B. Shamhart),

William Hamilton, Lewis M. Ordained Bapt. ministry, Dec. 1888; preached to country chs. in S.C., 1888-91, while attending coll.; city missionary, Washington, 1891-92; supply pastor First Bapt. Ch., Attica, N.Y., 1892-95; pastor 1st Ch., Canton, O., 1896-1900, 1st Ch., Spartanburg, S.C., 1900-12, 1st Ch., Petersburg, Va., 1912-20, Central Baptist Ch., Johnson City, Tenn., 1920-30, Waverly Ch., Jersey City, N.J., 1930—; also evangelical and radio service, Federated Churches of Greater New York, 1930—. Trustee Furman U., Anderson (South Carolina) Female Coll.; elected pres. Furman U., 1903, but declined; called to supply Met. Tabernacle, London (Spurgeon's old ch.), and accepted service for May 1911. Frequent evangelistic services in Richmond, Baltimore, Boston and other places. Author of pamphlets and mag. articles. Lecturer before college and high sch. classes. Mem. exec. bd. Tenn. Bapt. Conv. Democrat. Home: Jersey City, N.J. Died Apr. 26, 1938.

ROPER, William Winston, Princeton football coach; b. Phila., Pa., Aug. 22, 1880; s. Jourdan Wolfock and Rebecca (Gowen) R.; A.B., Princeton, 1902; student U. of Va. Law Sch., 1906-07; m. Elisabeth Binney Haines, June 7, 1910; children—Elisabeth Binney, William Winston. Football coach, Princeton, 1906-08, 1910-11, and 1919-29, U. of Mo., 1909. Practiced law, Phila., until 1926; mgr. Quaker City Agency of Prudential Ins. Co. of America. U.S. appraiser of merchandise, Port of Phila., 1912-16; mem. Phila. City Council, 1920—. Republican. Episcopalian. Author: Winning Football, 1921; Football—Today and Tomorrow, 1927. Home: Philadelphia, Pa. Died Dec. 10, 1933.

ROPES, Charles Joseph Hardy, clergyman; b. St. Petersburg, Russia (where father was U.S. consul), Dec. 7, 1851; s. William Hooper and Ellen Harriet (Hall) R.; Gymnasium, Arnstadt, Thüringen, Germany, 1868-69, Sorbonne, Paris, 1869; A.B., Yale, 1872; U. of Tübingen, 1872-73; Andover Theol. Sem., 1873-75, resident licentiate, 1875-76; Union Theol. Sem., 1876-77; D.D., Bowdoin, 1894, Yale, 1894; m. Annie Marvin Ladd, Oct. 4, 1877. Ordained Congl. ministry, Aug. 15, 1877; pastor Ellsworth, Me., 1877-81; prof. N.T. lang. and lit., 1881-1905, librarian, 1887-1901, and 1905—, Bangor Theol. Sem. Republican. Author: The Morality of the Greeks, 1872. Edited and translated latter half of Dr. Gerhard Uhlhorn's Conflict of Christianity with Heathenism, 1879. Address: Bangor, Me. Died Jan. 5, 1915.

ROPES, James Hardy, theologian; b. Salem, Mass., Sept. 3, 1866; s. William Ladd and Harriet Lawrence (Peirson) R.; A.B., Harvard, 1889, D.D., 1929; grad. Andover Theol. Sem., 1893, S.T.B., 1898; grad. study univs. of Kiel, Halle, and Berlin, 1893-95; D.D., Western Reserve U., 1905; m. Alice, d. Edward J. Lowell, Nov. 23, 1897; children—Harriet, Edward Jackson Lowell. Ordained Congl. ministry, 1901; instr. N.T. criticism and interpretation, 1895-98, asst. prof., 1898-1903, Bussey prof., 1903-10, Hollis prof. divinity, 1910—, Dexter lecturer on Bibl. lit., 1903—, dean in charge of univ. extension, 1910-22, and dean of special students, 1916-22, Harvard. Republican. Fellow Am. Acad. Arts and Sciences. Awarded medal for Biblical studies, British Acad., 1928. Author: Die Sprüche Jesu die in den kanonischen Evangelien nicht überliefert sind, 1896; The Apostolic Age in the Light of Modern Criticism, 1906; Commentary on the Epistle of St. James, 1915; The Text of Acts, 1925; The Singular Problem of the Epistle to the Galatians, 1929. Address: Cambridge, Mass. Died Jan. 8, 1933.

ROPES, John Codman, author; b. St. Petersburg, Russia (of American parentage), Apr. 28, 1836; grad. Harvard, 1857, LL.D., 1897; grad. Harvard Law Sch., 1861; practised law, 1861—. Author: The Army Under Pope (Campaigns of the Civil War); The First Napoleon; The Campaign of Waterloo; Atlas of Waterloo; The Story of the Civil War. Home: Boston, Mass. Died 1899.

ROPES, William Ladd, librarian; b. Newton, Mass., July 19, 1825; s. Hardy and Mary (Ladd) R.; A.B., Harvard, 1846, A.M., 1849; grad. Andover Theol. Sem., 1852; m. Harriet Lawrence Peirson, Sept. 5, 1865. Teacher Pub. Latin Sch., Boston, 1846-48; ordained Congl. ministry, Sept. 14, 1853; pastor First Ch., Wrentham, Mass., 1853-62; librarian Andover Theol. Sem., 1866-1905, librarian emeritus, 1905—. Address: Andover, Mass. Died Oct. 14, 1912.

RORABACK, Alberto T., judge; b. Sheffield, Berkshire County, Mass., Aug. 23, 1849; s. John C. and Maria L. (Hoysdradt) R.; ed. South Berkshire Inst., Mass., and Geneseo (N.Y.) Acad.; m. Minnie E. Hunt, Feb. 20, 1873. Admitted to Conn. bar, 1873; judge Ct. of Common Pleas of Litchfield County, 1889-97; mem. Conn. Ho. of Rep., 1885, 97 (chmn. judiciary com.); judge Superior Ct. of Conn., 1897-1908; justice Supreme Ct. of Conn., 1908-19. Republican. Methodist. Mason. Home: Canaan, Conn. Died Feb. 1, 1923.

RORABACK, J. Henry, Rep. nat. committeeman; b. Sheffield, Mass., Apr. 5, 1870; s. John C. and Maria (Hoysradt) R.; ed. high sch., Great Barrington, Mass.; m. Mary L. Parsons, Apr. 29, 1896; 1 son, Lewis P. Began practice at North Canaan, 1892; organizer, 1905, and pres. Berkshire Power Co., which built a hydroelectric sta. on Housatonic River nr. Canaan; organizer, 1907, and pres. Connecticut Light & Power Co., also Ousatonic Water Power Co., Bristol Traction Co.; dir. Aetna Life Ins. Co., Nat. Fire Ins. Co., Automobile Ins. Co. of Hartford, Aetna Casualty & Indemnity Co., Hartford-Conn. Trust, Eastern Machine Screw Co. Delegate 7 Rep. Nat. convs.; mem. Rep. State Com., 1898—, chmn., 1912—; mem. Rep. Nat. Com., 1920— (exec. com. and vice chmn). Home: Hartford, Conn. Died May 19, 1937.

RORER, Sarah Tyson, teacher of domestic science, editor and author; b. Richboro, Pa.; d. Charles Tyson and Elizabeth (Sagers) Heston; grad. East Aurora (N.Y.) Acad.; m. W. Albert Rorer, Feb., 1871 (dec.); children—William Albert, James Birch. Prin. Phila. Sch. Domestic Science; lecturer on Food in Health and Disease; author and editor for 53 yrs.; editor and partial owner Table Talk, 1886-92, Household News, 1893-97; staff Ladies' Home Journal, 1897-1911; later devoted time to writing and lecturing. Author: Mrs. Rorer's New Cook Book; Mrs. Rorer's Philadelphia Cook Book; Canning and Preserving; Home Candy Making; Salads; Bread-Making; Made Overs; Sandwiches; Hot Weather Dishes; Twenty Quick Soups; How to Use a Chafing Dish; Good Ways in Cooking; Dainties; Colonial Cookery; Good Cooking; A Book on Diet in Health and Disease; A Key to Simple Cookery. Home: Colebrook, Pa. Died Dec. 27, 1937.

RORIMER, Louis, artist, designer; b. Cleveland, O., Sept. 12, 1872; s. Jack and Minnie (Iglauer) R.; ed. Kunst. Gewerbe Sch. (Munich), Des Arts Decorative, and Académie Julian (Paris); m. Edith Joseph, Dec. 7, 1902; children—James J., Louise M. Began as teacher, 1886, later engaged in interior decorating and furnishing under name of Rorimer-Brooks Studios, of which became pres.; taught designing and modeling in Cleveland Sch. of Art 18 yrs., also lecturer at art institutes, etc.; exhibited drawings, sculpture and furniture at Cleveland Mus. of Art, and held architectural exhbns. in various parts of the country; decorator and designer of hotels, theatres and clubs. Mem. bd. dirs. Cleveland Sch. of Art. Home: Cleveland, O. Died Nov. 30, 1939.

RORTY, Malcolm Churchill, engineer; b. Paterson, N.J., May 1, 1875; s. Richard Mackay and Octa (Churchill) R.; grad. Walkill Acad., Middletown, N.Y., 1892; M.E. in E.E., Cornell U., 1896; m. Margaret McNaughten, Mar. 23, 1904; children—Margaret McNaughten, Malcolm McNaughten, James McNaughten (dec.). With J. G. White Co. and New York Telephone Co. until 1899; engr. and traffic engr. with Am. Bell Telephone Co., 1899-1903; gen. supt. traffic, etc., Central Dist. Telephone Co., Pittsburgh, Pa., 1903-10; comml. engr. Am. Telephone & Telegraph Co., 1910-13; asst. v.p. Western Union Telegraph Co., New York, 1913-14; spl. agt. Am. Tel. & Tel. Co., 1914-17, chief statistician, 1919-21; v.p. Bell Telephone Securities Co., 1921-22; asst. v.p. Am. Tel. & Tel. Co., 1922-23; pres. Internat. Telephone Securities Corp., 1923-27; v.p. Internat. Telephone & Telegraph Corp., 1923-30; v.p. American Founders Corp., 1930-31. President Am. Management Assn., 1934—. Served as lt. col. U.S.A., 1917-18; with Ordnance Dept. and Gen. Staff; attached to Interallied Munitions Council; participated in Meuse-Argonne offensive. Fellow Am. Statistical Assn. (pres. 1930-31); mem. Nat. Bur. Economic Research (pres. 1922-23, chmn. bd. 1924-25); corr. mem. faculty Univ. of Buenos Aires. Republican. Author: Some Problems in Current Economics, 1922; Bolshevism, Fascism, and Capitalism (with others), 1932. Home: Lusby, Md. Died Jan. 18, 1936.

ROSA, Edward Bennett, physicist; b. Rogersville, N.Y., Oct. 4, 1861; s. Rev. Edward David and Sarah G. (Rowland) R.; B.S., Wesleyan U., 1886, Sc.D., 1906; Ph.D., Johns Hopkins, 1891; m. Mary Evans, Mar. 22, 1894. Prof. physics, Wesleyan U., 1891-1902; physicist, 1901-10, chief physicist, 1910—, Nat. Bur. of Standards. Contbr. to Am. and European jours. of physics and electricity and the papers of the Nat. Bur. of Standards, making a specialty of theoretical and applied electricity and elec. measurements. In charge elec. div. of Bur. of Standards, including investigations on standards of service and safety for public utilities; sec. Internat. Com. on Elec. Units and Standards. Mem. Nat. Acad. Sciences. Died May 17, 1921.

ROSE, Edward Everley, dramatist; b. Stanstead, Que., Can., Feb. 11, 1862; s. George Henry and Nancy (Fox) R.; grad. Chauncy Hall Sch., Boston, 1881; studied Harvard, 1882-84. Engaged in dramatic authorship, 1884—. Plays: Pards; The Westerner; Senators from Gridley; The Rosary; Rock of Ages. Dramatizations: David Harum; To Have and to Hold; Richard Carvel; Janice Meredith; Eben Holden; Alice of Old Vincennes; Rupert of Hentzau; Gentleman from Indiana; Mr. Dooley; Fighting Bob; Kassia for Mrs. Leslie Carter. Address: New York, N.Y. Died Apr. 2, 1939.

ROSE, Frank Bramwell, chaplain U.S.N.; b. Tuckerton, N.J., Apr. 5, 1836; s. Francis Bodine and Sarah (Early) R.; ed. Central High Sch., Phila.; m. Mary Anna King, Apr. 2, 1851. Ordained 1862; chaplain 14th N.J. Inf., Sept. 1, 1862-June 18, 1865; apptd. from N.J., chaplain U.S.N., Feb. 3, 1870; retired Apr. 5, 1898; advanced to rank of rear admiral retired, June 29, 1906, for services during Civil War. Home: Swarthmore, Pa. Died 1910.

ROSE, Guy, artist; b. San Gabriel, Calif., Mar. 3, 1867; s. Leon John and Amanda (Jones) R.; studied art, San Francisco Art Sch., also at Julian Acad., Paris, France, under Doucet, Constant and Lefebvre; m. Ethel R. Boardman, Jan. 3, 1895. Hon. mention, Paris Salon, 1894; awarded medals, Buffalo, St. Louis and Atlanta Expns.; silver medal, San Francisco Expn., 1915; gold medal, San Diego Expn., 1915; two Black prizes and W. P. Harrison prize, Los Angeles. Represented in Los Angeles and Cleveland museums. Home: Pasadena, Calif. Died Nov. 17, 1925.

ROSE, Henry Martin, parliamentarian; b. Hornellsville (now Hornell), N.Y., Mar. 16, 1858; s. Henry Arnold and Zada Arminda (Martin) R.; Kalamazoo (Mich.) Coll., 1877-80; m. Mrs. Rena F. Mitchell, 1921. Editor and owner weekly newspapers in Mich., and later with editorial depts. Grand Rapids Herald, Detroit Journal, etc.; clk. U.S. Senate com. on revision of laws of U.S., 1895-1900; chief clk. U.S. Senate, 1900-05; asst. sec. and parliamentarian U.S. Senate, 1905 (office created in statute in which he is named). Republican. Episcopalian. Mason, K.P. Home: Washington, D.C. Deceased.

ROSE, John Carter, judge; b. Baltimore, Apr. 27, 1861; s. John and Mary Elizabeth (Hall) R.; Baltimore City Coll., 1873-76; L.B., U. of Md., 1882; LL.D., St. John's, 1915; m. Grace H. Beatson, Oct. 1886; children—Grace B., Jonathan, Douglas H. Admitted to bar, 1882, and practiced at Baltimore. Supervisor of the Census, Baltimore, 1890; U.S. atty., Dist. of Md., 1898-1910; U.S. dist. judge, Dist. of Md., 1910-22; U.S. circuit judge, 4th Circuit, Dec. 26, 1922—. Republican. Presbyn. Author: An Elementary Treatise on the Jurisdiction and Procedure of the Federal Courts, 1915. Home: Baltimore, Md. Died Mar. 26, 1927.

ROSE, John Marshall, congressman; b. Johnstown, Pa., May 18, 1856; A.B., Washington and Jefferson Coll., 1880; m. Fannie S. Slick, 1884. Admitted to Pa. bar, 1884; mem. Pa. Ho. of Rep., 1889; mem. 65th to 67th Congresses (1917-23), 19th Pa. Dist. Republican. Home: Johnstown, Pa. Deceased.

ROSE, Joseph Nelson, botanist; b. nr. Liberty, Ind., Jan. 11, 1862; s. George W. and Rebecca (Corrington) R.; A.B., Wabash Coll., 1885, A.M., 1887, Ph.D., 1889, LL.D., 1925; m. Lou B. Sims, 1888; children—Joseph Sims, Rebecca, Martha, Walter Deane (dec.), George. Asst. in botany, Wabash Coll., 1888-89; asst. and 1st asst., div. of botany, Dept. Agr., 1888-94; asst. curator, Dept. Botany, U.S. Nat. Mus., 1894-1905; asso. curator, U.S. Nat. Mus., Jan. 16, 1905-Jan. 16, 1912, and directly in charge of Nat. Herbarium; asso. in botany, U.S. Nat. Mus., 1912—, and research asso., Carnegie Instn. of Washington, 1912-23. Traveled extensively Mex. and S.A. Spl. study of cacti. In 1888 (with Dr. John M. Coulter) published a Revision of the Umbelliferæ of the U.S.; in 1905 (with Dr. N. L. Britton) published Revision N.A. Crassulaceæ; published numerous papers in tech. jours. on the order Umbelliferæ, Cactaceæ and Mexican plants; in 1899, Useful Plants of Mexico; in 1901, Monograph of North American Umbelliferæ; (with Dr. Britton) The Cactaceæ, 4 vols., 1919-23. In honor of his services in his spl. line of research Dr. Sereno Watson named the genus Rhodosciadium in 1890; Prof. Cogniaux the genus Roseanthus in 1896; Dr. Small the genus Roseanthus, 1910; Prof. Speggasini the genus Brittonrosea, 1923; Mr. Alwin Berger, Roseocactus, 1925. Presbyn. Home: Washington, D.C. Died May 4, 1928.

ROSE, Landon Cabell, banker; b. La Porte, Ind., Nov. 30, 1872; s. Landon Cabell and Nancy (Holbrook) R.; grad. Wabash Coll., 1893. Began banking business, 1893, firm of Rose & Co.; pres. North Avenue State Bank, 1906—; chmn. bd. Metropolitan Investment Co., Rose Realty Corp.; dir. Continental Casualty Co., Continental Assurance Co., Ochoco Timber Co., etc. Home: Chicago, Ill. Died 1931.

ROSE, Martha Emily Parmelee; b. Norton, O., Mar. 5, 1834; d. Theodore Hudson and Harriet (Holcombe) Parmelee; B.L., Oberlin, 1855; m. William G. Rose, Mar. 28, 1858. Teacher music in Mercer (Pa.) Acad. and Sch. of Music, 1855-58; resident Cleveland, O., 1865—. Actively identified for many yrs. with movements for improving conditions for working women of Cleveland. Founder, and 1st pres. Cleveland Sorosis; del. to 1st meeting Ohio Federation Women's Clubs, and framer of constn. of the federation. Author: The Centennial Album, 1876; Travels in Europe and Northern Africa, 1900; Character Building, 1906; Western Reserve of Ohio, 1914. Home: Cleveland, O. Died May 5, 1923.

ROSE, Mary D. Swartz, nutrition expert; b. Newark, O., Oct. 31, 1874; d. Hiram B. and Martha

(Davies) Swartz; B.Litt., Denison U., Granville, O., 1901; student Mechanics Inst., Rochester, N.Y., 1902; B.S., Teachers Coll. (Columbia), 1906; Ph.D., Yale, 1909; m. Anton Richard Rose, Sept. 15, 1910. Teacher in high sch., Wooster, O., 1899-1901, Fond du Lac, Wis., 1902-05; asst. in Dept. of Nutrition, Teachers Coll., 1906-07; traveling fellow, 1907-09; instr. in nutrition, 1909-11, asst. prof., 1910-18, asso. prof., 1918-21, prof., 1921—, Teachers Coll., Columbia. Dept. dir. Bur. of Conservation, Federal Food Board and N.Y. State Commn., 1918-19. Mem. Nutrition Commn. of Health Orgn. of League of Nations, 1935—, Council on Foods of A.M.A., 1933—; pres. Am. Inst. of Nutrition, 1937-38. Author: Laboratory Handbook for Dietetics, 1912; Feeding the Family, 1916; Everyday Foods in War Time, 1918; Foundations of Nutrition, 1927; Teaching Nutrition to Boys and Girls, 1932. Home: Edgewater, N.J. Died Feb. 1, 1941.

ROSE, Rufus Edwards, agrl. chemist; b. New Orleans, La., Mar. 19, 1847; s. Alfred James (M.E.) and Albina Stanhope (Johnston) R.; student Dolbear Tech. and Commercial Coll., New Orleans, 1862-64; m. Emeline Sahl, Mar. 20, 1871; children—Alfred Henry (dec.), Ruby Edwards; m. 2d, Mary Anna Morgan, July 18, 1894; children—Muriel Mary, Rufus Edwards. Supt. La. Reclamation Co., 1876-81, Disston Everglade Drainage Co., 1881-86, Disston-St. Cloud Sugar Company, 1886-89; state chemist of Fla., 1901—. Presbyn. Mason, K.P., Elk. Author: (brochures) The Sugar Industry of Florida; Everglades of Florida; Drainage of Farm Lands. Home: Tallahassee, Fla. Died Apr. 23, 1931.

ROSE, Thomas Ellwood, maj. U.S.A.; b. Bucks County, Pa., Mar. 12, 1830; common school edn.; became private 12th Pa., Apr. 1861; capt. 77th Pa., Oct. 1861; served at Shiloh, Corinth, Murfreesboro; col., Jan. 1863; taken prisoner at Chickamauga; escaped at Weldon, N.C.; recaptured next day; sent to Libby Prison, Oct. 1, 1863. With Maj. Hamilton, of 12th Ky., and working party of 15, cut through the stone wall of cellar and dug a tunnel 50 feet long, completing it in three months; 109 soldiers escaped; 48 were retaken, including Col. Rose; again confined in Libby until exchanged, Apr. 30, 1864; served until close of war; bvtd. brig. gen. vols. and col. U.S.A.; after war capt. and maj. U.S. inf., retired 1894. Address: Baltimore, Md. Died 1907.

ROSE, U. M., lawyer; b. Marion County, Ky., Mar. 5, 1834; s. Joseph and Nancy R.; LL.D., U. of Mo., 1888, and U. of Ark.; m. Margaret T. Gibbs, Oct. 25, 1853; children—George B. and William R. Practiced at Batesville, Ark., 1853-60; chancellor of Chancery Ct., Little Rock, Ark., 1860-65; in practice at Little Rock, 1865—. Mem. Dem. Nat. Com. several yrs.; pres. Am. Bar Assn., 1901-02; U.S. del. to 2d Hague Peace Conf., 1907, with rank as ambassador. Author: Rose's Digest of Arkansas Reports, 1867; also many articles on Am. and European jurisprudence in law jours. Address: Little Rock, Ark. Died Aug. 12, 1913.

ROSE, Wallace Dickinson, M.D.; b. Little Rock, Ark., Mar. 11, 1887; s. John M. and Lillie May (Kelly) R.; grad. Ark. Mil. Acad., 1907; M.D., U. of Ark., 1916; post-grad. work, Washington U. Med. Sch. and U. of Pa.; m. Kathryn Noble Nowlin, Jan. 21, 1911; children—U. M., Lillian May. Enlisted in U.S. Army, Aug. 11, 1917; went overseas Aug. 1918; assigned to U.S. Base Hosp., No. 115, Vichy, France; returned to U.S., July 1919 and practiced at Little Rock, 1919—; mem. staff Logan H. Roots Memorial Hosp., Bapt. State Hosp., St. Vincent's Infirmary; asso. prof. medicine, U. of Ark., and lecturer on physical diagnosis; demonstrator clin. medicine and chief of med. sect. Isaac Folsom Clinic. Democrat. Presbyn. Mason. Author: Physical Diagnosis, 1917. Home: Little Rock, Ark. Died Aug. 17, 1928.

ROSE, Walter Malins, lawyer; b. Toronto, Can., Nov. 25, 1872; s. Henry J. and C. E. R.; grad. Chaffey Coll., Ontario, Calif., 1891; Leland Stanford Jr. U., A.B., 1895, Coll. of Law, Cornell, LL.B., 1896 (law thesis prize); m. Mary Holt, Oct. 19, 1899. Admitted to bar Supreme Court Calif., Sept. 1896; Supreme Court U.S., Oct. 1899. Author: Notes on United States Reports (12 vols. and index), 1899-1901; Digest of U.S. Reports from the Beginning to Vol. 186, U.S. (3 vols.), 1903; A Code of Federal Procedure (3 vols.), 1907. Editor: Notes on Texas Reports (5 vols.), 1902. Residence: Los Angeles, Calif. Died 1908.

ROSE, Wickliffe, administrative officer; b. Saulsbury, Tenn., Nov. 19, 1862; s. Kinchen Langston and Jeanette (Cherry) R.; A.B., U. of Nashville, 1889, A.M., 1890; U. of Chicago Summer Sch., 1897-1902; LL.D., U. of Miss., 1910; A.M., Harvard, 1913; m. Ella Morio Sadler, Dec. 29, 1891; children—Ethel Lewis, Harold Wickliffe, Dorothy Taliaferro. Instr. history and math., Peabody Coll., 1891-92; prof. philosophy, Peabody Coll. and U. of Nashville, 1892-1902; prof. history and philosophy of edn., U. of Tenn., 1902-04; dean Peabody Coll. and U. of Nashville, 1904-07; gen. agt., Peabody Edn. Fund, 1907-15; administrative sec. and mem. Rockefeller Sanitary Commn., 1910-15; mem. Southern Edn. Bd., 1909-15 (exec. sec. 1909-13); trustee John F. Slater Fund, 1909-23; mem. Rockefeller Foundation, 1913-28; mem. Internat. Health Board, 1913-28 (gen. dir., 1913-23); mem. Gen. Edn. Bd., 1911-28, and pres., 1923-28, also pres. Internat. Edn. Bd., 1923-28; retired; mem. China Med. Bd.; mem. med. advisory bd. Am. Red Cross war council, 1917. Democrat. Member Church of the Disciples. Address: New York, N.Y. Died Sept. 5, 1931.

ROSENBAUM, Solomon Guedalia, corp. exec.; b. Raleigh, N.C., Feb. 12, 1868; s. Morris and Frances (Brasch) R.; ed. Raleigh Male Acad.; m. Bella Rosenthal, Feb. 15, 1894. Pres. Franmor Realty Corp., Yarboro Realty Corp., Frabel Corp.; dir. of the Woodbine Land & Improvement Co. Trustee United Hosp. Fund, Montefiore Hosp. for Chronic Diseases, Baron de Hirsch Fund. Author: Causes for the Loss of the Battle of Waterloo. Home: Roslyn, L.I. Died Dec. 26, 1937.

ROSENBERG, S. L. Millard, univ. prof.; b. Neudenan, Baden, Germany, Mar. 6, 1869; s. Leopold and Lina (Stiefel) R.; came to United States, 1885; B.S., U. of Pa., 1907, M.A., 1908, Ph.D., 1910; diplôme, U. of Grenoble, 1906; unmarried. Alliance Française traveling fellow, 1906; Harrison fellow, U. of Pa., 1906-09; U. of Pa. research fellow, 1909-15; del. Am. Traveling Fellow to Spain, 1933. Instr. Romance languages, Swarthmore Coll., 1910-12; prof. Romance langs., Girard Coll., 1912-22; prof. Spanish, U. of Calif. at Los Angeles, 1922—. Lecturer Nat. U., Mexico City, Mexico, summer, 1924. Author: La Española de Florencia, 1911; Las Burlas Veras, 1912; Life and Works of Julian de Armendariz, 1917; Baroja, Zalacain, el Aventurero (with L. D. Bailiff), 1925; Mexico Virreinal (with Romero de Terreros), 1925; Libro de Lectura, 1927; Espina, Talin y otros cuentos (with M. A. Zeitlin), 1927; Tradiciones y Leyendas Mexicanas (with Romero de Terreros), 1927; Rivas, Don Alvaro (with E. H. Templin), 1927; Baroja, Páginas Escogidas (with L. D. Bailiff), 1927; Anthology of Mexican Verse (with E. H. Templin), 1928; Anthology of Mexican Prose (with E. H. Templin), 1928; Páginas Misticas (with F. T. McKeon), 1929; León, Tipos y Paisajes, 1930; Heras, Horas Vividas (with H. P. Earle), 1931; Dario, Poetic and Prose Selections (with M. L. de Lowther), 1931; also magazine articles and reviews. Asso. editor Hispania; collaborator Modern Lang. Forum. Home: Los Angeles, Calif. Died July 10, 1934.

ROSENDALE, Simon Wolfe, lawyer; b. Albany, N.Y., June 23, 1842; s. Sampson R.; ed. Albany, and Barre (Vt.) Acad.; LL.D., Union U.; m. Helen Cone, Feb. 9, 1870. Admitted to bar, 1863; mem. law firm Rosendale and Dugan; asst. dist. atty., Albany County, 1864-67; recorder City of Albany, 1868-72; atty. gen. State of N.Y., 1892-94; corp. counsel of Albany several terms; commr. and v.p. State Bd. of Charities, 1899-1917; commr. on State Farm for Women. Pres. trustees Albany Med. Coll.; pres. bd. of governors Union U.; v.p. Am. Jewish Hist. Soc. Democrat. Wrote: The Involution of Wampum as Currency, New York Times (and pamphlet), 1896, and other monographs. Home: Albany, N.Y. Died Apr. 22, 1937.

ROSENFELD, Maurice (Bernard), pianist, music critic; b. Vienna, Austria, Dec. 31, 1867; s. David Louise (Mittler) R.; came to U.S., 1873; student, Coll. City of New York, 2 yrs., class of 1887; grad. Chicago Musical Coll., 1888, post-grad. degree, 1889 (Master of Music, 1896); m. Estelle Schlesinger, Aug. 28, 1907. Mem. faculty, piano dept., Chicago Mus. Coll., 1888-1911, Sherwood Music Sch., 1911-12; mem. bd. mus. dirs., Chicago Mus. Coll., 1912-16; established Maurice Rosenfeld Piano Sch., Chicago, Apr. 1916, reëstablished, Jan. 1, 1925. Music editor of Chicago Examiner, 1907-15. Gave many piano recitals; composer various pieces for orchestra and piano and contbr. to Musical Courier, New York, and Detroit Free Press; Chicago corr. Musical America, 1913-17, and Feb. 1, 1919-21; musical editor Chicago Daily News, 1917-31. Incorporated, Oct. 1923, and pres. Chicago Philharmonic Conservatory of Music; v.p. Chicago Conservatory, Sept., 1931—. Republican. Jewish religion. Mem. bd. exam. Ill. Music Teachers' Assn. Home: Chicago, Ill. Deceased.

ROSENFELD, Sydney, dramatist; b. Richmond, Va., Oct. 26, 1855; ed. pub. schs., Richmond and New York, and by pvt. tutors; m. Genie Holtzmeyer Johnson, 1883. First editor of Puck. Author: (plays) A Possible Case: Imagination; The Club Friend; The Politician; A Man of Ideas; A House of Cards; The Aero Club; The Senator (co-author). Operettas and musical plays: Lady or Tiger; The Mocking Bird; The Passing Show; The Giddy Throng; The King's Carnival; The Hall of Fame; The Vanderbilt Cup; Children of Destiny, 1910. Adapter: The White Horse Tavern; The Two Escutcheons; The Black Hussar; Prince Methusalem; Nanon. Died June 13, 1931.

ROSENGARTEN, George David, chemist; b. Phila., Pa., Feb. 12, 1869; s. Harry B. and Clara J. (Knorr) R.; B.S., U. of Pa., 1890; Ph.D., U. of Jena, 1892; hon. Sc.D., U. of Pa., 1927; m. Susan E. Wright, Apr. 23, 1895. V.p. Rosengarten & Sons, Inc., 1901-05; v.p. Powers, Weightman-Rosengarten Co., 1905-27, later dir. successors Merck & Co., Inc.; retired. Mem. Com. of Revision of United States Pharmacopœia, 1910-30. Mem. Am. Chem. Soc. (pres. 1927), Am. Inst. Chem. Engrs. (pres.). Republican. Episcopalian. Home: Malvern, Pa. Died Feb. 24, 1936.

ROSENTHAL, Albert, artist; b. Phila., Jan. 30, 1863; s. Max and Caroline (Rosenthal) R.; studied art under his father and at Pa. Acad.; studied also in Munich and in Paris under Gérôme, in the École des Beaux Arts. Painting portraits, 1893—; widely known as etcher and painter of portraits of famous Americans. Medals Chicago, Buffalo and San Francisco expns. Represented in museums of Brooklyn, N.Y., Youngstown, O., Dayton, O., Los Angeles, Calif., Kansas City, Mo., Dallas, Tex., Elgin, Ill., Buffalo, St. Louis, Detroit, Atlanta, Cleveland, Acad. of Fine Arts, Phila., Art Inst. Chicago, San Francisco Mus., Newport Art Assn., State Coll. (Pa.), New Hope (Pa.) High Sch., Salmagundi Club (New York), Hist. Society of Pa., New Yorkers Hist. Soc., U.S. Capitol, Washington, etc. Home: New Hope, Pa. Died Dec. 20, 1939.

ROSENTHAL, Herman, librarian, author; b. Friedrichstadt, Kurland, Russia, Oct. 6, 1843; s. Moritz and Pauline R.; ed. Progynasium of Jacobstadt; m. Anna Rosenthal, June 1864. Came to U.S., Aug. 16, 1881; started the 1st agrl. colony for Russian Jews in America in La.; organized 2 more colonies in S.D. and N.J. Contbr., 1885—, to New York Staatszeitung; sent by the Great Northern Ry. on mission to Japan and China, 1892-93; sec. of the German-Am. Reform Union, 1893-94; started the Russian Daily Zarya in 1880, and published and edited the Hebrew Monthly Intelligencer, New York; chief of Slavonic dept. New York Pub. Library, 1898—; editor Russian dept. Jewish Ency., 1900—. Mem. Imperial Russian Orphan Asylum, Red Cross Soc. (medal of latter, 1877-78). Author: Wrote des Sammlers, 1893; Lied der Lieder, 1893; Report on Japan, China and Corea, St. Paul, 1893; Spätherbstnebel Poems, 1906. Translator: Hugo Ganz' Land of Riddles (Russia), 1904; Prince Serge Urussov's Memoirs of a Russian Governor, 1908. Home: New York, N.Y. Died Jan. 27, 1917.

ROSENTHAL, Max, artist; b. Turck, Russian Poland, Nov. 23, 1833; studied lithography, drawing and painting in Paris, 1847-49; m. Caroline Rosenthal; father of Albert R. Came to Phila., 1849, and made chromo-lithograph plates for the 1st book fully illus. by the process in the U.S.; did much work as illustrator; made 1st facsimile of water colors reproduced in U.S. by lithographic process; artist for Govt. during Civil War making illustrations for report of U.S. Mil. Commn.; began etching, 1880; made many hist. portraits, more than 500 in Smithsonian Instn.; turned attention to messotints, 1890; made life size heads of Daniel Webster, Washington and many others; later years devoted to painting; completed painting of masterpiece, "Jesus at Prayer," 1904. Awarded various prizes, medals, etc. Address: Philadelphia, Pa. Died Aug. 8, 1918.

ROSENTHAL, Moritz, banker; b. Dixon, Ill., May 4, 1866; s. Sampson and Mina (Cahn) R.; B.Litt., U. of Mich., 1888; m. Virginia Moses, Apr. 12, 1897; children—Paul M., Jane (Mrs. Frederick M. Heimerdinger), John S. Admitted to Ill. bar, 1890; asst. state's atty. Cook County, Ill., 1893; asst. U.S. atty. Northern Ill., 1894-97; mem. firm Moses, Rosenthal & Kennedy, Chicago, 1897-1911; counsel for Standard Oil Co. in $29,000,000 fine case and 5 yr. dissolution suit; partner Ladenburg, Thalmann & Co., internat. bankers, N.Y. City, 1911—; chmn. bd. Duquesne Light Co., Phila. Co.; dir. Am. Gear & Mfg. Co., Hart, Schaffner & Marx, Hupp Motor Car Corp., Pittsburgh Motor Coach Co., Pittsburgh Rys. Co., Alliance Realty Co., Burns Bros., Broad-Exchange Co., Texarkana & Ft. Smith Ry. Co. Home: Riverdale-on-Hudson, N.Y. Died Nov. 12, 1934.

ROSENTHAL, Toby E., artist; b. New Haven, Conn., Mar. 15, 1848; s. Jacob and Ernestine (Germanus) R.; ed. pub. schs., New Haven and San Francisco; studied drawing under Henri Bacon and painting under Fortunato Arriola, San Francisco; student at Royal Academie, Munich, under Straehuber, Carl Raupp and Carl von Piloty, 1865-72; m. Sophie Ansbacher, July 26, 1880. Professionally engaged as painter, 1872—; repeatedly had classes in painting and composition, 1872-82. Paintings chiefly figural compositions and genre work; also painted many portraits in Calif., Eng. and Germany. Medals at Centennial Expn., Phila., 1876, Royal Acad., Munich, Internat. Expn., Munich (gold medal). Decorated Order Knight of St. Michael (Bavaria), 1914. Trustee Kunstgenossenschaft, München. Address: München, Bavaria. Died Dec. 1917.

ROSENWALD, Julius, merchant, philanthropist; b. Springfield, Ill., Aug. 12, 1862; s. Samuel and Augusta (Hammerslough) R.; pub. sch. edn., Springfield; m. Augusta Nusbaum, Apr. 8, 1890 (died 1929); m. 2d, Mrs. Adelaide Rau Goodkind, Jan. 8, 1930. With Hammerslough Brothers, wholesale clothing, New

York, 1879-85; pres. Rosenwald & Weil, Chicago, 1885-1906; v.p. and treas., 1895-1910, pres., 1910-25, later chmn. of bd. Sears, Roebuck & Co. Apptd. by Pres. Wilson, 1916, mem. Advisory Commn. of Council of Nat. Defense and chmn. com. on supplies; spl. mission in France for sec. of war, 1918; mem. 2d Nat. Indsl. Conf., 1919. Generous contbr. of time and money to civic, philanthropic and ednl. enterprises; stimulated constrn. and contributed part (about $600,000) of total cost of twenty-five Y.M.C.A. and three Y.W.C.A. buildings in twenty-five cities with about 2,000,000 Negro population; contributed $3,660,000 thereby stimulating constrn., at a total cost of $23,200,000, of 4,500 Negro rural public schools with capacity of 567,000 pupils and 12,600 teachers in the South, 339 of these built in 1929; donated $2,700,000 toward model housing project for Negroes in Chicago; pledged $3,000,000 for a Museum of Science and Industry in Chicago; pledged total of 6,000,000 for Jewish Colonization in Russia; contributed approximately $5,000,000 to U. of Chicago; established in 1917 Julius Rosenwald Fund with capital of $30,000,000 as of June 30, 1929, with chartered purpose, "the well-being of mankind." Hon. pres. Jewish Charities of Chicago; chairman Chicago Bureau of Public Efficiency; mem. executive committee Chicago Plan Commission; vice pres. Sinai Congregation (Chicago), Am. Jewish Com. (New York); trustee Rockefeller Foundation, Art Inst. Chicago, Tuskegee Inst., U. of Chicago, Hull House, Baron de Hirsch Fund. Home: Chicago, Ill. Died Jan. 6, 1932.

ROSEWATER, Andrew, civil and sanitary engr.; b. in Bohemia, Oct. 31, 1848; ed. in common and high schools, Cleveland, O.; m. Frances Meinrath, Oct. 18, 1883. Flagman engr. corps, Union Pacific Ry. explorations and surveys, 1864; later in other engring. position same road; asst. city engr., Omaha, 1868-70; city engr., 1870-75; mgr. and ad interim editor Omaha Bee, 1876-77; engr. in charge construction Omaha & Northwestern Ry., 1878-80; resident engr. Omaha Water Works Co., 1880-81; city engr., Omaha, 1881-87; 1887-91 cons. and designing engr. of sewerage for 25 cities; pres. elec. subway commn. of Washington, 1891-92; consulting engr. for cities in Colo., S.D., etc. City engr. Omaha, and pres. Bd. Public Works, 1897—. Wrote Report Elec. Commn. of D.C. to the President, 1891. Address: Omaha, Neb. Died 1909.

ROSEWATER, Edward, founder and editor, 1871—, Omaha Bee; b. Bukovan, a small village of Bohemia, 1841; ed. at village school and high school at Prague until 13 yrs. old; came to U.S., 1854; telegraph operator at 17; in U.S. mil. telegraph corps, 1862-63; went to Omaha, 1863, as mgr. Pacific Telegraph; mem. of Neb. legislature, 1871; mem. Rep. Nat. Com., 1892; mem. advisory bd. Nat. Com., 1896, 1900, 1904; received many votes on numerous ballots in Neb. legislature, 1901 for U.S. senator; mem. U.S. Mint Commn., 1897; representative of U.S. and v.p. Universal Postal Congress, Washington, 1897; original promoter Trans-Mississippi Expn. (Omaha), 1898, mem. exec. com. in charge of publicity and promotion; del. and mem. com. on resolutions, Am. Conf. Internat. Arbitration, Washington, 1904; mem. exec. com. Nat. Civic Federation. Home: Omaha, Neb. Died 1906.

ROSEWATER, Victor, journalist; b. Omaha, Feb. 13, 1871; s. Edward and Leah (Colman) R.; Ph.B., Columbia, 1891, A.M., 1892, Ph.D., 1893; m. Katie Katz, Jan. 27, 1904; children—Harriet Leah (Mrs. Percival M. Sax, Jr.), Edward. Began newspaper work on Omaha Bee, 1893, mng. editor, 1895, editor, 1906-20, editor and publisher, 1917-20. Regent Nebraska State U., 1896-97; del. White House Conf. on Conservation of Natural Resources, 1908; del.-at-large Rep. Nat. Conv., 1908; mem. Rep. Nat. Com., 1908-12 (chmn. 1912); mem. Advisory Com. Rep. Nat. Com., 1916; mem. advisory council Nat. Civic Federation; mem. Am. Jewish Com.; Neb. State Commn. on Workmen's Compensation, 1911. Pres. 1st home rule charter conv. for Omaha, 1913. Mem. com. on labor, Advisory Commn. of Council Nat. Defense, 1917-18; adminstr. for Neb. of paper and pulp sect. War Industries Bd., 1918-19; chmn. Neb. Constl. Conv. Survey Com., 1919. Spl. lecturer on municipal finance, U. of Neb., 1894, U. of Wis., 1904. Asst. to pres. Sesqui-Centennial Exhbn. Assn., 1921-25. Leader of Round Table on "The Press," in Inst. of Pub. Affairs, U. of Va., 1927-29, also at Inst. Statesmanship, Rollins Coll., 1930. Author: Special Assessments—A Study in Municipal Finance, 1898. Wrote title "Laissez Faire," Palgrave's Dictionary of Political Economy; title "Omaha," in Historic Towns of the Western States, 1901; History of the Liberty Bell, 1926; History of Co-operative News-gathering in the United States, 1930; Back Stage in 1912, 1932; also many mag. articles. Address: Philadelphia, Pa. Died July 12, 1940.

ROSING, Leonard August, retail mcht.; b. Malmö, Sweden, Aug. 29, 1861; s. August George and Charlotte Flintburg R.; moved to Minn., 1869; ed. dist. schs.; m. May B. Season, 1886. Lived on farm until 1882; clerk in gen. store, 1882-88; mem. firm of Rosing & Kraft, boots, shoes and furnishings, Cannon Falls, Minn., 1888—. Republican until 1890; left party because of McKinley bill; Dem. candidate for State senate, 1894; chmn. Minn. Dem. State Com., 1896-1900; Dem. nominee for gov. Minn., 1902; defeated. Private sec. to gov., 1899-1900; del. Nat. Dem. convs., 1900, 1904; chmn. exec. com. of Dem. State Com., 1904; mem. State Bd. of Control, 1905—; pres. Minn. Municipal and Commercial League, 1903-05. Home: St. Paul, Minn. Died 1909.

ROSS, Albert, see Linn Boyd Porter.

ROSS, Albert, officer U.S.N.; b. Clarion, Pa., Jan. 3, 1846; s. Dr. James and Mary A. (Wilson) R.; grad. U.S. Naval Acad., 1867; m. Alice Brewer, Mar. 1870. Midshipman, U.S.S. Minnesota, 1867-78; ensign, 1868; Powhatan, 1868-69; master, 1870; retired, 1871; Wachusett, 1873, Ossipee, 1874; restored to active list, 1874; lt., 1871; Worcester, flagship N. Atlantic sta., 1874-75; spl. duty, Annapolis, 1876; Passaic N. Atlantic sta., 1876-77; comd. Wyandotte, Washington, 1877-88; Portsmouth, apprentice training service, 1878-82; Navy Yard, Washington, 1882-83; Miantonomoh, 1883; torpedo instrn., Newport, R.I., 1883, 1889; U.S. Naval Acad., 1883-86; Alert, Pacific sta., 1887-89; Pensacola, 1889-90; training-ship Jamestown, 1890-92; lt. comdr., 1890; Naval Acad., 1892-98; comdr., Aug. 1897; comdg. Alliance, Jan. 1898-Dec. 1899; light house insp., 5th dist., 1900-02; capt., Apr. 1902; comdg. Buffalo, 1902-03; insp. naval colliers, 1904-05; comdt. Naval Training Sta., Great Lakes, Ill., and mem. Lighthouse Bd., July 1, 1905; rear admiral, Oct. 13, 1907; retired Jan. 3, 1908; continued on duty as comdt. Naval Training Sta., Great Lakes, until Nov. 1912. Gen. Insp. of naval training activities for regulars and reserves, Sept. 1917—. Comdr. Culver Summer Naval Sch., Culver, Ind., 1917—. Home: Coconut Grove, Fla. Died Jan. 23, 1926.

ROSS, Bennett Battle, chemist; b. Tuskegee, Ala., Dec. 25, 1864; s. Bennett Battle and Charlotte Augusta (Walker) R.; B.Sc., Ala. Poly. Inst., 1881, M.Sc., 1886; univs. Göttingen and Berlin, 1 semester each; LL.D., Southern U., 1917, Emory U., 1918; m. Letitia Roane Dowdell, Aug. 18, 1897. Asst. chemist, Ala. Poly. Inst., 1884-87; prof. chemistry, La. State U., 1887-93; prof. chemistry, 1893—, dean College of Agricultural Sciences, 1908-21; dean dept. of science, 1921—, Ala. Poly. Inst. (acting pres. during greater part of 1919-20). State chemist of Alabama, 1893—. Mem. State Bd. Industrial Preparedness, Ala., 1916; asso. mem. Naval Consulting Bd. of U.S. Democrat. Methodist. Co-author: Chemistry in Agriculture, 1926. Home: Auburn, Ala. Died Apr. 4, 1930.

ROSS, Clinton, author; b. Binghamton, N.Y., July 31, 1861; s. Erastus and Cornelia (Corbett) R.; A.B., Yale, 1884. Author: The Scarlet Coat; Chalmette and the Meddling Hussy (Am. historical tales); A Trooper of the Empress; Zuleka; The Puppet; The Countess Bettina; Heroes of Our War with Spain; Adventurers of Three Worthies; Improbable Tales; Two Soldiers and a Politician; The Break o' Day; Battle Tales; The Lady of the Blackfriars, or, The Old Play, 1909; A Tale of a Capitolene Venus, 1909; Tontelle; New Tale Book, The True Rosalind. Home: Binghamton, N.Y. Died Mar. 26, 1920.

ROSS, Denman Waldo, lecturer; b. Cincinnati, Jan. 10, 1853; s. John Ludlow and Frances (Waldo) R.; A.B., Harvard, 1875, A.M., Ph.D., 1880; unmarried. Lecturer on the theory of design, Harvard, 1899—. Fellow Am. Acad. Arts and Sciences, 1885—; trustee Mu. Fine Arts, Boston, 1895—; hon. v.p. India Soc. London; corr. mem. Gesellschaft für Ostasiatische Kunst (Berlin); hon. fellow Fogg Mus.; hon. keeper of Ross Study Series. Author: The Early History of Land-Holding Among the Germans, 1883; A Theory of Pure Design, 1907; On Drawing and Painting, 1912; The Painter's Palette, 1919. Home: Cambridge, Mass. Died Sept. 12, 1935.

ROSS, Erskine Mayo, judge; b. Bel Pré, Va., June 30, 1845; s. William Buckner and Elizabeth (Mayo) R.; grad. Va. Mil. Inst., 1865; m. Enez H. Bettis, May 7, 1874. Admitted to Calif. bar, 1869; justice Supreme Ct. of Calif., 1879-86; U.S. dist. judge, Southern Dist. of Calif., 1886-95; U.S. circuit judge, 9th Circuit, 1895-1911; judge U.S. Circuit Ct. of Appeals, Jan. 1, 1912—. Deceased.

ROSS, G(eorge) A(lexander) Johnston, theologian; b. Inverness, Scotland, Feb. 28, 1865; s. Rev. Donald and Helen (MacLeod) R.; gold medallist Royal Acad., Inverness; M.A., U. of Edinburgh, 1884; grad. United Presbyn. Coll., Edinburgh, 1888; D.D., Harvard U., 1919; D.D., Knox Coll., Toronto, 1919; m. Mary Louisa, d. Robert Campbell, of Edinburgh, Mar. 10, 1891; children—George Frank Dorean (dec.), Eliza Helen (Mrs. Marcus Spencer), Donald Neil Campbell (dec.), Mary Katharine, Anna Hildegard, Ian Hamilton; m. 2d, Carol, d. G. T. Barnes, Phila., June 14, 1916. Ordained Presbyn. ministry, 1890; pastor Bridge of Allan, Scotland, 1890-97, St. Paul's Ch., Westbourne Grove, London, 1897-1902, St. Columba's Ch., Cambridge, Eng., 1902-09, Bryn Mawr, Pa., 1909-11; prof. practical theology, Presbyn. Coll., Montreal, Can., 1911-12; prof. homiletics, Union Theol. Sem., 1912-26 (emeritus and lecturer). Mem. bd. preachers Harvard U., 1913-20. Author: The Universality of Jesus, 1908; The Cross, 1911; The God We Trust, 1913; Christian Worship and Its Future, 1927; Why Preach Christ?, 1929. Home: Honolulu, T.H. Died Jan. 22, 1937.

ROSS, James Delmage, elec. engr.; b. Chatham, Ont., Can., Nov. 9, 1871. Supt. municipal power system, Seattle, Wash., 1903—, on leave absence, 1933—; advisory engr. on power, Pub. Works Adminstrn., 1933-35; mem. Securities and Exchange Commn., Washington, D.C., 1935-37; adminstr. Bonneville Project, Columbia River, 1937—. Home: Seattle, Wash. Died Mar. 14, 1939.

ROSS, John Dawson, author; b. Edinburgh, Scotland, Oct. 23, 1853; s. David and Eliza (Ross) R.; ed. Dr. Bell's Sch. and Sch. of Arts, Edinburgh; came to U.S., 1873; LL.D., Waynesburg Coll., 1896; m. Ida Louise Forsberg, Dec. 10, 1879; children—Charles W., George W., Henrietta C., Ida L. Organized the Raeburn Book Co., New York, 1894, mgr. until 1910; mem. staff New York Pub. Library, 1920—, Library War Service, 1918-20. Fellow Soc. Antiquaries (Scotland); mem. Order of Scottish Clans, Burns Federation, Scotland (hon. v.p.). Democrat. Presbyn. Mason; hon. pres. Greater New York Masonic Assn. Author: Celebrated Songs of Scotland, 1887; Scottish Poets in America, 1889; Round Burns' Grave, 1891; Burnsiana, 1892; Stories of Prince Charlie, 1892; The Burns Scrap-Book, 1893; Highland Mary, 1894; All About Burns, 1896; Random Sketches on Scottish Subjects, 1896; Burns' Clarinda, 1897; A Cluster of Poets, 1897; Bonnie Jean, 1898; The Burns Almanac, 1898; The Memory of Burns, 1899; Early Critical Reviews on Robert Burns, 1900; All About Tam O'Shanter, 1900; Henley and Burns, 1901; The Burns Rosary, 1923; Burns' Blue Eyed Lassie, 1924; The Auld Clay Biggin, 1925; A Little Book of Burns Lore, 1926; Who's Who in Burns, 1927; Robert Burns and His Rhyming Friends, 1928; The Poems of Clarinda, 1929; The Burns Handbook, 1930; The Love Songs of Robert Burns, 1932; The Story of the Kilmarnock Burns, 1933. Home: Bellaire, L.I., N.Y. Died Oct. 29, 1939.

ROSS, J(ohn) Walker, editor; b. Gretna, La., Feb. 22, 1868; s. William and Christina (Witzman) R.; Tulane U., 1882-85; m. Julia Mary Murphy, Oct. 18, 1898; children—John Walker, Anna Virginia, Murphy William. Began as copyholder, Daily States, New Orleans, 1885, reporter, 1887-92, city editor, 1892-1909, mng. editor same, 1909-31, editor and pub., 1931-33, editor, 1933—. Maj. staff Gov. N.C. Blanchard, 1904-08; lt. col. staff Gov. J. Y. Sanders, 1908-12. Democrat. Lutheran. Mason. Home: New Orleans, La. Died Sept. 30, 1937.

ROSS, John Wesley, lawyer; b. Lewistown, Ill., June 23, 1841; s. Lewis Winans and Frances Mildred R.; attended Lewistown Sem., Ill. Coll., 1856-62, Harvard Law School, 1864-65 (LL.D., Georgetown U., 1885). Postmaster Washington, 1888-90; apptd. commissioner of the D.C., Sept. 1890, by Pres. Harrison, and was reapptd. by Pres. Cleveland, and twice by Pres. McKinley. He was pres. of the bd. of trustees of public schools of Washington 2 terms; pres. Rock Creek Park Commn. and Commn. for the erection of the Washington Public Library. Died 1902.

ROSS, John William, judge; b. Hardin Co., Tenn., s. Isaac Walker and Margaret Eunice (Cherry) R.; ed. Southern Normal U., Huntingdon, Tenn.; Cumberland U., Lebanon, Tenn., 1897-99; LL.B., law dept. same, 1900; m. Sara Frances Hord, Nov. 26, 1913. Practiced at Savannah, Tenn., 1900-13; chancellor 8th Chancery Dist. of Tenn., 1913-21; judge U.S. Dist. Court, Western Dist. of Tenn., June 11, 1921—. Republican. Home: Jackson, Tenn. Died July 9, 1925.

ROSS, Jonathan, lawyer; b. Waterford, Vt., Apr. 30, 1826; s. Royal and Eliza (Mason) R.; grad. Dartmouth, 1851 (LL.D.); worked on farm summers until 21 yrs. old; taught in common schools 7 successive winters, in acads. 3 yrs.; admitted to bar, 1856; practiced until 1870; mem. Vt. legislature, 1865, 1866 and 1867; State senator, 1870; State atty. for Caledonia Co., 1862-63; mem. State Bd. of Edn., 1866-70; mem. last Council of Censors, 1869; apptd. U.S. senator from Vt., Jan. 11, 1899, to fill vacancy caused by death of Justin S. Morrill; judge, Dec. 1, 1870-90; chief justice, 1890-1900, Supreme Court, Vt.; chmn. State R.R. Commn. Vt., 1900-02. Home: St. Johnsbury, Vt. Died 1905.

ROSS, Leonard Fulton, veteran soldier; b. Lewistown, Ill., July 18, 1823; s. Ossian M. R.; ed. common schools, Lewistown, Havana and Canton, Ill., and 1 yr. (1841-42) at Ill. Coll.; read law and was admitted to bar, Dec. 1844, at Springfield, Ill.; m. Catherine M. Sims, Nov. 13, 1845; m. 2d, Mary E. Warren, Jan. 10, 1865; now widower 2d time. Enlisted as pvt. Co. K, 4th regt., Ill. vol. inf., for Mexican war, July 18, 1846; promoted 1st lt., Sept. 1846; comd. co. at Vera Cruz and Cerro Gordo; elected probate justice, Fulton Co., Aug. 1847; co. clerk, same, Nov. 1849; raised co. for Civil war, elected capt.; commd. col. 17th regt., Ill. vols., May 1861; served in Mo., Ky. and Tenn.; promoted to brig. gen. vols., Apr. 1862; engaged in farming and stock-raising at Avon, Ill., Mar. 1866; apptd. collector internal revenue, 1867; unsuccessful candidate for Congress on

Rep. ticket, 1868; removed to Iowa City, Ia., 1882, and engaged importing and breeding cattle; visited England to examine the best herds of cattle, 1884; sold farm and stock, 1893, and in 1894 returned to Lewistown, Ill. Assisted in organizing the Lewistown Nat. Bank, served 2 yrs. as v.p. and mgr. of bank. Revisited Mexico, 1898, and visited Havana, Cuba; was in the city when the Maine was destroyed, Feb. 1898. Enlisted men enough in Fulton and adjoining counties for a regt. to serve in the Spanish war, but failed to get into the service. Was delegate to Nat. Dem. Convs., 1852, 1856, and Rep. Nat. Conv., 1872. Republican. Home: Lewistown, Ill. Died 1902.

ROSS, Leroy Williams, U.S. attorney; b. Brooklyn, N.Y., Apr. 30, 1883; s. James Stewart and Ella Mary (Griffith) R.; grad. Brooklyn Poly. Prep. Inst., 1900; LL.B., N.Y. Law Sch., 1903; m. Anna Mae Ehlen, Jan. 17, 1906. Began practice at Brooklyn, 1904; asso. in practice with James S. Ross until his decease, 1917. Asst. dist. atty., Kings Co., N.Y., 1909-11; U.S. atty., Eastern Dist. of N.Y., Sept. 4, 1919. Served in Secret Service, War Trade Board, World War; now capt. Judge Advocate Gen.'s Sect., U.S.R. Democrat. Episcopalian. Home: Brooklyn, N.Y. Died Oct. 8, 1921.

ROSS, Lewis P., merchant, mfr.; b. Tuscarora, N.Y., Jan. 30, 1843; s. Mahlon L. and Mary J. (Gager) R.; ed. in country schs.; m. Anna Conklin, May 31, 1866. Wholesale dealer in boots and shoes in Rochester, 1865—; pres. P. A. Field Shoe Co., Beverly, Mass., George H. Snow Co., Brockton, Mass.; chief partner in G. E. Thing & Co., whol. boots and shoes, Buffalo; pres. Fidelity Trust Co.; mem. F. M. Hodgdon, shoe mfrs., Haverhill, Mass. One of organizers, 3d pres., and trustee, 1883—, Rochester Chamber of Commerce. Pres. board trustees, U. of Rochester. Republican. Home: Rochester, N.Y. Died Dec. 1916.

ROSS, Patrick Hore Warriner; b. Bombay, India, Apr. 13, 1858; s. Frederick Torriano and Frances Ann (Johnson) R.; asso. in arts, Oxford U., 1873; m. Martha Emmeline Jackson, of London, Eng., 1875; children—Patrick W. Torriano, Douglas Walter, Lancelot Craigie, Frederick Sydenham, Evelyn; m. 2d, Florence Louise Kellett, 1922. In employ of Bank of England, 1875-81; visited Calif., New York and Europe, 1884; on sugar plantation in Hawaii, 1885-89; settled in Wash. Ty., 1889, and established The Nat. Bank of Ellensburg; moved to New York, 1911; founded, 1912, becoming pres. Nat. Marine League of U.S.A.; advocate of free ports in the U.S. Became a naturalized citizen of U.S., 1889. Trustee Seamen's Inst. of Brooklyn Y.M.C.A. Episcopalian. Author: Federation and the British Colonies, 1887; The Western Gate, 1911; The Blessings of War, 1917. Trade consultant to City of Newark. Home: Beachwood, N.J. Died Apr. 13, 1928.

ROSS, Perley Ason, prof. physics; b. Panacea, Mo., Apr. 6, 1883; s. William McKay and Zaida (Gittings) R.; A.B., Stanford, 1908, A.M., 1909, Ph.D., 1911; grad. study U. of Chicago, 1920; m. Olive Durbin, June 7, 1911; children—Ruth Eleanor, Betsy. Instr. in physics, Stanford, 1910-16, asst. prof. physics, 1916-24, asso. prof., 1924-26, prof., 1927—; acting asso. prof. physics, Cornell, 1926-27. Contributing scientist, Internat. Critical Tables. Fellow Am. Physical Society. Republican. Unitarian. Home: Palo Alto, Calif. Died Mar. 20, 1938.

ROSS, Robert Edwin, lawyer; b. Chicago, Ill., Sept. 19, 1871; s. Joseph P. (M.D.) and Elizabeth H. (King) R.; A.B., cum laude, Princeton, 1895; LL.B., Harvard U., 1899; m. Mary Lord, Aug. 6, 1914. Assisted the late Lambert Tree in organizing Illinois br. of Am. Red Cross, 1905, and was mem. of its 1st exec. com.; asst. to chmn. Chicago br. Am. Red Cross during World War. Pres. Presbyn. Social Union and Presbyn. Brotherhood of Chicago. Republican. Home: Chicago, Ill. Died Mar. 20, 1941.

ROSS, Walter L., ry. official; b. Bloomington, Ill., Jan. 1, 1865; s. Alexander I. and Margaretta (Clark) R.; ed. high sch.; m. Katherine Cox, Nov. 1888. Began as messenger boy Western Union Telegraph Co.; entered ry. service with Wabash Ry., 1887; with Toledo, St. Louis & Western Ry. from 1904, as gen. passenger agt., gen. frt. agt. and gen. traffic mgr. at Chicago, was v.p. in charge of traffic; became vice pres. Detroit & Toledo Shore Line R.R. Mason. Home: Cleveland, O. Died Apr. 5, 1939.

ROSS, William Bradford, governor; b. Dover, Tenn., Dec. 4, 1873; s. Ambrose B. and Sue (Gray) R.; ed. common schools, Dover, Tenn., and Peabody Normal Sch., Nashville; m. Nellie Davis Tayloe, Sept. 11, 1902. Settled in Cheyenne, Wyo., 1901; pros. atty. Laramie Co., Wyo., 1906-07; mem. Bd. Law Examiners, Wyo., 1910-22; gov. of Wyo., term 1923-27. Democrat. Vestryman P.E. Ch. Mason. Kiwanian. Home: Cheyenne, Wyo. Died Oct. 2, 1924.

ROSS, William McAllister, judge; b. Maine, N.Y., July 12, 1850; s. Alexander and Mary (Wilson) R.; studied law in office of Hon. Giles W. Hotchkiss, Binghamton, N.Y.; LL.B., Harvard, 1877; m. Jessie A. Johnson, 1880. Admitted to N.Y. bar, 1878, and began practice at Syracuse; elected justice of the peace, 1881, and later served full term of 5 yrs.; county judge of Onondaga Co., N.Y., 1894-1915; justice Supreme Court of N.Y., 5th Dist., 1915-Dec. 30, 1920. Republican. Home: Syracuse, N.Y. Died Mar. 19, 1934.

ROSS, Worth Gwynn, officer U.S. Coast Guard; b. Cleveland, O., Apr. 19, 1854; s. Gen. Samuel and Phebe (Wierman) R.; ed. Lititz (Pa.) Acad.; grad. Sch. of Instrn. Revenue Cutter Service, 1879; m. Hannah T. Gilbert, Jan. 11, 1882 (died 1888); m. 2d, Abby G. W. Bartlett, Oct. 29, 1895. Third lt., July 2, 1879; 2d lt., Oct. 24, 1884; 1st lt., Apr. 18, 1895; capt., June 3, 1902; capt. commandant, Apr. 25, 1908; chief of Revenue Cutter Service, Apr. 1, 1905-Apr. 30, 1911, when voluntarily retired on account of ill health. Served on Atlantic and Pacific coasts, Puget Sound, Behring Sea, Great Lakes, various foreign cruises, N. Atlantic Squadron during Spanish-Am. War, after which awarded medals by Congress; personally comd. fleet of revenue cutters in Gulf of Mexico, enforcing sanitary regulations, during the yellow fever epidemic of 1905. Home: New Bedford, Mass. Died Mar. 24, 1916.

ROSSEAU, Percival Leonard, artist; b. New Orleans, La., Sept. 21, 1859; s. Leon and Anna (Buford) R.; student Académie Julian, Paris, under Jules Lefebvre, Tony Robert Fleury and Herman Leon; m. Nancy Allena Bidwell, July 13, 1897; children—Leon Bidwell, Francis Vincent. Specializes in painting of animals, especially field dogs; exhibited at Salon, Paris, and in London, St. Petersburg and Milan; hon. mention Salon, Paris, 1900; gold medal, same, 1906. Home: Lyme, Conn. Died Nov. 29, 1937.

ROSSELL, John Settles, banker; b. Zion, Md., Jan. 9, 1856; s. John Settles and Lydia Mary (Janney) R.; ed. pvt. and pub. schs., and Elkton (Md.) Acad.; m. Sarah McCafferty, Nov. 11, 1877; children—Mary R. A., Joseph A., Paul F., Francis A., Leo A., Mrs. Ann Peters. Clk., printer, reporter, editorial writer and mgr. country newspaper; clk. and treas. Cecil County, Md., until 1888; with Security Trust Co., Wilmington, 1888—, pres., 1917-29, chmn. bd., 1929—. Chmn. finance com. Del. Anti-Tuberculosis Soc.; treas. Memorial Library Fund, U. of Del.; mem. Washington Memorial Bridge Commn. Prominent in Liberty Loan Drives and other war relief movements. Mem. Commn. to Prepare Old Age Pension Law. Democrat. K.C. Home: Wilmington, Del. Died Sept. 7, 1934.

ROSSELL, William Trent, army officer; b. Mt. Vernon, Ala., Oct. 11, 1849; s. Maj. William H. and Lucinda Gayle (Eastin) R.; apptd. from N.J., and grad. U.S. Mil. Acad., 1873; m. Jeanie Ellis, Dec. 27, 1881 (died 1897). Commissioned 2d lt. of engrs., June 13, 1873; promoted through grades to brig. gen. and chief of engrs. U.S.A., Aug. 12, 1913. Served on the Atlantic and Gulf Coast and on the Ohio and Miss. rivers; mem. Miss. River Commn., 1906-13; pres. bd. engrs. for rivers and harbors, 1909-13; pres. examining bd. for promotion engr. officers; sr. mem. Harbor Line Bd., New York harbor, and Bd. of Engrs. Fortification; div. engr. Eastern Div.; retired by operation of law, Oct. 11, 1913. Advisory engr. N.Y. State Highway Commn., 1914; fed. commr. N.Y. Harbor Line Commn., 1915. Called into active duty, Apr. 1917. Mem. Bd. Engrs. for Rivers and Harbors. Home: New Brighton, S.I., N.Y. Died Oct. 11, 1919.

ROSSER, Luther Zeigler, lawyer; b. Calhoun, Ga., Dec. 31, 1859; s. Rev. James A. and Temperance (Zeigler) R.; A.B., Emory Coll., Ga., 1878; m. Julia Connally, Nov. 1886. Admitted to Ga. bar, 1880; practiced Fairburn, until 1884, then at Atlanta; mem. Rosser, Slaton, Phillips & Hopkins; has been identified with many important causes in Georgia. Democrat. Methodist. Home: Atlanta, Ga. Died Mar. 13, 1923.

ROSSER, Thomas Lafayette, soldier, civ. engr.; b. Campbell Co., Va., Oct. 15, 1836; s. John and Martha M. (Johnson) R.; family removed to Tex., 1849; entered West Point, 1856, in class of 1861; class being ordered into army when Fort Sumter was fired upon, he resigned; went to Montgomery, Ala.; apptd. 1st lt. arty., C.S.A.; soon after capt. Co. D, Washington arty., New Orleans; severely wounded, Mechanicsville, Va., 1862; promoted lt. col. arty., and a few days later col. 5th Va. cav., in brigade of J. E. B. Stuart; brig. gen. cav. fall of 1863; maj. gen. cav. fall 1864; served in Army of Northern Va.; refused to surrender at Appomattox with Lee, but charged through lines and escaped; while endeavoring to reorganize scattered troops of the army was captured and made prisoner of war; was seriously wounded 4 times in battle; m. Betty B. Winston, 1863. Studied law after the war, but did not enter profession; was one of supts. Nat. Express Co. under Gen. Joe Johnston; later engr. in ry. service, including chief engr. Northern and Canadian Pacific railroads from 1870 until 1886, when he retired to an estate in Va.; apptd. brig. gen. U.S.V., June 10, 1898, and comd. 3d brigade, 2d div., 1st army corps, composed of 14th Minn., 2d Ohio and 1st Pa. regts., vol. inf., in war with Spain. Home: Charlottesville, Va. Died 1910.

ROSSITER, Edward Van Wyck, ry. official; b. St. Louis, Mo., July 13, 1844; s. Lucius Tuttle R. (of Mass.) and Mary (Wickes) R. (d. Gen. Van Wyck Wickes, of New York); ed. at Collegiate and Poly. Inst. of Brooklyn; m. Estelle, d. J. Lawrence Hewlett, of Great Neck, L.I., June 1869. Entered ry. service Sept. 1859; president's clerk Hudson River R.R.; clerk treasurer's office, same, 1860-67; cashier N.Y. & Harlem R.R., 1867-77; later treas. of same co.; June 1883, became treas. and from Nov. 1900, has been v.p. of N.Y.C.&H.R. R.R. Co., New York & Harlem R.R. Co., as well as of almost all the lines affiliated with the N.Y. Central Co., also Lincoln Nat. Bank, Lincoln Safe Deposit Co. Home: Flushing, L.I. Died 1910.

ROSSITER, Stealy Bales, clergyman; b. Berne, N.Y., May 22, 1842; s. John and Eva (Ball) R.; A.B., Union Coll., 1865; grad. Union Theol. Sem., 1869; (D.D., Union Coll., 1886); m. Mary Augusta Ropes, July 16, 1873. Ordained Presbyn. ministry, 1869; pastor Elizabethport, N.J., 1869-73, North Ch., New York, 1873-1901; sec. Am. McAll Assn., allied to the various McAll missions throughout France, 1901-04; pastor First Ch., Manila, P.I., 1904-11; acting pastor Calvary Presbyn. Ch., Newark, N.J., 1911—. Chaplain Grand Nat. Curling Club. Author: The Red Cord; Curlers' Sermons. Home: Newark, N.J. Died June 24, 1914.

ROSSITER, William Sidney, printer; b. Westfield, Mass., Sept. 9, 1861; A.B., Amherst Coll., 1884, M.A., 1924; m. Nellie C. Budd, Oct. 21, 1891; 1 dau., Marjorie (Mrs. Thomas Nugent Troxell). Bus. office N.Y. Tribune, 1884-88, N.Y. Press, 1888-89; treas. New York Printing Co., 1889-99; expert, printing and pub., U.S. Census, 1900-04; chief clerk, Census, 1904-09; v.p. Rumford Press, Concord, N.H., 1909-16, pres. 1916—. In 1908 selected by President Roosevelt to investigate Government Printing Office. Staff Central Bur. Planning and Statistics, War Industries Bd., 1918; chmn. joint advisory com. Am. Statis. Assn. and Am. Econ. Assn. to advise dir. of census. Author: The Population Problem of Vermont, 1911. Wrote report on Printing and Publishing for Census of 1900 and 1905; census report "A Century of Population Growth in the United States"; census monograph, Increase of Population, 1910 to 1920. Home: Concord, N.H. Died Jan. 23, 1929.

ROSZEL, Brantz Mayer, supt. mil. school; b. Baltimore, Md., Mar. 16, 1869; s. Stephan George and Anna Maria (Mayer) R.; A.B., Johns Hopkins U., 1889, Ph.D., 1896; certificate, Army War Coll., 1923; m. Christine Washington Chew, Feb. 2, 1905. Began as instr. mathematics, Johns Hopkins U., 1895; instr. in science, high schs., Washington, D.C., 1896-1903; headmaster Sewanee Grammar Sch. of U. of the South, 1903-08; supt. Shenandoah Valley Acad., Winchester, Va., 1908—. Commd. maj. Q.M.O.R.C., U.S.A., 1916; served in U.S. and France, 1917-18; promoted through grades to col. M.I. Res., Oct. 1925; now col. Aux. Res., U.S.A.; dir. R.O. Sch., Winchester, 1933-35. Mem. Constl. Conv. to repeal 18th amendment, 1934. Dir. Winchester Memorial Hosp. Companion Mil. Order of World War. Mil. Order Fgn. Wars of U.S. Democrat. Episcopalian. Mason. Author of the Commander's Tour, 1928. Also Fixing Commn. and Jewish Welfare Bd. for Army and Navy, World War. Pres. Zionist Orgn. America; co-chairman council Jewish Agency for Palestine. Democrat. Died Mar. 16, 1938.

ROTCH, A(bbott) Lawrence, meteorologist; b. Boston, Mass., Jan. 6, 1861; s. Benjamin Smith and Annie Bigelow (Lawrence) R.; pvt. schs. and tutor, Paris, Florence, Berlin, Boston, 1875-80; S.B., Mass. Inst. Tech., 1884; (hon. A.M., Harvard, 1891); m. Margaret Randolph Anderson, Nov. 22, 1893. In 1885 established and has since maintained the Blue Hill Meteorological Obs., nr. Boston, famous for its investigations of clouds, and for 1st use of kites to record meteorol. data; prof. meteorology, Harvard, 1906—. Mem. Internat. Jury Awards, Paris Expn., 1889, and then made Chevalier Legion of Honor; received Prussian Orders of the Crown, 1902, and Red Eagle, 1905, in recognition of efforts to advance knowledge of atmosphere; mem. various Am. and foreign scientific socs. and coms. Obtained 1st observations high above Atlantic Ocean with kites, 1901, 1st observations 5 to 10 miles above Am. Continent with registration balloons, 1904; 1st trigonometrical measurements of pilot balloons in U.S., 1909; collaborated with Teisserenc de Bort in sending a steam yacht to explore the tropical atmosphere, 1905-06; has taken part in scientific expdns. in U.S., S. America, Europe and Africa. Asso. editor of Am. Meteorological Journal, 1886-96; lectured before Lowell Inst. of Boston, 1891, 98; librarian Am. Acad. Arts and Sciences; trustee several ednl. instns., Boston. Editor: Observations and Investigations at Blue Hill, pub. in Annals Harvard Coll. Observatory. Author: Sounding the Ocean of Air, 1900; The Conquest of the Air, 1909; Charts of the Atmosphere for Aeronauts and Aviators (with A. H. Palmer), 1911. Home: Boston, Mass. Died Apr. 7, 1912.

ROTCH, Thomas Morgan, physician; b. Philadelphia, Pa., Dec. 9, 1849; s. Rodman and Helen (Morgan) R.; A.B., Harvard, 1870, M.D., 1874; m. Helen, d. William J. Rotch, of New Bedford, June 4, 1874. Med. house officer, Mass. Gen. Hosp., 1873-74; studied in European hosps., 1875-76; lecturer, 1878-88, asst. prof. diseases of children, 1888-93, prof., 1893-1903, prof. pediatrics, 1903—, Harvard; visiting phys. Children's Hosp. and Thomas Morgan

Rotch, Jr., Memorial Hosp. for Infants, Boston; apptd. consulting phys,. St. Francis' Hosp. for Infants, London, Eng., 1903. Author: Pediatrics (text-book); The Roentgen Ray in Pediatrics (text-book). Died Mar. 9, 1914.

ROTCH, William, engineer; b. New Bedford, Mass., July 22, 1844; s. William J. and Emily (Morgan) R.; A.B., Harvard, 1865; C.E., École Centrale des Arts et Manufactures, Paris, 1869; m. Mary Rotch Eliot, Sept. 6, 1873. Asst. engr., 1871-74, chief engr., 1875-80, Fall River Water Works; consulting engr. and purchasing agt. Mexican Central R.R. Co., Sonora R.R. Co., Atlantic & Pacific R.R. Co., and Southern Cal. R.R. Co., 1880-82; apptd., 1881, by Gov. John D. Long, one of commrs. who established boundary between Mass. and R.I.; consulting engr. several railway companies, 1882-90. President Fed. Wharf & Storage Co., Railroad Wharf & Storage Co., and Denbigh Mining Corp.; v.p. State Wharf & Storage Co.; treas. Broadway Storage Co. Dir. Adams Nervine Asylum, Infants' Hosp.; trustee Rotch Traveling Scholarship for Architects, etc. Home: Boston, Mass. Died Aug. 15, 1925.

ROTH, Filibert, forestry expert; b. Würtemberg, Germany, Apr. 20, 1858; s. Paul Raphael and Amalie (Volz) R.; early edn. in Würtemberg; came to U.S., 1871; on Western frontier, 1874-82; teacher, 1883-85; studied U. of Mich., 1885-93, B.S., 1890; m. Clara Hoffman, Oct. 7, 1888; 1 dau., Stella Rosa (wife of Prof. Orlan William Boston). Spl. expert on timber U.S. Dept. Agr., 1893-98; asst. prof. forestry, Cornell, 1898-1901; expert asst. Bur. Forestry, Dept. Agr., July-Nov. 1901; chief Div. Forest Reserves, Gen. Land Office, U.S. Dept. Interior, 1901; prof. forestry, U. of Mich., 1903-23, emeritus; LL.D., Marquette U., 1923. Author: Timber, 1895; Forest Conditions of Wisconsin, 1898; Cypress; The Annual Ring; Timber Physics, 1899; Uses of Wood, 1896; Grazing in Forest Reserves, 1902; First Book of Forestry, 1902; Forest Reserves Manual, 1902; Forest Regulation, 1914; Forest Valuation, 1915. Died Dec. 4, 1925.

ROTH, Henry Warren, clergyman; b. Prospect, Pa., April 5, 1838; s. Lewis and Lydia (Buechle) R.; A.B., with honors, Pa. Coll., 1861, A.M., 1864; studied Western Theol. Sem., Allegheny, Pa., 1861-64; (D.D., Westminister College, Pa., 1876; LL.D., Thiel College, Pa., 1913); m. Elizabeth T. Houston, June 15, 1876. Ordained Luth. ministry, 1861; pastor Grace Ch., Pittsburgh, 1861-70; pres. Thiel Coll., Greenville, Pa., 1870-87; pastor of Wicker Park Luth. Ch., Chicago, 1887-99; prof. practical theology, Chicago Luth. Theol. Sem., 1891-96; dir. and treas. Instn. Protestant Deaconesses, 1901; dir. Passavant Hosp., 1901—. Sec. Gen. Council Luth. Ch., 1866-70; pres. Pittsburgh Synod, 1871-73. Home: Greenville, Pa. Died Sept. 25, 1918.

ROTHERMEL, John Goodhart, educator; b. Philadelphia, Dec. 3, 1847; s. Peter Frederick and Caroline (Goodhart) R.; ed. pub. schs., Phila., Houllier Acad., Paris, and under pvt. tutors in Italy and Germany; m. Sallie C. Tobey, 1873. Engaged in mercantile business and civ. engring., 1868-94; on staff of Philadelphia Times, 1894-1902 (scientific editor, 1896-1902); dir. Wagner Free Inst. of Science, Phila., 1903-25, dir. emeritus, 1925—. Home: East Lansdowne, Pa. Died Apr. 1, 1928.

ROTHERMEL, John H., congressman; b. Richmond Tp., Berks Co., Pa., Mar. 7, 1856; s. John Y. and Louisa R.; acad. edn. Admitted to bar, 1881, and since in practice at Reading, Pa. Mem. 60th to 63d Congresses (1907-15), 13th Pa. Dist. Democrat. Home: Reading, Pa. Died Sept. 8, 1922.

ROTHROCK, Joseph Trimble, botanist; b. McVeytown, Pa., Apr. 9, 1839; s. Dr. Abraham and Phoebe B. R.; B.S., Harvard, 1864; M.D., U. of Pa., 1867; m. Martha E., d. Addison and Elizabeth Shafer May, May 27, 1869. Corpl. Co. D, 131st Pa. Inf. and capt. Co. E, 20th Pa. Cav., in Civil War; wounded at Fredericksburg. Prof. botany, U. of Pa., 1877-93; commr. of forestry for Pa., 1893-1905. Founded, 1903, and supt. until 1908, South Mountain Camp Sanatorium for Consumptives (state instn.). Author: Vacation Cruisings, 1884; Botany of the Wheeler Expedition, 1878, Vol. VIII; Flora of Alaska, 1867; Revision of North American Guarineæ, Proceedings of American Academy; Pennsylvania Forestry Reports, 1895, 1896, 1897. Home: West Chester, Pa. Died June 2, 1922.

ROTHSCHILD, Alonzo, author; b. New York, Oct. 30, 1862; s. John and Catherine (Meyer) R.; studied Coll. City of New York; spl. student Harvard; m. Meta Robitscheck, Sept. 11, 1895. In journalism and lit pursuits, 1884—. V.p. Lincoln Fellowship; dir. Free Religious Assn.; mem. Anti-Imperialist League, Mass. Reform Club, The Grange. Consulting editor on Am. history, Civil War, and Lincoln. Author: Lincoln, Master of Men, 1906. Home: East Foxboro, Mass. Died Sept. 29, 1915.

ROTHSCHILD, Marcus A., M.D.; b. Woodville, Miss., July 4, 1887; s. Morris H. and Emily Blanche R.; grad. Randolph-Macon Acad., Bedford City, Va., 1901, Horace Mann Sch., N.Y. City, 1904; A.B., Columbia, 1907; M.D., Coll. Phys. and Surg., N.Y. City, 1911; grad. study U. of Freiburg, Germany, 1912-13, Univ. Coll. Hosp., London, 1913-14; m. Edna E. Liebman, June 2, 1910; children—Edna Liebman, Marcus Adolphus. Began practice at N.Y. City, 1911; externe Mt Sinai Hospital, 1911-12, asso. physician, 1925-30, cardiographer, 1930-33; physician Beth Israel Hospital; cardiologist Broad Street-Pan American Hospital, 1930. Served as major Med. Corps, U.S.A., 1917-19. Director Am. Jewish Physicians Com. Fellow N.Y. Acad. Medicine. Democrat. Hebrew religion. Home: New York, N.Y. Died Feb. 16, 1936.

ROTHWELL, Richard Pennefather, editorial mgr. Engineering and Mining Journal, 1873—; b. Ingersoll, Ontario, Can., May 1, 1836; studied at Trinity Coll., Toronto; grad. Rensselaer Poly. Inst., 1858; Imperial School of Mines, Paris, France, 1862; practiced mining in France, 1863; telegraph cable and wire rope mfr., London, 1864-65; practiced as civil and mining engr. in Pa., 1866-73. Is pres. Scientific Publishing Co., publishers Engineering and Mining Journal, The Mineral Industry (annual), and books on mining metallurgy, etc. Author: The Mineral Industry: Its Statistics, Technology and Trade (for which he received, 1898, gold medal of the Societé d' Encouragement pour L'Industrie Nationale of Paris); Universal Bimetallism and an International Monetary Clearing House; etc. Died 1901.

ROTHWELL, Will A., lawyer; b. in Callaway Co., Mo., Jan. 4, 1863; s. Dr. W. A. and Sallie C. R.; grad. Mo. State Univ., with highest grade class honor, B.S., 1885; married. Admitted to bar, 1886, entered practice at Moberly, Mo.; pres. Jefferson Bldg. Co. City atty., Moberly, Mo., 1891-95; elected to Mo. legislature, 1894; pros. atty., Randolph Co., Mo., 1896-1900. Democrat; chmn. Dem. State Com. of Mo., 1902-04; mem. Dem. Nat. Com., 1904. Home: Moberly, Mo. Deceased.

ROTZELL, Willett Enos, physician, naturalist; b. Philadelphia, June 19, 1871; s. Dr. Joseph M. and Elizabeth (Whitehead) R.; ed. Eastburn Acad., Phila., also spl. studies in botany and zoölogy, especially ornithology; M.D., Hahnemann Med. Coll., Phila., 1892; (hon. B.S., Hiwassee Coll., Tenn., 1904); m. Amanda W. Lever, 1895. Lecturer on botany and zoölogy, 1895-1905, prof. med. botany, 1905-08, Hahnemann Med. Coll. Founder, 1903, and editor Atlantic Slope Naturalist. Author: Man—An Introduction to Anthropology, 2d edit., 1905. Home: Philadelphia, Pa. Died July 1913.

ROUND, William Marshall Fitts, corr. sec. Prison Assn. of New York, 1883—; b. Pawtucket, R.I., March 26, 1845; ed. public schools (A.M., Brown Univ.); studied Harvard Med. School; m. 1877, Ellen Miner Thomas; g.d. of Hon. Charles Miner. In charge New England dept., World's Fair, Vienna, 1873; became journalist and author; interested in prison reform; U.S. delegate to prison congresses, Rome and Paris, and Congrés d' Anthropologie Criminelle, Brussels. Reorganized and is dir. Nat. Prison Assn.; organized Burnham Industrial Farm, Canaan, N.Y.; devised and introduced "Mill" system of awards, adopted by many prominent institutions the world over; founded and organized Order of St. Christopher for training instnl. officers and employes, 1890. Author: Achsah, 1877; Hal, 1879; Child Marian Abroad, 1880; Rosecraft, 1884; Torn and Mended, 1885, etc. Home: Nantucket, Mass. Died 1906.

ROUNDS, Arthur Charles, lawyer; b. Cleveland, O., Dec. 28, 1862; s. Charles Collins and Kate Nixon (Stowell) R.; State Normal Sch., Farmington, Me.; Hallowell (Me.) Classical Acad.; A.B., Amherst Coll., 1887, A.M., LL.B., Harvard, 1890; hon. LL.M., New York U.; LL.D., George Washington U., 1921; unmarried. Admitted to N.Y. bar, 1891, and began practice in New York; mem. Hughes, Rounds, Schurman & Dwight. Dir. Union Buffalo Mills Co.; trustee Amherst Coll. Republican. Conglist. Home: Cannondale, Conn. Died Dec. 6, 1928.

ROURKE, Constance Mayfield, writer; b. Cleveland, O., Nov. 14, 1885; d. H. B. and Constance E. (Davis) R.; A.B., Vassar, 1907; holder of Borden Fund for foreign travel and study, 1907; student Sorbonne, 1908-09 ; reader Bibliothèque Nationale, British Mus., 1908-10. Instr. in English, Vassar, 1910-15. Author: Trumpets of Jubilee, 1927; Troupers of the Gold Coast, or the Rise of Lotta Crabtree, 1928; American Humor—A Study of the National Character, 1931; Davy Crockett, 1934; Audubon, 1936; Charles Sheeler: Artist in the American Tradition, 1938. Home: Grand Rapids, Mich. Died Mar. 23, 1941.

ROUSE, Adelaide Louise, author; b. Athens, N.Y.; d. John C. and Lydia L. (Whipple) R.; grad. Pennington (N.J.) Sem., 1885. Editorially connected with pub. houses, 1889—; compiled Nat. Documents and edited Mrs. Trollope's Domestic Manners of the Americans (Unit Books). Author: Frontier and City, 1889; Stephen Vane's Trust, 1890; Wendover House, 1892; Almost a Genius, 1895; The Deane Girls, 1895; Annice Wynkoop, Artist, 1895; Helen Beaton, College Woman, 1900; Under My Own Roof, 1902; Her Father's Family, 1903; The Letters of Theodora, 1905. Died 1912.

ROUSE, Henry Clark, ry. official; b. Cleveland, Mar. 15, 1853; s. Edwin Coolidge and Mary Miller R.; academic edn.; unmarried. Pres. and chmn. bd. dirs. M.,K.&T. Ry., 1891—; pres. Boonville R.R. Bridge Co., 1892—; receiver Northern Pacific Ry., 1893-96; was pres., 1894-96, Northern Pacific & Manitoba, Northern Pacific & Cascade, Central Washington, Wash. Shore Line, Rocky Fork & Cooke City, Sanborn Cooperstwn & Turtle Mtn., Tacoma, Orting & Southeastern Dak., Winnipeg Trans-County, Fargo & Southwestern Ry., Southeastern Dakota Ry., Coeur d'Alene Ry. and Navigation Co. Has also been dir. 27 other transportation cos. Home: Cleveland, O. Died 1906.

ROUSMANIERE, Edmund Swett, clergyman; b. Boston, Mass., Oct. 27, 1858; s. John Easton and Abby Whitmore (Swett) R.; A.B., Harvard, 1883; B.D., Episcopal Theol. Sch., Cambridge, Mass., 1886; D.D., Brown U., 1905; m. Sophie Knight, Nov. 5, 1890. Deacon, 1886, priest, 1887, P.E. Ch.; rector, All Saints' Ch., Pontiac, R.I., 1886-89, Grace Ch., New Bedford, Mass., 1889-99, Grace Ch., Providence, R.I., 1899-1909, St. Paul's Ch., Boston, 1910-12; dean Cathedral Ch. of St. Paul, Boston, Oct. 1, 1912—. Deputy to Gen. Conv., 1904, 07, 13, 16, 19; chmn. Bd. Examining Chaplains Diocese of Mass., 1914-19; pres. Standing Com. Diocese of Mass., 1922—. Home: Boston, Mass. Died Sept. 26, 1926.

ROUSS, Charles Broadway, merchant, philanthropist; b. Woodsboro, Md., Feb. 11, 1836; s. Peter Hoke and Belinda (Baltzell) R.; ed. Winchester, Va., Acad.; m. Maggie, d. James Keenan, 1859. In business, clerk and storekeeper, Winchester, Va., 1851-61; in C.S.A., 1861-65; in business New York, 1865—. Made large gifts to Winchester, Va., for various public purposes. Erected, Mt. Hope Cemetery, nr. New York, monument to dead Confederate Veterans' Camp, New York; founded physical laboratory, Univ. of Va.; founded Confederate Memorial Hall, Museum of Confederate Relics. Presented to New York replica of statues of Washington and Lafayette by Bartholdi; gave $100,000 for Confederate monument, Richmond, Va., etc. Home: New York, N.Y. Died 1902.

ROUSSEAU, Harry Harwood, rear adm., U.S.N.; b. Troy, N.Y., Apr. 19, 1870; s. William White and Jeanette (Parker) R.; C.E., Rensselaer Poly. Institute, 1891; m. Gladys Fargo Squiers, 1908. Draftsman and engineer for pvt. cos., 1891-98; apptd., after competitive exam., civ. engr. U.S.N., rank of lt., 1898; engr. Bur. of Yards and Docks, Washington, 1899-1903; engr. pub. improvements, Mare Island Navy Yard, Calif., 1903-07; apptd. chief Bur. of Yards and Docks, with rank of rear adm., Jan. 1907. Mem. Isthmian Canal Commn., 1907-14; engr. terminal constrn., Panama Canal, 1914-16; mem. Commn. on Navy Yards, 1916—; mgr. shipyard plants div. Emergency Fleet Corp., 1917-19. Given thanks of Congress and promoted to rank rear adm., Civil Engr. Corps, 1915. Dir. Panama R.R. Co.; v. chmn. U.S. Shipping Bd., Port Facilities Commn., 1918-20; dir. Naval Petroleum Reserves, 1927—; chief coordinator of Federal Service, 1928—. Episcopalian. Died July 25, 1930.

ROUTT, John Long, governor; b. Eddyville, Apr. 25, 1826; s. Daniel R.; went to Ill. in childhood; ed. dist. schs. Sheriff McLean Co., Ill., 1860-62; served, 1861-65, as capt. Co. E, 94th Ill. Vols.; in business, Bloomington, Ill., 1865; treas. McLean Co., 1865-69; U.S. marshal, Southern Dist. Ill., 1869-71; 2d asst. postmaster gen. U.S., 1871-75; apptd. gov. of Colo. Ty. by President Grant, 1875-76; elected 1st gov. of state, 1876; mayor of Denver, 1883-85; again gov., 1890-92. Republican. Home: Denver, Colo. Died 1907.

ROUTZAHN, Evart Grant, social worker; b. Dayton, O., Jan. 6, 1869; s. Josiah and Ella (Mathias) R.; ed. pub. schs.; m. Mary Brayton Swain, Mar. 7, 1914. Formerly engaged in Y.M.C.A. boys' and social work; dir. traveling exhibition campaign, Nat. Tuberculosis Assn., 1906-12, asso. dir. dept. of surveys and exhibits, Russell Sage Foundation, 1912-34 (retired). Editor education and publicity dept. Am. Jour. of Public Health, 1922—; instr. publicity methods, New York Sch. of Social Work, 1922-34; consultant in adult health edn. and social work publicity, 1935—. Fellow Am. Pub. Health Assn. (first chmn. edn. and publicity sect.); 1st chmn. Social Work Publicity Council. Author: (with Mary Swain Routzahn) A B C of Exhibit Planning, 1919; (with same) Publicity for Social Work, 1928. Home: New York, N.Y. Died Apr. 24, 1939.

ROUXEL, Gustave Augustin, auxiliary R.C. bishop of New Orleans, consecrated April 9, 1899; b. Redon, Ille et Vilaine, France, Feb. 2, 1840; s. James Rouxel and Scolastique Brécha; grad. Grand Seminary, Rennes, France. Came to U.S., 1863; ordained priest, Oct. 4, 1863; apptd. asst. priest Opelousas, La., for 6 months; pastor Lafayette, La., Oct. 1864; adminstr. Cathedral, New Orleans, 1872; pastor Annunciation Ch., 1885; apptd. canon and vicar-gen., 1878; apptd., 1899, bishop of Curium, and auxiliary bishop, New Orleans. Died 1908.

ROVERSI, Louis, author, editor; b. Bologna, Italy, Dec. 8, 1859; s. Paul and Enrica (Dozza) R.; grad. U. of Bologna, LL.D., with highest honors (graduation essay printed at expense of Italian Govt.), followed by spl. course on art at Royal Acad. Fine Arts, Bologna; m. Clara Nobbs, of Norwich, Eng., Aug. 10, 1888. Editor La Stella d'Italia, Bologna, 1882-85; editor Il Progresso Italo Americano, New York, 1885-98; sec. to dir. Met. Mus. of Art (late Gen. Louis P. di Cesnola) 1898-1904; editor of L'Araldo Italiano, 1907-11. Lectured for Bd. of Edn., New York, Newark, N.J., Jersey City, N.J., for Dante Alighieri Soc. of Boston, etc. Editorial writer and corr. various Italian newspapers. Secretary Am. Commission to first Internat. Expn. of Modern Decorative Art, Turin, Italy, 1902. Author: State and Church in Italy, 1880; Essays on Italian Art, 1883; L.P. di Cesnola and the Metropolitan Museum of Art, 1898; Ricordi Canavesani, 1900. Home: New York, N.Y. Died Jan. 5, 1927.

ROW, Robert Keable, publisher; b. Woodstock, Ont., Can., Aug. 28, 1858; s. Robert and Eliza (Keable) R.; prep. edn., St. Catharines Collegiate Inst., 1883-85; grad. Ottawa Normal Sch., 1880; A.B., Queen's U., Kingston, 1897; post-grad. work, U. of Chicago, 1901-03; m. Elizabeth, d. James Gillespie, of St. Catharines, Dec. 28, 1887 (died 1921); children—Gerald Gillespie (dec.), Wallace Keable (dec.), Kathleen Ethel, Margaret Elizabeth; m. 2d, Minnie Gregg Harper, Jan. 5, 1924. Prin. Normal Sch., Kingston, 1885-98; fellow in edn., 1901-03, instr. extension dept., 1903-06, U. of Chicago; supt. schs., Berwyn, Ill., 1903-06; pres. Row, Peterson & Co., pubs. ednl. books, 1906—, also chief editor. Mem. N.E.A., Chicago Council Foreign Relations, Chicago Association Commerce, Art Inst. Chicago (life). Republican. Methodist. Mason, Odd Fellow. Author: Graded Exercises in Arithmetic, 1883; Practical Language Training, 1892; The Natural System of Vertical Writing, 1895-96; Essential Studies in English (vols. I and II), 1907; The Educational Meaning of Manual Arts, 1909; Studies in English, 1916; Work and Play with Language, 1917; Triune Writing-Spellers, 1923; New National Spellers, 1926. Home: Evanston, Ill. Died Dec. 22, 1932.

ROWAN, Charles A., chmn. bd. Westinghouse Air Brake Co.; b. Pittsburgh, Pa., Sept. 27, 1874; s. William and Mary (Elder) R.; ed. pub. schs., Pittsburgh, and Parnassus (Pa.) Acad.; m. Alma Leitch, June 2, 1915; children—Charles A., Andrew Leitch, Eleanor Ward. Bookkeeper, Logan's Planing Mills, Parnassus, 1892-94, E. Pittsburgh Improvement Co., 1894-1903; asst. cashier E. Pittsburgh Nat. Bank, 1903; with Westinghouse Air Brake Co., 1903—, asst. auditor until 1910, auditor, 1910-16, comptroller, 1916-19, v.p. and comptroller after 1919, now chmn. bd.; also dir. many subsidiaries; pres. Westinghouse Internat. Brake & Signal Co. from 1927 to its dissolution in 1936; chmn., dir. First Nat. Bank of Wilmerding; dir. Union Trust Co. of Pittsburgh. Republican. Mason. Home: Edgewood, Pittsburgh, Pa. Died Sept. 13, 1940.

ROWAN, Joseph, congressman; b. N.Y. City, 1870; LL.B., Columbia, 1891; m. Cora Cook, 1905. Admitted to N.Y. bar, 1892; mem. 66th Congress (1919-21), 19th N.Y. Dist. Democrat. Home: New York, N.Y. Died Aug. 3, 1930.

ROWBOTTOM, Harry E., congressman; b. Aurora, Ind., Nov. 3, 1884; s. James and Ann R.; ed. pub. schs. and business coll.; m. Elizabeth Margaret Rosenberger, June 16, 1915. Mem. Ind. Ho. of Rep., 3 terms, 1919-24; mem. 69th to 71st Congresses (1925-31), 1st Ind. Dist. Republican. Home: Evansville, Ind. Died Mar. 22, 1934.

ROWE, Allan Winter, prof. chemistry; b. Gloucester, Mass., July 31, 1879; s. Arthur Howard and Lucy (Haskell) R.; B.S., Mass. Inst. Tech., 1901; M.S., Wesleyan U., 1904; Swett fellow of Mass. Inst. Tech, U. of Goettingen, Germany, 1904-06, Ph.D., 1906; grad. study Harvard, 1907-09, spl. research, 1909-14; unmarried. Asst. in chemistry, Wesleyan U., 1902-04; lecturer, Boston U. Sch. of Medicine, 1906-08, prof. chemistry, 1908—; mem. Evans Memorial, 1910—, dir. of research, 1921—; formerly pres. Boston Sch. Physical Edn. Trustee Boston Psychopathic Hosp. Mem. Am. Olympic Com.; dir. Sportsmanship Brotherhood. Fellow Am. Acad. Arts and Sciences, A.A.A.S., Am. Phys. Soc., Econ. Engring. Foundation (v. chmn.), Chem. Society (London); mem. Numerous scientific societies. Republican. Mason. Home: Boston, Mass. Died Dec. 6, 1934.

ROWE, Benjamin Ackley, chain store exec; b. Lee, Mass., Feb. 4, 1884; s. Charles Henry and Francis E. Allen) R.; ed. pub. schs.; m. Edna Mary Alexander, Sept. 6, 1912; children—Benjamin Ackley, Ruth Carroll (dec.). Began as store mgr. for W. T. Grant Co., chain stores, 1910, pres. of co., 1930—. Dir. New Rochelle Y.M.C.A., New Rochelle Hosp. Republican. Methodist. Home: New Rochelle, N.Y. Died Sept. 3, 1937.

ROWE, Henrietta Gould, author; b. East Corinth, Me., 1835; d. Aaron and Sarah Gould; acad. edn.; m. James Swett Rowe, Oct. 25, 1856. Writer of poems and stories for many mags.—principally relating to New England life and character. Educator of advanced pupils in history and literature, and a prominent clubwoman. Author: Re-told Tales of the Hills and Shores of Maine, 1892; Queenshithe, 1895; A Maid of Bar Harbor, 1902. Home: Bangor, Me. Died 1910.

ROWE, Henry Kalloch, educator, author; b. Boston, Mass., Nov. 30, 1869; s. Rev. Charles Henry and Frances (Kalloch) R.; A.B., Brown Univ., 1892, A.M., 1895, D.D., 1932; Ph.D., Boston Univ., 1905; m. Bertha W. Howard, 1893; 1 son, Howard Kalloch. Teacher Greek and history, Colby Acad., 1893-97, Monson Acad., 1897-1901, Frye Sch., Boston, 1902-04; instr. history, Boston U., 1903-06; asst. prof. ch. history, 1906-14, asso. prof. history and sociology, 1914-17, prof. social science and history, 1917-27, prof. history and social science, 1927-33, prof. church history, 1933—, Andover Newton Theol. School. Republican. Author: Landmarks in Christian History, 1912; Society, Its Origin and Development, 1916; History of Religion in the United States, 1924; Modern Pathfinders of Christianity, 1928; Tercentenary History of Newton, 1930; History of the Christian People, 1931; History of Andover Theological Seminary, 1933; History of Colby Junior College, 1937. Home: Newton Highlands, Mass. Died Sept. 16, 1941.

ROWE, Joseph Eugene, educator, mathematician; b. Emmitsburg, Md., Mar. 21, 1883; s. Charles Jacob and Cora (Hoke) R.; of Scotch-Irish and Huguenot ancestry; A.B., first honor, Gettysburg (Pa.) Coll., 1904, LL.D., 1930; student U. of Va., 1904-05; fellow in mathematics, Johns Hopkins, 1909-10, Ph.D., 1910; m. Nina King, Sept. 6, 1911; children—Joseph Eugene, Richard King. Instructor in mathematics, Goucher Coll., 1910-11, Haverford, 1911-12, Dartmouth, 1912-14; asst. prof., asso. prof., and prof. mathematics, Pa. State Coll, 1914-20; prof. and head dept. of mathematics, Coll. of William and Mary, 1921-28, dir. extension, 1924-28; pres. Clarkson Memorial Coll. of Technology, Potsdam, N.Y., 1928-32 (resigned); engaged in reseach in social sciences, Johns Hopkins U., 1932-33; apptd. mem. Bd. Veterans Appeals, Feb. 23, 1934. Asst. physicist Nat. Advisory Com., Aero, May 1917-Feb. 1918. Chief ballistician, Aberdeen Proving Ground, Ordnance Dept., U.S.A., 1920-21. Democrat. Episcopalian. Author: Introductory Mathematics. Co-author: History of Gettysburg College, 1931. Inventor mathematical instruments. Home: Baltimore, Md. Died Oct. 2, 1939.

ROWE, L(ouis) Earle, dir. art mus.; b. Providence, R.I., June 19, 1882; s. Thomas Richard and Arvilla (Pollard) R.; Ph.B., Brown U., 1904, A.M., 1906; Am. Sch. of Classical Studies, Athens, 1906-07; m. Margaret Talbot Jackson, June 19, 1917; children—John Howland, William Leavitt Jackson, Edith Talbot. Teacher, 1908-12, asst. in charge of Egyptian dept., 1909-12, Boston Mus. Fine Arts; asst. in history, Mass. Inst. Tech., 1910-12; mem. Harvard U. Mus. of Fine Arts Egyptian expdn., Feb.-June 1912; dir. of R.I. Sch. of Design, 1912-28, of mus. same, 1928—. Mason. Episcopalian. Home: Providence, R.I. Died Feb. 17, 1937.

ROWE, William Stanhope, banker; b. Cincinnati, O., July 30, 1857; s. Stanhope Sanderson and Frances Mary (Thomas) R.; ed. high sch., Cincinnati; m. Margaret Anna Richardson, June 12, 1879. Cashier Second Nat. Bank, Cincinnati, 1881-89; cashier First National Bank, 1889-1902, pres., 1902-29, retired; dir. The Fox Paper Co.; dir. Federal Reserve Bank of Cleveland 5 years; mem. Federal Advisory Council, Washington, D.C., 6 yrs. Republican. Episcopalian. Home: Madisonville, Cincinnati, O. Died May 20, 1941.

ROWELL, George Presbury, advertising agt. and publisher (retired); b. Concord, Vt., July 4, 1838; ed. Lancaster (N.H.) Acad. Founded, April 1865, at Boston, the advertising agency of George P. Rowell & Co.; removed to New York, 1867; began publishing Am. Newspaper Directory, 1869; established Printers' Ink, a weekly, 1888. Life mem. N.E. Society. Author: Forty Years an Advertising Agent, 1906. Died 1908.

ROWELL, John W., judge; b. Lebanon, N.H., June 9, 1835; acad. edn. at Randolph, Vt.; (LL.D., Vt. U., 1893); m. Mary L. Wheeler, Aug. 1, 1858. Admitted to bar, 1858; mem. Vt. Gen. Assembly, 1861-62; state's atty., Orange Co., 1862-63; mem. Vt. Senate, 1874-75; reporter decisions Supreme Ct., 1872-80; asso. judge, 1882-1902, chief judge, 1902—, Supreme Ct. of Vt. Republican. V.p. Randolph Nat. Bank from its organization, 1875. Home: Randolph, Vt. Died Feb. 13, 1924.

ROWELL, Jonathan Harvey, lawyer; b. Haverhill, N.H., Feb. 10, 1833; s. Jonathan B. and Cynthia (Abbott) R.; grad. Eureka Coll., Ill., 1861, (A.M., in course); law dept. Chicago Univ., 1865; m. Maria S. Woods, Oct. 23, 1866. Served lt. and capt. Co. G, 17th Ill. inf., 1861-64. Admitted to Ill. bar, 1865; State's atty. 8th jud. circuit, Ill., 1868-72; mem. Congress 4th Ill. dist., 1883-91. Home: Bloomington, Ill. Died 1908.

ROWELL, Joseph Cummings, librarian; b. Panama, S.A. (of Am. parents), June 29, 1853; s. Rev. Joseph and Hannah (Cummings) R.; B.A., U. of California, 1874, M.A., 1903, LL.D. from same school, 1935; m. Emma S. Fellows, June 11, 1876; children—Joseph Arthur, Clarence Fellows. Librarian U. of Calif. from 1875, emeritus. Mem. Board of Edn., Oakland, Calif., 1891-92. Home: Oakland, Calif. Died Nov. 13, 1938.

ROWLAND, Adoniram Judson, clergyman; b. Valley Forge, Pa., Feb. 9, 1840; s. Samuel Norton and Susanna (Suplee) R.; A.B., Bucknell U., 1862, A.M., 1865; grad. Rochester Theol. Sem., 1866; (D.D., Bucknell, 1880, LL.D., 1904); m. Harriet E. Frick, May 31, 1865; m. 2d, Kate S. Hershey, Oct. 29, 1878; father of Arthur John R. Ordained Bapt. ministry, 1862; chaplain U.S.A., 1862-63; pastor Mt. Auburn Ch., Cincinnati, 1866-68; pres. Mt. Auburn Inst., Cincinnati, 1868-70; pastor First Ch., Pittsburgh, 1870-72, Tenth Ch., Phila., 1872-84, Franklin Sq. Ch., Baltimore, 1884-95; gen. sec. Am. Bapt. Publication Soc., Feb. 1, 1895—. Sec. corp. Bucknell U., 1882—. Editor Our Young People from 1880, Senior Quarterly, 1883-95. Author: A Handbook on the Pentateuch, 1895. Home: Philadelphia, Pa. Died Jan. 31, 1917.

ROWLAND, Arthur John, engring. educator; b. Cincinnati, O., Feb. 19, 1867; s. Adoniram Judson and Harriet E. (Frick) R.; ed. pvt. schs., Phila.; freshman yr., U. of Pa.; partial course langs. and elec. engring., Johns Hopkins; m. Flora B. Dobler, May 16, 1895. Organized course in elec. engring., 1893, dir. Sch. of Engring., 1896-1913, dean, July 1913—, Drexel Inst., Phila. Author: Texts in Applied Electricity. Home: Philadelphia, Pa. Died 1934.

ROWLAND, Charles Leonard, engineer; b. Brooklyn, N.Y., Nov. 28, 1852; s. James and Mary E. R.; ed. common schs., Fairfield, Conn.; m. Alice Lucille Ackerly, Oct. 24, 1883; m. 2d, Kathryn Ethel Schweizer, July 20, 1917. Pres. Am. Welding Co., Dec. 1907—. Home: Carbondale, Pa. Died Apr. 18, 1926.

ROWLAND, Dunbar, historian; b. Oakland, Miss., Aug. 25, 1864; s. William Brewer and Mary Judith Moorman (Bryan) R.; desc. John Rowland, Eng., to America, 1635; B.S., Agrl. and Mech. Coll. of Miss., 1886; LL.B., U. of Miss., 1888, LL.D., 1906; m. Eron Opha, d. Maj. B. B. and Ruth Stovall (Rowland) Moore, Dec. 20, 1906. Practiced law at Memphis, Tenn., 1888-93, Coffeeville, Miss., 1893-1902; originator, and first dir. Miss. State Dept. Archives and History, Mar. 15, 1902—. Founder Miss. Hall of Fame and State Mus. Went abroad, 1906, for study of archive conditions in Europe, and investigation of original sources of Miss. history in archives of Eng., France, and Spain; secured transcripts of all European sources of the history of Miss. and Lower South; chmn. com. on coöperation of State Hist. Dept. and socs., which has developed a coöperative plan for the calendaring of French archives relating to history of Miss. Valley; originator of plan for the publication by the Nat. Govt. of an hist. roster of officers and men of the Union and Confed. armies, prepared by War Dept.; leader in movement for erection of Nat. Archives Bldg. in Washington. Mem. various hist. societies. Asst. sec. for Southern States of Am. Assn. for Internat. Conciliation, 1912-17; leader of movement for reformation of Am. Hist. Assn., 1913-15; dir. A.L.A. in United War Work Campaign, 1918; mem. Y.M.C.A. Bd. of Selection of war workers, 1918. Democrat. Episcopalian. Author: (editor or translator) Miss. Official and Statistical Register, 6 issues, 1904-24; Miss. Territorial Archives, 1905; Ency. of Miss. History, 1907; Miss. Provincial Archives English Dominion, 1911; Miss. Provincial Archives French Dominion (transl. Vol. I), 1927; Miss. Provincial Archives, French Dominion (transl. Vols. II, III; 10 vols. Ann. Repts. Dept. Archives and History, 1902-14; centennial edit. Ency. of Mississippi History, 1917; History of Mississippi, The Heart of the South, 2 vols., 1925; A Symposium of the Place of Discovery of the Mississippi River, by De Soto, 1927; Courts, Judges and Lawyers of Mississippi (1798-1935). Editor Official Correspondence of William C. Claiborne, 1801-16, 6 vols., and 5 vols. of the Centenary Series (Publs. Miss. Hist. Soc.); Jefferson Davis, Constitutionalist, His Letters, Papers and Speeches, 10 vols., 1923; Reviews of Jefferson Davis, Constitutionalist, 1924. Died Nov. 1, 1937.

ROWLAND, Henry Augustus, prof. physics Johns Hopkins, 1876—; b. Honesdale, Pa., Nov. 27, 1848; C.E., Rensselaer Poly. Inst., 1870 (Ph.D., Johns Hopkins, 1880); LL.D., Yale, 1895; LL.D., Princeton, 1896; engaged in railroad surveys, 1871; taught in Wooster Univ., 1871-72; instr., 1872-74, and asst. prof. physics, 1874-75, Rensselaer Poly. Inst.; studied abroad a year, then took present chair. Was member Electrical Congress at Paris, 1881; served on jury of electrical exhibition there, 1881; made chevalier, 1881, and in 1896 Officer Legion of Honor; m. Henrietta Harrison, June 4, 1890. Principal scientific work has been the discovery of magnetic action due to electric convection; the exact determination of the mechanical equivalent of heat; the discovery of concave grating and the machine for ruling gratings by which spectrum analysis has been revolutionized; also other papers on physical questions. Received Rumford, Draper and Mattenci medals for his discoveries. Home: Baltimore, Md. Died 1901.

ROWLAND, Henry Cottrell, author; b. New York, May 12, 1874; s. George and Maria Townsend (Durfee) R.; ed. pvt. schs., New York and Stanford, Conn., 1 yr. Williams Coll.; M.D., Yale Med. Sch., 1898; m. Mary Fulton Parkinson, June 22, 1910; children—Henry C., Peter Morgan (dec.), Diana. Able seaman, U.S. auxiliary cruiser Yankee, Spanish-Am. War; actg. asst. surgeon U.S.A., Philippine campaign, 1899-1900; physician in Vermenton and Accolay, France, 1914-15; dir. local mil. auxiliary hosp., 1916; allied publicity and propaganda work in U.S., 1917; war corr. Collier's Weekly and accredited special agent of the intelligence dept. U.S.N., in France, 1918. Episcopalian. Republican. Author: Across Europe in a Motor Boat, 1908; The Magnet, 1910; Duds, 1919; The Peddler, 1920; Mile High, 1921; Hirondelle, 1922; The Return of Frank Clamart, 1923; Of Clear Intent, 1923; Many Mansions. Home: Washington, D.C. Died June 6, 1933.

ROWLAND, Joseph Medley, clergyman, editor; b. Rowland, N.C., Jan. 9, 1880; ed. Weaverville Coll. (A.B., 1902) and Randolph-Macon Coll.; D.D., Asbury Coll., Wilmore, Ky., 1927; m. Lyde S. Lewis, Feb. 21, 1905; children—Claude Rogers, Ida Elizabeth, Joseph Stuart. Ordained ministry M.E. Ch., S.; successively pastor Laurel St. Ch., Richmond, Va., Park Place Ch., Norfolk, Rivermont Av. Ch., Lynchburg; editor Richmond Christian Advocate, Nov. 1, 1921—. Mem. Southern Meth. Press Assn. (pres. 2 terms). Alternate del. Gen. Conf. M.E. Ch., S., 1922; del. to Gen. Conf., 1930, 34, 38. Mason, Woodman. Author: A Pilgrimage to Palestine, 1915; Blue Ridge Breezes, 1916; Travels in the Old World, 1923; The Hill Billies, 1924; Bright Angel Trail, 1927. Dir. and conductor Pilgrimage Tours of Nashville, Tenn.; and conductor vacation tours abroad. Home: Richmond, Va. Died Aug. 17, 1938.

ROWLAND, Kate Mason, author; d. Maj. Isaac S. and Catherine Armistead (Mason) Rowland. Mem. Va. Hist. Soc., Assn. for Preservation of Va. Antiquities, Confed. Memorial Lit. Soc., U.D.C.; hon. mem. Woman's Lit. Club of Baltimore. Editor: Poems of Frank O. Ticknor, M.D. (Ga. poet), 1879; The Real Lincoln (by Dr. C. L.C. Minor), 1901. Author: The Life of George Mason, including his speeches, public papers and correspondence, 2 vols., 1892; The Life of Charles Carroll of Carrollton, with his correspondence and public papers, 2 vols., 1898. Home: Richmond, Va. Died June 28, 1916.

ROWLAND, William Samuel, pres. The Stanley Chemical Co.; b. Baltimore, Md., June 11, 1881; s. William and Ernestine H. (Stevens) R.; A.B., Cornell, 1907; m. Helen Rockwell Platt, Jan. 19, 1915; children—Hugh, William Platt, Jean, Helen. Chemist A. D. Little, Inc., Boston, 1908; chem. engr., The Stanley Works, New Britain, Conn., 1909-17; pres. The Stanley Chem. Co., 1913—; dir. various companies. Commd. maj. Chem. Warfare Service, World War; assigned development div. Am. Univ., Washington, D.C. Trustee Shuttle Meadow Sch. Republican. Conglist. Home: New Britain, Conn. Died Nov. 12, 1936.

ROWLEE, Willard Winfield, botanist; b. Fulton, N.Y., Dec. 15, 1861; s. George W. and Sarah C. (Distin) R.; B.L., Cornell, 1888, D.Sc., 1893; m. May Howard, Dec. 22, 1887. Instr. botany, 1888-93, asst. prof., 1893-1905, prof., 1905—, Cornell Univ. Author: Lieut. Heman Rowlee (1746-1818) and His Descendants, 1907. Home: Ithaca, N.Y. Died Aug. 8, 1923.

ROWLETT, Robert, newspaper editor; b. La Grange, Ky., Apr. 17, 1888; s. William Wirt and Sarah Rodman (White) R.; student Ohio State U., 1912-13; m. Helen Buford, Nov. 8, 1924; 1 dau., Betsy Anne. Social worker Neighborhood House, Louisville, Ky., Pine Mt. Sch., Hindman, Ky. and Godman Guild House, Columbus, O., 1906-13; actor with touring and stock cos., 1913-17; reporter, copy reader, state editor Courier-Journal, Louisville, 1920-23; copy reader The American, New York, 1923-24; city editor, news editor, mng. editor and editor The Nashville Tennessean, 1925—. Served as 1st Sergt. F.A., U.S.A., in France, World War. Democrat. Presbyn. Home: Nashville, Tenn. Died Jan. 3, 1937.

ROWLEY, John, taxidermist; b. Hastings-on-Hudson, N.Y., Mar. 11, 1866; s. John and Marianne (Preston) R.; Brooklyn Coll. and Poly. Inst., 1885-86; studied law, Columbia U., 1887-89; m. Rowena E. Thompson, 1906; children—John Stuart, William Preston, Robert Douglas. With Am. Mus. Natural History, New York, as asst. taxidermist and chief taxidermist, 1889-1904; taxidermist Stanford U., 1905-06; curator of mammals, Calif. Acad. Sciences, 1907-17; dir. Oakland Pub. Mus., 1917-21; chief taxidermist, Los Angeles Mus., 1921-27. Episcopalian. Author: The Art of Taxidermy; Taxidermy and Museum Exhibition. Home: Alhambra, Calif. Died Jan. 2, 1928.

ROY, Lillian Elizabeth, author; b. Morristown, N.J., Apr. 22, 1868; d. William Henry and Suzanne Marie (Wiffenback) Bäcker; ed. high sch., and under pvt. tutors; studied architecture and interior decorations; m. Harry Colin Roy, of Eng. and Toronto, Can., Jan. 27, 1887 (died 1901); children—Lillian (Mrs. G. B. Shults), Inez Rose (dec.), Mildred Ethel (Mrs. L. B. Tunison). Began marketing designs in art at 14; continued in husband's laboratory, N.Y. City, 1901-05; began writing for children, 1905; founded Loveland Magazine (juvenile), 1909, which was merged into "Children's Star," Washington, D.C., 1911, and office moved to New York; merged Star with Children's Blue Bird Magazine, of which was owner and editor until discontinued on account of war conditions, 1915. Republican. Author: Five Little Starrs' Series (8 books), 1912-18; Blue Bird Series, 1914-18; Woodcraft Girls and Boys Series, 1916-20; Alice in Beeland, 1919; Polly Brewster Series, 1920-32; Girl Scout Mountain Series, 1921; Girl Scout Country Life Series, 1921; (other juveniles) Little Indians; Seedlings Harvest; Principal Goodlove's Estates; Jacob's Ladder; Big Ben; The Prince of Atlantis, 1929. International lecturer on Atlantis and ancient civilizations. Died June 12, 1932.

ROYAL, George, M.D.; b. Alford, Mass., July 15, 1853; s. Ambrose and Mary Adelaide (Buchner) R.; educated Amherst (Mass.) Coll., hon. M.S., 1929; M.D., New York Homeopathic Medical College and Hospital, 1882; m. Ella J. Kingsbury, of Coventry, Conn., Nov. 27, 1879; children—Malcolm Allen, Wilmot Kingsbury, Paul Ambrose, Adelaide Janette (Mrs. H. J. Kroeger). Prof. materia medica and therapeutics, Coll. of Homeo. Medicine, State U. of Iowa, 1892-1922, and dean 18 yrs. Editor Ia. Homeo. Jour., 1918-24; corr. editor Jour. Am. Inst. Homeopathy. Progressive Republican. Conglist. Author: Textbook of Materia Medica, 1920; Theory and Practice of Medicine, 1923; Homeopathic Therapy of Disease of Brain and Nerve, 1928. Died Dec. 31, 1931.

"ROYAL, Ralph," see Jacob Ralph Abarbanell.

ROYALL, Tucker, banker; b. Palestine, Tex., Feb. 5, 1877; s. Nathaniel Royster and Annie (Richardson) R.; grad. Staunton Mil. Acad., 1896; grad. Eastman Nat. Business Coll., 1897; m. Fannie May Douglas, Jan. 29, 1901; 1 son, Nathaniel Royster. Pres. Royall Nat. Bank, Royall Loan & Investment Co., Michaux Park Land Co. (Palestine), Elkhart (Tex.) State Bank; chmn. bd. 1st Nat. Bank (Dallas). Chmn. Anderson Co. War Savings Com., and of 2d Liberty Loan Drive. Democrat. Mem. Christian Ch. Woodman. Home: Palestine, Tex. Deceased.

ROYALL, William Bailey, prof. Greek; b. Mt. Pleasant, S.C., Sept. 2, 1844; s. William and Elizabeth Venning (Bailey) R.; Furman U., Greenville, S.C., 1855-59; B.A., Wake Forest Coll., 1861, M.A., 1866; research work in British Museum, and at Rome and Athens, 1903-04; D.D., Judson Coll., 1887; LL.D., Furman, 1907; m. Sarah Hall, Sept. 6, 1871; children—Rena Hall (dec.), William, Margaret (dec.), John Hall, Robert Henry, James. Soldier C.S.A., Civil War; mem. Santee Arty., coast of S.C., 1861-62; commissary sergt., 55th N.C. Regt., 1862-65. Began teaching Greek, Wake Forest Coll., 1866; prof., 1871—; has taught Greek to presidents of 12 southern colls. and 2 theol. sems., etc. Ordained ministry Bapt. Ch., 1869. Democrat. Mason. Home: Wake Forest, N.C. Died Jan. 27, 1928.

ROYCE, Frederick Page, trustee; b. Newton, Mass., Oct. 5, 1868; s. Harrison A. R.; ed. Mass. Inst. Tech.; m. K. Eva Ames; children—Mrs. Catharine A. Hamlen, Mrs. Mary Baker, Frank Ames, Mrs. Harriet E. R. Theopold, Evelyn A. Formerly v.p. Stone & Webster, Inc.; dir. Boston Woven Hose & Rubber Co., Conn. Power Co., Hartford Electric Light Co., etc. Republican. Episcopalian. Home: Dedham, Mass. Died Nov. 5, 1933.

ROYCE, George Monroe, clergyman; b. Westmoreland Co., Va., Aug. 12, 1850; s. Col. John Harrison and Elizabeth (Monroe) R.; student Bethany Coll., Va., 1874, Harvard, 1875-77; grad. Union Theol. Sem., New York, 1878; studied and traveled in Europe, 1880-85; m. Eva Purdy Thomson, Apr. 16, 1914. Deacon, 1887, priest, 1888, P.E. Ch.; in charge St. Ambrose Ch., New York, 1887, Trinity, Paris, France, 1888-89, St. Paul's, Rome, Italy, 1889-90; rector St. James', Florence, Italy, 1890-93; founder, 1897, and rector, 1897-1902, Am. Ch., Munich; curate in sole charge Clanfield Hants, Eng., St. Marys, London, 1904-06; rector New Windsor-on-Hudson, N.Y.; retired. Founder Am. Circle in Nice (France), 1926. Author: The Little Bugler, 1881; Two Englishmen, by an American, 1885; The Decline of the American Pulpit, 1894; Americans in Europe, by One of Them, 1893; The Passing of the American, 1912; Notebook of an American Parson in England, 1918; Amye Robsart (five-act drama in blank verse); Base Born (five-act drama). Deceased.

ROYCE, Josiah, university prof.; b. Grass Valley, Calif., Nov. 20, 1855; A.B., U. of Calif., 1875; Ph.D., Johns Hopkins, 1878; (LL.D., U. of Aberdeen, 1900, Johns Hopkins, 1902, Yale University, 1911, St. Andrew's Univ., 1911; Litt.D., Harvard, 1911; D.Sc., Oxford, 1913); m. Katharine Head, Oct. 2, 1880. Instr. English literature and logic, U. of Calif., 1878-82; instr. philosophy, 1882-85, asst. prof., 1885-92, prof. history of philosophy, 1892-1914, Alford prof. natural religion, moral philosophy, and civil polity, Mar. 1914—, Harvey University. Fellow Am. Acad. Arts and Sciences. Author: Religious Aspect of Philosophy, 1885; History of California (in Am. Commonwealth series), 1886; The Spirit of Modern Philosophy, 1892; The Conception of God (joint author), 1897; The World and the Individual (2 vols.), 1900, 01; The Conception of Immortality, 1900; The Relation of the Principles of Logic to the Foundations of Geometry (Trans. Am. Math. Soc., July 1905); The Philosophy of Loyalty, 1908; Race Questions, Provincialism and Other American Problems, 1908; William James and Other Essays on the Philosophy of Life, 1911; Bross Lectures on The Sources of Religious Insight, 1912; The Problem of Christianity (2 vols.), 1913; War and Insurance, 1914. Died Sept. 14, 1916.

ROYCE, Luman Herbert, clergyman; b. Croton, O., June 6, 1868; s. LeRoy and Mary (Davis) R.; A.B., Ohio Wesleyan U., Delaware, O., 1890; D.D., Fairmount Coll. (now Municipal U.), Wichita, Kan., 1922; m. Mary Gardner, Sept. 3, 1891 (died 1928); children—Gardner, Polly (Mrs. J. Donald Myer), Paul, Donald. Ordained ministry Congl. Ch., 1891; pastor successively Vermilion, O., Camp Point and Mendon, Ill., Crestline, O., 1891-1903, Westminster Presbyn. Ch., Cleveland, 1903-09, Collinwood Congl. Ch., Cleveland, 1909-12; pastor East Congl. Ch., East Cleveland, also exec. sec. Congl. Union of Cleveland, 1912-18; nat. dir. city work, Congl. Ch. Extension Bds., 1918—. Republican. Home: Cleveland, O. Died July 19, 1935.

ROYSTER, James Finch, prof. English; b. Raleigh, N.C., June 26, 1880; s. Wisconsin Illinois and Mary Wills (Finch) R.; A.B., Wake Forest (N.C.) Coll., 1900; Ph.D., U. of Chicago, 1907; studied U. of Berlin, 1902-03; m. Carrie Belle Lake, June 17, 1908; children—Chauncey Lake, Martha Ellen. Instr. in English, U. of Colo., 1904-05; asst. in English, U. of Chicago, 1906-07; asso. prof. and prof. English, U. of N.C., 1907-14; prof. English, U. of Tex., 1914-21; Kenan prof. English philology, 1921—, dean Coll. Liberal Arts, 1922-25; dean of Grad. Sch., 1925—, U. of N.C. Democrat. Author: (with Stith Thompson) Guide to Composition, 1919; Practice Sheets for English Composition, 1920; Southern edition of Good English, 1921; Reading Report Blanks, 1922. Editor: A Middle English Tract on the Ten Commandments, 1911; Shakespeare's Love's (Labour's) Lost; American Short Stories, 1925; Studies in Philology, 1925. Home: Chapel Hill, N.C. Died Mar. 22, 1930.

RUBENS, Harry, lawyer; b. Vienna, Austria, July 7, 1850; grad. Poly. Sch., Vienna, 1867. Came to U.S., 1867; was city editor Westliche Post, St. Louis; asso. with Joseph Keppler, artist, in founding at St. Louis, 1871, comic journal "Puck" later of New York; pvt. sec. to U.S. Senator Carl Schurz, 1871-72; asst. sec. Mo. Senate, 1872-73; removed to Chicago, 1873; was local editor Chicago Freie Presse, later with Chicago Times, and Evening Mail; studied law; admitted to Ill. bar, June 8, 1877; mem., 1879-85, and pres., 1882-85, of the Chicago Public Library Board. Counsel Chicago Bd. of Edn., 1885-87; corp. counsel, Chicago, 1894-95; later gen. counsel, Republic Iron & Steel Co., United Breweries Co., United Iron & Steel Co., and other large corps.; counsel to consulate of Germany at Chicago. Founder, and many yrs. pres. Austro-Hungarian Benevolent Assn.; pres. Goethe Monument Com. Was judge advocate gen. Ill. State Militia, 1894-97. Pres. Germania Club, several terms. Decorated by Emperor of Germany with Order of the Crown, 1902, by Emperor of Austria with Order of the Iron Crown, 1907, and by King of Bavaria with Order of St. Michael, 1914. Home: Chicago, Ill. Died June 13, 1920.

RUBENS, Horatio Seymour, lawyer, corp. official; b. N.Y. City, June 6, 1869; s. Rudolph and Cecelia R.; B.S., Coll. City of New York, 1888; M.S., 1891; LL.B., Columbia, 1891. Studied law in office of Elihu Root and became his managing clerk; was counsel to Salvador and in other Spanish Am. affairs; gen. counsel of Cuban Junta in successful Cuban revolution against Spain, 1895-98; counsel to Am. Insular Commn. to Puerto Rico, 1900; counsel to U.S. Mil. Govt. in Cuba, 1900; mem. commn. for division of codes and laws in Cuba, 1901, also of tax, prison and electoral law commns. in Cuba; chmn. com. on alcohol, Council of Nat. Defense, 1917; pres. Consolidated Railroads of Cuba; pres. and chmn. bd. The Cuba R.R. Co.; chmn. bd. Cuba Northern Rys. Co.; director The Cuba Company. Colonel Auxiliary Res., U.S.A.; colonel Cuban Army of Liberation; Decorated Order Bust of Liberator (Venezuela), 1895; Grand Medal of Merit and Honor, 1922; given spl. vote of thanks by Cuban Revolutionary Congress, 1897; awarded spl. gold medal by Cuba, 1915, for services rendered during Cuban Revolution; was declared "Adopted Son of Havana," 1922; declared "Adopted Son of Camagüey," 1930; accorded, by act of Cuban Congress, title of "The Great Friend of Cuba," with spl. decoration created for this title; Comdr. Grand Cross of Carlos Manuel de Cespedas (Cuba); "Aodpted Son of Santa Clara" (Cuba), 1933; made hon. pres. of Cuba Vets. of Independence. Author: Liberty—The Story of Cuba. Home: Garrison, N.Y. Died Apr. 8, 1941.

RUBEY, Thomas Lewis, congressman; b. Lebanon, Mo., Sept. 27, 1862; A.B., U. of Mo., 1885, A.M., 1889; m. Fannie J. Horner, 1885. Supt. schs., Lebanon, 5 yrs.; teacher, Mo. Sch. Mines, Rolla; now engaged in banking at Lebanon. Was mem. Mo. Ho. of Rep., and Mo. Senate (pres. pro tem); lt. gov. of

Mo., 1903-05; mem. 62d to 66th and 68th to 70th Congresses (1911-21 and 1923-29), 16th Mo. Dist. Democrat. Home: Lebanon, Mo. Died Nov. 2, 1928.

RUBINKAM, Nathaniel Irwin, lecturer; b. Hartsville, Pa., Feb. 19, 1851; s. Nathaniel I. and Anna Maria (Wynkoop) R.; A.B., Princeton, 1874; U. of Halle, 1875; grad. Princeton Theol. Sem., 1878; studied Berlin, Basel, Paris, London, and traveled in Europe and Orient; Ph.D., Basel, 1891; m. Sarah Erety Shoemaker, April 24, 1880. Ordained Presbyn. ministry, 1878; pastor W. Pittston, Pa., 1878-80, Second Dutch Reformed Ch., Phila., 1880-85, Presbyn. Ch., Jamestown, N.Y., 1885-88, University Congl. Ch., Chicago, 1892-99; lecturer of Rubinkam Assn., Chicago, 1903—; extension lecturer in literature, U. of Chicago, 1893-1910. Mem. Chautauqua bd. of trustees, 1881-97; pres. C.L.S.C., 1900; pres. Internat. Folk-Lore Soc. of Chicago, 1898; pres. and sec., Univ. Ethical Soc., Chicago. Author: Zachariah, 1891. Editor and author: Hamlet, 1897; Masterpieces of Musical Art, 1906; Studies in Grand Opera, 1909; The Muses and Culture, 1910. Writer and editor of the University Forum, San Francisco. Died Sept. 29, 1919.

RUBINOW, Isaac Max, social worker; b. Grodno, Russia, Apr. 19, 1875; s. Max Simon and Esther (Shereshewsky) R.; came to America, 1893; A.B., Columbia U., 1895; student political science, 1900-03, Columbia U.; M.D., Univ. Medical College (New York U.), 1898; Ph.D., Columbia Univ., 1914; m. Sophie Himowich, July 9, 1899; children—Laura, Raymond S., Olga F. Practiced medicine, 1898-1903; examiner U.S. Civil Service Commn., 1903-04; econ. expert Bur. of Statistics, U.S. Dept. of Agr., 1904-07; mem. Bur. of Statistics, U.S. Dept. Commerce and Labor, 1907-08; mem. Bur. of Labor, 1908-11; chief statistician, Ocean Accident and Guarantee Corp., 1911-16; exec. sec. Social Ins. Com. of A.M.A., 1916-17; dir. Bur. of Social Statistics, Dept. Pub. Charities, N.Y. City, 1917. Dir. Am. Zionist Med. Unit in Palestine, 1919-22; dir. Jewish Welfare Soc., Phila., 1923-28; exec. dir. Zionist Orgn. America, 1928-29; sec. B'nai B'rith, Nov. 1929—. Lecturer on social insurance at New York Sch. of Philanthropy, 1912-15, Univ. of Chicago, summer 1930; contributing editor The Survey, 1911-16; editor Jewish Social Service Quarterly, 1925-29. Pres. Casualty Actuarial Soc., 1914-16; pres. Social Workers' Club of Phila., 1924-26; mem. Ohio Commn. on Unemployment Insurance, 1932; chmn. Advisory Bd. for Old Age Pension, Cincinnati, 1934-35. Awarded medal, 1907, from Russian minister of finance for "distinguished services to commerce and agriculture." Author: Russia's Wheat Surplus, 1906; Russia's Wheat Trade, 1908; Russian Wheat and Wheat Flour in European Markets, 1908; The Economic Condition of the Jews in Russia, 1908; Studies in Workmen's Insurance, Italy, Russia, Spain, 1911; Social Insurance, 1913; Was Marx Wrong?, 1914; Standard Accident Tables, 1915; Standards of Health Insurance, 1916; The Care of the Aged, 1931; The Quest for Security, 1934. Home: Cincinnati, O. Died Sept. 1, 1936.

RUBLEE, William Alvah, diplomat; b. Madison, Wis., 1861; grad. Harvard Univ. U.S. consul to Prague, Bohemia, 1890-94; editorial writer on Milwaukee Sentinel, 1894-1901; consul gen. to Hongkong, China, 1901-02; transferred to Havana, Oct. 1902; transferred to Vienna, Austria, 1903. Died 1910.

RUCKER, Daniel Henry, army officer; b. Belleville, N.J., Apr. 28, 1812; s. John A. and Sarah (Macomb) R.; m. Jane Curtis, 1850. Apptd. from Mich., 2d lt. 1st Dragoons, Oct. 13, 1837; 1st lt., Oct. 8, 1844; capt., Feb. 7, 1847; transferred to capt. asst. q.m., Aug. 23, 1849; maj. q.m. (14 yrs. service), Aug. 3, 1861; col. additional a.d.c. vols., Sept. 28, 1861; brig. gen., May 23, 1863; bvtd. maj. gen., Mar. 13, 1865; col. asst. q.m. gen., U.S.A., July 28, 1866; hon. mustered out of vol. service, Sept. 1, 1866; brig. gen. q.m. gen., Feb. 13, 1882; retired at own request, over 40 yrs.' service, Feb. 23, 1882. Bvtd. maj., Feb. 23, 1847, for battle of Buena Vista, Mex.; lt. col., col. and brig. gen., July 5, 1864, for services during the war; maj. gen. U.S.A., and U.S.V., Mar. 1865, for services during the war. Home: Washington, D.C. Died 1910.

RUCKER, Elbert Marion, prof. law; b. Anderson, S.C., Mar. 15, 1866; s. Elbert Marion and Sarah Frances (Whitner) R.; ed. Adger Coll., Walhalla, S.C.; A.B., U. of S.C., 1885, LL.B., 1887; m. Susan Elizabeth Kinard, 1886 (died 1913); children—Elizabeth (Mrs. George Rainsford Norris), Frances Louise (Mrs. William Webster Moore); m. 2d, Mary Mitchell Martin, Aug. 26, 1915. Admitted to S.C. bar, 1887, and began practice at Anderson; U.S. asst. atty., Washington, D.C., 1893-97; mem. S.C. Ho. of Rep., 1900-10 (chmn. ways and means com., 1908-10); prof. law, U. of S.C., 1910-26; served as lecturer summer schs. U. of Ga., U. of Ky., etc., and exchange prof. at U. of N.C.; was spl. asso. justice Supreme Court of S.C. various times. Democrat. Presbyn. Lived at Columbia, S.C. Died Aug. 16, 1926.

RUCKER, Louis H., soldier; b. in Illinois, Jan. 13, 1842. Entered Union Army, Apr. 19, 1861, as pvt., Capt. Barker's Chicago Dragoons, with which served to Aug. 18, 1861; pvt., sergt. and 1st sergt. Co. G, 8th Ill. Vol. Cav., Sept. 14, 1861-Feb. 8, 1864; 2d lt., Feb. 9, 1864, and 1st lt., Nov. 26, 1864, 8th Ill. Cav., serving until Apr. 21, 1865. Apptd. 2d lt. 9th U.S. Cav., July 28, 1866, 1st lt., July 31, 1867, capt., Mar. 20, 1879; maj. 4th Cav., Jan. 13, 1896, 6th Cav., Jan. 2, 1900; lt. col., Feb. 2, 1901; col. 8th Cav., Sept. 17, 1901, until retired as brig. gen. U.S.A., 1903. Died 1906.

RUCKER, William Colby, sanitarian; b. Kenney, Ill., Sept. 28, 1875; s. Hamline P. and Lydia Marie (Colby) R.; ed. U. of N.D.; U. of Minn., 1890-94; M.D., Rush Med. Coll., Chicago, 1897; M.S., Univ. of Calif., 1912, Dr.P.H., 1915; m. Annette Guequierre, July 19, 1902 (died 1910); m. 2d, Elizabeth Harwood Neff, Nov. 11, 1912. Asst. surgeon, 1902, passed asst. surgeon, 1907, surgeon, 1914, asst. surgeon gen., Apr. 1, 1912-Mar. 1, 1918, surgeon, Mar. 1, 1918-July 1, 1919, asst. surgeon gen., Reserve Corps, July 1, 1919-Sept. 15, 1920, surgeon, Sept. 15, 1920—, U.S., Public Health Service. Served at San Francisco, Boston, Vineyard Haven, Mass.; yellow fever campaign, New Orleans, 1905; Jamestown Expn., 1907; exec. officer plague campaign, San Francisco, 1907-10, and in command 1912; Rocky Mt. spotted fever campaign, Victor, Mont., 1911; comd. plague eradicative campaign, New Orleans, 1914. Fellow Am. Coll. Surgeons, Am. Coll. Physicians, A.M.A.; charter mem. Nat. Bd. Medical Examiners; member National Bd. on First Aid Standardization; life mem. Assn. Mil. Surgeons (Enno Sander gold medal, 1908; treas. 1917). Episcopalian. Has traveled extensively in Central and South America, making sanitary surveys and promoting public health work. Sec. com. on Hygiene and Sanitation Gen. Med. Bd. of Council Nat. Defense, 1917; detailed to army, and with A.E.F., Jan.-July 1918; port of embarkation, Newport News, Va., July 1918-June 1919; chief med. adviser, Bur. War Risk Ins., Washington, 1919-20; chief quarantine officer, the Panama Canal, Oct. 1920-Feb. 1924; med. officer in charge U.S. Marine Hosp. No. 14, New Orleans, La., June 7, 1925—. Died May 1930.

RUCKER, William Waller, congressman; b. nr. Covington, Va., Feb. 1, 1855; s. William P. and Margaret A. (Scott) R.; ed. country schs.; m. Fannie Applegate, May 20, 1880. Admitted to bar, 1876, and entered practice at Keytesville. Pros. atty. Chariton, Mo., 1886-92; judge Circuit Court, 12th dist., 1893-99; mem. 56th to 67th Congresses (1899-1923), 2d Mo. Dist. Democrat. Home: Keytesville, Mo. Died May 30, 1936.

RUCKMAN, John Wilson, army officer; b. Sydney, Ill., Oct. 10, 1858; s. Thomas and Mary (O'Brien) R.; grad. U.S. Mil. Acad., 1883, Arty. Sch., 1892, Army War Coll., 1915, Naval War Coll., 1916; m. May, d. of late Col. John Hamilton, U.S.A., June 16, 1887. Commd. 2d lt. 5th Arty., June 13, 1883; promoted through grades to col. C.A. Corps, Mar. 7, 1912; brig. gen., July 20, 1916; maj. gen. N.A., Aug. 5, 1917-May 1, 1918. First editor of Journal of U.S. Artillery, 1892-96; served in Havana, Cuba, with Army of Occupation, 1899-1901; instr. Sch. of Submarine Defense, 1901-04; in Philippine Islands, 1911-14, and insp. gen. there, 1911-12. Assigned to command 5th provisional regt. coast arty., Del Rio, Tex. border, July 3, 1916; later also comdg. dist. of El Paso Rio Grande, and dist. of Laredo, to July 1917; comd. S. Atlantic Coast Arty. Dist., Charleston, S.C., July-Aug. 1917, Southern Dept., Aug. 30, 1917-May 1, 1918, Northeastern Dept., Boston, May 23-July 20, 1918, N. Atlantic Coast Arty. Dist., Boston, July 21, 1918—. Wrote: The Command and Administration of the Fortress of Port Arthur during the Russo-Japanese War. Inventor many devices for use in war. Died June 7, 1921.

RUDD, Stephen A., lawyer; b. Brooklyn, N.Y., Dec. 11, 1874; s. Robert James and Mary Ann (Zeiser) R.; prep. edn., New York Prep. Sch.; student Brooklyn Law Sch., St. Lawrence U., 1910-12; m. Elizabeth Lindsay, 1895 (died 1923); children—Martha L., Stephen J., Lindsay H., Roy H.; m. 2d, Martha Lindsay; Admitted to N.Y. bar, 1914, and began practice at Brooklyn; associated with two sons under firm name of Rudd, Rudd & Rudd. Mem. Bd. of Alderman, N.Y. City, 1922-30; mem. 72d Congress (1931-33), at spl. election, Feb. 17, 1931, to fill vacancy occasioned by death of David J. O'Connell, 9th N.Y. Dist. and reëlected to 73d Congress (1933-35). Democrat. Home: Brooklyn, N.Y. Died Mar. 30, 1936.

RUDD, William Platt, judge; b. Albany, N.Y., June 9, 1851; s. William Tracy and Adeline Martha (Platt) R.; A.B., Union Coll., 1873, A.M., 1876; LL.B., Albany Law Sch., 1875; m. Aimee Pierson Allen, 1883. Admitted to bar, 1875, and practiced at Albany; was mem. Harris & Rudd; justice Supreme Ct. of N.Y., term 1910-24. V.p. Albany Co. Savings Bank. Mem. Albany Sch. Bd., 7 yrs.; corp. counsel, Albany, 1894-95. Trustee and pres. Home. Hosp., 1905-08; trustee, 1881—, Harmanus Bleecker and Pruyn Libraries (pres. bd.); pres. trustees Albany Law Sch.; mem. bd. govs., Union U.; trustee Chamber Commerce, Albany Hist. Soc. Vestryman St. Peter's Ch., Albany. Home: Albany, N.Y. Died Oct. 9, 1929.

RUDDY, Howard Shaw, editor; b. Bridgeport, Ill., Aug. 22, 1856; ed. Lawrenceville, Ill., pub. schs.; m. Alice A. Gosnell, Feb. 14, 1877. Entered on newspaper career, 1876; city editor Vincennes, Ind., Sun, 1878-88; lit. editor Rochester Herald, 1893—, also asso. editor, 1905—. Editor: Book Lovers' Verse, 1899. Home: Rochester, N.Y. Died Dec. 13, 1922.

RUDGE, William Edwin, printer, pub.; b. Brooklyn, N.Y., Nov. 23, 1876; s. William Edwin and Lavina (Knapp) R.; ed. pub. schs.; m. Lillie May Gould, Apr. 18, 1906; children—William Edwin, Frederick Gould. In printing and publishing business, New York, 1888—; pres. William Edwin Rudge, Inc. Awarded 2 gold, 2 silver and 2 bronze medals in ann. printing exhbns., New York; given 1st place in exhbn., Phila., 1925, hon. mention, Phila., 1926; apptd. by Herbert Hoover, sec. of commerce, to represent printing industry at Internat. Expn. of Modern Decorative and Industrial Art, Paris, 1925. Mem. advisory bd. New York Univ. course, given by Am. Inst. of Graphic Arts. Presbyn. Mason. Home: Mt. Vernon, N.Y. Died June 12, 1931.

RUDKIN, Frank H., judge; b. Vernon, O., Apr. 23, 1864; s. Bernard and Winifred (Leonard) R.; ed. common schools, and acad., Ohio; read law at Washington and Lee U.; m. Ellen Rose Doty, July 25, 1921. Admitted to bar, 1887, and began practice at N. Yakima, Wash.; judge Superior Ct., Wash., 1901-05, Supreme Ct., Wash., 1905-11 (chief justice, 1909-11); U.S. dist. judge, Eastern Dist. of Wash., 1911-23; U.S. Circuit judge, 9th Circuit, Jan. 9, 1923—. Republican. Died May 3, 1931.

RUDOLPH, Cuna H., banker; b. Baltimore, Md., June 26, 1860; s. Jacob and Elizabeth (Yeager) R.; ed. pvt. schs. and business coll.; m. Amy Edna Merz, June 8, 1901. Located at Washington, 1889, and engaged in hardware business; former pres. Rudolph & West Co.; pres. Second Nat. Bank, 1913-21. Pres. Bd. Commrs. of D.C., 1910-13 and 1921-24; re-appointed to same office by President Coolidge; resigned Oct. 1926; tendered a dinner by 1,000 citizens, Dec. 1926, and presented with silver service by the people of Washington. Opened first public playground in Washington, 1901. Mem. Washington Bd. of Trade (pres.); pres. Children's Hosp.; pres. Associated Charities; trustee Neighborhood House. Chmn. Clearing House Assn. D.C., 1914-21; chmn. George Washington Bicentennial Celebration. Republican. Home: Washington, D.C. Died Jan. 6, 1932.

RUDOLPH, Robert Livingston, bishop; b. N.Y. City, Dec. 29, 1865; s. Richard and Victoria (Schmadel) R.; B.A., New York U., 1892, M.A., 1896; B.D., Theol. Sem. (R.E.), Phila., 1896; Princeton Theol. Sem., 1894-95, U. of Erlangen, 1905; D.D. New York U., 1906; m. Anna Catherine Knight, Jan. 18, 1900; children—Katherine Elizabeth (dec.), Robert Knight. Lay Preacher, New York Orphan Asylum, 1891-95; ordained deacon, 1895; presbyter., 1896; asst. rector First Ch., New York, 1895-1903; apptd. prof. dogmatic theology and Christian ethics, Theol. Sem. R.E. Ch. Phila., 1903, then prof. systematic theology, bibl. theology and Christian ethics, also dean, 1925—; consecrated bishop R.E. Church, Jan. 12, 1909; bishop of New York and Phila. Synod; pres. Gen. Council R.E. Ch. and presiding bishop; v.p. bd. trustees Theol. Sem. R.E. Ch.; mem. exec. com. Fed. Council Chs. of Christ in America. Prohibitionist. Home: Philadelphia, Pa. Died Sept. 16, 1930.

RUE, Levi Lingo, banker; b. Phila., July 14, 1860; s. Francis J. and Mary Ellen (Lingo) R.; ed. pub. schs., Phila.; m. Mary McCurdy Gill, Oct. 6, 1887; children—Roberta (Mrs. Edward A. Steele), Florence (Mrs. W. Newton, Jackson), Francis Jamison. Began with Phila. Nat. Bank, 1878, elected pres. same, 1907; chmn. bd. Philadelphia-Girard Nat. Bank from merger, 1926, of Phila. and Girard Nat. banks, until merger of Phila.-Girard Nat. Bank, Apr. 1928, with the Franklin Fourth Street Nat. Bank with title of The Phila. Nat. Bank of which is chmn. bd.; dir. many companies; mgr. Western Saving Fund Soc. Pres. Phila. Clearing House Assn. Home: Chestnut Hill, Phila., Pa. Died June 7, 1931.

RUEDIGER, Gustav F(erdinand), pathology; b. Fountain City, Wis., June 9, 1876; s. Ernst and Augusta (Heise) R.; B.S., U. of Wis., 1900; M.D., Rush Med. Coll., Chicago, 1903; Ph.D., U. of Chicago, 1907; m. Abby Brayton, Aug. 20, 1908; children—Gustav Louis, Gretchen Elizabeth, William Karl. Prof. bacteriology and pathology, and dir. State Pub. Health Labs., U. of N.D., 1907-14; dir. Hygienic Inst. for LaSalle-Peru-Oglesby, Ill., 1914-17; dir. State Hygienic Lab., U. of Nev., 1917-21; engaged in pvt. practice of clin. pathology. Republican. Unitarian. Home: Pasadena, Calif. Died July 5, 1935.

RUFFNER, Charles Shumway, elec. engineer; b. Chicago, June 22, 1880; s. Vivion Whaley and Nellie (Shumway) R.; Centenary Coll., Palmyra, Mo., 1894-96; B.S. in E.E., U. of Mo., 1900; m. Hazel R. Wesson, June 5, 1911. With Telluride Power Co., until 1909; supt. operation Central Colo. Power Co.,

1909-11; at St. Louis, Mo., 1911-19; pres. and gen. mgr. Miss. River Power Distributing Co.; v.p. and gen. mgr. Elec. Co. of Mo., St. Louis County Gas Co., Arrow Engring. Co., Union Electric Light & Power Co., Union Colliery Co.; at New York, 1919-21, as v.p. North Am. Co. and subsidiaries; served as dir., v.p. and pres. Adirondack Power & Light Corp., 1921-26; pres. Mohawk Hudson Power Co., 1925-30, N.Y. Power and Light Corp., 1927-29; chmn. bd. Schenectady (N.Y.) Trust Co. Dir. N.Y. State Econ. Council, Boy Scout Council, Y.M.C.A., Bur. Municipal Research (treas.), Schenectady County Clearing House Assn. (pres.); chmn. group V, N.Y. State Bankers Assn., 1935-36. Fellow Am. Inst. E.E. (v.p. and mgr. 1919-20). Republican. Mason. Died Jan. 21, 1939.

RUFFNER, William Henry, educator, geologist; b. Lexington, Va., Feb. 11, 1824; s. Henry R., D.D., LL.D., pres. Washington Coll.; grad. Washington Coll. (now Washington and Lee Univ.), 1842, A.M., LL.D., same; m. Harriet A. Gray (dec.), 1850. Chaplain Univ. of Va., 1849-51; pastor 7th Presbyn. Ch., Phila., 1851-53; author of school law of Va. and 1st supt. public instruction, Va., 1870-82; founder State Female Normal School and prin. same, 1884-87. Was for yrs. editor official dept. Educational Jour. of Va. Author: School Reports of Virginia, 11 vols., 1871-82; Geological Report on Washington Territory; History of Washington and Lee Univ., 1893; Charity and the Clergy. Home: Lexington, Va. Died 1908.

RUGER, Thomas Howard, maj. gen. U.S.A., retired, 1897; b. Lima, N.Y., April 2, 1833; grad. West Point, 1854; assigned to engr. corps; resigned April 1, 1855; practiced law, Janesville, Wis., 1855-61; lt. col. 3d Wis. regt., June 1861; col., Aug. 20, 1862; brig. gen. vols., Nov. 29, 1862; served in Rappahannock campaign; comd. div. at Gettysburg; aided in suppressing draft riots, New York, 1863; served under Sherman and, Nov. 30, 1864 bvtd. maj. gen. for services in battle of Franklin; col. U.S.A., July 28, 1866; bvt. brig. gen. U.S.A., March 2, 1867, for services at battle of Gettysburg; mil. gov. Ga., 1868; supt. U.S. Mil. Acad., 1871-76; comd. dept. South, 1876-78; brig. gen., March 19, 1886; maj. gen., 1895. Home: Stamford, Conn. Died 1907.

RUGG, Arthur Prentice, judge; b. Sterling, Mass., Aug. 20, 1862; s. Prentice Mason and Cynthia (Ross) R.; A.B., Amherst, 1883; LL.B., Boston U., 1886; LL.D., Amherst, 1908, Harvard, 1914, Boston U., 1923, Williams, 1924; m. Florence May Belcher, Apr. 10, 1889; children—Charles Belcher, Arthur Prentice, Esther Cynthia, Donald Sterling (dec.). Admitted to bar, 1886; partner of Hon. John R. Thayer. Pres. Worcester Common Council, 1895; asst. dist. atty., Mass. Middle Dist., 1895-97; city solicitor, Worcester, 1897-1906; asso. justice of Supreme Jud. Court of Mass., Sept. 27, 1906-Sept. 20, 1911, chief justice same, Sept. 20, 1911—. Trustee Boston U., 1909-22, Clark U., 1909—, Amherst Coll., 1917—. Pres. Am. Antiquarian Society; mem. council Colonial Soc. of Mass. (v.p. 1918), Am. Law Inst.; fellow Am. Acad. Arts and Sciences (v.p. 1921-27). Republican. Unitarian. Delivered memorial address on Calvin Collidge at joint session of Congress, Feb. 1933. Home: Worcester, Mass. Died June 12, 1938.

RUGG, Frederic Waldo, banker; b. Rindge, N.H., Dec. 1, 1855; s. William Stickney and Clarissa (Sawtell) R.; ed. pub. schs.; m. Luella R. Billings, 1879 (died 1919); 1 son, Robert Billings; m. 2d, Mrs. Myra A. Knight, 1923. Began in business in Fitchburg, 1872; street ry. business, Boston, 1876-80; entered banking, 1880; cashier, 1898, and pres. Nat. Rockland Bank, 1907-32, chmn. bd., Jan. 1932—; trustee Instn. for Savings in Roxbury. Commr. statistics dept. City of Boston. Mem. bd. mgrs. Boston Provident Assn.; trustee Bank Officers' Assn., City of Boston, Highland Business Men's Assn., Roxbury Charitable Soc., Forest Hills Cemetery. Republican. Unitarian. Home: Cambridge, Mass. Died Nov. 5, 1932.

RUGG, Henry Warren, clergyman; b. Framingham, Mass., Sept. 3, 1833; s. Warren and Hannah (Smith) R.; ed. pub. schs. and by pvt. study; (S.T.D., Tufts Coll., 1888); m. Abby Nelson Howard, Dec. 25, 1853. Ordained Universalist ministry, 1854; pastor chs. in Mass. and Me., 1854-66, Ch. of Mediator, Providence, R.I., 1866-95; financial sec. Gen. Conv., 1895-99; trustee and sec. Corp. Tufts Coll., 1899—. Chmn. bd. of trustees Universalist Gen. Conv.; trustee and dir. Universalist Pub. House; sec. and supt. R.I. Universalist Conv. Mason; Grand Master Grand Encampment, K.T. of U.S.; for many years editor Free Masons Repository. Author: Lives of the Presidents, 1886; The Church, 1891; Our Word and Work, 1894. Home: Providence, R.I. Died 1910.

RUGGLES, Colden L'Hommedieu, army officer; b. Omaha, Neb., Mar. 18. 1869; s. George D. (brig. gen. U.S.A.) and Alma (L'Hommedieu) R.; grad. U.S. Mil. Acad., 1890; E.E., Lehigh U., 1903; grad. Army War Coll., 1922; m. Mary Appleton, d. Brig. Gen. Marcus P. Miller, U.S.A., Nov. 28, 1894; 1 dau., Colden (Mrs. E. L. Florance). Commd. add. 2d lt. 1st Arty., June 12, 1890; promoted through grades to col., May 15, 1917; brig. gen. (temp.), Aug. 8, 1918-Mar. 10, 1919. Duty Governor's Island, Ft. Monroe, Sandy Hook Proving Ground and Frankford (Pa.) Arsenal until 1900; insp. ordnace, U.S.A., Bethlehem Steel Co., 1900-03; at Watertown (Mass.) Arsenal, 1903-08; prof. ordnance and science of gunnery, U.S. Mill. Acad., 1908-11; comdg. officer Benicia (Calif.) Arsenal and ordnance officer Western Dept., 1911-13; comdg. officer Manila Ordnance Depot and ordnance officer Philippine Dept., 1913-15; comdg. officer Sandy Hook Proving Ground, 1915-18, also Aberdeen Proving Ground, 1917-18; chief of insp. div. Ordnance Dept., 1918; duty with A.E.F., Oct.-Dec. 1918; chief of tech. staff, Ordnance Dept., 1919-21; on duty as student officer, Army War Coll., Aug. 15, 1921-June 30, 1922; chief of tech. staff, Ord. Dept., Sept. 4, 1922-Aug. 27, 1923; apptd. asst. to the chief ordnance with rank of brig. gen., Mar. 28, 1923; became asst. chief ordnance and chief manufacture, Ord. Dept., 1923; retired. Delegate to Conf. for the Supervision of the International Trade in Arms and Ammunition, and in Implements of War, held in Geneva, Switzerland, May 4-June 17, 1925. Awarded D.S.M. Episcopalian. Died Apr. 2, 1933.

RUGGLES, George David, brig. gen. U.S.A., retired, Sept. 11, 1897; b. Newburgh, N.Y., Sept. 11, 1833; s. David and Sarah (Colden) R.; m. Alma Hammond L'Hommedieu. Entered West Point, Sept. 1, 1851; grad. July 1, 1855; commd. 2d lt. 2d inf.; became adj. of his regt., Sept. 10, 1857; asst. adj. gen. July 1, 1861. During war served as adj. gen. of brigade in 3-months' campaign; then assigned to duty in charge of the organization of vol. army; later became chief of staff, Army of Va.; later asst. chief of staff, Army of Potomac; then on spl. duty, under Sec. Stanton, in War Dept.; assisted Gen. Fry in organization of the conscription; served in spl. inspection service, and later as adj. gen. Army of the Potomac, under Gen. Meade, to end of war; reached bvtd. rank of brig. gen.; participated in many battles. After war adj. gen. of several divs. and depts. with successive promotions, becoming brig. gen. U.S.A., and adj. gen. of the army, Nov. 6, 1893, until retired. Under assignment of the President, was gov. Soldiers' Home, 1898-1903. Died 1904.

RUGGLES, Henry Joseph, lawyer, author; b. Poughkeepsie, N.Y., Aug. 16, 1813; s. Philo and Ellen (Bulkley) R.; grad. Columbia Coll.; entered practice at N.Y. City. Author: The Method of Shakespeare as an Artist, 1870; The Plays of Shakespeare Founded on Literary Forms, 1895. Died 1906.

RUGGLES, Oliver W., railway official. Errand boy to chief clerk pass. dept., clerk to chief clerk freight dept. Ohio & Miss. R.R.; baggageman, conductor, traveling pass. agt. and gen. pass. agt. St. Louis, Iron Mountain & Southern Ry.; asst. pass. agt. Mo. Pacific Ry. to 1881; gen. pass. and ticket agt. M.C. R.R., 1881—. Home: Chicago, Ill. Died Jan. 11, 1923.

RUHRAH, John, M.D.; b. Chillicothe, O., Sept. 26, 1872; s. Daniel Conrad and Mary (Fincknauer) R.; M.D., Coll. Phys. and Surg., Baltimore, 1894; post-grad. courses Johns Hopkins Hosp. Med. Sch., l'Institut Pasteur, Paris, 1897, univs. and hosps. of Vienna and Berlin and hosps. of Paris and London, 1900-01; unmarried. Asst. resident phys., 1894-95; resident phys., 1895-97, Mercy Hosp.; phys. in charge Pasteur Dept., Coll. Phys. and Surg., Baltimore, 1897; quarantine phys., port of Baltimore, 1898-1900; prof. diseases of children, Univ. of Md. Med. School; visiting physician to Mercy Hosp., Hosp. for Women of Md.; pres. Med. and Chirurg. Faculty, Md., 1919; pres. Am. Pediatric Soc., 1925; pres. Med. Library Assn., 1927, Research Soc., 1932, Am. Acad. Pediatrics, 1934, Osler Hist. Soc., 1933—. Commr. or pub. schs., Baltimore. Author: Diet in Health and Disease (with Julius Friedenwald); Dietetics for Nurses (with same); Manual of Diseases of Infants and Children; Poliomyelitis (with E. E. Mayer). Editor: Pediatrics of the Past; William Cadogan, His Essay on Gout. Home: Baltimore, Md. Died Mar. 10, 1935.

RULE, James Noble, educator; b. Manchester, Ia., Apr. 24, 1876; s. Henry William and Joan (Ruggles) R.; grad. Lewis Acad., Wichita, Kan., 1893; B.S., Washington and Jefferson Coll., 1898, M.S., 1901, Sc.D. for same coll., 1927; grad. study, U. of Wis., summer 1912; LL.D., Grove City Coll., 1931; Litt.D., Juniata Coll., 1932; LL.D., Temple U., U. of Pittsburgh, U. of Duquesne and Waynesburg Coll., 1932; LL.D., Ursinus Coll., 1933; Litt.D., U. of Pennsylvania, 1934; m. Cora Thompson, June 24, 1902; children—Margaret Agnes (Mrs. Leavitt D. Anders), William Thompson. Teacher high sch., Washington, Pa., 1898-1900; vice prin. Washington and Jefferson Acad., 1900-07, prin., 1907-12; head of dept. mathematics, high sch., Pittsburgh, Pa., Mar.-Sept. 1912; prin. Central High Sch., Pittsburgh, 1912-16; prin. Schenley High Sch., Pittsburgh, 1916-19; nat. dir. Jr. Am. Red Cross, 1919-21; dir. science, Pa. Dept. Pub. Instr., 1921-23; exec. sec. Pa. State Council Edn., 1923-31; acting supt. pub. instrn., Pa., Jan.-May 1931, supt. May 1931-35; principal Langley High Sch., Pittsburgh, 1935—. Dir. Ednl. Records Bur., N.Y. City; trustee Harrisburg Acad., Pa. State Coll.; chmn. Pa. Hist. Commn. Presbyn. Mason. Home: Pittsburgh, Pa. Died Apr. 11, 1938.

RULE, William, editor; b. Knox Co., Tenn., May 10, 1839; s. Frederick and Sarah Elisabeth (Brakebill) R.; ed. in common schs.; m. Lucy A. Maxey, Oct. 28, 1858; children—James Frederick (dec.), Cora (dec.), Alida (dec.), Stella (dec.), Lillian, William. Pvt. and officer in Union Army, 1862-65; edited a daily Republican newspaper, 1870—; editor Knoxville Chronicle, 1870-82, Knoxville Daily Journal and Tribune, 1885—. Clerk Knox Co. Ct. 2 terms; postmaster Knoxville 2 terms; mayor of Knoxville 2 terms, 1873, 98; mem. Rep. Nat. Com., 1876-84; trustee U. of Tenn. (sec. of bd. 40 yrs.; resigned and given hon. degree A.M.); U.S. pension agt., 1906-12. Home: Knoxville, Tenn. Died July 25, 1928.

RUMBOLD, Thomas Frazier, M.D.; b. Aberdeen, Scotland, Oct. 13, 1830; removed to Canada, 1834; to Iowa, 1839; ed. public schools and Iowa Coll.; grad. Jefferson Med. Coll., Phila., 1862; acting asst. surgeon U.S. army, 1862-65; took private courses on eye, ear and throat diseases; from 1866 he has limited his practice to these diseases. Member several nat. and foreign med. societies; author many medical papers and several books on his specialty; edited St. Louis Medical and Surg. Jour., 1878-84; invented numerous surgical appliances. Widower. Home: St. Louis, Mo. Died 1901.

RUMPLE, J. N. W., congressman; b. Fostoria, O., March 4, 1841; moved to Iowa, Sept. 1853; attended Ashland Sem., Western Coll. and normal dept., Iowa State Univ.; enlisted in 2d Iowa cav., Aug. 1861; mustered out as capt., Oct. 1865. Commenced study of law in Hon. H. M. Martin's office in Marengo, Ia., Dec. 1865; was admitted to practice Feb. 1867. Elected to State senate in 1873, and served in 14th, 15th, 16th and 17th gen. assemblies. Was Regent of State Univ. for several yrs.; also curator State Hist. Soc., co. atty., alderman, mayor, city solicitor and mem. bd. edn.; mem. Congress, 1901-03, 2d Ia. dist. Republican. Home: Marengo, Ia. Died 1903.

RUMSEY, Charles Cary, sculptor; b. Buffalo, N.Y., Aug. 29, 1879; s. Laurence Dana and Jennie (Cary) R.; A.B., Harvard, 1902; art student, Paris, 1902-06; m. Mary Harriman, May 26, 1910. Bronze medal, San Francisco Expn., 1916; exhibited "The Pagan," at Met. Mus. of Art, New York, 1921; executed frieze on arch, Manhattan Bridge, N.Y.; soldiers and sailors memorial, Brownsville (Brooklyn); statue of Pizarro, San Francisco Expn., etc. Served as capt. Hdqrs. Troop, 77th Div., and 40th Engrs., World War. Home: Westbury, L.I., N.Y. Died Sept. 21, 1922.

RUMSEY, Mary Harriman, philanthropy; d. Edward Henry (ry. pres.) and Mary (Averell) Harriman; m. Charles Carey Rumsey, sculptor (died 1922); 3 children. A founder Junior League, Community Councils; notable patron of arts; former owner chain of newspapers in the Southern States; an organizer Eastern Live Stock Coöperative Assn.; a developer Emergency Exchange Assn.; chmn. Consumers Advisory Com. of NRA. Home: Georgetown, D.C., and Sands Point, L.I., N.Y. Died Dec. 18, 1934.

RUMSEY, William, justice of Supreme Court, State of N.Y., 1880—; b. Bath, N.Y., Oct. 18, 1841; s. David and Jane E. (Brown) R.; grad. Williams Coll., 1861 (LL.D., 1888); m. Ella Moore, Feb. 1, 1872. Served during Civil War, 1861-65, in Peninsula, Shenandoah Valley, and other campaigns, engaging in many actions, severely wounded at Fair Oaks; promoted several times for bravery and distinguished services; retired with rank of lt. col. After war served for 2 yrs. with Robert E. Van Valkenberg, minister to Japan, as private sec. After return practiced law at Bath, N.Y., until elevation to bench; from March, 1895, asso. justice appellate div., Supreme Court, for 1st dept., State of N.Y. Republican. Received Republican nomination, 1888, for asso. judge, Court of Appeals, running ahead of his ticket. Author: Rumsey's Practice, 3 vols., 1887; joint author (with David Dudley Field) of A Codification of the Law of Evidence for the State of N.Y. Home: Bath, N.Y. Died 1903.

RUNCIE, Constance Fauntleroy, author, composer; b. Indianapolis, Jan. 15, 1836; d. Robert Henry and Jean Dale (Owen) Fauntleroy; g.d. Robert Owen, the father of coöperative socialism; English edn. at New Harmony, Ind., and studied in Germany 5 yrs.; m. James Runcie, D.D., P.E. clergyman, Apr. 9, 1861. Lived in Madison, Ind., 1861-71, then at St. Joseph, Mo. Organized, 1859, at New Harmony, Ind., the Minerva Club, said to be the 1st woman's club organized in America, 9 yrs. before Sorosis, New York; also founded the Bronté Club, Madison, Ind., 1867, and the Runcie Club, St. Joseph, Mo., 1894, of which she is "perpetual pres." Edited ch. paper 6 yrs.; was v.p. Social Science Club of Kan. and Western Mo.; chmn. com. on music and the drama to represent St. Joseph at Chicago Expn.; hon. v.p. Gen. Fedn. of Women's Clubs. Author: Children's Stories; Fables; Essay on Woman, 1904. Composer: Opera, Incognito; cantata, We Have Sinned Unto Death; Te Deum in G Major and Offertory Solos; songs, Take My Soul, O Lord, Invocation to Love, and many others; violin and piano solos, etc. Died 1911.

RUNKLE, Benjamin Platt, soldier; b. West Liberty, O., Sept. 3, 1837; s. Ralph Edwin and Hannah

Isabella (Piatt) R.; A.B., Miami U., 1857 (L.H.D., 1899); m. Lalla, d. Andrew McMicken, of Cincinnati, Feb. 10, 1894. Admitted to bar, 1859; practiced at Cincinnati, 1859-61; capt. 13th Ohio Inf., Apr. 22, 1861; maj., Nov. 8, 1861; col. 45th Ohio Inf., Aug. 19, 1862; hon. mustered out, July 21, 1864; lt. col. Vet. Reserve Corps, Aug. 22, 1864; bvtd. col., brig. gen. and maj. gen. vols., Nov. 9, 1865, "for meritorious services"; hon. mustered out, Oct. 5, 1866; maj. 45th U.S. Inf., July 28, 1866; bvtd. lt. col. U.S.A., Mar. 2, 1867, "for gallant and meritorious services at Shiloh" (wounded and left for dead on the field); col. U.S.A., Mar. 2, 1867, for same during the war. Editor Urbana (O.) Union, 1873-75. Ordained deacon P.E. Ch., Oct. 1882; ch. work, 1879-84; resigned diaconate, 1884; prof. mil. science, Kenyon Coll., 1879-81, Miami U., 1899-1901, U. of Me., 1901-02, Peekskill Mil. Acad., 1902-04, N.J. Mil. Acad., 1904-05, Germantown (Ohio) Mil. Inst., 1905-09; assigned to duty with N.G. of Ohio, 1909. A founder (grand consul, 1895-97) of Sigma Chi Fraternity, del. 1st and 22d and orator before 22d Grand chapters. Home: Hillsboro, Ohio. Died June 28, 1916.

RUNKLE, Delmer, banker; b. Boght, N.Y., Mar. 3, 1856; s. Henry H. and Margaret (Runkle) R.; ed. pub. schs. and Troy (N.Y.) Business Coll.; m. Mary E. Rosebrook, Oct. 18, 1898 (died 1921); m. 2d, Jessie Lillian Gardner, Dec. 6, 1924. Clerk Nat. State Bank, Troy, 1872-85; mgr. collection dept. Walter A. Wood Mowing & Reaping Machine Co., 1885-1901; organizer, 1901, Peoples Nat. Bank of Hoosick Falls, cashier until 1912, pres., 1912-28, chmn. bd., 1929-31; also pres. and dir. National City Bank of Troy, 1928—; formerly pres. Permanent Savings & Loan Assn., Industrial Bldg. & Mfg. Co., Hoosick Falls Cemetery Assn.; v.p. Hoosick Falls Mfg. Co.; former dir. The Peoples-First National Bank (Hoosick Falls), Noble & Wood Machine Co.; trustee Troy Savings Bank; county treas. Rensselaer Co., 1915-21. Chmn. Hoosick Falls Liberty Loan Drives, World War. Pres. Cheney Library and Hist. Rooms; pres. Samaritan Hosp. (Troy); trustee Hoosick Falls Pub. Schs.; mem. bd. govs. Marshall Sanitarium; trustee, elder, Hoosick Falls Presbyn. Ch. Republican. Elk. Trustee First Presbyn. Ch., Troy. Home: Troy, N.Y. Died Feb. 14, 1936.

RUNKLE, Erwin William, psychologist; b. Lisbon, Ia., May 20, 1869; s. Adam and Malinda Barbara (Sherk) R.; B.A., Coe College, Cedar Rapids, Ia., 1890; Ph.D., Yale, 1893; hon. fellow Clark U., 1899; m. May Middlekauff, 1894; 1 son, Lawrence M. Lecturer, Yale, 1893; prof. psychology and ethics, Pa. State Coll., 1893-1938, emeritus prof. philosophy, 1938—; also librarian Carnegie Library, 1904-24. Republican. Presbyn. Home: State College, Pa. Died Feb. 14, 1941.

RUNKLE, John Daniel, Walker prof. of mathematics, Mass. Inst. Tech., 1865—; b. Root, N.Y., Oct. 11, 1822; s. Daniel and Sarah (Gordon) R.; ed. public schools, acads. at Canajoharie, Ames and Cortland, N.Y.; grad. Lawrence Scientific School, Harvard, 1851 (A.M., Harvard; Ph.D., Hamilton; LL.D., Wesleyan); m. Catharine Robbins Bird, 1862. Apptd. asst. on Am. Ephemeris and Nautical Almanac, 1849; resigned, 1884; originated, 1858, Mathematical Monthly, and edited it until outbreak of Civil war; acting pres. Mass. Inst. Technology, 1868; pres. same, 1870-78; introduced manual training into U.S. from Russia, 1876. Author: Analytic Geometry. Wrote: New Tables for Determining the Values of the Coefficients in the Perturbative Function of Planetary Motion, Smithsonian Contributions, 1856; The Manual Element in Education; Report on Industrial Education. Home: Cambridge, Mass. Died 1902.

RUNNELLS, Clive, v.p. The Pullman Co.; b. Des Moines, Ia., Sept. 10, 1877; s. John Sumner and Helen R. (Baker) R.; student Harvard, 1896-1900; m. Mary Pierce Withers, Sept. 24, 1921. With the Chicago Junction Ry. Co. 4½ yrs.; commercial agt. P.M. R.R., Chicago, 1904-05; with Western Steel Car & Foundry Co., 1905-07; v.p. McCord & Co., ry. supplies, 1907-10; with the Am. Car & Foundry Co., 1910-11; partner Babcock, Rushton & Co., stocks and bonds, 1911-15; asst. to pres. Pullman Co., 1915-17, v.p., May 1917—. Republican. Episcopalian. Home: Chicago, Ill. Died Sept. 12, 1935.

RUNNELLS, John Sumner, lawyer; b. Effingham, N.H., July 30, 1844; s. John and Huldah (Staples) R.; A.B., Amherst, 1865; m. Helen R. Baker, Mar. 31, 1869 (died 1918); children—Mabel (Mrs. Robert Irving Jenks), Lucy (Mrs. Albert Atlee Jackson), Clive, Alice Rutherfurd (Mrs. William James). Pvt. sec. to Gov. Merrill, of Ia., 1868-69; consul at Tunstall, Eng., 1869-71; admitted to bar, 1871; practiced at Des Moines, 1871-87; reporter Supreme Ct. of Iowa, 1875-81; U.S. dist. atty., Ia., 1881-85; gen. counsel, 1887-1911, v.p., 1905-11, pres., 1911-22, chmn. bd., Jan. 1922—, The Pullman Co., Chicago. Chmn. Ia. State Rep. Com., 1879-81; mem. Rep. Nat. Com., 1880-84. Home: Chicago, Ill. Died July 11, 1929.

RUNNELS, Orange Scott, surgeon; b. Fredonia, O., June 11, 1847; s. Edwin and Lydia (Eaton) R.; ed. Oberlin Coll., 1864-68 (hon. A.M., 1894); M.D., Cleveland Homœ. Med. Coll., 1871; M.D., Med. Dept., Ohio State U., 1920; post-grad. courses Am. and European clinics; m. Dora Clark, June 20, 1872 (died 1891); children—Edwin Clark (dec.), Walter (dec.), Scott Clark, Clark (dec.); m. 2d, Mrs. Alice McCulloch, June 28, 1893. Gen. practice Indianapolis, 1871-90; surgeon-in-chief and propr. Runnels's Surg. Hosp., 1890—. Surgeon-general of Ind., 1897-1901; established and conducted Camp Mount Mil. Hosp. during Spanish-Am. War. Pres. Am. Inst. Homœopathy, 1886; nat. del. and v.p. World's Homœ. Congress, Basel, Switzerland, 1886; pres. Nat. Surg. and Gynecol. Soc., 1903; pres. Ind. Inst. Homœopathy, 1884; fellow Am. Coll. Surgeons. Home: Indianapolis, Ind. Died Aug. 15, 1929.

RUNYON, W(alter) Parker, shipbuilder; b. New Brunswick, N.J., Dec. 3, 1861; s. John and Anne (Beck) R.; ed. Rutgers Prep. Sch. and N.J. Business Coll.; m. Katherine Engle Hancock, Jan. 10, 1895. Began with Fairbanks, Martin & Co., commn. mchts., New York, 1880; later with Met. Life Ins. Co. 2 yrs., and in clothing mfg. business; connected with the Perth Amboy Dry Dock Co., 1894—, pres. more than 20 yrs.; v.p. Raritan Trust Co. V.p. Perth Amboy Hosp. Assn., Raritan Terminal and Waterways Assn.; mem. N.J. Bd. Commerce and Navigation, U.S. Chamber of Commerce, Nat. Security League, Maritime Assn. of Port of N.Y., Perth Amboy Chamber of Commerce, Y.M.C.A. of Perth Amboy (trustee), Nat. Marine League of U.S.A. (life mem. and trustee). Home: Perth Amboy, N.J. Died May 14, 1928.

RUNYON, William Nelson, judge; b. Plainfield, N.J., Mar. 5, 1871; s. Nelson and Wilhelmina Frances (Trow) R.; A.B., Yale, 1892; LL.B., New York Law Sch., 1894; m. Florence M. MacDonald, Jan. 1, 1913; children—Jane Trow, William Nelson, Frederic Walter (dec.), Florence Felicia. Mem. Common Council, Plainfield, 1897-98; city judge, 1899-1910; mem. N.J. House of Representatives, 1915-17, Senate, 1918-22 (pres. of Senate, 1919); acting gov. of N.J., May 16, 1919-Jan. 13, 1920; judge U.S. Dist. Court, Dist. of N.J., Jan. 27, 1923—. Republican. Chevalier Order of the Crown (Italian). Mason. Home: Plainfield, N.J. Died Nov. 9, 1931.

RUOFF, Henry Woldmar, editor, author; b. Brünn, Austria, Nov. 3, 1865, of German and English ancestry; direct desc. of Heinrich Ruoff, Margrove of Moravia (or Mähren); s. Frederick W. and Margaret Carey (Johnston) Ruoff; father killed in Austro-Prussian War; brought to U.S. at age of twelve; A.B., Indiana U., 1890; post-grad. student at Harvard, 2 yrs. in history, philosophy and comparative religions, and at Columbian (now George Washington) U., 2 yrs., in economics, politics and comparative jurisprudence; D.C.L., Columbian U., 1901, George Washington U., 1907; Litt.D., 1911; m. Anna Cordelia Allwein, Dec. 10, 1895; 1 dau., Helen Irmgard (Mrs. William C. Hitchcock). Asst. in ethnology, Chicago Expn., 1892-93; formerly instr. philosophy, Pa. State Coll. Spl. student Oxford U., U. of Berlin, and École des Sciences Politiques, Paris, in comparative politics and jurisprudence, 1901-02. Studied international law under W. E. Hall of Oxford and under Rudolf Sohm of Berlin. Asso. editor the Am. Spectator, 1904-06, Ridgway's, 1906-07, Nashville Tennesseean, 1907. Has traveled extensively, and made special study of comparative govt. internat. politics. Author: Home and State, 1898; Woman in the Middle Ages, 1899; Century Book of Facts, 1900; Constitution of the Pre-Christian Family, 1901; Capitals of the World, 1902; Leaders of Men, 1903; Universal Cyclopedic Handbook, 1904; The Standard Dictionary of Facts, 1908; Masters of Achievement, 1910; The Volume Library, 1911; The Human Interest Library, 1914; The Circle of Knowledge, 1917; Book of the War, 1918. Unitarian. Independent Democrat. Died July 2, 1935.

RUPP, Lawrence Henry, lawyer; b. New Tripoli, Pa., Sept. 26, 1881; s. Alvin and Mary Ellen (Miller) R.; A.B., Muhlenberg Coll., 1902, LL.D., from same coll.; studied law in office of John Rupp, Allentown; m. Maude Estelle Berlin, Nov. 28, 1907 (died 1932); 1 son, Lawrence Berlin; m. 2d, Florence Cole, July 1, 1933. Has practiced at Allentown, 1905—; mem. Butz & Ruppe. Dist. atty. Lehigh Co., 1912-16; chmn. Dem. State Com., 1919-20; candidate for nomination for U.S. senator, 1920; Dem. candidate for U.S. Senate, 1932. Formerly pres. Pa. Trust Co.; now trust officer Lehigh Valley Trust Co. Mem. Ref. Ch. Mason, Eagle; Grand Exalted Ruler Elks, 1930-31. Home: Allentown, Pa. Died May 29, 1936.

RUPP, William, prof. practical theology, Theol. Sem. Reformed Ch. in U.S., Sept. 30, 1893—; b. Lowhill tp., Lehigh Co., Pa., Apr. 17, 1839; s. Solomon and Maria Rupp; grad. Franklin and Marshall Coll., 1862 (A.M., D.D., same); grad. Theol. Sem., Mercersburg, Pa., 1864; m. Emma A. Hambright, Nov. 16, 1865. Ordained to ministry Reformed Ch. in U.S., Feb. 6, 1865; served charges at St. Clair, Schuylkill Co., Pa., 1865-66; Berlin, Somerset Co., Pa., 1867-77; Manchester, Md., 1877-88; Meyersdale, Pa., 1888-93. Regular contributor to Mercersburg Review; asst. editor Reformed Ch. Quarterly Review; editor of Reformed Ch. Review. Home: Lancaster, Pa. Died 1904.

RUPPERT, Jacob, Jr., congressman; b. New York, Aug. 5, 1867; s. Jacob and Anna (Gillig) R.; ed. Columbia Grammar Sch.; unmarried. Manager Jacob Ruppert Brewery, 1888—; pres. Astoria Silk Works; dir. Yorkville Bank, etc. A.d.c. with rank of col. on staff of Gov. Hill, 1889-92; sr. aid on Gov. Flower's staff, 1892-95. Mem. 56th to 59th Congresses (1899-1907). Democrat. Home: New York, N.Y. Died Jan. 13, 1939.

RUSBY, Henry Hurd, M.D., botanist; b. Franklin, N.J., Apr. 26, 1855; s. John and Abigail (Holmes) R.; Mass. State Normal Sch., 1872-74; M.D., Univ. Med. Col. (New York U.), 1884; hon. Pharm.M., Phila. Coll. Pharmacy and Science, 1923; Sc.D., Columbia, 1930; m. Margaretta Saunier Hanna, 1887. Awarded medal at Centennial Exhibition, 1876, for herbarium of plants of Essex Co., N.J.; made bot. explorations, N.M. and Ariz., 1880-81, and 1883, as agt. Smithsonian Instn., and S. America, 1885-87, interest of med. botany, crossing the continent; also on lower Orinoco River, 1896, and the Republic of Colombia, 1917; Bolivia and Brazil, 1921-22. Prof. of botany, physiology and materia medica, Dept. Pharmacy, Columbia, 1888-1930, and dean of faculty; prof. materia medica, U. and Bellevue Hosp. Med. Coll., 1897-1902. Hon. curator Economic Mus., New York Bot. Garden (chmn. bd. scientific directors, 1908-17, and mem. board of managers); Revision Com. 7th, 8th and 9th revisions, U.S. Pharmacopœia; mem. Revision Com. of Nat. Formulary; chmn. Commn. Pan-Am. Med. Congress for study of Am. medicinal flora; hon. mem. Pharm. Soc. of Great Britain; hon. mem. Instituto Medico Nacional of Mexico; pres. Torrey Bot. Club, 1905-12; pres. Am. Pharm. Assn., 1909-10. Expert in drug products in Bur. Chemistry, U.S. Dept. Agr., 1907-09; then pharmacognosist in same bur., 1912-17. Secured the vindication of Dr. Wiley and associates from charges, 1911. Fought successfully to stop the common use of decomposed ergot in those medicinal preparations for use in childbirth, from 1929 to 1935. Author: Essentials of Pharmacognosy, 1895; Morphology and Histology of Plants, 1899; Materia Medica of Buck's Reference Handbook of the Medical Sciences (8 volumes), 1899; National Standard Dispensatory, 1905; Wild Vegetable Foods of United States, 1906; Fifty Years of Materia Medica, 1907; Manual of Botany, 1911; Three Hundred New Species of South American Plants; A Guide to the Economic Collections of the New York Botanical Garden; Properties and Uses of Drugs, 1930; Jungle Memories, 1933. Introduced important drugs to Am. Materia Medica, among them pichi, cocillana, miré and caäpi. Awarded Hanbury medal, Brit. Pharm. Assn., 1929; Flueckiger medal, German Apothecaries Assn.; hon. mem. Brit. Pharm. Assn., 1930. Home: Sarasota, Fla. Died Nov. 18, 1940.

RUSH, Franklin Smithwick; b. Tompkinsville, Ky., Apr. 6, 1865; s. John Hagen and Elizabeth Sewell (Sartin) R.; ed. pub. schs.; m. Effie May Seymour, Dec. 24, 1895; 1 son, Edwin Franklin. Cowboy, later ranch foreman, 1890-95; farmer and stock raiser, 1895-1907; forest guard, Wichita Nat. Forest and Game Preserve, Okla., 1907-08, forest supervisor, 1908-23; owner and operator Craterville Park, 1923—; sponsor only all-Indian Agrl. Fair. Originator of 5-year farm working plan for Boys' and Girls' 4-H Clubs of Okla.; extensively identified with wild life conservation and Boy Scout work. Mem. Cherokee Strip Cow Punchers' Assn., Okla. Old Time Fiddlers' Assn. Republican. Baptist. Mason, Odd Fellow, Modern Woodman. Naturalist. Home: Craterville Park, Okla. Died Apr. 7, 1933.

RUSH, Sylvester R., lawyer; b. Morris Tp., Greene County, Pa., July 24, 1860; s. Calvin and Phoebe (Rush) R.; ed. Southwestern State Normal Sch., California, Pa., 1880-84; Mt. Union (O.) Coll., 1885-86; m. Edith M. Pindell, Sept. 6, 1899. Began practice at Omaha, Neb., 1888; chmn. Dem. County Central Com., Douglas County, Neb., 1892-94; asst. U.S. atty. for Neb., 1894-1907; spl. asst. to atty. gen. of U.S., 1907-22; again spl. asst. to atty. gen., Mar. 31, 1923—. Successfully represented U.S. Govt. in cases arising from unlawful enclosure of pub. lands in Neb., Wyo. and Colo.; in prosecution of fraudulent sales of swamp lands in Fla.; fraudulent entry of coal lands in Alaska; in case against Los Angeles Investment Co.; in Mabray foot and horse race swindling scheme; in case against Dr. Cook, alleged discoverer of the North Pole, on charge of fradudulent use of mails in sale of oil stocks; atty. for Internat. Harvester Co. Episcopalian. Mason. Home: Omaha, Neb. Died Mar. 1932.

RUSH, Thomas E., lawyer, author; b. N.Y. City, Jan. 16, 1867; s. Thomas E. and Delia (Connolly) R.; B.A., Coll. City of New York, 1886; LL.B., New York U., 1890; M.A., Coll. of St. Francis Xavier, 1900; LL.D., Fordham, 1920; m. Jessica Innis Brent, July 4, 1895 (died 1896). Began practice at N.Y. City, 1890; atty. for comptroller State of N.Y., 1911-14; surveyor of customs Port of New York, 1914—; dir. Internat. Motor Truck Corp., Mack Trucks Inc., Motor Car Abstract Co. Trustee St. Peter's Union for Seamen. Democrat. Catholic. Author: The Port of New York, 1920. Home: New York, N.Y. Died June 3, 1927.

RUSHMORE, David Barker, electrical engr.; b. Old Westbury, N.Y., Aug. 21, 1873; s. John Howard and Julia Anna (Barker) R.; B.S. in engring., Swarthmore Coll., 1894, C.E., 1897, Sc.D., 1923; M.E., Cornell U., 1895; unmarried. During vacations with Pond Machine Tool Co. and Westinghouse Electric & Mfg. Co., Newark, N.J.; with Westinghouse Electric & Mfg. Co., E. Pittsburgh, Pa., 1895, Royal Electric Co., Montreal, Can., 1897-99, Stanley Electric Mfg. Co., Pittsfield, Mass., 1899-1905; entered service Gen. Electric Co., 1905; chief engr. power and mining dept., 1907-22, and consulting engr., 1922-25 (resigned); pres. Español-Americano Co.; v.p. Spanish American Fruit Co. Dir. Northeastern Dispensary. Fellow American Inst. E.E. (v.p. 1911-13); mem. exec. com. Am. Sect. World Power Conf.; rep. of U.S. Govt. at World Power Conf., Barcelona, 1929; mem. bd. govs. Manhattan Council Boy Scouts America. Republican. Mem. Soc. of Friends. Mason. Home: New York, N.Y. Died May 5, 1940.

RUSHTON, Ray, lawyer; b. Montgomery, Ala., Dec. 19, 1868; s. Oliver Calvin and Margaret Snow (Graham) R.; ed. Highland Home Inst. and Howard Coll., Marion, Ala.; studied in law office of Jones & Falkner, Montgomery; m. Mary J. Wyatt, Jan. 3, 1893 (now dec.); children—Marion, Eugene, Rachel (Mrs. N. W. Upham), Mary (Mrs. Preston H. Haskett, Jr.), Graham; m. 2d, Luella J. Tillotson, Aug. 15, 1925 (now dec.). Admitted to Ala. bar, 1890, and practiced at Montgomery; mem. law firm Rushton & Rushton; dir. Alger Sullivan Lumber Co. City atty. Montgomery, 1901-02. Chief justice Spl. Supreme Court of Ala., 1933, under appmt. of the governor to decide cause in which all members of the court were disqualified. Pres. Montgomery Library Assn. Democrat. Baptist. Mason, K.P. Home: Montgomery, Ala. Died May 1, 1940.

RUSHTON, Richard Holt, banker; b. Dalton, Ga., June 8, 1851; s. Robert S. and Mary M. (Adams) R.; ed. at Dalton Acad., Ga., and in Phila.; married. Removed to Phila., 1869; entered employ Commercial Nat. Bank, 1870, became asst. cashier, 1878; assisted in organizing Tenth Nat. Bank and was its cashier, 1885-86; assisted in organizing Fourth St. Nat. Bank, and was its cashier, 1886-96, v.p., 1896-1902, pres. 1902—; was dir. in many corps. Was 1st pres. Pa. Bankers' Assn. Republican. Home: Wynnewood, Pa. Died 1910.

RUSK, John, clergyman; b. Ashton-under-Lyne, Eng., Aug. 19, 1849; s. James and Maria (Booth) R.; came to America, 1854; B.A., Marietta (O.) Coll., 1875, M.A., 1880; grad. Lane Theol. Sem., Cincinnati, 1878; Ph.D., U. of Wooster, 1885; m. Martha S. Kendall, May 23, 1878 (dec.). Ordained Presbyn. ministry, 1878; pastor Cincinnati, 1878-88 (Sixth Presbyn. Ch. built during his administration, and 3 other chs. organized), Fifth Av. Ch., Columbus, O., 1888-92, Fullerton Av. Ch., Chicago, 1892-95; founder, 1895, and pastor, independent organization in heart of Chicago, 1895—. Pres. Nat. Home Seekers' Assn., Soc. for Prevention of Crime. Author: Kant's Critique on the Ontological Argument, 1885; Critique on Sir William Hamilton's View of the Absolute, 1885; Four Thousand Years Ago, 1898; Life of Queen Victoria, 1902; Life of Rev. De Witt Talmage, D.D., 1902; The Life of Jesus and the Apostles, 1909. Died 1910.

RUSLING, James Fowler, lawyer; b. Washington, N.J., Apr. 14, 1834; s. Gershom and Eliza B. (Hankinson) R.; A.B., Dickinson Coll., 1854, A.M., 1857; LL.D., 1889; m. Mary F. Winner, Jan. 1, 1858; 2d, Emily W. Wood, June 30, 1870. Prof. natural science, Dickinson Sem., Pa., 1854-57; admitted to bar, Pa., 1857, N.J., 1859. First lt. 5th N.J. Inf., Aug. 24, 1861; capt. asst. q.-m. vols., June 11, 1862; lt. col., May 27, 1863; col., Apr. 29, 1865; bvtd. maj., lt. col. and col. vols., Mar. 13, 1865, "for faithful and meritorious services during the war"; brig. gen. vols., Feb. 16, 1866, for same; hon. mustered out, Sept. 17, 1867. U.S. pension agt., N.J., 1868-77; mem. Tex. Commn., N.J., 1896. Pres. N.J. Centennial Commn. to Tenn., 1897; trustee Dickinson Coll., 1861-83 and 1904—, Pennington Sem., 1869-99, and pres. bd. many yrs.; mem. gen missionary bd. M.E. Ch., 1891; del. Gen. Conf. M.E. Ch., 1896. Pres. Mercer County Soldiers' and Sailors' Monument Assn., 1891-1911. Author: Across America, or the Great West and Pacific Coast, 1874; History of State Street Methodist Episcopal Church, Trenton, N.J., 1886; History of Pennington Seminary, 1890; Men and Things I Saw in Civil War Days, 1899; European Days and Ways, 1902; History of Rusling Family, 1908. Died Apr. 1, 1918.

RUSSEL, Edgar, army officer; b. Pleasant Hill, Mo., Feb. 20, 1862; s. Richard and Elizabeth (Williams) R.; grad. U.S. Military Acad., 1887; m. Florence Kimball, Apr. 18, 1893; Commd. 2d lt. 3d Arty., June 12, 1887; 1st lt. 5th Arty., Nov. 2, 1893; trans. to 6th Arty., Mar. 8, 1898; capt. signal officer vols., June 20, 1898; maj. signal officer, Apr. 12, 1901; hon. discharged vols., June 30, 1901; 1st lt. Signal Corps, U.S.A., Aug. 30, 1900; capt., Feb. 2, 1901; maj., July 6, 1904; lt. col., July 1, 1916; col., Apr. 12, 1917; brig. gen. N.A., Oct. 2, 1917; brig. gen. U.S.A., Oct. 11, 1921; maj. gen., Dec. 5, 1922; retired from active service, Dec. 6, 1922. Instr. chemistry and asst. prof. chemistry, mineralogy and geology, U.S. Mil. Acad., 1893-98; comd. Signal Corps Co., Philippine Islands, 1898-1900; chief signal officer, Dept. Southern Luzon, 1900; duty Office of Chief Signal Officer, Washington, D.C., 1901-03; assisted in laying Wash.-Alaska Cable, 1903, and installing same, 1904; in charge Sitka-Valdez cable, 1904-05; asst. to chief of Signal Office, Washington, D.C., 1906-08; dir. Army Signal Sch., Ft. Leavenworth, Kan., 1908-12; duty Office of Chief Signal Officer, Washington, D.C., 1912-15; chief signal officer, Hawaii, 1916; same, Southern Dept., 1916-17; chief signal officer, A.E.F., with Gen. Pershing, May 29, 1917, until departure for U.S., July 15, 1919; hon. discharged as brig. gen. N.A., Aug. 15, 1919; brig. gen. U.S.A., Oct. 11, 1921; signal officer, Eastern Department, N.Y. City, Sept. 3, 1919—. Recommended for bvts. by Gen. Lawton and Maj. Gen. MacArthur, "for exceptionally skillful and meritorious services," in P.I. Awarded D.S.M., 1919; Companion of the Bath (British), 1919; Comdr. Legion of Honor (French), 1919. Del. Internat. Radio Conf., London, 1912; mem. Am. Inst. E.E., Inst. Radio Engs. Protestant. Home: New York, N.Y. Died Apr. 27, 1925.

RUSSEL, George Howard, banker; b. Detroit, Mich., Nov. 29, 1847; s. Dr. George B. and Anne E. (Davenport) R.; ed. public and private schools, Detroit; m. Frances E. Bagg, June 27, 1892. Yard foreman Detroit & Lake Superior Iron Mfg. Co. to 1866; elected sec. and treas. Hamtrouck Iron Works, 1867, and Detroit Car Works, 1872; began independently in mfr. of car wheels and castings, 1876; organized, with Walter S. Russel, the Russel Car Wheel & Foundry Co. (v.p.); elected pres. State Savings Bank, 1889, and on its consolidation with the People's Bank, 1907, was elected pres. People's State Bank; v.p. Great Lakes Engring. Works; dir. Detroit City Gas Co., Canada Life Assurance Co.; treas. Detroit United Ry. Was pres. Detroit Park and Boulevard Commn. Home: Grosse Pointe Farms, Mich. Died May 17, 1915.

RUSSEL, Henry, lawyer; b. Detroit, Mich., May 16, 1852; s. Dr. George B. and Anne E. (Davenport) R.; A.B., Univ. of Michigan, 1873, LL.B., 1875, A.M., 1876; m. Helen Muir, June 3, 1880 (dec.); m. 2d, Elanor Towle, Feb. 15, 1912. V.p. and gen. counsel M.C. R.R. Co., with legal dept., 1877—; pres. Detroit Mfrs.' R.R., Chicago, Kalamazoo & Saginaw R.R. Co.; dir. M.C. R.R. Co., Union Trust Co., People's State Bank, Mich. State Telephone Co., Detroit Steel Products Co., etc. Democrat. Presbyn. Died Feb. 25, 1920.

RUSSEL, Walter S.; b. Detroit, Mich., Mar. 12, 1855; s. Dr. George B. and Anne E. (Davenport) R.; C.E., U. of Mich., 1875 (hon. M.E., 1910); m. Mary E. Rumney, Apr. 24, 1880; children—Sydney, Gertrude, Marie D. With bros. George Howard and John R. R. founded Russel Wheel & Foundry Co., Detroit, 1877, of which was chmn.; dir. Detroit Steel Products Co., Am. Radiator Co., Detroit Lubricator Co., McCord Radiator & Mfg. Co., Hoskins Mfg. Co. Home: Detroit, Mich. Died Aug. 17, 1935.

RUSSELL, Addison Peale, author; b. Wilmington, O., Sept. 8, 1826; s. Charles and Mary (McNab) R.; ed. common schs.; hon. Litt.Doc., Ohio U., 1898; unmarried. Apprenticed to the printing trade at 15 and became editor and pub; mem. Ohio Legislature, 1855; sec. of state, Ohio, 1857-61; 6 yrs. in New York as financial agt. of Ohio. Republican. Author: Half Tints, 1867; Library Notes, 1879; Thomas Corwin, 1882; Characteristics, 1884; A Club of One, 1887; In a Club Corner, 1890; Sub-Cœlum, 1893. Deceased.

RUSSELL, Alexander Wilson, naval officer; b. in Md., Feb. 4, 1824. Apptd. purser U.S.N., Feb. 28, 1861; pay insp., Mar. 3, 1871; pay dir., Feb. 23, 1877; retired Feb. 4, 1886; advanced to rank of rear admiral retired, June 29, 1906, for services during Civil War. Home: Philadelphia, Pa. Died 1908.

RUSSELL, Alfred, lawyer; b. Plymouth, N.H., Mar. 18, 1830; s. William Wallace and Susan Carleton (Webster) R.; grad. Dartmouth Coll., 1850; LL.D., 1890; grad. Harvard Univ. Law Sch., 1852; m. Mrs. Ellen P. England (b. Wells), Oct. 28, 1857. Began practice, 1852; gen. atty. for Mich. and Canada Wabash R.R. Co.; U.S. dist. atty. for Mich., 1861-69. Republican. Author: The Police Power of the State, 1900. Was tendered German mission by Pres. Hayes, but declined. Home: Detroit, Mich. Deceased.

RUSSELL, Annie, actress; b. Liverpool, Eng., 1869; d. Joseph and Jane (Mount) R.; m. Oswald Yorke, English actor, Mar. 27, 1904. First stage appearance Montreal when 7; afterward at New York in juvenile "Pinafore" co.; went to S. America and West Indies in varied repertoire; returned to U.S. and joined Madison Sq. Theatre Co.; became famous in "Esmeralda" and George Parsons Lathrop's "Elaine"; retired for several yrs. on account of ill health; has appeared in several leading rôles, 1895—; 1st appearance in London, 1898. Has since appeared as a star in "Miss Hobbs," "A Royal Family," "The Girl and the Judge," "Mice and Men," "Jinny the Carrier," "Brother Jacques"; appeared in London, season 1906, creating title rôle of George Bernard Shaw's play, "Major Barbara"; played "Puck" in "Midsummer Night's Dream," Astor Theatre, New York, 1906. Became mem. New Theatre Co., 1910, playing Viola in "Twelfth Night," "Lady Teazle," etc. Prod. under own management, 1912-14, a repertoire of classical plays including "Much Ado About Nothing," Sheridan's "Rivals" and "School for Scandal," Goldsmith's "She Stoops to Conquer," a modern play by Paul Kester, "The Lady in the Case," and "His Royal Happiness" by Mrs. Everard Cotes; played Rosalie La Grange, in "The 13th Chair," for spl. Chicago engagement, Sept. 1917. Home: Petersburg, Fla. Died Jan. 16, 1936.

RUSSELL, Charles Addison, congressman; b. Worcester, Mass., March 2, 1852; grad. Yale, 1873; a.d.c. with rank of col. on Gov. Bigelow's staff, 1881-82; mem. Conn. legislature, 1883; sec. of State of Conn., 1885-86. Mem. Congress, 1887-1903, 3d Conn. dist. Mfr. of wool. Died 1902.

RUSSELL, Charles Edward, journalist, author; b. Davenport, Ia., Sept. 25, 1860, s. Edward and Lydia (Rutledge) R.; grad. St. Johnsbury (Vt.) Acad., 1881; LL.D., Howard, 1923; married; 1 son, John Edward. Was engaged on various newspapers; city editor New York World, 1894-97; mng. editor N.Y. American, 1897-99; pub. Chicago American, 1900-02; contbr. to mags. and lecturer on sociology and literature, 1904—. Socialist candidate for gov. N.Y., 1910, 12, for mayor of New York, 1913; for U.S. Senator, 1914; nominated, 1916, by party plebiscite for president (declined). Author: Such Stuff as Dreams, 1902; The Twin Immortalities, 1904; The Greatest Trust in the World, 1905; The Uprising of the Many, 1907; Lawless Wealth, 1908; Thomas Chatterton, the Marvelous Boy, 1908; Songs of Democracy, 1909; Why I Am a Socialist, 1910; Business, the Heart of the Nation, 1911; Stories of the Great Railroads, 1912; These Shifting Scenes, 1914; The Story of Wendell Phillips, 1915; Unchained Russia, 1918; After the Whirlwind, 1919; Bolshevism and the United States, 1919; The Outlook for the Philippines, 1922; Railroad Melons, Rates and Wages, 1922; The Hero of the Filipinos—José Rizal, 1923; Julia Marlowe—Her Life and Art, 1926; The American Orchestra and Theodore Thomas (Pulitzer prize for best biography of year), 1927; A-Rafting on the Mississipp', 1928; An Hour of American Poetry, 1929; From Sandy Hook to 62°, 1929; Haym Salomon and the Revolution, 1930; Blaine of Maine, 1931; Bare Hands and Stone Walls, 1933. Mem. special diplomatic mission sent to Russia by the U.S., 1917; commr. to Gt. Britain for U.S. Com. on Pub. Information, 1918; mem. President's Industrial Commn., 1919; pres. U.S. Civil Legion, 1932-33; hon. pres. Am. Assn. for Recognition of Irish Republic. Home: New York, N.Y. Died Apr. 23, 1941.

RUSSELL, Charles Howland, lawyer; b. New York, N.Y., Dec. 14, 1851; s. Charles H. and Caroline (Howland) R.; A.B., Harvard, 1872; LL.B., Columbia, 1874; m. Jane, d. Rt. Rev. Henry C. Poter, bishop of New York, 1890. Admitted to bar, 1874; mem. law firm Stetson, Jennings & Russell, 1894—. Pvt. sec. to William M. Evarts, Secretary of State, 1877-80; dir. Nat. Bank of Commerce, Mexican Telegraph Co. Trustee New York Pub. Library; pres. St. Luke's Hosp.; mem. Mun. Art Commn., New York, 1908-13. Pres. R.I. Soc. of the Cincinnati. Home: New York, N.Y. Died May 19, 1921.

RUSSELL, Charles Marion, artist; b. St. Louis, Mo., Mar. 19, 1865; s. Charles Silas and Mary (Mead) R.; ed. pub. schs.; LL.D., Mont. State Bd. of Edn., 1925, "for greatest historic accomplishment in an artistic way of any person in the state"; m. Nancy Cooper, 1896. Painting and modeling since early boyhood; moved to Mont., 1880. Has exhibited at London, New York, Chicago, San Francisco, Los Angeles and other cities. Democrat. Episcopalian. Elk. Author: Rawhide Rollins, 1921; More Rawhides, 1925. Home: Great Falls, Mont. Died Oct. 24, 1926.

RUSSELL, Charles Taze ("Pastor Russell"), independent minister; b. Pittsburgh, Pa., Feb. 16, 1852; s. Joseph L. and Ann Eliza (Birney) R.; ed. principally under pvt. tutors; m. Marie Frances, d. Mahlen and Salena Ackley, 1879. Began in independent ministry, Pittsburgh, 1878; served Brooklyn Tabernacle and N.Y. City Temple; disclaims being founder of a ministry, Pittsburgh, 1878; Brooklyn Tabernacle and N.Y. City Temple; disclaims being founder of a religious sect; interprets the punishment of the Bible as eternal death and not eternal torture. Author of a series of books, "Studies in the Scriptures," issued, 1886—; editor of The Watch Tower and Herald of Christ's Presence (semi-monthly jour.); pres. Watch Tower Bible and Tract Soc. of Pa., People's Pulpit Assn. of New York, Internat. Bible Students' Assn. (London, Eng.). Died Oct. 31, 1916.

RUSSELL, Charles Wells, lawyer, author; b. Wheeling, Va., Mar. 16, 1856; s. C. W. and Margaret Wilson (Moore) R.; student Georgetown Univ., 1870-73, LL.B., 1883, LL.M., 1884; m. Lucy Floyd Mosby, Feb. 19, 1879; children—Charles Wells (dec.), Margaret Moore (dec.), John Mosby; m. 2d, Lelia James Mosby, sister of 1st wife, Oct. 1, 1885. Entered Dept. of Justice, Washington, 1886, argued many French spoliation cases; legal adviser Dockery Joint Congressional Commn., 1893-95; gen. legal, including

Supreme Ct. work, 1895-1901; spl. asst. atty. gen. in charge insular and territorial affairs, 1902-1905; asst. atty. gen., U.S., 1905-10; E.E. and M.P. to Persia, 1910-14 (resigned); procured employment of Morgan Shuster and other Americans by Persian Govt. Constituted special ambassador, July 1914, to attend coronation of Shah Ahmad. Investigated and reported on reconcentrado starvation and military situation in Cuba, Dec. and Jan., 1897-98; legal adviser to P.R. Evacuation Commn., Aug.-Oct. 1898; successfully argued Maine Explosion cases, Spanish Claims Commn., 1901; sent by Atty. Gen. Knox to Paris, 1902, to investigate Panama Canal Co.'s title, and reported title clear, unencumbered and could be given as required by act of Congress; sent to Paris, Mar. 1904, to effect transfer of title and property of Panama Canal to U.S. and $40,000,000 gold to France, arranged for with J. Pierpont Morgan, in Paris; May 1904, sent to Panama as legal adviser to U.S. Govt. of Canal Zone; revisited Cuba to prepare case Countess O'Reilly vs. Gen. John R. Brooke concerning her Havana slaughter house monopoly; successfully defended General Brooke in the case; sent to investigate peonage slavery in southern states, Oct. 1906; prosecuted numerous peonage cases; sued several thousand persons at Muskogee, I.T., for illegally obtaining Indian lands, 1907-09, and successfully argued the cases in higher court. Author: Cuba Libre (play); Poems (privately printed), 1911, 12, 14; Poems, 1921. Editor: Memoirs of Col. John S. Mosby (his bro.-in-law), 1917. Home: Washington, D.C. Died Apr. 5, 1927.

RUSSELL, Daniel Lindsay, lawyer, gov.; b. Brunswick County, N.C., Aug. 7, 1845; s. Daniel Lindsay and Caroline Elizabeth (Sanders) R.; ed. Univ. of N.C., 1860-61; capt. C.S.A. in Civil War; admitted to bar, 1866; m. Sarah Amanda Sanders, Aug. 16, 1869. Mem. N.C. legislature, 1864-65, 1865-66 and 1876-77; judge 4th jud. circuit, 1868-74; mem. Congress, 1879-81; gov. N.C., 1897-1901. Republican. Died 1908.

RUSSELL, Edward Lafayette, lawyer; b. Franklin County, Ala., Aug. 19, 1845; s. George Daniel and Emily (Stovall) R.; ed. by father; worked on farm until Feb. 1862. Served in 41st Miss. Regt., C.S.A., pvt. and ensign; color bearer of regt.; when Confed. lines were broken at Nashville retreated to Franklin and swam Harper's Creek during night to save his colors; cotton planter after war; m. Emma Davis, Jan. 1869. Admitted to bar, 1871; practiced Verona, 1872; gen. counsel, May 1876, 1st v.p. and acting pres., Mar. 1897, Mobile & Ohio R.R.; later v.p. and gen. counsel same, Mobile, Ala. Presdl. elector, 1888, 1892, 1896; del. Ala. State Conv., on gold standard platform, 1896. Democrat. Died 1911.

RUSSELL, Frank, educator; b. Ft. Dodge, Ia., Aug. 26, 1868; s. D. C. and Elizabeth (Carleton) R.; grad. Univ. of Iowa, 1892, S. M., 1895; A.B., Harvard, 1896, A.M., 1897, Ph.D., 1898; married. Instr. Harvard, 1896—; ethnologist, Bureau of Am. Ethnology, 1901-02; spent 2½ yrs., 1892-94, in anthropol. and zoöl. work (alone) in Arctic America. Author: Explorations in the Far North, 1898; numerous scientific papers. Died 1903.

RUSSELL, George, cattle raiser; b. Bangor, Ireland, Apr. 15, 1837; s. James and Eliza (McMaster) R.; ed. in Ireland; m. Martha A. Marchand, Feb. 27, 1868. Was miner in early days of Calif.; in mercantile business early days in Nev.; nat. commr. Chicago Expn., 1893; chmn. of Live Stock Com., same; mem. Nev. Legislature, 1893; Dem. nominee for gov. Nev., 1898; pres. George Russell Co., Russell Land & Cattle Co., Elko, Nev. Democrat. Died May 10, 1924.

RUSSELL, George Harvey, insurance; b. Milwaukee, Nov. 3, 1866; s. Harvey and Mary Jane (Guilds) R.; pvt., pub. and high sch. edn., to 18; m. Laura Eustis, Jan. 18, 1893; children—Laura (Mrs. Bradlee Van Brunt), Marion (Mrs. Edgar J. Tapping, Jr.). In ins. business, 1887—; state agt. Standard Accident Ins. Co. of Detroit, 1892—; pres. George H. Russell Co.; dir. Standard Accident Ins. Co., Detroit; mgr. ins. dept. C.,M.&St.P. R.R. Co., 1913—. Republican. An organizer and sec. first young men's Republican club in Wis., 1888. Episcopalian. An organizer Cadet Light Inf., 1884, and advanced to capt.; insp. small arms practice 4th Wis. Inf.; was col. on staff of Gov. W. D. Hoard; apptd. as del. Ann. Conv. Nat. Civic Fedn., Washington, Mar. 1912; chmn. Local Bd., Div. 1, Milwaukee, under Selective Service Act, 1917-18. A.d.c. to Gov. E. L. Phillipp, with rank of col. in Wis. State Guard, 1917; commd. capt., Q.M.R.C., 1918. Mem. numerous underwriters assns. Made many trips abroad and has contbd. extensively on travel and ins. Home: Milwaukee, Wis. Deceased.

RUSSELL, Gordon, judge; b. Huntsville, Ala.; s. Henry A. and Mary (Gordon) R.; A.B., U. of Ga., 1878; m. Jennie Matthews; m. 2d, Annie Ford. Practiced at Dalton, Ga., to 1879, in Van Zandt County, Tex., 1879-95, Tyler, Tex., 1895—. Elected county judge, Van Zandt County, 1884; dist. atty. 7th Jud. Dist., 1892-96; judge 7th Jud. Dist., 1896-1902; elected 57th Congress, 1902, for unexpired term (1902-03) of R. C. De Graffenried, deceased; reëlected 58th to 61st Congresses (1903-11), 3d Tex. Dist.; resigned from Congress, June 1910, to become U.S. dist. judge, Eastern Dist. of Tex. Democrat. Died Sept. 14, 1919.

RUSSELL, Harry Newton, headmaster; b. London, Eng., July 13, 1862; s. John Archibald and Martha Holme (Bower) R.; grad. London Univ. Coll. Sch., 1879; pvt. study 3 yrs.; m. Constance Williams, of Tunbridge Wells, Kent, Eng., Oct. 9, 1889. Came to America, 1883; headmaster and trustee Kearney Mil. Acad., 1895-1913; headmaster, De Koven Hall, Tacoma, Wash., 1913-14, University School for Boys, Chicago, 1914-16; headmaster St. Alban's School, Knoxville, Ill., 1916—. Republican. Episcopalian. Died Feb. 15, 1936.

RUSSELL, Henry Moore, lawyer; b. Wheeling, W.Va., Apr. 5, 1851; s. Charles W. and Margaret Wilson (Moore) R.; A.B., Georgetown U., 1869, A.M., 1871; LL.B., U. of Va., 1870; m. Matilda Heiskell, Sept. 1876. In practice of law in Wheeling, 1871—. Del. Universal Congress of Lawyers and Jurists, St. Louis, 1904. Presbyn. Democrat. Home: Wheeling, W.Va. Died Oct. 7, 1915.

RUSSELL, Herbert Edwin, prof. mathematics; b. Paris, Me., Apr. 7, 1860; s. Charles and Asenath Howard (Willis) R.; A.B., Wesleyan U., Conn., 1884, A.M., 1887; studied Johns Hopkins; Sc.D., U. of Denver, 1914; m. Lena C. Rogers, June 18, 1885. Teacher mathematics and astronomy, Me. Wesleyan Sem., 1884-86; teacher mathematics, Boys' High Sch., Reading, Pa., 1887-91; asso. prof. mathematics, 1891-96, prof. pure mathematics, 1896—, and dean of Extra-Mural Coll., 1915—, U. of Denver. Republican. Methodist. Died May 31, 1927.

RUSSELL, Horace, lawyer; b. Bombay, N.Y., June 19, 1843; s. Charles and Hannah (Wright) R.; A.B., Dartmouth, 1865, LL.D., 1893; student Harvard Law Sch., 1866; m. Josephine Hilton, Feb. 26, 1878. Asst. dist. atty. of New York, 1873-80; judge advocate gen., N.Y., 1879-82; judge Superior Ct. of N.Y., 1880-83; receiver West Shore Ry. Co., 1884-86; gen. counsel to Stewart estate, 1880-99. Patron Met. Mus. of Art; pres. Gen. Alumni Assn. of Dartmouth Coll., 1909. Home: New York, N.Y. Died June 14, 1913.

RUSSELL, Isaac Franklin, judge; b. Hamden, Conn., Aug. 25, 1857; s. Rev. William H. and Susan (Voorhies) (Hiller) R.; A.B., New York U., 1875, LL.B., 1877, A.M., 1878; LL.M., Yale, 1879, D.C.L., 1880; LL.D., Dickinson, 1893; J.D., N.Y. U., 1904; m. Ruth Ferriss, May 8, 1886; children—William Morgan, Franklin Ferriss, George Phelps, Austin Abbott. Prof. polit. science, 1881-95, law, 1881—, New York U. Chief justice Ct. of Spl. Sessions City New York, 1910-16. Republican. Author: Outline Study of Law, 1894, 95, 1900; Encys., Cases on Measure of Damages, 1909. Home: Brooklyn, N.Y. Died Nov. 20, 1931.

RUSSELL, Israel Cook, prof. geology, U. of Mich., 1892—; b. Garrattsville, N.Y., Dec. 10, 1852; s. Barnabas and Louisa (Cook) R.; grad. New York U., 1872; post-grad. studies School of Mines, Columbia Coll.; M.S., C.E., LL.D., New York U.; m. J. Augusta Olmsted, Nov. 27, 1886. Mem. U.S. Transit of Venus expdn. to New Zealand, 1874-75; asst. prof. of geology, School of Mines, Columbia, 1875-77; asst. geologist U.S. Geog. and Geol. Survey West of 100th Meridian, 1878; traveled in Europe; geologist U.S. Geol. Survey, 1880—. Author: Lake Lahontan, 1885; The Newark System, 1892; Lakes of North America, 1895; Glaciers of North America, 1897; Volcanoes of North America, 1897; Rivers of North America, 1898; A View of the World in 1900—North America. Died 1906.

RUSSELL, James Solomon, clergyman, educator; b. Palmer's Springs, Va., Dec. 20, 1857; s. Solomon and Araminta (Russell) R.; student Hampton (Va.) Normal and Agrl. Inst., 1874-78; St. Stephen's Normal Training Sch., Petersburg, Va., 1878-82; studied langs. pvtly., 1879-82; Branch Theol. Sem. of Va., Petersburg, 1878-82; D.D., Theol. Sem. Va., 1917; LL.D., Coll. of Liberia, Monrovia, Africa, 1922; m. Virginia M. Morgan, Dec. 20, 1882 (died 1920); children—Mrs. Araminta Czarina Turner, James Alvin, Mrs. Otelia Virginia Deane, Herman Webster, Mrs. Charlotte Baylies Birchette. Deacon, 1882, priest, 1887, P.E. Ch.; at Lawrenceville, Va., 1882—, founder, 1888, and prin. St. Paul Normal and Industrial Sch. (colored); arch-deacon of colored work in Southern Va.; elected suffragan bishop Diocese of Ark., 1917 (declined), also of N.C., 1918 (declined). Awarded gold medal and $400, Harmon Foundation, 1928. Mason. Home: Lawrenceville, Va. Died Mar. 28, 1935.

RUSSELL, John Andrew, publisher; b. Sheboygan, Wis., Nov. 4, 1865; s. John and Alice (Brennan) R.; A.B., Detroit Coll., 1883, A.M., 1885; LL.D., U. of Detroit, 1916; unmarried. Pres. Manufacturer Pub. Co., pub. Mich. Mfr. and Financial Record, 1910—; dean Sch. of Commerce and Finance, U. of Detroit, 1916—; commr. Detroit Pub. Library. Chmn. U.S. Selective Service Bd. No. 7, Detroit, 1917-18; mem. Mich. St. Lawrence Waterway Commn.; mem. Mich. State Tax Inquiry Commn., 1929; receiver Detroit Bankers Co., 1935. Democrat. Roman Catholic. Author: Notes on Pre-historic Discoveries in Wayne County, Michigan, 1912; Germanic Influence in the Making of Michigan; Life of Joseph Warren Fordney. Writer on pub. utility and tax problems. Home: Detroit, Mich. Deceased.

RUSSELL, John Edward, college prof.; b. Walpole, N.H., Jan. 8, 1848; s. John B. and Lucy H. R.; student Dartmouth, 1869-71; A.B., Williams Coll., 1872; student Andover Theol. Sem., 1873-75; B.D., Yale, 1880; post-grad. studies Yale, and Berlin, 1883-84; m. Abbie Louise Baker, 1882. Lecturer history of philosophy, Williams Coll., 1885-86; prof. Bibl. theology, Yale Div. Sch., 1885-89; Mark Hopkins prof. philosophy, Williams College, Williamstown, Mass., 1889—. Lecturer philosophy of religion, Harvard Div. Sch., 1893-94; univ. preacher, U. of Chicago, 1906-07. Died Feb. 25, 1917.

RUSSELL, Joseph Ballister, merchant; b. Boston, Mass., Oct. 24, 1852; s. Charles Theodore and Sarah (Ballister) R.; ed. pub. and pvt. schs.; m. Lillian H. Tenney, May 20, 1880. In business at Boston, 1869—; pres. Boston Wharf Co.; dir. Boston Consolidated Gas Co., N.Y.,N.H.&H. R.R. Co., Conveyancers Title Insurance Co., Mass. Gas Co., Mystic Steamship Co., Boston Elevated Ry. Co., Mt. Auburn Cemetery; trustee N.E. Fuel & Transportation Co. V.p. Real Estate Exchange and Auction Bd. Dir. N.E. Fuel and Transportation. Democrat. Episcopalian. Home: Cambridge, Mass. Died Apr. 21, 1929.

RUSSELL, J(oseph) Henry, corp. officer; b. Cambridge, Mass., Feb. 21, 1855; s. Charles W. and Abigail M. (Orbeton) R.; ed. pub. and pvt. schs.; m. Adele E. Dow, Jan. 1, 1873; children—George H., Alice M. (Mrs. John W. Wood), A. Eloise (Mrs. Charles F. Shaw), Fannie S., Mildred W. (Mrs. E. F. Fish). Pres. Cambridge Electric Light Co., 1915—, also mem. exec. com.; pres. Woodbourne Co.; v.p. Home Savings Bank (investment com.), Boston; incorporator Cambridgeport Savings Bank; dir. Cambridge Trust Co., Cambridge Investment Corp.; trustee Bay State Associates. Was pres. Common Council of Cambridge, and Cambridge Sch. Bd. Republican. Conglist. Mason. Deceased.

RUSSELL, Lillian, actress, singer; b. Clinton, Ia., Dec. 4, 1861; d. Charles E. and Cynthia H. Leonard; removed to Chicago with parents, 1865; father later became mem. Chicago printing firm of Knight & Leonard; ed. Convent of the Sacred Heart, Chicago; studied vocal and violin music and sang in ch. choir, Chicago; studied for opera under Leopold Damrosch; m. Harry Braham, conductor Edward E. Rice's Pinafore Co.; m. 2d, Edward Solomon, conductor Casino Orchestra; m. 3d, John Chatterton, known to the stage as Signor Perugini, operatic tenor; m. 4th, Alexander P. Moore, editor Pittsbrugh (Pa.) Leader, June 11, 1912. First stage appearance was in chorus of Rice's Pinafore Co., 1879; later sang ballads at Tony Pastor's Theatre, taking stage name of "Lillian Russell"; sang at Casino Theatre until 1899; with Weber and Field's stock company several seasons; joined McCaull Opera Co., of which was prima donna until her own company was organized; starred in various opera rôles in U.S. and Eng.; frequently appeared in vaudeville; toured country delivering lecture, "How to Live a Hundred Years," 1913; active in Red Cross and Liberty Loan campaigns during world war. Home: Pittsburgh, Pa. Died June 6, 1921.

RUSSELL, Louis Arthur, composer, musician; b. Newark, N.J., Feb. 24, 1854; s. William Alexander and Frances Adeline (Blazier) R.; studied New York Coll. of Music, London (Eng.) Organ Acad.; studied theory and harmony with George Bristow and C. C. Mueller (New York), John Higgs and Berthold Tours (London), organ with S. P. Warren (New York), T. Y. Trotter (London), piano with Charles Fradel, Jan Pychowsky (New York); voice with John Howard, George Henschel, and William Shakespeare; unmarried. Organist and choirmaster South Park Presbyn. Ch., Newark, N.J., 17 yrs., Peddie Memorial Ch., Newark, 12 yrs., also Ch. of the Redeemer, and Clinton Av. Ref. Ch.; founder and condr. Oratorio Soc., Newark Symphony Orchestra; dir. Newark Coll. of Music, 1879—; dir. Normal Inst. of Music, Carnegie Hall, New York; dir. The Russell Studios, New York; mng. editor Essex Pub. Co. Mem. Am. Guild Organists (a founder). Gen. Sec. Nat. Acad. Vocal Arts. Mason. Author: Commonplaces of Vocal Art; English Diction for Singers and Public Speakers; The Singers' Control of Speech; The Body and Breath in Control; Plain Talk with American Singers; The Embellishments of Music; Complete Course in Hand Culture and Piano Playing; Pedal Independence at the Organ. Composer: (cantata) A Pastoral Rhapsody; (cantata) The Triumph of Freedom and Peace; (piano) Suite Fantastique, Suite Psychique; (violin) Suite Lyrique; also many songs. Died Sept. 5, 1925.

RUSSELL, Martin J., pres. Chicago Chronicle Co. and editor Chicago Chronicle, 1895—; b. Chicago, Dec. 20, 1845. Accompanied his uncle, Col. James A. Mulligan, with his regt. to Mo., 1861, was present at surrender of Lexington; on reorganization of regt. (23d Ill.) the following winter, enlisted and became 2d lt. in Co. A; later adj. gen. on staff of Col.

Mulligan. After death of latter in battle of Winchester the depleted regt. was consolidated into 5 companies and Lt. Russell was mustered out, Sept. 1864. Reporter on Chicago Evening Post, 1870-73; on city staff and later writing editor Chicago Times, 1873-83; editor Chicago Herald, 1883-87; on Chicago Times, 1887-91. Mem. bd. of visitors to West Point, 1887; was South Park commr., Chicago, 14 years; collector of customs, Chicago, 1894-98. Married. Home: Chicago, Ill. Died 1900.

"RUSSELL, Pastor," see Charles Taze Russell.

RUSSELL, Richard Brevard, judge, orator, publicist; b. nr. Marietta, Ga., Apr. 27, 1861; s. William John and Rebecca Harriette (Brumby) R.; A.B. and B.Ph., U. of Georgia, 1879, LL.B., 1880, LL.D., 1924; LL.D., Oglethorpe U., 1929; LL.D. from Atlanta Law Sch., 1936; m. Minnie L. Tyler, May 13, 1883 (died 1886); m. 2d, Ina Dillard, June 24, 1891; children—Mary Willie (Mrs. S. Gordon Green), Ina Dillard, Frances Marguerite (Mrs. James H. Bowden), Richard Brevard, Harriett Brumby (Mrs. S. Ralph Sharpton), Robert Lee, Patience Elizabeth (wife of Congressman Hugh Peterson, Jr. of Georgia), Walter Brown, William John, Fielding Dillard, Henry Edward, Alexander Brevard, Carolyn Lewis. Five children died in infancy—(3 by 1st marriage and 2 by 2d). Admitted to Ga. bar, 1880, and practiced at Athens; mem. Ga. Ho. of Reps., three terms, 1882-88, author of bill for Georgia State College for Women, 1887; solicitor gen., Western Circuit of Ga., 1888-97; judge Superior Cts., same circuit, 1898-1906 (resigned); one of 5 Dem. candidates for gov. of Ga., 1906, running 2d in field; elected judge Court of Appeals, State of Ga., 1906, reëlected, 1908 and 1914 for term ending 1921; chief judge of same, 1913-16; resigned to return to practice of law and care of personal interests; elected chief justice Supreme Court of Ga., 1922, by largest majority ever given a Georgian. Pres. Hoschton Telephone Co., Russell Mfg. Co.; large cotton planter. Asso. editor Athens Daily Banner, 1884-85; editor of Athens Daily Ledger, 1890-93; organizer Athens St. Ry. Co., 1886, Athens Savings Bank, 1887, N. Ga. Telephone Co., 1894. Mem. Bd. of Edn., Athens, 1885-95, Winder, Ga., 1897, Russell, Ga., 1903-17; trustee U. of Ga., 1887-90 and 1918-33 (chmn. bd., 1923—), Ga. Juvenile Protective Assn., 1907—; pres. bd. Ga. State Coll. for Women, 1918-33. Mason, Odd Fellow (Past Grand Master of Ga. and Rep. Sovereign G. Lodge), K.P. (Past Grand Rep.), mem. Royal Arcanum (Past Grand Regent of Ga., and Supreme Rep.). Pres. 1st Am. Congress of Agriculture, Feb. 1929. Delivered oration presenting statue of Crawford W. Long from Ga., placed in Nat. Hall of Fame, Washington, D.C., 1926. Home: Russell, Barrow County, Ga. Died Dec. 3, 1938.

RUSSELL, Robert McWatty, college pres.; b. Balm, Pa., Apr. 6, 1858; s. John Thompson and Jane (Williamson) R.; A.B., Westminster Coll., Pa., 1880; student Allegheny Theol. Sem.; D.D., Tarkio Coll., 1890; LL.D., Grove City Coll., 1907; m. Carolyn Belle Keech, June 6, 1888. Teacher McKeesport and Dayton acads., 1881-83; ordained U.P. ministry; pastor Caledonia, N.Y., Sixth Ch., Pittsburgh, Pa., 1890-1906; pres. Westminster Coll., New Wilmington, Pa., 1906-15; prof. Bible doctrine and homiletics, Moody Bible Inst., Chicago, 1915-19; Bible teacher and evangelist. Dir. Winona Assembly and S.S., Pa. Coll. for Women (1892-98). Contbr. for 3 yrs. series of articles to "The Midland" on "Truths for the Inner Life." Moderator U.P. Assembly, 1913-14. Died Aug. 21, 1921.

RUSSELL, Sol Smith, comedian; b. Brunswick, Me., June 15, 1848; followed Union army as drummer boy; left at Cairo, Ill., where he sang in a theatre, acted small parts and beat drum in the orchestra. Later joined a traveling co. and played at DeBar's Theatre, St. Louis, 1865; 1st appearance, New York, 1871; joined Daly's Co., 1874. For a number of yrs. has starred with his own co. in Edgewood Folks, Felix McCusick, A Poor Relation, Peaceful Valley, etc. Died 1902.

RUSSELL, Talcott Huntington, lawyer; b. New Haven, Conn., Mar. 14, 1847; s. William H. and Mary Elisabeth (Hubbard) R.; A.B., Yale, 1869; LL.B., Columbia, 1872; practiced at New Haven, 1872—; m. Geraldine Whittemore Low, Dec. 10, 1889. Apptd. receiver Am. Mut. Life Ins. Co., 1878, and wound up affairs of the co. after protracted litigation; sec. of independent Rep. organization in Conn. that secured vote of the state for Cleveland and defeat of James G. Blaine for pres., 1884; instr. Yale Law Sch., 1890-1900; treas. Nat. Conf. of Commrs. on Uniform State Laws and chmn. Bd. of Commrs. for Conn.; in general practice but has given much attention to the law of municipal corps. and law of life ins., including especially liability of dirs. and officers of ins. and other corps. Dem. nominee for atty. gen., Conn., 1910. Workmen's compensation commr. for 3d Congressional Dist., and chmn. bd. of commrs., 1913-15. Congregational. Died Oct. 20, 1917.

RUSSELL, Thomas Halbert, educator; b. Anderson, S.C., May 22, 1880; s. David Hamilton and Frances Elvira (Smith) R.; prep. edn. Patrick Mil. Inst., Anderson, S.C. (now defunct); grad. The Citadel, Charleston, S.C., 1902; LL.D., Hampden-Sydney Coll., Va.; m. Margaret Hartman Kable, d. of founder of Staunton Mil. Acad., June 20, 1905; children—William Kable, Thomas Halbert, Margarett Kable, David Hamilton. Comdt. cadets, Horner Mil. Sch., Oxford, N.C., 1902-04; with Staunton Mil. Acad., 1904—, pres. 1920—. Pres. City Council, Staunton, 2 yrs.; dir. Nat. Valley Bank, Staunton. Mem. bd. trustees Mary Baldwin Coll. Democrat. Presbyn. Mason. Maj. O.R.C. Home: Staunton, Va. Died May 26, 1933.

RUSSELL, William Hepburn, lawyer; b. Hannibal, Mo., May 17, 1857; s. Daniel L. and Matilda (Richmond) R.; ed. pub. and high schs. and commercial coll.; m. Mary Gushert, June 23, 1880. Served as reporter, city and mng. editor and asso. editor on the Courier, Clipper-Herald, and Journal, Hannibal. Admitted to bar, 1882; city atty., Hannibal, 1882-84; moved to Ind., 1884, and was gen. atty. Louisville, New Albany & Chicago R.R.; moved to Chattanooga, 1887, and lived in Tenn. until 1895; Dem. presdl. elector, 1892. Practiced in New York, 1895—; practiced in federal and state cts. Affiliated with Tammany Hall, 1895-97; but left it because of "Crokerism," and opposed its city tickets, 1897, 1902; voted Dem. ticket in Nat. and state elections. Supported Seth Low for mayor, 1902, and helped organize Greater New York Democracy, becoming chmn. exec. com.; apptd. sr. commr. of accounts, New York; resigned to support McClellan for Mayor, and Croker having been forced out as leader of Tammany, again became connected with the Dem. organization of New York; supported Civic Alliance (Fusion ticket) in campaign of 1909. Author: (with William Beverly Winslow) Russell and Winslow's Syllabus Digest of U.S. Supreme Court Reports (4 vols.), 1902. Home: New York, N.Y. Died Nov. 21, 1911.

RUSSELL, William T., bishop; b. Baltimore, Md., Oct. 20, 1863; s. William T. and Rose A. R.; student. St. Charles' Coll., Md., 5 yrs., Loyola Coll., Baltimore, 1 yr., Am. Coll. in Rome, 2 yrs., St. Mary's Sem., Baltimore, 4 yrs., Catholic U. of America, 2 yrs.; hon. D.D., St. Mary's Sem.; LL.D., Mt. St. Mary's Coll. Ordained R.C. priest, June 21, 1889; pastor St. Jerome's Ch., Hyattsville, Md., 1889-94; sec. to Cardinal Gibbons, Baltimore, 1894-1908; rector St. Patrick's Ch., Washington, 1908-17; elected, Dec. 7, 1916, and consecrated Mar. 15, 1917, bishop of Charleston. Created Domestic Prelate to Pope Pius X, June 20, 1911. Author: Maryland, The Land of Sanctuary, 1907; also History of the Archdiocese of Baltimore, in Catholic Ency. Home: Charleston, S.C. Died Mar. 18, 1927.

RUST, Henry Bedinger, corp. official; b. Rockland Farm, nr. Leesburg, Va., Dec. 1872; s. Armistead Thomson Mason and Ida (Lee) R.; ed. pub. schs. and by pvt. study; m. Elizabeth Sage Watkins, Nov. 5, 1901; 1 dau., Elizabeth Fitzhugh (Mrs. Stanley N. Brown). With Dept. Pub. Works, Pittsburgh, Pa., 1890-1901; supt. constrn. Colo. Fuel & Iron Co., Pueblo, Colo., 1901-03; v.p. and gen. mgr. Rust Boiler Co., Pittsburgh, Pa., 1903-08; with Babcock & Wilcox Co., 1908-15; pres. The Koppers Co., Pittsburgh, 1915-33, chmn. 1933; dir. Westinghouse Electric & Mfg. Co. Episcopalian. Home: Pittsburgh, Pa. Died Jan. 17, 1936.

RUSTON, John Edward, lawyer; b. N.Y. City, June 14, 1872; s. Charles and Elizabeth Miner (Purdy) R.; Brooklyn (New York) Boys' High Sch.; B.S., New York U., 1894, LL.B., 1895; m. May Frances Henderson, June 3, 1902. Admitted to N.Y. bar, 1896, and practiced at Brooklyn; mem. firm Ruston & Snyder; pres. Ocean View Development Corp.; counsel, trustee, mem. exec. com. Greater New York Savings Bank; dir. New York Dock Co., New York Trade Facilities Corp. Dist. atty. Kings County, N.Y., 1917-22. Chmn. draft bd. and sergt., Brooklyn Mounted Police Res., World War. Mem. Kings County Rep. Com. Dir. Brooklyn and Queens Young Men's Christian Assn. Republican. Conglist. Mason, Elk. Home: Brooklyn, N.Y. Died Feb. 1, 1932.

RUSTON, William Otis, educator; b. New York, Dec. 6, 1852; s. John and Mary Otis (Herring) R.; A.B., Coll. City of New York, 1872; grad. Union Theol. Sem., 1875; D.D., 1886, LL.D., 1907, Lenox Coll.; m. Mary Woods Crater, Oct. 5, 1876. Ordained Presbyn. ministry, 1875; pastor Fairmount, N.J., 1875-77, West Union, Ia., 1877-86, Dubuque, Ia., 1886-1903; prof. sacred language and lit., 1903-15, prof. Biblical theology, 1915—, pres., 1904-03, dean, 1908—, dir. 1887—, U. of Dubuque. Trustee Lenox Coll.; stated clerk Presbytery of Dubuque and Synod of Ia.; mem. Presbyn. Coll. Bd., 1894-1900. Home: Dubuque, Ia. Died May 27, 1922.

RUTAN, Charles Hercules, architect; b. Newark, N.J., Mar. 28, 1851; s. Nicholas Warren and Sarah Elizabeth (Marsh) R.; ed. schs. of Newark, 1857-67; in office of Gambrill & Richardson, architects, New York, 1867; m. Sarah E. Brower, Sept. 15, 1874. Draughtsman, Gambrill & Richardson, 1870-78; draughtsman with H. H. Richardson, Brookline, Mass., 1878-86; mem. firm of Shepley, Rutan & Coolidge, Boston, and Chicago, 1886—. Fellow Am. Inst. Architects. Pres. Am. Tract Soc. (Boston), 1895—, Congl. Ch. Union of Boston, 1903; chmn. Commn. of Union Conf. of Congl. Chs. of Boston, 1904; dir. Congl. S.S. and Publ. Soc., 1894—; Evangelistic Assn. of N.E., 1905—; trustee Fisk U., 1901—; trustee and treas. Am. Coll. for Girls, at Constantinople, Turkey, 1906—; pres. Internat. Inst. for Girls in Spain, 1907—. Home: Brookline, Mass. Died Dec. 17, 1914.

RUTH, Carl Douglas, newspaper corr.; b. Mazeppa, Minn., July 11, 1884; s. Reuben Eugene and Minnesota (Hyde) R.; B.S., Dak. Wesleyan U., Mitchell, S.D., 1905; spl. studies, Oberlin, 1905-06; m. Cora M. Walker, Mar. 9, 1911; 1 son, Robert Walker. Reporter Cleveland Leader, 1906-09; chief of Columbus bur., Cleveland Leader and Cincinnati Commercial-Tribune, 1909-15; Washington corr. Cleveland Leader, 1915-17, Cleveland News, 1915-29, Toledo Blade, Newark Star-Eagle and Duluth Herald, 1929—. Mem. standing com. of correspondents of Press Galleries of Congress, 1923-25. Capt. Mil. Intelligence Div. of Gen. Staff, U.S. Army, Aug.-Dec. 1918. Republican. Presbyn. Home: Washington, D.C. Died Jan. 25, 1936.

RUTHERFORD, Albert Greig, congressman; b. Watford, Ont., Can., Jan. 3, 1879; s. James and Elizabeth (Bailie) R.; brought to U.S., 1883; LL.B., U. of Pa., 1904; m. Iris Estelle Burns, Sept. 12, 1906 (dec.); children—Ira Burns, James; m. 2d, Jessica A. Robinson, Sept. 17, 1937. Admitted to Pa. bar, 1904; practiced in Scranton, Pa., 1904-18, Honesdale, Pa., 1918—; mem. 75th and 76th Congresses (1937-41), 15th Pa. Dist. Mem. Pa. Nat. Guard, advancing to maj., 1904-18; lt. col. Pa. Res. Militia, 1919. Republican. Presbyterian. Mason, Odd Fellow, Elk, K.P., Knight of Malta, Granger, Royal Arcanum. Home: Honesdale, Pa. Died Aug. 10, 1941.

RUTHERFORD, Clarendon, M.D.; b. Madrid, N.Y., June 22, 1854; s. Maj. John T. and Belinda Evelyn R.; Hobart Coll., N.Y., 1872-75; A.B., Union Coll., Schenectady, N.Y., 1876, A.M., 1879; M.D., C.M., McGill Med. Coll., Montreal, 1882; m. Jessie Haiselden, May 1885; 1 dau., Elizabeth Evelyn (Mrs. William C. Van Horne); m. 2d, Ella W. McCauley, Feb. 4, 1920. Practiced, Chicago, 1882—; prof. anatomy, Chicago Coll. of Physicians and Surgeons, 1888-93. Fellow Am. Acad. Medicine. Mason. Home: Chicago, Ill. Died Feb. 11, 1933.

RUTHERFORD, Mildred Lewis, author; b. Athens, Ga., July 16, 1851; d. Williams R. and Laura Battaille Rootes (Cobb) R.; grad. Lucy Cobb Inst., 1868; Litt.D., U. of Ga., 1923. Teacher of lit., co-prin. or prin., Lucy Cobb Inst., 1880-1908; pres. Lucy Cobb Inst., Athens, Ga., 1917-22, dir., 1925-26, chair of southern history and lit., 1917-26. Pres. Ladies' Memorial Assn., Athens, 1888—; state historian Georgia Div. U.D.C. (elected for life); historian-gen. U.D.C., 1911-16; historian-gen. Confederated Memorial Assns., 1921—. Editor and pub. Scrap Book, 1923—. Author: English Authors; American Authors; French Authors, 1907; Mannie Brown; Bible Question Book; The South in History and Literature, 1907; also many booklets on southern history. Home: Athens, Ga. Died Aug. 15, 1928.

RUTHERFORD, Samuel, congressman; b. Crawford County, Ga., Mar. 15, 1870; s. William and Julia R.; student Washington and Lee U.; LL.B., U. of Ga., 1894; m. Abigail Ponder, Dec. 14, 1897. Admitted to Ga. bar, 1894, and began practice at Forsyth; v.p. First Nat. Bank, Forsyth, 1901-16; served as mayor 3 terms and as city solicitor; was mem. Ga. Ho. of Rep., also of Senate; mem. 69th to 71st Congresses (1925-31), 6th Ga. Dist. Democrat. Home: Forsyth, Ga. Died Feb. 4, 1932.

RUTHERFORD, S(amuel) Morton, lawyer; b. Louisville, Ark., Feb. 16, 1859; s. Robert Bealle and Sallie Wallace (Butler) R.; A.B., Emory and Henry Coll., Va., 1883; m. Sallie Dillard, 1890. Began practice at Ft. Smith, 1888; mem. firm Rutherford & Cosgrove, Muskogee, Okla.; dir. First Nat. Bank, Guaranty Title & Trust Co. U.S. marshal, Northern Dist. of Ind. Ty., 1893-97; mayor of Muskogee, Okla., 1904-05; mem. Okla. Senate. Democrat. Episcopalian. Mason. Home: Muskogee, Okla. Died Dec. 16, 1922.

RUTHRAUFF, John Mosheim, college pres.; b. Stark County, O., Jan. 13, 1846; grad. Wittenberg Coll., O., 1871, A.M., D.D., from same; m. Sarah E. Morrison, May 28, 1879. Served 4 months in U.S. army, 1864 (100-day service). Ordained Luth. minister; preached at Louisville, Ky., 1872-74; Circleville, O., 1874-76; Washingtonville, O., 1876-80; Circleville, O., 1880-85; Dixon, Ill., 1885-95; pres. Carthage (Ill.) Coll., 1895-1901; pres. Wittenberg Coll., Springfield, O., 1901—. Was pres. Miami Synod, O., and twice pres. Synod of Northern Ill. (Luth. ch.). Pres. Rock Assembly, Dixon, Ill., 1888-95; 5 times delegate to gen. synod, Evang. Luth. Ch. in U.S.A. Died 1902.

RUTT, Christian Louis, newspaper editor; b. Milwaukee, Wis., Oct. 8, 1859; s. Christian and Katherina (Geiss) R.; ed. St. Benedict's parochial sch. and coll., Atchison, Kan., 1867-73; m. Annie Herbst, May 11, 1887 (died 1926); children—Helen Catherine (dec.), Maria Theresa (dec.), Frances Mary, Anna Catherine, Christian Louis (dec.). Began as printer with Atchison Champion, 1873; itinerant printer, reporter and editor in Ia., Neb., Kan. and Tex., 1878-83; settled in St. Joseph, Mo., 1883; telegraph editor and mng. editor, Gazette, 1883-1900; with Daily News, 1900-03; with News-Press as mng. editor and editorial writer, 1903—; co-pub. The News Corp.; as stockholder of Pearl Milling Co. developed formula, supplied name and placed on market Aunt Jemima Pancake Flour, 1889. Mem. and sec. St. Joseph Metropolitan Police Commn., 13 yrs.; mem. Buchanan County Soc. for Relief and Prevention of Tuberculosis, 1911— (pres. 8 yrs.); dir. Catholic Laymen's Corp. Democrat. K.C. Author: Buchanan County and St. Joseph, 1898; History of Buchanan County and City of St. Joseph, 1904. Home: St. Joseph, Mo. Died Sept. 1936.

RUTTENBER, Edward Manning, author; b. Bennington, Vt., July 17, 1825; private edn.; m. Matilda Ann McIntyre, June 10, 1837. Connected with Bureau of Mill. Records, 1863-65—supt. of div. in Govt. Printing Office; trustee common schools, printer, editor Newburgh Telegraph, Newburgh Register, Goshen Independent Republican; etc.; retired. Author: History of Newburgh, N.Y.; History of Orange County, N.Y.; History of Regimental Flags; History of Obstructions to Navigation of the Hudson River, 1776; History of Indian Tribes of Hudson River; etc. Home: Newburgh, N.Y. Died 1907.

RUTTER, Frank Roy, economist, statistician; b. Baltimore, Mar. 15, 1874; s. Frederick G. and Ella M. (Purvis) R.; A.B., Johns Hopkins, 1894 (Phi Beta Kappa), Ph.D., 1897; m. Janet Stevens Goodwin, Sept. 15, 1904; children—Ella Purvis, Janet Goodwin. With U.S. Dept. of Agr. (statis. research), 1899-1910; spl. European agt. for the dept. in London, 1907-09; chief Div. of Foreign Tariffs, Dept. of Commerce, 1910-14; asst. chief Bur. of Foreign and Domestic Commerce, same dept., 1914-17; commercial attaché, Tokyo, Japan, 1917-18; statistical advisor, Dept. of Commerce, 1919-20; prof. of foreign trade, U. of Ore., 1921-22; prof. of foreign commerce, Amos Tuck Sch., Dartmouth Coll., 1922—. Spl. lecturer on commerce, State U. of Ia., 1904; course on foreign tariff policy, Johns Hopkins, 1910; lecturer on commerce, George Washington U., 1913-17, Georgetown U., 1920-21; expert, U.S. Tariff Commn., in China and Japan, 1924. Author of numerous bulls. and articles on tariffs, foreign trade. Home: Hanover, N.H. Died 1926.

RUTTER, Henley Chapman, physician; b. Pearisburg, Va., Feb. 6, 1849; s. John Harrison and Lovinia (McDonald) R.; ed. high sch., Bellefontaine, O.; pvt. Co. B, 132d Ohio Inf., enlisting at age of 14; M.D., Med. Coll. of Ohio, Cincinnati, 1869; m. Margaret M. Cretcher, July 6, 1892. Interne, Good Samaritan Hosp., Cincinnati, 1869-70; asst. phys., Dayton Hosp. for Insane, 1871-72, supt. same, 1872-74; supt. Athens (O.) Hosp. for Insane, 1875-78, 1879-81; supt. Columbus Hosp. for Insane, 1882-84; mgr. Hosp. for Epileptics, 1893-1901; med. dir. Park View Sanatorium; in intervals engaged in gen. practice of Medicine at Bellefontaine, Cincinnati, and Columbus, O. Republican. Author: Criminal Responsibility of the Insane; also many essays and papers upon care and treatment of epileptics. Home: Columbus, O. Died 1910.

RUUD, Martin Bronn, prof. English; b. Fergus Falls, Minn., Aug. 2, 1885; s. Edward and Amunda (Jakobsen) R.; A.B., U. of N.D., 1906, A.M., 1907; Ph.D., U. of Chicago, 1915; fellow Am.-Scandinavian Foundation and U. of Chicago at Scandinavian univs., 2 yrs.; D.C.L., St. Thomas Coll., St. Paul, Minn., 1935; m. Christine Boyson, June 17, 1911. Instr. English, U. of N.D., 1907-10; instr. English and German, U. of Chicago, 1914-15; instr. English, U. of Minn., 1915-19, asst. prof., 1919-25, asso. prof., 1925-27, prof., 1927—, also chmn. dept. of Scandinavian. Lutheran. Author: A History of Shakespeare in Norway, 1917; A History of Shakespeare in Denmark, 1920; Thomas Chaucer, 1926. Editor: Norwegian Emigrant Songs and Ballads (with T. C. Blegen), 1936. Home: Minneapolis, Minn. Died Feb. 8, 1941.

RYAN, Daniel Joseph, lawyer; b. Cincinnati, Jan. 1, 1855; s. John and Honora (Ryan) R.; grad. Portsmouth (Ohio) High Sch., 1875; studied law, 1875-77; m. Myra L. Kerr, Jan. 10, 1884. Admitted to bar Supreme Ct. of Ohio, 1877; practiced at Portsmouth; city solicitor, Portsmouth, 2 terms; mem. 66th and 67th General Assemblies, Ohio (speaker pro tem. 67th); 1st pres. Ohio Rep. League, 2 terms; temporary chmn. 1st Nat. Conv. Rep. Clubs, New York, 1887; sec. state of Ohio, 1888-91; exec. commr. Ohio at Chicago Expn., and organized Ohio exhibit; mem. exec. com. Assn. of Am. Exhibitors, 1893, and its commr. to Antwerp Expn., 1893; del. from Ohio to Western Waterways Conv., Vicksburg. Pres. Central Ohio Land Co.; v.p., trustee Ohio Archæol. and Hist. Soc.; chmn. Ohio Tax Commn., 1920-21. Author: A History of Ohio (with E. O. Randall), 5 vols.; Arbitration Between Capital and Labor; article, "Ohio," in Encyclopedia Americana; The Civil War Literature of Ohio; Masters of Men; Ohio in Four Wars; Historic Failures in Applied Socialism. Home: Columbus, O. Died June 15, 1923.

RYAN, Edward William, sanitarian; b. Scranton, Pa., Dec. 14, 1884; s. Jerimiah E. and Bridget Ellen (Loftus) R.; M.D., Fordham U., 1912; unmarried. Spl. agt. Dept. of State, U.S., in Mexico, 1913-14, also surgeon Am. Embassy, Mexico City; with Am. Red Cross in evacuating Americans from troubled zone in Mexico; dir. Red Cross unit to Serbia, 1914; assigned to Salonika, 1917, instituting clean-up pub. health measures behind army as it advanced; dept. Red Cross commr. Germany after Armistice; also operating for Inter-Allied Commn., Berlin; assigned to Baltic States and continued there 1919-July 1922; stamped out epidemic in Esthonia, 1920. Mem. Legion of Honor. Awarded Croix de Guerre, Medaille des Epidemie (French); Comdr. White Eagle, Comdr. Order St. Sava, Charity Cross, Red Cross (Serbian); Comdr. St. Danilo (Montenegrin); Officer Order Savior (Grecian); Comdr. Order White Rose (Finnish); Comdr. Order St. Ann, Order St. Stanislaw (Russian); Officer 1st Class, Order of Liberty (Esthonian); Knight Order of Lithuania, etc. Home: Scranton, Pa. Died Sept. 1923.

RYAN, Harris Joseph, electrical engr.; b. Powell's Valley, Pa., Jan. 8, 1866; s. Charles W. and Louisa (Collier) R.; Baltimore City Coll., 1880-81; Lebanon Valley Coll., Annville, Pa., 1881-83; M.E., Sibley Coll. (Cornell U.), 1887; m. Katharine E. Fortenbaugh, Sept. 12, 1888. Instr. physics, 1888-89, prof. elec. engring., 1889-1905, Cornell; prof. elec. engring., Leland Stanford Jr. U. (now Stanford U.), 1905-31, prof. emeritus, 1931—, also hon. dir. Harris J. Ryan High Voltage Lab., Stanford U. Cons. engr. Los Angeles Aqueduct Power Bur., 1909-24. Mem. Jury of Awards, dept. electricity, Chicago Expn., 1893; del. Internat. Elec. Congress, St. Louis Expn., 1904; mem. jury, Panama-P.I. Expn., 1915. Fellow Am. Inst. E.E. (v.p., 1896-98; hon. v.p. representing Inst. at P.-P.I. Expn., 1915; pres. 1923-24). Author: (with H.H. Norris and G. L. Hoxie) Text-Book of Electrical Machinery, Vol. I, 1903. Contbr. to Trans. Am. Inst. Elec. Engrs.; numerous monographs on elec. subjects. Dir. Anti-submarine Supersonics Lab., of Nat. Research Council, Pasadena, Calif., 1918-19. Died July 3, 1924.

RYAN, James, bishop; b. Thurles, County Tipperary, Ireland, 1848; came to U.S. in childhood; studied for priesthood in sems. of St. Thomas and St. Joseph, Bardstown, Ky. Ordained R.C. ministry; prof. in St. Joseph's Sem.; pastor in Ky., Wataga, Danville, and Ottawa, Ill., to 1888; consecrated bishop of Alton, Ill., 1888. Died July 3, 1923.

RYAN, John D., mining man; b. in Mich., 1864; m. Nettie Gardner, 1896; 1 son, John C. Chmn. Anaconda Copper Mining Co., Chile Copper Co.; pres. United Metals Selling Co., Mont. Power Co.; dir. Nat. City Bank of New York, Emigrants Industrial Savings Bank. Apptd. dir. aircraft production by President Wilson, Apr. 1918, also chmn. Aircraft Bd.; 2d asst. sec. of war and dir. air service, Aug.-Nov. 1918. Mem. War Council Am. Nat. Red Cross (mem. Central Com.). Home: Butte, Mont. Died Feb. 11, 1933.

RYAN, Marah Ellis, author; b. Butler County, Pa., Feb. 27, 1866; d. Graham and Sidney (Mechling) Martin; wrote a few poems and stories under pen-name "Ellis Martin"; m. S. Erwan Ryan, actor, Sept. 23, 1883 (dec.). Author: In Love's Domain, 1889; Told in the Hills, 1890; Pagan of the Alleghenies, 1891; Squaw Eloise, 1892; A Flower of France, 1894; Comrades, 1896; The Bond-Woman, 1899; The Girl Montana, 1901; My Quaker Maid, 1906; For the Soul of Rafael, 1906; Indian Love Letters, 1907; The Flute of the Gods, 1909; Pagan Prayers, 1913; The Woman of the Twilight, 1913; The House of the Dawn, 1914; Treasure Trail, 1919; The Dancer of Tuluum, 1925. Home: Los Angeles, Calif. Died July 11, 1934.

RYAN, Martin Francis, pres. Brotherhood of Ry. Carmen; b. Coldwater, W.Va., Oct. 23, 1874; s. John and Mary (Call) R.; ed. pub. schs.; m. Sue Ellen Myers, Apr. 8, 1908; children—Martin, Mary, John Paul. Mechanic on S.P. Ry., later A.,T.&S.F. Ry., 1895-1903; elected mem. exec. bd. Brotherhood of Ry. Carmen of America, 1903, gen. v.p., 1905-09, gen. pres., 1909—. Mem. exec. council Ry. Employes' Dept. of Am. Federation of Labor, 6th v.p., 1927—; treas. A.F. of L., 1928—; an organizer, and treas. Union Labor Life Ins. Co., 1927—. Mem. of First Labor Mission to England, Ireland, Scotland, Wales and France, 1918; co-del. with Samuel Gompers to Pan-Am. Federation of Labor Conv., City of Mexico, 1924. Mem. Modern Woodmen of America, Elks. Catholic. Home: Kansas City, Mo. Died Jan. 17, 1935.

RYAN, Michael Sylvester, clergyman, educator; b. St. Louis, Mo., Dec. 22, 1875; s. John and Ellen (Ready) R.; grad. St. Mary's Sem., Perryville, Mo., 1890-97; Ph.D., U. of Rome, 1899, D.D., 1899. Joined Vincentians, 1891; ordained priest, R.C. Ch., 1898; pres. Kenrick Sem., Webster Groves, Mo., 1906-26; prof. moral and pastoral theology same instn. Home: Webster Groves, Mo. Died Aug. 10, 1931.

RYAN, O'Neill, judge; b. St. Louis, Jan. 5, 1860; s. Richard and Margaret (O'Neill) R.; ed. pub. schs. and Poly. Night Sch.; studied law in office of Given Campbell; LL.D., Christian Bros. Coll., St. Louis, 1907, St. Louis U., 1910; m. Mary Carmen Rashcoe, Nov. 24, 1897; children—O'Neill, Francis Campbell, Mary Carmen (Mrs. Marion L. J. Lambert), Kathleen (Mrs. John M. McTeer, Jr.), Margaret (Mrs. William F. Keeshan). Was admitted to practice law, 1880; partner in practice with Given Campbell, 1883-99; judge Circuit Court of City of St. Louis, 1901-07; mem. firm Ryan & Thompson (Guy A.), 1911-18; dean St. Louis U. Inst. of Law, 1908-15; judge Circuit Court, City of St. Louis, 1929-35, reëlected for term, 1935-41. Mem. Pub. Library Bd., 1899— (pres.). Declined apptmt. to Supreme Court of Mo. Supreme Chancellor Legion of Honor of Mo., 1890; mem. exec. com. Civic League, 1912-14; v.p. Catholic High Sch. Bd., 1915—; pres. Catholic Charities of St. Louis, 1919-25. Democrat. Home: St. Louis, Mo. Died Jan. 7, 1939.

RYAN, Patrick John, archbishop; b. Thurles, County Tipperary, Ireland, Feb. 20, 1831; grad. Carlow Coll., 1852; LL.D., Manhattan Coll., 1866, New York U. and U. of Pa. Ordained sub-deacon in Ireland; came to U.S.; became prof. English lit., Carondelet Theol. Sem., St. Louis; ordained deacon there, and, 1853, priest; served at the Cathedral, where he became rector, 1856. Acted as chaplain Gratiot St. Mil. Prison and Hosp., St. Louis, during the Civil War; while rector of Annunciation Ch. delivered Lenten lectures in English at Rome, 1868, on invitation of Pope Pius IX; consecrated, 1872, titular bishop of Tricomia in Palestine in partibus infidelium and made coadjutor bishop of St. Louis; promoted to archbishop, 1883, and June 8, 1884, transferred to See of Philadelphia. Author: What Catholics Do Not Believe; The Causes of Modern Religious Skepticism. Died 1911.

RYAN, Raymond Richard, lawyer; b. Chicago, Ill., Sept. 23, 1884; s. Richard and Mary (Ralph) R.; A.B., DePaul U., Chicago, 1904; student law U. of Colo., 1906-08; m. Helen Chandler, Dec. 3, 1917; children—Richard Raymond, Joseph Chandler, Charles Gardner. Admitted to N.M. bar, 1910, and began practice at Albuquerque; practiced at Silver City, N.M., 1911-17; judge Dist. Court 6th Dist., N.M., 1917-27; in practice at Albuquerque, 1927—. Home: Albuquerque, N.M. Died June 3, 1934.

RYAN, Thomas, assistant sec. of the interior; b. Oxford, N.Y., Nov. 25, 1837; reared on farm; ed. Dickinson Sem., Pa. Admitted to bar, 1861; served in Union Army, 1862-64; mustered out, with rank of capt., on account of wounds received in battle of the Wilderness. In practice at Topeka, Kan., from 1865; county atty., 8 yrs.; asst. U.S. atty., 1873-77; elected 45th to 51st Congresses (1877-91); resigned, 1889; U.S. minister to Mexico, 1889-93; apptd. 1st asst. sec. of the interior, Mar. 1897, serving several yrs. Republican. Died Apr. 5, 1914.

RYAN, Thomas Curran, lawyer; b. Utica, N.Y., July 4, 1841; s. Michael and Margaret (Ryan) R.; ed. in common sch. and by pvt. tutor; m. Emma Thurston, Feb. 14, 1876. Pvt. Co. G, 5th Wis. Inf., Civil War, 1861-63; practiced law, 1866—, at Wausau, Wis., 1881—. Universalist. Author: O'Hooligan's Fine Forms, 1903; Finite and Infinite, 1905; Intellectual Religion, 1912. Died Dec. 10, 1911.

RYAN, Thomas Fortune, financier; b. Nelson Co., Va., Oct. 17, 1851; m. Ida M. Barry, of Baltimore, Md., Nov. 25, 1873 (dec.); m. 2d, Mrs. Cornelius C. (Nicol) Cuyler, Oct. 29, 1917. Began in employ Baltimore dry goods house, 1868; entered Wall Street, 1870; mem. New York Stock Exchange, 1874, later interested in consolidation and extension of street ry. and lighting systems, New York, Chicago and other cities, and reorganizations of various rys. in the South; also had interests in coal properties in Ohio and W.Va., and coal and ry. cos. in Va.; said to be the largest individual owner of Congo diamond fields, Belgian Congo, Africa. Pruchased controlling interest of the Equitable Life Assurance Soc. of U.S., 1905; retired, Dec. 1908, as officer or dir. in more than 30 corps., in which was controlling factor; prominently identified with Am. Tobacco Co., 1898—, later with British Am. Tobacco Co.; identified with Belgian and Portuguese corps. engaged in development of mining activities in Belgian Congo, 1900—, and Portuguese Angola, 1912—; dir. Guaranty Trust Co., Carolina, Clinchfield & Ohio Railway Co. Delegate from Va. to Dem. Nat. Conv., 1904, 12. Home: New York, N.Y. Died Nov. 23, 1928.

RYAN, Timothy Edward, lawyer; b. Washington County, N.Y., Jan. 10, 1859; s. Jeremiah and Johannah R.; LL.B., U. of Wis., 1885; m. Mary E. Bannon, Oct. 5, 1887. Sr. mem. firm Ryan, Merton & Newbury, 1888—. City atty., Waukesha, 1888; pres. bd. edn., 1902-06; mem. Dem. Nat. Com., 1900-12. Home: Waukesha, Wis. Died 1911.

RYAN, William, editor; b. Maysville, Ky., Apr. 3, 1851; s. Michael and Maria Louisa (Richeson) R.; ed. pvt. schs., Maysville, to 16; unmarried. Pres.

The State (daily newspaper), Richmond, Va., 1889-93; removed to Birmingham, Ala., 1898; mng. editor Birmingham Age-Herald, 1903-16, and editorial writer same, 1917—. Member Dem. State Executive Com., Va., 1888-89. U.S. collector internal revenue, Richmond, 1893-97. Dir. Associated Charities, Birmingham, Birmingham Chamber Commerce. Was active in promotion of edn. and of music festivals. Catholic. Home: Birmingham, Ala. Died Nov. 9, 1920.

RYAN, William Henry, congressman; b. Hopkinton, Mass., May 10, 1860; s. Patrick and Jane (Cleary) R.; ed. Buffalo, N.Y., High Sch.; m. Ellen T. Cosgrove, Sept. 19, 1887. Engaged in boot and shoe business, 1878; pres. Ryan & Cable, Inc., gen. insurance and bonding agts. Mem. bd. supervisors, Erie Co., N.Y., 1894-99, chmn. same, 1898; mem. 56th to 60th Congresses (1899-1909); del. to Dem. Nat. Conv., St. Louis, 1904, New York, 1924; mem. Dem. State Com. Chmn. Buffalo Grade Crossing and Terminal Commn.; mem. Buffalo Terminal Commn., N.Y. State Council of Parks, Allegheny State Park Com. (chmn.); dir. Le Conteleaux St. Mary's Deaf Mute Instn. Treas. Catholic Charities of Diocese of Buffalo. Home: Buffalo, N.Y. Died Nov. 18, 1939.

RYAN, William Patrick, chem. engring.; b. West Medway, Mass., Mar. 11, 1895; s. John Henry and Catherine Maria (Hilferty) R.; grad. high sch., Medway, 1912, Phillips Acad., Andover, Mass., 1914; B.S., Mass. Inst. Tech., 1920 as of 1918; m. Pauline LaVerne Collins, Sept. 16, 1922; children—Mary Louise, Patricia Anne, Kathleen. Chem. engr. Nat. Lamp Co., Cleveland, O., Mar.-Sept. 1919; instr. in chem. engring., Mass. Inst. Tech., 1920-22, asst. prof., 1922-27, asso. prof., 1927-29, dir. Sch. of Chem. Engring. Practice, 1927—, prof. and head of dept., 1929—. Enlisted as pvt. Ordnance Dept., U.S.A., advancing to 2d lt. Chem. Warfare Service, World War. Catholic. Contbr. tech. articles to Jour. Industrial and Engring. Chemistry, Trans. Am. Inst. Chem. Engrs. Home: Wollaston, Mass. Deceased.

RYAN, William Thomas, electric power engring.; b. Bristol (now Joice), Ia., Feb. 28, 1882; s. Edward Thomas and Sarah (Slater) R.; E.E., U. of Minn., 1905; m. Ella I. Ryan, June 18, 1908. Connected with U. of Minn., 1906—, prof. electric power engring., 1922—. Mem. Am. Inst. Elec. Engineers (chmn. Minn. sect. 1912, 22; v.p. 1929-30) and other engring. socs. Mem. Minn. N.G., 1904. Catholic. Author: Design of Electrical Machinery (Vol. I), 1912 (Vol. II), 1912 (Vol. III), 1913; Electrical Problems, 1915. Contbr. over 40 papers pub. in tech. mags. Home: Minneapolis, Minn. Died Feb. 5, 1939.

RYBNER, Martin Cornelius, musician; b. Copenhagen, Denmark, Oct. 26, 1853; s. Johan William and Charlotte (Gosch) R.; ed. U. of Copenhagen; studied music Copenhagen Royal Conservatory and Leipzig Conservatory; studied composition with Gade and J. P. Hartmann, violin with Tofte and F. David, piano with E. Neupert, Reinecke, Von Bülow, A. Rubinstein and Liszt; m. Claudine Pezel de Corval, d. Dagmar de Corval (pianist). Début as pianist and violinist at Copenhagen and Leipzig; made concert tours through Scandinavia, Germany, France, Eng. and Italy; dir. Choral Soc., Baden-Baden, 1875; opera condr., associated with Felix Mottl, at Karlsruhe; dir. Coll. of Music and Philharmonic Choral Soc., Karlsruhe, 1886-1904; head Dept. of Music, Columbia, 1904-19; teacher of composition, New York Coll. of Music, 1924—. Gave first production in Germany of Massenet's "Marie Madeleine" and of F. Klose's "Grand Mass," at Karlsruhe, 1903. Knight orders of Dannebrog, Prussian Crown, Rose (Brazil), Zaehringer Lion (Baden); Grand Gold Medal for art and science, Baden; Chevalier of Danilo Order (Montenegro); court pianist of Denmark and Hesse. Author: Phases of Piano Study; N. W. Gade, Centenary of His Birth (Mus. Quarterly), 1917. Composer: Piano Trio in G Minor; songs for mixed chorus; violin and cello pieces; duets and songs; piano pieces (concert paraphrase) Meistersinger; (symphonic poem) Peace, Battle and Victory; Festival Overture in C major; Violin Concerto in G minor; (ballet in 3 acts) Prince Ador (prod. Royal Opera, Karlsruhe, 1903); Festival Cantata for solo, choir and orchestra. Arranged transcriptions for piano of Siegmund's Love-song, Wotan's Farewell and Fire Music, Liebestod, from "Tristan and Isolde," Siegfried's Funeral March. Home: New York, N.Y. Died Jan. 31, 1929.

RYDBERG, Per Axel, botanist; b. Odh, Sweden, July 6, 1860; s. Adolf Fredrik and Elfrida (Otterstrom) R.; grad. Royal Gymnasium, Skara, Sweden, 1881; B.S., U. of Neb., 1891, M.A., 1895; Ph.D., Columbia U., 1898; m. Alfrida Amanda Rydberg, Nov. 11, 1903; children—Arthur Alfred, Elsa Margreta (dec.), Lilly Irene, Linnea Astrid. Prof. natural sciences and mathematics, Luther Acad., Wahoo, Neb., 1884-90, 1891-93; at Upsala Inst., Brooklyn, 1895-96 and 1897-98; Upsala Coll., New Orange, N.J., 1898-99; fellow in botany, Columbia, 1896-97; asst. Bot. Lab., U. of Neb., 1894-95; field agt. dept. agr., divs. of botany and agrostology, summers of 1891-96; curator New York Botanic Garden, Bronx Park, 1899—. Author of monographs on Potentilleæ, Physalis, Saxifragaceæ, Rosaceæ, Carduaceæ and Fabaceæ; Catalogue of the Flora of Montana and the Yellowstone Park, 1900; Flora of Colorado, 1906; Flora of the Rocky Mountains and Adjacent Plains, 1917; Key to the Rocky Mountain Flora, 1919. Home: New York, N.Y. Died July 25, 1931.

RYDEN, George Herbert, univ. prof.; b. Kansas City, Mo., Jan. 26, 1884; s. August and Emma Sophia (Peterson) R.; A.B., Augustana Coll., Rock Island, Ill., 1909, Litt.D., 1938; M.A., Yale, 1911, grad. study, 1916-18 and 1926-27, Ph.D., 1928; awarded Currier fellowship, Yale, for 1911-12 (resigned). Clk., K.C.S. Ry., 1902-05; instr. history and social sciences, Bethany Coll., Lindsborg, Kan., 1911-12, prof., 1912-16; asst. in history, Yale, 1916-18; instr. in citizenship, Dartmouth, 1921-22; asso. prof. history and polit. science, U. of Del., 1922-28, prof., 1928—; prof. history, U. of Kan., summers 1930 and 36; prof. of history, U. of Minn., summer 1932. Mem. Delaware Dutch Tercentenary Committee, 1930-31, Del. Statues Commn., 1931-34; Sec. Del. Swedish Tercentenary Commn., 1935-38; State archivist of Delaware, 1930—; chmn. Historic Markers Commn. of Del., 1931-33. Ednl. sec. Y.M.C.A., army camps, Texas, and Italian front, Jan.-Nov. 1918, Paris until Aug. 1919; dir. South Russian Mission, Am. Red Cross, 1919-21. Awarded John Addison Porter prize (Yale), 1928; Italian War Cross, 1918; Orders of St. Stanislav and St. Anne (Russia), 1920; North Star (Sweden), 1938; medal of Russian Red Cross, 1920. Author: The Foreign Policy of the United States in Relation to Samoa; Delaware, The First State in the Union. Editor of Letters to and from Cæsar Rodney. Contbr. to 13th and 14th edits. Ency. Brit., to Dictionary Am. Biography and to hist. jours. Home: Newark, Del. Died Oct. 12, 1941.

RYDER, Albert Pinkham, artist; b. New Bedford, Mass., Mar. 19, 1847; s. Alexander Gage and Elizabeth (Cobb) R.; studied art under William E. Marshall and at Nat. Acad. of Design. Painter of pastoral landscapes, etc.; has been called "the last of the romanticists." N.A., 1906; mem. Nat. Inst. Arts and Letters. Died Mar. 28, 1917.

RYDER, Arthur William, coll. prof.; b. Oberlin, O., Mar. 8, 1877; s. William Henry and Mary Elizabeth (Bushnell) R.; grad. Phillips Acad., Andover, Mass., 1894; A.B., Harvard, 1897; univs. of Leipzig and Berlin, 1898-1901, Ph.D., Leipzig, 1901; unmarried. Instructor in Latin, Phillips Acad., 1897-98; asst. in Sanskrit, 1901-02; instr., 1902-06, Harvard; instr. in Sanskrit, 1906-08, asst. prof., 1908-19, asso. prof., 1919-25, prof., 1925—, U. of Calif., Berkeley. Translator: The Little Clay Cart (from the Sanskrit), 1905; Women's Eyes (verses from the Sanskrit), 1910; Kalidasa: translations of Shakuntala and other works, 1912; Twenty-two Goblins, 1917; Relatives (further verses from the Sanskrit), 1919; The Panchatantra, 1925; Gold's Gloom, 1925; The Ten Princes, 1927; The Bhagavad-Gita, 1929. Died Mar. 21, 1938.

RYDER, Charles Jackson, clergyman; b. Oberlin, O., Dec. 25, 1848; s. Oliver Roberts and Harriet Rachel (Jackson) R.; A.B., Oberlin Coll., 1875, B.D., 1880, A.M., 1887, D.D., 1894; m. Sarah H. Tenney, Aug. 20, 1876. Congl. minister; corr. sec. Am. Missionary Assn. Wrote on sociology, education, and missions, in various periodicals. Mem. Folk-Lore Soc.; trustee Oberlin Coll., Fisk U., Tougaloo U. Home: Stamford, Conn. Died Sept. 24, 1917.

RYDER, Frederick Milliachip, foreign service officer; b. Iberville, Can., Nov. 3, 1862; s. William Milliachip and Mary (Wadsworth) R.; ed. pub. schs. in Canada. Was on staff of the Springfield (Mass.) Union, Ansonia (Conn.) Sentinel, and New Haven Palladium; manager, sec., treas. New Haven Evening Leader, 1894-1902; Am. consul at Quebec, 1890-93; consul at San Juan del Norte, Nicaragua, 1905-08, at Rimouski, Que., June 10, 1908-Dec. 21, 1914; consul-gen. at Singapore, Straits Settlements, Dec. 22, 1914, at Winnipeg, Man., Mar. 2, 1915; consul-gen. at Vancouver, B.C., Sept. 11, 1919—. Died Jan. 5, 1939.

RYDER, Harry Osborne, prof. classics; b. Taunton, Mass., Jan. 4, 1880; s. Freeman Osborne and Annie Jane (Smith) R.; A.B., Boston U., 1902, A.M., 1905, Ph.D., 1908; m. Alice Viola McClure, Aug. 1913. Teacher, Wesleyan Acad., Wilbraham, Mass., 1902-03; Dickinson Sem., Williamsport, Pa., 1903-11; prof. classics, Western Md. Coll., Westminster, Md., 1911-19; prof. classics, Hamline U., 1919—, also faculty athletic rep. Republican. Methodist. Author: Essentials of Latin (from the functional point of view for coll. classes), 1928. Lecturer, on classical and philos. subjects. Home: St. Paul, Minn. Deceased.

RYDER, Robert Oliver, editor; b. Oberlin, O., Mar. 9, 1875; s. William Henry and Mary Elizabeth (Bushnell) R.; grad. Phillips Acad., Andover, Mass., 1894; student Yale and Williams colls.; m. Florence Wilson, Nov. 8, 1900. Began with Ohio State Journal, 1898, successively reporter and city editor until 1904, mng. editor, 1904-19, editor, 1919-30, asso. publisher, 1927-30; specialized as editorial paragrapher. Author: The Young Lady Across the Way, 1913. Home: Berkeley, Calif. Died Mar. 16, 1936.

RYDER, William Henry, theologian; b. Elyria, O., July 24, 1842; s. Oliver Roberts and Harriet Rachel (Jackson) R.; A.B., Oberlin Coll., 1866, A.M., 1888; grad. Andover Theol. Sem., 1869; D.D., Iowa (now Grinnell) Coll., 1891, Oberlin Coll., 1916. Corporal 150th Ohio Infantry, May-Aug. 1864; 2d lt. 5th U.S.C.T., 1864-65; was wounded in front of Richmond, Va., Oct. 27, 1864; m. Mary Elizabeth Bushnell, June 29, 1870 (died 1878); m. 2d, Ada Tripp, Oct. 12, 1881. Ordained Congl. ministry, 1869; pastor Watertown, Wis., 1869-70; prof. Greek lang. and lit., Oberlin Coll., 1870-77; pastor First Congl. Ch., Ann Arbor, Mich., 1877-88; prof. N.T. interpretation, Andover Theol. Sem., May 1888—, and Andover prof. same, Harvard U., Sept. 1908—. Home: Andover, Mass. Died Apr. 6, 1918.

RYERSON, Edward Larned; b. Chicago, Ill., Nov. 24, 1854; s. Joseph T. and Ellen Griffin (Larned) R.; Ph.B., Yale, 1876; m. Mary Pringle, d. Donald G. Mitchell ("Ik Marvel"), of New Haven, Conn., 1879; children—Joseph Turner, Mary Mitchell (Mrs. Donald M. Frost), Donald Mitchell, Edward Larned. In wholesale iron and steel business (established by father, 1842), 1876-1928; pres. same, 1888-1911, then chmn. bd.; was dir. Ill. Merchants Trust Co., pres. Newberry Library; trustee St. Luke's Hosp., Chicago Hist. Soc. Served as governing mem. Chicago Symphony Orchestra, Art Inst. Chicago; was hon. pres. Lake Forest Foundation for Architecture and Landscape Architecture. Republican. Episcopalian. Home: Lake Forest and Chicago, Ill. Died Jan. 19, 1928.

RYERSON, Martin Antoine; b. Grand Rapids, Mich., Oct. 26, 1856; s. Martin and Mary A. (Campau) R.; ed. Chicago pub. schs., Paris, France, Lake Geneva, Switzerland; LL.B., Harvard, 1878; hon. M.A., Yale, 1917; LL.D., Kenyon Coll., 1924, U. of Chicago, 1929; m. Carrie Hutchinson, Oct. 26, 1881. Dir. Northern Trust Co., Elgin Nat. Watch Co. Pres. and hon. pres. bd. trustees U. of Chicago; hon. pres. Art Inst. Chicago; v.p. Field Mus. Natural History; hon. trustee U. of Chicago; trustee O.S.A. Sprague Memorial Inst.; dir. Chicago Orphan Asylum. Home: Chicago, Ill. Died Aug. 11, 1932.

RYLANCE, Joseph Hine, clergyman; b. in England, June 16, 1826; grad. Kings Coll., London, A.K.C., 1860; D.D., Western Reserve Univ., 1866. Ordained deacon, 1861; priest, 1862, becoming asst. at St. Paul's, Lambeth, London, 1862-63; rector St. Paul's Cleveland, O., 1863-67; St. Jame's, Chicago, 1867-71; St. Mark's Ch., New York City, 1871—. Author: Preachers and Preaching; Essays on Miracles; Social Questions; Essay on Tennyson. Died 1907.

RYLAND, Joseph R.; b. San Jose, Calif., May 22, 1863; s. Caius Tacitus and Letitia M. (Burnett) R.; B.S., U. of Santa Clara, Calif., 1884; m. Cornelia T. O'Neal, Jan. 25, 1888; children—Reis J., Tass C. Pres. San Jose Water Works, 1911—; v.p. Nucleus Building & Loan Assn. Mem. Am. Water Works Assn. (pres. Calif. sect.). Mem. Soc. Calif. Pioneers. Democrat. Catholic. Elk. Home: San Jose, Calif. Died Jan. 27, 1928.

RYLAND, William Semple, clergyman; b. Richmond, Va., June 4, 1836; s. Rev. Robert R., D.D., and Josephine (Norvell) R.; A.B., Richmond Coll., 1855, A.M., 1869; grad. Rochester Theol. Sem., 1858; Ph.D., Mercer U.; D.D., Georgetown, Ky.; m. Mary E. Morton, Sept. 29, 1870. Bapt. pastor, Winchester, Va., and vicinity, 1859-61; teacher Clarke County, 1861-63; chaplain C.S.A., 1863-65; pastor and teacher Frederick County, Va., 1865-67; Grenada, Miss., 1867-73; Lexington, Ky., 1873-80. Pres. Lexington Female Coll., Ky., 1877-80; prof. natural science, 1880-93; chmn. faculty, 1887-89, and pres., 1889-98, Bethel Coll.; pastor Logan County, Ky., 1899—. Died 1906.

RYMAN, James H. T., banker; b. Milesburg, Pa., Aug. 15, 1855; s. Henry T. and Sarah J. (Parkhurst) R.; ed. Bellefonte (Pa.) Acad. Settled in Mont. Ty., 1879; mem. firm Wolf & Ryman, 1882—; with partner, organized, Feb. 1889, Western Montana Nat. Bank, Missoula, Mont. Mem. exec. bd. U. of Mont., 1895-1923; mem. Mont. State Bd. Edn.; pres. bd. trustees Missoula Pub. Library, 1893—; pres. bd. trustees Mont. Hist. Soc.; mem. bd. trustees Bellefonte (Pa.) Acad. Republican. Home: Missoula, Mont. Died June 1926.

RYNEARSON, Edward, educator; b. nr. Farmland, Ind., June 23, 1867; s. Sylvester and Mary Jane (Clark) R.; A.B., Ohio Wesleyan, 1893, A.M., 1896, D.Ped., 1919; work in biology, U. of Chicago, 1895-96; 7 summers at Marine Biological Laboratory, Woods Hole, Mass., and 1 summer, Columbia; m. Rosetta Ann Harper, July 5, 1899; children—Edward Harper, Sylvester Harper. Teacher of biology, Steele High Sch., Dayton, O., 1893-95; prof. biology, Central High Sch., Pittsburgh, 1896-98; head of acad. dept. Pittsburgh High Sch., 1898-1902; dir. high schs. of Pittsburgh, 1902-12; prin. Fifth Av. High Sch., Pittsburgh, 1912-28, and dir. vocational guidance, 1917—. Sent by Pittsburgh Bd. of Edn. to visit schs. in Great Britain and on the Continent, 1908.

Republican. Methodist. Mason. Was instructor in summer session Boston Univ., 1922, Teachers College (Columbia), 1923, Stanford U., 1924, Colo. State Teachers Coll., 1925, U. of Calif., 1927. Lecturer Cambridge U. (England) summer 1928. Home: Pittsburgh, Pa. Died May 25, 1932.

S

SAAR, Louis Victor Franz, composer, pianist; b. at Rotterdam, Holland, Dec. 10, 1868; s. Louis and Fanny (Jaquemar) S.; ed. Gymnasium, Strassburg; grad. Royal Acad. Music, Munich, 1889; m. Emilie Scholl, of Nürnberg, Germany, Oct. 7, 1897; children—Gertrude, Carl, Alice. Came to America as accompanist of Met. Opera Co., 1893; teacher piano, theory and composition, successively at Nat. Conservatory of Music, New York Coll. of Music, Inst. of Musical Art, 1898-1906; prin. theory dept. and dir. coll. chorus, Coll. of Music, Cincinnati, 1906-17; head of theory dept., Chicago Musical Coll., 1917-25; dean of faculty, Chicago College of Music, 1925-34. Composer of orchestral and chamber music, choral and piano music, songs, violin music, etc. Awarded the Mendelssohn stipendium, at Berlin, 1891; Tonkuenstler prize, Vienna, 1892; 1st prize for piano music, Boston, 1899; Kaiser prize, Baltimore, 1903; prizes in New York, Chicago, St. Louis, Washington, D.C., and Portland, Ore. Home: St. Louis, Mo. Died Nov. 23, 1937.

SABIN, Alvah Horton, chemist; b. Norfolk, N.Y., Apr. 9, 1851; s. Henry S. and Zaida (Vernal) S.; S.B., Bowdoin College, 1876, M.S., 1879; hon. D.Sc. from same college, 1917; m. Mary E. Barden, Oct. 29, 1880 (died 1934); children—Raymond E., Warren D. Prof. chemistry, U. of Vermont, 1880-86; state chemist Vt., 1882-86; varnish mfr. at New York, 1888-1905; consulting chemist, Nat. Lead Co., New York, 1910-37. Invented and patented, 1883, modern process for making sugar of milk. Lecturer New York Univ., 1896-1925; sect. editor, Chem. Abstracts Jour. of Am. Chem. Soc., 1907—. Republican. Author: Industrial and Artistic Technology of Paint and Varnish, 1904, 3d edit., 1927; House-painting, 1908, 4th edit., 1928; German and American Varnish-Making, 1911; Red Lead as Paint Material, 1917, 2d edit., 1933; White Lead, 1919; Painting Structural Steel, 1929. Home: Flushing, L.I., N.Y. Died July 11, 1940.

SABIN, Charles Hamilton, banker; b. Williamstown, Mass., Aug. 24, 1868; s. Thomas and Cordelia (Eldridge) S.; grad. Greylock Inst., S. Williamstown, Mass., 1885; (A.M., Williams); m. 2d, Pauline Morton, Dec. 1916. In employ of Henry Russell, flour mcht., Albany, 1887-89; with Nat. Commercial Bank, Albany, 1889-91, Park Bank, Albany, 1891-98; cashier Albany City Nat. Bank, 1898-1902; v.p. Nat. Comml. Bank, 1902-07; pres. Nat. Copper Bank, New York, 1907-10; v.p. Mechanics and Metals Nat. Bank, 1910; v.p., 1910-15, pres., 1915-21, chmn. bd., 1921-29, vice chmn. bd., 1929, chmn. bd., 1930—; Guaranty Trust Co. of New York; dir. numerous companies; trustee The Mackay Cos. (dir.). Pres. Boys' Club. Episcopalian. Home: Southampton, L.I. Died Oct. 11, 1933.

SABIN, Dwight May, U.S. senator; b. Manlius, Ill., April 25, 1845; ed. Windham, Conn., 1860-64; settled in Minn.; mem. legislature, 1871-83; U.S. senator, 1883-89; was chmn. Senate Com. on Railroads, and mem. Com. on Indian Affairs; mem. Nat. Rep. Com., 1878-84, and its chmn., 1882-84; from 1890 engaged in railroading and lumbering. Home: Stillwater, Minn. Died 1902.

SABIN, Elbridge Hosmer, author; b. Middletown-point, N.J., Jan. 10, 1865; s. late Henry and Esther F. (Hotchkiss) S.; bro. of Edwin Legrand S.; A.B., State U. of Iowa, 1886; unmarried. Admitted to bar 1888. Member Troop C, 1st Texas Cavalry, Spanish-Am. War. Author: Early American History for Young Americans, 1904; Stella's Adventures in Starland, 1907; The Magical Man of Mirth, 1910; The Queen of the City of Mirth, 1911; Prince Trixie, 1913. Home: Chula Vista, Calif. Died Jan. 30, 1934.

SABIN, Henry, educator; b. Pomfret, Conn., Oct. 23, 1829; s. Noah and Betsey (Cleveland) S.; A.B., Amherst, 1852; (LL.D., Drake U., Cornell Coll., Ia., State U. of Ia.); m. Esther F. Hotchkiss, 1858; father of Elbridge Hosmer and Edwin Legrand S. Engaged in teaching in Conn., N.J., Ill. and later in Ia.; state supt. pub. instrn., Ia., 1888-92, 1894-98. Republican. Pres. State Teachers' Assn., 1878; pres. dept. superintendence, 1893, chmn. com. of 12 on rural schs., 1895, and now mem. Nat. Ednl. Council of N.E.A. Author: Talks to Young People, 1899; Common Sense Didactics, 1903. Home: La Jolla, Calif. Died Mar. 22, 1918.

SABIN, Wallace Arthur, organist; b. Northamptonshire, Eng., Dec. 15, 1869; s. James and Annie Eliza (Parsons) S.; grad. Royal Coll. Organists, London, 1890; m. Kathryn Wells Rader, Apr. 1, 1913. Organist Magdalen Coll. Sch., Brackley, Eng., 1882-86, St. George's Ch., Oxford, 1887-89, S.S. Mary and John, Oxford, 1889-93; asst. organist Queen's Coll., Oxford, 1886-93; organist and choir master All Saints Ch., Warwick, 1893-94; organist St. Luke's Ch., San Francisco, Calif., 1894-1906, Temple Emanuel, 1896—, 1st Ch. of Christ, Scientist, 1906—. Formerly dir. Vested Choir Assn. of San Francisco and vicinity, Saturday Morning Orchestra of Ladies, Twentieth Century Music Club, San Francisco Musical Club Chorus. Gave organ recitals St. Louis Expn., 1904; official organist San Francisco Expn., 1915; dir. Exposition Chorus, Loring Club (men's voices), Wednesday Morning Choral Club of Oakland (women's voices), also of Étude Club (Berkeley). Fellow Am. Guild of Organists, Royal College Organists. Republican. Wrote music for Bohemian Club plays, St. Patrick at Tara, 1909, and Twilight of the Kings, 1918. Home: Berkeley, Calif. Deceased.

SABINE, Wallace Clement, physicist; b. Richwood, O., June 13, 1868; s. Hylas and Anna (Ware) S.; A.B., Ohio State U., 1886; A.M., Harvard, 1888; (D.Sc., Brown U., 1907; D.S., Harvard, 1914); m. Jane Downs Kelly, Aug. 22, 1900. Asst. physics, 1889-90, instr., 1890-95, asst. prof., 1895-1905, prof., 1905—, and dean of Scientific Sch., Harvard. Prof. Agrée a l'Université de Paris, 1916-17. Mem. Nat. Acad. Sciences; corr. mem. A.I.A.; fellow Am. Acad. Arts and Sciences, A.A.A.S. Author: Architectural Acoustics. Home: Boston, Mass. Died Jan. 10, 1919.

SABINE, William Tufnell, bishop; b. New York, Oct. 16, 1838; s. Gustavus A. (M.D.) and Julia H. (Tufnell) S.; A.B., Columbia, 1859, A.M., 1862; grad. Gen. Theol. Sem., New York, 1862; (D.D., New York U., 1890); m. Maria Theresa Schieffelin, Oct. 6, 1868. Deacon, 1862, priest, 1863, P.E. Ch.; pastor Ch. of the Covenant, Phila., 1863-66; Ch. of the Atonement, New York; became connected with R.E. Ch., 1874; pastor First R.E. Ch., New York, 1874-1907; elected bishop of New York and Phila. Synod, May 1902. Died Aug. 10, 1913.

SACHS, Julius, university prof.; b. Baltimore, July 6, 1849; s. Joseph and Sophia (Baer) S.; A.B., Columbia, 1867, A.M., 1871; post-grad. univs. of Würzburg, Berlin, Göttingen, Rostock, Ph.D., 1871; Litt.D. from Columbia Univ., 1929; m. Rosa Goldman, June 23, 1874; children—Dora (Mrs. Benjamin Sommers), Ernest (clin. prof. surgery, Washington Univ., St. Louis). Prin. Boys' Prep. Sch., 1872-1904; prin. Sch. for Girls, 1891-1907; prof. secondary edn., 1902-17, and prof. emeritus since 1917, Teachers Coll. (Columbia). Pres. Schoolmasters' Assn. of New York, 1889, Am. Philol. Assn.; 1891, Assn. Colls. and Secondary Schs. of Middle States, Headmasters' Assn. of U.S., 1899, New York Soc. of Archæol. Inst. America, 1900-03. Home: New York, N.Y. Died Feb. 2, 1934.

SACHSE, Julius Friedrich, author; b. Philadelphia, Nov. 22, 1842; s. J. H. Friedrich and Julianna D. W. (Buehler) S.; ed. in grammar schs. and old Lutheran Acad.; (Litt.D., Muhlenberg Coll.); m. Emma Caroline Lange, May 15, 1864. Librarian and curator Grand Lodge F. & A. M. of Pa., 1906—. Author: Benjamin Franklin as a Freemason, 1906; Freemasonry in Pennsylvania, 1727-1907, 1908 and 1909; Old Masonic Lodges of Pennsylvania, 1730-1800, 2 vols., 1912; Quaint Old Germantown (with J. Richards), 1913; History of Masonic Knights Templar in Pennsylvania, 1797-1919. Home: Philadelphia, Pa. Died Nov. 14, 1919.

SACKETT, Frederic Moseley, Jr., lawyer; b. Providence, R.I., Dec. 17, 1868; s. Frederic M. and Emma L. (Paine) S.; A.B., Brown U., 1890; LL.B., Harvard U., 1893; Dr. Oec., H. C. Handelshoch Schuler, Berlin; Dr. Rer. pol. honoris causa, Tübingen, Germany; LL.D., University of Louisville, 1937; m. Olive Speed, Apr. 12, 1898. Practiced law at Columbus, O., 1893-97, Louisville, Ky., 1898-1907; pres. Louisville Gas Co., and Louisville Lighting Co., 1907-12; pres. Pioneer Coal Co., Black Star Coal Company; federal food adminstr. for Ky. by appmt. U.S. Food Adminstrn., 1917. Pres. Louisville Bd. of Trade, 1917 and 1922-23; dir. Louisville Branch of Federal Reserve Bank until Dec. 1924. U.S. senator from Ky. for term 1925-31; resigned to become A.E. and P. to Germany, 1930, resigned, May 1933; now in practice in association with Bruce & Bullitt, Louisville, Ky. Republican. Unitarian. Home: Louisville, Ky. Died May 18, 1941.

SACKETT, Henry Woodward, lawyer; b. Enfield, N.Y., Aug. 31, 1853; s. Dr. Solon P. and Lovedy K. (Woodward) S.; A.B. from Cornell U., 1875; m. Elizabeth Titus, 1886 (died 1926). Admitted to New York bar, 1877; while pursuing law studies became law writer and later editorial writer and counsel for New York Tribune; became associated with Cornelius A. Runkle, counsel for Tribune, 1884, and after his death, partner of Charles Gibson Bennett, as Sackett & Bennett, 1888-94; now sr. mem. Sackett, Chapman, Brown & Cross; dir., counsel New York Tribune, Inc. Was member Troop A. and Squadron A, in New York, prior to Jan. 1, 1897, when he became aide, with rank of col., on staff of Gov. Black; during Spanish-Am. War did recruiting service and also served as asst. paymaster gen. S.N.Y. Trustee Cornell U., 1899—; sec. and trustee of Hudson-Fulton Celebration Commn.; commr. of Fire Island State Reservation; trustee and v.p. Am. Scenic and Historic Preservation Soc.; chmn. Cornell U. Semi-Centennial Celebration Com. Lecturer on libel law, Sch. of Journalism of Columbia U.; spl. lecturer, Coll. of Law of Cornell U. Republican. Episcopalian (sr. warden St. Thomas's Ch., Mamaroneck, N.Y.). Author: The Law of Libel for Newspaper Men, etc. Home: New York, and Mamaroneck, N.Y. Died Dec. 9, 1929.

SACKETT, William Edgar, publicist; b. N.Y. City, May 23, 1848; s. William E. and Josephine (Findlay) S.; ed. Anthon Sch. and New York Free Acad.; studied law with Chester A. Arthur (later pres. U.S.), 1865-68; m. Edith Freeman, Nov. 4, 1869 (died 1895); m. 2d, Mrs. E. M. Gulick, June 20, 1900. In charge N.J. bur. New York Times, 1874-82; founder Sunday Morning News (later Jersey City Daily News), 1882; N.J. editor New York Herald, 1885-96; free lance corr. at Washington, D.C., New York Herald, Spanish-Am. War, 1898; sec. U.S. Industrial Commn., 1898-1900; epigram editor for Dem. Nat. Cōm., 1908. Democrat. Episcopalian. Author: Modern Battles of Trenton, 1895; Vol. 2, in series, covering N.J. history, 1865-1915, 1915; How Wilson Became President, 1919; Empirical Newark, 1919. Publicity editor, Assn. Opposed to Nat. Prohibition, in N.J. gubernatorial campaign, 1919; with editorial dept. New York Times, Jan. 1920—. Editor of New Jersey's First Citizens, 1917. Home: Newark, N.J. Died Nov. 18, 1926.

SADLER, Lena Kellogg, M.D.; b. Abscota, Mich., June 9, 1875; d. Smith Moses and Susan Maria (Dickinson) Kellogg; ed. high sch., Mattoon, Ill.; student Cooper Med. Coll., San Francisco, Calif.; M.D., Am. Med. Missionary Coll. (U. of Ill.), 1906; post-grad. study in Europe, 1928; m. William Samuel Sadler, M.D., Dec. 3, 1897; children—Willis Kellogg (dec.), William Samuel, Jr. Practiced at Chicago, 1906—; asso. dir. Chicago Inst. Research and Diagnosis; attending gynecologist Columbus Hosp.; attending surgeon Women's and Children's Hosp.; instr. mental hygiene, Presbyn. Coll. of Christian Edn.; state chmn. pub. health and child hygiene Ill. Fedn. of Women's Clubs, 1924-27, 1931-33; med. dir. N. Side Rest Home. Fellow Am. Coll. Surgeons, A.M.A. Republican. Protestant. Author: The Mother and Her Child (with husband), 1916; How to Reduce and How to Gain (with same), 1920; How to Feed the Baby, 1925; Piloting Modern Youth (with husband), 1931; Psychiatric Nursing (with husband), 1937; The Sex Life Before and After Marriage (with husband), 1938. Lecturer on hygiene. Home: Chicago, Ill. Died Aug. 8, 1939.

SADLER, Reinhold, gov. Nev.; b. Prussia, Jan. 10, 1848; has long resided in Nev.; elected lt. gov., 1895, on ticket with J. E. Jones for gov. On latter's death, Apr. 10, 1896, succeeded to governorship; elected for 2d term, 1898-1903. Formerly Democrat; now Silver Party man. Married. Home: Carson City, Nev. Died 1906.

SADLER, Sylvester Baker, judge, author; b. Carlisle, Pa., Sept. 29, 1876; s. Wilbur Fisk and Sarah Ellen (Sterrett) S.; A.B., Yale, 1896; LL.B. and M.A., Dickinson, 1898, LL.D., 1920; unmarried. Began practice at Carlisle, 1898; pres. judge 9th Jud. Dist. of Pa., 1916-20; justice Supreme Court of Pa., term Jan. 1921-Jan. 1942. Republican. Presbyn. Author: Pennsylvania Criminal Procedure, 1903. Editor: Pennsylvania Supreme Court Cases, 1835-1889 (10 vols.), 1904. Home: Carlisle, Pa. Died Mar. 1, 1931.

SADLER, Wilbur Fisk, judge; b. Adams Co., Pa., Oct. 14, 1840; s. of Joshua and Harriet (Stehley) S.; ed. Centreville Acad., 1856-59; grad. Dickinson Sem., Williamsport, Pa., 1863; admitted to bar, Aug. 1864; began practice Carlisle, Pa.; m. Sarah E. Sterrett, Jan. 5, 1871 (dec.). Dist. atty. Cumberland Co., Pa., 1871; pres. judge 9th Jud. Dist. of Pa., 1884-94, and from 1904; present term expires 1914. Republican. Home: Carlisle, Pa. Died Nov. 11, 1916.

SADTLER, Samuel Philip, chemist; b. Pine Grove, Pa., July 18, 1847; s. Rev. Benjamin and Caroline (Schmucker) S.; A.B., Pa. Coll., 1867; Lehigh U., 1867-68; S.B., Harvard U., 1870; Ph.D., U. of Göttingen, 1871; (LL.D., Pa. Coll., 1902; Phi Beta Kappa); m. M. Julia Bridges, Dec. 17, 1872. Prof. natural science, Pa. Coll., 1871-74; prof. chemistry, Univ. of Pa., 1874-91, Phila. Coll. of Pharmacy, 1878-1916; consulting chem. expert. Fellow A.A.A.S. Author: Handbook of Chemical Experimentation for Lecturers, 1877; Handbook of Industrial Organic Chemistry, 5th edit., 1923 (also of German and Russian translations); Text-book of Pharmaceutical Chemistry (with Virgil Coblentz), 5th edit., 1917. Chem. editor 15th to 20th edits. of U.S. Dispensatory and mem. Com. of Revision of the U.S. Pharmacopœia, 1900-10, 1910-20. Home: Philadelphia, Pa. Died Dec. 20, 1923.

SAENGER, Oscar, vocal teacher; b. Brooklyn, N.Y., Jan. 5, 1868; s. S. Karl and Louise S.; grad. Brooklyn High Sch.; studied music and violin; later studied voice for 4 yrs. at Nat. Conservatory of Music, under Jacques Bouhy, and acting under Frederic Robinson; m. Charlotte Welles, Oct. 5, 1892. Began singing in concerts at age of 7; prof. vocal teaching Nat. Conservatory of Music, 1888-97; début in Grand Opera, with Am. Opera Co., 1891, singing leading baritone rôles; made tour of Germany and Austria; gave up concert work, 1892; engaged as teacher of voice, 1892—; inventor Oscar Saenger Vocal Training Records, Victor Co.; propr. Oscar Saenger Summer Sch., Chicago, Ill., and Oscar Saenger Studios, New York. Address: New York, N.Y. Died Apr. 20, 1929.

SAFFORD, Agnes Mabel, educator; b. Portland, Me.; d. Charles Forrester and Harriet (Moses) S.; ed. Emerson Coll., Boston, Mass.; unmarried. Teacher of English, Westbrook Sem., 1900-11, dean of girls, 1912-15; dean of girls and teacher of English, Goddard Sem., Barre, Vt., 1915-20; same, Westbrook Sem., Portland, 1920-25, prin., 1925—. Universalist. Home: Portland, Me. Died June 30, 1932.

SAFFORD, James Merrill, educator; b. Zanesville, O., Aug. 13, 1822; s. Harry and Patience (Van Horne) S.; grad. Ohio University, 1844; (Ph.D., A.M., Yale, 1866; M.D., Univ. of Nashville, 1872); m. Mrs. C. K. Owen, née Howard, 1859. Prof. natural science, Cumberland Univ., Lebanon, Tenn., 1848-72; prof. chemistry, med. dept., Univ. of Nashville and Vanderbilt Univ. (these depts. being united, 1894), 1874-94; prof. natural sciences, Vanderbilt Univ., 1875-1900; emeritus prof. geology. State geologist, Tenn., 1854-60 and 1871-1900. Over 30 yrs. mem. Tenn. State Bd. Health; mem. Geol. Soc. America. Presbyn. Author: Geological Reconnaissance of Tennessee, 1856; Geology of Tennessee (with map), 1869; Elements of the Geology of Tennessee, 1900. Home: Dallas, Tex. Died 1907.

SAFFORD, Truman Henry, Field Memorial prof. astronomy, Williams Coll., 1876—; b. Royalton, Vt., Jan. 6, 1836; grad. Harvard, 1854; (Ph.D., Williams, 1878); m. Elizabeth Marshall Bradbury, Mar. 8, 1860. Astronomer and mathematician; prof. astronomy, Univ. of Chicago, 1866-76. Author: Mathematical Teaching and Its Modern Methods. Fellow Am. Acad. Arts and Sciences; Asso. Royal Astron. Soc. of England; A.A.A.S. Home: Williamstown, Mass. Died 1901.

SAFFORD, William Edwin, botanist; b. Chillicothe, O., Dec. 14, 1859; s. Judge William Harrison and Pocahontas (Creel) S.; grad. U.S. Naval Acad., 1880; post-grad. studies, botany and zoölogy, Yale, 1883-85; marine zoölogy, Harvard, 1885; Ph.D., George Washington U., 1920; m. Clare, d. late Chief Justice Decius S. Wade, of Mont., Sept. 14, 1904; children—Decius Wade, Bernice Galpin. Served in U.S.N., 1880-1902; served in Spanish-Am. War, collecting for U.S. Nat. Mus. in the depts. of ethnology and ethnobotany, resigned Aug. 1, 1902, while on active duty in the Library and Naval War Records Office, Navy Dept.; asst. botanist, 1902-15, economic botanist, Apr. 1915—, Dept. Agriculture. Commr. to Peru and Bolivia, 1891-92, for Chicago Expn. (medal, 1893); v.gov. Island of Guam, 1899-1900; exec. officer U.S. receiving ship Independence, 1900-01; Smithsonian Instn., 1901-02. Author: A Year on the Island of Guam, 1902-04; Useful Plants of the Island of Guam, 1905; The Chamorro Language of the Island of Guam, 1905; Cactaceæ of Northeastern and Central Mexico, 1909; the classification of the genus Annona with descriptions of new and imperfectly known species, 1913; An Aztec Narcotic, 1915; Lignum nephriticum, 1916; Narcotics and Stimulants of the Ancient Americans; Chenopodium nuttaliæ, a food-plant of the Aztecs, 1918; Cosmos sulphureus, the Xochipalli, or Flower-paint of the Aztecs, 1918; Notes on the genus Dahlia, with descriptions of two new species from Guatemala, 1919; Natural History of Paradise Key and the nearby Everglades of Florida, 1919; Synopsis of the Genus Datura; Datura, an Inviting Genus for the Study of Heredity, 1921; Peyote, the narcotic Mescal Button of the Indians, 1921; Daturas of the Old World and New, 1922; Ant Acacias and Acacia Ants of Mexico and Central America, 1923; The Potato of Romance and of Reality, 1925. Home: Washington, D.C. Died Jan. 10, 1926.

SAGE, Eben Charles, educational dir.; b. Virden, Ill., Nov. 14, 1855; s. Charles Truman and Sophia Elizabeth (Gunnison) S.; A.B., Shurtleff Coll., 1878, D.D., 1897; B.D., Union Theol. Sem., 1882; Ph.D., Yale, 1890; m. Nora Amanda Cowen, Oct. 7, 1879; children—Mrs. Nora A. Dibble, Eben B., T. Bartlett. Ordained Bapt. ministry, 1882; pastor Geneseo, Ill., 1881-82, Urbana, 1883-86, Grand Av. Ch., New Haven, Conn., 1887-97, Hope Ch., New Haven, 1897-1902, First Ch., New Haven, 1902-04; asst. sec. Gen. Edn. Bd., 1904-19, then asst. dir. coll. and univ. edn. of Gen. Edn. Bd. Was associated with late Dr. William R. Harper (pres. U. of Chicago) in ednl. work; for many yrs. sec. Conn. Bapt. Edn. Soc.; pres. N.Y. State Colonization Soc.; trustee Suffield Acad., Conn. Home: East Haven, Conn. Died Oct. 4, 1927.

SAGE, Evan Taylor, prof. Latin; b. Sutton, Neb., May 16, 1881; s. Legene Selvy and Lillian Ophelia (Evans) S.; A.B., U. of Neb., 1902; A.M., U. of Chicago, 1904; Ph.D., U. of Chicago, 1908; fellow in Europe, 1906-07; m. Sophie Miriam Shanks, Aug. 25, 1909; children—Robert Legene, Evan Taylor. Instr. Latin and Greek, U. of Ida., 1907-11, U. of Wash., 1911-13, U. of Pittsburgh, summer 1910, 1913-14; asst. prof. Latin, U. of Pittsburgh, 1914-19, prof. and head of dept. of Latin, 1919-33, prof. of Latin and head dept. of Classics, 1933—; visiting prof. Latin, summers, U. of Colo., 1924, U. of Wash., 1927. With U.S. Air Service, 1917-19; now Adjt. Gen.'s Dept., O.R.C. Episcopalian. Author: Petronius, the Satiricon, 1929. Home: Pittsburgh, Pa. Died May 30, 1936.

SAGE, John Charles, bishop; b. Cleveland, Sept. 12, 1866; s. Jacob and Catharine (Evans) S.; pub. schs.; student Western Theol. Sem., Chicago, 1891; m. Harriet Louise Murphy, Sept. 1, 1891. Deacon, 1891, priest, 1893, P.E. Ch.; missionary Willoughby and Toledo, O., 1891-93; priest in charge St. Michael's and All Angels chs., Berwyn, Ill., 1893-96; rector St. Luke's Ch., Dixon, Ill., 1896-1902, St. John's Ch., Dubuque, Ia., 1902-11, St. John's Ch., Keokuk, Ia., 1911-18; elected missionary bishop of Diocese of Salina (Kan.), by House of Bishops, Oct. 19, 1917; consecrated as bishop, Jan. 1918. Editor the Iowa Churchman, 1903-13; mng. editor The Witness, 1917—; deputy to Gen. Conv. P.E. Ch., 1904, 07, 16. Died Oct. 3, 1919.

SAGE, John Davis, life ins.; b. Hartford, Conn., Sept. 14, 1877; s. Adoniram Judson and Eliza Given (Snowden) S.; prep. edn., Woodward High Sch. and Franklin Prep. Sch., Cincinnati; A.B., Brown U., 1899; m. Carmen Blow, Nov. 28, 1914; children—John Snowden, Barbara, Randolph Taylor, Sylvia. With Union Central Life Ins. Co., Cincinnati, 1899—, successively clk. in home office, editor of publs., asst. sec., sec., 3d, 2d, and 1st v.p., and pres., 1921—; dir. First Nat. Bank, Cincinnati Equitable Fire Ins. Co. Mem. Home Guard, World War; chmn. Cincinnati Community Chest, 1925. Trustee Brown U. Republican. Baptist. Home: Cincinnati, O. Died Dec. 4, 1928.

SAGE, John Hall, banker; b. Portland, Conn., Apr. 20, 1847; s. Charles Henry and Eliza (Hall) S.; ed. common and high schs., Portland and Bridgeport, Conn.; (hon. M.S., Trinity, 1901); m. Agnes Farwell Kellogg, Sept. 16, 1880. Engaged in banking business at Portland, 1873—. Fellow Am. Ornithologists' Union (sec., 1889-1917 and pres., 1917-20), and A.A.A.S. Author: Memorials and Other Gifts in Trinity Church, Portland, Conn., 1910; (with Dr. L. B. Bishop) The Birds of Connecticut, 1913. Trustee Berkeley Div. Sch. Home: Portland, Conn. Died Aug. 16, 1925.

SAGE, Russell, capitalist; b. Verona Tp., Oneida Co., N.Y., Aug. 4, 1816; s. Elisha and Prudence Risley S.; m. Margaret Olivia Slocum, of Syracuse, N.Y., Nov. 24, 1869. Brought up on farm; attended school winters; began business life as errand boy in his brother's grocery store at Troy; later clerk, salesman; retail grocer, 1837-39; wholesale grocer, 1837-57, at Troy. Alderman, 1847; later treas., Rensselaer Co.; mem. Congress, 1853-57, as Whig. Became interested in rys.; removed to New York, 1863, and engaged in buying and selling "privileges" in Wall St.; became large operator in ry. and other securities. Pres. and dir. Poughkeepsie & Eastern Ry. Co., Empire & Bay State Telegraph Co.; v.p., treas. and dir. Albia & Centerville Ry. Co.; dir. numerous railroads, telegraph companies, etc. Home: New York, N.Y. Died 1906.

SAGE, Mrs. Russell (Margaret Olivia Slocum Sage), philanthropist; b. Syracuse, N.Y., Sept. 8, 1828; d. Joseph and Margaret Pierson (Jermain) Slocum; grad. Troy Female Sem., 1847; (hon. degree Mistress of Letters, New York U., 1904); m. Russell Sage, Nov. 24, 1869 (died 1906). Founder Emma Willard Assn.; mem. Mayflower Descendants, Colonial Dames. Presbyterian. During 1907 gave $1,000,000 to Emma Willard Sem., Troy, N.Y.; $1,000,000 to Rensselaer Poly. Inst.; $115,000 to a pub. school at Sag Harbor, L.I.; $10,000,000 to be known as the Sage Foundation, for social betterment; $350,000 to Y.M.C.A., New York; $150,000 to Am. Seaman's Friend Soc., $150,000 to Northfield (Mass.) Sem.; $300,000 to Sage Inst. of Pathology of City Hosp., on Blackwell's Island; $250,000 to a home for indigent women; $100,000 to Syracuse U.; also various other donations; acquired ownership of Marsh Island in Gulf of Mexico and dedicated same as home for wild birds, 1912. Founded Russell Sage College of Practical Arts, Troy, N.Y., opened, 1916. Home: New York, N.Y. Died Nov. 4, 1918.

SAGE, William Hampden, army officer; b. in N.Y., Apr. 6, 1859; grad. U.S. Mil. Acad., 1882; Army War Coll., 1907. Commd. 2d lt. 5th Inf., June 13, 1882; promoted through grades to col. 12th Inf., Feb. 7, 1915; temporary maj. gen. N.G., Aug. 5, 1917. Prof. mil. science and tactics, Central U. of Ky., Richmond, Ky., 1892-93; garrison duty in Tex., 1894-98; a.d.c. to Gen. Ovenshine, in Philippine Islands, 1898; served as adj. gen. 1st and 2d brigades, 1st Div., 8th Army Corps; adj. gen. 3d Dist., Minanao and Jolo; duty at Malabang, P.I., 1903; duty at War Coll., Washington, D.C., 1906-07; adj. gen. Dept. of Columbia, 1907; duty on Mexican border, 1916-17; comdr. Camp Shelby, Hattiesburg, Miss., Sept. 1917-Mar. 1918; served with A.E.F. Medal of honor for action at Zapote River, P.I., June 13, 1899. Died June 4, 1922.

SAGEBEER, Joseph Evans, lawyer; b. Allentown, Pa., Apr. 4, 1861; s. Joseph Lybrand and Harriet (Keen) S.; A.B., Bucknell U., 1885; grad. Crozer Theol. Sem., 1888; Ph.D., U. of Pa., 1891; m. Catharine G. C. Cook, June 15, 1898; children—Richard Grafflin, Catherine Cook. Admitted to Pa. bar, 1900, began practice, Phila.; counsel Am. Bapt. Publ. Soc. Republican. Author: The Bible in Court—The Method of Legal Inquiry Applied to the Study of the Scriptures. Home: Berwyn, Pa. Died Dec. 18, 1940.

SAHLER, Charles Oliver, physician, surgeon; b. Ulster Park, N.Y., June 23, 1854; s. Solomon and Caroline (Winfield) S.; ed. common schs.; M.D., Coll. Phys. and Surg. (Columbia), 1878; m. Jennie Sahler, Apr. 20, 1880; 2d, Charlotte Atkins, Dec. 29, 1913. Founder, pres. and dir. of The Dr. C. O. Sahler Sanitarium, Kingston, N.Y. Mason. Author: Psychic Life and Laws. Home: Kingston-on-Hudson, N.Y. Died Sept. 17, 1917.

SAILER, Joseph, M.D.; b. Philadelphia, Oct. 1, 1867; s. John and Emily (Woodward) S.; Ph.B., U. of Pa., 1886, M.D., 1891; post-grad. studies in medicine, Paris, Zurich and Vienna, 1893-95; m. Mary Lowber Strawbridge, Feb. 5, 1901; children—Emily Woodward (dec.), Alice Welsh, Mary Lowber, Joseph, John, Priscilla Sparks, Elizabeth Wells, Albin Perington, Anne West (dec.). Practiced, Phila., 1891—; prof. diseases of the stomach and intestines, Phila. Polyclinic, 1902-09; demonstrator of pathology, 1899, instructor in clin. medicine, asso., asst. prof. and prof., U. of Pa., 1900—. Passed asst. surgeon U.S.N., 1898. Dir. Phila. Soc. for Organizing Charity; mgr. Babies' Hosp.; physician to Presbyn., University, and Phila. General hosps. In service during war as maj. and later lt. col. M.C., at Camp Wheeler as chief of med. service, Base Hosp., and at Vichy, France, as consultant in internal medicine, to the hosp. center. Fellow College Physicians of Phila. Home: Philadelphia, Pa. Died Dec. 31, 1928.

SAINT GAUDENS, Augustus, sculptor; b. Dublin, Ireland, Mar. 1, 1848; s. Bernard Paul Ernest S.; came to U.S. in infancy; learned trade of cameo cutter; studied drawing at Cooper Inst., 1861; student at Nat. Acad. Design, 1865-66; (hon. LL.D., Harvard; L.H.D., Princeton); at École des Beaux Arts, Paris, 1867-70; m. Augusta F. Homer, 1877. In Rome, 1870-72, producing there, 1871, his 1st figure, "Hiawatha"; settled in New York, 1872. Among his works are "Adoration of the Cross" (in St. Thomas Ch., New York), "The Puritan," "Diana" (on tower of Madison Square Garden, New York); statues of Abraham Lincoln and John A. Logan, Chicago; Admiral Farragut, New York; Peter Cooper, New York; Col. R. G. Shaw, Boston; monument to Gen. Sherman, New York. Corr. mem. Inst. of France; officer of the Legion of Honor. Received medal of honor, Paris, 1900; spl. medal of honor, Buffalo, 1901. Home: Windsor, Vt. Died 1907.

SAINT GAUDENS, Louis, sculptor; b. New York, Jan. 8, 1854; s. Barnard Paul Ernest S.; bro. of late Augustus S.; studied École des Beaux Arts, Paris, France, 1879-80. Assisted brother in numerous works. Home: Windsor, Vt. Died Mar. 8, 1913.

SAITO, Hirosi, Japanese ambassador; b. Gifu, Japan, Dec. 24, 1886; s. Shozaburo and Tsuruko (Kumamoto) S.; student Peers Coll., 1904-07, Tokyo Imperial U., 1907-10; Dr. of Humane Relations, Bates Coll., 1937; m. Miyoko Nagayo, Feb. 1918; 2 daughters, Sakiko, Masako. Attaché embassy, Washington, 1911, 3d sec., 1911-17; 3d and 2d sec. embassy, London, 1918-21; consul, Seattle, Wash., 1921-23; consul gen., N.Y. City, 1923-28; chief bur. information, Foreign Office, Tokyo, 1929-30; counselor embassy, London, 1931-32; charge d'affaires, embassy, Washington, 1932; minister, The Hague, 1933; ambassador to U.S., Washington, 1934—. Mem. Japanese delegation, Peace Conf., Paris, 1919, 1st Assembly League of Nations, 1920, Washington Naval Conf., 1921-22, London Naval Conf., 1930, Disarmament Conf., Geneva, 1931-33, Assembly League of Nations, Geneva, 1931-33, Econ. Conf., London, 1933. Decorated Order of Sacred Treasure, 2d class (Japan); Grand Cross of Order of Orange Nassau (Netherlands). Author: Life of Ramsey MacDonald, 1931; Japan's Policies and Purposes, 1935. Home: Tokyo, Japan. Died Feb. 26, 1939.

SAJOUS, Charles Euchariste de' Medici, M.D., author; b. at sea, near coast of France, Dec. 13, 1852; s. Count Charles E. and Marie Pierrette (Curt) de' Medici; ed. by pvt. tutors; M.D., Jefferson Med. Coll., Phila., 1878; LL.D., St. Joseph Coll., Phila., 1909; Sc.D., Temple U., 1915; m. Emma Christine Bergner, Jan. 30, 1884; 1 son, Louis Theodore de' Medici. Clin. lecturer Jefferson Med. Coll., 1881-90; dean and prof. laryngology, Medico Chirurg. Coll., 1897-98; prof. anatomy and physiology, Wagner Inst. of Science, 1880-82; prof. therapeutics, Medical Dept., Temple U., Phila., 1909-22; prof. endocrinology, U. of Pa., 1921—. Editor New York Medical Journal, 1911-19. Fellow Coll. of Physicians, Phila., Am. Coll. Physicians, and mem. of 22 scientific bodies; pres. Am. Assn. Study of Internal Secretions,

1917-18, Am. Therapeutic Soc., 1919-20. Lt. col. State Fencibles M.C., World War. Officer of the Acad. and Officer Legion of Honor, France; Knight Order Leopold, Belgium; gold medallist, 1922. Author: Curative Treatment of Hay Fever, 1884; Diseases of the Nose and Throat, 1885. Editor: Sajous' Analytical Cyclopædia of Practical Medicine (8 vols. and 10 edits.), 1898-1925, Sajous' Annual of the Universal Medical Sciences (5 vols. annually), 1888-96 (45 vols.); The Internal Secretions and the Principles of Medicine (2 vols.), 1903-22 (10 edits.); Strength of Religion as Shown by Science, 1926. Home: Philadelphia, Pa. Died Apr. 27, 1929.

SALE, Charles Partlow ("Chic"), actor; b. Huron, S.D., 1885; s. Frank Orvil (M.D.) and Lillie Belle (Partlow) S.; ed. pub. schs., Urbana, Ill.; m. Marie Bishop, Mar. 12, 1912; children—Cherry Virginia, Charles Bishop and Mary Clare (twins), Dwight Bishop. Character actor in vaudeville, 1908—; now starring in talking motion pictures; has appeared in "The Star Witness," "The Expert," "When a Fellow Needs a Friend," etc. Advertising writer. Republican. Mason. Author and pub. of the Specialist; I'll Tell You Why. Home: Beverly Hills, Calif. Died Nov. 7, 1936.

SALE, George, clergyman, educator; b. Toronto, Can., Sept. 13, 1856; s. Julian and Mary Ann (Tomlin) S.; A.B. (with silver medal in philosophy), U. of Toronto, 1884; studied Toronto Bapt. Coll. and theol. sem. of McMaster U.; (hon. A.M., Mercer Univ., Ga., 1895; D.D., Acadia Coll., N.B., 1906); m. Clara Beatrice Goble, of Goble's, Ont., Apr. 4, 1889. Ordained Bapt. ministry, 1889; pres. Atlanta Bapt. Coll., 1890-1906; supt. edn. Bapt. Home Missionary Soc. of New York, with schs. in Southern states, Okla., Mex., Cuba and P.R., May 1906—. Mem. Commn. of U.S.A. to Republic of Liberia, 1909. Home: Atlanta, Ga. Died 19—.

SALE, Samuel, rabbi; b. Louisville, Ky., Oct. 29, 1854; s. Isaac and Henrietta Sale; A.B., Univ. of Louisville, 1872; Univ. of Berlin and Rabbinical Seminary of Berlin, 1873-78; hon. D.H.L., Hebrew Union Coll., 1933; m. Rachel Goldenberg, Jan. 12, 1881 (died 1930). Rabbi of Har Sinai Congregation, Baltimore, 1878-83, Congregation Anshe Maarab, Chicago, 1883-87, Congregation Shaare Emeth ("Gates of Truth"), St. Louis, 1887-1918, rabbi emeritus, Jan. 1, 1919—. Has officiated as chaplain at all Nat. polit. convs. held in St. Louis during residence there. Home: St. Louis, Mo. Died May 19, 1937.

SALINGER, Benjamin I., judge; b. Wronke, Germany, May 14, 1861; s. Louis and Rosalie (Slimmer) S.; brought to America, 1872; ed. pub. schs. and 3 mos. at Cornell Coll., Mt. Vernon, Ia.; m. Lucy M. Boylan, June 5, 1881. Admitted to Ia. bar, 1882; practiced in Carroll Co. 32 yrs.; reporter Supreme Ct. of Ia. 8 yrs.; judge Supreme Ct. (nonpartisan selection), term 1915-21; apptd. spl. asst. to the atty. gen. in cases under the Sherman Act. Republican. Mason. Editor of Iowa Reports, vols. 90 to 117. Home: Carroll, Ia. Died July 10, 1931.

SALISBURY, Albert, normal sch. pres.; b. Lima, Wis., Jan. 24, 1843; s. Oliver and Emily (Cravath) S.; pvt. 13th Wis. Inf., 1863-65; A.B., Milton Coll., Wis., 1870, A.M., 1872, Ph.D., 1888; m. Abba A. Maxson, Nov. 20, 1866 (died 1881); m. 2d, Agnes Hosford, Aug. 28, 1883. Conductor of institutes for the Whitewater Normal Sch., 1873-82; supt. of schs. for Am. Missionary Assn. in the South and West, 1882-85; pres. State Normal Sch., Whitewater, Wis., 1885—. Author: Theory of Teaching and Elementary Psychology, 1905; School Management, 1911. Home: Whitewater, Wis. Died 1911.

SALISBURY, James Henry, physician; b. Scott, N.Y., Oct. 13, 1823; s. Nathan and Lucretia (Babcock) S.; grad. (B.N.S.) Polytechnic Inst., Troy, N.Y., 1846; grad. Albany Med. Coll., 1850 (A.M., 1852; LL.D., 1887, Union Coll.; LL.D., Amity Coll., Ind.); m. Clara Brasee. Asst. chemist, 1846-48; prin. chemist, 1849-52, N.Y. State Geol. Survey; lecturer on elementary and applied chemistry, N.Y. State Normal School, Albany, 1851-52. Conducted micros. investigations, which were published in Trans. A.A.A.S.; later devoted himself as specialist to the causes and treatment of chronic diseases, publishing his therapeutical discoveries in New York Jour. of Medicine. Practiced in Cleveland some yrs., later in New York. Author: Anatomy and Histology of Plants, 1848 (gold medal, essay Young Men's Assn., Albany); The Chemical and Physiological Examination of the Maize Plant, 1849 (prize essay, N.Y. Agrl. Soc.); Alimentation and Disease, 1886. Home: Dobbs' Ferry, N.Y. Died 1905.

SALISBURY, Rollin D., university dean; b. Spring Prairie, Wis., Aug. 17, 1858; s. Daniel and Lucinda (Bryant) S.; Ph.B., Beloit Coll., 1881, A.M., 1884 (LL.D., 1904). Instr. geology and biology, 1883-84, prof. geology, 1884-91, Beloit Coll.; student in Europe (chiefly at Heidelberg), 1887-88; prof. general and geographic geology, U. of Wis., 1891-92; prof. geographic geology, 1892—, dean of Univ. Colls., 1894-96, dean of Ogden (grad.) Sch. of Science, 1899—, head of dept. of geography, 1903-19, head of dept. of geology, 1919—, U. of Chicago. U.S. geologist, glacial div., 1882-94, geologist, 1894—, geologist in charge of Pleistocene geology of N.J., 1891-1915. Fellow Geol. Soc. America, Assn. Am. Geographers, A.A.A.S., Ill. Acad. Sciences. Died Aug. 15, 1922.

SALLMON, William Henry, educator; b. London, Ont., Sept. 6, 1866; s. Christopher and Mary (McMurdoch) S.; A.B., Yale, 1894, A.M., 1897; (D.D., Chicago Theol. Sem., 1904); m. Alice Bussey Trubee, Feb. 17, 1903. Ordained Congl. ministry, 1897; traveled in Australasia, Egypt, Palestine, and Southeastern Europe, 1897-1900; pastor South Ch., Bridgeport, Conn., 1902; pres. Carleton Coll., 1903-08; visited Yale Mission Coll. in China, and completed second tour of the world, 1908; asst. prof., sec. bur. of appmts., Yale U., 1908—; exec. sec., treas. Yale Mission Coll. in China, 1909—. Author: Studies in the Life of Jesus; Studies in the Parables and Miracles of Jesus; Studies in the Life of Paul; Among Australasian Students; Systematic and Proportionate Giving. Editor: The Culture of Christian Manhood; The Hymnal of Praise. Died Feb. 14, 1938.

SALMON, Daniel Elmer, veterinarian; b. Mt. Olive, N.J., July 23, 1850; s. Daniel Landon and Eleanor (Flock) S.; D.V.S., Cornell, 1872, D.V.M., 1876; m. Mary Thompson Corning, Oct. 17, 1872 (died 1902); m. 2d, Agnes Christina Dewhurst, Nov. 15, 1904. Connected with U.S. Dept. of Agr. as investigator, 1879-84, as chief Bur. Animal Industry, 1884-1906; dir. Nat. Veterinary School, Montevideo, 1906-12. Fellow A.A.A.S.; pres. U.S. Vet. Med. Assn., 1898; hon. asso. Royal Coll. Vet. Surgeons of Great Britain; hon. mem. Royal Agrl. Soc. of Eng., Epidemiol. Soc. of London; foreign asso. Société Centrale de Médicine Vétérinaire of France, etc. Home: Washington, D.C. Died Aug. 30, 1914.

SALMON, Joshua S., congressman (4th N.J. dist.); b. Schooley's Mt., Morris Co., N.J., Feb. 2, 1846; grad. Union Univ., law dept., 1873; m. Deborah Virginia Emmons, Oct. 13, 1869; 2d, Mrs. Emma L. (Mains) Richards, April 19, 1893. Admitted N.Y. bar, 1873; as atty., 1875, and later counsellor, N.J. bar; to bar of U.S. Supreme Court, 1894; mem. legislature, 1878; counsel for Morris Co. bd. of freeholders, 1880-93, and for numerous townships during most of time since admitted to bar; prosecutor of pleas, Morris Co., 1893-98; mem. 56th and 57th Congresses, 1899-1903. Democrat. Home: Boonton, N.J. Died 1902.

SALMON, Lucy Maynard, college prof.; b. Fulton, N.Y., 1853; d. George and Maria Clara (Maynard) S.; ed. Falley Sem., 1868-70; A.B., U. of Mich., 1876, A.M., 1883; fellow in history, Bryn Mawr Coll., 1886-87; student Paris and Florence, 1898-1900; L.H.D., Colgate U., 1912. Prin. McGregor (Ia.) High Sch., 1876-81; teacher of history, Ind. State Normal Sch., 1883-86; asso. prof., 1887-89, prof. hist., 1889—, Vassar Coll. Author: History of the Appointing Power of the President, 1885; Domestic Service (hist. and statis. study), 1897; Progress in the Household, 1906; The Newspaper and the Historian, The Newspaper and Authority (companion vols.), 1923. Home: Poughkeepsie, N.Y. Died Feb. 14, 1927.

SALMON, Thomas William, M.D.; b. Lansingburg, N.Y., Jan. 6, 1876; s. Thomas H. (M.D.) and Annie E. (Frost) S.; M.D., Albany Med. Coll., 1899; m. Helen Potter Ashley, Dec. 21, 1899; children—Thomas K., Edwin A., Richard, Russell G., Helen E., Barbara. Pvt. practice and Willard (N.Y.) State Hospital, 1899-1903; commd. asst. surgeon U.S. Marine Hosp. Service (now U.S. Pub. Health Service), Oct. 29, 1903; passed assistant surgeon, 1908, resigned Jan. 1, 1915; chmn. N.Y. State Bd. Alienists, 1911; med. dir. Nat. Com. for Mental Hygiene, 1915-21; staff Rockefeller Foundation, 1915-21; prof. psychiatry, Columbia U., 1921—; cons. psychiatrist, Presbyn. Hosp., 1922—. Maj., lt. col. and col., M.C. U.S.A., 1917-19; brig. gen. M.R.C.; sr. consultant in neuro-psychiatry, A.E.F. Awarded D.S.M. Mem. Permanent Inter-Allied Com. After-Care Disabled Soldiers; mem. Internat. Jury of Award, Panama-P.I. Expn. Author of chapter on "Immigration," in Modern Treatment of Mental and Nervous Diseases, 1913; chapter on "Mental Hygiene," Am. Year Book, 1917-20, and in Preventive Medicine and Hygiene, 1916-20; etc. Home: Larchmont, N.Y. Died Aug. 13, 1927.

SALMON, William Charles, congressman; b. Henry Co., Tenn., Apr. 3, 1868; s. Robert Henry and Sarah Elizabeth (Thomas) S.; L.I., Edgewood Normal Coll., Dickson Co., Tenn., 1890; student Dickson Coll., 1892, Valparaiso U., 1893; LL.B., Cumberland U., Lebanon, Tenn., 1897; m. Margaret M. Green, Dec. 7, 1905. Teacher and supt. pub. schs. until 1896; admitted to Tenn. bar, 1897, and practiced at Columbia; dir. Maury Nat. Bank (Columbia), Washington Mfg. Co. (Nashville). Pres. Bd. of Edn., Columbia, 1912, 22; spl. judge 11th Jud. Circuit, 1908; mem. 68th Congress (1923-25), 7th Tenn. Dist. Democrat. Mem. Christian (Disciples) Ch. Mason, Odd Fellow, Elk. Home: Columbia, Tenn. Died May 13, 1925.

SALMON, Wilmer Wesley, mfr.; b. Townsend, Del., Dec. 4, 1866; s. Daniel and Anna Maria (Hess) S.; A.B., Dickinson Coll., Carlisle, Pa., 1886, A.M., 1890; m. Belle C. Klink. With engr. corps, Pa. R.R., 1886, Phila. & Reading R.R., 1887-88; div. engr. Atlantic City R.R., 1889-90; asst. engr. C.&N.W. Ry., Chicago, 1890-92; with Hall Signal Co., 1893-1901, as engr., western agt., gen. agt. and v.p., representing the company in Europe, 3 yrs.; pres. Taylor Signal Co., Buffalo, 1901-04, Gen. Ry. Signal Co., Rochester, 1904—. Republican. Methodist. Home: Mamaroneck, N.Y. Died Jan. 23, 1936.

SALSBURY, Lant King, corp. officer; b. Saline, Mich., Mar. 11, 1867; s. George L. and Corintha (Edwards) S.; student Albion (Mich.) Coll., 1886-88; U. of Mich., 1889-90; m. Gertrude Shanks, Nov. 10, 1890 (dec.); 1 dau., Helen (wife of Dr. Shields Abernathy); m. 2d, Mrs. Margaret C. Graves. Originator of various companies in England; became pres. Sal-Mar Oil Corp., L. K. Salsbury & Co.; officer and dir. Ark. Timber Co.; etc. Democrat. Methodist. Mason. Home: Memphis, Tenn. Died July 12, 1938.

SALTER, Mary Turner, composer; b. Peoria, Ill., Mar. 15, 1856; d. Jonathan and Mary E. (Hinds) Turner; ed high sch., Burlington, Iowa; studied music, Coll. of Music, Boston, and with Mme. Erminia Rudersdorff; m. Sumner Salter, May 26, 1881; children—Edward Winthrop, Harold, Edith Marie, William Frost. Oratorio, concert and ch. singer, 1876-92; dramatic soprano, appearing with choral orgns. in Boston, New York, Chicago, etc., and soprano various chs., including St. Paul's, Boston, Broadway Tabernacle, New York, Trinity P.E. Ch., New Haven, and St. Paul's, Syracuse. Teacher of voice at Wellesley Coll., 1879-81. Composer: (songs) "The Cry of Rachel," "The Pine Tree," "Serenity," "Come to the Garden," (cycles) "Love's Epitome," and "Lyrics from Sappho," and others. Home: New York, N.Y. Died Sept. 12, 1938.

SALTER, William, clergyman; b. Brooklyn, Nov. 17, 1821; s. William Frost and Mary (Ewen) S.; A.B., New York Univ., 1840, A.M., 1843; Union Theol. Sem., 1840-42; grad. Andover Theol. Sem., 1843; (D.D., State U. of Iowa, 1864); m. Mary A., d. Deacon Eliab Parker Mackintire, of Charlestown, Mass., Aug. 25, 1846; father of William Mackintire S. Ordained Congl. ministry, 1843; home missionary Maquoketa, Iowa, 1843-46; pastor Burlington, Ia., April, 1846—. Author: Psalms for Worship and Instruction, Arranged in Order of Subjects, 1900; Words of Life for 1905, 1905; Iowa, 1673-1846, the First Free State in the Louisiana Purchase, 1905; Sixty Years, Sermons and Addresses, 1907. Home: Burlington, Ia. Died 1910.

SALTER, William Mackintire, lecturer; b. Burlington, Ia., Jan. 30, 1853; s. William and Mary A. (Mackintire) S.; A.B., Knox Coll., Ill., 1871, A.M., 1874; Yale Div. Sch., 1871-73; B.D., Harvard, 1876; Parker fellow of Harvard at U. of Göttingen, 1876-77; Columbia, 1881-82; m. Mary S. Gibbens, Dec. 2, 1885; children—Eliza Webb (dec.), John Randall (adopted). Lecturer Soc. for Ethical Culture of Chicago, 1883-92 and 1897-1907; lecturer Soc. for dept. of philosophy, U. of Chicago, 1909-13. Author: Ethical Culture of Phila., 1892-97; spl. lecturer for On a Foundation for Religion, 1879; Die Religion der Moral, Leipzig, 1885; Moralische Reden, Leipzig, 1889; Ethical Religion, 1889; First Steps in Philosophy, 1892; Anarchy or Government? An Inquiry in Fundamental Politics, 1895; Nietzsche, the Thinker, 1917; What is Americanism?, 1925. Home: Silver Lake, N.H. Died July 18, 1931.

SALTUS, Edgar, author; b. New York City, June 8, 1858; s. of Francis Henry and Eliza (Evertson) Saltus; ed. St. Paul's School, Concord, N.H., The Sorbonne, Paris; Columbia Univ., 1880. Author: Balzac, 1884; The Philosophy of Disenchantment, 1885; The Anatomy of Negation, 1887; Mr. Incoul's Misadventure, 1887; The Truth About Tristrem Varick, 1888; Eden, 1888; The Pace That Kills, 1888; A Transaction in Hearts, 1889; Mary Magdalen, 1892; Imperial Purple, 1893; When Dreams Come True, 1895; Purple and Fine Women, 1903; The Pomps of Satan, 1904; The Perfume of Eros, 1905; Historia Amoris, 1906; The Lords of the Ghostland, 1907; Daughters of the Rich, 1909; The Monster, 1913; Oscar Wilde—An Idler's Impression, 1917; The Paliser Case, 1919. Died July 31, 1921.

SALTZGABER, Gaylord Miller, commr. of pensions; b. Shelby, O., Mar. 14, 1846; s. Samuel and Jane (Van Horn) S.; ed. pub. schs. and business coll.; m. Eliza Little, Sept. 1, 1891. Mem. Troop I, 3d Ohio Cav., Sept. 1, 1861-Aug. 15, 1865; practiced law, Van Wert, O., 44 years; served as mayor, Van Wert, and mem. Sch. Bd.; mem. Ohio State Senate, 1876-80; U.S. commr. of pensions, 1913-21. Democrat. Methodist. Mason. Comdr. Ohio Dept. of G.A.R., 1922; comdr.-in-chief G.A.R., 1923. Home: Van Wert, O. Died Aug. 23, 1930.

SAMFIELD, Max, rabbi; b. Marktsteft, Bavaria, Germany, Jan. 23, 1844; s. Samuel and Rosa (Mendel) S.; Ph.D., U. of Würzburg, 1865; came to U.S., 1867; m. Pauline Frank, Jan. 26, 1873. Rabbi Congregation B'nai Zion, Shreveport, La., 1868-71, Congregation Children of Israel, Memphis, 1871—; elected rabbi same for life, May, 1911, after 40 yrs.' service.

Actively identified for many yrs. with charitable movements in Memphis and the South; a founder Tenn. Soc. for Prevention of Cruelty to Animals and Children, and of the non-sectarian United Charities, Hebrew Relief Assn. (pres.); mem. bd. govs. Hebrew Union Coll., Cincinnati. Supervisor Central Conf. Am. Rabbis. Scottish Rite Mason; mem. B'nai B'rith, 1869—. Founder, 1885, and editor Jewish Spectator. Home: Memphis, Tenn. Died Sept. 28, 1915.

SAMFORD, William Hodges, judge; b. Auburn, Ala., Aug. 7, 1866; s. Hon. William J. (gov. of Ala.) and Caroline E. (Drake) S.; g.s. William F. Samford, asso. editor New York Day-Book, and editor Warrick letters; student at Ala. Agrl. and Mech. Coll. (now Ala. Polytech. Inst.) through jr. yr., 1883; m. Kate C. Park, Dec. 18, 1890; children—William Connor (dec.), Frank Park, Yetta Glenn, James Drake, Mrs. Katherine Smith. Admitted to bar, 1894; practiced at Troy, in partnership with A. B. Foster and J. S. Carroll, 1894-1909; removed to Montgomery, Ala., Oct. 1, 1909; judge Alabama Court of Appeals, Mar. 1917—. Prosecuting attorney for Law Court of Pike County, 1895-1902; city attorney Troy, 1901-07; mem. Ala. Constl. Conv., 1901; mem. campaign com. for adoption of constn., 1901; Dem. presdl. elector from state at large, 1904; pres. Electoral Coll. of Ala., 1904. Methodist. Mason, K.P. Home: Montgomery, Ala. Died Feb. 2, 1940.

SAMMONS, Thomas, consul gen.; b. New York, N.Y., Feb. 7, 1863; s. John and Julia (Flynn) S.; ed. common schs., Albany (N.Y.) Law Sch. and George Washington U.; m. Elizabeth Wheeler, Oct. 30, 1888; 1 son, Wheeler. Farmer, 1874-79; telegraph operator, 1879-85; reporter, editor and pub., 1886-98; pvt. sec. to a U.S. senator, 1898-1905; consul gen. to Manchuria, 1905-06; assigned to Mukden and Antung, May 1906, in connection with negotiations for opening of these ports under treaty of 1903; consul gen. to Korea, 1907-09, to Japan, 1909-13, at Shanghai, 1913-19, at Melbourne, Australia, Sept. 1919-23. Home: Chicago, Ill. Died Oct. 15, 1935.

SAMPLE, Robert Fleming, Presbyn. clergyman; b. Corning, N.Y., Oct. 19, 1829; s. John and Jane (Wilson) S.; grad. Jefferson Coll., 1849; (D.D., Wooster Univ., 1876; LL.D., Washington and Jefferson Coll., 1898); m. Nannie M. Bracken, Mar. 31, 1853 (died 1902). Pastor, Mercer, Pa., 1853-56; Bedford, Pa., 1856-66; pastor-elect Andrew Ch., Minneapolis, 1866-68; Westminster Ch., Minneapolis, 1868-87; Westminster Presbyn. Ch., New York, 1887-1902, pastor emeritus, same. Has traveled in Europe, Palestine and Northern Africa. Asso. editor North and West, 1895-1902. Dir. McCormick Theol. Sem., 1876-89; trustee Macalester Coll., St. Paul, Minn., 1880-88; trustee Lincoln Univ., 1892—, and became prof. Christian ethics in same; mem. Bd. of Ch. Erection, 1887—; del. to Pan-Presbyn Councils, Belfast, 1884, and Washington, 1899; moderator gen. assembly, Presbyn. Ch. of the U.S.A. Dir. Western Div., Presbyn. Ch. of World, 1899—. Author: Beacon Lights of the Reformation, 1889; Christ's Valedictory, 1900; Spirit Grieved, 1890; Elements of Pulpit Power, 1901. Home: New York, N.Y. Died 1905.

SAMPSON, Alden, author; b. Manchester, Me., Mar. 13, 1853; s. Alden and Sarah Taber (Pope) S.; A.B., Haverford Coll., 1873, A.M., 1876; A.B., Harvard, 1876, A.M., 1877; student Harvard Law Sch., 1878-80; m. Mary Agnes Yarnall, June 10, 1890 (died 1911). Artist, explorer and traveler; game preserve expert, U.S. Biol. Survey, 1907, for establishment of game refuges in national forests; has lectured on literature, art and archeology, mountaineering and life of the forest before various socs. in the East and West; active in effort to protect Hetch Hetchy Valley, Calif., from conversion into reservoir. Author: Milton's Sonnets, 1886; A Bear Hunt in the Sierras, 1895; The Establishment of Game Refuges, 1900; Essay on the Wild Life, 1905; Studies in Milton and an Essay on Poetry, 1912. Home: Washington, D.C. Died Jan. 5, 1925.

SAMPSON, Archibald J., lawyer; b. nr. Cadiz, O., June 21, 1839; s. of Francis and Margaret Griffith (Evans) S.; bro. of Francis A. S.; pvt. to capt. in Union Army in Civil War; B.S., Mt. Union Coll., Ohio, 1861, A.M., 1865 (LL.D., 1890); LL.B., Cleveland Law Coll., 1866; m. Kate I. Turner, Sept. 18, 1866 (died 1886); m. 2d, Frances S Wood, Mar. 19, 1891. Admitted to bar, 1865; practiced at Sedalia, Mo., 1865-73, Cañon City, and Denver, Colo., 1873-93, Phoenix, Ariz., from 1893. Nominated for U.S. consul at Palestine, 1873, but declined; atty. gen. Colo., 1876-79; consul at El Paso del Norte, Mex., 1889-93; E.E. and M.P. to Ecuador, 1897-1907, being first person for over 80 yrs. living in a territory to receive a diplomatic appmt. Republican. Past dept. comdr. G.A.R. and now a.-a.-g. G.A.R. Mason. Died Dec. 24, 1921.

SAMPSON, Francis Asbury, lawyer; b. Harrison Co., O., Feb. 6, 1842; s. Francis and Margaret Griffith (Evans) S.; bro. of Archibald J. S.; A.B., Coll. City of New York, 1865, A.M., 1868; LL.B., New York U., 1868; m. Mrs. Harriette Maiden Lacey, July 23, 1869. V.p. Mo. Trust Co., Sedalia, 20 yrs., until consolidated with Mo. Trust Co., St. Louis; sec. and librarian, State Hist. Soc. of Mo., 1901-15, bibliographer, 1915—. Mason. Editor Mo. Hist. Review. Republican. Methodist. Home: Columbia, Mo. Died 1918.

SAMPSON, Martin Wright, univ. prof.; b. Cincinnati, Sept. 7, 1866; s. William S., Jr., and Virginia Ada (Wright) S.; U. of Munich, 1887-88; A.B., U. of Cincinnati, 1888, A.M., 1890; studied, Paris, 1891, England, 1896, 1899, Dublin, 1901, British Museum, 1901-02 and 1925, and Germany, 1906-07; m. Julia Dauchy Pattison, Dec. 1910; children—Stephen Hastings, Martin Wright, Margaret Virginia, Edward Coolidge. Instr. in English, 1889-91, asst. prof., 1891, U. of Iowa; asst. prof. English, Stanford U., 1892-93; prof. English, Ind. U., 1893-1906; prof. of English lit., 1907—, Cornell U. Joint author (with E. O. Holland): Written and Oral Composition, 1907. Translator: Singer's Dresden Gallery, 1907. Editor: Milton's Lyric and Dramatic Poems, 1901; Plays of John Webster, 1904; Gaskell's Cransford, 1905; Irving's Sketch Book, 1907; Milton's Minor Poems, 1911; Shakespeare's Two Gentlemen of Verona, 1912; Middleton's Plays, 1915; Selections from Milton, 1925; James's Daisy Miller, 1927; The Good Giant (children's stories), 1929. Trustee Wells Coll. Home: Ithaca, N.Y. Died Aug. 22, 1930.

SAMPSON, Thornton Rogers, theologian; b. Prince Edward, Va., Oct. 9, 1852; s. Rev. Francis S. and Caroline (Dudley) S.; A.B., Hampden-Sidney Coll., 1871; studied at univs. of Va. and Leipzig; theology at Edinburgh, and Union Theol. Sem., Va.; (D.D., Davidson Coll., N.C., 1893, LL.D., 1907); m. Ella S. Royster, Apr. 30, 1878. Ordained Presbyterian ministry, 1878; in mission work among the Greeks in Athens and Thessalonica, 1878-92; sec. foreign missions, 1892-94; pres. Assembly's Home and Sch., Fredericksburg, Va., 1894-97. Austin Coll., Sherman, Tex., 1897-1900; pres., 1900-05, Lutcher prof. ch. history and polity, 1905—, Austin Presbyn. Theol. Seminary. Home: Austin, Texas. Died Sept. 2, 1915.

SAMPSON, William Thomas, rear adm. U.S.N.; b. Palmyra, N.Y., Feb. 9, 1840; s. James and Hannah (Walker) S.; apptd. to navy, Sept. 24, 1857; grad. at head of class, U.S. Naval Acad., 1861 (LL.D., Harvard, 1899); m. Margaret Sexton, Aldrich, 1863; m. 2d, Elizabeth Susan Burling, 1882. Promoted to master, 1861; commd. lt., July 16, 1862; was exec. officer on ironclad "Patapsco" when it was blown up by a mine in Charleston harbor; he was blown into the water, but rescued; commd. lt. comdr., July 25, 1866; comdr., Aug. 9, 1874; capt., March, 1889; supt. Naval Acad., 1886-90. Has been in all branches of naval service; expert on ordnance, torpedoes, etc.; with Lt. Joseph Strauss, devised and perfected the superimposed turrets introduced into the navy, Feb. 1898, pres. bd. of inquiry as to cause of destruction of U.S.S. "Maine" in Havana harbor, Feb. 15, 1898; after declaration of war with Spain comd. N. Atlantic squadron, with rank of acting rear adm.; promoted to commodore, 1898, rear adm., 1899. In Spanish-Am. war his command numbered 125 vessels—the strongest ever organized for hostile purposes; this fleet captured many Spanish merchant vessels and blockade runners and finally defeated Spanish fleet under Admiral Cervera. Apptd., Sept. 1898, one of the 3 commrs. to Cuba; resumed command N. Atlantic fleet, Dec. 1898; commandant Boston Navy Yard, Oct. 14, 1899—. Died 1902.

SAMS, Oliver Newton, banker; b. Hillsboro, O., Oct. 19, 1862; s. Andrew J. and Ruth A. (Bell) S.; B.A., National Normal Univ., Lebanon, O., 1886; m. Mary E. George, Mar. 20, 1888; 1 son, Ralph G. Admitted to Ohio bar, 1887; practiced in Hillsboro, 1888-1907; pres. Merchants National Bank, Hillsboro, 1907—. Director Federal Reserve Bank of Cleveland, O. Prosecuting atty. Highland Co., 1900-06. Pres. Ohio State Bankers' Assn., 1915-16; mem. exec. council Am. Bankers' Assn. Trustee Wilmington (O.) Coll. Del. Gen. Conf. M.E. Ch., Baltimore, 1908. Mason. Home: Hillsboro, O. Died June 3, 1932.

SAMSON, George Clement, physician; b. Washington, D.C., Apr. 18, 1848; s. Rev. G. W. and Elizabeth (Smallwood) S.; A.B., Columbian Coll. (now George Washington U.), 1865, M.D., 1867; A.M., 1868; M.D., U. of Pa., 1869; studied U. of Edinburgh, 1867-68; m. Marianne Polkinhorn, Oct. 3, 1872. Physician in charge Soldiers' and Sailors' Orphan Home, Washington, 1870-79. Mem. bd. trustees pub. schs., D.C., 1878-82; mem. bd. mgrs. Y.M.C.A., 1891-97; mem. bd. mgrs. Washington City Bible Soc., 1888-99. Home: Washington, D.C. Died Feb. 10, 1922.

SAMSON, William Holland, author, editor, b. Le Roy, N.Y., Feb. 2, 1860; s. Russell L. and Mary Elizabeth (Parsons) S.; ed. common and high schs.; m. Mary Elizabeth Bixby, Dec. 25, 1882. Editorial writer Rochester Post Express, 1881-1911, mng. editor, 1896-1911; removed to New York, 1911. Editor: Private Journal of Aaron Burr (2 vols.), 1903; Letters from George Washington to Tobias Lear, with appendix containing miscellaneous Washington letters and documents, 1905; Letters of Zachary Taylor from the Battlefields of the Mexican War, 1908. Author: Mohican Point on Lake George, 1914. Home: New York, N.Y. Died June 24, 1917.

SAMUEL, Edmund William, congressman, physician; b. Blamavon, Wales, Nov. 27, 1857; s. Edmund and Mary Ann (Bower) S.; ed. pub. schs., Ashland, Pa., Jefferson Med. Coll., M.D., 1880; m. Alice Kiefer, Apr. 28, 1886. Engaged in practice of medicine, Mt. Carmel, Pa., 1880—; also in drug business, 1889—. Pres. Rich Hill Coal Co., Real Estate Exchange, Brush Valley Lumber & Timber Co.; dir. Samuel Realty Co., Peoples' Bldg. & Loan Assn. Methodist. Republican. Served 3 yrs. as sch. dir. Mt. Carmel Borough; mem. Congress, 16th Pa. dist., 1905-07. Mason; served 2 terms as Supreme Commander, Supreme Commandery of the Continent of America, Knights of Malta. Home: Mt. Carmel, Pa. Died Mar. 7, 1930.

SAMUEL, Henry Paul, judge; b. Mason Co., Ill., Oct. 2, 1886; s. Hickman B. and Sarah (Estep) S.; prep. edn., Whipple Acad., Jacksonville, Ill.; student Ill. Coll., Jacksonville, 1905-06, Ill. Wesleyan U., 1907-10; m. Millicent Rowe, June 15, 1918; 1 son, Paul Rowe. Admitted to Ill. bar, 1910; practiced in Montana, 1910-14; settled in Jacksonville, Ill., 1914; judge of County Court, Morgan Co., Ill., 1918-26; mem. Belatti, Samuell & Moriarity; judge Supreme Court, Ill., Oct. 1929-June 1930, to fill unexpired term of Justice Cyrus Deitz; apptd. mem. Ill. Commerce Commn., 1932-33; resumed private practice of law. Republican. Mason, Elk, K.P. Home: Jacksonville, Ill. Died Mar. 21, 1938.

SAMUELS, Arthur Hiram, editor; b. Hartford, Conn., Apr. 15, 1888; s. Louis L. and Minna Krotoshiner) S.; A.B., Princeton, 1909; m. Vivian Martin, Feb. 28, 1926. Reporter N.Y. Sun, 1909-13 (spl. corr. with Theodore Roosevelt); mgr. promotion dept. Curtis Pub. Co., 1913-16; partner Barrows, Richardson & Alley, 1920-28; exec. editor The New Yorker, 1928-30; editor Home and Field, 1930-31, Harper's Bazaar, 1931-34, House Beautiful, 1934—. Mng. editor for Food Adminstrn., Washington, D.C., 1916-17; served as capt. in office of surgeon gen., in charge of publicity in behalf of reconstruction of disabled soldiers, 1917-19. Composer musical comedy "Poppy" (with W. C. Fields), 1926. Home: New York, N.Y. Died Mar. 20, 1938.

SAMUELS, Edward Augustus, zoölogist; b. Boston, July 4, 1836; s. Emanuel and Abigail S.; common school edn.; has been engaged in literary work for about 50 yrs.; asst. sec. Mass. State Bd. of Agr., 1860-80; was 7 yrs. pres. Mass. Fish and Game Protective Assn. Author: Ornithology and Oölogy of New England; Among the Birds; With Fly-Rod and Camera; With Rod and Gun in New England and the Maritime Provinces; Mammalogy of New England; The Living World (2 vols., with Augustus C. L. Arnold). Home: Fitchburg, Mass. Died 1908.

SAMUELS, Samuel, seaman; b. Philadelphia, March 14, 1823; went to sea as cabin-boy at 11; advanced until he became merchant capt. at 21; for several yrs. capt. of the "Dreadnought," fastest of sailing packets; capt. U.S.S. "John Rice," 1863-64; gen. supt. q.-m.'s dept., New York, 1864; comd. "McClellan" at taking of Ft. Fisher, 1865; capt. "Fulton," last of Am. packet steamers between New York and Havre, 1866; afterward won the 1st ocean yacht race in the "Henrietta" against the "Fleetwing" and "Vesta," Dec. 1866; organized, 1872, the Samana Bay Co., of San Domingo, but his concession was revoked by new govt., 1874; later head of several large business enterprises in New York. Home: Brooklyn, N.Y. Died 1908.

SAMY, Mahmoud (Pasha), diplomat; b. Cairo, Egypt, Oct. 9, 1881; grad. Coppershill Engring. Coll., London, Eng.; m. Basna Hanem, June 1923. E.E. and M.P. from Egypt to U.S., July 16, 1925—. Died July 17, 1936.

SANBORN, Arthur Loomis, judge; b. Brasner Falls, N.Y., Nov. 17, 1850; s. Simpson E. and Harriet (Blount) S.; ed. pub. schs., Lake Geneva, Wis.; LL.B., Univ. of Wis., 1880; m. Alice E. Golder, Oct. 15, 1874. Register of deeds, Walworth Co., Wis., 1875-79; engaged in practice, 1880-1905; U.S. dist. judge, Western Dist. of Wisconsin, Jan. 10, 1905—. Congregationalist. Republican. Home: Madison, Wis. Died Oct. 18, 1920.

SANBORN, Benjamin H., publisher; b. Morrisville, Vt., May 11, 1851; s. Seth C. and Cornelia (Hyde) S.; prep. edn. Morrisville Acad.; entered Dartmouth Coll., but did not grad.; (A.M., Norwich U., 1894, Dartmouth, 1898); m. Ida A. Doty, Nov. 24, 1875. Began in text-book business with Robert S. Davis & Co., Boston; later with Messrs. Leach & Shewell; bought out the firm, 1884; withdrew, 1898, from firm of Leach, Shewell & Sanborn, and established corp. of Benjamin H. Sanborn & Co., of which was pres.; published more than 200 text-books; retired from active business, 1913. Congregationalist. Mem. N.E.A. Mason. Home: Southern Pines, N.C. Died Apr. 4, 1926.

SANBORN, Franklin Benjamin, journalist; b. Hampton Falls, N.H., Dec. 15, 1831; s. Aaron and

Lydia (Leavitt) S.; A.B., Harvard, 1855; m. Ariana Walker, Aug. 23, 1854; 2d, Louisa Leavitt, July 16, 1862. Editor Boston Commonwealth, 1863-67, Springfield Republican, 1868-1914, Jour. of Social Science, 1867-97. Has lectured at Cornell, Smith, and Wellesley, and at Concord (Mass.) Sch. of Philosophy. One of founders Am. Social Science Assn., Nat. Prison Assn., Nat. Conf. of Charities, Clarke Sch. for the Deaf, Mass. Infant Asylum, Concord Sch. of Philosophy, and sec. or pres. of most of these. Chmn. Bd. of State Charities, 1874-76; Mass. insp. of charities, 1879-88. Author: (biographies) Thoreau, 1872; John Brown, 1885; Dr. S. G. Howe, 1891; Alcott, 1893; Emerson, 1895; Dr. Earle, 1898; Personality of Thoreau, 1902; Personality of Emerson, 1903; A History of New Hampshire, 1904; Recollections of Seventy Years, 1909; Final Life of Thoreau, 1914. Edited for Bibliophile Soc., Boston, 5 vols. of Thoreau Manuscript, and a vol. each of Letters of Paul Jones, of J. H. Payne and Mrs. Shelley, and Letters and Fragments of T. L. Peacock, in all 8 vols. Home: Concord, Mass. Died Feb. 24, 1917.

SANBORN, Helen Josephine (Miss), author; b. Greene, Me., Oct. 6, 1857; d. J. S. Sanborn, of Chase & Sanborn, Boston; grad. Salem, Mass., Normal School, 1878; Wellesley Coll., 1884; mem. school bd., Somerville, Mass., 1890-93. Author: A Winter in Central America, 1886. Home: Somerville, Mass. Died Apr. 26, 1917.

SANBORN, Henry Nichols, librarian; b. Quincy, Mass., Mar. 5, 1879; s. Eben P. and Cora Frances (Nichols) S.; student Harvard, 1897-99; B.A., Dartmouth, 1902; M.A., Yale, 1903; student N.Y. State Library Sch., 1911-12; unmarried. Instr. English, Dartmouth, 1903-05, Phillips Acad., Andover, Mass., 1907-11; librarian University Club, Chicago, 1912-13; sec. Pub. Library Commn., Ind., 1913-18; librarian Bridgeport Pub. Library, 1918—. Dir. of Bridgeport Boy's Club. Home: Fairfield, Conn. Died Feb. 22, 1926.

SANBORN, John Bell, lawyer; b. Elkborn, Wis., May 12, 1876; s. Arthur Loomis and Alice (Golder) S.; B.L., U. of Wis., 1896, M.L., 1897, Ph.D., 1899; student U. of Wis. Law Sch., 1900-01; m. Gertrude Stillman, June 26, 1901; children—Katherine Yates, Arthur Craig, Stephen Blount (dec.). Practiced with father as Sanborn, Luse & Powell and Sanborn & Sanborn, 1901-05; sr. mem. Sanborn & Blake, 1905-19, and Sanborn, Blake & Aberg, since appmt. of father as U.S. dist. judge, 1905. Lecturer U. of Wis. Law Sch., 1908—; mem. Wis. Board of Bar Examiners, 1911-13; commissioner on Uniform State Laws, 1917-23 (sec. 1922); chmn. Wis. Central Legal Advisory Com. under Selective Service Law, 1917-19. Capt., 1921, maj., 1922, lt. col., 1923, Wis. N.G. (judge adv. 22d Cav. Div.); lt. col. J.A.G., Res. Republican. Conglist. Home: Madison, Wis. Died Dec. 31, 1933.

SANBORN, John Benjamin, veteran general; b. Epsom, N.H., Dec. 5, 1826; ed. Dartmouth Coll.; studied law; admitted to N.H. bar, July 1854; removed to St. Paul, Dec. 1854; engaged in practice; m. Catherine Hall, March 17, 1857, Newton, N.J.; m. 2d, Anna Nixon, Nov. 26, 1865; m. 3d, Rachel Rice, April 18, 1880. As adj. gen. and q.m. gen. organized and sent Minn. troops to war, 1861; col. 4th Minn., 1862; served to close of war, becoming brig. gen. and bvt. maj. gen.; participated in battles of Iuka, Corinth, Port Gibson, Raymond, Jackson, Champion's Hill, and in assault and siege of Vicksburg; in Oct. 1864 took command of Dist. of Southwest Mo., and fought the successful engagements of that period and section; fought against Indians of the Southwest in summer and fall of 1865; apptd. by President Johnson to settle difficulties with Indians in following winter; mem. Indian Peace Commn., 1867-68; has served in Minn. house and senate. Home: St. Paul, Minn. Died 1904.

SANBORN, J(ohn) Pitts, music critic, novelist, essayist; b. Port Huron, Mich.; s. John Pitts and Mary Ann (Wastell) S.; A.B., Harvard, 1900, A.M., 1902; unmarried. Musical editor New York Globe, 1905-23; foreign corr. Globe, summers 1912, 14, 15, 16 (in France, 1915, 16, 19, 20, 21, 22); foreign corr. New York Evening Mail, summer 1923; became musical editor New York Evening Mail, later musical editor New York World-Telegram. Decorated Cavaliere dell'Ordine della Corona d'Italia (Italian), Chevalier de la Légion d'Honneur (French). Episcopalian. Author: Vie de Bordeaux (poems), 1917; Prima Donna —A Novel of the Opera, 1929; Greek Night (novel), 1933; Metropolitan Book of the Opera, 1937. Home: New York, N.Y. Died Mar. 8, 1941.

SANBORN, Joseph Brown, soldier; b. Chester, N.H., Dec. 8, 1855; s. Josiah and Rachael S.; ed. pub. schs.; m. Julie F. Flanders (died 1922); children—Mrs. Helen F. Kline (dec.), Mrs. Katharine S. Boice; m. 2d, Willa Alice Week, Sept. 4, 1924. Moved to Chicago, 1877; pres. J. B. Sanborn Co., merc. agency, 1886-1925; mem. State Tax Commn., 1919-21. Identified with Ill. N.G. from 1879; maj. 1st Ill. Inf., Spanish-Am. War, 1898, serving in Santiago Campaign; col. same regt., 1899, and continued as col. same regt. (later 131st U.S. Inf.); arrived in France with regt., May 30, 1918; participated in Somme and Argonne-Meuse offensives, beginning Aug. 8, 1918, and closing Nov. 11, 1918, comprising in all 25 engagements. Decorated D.S.C., "for extraordinary heroism" nr. Gressaire, France, Aug. 9, 1918; D.S.M.; British D.S.O.; Officer Legion of Honor, France, and Croix de Guerre with palm; Officer Belgian Order of Leopold. Maj. gen. Ill. N.G., June 23, 1920; retired, June 20, 1921; lt. gen. retired, Apr. 6, 1931. Mem. Soc. of Santiago, Am. Legion. Mason. Republican. Home: Chicago, Ill. Died Dec. 22, 1934.

SANBORN, Katherine Abbott (Kate Sanborn), author; b. Hanover, N.H., July 11, 1839; d. Prof. Edwin D. and Mary Ann (Webster) S.; earned her first money by writing at 11 yrs. of age; has supported herself from age of 17. Teacher, consecutively, in Mary Inst., St. Louis; a day sch., Hanover, N.H.; teacher of elocution, Packer Inst., Brooklyn; lecturer on literary topics for past 20 yrs.; prof. lit., Smith Coll., several yrs. Author: The Wit of Women; Round Table Series of Literary Lessons; My Literary Zoo; Purple and Gold, and Grandmother's Garden (Christmas books); Our Calendar; "Children's," "Cupids," "Sunshine," "Rainbow" and "Starlight," Calendars; Old Time Wall Papers, 1905; Hunting Indians in a Taxi-Cab, 1911. Home: Metcalf, Mass. Died July 9, 1917.

SANBORN, Walter Henry, judge; b. Epsom, N.H., Oct. 19, 1845; s. Hon. Henry F. and Eunice (Davis) S.; A.B., Dartmouth, 1867, A.M., 1870, LL.D., 1893; m. Emily F. Bruce, Nov. 10, 1874; children—Nellie Grace (Mrs. Charles G. Hartin), Marian (Mrs. Grant Van Sant), Bruce Walter, Henry Frederick. Prin. high sch., Milford, 1867-70; practiced law, St. Paul, with his uncle, Gen. John B. Sanborn, 1871-92; U.S. circuit judge, 8th Jud. Circuit, Mar. 17, 1892—. Presiding judge U.S. Circuit Ct. of Appeals, 8th Circuit, June 4, 1903—. Conducted receivership U.P. R.R. Co., 1893-98, distributing $260,000,000, receivership of C.G.W. R.R. Co., 1908-09, receivership of Frisco R.R. Co., 1913-14, and receivership of D.&R.G. R.R. Co., 1918—. Wrote decision in Trans-Mo. Freight Assn. case, 1893, Standard Oil Co. case, 1909, Okla. gas case, 1911. Mem. City Council, St. Paul, 1878-80, 1885-92. Grand Comdr. K.T. of Minn., 1889; pres. Union League of St. Paul, 1890, St. Paul Bar Assn., 1890-91. Home: St. Paul, Minn. Died May 10, 1928.

SANCHEZ, Nellie Van de Grift; b. Indianapolis, Ind., Nov. 24, 1856; d. Jacob and Esther (Keen) Van de Grift; youngest sister of late Mrs. Robert Louis Stevenson; grad. Indianapolis High Sch., 1875; visiting student U. of Calif., 1905-10; m. Adulfo Sanchez, Sept. 12, 1880 (died 1890); 1 son, Louis Adulfo. Engaged in hist. research and transln. original Spanish documents. Progressive. Author: Spanish and Indian Place Names of California, Their Meaning and Their Romance, 1914; Life of Mrs. Robert Louis Stevenson; California Under Spanish and Mexican Rule; Spanish Arcadia (a study of social life in Calif. under Spain and Mexico), 1928; A Short History of California (with Dr. Rockwell D. Hunt). Home: Oakland, Calif. Died Jan. 4, 1935.

SANCHEZ-LATOUR, Francisco, diplomat; b. Quezaltenango, Republic of Guatemala, Aug. 21, 1876; s. Delfino Sanchez and Teresa Latour y La Torre; ed. in Eng. and France; m. Lillian Hall Davis, Oct. 6, 1920. Asst. dir. Nat. Inst. for Boys, Guatemala, 1906; nat. treas., 1907-11, mem. of Congress, 1907-11; 1st sec. spl. mission to U.S., 1908; del. to Deep Waterways Conv., New Orleans, 1909; chargé d'affaires of Guatemala, at Washington, D.C., 1910; 1st sec. to Legation, 1911-20; again chargé d'affaires, 1922; E.E. and M.P. from Guatemala to U.S., May 23, 1922—; also v.p. Pan Am. Union. Del. to Internacional High Commn. for Uniform Legislation, Buenos Aires, 1916; govt. del. and chmn. Guatemala delegation to Labor Conf., Washington, D.C., Oct. 1919; del. to 2d Pan-Am. Commercial Conf., Washington, D.C., June 1919; chairman Guatemala delegation to Central Am. Conf., Washington, D.C., Dec. 4, 1922-Oct. 7, 1923. Died Nov. 7, 1927.

SANDEFER, Jefferson Davis, univ. pres.; b. Sharp Co., Ark., Mar. 13, 1868; s. Samuel Butner and Mary Lucretia (Leverton) S.; grad. Parker Inst., Whitt, Tex., 1893; student U. of Tex. Summer Sch., 1899, 1900, 01; Ph.B., U. of Chicago, 1907; LL.D., Baylor U., 1917; m. Lucile Gilbert, Dec. 26, 1894; children—Jefferson Davis, Grace Elizabeth, Mary Louise, Gilbert Bryan. Pres. Strawn (Tex.) Coll., 1894-1900; supt. pub. schs., Granbury, Tex., 1900-01; prof. Latin and history, 1902-07, pres. 1908-09, John Tarleton Coll., Stephenville, Tex.; supt. of public schools, Stephenville, 1907-08; pres. Simmons College (now Hardin-Simmons Univ.), Abilene, Tex., July 1909—. Democrat. Baptist. Trustee Hendrick Memorial Hospital, Abilene, Tex.; mem. governing board Conf. for Education in Tex., Anti-Saloon League of Tex.; mem. Tex. Bapt. Gen. Conv. (pres. 1920-23); v.p. Southern Bapt. Conv., 1923-24. Mason. Home: Abilene, Tex. Died Mar. 22, 1940.

SANDERS, Archie D., congressman; b. Stafford, N.Y., June 17, 1857; s. John S.; ed. Le Roy Academy, and Buffalo Central High Sch. Began in produce business, with father; mem. N.Y. Assembly, 1895, 96; apptd. collector internal revenue, 28th Dist. of N.Y., by President McKinley, 1898, served 14 yrs.; mem. Rep. State Com., N.Y., 1900, 01; elected mem. N.Y. Senate, 1914; mem. 65th to 72d Congresses (1917-33), 39th N.Y. Dist.; chmn. com. on post office and post roads, 71st Congress. Home: Stafford, N.Y. Died July 15, 1941.

SANDERS, Daniel Jackson, pres. Biddle Univ., 1891—; b. Winnsboro, S.C., Feb. 15, 1847; ed. Brainerd Inst., Chester, S.C.; grad. Western Theol. Sem., 1874; (A.M., D.D., Lincoln Univ., Pa.; D.D., Biddle Univ., N.C.). Ordained Presbyn. minister, 1870; pastor Wilmington, N.C., 1874-86; abroad, 1875; m. F. T. Price, Sept. 16, 1880. Founder, 1879, editor and propr. Africo-Am. Presbyn. Mem. Gen. Council of Presbyn. chs., Toronto, 1892, and Washington, 1899; 5 times mem. Presbyn. Gen. Assembly. Home: Charlotte, N.C. Died 1907.

SANDERS, Frank Knight, author, editor; b. Batticotta, Jaffna, Ceylon, June 5, 1861; s. Marshall Danforth and Georgianna (Knight) S.; A.B., Ripon Coll., Wis., 1882; Ph.D., Yale, 1889; instr. Jaffna Coll., Ceylon, 1882-86; m. Edith Blackman, June 27, 1888; children—Helen, Morris Blackman, Frank Knight. Woolsey prof. Bibl. lit., 1891-1901, prof. Bibl. history and archæology and dean, Yale Divinity Sch., 1901-05; sec. Congl. S.S. and Pub. Soc., 1905-08; pres. Washburn Coll., Kan., 1908-14; dir. Missionary Preparation for Foreign Missions Conf. of North America, 1914-27. Author: The Teacher's Life of Christ, 1907; Studies in the Life of Paul, 1908; The Messages of the Sages, 1918; Outlines for Study of Biblical History and Literature (with Prof. H. T. Fowler), 1906; The Messages of the Earlier Prophets (with Prof. C. F. Kent), 1898; The Messages of the Later Prophets, 1899; History of the Hebrews, 1914, revised edit., 1929; The Program of Christianity, 1918; Old Testament Prophecy, 1921; Old Testament History, 1921. Co-editor: (with Prof. C. F. Kent) The Historical Series for Bible Students (9 vols.); The Messages of the Bible (12 vols.), 1897-1918; (with Prof. H. P. Beach) The World's Living Religions (10 vols.), 1923—; (with H. A. Sherman) The Life and Religion Series (10 vols.), 1921—. Home: Rockport, Mass. Died Feb. 20, 1933.

SANDERS, Henry Martin, clergyman; b. New York, N.Y., Nov. 20, 1849; s. Charles W. and Elizabeth (Barker) S.; A.B., Yale, 1872; grad. Union Theol. Sem., 1876; (D.D., U. of Rochester, 1891); m. Eleanor Butler, Nov. 20, 1883. Ordained Bapt. ministry, 1876; pastor Yonkers, N.Y., 1876-81; Central Ch., New York, 1882-88, Madison Av. Ch., New York, 1888-1901. Author: People's Praise Book, 1890; Bible Readings, 1890. Home: New York, N.Y. Died July 22, 1921.

SANDERS, Joseph M., judge; b. Wythe Co., Va., Aug. 26, 1866; s. John A. and Sallie (McDonald) S.; ed. common schs.; m. Mamie M. Crocket, Dec. 19, 1888. Admitted to bar, 1888; practiced at Bluefield, W.Va., 1888-96; judge Circuit Ct., 1896-1904; asso. justice Supreme Court of Appeals of W.Va., 1905-Oct. 1, 1907. Republican. Resumed practice at Bluefield. Home: Bluefield, W.Va. Died Feb. 17, 1927.

SANDERS, Louis Peck, lawyer; b. Helena, Mont.; s. Wilbur Fisk and Harriet Peck (Fenn) S.; grad. Phillips Exeter Academy, 1889; A.B., Harvard Univ., 1893; m. Natalie Rood Brown, Sept. 16, 1920; children—Helen, Wilbur Fisk, Louise Merris, Jean Edgerton. Admitted to Montana bar, 1900; mem. Kremer, Sanders & Kremer, Butte, 1907-34, when firm dissolved; now engaged in gen. practice. Served in Spanish-Am. War and Philippine Insurrection, 1898-99; with 1st Mont. Inf., as battalion adj., and capt. Co. B; was a.d.c. staff Brig. Gen. Harrison Gray Otis and staff Maj. Gen. Elwell S. Otis, comdg. 8th Army Corps in Philippines; organized 2d Mont. Inf., N.G., and served as first regt. adj.; civilian aide to sec. of War for Mont. C.M.T.C. Assn. Republican. Pub. first edit. Montana Codes. Home: Butte, Mont. Died July 21, 1940.

SANDERS, Newell, mfr.; b. Owen Co., Ind., July 12, 1850; s. John and Miriam (Coffey) S.; B.S., Indiana State Univ., 1873, LL.D., 1931; m. Corinne Dodds (also B.S., Indiana State U., 1873), 1873 (died 1929); children—Wendell (dec.), Norinne (Mrs. James Harvey Anderson), Mildred (Mrs. Walter Blair Wight), Sherman (dec.), Dot (dec.), Pansy (Mrs. Ben Matthews Allison). Merchant at Bloomington, Ind., 1873-77; began manufacture of plows at Chattanooga, Tenn., 1878; pres. and general manager of the Chattanooga Plow Company, 1882-1901, and again president, 1915-19, when sold to the Internat. Harvester Co.; established Newell Sanders Plow Co., 1901, was sole owner; dir. Nashville, Chattanooga & St. Louis Ry., Hamilton Nat. Bank. Chairman Rep. State Exec. Com. of Tenn., 1894-96, 1906-12. U.S. senator, Apr. 8, 1912-Feb. 2, 1913, only Rep. senator from Tenn. in 60 yrs.; mem. Rep. Nat. Com., 1912-16. Pres. Nat. Assn. Agrl. Implement and Vehicle Mfrs., 1907-08; vice-pres. Am. Soc. Mech. Engrs. Leader of statewide prohibition movement in Tennessee. Baptist. Home: Chattanooga, Tenn. Died Jan. 26, 1939.

SANDERS, Wilbur Fisk, lawyer; b. Leon, N.Y., May 2, 1834; s. Ira and Freedom (Edgerton) S.; common school edn.; removed to Ohio; taught school; admitted to bar, 1856; recruited a co. of inf. and a battery of arty. at beginning of war; apptd. 1st lt., 64th Ohio regt., and was acting asst. adj. gen., staff of Gen. James W. Forsyth; asst in construction of defenses along railroads south of Nashville, 1862; resigned of ill health and went to Montana (then Idaho); lawyer and interested in mines; was active in prosecution of robbers and murderers before the popular "law and order" tribunals; atty. for Northern Pacific R.R. Co., 1880-90; grand sec. Grand Lodge of A.F. and A.M., 1866-67-68, and grand master, 1868-69; Rep. candidate for delegate in Congress, 1864, 67, 80, 86; mem. legislative assembly, Mont., 1872-80; declined apptmt. of U.S. atty. for Mont., 1872; pres. Hist. Soc. of Mont., 1865-90; U.S. senator, 1890-93. Home: Helena, Mont. Died 1905.

SANDERS, William Brownell, lawyer; b. Cleveland, O., Sept. 1854; s. William D. and Cornelia R. (Smith) S.; A.B., Ill. Coll., 1873, A.M., LL.D., LL.B., Albany Law Sch.; m. Annie E. Otis, Apr. 30, 1884; 1 dau., Mary (Mrs. Harold T. Clark). Judge Ct. of Common Pleas, 1888-90; resigned; mem. Squire, Sanders & Dempsey, Cleveland, 1890—. V.p. Society for Savings; dir. Guardian Trust Co., Cleveland Stone Co., Kelly Island Lime and Transport Co. Trustee Cleveland Mus. of Art. Home: Cleveland, O. Died Jan. 25, 1929.

SANDERSON, Edwin Nash, engineer; b. Brooklyn, N.Y., Dec. 2, 1862; s. Elnathan Lawrence and Mary Elizabeth (Nash) S.; C.E., Rensselaer Poly. Inst., 1886; M.E., Cornell, 1887; m. Sarah E. Rogers, Apr. 19, 1889 (died 1905); children—Mrs. Helen Rogers Chamberlin, Mrs. Sibyl Edwina Sloane, Mrs. Katharine Mary McCaddon; m. 2d, Mildred Hays, Feb. 7, 1907. Mem. engring. firm Sanderson & Porter, New York; pres. Federal Light & Traction Co. and officer or dir. numerous pub. utility corps. Trustee Cornell U. Republican. Conglist. Home: New York, N.Y. Died Nov. 9, 1932.

SANDERSON, George Andrew, sec. U.S. Senate; b. Hamilton, O., Feb. 22, 1850; s. John and Amanda S.; grad. U.S. Naval Acad., 1871; m. Ella Dinsmore Phillips, May 5, 1896. Resigned from Navy, 1873; transportation business, 1873-92; at U.S. Yards, Chicago, 1892-1902; railroad constrn. in Mexico, 1904-19; became pres. Sonora Constrn. Co. Sec. U.S. Senate, May 19, 1919—. Republican. Christian Scientist. Died Apr. 24, 1925.

SANDERSON, George Augustus, judge; b. Littleton, Mass., July 1, 1863; s. George Webster and Charlotte Elizabeth (Tuttle) S.; A.B., Yale, 1885; LL.B., Boston U., 1887; m. Annie Sarah, d. Charles Curtis and Sarah Jane Sophia (Nutting) Bennett, Jan. 11, 1893; children—Bennett, Sylvia (dec.), Charlotte, Robert, George A. Began practice at Boston, 1887; asst. dist. atty., Middlesex Co., Mass., 1893-1902; dist. atty., 1902-07; justice of Superior Court of Mass., 1907-24; asso. justice Supreme Judicial Court of Mass., 1924—. Republican. Episcopalian. Home: Littleton, Mass. Deceased.

SANDERSON, Henry, banker; b. Titusville, Pa., Dec. 20, 1868; s. Edward Patterson and Elisa (Crassous) S.; ed. pub. and prep. schs.; m. Beatrice Walter (died 1921); children—James Reed, Henry G. Sec., later v.p. and pres. Mt. Morris Electric Light Co., 1890-98; pres. Union Trust Co., Newark, N.J., 1899-1900; pres. New York Transportation Co., Fifth Av. Stage Co., Met. Express Co., 1900-05; sr. partner Sanderson & Brown, members New York Stock Exchange, until 1911; sr. partner Charles D. Barney & Co., bankers, until 1920; dir. various corps. Installed first mechanically operated stage on Fifth Av.; instituted first trolley express in N.Y. State. Financial adviser to Am. Relief Assn. (Herbert Hoover), Paris, France, Jan.-June 1919. Republican. Episcopalian. Home: New York, N.Y. Died Mar. 24, 1934.

SANDERSON, Sibyl (Mrs. Antonio Terry), operatic singer; b. Sacramento, Calif.; d. Chief Justice Sanderson; ed. schools of San Francisco and in France; début as a professional singer at The Hague, 1888; gained fame in Massenet's operas in Paris; returned to U.S., Jan. 1895; sang with Abbey, Shoeffel & Grau Company, Metropolitan Opera House; appeared in leading soprano rôles in English, French and Italian operas; m. Antonio Terry, Cuban planter and millionaire, Dec. 1, 1897 (died 1899). Now living in Paris. Died 1903.

SANDOR, Mathias, painter; b. Hungary, July 10, 1857; ed. high sch. in Hungary, Art Students' League, New York, 1885-86, Académie Julian, Paris, 1889-90, under François Flameng and Gabriel Ferrier; unmarried. Came to U.S., 1881; began making designs for commercial purposes and painting portraits; now portrait, miniature and landscape painter. Exhibits in all important exhbns. Republican. Studio: New York, N.Y. Deceased.

SANDS, Benjamin Aymar, lawyer; b. New York, July 27, 1853; s. Samuel Stevens and Mary Emily (Aymar) S.; A.B., Columbia, 1874, A.M., 1877, LL.B., 1876; m. Amy K. Akin, Jan. 17, 1878. Admitted to bar, May 1876; mem. Webb & Sprague, 1876-82, Bowers & Sands, 1882—. Receiver Indianapolis, Decatur & Springfield R.R., 1886-92; v.p. Colo. Midland R.R., 1899-1901; v.p. Am. Mortgage Co., State Investing Co.; trustee Greenwich Savings Bank; chmn. bd. N. Brit. & Mercantile Ins. Co. of London; dir., exec. com. Terminal Warehouse Co., Lincoln Trust Co., Fidelity Bank, Commonweath Ins. Co.; dir., finance com. N. Brit. & Mercantile Ins. Co. of N.Y.; dir., auditing com. U.S. Safe Deposit Co. Presdl. elector, 1904. Fellow Met. Mus. of Art. Trustee Columbia U. Home: New York, N.Y. Died May 1, 1917.

SANDS, George Lincoln, ry. official; b. Brunswick, Me., Apr. 18, 1845; s. Jacob Waterhouse and Mary Jane (Dunlap) S.; ed. Brunswick, Me., pub. schs.; m. Theresa A. Doebler, June 26, 1874. Was brakeman, conductor, asst. supt., and div. supt. on various roads, 1865-79; resident engr. and div. supt. Internat. & Great Northern R.R., 1879-80; div. supt. and supt. Tex. & Pacific Ry., 1880-82; div. supt. various divs., A.,T.&S.F. R.R., 1882-87; supt. Atlantic & Pacific Ry., 1887; gen. supt. A.,T.&S.F. R.R., west of Mo. River, 1887-91; supt. transportation and gen. supt. San Antonio & Aransas Pass Ry., 1891-92; asst. mgr., 1892-94, mgr., Jan. 1894—, Wiggins Ferry Co., East St. Louis Connecting Ry. and St. Louis Transfer Co.; 2d v.p. and mgr. same Nov. 1899, to Feb. 1903; v.p. and mgr., 1900-02, St. Louis, Kansas City & Colo. R.R.; v.p. St. Louis & N. Ark. R.R., Aug. 1902—, and receiver same, Apr. 1912-Mar. 1914. Deceased.

SANDS, James Hoban, rear adm. U.S.N.; b. Washington, July 12, 1845; s. Benjamin F. and Henrietta M. (French) S.; apptd. from Md., and grad. U.S. Naval Acad., 1863; m. Mary Elizabeth Meade, Oct. 28, 1869; father of William Franklin S. Promoted ensign, May 28, 1863; advanced through grades to rear adm., Apr. 11, 1902. Served on Tuscarora, N. Atlantic Blockading Squadron, 1863-64; Juniata, May-Aug. 1864; Shenandoah, N. Atlantic Blockading Squadron, 1864-65; participated in evacuation of Charleston, and both attacks on Ft. Fisher; served on Hartford, E. India Squadron, 1865-68; Naval Obs., 1868, 1869-70; Richmond, 1869; Navy Yard, Washington, 1870; California, 1871-73; Hydrographic Office, 1873-75; Minnesota, 1875-76; Navy Yard, New York, 1877-79; spl. duty, Washington, 1880-82; comd. Iroquois, 1882-84; Navy Yard, Washington, 1884-86, 1892-93; comd. Monongahela, 1891-92; Navy Yard, Boston, 1893-95; comd. Columbia, 1895-97; Minneapolis, 1897-98; gov. Naval Home, Phila., 1898-1901; mem. Naval Retiring Bd., 1901, pres., 1902; comdt. Navy Yard, League Island, 1902-03; comd. Coast Squadron, N. Atlantic Fleet, 1903-05; supt. Naval Acad., 1905-07; retired, July 12, 1907. Died 1911.

SANDS, Lawrence Eyster, banker; b. Fairmont, Va., Aug. 4, 1859; s. Joseph Evans and Mary Virginia (Eyster) S.; ed. pub. schs. and Fairmont State Normal Sch.; m. Mary Eugenia Wagner, Oct. 25, 1883; children—John W., Mrs. Mary Virginia Paull. Began with Nat. Bank of W.Va., at Wheeling, 1880, advancing to asst. cashier; was made cashier Nat. Exchange Bank of Wheeling, 1895, pres., 1913-14; pres. First Nat. Bank, Pittsburgh, Pa., Apr. 1, 1914—; trustee Dollar Savings Bank. Episcopalian. Mason. Home: Pittsburgh, Pa. Died Oct. 19, 1928.

SANDT, George Washington, clergyman; b. Belfast, Pa., Feb. 22, 1854; s. Dr. John and Sophia (Frace) S.; A.B., Lafayette Coll., 1878, A.M., 1881; grad. Luth. Theol. Sem., Phila., 1883; D.D., Thiel Coll., Greenville, Pa., 1905, LL.D., 1922; m. Martha J. Kuntz, Aug. 16, 1883. Ordained Luth. ministry, 1883; prof. English lang. and literature, Augustana Coll., Rock Island, Ill., 1884-89; pastor Weisport, Pa., 1889-91, Wilkes-Barre, Pa., 1891-96; mng. editor The Lutheran, 1896-1907, editor in chief, 1907-28, then departmental contributor. Author: Ninety-five Theses for Protestant Church Doors, 1893; Luther's Ninety-five Theses, re-edited, 1911; Christian Science, Weighed and Tested, 1911; Another Fraud Exposed, 1913; Should Lutherans Get Together? 1913. Chmn. Inner Mission Com. of General Council and mem. Home Mission and Ch. Extension bds.; mem. bd. Phila. Motherhouse of Deaconesses and of Lankenau Hosp.; del. World Conf. of Lutherans, Upsala, Sweden, 1911, Conf. of League of Nations to Enforce Peace, Washington, 1915. Wrote Biography of Theodore E. Schmauk, D.D., LL.D., 1921. Home: Allentown, Pa. Deceased.

SANDYS, Edwyn William, editor, author; b. Chatham, Ont., June 9, 1860; s. Rev. Francis W. (D.D.) and Elizabeth A. B. (Moeran) S.; pvt. edn.; unmarried. Was editor Canadian Sportsman, Toronto; journalist to Canadian Pacific Ry.; removed to New York and became editor Outing, and spl. writer for other publs. Author: Upland Game Birds (Am. Sportsman's Library), 1902; Trapper Jim, 1903; Sportsman Joe, 1904; Sporting Sketches, 1905. Deceased.

SANER, Robert E(dward) Lee, lawyer, publicist; b. nr. Washington, Ark., Aug. 9, 1871; s. John Franklin and Susan Crawford (Webb) S.; student Searcy (Ark.) Coll. and Vanderbilt U.; LL.B., U. of Tex., 1896; LL.D., Centenary Coll., Southern Meth. U., 1926; m. Ileaine Marvin Smith, Mar. 31, 1903; 1 dau., Dorothy Lee. Admitted to Tex. bar, 1896; became sr. mem. law firm Saner, Saner & Jack, Dallas, Tex.; vice chmn. exec. com. Tex. Electric Ry., 1912-20; pres. United Securities Co., Tex. Mortgage & Investment Co.; v.p. Southern Loan & Security Co., Provident Loan Soc.; atty. for U. of Tex. for landed endowment comprising more than 2,000,000 acres, 1899-1930. Sec. Dem. State Exec. Com., 1899-1901. V. chmn. central legal advisory bd. of Tex. for selective draft, 1917; Tex. commr. on Uniform State Laws, 1920-34. As pres. of Am. Bar Assn., upon invitation of English and French bars, arranged trip to Eng. and France, for 2,000 mems. bar assn., 1924; presided, 1924, by invitation of President Coolidge, at first nat. contest of high schs.' orations on "The Constitution," in Continental Memorial Hall, in which judges were selected from members of Supreme Court of U.S. (this was the culmination of movement inaugurated by his report to Am. Bar Assn., 1922, "to re-establish the Constitution of the United States in the minds and hearts of the people." More than 1,000,000 students participating from 13,000 high schs. throughout U.S.). Presided at first nat. Inter-Collegiate Oratorical Contests, Los Angeles, 1925. Delivered address in Washington Memorial Chapel, Valley Forge, Pa., July 4, 1924. V.p. bd. trustees First M.E. Ch., S., Dallas. Mason. Sovereign St. Mark's Chapter Red Cross of Constantine; mem. Royal Order of Scotland. Author: Handbook for Citizenship Activities with Suggestions for the Celebration Thereof, 1924. Chmn. bd. of editors Am. Bar Journal, 1920—. Home: Dallas, Tex. Died Oct. 31, 1938.

SANFORD, Daniel Sammis, educator; b. Redding Ridge, Conn., Apr. 10, 1859; s. Daniel and Helen E. (Sammis) S.; A.B., Yale, 1882, A.M., 1885; course in edn., Harvard Grad. Sch., 1891, 92; study and observation of schs in France and Germany, 1898-99; m. Annie Bennett Tomlinson, July 7, 1898. Prin. Oil City (Pa.) High Sch., 1882-83; math. master, St. John's Sch., Ossining, N.Y., 1883-84; prin. High and Centre schs., Stamford, Conn., 1884-91; headmaster Brookline (Mass.) High Sch., 1891-1905; headmaster until 1925 of Sanford Sch., Redding Ridge, which was founded by him, Oct. 1905, on site of Redding Institute, founded by his father, 1847; chief clk. State Sch. Fund, Feb. 1935—. President Fairfield County (Conn.) Planning Assn.; dir. Regional Plan Assn. of New York. Episcopalian. Home: Redding Ridge, Conn. Died May 13, 1936.

SANFORD, Edmund Clark, univ. prof.; b. Oakland, Calif., Nov. 10, 1859; s. Edmund P. and Jennie E. (Clark) S.; A.B., U. of Calif., 1883; Ph.D., Johns Hopkins, 1888; (Sc.D., Hobart College, 1909; LL.D., U. of California, 1912); m. Florence Bartling, Dec. 28, 1901. Teacher Oahu Coll., Honolulu, 1883-85; fellow, 1887-88, instr. psychology, 1888, Johns Hopkins; instr. psychology, 1889-92, asst. prof., 1892-1900, prof. experimental and comparative psychology, 1900-09, prof. psychology and education, 1920—, Clark U.; pres. Clark Coll., 1909-20. Asso. editor Am. Jour. Psychology, 1895—; trustee Lyman and Industrial schs. (boys' and girls' reform schs. of Mass.), 1897-1905; pres. Am. Psychol. Assn., 1902; fellow A.A.A.S. Author: A Course in Experimental Psychology, 1898. Home: Worcester, Mass. Died Nov. 22, 1924.

SANFORD, Edward Terry, judge; b. Knoxville, Tenn., July 23, 1865; s. Edward J. and Emma (Chavannes) S.; A.B. and Ph.B., U. of Tenn., 1883; A.B., Harvard, 1885, A.M., LL.B., 1889; LL.D., U. of Cincinnati, 1908; Harvard Univ, 1904; m. Lutie Mallory Woodruff, Jan. 6, 1891; children—Dorothy (dec.), Anna Magee. Admitted to bar, 1888; asst. atty. gen. of U.S., 1907-08; U.S. dist. judge, Eastern and Middle dists. of Tenn., 1908-23; asso. justice Supreme Ct. of U.S., Feb. 1923—. Trustee U. of Tenn., 1897-1923; trustee Lawson McGhee Library; formerly mem. bd. of govs., Knoxville General Hosp.; charter mem. and chmn. bd. trustees, George Peabody Coll. for Teachers. Home: Washington, D.C. Died Mar. 8, 1930.

SANFORD, Elias Benjamin, clergyman; b. Westbrook, Conn., June 6, 1843; s. Isaac and Louisa (Weeks) S.; A.B., Wesleyan, 1865; hon. A.M., Yale, 1888; D.D., Wesleyan U., 1894; m. Martha Sanford, Oct. 10, 1870. Ordained Congl. ministry; pastor Cornwall, Thomaston and Westbrook, Conn., 1869-94; sec. Open and Institutional Church League, 1895-1900; gen. sec. Nat. Fedn. of Chs., 1900-08; corr. sec. Federal Council Chs. of Christ in America, 1908-13, hon. sec., 1913—. Author: History of Connecticut, 1887, revised and enlarged edition, 1923; Origin and History of the Federal Council of the Churches of Christ in America, 1916; History of the Reformation, 1917. Editor: Concise Cyclopedia of Religious Knowledge, 1890. Home: Middlefield, Conn. Died July 3, 1932.

SANFORD, George Bliss, col. U.S.A., retired; b. New Haven, Conn., June 28, 1842; s. Wm. Elihu and Margaret Louisa (Craney) S.; grad. Yale, 1863; m. Gertrude Minturn, Sept. 15, 1874. Entered service Apr. 26, 1861, as 2d lt. 1st U.S. Dragoons; promoted 1st lt., capt., maj., 1st U.S. Cav.; lt. col., 9th U.S. Cav.; col., 6th U.S. Cav.; served throughout the Civil War in cav. corps, Army of Potomac. In campaigns against hostile Indians, 1865-92. Pres. Conn. State soc. Soc. of the Cincinnati. Home: Litchfield, Conn. Died 1908.

SANFORD, Henry Lindsay, surgeon; b. Boston, Apr. 7, 1873; s. Henry Dean and Ellen Lucretia (Lindsay) S.; A.B., Harvard, 1896, M.D., 1900; post-grad. work in London, Paris, Berlin and Vienna, 1901-03; m. Mary Fairfield Coit, Mar. 17, 1909. Practiced in Cleveland, 1903—; asst. prof. in genito-urinary surgery, Western Reserve U. Sch. Medicine; asst. visiting genito-urinary surgeon, Lakeside Hosp.; urologist to St. Alexis Hospital; mem. Board of Health, Cleveland, 1914; mem. advisory com. Dept. Pub. Welfare, 1915. Mem. Troop A, O.N.G., 1903-06. Fellow Am. Coll. Surgeons. Episcopalian. Translator: (with Dr. R. C. Bryan) Casper and Richter's Functionelle Nierendiagnostik, 1903. Contbr. on med. topics. Mil. service in France, May 1917-June 1919; disch., June 19, 1919, with rank lt. col., M.C., U.S.A. Home: Cleveland, O. Died Feb. 5, 1938.

SANFORD, James Clark, army officer; b. in New York, Sept. 26, 1859; grad. U.S. Mil. Acad., 1884. Commd. 2d lt. engrs., June 15, 1884; 1st lt., Oct. 12, 1886; capt., Aug. 13, 1895; maj., Jan. 22, 1904; lt. col., July 6, 1908; col., Feb. 27, 1914. Sec. Mo. River Commn., 1890-94; in charge improvement upper Mo. and Yellowstone rivers, 1896-98; constrn. mil. rd., Ft. Washakie to Jackson's Lake, Wyo., 1898-99; in charge Charleston (S.C.) Engr. Dist. and engr. 6th Lighthouse Dist., 1900-03; constrn. seagoing self-propelling suction dredges, 1900-08; in charge Newport (R.I.) Engr. Dist., 1908; duty at New Orleans, La., 1916-17. Official del. of U.S. to Internat. Congress of Navigation, Milan, Italy, Sept. 1905, St. Petersburg, Russia, May-June 1908; mem. Permanent Internat. Com. of Navigation Congresses. Died Dec. 25, 1926.

SANFORD, John, manufacturer; b. Amsterdam, N.Y., 1851; A.B., Yale, 1872. Pres. Stephen Sanford & Sons; chmn. of bd. Amsterdam City Nat. Bank, Bigelow-Sanford Carpet Co. Home: Amsterdam, N.Y. Died Sept. 26, 1939.

SANFORD, Maria L., educator; b. Old Saybrook, Conn., Dec. 19, 1836; d. Henry and Mary (Clark) S.; grad. State Normal Sch., New Britain, Conn., 1855. Began teaching, 1852; prof. history, Swarthmore Coll., Pa., 1871-80; prof. rhetoric and elocution, U. of Minn., 1880-Jan. 1909 (retired). Lecturer upon lit. and history of art. Home: Minneapolis, Minn. Died Apr. 21, 1920.

SANFORD, Myron Reed, college prof.; b. Redding, Conn.; s. Francis A. and Lucy Hawley (Knap) S.; A.B., Wesleyan U., Middletown, Conn., 1880, A.M., 1883; student U. of Leipzig, 1893-94, also at Rome and Pompeii; L.H.D., U. of Vermont, 1910; unmarried. In charge of dept. of classics, Wyoming Conf. Sem., Kingston, Pa., 1880-86; prof. Latin, Haverford (Pa.) Coll., 1886-93, dean of faculty, 1890-93; prof. Latin lang. and lit., Middlebury (Vt.) Coll., 1894-1923 (emeritus). President Middlebury College War Service Committee, 1915-18. Conducted dramatization of Life of Cicero, 1899, 1900, 1910. Home: Bridgeport, Conn. Died Jan. 15, 1939.

SANGER, Alexander, merchant; b. Obenbreit, Bavaria, Germany, May 8, 1847; s. Elias and Babette S.; common school edn.; m. Fannie Fechenbach, May 11, 1879. Came to America, 1865; bookkeeper for Heller Bros., Cincinnati, 1871; partner Ochs, Lehman & Co., 1872; joined Sanger Bros., Corsicana, Tex., 1872, and opened store for firm at Dallas, Tex., same yr.; head dept. store employing 1,800 persons; pres. Sanger Bros. Dry Goods Co. Dir. Texas State Fair (pres. 1894), Dallas Chamber of Commerce and Mfrs.' Assn. (pres.); dir. Dallas Pub. Library; dir., pres. Temple Emanu-El; dir. Nat. Jewish Hosp. for Consumptives (Denver). Mason. Home: Dallas, Tex. Died Sept. 13, 1925.

SANGER, Charles Robert, chemist; b. Boston, Aug. 31, 1860; s. George Partridge and Elizabeth Sherburne (Thompson) S.; A.B., Harvard, 1881, A.M., cum laude, 1882, A.M., and Ph.D., 1884; m. Almira Starkweather Horswell, Dec. 21, 1886 (died 1905); m. 2d, Eleanor Whitney Davis, May 2, 1910. Asst. in chemistry, Harvard Univ., 1881-82, 1884-86; prof. chemistry, U.S. Naval Acad., 1886-92, Washington U., St. Louis, 1892-99; asst. prof. chemistry, 1899-1903, prof. and dir. chem. lab., Sept. 1, 1903—, Harvard Univ. Fellow Am. Acad. Arts and Sciences. Home: Cambridge, Mass. Died Feb. 25, 1912.

SANGER, Joseph Prentice, major gen. U.S.A.; b. Detroit, May 4, 1840; s. Henry Kirkland and Caroline (Prentice) S.; U. of Mich., 1858-60; (hon. A.M., Bowdoin, 1872); m. Frances E. Kent, Dec. 27, 1877. Served 2d lt. 1st Mich. Inf., May 1, 1861; mustered out of vol. service, Aug. 7, 1861; 2d lt. 1st U.S. Arty., Aug. 5, 1861; 1st lt., Oct. 26, 1861; with battery of light arty.; twice bvtd. for gallantry; orderly officer to President Lincoln 1 week, 1862. After war adj. of his regt.; in expdn. against Fenians, 1866; honor grad. Arty. Sch., 1869, and its first adj.; capt. 1st Arty., Feb. 7, 1875; maj. insp. gen., Feb. 12, 1889; comd. battery in Brooklyn "Whisky Riots," 1871; prof. mil. science, tactics and law, Bowdoin, 1872-75; admitted to bar, Portland, Me., Apr. 21, 1874; detailed to accompany Gen. E. Upton on tour of inspection of armies of Japan, China, Persia, India, Turkey, Italy, Russia, Austria, France and Eng., 1875-77; comd. battery, 1877-84, serving in r.r. riots; aide to Maj. Gen. Schofield, 1884-88; aide and acting sec. to President Harrison, 1891; mil. sec. to lt. gen., 1895; insp. S. Atlantic inspection dist. and prin. asst. to insp. gen. of army, 1895-98; lt. col. insp. gen. U.S.V., May 9, 1898; acting insp. gen. of the army; brig. gen. U.S.V., May 27, 1898; in command consecutively of 2d Brigade, 2d Div., 1st Corps, June 19, 1898; 3d Div., 1st Corps, June 29-Nov. 19, 2d Brigade, 2d Div., 1st Corps, to Dec. 12; 2d Div., 1st Corps, Dec. 4-Dec. 23; assigned to command dept. and subsequently Dist. of Matanzas, Cuba, Jan. 11, 1899; hon. disch., June 12, 1899, and assigned to duty with asst. sec. of war, July 3, 1899; apptd. by the president dir. census, Cuba and P.R., Aug. 9, and Sept. 8, 1899, respectively; apptd. mem. of War Coll. Bd., June 21, 1900; col. insp. gen., Feb. 2, 1901; insp. gen. and chief of the staff, Div. of the Philippines, July 4, 1901-Oct. 1, 1902; brig. gen., July 23, 1902; dir. Philippine Census, Oct. 6, 1902; maj. gen., Jan. 20, 1904; retired, Jan. 21, 1904. Mem. Brownsville Ct. of Inquiry, 1908-09. Mem. Medal of Honor Bd., 1916—. Died Mar. 15, 1926.

SANGER, William Cary, assistant sec. of war; b. Brooklyn, May 21, 1853; s. Henry and Mary E. (Requa) S.; grad. Poly. Inst. of Brooklyn, 1869; A.B., Harvard, 1874, A.M., 1875; LL.B., Columbia, 1878; (LL.D., Hamilton, 1902); m. Mary Ethel Cleveland, d. Gen. C. C. Dodge, Feb. 23, 1892. Mem. N.Y. Assembly, 1895-97; lt. col. 203d N.Y. Inf., Spanish-Am. War, 1898; asst. sec. of war, 1901-03. Pres. U.S. delegation to Internat. Conf., Geneva, 1906, to revise the treaty of 1864. Trustee Hamilton College. U.S. del. Internat. Red Cross Conf., London, 1907. Presdl. elector, 1908; mem. war relief bd. Nat. Red Cross; chmn. N.G. Commn. apptd. by Gov. Hughes, 1907; mem. N.Y. State Commn. in Lunacy, 1910-11; pres. State Hosp. Commn., 1911-13; was designated by the President to receive, on behalf of the U.S. Govt. the lighthouse at Crown Point, Lake Champlain, June 19, 1912. Chancellor N.Y. Chapter Colonial Order of Acorn; gov. N.Y. State Soc. of Colonial Wars; gov. gen. Order Founders and Patriots America; pres. Oneida Hist. Soc. Dir. mil. relief Potomac Div. Am. Red Cross, Washington, 1917-18, mgr., 1918-19. Author: The Reserve and Auxiliary Forces of England and the Militia of Switzerland (report to the President and the Secretary of War, prepared 1900), 1903. Home: Sangerfield, N.Y. Died Dec. 6, 1921.

SANGSTER, Margaret Elizabeth, author; b. (Munson) Ned Rochelle, N.Y., Feb. 22, 1838; private edn., chiefly in New York; m. George Sangster, 1858. Became contbr. to leading periodicals; asso. editor Hearth and Home, 1871-73, Christian at Work, 1873-79, Christian Intelligencer, 1879—; postmistress Harper's Young People, 1882-89; editor Harper's Bazar, 1889-99; staff contbr. Christian Herald, 1894—, Ladies' Home Journal, 1899-1905, Woman's Home Companion, 1905—. Author: Poems of the Household; Winsome Womanhood; Janet Ward; Eleanor Lee; Good Manners for All Occasions, 1905; The Story Bible, 1905; Happy School Days, 1909; and many others. Home: Glen Ridge, N.J. Died June 4, 1912.

SANKEY, Ira Allan, music publisher; b. Edinburgh, Scotland, Aug. 30, 1874; s. Ira David (evangelist) and Fanny (Victoria) S.; B.S., Princeton, 1897; spl. studies in civ. engring. and architecture; m. Frances Wann, Oct. 18, 1899. In music publishing business of Biglow & Main Co., Feb. 1, 1898—. Author: The Male Quartet, 1902; Hallowed Hymns, New and Old, 1908. Composer of sacred songs, including "Never Give Up," etc. Home: Brooklyn, N.Y. Died Dec. 30, 1915.

SANKEY, Ira David, evangelist and singer; b. Edinburgh, Pa., Aug. 28, 1840; s. Hon. David and Mary S.; moved to New Castle, Pa.; united with M.E. Ch. at 15; became choir leader, Sunday school supt. and pres. Y.M.C.A. there; at Indianapolis Y.M.C.A. Internat. Conv., 1870, met Dwight L. Moody, and became associated with him as a solo singer in evangelistic work in U.S. and abroad; of late years also lecturer. Gave to New Castle, as a free gift, a Y.M.C.A. and public library building; also gave a building site to M.E. Ch. there. Compiler: Gospel Hymns, 1875-95; Sacred Songs and Solos, 1873, pub. in England, which have had a circulation of over 50,000,000 copies, and have been translated into many languages; also "Winnowed Songs" for Sunday schools, 1890; Young People's Songs of Praise, 1902. He has composed many of the most popular gospel songs of his day, including "The Ninety and Nine" and "When the Mists Have Rolled Away." Author: The Gospel Choir; The Male Choir; Christian Endeavor Hymn-Book, 1894; Sankey's Story of the Gospel Hymns, 1906; My Life and Sacred Songs, 1906. Lost his eyesight, 1903. Home: Brooklyn, N.Y. Died 1908.

SANNO, James Madison Johnston, army officer; b. New Hampton, N.J., Dec. 10, 1840; s. William P. and Hannah (Zeller) S.; ed. in N.J.; asst. sergt.-at-arms, N.J. senate, 1858; apptd. cadet from N.J., 1859; grad. West Point, 1863; m. Mary Worth, d. Gen. John T. Sprague, U.S.A. (g.d. Gen. W. J. Worth, U.S.A.), June 10, 1868. Commissioned 2d lt. 7th Inf., June 11, 1863; promoted through grades to col. 18th Inf., Dec. 18, 1899; brig. gen. U.S.A. and retired, 1903. Provost marshal, adj. and insp. gen. Dept. Florida, 1865-69; frontier duty, 1869-78, insp. Indian supplies in Mont., 1877-78; in charge Dept. of Law, U.S. Inf. and Cav. Sch., Ft. Leavenworth, 1889-94; engaged June-Aug. 1896, collecting and deporting 537 refugee Canadian Cree Indians; insp. gen. depts. Mo., Dak. and the Lakes, April-Dec. 1898; pres. bd. claims against U.S., Manila, P.I., Jan.-Aug. 1900; organized 27th U.S. inf., 1901; comd. Dept. Colo., Nov.-Dec. 1901; comdg. regt. and Ft. D. A. Russell, Wyo., Jan. 1902—. Mem. various mil. organizations; insp. gen. A.A.S.R. (Masons), Southern Jurisdiction U.S. Died 1907.

SANSOM, Marion, livestock; b. Walker Co., Tex., June 20, 1852; s. R. P. and Susan (Manning) S.; ed. Trinity U., Tehuacana, Tex. (non-grad.); m. Eliza Powell, 1875. In livestock business from boyhood; owner of oil mills, cattle ranches, breeder of pure-bred cattle; pres. for 20 yrs. of First Nat. Bank of Alvarado, Tex.; settled at Ft. Worth, 1902; head of Cassidy-Southwestern Commn. Co., 1903-20; organizer, 1903, and first pres. Stockyards Nat. Bank, Fort Worth; dir. Federal Reserve Bank of Dallas; mgr. Fort Worth agency of agrl. loan agency of War Finance Corp., 1921-24. Pres. bd. Agrl. and Mech. Coll. of Tex. 8 yrs. Mason, Odd Fellow, K.P. Home: Fort Worth, Tex. Died Mar. 22, 1932.

SAN SOUCI, Emery John, governor; b. Saco, Me., July 24, 1857; s. Euzebe and Mary Louisa (Couette) S.; ed. pub. schs.; m. Minnie A. J. Duffy, Nov. 1, 1880. Began as back boy, Laconia Cotton Mills, Biddeford, Me., at age 11; clk., traveling salesman, mcht.; retired from active business, 1919; dir. Union Trust Co.; trustee Old Colony Coöperative Bank. Mem. Co. K, 1st Conn. N.G., 7 yrs.; 1st Co., Governor's Foot Guard, 2 yrs.; a.d.c. with rank of colonel on staff of Gov. Aran J. Pothier, 6 yrs. Mem. City Council, Providence, 1901-06; lt. gov. R.I., 1915-20, gov., 1921-22; collector Port of Providence, terms, 1923-27 and 1927-31. Trustee Olneyville Library, St. Vincent de Paul Infant Asylum. Republican. K.C., Elk, Eagle. Home: Providence, R.I. Died Aug. 10, 1936.

SANTEE, Ellis Monroe, M.D.; b. Hughesville, Pa., Aug. 13, 1862; s. John Clark and Elizabeth (Gray) S.; ed. Acad., New Columbus, Pa., 2 yrs. course Hahnemann Med. Coll., Phila.; M.D., Homœ. Med. Coll. of Mo., St. Louis, 1890; 1 yr. resident phys. Hahnemann Hosp., Rochester, N.Y.; m. Beulah H. Barber, Dec. 22, 1883 (died 1921); m. 2d, Jennie Wood, 1922. Formerly lecturer obstetrics, Cortland Hospital Training Sch. for Nurses; sec. Medico-Chirurg. Soc. of Central N.Y.; health commr., Cortland, dairy expert U.S. Dept. Agr., 1906-07; lecturer on sanitary subjects, N.Y. State Dept. Agr., 1908-17; retired. Author: Repertory of Convulsions, 1890; Santee Genealogy, 1900, 27; Farm Sewage, 1912. Home: Hunlock Creek, Pa. Died Dec. 22, 1931.

SANTEE, Harris Ellett, anatomist, neurologist; b. Snodes, O., Oct. 15, 1864; s. William B. and Catherine (Ellett) S.; A.B., Northeastern Ohio Normal Coll., 1889, hon. A.M., 1907; M.D., U. of Pa., 1892; A.M., Taylor U., 1900, Ph.D., 1901; m. Grace M. Brown, Aug. 28, 1895 (died 1903); children—Martha Boyle (Mrs. William Scott Walker), Mary Elizabeth (Mrs. George A. Langeler); m. 2d, Martha J. Pitt, Mar. 30, 1905. In practice at Chicago, 1892—; prof. anatomy, Harvey Med. Coll., 1896-1906, Jenner Med. Coll., 1906-18; prof. anatomy, Coll. of Phys. and Surg. (Univ. of Ill.), 1900-10; prof. nervous anatomy, Chicago Coll. Medicine and Surgery (med. dept., Valparaiso (Ind.) U.), 1910-17; dean and prof. diseases nervous system, Chicago Medical School, 1919-24. Republican. Conglist. Author: Anatomy of Brain and Spinal Cord (5th edit., 1915); Neurones and the Neurone Concept; The Brain of a Black Monkey; Important Anatomic and Physiologic Factors in Subarachnoid Medication; etc. Home: West Chicago, Ill. Died Feb. 28, 1936.

SANTOS, Epifanio de los, historian; b. Malabon, Rizal, P.I., Apr. 7, 1871; s. Escolastico and Antonina (Cristobal) S.; A.B., Ateneo de Manila, 1890; LL.B., U. of Sto. Tomas, Manila, 1897; m. Ursula Paez, 1899 (dec.); m. 2d, Margarita Torralba, 1908. Co-editor La Independencia and other papers and mags., 1898-1908; admitted to P.I. bar; dist. atty., Nueva Ecija, 1900; gov. of same, 1902-04; pros. atty., Bulacan and Bataan, 1906-25; tech. dir. Philippine census of 1918; dir. Philippine Library and Museum, 1925—. Mem. Hon. Commn. from Philippines to Louisana Purchase Expn., 1904 (mem. bd. awards on Philippine art). Author: Algo de Prosa, 1909; Filipinos y Filipinistas, 1909; Emilia Jacinto, 1910; Vida de Florante y Laura, 1916; Andres Bonifacio, 1918; Proceso de Rizal, 1913. Home: Manila, P.I. Died Apr. 18, 1928.

SAPIR, Edward, anthropologist, linguist; b. Lauenburg, Pomerania, Jan. 26, 1884; s. Jacob David and Eva (Sigel) S.; came with parents to U.S., 1889; A.B., Columbia, 1904, A.M., 1905, Ph.D., 1909, Sc.D., 1929; m. Florence Delson, 1911 (died 1924); children—Herbert Michael, Helen, Philip; m. 2d, Jean

V. McClenaghan, 1926; children—Paul Edward, James David. Research assistant in anthropology, U. of California, 1907-08; instr. in anthropology, U. of Pa., 1908-10; chief of division of anthropology, Can. Nat. Museum, 1910-25, asso. prof. anthropology, U. of Chicago, 1925-27, prof. same and gen. linguistics, 1927-31; Sterling prof. anthology and linguistics, Yale, 1931. Mem. Am. Acad. Arts and Sciences; mem. Am. Anthropol. Assn. (pres.). Author: Wishram Texts, 1909; Takelma Texts, 1909; Yana Texts, 1910; The Takelma Language of S.W. Oregon, 1912; Time Perspective in Aboriginal American Culture, 1916; Language, an Introduction to the Study of Speech, 1921 (with Marius Barbeau) Folk-Songs of French Canada, 1925; The Southern Paiute Language, 1931. Home: Hamden, Conn. Died Feb. 4, 1939.

SAPP, William Frederick, lawyer; b. Grand Rapids, Mich., Aug. 30, 1856; s. Rezin and Margaret E. (Peyre-Ferry) S.; ed. in pub. schs. of Grand Rapids, Coldwater and Kalamazoo, Mich.; m. Mary E. Wood, Oct. 29, 1885. Admitted to bar, 1879; walked into Kan. and began law practice at Galena, Kan., 1880; now mem. Sapp & Wilson. Was city atty. of Galena, and mem. of sch. bd.; Dem. candidate for Congress, 1894. Pres. and owner Battlefield Mining Co. Apptd. recruiting officer in Spanish-Am. War; chmn. of Dem. State Central Com. of Kan.; mem. Dem. Nat. Com. Home: Galena, Kan. Died Mar. 8, 1917.

SARD, Grange, stove mfr.; b. Albany, N.Y., Mar. 10, 1843; s. Grange and Lucy Ann (Cook) S.; ed. Albany Acad., and Albany Classical Inst.; m. Caroline S. Woolverton, Jan. 20, 1870. Began in stove mfg. business, 1860; was chmn. bd. Rathbone, Sard & Co., many yrs.; pres. Union Trust Co., Albany Cemetery Assn., Albany Home Bldg. Co.; trustee Albany Savings Bank; dir. Commercial Bank & Trust Co. Mem. exec. com. of 13 of Citizens' Assn., Albany; mem. Bd. Park Commrs., Albany, 17 yrs. Pres. Nat. Stove Mfrs.' Assn., Trust Co.'s Assn. State of N.Y.; trustee Dudley Observatory (Albany). Republican. Home: Albany, N.Y. Deceased.

SARGEANT, William H., life insurance; b. Springfield, Mass., Oct. 5, 1868; s. Thomas Henry and Annie Jay (Lawler) S.; ed. public schs.; m. Ida Belle Scott (died 1922). With Mass. Mut. Life Ins. Co., Springfield, 1884—; vice pres., 1909-28, pres., 1928—; chmn. board Morris Plan Co. of Springfield; dir. Instn. for Savings, Mutual Fire Ins. Co. Republican. Unitarian. Mason. Home: Springfield, Mass. Died Dec. 28, 1935.

SARGENT, Charles Sprague, dentrologist; b. Boston, Mass., Apr. 24, 1841; s. Ignatius and Henrietta (Gray) S.; A.B., Harvard, 1862, LL.D., 1901; m. Mary Allen, d. Andrew Robeson, of Boston, Nov. 28, 1873. First lt. 2d La. Inf., June 25, 1863; capt. a.d.c. vols., Mar. 15, 1865; bvtd. maj. vols., Mar. 26, 1865, "for faithful and meritorious services" during campaign against Mobile; hon. mustered out, Aug. 26, 1865. Prof. horticulture, 1872-73, dir. Botanic Garden, 1873-79, dir. Arnold Arboretum, 1872—, prof. aboriculture, 1879—, Harvard. Editor Garden and Forest, 1887-97. Planned Jesup collection of N. Am. woods for Am. Mus. Natural History, New York; was chmn. commn. for preservation of Adirondack forests, 1885; chmn. commn. apptd. by Nat. Acad. Sciences upon a forest policy for the forestry lands of the U.S., 1896-97; trustee Mus. Fine Arts, Boston; mem. Park Commn., Town of Brookline. Fellow Am. Acad. Arts and Sciences; pres. Mass. Soc. Promotion Agriculture, 1890—; trustee Mass. Hort. Soc. Author: Catalogue of the Forest Trees of North America; The Woods of the United States; The Forest Flora of Japan; Silva of North America; Report of the Forests of North America; Manual of the Trees of North America, 1905, 1922; Trees and Shrubs. Home: Brookline, Mass. Died Mar. 22, 1927.

SARGENT, Dudley Allen, dir. physical training; b. Belfast, Me., Sept. 28, 1849; s. Benjamin and Caroline (Rogers) S.; A.B., Bowdoin College, 1875, A.M., 1887; M.D., Yale, 1878; (hon. Sc.D., Bowdoin, 1894); m. Ella Fraser Ledyard, Apr. 7, 1881. Dir. Hemenway Gymnasium, 1879-1919, asst. prof. physical training, 1879-89, Harvard; dir. Normal School of Physical Training, Cambridge, Mass., 1881-1916, and pres. of its successor, Sargent Sch. for Physical Edn., 1916—; also pres. Sargent Camp, Peterboro, N.H. Inventor of modern gymnasium apparatus. Author: Universal Test for Strength, Speed and Endurance, 1902; Health, Strength and Power, 1904; Physical Educational, 1906. Home: Cambridge, Mass. Died July 21, 1924.

SARGENT, Frank Pierce, govt. official; b. East Orange, Vt., Nov. 18, 1854; s. Charles E. and Mary C. (Kinney) S.; ed. village sch.; m. Georgie M. McCullough. Became locomotive fireman; chief of Brotherhood of Locomotive Firemen, 1885 to Sept. 8, 1902. Apptd. by President McKinley, 1898, mem. Industrial Commn., resigned; declined position as chief of Bureau of Engraving and Printing, offered by President McKinley, 1900; U.S. Commr. Gen. of Immigration, July 1, 1902—. Republican. Mason. Home: Washington, D.C. Died 1908.

SARGENT, Franklin Haven, teacher; b. Boston, Mass., March 31, 1856; s. Rev. John Turner and Mary Elizabeth (Fiske) S.; A.B., Harvard, 1877; studied Boston Sch. of Oratory and under many pvt. teachers, U.S. and Europe. Began as dramatic teacher, 1878; instr. elocution, Harvard, 1880-82; dramatic dir. Madison Sq. Theatre, New York, 1882-84; pres. Am. Acad. Dramatic Arts, 1884—. Home: New York, N.Y. Died Aug. 28, 1923.

SARGENT, Fred Wesley, ry. president; b. Akron, Ia., May 26, 1876; s. Edgar Wesley and Abbie E. (Haskell) S.; LL.B., State U. of Ia., 1901; LL.D., Lawrence Coll., 1929, also from Huron Coll., S.D.; m. Mary Minier, Jan. 9, 1902; children—Minier, Haskell, Fredrica. Began practice at Sioux City, Ia., 1901; moved to Chicago, 1920; made v.p. and gen. counsel C.&N.W. Ry. Co. and C.,St.P.,M.&O. Ry. Co., 1923, pres. of both rys., June 1925—; dir. Continental Illinois Nat. Bank & Trust Co., Ill. Chamber of Commerce, Ill. Bell Telephone Co., Ind. Harbor Belt R.R. Co., Peoria and Pekin Union R.R. Co.; trustee Northwestern U., Corneil Coll., Lake Forest Acad., Field Museum of Natural History, Museum of Science and Industry. Republican. Methodist. Mason. Awarded Rosenthal Foundation medal "for outstanding civic service," 1933. Home: Evanston, Ill. Died Feb. 4, 1940.

SARGENT, Frederick, engineer; b. Liskeard, Cornwall, Eng., Nov. 11, 1859; s. Daniel and Jane (Yates) S.; ed. Anderson U., Glasgow; came to U.S., 1883; m. Laura S. Sleep, 1885. Consulting engr., Chicago, 1890—; mgr. mech. and elec. depts., World's Fair, Chicago, 1893 (awarded artists' medal); sr. mem. Sargent & Lundy, engrs. Home: Glencoe, Ill. Died July 26, 1919.

SARGENT, Frederick Le Roy, botanist, artist; b. Boston, Dec. 25, 1863; s. George Frederick and Mary Motley (Gavett) S.; Coll. City of New York, 1879-81; spl. course botany, Lawrence Scientific Sch. (Harvard), 1883-86; m. Helen M. C. Child, July 9, 1902; m. 2d, Bertha Taylor Parker, June 15, 1905. Teacher summer sch. of botany, Harvard, 1886; head dept. botany, U. of Wis., 1886-87; instr. botany, Med. Sch., Boston U., 1894-95; pres. Columbine Assn.; pres. Nat. Flower Conv., Asheville, N.C., 1896. Author: Guide to Cryptogams, 1886; Through a Microscope (joint author), 1886; A Key to North American Species of Cladonia, Cambridge, 1893; How to Describe a Flowering Plant, 1894; Corn Plants—Their Uses and Ways of Life, 1899; Omar and the Rabbi, 1919; Plants and Their Uses, 1913. Fellow A.A.A.S. Home: Cambridge, Mass. Died Jan. 16, 1928.

SARGENT, George Henry, writer; b. Warner, N.H., May 5, 1867; s. Walter and Addie C. (Morrill) S.; ed. Simonds High Sch.; m. Carrie Florence Dietz, Aug. 14, 1889. Began newspaper work at St. Paul, Minn., 1887; city editor St. Paul Pioneer Press, 1890-95; connected with Evening Transcript, Boston, 1895—; bibliographer, magazine writer and author. Republican. Conglist. Author: Modern Tendencies in Book Collecting, 1925; Amy Lowell, a Mosaic, 1926; Writings of A. Edward Newton, a Bibliography, 1927; A Busted Bibliophile and His Books, 1929. Compiler: Epigrams and Aphorisms of Oscar Wilde, 1906; (with Joseph Jackson) English Notes—a Review, 1919. Home: Warner, N.H. Died Jan. 14, 1931.

SARGENT, Henry Bradford, hardware mfr.; b. New York, Mar. 4, 1851; s. Joseph Bradford and Elizabeth Collier (Lewis) S.; Ph.B., Yale, 1871 (hon. M.A., 1907), now fellow emeritus, Yale; m. Harriet Amelia Oaks, Dec. 4, 1879. Has been connected with Sargent & Co., 1871— (pres. and gen. mgr.); dir. New Haven Bank (N.B.A.). Home: New Haven, Conn. Died Feb. 3, 1927.

SARGENT, Herbert Howland, officer U.S.A.; b. Carlinville, Ill., Sept. 29, 1858; s. Joseph True and Maria L. (Braley) S.; B.S., Blackburn U., 1878; grad. U.S. Mil. Acad., 1883; m. Alice C. Applegate, Aug. 11, 1886. Second lt. 2d Cav., June 13, 1883; 1st lt., June 19, 1890; capt., Mar. 2, 1899; maj., Jan. 8, 1909. Served on frontier (and prof. mil. science at U. of Ill., 1886-87) till outbreak Spanish-Am. War; served at Washington, May 1898, in organizing vols.; col. 5th U.S. Vol. Inf., May 20, 1898-May 31, 1899; organized regt. at Columbus, Miss.; at Santiago, Cuba., Aug. 12, 1898; comd. dist. of Guantanamo under Gen. Wood, 1899; lt. col. 29th U.S. Vol. Inf., July 5, 1899-May 10, 1901; fought insurgents on island of Luzon; comd. attacking forces Dec. 19, 1899, at battle of San Mateo in which Gen. Lawton was killed; recommended by Gens. Wood and Otis for bvts. for meritorious service in Cuba and Philippines, 1898-99. Prof. mil. science and tactics, Agrl. and Mech. Coll. of Tex., 1903-07; grad. Army War Coll., 1909; retired Nov. 1911. Recalled to active duty, June 27, 1917; asst. to dept. q.m. Western Dept., San Francisco, until Sept. 25, 1917; prof. mil. science and tactics, Princeton U., 1917-18; detailed to war plans div., Gen. Staff, Army War Coll., Washington, Mar. 28, 1918; lt. col. N.A., May 23, 1918; lt. col. U.S.A. retired, July 9, 1918; relieved from active duty and ordered home, Nov. 26, 1918. Recommended for command of a brigade in World War by Pres. Roosevelt and 24 gen. officers of regular army. Author: Napoleon Bonaparte's First Campaign, 1893; The Campaign of Marengo, 1897; The Campaign of Santiago de Cuba, 1907; The Strategy on the Western Front, 1919. Ordered to Washington, Nov. 1907, from S.D., to receive from President Roosevelt in person an especial compliment on his history of the Campaign of Santiago de Cuba. Home: Jacksonville, Ore. Died Sept. 16, 1921.

SARGENT, James, inventor; b. Chester, Vt., Dec. 5, 1824; s. William and Hannah S.; ed. dist. schs.; worked on farm and later foreman in woolen mill; m. Angeline M., d. Job and Hannah Foster, Apr. 29, 1847. Was traveling daguerreotyper, 1848-52; mfd. and sold an automatic apple-parer, 1852-57; partner Yale & Greenleaf Lock Co., 1857-65; invented burglar-proof locks and established in business in Rochester, 1865; invented Sargent time-locks, 1873; later added many styles of patented locks; pres. Sargent & Greenleaf Co., mfrs.; pres. Pfaudler Vacuum Fermentation Co., and inventor their glass enameled steel tanks and vacuum pump; inventor, automatic electric "semaphore" ry. signals, and pres. Gordon Railway Signal Co.; inventor automatic smoke consumer; pres. Waterloo Gold Mining Co., Calif. Home: Rochester, N.Y. Died 1910.

SARGENT, John Garibaldi, atty. gen. of U.S.; b. Ludlow, Vt., Oct. 13, 1860; s. John Henmon and Ann Eliza (Hanley) S.; A.B., Tufts Coll., 1887, A.M., 1912, LL.D., 1925; LL.D., Middlebury and Norwich Colls., 1925, Rutgers Univ. and Amherst Coll., 1928; m. Mary L. Gordon, Aug. 4, 1887; 1 dau., Mrs. Gladys Gordon Pearsons. Admitted to Vt. bar, 1890; mem. Stickney, Sargent & Skeels. State's atty., Windsor Co., Vt., 1898-1900; sec. civil and mil. affairs of Vt., 1900-02; atty. gen. of Vt., 1908-12; attorney general of U.S., 1925-29; mem. Stickney, Sargent & Chase, 1939—; pres. Ludlow Savings Bank and Trust Co., 1935. Republican. Trustee Black River Academy. Universalist. Home: Ludlow, Vt. Died Mar. 5, 1939.

SARGENT, John Singer, artist; b. Florence, Italy, 1856; s. Dr. Fitzwilliam S. (physician and author) of Boston, and Mary (Newbold) S.; ed. in Italy and Germany; studied painting at Acad. of Fine Arts, Florence, Italy, and in Paris under Carolus Duran; LL.D., Yale, 1916; D.Arts, Harvard, 1916, unmarried. Exhibited portrait of Carolus Duran in Paris Salon, 1877; traveled in Spain, 1879, and on return opened studio in Paris; removed to London, 1884, and has since resided there, but has visited U.S., 1876, 1887, 1889, 1895, 1903, painting and exhibiting paintings at leading exhibitions. Has painted many portraits, English and American, one of recent note being that of President Roosevelt, painted 1903; also various other pictures and mural paintings, of which made exhbn. at Royal Acad., London, and at Boston Pub. Library, 1903. A.N.A., 1894, N.A., 1897. Officier de le Legion l'Honneur, 1897; mem. de l'Institut, 1905; mem. Acad. of Berlin, 1900; Order Pour le Mirite, 1909. Asso. Royal Acad. (England), 1894; Royal Academician, 1897; mem. Am. Acad. Arts and Letters, Société Nationale des Beaux Arts. Died Apr. 15, 1925.

SARGENT, Ledyard Worthington, educator; b. Boston, Mass., June 29, 1882; s. Dudley Allen and Ella Fraiser (Ledyard) S.; A.B., Harvard U., 1905, A.M., from same univ., 1906; m. Etta same univ., 1906; m. Etta Lennox, Sept. 2, 1910 (died 1936); children—Jeanne, Lennox Ledyard, Cynthia Joy. Research asst. in physical chemistry, Mass. Inst. Tech., 1906-07; with wood utilization lab., U.S. Forest Service, Washington, D.C., 1907-08; asst. mgr. cyanide plant, Roesler & Hassler Chem. Co., Perth Amboy, N.J., 1908-09; in partnership with H. W. Morse, developing process for recovering potash from feldspar, 1909-10; teacher of chemistry, N.D. Agrl. Coll., 1910-11; farming nr. Stratham, N.H., 1911-13; v.p. The Sargent Sch., Cambridge, Mass., 1913-24, pres. from 1924 until retired. Editor: Autobiography of Dudley A. Sargent, 1927. Presented The Sargent School to Boston Univ., 1929. Home: Waveland, Mass. Deceased.

SARGENT, Nathan, naval officer; b. New York, Oct. 29, 1849; s. D. H. and Katherine (Sargent) Dustin; assumed name of grandfather, Nathan Sargent, by act of Congress, 1866; prep. edn., Emerson Inst. and Gonzaga Coll., Washington; apptd. to U.S. Naval Acad., from Mont., 1866, grad., 1870; m. Isabel Hill, Apr. 26, 1879. Promoted ensign, July 1871; master, July 1874; lt., Jan. 1881; lt. comdr., Mar. 1899; comdr., Sept. 1901; capt., May 13, 1906. Naval attaché at Rome, Berlin and Vienna, 1889-93; comdg. U.S.S. Scorpion and Machias, Atlantic Fleet, 1899-1901, U.S.S. Baltimore, Asiatic Fleet, 1904-06; mem. Gen. Bd. Home: Washington, D.C. Died 1907.

SARGENT, Walter, college prof.; b. Worcester, Mass., May 7, 1868; s. Lucius Manlius and Clara Fatima (Allen) S.; grad. Worcester Acad., 1885; studied art, Mass. Normal Art Sch., Boston, acads. of Colarossi and Delecluse, Paris; spl. student, Harvard U. (one course); m. Emma Florence Bailey, July 17, 1901. State supervisor of drawing, Mass., 1903-06; dir. drawing and manual training, Boston, 1906-09; prof. art edn., U. of Chicago, 1909-24, prof. and chmn. of Dept. of Art, 1924—. Lecturer on art topics. Has exhibited paintings Boston Art

Club, Soc. Am. Artists (New York), Am. Artists' Exhbn. (Chicago), Pa. Acad. (Phila.), Corcoran Gallery (Washington), Albright Galley (Buffalo, N.Y.). Author: Fine and Industrial Arts in Elementary Schools, 1912; How Children Learn to Draw, 1916; Art Education in the United States, 1918; The Enjoyment and Use of Color, 1923. Home: Chicago, Ill. Died Sept. 19, 1927.

SARGENT, William Durham; b. Lynn, Mass., June 16, 1863; s. George M. and Helen (Durham) S.; M.A., Northwestern U.; studied Mass. Inst. Tech.; m. May A. Pardridge; children—William Durham, Teresa Evelyn (Mrs. Ronald Gubelman). Has served as dir., mem. exec. and finance com. Am. Brake Shoe & Foundry Co.; and dir. and mem. exec. com. Am. Steel Foundries; dir., mem. exec. com. Crocker-Wheeler Electric Mfg. Co., and has been engaged in other enterprises, and is now chmn. bd. The Trucktor Corp. Republican. Home: Miami Beach, Fla. Died Feb. 15, 1940.

SARLES, Elmore Yocum, governor; b. Wonewoc, Wis., Jan. 15, 1859; s. Rev. Jesse D. and Margaret (Thompson) S.; ed. pub. schs. and 1 yr. at Galesville (Wis.) U.; m. Anna York, Jan. 10, 1886; children—Earle Redmon, Mrs. Doris York Mann, Duane York, Mrs. Eleanor Goodman. Engaged in banks and business, Wis., 1873-80; moved to N.D., 1881, and located at Hillsboro; organized Traill Co. Bank, 1881, which became First Nat. Bank of Hillsboro, 1885, of which is v.p.; general manager Sarles Real Estate Agency, Hillsboro; v.p. First Nat. Bank of Northwood, N.D. Was mayor of Hillsboro 2 yrs.; mem. bd. trustees Mayville (N.D.) Normal Sch., 6 yrs.; mem. Hillsboro High Sch. Bd. 15 yrs.; gov. of N.D., 1905-07. Republican. Mason, Elk. Home: Hillsboro, N.D. Died Feb. 14, 1929.

SARTAIN, Emily, painter; b. Philadelphia; d. John (artist) and Susannah Longmate (Swaine) S.; became engraver under her father and during professional career studied at Pa. Acad. Fine Arts, 1864-70; in Italy, and under Luminais, Paris, 1871-75. Engraved and etched numerous framing prints and book illustrations; painter of portraits and genre pictures; exhibited oil paintings at Paris Salon, 1875, 1883; received medal at Centennial Exhbn., 1876; Mary Smith prize, Pa. Acad., 1881, 1883, for best painting by women. Art editor Our Continent, 1881-83; mem. jury of awards, Art Dept., Chicago Expn., 1893; official del. from U.S. Govt. to Internat. Congress on Instruction in Drawing, Paris, 1900, Berne, 1904. Prin. Phila. Sch. of Design for Women, 1886-1919, prin. emeritus. Home: Philadelphia, Pa. Died June 17, 1927.

SARTAIN, Samuel, engraver on steel; b. Phila., Pa., Oct. 8, 1830; s. John Sartain, artist and engraver (died 1897). Began to engrave under his father at 16; from 1854 in business for himself; has engraved many framing and book plates. Home: Philadelphia, Pa. Died 1906.

SARTAIN, William, artist; b. Philadelphia, Pa., Nov. 21, 1843; s. John (artist) and Susannah Longmate (Swaine) S.; bro. of Emily S.; A.B., Central High School, Phila., 1861; studied painting under Schussele, Bonnât, and École des Beaux Arts, Paris; unmarried. Awarded silver medal, Boston, 1881; hon. mention, Philadelphia, 1887; bronze medal, Buffalo Exposition, 1901; silver medal, Charleston Expn., 1902; late prof. life classes, Art Students' League of New York; has painted many figure pieces, landscapes, etc., which are in pub. and pvt. collections; silver medal, Buenos Aires, 1910, and picture bought by Argentine Govt.; "Nubian Scheik," purchased for Luxembourg Gallery by French Govt. Occasional contbr. on art for jours. A.N.A.; pres. New York Art Club. Died Oct. 25, 1924.

SARTORI, Louis Constant, commodore U.S.N., retired June 3, 1874; b. Bloomsbury, Burlington Co., N.J., June 3, 1812; entered navy midshipman, Feb. 2, 1829; promoted lt., Sept. 8, 1841; served on bombbrig "Stromboli" during Mexican war, taking part in capture of Goatzacoalcas and Tabasco; while on Pacific squadron, 1855-56, commanded an expedition and had an engagement with Fijis; comdr., April 7, 1861; in blockading service during Civil war; capt., Sept. 26, 1866; commodore, Dec. 12, 1873. Home: Philadelphia, Pa. Died 1899.

SARTZ, Richard Sophus Nielsen, journalist, translator; b. Stryn, Norway, June 30, 1852; s. Hans Henrik Bödtker and Inger Charlotte (Brunn) S.; A.B., Christiania U., 1870; post-grad., 1871-72-73. Came to America, 1879; in mercantile business and newspaper writer, Phila., New York and Minneapolis, 1879-89; editor Minneapolis Daglig Tidende, 1889-92, Norden (Chicago), 1892-96; translator Dept. of Agr., Washington, 1898—; editor Am. division of Nordmandsforbundet, Christiania; asso. editor Illustreret Norsk konversations-leksikon, Christiania, 1906—; corr. various papers of Norway. Mem. Normandsforbundet, Am. Scandinavian Soc. (New York), Norwegian Soc. of D. of C. (hon. pres.). Awarded silver medal by Christiania U., 1911, for services in behalf of Scandinavian culture and lit. in America. Decorated by King of Norway as Knight, Class I, of the Order of St. Olav, 1912. Author: Norway's Contributions to Natural Sciences, 1905. Translator: E. Lilja's Mennesket, dets oprindelse, liv og bestemmelse, 1896. Home: Washington, D.C. Died June 1920.

SASLAVSKY, Alexander, violinist; b. Karkoff, Russia, Feb. 8, 1876; s. Michael and Anna (Gantz) S.; studied violin in Russia under Gorski, in Vienna under Prof. Gruen; grad. Vienna Conservatory of Music, 1893; m. C. Izolce Todd, June 18, 1906. Soloist, concert master and asst. condr., New York Symphony Orchestra, 1893-18; an organizer, 1904, and concert master 4 yrs., Russian Symphony Orchestra (resigned); conducts string quartette in own name; devoting time to chamber music and teaching, Los Angeles, Calif., 1918—. Besides Colo. series in summer, gives two series every winter in San Francisco and Los Angeles; conductor People's Symphony Orchestra, 1922-23, Bohemian Club Symphony Orchestra, 1921, Symphonic Ensemble of San Francisco, 1923—. First pres. The Bohemians (Los Angeles). Home: San Francisco, Calif. Died Aug. 3, 1924.

SASS, George Herbert ("Barton Grey"), author; b. Charleston, S.C., Dec. 24, 1845; grad. Coll. of Charleston, 1867 (LL.D., same, 1902); m. Anna E. Ravenel, Dec. 20, 1883. Contributes verses leading periodicals; many yrs. lit. editor Sunday News and Courier (Charleston); has delivered literary addresses; master in equity, Charleston Co., S.C. Author: The Hearst's Quest (poems), 1904. Home: Charleston, S.C. Died 1908.

SATER, John Elbert, judge; b. New Haven, O., Jan. 16, 1854; s. John J. and Nancy (Larason) S.; Miami U., 1871-73; A.B., Marietta Coll., 1875, A.M., 1878, LL.D., 1910; LL.D., Miami U., 1911; m. Mary S. Lyon, Oct. 9, 1889. Supt. schs., Wauseon, 1875-81; County School Examiner for 5 years; chief clerk in the office of state commr. of common schs., 1881-84; admitted to bar, 1884; mem. Columbus (O.) Bd. Edn., 1885-90 (pres. 1888-89); apptd. city solicitor of Columbus, 1899, but declined; trustee Pub. Library 4 yrs.; U.S. dist. judge, Southern Dist. of Ohio, Mar. 18, 1907; resigned Nov. 24, 1924, and returned to practice of law. Chmn. com. recommending law to transfer federal judges to circuits other than their own, 1921; pres. Columbus Chamber of Commerce, 1925; mem. Ohio Conv. to repeal 18th Amendment to U.S. Constitution. Republican. Mason. Author of Charter Law for Columbus, 1893; also article, Columbus Land Titles, in Lee's History, 1934. Home: Columbus, Ohio. Died July 18, 1937.

SATHRE, Jacob Cornelius, college pres.; b. Adams, Minn., Sept. 23, 1867; s. Stark Pederson and Elizabeth (Ronnebakken) S.; M.S., Valparaiso U., 1893; LL.B., U. of Minn., 1896; m. Tilla Anundson, Mar. 25, 1897. Taught sch. to pay expenses through coll.; pres. Crookston Coll., 1896—. Pres. Social Service League, Crookston; pres. Pub. Library Bd. Pres. Northwestern Commercial Schs. Assn., 1911-13. Mem. Rep. State Central Com., 1914-15. Methodist. Home: Crookston, Minn. Died July 20, 1922.

SATTERLEE, Eugene, banker; b. Glens Falls, N.Y., July 11, 1847; s. Leroy and Harriet (Hudnut) S.; A.B., U. of Rochester, 1867; LL.B., Albany Law Sch. (Union U.), 1872; student Heidelberg, Berlin, and Paris, 1868-70; m. Olivia Moore, Apr. 17, 1879. Began law practice at Rochester, 1874; mem. Satterlee & Yeoman, 1875-94, Satterlee & Taylor, 1894-95, Satterlee, Yeoman & Taylor, 1895-1902, Satterlee, Bissell, Taylor & French, 1902-05, retired. Pres. Lincoln Nat. Bank of Rochester, Rochester German Ins. Co. Pres. Village of Pittsford, 1904. Republican. Episcopalian. Pres. Alumni U. of Rochester, 1906. Home: Pittsford, N.Y. Died 1910.

SATTERLEE, George Reese, physician; b. Dobbs Ferry, N.Y., Nov. 3, 1873; s. Edward Rathbone and Joanna Meiser (Reese) S.; A.B., Columbia, 1894, A.M., 1898; M.D., Coll. Phys. and Surg. (Columbia), 1898; unmarried. Instructor in medicine, University and Bellevue Hospital Med. Coll., 1910—; pathologist, Gouverneur Hosp., 1907-09; visiting physician and pathologist, Washington Heights Hosp. Author: Outlines of Human Embryology, 1906. Home: New York, N.Y. Died Feb. 8, 1928.

SATTERLEE, Henry Yates, P.E. bishop; b. New York, N.Y., Jan. 11, 1843; s. Edward and Jane Anna (Yates) S.; A.B., 1863, A.M., 1866, Columbia; grad. Gen. Theol. Sem., 1866; (D.D., Union Coll., 1882, Princeton, 1896; LL.D., Columbia, 1897); m. Jane Churchill, June 30, 1866. Deacon, 1865; priest, 1867; asst., 1865-75, rector, 1875-82, Zion Ch., Wappinger's Falls, N.Y.; rector Calvary Ch., New York, 1882-96; elected bishop coadjutor of Ohio, 1887, and bishop of Mich., 1889; declined both; consecrated bishop of Washington, Mar. 25, 1896. Author: New Testament Churchmanship, 1899; The Building of a Cathedral; The Calling of a Christian and Christ's Sacrament of Fellowship, 1902. Died 1908.

SATTERLEE, Walter, artist; b. Brooklyn, N.Y., 1844; s. George Crary and Mary LeRoy (Livingston) S.; grad. Columbia, 1863; studied Nat. Acad. Design; also under Edwin White and Léon Bonnat. Paints figures in oil and water colors; teacher; book illustrator. Received Clarke prize, Nat. Acad., 1886. Associate, Nat. Acad., 1879—. Unmarried. Home: New York, N.Y. Died 1908.

SATTERTHWAITE, Thomas Edward, M.D.; b. New York, Mar. 26, 1843; s. Thomas Wilkinson and Ann Fisher (Sheafe) S.; A.B., Yale, 1864; Harvard Med. Sch., 1864-65; M.D., Coll. Phys. and Surg. (Columbia), New York, 1867; interne New York Hosp., 1867-69 (for 20 months), receiving diploma for surgery; LL.D., U. of Md., 1908; Sc.D., St. John's Coll., Md., 1912; m. Isabella, d. Dr. James Lenox Banks, of New York, 1884. Studied in Vienna, 1869-70; served in Franco-German War as asst. surgeon and surgeon Prussian Army. Microscopist and later pathologist at St. Luke's Hosp., N.Y. City, 1872-82; pathologist Presbyn. Hosp., 1873-88; one of the founders, sec. 2 yrs., prof. pathol. anatomy, 1 yr., and of gen. medicine, 7 yrs., v.p., 1890, prof. medicine, 1904-08, Post-Grad. Med. School; lecturer comparative pathology, Columbia Vet. Coll., 1881-82; organized med. and surg. staff, Chambers St. House of Relief (now Hudson St. Hosp.), 1875; a founder, and pres., 1894-99, Babies' Hosp.; now consulting physician to Post-Graduate, Orthopedic and Manhattan State hosps., New York. First lt., U.S.A.M.R.C., 1911-17. Pres. New York Pathol. Soc., 1880-81; one of founders and pres., 1902-03, Am. Therapeutic Soc.; a founder Am. Coll. Physicians; fellow N.Y. Acad. Medicine. Author: Manual of Histology, 1881; Practical Bacteriology, 1887; Diseases of the Heart and Aorta, 1905; Cardiovascular Diseases, 1912; Diseases of the Heart and Blood Vessels, 1918. Retired from practice, 1923. Died Sept. 19, 1934.

SATTLER, Eric Ericson, M.D.; b. Cincinnati, Nov. 4, 1859; s. Dr. George Sattler (one of the earliest practicing physicians in Cincinnati); M.D., Miami Med. Coll., 1882; studied univs. of Strassburg, Vienna, Berlin, London, Utrecht, New York, etc.; m. Blanche Wallingford, Feb. 1886. Splty. diseases of eye, ear, nose and throat, has held positions in Cincinnati Hosp., Miami Med. Coll., Elsberg Post-Grad. School, etc. Republican. Author: History of Tuberculosis, 1883. Has written numerous med. papers, etc. First called attention to nerve endings in cornea and corneal epithelium (original researches pub. from Strassburg Micros. Lab.). Home: E. Walnut Hills, Cincinnati, O. Died July 1926.

SATTLER, Robert, oculist; b. Cincinnati, July 23, 1855; s. George (M.D.) and Johanna L. Sattler; M.D., Miami Med. Coll., Cincinnati, 1875; post-grad. study N.Y. City and Europe, 1875-78; m. Agnes Maitland Mitchell, Mar. 2, 1902. Practiced in Cincinnati, 1878—; prof. ophthalmology, U. of Cincinnati, 1882—; exec. surgeon Ophthalmic Hosp., Cincinnati Hosp., etc. Home: Indian Hill, Cincinnati, O. Died Feb. 20, 1939.

SAULSBURY, Willard, senator; b. Georgetown, Del., Apr. 17, 1861; s. Willard and Annie Milby (Ponder) S.; ed. pvt. schs. and U. of Va.; m. May, d. Victor du Pont, of Delaware, Dec. 5, 1893. In practice at Wilmington, Oct. 1882—; with Victor du Pont, 1882-88; became sr. mem. Saulsbury, Morris & Rodney; consolidated Wilmington st. rys. and electric cos.; organized, and dir. Equitable Trust Co.; dir. Union Nat. Bank, etc. Chmn. Dem. State Com., 1900-06, Dem. Co. Exec. Com., 1892-98; mem. Dem. Nat. Com., 1908-20, and mem. exec. com.; Dem. caucus nominee for U.S. senator, 1899, 1901, 03, 05, 07, 11; elected U.S. senator for term 1913-19 (pres. pro tem. U.S. Senate, Dec. 1916-Mar. 4, 1919). On advisory com. Limitation of Armament Conf., Washington, 1921-22; Am. del Pan-Am. Conf., Santiago, Chile, 1923. Episcopalian. Home: Wilmington, Del., and Washington, D.C. Died Feb. 20, 1927.

SAUNDERS, Charles Francis, author; b. Bucks Co., Pa., July 12, 1859; s. Joseph and Mary (Parry) S.; grad. Friends' Central Sch., Phila., 1875; m. Elisabeth Moore Hallowell, Nov. 12, 1902; m. 2d, Mira Barrett Culin, May 11, 1921. Editor The United Friend, 1894-97; in business, 1875-1903; secretary Commercial Exchange of Phila., 1903-05. Quaker. Author: Under the Sky in California, 1913; With the Flowers and Trees in California, 1914; The California Padres and Their Missions (with J. Smeaton Chase), 1915; Finding the Worth While in California, 1916, rev. edit., 1937; Western Wild Flower Guide, 1917; Finding the Worth While in the Southwest, 1918, rev. edit., 1937; Useful Wild Plants of U.S. and Canada, 1920; the Southern Sierras of California, 1923; A Little Book of California Missions, 1925, rev. edit., 1938; Trees and Shrubs of California Gardens, 1926; The Wild Gardens of Old California, 1927; The Story of Carmelita, 1928; Capistrano Nights (with St. John O'Sullivan), 1930; Western Wild Flowers and Their Stories, 1933. Home: Pasadena, Calif. Died May 1, 1941.

SAUNDERS, Charles Gurley, lawyer; b. Lawrence, Mass., Oct. 3, 1847; s. Daniel and Mary Jane (Livermore) S.; A.B., Harvard, 1867, A.M., 1870, LL.B., 1870. Began practice in Boston with Daniel and Caleb Saunders (father and uncle); trustee N.E. Conservatory of Music; dir. Houston Oil Co. of Texas, Dartmouth Mfg. Co., Essex Co.; trustee Southwestern Settlement & Development Co. Judge of the Court of Review for the Dept. of N.E., of the P.E. Ch.; apptd. by Gen. Conv. held in Baltimore, 1892, mem. Commn. to Revise Constitution and Canons of P.E. Ch.; apptd. by the Gen. Conv., 1913, mem. of Commn. on the Revision of Enrichment of the Prayer Book;

deputy from Mass. to Triennial Gen. Conventions of P.E. Ch., 1895—; mem. standing com. Diocese of Mass., 1896—; chancellor Cathedral Corporation, Diocese of Mass. Home: Lawrence, Mass. Died Feb. 19, 1918.

SAUNDERS, Dudley Dunn, physician; b. Lawrence Co., Ala., Feb. 26, 1835; A.B., La Grange Coll., Ala., 1852, A.M., 1855; M.D., Univ. Medical Coll. (New York U.), 1856. Surgeon C.S.A., 1862-65; prof. surgery and descriptive anatomy, Med. Coll. of Memphis; prof. clin. medicine, physical diagnosis and forensic medicine, Memphis Hospital Medical Coll.; pres. Memphis Bd. Health, 1878. Home: Memphis, Tenn. Deceased.

SAUNDERS, Edward Watts, congressman; b. Franklin Co., Va., Oct. 25, 1860; s. Peter and Elizabeth (Dabney) S.; grammar and high sch. edn., Bedford Co., Va.; LL.B., U. of Va., 1882; m. Nancy D. Walker, Dec. 11, 1886. In practice at Rockymount, Va., 1882—. Mem. Va. Ho. of Rep., 1887-1901 (speaker, 1899-1901); judge Circuit Ct., 1901-06; elected 59th Congress, Nov. 1906, for unexpired term (1906-07) of Claude Augustus Swanson, resigned; reelected 60th to 66th Congresses (1907-21), 5th Va. Dist. Democrat. Died Dec. 16, 1921.

SAUNDERS, Eugene Davis, judge; b. Campbell Co., Va., July 25, 1853; s. Robert C. and Caryetta (Davis) S.; student U. of Va., 1869-74, LL.B., 1874; m. Laura M. Barelli, Feb. 17, 1884. Admitted to bar, 1876, and practiced at New Orleans. Prof. common law and equity, Tulane U.; U.S. dist. judge, Eastern Dist. of La., 1907-09. Democrat. Author: Saunders on Taxation, 1887; Saunders' Edition Civil Code of Louisiana, 1888; Notarial and Judicial Forms (with H. H. White). Home: New Orleans, La. Died 1914.

SAUNDERS, Frederick, librarian; b. London, England, Aug. 14, 1807; came to U.S., 1837, to establish a branch of his father's London publishing house; m. Mary Ann Farr, Sept. 18, 1833. Devoted his attention to efforts to secure internat. copyright law from Congress, but failed; became city editor New York Evening Post. Asst. librarian, 1859-76, librarian, 1876-96, of the Astor Library; was retired at his own request, but trustees voted to continue his salary during his lifetime; (A.M., Madison Univ., N.Y., 1853). Author: Salad for the Solitary and the Social; Pastime Papers; Evenings with the Sacred Poets; New York in a Nut Shell; Story of Some Famous Books; Stray Leaves of Literature; Memoir of the Great Metropolis; Character Studies; Story of the Discovery of the New World by Columbus; etc. Home: Brooklyn, N.Y. Died 1902.

SAUNDERS, John Monk, writer; b. Hinckley, Minn., Nov. 22, 1897; s. Robert Chancellor and Nancy (Monk) S.; B.A., U. of Wash., 1919; elected Rhodes scholar to Magdalen Coll., Oxford U., Eng., B.A. (Oxon.), 1921, M.A., 1925; m. Avis Hughes, Jan. 1922; divorced in Los Angeles, Apr. 1927; m. 2d, Fay Wray, June 15, 1927; one daughter, Susan Cary. Served on the editorial staff of the Los Angeles Times, 1922, New York Tribune, 1923; asso. editor Am. Magazine, 1924. Grad. U.S. Sch. of Mil. Aeronautics, Berkeley, Calif., 1917; commd. 2d lt. Air Service, U.S.A., May 16, 1917. Episcopalian. Author: Single Lady, 1931; Nikki (musical comedy). Wrote screen plays: Wings; Legion of the Condemned; The Dawn Patrol; The Last Flight; A Yank at Oxford. Home: Hollywood, Calif. Died Mar. 11, 1940.

SAUNDERS, John R., lawyer; b. King and Queen Co., Va., Dec. 19, 1869; s. Maj. William A. and Emeline (Motley) S.; student summers, U. of Va., 1892-93; m. Blanche Hoskins, Dec. 8, 1897; children—William Alexander, Emily Carter, John Richard. Began practice at Saluda, Va., 1893; pres. Bank of Middlesex; mem. Va. Senate, 1908-18 (resigned); atty. gen. of Va., Feb. 1, 1918—. Mem. staff Gov. A. J. Montague of Va., 1902-06, title of col. Democrat. Baptist. Odd Fellow, K.P., Elk, Eagle. Home: Saluda, Va. Died Mar. 17, 1934.

SAUNDERS, Kenneth James, educator, author; b. Cape Town, S. Africa, Jan. 10, 1883; s. Henry William (M.D., F.R.C.S.) and Jane Esther (Solomon) S.; ed. Clifton Coll., Bristol, Eng.; B.A., Emmanuel College, Cambridge, England, 1905, M.A., 1914, Litt.D., 1925; m. Babette Neugass, Nov. 20, 1921; children—Barbara, Thomas Wm., Madge. Studied Buddhism in Ceylon, 1908-12; with Y.M.C.A. in India as lit. sec., dir. of studies, etc., 1912-17; dir. of studies, Nat. Training Sch., London, 1917-19; prof. history of religion, Pacific Sch. of Religion, Berkeley, Calif., 1920-30. Lecturer U. of Calif.; Haskell lecturer U. of Chicago, 1921. Guggenheim traveling fellow, 1925 and 1926, for study in the field of religions in Asia; visiting prof., Columbia, 1928, Univ. of Hawaii, 1931-32, London U., 1933. Episcopalian. Author: The Buddha's Way of Virtue, 1910; The Heart of Buddhism, 1914; The Story of Buddhism, 1915; Adventures of the Christian Soul, 1915; Gotama Buddha, 1920; Buddhism in the Modern World; Epochs in Buddhist History, 1923; The Gospel for Asia, 1927; Buddhism, 1928; Ideals of East and West; Whither Asia, 1933; A Pageant of Asia, 1933. Home: Berkeley, Calif. Died Nov. 20, 1937.

SAUNDERS, Ripley Dunlap, newspaperman; b. Ripley, Miss., Dec. 17, 1856; s. Dr. Pascal Washington and Catherine (Kennelly) S.; ed. pvt. select schs. at Marianna, Ark.; Memphis, Tenn., and Pass Christian, Miss.; m. Mrs. Mary E. (Schinkel) Spearing, Aug. 3, 1903. Bookkeeper, 1874-89; with St. Louis Republic, 1889-90, St. Louis Post-Dispatch, 1890-92; corr. Post-Dispatch, in New York, 1892-93, Sunday editor, 1893-96; editorial writer, St. Louis Republic, to 1902, except during Spanish-Am. War; with Washington Times, Oct. 1902-Jan. 1903, then with St. Louis Republic until Aug. 1903; since then spl. writer and dramatic editor St. Louis Post-Dispatch. Was lt. in Light Battery A, 1st Mo. Arty., but resigned; re-enlisted in same at beginning of war with Spain, and served as gunner-corporal in P.R. campaign. Presbyn. Democrat. Author: John Kenadie, 1902; Colonel Todhunter of Missouri, 1911. Home: St. Louis, Mo. Died Mar. 16, 1915.

SAUNDERS, Robert Chancellor, lawyer; b. Campbell Co., Va., Dec. 24, 1864; s. Robert Chancellor and Caryetta L. (Davis) S.; LL.B., U. of Va., 1889; m. Nannie Mark, Oct. 15, 1896. Began practice at St. Louis, Mo., 1889; editorial writer West Pub. Co., law book pubs., St. Paul, Minn., 1890-91; practiced at Hickley, Minn., 1891-98, Pine City, Minn., 1898-1907; settled at Seattle, Wash., 1907. County atty., Pine Co., Minn., 2 terms, 1893-95, 1897-99; Dem. candidate for atty. gen. of Minn., 1898; U.S. dist. atty. Western Dist. of Wash., May 7, 1918—. Chmn. Wash. State Bd. Law Examiners. Life mem. Minn. Hist. Soc. Episcopalian. Mason. Home: Seattle, Wash. Died Jan. 31, 1922.

SAUNDERS, William Lawrence, engineer; b. Columbus, Ga., Nov. 1, 1856; s. W. T. (D.D.) and Eliza (Morton) S.; B.S., U. of Pa., 1876 (Sc.D., same, 1911); m. Bertha Louise Gaston, Aug. 4, 1886 (died 1906). In charge of hydrographic work, 1878, and sub-aqueous rock excavation, 1878-82, Nat. Storage Co., of Communipaw, N.J.; chmn. bd. Ingersoll-Rand Co.; pres. Stayley-Saunders Corp.; dir. A. S. Cameron Steam Pump Works, N.Y. & Honduras Rosario Mining Co. Gov., dir., dep. chmn. Fed. Res. Bank of N.Y., also mem. dist. com. on capital issues, Federal Reserve Bd., World War. Invented apparatus for sub-aqueous drilling, using tube and water jet system in gen. use in Baku oil fields, Russia; system of pumping liquids by compressed air; radialaxe system of coal mining; invented apparatus for Ingersoll track and bar channelers and gadders for quarrying stone. Apttd. mem. N.J. Harbor Commn.; mem. N.J. Bd. Commerce and Navigation; chmn. Permanent Group Com. for Nicaragua; mem. Naval Consulting Bd. of U.S., 1915—(chmn.). Was mem. N.J. State Dem. Com.; twice elected mayor of N. Plainfield, N.J.; mem. Dem. Nat. Campaign Com., 1916. Fellow Am. Geog. Soc., Acad. Polit. Science, Am. Acad. Polit. and Social Science; mem. numerous societies, civic orgns., etc. Del. as representative of A.I.M.E. at 1st Empire Mining and Metall. Congress, Wembly Expn., London, Eng., 1924. An organizer, and mem. during World War, of Mil. Engring. Com. which, at its own expense, equipped a regt. and sent it to France—the 1st regt. of engrs. to pass through London, and the 1st in action at the front. Episcopalian. Editor, now pres. Compressed Air Magazine. Author: Compressed Air Information; Compressed Air Production. Co-author: The Subways and Tunnels of New York; Rock Drilling. Founder, 1926, of Mining Medal, to recognize achievement in mining, by A.I.M.E. Home: Plainfield, N.J. Died June 25, 1931.

SAUREL, Paul (Louis), prof. mathematics; b. N.Y. City, May 10, 1871; B.S., Coll. City of New York, 1890; student Cornell U., 1890-92; Sc.D., Bordeaux, 1900. Instr. mathematics, Cornell U., 1892-96; tutor, 1896-98; instr. mathematics, 1900-05, asst. prof., 1905-06, asso. prof., 1906-14, prof., 1914—, head of dept., 1919—, Coll. City of New York. Home: New York, N.Y. Died Jan. 22, 1934.

SAUVEUR, Albert, univ. prof., b. Louvain, Belgium, June 21, 1863; s. Lambert and Hortense (Franquin) Sauveur (French parentage); ed. Athénée Royal (Brussels, Belgium), and in School of Mines (Liège), 1881-86; S.B., in mining and metallurgy, Mass. Inst. Tech., 1889; Sc.D., Case Sch. of Applied Science, 1921; Sc.D., U. of Grenoble, France, 1924, U. of San Marcos, Peru, 1925, Harvard, 1935, Dr. of Engring, Lehigh U., 1926; m. Mary Prince Jones, June 4, 1891; children—Hortense (Mrs. Romeyn Taylor), Mary Isabella (Mrs. George C. Eaton), Albert (dec.). Chemist and metallurgist various steel cos., 1889-97; instr. metallurgy, 1889-1900, asst. prof. metallurgy and metallography, 1900-05, prof. metallurgy, 1905, Gordon McKay professor, 1924-35, emeritus, 1935—, all of Harvard University. Editor The Metallographist, 1898-1903; editor Iron and Steel Magazine, 1903-06. Officier d'Académie; Officier Légion d'Honneur; Officer Order of Leopold (Belgium); awarded Elliott Cresson gold medal, Franklin Inst., Phila., 1913; Bessemer medalist, Brit. Iron and Steel Inst., 1924; first recipient of the Albert Sauveur Achievement medal, from the Am. Society for Metals. Fellow Am. Acad. Arts and Sciences, A.A.A.S.; pres. John Fritz Medal Bd. of Awards, 1916-17; hon. mem. Am. Inst. Mining and Metall. Engineers (v.p. 1910-12), Am. Society for Metals, Society Engineers Liège Sch. of Mines, Soc. Ingénieurs Civils de France, Society de l'Industrie Nationale; corr. mem. Society Encouragement Nat. Industry (France); pres. Salon Français (Boston), 1920-24. Metallurgist, Am. Aviation Commn. in France, 1917-19; metallurgical expert to the French Ministry of Munitions, 1917-19. Henry Marion Howe lecturer for 1924 (Am. Inst. Mining and Metall. Engrs.); Henry de Mille Campbell lecturer for 1929 (Am. Soc. for Steel Treating); Marburgh lecturer for 1938 (Am. Soc. for Testing Materials). U.S. del. 3d Pan.-Am. Scientific Congress, Lima, Peru, 1924. Author: The Metallography of Iron and Steel; Metallurgical Dialogues. Home: Cambridge, Mass. Died Jan. 26, 1939.

SAVAGE, Albert Russell, judge; b. Ryegate, Vt., Dec. 8, 1847; s. Charles W. and Eliza M. (Clough) S.; A.B., Dartmouth, 1871, A.M., 1874; (LL.D., Bates, 1898, Bowdoin, 1909); m. Nellie H. Hale, Aug. 17, 1871 (died 1912); m. 2d, Frances A. Cooke, Sept. 2, 1914. Admitted to bar, 1874; judge of probate, Androscoggin Co., 1885-89; speaker Me. Ho. of Rep., 1893; asso. justice Supreme Jud. Ct. of Me., 1897-1913; chief justice Apr. 10, 1913—. Republican. Home: Auburn, Me. Died June 13, 1917.

SAVAGE, Arthur William, founder Savage Arms Co.; b. Kingston, Jamaica, B.W.I., May 13, 1857; s. John Ashton and Jane (Henderson) S.; ed. at scs. of Leeds, England, and Baltimore, Md.; student South Kensington Art Acad., London, 1871-74; m. Annie Bryant, of England, 1879 (dec.); children—Alice Mary (Mrs. Harold von Briesen), Violet Jane (Mrs. William Steinemann), Arthur John, Mable Mascotte (Mrs. William Book), Harold George, Basil Henderson (dec.), Olive Annie (Mrs. Norman Peek), Eros Marshall; m. 2d. Ethel Bissell Doyle, 1919 (dec.). Came to U.S., 1886, naturalized, 1895. Went as hunter to expdn. to Australia, 1875; held prisoner by Australian Blacks 2 yrs.; mgr. cattle ranch and contbg. artist for London Graphic, 1883-86; coffee planter, Jamaica, B.W.I., 1884-86; supt. elec. railway, N.Y., 1888-91; mgr. Saratoga Springs (N.Y.) R.R., 1891-92; founded the Savage Arms Co., Utica, N.Y., 1893, mng. dir. until 1906; orange grower, 1906—; pres. Water Co. of Calif., Savage Tire Co., Savage Munition Co. Asso. with minister of munitions, England, during World War. Inventor of dirigible torpedo, magazine rifle improvements. Republican. Home: San Diego, Calif. Died Sept. 22, 1938.

SAVAGE, Francis Martin, banker; b. Louisa, Ky., May 2, 1855; s. Pleasant Martin and Sarah (Moore) S.; ed. Eastern Ky. Normal Sch.; m. Katherine Ogden, Dec. 27, 1905. Began as teller in home bank, Catlettsburg, Ky., 1875; organized a number of successful banks in the South and the Middle West; retired bank president but retained an active interest in the development of banks. A leader in building up the business portion of Gary, Ind.; extensive travels in Europe, Asia, Africa, 1907-08, Australia and New Zealand, 1916, South America, 1922, South Africa, 1923. Has devoted much time to social betterment of steel workers, improvement of edln. system, beautifying towns and cities. Republican. Episcopalian. Home: Washington, D.C. Died Feb. 18, 1934.

SAVAGE, George Martin, univ. prof.; b. nr. Rienzi, Tishomingo Co., Miss., Feb. 5, 1849; s. H. G. and E. J. S.; A.B., Southwestern Baptist (now Union) U., 1871; A.M., 1874, LL.D., 1890; m. Miss F. F. Williams, July 26, 1871; children—Kate, May (dec.), George H. (dec.), Emily, Louise (dec.), Maude (dec.), Lessie (dec.), Helen, Mary, Frances (dec.). Ordained Bapt. ministry, 1870; prin. Henderson Masonic Male and Female Inst., 1871-77 and 1880-84; prof. English and French, Southwestern Bapt. Univ., 1877-80; prin. Eagleville (Tenn.) High School, 1884-90; pres. S. Western Bapt. U., 1890-1904, prof. philosophy, 1904-05, again pres., 1906-07, prof. philosophy, 1907-08; prof., Hall-Moody Inst., 1908-09; prof. philosophy and Bible, Union Univ., Tenn., 1909-15, again pres. Union U., 1915-18, and prof. philosophy, Bible and French, 1918-35 (retired). Pres. Tenn. State Bapt. Conv., 1924-25 and 1925-26; pastor of various chs. from 1874. Author: Greece and Bible Lands. Home: Jackson, Tenn. Died June 1938.

SAVAGE, Giles Christopher, ophthalmologist; b. nr. Rienzi, Miss., Jan. 15, 1854; s. Rev. Hamilton Giles and Elenor Jane (Shields) S.; ed. pub. schs. in Miss., and Masonic Inst., Henderson, Tenn.; M.D., Jefferson Medical Coll., Phila., 1878; post-grad. work same, 1880-81, London and Vienna, 1884-85; LL.D., Union, 1919; m. Leslie Alice Jones, Oct. 4, 1881. Practiced in Jackson, Tenn., 1878-86, Nashville, 1886—; prof. ophthalmology, Vanderbilt U. Med. Dept., Nashville, 1886-1911; retired from teaching, 1911, to give entire time to pvt. practice and to writing. Mem. S.S. Bd. of Southern Bapt. Conv., Bapt. State Missionary Board, Tenn. Anti-Saloon

League, Union U., Jackson, Tenn.; pres. Tenn. Bapt. Conv., 1909, 10, 11. Pres. Nashville Acad. Medicine, 1891-92, Tenn. Med. Assn., 1896, Southern Med. Assn., 1909; 1st v.p. A.M.A., 1904-05 (chmn. ophthalmic sect., 1906-07). Founded Ophthalmic Record, 1891. Democrat. Author: New Truths in Ophthalmology, 1893; Ophthalmic Myology, 1902, 11; Ophthalmic Neuro-Myology, 1905, 26; Nervo Muscular Mechanism of the Eyes, and Routine in Eye-Work, 1916; Jesus, His Coming and His Going; Cycles of Time and Seasons; Time-and-Place; Harmony of the Gospels. Home: Nashville, Tenn. Deceased.

SAVAGE, Harlow Dow; b. Memphis, Tenn., Apr. 16, 1880; s. Samuel Summerfield and Frances B. (Dow) S.; ed. Kenyon Mil. Acad., Gambier, O.; m. Edna Stanhope Wood, Oct. 22, 1908; children—Samuel Summerfield, Alfred Hance, Nancy Wood (Mrs. Walter McCune Kelly), Harlow Dow. Formerly served as head of Ashland Fire Brick Co.; designed and installed the first completely electrified refractory plant in the world; elected v.p. Am. Arch Co., 1914, Locomotive Pulverized Fuel Co., 1916; in charge pulverized fuel div. of Combustion Engring. Corp., 1920-21, v.p., 1921-28; pres. Combustion Engineering Corp., 1928-30; pres. Dry Quenching Equipment Corp., Raymond Bros. Impact Pulverizer Co., Hedges-Walsh-Weidner Co., Heine Boiler Co., General Breweries Corp., Bismarck Brewing Corp. (Baltimore), Combustion Engring. Corp., Ltd. (Can.). Vice-pres. Baker & Spencer, Inc.; v.p. and dir. N.Y. Stocks, Inc., Manhattan Fund, Inc. Col. on staff of Gov. McCreery of Ky. An organizer, 1913, and 1st pres. Refractory Mfrs.' Assn. Democrat. Episcopalian. Mason. Home: Scarsdale, N.Y. Died Feb. 9, 1942.

SAVAGE, Henry Wilson, theatrical mgr.; b. New Durham, N.H., Mar. 21, 1859; s. Capt. M. Henry and Betsey T. (Woodhouse) S.; A.B., Harvard, 1880; m. Alice Louise Batcheler, Oct. 24, 1889; children—John Batcheler, Bettina True. Built Castle Sq. Theatre, Boston, 1894, and began as mgr. by presenting grand opera in English; first venture in N.Y. City was with grand opera at American Theatre, 1900; has devoted attention largely to musical comedy; pres. Henry W. Savage, Inc. Dir. Nat. Assn. Theatrical Producing Mgrs. (pres. 1907-09). Home: Ridgefield, N.J. Died Nov. 29, 1927.

SAVAGE, Hiram Newton, civil engr.; b. Lancaster, N.H., Oct 6, 1861; s. Hazen Nelson and Laura Ann (Newton) S.; B.S., New Hampshire Coll. Agr. and Mechanic Arts, 1887; C.E., Thayer Sch. of Civil Engring. (Dartmouth), 1891; D.Sc., Univ. of N.H., 1913; m. Linna Belle Clough, Dec. 1891 (died 1897); children—Lucy Eunice (Mrs. Robert L. Colthart), Laura Ada (Mrs. Laurence W. Hope); m. 3d, Eugenia Hurlock, 1927. Assistant engineer, East Tennessee, Virginia & Georgia R.R., Nashville & Tellico R.R. and Athens (Tenn.) Improvement Co., 1888; chief engr. Hydraulic Mining & Irrigation Co., N.M., 1889-90; engr. and supt. constrn. Billings Park and race track, White River Junction, Vt., and designed and located sewerage system for W. Randolph, Vt., 1890; chief engr. San Diego (Calif.) Land & Town Co., Sweetwater dam system, San Diego, 1891-1903; chief engr. Sweetwater Park and Race Track, 1893-94; cons. engr. San Diego & Cuyamaca R.R., San Diego & La Jolla R.R., Coronado Beach R.R., 1893-1903, Cuyamaca (Calif.) Water Co., 1896; chief engr. to contractor for U.S. Govt. San Diego Bay-Zuninga Shoals Jetty, 1894-98; cons. engr. Southern Calif. Mountain Water Co., Lower Otay Dam, Upper Otay Dam, Barrett Dam, Morena Dam & Carrying System to San Diego, 1893-1903; cons. engr. U.S. Govt. Reclamation Service, Aug. 12, 1903—; also supervising engr. Northern Div. in charge investigation, designs, construction, operation 12 irrigation projects and storage features, including Shoshone Dam (highest in the world), Corbett Tunnel, etc., total expenditures about $3,000,000 annually, 1904-15; cons. and constrn. engr. Sweetwater Water Co., enlargement extension Sweetwater Dam and Water Carrying System, 1916-17; hydraulic engr. City of San Diego (Calif.) Municipal Water System impounding and carrying features; designed and constructed with city forces, Lower Otay Dam, Barrett Dam, Morena Dam and Spillway enlargement, Rapid High Pressure Filtration Plant; directed investigation of all additional Water Supply resources in San Diego Co. and vicinity; field location and design all impounding and carrying features for fifty years future water requirements, estimated cost over $100,000,000, 1917-23. Toured world 3 times for engring. and architectural research; reported on tech. administrative matters and requirements to the President of U.S., 1925-26; cons. engr. The Research Service (internat.), Washington, also of Newell, Corse & McDaniel, Washington, D.C.; recalled to San Diego, 1928, to take charge of Municipal Bur. of Water Development. Mason. Home: San Diego, Calif. Deceased.

SAVAGE, John Houston, lawyer; b. McMinnville, Tenn., Oct. 9, 1815; s. George and Elizabeth (Kenner) S.; brought up on farm; ed. subscription schs. and Carroll Acad., McMinnville; studied law; admitted to Tenn. bar, Smithville, 1839; unmarried. Served 6 months as vol. in war with Seminole Indians, 1835; maj. 14th U.S. inf. and lt. col. 11th U.S. inf. in Mexican war; was in all the battles around the City of Mexico until wounded by a shell and disabled at Battle of Molino del Rey; later comd. dept. of Toluca until peace was declared. Resumed practice; was atty. gen. Tenn., 1842-47; elector on Polk ticket, 1844; mem. Congress, 1849-53 and 1855-59. Democrat. During Civil war was col. 16th Tenn. inf., C.S.A.; wounded at Perryville and at Murfreesboro; mem. Tenn. legislature, 1877, 1879 and 1887; again practicing in McMinnville. Died Apr. 5, 1904.

SAVAGE, Minot Judson, clergyman; b. Norridgewock, Me., June 10, 1841; s. Joseph L. and Ann S. (Stinson) S.; fitted for coll., but did not take course, because of poor health; grad. Bangor Theol. Sem., 1864; (D.D., Harvard, 1896); m. Ella A. Dodge, 1864 (died 1916). Congl. home missionary in California, 1864-67; pastor Framingham, Mass., 1867-69, Hannibal, Mo., 1869-73. Became Unitarian; pastor Third Unitarian Ch., Chicago, 1873-74, Ch. of the Unity, Boston, 1874-96; minister Ch. of the Messiah, New York, 1896-1906; retired. Author: The Minister's Hand-book; Life's Dark Problems, 1905; Life Beyond Death, 1901; The Passing and the Permanent in Religion, 1901; Living by the Day, 1901; Men and Women, 1902; Poems, 1905. Editor: Sacred Songs for Public Worship (with Howard M. Dow); Unitarian Catechism. Died May 22, 1918.

SAVAGE, Philip Henry, author; b. No. Brookfield, Mass., Feb. 11, 1868; s. Rev. Minot J. Savage; grad. Harvard, 1893 (A.M., 1896). Author: First Poems and Fragments (1895); Poems (1898). Home: Boston, Mass. Died 1899.

SAVAGE, Richard Henry, author, maj. U.S. vol. engrs.; b. Utica, N.Y., June 12, 1846; s. Richard and Jane Moorhead (Ewart) S.; apptd. from Calif., 1864, and grad. U.S. Mil. Acad., 1868; served, 2d lt., corps of engr., 3 yrs.; in Egyptian army, 1871-74; engr. on a ry. in South, 1874-84; then lawyer and author in New York; m. Anna Josephine Scheible, of Berlin, Germany, at German embassy, Washington, Jan. 2, 1873. Traveled in Turkey, Asia Minor, Russia, Siberia, Korea, China, Japan, Honduras, 1884-91. Apptd., May 1898, senior maj. 2d U.S. vol. engrs.; served through war with Spain; in Nov. 1898 went with his command to Havana, personally hoisting 1st Am. flag in Havana or Havana province; senior capt. (acting maj), 27th U.S. vol. inf., July 5 to Dec. 1, 1899; brig. gen. and chief engr. Spanish war veterans, Oct. 10, 1900; elected comdr.-in-chief Nat. Spanish-Am. War Vets., Washington, Oct. 11, 1903. Author: After Many Years; My Official Wife; For Love and Life; A Daughter of Judas; The Anarchist; Delilah of Harlem; The Little Lady of Lagunitas; The Flying Halcyon; Miss Devereaux of the Mariquita; In the Shadow of the Pyramids; The Last Days of Ismail Khedive; In the Swim; The Princess of Alaska, 1895; In the Old Chateau, 1896; His Cuban Sweetheart, 1896; The Hacienda on the Hill, 1900; The Shield of His Honor, 1900; The Midnight Passenger, 1900; Brought to Bay, 1900; Poems, 1900; In the House of His Friends, 1900; In the Esbekieyeh Gardens, 1900; The Mystery of a Shipyard, 1901; Special Orders for Commander Leigh, 1902; For a Young Queen's Bright Eyes, 1902; The Golden Rapids of High Life, 1903. Died 1903.

SAVAGE, Watson Lewis, M.D.; b. Cromwell, Conn., Nov. 26, 1859; s. Ralph B. and Sarah (Strickland) S.; A.B., Amherst, 1882, A.M., 1885; taught sch., Shattuck, Minn., 1882-83; M.D., L.I. College Hosp., 1885; m. Ella Whiting, Oct. 26, 1887; children—Helen Whiting (dec.), Dorothy Davis, John Whiting, Richard Billings, Watson Lewis, Kirkwood Hallock. Resident phys. and surgeon, St. Peter's Hosp., Brooklyn, 1885-87; med. dir. Berkeley Athletic Club, Lyceum and Sch., 1887-90; pres. and med. dir. Dr. Savage Physical Development Inst., Ltd., 1890—. Asst. dir. physical training, Brooklyn, Y.M.C.A., 1 yr.; dir. Gymnasium, Columbia Univ., 1897-1903; prof. New York Sch. Advanced Therapeutics. Organizer, 1895, becoming pres., N.Y. Normal Sch. of Physical Edn. (now the Savage School for Physical Edn.); organizer physical work in many schs. of New York; founded Down Town Exercise Rooms, New York, 1903, Dr. Savage Swimming Sch., 1907; director of athletics, Pittsburgh Athletic Assn.; organizer, and dir. dept. student health, Carnegie Inst. Tech., Pittsburgh, 1910-13; organizer and dir. dept. physical training, Pittsburgh Pub. Schs., 1912-13; organizer and dir. Dr. Savage Exercise Institute and Studio, 1913, New York. Author: Health and Success. Home: Mamaroneck, N.Y. Died Jan. 11, 1931.

SAVIDGE, Eugene Coleman, gynecologist; b. Allegany Co., Md., Oct. 21, 1863; s. Coleman Hall and Alcinda Harwood (Creager-Warfield) S.; bro. of Frank Raymond S.; B.S., B.L., U. of France, 1889; M.D., Univ. Med. Coll. (New York U.), 1891; m. Caroline, d. John S. Foster, Sept. 22, 1894. House gynecologist, 1891, asst. gynecologist out-door poor, 1892-1902, Roosevelt Hospital; resident phys. Sloane Maternity Hosp., 1892; attending gynecologist St. Mark's Hosp., 1903. Author: Wallingford, 1882; Gallery of Eminent Men, 1887; The Life and Times of Brewster, 1891; The American in Paris, 1895. Home: New York, N.Y. Died Oct. 10, 1924.

SAVIDGE, Frank Raymond, lawyer; b. Hancock, Md., May 22, 1866; s. Coleman Hall and Alcinda Harwood (Creager-Warfield) S.; ed. Baltimore City Coll., and Phila. High Sch.; LL.M., U. of Pa., 1895; m. Marie Louise, d. Nathan Robins, of Metuchen, N.J., July 31, 1902. Admitted to bar, 1888, and began practice at Phila.; was partner of late U.S. Atty. Gen. Benjamin Harris Brewster; now executor and trustee of his estate; solicitor of numerous corps. Author: Law of Boroughs, in Pennsylvania, 2d edit., 1903; Corporations in Pennsylvania, 1905, 26, Supplement, 1920. Public speaker. Home: Philadelphia, and Devon, Pa. Died Jan. 29, 1928.

SAVILLE, Bruce Wilder, sculptor; b. Quincy, Mass., Mar. 16, 1893; s. George Gurney and Caroline Elizabeth (Clark) S.; ed. pub. schs., Quincy; Boston Normal Art Sch.; studied with Theo. A. Ruggles Kitson 3 years; m. Beulah Margretta Kelley, children—William, Sally Wilder, Darrett Bruce. Opened studio in Quincy, Oct. 1911; exhibited at Nat. Acad. Design, Gorham Gallery (New York), Copley Gallery (Boston), Boston Art League, Art Inst. Chicago, Pa. Acad. Fine Arts, Nat. Sculpture Soc. Outdoor Exhibition, 1923, Phila. Art Alliance, Calif. Palace of Legion of Honor, San Francisco, Archtl. League, New York. Awarded first prize for sculpture, Columbus Gallery of Fine Arts, 1924. Head of dept. of sculpture, Ohio State U., 1921-25; also modeling class, Columbus Art Sch. until 1925. Unitarian. Drove French transport, July-Sept. 1917; in charge modeling dept. U.S. Army Camouflage, Paris, Sept. 1917-Feb. 1919. Home: Santa Fe, N.M. Died Feb. 27, 1939.

SAVILLE, Marshall Howard, archeologist; b. Rockport, Mass., June 24, 1867; spl. student in anthropology, Harvard, 1889-94; Sc.D., U. of San Marcos, Lima, Peru; m. Annie W. Lyon, June 14, 1893. Did field work under direction of Prof. Putnam; made important discoveries among the remains of the moundbuilders in Southern Ohio; made extensive explorations in Yucatan, 1890; among the Maya ruins of Copan, Honduras, 1891-92, for Peabody Mus., Harvard, and at the ruins of Palenque for the Am. Museum Natural History, 1897-98; 4 expeditions to ruins of Mitla and Oaxaca, 1899, 1902, 04; numerous expdns. to Peru, Ecuador, Colombia, Honduras, Guatemala, Central America; hon. curator of Mexican and Central Am. archeology, Am. Museum of Natural History, New York, 1908-10; prof. Am. archeology, Columbia, 1903—; staff of museum of the Am. Indian, Heye Foundation, 1918-32, Am. Museum of Natural History, New York, 1933; hon. prof. Museo Nacional, Mexico, 1933. Had charge of Central Am. exhibit, Chicago Expn., 1893. Has made explorations and discoveries of Aztec and Zapotec remains in Mexico. Founder of the Cortes Soc.; Officier de l'Academie Française; corr. mem. Royal Acad. History of Spain; hon. mem. Soc. de Geog. y Estadistica, Mexico, Instituto Historico, Peru; mem. Am. Anthrop. Assn. (pres. 1926-28). Capt., Mil. Intelligence Div., U.S.A., 1918. Home: New York, N.Y. Died May 7, 1935.

SAWIN, Theophilus Parsons, clergyman; b. Lynn, Mass., Jan. 14, 1841; s. Rev. Theophilus P. and Martha McIntyre (Mason) S.; ed. Kimball Union Acad. and Yale to sophomore years; (D.D., Williams); m. Emeline T. Farel, Sept. 28, 1864. Ordained Congl. pastor, Racine, Wis., Dec. 1, 1871; later called to Janesville, Wis., thence to Mystic Congl. Ch., Medford, Mass.; pastor First Presbyn. Ch., Troy, N.Y., 1886—. Author: The Transfiguring of the Cross, 1896; Liberty in the Presbyterian Church, 1899. Editor: Proceedings of the Centennial Anniversary of the First Presbyterian Church of Troy, N.Y., 1892. Chaplain N.Y. Soc. Founders and Patriots; asso. mem. Council of 70. Home: Troy, N.Y. Died 1906.

SAWTELLE, Charles Greene, brig. gen. U.S.A.; b. Norridgewock, Me., May 10, 1834; grad. U.S. Mil. Acad., 1854; m. Alice C. Munroe, 1869. Entered army as bvtd. 2d lt. inf., serving in Sioux expdn.; 2d lt. 6th Inf., Mar. 3, 1855; promoted through grades to col. asst. q.m. gen., Sept. 12, 1894; brig. gen. q.m. gen., Aug. 19, 1896; was q.m. gen. in Washington until retired, Feb. 16, 1897. In Civil War was engaged as chief q.m. in many of the more important operations of the war; remained in that branch of the service until retired at its head. Home: Washington, D.C. Died Jan. 4, 1913.

SAWTELLE, William Henry, jurist; b. Tuscumbia, Ala., Aug. 27, 1868; s. Benjamin Niles and India (Coburn) S.; student pvt. schools and Tuscumbia Classical and Mil. Acad.; m. Lulie Cristine Mhoon (died 1910); children—James Mhoon, William H.; m. 2d, Mary LaMotte Martin, June 25, 1915; 1 son, Benjamin Niles. Admitted to the Ala. bar, 1886; solicitor 8th Judicial Circuit, 1892-98, 11th Circuit, 1898-1905; removed to Tucson, Ariz., 1905; judge U.S. Dist. Ct. of Ariz., 1913-31; judge U.S. Circuit Ct. of Appeals, 9th Jud. Circuit, 1931—. Democrat. Presbyn. Mason. Home: Tucson, Ariz. Died Dec. 17, 1934.

SAWTELLE, William Luther, clergyman; b. Nineveh, N.Y., May 1, 1871; s. Rev. William Henry and Sally Martin (Smith) S.; grad. Susquehanna Collegiate Inst., Towanda, Pa., 1890; A.B., Williams Coll., 1894; D.D., 1919; grad. Auburn Theol. Sem., 1898;

m. Leila M. Perine, Sept. 15, 1903. Ordained Presbyn. ministry, 1898; pastor 1st Ch., Chittenango, N.Y., 1898-1902, Fulton, N.Y., 1902-10, First Ch., Elmira, N.Y., 1910-14, 2d Ch., Troy, N.Y., 1914-16, First Ch., Scranton, Pa., 1916—. Trustee Albright Memorial Library, Scranton; mem. bd. dirs. Pa. Assn. for the Blind. Republican. Home: Scranton, Pa. Died Apr. 9, 1926.

SAWYER, Charles E., physician; b. Nevada, O., Jan. 24, 1860; s. Alonzo N. and Harriet M. (Rogers) S.; ed. pub. schools, Nevada; M.D., Homœ. Hosp. Coll. (now Ohio State Homœ. Med. Coll. of Ohio State U.), 1881; m. May E. Barron, Aug. 11, 1879. Began practice at LaRue, O., 1881; established the Sawyer Sanatorium, 1890; removed to Marion, O., 1893, and established the Dr. C. E. Sawyer Sanatorium, later The Sawyer Sanatorium; gen. mgr. and consulting phys., C. E. & Carl W. Sawyer; v.p. Marion Nat. Bank; dir. Cleveland-Pulte Med. Coll., Masonic Temple Co. (Marion), etc. Commd. brig. gen. M.R.C., U.S.A., Mar. 12, 1921, and called to active duty same day as physician to the President (Harding); apptd. physician to President Coolidge, Aug. 11, 1923. Apptd. chief co-ordinator of Federal Bd. of Hospitalization by executive order; assigned a number of special services under the Veterans' Bureau. Trustee and chmn. exec. com. Harding Memorial Assn. Trustee Am. Inst. Homœpathy (gov.); fellow Am. Coll. Surgeons. Republican. Lutheran. Home: Marion, O. Died Sept. 23, 1924.

SAWYER, Charles Henry, gov.; b. Watertown, N.Y., March 30, 1840; s. Jonathan and Martha (Perkins) S.; with parents removed to Dover, N.H., 1850; ed. public schools and Franklin Acad. (hon. A.M., Dartmouth); m. Susan Ellen Cowan, Feb. 8, 1865. Learned business of woolen mfr.; supt. Sawyer Woolen Mills, 1865-81; later pres. same Co. until sale of the property to Am. Woolen Co., 1898; has been officially connected with rys., banks and other instns.; retired from business. Mem. N.H. legislature, 1869-70, 1876-77; gov. N.H., 1887-89; commr. N.H., Paris Expn. Home: Dover, N.H. Died 1908.

SAWYER, Charles Pike, music editor, critic; b. Newburyport, Mass., Nov. 5, 1854; s. Edward J. and Sarah Little (Thurlow) S.; Ph.B., Columbia, 1881; m. M. Elizabeth Amsden, Apr. 21, 1894. Began as music critic, 1870, and continued on various publs.; joined staff of Evening Post, New York, 1881, as sporting editor and asst. in music and drama; dropped sporting writing, 1920, dramatic work, 1924, and from then devoted entire time to music. Awarded medal "for distinguished service" by Columbia U. Home: Brooklyn, N.Y. Died May 8, 1935.

SAWYER, Donald Hubbard, civil engr.; b. Mt. Pulaski, Ill., Aug. 26, 1879; s. George Silas and Phoebe Content (Hubbard) S.; grad. Oak Park (Ill.) High School, 1897; B.S., U. of Ill., 1902; m. Elizabeth Osborn Merriam, Sept. 25, 1929; 1 son, George Osborn Sawyer (dec.). Began practice as civ. engr., 1902; city engr. Paris, Ill., 1903; chief engr. Ill. Traction System, 1904-09; mem. Sawyer Bros., Seattle and Spokane, Wash., 1910-17; with James Stewart & Co., N.Y. City, 1920-22; sec. Asso. Gen. Contractors of America, 1923-29; sec. Heating Bd. of Trade, New York, 1930; dir. Federal Employment Stabilization Bd. 1931-36; spl. asst. to Dir. of Procurement Div., Treasury Dept., 1936-39, since chief Real Estate Sect., Pub. Bldgs. Adminstrn.; chmn. Federal Real Estate Bd.; pres. U.S. Housing Corp. Served as maj., lt. col. Construction Div., U.S.A., 1917-20; charge constrn. Camp Grant, Rockford, Ill., nitrate plant, Cincinnati, and Camp Bragg, Fayetteville, N.C.; col. Q.M. Res. Baptist; chmn. bd. trustees Calvary Ch., Washington. Home: Alexandria, Va. Died June 21, 1941.

SAWYER, George Frederick, manufacturer; b. Boston, Mass., Sept. 9, 1875; s. George Frederick and Mary Elizabeth (Carlton) S.; ed. pub. schs., Chelsea, Mass.; m. Naomi Woodbury Babson, Nov. 15, 1899; children—Harold Babson, Edith Carlton (Mrs. Jay Danforth Edwards), Edson Woodbury, George Luere, Ruth. Began as office mgr., Attleboro, Mass., 1909; pres. and treas. Improved Seamless Wire Co., mfrs. rolled stock, 1919—; pres. Electric Chain Co.; treasurer Manufacturers Refining Co.; dir. Industrial Trust Co., Providence; mem. bd. mgrs. same co., Pawtucket. Mem. City Council, Quincy, Mass., 1905-07. Republican. Mason. Home: Edgewood, R.I. Died June 29, 1941.

SAWYER, J(ames) Estcourt, brig. gen. U.S.A.; b. Washington, D.C., July 3, 1846; s. Capt. H.B.S. (U.S.N.); grad. Arty. Sch., 1871; m. Elizabeth Thompson, June 1873. Apptd. from N.J., 2d lt. 5th Arty., Nov. 11, 1867; 1st lt., Nov. 10, 1874; capt. a.q.m., Dec. 1, 1893; maj. q.m. vols., May 12, 1898-Mar. 11, 1901; maj. q.m. U.S.A., Feb. 2, 1901; lt. col. deputy q.m. gen., July 10, 1904; col. a.q.m. gen., Apr. 21, 1910; brig. gen. U.S.A., July 3, 1910; retired by operation of law, July 3, 1910. Home: New York, N.Y. Died May 29, 1914.

SAWYER, Joseph Dillaway, author; b. Boston, Mass., Nov. 16, 1849; s. Joseph and Ann Maria (Dillaway) S.; grad. Chauncey Hall Sch., Boston, 1867; student Mass. Inst. Tech.; m. Mary Locke Wiggin, June 10, 1872. Dry goods commn. mcht., New York and Boston, many years, as mem. E. R. Mudge, Sawyer & Co., Sawyer, Burt & Manning, and Sawyer, Manning & Co.; with Joseph Sawyer, Sr.; imported the first Lister combers that ever arrived in America, enabling the Washington Mills, at Lawrence, Mass., to mfr. the first piece of worsted goods in America; suggested uniforming the police force throughout the country as well as all other official employes, and first manufactured cloth for this purpose, supplying it for many years; largely identified with real estate development on Long Island Sound, in L.I. and Conn. Author: How to Make a Country Place, 1914; The Pilgrim Spirit as Portrayed in the Plymouth Pageant of 1921, 1921; History of the Pilgrims and Puritans, Their Ancestry and Descendants, 3 vols., 1922; Washington (biography of George Washington), 2 vols., 1927. Home: Stamford, Conn. Died May 20, 1933.

SAWYER, Philetus, U.S. senator, mfr.; b. Rutland Co., Vt., Sept. 22, 1816; removed with parents, 1817, to Crown Point, Essex Co., N.Y.; brought up on farm; ed. dist. schools; became a saw-mill hand, then operated small saw-mill under contract; married, 1841, and, with wife and two sons, emigrated to Wis., 1847; in 1849 moved to Algoma, now Oshkosh; became one of the large mill and lumber operators of Wis. Member Wis. legislature, 1857 and 1861; mayor of Oshkosh, 1863-64; member Congress, 1865-75; U.S. senator, 1881-93. Republican. Home: Oshkosh, Wis. Died 1900.

SAWYER, Rollin Augustus, clergyman; b. Sawyerville, Que., Can., July 13, 1830; s. Rufus and Ruth (Alger) S.; ancestors landed in Mass., 1636; moved to Ohio, 1841; A.B., 2d honors, Western Reserve Coll., 1851 (Phi Beta Kappa); prin. Granville Acad., 1851-54; grad. Union Theol. Sem., New York, 1857; (D.D., Western Reserve U., 1872; Litt.D., Western Reserve U., 1911); m. Martha Elizabeth Linn, Aug. 18, 1857. Ordained Presbyn. ministry, 1858; pastor, Yonkers, N.Y., 1856-62, Newark, O., 1862-66, Dayton, 1866-70, Irvington, N.Y., 1870-79; stated supply, Greenwich, Conn., 1881-85; pastor Carmel, N.Y., 1885-88; stated supply, Hastings-on-Hudson, 1891-93, Montclair, N.J., 1893-1903; lecturer on lit., Bloomfield Theol. Sem., 1893-1908. Served as presiding officer in 3 synods. Progressive. Home: Montclair, N.J. Died Jan. 18, 1915.

SAWYER, Samuel Nelson, judge; b. Palmyra, N.Y., Oct. 6, 1858; s. Samuel William and Hannah (Nelson) S.; ed. Palmyra Classical Union Sch., and Phillips Acad., Andover, Mass.; LL.B., Albany Law Sch. (Union U.), 1883; LL.D. from Hobart College, Geneva, N.Y., 1929; m. Augusta Wells Webster, Oct. 20, 1885 (dec.); children—Charlotte Louise (Mrs. Ralph D. Sessions), Florence Isabel (dec.), Mary Nelson. In practice at Palmyra from 1883; dist. atty., Wayne Co., 2 terms, 1889-95; co. judge and surrogate, Wayne Co., 1898-1907; justice Supreme Court, N.Y., 1907-29, associate justice Appellate Div., 1926-29; became official referee of Supreme Ct. Republican. Episcopalian. Mason (Grand Master Grand Lodge, N.Y., 1908-10). Home: Palmyra, N.Y. Died May 1, 1939.

SAWYER, Thomas Jefferson, Universalist clergyman-teacher; b. Reading, Vt., Jan. 9, 1804; grad. Middlebury Coll., 1829 (A.M., S.T.D., Harvard, 1850; LL.D., Tufts, 1896); pastor in New York, 1830-45; m. Caroline M. Fisher, Sept. 21, 1831. Asso. editor The Christian Messenger, 1831-45; in charge Clinton, N.Y., Liberal Inst., 1845-52; pastor New York, 1852-61; editor The Christian Ambassador, 1863-66; on opening of Tufts Coll. Divinity School, 1869, became prof. systematic theology; prof. emeritus. Called the ednl. convention, 1847, which resulted in founding Tufts Coll.; was active in founding the Canton, N.Y., Theol. Sem.; suggested the Universalist Hist. Soc., 1834, and has been its sec. and librarian since that time. Author: Who Is God—the Son or the Father?; Endless Punishment in the Very Words of Its Advocates; etc. Died 1899.

SAWYER, Walter Hulme, M.D.; b. Lyme Tp., Huron Co., O., Aug. 10, 1861; s. George and Julia A. (Wood) S.; M.D., U. of Mich., 1884; LL.D. from Hillsdale (Mich.) College, 1926; house surgeon, Univ. Hosp., 1884-85; m. Harriet B. Mitchell, June 14, 1888; 1 son, Thomas Mitchell. Practiced Hillsdale, 1885—; surgeon L.S.&M.S. R.R. Regent U. of Mich.; trustee Hillsdale Coll.; mem. Hillsdale Sch. Bd. 32 yrs. Mem. Rep. State Central Com., 1894-98. Mem. Mich. State Bd. of Registration in Medicine, 1898-1906; pres. Mich. State Med. Soc., 1913. Fellow Am. College Surgeons. Episcopalian. Mason. Mem. Mich. State Com. Defense, 1917; mem. exec. com. of State Com. for Vol. Med. Service Corps during war; contract surgeon assigned to Hillsdale Coll. S.A.T.C.; mem. Hillsdale County Draft Bd. Home: Hillsdale, Mich. Died Apr. 28, 1931.

SAWYER, Walter Leon, editor, author; b. Cumberland, Me., Oct. 23, 1862; s. Joseph Smith and Abigail Pickles (Grannell) S.; ed. pub. and pvt. schs., Portland, Me.; m. Flora May Farmer, Nov. 12, 1884. Editorially connected with Portland Advertiser, Washington Post, etc., 1882-92; asst. editor Youth's Companion, 1892-1901; staff contbr. and contbr. to mags., 1901-09; editorial and spl. writer, Boston Evening Transcript, Aug. 1909—. Author: An Outland Journey, 1896; A Local Habitation, 1899. Home: Brookline, Mass. Died Jan. 1915.

SAXE, G(eorge) A(lexander) De Santos, physician; b. St. Petersburg, Russia, Feb. 22, 1876; s. Maximilian and Helen S.; ed. SS. Peter and Paul's Coll., St. Petersburg, to 1890; grad. Coll. Phys. and Surg. (Columbia) with high honors, M.D., 1898; unmarried. Asst. pathologist to Columbus Hosp., 1901-04; asst. to chair genito-urinary surgery, New York Post-Grad. Med. Sch. and Hosp., 1901—. Asst. editor New York Med. Jour., 1900—. Fellow N.Y. Acad. Medicine. Author: Examinations of the Urine, 1904; and a number of scientific articles in med. jours. Address: New York, N.Y. Died 1911.

SAXTON, Charles T., presiding judge N.Y. State Court of Claims for term 1898-1903; b. Clyde, N.Y., July 2, 1846; s. Daniel and Eliza A. S.; common school edn.; LL.D., Union Coll., 1891; m. Helen M. Field (deceased), Oct. 1, 1868. Served in Union army, 1861-66; admitted to bar, Dec. 1867; mem. assembly, 1887-89; State senator, 1890-94; lt. gov., 1895-96; delegate Rep. Nat. Conv., 1900. Dir. Union Trust Co. of Rochester; trustee Western N.Y. Instn. for Deaf Mutes. Address: Clyde, Wayne County, N.Y. Died 1903.

SAXTON, Francis Marion, lawyer; b. Burlington, Ky., Jan. 23, 1864; s. Francis and Sarah Ann (Swiggett) S.; student Central Normal Coll., Danville, Ind., 5 yrs., Sc.B., 1886, LL.B., 1889; m. Mary E. King, Aug. 6, 1890. Teacher Fla. Normal Sch., White Springs, Fla., 1889-91; teacher, Green Cove Spring, Fla., 1891-92; supt. Danville (Ind.) city schs., 1892-94; in law practice, at Baker City, Ore., 1895-1911; removed to Portland, 1911; practiced with Will R. King, 1895-1900, and 1911-13; U.S. attorney, Nome, Alaska, by appmt. of President Wilson, 1913-18; 1st U.S. atty. in Alaska to enforce the Sunday closing law. Democrat. State water commr. Ore., 1909-11. Home: Portland, Ore. Deceased.

SAXTON, Rufus, army officer; b. Greenfield, Mass., Oct. 19, 1824; s. Jonathan Ashley and Miranda (Wright) S.; ed. pub. schs. and acad., Deerfield, Mass.; grad. U.S. Mil. Acad., 1849; A.M., Amherst, 1853; m. Matilda Gordon Thompson, Mar. 11, 1863. Bvt. 2d lt. 3d Arty., July 1, 1849; commd. 2d lt. 4th Arty., Sept. 12, 1850; 1st lt., Mar. 2, 1855; capt. asst. q.m., May 13, 1861; brig. gen. vols., Apr. 15, 1862; hon. mustered out of vol. service, Jan. 15, 1866; maj. q.m. U.S.A., July 29, 1866; lt. col. deputy q.m. gen., June 6, 1872; col. asst. q.m. gen., Mar. 10, 1882; retired by operation of law after 43 yrs'. service, Oct. 19, 1888; advanced to rank of brig. gen. by act of Apr. 23, 1904. Bvtd. maj., lt. col. and col., Mar. 13, 1865, and brig. gen., Apr. 9, 1865, and maj. gen. vols., Jan. 12, 1865; awarded medal of honor, Apr. 25, 1893, for distinguished gallantry and good conduct in defense of Harper's Ferry, Va., May 26-30, 1862. Served on coast survey, 1853-61; chief q.m. on staff Gen. Lyon in Mo. campaign, of Gen. McClellan in western Va., and of Gen. Sherman's Port Royal expdn.; comd. forces at Harper's Ferry, 1862; mil. gov. Dept. of the South, 1862-65; comd. div. of 10th Army Corps and forces on Morris' and John's islands in attack on Charleston; commr. Freedmen's Bur. for S.C., Ga. and Fla. until end of war. Republican. Unitarian. Mem. Mil. Order of Medal of Honor Legion of U.S. Residence: Washington, D.C. Died 1908.

SAYERS, Joseph Draper, governor; b. Grenada, Miss., Sept. 23, 1841; s. David and Mary Thomas (Peete) S.; removed with father to Bastrop, Tex., 1851; ed. Bastrop Mil. Inst.; in C.S.A., 1861-65. Admitted to bar, 1866; mem. Tex. Senate, 1873; chmn. Dem. State Exec. Com., 1875-78; lt. gov. of Tex., 1879-80; elected 49th to 55th Congresses (1885-99); resigned from 55th Congress, Jan. 16, 1899; gov. of Tex., 2 terms, 1899-1903; chmn. Industrial Accident Bd. of Tex., 1913-15; mem. Bd. of Legal Examiners, Tex., 1922-26; mem. Bd. of Pardon Advisers, 1927—. Democrat. Grand Master Masons of Tex., 1875-76. Home: Austin, Tex. Died May 15, 1929.

SAYRE, Anthony Dickinson, judge; b. Tuskegee, Ala., Apr. 29, 1858; s. Daniel and Musidora (Morgan) S.; A.M., Roanoke Coll., Va., 1878; m. Minnie Buckner Machen, Jan. 15, 1884. Admitted to bar, 1881, and began practice at Montgomery, Ala. Clerk City Ct., Montgomery, 1883-89; mem. Ala. Ho. of Rep., 2 terms 1890-93, Senate, 1894-97 (pres. 1896-97); judge City Ct., 1897-1909; asso. justice Supreme Ct. of Ala., Feb. 6, 1909—. Democrat. Mem. Bd. Edn., Montgomery, 1891-1911. Mason. Home: Montgomery, Ala. Died Nov. 17, 1931.

SAYRE, Herbert Armistead, univ. prof.; b. Montgomery, Ala., Aug. 2, 1866; s. Paul Tucker and Eliza Rowe (Armistead) S.; student U. of Ala., 1884, U. of Va., 1892 (also asst. McCormick Obs.); Ph.D., Johns Hopkins, 1896; B.E., extra ordinem, U. of Ala., 1894; spl. studies in physics, U. of Chicago, 1898. Prof. mathematics, physics and astronomy, Ursinus Coll., Pa., 1897-98; prof. physics and astronomy, 1898-1906; prof. mathematics, 1907—.

U. of Ala. Address: University, Ala. Died Dec. 2, 1916.

SAYRE, Lewis Albert, M.D.; b. Bottle Hill (now Madison), Morris County, N.J., Feb. 29, 1820; grad. Transylvania U., 1839; Coll. Phys. and Surg., New York, 1842. Prosector in surgery Coll. Phys. and Surg., 1842-52; surgeon Bellevue Hosp., 1853-73, Charity Hosp., Blackwell's Island, 1859-73; consulting surgeon to both, 1873—; prof. orthopædic surgery and later of clinical surgery, Bellevue Hosp. Med. Coll.; later emeritus prof. orthopædic surgery Univ. and Bellevue Hosp. Med. Coll.; resident physician of city of New York, 1860-66; lectured in hospitals of Great Britain, 1877; was first Am. surgeon to successfully operate for hip-joint disease; introduced new methods of treatment in various diseases; m. Eliza Ann Hall, Jan. 25, 1849. Author: Practical Manual of the Treatment of Club-Foot; Lectures on Orthopædic Surgery; Spinal Curvature and Its Treatment. Address: New York, N.Y. Died 1900.

SAYRE, Lucius Elmer, univ. dean; b. Bridgeton, N.J., 1847; s. of David S.; Ph.G., Ph.M., Phila. Coll. Pharmacy; hon. B.S., U. of Mich., 1896; m. Ellen Platt, 1874. In business as mfg. chemist, 1882-85; instr., Phila. Coll. Pharmacy, 1880-85; dean Sch. of Pharmacy, U. of Kan., 1885—; mem. Revision Com. U.S. Pharmacopœia, 1890—; dir. drug analysis State Bd. of Health of Kan., 1907—; mem. bot. staff of Kansas State Bd. of Agr. Author: Chart of Materia Medica; Pharmacal Botany; Essentials of Pharmacy; Organic Materia Medica and Pharmacognosy; Essentials of Pharmacy (Sayre and Havenhill). Contbr. to most of the leading pharm. jours., principally Amer. Journal Pharmacy, Druggists' Circular and Merck's Report. Mem. com. on definitions and standards, connected with the Bur. of Chemistry, U.S. Dept. of Agr. Address: Lawrence, Kan. Died July 21, 1925.

SAYRE, Monell, corp. exec.; b. Morris County, N.J., Nov. 21, 1875; s. Monell and Marie (Stewart) S.; student Harvard, U., 1895-98; LL.D., Kenyon Coll., Gambier, O., 1932; adopted son, Francis Monell. Pension Expert, Carnegie Foundation, 1905-13; framed pension system of P.E. Ch., 1913; organized and directed (with Bishop Lawrence) campaign which raised $9,000,000 to establish Ch. Pension Fund of which was sec., later exec. v.p., 1913-33; exec. v.p. numerous corps.; pension adviser Fed. Res. System, 1920-27. Dem. candidate for Congress, 1922, 24 and 32. Chmn. finance com. Episcopal Diocese of New York, 1930-33. Home: Princeton, N.J. Died June 15, 1936.

SAYRE, Reginald Hall, surgeon; b. New York, Oct. 18, 1859; s. Dr. Lewis A. and Eliza Ann (Hall) S.; A.B., Columbia, 1881; M.D., Bellevue Hosp. Med. Coll. (New York U.), 1884; unmarried. Asst. to chair of surgery, Bellevue Hosp. Med. Coll., 1885-90; lecturer and orthopedic surgeon, 1890-97, adj. prof. orthopedic surgery, 1897-98, clin. prof., 1898-1910, prof., 1910—, Univ. and Bellevue Hosp. Med. Coll.; attending orthopedic surgeon, Bellevue Hosp., 1886-99; asst. attending surgeon, Bellevue Hosp., 1911—; etc. Editor dept. orthopedic surgery, Annals of the University Medical Sciences, 1890-96. Author: Immediate Reduction of Deformity after Tenotomy, 1887. Home: New York, N.Y. Died May 29, 1929.

SAYRE, Robert Heysham, civil engr., ry. official; b. Columbia County, Pa., Oct. 13, 1824; s. William H. S.; ed. common schs. and under James Nowlin, mathematician. Entered, 1840, engr. corps engaged in enlargement of Morris Canal, N.J.; on repairs of Lehigh Canal, 1841-43; on surveys and construction Back Track R.R., between Mauch Chunk and Summit Hill, 1844-45; later built the Switchback R.R. and inclined planes into Panther Creek Valley; development of coal mines, etc.; after 11 yrs. service with Lehigh Coal and Navigation Co. was elected chief engr. Delaware, Lehigh, Schuylkill & Susquehanna R.R. (later Lehigh Valley), serving 1852-82, and supervising extensions of system north and east; pres. and chief engr. S. Pa. R.R.; then 2d v.p. Lehigh Valley R.R. with oversight of traffic and engring. depts. and of extensions to Buffalo, and building branch roads. Pioneer in introduction of iron bridges, steel fire boxes, and the 1st to introduce the fish-bar track joint; began use of steel rails, 1864. One of promoters Bethlehem Iron Co.; dir., 1862 (gen. mgr., 1886; v.p., 1891); other large interests in corporations; chmn. bd. trustees Lehigh U.; chmn. exec. com., same, St. Luke's Hosp. Address: S. Bethlehem, Pa. Died 1907.

SAYRES, William Seaman, clergyman; b. Jamaica, N.Y., Oct. 16, 1851; s. Gilbert and Anna Leah (Seaman) S.; A.B., Dartmouth, 1876; studied theology, Berkeley Div. Sch., 1876-78; D.D., Dartmouth, 1904; m. Anna Stevens, Apr. 13, 1882; m. 2d, Mrs. Sarah L. Hunter, Sept. 7, 1912. Deacon, 1878, and priest, 1879, P.E. Ch.; one of founders, 1879, and prof. mathematics, St. John's Missionary Coll., Shanghai, 1879-80, 1882-85; sec. Standing Com. Am. Episcopal Jurisdiction of China, 1882-84; engaged in ednl. and evangelistic work, Wuchang and Hankow, 1880-82; rector New Lenox, Joliet, Morris, Ill., 1886-88; Montevideo, Minn., 1888-90, Broken Bow, Neb., 1890-93, Detroit, 1893-99. Sec. Detroit S.S. Inst., 1895-99; examining chaplain to bishop of Mich.; gen. missionary and arch deacon, Diocese of Mich., 1899—. Founder and mem. Ch. Unity Soc., Phila. Founded and edited The Platte (Neb.) Missionary, 1891-93; contbr. of ch. literature to newspapers and writer of tracts. Author: Forty Days; Things New and Old (reprints from Detroit Free Press). Regular contbr. to Detroit Sunday Free Press. Address: Detroit, Mich. Died May 5, 1916.

SBARBORO, Chevalier Andrea, banker; b. Acero Liguria, Italy, Nov. 26, 1839; s. Stefano and Maria (Torre) S.; brought to America at age of 4; ed. pub. schs., New York, and under pvt. tutors; m. Romilda Botto, Sept. 12, 1872. Began as clk. in grocery store, San Francisco, and became propr.; organizer and mgr. 5 mutual loan assns., beginning, 1875 (total receipts $6,500,000 in monthly installments, with which were built 2,500 homes for families, all fully paid); organizer and pres. Italian-Am. Bank; founder, sec. and mgr. Italian Swiss Agrl. Colony; founder and sec. San Francisco Sanitary Reduction Works. Organizer Mfrs.' and Producers' Assn., San Francisco (pres. 10 yrs.); organizer Calif. Promotion Com. Republican. Catholic. Mason. Anti-prohibitionist; delivered addresses against prohibition before committees of Calif. legislature and Congress of U.S. Founder and teacher of first Italian school, and publisher first Italian school book in Calif. Author of books on "True Temperance." Home: San Francisco, Calif. Died Feb. 28, 1923.

SCADDING, Charles, bishop; b. Toronto, Ont., Can., Nov. 25, 1861; s. Henry Simcoe and Elizabeth Winder (Wedd) S.; A.B., Trinity Coll., Toronto, 1885; m. Nellie Davy Donaldson, July 11, 1888 (died 1894); m. 2d, Mary R. Pomeroy, 1896. Deacon, 1885, priest, 1886, P.E. Ch.; asst. pastor St. George's Ch., New York, 1886-90; rector Christ Ch., Middletown, N.Y., 1890-91, Trinity Ch., Toledo, O., 1891-96, Emmanuel Church, La Grange, Ill., 1896-1906; consecrated bishop of Ore., Sept. 29, 1906. Deputation lecturer for London Soc. Propagation Gospel. Author: Dost Thou Believe, 1889; A Workable Graded System of Sunday School Instruction, 1896; Direct Answers to Plain Questions, 1899; also various tracts, etc. Address: Portland, Ore. Died May 29, 1914.

SCANLAN, Joseph D., newspaper pub.; b. Scranton, Pa., Mar. 9, 1876; s. Domnick and Mary (Kelly) S.; ed. high sch. and bus. coll., Superior, Wis.; m. Sarah M. McDougall, Nov. 28, 1918; children—Marjorie, Robert. Reporter Superior Evening Telegram, 1898, Duluth (Minn.) News Tribune, 1899, St. Paul Pioneer Express, 1900; advertising mgr. Grand Forks (N.D.) Herald, 1900-04; with Anaconda (Mont.) Standard, 1905, Daily Missoulian, Missoula, Mont., 1905-08; purchased Miles City (Mont.) Independent Weekly, 1909; established Miles City Daily Star, 1911. Register U.S. Land Office, Miles City, 1918. Chmn. Mont. State Rep. Com., 1920-24, 1930-32; Rep. presdl. elector from Mont., 1928; mem. Rep. Nat. Com., 1932—. Catholic. Elk. Home: Miles City, Mont. Died Aug. 9, 1939.

SCANLAN, Lawrence, bishop; b. County Tipperary, Ireland, Sept. 29, 1843; s. Patrick and Catharine (Ryan) S.; grad. All Hallows Coll., Dublin, 1868. Ordained priest R.C. Ch., June 24, 1868; asst. pastor St. Patrick's Ch., 1868-70, St. Mary's Cathedral, 1870-71, San Francisco; pastor, Woodland, Calif., 3 mos., Pioche, Nev., 1871-72, Petaluma, Calif., short time. Apptd. pastor Salt Lake City and of the whole Ty. of Utah, Aug. 1873; consecrated bishop of Laranda (Asia Minor) and vicar apostolic of Utah, June 29, 1887; apptd. 1st bishop of Salt Lake, 1891. Address: Salt Lake City, Utah. Died May 10, 1915.

SCANLON, Charles, general secretary; b. Three Churches, Hampshire County, W.Va., Oct. 5, 1869; s. Michael and Mary E. (Garrett) S.; B.S., Valparaiso (Ind.) U., 1895, A.M., 1899; U. of Minn., 1901; LL.D., Coll. of Wooster, O., 1916; m. Mary A. E. Walker, Apr. 2, 1894; children—Michael W., Mary B., Pauline R., Helen Ruth, Alice Walker, Ella Hill. Teacher pub. sch. and prin. town sch., W.Va.; teacher Normal Sch., Va., 1890-94; pastor Presbyn. Ch., Wheaton, Minn., 1895-99, Minneapolis, 1899-1903; prof. Macalester Coll., St. Paul, 1899-1901; nat. lecturer for Prohibition Party, 1903; gen. sec. Bd. Temperance Presbyn. Ch. U.S.A., 1904—. Nominated for gov. on Prohibition ticket, Minn., 1902; permanent chmn. Nat. Prohibition Conv., 1908; rep. U.S. Govt. at 12th to 16th Internat. congresses against alcoholism. Pres. Nat. Temperance Soc.; hon. treas. World Prohibition Fedn., and pres. Am. sect.; sec. Nat. Inter-Church Temperance Fedn.; trustee Nat. Prohibition Trust Fund. Editor Moral Welfare (Pittsburgh), National Advocate (New York). Home: Pittsburgh, Pa. Died Mar. 21, 1927.

SCANNEL, Richard, bishop; b. County Cork, Ireland, May 12, 1845; ed. coll. at Midleton, Cork; studied theology, All Hallows Coll.; ordained priest, 1871, coming to U.S.; pastor at St. Columbia's Ch., E. Nashville; rector of Nashville Cathedral, adminstr. Diocese of Nashville, 1880-83; rector St. Joseph's Ch., Nashville; consecrated 1st bishop of Concordia, Kan., Nov. 30, 1887; transferred to Omaha, Jan. 31, 1891. Address: Omaha, Neb. Died Jan. 7, 1916.

SCARBOROUGH, Dorothy, author; b. Mt. Carmel, Tex.; d. Judge John B. and Mary Adelaide (Ellison) S.; A.B. and A.M., Baylor U., Waco, Tex., Litt.D., 1923; studied U. of Chicago and Oxford U., Eng.; Ph.D., Columbia, 1917. Instr. in English, 1905-14, elected asst. prof., 1916, Baylor U.; instr. English, 1916-18, lecturer, 1919-22, asst. prof., 1923-31, asso. prof., 1931—, Columbia; on staff New York Sun, 1917-18. Baptist. Author: Fugitive Verses, 1912; The Supernatural in Modern English Fiction, 1917; From a Southern Porch, 1919; In the Land of Cotton, 1923; The Unfair Sex (a serial), 1925-26. Editor: Famous Modern Ghost Stories, 1921; Humorous Ghost Stories, 1921; On the Trail of Negro Folk-Songs, 1925; The Wind, 1925; Impatient Griselda, 1927; Can't Get a Red-bird, 1929; The Stretch-berry Smite, 1932; The Story of Cotton, 1933. Contbr. short stories, articles and verse to newspapers and mags. Address: New York, N.Y. Died Nov. 7, 1935.

SCARBOROUGH, Harold Ellicott, newspaperman; b. Bel Air, Md., Oct. 25, 1897; s. Harold and Frances Emily (Fanton) S.; A.B., Johns Hopkins, 1917; m. Gladys Mary Jones, Apr. 16, 1921; 1 dau., Elizabeth Anne. Began as reporter Baltimore (Md.) News, 1917, editorial writer, 1917-20; mem. London bur. New York Tribune, 1920-25; London corr. New York Herald Tribune, 1925-27, European editorial mgr., 1928—. Author: Stephen, the Well Beloved, 1923; The Immortals, 1924; England Muddles Through, 1932. Home: London, Eng. Died Apr. 7, 1935.

SCARBOROUGH, John, bishop; b. Castlewellan, Ireland, Apr. 25, 1831; s. John and Anna Bella Hannah S.; A.B., Trinity Coll., Conn., 1854, S.T.D., 1872; B.D., Gen. Theol. Seminary, New York, 1857; married. Deacon, 1857, priest, 1858, P.E. Ch.; asst. St. Paul's Ch., Troy, N.Y., 1857-60; rector Church of the Holy Comforter, Poughkeepsie, 1860-67, Trinity Ch., Pittsburgh, 1867-75; consecrated bishop of N.J., Feb. 2, 1875. Address: Trenton, N.J. Died Mar. 15, 1914.

SCARBOROUGH, William Sanders, educator; b. Macon, Ga., Feb. 16, 1854; s. Jeremiah and Frances S.; A.B., Oberlin College, 1875, A.M., 1878; Ph.D., Ky. State U., 1892; LL.D., Liberia Coll., W. Africa, 1882; Ph.D., Morris Brown Coll., Ga., 1908; F.Ph., St. Columba's Coll., Eng., 1909; m. Sarah C. Bierce, Aug. 2, 1881. Prof. classical Greek, Wilberforce U., 1877-91; prof. Hellenistic Greek, Payne Theol. Sem. (Wilberforce U.), 1891-95; prof. classical Greek, v.p. and head of Classical Dept., 1895-1908, pres., 1908-20, Wilberforce U.; asst. in farm studies, U.S. Dept. Agr., by appmt. of President Harding. Exegetical editor of the S.S. publs. A.M.E. Church; del. Ecumenical Meth. Conf., London, 1901, 21; del. Congress of Races, London, 1911. Mem. Am. Acad. Polit. and Social Science. Author: First Lessons in Greek, 1881; Theory and Functions of the Thematic Vowel in the Greek Verb; Our Political Status, 1884; Birds of Aristophanes, a Theory of Interpretation, 1886; also many articles on Negro folk-lore, the Negro question, classical, philol. and archæol. subjects. Rep. of Am. Philol. Assn. at Internat. Classical Conf., Cambridge U., 1921. Home: Wilberforce, O. Died Sept. 9, 1926.

SCARFF, Paul Brown, lawyer; b. Burlington, Ia., Aug. 9, 1871; s. Dr. John and Caroline (Chamberlain) S.; A.B., Hanover (Ind.) Coll., 1894; LL.B., Columbia, 1897; m. Edith Belle Roberts, Dec. 27, 1905; children—Dorothy Belle (Mrs. Peter Doelger), Virginia May (Mrs. Carl Hornung), Paul Brown. Admitted to N.Y. bar, 1897, and practiced in New York, 1897—; mem. firm Holm, Smith, Whitlock & Scarff (later Holm, Whitlock & Scarff), 1903—; v.p., sec., dir., mem. exec. com. and gen. counsel S. H. Kress & Co.; sr. v.p., dir. and mem. exec. com. Oakite Products, Inc.; mem. advisory bd. Chemical Bank and Trust Co.; v.p., trustee and mem. exec. com. Samuel H. Kress Foundation; v.p., sec., trustee Log Cabin Assn.; sec. and trustee Limited Price Variety Stores Assn. Served on Nat. Retail Bd. of NRA. Republican. Presbyn. Mason. Home: Westfield, N.J. Died Jan. 21, 1940.

SCARR, James Henry, meteorologist; b. nr. South Boston, Ionia County, Mich., Jan. 10, 1867; s. Francis O. and Joanna Eastman (Wilmarth) S.; student State Normal Sch., Emporia, Kan., 1887-89; studied law in office of Hon. John W. Sheafor, Concordia, Kan.; m. Laura E. Brown, Dec. 21, 1890; children—James Bernard (dec.), Francis Joseph. Teacher in pub. schs., Kan. and Okla., 1889-95; admitted to bar, 1892; practiced law, also newspaper and real estate business until 1898; entered service U.S. Weather Bur., 1898; stationed at St. Louis, Mo., and Cairo, Ill., 1898-1900, Helena and Havre, Mont., 1900-01; local forecaster, Sacramento, Calif., 1901-08, Tampa, Fla., 1908-09; dist. forecaster, New York, 1909-24; sr. meteorologist, New York, 1924-26, prin. meteorologist, 1926—. Fellow Am. Meteorol. Soc.; scientific mem. Inst. Aeronautical Sciences. Presbyn. Home: Hasbrouck Heights, N.J. Died Feb. 14, 1936.

SCARRITT, Winthrop Eugene, broker; b. Dorchester, Ill., June 17, 1857; s. Winthrop G. and Sarah E. (Meldrum) S.; B.A., DePauw, 1882, M.A., 1885; m. Lerria Tarbell, Sept. 20, 1887. Prof. belles lettres, U. of Colo., 1882-84; banker, 1885-93; mgr. bond dept. J. & W. Seligman, New York, 1894-1900; mem. firm E. R. Chapman & Co., 1900-02; pres. 1903-05, chmn. exec. com., 1905—; Commonwealth Trust Co. of New York; bond broker, 1906—; pres. Jones Taximeter Co. Mason. Republican. Methodist. Author: Three Men in a Motor Car, 1906. Contbr. to mags. on automobile and æronautic subjects. Home: E. Orange, N.J. Died 1911.

SCHAAF, Edward Oswald, M.D., composer; b. East New York, L.I., N.Y., Aug. 7, 1869; s. Rudolph Wilhelm Ludwig and Barbara (Sommer) S.; M.D., Bellevue Hosp. Med. Coll. (New York U.), 1894; spl. courses U. of Vienna, 1894-96; student Berlin, 1905-09; unmarried. Began practice in Newark, N.J., 1896. Attention given largely to music. Pres. Newark Philharmonic Concert Band Assn.; hon. mem. Am. Fedn. of Musicians. Wrote: Analysis of the Tannhauser Score (4 vols.); Twentieth Century Harmony Manual; The Art of Player-Piano Transcription (brochure), 1914; The Fundamental Principles Involved in the Composing and Arranging of Music for the Player-Piano, 1919; The Musical Individuality of the Player-Piano, 1922; The Art of Scoring for the Military Band; Treatise on Instrumentation; A Study of Modern Operatic Art (brochure); Music and the Photoplay, 1929; Analysis of the Tristan score (1 vol.); Analysis of The Maestersingers score (1 vol.). Among his principal musical compositions are (operas) Cymbeline (3 acts), The Maranas (2 acts), Choosing the Bride (2 acts), and one-act operas, Lucrèce, La Grande Bretéche, Little George, Cathleen Ni Hoolihan, The Merry Cuckoo, Margot; also 2 symphonies, 4 string quartets, 2 masses, and many songs; overtures, Colleoni, Festival, Weequahic, Branch Brook. Composer of state song, "Hail New Jersey"; Tone-poem, The Masque; Symphonic poem, In Memoriam. Made 120 arrangements for the player-piano, and 50 for military band. Home: Newark, N.J. Died June 25, 1939.

SCHAEBERLE, John Martin, astronomer; b. in Germany, 1853; s. Anton and C. Catherine (Voegele) S.; removed to Ann Arbor, Mich., 1854; apprentice in Chicago machine shop, 1868-71; became interested in astronomy; studied at Ann Arbor High Sch.; constructed a number of telescopes; C.E., U. of Mich., 1876; LL.D., U. of Calif., 1898; unmarried. Pvt. asst. to Prof. Watson, 1876-78; asst. Ann Arbor Obs., instr. in astronomy and acting prof. of astronomy, U. of Mich., 1878-88; astronomer Lick Obs., Mt. Hamilton, Calif., 1888-97, acting dir., 1897-98; had charge of eclipse expdns. of Lick Obs., 1889, 1893, Cayenne and Chile, and in 1896 to Japan; discovered 3 comets, and did much original work; extensive contbr. to astron. jours. Address: Ann Arbor, Mich. Died Sept. 17, 1924.

SCHAEFFER, John Ahlum, coll. pres.; b. Kutztown, Pa., May 31, 1886; s. Nathan Christ and Anna Matilda (Ahlum) S.; A.B., Franklin and Marshall Coll., Lancaster, Pa., 1904, A.M., 1905, Sc.D., 1929; Ph.D., U. of Pa., 1908; LL.D., Dickinson Coll., Carlisle, Pa., 1937; LL.D., Muhlenberg Coll., Allentown, Pa., 1938; m. Alice McConomy, Jan. 2, 1912 (dec.); children—Elizabeth (Mrs. Francis Bennett), John Nathan, Mary Helen, William Rathfon. Instr. chemistry, Carnegie Inst. Tech., 1908-11; with Eagle-Picher Lead Co., as chief chemist, dir. of manufacture, dir. of research and v.p., 1911-35; pres. Franklin and Marshall Coll., 1935—. Republican. Mem. Evang. and Ref. Ch. Mason. Author: Analysis of Paints and Painting Materials (with Henry A. Gardner), 1908; Experiments in Chemistry for Engineering Students (with Joseph H. James), 1910; The Chemical Analysis of Lead and Its Compounds (with Bernard S. White, and John H. Calback), 1912. Contbr. articles on industrial and engring. chemistry to jours. Address: Lancaster, Pa. Died Apr. 6, 1941.

SCHAEFFER, Nathan C., state supt. pub. instrn.; b. Maxatawny Tp., Berks County, Pa., Feb. 3, 1849; s. David and Esther Ann (Christ) S.; brother of William Christ S.; A.B., Franklin and Marshall Coll., Pa., 1867, Ph.D., 1879; D.D., LL.D., Dickinson, 1904; studied div. Theol. Sem. of the Reformed Ch.; finished edn. at univs. of Berlin, Tübingen, Leipzig; m. Anna Ahlum, July 8, 1880. Prof. Franklin and Marshall Coll., 1875-77; prin. Keystone State Normal Sch., 1877-93; state supt. of pub. instrn. of Pa., 1893—, and pres. State Bd. Edn. Clergyman of Reformed Ch. in U.S. (German Reformed). Mem. Commn. Industrial Edn.; sec. Bur. of Med. Edn. and Licensure, Dental Council of Pa.; sec. Coll. and Univ. Council Pa.; pres. Commn. that prepared the new sch. code of Pa.; chancellor Pa. Chautauqua at Mt. Gretna, 1902-05; pres. N.E.A., 1905-07. Author: Thinking and Learning to Think, 1900; History of Education in Pennsylvania. Editor: Bible Readings for Schools, 1897; Pennsylvania School Journal, 1893—. Prepared introduction to Hinsdale's Civil Government, Riddle's Nicholas Comenius, Life of Henry Harbaugh. Contbr. to ednl. and theol. jours. Mem. Simplified Spelling Bd. Home: Lancaster, Pa. Died Mar. 15, 1919.

SCHAEFFER, William Christ, prof. theology; b. Maxatawny, Berks County, Pa., Apr. 28, 1851; s. David and Esther Ann (Christ) S.; brother of Nathan C. S.; student State Normal Sch. Kutztown, Pa.; A.B., Franklin and Marshall Coll., Pa., 1871, A.M., 1876, Ph.D., 1889, D.D., 1903; Theol. Sem. Reformed Ch. in the U.S., Lancaster, Pa.; m. Mary H. Dreisbach, Jan. 11, 1881. Ordained Reformed Ch. ministry, 1874; pastor St. Paul's Ch., Waynesboro, Pa., 1874-76; prof. Latin and Greek, State Normal Sch., Kutztown, 1876-79; pastor Danville, Pa., 1879-84; pres. Palatinate Coll., Myerstown, Pa., 1884-91; pastor, Huntingdon, 1891-94, Chambersburg, 1894-1904; prof. N.T. science, Theol. Sem. Reformed Church, 1904—. Pres. dirs. Hood College, Frederick, Md.; v.p. Board of Home Missions Reformed Ch.; mem. Mercersburg Classic Synod of Potomac Reformed Ch. Author: Outlines of Life of Paul, 1908; Outline Studies on the Bible, New Testament, 1912; Catechetical Manual, 1913; The Supreme Revelation, 1914; The Greater Task, 1919. Contbg. editor Reformed Church Review; lesson editor S.S. Bd. Ref. Ch., 1898—. Address: Lancaster, Pa. Died Apr. 16, 1921.

SCHAFER, Joseph, historian; b. Muscoda, Wis., Dec. 29, 1867; s. Mathias and Anna J. (Bremmer) S.; B.L., U. of Wis., 1894, M.L., 1899, fellow, 1899-1900, Ph.D., 1906; LL.D., U. of Ore., 1933; m. Lily Abbott, Nov. 28, 1895; children—Max, Paul Abbott, Elizabeth, Sidney P., Joseph, Frederick. Teacher high sch., 1890-92; instr. history and civics State Normal Sch., Valley City, N.D., 1894-98; instr. history, 1900-01, asst. prof., 1901-04, prof. and head of dept., 1904-20, U. of Ore.; supt. State Hist. Soc. of Wis., 1920—; lecturer, U. of London, Feb.-Mar. 1936. Author: Origin of the System of Land Grants for Edn., 1902; History of the Pacific Northwest, 1905, 18; The Pacific Slope and Alaska, 1905; The Acquisition of Oregon Territory, 1908. Joint author and editor: Democracy in Reconstruction, 1919; A History of Agriculture in Wisconsin, 1922; Yankee and Teuton in Wisconsin, 1922-23; Francis Parkman, 1923; Wisconsin Domesday Book I, 1924; Four Wisconsin Counties, Prairie and Forest, 1927; Life of Carl Schurz, 1929; The Wisconsin Lead Region, 1931; Winnebago-Haricon Basin, 1927; The Social History of American Agriculture, 1936; also various essays. Editor: Intimate Letters of Carl Schurz, 1929; California Letters of Lucius Fairchild, 1931; Memoirs of Jeremiah Curtin, 1940. Editor: Wisconsin Magazine of History, 1922—. Home: Madison, Wis. Died Jan. 27, 1941.

SCHAFF, David Schley, clergyman; b. Mercersburg, Pa., Oct. 17, 1852; s. Rev. Philip S. (pres. Am. com. for revision of authorized version of the Bible); A.B., Yale, 1873; D.D., Ill. Coll., 1891, U. of Geneva, 1909; m. Lue M. Haynes; m. 2d, Elia Andrews; children—Philip H., Walter, Paul E., Norman, Mary Louise, Harold H., David S. Ordained Presbyterian ministry, 1877; pastor Hastings, Neb., 1877-81, Kansas City, Mo., 1883-88, Jacksonville, Ill., 1890-97; prof. ch. history, Lane Sem., 1897-1903; prof. ecclesiastical history and history doctrine, Western Theol. Sem., 1903-25; lecturer on Am. ch. history, Union Theol. Sem., 1925-29. Del. of Presbyn. Gen. Assembly to the celebration of the 400th anniversary of John Calvin's birth in Prague and Geneva, 1909, and Pan-Presbyterian Council, Aberdeen, Scotland, 1913. Author: Commentary on Acts, 1882; Life of Philip Schaff, 1897; Our Fathers' Faith and Ours, 1928. Co-editor: Schaff-Herzog Ency. (4 vols.), 1883; History of the Christian Church, vol. 1, 1050-1294, 1907, vol. 2, 1294-1517, 1910; John Huss—His Life, Teachings and Death—After Five Hundred Years, 1915; The Church—a Treatise by John Huss, transl., with notes, 1915; The Reformation and Its Influence, 1917. Chmn. com. Presbyn. Gen. Assembly to prepare the intermediate catechism, 1913; chmn. com. of Assembly to arrange celebration of 400th Anniversary of the Protestant Reformation, 1917. Address: New York, N.Y. Deceased.

SCHAFF, Morris, author; b. Kirkersville, O., Dec. 28, 1840; s. John and Charlotte (Hartzell) S.; grad. U.S. Mil. Acad., 1862; LL.D., Williams Coll., 1913; Litt.D., Otterbein U., 1914; m. Alice Page, Aug. 8, 1868. Second lt. Ordnance Corps, June 17, 1862; 1st lt., Mar. 3, 1863; capt., Mar. 7, 1867; bvtd. capt., May 6, 1864, "for gallant and meritorious service in battle of the Wilderness"; resigned, Dec. 31, 1871; insp. gen. Mass. Militia, 1882; mem. Board of Visitors to West Point, 1882. President West Point Alumni Assn., 1913. Democrat. Author: Etna and Kirkersville, 1905; Spirit of Old West Point, 1907; Battle of the Wilderness, 1908; Sunset of the Confederacy, 1912; Jefferson Davis, His Life and Personality, 1922. Address: Cambridge, Mass. Died Oct. 19, 1929.

SCHAFFER, Charles, physician; b. Phila., Feb. 4, 1838; s. of Charles (druggist) and Priscilla Morgan (Potts) S.; ed. by private tutor; M.D., U. of Pa., 1859; engaged in practice; m. Martha, d. Robt. T. Potts, 1862 (died 1878); m. 2d, Ellen E., d. Maj. David Zook, 1882 (died 1884); m. 3d, Mary T., d. Alfred Sharples, 1889. Contract surgeon U.S.A., in 1863; attending physician Bedford St. Mission, 1874, Mission Hosp. and Dispensary, 1875-80. Address: Philadelphia, Pa. Died 1903.

SCHAFFNER, John Henry, botanist; b. Agosta, Marion County, O., July 8, 1866; s. Daniel S., Jr., and Anna (Miller) S.; A.B., Baker U., Baldwin, Kan., 1893, M.S., 1896; A.M., U. of Mich., 1894; U. of Chicago, 1896-97; U. of Zürich, 1907-08; m. Cordelia Garber, 1916; children—Grace Odile, John Garber, James Daniel. Assistant in botany, U. of Mich., 1894-95; prof. natural science, S.D. U., 1895-96; asst. in botany, 1897-99, asst. prof. 1899-1902, asso. prof., 1902-11, prof., 1911-28, head of dept., 1908-18, research prof. of botany, 1928—, Ohio State U. Editor-in-chief Ohio Naturalist, 1900-15, of Ohio Jour. of Science, 1915-17. Presbyn. Author: Laboratory Outlines for General Botany, 1905; Trees of Ohio and Surrounding Territory, 1909; The Pteridophytes of Ohio, 1910; Field Manual of Trees, 1914; Catalog of Ohio Vascular Plants, 1914; The Grasses of Ohio, 1917; Field Manual of the Flora of Ohio and Adjacent Territory, 1928; Manual of Ohio Weeds (with H. A. Runnels), 1931; also numerous articles on cytology, morphology, the classification and evolution of plants, nature of sex, etc. Home: Columbus, Ohio. Died Jan. 27, 1939.

SCHALL, Thomas David, senator; b. Reed City, Mich., June 4, 1877; s. David and Mary Ellen S.; A.B., U. of Minn., 1902; LL.B., St. Paul Coll. of Law, 1904; m. Margaret H. Huntley, Nov. 5, 1902; children—Thomas D., Richard Burton, Peggy. Admitted to Minn. bar, 1904, and practiced at Minneapolis. Mem. 64th to 68th Congresses (1915-25), 10th Minn. Dist.; mem. U.S. Senate from 1925, 2d term expiring 1937. Republican. Lost his eyesight, 1907, but continued in practice of law. Home: Minneapolis, Minn. Died Dec. 11, 1935.

SCHALLER, Albert, judge; b. Chicago, Ill., May 20, 1856; s. Jean Michael and Barbara (Klein) S.; ed. Washington U., St. Louis; m. Kate E. Meloy, May 24, 1881; children—John C., Rose-Marie, Karl A., Josephine M., Marion E. Admitted to Minn. bar, 1879; county atty. Dakota County, Minn., 1879-91; city atty. Hastings, 1891-97, S. St. Paul, Minn., 1895-99; mem. Minn. Senate, 1895-1915; Dem. candidate for Congress, 3d Minn. Dist., 1900, and for judge of Dist. Court, 1914; asso. justice Supreme Court of Minn., by apptmt. of Gov. Hammond, 1915-17; practiced at St. Paul, 1895—. Mem. K.C., Elks. Home: Hastings, Minn. Deceased.

SCHAMBERG, Jay Frank, dermatologist; b. Phila., Pa., Nov. 6, 1870; s. Gustav and Emma (Frank) S.; A.B., Central High Sch., Phila., 1888; M.D., U. of Pa., 1892; post-grad. work, Vienna, Paris, Berlin and London; m. May Ida Bamberger, Oct. 11, 1905; children—Elizabeth, Ira Leo. Practiced at Phila., 1892—; prof. dermatology and syphilology, Grad. Sch. of Medicine, U. of Pa., 1919—; dir. Dermatol. Research Inst., Phila. Apptd. mem. Pa. Vaccination Commn., by Governor Tener, 1912. Mem. Am. Dermatol. Assn. (pres. 1920-21). Republican. Jewish religion. Author: Compend. of Diseases of Skin, 1898; Acute Contagious Diseases (with Dr. Welch), 1905; Skin Diseases and Eruptive Fevers, 1911. Associated with Drs. George W. Raiziss and John A. Kolmer, in research, early in World War I, which led to the first elaboration in U.S. of salvarsan, previously made only in Germany; donated profits arising from sale in U.S. as a permanent endowment for the Research Inst. of Cutaneous Medicine. Address: Philadelphia, Pa. Died Mar. 30, 1934.

SCHAUB, Frederick; b. nr. Lancaster, Wis., June 21, 1855; s. Philip J. and Mary K. (Biebricher) S.; grad. normal course, German-English Coll., Galena, Ill., 1878, A.M., 1884; D.D., Central Wesleyan Coll., Warrenton, Mo., 1907; m. Mary Strohn, Mar. 27, 1879. Ordained M.E. ministry, 1880; pastor Decorah, Ia., and Galena, Ill., until 1882; instr., later pres. German-English Coll., 1882-91; pres. Charles City (Ia.) Coll., 1891-94; pastor La Crosse, Wis., 1894-97; prof. Charles City Coll., 1897-1902; county supt. schs., Floyd Co., Ia., 1902-07; prof. Charles City Coll., 1907-14; prof. Bibl. and religious lit., Morningside Coll., 1914—. Mem. Northwest German Conf. M.E. Ch. Republican. Joint Author: History of Northwest German Conference of Methodist Episcopal Church, 1913. Home: Sioux City, Ia. Died Mar. 12, 1937.

SCHAUFFLER, Adolph Frederick, clergyman; b. Constantinople, Turkey, Nov. 7, 1845; s. William Gottlieb and Mary (Reynolds) S.; brother of Edward William S.; A.B., Williams Coll., 1867; Union Theol. Sem., 1868-69; grad. Andover Theol. Seminary, 1871; D.D., New York U., 1886, Williams College, 1909; m. Julia Baker, Aug. 1884. Ordained Congl. ministry, 1871; pastor Brookfield, Mass., 1871-72; city missionary, New York, 1872-87; pastor Olivet Ch., New York, 1873-87; supt. New York City Mission and Tract Soc., 1887-1902; pres. New York City Mission, 1902—. Author: Ways of Working, 1891; The Teacher, the Child and the Book, 1900; The Pastor as Leader of Sunday School Forces, 1903; Sparks from a Superintendent's Anvil, 1909. Address: New York, N. Y. Died Feb. 18, 1919.

SCHAUFFLER, Edward William, physician; b. Vienna, Austria, Sept. 11, 1839; s. William Gottlieb and Mary (Reynolds) S.; brother of Adolph Frederick S.; A.B., Williams College, 1862, A.M., 1875. First lt. and adj. and later capt., 127th N.Y. Vols., 1862-65; M.D., Coll. Phys. and Surg. (Columbia), 1868. In practice at Kansas City, 1868—; one of organizers, 1869, and later teacher, Kansas City Med. Coll.; prof. internal medicine, Med. Sch., U. of Kan. Presbyterian. Republican. One of translators Ziemssen's Ency. of Medicine. Contbr. numerous articles to 1st and 2d edits. Wood's Reference Handbook of the Medical Sciences. Home: Kansas City, Mo. Died Oct. 29, 1916.

SCHAUFFLER, Henry Park, clergyman; b. Constantinople, Turkey, May 3, 1870; s. Henry A. (D.D.) and Clara Eastham (Gray) S. (missionaries); A.B., Amherst, 1893; grad. Hartford Theol. Sem., 1897; m. Grace M. Jarvis, Jan. 14, 1909. Ordained Congl. ministry, 1898; pastor 2d Ch., Berlin, Conn., 1897-1904, Olivet Memorial Ch., N.Y. City, 1905-12; supt. Brooklyn City Mission, 1913-18; dir. New York met. survey and program constrn. of Interch. World Movement, 1919. Sec. Greater N.Y. City Missions Council; one of organizers of Child Welfare Exhibit Movement; mem. exec. com. New York Child Welfare Com., N.Y. State S.S. Assn. Trustee Hartford Theol. Sem. Died July 6, 1930.

SCHAUFFLER, William Gray, M.D.; b. of Am. missionary parents, Constantinople, Turkey, Oct. 28, 1863; s. Henry Albert (D.D.) and Clara Eastham (Gray) S.; B.A., Amherst, 1886, M.A., 1903; M.D., Coll. Phys. and Surg. (Columbia), 1889; m. Eleanor H. Hawkes, Jan. 14, 1891 (died 1891); 1 son, William Gray; m. 2d, Lilian Miner Boswell, Sept. 5, 1894. Prof. of physiology and diseases of women, med. dept. Am. Univ., Beirût, Syria, 1891-96; practiced, Lakewood, N.J., 1896-1917, Princeton, 1920—; med. adviser to Princeton Theol. Sem. Mem. N.J. N.G., 1905—; lt. col. M.C., surgeon gen. N.J., 1911-17; a.d.c. to 3 govs. of N.J.; lt. col., sanitary insp., 39th Div., Camp Beauregard, La., and in France; col. M.C., U.S.A.; information officer Advance G.H.Q., Germany; attached to High Rhineland Commn., Germany. Republican. Presbyn. Mason. Home: Princeton, N.J. Died Apr. 30, 1933.

SCHAYER, Milton M(incha), banker; b. Denver, Colo., Apr. 30, 1876; s. Charles M. and Rika (Saft) S.; ed. grammar sch.; m. Elsie Reinach, Jan. 8, 1908 (dec.); m. 2d, Jane S. Bear, Jan. 11, 1921. Pres. Bankers Bldg. & Loan Assn., Denver; mem. bd. govs. Colo. Bldg. & Loan Inst.; pres. Colo. State League of Bldg. & Loan Assns.; mem. U.S. Bldg. & Loan League (nat. pub. relations com.; nat. exec. com.; state historian of commemorative vol.), Internat. League of Bldg. & Loan Assn. (exec. com.); pres. Southwestern Group of Bldg. & Loan Assns. Sec. Denver Community Chest 3 yrs. Organizer and author of ritual of Jr. Order B'nai B'rith (exec. com.); Colo. state chmn. Jewish Welfare campaign. Jewish religion. Mason; mem. B'nai B'rith. Awarded silver plaque, Denver Chamber Commerce, as most valuable citizen, 1925. Author of syndicated column "Things to Think About." Contbr. to financial and Masonic jours. Lecturer. Awarded citation by Gov. for work done in building better religious spirit, 1933. Home: Denver, Colo. Died Dec. 11, 1935.

SCHECHTER, Solomon, theologian, author; b. Fokshan, Roumania, Dec. 7, 1847; s. Isaac and Rachel S.; ed. univs. Vienna and Berlin; grad. as rabbi, Vienna, 1887; specialized in divinity and Semitics; A.M., U. of Cambridge, Eng., 1891, Litt.D., 1898; Litt.D., honoris causa, Harvard U., 1911; m. Matilda Roth, 1887. Reader of Rabbinic, Univ. of Cambridge; prof. Hebrew, Univ. Coll., London, Eng., 1899-1901; traveled in Italy, Egypt, Palestine and elsewhere; sent by U. of Cambridge to examine Hebrew lit.; made various discoveries; came to U.S., 1902; pres. Jewish Theol. Sem. of America, 1902—. Author: Abot de Rabbi Nathan, 1887; Studies in Judaism (1st series), 1896; Wisdom of Ben Sira, 1899; Midrash Ha-Gadol, 1902; Saadyana, 1902; Studies in Judaism (2d series), 1908; Some Aspects of Rabbinic Theology, 1909; Documents of Jewish Secretaries (2 vols.), 1911; also various papers in English, German, French and Hebrew periodicals. Home: New York, N.Y. Died Nov. 19, 1915.

SCHEFFAUER, Herman George, author; b. San Francisco, Feb. 3, 1878; s. John George and Maria Theresa (Eisele) S.; ed. public and pvt. schs., Calif., art course, U. of Calif.; m. Ethel, d. William W. Talbot, 1912. Engaged with architects of San Francisco as designer and water colorist, teacher of draughting, meanwhile writing poetry; gave up architecture, May 1904, traveled in Europe and in northern Africa 1 yr.; spent 2 yrs., 1905-07, in London, Eng.; returned to San Francisco, later became resident worker Univ. Settlement, New York; returned to London, Dec. 1910. Author: Of Both Worlds (poems), 1903; Looms of Life (poems), 1907; Sons of Baldur (forest play, Bohemian Club, San Francisco), 1908; The Masque of the Elements, 1911; Drake in California, 1912; The New Shylock (a play), 1913. Translator: Survey of the Woman Problem (from German), 1913; Heine's Atta Troll, 1913, etc. Contbr. to leading Am. revs. and mags. Died 1927.

SCHEIBLE, Charles Frederick, mayor; b. Youngstown, May 29, 1869; s. John and Christina (Myers) S.; ed. pub. schs.; m. Cora B. Williams, May 11, 1894; children—Mrs. Jaunita Kinden, Charles R. Constructing engr., especially highways and ry. bridges; dir. of service, Youngstown, 1921, 22; mayor, Youngstown, 1924-27 inclusive; later construction engr., Truscon Steel Co. Republican. Mem. German Ref. Ch. Mason, K.P., Elk. Address: Youngstown, O. Died Sept. 5, 1935.

SCHELL, Edwin Allison, coll. pres.; b. Deer Creek, Ind., Nov. 25, 1859; s. Jacob and Elizabeth (Zeller) S.; A.B., Northwestern U., Ill., 1886 (winner Kirk oratorical prize); B.D., Garrett Bibl. Inst., 1889; Ph.D., Ill. Wesleyan U., 1891; D.D., Hedding Coll., Ill., 1892; m. Emma Wright, July 14, 1886. Ordained M.E. ministry, 1883; pastor Hammond, Ind., 1883-86, St. Paul's Ch., South Bend, Ind., 1886-90, First Ch., Yonkers, N.Y., 1890-93; gen. sec. Epworth League, 1892-99; presiding elder Crawfordsville, Ind., 1901-07; pastor Laporte, Ind., 1908; pres. Iowa Wesleyan Coll., 1908-18; Red Cross worker in France and Serbia, 1918-19; Chautauqua and lyceum lecturer, 1920-24; pastor of the Country Club, Kansas City; Mo. Pres. bd. of trustees Epworth Assembly; del. Ind. State Rep. convs., 1886, 88, 1904, 06, 08. Lectured in every state and ty. of the Union, including Alaska; government lecturer Philippine Teachers' Assembly, 1913. Author: The New Generation, 1893; Concerning the Collection, 1895; Epworth League Bible Studies, 1894-99; Traits of the Twelve, 1911; In Ports Afar, 1914. Home: Glendale, Calif. Died 1937.

SCHELL, William Elias, educator; b. Carroll County, Ind., Oct. 25, 1861; s. Jacob and Elizabeth (Zeller) S.; A.B., Western Coll., Toledo, Ia., 1890, A.M., 1893; D.D., Lane U., Kansas, 1902; LL.D., Kansas City U., 1923; m. Alice L. Pierson, Jan. 3, 1880; children—Gracie Lelia, Lena Elizabeth, Winnie Ermine (dec.), Louis Irving, Ruth Alice. Licensed minister, 1890; ordained ministry United Brethren in Christ, 1893; pastor DuBois, Neb., 1890-93, York, Neb., 1893-95, presiding elder, York dist., 1895-97; pres. York (Neb.) Coll., 1897-1913; gen. sec. of edn. U.B. Ch., 1913-29; v.p. and dir. finance Kansas City U., 1920—. Pres. Nat. Bd. of Edn. U.B. Ch., 1905-13. Home: Kansas City, Kan. Died July 31, 1935.

SCHELLING, Ernest Henry, pianist, composer and conductor; b. N.J., July 26, 1876; s. of Felix and Rose (White) S.; studied music under Mathias Moszkowski (Paris), Huber (Basel), Paderewski (Switzerland); Doctor of Music, U. of Pa., 1928; m. Lucie How Draper, May 3, 1905. Composer: Légendes Symphoniques, 1904; Symphony Fantastic Suite, piano and orchestra; Impressions, variations for piano and orchestra (Boston Symphony, 1915); Violin Concerto (Kreisler, Boston Symphony, 1916); Victory Ball (after poem by Noyes), first perf. in New York with Phila. Philharmonic Orchestra, Feb. 1923; "Morocco" for orchestra (N.Y. Philharmonic, 1927); divertimento for string quartet and piano (Flonzaley, New York, 1925). Conductor children's and young people's concerts, N.Y. Philharmonic, Boston, Phila., Baltimore, San Francisco, Los Angeles, Hollywood Bowl and Cincinnati orchestras, etc., comdr. Baltimore Symphony Orch., 1936, 37, 38. Commd. capt. of cavalry, Aug. 5, 1917, promoted maj., Nov. 10, 1918; served with army abroad, Oct. 1917-Apr. 1920. Decorated French Legion of Honor, 1919; D.S.M. (U.S.), 1923; Comdr. Alphonso XII (Spain); Officer Polonia Restituta (Poland). Home: New York, N.Y. Died Dec. 8, 1939.

SCHENCK, Benjamin Robinson, surgeon; b. Syracuse, N.Y., Aug. 19, 1872; s. Adrian A. and Harriet (Robinson) S.; A.B. Williams, 1894; M.D., Johns Hopkins, 1898; m. Jessie McCallum, Aug. 17, 1904. Resident gynecologist to Johns Hopkins Hosp. 1898-1903, instr. in gynecology, 1901-03; removed to Detroit, 1903; became gynecologist to Harper Hosp.; cons. obstetrician to Woman's Hosp., Detroit; asso. prof. gynecology, Detroit Coll. of Medicine. Republican. Presbyn. Author: Ancestors and Descendants of Rulef Schenck, 1911. Contbr. numerous articles in contemporary med. lit. and to several systems of surgery. Home: Detroit, Mich. Died June 30, 1920.

SCHENCK, Charles Meigs, corp. exec.; b. Franklin, O., Jan. 3, 1850; s. Washington Lafayette and Julia (Bliss) S.; educated at Antioch Coll., Yellow Springs, O., 1868-71; m. Mary Elizabeth Stone, Sept. 8, 1875 (died 1929); children—Julia (Mrs. S. B. Foote), Martha, Charles (dec.), Paul A., Gertrude (Mrs. H. W. Hochbaum), Harriet (dec.). Clerk in local freight office C.,B.&Q. R.R., Burlington, Ia., 1871-72; bookkeeper and gen. salesman William Bell & Co., wholesale dry goods, Burlington, 1872-77; successively cashier, sec., v.p. and treas., Whitebreast Coal & Mining Co. and its successors, the Whitebreast Co. and Whitebreast Fuel Co., Ia. and Chicago, 1877-91; pres. Western Supply Co., 1884-94; sec. and gen. auditor Colo. Fuel & Iron Co., Denver, 1892-93; pres. Colo. & Wyo. Ry. Co. and v.p. Crystal River R.R. Co., 1902; pres. and treas. Colo. Supply Co. (operating 30 gen. mdse. stores in Colorado and Wyoming), 1893-1915; dir., v.p. Merchants Fire Ins. Co., Denver, 1915—. Mem. and treas. Bd. of Edn., Denver pub. schs., 1917-29, pres., 1920—. Clerk provost marshal's office, Dayton, O., Feb.-June, 1865; mem. Ia. State Militia, 1873-74. Republican. Mason. Unitarian. Home: Denver, Colo. Died Nov. 9, 1933.

SCHENCK, Ferdinand Schureman, theologian; b. Ulster County, N.Y., Aug. 6, 1845; s. Rev. Martin L. and Abby (Van der Veer) S.; A.B., Princeton, 1865, A.M., 1868; LL.B., Albany Law Sch., 1867; grad. New Brunswick Theol. Sem., 1872, D.D., 1891, LL.D., 1906, Rutgers; m. Ellie S. Haring, Aug. 26, 1874. Practiced law, 1867-69; licensed by classis of Ulster, Ref. Ch. in America, 1872; pastor Clarkstown, 1872-77, Montgomery, 1877-90, Hudson, N.Y., 1890-97, University Heights, New York, 1897-99; prof. practical theology, New Brunswick Theol. Sem., 1899—. Acting prof. philosophy, 1904-05, acting prof. ethics and evidences of Christianity, 1906-07 and 1916-17, Rutgers; actg. prof. homiletics, Princeton Theol. Sem., 1909-10. Author: The Ten Commandments in the Nineteenth Century, 1889; The Bible Reader's Guide, 1896; The Ten Commandments and the Lord's Prayer, 1902; Modern Practical Theology, 1903; The Sociology of the Bible, 1909; Christian Evidences and Ethics, 1910; A Young People's History of the Christian Church, 1911; The Oratory and Poetry of the Bible, 1915; The Apostles Creed in the 20th Century, 1918; Expository Sermons on the Heidelberg Catechism, 1920; A Guide Book to the Stars, 1922. Address: New Brunswick, N.J. Died Aug. 6, 1845.

SCHENCK, William Edward, clergyman; b. Princeton, N.J., Mar. 29, 1819; s. John C. and Annie B. (Hutchinson) S.; grad. Princeton, 1838; Theol. Sem., 1841; D.D., Jefferson Coll., Pa., 1861; m. Jane Whittemore Torrey, Apr. 18, 1843 (died 1856); m. 2d, Mary B. Kittle (died 1900). Missionary in Pa. coal region, 1841-42; ordained, 1843; held pastorates, Manchester, N.J., New York, and Princeton, N.J., until 1852; supt. ch. extension for Presbytery of Phila., 1852-54; sec. Presbyn. Bd. of Publn., 1854-86, editor, 1862-70; permanent clerk gen. assembly (old school), 1862-70, and mem. Reunion Com., 1867-70; dir. Princeton Theol. Sem., 1865— (sec., 1870-98); trustee of Gen. Assembly, 1865-87, and v.p. bd.; v.p. Pa. (Auxiliary) Colonization Soc., 1865—, and of Am. Colonization Soc., 1877—. Author: Historical Account of the First Presbyterian Church of Princeton, New Jersey, 1851; Church Extension for Cities, 1854; Aunt Fanny's Home, 1861; Nearing Home, 1863; The Fountain for Sin, 1864; Children in Heaven, 1867; etc. Address: Oakmont, Allegheny County, Pa. Died 1904.

SCHEPPEGRELL, William, laryngologist; b. (of American parents) Hanover, Germany, Sept. 22, 1860; high sch. and coll. edn.; A.M., 1884; M.D., Med. Coll. State of S.C.; spl. course, 1887-89; m. Jessie A., d. Prof. Allessandro Gambati, 1882. In practice at Charleston, S.C., until 1890, at New Orleans, 1890—; asst. surgeon, Eye, Ear, Nose and Throat Hosp.; chief of hay fever clinic, Charity Hospital. Inventor of many appliances in ear, nose and throat specialty. Pres. Audubon Park Commn. Asso. editor The Laryngoscope; co-editor Annals of Otology, Rhinology and Laryngology. Author: Hay Fever and Asthma, Cause, Treatment and Cure; Electricity in Diseases of the Nose, Throat and Ear; Non-Malignant Tumors of the Throat; and other works. Home: New Orleans, La. Deceased.

SCHERER, Melanchthon G. G., clergyman; b. Catawba County, N.C., Mar. 16, 1861; s. Rev. Simeon and Sarah S.; A.B., Roanoke Coll., Salem, Va., 1881, A.M., 1886, D.D., 1902; m. Alice M. Ehrman, Oct. 20, 1886; 1 son, Rev. Paul E. (D.D.). Ordained ministry Evang. Luth. Ch., 1883; pastor Grafton, W.Va., 1886-90, Mt. Holly Springs, Pa., 1890-93, Concord, N.C., 1893-96; pres. N.C. Coll., 1896-99; pastor Newberry, S.C., 1899-1901; theol. prof., 1901-04; pastor Charleston, S.C., 1904-18; pres. United Synod Evang. Luth. Ch. in the South, 1914-18; sec. United Luth. Ch. in America, 1918—. Del. to World Conf. on Faith and Order, Lausanne, Switzerland, 1927 (mem. continuation com.). Democrat. Author: (with Frederick H. Knubel) Our Church, 1924. Home: New York, N.Y. Died Mar. 9, 1932.

SCHERESCHEWSKY, Joseph Williams, M.D.; b. Peking, China, Mar. 6, 1873; s. Samuel I. J. and Susan Mary (Waring) S.; brought to U.S. in infancy; A.B., Harvard, 1895; M.D., Dartmouth Med. Sch., 1899; m. Bessie Berry Conklin, June 27, 1899; children—Dorothy Duncan, Mary Elizabeth, Henry Waring, Catherine Chapman, Helen Louise (dec.), John Forby, Benjamin Berry. Served as pvt., and acting hosp. steward, U.S.A., in Cuba, Spanish-Am. War, 1898; apptd. asst. surgeon U.S.P.H.S., Nov. 4, 1899; promoted through grades to med. dir., 1930. Specialized in indsl. hygiene and occupational diseases; in charge Office of Field Investigations of Occupational Diseases, U.S.P.H.S., 1913-18; asst. surgeon gen. in charge of div. of scientific research, Bur. of Pub. Health Service, 1918-22; later in charge investigations in cancer of P.H.S. In charge of organizing of Ga. Cancer Control Program, 1937. Associate editor Journal of Industrial Hygiene. Awarded Distinguished Service Key by Am. Conf. of Phys. Therapy, 1936. Episcopalian. Home: Belmont, Mass. Died July 9, 1940.

SCHERESCHEWSKY, Samuel Isaac Joseph, P.E. bishop; b. Tanroggen, Russian Lithuania, May 6, 1831; Jewish parentage; studied at home in different Rabbinical schs.; then in Germany, chiefly at Breslau; went, 1854, to U.S., where he embraced Christianity; studied Western Theol. Sem. Presbyn.), Allegheny, Pa., 1855-58; joined P.E. Ch., 1858; studied Gen. Theol. Sem., New York, 1858-59; D.D., Kenyon, 1876; S.T.D., Columbia, 1877; m. 1868. Ordered deacon, July 7, 1859, in New York; ordained priest at Shanghai, China, Oct. 28, 1860; missionary in Shanghai, 1860-63, in Peking, 1863-75; in U.S., 1875-77; elected bishop, 1875, 1876, 1877; declined 1st two elections; accepted 3d; consecrated Oct. 31, 1877, 3d P.E. bishop of China; resigned, 1883, because of impaired health; lived in U.S., 1886-95, in China, 1895-97, in Japan, 1897—. Translated Book of Common Prayer into Mandarin (with Rev. J. S. Burden) while at Peking; revised the entire Mandarin Bible, 1887-95, 1895; made entirely new transl. of Bible into Wenli (the classical language of China), 1888-1902, 1902. Died 1906.

SCHERGER, George Lawrence, clergyman; b. Lawrenceburg, Ind., Oct. 21, 1874; s. Christian and Marguerite (Rush) S.; A.B., Ind. U., 1894; U. of Leipzig, 1895-96; U. of Berlin, 1896-98; Ph.D., Cornell U., 1899; m. Bertha Mittelstaedt, January 18, 1898. Instr. history, 1899-1901, asst. prof., 1901-03, prof. history, 1903—, Armour Inst. Tech., Chicago. Pastor and supt. of Armour Mission, 1905-31; pastor St. Paul's Evang. Luth. Ch., 1929—. Pres. Asso. Ch. Charities of Chicago. Republican. Author: Evolution of Modern Liberty, 1904: Men of the Hour, 1932; also numerous papers and revs. Home: Chicago, Ill. Died Mar. 31, 1941.

SCHERMERHORN, Frederick Augustus, capitalist; b. New York, N.Y., Nov. 1, 1844; E.M., Columbia School of Mines, 1868. Commd. 2d lt., 185th N.Y. Inf., Dec. 27, 1864; 1st lt., Jan. 25, 1865; served in Army of the Potomac; mustered out, May 30, 1865; bvtd. capt. "for gallant conduct at battle of Five Forks, Apr. 1, 1865"; served N.G.S.N.Y., pvt. to 1st lt., 7 yrs. Trustee Columbia Coll.; treas. N.Y. Trade Sch. Home: New York, N.Y. Died Mar. 20, 1919.

SCHERZER, Albert H., engr.; b. Peru, Ill., July 22, 1865, s. William and Wilhelmina S.; ed. Peru (Ill.) High Sch. and Tech. Sch., Zürich, Switzerland; LL.B., Union Coll. of Law, Chicago, 1892; m. Donna G. Adair, May 8, 1902. Engaged in law practice, Chicago, until death of his brother, William, inventor of the Scherzer rolling lift bridge, becoming pres. and chief engr. of The Scherzer Rolling Lift Bridge Co.; designed and built many large and important ry., electric ry. and highway bridges in U.S. and abroad; also invented improvements in bridges. Office: Chicago, Ill. Died Jan. 28, 1916.

SCHEVE, Edward Benjamin, musician; b. Herford, Germany, Feb. 13, 1865; s. Edward and Adelaide (Schoneborn) S.; came to America, 1883; ed. Kullaks Acad. of Music, Berlin, 1885-88; organ under F. Grunicke; piano, A. Konig, and composition, Alb. Becker; hon. Mus.D., Grinnell College, Iowa; m. Lina Grosch, October 9, 1890. Instr. Kullaks Acad. of Music, 1886-88; organist and teacher, Rochester, N.Y., 1888-92; concert organist and dir. of a conservatory of music, Chicago, 1892-1906; prof. theory and composition and instr. in organ and piano, Grinnell Coll. Sch. of Music, 1906—. Baptist. Author: Death and Resurrection of Christ (oratorio), 1906; Requiem, 1909; Festival March (orchestra, organ and chorus), 1909; Conzerto for Piano and Orchestra, 1913; Sonata for Violin and Piano, 1913; suite, In Trying Times, for orchestra, 1914; suite religioso for organ and orchestra, 1915; sonata for organ, 1915; Symphony in D-minor, for Orchestra, 1917; Meditations on Quotations from the Psalms, for piano and violin, 1917; symphonic poem for orchestra, A Day in Elkanah Valley, 1920; Song of Triumph, intermezzo for orchestra, 1921; also numerous compositions for piano, organ, voice and religious service. Address: Grinnell, Ia. Died June 18, 1924.

SCHICK, John Michael, clergyman; b. Richmond, Va., Nov. 8, 1848; s. Peter and Mary (Schowe) S.; A.B., Mercersburg Coll., Pa., 1873; theol. course, same, 1873-76, A.M., 1876; D.D., Heidelberg U., Ohio, 1891; m. Mary J. Lloyd, Oct. 15, 1879. Ordained ministry Ref. Ch. in U.S., 1876; pastor, Orbisonia, Pa., 1876-81, Meyersdale, 1881-88, Shenango, 1888-94, Tiffin, O., 1894-1900, Grace Ref. Church, Washington, of which President Roosevelt was a member, 1900—. Mem. com. to prepare Hymnal of the Reformed Ch., 1890; sec.-treas. Bd. of Ministerial Relief Ref. Ch. Author: The Catechumens' Counsellor, 1901. Address: Washington, D.C. Died July 22, 1913.

SCHIEFFELIN, Bradhurst, wholesale druggist; b. New York, N.Y., Sept. 21, 1824; s. Henry Hamilton and Maria Teresa (Bradhurst) S.; partner in Schieffelin Bros. drug house, established by his grandfather, 1794; m. Lucy, d. Thomas Dodge. Became known as supporter of equal suffrage for all males in N.Y., 1846. Introduced petroleum to the world, commercially, 1860. Formed com. of prominent citizens to advise with and support President Lincoln during war. During commercial crisis following war sheltered and fed thousands of destitute persons at his own expense. Formulated, and with Horace Greeley and Charles O'Connor, signed petition to Congress, introduced by Roscoe Conkling, to prevent appropriation of public money or property to religious sectarian corps. Organized Bread and Shelter Soc. to remove destitute persons from cities to rural dists. for their self support. Composer of numerous melodies. Advocate of limitation of inheritances and for several yrs. published a periodical in that interest. Address: New Dorp, N.Y. Deceased.

SCHIEFFELIN, Samuel Bradhurst, merchant, author; b. New York, N.Y., Feb. 24, 1811; ed. private schools; mem. firm of Schieffelin Bros., drugs; began to contribute to religious press when a young man. Author: Message to Ruling Elders, their Office and their Duties; The Foundations of History: a Series of First Things; Milk for Babes: a Bible Catechism; Children's Bread: a Bible Catechism; Words to Christian Teachers; People's Hymn Book; Children of God, and Union with Christ; After Death and Other Mysteries; etc. Address: New York, N.Y. Died 1900.

SCHIEREN, Charles Adolph, mayor; b. province of Rhein, Prussia, Feb. 28, 1842; came to U.S., 1856; employed in father's cigar and tobacco store until 1864; clerk in belting factory, 1864-68; established on small scale, 1868, business known as Charles A. Schieren Co., tanners and belting mfrs., one of the largest in U.S.; 1st vice-pres. and trustee Germania Savings Bank, Brooklyn; trustee Brooklyn Trust Co.; dir. Germania Life Ins. Co., Nassau Nat. Bank. Pres. and dir. Brooklyn Acad. Music; 1st v.p. and trustee Brooklyn Inst. Arts and Sciences. Elected, 1893, mayor of Brooklyn, that city being merged in Greater New York, Jan. 1, 1898. Home: Brooklyn, N.Y. Died Mar. 10, 1915.

SCHIFF, Jacob Henry, banker; b. Frankfort-on-the-Main, Germany, 1847; s. M.S.; ed. schs. of Frankfort; came to U.S., 1865; settled in New York; m. Theresa Loeb, 1875; father of Mortimer L. S., and father-in-law of Felix Warburg. Member firm Kuhn, Loeb & Co., bankers, New York; dir. Central Trust Co., Western Union Telegraph Co., Wells Fargo & Co. Pres. Montefiore Home for Chronic Invalids; v.p., trustee Baron de Hirsch Fund; dir. New York Foundation; v.p. New York C. of C.; founded Jewish Theol. Sem., the Semitic Mus. (Harvard), Nurses' Settlement, New York. Home: New York, N.Y. Died Sept. 25, 1920.

SCHIFF, Mortimer L., banker; b. New York, N.Y., June 5, 1877; s. Jacob Henry and Theresa (Loeb) S.; student Amherst Coll., class of 1896, hon. A.M., 1906; m. Adèle G. Neustadt, Apr. 30, 1901. Studied railroading with N.Y., Ont. & Western Ry. and G.N. Ry., then spent 2 yrs. at Hamburg and London, studying European banking methods; partner banking firm of Kuhn, Loeb & Co., New York, 1900—. Dir. Am. & Continental Corp., L.A. & Salt Lake R.R., New York Foundation, Western Union Telegraph Co., Pacific Oil Co., Chemical Bank & Trust Co., Chemical Safe Deposit Co. Mem. N.Y. Stock Exchange; v.p. Chamber Commerce N.Y. State; trustee Baron de Hirsch Fund, Provident Loan Soc. of New York. Pres. Jewish Board of Guardians; v.p. Boy Scouts of America. Home: New York, N.Y. Died June 4, 1931.

SCHILDER, Paul Ferdinand, M.D., psychiatrist; b. Vienna, Austria, Feb. 15, 1886; s. Ferdinand and Berta (Fürth) S.; M.D., U. of Vienna, 1909, grad. student, 1909-10; Ph.D., U. of Halle, 1911; m. Mitzi Moser, July 1919; m. 2d, Lauretta Bender, M.D., Nov. 1936; children—Michael, Peter. Asst. in psychiatry, Univ. Hosps., Halle, 1910-12, Leipzig, 1912-14; physician in Austrian Army, 1914-18; 1st asst. in psychiatry, Univ. Hosp., Vienna, 1918-28; extraordinary prof., U. of Vienna, 1925; clin. dir. psychiatric div., Bellevue Hosp., New York, 1929—; research prof. of psychiatry, New York U., 1929—. Author: Hypnosis (with O. Kauders), 1926; Introduction to a Psychoanalytic Psychiatry, 1928; Brain and Personality, 1931; The Image and Appearance of the Human Body, 1935; Psychotherapy, 1938; also several books published in Berlin and Vienna. Home: New York, N.Y. Died Dec. 8, 1940.

SCHILLER, William Bacon, mfr.; b. Pittsburgh, Pa., July 7, 1859; s. John G. and Anne J. (Queen) S.; ed. pub. schs.; m. Margaret Patterson Burdett, June 6, 1900; children—Morgan B., William B., Frederic C. Began as office boy with R. W. Hitchcock & Co., Youngstown, Pa., 1876; bookkeeper 2d Nat. Bank, Youngstown, 1879-83; sec. Brier Hill Iron & Coal Co., 1883-86; treas., gen. mgr. Youngstown Coal & Coke Co., Ltd., and Bessemer Limestone Co., 1886-89; gen. mgr. Monongahela Furnace Co., 1889-92, until it was consolidated with Nat. Tube Works Co.; mgr. blast furnaces and steel works, Nat. Tube Works Co., until orgn., 1899, of Nat. Tube Co., with which continued as mgr. nat. dept.; 1st v.p. same, 1901, pres. 1902-26 (retired); dir. Union Trust Co., Mellon Nat. Bank, Union Savings Bank, Bell Telephone Co. of Pa., Nat. Union Fire Ins. Co. Republican. Episcopalian. Home: Pittsburgh, Pa. Died July 25, 1935.

SCHILLING, Hugo Karl, univ. prof.; b. Saalfeld, Thuringia, Germany, Mar. 28, 1861; ed. schs. and coll., Saalfeld; A.M., Ph.D., U. of Leipzig, 1885; came to America, 1886; m. Theresa T. Stitt, July 14, 1887; children—Mrs. Elsa Margaret Douglas (dec.), Mrs. Elisabeth Frances Drury, Karl Howard, Hugh Edward. Prof. modern langs., Wittenberg Coll., Springfield, O., 1886-91; asst. prof. German, Harvard, 1891-1901; prof. German lang. and lit., U. of Calif., 1901-29 (emeritus). Editor Modern Lang. Notes, 1899-1901, U. of Calif. Publs. in Modern Philology, 1909—. Author: König Alfreds angelsächsische Bearbeitung der Weltgeschichte des Orosius, 1886; also numerous philol., lit., hist. and ednl. articles in Am. and European jours. Home: Berkeley, Calif. Died July 12, 1931.

SCHINDEL, John Randolph, lawyer; b. Ft. Stevenson, Dakota Ty., June 8, 1875; s. Jeremiah Peter and Martha Pintard (Bayard) S.; LL.B., U. of Cincinnati, 1899; m. Ella Baker, June 15, 1918. Began law practice with Maxwell & Ramsey, Cincinnati, 1899; asst. city solicitor, Cincinnati, 1906-08; mem. firm Waite & Schindel, later Waite, Schindel & Bayless, 1909—; dir. and member exec. com., Union Central Life Ins. Co.; dir. and gen. counsel Columbia Life Ins. Co.; dir., sec. and counsel Holmes Darst Coal Corp.; dir., counsel Chemical Products Corp.; dist. atty. B.&O. R.R. Company; atty. Postal-Telegraph Cable Co., Conn. Gen. Life, Phoenix Mut., Midland Mut., Lincoln Nat., Mass. Mut. ins. cos., and Med. Protective Co. Member Cincinnati Charter Commn., 1913-14; chmn. bd. trustees Cincinnati Bur. Municipal Research, 1911-17; trustee Babies Milk Fund Assn. Mem. Am. Acad. Polit. and Social Science, Acad. Polit. Science. Episcopalian (junior warden Christ Ch.). Home: Cincinnati, O. Died Oct. 29, 1941.

SCHINDEL, S(amuel) John Bayard, army officer; b. Camden, N.J., June 3, 1871; s. J. P. (capt. U.S. Army) and Martha Pintard (Bayard) S.; grad. U.S. Mil. Acad., 1893; Army War Coll., 1908; m. Isa Urquhart Glenn, Nov. 11, 1903. Commd. add. 2d lt. 3d Arty., June 12, 1893; 2d lt., Nov. 2, 1893; trans. to 16th Inf., Feb. 25, 1895, to 6th Inf., Apr. 12, 1895; 1st lt. 3d Inf., Apr. 26, 1898; trans. to 6th Inf., Dec. 19, 1898; capt., Feb. 2, 1901; maj., June 12, 1916; lt. col., June 30, 1917; col. N.A., Aug. 5, 1917; brig. gen. (temp.), Aug. 8, 1918. With regt. at Ft. Thomas, Ky., 1895-98; in Santiago Campaign, 1898, participated in Battle of San Juan Hill and Siege of Santiago; in Philippines, 1899-1902, and 1905-06, participating in engagement at Valdes, July 1899, and Bud Dajo, Mar. 4-9, 1906; attended Swiss autumn maneuvers, 1907; duty Gen. Staff, 1912 to 1916, June-Aug. 1918; assigned to Camp Meade, Md., Aug. 26, 1918; duty Gen. Staff, Mar.-Sept. 1919, later at Ft. Leavenworth. Episcopalian. Home: Allentown, Pa. Died Mar. 11, 1921.

SCHINDLER, Jacob John, editor; b. Monroe, Wis., July 13, 1868; s. Henry and Katharine (Zopfi) S.; B.Litt., U. of Wis., 1889; m. Grace Alma Lamb, Aug. 17, 1898. Connected successively with La Crosse Republican and Leader, Green Bay Gazette, and Oshkosh Northwestern, Milwaukee Journal (city editor); removed to St. Paul, 1896, as asst. city editor Pioneer Press; later served 1 yr. as telegraph editor Minneapolis Journal and for short time as mng. editor St. Paul Dispatch; was city editor, night editor and mng. editor, Pioneer Press; mng. editor, 1913-20, asst. to the editor, Dec. 1920—, The Milwaukee Journal. Home: Milwaukee, Wis. Died 1922.

SCHINDLER, Kurt, composer, dir.; b. Berlin, Germany, Feb. 17, 1882; ed. univs. of Berlin and Munich and under masters in music; m. Vera Andeuchevitch, actress. Asso. condr. at Met. Opera House, New York, 1905-07; reader for G. Schirmer, music pub., 1907—. Founded MacDowell Chorus, 1908; choir dir. Temple Emanuel. Composer many songs; editor of A Century of Russian Song, etc. Address: New York, N.Y. Died Nov. 16, 1935.

SCHINDLER, Solomon, author; b. Neisse, Germany, Apr. 24, 1842; grad. Breslau, Germany, 1862; post-grad. course in Teachers' Normal Sch., Buren, Germany; m. Henrietta Schutz, June 24, 1868. Came to U.S., 1871; became minister Congregation Adath Emuno, Hoboken, N.J., later of Congregation Adah Israel, Boston, 1874-94; mem. Boston Sch. Bd. by popular election, 1888-94; resigned position as rabbi, 1894; became supt. Fedn. of Jewish Charities of Boston, 1895-99; supt. Leopold Morse Home, 1899-1909; resigned and retired, 1909. Author: Messianic Expectations and Modern Judaism; Dissolving Views of the History of Judaism; Young West, a Sequel to Bellamay's Looking Backward. Contbr. many articles in The Arena. Address: Dorchester, Mass. Died May 5, 1915.

SCHINNER, Augustin Francis, bishop; b. Milwaukee, Wis., May 1, 1863; s. Michael and **Mary**

(Koenig) S.; ed. St. Francis Sem., nr. Milwaukee. Ordained priest, R.C. Ch., 1886; pastor Richfield, Wis., 1886-87; mem. faculty, St. Francis Sem., 1887-93; sec. to Archbishop Katzer, and chancellor and vicar gen. Archdiocese of Milwaukee, 1893-1905; consecrated 1st bishop of Superior, Wis., July 25, 1905; resigned, 1913, and apptd. 1st bishop of Spokane, Mar. 18, 1914; apptd. titular bishop, Dec. 17, 1925. Address: Milwaukee, Wis. Died Feb. 7, 1937.

SCHLACKS, Charles Henry, corp. official; b. Chicago, Ill., Nov. 12, 1865; s. Henry and Christine (Thielen) S.; ed. pub. schs.; m. Laura N. Pierson, Jan. 18, 1893. Asst. gen. mgr. D.&R.G. R.R., 1893-1900; gen. mgr. Colo. Midland R.R., 1901-04; v.p. D.&R.G. R.R., 1904-13, Western Pacific R.R., 1910-13; pres. Hale & Kilbourn Co., Phila., 1914; gen. mgr. Eddystone Rifle Plant of Midvale Steel & Ordnance Co., 1915-19; pres. Union Oil Co. of Del., 1919-22; dir. Barber Asphalt Co., Am. Pulley Co., Keystone Watch Case Corp., Riverside Metals Co., Baldwin Locomotive Works, Midvale Steel Corp. Home: Bryn Mawr, Pa. Died Mar. 3, 1941.

SCHLADERMUNDT, Herman T., artist; b. Milwaukee, Wis., Oct. 4, 1863; s. Joachim and Caroline (Widman) S.; ed. in art, Delacluse and Julian Acads., Paris, France; m. Anna R. Gardner, 1897; children—Rosaline, Peter. Medal, Chicago Expn., 1893; Allied Arts prize, Architectural League, N.Y., 1898. Mural decorations: Thomas Ryan Art Gallery, New York; Grand Jury Room, Newark (N.J.) Court House; corridor, Denver Post Office; also stained glass, Congressional Library, Washington, D.C.; Missouri Capitol, Jefferson City; Flagler Memorial, St. Augustine, Fla.; etc. Home: Bronxville, N.Y. Died Jan. 26, 1937.

SCHLADITZ, E., engraver; b. Leipzig, Germany, 1862; studied in many art centres of Europe, then came to New York. Diplomas in Boston, Phila., and Vienna, Austria; medal, Chicago Expn., 1893; silver medal, Paris Expn., 1900; medal, Buffalo Expn., 1901. Address: New York, N.Y. Died 1910.

SCHLAKE, William E., brick mfr.; b. York, Pa., Sept. 11, 1863; s. Henry and Mary (Schleeter) S.; ed. pub. schs.; m. Miss Mueller, Mar. 17, 1887; children—Elsa, Helen, William F., Theodore H., Edwin C. Settled at Chicago, 1884; taught sch. until 1890; began in business as a brick mfr.; became sec. Ill. Brick Co., 1900, and pres., 1909—. Alderman 26th Ward, 3 terms, 1894-1900, and chmn. finance com. Chicago City Council, 1899-1900. Apptd. mem. Bd. of Commrs. of Chicago Fair, 1935. Mem. Draft Registration Bd., 1917. Mem. Common Brick Mfrs.' Assn. (pres. 1918-21, 1925-29). Democrat. Lutheran. Home: Chicago, Ill. Died May 5, 1940.

SCHLAPP, Max Gustav, neurologist; b. Fort Madison, Ia., Nov. 4, 1869; s. George and Marie (Dupuis) S.; student Cornell U., 1891-93; Bellevue Med. Sch. (New York U.); studied in Germany 6 yrs., M.D., U. of Berlin, 1896; unmarried. Specialist in mental and nervous diseases; asst. prof. neuropathology, Cornell U., until 1914; prof. neuropathology, Post-Grad. Med. Sch. Hosp., 1911—; mem. N.Y. State Commn. to investigate Provision for the Mentally Deficient, by apptmt. of Gov. Glynn, 1914. Protestant. Author of numerous tech. papers pertaining to neurol. topics, causes of feeble-mindedness, etc. Chmn. med. bd. Children's Courts, N.Y. City. Office: New York, N.Y. Died Mar. 5, 1928.

SCHLEGEL, H. Franklin, clergyman; b. Mauch Chunk, Pa., Oct. 25, 1867; s. William and Christena (Stahl) S.; B.E., Albright Coll., Pa., 1897, Ph.D., 1906, D.D., 1935; m. Jean M. Herb, Mar. 30, 1916; children—William Franklin, Franklin Kehler, Sarah Christene, Jean Elizabeth. Ordained ministry United Evang. Ch., 1893; pastor Freemansburg, Pa., 1891-94, Wilkes-Barre, 1894-95, Albright Coll., 1895-97, Williamstown, 1897-99, Harrisburg, 1899-1903, Shamokin, 1903-07, Albright Coll., 1907-11, Mt. Carmel, 1911-15, Lancaster, 1915-18; presiding elder, 1918-22; pastor Trinity Evangelical Ch., Easton, Pa., 1922—. Chmn. Forward Movement; chmn. Permanent Commn. on Temperance; pres. Ednl. Aid Soc.; mem. exec. com. Nat. Service Commn., Evang. Ch.; del. Gen. Conf. 8 times to 1938; mem. Commn. on Ch. Union and Federation of Evang. Ch.; mem. Commn. on Worship, Fed. Council of Chs. of Christ in America; exec. sec.-treas. Bd. of Ch. Extension of Evang. Ch. Chmn. exec. com. Albright Coll., also trustee and sec. bd. of trustees; trustee Bibl. Sem. (New York), Harrisburg State Hosp.; 1st v.p. Pa. State Anti-Saloon League; pres. Assn. of Trustees of Colls. of Liberal Arts of Pa. Republican. Mason. Maj., chaplain, retired U.S.A. Home: Easton, Pa. Died Apr. 28, 1941.

SCHLESINGER, Elmer, lawyer; b. Chicago, Ill., Nov. 20, 1880; s. Leopold and Henrietta (Mayer) S.; A.B., Harvard, 1901, LL.B., 1903; m. Halle Schaffner, 1911 (divorced, 1921); children—Halle, Elmer; m. 2d, Eleanor Patterson Gizycka, Apr. 1925. Mem. firm, Mayer, Meyer, Austrian & Platt, Chicago, 1908-21; v.p. and gen. counsel U.S. Shipping Bd., Washington, D.C., June 15, 1921-Sept. 1, 1922; later mem. Chadbourne, Stanchfield & Levy, New York; organizer of many large industrial corps.; mem. bd. dirs. Chicago Tribune, The News (New York), Liberty Magazine, Fifth Av. Coach Co., New York Rys. Corp., etc. Republican. Jewish religion. Home: New York, N.Y. Died Feb. 20, 1929.

SCHLESINGER, Louis, real estate, insurance; b. Newark, N.J., Dec. 16, 1865; s. Alexander and Fanny (Fleischer) S.; ed. pub. schs. of Newark; m. Sophie Levy, Oct. 8, 1890 (died 1937); children—Alexander L. (dec.), Joel L. Began as office boy, Brown & Volk, real estate, Newark, 1880; in real estate and insurance business, 1890—; pres. Louis Schlesinger, Inc., 1911—; pres. Schlesinger-Heller Agency; dir. United States Trust Company; sec.-treas. Union Bldg. Co., 1904-28. Nat. chmn. state bd. dirs. Nat. Farm Sch., Bucks County, Pa. Organizer Newark Real Estate Bd.; past pres. N.J. Assn. Real Estate Bds.; mem. N.Y. Real Estate Bd.; mem. exec. bd. Union of Am. Hebrew Congregations, 1913—; mem. admission com. Jewish Children's Home, Newark; mem. Congregation B'nai Jeshurun (Ref. Hebrew). Mason (Shriner). Home: West Orange, N.J. Died Sept. 15, 1942.

SCHLEY, Grant Barney, banker; b. Chapinsville, N.Y., Feb. 25, 1845; s. Evander S.; ed. Canandaigua Acad.; m. Elizabeth, d. George E. Baker, 1879. Began business life as clerk in express office of Wells, Butterfield & Co., Syracuse, 1861-63; agt. same at Suspension Bridge, N.Y., 1863-66; in money dept. of firm's successor, Am. Express Co., at New York, 1866-74; with 1st Nat. Bank, New York, 1874-80; mem. New York Stock Exchange, 1880, and mem. banking and brokerage firm Groesbeck & Schley, succeeded 1885 by Moore & Schley, one of the largest in U.S., of which he became senior mem. 1899. Pres., dir. Coal Creek Mining & Mfg. Co., Crœsus Gold Mining & Milling Co., El Potosi Mining Co., Tintic Co., Howe Sound Co.; 1st v.p. Electric Storage Battery Co.; pres., dir. Chihuahua Mining Co.; chmn. bd. Elliott-Fisher Co.; dir. Am. Smelting & Refining Co., N.P. Railway Co., Republic Iron & Steel Co. of New Jersey, Pittsburgh Coal Company, etc. Home: New York, N.Y. Died Nov. 2, 1917.

SCHLEY, Winfield Scott, rear admiral U.S.N.; b. nr. Frederick City, Md., Oct. 9, 1839; s. John Thomas and Georgiana Virginia (McClare) S.; apptd. to U.S. Naval Acad. from Md., 1856, grad. 1860; m. Annie R. Franklin, Sept. 10, 1863. Promoted midshipman, June 15, 1860; master, Aug. 31, 1861; lt., July 16, 1862; lt. comdr., July 25, 1866; comdr., June 10, 1874; capt., Mar. 31, 1888; commodore, Feb. 6, 1898; rear admiral, Mar. 3, 1899. Served on Niagara, 1860-61; Keystone State, 1861; Potomac, storeship, at Ship Island, 1861-62; Winona, W. Gulf Blockading Squadron, 1862-63; participated in engagement with a battery near Port Hudson, Dec. 14, 1862; all engagements which led to capture of Port Hudson, Mar.-July 1863; served on Wateree, Pacific Squadron, 1864-66; on duty Naval Acad., 1866-69, 1872-76; served on Benicia, 1869-72; participated in attack on Salee River forts in Korea, 1871; comd. Essex, 1876-79; light house insp. 2d dist., 1880-83; comd. the Thetis and Greely expdn., 1884, and rescued Lt. Greely and 6 survivors at Cape Sabine, for which was awarded a gold watch and vote of thanks of Md. legislature and gold medal from Mass. Humane Soc.; chief Bur. of Equipment and Repair, 1884-89; comd. Baltimore, 1889-92; mem. Bd. Inspection and Survey, 1896-97; chmn. Lighthouse Bd., 1897-98; during war with Spain comd. Flying Squadron, 1898; was in immediate command in battle of Santiago de Cuba, July 3, 1898, which resulted in the destruction of Admiral Cervera's Fleet; commander-in-chief S. Atlantic Squadron, 1899-1901; retired, Oct. 9, 1901. Presented with gold sword by people of Pa., a silver sword by Royal Arcanum, a gold and jeweled medal, with the thanks of Md. legislature, a silver service, etc., for services at battle of Santiago. Author: The Rescue of Greely, 1885; Forty-Five Years Under the Flag, 1904. Address: Washington, D.C. Died 1911.

SCHLOTTERBECK, Julius Otto, pharmacognosist; b. Ann Arbor, Mich., Sept. 1, 1865; s. Hermann William and Rosina Christina Schlotterbeck; Ph.C., U. of Mich., 1887, B.S., 1891; Ph.D., U. of Berne, Switzerland, 1896; m. Eda May Clark, Aug. 11, 1898. Asst. in pharmacognosy and pharmacy, 1888-90, in pharmacognosy, 1891-92, instr. pharmacognosy and botany, 1893-95, asst. prof., 1896-1904, jr. prof., 1904-07, prof., 1907—, dean Sch. Pharmacy, 1905—, U. of Mich. Discoverer of several new vegetable alkaloids. Mem. Com. Revision U.S. Pharmacopœia, 1910—. Address: Ann Arbor, Mich. Died June 1, 1917.

SCHLUNDT, Herman, chemist; b. Two Rivers, Wis., July 16, 1869; s. Carl and Maria (Dryer) S.; B.S., U. of Wis., 1894, M.S., 1896, Ph.D., 1901; U. of Leipzig, 1899-1900; Cavendish Lab., 1921; m. Martha A. McMinn, July 27, 1899; children—Anna, Esther. Asst. in chemistry, U. of Wis., 1894-96; instr. physics and chemistry, high schs., Milwaukee, 1896-99; fellow in chemistry, U. of Wis., 1901-02; instr. chemistry, 1902-05, asst. prof. physical chemistry, 1905-07, prof., 1907—, U. of Mo. Mem. Wis. Acad. Sciences, Arts and Letters. Kiwanian. Home: Columbia, Mo. Died 1937.

SCHMAUK, Theodore Emanuel, theologian, editor; b. Lancaster, Pa., 1860; s. Rev. Benjamin W. and Wilhelmina C. (Hingel) S.; grad. U. of Pa., 1880. Ordained Evang. Lutheran ministry, 1883; editor-in-chief Luth. Ch. Review, 1895—; editor Luth. S.S. Lessons and General Council Graded Series, 1896—; lit. editor The Lutheran, 1889—; prof. Christian faith, apologetics, ethics, Luth. Theol. Sem., 1911—. Pres. Gen. Council of Evang. Luth. Ch. in N. America, 1903—; pres. trustees of Gen. Council, 1907—; pres. bd. of dirs. Phila. Theol. Sem., 1908—; chmn. com. on degrees Muhlenberg Coll.; exec. com. Internat. Luth. Conf., 1903—; chmn. ways and means com. for orgn., mem. exec. bd., publn. bd., and pres. S.S. Board of United Luth. Ch., 1918—. Pres. Pa. German Soc. (chmn. exec. com.); life mem. Hist. Soc. Pa. Author: Bible History, 1899; Manual of Bible Geography, 1901; The Early Churches of the Lebanon Valley, 1902; History of the Lutheran Church in Pennsylvania from the Original Sources, 1903; Bible Scenes, 1905; The Christian Kindergarten, 1906; The Confessions and Confessional Principle of the Lutheran Church, 1909; Annotated Edition of Benjamin Rush's Account of the German Inhabitants of Pennsylvania, 1910; In Mother's Arms: Child-Training, 1911; Christianity and Christian Union, 1913; The Art of Teaching in Sunday-School, 1919. Address: Lebanon, Pa. Died Mar. 23, 1920.

SCHMIDLAPP, Jacob Godfrey, banker; b. Piqua, O., Sept. 7, 1849; s. Jacob Adam and Sophia F. (Haug) S.; ed. pub. schs., Piqua; m. Emelie Balke, Dec. 6, 1877 (died 1900). In cigar and whiskey business, Memphis, 1868-74; removed to Cincinnati, 1874, and added distillery and malting business; later organized Export Storage Co.; organized Union Savings Bank & Trust Co., 1890, pres., 1890-1907, chmn. bd., 1907—; dir. Equitable Life Assurance Soc., Am. Security Co., Electric Securities Company, Degnon Construction Company, White Rock Springs Co. (New York), Mont. Power Co., B.&O. R.R., Piqua (O.) Malt Co. Trustee Coll. of Music, Cincinnati Art Sch., Cincinnati Law Sch., Cincinnati Art Mus., May Festival Assn., Music Hall Assn., McCall Colored Industrial Sch.; pres. Cincinnati Model Homes for Wage Earners; dir. Carnegie Peace Fund; treas. Am. Soc. Jud. Settlement of Internat. Disputes. Home: Cincinnati, O. Died Dec. 18, 1919.

SCHMIDT, George Small, lawyer; b. Carlisle, Pa., Feb. 5, 1861; s. Henry Daneman and Mary Louise (Carson) S.; prep. edn., York Collegiate Inst.; A.B., Princeton, 1881, A.M., 1884; LL.B., U. of Pa., 1884; m. Mary Richardson Small, June 16, 1891; children—Mary Richardson (Mrs. William H. Kurtz), George Small, Samuel Small. Admitted to Pa. bar, 1884, and practiced at York, 1884—, mem. firm Schmidt, Keesey, Stair & Kurtz; pres. Steacy Schmidt Mfg. Co., York, 1900-15, Ruggles-Coles Engring. Co., 1912-15; gen. counsel York Ry. Co., Edison Light & Power Co., York Telephone & Telegraph Co.; pres. and counsel Baltimore & Cumberland Valley R.R. Extension Co., Somerset Coal Ry. Co.; v.p. and trust officer York County Nat. Bank; treas. and counsel York Safe & Lock Co.; dir. and counsel Md. Bolt & Nut Co., Miller Safe Co., Schmidt & Ault Paper Co. Pres. Children's Home, York; trustee York Collegiate Inst., York Benevolent Assn. Del. to Rep. Nat. Conv., 1888. Episcopalian. Author: Vagrant Verses, 1926; Random Rhymes, 1928. Home: York, Pa. Died Jan. 9, 1935.

SCHMIDT, Joseph Martin, coll. prof.; b. Altenburg, Perry County, Mo., Mar. 25, 1846; s. Gottfried and Christiana (Poppitz-Schlimpert) S.; A.B., Concordia Coll., Ft. Wayne, Ind., 1865; grad. Concordia Sem., St. Louis, 1868, D.D., 1921; m. Sarah Theisen, Feb. 19, 1871. Ordained Lutheran ministry, 1868; pastor, Weston, Mo., 1868-69, Dallas, Mich., 1869-72, Saginaw, 1872-94; visitor Mich. Dist., Evang. Luth. Synod of Mo., Ohio, and Other States, 1880-82; pres. same dist. 1882-91; pres. 1894-1903, prof. Hebrew and history, 1903-17, Concordia Coll., Ft. Wayne, Ind.; retired. Author of addresses, sermons and articles on religious subjects. Home: Ft. Wayne, Ind. Died May 1, 1931.

SCHMIDT, Nathaniel, univ. prof.; b. Hudiksvall, Sweden, May 22, 1862; s. Lars Peter Anderson and Fredrika Wilhelmina S.; studied Stockholm U., 1882-84, Madison (now Colgate) U., 1884-87, A.M., 1887, U. of Berlin, 1890; D.H.L., Jewish Inst. of Religion, 1931; m. Ellen Alfvén, Sept. 26, 1887; children—Dagmar Alfvén (Mrs. Oliver Sanford Wright), Thord Alfvén (dec.). Prof. Semitic langs. and lits., Colgate U., 1888-96, prof. Semitic lang. and Oriental history, Cornell U., 1896-1932 (prof. emeritus). Lecturer history Columbia, summers, 1925-35. Dir. Am. Sch. Archæology in Jerusalem, 1904-05; mem. board of trustees of Am. Schs. of Oriental Research in Jerusalem and Baghdad. Author: Introduction to the Hexateuch, 1896; Biblical Criticism and Theological Belief, 1897; Syllabus of Oriental History, 1897; The Republic of Man, 1899; Outlines of a History of Egypt, 1901; Outlines of a History of India, 1902; Outlines of a History of Syria, 1902; The Prophet of Nazareth, 1907; The Messages of the Poets, 1911; Ibn Khaldun, Historian, Sociologist, Philosopher.

1930; The Coming Religion, 1930. Editor: Ecclesiasticus (with intro. and notes—in Temple Bible), 1903. Contbr. of more than 1500 articles in New Internat. Ency., 2d edit., 1914-17; also articles in several encys. and in many theol. publs. Address: Ithaca, N.Y. Died June 29, 1939.

SCHMIDT, Otto L., M.D.; b. Chicago, Ill., Mar. 21, 1863; s. Dr. Ernst S.; grad. Central High Sch., 1880; M.D., Chicago Med. Coll., 1883; post-grad. work, univs. of Würzburg and Vienna; m. Emma Seipp. Practiced at Chicago, 1883—; phys. to Alexian Bros. Hosp.; chmn. Ill. Centennial Commn., 1915-19. Mem. Ill. State Hist. Soc. (pres. 1914-32) Ill. State Historical Library (pres. 1923-32), Chicago Historical Soc. (trustee 1899-1932; pres. 1923-27), Inland Lake Yachting Assn. (pres. 1916-32). Mem. Bd. of Edn., Chicago, 1927-28. Home: Chicago, Ill. Died Aug. 20, 1935.

SCHMIDT, William, clergyman; b. Hermannsburg, Hanover, Germany, July 26, 1855; s. P.H. and Dorothea (Petersen) S.; ed. in Hermannsburg, Germany, and Capital U., Columbus, O., A.M., 1876; Litt.D., 1918; m. Anna Haeffner, Sept. 4, 1879. Ordained Evang. Luth. ministry, Aug. 11, 1878; prof. history, 1886—; later in Evang. Luth. Sem., St. Paul. Author: Bleibe Daheim; Sighard the Centurion (published in 5 languages), 1897; Aethelburga, 1900; Geschichte der Ohio Synode, 1901; Ramuldu, 1903; Sternenauge, 1906; Goldene Quelle, 1907; Landolf, 1910; Durch Luther befreit (Through Luther to Liberty), 1913; Der Herr ist Gott, 1917; Gedenkschrift der Ohio Synode, 1918; Friedensklaenge, 1921; Christ Conquers, 1925; Ben Juda the Shepherd, 1926; Pantherleap, 1928—all but three in German and English. Address: St. Paul, Minn. Died May 31, 1931.

SCHMUCK, Elmer Nicholas, bishop; b. Peoria, Ill., July 27, 1882; s. George and Rosa Bertha (Kreuter) S.; grad. Seabury Div. Sch., Faribault, Minn., 1905, D.D., 1927; m. Katharine Fay Currie, Sept. 7, 1905; children—Marion Louise, George Gordon, Rosemary Fay, Roger Currie. Deacon, 1905, priest, 1906, P.E. Ch.; rector St. Peter's Ch., New Ulm, Minn., and All Souls' Ch., Sleepy Eye, Minn., 1905-06, St. Paul's Ch., Owatonna, Minn., 1906-11, St. John's Ch., Minneapolis, Minn., 1911-23, St. Mark's Ch., Denver, Colo., 1923-25; gen. sec., field dept., Nat. Council P.E. Ch., 1925-29; consecrated bishop of Wyo., Dec. 13, 1929. Trustee Seabury Div. Sch. Mason. Home: Laramie, Wyo. Died Apr. 28, 1936.

SCHMUCKER, Samuel D., judge; b. Gettysburg, Pa., Feb. 26, 1844; s. Rev. Dr. S. S.; A.B., Pa. Coll., 1863; LL.B., New York U., 1865; LL.D., Pa. Coll., 1898, St. John's, Md., 1904; m. Helen J. Bridges, Nov. 16, 1869. Sergt. 26th Pa. Regt. in Union Army, 1863; practiced law at Baltimore, 1865-98; judge Ct. of Appeals of Md., 1898—. Republican. Mem. commn. which prepared present charter of Baltimore. Home: Baltimore, Md. Died 1911.

SCHNABEL, Charles J., lawyer; b. Pittsburgh, Aug. 17, 1867; s. Robert A. and Elizabeth M. (Becker) S.; ed. pvt. and pub. schs.; LL.B., Law Dept., U. of Ore., 1891; m. Elsa Anne Smith, Oct. 6, 1896. Pvt. sec. to gen. supt. Pullman Co., Chicago, 1888-89; located in Portland, Ore., 1889; admitted to Ore. bar, 1891; pres. Schnabel Investment Co.; sec. Smith & Watson Iron Works. Mem. Mich. N.G., 1885-87. Asst. U.S. atty. for Ore., 1893-98. Unitarian. Mason. Home: Portland, Ore. Deceased.

SCHNECKER, Peter August, organist, composer; b. in Germany, Aug. 26, 1850; s. John and Philippine S.; studied piano and violin; came to U.S., 1865; studied organ, harmony and counterpoint under Samuel P. Warren, organist of Grace Ch., New York; studied composition in Leipzig Conservatory, 1874. Married, 1873. Asst. organist St. Thomas Ch., New York, 1870-80; organist and musical dir. West Presbyn. Ch., New York, 1872—; prolific as composer, said to have composed more ch. music than any other Am. composer; prominent mem. New York Manuscript Soc. Address: New York, N.Y. Died 1903.

SCHNEDER, David Bowman, missionary; b. Bowmansville, Pa., Mar. 23, 1857; s. Baltzer and Elizabeth (Bowman) S.; A.B., Franklin and Marshall Coll., 1880, D.D., 1899; grad. Lancaster (Pa.) Theol. Sem., 1883; LL.D., Ursinus Coll., 1924; m. Anna M. Schoenberger, 1887; children—John Baltzer (dec.), Mary Elizabeth (dec.), Anna Margaret (wife of Rev. Alfred Ankeney), Clara Katherine (wife of Dr. C. G. Burn). Ordained ministry Reformed Church in United States, 1883; pastor Marietta, Pennsylvania, 1883-87; sent as missionary Ref. Church to Japan, 1887; prof. systematic theology, North Japan Coll., 1887-1901; pres., 1901-36; president emeritus, 1936—. Visited Germany, 1897, also visited both England and Germany for educational investigation, 1907; delivered course of lectures on Buddhism, at Lancaster Theol. Sem., 1897-98. Del. from Japan to Internat. Missionary Meeting, Williamstown, Mass., 1929. Decorated Fourth Order of Rising Sun, Japan, 1916; Third Order of Sacred Treasure, 1924; Third Order of Rising Sun, 1936; presented medal by Imperial Ednl. Assn. of Japan, 1918, "for meritorious service" in the cause of education in Japan; presented a second medal on the Fiftieth Anniversary of Imperial Ednl. Assn. of Japan, 1933; presented to the Prince Regent of Japan "in recognition of long and meritorious service in education," 1928. Mem. Am. Acad. Polit. and Social Science, Internat. Commn. for Christian Edn. in Japan. Died Oct. 5, 1938.

SCHNEIDER, Albert, bacteriologist; b. Granville, Ill., Apr. 13, 1863; s. John and Elizabeth (Burcky) S.; M.D., Coll. of Phys. and Surg. Chicago, 1887; B.S., U. of Ill., 1894; M.S., U. of Minn., 1894; Ph.D., Columbia, 1897; m. Marie Louise Harrington, June 28, 1892; 1 dau., Cornelia Elizabeth. Instr. botany, U. of Minn., 1893; prof. pharmacognosy and bacteriology, Northwestern U. Sch. of Pharmacy, Chicago, 1897-1903; prof. pharmacognosy and bacteriology, 1903-19, materia-medica and therapeutics, 1904-06, U. of Calif.; dir. expt. sta. Spreckels Sugar Co., 1906-07; pharmacognosist, U.S. Dept. Agr., 1909-15; micro-analyst, Calif. State Food and Drug Lab., 1915-19; prof. pharmacognosy, Coll. Pharmacy of U. of Neb., 1919-21. Editor-in-chief of Pacific Pharmacist, 1910-15. Author: Primary Microscopy and Biology, 1890; A Text-book of General Lichenology, 1897; Guide to the Study of Lichens, 1898; Microscopy and Micro-Technique, 1899; Hints on Drawing for Students of Biology, 1899; General Vegetable Pharmacography, 1900; The Limitations of Learning, and Other Science Papers, 1900; Powdered Vegetable Drugs, 1920; Bird and Nature Study Chart Manual, 1903; Medicinal Plants of California, 1909; Drug Plant Culture in California, 1912; Pharmaceutical Bacteriology, 1920; Bacteriological Methods in Food and Drugs Laboratories, 1915; The Microbiology and Microanalysis of Foods, 1920; Microscope in Detective Work (rept., Office of Naval Intelligence), 1918; Laboratory Pharmacology and Toxicology, 1925. Translator: Westermaier's Compendium der Allgemeinen Botanik, 1896. Contbr. many papers to scientific jours. Mem. Internat. Jury of Awards, Panama P.I. Expn., 1915. Inventor of car ventilating system. Dean, School of Pharmacy, N. Pacific Coll., Portland, Ore., 1922—. Lecturer on crime investigation, U. Calif. summer sessions. Address: Portland, Ore. Died Oct. 27, 1928.

SCHNEIDER, Charles Conrad, engr.; b. Apolda, Saxony, Apr. 24, 1843; s. Julius and Emilie (Bengel) S.; grad. Royal Sch. Tech., Chemnitz, 1864; m. Katharine Clyde Winters, Jan. 8, 1880. In machine-shop practice in Germany, 1864-67; draughtsman Rogers Locomotive Works, Paterson, N.J., 1867-70; asst. engr. Mich. Bridge & Construction Co., Detroit, 1870-73, Erie Ry., New York, 1873-75; engaged on proposed Blackwell's Island Bridge across East River, New York, 1876; designer Del. Bridge Co., New York, 1876-78; civ. engr. in pvt. practice, New York, 1878-86, designing and superintending structural work for bridges and bldgs.; chief engr. bridge and constrn. dept., Pencoyd Iron Works, Phila., 1886-1900; v.p. Am. Bridge Co., in charge of engring., 1900-03; cons. engr., with splty. in bridges and structural steel work, 1903; mem. bd. of engineers, Quebec Bridge, 1911—. During period 1878-86 designed and constructed several long-span bridges, the most prominent being the Fraser River (Cantilever) Bridge, Can. Pac. Ry., 1882, and the Niagara Cantilever Bridge, 1883. Awarded Rowland prize, Am. Soc. C.E., 1886, for paper on constrn. of the Niagara Bridge. Norman medal, same, 1905, for paper on Structural Design of Buildings, and Norman medal, same, 1908, for paper on Movable Bridges; also, 1886, 1st prize on design for Washington Bridge across Harlem River, New York. Mem. Am. Society C.E. (dir. 1887, 1898-1900, v.p. 1902-03, pres. 1905). Author: General Specifications for Railroad Bridges, 1886; General Specifications for Highway Bridges, 1901; General Specifications for Structural Steel Work in Buildings, 1905. Home: Wissahickon, Phila. Died Jan. 8, 1916.

SCHNEIDER, George J., congressman; b. Grand Chute, Outagamie County, Wis., Oct. 30, 1877; ed. pub. schs. Paper maker by trade; 2d v.p. Internat. Brotherhood of Paper Makers' Union; mem. exec. bd., Wis. State Fed. of Labor; mem. 68th to 72d and 74th and 75th Congresses (1923-33 and 1935-39), 8th Wis. Dist. Progressive. Home: Appleton, Wis. Died Mar. 12, 1939.

SCHNEIDER, Herman, univ. dean; b. Summit Hill, Pa., Sept. 12, 1872; s. Anton and Sarah (Wintersteen) S.; B.S., Lehigh U., 1894; Sc.D., U. of Pittsburgh, 1911; LL.D., U. of Cincinnati, 1933; m. Louise Bosworth, July 27, 1904. Engaged in structural iron work, 1894-97; on engring. staff Oregon Short Line R.R., 1897-99; instr. civ. engring., Lehigh U., 1899-1903; asst. prof. civ. engring., U. of Cincinnati, 1903-04, prof., 1904-29, dean Coll. Engring., 1906-19, dean Coll. Engring. and Commerce, 1919—, dir. Sch. of Applied Arts, 1922—, dir. Inst. Scientific Research, 1924—, acting pres. U. of Cincinnati, 1928-29, pres., 1929-32 (pres. emeritus), later dean. Originator coöp. system of tech. edn. whereby radical changes have been made in engring. and trade instrn. Mem. Com. on School Inquiry, City of N.Y., 1911-13; cons. expert, Bd. of Edn., City of N.Y., 1914-15. Chief of indsl. service sect., War Dept., 1917-18; mem. advisory bd., com. on edn. and spl. training, Gen. Staff U.S.A., 1918. Lamme Medalist, 1936. Adv. Council on Applied Physics, Am. Inst. of Physics, 1936-37. Author: Education for Industrial Workers; Arthur McQuaid, American; also pamphlets on ednl. subjects. Presbyn. Home: Cincinnati, O. Died Mar. 28, 1939.

SCHNEIDER, Joseph, oculist; b. Weigsdorf, Silesia, Germany, Dec. 10, 1845; prep. edn., univs. of Breslau and Würzburg, 1874; post-grad. studies, Würzburg, Vienna, Halle. Came to U.S., 1881, and in practice at Milwaukee, 1881—; specialist in ophthalmology and otology. Del. Internat. Med. Congress, Berlin, 1890. Recipient of gold medal and hon. Doctor and Senator, U. of Würzburg. Home: Milwaukee, Wis. Died June 4, 1927.

SCHNEIDER, Samuel Hiram, exec. sec. Assn. Western Rys.; b. New Albany, Ind., Oct 19, 1886; s. Charles and Pauline (Nemeroff) S.; ed. pub. schs. at Huntingburg, Rockport and Princeton, Ind., and business coll. at Louisville, Ky.; m. Eva Smith, June 6, 1922; children—Charles Ivan, Paul Eugene, Eloise Sylvia. Began railway service as stenographer-clerk with Southern Ry., 1903, continuing until 1911; with Mo. P. R.R. in various capacities, 1911-15; 1915—, served with Assn. of Western Rys., Gen. Mgrs. Assn. of Chicago, Chicago Railroad Presidents' Conf. and Western Assn. of Ry. Execs. apptd. sec. Assn. Western Rys., and Gen. Mgrs. Assn. of Chicago, 1916, also sec. Chicago Railroad Presidents Conf., 1930, asst. to chmn. Western Assn. Ry. Execs., 1933; exec. sec. Assn. Western Rys., June 1, 1936—. Home: Chicago, Ill. Deceased.

SCHNITZLER, John William, banker; b. Mildmay, Ont., Can., Feb. 11, 1882; s. Lawrence and Elizabeth (Schuette) S.; ed. high sch., Mildmay; m. Catherine White, June 12, 1906; children—(adopted) Helen Patricia, Margaret. Came to U.S., 1898, naturalized citizen, 1908. Engaged in newspaper work 1899-1911; pres. Schnitzler Corp., First State Bank, Froid, Mont., Culbertson (Mont.) State Bank; wheat farmer, operating 10,000 acres. Mem. Mont. State Senate, 1924-31; mem. Rep. Nat. Com., 1928—, term 1928-32. Mason. Home: Froid, Mont. Deceased.

SCHNUR, George Henry, Jr., clergyman; b. Vandalia, Ill., Jan. 24, 1861; s. George Henry and Marie (Esbjoern) S.; A.B., Carthage (Ill.) Coll., 1882, A.M., 1888; Lutheran Theol. Sem., Gettysburg, Pa., 1886; D.D., Wittenberg (O.) Coll., 1920; m. Nina L. Charles, July 30, 1889; children—Faith (Mrs. Walter F. Erickson), Carl Esbjoern, Marie (Mrs. John M. Hedlund), George Luther, Rev. Paul Newton. Teacher pub. schs., 1879-83; ordained Luth. ministry, 1886; home mission work, 1886-1906, founding congregations at Omaha, Nevada, Ia., Evansville, Ind., and Chillicothe, O.; pastor St. Paul, Minn., 1906-14 (built Ch. of the Reformation), Zelienople, Pa., 1914-18, Grace Ch., Erie, 1918—. Compiler and editor of Lutheran Parish Register, 1925; editor Luther League Topics, 1898-1917; editor Lutheran Year Book, 1926-33; chmn. Year Book and Statistical Com., United Lutheran Ch., 1922-34; sec. of statistics, Pittsburgh Synod (Luth.), 1916-38. Republican. Home: Erie, Pa. Died Oct. 26, 1939.

SCHODDE, George Henry, univ. prof.; b. Allegheny, Pa., Apr. 15, 1854; s. George F. and Mary Louise (Tücke) S.; A.B., Capital U., Columbus, O., 1872; Ph.D., U. of Leipzig, 1877; D.D., Pa. Coll., Gettysburg, 1885; m. Mary Dorsch, Dec. 22, 1881. Prof. Greek and theology, Capital U., 1880—. Editor Theol. Mag. 1897—, and Luth. Standard, 1880—. Author: The Protestant Church in Germany, 1903. Translator: Book of Enoch and Book of Jubilees (from Ethiopic); Delitzsch's Day in Capernaum, 1890; Weiss' Religion of the New Testament, 1905; Weiss' Commentary on the New Testament (4 volumes), from German, 1906. Contbr. for many yrs. to Independent Sunday School Times, etc. Home: Columbus, O. Died Sept. 15, 1917.

SCHOENFELD, Hermann, univ. prof.; b. Oppeln, Prussia, Jan. 21, 1861; s. Emanuel and Jeannette S.; graduate gymnasium, Strehlen (Silesia); studied univs. of Berlin, Breslau, Leipzig and Paris (École de Droit), and Petrograd; (Ph.D., LL.D.); m. Johanna Richter, Mar. 20, 1888; children—Hans Frederick Arthur, Herbert Hermann, Rudolf Emil, Margaret Hertha. Instr. modern langs., Providence, R.I., and New Bedford, Mass., 1888-90; instr. German, Johns Hopkins, 1891-93; U.S. consul at Riga, Russia, and del. U.S. Bur. Edn. for investigation higher edn. in Poland, 1893-94; prof. Germanics, George Washington U., 1894—. Lecturer Catholic U., 1895, Cornell U., 1901, U. of Kansas, 1913; Ottoman consul-general at Washington, 1899-1910; asso. commr. gen. of Turkey at St. Louis Expn., 1904. Officer and comdr. Turkish, Persian and Venezuelan orders, and gold medal of Instruccion Popular. Contbr. Brockhaus' Conversations Lexicon, Johnson's Universal Cyclo., Appleton's Ann. Cyclo. Ency. Americana, Am. and European mags. Corr. on Am. Edn. for Ped. Archive in Brunswick. Author: Brant and

Erasmus, 1892; Erasmus and Rabelais, 1903; Higher Education in Poland, 1896; History of Teutonic and Slavic Women, 1906; Essays on Universal Peace and German Armaments, 1913; Causes of European Conflagration, 1914-15. Editor: German Historical Prose, 1896; Leopold von Ranke, 1899; Schiller's Maria Stuart, 1899; Wilhelm Tell, 1912; Bismarck's Letters and Orations, 1905. Address, Washington, D.C. Died July 4, 1926.

SCHOEPF, W(illiam) Kesley, traction pres.; b. Ft. Delaware, Del., May 20, 1864; s. Gen. Albin and Julia (Kesley) S.; m. Albertine Odell, 1891; children—Albin Kesley, Mrs. Elizabeth Huebscher. Was prin. asst. engr. of D.C. and engaged in constrn. underground trolley system, Washington; v.p. and gen. mgr. Belt Ry. and Eckington & Soldiers' Home Ry. Co., Washington, 1893; v.p. and gen. mgr. Consolidataed Traction Co., Pittsburgh, 1899; chmn. exec. com. Cincinnati Traction Co., 1901, and pres., 1902; pres. Ohio Traction Co., 1905; pres. Cincinnati Car Co., 1913. Owner of Sheffield Farm, Glendale, O. Episcopalian. Mason. Home: Cincinnati, O. Died May 6, 1927.

SCHOETZ, Max, lawyer; b. Menasha, Wis., Dec. 27, 1884; s. M. M. and Barbara (Landgraf) S.; grad. high sch., Menasha, 1898; B.A., Lawrence Coll., Appleton, Wis., 1902; LL.B., U. of Wis., 1908; m. Mollie Knoernschild, June 27, 1912; children— Barbara, Max, David, Carl (dec.). Law clk. various firms in Oshkosh, Madison and Milwaukee until 1912; mem. firm Schoetz, Williams & Gandrey, Milwaukee, 1913—; served as 2d and 1st asst. city atty. of Milwaukee; counsel City of Milwaukee in street car fare and telephone litigation; prof. public law and dean of Law Sch., Marquette U., 1911—; v.p. Vliet Street State Bank; dir. Community Bldg. & Loan Assn.; dir. and treas. Inter State Exchange. Mem. Co. B, Wis N.G.; prof. military law. S.A.T.C. Mem. Wis. Commn. on Uniform State Laws. Catholic. Author: Docket and Note Book Moot Court, 1917; also articles in law reviews. Home: Milwaukee, Wis. Died June 8, 1927.

SCHOFF, Hannah Kent, philanthropist; b. Upper Darby, Pa.; d. Thomas and Fannie (Leonard) Kent; ed. boarding sch. and pvt. courses; m. Frederic Schoff, Oct. 23, 1873; children—Wilfred Harvey, Mrs. Edith Boericke, Mrs. Louise Ehrman, Leonard Hastings, Harold Kent, Mrs. Eunice Simmons, Albert Lawrence. First pres. Pa. Congress of Mothers, 1899-1902; v.p., 1897-1902, pres., 1902-20, hon. pres., Nat. Congress of Mothers, which, with the aid of President Roosevelt and Dept. of State, held at the White House, Mar. 1908, the 1st Internat. Congress in America on the Welfare of the Child; held 2d Internat. Congress on Child Welfare, Washington, 1911; chmn. com. on social service, etc., New Century Club, 1900-03; hon. pres. Nat. Congress of Parents and Teachers. Organized and led a movement to obtain juvenile ct. and probation system in Pa., passed by legislature, 1901; led movement leading to enactment of same laws, 1903, after Superior Ct. had declared the laws passed in 1901 unconstitutional because of tech. errors; chmn. com. which raised salaries and recommended for appmt. 1st probation officers in Pa.; pres. Phila. Juvenile Ct. and Probation Assn., 1901-23; delegate from U.S. Dept. of State to the 3d Home Edn. Congress, Brussels, 1910. Special collaborator Home Edn. Div. Bur. of Edn., 1913-19; founder and sec. bd. United Service Club for Enlisted Men, Phila.; hon. trustee Nat. Kindergarten Coll., Chicago; dir. Nat. Kindergarten Assn. Compiled: Laws of Every State in the United States Concerning Dependent and Delinquent Children, 1900. Editor Child Welfare Magazine 16 yrs., and contbr. numerous articles to mags. Author: The Wayward Child; The Evolution of the Mother's Pension; Wisdom of the Ages in Bringing Up Children, 1933. Home: Philadelphia, Pa. Died Dec. 10, 1940.

SCHOFF, Stephen Alonzo, engraver; b. Danville, Vt., 1818; s. John Chase and Eunice (Nye) S.; ed. common schools, Newburyport, Mass.; studied and worked at line engraving, Boston, 1834-39; drawing and line engraving at Paris, France, 1839-41; worked for bank note cos. at New York; was 2 yrs. in Bur. of Engraving, Washington; afterward at Boston, New York, Newtonville, Mass., and Brandon, Vt., as engraver. Notable among his art engravings are the large plate from Wm. M. Hunt's "Bathers" and from S. W. Rowse's portrait of Ralph W. Emerson. Address: Brandon, Vt. Died 1904.

SCHOFF, Wilfred Harvey, sec. Commercial Museum; b. Newtonville, Mass., Nov. 27, 1874; s. Frederic and Hannah (Kent) S.; A.B., Harvard, 1894; A.M., U. of Pa., 1896; m. Ethelwyn McGeorge, June 20, 1900; children—Muriel (Mrs. John Owen Clark), Wilmot, Beatrice Leonard (Mrs. John Stanley Carver), Mary Corona, Elinor; m. 2d, Marie Magdalene Gertrude Gallagher, July 22, 1925. Made tour of S.Am. republics, Portugal, Spain and France, 1899, as commr. for Export Expn. of Phila.; U.S. commr. to Congress of Commerce, Comml. Geography and Colonial Adminstrn., Paris, 1900; lecturer on foreign commerce, U. of Wis., 1901, U. of Ill., 1903, Harvard, 1908-11; sec. and asst. treas. Commercial Mus., Phila., 1900—. Consul for Bolivia in Phila. Author: Descendants of Jacob Schoff, 1910; The Periplus of the Erythræan Sea, 1912; The Periplus of Hanno, 1913; The Parthian Stations of Isidore of Charax, 1914; The St. Mary's Falls Canals, 1915; The Delaware River, 1915; The Ohio River Improvement, 1915; The Mississippi River Improvement, 1915; The Hudson River Improvement, 1916; The Warrior River Improvement, 1916; The Ship "Tyre," 1920; The Periplus of Marcian of Heraclea, 1922. Collaborated with 5 others in a symposium on the Song of Songs, 1924. Trustee and asso. sec. Am. Schools of Oriental Research. Home: Cynwyd, Pa. Died Sept. 14, 1932.

SCHOFIELD, Frank Lee, lawyer; b. Moundsville, Va., Oct. 1, 1849; s. William and Phoebe (Jones) S.; A.M., Christian U., Canton, Mo., 1870; m. Anna E. High, Nov. 14, 1872. Admitted to Mo. bar, 1870; supt. pub. schs., Lewis County, Mo., 1871; pros. atty., Lewis County, Mo., 1873-76; standing master in chancery, U.S. Circuit Ct. for Northern Div., Eastern Dist. of Mo., 1887— (retired). Non-resident lecturer on jurisdiction and procedure of fed. courts, U. of Mo., 1904-10. Dir. Farmers' and Merchants' Bank, Hannibal, Mo. Del. Universal Congress Lawyers and Jurists, St. Louis, 1904; mem. Mo. Bar Assn. (pres. 1903-04). Past Eminent Comdr. K.T. Chmn. Mo. Mark Twain Monument Commn.; pres. Hannibal Bd. of Edn.; dir., pres. Hannibal Free Public Library, retired. Christian (Disciples) Ch. (pres. emeritus official bd.). Address: Hannibal, Mo. Died July 9, 1925.

SCHOFIELD, Harvey A., educator; b. Augusta, Wis., Mar. 28, 1877; s. John and Eliza Ann (Horel) S.; grad. high sch., Augusta, 1896, Stevens Point (Wis.) State Teachers Coll., 1901; Ph.B., U. of Wis., 1904; m. Dorothy Burnham Packard, Aug. 20, 1908 (died 1931); children—John P., Elizabeth Lou; m. 2d, Frances Jagoditsch, July 15, 1933. Teacher rural schs., 1896-98; prin. ward sch., Wausau., Wis., 1901-02; teacher history and athletics, Madison (Wis.) High Sch., 1904-05; prin. schs., Ellsworth, Wis., 1905-07, Neillsville, 1907-09; prin. high sch., Superior, Wis., 1909-13, Central High Sch., St. Paul, Minn., 1913-16; pres. State Teachers Coll., Eau Claire, 1916—. Methodist. Mason. Home: Eau Claire, Wis. Died Aug. 3, 1941.

SCHOFIELD, Henry, prof. law; b. Dudley, Mass., Aug. 7, 1866; s. John and Margaret (Thompson) S.; A.B., Harvard, 1887, A.M., 1890, LL.B., 1890; m. Marie Therese Stehlin, 1901. Admitted to Ill. bar, 1890; in office of Charles H. Aldrich, solicitor gen. of U.S., Washington, D.C., 1891-92; practiced, Chicago, 1892-1900; asst. corp., counsel of Chicago, 1900-01; prof. law, Northwestern U. Law Sch., 1902—. Democrat. Home: Chicago, Ill. Died Aug. 15, 1918.

SCHOFIELD, John McAllister, lt. gen. U.S.A.; b. Gerry, N.Y., Sept. 29, 1831; s. Rev. James and Caroline (McAllister) S.; ed. there and in Bristol and Freeport, Ill.; entered West Point, 1849; grad. 1853; LL.D., Chicago U. Served in garrison in S.C. and Fla. until 1855; asst. prof. natural philosophy West Point, 1855-60; under leave of absence, prof. physics, Washington U., St. Louis, until April 1861; in Civil War became brig. gen., Nov. 1861, and maj. gen., Nov. 1862, of vols.; comd. a dept. and army in the field; in the Atlanta campaign and later comd. at battle of Franklin, Tenn., for which he was made brig. gen. and bvt. maj. gen. in regular army. After war became div. comdr.; was sec. of war, 1868-69; comd. the Army of the U.S., 1888-95; was made lt. gen., 1895; retired from active service by operation of law, Sept. 29, 1895. Comdr.-in-chief Mil. Order Loyal Legion, 1900; re-elected, 1902. Author: Forty-six Years in the Army, 1897. Address: Bar Harbor, Me. Died 1906.

SCHOFIELD, William, judge; b. Dudley, Mass., Feb. 14, 1857; s. John and Margaret (Thompson) S.; grad. Nichols Acad., Dudley, 1879; student, Harvard, 1879-80; LL.B., Harvard Law Sch., 1883; m. Edna M. Green, Dec. 1, 1892. Pvt. sec. Justice Gray, U.S. Supreme Court,, 1883-85; practiced in Boston, 1885—. Assisted in drafting Act of Registering and Confirming Titles to Land, passed by Mass. Legislature, 1898; mem. Mass. Ho. of Rep., 1899-1902; instr. in torts, 1886-90, Roman law, 1888-92, Harvard Law Sch.; asso. judge Mass. Superior Court, 1903-11; U.S. circuit judge, 1st Circuit, May 1911—. Republican. Home: Malden, Mass. Died June 10, 1912.

SCHOFIELD, William Henry, univ. prof.; b. Brockville, Ont., Apr. 6, 1870; s. Rev. William Henry and Anna (Parker) S.; A.B., Victoria Coll., U. of Toronto, 1889; A.M., Harvard, 1893, Ph.D., 1895; studied at Paris, Christiania, Copenhagen, and elsewhere in Europe, 1895-97; m. Mary Lyon Cheney, Sept. 4, 1907. Master of modern langs., Collegiate Inst., Hamilton, Ont., 1889-92; instr. English, 1897-1902, asst. prof. English, 1902-06, prof. and chairman dept. comparative lit., 1906—, Harvard. Lecturer in English lit., U. of Chicago, summer, 1902; Harvard exchange prof. at U. of Berlin, 1907-08; lecturer at The Sorbonne, Paris, and at U. of Copenhagen, 1911; Harvard exchange lecturer to western colls., 1918; lecturer for Nat. Security League, 1918. Pres. Am. Scandinavian Foundation, New York; mem. admin. bd. Inst. of Internat. Edn.; pres. Men's Club, Peterborough, N.H., 1913—. Author: Studies on the Libeaus Desconus, 1895; The Home of the Eddic Poems (from Norwegian of Sophus Bugge), 1899; English Literature from the Norman Conquest to Chaucer, 1905; Chivalry in English Literature, 1912; Mythical Bards and the Life of William Wallace, 1919. Also articles in Harvard Studies and Notes, Publs. of the Modern Lang. Assn. of America, and various French, German, Danish and Am. reviews. Editor-in-chief, Harvard Studies in Comparative Literature. Address: Cambridge, Mass. Died June 24, 1920.

SCHOLZ, Richard Frederick, coll. pres.; b. Milwaukee, Wis., Oct. 24, 1880; s. Gustav and Ernestine (Asmann) S.; B.A., U. of Wis., 1902, M.A., 1903, Ph.D., 1911; Rhodes scholar, Oxford U., 1904-07; studied at U of Berlin, 1905-06; m. Cheryl Alice Merrill, Dec. 7, 1911. Teaching fellow in Latin, 1902-03, in history, 1903-04, instr. history, 1907-08, U. of Wis.; asst. prof. ancient history, 1908-18, asso. prof. history, 1918, U. of Calif.; prof. history, U. of Wash., 1918-21; pres. and prof. history, Reed Coll., Apr. 1, 1921—. Lecturer in history, U. of Wis., summer, 1912, Harvard, June 1913-Feb. 1914. Mem. editorial bd., Pacific Review, 1918-21. Fellow Royal Hist. Soc.; mem. Nat. Council of Nat. Econ. League, Acad. Polit. Science. Author: (with Stanley K. Hornbeck) Oxford and the Rhodes Scholarships, 1907. Contbr. on philol. and hist. topics. Address: Portland, Ore. Died July 23, 1924.

SCHOONHOVEN, John James, biologist; b. McIntyre, N.Y., July 3, 1864; s. George W. and Maria (Mead) S.; A.B., St. Francis Coll., Brooklyn, 1893; A.M., Coll. of St. Francis Xavier, New York, 1894; L.I. Coll. Hosp., 1888-90; post-grad., philosophy, New York U., 1900-01; m. Helen E. Butterfield, June 16, 1897; 1 son, George Otis (dec.). Staff lecturer New York, Newark and Jersey City bds. of edn.; lecturer Brooklyn Inst. Arts and Sciences; apptd. spl. lecturer, instr. in edn. N.Y. Univ., 1930—. Specialist on subject of parasitism (animal parasites, entomogenous fungi and trypanosomiasis). Pres. dept. zoölogy, mem. council and fellow Brooklyn Inst. Arts and Sciences. Pres. Am. Assn. for Planting and Preservation of City Trees, 1910-12; del. 15th Internat. Congress on Hygiene and Demography; dir. Brooklyn Zoöl. Assn., 1915-25. Republican. Conglist. Contbr. articles to magazines and papers, scientific socs. Home: Brooklyn, N.Y. Died June 1936.

SCHOONMAKER, Edwin Davies, writer; b. Scranton, Pa., Feb. 1, 1873; s. Jacob and Katherine (Davies) S.; student Ky. Wesleyan Coll.; A.B., Transylvania U., Lexington, Ky., 1897 (A.M., 1906); m. Nancy Musselman, Nov. 30, 1904; children—Frank, Thorsten Burgess (dec.). Prof. ancient langs., Eureka (Ill.) Coll., 1897-99; engaged in research and lit. work, N.Y. City, 1900—. Mem. U.S. Mission to Russia, 1918-19. Author: The Saxons, 1905; The Americans, 1913; The World Storm and Beyond, 1915; Our Genial Enemy, France, 1932; Democracy and World Dominion, 1939. Contbr. essays, stories and poems to leading mags., and lecturer on various phases of Russian life and development. Home: Woodstock, N.Y. Died May 4, 1940.

SCHOTT, Charles Anthony, asst. U.S. Coast and Geodetic Survey; b. Mannheim, Baden, Germany, Aug. 7, 1826; grad. Polytechnic Sch., Carlsruhe, C.E., 1847. Came to U.S., 1848; entered U.S. Coast and Geodetic Survey, asst., 1856—. Mem. Govt. parties to observe total eclipse of the sun, Aug. 1869 (Springfield, Ill.), and Dec. 1870 (Cantania, Sicily); del. to Internat. Conf. on Terrestrial Magnetism, Bristol, Eng., 1898. Mem. Nat. Acad. of Sciences; Washington Acad. of Sciences. Author of many papers on hydrography, geodesy and particularly on terrestrial magnetism in reports of the Survey, and on tides, meteorology and physics of the globe in Smithsonian Instn. publs. between 1858 and 1881. Address: Washington, D.C. Died 1901.

SCHOTT, Henry; b. Leavenworth, Kan., June 11, 1873; s. Henry and Marie Luise (Beckman) S.; U. of Kan., 1890-92; m. Frances, d. Gardiner Lathrop, Sept. 15, 1910. Mem. editorial staff Kansas City Star, 1897-1911; pres. of advertising business, 1911-15; with Montgomery Ward & Co., Chicago, as v.p., in charge of sales and adv., 1915-21; v.p. Seaman Paper Co., 1921-24. Spent 1914 in travel in Europe, contributing monthly articles to Nation's Bus. Mag.; on staff of same, 1925; resigned as asst. to the publisher, to become adv. and sales promotion counsel for West Coast Lumbermen's Assn., hdqrs. Seattle. Wash. Republican. Lutheran. Address: Seattle, Wash Died Nov. 27, 1926.

SCHOULER, James, lawyer, author; b. Arlington, Mass., Mar. 20, 1839; s. William and Frances (Warren) S.; brother of John S.; A.B., Harvard, 1859 LL.D., Nat. Univ., 1891, Johns Hopkins, 1902; m. Emily F. Cochran, Dec. 14, 1870 (died 1904). Admitted to Mass. bar, 1862, Supreme Ct. of U.S., 1867; non-resident prof. of law, Nat. U., Washington 1888-1908; prof. law Boston U., 1882-1902; lecturer

Johns Hopkins, Baltimore, 1891-1908. Pres. Am. Hist. Assn., 1897; Am. Acad. Polit. and Social Science, Nat. Inst. Arts and Letters. Author: The Law of Domestic Relations; The Law of Bailments; The Law of Personal Property; The Law of Husband and Wife; Law of Executors and Administrators; Law of Wills, 1900; Life of Thomas Jefferson; Historical Briefs; History of the United States (1783-1877), 7 vols., 1913; Alexander Hamilton, 1901; Eighty Years of Union, 1904; Americans of 1776, 1905; Ideals of the Republic, 1908; also various magazine articles, etc. Home: Intervale, N.H. Died Apr. 16, 1920.

SCHOULER, John, rear admiral U.S.N.; b. Lowell, Mass., Nov. 30, 1846; s. William and Frances (Warren) S.; brother of James S.; apptd. to U.S. Naval Acad. from Mass., 1861, grad. 1864; m. Hope Day, Aug. 31, 1881. Promoted ensign, Nov. 1, 1866; master, Dec. 1, 1866; lt., Mar. 12, 1868; lt. comdr., June 3, 1869; comdr., June 8, 1885; capt., June 5, 1898; retired with rank of rear admiral, Nov. 21, 1899. Summer of 1864, was attached to the Marblehead, in pursuit of the Confederate steamers Florida and Tallahassee; served on Colorado, 1865-67; Frolic, 1867-68; Portsmouth, 1869-70; exec. officer of Terror, 1871-72; in Hydrographic Office, 1872-73; Naval Acad., 1873-76, 1880-84, 1885-88; exec. officer Essex, 1876-79, Lancaster, 1884-85; comd. Portsmouth, 1889-91; Bureau of Navigation, 1891-92; mem. Naval Examining and Retiring Bds., 1893-95; chief of staff, N. Atlantic Fleet, flagship New York, 1895-97; spl. duty Bureau of Navigation, 1897-99. Home: Catskill, N.Y. Died Dec. 26, 1917.

SCHRECKENGAST, Isaac Butler, clergyman; b. Danville, Ia., Oct. 5, 1864; s. Isaac and Sarah Schreckengast; B.Sc., Ia. State Coll., Ames, Ia., 1885; student Iowa Wesleyan U., 1886-87; S.T.B., Boston Univ. Sch. of Theology, 1895; D.D., Simpson Coll., Ia., 1906; Ph.M., Ia. State Coll., 1906; m. Genevieve Clarke, May 1, 1889; children—Mrs. Joy Ruth Jones, Mrs. Carita Clarke Taylor, Mrs. Dorothy Hansen. Ordained Meth. Episcopal ministry, 1887; pastor Sweetland, Ia., 1888-91; student pastor Boston, 1891-95; pastor West Liberty, Ia., 1895-99, Washington, Ia., 1899-1905, 1st Ch., Burlington, Ia., 1905-10, College Ch., Univ. Pl., Neb., 1910-13; vice-chancellor and treas., 1913-17, actg. chancellor, 1917-18, chancellor, 1918-32, prof. English Bible and chancellor emeritus, 1932—, Neb. Wesleyan U. Mem. S.S. Bd. of M.E. Ch., 1908-24; mem. Bd. of Edn., M.E. Ch., 1924—. Address: University Place, Neb. Died Sept. 10, 1935.

SCHREYVOGEL, Charles, artist; b. New York, Jan. 4, 1861; s. Paul and Theresa (Erbe) S.; ed. New York pub. schs.; apprenticed to gold engraver, then to die sinker, and later to lithographer; student in Munich, 1886-89, under Frank Kirchbach and Carl Marr; m. Louise Walther, Aug. 20, 1894. Thomas B. Clarke prize, Nat. Acad. Design, 1900, for oil painting "My Bunkie"; medals, Paris Expn., 1900, Buffalo Expn., 1901, St. Louis Expn., 1904. A.N.A., 1901. Address: Hoboken, N.J. Died 1912.

SCHROEDER, Ernest Charles, veterinarian; b. Baltimore, Apr. 3, 1865; s. Henry A. and Hermine (Wandscher) S.; ed. Baltimore City Coll., and Md. Agrl. Coll.; M.D.V., Harvard, 1887; specialized in scientific agr. and vet. medicine; m. Florence R. Brett, 1889; 1 son, Robert Brett. Attention devoted to experimental medicine. Contbr. to reports and bulls. U.S. Dept. Agr. concerning original investigations of various contagious and infectious diseases; also to various med. jours. Nat. del. Internat. Congress Tuberculosis, Rome, 1912. Home: Bethesda, Md. Deceased.

SCHROEDER, Frederick A., mayor of Brooklyn; b. Trier, Rhenish Prussia, Mar. 9, 1833; came with father to U.S., 1849; learned cigar making; established for himself as cigar mfr. but abandoned that, 1868, becoming importer and dealer in leaf tobacco; one of founders, 1867, and pres. Germania Savings Bank of Kings County, 1867—; comptroller of Brooklyn, 1771; mayor, 1876-78; State senator, 1879-81; nominated for mayor, 1888, but declined. Republican. Married Mary Jane Rusher, 1854. Address: Brooklyn, N.Y. Died 1899.

SCHROEDER, Seaton, rear admiral U.S.N.; b. Washington, Aug. 17, 1849; s. Francis and Caroline (Seaton) S.; apptd. to U.S. Naval Acad. from S.C., 1864, grad. 1868; m. Maria C. B. Wainwright, Jan. 16, 1879. Promoted ensign, Apr. 19, 1869, master, July 12, 1870; lt. Oct. 29, 1872; lt. comdr., Sept. 27, 1893; comdr. Mar. 3, 1899; capt., Aug. 10, 1903; rear admiral, July 11, 1908. Served on Saginaw, Pensacola and Benicia, 1868-72. Mem. Commodore John Rodgers' expdn. against Korean forts, 1871, being in landing party and taking part in the several engagements; Canandaigua, Pinta, Mayflower and Swatara, 1873-75; Hydrographic Office, 1875-76, 1880-81; Gettysburg, 1876-78; on leave associated with H. H. Gorringe in removing obelisk from Egypt to New York, 1879-80; Despatch, 1881-82; fish commn. steamer Albatross, 1882-85; Bur. of Navigation, Navy Dept., 1886-88; spl. duty with building dynamite cruiser Vesuvius, 1888-90; comd. Vesuvius, 1890-93; Navy Yard, Washington, 1893; mem. Bd. of Inspection and Survey, 1894-96; exec. officer Massachusetts, 1897-99; was advanced 3 numbers in rank "for eminent and conspicuous conduct" in the war with Spain, 1898; duty Navy Yard, Washington, 1899-1900; naval gov. Island of Guam and comdg. Yosemite, 1900-03; chief intelligence officer, 1903-06; comdg. Virginia, 1906-08; comdg. a div. of Atlantic Fleet, 1908-09; comdr.-in-chief Atlantic Fleet, Mar. 1909-June 1911; mem. Gen. Bd. to Aug. 17, 1911, when retired for age; continued on spl. duty in Navy Dept. for 3 yrs. after retirement; hydrographer, Oct. 1917-Mar. 1919. Author: Fall of Maximilian's Empire, 1887. Prize essayist U.S. Naval Inst., 1894; writer of other essays and contbr. to mags. Home: Washington, D.C. Died Oct. 19, 1922.

SCHROEDER, William Edward, surgeon; b. Cook County, Ill., Dec. 25, 1867; s. Martin and Elizabeth S.; ed. U. of Ill.; M.D., Chicago Med. Coll., 1891. In practice of surgery at Chicago, 1891—; prof. surgery and clin. surgery, Northwestern U. Med. Sch., 1906-14; chief of staff and sr. surgeon, Wesley Hosp.; surgeon German Deaconess Hosp. Home: Chicago, Ill. Died Mar. 5, 1926.

SCHUCHARDT, Rudolph Frederick, elec. engr.; b. Milwaukee, Wis., Dec. 14, 1875; s. Louis and Rose (Winkler) S.; B.S. and E.E., U. of Wis., 1897; m. Ada L. Briggs, June 6, 1906 (dec.); children—John William, Elizabeth Ann. With Janesville (Wis.) Electric Light & Power Co., 1897; engr. with Meysenberg & Badt, Chicago, 1897-98; entered employ of Commonwealth Edison Co. (then Chicago Edison Co.) as sub-station operator, June 1898, chief elec. engr., July 1909. Served as expert in Colorado Springs street lighting controversy, 1907; v.pres. and dir. Associated Engineers. Mem. administrative bd. and chmn. public affairs com. Am. Engring. Council. Fellow Am. Inst. Elec. Engrs., 1912 (pres. 1928-29); mem. Illuminating Engineering Soc. (chmn. Chicago sect., 1911-12), Nat. Electric Light Assn. (pres. Chicago sect., 1911-12; chmn. tech. nat. sect., 1922-23; chmn. power survey com.), Am. Acad. Polit. and Social Science, Western Soc. Engrs. (chmn. elec. sect., 1913), Chicago Elec. Assn. (pres. 1901). Awarded Chanute Medal, Western Soc. Engrs., 1907. Del. to World Engring. Congress, Japan, 1929. Congregationalist. Wrote booklet, "Panama and the Isthmian Canal," 1912; also papers read before Am. Inst. E.E. and other socs.; contbr. to tech. mags. Mem. Instn. of E.E. of Great Britain. Home: Glencoe, Ill. Died Oct. 25, 1932.

SCHUERMAN, William Henry, engr.; b. Cincinnati, Nov. 8, 1859; s. C. Frederic and Henrietta (Woesten) S.; U. of Cincinnati, 1881; Johns Hopkins U., 1882-83. Engaged in ry. engring., summer 1880, and 1881-82; asst. in physics, 1883-85; asst. prof., 1885-88, U. of Mo.; engaged in water supply and irrigation engring., Covington, Ky. and Kern County, Calif., 1888-93; prof. civ. engring., 1894-1912, prof. pure and applied mathematics, 1912-21, prof. applied mechanics and structural engring., 1921—, dean Sch. of Engring., 1895—, Vanderbilt U. Contbr. to Proceedings of Engring. Assn. of the South, and bulls. Am. Ry. Engring. Assn. Address: Nashville, Tenn. Died 1932.

SCHUETTE, Conrad Herman Louis, clergyman; b. Hanover, Germany, June 17, 1843; s. Dietrich and Dorothy S.; brought to U.S. in boyhood; A.B., Capital U., Columbus, O., 1863, D.D., 1898; grad. Evang. Luth. Sem., Columbus, 1865; m. Miss V. M. Wirth, Sept. 1865; children—Jesse R., Walter E., Winifred M., Gertrude H., Dorothy M. Ordained Luth. ministry, 1865; pastor St. Mark's Ch., Delaware, O., 1865-73; prof. mathematics, Capital U., 1873-80; prof. comparative theology and Christian ethics, Evang. Luth. Sem., 1880-95; gen. pres. Evang. Luth. Synod of Ohio and Other States, 1895-1925; pres. Nat. Luth. Council, 1923-24. Author: Church Members' Manual, 1870; State, Church and School, 1883; Before the Altar, 1894; Daily Exercises unto Godliness; Testimonies Unto Church Union; "Wiggie." Address: Columbus, O. Died Aug. 11, 1926.

SCHUHMANN, George William, clergyman; b. Louisville, Ky., Feb. 12, 1865; s. George Sebastian and Mary (Nold) S.; A.B., Louisville High Sch., 1883; D.D., Innsbruck U., Austria, 1890. Ordained priest R.C. Ch., 1889; asst. pastor of cathedral, Louisville, 1891-1908; pastor St. John's Ch., Louisville, 1908—; chancellor Diocese of Louisville, 1910—; adminstr. of diocese, 1923; vicar general, June 1923—; Papal domestic prelate, 1924. Mem. Louisville Vice Commn., 1916. Trustee Louisville Pub. Library. Home: Louisville, Ky. Died Nov. 29, 1931.

SCHULTE, Hermann von Wechlinger, anatomist; b. Utica, N.Y., Aug. 9, 1876; s. Bernard and Julia Low (Nelson) S.; A.B., Trinity Coll., Conn., 1897; M.D., Coll. Phys. and Surg. (Columbia), 1902; summer course, U. of Berlin, 1905; m. Susan Augusta Embury, Sept. 11, 1907. Interne, Presbyn. Hosp., New York, 1902-04; successively instr. anatomy, asst. demonstrator, demonstrator, adj. prof., asst. prof., asso. prof., Coll. Phys. and Surg. (Columbia), 1904-16; prof. anatomy, 1916—, jr. dean, 1916-17, dean, 1917—, Creighton U. Sch. of Medicine, Omaha, Neb.; chief of staff, St. Joseph's Hosp.; pres. State Anatomical Bd. of Neb., 1916—; mem. Omaha Pub. Library Bd., 1927-30. Lt. col. Med. Res., comdg. Gen. Hosp. No. 55, 1922—. Mem. exec. com. Omaha Community Chest; trustee Soc. for Relief of Disabled; mem. bd. Omaha Social Settlement. Fellow A.A.A.S., New York Acad. Science, Neb. Acad. Science (pres. 1922). Mem. Am. Acad. Polit. and Social Science, Omaha Council Social Agencies (pres. 1925-29), Nebraska Conf. for Social Work (pres. 1928-29). Episcopalian. Home: Omaha, Neb. Died July 13, 1932.

SCHULTZ, Ernst William, furniture mfr.; b. Manitowoc County, Wis., Jan. 11, 1877; s. Joachim and Otilie (Krueger) S.; grad. Oshkosh (Wis.) State Normal Sch., 1898; m. Clara Haese, June 1, 1912; children—Ernst William, Carolyn. Pres. The Northfield Co., 1905—; dir. of Bank of Sheboygan, Wis.; mem. bd. govs. Am. Furniture Mart. Pres. Wis. State Bd. Vocational Edn.; pres. bd. trustees Stout Inst., Menominee; dir. Sheboygan Memorial Hosp. Republican. Lutheran; mem. bd. govs. Lutheran Laymen's League. Home: Sheboygan, Wis. Died May 4, 1938.

SCHULTZE, Augustus, theologian; b. Nowawes, Brandenburg, Germany, Feb. 3, 1840; s. C. Louis and D. Frederica (Haeseler) S.; grad. Moravian Coll., Niesky, 1858; Theol. Sem., Gnadenfeld, Silesia, 1861; D.D., Lafayette Coll., 1893; L.H.D., Columbian U., 1901; m. Addie E. Peter, July 5, 1876. Taught in French acad. at Lausanne, Switzerland, 1861-62; instr. classics, Moravian Coll., Niesky, 1862-70; became prof., 1870, pres. Moravian Coll., 1885—, and Theol. Sem., Bethlehem, Pa. One of the 3 mems. governing bd. Moravian Ch. in America, 1881-93; many yrs. editor Der Brüder Botschafter; compiled new liturgy and hymns, German Moravian Hymn Book; wrote English and German Catechisms, Moravian Ch. Author: History of the Widow's Society of Bethlehem, 1880; Aarlig Dagbog (1st Moravian Text-book in the Danish language), 1888; Die Missionsfelder der Erneuerten Brüderkirche, 1890; Grammar and Vocabulary of the Eskimo Language of N. Western Alaska, 1894; The Theology of Peter and Paul, 1896; Guide to the Old Moravian Cemetery at Bethlehem, 1898; The Books of the Bible Analyzed, 1902; Christian Doctrine and Systematic Theology, 1909. Pres. Moravian Ednl. Assn. Address: Bethlehem, Pa. Died Nov. 12, 1918.

SCHULTZE, Carl Emil ("Bunny"), newspaper artist; b. Lexington, Ky., May 25, 1866; s. Charles and Jane (Delph) S.; ed. in Cassel, Germany, and Lexington, Ky., pub. schs.; m. Mary Greenlee Brown, Nov. 1899. Began drawing for newspapers under name of "Bunny," Jan. 1900; introduced "Foxy Grandpa" series, first published in New York Herald, Jan. 7, 1900, continued in New York American from Feb. 17, 1902; New York Evening Journal, International Feature Service, Inc., 1923-27 (retired). Author of the "Foxy Grandpa" books. Died Jan. 18, 1939.

SCHUMACHER, Ferdinand, miller; b. Celle, Hanover, March 30, 1822; ed. high school; apprentice to wholesale grocer, Harburg, Germany, 1837-42; clerk, 1842-44, shipping mgr. for sugar refinery, 1844-50. Came to U.S., 1850; farmed nr. Cleveland, 1 yr.; established as grocer at Akron, 1851. In 1856 became pioneer mfr. of oatmeal in U.S.; consolidated large oatmeal interests in The Am. Cereal Co., of which he was pres. until March 8, 1899. Address: Akron, O. Died 1908.

SCHUMANN-HEINK, Ernestine (Madame Schumann-Heink), prima donna; b. Lieben, nr. Prague, Austria, June 15, 1861; d. Maj. Roessler; ed. Ursuline Convent, Prague; m. Mr. Heink, 1882; m. 2d, Paul Schumann; m. 3d, William Rapp, Jr., May 1905 (divorced 1914). Prin. contralto, Dresden Court Opera, at 17, and made first appearance on stage as Azucena in "Il Trovatore," Oct. 13, 1878; appeared as Ernestine Heink in Hamburg, 1883, and later sang a star engagement at Kroll's Theatre, Berlin; gained nat. reputation at Bayreuth; mem. Met. Opera Co., New York, for several seasons; starred in "Love's Lottery," 1905-06; reappeared at age of 64 with Metropolitan Opera Co., Feb. 25, 1926, in "Das Rheingold." Widely known as concert singer. Toured in vaudeville, 1932-33; radio work, 1933-35; made first screen picture "Here's To Romance," 1935. Home: Coronado, Calif. Died Nov. 17, 1936.

SCHURMAN, George Wellington, lawyer; LL.M., Cornell U., 1893; m. Helen I. Munro. Mem. Hughes (Charles E.), Rounds, Schurman & Dwight, later Hughes, Schurman & Dwight; atty. for Dorothy Gould in suit to remove Edwin Gould as trustee Gould properties. Dir. Brearly School. Republican. Home: New York, N.Y. Died Jan. 9, 1931.

SCHURZ, Carl, publicist; b. Liblar, nr. Cologne, March 2, 1829; s. Christian and Marianne S.; ed. gymnasium, Cologne, Univ. of Bonn; LL.D., Harvard, and of U. of Mo.; LL.D., Columbia, 1899. Published liberal newspaper at Bonn; took part in revolutionary movements in 1848-49, and was compelled to leave Bonn, 1849; joined revolutionary army, but finally had to flee to Switzerland. Newspaper corr., Paris, 1851; teacher in London; m. Margaretta Meyer, July 1852. Came to U.S., 1852; settled in Watertown, Wis.; defeated as Rep. candidate for lt. gov. Wis., 1857; mem. Nat. Rep. Conv., 1860; U.S. minister to Spain, 1861; resigned to enter army; apptd. brig. gen., April 1862; maj. gen., March 14, 1863; comd. div. at Second Bull Run and at Chancellorsville, and a corps of Gettysburg. Washington corr. New York Tribune, 1865-66; founded Detroit Post, 1866; editor St. Louis Westliche Post, 1867; temp. chmn. Rep. Nat. Conv., Chicago, 1868; U.S. senator from Mo., 1869-75; one of organizers Liberal party, 1872; presided over conv. at Cincinnati which nominated Greeley for President; supported Hayes, 1876; Sec. of the Interior, 1877-81; editor New York Evening Post, 1881-84. One of leaders Independent movement, 1884; supported Cleveland for President; contbr. to Harper's Weekly, 1892-98; pres. Nat. Civil Service Reform League, 1892-1901. Author: Speeches, 1885; Life of Henry Clay, 1887; Abraham Lincoln, an Essay, 1889; etc. Home: New York, N.Y. Died 1906.

SCHURZ, Carl Lincoln, lawyer; b. Washington, D.C., Feb. 28, 1871; s. Hon. Carl and Margarete (Meyer) S.; A.B., Harvard, 1893; student Harvard Law Sch. 1 yr.; LL.B., New York Law Sch., 1895; studied U. of Heidelberg, summer 1900; m. Harriet Tiedemann, Oct. 20, 1897; m. 2d, Marie (Leroy) Hart, Aug. 2, 1922. Clk. in Law offices of Parsons Shepard & Ogden, New York, 2 yrs.; chief atty., Legal Aid Soc., New York, 1897-1901; became mem. Oakes, Van Amringe & Schurz, 1907, later Oakes & Schurz, to 1913; apptd. gen. counsel Hamburg Am. Line, 1913; trustee Central Savings Bank of New York, Herman Knapp Memorial Eye Hosp., Deutsche Gesellschaft. Democrat. Home: New York, N.Y. Died May 19, 1924.

SCHUYLER, Aaron, univ. prof.; b. Seneca County, N.Y., Feb. 7, 1828; s. John B. and Elizabeth (Turner) S.; ed. Seneca Acad. and Ohio Wesleyan U., hon. A.M., 1860; LL.D., Otterbein U., 1875; m. Amanda Pearce, Nov. 13, 1851; m. 2d, Mrs. Josephine Campbell, July 29, 1886. Prin. Seneca Acad., 1851-62; prof. mathematics, 1862-75, pres. 1873-85, Baldwin U.; prof. mathematics and mental philosophy, Kansas Wesleyan U., 1885—. Mem. Am. Acad. Polit. and Social Science. Author: Higher Arithmetic, 1877; Complete Algebra, 1870, revised, 1883; Elements of Geometry, 1876; Surveying, 1873; The Principles of Logic, 1869; Empirical and Rational Psychology, 1882; Outlines of Psychology, 1893; Systems of Ethics, 1902. Address: Salina, Kan. Died Feb. 1, 1913.

SCHUYLER, Hamilton, clergyman, writer; b. Oswego, N.Y., Apr. 3, 1862; s. Anthony and Mary (Allen) S.; ed. Gen. Theol. Sem., N.Y. City, 1890-92, Oxford U., Eng., 1892-93; hon. Litt.D., Rutgers U., 1928; m. Irma Chandor, Oct. 19, 1898. Ordained deacon, 1892, priest, 1893, P.E. Ch.; asst., Calvary Ch., N.Y. City, 1893-94, Trinity Ch., Newport, R.I., 1894-95; dean of Cathedral, Davenport, Ia., 1896-98; rector Trinity Ch., Trenton, N.J., 1900-30, hon. canon of Trinity Cathedral, 1930—. Trustee Free Public Library, Trenton, 1905—. Author: Studies in English Church History, 1898; A Fisher of Men, 1906; The Intellectual Crisis Confronting Christianity, 1913; Within the Cloister's Shadow and Other Poems, 1915; Liturgical Hymns for the Church's Season's, and 1915; The Battle of Trenton (verse), 1926; The Roeblings, A Century of Engineers, Bridge Builders and Industrialists, 1931. Contbr. Am. Ch. Monthly. Winner of Collis P. Huntington prize for best poem in reply to Edwin Markham's "Man With the Hoe," 1900. Editor: A History of Trenton, 1929. Home: Trenton, N.J. Died Jan. 23, 1933.

SCHUYLER, James Dix, engr.; b. Ithaca, N.Y., May 11, 1848; s. Philip Church and Lucy M. (Dix) S.; ed. Friend's Coll., 1863-68; self-ed. after that; m. Mrs. Mary Ingalls Tuliper, July 1889. Engaged in ry. constrn. in Colo., 1869-73; removed to Calif., 1873; asst. state engr. Calif., 1878-82; chief engr. and supt. Sinaloa & Durango R.R., Mexico, 1882-84; built section of great sea-wall, San Francisco, 1884-85; built Sweetwater dam, 1887-88, and later the Hemet dam. Built water works in Denver, Portland, Ore., etc., and irrigation works in West. Cons. engr. in water-right litigation and water works constrn., from Hawaii to Ohio and from British Columbia to City of Mexico; also cons. hydraulic engr. Am. Beet Sugar Co. Engaged in bldg. large power plants in Calif. and Mex., and extensive works for irrigation and power development in Mex., Brazil, N.M., Colo., and other Western states; mem. of commn. of engrs. on Los Angeles City Aqueduct; cons. engr. to Territorial Govt. of Hawaii on constrn. of Nuuanu dam; to Monterey Water Works and Sewer Co. Ltd., Mex.; to Kobe Syndicate, on extensive power project in Japan, involving very high dam; to Mexican Light & Power Co., Ltd., on building of four large dams for power in Necaxa Valley, State of Puebla, Mex.; to Vancouver Power Co., Ltd., Vancouver, B.C., building dam at Coquitlam Lake. Mem. commn. of engrs. apptd. by President Roosevelt to accompany President-elect Taft to Panama, Jan. 1909, to finally decide type of canal. Author: Reservoirs for Irrigation, Water Power and Domestic Water Supply, 1901. Contbr. to Engineering News and other scientific jours. Twice winner of Rowland prize, 1888 and 1896, for best papers of yr. read before Am. Soc. C.E. Home: Ocean Park, Calif. Died Sept. 13, 1912.

SCHUYLER, Karl Cortlandt, lawyer; b. Colorado Springs, Colo., Apr. 3, 1877; s. Frederick and Nellie M. (Farnan) S.; U. of Denver, 1897-98; m. Alsena Shepard, June 21, 1905; children—Eleanor, Karl Cortlandt. Practiced law at Denver, Colo., 1903—; pres. Kinney-Coastal Oil Co.; dir. Denver Nat. Bank; Denver chmn. 4th and 5th Liberty Loan Drives; chmn. Triangle War Fund; chmn. Colo. Com. for Relief of Ex-Service Men; pres. Denver Community Chest. Trustee U. of Denver, Colo. Woman's Coll. Mem. Acad. Political Science. Republican. Conglist. Home: Denver, Colo. Died July 31, 1933.

SCHUYLER, Livingston Rowe, clergyman; b. New York, N.Y., 1868; B.A., Coll. City of New York, 1889, M.A., 1893; B.D., Gen. Theol. Sem., 1894; fellow in eccles. history, Ch. Univ. Bd. of Regents, 1894-97; student U. of Oxford, Eng., 1895-96, U. of Paris, 1896-97; Ph.D., New York U., 1904; m. Leonora St. George, d. Col. St. George Rogers, 1894. Deacon, 1894, priest, 1894, P.E. Ch.; acting chaplain U.S.A., Willetts Pt. (Ft. Totten), N.Y., 1894-95; asst. minister Holy Trinity Ch., Paris, France, 1896-97; rector Ch. of St. James the Less, Scarsdale, N.Y., 1901-08; rector Ch. of St. Andrew-by-the-Sea, Allenhurst, N.J., 1908-16; asso. prof. of history, 1916—, Coll. City of New York. Author: The Liberty of the Press in the American Colonies, 1905. Address: New York, N.Y. Died Jan. 1, 1931.

SCHUYLER, Montgomery, journalist, author; b. Ithaca, N.Y., Aug. 19, 1843; s. Rev. Anthony and Eleanor (Johnson) S.; student Hobart Coll., 1858; m. Katherine Beeckman Livingston, Sept. 16, 1876; 1 son, Montgomery S., Jr. With the New York World, 1865-83, New York Times, 1883-1907, New York Sun, 1912—. Mng. editor Harper's Weekly, 1885-87; reader for Harper & Bros., 1887-94. Contbr. poems and critical papers on architecture and literature to leading mags. Mem. Nat. Inst. Arts and Letters. Author: The Brooklyn Bridge (with W. C. Conant), 1883; Studies in American Architecture, 1892; Westward the Course of Empire, 1906. Address: New Rochelle, N.Y. Died July 16, 1914.

SCHUYLER, Walter Scribner, brig. gen. U.S.A.; b. Ithaca, N.Y., Apr. 26, 1850; s. George Washington and Matilda (Scribner) S.; grad. U.S. Mil. Acad., 1870; m. Mary Miller Gardiner, Dec. 20, 1883 (died 1902); m. 2d, Elizabeth Stanton, Mar. 3, 1921. Commd. 2d lt. 5th Cav., June 15, 1870; promoted through grades to brig. gen. U.S.A., Jan. 5, 1911. Bvtd. capt. U.S.A., Feb. 27, 1890, for services in Indian campaigns in Ariz., Wyo., Mont., Colo., 1871-79; prof. mil. science, Cornell U., 1883-86, 1896-98; col. 203d N.Y. Inf., July 3, 1898-Mar. 25, 1899; col. 46th U.S. Inf., Aug. 17, 1899-May 31, 1901; served in P.R., P.I., and Cuba, 1899-1902; mil. observer with Russian army in Manchuria, 1904; mem. Gen. Staff U.S.A., 1904-06, 1910; comdr. Mil. Dist. Hawaii, 1909-10, Dept. of the Colo., Feb. 6-Mar. 8, 1911; comd. independent cav. brigade, San Antonio, Tex., Mar. 12-July 15, 1911; comdg. Ft. Riley, Kan., July 1911-June 1912; comdg. Dept. of Calif., June-Dec. 1912; 8th Brigade, Dec. 1912-Apr. 1913; retired Apr. 26, 1913. Home: Carmel, Calif. Died Feb. 17, 1932.

SCHUYLER, William, teacher; b. St. Louis, May 4, 1855; s. Montgomery (D.D.) and Sophia Elizabeth (Norton) S.; B.A., Washington U., 1874, M.A., 1877; studied music and composition with pvt. instrs., drawing and painting, St. Louis Sch. of Fine Arts, 1876-80; m. Hidee Remington, Dec. 24, 1881 (died 1897). Teacher, lecturer and writer, gen. and pedagog. subjects, 1877—; asst. prin. in high schs., St. Louis, 1895-1913; prin. McKinley High Sch., St. Louis, 1913—. Wrote spl. articles, editorials and mus. criticisms, St. Louis Post-Dispatch, 1890-97; dramatic and mus. critic, The Criterion, 1896-97. Democrat. Episcopalian. Author: An Ambassador of Christ, 1901; Under Pontius Pilate, 1906; The Art of Composition (with Philo M. Buck, Jr.); Mona Lisa (under the nom de plume of Guglielmo Scala), 1911. Editor: Macaulay's Life of Samuel Johnson, 1903. Composer: Now the Shadows Darken (song); Song Cycle from Black Riders (5 songs); The Golden Fullness (song with 'cello obligato); An Idyl of Spring (piano solo); The Light of the World (song); Parted Love (2 songs); A Memory (piano solo). Home: St. Louis, Mo. Died July 7, 1914.

SCHWAB, Charles M., steel mfr.; b. Williamsburg, Pa., Feb. 18, 1862; childhood from 5th year at Loretto, Pa.; s. of John A. and Pauline (Farabaugh) S.; ed. village sch. and St. Francis Coll.; hon. Dr. Engring., Lehigh, 1914, Stevens Inst. Tech., 1921; LL.D., Lincoln Memorial U., 1917, St. Francis Coll., Loretto, Pa., 1923, Franklin and Marshall Coll., 1924, Juniata Coll., 1926; D.C.S., New York U., 1918; Sc.D., U. of Pa., 1927; m. Emma Eurana Dinkey, 1883. As a boy drove stage from Loretto to Cresson, Pa., 5 miles; entered service of Carnegie Co. as stake-driver in engring, corps of Edgar Thompson Steel Works, serving as chf. engr. and asst. mgr., 1881-87; supt. Homestead Steel Works, 1887-89; gen. supt. Edgar Thompson Steel Works, 1889-97, Homestead Works, 1892-97; pres. Carnegie Steel Co., Ltd., 1897-1901; pres. U.S. Steel Corp., 1901-03; later chmn. bd. Bethlehem Steel Corp., Bethlehem Steel Co.; dir. Metropolitan Life Ins. Co. Director general shipbuilding, U.S. Shipping Bd. Emergency Fleet Corp., Apr.-Dec. 1918. Pres. Am. Iron & Steel Inst., 1926-32, chmn., 1932-34. Awarded Melchett Medal (British) "for distinguished service in industry," 1932. Home: New York, N.Y. Died Sept. 18, 1939.

SCHWAB, Gustav Henry, merchant; b. New York, May 30, 1851; s. Gustav and Catharine Elizabeth (von Post) S.; brother of John Christopher S.; ed. New York and Germany; m. Caroline Wheeler, Oct. 25, 1876. Mem. firm Oelrichs & Co., shipping mchts., importers and Am. agts. North German Lloyd Steamship Co.; dir. U.S. Trust Co., Merchants' Nat. Bank, Atlantic Mut. Ins. Co., and other corps.; chmn. com. on foreign commerce and the revenue laws, Chamber of Commerce State of N.Y.; 1st v.p. Merchants' Assn., New York. Served as mem. com. of 70, 1894; decorated order SS. Lazaro and Maurizio, by King of Italy, 1895; Red Eagle of 3d class by German Emperor, 1902. Home: New York, N.Y. Died Nov. 12, 1912.

SCHWAB, John Christopher, librarian; b. New York, Apr. 1, 1865; s. Gustav and Eliza Catharine (von Post) S.; brother of Gustav Henry S.; A.B., Yale, 1886, A.M., 1888; U. of Berlin, 1887-88; A.M., Ph.D., Göttingen, 1889; m. Edith A. Fisher, Oct. 5, 1893. Instr. polit. economy, 1890-93, asst. prof., 1893-98, prof., 1898-1905, librarian, 1905—, Yale U. Editor Yale Review, 1892—. Mem. Co. F, 2d Regt., Conn. N.G., 1891-94. Episcopalian. Author: History of New York Property Tax, 1880; The Confederate States of America, 1901. Contbr. to hist. revs. and mags. Address: New Haven, Conn. Died Jan. 12, 1916.

SCHWABE, H. August, artist; b. Oberweissbach, Thüringen, Germany, Feb. 2, 1843; s. Christian and Christiana (Welsche) S.; learned drawing and china decorating and at 18 worked as painter and designed stained glass, Stuttgart; studied in Poly. Sch., Royal Acad. Fine Arts, Munich and Cologne; came to U.S., 1871, and later studied at old Acad. of Design, New York, and under William Chase, also at Munich, Paris, and in Julien Acad. Designed and painted ch. windows in New York, Pittsburgh, Chicago, etc. Awarded gold medal for stained glass design and execution, St. Louis Expn., 1904; exhibited New York Acad. Design, Art Assn., etc.; also portrait figure painter. Home: Newark, N.J. Died Feb. 8, 1916.

SCHWAN, Theodore, major general U.S.A.; b. Hanover, Germany, July 9, 1841; s. Rev. H. C. S.; ed. gymnasium in Germany; came to U.S., 1857; m. Elizabeth M. Steele (dec.). Served as pvt., corporal, sergt. and 1st sergt., C. K, and q. m. sergt. 10th U.S. Inf., June 12, 1857-Nov. 6, 1863; 2d lt. 10th Inf., Oct. 31, 1863; 1st lt., Apr. 9, 1864; capt., Mar. 14, 1866; assigned to 11th Inf., Dec. 13, 1869; maj. a.-a.-g., July 6, 1886; lt. col. a.-a.-g., Feb. 19, 1895; brig. gen. vols., May 4, 1898; col. a.-a.-g. U.S.A., May 18, 1898; hon. discharged from vol. service, Apr. 14, 1899; brig. gen. vols., Apr. 14, 1899; brig. gen. U.S.A., Feb. 2, 1901; hon. discharged from vol. service, Feb. 21, 1901; retired at own request after 40 yrs.' service, Feb. 21, 1901. Bvtd. captain, Oct. 1, 1864, "for gallant services" in battle of Chapel House, Va.; maj., Mar. 2, 1867, "for gallant and meritorious services," during the war; awarded medal of honor, Dec. 12, 1898, "for most distinguished gallantry" in action at Peebles Farm, Va., Oct. 1, 1864. Attached to Am. Embassy, Berlin, Germany, 1892-93. Comd. 1st Div., 9th Army Corps, May-July 1898; comd. western column in Puerto Rican campaign; chief of staff, Div. of P.I. and prin. asst. to mil. gov., also in command of Southern Luzon expdns., 1899-1900; promoted maj. gen. U.S.A., Aug. 29, 1916. Author Report on the Organization of the German Army with supplement showing the orgn. of the German Gen. Staff. Address: Washington, D.C. Died May 27, 1926.

SCHWARTZ, Karl, clergyman; b. Canadice, N.Y., Nov. 21, 1863; s. Seymour T. and Mary E. (Swift) S.; A.B., Syracuse U., 1886, A.M., 1897; grad. Berkeley Div. Sch., Conn., 1899; Ph.D., Syracuse, 1909; m. Elizabeth Gill, July 6, 1904. Deacon, 1887, priest, 1889, P.E. Ch.; rector of Trinity Ch., Lowville, N.Y., 1889-91; asst. rector Ch. of Zion and St. Timothy, New York, 1891-98; chaplain 1st N.Y. Vols. in war with Spain, 1898-99; dean Cathedral of the Savior, Syracuse, N.Y., 1904, rector, 1904—. Author: A Catechism, 1900; A Message, 1900; The Church Year, 1901; Inherited Criminal Tendencies and How Nature Deals With Them, 1902; The Degenerate and Society, 1909. Contbr. to various periodicals. Address: Syracuse, N.Y. Died Dec. 8, 1924.

SCHWARZ, George Frederick, forester; b. Baltimore, Apr. 13, 1868; s. Frederick A. O. and Caroline (Clausen) S.; ed. Harvard Coll. and Law Sch., 1891-95; nat. forest schs. of Germany and France, 1895-97; unmarried. Expert in Forest Service, U.S. Dept. Agr., 1899-1904. Author: Forest Trees and Forest Scenery, 1901; The Rock River and Its Relation to the Surrounding Forests, 1903; The Longleaf Pine in Virgin Forest, 1907. Consulting forester, retired. Home: Bronxville, N.Y. Died Jan. 1, 1931.

SCHWATT, Isaac Joachim, coll. prof.; b. Mitau in Kurland, Russia, June 18, 1867; s. Joachim and

Doris (Nibur) S.; grad. Mitau Coll., 1883; Ph.D., U. of Pa., 1893; m. Rose Eichman, July 31, 1896. Instr. mathematics, 1893-97, asst. prof., 1897-1908, prof., 1908—, U. of Pa. Transl. Durege's Theory of Functions, from the German (with Prof. Fisher); Geometrical Treatment of Curves; a series of Five Text-Books on Algebra (with Prof. Fisher). Address: Philadelphia, Pa. Died 1934.

SCHWEBACH, James, bishop; b. Platen, Duchy of Luxemburg, Aug. 15, 1847; s. Nicholas and Margaret S.; classical studies under pvt. tutors and at Coll. of Diekirch; came to U.S. in 1864; philos. and theol. course, St. Francis Sem., nr. Milwaukee. Deacon, 1869, priest, 1870, R.C. Ch.; pastor St. Mary's, La Crosse, 1870-92; vicar-gen., 1882, and later adminstr., Diocese of La Crosse; consecrated bishop of La Crosse, Feb. 24, 1892. Address: La Crosse, Wis. Died June 6, 1921.

SCHWEIKERT, Harry Christian, author; b. Bernville, Berks County, Pa., Feb. 24, 1877; s. Christian and Cornelia (Altmaier) S.; A.B., Princeton, 1903, A.M., 1908; studied U. of Chicago, Alliance Française, Paris, 1913, and Columbia U.; also U. of Seville, 1923; m. Alice Josephine Squires, March 31, 1930. Teacher of English, Central High Sch., St. Louis, 1903—; lecturer on English lit., Collegiate Dept., Benton Coll. of Law, St. Louis., 1906—, prin. until 1927. Wilson Democrat. Author: French Short Stories, 1918; Russian Short Stories, 1919; Short Stories, 1925; Five Plays of Shakespeare, 1926; Frank T. Bullen's Cruise of the Cachalot, 1926; Early English Plays, 1927; Adventures in Literature, Book 9 (with Dr. J. M. Ross), 1928; Adventures in Prose and Poetry (with Mary E. Lowe and H. Augustus Miller, Jr.), 1929; Adventures in American Literature (with Rewey Belle Inglis and John Gehlmann), 1930; Adventures in English Literature (with Alice C. Cooper and Marion E. Sturdevant), 1930. Editor of school edit. of Stevenson's Black Arrow, 1930. Translations of Spanish and Italian short stories in mags. Home: St. Louis, Mo. Died June 5, 1937.

SCHWEINFURTH, Charles Frederick, architect; b. Auburn, N.Y., 1856; acad. edn. there, graduating 1872; traveled in Eng., France, Italy and Spain; studied architecture, New York, Boston, and Phila.; m. Mary Ella, d. Samuel Griggs, 1879. Practiced New York, 1880-83; in Cleveland, O., 1883—; practice mostly in residence, collegiate and ch. structures; architect of Trinity Cathedral, Cleveland. Home: Cleveland, O. Died Nov. 8, 1919.

SCHWEINFURTH, Julius Adolph, architect; b. Auburn, N.Y., Sept. 20, 1858; s. Charles J. and Katherine (Ammon) S.; studied architecture in Boston, London, Paris, Rome and Florence, Italy; m. M. Fannie Bellows, Mar. 29, 1889; 1 son, Charles. With Peabody & Stearns, architects, Boston, 13 yrs.; partner of C. F. Schweinfurth, architect, of Cleveland, O., 1884-86; foreign travel, 1886-88; practiced architecture in Boston, 1895—. Fellow Am. Inst. Architects. Episcopalian. Author: Sketches Abroad, 1887. Made spl. study of early Greek and Etruscan sculpture. Contbr. to archtl. jours. Home: Wellesley Farms, Mass. Died Sept. 29, 1931.

SCHWEINITZ, Emil Alexander de, bacteriologist; b. Salem, N.C., Jan. 18, 1866; s. Bishop E. A. and Sophia A. (Herman) de S.; ed. at Nazareth Hall and Bethlehem, Pa.; grad. U. of N.C., 1882; Ph.D., Göttingen, Germany; M.D., Columbian U., Washington. Dir. biochemic lab., U.S. Dept. Agr.; dean and prof. Columbian Med. Sch. U.S. del. to 4th Internat. Congresses on Tuberculosis, Paris, 1898, and Berlin, 1899; U.S. del. to Internat. Med. Congress and Congress for Hygiene, Paris, 1900. Made many original investigations and published many papers on the products of bacteria, preparation of tuberculins, various antitoxins, the composition of bacilli, especially those of tuberculosis; the comparative virulence of tubercle bacilli and virulence of bovine tubercle bacilli for man; also on disinfectants and hygienic problems. Address: Washington, D.C. Died 1904.

SCHWEINITZ, George Edmund de, M.D.; b. Phila., Oct. 26, 1858; s. Rt. Rev. Edmund and Lydia de S.; A.B., A.M., Moravian, 1876; M.D., U. of Pa., 1881, LL.D., 1914; L.H.D., Moravian Coll.; D.Sc., U. of Mich., 1922, Harvard, 1927. Prof. ophthalmology, U. of Pa. Grad. Sch. of Medicine, 1902-24, emeritus, 1924—; cons. ophthalmologist Phila. Hosp. Maj. Med. R.C., 1917; active service, Sept. 29, 1917-Apr. 1, 1919; lt. col. M.C., U.S.A., in France, Oct. 1917-Mar. 1918; on duty in U.S. as officer in charge of and consultant in ophthalmology, Surgeon Gen.'s Office; brig. gen. Aux. Med. Res.; mem. editorial bd. for med. and surg. history of the war. V.p. Pa. Inst. for Instrn. of Blind; trustee U. of Pa. Mem. A.M.A. (pres. 1922-23), Am. Ophthal. Soc. (pres. 1916). Author: Diseases of the Eye, 1924; Diseases of the Eye, Ear, Nose and Throat (with Dr. Randall), 1899; Toxic Amblyopias, 1896 (Alvarenga prize essay). Am. editor Haab's Ophthalmoscopy and External Diseases of Eye and Operative Ophthalmology; Pulsating Exophthalmos (with Dr. Holloway); Ophthalmic Year Book (with Dr. Jackson), 1905-09. Contbr. numerous articles and monographs on ophthal. and neurol. subjects. Bowman lecturer, London, 1923. Awarded plaque from Soc. Française D'Ophthalmologie, 1924; Howe prize medal in ophthalmology, 1927; Huguenot Cross, 1928; Leslie Dana medal for prevention of blindness, 1930. Address: Philadelphia, Pa. Died Aug. 22, 1938.

SCHWEITZER, (Johann) Paul, chemist; b. Berlin, Germany, Mar. 16, 1840; s. A. F. T. and Julia (Hoehne) S.; Ph.D., U. of Göttingen, 1869; LL.D., U. of Mo., 1897; m. Sarah Howard, June 18, 1870. Asst. to H. Rose, Berlin, 1863, Poly. Inst., Phila., 1865, Sch. of Mines (Columbia), 1866; prof. chemistry, 1872-94, prof. agrl. chemistry, 1874-1906, chemist, Expt. Sta., 1887-1906, U. of Mo. Gold medal Paris Expn., 1900. Author of numerous papers on chem. subjects in scientific jours. and Agrl. Sta. bulls. Address: Columbia, Mo. Died 1911.

SCHWEPPE, Charles Hodgdon, banker; b. Alton, Ill., Nov. 18, 1880; s. William E. and Eva (Jewett) S.; A.B., Harvard, 1902; m. Laura A., d. John G. Shedd, Feb. 22, 1913 (died 1937); children—Jean Shedd (Mrs. A. Watson Armour, III), John Shedd. With Lee, Higginson & Co., bankers, Boston, 1902—, opened Chicago office for the firm, 1905, partner, 1913—; chmn. bd. Public Welfare Commrs. State of Ill.; pres. Lee, Higginson Corp.; dir. Marshall Field & Co., Fairbanks, Morse & Co. Pres. St. Luke's Hosp.; v.p. Old People's Home; mem. bd. trustees Home for Friendless, Shedd Aquarium Society, Chicago Zoöl. Soc., Ferry Hall (Lake Forest, Ill.), Chicago Boys Club. Republican. Episcopalian. Home: Lake Forest, Ill. Died Aug. 26, 1941.

SCHWERT, Pius Louis, congressman; b. Angola, N.Y., Nov. 22, 1892; s. Julius Marcus and Louisa Elizabeth (Ahlers) S.; B.S. in Economics, U. of Pa., 1914; m. Hattie E., Feb. 12, 1922. Baseball player with New York Yankees, 1914, 15, 16; financial sec. U.P. Christian Assn., winters of same yrs.; owner gen. store, Angola, N.Y., 1916-21; successively clk., v.p. and pres. Bank of Angola, 1921-31; mgr. of employment bur., 1933; mem. President Roosevelt's Spl. Review Bd., 1933; elected county clk., Erie County, 1933, 1936; mem. 76th Congress (1939-41), 42d N.Y. Dist.; dir. Automobile Club of Buffalo, Evans Land Corp., Angola Development Co. Commd. ensign, U.S. Naval Res., World War I. Democrat. Lutheran. Mason, Odd Fellow, Elk, Eagle, Moose. Home: Buffalo, N.Y. Died Mar. 11, 1941.

SCHWERTNER, August John, bishop; b. Canton, O., Dec. 23, 1870; s. Anton and Christina (Richart) S.; ed. Canisius Coll. (Buffalo, N.Y.), St. Mary's Sem. (Cleveland, O.). Ordained priest R.C. Ch., 1897; curate St. Columba's Ch., Youngstown, O., 1897; pastor St. Anthony's Ch., Milan, O., 1897-1903, St. Mary's Ch., Rockport, 1903-07, St. John's Ch., Lima, 1907-13; chancellor Diocese of Toledo, 1913-21; named domestic prelate by Pope Benedict XV, 1916; consecrated bishop of Wichita, June 8, 1921. Home: Wichita, Kan. Died Oct. 10, 1939.

SCIDMORE, Eliza Ruhamah, author; b. Madison, Wis., Oct. 14, 1856; ed. at boarding schs.; (Litt.D.). Fgn. sec. Nat. Geog. Soc. Author: Alaska, the Southern Coast and the Sitkan Archipelago, 1885; Jinrikisha Days in Japan, 1890; Guide to Alaska and the Northwest Coast, 1890; Java, the Garden of the East, 1897; China, the Long-Lived Empire, 1900; Winter India, 1903; As The Hague Ordains, 1907. Address: Washington, D.C. Died Nov. 3, 1928.

SCIDMORE, George Hawthorne, consul gen.; b. Dubuque, Ia., Oct. 12, 1854; s. George Bolles and Eliza Catherine (Scidmore) S.; ed. pvt. schs., Madison, Wis., and Washington; LL.B., Nat. U., Washington, 1876; admitted to bar, 1876; unmarried. Consular clerk at Liverpool, 1876; vice-consul at Dunfermline, 1877; consular clerk, Paris, 1878-80; v.-consul, Osaka, and Hiogo, 1884; v. consul gen., Shanghai, June-Dec. 1885; vi and dep. consul gen., Kanagawa, 1885-91; spl. agt. to investigate claims of Am. citizens to lands in Fiji Islands, 1891; deputy consul gen., Kanagawa, 1894-1902, Yokohama, 1902-04; legal adviser to Am. Legation and Embassy, Tokyo, 1904-07; apptd. consul at Nagasaki, Mar. 30, 1907, at Kobe, June 2, 1909; consul gen. at Seoul, Aug. 27, 1909, at Yokohama, Nov. 25, 1913—. Barrister and solicitor of Brit. Ct. for Japan, 1893; lecturer several yrs. on Am. and English law, Tokyo English Law Sch. Author: American Consular Courts in Japan; also numerous reports to Dept. of State. Home: Washington, D.C. Died Nov. 27, 1922.

SCOFIELD, Cyrus Ingerson, clergyman; b. Lenawee County, Mich., Aug. 19, 1843, and reared in Wilson County, Tenn.; s. Elias and Abi (Goodrich) S.; educated privately; m. Hettie van Wart, July 14, 1884. Pvt., Co. H, 7th Tenn. Inf., May 1861, in Army of Northern Va. under Gen. Lee; Confed. Cross of Honor; admitted to Kan. bar, 1869; mem. Kan. Ho. of Rep., from Atchison and Nemaha counties, 1870-71; apptd. U.S. atty. for Kan. by President Grant, 1873. Converted to Christian religion at St. Louis, 1879; ordained Congregational ministry, 1882; pastor First Ch., Dallas, Tex., 1882-95, Moody Ch., Northfield, Mass., 1895-1902, again First Ch., Dallas, 1902-07. Lectured extensively on Biblical subjects in Europe and America. Author: Rightly Dividing the Word of Truth, 1885; Addresses on Prophecy, 1900; The Doctrine of the Holy Spirit, 1906; Lectures on Galatians, 1907. Editor: Scofield Reference Bible. 1910; Bible of 1911, 1911. Head of Scofield Corr. Bible Sch. Home: Douglaston, L.I., N.Y. Died July 24, 1921.

SCOFIELD, Edward, governor; b. Clearfield, Pa., Mar. 28, 1842; ed. dist. sch.; worked in printing offices, 1855-61; served pvt. to maj. 11th Pa. Regt., 1861, until captured, May 1864; prisoner of war 10 months. Worked on ry. surveys, 1865-68, in Pa.; went to Oconto, Wis., 1868; foreman of lumber mill, 1868-76; lumber mfr. on large scale, 1876—. Mem. Wis. Senate, 1887-91; gov. of Wis., 1896-1900. Republican. Address: Oconto, Wis. Died Feb. 3, 1925.

SCOFIELD, Walter Keeler, med. dir. U.S.N.; b. Stamford, Conn., Apr. 28, 1839; s. Alfred and Maria S.; M.D., Coll. Phys. and Surg. (Columbia), 1868; m. Mary Candee, Jan. 14, 1876. Asst. surgeon U.S.N., July 12, 1861; passed asst. surgeon, June 22, 1864; surgeon, Apr. 7, 1866; med. insp., Nov. 21, 1883; med. dir., Feb. 8, 1890; retired with rank of rear admiral, Apr. 28, 1901. Home: Stamford, Conn. Died 1910.

SCOFIELD, William Bacon; b. Hartford, Conn., Feb. 8, 1864; s. James M. and Madilia N. (Hoche) S.; student Harvard; studied modeling with Gutzon Borglum; m. Myrtis Sigourney, Dec. 31, 1919. Officer and part owner Worcester Thread Co., Crompton-Thayer Loom Co.; dir. in other mfg. cos. Sculptor and writer. Mem. Am. Federation of Arts. Republican. Author: Verses, 1914 (including John, The Orange Man, a famous Harvard poem); Poems of War, 1919; A Forgotten Idyll, 1921. Address: Worcester, Mass. Died Jan. 22, 1930.

SCOLLARD, Clinton, author; b. Clinton, N.Y., Sept. 18, 1860; s. of James I. and Elizabeth (Stephens) S.; A.B., Hamilton, 1881; student Harvard, and Cambridge, Eng.; m. Georgia Brown, July 3, 1890; 1 dau., Elisabeth; m. 2d, Jessie B. Rittenhouse, author, 1924. Prof. English lit., Hamilton Coll., 1888-96 and 1911—. Mem. Nat. Inst. Arts and Letters. Author: The Cloistering of Ursula, 1902; Lyrics of the Dawn, 1902; Count Falcon of the Eyrie, 1903; Footfaring, 1904; The Lyric Bough, 1904; Ballads of Valor and Victory (with Wallace Rice), 1904; Lyrics and Legends of Christmas-tide, 1904; Odes and Elegies, 1905; A Southern Flight (with Frank Dempster Sherman), 1906; Easter Song, 1907; Voices and Visions, 1908; Pro Patria, 1909; Chords of the Zither, 1910; The Vicar of the Marches, 1910; Songs of a Syrian Lover, 1911; From the Lips of the Sea, 1911; Lyrics from a Library, 1913; Poems—Selected, 1914; The Vale of Shadows and Other Verses of the Great War, 1915; Italy in Arms and Other Verses, 1915; Ballads, Patriotic and Romantic, 1916; Let the Flag Wave and Other Verses, 1917; Elegy in Autumn, 1917; War Voices and Memories, 1919; Epic of Golf, 1923; Songs of Summer, 1927; Lyrics of Life, 1928; Lyrics of Florida, 1929; The Crowning Years, 1929; Songs Out of Egypt, 1930. Editor: Ford's Broken Heart, 1894; Ballads of American Bravery, 1900; Poems of Frank Dempster Sherman; Bird Lovers' Anthology (with Jessie B. Rittenhouse), 1930. Address: Kent, Conn. Died Nov. 19, 1932.

SCOTSON-CLARK, George Frederick; b. Brighton, Sussex, Eng., Feb. 9, 1872; s. Rev. Frederick (Mus. Bac., Oxon.) and Catherine Eliza (Brown) S-C.; ed. Brighton Grammar Sch.; m. Ethel, d. Emanuel Crabb, July 5, 1902. First came to U.S., 1891; art dir. Cassell & Co., London, Eng., 1907-12, McCaw, Stevenson & Orr, Belfast, Ireland, 1912-13, Cheltenham Adv. Service, New York, 1913-18, Century Co., 1918-21. Member advisory com. London County Council Art Schs., 1911-14. Mem. K Co., 7th N.Y. Inf., World War I. Author: The Halls; Eating Without Fears; An Amazing Ancestor; Half-Hours in the Kitchenette. Home: Norwalk, Conn. Died Dec. 21, 1927.

SCOTT, Alfred James, Jr., M.D.; b. Paw Paw, Mich., Sept. 28, 1881; s. Alfred James (M.D.) and Annis Jane (Brown) S.; grad. high sch., Milwaukee, Wis., 1900; M.D., Coll. of Medicine, Los Angeles Dept. of U. of Calif., 1909; student U. of Southern Calif., summer 1907; m. Loretta Riddell, June 17, 1908; children—Loretta (Mrs. J. Frederick Davaly), Alfred James, III. Telegraph operator, 1900-05; began practice of medicine at Los Angeles, 1909; clin. instr. in pediatrics, Med. Coll. U. of Calif., Los Angeles Dept., 1909-12; same, U. of Southern Calif., 1912-13, asst. prof. pediatrics, 1914-18, asso. prof., 1918-19, prof., 1919-20; prof. clin. pediatrics, Coll. Med. Evangelists, Los Angeles, 1920-34, prof. pediatrics, 1934-38, prof. emeritus, 1938—; mem. attending staff Los Angeles Gen. County Hosp., 1910-24, mem. cons. staff, 1924-36, hon. emeritus staff, 1938—; mem. Calif. State Dept. Pub. Health, 1922-32; mem. cons. heart bd. Los Angeles Pub. Schs., 1925-30; mem. sr. staff Calif. Hosp., mem. med. advisory bd., 1923-37; retired from active practice, July 10, 1936. Mem. professional Advisory com. Bur. of Child Hygiene, Calif. State Dept. of Pub. Health, 1937—. Examiner, Selective Service Draft Bd., Glendale Dist., 1918-19; mem. Voluntary Service Med. Corps. Pres. Calif Babies Hosp., 1920-31 (a founder). Licentiate Am. Bd. Pediatrics, 1934. Republican. Conglist. Mason. Home: Los Angeles, Calif. Died Apr. 16, 1940.

SCOTT, Arthur Carroll, surgeon; b. Gainesville, Tex., July 12, 1865; s. Rufus Franklin and Martha Helen (Moran) S.; ed. high sch., Gainesville; M.D., Bellevue Hosp. Med. Coll., New York, 1886; LL.D., Trinity U., Waxahachie, Tex., 1935; m. Maud Sherwood, Oct. 30, 1889; children—Arthur Carroll, Lucile (Mrs. Preston A. Childers), Helen (Mrs. Walker Saulsbury). Interne and res. surgeon Western Pa. Hosp., Pittsburgh, 1886-88; practiced at Gainesville, 1888-92; chief surgeon Gulf, Colo. & Santa Fe Hosp. Assn. and Ry. Co., 1892—; organized, with associate, Dr. R. R. White, Kings Daughters Hosp., Temple, Tex., and supervised its development, 1898-1904; sr. surgeon and pres. Scott & White Hosp., Temple, 1904—. Mem. State Prison Bd., Tex.; chmn. Tex. com. of Am. Soc. for Control of Cancer, 1913-25. Author of many papers and articles on med. subjects, especially cancer. Home: Temple, Tex. Died Oct. 27, 1940.

SCOTT, Austin, coll. prof.; b. Maumee, O., Aug. 10, 1848; s. J. Austin and Sarah (Ranney) S.; A.B., Yale, 1869; A.M., U. of Mich., 1870; univs. of Leipzig and Berlin, 1870-73; Ph.D., Leipzig, 1873; LL.D., Princeton, 1891; m. Anna Prentiss Stearns, Feb. 21, 1882. Pvt. sec. to George Bancroft, the historian, 1872-73; taught German, U. of Mich., 1873-75; with Mr. Bancroft arranging materials for History of the Constitution of the U.S., 1875-82; asso. in history, Johns Hopkins, 1875-81; acting prof. history, 1883, Voorhees prof. history, polit. economy and constl. law, 1883-90, pres., 1890-1906, prof. history and polit. science, 1906—, Rutgers College. Contbr. to revs. Address: New Brunswick, N.J. Died Aug. 16, 1922

SCOTT, (Robert) Bruce, lawyer; b. Kaneville, Ill., March 18, 1874; s. John H. and Martha J. (Ostrander) S.; Ph.B., U. of Pa., 1895; post-grad. work, univs. of Chicago, Wis. and Berlin, 1905-07; m. Alice Downing, 1897; children—Martha Louise (dec.), Janet Downing, (Alice) Roberta. Admitted to Ill. bar, 1897; practiced in Aurora, 1897-1905; mem. polit. science and law faculties, U. of Wisconsin. 1906-11 (resigned as prof. of law); local atty. C.,B.&Q. R.R. Co., Aurora, 1900-05, gen. atty., 1911-17, gen. solicitor, 1917-24 (except war period, Jan. 1, 1918-Mar. 1, 1920, gen. solicitor U.S. Railroad Adminstrn.); gen. counsel and dir. C.,B.&Q. R.R. Co., 1924-28, v.p., gen. counsel and dir. from Dec. 10, 1928 to July 1, 1937, v.p., spl. counsel and dir., July 1, 1937—; gen. counsel C.&S. Ry. Co., 1924-28, v.p. and gen. counsel from Dec. 10, 1928 to July 1, 1937, v.p. and spl. counsel, July 1, 1937—; dir., 1932—; v.p. and spl. counsel of all Burlington Lines, including C.,B.&Q. R.R. Co., C.&S. Ry. Co., Ft. Worth & Denver City Ry. Co., Wichita Valley Ry. Co., July 1, 1937—. Home: Evanston, Ill. Died Mar. 14, 1939.

SCOTT, Charles, lawyer, cotton planter; b. Jackson, Miss., Nov. 7, 1847; s. Charles and Elizabeth M. (Bullus) S.; ed. pub. and pvt. schs. to 15; admitted to bar under spl. license before reaching 21; m. Malvina Yerger, Mar. 10, 1870. Enlisted in C.S.A. as pvt., 1862, in Capt. Yerger's co., Adams' Cav. regt.; later detailed as vol. a.-d.-c. under Gen. Daniel W. Adams to participate as mem. of his staff in relief of Vicksburg; joined Capt. W. E. Hunt's co., 28th Miss. Cav., and continued in war until surrendered under Forrest at Gainesville, Ala., May 9, 1865. Practiced 1867-1913; mem. firm of Charles Scott, Sykes & Somerville, Rosedale and Cleveland, Miss.; declined circuit judgeship, offered by Gov. Robert Lowry, and chancellor of dist., by Gov. Stone; became largest cotton planter in the South. Democrat. Episcopalian. Pres. Bd. of Miss. Levee Commrs. one term and declined reëlection; organized, 1890, and pres., 1890—, Interstate Miss. River and Levee Improvement Assn.; chmn. Western Waterways Conv., Memphis, 1906; Dem. candidate, before primary, for gov. of Miss., 1907; dir. and mem. bd. of govs. Lakes to Gulf Deep Waterway Assn. (several times chmn. com. on resolutions); dir. Internat. League for Highway Improvement, Nat. Rivers and Harbors Congress, Southern Commercial Congress, etc. Mem. Am. Acad. Polit. and Social Science, Am. Polit. Science Assn., Baltimore. Pres. Miss. Com. on Monuments in Honor of Women of the Confederacy. Maj. gen. comdg. 2d Div. Forrest's Cav. Corps, U.C.V. Home: Rosedale, Mississippi. Died Oct. 26, 1916.

SCOTT, Charles Frederick, congressman; b. on farm Allen County, Kansas, Sept. 7, 1860; s. John W. and Maria (Protsman) S.; B.S., U. of Kansas, 1881, M.S., 1888; LL.D., Kan. Agrl. Coll., 1910; m. May Brevard Ewing, June 15, 1893 (died 1929); children—Ewing C., Angelo C., Ruth M., Charles F.; m. 2d, Helen Bay Raymond, Mar. 7, 1937. Acquired interest in Iola Register, 1882, became owner, 1887, made it a Daily, 1897, which edited, 1897—. Mem. Kan. Senate, 1892-96; presdl. elector, 1896; mem. 57th to 59th Congresses (1901-07), Kan. at-large, 60th and 61st Congresses (1907-11), 2d Dist. Republican. Regent U. of Kan. Acting pres. Coll. of Emporia, Kan., 1917. Author: Letters (a small volume of letters written in Mexico and Europe); History of Allen and Woodson Counties, Kansas; In the Far East. Home: Iola, Kan. Died Sept. 18, 1938.

SCOTT, Charlotte Angas, coll. prof.; b. Lincoln, Eng., June 8, 1858; d. Caleb (D.D.), and Eliza Ann (Exley) S.; completed course at Girton Coll., Cambridge, Eng.; B.Sc., London U., 1882, D.Sc., 1885; unmarried. Came to U.S., Sept. 1885, as head dept. mathematics, Bryn Mawr Coll. Author: An Introductory Account of Certain Modern Ideas and Methods in Plane Analytical Geometry, 1894; Cartesian Plane Geometry, Part I (analytical cones), 1907. Edited Am. edit. Arithmetic for Schools, by Rev. J. B. Lock (Cambridge, Eng.), 1891. Contbr. to math. jours. Address: Bryn Mawr, Pa. Died 1931.

SCOTT, Colin Alexander, psychologist; b. Ottawa, Ont., Can., Feb. 11, 1861; s. Robert and Isabella S.; Coll. City of New York, 1877; B.A., Queen's U., Kingston, Ont., 1885; studied Ontario Art Sch., 1887; Ph.D., Clark U., Worcester, Mass., 1896; m. Helen McColl, Oct. 1881. Head dept. of psychology, Chicago Normal Sch., 1897-1901; editor Child Study Quarterly, 1899-1901; prof. edn., Miami U., Oxford O., 1902; head dept. of psychology, Boston Normal Sch., 1902-10; prof. psychology and edn., Tufts Coll., 1910-11, Boston Normal Sch., 1911-15; prof. edn. Mt. Holyoke Coll., 1915—. Also head of dept. of records and results, Springfield schs. Writer, lecturer, exhibitor at various art exhbns. Author: Social Education. 1908. Home: South Hadley, Mass. Died 1925.

SCOTT, Earl Francis, mech. engr.; b. Marshall, Tex., Dec. 31, 1874; s. Francis Marion and Lucy Muncton (Duncan) S.; B.E., Vanderbilt, 1903, M.E., 1906; m. Nina Viola Elmer, Nov. 21, 1906; children—Elizabeth Elmer, Margueryte Elmer, Fred, William Elmer. Instr. in shop work, Vanderbilt U., 1897-1903; in the North and with consulting engrs., Miss., 1903-05; in employ A. M. Lockett & Co., New Orleans, 1905-08; in charge engring. dept. Gen. Fire Extinction Co., Atlanta, Ga., 1908-13; asst. mgr. Griscom Russell Co., Atlanta, 1913-14; pres. and mgr. Earl F. Scott & Co., contracting mech. engrs., Atlanta, 1914—. Mem. Bd. Mech. Engrs., City of Atlanta. Fellow Am. Soc. Mech. Engrs. (mgr. 1920-23, v.p. 1923-25). Episcopalian. Mason (32°, Shriner). Home: Atlanta, Ga. Died Dec. 18, 1940.

SCOTT, Ellen C., author; b. Kensington, Conn., July 27, 1862; d. William J. and Anne (Drew) Corrigan; ed. pub. and pvt. sch.; m. Julius E. Scott, Mar. 4, 1886; 1 dau., Anna Drew. Catholic. Author: Elizabeth Bess, 1917; The Loyalty of Elizabeth Bess, 1918; That Fool Moffett, 1925. Contbr. to mags. and newspapers. Home: Milford, Del. Died June 18, 1936.

SCOTT, Ernest, prof, pathology; b. Athens, O., July 30, 1875; s. William H. and Sarah Ann (Felton) S.; B.S., Ohio State U., 1897, M.D., 1900; studied U. of Freiburg, Germany, 1901, U. of Vienna, Austria, 1902; m. Mabel Huddleson, Oct. 14, 1908; children—Dorothy DeLong, Jane Lee (Mrs. Robert Keyes). Prof. histology, Ohio Med. U., 1903-04, prof. pathology, 1904-07; prof. pathology, Starling-Ohio Med. Sch., 1907-14; prof. pathology, Coll. of Medicine, Ohio State U., 1914—. Republican. Presbyn. Home: Westerville, O. Died Mar. 6, 1934.

SCOTT, Francis Markoe, judge; b. New York, Mar. 14, 1848; s. Thomas and Eleanor A.S.; A.B., Coll. City of New York, 1867, A.M., 1869; LL.B., Columbia, 1869; m. Lucy Parkman Higgins, Oct. 2, 1878. Asst. corp. counsel, New York; aqueduct commr., 1888-95; corp. counsel, 1895-97; justice Supreme Ct. of N.Y., 1st Dist., 1898-1918 (resigned); resumed practice as mem. firm Scott, Gerard & Bowers. Democrat. Home: New York, N.Y. Died Feb. 5, 1922.

SCOTT, Frank Hall, publisher; b. Terre Haute, Ind., Apr. 7, 1848; s. William Clement and Maria Frances (Crawford) S.; ed. Richmond (Ind.) pub. schs. to 1865, Pa. Mil. Acad.; L.H.D., Marietta Coll., O., 1894; m. Julia Draper Davis, March 27, 1878. Entered office of Scribner's Monthly, 1870; pres. The Century Co., pubs., 1893—. Home: New York, N.Y. Died Nov. 25, 1912.

SCOTT, Frank Hamline, lawyer; b. Tipton, Ia., Jan. 1, 1857; s. Washington and Amelia (Kline) S.; A.M., Northwestern U., 1876; LL.B., Union Coll. of Law, Chicago, 1878; m. Edith Kribben, 1882; children—Bertram Delafield, Marion Sturges (wife of Capt. Julian A. Soames). Engaged in general practice of law at Chicago, 1878—; mem. Scott, Bancroft, Martin & MacLeish. Democrat. Home: Chicago, Ill. Died Oct. 11, 1931.

SCOTT, Fred Newton, univ. prof.; b. Terre Haute, Ind., Aug. 20, 1860; s. Judge Harvey D. and Mary (Bannister) S.; A.B., U. of Mich., 1884, A.M., 1888, Ph.D., 1889; m. Isadore Thompson, 1887; children—Harvey Davis, Mrs. Marion Lynd Goodrich, Richard Cushman; m. 2d, Georgia Jackson, 1923. Asst. librarian, 1884-85, 1887-89, instr. English, 1889-90, asst. prof. rhetoric, 1890-96, jr. prof., 1896-1901, prof., 1901-21, prof. rhetoric and journalism, 1921-27; emeritus prof. of rhetoric, 1927—, U. of Mich.; univ. editor, 1897-1900. Pres. Modern Lang. Assn. America, 1907, Nat. Council of Teachers of English, 1911-13, N. Central Assn. Colls. and Secondary Schs., 1913, Am. Assn. Teachers Journalism, 1917. Author: Memorable Passages from the Bible, 1906; Selections from the Old Testament, 1910. Joint author: Paragraph Writing, 1893; Composition-Rhetoric, 1897; Introduction to Literary Criticism, 1899; Elementary English Composition, 1900; Composition-Literature, 1902; The Teaching of English, 1903; Aphorisms for Teachers of English Composition, 1905; Brief English Grammar, 1905; Lessons in English, Books I and II, 1906; The Standard of American Speech, 1926. Editor: Contributions to Rhetorical Theory. Contbr. to mags. and philol. jours. and to Internat. Ency. Translator: (with C. L. Meader) Plays by Leonid Andreyeff, 1915. Mem. Conf. of Am. and Brit. Professors of English, U. of London, 1920; mem. Internat. Council on English. Home: Ann Arbor, Mich. Died May 29, 1930.

SCOTT, Frederic William, banker; b. Petersburg, Va., Aug. 30, 1862; s. Frederic Robert and Sarah Frances (Branch) S.; student Princeton, 1881-82; m. Elisabeth Strother, Oct. 18, 1893; children—Buford, Mrs. Edward C. Anderson, Mrs. John H. Bocock, Fred W., Jr., Mrs. William T. Reed, Jr. Mem. firm Arrington & Scott, tobacconists, Richmond, Va., 1884-90, Shelburne & Scott, leaf tobacco, 1893-1900; Thomas Branch & Co., bankers and brokers, 1889-91, Scott & Stringfellow, 1893—. Widely known in connection with reorganization of various concerns, among them the M. Rumely Co., the Chesapeake & Ohio Ry., the Internat. Mercantile Marine Co.; dir. Atlantic Coast Line R.R. (finance com.), L.&N. R.R. Co. (finance com.), General Am. Investors Co. Apptd. Mar. 1918, mem. Division Finance and Purchases, under U.S. Railway Adminstrn. Rector of U. of Va. Mem. Va. Vols. (state militia), 1883-90, advancing to capt. on staff. Democrat. Episcopalian. Home: Richmond, Va. Died Sept. 24, 1939.

SCOTT, George Eaton, pres. Am. Steel Foundries; b. St. Louis, Mo., 1871. Began with Simmons Hardware Co., St. Louis, 1887; settled in Chicago, 1901; v.p. Simplex Ry. Appliance Co., 1901-05; v.p. Am. Steel Foundries, 1905-29, pres., 1929—; dir. Harris Trust and Savings Bank, Chicago Daily News, Griffin Wheel Co., The Wahl Co., Personal Loan and Savings Bank. Gen. mgr. and mem. Am. Red Cross War Council, 1917-19; mem. exec. com. Am. Red Cross, 1919—. Pres. Izaak Walton Conservation Foundation. Republican. Home: Lake Forest, Ill. Died Jan. 11, 1939.

SCOTT, Guy Charles, jurist; b. Henderson County, Ill., Aug. 14, 1863; s. Samuel and Sarah E. (Wilson) S.; ed. pub. schs. and student Knox Coll.; admitted to bar, 1886; m. Jessie Irvin, June 11, 1891. County clerk, Mercer County, Ill., 1887; mayor Aledo, Ill., 1895-99 and 1901-03; del. Nat. Dem. Conv., 1892; justice Sup. Ct. of Ill., 1903—, chief justice, 1906-07. Democrat. Mason. Home: Aledo, Ill. Died 1909.

SCOTT, Harriet Maria, educator; ed. at home and in private schools and Ind. State Normal Sch., unmarried. Prin. Detroit Normal Training Sch., 1886-99, with the exception of 1 yr., 1890-91; acting prof. pedagogy, Throop Poly. Inst., 1902-03. One of State officers Calif. Congress of Mothers and Child Study Circles; lecturer on ednl. topics. Author: Organic Education, 1897, 99. Address: Pasadena, Calif. Died 1906.

SCOTT, Harvey W., newspaper editor; b. in Tazewell County, Ill., Feb. 1, 1838; removed to Ore., 1852; reared on farm; worked at various occupations; classical edn. Editor, 1865—, also part owner, Portland Oregonian. Republican. Address: Portland, Ore. Died 1910.

SCOTT, Henry Tiffany, mfr.; b. on farm, Baltimore County, Md., Sept. 20, 1846; s. John and Elizabeth (Lettig) S.; ed. country schs. and Lamb's U.; worked on farm and later engaged in mercantile business in Baltimore, Md.; removed to San Francisco, Calif., 1867; m. Elsie Horsley. Entered employ of Union Iron Works as timekeeper, continuing in various positions until 1875, when became mem. and pres. Prescott, Scott & Co., purchasers of the works; co. incorporated, 1883, of which became 1st v.p., pres. and chmn. of the bd., pres. Mercantile Nat. Bank; chmn. bd. Pacific Telephone & Telegraph Co. Home: Burlingame, Calif. Died June 27, 1927.

SCOTT, Hugh Lenox, officer U.S.A.; b. Danville, Ky., Sept. 22, 1853; s. Rev. Wm. M. Scott and Mary E. Hodge, g.g.d. of Benjamin Franklin; grad. U.S. Mil. Acad., 1876; L.H.D., Princeton, 1910; LL.D., Columbia; L.M.S., Chester (Pa.) Mil. Acad., 1916; m. Mary, d. Gen. Lewis Merrill, June 1880; children—David Hunter, Anna Merrill, Lewis Merrill, Mary Blanchard, Sarah H. Merrill. Second lt. 9th Cavalry, June 15, 1876; transferred to 7th Cavalry, June 26, 1876; promoted through grades to maj. gen. U.S.A., April 30, 1915. Served in the Sioux expedition, 1876; Nez Percé expedition, 1877; Camp Robinson, Neb., and Cheyenne expdn., 1878; routine duty, principally with Indians of the Plains, 1878-91; hon. mention from War Dept., Okla., 1891; in charge in investigation of Ghost Dance distubrances, 1890-91; enlisted and comd. Kiowa, Comanche and Apache Indians, troop L, 7th Cav., 1892, until mustered out after 5 yrs.' enlistment (last Indian troop mustered out); in charge Geronimo's band Chiricahua Apaches, 1894-97. On duty at Bur. Ethnology, Smithsonian Instn., writing work on sign language, Plains Indians, N. America, Nov. 1897; adj. gen. of Cuba, 1898-1903; gov. Sulu Archipelago and comdg. military post of Jolo, P.I., 1903-06; abolished slavery and the slave trade in the Sulu Archipelago; supt. and comdt. U.S. Mil. Acad., with rank of col., Sept. 1, 1906-Aug. 31, 1910. On duty, Mar. and Apr. 1908, settling troubles of Navajos in N.M. and Mexican Kickapoos in Ariz. for Interior Dept.; again in 1911, for same dept., trouble with Hopi Indians at Hotevilla, Ariz.; engaged in settlement, for War and Interior depts., of Apache prisoners of war, Okla. and N.M., 1912; comdg. 3d Cav., Ft. Sam Houston, Tex., 1912; comdg. 2d Cav. Brigade and patrol on Mexican border, 1913-14. Settled by diplomacy Navajo Indian trouble at Beautiful Mountain, Ariz., Nov. 1913; asst. chief of Gen. Staff, U.S.A., Apr. 22, 1914; settled by diplomacy impending conflict on Mexican border at Naco, Ariz., Jan. 1915, as well as on two other occasions at El Paso, Tex.; settled Piute Indian trouble, Bluff, Utah, Mar. 1915; recovered property of foreigners confiscated by General Villa in Mexico, Aug. 1915. Chief of staff U.S.A., Nov. 17, 1914-Sept. 22, 1917 (laid basis for participation of U.S. in war with Germany); retired by operation of law, Sept. 22, 1917, but retained on active duty to May 12, 1919; chmn. State Highway Commn. of N.J., 1923—. Mem. U.S. Commn. to Russia, 1917; apptd. comdr. 78th Div. and Camp Dix, N.J., Dec. 26, 1917; served with a British div. in the front line at Arras and with a French div. in front line at Chalons; present at battle for Passchendal Ridge, 1917; inspected line from Verdun to Ypres. Awarded D.S.M., 1918. Mem. Bd. of Indian Commrs., 1919—. Hon. mem. many socs. and clubs, and of various Indian tribes. Mason (33°). Author: Some Memories of a Soldier, 1928; also various monographs and reports relating to Plains Indians. Home: Princeton, N.J. Died Apr. 30, 1934.

SCOTT, Hugh McDonald, Congl. clergyman; b. Guysborough, N.S., March 31, 1848; s. John Henry and Sarah (McDonald) S.; grad. Dalhousie Coll., Halifax, N.S., 1870; grad. in divinity, U. of Edinburgh, Scotland, 1873; studied in Berlin, 1873, and in Leipzig, 1878-81; D.D., Beloit Coll., 1884; ordained to ministry, 1874; m. Helen Grace Galdwin, May 3, 1883. Pastor Presbyn. Ch., Merigomish, N.S., 1874-78; prof. eccles. history, Chicago Theol. Sem., 1881—. Author: Section on Church History, in Current Discussion in Theology, annual published 1883-90; The Nicene Theology (Stone lectures before Princeton Theol. Sem.), 1896, Chicago Sem. Press. Cntbr. to theol. reviews and mags. on church history. Address: Chicago, Ill. Died 1909.

SCOTT, Irving Murray, v.p. and gen. mgr. Union Iron Works, San Francisco; b. of Quaker parentage, Hebron Mills, Baltimore County, Md., Dec. 25, 1837; ed. Milton, Md., Acad., and Baltimore Mechanics' Inst.; entered factory of Obed Hussey, mfr. reaping machinery, Baltimore, later in other works; became expert draftsman and engr. and went to Calif.; draftsman, supt. and later partner in Union Iron Works, San Francisco; designed machinery for working Comstock mines; invented improved cut-off engines and other machines; several terms pres. Mechanics' Inst., and of the Art Assn. of San Francisco; regent U. of Calif., and trustee of Leland Stanford, Jr., U. Builder of battleship Oregon and others for U.S. navy; went to St. Petersburg, 1898, to advise Russian govt. in regard to building of war ships. Address: San Francisco, Calif. Died 1903.

SCOTT, Isaiah Benjamin, bishop; b. Woodford County, Ky., Sept. 30, 1854; s. Benjamin and Polly (Anderson) S.; student Clark Sem. (now Coll.), Atlanta, Ga., 1874-77; A.B., Central Tenn. Coll. (now Walden U.), Nashville, 1880, A.M., 1883; studied theology, 1880-81; D.D., New Orleans U., 1893; m. Mattie J. Evans, May 1881; children—Evans Braden (dec.), Annie Laura (dec.), Cornelia Belle, Marie Adele (dec.), Mabel Etta, Ira Benjamin. Entered Tenn. Conf., M.E. Ch., 1881, then transferred to Texas Conf.; prof. in Prairie View State Normal and Industrial Coll., 1881; pastor, Houston, Galveston, Austin, Simpson and Marshall, Tex., 1882-87; presiding elder, Marshall and Houston dists., 1887-93; pres. Wiley U., Texas, 1893-96; editor Southwestern Christian Advocate, New Orleans, 1896-1904; elected bishop for Africa, May 1904. Elected to Gen. Conf., 1888, 92, 96, 1900 and 04 by Tex. Ann. Conf.; mem. Ecumenical Confs., Washington, D.C., 1891, London, Eng., 1901, Toronto, Can., 1911. Retired from active work, 1916. Home: Nashville, Tenn. Died July 4, 1931.

SCOTT, Jeannette, artist; b. Kincardine, Ont., Sept. 26, 1864; d. of John and Jeanette (Brown) S.; ed. West Phila. pub. schs., and later studied drawing at Sch. of Design for Women, Pa. Acad. Fine Arts; studied in Paris, 1889-94, and during that time exhibited pictures in Salon de Champs de Mars (now Société Nationale des Beaux Arts); hon. A.M., Syracuse, 1909, Dr. Fine Arts, 1927. Returned to New York, 1894; prof. painting, 1895, head painting dept., 1902, Syracuse U. (emeritus, 1927). Spent year, 1902-03, in Paris, and again exhibited at Société Nationale; exhibited Chicago Expn., 1893, and later at Pa. Acad. Fine Arts, New York Acad. and local exhbns. Rep. in permanent collection of Syracuse Mus. Fine Arts. Address: Skaneateles, N.Y. Died Nov. 16, 1937.

SCOTT, John, farmer; b. Jefferson County, O., Apr. 14, 1824; s. John S. (of Scotch-Irish ancestry); ed. Franklin Coll., New Athens, O.; studied law, Steubenville, O.; admitted to practice by Supreme Court, 1845; m. Mary S. Wright, Nov. 24, 1863. Pvt. Ky. mounted vols., 1846-47; captured at Encarnaçion with Cassius M. Clay, Jan. 1847; mem. Iowa State senate, 1860; lt. col. 3d Iowa inf., 1861; col. 32d Iowa inf., 1862-64; lt. gov. Iowa, 1868; U.S. assessor internal revenue, 1870-71; pres. State Agrl. Soc., 1872-73; pres. State Improved Stock Breeders' Assn., State Road Improvement Assn. Mem. State senate in 1886; pres. State Soc. of Scotch-Irish; pres. Pioneer Law Makers' Assn. Republican. Publisher Kentucky Whig, Mt. Sterling, Ky., 1852-54; Farmers' Journal, Cedar Rapids, Ia., 1872. Mason; grand master, Iowa, 1870. Author: Encarnacion, or the Prisoners in Mexico, 1848; Hugh Scott and His Descendants; History of the Thirty-second Iowa Infantry. Address: Des Moines, Ia. Died 1903.

SCOTT, John Prindle, composer; b. Norwich, N.Y., Aug. 16, 1877; s. Warren L. and Delia (Prindle) S.; student Oberlin Conservatory and Coll. 4 yrs.; unmarried. Teacher of singing, Saginaw, Mich., 2 yrs.; concert singer 10 yrs. Composer of about 70 published works, including songs, ensemble numbers, piano pieces, etc.; active as a leader in community singing, and leader in choruses of settlement houses. Awarded prize from State of Neb., for musical setting for Ode, from Ohio U., for college song. Home: MacDonough, N.Y. Died Dec. 2, 1932.

SCOTT, John William, merchant; b. Ottawa, Ill., Mar. 24, 1870; s. John Edwin and Harriet Emma (Hossack) S.; Brown U., 1886-87; m. Emilie Cluett, Oct. 3, 1899; children—Elizabeth Cluett (Mrs. Edward Kenneth Welles), Barbara (Mrs. Donald P. Welles). Entered service of Carson Pirie Scott & Co., wholesale and retail dry goods, Chicago, 1889; admitted to partnership in firm Jan. 1, 1901; dir. Internat. Harvester Co. Served as dir. Textile and Rubber Div. of War Industries Bd., World War I. Vice pres. Presbyn. Hosp., Newberry Library; vice chmn. Chicago Chapter Am. Red Cross. Republican. Conglist. Home: Hubbard Woods, Ill. Died May 6, 1932.

SCOTT, Julia Green (Mrs. Matthew T. Scott), president gen. D.A.R.; b. Danville, Ky.; d. Rev. Lewis Warner (D.D., LL.D.) and Mary Peachy (Fry) Green; ed. at Richmond, Va., and New York; m. Matthew T. Scott (died 1891). Managed an estate of 8,000 acres in Central Ill. and 4,000 acres in Ia., 1891—; pres. McLean County Coal Co., Bloomington, Ill. Elected pres. gen. Nat. Soc. D.A.R., Apr. 1909, reëlected Apr. 1911. Established the Matthew T. Scott Inst. at Phelps, Ky., as a memorial to her husband; interested in promoting welfare of mountain whites in various Southern states; state and nat. chmn. Ft. Massac Commn.; sec. Home Missionary Bd. of Presbyn. Ch. of Ill.; mem. Woman's Council of George Washington U. Sec. war relief service com. and chmn. Fatherless Orphans of France and Restoration of Tilloloy, of Nat. Soc. D.A.R.; chmn. peace com. Washington Fed. Woman's Clubs; mem. U.D.C., and mem. or hon. mem. many other orgns. Home: Bloomington, Ill. Died Apr. 29, 1923.

SCOTT, Julian, battle and figure painter; b. Johnson, Vt., Feb. 14, 1846; in Union army, 1861-63; awarded a medal of honor by Congress; studied art at Nat. Acad. of Design and under Emanuel Leutzè; assoc. Nat. Acad., 1870—; m. Mary, dau. William Burns, founder New York Sunday Despatch, Oct. 12, 1870. Apptd., 1890, spl. Govt. agt. to report upon condition of Kiowa, Comanche, Wichita and other Indians in Okla., the Pueblos of N.Mex. and Ariz. and the Navajos. Spent 3 years at this work with results embodied in the Report of Indians Taxed and Indians Not Taxed of the United States at the Eleventh Census. Address: Plainfield, N.J. Died 1901.

SCOTT, Leroy, author; Fairmount, Ind., May 11, 1875; s. Eli J. and Eleanor (Reader) S.; A.B., Ind. U., 1897; m. Miriam Finn, June 24, 1904; children—Helen, Hilda, David. In newspaper work, 1897-1900; asst. editor Woman's Home Companion, 1900-01; asst. headworker Univ. Settlement, New York, 1902-03; devoted entire time to writing, New York, 1904—. Author: The Walking Delegate, 1905; To Him That Hath, 1907; The Shears of Destiny, 1910; Counsel for the Defense, 1912; No. 13 Washington Square, 1914 (dramatization, 1915); Partners of the Night, 1916; Mary Regan, 1918; A Daughter of Two Worlds, 1919; Children of the Whirlwind, 1921; Cordelia the Magnificent, 1923; The Heart of Katie O'Doone, 1925; The Trail of Glory, 1926. Contbr. many serials and short stories to mags. Home: New York, N.Y. Died July 21, 1929.

SCOTT, Llewellyn Davis, educator; b. Caroline County, Va., Nov. 6, 1871; s. Frank Woolfolk and Julia Isabel (Mann) S.; grad. Randolph-Macon Coll., Ashland, Va., 1890; post-grad. work, Harvard, 1 term, 1897; m. Lila Lovelace, 1894 (died 1902); children—Llewelyn Davis (dec.), Francis Wyatt, Kendrick Lovelace (dec.); m. 2d, Josephine Lovelace, 1904 (died 1929); children—Alice Chandler (dec.), Josephine Lovelace, Mary Wyatt (Mrs. Gardner Cushman); m. 3d, Marguerite A. Cooper. Prof. Latin, Marion (Ala.) Mil. Inst., 1890-94; asso. prin., 1894-1904, prin., and pres., 1904—, Washington Sem. Democrat. Methodist; steward St. Mark's Ch. Address: Atlanta, Ga. Died June 5, 1939.

SCOTT, Lon Allen, congressman; b. Cypress Inn, Tenn., Sept. 25, 1888; s. Daniel E. and Mattie (Cash) S.; ed. Savannah Inst.; LL.B., Cumberland U., 1915 (valedictorian); unmarried. Jr. mem. firm D. E. Scott & Son, Savannah, Tenn., 1909—; pres. and mgr. Scott Land & Lumber Co., 1919—; pres. Tenn. River Lumber Co., Dixie Oil Co. of Savannah, Ga., and Selmer, Tenn. Mem. Tenn. Ho. of Rep., 1913-17; minority leader Rep. Party in Tenn., 1915-17; mem. 67th Congress (1921-23), 8th Tenn. Dist. Enlisted as pvt. World War I; commd. lt. and assigned as instr. at Quantico, Va. Republican. Mem. Christian (Disciples) Ch. Mason, K.P., Woodman, Moose. Home: Savannah, Tenn. Died Feb. 11, 1931.

SCOTT, Lucy Jameson, editor; b. Irasburg, Vt., Nov. 27, 1843; d. Alexander and Sarah Knowles (Locke) Jameson; grad. Newbury (Vt.) Sem. and Collegiate Inst., 1866 (valedictorian); m. Rev. Orange W. Scott, July 17, 1867. Taught dist. schs., summers, 1862-64, and 1 yr. in sem.; identified for many yrs. with W.C.T.U. and Woman's Foreign Missionary Soc. of M.E. Ch. Editor Junior Missionary Friend, pub. by Woman's Foreign Missionary Soc. of M.E. Ch. Author: Santa Claus Stories, 1875; David Douglas and His Wife, 1889; Gilead Guards, 1890; The Upstairs Family, 1898; Twelve Little Pilgrims Who Stayed at Home, 1900; In Circles of Light, 1907; also many booklets and leaflets. Home: Brooklyn, N.Y. Died Feb. 2, 1920.

SCOTT, Mary Augusta, coll. prof.; b. Dayton, Ohio, Dec. 29, 1851; d. Abraham MacLean and Julia Anne (Boyer) S.; sister of William Forse S. and Charles Payson Gurley S.; kinswoman of John Scott; cousin of Charles Thomas Forse; A.B., A.M., Vassar Coll.; mem. Newnham Coll., U. of Cambridge, Eng. (Moral Sciences Tripos), 1886-87; student in Romance langs., Johns Hopkins U., 1889-90; first woman fellow, Yale U., 1892-94, Ph.D., 1894. Prof. English lang. and lit., Smith Coll., 1902—. Author: Hugh Scott, an Immigrant of 1670, and His Descendants (with John Scott), 1895; The Book of the Courtyer; A Possible Source of Benedick and Beatrice, 1901; The Essays of Francis Bacon, with Introduction, Notes, and Index, 1908; The Italian Novella, 1911; Elizabethan Translations from the Italian, 1916; Ballads and Songs of the United States, 1916. Editor: Operative Gynecology, by Dr. Howard A. Kelly, 1898; Walter Reed and Yellow Fever, by Dr. Howard A. Kelly, 1906. Contbr. to The Dial, 1898—; also many review and critiques in lit. and academic jours., Am. and foreign. Address: Northampton, Mass. Died Mar. 28, 1918.

SCOTT, Nathan Bay, senator; b. Guernsey County, O., Dec. 18, 1841; s. David and Mary (Bay) S.; common sch. edn.; served in Union Army, 1862-65; settled at Wheeling after the war and engaged in mfr. of glass; pres. Central Glass Works for 42 yrs.; organized and became v.p. Dollar Savings & Trust Co. Pres. city council (2d branch), 1880-82; mem. W.Va. Senate, 1882-90; member Rep. Nat. Com., 1886-1912 (exec. com. most of time); collector internal revenue, 1898-99; U.S. senator from W.Va., 2 terms, 1899-1911. Mem. Lincoln Memorial Commn. Address: Washington, D.C. Died Jan 2, 1924.

SCOTT, Richard H., judge; s. Charles and Margaret (Hamilton) S.; m. Agnes C. Scott, July 1, 1885. Asso. justice Supreme Ct. of Wyo., Feb. 23, 1906—. Republican. Home: Cheyenne, Wyo. Died Sept. 26, 1917.

SCOTT, Richard John Ernst, M.D., writer, editor; b. Whitchurch, Hampshire, Eng., Jan. 7, 1863; s. Gerald Lewis and Marie (Lerche) S.; B.A., U. of Durham, Eng., 1885, M.A., 1889, B.C.L., 1893; M.D., Cornell U. Med. Coll., New York, 1899; m. Mary Josephine Platt Blackmore, Feb. 19, 1889. Practiced in New York, 1899—; attending phys., heart and lung dept., outdoor div. Bellevue Hosp., 1899-1903; gynecologist, Demilt Dispensary, 1901-12. Fellow New York Acad. Medicine. Author: State Board Examination Series (7 vols.), 1903-06. Contbr. Reference Handbook of the Medical Sciences. Editor and reviser of Witthaus' and Scott's Textbook of Chemistry, Witthaus' Essentials of Chemistry and Toxicology, Hughes' Practice of Medicine, Cyclo. of Practical Medicine and Surgery, Pocket Cyclo. of Medicine and Surgery, Gould's Practitioner's Medical Dictionary, Gould's New Medical Dictionary, Pocket Cyclo. of Nursing, Potter's Therapeutics, Materia Medica and Pharmacy. Contributing editor (med. topics) Winston's Cumulative Loose-leaf Ency.; spl. dept. editor (medicine), Winston's Simplified Dictionary. Mem. editorial staff Medical Record, 1905-22. Address: Brooklyn, N.Y. Died Oct. 24, 1932.

SCOTT, Robert Kingston, governor; b. in Armstrong County, Pa., July 8, 1826; ed. at common schools in Pa. and Central Coll. of Ohio; studied medicine at Navarre, O., and subsequently attended lectures at Starling Med. Coll., Columbus, O. In Calif., 1850-51; engaged in milling and medical practice; 1851-57 practiced medicine in Henry County, O.; then a merchant until 1861. Served in Union army, 1861-65 maj. to bvt. maj. gen.; then, Jan. 2, 1866 to 1868, asst. commr. Freedmen's Bur. in S.C.; gov. of S.C., 1868-72; in real estate business in Columbia, S.C., 1872-77; in like business in Ohio, 1877—. Address: Napoleon, Henry County, O. Died 1900.

SCOTT, Samuel Parsons, lawyer, author; b. Highland County, O., July 8, 1846; s. William and Elizabeth Jane (Parsons) S.; A.B., Miami (valedictorian, youngest in his class), 1866, A.M., 1887; m. Elizabeth Woodbridge Smart, Oct. 10, 1895. Admitted to bar, 1868, and in active practice at Leavenworth, Kan., and San Francisco, Calif., until 1875. Mem. Comparative Law Bur. of Am. Bar Assn. and editor of its Spanish department 20 years. Author: Through Spain, 1886; History of the Moorish Empire in Europe, 1904. Translator and editor of many works of ancient Spanish jurisprudence, including the Forum Judicum, 1910; Las Siete Partidas, 1912; El Fuero Viejo de Castilla; El Fuero Real; Las Leyes del Estilo; El Ordenamiento de Alcalá; Las Leyes Nuevas; El Ordenamiento de las Tafurerias; Las Leyes de Toro; Leyes para los Adelantados Mayores, 1913; El Código Penal de España, 1914; Corpus Juris Civilis. Home: Hillsboro, O. Died May 30, 1929.

SCOTT, Sutton Selwyn, lawyer, farmer; b. Huntsville, Ala., Nov. 26, 1829; s. James G. and Ann (Biddle) S.; grad. East Tenn. Univ. (now U. of Tenn.), 1850; m. Loula Marie Hurt, Nov. 10, 1864. Mem. Ala. legislature from Madison County, 1857-58 and 1859-60; trustee U. of Ala., 1860; Confederate Commr. of Indian Affairs, 1863; del. to Ala. Constitutional Conv., 1875; del. to Nat. Dem. Conv., Cincinnati, 1880; mem. legislature from Russell County, Ala., 1884 and 1890; U.S. commr. to adjudicate claims in N. Mex. and Colo., 1885-87; chmn. commn. to the Indians of Utah, 1894-96. Democrat. Author: Southbooke—Southern Tales and Sketches, 1880; The Mobilians: or Talks about the South, 1897; and numerous articles to periodicals over his own signature and different pen-names. Address: Auburn, Ala. Died 1907.

SCOTT, Thomas Morton, soldier; b. Cadiz, O., June 25, 1824; s. James and Harriet (Arnold) S.; lineal descendant of Thomas Scott, mem. English Parliament, and one of com. which signed death warrant of Charles I; acad. edn.; moved to Louisville, Ky., 1844; m. sister of Capt. Z. M. Shirley, May 1851. Sergt. maj., 1st Ky. Inf., in Mexican War: participated in battles of Monterey and Buena Vista; in Calif., 1849-51; comd. troop of vols. against hostile Indians. Lived in Tex., 1852—; raised Co. I, 9th Tex. Inf., C.S.A.; served through war as capt. and a.a.g.; assisted in making peace treaties with 160 wild Indian tribes who had been depredating in Tex., May 1865. Mem. bd. of dirs. State Agrl. and Mech. Coll. and Prairie View Normal Sch., 1876-86; bus. agt. same, 1886-90; col. on Gov. Roberts' staff 2 yrs.; mem. bd. trustees and financial agt. Add Ran Christion U., Texas, 1892-97—; again mem. bd. of trustees, June 1898—. Apptd. lt. col. and a.d.c. on staff Gov. Lanham, 1903; lt. col. and chief q.m. on staff Maj. Gen. K. M. Van Zandt, comdg. Tex. Div. U.C.V.; v.p. for Tex. Nat. Assn. Mexican War Vets.; bvtd. maj. gen. U.C.V., 1906. Address: Melissa, Collin County, Tex. Died Mar. 6, 1911.

SCOTT, Tully, judge; b. St. Paris, O., July 12, 1857; s. David and Mary J. (Lippincott) S.; ed. high sch., St. Paris; Kansas State Agrl. Coll. (non grad.); m. Harriet I. Hunter, Dec. 24, 1891. Admitted to Kan. bar, 1880; practiced at Beloit; receiver pub. moneys, Oberlin, Kan., under appmt. of President Cleveland, 1885-89; removed to Cripple Creek, Colo., 1901; mem. Colo. State Senate, 1907-11; apptd. presiding judge Colo. Ct. of Appeals, 1911-12; asso. justice Supreme Ct. of Colo., 1913-23. Democrat. Baptist. Home: Denver, Colo. Died May 4, 1924.

SCOTT, Walter, merchant, philanthropist; b. Montreal, Can., Dec. 22, 1861; s. Walter and Mary (Sharp) S.; moved to Boston with parents, 1864; ed. pub. schs. With Butler Bros., wholesale general mdse., 1877, mgr. New York br. 1889-1932; retired. Long a leader in Order of Scottish Clans of U.S. and Can., and active mem. many other Scottish socs.; colonel of the New York Scottish Highlanders. Endowed scholarships in Smith Coll., Stevens Inst. Tech., Am. Internat. Coll., etc.; large donor of prizes for Scottish events, also, Walter Scott medals for valor for members of police and fire depts. in leading cities of U.S., also in the Argentine and Ireland. Pres. Walter Scott Free Industrial Sch. for Crippled Children, New York; a founder of Broad Street Hosp. Pres. Stevenson Soc. of America. Hon. police commr. of N.Y. City. Chevalier Legion of Honor (France); mem. Order of Leopold (Belgium). Awarded Silver Grand Cross of Austria. Republican. Baptist. Office: New York, N.Y. Died Nov. 28, 1935.

SCOTT, Wilfred Welday, prof. chemistry; b. Zanesville, O., Aug. 13, 1876; s. Thomas Jefferson and Mary Elizabeth (Worthington) S.; A.B., Ohio Wesleyan U., 1897, A.M., 1901; studied Cornell U., 1903-05, U. of Chicago, summer 1909; Sc.D., Colo. Sch. of Mines, 1923; m. Harriet Eleanora Torbet, July 30, 1907; children—Margaret Elizabeth, Winifred Harriet. Instr. Philander Smith Coll., Naini Tal, India, 1898-1901; prof. chemistry, Morningside Coll., Sioux City, Ia., 1905-10; chief chemist Baldwin Locomotive Works, Phila., 1910-11; chemist Gen. Chem. Co., New York, 1911-21; prof. chemistry, Colo. Sch. of Mines, 1921-25; prof. chemistry, U. of Southern Calif., 1925—. Republican. Methodist. Author: Qualitative Chemical Analysis, 1910; Standard Methods of Chemical Analysis (2 vols.), 1917; Technical Methods of Metallurgical Analysis, 1923; Inorganic Quantitative Chemical Analysis, 1926; Chemical Methods of Metallurgical Analysis, 1927; Elements of Qualitative Chemical Analysis, 1932; Essentials of Quantitative Chemical Analysis, 1930; also various tech. monographs. Co-editor: Our Clan—Scott, 1921. Address: Los Angeles, Calif. Died May 3, 1932.

SCOTT, Will, prof. zoölogy; b. Houston, Ind., Apr. 20, 1877; s. Adam and Priscilla Ann (Clark) S.; grad. Ind. State Normal Sch., Terre Haute, 1905; Donaldson fellow in zoölogy, Ind. U., 1907-08, A.B., A.M., 1908, Ph.D., 1911; m. Naomi Florence Crumbaugh, June 18, 1907; 1 dau., Mary Frances. Instr. in zoölogy, Ind. U., 1908-11, asst. prof. zoölogy, 1911-19, asso. prof., 1919-21, prof., 1921—. Investigator of fisheries problems, Ind. Conservation Commn., 1926—; dir. Ind. U. Biol. Sta., 1920—. Fellow A.A.A.S., Ind. Acad. Science. Democrat. Methodist. Mason. Home: Bloomington, Ind. Died Oct. 17, 1937.

SCOTT, William lawyer; b. Huntingdon, Pa., May 8, 1850; s. John and Annie E. (Eyster) S.; grad. Princeton, 1868; studied law; admitted to bar, 1878; m. Annie L. King, Sept. 16, 1880. Practiced law in Pittsburgh, 1878—. Home: Pittsburgh, Pa. Died 1906.

SCOTT, William Earl Dodge, naturalist; b. Brooklyn, N.Y., Apr. 22, 1852; s. Moses Warren (U.S.A.) and Juliet Ann (Cornell) S.; A.B., Harvard, 1873; m. Marian, d. James Johonot, June 22, 1877. Curator, Princeton, 1874-85, curator dept. ornithology, Princeton, 1897—. Did field work for Brit. Mus., Am. Mus. Natural History, Mus. of Comparative Zoölogy, etc. Author: Bird Studies, 1897; Story of a Bird Lover, 1902; Birds of Patagonia, Part I, 1903, Part II, 1910; also 60 tech. papers on birds in scientific jours., and popular articles in mags. Address: Princeton, N.J. Died 1910.

SCOTT, William Henry, printing; b. Phila., Pa., May 4, 1846; s. John and Elizabeth (McFee) S.; ed. Central High Sch., Phila.; m. Martha J. Parr, Dec. 22, 1874. Organized firm of Allen, Lane & Scott, book and job printers, 1872, and became sole propr.; dir. Germantown Trust Co. Especially interested in S.S., ch., and charitable instns.; trustee Germantown Hosp., Lincoln U., Presbyn. Bd. of Publ., Whosoever Gospel Mission. Republican. Presbyn. Home: Germantown, Phila., Pa. Died Apr. 12, 1920.

SCOTT, William R., ry. official; b. Nov. 8, 1860; ed. public schools. Began as locomotive fireman, A.,T.&S.F. Ry., 1881; locomotive engr., 1884-91, traveling engr., 1891-98, same rd.; trainmaster Northern div., Gulf, Colo. & Santa Fe Ry., 1898-1900; div. supt. same rd., at Cleburne, Tex., 1900-01; gen. supt. Ft. Worth & Denver City Ry., 1901-03; asst. supt. Sacramento div. S.P. Co., Sept.-Nov. 1903; supt. Salt Lake div., 1903-05, Western div., 1905-07, gen. supt. Northern dist., Sept.-Nov. 1907, asst. gen. mgr., 1907-12, gen. mgr., 1912, later v.p. and gen. mgr. S.P. Co.; apptd. federal mgr. S.P. Western Pacific, Deep Creek, and Tidewater Southern rys., July 1, 1918; pres. S.P. Tex. and La. lines, Mar. 1, 1920—. Office: Houston, Tex. Died Dec. 20, 1926.

SCOTT, William Sherley, army officer; b. McKinney, Tex., Jan. 12, 1856; s. Col. Thomas M. and Elizabeth M. (Sherley) S.; m. Nelle Z. Hastings, Nov. 30, 1887 (dec.). Grad. U.S. Mil. Acad., 1880, Inf. and Cav. Sch., 1887; Army War Coll., 1908. Commd. 2d lt. 1st Cav., June 12, 1880; promoted through the grades successively to rank of brig. gen. U.S.A., Oct. 14, 1918; retired by operation of law, Jan. 12, 1920, age of 64. Commd. capt. asst. adj. gen. vols., May 9, 1898; maj. A.A.G., Sept. 17, 1898-May 12, 1899; lt. col. 44th Vol. Inf., 1899-1901; col. and asst. chief Philippine Constabulary, 1903-06; brig. gen. N.A., Aug. 5, 1917, vacated by apptmt. to brig. gen. regular army, Oct. 1918. Sec. Inf. and Cav. Sch., 1890-94; adj. 1st Cav., 1894-98; asst. adj. gen. 7th Army Corps, 1898-99, of Philippine Div., 1902-03; adj. gen. Dept. of Tex., 1910-13; in charge militia affairs Southern Dept., adj. 1st Cav. Brigade, and chief of staff 15th Militia Div., 1913-16; comdg. 1st O.T.C., Leon Springs, Tex., May-Aug. 1917. Participated in Sioux Indian Campaign, 1890-91, in Cuba and Puerto Rico, Spanish-Am. War, 1898-99, Philippine Insurrection, 1899-1901; recommended for brig. gen. vols. for suppressing insurrection and securing surrender insurgent forces, World War I; comdg. 59th Brigade Aug.-Sept. 22, and 30th div., Camp Seiver, Greenville, S.C., to Nov. 8, 1917; comdg. Base Sect. 2, Bordeaux, France, Dec. 3, 1917-Aug. 10, 1918; in charge constrn. and training area of S.W. France. commdg. 41st Div. in France, Aug.-Nov. 1918, 153d Depot Brigade, Camp Dix, N.J., to Dec. 15, 1918; comdg. Ft. Oglethorpe, Ga., and demobilization center, Dec. 18, 1918-Oct. 26, 1919; comdg. Ft. Sam Houston, Tex., to Jan. 12, 1920. Decorations: Gold Medalist Army Team; medals Indian Wars, Spanish-Am. War, Cuban Occupation, Puerto Rican Campaign, Mexican Border, World War; Officer Legion of Honor (France), 1919. V.p. Sam Houston State Bank & Trust Co., 1920-23, pres., 1923-32; chmn. bd. Nat. Bank of Fort Sam Houston, 1932—. Address: San Antonio, Tex. Died Aug. 31, 1941.

SCOTTEN, Samuel Chatman, commission mcht.; b. Burlington, Ia., Oct. 31, 1851; s. Samuel C., Sr., and Mary (Campbell) S.; ed. pub. schs.; m. Susie Colman. Began as clk. in grocery store, 1861; in grain and commn. business, Chicago, 1878—; mem. J. F. Harris & Co., later Harris, Gates & Co., Inc., 1903, as Harris, Scotten Co., of which became pres.; mem. Scotten & Snydacker, 1907—; dir. Nat. Bank of Republic, C.,B.&Q. R.R., Pacific Fisheries Co., Colonial Land Co., Ill. Timber Co., etc. Home: Chicago, Ill. Died Aug. 5, 1920.

SCOTTI, Antonio, baritone; b: Naples, Italy, Jan. 25, 1868; s. Domenico and Luisa S.; studied under Mme. Trifari Paganini, Naples (his only teacher); unmarried. Début as Amonarso in "Aïda," at Teatro Reale, Malta, 1889; appeared in many other theatres of Italy and spent 6 seasons in S. America; engagements in Madrid, St. Petersburg, Moscow, Warsaw and Odessa; sang in "Don Giovanni," in London, under management of Maurice Grau, 1899, and was engaged for the Met. Opera Co., New York for season 1899-1900, and later returned to appear for many yrs. as Don Giovanni, Scarpia, Tonio, Falstaff, Iago, Amonasro, and in many other leading parts of best known operas. Home: Naples, Italy. Died Feb. 26, 1936.

SCOULLER, James Brown, United Presbyn. clergyman; b. Newville, Pa., July 12, 1820; grad. Dickinson Coll., 1839, A.M., Dickinson; D.D., Muskingum Coll., Ohio; m. Helen I. Niven, June 21, 1848; in active pastorates 20 years; wrote regularly for papers of United Presbyn. church, 1844—. Author: A Manual of the United Presbyn. Church; also histories of the Big Spring and Argyle Presbyteries and New York Synod of the same church. Address: Newville, Pa. Died 1899.

SCOULLER, John Crawford, clergyman; b. Fair Haven, O., Nov. 3, 1858; s. Rev. John Young (D.D.) and Eleanor (Beckett) S.; A.B., Washington and Jefferson Coll., Washington, Pa., 1880; grad. Pittsburgh Theol. Sem., 1883; m. Mary Fulton, Sept. 16, 1884. Ordained ministry U.P. Ch., 1883; pastor Uniontown, O., 1883-88, Greenville, Pa., 1888-96, 4th Ch., Phila., 1896-1918; sec. Bd. Ministerial Relief, U.P. Ch. of N.A., May 30, 1907—. Moderator Gen. Assembly U.P. Ch., 1911. Trustee Franklin (O.) Coll., Deaconess Sch. of Presbyn. and Ref. Chs., Phila. Republican. Home: Philadelphia, Pa. Died Jan. 11, 1925.

SCOVEL, Sylvester, engr. and promoter Cuban enterprises; b. Denny Station, Allegheny County, Pa., July 29, 1869; s. Rev. Sylvester F. and Caroline (Woodruff) S.; ed. pub. sch., Pittsburgh, and U. of Wooster, O.; grad. Mich. Mil. Acad., 1887; spent portions of 4 yrs. at U. of Mich., working between times; m. Frances, d. S. Carr Cabanné, Apr. 5, 1897. From 19 to 26 yrs. of age continuously time-keeper in blast furnace constrn., Tenn.; asst. supt. water works constrn., Ky.; mech. draughtsman, Pittsburgh; promoter, Chicago, and Cleveland, O., Oct. 5, 1895; sent to Cuba as war corr. Pittsburgh Dispatch and New York Herald; made prisoner, Havana, Jan. 1896; escaped; entered employ New York World; injured in field; lived with insurgents 11 months at different visits; ran Spanish mil. and police lines 20 times, going and coming from field; captured, Feb. 7, 1897, and imprisoned by Spaniards at Sancti Spiritus, Cuba; released by pressure of U.S. Govt., after legislatures of 13 States and U.S. senate had requested his release. Sent by The World to Turco-Greek war; then Spain; then to the Klondike; thence to Havana just before blowing up the "Maine"; then with U.S. navy and army until Am. occupation of Santiago and Spanish evacuation of Havana, Jan. 1, 1899; consulting engr. for U.S. mil. govt., Cuban customs service, 1899-1902. Address: Havana, Cuba. Died 1905.

SCOVEL, Sylvester Fithian, univ. prof.; b. Harrison, O., Dec. 29, 1835; s. Rev. Sylvester S. (pres. Hanover Coll., Ind.) and Hannah Cook (Matlack) S.; A.B., Hanover Coll., 1853, A.M., 1856; m. Caroline Woodruff, Oct. 6, 1857. Ordained Presbyn. ministry, 1857; pastor, Jeffersonville, Ind., 1857-61, Springfield, O., 1861-66, First Ch., Pittsburgh, Pa., 1866-83; Hoge prof. morals and sociology, 1883—, pres., 1883-98, acting pres., 1899, U. of Wooster, Del. Pan-Presbyn. Council, Phila., 1880, Glasgow, 1896, Jubilee meeting of Evang. Alliance, London, 1896, World's Parliament of Religions, 1893. Lecturer at Winona and Chautauqua (N.Y.), 1899. Pres. Nat. Reform Assn., 1897—; v.p. Am. Peace Assn., Am. Polit. Science Assn. Address: Wooster, O. Died 1910.

SCOVELL, Melville Amasa, chemist; b. Belvidere, N.J., Feb. 26, 1855; s. Nathan and Hannah (Aller)

S.; B.S., U. of Ill., 1875, M.S., 1877, Ph.D.; m. Nannie D. Davis, Sept. 8, 1880. Instr. of chemistry, 1875-76, asst. prof., 1876-80, prof. agrl. chemistry, 1880-84, U. of Ill.; mgr. sugar factories, 1884; spl. agt. U.S. Dept. Agr., 1884-85; dir. Ky. Agrl. Expt. Sta., 1885-1910; dir. Agrl. Expt. Sta. and dir. Agrl. Coll., State U., 1910—. Pres. park commn. of Lexington, Ky.; mem. Ky. State Fair Com.; mem. U.S. Food Standard Com.; in charge pure food control, fertilizer control, concentrated feed control and seed control work of State of Ky. Invented a process of clarifying cane juices by superheating (with Henry A. Weber), a method now extensively used; also modification in the Kjedahl method where nitrates are present. Fellow A.A.A.S., Soc. Chem. Industry, London; mem. Am. Acad. Polit. and Social Science; past pres. Assn. Official Agrl. Chemists; past pres. Am. Assn. Agrl. Colls. and Expt. Stas. Address: Lexington, Ky. Died 1912.

SCOVILLE, Robert; b. Buffalo, N.Y., Jan. 4, 1876; s. Nathaniel Church and Frances (Wasson) S.; ed. Berkeley Sch., N.Y. City; M.S., Conn. Agrl. Coll., 1918; M.A., Yale, 1918; m. Virginia Busen Benz, 1928. Mem. Conn. Ho. of Rep., 1901, 03; apptd. fed. food adminstr. for Conn., 1917. Pres. Salisbury Bank & Trust Co., Lakeville, Conn. Trustee and treas. Hotchkiss Sch., Lakeville, Conn., Agrl. Coll. Republican. Episcopalian. Mason, K.P., Elk. Home: Salisbury, Conn. Died Nov. 8, 1934.

SCREWS, William Wallace, editor; b. in Barbour, County, Ala., Feb. 25, 1839; s. Benjamin and Moning J. S.; ed. pvt. schs., Glennville, Ala.; studied law, 1858-59, in office of Watts, Judge & Jackson, Montgomery, Alabama; admitted to bar, 1859 (age 20), and practiced until 1861; m. Emily F. Holt, Apr. 25, 1867. Was opposed to secession, but went with his state. Went with 1st troops to Pensacola; took part in capture navy yard and Ft. Barancas; later lt. Co. G, 59th Ala. Regt.; saw hard service with Bragg's army in Ky., at Chickamauga, Knoxville and last 12 months of war with Lee in Va. Wrote letters to Montgomery Advertiser from army, and became identified with that paper after war. It was suppressed by Federal troops from Apr. 20 until July 20, 1865; connected with the editorial dept., 1865—; becoming pres. Advertiser Co. and editor-in-chief. Sec. of State of Ala., 1878-82; postmaster Montgomery, 1893-97; pres. Nat. Editorial Assn. Mem. standing com. P.E. Ch., Diocese of Ala.; lay del. from Ala. to P.E. Gen. Conv., Boston, 1904, Richmond, Va., 1907, Cincinnati, 1910. Grand high priest, Grand Chapter, Royal Arch Masons of Ala. Address: Montgomery, Ala. Died Aug. 8, 1913.

SCRIBNER, Arthur Hawley, publisher; b. New York, Mar. 15, 1859; s. Charles and Emma L. (Blair) S.; brother of Charles S.; A.B., Princeton, 1881; m. Helen C. Annan, Jan. 29, 1900. V.p. Charles Scribner's Sons (founded by his father, 1846), upon the incorporation of the business, 1903, pres., 1928—. A founder and 1st pres. Ivy Club, Princeton. Home: New York, N.Y. Died July 3, 1932.

SCRIBNER, Charles, publisher; b. New York, Oct. 18, 1854; s. Charles and Emma E. (Blair) S.; A.B., Princeton, 1875, Litt.D., 1925; m. Louise, d. Rev. Jared Bradley Flagg, Oct. 5, 1882; children—Mrs. Louise Schieffelin, Charles. Identified with Charles Scribner's Sons (founded by his father, 1846), 1875—, and became pres.; founded Scribner's Magazine; dir. Nat. Park Bank. Trustee Princeton U., Skidmore Coll. Republican. Home: New York, N.Y. Died Apr. 19, 1930.

SCRIBNER, Charles Ezra, elec. engr.; b. Mt. Vernon, O., Feb. 16, 1858; s. Charles Harvey and Mary Elizabeth (Morehouse) S.; ed. Toledo High School; D.Engring., U. of Vt., 1920; m. Marietta Margaret Brown, Dec. 1, 1880 (died 1920); children—Charles Harvey, Margaret Belle, Mary Etta (dec.). Began with Western Electric Mfg. Co., Chicago, 1876, firm name changed, 1882, to Western Electric Co., connected with New York office, 1908-16, as chief engr. in charge of development and experimental work; retired. Took out between 400 and 500 U.S. patents (3d in elec. field in U.S.) and filed between 600 and 700 applications; prin. inventions relate to telephone switchboards. Awarded Gold Medal, Paris Expn., 1900. Fellow Am. Inst. E.E. (mgr. 1912-13, v.p. 1913-15). Republican. Mem. Evangelical Ch. Home: Jericho, Vt. Died June 25, 1926.

SCRIBNER, Frank Kimball, author; b. New York, Feb. 22, 1867; s. Walter and Harriet A. (Kimball) S.; A.B., Williams, 1890; student Harvard Law Sch., 1893; m. Alice Margaret Hill, June 26, 1900. On staff New York Sun 4 yrs. Contbr. short stories, etc., to mags., 1889—. Author: The Honor of the Princess, 1897; The Love of the Princess Alice, 1898; The Fifth of November, 1898; In the Land of the Loom, 1899; A Maid of the Colonies, 1900; A Continental Cavalier, 1900; The Secret of Frontellac; also series Adirondack and Canadian hunting and fishing stories. Address: Cornwell-on-Hudson, New York. Died Nov. 10, 1935.

SCRIBNER, Gilbert Hilton, lawyer; b. Monroe County, N.Y., June 23, 1831; s. Sewell B. S.; ed. Oberlin Coll., O.; studied law under Hon. Daniel B. Taylor, of New York; practiced law, 1856-68; m. Sarah Woodbury, d. Hon. James O. Pettengill, Oct. 22, 1856. Mem. N.Y. legislature, 1869; sec. State N.Y., 1870-73; v.p. Central Park North and East River R.R. Co., 1873-80, pres., 1880-93; pres. Palisade Bank, Yonkers, N.Y., 1863. Was Whig; Republican, 1856—; pres. Young Men's State Rep. Assn., 1870; pres. New York Skin and Cancer Hosp., 1883-87; trustee Rochester Theol. Sem., 1871-78; dir. Bank of New Amsterdam from organization to 1893. Author: Where Did Life Begin? (monograph), 1883, in which he was first to originate, formulate and defend the theory of the circumpolar origin of life, which is being confirmed in many ways—particularly by the discovery of fossil remains in the eocene deposits of Wyo. Also writer of pamphlets on Taxation of Corporate Property, 1880-90; occasional contbr. to Popular Science Monthly, 1883—. Address: Yonkers, N.Y. Died 1910.

SCRIBNER, Harvey, lawyer; b. Mt. Vernon, O., Mar. 19, 1850; s. Judge Charles H. and Mary E. S.; grad. pub. school; removed with parents to Toledo, 1869; studied law in his father's office; admitted to bar, 1871; m. Mrs. Jennie B. Bullad, Sept. 23, 1880. Trustee Pub. Library and pres. of bd.; bank dir.; identified with many important cases, especially in suits against rys. Democrat. Author: My Mysterious Clients; A Messenger from Santa Claus, 1904; Memoirs of Lucas County, 1910. Address: Toledo, O. Died Jan. 21, 1913.

SCRIBNER, Mrs. Lucy Skidmore, philanthropist; b. N.Y. City, July 4, 1853; d. Joseph Russell and Lucy Ann (Hawley) Skidmore; ed. pvt. schs.; hon. M.A., Mt. Holyoke Coll., 1916; m. John Blair Scribner, publisher, May 13, 1875 (died 1879). Founder, 1911, and trustee Skidmore Coll. (professional coll. for women), Saratoga Springs, N.Y. Presbyn. Home: Saratoga Springs, N.Y. Died May 2, 1931.

SCRIPPS, Edward Wyllis, newspaper pub.; b. Rushville, Ill., June 18, 1854; s. James M. and Julia (Osborne) S.; ed. pub. schs. and under pvt. tutors; m. Nackie Holtsinger, Oct. 5, 1885. Began in newspaper bus. in Detroit, 1874; held controlling interest in 28 daily newspapers in 15 states of U.S., including Cleveland Press (founder and first editor), Cincinnati Post, Toledo News-Bee, Columbus Citizen, Pittsburgh Press, etc., these papers being members of Scripps-Howard Newspapers, including the Scripps-McRae League, Cincinnati; controlling owner United Press Assns. N.Y. City, serving news to nearly 900 daily newspapers in U.S.; controlling dir. Newspaper Enterprise Assn., Cleveland, furnishing illustrations, features, etc., to several hundred daily newspapers. Owner 10,000-acre ranch, Calif. World traveler. Endowed nat. orgn. for furnishing scientific news in popular form. Home: West Chester, O. Died Mar. 12, 1926.

SCRIPPS, James Edmund, newspaper publisher; b. London, Eng., March 19, 1835; s. James M. and Ellen M. (Saunders) S.; ed. at Rushville, Ill.; m. Harriet J. Messinger, Sept. 16, 1862. Began career of journalism on Chicago Tribune, 1857; established Detroit Evening News, Aug. 23, 1873; later participated in establishing Cleveland Press, 1878; St. Louis Chronicle, 1880; Cincinnati Post, 1881. Projected Detroit Museum of Art and presented it with collection of works of the old masters, 1884-89; built ch. for Reformed Episcopal denomination, 1890-93; park commr., Detroit, 1892-94; mem. Detroit Public Library Commn., 1900; State senator, 1903. Author: Memorials of the Scripps Family, 1891; Five Months Abroad, 1882. Home: Detroit, Mich. Died 1906.

SCRIPPS, Robert Paine, journalist; b. San Diego, Calif., Oct. 27, 1895; s. Edward Wyllis and Nackey (Holtsinger) S.; educated under pvt. tutors and at Pomona (Calif.) College; m. Margaret Lou Culbertson, Mar. 21, 1917; children—Robert Paine, Charles Edward, Margaret Ellen, Nackey Elizabeth, Samuel Holtsinger, Edward Wyllis III. Reporter and newspaper corr. at age of 16; editorial dir., 1917—, of Scripps-Howard and Scripps-McRae Newspapers, including Times-Press (Akron, O.), Cleveland Press, Cincinnati Post, Kentucky Post (Covington, Ky.), Columbus Citizen, Toledo News-Bee, Telegram (Youngstown, O.), Pittsburgh Press, Evansville Press, Indianapolis Times, Oklahoma City News, Rocky Mountain News, Houston Press, Fort Worth Press, El Paso Herald-Post, New Mexico State Tribune (Albuquerque, N.M.), Memphis Press-Scimitar, Birmingham Post, Knoxville News-Sentinel, Buffalo Times, Daily News (Washington, D.C.), San Diego Sun, Daily News (San Francisco), World-Telegram (New York). Pres. and treas. E. W. Scripps Company; dir. N.E.A. Service, Newspaper Information Service, United Press Assn. Trustee Miami U. (Oxford, O.), Science Service (Washington, D.C.). Home: West Chester, O. Died Mar. 2, 1938.

SCRIPTURE, William Ellis, judge; b. Westmoreland, Oneida County, N.Y., Nov. 2, 1843; s. Parker A. and Harriet Standish (Snow) S.; grad. Whitestown Sem., 1865; entered Hamilton Coll., 1865; later entered Albany Law Sch.; m. Emma C. Goodwin, Aug. 1867. Admitted to bar, May 1867; justice Supreme Ct. of N.Y., 1896-1909. Republican. Address: Rome, N.Y. Died Jan. 4, 1933.

SCRIVEN, George Percival, army officer; b. Philadelphia, Pa., Feb. 21, 1854; s. Charles Henry and Elizabeth (Shuff) S.; entered U. of Chicago, class 1875, Rensselaer Poly., Troy, N.Y., class 1876, leaving after 2 yrs. to enter U.S. Mil. Acad., from which grad. 1878 (5th in class); m. Bertha, d. Gen. Edward S. Bragg, Feb. 7, 1891 (died 1914); m. 2d, Elizabeth, d. Peter McQuade, Oct. 6, 1915. Second lt. 8th Infantry, June 14, 1878; trans. to Arty. and to the Signal Corps, Dec. 18, 1890; capt., June 14, 1892; maj. Signal Corps; promoted through grades to brig. gen., and chief signal officer of the Army, Mar. 5, 1913; retired Feb. 3, 1917. Served at various posts; mil. attaché, Mexico City, 1894, Rome, 1894-97; present at coronation of Emperor of Russia, 1896; detailed with Turkish forces, 1897; chief signal officer, Dept. of Gulf, Spanish-Am. War, May-June 1898; with 4th Philippine Expdn., 1898; on staff of Gen. Wesley Merritt, in Philippines; served in Cuba, 1899, and in Philippines; chief signal officer of the Visayas, and chief signal officer China Relief Expdn., Aug.-Nov. 1900; in Philippines to May 1901; on duty St. Louis Expn., 1904; chief signal officer Dept. of East, 1904-09, Philippines Div., 1909-11; asst. to chief signal officer of the army, July 1911-Feb. 1913. Cited "for gallantry in action" against Chinese Boxer forces at Yang-Tsun, Aug. 6, 1900, and "for gallantry in action" against Boxer forces at Peking August 14-15, 1900; medal, War Dept., for gallantry in the field. Catholic. Mem. orders of the Dragon and the Carabao; badges: Spanish-Am. War, Philippines, Army of Cuban Occupation, China Relief Expdn. (with 2 silver stars), Mexican Expdn., foreign service Great War. Recommended by Gen. Chaffee for bvtd. lt. col. "for gallant conduct" at Yang-Tsun, Aug. 6, 1900, and at Peking, Aug. 14 and 15, 1900. Apptd. by the President mem. Nat. Advisory Com. for Aeronautics, and elected chmn. Applied for retirement after more than 42 yrs.' service, Dec. 30, 1916; retired Feb. 13, 1917; applied for active service in case of war, same date; on active duty under instructions from the President, Sept. 17, 1917; designated by Sec. of State at request of Sec. of War, Sept. 24, 1917, as mil. attaché to Am. Embassy at Rome, Italy; reported at Rome, Nov. 15, 1917, proceeded to the Italian front along the Piave River, later detailed as observer with the Italian armies; served with Italian troops in the Balkans, and awarded decoration Grand Officer Crown of Italy; on duty War Coll., Washington, July 1-Sept. 27, 1918. Awarded gold medal by Mil. Service Instn. for article "Nicaragua Canal and Its Military Aspects," 1893; wrote (brochure) "Transmission of Military Information, 1908; "The Story of the Hudson Bay Company." Address: Washington, D.C. Died Mar. 7, 1940.

SCRUGGS, William Lindsay, lawyer, author; b. nr. Knoxville, Tenn., Sept. 14, 1836; s. Frederick and Margaret (Kimbrough) S.; student Strawberry Plains Coll., Tenn., 1854-57; LL.D., Furman U., S.C., 1907; admitted to bar, 1858; m. Judith Ann, d. John H. S. Potts, Aug. 3, 1858 (died 1897). Chief editor Columbus (Ga.) Daily Sun, 1862-66, Atlanta New Era, 1870-72; E.E. and M.P. to Colombia, 1872-77 and 1882-87; consul gen. in China, 1878-82; E.E. and M.P. to Venezuela, 1889-93; legal adviser and special agent Venezuelan Govt., charged with settlement Anglo-Venezuelan boundary dispute, 1894-98; brought it to arbitration, 1897. Independent Republican. One of founders of Atlanta pub. sch. system, 1869-70, and of the Y.M. Library, Atlanta (now Carnegie), 1867. Author: British Aggressions in Venezuela, or the Monroe Doctrine on Trial, 1894; Official History of the Guayana Boundary Dispute, 1895; Lord Salisbury's Mistakes, 1896; Fallacies of the British Blue Book, 1896; The Colombian and Venezuelan Republics (2d edit.), 1905; Evolution of American Citizenship, 1901; Origin and Meaning of the Monroe Doctrine, 1902; Evolution of the XIVth and XVth Amendments. Contbr. to hist., econ., and legal revs. Address: Atlanta, Ga. Died July 18, 1912.

SCRYMSER, James Alexander, capitalist; b. New York, N.Y., 1839; ed. College Hill Acad., Poughkeepsie, N.Y. Served in Civil war in 12th N.Y. Vols., and took part in all battles of Army of Potomac until June 1864. Projected and organized, 1865, Internat. Ocean Telegraph Co., which laid 1866-70, and operates submarine cables between U.S. and Cuba and other W. Indian Islands; projected, 1879, and established, 1881, Mexican Telegraph Co., and later the Central and S. Am. Telegraph Co., connecting U.S., via Galveston, Tex., with 16 nationalities in Mexico, and Central and S. America. Pres. and dir. Central and S. Am. Telegraph Co., Mexican Telegraph Co. Home: New York, N.Y. Died Apr. 1918.

SCUDDER, Horace Elisha, author; b. Boston, Mass., Oct. 16, 1838; s. Charles and Sarah Lathrop (Coit) S.; grad. Williams, 1858; Litt.D., Princeton; taught, New York, 3 yrs.; reader for Hurd and Houghton; editor Riverside Mag. for Young People, 1867-70; editor Atlantic Monthly, 1890-98; m. Grace Owen, 1873. Author: Seven Little People and Their Friends; Dream Children; Stories from My Attic; The Dwellers in Five-Sisters Court; Stories and Romances; Boston Town; Life of Noah Webster; A History of the United States; A Short History of the United States; The Book of Fables; The Book of Folk Stories; Book of

Legends; Fables and Folk Stories; George Washington; The Bodley Books (juveniles, 8 vols.); Life of Bayard Taylor; Men and Letters (essays); Childhood in Literature and Art; Recollections of Samuel Breck; Literature in School; The Children's Book; etc. Address: Cambridge, Mass. Died 1902.

SCUDDER, Janet, sculptor and painter; b. Terre Haute, Ind., Oct. 27, 1873; d. William Hollingshead and Mary (Sparks) S.; ed. pub. schs.; Cincinnati Art Acad.; Art Inst. Chicago; Vittis Acad., Colarossi's Acad., and MacMonnies' Studio, Paris; unmarried. Awards: bronze medal, Chicago Expn., 1893; medal, St. Louis Expn., 1904; hon. mention, Salon, Paris, 1911; silver medal San Francisco Exposition, 1915; olympiade medal, Amsterdam, 1928. Awarded silver medal at Paris, Exposition, 1937. Principal works: Frog Fountain, in Met. Mus. Art, New York; Young Diana, hon. mention, Salon, 1911; Little Lady of the Sea, in Salon, 1913; Fighting Boys' Fountain, Art Inst., Chicago. Represented in Musée du Luxembourg, Paris; Met. Mus., Numismatic Mus., N.Y. City; Congressional Library, Washington; Peabody Inst.; John Herron Inst., Indianapolis; Art Inst., of Chicago; Philips Art Mus., Okla.; Swope Art Mus., Terre Haute, Ind. Chevalier de la Légion d'Honneur, 1925. Exhibited paintings at Macbeth Galleries, New York, 1933. A.N.A. Author: Modeling My Life (autobiography), 1925. Address: New York, N.Y. Died June 9, 1940.

SCUDDER, Moses Lewis; b. in Mass., 1843; s. Rev. M. L. and Sarah A. (Pratt) S.; grad. Poly. Inst. of Brooklyn, 1860; A.B., Wesleyan U., 1863; m. Clarine Williams, 1873 (died 1904). Pres. St. Joseph, South Bend & Southern R.R., The Investors' Agency, Inc. Author: (novel) Almost an Englishman, 1879; National Banking, 1878; Congested Prices, 1884; The Labor Value Fallacy, 1885. Pres. Scudder Assn. America. Home: Huntington, L.I., N.Y. Died Oct. 29, 1917.

SCUDDER, Myron Tracy, educator; b. Palamanir, India, Sept. 28, 1860; s. Ezekiel Carman and Sarah Ruth (Tracy) S.; grad. Adelphi Acad., Brooklyn, 1877; A.B., Rutgers, 1882, A.M., 1886; Clark U. Summer Sch., 1897; Yale, 1898-99; m. Martha Dumont, June 23, 1897; children—Elizabeth M. (Mrs. Alfred Max Slagle), Dorothy D. (Mrs. Oliver C. Walker). Teacher in Fort Plain pub. schs., 1882-83; gen. sec. Y.M.C.A., Yonkers, N.Y., 1883-84; prin. Fort Plain schs., 1884-88, Rome Free Acad., 1888-90; teacher classics, Plattsburg State Normal Sch., 1890-92; insp. Regents Schs., N.Y. State, 1892-97; prin. Hillhouse High Sch., New Haven, Conn., 1897-99; prin. State Normal School, New Paltz, N.Y., 1899-1908; prof. edn., Rutgers, 1908-12; pres. The Scudder School for Girls, New York, Sept. 1911—; lecturer New York U., 1903-04, summer sch. U. of Me., 1909, U. of Va., 1911-16. Author: New York—Its State and Local Government, 1895; Recreations for Rural Communities, 1912; also numerous monographs on edn. Republican. Presbyn. Mason. Treas. and dir. Camp Fire Girls of America; treas. Nat. Bd. of Review of Motion Pictures. Home: New York, N.Y. Died Dec. 28, 1935.

SCUDDER, Samuel Hubbard, naturalist; b. Boston, Apr. 13, 1837; s. Charles and Sarah Lathrop (Coit) S.; A.B., Williams, 1857, A.M., 1860; B.S., Lawrence Scientific School (Harvard), 1862; Sc.D., Williams, 1890; LL.D., Western U. of Pa., 1890; m. Jeannie Blatchford, June 25, 1867. Assisted Louis Agassiz in Mus. Comparative Zoölogy, 1862-64; sec. Boston Soc. of Natural History, 1862-70, custodian, 1864-70, pres., 1880-87; asst. librarian, Harvard, 1879-82; palæontologist of U.S. Geol. Survey, 1886-92. Mem. Nat. Acad. Sciences, 1877—; Am. Philos. Soc.; fellow Am. Acad. Arts and Sciences, A.A.A.S. (gen. sec., 1875). Author: A Century of Orthoptera, 1879; Catalogue of the Scientific Serials of All Countries, 1879; Butterflies, Their Structure, Changes and Life Histories, 1881; Nomenclator Zoölogicus, 1884; The Winnipeg Country, 1886; Butterflies of the Eastern United States and Canada, 1889; A Classed and Annotated Bibliography of Fossil Insects, 1890; The Fossil Insects of North America, 1890; Index to the Known Fossil Insects of the World, 1891; Tertiary Rhynchophorous Coleoptera of the United States, 1893; Brief Guide to the Common Butterflies, 1893; The Life of a Butterfly, 1893; Frail Children of the Air, 1895; Revision of the American Fossil Cockroaches, 1895; Guide to the Genera and Classification of N.A. Orthoptera, 1897; Revision of the Orthopteran Group, Melanopli, 1897; Everyday Butterflies, 1899; Catalogue of the Described Orthoptera of the United States and Canada, 1900; Adephagous and Clavicorn Coleoptera from the Tertiary Deposits at Florissant, Colo., 1900; Index to North Am. Orthoptera, Described in the 18th and 19th Centuries, 1901 (Boston Soc. Natural History). Address: Cambridge, Mass. Died 1911.

SCUDDER, Wallace McIlvaine, editor, pub.; b. Trenton, N.J., Dec. 26, 1853; s. Judge Edward Wallace and Mary Louisa (Drake) S.; prep. edn. State Model Sch., Trenton; M.E., Lehigh U., 1873; Harvard Law Sch., 1875-76; admitted to N.J. bar, 1876; Litt.D. from Rutgers Coll., 1926; m. Ida Quinby, Oct. 1880 (died Jan. 1903); children—Edward Wallace, Antoinette Quinby; m. 2d, Gertrude Witherspoon, Apr. 17, 1906; 1 son, Wallace McIlvaine. Editor and pub. Newark Evening News, Sept. 1, 1883—. Home: Newark, N.J. Died Feb. 24, 1931.

SCULLY, James Wall, brig. gen. U.S.A.; b. Kilkenny, Ireland, Feb. 19, 1838; s. Thomas Sadlier and Eleanor Cairns (Wall) S.; ed. St. Kiernan's Coll., Kilkenny, 1848-51; studied surveying under father, in Ulster County, N.Y., and Gallatin, Tenn., 1852-56; m. Mary Adelaide Cuddy, 1862. Served pvt., corporal and sergt., Co. K, 1st Arty., 1856-61; in vols. as 1st lt. and regimental q.m., 10th Tenn. Inf., July 14, 1862; lt. col., Aug. 21, 1863; col., June 6, 1864; hon. mustered out of vol. service, May 25, 1865; apptd. capt. a.q.m. U.S.A., Sept. 27, 1865; maj. q.m., Jan. 25, 1883; lt. col. deputy q.m. gen., Sept. 12, 1894; col. a.q.m. gen., Feb. 4, 1898; retired at own request, Nov. 1, 1900; advanced to rank of brig. gen. retired, by act of Apr. 23, 1904. Bvtd.: maj. (for Mill Springs, Ky.), lt. col. (for Shiloh), and col. (for Nashville), Sept. 27, 1865. Roman Catholic. Address: Atlanta, Ga. Died June 2, 1918.

SCULLY, Thomas J., congressman; b. S. Amboy, N.J., Sept. 19, 1868; ed. pub. schs., and Seton Hall Coll., S. Orange, N.J. Engaged in towing and transportation business. Presdl. elector, 1908; mayor South Amboy, 1909-10; mem. 62d to 66th Congresses (1911-21), 3d N.J. District. Democrat. Home: South Amboy, N.J. Died Dec. 14, 1921.

SCULLY, William Augustine; b. New York City, Aug. 24, 1886; s. Daniel Joseph and Julia (Browne) S.; ed. pub. schs., business coll., under pvt. tutor and Georgetown U.; m. Asenath Genevieve Hall, June 1913; children—Kate Hyde, William Hall. Began as bank and stock broker, New York, later newspaper reporter and special newspaper corr.; officer or dir. mfg. and banking corps.; v.p. Ridgway Pub. Co.; dir. Washington Rapid Transit Co.; advisory editor Text Book of Aerial Laws. Spl. attaché for polit.-economic affairs, Div. of Western European Affairs, Dept. of State, 1919-20; Eastern dir. Foreign Language Bur. of Rep. Nat. Com., 1923. Sec. El Paso County (Colo.) Rep. Com., 1910; asst. Eastern dir. of publicity under Republican Nat. Com., campaign, 1923; alternate del. Rep. Conv., N.Y. State, from 1st Assembly Dist., 1926, 27. Served 3 yrs. as mem. 3d Battery, F.A., 2 yrs. with Troop C, Cav. N.Y.N.G., and of Denver City Troop, 2 yrs. Capt. Aviation Sect., Signal Corps, and maj. Air Service, assigned to Gen. Staff, World War I, served 1917-20 as spl. operative, Office of Naval Intelligence; mem. Clearance Com. of War Industries Board, Washington, and mem. Council Nat. Defense, Washington, 1917; lt. col. Mil. Attaché Sect., Mil. Intelligence, O.R.C., 1921—. Mem. American Acad. of Political and Social Science, Am. Political Science Association. Catholic. Home: Washington, D.C. Deceased.

SEABROOKE, Thomas Q., actor; b. Mt. Vernon, N.Y., Oct. 20, 1860. Employed in East Chester Nat. Bank, 1871-80; engaged in theatrical venture at a Newark, N.J., house, which failed; début in Sept. 1880, as Bertie Cecil in "Cigarette"; later played with various cos. in comedy rôles; took star part in "The Isle of Champagne," 1892; later appeared at head of his own and other opera and comedy cos. Home: New York, N.Y. Died Apr. 3, 1913.

SEABURY, William Jones, clergyman; b. New York, Jan. 25, 1837; s. Rev. Samuel and Hannah Amelia (Jones) S.; A.B., Columbia, 1856, A.M., 1859; admitted to New York bar, 1858, and engaged in practice; grad. Gen. Theol. Sem. of New York, 1866; (D.D., Hobart, 1874, ad eundem, Gen. Theol. Sem., 1885); m. Alice Van Wyck, d. Thomas Marston and Mary Susan (Saltonstall) Beare, Oct. 29, 1868. Deacon and priest P.E. Ch., 1866; rector Ch. of the Annunciation, New York, 1868-98; prof. ecclesiastical polity and law, General Theol. Seminary, 1873—. Author: Manual for Choristers, 1878; Lectures on Apostolical Succession, 1893; An Introduction to the Study of Ecclesiastical Polity, 1894; Notes on the Constitution of 1901, 1902; Memoir of Bishop Seabury, 1908. Editor: Memoir, 1873, and Discourses, 1874, of Rev. Samuel Seabury, D.D. Died Aug. 30, 1916.

SEAGER, Henry Rogers, economist; b. Lansing, Mich., July 21, 1870; s. Schuyler F. and Alice (Berry) S.; Ph.B., U. of Mich., 1890; Ph.D., U. of Pa., 1894; Johns Hopkins, 1890-91, Halle, 1891-92, Berlin, 1892, Vienna, 1893; m. Harriet Henderson, June 5, 1899; 1 son, Schuyler Fiske. Assistant prof. of political economy, U. of Pennsylvania, 1896-1902; adj. prof. polit. economy, 1902-05, prof., 1905—, Columbia. Member board editors Polit. Science Quarterly. Author: Introduction to Economics, 1904; Economics. Briefer Course, 1909; Social Insurance, 1910; Principles of Economics, revised edition, 1923; History of the Shipbuilding Labor Adjustment Board, 1917-19, 1921; Practical Problems in Economics, 1923; Trust and Corporation Problems, 1929. Sec. Shipbuilding Labor Adjustment Bd., Washington, 1917-19; pres. Am. Assn. for Labor Legislation, 1911-13, Am. Econ. Assn., 1922; exec. sec. President's Industrial Conf., 1919-20. Home: New York, N.Y. Died Aug. 23, 1930.

SEAGER, Lawrence H., bishop; b. Fremont, O., Apr. 19, 1860; s. Charles D. and Caroline (Hoover) S.; A.B., Ohio Northern U., 1886, LL.D., 1928; A.B., Northwestern Coll., Naperville, Ill., 1887; grad. Evang. Theol. Sem., Naperville, 1888; D.D.; m. Mary G. Twigg, Sept. 16, 1896. Ordained ministry Evang. Ch., 1888; pastor Cleveland, Akron, and Fremont, O., 1889-1900; editor denominational S.S. lit., 1900-11; pres. Northwestern Coll., 1911-16; bishop Evangelical Ch., Oct. 1915—. Republican. Home: Le Mars, Ia. Died Aug. 30, 1937.

SEAGRAVE, Frank Evans, astronomer; b. Providence, R.I., Mar. 29, 1860; s. George Augustus and Mary Greene (Evans) S.; ed. sch. of Rev. Charles H. Wheeler, 1869-74; Harvard Coll. Obs., 1875-77; M.A., Brown U., 1911; unmarried. During period 1878-1901 went on 3 total solar eclipse expdns. and observed visually and photographically many phenomena, such as the reversing layer, corona and prominence spectra; photographed transit of Venus, at Providence, R.I., Dec. 6, 1882; accomplished important work in relation to Halley's comet which appeared in 1909, 1910. Has made numerous observations of comets, and computations and observations of variable stars of different types to determine their periods and forms of their light curves; also orbits of comets, asteroids, the planet Pluto, etc. Owner and dir. of a new obs., N. Scituate, R.I. Died July 15, 1934.

SEALOCK, William Elmer, educator; b. Rural Dale, O., Feb. 9, 1877; s. Wesley and Catherine (Miller) S.; A.B., Ohio State U., 1905; studied U. of Wis. 4 summers; Ph.D., Columbia, 1914; m. Nancy M. Whitney, May 1, 1898. Supt. schs., Circleville, O., 1906-12; supervisor high schs., State Dept. of Edn., Ohio, 1914-15; asso. prof. vocational edn., Iowa State Coll., Ames, Ia., 1915-18; head dept. of history and principles of edn., 1918-21, dean Coll. of Edn., U. of Neb., 1921-31; pres. Municipal U. of Omaha, 1931—. Republican. Unitarian. Mason. Home: Omaha, Neb. Died July 7, 1935.

SEALY, Frank L., organist, condr.; b. Newark, N.J., Sept. 13, 1858; s. John and Lydia (Tuttle) S.; studied under Frank Illsley, Jan Pychowski, Dudley Buck, and in Europe; m. Emma Grace Farrington, Sept. 7, 1893; 1 son, Donald F. Organist with N.Y. Symphony Soc., 1885—, N.Y. Oratorio Soc., 1885-1921, Fifth Av. Presbyn. Ch., 1900-18. Pres. New York Manuscript Soc., 1903-09; warden Am. Guild Organists, 1922-32. Organizer and was condr. Newark Madrigal Club. Home: Scarsdale, N.Y. Died Dec. 13, 1938.

SEAMAN, Arthur Edmund, geologist; b. Casnovia, Mich., Dec. 29, 1858; s. George Washington and Sarah Melissa (Moore) S.; B.S., Mich. Coll. Mines, 1895, E.M., 1915; m. Mary Annette Brotherton, Nov. 11, 1885 (dec.); children—Wyllys Arthur, Mary Lucile. Connected with Mich. Coll. of Mines, 1889—, prof. geology, 1899—. Republican. Episcopalian. Mason. Home: Houghton, Mich. Died 1937.

SEAMAN, George Milton, paper mcht.; b. St. Joseph, Mo., June 24, 1876; s. Charles H. and Kate (Porter) S.; ed. high sch., St. Joseph; m. Adelaide M. Herzberg, Nov. 30, 1905. In paper business, 1895—; treas. and dir. Bermingham & Seaman Co., 1905-14, then pres; pres. Seaman Paper Co. Republican. Episcopalian. Home: Chicago, Ill. Died May 11, 1936.

SEAMAN, Gilbert Edmund, M.D.; b. Alpena, Mich., Sept. 19, 1869; s. Ami L. and Jessie (Gordon) S.; grad. Episcopal Acad. of Michigan, 1886; student Detroit College of Medicine; M.D., Mich. College of Medicine and Surgery, 1889; studied univs. of Würzburg and Berlin. Began practice at Milwaukee, 1892; now med. supt. Winnebago State Hosp. Captain and asst. surgeon, U.S. Vols., Spanish-Am. War, serving in P.I.; maj. and surgeon, Wis. N.G., 1903-13; surgeon gen. of Wis., 1913—; col. Med. Corps, chief surgeon 32d Div. and chief surgeon, 6th Army Corps, A.E.F. Regent at-large U. of Wis.; mem. Wis. State Bd. Edn.; dir. Div. Mental Hygiene State Dept. Public Welfare; former clin. dir. Shorewood Hosp. Sanitarium. Fellow Am. Coll. Surgeons, Royal Inst. Public Health. Awarded D.S.M. (U.S.); mem. Legion of Honor (France). Republican. Protestant. Author: Compendium for Medical Officers, 1917; History Medical Dept. 32d Division; Lister as a Scientist; Problems Relating to Care of Insane in Wisconsin. Home: Madison, Wis. Died May 25, 1941.

SEAMAN, Henry Bowman, engineer; b. New York, Jan. 20, 1861; s. Valentine H. and Rebecca (Cromwell) S.; B.S., Swarthmore Coll., 1881, C.E., 1884; m. Grace Dutton, Apr. 7, 1904; children—Ayres Cromwell, Henry Bowman. Admitted to N.Y. bar; in practice as civ. engr.; was asst. engr. Kings Co. Elevated Ry., Brooklyn; bridge engr. Erie Ry. system; resident engr. of constrn., N.Y.,N.H.&H. R.R. at Mt. Vernon, N.Y.; chief of engrs. Audit Co. of New York, 1898; engr. abolition of grade crossings, Syracuse, N.Y., 1898; chief engr. (for contractors) 4th Av. sect. Underground R.R., New York, 1900; reconstruction of bridges, N.Y.,N.H.&H. R.R., 1903; consulting engr. dept. bridges, New York; chief engr. Public Service Commn., New York; contractor's engr. for foundation and masonry Hell Gate Bridge, New York; supervising engr. shipbuilding plant, U.S.N.; chief engr. Steinway Tunnel Extension, Manhattan, New York. Home: Brooklyn, N.Y. Died Oct. 24, 1940.

SEAMAN, Louis Livingston, surgeon; b. Newburgh, N.Y., Oct. 17, 1851; s. Valentine and Anna Amelia (Ferris) S.; A.B., Cornell, 1872; M.D., Jefferson Med. Coll., Phila., 1876; M.D., Univ. Med. Coll. (New York U.), 1877; LL.B., New York U., 1884; F.R.C.S., London, 1908; LL.D., Lincoln U.; m. Fannie Blackstone Freeman, 1889 (died 1895); m. 2d, Mary Stuart Huntington, Dec. 12, 1907 (died 1926). Resident surgeon New York State Emigrant Hospital, 1877-79; supt. of State Emigrant Insane Asylum, 1879-81; chief of staff of various hosps. and the Training Sch. for Nurses, Blackwell's Island, until 1885; made tour around the world, 1886, with spl. study, in hosps. of India, of contagious and epidemic diseases peculiar to the Orient. Del. to Internat. Congresses, London, 1881, Berlin, 1894, Moscow, 1897, Paris, 1900, Madrid, 1903, Lisbon, 1906, Budapest, 1910, London, 1913. Emeritus pres. China Soc. America; pres. Brit. War Relief Assn., Phys. and Surg. Travel Club U.S. Trustee Sulgrave Instn., Eng. (ancestral home of Washington), Cornell U. With 2d Imperial Army of Japan, at the front in Manchuria, 1905; spl. corr. of The Independent at the front in the European War. Knight Order of Leopold (Belgian); Comdr. Order of the Crown (Rumanian); Order Rising Sun, Order of the Treasury (Japan); Order of Special Merit, and mem. Red Cross of Japan; service medals Spanish-Am. War, Philippines, China, by France and England in the World War. Author: From Tokio Through Manchuria with the Japanese, 1905; The Real Triumph of Japan, 1906. Home: New York, N.Y. Died Jan. 31, 1932.

SEAMAN, William Henry, examiner U.S. Patent Office; b. New York, Nov. 1, 1837; s. John G. and Ann R. (Wall) S.; ed. Friends' Sch., New York; LL.B., Columbian (now George Washington) U., 1872; M.D., Howard U., 1882; m. Marianna P. Clark, Aug. 27, 1873. Admitted to bar, 1872; prof. botany, 1871-73, chemistry, 1874-1910, Howard U. Med. Sch.; examiner, 1879—, prin. examiner, 1906—, U.S. Patent Office. Home: Washington, D.C. Died 1910.

SEAMAN, William Henry, judge; b. New Berlin, Wis., Nov. 15, 1842; s. Williams and Arelisle (Crane) S.; ed. pub. schs., Sheboygan, Wis.; worked as printer, 1859-61; served in 1st Wis. Inf., 1861-64, in Civil War; m. Mary A. Peat, Dec. 17, 1868. Admitted to bar, 1868, and engaged in practice until 1893; U.S. dist. judge, Eastern Dist., Wis., 1893-1905; U.S. circuit judge, 7th Circuit, Feb., 1905—. Home: Sheboygan, Wis. Died Mar. 8, 1915.

SEAMANS, Clarence Walker, mfr.; b. Ilion, N.Y., June 5, 1854; s. Abner Clark and Caroline (Williams) S.; ed. pub. schs., Ilion; m. Gertrude Watson, Feb. 20, 1879. In employ, E. Remington & Sons, Ilion, 1869-75; mine supt. in Utah, 1875-78; mgr. sales, Fairbanks & Co. and E. Remington & Sons, 1878-82; organized, 1882, Wyckoff, Seamans Benedict, incorporated as Remington Typewriter Co., 1886, of which was treas. and gen. mgr. to 1893; pres., 1893-1910, chmn. bd., 1910—, Union Typewriter Co. Trustee Syracuse U., 1895-1911, Brooklyn Inst. Arts and Sciences. Home: Brooklyn, N.Y. Died May 30, 1915.

SEARCH, Preston Willis, educator; b. Marion, O., Apr. 10, 1853; s. Thomas and Matilda Clark (Sharpless) S.; ed. U. of Wooster, O.; advanced work in Clark U., Worcester, Mass., and univs. of Lausanne, Switzerland, and Jena, Germany; m. Margaret S. Fitzgerald, Aug. 1, 1883 (died 1927); 1 son, Frederick Preston. Principal Millersburg (O.) Academy, 1874-75; supt. pub. schs., W. Liberty, O., 1877-83, Sidney, O., 1883-88, Pueblo, Colo., 1888-94, Los Angeles, Calif., 1894-95, Holyoke, Mass., 1896-99. Traveler and student of edn. in many lands; founder of industrial schs., music festival assns., students' aid socs. and travel clubs; past pres. of local and State Y.M.C. Assns.; pres. of European Schs. of Travel, Study and Conf. for Am. Young People. Music and art critic; lecturer before univs., colls., state normal schs., lit. socs., ednl. congresses, chautauquas, lyceums, etc., having given over 7,000 lectures. First to organize city system of schs., as at Pueblo and Los Angeles, on a basis of fundamental recognition of the individual. Formerly editor of The Advance in Education. Pres. Literary Art Community, Carmel-by-the-Sea, 1914—; pres. Carmel Municipal Advisory Bd., Carmel Acad. Music and Fine Arts, Carmel Summer Musical Festival; mem. civic, state and nat. commns., also civic, ednl., lit. and scientific assns. Mem. Phi Delta Theta, 1872—; editor of its first songbook, poet laureate of nat. conventions, 1878 and 1930, "golden legionnaire," "hon. choragus." Prohibitionist. Presbyn. Author: An Ideal School, 1901; Foundations of Belief; The Individual in Mass Education; The Ethics of the Public Schools; Motives in Education; Budget of Christmas Stories. Home: Carmel-by-the-Sea, Calif. Died Dec. 12, 1932.

SEARCH, Theodore Corson, manufacturer; b. Southamptom, Pa., 1841; s. Jacob M. and Nancy M. S.; ed. Pa. State Normal Sch. and Chester Normal and High Sch.; (hon. A.M., Brown, 1895); m. Anna L. White, Dec. 25, 1862. Treas. and gen. mgr. John B. Stetson Co., 1893-1900; pres. Cold Spring Bleaching and Finishing Works. Pres. National Assn. of Manufacturers, 1897-1902; pres. Pa. Mus. and Sch. of Industrial Art. Home: Langhorne, Pa. Deceased.

SEARCY, Chesley Hunter, lawyer; b. Louisville, Ky., Dec. 14, 1881; s. John and Rosa (Colter) S.; student Vanderbilt U., 1901-03; LL.B., U. of Louisville, 1904; m. Mary Lillian Black, Feb. 16, 1906. Practiced at Louisville, 1904—; asst. co. atty. Jefferson Co., 1908-10; Rep. nominee for Ky. Senate, 1911; chmn. Rep. com., Louisville, 1917-18, Rep. State Com., 1918-20; mem. Rep. Nat. Com., 1921-24; now mem. from state at large Rep. State Exec. Com.; pres. Bd. Sinking Fund Commrs., Louisville, 1918—. Mem. Christian (Disciples) Ch. Mason, Elk. Home: Louisville, Ky. Died May 9, 1935.

SEARLE, Arthur, astronomer; b. London, Eng., Oct. 21, 1837; s. Thomas and Anne (Noble) S.; brother of George Mary S., came to U.S., 1840; A.B., Harvard, 1856, A.M., 1859; m. Emma Wesselhoeft, Jan. 1, 1873. After 12 yrs. in other places became asst. in Harvard Coll. Obs., 1869-83; asst. prof. of astronomy, 1883-87, Phillips prof., 1887-1912 (emeritus), Harvard U. Fellow Am. Acad. Arts and Sciences. Author: Outlines of Astronomy, 1874; Essays, I-XXX, 1910. Died Oct. 24, 1920.

SEARLE, Charles James, judge; b. Ft. Smith, Ark., May 16, 1865; s. Elhanan J. and Cassarilla (Pierce) S.; student Campbell Coll., Holton, Kan., 1886-87; LL.B., State U. of Iowa, 1889; m. Mary Pryce, Apr. 7, 1898; children—Franklin P., Margaret, Charles J. Admitted to Ill. bar, 1889, and began practice at Rock Island; state's atty. Rock Island Co., 1892-1900; judge Court of Claims, Ill., 1902-07; mem. staff of U.S. atty. gen., war fraud investigation, 1921-23; judge Circuit Court, Ill., 1923—. Pres. bd. trustees Western Ill. State Normal Sch., 1898-1902. Republican. Home: Rock Island, Ill. Died Feb. 7, 1933.

SEARLE, Charles Putnam, lawyer; b. New Marlboro, Mass., July 21, 1854; s. Richard T. and Emily A. (Putnam) S.; A.B., Amherst, 1876; studied Nat. Law Sch., Washington; admitted to bar, 1884; m. Cora Hogg, 1885. Has practiced at Boston, 1884—; splty. customs and revenue law; pres. and dir. Calvin Putnam Lumber Co., and many corps. and assns. Episcopalian. Home: Boston, Mass. Died Jan. 17, 1917.

SEARLE, George Mary, clergyman, astronomer; b. London, England, June 27, 1839; s. Thomas and Anne (Noble) S.; bro. of Arthur S.; came to U.S., 1840; A.B., Harvard, 1857, A.M., 1860; (hon. Ph.D., Catholic U., Washington, 1896). Asst. Dudley Obs., Albany, 1858-59; discovered the asteroid "Pandora"; with U.S. Coast Survey, 1859-62; asst. prof. U.S. Naval Acad., 1862-64; asst. Harvard, Obs., 1866-68. Converted to Roman Catholic faith, 1862; joined Paulists, March 1868; ordained priest, 1871; became teacher of science in Paulist Sem.; apptd. chief prof. mathematics, Catholic U., Washington, Oct. 1895. Superior gen. of the Paulist Fathers, 1904-09. Author: Elements of Geometry, 1877; Plain Facts for Fair Minds, 1895; How to Become a Catholic, 1906; The Truth About Christian Science, 1916. Retired. Died July 7, 1918.

SEARLE, John Preston, teacher; b. Schuylerville, N.Y., Sept. 12, 1854; s. Reverend Samuel Tomb and Cornelia Fonda (Southworth) S.; A.B., Rutgers Coll., 1875, A.M., 1878; grad. New Brunswick (N.J.) Theol. Sem., 1878; (D.D., Rutgers, 1893); m. Susie Bovey, Dec. 12, 1882. Ordained in ministry Ref. Ch. in America, 1878; pastor, Griggstown, N.J., 1878-81. First Ch., Somerville, N.J., 1881-93; prof. systematic theology, New Brunswick Theol. Sem., 1893—, and pres. of faculty, 1902—. V.p. Bd. Foreign Missions, Ref. Ch. in America; trustee Rutgers Coll., 1898—; trustee Arabian Mission. Mem. exec. commn. Alliance Ref. and Presbyn. chs. (pres. 1915-16); chmn. Conf. Ch. Unity Coms. of Ref. and Presbyn. Chs., 1902, 03, 04, 06; pres. Gen. Synod Ref. Ch. America, 1917. Author: An Outline of Theological Encyclopedia; Life of Talbot Wilson Chambers, S.T.D., LL.D. Home: New Brunswick, N.J. Died July 27, 1922.

SEARLES, John Ennis, pres. and dir. Tenn. Northern Ry. Co., Hyatt Roller Bearing Co., Cornucopia Mines Co. of Ore., Phoenix Securities Co.; v.p. and dir. Terminal Warehouse Co., Am. Universal Mill Co.; dir. Iowa Central Ry. Co., Minneapolis & St. Louis R.R. Co. Home: New York, N.Y. Died 1908.

SEARLES, John William, coal operator; b. Venango City, Pa., Jan. 19, 1870; s. Edward Bigelow and Mary Elizabeth (Bixby) S.; ed. pub. schs., Buffalo and Baltimore; m. Maria Williams Marshall, Oct. 14, 1897; children—Edward Randolph, Eleanor Duncan (dec.). Identified with coal and coke business, 1901—; pres. Pa. Coal & Coke Corp. and abt. 20 subsidiary cos., Dec. 20, 1922—; pres. North River Coal & Wharf Co., Cresson Electric Light Co., Reilly Canon Fuel Co. Vice pres. Nat. Coal Assn. Republican. Episcopalian. Home: West Orange, N.J. Died Oct. 15, 1933.

SEARLES, William Henry, engineer; b. Cincinnati, O., June 4, 1837; s. Asbury M. and Rachel (Mitchell) S.; student Wesleyan Univ., 1856-57; C.E., Rensselaer Poly. Inst., 1860; m. Mary L. Doolittle, June 8, 1870. Prof. geodesy and road engring., Rensselaer Poly Inst., 1862-64; locating and constructing rys. in Ohio, Mich., Pa., Ind., and N.Y., 1864-85; engr. N.Y. state canals, 1876-78; cons. engr. in gen. practice, 1880—. Author: Field Engineering, 1880; The Railroad Spiral, 1882. Home: Elyria, O. Died Apr. 25, 1921.

SEARS, Clinton Brooks, brig. gen. U.S.A.; b. Penn Yan, N.Y., June 2, 1844; s. Clinton William and Angeline (Brooks) S.; ed. pub. and high schs., and Ohio Wesleyan U., to 1862; grad. U.S. Mil. Acad., 3d in class of 63, 1867; (hon. A.B., Ohio Wesleyan, 1881, A.M., 1884); m. Lydia Evelyn Smith, Oct. 22, 1873; 2d, Mrs. Alice (Bullock) Peevers, Feb. 11, 1902. Served as pvt., corporal and acting color sergt. Co. G, 95th Ohio Inf., July 24, 1862-Sept. 15, 1863; commd. 2d lt. and 1st lt., U.S. Engrs., June 17, 1867; capt., Apr. 9, 1880; maj., Sept. 20, 1892; lt. col., Apr. 21, 1903; col., Jan. 11, 1907. Recommended to the President as cadet to U.S. Mil. Acad. by Gens. Grant and Sherman, after competitive exam. from 15th Army Corps; has served in U.S. and P.I. in constrn. of river and harbor works, fortifications, roads, bridges, canals, locks, dams, etc.; asst. prof. civ. and mil. engring., 1876-77, geography, history and ethics, 1877-78, mechanics, acoustics, optics and astronomy, 1878-82, U.S. Mil. Acad.; instr. submarine mining, U.S. Engr. Sch., Willets Point, N.Y., 1891-92; chief engr div. of the Philippines, 1901-03; mem. and pres. Miss River Commn., engr. 15th light house dist. and in charge of improvement of Miss. River from St. Louis to Cairo; pres. spl. bd. to report upon 14 ft. water way project from Chicago to the Gulf; retired, June 2, 1908, with rank of brig. gen. U.S.A. Fellow Nat. Acad. Design. Author of numerous official reports, 1870—, and of Ransom Genealogy. Home: Newton Centre, Mass. Died 1912.

SEARS, Frederic William, neurologist; b. Morristown, N.J., June 30, 1859; s. Hector and Susan T. (Gustin) S.; grad. Adelphi Acad., 1876; student Yale; A.B., Amherst, 1881; M.D., U. of Vt., 1888; post-grad. course, Coll. Phys. and Surg. (New York U.), 1889, Roosevelt Hosp., 1891, London, Eng., 1904, Paris, 1905, Berlin and Munich, 1906, Harvard, 1907, Johns Hopkins, 1908, Harvard, 1909; m. Mary E. Hollis, 1881. In business, Jamestown, N.Y., 1885-86; farming, South Hero, Vt., 1886-90; began practice of medicine, Waterbury, Vt., 1890; prof. nervous diseases, Coll. of Medicine, U. of Vt., 1912—. Owner and supt. Lakeview Sanatorium, 1917-20. Neurologist, Mary Fletcher, Fanny Allen and Bishop de Goesbriand hosps.; pres. Burlington Health Commn., 1914-17. Republican. Episcopalian. Mason. Home: Burlington, Vt. Died Jan. 2, 1934.

SEARS, Frederick W., M.D.; b. Homer, N.Y., Dec. 19, 1858; s. Henry and Mary (Hatch) S.; prep. edn., Colgate Acad., Hamilton, N.Y., and Cazenovia (N.Y.) Sem.; M.D., Syracuse Med. Coll., 1886; m. Jessie Pratt, June 7, 1882; children—Nathan P., Kathryn. Began practice at Syracuse, 1886; instr. in histology and asso. prof. gynecology, Syracuse Med. Coll., 1886-96; now prof. emeritus public health and hygiene, medical dept. of the univ.; surgeon Syracuse Memorial Hosp., 1894-1914; health officer Syracuse, 1895-98, 1914-18; dist. state health officer, 1914—. Surgeon N.G.N.Y. Republican. Presbyn. Home: Syracuse, N.Y. Died Aug. 1934.

SEARS, George Gray, M.D.; b. Boston, Mass., Oct. 22, 1859; s. George O. and Sarah G. (Richards) S.; A.B., Amherst, 1880, D.Sc., 1925; M.D., Harvard U., 1885, LL.D. from same, 1926; m. Ruth Williams, Feb. 2, 1904; 1 dau., Ruth. Practicing medicine at Boston, 1886—; visiting physician, Boston City Hosp., 1902-19, consulting phys., 1919—; instr. 1897, asst. prof. clin. medicine, 1901, clin. prof., 1911, prof. clin. medicine, 1912, emeritus prof., 1919, Harvard. V.p. Boston Med. Library, 1928-35. Trustee Boston City Hosp., 1918-39; trustee Forsythe Dental Infirmary, 1924—. Republican. Home: Boston, Mass. Died May 27, 1940.

SEARS, James Hamilton, commodore U.S.N.; b. Binghamton, N.Y., Jan. 6, 1855; s. Charles William and Augusta (Howe) S.; grad. U.S. Naval Acad., 1876; m. Rosa Helen Ranlett, Feb. 4, 1885. Promoted ensign, Apr. 1879; lt., jr. grade, Dec. 1884; lt., Sept. 1892; lt. comdr., May 1899; comdr., Jan. 1905; capt., August 1908; commodore and voluntarily retired, June 30, 1910. Served in Yantic, Kearsarge and Tennessee, China squadron, 1876-78; Kearsarge, N. Atlantic squadron, U.S. Naval Acad. and Navy Yard, Boston, 1879-81; Monitor Montauk, 1881-82; Training Ship Portsmouth, 1883-85; Naval Observatory, 1885-86; Schoolship St. Mary, 1887-89; Baltimore, 1890-92; spl. duty, Navy Dept. and Staff War College, Newport, R.I., 1892-93; U.S. Coast and Geod. Survey, 1894-97; U.S. Naval Home, Phila., 1897-98; flag lt. Brooklyn, on staff Commodore W. S. Schley, in W.I. and spl. duty with Puerto Rico Commission during and afterwards, Spanish-Am. War, 1898; U.S.S. Indiana, torpedo sta., Newport, 1898-99; flag lt., staff Rear Admiral W. S. Schley on Chicago, S. Atlantic sta., 1900-01; in charge hydrographic office, New York, 1901-02; exec. officer Brooklyn, Mediterranean Squadron, and in command Alliance, Vixen, Gloucester, 1903-04; insp. 8th lighthouse dist., Gulf of Mex., 1905-07; China squadron, 1907-08, naval attaché, U.S. Embassy, Tokyo and Am. Legation, Peking, 1909-10. Author: The Chilian Revolution of 1891; War on the Coast. Died Dec. 8, 1915.

SEARS, Lorenzo, university prof.; b. Searsville, Mass., Apr. 18, 1838; s. Nathaniel and Cordelia (Morton) S.; A.B., Yale, 1861; grad. Gen. Theol. Sem., New York, 1864; (hon. A.M., Trinity, 1887, Litt.D., 1892); m. Adeline Harris, Jan. 2, 1866. Deacon, 1864, priest, 1865, P.E. Ch.; rector in Conn., R.I., N.H., 1864-85; prof. rhetoric and English lit., U. of Vt., 1885-88; prof. rhetoric, 1890-95, Am. lit., 1895-1906, Brown University. Author: Principles and Methods of Literary Criticism, 1898; American Literature in the Colonial and National Periods, 1902; Seven Laws of Literary Composition, 1904; The Makers of American Literature, 1904; Wendell Phillips, Orator and Agitator, 1909; John Hancock, the Picturesque Patriot, 1912; John Hay, Author and Statesman, 1914. Died Mar. 1, 1916.

SEARS, Nathaniel Clinton, lawyer; b. Gallipolis, O., Aug. 23, 1854; s. Amos Gould and Susan (Davis) S.; A.B., Amherst, 1875, A.M., 1878; law student, U. of Berlin, 1875-76; (LL.D., Northwestern U., 1898); m. Laura Raymond Davidson, May 26, 1887. Admitted to Ill. bar, Jan. 1, 1878; elected judge Superior Ct. of Cook Co., Ill., 1893; apptd. asso. justice Appellate Ct. of Ill., 1897; reapptd., 1900, chief justice Appellate Ct., 1902; resigned Apr. 1, 1903, to enter firm of Sears, Meagher & Whitney, Chicago, retired. Rep. candidate for mayor of Chicago, 1897. Was mem. Chicago Bd. of Education. Died May 7, 1934.

SEARS, Richard Warren; b. Stewartville, Minn., Dec. 7, 1863; s. James Warren and Eliza A. (Benton) S.; ed. common schs. of Minn.; m. Anna Lydia Meckstroth, June 20, 1895. Began as railroad employe at St. Paul, in 1880; started in mail order business in Minneapolis, 1886; organized Sears, Roebuck & Co., in 1890, in Minneapolis, of which was the sr. mem. until 1895, when business was transferred to Chicago and incorporated, becoming pres.; in 1908 retired from active business and engaged in farming. Republican. Home: Oak Park, Ill. Died Sept. 28, 1914.

SEARS, Russell Adams, lawyer; b. Brooklyn, N.Y., Oct. 13, 1869; s. Samuel Davis and Ella Evelyn (Hayden) S.; ed. pub. schs.; m. Jennie Crocker, 1890; children—Percival Adams, Winslow, Samuel Powers, Constance (Mrs. Oliver Middleton Read), Barbara (Mrs. Randolph Packard Rice), Eleanor (Mrs. George Howe Phillips), Joan. Admitted to Mass. bar, 1890, and began practice at Boston; atty. for Boston Elevated Ry., 1902—; pres. Transit Mutual Ins. Co. Served as mayor, city solicitor and mem. City Council, Quincy; vice chmn. Governor's Com. on Highway Safety. Dir. Am. Red Cross, Quincy. Republican. Unitarian. Home: Quincy, Mass. Died July 1932.

SEARS, Sarah Choate, artist; b. Cambridge, Mass., May 5, 1858; d. Charles Francis and Elizabeth W. (Carlile) Choate; pupil Cowles Art Sch. and Mus. of Fine Arts, Boston; m. Joshua Montgomery Sears, Sept. 18, 1877. Awarded William T. Evans prize, 1892; medal, Chicago Expn., 1893; hon. mention, Paris Expn., 1900; bronze medal, Buffalo Expn., 1901; silver medal, Charleston Expn., and St. Louis Expn., 1904. Home: Boston, Mass. Died Sept. 26, 1935.

SEARS, Walter Herbert, engineer; b. Plymouth, Mass., Dec. 8, 1847; s. Thomas Bartlett and Louisa (Churchill) S.; C.E., Mass. Inst. Tech., 1868; m. Ella M. Blackmer, Nov. 18, 1897. As chief or prin. asst. engr. has built water works at Winchester, Beverly, Plymouth, Mass., Pawtucket, R.I., Newark, N.J., Rochester, N.Y., Stillwater, Minn.; also new water supply for New York, etc. Home: Plymouth, Mass. Died Oct. 7, 1911.

SEARS, Walter James; b. Douglas Co., Kan., July 10, 1869; s. Charles May and Mary Ann (Smith) S.; grad. high sch., Chillicothe, O., 1889; B.Ph., Ohio State U., 1894; m. Jessie M. Carpenter, Dec. 20, 1904; children—Lorine C., Walter James, Mary P. Reporter and editor, 1894-97; advertising and sales mgr. Sears & Nichols Co., food mfrs., 1897-1910; pres. Sears & Simpson Co., printers and publishers, 1911-20; pres. Sears & Nichols Co., 1915-22; pres. Sears & Derr Co., food mfrs., 1924—. Served as pvt. Ohio Vol. Inf., Spanish-Am. War; chmn. War Camp Com. Service, pres. Ross Co. Council of Defense and Ross Co. Food Administrator, World War. Pres. City Council and vice-mayor Chillicothe, 1896-98, 1905-07; Rep. candidate for mayor, 1907; Rep. presdl. elector, 1904. Trustee Ohio State U., 1907-15. Episcopalian. Mason, Elk. Home: Chillicothe, O. Died Feb. 13, 1929.

SEARS, Willard Thomas, architect; b. New Bedford, Mass., Nov. 5, 1837; s. Willard and Ruth Barker (Cushman) S.; ed. Phillipps Acad., New Bedford, Mass.; Allen's Sch., West Newton; studied architecture with Solomon K. Eaton, New Bedford, 1856-57; with Gridley J. F. Bryant, Boston, 1858-59; m. May, d. Rev. Mellish Irving Motte, of Boston, Jan. 1, 1862. Began practice in Boston on own account, 1860; in 1864, with Charles A. Cummings, formed partnership of Cummings & Sears; work of firm in many cities of U.S., also South America and Hayti; rebuilt cathedral at Cape Haitien, 1878 (originally erected by French architects, 1748-74, destroyed by earthquake, 1842). Republican. Unitarian. Fellow Am. Inst. Architects, 1889. Home: Boston, Mass. Died May 21, 1920.

SEARS, William Henry, lawyer; b. Shellsburg, Ia., Mar. 7, 1858; s. Charles May and Mary Ann (Smith) S.; student normal dept. University of Kan., 1882; studied international law and diplomacy under Prof. James H. Canfield, U. of Kan., 1885, 88, 89; LL.B., U. of Kan., 1890; LL.M., U. of Mich., 1892; m. Alice Hibbard Peabody, June 25, 1884; 1 son, Burton Peabody. Buffalo hunter, cowboy and teamster until 1877; later coal miner, teacher, and in business of evaporating sweet corn, in Kan.; admitted to Kan. bar, 1890, later to bar Supreme Court of Kan., of Mich. and Supreme Court of U.S.; practiced at Lawrence, Kan., Washington, D.C., etc.; pres. and atty. Pentwater (Mich.) Machinery Co.; trustee Magoffin Oil Royalty Syndicate, Washington, D.C. Enlisted in Kan. N.G., 1884; brig. gen., 1893-95; judge advocate gen., 1897-99. Asst. supt. Indian Industrial Sch., Lawrence, Kan., 1887-88. Pvt. sec. to U.S. Senator William A. Harris, 1897-1900; field agt. and sec. to Clara Barton, pres. Am. Nat. Red Cross, 1900-05; chmn. Mich. delegation to Progressive Nat. Conv., Chicago, 1912; Prog. candidate for Congress, 9th Mich. Dist., 1912, 14. Organized first school in U.S. for training Nat. Guard officers, 1894, and secured first appropriation for that purpose from Kan. legislature; active in securing passage, in Congress, of charter for Am. Nat. Red Cross, 1900; author amendment to Nat. Bank Act, fixing $25,000 minimum capitalization. Trustee Clara Barton Nat. Memorial Assn. Hoover Republican. Unitarian. Mason. Home: Lawrence, Kan. Died Oct. 5, 1933.

SEARS, Zelda, actress; b. Brockway, Mich., Jan. 21, 1873; d. Justin Louis and Roxa (Tyler) Paldi; ed. pub. schs., Port Huron, Mich.; m. Herbert E. Sears, Apr. 13, 1892; m. 2d, L. C. Wiswell. For 10 years appeared under the management of Charles Frohman; starred in "The Nest Egg." Author: (mus. comedies) Lady Billy; The Clinging Vine; The Magic Ring; Lollipop. Home: Wilton, Conn. Died Feb. 19, 1935.

SEARSON, James William, prof. English; b. Grand Island, Neb., Sept. 12, 1873; s. Edwin and Jane (Burkett) S.; A.B., U. of Neb., 1896, A.M., 1899; work toward Ph.D., 1910; graduate work, Columbia U., 1917-18; m. Martha Ellen Chappell, July 25, 1901; 1 dau., Wilma Ruth. Prin. Weeping Water (Neb.) High Sch., 1894-95; fellow and asst. Dept. of History, U. of Neb., 1896-98; supt. schs., Wahoo, Neb., 1899-1905; lecturer Summer Sch., U. of Neb., 1904, 24; prof. rhetoric and lit., State Normal Sch., Peru, Neb., 1905-10; asso. prof. English lang. and lit., 1910, prof. English, 1911-21, Kan. State Agrl. Coll.; prof. English, Univ. of Nebraska, 1921—. Democrat. Methodist. Fellow Royal Soc. of Arts (London). Mason. Author: (with George E. Martin) Studies in Reading (series), 1910-13; Kansas Readers, 1916-17; Self-Correction in English. Editor: The American Educational Digest (with Dr. Frank A. Weld); classics, Macbeth, Merchant of Venice, Idylls of the King (with Harriet E. Towne), and Lady of the Lake (University Classics, 1923); Julius Cæsar, 1924; Silas Marner, 1924; Treasure Island, 1925. Spl. Text-book editor Kan. School Book Commn., 1916-17; mng. editor Nat. School Service, Washington, 1918-19; publs. editor University Pub. Co., 1921. Home: Lincoln, Neb. Died July 7, 1927.

SEASHORE, August Theodore, coll. pres.; b. nr. Dayton, Ia., Dec. 24, 1871; s. Carl Gustaf and Emily Charlotta (Borg) S.; grad. Gustavus Adolphus Bus. Coll., St. Peter, Minn., 1892; A.B., Gustavus Adolphus Acad. and Coll., 1900, D.D., 1925; student Mt. Airy Sem., Phila., Pa., 1900-02, Augustana Theol. Sem., Rock Island, Ill., 1902-03, D.D., 1925; student U. of Minn., 1904-05, and in absentia, 1919-20; m. Jennie Caroline Rose, Sept. 2, 1903; children—Rosel Theodore, Gustav Harold, Colin Mauritz, Selma Lillian, Stanley Emanuel, Sylvia Christine. Ordained ministry Lutheran Ch., 1903; pastor Swea City, Ia., 1903-06, Minneapolis, Minn., 1906-11, Swedeburg, Neb., 1911-15; pres. Luther Coll., Wahoo, Neb., 1915—. Trustee Bd. of Edn. of Neb. Conf. of Lutheran Ch. (pres.; mem. pension com.). Republican. Editor Luther Coll. Advocate. Home: Wahoo, Neb. Died Feb. 26, 1934.

SEASTONE, Charles Victor, civil engr.; b. New Boston, Ill., Apr. 18, 1872; s. John August and Eva Sophia (Hillmore) S.; B.S., in Civ. Engring., U. of Ill., 1895; m. Susan Sarah Bouton, June 25, 1900; children—John Bouton, Charles Victor. Began in employ of U.S. Govt. on Mississippi River Survey, 1895; asst. dept. of theoretical and applied mechanics, U. of Illinois, 1898-1900; successively instr., asst. prof. and asso. prof. municipal and sanitary engring., Purdue U., 1900-07; cons. engr., Madison, Wis., 1907—; now asso. consultant Mead, Ward & Hunt, hydro-electric developments and power plants; pres. Madison Metropolitan Sewerage Commn. Republican. Home: Madison, Wis. Died Sept. 26, 1940.

SEAVER, Edwin Pliny, educator; b. Northborough, Mass., Feb. 24, 1838; s. Samuel and Julia (Conant) S.; A.B., Harvard U., 1864, A.M., 1867, LL.B., 1870, but never practiced law; m. Margaret Wiley Cushing, Sept. 10, 1872. Teacher Friends' Acad., New Bedford, Mass., 1857-60, 1864, 1865; tutor and asst. prof. mathematics, Harvard, 1865-74; head master, English High Sch., Boston, 1874-80; supt. pub. schs., Boston, 1880-1904; retired. Mem. Bd. of Overseers of Harvard, 1877-1908, except 1890-91. Fellow Am. Acad. Arts and Sciences. Unitarian. Author: The Franklin Arithmetics, Algebra, Trigonometry, 1877; Mathematical Handbook, 1907. Home: New Bedford, Mass. Died Dec. 7, 1917.

SEAWELL, Emmet, judge; b. Yountville, Calif., Apr. 5, 1862; s. William N. and Sarah A. (Rickman) S.; A.B., Pacific Methodist Coll., Santa Rosa, Calif., 1887; LL.D., Coll. of the Pacific, Stockton, Calif.; m. Ida S. Graeter, Mar. 20, 1892; children—Dorothea, Emmet James. Admitted to Calif. bar, 1890, and began practice at Santa Rosa; dist. atty. Sonoma Co., 1892-98; judge, Superior Court, Sonoma Co., 1902-22, elected asso. justice Supreme Court of Calif. for term 1922-28. Chmn. Sonoma div. Calif. State Council Defense and chmn. Legal Advisory Bd., World War. Democrat. Mason, Elk. Home: Berkeley, Calif. Died July 7, 1939.

SEAWELL, Molly Elliott, author; b. Gloucester Co., Va.; d. John Tyler (a nephew of President Tyler) and Frances Jackson S.; ed. at home. Her father died and she and her mother removed to Washington, D.C. Began writing sketches and stories in 1886; published 1st novel, 1890. In 1890 her "Little Jarvis" took a prize of $500 offered by Youth's Companion for the best story for boys; in 1895 her "Sprightly Romance of Marsac" took a prize of $3,000 offered by the New York Herald; in 1908 took prize of $1,900 offered by New York Herald, for a short story, "John Mainwaring, Financier." Author: Little Jarvis, 1890; Paul Jones, 1892; Maid Marian, Decatur and Somers, 1894; The Sprightly Romance of Marsac, 1896; A Virginia Cavalier, 1896; The Rock of the Lion, 1897; Twelve Naval Captains (text-book at U.S. Naval Acad.), 1897; Gavin Hamilton, 1899; and many others. Plays: Maid Marian, 1894; Sprightly Romance of Marsac, 1900. Died Nov. 15, 1916.

SEAY, Abraham Jefferson, governor; b. Amherst Co., Va., Nov. 28, 1832; s. Camm and Lucy Jane (Tiller) S.; parents removed to Osage Co., Mo., 1835; acad. edn.; elected co. sch. commr., 1858; afterward studied law. Served pvt. to col. 32d Mo. Inf., 1861-65; served in 11 Southern States, fought in 7, and was engaged in 28 battles and skirmishes, including campaigns of Vicksburg, Chattanooga, Atlanta, etc. Rep. candidate for Congress, 1872, 1874, defeated by "Silver Dick" Bland; circuit judge, 1875-87; Rep. nominee for judge Ct. of Appeals, Eastern Dist. of Mo., 1888; judge Supreme Ct. of Okla. Ty., 1890-92; gov. of Okla. Ty., 1892-93. Pres. 3 banks. Died Dec. 22, 1915.

SEAY, Frank, clergyman; b. New Orleans, Dec. 17, 1881; s. Thomas (gov. Ala., 1886-90) and Clara (De Lesdernier) S.; A.M., Southern U., 1899; Vanderbilt U., 1900-01, 1901-02; U. of Chicago (summer), 1902; Harvard U., 1902-03, A.M., 1903; U. of Berlin, Germany, 1906; unmatriculate student by courtesy Oxford U., England, fall of 1906; m. Clara Callaway, Oct. 27, 1908. Ordained M.E., South, ministry, 1903; pastor Forest Av. Ch., Montgomery, Ala., 1903-05, St. Stephens Road Ch., Mobile, 1907-08, Uniontown, 1909; prof. theology and N.T. Greek, 1909-12, prof. philosophy and N.T. Greek, 1912-15, Southwestern U., Georgetown, Tex.; prof. N.T. Greek and interpretation, Southern Meth. U., Dallas, Tex., 1915—. Author resolution on Tri-Conf. Preachers' Inst., 1907, and sec. commn. to establish same; mem. Ala. Conf. Commn. on Centennial of Ala. Methodism, 1907; mem. original com. of three on associated charities for Mobile and sec. larger com. to establish same. Author: Gist of the Old Testament, 1905; The Story of the Old Testament, 1912; An Outline for the Study of Old Testament History (written at request of the College of Bishops of M.E. Ch., S., for conf. course of study for young ministers), 1917; An Outline for the Study of Old Testament Philosophy, Wisdom and Worship, 1919. Home: Dallas, Tex. Died Feb. 14, 1920.

SEBASTIAN, John, ry. official; b. Newport, Ky., Jan. 28, 1849. Served as clerk, chief clerk and traveling agt. in pass. dept. A.,T.&S.F. R.R., 1869-80; gen. Southwestern pass. agt. C.,R.I.&P., 1880-87; gen. ticket and pass. agt. Chicago, Kan. & Neb. div. same, 1887-89; gen. pass. and ticket agt. C.,R.I.&P. Ry., 1899 to July 1, 1902; pass. traffic mgr., 1902-

Jan. 20, 1903, pass. traffic mgr. R.I. System, 1903-06, of R.I. Lines, Frisco Lines and C.&E.I. R.R., Feb. 1906-Dec. 1909; 3d v.p. C.,R.I.&P. Ry., Dec. 1909—. Home: Evanston, Ill. Died Mar. 1, 1914.

SEBENIUS, John Uno, mining engr.; b. Sweden, Sept. 10, 1862; s. Carl William and Josephine Christine (Creutzer) S.; grad. Royal Tech. Inst. and Sch. of Mines, Stockholm, 1886; came to America, 1888; m. Susan May A. Manning, 1895 (died 1918); children—William Hobbs Manning, Carl Harald. Asst. supt. Witherbee, Sherman & Co., mines, Lake Champlain, N.Y., 1890-92; spl. exploration on Missabe Range, 1892-94; mining engr. for Rouchleau Ray Iron Co., 1894-98, for Lake Superior Consolidated Iron Mines, 1898, until U.S. Steel Corp. was formed, 1901; became mining engr. and supt. explorations and mineral lands on Missabe Range, for Oliver Iron Mining Co., 1901; gen. mining engr. for same company, 1905-30. Served as maj. on staff of Gov. John A. Johnson and as col. staffs Govs. Eberhardt, Hammond and Burnquist. Home: Duluth, Minn. Died Dec. 18, 1932.

SEBREE, Uriel, rear admiral U.S.N.; b. Fayette, Mo., Feb. 20, 1848; s. John P. and Louisa (Daly) S.; early edn. in schools of Fayette, Mo.; grad. U.S. Naval Acad., 1867; m. Annie Bridgman, June 16, 1886. Leaving Naval Acad. as midshipman in June 1867, served in divers duties and grades as naval officer in various parts of the world until promoted capt., Oct. 9, 1901; rear admiral, July 8, 1907. Was on Arctic relief expdn. on S.S. Tigress, 1873, under Comdr. Greer; on Greely relief expdn., 1884, under Comdr. Schley; on U.S.S. Baltimore, under command of Capt. Schley, 1889-92; light house insp., Portland, Ore., 1885-89, San Francisco, 1898-1901; comd. gunboat Wheeling, in Behring Sea, 1897-98; comd. Naval sta., Samoan Islands, 1901-02; comd. battleship Wisconsin, 1903-04; naval sec., Lighthouse Bd., 1904; comdg. 2d div. Pacific Fleet, 1907-09; comdr.-in-chief Pacific Fleet, 1909-10; retired, Feb. 20, 1910. Home: Coronado, Calif. Died Aug. 6, 1922.

SECKENDORFF, Max Gebhard, newspaperman; b. Brussels, Belgium, Dec. 1, 1852; pvt. sch. edn. in Germany. Entered the German Navy in 1868 and served in it during the Franco-German War, 1870-71. In newspaper work, 1880—; chief Washington bur. of New York Tribune, 1883-1902. Home: New York, N.Y. Died 1911.

SEDDON, William Little, civil engr.; b. Stafford Co., Va., Oct. 14, 1862; s. John Seddon and Mary A. (Little) S.; student U. of Mo., 1880-81; m. Kate McD. Martin, Nov. 7, 1888; 1 dau., Mary Alexander. With Seaboard Airline Ry., 1898—, consecutively as instrument-man, resident engr. and asst. engr. until 1905, chief engr., 1905-13, asst. to pres., 1913-15; v.p. in charge of operation, 1915-18, gen. mgr., 1918-20, v.p. and cons. engr. Mar. 1, 1920—. Democrat. Presbyn. Home: Portsmouth, Va. Died July 10, 1937.

SEDGWICK, Anne Douglas, author; b. Englewood, N.J., Mar. 28, 1873; d. George Stanley and Mary (Douglas) S.; ed. by governess, at home. Left America when 9 yrs. of age and has since lived abroad, chiefly in Paris and London; while in Paris studied painting for several yrs., exhibiting at Champs de Mars; m. Basil de Selincourt, of Far End, Kingham, Oxon, Eng., Dec. 11, 1908. Member National Institute of Arts and Letters. Author: The Dull Miss Archinard, 1898; The Confounding of Camelia, 1899; The Rescue, 1902; Paths of Judgment, 1904; The Shadow of Life, 1906; A Fountain Sealed, 1907; Amabel Channice, 1908; Franklin Winslow Kane, 1910; Tante, 1911; The Nest, 1912; The Encounter, 1914; A Childhood in Brittany Eighty Years Ago, 1918; Christmas Roses, 1920; The Third Window, 1920; Adrienne Toner, 1922; The Little French Girl, 1924; The Old Countess, 1927; Dark Hester, 1929; Philippa, 1930. Died July 19, 1935.

SEDGWICK, Arthur George, lawyer and writer; b. New York, Oct. 6, 1844; s. Theodore and Sarah (Ashburner) S.; A.B., Harvard, 1864, LL.B., 1866, A.M., 1870; m. Lucy Tuckerman, Nov. 16, 1882 (died 1904). First lt., 20th Mass. Regiment, 1864; taken prisoner at Deep Bottom, Va.; in Libby prison contracted an illness which disabled him from further service. Practiced at Boston till 1872, and (with O. W. Holmes, Jr.) edited Am. Law Review; admitted to bar, New York, in 1875, and practiced there until 1881; on editorial staff of Evening Post and The Nation; contbr. to the press, 1865-1905. Lecturer on law before Lowell Institute, Boston, 1885-86; Godkin lecturer at Harvard, 1909. Author: (with F. S. Wait) A Treatise on the Principles and Practice Governing the Trial of Title to Land; Elements of Damages, 2d edit., 1909; (alone) The Democratic Mistakes, 1912. Edited 5th, and coeditor of 7th, 8th and 9th edits. of his father's Measure of Damages. Home: New York, N.Y. Died July 14, 1915.

SEDGWICK, Henry Dwight, lawyer; b. Stockbridge, Mass., Aug. 16, 1824; s. Henry Dwight and Jane (Minot) S.; grad. Harvard, 1843; studied Harvard Law Sch., 1845-46; m. Henrietta Ellery, Oct. 15, 1857. Admitted to bar, 1846. Author: Sedgwick on Damages, 1868, 1874: Sedgwick's Leading Cases on Damages, 1878. Home: Stockbridge, Mass. Died 1903.

SEDGWICK, Julius Parker, pediatrist; b. Wrightstown, Wis., May 27, 1876; s. David Ernest and Jennie (Treat) S.; B.Sc., U. of Neb., 1896; M.D., Rush Med. Coll., Chicago, 1899; studied U. of Berlin, 1904-05; m. Emily Weeks, July 28, 1901. Interne, Alexian Bros. Hosp., Chicago, 1899-1900, Presbyn. Hosp., 1900-01; asst. phys., Fabiola Hosp., Eveleth, Minn., 1901-04; in practice of pediatrics, at Minneapolis, Minn., 1905—; teaching, U. of Minn., 1906—, prof. pediatrics and chief of dept., 1915—, pediatrist University Hosp.; served as maj. Am. Nat. Red Cross, work in France, 1917, returning to U.S., Jan. 1918. Died Feb. 1923.

SEDGWICK, Samuel Hopkins, judge; b. Bloomingdale, Ill., Mar. 12, 1848; s. Parker (M.D.) and Hepsibah (Goodwin) S.; A.B., Wheaton (Ill.) Coll., 1872, A.M., 1874; law student U. of Mich., 1871-72; m. Clara M. Jones, Sept. 25, 1878. Practiced at Kewaunee, Wis., 1874-78; at York, Neb., 1878—; judge District Ct., 5th Dist., Neb., 1896-1900; Supreme Ct. commr., 1901-02; judge Supreme Ct. of Neb., 1902—, present term expires 1923 (chief justice 1906-08). Republican. Home: Lincoln, Neb. Died Dec. 1919.

SEDGWICK, William Thompson, biologist; b. West Hartford, Conn., Dec. 29, 1855; s. William and Anne Thompson (Barbour) S.; Ph.B., Sheffield Scientific Sch. (Yale), 1877; Ph.D., Johns Hopkins, 1881; (hon. Sc.D., Yale, 1909); m. Mary Katrine Rice, Dec. 29, 1881. Instr. physiol. chemistry, Sheffield Scientific Sch., 1878-79; fellow, and asso. biology, Johns Hopkins, 1879; asst. prof., asso. prof. and prof. biology, now prof. biology and public health, Mass. Inst. of Technology, 1883—. Biologist Mass. State Board of Health, 1888-96; curator Lowell Inst., Boston, 1897—; chmn. Pauper Instns.' Trustees, 1897-99, and (1899-1900) Instns.' Registrar, City of Boston. Trustee Simmons Coll., 1899—; pres. bd. dirs. Sharon Sanatorium, 1902—; mem. advisory bd. Hygienic Laboratory U.S. Public Health Service, 1902—. V.p. Boston Society Municipal Officers, 1898-1900; pres. Boston Civil Service Reform Assn., 1900, Mass. Civil Service Reform Assn., 1901, Soc. Am. Bacteriologists, 1900; fellow Am. Acad. Arts and Sciences, A.A.A.S. (v.p. 1905); mem. State Dept. Health of Mass., Internat. Health Bd., Rockefeller Foundation; chmn. Harvard Tech. Sch. of Pub. Health. Author: General Biology (joint author), 1886; Life and Letters of William Barton Rogers (asst. editor), 1896; Principles of Sanitary Science and Public Health, 1902; The Human Mechanism (joint author), 1906; A Short History of Science (joint author), 1917. Home: Boston, Mass. Died Jan. 26, 1921.

SEDLEY, Henry, author; b. Boston, Apr. 4, 1831; ed. there; studied civil engring. at Rensselaer Polytechnic Inst.; practiced in San Francisco; later in journalism in New York on editorial staff of Times, Evening Post, Commercial-Advertiser, etc. Author: Dangerfield's Rest; Marion Rooke; etc. Died 1899.

SEE, Horace, naval architect; b. Philadelphia, July 17, 1835; s. Richard Colhoun and Margarita (Hilyard) S.; academic edn.; learned trade of machinist; supt. engr. William Cramp & Sons, Phila.; m. Ruth Ross Maffet, Feb. 20, 1879. Had much to do with introduction of triple-expansion engines into vessels of U.S. Navy; designed engines of cruisers Yorktown, Concord, Bennington, Philadelphia, Newark and Vesuvius; yachts, Atalanta, Corsair, Stranger, Peerless; steamer Monmouth; steamships, Mariposa, Queen of the Pacific, Caracas, Olivette; designed hull and machinery of steamships El Rio, El Valle, El Alba, Comus, Proteus, U.S. cruisers Yankee, Dixie, hosp. ship Solace; wrecking steamers Relief and Tasco, New York police launches, etc., into which many of his inventions were introduced, such as the hydropneumatic ash ejector, folding hatch cover, etc.; also inventor cylindrical mandrel for face bearings, which makes it possible to produce with certainty a true bearing and journal, double furnace water tube boiler, pneumatic siphon fire hydrant, etc. Superintends the constn., performance and maintenance of vessels and machinery; established at New York, 1889; consulting engr. Newport News Shipbuilding Co. and other corps. Private Gray Reserves early part of Civil War; corpl. 7th Regt. Pa. militia in Md., 1862; adj. 20th Regt. N.G. Pa. during July riots, 1877, and later capt. 1st Regt. N.G., Pa. Home: Glen Summit Springs, Pa. Died 1909.

SEEGERS, John Conrad, clergyman; b. Columbia, S.C., Oct. 6, 1867; s. John C. and Mary Dorothea (Schroeder) S.; Ph.B., Newberry (S.C.) Coll., 1888, D.D., 1909; grad. Mt. Airy (Phila.) Theol. Sem., 1891; hon. A.M., Muhlenberg Coll., Pa., 1907; m. May Erwin Idé, Feb. 14, 1893; children—John Conrad, Theodore Idé (dec.), Virginia May, Francis H. (dec.), Florence M., L. Walter, Sarah D., Ernest F. M. Ordained Luth. ministry, 1891; pastor Richmond, Va., 1891-94, Albany, N.Y., 1895-1901, Easton, Pa., 1901-11, Reading, Pa., 1911-14, Wilmington, N.C., 1918-21; prof. practical theology, Lutheran Sem., Columbia, S.C., 1914-18, Luth. Sem., Mt. Airy, Phila., 1921—. Served as chmn. English mission div. Bd. of Am. Missions, United Luth. Ch. in America; elected v.p. Bd. of Am. Missions, Oct. 1933. Democrat. Co-author: Explanation of Common Service, 1908; The Church for the Ages, 1922. Co-editor of Gospel Preaching for the Day (2 vols.). Home: Philadelphia, Pa. Died June 23, 1936.

SEEGMILLER, Wilhelmina, art dir.; b. Fairview, Ont., Can., Dec. 6, 1866; d. Frederick and Dolena (Gordon) S.; pub. schs., Goderich, Can.; art training in studios, Toronto; training for teaching in schs. of Grand Rapids, Mich.; grad. Pratt Inst., Brooklyn, 1899; unmarried. Dir. of art, Indianapolis pub. schs., Sept. 1895—. Pres. Western Drawing and Manual Training Assn., Grand Rapids, Mich., May 1900. Author: Little Rhymes for Little Readers, 1903; Primary Hand Work, 1906; Applied Arts Drawing Books (16 in number), 1908; A Hand Clasp, 1911; Other Rhymes for Little Readers, 1911; Riverside Readers, 1911. Home: Indianapolis, Ind. Died May 24, 1913.

SEELER, Edgar Viguers, architect; b. Phila., Pa., Nov. 18, 1867; s. George W. and Anna Maria (Viguers) S.; grad. Central High Sch., Phila., 1884; office work as archtl. draftsman and student night classes, Sch. of Indst. Art, Phila., 4 yrs.; student Mass. Inst. Tech., 1888-90; pupil Victor Laloux, École des Beaux Arts, Paris, 1890-93; m. Martha Page Laughlin, June 29, 1905; children—Sidney Page, Edgar Viguers, Josephine Page. Asst. prof. archtl. design, U. of Pa., 1893-98; began practice at Phila., 1895; architect of Bulletin Bldg., Real Estate Trust Bldg., Hallowell Bldg., First Baptist Ch., Dept. of Architecture Bldg. (U. of Pa.), Curtis Publishing Co. Bldg., Penn Mutual Life Ins. Co.'s Home Office Bldg., Fire Assn. Bldg.—of Phila.; James V. Brown Memorial Library, Williamsport, Pa.; Cannon Club, Princeton, N.J.; retired from practice, 1926. Architect for U.S. Ordnance Dept., Phila. Dist., and U.S. Housing Corp., Dept. of Labor, Ridley Park Project, Pa., World War. Trustee Pa. Mus. and Sch. of Industrial Art. Fellow Am. Inst. Architects. Awarded medal, Art Club of Phila., Exhbn. of 1895. Republican. Unitarian. Home: Philadelphia, Pa. Died Oct. 26, 1929.

SEELEY, Levi, normal sch. prof.; b. N. Harpersfield, N.Y., Nov. 21, 1847; s. Levi and Hannah (Thorpe) S.; grad. Albany Normal Sch., 1871; Ph.D., U. of Leipzig, 1886; (hon. A.M., Williams, 1871); m. Marie Hesse, of Oberrossla, Germany, July 24, 1886. Principal pub. schs., Orient, N.Y., 1871-74, New Hamburgh, 1874-75, Patchogue, 1875-81; supt. of schs., Lansingburg, N.Y., 1881-83; student in Germany, 1883-86; prin. pub. sch., Cobleskill, N.Y., 1886-87, Ferry Hall Sem., Lake Forest, Ill., 1887-94; traveled and studied in Europe, 1894-95; prof. pedagogy, Trenton Normal Sch., 1895—. Author: The American Common School System, 1886 (thesis for degree at Leipzig); The Grube System of Numbers, 1887; The Grube Idea, 1890; The German Common School System and Its Lessons to America, 1896; History of Education, 1899; The Foundations of Education, 1901; A New School Management, 1903; Seeley's Question Book, 1905; Elementary Pedagogy, 1906; Teaching, Its Aims and Methods, 1915. Home: Trenton, N.J. Died Dec. 23, 1928.

SEELY, Henry Martyn, college prof.; b. S. Onondaga, N.Y., Oct. 2, 1828; s. Joseph Owen and Susanna (Stearns) S.; Ph.B., Yale, 1856, A.M., 1860; M.D., Berkshire Med. Instn., 1857; studied at Freiberg and Heidelberg, 1867-68; m. Adelaide E. Hamblin, Sept. 1, 1858 (died 1865); 2d, Sarah J. Matthews, June 11, 1867. Prof. chemistry, Berkshire Med. Instn., 1857-62, U. of Vermont, 1860-67; prof. chemistry and natural history, 1861-92, natural history, 1892-95, emeritus prof., 1895, Middlebury Coll. Sec. Vt. Bd. of Agr., 1875-78; edited 3 vols. of reports. Prohibition candidate for gov. of Vt., 1886, 1888. Home: Middlebury, Vt. Died May 4, 1917.

SEELY, Walter Hoff; b. Middletown, N.J., Oct. 24, 1873; s. Col. Uriah and Nancy (Hopping) S.; grad. Colgate Acad. and Rutgers Coll.; m. Blanche Stoddard, Dec. 24, 1910; children—Nancy Stoddard, Jane Stoddard. With Springfield (Mass.) Republican, 1895-96; night editor Philadelphia (Pa.) Press, 1896-1900; editor-in-chief Newark (N.J.) Evening News, 1900-02; with New York World, 1902-05; asst. to president and agency dir. Pacific Mut. Life Ins. Co. at San Francisco, 1905-11; writer and lecturer; pub. Success Magazine, 1922, succeeding Orison Sweet Marden as editor same, 1923, resigned 1926; pres. Florida Service Corp., 1926—. Served in Intelligence Service, U.S.A., in America and Europe, 1917-18. Republican. Episcopalian. Mason. Home: Hollywood, Fla. Died June 23, 1936.

SEELYE, L(aurenus) Clark, educator; b. Bethel, Conn., Sept. 20, 1837; s. Seth and Abigail (Taylor) S.; A.B., Union Coll., 1857; Andover Theol. Sem., 1858-59; univs. of Berlin and Heidelberg, 1860-62; (D.D., Union, 1875; LL.D., Amherst Coll., 1894, Union Coll., 1913, Smith Coll., 1913); m. Henrietta Sheldon Chapin, Nov. 17, 1863. Ordained Congl. ministry, 1863; pastor North Ch., Springfield, Mass.,

1863-65, prof. rhetoric and English lit., Amherst, 1865-73; 1st pres. Smith Coll., 1873-1910, pres. emeritus, 1910—. Home: Northampton, Mass. Died Oct. 12, 1924.

SEEM, Ralph Berger, hosp. administrator; b. Bangor, Pa., June 16, 1880; s. Thomas Harrison and Emma Cecelia (Hartzell) S.; Ph.B., Lafayette Coll., Easton, Pa., 1902; M.D., Johns Hopkins, 1906; unmarried. Interne and resident phys., St. Luke's Hosp., Bethlehem, Pa., 1906-08; med. supt. James Walker Memorial Hosp., Wilmington, N.C., 1908-12; asst. supt. Johns Hopkins Hosp., Baltimore, 1912-20, acting supt., 1917-19; dir. Albert Merritt Billings Hosp., U. of Chicago, 1919-20; supt. Peking (China) Union Med. Coll. Hosp., 1920-21; physician supt. Stanford U. Hosp., Sept. 1, 1929—. Home: San Francisco, Calif. Died May 14, 1941.

SEESTED, August Frederick, newspaper mgr.; b. Tondern, Denmark, Mar. 26, 1864, came to U.S., 1880; m. Mary Irwin, Aug. 13, 1888. Newspaper work with Kansas City Star, 1881—; gen. mgr., 1902-27; pres. Kansas City Star Co., Sept. 1927—. Home: Kansas City, Mo. Died Oct. 2, 1928.

SEGER, Charles Bronson; b. New Orleans, Aug. 29, 1867; s. Augustin Bronson and Louise Juliette (Ham) S.; ed. pub. schs.; m. Marie Louise Knee. With S. P. Co. as office boy Morgan's La. & Tex. Ry. & Steamship Co., later clk., steamship auditor, traveling auditor, and chief clk. to gen. auditor; auditor and sec. Galveston, Harrisburg & San Antonio Ry., Tex. & New Orleans R.R., and Direct Navigation Co., 1893-1904; also auditor and sec. Galveston, Houston & Northern Ry., 1900-04; auditor Pacific System of S.P. Co., at San Francisco, 1904-09; gen. auditor, U.P. System and S.P. Co., 1910-11; deputy comptroller same, 1911-13; v.p. and comptroller, U.P. System, 1913-18, and pres., 1918-19; dir., 1916—, mem. exec. com., 1918—, U.P. R.R.; dir. and mem. exec. com. Ore. Short Line R.R., and Ore.-Wash. R.R. & Navigation Co., 1913—; dir. 1921—, mem. exec. com., 1922—, Los Angeles & Salt Lake R.R.; pres. U.S. Rubber Co., 1919-29, also chmn., 1921-29; pres. Dominion Rubber Co., Ltd., 1919-22, chmn. bd., 1922-29; officer or dir. many other cos. Home: New York, N.Y. Died Nov. 11, 1940.

SEGER, George N., congressman; b. N.Y. City, Jan. 4, 1866; ed. pub. schs. Engaged in building business, Passaic, N.J.; mem. Sch. Bd., 1906-11; mem. City Commn. 3 terms, 1911-23, serving 8 yrs. as mayor and 4 yrs. dir. finance; mem. 68th to 72d Congresses (1923-33), 7th N.J. Dist., and 73d to 76th Congresses (1933-41), 8th N.J. Dist. Mem. Council Nat. Defense, World War. Home: Passaic, N.J. Died Aug. 26, 1940.

SEIBERT, John F., clergyman; b. Chambersburg, Pa., Aug. 29, 1868; s. William and Mary (Rader) S.; student Pennsylvania Coll., Gettysburg, 1887-89; grad. Luth. Theol. Sem., Gettysburg, 1892; D.D., Carthage Coll., 1916; m. Florence A. Eliker, July 26, 1892; children—Edith M. (Mrs. Earl L. Lambert), Wm. Roy, Florence G. (Mrs. Thomas D. Elliott), Ruth M. (Mrs. Edw. M. Meltzer), Luther Y., Charles A. Ordained Luth. ministry, 1892; successively pastor Ft. Madison, Ia., Sedalia, Mo., North Platte, Neb.; mgr. Chicago office Luth. Pub. Soc., 1912-23; supt. of missions Lutheran Synod of Northern Ill., 1909-20; pres. Ill. Synod United Lutheran Ch., 1920-21; gen. supt., Central Dist. Bd. of Home Missions and Ch. Extension, United Luth. Ch., 1921-23; gen. sec. Bd. of Home Missions and Ch. Extension of United Luth. Ch. in America, 1923-26; sec. English div. Bd. Am. Missions of United Luth. Ch., 1927-36, then gen. asst. supt. same. Home: Chicago, Ill. Died Apr. 19, 1939.

SEIBERT, William Adam, physician; b. Lowhill, Pa., Feb. 10, 1859; s. Owen and Matilda (Miller) S.; A.B., Lafayette Coll., Easton, Pa., 1882, A.M., 1885; M.D., Boston U. Sch. of Medicine, 1885; m. Adelaide Koondoerfer, Feb. 18, 1905. Practiced at Easton, 1885—. Trustee Homœ. State Hosp., Allentown, Pa. Republican. Lutheran. Home: Easton, Pa. Died 1919.

SEIDERS, George Melville, lawyer; b. Union, Me., Jan. 15, 1844; s. Henry and Mary W. (Starrett) S.; A.M., Bowdoin Coll., 1872; read law under Hon. Thomas B. Reed; admitted to bar, 1878; m. Clarice S. Hayes, Nov. 24, 1874. In practice at Portland, 1878—; asst. U.S. council, Ala. Court of Claims, 1883, until the work of the court was completed; co. atty. Cumberland Co., 1885-89; mem. Me. Ho. of Rep., 1878, Senate, 1892, 1893, 1894, 1895 (pres. last 2 sessions); atty. gen. of Me., 1900-05; mem. Rep. State Com., 1901-05. Corp. 24th Me. Vols., 1862. Conglist. Home: Portland, Me. Died May 26, 1915.

SEIF, William Henry, capitalist; b. Ross, Pa., Sept. 11, 1859; s. Philip and Dorothy (Roth) S.; ed. public schools and Duff's Coll.; m. Annie Graitge, Mar. 26, 1885. Cashier Pittsburgh Dispatch, 1880-84; pres., treas. and mgr. Times, 1884-1906; dir. Bank of Pittsburgh, N. Am. Guarantee Title & Trust Co., Pittsburgh Life & Trust Co. Mem. exec. com., Am. Newspaper Publishers' Assn., 1894-1900; elected mem. bd. mgrs. Western Pa. Hosp., 1899; elected mem. bd. mgrs. Allegheny Co. Work House, 1900; pres. bd. of trustees Elizabeth Steel Magee Hosp. Home: Pittsburgh, Pa. Died Sept. 11, 1921.

SEIP, Theodore Lorenzo, pres. Muhlenberg Coll., Jan. 1, 1886—; b. Easton, Pa., June 25, 1842; s. Reuben L. and Sarah A. S.; grad. Pa. Coll., Gettysburg, 1864 (A.M.; D.D., Univ. of Pa.); grad. Lutheran Theol. Sem., Phila., 1867. One of the founders of Muhlenberg Coll.; prof. Latin and Greek there until 1886. Pres. of Evang. Luth. Ministerium of Pa. and adjacent States, the oldest Lutheran Synod in America, 1895-98; mem. Coll. and Univ. Council of the State of Pa. Home: Allentown, Pa.

SEISS, Joseph Augustus, clergyman; b. Frederick Co., Md., Mar. 18, 1823; s. John and Eliza (Schuler) S.; ed. Pa. Coll. (A.M., D.D., LL.D., L.H.D.); entered Luth. ministry in Va., 1842; pastor in Martinsburg and Shepherdstown, W.Va., Cumberland and Baltimore, Md., and from 1858 in Phila.; pastor Ch. of the Holy Communion; distinguished as a preacher; prominent in affairs of Luth. Ch.; 12 yrs. editor The Lutheran, and of The Prophetic Times. Author: Baptist System Examined, 1858; Parable of the Ten Virgins, 1862; Lectures on Apocalypse, 3 vols., 1866-1881; Ecclesia Lutherana, 1868; Lectures on the Gospels, 2 vols., 1868, 1870; Truth Made Plain, 1870; Uriel, Occasional Discourses, 1874; A Miracle in Stone, 1877; Voices from Babylon, 1879; Blossoms of Faith, 1880; The Gospel in the Stars, 1882-85; The Golden Altar, 1882-98; Lectures on the Epistles, 2 vols., 1885; Letters of Jesus, 1889; Lectures on Gospels and Epistles for Minor Festivals, 1893; Beacon Lights, 1900; Lenten and Passiontide Sermonettes, 1901; The Christ and His Church, 1902. Home: Philadelphia, Pa. Died 1904.

SEITZ, Don Carlos, newspaper mgr.; b. Portage, O., Oct. 24, 1862; s. Rev. J. A. S.; grad. Liberal Inst., Norway, Me., 1880; hon. A.M., St. Lawrence U., 1906; D.Litt., Bowdoin Coll., 1921; m. Mildred E. Blake, Apr. 15, 1890. Albany corr. Brooklyn Eagle, 1887-89; city editor, same, 1889-91; asst. publisher New York Recorder, 1892-93; mng. editor Brooklyn World, 1893-94; advertising mgr., 1895-97, business mgr., 1898-1923, New York World; mgr. Evening World, 1923-26; associate editor Outlook, 1926-27; asso. editor The Churchman, 1929-32. Trustee and secretary Authors Club Carnegie Fund. Author: Writings By and About James McNeill Whistler, 1910; Elba and Elsewhere, 1910; Surface Japan, 1911; Letters from Francis Parkman to E. G. Squier, with Bibliog. Notes and a Bibliography, 1911; The Buccaneers, 1912; Whistler Stories, 1913; Training for the Newspaper Trade, 1916; The Unprecedented Invasion of Althuria, 1917; Paul Jones—His Campaigns in English Seas, 1778-79, 1917; In Praise of War, 1917; Farm Voices, 1918; Brains in Chains, 1919; The Tryal of William Penn, 1919; Artemus Ward, 1919; Braxton Bragg, 1923; Joseph Pulitzer; His Life and Letters, 1924; Monogatari, 1924; Under the Black Flag, 1925; Uncommon Americans, 1925; The Dreadful Decade, 1926; A Chapter on Autography, 1926; The Great Island, 1926; Horace Greeley, 1926; The James Gordon Bennetts, 1928; From Kaw Tepee to Capital, 1928; The Also Rans, 1928; Famous American Duels, 1929; Lincoln, the Politician, 1931; The Tryal of Captain William Kidd, 1933. Home: Brooklyn, N.Y. Died Dec. 4, 1935.

SELBY, Augustine Dawson, botanist; b. in Athens Co., O., Sept. 2, 1859; s. Warren and Emily (Garretson) S.; B.S., Ohio State Univ., 1893; Washington U. and Shaw Sch. of Botany, 1899; Columbia, 1902-03; m. Libbie Glover, Dec. 15, 1883. Supt. schs., Huntington, W.Va., 1884-86; prin. high sch., Ironton, O., 1886-87, Garfield Sch., Columbus, O., 1887-89; teacher botany, Columbus High Sch., 1889-94; sec. Columbus Hort. Soc., 1888-94; botanist and chemist, Ohio Agrl. Expt. Sta., 1894-1902; botanist and chief of dept. of botany in same, 1902-23. Interested chiefly in diseases of plants and their remedies and in plant breeding; also commercial apple growing. Propr. Selby Heights Fruit Farm, Sharpsburg, O. Writer in reports, Ohio Agrl. Expt. Sta. (Wooster, O.), and in scientific jours. Dir. Ohio State Life Ins. Co. Mason. Home: Wooster, O. Died May 7, 1924.

SELBY, Charles Baxter, lawyer; b. Osceola, Ia., Feb. 8, 1872; s. John N. and Judith W. (Webster) S.; student Lane U., Lecompton, Kan.; B.S., Kan. State Agrl. Coll., 1895; m. Alice V. Larimer, June 1904. Admitted to Tenn. bar, 1898, and began practice at Knoxville; moved to Oklahoma City, Okla., 1901; practiced in Ore., 1908-13; U.S. commr. under Federal Judge Charles H. Wolverton, Ore., 1909-14; county atty., Oklahoma Co., 1917-18; spl. asst. to atty. gen. of U.S., 1925—. Republican. Home: Oklahoma City, Okla. Died Nov. 6, 1933.

SELFRIDGE, Thomas Oliver, rear admiral, U.S.N.; b. Boston, Apr. 24, 1804; m. Louisa Cary, d. John Soley, Charlestown, Mass., 1834. Apptd. to navy, Jan. 1, 1818; commissioned lt., Mar. 3, 1827; comdr., Apr. 11, 1844; capt., Sept. 14, 1855; commodore, July 16, 1862; placed on retired list, Apr .24, 1866; promoted rear admiral, July 25, 1866. Comd. the sloop "Dale" of the Pacific squadron, 1847-48; he took part in engagement and capture of Matanzas and Guaymas; at latter place received a severe wound, which incapacitated him for sea duty. During Civil war comd. a few months the steam-frigate "Mississippi" in Gulf squadron; later comd. Mare Island Navy Yard, San Francisco; pres. examining bd., 1869-71; now senior officer on navy retired list. Home: Washington, D.C. Died 1902.

SELFRIDGE, Thomas Oliver, rear admiral U.S.N.; b. Boston, Feb. 6, 1836; s. late Rear Admiral Thomas Oliver and Louisa Cary (Soley) S.; apptd. acting midshipman U.S. Naval Acad., from Mass., Oct. 3, 1851, grad. 1854; m. Ellen F., d. Judge George F. Shepley, of Portland, Me., Aug. 1895. Promoted passed midshipman, Nov. 22, 1856; advanced through grades to commodore Apr. 11, 1894; rear admiral, Feb. 28, 1896. Served on Independence and Nautilus, 1854-57; on Vincennes as acting master on the coast of Africa, 1858-60; on Cumberland, 1860-61, was on board when she was sunk by Confederate Iron Clad Merrimac; flag lt. N. Atlantic Sta. and comd. submarine boat Alligator, 1862; comd. Cairo, Miss., Squadron, which was blown up by torpedo; comd. a battery at capture of Vicksburg; comd. Huron at engagements at Ft. Fisher; on duty Naval Acad., 1865-68; comd. Nipsic, 1868-70; comd. survey of the Isthmus of Darien to select a route for an interoceanic ship canal, 1869-74; Navy Yard, Boston, 1873-75; torpedo instrn., 1877; comd. Enterprise, 1878-80; in charge Torpedo Sta., Newport, 1881-84; comd. Omaha, 1885-87; spl. duties, 1888-90; commandant Navy Yard, Boston, 1890-93; pres. Bd. Inspection and Survey, 1894-95; comdr.-in-chief European Squadron, 1895-97; retired, Feb. 6, 1898. Chevalier Legion of Honor, France; awarded gold medal by Czar of Russia in honor of his coronation. Home: Washington, D.C. Died Feb. 4, 1924.

SELIGMAN, Albert Joseph, banker; b. New York, Feb. 24, 1859; s. Jesse and Henrietta S.; C.E., Rensselaer Poly. Inst., 1878; Royal Berg-Academie, Freiberg, Saxony, 1878-80; Royal Sch. of Mines, Liège, Belgium, 1880-81; m. Lillie Glazier, Dec. 22, 1886. Interested in mines nr. Helena, Mont., 1881—; mem. Seligman & Meyer, bankers and brokers, New York, 1899-1919; became mem. A. J. Seligman & Co., 1919; pres. Butte Copper & Zinc Co. Mem. Territorial Legislature, 1884-85; chmn. Rep. State Com., 1889-90; chmn. Mont. delegation Minneapolis Convention, 1892. Grand Chancellor, Knights of Pythias of Mont., 1888-90; Exalted Ruler, Helena Lodge, No. 193, B.P.O. of Elks, 1897, 98. Republican. Home: New York, N.Y. Died Apr. 13, 1935.

SELIGMAN, Arthur, governor; b. Santa Fe, N.M., June 14, 1873; s. Bernard and Frances (Nusbaum) S.; grad. Swarthmore (Pa.) Coll. Prep. Sch., 1887, also Pierce's Coll. Bus., Phila.; m. Frankie E. Harris, July 4, 1896; children—Frankie Richardson March, Otis Perry. Entered mercantile business, Santa Fe, N.M., 1888; pres. Seligman Bros., 1903-26; pres. La Fonda Building Corp., 1920-26; pres. First Nat. Bank, 1924—; dir. Northern N.M. Loan Assn. Has held many public offices, among them: Mayor of Santa Fe; mem. bd. Pan Am. and St. Louis expns.; mem. Bd. of Equalization of N.M.; chmn. Santa Fe County Commrs.; mem. Bd. Irrigation Commn., 1910; pres. Ednl. Survey Commn., 1923. Chmn. Dem. County Central Com. 6 yrs., City Central Com. 8 yrs., Territorial Dem. Com., 1895-1911, Dem. State Com., 1912-22 (sec. 1910-12); mem. of Dem. Nat. Com., 1920—; gov. of N.M., 1931— for term, 1931-33. Mason, Elk. Home: Santa Fe, N.M. Died Sept. 25, 1933.

SELIGMAN, Edwin Robert Anderson, economist; b. New York, Apr. 25, 1861; s. Joseph and Babette (Steinhardt) S.; A.B., Columbia, 1879, A.M., LL.B., 1884, Ph.D., 1885, LL.D., 1904; univs. of Berlin, Heidelberg, Geneva and Paris 3 yrs.; hon. Doc., Univ. of Paris, 1925, Univ. of Heidelberg, 1927, University of Havana, 1932; L.H.D., Rollins Coll., 1938; m. Caroline Beer, Apr. 4, 1888; children—Eustace, Mabel (dec.), Violet (dec.), Hazel. Lecturer on economics, 1885, adj. prof. polit. economy, 1888-91, prof. polit. economy and finance, 1891-1904, McVickar prof., 1904-31, prof. emeritus in residence, 1931—, Columbia U. Was mem. Com. of 70, and Com. of 250, and sec. Com. of 15, New York; mem. mayor's advisory com. on taxation and finance, 1905, and spl. State Tax Com., 1906; mem. President Roosevelt's Com. on Statistical Reorganization, 1908; chmn. trustees Bur. of Municipal Research, 1905-10; chmn. Mayor's Tax Com., 1914-16; expert adviser to Joint Legislative Tax Com. of 1919-22; mem. Advisory Com. on U.S. Census, 1919-22; mem. N.Y. State Tax Commn., 1929-31; financial adviser to Cuba, 1931; adviser to com. of ways and means, U.S. Congress, 1918-25; mem. Pres.'s Unemployment Conf., 1921; expert to League of Nations com. on econs. and finance, 1922-23. Comdr. Order of the Crown of Roumania; Commander Order of Manuel de Cespedes, Cuba. Clubs: Authors, City, National Arts, Columbia, Sculpture, Municipal Art. Editor: Columbia Series in History, Economics and Public Law, Political Science Quarterly, Encyclopedia of the Social Sciences (15 vols.). Author: Finance Statistics of American Commonwealths, Am. Statistical Association, Boston, 1889; The Shifting and Incidence of Taxation (5th edit.), 1927, Progressive Taxation in Theory and Practice (2d edit.), 1908; Essays in Taxation (10th edit.), 1925; Two Chapters on Mediæval Guilds of England, 1887; Economic Interpretation of History (2d edit.), 1937; Principles of Economics (12th edit.), 1929; The Income Tax (2d edit.), 1914; Currency Inflation and Public Debts, 1921; Essays in Economics, 1925; Studies in Public Finance, 1925; The Economics of Installment Selling, 1927; Double Taxation and International Fiscal Coöperation, 1928; The Economics of Farm Relief, 1929; Price Cutting and Price Maintenance, 1932. Died July 18, 1939.

SELIGMAN, Henry, banker; b. San Francisco, Calif., Mar. 31, 1857; s. Jesse and Henrietta (Hellman) S.; A.B., New York U., 1875; m. Addie Walter, Mar. 11, 1899; children—Mrs. Gladys van Henkelom, Mrs. Frederick Lewisohn, Walter. With Anglo-California Bank, San Francisco, 1875-80; returned to N.Y. City, and became partner of firm of J. & W. Seligman & Co. Republican. Home: New York, N.Y. Died Dec. 23, 1933.

SELIGMAN, Isaac Newton, banker; b. Staten Island, N.Y., July 10, 1856; s. Joseph and Babette (Steinhardt) S.; brother of Edwin Robert Anderson S.; A.B., Columbia, 1876; m. Guta, d. of Solomon and Betty Loeb, 1883. Was mem. of the victorious Columbia "eight," which defeated Harvard, Yale and other crews on Saratoga Lake, 1874. In banking business, 1876—; mem. J. & W. Seligman & Co., bankers, New York, 1878—; trustee Munich Reinsurance Co., Russia Reinsurance Co., U.S. Savings Bank, Lincoln Trust Co.; mem. advisory com. Audit Co. of New York; treas. and dir. City & Suburban Homes Co. V.p. United Hebrew Charities, St. John's Guild (treas.), Nat. Child Labor Com. (chmn. finance com.), McKinley Memorial Assn. (exec. com.), Gen. Grant Tomb Assn., Carl Schurz Memorial Com. (treas.), Chamber of Commerce (tax com.), Legal Aid Society, City Club (chmn. finance com.); treas. Citizens' Union; treas. Hudson-Fulton Memorial Com. (exec. com.); v.p. and treas. Andrew H. Green Memorial Assn.; mem. com. of nine for police investigation; trustee Civic Forum, etc. Home: New York, N.Y. Died Sept. 30, 1917.

SELIGMAN, Jefferson, banker; b. New York, N.Y., Nov. 26, 1858; s. James and Rosie (Content) S.; A.B., Columbia, 1878; also med. student Göttingen, Germany; unmarried. Started in banking business as cashier, 1880, partner J. & W. Seligman & Co., 1878—. Decorated Chevalier Légion d'Honneur (France). Home: New York, N.Y. Died June 18, 1937.

SELINGER, Jean Paul, portrait painter-artist; b. Boston, June 24, 1850; s. Clement and Dorothea S.; ed. pub. schs., Boston, Lowell Inst. of Fine Art, Art Acad. of Stuttgart, Germany, Acad. of Fine Arts, Munich; pupil of Wilhelm Liebl, Munich; m. Emily Harris McGary, 1882. Hon. mention, Munich Expn., 1881; large medal, expn., Boston; winner of $1,000 Osborne prize for most popular picture in New York Exhbn. of Paintings. Home: Boston, Mass. Died 1909.

SELL, Edward Herman Miller, physician; b. Upper Saucon Tp., Lehigh Co., Pa., Aug. 16, 1832; s. Samuel and Mary (Miller) S.; A.B., Pa. Coll., Gettysburg, 1856, A.M., 1859; grad. Gettysburg Theol. Sem.; was in active Luth. ministry, 1858-63; M.D., Bellevue Hosp. Med. Coll. (New York U.), 1866; studied several yrs. in Europe; in Paris during siege, 1870-71; grad., master of obstetrics, U. of Vienna, 1872; m. Anna J. Lloyd, Jan. 17, 1894. In 1871 organized 1st practical gynecol. operative course of the world at U. of Vienna; discovered cure of morphine habit. One of 7 organizers Am. Acad. Medicine, 1876. Fellow N.Y. Academy of Medicine; del. Internat. Med. Congresses, 1890, 94, British Med. Assn., 1870, 73, 76; life mem. Huguenot Soc. America. Editor Physician and Pharmacist, 1869-80. Died June 7, 1920.

SELL, Henry Thorne, clergyman; b. Brooklyn, Sept. 30, 1854; s. Henry T. and Martha A. (Fordham) S.; A.B., Wesleyan U., 1873, A.M., 1876; B.D., Yale, 1877; D.D., Ripon Coll., 1902; m. Mary Blackman, Nov. 21, 1888; children—Henry B., Charles J. (dec.). Prof. mathematics and German, Chamberlain Inst. and Female Coll., Randolph, N.Y., 1873-74; ordained Congl. ministry, 1877; pastor, Lysander, N.Y., 1877-81, Cortland, 1881-86; dist. sec. for Ill. and Wis. Nat. Congl. S.S. and Publ. Society, Chicago, 1886-92; pastor Auburn Park (1892-96) and Covenant (1898-1901) chs., Chicago. Editor The Advance, Chicago, 1901-03; preaching, lecturing and writing books, 1903-06; pastor Plymouth Ch., Ft. Wayne, Ind., 1906-10, Union Ch., Jacksonville, Fla., 1912-16; moderator Fla. Congl. State Conf., 1915, 16; pastor 1st Ch., Kenosha, Wis., 1918-23. Lecturer for The Independent and Redpath-Horner Chautauqua Systems, etc. Mason. Mem. N.Y. City Congl. Assn. Author: Supplemental Bible Studies, 1890; Bible Study by Books, 1896; Bible Study by Doctrines, 1897; Bible Study by Periods, 1899; Bible Studies in the Life of Christ, 1902; Bible Studies in the Life of Paul, 1904; Bible Studies in the Life of the Christian, 1905; Studies in Early Church History, 1906; Bible Studies in Vital Questions, 1916; The Twentieth Century Story of The Christ, A Harmony of The Four Gospels, 1917; Studies in The Four Gospels, 1917; Sermons in Stories, 1923; Studies of Great Bible Characters, 1923; Sermons in Objects, 1924; Studies of Famous Bible Women, 1925; Sermons in Action, 1926; Studies of Great Bible Cities, 1927; Preaching and Lecturing in New York Churches, 1923, 1927. Died July 20, 1928.

SELLERS, Coleman, consulting engr.; b. Phila., Jan. 28, 1827; s. Coleman and Sophonisba (Peale) S.; ed. private schools and Bolmar's Acad., West Chester, Pa.; E.D., Stevens Inst. of Technology; prof. engring. practice same, 1886—; Sc.D., Univ. of Pa., 1899; m. Cornelia, d. Horace Wells, of Cincinnati, Oct. 8, 1851. Chief engr. Niagara Falls Power Co., and chief mech. engr. Canadian Niagara Power Co. The engring. work of development of the power of Niagara Falls was undertaken under his advice and direction. Knight of the Royal Norwegian Order of St. Olaf. Mem. numerous scientific societies. Home: Philadelphia, Pa. Died 1907.

SELLERS, Coleman, Jr., engineer; b. Cincinnati, Sept. 5, 1852; s. Coleman and Cornelia (Wells) S.; B.S., U. of Pa., 1873, M.S., 1876; spl. studies mech. engineering in works of Wm. Sellers & Co., Philadelphia; m. Helen Graham Jackson, June 3, 1880. Asst. mgr., 1886-1902, engr., 1902-19, and pres., 1919—, Wm. Sellers & Co., Inc. One of Pa. commrs. of navigation for River Delaware, 1907—. Pres. Phila. Chamber Commerce, 1908-12. Home: Philadelphia, Pa. Died Aug. 15, 1923.

SELLERS, Horace Wells, architect; b. Philadelphia, July 21, 1857; s. Coleman and Cornelia (Wells) S.; grad. Eastburn Acad., Phila., 1873; B.Sc., U. of Pa., 1877; m. Cora Wells, d. late Charles Wells, of Cincinnati, Nov. 22, 1899; children—Lester Hoadley, Charles Coleman, Jessie. Entered the office of Joseph M. Wilson (fellow A.I.A.), then engr. bridges and bldgs., Pa. R.R., 1877, and with Wilson Bros. & Co., engrs. and architects; engaged on architectural engring. and executive details connected with r.r., electric light and other developments and machine works, 1882-92; associated after 1892 with late Coleman Sellers who was pres. and chief engr. Niagara Falls Power Co., and in his gen. practice as consulting engr., at same time conducting individual architectural practice. Fellow A.I.A. (ex-dir.; pres. Philadelphia Chapter), Royal Soc. of Arts (Gt. Britain). Republican. Episcopalian; mem. Commn. on Ch. Architecture, Diocese of Pa. Home: Ardmore, Pa. Died Nov. 26, 1933.

SELLERS, James Freeman, educator; b. Starkville, Miss., June 1, 1862; s. Thomas George and Mary Elizabeth (Crenshaw) S.; B.A., U. of Miss., 1885, M.A., 1890; student U. of Va., 1892; teaching fellow U. of Chicago, 1896-98; LL.D., Mississippi College, 1917; Sc.D., Mercer University, Macon, Ga., 1933; m. Dora Fort, Dec. 20, 1888; children—Thomas Fort, William LeRoy, James Freeman, Erle Dees, Mark Ashley, Abbott Mannie. Prof. chemistry, Mississippi Coll., 1888-93; same, Mercer U., 1893-1918, acting pres., 1913-14, dean, 1914-18; dean Oglethorpe U. Sch. of Science and of the university, July 1, 1919—. Served as Y.M.C.A. area educational secretary in Great Britain, 1918; prof. chemistry, Army Ednl. Corps, A.E.F. Univ., Beaune, France, 1919. Democrat. Baptist. Author: Treatise on Analytical Chemistry, 1900. Home: Atlanta, Ga. Died May 19, 1936.

SELLERS, Kathryn, lawyer; b. Broadway, O., Dec. 25, 1870; d. John Henry and Nancy J. (Alexander) S.; ed. pub. and high schs., Marysville, O.; LL.B., Washington Coll. of Law, 1913, LL.M., 1914. Clerk U.S. Weather Bur., Washington, D.C., 1891-1900; asst. in Dept. of State Library, 1900-11; bibliographer and librarian, Carnegie Endowment for Internat. Peace, 1911-18; began law practice 1913; prof. law, Washington Coll. of Law, 1914-21. Compiler of periodical lit. of internat. law and chronicle of internat. events in Am. Jour. of Internat. Law, 1911-19. Judge Juvenile Court of D.C., 1918-34. Mem. D.C. Bd. of Charities, 1924-27. Episcopalian. Home: Washington, D.C. Died Feb. 23, 1939.

SELLERS, Matthew Bacon, aerodynamics; b. Baltimore, Mar. 29, 1869; s. Matthew Bacon and Annie L. (Lewis) S.; ed. pvt. schs. and under pvt. tutors, including 1 yr. in Göttingen, Germany, and 1 yr. in Evreux, France; LL.B., Harvard, 1892; spl. courses later, Lawrence Scientific Sch. (Harvard), and Drexel Inst., Phila.; m. Ethel Clark, June 18, 1918; children—Matthew B., John C. Research in aerodynamics, 1900—; in practice as cons. aeronautical engr.; apptd. by President Taft mem. Aerodynamic Lab. Com., 1912; mem. Navy Consulting Bd., Sept. 1915—. Dir. and mem. tech. bd. Aeronautical Soc. America. Inventor of lightest aeroplane in world, flying with least horsepower; first to determine lift and drift of arched surfaces by means of the "wind tunnel." Home: Ardsley-on-Hudson, N.Y. Died Apr. 5, 1932.

SELLERS, Sandford, president military acad.; b. Anderson Co., Ky., July 24, 1854; s. John Newton and Marcia Jane (McBrayer) S.; A.B., Centre Coll., Danville, Kentucky, 1877, A.M., 1880; LL.D., Westminster Coll., Fulton, Mo.; m. Lucia V. Rogers, Dec. 27, 1882; children—Ovid Rogers, Mrs. Marcia Davis, Mrs. Pauline Richardson, Sandford, J. M. Prof. English, Austin Coll., Sherman, Tex., 1879-80; became supt. Wentworth Mil. Acad., Lexington, Mo., 1880, then pres. Commd. as maj. and col. Mo. N.G., as supt. Wentworth Mil. Acad. V.p. Lexington Savings Bank; pres. Wentworth Mil., Lit., Scientific and Ednl. Co. Democrat. Presbyn. Home: Lexington, Mo. Died Mar. 4, 1938.

SELLERS, William, mfr., mech. engr.; b. Delaware Co., Pa., Sept. 19, 1824; s. John and Elizabeth (Poole) S.; ed. private school; apprenticed to machinists' trade at 14; at 21 became foreman for Fairbanks, Bancroft & Co., Providence, R.I.; started in 1847 business now known as William Sellers & Co., incorporated, of which he is pres. and engr.; also pres. Edgemoor Iron Co., 1868—, and of Midvale Steel Co., 1873-87; dir. Phila., Wilmington & Baltimore R.R., 1865—; pres. Franklin Inst., 1864-67; park commr., Phila., 1867-72; mem. Nat. Acad. Sciences, from 1873; v.p. Centennial Bd. of Finance, for exhbn. of 1876. Chevalier Legion d'Honneur, 1889. Read paper before Franklin Inst., 1864, on "Screw Threads and Nuts," which has since become the standard for the U.S. and the form of thread for the continent of Europe. Home: Phila., and Edgemoor, Del. Died 1905.

SELLEW, Walter Ashbel, bishop; b. Gowanda, N.Y., Feb. 27, 1844; s. Ashbel R. and Jane M. (Tucker) S.; A.B., Dartmouth, 1866, A.M., 1869; m. Jennie R. Peters, June 4, 1873 (died 1895); children—Mrs. Ada Virginia Layman, Mrs. Cora R. DeWitt; m. 2d, Mrs. Rebecca E. Muse, Mar. 31, 1897. Ordained ministry Free Meth. Ch., 1872; pastor successively, Tonawanda, Rochester, N.Y., Spring Arbor, Mich., Dunkirk, N.Y., Gerry, Allegany, N.Y., Buffalo; presiding elder Chautauqua, Allegany, Buffalo, Oil City, Bradford and Pittsburgh districts, 1887-98; elected bishop Oct. 15, 1898. Treas. The Gerry (N.Y.) Home for Aged Persons and the Gerry Orphanage; also treas. The A.M. Chesebrough Sem., North Chili, N.Y. Treas. Free Meth. Pub. House and pres. trustees Free Meth. Ch. of N.A. Officially made a missionary tour of inspection around the world, 1906, visiting all foreign missionary stas. of Free Meth. Ch.; visited China and Japan, 1910, and again visited Japan in 1926 to preside at the Annual Conf. at Osaka; chmn. finance com. Gen. Missionary Bd.; reëlected bishop for 8th consecutive term of 4 yrs. each, in 1927, although past 83 yrs. of age. Author: Clara Leffingwell, A Missionary. Home: Jamestown, N.Y. Died Jan. 16, 1929.

SELLS, Elijah Watt, accountant; b. Muscatine, Ia., Mar. 1, 1858; s. Elijah and Isabel (Watt) S.; educated Baker U., Kansas (M.A., 1909; D.C.S., New York U., 1916); m. Mabel Graves, Apr. 24, 1884. In service of different rys. in various depts. till 1893; with late Charles Waldo Haskins, was selected by joint commn. of 53d Congress, 1893, to effect a revision of the accounting system of U.S. Govt. with a view to simplifying and expediting public business (the most extensive and important undertaking of the kind in the history of the country). At the conclusion of this work, 1895, established firm of Haskins & Sells, of which is now sr. mem.; reported on a system of accounting for P.I. to U.S. Govt., 1908; etc. Home: Greenwich, Conn. Died Mar. 19, 1924.

SELLSTEDT, Lars Gustaf, artist; b. Sundsvall, Sweden, Apr. 30, 1819; ed. there and at Hernösand, Sweden; went to sea, 1832; came to U.S., 1834, as cabin boy on barque "Prudent," of New York; served on U.S. man-of-war, 1837-40; settled in Buffalo, 1842, and began to study art, earning money to pay his way by occasional trips on Lake Erie vessels; m. Caroline, d. William K. Scott, M.D., of Buffalo, 1856. One of founders (dir. 26 yrs., pres. 1876-77) Buffalo Fine Arts Academy, A.N.A., 1873, N.A., 1875. Author: From Forecastle to Academy (autobiography), 1905. Home: Buffalo, N.Y. Died 1911.

SELTZER, Charles Alden, author; b. Janesville, Wis., Aug. 15, 1875; s. Lucien Bonaparte and Oceanna (Hart) S.; ed. pub. schs., Columbus, O.; m. Ella Alberts, July 28, 1896; children—Louis B., Robert M., Helen G., Charles A., Edna E. Author: The Range Riders, 1911; The Two-Gun Man, 1911; The Coming of the Law, 1912; The Trail to Yesterday, 1913; The Boss of the Lazy Y, 1915; The Range Boss, 1916; The Vengeance of Jefferson Gawne, 1917; Firebrand Trevison, 1918; The Man With a Country (patriotic serial), 1919; The Ranchman, 1919; The Trail Horde, 1920; Drag Harlan, 1921; Beau Rand, 1921; Square Deal Sanderson, 1922; West, 1922; Brass Commandments, 1923; Lonesome Ranch, 1924; The Way of the Buffalo, 1924; Last Hope Ranch, 1925; Trailing Back, 1925; Channing Comes Through, 1925; The Valley of the Stars, 1926; A Gentleman from Virginia, 1926; Slow Burgess, 1926; Land of the Free, 1927; Mystery Range, 1928; The Mesa, 1928; The Raider, 1929; The Red Brand, 1929; Gone

North, 1930; A Son of Arizona, 1931; Double Cross Ranch, 1932; Clear the Trail, 1933; Breath of the Desert, 1934; West of Apache Pass, 1934; Silverspurs, 1935; Kingdom in the Cactus, 1936; Open Range Omnibus, 1936; Parade of the Empty Boots, 1937; Coming of the Law, 1938; Treasure Ranch, 1940. Mayor of North Olmstead, O. Home: North Olmstead, O. Died Feb. 9, 1942.

SEMBRICH, Marcella, operatic soprano; b. Lemberg, Austria, 1858; d. Casimir Kochanski (musician); adopted mother's maiden name, Sembrich; began learning piano and violin at 4; played for dances to assist in support of family at 12; studied at Lemberg Conservatory of Music; m. her teacher, Prof. W. Stengel, May 5, 1877 (died 1917). She made her début as Elvira, at Athens, Greece, June 3, 1877; engaged for Dresden Opera House, 1878; gained prominence by singing Lucia at Covent Garden, London, 1880, and later sang in leading European opera houses; made first appearance in America, in "Lucia di Lammermoor," at Metropolitan Opera House, New York, Oct. 24, 1883, and afterwards sang as Elvira, Violetta, Ophelia, Rosina and Gilda; sang in the leading cities of the U.S. for many seasons; retired from stage, Feb. 6, 1909, and retired from concert stage Jan. 15, 1916; dir. vocal dept., Curtis Inst., Phila., 1924—; also instr. Juillard Grad. Sch. of Music, New York. Home: New York, N.Y. Died Jan. 11, 1935.

SEMPLE, Ellen Churchill, anthropo-geographer; b. Louisville, Ky., 1863; d. Alexander Bonner and Emerine (Price) S.; B.A., Vassar Coll., 1882, A.M., 1891; studied at U. of Leipzig, 1891-92, 1895; LL.D., U. of Ky., 1923; unmarried. Special field of work in anthropo-geography, or the study of the influence of geog. conditions upon the development of society, a new science in which she was a pioneer in America. Professor anthropo-geography, Clark Univ., Worcester, Mass., 1921-28. Pres. Assn. Am. Geographers, 1921. Contributor scientific articles to Bulletin of Am. Geog. Soc., Journal of Geography, New York, and Geog. Journal of London. Author: American History and Its Geographic Conditions, 1903; The Influences of Geographic Environment, 1911. Gold medalist, Am. Geog. Soc., 1914. Died May 8, 1932.

SEMPLE, Henry Churchill, clergyman, educator; b. Montgomery, Ala., Oct. 18, 1853; s. of Maj. Henry Churchill and Emily Virginia (James) S.; A.B., Mt. St. Mary's, Md., 1871, A.M., 1873; studied philosophy and theology, Bardstown, Ky., 1871-72; Am. Coll., Rome, 1872-76; Clermont-en-Auvergne, 1876-77; Aix-en-Provence, 1877-79. Joined Soc. of Jesus (Jesuits), 1876; ordained R.C. priest, 1879; was prof. lit., Spring Hill., Ala., Macon, Ga., and Georgetown U., D.C.; pres. Coll. of Immaculate Conception, New Orleans, 1895-99; moderator of theol. conferences of Archdiocese of N.Y., 1906-19, of New Orleans, 1919—. Author: Anglican Ordinations, 1906; What Times! What Morals!, 1908; Heaven Open to Souls, 1917; American Liberty Enlightening the World, 1920. Died June 26, 1925.

SENEFF, Edward H., lawyer; b. Mt. Eaton, O., Sept. 25, 1867; s. Philip and Mary Adaline (Sleighbaugh) S.; B.S., Valparaiso U., 1889; LL.B., Lake Forest (Ill.) Coll., 1896; m. Lyda Lawson, 1891; children—George Philip, Thomas Ellsworth. Entered law dept. C.&E.I. R.R. Co., 1897, gen. atty., 1901, gen. solicitor, 1911; apptd. gen. solicitor Pa. Lines West of Pittsburgh, 1914; gen. solicitor Pa. R.R. Co., Pittsburgh, 1920, trans. to Phila., 1923. Republican. Presbyn. Home: St. Davids, Pa. Died May 30, 1932.

SENIOR, Harold Dickinson, anatomist; b. Croydon, Eng., Oct. 30, 1870; s. Joseph and Amy (Westall) S.; Chatham House College, Ramsgate, Eng.; Charing Cross Hosp. Med. Coll. Sch., London; L.R.C.P., 1892; M.R.C.S., London, 1892, and fellow, 1895; M.B., Durham U., 1895, M.D. (gold medalist), 1918; D.Sc., Syracuse U., 1910; m. Jean Headley, of Halifax, N.S., June 29, 1901. House surgeon and phys. Charing Cross Hosp., London, and various other clin. appmts., 1892-93; asst. demonstrator anatomy, Durham U., 1893; jr. demonstrator anatomy, Charing Cross Hosp. Med. Sch., 1894-95; demonstrator anatomy, Medico-Chirurg. Coll., Phila., 1902-04; asso. in anatomy Wistar Inst. of Anatomy and Biology, 1904-07; prof. anatomy, Syracuse U., 1907-10; prof. anatomy New York U., 1910-36 (emeritus). Fellow A.A.A.S., N.Y. Acad. Medicine. Home: Salisbury, Cove, Me. Died Aug. 6, 1938.

SENN, Nicholas, physician, surgeon; b. Buchs, Canton of St. Gall, Switzerland, Oct. 31, 1844; brought to U.S. by parents, 1853; settled at Ashford, Fond du Lac Co., Wis.; grad. Fond du Lac High School, 1864; taught school; grad. Chicago Med. Coll., 1868; Univ. of Munich, 1878; house physician, Cook Co. Hosp., 1868-69; practiced medicine, Fond du Lac, 1869-74; Milwaukee, 1874-93; was surgeon-gen. of Wis.; engaged in practice at Chicago; surgeon-gen. Ill. Nat. Guard; well known specialist in surgery; attending surgeon, Presbyn. Hosp., and surgeon-in-chief, St. Joseph's Hosp., Chicago, until apptd., May 1898, chief surgeon 6th army corps, with rank of lt. col., U.S. vols., and chief of operating staff with army in the field; served until Sept.; prof. surgery, Coll. of Phys. and Surg., Chicago, 1884-87; prof. principles of surgery, 1887-90; from 1890 prof. practical and clinical surgery, Rush Med. Coll., also prof. surgery, Chicago Policlinic; professorial lecturer on mil. surgery, Chicago Univ.; del. Internat. Med. Congress, Berlin, 1890, Moscow, 1897, Madrid, 1903. Author: Four Months Among the Surgeons of Europe; Experimental Surgery; Intestinal Surgery; Surgical Bacteriology; Principles of Surgery; Pathology and Surgical Treatment of Tumors; Tuberculosis of Bones and Joints; Tuberculosis of the Genito-Urinary Organs; Syllabus of Practice of Surgery; Practical Surgery; Surgical Notes on the Spanish-American War; Medico-Surgical Aspects of the Spanish-American War; Practical Surgery; Nurse's Guide for the Operating Room, 1902; Around the World via Siberia; Our National Recreation Parks; Around the World via India—A Medical Tour. Home: Chicago, Ill. Died 1908.

SENNER, Joseph Henry, journalist; b. in Austria, Sept. 30, 1846; ed. gymnasium at Brunn; grad. in law Univ. of Vienna, 1867 (Doctor Juris); practiced law in Brunn, 1867-80; came to U.S., 1880, as corr. German and Austrian newspapers; on staff New Yorker Staats Zeitung, 1881-82; editor-in-chief Milwaukee Herold, 1882-85; foreign editor New York Staats Zeitung, 1885-93; U.S. commr. of immigration port of New York, 1893-97. Democrat. Pres. The Food Trade Pub. Co., publishers of The Nat. Provisioner, and of Cold Storage and Ice Trade Journal. Delivered, Jan. to Apr. 1882, weekly pub. lectures (in German) on history of civilization. Was 5 yrs. pres. German Social Scientific Soc.; 4 yrs. pres. Nat. Organization German-Am. Journalists; v.p. German Liederkranz, New York; 7 yrs. pres. Autrian Soc., New York. Home: New York, N.Y. Died 1908.

SENSENIG, David Martin, educator, author; b. Lancaster Co., Pa., Dec. 17, 1840; s. Michael and Barbara (Martin) S.; grad. in elementary course, 1867, and in scientific course, B.S., 1870, M.S., 1872, State Normal Sch., Millersville, Pa.; m. Annie M. Gillingham, Aug. 9, 1870. Worked on father's farm until 1860; taught dist. sch., 1860-63; mem. mercantile firm, M. Sensenig & Son, 1863-65; student, 1865-67, teacher and student, 1867-70, prof. mathematics, 1870-75, Millersville (Pa.) State Normal Sch.; prof. mathematics, 1875-76, prin. 1876-79, State Normal Sch., Indiana, Pa.; prof. mathematics, West Chester (Pa.) State Normal Sch., 1879—. Republican. Was mem. Rep. Co. Com., Lancaster Co., Pa., 1864. Mem. Free Museum of Science and Art, Dept. Archeology, Univ. of Pa. Inst. lecturer, 1875-90. Author: Numbers Symbolized (elementary algebra), 1888; Numbers Universalized (advanced algebra), 1890; Key to Elementary Algebra, 1890; Key to Advanced Algebra, 1891; also the Sensenig-Anderson Series (New Complete Arithmetic, 1900, Key, 1904, Essentials of Arithmetic, 1902, Key, Introductory Arithmetic, 1903). Died 1907.

SENTER, John Henry, lawyer; b. Cabot, Vt., Nov. 11, 1848; s. Dearborn Bean and Susan C. (Lyford) S.; ed. pub. schs., Vt., and Concord (N.H.) High Sch.; m. Addie G. Martin, Nov. 1, 1875. Has been sec. Dem. State Com. for 27 yrs.; chmn. same, 1898-1900; mem. Dem. Nat. Com., Vt., 1900-04; Dem. candidate for gov. of Vt., 1900; nat. bank examiner, 1885-89; U.S. atty., 1893-97; has held numerous local offices; mayor of City of Montpelier, 1898, 1899; state's atty., Washington Co., 1903-04; mem. Vt. Legislature, 1906. Home: Montpelier, Vt. Died Jan. 20, 1916.

SERGEL, Charles Hubbard, publisher; b. Muscatine, Ia., Sept. 25, 1861; s. John Henry and Jean G. (Pocock) S.; grad. high sch., Mansfield, O.; m. Annie E. Myers, Mar. 3, 1891. Began, 1882, with Western News Co., Chicago, resigning 1890, as head of its book dept.; organized, 1886, and pres. The Dramatic Pub. Co.; organizer and propr. Charles H. Sergel & Co., pubs. Peruvian consul at Chicago, 1893-1901. City treas. of Chicago, 1915-17; pres. Sanitary Dist. of Chicago, 1916-20 and trustee, 1920-22; treas. Rep. State Central Com., 1918-20. Wrote: Sound Money, 1895. Home: Chicago, Ill. Died Jan. 7, 1926.

SERPELL, Susan Watkins, artist; b. in California; d. James Thomas and Susan E. (Owens) Watkins; ed. in Calif. and N.Y. City; m. Goldsborough Serpell, Jan. 16, 1912. Widely known as painter of interiors; hon. mention Paris Salon, 1899, gold medal, same, 1900; silver medal, St. Louis Expn., 1904; Julia A. Shaw Memorial Prize, Nat. Acad. Design, 1910; McMillan Prize, Woman's Art Club, New York, A.N.A., 1912. Episcopalian. Home: Norfolk, Va. Died June 1912.

SERRELL, Edward Wellmann, civil and mil. engr.; b. abroad (but a citizen of U.S. by birthright), Nov. 5, 1826; academic edn.; m. Jane, d. Rev. Jesse Pound, Apr. 6, 1848 (died 1896); 2d, Marion Seaton Roorbach, Sept. 6, 1900 (died Nov. 1904). Began engring. profession under his father and elder brother. Was asst. engr. to commrs. of Erie R.R.; asst. to chief of Topog. Engrs., U.S.A.; asst. engr., 1848, Panama Survey; engr. Central R.R. of N.J.; chief engr. Niagara bridge, 1850; chief engr. St. John bridge, Hoosac tunnel and many other public works. In Civil War organized and comd. 1st regt. vol. engrs, U.S.A., becoming col. engrs.; chief engr. 10th corps, U.S.A.; chief engr. and chief of staff, Army of the James; chief engr. Dept. of the South, U.S.A.; was at capture of Fort Wagner; devised and built Swamp Angel batteries; was in 126 actions, becoming bvt. brig. gen. Made many useful inventions, in long wire, armor plate, impromptu gun carriages, electric coast defenses, iron viaducts, etc. Published many reports on railroads and canals. Is consulting engr. to several corps.; has projected an interoceanic canal from San Blas to Pearl Island Harbor. Consulting engr. Am. Isthmus Ship Canal Co. Home: West New Brighton, N.Y. Died 1906.

SERVISS, Garrett Putman, author; b. Sharon Springs, N.Y., Mar. 24, 1851; s. Garrett Putman and Katharine (Shelp) S.; B.S., Cornell U., 1872; LL.B., Columbia, 1874; m. 2d, Henriette Gros le Blond, of Bourgogne, France, 1907. Editorial writer on New York Sun until 1892; then lecturer on travel, history and astronomy. Author: Astronomy with an Opera Glass, 1888; Astronomy with the Naked Eye, 1908; Curiosities of the Sky, 1909; Round the Year with the Stars, 1910; Astronomy in a Nutshell, 1912; Eloquence, 1912; The Moon Maiden (scientific mystery story), 1915. Home: Tenafly, N.J. Died May 25, 1929.

SESSIONS, Clarence William, judge; b. Ionia Co., Mich., Feb. 8, 1859; s. William and Julia (Jennings) S.; student U. of Mich., 1877-80; m. Mary S. Foote, of Ionia, Mich., July 5, 1882 (died 1925); m. 2d, Mary L. Lovell, May 7, 1911. Admitted to Mich. bar, 1883; practiced at Ionia, 1883-85; moved to Muskegon, Mich., 1885, and became partner Frank H. Bassett, as Sessions & Bassett; judge Circuit Court, Mich., 1906-11; judge U.S. Dist. Court, Western Dist. of Mich., Oct. 3, 1911—. Presbyn. Home: Grand Rapids, Mich. Died Apr. 1, 1931.

SESSIONS, William Edwin, manufacturer; b. Bristol, Conn., Feb. 18, 1857; s. John Humphrey and Emily (Bunnell) S.; grad. Hartford High Sch., 1876; m. Emily Brown, June 12, 1878. Began in mfg. business at Bristol, 1879; pres. and treas. (organizer and prin. owner), The Sessions Foundry Co.; pres. Sessions Clock Co., Bristol Trust Co. Methodist; supt. Prospect M.E. S.S.; trustee Wesleyan U., Conn., 1900—. Home: Bristol, Conn. Died Aug. 27, 1920.

SESSUMS, Davis, bishop; b. Houston, Tex., July 7, 1858; s. Alexander and Mary (Runnels) S.; A.B., U. of the South, Tenn., 1878, A.M., 1878 (D.D., 1891); m. Alice C., d. Rt. Rev. J. N. Galleher, bishop of La., Dec. 18, 1890. Deacon, 1882, priest, 1882, P.E. Church; rector Grace Ch., Galveston, Tex., 1882; asst. and rector Calvary Ch., Memphis, Tenn., 1883-87; rector Christ Ch., New Orleans, 1887-91; consecrated coadjutor bishop of La., 1891, bishop of Louisiana, 1891. Home: New Orleans, La. Died Dec. 24, 1929.

SETON, Robert, archbishop; b. Pisa, of American parents, Aug. 28, 1839; s. William and Emily (Prime) S.; head of the ancient Scottish family of Setons of Parbroath; grad. Ecclesiastical Acad., Rome, 1867; (D.D., Roman U., 1867; LL.D., U. of Notre Dame, Ind., 1893). Was raised, 1866, to rank of pvt. chamberlain to Pope Pius IX; is dean of all the Monsignori in U.S. Was made prothonotary apostolic, 1867; rector St. Joseph's Church, Jersey City, from 1876 until recently, when he went to Rome to remain; archbishop of Heliopolis, June 1903—. Some time Roman corr. N.Y. Times under pen-name "Fyvie." Lecturer Catholic Univ., Washington, and at Seton Hall Coll., S. Orange, N.J. Author: Memoir, Letters and Journal of Elizabeth Seton, 1869; Roman Essays, 1882; The Dignity of Labor, 1893; An Old Family, 1899. Died Mar. 22, 1927.

SETTLE, Evan E., congressman-lawyer; b. Frankfort, Ky., Dec. 1, 1848; grad. Louisville High School, 1864; admitted to bar, 1870; entered practice at Owenton; co. atty., Owen Co., 1878-87; member Ky. legislature, 1887-88 and 1889-90; elected to Congress, 1896, as Democrat, defeating W. C. P. Breckinridge, fusion candidate of Republicans and Gold Democrats; reëlected, 1898. Home: Owenton, Ky. Died 1899.

SETTLE, George Thomas, librarian; b. Russellville, Ky., Apr. 21, 1865; s. Rev. Henry Clay and Isabella (Kerr) S.; ed. pub. schs. Owensboro and Louisville, Ky.; student Bethel Coll., Russellville; studied law; m. Anna Florence Hubbuch, Apr. 10, 1913. Head of book dept. and buyer, John P. Morton & Co., 1887-1905; head of order and accession dept., 1905-12, asst. librarian, Apr.-Nov. 1912, librarian, Nov. 1912—, Louisville Free Pub. Library. Mem. A.L.A (library revenues com.), Ky. Library Assn. (pres. 1917). Mem. Ky. Library Commn., 1912-15; mem. library dept. Southern Conf. Edn. and Industry (pres. 1915); mem. Ky. Assn. Perry Centennial Celebration, 1913; mem. Louisville Council Boy Scouts, Ky. Com. on Inter-racial Coöperation. Camp Librarian (A.L.A

Library War Service), Camp Zachary Taylor, Ky., Dec. 1917-Nov. 1919. Home: Louisville, Ky. Died Dec. 29, 1930.

SEVERANCE, Caroline Maria Seymour, philanthropist; b. Canandaigua, N.Y., Jan. 12, 1820; d. Orson and Caroline M. (Clarke) Seymour; grad. Female Sem., Geneva, N.Y., 1835; m. Theodoric C. Severance, Aug. 27, 1840 (died 1892). Lived in Cleveland until 1855, in Boston 1855-75, then in Los Angeles. One of founders and 1st pres., 1868, of N.E. Woman's Club, Boston, a few weeks before Sorosis of New York was organized—so sometimes called "the mother of women's clubs." Active in woman suffrage agitation in Cleveland and Boston, and lectured at various places. Prepared several memorials and appeals for suffrage, also papers before Women's Congress; was on bd. of Hosp. for Women and Children, Boston. Has founded clubs in Calif. at Los Angeles and Santa Barbara; and has been trustee of Unitarian Ch. and Pub. Library. Founder and pres. Los Angeles Free Kindergarten Assn. Pioneer suffragist. Home: Los Angeles, Calif. Died Nov. 10, 1914.

SEVERANCE, Cordenio Arnold, lawyer; b. Mantorville, Minn., June 30, 1862; s. Erasmus C. and Amanda Julia (Arnold) S.; ed. Carleton College, Minn., 1877-80 (LL.D., 1919); m. Mary Frances Harriman, June 26, 1889. Admitted to bar, 1883; mem. firm of Davis, Kellogg (Frank B.) & Severance, St. Paul, 1887-1917, Davis, Severance & Olds, 1917-19, Davis, Severance & Morgan, 1919-23, Davis, Kellogg, Severance & Morgan, 1923—. Mem. Nat. Conf. of Commrs. on Uniform State Laws, 1910—; pres. Minn. Bar Assn., 1911, Am. Bar Assn., 1921. Chmn. Am. Red Cross Commn. to Serbia, 1917. Trustee Carnegie Endowment for Internat. Peace, 1919—, Carleton Coll., 1920—. Republican. Home: Cottage Grove, Minn., and St. Paul. Died May 6, 1925.

SEVERANCE, Frank Hayward, author; b. Manchester, Mass., Nov. 28, 1856; s. Lucius Warren and Maria Lucretia (Hayward) S.; B.S., Cornell, 1879; L.H.D., U. of Vt., 1911; LL.D., U. of Toronto, 1920; m. Lena Lillian Hill, Aug. 19, 1885; children—Hayward M., Mildred, Edith Lilian. Reporter and city editor Erie (Pa.) Gazette, 1879-80, Buffalo Express, 1881-86; mng. editor Illustrated Buffalo Express, 1886-1902. Lecturer on history. Author: Old Trails on the Niagara Frontier (2 edits.), 1899, 1903; Studies of the Niagara Frontier, 1911; Peace Episodes on the Niagara, 1915; An Old Frontier of France, 2 Vols., 1917; also editor of volumes 4 to 29, Publ. Buffalo Hist. Soc. Editor: The Gilbert Family Captivity, 1904. Home: Buffalo, N.Y. Died Jan. 26, 1931.

SEVERANCE, John Long; b. Cleveland, O., May 8, 1863; s. Louis Henry and Fannie (Benedict) S.; A.B., Oberlin (O.) Coll., 1885; m. Elisabeth Huntington DeWitt, Nov. 3, 1891 (dec.). Chmn. bd. Youngstown Steel Door Co., Colonial Salt Co.; pres. Cleveland Arcade Co. Pres. Cleveland Mus. of Art, Cleveland Orchestra Co.; trustee Nanking (China) Univ., Oberlin Coll., Western Reserve U.; sponsor of Severance Union Med. Sch. and Hosp., Seoul, Korea (founded by father). Republican. Home: Cleveland Heights, O. Died Jan. 16, 1936.

SEVIER, Henry Hulme (Hal Sevier), ambassador; b. Columbia, Tenn., Mar. 16, 1878; s. Theodore Frances and Mary (Douglas) S.; self-educated; m. Clara Driscoll, July 31, 1906. Began career as the editor of a country newspaper, 1895; mem. Tex. House of Representatives 2 terms, 1902-06; founder, owner and editor Austin (Tex.) American until 1917; apptd. to visit S. America to conduct educational and informative campaign to combat propaganda against United States at time of World War; apptd. A.E. and P. to Chile, 1933; v.p. Corpus Christi (Tex.) Bank & Trust Co.; mem. bd. of dirs. Corpus Christi Nat. Bank. First pres. Austin Pub. Library Assn. Democrat. Episcopalian. Mason; mem. Woodmen of the World. World traveler. Home: Corpus Christi, Tex. Died Mar. 10, 1940.

SEWALL, Arthur, ship owner and ship builder; b. Bath, Me., Nov. 25, 1835; apprenticed in ship yards of his father, William D. Sewall. In 1854, with a brother, established E. & A. Sewall, ship-builders and commn. merchants, which later became Arthur Sewall & Co., now the largest managers and probably the largest owners of sailing tonnage in the U.S.; also owning plant for building iron ships; was pres., 1884-93, of Maine Central R.R.; is pres. Bath Nat. Bank. Was mem. Dem. Nat. Committee, 1888-96; Dem. nominee for Vice President of U.S., 1896; defeated. Home: Bath, Me. Died 1900.

SEWALL, Arthur Wollaston, pres. General Asphalt Co.; b. Mobile, Ala., Nov. 19, 1860; s. Kiah Bayley and Lucretia (Day) S.; ed. high sch.; m. Cynthia Pope Yeatman, Dec. 29, 1897. In asphalt business, 1900—; became pres. Gen. Asphalt Co., 1912, now dir.; dir. Baldwin Locomotive Works, Federal Reserve Bank, 3d Dist., Ins. Co. of N. America, Mut. Assurance Co., Am. Pulley Co. Dir. Zoöl. Soc. Republican. Episcopalian. Home: Philadelphia, Pa. Died Aug. 1, 1939.

SEWALL, Edmund Devereux, ry. official; b. Wilmington, Del.; s. Edmund Q. and Louise L. (Lovett) S.; ed. Taylor and Jackson's Acad., Wilmington. With engr. corps Wicomico & Pocomoke, N.P., Chicago & Can. Southern, St. Paul, Minn. & Man., and St. Paul & Duluth rys. prior to 1882; joint agent St. Paul & Duluth and C.,M.&St.P. cos. at Stillwater, Minn., 1882; with C.,M.&S.P. Ry. Co., 1883—, as agt. at Stillwater, 1883, traveling lumber agt., Milwaukee, 1888, commercial agt., St. Paul, 1889-95, asst. gen. frt. agt., Milwaukee, 1895-98, gen. Northwestern agt., 1898-1902 and asst. gen. supt. 1902-06, Minneapolis; asst. to the president, Chicago, 1906-13, and v.p., at Chicago, 1913—. Home: Chicago, Ill. Died Mar. 30, 1923.

SEWALL, Frank, clergyman; b. Bath, Me., Sept. 24, 1837; s. of William Dunning and Rachel Allyn (Trufant) S.; A.B., Bowdoin Coll., Brunswick, Me., 1858, A.M., 1862 (S.T.D., 1902); studied in Tübingen and Berlin; attended lectures at Sorbonne, Paris; m. Thedia Redelia Gilchrist, 1869. Ordained New Ch. (Swedenborgian) ministry, 1863; pastor, Glendale, O., Urbana, O. (pres. Urbana U., 16 yrs.), Glasgow, Scotland, and Washington, D.C., 1890—; gen. pastor Maryland Assn., 1893—; pres. Swedenborg Scientific Assn., 1898—. Author: The New Metaphysics, 1888; The Ethics of Service, 1889; Dante and Swedenborg and Other Essays in the New Renaissance, 1893; Swedenborg and Modern Idealism, 1902; Pulpit and Modern Thought, 1905; Reason in Belief, 1906; Being and Existence—a Philosophical Discussion, 1909; Swedenborg and the Sapientia Angelica, 1910; Life on Other Planets, according to Swedenborg, 1911; Spirit as Object, 1912; Ericken and Borgeson: Have Their Teachings a Spiritual Content?, 1913. Died Dec. 7, 1915.

SEWALL, Harold Marsh, lawyer; b. Bath, Me., Jan. 3, 1860; s. of late Hon. Arthur and Emma Duncan (Crooker) S.; A.B., Harvard, 1882, and LL.B., 1885; (hon. A.M., Bowdoin College, 1919); m. Camilla Loyall Ashe, Sept. 14, 1893. Vice-consul at Liverpool, 1885-87; consul-gen. at Samoa, 1887-89; opposed German pretensions there; attaché of commission which negotiated Berlin treaty of 1889, for joint govt. of Samoa by the powers; reapptd. consul-gen. at Samoa, 1889-92; secured site to naval sta. at Pago-Pago; admitted to Me. bar, 1892. Del. Rep. Nat. Conv., 1896; mem. Me. Ho. of Rep., 1896; U.S. minister to Hawaii, 1897; received transfer sovereignty of islands, 1898; spl. agt. U.S. until orgn. of the territory; was first member Rep. Nat. Com. for Hawaii; mem. Me. Ho. of Rep., 1903-07, Senate, 1907-09; Rep. candidate for Congress, 1914. Chmn. Me. Com. of Public Safety; mem. advisory com. of Conf. for Limitation of Armament, 1921; mem. Rep. Nat. Com. Home: Bath, Me. Died Oct. 28, 1924.

SEWALL, Henry, M.D.; b. Winchester, Va., May 25, 1855; s. Thomas and Julia Elizabeth (Waters) S.; B.S., Wesleyan U., Conn., 1876; Ph.D., Johns Hopkins, 1879; hon. M.D., U. of Mich., 1888, Sc.D., 1912; M.D., U. of Denver, 1889; Sc.D., Wesleyan, 1926; U. of Colorado, 1927; m. Isabel Josephine Vickers, of Toronto, Ont., Sept. 21, 1887. Asst., fellow and asso. in biology, Johns Hopkins, 1876-81; prof. physiology, U. of Mich., 1882-89; prof. physiology, Denver and Cross Coll. of Medicine, 1890-1908; prof. medicine, 1911-17, prof. and lecturer in medicine, 1917-19, U. of Colo., prof. medicine emeritus. Mem. Nat. Bd. Med. Examiners until 1919; secretary Colo. State Board of Health, 1893-99. Trudeau medalist, Nat. Tuberculosis Assn., 1930; Kober medalist, Assn. Am. Physicians, 1931. Author researches in physiology, published mostly in the Jour. of Physiology, 1877-90, and later in tuberculosis, immunology and clinical medicine. Home: Denver, Colo. Died July 8, 1936.

SEWALL, John Smith, theologian; b. New Castle, Me., March 20, 1830; s. Jotham, Jr. and Rachel Crosby (Bradbury) S.; A.B., Bowdoin Coll., 1850, A.M., 1855; grad. Bangor Theol. Sem., 1858; (D.D., Bowdoin, 1878); m. Louise, d. Samuel Page Benson, M.C., of Winthrop, Me., Aug. 7, 1858. Capt.'s clerk U.S.N., 1850-54; mem. Commodore Perry's Japan expedition. Ordained Congl. ministry, 1859; pastor Wenham, Mass., 1859-67; prof. of rhetoric, oratory and English lit., Bowdoin Coll., 1867-75; prof. homiletics and sociology, 1875-1903 (emeritus), Bangor Theol. Sem. Author: Logbook of the Captain's Clerk, 1906. Home: Bangor, Me., Died 1911.

SEWALL, May Wright, lecturer; b. Milwaukee, May 27, 1844; d. Philander Montague and Mary Weeks (Brackett) Wright; B.L., Northwestern U., 1866, A.M., 1868; m. Theodore Lovett Sewall, Oct. 30, 1880 (died 1895). Prin. of Girls Classical Sch., founded by her husband, at Indianapolis. Prominent in woman suffrage cause and edn. of women; life mem. and officer Nat. Am. Woman Suffrage Assn.; hon. pres. Internat. Council of Women, and Nat. Council of Women, U.S.; del. Universal Congress of Women, Paris, 1889; traveled, 1891-92, in France, Italy, Germany, Belgium, Switzerland, in interest of Congress of Representative Women, Chicago Expn. (of which she was chmn.), 1893; officer in many orgns. (literary, artistic and reform) in America and Europe; commn. by President McKinley to congresses held in Paris, 1900; chmn. Internat. Council, Com. on Peace and Arbitration, 1904-14; commd. by Bd. of Mgrs. Panama P.I. Expn. to carry its invitation to many internat. bodies to convene in San Francisco, 1915, and organized and was pres. Internat. Conf. of Women Workers for Permanent Peace, San Francisco, July 1915. Author: Higher Education of Women in the Western States of the U.S.A.; History of the Woman Suffrage Movement in Indiana; Historical Résumé of the World's Congress of Representative Women (2 vols.); The International Council of Women (2 vols.); Women, World War and Permanent Peace (1 vol.), 1915. Address: Eliot, Me. Died July 22, 1920.

SEWALL, Rufus King, lawyer, author; b. Edgecombe, Me., Jan. 22, 1814; grad. Bowdoin, 1837 (A.M.), Bangor Theol. Sem., 1841; supplied pulpits in Vt. and Mass., but could not accept permanent pastorate because of ill-health; lived in San Augustine, Fla., 5 yrs.; studied law, Mobile, Ala.; returned to Me., practiced at Wiscasset; was admitted to bar, U.S. Supreme Court; chmn. examining com. Lincoln Co. bar; v.p. Me. Hist. Soc. Author: Ancient Dominion of Maine; Ancient Voyages to the Western Continent; Memoir of Joseph Sewall, D.D.; Lectures on the Holy Spirit; Sketches of St. Augustine. Home: Wiscasset, Me. Died 1903.

SEWARD, Coy Avon, artist; b. Chase, Kan., Mar. 4, 1884; s. Roscoe Conkling and Hettie Ann (Bohrer) S.; prep. edn., high sch., Chase; art study, Washburn Coll., Topeka, Kan., and Bethany Coll., Lindsborg, Kan.; m. Mabel E. Drew, May 11, 1908; children—Dorothy Maurine, Helen Margaret, Mildred Avon, Virginia Ruth. With Western Lithograph Co., Wichita, Kan. Works on permanent exhbn. at Los Angeles (Calif.) Mus.; Calif. State Library; Grand Lodge A.F. and A.M. and Mulvane Mus., Topeka; John Vanderpoel Memorial Sch., Chicago; Bethany Coll., Lindsborg, Kan.; Wichita High Sch. and Twentieth Century Club, Wichita; Library of Congress; Chicago Art Inst., U. of Kan.; R.I. Sch. of Design; Honolulu Acad. of Fine Arts; Bibliotheque Nationale, Paris, France; Tulsa U.; Wichita U. Awarded 1st prize, Mid West Artists, Kansas City, Mo., 1923, bronze medal 1926, gold medal, 1927, graphic arts prize, Delta Phi Delta, 1936. Republican. Mem. Christian (Disciples) Ch. Mason. Home: Wichita, Kan. Died Jan. 31, 1939.

SEWARD, Frederick William, lawyer; b. Auburn, N.Y., July 8, 1830; s. William Henry (Sec. of State) and Frances A. (Miller) S.; brother of William Henry S.; A.B., Union College, 1849 (LL.D., 1878); m. Anna M. Wharton, Nov. 9, 1854. Admitted to bar, 1851; one of editors and owners Albany Evening Journal, 1851-61. Was sent to warn Abraham Lincoln of plot to assassinate him in Baltimore, 1861; asst. secretary of state, 1861-69, 1877-81; as acting sec. of state, sat in cabinets of Presidents Lincoln, Johnson and Hayes; was nearly murdered in his father's defense, Apr. 14, 1865; was sent on spl. mission with Admiral Porter to negotiate W. Indian treaties, 1867; participated in purchase of Alaska, and negotiation for Pago-Pago Harbor, Samoa; mem. N.Y. Assembly, 1875; Rep. nominee for sec. of state of N.Y., 1875; state commr. at Yorktown Centennial celebration, 1881. Pres. Union Coll. Alumni Assn., 1900, Soc. of the Cayugas, 1902; pres. at Semi-Centennial of Rep. party, Saratoga, 1904; mem. Internat. Arbitration Conf., Washington, 1904; v.p. Hudson-Fulton Commn. and chmn. of Plan and Scope Com., 1908-09. Author: Life and Letters of William H. Seward, 1891; A West Indian Cruise (serial in Godey's mag.), 1894. Home: Montrose, N.Y. Died Apr. 25, 1915.

SEWARD, George Frederick, financier; b. Florida, N.Y., Nov. 8, 1840; s. George W. and Tempe Wicke (Leddell) S.; bro. of Samuel Swayze S.; ed. Seward Inst., and Union Coll. (LL.D., Union, 1904); m. Kate Sherman, Aug. 4, 1870. Consul, 1861-63, consul gen., 1863-78, at Shanghai, China; apptd. minister to Korea, 1869, but, at his suggestion, the sending of a mission to that country was deferred; minister to China, 1876-80; but, declining to undertake negotiation of a treaty restricting Chinese immigration, was recalled. During service in China was active in checking piracy and suppressing riots. Was pres. North China Branch, Royal Asiatic Soc., 1865-66. Became v.p., 1887, pres., 1893—, The Fidelity & Casualty Co. of New York; pres. Va. Electrolytic Co., Tin Products Co.; v.p. Va. Laboratory Co. V.p. New York Chamber of Commerce; trustee Union Coll.; gov. Union Univ. Decorated Knight of Dannebrog by Denmark; Order Commander of Dragon of Annam by France. Author: Chinese Immigration in Its Social and Economical Aspects; Digest of System of Taxation of New York, 1902. Home: East Orange, N.J. Died 1910.

SEWARD, John Perry, M.D.; b. Phila., Pa., Dec. 20, 1868; s. Rev. Samuel S. and Christiana F. (Kimber) S.; A.B., Columbia, 1890; M.D., New York Homœ. Med. Coll. and Hosp., 1893; m. Edith de Charms Hibbard, June 2, 1900 (died 1920); children—Ruth de Charms, Christine Kimber, John Perry, Ralph Theodore; m. 2d, Gertrude Cornwell Hopkins, Dec. 2, 1922. Demonstrator and lecturer in anatomy, New York Homœ. Med. Coll., 1891-96; prof. hygiene and dietetics, New York Med. Coll. and Hosp. for Women, 1896-98; prof. materia medica, New York Homœ. Med. Coll., 1898-1902; prof. practice, New York Med. Coll. and Hosp. for Women, 1909-16; cons. phys. Laura Franklin Hosp., 1896-1922; attending phys. Hahnemann Hosp., 1899-1922, Met. Hosp., 1902-14, Fifth Av. Hosp., 1922-29; cons. phys. Metropolitan, N.Y. Ophthalmic and Broad Street hosps. Alumnus trustee New York Homœ. Med. Coll., 1931—. Democrat. Swedenborgian. Home: New York, N.Y. Died May 22, 1933.

SEWARD, Samuel Swayze, clergyman; b. Mendham, N.J., Apr. 16, 1838; s. George W. and Tempe Wicke (Leddell) S.; bro. of George Frederick S.; entered Union Coll., 1853, but did not graduate; admitted to Calif. bar, 1861; grad. New Church Theol. Sch., Waltham, Mass., 1868; m. Crissie F. Kimber, Oct. 13, 1864. Lt. 3d N.Y. Heavy Arty., 1861; a.d.c. on staff of Brig. Gen. E. O. C. Ord throughout the war; promoted capt. and maj., with two bvts., lt. col. and col., resigning Oct. 1865. Ordained New Jerusalem (Swedenborgian) ministry, 1869; pastor Poughkeepsie, N.Y., 1868-69, N. Bridgewater, Mass., 1870-75, Wilmington, Del., 1875-78, New York, 1878-97. Sec. Gen. Conv. of the New Jerusalem in the U.S.A., 1877-92; chmn. Council of Ministers, 1892-97 (v.p., 1897-1900, pres., 1900-1911); mem. bd. mgrs. Am. Swedenborg Printing & Pub. Co., 1878— (pres. 1900—); dir. Bd. of Publication, New Jerusalem Ch.; mem. bd. mgrs. New Ch. Theol. Sch. Home: Pittsfield, Mass. Deceased.

SEWARD, Samuel Swayze, Jr., prof. English; b. Wilmington, Del., Apr. 28, 1876; s. Samuel Swayze and Christiana Fredericka (Kimber) S.; grad. Irving Sch. for Boys, 1892; A.B., Columbia, 1896, A.M., 1897; Exeter Coll., Oxford U., Eng., 1899-1900; m. Amy M. Holman, of Dunsford, Devonshire, Eng., Aug. 31, 1919; children—Margaret, Jean. Asst. in English lit., Columbia, 1897-99; with Stanford U., 1900—, now professor English. With Commn. for Relief in Belgium, Prov. of Limbourg, June-Dec. 1915; enlisted in Ambulance Service, U.S.A., June 6, 1917; commd. 1st lt., Sept. 21, 1917; comd. Sect. 643, U.S.A.A.S., attached to 20th Div. Inf. (French), Mar. 1918-Mar. 1919; hon. discharged, Apr. 26, 1919. Decorated Chevalier Legion of Honor and Croix de Guerre (French), 2 citations; medal of King Albert (Belgium). Democrat. Swedenborgian. Author: Rhetoric in Practice (with A. G. Newcomer), 1905; Poems, Lyric and Narrative, 1909; Note-Taking, 1910; Reference Sheets, 1922; English Grammar—Correct and Effective Use (with K. Smith and E. B. Magee), 1928; The Paradox of the Ludicrous, 1930; Handbook of the English Sentence, 1932. Home: Palo Alto, Calif. Died Aug. 28, 1932.

SEWARD, Theodore Frelinghuysen, author, pres. Brotherhood of Christian Unity; b. Florida, N.Y., Jan. 25, 1835; s. Israel and Mary (Johnson) S.; studied music under Lowell Mason and Thomas Hastings. Organist of a ch. in New London, Conn., 1857-59; in Rochester, N.Y., 1859-62, then in New York; m. Mary H. Coggeshall, June 12, 1860. Edited The Musical Pioneer and the New York Musical Gazette; introduced "Tonic Sol-fa" system of musical notation and instruction into U.S. and prepared series of text-books; founded Am. Tonic Sol-fa Assn.; founded Brotherhood of Christian Unity, 1891, and World's Neighbor-chain, 1898. Author: The School of Life, 1894; Heaven Every Day, 1896; Don't Worry, 1897; Spiritual Knowing, 1900. Home: New York, N.Y. Died 1902.

SEWARD, William, bvt. brig. gen. N.G.N.Y.; b. New Hackensack, Dutchess Co., N.Y., Aug. 19, 1837; s. Wm. S.; ed. high school, Newark, N.J.; m. Louisa M. Lockwood, Oct. 11, 1864. Joined N.Y. Nat. Guard, Oct. 1, 1858; served in Civil war, 1861-63; commd. 1st lt. while in service of U.S., 1862; adj. 9th regt., 1866; maj. same, 1868; asst. adj. gen. 3d brigade, N.Y.N.G., Apr. 1870; bvt. col., Jan. 31, 1879; col. 9th regt., N.G.N.Y., Apr. 1882; brig. gen. bvt., May 1898; retired at own request (total service, 38½ yrs.). Republican. Home: New York, N.Y. Died 1905.

SEWARD, William Henry, soldier, banker; b. Auburn, N.Y., June 18, 1839; s. William Henry (Sec. of State) and Frances A. (Miller) S.; bro. of Frederick William S.; pvt. edn.; m. Janet M. Watson, June 27, 1860 (died 1913). Apptd. Sept. 12, 1862, lt. col., 138th N.Y. Vols.; afterward col. 9th N.Y. Heavy Arty.; participated in battles of Monocacy, Petersburg, Cold Harbor, Opequan and others; promoted for gallantry, Sept. 1863, to brig. gen. comdg. 1st Brigade, 3d Div., Dept. of Shenandoah; resigned, June 1, 1865. Head of banking firm of William H. Seward & Co., 1860—; trustee Cayuga Co. Savings Bank. Pres. Seymour Library. Republican. Pres. N.Y. electoral coll., 1888. Home: Auburn, N.Y. Died Apr. 26, 1920.

SEWELL, Albert Henry, judge; b. Hamden, N.Y., Oct. 30, 1847; s. William H. and Celinda S.; student Union Coll., 1867-68; A.B., Cornell U., 1871; LL.B., Albany Law School, 1873; m. Mary E. Wright, 1889. Admitted to bar, 1873; mem. N.Y. Assembly, 1878; co. judge and surrogate, Delaware Co., N.Y., 1889-99; apptd. by Gov. Roosevelt to fill vacancy, Aug. 1899, and elected Nov. 1899, justice Supreme Ct. of N.Y.; was asso. justice Appellate Div., 2d dept., 1900-01, 3d dept., 1907-12, and 1916-17; retired on reaching age limit, Jan. 1, 1918; apptd. official referee, Jan. 18, 1918. Trustee Cornell U., 1908-13. Republican. Home: Walton, N.Y. Died July 13, 1924.

SEWELL, (Lydia) Amanda Brewster, artist; b. Essex Co., N.Y.; d. Benjamin T. and Julia Anne (Washburn) Brewster; studied Art Students' League, New York, and under Julian and Carolus Duran, Paris; m. Robert van Vorst Sewell, Apr. 12, 1888. Began painting in Paris, 1886; exhibited at Paris Salon, 1886, 1887, 1888; awarded Dodge prize, Nat. Acad. Design, 1888; Clarke prize, same, 1903; bronze medal, Chicago Expn., 1893, Buffalo Expn., 1901, St. Louis Expn., 1904; silver medal, Charleston Expn. Prin. works, portraiture in the style and spirit of the early English masters, A.N.A. Died Nov. 15, 1926.

SEWELL, John Stephen; b. Butler's Landing, Tenn., Jan. 16, 1869; s. Caleb Witt and Sarah Seaton (Miller) S.; grad. U.S. Mil. Acad., 1891; m. Agnes Temple Lyon, July 6, 1894. Commd. 2d lt. Engr. Corps, U.S.A., 1891; served as maj. and lt. col. 1st Vol. Engrs., Puerto Rican Expdn., Spanish-Am. War; resigned from U.S.A., Jan. 31, 1908; v.p. and gen. mgr. Ala. Marble Co., 1907-19 (on leave of absence during World War), pres., 1919—; col. Engr. Corps, Nat. Army, 1917-18; sect. engr., St. Nazaire, France, Aug. 1917-Aug. 1918; comdg. officer Base Sect. No. 1, St. Nazaire, Aug. 1918-Feb. 1919, Base Sect. No. 9, Antwerp and Rotterdam, Feb.-July 1919; col. Engr. R.C., 1919—. Served under Charles G. Dawes during orgn. of U.S. budget, 1921; mem. Budget Commn. to Dominican Republic, 1929; became dir. of exhibits, Century of Progress Expn., Chicago, 1931. Awarded D.S.M. (U.S.); Officer Legion of Honor (France); Officier Order of Leopold (Belgium); Norman medal, Am. Soc. C.E., 1906. Republican. Home: Birmingham, Ala. Died Apr. 1940.

SEWELL, Oscar Marion, ry. official; b. Campbell Co., Ga., Dec. 9, 1866; s. James Wiley and Elizabeth Amelia (Chapman) S.; ed. pub. schs. and corr. course, Alexander Hamilton Inst.; m. Jessie Lee Williams, Sept. 3, 1890; children—Jessie Marion (dec.), Amelia Catherine (Mrs. Sewell Browne), Oscar Mather, Horace Latura, Cassius Finley, Benjamine Williams, Fortuno Chapman. Successively brakeman, freight condr., yard dispatcher, passenger condr., L.&N. R.R. Co., 1885-96; condr. Chesapeake, Ohio & Southwestern Ry. (now br. of I.C. R.R.), 1896-1902, trainmaster Paducah & Fulton dist., 1902-03; agt. and gen. yardmaster Tenn. Central R.R. Co., later asst. supt., 1903-05, chief clk. to v.p. and gen. mgr., 1905-06; supt. White River div. Mo. P. R.R. Co., Feb.-Aug. 1906; gen. supt. Mo., Okla. & Gulf Ry., 1906-07; supt. transportation, Guanica Centrale, Puerto Rico, 1907-12; v.p. and asst. gen. mgr. Puerto Rico Rys. Co. and subsidiaries, later pres. and gen. mgr., 1912-20; spl. rep. of exec. dept., Okla. Southwestern Ry., Miami Mineral Belt Ry., Okla. Union R.R. Co., 1923-25, became v.p. of same and Union Transportation Co., 1925; pres. Tulsa (Okla.) Rubber Products Co., 1927—; in investment and ins. business under own name, 1931—; pres. Tex. Gulf Securities Corp., Seneca Life Ins. Co.; exec. v.p. Slick Townsite Co., Slick Gas Co., Interurban Constrn. Co. Chief of Am. Protective League, Puerto Rico, World War; cited by President Wilson in behalf of Am. Red Cross. Democrat. Baptist. Mason. Home: Tulsa, Okla. Died Mar. 29, 1936.

SEWELL, Robert van Vorst, painter; b. New York, 1860; s. Robert and Sarah (van Vorst) S.; A.B., Columbia, 1883; studied under Lefebvre and Boulanger, Paris, 1883-87; m. Lydia Amanda Brewster, Apr. 12, 1888. Won 1st Hallgarten prize, Nat. Acad. Design, 1888; silver medal, Buffalo Expn. for exhibit of designs of mural paintings, etc. His mural painting, The Canterbury Pilgrims, in great hall of Georgian Court, Lakewood, and several others are widely known; painted The Story of Psyche, a series of lunette decorations of the Palm Room of the St. Regis Hotel, New York. A.N.A., 1902. Home: Oyster Bay, L.I., N.Y. Died Nov. 18, 1924.

SEWELL, William Joyce, U.S. senator, capitalist; b. Castlebar, Ireland, Dec. 6, 1835; came to U.S., 1851; served in Union army, 1861-65, capt. to bvt. maj. gen. of vols.; after war became connected with r.r.'s in N.J., branches of Pa. R.R. system; now v.p. W. Jersey and Seashore R.R. and dir. Pa. R.R.; has banking and other interests in N.J.; also in command 2d brigade, Nat. Guard of N.J. State senator from Camden Co., 1872-81, and pres. N.J. senate, 1876, 1879 and 1880; U.S. senator, 1881-87, and 1895-1907. Was one of the nat. commrs. of N.J. for World's Columbian Expn. Home: Camden, N.J. Died 1901.

SEXTON, George Samuel, clergyman; b. Middleburg, Tenn., June 10, 1867; s. James R. and Mary J. (Justice) S.; student Hendrix Coll., Ark.; D.D., Ky. Wesleyan U., 1910; m. Sallie Gray Moseley, Aug. 30, 1893; 1 son, George Samuel. Ordained M.E. Ch., South, ministry, 1888; pastor Texarkana, Ark., 1888-92, St. Jo, Texas, 1893, Henrietta, 1894, Gainesville, 1895-96, Plano, 1897-99, Terrell, 1900-01; presiding elder Gainesville dist., 1902-03; pastor, Galveston, 1904-05, St. Paul's Ch., Houston, 1906-09; asst. corr. sec. Bd. Ch. Extension, June 1, 1909; pastor First Church, Shreveport, La.; pres. emeritus Centenary Coll. of La., Shreveport. Completed St. Paul's Ch., Houston, 1909, cost $212,000; in charge erection Representative and Monumental Ch., Washington, under Gen. Conf., to cost $500,000. Capt. and chaplain 6th Tex. Inf.; later chaplain 1st Tex. U.S.V., during Spanish-Am. War; chaplain La. Div. United Spanish War Vets. Leader of delegation from Tex. Annual Conf. to Gen. Conf. M.E. Ch., S., Asheville, N.C., May 1910; del. from La. to Gen. Conf., 1923-26. Mason; Grand Prelate Grand Commandery K.T. of Tex.; Grand High Prelate for U.S. of Grand Imperial Council of Red Cross of Constantine. Democrat. Home: Shreveport, La. Died July 4, 1937.

SEXTON, John Chase, M.D.; b. Rushville, Ind., Jan. 21, 1859; s. Dr. Marshall and Elizabeth S.; ed. Rushville High Sch. and Hanover Coll.; M.D., Med. Coll. of Ohio, 1882; post-grad. work, Phila., New York, Chicago; m. Hannah Cullen, Sept. 27, 1882. Prof. gastro-intestinal surgery, Ind. U. Med. Coll. Fellow Am. Assn. Obstetricians and Gynecologists. Home: Rushville, Ind. Died Dec. 26, 1936.

SEXTON, Lawrence Eugene, lawyer; b. Cleveland, July 26, 1859; s. David Botsford and Caroline Elizabeth (Hale) S.; grad. Phillips Acad., Exeter, N.H., 1880; A.B., cum laude, Harvard, 1884; LL.B., Columbia, 1887; unmarried. In practice at New York, 1887—; mem. firm Wetmore (Edmund) & Jenner, 1889—; dir. Ramapo Foundry & Wheel Works. Judiciary nominators' and Rep. nominee for justice Supreme Ct. N.Y., 1906. Overseer, Harvard U., 1909—. Democrat. Mem. various civic orgns., societies, etc. Home: New York, N.Y. Died Aug. 30, 1919.

SEXTON, Lewis Albert, M.D.; b. Tenn., Mar. 25, 1876; s. William Robert and Mary (Sparkman) S.; student acad. and pharm. depts. Vanderbilt U., Nashville, Tenn., 1899-1901; M.D., Vanderbilt, 1906; m. Henrietta Stenz, Apr. 19, 1916. Asst. chemist, Spurlock-Neal Co., Nashville, 1901-02; interne, Nashville City Hosp., 1906-07, Riverside Hosp., New York, 1907-08; resident phys. Willard Parker Hosp., New York, 1908-14; asst. supt. Johns Hopkins Hosp., Baltimore, Md., 1914-17; supt. Hartford (Conn.) Hosp., 1917—. Mem. Camp Fire Club of America. Republican. Presbyn. Home: Hartford, Conn. Died Dec. 3, 1936.

SEXTON, Pliny Titus, lawyer, banker; b. Palmyra, N.Y., June 12, 1840; s. Pliny and Hannah (Van Alstine) S.; ed. pvt. schs. Palmyra Classical Union Sch., Rensselaer Poly. Inst.; LL.B., State and Nat. Law Sch., Poughkeepsie, N.Y., 1859; (LL.D., Union Univ., 1893); m. Harriot Hyde, 1860. Admitted N.Y. bar, 1861, Supreme Ct. of U.S., 1882; pres. First Nat. Bank, Palmyra, 1876—. Pres. Village of Palmyra, 1879-83, and of its bd. of edn., 1883-89; Rep. candidate for treas. of N.Y., 1883; regent, 1890—, vice-chancellor, 1913-15, chancellor, 1915-21, chancellor emeritus, 1921—, U. of the State of N.Y.; hon. chancellor Union U., 1893; procured appropriation and authority for univ. extension work by U. State of N.Y.—first legislation on that subject in U.S. Home: Palmyra, N.Y. Died Sept. 5, 1924.

SEYMOUR, Arthur Bliss, botanist; b. Moline, Ill., Jan. 3, 1859; s. Frank and Mary Elizabeth (Bliss) S.; B.S., U. of Ill., 1881, M.S., 1886; m. Anna Julia Conkling, May 6, 1886; children—Mary Elizabeth, Rosa Margaret, Frank Conkling, Edith Katharine. Botanist to Ill. State Lab. Natural History, 1879, 1881-83; pvt. asst. in Cryptogamic Herbarium and Gray Herbarium, Harvard Univ., 1883-85; instr. in charge bot. dept., U. of Wis., 1885-86; asst. in Cryptogamic Herbarium, Harvard, 1886—; teacher of cryptogamic botany, Radcliffe Coll., 1890-91, and summer classes, 1890, 92. Fellow Am. Acad. Arts and Sciences, and A.A.A.S. Compiler: A Provisional Host-Index of the Fungi of the United States (with W. G. Farlow), 1888-91; Host Index of the Fungi of North America, 1929. Editor and publisher (with F. S. Earle) Economic Fungi and Economic Fungi Supplement. Home: Belmont, Mass. Died Mar. 31, 1933.

SEYMOUR, Augustus Theodore, lawyer; b. Nebraska City, Neb., Aug. 22, 1873; s. Theodore Holly and Elizabeth (Barriball) S.; student, Oberlin, 1890-93; Ohio State U. Sch. of Law, 1894-95; m. Evelyn Owens, June 5, 1902; children—James Owens, Augustus T. Admitted to Ohio bar, 1894, and began practice at Columbus; mem. Vorys, Sater, Seymour & Pease. Asst. pros. atty., Franklin Co., O., 1900-05, pros. atty., 1905-06; asst. to the atty. gen. of U.S., Nov. 10, 1922-Mar. 1925. Pres. Columbus Chamber of Commerce, 1914-15. Republican. Conglist. Home: Columbus, O. Died Mar. 11, 1926.

SEYMOUR, Frederick, lawyer; b. Whitney's Point, N.Y., Aug. 2, 1856; s. George W. and Mary (Freeman) S.; bro. of John Sammis S.; grad. Yale, 1881, A.B., 1895; studied Columbia Law Sch.; m. Julia C., d. Nathan Dikeman, of Waterbury, Conn., Oct. 14, 1885. In practice at New York, 1882—; mem. Seymour, Seymour & Megrath. Home: E. Orange, N.J. Deceased.

SEYMOUR, George Franklin, first P.E. bishop of Springfield, consecrated June 11, 1878; b. New York, Jan. 5, 1829; s. Isaac Newton and Elvira (Belknap)

S.; grad. Columbia, 1850 (LL.D., 1878; S.T.D., Racine Coll., Wis., 1867); grad. Gen. Theol. Sem., 1854; ordered deacon, Dec. 17, 1854; ordained priest, Sept. 23, 1855; m. Mrs. Harriet Atwood (Downe) Aymar, July 23, 1889. Was pastor in charge of a mission at Annandale on the Hudson, N.Y., from 1854, and founded there, 1855, St. Stephen's Coll., being its first warden, 1855-61; rector St. Mary's Ch., Manhattanville, N.Y., 1861-62; rector Christ Ch., Hudson, Columbia Co., N.Y., 1862-63; St. John's, Brooklyn, 1863-67; prof. ecclesiastical history, Gen. Theol. Sem., 1865-79; dean of same, 1875-79; chaplain of the House of Mercy, New York, 1867-79; supt. Soc. for Promoting Religion and Learning, New York, 1871-79. Author: What Is Modern Romanism?, 1885; Amusements in Their Relation to Religion, 1890; Marriage and Divorce, 1893; The Church Idea of the Family, 1899; "Money, What It Really Is," 1896; Sacraments and Principles of the Church, 1 vol., 1903; etc. Home: Springfield, Ill. Died 1906.

SEYMOUR, Horatio Winslow, editor; b. in Cayuga Co., N.Y., 1854; s. Andrew Milliken and Louisa Maria (Goodyear) S.; ed. in pub. schs., Racine, Wis.; m. Annie E. Jones, 1876. Learned printer's trade in offices of Racine Advocate and Journal; city editor Milwaukee News, 1873-75; telegraph editor, 1875-79, night editor, 1879-83, Chicago Times; editorial writer, 1883-87, editor and mng. editor, 1887-95, Chicago Herald; editor and pub. Chicago Chronicle, 1895-1907; editorial writer and editorial supervisor New York World, 1908-11; editor The Republic, St. Louis, Aug. 15, 1911-May 1, 1912, from which time has been a writer for the World, New York. Author: Government & Co., Limited, 1895. Died Dec. 17, 1920.

SEYMOUR, John Sammis, lawyer; b. Whitney's Point, N.Y., Sept. 28, 1848; s. George W. and Mary (Freeman) S.; brother of Frederick S.; A.B., Yale U., 1875, LL.B., 1878; m. Clara E., d. Gen. Charles Olmstead, of Norwalk, Conn., Sept. 10, 1879. In practice at New York, 1897—. Mem. Conn. Senate, 1891-93; U.S. commr. of patents, 1893-97. Home: Norwalk, Conn. Died June 16, 1931.

SEYMOUR, Morris Woodruff, lawyer; b. Litchfield, Conn., Oct. 6, 1842; s. Origen Storrs (late chief justice Supreme Ct., Conn.) and Lucy Morris (Woodruff) S.; A.B., Yale, 1866; LL.B., Columbia Law School, 1867; (LL.D., Trinity College, Conn., 1916); m. Charlotte Sanford, Sept. 15, 1869. Practiced Bridgeport, Conn., 1867—, specializing in corp. and patent law; lecturer Law Dept., Yale. Judge of City Ct., Bridgeport, 1879-80; corp. counsel, 1880-82; mem. Conn. State Senate, 1881, 1882; col. on staff of Gov. English, 1867-69, 1870-71. Democrat. Episcopalian. Pres. State Reformatory; mem. Bd. of Pardons, 1883—; trustee Conn. Industrial Sch., Cheshire Acad.; pres. Hotchkiss Sch., Lakeville, Conn.; chancellor diocese of Conn. President Conn. Soc. Mil. Order Foreign Wars, Conn. Soc. Colonial Wars; v.p. Conn. Soc. of the Cincinnati, Conn. Hist. Society. Home: Litchfield, Conn. Died Oct. 28, 1920.

SEYMOUR, Robert Gillin, clergyman; b. New York, Feb. 27, 1841; s. James W. and Katharine (Fitzgerald) S.; A.B., Colgate, 1866, A.M., 1871; (D.D., Univ. of Chicago, 1882); m. Annie E. Hadden, Oct. 2, 1865. Served as 2d lt. Co. D, 79th U.S.C.T., in Civil War; ordained Baptist ministry, 1864; pastor New Orleans, 1864-66, Great Falls, N.H., 1866-69, Boston, Mass., 1869-89, Auburn, N.Y., 1889-91; dist. sec. Am. Bapt. Missionary Union, 1891-93; pastor Lowell, Mass., 1893-95; sec. Am. Bapt. Publ. Soc., Phila., 1895—. Chaplain Mass. Ho. of Rep., 1878-84; trustee Colgate U. Author: Light for the Journey, 1894; Pastor's Companion, 1900; Fresh Water from Old Wells, 1907. Home: Narberth, Pa. Died Sept. 20, 1912.

SEYMOUR, Thomas Day, prof. of Greek, Yale, 1880—; b. Hudson, O., April 1, 1848; s. Prof. Nathan Perkins and Elizabeth (Day) S.; grad. Western Reserve Coll., 1870, LL.D., 1894 (LL.D., Univ. of Glasgow, Scotland, 1901); studied at Leipzig and Berlin; m. July 2, 1874, Sarah M., d. Pres. Henry L. Hitchcock, D.D. Prof. Greek, Western Reserve Coll., 1872-80; chmn. mng. com. Am. School of Classical Studies, Athens, Greece, 1887-1901. Pres. Archæol. Inst. of America; asso. fellow Am. Acad. Arts and Sciences. Co-editor of the "College Series" of Greek authors. Am. co-editor of the classical Review, G1. Editor: Selected Odes of Pindar, with Notes, 1882; Introduction to the Language and Verse of Homer, 1885; Homer's Iliad, books i-vi, in "College Series," 1887-90; Introduction and Vocabulary to School Odyssey, 8 books, 1897; Homeric Vocabulary, 1889. School Iliad, books i-vi, 1889, 1901. Home: New Haven, Conn. Died 1907.

SEYMOUR, William, actor, stage mgr.; b. New York, Dec. 19, 1855; s. James and Lydia Eliza (Griffith) S., both then members Burton's Chambers St. Theatre Co.; ed. pub. and pvt. schs., New York and New Orleans; m. May, d. E. L. Davenport (and sister of Fanny Davenport), Jan. 8, 1882; children—May Davenport (Mrs. W. Stanley Eckert), Edward L. Davenport, Fanny Davenport (wife of Prof. R. M. Field), James W. Davenport, John Davenport. Began at Varieties Theatre, New Orleans, 1862-65; played with Joseph Jefferson, New York and Phila., 1866-67, and at Booth's Theatre, New York, 1869-71, Globe Theatre, Boston, 1871-72; stage mgr. Varieties Theatre, New Orleans (with Lawrence Barrett), 1872-75, Union Square Theatre, New York (with A. M. Palmer), 1875-77, California Theatre, San Francisco (with John McCullough), 1877-79; acting and stage mgr., Boston Mus., 1879-89, Tremont Theatre, Boston (with Abbey & Schoeffel), 1889-98; toured country with Sol Smith Russell, 1898-99; with Maurice Grau, Met. Opera House, 1900-01; gen. stage dir., 1904-11, antiquarian, 1911-16, for Charles Frohman; stage dir. Punch and Judy Theatre, N.Y. City, 1916-17; with George C. Tyler, seasons, 1919-23, and 1925-26; with Dramatists Theatre, Inc., 1923-25. Episcopalian. Republican. Home: South Duxbury, Mass. Died Oct. 2, 1933.

SEYMOUR, William Wolcott, investment banker; b. St. Albans, Vt., July 20, 1861; s. Henry Edmund and Susan Catherine (Hubbell) S.; B.A., Williams Coll., 1884; Göttingen and Berlin, 1884-86; m. Emily Wells Risley, Jan. 4, 1910; children (adopted)—William Seymour Leake, Jane Seymour Leake, Virginia Leake, Barbara Leake. With Seymour, Barto & Co., Tacoma, Wash., 1890-96, Seymour Bros. & Co., 1896-1900; pres. Tacoma Gas Co., 1900-06; now pres. N. Pacific Pub. Service Co., Ellensburg Gas & Water Co., Seymour Land & Timber Co., Washington State Land Co., Eaton Land Company; dir. Shaffer Box Company, Tacoma. Pres. Park Board, Tacoma, 1909-11; mayor of Tacoma, 1911-14. Trustee Whitman Coll., Tacoma Chamber Commerce, Ferry Museum (Tacoma), Washington Children's Home (Seattle); chmn. War Camp Community Service, and Soldiers' and Sailors' Club House, Tacoma, during first year of war. Republican. Conglist. Presented Tacoma with Conservatory in Wright Park; inaugurated Boys' Club at St. Albans, Vt., and Y.M.C.A. Camp at Glen Cove, Wash. Mem. at large of Nat. Council Boy Scouts of America. Home: Tacoma, Wash. Died Oct. 1, 1929.

SEYMOUR, William Wotkyns, physician; b. Troy, N.Y., July 29, 1853; s. William Pierce and Helen Hughes (Wotkyns) S.; grad. Yale, 1875; Harvard, M.D., 1878; m. Frances Minturn, Jan. 23, 1883. House surgeon, Boston City Hosp., 1878-79; in Vienna and London, 1879-80; formerly prof. diseases of women, U. of Vermont; surgeon to Samaritan Hosp., Troy, N.Y. Democrat (hard money). Translator: Kehr's Diagnosis of Gallstone Disease (from German), 1901. Home: Troy, N.Y. Died 1904.

SHAAD, George Carl, electrical engr.; b. Stratford, N.Y., May 5, 1878; s. George and Christina (Ernst) S.; B.S. in Elec. Engring., Pa. State Coll., 1900, E.E., 1905; m. Merthyr Tydvil Evans, Sept. 1, 1906; children—Margaret Louise (dec.), George Carl (dec.), Dorothy, Paul, George Ernst, David. With Gen. Electric Co., Schenectady, N.Y., 1900-02; instr. elec. engring., 1902-04, asst. prof., 1904-06, U. of Wis.; with Bur. of Standards, Washington, summer, 1905; asst. prof. elec. engring., 1906-07, asso. prof., 1907-09, Mass. Inst. Tech.; prof. elec. engring., U. of Kan., 1909—, and acting dean School of Engineering, 1917-18, dean of Sch. Engring. and Architecture, 1927; also cons. engr. Fellow Am. Inst. Electrical Engrs. Died July 9, 1936.

SHACKELFORD, James M., lawyer; b. Lincoln Co., Ky., July 7, 1827; s. Edmund and Susan S.; academic edn. at Springfield, Ky.; admitted to bar, 1853; was lt. Co. I, 4th Ky. regt., in Mexican war; admitted to Ky. bar, 1853; col. 25th Ky. inf., and later of 8th Ky. cav., in Union army; became brig. gen., March 17, 1863; captured Confederate Gen. John H. Morgan and command, July 20, 1863, and later comd. a cav. army corps, the Army of the Ohio, consisting of 16 regts. Was Rep. elector for Ind., 1880 and 1888; judge U.S. court, Ind. Ty., 1889-93, then engaged in law practice there; atty. for the Choctaw Nation. Republican. Died 1909.

SHACKLEFORD, Thomas Mitchell, judge; b. Fayetteville, Tenn., Nov. 14, 1859; s. Daniel Park and Aletha (Young) S.; ed. pvt. schs., Fayetteville, and Burritt Coll., Spencer, Tenn.; LL.D., U. of Fla., 1910; m. Nannie Clopton Rhea, Sept. 21, 1882 (died 1887); 1 son, Thomas M.; m. 2d, Lena Aumerle Wooten, Dec. 13, 1888; 1 son, Robert W. Removed from Tenn. to Fla., 1882; engaged in orange culture, Marion Co., 1882-83; admitted to bar, 1882; practiced law, Brooksville, 1883-93, Tampa, 1893-1902. Candidate for Congress, 1890; presdl. elector for Fla., 1892; city atty. Tampa, 1900-02; elected justice Supreme Ct. of Fla. for term 1902-21 (chief justice 1905-09, 1913-15); resigned Sept. 1, 1917, and resumed law practice at Tampa, as sr. mem. Shackleford & Shackleford. Edited Register and Crescent, while at Brooksville; has been corr. Louisville Courier-Journal and Nashville American. Author: Amos Kohegan, 1883; By Sunlit Waters (with Rev. William Wilson DeHart). Home: Tampa, Fla. Died Sept. 21, 1927.

SHACKLETON, Robert, author; b. Mazomanie, Wis., Dec. 26, 1860; s. Robert and Sarah S.; ed. Cleveland, O.; law student U. of Mich., 1879-80; admitted to Ohio bar, 1881; m. Elizabeth H. Fleming, Aug. 6, 1890. In newspaper work, New York, 1895-1900; an asso. editor The Saturday Evening Post, Phila., 1900-02. Author: Toomey and Others, 1900; The Quest of the Colonial (with Elizabeth Shackleton), 1907; Strange Stories of the Civil War (part author), 1907; Adventures in Home-Making (with Elizabeth Shackleton), 1910; Unvisited Places of Old Europe, 1913; The Charm of the Antique (with Elizabeth Shackleton), 1914; Touring Great Britain, 1914; The Life of Russell H. Conwell, 1915; The History of Harper's Magazine, 1916; The Book of Boston, 1916; The Book of New York, 1917; The Book of Philadelphia, 1919; The Book of Chicago, 1920; The Book of Washington, 1921. Home: Fairfield, Conn. Died Mar. 1923.

SHAFER, John Douglas, judge; b. Allegheny Co., Pa., Dec. 5, 1848; s. Alexander Geary and Maria D. (Harper) S.; A.B., Washington and Jefferson Coll., 1866; m. Mrs. Maud B. Gifford, June 25, 1901. Teacher at W. Alexander and McKeesport, Pa., 1866-71; prof. Greek, Westminster Coll., 1871-73; admitted to bar, 1874; practiced at Pittsburgh; dean, Pittsburgh Law Sch. from its foundation, 1895-1920, dean emeritus. Apptd. by gov. judge Ct. of Common Pleas, Allegheny Co., May 1897; elected 1897, and reëlected, 1907 and 1917; apptd. president judge, 1915, for term ending 1927. Trustee and v.p. Carnegie Inst. of Pittsburgh. Republican. Presbyn. Home: Pittsburgh, Pa. Died Oct. 12, 1926.

SHAFER, Sara Andrew, author; b. La Porte, Ind., d. Dr. George Lafferty and Catherine Piatt (Andrew) Andrew; ed. pvtly.; m. Carlton Shafer, Nov. 19, 1884 (died 1906). Episcopalian. Author: In "Historic Town Series," Annapolis, 1900, Frederick, 1900, Mackinac, 1901; The Day Before Yesterday, 1904; Beyond Chance of Change, 1905; A White Paper Garden, 1910. Home: La Porte, Ind. Died 1913.

SHAFFER, Cornelius Thadeus, bishop; b. Troy, O., Jan. 3, 1847; s. John Shelby and Margaret (Otis) S.; ed. Berea (Ky.) Coll., 1867-69; spl. course, Cadiz, O., 1873; spl. course in Hebrew, Brooklyn, 1878-79; M.D., Jefferson Med. Coll., Phila., 1888; (D.D., Allen U., S.C., 1890, Wilberforce, 1905); m. Annie Marie Taylor, Oct. 26, 1870. Served in 23d Ohio Colored Inf. and 100th U.S. Colored Inf., 1864-65. Ordained A.M.E. ministry, 1870; held various pastorates in Ohio, N.Y., Md., Pa. Presiding elder 3 yrs.; sec. and treas. Ch. Extension Bd. A.M.E. Ch., 1892-1900; bishop A.M.E. Ch., 1900—; pres. Western U., Quindaro, Kan., 1901-03. State sec. of N.Y., Good Templars of the World, 1878-79; del. Ecumenical Conf., London, 1901, Toronto, 1911; held two confs. in Africa, 1902. Mem. Chicago Vice Commn.; pres. trustees Wilberforce U., 1912-16. Author: Pastors Visiting Companion and Diary, 1885. Home: Chicago, Ill. Died Mar. 28, 1919.

SHAFFER, Newton Melman, orthopedic surgeon; b. Kinderhook, N.Y., Feb. 14, 1846; s. Rev. James Newton and Jane Emeline (Hale) S.; ed. Claverack Acad. and Free Acad. (now Coll. of the City of New York); student at the Hosp. for Ruptured and Crippled, New York, 1863-67; M.D., Univ. Med. Coll. (New York U.), 1867; m. Margaret H. Perkins, Oct. 15, 1873; children—Newton Melman (dec.), Newton Melman (adopted grandson). Student, clin. recorder, asst. res. surgeon, N.Y. Hosp. for Relief of Ruptured and Crippled, 1863-68; asst. surgeon and surgeon in chief N.Y. Orthopædic Dispensary and Hosp., 1870-98; orthopedic surgeon to St. Luke's Hosp., 1872-87; was prof. orthopedic surgery, New York U. Med. Coll.; same, Cornell U. Med. Coll. (emeritus); was founder and surgeon in chief N.Y. State Orthopædic Hosp., and cons. orthopedic surgeon, Presbyn. Hosp. Chmn. com. which secured admission of Am. Orthopædic Assn. to Congress Am. Phys. and Surg., 1888; chmn. of com. which secured recognition of orthopedic surgery at 10th Internat. Med. Congress, 1900; first chmn. orthopedic sect. A.M.A., 1913; an exec. officer Congress Am. Phys. and Surg. over 25 yrs.; now cons. orthopedic surg. St. Luke's Hosp.; cons. orthopedic surg. N.Y. State Orthopædic Hosp. for Children. Fellow Am. Coll. Surgeons. Author: Selected Essays on Orthopædic Surgery, 1923. Home: New York, N.Y. Died Jan. 3, 1928.

SHAFROTH, John Franklin, senator; b. Fayette, Mo., June 9, 1854; s. John and Anna (Awl) S.; B.S., U. of Mich., 1875 (LL.D., 1909); m. Virginia Morrison, Oct. 26, 1881. Admitted to Mo. bar, 1876; practiced law at Fayette, Mo., 1876-79, Denver, 1879—; city atty., 1887-91; mem. 54th to 58th Congresses (1895-1905), 1st Colo. Dist.; refused to retain seat in 58th Congress, Feb. 15, 1904, as the general election at which he was a candidate had been tainted by fraud; gov. of Colo., terms, 1909-11, 1911-13; U.S. senator, 1913-19. Democrat. Mem. law firm of Shafroth & Shafroth. Home: Denver, Colo. Died Feb. 20, 1922.

SHAFTER, William Rufus, maj. gen. U.S.A., retired; b. Galesburg, Mich., Oct. 16, 1835; s. Hugh M. and Eliza (Sumner) S.; lived on farm and attended com. schs.; taught sch. 3 yrs. prior to 1861; m. Harriet Grimes, Sept. 11, 1862 (died 1898). Entered Union army as 1st lt. 7th Mich. inf., Aug. 22, 1861; maj. 19th Mich. inf., Sept. 5, 1862; lt. col., June 5, 1863; col. 17th U.S. colored inf., Apr. 19, 1864; bvt. brig. gen., Mar. 13, 1865, for gallant and meritorious services during the war; mustered out of vol. service, Nov. 2, 1865; entered regular army as lt. col., Jan. 26, 1867; bvtd. col., U.S.A., Mar. 2, 1867, and given Congressional medal of honor for gallant and meritorious services at battle of Fair Oaks, Va.; assigned to 24th inf., Apr. 14, 1869; col., Mar. 4, 1879; assigned to 1st inf.; brig. gen., May 3, 1897, in charge dept. of Calif.; maj. gen. vols., May 1898; went to Tampa, Fla.; thence to Cuba, where he comd. the mil. operations ending in capitulation of Gen. Linares' army and surrender of Santiago de Cuba, July 1898; comdg. Depts. of Calif. and Columbia, 1899-1901; retired June 30, 1901, as maj. gen. Home: Bakersfield, Calif. Died 1906.

SHAHAN, Thomas Joseph, bishop, rector; b. Manchester, N.H., Sept. 11, 1857; s. Maurice Peter and Mary Anne (Carmody) S.; student Montreal Coll., Can., 1872; Am. Coll., Rome, 1878-82; S.T.D., Propaganda, Rome, 1882; J.U.L., Roman Sem., 1889; student of history, U. of Berlin, 1889-91, The New Sorbonne and Institut Catholique, Paris, 1891; J.U.D., Georgetown U. Ordained R.C. priest, 1882; chancellor and sec. Diocese of Hartford, 1883-88; prof. ch. history and patrology, 1891-1909; rector, 1909-28, Catholic U. of America. Lecturer on history and elements of Roman law, 1895-1909; editor Catholic U. Bulletin, 1895-1909; lecturer on history of edn. in Catholic U. Inst. of Pedagogy, New York, 1902-03; mem. bd. of judges for Hall of Fame, Univ. Heights, New York. Pres. Catholic Edn. Assn., 1909-28, Nat. Conf. of Catholic Charities, 1910-14; created domestic prelate of Pontifical Court (Rome) with rank of monsignor, 1909; consecrated titular bishop of Germanicopolis, Nov. 15, 1914; asst. at pontifical throne, 1928. Author: The Blessed Virgin in the Catacombs, 1892; Giovanni Battista de Rossi, 1900; The Beginnings of Christianity, 1903; The Middle Ages, 1904; The House of God and Other Addresses and Studies, 1905; St. Patrick in History, 1905. Translator: Patrology, by Otto Bardenhewer, 1908. Asso. editor Catholic Encyclopedia, 1905-29, Universal Knowledge Foundation, 1927—. Officer Legion of Honor, 1919. Home: Baltimore, Md. Died Mar. 9, 1932.

SHALER, Alexander, soldier; b. Haddam, Conn., Mar. 19, 1827; s. Ira and Jerusha (Arnold) S.; grad. Brainerd Acad., Haddam, Conn., 1844; m. Mary McMurray, Mar. 31, 1847. At 17 employed by his father, and 3 yrs. later became propr. of a stone business, continuing until 1861. Joined Washington Grays (later 8th Regt., N.Y. State Militia), 1845; transferred to 7th Regt., 1848; promoted sergt., and 1st lt., and took part in suppressing Astor Place riots, 1849; captain, 1850-60; major 7th Regt., N.G.S.N.Y., 1860-61. Commd. of President lt. col. 1st U.S. Chasseurs, afterward 65th N.Y. Vols., June 1, 1861; col., July 17, 1862; brig. gen., May 26, 1863; maj. gen. U.S.V., July 27, 1865, "for meritorious services during war." Maj. gen. 1st Div. N.G.S.N.Y. and mem. bd. to provide armories for city troops; hon. disch., May 21, 1886. Awarded Congressional Medal of Honor, Nov. 25, 1893, "for distinguished gallantry at battle of Marye's Heights"; was 3 mos. in Confed. prison, 1864. Founder and propr. Hudson Heights, N.J., and of other properties at Ridgefield, N.J. Mem. New York bd. supervisors, 1866; fire commr., 1867-73, and pres., 1867-70, fire dept., New York; spent 3 mos. after great fire of 1871 reorganizing Chicago Fire Dept. at invitation of city authorities; pres. New York Bd. Health, 1883; mayor Borough of Ridgefield N.J., 1899-1901; pres. N.Y. City Assn. Union Ex-Prisoners of War, 1887-96; one of organizers (4 yrs. v.p. and pres.) Nat. Rifle Assn.; comdr. Mil. Order Loyal Legion. Home: Ridgefield, N.J. Died 1911.

SHALER, Charles, brigadier gen. U.S.A.; b. Pittsburgh, May 23, 1843; s. Charles and Mary Anne (Riddle) S.; ed. U.S. Mil. Acad.; m. Florence Stidham, Apr. 27, 1896. Enlisted as sergt. Co. I, 12th Pa. Inf., Apr. 25, 1861; discharged, Aug. 5, 1861; cadet U.S. Mil. Acad., 1863-67; commd. 2d lt. 5th U.S. Arty., June 17, 1867; transferred to Ordnance Dept., July 5, 1867; 1st lt., June 23, 1874; capt., Mar. 4, 1879; maj., Feb. 22, 1897; lt. col., Feb. 18, 1903; col., Sept. 17, 1904; brig. gen. and retired at own request after 40 years' service, Jan. 19, 1905. Episcopalian. Home: Indianapolis, Ind. Died Mar. 26, 1915.

SHALER, Nathaniel Southgate, dean Lawrence Scientific School and prof. geology, Harvard; b. Newport, Ky., Feb. 20, 1841; grad. Lawrence Scientific School, Harvard, 1862, Sc.D., 1865; served 2 yrs. as arty. officer in Union army during Civil war; instr. zoölogy and geology, Lawrence Scientific School, 1868-72; prof. palæontology, 1868-87, then prof. geology Harvard; dir. Ky. geol. survey, 1873-80, devoting part of each year to that work; from 1884 geologist in charge Atlantic div., U.S. Geol. Survey; mem. Nat. Acad. Sciences, etc. Author: A First Book in Geology; Kentucky, a Pioneer Commonwealth; The Nature of Intellectual Property; The Story of Our Continent; The Interpretation of Nature; Illustrations of the Earth's Surface; Sea and Land; The United States of America: a Study of the American Commonwealth; Fossil Brachiopods of the Ohio Valley; American Highways; Features of Coasts and Oceans; Domesticated Animals: their Relation to Man; The Individual: Study of Life and Death, 1900; The Neighbor, 1904; The Citizen, 1903; etc. Died 1906.

SHALLENBERGER, Ashton C., congressman; b. Toulon, Ill., 1862; s. Martin and Eliza (Hall) S.; ed. U. of Ill.; m. Eliza Zilg, 1885; children—Martin C., Grace Pauline, Barbara Dorothea. Removed to Neb., 1881, and engaged in cattle raising and farming; organizer, 1887, since cashier and pres. Bank of Alma. Mem. 57th Congress (1901-03), 5th Dist. of Neb.; gov. of Neb., 1909-11; Dem. primary nominee for U.S. senator, 1912; mem. 64th, 65th and 68th to 72d Congresses (1915-19, 1923-33), 5th Neb. Dist., and 73d Congress (1933-35), 4th Neb. Dist. Mason. Home: Alma, Neb. Died Feb. 22, 1938.

SHALLENBERGER, William Shadrach, asst. postmaster gen.; b. Mt. Pleasant, Pa., Nov. 24, 1839; s. Abraham and Rachel S.; ed. at Mt. Pleasant and at Lewisburg U. (hon. A.M., Lewisburg, 1880); m. Josephine Power, Dec. 1, 1864. First lt. and adj. 140th Pa. Vols., 1862-64; wounded at Gettysburg and Todd's Tavern. Mem. 45th to 47th Congresses (1877-83), 24th Pa. Dist.; 2d asst. postmaster gen., 1897-1907. Republican. Home: Rochester, Pa. Died Apr. 15, 1914.

SHAMBAUGH, Benjamin Franklin, univ. prof.; b. Elvira, Ia., Jan. 29, 1871; s. John and Eve Anna (Ressler) S.; Ph.B., State U. of Ia., 1892, A.M., 1893; Ph.D., U. of Pa., 1895; m. Bertha M. Horak, Aug. 11, 1897. Prof. polit. science, State U. of Iowa, 1895—, head dept. polit. science, 1897—. Editor Iowa Journal of History and Politics. Supt. State Hist. Soc. of Iowa, 1907—. Author: History of the Constitutions of Iowa, 1902; The Constitutions of Iowa, 1934. Editor: Documentary Material Relating to the History of Iowa, 1895; Fragments of Debates of the Constitutional Conventions of 1844 and 1846, Ia., 1900; Messages and Proclamations of the Governors of Iowa, 1903; The Old Stone Capitol Remembers, 1939. Editor Iowa Biographical Series, Iowa Economic History Series, Iowa Social History Series, Iowa Applied History Series, and the Iowa Chronicles of the World War Series. Died Apr. 7, 1940.

SHANAHAN, David Edward, realtor; b. Lee Co., Ill., Sept. 7, 1862; s. George and Katherine Vale (Power) S.; grad. South Div. High Sch., Chicago; LL.B., Chicago Coll. of Law, 1896; unmarried. Engaged in real estate and banking business; director, Terminal Nat. Bank, E. L. Essley Machinery Company. South Town supervisor, 1885-87; mem. Ill Ho. of Rep., 1894-1931 (temp. speaker, 1903; speaker, 1915-31). Has served as del. to city, county, state and nat. Rep. convs.; mem. Chicago Charter Conv., 1905; mem. Ill. Commn. to San Francisco Expn., 1915; mem. State Council of Defense, 1917. Mem. K.P., Royal Arcanum, Elks, Woodmen. Home: Chicago, Ill. Died Oct. 18, 1936.

SHANAHAN, Edmund Thomas, theologian; b. Boston, Mass., Nov. 22, 1868; s. Michael F. and Ellen M. S.; A.B., Boston Coll., 1888; S.T.D., Propaganda, Rome, 1893; J.C.L., Roman Sem., 1895; Ph.D., Roman Acad., 1895. Ordained R.C. priesthood, 1893; instr. philosophy and dogmatic theology, Am. Coll., Rome, 1894-95; student Louvain U., Belgium, 1895; asso. prof. philosophy, 1895-1901, prof. dogmatic theology, 1898-1920, dean faculty of theology, 1901-03, 1907-09, 1915-17, Catholic U. of America; parish priest, Sacred Heart Ch., Watertown, Mass., Dec. 1920—. Lecturer before Am. Soc. Extension of Univ. Teaching, Phila., 1897, U. of Pa., 1898-99. Home: Watertown, Mass. Died Mar. 19, 1929.

SHANAHAN, John W., D.D., Roman Catholic, bishop of Harrisburg (Pa.); consecrated May 1, 1899. Died Feb. 19, 1916.

SHANDS, Aurelius Rives, surgeon; b. Petersburg, Va., Nov. 5, 1860; s. Aurelius Rives and Martha (Wood) S.; grad. Univ. Sch., Petersburg, 1880; M.D., U. of Md., 1884; m. Agnes Horner Eppes, Dec. 31, 1895. Prof. orthopedic surgery, Columbian (now George Washington) U., from 1894, emeritus. Home: Washington, D.C. Died Apr. 27, 1941.

SHANDS, Garvin Dugas, lawyer; b. Spartanburg Dist., S.C., Dec. 5, 1844; s. Anthony Capel and Frances Jane (Ferguson) S.; ed. Wofford Coll., S.C., through jr. yr.; LL.B., U. of Ky., 1870; (LL.D., Wofford, 1897); m. Mary E. Roseborough, Dec. 14, 1870. Served pvt. and non-commd. officer in S.C. regts., Hampton's corps, Lee's army, C.S.A., 1861-65, in S.C. and Va. Admitted to bar, 1870, and engaged in practice in Miss.; mem. Miss. Ho. of Rep., 1876-80; lt. gov. of Miss. and pres. Senate, 1882-90. Democrat. Dean of Law Sch., U. of Miss., 1894-1906; prof. common law, Tulane U., Oct. 1906—. Mem. M.E. Ch., South, and mem. Gen. Confs., Nashville, 1882, Richmond, 1886, St. Louis, 1890, Memphis, 1894, Birmingham, 1906. Home: New Orleans, La. Died July 1, 1917.

SHANKLAND, Edward Clapp, civil engr.; b. Pittsburgh, Pa., Aug. 2, 1854; s. Edward Russell and Emeline F. (Clapp) S.; pub. sch. edn.; C.E., Rensselaer Poly. Inst., 1878; (hon. M.A., Cornell Coll., Ia., 1904); m. Harriet Graham, July 19, 1881. Engaged on U.S. improvement of Mo. and Miss. rivers, 1878-83; bridge work, Canton, O., 1883-89; designing steel work for bldgs., 1889—; engr. for Burnham & Root, architects, 1889-94; engr. of constrn. and chief engr. of works, Chicago Expn., 1891-93; mem. D. H. Burnham & Co., 1894-98, of E. C. & R. M. Shankland, 1898—. Mem. Harbor Subway Commn., Chicago, 1911-16. Home: Chicago, Ill. Died June 3, 1924.

SHANKLIN, John Gilbert; b. Evansville, Ind.; s. John and Philura (French) S.; ed. Kenyon, Coll., Gambier, O.; attended Univ. of Berlin, Germany, 1867-68; m. Gertrude Avery, 1879. Sec. State of Ind., 1879-81; defeated for nomination for gov. in 1892, by small majority; mem. (from Ind.) of Dem. Nat. Com., 1896-1900. Editor and propr. Evansville (Ind.) Daily Courier, 1871-97. Died 1903.

SHANKLIN, William Arnold, university pres.; b. at Carrollton, Mo., Apr. 18, 1862; s. of Wesley Dunscombe and Locke (Arnold) S.; bro. of Arnold S.; A.B., Hamilton Coll., 1883; S.T.B., Garrett Bibl. Inst., Evanston, Ill., 1891; (hon. A.M., Hamilton, 1893, Wesleyan U., 1912; D.D., U. of Wash., 1895, Allegheny Coll., 1910; LL.D., Baker U., 1906, Trinity Coll., Conn., 1910, U. of Vt., 1911, Hamilton Coll., 1913, Allegheny Coll., 1915; L.H.D., Upper Ia., 1909; S.T.D., Garrett Bibl., 1922); m. Emma Elizabeth Brant, Oct. 14, 1891. Entered M.E. ministry, 1887; pastor, Peru, Kan., 1887-89, Ft. Scott, 1889-90, Spokane, Wash., 1890-93, Seattle, Wash., 1893-96, Dubuque, Ia., 1896-1900, Reading, Pa., 1900-05; pres. Upper Iowa U., 1905-09, Wesleyan U., 1909-23, pres. emeritus, 1923—. Mem. Univ. Senate of M.E. Ch.; mem. Conn. State Bd. of Edn.; trustee and mem. administrative bd. Am. U. Union in Europe; mem. Conn. Geol. Commn. Pres. Assn. Am. Colls., 1919, Meth. Ednl. Assn., 1921-22; exec. com. Am. Council on Edn., 1918. Home: Middletown, Conn. Died Oct. 6, 1924.

SHANKS, David Carey, army officer; b. Salem, Va., Apr. 6, 1861; s. David Carey and Sarah (Boone) S.; student Roanoke Coll., Salem, Va., 1874-78; grad. U.S. Mil. Acad., 1884; m. Nancy Chapman, Oct. 5, 1893; children—Katharine Chapman (wife of William E. Malloy, U.S.N.), Sarah Chapman (wife of Stephen J. Chamberlin, U.S.A.). Commd. 2d lt. 18th Inf., June 15, 1884; brig. gen., May 15, 1917; maj. gen. N.A., Aug. 5, 1917; maj. gen. U.S.A., Mar. 7, 1921; retired Jan. 17, 1925. Hon. sec. Am. Foundation for the Blind. Adj. 18th Inf., 1890-94; participated in campaigns, Philippine Insurrection, islands of Negros and Panay, 1899-1901; gov. Cavite Province, P.I., 1903-05; comdr. Port of Embarkation, Hoboken, N.J., Aug. 1, 1917-Sept. 9, 1918, and Dec. 5, 1918—; comd. 16th Div., Camp Kearny, Calif., Sept.-Nov. 30, 1918. Awarded D.S.M. (army), 1919, D.S.M. (navy), 1920. Author: Management of the American Soldier; As They Passed Through the Port, 1927. Home: Washington, D.C. Died Apr. 10, 1940.

SHANKS, Lewis Piaget, educator, author; b. Albany, N.Y., Mar. 24, 1878; s. Robert Lewis and Sophia Harriet Ann (Piaget) S.; Ph.B., Cornell, 1899, Ph.D., 1908; A.M., Columbia U., 1904; studied in Paris; m. Ethel Rollins, 1904; 1 son, Walter Rollins; m. 2d, Carrie Lewis, 1919; m. 3d, Louise Newhall Johnson, 1932. Began as master in pvt. sch., 1902; instr. Romance langs., U. of Wis., 1906-08; asst. prof. Romance langs., U. of Idaho, 1908-09, U. of Tenn., 1909-12, U. of Pa., 1912-18; prof. and head of dept., U. of Western Ontario, 1919-25; asso. prof., later prof. Romance langs., Johns Hopkins, 1925—. Democrat. Author: Anatole France, 1919; French Composition for Colleges (with E. A. Méras), 1924; Flaubert's Youth (1821-1845), 1927; Baudelaire, Flesh and Spirit, 1930. Translator: Complete Poems of Charles Baudelaire (metrical transl.), 1925; Baudelaire's Flowers of Evil, 1931; Anatole France—The Mind and the Man, 1932. Editor: Selections from Anatole France, 1932. Died Jan. 28, 1935.

SHANKS, William Franklin Gore, journalist; b. Shelbyville, Ky., Apr. 20, 1837; s. Sanders and Maria (Gore) S.; ed. Louisville, Ky.; m. Mary R. Lynn, June 24, 1863. War corr. New York Herald, 1861-65; editorial writer same, 1865-67; mng. editor Harper's Weekly, 1867-69; city editor New York Times, 1869; foreign editor, 1870-71, and city editor, 1871-80, New York Tribune; editor Daily Star, New York, 1889-90. In 1885 organized the Nat. Press Intelligence Co. (clipping bureau), of which he is pres.; in 1891 established The Daily and Weekly Bond Buyer, which he owns and edits. Author: Personal Recollections of Distinguished Generals; A Noble Treason (tragedy); The Ring Master (a novel). Was during war volunteer a.d.c. (without pay) on staffs of Gens. Rousseau and Thomas; wounded at battle of Chickamauga. Home: Brooklyn, N.Y. Died 1905.

SHANLEY, John, R.C. bishop; b. Albion, N.Y., Jan. 4, 1852; s. John and Nancy (McLean) S.; family removed to St. Paul, 1857; student Coll. of the Propaganda, Rome, 1869-74 (D.D., 1874). Ordained, Rome, May 30, 1874; asst., 1874-75, pastor,

1875-89, Cathedral of St. Paul; consecrated bishop of Fargo (N.D.), Dec. 27, 1889. Died 1909.

SHANNAHAN, John Newton, pub. utility exec.; b. Troy, N.Y., Aug. 8, 1872; s. Wm. and Jennie (Deane) S.; C.E., Rensselaer Poly. Inst., 1894; m. Mary Helena Brayton, Dec. 23, 1897; children—William Dean, Ruth. Began as batteryman, block signal dept., N.Y.C.&H.R. R.R., 1895, insp. signals, 1895-99; chief engr. Fonda, Johnstown & Gloversville R.R. Co., 1899-1903, gen. superintendent, 1903-07; v.p. and gen. mgr. Washington, Baltimore & Annapolis Electric R.R. Co., 1907-11; mgr. ry. operations, J. G. White & Co., 1911-12; v.p. and gen. mgr. Newport News & Hampton Ry., Gas & Electric Co., 1912-16, pres., 1916-26; pres. Old Dominion Land Co., 1925-27; pres. Omaha & Council Bluffs Street Ry. Co., 1927-32; pres. Midland United Co. of Ind., 1933—. Trustee Rensselaer Poly. Inst. Unitarian. Home: Indianapolis, Ind. Died Aug. 17, 1938.

SHANNON, Edgar Finley, univ. prof.; b. Bourbon Co., Ky., Sept. 19, 1874; s. James Butler and Lois Vashti (McCain) S.; A.B., Centre Coll., Ky., 1893; studied U. of Leipsic, 1898; A.M., Harvard, 1910, Ph.D., 1912; m. Mary Eleanor Duncan, Dec. 28, 1904; children—Robert Duncan (dec.), Edgar Finley. Asso. prof. ancient langs., 1895-1902, asso. prof. English and modern langs., 1902-06, prof. English, 1906-14, dean Coll. of Arts and Sciences, 1913-14, U. of Ark.; prof. English, Washington and Lee U., 1914—; prof. English, Peabody Coll. for Teachers, summer session, 1916, U. of Virginia, summer session, 1924, 25, 28-32, 34, Northwestern Univ., 1936. Presbyn. Author: An Atlas of English Literature; Chaucer and the Roman Poets. Home: Lexington, Va. Died May 2, 1938.

SHANNON, Nellie, financier; b. San Francisco, Calif., Oct. 26, 1863; s. Samuel Oliver and Mary J. (Norris) Holmes; ed. San Francisco High Sch. and San Jose Normal Sch.; m. Michael Shannon, of County Clare, Ireland, Nov. 25, 1883. Interested in philanthropy and music. Republican. Catholic. Home: Los Angeles, Calif. Died June 21, 1924.

SHANNON, Richard Cutts, congressman; b. New London, Conn., Feb. 12, 1839; s. Charles Tebbets and Jane Randell (Stanwood) S.; A.B., Colby Coll., 1862, A.M., 1866; LL.B., Columbia, 1885; (LL.D., Colby, 1892); m. Martha A. Greenough, Sept. 19, 1887. Sergt. Co. H, 5th Me. Inf., June 24, 1861; 1st lt., Oct. 10, 1861; capt. a.a.g. vols., Oct. 2, 1862; bvtd. maj. and lt. col. of vols. for his services. Sec. U.S. Legation to Brazil, 1871-75; asst. treas., v.p. and gen. mgr. and later pres., Botanical Garden R.R. Co., An Am. enterprise in Brazil, 1876-83; admitted to N.Y. bar, 1886; E.E. and M.P. to Nicaragua, Costa Rica and Salvador, 1891-93; mem. 54th and 55th Congresses (1895-99). Republican. Alumni trustee Colby College. Home: Brockport, N.Y. Died Oct. 7, 1920.

SHANNON, Robert Thomas, law book writer; b. nr. Lobelville, Tenn., May 5, 1860; s. Joseph J. and Nancy (Young) S.; student Vanderbilt, 1882; M.A., Cloverdale (Tenn.) Sem., 1884; LL.B., Cumberland U., 1884; m. Nannie A. Bell, Sept. 3, 1890 (died 1891); 1 dau., Nannie Bell; m. 2d, Florence B. McDonald, June 2, 1898; children—Emma E. (Mrs. A. R. Gray), William M. Admitted to Tenn. bar, 1884, and began practice at Waverly; settled at Nashville, 1893; apptd. mem. Tenn. Code Commn., 1929. Democrat. Mem. Christian (Disciples) Ch. Author: Tennesee Code Supplements, 1893, 95, 1904, 25; Annotated Code of Tennessee, 1896, 1917; Annotations on Tennessee Cases, with Table of Cases and Digest, 1929. Home: Nashville, Tenn. Died Sept. 6, 1931.

SHAPLEIGH, Frank Henry, artist; b. Boston, Mar. 7, 1842; s. John H. and Harriet N. (Powers) S.; ed. Boston public schools; prep. study for landscape painting, Old Lowell Inst. Drawing School; m. Boston, Oct. 19, 1870, Mary A., d. E. B. Studley. Enlisted in 45th Mass. regt., served in campaign in N.C.; after service completed, opened studio in Boston. Studied in studio of Emile Lambinet, Paris, 1866-88; returned to Boston. Has a studio at Crawford Notch, White Mountains. For several winters has occupied studio at the Ponce de Leon, St. Augustine, Fla. Most of his paintings have been in oil. Home: Boston, Mass. Died 1906.

SHAPLEIGH, Waldron, chemist; b. in Philadelphia, Jan. 25, 1848; s. Marshall S. and Elizabeth M. (Blandy) S.; ed. Episcopal Acad., Phila.; grad. Lehigh Univ., 1871; student chemistry, Paris and Vienna; m. Mary H. DuPuy, Dec. 23, 1880. Asst. prof. chemistry, Lehigh Univ., 1868-72; studied in Europe, 1872-74; supt. Kings Co. Refining Co., 1874-83; chemist Welsbach Light Co., 1887—; commr. from Pa. to Vienna Expn., 1873; judge awards World's Columbian Expn., 1893. Home: Philadelphia, Pa. Died 1901.

SHARP, Benjamin, zoölogist; b. Germantown, Phila., Nov. 1, 1858; s. Benjamin and Hannah Ballinger (Leedom) S.; ed. Swarthmore Coll., 1871-76; M.D., U. of Pa., 1879, Ph.D., 1880; Ph.D., Univ. of Würzburg, 1883; univs. of Berlin and Leipzig, and Zoöl. Sta., Naples, 1879-83; m. Virginia May Guild, Sept. 15, 1881. Prof. invertebrate zoölogy, Acad. Natural Sciences, Phila., 1883, U. of Pa., 1884-86; life mem. and corr. sec., 1890-1901, Acad. Natural Sciences, Phila., for which made expdns., collecting in Caribbee Islands in winter, 1888-89; to H.I., collecting archæol. and zoöl. specimens summer of 1893; also in Arctic, 1895, on U.S. revenue cutter "Bear," in Alaska and Siberia. Had charge zoölogy in First Arctic Expedition, Lt. R. E. Peary, 1891. Vice-pres. Nantucket Hist. Assn. Mem. Soc. of Friends. Lecturer. Rep. in Gen. Court of Mass. for Nantucket, 1910-13. Home: Nantucket Island, Mass. Died Jan. 24, 1915.

SHARP, Dallas Lore, univ. prof.; b. Haleyville, N.J., Dec. 13, 1870; s. Reuben Lore and Mary Den (Bradway) S.; A.B., Brown U., 1895; S.T.B., Boston U., 1899; (hon. Phi Beta Kappa, Boston U., 1914, and Brown U., 1916; Litt.D., Brown, 1917); m. Grace Hastings, Aug. 4, 1895; children—Dallas Lore, Waitstill, Morrison, Huntington. Ordained M.E. ministry, 1895; pastor Porter, Mass., 1896-98, Brockton Heights, 1898-99; asst. librarian, 1899-1902, asst. prof. English, 1902-09, prof. English, 1909, Boston U. On staff Youth's Companion, 1900-03. Author: Wild Life Near Home, 1901; Watcher in the Woods, 1903; Roof and Meadow, 1904; The Lay of the Land, 1908; The Face of the Fields, 1911; The Fall of the Year, 1911; Winter, 1912; The Spring of the Year, 1912; Summer, 1913; Beyond the Pasture Bars, 1913; Where Rolls the Oregon, 1914; The Hills of Hingham, 1916; The Seer of Slabsides, 1921; Education in a Democracy, 1922; Highlands and Hollows, 1923; The Magical Chance, 1923; The Spirit of the Hive, 1925. Sanctuary! Santuary! 1926; The Better Country, 1928. Home: Hingham, Mass. Died Nov. 29, 1929.

SHARP, Edwin Rees, banker; b. Groveport, O., Oct. 24, 1858; s. Abram and Harriet (Rees) S.; ed. pub. schs.; m. Flora Field, Nov. 22, 1882: children—Edwin Rees, Esther Davidson (Mrs. George T. Johnson). Began as messenger boy with bank, Columbus, O., 1874; now chmn. bd. Huntington Nat. Bank; v.p. and treas. Scioto Valley Ry. & Power Co. Republican. Home: Columbus, O. Deceased.

SHARP, George Matthews, judge; b. Baltimore, Md.; s. A. P. and Anna (Matthews) S.; ed. private schs., Baltimore; LL.B., Yale, 1875; spl. student, 1874-76; (hon. A.M., Yale, 1889; LL.D., Washington Coll., 1907); unmarried. Admitted to bar, 1875; judge Supreme bench of Baltimore City, 1897—. Lecturer Yale Law Sch., 1889-1900, Georgetown U. Law Sch., 1901-02. Republican. Mem. Soc. of Friends. Home: Baltimore, Md. Died July 7, 1911.

SHARP, Hunter, consul; b. Hertford Co., N.C., Oct. 5, 1861; s. Starkey and Jane Trimble (Lewis) S.; ed. Trinity Coll., N.C., Bingham's Mil. Acad., N.C., U. of N.C., and U. of Md.; m. May Adelaide Suydam, June 27, 1900. Marshal and v.consul at Osaka and Hioga, Japan, 1886-99; vice and deputy consul and interpreter, same, 1900-02; vice and deputy consul and interpreter at Kobé, Japan, 1902-05, consul, 1905-08; consul gen. at Moscow, Russia, 1908-09; consul at Lyons, France, 1909-10, at Belfast, Ireland, 1910-20, at Edenburgh, Scotland, Apr. 1920—. Home: Harrellsville, N.C. Died Dec. 17, 1923.

SHARP, Mrs. John C. (Nellie M. Sharp); b. Hillside Farm, Mich.; d. Dwight and Mary W. Merriman: m. Hon. John C. Sharp, 1881 (died 1907). Owner and mgr. Hillside Farm of several hundred acres, specializing in fattening steers for market. Prominent in club work, reforestation, etc. Mem. and officer Mich. State Fedn. of Women's Clubs since its orgn.; pres. Improvement Soc. of Jackson; widely known as speaker on social and civic topics; del. by apptmt. of 900 to 3d Nat. Conservation Congress, Kansas City, Mo., 1911; del. Gen. Fedn. of Women's Clubs, San Francisco, 1912. Home: Jackson, Mich. Died Nov. 9, 1912.

SHARP, John Fletcher, lawyer; b. Camp Point, Ill., Mar. 2, 1865; s. James and Parmelia J. (Bates) S.; student Chaddock School, Quincy, Ill., 1886-88; LL.B., U. of Mo., 1889; m. Bessie Constance Grady, Nov. 23, 1892 (dec.); children—Helen Irene, John Fletcher. Began practice at Purcell, I.T., 1889; mem. Supreme Court Com. of Okla., 1911-15; elected asso. justice Supreme Court of Okla., Nov. 1914; chief justice, 1917-19; resigned to re-enter law practice, Oct. 1, 1919; mem. Stuart, Sharp & Cruce. Okla. atty. for St.L.&S.F. Ry. Co. Democrat. Episcopalian. Home: Oklahoma City, Okla. Died Mar. 9, 1927.

SHARP, Katharine Lucinda, librarian; b. Elgin, Ill., May 21, 1865; d. John William and Phebe (Thompson) S.; Ph. B., Northwestern U., 1885, Ph.M., 1889; B.L.S., N.Y. State Library Sch., 1892, M.L.S., 1906; A.M., U. of Illinois, 1907. Teacher, 1886-88; asst. librarian Scoville Inst., Oak Park, Ill., 1888-90; library organizer, Wheaton, Ill., 1891, Xenia, O., 1892; in charge Comparative Library Exhibit, Chicago Expn., 1893; dir. dept. library science, Armour Inst. Tech., Chicago, 1893-97; head librarian and dir. State Library Sch., U. of Ill., 1897-1907. Dir. Summer Sch. of Library Science, U. of Wis., 1895-96; lecturer on library economy, U. of Chicago, 1896. Mem. Ill. State Library Assn. (pres. 1903-04), A.L.A. (council, 1895-1905; v.p., 1898, 1907); fellow Am. Library Inst., 1906—. Died June 1, 1914.

SHARP, Robert, univ. pres.; b. Lawrenceville, Va., Oct. 24, 1851; s. Richard Henry and Lucy (Hardy) S.; A.B., Randolph-Macon Coll., Va., 1876, later A.M.; Ph.D., U. of Leipzig, Germany, 1879; LL.D., Tulane U., 1919; m. Blanche Herndon, Dec. 22, 1881. Prof. English, U. of Louisiana, 1880-84; prof. English, 1884-1913, pres., 1913-18 (pres. emeritus), Tulane U. Editor: Beowulf (Anglo-Saxon poem) and The Fight at Finsburh (with James A. Harrison), 1885; Shakespeare's Merchant of Venice, 1903. Writer on Anglo-Saxon lit. Home: Biloxi, Miss. Died Jan. 23, 1931.

SHARP, Robert Sherman, chief postoffice insp.; b. Chattanooga, Tenn., Nov. 5, 1869; s. Col. Alonzo G. S.; Grant U., Chattanooga, Tenn. Postmaster, Chattanooga, 1897-1903; resigned to become gen. mgr. textile mills at Chattanooga; apptd. U.S. revenue collector, with headquarters at Nashville, Tenn.; chief postoffice insp. of U.S., Apr. 7, 1910—. Died Mar. 8, 1932.

SHARP, Waldo Z., banker; b. Columbus, O., Mar. 23, 1870; s. John Patterson and Abigail (Vesey) S.; ed. dist. sch.; m. Maude Fairfield, July 1894; children—Esta L., Margaret A., Lester J. (died 1928). In banking business, 1902—; pres. Security Nat. Bank, Sioux Falls, 1919—. Republican. Mason, Elk. Home: Sioux Falls, S.D. Died Dec. 8, 1933.

SHARP, William Graves, ambassador; b. Mt. Gilead, O., Mar. 14, 1859; s. George and Mahala (Graves) S.; LL.B., U. of Mich., 1881; (LL.D., Allegheny Coll., U. of Mich., Oberlin Coll., 1919); m. Hallie M. Clough, 1895. Practiced law at Elyria, Ohio; many yrs. interested in iron and chem. mfg. Prosecuting atty. Lorain Co., O., 1885-88; Dem. presdl. elector, 1892; Dem. nominee for Congress, 1900; mem. 61st to 63d Congresses (1909-15), 14th Ohio Dist. (resigned July 23, 1914); ambassador extraordinary and plenipotentiary to France, Dec. 2, 1914-Apr. 14, 1919 (1st Am. ambassador to become dean of the diplomatic corps at Paris). Elected foundation mem. Société Astronomique de France, of which science has been a life-long student. Grand Cross of the Legion of Honor of France. Home: Elyria, O. Died Nov. 17, 1922.

SHARPE, Alfred Clarence, army officer; b. Delaware, O., Sept. 12, 1850; s. George Washington and Caroline Rebecca (Snider) S.; bro. of (Anne) Virginia Sharpe Patterson; ed. Ohio Wesleyan U.; cadet U.S. Mil. Acad., 1872-75; (hon. A.M., U. of Wooster, 1888; LL.D., U. of S.D., 1905); m. Margaret Plunket Richardson, Dec. 27, 1877. Commd. 2d lt. 10th Cav., June 21, 1876; transferred to 22d Inf., July 28, 1876; 1st lt., June 30, 1881; capt., Feb. 1, 1893; maj. a.a.g. vols., May 12, 1898; hon. disch., Apr. 17, 1899; maj. insp. gen. vols., Apr. 17, 1899; maj. a.a.g. U.S.A., Feb. 2, 1901; lt. col. inf., Mar. 29, 1904; a.a.g., Apr. 7, 1904; assigned to 30th Inf., Mar. 16, 1905; detailed General Staff, June 27, 1907; col., May 9, 1908, assigned to 23d Inf. Brevetted 1st lt., Feb. 27, 1890, for action against Indians at Spring Creek, Mont., Oct. 15, 16, 1876; recommended for bvts. lt. col., and col. for action in battles before Santiago, 1898. Admitted to Mich. bar, 1879; prof. mil. science, U. of Wooster, 1884-88, U. of South Dakota, 1891-93; judge advocate Dept. Ariz. and Colo., 1893-97; sec. of justice of P.R. during reconstruction period, 1899-1900; comd. Dist. of Zamboanga, Mindanao, 1908-09. Post of Parang, 1909-10, Dist. of El Paso, Tex., during Madero revolution, 1911; on duty with gov. of Ohio, 1911-12; with gov. of Colo., 1913-14. Retired, age limit, Sept. 12, 1914. Recalled to active duty in war with Germany, Sept. 1918-Mar. 1919. After retirement engaged in orange growing in Calif. Gold medalist and life mem. Mil. Service Instn., 1887. Home: Palo Alto, Calif. Died 1922.

SHARPE, Henry Augustus, judge; b. nr. Decatur, Ala., June 10, 1848; s. William and Lucy Gayle (Reese) S.; ed. pub. schs., Ala.; LL.B., Cumberland U., 1870; m. Mary M. Hansell, May 19, 1875. Register in chancery, Morgan Co., Ala., 1871; mem. Ala. Ho. of Rep., 1878-79; judge City Ct., Birmingham, 1884-98 and, 1907—; asso. justice Supreme Ct., Ala., 1898-1904. Democrat. Home: Birmingham, Ala. Died Aug. 10, 1919.

SHARPE, Nelson, judge; b. Northumberland Co., Ont., Can., Aug. 25, 1858; s. Nelson and Eunice (McColl) S.; ed. Albert Coll., Belleville, Ont.; LL.B. from U. of Michigan; m. Frances Lean, of Ontario, Oct. 24, 1883 (dec.). Naturalized citizen of U.S., 1885; pros. atty. Ogemaw Co., Mich., 1891-93; judge 34th Jud. Circuit, Mich., 1893-1919; apptd. asso. justice Supreme Court of Mich. to fill vacancy, 1919, elected to same office Nov. 1920, reëlected, Apr. 1927, and Apr. 1935. Republican. Episcopalian. Mason, K. of P. Home: West Branch, Mich. Died Oct. 20, 1935.

SHARPLES, Stephen Paschall, chemist; b. West Chester, Pa., Apr. 21, 1842; s. Philip P. and Mary A. (Paschall) S.; S.B., Lawrence Scientific Sch. (Harvard), 1866; (hon. M.S., Pa. State Coll., 1915); m.

Abbie M. Hall, June 16, 1870 (died 1914). Prof. chemistry, Boston Dental Coll., 1875-93; cons. chemist, 1872—. Insp. and assayer of liquors for Mass., 1885-1902; was expert on census, 1880; a judge of awards, Chicago Exposition, 1893. Fellow Am. Acad. Arts and Sciences, A.A.A.S., Soc. of Industrial Chemistry, Eng. Editor: Genealogical Magazine. Author: Chemical Tables, 1866. Joint editor: History of the Kimball Family, 1897; editor Records of the Church of Christ in Cambridge, 1906; etc. Home: Cambridge, Mass. Died Aug. 21, 1923.

SHARPLESS, Isaac, educator; b. Chester Co., Pa., Dec. 16, 1848; s. Aaron and Susanna (Forsythe) S.; B.S., Harvard, 1873; (Sc.D., U. of Pa., 1883; LL.D., Swarthmore, 1889; L.H.D., Hobart College, 1903; LL.D., Harvard U., 1915); m. Lydia Trimble Cope, Aug. 10, 1876. Instr. mathematics, 1875-79, prof. mathematics and astronomy, 1879-84, dean, 1884-87, pres., 1887-1917, Haverford Coll.; resigned to become dean of T. Wistar Brown Grad. Sch., same. Author: (Textbooks) Astronomy, Geometry, English Education (in Internat. Edn. Series); A Quaker Experiment in Government, 1898; Two Centuries of Pennsylvania History, 1900; Quakerism and Politics, 1906; The American College, 1915. Home: Haverford, Pa. Died Jan. 16, 1920.

SHATTUC, William B., congressman; b. North Hector, N.Y., June 11, 1841; removed to Ohio, 1852; ed. in public schools; was commd. officer in Union army during Civil war, serving in the Army of the Frontier; in ry. service, 1864-95; retired; served as State senator; mem. Congress from 1st Ohio dist., 1897-1903. Republican. Home: Madisonville, O. Died 1911.

SHATTUCK, Aaron Draper, artist; b. Francestown, N.H., Mar. 9, 1832; s. Jesse and Harriet (Williams) S.; ed. at Lowell, Mass.; studied art at Nat. Acad. Design; m. Marian Colman, June 4, 1860; children—William, Walter, Isabel, Bertha, Edwin H., Helen Howard. Specialty, landscapes, cattle and sheep. Invented "Shattuck" stretcher frame for artists' canvas. N.A., 1861. Died July 30, 1928.

SHATTUCK, Charles Houston, forester, botanist; b. Vandalia, Mo., Nov. 21, 1867; s. Warren Charles and Matilda Catherine (Houston) S.; B.S., Campbell Coll., Holton, Kan., 1894, M.S., 1898; Ph.D., U. of Chicago, 1908; studied Woods Hole, Mass., and Biltmore (N.C.) Sch. of Forestry; m. Maud Elizabeth Stackhouse, Aug. 15, 1895. Prof. physical sciences, 1895-98, prof. biology and geology, 1898-1903, v.p., 1897-1903, Campbell Coll.; prof. natural history, Washburn Coll., Topeka, Kan., 1904-07; research and teaching fellow, U. of Chicago, 1908; instr. in botany, Woods Hole, Mass., summer, 1908; prof. botany and forestry, Clemson Coll., S.C., 1908-09; prof. forestry and bot. morphology, 1909-17, dean Coll. Letters and Sciences, 1914-17, U. of Idaho; also forester, U. of Idaho Expt. Sta., 1909-17, and with U.S. Forest Service, summers 1910-17; prof. forestry in charge grazing U. of Calif., 1917—. Republican. Methodist. Home: Berkeley, Calif. Died 1931.

SHATTUCK, Frederick Cheever, M.D.; b. Boston, Mass., Nov. 1, 1847; s. George Cheyne and Anne Henrietta (Brune) S.; A.B., Harvard, 1868, A.M., 1872, M.D., 1873; LL.D., U. of Cincinnati, 1908; Sc.D., Harvard, 1912; m. Elizabeth Perkins Lee, June 19, 1876; children—George Cheever, Henry Lee, Mrs. Elizabeth Perkins Bigelow, Mrs. Clara Lee Richardson (dec.). Has practiced at Boston, 1875—; clin. instr. auscultation and percussion, 1879-84, instr. theory and practice of physic, 1884-88, Jackson prof. clin. medicine, 1888-1912, emeritus, 1912, Harvard; consulting phys. to Mass. Gen. and various other hosps.; 1st lt. U.S.A. Med. Reserve Corps, retired. Overseer Harvard, 1913-19. For many yrs. trustee St. Paul's Sch.; pres. of bd. (resigned 1924). Fellow Am. Acad. Arts and Sciences; mem. Mass. Hist. Soc., etc. Home: Boston, Mass. Died Jan. 11, 1929.

SHATTUCK, George Brune, physician; b. Boston, Mass., Aug. 18, 1844; s. George Cheyne and Anne Henrietta (Brune) S.; bro. of Frederick Cheever S.; A.B., Harvard, 1863, A.M., 1867, M.D., 1869; m. Amalia Schutte, June 6, 1872. In practice at Boston, 1869-1911; sr. physician to Boston City Hospital; editor Boston Medical and Surgical Journal; instr. clin. medicine, Harvard Med. Sch., 1886-88; pres. Mass. Charitable Eye and Ear Infirmary. Overseer Harvard, 1890-1901, 1903-12. Home: Boston, Mass. Died Mar. 12, 1923.

SHATTUCK, George Burbank, geologist; b. Lowell, Mass., 1869; s. Horace B. and Mary L. (Comins) S.; B.S., Amherst, 1892; Ph.D., Johns Hopkins, 1897; m. Annie B. Gibson, 1896. Asst., asso. and asso. prof. geology, Johns Hopkins, 1897-1905; prof. geology, Vassar Coll., 1906—. Home: Poughkeepsie, N.Y. Died 1934.

SHATTUCK, Lemuel C., banking, mining; b. Erie, Pa., Jan. 5, 1866; s. Henry and Phoebe (Coover) S.; ed. pub. schs.; m. Isabella Grenfell, 1891 (died 1924); children—Henry (dec.), Warner Austin, Edward (dec.), Carl (dec.), Spencer, Isabelle Fern, Dorothy Irene; m. 2d, Olive Wilson, 1927; 1 son, Lemuel C. Began mining at Bisbee, Ariz., 1886; pres. Shattuck Denn Mining Corp.; organizer and now pres. Miners & Merchants Bank; treas. Bar Boot Cattle Co., O.K. Cattle Co., 79 Lead Copper Co. Formerly supervisor Cochise County; also mem. City Council, Bisbee; mem. Ariz. Copper Tariff Commn. Democrat. Episcopalian. Elk, Rotarian. Home: Bisbee, Ariz. Died Sept. 7, 1938.

SHATTUCK, Samuel Walker, univ. prof.; b. Groton, Mass., Feb. 18, 1841; s. Walter and Roxana (Fletcher) S.; B.S., Norwich U., 1860; A.M., 1867, C.E., 1871 (LL.D., Norwich U., 1907, U. of Illinois, 1912); m. Adelaide L. White, Aug. 14, 1866. Served in U.S.V., 1861-65; sergt. maj. 6th Mass. Vols.; capt. 8th Vt. Vols.; brigade adj. and insp. gen. on several staffs; insp. gen. of Vermont, 1867-68. Instr. mathematics, 1860, adj. prof. mathematics and mil. tactics, 1865-66, pres. pro tem, 1865-66, v.p., 1866-68, Norwich U., Vt.; asst. prof. mathematics and instr. mil. tactics, 1868, prof. civ. engring., 1870, head dept. mathematics, 1868-1906, prof. mathematics, 1871-1912 (emeritus), comptroller, 1905-12, U. of Illinois. Home: Urbana, Ill. Died Feb. 13, 1915.

SHAUCK, John Allen, judge; b. Richland Co., O., Mar. 26, 1841; A.B., Otterbein U., 1866, A.M., 1869 (LL.D., 1897); LL.B., U. of Mich., 1867; m. Ada May Phillips, June 1, 1876. Practiced law, Dayton, O., 1869-85; judge Circuit Ct., 1885-95; asso. justice Supreme Ct., Ohio, Feb. 9, 1895— (chief justice, 1906-07). Republican. Lecturer supreme ct. practice, 1898-1900, prof. law, 1900—, Ohio State U. Home: Columbus, O. Died Jan. 3, 1918.

SHAUGHNESSY, Sir Thomas George, ry. pres.; b. Milwaukee, Wis., Oct. 6, 1853; common sch. edn.; m. Elizabeth Bridget, d. of M. Nagle, of Milwaukee, 1880. Entered ry. service 1869, in purchasing dept. C.,M.&St.P. Ry.; gen. storekeeper, same, Jan. 1879-Oct. 1882; gen. purchasing agt., Oct. 1882-Jan. 1884, asst. to gen. mgr., Jan. 1884-Sept. 1885, asst. gen. mgr., Sept. 1885-Sept. 1889, asst. to pres., Sept. 1889-June 24, 1891, v.p. and dir., June 24, 1891-June 12, 1899, pres., June 12, 1899—, Canadian Pacific Ry.; pres., dir. of a number of R.R. cos., all of which are directly or indirectly connected with C.P. Ry. Knighted by Queen Victoria, 1901; K.C.V.O., 1907; apptd. to baronetcy by King George V, 1915. Catholic. Home: Montreal, Que., Can. Died Dec. 10, 1923.

SHAW, Albert Duane, pres. Canadian Niagara Power Co.; b. Town of Lyme, N.Y., Dec. 27, 1841; grad. St. Lawrence Univ., Canton, N.Y., 1867. While a student at Union Acad., Belleville, N.Y., he volunteered, May 1861, in 35th N.Y. vols.; served as private and non-commissioned officer until 1863; then as recruiting officer. Member N.Y. assembly, 1866; consul at Toronto, 1868-78; at Manchester, Eng., 1878-86; col. 36th regt., Nat. Guard N.Y., 1867-68. Home: Watertown, N.Y. Died 1901.

SHAW, Anna Howard, woman suffragist; b. Newcastle-on-Tyne, Eng., Feb. 14, 1847; d. of Thomas and Nicolas (Stott) S.; arrived in America with parents at 4 yrs. of age; studied Albion (Mich.) Coll., 1872-75; grad. Theol. School of Boston U., 1878; M.D., Boston U., 1885; (D.D., Kansas City U., 1902; LL.D., 1917). Was granted local preacher's license by dist. conf. of Methodist Ch. and paid expenses by preaching and lecturing while at college and univ.; pastor M.E. Ch., Hingham, Mass., 1878, East Dennis, 1878-85; was refused ordination by N.E. Conf. M.E. Ch., on account of sex; case appealed to Gen. Conf. at Cincinnati, 1880, and refusal confirmed; ordained by M.P. Ch., Oct. 12, 1880, being first woman to receive ordination by that denomination; resigned from pulpit and was chosen lecturer for Mass. Woman's Suffrage Assn., 1885; nat. supt. of franchise W.C.T.U., 1886-92; nat. lecturer, 1886-1904, v.p.-at-large, 1892-1904, pres., 1904-1915, now hon. pres., Nat. Am Woman Suffrage Assn. Has spoken in every state of the Union, before many state legislatures and before coms. of both houses of Congress. Only woman who ever preached in Gustav Vasa Cathedral, state ch. of Sweden, and first ordained woman to preach in Berlin, Copenhagen, Christiania, Amsterdam and London. Chmn. Woman's Com. of Council Nat. Defense, 1917—. Author: The Story of a Pioneer. Home: Moylan, Pa. Died July 2, 1919.

SHAW, Charles Frederick, soil science; b. West Henrietta, N.Y., May 2, 1881; s. Frederick Franklin and Mary Anna (Tabolt) S.; B.S. in Agr. Cornell U., 1906; m. Helen Susannah Hosterman, June 19, 1909. Entered Bur. of Soils, U.S. Dept. of Agr., as scientific asst., Feb. 1, 1906; instr., 1907-09, asst. prof. agronomy, 1909-13, Pa. State Coll.; also soil scientist Bur. of Soils in charge soil survey of Pa.; prof. soil technology, U. of Calif., Jan. 1, 1913—, also in charge soil survey of Calif.; visiting prof. of soils, U. of Nanking (China), 1930. Fellow Am. Soc. Agronomy, A.A.A.S., Am. Geog. Society. Republican. Mason. Author: Laboratory Guide in Soil Physics, revised edit., 1911; Soils of Pennsylvania, 1912; Key to Soils of California, 1928; Soils of China, 1931. Consulting engr. U.S. Reclamation Service, 1919-26; cons. engr. Nat. Commn. de Irrigacion, Mexico, 1926-28. Home: Berkeley, Calif. Died Sept. 12, 1939.

SHAW, Edgar Dwight, newspaper mgr.; b. Leominster, Mass., Aug. 22, 1871; s. Francis Henry and Isabella Rhoda (Warfield) S.; grad. Phillips Exeter Acad., 1889; A.B., Harvard, 1893; m. Gertrude Stevenson, May 12, 1921. Began as reporter Springfield (Mass.) Union, 1893; mng. editor Boston Journal, 1903-04; mng. editor, later gen. mgr. Washington (D.C.) Times, 1904-12; mng. editor Boston Herald, 1912-13, Boston Traveler, 1913-14, Boston Journal, 1914-17; with W. R. Hearst orgn., 1919-27, pub. successively Washington Times, Detroit Times, Boston American, Boston Advertiser, establishing Rochester (N.Y.) Journal and Syracuse (N.Y.) Telegram; now associated with Arthur Brisbane. Mem. Business Hist. Society. Home: New York, N.Y. Died Apr. 13, 1931.

SHAW, Edward Richard, prof. pedagogy, New York Univ.; b. Bellport, L.I., 1855; s. Joseph M.S.; grad. Lafayette Coll., B.Ph. (New York Univ., Ph.D., 1890); m. Huldah M. Greene. Author: Physics by Experiment; English Composition by Practice; Legends of Fire Island Beach. Home: New York, N.Y. Died 1903.

SHAW, Eugene Wesley, geologist; b. Delaware, O., July 29, 1881; s. William Bigelow and Irene (Gardner) S.; B.S., Ohio Wesleyan U., 1905, D.Sc., 1927; U. of Chicago, 1905-07; m. Abbie Potter Haylett, Oct. 18, 1907. With U.S. Geol. Survey most of time, 1907-21; consulting geologist, 1921-29; chief geologist Iraq Petroleum Co., London, 1929—. Has made extensive investigations for oil corporations in various countries; in charge of natural gas valuation, U.S. Treasury Dept., 1918-19; chief of sub-sect. of sedimentation, U.S. Geol. survey, 1919-20. Has devoted attention principally to estimation of underground reserves of oil and natural gas, appraisal of oil and gas properties, developed and prospective; behavior of streams as involved in certain law suits and problems of river improvements; investigation of geologic history of mountain ranges, coasts and deltas of N. and S. America, Europe, Asia and Africa; studies of geophysics of the great sedimentary basins. Mem. various professional societies. Methodist. Author: Coal, Oil and Gas of Foxburg Quadrangle, Pa. (U.S. Geological Survey), 1909; Mud Lumps at Mouth of the Mississippi River, 1912; Natural Gas of North Texas, 1916; Oil Fields of Allen County, Ky., 1919; also about 100 other publs. Explored and mapped 100,000 sq. miles along east base of Andes, S. America. Home: Chevy Chase, Md. Died Oct 7, 1935.

SHAW, Frances Wills, writer; b. Chicago, Apr. 10, 1872; d. Moses D. and Fannie (Searls) Wells; ed. Dearborn Sem., Chicago, and at Farmington, Conn.; m. Howard Van Doren Shaw, Apr. 20, 1893 (dec.); children—Evelyn (Mrs. John T. McCutcheon), Sylvia (Mrs. Clay Judson), Frances Theodora (Mrs. John L. King). Member of the board of directors of the Chicago Orphan Asylum. Presbyn. Author: Songs of a Baby's Day, 1917; also one-act plays. Home: Chicago, Ill., and Lake Forest, Ill. Died Oct. 12, 1937.

SHAW, George Elmer, lawyer; b. Pittsburgh, Pa., Apr. 3, 1861; s. Dr. Thomas Wilson and Catherine Wolf (Stoner) S.; LL.B., U. of Mich., 1883; m. Mary E. Ewing, Dec. 19, 1893; children—Elizabeth (wife of George M. Laughlin III), Mary Ewing (Mrs. Rees Townsend Scully), Thomas Ewing. Admitted to Pa. bar, 1884, and began practice at Pittsburgh; dir. Mellon Nat. Bank, Union Trust Co. of Pittsburgh, Union Savings Bank, Crucible Steel Co. of America, Pittsburgh & Lake Erie R.R. Co. Trustee Carnegie Inst., Carnegie Inst. Tech. Republican. Presbyn. Home: Pittsburgh, Pa. Died June 14, 1938.

SHAW, Harriett McCreary Jackson, artist; b. Fayetteville, Ark., Mar. 17, 1865; d. Rev. Cortes and Julia (Waters) Jackson; ed. U. of Ark.; grad. Denver Sch. of Fine Arts, 1893 (highest honors); pupil of G. W. Platt (Art Inst. Chicago), Magda Heuerman (Chicago), Samuel Richards (Munich, Germany); m. Hon. Thomas W. Shaw, 1885 (died 1890); 1 dau., Mrs. Helen McGregor (dec.). Instr. Denver Sch. of Fine Arts, 1894-95; prin. of art, William Woods Coll. for Girls, Fulton, Mo., 1895-98; dir. of exhibits, Woman's Bldg., and lectured in Fine Arts Bldg., Seattle Expn., 1909; has lectured extensively on art in the Northwest, 1909—. Painted life-size portrait of Rev. J. B. Jones, for J. B. Jones Hall, William Woods Coll. Silver medal for ivory miniatures, St. Louis Expn., 1904; gold and silver medals, for life portraits, Seattle Expn.; awarded fellowship for advanced study abroad, John Simon Guggenheim Memorial Foundation. Chmn. art com. Wash. State Fedn. Women's Clubs, 1909-10; mem. art com. Gen. Federation Women's Clubs, 1910-12. Democrat. Christian Scientist. Author: Outlines of American Painting. Assisted in compiling Handbook Municipal Art in America, and Reader's Guide to Modern Art, for San Francisco Expn. Mem. faculty and prin. of fine arts course, Seattle Industrial and Commercial Art School. Home: Seattle, Wash. Died Nov. 3, 1933.

SHAW, Henry Larned Keith, M.D.; b. Chaumont, N.Y., Aug. 8, 1873; s. Col. Albert D. and Mary Sherwood (Keith) S.; C.E., Pa. Mil. Coll., 1890; A.B., Cornell, 1893; M.D., Albany Med. Coll., 1896, m. Susanne Sturtevant Burrell, Mar. 27, 1906; children—Elizabeth Burrell Carr, Mary Keith Bossi. Practiced Albany, 1900—; prof. diseases children, Albany Med. Coll., 1905—; consultant in child hygiene, N.Y. State Dept. of Health; pediatrician-in-chief Albany Hospital, Lieutenant Colonel Med. Sect. O.R.C., U.S.A. Del. Internat. Med. Congress, Lisbon, Portugal, 1906. Author: The Happy Child, 1924; The Young Child's Health, 1925; Communicable Diseases in Children, 1927. Translator: Pfaunder and Schlossmann's Diseases of Children, 1907. Home: Albany, N.Y. Died Mar. 26, 1941.

SHAW, Howard Van Doren, architect; b. Chicago, Ill., May 7, 1869; s. Theodore A. and Sarah (Van Doren) S.; B.A., Yale, 1890; Mass. Inst. Tech., 1893; m. Frances Wells, 1893. Practiced at Chicago, 1893—. Fellow A.I.A.; mem. exec. art com. of Art Inst. Chicago; chmn. Ill. State Art Commn.; trustee Art Inst., United Charities of Chicago. Republican. Presbyn. Homes: Chicago, and Lake Forest, Ill. Died May 6, 1926.

SHAW, J(ohn) W(illiam), archbishop; b. Mobile, Ala., Dec. 12, 1863; Acad. Brothers Sacred Heart, Mobile; classical studies St. Finian's Sem., Navan, Ireland; philos. and theol. studies, U. of the Propaganda, Rome; student N.A. Coll., Rome, 1882-88; ordained R.C. priest, May 26, 1888. Asst. Cathedral, Mobile, July 1888-Feb. 1889; asst. and missionary, St. Peter's Ch., Montgomery, Ala., 1889-91; rector Cathedral of Mobile and chancellor of the diocese, 1891-1910; apptd. coadjutor bishop of San Antonio, Tex., Feb. 7, 1910, consecrated, Apr. 14, 1910; succeeded to the bishopric of San Antonio, Mar. 11, 1911; archbishop of New Orleans (La.), Jan. 25, 1918. Died Nov. 3, 1934.

SHAW, Joseph Alden, educator; b. Athol, Mass., Jan. 4, 1836; s. the Rev. Linus Hall and Louisa Alden (Jones) S.; grad. Phillips Exeter Acad., 1855. A.B., Harvard, 1858, A.M., 1866; M. Eliza Antoinette Thompson, Nov. 18, 1863; father of Robert Kendall S. Prin. New Salem (Mass.))Acad., 1858; teacher, 1867, head master, 1888-1912, Highland Mil. Acad., Worcester. Republican. Episcopalian. Councillor Mass. Fedn. of Chs. Home: Worcester, Mass. Died May 22, 1915.

SHAW, Leslie Mortier, sec. treasury; b. Morristown, Vt., Nov. 2, 1848; s. Boardman O. and Lovisa (Spaulding) S.; B.S. and M.S., Cornell Coll., Ia., 1874; LL.B., Ia. Coll. of Law, 1876; LL.D., Simpson Coll., 1898, Cornell Coll., 1899, Wesleyan U., 1904, Dickinson Coll., 1908; m. Alice, d. James Crawshaw, of Clinton Co., Ia., Dec. 6, 1877. Practiced law, Denison, Ia., 1876-97; engaged in banking at Denison, Manilla, and Charter Oak, Ia., 1880; gov. of Ia., two terms, 1898-1902; sec. of the treasury in cabinet of President Roosevelt, Feb. 1, 1902-Mar. 4, 1907. Permanent chmn. Internat. Monetary Conv., Indianapolis, 1898; lay del. Gen. Confs. M.E. Ch., 1888, 92, 96, 1900. Lecturer and author: Home: Washington, D.C. Died Mar. 28, 1932.

SHAW, Lucien, judge; b. Vevay, Ind., Mar. 1, 1845; s. William and Linda (Rous) S.; ed. Vevay Acad.; LL.B., Indianapolis Law Coll., 1869; LL.D., Univ. of Calif., 1922, Univ. of Southern Calif., 1922; m. Hannah J. Hartley, July 29, 1873; 1 son, Hartley. Admitted to Indiana bar, 1869; practiced at Bloomfield, Ind., 1869-83, at Fresno, Calif., 1884-86, at Los Angeles, Calif., 1886-89. Judge Superior Court, Los Angeles Co., 1889-1902; associate justice Supreme Court of Calif., 1903-23 (chief justice, 1921-23), retired. Republican. Home: Glendale, Calif. Died Mar. 19, 1933.

SHAW, Mary, actress; b. Boston, Mass., 1860; ed. pub. schs. First appeared on stage in Boston, 1878; played Lady Sneerwell, in "School for Scandal," Haverley's Theatre, New York, 1881; toured with Julia Marlowe; scored pronounced success as Mrs. Arling, in "Ghosts" and as Mrs. Warren, in "Mrs. Warren's Profession." Home: New York, N.Y. Died May 18, 1929.

SHAW, Robert Anderson, lawyer; b. Marietta, O., Dec. 19, 1870; s. Rodney Keene and Lovina (Clark) S.; student Marietta (O.) Coll. Acad., 1883-86; A.B., Marietta, 1890; m. Myrtie Grace Wilhelm, Sept. 26, 1901; children—Elizabeth S. Milton, Marian Chandler (dec.). Studied law in offices of Merrell, Ryel & Merrell, Lowville, N.Y., 1891-94; admitted to N.Y. bar, 1893; law clk. offices of Roswell W. Keene, N.Y. City, 1894-95, Truax & Crandall, 1895-97; law clk. Phillips & Avery, 1897-1907, mem. of firm, 1907—. Mayor, Teaneck, N.J., 1911-13, mem. sch. bd., 1915-22, mem. Welfare Com., 1918-35; v.p. Northern Valley Chapter Am. Red Cross, Englewood, N.J., 1934-35; former mem. N. Bergen Co., N.J., Council of Boy Scouts. Trustee Marietta Coll. Republican. Baptist. Home: New York, N.Y. Died Aug. 2, 1941.

SHAW, Sterling Price, clergyman; b. Adams Co., Ia., Apr. 18, 1872; s. Stephen Hamilton and Lamira (Moore) S.; B.O., Central U. of Ia., 1901; grad. theol. dept. same, 1902; B.A., Ewing (Ill.) Coll., 1908, Ph.D., 1910; D.D., Sioux Falls (S.D.) U., 1917; m. Louise G. Crow, Apr. 16, 1894; children—Sterling Chester (dec.), Lowell Everett, Mary Irene, Louise; m. 2d, Ida Mae Dibley, Oct. 8, 1925. Ordained Bapt. ministry, 1894; pastor various chs. while securing edn., 1st Bapt. Ch., Marion, Ia., 1904-07; chancellor Central U., Pella, Ia., 1907-10; gen. supt. S.D. Bapt. Conv., 1910-25; editor S.D. Bapt. Bulletin, 1910-25; church edifice missionary, N.D. Bapt. Conv., 1925—. Traveled in Egypt, Palestine, Turkey, Africa and western Europe, winter 1930. Pres. board of Sioux Falls University, 1911-25; trustee Kansas City Baptist Theol. Sem., Northwestern Bapt. Hosp. Assn., St. Paul, Minn.; mem. gen. bd. promotion Northern Bapt. Conv., etc. Sent by S.D. Bapt. Conv. to western Europe, to investigate social and religious conditions, 1919. Republican. Mason, Rotarian. Home: Fargo, N.D. Died Aug. 4, 1934.

SHAW, Walter Keith, cotton mcht.; b. Abington, Mass., Mar. 13, 1868; s. Elijah Anderson and Frances Emma (Dyer) S.; B.S., Mass. Inst. Tech., 1888; m. Mary Groom Hutchins, Nov. 4, 1897; children—Gordon Hutchins (dec.), Walter Keith. Began in cotton merchandising business as mem. firm E. A. Shaw & Co., Boston, 1895, becoming sole owner, 1897; formed partnership with Henry G. Brooks, 1905, pres. from incorporation of firm. Episcopalian. Home: Concord, Mass. Died July 6, 1933.

SHAWKEY, Morris Purdy, coll. pres.; b. Sigel, Pa., Feb. 17, 1868; s. George and Elizabeth (Witherspoon) S.; Oberlin Coll.; A.B., Ohio Wesleyan U., 1894, A.M., 1909, Ped.D., 1918; LL.D., W.Va. Wesleyan University, 1927; m. Elizabeth Carver; children—Morris Carver, John W., Leonard Asbury. Asst. state supt. schs., W.Va., 1897-1905; mem. W.Va. Legislature, 1902-04 (chmn. com. on edn.); supt. schs., Kanawha Co., W.Va., 1907-09 (resigned); state supt. schs., W.Va., Mar. 4, 1909-21; pres. Marshall Coll., Huntington, W.Va., until 1935; pres. Charleston (W.Va.) Edni. Centre; business mgr. Morris Harvey Coll. Editor W.Va. Sch. Journal and Educator. President State Bd. of Education. Republican. Methodist. Author: A Geography of West Virginia, 1901; Story of West Virginia, 1913; West Virginia in History, Life, Literature and Industry, 1928. Home: Charleston, W.Va. Died Feb. 6, 1941.

SHEA, Daniel William, physicist; b. Portsmouth, N.H., Nov. 27, 1859; s. of Timothy and Margaret (McCarthy) S.; A.B., Harvard, 1886, A.M., 1888, Ph.D., Friedrich Wilhelm's Universität, Berlin, 1892, unmarried. Mem. N.H. Ho. of Rep., 1886-88; asst. in physics, Harvard, 1889, 1892; asst. prof. physics, 1892-94, prof., 1894-95, U. of Illinois; prof. physics, 1895—, dir. School of Technology, 1897-1906, dean Faculty of Sciences, 1906-09 and 1911-15, Catholic U. of America. Fellow A.A.A.S., Am. Phys. Society. Democrat. Author: Instruction Sheets for Experiments in Physics, 1913, revised edit., 1921. Home: Greenland, N.H. Died Oct. 1930.

SHEA, Joseph Bernard, merchant; b. Allegheny, Pa., June 2, 1863; s. Christian Bernard and Elizabeth (Galway) S.; B.A., Princeton, 1885; m. Clara Bell Morgan, June 11, 1891; children—C. Bernard, Sidney Morgan. In employ of Long & Co., operating Vulcan Forge & Iron Works, Pittsburgh, 18 mos., 1885-87; with Pittsburgh Dry Goods Co., 1887-1901, pres., 1897-1901; resigned to become dir. Joseph Horne Co., the oldest dept. store in Western Pa., now pres.; dir., treas., Western Pa. Expn. Soc.; dir., treas. Retail Research Assn., Asso. Merchandising Corp.—both New York. Life trustee Princeton U.; pres. Pittsburgh Orchestra; v.p., dir. Pittsburgh Chamber Commerce. Independent Republican. Methodist. Served in Signal Corps and Bur. of Aircraft Production, Feb. 20-Dec. 24, 1918, resigning as chief of raw materials dept. procurement div., Bur. of Aircraft Production, in charge of all non-metal materials. Home: Pittsburgh, Pa. Died Jan. 6, 1930.

SHEA, Joseph Hooker, judge; b. Lexington, Ind., July 24, 1863; A.B., Ind. U., Bloomington, Ind., 1889. Admitted to Ind. bar, 1889; practiced at Scottsburg, 1889-99; removed to Seymour, 1900; pros. atty. 6th Judicial District, Ind., 1891-95; mem. State Senate, 1896-1900; elected judge Circuit Court, 4th Jud. Circuit, 1905-12; judge Ind. Appellate Court, 1913-16; A.E. and P. to Chile, 1916-21; resumed law practice at Indianapolis, 1922. Trustee Indiana U., 1893-1916. Catholic. Home: Seymour, Ind., and Indianapolis. Died Dec. 28, 1928.

SHEAN, Charles M., painter; b. Brooklyn; s. Edward A. and Sarah A. (Burr) S.; studied Art Students' League, New York and Paris; married. Portrait and mural painter. Medal, mural painting, St. Louis Expn., 1904. Wrote: A Plea for Americanism in the Decoration of Public Buildings, 1901; Mural Painting from the American Point of View, 1904. Home: Brooklyn, N.Y. Died Oct. 7, 1925.

SHEARD, Titus, mfr.; b. Batley, England, Oct. 4, 1841; parents died and he came to U.S., 1856, settling in Little Falls, N.Y.; ed. common schools; m. Helen M. Waite, 1863. Represented Herkimer Co. in N.Y. State assembly, 1878-79, and again in 1884, when he was elected speaker, defeating Theodore Roosevelt for Rep. caucus nomination; State senator, 1890-91. Mfr. knitted cotton and woolen underwear. Home: Little Falls, N.Y. Died 1904.

SHEARER, Andrew, farmer; b. nr. Glasgow, Scotland, Mar. 10, 1850; s. James Shearer and Mary (Marshall) S.; ed. high sch., Scotland; m. Mary B. Walker, Mar. 26, 1880 (died 1927); children—George W., David W., Herbert A., Winifred, Maynie. Came to U.S., 1870, naturalized, 1876. Farmer in Kan., 1870—; mem. Kan. Ho. of Rep., 1911-12. Mem. exec. bd. Kan. State Farm Bur. (life). Awarded gold medals "for distinguished unselfish service to organized agriculture," by Kan. State Farm Bur. and Am. Farm Bur. Federation. Mem. Rosicrucian Brotherhood. Democrat. Patentee of farm machinery. Home: Frankfort, Kan. Died Oct. 12, 1934.

SHEARER, Augustus Hunt, librarian; b. Phila., Pa., Feb. 21, 1878; s. Isaac Davis and Sarah Williamson (Hunt) S.; A.B., Rutgers, 1899, A.M., 1902, Litt.D., from the same college, 1934; A.B., Harvard Univ., 1900, A.M., 1901, Ph.D., 1903; m. Inez Ardelle Rogers, Dec. 4, 1915; children—Mary Ardelle, Sarah Hunt, Anne Francis, David Hunt. Teacher history, Trinity Coll., Conn., 1904-06, Dartmouth Coll., 1906-09, Hamilton Coll., 1909-12, Northwestern U., 1916-17; at Newberry Library, Chicago, 1912-17; librarian Grosvenor Library, Buffalo, N.Y., 1917—. Lecturer in history, 1918—, dir. library science course, 1920—, U. of Buffalo. Dir. Buffalo Soc. Natural Sciences; trustee Buffalo Symphony Soc.; mem. Library Council of State of New York; pres. N.Y. Library Assn., 1922-23, 1927-28. Republican. Mem. Reformed Ch. Co-author: Guide to Historical Literature, 1931; History of New York State (Alexander C. Flick, editor), 1933. Home: Buffalo, N.Y. Died May 31, 1941.

SHEARER, George Lewis, clergyman; b. Dillsburg, Pa., Oct. 16, 1835; s. Dr. George Lewis and Eliza (Eichelberger) S.; A.B., Lafayette Coll., 1857; grad. Princeton Theol. Sem., 1864; (D.D., Lafayette, 1883); m. Mary Wing Ketchum, Dec. 27, 1865. Taught Monroeville, Ala., 1857-59, Academie, Pa., 1859-61; during vacations missionary of the Am. Tract Soc. at Washington and in the Army of Northern Va., 1862-65; licensed to preach, 1864; ordained evangelist, Presbyn. Ch., Oct. 3, 1865; dist. sec. Am. Tract Soc. at Phila., 1864-65, Richmond, Va., 1865-68, San Francisco, 1869, asst. sec. at New York, 1868-72, corr. sec., 1872-1902, gen. sec., 1902-07, sec. emeritus, 1908—, Am. Tract Soc. Reorganized the southern work of the Am. Tract Soc., 1865-68, at Richmond, Va., and organized its agency on Pacific Coast, 1869. V.p. Evang. Alliance; one of founders Presbyn. Union of New York, 1887; v.p. Citizens' Eastside Improvement Assn., New York, 1902—; chmn. exec. com. Soc. for Publishing Evang. Lit. for the Blind, for whom he has prepared devotional books, out of the Am. Standard Revised Bible. Home: Carlisle, Pa. Died Mar. 10, 1919.

SHEARER, John Bunyan, college pres.; b. Appomattox Co., Va., July 19, 1832; s. John A. and Ruth Akers (Webber) S.; A.B., Hampden-Sidney Coll., Va., 1851; A.M., U. of Va., 1854; studied Union Theol. Sem., Va., 1854-58; (D.D., Hampden-Sidney Coll., 1872; LL.D., Southwestern Presbyn. U., 1889); m. Mrs. Lizzie Gessner, Sept. 5, 1854. Ordained Presbyn. ministry, 1859; pastor Chapel Hill, N.C., 1858-62, Spring Hill, Va., 1862-70; prin. Cluster Springs High Sch., 1866-70; prof. Bibl. instrn. and moral philosophy, and pres., 1870-75, Stewart Coll., Clarksville, Tenn.; pres., 1875-79, prof. Bibl. instrn., 1879-88, Southwestern Presbyn. U.; prof. Bibl. instrn., 1888—, pres., 1888-1901, v.p., 1901—, Davidson Coll. Author: Bible Course Syllabus (3 vols.), 1895; Modern Mysticism, 1905; Sermon on The Mount, 1906; Studies in the Life of Christ, 1907; The Scriptures, Fundamental Facts and Features, 1908; Selected Old Testament Studies, 1909; Hebrew Institutions, Social and Civil, 1910; Selected O.T. Studies, 1911; One Hundred Brief Bible Studies, 1912. Home: Davidson, N.C. Died June 14, 1919.

SHEARER, John Sanford, physicist; b. New York, Oct. 20, 1865; B.S., Cornell, 1893, Ph.D., 1900; m. Minnie Lee, June 20, 1888. Instr. physics, 1893-1902, asst. prof., 1902-09, Cornell; prof. physics, Columbia, 1909-10, Cornell, 1910—. Pres. Cornell Coöperative Soc. Commd. maj., Sanitary Corps N.A., 1917, lt. col., 1918; consultant in roentgenology, A.E.F., France. Republican. Conglist. Author: Notes and Questions on Physics, 1900; Lecture Outlines and Notes, 1906. Joint author: U.S.A. X-Ray Manual. Asso. editor Am. Jour. of Roentgenology. Home: Ithaca, N.Y. Died May 1922.

SHEARIN, Hubert Gibson, university dean; b. Boyle Co., nr. Danville, Ky., May 5, 1878; s. Henry Harper and Georgia Anna (Gibson) S.; A.B., Centre Coll., Danville, 1897, A.M., 1899; studied in Europe, 1900; fellow in English, Yale, 1900-02, Ph.D., 1902; informal attendance at various instns., 1902—; m. Ruth Marguerite Bené, Sept. 2, 1903. Prof. English, Ripon Coll., Wis., 1902-05; prof. English lang. and lit., Transylvania P., 1905-09; prof. English philology and dean of Hamilton Coll., Lexington, Ky., 1909-14; head of English dept., Occidental Coll., Los Angeles, 1914—. Author: The Expression of Purpose in Old English Prose, 1903; The That-Clause in the Authorized Version of the Bible, 1910; Syllabus of Kentucky Folk-Songs, 1911. Collaborator on The Wordsworth Concordance, 1910, and The Encyclopedia of Southern Literature (15 vols.), 1910. Home: Los Angeles, Calif. Died Aug. 11, 1919.

SHEARMAN, Thomas Gaskell, lawyer; b. Birmingham, England, Nov. 25, 1834; came with parents to

New York, when 9 years old; private edn.; settled in Brooklyn, 1857; admitted to bar, 1859; m. Ella Partridge, 1859. Managing counsel for Henry Ward Beecher in the actions brought against him by Theodore Tilton and F. D. Moulton; prominent free-trade advocate; supt. Plymouth Ch. Sunday School. Author: Shearman and Redfield on Negligence (with Amasa A. Redfield); Tillinghast and Shearman's Practice; Natural Taxation; Crooked Taxation; Does Protection Protect?; Pauper Labor of Europe; The Single Tax; Distribution of Wealth; Who Own the United States? Home: Brooklyn, N.Y. Died 1900.

SHEATS, William Nicholas, state supt. of schs.; b. Auburn, Ga., Mar. 5, 1851; s. John Lemuel and Ann Elizabeth (Jackson) S.; A.B., Emory Coll., Ga., 1873, A.M., 1876; LL.D., Stetson U., 1913; m. Mary Susan Williams, Nov. 14, 1877. Went to Fla., 1866; high sch. prin. in Fla., 16 yrs.; co. supt. schs., 12 yrs.; state supt. pub. instrn., 1893-1905 and 1913-25. Del. State Constl. Conv., Fla., 1885. Democrat. Mem. M.E. Ch., S. Mason, K.P., etc. Home: Tallahassee, Fla. Died July 19, 1922.

SHEDD, Fred Fuller, newspaper editor; b. New Boston, N.H., Feb. 9, 1871; s. Daniel Fuller and Clara Ellen (Fogg) S.; grad. high sch., Haverhill, Mass., 1886; m. Frances Martha Hodgdon, Feb. 27, 1891; children—Harold Hodgdon, Clifford Ernest, Karl Eastman. Began as bookkeeper, Haverhill Gazette, 1886, reporter, 1889; editor Haverhill Evening Gazette, 1899-1907; editorial writer, Boston Herald, 1907-09, editor, 1909-11; editorial writer, Phila. Evening Bulletin, 1911-21, editor in chief, 1921—; lecturer, Sch. of Journalism, Pa. State Coll., 1930—. Pres. Am. Soc. Newspaper Editors, 1930-32. Republican. Conglist. Home: Philadelphia, Pa. Died Apr. 2, 1937.

SHEDD, George Clifford, author; b. Ashland, Neb., Nov. 19, 1877; s. Hibbard Houston and Katharine Leigh (Graves) S.; A.B., U. of Neb., 1900; m. Apr. 27, 1921. Republican. Conglist. Author: Miniatures, 1900; Princess of Forge, 1910; The Incorrigible Dukane, 1911; The Isle of Strife, 1912; The Lady of Mystery House, 1917; The Invisible Enemy, 1918; In the Shadow of the Hills, 1919; The Iron Furrow, 1920; Cryden, 1922; Canyon of Conflict, 1928; Silver Skull, 1929. Home: Los Angeles, Calif. Died Jan. 8, 1937.

SHEDD, J(oel) Herbert, engineer; b. Pepperell, Mass., May 31, 1834; s. Joel and Eliza (Edson) S.; ed. Bridgewater Acad.; took 3 yrs.' course civ. engring. in a Boston office; (hon. A.M., Brown U., 1894); m. Julia A. Clark, Aug. 26, 1856 (died 1897); 2d, Sarah Marble, June 29, 1905. Practiced civ. engring. at Boston, 1856-69, Providence, 1869—. Has served on numerous commns. of Mass. and R.I. on river and harbor improvement. As engr. for the city of Providence, designed and built Providence water works, costing $4,500,000, the sewerage system, costing $5,500,000, and other large engring. works; chmn. State Bd. of Harbor Commrs. since its organization, 1876; engr. for many large water power developments; commr. for State of R.I. to Paris Expn., 1878. Mem. advisory com. Brown U. Home: Providence, R.I. Died Nov. 27, 1915.

SHEDD, John Cutler, prof. physics; b. of Am. parents, Uramia, Persia, June 30, 1868; s. John Haskell and Sarah Jane (Dawes) S.; A.B., Princeton, 1891; M.S., Cornell U., 1892; Ph.D., U. of Wis., 1899; m. Katherine Stockton Blayney, Aug. 25, 1896; children—John Stockton (dec.), Catherine Cutler. Prof. physics, Marietta (O.) Coll., 1893-97; fellow in physics, U. of Wis., 1897-99, instr., 1899-1900; prof. physics, Colorado Coll., Colorado Springs, Colo., 1900-07; prof. physics and dean Westminster Coll., Denver, 1907-09; prof. physics, Olivet (Mich.) Coll., 1909-16 (dean 1915-16), Occidental Coll., Los Angeles, Calif., 1916—; prof. physics, U. of Calif., Southern Br., summers 1919, 21, 23. Served as food administrator part of Los Angeles Co., 1917-18, also as capt. Am. Protective League, mem. Liberty Loan Com., etc. Fellow Am. Phys. Soc., A.A.A.S. Author (with others) Shop and Road Testing Dynamos and Motors, 1898, 1901; Shop Tests of Electrical Car Equipment, 1909; Miscellaneous Tests on Electrical Car Equipment, 1910. Home: Los Angeles, Calif. Died May 20, 1933.

SHEDD, John Graves, merchant; b. Alstead, N.H., July 20, 1850; s. William and Abigail (Wallace) S.; ed. common schs., Alstead and Langdon, N.H.; m. Mary R. Porter, May 15, 1878; children—Laura Abbie (Mrs. Charles H. Schweppe), Helen May (Mrs. Kersey Coates Reed). Employed in gen. stores at Bellows Falls, Vt., 1867-72; removed to Chicago and entered employ of Field, Leiter & Co., Aug. 7, 1872, remaining with that firm and its successor, Marshall Field & Co., of which became chmn. of bd.; trustee Mut. Life Ins. Co. (New York). Dir. First State Pawners' Soc. (Chicago). Donor of Shedd Aquarium ($2,000,000) to city of Chicago, 1924. Republican. Home: Chicago, Ill. Died Oct. 22, 1926.

SHEDDEN, Lucian Love, lawyer; b. Mooers, N.Y., Oct. 13, 1849; s. James S. and Ann (Perry) S.; ed. Ft. Edward Collegiate Inst.; LL.B., Albany Law Sch., 1872; (LL.D., Wesleyan U., Conn.); m. Kathrine A. Alden, Apr. 22, 1879. Practiced at Mooers, N.Y., 1872-88, then at Plattsburg; mem. Shedden & Shedden (father and son), Mar. 1, 1909—; dir. City Nat. Bank. Dist. atty. Clinton Co., N.Y., 1878-84; co. judge Clinton Co., 1892-1903; corp. counsel, Plattsburg; mem. local bd. State Normal Sch.; regent U. State of N.Y., 1905-16; apptd. by Gov. Higgins commr. of gas and electricity, 1905. Republican. Methodist. Pres. S. F. Vilas Home for Aged; trustee Y.M.C.A. Plattsburg, N.Y. Died Jan. 19, 1912.

SHEEDY, Dennis, banker; b. in Ireland, Sept. 26, 1846; s. John and Margaret S.; came with parents to Mass. while still a small child; removed to Ia., 1858; common sch. edn.; m. Katherine V. Ryan (died 1895); 2d Mary Teresa Burke, 1898. Crossed the plains to Denver, 1863, walking most of the way; went to Mont., 1864, and began mining, soon entering grocery business in mining camp; sold out in 7 mos., and removed to Utah; took course in commercial law at Chicago, afterwards returning to Utah over the Overland route (then beset by hostile Indians), as capt. of a band of emigrants; engaged extensively in merchandise and freighting business in Utah, Mont., Ida., and Nev.; entered cattle business, 1869, and operated on a large scale with headquarters in Kansas City and camps in Kan., Neb., Indian Ty., and Nev.; sold out, as free range became restricted, in 1884; returned to Denver, 1881; v.p. Colo. Nat. Bank, Denver, 1883—; one of founders and pres. and gen. mgr., Globe Smelting & Refining Co.; dir. and mem. exec. bd. Am. Smelting & Refining Co., 1898-1908; v.p. Internat. Smelting & Refining Co. of N.Y., Jan. 1909 until absorbed into Anaconda Copper Co.; one of organizers and president of Denver Dry Goods Co. Has patented 18 inventions in smelting. Home: Denver, Colo. Died Oct. 16, 1923.

SHEEDY, Morgan M., clergyman; b. Ireland, Oct. 8, 1853; s. Michael and Mary (Madden) S.; LL.D., Notre Dame U., 1906, Mount St. Mary's (Md.) Coll., 1908. Ordained R.C. priest, 1876; rector St. John's Ch., Altoona, Pa., Dec. 1894—. First pres. and treas. Catholic Summer Sch. (dir. Reading Circle Union); v.p. Catholic Total Abstinence Union of America 4 yrs. Rector Cathedral of the Blessed Sacrament, Altoona; mem. of the Bishop's Council; dean of the Diocesan Clergy. Editor and pub. The Altoona Monthly. Popular lecturer. Author: Christian Unity, 1895; Social Problems, 1896; Briefs for Our Times, 1906; etc. Home: Altoona, Pa. Died Oct. 25, 1939.

SHEEHAN, John Charles, lawyer, contractor; b. Buffalo, N.Y., Aug. 5, 1848; s. William and Hanora (Crowley) S.; ed. St. Joseph's Coll., and Commercial Coll. of Buffalo; m. Minnie Mulhall, June 2, 1892. Prominent Tammany Hall leader; police commr., New York, 1892-95. Home: New York, N.Y. Died Feb. 9, 1916.

SHEEHAN, Joseph Raymond, pres. Am. President Lines; b. Boston, Mass., Nov. 22, 1888; s. David James and Elizabeth Agnes (Cody) S.; grad. Boston Latin Sch., 1906; A.B., Harvard, 1910; m. Reina Jane Finn, June 24, 1925; children—Jane Patricia, Virginia. Clerk Foreign Office, Jordan Marsh Co., Boston, 1910-11; clerk Burton Pierce Co., Boston, 1911-12; mgr. D. J. Sheehan & Co., Boston, 1912-17; personnel mgr. and asst. to v.p. All America Cables, Inc., New York, 1920-34; administrative co-ordinator Securities and Exchange Commn., Washington, D.C., 1934-36; asst. to Joseph P. Kennedy, New York, 1936-37; exec. dir. U.S. Maritime Commn., Washington, D.C., 1937-38; pres. Am. President Lines, Ltd. (formerly Dollar Steamship Lines, Ltd., Inc.), 1938—. Served in Harvard Regt., May-Aug. 1917, Plattsburg O.T.C., Aug.-Nov. 1917; capt. 304th Inf., 76th Div., U.S. Army, later capt. 320th Inf., 80th Div., 1917-19, with A.E.F., July 1918-June 1919. Democrat. Catholic. Home: San Francisco, Calif. Deceased.

SHEEHAN, William Francis, lawyer; b. Buffalo, N.Y., Nov. 6, 1859; s. William and Hanora (Crowley) S.; A.B., St. Joseph's Coll.; m. Blanche Nellany, Nov. 27, 1889. Admitted to bar, 1881; practiced at Buffalo, 1881-95, New York, 1895—; mem. Parker (Alton Brooks), Hatch (Edward Wingate) and Sheehan, 1905—; dir. Kings County Electric Light & Power Co., Albany & Southern R.R. Co., Louisville Lighting Co., Western N.Y.&Pa. Traction Co., etc. Mem. N.Y. Assembly, 1885-91 (speaker of House, 1891); lt. gov., 1892-95; mem. Dem. State Com., 1889-93; mem. Dem. Nat. Com., 1891, 1896. Home: New York, N.Y. Died Mar. 14, 1917.

SHEERIN, James, clergyman, writer; b. Armadale, Scotland, May 6, 1865; s. William and Mary (Lecky) S.; brought by parents to U.S., 1870; student St. Stephen's Coll., N.Y. City, 1885-88, St. John's Coll., Denver, Colo., 1888-90; B.D., Kenyon Coll., Gambier, O., 1892; B.A., Columbia, 1901; B.D., Episcopal Theol. Sch., Cambridge, 1903; summer schs., Harvard and Oxford U., 1901-08; m. Mary Elisabeth Picking, June 28, 1892; children—Mary Elisabeth (Mrs. William Benfield Pressey), Charles Wilford, Florence Gertrude (Mrs. Theodore Melville Lay). Newspaper reporter, 1883-85; master, Jarvis Hall, Denver, 1888-90; deacon, 1892, priest, 1892, P.E. Ch.; asst. rector Trinity Ch., Pittsburgh, Pa., 1892-93; rector St. Peter's Ch., Ashtabula, O., 1893-95; warden of Episcopal Hall, W.Va. Univ., 1895-98; vicar Ascension Parish, N.Y. City, 1898-1900; asso. rector St. James' Ch., Cambridge, Mass., 1901-04; rector Ch. of the Good Shepherd, Clinton, Mass., 1904-09, Christ Ch., Warren, O., 1909-11, St. Matthew's Ch., Boston, Mass., 1911-17; vicar St. Thomas Chapel, N.Y. City, 1917-19; supt. Orphans' Home, N.Y. City, 1919-26; rector Am. Ch., Munich, Germany, 1926-30; retired. Provisional dep. from Western Mass., Gen. Conv., 1907; del. to Pan Anglican Congress, London, 1908. Pres. Mass. Clerical Assn. 1915-17. Mason. Author: Church, State and University, 1906; The Religion of Parsifal, 1925; The Universal Prayer, 1929. Cofounder and asso. editor The Witness, 1917-22; European corr. Living Church, 1913-14. Contbr. to The Churchman. Home: Bucyrus, O. Died Dec. 24, 1933.

SHEFFEY, Edward Fleming, businessman; b. Giles Co., Va., Nov. 12, 1865; s. Rev. Robt. Sawyers (evangelist) and Eliza W. (Stafford) S.; ed. pub. and pvt. schs.; m. Mattie Elizabeth Mahood, Dec. 10, 1890 (died 1927); children—Robert Alexander, Edward Fleming, Charles Phillips Mahood, Grace Stafford, Max Hugh, John Mahood, Coke Smith. With Guggenheimer & Co., wholesale dry goods, Lynchburg, 1882-1904, becoming v.p., sec. and treas.; with Craddock-Terry Company, Oct. 1, 1904—. Member Common Council, 1915-18; pres. Bd. Aldermen, 1918-20, Lynchburg. Trustee Randolph-Macon Coll.; chmn. exec. com. Randolph-Macon Woman's Coll. Democrat. Mem. M.E. Ch. S.; supt. Court St. S.S., 1891-1927; director and pres. Lynchburg Y.M.C.A.; v.p. Va. State S.S. Assn., 1915-16; dir. Nat. Assn. Credit Men, 1914-17. Mason, Odd Fellow; mem. Jr. O.U.A.M. Home: Lynchburg, Va. Died Jan. 10, 1933.

SHEFFIELD, Devello Z., missionary; b. Gainesville, N.Y., Aug. 13, 1841; s. Asa Campbell and Caroline (Murry) S.; ed. Warsaw (N.Y.) Acad.; served 2 yrs. in Civil War; grad. Auburn Theol. Sem., 1869; m. Eleanor Woodhull Sherrill, July 27, 1869. Ordained Presbyn. ministry, 1869; missionary in China, 1869—; pres. Union Coll., Tungchou, nr. Peking, 1890—. Pres. China Ednl. Assn., 1896-99; chmn. Bible Revision Com. in higher classical style. Author: Universal History, 1881; Church History, 1889; Systematic Theology, 1893; Political Economy, 1896; Principles of Ethics, 1907; Psychology, 1907; Political Science, 1909. Died July 1, 1913.

SHEFFIELD, James Rockwell, ambassador; b. Dubuque, Ia., Aug. 13, 1864; s. Frederick W. H. and Sarah (Kellogg) S.; A.B., Yale, 1887 (class orator), LL.D., 1925; LL.B., Harvard, 1889; m. Edith Tod, Nov. 2, 1898; 1 son, Frederick. Pvt. sec. to U.S. Senator William B. Allison, of Ia., 1888; settled in practice in N.Y. City; mem. N.Y. Assembly, 1893; apptd. fire commr. N.Y. City, by Mayor Strong, 1895, and elected pres. bd. 1896; A.E. and P. from U.S. to Mexico, 1924-27, retired. Appointed special ambassador to Venezuela, 1930. Trustee Carnegie Endowment for Internat. Peace; trustee Presbyn. Hosp., Trudeau Sanatorium, and various religious, charitable and ednl. socs. and instns., including Barnard Coll. of which is chmn. of board of trustees. Presbyn. Home: New York, N.Y. Died Sept. 2, 1938.

SHEFFIELD, William Paine, lawyer; b. on Block Island, R.I., Aug. 30, 1819; s. George Gardner and Eliza (Paine) S.; academic edn.; studied law at Harvard (LL.D., Brown, 1868); admitted to bar, 1844; began practice in Mass.; m. Lilias White, d. Samuel Sanford, Boston, 1847. Author of numerous hist. monographs. Mem. R.I. Constl. Convs., 1841, 1842; more than 25 yrs. mem. R.I. legislature; chmn. of commn. to revise State laws, 1872; mem. of Congress, 1861-63; U.S. senator, by exec. apptmt. to fill unexpired term of H. B. Anthony, 1884-85. Dir. Redwood Library over 40 yrs.; pres. bd. trustees People's Free Library from its institution. Home: Newport, R.I. Died 1907.

SHEFFIELD, William Paine, congressman; b. Newport, R.I., June 1, 1857; s. William P. and Lilias White (Sanford) S.; A.B., Brown U., 1877, A.M., 1880; law student at Paris, and at Harvard, 1878-79; m. Mary Stevens Burdick, Oct. 16, 1889. In practice at Newport, 1880—; mem. sch. com., 1883-1902; mem. R.I. Ho. of Rep., 1885-87, 1889-90, 1894-96, 1899-1901; mem. 61st Congress (1909-11), 1st R.I. Dist.; mem. Rep. Nat. Com., May 1911—. Episcopalian. Home: Middletown, R.I. Died Oct. 19, 1919.

SHELBY, David Davie, judge; b. Madison Co., Ala., Oct. 24, 1847; s. Dr. David and Mary (Bouldin) S.; studied law at Cumberland U., Lebanon, Tenn.; m. Annie Davis, Aug. 8, 1872. Admitted to bar, 1870, to Supreme Court of U.S., 1882; practiced at Huntsville, 1870-99. Mem. Ala. Senate, 1882-84; U.S. circuit judge, 5th Jud. Circuit, Mar. 2, 1899—. Republican. Home: Huntsville, Ala. Died Aug. 22, 1914.

SHELBY, Gertrude Singleton Mathews, author; b. Momence, Ill., Apr. 13, 1881; d. William Frank and

Gertrude (Magoffin) Singleton; ed. high sch.; m. John L. Mathews, author, Sept. 10, 1900 (died 1915); m. 2d, Edmund P. Shelby, M.D., Aug. 31, 1917. Contbr. to mags., 1915—, including Harper's, Century, Outlook, New Republic, Theatre Arts Monthly, Bookman, Nation, also lecturer; mng. editor (1917-18) News Letter, nat. publ. Woman's Council of Nat. Defense, and head of its news dept.; specialist on coöperative credit; organizer and exec. sec. Nat. Com. for Cooperative Banks; testified before Senate Banking and Currency committee, 1925, on farm credits; reported on same to Am. Farm Bureau Fedn., and Dem. Nat. Committee, 1928; wrote series for magazines; specialist on negroid peoples and folklore, Africa, Dutch Guiana and southern U.S. Author: Treasure (novel, under name of Gertrude S. Mathews), 1917; Galusha A. Grow (biography, with James T. Dubois), 1917; How to Face Peace (community programs, under name of Gertrude Mathews Shelby), 1918; Deporté (fiction), 1927; Black Genesis (with S. G. Stoney), 1930; Po' Buckra (with same), 1930. Hist. research 16th and 17th Century America, 1930-35. Home: Venice, Fla. Died Nov. 1, 1936.

SHELBY, John Todd, lawyer; b. Springfield, Ill. (parents being residents of Fayette Co., Ky.), Jan. 25, 1851; s. Thomas Hart and Frances Stuart (Todd) S.; Center Coll., Danville, Ky., 1866-67; Kentucky U. (now Transylvania U.), Lexington, K., 1867-88; A.B., Princeton, 1870, A.M., 1873; (LL.D., Agrl. and Mech. Coll. of Ky. [now State U. of Ky.], 1904); m. Lizzie M. Craig, Nov. 7, 1872. Admitted to Ky. bar, 1872; mem. Breckinridge & Shelby, 1875-1904 (dissolved by death of sr. partner), Shelby & Shelby, 1907-13, Shelby, Northcutt & Shelby, 1913—; dir. First and City Nat. Bank, Lexington, and Y.M.C.A., Lexington. Republican. Episcopalian. Home: Lexington, Ky. Died Mar. 2, 1920.

SHELBY, William Read, ry. official; b. Lincoln County, Ky., Dec. 4, 1842; s. John Warren and Mary Humphreys (Knight) S.; educated Centre College, Ky., to end of sophomore year, 1861; prevented by Civil War from graduating; m. Mary K., d. Gen. George W. Cass, of Pittsburgh, June 16, 1869. Sec. and treas. Continental Improvement Co., 1869-87, Southern Ry. Security Co., 1870-73; treas., 1871-87, v.p. and treas., 1887—, Grand Rapids & Ind. R.R. Co.; reorganized as Grand Rapids & Ind. Ry. Co., 1896; pres. Cincinnati, Richmond & Fort Wayne R.R. Co., 1899—, Muskegon, Grand Rapids & Ind. R.R. Co., 1899—, Traverse City R.R., 1899—. Chmn. State Central Com. Gold Democrats, Mar. 1896; mem. exec. and Nat. Com. of Nat. Dem. party, 1896. Home: Grand Rapids, Mich. Died Nov. 30, 1930.

SHELDEN, Carlos Douglas, congressman 12th Mich. dist.; b. Walworth, Wis., June 10, 1840; removed with his parents to Houghton Co., Mich., 1847; ed. Union School, Ypsilanti, Mich.; served through Civil War as capt. 23d Mich. inf. Mem. Mich. legislature, 1892-94; State senate, 1894-96; mem. of Congress, 1897-1903, 12th Mich. dist. Republican. Home: Houghton, Mich. Died 1904.

SHELDON, Arthur Frederick, author, teacher; b. Vernon, Mich., May 1, 1868; s. Elsworth and Helen Mary (Woodward) S.; grad. Vernon High Sch., 1885; Fenton (Mich.) Normal Sch. 1 term; LL.B., U. of Mich., 1892; m. Anna Griffiths, Jan. 1, 1895; children—Rachel Miriam, Helen Muriel, Arthur Frederick. Taught dist. sch. 2 yrs., became book salesman at 19 and paid way through coll.; entered employ of Werner Co., pubs., 1893; pres. and gen. mgr. Sheldon Pub. Co., Chicago, 1899-1902; founded, 1902, and was pres., becoming pres. emeritus, the Sheldon Sch. (business science); formulator of "Science of Salesmanship." Mason. Author: Science of Successful Salesmanship (25 vols.), 1902; Science of Industrial Success (10 vols.), 1905; The Science of Service (7 vols.), 1909; The Science of Business Building (32 vols.), 1910; The Science of Business, 1915; Talks About Business, 1919. Founder and dir. The Forum of Fundamentals and the Natural Law Legion. Homes: Kingston, N.Y., and New York, N.Y. Died Dec. 21, 1935.

SHELDON, Caroline M., educator; b. Potsdam, N.Y., Jan. 22, 1860; d. Noah Buttolph and Maria (Billings) S.; grad. State Normal Sch., Potsdam, 1878; A.B., Iowa (now Grinnell) Coll., 1893, A.M., 1895; studied U. of Chicago and U. of Calif., also in Paris, Italy, Spain; has spent considerable time in England and Scotland. Teacher in New York and Iowa pub. and high schs. for a number of yrs.; registrar and prof. Romance langs., Mills Coll., Calif., 1902-04; teacher French and Spanish, Seattle High Sch., 1904-06; instr. French, 1906-08, acting dean of women, 1907-09, asst. prof. modern langs., 1909-11, asso. prof., 1911-13, prof. Romance langs., 1913-26 (emeritus), Grinnell Coll. Mem. Huguenot-Walloon Tri-centenary Commn., 1924. Author: Princess and Pilgrim in England, 1904. Home: Potsdam, N.Y. Died June 16, 1929.

SHELDON, Charles, author; b. Rutland, Vt., Oct. 17, 1867; s. John A. and Caroline A. (Eastman) S.; grad. Phillips Acad., Andover, Mass., 1887; A.B., Yale, 1890; m. Louisa Walker Gulliver, May 12, 1909. Asst. supt., Toledo div., L.S.&M.S. Ry., 1893; gen. mgr., Consolidated Car Heating Co., Albany, N.Y., 1894-98, Chihuahua & Pacific Ry., Mex., 1898-1902; exploring and hunting in Yukon Ty., Alaska and Mexico, from 1902. Author: The Wilderness of the Upper Yukon, 1911; The Wilderness of the North Pacific Coast Islands, 1912. Home: Washington, D.C. Died Sept. 21, 1928.

SHELDON, Charles Mills, artist, corr.; b. Lawrenceburg, Ind., June 24, 1866; s. George and Jeannette (Mills) S.; pub. sch. edn.; studied in Paris, under Constant and Lefebvre, at Acad. Julian, 1890-91; m. Grace Garland Fitch, Nov. 26, 1896; children—Jeannette (dec.), Eugene. Traveled in Southern States, illustrating articles for Associated Press, 1889; illustrator on Pall Mall Budget, 1892-95; artist and corr. Black and White, London, in S. Africa during time of Jameson raid, and through Dongola Expdn., Soudan, 1896; artist corr. Frank Leslie's and Black and White in Cuba, 1898; artist and corr. to opening of Assouan Barrage and Delhi Durbar, 1903. Spl. artist on British front for Northcliffe Press, 1918. Fellow Royal Geog. Society. Died Mar. 15, 1928.

SHELDON, Charles Stuart, M.D.; b. New York Mills, N.Y., Jan. 14, 1842; s. Stephen S. and Lemira Wheaton (Harris) S.; grad. Brockport Collegiate Inst., 1858, Phillips Acad., Andover, Mass., 1859; A.B., Yale, 1863, A.M., 1866; M.D., U. of Buffalo, 1867; M.D., Coll. Phys. and Surg. (Columbia), 1868; m. Emma L. Hodge, Oct. 30, 1868; children—William Hodge (dec.), Sidney Roby, Walter Hodge, Stuart Harris, Helen Miriam. Resident phys. Buffalo Gen. Hosp., 1865-67; practiced at Winona, Minn., 1868-71, Greenville, Mich., 1871-84, Madison, Wis., 1884—. Dir. Commercial Nat. Bank and Commercial Trust Co. Home: Madison, Wis. Died Apr. 20, 1929.

SHELDON, Edward Stevens, university prof.; b. Waterville, Me., Nov. 21, 1851; s. Rev. David Newton and Rachel Hobart (Ripley) S.; brother of Henry Newton S.; A.B., Harvard, 1872; studied Berlin, Paris and Leipzig, 1874-77; m. Catherine Hamlin Hinckley, Apr. 2, 1884. Instr. modern langs., 1877-84, asst. prof. Romance philology, 1884-94, prof., 1894-1921, prof. emeritus, 1921, Harvard U. Fellow Am. Acad. Arts and Sciences. Author: A Short German Grammar, 1879; (with A. C. White) Concordanza delle Opere Italiane in Prosa e del Canzoniere di Dante Alighieri, 1905; revision of etymologies in Webster's International, 1890, 1900, and New Internat. Dictionary, 1910. Home: Cambridge, Mass. Died Oct. 16, 1925.

SHELDON, Edward Wright, banker, lawyer; b. Plainfield, N.J., Dec. 17, 1858; s. Rev. George (D.D.) and Martha (Lyman) S.; A.B., Princeton, 1879, A.M., 1882; LL.B., Columbia, 1881. Chmn. bd. trustees U.S. Trust Co. of New York; dir. Milbank Memorial Fund, Louisville & Nashville R.R. Co., Royal Ins. Co., Ltd., Royal Indemnity Co., Queen Ins. Co. of America, Eagle Indemnity Co., Am. & Foreign Ins. Co., and many other companies. Governor and pres. Soc. of New York Hosp., Soc. of Lying-In Hosp. of City of New York; chmn. Joint Administrative Bd. of New York Hosp.-Cornell Med. Coll. Assn.; trustee Roosevelt Hosp., Princeton U., Barnard Coll.; trustee and treas. New York Pub. Library. Home: New York, N.Y. Died Feb. 14, 1934.

SHELDON, Frederick Beaumont, ry. official; b. Manchester, Eng., Jan. 27, 1856; s. Stephen and Ruth (Beaumont) S.; ed. in Endowed Grammar Sch. at Lymm, Cheshire, Eng.; m. Harriet Ellen Thrall, Sept. 8, 1881; children—Walter Thrall, Stephen, Mary Lees (Mrs. C. F. Long), Ruth Beaumont (Mrs. A. D. Hall), Harriet, Anne Edith (Mrs. E. S. Morton). Came to U.S., 1870; began as rear flagman on survey of Ark. Central R.R., Nov. 1870; draftsman same rd., 1871-72; topographer, draftsman and asst. engr. Columbus & Toledo R.R., 1872-77; engr. same rd., 1877-81; also engr. Ohio & W.Va. rd., Jan.-Aug. 1881; engr. Toledo, and Ohio River divs., Columbus, Hocking Valley & Toledo Ry., 1881-88; chief engr. same, and reorganized rd., the Hocking Valley Ry., 1888-1900; asst. to pres. of H.V.,T.& O.C. and K.&M. rys., 1900-10; pres. Kanawha & Mich. Ry., 1910-15; v.p. Toledo & Ohio Central, Zanesville & Western, and Kanawha & Mich. rys., 1915-22, also v.p. Kanawha & W.Va. R.R. (all N.Y.C. lines), 1916-22; resident v.p. Ohio Central Lines, Aug. 1922—. Republican. Episcopalian. Home: Columbus, O. Died Mar. 1, 1927.

SHELDON, George Preston, underwriter; b. New York, Jan. 17, 1847; s. Charles and Janet (Reid) S.; A.B., Yale, 1867; LL.B., Columbia, 1869; m. Frances Pendleton, July 2, 1872 (died 1885); m. 2d, Carolyn Pendleton, May 21, 1890. Pres. Phœnix Ins. Co., Apr. 19, 1888—; dir. Brooklyn Bank. Home: Greenwich, Conn. Died 1909.

SHELDON, George Rumsey, banker; b. Brooklyn, Apr. 16, 1857; s. William C. and Mary (de Forest) S.; A.B., Harvard, 1879; m. Mary R. Seney, Dec. 16, 1881. Engaged in banking, 1879—; treas. and chmn. bd. North Am. Co.; chmn. exec. com. and treas. Milwaukee Elec. Ry. & Light Co.; pres. Elec. Securities Co.; treas. and dir. Detroit Edison Co.; dir. numerous corporations. New York mem. Rep. Nat. Com., 1903-04; treas. N.Y. Co. Com., 1899-1903, N.Y. State Com., 1906, Rep. Nat. Com., 1908-16. Trustee St. Paul's Sch. Episcopalian. Home: New York, N.Y. Died Jan. 14, 1919.

SHELDON, George William, author; b. Summerville, S.C., Jan. 28, 1843; s. George (D.D.) and Martha (Lyman) S.; bro. of Edward Wright S.; A.B., Princeton, 1863, A.M., 1866 (L.H.D., 1896). Tutor in Latin and belles lettres, Princeton, 1865-67; instr. Oriental langs., Union Theol. Sem., 1867-73; afterward art editor New York Evening Post; lit. adviser at London, of D. Appleton & Co., 1890-1900. Author: American Painters; Story of the Volunteer Fire Department of New York City; Hours with Art and Artists; Artistic Homes; Artistic Country Seats; Recent Ideals of American Art; Ideals of Life in France. Home: Summit, N.J. Died Jan. 29, 1914.

SHELDON, Henry Clay, theologian; b. Martinsburg, N.Y., Mar. 12, 1845; s. Ira and Fanny Maria (Bingham) S.; A.B., Yale, 1867, A.M., 1870; S.T.B., Boston U., 1871; D.D., Lawrence, 1887; m. Louise McLellan, Sept. 16, 1875; children—Herbert Prescott, Ernest McLellan. Ordained M.E. ministry; pastor St. Johnsbury, Vt., 1871-72, Brunswick, Me., 1872-74; prof. hist. theology, 1875-95, systematic theology, 1895-1921, Boston U. Author: History of Christian Doctrine (2 vols.), 1886; History of the Christian Church (5 vols.), 1894; System of Christian Doctrine, 1903; History of Unbelief in the Nineteenth Century, 1907; Sacerdotalism in the Nineteenth Century, 1909; New Testament Theology, 1911; Christian Science So-Called, 1913; A Fourfold Test of Mormonism, 1914; Studies in Recent Adventism, 1915; Theosophy and New Thought, 1916; The Mystery Religions and the New Testament, 1918; Pantheistic Dilemmas and Other Essays in Philosophy and Religion, 1920; The Essentials of Christianity, 1922. Home: West Newton, Mass. Died Aug. 4, 1928.

SHELDON, Henry Newton, judge; b. Waterville, Me., June 28, 1843; s. David Newton and Rachel Hobart (Ripley) S.; bro. of Edward Stevens S.; A.B., Harvard, 1863 (LL.D., 1908); 2d and 1st lt. 55th Mass. Inf., 1864-65; m. Clara P. Morse, Dec. 31, 1868. Practiced law at Boston, 1866-94; justice Superior Ct. of Mass., 1894-1905; justice Supreme Jud. Ct. of Mass., from Oct. 18, 1905-Jan. 4, 1915; resigned. Independent Republican. Unitarian. Author: The Law of Subrogation, 1882. Mem. Mass. Judicature Commn., 1919—. Home: Boston, Mass. Died Jan. 14, 1926.

SHELDON, Joseph, lawyer; b. Watertown, N.Y., Jan. 7, 1828; s. Joseph and Hepzibah (Richardson) S.; A.B., Yale, 1851, A.M., LL.B., 1853; studied law; as mem. of com. representing Yale composed speech of invitation and welcome delivered to Louis Kossuth, 1852; m. Abby E., d. S. Elbridge Barker, of Syracuse, N.Y., Sept. 7, 1861. Began practice at New Haven, 1853; partner Hon. L. E. Munson, 1859-65; instituted and managed earliest Conn. lecture courses on anti-slavery lines; made many speeches advocating election of Abraham Lincoln; organized and drilled colored mil. co. during the war; in Eng. mfg. machine-made brushes, 1868-74; resumed law practice, New Haven, 1874. Alderman, New Haven, 1879-82; judge of city ct., 1881-83; del. and one of speakers, Red Cross Conf., Geneva, Switzerland, 1884; Peoples party candidate for gov. of Conn., 1904. Universalist. Home: New Haven, Conn. Died Oct. 25, 1911.

SHELDON, Lionel Allen, governor; b. Worcester, N.Y., Aug. 30, 1831; s. Allen and Anna Maria (de les Dernier) S.; Oberlin Coll., 1848-50; admitted to bar, 1853; LL.B., Fowler Law Sch., Poughkeepsie, N.Y., 1853; m. Mary Greene Miles, Dec. 29, 1868. Probate judge, Lorain Co., O., 1856-57; practiced law, 1857-61; lt. col. 42d Ohio Inf., Nov. 27, 1861 (James A. Garfield, col.); col., Mar. 14, 1862; bvtd. brig. gen. vols., Mar. 13, 1865, "for faithful and meritorious services during the war"; served in W.Va., Ky., E. and W. Tenn., Ark., Miss. and La.; was in battles of Middle Creek, capture Cumberland Gap, Chickasaw Bayou, Arkansas Post, Port Gibson (wounded), Champion Hill, Big Black, Siege of Vicksburg, and (in command) Comite River, La.; mustered out at New Orleans, Dec. 2, 1864. Practiced law, New Orleans, 1864-79; mem. 41st to 43d Congresses (1869-75), 2d La. Dist.; represented govt. as atty. in cases from Gulf Coast before Alabama Claims Commn., and commn. to revise customs regulations for Gulf Coast; presdl. elector, 1876; gov. of N.M., 1881-85; receiver of Tex. & Pacific Ry., 1885-87; sold it Nov. 1887, and removed to Calif.; in practice at Los Angeles, 1887—. Home: Pasadena, Calif. Died Jan. 17, 1917.

SHELDON, Ralph Edward, anatomist; b. Lisle, N.Y., Mar. 28, 1883; s. Herbert Clayton and Rosalia (Reed) S.; A.B., Cornell U., 1904, A.M., 1905; S.M., Harvard, 1907; Ph.D., U. of Chicago, 1908; m. Emily Evans, Aug. 13, 1908. Asst., U.S. Forest Service, summers, 1902, 1903; scholar in neurology, 1904-05, Goldwin Smith fellow in neurology, 1905-06, asst. in zoölogy, summers, 1904-07, Cornell U.; Edward Austin fellow, Harvard, 1906-07; asst. in anatomy, 1907-09, asso., 1909, U. of Chicago; scienific asst. and investigator, U.S. Bur. Fisheries, Woods Hole, Mass., summers, 1908, 1910; asst. prof. anatomy, 1909-12, asso. prof., 1912-14, prof. and head of dept., 1914—, U. of Pittsburgh. Home: Pittsburgh, Pa. Died July 9, 1918.

SHELDON, Rowland Caldwell, sociol. worker; b. Camden, N.J., June 24, 1876; s. Norman and Letitia Anne (McClenthen) S.; U.S. Mil. Acad., 1895-98; Harvard U., 1899, 1900; m. Grace L. Flint, 1911; children—John F., Carol McC. Comdt. Montclair Acad., 1900-11; gen. sec. Big Brother Movement, New York, 1912-24; exec. sec. Big Brother and Big Sister Fedn. (internat.), 1920—; organized Nat. Crime Prevention Inst., Inc., 1936, became 1st exec. dir. Episcopalian. Has delivered pub. addresses throughout U.S. and Canada. Supervised study of problem children in 26 N.Y. towns and 6 N.J. cities for prevention juvenile delinquency and crime. Died Dec. 5, 1936.

SHELDON, Samuel, electrical engr.; b. Middlebury, Vt., Mar. 8, 1862; s. Harmon Alexander and Mary (Bass) S.; A.B., Middlebury Coll., 1883, A.M., 1886; Ph.D., U. of Würzburg, 1888; asst. to Kohlrausch, distinguished physicist, with whom he was associated in his celebrated determination of the ohm; (D.Sc., U. of Pennsylvania, 1906; D.Sc., Middlebury Coll., 1911); m. Frances Warner Putnam, June 18, 1891. Asst. in physics, Harvard, 1888-89; prof. physics and elec. engring., Poly. Inst. of Brooklyn, 1889—; pres. dept. electricity Brooklyn Inst. Arts and Sciences; consulting engr. and frequently called to give expert testimony in state and federal cts.; expert of Swiss Dept. of Justice and Police, 1903—; sec. sect. B, Internat. Elec. Congress, 1904; mem. Internat. Elec. Jury of Awards, St. Louis Expn., 1904. Fellow A.A.A.S., Brooklyn Inst. Arts and Sciences; hon. fellow Am. Electro-Therapeutic Assn. Dir. John Fritz Medal Assn. (pres. 1910-11). Author: Dynamo Electric Machinery, 1900-03; Alternating Current Machines (joint author), 1902; Electric Traction and Transmission Engineering (joint author), 1911; Physics Laboratory Experiments (joint author). Home: Brooklyn, N.Y. Died Sept. 4, 1920.

SHELDON, Walter L., founder, and from 1886 lecturer, Ethical Soc. of St. Louis; b. W. Rutland, Vt., Sept. 5, 1858; s. Preston and Cornelia Hatch S.; ed. high school, Middlebury, Vt.; grad. Princeton, 1880; studied in dept. of philosophy and science 2 yrs., at Berlin and Leipzig univs.; m. Anna, d. Charles Hartshorne of Phila, May 18, 1892. Connected with various ednl. efforts, St. Louis; founder and from 1888 to 1905 dir. Self Culture Hall Assn. Author: An Ethical Movement (lectures), 1896; An Ethical Sunday School, 1900; Story of the Bible, 1899; A Graded Course of Ethical Instruction for the Young (4 vols.). Has written for the Internat. Jour. of Ethics. Chmn. social science dept. World's Congress of Arts and Sciences, St. Louis, 1904. Home: St. Louis, Mo. Died 1907.

SHELTON, Charles Eldred, college pres.; b. Mt. Pleasant, Ia., June 16, 1859; s. Rev. Orville Clarkson and Lucy (Carnifex) S.; A.B., Iowa Wesleyan U., 1879, A.M., 1881 (LL.D., 1902); admitted to bar, 1880; m. Julia Woodward, Oct. 28, 1880. Engaged in Bishop William Taylor's ednl. missionary work in Brazil, 1880-82, organizing schs. in Pernambuco and Bahia; prin. DeWitt (Ia.) pub. schs., 1885-89; teacher Western Normal Coll., Shenandoah, Ia., 1889-92, Lincoln (Neb.) Normal U., 1892-93; supt. pub. schs., Burlington, Ia., 1893-99; pres. Simpson Coll., Indianola, Ia., 1899-1910; supt. Mt. Lake Park (Md.) Summer Resort and Assemblies, Feb. 1911—. Pres. Ia. State Ednl. Assn., 1901-02. Home: Mt. Lake Park, Md. Died May 13, 1940.

SHELTON, Don Odell, educator, editor; b. Odessa, N.Y., May 5, 1867; s. Charles and Amanda (Thompson) S.; ed. pub. schs. and later pursued systematic courses of study for yrs., devoting special attention to Bibl. and theol. subjects; LL.D., Wheaton Coll., Ill., 1926; m. Matilda Kay, Sept. 12, 1901. Sec. of religious work, Y.M.C.A., Elmira, N.Y., 1887-89; founded, and edited Young Men's Journal, Elmira, N.Y., 1886-87; sec. East Side Br. Y.M.C.A., New York, 1889-98; edited The Bible Student, New York, 1897-98. Teacher Bible classes, New York, and speaker at religious convs., 1889-98; teacher of Bible at College Students' Summer Confs., 1901-02; conducted Bible Confs. in large Am. cities, 1899, 1900; sec. religious work dept., Internat. Com. Y.M.C. Assns., New York, 1900-02; sec. Congl. Home Missionary Soc., 1903-07; pres. Nat. Bible Inst., New York, 1906—; founded, 1907, editor The Bible To-Day. Author: Personal Work and the Personal Worker, 1896; Higher Ideals of Christian Stewardship, 1897; The Public Use of the Bible, 1898; The Greatest of Books, 1900; Raising the Average, 1906; The Bible and Modern Civilization, 1921; Aggressive Evangelism and the Christian Fundamentals, 1921; Better Than Gold, 1927; Guidance Through Life's Contradictions, 1927. Home: Briarcliff Manor, N.Y. Died Jan. 29, 1941.

SHELTON, Louise, author; b. N.Y. City, Mar. 28, 1867; d. William Henry and Charlotte Johnes S. Pres. Morris County Soc. for Prevention of Cruelty to Children and Animals. Author: Seasons in a Flower Garden, 1906; Continuous Bloom in America, 1915; Beautiful Gardens in America, 1915. Home: Morristown, N.J. Died Mar. 26, 1934.

SHELTON, Thomas Wall, lawyer, publicist; b. Ringgold, Va., Dec. 8, 1870; s. Thomas Jefferson and Sarah Elizabeth Williams (Motley) S.; prep. edn. Denna's Prep. Sch., Highland Falls, N.Y., and Va. Mil. Inst.; B.L., Washington and Lee U., Lexington, Va., 1893; unmarried. Admitted to Va. bar, 1893; city atty., Norfolk, Va., 1894-96; specializes in constl. law, law of corps.; and statutory and common law liens. Member board visitors Virginia Military Institute 7 years; capt. 4th Regt. Va. Inf.; judge advocate gen. Va. N.G., 1907-17. Conceived and organized Nat. Conf. of Judges (now the jud. sect. of Am. Bar Assn.) and known as "father" of the Interstate Conf. of Judges; originated campaign for uniformity of procedure in courts, federal and state, and its simplification through rules of court. Mem. Nat. Conf. Commrs. on Uniform State Laws (chmn. com. on jud. opinions). Mem. Rules Com. of Supreme Court of Va. Democrat. Episcopalian. Wrote: Spirit of the Courts. Home: Norfolk, Va. Died Mar. 17, 1931.

SHENEHON, Francis Clinton, hydraulic engr.; b. Brooklyn, N.Y., Dec. 20, 1861; s. Ellsworth S. and Ella (Dalley) S.; B.C.E., U. of Minn., 1895, C.E., 1900; m. Kate Bird Cross, May 14, 1891. Engr. U.S. War Dept., on building of New Ft. Brady, Sault Ste. Marie, Mich., 1890-91; on building of ship lock and canal, and channelization of St. Mary's River, 1891-98; on Lake Survey, at Buffalo, Ogdensburg and Detroit, 1898-1909; dean Coll. of Engring., U. of Minn., and consulting engr., 1909-17; engring. practice, May 1917—. Consulting engr. Sanitary District Chicago for regulating works in St. Clair, Niagara and St. Lawrence rivers up to 1924; for Northern States Power Co., for water power development in Miss. and St. Croix rivers; engr. v.p. Byllesby Engring. & Management Corp., Chicago, 1923-24; consulting hydraulic engr. Author of Preservation of Niagara Falls, and The St. Lawrence Waterway to the Sea, and other tech. papers. Studied water power development in Norway, Sweden, Germany and Switzerland, 1927. Home: Minneapolis, Minn. Died Oct. 3, 1939.

SHENTON, Herbert Newhard, sociologist; b. Pottstown, Pa., July 9, 1884; s. Robert M. and Helen Louise (Scheck) S.; Ph.B., Dickinson Coll., Carlisle, Pa., 1906, M.A., 1909, L.H.D., 1926; B.D., Drew Theol. Sem., 1910; Union Theol. Sem., 1910-12; Ph.D., Columbia, 1925; m. Edna Mae Logan, June 27, 1919. Student pastor, various times, in Pa. and N.J., 1905-15; ordained M.E. ministry, 1910; instr. sociology, Columbia, 1912-25, asst. prof., 1925-27; prof. sociology and head of dept., Syracuse U., 1927—; asst. to Josiah Macy, Jr. Foundation, 1934—. Chief of reconstruction research div. U.S. Council Nat. Defense, World War, acting dir. same, and dir., June-Oct. 1920. Exec. sec. U.S. Bituminous Coal Commn., 1920; organizing sec. U.S. Anthracite Coal Commn., 1920; lecturer, Gen. Staff War Coll., 1920-21; dir. of reconnaissance study Y.M.C.A. and Y.W.C.A. relations throughout United States, 1929-30. Mem. exec. com. Meth. Fedn. for Social Service; vice chmn. dept. of research and edn. Federal Council of Chs. Executive sec. Internat. Auxiliary Lang. Assn. in U.S.; mem. Nat. Council and Internat. Com. of Y.M.C.A. Mason. Author: The Practical Application of Sociology, 1926; Cosmopolitan Conversation, 1933. Co-author: International Communication, 1931. Home: Syracuse, N.Y. Deceased.

SHEPARD, Andrew N., tobacco grower; b. Portland, Conn., May 5, 1862; s. Nelson and Elizabeth (Tryon) S.; ed. Glastonbury Acad. and Cheshire Mil. Acad., Conn.; m. Harriet Stockwell, May 1, 1889; children—Dorothea (Mrs. Gordon W. Stewart), Nelson A. In tobacco business, 1884—, mem. A. N. Shepard & Son, growers and packers of Conn. tobacco, Hartford; pres. Portland Trust Co., 1924—. Mem. Conn. Ho. of Rep., 1901 and 1923, Conn. Senate, 1907-08. Episcopalian. Mason. Home: Portland, Conn. Died 1934.

SHEPARD, Charles Edward, lawyer; b. Dansville, N.Y., Mar. 14, 1848; s. Charles and Katherine Rochester (Colman) S.; A.B., Yale, 1870 (Phi Beta Kappa); studied law offices, Dansville and Rochester, N.Y.; m. Alice Maria Galloway, June 15, 1881. Practiced Fond due Lac, Wis., 1872-83, at Milwaukee, Wis., 1883-91, and at Seattle, Wash., until retired. A founder and dir. Fond du Lac Public Library, 1875-80; mem. Wis. Ho. of Rep., 1881-82; trustee Seattle Pub. Library, 1895-1900 and 1901-08; mem. Uniform Law Commn. State of Wash., 1905—; candidate on non-partisan ticket for justice Sup. Ct., Wash., 1910 (defeated). Republican. Chancellor Diocese of Olympia, P.E. Ch. Author: Shepard's Wisconsin Digest, 1884; Golden Lives, 1905. Home: Spokane, Wash. Died Mar. 31, 1928.

SHEPARD, Charles Henry, physician; b. Canada, Sept. 28, 1825; s. Timothy and Betsey (Vail) S.; acad. edn. at Ogdensburg, N.Y.; M.D., New York Med. Coll., 1859; twice married. Established, 1863, in Brooklyn, the first Turkish bath in America, which he still conducts. Has written several monographs. Home: Brooklyn, N.Y. Died 1910.

SHEPARD, C(harles) Sidney, capitalist; b. Buffalo, N.Y., July 29, 1856; s. Sidney and Elizabeth De Angelis (Wells) S.; A.B., Yale, 1878; LL.B., Hamilton Coll., 1879; unmarried. Admitted to bar, 1879; after death of father, 1893, succeeded to many of latter's positions of trust. Resigned from most directorates, 1910; dir. Mobile & Ohio R.R. Co., S.A.L. Ry. Co., Ft. Dodge, Des Moines & Southern R.R. Co. Republican. Presbyn. Home: New Haven, N.Y. Died Apr. 26, 1934.

SHEPARD, Edward Martin, geologist; b. West Winsted, Conn., May 15, 1854; s. Samuel and Mary Isabella (Dennis) Shepard; Williams Coll., class of '78, A.M., 1881; Sc.D., Waynesburg Coll., Pa., 1902; LL.D., Drury Coll., Springfield, Mo., 1923; m. Harriett Elma Ohlen, June 28, 1881. Prof. natural science, Waynesburg Coll., 1878; prof. biology and geology, 1879-1908, acting pres., 1893-94, dean, 1903-08, Drury Coll. Spl. asst. Mo. Geol. Survey, 1894-95; state geologist, 1901; field asst. dept. hydrology, U.S. Geol. Survey, 1903-07. Mem. bd. mgrs., 1893-1911 and 1913—, v.p., 1903-06, sec., 1919—, Mo. Bur. of Geology and Mines. Mem. 10th Internat. Congress of Geologists, City of Mexico, 1906. Mem. numerous geog. and hist. societies. Mem. Springfield Park Bd., 1919-23, Springfield Chamber of Commerce; mem. bd. of mgrs. Springfield Children's Home. Author: Systematic Mineral Record, 1883. Conglist. Democrat. Died Apr. 28, 1934.

SHEPARD, Edward Morse, lawyer; b. in New York, July 23, 1850; s. Lorenzo B. S.; A.B., Coll. City of New York, 1869; (LL.D., Tulane U., 1903, Washington and Lee, 1904, Williams, 1907); unmarried. Admitted to bar, 1871, and entered practice at New York; dir. in numerous ry. and other corps. Civil service commr., Brooklyn, 1883-85 (chmn. bd., 1888-90); N.Y. state forestry commr., 1884-85; Dem. candidate for mayor of Greater New York, 1901; since proposed for gubernatorial and other nominations of his party. Chmn. bd. trustees Coll. City of New York; trustee Packer Collegiate Inst. Author: Martin Van Buren (American Statesmen Series); Memoirs of Dugdale. Home: Brooklyn, N.Y. Died 1911.

SHEPARD, Edwin M., rear admiral U.S.N., retired; b. Oswego, N.Y., Sept. 16, 1843; s. Elisha H. and A. K. (Gray) S.; ed. Naval Acad., 1859-61; m. Alice Stevens, Dec. 9, 1868. Apptd. ensign, Nov. 22, 1862; lt., Feb. 22, 1864; lt. comdr., July 25, 1866; comdr., June 1878; capt., May 15, 1893; rear admiral, Mar. 3, 1901; retired, 1902, after 40 yrs. service as officer. Served on sloop Vincennes, 1861-62, at passes of Mississippi River; on sloop Mississippi, 1862-63, until her destruction; on gunboat Essex in siege of Port Hudson and with naval battery of 9-inch guns on shore for several weeks; on monitor Mahopac at siege of Charleston, S.C., and on James River; on Wachusett, capture of privateer Florida, Oct. 7, 1864; varied services on sea and land, after the war; light-house insp., Apr. 1898. Home: Washington, D.C. Died 1904.

SHEPARD, Fred Douglas, medical missionary; b. Ellenburg, N.Y., Sept. 11, 1855; s. Rufus George and Charlotte M. (Douglas) S.; student Cornell U., 1876-78; M.D., U. of Mich., 1881; post-grad. study New York, 1881-82; m. Fanny P. Andrews, July 2, 1882. Prof. surgery, Central Turkey Coll., 1882-88, acting pres. same, 1884-85, 1895-96; dir. and surgeon Azariah Smith Memorial Hosp., 1883—. Medal "for specially meritorious vol. service" from Am. Nat. Red Cross, 1909; decorated with the Order of the Medjidieh by Sultan of Turkey, 1910. Mem. Med. Missionary Assn. of Turkey. Republican. Conglist. Home: Aintab, Turkey. Died Dec. 18, 1915.

SHEPARD, Frederick Job, librarian; b. Essex, Conn., Jan. 23, 1850; s. Dr. Frederick W. and Maria Theresa (Green) S.; A.B., Yale, 1873; m. Ellie J. Sumner, Nov. 10, 1881 (died 1929). Connected with Worcester Press, 1873-74, Indianapolis Sentinel, 1874-76, Hartford Courant, 1876, New York World, 1876-80, Buffalo Courier, 1880-97; reference librarian Buffalo Pub. Library, 1897-1925. Contbr. J. N. Larned's Literature of American History; editor reprint Thomas Budd's Good Order Established in Pennsylvania, 1902; compiler Index to Illustrations and several histories of coll. class. Home: Buffalo, N.Y. Died Jan. 12, 1934.

SHEPARD, Guy Conwell, investment counsel; b. in Mondamin, Iowa, Dec. 21, 1873; s. of Nathaniel and Ruth Elizabeth (Fouts) Shepard; descendant of Edward Shepard, who came from England to Cambridge, Mass., 1630; ed. in public and high schs., Council Bluffs, Ia.; m. Gertrude Gleason, May 9, 1900; children—Fayette Gleason, Jeanette Ruth (Mrs. Charles M. French). Started in packing business as office boy with Cudahy Packing Co., Omaha, Oct. 14, 1891, advancing through various positions; came to Chicago in 1911; v.p. Cudahy Packing Co., 1915-32. Apptd. administrator in charge of packing house products, under farm relief act, serving 1933-34. Dir. Evanston

Pub. Library; commr. First Park Dist., Evanston, Ill. Episcopalian. Home: Evanston, Ill. Died Sept. 4, 1938.

SHEPARD, Harvey Newton, lawyer; b. Boston, Mass., July 8, 1848; s. William and Eliza (Crowell) S.; A.B., Harvard, 1871; Harvard Law Sch., 1871-72; m. Fannie May Woodman, Nov. 25, 1873; children—Grace Florence, William Harold (dec.), Marion (dec.), Alice Mabel, Edith. Practiced at Boston from 1873; pres. Boston Common Council, 1880; mem. Mass. Ho. of Rep., 1881, 82; 1st asst. atty. gen. of Mass., 1883-86; mem. Mass. Civil Service Commn., 1914-19; mem. Mass. State Forest Commn., 1914-19; mem. Nat. Forestry Policy Commn. of Chamber of Commerce U.S. Democrat. Methodist. Mason. Home: Roxbury, Boston, Mass. Died Apr. 14, 1936.

SHEPARD, Helen Miller (Gould); b. New York, N.Y., June 20, 1868; d. late Jay and Helen Day (Miller) Gould; honorary L.H.M., New York U., 1902; LL.D., Am. Coll. for Girls, Turkey, 1910; m. Finley Johnson Shepard, Jan. 22, 1913; children—Olivia Margaret, Finley Jay, Helen Anna. Has been identified with philanthropic work for many yrs.; has made many notable gifts, including: library bldg. to New York U., 1895, and Hall of Fame, same university, in 1900; $100,000 to U.S. Govt. for war purposes, 1898; $10,000 Rutgers Coll., 1898; $10,000 Engring. Sch., New York U., 1898; a building to naval branch, Brooklyn Y.M.C.A., 1900; a dormitory for Northfield Seminary, and numerous other donations for educational and charitable purposes. Gave personal attention to care of sick and convalescent soldiers at Camp Wikoff, 1898, at time of Spanish-Am. War, and gave $50,000 for needed supplies. Mem. bd. Russell Sage Foundation. Mem. numerous societies. Homes: Tarrytown, N.Y., and New York, N.Y. Died Dec. 21, 1938.

SHEPARD, Irwin, secretary; b. Skaneateles, N.Y., July 5, 1843; s. Luman and Betsy J. S.; A.B., Olivet (Mich.) Coll., 1871, A.M., 1874 (hon. Ph.D., 1893; Pd.M., Mich. Normal Coll., 1912); m. Mary Bassett Elmer, Aug. 23, 1871. Served in 17th Mich. Inf., 9th Army Corps, 1862-65; discharged for wounds received in the Battle of the Wilderness, May 6, 1864; received Congressional Medal of Honor "for meritorious services at Knoxville, Tenn., Nov. 21, 1863." Supt. city schs., Charles City, Ia., 1871-75; prin. high sch., 1875-78, supt. city schs., 1878-79, Winona, Minn.; pres. State Normal Sch., Winona, 1879-98; permanent sec. N.E.A., Mar. 1, 1898-Aug. 1912; nat. sec. Bur. Conventions and Societies, Panama-Pacific Internat. Expn., July 1, 1913-Oct. 1, 1914. Home: Winona, Minn. Died Apr. 17, 1916.

SHEPARD, James Henry, chemist; b. Lyons, Mich., Apr. 14, 1850; s. Daniel Ensign and Lydia Maria (Pendell) S.; student Albion (Mich.) Coll., through sophomore yr.; B.S., U. of Mich., 1875; post-grad. study, same, 1881; m. Clara R. Durand, June 28, 1888. Supt. schs., Holly, Marquette, and Saline, Mich., 1875-80; instr. natural science, Ypsilanti (Mich.) High Sch., 1882-88; prof. chemistry, S.D. Agrl. Coll., and chemist Agrl. Expt. Sta. of S.D., 1888—. V.p. S.D. Agrl. Coll., 1890-1900; dir. Expt. Sta. of S.D., 1895-1901; chemist S.D. Pure Food Commn., 1901—. Republican. Presbyn. K.T. Author: Shepard's Elements of Chemistry, 1885; same (briefer course), 1890; Notes on Chemistry, 1886. Home: Brookings, S.D. Deceased.

SHEPARD, Luther Dimmick, dentist; b. Windham, Me.; s. John William and Elisa (Burns) S.; A.B., Amherst, 1862, A.M., 1868; D.D.S., Baltimore Coll. Dental Surgeons, 1861; (hon. D.M.D., Harvard, 1879); m. Josephine Bailey, Oct. 5, 1871. Adj. prof. operative dentistry, 1868-79, prof. operative dentistry, 1879-82, Harvard. Pres. Am. Dental Assn., 1879; pres. World's Columbian Dental Congress, Chicago, 1893; pres. N.E. Amherst Alumni Assn., 1906. Home: Boston, Mass. Died 1911.

SHEPARD, Seth, judge; b. Washington Co., Tex., Apr. 23, 1847; s. Chauncey Berkeley and Mary Hester (Andrews) S.; B.L., Washington Coll. (now Washington and Lee U.), 1868; (LL.D., Georgetown U., 1895); m. Caroline Nelson Goree, Jan. 18, 1882; 2d, Etta K. Jarvis, Mar. 25, 1890. Was pvt. Co. F, 5th Tex. mounted vols., C.S.A., July 4, 1864, to end of war. Practiced law at Brenham, Galveston, and Dallas, Tex., 1869-93; mem. Tex. Senate, 1874; asso. justice, 1893-1905, chief justice, Jan. 5, 1905—, Ct. of Appeals of D.C. Lecturer in constl. law, equity, jurisprudence, and law of corps., Sch. of Law, Georgetown U., Jan. 1895—. Regent U. of Tex., 1883-91. Fellow Texas Hist. Assn. Home: Washington, D.C. Died Dec. 3, 1917.

SHEPARD, Stuart Gore, lawyer; b. Chicago, Jan. 21, 1874; s. Hon. Henry M. and Frances (Welles) Shepard; desc. Ralph Shepard, Mass., about 1640; B.L., Hobart Coll., Geneva, N.Y., 1893, later M.L.; LL.B., Chicago-Kent Coll. of Law, 1895. Admitted to bar, Mar. 1895, and became connected with office of Shope & Mathis; asst. corp. counsel, Chicago, 1896; became mem. Browning & Shepard, 1897; dem. candidate for Judge Superior Court, 1905; partnership with Robert R. McCormick and S. E. Thomason, 1909, title of firm later Shepard, McCormick, Thomason, Kirkland & Patterson; gen. counsel for Chicago Tribune, 1910-19, afterwards with Taylor, Miller, Dickinson & Smith; now alone. Formerly officer in Chicago Div., Ill. Naval Reserve. Democrat. Episcopalian. Died Sept. 25, 1936.

SHEPARD, Walter James, educator; b. Salt Lake City, Utah, Nov. 10, 1876; s. James Rea and Josephine Amelia (Lockley) S.; A.B., Willamette U., Salem, Ore., 1900, and Harvard, 1902; grad. study Harvard, Heidelberg U. and U. of Berlin, 1903-07; m. Emma Alice Adams, June 26, 1903; children—Max Adams, Mildred Martha. Instr. polit. science, U. of Wis., 1907-09; asst. prof. polit. science, Ohio State U., 1909-11; successively asst. prof. polit. science, asso. prof., U. of Mo., 1911-21; prof. polit. science, Ohio State U., 1921-23, Washington U., 1923-24, Robert Brookings Grad. Sch. of Economics and Govt., Washington, D.C., 1924-28; dean of Coll. Arts and Sciences, Ohio State U. Mem. City Council, Columbia, Mo., 1914-16. Served as 1st lt. and capt., Ordnance Dept., U.S.A., 1917-18. Chmn. Ohio State Planning Bd. Co-author and co-translator of H. Krabbe's The Modern Idea of the State, 1922. Home: Columbus, O. Died Jan. 25, 1936.

SHEPARD, William Orville, bishop; b. Sterling, Ill., Apr. 11, 1862; s. William Harrison and Caroline L. (Reed) S.; A.B., DePauw U., Greencastle, Ind., 1885; B.D., DePauw Sch. of Theology, 1886; Ph.D., Syracuse U., 1895; D.D., DePauw, 1896; LL.D., same, 1912; m. Emily Odell, Aug. 15, 1883. Ordained M.E. ministry, 1886; pastor of chs. in Chicago and vicinity, 1886-1909; dist. supt., Chicago Northern Dist., 1909-12; bishop M.E. Ch., May 1912—. Author: Oakland Sermons, 1896. Died Nov. 30, 1931.

SHEPARDSON, Francis Wayland; b. Cheviot (now Cincinnati), O., Oct. 15, 1862; s. Daniel (D.D.) and Eliza (Smart) S.; A.B., Denison U., 1882, A.M., 1886, LL.D., 1906; A.B., Brown U., 1883; Ph.D., Yale, 1892; m. Cora Lenore Whitcomb, Sept. 3, 1884; 1 son, John Whitcomb (dec.). Teacher at Young Ladies' Inst., Granville, O., 1883-87; editor Granville Times, 1887-90; docent, 1892-93, extension asst. in history, 1893-95, instr. Am. history and sec. lecture study dept. of university extension div., 1895-97, acting recorder, 1897-98, asst. prof. Am. history, 1897-1901, sec. to pres., 1897-1904, dean of sr. colls., 1904-07, asso. prof. Am. history, 1906-17, U. of Chicago; dir. Dept. of Registration and Edn., State of Ill., and chmn. Ill. Board for Vocational Education, 1917-21; director The Julius Rosenwald Fund, 1921-26; vice chmn. Chicago Commn. on Race Relations, 1919-20; engaged in literary work, 1926—. Editorial writer Chicago Tribune, 1906-10. Lecturer to Am. teachers, in P.I., 1911, 14. Sec. Nat. Interfraternity Conf., 1909-14, chmn., 1914. Mem. Beta Theta Pi (trustee 1906-07; gen. sec. 1907-17; pres., 1918—; editor 1917-31); Phi Beta Kappa (senator United Chapters, 1913—; v.p. 1919-28). Trustee Denison U. Republican. Baptist. Mason. Author: The Beta Book, 1927, revised edit., 1930, 35; Beta Lore, 1928; Beta Life, 1929; Denison University, 1831-1931, A Centennial History, 1931. Editor 11th, 12th and 13th edits. Baird's Manual American College Fraternities, 1927, 29, 35. Home: Granville, O. Died Aug. 9, 1937.

SHEPARDSON, George Defrees, engineer; b. Cheviot, O., Nov. 20, 1864; s. Daniel (D.D.) and Eliza (Smart) S.; A.B., Denison Univ., 1885, A.M., 1888; M.E., Cornell U., 1899; D.Sc., Harvard, 1912; m. Harriet B. King, 1892; 1 dau., Mary King. Prof. elec. engring., U. of Minn., 1891—. Mem. jury of awards, Buffalo Expn., 1901, St. Louis Expn., 1904. Author: Electrical Catechism, 1901, 1908; Electric Train Lighting, 1901; Theory of Telephone Apparatus, 1917; Elements of Electrical Engineering, 1924; An Engineer's Religion, 1926. Home: Minneapolis, Minn. Died May 26, 1926.

SHEPERD, James Edward, lawyer; b. Mintonsville, Va., July 21, 1847; s. Thomas and Ann Eliza (Browne) S.; grad. High Sch., and law dept. Univ. of N.C., 1867 (LL.D.); m. Elizabeth Brown, Feb. 1, 1871. Elected judge Superior Court N.C., 1881; asso. justice Supreme Court N.C., 1886, chief justice same, 1890; at end of term resumed practice. Prof. law, Summer Law Sch., Univ. of N.C., 8 yrs. Democrat. Home: Raleigh, N.C. Died 1910.

SHEPHERD, Alexander R.; b. Washington, Jan. 30, 1835; his father's death led him to engage in business while a boy, and he was successful; enlisted, 1861, in Washington vols.; elected pres. city council, 1861; was a strong advocate of public improvements; became chmn. of Citizen's Reform Assn. which secured legislation establishing Territorial govt. in D.C.; was apptd. gov. of D.C. by President Grant; he planned and carried out large public improvements and charges of corruption were made against him, which an investigation failed to sustain. Congress changed the dist. govt. to one by 3 commrs.; President Grant nominated him as a commr., but Senate refused confirmation. Later as v.p. and gen. mgr. of a co. he developed at Batopilas, Mexico, a large silver mine. Address unknown. Died 1902.

SHEPHERD, Clifford John, banker; b. Arcanum, O., Apr. 14, 1879; s. Fremont and Minerva (Fleck) S.; ed. high sch., Arcanum; m. Rolena Bennett, Nov. 27, 1903; children—Elizabeth Edna, Lucy Bennett. Began in banking business, Indianapolis, Ind., 1901; with First Nat. Bank, Richmond, Calif., 1912-14; dir. Los Angeles Br. Federal Reserve Bank of San Francisco, 1914-25; pres. Peoples Nat. Bank, Los Angeles, 1925-28; mem. Ramboz & Shepherd, financial adminstrs., 1928-37; dir. and mem. of exec. com. J. W. Robinson Co. Republican. Methodist. Mason. Home: Glendale, Calif. Died Sept. 17, 1939.

SHEPHERD, Henry Elliot, author; b. Fayetteville, N.C., Jan. 17, 1844; s. Jesse George and Catharine Isabella (Dobbin) S.; Davidson Coll., N.C.; U. of Va., 1860-61; M.A., Lafayette Coll., Pa., 1875; LL.D., Davidson, 1883, U. of N.C., 1883; m. Kate MacGregor Pinkerton Goodridge, June 25, 1867 (died 1920). Entered Confederate Army at 17; severely wounded at Gettysburg, July 3, 1863. Prof. English and history, Baltimore City Coll., 1868-75; supt. of instruction, Baltimore, 1875-82; pres. Coll. of Charleston, S.C., 1882-97. Democrat. Presbyn. Author: History of the English Language, 1874; Study of Edgar Allan Poe, Poe Memorial Vol., 1877; Grammar of the English Language, 1881; Historical Reader, 1881; Life of Robert E. Lee, 1906; Commentary on Tennyson's "In Memoriam," 1908; Representative Maryland Authors, 1911. Editor: Nelson's History of Baltimore, 1899; Narrative of Prison Life at Baltimore and Johnson's Island, Ohio, 1917. Home: Baltimore, Md. Died May 29, 1929.

SHEPHERD, Theodosia Burr, seed grower, florist, originator of new flowers; b. Keosauqua, Ia., Oct. 14, 1845; d. Augustus Hall (congressman from Iowa and later chief justice Neb.) and Ellen P. Lee Hall; ed. in Iowa and, 1857-59, at Mrs. Bryan's Sem., Batavia, N.Y.; m. William Edgar Shepherd, lawyer, Sept. 4, 1867. Went to Calif., 1873, on account of ill-health; engaged in growing seeds in a small way in 1885; commenced spl. work of hybridizing and creating new varieties of plants some yrs. later; has sent out many novelties of own creation, in begonias, nasturtiums, poppies, calleopsis, cosmos, etc.; was first one to grow flower seeds for Eastern trade in Calif.; is called "Pioneer flower seed grower of California," now pres. Theodosia B. Shepherd Co. Writer and lecturer on floriculture. Home: Ventura, Calif. Died 1906.

SHEPHERD, William Gunn, newspaper and magazine writer; b. Springfield, O., June 13, 1878; s. Harrison T. and Sarah (Leming) S.; ed. high sch., St. Paul, Minn., and summer schs. U. of Minn.; m. Elizabeth Striebinger, Dec. 12, 1917; children—William Gunn, Robert Suclare. Began as reporter, St. Paul Dispatch, 1898; went to New York, 1908; wrote fiction for Munsey's Mag.; in Mexico, Madero revolution, entering Mexico City with Madero; became European corr. Newspaper Enterprise Assn., 1912, covering Olympic Games at Stockholm, polit. and other news in capitals of Europe; returned to Mexico for United Press and there at time of Huerta's downfall; with U.S. Army at Vera Cruz; in Europe intermittently, 1914-21, in every capital or with every army, both sides, except Turks, Bulgars and Rumanians, writing articles for Everybody's, Collier's, Harper's, Metropolitan, etc.; in Russian revolution, as corr. United Press Assn. of America, Exchange Telegraph of London, England, and Everybody's Mag.; attended Paris Peace Conf. and signing of treaty at Versailles for Everybody's Mag. and New York Evening Post; investigated and wrote on reconstruction problems in Germany, France and England, 1921; covered Rep. and Dem. nat. convs. for newspaper syndicate, 1920, 24; staff corr. Collier's Weekly, 1924—, investigating prohibition enforcement, state penitentiary systems, law violations, organized crime, also commercial and financial situations and methods. Author: The Confessions of a War Correspondent, 1917; The Scar That Tripled, 1918; Boy's Own Book of Politics, 1923; Great Preachers as Seen by a Journalist, 1925. Home: Locust, N.J. Died Nov. 4, 1933.

SHEPHERD, William R., historian; b. Charleston, S.C., June 12, 1871; s. William and Leonora Adaline (Brown) S.; A.B., Columbia, 1893, A.M., 1894, Ph.D., 1896, Litt.D., from same university, 1929; L.H.D., Chile, 1910; LL.D., U. of S.C., 1930; studied U. of Berlin; Hon.D., Madrid, 1934. Seth Low prof. history, Columbia, 1926—; visiting Carnegie prof., U. of Vienna, 1932; lectured at univs. in Spain, Gt. Britain and Germany; rep. of U.S. Govt. on missions in Hispanic America; Round Table leader Williamstown (Mass.) Inst. of Politics, 1927. Mem. various Am. and fgn. hist. societies. Awarded Comendador con Placa Real Orden de Isabel la Católica; Grosses Goldenes Ehrenzeichen für Verdienste um die Republik Oesterreich. Author: Historical Atlas; Atlas of Medieval and Modern History; History of Proprietary Government in Pennsylvania, 1896; Guide to Materials for the History of the United States in Spanish Archives, 1907; Latin America, 1914; The Hispanic Nations of the New World; The Story of New Amsterdam, 1926. Died June 7, 1934.

SHEPLEY, George Foster, architect; b. St. Louis, Mo., Nov. 7, 1860; attended Washington Univ.; grad.

Mass. Inst. Tech., 1882; m. Julia Hayden Richardson, d. late H. H. Richardson, architect, June 1886. Is of Shepley, Rutan & Coolidge, successors to business of the late H. H. Richardson. Among bldgs. they have designed are: Ames Bldg., Chamber of Commerce, Southern Terminal Sta., New Congregational House, Mercantile Bldgs., Boston; New Public Library, Art Inst., Chicago; Leland Stanford, Jr., Univ., Calif.; new Union Sta., Albany, N.Y.; etc. Home: Brookline, Mass. Died 1903.

SHEPLEY, George Leander, insurance; b. Dover, N.H., Oct. 11, 1854; s. John and Sarah Elizabeth (Huntress) S.; ed. high sch.; (hon. A.M., Brown U., 1921); m. Carolyn Lisbeth Peck, Sept. 15, 1880 (died 1912). Now pres. Starkweather & Shepley, ins., estab. 1871; also pres. Shepley Land Co., R.I. Ins. Co.; 2d v.p. Am. Woolen Co., Mass. Colonel on staff of Gov. Dyer, 1898-1900; lt. gov. of R.I., 1903. Dep. gov. gen. Soc. Colonial Wars. Republican. Universalist. Mason; Past Grand Comdr. Grand Commandery K.T., Mass. and R.I. Owner of rare collection N.E. Americana. Home: Providence, R.I. Deceased.

SHEPPARD, James J., educator; b. Panola, Ill., Jan. 1, 1868; s. David and Nancy (Hayes) S.; A.B., Harvard, 1894; Columbia, 1897-1900, New York U., 1900-02; m. Rena French Masters, July 12, 1905. Teacher in Minn., Ia. and Ill., 1884-86; prin. high sch., Decatur, Ill., 1894-97; head history dept., DeWitt Clinton High Sch., New York, 1897-1902; acting prin. Annex, DeWitt Clinton High Sch., 1900-02; prin. from 1902, and organized new High Sch. of Commerce, New York (1st instn. of kind in U.S.). Pres. high sch. sect. Ill. State Teachers' Assn., 1897; pres. N.Y. City High Sch. Teachers' Assn., 1902-04; mem. bd. dirs. New York City Teachers' Assn., 1900—; pres. Interborough Council, New York, 1904—; pres. New York City High Sch. Principals' Assn., 1908-09; chmn. Com. on Instrn. in Municipal Govt. in Am. Ednl. Instns., Elementary and Secondary Sch. Sect. of Nat. Municipal League; chmn. Com. on Commercial Exams., N.Y. State Exam. Bd., 1906-08. Editor: Appleton's Series of Texts for Commercial Schools. Home: New York, N.Y. Died Mar. 13, 1914.

SHEPPARD, John Calhoun, governor; b. Edgefield County, S.C., July 5, 1850; s. James and Sarah Louise (Mobley) S.; ed. Furman U., Greenville, S.C., LL.D., 1925; m. Helen Wallace, May 22, 1879; children—William Wallace, Helen Wallace (Mrs. B. E. Nicholson), Henrietta (Mrs. D. D. McColl), Sarah Maxwell (Mrs. B. L. Mims), John Calhoun (dec.), James Orlando, George Lamb Buist (dec.), Francis Wilkerson Pickens. Admitted to S.C. bar, 1871; practiced as mem. firm of Youmans & Sheppard, 1871-75, since with bro. as Sheppard Bros.; pres. Bank of Edgefield, 1890—. Mem. S.C. Ho. of Rep., 3 terms, 1876-1882 (speaker 1877-1882); elected lt. governor, 1882, reëlected, 1884, serving as gov., 1886, completing term of Gov. H. S. Thompson, resigned; mem. State Senate 2 terms, 1898-1902; mem. State Constl. Conv., 1895. Democrat. Baptist. Chairman bd. trustees Edgefield Male Acad., 1891—. Supreme Dictator Knights of Honor, 2 terms, 1906-10. Elected to State Senate for an unexpired term, 1919. Home: Edgefield, S.C. Died Oct. 17, 1931.

SHEPPARD, John Levi, congressman; b. Apr. 13, 1854, Chambers Co., Ala.; s. John Levi and Amanda (Morris) S.; removed with mother to Morris Co., Tex., about 1859; attended country schools; m. Alice Eddins, Sept. 1873. Began practice of law, 1879; dist. atty. 5th jud. dist., 1882-88 (twice reelected); judge same dist., 1888-96, retiring; temporary chmn. State Dem. Conv., 1892; del. to Bimetallic Conv., Chicago, 1893; Dem. Nat. Conv., 1896, chosen mem. Presidential Notification Com.; mem. Congress from 4th Tex. Dist., 1899-1903. Home: Texarkana, Tex. Died 1902.

SHEPPARD, Lucius Elmer, labor official; b. Bridgeton, N.J., Feb. 10, 1863; s. Ephraim E. and Cinderilla (Bonham) S.; ed. dist. schs.; m. Annie J. Crane, Oct. 19, 1885. Entered service Pa. R.R., 1881, conductor, 1883; pres. Order Ry. Conductors, 1919-28, asst. pres., 1928—. Mem. Govt. Arbitration Bd. between Eastern rys. and conductors and trainmen, 1913; mem. Pres. Wilson's 1st Industrial Conf., 1917; mem. Ry. Adjustment Board, Jan.-July 1918. Chmn. federal commn. to investigate unskilled labor conditions in H.T., 1922. Episcopalian. Mason, Odd Fellow, Elk. Home: Cedar Rapids, Ia. Died Sept. 26, 1934.

SHEPPARD, Walter Wade, lawyer; b. Liberty Co., Ga., Aug. 31, 1856; s. David B. M. and Marion C. (Frazier) S.; A.B., U. of Ga., 1889, B.L., 1893; M.L., Georgetown U., 1894; m. Hattie Tillman Clements, June 21, 1911; children—Harriet Clements, Martha Virginia, Marion Elizabeth. Admitted to Ga. bar, 1893; in practice at Savannah, Ga., 1896-1911; sec. to Congressman Lester, 1893-1902; judge Superior Court, Atlantic Circuit of Ga., 1911-27; U.S. dist. atty., Southern Dist. of Ga., Sept. 15, 1932-Mar. 4, 1933; senator 2d Dist. of Ga., 1894-96. Mem. bd. of selectmen Midway Soc. (historical). Presbyn. Mason, Junior Order United Mechanics of America. Home: Savannah, Ga. Died June 27, 1935.

SHEPPARD, Warren, marine artist; b. Greenwich, N.J., Apr. 10, 1858; s. Josiah and Mary (Harding) S.; ed. Central High Sch., Phila.; pupil of M.F.H. de Haas; m. Annabella McIntyre, 1879 (died 1889); 1 son—J. Warren. Works on permanent exhbn.: "Restless Sea," Buffalo Mus., shown at World's Fair, Chicago, 1893; "Restless Ocean," Toledo Mus., shown at St. Louis Exposition, 1904; clipper ship "Flying Cloud," India House, New York; "South Street (New York) in the Eighties," Phillips Acad., Andover, Mass.; also paintings on exhibition in Albright Gallery (Buffalo), Pub. Library (Springfield, Mass.), Addison Gallery (Phillips Acad., Andover, Mass.), etc. Awarded gold medal, Industrial and Mining Expn., Denver, 1884; hon. mention, Chicago Expn., 1934. Author: Practical Navigation (adopted by U.S. Navy); A Tale of the Sea. Home: Brooklyn, N.Y. Died Feb. 21, 1937.

SHEPPARD, William Bostwick, judge; b. Bristol, Fla., Oct. 4, 1860; s. Joseph and Cynthia (McAliley) S.; studied U. of N.C., 1881-82; m. Mary Emily Gibson, May 10, 1890. Admitted to bar, 1891, and practiced at Apalachicola, Fla., 1891-1903; candidate for state senator, 1888, for atty. gen., 1896; collector of customs at Apalachicola, 1889-94, 1897-1901; mayor of Apalachicola, 1894; U.S. dist. atty., Northern Dist. of Fla., 1903-07; U.S. dist. judge, Northern Dist. of Fla., Sept. 5, 1907—. Republican. Unitarian. Home: Pensacola, Fla. Died Apr. 21, 1934.

SHEPPERD, John Henry, coll. pres.; b. Chariton, Ia., Jan. 12, 1869; s. John Wesley and Clerenda Jane (Sanderson) S.; B.Agr., Iowa State Coll., 1891, D.Agr., 1928; student U. of Minn. ½ yr., 1890-91; M.S.A., U. of Wisconsin, 1893; m. Adele Taylor, July 3, 1895. Prof. agriculture, N.D. Agrl. Coll., 1893-1904, dean of agr. and vice dir. experiment station, 1904-14, chmn. animal husbandry dept., 1914-29, acting president, 1929-30, pres., 1930-37 (pres. emeritus). Dir. N.D. Grimm Alfalfa Seed Assn., Fargo Bldg. & Loan Assn. Formulator of rules and system for conducting live stock judging contests. Co-author: (with J. C. McDowell) Elements of Agriculture, 1905. On editorial staff Orange Judd Farmer, 1893. Home: North Fargo, N.D. Died Jan. 22, 1939.

SHERIDAN, Michael Vincent, brig. gen. U.S.A.; b. Somerset, O., May 24, 1840; s. John and Mary (Miner) S.; youngest brother of late Gen. Philip H. S.; ed. St. Joseph's Coll., Somerset. Served as vol. aide to Gen. P. H. S., at battles of Perryville, Ky., and Stone River, Tenn., Oct. 1862-Jan. 1863; apptd. 1st lt. 2d Mo. Inf., Sept. 7, 1863; capt. a.d.c., May 18, 1864; hon. mustered out of vol. service, Aug. 1, 1866; apptd. 2d lt. 5th U.S. Cav., Feb. 23, 1866; capt. 7th Cav., July 28, 1866; maj. a.a.g., June 7, 1883; lt. col., July 9, 1892; col., Jan. 25, 1897; brig. gen. vols., May 27, 1898; hon. disch. from vols., May 12, 1899; brig. gen. U.S.A., Apr. 15, 1902; retired at own request, over 30 yrs.' service, Apr. 16, 1902. Bvtd.: maj. vols., Mar. 13, 1865, "for gallant and meritorious services"; maj., Mar. 2, 1867, for battle of Opequan, Va.; lt. col., Mar. 2, 1867, for battle of Fisher's Hill, Va. Participated in battles of Chickamauga, Missionary Ridge, in Grant's campaign around Richmond, in Shenandoah, Appomattox campaigns, etc. Lt. col. a.d.c. to Lt. Gen. Sheridan, 1870-78, and his mil sec., 1878-88; adj. gen. Dept. of the Platte, 1889-93; a.a.g. Dept. of the Mo., 1897-98; adj. gen. vols. at Camp Thomas, Ga., Apr.-July 1898; chief of staff to Gen. Brooke in P.R. expdn., July-Dec. 1898, and in charge civil affairs, Aug.-Dec. 1898; comd. Dept. of the Lakes, 1898-99, adj. gen. same, 1899-1900, Dept. of the East, 1900-02. Died Feb. 21, 1918.

SHERIDAN, Wilbur Fletcher, clergyman; b. Rossville, Ind., Dec. 5, 1863; s. Rev. Andrew Jackson and Mary Anne (Merrill) S.; A.B., De Pauw U., 1885, A.M., 1888; S.T.B., Boston U., 1891; (D.D., DePauw, 1904); m. Effie L. Lamar, June 21, 1893. Pastor Indianapolis, 1885-89; ordained M.E. ministry, 1887; pastor Washington, Ind., 1891-93, Detroit, 1893-96, Pontiac, Mich., 1896-1900, Saginaw, Mich., 1900-01, Trinity Ch., Louisville, Ky., 1901-04, Mt. Vernon Pl. Ch., Baltimore, 1904-09, Howard Memorial Ch., Kansas City, Mo., 1909-12; gen. sec. Epworth League of M.E. Ch., 1912—. Del. Gen. Conf., 1900, 12, 16. Author: Talks to Probationers, 1900; The Sunday Night Service, 1903; Life of Bishop Isaac Wilson Joyce, 1907; The Experimental Note. Home: Evanston, Ill. Died Mar. 10, 1920.

SHERLEY, Swagar, lawyer; b. Louisville, Ky., Nov. 28, 1871; s. Thomas H. and Ella (Swagar) S.; A.B., Louisville Male High Sch., 1889; B.L., U. of Va., 1891; m. Mignon Critten, Apr. 21, 1906. Admitted to bar, 1891. Mem. 58th to 65th Congresses (1903-19), 5th Ky. Dist.; dir. div. of finance U.S. R.R. Administration, Mar. 1919-Sept. 1920. Mem. Sherley, Faust & Wilson. Democrat. Home: Washington, D.C. Died Feb. 13, 1941.

SHERLOCK, Chesla C., writer, editor; b. Keswick, Ia., May 24, 1895; s. Wallace E. and Melva May (Long) S.; grad. West Des Moines High Sch., 1913; LL.B., Drake U., 1916; m. Lucile Peck, May 26, 1917 (divorced 1935); children—Marilee Altha (Mrs. Carey P. Williams, Jr.), Ellen Lorraine, Susan, Judith; m. 2d, Kathleen Mullen, Aug. 7, 1935. Began writing for magazines and newspapers, 1912; supplied articles for more than 175 publications; co-editor Iowa Homestead, agricultural mag., 1921-22; editor Better Homes and Gardens, 1922-27; asso. editor The Ladies' Home Journal, 1927-29, mng. editor, 1929-33; purchased half-interest in Marshalltown (Ia.) News, 1933, and became sole owner, Jan. 1934. Founded The Scratch Pad (nat. monthly of militant Americanism), July 1933. In campaign of 1934 delivered 62 speeches in Iowa, opposing New Deal; editor St. Nicholas Mag., 1935-37. Practiced law in Des Moines, 1916-17. Secretary Iowa Industrial Commn., Apr.-Dec., 1917. Served as aviation cadet, Signal R.C., U.S.A., 1917-18. Received Distinguished Service Award from Am. Assn. of Nurserymen, 1931. Mason. Republican. Presbyterian. Author: Principles of Highway Law, 1915; Vest Pocket Lawyer, 1919; Know Your Compensation Liability (pub. serially), 1920-21; Modern Farm Coöperative Movement, 1922; Modern Farmyard Buildings, 1922; Bulb Gardening, 1922; Successful Rose Culture, 1924; Homes of Famous Americans (2 vols.), 1926; Tall Timbers, a Series of American Biographical Contrasts, 1926; City and Suburban Gardening, 1928; The World's Debt to the United States, 1929; The Gardener's How Book, 1935; The Utility Gardener's How Book, 1936; Fingertip Facts About Gardening, 1937; Farewell to Worry, 1937; and seven other books. Died June 30, 1938.

SHERMAN, Andrew Magoun, clergyman; b. Marshfield, Mass., May 5, 1844; s. Aaron Simmons and Lydia (Whitney) S.; ed. Birmingham (Conn.) pub. scvh.; pvt. instrn. and study; m. Arrabella Malvern Woodruff, Jan. 24, 1864. Served pvt. U.S.V., 1862-65. Entered M.E. ministry, 1869; pastor M.E. chs. in Conn. and Mass., 1869-77; ordained to Congregational ministry, 1878; pastor Congregational churches in N.Y., Mass. and N.J., 1878-90. Editor The Welcome Guest (monthly), 1889-92. Member Am. Irish Hist. Society, I.O.O.F., 1868—, G.A.R.; a.-d.-c. on staff of national comdr. G.A.R., 1908-09. Author: Historic Morris County (N.J.) Buildings, 1913; The Story of Fort Nonsense, Morristown, N.J., 1914; Revolutionary Camping Grounds of the Connecticut Brigades in Morris County, N.J., the Winter of 1779-80, 1914; The Meeting of Anthony Wayne's Pennsylvania Troops in Morris County, N.J., January 1, 1781, 1914; Recollections of a Half Century and More, 1915. Home: Morristown, N.J. Died Dec. 28, 1921.

SHERMAN, Buren Robinson, lawyer; b. Phelps, N.Y., May 28, 1836; grad. Elmira, N.Y., 1853 (LL.D., Univ. of State of Iowa, 1883). Removed to Iowa, April 1855; admitted to bar, April 1859, locating at Vinton, Benton Co. Entered Union army, July 1861, as 2d lt. Co. E, 13th Iowa vol. inf.; severely wounded at Shiloh, April 6, 1862; promoted capt., April 11, 1862; resigned on account of wounds received in battle, April 11, 1863. Auditor of State, Iowa, 1875-81; gov. Iowa, 1882-86. Republican. Home: Vinton, Ia. Died 1904.

SHERMAN, Charles Colebrook, editor; b. Syracuse, N.Y., Dec. 18, 1860; s. Charles Wager and Mary Harriet (Colebrook) S.; A.B., Yale, 1883; Yale Div. Sch., 1886-88, U. of Chicago, 1895-96, 1899-1900, U. of Berlin, 1897-98; m. Mary Louise Colebrook, Nov. 11, 1908. Taught in Hopkins Grammar Sch., New Haven, Conn., 1883-84, Syracuse, N.Y., 1884-86, 1890-94; on staff Syracuse Journal, 1889-90; editor dept. of religion, New Internat. Ency., 1902-03; mng. editor New Schaff-Herzog Religious Ency., 1903-07. Home: New Rochelle, N.Y. Died May 9, 1927.

SHERMAN, Christopher Elias, civil engr.; b. Columbus, O., Dec. 28, 1869; s. Sylvester Morrill and Lemyra Ann (Shoemaker) S.; grad. Columbus (O.) Central High Sch., 1887; 4 yrs. in civ. engring. (3 years in the field), Ohio State Univ., C.E., 1894; m. Elonora Bruning, June 22, 1897. In college and in gen. engring. work, 1888-94, chief draftsman, Ohio Geol. Survey, 1892; chief draftsman U.S. Barge Canal Survey, in Ohio, 1895-96; asst. prof. and prof. civ. engring., Ohio State U., from Sept. 1896, 1st U.S. asst. engr. 4th Army Corps, 1898; U.S. asst. engr. in Yellowstone Park, summers, 1899, 1900; rep. of govs. of Ohio in State Topographic Survey, 1902-36; also consulting work for State of Ohio; Ohio-Michigan boundary commr., 1915. Chief engineer Scioto-Sandusky Conservancy, 1935, pres. bd. dirs., 1937. Republican. Conglist. Author: Theory and Practice of Lettering, 1895; Preliminary Report on Topographic Survey of Ohio, 1904; A Commemorative Bulletin, 1910; Progress Report on Ohio Topographic Survey, 1910; The Ohio Water Problem, 1915; Final Report, Ohio Topographic Survey, Vols. 1 to 4, 1916 to 1933; Ohio Stream Flow, 1932; Land of Kingdom Come, 1936. Died May 6, 1940.

SHERMAN, Edward Augustine, forester, lawyer; b. Humboldt Co., Ia., Mar. 5, 1871; s. Edward and Sarah (White) S.; B.S., Ia. State Coll. of Agr. and

Mechanic Arts; also M.S. and Sc.D. from same institution; m. Eleanor Elizabeth Owen, June 14, 1905. Formerly in newspaper business in Ia., and Hamilton, Mont.; apptd. supervisor Bitter Root Forest Reserve, 1903; trans. to forest service, Dept. of Agr., 1905; supervisor Hell Gate, Lolo, Big Hole reserves, 1907, and apptd. chief insp. Dist. 1 same yr.; forest supervisor Sequoia Nat. Forest, Calif., 1908-10; dist. forester, Ogden, Utah, 1910-15; asst. forester in charge of lands, Washington, D.C., 1915-20; asso. chief forester, 1920-35, asst. chief and adviser, 1935—. Admitted to Utah bar, 1915. Formulated land classification system for nat. forests. Mem. 52d Iowa Vol. Inf., Spanish-Am. War. Home: Washington, D.C. Died Mar. 28, 1940.

SHERMAN, Elijah Bernis, master chancery U.S. Circuit Court, 1879—; b. Fairfield, Vt., June 18, 1832; s. Elias Huntington and Clarissa (Wilmarth) S.; grad. Middlebury Coll., 1860 (A.M.; LL.B., Univ. Chicago, 1864; LL.D., Middlebury, 1885). Prin. Brandon Sem., 1861-62; lt. 9th Vt. inf., 1862-63; m. Hattie G. Lovering, 1866. Admitted to bar, Chicago, 1864; mem. Ill. legislature, 1876-80; lt. col. and judge advocate, 1st brigade, Ill. Nat. Guard, 1877-84; atty. for auditor of public accounts of Ill., 1877-89; chief supervisor elections, Northern dist. Ill., 1884-95; trustee Middlebury Coll., 1892—; grand master of Ill., I.O.O.F., 1874; Mason. Home: Chicago, Ill. Died 1910.

SHERMAN, Frank Asbury, college prof.; b. Knox, Me., Oct. 4, 1841; s. Harvey Hatch and Eliza Dudley (Doty) S.; B.S., Dartmouth, 1870, M.S., 1873; m. Lucy R. Hurlbutt, Jan. 18, 1872. Served in Civil War as corporal in 4th and 19th Me. regts., 1862-65; wounded several times and lost left arm at Battle of Wilderness, May 1864; instr. mathematics, Worcester Poly. Inst., 1870-71; prof. mathematics, Dartmouth, 1871-1911 (emeritus). Home: Hanover, N.H. Died Feb. 26, 1915.

SHERMAN, Frank Dempster, university prof.; b. Peekskill, N.Y., May 6, 1860; s. John Dempster and Lucy (McFarland) S.; Ph.B., Columbia, 1884; m. Juliet Mersereau Durand, Nov. 16, 1887. Asst. in architecture, 1887-88, instr., 1888-91, adj. prof., 1891-1904, prof. graphics, 1904—, Columbia. Author: Madrigals and Catches, 1887; Lyrics for a Lute, 1890; Little-Folk Lyrics, 1892; Lyrics of Joy, 1904; A Southern Flight (with Clinton Scollard), 1906. Home: New York, N.Y. Died Sept. 19, 1916.

SHERMAN, Gordon Edward, lawyer, educator; b. Morristown, N.J., Aug. 11, 1854; s. Byron and Julia Antoinette (Burnham) S.; prep. edn. in Switzerland; Ph.B., Sheffield Scientific Sch. (Yale), 1876 (class poet); LL.B., Washington U., 1878; m. Harriet Emmons Shelton, June 12, 1894. Asst. prof. comparative and internat. law, Yale, 1911-16 (resigned). Del. from Conn. Internat. Prison Congress, Washington, D.C., 1910; Yale del. to Conf. of Teachers of Internat. Law, Washington, 1914, and to 2d Pan Am. Scientific Congress, Washington, 1915, delivering address on "Evolution of Public Law." Republican. Presbyn. One of revisers of English transl. Swiss Civil Code, 1915. Editor of Elements of International Law (by George B. Davis), 4th edit., 1916; editor for Switzerland in Comparative Law Bureau of Am. Bar Assn. Home: Morristown, N.J. Died Nov. 28, 1925.

SHERMAN, Harry Mitchell, surgeon; b. Providence, R.I., Nov. 23, 1854; s. Richard Mitchell and Sally Smith (Mauran) S.; A.B., Trinity Coll., 1877, A.M., 1880; M.D., Coll. Phys. and Surg. (Columbia), 1880; m. Matilda A. Barreda, Apr. 8, 1890 (died 1895); m. 2d, Lucia Hamilton Kittle, July 7, 1900. Mem. house staff Bellevue Hosp., New York, 1880-81; asst. surgeon West Point Foundry, Cold Spring, N.Y., 1881-84; orthopedic surgeon Children's Hosp., San Francisco, 1886—; clin. prof. orthopedic surgery, 1896-99, prof. principles and practice of surgery, 1899-1912, U. of Calif.; surgeon to St. Luke's Hosp., 1901—, to Univ. of Calif. Hospital, 1907-12. Fellow Am. Surg. Assn., A.M.A. Maj., M.C. U.S.A., Apr. 1917-Dec. 1918; chief of surg. service, Ft. Rosecrans, Calif., July-Dec. 1918. Home: San Francisco, Calif. Died May 15, 1921.

SHERMAN, Hoyt, banker; b. Lancaster, O., Nov. 1, 1827; s. Charles R. and Mary (Hoyt) S., brother Gen. W. T. and Senator John Sherman; grad. Howes Acad., Lancaster, O., 1842; studied law, 1848-50, admitted to practice by Ia. Supreme Court, 1850; m. Sarah Moulton, Dec. 25, 1855. In early life learned printer's trade; followed it until 1847 in office of Cincinnati Gazette; postmaster Des Moines, 1849-53; clerk of court 2 terms; maj. and paymaster, 1861-64. Aided in establishing a leading life ins. co. for many yrs.; mem. 11th gen. assembly Iowa, 1865-66. Author of statute regulating life ins. cos., and pres. Equitable Life of Iowa, 1874-88. Republican. Comdr. Iowa Commandery Loyal Legion, U.S.A., 1889-91. Home: Des Moines, Ia. Died 1904.

SHERMAN, James Schoolcraft, Vice-President of the United States; b. Utica, N.Y., Oct. 24, 1855; s. Gen. Richard U. and Mary Frances (Sherman) S.; ed. pub. schs., New Hartford, N.Y., Utica Acad., and grad. Whitestown (N.Y.) Sem., 1874; A.B., Hamilton Coll., 1878, LL.B., 1880 (LL.D., 1903); m. Carrie Babcock, Jan. 26, 1881. Admitted to bar, 1880, and entered practice at Utica; pres. Utica Trust & Deposit Co. Mayor of Utica, 1884-85; mem. 50th and 51st Congresses (1887-91), 23d N.Y. Dist., and 53d to 60th Congresses (1893-1909), 25th and later 27th Dist.; chmn. Rep. State convs., 1895, 1900, 1908; chmn. Rep. Nat. Congressional Com., 1906; elected Vice-President of the U.S., Nov. 3, 1908, for term 1909-13. Trustee Hamilton Coll., 1905—. Mem. Elks, Royal Arcanum. Mem. Dutch Ref. Ch. Home: Utica, N.Y. Died Oct. 30, 1912.

SHERMAN, John, sec. of state of U.S.; b. Lancaster, O., May 10, 1823; ed. Howe's Acad. there; admitted to bar, May 11, 1844; m. Cecilia, dau. Judge Stewart, Mansfield, O., Aug. 30, 1848. Delegate to Nat. Whig convs., 1848, 1852; pres. of the first Rep. conv. in Ohio, 1855. Mem. Congress, 1855-61; U.S. senator, 1861-77, 1881-97; Sec. of the Treasury, U.S., 1877-81; sec. of state, 1897-98. Republican. Long a Republican leader, especially on financial questions. Author of specie resumption plan of the Sherman act, 1879, and other laws. Author: Recollections of Forty Years in the House, Senate and Cabinet; Selected Speeches and Reports on Taxation; etc. Home: Mansfield, O., and Washington, D.C. Died 1900.

SHERMAN, John Dickinson, editor; b. Chicago, Aug. 30, 1859; s. Penoyer L. and Louise (Dickinson) S.; A.B., Hamilton Coll., 1881; m. Mary Belle King, 1887; 1 son, John King. Began newspaper work, as Hyde Park corr. Chicago Tribune, 1882, city editor same, 1889-96, Sunday editor, 1896; on editorial staff Chicago Record Herald, 1897; city editor Inter Ocean, 1898-1902, lit. editor, 1902-06; asso. editor Inter Ocean and editor Weekly Inter Ocean and Farmer, 1906-14, when Inter Ocean and Record Herald merged as Chicago Herald; became editor Western Newspaper Union. Republican. Episcopalian. Home: Estes Park, Colo. Died Mar. 19, 1926.

SHERMAN, John Francis, corp. executive; b. Feb. 25, 1888; s. Louis and Nettie (Greenspoon) S.; ed. pub. schs.; m. Sarah Alman, Aug. 1908; children—John Francis, Robert Alman, Phyllis Emily. Organizer, predecessor of The Sherman Corp., management and business engrs., 1910 (pres.); dir. Bankers' Securities Corp., Bankers' Bond & Mortgage Co., Industrial Rayon Corp., McLellan Stores Co., Ritz-Carlton Hotel Co., Consol. Chain Stores Co., Green Hamilton Co., Leavitt Stores Co., Utilities Hydro & Rail Shares Corp. Home: New York, N.Y. Died Mar. 18, 1934.

SHERMAN, Lawrence Y., senator; b. Miami Co., Ohio, Nov. 8, 1858; s. Nelson and Maria (Yates) S.; removed with parents to Ill., 1859; ed. common schs., and Lees Academy, Coles County, Ill.; LL.B., McKendree College, Ill., 1882; m. Ella M. Crews, 1891 (died 1893); m. 2d, Estelle Spitler, Mar. 4, 1908 (died 1910); 1 dau., Virginia. Practiced law at Macomb, Ill., Springfield, Ill., and Daytona Beach, Fla., 1882-1929; one of organizers First Atlantic National Bank of Daytona Beach, 1924, pres., 1925, chmn. of bd., 1925-27; merged with Atlantic National Bank of Jacksonville, 1930, of which was director until retirement, 1933. County judge McDonough Co., Ill., 1886-90; mem. Ill. House of Rep., 1897-1905, speaker of House, 1899-1901, 1901-03; lt. gov. of Ill., 1905-09; apptd. mem. Spanish Treaty Claims Commission, 1907, but declined; pres. Bd. of Administration of State of Ill., having control of 17 state charities, 1909-13; elected U.S. senator, Mar. 26, 1913, to fill unexpired term (1913-15) of William Lorimer; reëlected for term 1915-21; $1.00 year man under Hon. Charles G. Dawes, dir. of the budget, in installation of that system. Mem. Rep. Nat. Com., 1916-24. Republican. Mason. Home: Daytona Beach, Fla. Died Sept. 15, 1939.

SHERMAN, Lucius Adelno, university dean; b. Douglas, Mass., Aug. 28, 1847; s. Asahel and Eunice (Walker) S.; A.B., Yale U., 1871, Ph.D., 1875; LL.D., Neb. Wesleyan U., 1910; m. Antoinette Whittlesey (died 1876); 1 son, Lucius Whittlesey; m. 2d, Anna Barber Williston (died 1900); children—Horace Williston, Mrs. Winifred Sherman Updike; m. 3d, Mrs. Josephine Fisher, June 26, 1902. Prof. English lang. and lit., 1882—, dean of the general faculty, 1887-1901, and of Grad. Coll., 1901-26, Univ. of Neb.; retired. Author: Onalytics of Literature, 1893; What Is Shakespeare?, 1902; Elements of Literature and Composition, 1908; How to Describe and Narrate Visually, 1925. Editor: Shakespeare's Macbeth, 1899; Tennyson's The Princess, 1900; Shakespeare's Hamlet, 1903; Massinger (in Masterpieces of the English Drama series), 1912. Translator de luxe edit. of Frithiof's Saga, 1878. Home: Lincoln, Neb. Died Feb. 13, 1933.

SHERMAN, Mary Belle King, club woman; b. Albion, N.Y.; d. Rufus and Sarah E. (Whitney) King; ed. pub. schs., Rochester, N.Y., and Park Inst., Chicago; m. John Dickinson Sherman, Feb. 10, 1887; 1 son, John King. Served as instructor in parliamentary law, John Marshall Law School, Chicago; former sec. Chicago Woman's Club; pres. Gen. Fedn. of Women's Clubs, 1924-26, reëlected for term, 1926-28. elected hon. pres., 1930; chmn. Am. Home Dept., Gen. Fedn. Women's Clubs, 1928-32; nat. consultant Home Owner's Protective Enterprise. Mem. Nat. War Gardens Commn. and asst. to dir. of School Garden Army of the Bur. of Edn., Dept. of Interior, during World War; presdl. commr. of U.S. George Washington Bicentennial Commn., in charge of women's organizations. Mem. advisory council Nat. Broadcasting Co., New York. Trustee Nat. Parks Assn. Mem. D.A.R. Active in establishment of Rocky Mountain and other nat. parks and for recognition of the home-maker in the 1930 census. Author: Parliamentary Law and Rules of Procedure. Died Jan. 15, 1935.

SHERMAN, Merritt Masters, stockman; b. Salem, N.Y., Nov. 9, 1854; s. Josiah Rising and Lydia (Walker) S.; student Cornell U., 1873-76; m. Lisette F. Jones, Nov. 23, 1886 (died 1917). Went to Kan.; has a 24,000-acre farm in Central Kan., with 10,000 acres under plough; gave up farming, 1934 (farm managed by son, Carl). Author: Autocracy of Class, 1934. Home: Crawford, Kan. Died June 12, 1937.

SHERMAN, Moses Hazeltine, pres. Los Angeles Steamship Co.; b. West Rupert, Vt., Dec. 3, 1853; s. Enoch Sterling and Miranda Wright (Warner) S.; grad. Oswego (N.Y.) Normal Sch.; m. Harriet Pratt, June 2, 1885 (dec.); children—Robert P., Hazeltine (Mrs. Frank B. Keever), Lucy Pratt. Teacher, pub. schs., Prescott, Ariz., 1874-76; Ariz. rep. at Centennial Expn., Phila., Pa.; territorial supt. pub. instruction, Ariz., 1878-81; adj. gen. Ariz. Ty., 1881; organizer Valley Bank of Phoenix, 1884; moved to Los Angeles, Calif., 1889; with Eli P. Clark built Los Angeles Electric Ry. and Los Angeles & Pasadena Electric Ry., 1889-95; with Los Angeles Steamship Co., 1920—, pres., 1926—; pres. El Tejon Ranchos, Inc., Lower Colorado River Ginning Co.; v.p. Del Rey Co.; dir. various companies. Republican. Mason. Author of the school laws of Arizona. Home: Los Angeles, Calif. Died Sept. 9, 1932.

SHERMAN, Stuart Pratt, editor, author; b. Anita, Ia., Oct. 1, 1881; s. John and Ada Martha (Pratt) S.; A.B., Williams, 1903; A.M., Harvard, 1904, Ph.D., 1906; L.H.D., Williams, 1922; m. Ruth Bartlett Mears, Dec. 25, 1906; 1 son, John Mears. Instr. in English, Northwestern U., 1906-07; asso. in English, 1907-08, asst. prof., 1908-09, asso. prof., 1909-11, prof., 1911-24, U. of Illinois; lit. editor N.Y. Herald Tribune, 1924—. Mem. Am. Acad. Arts and Letters, 1923. Treasure Island, 1911; Coriolanus (in Tudor Shakespeare), 1912; A Book of Short Stories, 1914; Ford's 'Tis Pity and the Broken Heart, 1915. Asso. editor Cambridge History of American Literature, 1917; The Scarlet Letter, 1919; The Sand-Flaubert Letters (with A. L. Mackenzie), 1921; Essays and Poems of Emerson, 1921; Leaves of Grass, 1922; The Poetical Works of Joaquin Miller, 1923; American Prose Masters, 1923; Letters to a Lady in the Country, 1925. Author: Matthew Arnold, 1917; On Contemporary Literature, 1917; Americans, 1922; The Genius of America, 1923; Men of Letters of the British Isles (with Theodore Spicer-Simson), 1924; My Dear Cornelia, 1924; Points of View, 1924. Died Aug. 21, 1927.

SHERMAN, Thomas Townsend, lawyer; b. of Am. parents, London, Eng., July 28, 1853; s. Edward Standish and Catharine Augusta (Townsend) S.; prep. edn., Dwight Sch., N.Y. City, and Fairfield (Conn.) Acad.; B.A., Yale, 1874; LL.B., Columbia, 1876; m. Anne Wiggin Sherman, Oct. 19, 1887; 1 dau., Emily Balch (Mrs. Arthur Talbot). Admitted to N.Y. bar, Dec. 13, 1876, and began practice at N.Y. City; mem. Evarts, Choate, Sherman & Leon. Dir. and pres. James Gordon Bennett Memorial Home for New York Journalists. Republican. Episcopalian (sr. warden and clerk of vestry, Christ Ch., Rye, N.Y.; mem. of vestry, 1883—). Author: Sherman Genealogy, 1920. Home: New York and Rye, N.Y. Died Aug. 27, 1931.

SHERMAN, Wells Alvord, marketing specialist; b. Ash Grove, Va., July 19, 1868; s. Franklin and Caroline Matilda Clapp (Alvord) S.; grad. Greylock Inst., South Williamstown, Mass., 1887; m. Elsie M. Besley, May 23, 1895; children—Caroline Elizabeth, Mary Collins, Elsie Besley, Martha Thatcher, Wells Alvord, Grace Whitney. State statis. agt. U.S. Dept. Agr., 1895-1900; scientific asst. in statistics, same, 1900-03; examiner U.S. Civil Service Commn., 1903-10; asst. in cotton standardization, and investigations in handling and marketing cotton, U.S. Dept. Agr., 1910-12; with Bur. Markets (now Bur. of Agrl. Economics), U.S. Dept. Agr., 1913—; in charge fruit and vegetable div., 1920-27; initiated and organized, 1922, nation-wide shipping point inspection service for fruits and vegetables; chief marketing specialist, U.S. Dept. Agr., and chief of Calif. Div. of Markets, 1927-28; principal marketing specialist in charge fruit and vegetable div. B.A.E., U.S. Dept. of Agr., 1929-38, in charge adminstrn. of the Perishable Agrl. Commodities Act of 1930 to 1938; retired July 31, 1938. Methodist. Author: Merchandising Fruits and Vegetables, 1929. Home: McLean, Va. Died Aug. 2, 1939.

SHERMAN, William Winslow, banker; b. New York, N.Y., Mar. 12, 1833; s. Jahaziel and Ann Maria King S.; family removed to Vt.; ed. Castleton and Burlington, Vt.; m. Mrs. Henrietta Tysen, 1857. Returned to New York; held clerkship, Bank of Commerce, 1858-63, paying teller, 1863-78, asst. cashier, 1878-82, cashier, 1882-91, pres. and dir., 1891-99; retired. Home: New York, N. Y. Died 1908.

SHERRARD, Thomas Herrick, forester; b. Brooklyn, Mich., May 17, 1874; s. Thomas and Valeria (Gray) S.; Dr. Holbrooks' Mil. Sch., Sing Sing, N.Y., 1886-92; A.B., Yale, 1897; at Harvard Grad. Sch., 1897-98; studied forestry under various officers in German Forest Service, 1898-99; Forest Sch., U. of Munich, semester, 1899; m. S. Drew Bennett, Apr. 22, 1908; children—Valeria (dec.), Margaret, Thomas Drew. Agt. Bur. of Forestry, U.S. Dept. Agr., 1899-1903; asst. forester, Forest Service, U.S. Dept. Agr., July 1903—; supervisor Ore. Nat. Forest, Feb. 1, 1908—; senior forester, Jan. 1939. Presbyn. Author: A Working Plan for Forest Lands in South Carolina (Bull. 43, Bur. of Forestry). Home: Portland, Ore. Died Jan. 22, 1941.

SHERRIFF, Andrew Rothwell; b. Washington, D.C., Apr. 8, 1872 (surname formerly Sheriff); s. George Lewis and Susan Burrows (Rothwell) S.; g.g.g.s. of Col. Wm. Dewers, of Valley Forge; attended public graded and high schs., Washington, D.C., 1878-89; LL.B., Georgetown U., 1892; A.B., A.M., LL.B., Harvard (finished 1896); m. Marguerite, d. William Hamilton Mitchell, Oct. 17, 1900; children—Rothwell Mitchell, William H. M., Kathleen; m. 2d, Mrs. Virginia Listemann Baxter, d. Bernhard Listemann, Oct. 25, 1924. Document clk., Smithsonian Instn., Washington, D.C., 1889-92; admitted to D.C. bar, 1894, to Ill. bar, 1896, to U.S. Supreme Court, 1907; asst. instr. constl. law, Harvard, 1895-96; settled in Chicago 1896, and from then actively engaged in practice of law; first associated with Alfred E. McCordic and James J. Barbour, later with Louis L. Dent, Fletcher Dobyns, Charles Y. Freeman, and Senator James Hamilton Lewis; mem. legal dept. Reconstruction Finance Corp. Served many yrs. as vestryman Trinity Ch. and as trustee St. Luke's Hospital, also as chairman or mem. of many professional, pub. welfare and wartime committees. Roosevelt Democrat. Episcopalian. Home: Chicago, Ill. Died Mar. 18, 1935.

SHERRILL, Charles Hitchcock, former American ambassador to Turkey; b. at Washington, D.C., Apr. 13, 1867; s. Charles Hitchcock and Sarah Fulton (Wynkoop) S.; A.B., Yale U., 1889, LL.B., 1891, A.M., 1892; LL.D., New York U., 1918; m. Miss George Barker, d. late Edward N. Gibbs, of New York, Feb. 8, 1906. Practiced law at New York, 1891-1909; U.S. minister to Argentina, Mar. 25, 1909-July 27, 1911, when ill health forced him to decline Embassy to Japan and to retire from the diplomatic service. Resumed practice of law, Sept. 1912. Vice pres. Berkshire Fine Spinning Associates. American ambassador to Turkey, 1932-33. Trustee New York Univ. 12 years (founder College of Fine Arts). Grand Cross Order of Crown (Italy); Comdr. Legion of Honor (France); Comdr. Order of Leopold I (Belgium); Grand Cross Order of White Eagle (Yugo-Slavia); Grand Officer Order of White Lion (Czechoslovakia); Comdr. Order of Polar Star (Sweden); Comdr. Order of Orange Nassau (Holland); Grand Officer Order of Merit (Austria); Grand Officer Order Pour le Mérite (Hungary). Originator of a series of international inter-university track athletic matches that began with Yale vs. Oxford, 1894; Am. 100-yard champion, 1887, also won 7 inter-collegiate championships. Brig. gen. and adj. gen. State of N.Y. in charge United States draft, 1917-18. Col. and a.-d.-c. on staffs of Governors Odell and Higgins, of N.Y. Chairman aviation committee of the New York Chamber of Commerce; mem. International Olympic Sports Committee. Presbyterian. Republican. Author: Stained Glass Tours in France, 1908; Stained Glass Tours in England, 1909; Stained Glass Tour in Italy, 1913; French Memories of 18th Century America, 1915; Modernizing the Monroe Doctrine, 1916 (also Spanish and Japanese edits.); Have We a Far Eastern Policy?, 1920; Prime Ministers and Presidents, 1922; Stained Glass Tours in Spain and Flanders, 1924; The Purple or the Red, 1924; Stained Glass Tours in Germany, 1927; Bismarck and Mussolini, 1931 (also Italian edit.); Sherrill Genealogy, 1932; Mosaics, 1933; A Year's Embassy to Mustafa Kemal, 1933 (also French edit.); Kemal, Roosevelt and Mussolini. Died June 25, 1936.

SHERRILL, John Bascom, editor, pub.; b. Iredell Co., N.C., Feb. 23, 1864; s. Martin Van Buren and Martha Jane (Douglass) S.; ed. high sch., Olin, N.C.; m. Anna S. Montgomery, Jan. 5, 1887; children—Mrs. Mary Lilly Privett, Mrs. Anna D. Archibald, William Montgomery, Cottrell. Editor and pub. Concord Times, 1885—; Concord Daily Tribune, 1910—. Postmaster of Concord, 1894-98; mem. Sch. Bd. Concord, 8 yrs. Sec.-treas. N.C. Press Assn., 1888-1920 (pres. 1921-23). Trustee Duke U. Mem. N.C. General Assembly, lower house, 1923-24. Democrat. Mem. M.E. Ch., S. Home: Concord, N.C. Died Feb. 28, 1934.

SHERRILL, Miles Osborne, librarian; b. in Catawba Co., N.C., July 26, 1841; s. of Hiram and Sarah (Osborne) S.; ed. Rhehobeth Acad. and Catawba Coll. (non-grad.); m. Sarah R. Bost, May 1, 1867. Enlisted in Confederate Army, Apr. 1861; served as corporal, sergt. and 1st lt.; wounded at Spottsylvania C.H., May 1864, and lost right leg; spent next 10 mos. in northern prison; clk. Superior Ct. and judge Probate Ct., of Catawba Co., 14 yrs., 1868-83; mem. N.C. Ho. of Rep., 1883, Senate, 1885, 1893; cashier in office of collector internal revenue, Western Dist. of N.C., 1885-89; state librarian of N.C., 1899-1917. Trustee Female Coll., Lenoir, N.C. Democrat. Del. annual confs. and to Gen. Conf. M.E. Ch., South. Home: Greensboro, N.C. Died Apr. 8, 1919.

SHERWELL, Guillermo Antonio; b. of Am. parents, Paraje Nuevo, State of Veracruz, Mex., June 5, 1878; s. William and Beatriz González (Clavijo) S.; high sch., Orizaba; J.D., Nat. U. of Mex., 1909; Ph.D., Georgetown U., 1922; m. Luisa Velázquez, of Mexico, June 30, 1896. Prof. psychology and science of edn., Normal Sch., Jalapa, 1902; prof. history and Spanish lit., Coll. of Jalapa, 1903-12, dean, 1912; head of grammar schs., normal schs. and vocational schs. system, Mexico City, 1913; counsellor Mex. Nat. U., 1913-14; in charge dept. pub. instrn. and fine arts, Mexico, 1914; teacher Spanish, high schs., N.Y. City, 1915-18; juristic expert, Inter-Am. High Commn., Washington, D.C., 1918-22, sec. same, 1922—; prof. Spanish and foreign laws, Georgetown U., 1918—. Decorated Order of El Libertador and Medal Pub. Instrn., Venezuela. Catholic. Author: Secondary Education in the United States, 1905; Simon Bolivar, 1921; Sucre, 1924; etc. Died July 7, 1926.

SHERWIN, Henry Alden, paint mfr.; b. Baltimore, Vt., Sept. 27, 1842; s. Alden W. and Rachel (Bachelder) S.; ed. pub. schools; m. Frances Smith, 1865. Connected with dry goods and wholesale grocery business, Cleveland, 1860-66; entered paint business, Cleveland, 1866, under title of Dunham & Co.; admitted E. P. Williams to partnership, 1870, and firm became Sherwin, Williams & Co.; business incorporated, 1884, as Sherwin-Williams Co., of which became chmn. bd. dirs.; dir. 1st Nat. Bank, Cleveland Trust Co.; trustee Soc. for Savings. Home: Willoughby, O. Died June 26, 1916.

SHERWIN, John Collins, judge; b. Berlin, Erie Co., O., Feb. 6, 1852; s. John C. and Virginia A. S.; ed. Ripon and Beloit colls., Wis.; LL.B., U. of Wis., 1875; admitted to bar, 1875; married. Dist. atty. 12th Jud. Dist., Ia., 1885-86; judge Dist. Ct., same dist., 1888-99; justice Supreme Ct. of Ia., term 1900-12. Republican. Home: Mason City, Ia. Died Feb. 3, 1919.

SHERWIN, Thomas, businessman; b. Boston, July 11, 1839; s. Thomas and Mary King (Gibbens) S.; ed. Boston Latin Sch. and Harvard; m. Isabel Fiske Edwards, Jan. 18, 1870. First lt. and adj. 22d Mass. Inf., Oct. 8, 1861; maj., June 28, 1862; lt. col., Oct. 17, 1862; bvtd. col. vols., Sept. 30, 1864, "for gallant services at battle of Peebles Farm, Va."; brig. gen. vols., Mar. 13, 1865, "for distinguished gallantry at battle of Gettysburg, and for gallant and meritorious services during the war"; hon. mustered out, Oct. 17, 1864. Chmn. bd. N.E. Telephone & Telegraph Co., 1909—; officer or dir. in other corps. Home: Jamaica Plain, Mass. Died Dec. 20, 1914.

SHERWOOD, Andrew, geologist; b. Mansfield, Pa., July 16, 1848; s. Albert and Julia A. (Clark) S.; desc. in 8th generation from Thomas S., the pioneer (b. in Eng., 1586, died, Fairfield, Conn., 1655); ed. State Normal Sch. and old U. of Chicago; m. Jennie L. Knapp, Apr. 17, 1872; children—Anna Leona, Hugh Miller, Mrs. Mattie Julia Beach, Mrs. Lola Inez Williams, Mrs. Jennie Elizabeth Marvin. With J. S. Newberry one year on the geol. survey of Ohio; in charge of field work under James Hall, 5 yrs., on geol. survey of N.Y.; asst. state geologist under J. P. Lesley, 5 yrs. on the 2d geol. survey of Pa.; in charge Pa. mineral exhibit, Chicago Expn., 1893; leader of expdn. to headwaters of the Yukon, 1898; apptd. U.S. dep. mineral surveyor for Ore., Ida. and Ariz., 1900. Prohibition candidate for Congress, 1894. Baptist. Author of geol. works and maps published by the state. Home: Portland, Ore. Died Oct. 31, 1933.

SHERWOOD, Carl G., judge; b. nr. Whitney Point, N.Y., Jan. 18, 1855; s. George and Mary Ann (Jeffords) S.; ed. high sch., Binghamton, N.Y., 2 yrs.; m. Nellie C. Fountain, Feb. 10, 1885; children—George Fountain, Harry Allen (dec.), Mary Carleton, Dorothy Viola. Admitted to S.D. bar, 1881; register of deeds, Clark Co., S.D., 1882-86; del. S.D. Constl. Conv., 1883, 1889; mem. S.D. Senate, 1889-91; circuit judge, 3d Jud. Circuit of S.D., 1912-17; asso. justice Supreme Court, 3d Dist., S.D., 1922-25 (presiding judge, 1924); reëlected for term of 6 yrs., Nov. 1925 (presiding judge, 1929). Republican. Methodist. Mason, Odd Fellow, K.P., Elk, Woodman. Home: Clark, S.D. Died Aug. 18, 1938.

SHERWOOD, George Herbert, museum dir.; b. Richmond, Me., Mar. 28, 1876; s. Benjamin Atherton and Elizabeth May (Murray) S.; A.B., Brown U., 1898, A.M., 1899, Ed.D., 1928; m. Alverda Laura Brown, Oct. 21, 1902. Assistant in Biol. Laboratory, U.S. Fish Commission, Woods Hole, Mass., 1898-1902; with Am. Mus. Natural History, New York, 1901—, was asst. curator dept. invertebrate zoölogy, until 1906, curator-in-chief, department edn., 1906—, asst. sec. and asst. treas., 1906-11, asst. sec., 1911-21, exec. sec., 1921-34, acting dir. 1924-26, dir., 1927-34, hon. dir., 1935—. Pres. and life member New York Acad. of Sciences (treas.). Dir. Alice Rich Northrop Memorial. Fellow New York Zoöl. Society. Republican. Baptist. Home: New York, N.Y. Died Mar. 18, 1937.

SHERWOOD, Granville Hudson, bishop; b. Elgin, Ill., Dec. 6, 1878; s. David Burton and Lura (Trowbridge) S.; prep. edn. St. Paul's Sch., Concord, N.H., 1894-96; student Trinity Coll., Conn., 1896-98 (S.T.D., 1918); U. of Chicago, 1898-99; Western Theol. Sem., 1903 (D.D., 1917); m. Lucy Galt Kinney, Sept. 10, 1902. Deacon and priest P.E. Ch., 1903; rector Christ Ch., Streator, Ill., 1903-05, Trinity Ch., Rock Island, 1905-17; bishop of Springfield (Ill.), Apr. 25, 1917—. Died Nov. 22, 1923.

SHERWOOD, Herbert Francis, civic organizer; b. West Cornwall, Conn., Oct. 9, 1872; s. John Cotter and Ellen Clarissa (Hart) S.; ed. Gunnery Sch., Washington, Conn., 1888-89; studied at Columbia and at Sch. of New York Bur. Municipal Research; hon. A.M., for work done on immigration, 1911; m. Lillian Hammond, Mar. 6, 1901; 1 son, John Hammond Bradford. Reporter, Stamford Advocate, 1892-97; spl. writer New York Tribune, 1899-1915, also lecturer on community questions; asst. sec. Nat. Bd. Review, 1916-18; mgr. Fall River Chamber Commerce, 1923-28; industrial commr., Scranton Chamber Commerce, 1928—; lecturer New York Bd. of Edn. many years. Pres. Dept. of Sociology, Brooklyn Inst. Arts and Sciences; sec., 1924-25, pres., 1926-27, N.E. Assn. Commercial Executives; chmn. advisory com. N.E. Council, 1926-28. Mem. Conn. S.G., 1917-18. Independent Republican. Congfist. Home: Scranton, Pa. Deceased.

SHERWOOD, Isaac R., congressman; b. Stanford, N.Y., Aug. 13, 1835; s. Aaron and Maria (Yeomans) S.; student Antioch Coll., O., 1854-56, LL.B., Ohio Law Coll., Cleveland, 1859; m. Katharine Margaret Brownlee, Sept. 1, 1859. Pvt. 14th Ohio Inf., Apr. 22-Aug. 13, 1861; 1st lt. adj. 111th Ohio Inf., Sept. 6, 1862; maj., Feb. 13, 1863; lt. col., Feb. 12, 1864; bvtd. brig. gen. vols., Feb. 27, 1865, "for gallant and meritorious services" at Resaca, June 14, 1864, Franklin, Tenn., Nov. 30, 1864, and at Nashville, Dec. 15, 1864; hon. mustered out, Oct. 8, 1865. Editor Toledo Commercial, 1865, Cleveland Leader, 1865-66, Toledo Journal, 1874-83, Canton News-Democrat, 1888-98. Sec. of state of Ohio, 1869-73; mem. 43d Congress (1873-75), 6th Ohio Dist.; probate judge, 1878-84; mem. 60th to 66th Congresses (1907-21) and 68th Congress (1923-25), 9th Ohio Dist. Author of the "Sherwood Dollar-a-Day Bill" and "Medal of Honor Bill." Elk. Home: Toledo, O. Died Oct. 15, 1925.

SHERWOOD, Katharine Margaret Brownlee, author; b. Poland, Ohio, Sept. 24, 1841; d. Judge James and Rebecca (Mullen) Brownlee; ed. at Union Sem., Poland; m. Isaac R. Sherwood, Sept. 1, 1859. Nat. organizer Woman's Relief Corps G.A.R., and 2d nat. pres.; chmn. com. citizenship Nat. Council Women U.S.; active in women's clubs and D.A.R.; hon. pres. Ohio Newspaper Women's Assn.; sec. Toledo Centre Univ. Extension. Author: Camp Fire and Memorial Poems; Dream of the Ages, a Poem of Columbia, 1893. Other poems appear in the following books: Through the Year With the Poets; Tributes to Shakespeare; Every Day in the Year; Ballads of Bravery, etc. Home: Toledo, O. Died Feb. 15, 1914.

SHERWOOD, Mary Elizabeth Wilson, author; b. (Wilson) Keene, N.H., 1830 (d. James Wilson, congressman from N.H.). When her mother died she assumed care of the large family in Washington; m. John Sherwood, a New York lawyer. Prominent as social leader; also writer for newspapers and magazines, and reader. Best known as "Mrs. John Sherwood"; many of her poems were published under her initials "M. E. W. S." Author: The Sarcasm of Destiny; A Transplanted Rose; Home Amusements; Amenities of Home; Manners and Social Usages; Royal Girls and Royal Courts; Sweet Brier; An Epistle to Posterity; Here and There and Everywhere; The Art of Entertaining; 300 short stories in Harper's and other mags. Died 1903.

SHERWOOD, Sidney, asso. and asso. prof. political economy Johns Hopkins, 1892—; b. Saratoga County, N.Y., May 28, 1860; s. Thomas B. and Mary F. (Beattie) S.; grad. Princeton, A.B., 1879; studied law in offices and 1884-85, Columbia Law School, practiced law, New York, 1885-88; post-grad. student Johns Hopkins, 1888-91; Ph.D., 1891; instr. in finance, Univ. of Pa., 1891-92; m. Mary A. Beattie, Sept. 3, 1891. Author: History and Theory of Money, 1893. Contbr. numerous articles on economics, etc., to educational journals. Died 1901.

SHERWOOD, William Hall, composer, pianist; b. Lyons, N.Y., Jan. 31, 1854; s. Rev. Lyman H. and Mary (Balis) S.; grad. Lyons Musical Acad., of which his father was founder and prin.; studied in

U.S. under Edward Heimburger, Pychowski, William Mason; in Europe with Kullak, and Deppe, Berlin, and finally with Liszt, at Weimar; also studied organ; was organist English Ch., Stuttgart, and English Chapel, Berlin; m. Estelle F. Abrams, 1882. Has played in principal cities of Europe and Can., and all parts of the U.S.; dir. Sherwood Music Sch. Composer of some high grade music for piano. Author: University Extension Course of Music Study and Piano Playing (a new departure in fundamental respects for the best modern principles of interpretation, technic and touch); Music Study and the Mutual Relations of Interpretation and Technic. Home: Chicago, Ill. Died 1911.

SHERZER, William Hittell, coll. prof.; b. Franklin, O., Sept. 6, 1860; s. Jacob Weinland and Mary (Firman) S.; S.B., U. of Mich., 1889, M.S., 1890, Ph.D., 1901; m. Maude Jerome, Sept. 4, 1889; children—Allen Firman, Josephine, Mrs. Gertrude Lamb, Jerome Hittell. Prin. of Saginaw (West Side) High Sch., 1886-89; instr. geology, U. of Mich., 1891-92; prof. natural sciences, Mich. State Normal Coll., 1892—; spl. study in anthropology, U.S. Nat. Mus., 1927-28; research asst. in anthropology, U. of Mich., 1928—. Has filled summer engagements at the Natural Science Camp, Canandaigua Lake, N.Y., 1892, 1893, 1898. Chautauqua, N.Y., 1897, 1898; asst. upon Mich. State Geol. Survey, 1896-1913; spent 1900-01 in U. of Berlin. In charge Smithsonian Glacial Expdn. to Canadian Rockies and Selkirks, summer 1904 and 1905. Spent fall 1920 and winter 1921, in field studies in Hawaiian Islands, spl. investigation of the explosive eruptions of Kilauea. Home: Ypsilanti, Mich. Died 1932.

SHETTER, Stella Cross, writer; b. Fairview, Pa., Apr. 10, 1880; d. Lycurgus Pollock and Agnes (Hindman) Cross; grad. high sch., Pittsburgh, 1898; Home Corr. Sch., Springfield, Mass.; m. Fred E. Shetter, May 21, 1902; children—Sarah (dec.), Katherine Louise, Virginia Cross, Egbert Passavant, Agnes Ray. V.p. for W.Va., League of Am. Pen Women, 1928-32. Republican. Presbyn. Author: Early Candlelight Stories, 1922; When Grandma Was a Little Girl, 1926. Winner of prize by League of Am. Pen Women for best short-short story, 1932. Home: Clarksburg, W.Va. Died Dec. 31, 1936.

SHIDY, Leland Perry, tidal expert; b. St. Louis, Mo., July 27, 1851; s. William and Mary T. (Bowers) S.; grad. Mo. State Normal Sch., 1871; attended Mo. State U., 1870-73, left senior class without graduation; received degree of analyt. chemist, Columbian U., 1887; m. Margaret Warren, Sept. 21, 1911. Tidal computer in Coast Survey Office, May 27, 1873-Nov. 18, 1897; chief of Tidal Div., U.S. Coast Survey, Nov. 19, 1897-Oct. 15, 1915, when Tidal Div. became sect. of Div. of Hydrography and Topography; retired, 1930. Introduced methods of saving labor in tidal computations; had annual volume of tide tables extended to the world, 1896; has published various annual reports; biographies of R. S. Avery and F. M. Little; results of tide observations at Nassau, New Providence Island, Bahamas; results of tide observations at Spitzbergen; "Present State of Our Knowledge of Tides," etc. Home: Stockton, Calif. Died Oct. 2, 1935.

SHIELDS, Charles R., banker; b. Newark, O., May 10, 1861; s. William and Elizabeth (Duncan) S.; ed. high sch., Newark, O.; m. Mary La Salle Wing, June 17, 1885; children—Elizabeth D. (Mrs. Myron B. Kauffman), Mayhew W., Mary M., Helen J. (Mrs. Phil. S. Bradford), Arminie L. (Mrs. Robert A. Hammond), Robert D. Began with Franklin Bank, Newark, 1881; asst. cashier New First Nat. Bank, Columbus, 1899-1912, cashier, 1912-18, v.p., 1918-26; pres. First Nat. Bank, Columbus, 1926-28; pres. First-Citizens Trust Co., 1928-31; chmn. bd. Ohio Nat. Bank, 1931-37; retired, 1937. Conglist. Home: Columbus, O. Died Feb. 11, 1939.

SHIELDS, Charles Woodruff, clergyman, prof. harmony of science and revealed religion, Princeton, 1865—; b. New Albany, Ind., Apr. 4, 1825; s. James Read and Hannah (Woodruff) S.; grad. Princeton, 1844; (D.D., 1861; LL.D., Columbian Univ., 1871). Took 4 yrs. course, Princeton Theol. Sem., 1844-88; licensed to preach, 1848; ordained, 1849; pastor Presbyterian Ch., Hempstead, L.I.; pastor 2d Presbyn. Ch., Phila., 1850-65; ordained minister in P.E. Ch., Dec. 13, 1898, retaining chair at Princeton; m. Charlotte Elizabeth, d. Peter Bain, Albany, N.Y., Nov. 22, 1848; m. 2d, Elizabeth, d. Hon. John K. Kane, Phila., Apr. 25, 1861. Author: The Historic Episcopate, 1892; The Presbyterian Book of Common Prayer, 1893; The United Church of the United States, 1896; The Reformer of Geneva, 1898; The Scientific Evidences of Revealed Religion, 1900. Home: Princeton, N.J. Died 1904.

SHIELDS, G. O. ("Coquina"), editor; b. Batavia, O., Aug. 26, 1846; s. John F. and Eliza J. S.; ed. common sch., Delaware Co., Ia., 3 mos.; beyond that self-ed.; unmarried. In Civil War, 1863-65. Editor and mgr. Recreation, 1894-1905; editor Shields' Magazine, 1905—. Contbr. to mags. and newspapers, 1866-94. Organized, 1898, pres. 1898-1919, League of Am. Sportsmen; organized, 1897, and pres., 1897-1902, Camp Fire Club; devoting whole life to protection of song-birds, game and game fishes. Author: The Big Game of North America; Cruisings in the Cascades; American Game Fishes; Hunting in the Great West; The American Book of the Dog; Camping and Camp Outfits; The Battle of the Big Hole. Died Nov. 12, 1925.

SHIELDS, George Howell, judge; b. Bardstown, Ky., June 19, 1842; s. George W. and Martha A. (Howell) S.; Westminster Coll., Fulton, Mo., 1859-60; Louisville (Kentucky) Law Sch., 1865; (LL.D., Westminster, 1891); m. Mary Harrison Leighton, Feb. 1, 1866. In practice at St. Louis, 1873—; law partner of John B. Henderson, 1873-83, John W. Noble, 1895-1903; mem. Mo. Ho. of Rep., 1871, Mo. Constl. Conv., 1875; pres. Bd. of Freeholders, which framed the St. Louis charter, 1876; candidate for judge Supreme Ct. of Mo., 1872; chmn. Rep. State Com., 1876-80; asst. atty. gen. of U.S., 1889-93; counsel and agt. of U.S. before U.S. and Chilean Claims Commn., 1893-94; judge St. Louis Circuit Ct., terms 1907-13, 1915-20. Home: St. Louis, Mo. Deceased.

SHIELDS, John Knight, senator; b. Clinchdale, Tenn., Aug. 15, 1858; s. Judge James T. and Elizabeth (Simpson) S.; studied under pvt. tutors; m. Mary Fulkerson, June 1883 (dec.); m. 2d, Mrs. Jeannette Swepson Dodson Cowan, Dec. 7, 1912. Admitted to bar, 1879; partner with father until latter retired, 1890; partner with R. E. L. Mountcastle, 1890-92, and 1894-1902; chancellor 12th Chancery Div. of Tenn., 1892-94; asso. justice Supreme Ct., Tenn., for terms 1902-10, 1910-18; chief justice, 1910-13; U.S. senator, 2 terms, 1913-25. Democrat. Home: Clinchdale, Tenn. Died Sept. 30, 1934.

SHIELDS, Thomas Edward, college prof.; b. Mendota, Minn., May 9, 1862; s. John and Bridget (Burke) S.; St. Francis Sem., Milwaukee, 1882-85; St. Thomas Sem., St. Paul, 1885-91; A.M., St. Mary's Sem., Baltimore, 1892; Ph.D., Johns Hopkins, 1895; (LL.D., Manhattan Coll., New York, 1908). Master discipline and prefect studies, St. Thomas Coll., St. Paul, 1888-90; ordained R.C. priest, 1890; asst. pastor Cathedral, St. Paul, 1891-92; prof. biology and psychology, St. Paul Sem., 1895-98; asst. pastor St. Joseph's Ch., St. Paul, 1898-1902; instr. psychology, 1902-06, asst. prof. physiol. psychology, 1906-07, asso. prof. psychology, 1907-09, prof. psychology and edn., 1909—, dean Catholic Sisters Coll., Catholic U. of America. Founded, 1905, and became pres. Catholic Corr. Sch.; founded, 1909, becoming pres. Catholic Edn. Press; founded, 1911, from then editor Catholic Ednl. Review. Perfected plethysmograph, 1905. Hon. mem. Minn. Acad. Medicine. Author: Index Omnium, 1888; The Education of Our Girls, 1907; The Making and the Unmaking of a Dullard, 1909; Religion, First Book, 1908, Second Book, 1909, Third Book, 1910; Third Reader, 1910; The Teacher's Manual of Primary Methods; Fourth and Fifth Readers (Catholic edn. series), 1915; The Philosophy of Education, 1917; Religion, Fourth Book, 1918. Home: Washington, D.C. Died Feb. 16, 1921.

SHIELDS, William S., banker, mcht.; b. Clinchdale, Tenn., Oct. 13, 1853; s. James Thomas and Elizabeth (Simpson) S.; ed. pvt. schs.; m. Alice Watkins, Oct. 30, 1890. Began in banking business, 1888; became pres. City Nat. Bank, Knoxville, Tenn., 1895; retired. Trustee U. of Tenn., Washington Coll., Tenn., Lawson-McGee Library. Col. on staff of gov. of Tenn. Presbyn. Elk. Home: Knoxville, Tenn. Died Dec. 2, 1933.

SHIELS, Albert, educator; b. N.Y. City, July 9, 1865; s. George E. and Alberta S.; A.B., Coll. City of New York, 1886, Pd.M., 1896, A.M., 1899; (L.H.D., Muhlenberg Coll., Allentown, Pa.); m. Frances O'Keefe, Apr. 1890. Cashier Panama R.R., 1887-90, also consul for Mexico at Panama and Colon and acting consul for Great Britain; teacher various grades and prin. evening sch., N.Y. City, 1890-99; apptd. 1st prin. in Greater New York, 1899; dist. supt. schs., 1906-13, in charge of all evening schs., 1911-13; dir. Div. of Reference and Research, Dept. of Edn., N.Y. City, 1913-16; supt. schs., Los Angeles, Calif., 1916-19. Dir. Community Councils, New York, 1919—; asso. dir. Inst. Ednl. Research, Teachers College, Columbia U., 1921. Chmn. Nat. Am. Council. Actively identified with movements affecting the immigrant and assimilation of foreign population; was 1st chmn. Nat. Bd. of Censorship of Moving Pictures. Officer d'Académie, France. Lecturer Teachers Coll. (Columbia), Dartmouth Coll., U. of Calif. Presbyterian. Mason. Home: New York, N.Y. Died Mar. 14, 1940.

SHILLING, Alexander, painter, lawyer; b. Chicago, Ill.; s. Gustav and Bertha S.; ed. America and abroad. Landscape painter and painter-etcher. Gold medal, Phila. Art Club; silver medal, St. Louis Expn., 1904; Shaw prize for etching, 1913; oil painting, "Walcheren," purchased by Met. Mus., 1921. Rep. by dry points and etchings in prints dept. Willamette U., Salem, Ore., 1906; B.A., Willamette U., 1910; LL.B., Willamette U. Sch. of Law, 1910; m. June Patty, Sept. 20, 1911; children—Mildred, Evelyn and Adelyn (twins), Franklin. Admitted to Ore. bar, 1910, and began practice at Portland; asst. atty. gen. of Ore., 1911 and 1912; mem. McNary, Smith & Shields, 1913-15, Smith & Shields, 1915-23, Maguire, Shields & Morrison, 1933—; asst. atty. gen. U.P. R.R. System, 1923-33, now gen. atty. Northwest Dist. U.P. R.R.; dir. Ore. & Wash. R.R. Co. Mem. bd. dirs. Pub. Schs. of Portland. Mem. Ore. Bd. of Bar Examiners, 1923— (chmn.); served as spl. master in chancery; mem. Regional Labor Bd., 1934; mem. Ore. N.G. 3 yrs. Republican. Elk. Home: Portland, Ore. Died Jan. 19, 1937.

SHIMEK, Bohumil, botanist; b. nr. Shueyville, Ia., June 25, 1861; s. Francis Joseph and Maria Theresa (Tit) S.; C.E., State U. of La., 1883, M.S., 1902; hon. Ph.D., U. of Prague, 1919; m. Anna E. Konvalinka, June 23, 1886 (died 1922); children—Ella, Bertha (Mrs. P. J. Hanzlik), Anna (Mrs. M. O. Hanzlik), Vlasta (Mrs. George Krepelka), Frank; m. 2d, Marguerite Meerdink, Mar. 6, 1924. Teacher sciences, in secondary schs. of Ia., 1883-88; instr. zoölogy, U. of Neb., 1888-90; instr. botany, 1890-93, asst. prof., 1893-1903, prof. physiol. botany, 1903-14, prof. botany and head of dept., 1914-19, research prof., 1919—, State U. of Ia. Lecturer (exchange prof.) U. of Prague, 2d semester, 1913-14; spl. asst. Ia. Geol. Survey, 1908—. Served at various times as dir. Ia. Lakeside Lab. Hon. chmn. geol. sect. Scientific Congress, Prague, 1914; fellow A.A.A.S. (v.p. sect. E, 1911), Geol. Soc. America, Ia. Acad. Sciences (pres.). Author of about 160 scientific papers. Home: Iowa City, Ia. Deceased.

SHIMER, Porter William, chemist, metallurgist; b. Shimerville, Pa., Mar. 13, 1857; s. Peter A. and Ellen (Werkheiser) S.; E.M., Lafayette Coll., 1878, Ph.D., 1899; m. Elizabeth Sandt, Oct. 12, 1880; children—Katharine (Mrs. J. Willard Paff), William Robert, Edward Bernard, Margaret (Mrs. Paul Hoffman). Propr. chem. and metall. lab., Easton, Pa., 1885—; pres. Shimer Chem. Co., 1924—; in analytical, consulting and investigation work; lecturer iron and steel, Lafayette Coll., 1894-1902. Discovered titanium carbide; awarded John Scott medal, Franklin Inst., 1901, for invention of combustion crucible. Mem. Int. Steel Standards Com. Author of papers on new methods and apparatus used in analytical chemistry; application of chemistry to metall. and other problems. Inventor of a new process for case-hardening iron and steel, molten baths for steel treating, chaplet alloy used in iron founding, etc. Home: Easton, Pa. Died Dec. 7, 1938.

SHINE, Francis Eppes, surgeon; b. St. Augustine, Fla., Jan. 13, 1871; s. William Francis and Maria Jefferson (Eppes) S.; g.g.g.s. Thomas Jefferson; A.B., U. of South, Sewanee, Tenn., 1892; U. of Virginia, 1895; M.D., New York Hosp., New York, 1899; m. Anne Barker, of Toronto, Can., Aug. 2, 1904. Surgeon Chinese Relief Expdn., Hosp. Ship, Maine, 1900; instr. and chief of clinic, Med. Dept., Cornell U., 1901-02; removed to Ariz., 1903; chief surgeon El Paso & South Western R.R., Copper Queen Consolidated Mining Co. Episcopalian. Major, Med. O.R.C., 1917. Mem. Am. Legion, Am. Officers of the Great War. Removed to Los Angeles, Calif., Jan. 1920. Home: Los Angeles, Calif. Died Sept. 8, 1922.

SHINN, Charles Howard, forester, author; b. on farm in Williamson Co., Tex., Apr. 29, 1852; s. James and Lucy E. (Clark) S.; brother of Milicent Washburn S.; moved to Calif., 1858; ed. U. of Calif., and Johns Hopkins U.; m. Julia C. Tyler, 1888. Taught sch. several yrs.; engaged in newspaper and mag. work San Francisco, Baltimore, and New York, 1878-89; insp. California agrl. expt. stas. (U. of Calif.), 1890-1901; collaborator for Calif. of U.S. Div. of Forestry, 1899-1900; agt. and expert U.S. Bur. of Forestry, 1902; apptd., 1902, head forest ranger Dept. Interior; assigned to Sierra Nat. Forest, Calif.; supervisor same, 1904; forest examiner, district five, 1911-23. Author: Pacific Rural Handbook, 1879; Land Laws of Mining Districts, 1884; Mining Camps, 1885; Coöperation on the Pacific Coast, 1888; Story of a Mine, 1890. Editor of Fresno Republican book page, and writer of reviews for San Francisco periodicals. Home: Ukiah, Calif. Died Dec. 2, 1924.

SHINN, Florence Scovel, illustrator; b. Camden, N.J.; d. Alden Cortlandt and Emily (Hopkinson) Scovel; ed. Friends' Central Sch., Phila.; studied art at Pa. Acad. of Fine Arts; m. Everett Shinn, Jan. 26, 1898. Illustrator, 1897—. Illustrator: Four-Masted Catboat, 1899; The Loom of Destiny, 1899; Autobiography of a Tomboy, 1900; The Van Dwellers; A Drone and a Dreamer, and Stepping Heavenward, 1901; The Flight of Pony Baker, 1902; The New Boy at Dale, 1903; Lovey Mary, 1903; Mrs. Wiggs of the Cabbage Patch; Coniston; etc. Home: New York, N.Y. Died Oct. 17, 1940.

SHINN, George Wolfe, clergyman; b. Philadelphia, Pa., Dec. 14, 1839; s. William Hooton and Sarah (Wolfe) S.; grad. Phila. Div. Sch., 1863; (D.D., William and Mary, 1883); m. Elizabeth Mills, 1863. Deacon, 1862, priest, 1863, P.E. Ch.; asst. St. Paul's, Phila., 1862-63; rector Ch. of Our Savior, Phila., 1863-65, Trinity, Shamokin, Pa., 1865-67, St. Paul's, Lock Haven, Pa., 1867-70, St. Luke's, Troy, N.Y., 1870-73; head master St. Paul's Sch., Troy, 1873-75; rector Grace Ch., Newton, Mass., 1875-1906. Hon. v.p. and pres. Boston Chapter Actors' Ch. Alliance, 1903. Author: Manual of the Prayer Book; **Manual of**

Church History; Questions About Our Church; Friendly Talks About Marriage; Confirmation; The Episcopal Church; Stories for the Happy Days of Christmas-tide. For 25 yrs. editor of the Whittaker Series of Sunday School Instructions, Teachers' Assistants, etc.; one of editors of Am. Church Sunday School Magazine; editor of Temperance. Home: Summit, N.J. Died 1910.

SHINN, Milicent Washburn, author; b. Niles, Calif., Apr. 15, 1858; d. James and Lucy E. (Clark) S.; A.B., U. of Calif., 1880, Ph.D., 1898. Teacher dist. schs., 1875-76 and 1881; editor San Francisco Commercial Herald during sr. yr. in coll., and later, 1880-81; editor Californian, 1882, Overland Monthly, 1883-94. Active on coms. and official bds., Assn. of Collegiate Alumnæ, 1885-1910. Author: Notes on the Development of a Child, 1894-99 (pub. in German, 1905); The Biography of a Baby, 1901; The Development of the Senses in the First Three Years of Childhood (continuation of "Notes on the Development of a Child"), 1907; etc. Home: Niles, Calif. Died Aug. 14, 1940.

SHIPLEY, (Howard) Maynard, writer, lecturer; b. Baltimore, Md., Dec. 1, 1872; s. Elmon Allen and Sarah Armitage (Jerome) S.; student Stanford U., 1901-03; m. Josephine M. Beede, 1893; m. 2d, Eugenie M. Haag, 1902 (dec.); m. 3d, Miriam Allen de Ford (writer), 1921. Founded, 1898, and 2d pres. Seattle Acad. Science; founder, 1924, and pres. Science League of America, Inc. (nat. assn. to protect freedom in teaching and to resist attempts to unite ch. and state in the U.S.). Lecturer on astronomy and evolution for 20 yrs.; radio lecturer on science. Author: The War on Modern Science, 1927; The Key to Evolution, 1929; also of 33 "Little Blue Books" on physics, astronomy and other scientific subjects. Contbr. This Amazing World (syndicate feature). Mem. Am. advisory council Yenching U.; mem. nat. laymen's advisory council Nat. Conf. of Jews and Christians. Died June 18, 1934.

SHIPLEY, Samuel R., financier, life underwriter; b. Philadelphia, Pa., Jan. 8, 1828; s. Thomas S. (Quaker ancestry); ed. Friends' Boarding Sch., Westtown, Pa. At early age became mem. C. W. Churchman & Co., importers, Phila., later of Shipley, Hazard & Hutchinson; organized, 1865, and pres., 1865-1905, Provident Life and Trust Co. of Phila. Identified with various financial interests and benevolent instns. of Phila. Home: Philadelphia, Pa. Died 1908.

SHIPMAN, Arthur Leffingwell, lawyer; b. Hartford, Conn., Nov. 19, 1864; s. Nathaniel and Mary C. (Robinson) S.; Yale, 1886, LL.B., 1888; m. Melvina Van Kleeck, June 27, 1901; children—Natalie, Anne V. K. (dec.), Arthur L., Mary C. Corp. counsel, Hartford, 1904-08, 1910-12; mem. Shipman & Goodwin; dir. Aetna Ins. Co., Travelers Ins. Co., Travelers Indemnity Co., Travelers Bank & Trust Co., Conn. River Banking Co., Collins Co., Capewell Horse Nail Co., Sanborn Map Company, etc. Republican. Conglist. Home: Hartford, Conn. Died Oct. 16, 1937.

SHIPMAN, Herbert, bishop; b. Lexington, Ky., Aug. 3, 1869; s. Jacob S. and Anne Louisa (Gold) S.; B.A., Columbia, 1890; B.D., Gen. Theol. Sem., 1894. Deacon, 1894, priest, 1895, P.E. Ch.; rector Ch. of Heavenly Rest, N.Y. City, 1907-21; elected suffragan bishop, Diocese of N.Y., May 13, 1921. Chaplain U.S.A., 1896; chaplain 104th F.A., 1917-18; sr. chaplain 1st A.C., 1918-19. Home: New York, N.Y. Died Mar. 23, 1930.

SHIPMAN, Louis Evan, author, playwright; b. Brooklyn, N.Y., Aug. 2, 1869; s. Hamilton W. and Caroline Townsend (Hoopes) S.; ed. Polytechnic Inst. of Brooklyn, and 1892-93, Harvard University; m. Ellen Biddle, 1893; children—Ellen Biddle, Evan Biddle, Mary Pamela; m. 2d, Lucile Watson, 1928. Editorial writer Leslie's Weekly, 1895-96; contbr. to Life and Collier's Weekly; editor of Life, May 1922-24. Author: Urban Dialogues, 1896; A Group of American Theatrical Caricatures, 1898; D'Arcy of the Guards, 1899; Predicaments, 1899; The Curious Courtship of Kate Poins, 1901; The Quality of Youth, 1904; The True Adventures of a Play, 1914; Three Comedies, 1923. Plays produced: The Head of the House, 1898; D'Arcy of the Guards, 1901, and 1910; The Crisis (with Winston Churchill), 1902; John Ermine of the Yellowstone (with Frederic Remington), 1903; The Crossing (with Winston Churchill), 1905; On Parole, 1906; The Admiral, 1909; The Grain of Dust, 1911. Opened the Henry Miller Theatre, New York, with "The Fountain of Youth," 1918; Fools Errant, 1921; Poor Richard, 1924; Le Bonhomme Richard (in French), Theatre National de l'Odeon, Paris, 1928. During the war was member N.H. State Committee of 100 of Public Safety; state director of "Four-Minute-Men," and local food administrator. Decorated Chevalier Legion of Honor (France), 1930. Died Aug. 2, 1933.

SHIPMAN, Nathaniel, U.S. judge 2d circuit, 1892-1902; b. Southbury, Conn., Aug. 22, 1828; s. Rev. Thomas L.S.; prepared at Norwich, Conn., Acad., and at Plainfield, Conn.; grad. Yale, 1848 (LL.D., 1885); m. Mary C. Robinson, May 25, 1859. Practiced law at Hartford until 1873; U.S. dist. judge for Conn., 1873-92. Home: Hartford, Conn. Died 1906.

SHIPMAN, Samuel, dramatist; b. N.Y. City; s. Nathan and Anna S.; ed. Columbia Univ.; unmarried. Author: (plays) Love and Art; A Social Outcast; A Spiritual Vulture; The Spell; She Means Business; Cheaper to Marry; Lawful Larceny. Co-author: It Depends on the Woman; The Royal Maid; Some Warriors; Children of Today; The Good-for-Nothing; Two Sweethearts; Exemption; Right or Wrong; Woman in Room 13; Crooked Gamblers; Nature's Nobleman; Elevating a Husband; The Kreutzer Sonata; The Unwritten Chapter; The Crooked Square; First Is Last; East Is West; Friendly Enemies; Crime; Creoles; Trapped; Fast Life; Scarlet Pages; Drink for Drink; The Mighty Weak; A Lady Detained. Died Feb. 9, 1937.

SHIPMAN, William Rollin, clergyman, educator; b. Granville, Vt., May 4, 1836; s. Harvey and Betsey (Eaton) S.; A.B., Middlebury Coll., 1859, A.M., 1862; (D.D., St. Lawrence, 1882; LL.D., Tufts, 1899, Middlebury, 1900); m. Martha F. Willis, July 28, 1868 (died 1894). Ordained to Universalist ministry, 1865; prof. rhetoric and logic, 1864-1907, dean, 1900-07, Tufts Coll.; emeritus, July 1907—. Died 1908.

SHIPP, Frederic B., Y.M.C.A. officer; b. Swaffham, Norfolk Co., Eng., Jan. 2, 1868; s. Thomas and Susan (Margetson) S.; grad. Ridgetown (Ont.) Collegiate Inst., 1886; m. Lotta J. Hayne, Apr. 6, 1894. Asst. state sec. Y.M.C.A., Minn., 1889, Kan., 1890-94, Pa., 1895-97; with Internat. Com. Y.M.C.A., 1898—; railroad sec., 1898-1906, exec. sec., 1907-14, asso. gen. sec., 1915, and general secretary at Pittsburgh, 1916-28. Organized, and directed Y.M.C.A. work for soldiers during Spanish-Am. War, 1898; made preliminary study and directed initial steps in establishing Y.M.C.A. work in Mexico, 1901; treas. Y.M.C.A. with A.E.F. in France, 1917-18. Nat. dir. China famine fund campaign raising over $8,000,000 for relief in N. China, 1921. V.p. and dir. of Standard Life Ins. Co., Homewood-Peoples Bank. Trustee Pa. Coll. for Women; mem. gen. bd. Nat. Council Y.M.C.A.; mem. Gen. Council Presbyn. Ch. in U.S.A.; treas. Pittsburgh Y.M.C.A. Home: Pittsburgh, Pa. Died Nov. 20, 1932.

SHIPP, Scott, educator; b. Warrenton, Va., Aug. 2, 1839; student Westminster Coll., Mo.; grad. Va. Mil. Inst., 1859 (Litt.D., 1883; LL.D., Washington and Lee U., 1890); m. Anne Alexander, d. Arthur A. Morson, Aug. 19, 1869. Asst. prof. mathematics, later of Latin, Va. Mil. Inst.; lt., capt., maj. and lt. col., C.S.A.; ordered, 1862, by Confed. sec. of war to report as commandant of cadets and instr. of Va. Mil. Inst.; comd. cadets at battle of New Market, where was wounded; after war, grad. in law; reapptd. to Va. Mil. Inst., was supt. same (supt. emeritus). Declined presidency Va. Agr. and Mech. Coll.; mem. bd. of visitors U.S. Mil. Acad., 1890; pres. bd. of visitors U.S. Naval Acad., 1894. Retired under Carnegie Foundation, July 1907. Home: Lexington, Va. Died Dec. 7, 1917.

SHIPPEN, Edward, medical dir. U.S.N.; b. in N.J., June 18, 1826; A.B., Princeton, 1845, A.M., 1848; M.D., U. of Pa., 1848. Apptd. to U.S. Navy, from Pa., 1849, as asst. surgeon, commd. surgeon, Apr. 26, 1861; promoted med. dir., Mar. 17, 1876; retired June 18, 1888; rear admiral retired, 1907. Principal naval service in China and on coasts of Africa and S. America; on European sta. 4 yrs.; was on the Congress when destroyed by Merrimac; on New Ironsides in both battles of Fort Fisher; at Bermuda Hundred, defending Grant's right flank; chief med. officer, Naval Acad., Annapolis; fleet surgeon, European squadron; nearly 7 yrs. in charge of Naval Hosp., Phila. Companion Mil. Order Loyal Legion; fellow Coll. Physicians of Phila.; gov. Pa. Soc. of Colonial Wars; pres. Geneal. Soc. Pa. Author: Thirty Years at Sea; A Christmas at Sea; Naval Battles of America, 1905; Naval Battles of the World, 1905. Home: Philadelphia, Pa. Died 1911.

SHIPPEN, Joseph, lawyer; b. Meadville, Pa., Sept. 10, 1839; s. Judge Henry and Elizabeth Wallis (Evans) S.; bro. of Rush Rhees S.; A.B., Harvard, 1860, A.M., 1867; m. Elizabeth Jones Winslow; m. 2d, Marian Virginia Williamson, Nov. 29, 1884 (died 1906); m. 3d, Elizabeth W. Gilmer, Apr. 2, 1907. Began study of law at Meadville, 1860; admitted to Pa. bar, 1862, Supreme Ct. of U.S., 1878; commd. by state of Pa. to visit, relieve and report as to sick and wounded Pa. soldiers in Civil War; agent and secretary U.S. Sanitary Commn. for Western Pa., at Pittsburgh; taught in high sch., Worcester, Mass., 1863-64; master in chancery U.S. Circuit Ct., Eastern Dist. of Mo., 1872-79. Trustee Meadville Theol. Sch. (1 yr. instr. and lecturer); pres. Western Unitarian Conf.; Pacific Coast Unitarian Conf.; chmn. gen. conf. com. of local improvement clubs of Seattle; pres. Western Fedn. of Improvement Clubs. Del. 16th Internat. Peace Congress, Munich, 1907; del. Lake Mohonk Internat. Peace Conf. Republican. Home: Seattle, Wash. Died June 15, 1923.

SHIPPEN, Rush Rhees, clergyman; b. Meadville, Pa., Jan. 18, 1828; s. Judge Henry and Elizabeth Wallis (Evans) S.; brother of Joseph S.; A.B., Allegheny Coll., Pa., 1843, A.M., 1856; grad. Meadville Theol. Sch., 1849; m. Zoe Rodman, Oct. 10, 1855. Ordained Unitarian ministry, 1849; pastor First Ch.,

Chicago, 1849-57, Meadville, Pa., 1857-58, Unity Ch., Worcester, Mass., 1858-71; sec. Am. Unitarian Assn., Boston, 1871-81; pastor All Souls' Ch., Washington, 1881-95, Unity Ch., Brockton, Mass., 1895-1905, in Italy, 1905-06; pastor, Atlanta, Ga., 1906-07. Home: Brockton, Mass. Deceased.

SHIPTON, James Ancil, army officer; b. Ohio, Mar. 10, 1867; grad. U.S. Mil. Acad., 1892, Sch. of Submarine Defense, 1906. Commd. add. 2d lt. 4th Arty., June 11, 1892; promoted through grades to brig. gen. N.A., Aug. 5, 1917; col. Coast Arty. Corps, May 29, 1918. Served with battery during railroad strikes, Chicago, 1894; mil. attaché Am. Legation, Petropolis, Brazil, 1898-99; in Philippine Islands, 1899-1901; participated in Gen. Kobbe's expdn. to open hemp ports of Luzon; comdg. various dists., P.I., 1900-01; comd. 52d Co., Coast Arty., Governor's Island, N.Y., 1901-02; spl. instrn., Gen. Electric Co., Schenectady, N.Y., 1906-07; comdr. Torpedo Depot and disbursing officer same, 1908; mil. attaché, Argentina, 1912-14; grad. Army War Coll., 1915-16; instr. same, 1916-17; served in France, July 1917-Aug. 1919; organized Anti-Aircraft Service and chief of same until July 1, 1918; comd. 55th Brig. F.A.; comd. divisional arty., 89th Div. in attack on St. Mihiel and divisional arty. 37th Div. in attack in Meuse-Argonne; comd. S.O.S. troops, region of Nancy, to June 1, 1919. Retired at own request, after 30 yrs.' service, Feb. 20, 1920. Officer French Legion of Honor. Married Georgia L. Lincoln, Dec. 17, 1902. Died Feb. 15, 1926.

SHIRAS, George, Jr., jurist; b. Pittsburgh, Pa., Jan. 26, 1832; s. George and Eliza (Herron) S.; bro. of Oliver Perry S.; A.B., Yale, 1853, LL.B., 1854 (LL.D., 1883); m. Lillie E. Kennedy, Dec. 31, 1857; father of George S., 3d. Admitted to Pa. bar, 1856, and practiced in Pittsburgh until apptd. asso. justice Supreme Ct. of U.S., Oct. 10, 1892; retired Feb. 24, 1903; presdl. elector, 1888. Home: Marquette, Mich. Died Aug. 2, 1924.

SHIRAS, Oliver Perry, judge; b. Pittsburgh, Pa., Oct. 22, 1833; s. George and Eliza (Herron) S.; bro. of George, Jr.; A.B., Ohio U., Athens, O., 1853, A.M., 1856; LL.B., Yale, 1856 (LL.D., 1886); m. Elizabeth Mitchell, Feb. 26, 1857. Practiced law at Dubuque, Ia., 1856-82; U.S. dist. judge, Northern Dist. of Ia., 1882-1903. Republican. A.d.c. on staff Gen. Herron, in army of frontier; served in Mo., Ark., and La., until 1864. Author: Equity Practice in Circuit Courts of U.S. Home: Dubuque, Ia. Died Jan. 7, 1916.

SHIRLAW, Walter, artist; b. Paisley, Scotland, Aug. 6, 1838; brought to U.S. 1840; became banknote engraver; exhibited at Nat. Acad., 1861; engaged in art work; academician, Chicago Acad. of Design, 1868; studied in Munich, 1870-77; specialty, genre pictures; has also done much noteworthy decorative work and illustrations for books and mags.; one of founders and 1st pres. Soc. of Am. Artists; taught in Art Students' League; asso., 1887, academician, 1888—, Nat. Acad. Design. Died 1909.

SHIVELY, Benjamin Franklin, senator; b. St. Joseph Co., Ind., Mar. 20, 1857; s. Joel and Elizabeth S.; ed. Northern Ind. Normal Sch.; LL.B., U. of Mich., 1886; m. Laura Jenks, June 19, 1889. In practice at South Bend, Ind., 1886—. Elected to 48th Congress, 1884, for unexpired term (1884-85) of William H. Calkins, resigned; reëlected to 50th, 51st and 52d Congresses (1887-93), 13th Ind. Dist. Dem. nominee for gov. of Ind., 1896; received Dem. vote in Ind. Legislature, for U.S. senator, 1903, 05; elected U.S. senator for term, 1909-15. Pres. trustees Indiana U., Bloomington. Home: South Bend, Ind. Died Mar. 14, 1916.

SHIVERICK, Asa, merchant; b. Omaha, Neb., Jan. 8, 1877; s. Charles and Jane (Bancroft) S.; grad. St. Paul's Sch., Concord, Mass., 1895; m. Jane Bancroft, Feb. 1912; children—Jane, Asa, Charles. Pres. The Higbee Co., dept. store, Cleveland; dir. Erie R.R. Co. Episcopalian. Home: Cleveland Heights, O. Died July 1, 1937.

SHOEMAKER, Charles Frederick, captain and chief U.S. Revenue Cutter Service; b. Glendale, Ia., Mar. 27, 1841; s. Capt. William R. (U.S.A.) and Julia (Hepburn) S.; ed. U.S. Naval Acad., 1858-60, self-taught after that; m. Mary A. Cole, May 13, 1862; m. 2d, Rita Miller, Sept. 2, 1881. Acting midshipman U.S.N., Sept. 1858-Sept. 1860; entered U.S. Revenue Cutter Service, Nov. 20, 1860, as 3d lt.; resigned at close of Civil War; recommd. 3d lt., June 1868, in U.S. Revenue Cutter Service; 2d lt., Mar. 12, 1872; 1st lt., Mar. 25, 1878; capt., Mar. 18, 1895; retired from active service on account of age, Mar. 27, 1905. While lt. performed all duties of line officer on shipboard and on all stas. from Mass. to Gulf of Mexico; insp. life saving stas. 13 yrs.; on being promoted to capt., 1895, assigned to be chief Revenue Cutter Service; reorganized and rebuilt service; added 19 new vessels to it; sent relief expdn. to Point Barrow which rescued ice-bound whaler in winter of 1897-98; placed fleet of revenue cutters in cooperation with navy in Spanish-Am. War; promoted and commd. captain commandant retired, May 5, 1908. Democrat (of Tilden and Cleveland school). Home: Woodstock, Va. Deceased.

SHOEMAKER, Henry Francis, retired railway official; b. Orwigsburg, Pa., Mar. 28, 1845; s. John W. and Mary (Brock) S.; ed. Genesee Sem., Lima, N.Y.; m. Blanche, d. Col. James W. Quiggle, of Phila. Apptd. to U.S. Naval Acad., 1861; resigned same year to go on staff of Gen. McClernand in western army, 1861-63; served 1st lt. 27th Pa. Vols., 1863. Became interested in mining anthracite coal in Pa., 1868, and later in bituminous coal mining in W.Va. and Ohio. Elected sec. and treas. Central R.R. of Minn., 1878; pres. Mineral Range R.R., 1887, Cincinnati, Dayton & Ironton R.R., 1889, Dayton & Union R.R., 1890; chmn. exec. com. C.,H.&D. Ry., 1890; v.p. Ind., Decatur & Western Ry., 1893; v.p. Cincinnati, Indianapolis & Western Ry., 1902; chmn. bd. dirs. Cincinnati, New Orleans & Tex. Pacific, 1899; chmn. bd. dirs. C.,H.&D.Ry., 1890. Home: New York, N.Y., and Riverside, Conn. Died July 2, 1918.

SHOEMAKER, John Vietch, physician; b. Chambersburg, Pa., Mar. 18, 1852; s. Lewis A. and Mary M. (Greenawalt) S.; A.B., Dickinson Coll., Pa., 1872, A.M., 1875; M.D., Jefferson Med. Coll., 1874; LL.D., Dickinson, 1895; m. Jennie M. Logan, 1874. Demonstrator and lecturer on anatomy and lecturer on cutaneous affections, Jefferson Med. Coll., 1874-86; prof. cutaneous diseases and prof. materia medica and therapeutics, 1886—, pres., 1890—, Medico-Chirurg. Coll., Phila. A founder of Medical Bulletin, 1879, Medical Register, 1887, and later editor Medical Times and Register. Was pres. Am. Med. Editors' Assn.; fellow London Med. Soc.; del. 9th, 10th and 11th Internat. Med. Congresses; surgeon gen. N.G. Pa., 1898-1902; commr. state of Pa. to Paris Expn., 1900; pres. Bd. Charities and Corrections City and County of Phila., 1901—. Apptd. surgeon Med. Reserve Corps U.S.A., 1908. Author: Poisons and Antidotes; Ointments and Oleates; Treatise on Materia Medica and Therapeutics; Heredity, Health and Personal Beauty; A Practical Treatise on Diseases of the Skin, 1898. Died 1910.

SHOEMAKER, Michael Myers, author; b. Covington, Ky., June 26, 1853; s. Robert Myers and Mary Colegate (Steiner) S.; student 2 yrs. Cornell Univ., class 1874; m. Helen Parmelee, Feb. 19, 1910. Traveled the world over in the study of the people of the earth. Founder Ohio Soc. Colonial Wars. Author: Eastward to the Land of the Morning, 1893; Kingdom of the White Woman, 1894; Sealed Provinces of the Tsar, 1895; Island of the Southern Seas, 1897; Quaint Corners of Ancient Empires, 1899; Palaces and Prisons of Mary Queen of Scots, 1901; The Great Siberian Railway, 1903; Heart of the Orient, 1904; Winged Wheels in France, 1906; Wanderings in Ireland, 1908; Islam Lands, 1910; Indian Pages and Pictures, 1912. Home: Cincinnati, O., and Bennington, Vt. Died Aug. 11, 1924.

SHOEMAKER, Rachel Hinkle, elocutionist; b. Plumstead, Pa., Oct. 1, 1838; d. William Marshall and Elizabeth (Walter) Hinkle; attended State Normal Sch., Millersville, Pa.; later specialized in elocution, platform delivery, German, French and literature; m. J. W. Shoemaker, June 27, 1867 (died 1880). Established, 1874, and instr. and prin. Nat. Sch. of Elocution and Oratory, Phila., 1874—. Author: Delsartian Pantomimes, 1891; Advanced Elocution, 1895. Compiled 12 vols. of Best Selections, 2 vols. Young Folks' Recitations, and Classic Dialogues. Home: Cynwyd, Pa. Died Feb. 1, 1915.

SHOEMAKER, Waite Almon, normal sch. pres.; b. Willoughby, O., Mar. 24, 1860; s. Abraham and Achsah (Waite) S.; grad. State Normal Sch., St. Cloud, Minn., 1881; student U. of Minn., 1896, 1897; Pd.M., New York U., 1898, Pd.D., 1899; m. Louise Polley, June 2, 1884. Began as teacher in country schs., 1875; supt. pub. schs., St. Cloud, Minn., 1900-01; became mem. faculty State Normal Sch., St. Cloud, 1881, pres., 1902—. Republican. Unitarian. Home: St. Cloud, Minn. Died 1916.

SHOEMAKER, William Rawle, naval officer; b. Staten Island, N.Y., Feb. 10, 1863; s. Capt. Comdt. Charles F. (U.S.R.C.S.) and Mary Augusta (Cole) S.; grad. U.S. Naval Acad., 1884; post-grad. work in electricity, Johns Hopkins, 1889-92; m. Jennie D., d. Morton Cheeseman, of N.Y. City and San Francisco, June 2, 1896; children—William Rawle, Carolyn (Mrs. A. B. Hepler), Katherine (Mrs. Arthur Caley Davis). Commissioned ensign, U.S.N., July 1, 1884; promoted through grades to rear adm., Dec. 24, 1917. Instr. U.S. Naval Acad., 1896-98; comdr. U.S.S. Talbot, Spanish-Am. War, 1898-99, U.S.S. Arayat, Philippine Insurrection, 1900-02; instr. Naval Acad., 1902-04; navigator U.S.S. Alabama; exec. officer U.S.S. Maine and Connecticut; in charge enlisted personnel of navy, Bur. Navigation, 1907-09; comd. scout cruiser Chester, 1909-10; chief-of-staff, Atlantic Fleet, 1910-12; mem. Gen. Bd. of Navy, 1912-14; comd. U.S.S. Arkansas, 1914-16; mem. Gen. Bd., 1917-19; apptd. comdr. battleship div. 3, Atlantic Fleet, Jan. 29, 1919, battleship force 1, Atlantic Fleet, Apr. 1, 1919, battleship div. 3, Pacific Fleet, July 1, 1919, cruiser force, Pacific Fleet, July 8, 1920; comdt. 14th Naval Dist. (Hawaii), Jan. 14, 1921; v. adm. and comdr. battleship force, Pacific Fleet, July 8, 1921—; dir. war plans operations, Navy Dept., June 26, 1923-24; chief of Bur. of Navigation, June 7, 1924-Feb. 10, 1927, retired. Died May 30, 1938.

SHONTS, Theodore Perry, railway official; b. Crawford County, Pa., May 5, 1856; s. Dr. Henry Daniels and Margaret Nevin (Marshall) S.; removed with parents in boyhood, to Appanoose County, Ia.; A.B., Monmouth (Ill.) Coll., 1876; m. Harriet Amelia, d. Gen. (afterwards Gov.) Francis M. Drake, of Centerville, Ia., 1882. After graduation became an accountant, and employed by nat. banks in Ia. to standardize and simplify their methods of bookkeeping; studied law and practiced a short time at Centerville; became associated with General Drake, who had large financial and railroad interests, and who placed much of the work of management and constrn. in his hands; had charge of constrn. of part of Ia. Central R.R.; afterwards built the Mo., Ia. & Neb. R.R. and was its controlling owner; with associates secured control of Toledo, St. Louis & Western R.R. and rehabilitated same; selected by Pres. Roosevelt, spring of 1905, as chmn. Isthmian Canal Commn., formulating the plans for that work; continued at its head until Feb. 1907; pres. Interborough-Met. Co. of New York (now Interborough Consolidated Corp.). Became pres. Toledo, St. Louis & Western R.R., Jan. 15, 1904; pres. C.&A. R.R., 1909-12, Ia. Central Ry. and Minneapolis & St. Louis R.R., 1909-11; also pres. and dir. Interborough Rapid Transit Co., N.Y. Rys. Co., Rapid Transit Subway Constrn. Co., Subway Realty Co.; chmn. exec. com. and dir. N.Y. & Queens County Ry. Co.; dir. Am. Trust & Savings Bank (Chicago), C.&O. Ry. Co., Des Moines & Ft. Dodge R.R., Co., 5th Av. Coach Co., Ia. Central Ry. Co., L.I. Electric Ry. Co., N.Y.&L.I. Traction Co., N.Y. Transportation Co., Pittsburgh & Shawmut R.R. Co., Realty Trust Co. (Atlanta, Ga.), Toledo, St. Louis & Western R.R. Co., White Sulphur Springs, Inc. Died Sept. 21, 1919.

SHOOK, Alfred M., financier; b. Winchester, Tenn., July 16, 1845; s. James K. and Eliza (Green) S.; ed. 5 mos. in pub. sch., Franklin County, Tenn.; m. Terresa Estill, July 17, 1871. With Tenn. Coal, Iron & R.R. Co., 1866-1903, filling all positions including v.p. and gen. mgr.; pres. First Savings Bank and Trust Co., Brush Creek Coal Co.; dir. First Nat. Bank (Nashville), Nashville Ry. & Light Co., Nashville Trust Co.; trustee Mut. Life Ins. Co. (New York). Pres. Monteagle S.S. Assembly. Home: Nashville, Tenn. Died Mar. 18, 1923.

SHOOP, John Daniel, educator; b. Sabina, O., Mar. 3, 1857; s. Jonathan M. and Margaret (Snider) S.; ed. high sch., Washington C.H., O., Bloomingburg (O.) Acad., Ind. Normal U., Cook Co. (Ill.) Normal Sch., Lake Forest U. (A.B.), U. of Chicago; LL.D., Chicago Coll. of Law, 1916; m. Jennie B. Perrill, Sept. 1, 1887. Country sch. teacher in Ohio, 1878; supt. schs., Bloomingburg, O., 1886-88, Saybrook, Ill., 1889-90, Gibson City, Ill., 1891-96, Paris, Ill., 1897-1901; with city schs., Chicago, 1901—, becoming asst. supt., 1909, supt., 1915—. Republican. Mason. Home: Chicago, Ill. Died Aug. 9, 1918.

SHOPE, Simeon P., lawyer; b. Akron, O., Dec. 3, 1837; s. Simeon P. and Lucinda (Richmond) S.; parents removed to Marseilles, Ill., 1839; common sch. and academic edn.; taught dist. sch.; m. Sarah M. Jones, 1858 (died 1883). Admitted to bar, 1858; practiced at Metamora, and Lewiston, Ill., 1858-77; judge Circuit Ct., 10th Ill. Circuit, 1877-85; asso. justice Supreme Ct., Ill., 1885-94; declined renomination; in practice at Chicago, 1894—; sr. mem. Shope, Zane, Busby & Weber. Democrat. Home: Chicago, Ill. Died Jan. 23, 1920.

SHORE, Clarence Albert, dir. hygienic lab.; b. Salem, N.C., Nov. 26, 1873; s. Henry Washington and Lavinia Elizabeth (Boyer) S.; B.S., U. of N.C., 1901, M.S., 1902, LL.D., 1929; M.D., Johns Hopkins, 1907; m. Ellen Dortch, May 27, 1914. Instr. in biology, U. of N.C., 1901-04; dir. State Lab. of Hygiene, N.C., 1908—. Mem. Moravian Ch. Home: Raleigh, N.C. Died Feb. 10, 1933.

SHOREY, Paul, university prof.; b. Davenport, Ia., Aug. 3, 1857; s. Daniel L. and Maria A. (Merriam) S.; A.B., Harvard, 1878; U. of Leipzig, 1881-82, U. of Bonn, 1882, Am. Sch. of Classical Studies, Athens, 1882-83; Ph.D., U. of Munich, 1884; LL.D., Ia. Coll., 1905, U. of Mo., 1913, Johns Hopkins, 1915, U. of Mich., 1915, U. of Colorado, 1917, Princeton, 1920, Univ. of Pa., 1921; Litt.D., Univ. of Wis., 1911, Brown, 1914; D.Letters and Philosophy, U. of Liège, 1924; Litt.D., Harvard, 1925; admitted to bar, Chicago, 1880; m. Emma L. Gilbert, June 1895. Prof. Greek, Bryn Mawr Coll., 1885-92; prof. Greek 1892—, head dept., 1896—, U. of Chicago. Annual asso. dir. Am. Sch. Classical Studies, Athens, 1901-02; mng. editor Classical Philology, 1908—. Turnbull lecturer in poetry, Johns Hopkins U., 1912; Roosevelt prof. U. of Berlin, 1913-14. Pres. Am. Philol. Assn., 1910; mem. Nat. Inst. Arts and Letters; associé de l' Académie Royale de Belgique, 1929. Author: De Platonis Idearum Dostrina, 1884; The Idea of Good in Plato's Republic, 1895; The Odes and Epodes of Horace, 1898; The Unity of Plato's Thought, 1903; The Assault on Humanism, 1917. Mem. Acad. Arts and Letters. Home: Chicago, Ill. Died Apr. 24, 1934.

SHORT, Francis Burgette, denominational sec.; b. nr. Georgetown, Del., Dec. 20, 1868; s. Isaac B. and Julia (Knowles) S.; grad. Wilmington Conf. Acad., 1889; A.B., U. of Del., 1891; student Drew Theol. Sem., 1899; D.D., Puget Sound Coll., 1913; LL.D., Kan. Wesleyan U.; m. Mabel L. Hart, 1902; 1 son, Isaac Dolphus. Ordained M.E. ministry, 1892; pastor Mt. Pleasant, Md., 1890-92, Harrison St. Ch., Wilmington, Del., 1892-97, Epworth Ch., Wilmington, 1897-1902; sec. Y.M.C.A.; Wilmington, 1902; v. chancellor U. of the Pacific, 1903, 04; pastor Portland, Ore., 1904-07, Salt Lake City, Utah, 1907-13, Spokane, Wash., 1913-18; extension sec. Bd. of Temperance, Prohibition and Pub. Morals, M.E. Ch., 1920—. Was with J. C. Penney Co. 10 yrs. Republican. Mason (Past Potentate El Katif Temple, Spokane). Writer on religious and travel topics; lecturer. Home: Milford, Del. Died 1936.

SHORT, Frank Hamilton, lawyer; b. Shelby County, Mo., Sept. 12, 1862; s. Joshua Hamilton Bell and Emily (Wharton) S.; ed. common schs.; read law in law offices; m. Nellie Curtis, Mar. 17, 1897. In practice at Fresno, Calif., 1885—; chiefly atty. for irrigation, electric power and oil cos.; dir. Fresno Nat. Bank; v.p. Fresno Canal & Irrigation Co., Yosemite commr., 1896-1904; trustee State Normal Sch., San José, Calif., 1896-1901; mem. State Conservation Commn., 1905—. Del. many Rep. state convs., 1888—; del. Rep. Nat. Conv., St. Louis, 1896, Chicago, 1904. Delivered many addresses on pub., polit. and other subjects. Mason, K.T. Died June 5, 1920.

SHORT, Josephine Helena, author; b. Urbana, Ill.; d. Joseph S.; collegiate edn.; A.B., Boston U., 1886. Extensive traveler; chaperoned many parties in Europe. Lecturer. Author: Oberammergau, 1910; Chosen Days in Scotland, 1911; Reading Journey Through Scotland, 1913. Speaker for Flying Squadron (war work). Home: White Plains, N.Y. Deceased.

SHORT, William Harrison, clergyman; b. on farm, nr. College Springs, Ia., Dec. 4, 1868; s. James Black and Eugenia (Noe) S.; B.S., Amity Coll., College Springs, Ia., 1887; B.A., Beloit Coll., Wis., 1894, M.A., 1897; B.D., Yale Theol. Sch., 1897; Harvard U., summer, 1900; m. Caroline Sleight Steuart, Oct. 17, 1900; children—Elizabeth Dering (dec.), James Steuart, Frederick Wallace, Frances Eugenia, Robert Dering, Douglas Fosdick. Ordained Congl. ministry, 1897; pastor in Wis. and Minn., 1897-1908; sec. New York Peace Soc., 1908-17; sec. and mem. exec. com. League to Enforce Peace, 1915-23, director gen. com. on limitation of armament during internat. conf. that met at Washington, D.C., Nov. 11, 1921; sec. 20th Century Fund, 1922-23; exec. dir. League of Nations Non-Partisan Assn., 1923-25; dir. Doane Corp., 1925; treasurer Rollins Coll., 1926-27; dir. of Motion Picture Research Council, Incorporated, 1927—. Delegate to 19th Internat. Peace Congress, Stockholm, Sweden, 1910, 20th Congress, Geneva, Switzerland, 1912; mem. Mohonk Conf., 1909—; mem. and sec. exec. com. American Peace Centenary Committee; trustee American-Scandinavian Foundation, 1911-27; mem. Council on Foreign Relations, Nat. Council Boy Scouts of America, 1924-28. Was mem. com. that drafted covenants for the League of Nations as follows: the original covenant 1914-15, that launched the idea in U.S. and abroad; an elaboration of the original draft, 1916-17; a revised covenant under chairmanship of President Taft, 1918. Mason. Author: A Generation of Motion Pictures, 1928; also pamphlets on internat. subjects. Editor League of Nations Herald, 1923-25. Home: Amityville, L.I., N.Y. Died Jan. 10, 1935.

SHORTALL, John G., lawyer, humanitarian; b. Dublin, Ireland, Sept. 20, 1838; s. John and Charlotte (Towson) S.; removed to New York, 1841; m. Mary Dunham Staples, Sept. 5, 1861. In Chicago, 1854—; studied law; admitted to Ill. bar. In 1861 became owner of real estate abstracts which acquired exceptional value after destruction of pub. records of deeds, etc., by fire of 1871; one of founders Ill. Humane Soc., 1869; pres. same, 1877-1906; organized Am. Humane (Nat.) Assn., 1877; pres. thereof many terms; presided over Humane Congress, World's Columbian Expn., 1893, and presented association's exhibit (award). In 1880 apptd. appraiser sch. lands, City of Chicago; 10 yrs. dir. and 3 terms pres. Chicago Pub. Library; as such obtained in 1890 consent of abutting owners and acquired possession of Dearborn Park site for library. Home: Lakeside, Ill. Died 1908.

SHORTLE, Abraham Given, physician; b. Tipton, Ind., Feb. 14, 1871; s. George M. and Margaret (Bell) S.; grad. Northern Ind. Normal Sch., 1887; M.D., Baltimore (Md.) Med. Coll., 1896; studied Post-Grad. Med. Sch. Chicago, 1900, 01, U. of Chicago, summer 1907, U. of Heidelberg, Germany, 1907, 08; m. Alice Stanley Mitchell, Aug. 18, 1903. Practiced at Yorktown, Ill., 1897-98, Chicago, 1898-1905, Albuquerque, N.M., 1908—; founder, pres. and med. dir. Albuquerque Sanatorium. Sec. N.M. State Bur. of Health, and State Bureau of Child's Welfare. Republican. Presbyterian. Mason. Home: Albuquerque, N.M. Died May 1922.

SHORTLIDGE, Jonathan Chauncey, educator; b. Concordville, Pa., Aug. 2, 1872; s. Joseph and Caroline Bailey (Gause) S.; A.B., Swarthmore Coll., 1896; A.B., Harvard, 1898; m. Helen Wood, June 14, 1923. Prin. Friends Acad, Locust Valley, N.Y., 1896-97; teacher, Maplewood Inst., Concordville, Pa., 1898-1920; prin. Maplewood Sch. for Boys, Chester Heights, Pa., 1920—; dir. Maplewood Summer Camp. Mason. Home: West Chester, Pa. Died Jan. 30, 1941.

SHORTRIDGE, N. Parker, capitalist; b. Portsmouth, N.H.; ed. pub. and pvt. schs. With David S. Brown & Co., cotton and woolen goods commn., Phila., 12 yrs.; became mem. firm of George F. Peabody & Co., succeeded by Harris Shortridge & Co. and Shortridge, Borden & Co.; retired from commn. business, 1877, and devoted attention to corps.; mem. Centennial Bd. of Finance, 1873-93; dir. Pa. R.R., 1874—, and served as head of many important coms.; dir. Phila. Nat. Bank; trustee Union Trust Co. of New York, Phila. Trust, Safe Deposit & Ins. Co. Home: Wynnewood, Pa. Died Jan. 1915.

SHOUP, George Laird, stock raiser, merchant; b. Kittanning, Pa., June 15, 1836; ed. public schools; farmer and stock raiser nr. Galesburg, Ill., 1852-59; miner and mcht., Colo., 1859-61; enlisted in a co. of scouts, Sept. 1861; served in Colo. and N.Mex.; later lt. 1st Colo. cav., promoted until he became col. 3d Colo. cav.; on leave of absence, 1864, to serve 30 days as mem. Colo. constitutional conv.; established stores, 1866, at Virginia City, Mont., and Salmon City, Ida.; 2 terms mem. Idaho legislature; gov. of Territory, 1889-90; elected gov. of State, 1890; U.S. senator, 1890-1901. Republican. Died 1904.

SHOUP, Oliver Henry; b. Champaign County, Ill., Dec. 13, 1869; s. William R. and Delia J. (Ferris) S.; student Colo. Coll., Colorado Springs, Colo., 1886-88; m. Unetta Small, Sept. 18, 1891 (died 1927); children—Mrs. Reba Leeming (dec.), Oliver Henry, Merrill E., Verner R.; m. 2d, Mary Alice Hackett, Mar. 3, 1930. Moved to Colorado Springs at 13; employed by Colorado Springs Company (original town company); with the late Verner Z. Reed and others organized Midwest Oil Co.; first pres. same, and Midwest Refining Co.; pres. Westland Securities Co., identified for many yrs. with irrigation, land, oil development and mining enterprises, banking and real estate business. Trustee Colo. Coll., 1917-31; mem. Colorado Springs Sch. Bd., 1917-18. Gov. of Colo., 2 terms, 1919-23. Organized Presbyn. Hosp. of Denver and was pres. many years. Republican. Presbyterian. Died Sept. 30, 1940.

SHOVE, Eugene Percy, banking, mining; b. Town of Green, N.Y., July 25, 1855; s. Benjamin and Cornelia (Terwiliger) S.; prep. edn., Ithaca (N.Y.) Acad. and Cazenovia (N.Y.) Sem.; and student Syracuse U.; LL.D., Colorado College, 1931; m. Eva Louise Steele, Feb. 19, 1885. Cashier, 1st Nat. Bank, Gunnison, Colo., 1885-95; engaged in banking and gold and copper mining, 1895—; pres. El Paso Nat. Bank of Colorado Springs, Colo., 1916-18; chmn. bd. First Nat. Bank, Colorado Springs, 1918-24, and 1933—; v.p. Golden Cycle Corp.; treas. Cresson Gold Mining & Milling Co., Holly Sugar Corp.; dir. Holly Oil Co. Mayor of Gunnison, 1893-96; former city treasurer; mem. bd. trustees, city schools, Colorado Springs. Vice pres. Colo. Coll. Republican. Quaker. Mason. Elk. Home: Colorado Springs, Colo. Died Feb. 17, 1939.

SHOW, Arley Barthlow, university prof.; b. Wenona, Ill., Aug. 10, 1856; s. Joseph Lewis and Katherine (Jackson) S.; A.B., Doane Coll., Neb., 1882, A.M., 1887; grad. Andover Theol. Sem., 1885; grad. student in history, Harvard, 1892, U. of Leipzig, 1900-01, 1909; m. Bucephalia Wolph, June 17, 1885. Ordained Congl. ministry, 1885; pastor Waco, Neb., 1885-87; prof. history and English lit., Doane Coll., 1887-92; asst. prof. European history, 1892-93, asso. prof., 1893-95, prof., 1895-1901, mediæval history, 1901—, Leland Stanford Jr. U. Lecturer on ch. history, Pacific Theol. Sem., Calif., 1905-07. Wrote history of Congregational Institutions, in Caldwell's Education in Nebraska, 1902; The Movement for Reform in the Teaching of Religion in the Public Schools of Saxony (U.S. Bur. of Edn., Bull. No. 1, 1910); The New Culture-History in Germany, 1912. Home: Palo Alto, Calif. Died Oct. 28, 1920.

SHOWALTER, Anthony Johnson, composer, pub.; b. Rockingham Co., Va., May 1, 1858; s. John A. and Susanna (Miller) S.; ed. pub. and pvt. schs.; studied music with B. C. Unseld and H. R. Palmer, New York, P. J. Merges, Phila., Dr. George F. and F. W. Root, Chicago, and others; studied methods in Eng., France and Germany one summer; m. Callie Walser, Nov. 1881; m. 2d, Mrs. Eleanor Dorsey, née Gillen, June 1912. Began, 1880, as teacher, compiler singing school books and composer, and as publisher, Dalton, Ga., 1884; pres. The A. J. Showalter Co., Dalton, Ga., Texarkana, Ark.-Tex., Chattanooga, Tenn., dir., mem. exec. com. Interstate Life & Accident Co., Chattanooga. Democrat. Presbyn. Mason. Author or Composer: Work and Worship, 1886; Rudiments of Music, 1886; Class Choir and Congregation, 1888; Complete Rudiments of Music, 1896; Showalter's Practical Harmony, 1907; Showalter's Practical Harmony Tablet, 1907; Practical Rudiments and Music Reader, 1909, and many others—over 100 books in all. Most popular composition, the gospel song, "Leaning on the Everlasting Arms," pub. in more than a thousand music books and translated into practically every language of the world where the Christian religion is known. Home: Chattanooga, Tenn. Died Sept. 15, 1924.

SHOWALTER, Jackson Whipps; b. Minerva, Ky., Feb. 4, 1860; s. Freeman Benoni and Margaret Rachel (Whipps) S.; student Kenyon Coll., O., 3 yrs., 1875-78; B.A., Ky. Mil. Inst., Frankfort, 1881; m. Nellie Love Marshall, Feb. 28, 1887. Engaged in farming, 1905—. Won title of chess champion of America, 1888, and held it until defeated by Pillsbury some 10 yrs. later; finished 4th in Internat. Tournament, 1904; defeated by F. J. Marshall, Am. champion, 1909. Republican. Episcopalian. Home: Georgetown, Ky. Died Feb. 2, 1935.

SHOWALTER, Noah David, state supt. edn.; b. Cass Co., Neb., Feb. 22, 1869; s. Noah and Nancy (Shoopman) S.; student U. of Ida., 1893-96; grad. Lewiston (Ida.) State Normal Sch., 1899; A.B., State Coll. of Wash., 1907, A.M., 1908; LL.D., College of Puget Sound, 1930; m. Arra Belle Thomas, Mar. 12, 1891. Teacher Whitman County, Wash., 1894; county supt. schools, Whitman County, 2 terms, 1905-09; pres. State Normal Sch., Cheney, Wash., May 1910-26. Mem. State Code Commn., 1907-08, later mem. Wash. State Bd. Edn.; state superintendent of public instruction, Olympia, Wash. Organized first rural sch. dept. in the Northwest, 1908, and established 6 rural demonstration schs. in 6 counties. Attended Teachers Coll. (Columbia U.) summer 1916, Stanford U., summer 1920, 23. Trustee World Federation of Ednl. Assns. Republican. Methodist. Author: A Handbook for Rural School Officers. Died Aug. 4, 1937.

SHOWALTER, William Joseph, editor; b. Dale Enterprise, Va., July 10, 1878; s. David Bowman and Susan Catherine (Swope) S.; student Bridgewater (Va.) College, 1894-96; LL.D. from same college, 1930; hon. Sc.D., Pennsylvania Coll., 1921; m. Effie Caldwell Coyner, Nov. 12, 1902. Teacher, pub. schs., Va., 1896-98; city editor Harrisonburg Daily News, 1898-1901; joined Washington (D.C.) Bur. New York Journal, 1901; editorial writer Dem. Congressional Com., 1902; Washington corr. Va. and W.Va. newspapers, 1902-07; writer for Haskin Syndicate, 1907-13; editor Staunton (Va.) Daily News and Harrisonburg (Va.) Daily News Record; 1913-15; asst. to editor, asst. editor, staff writer and chief of the division of research, National Geog. Magazine, 1914—. Decorated Order of Bolivar by Govt. of Venezuela, 1912, as writer on Latin-Am. topics. Asso. editor History of the Panama Canal. Mem. bd. trustees American Univ.; chmn. commn. to draft a statement on the relationship between religion and science, for the United Luth. Ch. in America. Home: Harrisonburg, Va. Died Oct. 13, 1935.

SHOWER, George Theodore, physician; b. Manchester, Md., Aug. 20, 1841; s. Adam and Mary Ann (Geiger) S.; A.B., Franklin and Marshall Coll., Pa., 1860, A.M., 1895; M.D., Hahnemann Med. Coll., Phila., 1882; m. Ida M. Leslie, Dec. 5, 1890 (died 1895). Mem. Co. D, 1st Md. Cav., C.S.A., during Civil War. Practiced in Baltimore, 1882—; prof. physiology, 1894-99, prof. materia medica, 1899-1908, also dean, 1900-06, Southern Homœ. Med. Coll. (later Atlantic Med. Coll.), Baltimore. Trustee Catawba Coll., N.C., 1903-06; elder and treas. Trinity Reformed Ch., Baltimore, 1884—; treas. Reformed Ch. Extension Soc. Democrat. Home: Baltimore, Md. Died Feb. 2, 1923.

SHOWERMAN, Grant, univ. prof.; b. Brookfield, Wis., Jan. 9, 1870; s. Hiram and Ellen Augusta (Parker) S.; A.B., U. of Wis., 1896, A.M., 1897, fellow in Latin, 1896-98, Ph.D., 1900; fellow Archæol. Inst. of America at Am. Sch. of Classical Studies, Rome, 1898-1900; m. Zilpha Marie Vernon, at Rome, Aug. 10, 1899. Prof. classics, U. of Wis., 1900—. Mem. many professional societies. Decorated Cavalier of the Crown of Italy. Presbyterian. Author: With the Professor, 1910; Translation of Ovid's Heroides and Amores, Loeb Classical Library, 1914; The Indian Stream Republic and Luther Parker, 1915; A Country Chronicle, 1916; A Country Child, 1917; Horace and His Influence, 1922; Eternal Rome, 1924; Century Readings in Ancient Classical Literature, 1925; Rome and the Romans, 1931. Annual prof. Am. Acad. in Rome, 1922-23, dir. summer session, 1923-32. Home: Madison, Wis. Died Nov. 13, 1935.

SHRADY, George Frederick, physician; b. New York, Jan. 14, 1837; ed. Coll. City of New York (A.M., Yale); grad. Coll. Phys. & Surg., New York, 1858; m. Mary Lewis (died 1883); m. 2d, Hester E. Cantine, 1888. Editor Medical Record, New York; consulting surgeon to St. Francis, Columbus, Gen. Memorial and Health Dept. hosps., New York. Acting asst. surgeon, U.S.A., during Civil war; attended Gen. Grant, as cons. surgeon, in last illness. Home: New York, N.Y. Died 1907.

SHRADY, Henry Merwin, sculptor; b. New York, N.Y., Oct. 24, 1871; s. Dr. George Frederick and Mary (Lewis) S.; A.B., Columbia, 1894; studied law, but never practiced, and was engaged in business, 1895-1900; self-taught in art; m. Harrie E. Monroe, Nov. 18, 1896. Won competition for equestrian statue of General George Washington, for Brooklyn, N.Y. ($50,000), 1901; won competition for Grant Memorial for Washington, 1902 ($250,000); commd., 1903, by Holland Soc. of New York, to make equestrian statue of William the Silent; executed equestrian statues of Gen. Williams (Detroit), Gen. Lee (Charlottesville, Va.); statue of Jay Cooke (Duluth). A.N.A., 1909. Home: Elmsford, N.Y. Died Apr. 12, 1922.

SHREVE, Milton William, congressman; b. Venango Co., Pa., May 3, 1858; s. Rev. Cyrus and Florella (Nourse) S.; Allegheny College, Pa., 2 yrs.; Ph.B., Bucknell U., Pa., 1884, A.M., same; m. Mary Hill, 1885. Admitted to Pa. bar, 1893; dist. atty., Erie Co., Pa., 1899-1902; mem. Pa. Ho. of Rep., 3 terms, 1906-12 (speaker 1911); member 63d Congress (1913-15), and of 66th and 67th Congresses (1919-23), 25th Pa. Dist., and 68th to 72d Congresses (1923-33), 29th Dist.; practice of law, 1933—. Republican. Presbyn. Mason. Home: Erie, Pa. Died Dec. 23, 1939.

SHRIVER, Alfred Jenkins, lawyer; b. Baltimore, Md., June 5, 1867; s. Albert and Annie (Jenkins) S.; won intercollegiate thesis prize over 2,500 competitors in 1887; A.B., Johns Hopkins, 1891; post-grad. course same, 1892; LL.B., U. of Md., 1893; hon. A.M., Loyola Coll., 1894; unmarried. In law practice at Baltimore, 1893—; has been prominently identified with many estates and will contests. Author: Res Gestæ as a Rule of Evidence; Law of Wills of Personal Property in Maryland Prior to Aug. 1, 1884; Status of the Original Preferred Stock of the Baltimore & Ohio R.R. Co. and other legal publications. Home: Baltimore, Md. Died Sept. 3, 1939.

SHRIVER, John Shultz, journalist; b. Baltimore, Md., June 17, 1857; s. J. Alexander and Olivia B. S.; B.S., Princeton, 1878. Actively engaged in journalism, 1878—; Washington corr. Baltimore American and Baltimore Star, 1885—. Author: Almost (romance), 1890; Through the South and West with President Harrison, 1894. Home: Washington, D.C. Died Apr. 11, 1915.

SHRYOCK, Henry William, educator; b. nr. Olney, Ill., Mar. 25, 1861; s. William and Elizabeth Ann (Woods) S.; Ph.B., Ill. Wesleyan U., 1894; spl. work U. of Chicago; m. Jessie Burnett, 1886; 1 son, Burnett Henry. Prin. high sch., Olney, Ill., 1885-94; head of English Dept., Southern Ill. State Normal Sch., 19 years; v.p. same, 16 yrs., pres., 1912—. Mem. Ill. State Teachers' Assn. (pres. 1911), Southern Ill. Teachers' Assn. (pres. 1904). Elk. Traveled in Europe, 1902, 09, 14. Editor: Tennyson's Princess, 1896; Reading-Literature (8th grade), 1914. Translator: Molière's A Doctor in Spite of Himself, 1908. Lecturer in 12 states of the Middle West. Home: Carbondale, Ill. Died Apr. 11, 1935.

SHUEY, Edwin Longstreet, manufacturer; b. Cincinnati, O., Jan. 3, 1857; s. Rev. William J. and Sarah (Berger) S.; A.B., Otterbein Coll., 1877, A.M., 1880 (LL.D., 1918); m. Effie Mitchell, Aug. 15, 1882. Prof. in Otterbein Coll., 1881-85; publishing and mfr. paint (Lowe Brothers Co.), 1885-1918; retired. Mem. Internat. Com. Y.M.C.A., New York, 1893—; mem. Ohio State Com. Y.M.C.A., 1895—; trustee Dayton Y.M.C.A., 1887—, Dayton Pub. Library, 1897-1914; pres. trustees Otterbein Coll., 1919—. Mem. labor com. of Advisory Commn. of Council Nat. Defense, 1917; mem. Nat. War Work Council Y.M.C.A., 1917-20; in charge of training Y.M.C.A. workers for overseas service, 1918. Republican. United Brethren. Author: Handbook of the United Brethren in Christ, 1885; Factory People and Their Employers, 1900. Am. editor in chief The Bible Readers' Aids of the International Bible, 1895. Mem. commn. on councils of churches of Fed. Council of Chs. of Christ. Pres. Dayton Council of Churches, 1920—. Home: Dayton, O. Died Sept. 27, 1924.

SHUEY, William John, clergyman, publisher; b. Miamisburg, O., Feb. 9, 1827; s. Adam and Hannah (Aley) S.; ed. pub. schools and Ohio Conf. High Sch., Springfield, O.; m. Sarah Berger, Mar. 7, 1848 (died 1901). Ordained U.B. ministry, 1848; pastor Lewisburg, O., 1849-51, Cincinnati, 1851-54, 1855-59, 1861-62, Dayton, O., 1859-61; presiding elder, 1862-64; missionary in Africa, 1854-55; publisher U.B. Publishing House, Dayton, 1864-97; mgr. Bonebrake Theol. Sem., 1897-1901; retired from active labors, 1901. Pres. Dayton Hist. Soc.; mem. Bd. of Edn., Dayton. Dir. Fourth Nat. Bank; mem. bd. of Trustees Otterbein U., Miami Valley Hospital, Asso. Charities (Dayton). Home: Dayton, O. Died Feb. 21, 1920.

SHUFELDT, Robert Wilson, author; b. New York, Dec. 1, 1850; s. Rear Adm. Robert Wilson and Sarah H. (Abercrombie) S.; Cornell, class of '74; M.D., Columbian (now George Washington) U., 1876; m. Catherine Babcock, Sept. 12, 1876; m. 2d, Florence, g.d. J. J. Audubon, Sept. 5, 1895; m. 3d, Alfhild Dagny Lowum, Mar. 14, 1898. Served on U.S.S. "Proteus" in E. Gulf Squadron, Civil War, 1864-65, as captain's sec. and signal officer, with the rank of midshipman; commd. 1st lieut. medical dept. U.S.A., Aug. 5, 1876; capt., 1881; maj., Apr. 23, 1904; retired for disability, 1891. Surgeon with Gens. Merritt, Crook and Sheridan in frontier Indian wars, 1876-81; curator Army Med. Mus., Washington, 1882; hon. curator Smithsonian Instn., under Baird, and in 1895; judge Chicago Expn. Active list M.C. U.S.A., Jan. 8, 1918-Jan. 9, 1919, and in charge classification of war collections of Army Med. Museum. Mem. numerous scientific societies. Author: Contributions to the Anatomy of Birds, 1882; The Osteology of Amia calva, 1885; Outlines for a Museum of Anatomy, 1885; Contributions to the Study of Heloderma, 1890; The Myology of the Raven, 1890; Scientific Taxidermy for Museums, 1894; Lectures on Biology, 1892; Chapters Natural History of U.S., 1897; Osteology of Owls, 1900; Osteology of Herodiones, 1901; Osteology of Pigeons, 1901; Studies of the Human Form, 1907; The Negro, 1907; Osteology of Birds, 1909; (with present wife) Folk-Lore Tales of Moe and Asbjornsen; An Arrangement of the Families and the Higher Groups of the Mammalia, 1911; Racial Types of Beautiful Women as So Considered by Their People, 1911; Review of the Fossil Fauna of the Desert Region of Oregon, 1913; Further Studies of Fossil Birds with Descriptions of New and Extinct Species, 1913; America's Greatest Problem—The Negro, 1915. Editorial naturalist of Nature Magazine, Washington, 1923—. Home: Washington, D.C. Deceased.

SHULL, Deloss Carlton, lawyer; b. Pella, Ia., Mar. 28, 1858; s. Jacob Henry and Martha (Cutler) S.; A.B., Des Moines U., 1881; LL.B., Drake U., 1882; m. Fannie Edith Mitzell, Oct. 24, 1889; children—Deloss Perkins, Henry C., Laurens Corning (lt. U.S.A., killed in action at Chateau Thierry, World War). Began practice at Vermilion, S.D., 1882; moved to Sioux City, Ia., 1887; became mem. Shull and Stilwill; atty. for C.,M.,St.P.&P. R.R. Co. Pres. Northern Bapt. Conv., 1919-20. Trustee Univ. of Chicago. Republican. Mason. Home: Sioux City, Ia. Died June 7, 1938.

SHULTERS, Hoyt Volney, banker; b. Ellington, N.Y., Dec. 3, 1868; s. Edwin and Martha (Camp) S.; ed. pub. schs. and business coll.; m. Mary Courtright, Aug. 20, 1890. Sec.-treas. Northwestern Ohio Natural Gas Co., Toledo, 1895-1902; sec.-treas. East Ohio Gas Co., Cleveland, 1902-18; pres. Nat. City Bank, Cleveland, 1918—; dir. Cleveland Union Stock Yards Co., The S. Korach Co. Breeder of Guernsey cattle and Shropshire sheep. Trustee Andrews Inst. for Girls, Willoughby, O. Republican. Mason. Home: Cleveland, O. Died Sept. 28, 1932.

SHUMAKER, Edward Seitz, supt. Indiana Anti-Saloon League; b. Greenville, O., July 30, 1867; s. David W. and Sarah Ann (Seitz) S.; A.B., DePauw U., 1895, D.D., 1918; m. Lena Belle Truax, Sept. 11, 1896 (died 1899); m. 2d, Flora May Holliger, Sept. 12, 1900; children—Lois Willard, Albert Edmund, Paul Russell, Charles Wayne, Arthur Wesley. Ordained ministry M.E. Ch., 1890; pastor successively Bainbridge, Knightsville, Plainfield, Terre Haute, Williamsport (all of Ind.), until 1903; field sec. Ind. Anti-Saloon League, 1903-04, supt. South Bend dist., 1904-07, supt. Ind., 1907— (sr. supt. in U.S.). Mem. Legal Hnudred, Taylor U., Upland, Ind. Republican. Author: Descendants of Henry Keller, 1924. Leader of Ind. drys in fight which secured county option in 1908, state prohibition, 1917, national prohibition, 1919. Home: Indianapolis, Ind. Died Oct. 25, 1929.

SHUMAN, Abraham, merchant; b. May 31, 1838; (hon. M.A., Tufts Coll.); m. Hattie Lang, Nov. 3, 1861. Founder and sr. mem. A. Shuman & Co., Boston; dir. Commonwealth Trust Co., Puritan Trust Co., U.S. Trust Co. Dir. Boston Merchants' Assn.; mem. Boston Chamber of Commerce and representative of that body in Mayor Quincy's "Advisory Cabinet," 1896; pres. bd. trustees Boston City Hosp.; trustee Mus. Fine Arts. Donor of marble busts of Wendell Phillips to Boston Pub. Library and Faneuil Hall, and of bronze bust of Pres. Capen, to Tufts College, 1906. Home: Boston, and Beverly, Mass. Died June 26, 1918.

SHUMAN, Edwin Llewellyn, author; b. Lancaster Co., Pa., Dec. 13, 1863; s. William C. and Rebecca (Fertig) S.; Ph.B., Northwestern U., 1887, Ph.M. from same univ., 1890; m. Emma Thompson, Dec. 25, 1895 (died 1937). Editor Evanston Press, 1889-90; traveled in Alaska, 1891; reporter and editor on Chicago Journal, 1892-95; lit. editor and editorial writer Chicago Tribune, 1895-1901; lit. editor Chicago Record-Herald, 1901-13; asst. gen. mgr. Associated Sunday Mags., New York, 1915; mng. editor Current History Magazine of New York Times, 1916-22; associate editor Internat. Book Review, 1922-26; staff editor of Literary Digest, 1926-33; editor of The Homiletic Review, 1933; book editor Funk & Wagnalls Co. Author: Steps Into Journalism, 1894; Practical Journalism, 1903; How to Judge a Book, 1910. Editor: A Decade of Oratory, 1888. Translator: Trail Blazers of Science (from German), 1936. Home: Yonkers, N.Y. Died Dec. 13, 1941.

SHUMWAY, Daniel Bussier, university prof.; b. Phila., May 5, 1868; s. Lowell and Anna Sarah (Bussier) S.; B.S., U. of Pa., 1889; student Grad. Sch., same, 1889-92; Ph.D., U. of Göttingen, 1894; U. of Berlin, winter semester, 1894-95, U. of Munich, summer semester, 1895; m. Elsbeth Lorenz, of Göttingen, Aug. 22, 1895. Instr. English, 1889-92, German, 1895-1901, asst. prof. German, 1901-08, prof. German philology, 1908—, U. of Pa. Republican. Translator: The Nibelungenlied, 1909. Home: Philadelphia, Pa. Died Jan. 11, 1940.

SHUMWAY, Edgar Solomon, educator; b. Belchertown, Mass., June 6, 1856; s. Solomon and Susan (Perry) S.; A.B., Amherst, 1879, A.M., 1882; Ph.D., Rutgers, 1893; studied Roman law, etc., Berlin, and Marburg univs., 1886-87, and at Archæologische Institut, Athens, Greece, Archæologische Institut, Rome, Italy; m. Florence Snow, June 18, 1890; children—Waldo, Lowell, Conrad, Eric. Teacher, Cheltenham Mil. Acad., Phila., 1880-82; prof. Latin and Greek, Potsdam (N.Y.) State Normal Sch., 1882-83; adj. prof., and prof. Latin lang. and lit., Rutgers College, 1883-1900; purchased Rutgers art collection; lecturer on Roman law, U. of Pa., 1900-04; head of classical dept., Manual Training High Sch., Brooklyn, 1904-26; in charge of Annex High Sch., 1909-10. Univ. extension lecturer for N.Y. and N.J. on Greek, Hellenistic and Roman art; mem. mng. com. Am. Sch. Classical Studies in Rome. Author: A Day in Ancient Rome; Latin Synonyms; Syllabus of Classical Archæology; Synopsis of Sources, Literature and Language of Roman Law. Editor Latine, a monthly jour. Editor Conington's Virgil, and Pope's Homer's Odyssey. Contbr. to jours. and mags. Second lt. 14th Inf. N.Y.G., retired; mil. instr. Boyce's Tigers and N.Y. State Cadets. Home: Brooklyn, N.Y. Died Apr. 18, 1928.

SHUMWAY, Walter Bradley, clergyman, educator; b. Phila., Pa., Dec. 31, 1852; s. Lowell and Laura (Bradley) S.; ed. Central High Sch., Phila.; in business 20 yrs.; grad. Newton Theol. Sem., 1894, B.D., 1910; D.D., Temple U., 1909; m. Louise B. Henderson, May 15, 1901; children—Adelaide Katherine, Margaret Henderson. Ordained Bapt. ministry, 1894; pastor Springvale, Me., 1894-99, Swampscott, Mass., 1900-09, Bryn Mawr, Pa., 1910-14; dean theol. dept. Temple U., 1909-28, also prof. ch. history (dean emeritus). Republican. Home: Bryn Mawr, Pa. Died Mar. 13, 1934.

SHUNK, Joseph Lorain, college prof.; b. Wilmot, O., Sept. 14, 1844; s. Josiah and Christena (Putman) S.; A.B., Mt. Union Coll., Alliance, O., 1877, A.M., 1880, Ph.D., 1889; (D.D., Ohio Wesleyan U., 1915; LL.D., Baldwin-Wallace Coll., and Mt. Union Coll., 1917); m. Uretta S. Wolf, Dec. 16, 1869. Served in 163d Ohio N.G., and in 86th and 184th Ohio Inf., during Civil War; instr. Latin and Greek, 1877-84, prof. Greek lang. and lit., 1884-1921, prof. emeritus, 1921, sec. of faculty, 1884-1908, trustee, 1889-1913, v.p., 1898-1911, acting pres., Nov. 1, 1908-Apr. 8, 1909, Mt. Union Coll. Dir. 1887-1905, v.p., 1890-95, pres. 1895-1905, First Nat. Bank, Alliance, O. Republican. Clergyman M.E. Church. Home: Wilmot, O. Died Oct. 12, 1936.

SHUNK, William Alexander, army officer; b. Westville, Ind., Dec. 23, 1857; s. Francis Rawn and Cannarissa (Logan) S.; grad. U.S. Mil. Acad., 1879; honor grad. Inf. and Cav. Sch., Ft. Leavenworth, Kan., 1887; grad. Army War Coll., Washington, D.C., 1912; m. Caroline S. Merrill Pratt, June 14, 1885. Commd. 2d lt. 8th Cav., June 13, 1879; 1st lt., July 23, 1885; capt., Oct. 5, 1892; maj. engr. officer vols., May 19, 1898; hon. disch. vols., Mar. 13, 1899; maj. 34th Vol. Inf., July 5, 1899; hon. mustered out vols., Apr. 17, 1901; maj. U.S. Army, June 28, 1902; lt. col. 1st Cav., Nov. 20, 1908; col., Aug. 2, 1912; assigned to 15th Cav., Aug. 15, 1915. Served in campaigns against Victorio in Tex. and N.M., against Geronimo in N.M., also many minor Indian operations; instr. in mil. art, Inf. and Cav. Sch., Ft. Leavenworth, Kan., 1889-93; participated in suppressing Philippine Insurrection, 1899-1901; in Cuba, 1901-02; comd. Central Dept., Chicago, 1913-14. Medals for Indian Wars, Cuban Service, Philippine Insurrection. Home: Fort Leavenworth, Kan. Died Dec. 23, 1921.

SHUNK, William Findlay, civ. engr.; b. Harrisburg, Pa., Sept. 6, 1830; s. Francis R. and Jane (Findlay) S.; ed. pub. schs., Harrisburg, Harrisburg Acad., and Dickinson Coll.; midshipman, U.S.N., 1846-50; m. Gertrude Wyeth, Apr. 7, 1852. In Pa. R.R. service, 1851-56; in U.S. Coast Survey, 1856; asst. engr. Lewisburg & Spruce Creek R.R., 1856-57; clerk in State Dept., Washington, 1861-65; Rock Island U.S. Govt. surveys, 1865-66; asst. engr. Dutchess & Columbia R.R., 1867; chief engr. Conn. Western R.R., 1868-74; chief engr. Met. Elevated R.R., New York, during construction and of Manhattan Elevated R.R. after construction of roads, 1876-82; chief engr. S.Pa. R.R., 1882-85; chief engr. Kings Co. Elevated R.R., Brooklyn, 1887-89; engr. in charge Intercontinental R.R. Surveys, 1890-92; chief engr. Guayaquil & Quito R.R., Ecuador, 1898-1902; retired. Author: Shunk on Railway Curves, 1854; The Field Engineer (15 edits.), 1879-1903. Home: Harrisburg, Pa. Died 1907.

SHUPE, Henry Fox, clergyman, editor; b. nr. Scottdale, Pa., Mar. 18, 1860; s. Daniel W. and Mary Ann (Fox) S.; student Otterbein Coll., Westerville, O., 1 yr.; grad. Bonebrake Theol. Sem., Dayton, O., 1885; grad. Chautauqua Lit. and Scientific Circle, 1891; D.D., York (Neb.) Coll., 1905; m. Susan Stoner, Aug. 13, 1885 (died 1894); children—Erma, Mary Catherine, Nellie (dec.); m. 2d, Ellwyn Billheimer, Nov. 20, 1895 (died 1896); m. 3d, Margaret Faist, July 3, 1899; 1 son, Frederick Henry. Ordained U.B. ministry, 1886; pastor Tyronne, Pa., 1884-88, Williamsport, 1889, Braddock, 1890-93; editor The Watchword (organ of Christian Endeavor Socs. of U.B. Ch.), 1893—; sec. Christian Endeavor work of the U.B. Ch., 1893-1900, 1905-09. Trustee United Soc. Christian Endeavor, Boston, 1894—; mem. exec. com. C.E. Union of U.B. Ch., 1890—. Republican. Author: Effective Endeavor, 1915; Hunger of the Teens, 1918. Home: Dayton, O. Died Oct. 13, 1926.

SHURTLEFF, Charles Allerton, lawyer; b. Shasta, Calif., Apr. 4, 1857; s. Benjamin (M.D.) and Ann M. (Griffith) S.; A.B., Napa Coll. (now Coll. of the Pacific), 1879; LL.B., Hastings Coll. Law (U. of Calif.), 1882; LL.D. from the Coll. of the Pacific, 1926; m. Ada S. West, Oct. 14, 1886 (died 1925); m. 2d, Nellie V. Crockett, July 25, 1927 (died 1934). Admitted to Calif. bar, 1882, and entered practice at San Francisco; asst. U.S. atty., Northern Dist. Calif., 1891-93; asso. justice Supreme Court of Calif., July 1921-Jan. 1923; dir., sec. and treas. Mendocino Redwood Co.; dir. and sec. Curtis, Collins and Holbrook Co. Trustee Nat. Board of Stanford Univ., Hastings Coll. Law, Coll. of the Pacific, Children's Hosp. (San Francisco); mem. first Bd. of Bar Examiners of Calif. Pres. Calif Bar Assn. (now State Bar of Calif.), 1925-26. Republican. Protestant. Home: Menlo Park, Calif. Died Apr. 14, 1941.

SHURTLEFF, Ernest Warburton, clergyman; b. Boston, Apr. 4, 1862; s. Asahel M. and Sarah Ann (Keegan) S.; Harvard, 1881-82; New Ch. Theol. Sem., 1884; grad. Andover Thoel. Sem., 1888; post-grad. scholarship course, Andover, 1890; also received complete musical edn.; (D.D., Ripon Coll., 1905); m. Helen S. Cramer, July 20, 1899. Ordained Congl. ministry, 1889; pastor at Ventura, Calif., 1889-90, Plymouth, Mass., 1891-98, First Church, Minneapolis, 1898-1905; organized American Ch. in Frankfort-on-the-Main, Germany, 1905-06; in charge of the Students' Atelier Reunions, Paris, France, 1906—. Author; Poems, 1883; Easter Gleams, 1883; New Year's Peace, 1885; Song of Hope; When I Was a Child, 1886; Shadow of the Angel, 1896, 6th edit., 1909; Easter in Heaven, 1896; Heaven in Easter, 1896, etc. Died Aug. 1917.

SHURTLEFF, Glen Kassimer, gen. sec. Y.M.C.A.; b. Watkins, N.Y., Nov. 21, 1860; s. Rev. Alonzo H. and Julia M. (Phinney) S.; ed. pub. sch., Warners, N.Y., 1874-75, Elbridge Collegiate Inst., 1875-76, Phœnix Acad., 1877, Syracuse Classical Sch., 1877-79, Syracuse Univ., 1878-81. m. Gertrude E. Packard, Oct. 8, 1884. Gen. sec. Y.M.C.A., Utica, N.Y., 1883-90, Denver, 1890-93, Cleveland, 1893—. Mem. exec. com. Cleveland Municipal Assn.; exec. com. Council of Sociology; trustee Cleveland Sch. of Art; trustee Goodrich House (Cleveland). Episcopalian. Republican. Home: Cleveland, O. Died 1909.

SHURTLEFF, Roswell Morse, artist; b. Rindge, N.H., June 14, 1838; s. Asahel Dewey and Eliza (Morse) S.; grad. Dartmouth Coll., 1857 (hon. B.S., 1882); took charge architect's office, Manchester, N.H., 1857; worked at lithography, Buffalo, 1858-59; in Boston, drawing on wood and attending evening classes Lowell Inst., 1859; worked as illustrator and attended Acad. of Design, New York, 1860-61; enlisted Apr. 16, 1861, 99th N.Y. Vols.; promoted lt. and adj.; 1st federal officer to be shot and taken prisoner (July 19, 1861); in Southern hosps. and prisons nearly 8 months; released on parole; m. Clara E., d. Joseph B. and Eleanor (Carrier) Halliday, of Hartford, Conn., June 14, 1867. Began to paint in oil, 1870, at first animal pictures, later landscapes in both oil and water colors. Home: New York, N.Y. Died June 6, 1915.

SHUTE, Daniel Kerfoot, M.D.; b. Alexandria, Va., Oct. 22, 1858; s. Samuel Moore and Jane Cecelia (Kerfoot) S.; A.B., Columbian (now George Washington) U., 1879, M.D., 1883; post-grad. course in clin. ophthalmology, Royal London Ophthalmic Hosp., and at Univ. of Berlin; hon. D.Sc., George Washington Univ., 1932; m. Augusta Pettigrew, Aug. 19, 1896. Prosector to chair of anatomy, 1886-87, lecturer, 1887-88, prof. anatomy, 1888-1910, and (formerly) clin. prof. ophthalmology, George Washington U.; ophthalmologist Providence Hospital, Central Dispensary and Emergency Hosp., Columbia Hosp., Govt. Hosp. for the Insane, George Washington Hosp., D.C. Fellow A.A.A.S., Va. Med. Soc. Author: A First Book in Organic Evolution, 1899. Home: Washington, D.C. Died Oct. 21, 1935.

SHUTE, Samuel Moore, prof. English lang. and lit., Columbian Univ., 1859—; b. Philadelphia, Jan. 24, 1823; grad. Univ. of Pa., 1844; studied theology in Sem. of Reformed Ch., Phila.; pastor Bapt. Ch., Pemberton, N.J., 1853-56; Alexandria, Va., 1856-59. Author: Manual of Anglo-Saxon; etc. Home: Kerfoot, Va. Died 1902.

SHUTTER, Marion Daniel, clergyman; b. New Philadelphia, O., Aug. 4, 1853; s. Peter K. and Alethia M. (Haag) S.; A.B., U. of Wooster, 1876, A.M., 1879; B.D., Bapt. Theol. Sem., Chicago, 1881; D.D., Canton Theol. Sem., New York, 1900; LL.D., Fargo (N.D.) Coll., 1921; m. Mary E. Wilkinson, June 30, 1887; 1 son, Arnold Wilkinson. Ordained Bapt. ministry, 1881; pastor Olivet Bapt. Ch., Minneapolis, 1881-86; changed views and pastor First Universalist Ch., Minneapolis, 1886, 1934-38. Founded Unity Settlement, 1897, pres. bd., 1897-1938. Pres. Minneapolis Vice Commn., 1910-11, Morals Commn., 1911-12, Univeralist Gen. Conv., 1911-15. Pres. Minn. Charter Commn., 1920-32. Author: Wit and Humor of the Bible, 1892; Justice and Mercy, 1894; A Child of Nature, 1896. Joint editor: Progressive Men of Minnesota, 1897; Applied Evolution, 1900; The Way the Preachers Pray, 1900; Life of James Harvey Tuttle, 1905; Report of Minneapolis Vice Commn., 1911. Editor: History of Minneapolis, 1922. Mem. Bd. of Lectureship, Universalist Ch., 1919; v.p. Internat. Congress of Religious Liberals, 1927. Home: Minneapolis, Minn. Died Aug. 31, 1939.

SIBERT, William Luther, army officer; b. Gadsden, Ala., Oct. 12, 1860; s. William J. and Marietta (Ward) S.; U. of Ala., 1878-80; grad. U.S. Mil. Acad., 1884; m. Mary Margaret Cummings, Sept. 1887; children—William Olin, Franklin Cummings, Harold Ward, Edwin Luther, Martin David, Mary Elizabeth; m. 2d, Evelyn Clyne Bairnsfather, of Edinburgh, Scotland, June 8, 1922. Apptd. 2d lt. engrs., June 15, 1884; grad. Engr. Sch. of Application, 1887; 1st lt., Apr. 7, 1888; capt., Mar. 31, 1896; maj., Apr. 23, 1904; lt. col., 1909; brig. gen. U.S.A. and extended the thanks of Congress by act approved Mar. 4, 1915; maj. gen., June 28, 1917; retired, Apr. 4, 1920. Asst. engr. river work in Ky., 1887-92; in constrn. ship channel connecting Great Lakes, 1892-94; in charge engring. river and harbor dist. (Ark.), 1894-98; instr. civ. engring., Engr. Sch. of Application, 1898-99; chief engr. 8th Army Corps, and chief engr. and gen. mgr. Manila & Dagupan R.R., 1899-1900; in charge engring. river and harbor dists. (hdqrs. Louisville and Pittsburgh), 1900-07; mem. Isthmian Canal Commn., Mar. 1907-Apr. 1914. Built the Gatun Locks and Dam, Panama Canal, the west breakwater, Colon Harbor, and excavated channel from Gatun to Atlantic Ocean. Under the joint auspices of the Am. Nat. Red Cross and the Chinese Govt., served as chmn. bd. engrs. on flood prevention problem, Huai River Valley, China, June-Oct. 1914. Assigned as comdr. 1st Div., Am. troops in France, under Maj. Gen. Pershing, June 1917; comdr. Southeastern Dept., at Charleston, S.C., Jan.-May 1918; dir. Chem. Warfare Service, U.S.A., which he organized, May 1918-Feb. 1920. Chmn., chief engr. Ala. State Docks Commn., Nov. 26, 1923—; chmn. bd. engrs. and geologists apptd. July 1928, with approval of President of the U.S., to report on economic and engineering feasibility of Boulder Dam. Pres. Am. Assn. of Port Authorities, 1929-30. D.S.M. (U.S.); Comdr. Legion of Honor (French). Home: Bowling Green, Ky. Died Oct. 16, 1935.

SIBLEY, Frederick Hubbard, prof. mech. engineering; b. Oxford, Mass.; s. Sumner and Maria F. (Miller) S.; Ph.B., Brown U., 1898; student night schs., Mass. Inst. Tech.; M.E., Case Sch. Applied Science, 1905; m. Annabelle Pearson, June 10, 1909; children—Alden Kingsland, Julia Pierson. Apprenticeship machine shop and surveyor's office; draftsman and asst. engr., Westinghouse Elec. Mfg. Co., and N.Y.C.& H.R. R.R., 1899-1903; instr. and asst. prof. mech. engring., Case Sch. Applied Science, Cleveland, O., 1903-08; prof. mech. engring., U. of Ala., 1908-12; asso. prof., later prof. mech. engring. and head of the dept., U. of Kan., 1912-20; dean Coll. of Engring., U. of Nev., 1920—. Mem. various engring. societies, etc. Unitarian. Author: Elementary Mechanical Drawing (with W. D. Browning), 1905; A Text Book of Pure Mechanism, 1914; Engineering Thermo-dynamics, 1930; Manchaug—A Historical Novel, 1936. Research work on flow of stream through nozzles, mfr. of synthetic gasoline, strength of steel at high temperatures. Home: Reno, Nev. Died Apr. 2, 1941.

SIBLEY, Frederick W., colonel U.S. Army; b. at Ft. Phantom Hill, Texas, Oct. 17, 1852; s. Gen. C. C. (U.S.A.) and Nancy (Davenport) S.; grad. U.S. Mil. Acad., 1874; m. Fannie, d. Col. E. D. Lane, U.S.A., 1877. Second lt. 2d Cav., June 17, 1874; promoted through grades to col. 14th Cav., Mar. 3, 1911. Served for ten years against the Indians, in Rocky Mountains and on the plains; participated in nearly all of General Crook's engagements with the Sioux and Cheyennes, breveted, "for gallantry in action on the Little Big Horn River," in July 1876, and later "for distinguished gallantry in action against Crazy Horse's camp" on Powder River, Mont., Mar. 17, 1876; was recommended for medal of honor; adj. 2d Cav., 1889-93, 1899-1900; insp. gen. Dept. of Tex., 1900-01. During war with Spain commanded headquarters guard, 4th Army Corps under Maj. Gen. John Coppinger; adj. gen. and a.a.g. Dept. of Luzon, P.I., 1903, 1904; in com-

mand of squadron of 2d Cav. and battalion of 7th Inf., which suppressed the Ladrones of Cavite and Bantangas provinces, 1905, returning invalided to U.S.; selected for detail on Gen. Staff, declined, Dec. 1908; comdt. U.S. Mil. Acad., Feb. 1, 1909-Feb. 1, 1911. Died Feb. 17, 1918.

SIBLEY, Hiram Luther, lawyer; b. Trumbull Co., O., May 4, 1836; s. Rev. Ezekiel and Phebe (Simons) S.; ed. common schs. and 1 yr. in spl. schs.; (hon. M.A., Marietta Coll., 1878; LL.D., Claflin U., 1905); m. Esther Ann Ellis, Apr. 20, 1858 (died 1916). Was elected county clerk of Meigs Co., Ohio, 1860; lt. 116th Ohio Inf., 1862-65; admitted to bar, 1865; began practice at Marietta, O., 1866; judge Ct. of Common Pleas, 1883-97, judge of Circuit Ct., 1897-1908, apptd. mem. commn. to revise and consolidate laws of Ohio, 1906; revision completed and adopted by State. Del. Ecumenical Conf., M.E. Ch., Washington, 1891, Gen. Conf., 1884, 1904, 12; attended and proposed important change in church polity. Mason. Author: Organic Law M.E. Ch., 1894; Right to and Cause for Action, 1896. Editor: Nash's Pleading and Practice, 1906-07. Gen. legal adviser Internat. Telephone Co., Columbus, O. Lecturer. Home: Marietta, O. Died Nov. 5, 1920.

SIBLEY, Joseph Crocker, congressman; b. Friendship, N.Y., Feb. 18, 1850; s. Joseph C. (M.D.) and Lucy Elvira (Babcock) S.; acad. edn., Springville and Friendship, N.Y.; LL.D., twice; m. Metta E. Babcock, Mar. 17, 1870 (died 1911); children—Mrs. Josephine Heathcote, Mrs. Celia Wilson; m. 2d, Ida Rew, Dec. 6, 1913. Formerly mfr. of lubricating oils, and interested in various business enterprises. After three years' experimental work made the first successful substitute for petroleum for use in valves and cylinders of steam locomotives; this product was used on practically every locomotive in America and many foreign lands; retired from business 1910; from then devoted his attention exclusively to experimental work in soil fertility and investigation of plant life and its improvement; for many years prominent as breeder of trotting horses and Jersey cattle. Pres. Pa. State Dairymen's Assn.; mem. State Bd. of Agr.; trustee Bucknell U.; one of the organizers American Trotting Register Assn.; mem. bd. review of Nat. Trotting Assn. First to propose the hosp. at Franklin, Pa., and was first and largest individual contbr. toward erecting the bldg.; gave Sibley Law Library to Venango Co. (Pa.) Bar Assn. Mayor of Franklin, Pa.; mem. 53d Congress (1893-95) and 56th and 57th Congresses (1899-1903), 27th Pa. Dist., and 58th and 59th Congresses (1903-07), 28th Pa. Dist. Democrat until 1900; became Republican. Home: Franklin, Pa. Died May 19, 1926.

SIBLEY, William Giddings, editor; b. Racine, O., Feb. 29, 1860; s. Hiram Luther and Esther Ann (Ellis) S.; B.A., Marietta Coll., 1881, hon. M.A., 1906; L.H.D., Rio Grande College, 1926, Marietta, 1928; m. Miss Frank Roberts, Aug. 26, 1886; 1 son, Hiram Ellis. Clerk in gen. store, 1881-87; founder, and editor Meigs County Tribune, 1887-90; editor and pub. Gallipolis (O.) Tribune, 1890-1920; editor Omaha Bee, Feb.-Oct. 1920; chief editorial writer Chicago Daily Journal of Commerce, Oct. 1920-24; writer "Along the Highway" editorial column, same, 1924—. State librarian of Ohio, 1889-90; capt. and q.m. 7th Regt. O.N.G., 1902-03. Republican. Methodist. Mason. Mem. Loyal Legion. Author: The French Five Hundred and Other Papers, 1901; The Story of Freemasonry, 1904. Home: Gallipolis, O. Died Jan. 30, 1935.

SICARD, Montgomery, rear admiral U.S.N., retired Sept. 30, 1898; b. New York, N.Y., Sept. 30, 1836; apptd. to navy Oct. 1, 1851; Naval Acad., 1851-55; promoted master Nov. 4, 1858; commd. lt., 1861; lt. commander, July 16, 1862; comdr., 1870; capt., Aug. 1881; commodore, 1894; rear admiral, April 1897. Served as executive officer Oneida, West Gulf squadron, 1862-63, taking part in bombardment and passage of Forts Jackson and St. Philip; destruction of Confederate flotilla and gunboats; capture of Chalmette batteries; capture of New Orleans; engagements with Vicksburg batteries, with Confederate ram Arkansas, July 1862; commanded Seneca at both attacks and capture of Fort Fisher and left wing 2d div. in naval land assault on same, Jan. 15, 1865; bombardment of Ft. Anderson, etc.; chief of Bureau of Ordnance, 1881-90, and introduced steel high-power ordnance into the navy; comdr.-in-chief, 1897-98, U.S. naval force North Atlantic station; placed on sick leave; after partial recovery pres. Naval War Bd. for war with Spain. Home: Westernville, N.Y. Died 1900.

SICKEL, William George, ocean transportation: b. Baltimore, Md., Nov. 30, 1868; s. John L. and Emily (Brooks) S.; grad. Baltimore High Sch., 1885; m. Ruby Allen, Apr. 22, 1896. Began as clk. in Chicago office of Atlantic Transport Line, 1887; southwestern agt., same, at St. Louis, 1889-93, asst. western frt. agt., Chicago, 1894-1901; asst. western frt. mgr. and western frt. mgr. Internat. Merchant Marine Co., Chicago, 1902-06; asst. to gen. mgr., 1906-12, and became vice-dir., 1912, Hamburg-Am. Line, New York; dir. N.Y. & Hanseatic Corp. Democrat. Home: New York, N.Y. Died May 1, 1929.

SICKELS, David Banks, author; b. New York, N.Y., Feb. 8, 1837; s. Dr. John and Hester Ann (Ellsworth) S.; ed. by pvt. tutors; grad. Kennett Square Inst., Pa., as civ. engr., which profession he followed for several yrs. War corr. for Eastern and Western newspapers during Civil War; apptd. a.d.c. on staff of gov. of Ark., 1870, with rank of col.; was intimate friend of Gen. Sheridan; mem. and represented banking firm of Clark, Walcott & Co., abroad several yrs.; fiscal agt. State of Ark., 1866-70; traveled extensively in Far East and was diplomatic rep. of U.S. to Siam, 1876-81; also acting consul of Royal Netherlands Govt.; with Lyman W. Briggs, founded Am. Surety Co., 1882, of which was 1st sec., then treas. and v.p. until retired, 1906, to engage in lit. work; now v.p. 23d Ward Bank of New York, which he organized; treas. Universal Trust Co. Lecturer on Oriental subjects and Eastern religions. Life mem. Y.M.C.A. (parent soc.); mem. numerous societies. Mason. Author: Leaves of the Lotos, 1896; Land of the Lotos, 1899; Flowers from the Wayside, 1914. Eastern corr. of western newspapers. Home: Paterson, N.J. Died Dec. 19, 1918.

SICKLES, Daniel Edgar, major gen. U.S.A.; b. New York, N.Y., Oct. 20, 1825; s. George Garrett and Susan (Marsh) S.; ed. New York U.; learned printer's trade; studied law, and admitted to bar, 1846. Practiced in New York, 1846-53; mem. legislature, 1847; maj. 12th Regt. N.G.S.N.Y.; corp. atty., New York, 1853; resigned to become sec. of legation at London, 1853-55; state senator, 1856-57; mem. Congress, 1857-61. Apptd. col. 1st Regt. U.S.V., June 20, 1861; brig. gen. vols., Sept. 3, 1861; maj. gen. vols., Nov. 29, 1862; hon. mustered out of vol. service, Jan. 1, 1868; col. 42d U.S. Inf., July 28, 1866; retired with rank of maj. gen. U.S.A., Apr. 14, 1869. Comd. 2d Brigade, 2d Div., 3d Army Corps, under Gen. Hooker, later succeeded him as comdr. 2d Div., 3d Corps; served in battles of Fair Oaks, Malvern Hill, Antietam, 7 days' battle before Richmond, etc.; comd. 3d Army Corps, Army of the Potomac, participating in Chancellorsville campaign and battle of Gettysburg. Bvtd. brig. gen., Mar. 2, 1867, "for gallant and meritorious services at battle of Fredericksburg, Va."; maj. gen., Mar. 2, 1867, for same at battle of Gettysburg, Pa (wounded in right leg, necessitating amputation); awarded Congressional Medal of Honor, Oct. 30, 1897, "for most distinguished gallantry in action at Gettysburg, July 2, 1863, displayed on the field of battle before and after the loss of his leg, while comdg. 3d Army Corps." Sent on spl. mission to S. America, 1865; comd. Mil. Dept. of the South, 1865, Dept. of the Carolinas, 1866-67; apptd. U.S. minister to Holland, 1866, to Mexico, 1869, declined; U.S. minister to Spain, 1869-73; mem. Congress, 1892-94; pres. N.Y. State Bd. of Civil Service Commrs., 1888-89; sheriff New York, 1890. Comdr. Medal of Honor Legion, 1902; decorated by Republic of France Commander Legion of Honor of France, 1879. Home: New York, N.Y. Died May 2, 1914.

SIDDALL, John MacAlpine, editor; b. Oberlin, O., Oct. 8, 1874; s. Dr. James F. and Orinda Sarah (Candee) S.; Ph.B., Oberlin, 1898; A.B., Harvard, 1899; m. Jean Harriet Joiner, Nov. 22, 1904. Reporter and asst. city editor Cleveland Plain Dealer, 1899-1901; asst. editor Chautauquan Magazine, 1901-02; sec. of pub. schs., Cleveland, 1902-04; on editorial staff, McClure's Magazine, 1904-06; asso. editor American Magazine, 1906-15. and editor-in-chief, 1915—. Author: Sid Says, 1917. Home: New York, N.Y. Died July 16, 1923.

SIDDONS, Frederick Lincoln, judge; b. London, Eng., Nov. 21, 1864; s. Joachim H. and Mary A. S.; ed. principally at home; LL.B., Columbian (now George Washington) U., 1887, LL.M., 1888; admitted to bar, 1887; m. Harriet C. Van Auken, Apr. 26, 1892; children—Mary Elizabeth (Mrs. George Starr Lasher), Frederick Philip Heyward. Prof. law Nat. U., 1898—; Asso. Justice Supreme Court, D.C., 1915—. Democrat. Was for 6½ yrs. a commr. on Uniform State Laws for the D.C., one of 3 commrs. of D.C. and chmn. Commn. on Pub. Welfare Legislation of D.C. Home: Washington, D.C. Died June 19, 1931.

SIDERS, Walter Raleigh, educator; b. nr. Knoxville, Ia., Dec. 4, 1870; s. Cyrus W. and Mary Jane (Whiteman) S.; B.S., Fremont Coll., 1891; Pd.D., U. of Ida., 1927; m. Ethel Vinita Sparks, Dec. 26, 1904; children—Walter R., Bernard (dec.), Carol Knox. Prin. pub. schs., Crawford, Neb., 1891-94; supt. schs. Alliance, Neb., 1894-98; prin. high sch., Wahoo, Neb., 1898-99; supt. schs., Pocatello, Ida., 1899-1927; field rep. World Fedn. of Education Assns. 1927-32; asst. in adminstrn. of N.J. junior colls., 1934-35; sec. and ednl. adviser to Omaha teachers, 1937—; lecturer, specialist in school orgn. Developed a system of whole-class, group and individual instruction which was first reported to N.E.A. at Chicago in 1909. Mem. Nat. Council of Edn., 1910-31. Conglist. Author: Course of Study Public and High Schools, State of Idaho, 1903; Code School Laws for Idaho, 1911; Report on Situation of Public Education in Omaha, 1927. Home: Montclair, N.J. Died Oct. 25, 1940.

SIDIS, Boris, psychopathologist; b. in Russia, Oct. 12, 1867; came to America, 1887; A.B., Harvard,

1894, A.M., 1895, Ph.D., 1897, M.D., 1908. Associate psychologist and psychopathologist, Path. Inst., N.Y. State hosps., 1896-1901; dir. Psychopathological Hosp. and Psychopath. Lab. of N.Y. Infirmary for Women and Children, 1901; in practice at Boston. Med. dfr. Sidis Psychotherapeutic Inst., Portsmouth, N.H. Investigator and writer on psychol. subjects. Formerly asso. editor Archives of Neurology and Psychopathology; asso. editor Jour. of Abnormal Psychology. Author: Psychology of Suggestion; Multiple Personality (Sidis and Goodhart), 1905; Philistine and Genius, 1911; The Psychology of Laughter, 1913; The Foundations of Normal and Abnormal Psychology, 1914; Symptomatology, Psychognosis and Diagnosis of Psychopathic Maladies, 1914; The Causation and Treatment of Psychopathic Diseases, 1916; The Source and Aim of Human Progress (A Study in Social Psychology and Social Pathology), 1919. Home: Portsmouth, N.H. Died Oct. 24, 1923.

SIDNEY, Margaret. See Harriet M. Lothrop.

SIDWELL, Thomas Watson, school prin.; b. Johnsville, Md., May 16, 1859; s. Dr. Reuben and Sarah A. S.; ed. New Windsor Coll., 1874-76; hon. M.A., U. of Pa., 1907; m. Frances M. Haldeman, June 29, 1887. Taught in pub. schs., 1876-80, Friends' Elementary and High Sch., Baltimore, 1880-83; founded, 1883, and became principal, Sidwells' Friends Sch., Washington, D.C. Died Apr. 11, 1936.

SIEBECKER, Robert George, judge; b. in Sauk Co., Wis., Oct. 17, 1854; s. William and Christiana (Graff) S.; B.S., U. of Wis., 1878, LL.B., 1880; m. Josephine, d. Josiah and Mary La Follette, of Madison, Wis., May 15, 1879. In practice at Madison, 1879-90; mem. La Follette, Siebecker & Harper, 1885-90; city atty., 1886-90; judge Circuit Ct., 9th Jud. Circuit, 1890-1903; asso. justice Supreme Ct. of Wis., Apr. 9, 1903—. Republican. Unitarian. Home: Madison, Wis. Died Feb. 12, 1922.

SIEBEL, John Ewald, chemist; b. Hofkamp bei Wermelskuchen, Germany, Sept. 18, 1845; s. Peter and Lisetta (Reininghaus) S.; A.B., Realgymnasium, Hagen, 1862; Ph.D., U. of Berlin, 1865; came to America, 1865; m. Anna Regina Schaeffer, 1870. Chief chemist Belcher's Sugar Refining Co., Chicago, 1866-67; established laboratory, 1868; analyt. and forensic chemist Cook Co. and chemist Bd. of Pub. Works and other city bds., 1869-73; prof. chemistry and physics, German High Sch., 1871; city gas insp. and acting city chemist, 1873-80; pub. and editor Am. Chem. Review, 1880-86; pub. and editor Original Communications of Zymotechnic Inst., 1890-1900; dir. Zymotechnic Inst. from incorporation, 1901, when Siebel's Brewing Acad. was added. Protestant. Author: Newton's Axiom Developed, 1868; Preparation of Dialized Iron, 1869; New Methods for Manufacture of Soda, 1874; New Methods for Manufacture of Phosphates, 1878; Compend of Mechanical Refrigeration, 1895, 9th edition, 1915; Thermo- and Electro-dynamics of Energy Conversion. Home: Chicago, Ill. Died Dec. 20, 1919.

SIEBENTHAL, Claude Ellsworth, geologist; b. Vevay, Ind., Apr. 16, 1869; s. John Amie and Annie (McKay) S.; desc. of John Francis de Siebenthal, one of the Swiss founders of Vevay and Switzerland Co., Ind., 1801; student Ind. U., 1889-91, 1893-94; A.B., Stanford, 1892, A.M., 1893; fellow U. of Chicago, 1897-99, 1900-01; m. Myrtle Madden, Dec. 14, 1904. Asst. geologist Ark. Geol. Survey, 1889-93; instr. geology, Ind. U., 1891; asst. geologist Ind. Geol. Survey, 1896-99; instr. physiography and geology, Indianapolis Manual Training Sch., 1899-1900; asst. geologist, 1901-10, geologist, 1911—, U.S. Geol. Survey. Republican. Author: Joplin (Mo.) District Folio (with W. S. T. Smith), 1907; Geology and Water Resources of the San Luis Valley, Colo., 1910; Origin of the Zinc and Lead Deposits of the Joplin Region, 1915. Died Mar. 1, 1930.

SIEDENBURG, Frederic, clergyman, educator, sociologist; b. Cincinnati, O., Jan. 28, 1872; s. Frederic and Barbara (Kaelin) S.; B.A., St. Xavier's Coll., Cincinnati, 1893; joined Soc. of Jesus (Jesuits), 1893; M.A., St. Louis U., 1899; divinity student St. Louis U., 1904-08; sociology and economics, univs. of Innsbruck and Vienna, 1909-11. Prof., St. Ignatius Coll., Chicago, 1900-03, St. Louis U., 1903-04; ordained R.C. priest, 1907; with Loyola U., Chicago, 1911-32, dean School of Sociology, 1914-32; exec. dean U. of Detroit, 1932—. Trustee Detroit Council of Social Agencies; pres. Mich. Conf. of Social Service. Home: Detroit, Mich. Died Feb. 20, 1939.

SIES, Raymond William, university prof.; b. Oxford, Ia., Oct. 14, 1878; s. Charles Henry and Anna Elizabeth (Kortum) S.; student, Ia. State Coll., 1898-1900; A.B., U. of Iowa, 1907, A.M., 1908; Ph.D., Columbia, 1913; m. Alice Mae Corbin, June 20, 1914. Teacher pub. schs., Newhall, Ia., 1901-02; supt. schs., Oxford, Ia., 1902-05; prof. ednl. administration, U. of Pittsburgh, 1910-18; prof. ednl. administrn. and supervision, U. of Minn., 1918-21; prof. ednl. administration, U. of Ky., 1921—. Author: Teachers' Pension Systems in Great Britain (U.S. Bur. Edn.), 1913. Home: Lexington, Ky. Died Jan. 29, 1922.

SIFTON, Harry Austin, surgeon; b. Oil Springs, Ont., Can., May 20, 1867; s. Henry and Margaret (Watkins) S.; M.D., U. of Mich., 1886; m. Mary Ellen Evans, Apr. 17, 1895. Began practice at Suttons Bay, Mich., 1886; chief of staff, Milwaukee Hosp., 1906-27; consultant on staff same and Milwaukee County Hosp., Columbia Hosp., Johnston Emergency Hosp.; cons. surgeon C.&N.W. Ry. Co. Fellow A.C.S.; mem. various Med. Societies. Home: Milwaukee, Wis. Died Feb. 27, 1935.

SIGEL, Franz, soldier; b. Sinsheim, Baden, Nov. 18, 1824; grad. Mil. School, Carlsruhe, 1843; lt. in army of Baden, 1843-47; challenged to a duel, 1847; severely wounded his antagonist and resigned from army for political reasons; was a leader in Baden revolution, 1848 and 1849, becoming sec. of war; adj. gen. with Gen. Microslawski, then chief in command, and leading retreat of defeated army to Switzerland; was in Switzerland, 1849-51; in England, 1851-52; came to U.S. in May 1852; taught and published a mil. mag., New York, 1852-58; teacher and elected dir. of public schools, St. Louis, 1858-61; organized a regt. and a battery at beginning of Civil war; commd. brig. gen., May 1861; maj. gen., March 1862; served 1st in Mo.; instrumental in gaining the battle of Pea Ridge; in 1862 comd. troops at Harper's Ferry; comd. reserve army of Pa., June 1863; dept. and Army of W.Va., 1864; participated in many battles; resigned commn., May 1865; edited Baltimore Wecker, 1865-67; removed to New York; Republican candidate for sec. of State of N.Y., 1869; apptd. collector internal revenue, May 1871; elected register of city of New York for the term of 1871-74; lectured and edited a weekly paper after that; affiliated with Democratic party, 1876-96, but took sides with McKinley in latter year. He became an advertising bureau and publisher and editor of the New Yorw Monthly. Home: New York, N.Y. Died 1902.

SIGEL, Franz, lawyer; b. N.Y. City, Sept. 23, 1872, s. Franz and Elise (Dulon) S.; father served as gen. Revolutionary army, Baden, Germany, 1848-49, and as maj. gen. U.S. Vols., Civil War; B.S., Coll. City of New York, 1892; LL.B., New York U., 1896; m. Eleanor M. Record, June 4, 1907. Practiced in N.Y. City, 1896—. Prominent in patriotic propaganda, as speaker and writer, during World War. Mem. League to Enforce Peace (exec. com.), Am. Friends of German Democracy (pres.), Bronx County Chapter Am. Red Cross (exec. com.); Mayor's Com. of Nat. Defense (N.Y. City); chmn. Red Cross membership drive of Bronx County, 1917, also chmn. canteen div., Bronx Co. Red Cross, 1917, 18; chmn. Speaker's Com. of Mayor's Com., recruiting, 1917; mem. Speaker's Com. of all Liberty Loan drives. Democrat. Protestant. Home: New York, N.Y. Died Feb. 19, 1922.

SIGMUND, Jay G., writer; b. Waubeek, Ia., Dec. 11, 1885; s. Herman R. and Sarah Jane (Bruce) S.; ed. high sch., Central City, Ia.; m. Louise B. Heins, Aug. 9, 1910; children—James Bruce, Mary Louise, Jane Elizabeth. General agent of Minn. Mutual Life Insurance Co.; lecturer on lierature. Democrat. Author: Frescoes (verse), 1921; Pinions (verse), 1923; Land O. Maize Folk (verse), 1924; Drowsy Ones (verse), 1926; Wapsipinicon Tales (short stories), 1927; Merged Blood (short stories), 1929; Ridge Road (stories and verse), 1930; Altar Panels (verse), 1931; The Least of These (short stories), 1935; Burr Oak and Sumac (verse), 1935; also 1-act plays, "Barabbas Released," "The Unnatural Man," "The Wapsipinicon," "The Guest of Honor," "The Inventor," "A Tomb for Poets," "Saints at the Board," "The Ghoul," "Lumber for the Dead"; "Heron at Sunset" (poems), 1937. Co-author (with Betty Smith) one act plays: "The Saints Get Together," "Folk Stuff," "Trees of His Father," "Vine Leaves," "Common Ground," "The Silvered Rope." Winner Gypsy Magazine poetry prize of $100, 1932. Home: Cedar Rapids, Ia. Died Oct. 29, 1937.

SIGSBEE, Charles Dwight, rear adm. U.S.N.; b. Albany, N.Y., Jan. 16, 1845; s. Nicholas and Agnes (Orr) S.; apptd. to U.S. Naval Acad. from N.Y., 1859, grad. 1863; m. Eliza Rogers Lockwood, Nov. 1870. Ensign, Oct. 1, 1863; master, May 10, 1866; promoted through grades to rear adm., Aug. 11, 1903—. Served on the Monongahela and Brooklyn, W. Gulf Blockading Squadron, 1863-64; participated in battle of Mobile Bay, Aug. 5, 1864; N. Atlantic Blockading Squadron, 1865; both attacks, and final assault, on Ft. Fisher; Wyoming and Ashuelot, Asiatic Squadron, 1865-69; Naval Acad., 1869-71, 1882-85, 1887-90; Worcester, 1871-73; Hydrographic Office, 1873-74, 1878-82; coast survey, 1874-78, sounded and explored Gulf of Mex.; comd. practice ship Dale, during practice cruises, 1883-84; comd. Kearsarge, 1885-86; spl. duty, Navy Dept., 1887; mem. Examining and Retiring Bds., 1887; comd. training-ship Portsmouth, 1891-93; hydrographer, Navy Dept., 1893-97; comd. Maine, Apr. 10, 1897, until she was blown up and destroyed in Havana harbor, Feb. 15, 1898; comd. St. Paul in Cuban and Porto Rican waters, 1898-1900; advanced 3 numbers in rank "for extraordinary heroism displayed during war with Spain, and on the occasion of the wreck of Maine"; chief intelligence officer, 1900-03; comdt. Navy Yard, League Island, 1903-04; comd. S. Atlantic Squadron, 1904-05, 2d Div. of N. Atlantic Fleet, 1905-06; spl. duty, 1906; retired Jan. 16, 1907. Introduced numerous inventions and new methods in deep sea exploration, for which he later received decoration of Red Eagle of Prussia from Emperor William I, and received gold medal from abroad. Author: Deep Sea Sounding and Dredging, U.S. Coast Survey, 1880; Personal Narrative of the Battleship Maine, 1899. Home: New York, N.Y. Died July 19, 1923.

SIHLER, Ernest Gottlieb, univ. prof.; b. Fort Wayne, Ind., Jan. 2, 1853; s. Rev. William S. and Susannah (Kern) S.; grad. Concordia Coll., Ind., 1869; studied divinity Concordia Lutheran Sem., St. Louis; univs. of Berlin and Leipzig, 1872-75; fellow Greek, Johns Hopkins, 1876-79, Ph.D., 1878 (1st Ph.D. in Greek there); Litt.D., Lafayette Coll., 1915; m. Emily Birkner, Sept. 5, 1881 (died 1928); children—Henry John, Florence (dec.), Howard Crosby. Classical instr., New York, 1879-91; prof. in Concordia Coll., Milwaukee, 1891-92; prof. Latin, and lecturer in Grad. Sch., New York U., 1892-1923 (emeritus). Visited Pompeii, Rome, Oxford, 1897, Cambridge, 1909; active in securing transfer to New York U. of classical library of late Prof. Hübner of U. of Berlin. Author: Lexicon to Latinity of Cæsar's Gallic War, 1891; Testimonium Animæ (The Spiritual Elements of Classical Civilization), 1908; Annals of Cæsar, a critical biography, 1911 (German version, Teubner, Leipzig, 1912); Cicero of Arpinum, 1914; Hellenic Civilization (with G. W. Botsford), 1915. Editor: Edition of Plato's Protagoras, 1881, 1892; Edition of Cicero's Second Philippic, 1901. Collaborator with Chancellor MacCracken on Memorial Vol. of Hall of Fame of New York U., 1901; History of New York University (co-author), 1901; From Augustus to Augustine, 1923; From Maumee to Thames and Tiber, 1930. Home: Mt. Vernon, N.Y. Died Jan. 7, 1942.

SIKES, Enoch Walter, coll. pres.; b. Union Co., N.C., May 19, 1868; s. John C. and Jane (Austin) S.; M.A., Wake Forest Coll., N.C., 1891; Ph.D., Johns Hopkins, 1897; m. Ruth Wingate, Aug. 1, 1900. Teacher, 1891—; prof. history and polit. economy, 1897-1916, dean, 1915-16, Wake Forest (N.C.) Coll.; pres. Coker Coll., Hartsville, S.C., 1916-25; pres. Clemson Agrl. Coll., Clemson, S.C., July 1, 1925—. Mem. N.C. Senate, 1911. Gov. Carolinas Kiwanis Dist., 1925. Author: From Colony to Commonwealth, 1897; The Confederate Congress, 1904; Joseph Hewes, 1904; Sketches in Biographical History of North Carolina, 1909; The First Constitution of North Carolina, 1909. Died Jan. 8, 1941.

SIKES, George Cushing, publicist; b. Dodge Center, Minn., June 4, 1868; s. Henry Chauncey and Eleanor (Shepard) S.; B.S., U. of Minn., 1892; Ph.M., U. of Chicago, 1894; m. Madeleine, d. Hon. Alfred Wallin, Feb. 6, 1897; children—Alfred Wallin, Eleanor Shepard. Learned printer's trade; was one time pres. Minneapolis Typographical Union; did newspaper work in Minneapolis and Chicago; editorial writer on Chicago Record, 1895-1900; sec. Chicago St. Ry. Commn., 1900-02; asst. sec., 1903-05, sec., 1906-08, Municipal Voters' League, Chicago; expert investigator for Chicago Harbor Commn., May 1908-Feb. 1909, and for John M. Ewen, Chicago harbor commr., during summer and fall of 1909. Sec. Chicago Bur. of Pub. Efficiency, Aug. 1910-Oct. 1, 1915; engaged by the bur. to assist in preparation of reps., issued 1917, Unification of Local Governments in Chicago, and City Manager Plan for Chicago; also by Taxpayers' Assn. of Calif. on rep. City and County Consolidation for Los Angeles. Several yrs. writer of editorial and spl. articles for Chicago Daily News. Spl. student of municipal questions; dir. of Policemen's Annuity and Benefit Fund of Chicago, 1923-26; sec. Chicago Pension Commn., created to study Chicago public pension problems, until July 1927. Home: Chicago, Ill. Died July 20, 1928.

SILCOX, Ferdinand Augustus, chief U.S. Forest Service; b. Columbus, Ga., Dec. 25, 1882; s. Ferdinand Augustus and Carrie Olivia (Spear) S.; B.S., Coll. of Charleston (S.C.), 1903; M.F., Yale, 1905; LL.D. (hon.), College of Charleston, 1935, Syracuse U., N.Y., 1938; m. Marie Louise Thatcher, Mar. 4, 1908. Forest assistant U.S. Forest Service, 1905, advancing through successive stages to dist. forester, 1910-17; joint apptmt. by U.S. Dept. Labor and U.S. Shipping Board to handle labor relations in Seattle shipyards and spruce production for airplanes, and to arrange, in coöperation with War Dept., for mobilization of labor for N.J. munitions and airplane constrn., 1917-19; dir. industrial relations U.S. Typothetae of America, 1919-22; dir. industrial relations of N.Y. Employing Printers Assn. (organized apprenticeship schs. in coöperation with Bd. of Edn.), 1922 to 1933; apptd. chief U.S. Forest Service, Nov. 15, 1933; arbitrator between Realty Advisory Bd. of Labor Relations, Inc., and Building Service Employees Internat. Union, N.Y. City, 1936. Capt. 20th Engrs., U.S.A., World War. Democrat. Died Dec. 20, 1939.

SILL, John Mahelm Berry, diplomat, educator; b. Black Rock, N.Y., Nov. 23, 1831; was 1st graduate of Mich. State Normal School, 1854 (A.M., Univ. of Mich., 1871; master of pedagogics, Mich. State Normal Coll., 1892); m. Sally Beaumont, Mar. 22, 1854; prof. in State Normal, 1854-63; prin. same, 1886-94; also twice supt. schools Detroit; ordained minister P.E. Ch., 1890; U.S. minister to Korea, 1894-97; mem. State Bd. Regents, Univ. of Mich., 1867-70. Author: Synthesis of the English Sentence, 1856; Lessons in English, 1879. Home: Detroit, Mich. Died 1901.

SILLIMAN, Charles Augustus, lawyer; b. Troy, N.Y., Nov. 17, 1830; s. Robert Davis and Lorenda (Covell) S.; ed. Burnett Sch., Troy, 1842-44, Troy Acad., 1844-45, Anthon Grammar Sch., New York, 1845-46, Columbia Coll., 1846-50, A.B., 1850 (later A.M.); student Columbia Law Sch., 1858-60, LL.B., 1860; m. Mary Alice Rossiter (dec.); m. 2d, Maria Elizabeth Harper (dec.). Was mem. forwarding and mercantile firm of Silliman, Matthews & Co. (established by father), owning and running steamboats, barges and canalboats on Erie Canal and Hudson River, afterward changing name to Silliman & Co. (dissolved 1878); also head of commn. firm of Silliman, Martindale & Dix, of New Orleans, 1863-64. Practiced law, New York, 1860-99, Troy, N.Y., 1899—; recent practice principally in Albany before gov. and legislative com. Apptd. commr. of docks, New York, by Mayor Abram S. Hewitt, 1888. Trustee Columbia Univ., 1876—; life mem. N.Y. Hist. Soc., New England Soc. of City of New York. Presbyn. Independent Republican. Active in Christian Endeavor movement in Rensselaer and Albany cos. (pres. Troy Local Union, 1899-1900). Home: Troy, N.Y., and New York City. Died 1906.

SILLOWAY, Thomas William, architect; b. Newburyport, Mass., Aug. 7, 1828; after spl. edn. established as architect in Boston, 1851; architect of the Vermont Capitol; Buchtel Coll., Akron, O.; Soldiers' Monument, Cambridge, Mass., and more than 450 chs., etc.; restored 6 chs. in Charleston, S.C., which had been partially destroyed by the earthquake, 1886. Began to preach to Universalist congregations in 1852, and was ordained minister, 1862. Unmarried. Author: Theogonis; Text-book of Modern Carpentry; Warming and Ventilation; The Conference Melodist; Cantica Sacra; Cathedral Towns of England, Ireland and Scotland (with Lee L. Powers); editor (with Harding) of 6th edit. of Shaw's Civil Architecture. Home: Boston, Mass. Died 1910.

SILLS, Milton, actor; b. Chicago, Ill., Jan. 12, 1882; s. William Henry and Josephine Antoinette (Troosst) S.; A.B., U. of Chicago, 1903; scholar and fellow in philosophy same univ., 1½ yrs.; m. Gwladys Edith Wynne, of London, Eng., May 26, 1910 (divorced); 1 dau., Dorothy Gardyne; m. 2d, Doris (Margaret) Kenyon, actress Oct. 12, 1926; 1 son, Kenyon Clarence. Début in "Dora Thorne," at New Palestine, O., 1906; played in Donald Robertson's Art Theatre, Chicago, 1907-08, later in New Orleans; leading man in "This Woman and This Man," at Maxine Elliott Theatre, New York, 1909, also appeared in "A Happy Marriage," by Clyde Fitch, under management of Charles Frohman; appeared in "The Servant in the House," Belasco's "The Fighting Hope"; played in "Diplomacy," "Mother," "The Rack," under William A. Brady; then in "The Governor's Lady," "The Law of the Land," etc. First screen work, 1914, in "The Pit"; has taken leading parts in "Behold My Wife," "The Great Moment," "Adam's Rib," "As Man Desires," "Skin Deep," "The Sea-Hawk," "The Knock-out," "Men of Steel," "Hard Boiled Haggerty," etc. Also author "Men of Steel." Republican. Frequent speaker on screen art, literature and religion; gave lecture at Coll. of Business Administration, Harvard, 1927. Home: Los Angeles, Calif. Died Sept. 15, 1930.

SILSBEE, Arthur Boardman; b. Salem, Mass., Jan. 19, 1854; A.B., Harvard, 1875; traveled in Europe, 1875-78; unmarried. Pres. Merchants Nat. Bank, Boston; dir. Ipswich Mills; pres. Salmon Falls Mfg. Co.; trustee Provident Instn. for Savings. Home: Boston, Mass. Died Apr. 1924.

SILVER, Gray, farmer, agrl. economist; b. Whitehall, Va., Feb. 17, 1871; s. Francis III (C.S.A.) and Mary Ann (Gray) S.; ed. pub. and pvt. schs.; Master Farmer, conferred by W.Va. U., 1930; m. Kate Bishop, Dec. 5, 1908; children—Mary Gray, Gray, Anne Beall, Francis 5th, Catherine du Bois. Engaged in farming in Shenandoah Valley, also in Ill. and Ark.; breeder Shorthorn cattle and Shropshire sheep; pres. John W. Bishop Co., Martinsburg, W.Va.; pres. Potomac Farm Loan Bank; dir. Merchants & Farmers Bank; mem. State Senate, Va., 1907-15; lt. gov. of Va., 1911-13; mem. State Tax Commn., 1926-27; mem. Legislative Commn. of W.Va., investigating state instns. and providing fiscal system for the state; mem. Federal Unemployment Commn., 1930; mem. Nat. Park Bd. Represented W.Va. at organization meeting of Am. Farm Bur. Fedn., 1919, dir. and mem. exec. com., 1919-26; organizer agrl. bloc in Congress. Pres. Inwood Fruit Growers (cooperative). Grain Marketing Co. (nat. cooperative), Berkeley (W.Va.) Fruit Growers, Eastern Grain Growers Coop. Corp., operating in soft wheat; mem. commn. apptd. by President Taft to study tariff relations to wool industry and report to Tariff Commn.; mem. Farm Bur. Federation group visiting Europe, 1924; mem. Fact Finding Commn. on Distribution Cost, Nat. Unemployment Conf. Col. on staff of Gov. H. D. Hatfield; official rep. of Am. Farm Bur. Federation at Rep. and Dem. nat. convs., 1920, 24. Decorated by French Govt. for "distinguished service in agriculture." Presbyn. Mason. Author and patron of 7 companion bills constituting W.Va. good roads system and laws. Home: Martinsburg, W.Va. Died July 28, 1935.

SILVER, H(orace) Percy, clergyman; b. Philadelphia, Pa.; s. Joseph S. and Harriet L. (Robinson) S.; pub. schs. of Phila.; grad. Gen. Theol. Sem., N.Y., 1894; LL.D., Hobart College; S.T.D., General Theological Seminary; Litt.D., Middlebury (Vt.) College; unmarried. Was with J. B. Lippincott Co., Phila., 4½ yrs.; deacon, 1894, priest, 1895, P.E. Ch.; in charge St. Andrew's Ch., Omaha, Neb., 1894-96; rector Holy Trinity Ch., Lincoln, Neb., 1896-99, Ch. of Good Shepherd, and canon of Trinity Cathedral, Omaha, 1899-1901; chaplain U.S.A., 1901-10; sec. Missionary Dept. of the Southwest, 1910-13; elected bishop coadjutor of Kan. (withdrew); elected bishop coadjutor of Tex. (declined); chaplain U.S. Mil. Acad., Sept. 1913-18; rector Ch. of the Incarnation, New York, Oct. 1918—; elected bishop of Wyo., 1927 (declined). Mem. Nat. Council. Mason, K.C.C.H. Home: Bedford Hills, N.Y. Died Dec. 15, 1934.

SILVERMAN, Joseph, rabbi; b. Cincinnati, O., Aug. 25, 1860; s. M. H. and Ulrika (Piorkowsky) S.; A.B., U. of Cincinnati, 1883; studied Hebrew Union Coll., D.D., 1887; D.H.L., University of N.Y., 1924; m. Henriette Block, Dec. 5, 1886; 4 children. Ordained rabbi, 1884; minister Temple Emanu-El, Dallas, Tex., 1884-85, Congregation Benai Israel, Galveston, 1885-88, Temple Emanu-El, New York, 1888-1922 (rabbi emeritus); hon. rabbi Temple Emanu-El, Boro Park, Brooklyn, 1925. Member Council of Religious Congress, Chicago Exposition, 1893; pres. Central Conf. Am. Rabbis, 1900-03; founder, 1903, and pres. Emanu-El Brotherhood; mem. Am. Jewish Com.; former gov. Hebrew Union Coll.; Grand Chaplain Masons of N.Y., 1906-08; pres. Order B'nai B'rith, Dist. I, 1913-15; mem. General Com. Order of B'nai B'rith; mem. exec. com. Nat. Assn. Advancement of Colored Race, 1909-12; v.p. Internat. Peace Forum and asso. editor Peace Forum Mag., 1913; mem. Mohawk Peace Conf., 1911-13. Hon. pres. Assn. Reform Rabbis of N.Y.; hon. pres. N.Y. Bd. Jewish Ministers; pres. Eastern Council Reform Rabbis, 1917-19; sec. Emanu-El Theol. Sem. Assn.; trustee Emanu-El Sisterhood for Personal Service; hon. v.p. Palestine Foundation Fund; mem. nat. exec. com. Zionist Orgn. America, Masonic Palestine Foundation; mem. Am. com. Jewish Palestine Exploration Soc. Author: Catechism on Judaism, 1886. Home: New York, N.Y. Died July 26, 1930.

SILZER, George S., governor; b. New Brunswick, N.J., Apr. 14, 1870; s. Theodore C. and Christina (Zimmerman) S.; ed. pub. and high schs.; LL.D., Rutgers, 1923; m. Henrietta T. Waite, Apr. 18, 1898. Admitted to N.J. bar, 1892; mem. Bd. of Aldermen, Brunswick, N.J., 1892-96; chmn. Dem. Co. Com., Middlesex Co., 10 yrs.; mem. N.J. Senate, 1907-12; prosecutor of pleas, Middlesex Co., 1912-14; circuit judge, by apptmt. of Gov. Fielder, later by apptmt. Gov. Edwards, 1914-22 (resigned); gov. of New Jersey, 1923-26. Chmn. bd. New Brunswick Trust Co.; chmn. bd. and dir. Interstate Trust Co., New York, 1929-30; trustee Central Savings Bank in the City of New York. Chmn. Port of New York Authority, 1926-28. Episcopalian. Mason, Elk. Home: Metuchen, N.J. Died Oct. 16, 1940.

SIM, John Robert, coll. prof.; b. Morgan Co., Va. (now W.Va.), Feb. 15, 1849; s. Robert and Margaret (Couthill) S.; A.B., Coll. City of New York, 1868; m. Mary Adelaide Duff, Nov. 23, 1881; children—Robert Lee, Marjorie Duff, Adelaide Margaret. Tutor in mathematics, Coll. City of New York, 1870; taught in Cooper Union Tech. Sch., Harlem Evening High Sch.; instr. pure mathematics, 1890-95, asst. prof., 1895-1904, prof., 1904-19, and prof. in charge academic dept., 1901-19, prof. emeritus, Nov. 1, 1919, Coll. City of New York, trustee Teachers' Assn. City of New York. Chmn. bd. trustees Students' Aid Assn. of Coll. City of N.Y. Independent Democrat. Presbyn. Home: New York, N.Y. Died Dec. 22, 1925.

SIMKINS, Henry Walter, editor; b. nr. Columbus, O., Oct. 29, 1868; s. John Harvey and Elizabeth (Colwell) S.; Nat. Normal U., Lebanon, O., 1887-88; business coll., San Francisco, 1892; Stanford U., 1892-94; m. Eleanore H. Abbott, June 30, 1902. Taught sch. in Calif., 1888-92; owned book and stationery store, Palo Alto, 1892-1907; owner and editor Palo Alto Times (daily), 1898-1919; established "The Altrurian," a mag. devoted to ethics, religion and industrial reform, 1911; dir. First Nat. Bank. City clerk, Palo Alto, 1894-1904; councilman, 1908-09; mem. Bd. of Freeholders, 1909; pres. Bd. of Trade, 1906-07, Santa Clara Co. Editorial Assn., 1913-14. Inventor of the revolving bond fund for financing street paving adopted by San Francisco and other cities. Founder and owner Peninsula Newspaper Syndicate. Chief editorial writer San Francisco Journal, 1920—. Methodist. Home: Palo Alto, Calif. Died Jan. 14, 1925.

SIMKINS, William Stewart, prof. law; b. Edgefield, S.C., Aug. 25, 1842; s. Eldred James and Martha (Bythewood) S.; grad. Mil. Acad. of S.C., Charleston, S.C., 1861; D.C.L., U. of the South, June 1913; m. Lizzie Ware, Feb. 10, 1870 (died 1911). Joined S.C. troops, Dec. 1860; transferred to C.S.A. after its organization, 1861, as 1st lt. of arty.; served through Civil War and surrendered with Johnson's Army, in N.C., Apr. 1865. Admitted to bar, 1870; practiced at Monticello, Fla., 1870-73, Corsicana, Tex., 1873-85, Dallas, 1885-99; prof. law U. of Tex., 1899—. Episcopalian. Mason. Author: Simkins on Equity, 1903; Contracts and Sales, 1905; Administration of Estates in Texas, 1908; A Federal Suit in Equity, 1909; A Federal Suit at Law, 1912; Title by Limitation in Texas. Lectures on legal ethics. Home: Austin, Tex. Died Feb. 27, 1929.

SIMMONS, Edward, artist; b. Concord, Mass., Oct. 27, 1852; s. George Frederick and Mary Emerson (Ripley) S.; A.B., Harvard, 1874; studied painting under Lefebvre, and Boulanger, Paris; m. Vesta Schallenberger, Dec. 1883; children—William, George Bradford; m. 2d, Alice Ralston Morton, Sept. 1903; 1 son, Peter. Professional painter, 1879—; prize from Municipal Art Soc. of New York for mural decoration in Criminal Ct. Bldg.; decorations in Mass. State House, Minn. Capitol, Appellate Ct., New York, Library of Congress, Washington, D.C., S.Dak. Capitol, Waldorf Astoria Hotel, Law Ct. of Des Moines, Ia., Court House, Mercer, Pa., also pvt. homes of Frederick Vanderbilt, Hyde Park, N.Y., John D. Rockefeller, Tarrytown, N.Y., etc.; mural decorations, Panama P.I. Expn. Mem. Nat. Inst. Arts and Letters, Ten Am. Painters. Author: From Seven to Seventy, Memories of a Painter, 1922. Died Nov. 17, 1931.

SIMMONS, Edward Alfred, publisher; b. Brooklyn, N.Y., Mar. 20, 1875; s. John Wesley and Agnes Anne (Owers) S.; ed. pub. schs., Brooklyn; m. Ida Boone Rines, Oct. 12, 1914; children—Aline, Doris, Elizabeth. Entered employ of Simmons-Boardman Pub. Co., 1889, sec. 1898, dir., treas. and v.p. 1903, pres., 1911—; chmn. bd. Am. Saw Mill Machinery Co., Corley Mfg. Co.; pres. Am. Saw Works. Served in Construction Div., U.S.A., Feb. 1918-Feb. 1919, World War; now col. Q.M. Res. Affiliate mem. Am. Soc. C.E.; asso. mem. Am. Soc. Mech. Engrs. Republican. Episcopalian. Mason, Elk. Home: Brooklyn, N.Y. Died Oct. 1, 1931.

SIMMONS, Edward Campbell, merchant; b. Frederick, Md., Sept. 21, 1839; s. Zachariah T. and Louisa C. S.; high sch. edn., St. Louis; m. Garrie Welch, Nov. 24, 1866. Engaged in hardware business in St. Louis, Jan. 1, 1856—; now chmn. bd. dirs. Simmons Hardware Co.; dir. Bank of Commerce, St. Louis Union Trust Co., Mo.P. Ry. Police commr., 1881. Cleveland Democrat. Episcopalian. Home: St. Louis, Mo. Died Apr. 18, 1920.

SIMMONS, Franklin, sculptor; b. Webster, Me., Jan. 11, 1839; ed. Bates Coll., Lewiston, Me.; (hon. A.M., Bates, Colby, 1885, Bowdoin, 1888); m. Baroness von Jeinsen, née Slocum, of Providence, R.I., June 9, 1892. After some preliminary work in portraiture in Me., spent winters of 1865 and 1866 in Washington; had sittings from Admirals Farragut and Porter, Generals Grant, Meade, Sheridan, Sherman, Thomas, Hooker and others. From 1868 has lived mostly in Rome. Has executed about 100 portrait busts in marble; about 15 public monuments, including statues of William King, Roger Williams, Gov. Pierpont of Va., and G.A.R. monument of Gen. Grant for National Capitol, and equestrian monument of Gen. Logan in Iowa Circle, Washington; Longfellow, and Soldiers' monuments, Portland, Me.; O. P. Morton, Indianapolis; monument to Roger Williams, Providence, R.I., etc.; also ideal statues, including Penelope, Medusa, Seraph Abdiel, Galatea, The Mother of Moses, Benjamin; bronze statue of Alexander Hamilton for Paterson, N.J.; etc. Thrice decorated by King of Italy, the last, Commendatore of the Crown of Italy. Studio: Rome, Italy. Died Dec. 8, 1913.

SIMMONS, Furnifold McLendell, senator; b. Jones Co., N.C., Jan. 20, 1854; s. Furnifold Greene and Mary (McLendell) S.; A.B., Trinity Coll., N.C., 1873; LL.D., Trinity, 1901, and University of N.C., 1915; m. Eliza Humphrey, 1875; m. 2d, Belle Gibbs, 1886. Admitted to bar, 1875, and practiced at New Bern and Raleigh, N.C., until 1901. Mem. 50th Congress (1887-89), 2d N.C. Dist.; collector internal revenue, 4th Dist., 1893-97; chmn. Dem. Exec. Com. of N.C., 1892, 98, 1900, 02, 04, 06; U.S. senator from N.C., 5 terms, 1901-31; chmn. Senate Finance Com., 1913-19; former mem. Dem. Nat. Com., resigning 1928. Co-author of Underwood-Simmons Tariff Act, 1913-21. Home: New Bern, N.C. Died Apr. 30, 1940.

SIMMONS, George H., editor; b. Moreton, Eng., Jan. 2, 1852; s. George and Sarah Louise (Clifford) S.; came to U.S., 1870; student Tabor Coll., Ia., 1871-72, U. of Neb., 1872-76; M.D., Hahnemann Medical College, Chicago, 1882; M.D., Rush Medical College, 1892; L.M., Rotunda Hospital, Dublin, 1884; post-grad. work in Europe, 1883-84; (hon. A.M., Tabor, 1899; LL.D., Northwestern U., 1907). Practiced medicine and surgery, Lincoln, Neb., 1884-99; gen. sec. A.M.A., 1899-1911; editor Jour. Am. Med. Assn., 1899-1924, editor and general manager emeritus, 1924—; established Western Medical Review, 1896. Commd. 1st lt. Med. R.C., U.S.A., 1908, maj., 1917. Sec. Neb. State Med. Soc., 1895-99, Western Surg. and Gynecol. Soc., 1896-99; pres. Inst. of Medicine, Chicago, 1921. Home: Hollywood, Fla. Died Sept. 1, 1937.

SIMMONS, George Welch, merchant, capitalist; b. St. Louis, Aug. 12, 1878; s. Edward C. and Garafelia (Welch) S.; A.B., Yale, 1900; m. Virginia Wright, Nov. 21, 1903; children—Richard W., Virginia, Lulie, George W. Began in warehouse, firm of Simmons Hardware Co., 1900, becoming gen. mgr., 1904; when Simmons business merged with Winchester interests, was made pres. of Winchester-Simmons Co. from which retired Jan. 1, 1924, to become v.p. Mechanics & Metals Nat. Bank; on merger with Chase Nat. Bank became v.p. later; resigned, 1927, to become pres. George W. Simmons Corp.; dir. Simmons Hardware Co., Winchester-Simmons Co. (Del.), Southwestern Bell Telephone Co., Southern Wheel Co. Republican. Episcopalian. Mgr. Southwestern Div. Am. Red Cross, 1917-19. Spl. commr. A.R.C., to France, 1918; to Siberia, 1919. Homes: New York City and Manhasset, L.I., N.Y. Died May 22, 1930.

SIMMONS, Henry Clay, pres. Fargo Coll., 1894—; b. Hartford, N.Y., Feb. 15, 1845; removed to Beloit, Wis., when 9 years old; grad. Beloit Coll., 1869 (D.D., 1897); Chicago Theol. Sem., 1872; pastor in Fond du Lac Co., Wis., 1872-74; married there, Aug. 11, 1874. Pastor Marshall, Minn., 1874-79; Walnut Grove and Tracy, Minn., 1879-82; supt. Congl. Home Missionary Society's work in N.Dak., 1882-97; also in Eastern Mont., 1882-88. Home: Fargo, N.Dak. Died 1899.

SIMMONS, Henry Martyn, Unitarian minister; b. Paris, N.Y., 1841; s. Philip T. and Miranda (Head) S.; grad. Hamilton Coll., 1864, and Auburn Theol. Sem.; m. 1868, Florence A. Head. Preached at Syracuse and Ilion, N.Y., at Kenosha and Madison, Wis., and for 24 yrs. at Minneapolis; supt. schools in Kenosha several yrs.; was editor of Unity, Chicago, 1 yr. Author: The Unending Genesis, 1882; New Tables of Stone, 1904. Home: Minneapolis, Minn. Deceased.

SIMMONS, J(oseph) Edward, banker; b. Troy, N.Y., Sept. 9, 1841; s. Joseph Ferris and Mary Sophia (Gleason) S.; A.B., Williams Coll., 1862; LL.B., Albany Law Sch., 1863; m. Julia Greer, Apr. 12, 1866. Practiced law at Troy, and New York; became mem. of a Wall St. commn. house; pres. N.Y. Stock Exchange, 1884-85; pres. Fourth Nat. Bank of New York, 1888—; pres. Panama R.R. Co., Columbia Steamship Co. President New York Clearing House; pres. Chamber of Commerce of State of New York, 1907—. Grand Master of Masons, N.Y., 1883-84; pres. Bd. of Edn., New York, 1885-90; gov. and treas. New York Hosp.; trustee Williams Coll. Home: New York, N.Y. Died 1910.

SIMMONS, Lessie Southgate, musician; b. Louisburg, N.C., July 5, 1863; d. James and Delia Haywood (Wynne) Southgate; educated Staunton (Va.) Wesleyan Female Inst., Grand Conservatory of Music, New York; pupil of Murio-Celli, S.B. Mills, Samuel P. Warren; studied voice with Frau Nicholas Kempner, Berlin, and E. Delle Sedie, Paris; m. Thomas J. Simmons, LL.D., Nov. 11, 1891. Before marriage was dir. Durham (N.C.) Sch. of Music; dir. of music in her husband's coll., Eufaula, Ala., 1893-98; and at the same time dir. of music, Georgia Chautauqua, Albany, Ga.; dir. of music Shorter Coll., Rome, Ga., 1898-1910, Brenau Coll., 1910—. Lecturer on music, art, temperance, ancient religions, travels in far Eastern lands, etc. Methodist. Home: Gainesville, Ga. Died May 19, 1914.

SIMMONS, William Marvin, lawyer, educator; b. Stanwood, Ia., Apr. 20, 1885; s. Marvin Lewis and Nellie (Bush) S.; B.S., Cornell Coll., Mt. Vernon, Ia., 1906; LL.B., Harvard, 1911; unmarried. Admitted to Calif. bar, 1911, and began practice in legal dept. Western Pacific Ry. Co., San Francisco; practiced with William C. Crittenden, 1912-14, partner Crittenden & Simmons, 1914-17; in U.S. Army, May 1917-July 1919; hon. discharged as capt.; mem. Bell, Brookman, Simmons & Creech, 1919-24; dean Hastings Coll. of Law, July 1, 1925—. Home: San Francisco, Calif. Died July 25, 1940.

SIMMS, Joseph, physiognomist; b. Plainfield Center, N.Y., Sept. 3, 1833; s. of Ephraim Fitch and Florinda Johnson (Norton) S.; ed. dist. schs. and acad.; Med. Dept., New York U., 1866-67; Coll. Phys. and Surg. (Columbia), 1868-69; M.D., Eclectic Med. College, New York, 1871; m. Jemima Sinclair, of Edinburgh, Scotland, Apr. 7, 1885. Pub. sch. teacher, 1850-54; began lecturing on physiognomy and other subjects, 1854; served in Union Army under Generals Sherman and Grant, 1861-63. Traveled extensively in all the continents; lectured in all principal cities of U.S., Great Britain and Australia, delivering extensive courses in larger centers; spent over 3 yrs. in the islands of the Pacific, and journeyed in America from Alaska to Patagonia, studying birds, fishes, animals and races of men; retired from lecture platform, 1884, after acquiring a fortune. Republican. Elected mem. Anthropol. Inst. Great Britain and Ireland, 1875. Mason. Author: Physiognomical and Physiological Chart, 1867; An Original and Illustrated Physiological and Physiognomical Chart, 1873, 4th edit., 1888; Nature's Revelations of Character, 1874, 10th edit., 1891; Practical and Scientific Physiognomy, 1884. Died Apr. 11, 1920.

SIMMS, S(tephen) Chapman, ethnologist; b. Georgetown, D.C., Mar. 22, 1863; s. Joseph Libbey and Rosa Margaret (Edmonston) S.; pvt. sch. edn.; m. Margaret Elizabeth, d. Ephraim Whitlock, of Brooklyn, Apr. 23, 1891. Reporter, corr., asst. mng. editor, 1884-90; asst. sec. and chargé d'affaires, dept. foreign affairs, Chicago Expn., 1891-94; Royal Portuguese vice-consul, Chicago, 1892, consul, 1918—; representative of late Sultan of Johore, Straits Settlement, during Chicago Expn.; apptd. asst. curator of industrial arts, Field Mus. of Natural History, Chicago, 1894, and continued with the Museum, as asst. curator of ethnology, 1894-1912, curator of N.W. Harris pub. sch. extension, 1912-28, dir. of the Museum, July 1928—. Ethnologist in charge div. of ethnology, dept. anthropology, St. Louis Expn., 1904; mem. Superior Jury of Internat. Jury of Awards, Panama P.I. Expn., 1915; v.p. and sec. Internat. Jury of Awards, Sesquicentennial Internat. Expn., 1926. Decorated by Chinese Republic with Order of Kia-ho, 1915; by Czecho-Slovakian Govt. with Order of White Lion, 1928. Home: Chicago, Ill. Died Jan. 28, 1937.

SIMON, Abram, rabbi; b. Nashville, Tenn., July 14, 1872; s. David and Rachel (Lederhandler) S.; B.Litt., U. of Cincinnati, 1894; rabbi, Hebrew Union Coll., Cincinnati, 1894, D.H.L., 1925; Ph.D., George Washington U., 1917; m. Carrie Obendorfer, Aug. 5, 1896; children—Leo W. (dec.), David R. Rabbi, Sacramento, Calif., 1894-99, Omaha, Neb., 1899-1904, Washington, D.C., 1904—. Served as Red Cross searcher, nr. Verdun, World War. Pres. Bd. of Edn., Washington, 1920-23, now mem. same. Trustee Columbia Hosp., Free Pub. Library, Jewish Chautauqua Soc. Mem. Central Conf. Am. Rabbis (pres.), Synagogue Council America (chmn.). Republican. Mason; mem. B'nai B'rith. Author: History of Jewish Education, 1912. Home: Washington, D.C. Died Dec. 24, 1938.

SIMON, Charles Edmund, M.D.; b. Baltimore, Sept. 23, 1866; s. Charles, Jr., and Helen (Kirchner) S.; A.B., Johns Hopkins, 1888; student medicine, U. of Pa., 1888-89; M.D., U. of Md., 1890; m. Lina Stumm, of Basel, Switzerland, Apr. 22, 1892; 1 son, Charles Henry. Asst. resident phys. Johns Hopkins Hosp., 1890-91; opened 1st clin. lab., Baltimore, 1897; teacher of clin. lab. methods to post-grads. in medicine; prof. clin. pathology and physiol. chemistry, U. of Maryland, 1910-20; fellow by courtesy, Sch. of Hygiene and Pub. Health of Johns Hopkins U., 1920-21; lecturer med. zoölogy, 1921-23, resident lecturer med. zoöl. div. of filterable viruses, 1923—. Mng. editor Am. Jour. of Hygiene. Author: Clinical Diagnosis, 1896; Physiological Chemistry, 1901; Infection and Immunity, 1911; Human Infection Carriers, 1919. Home: Baltimore, Md. Died Nov. 8, 1927.

SIMON, Franklin, merchant; b. N.Y. City, Feb. 7, 1865; s. Henri and Hellene (Scheier) S.; ed. pub. schs.; m. Frances Carroll, Aug. 20, 1892; children—Arthur J., Helene S. (Mrs. Laurence M. Lloyd), George D. Pres. Franklin Simon & Co., specialty shop, N.Y. City, 1903—. Dir. Hosp. for Joint Diseases; mem. bd. govs. Stuyvesant Sq. Hosp. Home: New York, N.Y. Died Oct. 4, 1934.

SIMON, Joseph, senator; b. 1851; a resident of Portland, Ore., 1857—; ed. pub. schs., Portland, Ore.; unmarried. Admitted to Ore. bar, 1872; mem. City Council, Portland, 1877-80; sec. Rep. State Central Com., 1878; chmn. same, 1880, 84, 86; mem. Rep. Nat. Com., 1892-96; mem. Ore. Senate, 1880-98 (pres. 5 sessions); U.S. senator, 1898-1903; mayor of Portland, 1909-11. Home: Portland, Ore. Died Feb. 14, 1935.

SIMON, William, chemist; b. Eberstadt, Hessen, Germany, Feb. 20, 1844; s. Rev. William and Agnes (Briegleb) S.; ed. at Giessen, 1852-60; in a drug store, 1860-66; Ph.D., U. of Giessen, 1869; (hon. M.D., Coll. Phys. and Surg., Baltimore, 1880; (Sc.D., U. of Pennsylvania, 1915); asst. to Prof. H. Will, 1869-70; in Franco-Prussian War, 1870; came to U.S., 1870; opened 1st chem. lab. for instrn. at Baltimore, 1871; m. Paula Driver, May 13, 1873. Chemist to Baltimore Chrome Works, 1870-1907; prof. chemistry, Md., Coll. Pharmacy, 1872-1902, Coll. Phys. and Surg., Baltimore, 1880—, Baltimore Coll. Dental Surgery, 1888—. Pres. Md. Pharm. Assn., 1887-88; fellow, mem. or hon. mem. of many chem. and pharm. socs. Author: Manual of Chemistry, 1884, 10th edit., 1912. Home: Catonsville, Md. Died July 19, 1916.

SIMONDS, Alvan Tracy, mfr.; b. Fitchburg, Mass., Dec. 23, 1876; s. Daniel and Ellen M. (Gifford) S.; A.B., Harvard, 1899; hon. Sc.D., Boston U., 1931; studied at School of Metallurgy, Sheffield, Eng., 1900; m. Susan Gansevoort Lansing, Apr. 16, 1901; m. 2d, Virginia Chalavaya Fildes, Sept. 4, 1926. Pres. Simonds Saw & Steel Co., 1913—; pres. Abrasive Company, Phila., 1927—. Captain Ordnance Dept., U.S.A., Washington, D.C., in charge purchase and production of helmets and body armor, World War, 1917. Assistant Chief of Ordnance of 1st Dist., 1938. Member advisory com. Grad. Sch. of Business Administration, Harvard. Has offered prizes annually for best essays on economic subjects by pupils high schs., normal schs. and trade schs., U.S. and Can., 1921—. Republican. Conglist. Author: Business Fundamentals, 1923. Lecturer. Home: Jamaica Plain, Mass. Died Sept. 2, 1941.

SIMONDS, Frank H(erbert), journalist; b. Concord, Mass., Apr. 5, 1878; s. William Henry and Jennie E. (Garty) S.; A.B., Harvard, 1900; Litt.D., Dartmouth Coll., 1918; m. Mary France Gledhill, Dec. 25, 1902; children—Katharine (Mrs. Lovell Thompson), James G. Began, 1901, as reporter New York Tribune, and continued with same at Washington bur., 1903, and as Albany corr., 1904-05; Albany corr. New York Evening Post, 1906-08; editorial writer, The Sun, 1908-13; editor The Evening Sun, 1913-14; asso. editor The Tribune, Mar. 1915-Dec. 1918; contbg. editor Review of Reviews, 1914-33; contbr. to syndicate of 50 Am. and foreign newspapers, 1918—. Chevalier Légion d'Honneur (French), 1919; Commander of Order of the Phoenix (Greek); Officer Star of Rumania; Officer Polonia Restituta (Polish); Officer Order of the Crown (Belgian); Order of Merit (Hungarian). Served as pvt. Co. I, 6th Mass. Regt., Spanish-Am. War. Author: They Shall Not Pass—Verdun, 1916; History of the World War, 5 vols.; How Europe Made Peace without America, 1927; Can Europe Keep the Peace, 1931; They Won the War, 1931; Can America Stay at Home, 1932; ABC of the War Debts, 1933. Homes: Washington, D.C., and Snowville, N.H. Died Jan. 23, 1936.

SIMONDS, Frederic William, univ. prof.; b. Charlestown, Mass., July 3, 1853; s. Andrew Wait and Ellen R. (Cox) S.; B.S., Cornell, 1875, M.S., 1876; Ph.D., Syracuse U., 1879; D.Sc., U. of Ark., 1893; m. Norma A. Wood, Aug. 21, 1877 (died 1915); children—Fred Hartt (dec.), Anna Wood, Andrew Warren. Instr. geology and palæontology, Cornell, 1875-77; prof. geology, zoölogy, and botany, U. of N.C., 1877-81; spl. agt. 10th Census, dept. mining statistics, 1880; lecturer economic geology, Cornell, 1887; prof. geology and biology, U. of Ark., 1887-90; asst. geologist Ark. Geol. Survey, 1887-92; asso. prof. geology, 1890-95, prof., 1895—, U. of Tex. Mason. Author Annual Report of the Geological Survey of Arkansas, 1888, Vol. 4, 1891; Annual Report of the Geological Survey of Arkansas, 1891, Vol. 2, 1893; A Record of the Geology of Texas for the Decade Ending Dec. 31, 1896, 1900; The Minerals and Mineral Localities of Texas, 1902; The Geography of Texas—Physical and Political, 1905; The Maury-Simonds Physical Geography, 1908. Home: Austin, Tex. Died Mar. 27, 1941.

SIMONDS, George Sherwin, army officer; b. Cresco, Ia., Mar. 12, 1874; s. William O. and Ellen Augusta (Sherwin) S.; grad. U.S. Mil. Acad., 1899; grad. Inf. and Cav. Sch., 1904; grad. Army War Coll., 1920; m. Minnette Lomas, July 7, 1903 (died 1904); m. 2d, Florence Page, May 9, 1906; children—Marjorie Louise (wife of William F. Ryan, officer of U.S. Army), Frances Page (wife of N. A. Costello, officer of U.S. Army). Commd. 2d lt. 22d Inf., Feb. 15, 1899; promoted through grades to maj. gen., Feb. 11, 1933; served as maj., lt. col., col. and brig. gen. N.A., World War. With regt. in Philippines, 1899; comdg. gunboat Oeste, in Philippines, 1899, gunboat Florida, 1900, gunboat Laguna de Bay, 1900-01; in China, Jan.-May 1901; returned to U.S., Feb. 1902; with regt. in Neb. and Okla., 1902-03; at Inf. and Cav. Sch., 1903-04; instr. dept. of law and history, U.S. Mil. Acad., 1904-05, dept. of tactics, 1905-08; in Alaska, 1908-10; on Mexican border, 1910-15; instr. dept. of tactics, U.S. Mil. Acad., 1915-17; arrived in France, June 1917; served as adj. 26th Div., on Gen. Staff at Gen. Hdqrs. as chief of staff, 2d Army Corps, and as chief of staff, and in comd Am. Embarkation Center, at Le Mans; participated in major operation, Somme defensive, Mar.-Apr. 1918, Lys defensive, Apr., Ypres-Lys offensive, Sept., and in Somme offensive, Aug. 1919; served as student officer, instr. and asst. comdt. Army War Coll., 1919-24; comdr. Tank School, Camp Meade, Md., Sept.-Dec. 1924; comdg. inf. brigade in Canal Zone, Jan. 1925-Sept. 1927; asst. chief of staff, War Plans Div., War Dept., 1927-31; duty with Geneva Disarmament Conf., 1931-32; comdt. Army War Coll., 1932-35; deputy chief of staff War Dept., 1935-36; comdg. gen. 4th Army and 9th Corps Area, June 20, 1936—. Awarded D.S.M. (U.S.); Companion of the Bath (British); Order of the Crown (Italian); Officer Legion of Honor (French). Home: Cresco, Ia. Died Nov. 1, 1938.

SIMONDS, Gifford Kingsbury, gen. mgr. Simonds Saw Co.; b. Fitchburg, Mass., Nov. 29, 1880; s. Daniel and Ellen (Gifford) S.; ed. pub. schs., Fitchburg, and Hopkinson Acad., Boston; m. Ruth Woodward, Oct. 12, 1910; children—Priscilla, Gifford K., John Howland, Ruth. With Simonds Saw Co., 1898—, gen. mgr., 1914; pres. Waltham Watch Co., 1921-22; pres. Hunter Arm Co., Fulton, N.Y., 1922-25; pres. Marschalk & Pratt, advertising agts., N.Y. City, 1924-29. Conglist. Author: The American Way to Prosperity, 1928; Forecasting for Business (lecture), 1930. Home: Brookline, Mass. Died Mar. 20, 1941.

SIMONDS, Ossian Cole, landscape gardener; b. Grand Rapids, Mich., Nov. 11, 1855; s. Joel A. and Harriet Newell (Garfield) S.; C.E., U. of Mich., 1878; hon. M.A. from same university in 1929; m. Martha E. Rumsey, May 12, 1881; children—Gertrude (Mrs. William E. Walker), Herbert, Marshall, Donald, Robert. Mem. Holabird, Simonds & Roche, architects, Chicago, 1880-83; supt. Graceland Cemetery, 1881-1898; mem. bd. of mgrs., and landscape gardener, same, 1898—; formerly mem. O. C. Simonds & Co., now Simonds & West. Author of book on landscape gardening, and occasional lecturer on same subject at the U. of Mich. and elsewhere. Home: Chicago, Ill. Died Nov. 20, 1931.

SIMONDS, William Edgar, lawyer; b. Canton, Conn., Nov. 25, 1841; s. John and Hyphena S.; grad. State Normal School, New Britain, Conn., 1860 (hon. A.M., Yale, 1890); taught, 1860-62; served, 1862-63, pvt. to lt., 25th Conn. vols., and received Congressional medal for gallantry at battle of Irish Bend., La.; grad. Yale Law School, 1865; entered practice at Hartford; mem. Conn. legislature, 1883, 1885 (speaker); lecturer on patent law, Yale Law School, 10 yrs., and Columbian Univ. 4 yrs.; mem. Congress, 1889-91; commr. of patents, 1891-93; Chevalier Légion d'Honneur of France, 1893—. Author: Design Patents, 1874; Digest of Patent Office Decisions, 1880; Digest of Patent Cases, 1888; Whither, a Study of Immortality, 1900. Home: Hartford, Conn. Died 1903.

SIMONS, James, lawyer; b. Charleston, S.C., Nov. 20, 1839; s. James and Sarah L. (Wragg) S.; ed. S.C. Coll. and U. of Leipzig; (LL.D., Hobart Coll., also U. of S.C.); m. Elizabeth Potter Schott, Oct. 16, 1890. Studied law father's office; admitted to bar, 1860; inf. officer and afterward arty. officer, 1861-65, C.S.A.; resumed practice after war; pres. Charleston (S.C.) News and Courier Co., 1894—. Member S.C. Ho. of Rep., 1878-91 (speaker 1882-90); chmn. Bd. Pub. School Commrs., Charleston; pres. trustees High Sch., Charleston. Pres. Carolina Art Assn.; v.p. gen. Soc. of the Cincinnati, 1902—; pres. Soc. of the Cincinnati in S.C., 1898—. Home: Charleston, S.C. Died July 4, 1919.

SIMONS, Minot, clergyman; b. Manchester, N.H., Sept. 24, 1868; s. Langdon and Sarah Frances (Shephard) S.; Phillips Exeter Acad.; A.B., Harvard, 1891, A.M., S.T.B., 1894; D.D., Meadville Theol. Sch., 1921; m. Helen Louise Savage, Dec. 18, 1894; 1 son, Langdon Savage. Ordained Unitarian ministry, 1895; pastor First Parish, Billerica, Mass., 1895-1900; First Unit. Ch., Cleveland, O., 1900-19; sec. Ch. Extension Dept., Am. Unit. Assn., 1919-23; pastor All Souls Ch., New York, 1923—. Preacher Western Reserve U., 1904-19; mem. bd. preachers, Harvard U., 1912-13. Chmn. Council of Gen. Conf. Unitarian Chs., 1915; trustee Meadville Theol. Sch., 1912-28; trustee Phillips Exeter Acad., Hackley Sch., Tarrytown, N.Y.; mem. Bd. of Overseers, Harvard Univ., 1932-38. Republican. Author: Vexed Questions, 1913; Working Faiths, 1914; A Modern Theism, 1931. Died May 25, 1941.

SIMONSON, William A., banker; b. Newark, N.J., Apr. 27, 1865; s. Frederick and Ann (Knights) S.; ed. pub. schs.; m. Elizabeth Ball, Apr. 8, 1896; children—Douglass B., Elizabeth Downes. Senior v.p. and dir. National City Bank; dir. New Amsterdam Gas Co., Lincoln Safe Deposit Co., Internat. Banking Corp. Republican. Episcopalian. Home: New York, N.Y. Died Mar. 5, 1937.

SIMONTON, Charles H., U.S. judge 4th circuit, 1893—; b. Charleston, S.C., July 11, 1829; s. Charles S. and Elizabeth (Ross) S.; grad. S.C. Coll. with 1st honors of class (LL.D.; also D.C.L., U. of the South); taught school 1 yr.; studied law; practiced at Charleston; mem. S.C. legislature, 1853-86 (except during Civil war and Reconstruction period); was speaker and later chmn. judiciary com. Served in C.S.A., capt. Washington light inf.; later col. 25th S.C. vols.; prisoner at Ft. Delaware during last 6 months of war. U.S. dist. judge, Dist. of S.C., 1886-93. Author: Lectures on Jurisdiction and Practice of U.S. Courts; Digest of the Equity Decisions, State of S.C., 1857; The Federal Courts, Organization, Jurisdiction and Procedure, 1898. Home: Charleston, S.C. Died 1904.

SIMONTON, Ida Vera, traveler, lecturer; b. Pittsburgh, Pa., Sept. 13, 18—; d. Jefferson Wilson and Lydia Ellen (Hoover) S.; ed. high sch., Pittsburgh; studied in London, Eng., and Paris, France. Went alone to W. Africa, 1906, and lived among the savages of the French Congo and other parts of Africa for 3 yrs.; also voyaged in the Nigerias, the Kamerun, Togoland, Liberia, Portuguese Angola, Belgian Congo, Dahomey and Sierra Leone; staff lecturer on savage Africa for Bd. of Edn., N.Y. City. Speaker for Am. Nat. Red Cross, Nat. Woman Suffrage, the Liberty Loan, etc.; sec. and gen. organizer Am. Woman's League for Self-Defense. Pres. Women's Mil. Reserve of U.S. Author: Hell's Playground, 1912. Home: New York, N.Y. Died July 5, 1931.

SIMONTON, John Wiggins, pres. judge 12th jud. dist. Pa., Jan. 1881—; b. Hanover Tp., Pa., Dec. 2, 1826; s. Hon. William and Martha (Snodgrass) S.; prep. edn. Strasburg, Pa., Acad. and Lafayette Coll.; grad. Princeton, 1850 (A.M., Princeton; LL.D., Franklin and Marshall); m. Sarah Hoyer Kunkel, July 8, 1855. Admitted to bar, 1853; practiced law, State and U.S. courts; dist. atty., Dauphin Co., 1865-68; pres. Pa. State Bar Assn., 1895; pres. Hist. Soc. of Dauphin Co. Republican. Home: Harrisburg, Pa. Died 1903.

SIMPSON, Albert B., clergyman; b. Dec. 15, 1844; s. James and Jane (Clark) S.; ed. Knox Coll., Toronto, Can.; m. Miss Henry, of Toronto, Sept. 13, 1865. Ordained Presbyn. ministry, 1865; pastor Hamilton, Ont., 1865-74, Louisville, Ky., 1874-81, New York, 1881—. Founder, 1887, the Christian Alliance, which combined with Internat. Missionary Alliance, 1897, as the Christian and Missionary Alliance, of which became pres. and gen. supt.; has sent out hundreds of foreign missionaries, and maintains Missionary Training Inst., Inst. for Training of Home Workers, Berachah Home, college and academy, all at Nyack, N.Y.; is pastor Gospel Tabernacle, New York, holding daily services, relieving the destitute, and doing rescue work in the slums; has raised large sums for the work. Author: The Gospel of the Kingdom, 1893; Outlook on Missionary Lands, 1897; The Holy Spirit in the Old and New Testaments, 1899; Christ in the Bible (16 vols.), 1902-09; Echoes of the New Creation, 1903; The Cross of Jesus, 1910; We Would See Jesus, 1910; When the Comforter Came, 1911; The Old Faith and the New Gospel, 1911; Christ Life, 1911. Editor The Alliance Weekly; prop. Alliance Press Co. Home: Nyack, N.Y. Died Oct. 29, 1919.

SIMPSON, Alex, Jr., judge; b. Phila., Pa., Jan. 7, 1855; s. John Alexander and Mary A. (Atmore) S.; A.B., Central High Sch., Phila., 1871, A.M., 1876; hon. M.A., Wesleyan U., Conn., 1912; LL.D., Dickinson, 1912; LL.D., Pa. Military College, Chester, Pa., 1921; m. Ella F. Trau, Mar. 3, 1909. Admitted to Pa. bar, 1879, and practiced at Phila. Now justice Supreme Court of Pa. V.p. Dickinson Coll.; pres. Meth. Episcopal Hosp.; trustee Phila. City Missionary Soc. of M.E. Ch. Republican. Home: Philadelphia, Pa. Died July 1935.

SIMPSON, Charles Torrey, naturalist; b. Tiskilwa, Ill., June 3, 1846; s. Jabez and Matilda (Cook) S.; student zoölogy and botany; Sc.D., U. of Miami, Fla., 1927; m. Cornelia Couch (dec.); m. 2d, Flora G. Roper, Sept. 17, 1902. On scientific staff, U.S. Nat. Mus., 1889-1902; collaborator U.S. Dept. Agr., 1914—. Some time lecturer in Georgetown U. Author: Geographical Distribution of the Land and Freshwater Mollusks of the West Indies, 1895; Synopsis of the Naides or Pearly Freshwater Mussels, 1900; Report on the Mollusks of the Fish Hawk Expdn. to Puerto Rico, 1901; Descriptive Catalogue of the Pearly Freshwater Mussels, 1913; Native and Exotic Plants of Dade County, Florida, 1913; Ornamental Gardening in Florida, 1915; In Lower Florida Wilds, 1920; Out of Doors in Florida, 1923; Florida Tree Snails of the Genus Liguus, 1929. Awarded Meyer medal for plant introduction, 1932. Home: Miami, Fla. Died Dec. 17, 1932.

SIMPSON, David Ferguson, judge; b. Dodge Co., Wis., June 13, 1860; s. William and Catherine (Goodsir) S.; B.L., U. of Wis., 1882, LL.B., 1884; LL.B., Columbia U., 1884; m. Josephine Sarles, Jan. 14, 1886. In law practice at Minneapolis from 1884; asst. city atty., 1891-93, city atty., 1893-97; judge Dist. Ct., Hennepin Co., Minn., 3 terms, 1897-1910; justice Supreme Ct., Minn., Jan. 1, 1911-Jan. 1, 1912; resigned; mem. Lancaster, Simpson, Junell & Dorsey. Republican. Unitarian. Mason, Elk. Home: Minneapolis, Minn. Died Oct. 11, 1925.

SIMPSON, Edward, naval officer; b. Annapolis, Md., Sept. 16, 1860; s. Edward (rear admiral U.S.N.) and Mary Ann (Ridgely) S.; grad. U.S. Naval Acad., 1880; m. Camilla M. Ridgely, Dec. 3, 1890; 1 son, Edward Ridgely. Ensign, jr. grade, Mar. 3, 1883; promoted through grades to rear admiral U.S. Navy, July 1, 1919; retired Sept. 16, 1924. Served on Brooklyn during Spanish-Am. War, 1898; assisted in subduing Philippine Insurrection, 1899-1901; exec. officer, Arkansas, 1902-05; duty with Bur. of Ordnance, Navy Dept., 1905-08; comd. Montgomery, 1908-09; naval attaché Am. Embassy, London, Eng., 1909-12; comd. Minnesota, 1912-14; at Naval War Coll., Newport, R.I., 1915; apptd. comdt. naval stas., Olongapo and Cavite, P.I., Feb. 7, 1916. Apptd. hydrographer of the Navy, 1919. Comdr. train, Atlantic Fleet, 1920-21; comdt. 14th Naval Dist., T.H., 1921-23; comdt. 12th Naval Dist., San Francisco, 1923-24. Episcopalian. Home: Ruxton, Md. Died Sept. 6, 1930.

SIMPSON, Frienche, banker; b. on Bull Run, Va., Feb. 13, 1848; s. James Hendley and Emily (Dye) S.; ed. Leesburg (Va.) Acad. and common schs., Colorado Co., Tex.; admitted to bar, 1877; m. Jennie Harbert, Feb. 11, 1877. Pvt. Co. A, 13th Texas Inf., 1865; farmer, 1866-73; banker from 1888; organized First Nat. Bank, Hallettsville, Tex., and was cashier of same for 25 yrs.; retired. With Tex. State Geol. Survey, 1874-75; mayor, Columbus, Tex., 1884; mem. Tex. State Senate, 1893-97. Methodist. Director Masonic Orphans' Home, Ft. Worth, 1890-1900; grand treasurer Masonic Grand Lodge, Tex., 1900. Author: A Study of Nature, 1900; A Paraphrase of Quatrains of Omar Khayyam, 1909. Chmn. Local Selective Service Bd., Lavaca Co., Tex., 1917-19. Home: Hallettsville, Tex. Died Mar. 23, 1923.

SIMPSON, Howard Edwin, geologist; b. Clarence, Ia., July 9, 1874; s. Hiram Garrison and Frances Abigail (Carter) S.; Ph.B., Cornell Coll., Mt. Vernon, Ia., 1896, Sc.D., 1930; student Univ. of Chicago 3 summers; A.M., Harvard U., 1905; m. Carrie Esther Bonebrake, Dec. 30, 1903; children—Jessie Frances, Robert Bonebrake, Carolyn Cradock (dec.), Howard Edwin. Science teacher, later prin. high sch., Knoxville, Ia., 1897-1900; supt. schs., Columbus Jct., Ia., 1900-03; field and lab. asst., 1903-04, asst. in physiography and meteorology, 1904-05, Harvard; instr. and asso. prof. geology, Colby Coll., 1905-09; asst. prof. geology, 1909-14, asso. prof., 1914-19, prof. geographic geology, 1919—, head dept. geology and geography and state geologist, 1933—, U. of N.D. Visiting prof., U. of Chicago, summer 1918, U. of Southern Calif., summer 1920. Served as asst. U.S. Geol. Survey, various seasons, and as water geologist Can. Geol. Survey, summer 1929; water geologist, National Resources Board, 1934; spl. meteorol. observer, U.S. Weather Bur. Fellow Geol. Soc. of America, Assn. Am. Geographers, A.A.A.S., Am. Meteorol. Soc., Am. Geog. Society. Mem. Gen. Conf. M.E. Ch., 1920, 28, 32, 36; mem. World Service Commn., M.E. Ch.; mem. Nat. Council Y.M.C.A.; mem. bd. trustees Wesley Coll. Mem. N.D. State Geographic Bd. and N.D. State Planning Bd. Author or joint author of Geography of North Dakota; Underground Water Resources of Iowa; Ground Water Resources of N.D.; Conservation of Artesian Waters; A Method of Prospecting for Water; etc. Home: Grand Forks, N.D. Died Jan. 31, 1938.

SIMPSON, James, utility executive; b. Glasgow, Scotland, Jan. 26, 1874; s. William and Isabella (Brechin) S.; brought to U.S. in 1880; ed. pub. schs. and business coll., Chicago; m. Jessie, d. of John McLaren, of Chicago, 1903; children—James, John McLaren, William. Began as clerk in cashier's office of Marshall Field & Co., 1891; confidential clerk in Mr. Field's office, 1892, 2d v.p. and asst. to pres., 1906, 1st v.p., 1918, pres., 1923, chmn. bd. 1930, resigned, 1932, now dir.; chmn. and director Commonwealth Edison Co., Commonwealth Subsidiary Corp., Public Service Co. of Northern Ill.; dir. Super Power Co. of Ill., Western United Gas & Electric Co., A.M. Castle & Co., N.Y.C. R.R.; trustee J. N. Field Estate & Trusts; mem. advisory com. Chicago Community Trust. Dir. Am. Red Cross (Chicago chapter), Children's Memorial Hosp. (chmn. finance com.); trustee Chicago Sunday Evening Club, Chicago Zoöl. Soc., Field Mus. of Natural History, Shedd Aquarium, Otho S. Sprague Inst.; mem. bd. govs. Scottish Old People's Home. Served as civilian aide to sec. of war for 6th Corps Area, World War; mem. Capital Issues Com.; in France as commr. Am. Red Cross, 1918. Homes: Glencoe, Ill., and Chicago. Died Nov. 25, 1939.

SIMPSON, Jerry, congressman, farmer; b. New Brunswick, Mar. 31, 1842; removed to Oneida Co., N.Y., 1848; began life as a sailor at 14 yrs. of age; followed that pursuit 23 yrs., comdg. many large vessels on the Great Lakes; served for a time in 12th Ill. inf. in Civil War; went to Kan., 1878; now lives in N.M. Originally Republican, but became Greenbacker and later Populist. Mem. Congress, 1891-95 and 1897-99, from Kan., nominated last time by both Democrats and Populists. Home: Roswell, N.M. Died 1905.

SIMPSON, John, brigadier gen. U.S.A.; b. Bethel, O., Jan. 21, 1840; s. Samuel and Elizabeth (Griffith) S.; ed. pub. schs. of Ohio; m. Laura S. Chafee, Oct. 21, 1869. Enlisted pvt. 5th Ohio Cav., Sept. 27, 1862, and served until May 25, 1865; from July 1863, to close of war on duty at hdqrs. Dept. of the Tenn., and Mil. Div. of the Mississippi. Apptd. 2d lt. 4th Arty., Aug. 17, 1867; promoted through grades to col. and asst. q.m. gen., Feb. 2, 1901; brig. gen. U.S.A., Aug. 17, 1903; retired Aug. 18, 1903. Died Oct. 30, 1914.

SIMPSON, John A., pres. Nat. Farmers' Union; b. Salem, Neb., July 4, 1871; s. William J. and Sarah Catharine (Cornell) S.; grad. U. of Kan., 1896; m. Millie Berlet, June 21, 1896; children—William B., Ellen Catharine (Mrs. A. H. Bergthold), Dorothy, Mildred, John B., Irma (Mrs. Pursell Graham). Teacher pub. schs., Neb. and Kan., 4 yrs.; state accountant, Neb., 1897-1901; in banking business, 1907-11; state pres. Okla. Farmers' Union, 1917-31; pres. Nat. Farmers' Union, 1931—. Home: Oklahoma City, Okla. Died Mar. 15, 1934.

SIMPSON, John Woodruff, lawyer; b. Craftsbury, Vt., Oct. 13, 1850; s. James W. and Jean B. (Simpson) S.; A.B., Amherst Coll., 1871 (LL.D., 1903); LL.B., Columbia, 1873; m. Kate, d. George I. Sevey, May 15, 1889. Admitted to bar, 1873, and entered practice at New York; with Alexander & Green 10 yrs.; mem., 1884—, successively: Simpson, Thacher & Barnum; Reed, Simpson, Thacher & Barnum; Simpson, Thacher, Barnum & Bartlett; and Simpson, Thacher & Bartlett. Presidential elector, 1904. Trustee Amherst Coll., 1904—, and mem. Corp. Home: New York, N.Y. Died May 1920.

SIMPSON, Kenneth Farrand, lawyer; b. New York, N.Y., May 4, 1895; s. William Kelly (M.D.) and Anna (Farrand) S.; student Hill Sch., Pottstown, Pa., 1910-13; B.A., Yale, 1917; LL.B., Harvard, 1922; m. Helen Louise Knickerbacker Porter, June 25, 1925; children—William Kelly, Helen-Louise Knickerbacker, Elizabeth Carroll, Sarah Pierpont Fleurnoy. Admitted to N.Y. bar, 1922; associated with Cadwalader, Wickersham & Taft, 1922-25; asst. U.S. atty., Southern Dist. of N.Y., 1925-27; mem. Barnes, Richardson & Halstead, 1928-33, Hunt, Hill & Betts, 1934-39; sr. partner Simpson, Brady & Noonan, 1939—. Chmn. Rep. County Com., N.Y., 1935—; mem. Rep. Nat. Com., N.Y. State, 1937—; Rep. dist. leader 15th Assembly Dist., N.Y. County, 1933-38; del. Rep. Nat. Conv., 1936; mem. N.Y. Rep. State Com. and Rep. State Exec. Com., 1935—. Served as capt. F.A., U.S. Army, 1917-19, with A.E.F., 1 yr.; comdt. Am. Sch. Detachment, U. of Aix-Marseilles, 1919. Decorated Palmes Academiques, by French Minister of Pub. Instrn. and Beaux Arts. Former trustee Pub. Edn. Assn. Episcopalian. Home: New York, N.Y. Died Jan. 25, 1941.

SIMPSON, Marcus De Lafayette, army officer; b. Esperance, N.Y., Aug. 28, 1824; s. William and Lydia S.; grad. U.S. Mil. Acad., 1846; m. Clara B. Barnum, Sept. 29, 1892. Bvt. 2d lt. 2d Arty., July 1, 1846; 2d lt., Mar. 3, 1847; promoted through grades to col. asst. commissary gen. of subsistence, June 23, 1874; retired by operation of law, Aug. 28, 1888; advanced to rank of brig. gen. retired, by act of Apr. 23, 1904. Bvtd. 1st lt., Aug. 20, 1847, for battles of Contreras and Churubusco, Mex.; capt., Sept. 13, 1847, for battle of Chapultepec, Mex.; col., brig. gen. and maj. gen., Mar. 13, 1865, for services during Civil War. Home: Riverside, Ill. Died 1909.

SIMPSON, Robert, author, editor; b. Strathy, Scotland, Oct. 12, 1886; s. Robert and Mary Ann (Smith) S.; ed. pub. schs., Glasgow; m. Marie A. Socin, Aug. 14, 1915; children—Peggy, Robert, Kenneth MacKenzie. Palm oil trade, West Africa, 1905-07; came to U.S., 1907; joined editorial staff of Frank A. Munsey Co., 1916; mng. editor Argosy, 1917-20; free lance, 1920-25; editor Mystery Magazine, 1925-27; free lance, 1927—. Author: The Bite of Benin, 1919; Swamp Breath, 1921; The Gray Charteris, 1923; Eight Panes of Glass, 1924; Calvert of Allobar, 1925. Home: New York, N.Y. Died Jan. 7, 1934.

SIMPSON, Robert Tennent, judge; b. Florence, Ala., June 5, 1837; s. John and Margaret (Patton) S.; A.B., Princeton, 1857, A.M., 1887; LL.B., Cumberland U., Lebanon, Tenn., 1859; m. Mattie Collier, Sept. 2, 1861. Began practice at Des Arc, Ark., 1859; entered C.S.A. as pvt. 4th Ala. Regt., Apr. 1861; in service during entire war, until paroled as capt. 63d Ala. Regt., May 10, 1865. Practiced at Camden, Ala., 1865-70, at Florence, 1870-1904; mem. Ala. Ho. of Rep., 1882-83 and 1903, Senate, 1884-87; asso. justice Supreme Ct. of Ala., 1904—. Dir. Ala. Trust and Savings Bank, Florence. Democrat. Presbyn. Home: Florence, Ala. Deceased.

SIMPSON, Sutherland, physiologist; b. Orkney Islands, Scotland, Feb. 3, 1863; s. Sutherland and Margaret (Taylor) S.; ed. Heriot-Watt Coll., Edinburgh, 1882-85; B.Sc., Edinburgh U., 1894, M.B., Ch.B., 1899, M.D. (gold medal), 1901, D.Sc., 1903; m. Catherine Graham Pettigrew Anderson, of Edinburgh, Aug. 6, 1908. Prof. and head dept. physiology and biochemistry, Cornell U., 1908—. F.R.S., Edinburgh. Author original research papers on central nervous system, animal heat and body temperature, secretory glands, bile secretion, etc. Home: Ithaca, N.Y. Died Mar. 3, 1926.

SIMPSON, William James, banker; b. Rochester, N.Y., Oct. 13, 1877; s. Joseph T. and Isabelle (Tytler) S.; ed. pub. schs.; m. Helen E. Van Vechten, June 7, 1904; children—Helen Fenn (Mrs. W. Moreau Smith), Margaret Elizabeth (wife of Dr. Henry Ward Williams), Jean Isabella. Successively messenger, bookkeeper, teller, cashier and v.p. Lincoln-Alliance Bank, Rochester, 1896-1922; pres. Genesee Valley Trust Co., Rochester, 1922—. Republican. Presbyn. Mason. Home: Brighton, N.Y. Died Aug. 25, 1932.

SIMPSON, William Kelly, physician, surgeon; b. Hudson, N.Y., Apr. 10, 1855; s. George Nicholas and Caroline (McCann) S.; Cornell U., 1876; M.D., Coll. Phys. and Surg. (Columbia), 1880; m. Anna Farrand, Oct. 25, 1882. Practiced, New York, 1880—; prof. laryngology, Coll. Phys. and Surg., 1904—; cons. laryngologist, Presbyn. Hosp., and others. Fellow Am. Laryngol. Assn., New York Acad. Medicine. Progressive. Episcopalian. Home: New York, N.Y. Died Feb. 6, 1914.

SIMRELL, William Le Grand, life insurance; b. Great Bend, Pa., Mar. 24, 1863; s. William Wallace and Marion Eudoxia (Sampson) S.; LL.B., New York U., 1899; m. Matie Elizabeth Bishop, Jan. 1, 1899; children—Alma Idell (Mrs. T. J. Selkirk), Helen Marion (Mrs. Richard S. Young), William Le Grand. In mfg. business, Great Bend, 1882-86; mercantile business, Montrose, Pa., 1886-90; mercantile business, Brooklyn, N.Y., 1890-93; with The Mutual Life Ins. Co. of New York, 1893—, pvt. sec., 1893-1906, auditor, 1906-24, secretary, 1924—. Mem. bd. mgrs. Central Br. Y.M.C.A. (com. on edn. and com. on vocation). Mem. Rep. County Com., Kings County. Pres. Prosperity Fund Credit Union. Conglist. Admitted to New York bar, 1902. Home: Brooklyn, N.Y. Died May 31, 1933.

SIMS, Clifford Stanley, ry. official; b. Prairie Ridge Plantation, Abercrombie's Landing, Desha Co., Ark., Jan. 12, 1868; s. Clifford Stanley and Mary Josephine (Abercrombie) S.; ed. Mt. Holly, N.J., grad. 1885; m. Martha Lee Jenkins, Dec. 8, 1909; 1 dau., Martha Lee Jenkins. In engring. depts. Pa. R.R. and other rys., 1885-88; apptd. asst. supervisor C. and P. div. Pa. Lines West of Pittsburgh, headquarters at Cleveland, 1888, and later asst. engr. and engr. maintenance of way, at Toledo, O., Allegheny, Pa., and Chicago; supt. Pa. Lines West of Pittsburgh, at Chicago, 1901-02; gen. supt. B.&O. R.R., at New York, 1902-03, and gen. mgr., same, at Baltimore, 1903-05; asst. to pres. Erie R.R., at New York, 1905-07; 2d v.p. and gen. mgr. D.&H. Co., at Albany, N.Y., 1907-17; resident v.p. D.&H. Co., Montreal, Can., June 1, 1917, furloughed, May 1, 1923; pres. Hudson River Navigation Corp., 1926-27; furloughed v.p. Delaware & Hudson Co., 1927—. Home: New York, N.Y. Died Jan. 30, 1935.

SIMS, Frederick Wilmer, judge; b. Louisa Co., Va., July 23, 1862; s. Frederick H. (M.D.) and Maria Louisa (Kimbrough) S.; student U. of Virginia 1 session; m. Lucy Payne Winston, Sept. 8, 1888. Worked as a farmer, clk. in store, saw-mill laborer and mgr., carpenter and fireman on ry.; admitted to Va. bar, 1886, and began practice at Louisa, Va.; judge Louisa Co. Court, 1890-1904; mem. Va. Senate, 1906-12; judge Supreme Court of Appeals of Va., 1916-19. Democrat. Presbyn. Mason. Home: Louisa, Va. Died Feb. 8, 1925.

SIMS, John Francis, normal sch. pres.; b. Buffalo, N.Y., Apr. 21, 1862; s. Joseph and Mary (Mangin) S.; student U. of Wis. and U. of Chicago; holds teacher's life certificate in Wis.; m. Georgine Engelhard, Oct. 15, 1887. Began teaching in Wis., 1879; mem. faculty, State Normal Sch., River Falls, Wis., 1896-1906; pres. State Normal Sch., Stevens Point, Wis., Aug. 1906—. Pres. Pittsville State Bank. Democrat. Home: Stevens Point, Wis. Died May 29, 1926.

SIMS, Richard Maury, banker; b. Rock Hill, S.C., Nov. 14, 1874; s. Robert Moorman and Ada Walton (Sims) S.; B.S., U. of S.C., 1893; m. Louise Bundschu, Sept. 9, 1904; children—Leora (Mrs. Lee Aydelot), Richard Maury, Robert Lee. Teacher Sonoma (Calif.) High Sch., 1893-94, admitted to Calif. bar, 1895, one of asst. city attys., San Francisco, 1895-98; mem. Morrison, Cope & Brobeck, 1906-09; trust officer Mercantile Trust Co. (now Am. Trust Co.), 1909—, v.p., 1920—. Democrat. Mason. Author: California Corporation Law, 1903. Edited Calif. codes and digests. Home: Berkeley, Calif. Died May 9, 1935.

SIMS, Thetus Wilrette, congressman; b. Wayne Co., Tenn., Apr. 25, 1852; s. G. W. and Jennie (Whitson) S.; reared on farm; ed. Savannah (Tenn.) Coll.; LL.B., Cumberland U., 1876; m. Nannie H. Kittrell, Dec. 26, 1877; 7 children. In practice at Linden, Tenn., 1876—; supt. public instrn., Perry Co., Tenn., 1882-84. Dem. presdl. elector, 1892; mem. 55th to 66th Congresses, inclusive (1897-1921), 8th Tenn. Dist.; chmn. Com. on Interstate and Foreign Commerce. Home: Lexington, Tenn. Died Dec. 17, 1939.

SIMS, William Sowden, naval officer; b. Port Hope, Can., Oct. 15, 1858; s. Alfred William and Adelaide (Sowden) S.; apptd. from Pa. to U.S. Naval Acad. and grad., 1880; LL.D., Yale, Harvard, Tufts, and Juniata, 1919, U. of Pa., Columbia and Williams, 1920, Cambridge (Eng.), 1921; Sc.D., Stevens, 1921; LL.D., Union, McGill, and Queen's (Can.), 1922, U. of Calif., Wesleyan, 1923; m. Anne, d. late Sec. of Interior Ethan Allen Hitchcock, of St. Louis, Nov. 21, 1905. Promoted through grades to rear adm., Jan. 5, 1917; vice adm., May 28, 1917; admiral, Dec. 4, 1918 (reverting to permanent rank of rear adm. upon relinquishment of command U.S. naval forces operating in European waters, Mar. 31, 1919); retired Oct. 15, 1922. Naval attaché, Am. embassies, Paris and St. Petersburg, Mar. 1897-Nov. 1900; Kentucky, China Sta., Nov.-Mar. 1900-01; Monterey, China Sta., Mar.-Oct. 1901; Brooklyn, aide on staff comdr. in chief Asiatic Fleet, Oct. 1901-Feb. 1902; fleet intelligence officer and insp. target practice, Asiatic Fleet, on bd. New York, Feb.-Oct. 1902; Bur. Navigation, Navy Dept., Nov. 1902-Feb. 1909; additional duty as naval aide to the President, Nov. 1907-Feb. 1909; comdg. Minnesota, Mar. 1909-Apr. 1911; Naval War Coll., Newport, R.I. (student), May 1911-June 5, 1913; comdg. Atlantic Torpedo Flotilla, 1913-15; battleship Nevada, Nov. 22, 1915-Dec. 31, 1916; pres. Naval War Coll., Feb. 1917 to commencement of hostilities; comdg. Am. naval operations in European waters, Apr. 28, 1917, until end of war; resumed presidency of Naval War Coll., Apr. 7, 1919. Made extensive report, 1920, to U.S. Senate naval affairs sub-com., alleging grave errors on the part of U.S. Navy Dept. in management of naval operations during the war. Declined D.S.M. (U.S.), 1919; awarded Grand Cross Order St. Michael and St. George (British), 1918; Grand Officer Legion Honor (French), 1919; Grand Cordon, First-Class, Order Rising Sun (Japan), 1920; Grand Cordon Order Leopold (Belgium), 1920; Grand Officer Crown of Italy, 1921. Episcopalian. Home: Newport, R.I. Died Sept. 25, 1936.

SIMS W(infield) Scott, inventor; b. New York, Apr. 6, 1844; s. Capt. Lindsay D. and Catherine B.S.; grad. high sch., Newark, N.J.; served in 37th N.J. Regt. in Civil War; m. Lida Leek, June 11, 1867 (died 1888); 2d, Mrs. Josephine Courter French, June 24, 1891. Invented various devices in electro-magnets; constructed an electric motor for light work in 1872, weighing 45 pounds, and having a battery of 20 half-gallon Bunsen cells, by means of which he was enabled to propel an open boat 16 feet long, with 6 persons on board, at the rate of 4 miles an hour; was first to apply electricity for propulsion of torpedoes, his device of a torpedo being a submarine boat with a cylindrical hull of copper and with conical ends, furnished with screw propeller and a rudder, the power being electricity generated on shore or on shipboard, by means of which the torpedo is propelled, guided and exploded; subsequently he devised a boat with a speed of 22 miles an hour and to carry a 500-lb. charge of dynamite; also invented the wireless dirigible torpedo, of which sold 5 to Japanese Govt., 1907; invented the Sims-Dudley Dynamite Gun, used by Cuban insurgents, and by the "Rough Riders" at battle of Santiago; now designing a dynamite cruiser to carry 100 tons of high explosives, controlled by an operator on ship or shore; has also designed a dynamite gun for use with dirigible warships, and an aeroplane dynamite gun. Home: Newark, N.J. Died Jan. 7, 1918.

SINCLAIR, Alexander Grant, physician; b. Glengarry Co., Ont., Can., July 30, 1842; s. Archibald and Mary (Grant) S.; student med. dept., U. of Mich.; M.D., Coll. Phys. and Surg. (Columbia), 1869; U. of Vienna, 1872; (LL.D., Ark. Normal Coll., 1901); unmarried. Resident surgeon New York Eye and Ear Infirmary, 1869-72; ophthalmic and aural surgeon Harper Hosp., Detroit, 1875-78; prof. ophthalmology and otology, 1878-1907, materia medica and therapeutics, 1883-85; dean of faculty, 1884-86, prof. hygiene, 1898-1907, prof. emeritus, 1907, Memphis Hosp. Med. Coll. V.p. Continental Savings Bank. Asso. editor Peninsular Jour. of Medicine, Detroit, 1873-76; editor Memphis Medical Monthly, 1895. Originated movement in Southern Med. Coll. Assn., 1896, to require candidates for graduation to attend 4 sessions of 6 mos. each, which became operative, 1899. Baptist. Home: Memphis, Tenn. Died Nov. 19, 1915.

SINCLAIR, Angus, editor, engr.; b. in Scotland, 1841; s. Alexander and Margaret (McLeay) S.; ed. at Lawrencekirk, Scotland; spl. studies in chemistry State U. of Ia.; m. Margaret A. Moore, 1877. Engaged in editorial work, 1883—; editor Automobile Magazine, and of Railway Engineering. Writer on railway and automobile subjects. Author: Locomotive Engine Running, 1884; Combustion in Locomotive Fire Boxes, 1890; Combustion and Smoke Prevention, 1896; Burning Soft Coal Without Smoke, 1899; Firing Locomotives, 1901; Twentieth Century Locomotives; History of the Development of the Locomotive Engine, 1907; Railroad Men's Catechism, 1907, etc. Home: Milburn, N.J. Died Jan. 2, 1919.

SINCLAIR, John Elbridge, educator; b. Brentwood, N.H., Mar. 28, 1838; s. Harry and Eliza Ann (Robinson) S.; B.S., Dartmouth, 1858, A.M., 1879, Ph.D., 1883; (hon. A.M., Washington U., St. Louis, 1862); m. Isabella Aiken Noyes, Nov. 1864 (dec.); 2d, Marietta S. Fletcher, Nov. 21, 1870. Began teaching at Adrian, Mich., 1858; tutor Washington U., 1859-63; asst. prof., 1863-66, prof. mathematics, 1866-69, Chandler Sch., Dartmouth; prof. mathematics, Worcester Poly. Inst., 1869-1908, prof. emeritus, 1908—. Deacon Congl. Ch. Home: Worcester, Mass. Died Sept. 12, 1915.

SINCLAIR, Lee Wiley, capitalist; b. Cloverdale, Ind., Feb. 18, 1836; s. Isaac R. and America S.; reared on farm; ed. in country schs.; m. Caddie Persise, 1866. In woolen mill business at Greencastle and Salem, Ind., and South Chicago, Ill., until 1888; in 1880 bought one-third interest in West Baden Springs, and in 1901 acquired entire interest of partnership; organized West Baden Springs Co. (pres.); pres. West Baden Nat. Bank; pres. Bank of Salem (Ind.), 1880—. Was first to bring West Baden Springs to gen. notice, and in 1902 erected there a hotel costing $1,000,000. Home: West Baden, Ind. Died Sept. 7, 1916.

SINCLAIR, Robert Soutter, packer; b. Cedar Rapids, Ia., Oct. 9, 1872; s. Thomas M. and Caroline C. (Soutter) S.; prep. edn., William Penn Charter Sch., Phila.; B.A., U. of Pa., 1894; m. Elizabeth J. Alexander, Jan. 28, 1903 (died 1908); children—Mary, Thomas G., Elsie C., Caroline E. (Mrs. Philip Will, Jr.); m. 2d, Ethel Heywood Bennett, Jan. 23, 1923. With father's meat packing firm, T. M. Sinclair & Co., Cedar Rapids, 1895-1930, v.p., 1899-1917, pres., 1917-30; pres. Kingan & Co., meat packers, Indianapolis, 1930—; elected dir. C.,C.C.& St.L. Ry., Oct. 30, 1935; pres. Universal Crusher Co. Trustee Coe College, Cedar Rapids. Dir. Inst. of Am. Meat Packers. Republican. Presbyn. Home: Indianapolis, Ind. Died May 14, 1937.

SINCLAIR, William, brig. gen. U.S.A., retired; b. nr. St. Clairville, O., Feb. 15, 1835; s. John and Mary A. S.; grad. West Point, 1857; m. Eugenia McDonald, Dec. 11, 1865. Bvt. 2d lt. arty., July 1, 1857; 2d lt., 1858; 1st lt., 1861; bvt. capt., May 4, 1862, for gallant and meritorious services at siege of Yorktown, Va.; col., 6th Pa. Reserve vols., June 27, 1862; bvt. maj., Dec. 13, 1862, for gallantry at battle of Fredericksburg; resigned vol. commn., June 6, 1863; lt. col., staff U.S.V., 1863-65; capt., 3d arty., Dec. 11, 1865; maj., 2d arty., Apr. 6, 1886; lt. col., 5th arty, June 6, 1896; col., 7th arty., Mar. 8, 1898; brig. gen., U.S.A., Feb. 8, 1899; retired at own request after 40 yrs. service, Feb. 13, 1899. Took part in principal battles of Army of Potomac, 1861-62, and afterward in Vicksburg campaign, Army of Western La., etc.; wounded at Manassas, Aug. 29, 1862, and at Fredericksburg, Dec. 13, 1862; was in service in Pa., quelling ry. disturbances, 1877. Home: Washington, D.C. Died 1905.

SINGER, Frederic, rear admiral U.S.N.; b. Carlsruhe, Baden, Germany, May 3, 1847; s. Joseph and Frederica (Winterwerber) S.; came to America with parents, 1848; grad. U.S. Naval Acad., 1868; unmarried. Midshipman on U.S. frigate Macedonian, 1864; served on Nipsic, 1868-69; commd. ensign, Apr. 19, 1869; promoted through grades to capt., Feb. 4, 1904. rear admiral and retired, June 26, 1906. Served in various capacities; in naval intelligence office, Washington, 1888-90, 1893-94; in charge of diplomatic corps on board coast survey steamer Blake, representing Navy Dept. at Internat. Naval Review, New York, Apr. 1893; chief intelligence officer of the navy and mem. Bd. of Constrn., 1895-96; took part in battle of Manila Bay, as exec. officer cruiser Raleigh, May 1, 1898; comd. captured transport, Manila, fitted her as a gunboat with 8 guns taken from wrecks of Spanish fleet, July 1898-June 1899; commandant, U.S. naval sta., New Orleans, June 1, 1904-June 1, 1909. Received medal voted by Congress and was promoted 5 numbers for eminent and conspicuous conduct in battle of Manila Bay; Civil, Spanish and Philippine war medals. Died Jan. 4, 1923.

SINGER, Harold Douglas, M.D.; b. London, Eng., Jan. 7, 1875; s. Charles Douglas and Edith Eleanor (Godden) S.; student Merchant Taylors' Sch., London, 1886-93; ed. in medicine at U. of London, St. Thomas' Hosp. and Royal Coll. Phys., degrees M.B., and M.D.; m. Edith M. Day, of London, 1904 (died 1923); children—Eleanor Douglas, Daisy Douglas, Charles Douglas; m. 2d, Rhoda Worthington, 1925. House phys., St. Thomas' Hosp., London, 1898, asst. supt. Clin. Lab., 1899; jr. resident Nat. Hosp., Queen Sq., London, 1900, sr. res., 1901; res. asst. phys. St. Thomas' Hosp., 1902-04; came to U.S., 1904, naturalized citizen, 1912; asso. prof. neurology, Creighton U., Omaha, Neb., 1904-06; asso. prof. psychiatry, U. of Neb., 1906-07; also asst. supt. Norfolk (Neb.) State Hosp., 1906-07; dir. Ill. State psychopathic Inst., 1907-20; state alienist, Ill., 1917-20; spl. examiner Ill. Exemption Bd., 1917; advisory consultant in neuropsychiatry to surgeon gen. U.S.P. H.S. and later to dir. U.S. Vets. Bur., 1919-22; prof. psychiatry, Coll. of Medicine, U. of Illinois, 1919—. Fellow Royal Soc. Medicine, and Royal College of Physicians. Republican. Episcopalian. Mason. Home: Chicago, Ill. Died Aug. 29, 1940.

SINGER, Isidore, editor, author; b. Weisskirchen, Moravia, Austria, Nov. 10, 1859; s. Joseph and Charlotte S.; ed. univs. of Vienna and Berlin; Ph.D. Founded and published Allgemeine Österreichische Literaturzeitung, Vienna, 1884-85; went, 1887, as sec. and librarian to the late French ambassador at Vienna, Count Alexandre Foucher de Careil (editor of Leibniz's works), to Paris; became employe French Foreign Office in Bureau de la Presse. Founder and editor-in-chief of La Vraie Parole (paper founded to counteract Ed. Drumont's anti-Semitic La Libre Parole); went to Italy, 1891; came to New York, 1895, to carry out his life work, Jewish Ency. (12 vols.), 1901-05; mng. editor Internat. Ins. Ency., 1909; German Classics of the XIXth and XXth Centuries (20 vols.; Vol. XX, 1914). Author: Berlin, Wien und der Antisemitismus, 1882; Presse und Judenthum, 1882; Sollen die Juden Christen Werden?, 1884; Briefe Berühmter Christlicher Zeitgenossen über die Judenfrage, 1884; Die Beiden Elektren—Humanistische Bildung und der Klassische Unterricht, 1884; Auf dem Grabe Meiner Mutter (transl. into Hebrew by Solomon Fuchs), 1888; Le Prestige de la France en Europe, 1889; La Question Juive, 1893; Anarchie et Antisémitisme, 1894; Der Juden Kampf uns Recht, 1902; Russia at the Bar of the American People, 1904; Christ or God?, 1908; Social Justice, 1923; A Religion of Truth, Justice and Peace, 1924; Theology at the Crossroads, 1928; One God, One Mankind, 1935; also numerous transls. of French works into German. Founder (1922) and sec. Am. League of The Brotherhood of Man. Home: New York, N.Y. Died Feb. 20, 1939.

SINGLETON, Esther, author, editor; b. Baltimore; d. Horace Leonard and Martha Colgate (Morling) S. Has resided in New York, 1887—. Author: A Guide to the Opera, 1899, 1909; The Furniture of Our Forefathers (2 vols.), 1900; London, 1902; French and English Furniture; Historic Buildings, 1903; Great Events of the World's History (5 vols.), 1903; Russia, 1904; Japan, 1904; Venice, 1905; The Story of the Universe (4 vols.), 1905; The Wild Flower Fairy Book, 1905; Great Portraits, 1905; Rome, 1906; Holland, 1906; Historic Buildings of America, 1906; Dutch and Flemish Furniture, 1907; Germany, 1907; The White House, 1907; Switzerland, 1908; Standard Galleries, Holland, 1908; Famous Cathedrals, 1909; The Art of the Belgian Galleries, 1909; A Guide to the Modern Operas, 1909; Dutch New York, 1909; Florence, 1910; How to Visit the Great Picture Galleries, 1911; The Children's City, 1911; Egypt, 1911; Modern Pictures, 1911; Furniture, 1911; How to Visit the English Cathedrals, 1912; China, 1912; A Daughter of the Revolution (novel), 1915; The Orchestra and Its Instruments, 1917; Amérique (in French) for the Histoire de la Musique, Paris Conservatoire, Paris, 1921; The Shakespeare Garden, 1922; The Collecting of Antiques, 1926; Dolls, 1928; Old World Masters in New World Galleries, 1929; Shakespearean Fantasias, 1929. Translator: Albert Lavignac's Music Dramas of Richard Wagner. Mem. Colonial Dames State of N.Y. Home: New York, N.Y. Died July 2, 1930.

SINGLETON, Marvin Edward, investments; b. Ellis Co., Tex., Jan. 6, 1872; s. John Hawkins and Rebecca Ann (Barker) S.; ed. country sch.; m. Susie Clary, Jan. 6, 1897 (died 1920); children—Edward C., John H., Susie S., Elizabeth R., Marvin E., Joe R., June; m. 2d, Mary Perry, June 22, 1922; children—Mary, Perry. Organizer, 1898, mgr., 1898-1902, Ft. Worth Cotton Oil Co.; organizer, 1902, pres. and gen. mgr., 1902-18, E. St. Louis Cotton Oil Co.; pres. Mo. State Life Ins. Co., 1919-28; chmn. bd. and pres. Citizens Nat. Bank (Waxahachie, Tex.); pres. Munger Cotton Oil Co. (Mexia, Tex.), First Nat. Bank (Farmersville, Tex.), Utah-Ida. R.R., Mich. Davis Co., E. Tex. Cotton Oil Co.; owner and pres. Singleton Farm, Inc. (Midlothian, Tex.). Ordnance chief, U.S.A., St. Louis District, 1918—; col. Ordnance Reserve. Awarded D.S.M. (U.S.). Methodist. Mason. Home: St. Louis, Mo. Died Jan. 29, 1938.

SINGMASTER, John Alden, theologian; b. Macungie, Pa., Aug. 31, 1852; s. of James and Sarah Ann (Mattern) S.; A.B., Pa. College, Gettysburg, 1873; grad. Luth. Theol. Sem., 1876; (D.D., Pa. Coll., 1894, LL.D., 1920); m. Caroline Hoopes, Nov. 1, 1877; father of Elsie S. Ordained Luth. ministry, 1875; pastor, Schuylkill Haven, Pa., 1876-82, Macungie, Pa., 1882-86, Brooklyn, N.Y., 1887-90, Allentown, Pa., 1890-1900; prof. Bibl. theology, 1900-03, systematic theology, 1903—, pres., 1906—, Luth. Theol. Sem. Sr. editor Lutheran Quarterly, Gettysburg; writer exegetical comments on S.S. lessons in Lutheran Observer, Phila., 20 yrs. Pres. Gen. Synod Evang. Luth. Ch. in U.S., 1915. A founder United Luth. Ch. in America, 1918. Home: Gettysburg, Pa. Died Feb. 27, 1926.

SINKLER, Wharton, neurologist; b. Philadelphia, Aug. 7, 1845; s. Charles and Emily (Wharton) S.; S.C. Coll., 1862-63; M.D., U. of Pa., 1868; m. Ella Brock, Feb. 10, 1872. Served in 2d S.C. Cav., C.S.A., during Civil War; physician in Phila., 1868—; specialist in nervous diseases. Pres. Colony Farm for Epileptics of Pa., 1892—. Trustee U. of Pa. Contbr. to text-books, cyclopedias and med. jours. Fellow Coll. Physicians of Phila. Home: Philadelphia, Pa. Died 1910.

SINNOTT, Nicholas John, judge; b. The Dalles, Oregon, Dec. 6, 1870; s. Nicholas Byrne and Bride Mary (Brass) S.; A.B., Notre Dame U., Ind., 1892; m. Isidore Irene Purcell, Sept. 4, 1901. Admitted to Ore. bar, 1895; mem. Bennett & Sinnott, The Dallas, Ore., 1901-12; mem. Ore. State Senate, 1909, 11; mem. 63d to 70th Congresses (1913-29), 2d Ore. Dist.; resigned to become judge Court of Claims of U.S., 1928. Chmn. Com. on Public Lands, 66th to 69th Congresses. Republican. Catholic. Home: The Dalles, Ore. Died July 20, 1929.

SIPPY, Bertram Welton, physician; b. Neptune, Wis., Oct. 30, 1866; s. Thomas and Laura (Welton) S.; U. of Wis., 1884-87; M.D., Rush Med. Coll., Chicago, 1890; interne Cook Co. Hosp., Chicago, 1890-92; U. of Vienna, 1895-96, U. of Berlin, 1902; m. Mabel Lamberson, June 25, 1895. In practice at Chicago from 1897; asst. chief surgeon N.P. R.R., 1892-95; instr. and asst. prof. medicine, 1897-1906, prof. medicine, 1906—, Rush Med. Coll. (U. of Chicago); attending phys. Presbyn. Hospital. Home: Chicago, Ill. Died Aug. 15, 1924.

SIQUELAND, Tryggve Albert, banking, lawyer; b. Stavanger, Norway, June 16, 1888; s. Ludwig Albert and Hanna (Aske) S.; grad. Latin Sch., Stavanger; grad. Chicago Law Sch., 1909; LL.B. cum laude, Northwestern Sch. of Commerce, 1912; m. Lovey Mabel Ida Thorp, Dec. 24, 1910; children—Alyce Victoria, Margo Ida. Came to U.S., 1904, naturalized citizen, 1910. Admitted to Ill. bar, 1909, then in pvt. and corp. practice at Chicago; mgr. foreign dept. and 2d v.p. State Bank of Chicago, 1919-29; v.p. Foreman-State Nat. Bank, 1929-31; asst. v.p. First Nat. Bank of Chicago, 1931—. Mem. I.N.G., 1905-14; served as capt. and promoted to maj. and lt. col. U.S.A., World War; now col. cav., U.S. Army, commanding 317th Cav. Regt.; mem. advisory council 6th Corps Area, U.S.A. Military attaché U.S. Legation, Copenhagen, Denmark, and Oslo, Norway, 1917-19. Treas. and dir. Henry Booth House, Chicago. Decorated Victory Medal (U.S.); Comdr. Mil. Div. Order of British Empire; Comdr. Order of Vasa (Sweden); Comdr. Order of Crown (Roumania); Commander of the Order of Saint Olav (Norway); Knight Order of Dannebrog, and Slesvig Medal (Denmark); Officer Order Crown of Italy; Officier d'Instruction de Perse (Persia); Officier Cruz de Melba de Portuguese (Portugal); gold medal of merit Cross of Malta of the Order of St. John of Jerusalem; Order of the Red Cross (Japan); gold medalist, Geog. Soc. of Persia. Chairman Chicago George Washington Bi-Centennial Commission; awarded George Washington Bi-Centennial gold medal. Lutheran; trustee Lutheran Deaconess Home and Hospital. Mason. Aide de camp to Queen Marie of Rumania during visit to U.S., 1926, to Crown Prince Gustav Adolf of Sweden during visit to U.S., 1926, to the Maharajah of Karputhala of India, during visit to U.S., 1929, to Gen. Italo Balbo and Maharajah of Baroda, 1933. Lecturer on mil., econ., financial, commercial and art subjects. Home: Bridgman, Mich. Died Feb. 7, 1937.

SIROVICH, William I., M.D., congressman; b. York, Pa., Mar. 18, 1882; s. Rev. Jacob and Rose (Weinstock) S.; B.A., Coll. of City of New York, 1902; M.D., M.A., Columbia, 1906; unmarried. Began practice at N.Y. City, 1906; supt. Peoples Hosp., 1917—; lecturer for New York Bd. of Edn., 1918-28; elected pres. Industrial Nat. Bank of New York, July 1928. Supt. Peoples Hosp., 1911-29; served as mem. bd. mgrs. Mohansic State Hosp. Commn., Widows' Pension Commn., New York Child Welfare Bd., etc.; official arbitrator in labor disputes. Mem. of 70th to 75th Congresses (1927-39), 14th N.Y. Dist. Fellow Am. Coll. Surgeons. Mason, Odd Fellow. Home: New York, N.Y. Died Dec. 17, 1939.

SISLEY, Lyman A., editor; b. Chicago; s. John James and Anna (Lyman) S.; ed. pub. schs.; m. Helen Meiklejohn, Aug. 27, 1890; 1 son, Lyman Noyes. Admitted to Neb. bar, 1882, and practiced several yrs.; founded Mining World (weekly publ.), at Butte, Mont., Sept. 22, 1894, and editor same; moved paper to Chicago, 1902; pres. Mining World Co.; v.p., sec. and editor in chief International Trade Press, Inc.; v.p., sec. Magazines, Inc. Home: Chicago, Ill. Died Oct. 21, 1927.

SISSON, Francis Hinckley, banker; b. Galesburg, Ill., June 14, 1871; s. William Pardon and Harriet (Hinckley) S.; A.B., Knox Coll., 1892, LL.D., 1921; A.B., Harvard, 1893; m. Grace Lass, June 16, 1897. Newspaper reporter and editorial writer, 1893-98; editor Evening Mail, Galesburg, 1898-1903; staff, McClure's Mag., New York, 1903-04; adv. mgr. Am. Real Estate Co., 1904-12; v.p. and gen. mgr. H. E. Lesan Adv. Agency, 1912-16; asst. chmn. Assn. of Ry. Executives, 1916-18; v.p. Guaranty Trust Co. of New York, 1917—; dir. Guaranty Co. of New York. Home: Yonkers, N.Y. Died Sept. 17, 1933.

SISSON, Septimus, comparative anatomist; b. Gateshead, Eng., Oct. 2, 1865; s. George and Mary (Arnott) S.; came to America, 1882; S.B., U. of Chicago, 1898; V.S., Ont. (Can.) Vet. Coll., 1891; Univ. of Berlin, 1905-06; (D.V.Sc., U. of Toronto, 1921); m. Katherine Oldham, Oct. 5, 1892. Prof. comparative anatomy, Ohio State University, Sept., 1901—. Author: A Text-Book of Veterinary Anatomy, 1910; A Veterinary Dissection Guide, Part I, 1911; The Anatomy of the Domestic Animals, 1914. Translator: Ellenberger, Baum und Dittrich's Anatomie der Tiere für Künstler, 1906. Prin. contribution to anatom. knowledge consists of first descriptions of natural form and topography of the plastic organs and viscera of the chief domestic animals as determined by fixation in situ by means of intravascular injection of formalin or other hardening fluid. Unitarian. Home: Columbus, O. Deceased.

SISSON, Thomas Upton, congressman; b. Attala Co., Miss., Sept. 22, 1869; A.B., Southwestern

Presbyn. U., Clarksville, Tenn., 1890; m. Mamie Purnell, June 5, 1901. Prin. pub. schs., Carthage, Miss., 1890-91, graded schs., Kosciusko, Miss., 1891-93; admitted to bar, 1894; practiced at Memphis, Tenn., 1894-95, then at Winona. Was mem. Miss. Senate; Dem. elector for state at-large, 1900; elected dist. atty. 5th Jud. Dist., 1903; defeated for nomination for gov., 1907; mem. 61st to 67th Congresses (1909-23), 4th Miss. Dist. Grand Master Masons in Miss., 1905. Home: Winona, Miss. Died Sept. 1923.

SIVITER, Anna Pierpont, author; b. Fairmont, Va.; d. Francis Harrison (gov. Va., 1861-67) and Julia A. (Robertson) Pierpont; ed. Washington (Pa.) Sem. and Pittsburgh Coll., and by pvt. tutors; m. William Henry Siviter, June 24, 1886; 1 dau., Frances Pierpont (wife of James Chambers Pryor, U.S.N.). Asso. editor Our Young People, 1888-93; editorial charge of S.S. periodicals, Meth. Protestant Ch., 1899. Many yrs. active in church, civic and charitable work. Mem. D.A.R., U.S. Daughters of 1812. Presbyn. Author: Nehe, A Tale of the Times of Artaxerxes, 1903; The Sculptor and Other Poems, 1903; Songs of Hope, 1906; Four Christmas Days, 1912; On Parole, 1916; Songs Sung Along Life's Way, 1921. Home: Pittsburgh, Pa. Died Mar. 12, 1932.

SIVITER, William Henry, journalist; b. Dudley, Eng., May 25, 1858; s. Rev. Henry and Sarah Jane (Boden) S.; came to America, 1869; ed. pub. schs. and Fairmont (W.Va.) State Normal Sch.; m. Anna Pierpont, June 24, 1886; 1 dau., Frances Pierpont (wife of James Chambers Pryor, rear adm. U.S.N.). Editor, mgr. Oil City Derrick, 1882-85; on staff Pittsburgh Chronicle-Telegraph, 1885-1927; widely known as a humorist, contributing to many mags. and periodicals in that capacity. Mem. Pittsburgh Stock Exchange (former dir., chmn. securities com. and chmn. arbitration com.). Home: Pittsburgh, Pa. Died May 4, 1939.

SKEEL, Franklin Deuel, ophthalmologist; b. Sterling Valley, N.Y., Feb. 1851; s. Rev. H. and Lucy L. S.; A.B., Wesleyan U., Conn., 1875, A.M., 1879; M.D., Univ. Med. Coll. (New York U.), 1881; m. Mary A. Robertson, Dec. 7, 1882. Asst. surgeon, 1885-94, surgeon to New York Eye Infirmary, 1895—. Mem. N.Y. Acad. Sciences, New York Acad. Medicine, New York Ophthal. Soc.; pres. New York Micros. Soc., 1897-99. Home: Bedford Hills, N.Y. Died Jan. 15, 1923.

SKEEL, Roland Edward, physician; b. Fulton, N.Y., Feb. 9, 1869; s. Francis Adelbert and Hattie (Butler) S.; ed. Cleveland pub. schs.; M.D., U. of Mich., 1890, A.M., 1915; M.S., Ohio Wesleyan, 1915; m. Alva P. Boepple, 1893. Dean, Cleveland Coll. Phys. and Surg., 1902-10; prof. gynecology, same, 1910-11; asso. clin. prof. gynecology, 1911-20, Western Reserve U. Fellow Am. Assn. Obstetricians, Gynecologists and Abdominal Surgeons (pres. 1921-22), A.M.A. Service in France, 1917-19. Republican. Died Sept. 4, 1925.

SKEELE, Walter Fisher, musician; b. Hartford, Conn., Sept. 26, 1865; s. John P. and Elizabeth (Blodgett) S.; student Oberlin Coll. 1 yr., Oberlin Conservatory of Music, 3 yrs.; A.B., Amherst, 1888; m. Mary A. Bosworth, Feb. 4, 1891; children—Franklin Bosworth, Mary Thurston. Organist 1st Congl. Ch., Chicago, 1888-90, Plymouth Congl. Ch., 1890-93, 1st Congl. Ch., Los Angeles, Calif., 1896-1925, then 9th Ch. of Christ, Scientist. With Coll. of Music, U. of Southern Calif., 1898-1933, dean emeritus and prof. of organ and piano. Republican. Conglist. Home: Los Angeles, Calif. Died Apr. 18, 1935.

SKELTON, Henrietta, nat. lecturer and organizer W.C.T.U., 1881—; b. Heidelberg, Germany, 1842, her father being pres. Heidelberg Univ.; ed. in Collegiate Inst., Heidelberg; her father dying when she was 15 years old, she removed with an uncle to Toronto, Canada; taught German language 2 years in Bishop Strong's Young Ladies' Coll.; m. Samuel Murray Skelton, supt. Northern R.R. of Canada, 1859 (died 1873). Lectures in English and German on temperance and on subjects of today. Home: Pacific Grove, Calif. Died 1900.

SKELTON, Leslie James, artists; b. Montreal, Can., Apr. 27, 1848; s. James Welsh and Mary (Gault) S.; ed. pvt. and high schs., Montreal; studied in Paris several yrs.; pupil of Iwill; m. A. Rachel Bulley, of New Brighton, Cheshire, Eng., July 11, 1878. Landscapes in oil and pastel exhibited: Salon, Paris, 1901; Liverpool Autumn Exhbn., 1902; British and Colonial Exhbn., at time of King Edward's coronation, 1902; Royal Inst., London, Royal Acad., London, 1904; Nat. Acad. Design, New York, 1908; Royal Canadian Acad.; Denver Artists Club; Montreal Art Assn.; Colorado Springs Art Society. Represented in the permanent collection of Colorado College, Nat. Gallery, Ottawa, Can., Montreal Art Assn. One of his most noted productions entitled "Gathering Storm in Estes Park," reproduced in colors in Brush and Pencil, Feb. 1903. Loaned, without remuneration, 16 of his pictures of Colorado scenery for reproduction by 3 color ½-tone process on postal cards. Mem. Professional Artists of the Broadmoor Art Acad.; pres. Coburn Library Book Club, Colorado Springs; 2d v.p. Winter Night Club, 1911; v.p. Colorado Springs Art Soc., 1913—. Chmn. exhibition com. Broadmoor Art Acad. Home: Colorado Springs, Colo. Died Jan. 10, 1929.

SKENE, Alexander Johnston Chalmers, M.D.; b. Fyvie, Aberdeenshire, Scotland, June 17, 1837; ed. in schools of Aberdeen; studied medicine in King's Coll., Scotland; Univ. of Mich., and (grad., 1863) Long Island Coll. Hospital; acting asst. surgeon U.S. army, 1863-64; has practiced in Brooklyn, 1864—; adjunct prof. Long Island Coll. Hospital, 1864; prof. gynecology, 1872; dean of the faculty, 1886; introduced many important operations and has invented several surgical instruments. Author: Uro-Cystic and Urethral Diseases in Women; Treatise on Diseases of Women, for the Use of Students and Practitioners; Medical Gynecology; Electro-Hemostasis and Electro-Cautery in Surgery. Died 1900.

SKIFF, Frederick James Volney, museum dir., expn. mgr.; b. Chicopee, Mass., Nov. 5, 1851; s. James Martin and Angeline C. (Winchell) S.; ed. Springfield, Mass., and Brooklyn; (M.A., Colorado Coll., 1905; LL.D., George Washington U., 1908, Washington U., St. Louis, 1908); m. Mary R., d. Dr. Otis Everett French, of Garnett, Kan., June 3, 1876. Removed to Kan., 1870; in newspaper work, Lawrence, Kan., 1870-77; on staff Denver Tribune, 1877, and advanced until became mgr., 1881. Mem. Colo. Legislature, 1885-86; apptd. commr. of immigration and statistics for Colo., 1889; prepared exhibits resources of Colorado at Chicago Interstate Expn., 1889, St. Louis Interstate Expn., 1890; apptd., 1890, mem. Chicago World's Expn. Commission; chmn. com. mines and mining, same; also, apptd. by act of legislature, 1891, mem. Colo. State Bd., Columbian Fair Mgrs.; chief dept. mines and mining, 1891-93, and deputy dir. gen., 1892-93, Chicago Expn. Dir. Field Mus. of Natural History, Chicago, 1894—. Assisted in organizing the jury of awards, Nashville (Tenn.) Expn., 1897; dir.-in-chief U.S. exhibits, Paris Expn., 1898-1901; dir. of exhibits, St. Louis Expn., 1901-05; apptd., 1908, U.S. commr. gen. Japanese Exposition, 1917; apptd., 1911, dir.-in-chief Panama-Pacific Expn., San Francisco, 1915. Received bronze medal from France and gold medal from Germany; comdr. Legion d'Honneur, France; comdr. Leopold, Belgium; Crown, Italy; Red Eagle, Germany; Francis Joseph, Austria; comdr. Double Dragon, China; grand cross Sacred Treasure, Japan; etc. Mem. Am. Mus. Assn. (past pres.), N.E.A., etc. Home: Chicago, Ill. Died Feb. 24, 1921.

SKILES, William Woodburn, congressman, 14th Ohio dist., 1901-05; b. Stoughstown, Pa., Dec. 11, 1849; s. John G. S.; grad. Baldwin Univ., 1876; m. E. Dora Matson, Oct. 3, 1878. While taking coll. course taught dist. school part each coll. year; kept up course at home. Read law at Mansfield, O.; started practice at Shelby, 1878. Pres. Citizens' Bank and Shelby Electric Co.; stockholder Shelby Steel Tube Co.; pres. Shelby bd. of edn., 16 yrs. Republican. Home: Shelby, O. Died 1904.

SKILLERN, Ross Hall, M.D.; b. Phila., Nov. 13, 1875; s. Samuel Ruff (M.D.) and Sarah H. (Ross) S.; A.B., U. of Pa., 1894; M.D., Med. Dept., U. of Pa., 1897; post-grad. work, U. of Vienna, 1907; Sc.D., Ursinus College, Pa., 1925; m. Eliza Michler Porter, June 3, 1903; children—Ruth Porter, Sara Ross, Ross Porter, Andrew Porter. Began gen. practice with father, 1897; began specializing in diseases of nose, throat and ear, 1900; largyngologist Rush Hosp., 1900-13; prof. laryngology, Medico-Chirurg. Coll., 1912-18; prof. laryngology Post Grad. Sch. of Medicine, U. of Pa., 1918—. Mem. Am. Bd. Examiners in Oto-Laryngology. Capt. and asst. surgeon, 2d Regt. N.G., Pa., 1904-09. Episcopalian. Fellow Am. Coll. of Surgeons; mem. numerous med. societies. Commd. maj., in charge div. head surgery, Base Hosp., Camp Sheridan, Ala., 1917-18; lt. col. comdg. Base Hosp. 89, Mesves sur Loire, France, 1918-19. Author: The Accessory Sinuses of the Nose, 4 edits., 1916-23. Home: Ardmore, Pa. Died Sept. 20, 1930.

SKILLMAN, Thomas Julien, civil engr.; b. Trenton, N.J., Nov. 6, 1876; s. Luther S. and Mary B. S.; C.E., Princeton, 1898; m. Louise E. Jenkinson, Oct. 26, 1904; children—Margaret B., Thomas J., Richard J., Charlotte L. Began as rodman Pa. R.R., Mar. 1, 1899, and continued with same rd. successively as transitman, 1902; asst. supervisor, 1902-05; supervisor, 1905-13; div. engr., N.Y., Phila. & Norfolk R.R., 1913-14, West Jersey & Seashore R.R., 1914-17, Pa. R.R., 1917-19; prin. asst. engr., Eastern Pa. Div., Pa. R.R., 1919-20; chief engr. maintenance of way, Northwestern Region, and later Western Region, Pa. R.R., Chicago, 1920-26; asst. chief engr. of constrn., Western Region, Pa. R.R., Chicago, 1926; chief engr. Long Island R R., July 1926-Feb. 1927; chief engr. Pa. R.R., Phila., 1927-36, chief engr., consultant, Oct. 1, 1936—. Republican. Presbyn. Home: Ardmore, Pa. Died Sept. 24, 1939.

SKILTON, Charles Sanford, composer, organist; b. Northampton, Mass., Aug. 16, 1868; s. Otis Avery and Adeline Maria (Sanford) S.; A.B., Yale, 1889; studied music with Bargiel and Boise, Berlin, Germany, 2 yrs., 1891-93; with Buck and Shelley, New York, 1897-98; Dr. of Music from Syracuse U., 1933; m. Maud H. Grignard, Dec. 30, 1903; children—Helen Marie, Vivian Maud, Sanford Albert. Instr. langs., Siglar's Prep. Sch., Newburgh, N.Y., 1889-91; dir. music, Salem (N.C.) Acad. and Coll., 1893-96; instr. music, N.J. State Normal Sch., Trenton, N.J., 1898-1903; prof. of organ, theory of music, history of music, U. of Kan., 1903—, also dean Sch. of Fine Arts, 1903-15. Fellow Am. Guild Organists (dean Kan. Chapter 1915, 1935). Composer: Music to "Electra" (Smith College, 1889); Sonata for Violin and Piano (½ first prize, Music Teachers' Nat. Assn, 1897); (first prizes with Kan. Fedn. of Music Clubs) Chorus, 1922, Song, 1931; Two Indian Dances, for string quartet and orchestra; sonata and fantasy for organ; (cantatas) The Witch's Daughter, Ticonderoga; (oratorio) The Guardian Angel; (suites) Primeval and East and West for orchestra; (operas) Kalopin, The Sun Bride, The Day of Gayomair. Home: Lawrence, Kan. Died Mar. 12, 1941.

SKILTON, DeWitt Clinton, fire underwriter; b. Plymouth Hollow (now Thomaston), Conn., Jan. 11, 1839; s. John Chester and Anna (Headton) S.; ed. Thompson Acad.; m. Ann Jeanette Andrews, Aug. 1865. Entered mercantile business, Hartford, 1855; entered ins. business as clerk in Hartford Fire Ins. Co., Oct. 24, 1861; entered vol. service in Civil War, Aug. 1862, as 2d lt. Co. B, 22d Conn. Vols.; promoted 1st lt., Feb. 1863. Sec. Phœnix Ins. Co., Dec. 1867, became v.p. Aug. 1888, pres., Feb. 1891—; pres. Nat. Bd. of Fire Underwriters, 1891, 1892, 1893; member com., of 20 which prepared the Standard Policy of Fire Insurance for the state of N.Y., now in gen. use throughout the country. Dir. Hartford Nat. Bank; trustee State Savings Bank, Hartford. Home: Hartford, Conn. Died Dec. 27, 1913.

SKINNER, Aaron Nichols, astronomer; b. Boston, Aug. 10, 1845; s. Benjamin Hill and Mercy (Burgess) S.; student Beloit Coll., 1867-68; spl. course in astronomy, U. of Chicago, 1867-70; m. Sarah Elizabeth Gibbs, Feb. 9, 1874. Asst. at Dearborn Obs., Chicago, 1867-70; asst. astronomer U.S. Naval Obs., Washington, 1870-98; prof. mathematics, U.S.N., 1898—; astronomer in charge of 9-inch Transit Circle, U.S. Naval Obs., 1893-1902; in charge 26-inch equatorial, 1902, 1903; div. of equatorials, 1903—. In 1894-95 determined places of 8,824 stars in zone 14 degrees to 18 degrees south declination as a contbn. to the great Star Catalogue of Astronomische Gesellschaft, from 23° south declination to 80° north declination. Discoverer of 4 variable stars; active participant in all the meridian circle work of Naval Obs., 1871—chief U.S. Naval Obs. expdn. to Sumatra to observe total solar eclipse of May 17, 1901; retired from active service with rank of comdr. U.S.N., 1907. Fellow A.A.A.S., Astronomische Gesellschaft, Astron. and Astrophys. Soc. of America. Author: Washington Zone Observations; Katalog der Astronomische Gesellschaft Zone 14° bis 18° (Leipzig), 1908. Home: Washington, D.C. Died Aug. 14, 1919.

SKINNER, Avery Warner, educator; b. Mexico, N.Y., Aug. 18, 1870; s. Timothy W. and Sarah L. (Rose) S.; grad. Mexico (N.Y.) Acad., 1887; A.B., Syracuse U., 1892; grad. study in history and school administration, Columbia U., 1915; Ph.D., N.Y. State Coll. for Teachers, 1924; m. Nancy Brown Bates, Aug. 24, 1893; children—Margaret Rose (Mrs. Harold O. Fullerton), Charlotte Huntington (Mrs. Willard G. Taylor). Prin. Andes (N.Y.) Collegiate Inst., 1892-94; prin. Mexico Acad., 1895-99; instr. in history, State Summer Sch., Thousand Island Park, N.Y., 1896-1904; supt. schs., Oneida, N.Y., 1899-1909; insp. schs., N.Y. State Edn. Dept., 1909-15; supervisor of history, same dept., 1915-20; dir. examinations and inspections div., same dept., 1920—; lecturer on methods of teaching history, summer sessions, Syracuse U., 1918-26, on school administration, Ore. Agrl. Coll., 1927. Trustee Mexico Academy. Republican. Presbyn. Mason. Author: (with Anna Elizabeth Foote) Explorers and Founders of America, 1907, 29; (with Anna E. Foote) Makers and Defenders of America, 1910, 29; History and Government of New York State, 1918; Community Life in New York, 1928. Editor and compiler of Selections for Memorizing, 1906. Asso. editor High School Quarterly. Homes: Albany, N.Y., and Mexico, N.Y. Died Dec. 13, 1937.

SKINNER, Belle; b. Skinnerville, Mass.; d. William and Sarah E. (Allen) S.; A.B., Vassar. Rebuilt devastated village of Hattonchâtel, France, giving it a water system, electrical system, school house and circulating library. Chevalier Légion d'Honneur, Officier de l'Instruction Publique, Médaille de la Reconnaissance Française. Conglist. Collector and owner of the "Belle Skinner Collection of Musical Instruments." Home: Holyoke, Mass. Died Apr. 9, 1928.

SKINNER, Charles Montgomery, editor on staff Brooklyn Eagle; b. Victor, N.Y., Mar. 15, 1852; common school edn. Cambridge, Mass., and Hartford, Conn.; married in 1876. Author: Villon, the Vagabond, and adapter of Richepin's "Le Chemineau" (dramas, played by his brother, Otis Skinner); Myths and Legends of Our Own Land; Myths and Legends Beyond Our Borders; Nature in a City Yard; With Feet to the Earth; Do-Nothing Days; Myths and Legends of Our New Possessions; American Myths and Legends, 1903; Little Gardens, 1904. Represented Brooklyn Eagle on the relief expdn. of the Dixie to Martinique. Died 1907.

SKINNER, Charles Rufus, educator; b. Union Square, N.Y., Aug. 4, 1844; s. Avery and Charlotte Prior (Stebbins) S.; ed. Mexico Acad., Clinton Liberal Inst.; hon. A.M., Hamilton, 1889; LL.D., Colgate, 1895; Litt.D., Tufts, 1901; m. Elizabeth Baldwin, Oct. 16, 1873 (died 1918) children—Grace Alice (dec.), Harold Baldwin, Albert Merriman, Charles Rufus, Bessie (dec.), Elizabeth. In business in New York, 1867-70; mgr. and city editor Watertown, N.Y., Daily Times, 1870-74; mem. N.Y. Assembly, 1877-81; mem. 47th and 48th Congresses (1881-85); deputy state supt. pub. instr., 1886-92; supervisor teachers' institutes and teachers' training classes, 1892-95; state supt. pub. instrn., 1895-1904; asst. appraiser port of New York, 1906-11; librarian of N.Y. Assembly, Albany, 1914; legislative librarian, Albany, 1915-25; retired Oct. 31, 1925. Republican. Pres. N.E.A., 1897. Author: Commercial Advantages of Watertown, N.Y., 1876; New York Question Book, 1890; Arbor Day Manual, 1891; Manual of Patriotism for the Schools of New York, 1900; The Bright Side, 1909. In 48th Congress, 1883, introduced a bill providing for special delivery stamp, which bill became a law, Mar. 4, 1885; put in force law requiring U.S flags to be displayed over or near every pub. sch. in state. Home: Albany, N.Y. Died June 30, 1928.

SKINNER, Constance Lindsay, writer; b. Canadian Far North; d. Robert James and Anne (Lindsay) S.; ed. in pvt. sch., Vancouver, and under tutors. Began writing as a schoolgirl for local newspapers; later engaged as polit. reporter and editorial writer for British Columbian papers; was dramatic and musical critic and spl. feature writer, Los Angeles Times, Los Angeles Examiner, and Chicago American. Author: Builder of Men (pub. in Germany only), 1913; Good Morning, Rosamond (novel), 1917; Silent Scot, Frontier Scout, 1925; The Search Relentless (novel), 1925; The White Leader, 1926; Becky Landers, Frontier Warrior, 1926; The Pageant of America (Vol. I), 1926; The Tiger Who Walks Alone, 1927; Roselle of the North, 1927; Debby Barnes, Trader, 1932; (plays) David, prod. Forest Theatre, Carmel, Calif., 1910; Good Morning, Rosamond, prod. New York, 1917; also Songs of the Coast Dwellers (poems); Pioneers of Old Southwest and Adventurers of Oregon in Yale U. Series of Chronicles of America, 1919; Andy Breaks Trail, 1928; The Ranch of the Golden Flowers, 1928; Red Willows (novel), 1929; Red Man's Luck, 1931; Debby Barnes, Trader, 1932; Beaver, Kings and Cabins (history of the fur trade), 1933; Rob Roy, The Frontier Twins, 1934. Editor "The Rivers of America" series. Home: New York, N.Y. Died Mar. 27, 1939.

SKINNER, Ernest Brown, univ. prof.; b. Perry Co., O., Dec. 12, 1863; s. Thomas Peter and Harriet Newell (Brown) S.; A.B. Ohio U., Athens, 1888; scholar in mathematics, Clark U., 1891-92; Ph.D., U. of Chicago, 1900; LL.D. from Ohio U., 1932; m. Adda C. Coe, Aug. 8, 1888; children—Merrill Edmund, Helen Harriet, Edith Virginia. Prof. mathematics, Amity Coll., 1888-91; instr. mathematics, 1892-95, asst. prof., 1895-1910, asso. prof., 1910-20, prof., 1920—, Univ. of Wis.; dir. University Avenue Bank, Madison, Wis. Mem. Madison Bd. Education, 1919-29 (pres., 1920-29). Dir. McCormick Theol. Seminary; mem. Permanent Judicial Commn. of the General Assembly Presbyn. Ch. in U.S.A., 1926-29. Author: The Mathematical Theory of Investment, 1913, rev. edit., 1924; High School Course in Mathematics, 1910; College Algebra, 1917; Introduction to Trigonometry and Analytic Geometry, 1932. Home: Madison, Wis. Died Apr. 3, 1935.

SKINNER, Henrietta Channing Dana, author; b. Cambridge, Mass., Feb. 22, 1857; d. Richard Henry Dana, Jr., and Sarah (Watson) Dana; pvt. schs. Boston and Germany, Convent of the Assumption, Paris, Radcliffe Coll., 1886-88; music, Artists' Sch., Stuttgart Conservatory, and with César Franck, Paris; m. Henry Whipple Skinner, June 25, 1892 (dec.); 1 son, Richard Dana. Hon. gov. gen. Order Descendants of Colonial Governors; mem. Colonial Dames of Mass., D.A.R., etc. Catholic. Author: Espiritu Santo, 1899; Heart and Soul, 1901; Faith Brandon, 1911; Their Choice, 1913. Home: Boston, Mass. Died Jan. 29, 1928.

SKINNER, Henry, entomologist; b. Philadelphia, Mar. 27, 1861; s. William S. and Sarah (Irvin) S.; B.S., U. of Pa., 1881, M.D., 1884; Sc.D., U. of Pittsburgh; m. Celia Angela Beck, July 14, 1886; children—Marion (Mrs. Harvey Wilson Madara), William Henry. Associated with Dr. William Goodell in practice of medicine, 1884-1900; devoted entire attention to entomology from 1900; state entomologist of Pennsylvania; prof. entomology, Pa. Hort. Soc.; in charge entomol. dept. and chmn. publn. com. and mem. council. Acad. Natural Sciences,

Phila.; v.p. Acad. Natural Sciences of Phila.; mem. various scientific societies. Editor Entomological News, 1890-1911. Mem. com. on nomenclature, Internat. Zoöl. Congress. Home: Narberth, Pa. Died May 29, 1926.

SKINNER, Hubert Marshall, educator, author; b. Valparaiso, Ind., Jan. 15, 1855; s. Hon. John N. and Joanna E. (Marshall) S.; A.M., DePauw U., 1877 (Ph.D., Chattanooga U., 1902, Valparaiso U., 1907); m. Emily S. Ogden. Supt. city schools, Brookville, Ind., 1880-83; deputy state supt. pub. instrn., 1883-86, and sec. Teachers' Reading Circle of Ind.; in charge of reading circle correspondence of Am. Book Co., 1892-1911; dean, collegiate dept. Lincoln-Jefferson U. Lecturer, Chautauqua, N.Y., 1906. Originated celebration of "Lincoln Day." Editor-in-chief of Collegiate Course for Home Study (12 vols.), 1908-09. Author: Story of the Britons, 1903; Calderon's La Vida Es Sueño (edited), 1904; Santillana's El Centiloquio (edited, 1902, transl. 1907); The Story of the Letters and Figures, 1906; Practical Agriculture, 1915. Home: Morgan Park, Ill. Died June 4, 1916.

SKINNER, Otis, actor; b. Cambridge, Mass., June 28, 1858; s. Rev. Charles A. and Cornelia B.S.; ed. Hartford, Conn.; hon. A.M., Tufts Coll., 1895; D.H.L., St. Lawrence U., 1930, U. of Pa., 1936; m. Maud Durbin, Apr. 21, 1895 (dec.); 1 dau., Cornelia Otis. Amateur reader and actor, Hartford, Conn.; professional début as Jim in "Woodleigh," Phila. Mus., Nov. 1877; later in Walnut St. Theatre Stock Co., Phila.; New York début at Niblo's in Kiralfy's "Enchantment," 1879; successively took important rôles at Booth's Theatre, Boston Theatre and with Lawrence Barrett; with Augustin Daly in New York, London, Paris, Berlin, etc., 5 yrs.; leading man with Mme. Modjeska, 1892-95; since then starring in romantic plays and as mgr. and producer. Starred in "His Grace de Grammont," 1894; "Hamlet," 1896; "Prince Otto," 1900; "Francesca da Rimini," 1902; "The Harvester," 1904; "The Duel," 1906; "Kismet," 1911, 12, 13, 14; "The Silent Voice," "A Celebrated Case," 1914-15; "Cock o' the Walk," 1915-16; "Mister Antonio," 1916, 17, 18; "The Honor of the Family," 1918-19; "Pietro," 1919-20; "At the Villa Rose," 1920-21; "Blood and Sand," 1921-22; "Sancho Panza," 1923, 24, 25; "Merry Wives of Windsor," 1927-28; "A Hundred Years Old," 1929-30; "Merchant of Venice," 1931-32. Wrote: Footlights and Spotlights; Mad Folk of the Theatre; One Man in his Time; etc. Home: New York, N.Y. Died Jan. 4, 1942.

SKINNER, Stella, prof. of art; b. Grand Rapids, Mich., Oct. 18, 1857; d. Aaron Sheldon and Maria (Wright) S.; grad. Art Dept., Pratt Inst., Brooklyn, N.Y., 1890; grad. work same, 1899-1901; attended Yale Art School lectures; extended study in European art galleries. Supervisor drawing, pub. schs., New Haven, Conn. 1891-99; instr. art, State Normal Sch. New Paltz, N.Y., 1901-08, lecturer and dir. art dept., Northwestern U., 1908—, prof. art, 1918—. Instr. summer session, Teachers Coll. (Columbia), 1912; spl. lecturer Art Inst. Chicago; has lectured widely throughout U.S. Conglist. Home: Evanston, Ill. Died Dec. 26, 1922.

SKINNER, Thomas Clagett, clergyman; b. Upperville, Va., May 22, 1869; s. Nathaniel Jackson and Julia Augusta (Nixon) S.; La Grange (Mo.) Coll., 1888-90; Richmond (Va.) Coll., 1893, D.D., 1908; grad. Crozer Theol. Sem., Chester, Pa., 1896; m. Florence Frances Burnett, Oct. 15, 1901 (died 1928); 1 dau., Mary Elizabeth. Ordained Bapt. ministry, 1896; pastor Lansdowne, Pa., 1896-98, Berkley Av. Ch., Norfolk, 1898-1901, North Av. Ch., Baltimore, 1901-07, 1st Ch., Roanoke, Va., 1907-12, 2d Ch., Richmond, Va., 1912-20, First Ch., Columbia, S.C., 1920-26, First Ch., Lynchburg, Va., 1926— Elected pres. Va. Bapt. Gen. Assn., 1929, 30. Democrat. Home: Lynchburg, Va. Died Jan. 19, 1934.

SKIPPER, Glenn Blount; b. Bartow, Fla., Dec. 22, 1887; s. Enoch Everett and Mattie Elizabeth (Blount) S.; ed. Summerlin Inst. and S. Fla. Mil. Coll., Bartow, and Alamo City Commercial Coll., San Antonio, Tex.; m. Nina Belle Bigham, Apr. 17, 1907; 1 son, James Everett. Associated in cattle, land, mercantile and banking business with father until latter's death, 1920, then in business alone. Served as corpl. inf., U.S.A., World War. Mem. Rep. Nat. Com., term 1928-32. Methodist. Mason. Home: Bartow, Fla. Deceased.

SKOOG, Karl Frederick, sculptor; b. Vermland, Sweden, Nov. 3, 1878; s. Anders Frederick and Anna (Johannson) S.; came to U.S., 1902, naturalized citizen, 1919; studied art with Bella L. Pratt and Prof. Andrew Garbutt, Boston, Mass., and with Junghanel and Richter, Gothenburg, Sweden. Exhibited at Albright Gallery, Buffalo; Pa. Acad. Fine Arts; Nat. Acad. Design, New York; Art Inst. Chicago; Boston Art Mus. and Boston Art Club; Conn. Acad. Fine Arts; etc. Awarded 4 first prizes, 1 second prize and 4 hon. mentions. Works: Soldiers World War Monument, Cambridge, Mass.; Soldiers World War Monument, Cromwell, Conn.; Perry Monument, Malden, Mass.; sculptured bronze doors,

"Light" and "Charity" for Masonic Temple, Goshen, Ind.; bust of John Ericsson, Brockton, Mass.; memorial reliefs at Malden, Cromwell, and Newton, Mass., panels, Empire Theatre, Springfield, Mass.; memorial relief and Masters of Destiny group of 8 figures, John Morton Memorial Mus., Phila., Pa.; etc.; rep. in Museum of Numismatic Soc., N.Y. City, John H. Vanderpool Memorial Collection, Chicago, Museum of Foring Swedes, Gothenburg, Sweden. Republican. Truth Student. Home: Boston, Mass. Died Mar. 26, 1936.

SLACK, Leighton P., judge; b. Woodstock, Vt., June 18, 1867; s. Joel B. and Mary A. (Fullam) S.; ed. Black River Acad., Ludlow, Vt.; m. Leah E. Mears, July 11, 1899; 1 dau., Ruth Estelle. Admitted to Vt. bar, 1892, and to U.S. cts., 1894; practiced, Barre, 1892-95; removed to St. Johnsbury, 1895; mem. Dunnett & Slack, 1895-1913; state's atty. Caledonia Co., 1898-1900; mem. Vt. State Senate, 1904-06; lt. gov. of Vt., 1910-12; chmn. Rep. presdl. electors, Vt., 1912, judge Superior Court of Vt., Oct. 1913-May 5, 1919; asso. justice Supreme Court, May 1919—. Republican. Conglist. Home: Montpelier, Vt. Died April 2, 1938.

SLACK, Munsey, newspaper pub.; b. Bristol, Tenn., Dec. 10, 1877; s. John and Julia (Holston) S.; student King Coll., Bristol, Tenn.; Ph.B., Franklin (Ind.) Coll., 1899; m. Maxie Cox, Dec. 31, 1902; children—Mary Amelia (wife of Dr. Nat. Copenhaver), John Charles, James Abraham, Julia (wife of Dr. P. D. Stout), Embree (Mrs. James A. Booher), Munsey, Thad Cox; m. 2d, Mary E. Trolinger, Nov. 28, 1936. Began as publisher Abingdon Virginian, 1901; pub. Johnson City Staff, 1903-24; asso. pub. Bristol (Va. and Tenn.), Herald Courier and News Bulletin, 1919—; pres. Bristol Pub. Corp. Chmn. Washington County (Tenn.) Exemption Bd. World War. Gen. chmn. com. that raised $513,000 for a hotel in Johnson City, and of com. of So. Methodist Ch. that raised $200,000 for a Centenary fund and Christian edn., in Morristown dist. Home: Bristol, Tenn. Died Dec. 7, 1939.

SLADE, George Theron, railway official; b. N.Y. City, July 22, 1871; s. George P. and Cornelia W. (Strong) S.; A.B., Yale, 1893; m. Charlotte E., d. James J. Hill, of St. Paul, Minn., Oct. 9, 1901 (died 1923); children—George Norman, Georgiana Mary. Entered service G.N. Ry., 1893; supt. Eastern Ry. of Minn., 1897-99; gen. manager Erie & Wyo. Valley Ry., 1899-1901; supt. Wyo. and Jefferson divs. of Erie R.R., Mar.-Aug. 1901; gen. supt. Erie div., same rd., 1901-03; gen. supt. G.N. Ry., 1903-07; gen. mgr. N.P. Ry., 1907-09, 3d v.p. same rd., 1909-13, 1st v.p. in charge operation, 1913-18; resigned Feb. 1918, to become dep. dir. gen. of transportation A.E.F. in France, rank of col. Spl. work for U.S. Govt. in Alaska and France, 1919; mem. President Wilson's 2d Industrial Conf., 1920; pres. Absaroka Oil Development Co., 1920-22; Tide Water Oil Co., 1923-24; now inactive. Home: New York, N.Y. Died Jan. 24, 1941.

SLAFTER, Edmund Farwell, P.E. clergyman, author; b. Norwich, Vt., May 30, 1816; s. Sylvester and Mary Armstrong (Johnson) S.; grad. Dartmouth, 1840 (A.M.; D.D.); studied at Andover Theol. Sem.; deacon, 1844; priest, 1845; m. Mary Anne Hazen, Aug. 16, 1849. Rector St. Peter's, Cambridge, Mass., 1844-46; St. John's Jamaica Plain, 1846-53; asst. rector St. Paul's, Boston, several yrs.; supt. for P.E. Ch. in Am. Bible Soc., 1857-77, resigned; now registrar Diocese of Mass. From 1877 devoted himself to management of property and hist. studies. Author: Sir William Alexander and American Colonization; 1873; Voyages of the Northmen to America, 1877; History and Causes of Incorrect Latitudes as Recorded in the Journals of Early Writers, Navigators and Explorers, 1882; John Checkley, or, the Evolution of Religious Tolerance in Massachusetts Bay, 1897. Home: Boston, Mass. Died 1906.

SLAGHT, William Ernest Andrew, coll. prof.; b. Woodstock, Can., Nov. 3, 1875; s. Philander and Catherine (Malcolm) S.; B.A., Toronto U., 1898; S.T.B., Yale Div. Sch., 1902; grad. work in theology, 1903, philosophy, 1905-07, M.A., 1907; grad. study State U. of Iowa, 1924-25, Ph.D., 1926; D.D., Baker U., 1921; m. Minnie Edith Deacon, June 23, 1902; children—Morley Frederick, Leonard Malcolm, William Henry. Pastor Westville M.E. Ch., New Haven, Conn., 1906-08; asso. pastor 1st Ch., Middletown, Conn., 1909; prof. philosophy, Baker U., 1910-20; prof. psychology, Cornell Coll., 1921—. Republican. Mason. Author: Untruthfulness in Children, 1928. Home: Mount Vernon, Ia. Died Mar. 26, 1932.

SLAGLE, Robert Lincoln, coll. pres.; b. Hanover, Pa., Mar. 17, 1865; s. William Augustus and Margaret (Stine) S.; A.B., Lafayette, 1887, A.M., 1890, LL.D., 1922; Ph.D., Johns Hopkins, 1894; hon. Sc.D., U. of South Dakota, 1927; m. Gertrude Anna Riemann, May 28, 1896 (died 1915). Asso. with the late Prof. W. O. Atwater in food studies at Middletown, Conn., 1894-95; prof. chemistry, S.D. Agrl. Coll. (now S.D. State Coll. of Agr. and Mechanic Arts), 1895-97; prof. chemistry, 1897-98, pres. 1898-1905, S.D. Sch. of Mines; pres. S.D. State Coll. of Agr. and Mechanic

Arts, 1906-14; pres. U. of S.Dak., Feb. 1, 1914—. Mason. Republican. Episcopalian. Home: Vermilion, S.D. Died Jan. 29, 1920.

SLATE, Frederick, physicist; b. London, Eng., Jan. 21, 1852; B.S., Poly. Inst. of Brooklyn, 1871; studied univs. of Berlin and Strassburg, 1877-79; LL.D., U. of Calif., 1925; m. Ella H. DeWolfe, 1884. Instr. chemistry, 1874-77, prof. physics, 1891-1918, U. of Calif. (emeritus). Author: Principles of Mechanics, 1900; Elementary Physics, 1902; Fundamental Equations of Dynamics, 1918. Home: Berkeley, Calif. Died Feb. 26, 1930.

SLATTERY, Charles Lewis, bishop; b. Pittsburgh, Pa., Dec. 9, 1867; s. Rev. George and Emma McLellan (Hall) S.; A.B., Harvard, 1891; D.B., Episcopal Theol. Sch., Cambridge, 1894; D.D., Cambridge, 1907, U. of the South, 1918, Trinity Coll., Conn., 1922, Harvard U., 1923; m. Sarah Lawrence, 1923. Deacon, 1894, priest, 1895, P.E., Ch.; master Groton Sch., and rector of St. Andrew's, Ayer, Mass., 1894-96; dean Cathedral of Our Merciful Saviour, Faribault, Minn., 1896-1907; rector Christ Ch., Springfield, Mass., 1907-10; rector Grace Ch., New York, 1910-22; bishop coadjutor of Mass., 1922-27, bishop of Mass., 1927—. Gen. chmn. Church Congress in U.S.; chmn. Commn. for Revision and Enrichment of the Book of Common Prayer; pres. bd. trustees Wellesley Coll.; trustee Boston U., Brooks School. Lecturer in Seabury Div. Sch., Faribault, Minn., 1905-07, Berkeley Div. Sch., 1909-10; Paddock lecturer, Gen. Theol. Sem., 1911-12; West lecturer, Stanford U., 1915; preacher at Harvard U., 1921-27. Author: Felix Reville Brunot, 1901; The Master of the World—a Study of Christ, 1906; Life Beyond Life—a Study of Immortality, 1907; The Historic Ministry and the Present Christ, 1908; Present-Day Preaching, 1909; Alexander Viets Griswold Allen, 1911; The Authority of Religious Experience, 1912; The Light Within, 1915; Why Men Pray, 1916; The Gift of Immortality, 1916; A Churchman's Reading, 1917; David Hummell Greer, Eighth Bishop of New York, 1921; The Ministry, 1921; The Holy Communion, 1922; The Spirit of France, 1923; William Austin Smith, 1924; Bible Lessons for the Sunday Mornings of the Christian Year, 1925; In Times of Sorrow—A Book of Consolation, 1927; Words from His Throne—A Story of the Cross, 1927; Following Christ, 1928. Home: Boston, Mass. Died Mar. 12, 1930.

SLATTERY, John Theodore, clergyman; b. Albany, N.Y.; s. Michael J. and Catherine (Milerick) S.; prep. edn., Christian Bros. Acad., Albany, N.Y.; A.B., Manhattan Coll., 1886; A.M., New York State Coll. for Teachers and Columbia U.; Ph.D., Villanova Coll.; also studied U. of Chicago and University Coll., Oxford, Eng.; theol. studies, St. Joseph's Provincial Seminary, Troy, N.Y.; Litt.D., Fordham U., New York City. Ordained priest R.C. Ch., 1891; pastor Ch. of the Sacred Heart, Stamford, N.Y., 1904-06, St. Columbia's Ch., Schenectady, 1906-09 (built the ch. and organized the parish), St. Patrick's Ch., Watervliet, 1909-21, St. Joseph's Ch., Troy, 1922—. Chairman Watervliet branch Am. Red Cross, 1910-21; pres. Capital District Conf. on Social Welfare; atty. for Catholic Diocese of Albany. Domestic prelate to the Pope, with title of Monsignor. Commendatore of Order of the Crown of Italy. Author: A System of Mnemonics, 1896; Dante, the Central Man of the World, 1920; Dante's Attitude Towards the Church and Clergy of His Time, 1921; My Favorite Passage from Dante, 1928; Aids to the Study of the Divine Comedy, 1929. Home: Troy, N.Y. Deceased.

SLAUGHT, Herbert Ellsworth, university prof.; b. Watkins, N.Y., July 21, 1861; s. Abram and Helen (Hanly) S.; A.B., Colgate U., 1883, A.M., 1886, D.Sc., 1911; Ph.D., U. of Chicago, 1898; studied in Europe, 1902-03; m. Mary Laura Davis, July 23, 1885 (died 1919); 1 dau., Katharine May. Instr. mathematics, Peddie Inst., N.J., 1883-92; fellow in mathematics and asst. in various grades, 1892-96, instr. mathematics, 1896-1900, asst. prof., 1900-08, asso. prof., 1908-13, prof., 1913-31, in charge of bd. for recommendation of teachers, 1900-14, U. of Chicago; prof. emeritus. Hon. life pres. Nat. Council Teachers of Mathematics, Math. Assn. of America. Editor and co-author series of textbooks in mathematics for schools and colleges. Editor, 1912-17, mgr., 1918—, Am. Math. Monthly. Co-editor of the Carus Mathematical Monographs (series for the non-tech. reader). Home: Chicago, Ill. Died. May 21, 1937.

SLAUGHTER, Christopher C., cattle raiser; b. Sabine Co., Tex., Feb. 9, 1837; s. George Webb and Sarah (Mason) S.; said to be 1st male child born of a marriage contracted under the Republic of Texas; ed. at home; m. Cynthia A. Jowell, 1861; m. 2d, Carrie A. Averill, 1877. Began cattle business, 1857; entire capital $500; capt. Texas Rangers and bvtd. col. C.S.A., 1861-65; after war reëntered cattle business, very small capital, became noted as pioneer in cattle industry and Indian fighter; has been called for years the "Cattle King of Texas." One of largest individual land owners in America, owning over 500,000 acres of land in Tex. Was v.p. City Bank of Dallas, 1877; v.p. City Nat. Bank, Dallas, 1880; organized Am. Nat. Bank, 1884, became its vice-pres. Organized Cattle Raisers' Assn. of Tex., 1877, and was its 2d pres.; 1st pres. and organizer Beef Producers' and Butchers' Nat. Assn. America, 1884. Democrat. Baptist; pres. bd. dirs. Bapt. Gen. Conv. of Texas. Has made large gifts to schs., colls. and hosps. in Texas. Founder Bapt. Memorial Sanitarium at Dallas. Home: Dallas, Tex. Died Jan. 25, 1919.

SLAUGHTER, Moses Stephen, prof. of Latin; b. Brooklyn, Ind., Oct. 3, 1860; s. John and Sarah Louisa (Rider) S.; B.A., DePauw U., 1883; scholar in Latin, 1884-85, and fellow in Latin, Johns Hopkins U., 1885-86, Ph.D., 1891; univs. Berlin and Munich, 1893-94; m. Gertrude Elizabeth Taylor, June 28, 1893. Instr. in Latin, Bryn Mawr Coll., 1887-88; prof. Latin, Collegiate Inst., Hackettstown, N.J., 1888-89; Iowa Coll., 1889-96; prof. Latin, U. of Wis., 1896—; ann. prof. Latin Am. Sch. of Classical Studies, at Rome, 1909-10. Conglist. Author: The Story of Turnus, 1896. Democrat. With Italian Commn. of Am. Red. Cross, 1918-19; in charge of Venice dist., rank of maj. Silver medal of Italian Red Cross; Croce di Guerra; Cavaliere della Corona d'Italia. Home: Madison, Wis. Died Dec. 29, 1923.

SLAVEN, Henry Bartholomew, contractor; b. nr. Picton, Ont., Oct. 19, 1853; reared on farm; ed. common schools; became druggist's asst.; grad. Ontario Coll. of Pharmacy at 17; attended med. coll., Phila., 2 yrs.; mgr. wholesale drug house in Canada, 1873-76; in drug and mfg. business in San Francisco, 1876; with a brother established, 1878, firm of Slaven Bros., contractors of public works and contractors, 1880-89, on Panama Canal. Incorporated business, 1882, as Am. Contracting & Dredging Co., of which he is pres. Treas. Nicaragua Canal Co., 1889—; pres. Chase Granite Co., Bluehill, Me. Home: New York, N.Y. Died 1904.

SLAYDEN, James Luther, congressman; b. Graves Co., Ky., June 1, 1853; s. Thomas A. and Letitia E. (Beadles) S.; student Washington and Lee U., Va., 1872-73; m. Ellen Maury, June 12, 1883. Formerly cotton mcht. Mem. Tex. Ho. of Rep., 1892; declined reëlection; mem. 55th to 57th Congresses (1897-1903), 12th Texas Dist., and 58th to 65th Congresses (1903-19), 14th Dist. Democrat. Chmn. Am. group of Interparliamentary Union; pres. Am. Peace Soc.; trustee Carnegie Endowment for Internat. Peace; mem. World Court League. Home: San Antonio, Tex. Died Feb. 24, 1924.

SLEDD, Andrew, coll. prof.; b. Lynchburg, Va., Nov. 7, 1870; s. Robert Newton and Frances Carey (Greene) S.; A.B., and A.M., Randolph-Macon Coll., 1894; A.M., Harvard, 1896; Ph.D., Yale, 1903; LL.D., U. of S.C., 1905, Rollins Coll., 1909; D.D., U. of Fla., 1909; m. Annie Florence, d. Warren A. Candler, Mar. 14, 1899. Prin. high school, Arkadelphia, Ark., 1892-93; instr. Randolph-Macon Acad., Bedford, Va., 1894-95; teaching fellow, Vanderbilt U., 1897; prof. Latin, Emory Coll., Ga., 1898-1902; prof. Greek, Southern U., Greensboro, Ala., 1903-04; pres. U. of Fla., 1904-09, Southern U., Greensboro, Ala., 1910-14; prof. N.T. Greek, Emory U., Atlanta, Ga., and librarian theol. dept. same, 1914—. Writer of St. Mark's Life of Jesus, The Canon of the Scriptures, His Witnesses. Democrat. Home: Decatur, Ga. Died Mar. 16, 1939.

SLEDD, Benjamin, coll. prof.; b. Bedford Co., Va., Aug. 27, 1864; s. William and Arabella (Hobson) S.; M.A., Washington and Lee U., 1886, hon. Litt.D., 1907; spl. student Johns Hopkins, 1886-87, but took no degree on account of failing eyesight; m. Neda Purefoy, June 11, 1889; children—Arthur Purefoy, Gladys Hobson, Elva Douglas. Prof. English, Wake Forest Coll., 1888—. Author: (poems) From Cliff and Scaur, 1897; The Watchers of the Hearth, 1901; When Freedom Came, 1910; At Lexington, A Memorial Poem, 1913; A Virginian in Surrey, 1914; To England; Afterthought, 1919; The Dead Grammarian, 1924; The Modernist and The Megatherium, 1927. Editor: La Princesse de Clèves, 1892. Traveling fellow of Albert Kahn Foundation, 1914-15. Died Jan. 4, 1940.

SLEEPER, Albert E., gov.; b. Bradford, Vt., Dec. 31, 1862; s. Joseph Edson and Hannah S.; ed. Bradford Acad.; m. Mary C. Moore, July 30, 1901. Removed to Lexington, 1884; engaged in mercantile business and as traveling salesman, later in banking and real estate business; pres. First Nat. Bank (Yale, Mich.), State Savings Bank (Bad Axe), Commercial State Bank (Marlette), Citizens State Bank (Ubley), Clark & McCaren Co., wholesale grocers (Bad Axe). Mem. Mich. Ho. of Rep., 1901-02, 1903-04; mem. Rep. State Com., 1905-07; state treas. of Mich. 2 terms, 1909-13; gov. of Mich. 2 terms, 1917-20 inclusive. Episcopalian. Mason. Home: Bad Axe, Mich. Died May 13, 1934.

SLEICHER, John A., editor; b. Troy, N.Y., Oct. 4, 1848; s. William S.; ed. Troy High Sch.; (LL.D., Syracuse U.); m. Ella S. Peckham, 1873. City editor Troy Whig, Press, and Times; part propr. Troy Times; was mgr. at New York of N.Y. State Assn. Press; propr. Schenectady (N.Y.) Union; editor-in-chief and part owner Albany Evening Journal; editor-in-chief New York Mail and Express and civ. service commr. of State of N.Y., 1889-93; became editor-in-chief Leslie's Weekly, and pres. of the Leslie-Judge Co. Mem. N.Y. Bd. Trade and Transportation (dir.), Civ. Service Reform Assn. (exec. com.). Trustee Syracuse U. Mem. N.Y. State Water Supply Commission, 1905-11. Home: New York, N.Y. Died May 5, 1921.

SLEMP, Campbell, congressman; b. Turkey Cove, Va., Dec. 2, 1839; s. S. S. and Margaret (Read) S.; ed. Turkey Cove, until 1856, Emory and Henry Coll., 1856-59; m. Nannie B. Cawood, June 9, 1865. Entered C. S. A., 1861; served as capt., lt. col. and col. 64th Va. regt. Mem. Va. legislature, 1879-83; was on Mahone ticket for lt. gov. in 1889, on Harrison ticket as elector, 1888; on McKinley electoral ticket, 1896; mem. Congress, 9th Va. dist., 1903-07. Republican. Farmer and real estate dealer. Home: Big Stone Gap, Va. Died 1907.

SLENKER, Elmina Drake ("Aunt Elmina"), author; b. La Grange, N.Y., Dec. 23, 1827; d. Thomas Drake (a Quaker preacher, who was expelled from the ministry for heresy, and became a Freethinker, as did his daughter) and Eliza (Pinkham) Drake; m. Isaac Slenker, 1856. Author: Little Lessons for Liberal Sunday School; Studying the Bible, 1870; The Infidel School Teacher, 1885; The Handsomest Woman, 1885; The Darwins; Little Lessons for Little Folks, 1887. Editor: The Little Freethinker, etc. Home: Snowville, Va. Deceased.

SLICER, Thomas Roberts, clergyman; b. Washington, D.C., Apr. 16, 1847; s. Rev. Henry S.; ed. in Baltimore; (hon. A.M., Dickinson Coll., 1872); m. Adeline E., d. Theodore C. Herbert, U.S.N., Apr. 5, 1871. In Methodist ministry, 10 yrs. in Md., Colo., and N.Y.; entered Unitarian ministry, 1881; pastor Providence, R.I., 1881-90, Buffalo, N.Y., 1890-97, Ch. of All Souls, New York, 1897—. Author: Doctrine of the Unity of God in the First Three Centuries, 1893; The Great Affirmations of Religion, 1900; The Power and Promise of the Liberal Faith, 1900; One World at a Time, 1902; Shelley—An Appreciation, 1904; The Way to Happiness, 1907; From Poet to Premier, Centennial of 1909. Home: New York, N.Y. Died May 29, 1916.

SLIFER, Hiram Joseph, civil engr.; b. Colmar, Pa., Oct. 12, 1857; s. John and Lydia (Huttel) S.; grad. in course of mining and civ. engring., Polytechnic Coll. of Pa., 1876; m. Mary A. Beatty, Oct. 11, 1882. Engaged as rodman, leveler, and transitman, Mexican Nat. Constrn. Co., 1879-82; asst. engr. Phila. div. Pa. R.R., 1882-91; prin. asst. engr. Milwaukee, West Shore & Western Ry., 1891-93; div. engr. Ashland div., C.&N.W. Ry., at Kaukauna, Wis., 1893-97; successively div. engr., engr. of 2d track in Iowa, and supt. Ia. div., same rd., 1897-1902; gen. supt. eastern dist., C.,R.I.&P. R.R., 1902-03, central dist., 1903-05; steam ry. expert and business mgr. constrn. dept., J. G. White & Co., New York, 1905-07; gen. mgr. Panama R.R. & S.S. Lines, at Colon, Panama, 1907-09; gen. mgr. C.G.W. Ry., 1909-12. Mason. Commd. lt. col. 21st Engrs. and with A.E.F. in France. Home: Chicago, Ill. Died Feb. 3, 1919.

SLINGERLAND, Mark Vernon, asst. prof. econ. entomology, Cornell Univ., Jan. 3, 1899—; b. Otto, N.Y., Oct. 3, 1864; s. Jacob A. and Mary (Ballard) S.; grad. Cornell, B.S., 1892; m. Effie B. Earll, Sept. 10, 1891. Asst. entomologist, staff of Agrl. Expt. Sta., Cornell, 1889—. Has published many bulletins on injurious insects. Home: Ithaca, N.Y. Died 1909.

SLOAN, Edwin P., surgeon; b. Neosho, Mo., Feb. 13, 1878; s. George S. and Hannah O. (Plummer) S.; grad. high sch., Neosho, 1893; M.D., Univ. Med. Coll., Kansas City, Mo., 1898; post-grad. work, Chicago Polyclinic, N.Y. Post-Grad. Med. Sch., U. of Berlin; m. Dec. 23, 1899 (wife died 1908); children—George E., Howard P., Ralph E.; m. 2d, Mary A. Bell, Oct. 25, 1916. Practiced Danvers, Ill., 1898-1903; settled in Bloomington, Ill., 1905; specialized in goiter and stomach surgery; mem. Sloan, Deneen & Sloan, diagnosis and abdominal and goiter surgery; surgeon-in-chief, Sloan Clinic, Bloomington, Ill. Pres. advisory bd. Ill. State Bd. of Health. Presbyn. Mason. Home: Bloomington, Ill. Died Sept. 13, 1935.

SLOAN, George Beale, banker; b. Oswego, N.Y., June 20, 1831; s. James S.; ed. pub. schs.; entered mercantile life at early age; later was partner in various firms until 1864, when he, with Theodore Irwin, established grain and flour commn. firm of Irwin & Sloan; that firm retired from business in 1884; then pres. 2d Nat. Bank, Oswego, and dir. in bds. of trustees of several mfg. cos. Was mem. N.Y. assembly, 1874, 1876, 1877, 1879 (speaker, 1877); State senator, 1886-91, and chmn. finance com. during entire term of service. Presidential elector, 1896. Republican. Was one of the commrs. for State of New York at World's Columbian Commn., 1892-93. Home: Oswego, N.Y. Died 1904.

SLOAN, Richard E., governor; b. Preble Co., O., June 22, 1857; s. Dr. Richard and Mary (Caldwell) S.; A.B., Monmouth Coll., 1877, A.M., 1889; LL.B., Cincinnati Law Sch., 1884; LL.D., Monmouth, 1906, U. of Arizona, 1925; m. Mary Brown, Nov. 22, 1887 (died 1921); children—Eleanor B., Richard E. (dec.), Mrs. Mary C. Wilbur. Practiced at Phoenix and Florence, Ariz., 1884-89; mem. territorial council, 1888-89; asso. justice Supreme Ct., 1889-94 and

1897-1909; gov. of Ariz., 1909-12. Republican. Home: Phoenix, Ariz. Died Dec. 14, 1933.

SLOAN, Samuel, capitalist; b. in Ireland, Dec. 25, 1817; grad. Columbia Coll. Grammar Sch., 1831; entered ry. service, Dec. 1854; dir., 1854-55, pres., 1855-65, Hudson River R.R.; commr. for trunk lines, 1865-67; dir., 1864-67, pres., 1867-99, Delaware, Lackawanna & Western; pres. for several yrs. of about 16 smaller railroads; v.p. Nat. City Bank; chmn. bd. mgrs. Del., Lackawanna & Western R.R. Co.; dir. Bank of the Metropolis, Western Union Telegraph Co., Tex. & Pacific Ry. Co., etc. Served 1 term in State senate, N.Y. Republican. Home: New York, N.Y. Died 1907.

SLOAN, Samuel; b. Garrison, N.Y., Oct. 3, 1864; s. Samuel and Margaret (Elmendorf) S.; B.A., Columbia, 1887; m. Katharine S. Colt, 1888. Began with Farmer's Loan & Trust Co., 1887, v.p., 1907-30, then dir. City Bank Farmers Trust Co.; pres. and dir. Cayuga & Susquehanna R.R., Naols Corp.; dir. D.L.&W. R.R., Atlanta & Charlotte Air Line, N.Y. Lackawanna & Western R.R., Nat. City Bank of New York, etc.; trustee and v.p. Seaman's Bank for Savings; trustee Atlantic Mut. Ins. Co.; chmn. trustees Y.M.C.A. Republican. Mem. Ref. Dutch Ch. Home: Garrison, N.Y. Died Nov. 26, 1939.

SLOANE, Alfred Baldwin, composer; b. Baltimore, Aug. 28, 1872; s. Francis James and Emma (Baldwin) S.; ed. pvt. tutors and pub. schs.; m. Mae Auwerda, Feb. 15, 1900. Composer of music, 1890—, including music of "Jack and the Beanstalk," "Excelsior, Jr.," music of many of late Charles Hoyt's farces, "Sergeant Kitty," "The Mocking Bird," Lillian Russell's "Lady Teazle" (comic opera founded on Sheridan's "School for Scandal"), "Mama's Papa," "All Around Chicago," "The Gingerbread Man," "Coming Thro' The Rye," etc. Pres. Composers' Pub. Co.; v.p. Authors' and Composers' Pub. Co. Episcopalian. Home: New York, N.Y. Died Feb. 21, 1924.

SLOANE, Charles Swift, geographer; b. Ashland, Pa., July 7, 1859; s. Thomas J. and Mary (Swift) S.; B.S., Dartmouth, 1880; m. Christine Engebretson, Oct. 1885. Sec. U.S. Geog. Bd., Apr. 6, 1904—; apptd. geographer 13th Census, July 2, 1909. Home: Washington, D.C. Died Nov. 3, 1923.

SLOANE, John, merchant; b. Edinburgh, Scotland, Mar. 14, 1834; s. William and Euphemia S.; ed. in schs. of New York; m. Adela Berry, Nov. 20, 1867. Engaged in mercantile business, Feb. 15, 1849—; pres. W. & J. Sloane, carpet mchts.; mem. W. & J. Sloane & Co., San Francisco; dir. Equitable Life Assurance Soc. of U.S., Bank of the Manhattan Co., 2d Nat. Bank, Hudson Trust Co., New Amsterdam Gas Co., and other corps. Presbyn. Republican. Home: New York City, and Lenox, Mass. Died 1905.

SLOANE, Thomas Morrison, lawyer; b. Sandusky, O., July 28, 1854; s. Rush Richard and Sarah E. (Morrison) S.; attended Episcopal Acad. of Conn., 1869; grad. Phillips Exeter Acad., Exeter, N.H., 1873; A.B., Harvard, 1877; LL.B., Law Sch., U. of Mich., 1880; m. Sarah Maria Carswell Cooke, June 22, 1881. Practiced, Sandusky, O., 1880—; pres. City Council, 2 terms; probate judge, Erie Co., O., Feb. 1906-Feb. 9, 1917 (now serving 3d term); mem. Sch. Bd., Sandusky. Mem. Ohio N.G. 12 yrs., serving last 7 yrs. as adj. 16th Regt. Democrat. Episcopalian. Mem. bd. trustees, and chancellor Diocese of Ohio; deputy to Gen. Conv. P.E. Ch. V.p. Firelands Hist. Soc. Mason. Home: Sandusky, O. Deceased.

SLOANE, T(homas) O'Conor, scientific expert; b. New York, Nov. 24, 1851; s. Christian S. and Eliza M. (O'Conor) S.; A.B., St. Francis Xavier Coll., 1869, A.M., 1873, LL.D., 1912; E.M., Columbia, 1872, Ph.D., 1876; m. Isabel X. Mitchel, Sept. 18, 1877; 1 son, T(homas) O'Conor; m. 2d, Alice M. Eyre, of Dublin, Ireland, Apr. 16, 1884; children—Charles O'Conor, John Eyre, Alice Mary. Prof. natural sciences, Seton Hall Coll., S. Orange, N.J., 1888-89; has given many scientific lectures and acted as expert in many lawsuits about patents. Invented Self-Recording Photometer, first instrument that ever recorded mechanically on an index card the illuminating power of gas. Described in 1877 new process for determining sulphur in illuminating gas, which was found on exhaustive trial to be scientifically accurate. Has been on editorial staff of Plumber and Sanitary Engineer, Scientific American, Youth's Companion, Everyday Engring., Practical Electrics, and mng. editor The Experimenter; editor Amazing Stories. Mem. adv. bd. N.Y. Electrical Sch. Mem. State Bd. Edn., N.J., 1905-11. Author: Home Experiments in Science, 1888; Rubber Hand Stamps and the Manipulation of India Rubber, 1891; Arithmetic of Electricity, 1891; Electricity Simplified, 1891; Standard Electrical Dictionary, 1892; Electric Toy Making for Amateurs, 1892; How to Become a Successful Electrician, 1894; Liquid Air and the Liquefaction of Gases, 1899; The Electrician's Handy Book, 1905; Elementary Electrical Calculations, 1909; Motion Picture Projection, 1921; Rapid Arithmetic, 1922. Compiler: Facts Worth Knowing, 1890. Translator: Electric Light (Alglave & Boulard), 1884; Jörgensen's Life of St. Francis of Assisi. Home: South Orange, N.J. Died Aug. 7, 1940.

SLOANE, William, merchant; b. New York, Feb. 18, 1873; s. John and Adela (Berry) S.; grad. Cutler Sch., New York, 1891; B.A., Yale, 1895; m. Frances Church Crocker, Nov. 22, 1904. Pres. W. & J. Sloane, Inc., floor coverings and furniture; v.p. Nairn Linoleum Co., Kearny, N.J.; trustee U.S. Trust Co.; dir. Manhattan Co.; trustee Bank for Savings, Provident Loan Soc. Mem. Squadron A, N.G.N.Y., disch., Dec. 2, 1901. Trustee Robert Coll., Constantinople. Trustee and sec. N.Y. Pub. Library; mem. Internat. Com. Y.M.C.A.; pres. and mgr. Presbyn. Hosp. (New York); chmn. Nat. War Work Council Y.M.C.A.; dir. Burke Foundation. Vestryman St. Mark's P.E. Ch., Mt. Kisco, N.Y. Home: Mt. Kisco, N.Y., and New York, N.Y. Died Aug. 11, 1922.

SLOANE, William A., judge; b. Rockford, Ill., Oct. 10, 1854; s. Hampton P. and Adeline (Grand-Girard) S.; A.B., Grinnell (Ia.) Coll., 1877; m. Annie B. Kimball, May 1, 1882; children—Harrison G., Paul Edward, Hazel Hortense. Admitted to Mo. bar, 1878; practiced in Sedalia; editor Eagle-Times, Sedalia, 2 yrs.; mng. editor Daily Banner, Carthage, Mo., 4 yrs.; removed to San Diego, Calif., 1886, and reëntered practice of law; judge Municipal Court, San Diego, 1888-92; judge Superior Court of Calif. for San Diego Co., 1911-18; asso. justice Calif. Court of Appeal, 1918; asso. justice Supreme Court of Calif., 1918-23 (retired); mem. Sloane & Sloane, 1923-29; apptd. presiding justice 4th Dist. Court of Appeal, Sept. 1929. An organizer of Prog. movement in Calif., 1912, and mem. Prog. State Exec. Com., 1911-12. Dir. and mem. exec. bd. Panama-Calif. Expn., 1915. Conglist. Home: San Diego, Calif. Died Apr. 21, 1930.

SLOANE, William Milligan, univ. prof.; b. Richmond, O., Nov. 12, 1850; s. Rev. James Renwick and Margaret (Milligan) S.; A.B., Columbia, 1868, L.H.D., 1887; Ph.D., Leipzig, 1876; A.M., Princeton, 1896; LL.D., Rutgers, 1898, Princeton, 1903; m. Mary Espy Johnston, Dec. 27, 1877; children—Mary Renwick (Mrs. Joseph L. Delafield), James Renwick, Francis Johnston, Margaret Milligan (Mrs. Benson B. Sloan). Taught Newell Sch., 1868-72; sec. to George Bancroft, the historian, in Berlin, 1873-75; prof. Princeton, 1876-96; Seth Low prof. history, Columbia, 1896—. Editor Princeton Review, 1886-89. Officer Legion of Honor, France and Swedish North Star. President Am. Acad. Arts and Letters; pres. Am. Hist. Assn., 1911; pres. Nat. Inst. Arts and Letters. Author: Life and Work of James Renwick Wilson Sloane (his father), 1888; The French War and the Revolution, 1893; Life of James McCosh, 1896; Napoleon Bonaparte, a History (4 vols.); French Revolution and Religious Reform, 1901; Parteiherrschaft in Amerika, 1913; The Balkans, a Laboratory of History, 1914; Party Government in the United States of America, 1914; The Powers and Aims of Western Democracy, 1919; Greater France in Morocco, 1924. Home: Princeton, N.J. Died Sept. 11, 1928.

SLOCTEMEYER, Hugo Ferdinand, dir. vocations; b. Cincinnati, May 22, 1884; s. John Frederick and Mary Elizabeth (Vogt) S.; student St. Xavier Coll., Cincinnati, 1900-02, LL.D., 1931; A.B., St. Louis U., 1904, A.M., 1908, M.S., 1910. Instr. mathematics, Marquette Acad., Milwaukee, 1906-07; instr. physics and mathematics, St. John's Coll., Toledo, O., 1910-14; prof. physics, U. of Detroit, 1918-19, St. Louis U., 1920-30; pres. St. Ignatius Coll., Chicago, 1930-31, Xavier U., Cincinnati, 1931-35. Mem. St. Louis U. Geol. expdns., 1910, 11, 13, 15, dir. expdn., 1915. Mem. Soc. of Jesus; founder Jesuit Edn. Assn., 1921. Catholic. Home: Milford, Ohio. Died Feb. 7, 1937.

SLOCUM, Arthur Gaylord, educator; b. Steuben, N.Y., Oct. 10, 1847; s. Henry and Sally R. S.; A.B., U. of Rochester, 1874, A.M., 1877 (LL.D., 1892); m. Mary M. Calvert, July 1875. Prin. Collegiate Inst., Rochester, 1874-75, Riverside Collegiate Inst., Wellsville, N.Y., 1875-76; supt. pub. schs. and prin. Free Acad., Corning, N.Y., 1876-92; became pres. Kalamazoo Coll., Mich., 1892 (resigned). Home: Rochester, N.Y. Died Oct. 18, 1924.

SLOCUM, Charles Elihu, physician, surgeon; b. Northville, N.Y., Dec. 30, 1841; s. Capt. Caleb Wright and Elizabeth (Bass) S.; acad. edn.; chemistry and mineralogy, U. of Mich.; M.D., Coll. Phys. and Surg. (Columbia), 1869; M.D., Jefferson Med. Coll., 1876; Ph.D., U. of Pa., 1877; studied in Vienna, 1879; (LL.D., Defiance Coll., 1903); m. Sophia B. Craver, M.D., Apr. 5, 1900. Prof. psychology and ethics Cleveland Coll. Phys. and Surg., 1896-1900; prof. chemistry, 1900-01, biology and geology, 1902-11, Defiance Coll. (prof. emeritus); pres. The Slocum Pub. Co., from Sept. 15, 1909. Founder Charles Elihu Slocum Library, Ohio Wesleyan U., and reference library with scientific and hist. collections, Defiance Pub. Library. Author: A History of the Slocums, Slocumbs and Slocombs of America, Genealogical and Biographical, Vol. I, 1882, Vol. II, 1908; History of the Maumee River Basin, 1905; Frances Slocum, the Captive, 1906; History of the Ohio Country Between the Years 1783-1815, 1909; Life and Services Maj. Gen. Henry W. Slocum, 1913, etc. Home: Toledo, O. Died June 7, 1915.

SLOCUM, Clarence Rice, consul; b. Brooklyn, June 22, 1868; s. Henry Warner and Clara (Rice) S.; A.B., Williams Coll., 1893; m. Anne Louise Boyle, Apr. 26, 1893. Am. consul at Warsaw, 1903-05, at Weimar, 1905-06; consul gen. at Boma, 1906-07; consul at Zittau, 1907-08, at Fiume, June 10, 1908—. Home: New York, N.Y. Died Feb. 25, 1912.

SLOCUM, Herbert Jermain, army officer; b. in Ohio, Apr. 25, 1855; grad. U.S. Mil. Acad., 1876, Inf. and Cav. Sch., 1883. Commd. 2d lt. 25th Inf., June 21, 1876; trans. to 7th Cav., July 28, 1876; 1st lt., Sept. 22, 1883; capt., Aug. 26, 1896; maj. insp. gen. vols., May 12, 1898; hon. disch. vols., May 12, 1899; q.m. U.S.A., July 25, 1902; maj. 1st Cav., Aug. 26, 1903; trans. to 2d Cav., Oct. 16, 1903, to 7th Cav., Feb. 26, 1908; lt. col. of cav., Mar. 3, 1911; col., Aug. 2, 1912; assigned to 13th Cav., Sept. 1, 1914; duty on Mexican border, 1916-17. Died Mar. 29, 1928.

SLOCUM, Thomas Williams, merchant; b. Boston, Mass., Jan. 26, 1867; s. William Henry and Sarah Elizabeth (Williams) S.; grad. Roxbury Latin Sch., 1886; A.B., Harvard, 1890; unmarried. In employ Lyman Mills, Holyoke, Mass., 1891-94; became connected with Minot Hooper & Co., dry goods commission, New York, 1894, member of the firm, 1896—; pres. Minot Hooper & Co., Inc., dir. Virginia Hot Springs Co.; trustee Greenwich Savings Bank (New York); dir. Technicolor. Decorated Chevalier Order of the Crown (Belgium). Director of hearings War Trade Bd. and U.S. Shipping Bd., Washington, 1917-18. Pres. Downtown Dry Goods Assn. of N.Y. City; overseer, Harvard Univ., 1914-20, and 1923-29; trustee for life of Roxbury Latin School. Pres. Associated Harvard Clubs, 1909-10. Republican. Unitarian. Home: New York, N.Y. Died June 24, 1937.

SLOCUM, William Frederick, coll. pres.; b. Grafton, Mass., July 29, 1851; s. William F. (lawyer) and Margaret (Tinker) S.; A.B., Amherst, 1874; studied Germany, 1874-75; B.D., Andover Theol. Sem., 1878; LL.D., Amherst, 1893, U. of Neb., 1894, Illinois Coll., 1904, Harvard, 1912, and Colorado Coll., 1917; D.D., Beloit Coll., 1901; m. Mary Goodale Montgomery, July 29, 1880. Ordained Congl. ministry, 1878; pastor, Amesbury, Mass., 1878-83, First Ch., Baltimore, 1883-88; pres. and head prof. philosophy, Colo. Coll., Sept. 1, 1888-Oct. 1, 1917 (pres. emeritus); mem. staff and of exec. com. League to Enforce Peace, 1917—. Organizer, and pres. 5 yrs., State Bd. Charities and Corrections of Colo., also pres. State Bd. of Pardons, Colo. Mem. Carnegie Foundation Advancement of Teaching, 1907-17 (chmn. bd. 1914-17); mem. Hague Peace Congress, 1913. Home: Newton Center, Mass. Died May 1, 1934.

SLOPER, Andrew Jackson, banker; b. Southington, Conn., July 14, 1849; s. Lambert E. and Emma (Barnes) S.; grad. high sch., New Britain, Conn., 1865; m. Ella B. Thomson, Oct. 8, 1873; children—Harold T., William T., Kenneth T.; m. 2d, Myra Wilcox, Sept. 30, 1911; 1 son, Erwin W. Dry goods clk., 1865-66; discount clk., 1867-68, teller, 1868-73, asst. cashier, 1873-85, cashier, 1885-95, pres., 1895—, New Britain Nat. Bank; pres. and treas. New Britain Gas Light Co. Pres. New Britain Inst. (pub. library); dir. Y.M.C.A. of New Britain. Has served as councilman, alderman, sewer commr. and police commr.; state senator, 1901; chmn. Bd. of Park Commrs., Bd. of Cemetery Commrs. Republican. Baptist. Mason. Home: New Britain, Conn. Died June 2, 1933.

SLOSSON, Annie Trumbull, author; b. Stonington, Conn., May 18, 1838; d. Gurdon and Sarah A. Trumbull; ed. Hartford, Conn.; m. Edward Slosson, June 27, 1867 (dec.). Writer short stories; also naturalist, especially interested in entomology and botany. Patron Am. Mus. Natural History and present to same of 35,000 specimens of insects, 1925. Author: China Hunters' Club, 1878; Fishin' Jimmy, 1889; Seven Dreamers, 1891; The Heresy of Mehetable Clark, 1892; Dumb Foxglove, 1898; Story-tell Lib, 1900; White Christopher, 1901; Aunt Abby's Neighbors, 1902; Simples from the Master's Garden, 1907; A Dissatisfied Soul, 1908; A Local Colorist, 1912; A Little Shepherd of Bethlehem, 1913; Puzzled Souls, 1915; And Other Folks, 1918. Died Oct. 4, 1926.

SLOSSON, Edwin Emery, editor; b. Albany, Kan., June 7, 1865; s. William B. and Louise (Lilly) S.; B.S., U. of Kan., 1890, M.S., 1892; Ph.D., U. of Chicago, 1902; m. May Preston (Ph.D., Cornell), Aug. 12, 1891; children—Preston, Alfred (dec.). Prof. chemistry, U. of Wyo., and chemist, Wyo. Agrl. Expt. Sta., 1891-1903; lit. editor The Independent, 1903-20. Asso., Columbia Sch. of Journalism, 1912-20; dir. of Science Service. Author: Great American Universities, 1910; Major Prophets of Today, 1914; Six Major Prophets, 1917; Creative Chemistry, 1919; Easy Lessons in Einstein, 1920; The American Spirit in Education, 1921; Plots and Personalities, 1922; Chats on Science, 1923; Sermons of a Chemist, 1925. Home: Washington, D.C. Died Oct. 15, 1929.

SLUSS, Homer Oscar, educator; b. Louisville, O., July 16, 1871; s. William McLaughlin and Catherine Brandt (Youtz) S.; grad. Western Reserve Acad., Hudson, 1891; A.B., Western Reserve U., 1895; studied summer, Harvard, 1905; M.A., Columbia, 1925; m. Rose Eloise Rankins, Aug. 19, 1913; children—Jane, William. Teacher Greek and German, Western Reserve Acad., 1895-1903, Dummer Acad., South Byfield, Mass., 1903-04; prin. high sch., Covington, Ky., 1904-07; supt. pub. schs., Covington, 1907-17; prin. Western Reserve Acad., 1917-24; instr. history, Hughes High Sch., Cincinnati, O., 1925—. Mem. Bd. Teachers' Examiners, Ky., 1910-12. Conglist. Home: Covington, Ky. Died June 7, 1929.

SLUTER, George, Presbyn. clergyman; b. St. Louis, Mo., May 5, 1837; s. Frederick Ludwig and Dorothy (Krafts) S.; grad. Westminster Coll., 1860; Princeton Theol. Sem., 1863. Pastor Rensselaer, Mo., 1863-65; Webster St. Ch., St. Louis, 1865-70; First Ch., Duluth, Minn., 1870-71; First Ch., Shelbyville, Ind., 1871-81; First Ch., Arlington, N.J., 1881-93. Was sec. missions Southern Presbyn. Synod of Mo.; asso. editor Missouri Presbyterian. New York corr. Cincinnati Herald and Presbyter. Sec. Presbyn. Ministers' Assn. of New York and vicinity, 1885-1900. Author: Instruction of the Deaf and Dumb, 1868; Values of a Religious Literature, 1874; A Eulogy of Masonry, 1878; Historical and Critical Essay Acta Pilati, 1879; The Religion of Politics, 1880; Life of Emperor Tiberius, 1881; Family Religion, 1883; Walking with God, 1884. Home: Stirling, N.J. Died 1909.

SLY, William James, prof. religious edn.; b. London, Eng., May 18, 1867; s. David C. and Susan Ann (Morse) S.; came to U.S., 1880; B.A., U. of Rochester, 1892, M.A., 1895; grad. Rochester Theol. Sem., 1895; Ph.D., Denver U., 1914; m. Grace Pierson Taintor, Sept. 1, 1896. Ordained Bapt. ministry, 1895; pastor Third Ch., Kansas City, Kan., 1895-99, 1st Ch., Springfield, O., 1899-1907, Garfield Park, Ch., Chicago, 1907-10, Delta, Colo., 1910-11; dir. religious edn. of Bapt. denomination for Colorado, at Denver, Colo., 1911-15; dir. same for Conn., 1915-19 and of New Americans for Am. Bapt. Publ. Soc., Phila., 1919-22; specialist in religious edn. for Inter Ch. World Movement, New York, Mar.-June 1921; first prof. religious edn., Linfield Coll., McMinnville, Ore., 1922-29; dist. supt. for N.E., Edn. Extension Service and pastor Third Bapt. Ch., Norwich, Conn., 1929-35; peace edn. lecturer in churches, colls., high schools, 1935—; mem. Conn. Bapt. State Conv. Bd., 1932-35. Author: World Stories Retold, 1914; More World Stories Retold, 1937. Parish minister of Metropolitan Presbyn. Church, Washington, D.C. Home: Avon, N.Y., and Washington, D.C. Died Jan. 24, 1940.

SMALL, Albion Woodbury, university dean; b. Buckfield, Me., May 11, 1854; s. Rev. Albion K. P. and Thankful (Woodbury) S.; A.B., Colby, 1876, A.M., 1879; Newton Theol. Instn., 1876-79; univs. of Berlin and Leipzig, 1879-81; Ph.D., Johns Hopkins, 1889; (LL.D., Colby, 1900); m. Valeria von Massow, of Berlin, June 20, 1881. Prof. history and polit. economy, Colby Coll., 1881-88; reader in history, Johns Hopkins, 1888-89; pres. Colby Coll., 1889-92; prof. and head dept. sociology, 1892—, dean Grad. Sch. Arts and Lit., 1905—, U. of Chicago. Editor Am. Jour. of Sociology, 1895—. V.p. and Lit., 1905-1923, U. of Chicago. Editor Arts and Sciences, St. Louis Expn., 1904. Author: General Sociology, 1905; Adam Smith and Modern Sociology, 1907; The Cameralists, 1909; The Meaning of Social Science, 1910; Between Eras, from Capitalism to Democracy, 1913. Died Mar. 25, 1926.

SMALL, Elden, author; b. Marshall, Mich., July 22, 1876; s. Harry L. and Mary (Pattee) S.; ed. Valparaiso U. and Northern Ind. Law Sch.; m. Florence Kingsley, 1901. Began as reporter Valparaiso (Ind.) Messenger, 1894; became connected with South Bend Morning Post, 1894, Indianapolis Sentinel, 1903; feature writer and dramatic critic Detroit Times, 1904-07; reporter and dramatic critic Detroit News, 1907-09; asst. mng. editor Detroit Evening Journal, 1909-11; dramatic and music editor, 1920-23; syndicate writer, 1917-27; feature writer Detroit Free Press, 1923-25; lecturer journalism, Adrian Coll., 1926. Mem. Ind. Ho. of Rep., 1901-03; mem. Bd. of Edn., Detroit, 1911-15. Mem. Internat. League of Press Clubs (internat. v.p., 1908-16). Republican. Unitarian. Mason. Author: At the Court of Bohemia, 1903; Little Sermons, 1917; Songs at Twilight, 1919; The Singing Woman, 1925; The Story of Detroit Commandery No. 1, K.T., and the Old Guard, 1932. Editor The Loyalist (monthly Masonic mag.); editor and pub. Metropolitan Search Light (monthly). Home: Detroit, Mich. Deceased.

SMALL, John Kunkel, botanist; b. Harrisburg, Pa., Jan. 31, 1869; s. George H. and Catharine K. S.; A.B., Franklin and Marshall Coll., 1892, Sc.D., 1912; Ph.D., Columbia Univ., 1895; m. Elizabeth Wheeler, 1896; children—George Kunkel, Kathryn Wheeler, Elizabeth, John Wheeler. Curator, Herbarium of Columbia U., 1895-99; spl. agt. Ga. Geol. Survey, 1895; curator, Herbarium of New York Bot. Garden, 1898-1906, head curator, 1906-32, chief research asso. and curator, 1932—. Author: A Monograph of the North American Species of the Genus Polygonum, 1895; Flora of the Southeastern States, 1903, 2d edition, 1913; Flora of Miami, 1913; Flora of Lancaster County, 1913; Florida Trees, 1913; Flora of the Florida Keys, 1913; Shrubs of Florida, 1913; Ferns of Tropical Florida, 1918; Ferns of Royal Palm Hammock, 1918; From Eden to Sahara—Florida's Tragedy, 1929; Ferns of Florida, 1932; Manual of Southeastern Flora, 1932; Ferns of Vicinity of New York (illustrated), 1935. Interested in bot. exploration of southeastern U.S., the interpretation and classification of its flora and its phytogeography, with special reference to its native palms, irises, flowering epiphytes, cacti, and ferns. Home: New York, N.Y. Died Jan. 20, 1938.

SMALL, Len(nington), governor; b. Kankakee, Ill., June 16, 1862; s. Abram Lennington (M.D.) and Calista (Currier) S.; ed. pub. schs., normal sch. and business coll.; m. Ida Moore, Nov. 21, 1883 (died 1922); children—Budd L., Leslie C., May (Mrs. A. E. Inglesh). Farmer; sec. Kankakee Interstate Fair many years; formerly mem. Bd. Supervisors Kankakee County, clk. Circuit Court; pres. bd. trustees Kankakee State Hosp.; pres. First Trust & Savings Bank, Kankakee. Mem. Ill. State Senate 1 term; state treas., 1905-07 and 1917-19; asst. treas. in charge U.S. Sub-treasury at Chicago, under President Taft; elected gov. of Ill. for term 1921-25; reëlected, 1924, for term 1925-29; defeated for renomination, 1928, renominated, Apr. 1932. Republican. Home: Kankakee. Ill. Died May 17, 1936.

SMALL, Robert Scott, banker; b. Charleston, S.C., May 20, 1891; s. James H. and Charlotte C. (Whaley) S.; ed. pub. schs.; m. Louise Johnson, 1914. Began in employ Bank of Charleston, Nov. 23, 1906, pres., May 15, 1923—; pres. S.C. Security Co., S.C. Savings Bank, The S.C. Co.; vice-pres. Savannah Fire Ins. Co.; dir. Southern Home Ins. Co., Equitable Fire Ins. Co. of Charleston, Gen. Asbestos and Rubber Co., Cameron and Barkley Co., First Carolinas Joint Stock Land Bank (Columbia, S.C.), Raybestos Co. (Bridgeport, Conn.), Raleigh and Charleston Ry. Co., Williamson Mills Co., Central R.R. of S.C. Trustee Coll. of Charleston, Porter Acad. Presbyn. Home: Charleston, S.C. Died Feb. 20, 1931.

SMALL, Sam(uel) (White), journalist; b. Knoxville, Tenn., July 3, 1851; s. Alexander Benson and Elizabeth Jane (White) S.; A.B., Emory and Henry Coll., Va., 1871, A.M., 1887; Ph.D., Taylor U., Upland, Ind., 1894; D.D., Ohio Northern U., 1894; m. Annie I. Arnold, 1873 (died 1915); children—Sam W., Robert Toombs. Stenographer and newspaper reporter; sec. President Andrew Johnson during his post-presidential political campaigns; on the editorial staff of Atlanta Constitution, 1875—, and now its editorial writer. Official reporter, Georgia Constl. Conv., 1877; sec. Am. Commn. to Paris Expn., 1878; com. reporter U.S. Senate, 1879-81; was founder the Norfolk (Va.) Daily Pilot, later founded Daily Oklahoman, Oklahoma City, Okla. Entered evangelistic work at Atlanta, Ga., Sept. 15, 1885; associated in many campaigns with Sam Jones, later alone, and as reform lecturer. Reserve soldier C.S.A., Jan. 19-Apr. 20, 1865; lt. col. and a.d.c. Ga. N.G.; capt. and chaplain 3d U.S. Vol. Engrs., Spanish-Am. War in Cuba, 1898-99. Chaplain in chief Naval and Mil. Order Spanish-Am. War. Democrat. Methodist. Mason, Odd Fellow, K.P., Red Man. Author: Old Si's Savings, 1886; Pleas for Prohibition, 1889; The White Angel of the World, 1891. Home: Livingston Heights, Va. Died Nov. 21, 1931.

SMALLEY, Bradley Barlow, lawyer; b. Jericho, Vt., Nov. 26, 1835; s. Judge David A. and Laura (Barlow) S.; common school edn. at Burlington, Vt.; academic edn., Browington, Vt., and at Chambly, P.Q., Canada. Has long been mem. of the Nat. Dem. Com., and at one time was its sec. Clerk U.S. Circuit and Dist. courts for the Dist. of Vt., from Jan. 1, 1861, to July 1, 1885; U.S. commr., 1861-96; collector of customs, Dist. of Vt., from Sept. 1885-89, and from Sept. 1, 1893, to Oct. 1, 1897; commr. World's Columbian Expn. from Vt. Pres. at various times of the Montpelier & White River R.R. Co., the Ogdensburg & Lake Champlain R.R. Co., and the Montreal & Province R.R. Co.; now pres. Burlington Trust Co. Home: Burlington, Vt. Died 1909.

SMALLEY, Eugene Virgil, journalist; b. Randolph, O., July 18, 1841; ed. in Ohio and N.Y. public schools and N.Y. Central Coll., McGrawsville; m. Josephine M. Conday, 1873. Served in 7th Ohio inf. during Civil war; corr. and editorial writer New York Tribune, 1871-82; now editor Northwest Magazine, St. Paul, Minn., and sec. Nat. Sound Money League, Chicago. Author: A History of the Republican Party; Political History of Minnesota; etc. Home: St. Paul, Minn. Died 1899.

SMALLEY, Frank, coll. dean; b. Towanda, Pa., Dec. 10, 1846; s. Isaac and Sarah (Compton) S.; student Northwestern U., 1870-71; A.B., Syracuse U., 1874, A.M., 1876, Ph.D. (in Latin), 1891; LL.D., Colgate U., 1909, Union U., 1909; m. Jennie Mather, Sept. 7, 1876; children—Frank Mather, Carrie Elizabeth (dec.). Instr. geology, zoölogy and botany, 1874-77, adj. prof. Latin, 1877-81, prof. Latin lang. and lit., 1881-93, Gardner Baker prof. same, 1893-1924, registrar, 1894-1900, lecturer on Roman law, Coll. of Law, 1895-1902, dean Coll. of Liberal Arts, 1900-17, acting chancellor, summer 1903 and year 1908-09, and vice chancellor emeritus, 1917—, historian of the university, 1924—, all Syracuse U. Mem. Archæol. Inst. America, Am. School Classical Studies in Rome, Italy (mng. com.). Republican. Methodist. Author: Analysis and Formation of Latin Words, 1879; Latin Verse, 1884; Introduction and Notes to Fifth Book of Cicero's Tusculan Disputations, 1892, 1894; Brief Selections to Illustrate Roman Literature, 1894; Libretto, "Plauti Trinummus," 1895; Syllabus of Lectures in Roman History, 1895. Editor: Alumni Record and General Catalogue of Syracuse University, Vols. I-IV, 1899-1923; The Golden Jubilee, Syracuse University, 1870-1920. Home: Syracuse, N.Y. Died Apr. 3, 1931.

SMALLEY, George Washburn, American corr. London Times, July 1895—; b. Franklin, Mass., June 2, 1833; s. Rev. E. and Louisa (Washburn) S.; grad. Yale, 1853 (A.M.); Harvard Law School, 1855; practiced law in Boston, 1856-61. In Civil war, 1861-62, war corr. New York Tribune; organized European Bureau, New York Tribune, 1866-67; in charge of its European corr. until 1895; spl. U.S. commr. at Paris Expn., 1878. Author: London Letters, 1890; Studies of Men, 1895. Died Apr. 4, 1916.

SMALLEY, Harrison Standish, political economist; b. Chicago, Ill., Apr. 18, 1878; s. Joseph Henry and Jennie (Buffum) S.; A.B., Univ. of Mich., 1900, Ph.D., 1903; spl. student in law, same, 1903-06; fellow in polit. economy and finance, Cornell U., 1901-02; m. Winifred Ernestine, d. Prof. Wooster W. Beman, of Ann Arbor, Mich., Sept. 12, 1905. Asst. in polit. economy, 1902-03, instr., 1903-07, asst. prof., 1907-11, prof., 1911—, U. of Mich. Vice-pres. Mich. Acad. of Science, 1910—. Co-author: State Regulation of Railways, 1903. Author: Railroad Rate Control in Its Legal Aspects, 1906; Transportation in the United States, 1910. Asso. editor Mill Supplies, 1911—. Home: Ann Arbor, Mich. Died Sept. 23, 1912.

SMART, Charles, soldier, physician; b. Aberdeen, Scotland, Sept. 18, 1841, s. Alexander and Anne (Kelman) S.; ed. Keith, Banffshire and Marischal Coll.; grad. Univ. of Aberdeen, M.B., C.M., 1862; m. Dora, d. Dr. John Purcell, New York, 1869. Came to U.S., 1862; enlisted as asst. surgeon, 63d N.Y. vols., 1862; served with Army of Potomac, 1863-64; apptd. asst. surgeon, U.S.A., Mar. 30, 1864; btvd. capt., Dec. 2, 1864, for meritorious services in the field being the 1st asst. surgeon in U.S.A. to receive the honor; capt., 1866; maj., 1882; later lt. col., and col., Feb. 2, 1902—; served various stas. after Civil War; now asst. surgeon gen. U.S.A. Author: (novel) Driven from the Path, 1872; Handbook for Hospital Corps, U.S.A., 1898. Home: Washington, D.C. Died 1905.

SMART, Frank Leroy, supt. of schs.; b. Iberia, O., Oct. 1, 1862; s. James Taylor and Lydia Ann (Boyer) S.; A.B., Northern Ind. Normal Sch., Valparaiso, 1889; A.B., Harvard, 1896; student U. of Chicago, 1900; m. Martha Foster, Dec. 22, 1890; children—Robert Leroy, Dorothy Hathaway (Mrs. John C. Blied). Teacher various village schs., Ill., Tex., Ariz., 1882-93; prin. high schs., Dubuque, Ia., 1896-1900 and 1902-06, Winnetka, Ill., 1900-01, Davenport, Ia., 1906-07; supt. city schs., Davenport, 1907—. Democrat. Unitarian. Rotarian. Home: Davenport, Ia. Deceased.

SMART, George Thomas, clergyman, educator; b. Leicester, Eng., Sept. 21, 1863; s. Stephen and Emma (Smith) S.; came to U.S., 1881; A.B., Harvard, 1895; (D.D., Middlebury Coll., 1900); m. Charlotte Hurlburt, of Yarmouth, N.S., Aug. 22, 1888; children—Stephen Bruce, Paul Hurlburt. Ordained Congl. ministry, 1888; pastor West Pawlet, Vt., 1888-89, West Rupert, Vt., 1889-91, Manchester, Vt., 1894-1902, Newton Highlands, Mass., 1902-21. Lecturer upon English lit., philosophy and art, 1895—; lecturer, Andover Theol. Sem., 1921, Middlebury Coll. Sch. of English, 1921; studied art in Europe 1923-24; acting pres. Wheaton Coll., 1925-26. Author: Studies in Conduct, 1905; The Mystery of Peace, 1909; The Golden Bond, 1909; If I Should Meet the Master, 1910; The Temper of the American People, 1912. Trustee Wheaton Coll. Home: Noroton, Conn. Died Mar. 13, 1928.

SMART, James Henry, pres. Purdue Univ., 1883—, b. Center Harbor, N.H., June 30, 1841; academic edn.; (A.M., Dartmouth; LL.D., Univ. of Ind.). Taught in Concord, N.H., 1858, and in other New England schools until 1861; then taught in Toledo, O., public schools, and in 1865 became supt. schools, Ft. Wayne, Ind.; m. Mary H., dau. Prof. Swan, Grinnell Coll., Iowa, July 21, 1870. Member Ind. State bd. of edn. 27 years; thrice State supt. of public instruction; trustee State Univ., 1883; 6 years trustee State Normal School. Asst. commr. of Ind. to Vienna Expn., 1872; U.S. commr. to Paris Expn., 1878; commr. from U.S. Dept. of Agr. to Agrl. Congress at The Hague, 1891. Pres. Ind. Teachers' Assn., 1871, Nat. Ednl. Assn., 1880; Am. Assn. of Agrl. Colleges and Experiment Stations, 1890. Author: An Ideal School System for a State; The Institute System for the United States; Commentary on the School Laws

Republican. Soc. of Friends. Trustee Vassar Coll., of Indiana; The Schools of Indiana; Books and Reading for the Young, etc. Home: Lafayette, Ind. Died 1900.

SMEDLEY, William Thomas, artist; b. in Chester Co., Pa., Mar. 26, 1858; s. Peter and Amy A. S. (Quaker parentage); pub. sch. edn.; entered a newspaper office at 15; studied engraving in Phila. and art in Pa. Acad. Fine Arts; went to New York, 1878, and later to Paris; studied under Jean Paul Laurens; opened studio, New York, 1880; has since been actively engaged as illustrator for Harper's and other standard periodicals; m. May Rutter Darling, 1892. In 1882 engaged by pubs. of Picturesque Canada to travel with Marquis of Lorne through West and Northwest Canada and illustrate the work; later made several sketching tours in U.S. and in 1890 around the world; exhibited Paris Salon, 1888. Principal productions are: "An Indiscreet Question"; "A Thanksgiving Dinner"; "A Summer Occupation." N.A., 1905. Home: New York, N.Y. Died Mar. 26, 1920.

SMILEY, Albert Keith, educator, humanitarian; b. Vassalboro, Me., Mar. 17, 1828; s. Daniel and Phoebe (Howland) S.; A.B., Haverford Coll., Pa., 1849, A.M., 1859; (hon. A.M., Brown U., 1875; LL.D., Haverford, 1906); m. Eliza Phelps Cornell, July 8, 1857. Instr. Haverford Coll., 1848-53; joint founder, with twin brother, and prin. English and Classical Acad., Phila., 1853-57; prin. Oak Grove Sem., Vassalboro, Me., 1858, 1859, Friends' Boarding Sch. (now Moses Brown Sch.), Providence, R.I., 1860-79. In 1869 purchased property at Lake Mohonk, Ulster Co., N.Y., which by subsequent additions now contains 5,500 acres, and built a hotel (summer resort), 1870. The estate is laid out as a private park, has more than fifty miles of roads, 25 miles of paths and trails, and is open to the public. Mem. Bd. of U.S. Indian Commrs., 1879—. Each autumn from 1882, upwards of 200 persons have been invited as his personal guests for 4 days to discuss the Indian question; from 1904 the question of other dependent peoples (Philippines, Puerto Rico and Hawaii) has been included. Each spring, from 1894, a similar conf. has been called in the interest of internat. arbitration; to this upwards of 300 personal guests are invited for 4 days. In 1889 he purchased jointly with his twin brother, Alfred Homans S., large property in Redlands, Calif., for use as winter residence (became sole owner when bro. died in 1903). This property, Canon Crest Park (popularly called Smiley Heights), is visited yearly by many thousands of tourists. In 1898 he presented to the City of Redlands, Calif., a public library and adjoining park at a cost of $60,000, and in 1906 enlarged the library by adding wing costing $11,000. Men. bd. trustees Brown U., 1875; mem. original bd. trustees Bryn Mawr Coll.; pres. bd. trustees N.Y. State Normal Sch., New Paltz, N.Y., from its establishment, 1884. Mem. many societies and orgns. (An entrance gateway and keeper's lodge which cost over $19,000, located at the main entrance of Lake Mohonk estate, was presented Mr. and Mrs. Smiley, on July 8, 1907, the 50th anniversary of their marriage, by 1,400 guests of Lake Mohonk Mountain House as a testimonial of their esteem). Home: Mohonk Lake, N.Y. Died Feb. 2, 1912.

SMILEY, Charles Wesley, researcher; b. Fitchburg, Mass., Sept. 10, 1846; s. Charles Milton and Elmira Lydia Mitchell (Peirce) S.; M.Ac., Eastman Nat. Business Coll., 1867; A.B., Wesleyan U., Conn., 1874, A.M., 1877; spl. student and asst. librarian, Drew Theol. Sem., Madison, N.J., 1874-75; traveled and studied in Europe, summers, 1901, 1902, 1905 and 1906; m. 1890, divorced, 1898. Teacher in Hackettstown Collegiate Inst., 1875-76, Drew Female Sem., 1876-77; edited Berean Sunday School Lessons, 1875-77, biog. catalogue of Psi Upsilon fraternity, 1877-79; spl. agt. 9th Census, 1879-91; editor for U.S. Fish Commn., 1881-89; spl. agt. 10th Census in charge fishery statistics, 1889-91; editor and pub. Am. Monthly Microscopical Journal, 1887-1902, The Microscope, 1895-98, Occult Truths, 1899-1902; editor Wesleyan U. Alumni Record, 1888; edited 6 reports and 3 annual bulls. U.S. Fish Commn.; asso. editor The Fishing Industries of the U.S., 1879-89. Republican. Platonist. Prin. work consists of original researches in Greek philosophy and rendering of N.T. Greek, 1902-09. Author: La Petite Géographie de San Francisco, 1913; Occult Expositions of the N.T., 1915. Died Apr. 12, 1926.

SMILEY, Daniel, humanitarian; b. Vassalboro, Me., Nov. 29, 1855; s. Daniel and Dorcas Burnham (Hanson) S.; A.B., Haverford Coll., Pa., 1878; m. Effie Newell, June 18, 1881; children—Albert Keith, Hugh, Francis Gerow, Ruth (Mrs. Thomas Sanborn). Instr. in Greek and Latin, William Penn Charter Sch., Phila., 1878-81; joined brother, the late Albert K. Smiley, in management of property at Lake Mohonk, N.Y., succeeding, 1912, to ownership of Lake Mohonk estate, and Cañon Crest Park, Redlands, Calif. Associated in management from the beginning, 1882, now in sole charge, Conf. on Internat. Arbitration, and Conf. of Friends of the Indians and Other Dependent Peoples, held at Lake Mohonk each

1902-22 (chmn. bd. 1920-22), Haverford Coll., New Paltz (N.Y.) State Normal Sch. (pres. bd.), U. of Redlands, Calif. Mem. exec. com. Nat. Peace Conf., New York, 1907, Chicago, 1909. Died Feb. 14, 1930.

SMILEY, Elmer Ellsworth, clergyman; b. Syracuse, N.Y., Aug. 6, 1862; s. Alpheus and Rosetta (Kathan) S.; A.B., Syracuse U., 1885; B.D., Yale, 1890, A.M., 1901; (D.D., Syracuse, 1899); m. Edith Constance House, June 17, 1891. Prin. E. Bloomfield Acad., N.Y., 1885-87; ordained Congl. ministry, 1891; pastor Pilgrim Ch., Vancouver, Wash., 1891-94, First Ch., Cheyenne, Wyo., 1894-98; chaplain of Wyo. Legislature, 1896-97; pres. U. of Wyo., 1898-1903; pastor Groton, N.Y., 1903. Home: Groton, N.Y. Died 1911.

SMILEY, William Brownlee, clergyman; b. Robinson Twp., Washington Co., Pa., Dec. 7, 1856; s. David and Elizabeth Jane (McBride) S.; A.B., Westminster Coll., New Wilmington, Pa., 1879, D.D., 1898; grad. Pittsburgh Theol. Sem., 1882; m. Margaret Fergus, June 7, 1882; children—Olive Bell (Mrs. G. A. Lewis), Thomas Fergus, Howard Brownlee, Margaret Pauline (dec.). Ordained U.P. Ministry, 1882; pastor Charities Ch., Canonsburg, Pa., 1882-1909; sec. S.S. work, U.P. Denomination, 1909-13; pastor Oneonta, N.Y., 1913-18, Rochester, Pa., 1918—. Del. U.P. Ch. to Psalmody Conv., Belfast, Ireland, 1902; moderator Gen. Assembly U.P. Ch., 1916. Mem. Bd. Publishers U.P. Ch., 1890-1909; mem. bd. dirs. Pittsburgh Theol. Sem., 1902-16; represented Gen. Assembly U.P. Ch. in the World Conf. on Faith and Order, at Lausanne, Switzerland, Aug. 1927, and made mem. continuation com. of conf. Prohibitionist. Author: Teacher Training Manual for Bible Students, 1911. Home: Rochester, Pa. Died Dec. 10, 1931.

SMILEY, William Henry, supt. emeritus pub. schs.; b. Malden, Mass., Apr. 28, 1854; s. Henry Lyman and Mina Abigail (Grover) S.; A.B., Harvard, 1877; hon. A.M., U. of Denver, 1906; Litt.D., Colo. Coll., 1913; LL.D., U. of Colorado, 1913, U. of Denver, 1914; m. Mary S. Chandler, June 26, 1884. Prin. New Salem Acad., Sept. 1877; instr. Latin and Greek, St. John's (boys') Sch., Boston, 1880; prin. Jarvis Hall, boys' sch., Denver, 1883-86; instr. Latin and Greek, Denver High Sch., dist. No. 1, 1886-92, prin., 1892-1912; supt. pub. schs., City and County of Denver, 1912-15; supervisor, high school education, same, 1915-16, asst. supt. of schools, 1917-23, supt. emeritus, 1924—. Mem. Conf. on Secondary Instrn. in Greek, U. of Mich., Dec. 1892; mem. N.E.A. (pres. dept. secondary edn.), 1895; sec. com. on coll. entrance requirements, rep. pub., 1899; v.p. dept. higher edn., 1902, dept. secondary edn., 1904); mem. com. Nat. Council Edn., of N.E.A., 1909; pres. Ednl. Council of Colo.; mem. Art Commn. City and Co. of Denver, 1906-12; pres. Colo. State Teachers' Assn., 1907; mem. Nat. Inst. Social Sciences, Denver Art Museum Assn. Trustee Colo. Sch. of Mines, 1922-27, pres. of bd., 1925—. Home: Denver, Colo. Deceased.

SMILLIE, George Frederick Cumming, picture engraver; b. N.Y. City, Nov. 22, 1854; s. George (D.D.S.) and Olivia M. (Duy) S.; ed. pub. and pvt. schs.; m. Clara M. Ward, 1878 (died 1899); m. 2d, Mrs. Lily Brandon Munroe, Apr. 6, 1901. Pupil Nat. Acad. Design, 1871; acquired profession under uncle, James Smillie (N.A.), the engraver, in Am. Bank Note Co., 1871-87; v.p. and mgr. Canada Bank Note Co., Montreal, 1887, Homer Lee Bank Note Co., New York, 1888; prin. engraver U.S. Bur. Engraving and Printing, 1894, and supt. picture engraving dept., Feb. 1918—. Engraved portraits and vignettes appearing on U.S. currency and other securities, postage and revenue stamps. Chief works: silver certificates of 1895; large official portraits of the Presidents; Kenyon Cox design, "America," "Spirit of Liberty," appearing on Liberty Bonds. Mem. exec. com. N.Y. Free Trade Club, 1884-88; foundation mem. Reform Club, 1888, Nat. Soc. Fine Arts; mem. Am. Fedn. Arts. Died 1924.

SMILLIE, George Henry, painter; b. New York, Dec. 29, 1840; s. James S. (N.A.) and Catharine (Van Valkenburgh) S.; brother of James David Smillie; studied and traveled in Europe and America; m. Nellie Sheldon Jacobs, June 28, 1881. Splty. landscapes; many of his paintings are in pub. and pvt. galleries, Am. and European. A.N.A., 1866, N.A., 1882; rec. sec. Nat. Acad. Design, 1892-1902. Home: Bronxville, N.Y. Died Nov. 10, 1921.

SMILLIE, Helen Sheldon Jacobs, painter; b. N.Y. City, Sept. 14, 1854; d. Samuel J. and Helen (Sheldon) Jacobs; studied under Joseph O. Eaton and James D. Smillie; m. George Henry Smillie, June 28, 1881; children—Sheldon, Charles Van V., Gordon Swift. Painter of genre pictures in oils and water colors. Home: Bronxville, N.Y. Died July 31, 1926.

SMILLIE, James David, artist; b. New York, Jan. 16, 1833; s. James S. (N.A.) and Catharine (Van Valkenburgh) S.; ed. academic dept., New York Univ., and private schools; studied art under his father, and at schools of Nat. Acad. of Design; m. yr. Mem. U.S. Bd. of Indian Commrs., 1912—.

May, 1881, Anna C. Cook (died 1895). Made reputation as landscape engraver before becoming painter. Asso. 1865, and academician, 1876, Nat. Acad. of Design, and its treas., 1894-99. One of founders, 1866, treas., 1866-71, and pres., 1871-77, Am. Water Color Soc.; also a founder, sec., and later pres., New York Etching Club. One of the "original fellows" of the Painter-Etcher Soc. of London, Eng. Studio: New York, N.Y. Died 1909.

SMISER, James A., lawyer; b. Helena, Ark., Feb. 22, 1862; s. James and Charlotte Page (Booker) S.; student Southwestern Presbyn. U., Clarksville, Tenn.; LL.B., Vanderbilt U., 1885; m. Mary G. Williamson, June 6, 1900. Admitted to Tenn. bar, 1885, and practiced at Columbia; county atty., Maury Co., Tenn., 1890-98; city atty., Columbia, 1898-1905; chmn. Dem. Com. for Maury Co., most of time for 10 yrs.; U.S. atty., 1st Div., Alaska, Jan. 20, 1915-Aug. 31, 1921; engaged in practice of law at Columbia. Democrat. Episcopalian. Odd Fellow, K.P. Home: Columbia, Tenn. Deceased.

SMITH, Abraham E., consul; b. Royston, Cambs, Eng., Apr. 6, 1848; s. Abraham and Mary (Millard) S.; ed. prep. sch.; came to America, 1850; m. Frances J. Rice, Feb. 26, 1869. Editor of the Woodstock (Ill.) Sentinel, 1859-65, Indianapolis (Ind.) Gazette, 1866, Rockford (Ill.) Gazette, 1869-93, Ft. Madison (Ia.) Plaindealer, 1895. Postmaster, Woodstock, 1861-65; mem. Rep. State Com., Ill., 1870-72; del. Rep. State convs., Ill., each alternate yr., 1870-90, and 1896; postmaster, Rockford, 1875-79; Am. consul at Victoria, B.C., July 1897—. Trustee U. of Ill., 1872-73; hon. Ill. commr. World's Fair, Paris, 1889; del. World's S.S. Conv., London, 1889. Methodist. Died Jan. 19, 1915.

SMITH, A(bram) Alexander, physician; b. Wantage, N.J., Mar. 25, 1847; s. James Alexander and Mary A. (Corbin) S.; A.B., Lafayette Coll., 1868, A.M., 1871; M.D., Bellevue Hosp. Med. Coll. (New York U.), 1871; (hon. A.M., Princeton, 1892; LL.D., Lafayette, 1892); m. Sue L. Bender, Dec. 24, 1873. Interne Bellevue Hosp., 1871-72; attending phys. Demilt Dispensary, 1873-79; asst. phys. and surgeon, N.Y. State Woman's Hosp., 1875-79; adj. lecturer clin. medicine, 1875-77, lecturer materia medica and therapeutics, 1879-80, prof., 1880-92, Bellevue Hosp. Med. Coll., prof. principles and practice of medicine and clin. medicine, Univ. and Bellevue Hosp. Med. Coll., 1898—. Home: New York, N.Y. Died Dec. 13, 1915.

SMITH, Albert Edwin, univ. pres.; b. New Richmond, O., Dec. 16, 1860; s. Hugo Edwin and Mary Ann (Smith) Smith; A.B., Ohio Wesleyan, 1887, Ph.D., 1897, D.D., 1907; D.D., Ohio Northern U., 1905; LL.D., 1927; m. Harriet Vergon, Oct. 26, 1887; children—Rachel V., Edwin V., Paul V., Seth V. (dec.), Harriet V., Esther V. (dec.), Benjamin V. Ordained M.E. ministry, 1887; pastor York, O., 1887-91, Celina, 1891-94, Toledo, 1894-95, Defiance, 1895-99, Marion, 1899-1905; pres. Ohio Northern U., 1905-30 (pres. emeritus). Mem. Gen. Conf. M.E. Ch. 4 times; mem. Bd. Edn. M.E. Ch. Home: Lakeside, O. Died Aug. 26, 1941.

SMITH, Albert William, chemist; b. Newark, O., Oct. 4, 1862; s. George H. and Mary (Sanborn) S.; Ph.C., U. of Mich., 1885; B.S., Case Sch. Applied Science, Cleveland, 1887; Ph.D., U. of Zürich, 1891; m. Mary Wilkinson, of Cleveland, June 5, 1890. Prof. metallurgy and chemistry, Case School Applied Science, 1891-1907, prof. metallurgy and head of dept. metall. engring., 1907-11, prof. chemistry and head of dept., 1911-27. Fellow A.A.A.S., Chem. Soc. London; mem. Am. Chem. Soc. (councillor), Franklin Inst., Am. Inst. Mining and Metall. Engrs., Am. Electrochem. Soc., Soc. Promotion Engring. Edn., Am. Inst. Chem. Engrs., Soc. Chem. Industry, French Soc. Industrial Chemists, Deutsche Chemische Gesellschaft, Phi Chi, Tau Beta Psi, Sigma Xi, Alpha Chi Zeta. Presbyterian. Clubs: University, Union. Contbr. to tech. papers. Home: Cleveland, O. Died Mar. 4, 1927.

SMITH, Alexander, chemist; b. Edinburgh, Scotland, Sept. 11, 1865; s. Alexander W. and Isabella (Carter) S.; B.Sc., U. of Edinburgh, 1886; Ph.D., U. of München, 1889; LL.D., U. of Edinburgh, Scotland, 1919; m. Sara Bowles, Feb. 16, 1905. Asst. in chemistry, U. of Edinburgh, 1889-90; prof. chemistry and mineralogy, Wabash Coll., 1890-94; asst. prof. chemistry, 1894-98, asso. prof., 1898-1903, prof. and dir. of gen. and physical chemistry, 1903-11, dean Jr. Colls., 1900-11, U. of Chicago; prof. and head of dept. chemistry, Columbia U., N.Y., 1911-July 1, 1921. Author: Lassar-Cohn Laboratory Manual of Organic Chemistry (translated), 1895; Laboratory Outline of General Chemistry, 1899 (transl. into German, Russian, Italian, Portuguese); The Teaching of Chemistry and Physics (with E. H. Hall), 1902; Introduction to General Inorganic Chemistry, 1906 (transl. into German, Russian, Italian, Portuguese); General Chemistry for Colleges, 1908; Text-book of Elementary Chemistry, 1914; Intermediate Chemistry, 1919. Home: Edinburgh, Scotland. Died Sept. 9, 1922.

SMITH, Alexander Coke, bishop of M.E. Ch., South; b. Sumter Co., S.C., Sept. 16, 1849; s. Rev. W. H. and Isabella (McLeod) S.; grad. Wofford

Coll., Spartanburg, S.C., 1872, A.M., 1874 (D.D., Erskine Coll., Due West, S.C., 1887); m. Kate Kinard, Dec. 22, 1875. Prof. mental and moral philosophy, Wofford Coll., 1886-90; prof. practical theology Vanderbilt Univ., 1890-92; resigned 1892 to return to pastorate; del. to Ecumenical Conf., Washington, 1891, and read essay on Christian Coöperation; fraternal delegate gen. conf. Methodist Ch. of Can., Toronto, Sept. 1898; del. Ecumenical Conf., London, Sept. 1901. Elected bishop at Gen. Conf., Dallas, Tex., May 1902. Home: Norfolk, Va. Died 1906.

SMITH, Alexander Wyly, lawyer; b. Habersham Co., Ga., June 24, 1861; s. Henry Lamar and Sarah Amelia (Wyly) S.; student U. of Georgia, through junior yr., 1876-78; m. Ida Kendrick, Sept. 10, 1885. Admitted to Ga. bar, 1883, and began practice at Atlanta; mem. Abbott & Smith, 1885-92, Alexander W. and Victor L. Smith, 1892-99, Smith, Hammond & Smith, 1899—. Spl. counsel to the dir. gen. of railroads, Washington, Apr. 1, 1920—. Mem. of standing coms. on railroads, tariff and federal trade of Chamber Commerce U.S.A. Maj., U.S.R. Ordnance Div. Gen. mgr. Cotton States and Internat. Expn., Atlanta, 1895. Democrat. Episcopalian. Home: Atlanta, Ga. Died Jan. 12, 1925.

SMITH, Alfred H., ry. president. Entered service of L.S.&M.S. Ry. at Cleveland, as messenger boy, 1879; served in various depts. to foreman constrn. work till 1890; continued with L.S.&M.S. Ry. until 1902, as supt. Kalamazoo div., Oct. 1890-Oct. 1891; supt. Lansing div., Oct. 1891-Feb. 1893; supt. Franklin division, at Youngstown, Ohio, Feb. 1893-July 1897; supt. Mich. div., at Toledo, O., July 1897-Apr. 1, 1901; asst. gen. supt., Apr. 1-June 17, 1901, and gen. supt., June 17, 1901-Feb. 1902, at Cleveland; with N.Y.C.&H.R. R.R., Feb. 1902—, as general supt., Feb. 1902-July 1, 1903; gen. mgr., July 1, 1903-Apr. 15, 1912, also v.p., June 1906-Apr. 15, 1912; v.p. N.Y. Central Lines east and west of Buffalo, Apr. 15, 1912-Mar. 1913; sr. v.p. in charge of operation, maintenance and constrn., Mar.-Dec. 1913, and pres. N.Y. Central Lines, Jan. 1, 1914. Apptd., Dec. 29, 1917, asst. dir. gen. of railroads in charge transportation in trunk line territory east of Chicago and north of Ohio and Potomac rivers, apptd. regional dir. of eastern dist., Jan. 18, 1918; re-elected pres. N.Y. Central Lines, June 1, 1919. Home: New York, N.Y. Died Mar. 8, 1924.

SMITH, Alfred Theodore, army officer; b. Washington, D.C., Nov. 25, 1874; s. Theodore Smith and Lydia Justine (Kilp) S.; ed. pub. and pvt. schs., Washington, D.C.; grad. army Sch. of the Line, 1915, Gen. Staff Coll., 1922, Army War Coll., 1921; m. Anne Yvonne Pike, Feb. 24, 1903. Successively pvt., corpl. and sergt., U.S.A., 1894-97; commd. 2d lt., 1897; promoted through all grades to brig. gen., May 24, 1933. Served in Santiago Campaign in Cuba, 1898, in Philippine Insurrection, 1899-1901, Philippine Samar Expdn. against bandits, 1905, Mexican border, 1912-14; mil. attaché U.S. Embassy, Buenos Aires, Argentina, 1916-19, The Hague Conf., 1919; comdg. 54th U.S. Inf., 1919-20; gen. staff, hdqrs. 3d Corps Area, 1922-26; in charge N.G. affairs, same hdqrs., 1926-28; comdg. 34th U.S. Inf., 1928-31; asst. chief of staff and chief mil. intelligence div., War Dept. Gen. Staff, 1931—. Awarded Silver Star and cited for gallantry in action at El Caney, Cuba; Comdr. Order of the Crown (Italian). Died Nov. 27, 1939.

SMITH, Allard, banking; b. Eau Claire, Wis.; s. W. H. and Catherine (Fox) S.; B.L., U. of Wis., 1900; m. Margaret E. Butt. In engring. constrn., financial and exec. positions with Bell Telephone Co., Chicago, Ohio, Ind., Ill., Mich. and Wis., 1900-14, gen. mgr., Cleveland, O., 1914-20; v.p., later exec. v.p. Citizen's Savings & Trust Co., Cleveland, merged, 1921, with Union Trust Co. Organizer and chmn. Industrial Div., Liberty Bond campaigns, Cleveland. Chmn. Federal County Highway Commn.; mem. exec. com. and vice chmn. Community Fund; chmn. com. which guaranteed opening of Cleveland Pub. Auditorium; was mem. exec. com. Civic League, Cleveland Regional Plan Com., Assn. to Promote Criminal Justice. Mem. Cleveland Chamber Commerce (pres.; dir.; chmn. industrial com.). Republican. Home: Cleveland, O. Deceased.

SMITH, Allen, brigadier gen. U.S.A.; b. Ft. Marion, St. Augustine, Fla., Apr. 21, 1849; s. Maj. Gen. Charles Ferguson (U.S.A.) and Fanny (Mactier) S.; cadet U.S. Naval Acad., 1863-66; m. Julia Stephens, July 2, 1874. Apptd. from Pa., 2d lt. 1st Inf., July 18, 1866; 1st lt., Apr. 22, 1868; capt., May 21, 1880; transferred to 4th Cav., Dec. 6, 1880; maj. 1st Cav., Nov. 21, 1897; lt. col., Feb. 2, 1901; col. 6th Cav., June 28, 1902; brig. gen. and retired at own request after 40 yrs.' service, Mar. 18, 1905. Home: Spokane, Wash. Died Oct. 30, 1927.

SMITH, Allen John, M.D.; b. York, Pa., Dec. 8, 1863; s. Gibson and Susan (Fahs) S.; A.B., Pa. Coll., 1883, A.M., 1886, Sc.D., 1910, LL.D., 1921; LL.D., McGill, 1911; M.D., U. of Pa., 1886; m. Harriet W. Brooke, 1888 (died 1896); 1 son, Gibson; m. 2d, Pearl L. Pierce, 1899. Resident phys., Phila. Hosp., 1886-87; asst. demonstrator pathology, U. of Pa., 1887-91; prof. pathology, etc., med. dept. U. of Texas, 1891-1903; prof. pathology, 1903-10, prof. comparative pathology and dir. courses in tropical medicine, 1910—, prof. pathology, 1911—, U. of Pa. Commd. maj., M.R.C., U.S.A., Apr. 11, 1917; active service, base hosps., Camp Dix, N.J., and Camp Pike, Ark., June 20, 1918-Mar. 22, 1919; lt. col., May 19, 1919. Author: Lessons and Laboratory Exercises in Bacteriology, 1902, etc. Home: St. Davids, Pa. Died Aug. 19, 1926.

SMITH, Alphonse J., bishop; b. Madison, Ind., Nov. 14, 1883; s. George J. and Mary (Dittgen) S.; A.B., St. Mary's (Kan.) Coll., 1904; D.D., North Am. Coll., Rome, Italy, 1908. Ordained priest R.C. Ch., 1908; asst. pastor S.S. Peter and Paul Cathedral, Indianapolis, 1908-21; pastor St. Joan of Arc Ch., Indianapolis, 1921-24; consecrated bishop of Nashville (Tenn.), Mar. 25, 1924. Died Dec. 16, 1935.

SMITH, Alva J., gen. passenger and ticket agt., Lake Shore & Mich. Southern Ry., March 1, 1887—; b. Churchville, Monroe Co., N.Y., Sept. 30, 1840; common school edn.; served clerk and asst. gen. passenger agt., 1866-78, gen. passenger agt., 1878-87, Cleveland, Columbus, Cincinnati & Indianapolis Ry., Indianapolis & St. Louis Ry., 1881-87, Cincinnati, Hamilton & Dayton R.R., 1881-82, Dayton & Union R.R., 1882-87. Home: Cleveland, O. Died 1906.

SMITH, Andrew Heermance, physician; b. Charlton, N.Y., Aug. 27, 1837; s. Archibald and Cornelia (Heermance) S.; ed. Ballston Spa Inst., Union Coll., A.M., Coll. Phys. and Surg., New York, M.D., 1858; univs. of Göttingen and Berlin; m. Jane T. Sheldon, 1884. Practiced medicine, 1859-61; entered army as asst. surg. 43d N.Y. vols., 1861; surg. 94th N.Y. vols., 1862; asst. surg. U.S.A., 1862-68; bvtd. maj., U.S.A., 1867. Began practice of medicine in New York in 1868. Has been physician to St. Luke's and Presbyn. hosps., and surgeon to Manhattan Eye, Ear and Throat Hosp. Now cons. physician St. Luke's, Presbyn., St. Mark's, Woman's, Post-Graduate and Ruptured and Crippled hosps.; v.p. Post-Grad. Med. Sch. and Hosp. Pres. N.Y. Acad. Medicine, 1903-04; del. to Internat. Med. Congress, Berlin, 1890, Madrid, 1903. Episcopalian. Republican. Home: New York, N.Y. Died 1910.

SMITH, Andrew Thomas, normal sch. prin.; b. nr. Norristown, Pa., Sept. 10, 1862; s. Erasmus P. and Elizabeth (Baker) S.; grad. State Normal Sch., West Chester, Pa., 1883; Pd.D., New York U., 1893; spl. student in philosophy, U. of Pa., and pedagogy with Dr. William H. Payne, of U. of Mich.; hon. A.M., Lafayette Coll., 1903; m. Elizabeth Fenton Ogden, Aug. 7, 1888. Teacher in dist. sch., Pa., 1881, Soldiers' Orphan Sch., 1883-85; prof. pedagogy, West Chester State Normal Sch., 1885-99, v.prin. last 7 yrs.; prin. Mansfield (Pa.) State Normal Sch., 1899-1913, Clarion (Pa.) Normal Sch., Jan.-July 1914, Thomas Normal Training Sch., Detroit, 1914-17; prof. pedagogy, 1917-20, prin., Apr. 26, 1920—, West Chester Normal Sch. Lecturer in teachers' institutes, 1887—. Republican. Elder Presbyn. Ch. Mason. Author: Quarto-Centennial History of West Chester State Normal School, 1896; Mind Evaluations for Teaching Purposes, 1893; Systematic Methodology, 1900. Home: West Chester, Pa. Died Feb. 8, 1928.

SMITH, Anna Tolman, specialist in edn.; b. Boston, Mass.; d. Tolman Gore and Abigail (Dyer) S.; ed. Boston High and Normal School, Albion (N.Y.) Female Sem. and under pvt. tutors; unmarried. Specialist foreign ednl. systems, U.S. Bur. of Edn., 1879—; mem. Jury of Awards, Edn., Paris Expn., 1900; same, St. Louis Expn., 1904; decorated Officier de l'Instruction publique by French Govt., 1900. Departmental editor Cyclopedia of Education. Home: Washington, D.C. Died Aug. 28, 1917.

SMITH, Archibald Cary, naval architect; b. New York, N.Y., Sept. 4, 1837; s. Rev. E. Dunlap and Jane B. (Cary) S.; ed. Univ. Grammar Sch., New York. Learned boat building trade under Robert Fish; built, 1860, the "Comet," which was champion for several yrs. Studied marine painting under Maurice F. H. de Haas, and painted pictures of many noted yachts. Built the Vindex, an iron yacht of novel design, which attracted much attention; abandoned painting and has since been engaged in designing and altering yachts and other boats, including: Schooners—Intrepid, Norma, Fortuna, Whim, Iroquois, Yampa, Lasca, Ariel, Oriole, Harbinger, Katrina, Elsemarie, Amorita, Carlotta, Helene, Vigil, Uncas, Clorita, Tekla, Laurus, Winona; sloops and yawls—Vindex, Madcap, Mischief (defended America's cup, 1887), Indolent, Meteor, Gorilla, Banshee, Cinderella, Montecito, Katona, Julnar, Polly, Vela, Sapho, Edith, Rover, Sakana, Priscilla, Myeera; steamboats—Richard Peck, City of Lowell, Chester W. Chapin, Refuge, Free Lance, pilot-boat New York, Espadon. Died 1911.

SMITH, Arthur Cosslett, lawyer, author; b. Jan. 19, 1852; s. James Cosslett (justice Supreme Court) and Emily Ward (Adams) S.; A.B., Hobart Coll., Geneva, N.Y., 1872, A.M., 1875 (L.H.D., 1905); LL.B., Columbia, 1875; m. Elizabeth Storer Atkinson, June 19, 1879. In practice, Rochester, N.Y. Episcopalian. Author: The Monk and The Dancer, 1900; The Turquoise Cup, 1903. Home: Rochester, N.Y. Died 1926.

SMITH, A(rthur) Donaldson, explorer; b. Andalusia, Pa., April 27, 1864; A.B., U. of Pa., 1885, M.D., 1889; post-grad. studies at Harvard, Johns Hopkins, and Heidelberg. Engaged in African exploration, 1890—, with scientific staff provided by British Mus.; exploration between Berbera and the Nile, and in Mongolia. Was awarded Cullum gold medal, Am. Geog. Soc.; Kane gold medal, Phila. Geog. Soc.; patron's medal by Royal Geog. Soc., London, May 21, 1902. Author: Through Unknown African Countries. Home: Kaolin, Pa. Died Feb. 18, 1939.

SMITH, Arthur George, mathematician; b. Wayne, Ia., Nov. 27, 1868; s. Charles Alvord and Margaret (Young) S.; Ph.B., State U. of Ia., 1891, M.A., 1894; grad. student Cornell U., U. of Göttingen, Germany, and Univ. of Cambridge, Eng.; m. Grace Otis Partridge, Aug. 18, 1896. Instr. in mathematics, 1893-96, asst. prof., 1896-1904; prof. mechanics and physics, 1904-09, prof. and head of dept. of mechanics, 1909-11, prof. and head dept. of mathematics and astronomy, 1911—, State U. of Iowa. Home: Iowa City, Ia. Died Nov. 5, 1916.

SMITH, Arthur Henderson, missionary; b. Vernon, Conn., July 18, 1845; s. Albert (D.D.) and Sarah Tappan (Stoddard) S.; mem. Co. B, 40th Wis. Vol. Inf., May-Sept. 1864; A.B., Beloit Coll., 1867, A.M., 1870; Andover Theol. Sem., 1867-69; Union Theol. Sem., 1869-70; Coll. Phys. and Surg., New York, 1870-71; D.D., Beloit, 1894; LL.D., Whitman, 1906; m. Emma Jane Dickinson, Sept. 8, 1871; children—Florence Dickinson (dec.), Marie Jessica (dec.), Henry Dickinson (dec.). Went to China, 1872, under A.B.C.F.M.; located at Tientsin, 1872-80; apptd. to P'ang Chuang Sta., Shantung Province, 1880; in winter of 1885-86, first acting pastor First Congl. Ch., Pasadena, Calif. Was in siege in Peking, June to Aug. 1900; acting pastor Union Ch., Tientsin, China, Oct. 1900-July 1901; missionary-at-large of A.B.C.F.M., June 1906—; Am. chmn. China Centenary Conf., 1907; one of Am. bd. delegates to World's Missionary Conf., Edinburgh, June 1910; 1st asst. moderator National Council Congl. Chs., Oct. 1910. Mem. China Continuation Committee, 1913, and of exec. com. same, 1915-18; mem. editorial bd. Chinese Recorder from formation until 1926. Author: Proverbs and Common Sayings of Chinese, 1888, 1902 (Shanghai); Chinese Characteristics, 1890 (transl. into French, German, Chinese and Japanese); Village Life in China, 1899; China in Convulsion, 1901; Rex Christus, An Outline Study of China (for United Woman's Bds. of Missions), 1903; The Uplift of China, 1907 (several English edits., also transl. into German, Danish, Norwegian, and Swedish); China and America Today, 1907. Editor (and chief author) Manual for Young Missionaries in China. Home: Claremont, Calif. Died Aug. 31, 1932.

SMITH, Augustus Wardlaw, cotton mfr.; b. Abbeville, S.C., April 29, 1862; s. Lt. Col. Augustus M. and Sarah (Wardlaw) S.; U. of the South, Sewanee, Tenn.; m. Mary Noble, Jan. 5, 1887 (dec.); m. 2d, Belle Perrin, June 5, 1901. Began as clk. in uncle's store, at Abbeville, 1881; mercantile business on own account, 1883; moved to Woodruff, S.C., 1900, Spartanburg, about 1905; organizer, 1900, Woodruff Cotton Mills; became pres. and treas. the Brandon Corp., head office at Greenville, formed by merger of Brandon Mills, Brandon Duck Mills, Painsett Mills and Woodruff Cotton Mills; also pres. and treas. Aug. W. Smith Co. (mercantile business), of Spartanburg. Col. 3d S.C. Regt., 1890-91, mayor of Abbeville, 1891-92. Democrat. Episcopalian. K.P. Home: Greenville, S.C. Died June 13, 1934.

SMITH, B. Holly, oral surgeon; b. in Prince Georges Co., Md., Mar. 17, 1858; s. Rev. Bennett Holloway and Matilda C. (Janney) S.; ed. pvt. tutors; D.D.S., Baltimore Coll. Dental Surgery, 1881; M.D., Coll. Phys. and Surg., 1883; m. Frances Gist Hopkins, June 6, 1883. Practiced, Baltimore, 1881—; has served as prof. oral surgery, Baltimore Coll. of Dental Surgery and Coll. Phys. and Surg. Mem. exec. com. Nat. Assn. Dental Faculties; chmn. Oral Hygiene Council of Md. Democrat. Conglist. Mason. Home: Baltimore, Md. Died Jan. 22, 1920.

SMITH, Barton, lawyer; b. Channahon, Ill., June 2, 1852; s. Charles Claibourne and Corinza (Burr) S.; g.s. of Barton Smith and desc. on mother's side of Burr family, Hartford, Conn., 1630; B.S., U. of Mich., 1872, LL.B., 1875; m. May Searles, Dec. 25, 1877; children—Clifford Charles (dec.), Mildred (Mrs. Maurice Allen). Mem. Smith & Geddes, Toledo, 1875-81, Baker, Smith & Baker, 1881-94, Smith & Baker, 1894-1914, Smith, Baker, Effler & Allen, 1914-20, Smith, Baker, Effler, Allen & Eastman, 1920-24, Smith, Baker, Effler and Eastman, 1925—; pres. Toledo Blade Co., 1920-26, and chmn. bd. dirs. Toledo Blade, Sept. 1926-27. Democrat. Active in politics until 1896, when was one of 5 Gold Democrats from Ohio to Dem. Nat. Conv. that nominated William J. Bryan for President. Charter mem. Toledo Museum of Art. Mason; Past Master Grand Lodge F.&A.M. of Ohio; Past Grand Comdr. Grand Commandery K.T. of Ohio; Past Thrice Potent Master of Mi-A-Mi Lodge of Perfection, Toledo; First Comdr.-in-Chief of Toledo Consistory S.P.R.S.; was del. to Conf. of

Supreme Councils of the World at Brussels, 1907, Washington, 1912 (v.p.), Lausanne, Switzerland, 1922; Most Puissant Sovereign Grand Comdr. of Supreme Council 33° of A.A.S.R. for the Northern Masonic Jurisdiction U.S.A., 1910-21. U.S. rep. on Internat. Arbitral Commn. for determination of Landreau claim against Republic of Peru, 1922. Home: Toledo, O. Died Nov. 16, 1935.

SMITH, Benjamin Eli, editor; b. Beirut, Syria, Feb. 7, 1857; s. Rev. Eli and Hetty S. (Butler) S.; A.B., Amherst, 1877, A.M., 1881 (L.H.D., 1902); m. Cora Shelton Cheesman, Oct. 13, 1883. Translated Schwegler's History of Philosophy, 1879; mng. editor, 1889-91, editor, 1894—, Century Dictionary; editor Century Cyclopedia of Names, 1894, Century Atlas, 1897, Century Dictionary Supplement (2 vols.), 1909; rev. ed. of Century Dictionary, Cyclopedia and Atlas (12 vols.), 1911; translated Cicero's De Amicitia (Lælius), 1897; edited Franklin's Poor Richard's Almanac, 1898; Selections from Marcus Aurelius, 1899, and from Epictetus, 1900, and from Pascal, 1902. Home: New Rochelle, N.Y. Died Feb. 24, 1913.

SMITH, Bolton; b. Indianapolis, Ind., July 25, 1861; s. Francis and Sarah (Bolton) S.; student, Dresden, Germany, 2 yrs.; grad. Collège de Genève, Switzerland, 1878; LL.B., Central Law Sch., Indianapolis, 1882; post-grad. work in law, summer, U. of Virginia; m. Grace Carlile, June 20, 1889; children—Louise Bolton-Smith (dec.), Carlile Bolton-Smith. Investment banking business, Memphis, 1885-1932 (retired). Vice pres. Nat. Council Boy Scouts of America; chmn. advisory com. on interracial activities, and mem. exec. com. Board of Trustees of George Peabody College for Teachers; trustee Brookings Instn. (Washington, D.C.). Democrat. Episcopalian. Mason. Author of article, A Philosophy of Race Relation (printed in Congressional Record, Dec. 1919). Home: Washington, D.C. Died Mar. 27, 1935.

SMITH, Bridges; b. Wilmington, N.C., Sept. 19, 1848; s. James Harvey and Mary Louisa (Reeves) S.; ed. Bibb Co. Acad., Macon, Ga., and in printing offices; m. Annie S. Wade, 1868; m. 2d, Katrina Goelz, 1886; m. 3d, Margaret Goelz, Apr. 10, 1919 (all of Macon). In army of C.S.A., 1861-Apr. 23, 1865; detailed to mfr. ammunition. City clk. of Macon 15 yrs., mayor 12 yrs.; judge Juvenile Court. Pres. Washington Memorial Library; sec. and treas. Price Free Library, Alexander Free Sch. Bd. Democrat. Presbyn. Adj. Ga. Div. U.C.V. Odd Fellow, K.P., Elk, Eagle, Red Man. Short story writer; conductor column, "Just Twixt Us," in Macon Daily Telegraph. Home: Macon, Ga. Died Oct. 5, 1930.

SMITH, Byron Laflin, banker; b. Saugerties, N.Y., May 9, 1853; s. Solomon Albert and Maria (Laflin) S.; U. of Chicago, 1874; m. Carrie Cornelia Stone, May 24, 1876. Began in banking business at Chicago, 1871; pres. Northern Trust Co.; dir. C.&N.W. Ry., C.,St.P.,M.&O. Ry., A.,T.&S.F. Ry., Chicago Telephone Co., Commonwealth Edison Co., Chicago. Independent Democrat. Presbyn. Home: Chicago, Ill. Died Mar. 22, 1914.

SMITH, Cameron C., steel mfr.; b. Butler Co., Pa., Apr. 24, 1861; s. Joseph and Mary Ann (Watson) S.; prep. edn., Sharpsburg (Pa.) Acad.; student Waynesburg (Pa.) Coll.; m. Maude Forsaith, May 26, 1902; 1 dau., Dorothy Forsaith (Mrs. Jay Willard Badgley). Clerk Carnegie Steel Co., 1883-93; asst. to pres., Reliance Steel Casting Co., 1893-99; organizer Union Steel Casting Co., 1899, pres., 1899-1917, chmn. bd., 1917—; treas. Duncan Land & Improvement Co. Served as business mgr. N.Y. Dist. for Ordnance and mem. War Claims Bd., World War, title of lt. col. Trustee Waynesburg Coll. Republican. Presbyn. Mason; mem. Royal Arcanum. Died May 2, 1932.

SMITH, C(harles) Alphonso, prof. English; b. Greensboro, N.C., May 28, 1864; s. Rev. J. Henry and Mary Kelly (Watson) S.; brother of Henry Louis and Egbert Watson S.; A.B., Davidson Coll., N.C., 1884, A.M., 1887; Ph.D., Johns Hopkins, 1893; (LL.D., U. of Miss., 1905, Univ. of N.C., 1913; L.H.D., U. of Cincinnati, 1916); m. Susie McGee Heck, Nov. 8, 1905. Instr. English, Johns Hopkins, 1890-93; prof. English lang. and lit., La. State U., 1893-1902; studied abroad, 1900-01; lecturer, Summer Sch. of the South, Monteagle, U. of Calif., U. of Kan., Chautauqua, Brooklyn Inst. of Arts and Sciences, etc.; prof. English, 1902-07, head English dept., 1907-09, dean grad. dept., 1903-09, U. of N.C.; Edgar Allan Poe prof. English, U. of Virginia, 1909-17; head of dept. of English, U.S. Naval Acad., 1917—. Roosevelt prof. Am. history and instns., U. of Berlin, 1910-11. Democrat. Presbyn. Author: Old English Grammar and Exercise Book, 1896; Elementary English Grammar, 1903; Studies in English Syntax, 1906; The American Short Story, 1912; What Can Literature Do for Me?, 1913; O. Henry Biography, 1916; Keynote Studies in Keynote Books of the Bible, 1919; New Words Self-Defined, 1919; Poe—How to Know Him. Editor: Selections from Huxley, 1911; Pericles, 1913; Short Stories Old and New, 1916; Selected Stories from O. Henry, 1922; Essays on Current Themes, 1923. Asso. editor World's Orators, 1901. Joint author Krüger-Smith's German Conversation Book, 1902; Smith-McMurry Language Series (3 books), 1919. Editor in chief Library of Southern Literature. Lecturer. Died June 14, 1924.

SMITH, Charles Axel, lumber mfr.; b. in Sweden, Dec. 11, 1852; came to U.S. and settled in Minneapolis, 1867; attended pub. schs. to 1871; U. of Minn., 1872-73; m. Johanna Anderson, Feb. 14, 1878. Worked while getting edn.; in business handling wheat, lumber and farm machinery in western Minn., 1878-84; in lumber business with hdqrs. at San Francisco, Calif., 1884—; pres. Pacific States Lumber Co., Coos Bay Lumber Co., Western Lumber & Mfg. Co., Compo Board Co. Republican; McKinley elector, 1896. Treas. Gen. Council Luth. Ch. in N. America, 1909-15. Col. Minn. N.G. on staff of Gov. David Clough, 1894. Regent U. of Minn., 2 terms (resigned 1913). Comdr. 2d degree Order of Vasa, conferred by King Oscar of Sweden. Home: Berkeley, Calif. Died Dec. 9, 1925.

SMITH, Charles Bennett, congressman; b. Wyoming Co., N.Y., Sept. 14, 1870; s. James and Mary (Barnes) S.; ed. country schs. and Arcade Acad., N.Y., 1884-87; m. Frances G. Stanton, of Buffalo, N.Y., June 10, 1902 (died 1931); m. 2d, Frances Elizabeth Meyer, July 1932. Reporter staff of Buffalo Courier, 1889-91; legislative corr. Buffalo Times, 1892-94; editor Buffalo Times, 1895-96; editor Buffalo Enquirer (evening) and Buffalo Courier (morning), 1897-1911; pub. and editor Niagara Falls Journal, 1910-14. Mem. and chmn. Bd. Sch. Examiners, Buffalo, 1908-11; mem. 62d Congress (1911-13), 36th N.Y. Dist., and 63d to 65th Congresses (1913-19), 41st N.Y. Dist.; became supt. of Div. of Standards and Purchases of State of New York. Democrat. Home: Albany, N.Y. Died May 21, 1939.

SMITH, Charles Blood, lawyer; b. Kendall Co., Ill., June 26, 1850; s. William and Rebecca (Blood) S.; student Cornell U., 1868-69; student law in offices of McCagg, Fuller & Culver, Chicago; m. Abigail Holt, 1876 (died 1890); children—Louise (Mrs. Eugene Sallee, dec.), Helen (wife of Dr. Forrest Loveland), Eva (Mrs. A. C. Bartell), Isabel (wife of John A. Robenson, U.S.A.); m. 2d, Miriam Redden, 1893. Mem. Rossington & Smith, 1873—, and successor to firms of Rossington, Johnston & Smith, Rossington, Smith & Dallas, Rossington, Smith & Histed and successor to the late firm of Rossington, Smith & Barnum, of Topeka. Republican. Episcopalian (lay chancellor Diocese of Kansas). Mem. bd. trustees and v.p. Christ's Hosp. Home: Topeka, Kan. Deceased.

SMITH, Charles Card, writer; b. Boston, Mar. 27, 1827; s. George and Harriet (Card) S.; ed. pub. and pvt. schools, Gloucester, Mass.; (hon. A.M., Harvard U., 1887); m. Georgiana Whittemore, Aug. 22, 1853. Sec. Boston Gas Light Co., 1853-89. Treas. Am. Unitarian Assn., 1862-71; treas. Mass. Hist. Soc., 1877-1907, and editor of publs., 1889-1907. Fellow Am. Acad. Arts and Sciences. Home: Boston, Mass. Died Mar. 20, 1918.

SMITH, Charles Dennison, physician; b. Portland, Me., Nov. 8, 1855; s. Lewis B. and Julia A. S.; A.B., Colby, 1877, A.M., 1890; M.D., Bowdoin, 1879-80 (A.M., 1895); interne Me. Gen. Hosp., 1879-80; m. Albertina M. Means, Nov. 8, 1882. In gen. practice, 1881-1902; prof. physiology, 1891-1921, Bowdoin Coll.; visiting phys., 1895-1902, supt. and resident phys., 1902—, Me. Gen. Hosp.; pres. Me. State Bd. of Health, 1892-1914. Home: Portland, Me. Died Oct. 11, 1925.

SMITH, Charles Emory, journalist; b. Mansfield, Conn., Feb. 18, 1842; s. Emory Boutelle and Arvilla Topliff (Royce) S.; removed to Albany, N.Y., with parents, 1849; grad. Union, 1861 (LL.D., Union, 1889, Lafayette, 1900, Knox, 1900, Wesleyan, 1901); m. Ella Huntley, June 30, 1863; m. 2d, Nettie Nichols, Oct. 3, 1907. Actively engaged during Civil War in raising and organizing Union vol. regt. Editor Albany Express, 1865-70, Albany Journal, 1870-80, Phila. Press, 1880—. U.S. minister to Russia, 1890-92; Postmaster Gen. U.S., Apr. 21, 1898, to Jan. 15, 1902. Chmn. com. on resolutions, Rep. State convs., 1874-80, pres. 1879. Pres. N.Y. State Press Assn., 1874; regent Univ. of State of N.Y., 1879-80; trustee Union Coll., 1881. Died 1908.

SMITH, Charles Ernest, clergyman; b. County of Cheshire, Eng.; s. W. J. and A. E. S.; B.A., with honors, Univ. Coll., Durham, 1887; hon. M.A., St. John's, Md., 1891, D.D., 1896; D.D., U. of the South, 1896; D.C.L., Bishop's Coll., Lenoxville, P.Q., 1901; m. Flora Woods, of Surrey, Eng., June 29, 1882. Deacon, 1880, priest, 1882, Angelican Ch.; asst. Harbor Grace, Newfoundland, 1880-81; rector Heart's Content, Newfoundland, 1881-89, St. Paul's Parish, Aquasco, Md., 1889-92, St. Michael and All Angels', Baltimore, 1892-1902, St. Thomas' Ch., Washington, 1902-36. Author: Old Church in New Land (2d edit.), 1894; In the Household of Faith, 1895; Call to Confirmation (8th edit.), 1895; Readings and Prayers for Communicants, 1897; Religion Under the Barons of Baltimore, 1899; Ten Years in the Parish, 1902; Altar Devotions, 1908; Another Ten Years, 1923; Under the Northern Cross, 1925. Home: Washington, D.C. Died June 2, 1939.

SMITH, Charles Forster, univ. prof.; b. Abbeville Co., S.C., June 30, 1852; s. Rev. James F. and Julia (Forster) S.; A.B., Wofford Coll., S.C., 1872; studied Harvard, 1874, univs. of Leipzig and Berlin, 1874-75, Leipzig, 1879-81, Ph.D., 1881; LL.D., U. of Ark. and Wofford Coll., 1910; m. Anna L. Du Pré, Aug. 21, 1879 (died 1893); children—Warren Du Pré, Mrs. Julia Forster Harvey, Mrs. Anna Bell Blakeman, Charles Forster, Daniel Du Pré (dec.). Prof. Classics and German, Wofford Coll., 1875-79; asst. prof. Latin and Greek, Williams Coll., Mass., 1881-82; prof. modern langs., Vanderbilt, 1882-83, prof. Greek, 1883-94; prof. Greek and Classical philology, U. of Wis., 1894-1917, prof. emeritus, 1917—. Author: Reminiscences and Sketches, 1909; Life Sketch of former President Charles Kendall Adams of the University of Wisconsin, 1925. Editor: Thucydides, Vol. VII, 1886, Vol. III, 1894, Vol. VI, 1913; Xenophon's Anabasis, 1905; Herodotus, Vol. VII, 1907. Translator: Hertzberg's Geschichte, Griechenlands, 1900; Thucydides, for Loeb Classical Library, 1919-23. Home: Racine, Wis. Died Aug. 3, 1931.

SMITH, Charles Henry ("Bill Arp"), author; b. Lawrenceville, Ga., June 15, 1826; s. A. R. and Caroline Ann (Maguire) S.; grad. Franklin Coll., Athens, Ga., 1848; studied law, 1849; m. Octavia, d. Judge Hutchins, 1849. Removed to Rome, Ga.; practiced there 27 yrs.; now lives in Cartersville. Has been writing weekly letters to Atlanta Constitution and Home and Farm of Louisville for 30 yrs.; served in C.S. army, 1861-65, becoming maj. on staff Brig. Gen. G. T. Anderson, 3d Ga. brigade. Author: Bill Arp's Letters; Bill Arp's Scrap-Book; The Farm and the Fireside; A Side Show of the Southern Side of the War; Fireside Sketches, 1890; Georgia as a Colony and State, 1733-1893, 1890. Home: Cartersville, Ga. Died 1903.

SMITH, Charles Henry, col. and bvt. maj. gen., U.S.A., retired; b. Hollis, Me., Nov. 1, 1827; s. Aaron and Sally (Gile) S.; grad. Waterville Coll. (now Colby), Me., 1856 (A.M.); taught school; studied law at Eastport, Me.; m. Mary Richards Livermore, July 28, 1864. Entered vol. service, 1861; served until 1865; capt. to bvt. maj. gen. Was in 63 battles and engagements and 3 times wounded; mustered out, Aug. 11, 1865. Admitted to bar, 1865; State senator, Me., 1866. July 28, 1866, apptd. col. 28th U.S. inf.; transferred to 19th U.S. inf., 1869; promoted to bvt. brig. gen. and bvt. maj. gen., U.S.A.; retired from active service, Nov. 1, 1891. Died 1902.

SMITH, Charles Henry, univ. prof.; b. Beirut, Syria, May 14, 1842; s. Rev. Eli and Maria Ward (Chapin) S.; A.B., Yale, 1865; (LL.D., Bowdoin, 1894); m. Sarah Elizabeth Munn. Tutor, Yale, and teacher various schs., 1865-74; prof. Bowdoin, 1874-90; prof. Am. history, Yale, 1890-1910, prof. emeritus, 1910—. Fellow Royal Hist. Society; mem. several hist. societies. Author: History of Yale University, 1898. Home: Rochester, N.Y. Died Feb. 14, 1933.

SMITH, Charles Manley, governor; b. West Rutland, Vt., Aug. 3, 1868; s. Hiram Alonzo and Ellen (Manley) S.; grad. St. Johnsbury Acad., 1887; A.B., Dartmouth Coll., 1891; m. Mary Stark, Nov. 1, 1893 (dec.); children—Dorothy (Mrs. Andrew C. Mathews), Charlotte (Mrs. Theodore Nicolet), Stark (dec.). Mem. State Senate, Vermont, 1927-31, House, 1931-32; lt. gov., 1932-34, gov. of Vt., for term ending Jan. 1937; pres. and trustee Marble Savings Bank. Dir. Vt. Children's Aid Soc.; trustee Vt. Hist. Society. Republican. Episcopalian. Mason, K.P.; mem. Grange. Home: Rutland, Vt. Died Aug. 12, 1937.

SMITH, Charles Sidney, brigadier gen. U.S.A.; b. St. Albans, Vt., Dec. 26, 1843; s. Rev. Worthington and Mary Ann (Little) S.; apptd. to U.S. Mil. Acad. from Ill., 1862, grad. 1866; m. Miss E. L. Northrop, 1891 (died 1891). Apptd. 2d lt. 4th Arty., June 18, 1866; 1st lt., July 28, 1866; transferred to ordnance dept., Nov. 1, 1874; capt., Aug. 2, 1879; maj., July 7, 1898; lt. col., Apr. 5, 1903; col., Jan. 19, 1905; brig. gen., Oct. 9, 1907; retired Dec. 26, 1907. Died Nov. 9, 1922.

SMITH, Charles Spencer, bishop; b. Colborne, Can., Mar. 16, 1852; s. Nehemiah Henry and Catherine S.; ed. in pub. schs. of Can.; M.D., Meharry Med. Coll., Nashville, Tenn., 1880; (D.D., Wilberforce U., also Victoria Coll., Can., 1911; LL.D., Wilberforce, 1913); m. Katie Josephine Black, Mar. 1876; m. 2d, Christine Shoecraft, Dec. 31, 1888. Ordained ministry A.M.E. Ch., 1872; mem. Ala. Ho. of Rep., 1874-76; founded, Aug. 11, 1882, sec. and treas, 1882-1900, S.S. Union A.M.E. Ch.; visited W. and S.W. coast of Africa, 1894; elected bishop, May 1900; presiding bishop A.M.E. Ch. in Mich., Can., and West Indies. Author: Glimpses of Africa, West and Southwest Coast, 1895. Home: East Detroit, Mich. Died Feb. 1, 1923.

SMITH, Charles Sprague, educator, lecturer, writer; b. Andover, Mass., Apr. 27, 1853; s. Charles and Caroline L. (Sprague) S.; ed. Amherst Coll., 1870-75, Berlin, Paris, Rome, Madrid, Oxford, Scandinavia, 1875-80; m. Isabelle J. Dwight, 1884. Prof. modern langs. and foreign lit., 1880-91, Columbia Univ., lecturer from 1887. Organizer, 1895, and pres. Comparative Literature Soc.; organizer, 1897, and mng. director The People's Inst.; mem. Com. of 15, 1901. Author: Barbizon Days, 1902; Working With the People, 1904. Home: New York, N.Y. Died 1910.

SMITH, Charles Stewart, merchant; b. Exeter, N.H., Mar. 2, 1832; s. Rev. John and Esther Mary (Woodruff) S.; ed. country schs. until 15 yrs. old; m. Eliza Bradish (died 1863); m. 2d, Henrietta H. Caswell; m. 3d, Anna Walton Brown. Went to New York at age of 15, becoming boy in wholesale dry goods store, and in 1863 became partner in dry goods firm of S. B. Chittenden & Co. and for several years their European buyer. Later one of founders of the dry goods commn. house of George C. Richardson & Co., later George C. Richardson, Smith & Co., and Smith, Hogg & Garden, retiring, 1887. Was for 7 yrs. pres. New York Chamber of Commerce; declined nomination as mayor of New York which he was urged by Com. of 70 to accept, 1894; became chmn. exec. com. of 70, which overthrew Tammany, and chmn. com. of Chamber of Commerce that instigated police investigation which resulted in election of Mayor Strong, 1894; also chmn. Citizens Union Exec. Com. that conducted Seth Low campaign of 1897. One of founders of 5th Av. Nat. Bank; dir. German Am. Ins. Co., U.S. Trust Co., 4th Nat. Bank, Merchants Bank, Presbyn. Hosp., Greenwich Savings Bank. Home: New York, N.Y. Died 1909.

SMITH, Charles Sumner, mining man; b. Lincoln, Mass., Dec. 19, 1857; s. Francis and Abigail (Baker) S.; ed. Phillips Acad., Andover, Mass.; m. Mary Isabel Smyth, Mar. 6, 1888. Farmer for many yrs.; came into prominence, 1902, through suit in relation to sale of the Old Dominion Copper Mining & Smelting Co., resulting in verdict in favor of stockholders, of $2,000,000 (largest damages ever awarded up to that time in Mass. court); pres. Arizona Commercial Mining Co., Old Dominion Co.; chmn. Abington Textile Machinery Trustees. Mem. Mass. Senate, 1917, 18, 19; mem. Gov.'s Council, 5 yrs.; chmn. Bd. of Selectmen of Lincoln, Mass., 20 yrs. Republican. Conglist. Home: Lincoln, Mass. Died Aug. 28, 1927.

SMITH, Charles Theodore, banker, nurseryman, farmer; b. Wildwood, Ga., June 12, 1865; s. Philip and Mary Jane (Basden) S.; ed. common schs. and by spl. study; m. Effie Richter, Dec. 1, 1892; 1 son, Charles Richter. Associated with brother, J. H. Smith, in establishing Concord Nurseries, 1887, of which is pres. and gen. mgr.; pres. Concord Banking Co., 1903—. Mem. County Bd. of Edn., 1898-1922; mayor of city of Concord, 3 terms. Mem. Southern Nurserymen's Assn. (pres. 3 terms), Country Bankers' Assn. (pres. 1916, 17, 18); Ga. Hort. Soc. (pres. 1936, 37). Democrat. Mem. Christian (Disciples) Ch.; pres. Dist. Mission Bd., 12 terms. Home: Concord, Ga. Died Apr. 24, 1939.

SMITH, Charles Wenham, organist, composer; b. London, Eng., Dec. 25, 1851; s. Charles and Margaret (Fitzgerald) S.; studied under Sir George Elvey, E. Hopkins, Meyer Lutz and Charles Steggall; m. Eliza Street, of Sussex, Eng., Aug. 8, 1876. Organist parish ch., Banstead, Surrey, Eng., 1866-68, Holy Trinity Ch., Barnes, Surrey, 1868-70, St. Patrick's Cathedral, Newark, N.J., 1880-85, First Bapt. Ch., Brooklyn, 1885-86, St. James R.C. Ch., N.Y. City, 1886-88, 1890-92, Plymouth Ch., Brooklyn, 1888-90; organist and choir master First Presbyn. Ch., Elizabeth, N.J., 1892—; organist, Temple B'nai Jeshuran, Newark, N.J. Condr. Newark Opera Co., 1892-95. Composer: Mass in G, 1877; Mass in F, 1879; also anthems, part songs, songs, piano and organ works. Home: Newark, N.J. Died Sept. 6, 1920.

SMITH, Charles William, bishop; b. Fayette Co., Pa., Jan. 30, 1840; s. Rev. Wesley and Mary E. (Ford) S.; ed. various schs. but did not grad.; (hon. M.A., Allegheny Coll., 1872; D.D., Scio Coll., 1879; LL.D., Mt. Union Coll.); m. Caroline L. Lindley, Dec. 5, 1865. Ordained M.E. ministry, 1859; pastor various chs. in and nr. Pittsburgh, Pa., 1859-79; presiding elder Pittsburgh Dist., 1880-84; editor Pittsburgh Christian Advocate, 1884-1908; bishop M.E. Ch., May 1908—. Trustee Woman's Coll. (Baltimore), Puget Sound U. (Wash.). Eight times a mem. Gen. Conf. M.E. Ch.; mem. Centennial Conf., Baltimore, 1884, Ecumenical Conf., Washington, 1891, London, 1901, Toronto, 1911; mem. and v.-chmn. commn. to revise constitution of the ch., 1896-1900; mem. commn. which compiled joint hymnal of M.E. Ch. and M.E. Ch., S.; mem. joint commn. on unification of Japan Methodism by which members of these chs. in Japan were organized into an independent ch.—the Methodist Church of Japan. Republican. Died Oct. 31, 1914.

SMITH, Chauncey Wayland, State supt. pub. instrn.; b. New York, N.Y., Aug. 10, 1885; s. Reuben and Cora (Philbrook) S.; grad. Kimball Union Acad., Meriden, N.H., 1903; B.A., Dartmouth, 1907; post grad. study, summer sessions U. of Mont., U. of Utah, U. of Wash., U. of Calif.; m. Harriett Burnett, Feb. 24, 1922. Began as teacher, Bright, Wash., 1907; served successively as prin. or supt. schs. at Ephrata and Startup, Wash., Neihart, Mont., and Tonopah, Virginia City, Fallon (deputy state supt.), Elko, Hawthorne, Ely (deputy state supt.), and Eureka, Nev.; elected State supt. pub. instrn., Nev., term 1935-39. Chmn. bd. Nev. Orphans Home; mem. bd. Nev. Pub. Health. Mem. state com. of Nat. Youth Adminstrn., Nev. Professional Engring. Assn. (mem. advisory bd.), Nev. Ednl. Assn. (v.p. 1932-34), State Bd. of Edn., N.E.A. Democrat. Mason; mem. O.E.S. Editorial corr. N.Y. Sunday Times. Home: Carson City, Nev. Deceased.

SMITH, Clarence James, newspaperman; b. Easton, Pa., July 29, 1874; s. John Jackson and Sue (Bonstein) S.; grad. high sch., Easton, 1891; m. Edith Clappison, Apr. 30, 1906; children—Jack Clappison, Clarence James. Reporter Easton Daily Argus, 1893-1904, editor, 1904-10; city editor Allentown (Pa.) Morning Call, 1910-19, owner, v.p. and mng. editor, 1920-34; now connected with Pa. Power & Light Co.; founder and pub., 1919, Allentown Morning Herald. Served as 1st sergt. Pa. Inf., Spanish-Am. War, capt. and regtl. q.m., 1912-17; capt. on Mexican border, 1916; organizer 103d Am. Train, 28th Div., A.E.F., serving as maj. inf. in France, 1918-19; lt. col. inf., Pa. N.G., 1920-23; col. C.A., 1923—. Mem. Pa. Editorial Assn. (pres.), Interstate Circulation Mgrs. Assn. (pres.), Allentown Chamber Commerce (pres.). Republican. Episcopalian. Odd Fellow, Elk. Home: Allentown, Pa. Died Aug. 28, 1940.

SMITH, Clay, musician, composer; b. Bainbridge, Ind., Aug. 6, 1876; studied music with pvt. teachers; m. Coyla M. Spring (soprano), May 8, 1915. Began on cornet at 14 later taking up trombone and saxophone; has traveled widely as soloist with leading bands and orchestras, and various musical orgns. and in extension work of univs. of Wis., Minn. and Kan.; was trombone soloist and asst. dir. Liberati Band; mgr. Smith-Spring-Holmes Orchestral Quintet. Mason. Composer of numerous songs, best known being "Sorter Miss You"; also band and orchestra selections, instrumental solos and duets for various instruments—about 200 published compositions. Writer on musical subjects. Home: Chicago, Ill. Died July 18, 1930.

SMITH, Clement Lawrence, prof. Latin Harvard Univ., 1883-1904; b. Upper Darby, Pa., April 13, 1844; s. George and Mary (Lewis) S.; grad. Haverford Coll., Pa., 1860 (A.M., 1863; hon. LL.D., 1888); grad. Harvard, A.B., 1863; m. Emma G. Griscom, Aug. 25, 1870. Asst. prof. classics and mathematics, Haverford Coll., 1863-65; student Univ. of Göttingen, 1865-66; traveling in Greece and Italy, 1866-67; prof. Greek and German, Swarthmore Coll., Pa., 1869-70; tutor Latin, Harvard, 1870-73; asst. prof. Latin, 1873-83; dean of Harvard Coll., 1882-91; dean faculty arts and sciences, Harvard, 1898-1902. Dir. Am. Sch. of Classical Studies, Rome, 1897-98; pres. Am. Philol. Assn., 1898-99. Editor: Odes and Epodes of Horace, 1894. Home: Cambridge, Mass. Died 1909.

SMITH, Clinton De Witt, agriculturist; b. Trumansburg, N.Y., Mar. 7, 1854; s. Reuben S. and Clarissa G. (Pease) S.; B.S., Cornell, 1873, M.S., 1875; m. Anna Cora Smith, June 16, 1892. Prize capt. cadets, Cornell, 1873; comdt. Star Mil. Inst., New York, 1879; practiced law, Trumansburg, 1888-90; asst. agriculturist, Cornell U., 1890, Ark. Expt. Sta., 1891; dir. expt. sta. and prof. dairy husbandry, U. of Minn., 1891-93; prof. agr. and dir. expt. sta., 1893-1900, dir. expt. sta. and dean of special courses, 1900-08, Mich. Agrl. Coll.; pres. Escola Agricola ("Luiz de Queiroz"), Piracicaba, Sao Paulo, Brazil, 1908-13; in extension work, Cornell U., 1913—. Owner and mgr. of farm. Apptd. dean of Coll. of Agr., U. of Ill., 1897; elected pres. N.M. Agrl. Coll., 1902. Originated spl. courses and built dairy bldgs., both at U. of Minn. and Mich. Agrl. Coll. Baptist. Republican. Mem. teaching staff, Extension Div. Cornell U., and farmer at Trumansburg, N.Y. Home: Trumansburg, N.Y. Died Aug. 4, 1916.

SMITH, Clyde Harold, congressman; b. Harmony, Me., June 9, 1876; s. Willard F. and Angie (Bartlette) S.; ed. rural schs. and Hartland (Me.) Acad.; m. Margaret Chase, May 14, 1930. Supt. schs., Hartland, Me., 1903-04; selectman, Hartland, 1904-07; sheriff Somerset Co., 1905-09; mem. Me. Ho. of Reps., 1899-1903, 1919-23; selectman, Skowhegan, 1914-27; 1928-32; state senator, 1923-29; chmn. State Highway, 1926-30; mem. Gov's. Council, 1932-36; mem. 75th and 76th Congresses (1937-41), 2d Me. Dist., pres. Steward Goodwin Co., Bangor, Me. Chmn. bd. trustees Reformatory for Women, 1916-26. Republican. Odd Fellow. Home: Skowhegan, Me. Deceased.

SMITH, Daniel Appleton White, missionary; b. Waterville, Me., June 18, 1840; s. Samuel Francis (author of "My Country 'Tis of Thee") and Mary (White) S.; A.B., Harvard, 1859; grad. Newton Theol. Instn., 1863; (D.D., Bapt. Union Theol. Sem. (now Div. Sch. U. of Chicago), 1883); m. Sarah Lincoln Stevens, Aug. 19, 1863. Ordained Bapt. ministry, July 26, 1863; missionary, 1863—; pres. Karen Theol. Sem., Insein, Burma, 1876-1916 (pres. emeritus). Editor the Morning Star, a Karen monthly, 1868—. Author: (in Karen) Principles of Logic, 1883; Sermonizing and Preaching, 1904; (in English) Sketch of the Life of Edward Abiel Stevens, 1886; Sound Principles of Interpretation, 1902. Translator: Wayland's Moral Science, 1885; annotations of the Annotated Para Bible of the London Religious Tract Society, 1887, 2d edit. revised and enlarged, completed 1913. Home: Insein, Burma. Died Dec. 12, 1921.

SMITH, David Morton, publishing agent; b. Knoxville, Tenn., Oct. 14, 1854; s. Jeremiah Ramsey and Thurza (Young) S.; ed. pub. schs. and business coll.; m. Virginia Cunnyngham, Dec. 9, 1879. In charge gen. office of Thompson Bros. & Kelley, Nashville, 1875-88; business mgr. Methodist Pub. House, 1888-90; elected pub. agt. by Gen. Conf. M.E. Ch., S., May 1890, and reelected every 4 yrs. until elected agt. emeritus, 1922. Mem. M.E. Ch., S. Home: Nashville, Tenn. Died Aug. 2, 1931.

SMITH, David Thomas, lawyer; b. Hardin Co., Ky., Nov. 12, 1840; s. George W. and Hannah (Ashcraft) S.; ed. pub. schs., and acads.; M.D., U. of Louisville, 1870; m. Katherine Baird, 1875; 2d, Anna Stallard Penick, 1884. Prin. male dept. Los Angeles (Calif.) pub. sch., 1864-65; practiced medicine, 1870-1903; admitted to bar, 1881, and engaged in law practice, 1903—. Coroner and health officer Jefferson Parish, La., 1881-84; asso. editor Am. Practitioner and News, 1885-89; lecturer on med. jurisprudence and hygiene, U. of Louisville. Author: Obstetric Problems, 1892; The Philosophy of Memory and Other Essays, 1899; Vibration and Life, 1912; Essays in Physics and Philosophy, 1912. Home: Louisville, Ky. Deceased.

SMITH, Dean Tyler, surgeon; b. Portland, Mich., Sept. 9, 1860; s. John E. (M.D.) and Amelia J. (Tyler) S.; B.S., U. of Neb., 1887; M.D., Chicago Homœ. Med. Coll., 1889; student New York Post-Grad. Coll., 1894, Johns Hopkins Med. Coll., 1900; m. Ella A. Snook, Jan. 17, 1894. Prof. surgery and clin. surgery, U. of Mich. Homœ. Coll., 1901—. Republican. Baptist. Author: Before and After Surgical Operations, 1906. Home: Ann Arbor, Mich. Died Jan. 30, 1933.

SMITH, Delavan, journalist; b. Cincinnati, Dec. 28, 1861; s. William Henry and Emeline (Reynolds) S.; ed. Lake Forest (Ill.) Acad., Lake Forest Coll. and Mass. Inst. Tech., unmarried. Pub. Indianapolis News; v.p. Oliver Typewriter Co. Presbyterian. Independent. Republican. Home: Lake Forest, Ill., and Indianapolis, Ind. Died Aug. 25, 1922.

SMITH, E. Otis, urologist; b. Rushville, Ind., Feb. 2, 1871; s. George W. and Josephine (Payne) S.; student Valparaiso Normal Sch., 1887-88, De Pauw U., 1888-93; M.D., Med. Coll. of Ohio, Cincinnati, O., 1896; m. Eugenia Bradley, Sept. 4, 1901; children—Elizabeth Lucille, Bradley Haddon, Eugenia Josephine. Practiced at Cincinnati, 1897—; prof. urology, U. of Cincinnati, 1908-33 (emeritus); dir. urol. service Cincinnati Gen. Hosp. Democrat. Methodist. Contbr. chapters to Regional Surgery (by Binnie), 1915. Home: Cincinnati, O. Died Dec. 26, 1934.

SMITH, Edgar, playwright, librettist; b. Brooklyn, N.Y., Dec. 9, 1857; s. Edgar M. and Amanda (McPhail) S.; ed. Pa. Mil. Academy, Chester; m. Nanette B. Nixon, Nov. 5, 1895. Actor various New York cos., 1878-86; librettist and occasional actor with New York Casino Co., 1886-92; writer of Weber and Fields' extravaganzas and burlesques, 1896-1904. Republican. Episcopalian. Mason, Elk. Writer and adapter of upwards of 160 plays, travesties, burlesques, musical comedies and operas, among them (adaptations) Nadjy, Grande Duchesse, Madelon, Poor Jonathan, The Brigands, The Peasant Girl, Alone at Last, The Girl from Paris, The Girl Behind the Counter, The Girl from Brazil, etc.; (original) Spider and Fly, Pousse Café, Catherine, Barbara Fidgety, Tillie's Nightmare, Old Dutch, The Mimic World, The Sun Dodgers, Hands Up, Robinson Crusoe, Jr., The Blue Paradise, Oh What a Girl, Home Sweet Home, Hotel Topsy Turvy, Dream City, Up and Down Broadway, Mr. Hamlet of Broadway, Step This Way, Hello Alexander, Red Pepper, The Merry World, etc. Co-Author: Peggy Ann. Home: Elmhurst, L.I., N.Y. Died Mar. 8, 1938.

SMITH, Edgar Bronson, surgeon; b. Winsted, Conn., Dec. 23, 1853; s. Jesse and Priscilla Jane (Bradford) S.; grad. Lapham Inst., N. Scituate, R.I., 1874; student Brown U., 1874-76; M.D., Coll. Phys. and Surgeons, Columbia, 1880; m. Harriet Lindsay, June 1, 1925. Began practice at Providence, 1880; visiting surgeon R.I. Hosp. and St. Joseph's Hosp., Providence, and Memorial Hosp., Pawtucket, R.I., 1895-1914; cons. surgeon to nearly all hosps. in state. Fellow Am. Coll. of Surgeons. Home: Providence, R.I. Died Apr. 9, 1937.

SMITH, Edgar Fahs, chemist, educator; b. York, Pa., May 23, 1856; s. Gibson and Susan (Fahs) S.; B.S., Pa. Coll., 1874; A.M., Ph.D., Göttingen, 1876; hon. degrees from various colls. and univs.; m. Margie A. Gruel, 1879. Instr. chemistry, U. of Pa., 1876-81; prof. chemistry, Muhlenberg Coll., 1881-83, Wittenberg Coll., 1883-88; prof. chemistry, 1888-1920; v.provost, 1899-1911, provost, 1911-20, U. of Pa.; pres. electoral course for Pa., 1925. Mem. Jury of Awards, Chicago Expn., 1893; mem. U.S. Assay Commn., 1895, 1901-05; adviser in chemistry, Carnegie Inst., 1902; trustee Carnegie Foundation, 1914-

20; pres. Wistar Inst., Phila., 1911-22. Mem. Electoral Coll., Pa. (1915), Com. Pub. Safety, Commn. for Revision of Constn. of Pa. (1919), Coll. and Univ. Council (1911-20), State Council Edn. (1920-22); research asso. Carnegie Inst. (1915, 18). Apptd. by President Harding to bd. of tech. advisers, Disarmament Conf., 1921. Officer Legion of Honor of France, 1932. Awarded Elliott Cresson medal, Franklin Inst., 1914, Chandler medal, Columbia U., 1922. Mem. Nat. Acad. Sciences, Am. Philos. Soc. (pres. 1902-06), Am. Chem. Soc. (pres. 1898, 1921, 22). Author (or editor): Classen's Quantitive Analysis, 1878; Clinical Analysis of Urine (with John Marshall), 1881; Richter's Inorganic Chemistry (5th edit.), 1900; Smith & Keller's Chemical Experimentation, 1902; Richter's Organic Chemistry, 1900; Smith's Electro-Chemical Analysis, 1911; Oettel's Practical Exercises in Electro-Chemistry, 1897; Oettel's Electro-Chemical Experiments, 1897; Elements of Chemistry, 1919; Shorter Course Chemical Experiments, 1913; Theories of Chemistry, 1913; Elements of Electrochemistry, 1913; also numerous books and pamphlets relating to the history of chemistry in America, and investigations in inorganic chemistry, including the determination of atomic weights. Address: Philadelphia, Pa. Died May 3, 1928.

SMITH, Edmund Kirby, banker; b. Hernando, Miss., Feb. 25, 1871; s. Lemuel B. and Annie (Campbell) S.; ed. pub. and high schs., Miss., and U. of Miss.; m. May Pauline Rerdell, 1892. Began career with First Nat. Bank, Orlando, Fla., 1888, later apptd. city treas.; founded Merchants Bank, Orlando; in banking business in Ark. and Tex., organizing State Nat. Bank and State Savings & Trust Co., Texarkana, Ark.; pres. Ark. Bankers' Assn., 1905-06; exec. council, American Bankers Assn., 1907-10, and of Nat. Bank sect., 1912-14; moved to Shreveport, La., 1910; 1st pres. Shreveport Chamber of Commerce, 1910-13; mem. Nat. Currency Assn. for La. and Miss., 1914; mem. La. Loan Commn. (for distribution of $135,000,000 cotton loan fund), 1914; dir. Kansas City, Shreveport & Gulf Ry., 1917-18; chmn. bd. Caddo Central Oil & Refining Corp. (N.Y. City and Shreveport); chmn. bd. Commercial Nat. Bank, Shreveport; pres. and owner Shreveport Hotel Co., Washington Hotel Co., Shreveport; owner Meridian Mansions Hotel, Washington, D.C. Home: Shreveport, La. Died Nov. 12, 1929.

SMITH, Edward B., banker; b. Phila., Sept. 23, 1861; s. Albert H. and Emily (Kaighn) S.; ed. William Penn Charter Sch., Phila., and U. of Pa., class of 1882; m. Laura Howell Jenks, Apr. 11, 1888. In banking business, Phila., 1886—; organized, 1892, and head of Edward B. Smith & Co., bankers, 1892—: dir. Lehigh Valley R.R. Co., Lehigh Valley Transit Co., Girard Fire Ins. Co., etc. Mem. bd. dirs. City Trusts, Phila., 1906—. Republican. Served in 1st Troop, Phila. City Cav., 1882-89. Home: Philadelphia, Pa. Died Jan. 7, 1918.

SMITH, Edward Curtis, governor; b. St. Albans, Vt., Jan. 5, 1854; s. John Gregory and Anna Eliza (Brainerd) S.; A.B., Yale, 1875; LL.B., Columbia, 1877; LL.D., Norwich U., 1901; m. Anna B. James, Oct. 3, 1888; children—James Gregory, Edward Fairchild, Curtis Ripley, Mrs. Dorothea B. Castles. Admitted to Vt. bar, 1877; gov. of Vt., 1898-1900. Republican. Home: St. Albans, Va. Died Apr. 6, 1935.

SMITH, Edward Laurence, U.S. attorney; b. Hartford, Conn., Jan. 22, 1875; s. Andrew and Julia Agnes (Burke) S.; A.B., Yale, 1897, LL.B., 1899; hon. M.A., Trinity, 1912; m. Grace M. Lynch, Feb. 6, 1909. Began practice at Hartford, 1899; mayor of Hartford, 1910-12; judge Court of Common Pleas, 1912-20; apptd. U.S. atty., Dist. of Conn., 1920. Trustee Hartford Pub. Library, Conn. Coll. for Women; dir. Nat. Catholic Welfare Council; chmn. Catholic Social Service Bur. (Hartford). Democrat. K.C. Home: Hartford, Conn. Died Feb. 9, 1923.

SMITH, Edward Laurence, educator; b. Newark, Del., Mar. 19, 1877; s. Hosea R. and Mary Louisa (Sentman) S.; B.A., Delaware Coll., Newark, Del., 1896, M.A., 1899; univ. scholar; 1898-99, univ. fellow, 1899-1900, grad. student in Romance langs., 1901-02, Columbia; studied U. of Paris, 1900-01; m. Deborah Chambers Johnston, Aug. 19, 1903. Instr. French, German and Spanish, Brooklyn Poly. Inst., 1901-02; instr. Romance langs., 1902-04, prof. modern langs., 1904—, acting sec. and sec. faculty, 1911, dean, 1915—, U. of Delaware. Democrat. Presbyn. Home: Newark, Del. Died Jan. 23, 1923.

SMITH, Edward Lincoln, clergyman; b. Montpelier, Vt., Apr. 6, 1865; s. Carlos Lilley and Catherine Holden (Chapin) S.; A.B., Yale, 1886; B.D., Yale Div. Sch., 1890; D.D., Whitman Coll., 1904; m. Rosalia I. Baker, Oct. 26, 1898. Ordained Congl. ministry, 1890; pastor Genesee, Ida., 1890-93, Walla Walla, Wash., 1893-98, Pilgrim Ch., Seattle, 1899-1912 and 1921-23, Queen Anne Congl. Ch., Seattle, 1924-30. Mem. Sch. Bd., Seattle, 1903-06, 24-30. Corporate mem. A.B.C.F.M. (corr. sec. 1912-21); mem. bd. dirs. Congl. State Conf., Congl. Ch. Extension Soc. (Seattle), Pilgrim Foundation (U. of Wash.). Republican. Author: Two Warriors; Six Studies in Acts; Meditations on Five Psalms. Home: Seattle, Wash. Died June 24, 1940.

SMITH, Edward Parson, mayor; b. Winfield, Henry County, Ia., Sept. 30, 1860; s. Edward and Celia (Shockley) S.; prep. edn. Howe's Acad., Mt. Pleasant, Ia.; LL.B., State U. of Ia., 1885; m. Margaret E. Wertman, Nov. 1884. Began practice at Seward, Neb., 1885; removed to Omaha, 1890; partner, 1897-1917, of Hon. Constantine J. Smyth, former justice Ct. of Appeals, Washington; atty. for Omaha Grain Exchange 15 yrs., specializing in commerce cases before Interstate Commerce Commn., and established rates that made Omaha a grain market; mem. firm Smith, Schall & Howell; pres. Prudential Savings & Loan Assn.; pres. Omaha Cooperage Co. Asst. atty. gen. of Neb., 1896-98; mayor of Omaha, 1918-21. Democrat. Conglist. Home: Omaha, Neb. Died May 21, 1930.

SMITH, Edwin, astronomer, geodesist; b. New York, Apr. 13, 1851; s. Edwin and Adelia O. (McIntyre) S.; ed. Coll. City of New York to jr. yr., class of '71; self-study in astronomy and geodesy; m. Lucy S. Black, Nov. 17, 1885. Entered U.S. Coast and Geod. Survey, 1870, asst., 1874; astronomer in charge party to observe transit of Venus at Chatham Islands, S. Pacific, 1874; same, Auckland, New Zealand, 1882; next determined force of gravity at Auckland, N.Z., Sydney, New South Wales, Singapore, Tokio, Japan, San Francisco and Washington, with the 3 Kater pendulums belonging to the Royal Soc. of England, which had been used in the Great Indian Survey; in charge instrument div. U.S. Coast and Geod. Survey, 1879-94, during which time also carried on observations for variation of latitude at Rockville, Md., in cooperation with the work of the Internat. Geod. Assn. Left Coast and Geod. Survey, 1895, and was with the N.Y. State Land Survey till end of 1897, when was again apptd. asst. Coast and Geod. Survey. In 1899 established Internat. Geod. Assn. Latitude Obs. at Gaithersburg, Md., and made observations for variation of latitude from Oct. 1899, to Jan., 1901; engaged on astron., magnetic, and geodetic work of the survey, 1901—. Wrote several papers pub. as appendices to Coast and Geodetic Service Reps. Address: Rockville, Md. Died Dec. 2, 1912.

SMITH, Edwin Burritt, lawyer; b. Spartansburg, Pa., Jan. 18, 1854; s. Henry and Emily (Kinney) S.; orphaned in early life, lived with an uncle at Cerro Gordo, Ill., 1860-64; uncle died and he worked at farm work, 1864-72; taught school, studied at Oberlin Coll. (A.M., 1893); LL.B., Union Coll. of Law, Chicago, 1879; M.L., Yale, 1880; practiced at Chicago, 1881—; mem. firm Peckham, Smith, Packard & ApMadoc; spl. counsel for City of Chicago in traction matters, 1903-05; m. Emma J. Dauman, Nov. 8, 1883. Active in polit. reform movements; mem. Ill. Commn. for Promotion of Uniform Legislation in U.S., 1893—; prof. law, Northwestern U., 1894-1902; active in Anti-Imperialist League. Reported vols. 114-122 U.S. Supreme Ct. Reports for "Law Edition"; also vols. 21-47 Ill. Appellate Ct. Reports. Edited A Great Chancellor and Other Papers, by James L. High, 1902. Contbr. to leading mags. Residence: Chicago, Ill. Died 1906.

SMITH, Edwin E., newspaper pub.; b. Meriden, Conn., Jan. 7, 1862; s. Willis L. and Melissa Charlotte (Way) S.; ed. pub. schs.; m. Jennie J. Lee, Jan. 1, 1883; children—Isabel Lee (Mrs. C. R. Bickford), Wayne C. Began as bus. mgr. Meriden Morning Record, 1885; v.p. and treas. Republican Pub. Co.; v.p. Puritan Bank & Trust Co. (mem. exec. bd.). Republican. Universalist. Home: Meriden, Conn. Died Jan. 24, 1934.

SMITH, E(dwin) Sumter, teacher; b. Broad Run, Va., Apr. 13, 1861; s. Henry and Frances Ella (Foote) S.; student Bethel (Va.) Mil. Acad., 1871-79; grad. in mathematics and modern langs., U. of Va., 1882; m. Elizabeth Walter Quinby, June 28, 1893. Instr. modern langs., Augusta Mil. Acad., 1882-83, Onancock Acad., 1883-84; instr. mathematics and modern langs., Bethel Mil. Acad., 1884-90; instr. modern langs., 1890-1921, asso. prin., 1890-98, prin., 1898-1921 (emeritus), Randolph-Macon Acad.; dir. Peoples Bank. Democrat. Methodist. On honor list war activities, Bedford County. Home: Bedford, Va. Died Jan. 26, 1926.

SMITH, Edwin Whittier, lawyer; b. Pittsburgh, Pa., Oct. 23, 1857; s. Curtis Benjamin Miner and Hannah Jacobs (Washburn) S.; B.A., Yale, 1878; LL.D., U. of Pittsburgh, 1930; LL.D., Allegheny Coll., Meadville, Pa., 1934; unmarried. Admitted to Pa. bar, 1881, practiced at Pittsburgh, 1881—; with Knox & Reed until 1901; became mem. Reed, Smith, Shaw & Beal, 1902, later Reed, Smith, Shaw & McClay; pres. South Hills Trust Co., Mt. Lebanon Cemetery Co.; dir. Philadelphia Co., Duquesne Light Co., Pittsburgh Rys. Co., Reliance Life Ins. Co., Nat. Union Fire Ins. Co., Nat. Union Indemnity Co., Monongahela Inclined Plane Co. Del. to Internat. Congress on Maritime Law, Brussels, 1909, 10; apptd. mem. Election Law Commn. of Pa., 1927, to codify, amend and revise election laws of the state; mem. Citizens' Com. on Teachers' Salaries (Pittsburgh); v.p. Welfare Fund of Pittsburgh; trustee Children's Service Bur. Republican. Home: Pittsburgh, Pa. Died Nov. 17, 1937.

SMITH, Elbert Sidney, judge; b. Twinsburg, O., Mar. 8, 1847; s. Richard Thaddeus and Louisa (Herrick) S.; A.B., Willoughby (Ohio) Coll., 1868; m. Elsy Jane, d. of Rev. Hiram Kinsley, June 19, 1879 (died 1925); children—Elda Louisa, Elberta Thalia, Sidney Benjamin. Admitted to Ill. bar, 1874, and began practice in Champaign County; asst. to atty. gen. of Ill., 1881-83, 1885-93, 1901-05; state's atty. for Sangamon County, Ill., 1896-1900; mem. Ill. Senate, 1915-17; del. Rep. Nat. Conv., 1916, 20; elected judge Circuit Court, 7th Jud. Circuit, to fill vacancy, Mar. 1917, and reëlected June 1921, for term ending June 1927; declined reëlection; mem. law firm Smith & Friedmeyer, 1900-17. Mason, Odd Fellow, Woodman. Home: Springfield, Ill. Died Feb. 18, 1934.

SMITH, Ellen M. Cyr, author; b. Montreal, Can.; d. Prof. Narcisse and Ellen S. (Howard) Cyr; grad. high sch., normal schs., Cambridge, Mass.; m. Ruel Perley Smith, June 19, 1896. Taught for 15 yrs. in Cambridge, Mass. Author: Cyr's Readers. Address: Flatbush, L.I., N.Y. Died July 26, 1920.

SMITH, Ellison Griffith, judge; b. Noble County, O., Dec. 5, 1854; s. Amos Griffith and Mary A. (Ellison) S.; student Lenox Coll., Ia., 1865-71, State U. of Ia., 1872-74; LL.B., State Univ. of Ia., 1874; LL.D., U. of South Dakota, 1927; m. Anna F. Kirkwood, Oct. 18, 1877 (dec.); children—Mrs. Agnes Graeme Kennedy (dec.), Ellison Griffith, Amos Campbell; m. 2d, Florence Pearl Hunkins, Jan. 3, 1922; m. 3d, Alberta Green, July 27, 1927. Began practice, Yankton, S.D., 1876; reporter, Territorial Supreme Ct., 1879-88; asst. U.S. dist. atty., 1883-86; dist. atty., 1881-85; mem. Territorial Legislative Council, 1887-89; circuit judge 1st Circuit, 1889-1909; asso. justice Supreme Ct. of S.D., 1909-22 (presiding judge, 1911-22); prof. law U. of S.D., Mar. 1, 1923—. Republican. Conglist. Home: Vermilion, S.D. Died Sept. 3, 1935.

SMITH, Erastus Gilbert, chemist; b. S. Hadley, Mass., Apr. 30, 1855; s. Byron and Nancy (Dwight) S.; A.B., Amherst, 1877, A.M., 1880; Ph.D., U. of Göttingen, 1883; LL.D., Beloit, 1921; m. Elizabeth Mayher, Dec. 26, 1883; children—Gilbert M., Philip M., Elizabeth, Rebecca, Eleanor (dec.). Prof. chemistry, 1881-1921, prof. emeritus, 1921, dean, 1903-04, Beloit Coll. Mayor of Beloit, 1887-89, 1890-91, 1924-26; pres. Beloit Savings Bank, 1913-21, chmn. bd., 1929—. Mem. Wis. Assembly three terms, 1927-1932. Fellow A.A.A.S. Mem. Wis. Acad. Sciences, Arts and Letters. State consul Modern Woodmen, 1922-29. Author: Determination of the Rock-forming Minerals, 1885; Manual of Qualitative Analysis; also various chem. monographs. Home: Beloit, Wis. Died June 19, 1937.

SMITH, Ernest Ashton, educator; b. Fletcher, O., July 4, 1868; s. Samuel DeHaven (M.D.) and Martha Jane (Singles) S.; A.B., Ohio Wesleyan U., 1888, A.M., 1891; Ph.D., Johns Hopkins, 1900; Oxford U., Eng., 1906, U. of London, 1907; m. Rosalie Bork, June 17, 1916. Prof. history and economics, Allegheny Coll., 1898-1910; asst. prof., Princeton, 1910-13; prof., Allegheny, 1913-16; supt. of schools, Salt Lake City, Utah, 1916-20, Evanston, Ill., 1920-25; pres. State Normal Sch., La Crosse, Wis., 1925—. Albert Shaw lecturer in diplomatic history, Johns Hopkins, 1908; lecturer in edn., Northwestern U., 1920-25. Methodist. Author: The History of the Confederate Treasury, 1901; Hildebrand the Builder, 1908; The Diplomatic Contest for the Ohio Valley, 1909; Allegheny, a Century of Education, 1915; Martin Ruter, 1915; Bishop Calvin Kingsley, 1921 Address: La Crosse, Wis. Died Dec. 28, 1926.

SMITH, Ernest Ellsworth, M.D., chemist; b. New Haven, Conn., Dec. 20, 1867; s. Henry Ellsworth and Ellen Louise (Shares) S.; Ph.B., Sheffield Scientific Sch. (Yale), 1888, Ph.D., 1891; M.D., Bellevue Hosp. Med. Coll. (New York U.), 1898; m. Lillian I. Church, 1890; 1 son, Harold Ellsworth. Asst. in physiol. chemistry, Yale, 1888-91; research asso. Dr. C. A. Herter's pvt. labs., New York, 1891-95; prof. physiology and organic and biol. chemistry, Fordham U. Med. Sch., New York, 1906-11. Specialist in experimental medicine and clin. pathology. Fellow N.Y. Acad. Medicine, N.Y. Acad. Sciences (pres. 1918, 19), A.A.A.S. Author of Aluminum Compounds in Food; also many papers and monographs on chem. and med. subjects. Home: Richmond Hill, N.Y. Deceased.

SMITH, Erwin F., plant pathologist; b. Gilbert's Mills, N.Y., Jan. 21, 1854; s. R. K. and Louisa (Frink) S.; B.S., in biology, U. of Mich, 1886, Sc.D., 1889; Sc.D., U. Wis., 1914; LL.D., U. Mich., 1922; m. Charlotte M. Buffett, Apr. 13, 1893 (died 1906); m. 2d, Ruth Annette Warren, Feb. 21, 1914. Expert pathologist U.S. Dept. of Agr., 1899—; later in charge lab. of plant pathology, Bur. of Plant Industry. Asso. editor Centralblatt für Bacteriologie (2 Abt., first 25 vols.); contbr. to Standard Dictionary (1st edit.). Trustee Marine Biol. Lab., Woods Hole, Mass. (3 terms). Certificate of honor, A.M.A., 1913, for cancer in plants. Mem. Council Nat. Defense. Mem. Nat. Acad. Sciences (chmn. bot. sect. 3 yrs.), Am. Philos. Soc.; fellow Am. Acad. Arts and Sciences, A.A.A.S. (pres. Sect. G, 1906); pres. Soc.

Plant Morphology and Physiology, 1902, Soc. Am. Bacteriologists, 1906, Bot. Soc. America, 1910, Am. Phytopathol. Soc., 1916. An incorporator of Nat. Carillon Assn. Author: Bacteria in Relation to Plant Diseases, Vol. I, 1905, Vol. II, 1911, Vol. III, 1914; various papers on general botany, mycology, sanitary science and bacteriology; For Her Friends and Mine (sonnets, issued pvtly.), 1915; Pasteur—the history of a Mind (transl. with Florence Hedges), 1920; An Introduction to Bacterial Diseases of Plants, 1920. Home: Washington, D.C. Died Apr. 6, 1927.

SMITH, Erwin Jesse, U.S. atty.; b. Celina, Tenn., Nov. 27, 1866; s. Nathaniel and Belle (Langford) S.; grad. Agrl. and Mech. Coll. of Tex., 1888; m. Nannie Weir, Aug. 14, 1889 (died 1894); m. 2d, Claire L. Person, July 12, 1905. Began practice at Denison, Tex., 1890; U.S. atty., Eastern Dist. of Tex., 1920-21. Served as capt. Denison Rifles, Tex. N.G., 1890-92. Democrat. K.P., Elk. Home: Denison, Tex. Died June 23, 1925.

SMITH, Ethan Henry, surgeon; b. Berrien County, Mich., Mar. 14, 1864; s. James and Malvina (Babcock) S.; prep. edn. high sch., Niles, Mich.; student U. of Mich. Med. Dept., 1883-84; M.D., Bellevue Hosp. Med. Coll. (New York U.), 1889; m. Mrs. Mary J. Cook Saxe, Jan. 25, 1894. Prof. orthopedic surgery and clin. surgery, 1904—, trustee and dean of faculty, 1908-13, Coll. Phys. and Surg., San Francisco; surgeon to San Francisco Hosp.; orthopedic surgeon Northwestern Pacific Ry. Protestant. Home: San Francisco, Calif. Deceased.

SMITH, Eugene, engineer, zoölogist; b. New York, N.Y., Nov. 25, 1860; ed. pub. and high schs., Jersey City, and by pvt. instrn.; m. Sept. 1888. City surveyor and engr., Hoboken, N.J. Author: The Home Aquarium, 1902; also papers on The Fishes of the Fresh and Brackish Waters in the Vicinity of New York City, 1897, and The Turtles and Lizards in Proceedings Linnæan Society, New York. Address: Hoboken, N.J. Died Dec. 25, 1912.

SMITH, Eugene Allen, geologist; b. Autauga County, Ala., Oct. 27, 1841; s. Dr. Samuel P. and Adelaide Julia (Allen) S.; A.B., U. of Ala., 1862; Ph.D., Heidelberg, 1868; attended one semester in Berlin, one in Göttingen, 1865-66, and two in Heidelberg, 1866-68; LL.D., U. of Miss., 1899, U. of Ala., 1906; m. Jennie H., d. of Chancellor Landon C. Garland, of U. of Ala., July 10, 1872. Second lt. Co. K, 33d Ala., C.S.A., 1862; capt. and instr. tactics, 1862-65, prof. geology and mineralogy, 1871-74, chemistry, geology and natural history, 1874-78, chemistry, mineralogy and geology, 1878-90, mineralogy and geology, 1890—, U. of Ala. State geologist of Ala., 1873—. Hon. commr. to Paris Expn., 1878; spl. agt. on cotton culture, 10th Census, 1880; mem. Am. Com. Internat. Geol. Congress, 1884-89; mem. jury of awards, expns. at Atlanta, 1895, Nashville, 1897, St. Louis, 1904. Fellow A.A.A.S. (chairman Sect. E, 1904), Geol. Soc. America (council, 1892-95, 2d v.p. 1906, pres. 1913). Mem. State Highway Commn., 1911-23. Home: University, Ala. Died Sept. 7, 1927.

SMITH, Eugene Hanes, dean dental sch.; b. Oldtown, Me., Oct. 23, 1853; s. Asa and Mary (Crosby) S.; ed. Allen English and Classical Sch., Newton, Mass.; D.M.D., Harvard, 1874; hon. A.M., Howard; m. Carrie Maria Shaw, Oct. 12, 1876. Prof. clin. dentistry and dean, 1895—, Harvard Dental Sch. Contbr. numerous professional papers to proc. of dental socs. Address: Boston, Mass. Died May 7, 1925.

SMITH, Francis Asbury, lawyer; b. E. Salisbury, Mass., Nov. 29, 1837; s. James Gilman and Polly (Leavitt) S.; A.B., Wesleyan U., Conn., 1859; m. Julia M. Scott, Apr. 11, 1863. Served 2 yrs. in Civil War as 2d lt. 3d N.Y. Inf.; began practice 1864; county judge Essex County, N.Y., 1879-91; mem. law firm of Smith & Wickes, 1898—. Author: The Critics versus Shakspere, 1907. Address: Elizabethtown, N.Y. Died Oct. 12, 1915.

SMITH, Francis Henry, educator; b. Leesburg, Va., Oct. 14, 1829; s. Daniel G. and Eleanour (Buckey) S.; M.A., U. of Va., 1851; LL.D., Hampden-Sidney, Emory and Henry, and Randolph-Macon colls.; D.C.L., Sewanee; m Mary Stuart Harrison, July 21, 1853; children—Eleanor (Mrs. Chas. W. Kent), Capt. George Tucker (U.S.N.), Rosalie (Mrs. Carrington Harrison), Denton. Asst. to prof. of mathematics, 1851-53, prof. natural philosophy, 1853-1907, prof. emeritus, 1907—, U. of Va. Visitor Miller Manual Labor Sch. (with exception of 3 yrs.), 1886-1909. Author: Thoughts on the Discord and Harmony of Science and the Bible, 1888; Outlines of Physics, 1894; Christ and Science, 1906; Nature, a Witness for the Unity, the Power and the Goodness of God. Address: University, Va. Died July 5, 1928.

SMITH, F(rancis) Hopkinson, artist, author; b. Baltimore, Md., Oct. 23, 1838; s. Francis Hopkinson and Susan (Teackle) S.; when quite young was clerk in iron works; later ed. as mech. engr.; L.H.D., Yale, 1907; m. Josephine Van Deventer; father of F. Berkeley S. Became engr. and contractor; built govt. seawall around Governor's Island; another at Tompkinsville, S.I.; the Race Rock light house off New London; foundation for Bartholdi Statue of Liberty, etc. Did much landscape work in water colors, charcoal work and illustrations; represented in Walter's Gallery, Baltimore, Marquand Collection, etc.; lecturer on art subjects. Awarded bronze medal, Buffalo Expn., 1901; silver medal, Charleston Expn., 1902; gold medal, Phila. Art Club, 1902; gold medal, Am. Art Soc., 1902. Comdr. Order of the Mejidieh, 1898, and of the Order of Osmanieh by Sultan of Turkey, 1900. Mem. Am. Acad. Arts and Letters. Author: Old Lines in New Black and White, 1885; Well-Worn Roads, 1886; A White Umbrella in Mexico, 1889; A Book of the Tile Club, 1890; Col. Carter, of Cartersville, 1891; A Day at Laguerre's, 1892; American Illustrators, 1892; A Gentleman Vagabond and Some Others, 1895; Tom Grogan, 1896; Gondola Days, 1897; Venice of To-day, 1897; Caleb West, 1898; The Other Fellow, 1899; The Fortunes of Oliver Horn, 1902; The Under Dog, 1903; Col. Carter's Christmas, 1904; At Close Range, 1905; The Wood Fire in No. 3, 1905; The Tides of Barnegat, 1906; The Veiled Lady, 1907; The Romance of an Old-Fashioned Gentleman, 1907; Peter, 1908; Forty Minutes Late, 1909; Kennedy Square, 1911; Arm-Chair at the Inn, 1912; Charcoals of New and Old New York, 1912, In Thackeray's London, 1913. Address: New York, N.Y. Died Apr. 7, 1915.

SMITH, Francis Marion, capitalist; b. Richmond, Wis., Feb. 2, 1846; s. Henry G. and Charlotte P. S.; A.B., Milton (Wis.) Coll., 1863; m. Evelyn Ellis, Jan. 23, 1907. At home on father's farm until 21; went West; discovered Teel's Marsh Borax Mines, Nevada, 1872; pres. Realty Syndicate, Oakland, Calif. Rep. presdl. elector, 1904, 1909, Calif. Mem. S.A.R. Home: East Oakland, Calif. Died Aug. 27, 1931.

SMITH, Frank, zoölogist; b. Winneconne, Wis., Feb. 18, 1857; s. Samuel Franklin and Aurelia (Shepard) S.; Ph.B., Hillsdale Coll., Mich., 1885 (D.Sc., 1923); A.M., Harvard, 1893; m. Edith M. Fox, Sept. 8, 1887 (died 1888); 1 son, Donald Fisk (dec.); m. 2d, Isadora Stamats, July 12, 1890. Prof. chemistry and biology, Hillsdale Coll., 1886-92; instr. in biology, Trinity Coll., Hartford, Conn., 1892-93, instr. in zoölogy, 1893-96, asst. prof., 1896-1900, asso. prof., 1900-13, professor zoölogy, 1913-26 (emeritus), U. of Ill. Fellow A.A.A.S. Unitarian. Contbr. chiefly to morphology and taxonomy of land and fresh water annelids, of fresh water sponges, and on migration of birds. Home: Hillsdale, Mich. Died Feb. 3, 1942.

SMITH, Frank Bulkeley, lawyer, mfr.; b. Worcester, Mass., Aug. 25, 1864; s. Charles Worcester and Josephine Caroline (Lord) S.; A.B., Harvard, 1886, A.M., 1888, student Harvard Law Sch., 1886-87; m. Nancy H. Earle, June 5, 1890. Admitted to Mass. bar, 1889, and practiced in Worcester; largely interested in mfg.; trustee Estate of H. N. Slater, 1899-1911; treas. S. Slater & Sons, 1890-1911; treas. New England Cotton Yarn Co., 1911-17. Republican. Home: Worcester, Mass. Died Oct. 13, 1918.

SMITH, Frank Marshall, mining engr.; b. Phila., Pa., Aug. 16, 1866; s. William Marshall and Mary Alice (Beath) S.; grad. High Sch., 1884; E.M., Sch. of Mines (Columbia), 1889; m. Clara Thatcher Everhart, June 21, 1893; children—Aldridge Everhart, Dorothy Alice (Mrs. Irving T. Atwater), Marjorie Helen (wife of Augustus D. Sanders, U.S.A.). With U.S. Geological Survey, 1889-90; assayer and asst. supt. Colo. Smelting Co., Pueblo, Colo., 1891-93; supt., later mgr., United Smelting and Refining Co., Great Falls, Mont., 1893-1901; asst. mgr. Utah dept., Am. Smelting & Refining Co., 1901-02; asst. mgr. E. Helena Plant, same company, 1902-05, mgr., 1905-19; asst. dir., Bunker Hill Smelter, Kellogg, Ida., 1919-20, dir. 1920-35; pres. Northwest Lead Co. (Seattle, Wash.), 1930-35; dir. Spokane Gas & Fuel Co.; cons. metall. engr. Treadwell Yukon Co., 1930. Mem. Am. Inst. Mining and Metall. Engrs. (chmn. Mont. sect., 1915; v.p., 1923-26; chmn. Columbia sect., 1927), Mont. Soc. Engrs. (pres. 1910), Am. Silver Producers Assn. (v.p. 1924—), Associated Engrs. of Spokane (pres. 1925), Northwest Mining Assn. (pres. 1929), Am. Mining Congress (chmn. Western div. 1929). Pres. Spokane Community Welfare Federation, 1929-30. Republican. Mason. Home: Spokane, Wash. Died June 1, 1937.

SMITH, Frank O., congressman; b. Smithville, Md., Aug. 27, 1859; s. Dr. John S. and Ruth Ellen (Owens) S.; educated North Mount Inst., W.Va., and Bethel Mil. Acad., Va.; m. Mrs. Lillie Griffith, Mar. 25, 1885. In U.S. Internal Revenue Service, first Cleveland adminstrn. resigning, 1889; organized Calumet Canning Co., 1889, Frank O. Smith & Co., gen. mdse., 1890; engaged in mfr. flour, feed, etc., 1898-1910; afterward fruit grower. Apptd. state tobacco insp. by Gov. Edwin Warfield, 1904, reapptd., 1906; candidate for State Senate, 1911; mem. 63d Congress (1913-15), 5th Md. Dist. Democrat. Methodist. Mason. Address: Dunkirk, Md. Died Jan. 29, 1924.

SMITH, Frank Sullivan, lawyer; b. Granger, N.Y., Oct. 14, 1851; s. Gen. William M. S. (M.D.) and Adeline (Weeks) S.; grad. Angelica (N.Y.) Acad.; A.B., Yale, 1872; LL.D., Alfred (N.Y.) U., 1903; m. Clara A. H. Higgins, Oct. 17, 1877. In practice at New York. Pres. Shawmut Coal & Coke Co., Shawmut Commercial Co., Shawmut Mining Co., Kersey Mining Co.; acting pres., v.p., gen. counsel, receiver and dir. Pittsburgh, Shawmut & Northern R.R. Co.; trustee Hamilton Trust Co.; dir. and mem. exec. com. Am. Light & Traction Co.; dir. Manhattan Life Ins. Co. Mem. N.Y. State Bd. Law Examiners, 1902—; trustee Alfred Univ. Del. Rep. Nat. Conv., 1884, 1912, 1916; sec. Rep. State Com. N.Y., 1887-91. Home: Angelica, N.Y. Died Nov. 15, 1920.

SMITH, Franklin Guest, brig. gen. U.S.A.; b. nr. Blossburg, Pa., Feb. 16, 1840; s. Franklin R. (M.D.) and Mary (Guest) S.; C.E., Rensselaer Poly. Inst., 1859; m. Frances L. Dauchy, Feb. 8, 1866; m. 2d, Georgiana Dauchy, of San Francisco, Sept. 4, 1881. Pvt. sec. to gen. supt. Ohio & Miss. R.R., 1860-61; pvt. sec. Maj. Gen. George M. McClellan, spring of 1861-Aug. 5, 1861, when apptd. 2d lt. 4th U.S. Arty.; promoted 1st lt., as of same date, and joined army comd. by Gen. D. C. Buell at Louisville, Ky., Jan. 1862; served with that army under Gens. Buell, Rosecrans and Thomas until close of Civil War. Bvtd. capt., Dec. 31, 1862; maj., Sept. 20, 1863. Capt. U.S.A., Feb. 5, 1867; maj. 2d Arty., Aug. 28, 1891; lt. col. 6th Arty., Mar. 8, 1898; col. Arty. Corps, Feb. 2, 1901; brig. gen., Aug. 3, 1903; retired Aug. 4, 1903. Participated in Indian campaigns against Sioux and Cheyennes, 1876-77, against Bannocks, 1878, and against Apaches, 1881; during war with Spain arty. insp., Dept. of the South, and in command of siege train of 100 guns organized at Port Tampa, Fla., for possible use in siege of Havana, but which never left U.S., owing to sudden close of war. From Jan. 1894, to July 1908 (except during war with Spain), commr. and sec. Chickamauga and Chattanooga Nat. Park Commn. Home: Washington, D.C. Died Oct. 7, 1912.

SMITH, Franklin Orion, psychologist; b. Macon County, Ill., Feb. 22, 1867; s. Charles Davis and Lucinda Jane (Kerby) S.; M.Di., Ia. State Teachers Coll., Cedar Falls, Ia., 1903; A.B., State U. of Ia., 1906, A.M., 1907, Ph.D., 1912; studied U. of Chicago, summer quarter, 1910; fellow by courtesy Johns Hopkins, 1 semester, 1921; research fellow, Harvard, 1 semester, 1922; m. Agnes Wallace, 1907; children—Eleanor Isabel, Jean Wallace. Teacher rural schs., Macon Co., Ill., 1889-95; prin. schs. in Hamilton County, Ia., 1897-1900; prin. Twp. Consolidated Sch., Buffalo Center, Ia., 1903-04; instr. psychology and edn., Woodbine (Ia.) Normal Sch., 1907-10; fellow in psychology, State U. of Ia., 1910-12; asst. prof. edn. and psychology, U. of Utah, 1912-15; prof. psychology, U. of Mont., 1915—; prof. ednl. psychology, Cornell U., summer 1922, U. of Colo., 5 summers to 1929. Congregationalist. Odd Fellow. Contbr. to Psychol. Monographs, Jour. Experimental Psychology, British Jour. Psychology, etc. Home: Missoula, Mont. Died July 13, 1941.

SMITH, Fred B.; b. Lone Tree, Ia., Dec. 24, 1865; s. Robert A. and Endora (Dinwiddie) S.; State U. of Ia., 1882-83; LL.D., Ursinus Coll., Pa; S.T.D., Syracuse U.; m. Minnie A. Colvin, June 2, 1886; children—F. Gordon, Martha Lucile Cross, Helen Read, Dorothy Ryan, Richard M.; m. 2d, Lillian Eberenz, Oct. 13, 1917. Secretary Y.M.C.A., Sioux Falls, 1888-91; gen. sec. Y.M.C.A., Dubuque, Ia., 1891-96; in evangelistic work, 1896-98; sent by Internat. Com., Y.M.C.A., to army camp at Chickamauga, 1898, later going to Cuba on mission among the soldiers; visited various cities, 1899-1901, urging greater emphasis on religious work in Y.M.C.A., a feature being the Jubilee Conv. at Boston, June 1901; Internat. sec. Y.M.C.A., 1910; originator, 1910, and leader in "The Men and Religion Forward Movement"; chmn. Citizens Com. of 1,000 for Law Enforcement; chmn. Am. sect. World Alliance for Internat. Friendship; moderator Nat. Council of Congl. Chs. of America, and chmn. exec. com. Republican. Author: Men Wanted, 1911; A Man's Religion, 1916; Observations in France, 1918; On the Trail of the Peacemaker, 1923; Must We Have War?, 1929. Home: White Plains, N.Y. Died Sept. 4, 1936.

SMITH, Frederick Appleton, brig. gen. U.S.A.; b. Craigville, N.Y., May 15, 1849; apptd. from N.Y., and grad. U.S. Mil. Acad., 1873; m. Wilhelmina Fowler, Oct. 3, 1878. Commd. 2d lt. 12th Inf., June 13, 1873; 1st lt., June 28, 1878; capt., Dec. 29, 1890; maj. chief commissary subsistence vols., July 16, 1898-June 13, 1899; maj. 1st U.S. Inf., June 20, 1899; detailed insp. gen., Feb. 28, 1901; lt. col. 29th Inf., July 14, 1902; detailed insp. gen., July 30, 1902; col. 8th Inf., Jan. 24, 1904; brig. gen. U.S.A., Oct. 24, 1908. Served in Indian campaigns on Western frontier in Ariz., Dakotas and Nev. Acting asst. adj. gen., hdqrs. Div. of Cuba, July 28-Oct. 1899; comdg. Dist. of Guanajay, Cuba, Oct. 11, 1899-Aug. 1900; in P.I., Sept. 1900-Feb. 1903; detailed insp. gen., Feb. 28, 1901, Dept. Visayas, Aug. 2, 1901, Dept. S. Philippines, Dec. 1901, Dept. Visayas, Sept. 1902-Feb. 1903; insp. gen.'s office, Washington, Feb.-Apr. 1903; gen. staff, Apr. 17, 1903; revising inf. drill regulations, Sept. 9, 1903-July 1904; at Govs. Island, N.Y., July 1904-Feb. 1906; in P.I., Apr. 1906-Apr. 1908; Ft. Mc-

Dowell, Angel Island, Calif., May 12-Sept. 1908; comdg. Dept. Calif., Oct. 26, 1908-Jan. 13, 1909; Ft. D. A. Russell, Wyo., Apr. 25, 1909-Mar. 16, 1910; Dept. of the Mo., Mar. 18, 1910-Feb. 15, 1913; Central Div., Chicago, Oct. 31-Nov. 29, 1912; 5th Brig., 2d Div., Feb. 15-Apr. 29, 1913; retired May 15, 1913. Home: New York, N.Y. Died Feb. 4, 1922.

SMITH, Frederick Augustus, judge; b. Norwood Park, Cook County, Ill., Feb. 11, 1844; s. Israel G. and Susan (Pennoyer) S.; pvt. Co. G, 134th Ill. Inf., 1863-65; B.S., U. of Chicago, 1866; LL.B., Union Coll. of Law, Chicago, 1867; m. Frances B. Morey, July 26, 1871. In practice at Chicago, 1867—; mem. firm Smith & Kohlsaat, 1867-69, Smith, Helmer, Moulton & Price, 1890-1902; Rep. nominee for judge Superior Ct., 1898; judge Circuit Ct., Cook County, Ill., 1908— (now chief justice). Republican. Trustee U. of Chicago, Rush Med. Coll. Home: Chicago, Ill. Died July 31, 1919.

SMITH, Frederick H., capitalist; b. Buffalo, N.Y.; 1869; s. W. H. and Elizabeth Cathcart (Brown) S.; A.B., De Veaux Coll.; m. Sarah Brockway, 1893. V.p. Dime Savings Trust Co., Merchants' Nat. Bank; dir. Peoria Ry. Terminal Co., Peoria Gas & Electric Co., McCoy Wholesale Grocery Co., and other corps. Col. on staff of Gov. John R. Tanner, 1897-1900, on staff of Gov. Richard Yates, 1900-04; del. Rep. Nat. Conv., 1900; presdl. elector, 1904; chmn. Rep. Central Com., Peoria Co., many years; chmn. finance com. Rep. Nat. Com., campaign of 1908. Pres. Ill. Commn. S.C. and West Indian Expn., 1901-02 (awarded gold medal "for distinguished services" by dirs. of expn.); trustee Ill. State Insane Asylum, Bartonville, Ill., 1907. K.T. Mason. Home: Peoria, Ill. Deceased.

SMITH, George Albert, M.D.; b. Wakefield, N.H., Nov. 9, 1858; s. Alfred F. and Susan E. (Mordeaugh) S.; M.D., Bellevue Hosp. Med. Coll. (New York U.), 1881; m. Amelia M. Kaus, Dec. 8, 1886; children—Alfred J., Mrs. Susan Reilly, George A. Asst. phys., asst. supt. and supt., New York Asylum for the Insane, Harts Island, N.Y., 1882-95; med. supt. Central Islip State Hosp. for the Insane (7247 beds), 1895-1932 (emeritus). Mason. Address: Bay Shore, L.I., N.Y. Died Jan. 6, 1942.

SMITH, George Carson, railway official, financier; b. Granville, N.Y., Mar. 4, 1855; s. Harvey J. and Olivia Cordelia (White) S.; A.B., Adrian (Mich.) Coll., 1877; m. Jennie Prosser, May 15, 1878; father of Olivia Smith Cornelius. Pvt. sec. to gov. of Mich., 1877-81, during which time studied law; sec. to gen. mgr. Internat. & Great Northern, and Tex. & Pacific rys., 1881-89; asst. to v.p., 1889-91, asst. gen. mgr., 1891-94, Mo. P. Ry. System; pres. Atlanta & W. Point R.R., and Western Ry. of Ala., 1894-1900; identified with Westinghouse interests, 1900-11, as pres. Lackawanna & Wyoming Valley Rapid Transit Co., Grand Rapids, Grand Haven & Muskegon Ry., Westinghouse Inter-Works Ry.; v.p. Security Investment Co., Niagara, Lockport & Ontario Power Co., Electric Power Securities Co. of Niagara Falls, E. Pittsburgh Improvement Co., Manila Electric R.R. & Lighting Corp.; dir. Interstate Investment Co., and many Westinghouse and other corps. Dir. Merchants and Mfrs. Exchange New York. Home: New York, N.Y. Died May 30, 1916.

SMITH, George Henry, coll. prof.; b. Lancaster, O., Dec. 21, 1847; s. John C. and Catherine (Myers) S.; A.B., Wittenberg Coll., Springfield, O., 1870, A.M., 1872; B.D., Pacific Theol. Sem., Oakland, Calif., 1875; D.D., Wheaton Coll., 1923; m. Rachel Mooar, June 28, 1877; children—Sarah K., Winifred (Mrs. O. M. Olson), George M., Larmon L. Ordained Congl. ministry, 1877; pastor Rio Vista, Calif., 1877-79, Redwood City, Calif., 1880, Kohalo, Hawaii, 1880-83, Cincinnati, O., 1884-87, St. Charles, Ill., 1887-98; prof. Latin, 1899, prof. Greek and Latin, 1916-20, became prof. Greek, 1920, also vice-pres. of faculty, 1927, Wheaton Coll., emeritus, 1927—. Alderman, City of Wheaton, 1906-10. Asso. editor Wheaton Progressive. Home: Wheaton, Ill. Died Jan. 2, 1937.

SMITH, George M., univ. prof.; b. Belgrade, Me., May 30, 1847; s. George and Mary S.; A.B., Colby, 1873, A.M., 1878; U. of Giessen, 1898-99; m. Mary E. Hall, Mar. 18, 1876. Taught high schs. in Mass., 1873-87, Canton, N.Y., 1887-91; prof. Greek, 1891-94, Greek and pedagogy, 1894-99, modern langs. and pedagogy, 1899-1909, German and Romance languages, 1909-18, Spanish language, 1918—, U. of South Dakota. Author: A Vocabulary to Cæsar, book II, 1890, Syracuse, N.Y.; Outlines of Civics for South Dakota, 1892, The State and Nation (Smith and Young), 1894; History and Civil Government of South Dakota (Smith and Young), 1895; Outlines of Pedagogy (Smith and Young), 1897. Editor: History of South Dakota, 1915. Editor South Dakota Educator, 1908-14. Address: Vermilion, S.D. Died June 25, 1920.

SMITH, George Theodore, exec.; b. N.Y. City, Apr. 29, 1855; s. Charles Tappan and Martha Elizabeth S.; student Coll. City of New York; m. Hattie Louise Young, Apr. 25, 1882; children—Edward Young (dec.), Natalie Young (Mrs. L. Fred Bruce). Pres. Am. Graphite Co., Joseph Dixon Crucible Co.; v.p. Colonial Life Ins. Co. of America, Raritan River R.R.; mem. bd. mgrs. Provident Instn. for Savings. Home: Jersey City, N.J. Died Dec. 19, 1940.

SMITH, George W., congressman, lawyer; b. Putnam County, O., Aug. 18, 1846; grad. McKendree Coll., Lebanon, Ill., 1868; grad. law dept., same univ. at Bloomington, Ill., 1870; admitted to bar, 1870; in active practice at Murphysboro, 1870—. Presidential elector, 1880; mem. Congress from 22d Ill. dist., 1889-1903, and 25th dist., 1903-07. Republican. Home: Murphysboro, Ill. Died 1907.

SMITH, George Walter Vincent; b. New York, June 14, 1832; s. George Wilson and Sarah Henrietta (Wheeler) S.; ed. Amenia Sem., Dutchess County, N.Y., 1845-48, and under pvt. tutors; m. Belle Townsley, June 22, 1869. Began active career with Babcock, Gould & Co., importers, New York, 1850; mem. firm of Stivers & Smith, mfrs. fine carriages, New York, 1857-67 (retired). Founder, 1893, donor and dir. Art Museum, Springfield, Mass.; dir. City Library Assn., Springfield. Republican. Address: Springfield, Mass. Died Mar. 28, 1923.

SMITH, George Weissinger, mayor; b. Louisville, Ky., Oct. 10, 1864; s. Capt. Thomas F. (U.S.A.) and Blanche (Weissinger) S.; student U. of Va., 1883-86; LL.B., U. of Louisville, 1887; m. Ellen Hunt, Oct. 30, 1890. Practiced in Louisville, 1887—; mem. Ky. Ho. of Rep., 1898; mayor of Louisville, 1917-21. Later pres. Louisville Water Co. Pres. Parental Home and Sch. Com., Jefferson County, Ky.; trustee Louisville Sch. of Reform. Served as pvt. Co. F, Louisville Legion, 3 yrs. Republican. Presbyn. Home: Louisville, Ky. Deceased.

SMITH, G(eorge) Williamson, educator; b. Catskill, N.Y., Nov. 21, 1836; s. George and Catherine (Williamson) S.; A.B., Hobart Coll., 1857, A.M., 1860; S.T.D., 1880, Columbia, 1887; LL.D., Trinity, 1887, Williams, 1889; D.D., Yale, 1901; m. Susanna Duvall, Oct. 10, 1859. Prin. Bladensburg Acad., 1858-59; clerk, U.S. Navy Dept., 1861-64; deacon, 1860, priest, 1864, P.E. Ch.; chaplain U.S.N., July 1864; acting prof. mathematics, U.S. Naval Acad., Newport, 1864-65; chaplain Naval Acad., Annapolis, 1865-68; chaplain U.S.S. Franklin, 1868-71; rector Grace Ch., Jamaica, L.I., N.Y., 1872-81, Ch. of the Redeemer, Brooklyn, 1881-83; pres., 1883-1904, emeritus prof. metaphysics, 1904—, Trinity Coll., Hartford, Conn.; asst. minister St. John's Ch., Washington, 1905—. Address: Washington, D.C. Died Dec. 27, 1925.

SMITH, Gerald Birney, univ. prof.; b. Middlefield, Mass., May 3, 1868; s. Metcalf John and Harriet Louise (Eldredge) S.; A.B., Brown U., 1891; A.M., Columbia, 1898; D.B., Union Theol. Sem., 1898; univs. of Berlin, Marburg, and Paris, 1898-1900; D.D., Brown, 1909; m. Inez Michener, July 10, 1894; children—Phyllis Gray, Cecil Michener. Tutor in Latin, Oberlin Acad., 1891-92; instr. mathematics and modern langs., Worcester Acad., 1892-95; instr. systematic theology, 1900-04, asst. prof., 1904-06, asso. prof. dogmatic theology, 1906-13, prof. Christian theology, 1913—, U. of Chicago. Ordained Bapt. ministry, 1902. Nathaniel William Taylor lecturer, Yale, 1912. Earle lect., Berkeley, Calif., 1920. Mng. editor Am. Jour. Theology, 1909-20; editor Jour. of Religion, 1921-27. Author: Practical Theology, 1903; Biblical Conception of Atonement (with Ernest D. Burton and John Merlin Powers Smith), 1909; Social Idealism and the Changing Theology, 1913; Principles of Christian Living, 1924; Current Christian Thinking, 1927. Editor: (and part author) A Guide to the Study of the Christian Religion, 1916. Editor: (with Shailer Mathews) A Dictionary of Religion and Ethics, 1921. Home: Chicago, Ill. Died Apr. 3, 1929.

SMITH, Gerrit, composer, organist; b. Hagerstown, Md., Dec. 11, 1859; s. Gerrit Henry and Marie Antoinette (Fitz Hugh) S.; g.s. Col. William Fitzhugh of Md., g.g.s. Col. James Livingston, grandnephew Gerritt Smith, abolitionist and philanthropist; ed. Hobart Coll.; studied music and architecture abroad; Mus. Doc., Hobart, 1891; m. Caroline Butterfield, 1887. Organist St. Paul's Cathedral, Buffalo, and St. Peter's Ch., Albany; organist Old South Ch., New York, 1885—; later prof. music, Union Theol. Sem.; prof. theory, Master Sch., Brooklyn. Gave 285 free organ recitals in that ch. and played abroad. Founder, and 6 yrs. pres. Manuscript Soc. of Composers; pres. New York State Music Teachers' Assn.; hon. pres. Am. Guild of Organists. Well-known composer and writer on musical topics. Compositions: King David (cantata); Song Cycle; "Thistledown"; also over 75 songs, numerous piano pieces, carols and ch. anthems. Home: New York, N.Y. Died July 21, 1912.

SMITH, Gertrude, author; b. Coloma, Eldorado County, Calif.; d. Rev. W. N. and Jane (Letts) S.; sister of Minna Carolina S.; early life in West; ed. at Boston and in Europe. Author: The Rousing of Mrs. Potter, and Other Stories; The Arabella and Araminta Stories, 1895; Dedora Hayward; Ten Little Comedies; The Boys of Marmiton Prairie, 1899; The Wonderful Stories of Jane and John, 1899; The Roggie and Reggie Stories, 1900; The Boo Boo Book, 1900; The Queen of Little Barrymore Street, 1902; The Lovable Tales of Janey and Josey and Joe, 1902; Stories of Peter and Ellen, 1903; Little Precious, 1904; The Baby Bible Stories, 1904; Little Mother and Georgie, 1905; Robbie Bible Stories, 1905; The Beautiful Story of Doris and Julie, 1906; Little Girl and Philip, 1907; Delight, 1908; When Roggie and Reggie Were Five, 1909; Bed-time Bible Stories, 1914. Died 1917.

SMITH, Goldwin, author; b. Reading, Eng., Aug. 23, 1823; s. Richard S. (M.D.); A.B., Magdalen Coll. (Oxford U.), 1845, also A.M.; fellow Univ. Coll., Oxon, 1847; LL.D., Brown U., 1864, Princeton, 1896; D.C.L., Oxford, 1882; also L.H.D.; m. Mrs. Harriet (Dixon) Boulton, d. Thomas Dixon, 1875. Called to English bar, 1847; Regius prof. modern history, Oxford, 1858-66; active champion of North during Am. Civil War; visited U.S., 1864; came to U.S., 1868; lecturer, 1868-71, and later hon. prof. English and constl. history, Cornell. Lived in Toronton, 1871—. Active in ednl. assns.; v.p. Canadian Land Law Amendment Assn.; pres. Modern Lang. Assn. America, etc. Prominent exponent of idea that Canada is destined to merge her polit. life in that of U.S. Author: William Cowper, 1880; Jane Austen, 1890; Lectures and Essays, 1881; The Conduct of England to Ireland, 1882; False Hopes, 1883; Loyalty, Aristocracy and Jingoism, 1891; The Political Destiny of Canada, 1878; Canada and the Canadian Question, 1891; William Lloyd Garrison—a Biographical Essay, 1892; A Trip to England, 1892; History of the United States, 1893; Oxford and Her Colleges, 1894; Bay Leaves—Translations from the Latin Poets, 1894; Specimens of Greek Tragedy, 1894; Essays on Questions of the Day, 1894; Guesses at the Riddle of Existence, 1896; The United Kingdom, 1899; Shakespeare—The Man, 1900; Commonwealth or Empire, 1902; In the Court of History, 1902; The Founder of Christendom, 1903; Lines of Religious Inquiry, 1904; My Memory of Gladstone, 1904; Irish History and the Irish Question, 1905; Labour and Capital, 1907; also numerous articles in mags. Address: Toronto, Can. Died 1910.

SMITH, Gregory L., lawyer; b. Baldwin County, Ala., July 7, 1853; s. Robert and Helen (Herndon) S.; student U. of Va., 1874; LL.B., 1875; m. Gertrude C., d. Sydenham Moore, Apr. 16, 1879; children—Helen Herndon, Hattie Beverly, Gertrude Creswell, Gregory Little (dec.), Harry Hardy. Admitted to bar, 1875, and in practice at Mobile, 1875—. Prominent in criminal practice until retired from that branch, 1893; engaged in civil cases, principally corporate, 1893—. Home: Mobile, Ala. Died June 6, 1929.

SMITH, Hamilton Lamphere, educator; b. New London, Conn., Nov. 5, 1818; s. Anson and Amy C. (Beckwith) S.; ed. Union Sch., New London, Conn., until 1834; grad. Yale, 1839; A.M., Yale; LL.D., Trinity Coll.; L.H.D., Hobart Coll.; m. Julia Buttles, 1847. Prof. astronomy and natural philosophy, Kenyon Coll., 1849-67; same, Hobart Coll., 1867-1900; retired, 1900. Author: Natural Philosophy for Schools and Academies, 1842; The World, 1845. Editor Annals of Science, monthly jour., Cleveland, 1842-44. Writer numerous papers in Silliman's Jour., Am. Jour. of Microscopy, Boston Lyceum Natural History, Jour. N.Y. Micros. Soc., Trans-Am. Micros. Soc., chiefly on diatomaceæ and marine algæ. Address: Yonkers, N.Y. Died 1903.

SMITH, Harlan Ingersoll, anthropologist; b. E. Saginaw, Mich., Feb. 17, 1872; s. Harlan Page and Alice Elvira (Ingersoll) S.; ed. at pub. and high schs. and U. of Mich. 2 yrs.; prior to 1890 studied archæology of Saginaw Valley; m. Helena E. Oakes, Nov. 25, 1897; children—Elizabeth Alice (Mrs. Allan T. Powell), Marjorie Oakes (Mrs. G. Douglas Mallory). Asst. Peabody Mus., Harvard, 1891; field asst., dept. anthropology, Chicago Expn., 1891-93; explored ancient mounds in Ohio, Ky., Wis., N.Y., Mich., etc.; in 1891-93 had charge anthrop. collections in Museum of U. of Mich.; explored ancient garden beds nr. Kalamazoo, Mich., for Archæol. Inst. America, 1894; became connected with Am. Mus. Natural History, New York, 1895, mem. faculty, 1896-1914, asst. curator of archæology, 1900-1910, asso. curator of anthropology, 1910-11, hon. curator of archæology, 1912-14; archæologist, Geol. Survey of Can., June 15, 1911-20; archæologist Nat. Mus. of Canada (formerly Victoria Memorial Mus.), 1920-37. Am. archæologist Jesup North Pacific expdn.; instr. evolution of industries, Pratt Inst., Brooklyn, 1906-07; lecturer New York Bd. of Edn., 1898-1911. Archæol. exploration in B.C., 17 seasons, 1897-1929, in N.S., 1914, other parts of Can., 1911-21. Fellow A.A.A.S. Author: Archæology of Lytton, 1899; Archæology of the Thompson River Region, 1900; Cairns of British Columbia and Washington, 1901; Shell Heaps of the Lower Fraser River, British Columbia, 1903; Archæology of the Gulf of Georgia and Puget Sound, 1907; Archæology of the Yakima Valley, Washington, 1910; The Prehistoric Ethnology of a Kentucky Site, 1910; An Album of Prehistoric Canadian Art, 1923; The Archæology of Merigomish Harbour, Nova Scotia, 1929; also numerous papers on anthrop. and mus. subjects. Made motion pictures of Indians in British Columbia and Alberta, 1923-29. Home: Ottawa, Ont., Can. Died Jan. 28, 1940.

SMITH, Harmon, M.D.; b. McDonough, Ga., Mar. 20, 1872; s. S. O. and Alice Cloud (Stokes) S.; A.B., U. of Ga., 1892, Sc.D., 1922; M.D., Bellevue Hosp. Med. Coll., 1897; m. Janet Williams, June 1915; 1 son, Harmon. Interne Kings County Hosp., 1897-98, Loomis Sanitarium, 1898; surgeon dir. Manhattan Eye & Ear Hosp.; consultant laryngologist Memorial and Babies hosps., New York; cons. aurist Monmouth Memorial Hosp. (Long Branch, N.J.). Fellow Am. College Surgeons. Democrat. Home: New York, N.Y. Died 1934.

SMITH, Harold Babbitt, elec. engr.; b. Barre, Mass., May 23, 1869; s. Samuel Francis and Julia Asenath (Babbitt) S.; M.E., Cornell U., 1891; post-grad. student Cornell, 1891-93; m. Laura Bertha Smith, June 15, 1894; m. 2d, Persis H. Smith, September 28, 1911; children—P. Nancy, Margaret S., Richard S. Prof. elec. engring., U. of Ark., 1892; head designer and elec. engr. Elektron Mfg. Co., Springfield, Mass., 1893; prof. elec. engring., Purdue U. (dir. Sch. of Elec. Engring.), 1893-96; prof. elec. engring. and dir. dept. elec. engring., Worcester Poly. Inst., 1896—; elec. engr., designer, cons. engr., Westinghouse Electric & Mfg. Co., Pittsburgh, 1905—. Fellow Am. Inst. E.E. (dir. 1920-24; v.p. 1924-26; pres. 1929-30), A.A.A.S. Chmn. Internat. Group Jury of Awards in elec. engring., St. Louis Expn., 1904. Asso. mem. Naval Consulting Bd. U.S. and cons. engr. with spl. bd. of U.S. Navy on anti-submarine devices, 1917-19; mem. Am. Engring. Council, 1930-32. Writer of many monographs and contributions to transactions of socs. and engring. publs. Study and travel through Europe, Africa, India, China, Japan, etc., 1911-13. Address: Worcester, Mass. Died 1932.

SMITH, Harry Alexander, army officer; b. Atchison, Kan., June 18, 1866; s. Henry T. and Anna S.; grad. U.S. Mil. Acad., 1891; distinguished grad. Army Sch. of the Line, 1908; grad. Army Staff Coll., 1909; m. Harriet Newcomb, Oct. 27, 1892; children—Newcomb, William A. Commd. 2d lt. 1st Inf., June 12, 1891; promoted through grades to col., Aug. 5, 1917; brig. gen. N.A., June 26, 1918-July 31, 1919; brig. gen. regular army, May 10, 1922; maj. gen., Sept. 20, 1926. With regt. in Calif., 1891-96; on duty with Kan. Nat. Guard, 1896-98, maj. 21st Kan. Vols., Apr. 26-Dec. 10, 1898; in Cuba, 1899-1900; in Philippines, 1900-02, 1905-07; sr. instr., dept. of law, Army Service Schs., 1909-12; instr. dept. of mil. art, Army Service Schs., 1912-14; in charge dept. of justice and of pub. safety, Vera Cruz, Mexico, May 1-Nov. 21, 1914; adj. 5th Brigade, Galveston, Tex., Jan.-Oct. 1915; in China, Apr. 1916-Aug. 1917; duty Gen. Staff, War Dept., Sept. 26-Nov. 19, 1917; arrived in France, Nov. 26, 1917; asst. comdt. Army Service Schs., France, Feb.-May 1918, comdt. May 1-Nov. 11, 1918; in charge civil affairs, Germany, Nov. 11, 1918-July 9, 1919; asst. comdt. Gen. Staff Coll., Washington, D.C., Aug. 1, 1919-Oct. 1, 1922; comdg. 16th Inf. Brig., Oct. 1, 1922-June 30, 1923; comdt. Gen. Service Schs., Ft. Leavenworth, Kan., 1923-25; apptd. asst. chief of staff, War Plans Div., July 1, 1925; mil. del. to Limitation of Arms Conf., Geneva, May 1926; rep. of U.S. Government at coronation of Shah of Persia, Apr. 26, 1926; comdg. gen. 7th Corps Area, June 1, 1927—. Awarded D.S.M.; Legion of Honor (French); Companion of the Bath (British); Comdr. Order of the Crown of Oak (Luxemburg); Comdr. Order of Solidaridid (Panama). Presbyn. Home: Atchison, Kan. Died May 26, 1929.

SMITH, Harry Alexander, insurance pres.; b. Springfield, Mass., May 24, 1869; s. Alexander and Charlotte (Smith) S.; A.B., Amherst, 1890; m. Helen C. Nichols, Dec. 24, 1890; children—James Nichols, Mrs. Harriet Helen Walker, Malcolm Keith. Began at Rochester, N.Y., as local agt. Nat. Fire Ins. Co. of Hartford, 1890; continued with same company, successively as spl. agt., state agt., asst. sec., 1900-07, v.p., 1907-15, pres., Feb. 1915—; pres. Mechanics & Traders Ins. Co. of New Orleans, Colonial Securities Co. (Hartford), Franklin Nat. Ins. Co. of New York, Transcontinental Ins. Co. of New York; dir. Phoenix-State Bank & Trust Co. (Hartford), Bush Terminal Co., Ala., Tenn. & Northern R.R., Rossia Ins. Co. of America, Fire Reassurance Co. of New York, Lincoln Ins. Co. of New York, First Reinsurance Co. of Hartford, Central Nat. Bank (New York). Dir. Chamber of Commerce U.S.A. Home: Hartford, Conn. Died Dec. 17, 1928.

SMITH, Harry Bache, dramatic author; b. Buffalo, N.Y., 1860; s. Josiah Bailey and Elizabeth (Bache) S.; ed. pub. schs., Chicago; m. Lena Reed, Oct. 1887; 1 son, Sydney R.; m. 2d, Irene Bentley, Nov. 1906. Dramatic and lit. critic for newspapers before writing for the stage. Author: Robin Hood; Rob Roy; Little Corporal; Fortune Teller; Highwayman; Serenade; Wizard of the Nile; Idol's Eye; Half a King; Fencing Master; Knickerbockers; Three Graces; Begum; Jupiter; Tar and the Tartar; Tzigane; Crystal Slipper; Foxy Quiller; Casino Girl; Belle of Bohemia; Cadet Girl; Wild Rose; Billionaire; Office Boy; A Madcap Princess; Liberty Belles; Papa's Wife; Little Duchess; Babette; Parisian Model; Rich Mr. Hoggenheimer; Tattooed Man; Dolly Dollars; Free Lance; Silver Star; Little Miss Fix-It; Miss Innocence; Nearly a Hero; Golden Butterfly; Bachelor Belles; Little Nemo; Follies of 1907, of 1908, of 1909, of 1910; Mandarin; Maid Marian; Rounders; Paradise of Mahomet; Soul Kiss; Girl in the Train; Belle of Mayfair; Strollers; Singing Girl; Girl from Dixie; Second Fiddle; Spring Maid; Red Rose; Watch Your Step; Springtime of Youth; Caroline; Sirens; Gypsy Love; Doll Girl; Girl from Utah; The Enchantress; Angel Face; The Love Song; Naughty Riquette; Princess Flavia; The Circus Princess; Countess Maritza; The Red Robe; White Lilacs; Three Little Girls; Marching By; Rogues and Vagabonds; etc. Books: A Sentimental Library; Lyrics and Sonnets; Early Letters of Charles Dickens; Stage Lyrics; Will Shakespeare, Player; First Nights and First Editions; etc.; also articles in mags. Address: New York, N.Y. Died Jan. 1, 1936.

SMITH, Harry Eaton, naval officer; b. Fremont, O., Dec. 28, 1869; s. Henry Bishop and Eta Beary (Dalton) S.; grad. U.S. Naval Acad., 1891; m. Fanny, d. of ex-President Hayes, Sept. 1, 1897; 1 son, Dalton Hayes; m. 2d, Olga, d. C. A. Bengtson, 1920; children—Harry Eaton, Robert Giesé. Commissioned ensign U.S.N., 1893; lt. (j.g.), 1899; lt., 1900; lt. comdr., 1906; transferred to corps of profs. of mathematics, 1906; comdr., Aug. 10, 1907; capt., 1919. Duty U.S. Naval Acad., 1903-15, and head of dept. mathematics, 1912-15; U.S. Naval Obs., 1915; retired, Mar. 30, 1920. In charge of a group of gold mines, Shasta, Calif. Author: Strength of Material, 1908; Theoretical Mechanics (text-books for midshipmen). Home: Shasta, Calif. Died Mar. 26, 1931.

SMITH, Harry James, author; b. New Britain, Conn., May 24, 1880; s. John B. and Lucy F. (Nichols) S.; A.B., Williams Coll., 1902; A.M., Harvard, 1904; unmarried. Instr. Williams Coll., 1902-03, Oberlin Coll., 1904-05; asst. editor Atlantic Monthly, 1906-07; in journalistic and lit. work, 1907—. Author: Amédée's Son, 1908; Enchanted Ground, 1910; Mrs. Bumpstead-Leigh (play, prod. by Mrs. Fiske), 1911; Blackbirds (play), 1913. Address: Berlin, Conn. Died Mar. 17, 1918.

SMITH, Hay Watson, clergyman; b. Greensboro, N.C., Feb. 18, 1868; s. Rev. J. Henry and Mary Kelly (Watson) S.; A.B., Davidson (N.C.) Coll., 1890; student Union Theol. Sem., Richmond, Va., 3 yrs., Union Theol. Sem., New York, 1 yr.; D.D., Oglethorpe U., 1920; m. Jessie Alice Rose, Oct. 22, 1902; children—Mrs. Allan S. Glenn, Virginia Watson (Mrs. Eugene Zemp DuBose), Hay Watson, George Rose, Norris Kelly. Licensed ministry, Presbyterian Ch., 1897; served in various pastorates including Brooklyn and Port Chester, N.Y., until 1911; pastor Second Ch., Little Rock, 1911—. Democrat. Wrote: (brochures) Evolution and Presbyterianism, 1923; Some Facts About Evolution, 1927. Home: Little Rock, Ark. Died Jan. 20, 1940.

SMITH, Henry A. M., judge; b. Charleston, S.C., Apr. 30, 1853; s. John Julius Pringle and Elizabeth (Middleton) S.; B.A., Coll. of Charleston, 1872, LL.D., 1911; m. Emma B. Rutledge, June 24, 1879. Admitted to bar, 1874, and practiced at Charleston; mem. firm Mitchell & Smith, 1877-1911; U.S. dist. judge, Dist. S.C., June 14, 1911-23. Democrat. Episcopalian. V. chmn. Hist. Commn. S.C.; v.p. trustees Coll. of Charleston; v. chmn. Bd. Pub. Sch. Commrs. Frequent contbr. to S.C. Hist. and Geneal. Mag. Address: Charleston, S.C. Died Nov. 23, 1924.

SMITH, Henry Bradford, prof. philosophy; b. Phila., Pa., Jan. 14, 1882; s. Henry Augustus and Martha Louise (Stevenson) S.; A.B., U. of Pa., 1903, Ph.D., 1909; studied Harvard, 1904-05, Munich, 1 semester, 1906; m. Mary Follett Perkins, Sept. 13, 1915 (died 1925). Harrison scholar in philosophy, U. of Pa., 1903-04, 1905-06, fellow in philosophy, 1906-07, research fellow, 1910; instr. mathematics, Tufts Coll., 1904-05, Carnegie Inst., Pittsburgh, 1907-10; instr. mathematics, U. of Pa., 1911, in philosophy, 1911-16, asst. prof., 1916-24, prof., 1924—; sometime acting prof. philosophy, U. of Del., U. of Wash. and Bryn Mawr Coll. Mem. advisory bd. Philosophy of Science (mag.). Mem. Am. Philos. Assn., Am. Acad. Polit. and Social Science. Author: A First Book in Logic, 1922; How the Mind Falls into Error, 1923; The Collective Mind, 1924; A System of Formal Logic, 1926; Symbolic Logic, 1927; Science of Modality, 1934; also monographs and numerous articles in jours. Address: Philadelphia, Pa. Died Nov. 17, 1938.

SMITH, Henry Cassorte, congressman, lawyer; b. Canandaigua, N.Y., June 2, 1859; s. Wanton G. S.; grad. Adrian Coll., 1878 (B.S.); m. Emma Watts, Dec. 20, 1887; m. 2d, Grace Virginia Bassett, Sept. 20, 1904. Admitted to bar, 1880; city atty. Adrian, 1880; asst. pros. atty., 1881-83; delegate (alternate) Rep. Nat. Conv., 1896; won family mileage ticket case against L.S.&M.S. R.R. in lower courts; mem. Congress from 2d Mich. dist., 1899-1903. Republican. Address: Adrian, Mich. Died 1911.

SMITH, Henry Justin, newspaper editor; b. Chicago, Ill., June 19, 1875; s. Justin A. and Mary L. (Grose) S.; prep. edn., Morgan Park (Ill.) Acad.; A.B., U. of Chicago, 1898; m. Katharine A. Smith, Sept. 9, 1899. Began as reporter Chicago Daily News, 1899, city editor, 1901-06, asst. mng. editor, 1906-13, news editor, 1913-24; asst. to pres. U. of Chicago, 1924-26; mng. editor Chicago Daily News, 1926—. Author: The Other Side of the Wall, 1919; Deadlines, 1922; Josslyn, 1924; Innocents Aloft, 1927; Poor Devil, 1929, Senor Zero, 1931; Chicago—A Portrait, 1931; Chicago's Great Century, 1933; Young Phillips, Reporter, 1933. Co-Author: Chicago—The History of Its Reputation, 1929. Awarded Chicago Foundation for Literature prize, for fiction, 1931. Home: Glencoe, Ill. Died Feb. 9, 1936.

SMITH, Henry Leavitt, publisher; b. New York, Feb. 19, 1848; s. Rev. Dr. Asa D. Smith (pres. Dartmouth Coll.) and Sarah Ann (Adams) Smith; grad. Phillips Andover Acad., 1865; A.B., Dartmouth, 1869, A.M., 1872; m. Jane Isabelle Noyes, June 1, 1871. An incorporator, 1904, and dir. Charles Scribner's Sons; retired, 1912. Republican. Officer The Brick Presbyn. Church; treas., 1912-17, and mem. of exec. com. Coll. Bd. Presbyterian Ch.; pres. New York Bible Soc.; dir. and sec. N.Y. City Mission Soc. Home: New York, N.Y. Died Sept. 7, 1918.

SMITH, H(enry) M(arston), Jr., lawyer; b. Richmond, Va., July 19, 1859; s. Hiram Moore and Elizabeth (Ames) S.; grad. Va. Poly. Inst., 1877; student Richmond Coll., 1877-78; B.L., U. of Va., 1880 (classmate of Woodrow Wilson); m. Lucy Conway Gordon, Nov. 7, 1883; children—Hiram Moore, James Gordon, May St. Claire (Mrs. Walter L. Lefew). Admitted to Va. bar, 1880, and practiced at Richmond, 1880—; commonwealth's atty., Richmond, 1890-96; mem. firm Smith & Gordon; specialized in jury trials and widely known for connection with prominent criminal cases; dir. Union Bank & Federal Trust Co., Spotless Co. Capt. Home Guard, World War I. Del. Dem. Nat. convs., Baltimore and St. Louis; Dem. presdl. elector, 1909. Mem. bd. visitors Va. Poly. Inst. 15 yrs. Presbyterian. Home: Richmond, Va. Died June 21, 1936.

SMITH, Henry Preserved, educator, author; b. Troy, O., Oct. 23, 1847; s. Preserved and Lucy (Mayo) S.; A.B., Amherst, 1869; Lane Theol. Sem., 1869-72, U. of Berlin, 1872-74, U. of Leipzig, 1876-77; D.D., Maryville, 1883, Amherst, 1886, Princeton, 1888; m. Anna Macneale, Dec. 27, 1877. Ordained Presbyn. ministry, 1875; instr. ch. history and prof. Hebrew and O.T. exegesis, Lane Theol. Sem., Cincinnati, 1874-93; prof. Bibl. lit. and asso. pastor, Amherst, 1898-1906; prof. O.T. lit. and history of religions, Meadville (Pa.) Theol. Sch., 1907-13; chief librarian and prof., Union Theol. Sem., 1913-25, emeritus, 1925—. Author: Inspiration and Inerrancy, 1893; The Bible and Islam, 1897; A Commentary on the Books of Samuel (Internat. Critical Commentary), 1899; Old Testament History (Internat. Theol. Library), 1903; The Religion of Israel, 1914; Essays in Biblical Interpretation, 1921. Home: Poughkeepsie, N.Y. Died Feb. 26, 1927.

SMITH, Henry Tomlinson, dentist; b. Cincinnati, O., Jan. 24, 1866; s. Henry A. and Lucy (Tomlinson) S.; ed. Woodward High Sch.; D.D.S., Ohio Coll. of Dental Surgery, 1888; m. Clara Goshorn, Nov. 21, 1901; 1 son, Willard M. (dec.). Prof. dental pathology, Ohio Coll. of Dental Surgery (Dental Dept. of U. of Cincinnati), 1896—, also dean faculty and mem. bd. trustees. Editor Am. Jour. of Dental Science, Cincinnati. First lt. Cincinnati Home Guards, 1918-19. Mem. Med. Advisory Bd., Cincinnati Dist., 1918; examiner for dental R.C., 1918. Mem. Med. staff Episcopal Children's Hosp., Mt. Auburn Orphan Asylum. Treas. Soc. Colonial Wars in State of Ohio. Regular contbr. to dental jours. Home: Cincinnati, O. Died Mar. 11, 1930.

SMITH, Herbert Eugene, univ. dean; b. Hartford, Conn., Oct. 21, 1857; s. Henry Hart and Mary Buckley (Morgan) S.; Ph.B., Yale, 1879; M.D., U. of Pa., 1882; studied U. of Heidelberg, 1883; m. Emily Scull Dinnin, June 30, 1885; children—Emily Dinnin, Mary Morgan, Elizabeth B. Instr. chemistry, 1882-85, prof. and dean Med. Sch., 1885-1910, prof. emeritus, 1910—, Yale U. Home: Los Gatos, Calif. Died Oct. 9, 1933.

SMITH, Herbert Huntington, naturalist; b. Manlius, N.Y., Jan. 21, 1851; s. Charles and Julia Maria (Huntington) S.; studied Cornell U., 1868-72; m. Amelia Woolworth Smith, Oct. 5, 1880. Best known as collector of natural history specimens; traveled in Brazil, 1871, 1873-77, 1881-86, Mexico, 1889, W.I., 1890-95, Colombia, 1898-1901. In Mexico employed for the Biologia Centrali-Americana, in W.I. for W. Indian Com. of the Royal Soc. and Brit. Assn. Collections (at least 500,000 specimens) are in nearly every large museum in the world. Collaborated in Century Dictionary, Century Cyclo. of Names and Johnson's Cyclo. Curator Carnegie Museum, Pittsburgh, 1896-98, and connected with that instn., 1902; curator, Ala. Mus. of Natural History, 1910—. Author: Brazil—the Amazons and the Coast, 1880; De Rio de Janeiro á Cuyabá, 1886 (in Portuguese). Published His Majesty's Sloop Diamond Rock, over the pen-name, H. S. Huntington, 1904. Address: University, Ala. Died Mar. 22, 1919.

SMITH, Herbert Knox, lawyer; b. Chester, Mass., Nov. 17, 1869; s. Edward Alfred and Melissa E. (Knox) S.; A.B., Yale, 1891, post-grad., 1891-93, LL.B., 1895; m. Gertrude E. Dietrich, Sept. 29, 1908. Practiced law at Hartford, Conn., 1895-1903 and 1912—. Mem. Hartford Common Council, 1900-02; chmn. Hartford Rep. Town Com., Jan.-Dec. 1903; mem. Conn. Ho. of Rep., 1903-05; deputy commr. of corps., Dept. of Commerce and Labor, 1903-07; commissioner of corporations, 1907-12. Prog. candidate for gov. of Conn., 1912; maj. Q.M.C., U.S. Army, 1918-19. Dir. Farmington (Conn.) Savings Bank, Hartford-Empire Co. Conglist. Home: Farmington, Conn. Died Dec. 17, 1931.

SMITH, Hoke, senator; b. Newton, N.C., Sept. 2, 1855; s. Hosea Hildreth Smith (LL.D.) and Mary Brent (Hoke) S.; educated by father; moved to Ga., 1872; m. Birdie, d. Gen. T. R. R. Cobb, Dec. 19, 1883; children—Marion, Mrs. Mary Brent Ransom, Mrs. Lucy Hoke Smith Grant, Mrs. Callie Hoke Smith May; m. 2d, Mazie Crawford, Aug. 27, 1924. Admitted to Ga. bar, 1873; practiced at Atlanta, 1873-93, and 1896-1907; propr. of the Atlanta Journal, 1887-96. Del. Dem. State Conv., 1882; pres. Young Men's Library, Atlanta, 1881-83; pres. Atlanta Bd. Edn., 1896-1907; del. Dem. Nat. Conv., 1892; sec. of the interior, in cabinet of President Cleveland, Mar. 4, 1893-Sept. 1, 1896, resigning to support Bryan for the presidency; gov. of Ga., 1907-09; reëlected for term 1911-13; elected U.S. senator to fill unexpired term (1911-15) of A. S. Clay, deceased, and resigned as gov.; began service as U.S. senator, Dec. 1, 1911; reëlected for term 1915-21; later practiced law at Atlanta. Home: Atlanta, Ga. Died Nov. 27, 1931.

SMITH, Holmes, coll. prof.; b. Keighley, Yorkshire, Eng., May 9, 1863; s. Solomon and Margaret (Myers) S.; educated schs. in England, including the Normal Sch. of Science, later the Royal Coll. of Science, South Kensington, 1880-84; studied art and its history in U.S. and Europe; hon. A.M., Washington U., 1907; Dr. Fine Arts, U. of Neb., 1928; came to U.S., 1884, naturalized, 1896; m. Rose Greenleaf Eliot, Feb. 9, 1897; 1 dau., Abigail Eliot, M.D. Instr. drawing, 1884-1903, asst. prof., 1903-07, prof. drawing and history of art, 1907-30, prof. of history of art, 1930-33 (prof. emeritus, 1933—), Washington U. (asst. to the dir. of St. Louis Sch. and Mus. of Fine Arts, 1892-94). Painter of water colors and exhibitor in various exhbns. Lecturer and contbr. to literature on art and ednl. topics. Joint Author: College Teaching (chap. on teaching of art). Home: St. Louis, Mo. Died June 1, 1937.

SMITH, Homer, prof. English; b. Boston, Mass., June 27, 1867; s. George and Anne Eliza (Richards) S.; A.B., Amherst, 1891; Ph.D., U. of Pa., 1895; m. Julia Perry, 1905. Instr. English, U. of Pa., 1892-98; prof. English, Amherst, 1900-02, Ursinus Coll., 1903—. Republican. Episcopalian. Author: Pastoral Influence in the English Drama, 1897. Home: Collegeville, Pa. Died Aug. 26, 1934.

SMITH, H(omer) A(mos) A(rthur), chief Washington, D.C., Office, Panama Canal; b. Weston, Vt., Mar. 4, 1875; s. Amos Adoniram and Clara A. (Priest) S.; Ph.B., U. of Colo., 1899; LL.B., Columbian (now George Washington) U., Washington, D.C., 1901; LL.M., Nat. U. Law School, Washington, D.C., 1902; m. Hazel Grove, July 23, 1902; children—Carla (Mrs. Donald L. Turner), Frances Winfield (Mrs. E. David Haas), Homer Grove, Angeline (Mrs. James W. Eastwood). Librarian U.S. Treasury Dept., 1900-02; clk. office of auditor for War Dept. and Isthmian Canal Commn., 1902-08; treas. Canal Zone, 1908; asst. examiner of accounts Isthmian Canal Commn., 1908-11, head accounting dept., 1911-22; mem. Joint Land Commn. U.S. and Panama, 1920; chief investigations Gen. Accounting Office, 1922-27; chief accountant Employees Compensation Commn., 1927-28, commr., 1928-29; accountant and legal adviser Bur. Industrial Alcohol, 1929-30; asst. comptroller Panama Canal, 1930-36, comptroller, 1936, chief Washington Office and gen. purchasing officer, 1936—; dir. Panama R.R. Co. Pres. Union Ch. of the Canal Zone, 1914-22. Presbyterian. Home: Takoma Park, Md. Died Mar. 20, 1940.

SMITH, Hugh McCormick, ichthyologist; b. Washington, Nov. 21, 1865; s. Thomas Croggon and Cornelia Frances (Hazard) S.; ed. pub. and high schs., Washington; M.D., Georgetown U., D.C., 1888; post-grad. med. study, New York; LL.D., Dickinson, 1908; m. Emma Hanford, Mar. 12, 1899. Entered U.S. Fish Commn. (now Bur. of Fisheries), as asst., 1886; asst. in charge scientific inquiry, 1897-1903; dir. biol. lab., U.S. Fish Commn., Woods Hole, Mass., 1901-02; co-spl. agt. in charge of fisheries, 10th Census; deputy commr. of fisheries, 1903—. Editor Bur. of Fisheries, 1904—. Mem. med. faculty, Georgetown U., 1888-1902, prof. normal histology, 1895-1902. Visited many foreign countries to study their fisheries; represented U.S. at various internat. fishing congresses; published numerous reports and papers on ichthyology, economic fisheries and pisciculture, in govt. reports and elsewhere; contbr. to tech. and popular periodicals. Fellow A.A.A.S. Home: Washington, D.C. Died Sept. 28, 1941.

SMITH, Huron H(erbert), curator of botany; b. Danville, Ind., July 26, 1883; s. Wesley Orrison and Emma Lavina (McCurdy) S.; grad. high sch., Winchester, Ind., June 1902; B.S., De Pauw U., 1905; studied Cornell U., 1905-07; m. Ethel Auretta Clark, June 15, 1910; 1 dau., La Vaughn Chenewah. Asst. curator of botany, Field Mus., Chicago, worked on a dictionary, and collected N. Am. Dendrographic Display, 1907-17; curator of botany, Milwaukee Pub. Mus.; spl. research and publs. in ethnobotany of Wis. Indian tribes. Physical and ednl. sec. Y.M. C.A., World War I; troop transport sec. U.S. to France. Fellow A.A.A.S.; mem. Wis. Acad. Science, Arts and Letters. Sixth recipient of Increase A. Lapham medal, Wis. Archæol. Soc. Republican. Methodist. Author: Ethnobotany of Menomini Indians, 1924; Ethnobotany of Meskwaki Indians, 1927; Ethnobotany of Ojibwe Indians; Mushrooms of Milwaukee Region; also year books Milwaukee Pub. Mus. and many articles in mags. Lecturer. Home: Milwaukee, Wis. Died 1933.

SMITH, Isabel E., miniature painter; b. Smiths Landing, O.; d. Capt. Alexander and Rachel (McClain) S.; m. Carl F. Smith, 1895. Painted miniature of President McKinley (on brooch daily worn by Mrs. McKinley); also miniature of Queen Wilhelmina of Holland from life, Queen Victoria, President Faure of France, and other notables. Mem. Nat. Woman's Indian Assn. Auxiliary. Home: Pasadena, Calif. Died Oct. 4, 1938.

SMITH, J(abez) Burritt, lawyer; b. Sherburn, N.Y., Mar. 17, 1852; s. Martin Hubbard and Mary Ann (Holmes) S.; grad. State Normal Sch., Winona, Minn., 1875; m. Marcia Alice Bradford, Mar. 17, 1876. Admitted to Wis. bar, 1880; practiced, Hudson, 1881-88; at Madison, 1888—; owner The Peerless Press. State sec. Prohibition Party State Central Com., 1888-94, chmn. same com., 1909—; mem. Prohibition Nat. Com., 1910—; Prohibition candidate for gov. of Wis., 1900. Conglist. Author: High Joe, or The Logger's Story, 1892; Barriers Broken, 1894. Home: Madison, Wis. Died Dec. 31, 1914.

SMITH, Jacob Hurd, brig. gen. U.S.A.; b. Jackson, Iron Furnace, O., Jan. 29, 1840; s. J. M. G. S.; grad. Collegiate and Commercial Inst., New Haven, Conn., 1858; m. Adelaide M. Hall, of Topeka, Kan., Feb. 4, 1885. Enlisted for Civil War, May 8, 1861; 1st lt. 2d Ky. Inf., June 5, 1861; capt., Jan. 28, 1862; hon. mustered out, June 29, 1863; capt. Veteran Reserve Corps, June 25, 1863; hon. mustered out, Oct. 21, 1865; capt. 13th Inf. U.S.A., Mar. 7, 1867; maj. judge advocate May 25, 1869; maj. 2d Inf., Nov. 26, 1894; lt. col. 12th Inf., June 30, 1898; lt. col. 17th Inf., Oct. 20, 1899; brig. gen. vols., June 1, 1900; brig. gen. U.S.A., Mar. 30, 1901; retired, July 17, 1901. Bvtd. maj. Mar. 7, 1867, "for gallantry in battle of Shiloh, Tenn., Apr. 6, 1862"; twice wounded; in Indian wars of frontier, 1867-98; participated in Spanish-Am. War, 1898, in Philippines, 1899. Address: Washington, D.C. Died Mar. 2, 1918.

SMITH, James, Jr., senator; b. Newark, N.J., June 12, 1851; ed. pvt. schs. and coll. at Wilmington, Del. Engaged in dry goods and importing business, and later mfr. of patent and enameled leather; pres. Federal Trust Co., Newark. Alderman Newark, 1883-87; declined unanimous nomination for mayor; later pres. 1st bd. of works of Newark. Mem. of Dem. Nat. Com., and chmn. N.J. delegations to Dem. Nat. convs., 1884, 1892, 1896; U.S. senator from N.J., 1893-99. Home: Newark, N.J. Died Apr. 1, 1926.

SMITH, J(ames) Allen, univ. prof.; b. Pleasant Hill, Mo., May 5, 1860; s. Isaac James and Naomi (Holloway) S.; A.B., U. of Mo., 1886, LL.B., 1887, A.M., 1892; Ph.D., U. of Mich., 1894; m. Doris J. Lehmann, Nov. 26, 1890. Prof. economics and sociology, Marietta Coll., O., 1895-97; prof. polit. science, 1897—, dean Grad. Sch., 1909-20, U. of Wash. Actg. prof. polit. science, Stafford U., 1918-19. Author: The Multiple Money Standard, 1896; The Spirit of American Government, 1907. Address: Seattle, Wash. Died Jan. 30, 1926.

SMITH, James Allwood, consul gen.; b. Grand Rapids, Mich., Nov. 3, 1865; s. Rev. Joseph Morgan and Cordelia (Root) S.; ed. Williston Sem., Easthampton, Mass.; m. Marguerite A. Ransom, Dec. 18, 1890. Mgr. extensive marble property in Vt., 1891; Am. consul at Leghorn, Italy, 1897-1907; consul gen. at Boma, Kongo Free State, 1907-08, at Genoa, Italy, 1908-13, at Calcutta, India, Sept. 1913—. Republican. Conglist. Mason. Home: Middlebury, Vt. Died Oct. 2, 1920.

SMITH, James Dickinson, banker, yachtsman; b. Exeter, N.H., Nov. 24, 1832; s. Rev. John and Esther Mary (Woodruff) S.; ed. public schools; m. Elizabeth, d. Archibald Henderson, 1857. Established banking firm of Jameson, Smith & Cotting, later James D. Smith & Co., New York; pres. of New York Stock Exchange, 1885-86; treas. State of Conn., 1881; pres. city council, Stamford, Conn., 1894-97; dir. in several corporations. Mem. N.Y. Yacht Club, Mar. 27, 1873—, of which he was rear-commodore, 1880, vice-commodore, 1881, commodore, 1882-83; for 13 yrs. chmn. America's cup com. of the club; owned several famous yachts. Address: New York, N.Y. Died 1909.

SMITH, James Ellwood, business man; b. Schellsburg, Pa., Feb. 12, 1851; s. John and Jane (Rea) S.; ed. pub. schs., Schellsburg; m. Sallie Bryant, Dec. 15, 1880. Located at St. Louis, 1875; with Simmons Hardware Co., 1875-1911, dir., 1889, sec., 1893-98, v.p., 1898-1911; dir. of First National Bank, St. Louis, 1900-35. Dir. of the Louisiana Purchase Expn., 1904 (chmn. com. electricity; mem. com. fine arts and internat. jury awards); hon. commr. of expdn. to Japan, 1902, and decorated with Order Rising Sun, 1904; Imperial Order of Sacred Treasure, 1932; consul honoraire for Japan at St. Louis, 1904-32. Mem. inland water transportation com. of Council Nat. Defense, June 1917-19; mem. advisory bd. Inland Waterways Corp., 1924-34. Democrat. Presbyterian. Home: St. Louis, Mo. Died May 3, 1936.

SMITH, James Francis, judge; b. San Francisco, Calif., Jan. 28, 1859; s. Patrick and Anne S.; grad. Santa Clara Coll., 1878, A.M.; studied law Hastings Law Sch., Calif.; admitted to bar, Jan. 1881; m. Lillie A. Dunnigan, Aug. 13, 1885 (dec.); 1 son, Cyril J. Became col. 1st Calif. Regt., U.S.V., Apr. 1898; served 1st expdn. to Philippines, arriving June 30, 1898; was in battle of Malate Trenches, July 31, 1898, taking of Manila, Aug. 13, 1898; dep. provost marshal, Manila, Aug. 1898; pres. Mil. Commn., Oct. 12, 1899; comd. 1st Brigade, 1st Div. 8th Army Corps, Oct. 22, 1898; mem. commn. to confer with commn. from Aguinaldo, Jan. 1899; in battle of Santa Aña, Feb. 5, 1899; in fighting at San Pedro Mecati, Pateros and Taguig, Feb. 15 to Mar. 1, 1899; commended for gallantry in dispatches; in command Island of Negros, March 1, 1899; brig. gen. U.S.V., Apr. 24, 1899; comd. Dept. Visayas, Apr. 1899; mil. gov. Island of Negros, July 24, 1899; collector customs, Philippine Archipelago, Oct. 1900; hon. discharged, June 17, 1901. Asso. justice Supreme Court of P.I., June 17, 1901; mem. Philippine Commn. and sec. of Pub. Instrn., P.I., Jan. 1, 1903-06; gov. gen. of P.I., Sept. 20, 1906-Nov. 11, 1909 (resigned); apptd. asso. judge U.S. Ct. of Customs Appeals, 1910. Home: Cloverdale, Calif. Died June 29, 1928.

SMITH, J(ames) Frank(lin), clergyman; b. Gadsden, Tenn., Dec. 24, 1868; s. John Wesley and Emily Elizabeth (Combs) S.; A.B., Bethel Coll., McKenzie, Tenn., 1892; B.D., Cumberland U., Lebanon, Tenn., 1895; grad. Union Theol. Sem., New York, 1896; A.M., Columbia U., 1896; D.D., Trinity U., Tex., 1906; m. Lillian Duff Neal, of Louisville, Ky., Sept. 9, 1903. Ordained ministry Cumberland Presbyn. Ch., 1892; pastor City Temple—Central Presbyn. Ch., Dallas, Tex., 1896—. Moderator Tex. Synod, 1901; mem. Council of Chs. holding the Reformed Faith; del. Federal Council Chs. of Christ in America; moderator Gen. Assembly of Presbyn. Ch. in U.S.A., 1918-19. Progressive Democrat. Author: My Father's Business and Mine, 1914. Address: Dallas, Tex. Died July 15, 1920.

SMITH, James Henry Oliver, clergyman; b. Warren County, O., Dec. 27, 1857; s. Edward Mosely and Sarah (Wilson) S.; B.A., Butler U., M.A., 1884; D.D., LL.D.; m. Mary Elmina Coe, Aug. 31, 1880. State evangelist of Christian (Disciples) Ch., Ind., and editor Central Christian, 1885-88; pastor, Valparaiso, Ind., 1888-95, and of Union Christian Ch., Chicago, People's Inst., Chicago; afterwards lectured in West, Calif. and Tex.; pastor First Ch., Oklahoma City, later First Ch., Little Rock, Ark., Met. Ch. of Christ, Chicago, then at Pittsburg, Kan., and as pastor First Ch., Okmulgee, Okla.; engaged in evangelistic service. Pres. Christian Endeavor Union of Ind., 1893; corr. sec. Ind. Christian Missionary Soc. 3 yrs.; dir. Foreign Christian Missionary Soc., Am. Missionary Soc., Provident Assn.; served as dir. Carnegie Library, Oklahoma City. Dir. McGarvey Bible Coll. and Internat. Bible Coll. Home: Oklahoma City, Okla. Died Dec. 27, 1935.

SMITH, James McLain, farmer, breeder; b. Troy, O., Nov. 4, 1838; s. T. J. S. and Jane Bacon S.; A.M., Miami U., 1859; studied law in father's office; admitted to bar, 1861; never practiced; unmarried. Elected to legislature, 1870; trustee Miami U., 1872-97; trustee Ohio State U., 1897—; editor and propr. Dayton Daily Ledger, 1875-76; editor of Dayton Democrat, 1877-79; editor Farmers' Home, 1890-97. Established 1st herd of Red Polled cattle in Ohio, and made 1st importation of the breed to that State, 1886. Sec. Red Polled Cattle Club of America, 1888—; gold standard Democrat. Contbr. to revs. on econ. topics. Address: Dayton, O. Died 1905.

SMITH, James Perrin, paleontologist; b. Cokesbury, S.C., Nov. 27, 1864; s. Rev. James Francis and Julia (Forster) S.; A.B., Wofford Coll., S.C., 1884; A.M., Vanderbilt U., Tenn., 1886; Ph.D., Univ. of Göttingen, Germany, 1892; LL.D., Wofford Coll., S.C., 1916; m. Frances Norris Rand, Aug. 19, 1896; children—Forster Rand, Mary Norris, Howard Carlisle, Charles Kirtland. Prof. paleontology, Stanford U., 1892—; geologist U.S. Geol. Survey, 1895—. Democrat. Protestant. Author numerous monographs on scientific topics. Address: Palo Alto, Calif. Died Jan. 1, 1931.

SMITH, James Porter, prof. of theology; b. of Am. parents, Recife, Brazil, S. America, Aug. 19, 1882; s. John Rockwell and Susan Caroline (Porter) S.; parents missionaries in Brazil; student Central Coll., Danville, Ky., 1901-02, U. of Va., 1902-07; Union Theol. Sem., Richmond, 1907-09; D.D., Hampden-Sidney Coll., 1923; m. Sarah Miller Hall, Dec. 29, 1909; children—Rockwell Hall, James Warfield, Carolyn Miller, Charles Emerson. Ordained missionary of Presbyn. Ch. in U.S., 1909; field and pastoral work, Brazil, 1909-19; prof. church history and history of philosophy, Theol. Sem. of Presbyn. Ch. of Brazil, 1919-24, prof. systematic theology, 1924-30, pres., 1926-30; prof. theology Union Theol. Sem., Richmond, 1930—. Editor: An Open Door in Brazil, 1925. Home: Richmond, Va. Died July 31, 1940.

SMITH, James Sheppard, banker; b. St. Louis, Mo., Feb. 3, 1871; s. Elsworth Fayssoux and Isabelle (Chenie) S.; student St. Louis U.; m. Susan Mitchell Cabanne, Oct. 15, 1893; children—Sunie C., Elsworth F., J. Sheppard, Charless, Cabanne, Mary Ambrose. Pres. Miss. Valley Trust Co., 1925—; pres. de Mun Estate Corp.; dir. Smith & Davis Mfg. Co., Mo. State Life Ins. Co., Mo. Portland Cement Co., Am. Credit Indemnity Co., St. Louis Public Service Co. Republican. Catholic. Home: St. Louis, Mo. Died Oct. 9, 1931.

SMITH, Jeanie Oliver Davidson ("Temple Oliver"), author; b. Troy, N.Y.; d. Richard and Margaret Oliver (Amos) Davidson; ed. Troy, N.Y., and Edinburgh, Scotland; m. Horace E. Smith, LL.D., dean Albany Law Sch. (died 1902). Lived several years in Scotland; contbr. to Brit. and Am. periodicals. Presbyterian. Author: Day Lilie (poems), 1889; Mayor of Kanemeta, 1891; Donald Moncrief, 1893; Story of Blackie (juvenile), 1894; Stories of Fido and Hunter (juvenile), 1896; Blackie's Diary (juvenile), 1899; The Christ (poems), with O. C. Auringer, 1899; Blackie's Companions, 1907; Dun Edin—an International Story, 1909; His Heart's Desire, 1909; The Midnight Journey (poem), 1909; Sonnets of Life, 1911; A Forest Idyl, 1913; (Easter brochure) The Ascension, 1913; The New York Stock Exchange, 1913; The Seal of Hellas (poetic drama), 1915; Things of To-day (essays and revs.), 1916; The Story of Zephyr (juvenile Christmas story), 1917; Poems (brochure), 1919; The Art of Letters, 1919. Address: Johnstown, N.Y. Died Nov. 16, 1925.

SMITH, Jeremiah, judge; b. Exeter, N.H., July 14, 1837; s. Jeremiah and Elizabeth (Hale) S.; A.B., Harvard, 1856, A.M., 1859; LL.D., Dartmouth, 1883; m. Hannah Webster, Apr. 5, 1865 (died 1904); father of Jeremiah, Jr. Admitted to bar, 1861; practiced at Dover, N.H., 1861-67; justice Supreme Ct. of N.H., 1867-74; Story prof. law, Harvard, 1890-1910 (resigned to take effect Sept. 1, 1910). Visitor Chandler Scientific Sch., Dartmouth, 1885-92; trustee Phillips Exeter Acad., 1868-74, and 1898-1902. Address: Cambridge, Mass. Died Sept. 3, 1921.

SMITH, Jeremiah, Jr., lawyer; b. Dover, N.H., Jan. 14, 1870; s. Jeremiah and Hannah (Webster) S.; A.B., Harvard, 1892, LL.B., 1895; unmarried. Sec. to Justice Gray, of Supreme Ct. of U.S., 1895-96; practiced in Boston, 1896—; mem. firm of Herrick, Smith, Donald & Farley. Served with A.E.F. as capt. Q.-M. Corps; with Am. Mission to Negotiate Peace as counsel to Treasury Dept. and an adviser on financial questions; commr. gen. League of Nations for Hungary, 1924-26, in charge of financial reconstruction of Hungary. Trustee Phillips Exeter Acad., N.H.; fellow Harvard Coll. Democrat. Home: Cambridge, Mass. Died Mar. 12, 1935.

SMITH, Jesse Merrick, engineer; b. Newark, O., Oct. 30, 1848; s. Henry and Lucinda (Salisbury) S.; ed. Philo Patterson's Sch., Detroit, Mich., Rensselaer Poly. Inst., Troy, N.Y., 1865-68, École Centrale des Arts et Manufactures, Paris, 1869-72, M.E., 1872; m. Ella A. Moore, Feb. 5, 1879 (deceased); m. 2d, Annie Coffin, Nov. 26, 1903 (deceased); m. 3d, Mabel A. MacKinney, June 24, 1916. Engaged in building iron blast furnaces, and in coal mines in Hocking Valley, O., 1874-80; cons. engr., Detroit, designing spl. machinery and mfg. and elec. power plants, and expert in patent litigation, 1880-98; cons. engr. and expert in patent litigation in New York, 1898-1914. Address: New York, N.Y. Died Apr. 1, 1927.

SMITH, Jessie Willcox, artist; b. Phila., Pa.; ed. pvt. schs., Phila.; d. Charles Henry and Katherine DeWitt (Willcox) S.; studied at Pa. Acad. Fine Arts, and under Howard Pyle, at Drexel Inst.; unmarried. Portrait painter of children. Illustrator: Stevenson's Child's Garden of Verses; Kingsley's Water Babies; At the Back of the North Wind; also other books and much mag. work. Address: Philadelphia, Pa. Died May 3, 1935.

SMITH, Joel West, educator; b. East Hampton, Conn., Sept. 17, 1837; s. John William Burke and Delia Elliott (West) S.; ed. common and pvt. schs., Conn.; unmarried. Teacher pub. schs. of Ill., 1854-55; lost eyesight, 1862, by premature discharge of cannon in firing salute on 4th of July; became connected with Perkins Instn. for the Blind, Boston, Mass., May 1863; teacher in Royal Normal Coll. for the Blind, Sydenham, Eng., 1872-75; recalled to Perkins Instn., 1875, as supervisor boys' dept. and mgr. tuning dept. Revised the Braille system of writing and printing for the blind, by introducing the principle of recurrence of letters; first blind person to use a typewriter; secured contract from City of Boston for tuning and repairing pianos in all pub. schs., the work to be done by blind graduates of Perkins Instn.; pub. of The Mentor. Republican. Conglist. Home: East Hampton, Conn. Died May 9, 1924.

SMITH, John Addison Baxter, rear admiral U.S.N.; b. Baltimore, Mar. 21, 1845; s. John A. and Sophia F. S.; ed. Dickinson Sem., Pa.; served apprenticeship, machine shop, Baltimore; course of engring., Baltimore; m. Ella E. Smith. Apptd. 3d asst. engr. U.S.N., Apr. 21, 1863; promoted 2d asst. engr., Sept. 28, 1864; 1st asst. engr., 1868; chief engr., 1892; comdr., 1899; capt., June 1902; retired, Mar. 21, 1905, with rank of rear admiral, and apptd. gen. insp., Bur. Steam Engring., Navy Dept. Served off Charleston, S.C., during Civil War; attached to U.S.S. Housatonic when that vessel was blown up by Confederate torpedo. Served with Shufeldt Expdn., surveying Isthmus Tehuantepec; head of dept. steam engring., Norfolk Navy Yard, 1896-99; same New York Navy Yard, 1899-1905; had full charge of reconstructing the building and machinery of the dept.; built machinery of battleship Connecticut. Served on following vessels: Housatonic, Paul Jones, Wabash, Mohongo, Saco, Seminole, Mayflower, Hartford, Saugus, Wyandotte, Tallapoosa, Atlanta, Montgomery, Texas; served as gen. insp. of machinery, and pres. bd. on changes in machinery of vessels building on Atlantic Coast until Aug. 1908. Republican. Address: Atlantic City, N.J. Died Mar. 9, 1918.

SMITH, John Bernhardt, entomologist; b. New York, Nov. 21, 1858; s. John and Elizabeth S.; pub. sch. edn.; hon. Sc.D., Rutgers, 1891; m. Marie von Meske, June 22, 1886. Admitted to bar, 1879; spl. agt. Entomol. Div., U.S. Dept. Agr., 1884; asst. curator U.S. Nat. Mus., 1886; state entomologist of N.J., 1898; prof. entomology, Rutgers Coll., and entomologist N.J. Agrl. Coll. Expt. Sta., 1889—. In charge of N.J. State campaign against the mosquito pest, with an appropriation of $350,000. Fellow A.A.A.S. Editor Bulletin Brooklyn Entomol. Soc. and Entomologia Americana, to 1890; contbr. of several hundred articles to govt. and tech. publications. Author: Economic Entomology for the Farmer and Fruit-Grower, and for Use as a Text Book in Agricultural Schools and Colleges, 1896; Our Insect Friends and Enemies, 1909. Address: New Brunswick, N.J. Died Mar. 12, 1912.

SMITH, John Butler, governor; b. Saxton's River, Vt., Apr. 12, 1838; acad. edn. Began manufacture of hosiery and knit goods, 1864; permanently located at Hillsboro, 1866; built up large business, which was incorporated in 1882, he and a nephew being chief owners. Rep. presdl. elector, 1884; mem. Exec. Council of N.H., 1887-89; chmn. Rep. State Com., N.H., 1890; gov. of N.H., 1893 and 1894. Address: Hillsboro Bridge, N.H. Died Aug. 10, 1914.

SMITH, John Corson, soldier; b. Phila., Feb. 13, 1832; s. Robert and Sarah (Harvey) S.; ed. pub. schs., Phila.; m. Charlotte A. Gallaher, Mar. 24, 1856. Enlisted pvt. 74th Ill. Vols., 1862; raised Co. I, 96th Ill. Inf., and elected maj., Sept. 6, 1862; lt. col., Sept. 20, 1863; bvtd. col. vols., Feb. 20, 1865; brig. gen. vols. "for meritorious services," June 20, 1865; hon. mustered out, June 10, 1865. Participated in 2d battle of Fort Donelson, battles of Franklin, Liberty Gap, Chickamauga, Lookout Mountain, Missionary Ridge, Resaca, Kingston, Cassville, New Hope Church, Dallas, Pumpkinvine Creek, Pine Mountain, and at Kenesaw Mountain, where was severely wounded, also Nashville. In internal revenue service, 1865-74; chief insp. grain, Ill., 1875-77; commissioner Centennial Exposition, 1876; state treas., 1879-81, 1883-85, lt. gov. of Ill., 1885-89; del. Rep. Nat. convs., 1872, 76. Republican. 33° Mason; Past Grand Master Grand Lodge of Ill. A.F. & A.M., and I.O.O.F. Author: History of Freemasonry in Illinois, 1903; also many pamphlets. Home: Chicago, Ill. Died 1910.

SMITH, John Day, judge; b. Litchfield, Me., Feb. 25, 1845; s. Edward G. and Elizabeth B. (Lord) S.; A.B., Brown U., 1872, A.M., 1875; LL.B., Columbian (now George Washington) U., 1878, LL.M., 1881; m. Mary H. Chadbourne, July 20, 1872 (died 1874); m. 2d, Laura Bean, Sept. 16, 1879. Served in Civil War in Co. F, 19th Me. Vols., 2d Army Corps; was in all battles of Army of Potomac from Antietam until June 22, 1864, when he was severely wounded in action at Petersburg, Va. Prin. Worcester (Mass.) Acad., 1872-76. Admitted to bar, 1880; mem. Minn. Ho. of Reps., 1889, Senate, 1891-95; judge 4th Judicial District Minn., terms 1905-11, 1911-17; resigned because of serious illness, May 5, 1913. Republican. Lecturer on law of torts and criminal law, Howard U., 1881-86, on Am. constl. law, U. of Minn., 1888-1905. Baptist. Author: Cases on Constitutional Law, 1897; History of Nineteenth Maine Regiment, 1909; Reminiscences and Sunset Memories, 1923. Home: Minneapolis, Minn. Died Mar. 5, 1933.

SMITH, John Hammond, prof. civil engring.; b. Wellsville, O., Oct. 14, 1867; s. John William and Almira (Hart) S.; E.E., Western U. of Pa. (now U. of Pittsburgh), 1898; post-grad. work, Cornell U., summer of 1900; m. Anna D. Coleman, July 3, 1901 (died 1906); children—Anna Virginia, Lillian Isabella; m. 2d, Gertrude M. Smith, June 23, 1909 (died 1918); m. 3d, Helen C. Dalrymple, June 25, 1919; children—Helen Ilene, Evelyn Almira, Martha Louise. With Julian Kennedy, Riter-Conley Mfg. Co., Am. Bridge Co. and Concrete Products Co., Pittsburgh, 1896-1910; supt. shops and instr., 1898-1900, prof. drawing, 1900-09, prof. civ. engring., 1909—, U. of Pittsburgh. Republican. Presbyn. Contbr. many papers on engring. and photo-sculpture. Inventor of new photo-sculpturing process and instruments for testing materials. Home: Pittsburgh, Pa. Died 1932.

SMITH, John M. C., congressman; b. Belfast, Ireland, Feb. 6, 1853; s. Richard and Barbara (McMunn) S.; brought to America by parents, 1855; student lit. dept., 1878-79, law dept., 1879-80, U. of Mich.; m. Lena Parkhurst, Oct. 6, 1887. Admitted to bar, 1882, and in practice at Charlotte, 1882—; pres. First Nat. Bank, Charlotte, 1898—; also interested in farming and stock raising. Alderman and pros. atty., Charlotte; mem. Mich. Constl. Conv., 1908; mem. 62d to 67th Congresses (1911-23), 3d Mich. Dist. Republican. Mason. Address: Charlotte, Mich. Died Mar. 30, 1923.

SMITH, J(ohn) M(erlin) Powis, educator; b. London, Eng., Dec. 28, 1866; s. William and Anne (Powis) S.; A.B., Des Moines (Ia.) Coll., 1893; Ph.D., U. of Chicago, 1899; D.D., Meadville Theological School, 1931; m. Catherine McKlveen, Sept. 19, 1899; 1 dau., Mrs. H. E. Gates. Instr. Greek, Des Moines Coll., 1891-92, Cedar Valley Sem., Osage, Ia., 1893-95; grad. student and fellow, U. of Chicago, 1895-99; lit. sec. to Pres. William R. Harper, 1899-1906; docent in Semitic langs. and lits., 1899-1901, asst., 1901-02, asso., 1902-05, instr., 1905-08, asst. prof., 1908-12, asso. prof., 1912-15, prof., 1915—, U. of Chicago. Asso. editor Bibl. World, 1906-20, Am. Jour. Theology, 1907-20, Jour. of Religion, 1920—; asso. editor, 1907-15, editor, 1915—, Am. Jour. Semitic Langs. and Lits. Progressive Rep. Bapt. Author: Biblical Ideas of Atonement (with E. D. Burton and G. B. Smith), 1909; Commentaries on Micah, Zephaniah, Nahum and Malachi (Internat. Critical Series), 1911-12; Commentaries on Amos, Hosea and Micah (Bible for Home and School), 1914; The Prophet and His Problems, 1914; A Guide to the Study of the Christian Religion (with G. B. Smith, et al.), 1916; Harper-Smith's Hebrew Method and Manual, 1921; Harper-Smith's Elements of Hebrew, 1921; The Religion of the Psalms, 1922; The Moral Life of the Hebrews, 1923; The Prophets and Their Times, 1925; The Psalms, 1926; The Old Testament—An American Translation (with A. R. Gordon, T. J. Meek and L. Waterman), 1927; The Bible—An American Translation (with E. J. Goodspeed), 1931. Contbr. to University of Chicago Sermons, 1915; to Hastings' Dictionary of the Bible (one vol.), 1909; to Dictionary of Religion and Ethics (Matthews and G. B. Smith), 1921; to Standard Bible Dictionary, 1925, and Ency. Britannica, 1929. Mem. Commn. apptd. by Internat. Council of Religious Edn. to revise the American Revision of the Bible, 1930. Home: Chicago, Ill. Died Sept. 26, 1932.

SMITH, John Talbot, clergyman; b. Saratoga, N.Y., Sept. 22, 1855; acad. edn., Albany, N.Y.; grad. div. dept., St. Michael's Coll., Toronto, Can.; LL.D., Mt. St. Mary's Coll., Emmitsburg, Md., 1896, Notre Dame U., 1907. Ordained R.C. priest, 1881; missionary in Adirondacks, 1881-89; pastor Dobbs Ferry, N.Y., 1908—. Editor New York Catholic Review, 1889-92; contbr. to various mags. Author: A Woman of Culture, 1881; Solitary Island, 1884; History Diocese of Ogdensburg, 1885; The Prairie Boy, 1886; His Honor, the Mayor, 1891; Saranac, 1893; Training of a Priest, 1896; The Chaplain's Sermons, 1896; Brother Azarias, 1897; Lenten Sermons, 1899; The Black Cardinal (drama), 1900; The Man Who Vanished, 1904; History of Catholics of New York (2 vols.), 1907; The Black Cardinal (novel), 1909; The Boy Who Looked Ahead, 1920; The Boy Who Came Back, 1921. Founder Catholic Actors' Guild, 1914; The Parish Theatre, 1918; Catholic Writers Guild, 1920. Address: Dobbs Ferry, N.Y. Died Sept. 24, 1923.

SMITH, John Walter, senator; b. Snow Hill, Md., Feb. 5, 1845; s. John Walter and Charlotte (Whittington) S.; ed. pvt. tutors and Washington Acad.; m. Mary Frances Richardson, 1869. In lumber business, Md., Va., and N.C., 1865—; pres. First Nat. Bank of Snow Hill. Mem. Md. Senate, 1889-99 (pres. 1894); nominee for U.S. senator, 1896; mem. 56th Congress (1899-1901), 1st Md. Dist., resigned 1900; gov. of Md., 1900-04; elected U.S. senator, Mar. 24, 1908, for unexpired term (1908-09) of William Pinkney Whyte, deceased; reëlected for terms 1909-15 and 1915-21. Chmn. Dem. State Com.,

1895; del.-at-large Dem. Nat. Conv., 1900, 04, 12, 16. Address: Snow Hill, Md. Died Apr. 19, 1925.

SMITH, J(ohn) Warren, meteorologist; b. Grafton, N.H., Sept. 21, 1863; s. John R. and Mary E. (Wadleigh) S.; B.S., N.H. Coll. Agr. and Mechanic Arts, 1888, M.S., 1900; Lawrence Scientific Sch. (Harvard), 1891-92; grad. Summer Sch. of Agr., Ohio State U., 1902; married twice; children—(by 1st marriage) Ruth Eaton, Russell Wellington; (by 2d marriage) Audrey. Began with U.S. Weather Bur., 1888; dir. N.E. sect., 1890-96, Mont. sect., 1896-97, Ohio sect., 1898-1900; dist. forecaster at St. Louis, 1909-10; prof. meteorology and dir. Ohio sect., 1910-15, also prof. meteorol. science, Ohio State U., 1910-15; apptd. chief of div. agrl. meteorology, Weather Bur., Washington, 1916. Pres. Ohio Acad. Science, 1914-15. Author: Agricultural Meteorology, a Study in Weather and Crops (Rural Text Book Series), 1920. Home: Columbus, O. Died Jan. 21, 1940.

SMITH, John Wesley, state commr. agr.; b. Monongalia County, W.Va., Feb. 22, 1863; s. G. W. and Dorcas (Amos) S.; ed. Buckhannon (W.Va.) Acad. and Glenville Normal Sch.; m. Annie Laura Conrad, Sept. 30, 1890; children—Edward Conrad, Mrs. Elta Garrett, Mrs. Eva Weaver, George Emerson. Farmer; commr. of County Court, Lewis County, W.Va., 1899-1905; field agt. for state tax commr., W.Va., 1905-06; mem. Bd. of Review and Equalization, Lewis County, 1909-25; mem. W.Va. Ho. of Del., 1922-24, state commr. of agr., West Virginia, 1925—. Republican. Methodist. Leader in securing passage of coöperative marketing law, also of law coördinating work of Coll. of Agr. and State Dept. of Agr. Home: Charleston, Va. Died Jan. 1931.

SMITH, J(onas) Waldo, civil engr.; b. Lincoln, Mass., Mar. 9, 1861; s. Francis and Abigail Prescott (Baker) S.; Phillips Acad., Andover, Mass.; C.E., Mass. Inst. Tech., 1887; D.Engring., Stevens Inst. Tech., 1918; D.Sc., Columbia, 1918. Chief engr. water works of his home town at 17; asst. in office of Essex Co., Lawrence, 1881-83; asst., summers, Holyoke Water Power Co., 1884, 85, and 1887-90; joined staff of Clemens Herschel, 1890; res. engr. E. Jersey Water Co., looking after constrn. of 4 reservoirs and dams on Pequannock watershed, 1890-92; prin. asst. engr., same co., in charge Passaic Water Co., Paterson, and also engr. Montclair Water Co. and Acquackanonk Water Co., of Passaic, 1892-1900; chief engr. E. Jersey Water Co., 1900-1903; chief engr. aqueduct commrs. of New York, 1903-05; completed constrn. of new Croton dam (largest masonry dam in the world); chief engr. Bd. of Water Supply of New York, 1905-22, cons. engr., 1922; cons. engr., Moffat Tunnel Commn., Denver, Boston and Providence Water Supplies, etc. Awarded John Fritz medal, 1918, "for achievement as engineer in providing the City of New York with a water supply"; Washington Award of Western Soc. Engrs., 1925. Conglist. Home: New York, N.Y. Died Oct. 14, 1933.

SMITH, J(onathan) Ritchie, clergyman; b. Baltimore, Md., June 23, 1852; s. Joseph T. and Elizabeth C. (Letterman) S.; Baltimore City Coll.; A.B., Princeton, 1872, A.M., 1875; studied law, U. of Md., 1872-73; grad. Princeton Theol. Sem., 1876; D.D., Franklin and Marshall, 1903; m. Louise Hasbrouck, June 12, 1883; children—Ritchie Hasbrouck (dec.), Louise Letterman, Dudley Cooke, Craig Ritchie. Ordained Presbyn. ministry, 1876; pastor 1st Ch., Peekskill, N.Y., 1876-98, Market Sq. Ch., Harrisburg, Pa., 1900-14; lecturer, Union Theol. Sem., New York, 1913-14; prof. homiletics, Princeton Theol. Sem., 1914-29 (emeritus). Democrat. Author: Teaching of the Gospel of John, 1904; The Wall and the Gates, 1919; The Holy Spirit in the Gospels, 1926. Contbr. many papers to revs. and mags. Address: Englewood, N.J. Died Feb. 23, 1936.

SMITH, Joseph, pres. Reorganized Ch. of Jesus Christ of Latter-Day Saints; b. Kirtland, Lake County, O., Nov. 6, 1832; s. Joseph S. (founder of the Mormon Ch.) and Emma (Hale) S.; common sch. edn. at Nauvoo, Hancock County, Ill.; m. Ada Rachel Clark. After removal of the main body of Mormons to Utah, remained with his mother's family; kept hotel and farmed until manhood; studied law, but did not seek admission to bar. In 1860 became pres., as above, of—"Reorganized Church," being opposed to polygamy and not affiliating with the ch. in Utah. Editor Saints' Herald, organ of his denomination, 1863—. Address: Independence, Mo. Died Dec. 10, 1914.

SMITH, Joseph, newspaperman; b. Dublin, Ireland, Aug. 15, 1853; s. Patrick Gerald and Mary (Thornton) S.; grad. Royal Mil. Sch., Dublin; m. Janet Wright Worthen, Jan. 13, 1886. In U.S. cav. service in N.M., Ariz. and Tex., 1873-78; traveled in Brazil, Uruguay and Argentina, 1878-80; founded and edited Sunday Arena, Lowell, 1892; spl. corr. Illustrated American, Chicago Expn., 1893; sec. Lowell Police Commn., 1896-1906; became asso. editor Boston Traveler, 1907. Editor Boston Truth, 1913-14; sec. of publicity for City of Boston, 1922-25. Author: The "Scotch-Irish" Shibboleth (pub. by Am. Irish Hist. Soc., Washington), 1898. Contbr. papers on hist. and ethnol. subjects to Pilot. Wrote: The Algerine, Criterion, 1899; Tales of a Trooper, Illustrated American, 1893; Story of the Bones, and Rory Lynch, Harper's Weekly, 1894-97; Personally Conducted Tours, Life, 1897; also numerous sketches in "Life," 1897—. Home: Roxbury, Mass. Died July 15, 1929.

SMITH, Joseph Adams, rear admiral, U.S.N.; b. Machias, Me., Sept. 1, 1837; s. George S. and Delia P. (Adams) S.; ed. Machias pub. sch., Bucksport Sem., Me., Plymouth, N.H., and at Harvard Law Sch., LL.D.; m. May Hamlin Bartlett, Jan. 26, 1881. Apptd. to U.S.N. from Me., 1861, as asst. paymaster; served Kearsarge, comd. powder div., in fight with Confederate Stmr. Alabama, July 19, 1864; paymaster, 1862; pay inspector, 1879; paymaster-gen., U.S.N., 1882-86; pay dir., 1891; retired with rank rear admiral, Sept. 1, 1899. Died 1907.

SMITH, Joseph Fielding, pres. Ch. of Jesus Christ of Latter-Day Sains; b. Far West, Mo., Nov. 13, 1838; s. Hyrum and Mary (Fielding) S.; (nephew of Joseph Smith, "Mormon" prophet); drove an ox-team in the Exodus of 1846 to Winter Quarters on Missouri River; crossed plains and drove ox-team to Salt Lake Valley, 1848; worked as manual laborer, 1848-54; missionary to Sandwich Islands, 1854-58; sergeant-at-arms, Territorial legislature, 1858-59; ordained a seventy, Mar. 20, 1858; high priest and mem. High Council, Oct. 16, 1858; missionary to Great Britain, 1860-63, 1874-75, and 1877, and missionary to European Continent and Sandwich Islands. Presided over European mission, and edited "The Millennial Star." Ordained apostle, July 1, 1866; mem. council of 12, 1867; second counselor in First Presidency of Ch., 1880-1901; pres. of the ch. after Lorenzo Snow, 1901—. Several times mem. Utah Legislature; several times mem. city council Salt Lake City; council (or senate) in Utah Legislature, 1882; presided over Constl. Conv., 1882, which framed constn. for State of Utah, and petitioned Congress for admission into the Union. Pres. of Zion's Coöperative Mercantile Instn., State Bank of Utah, Zion's Savings Bank & Trust Co., Utah Sugar Co., Consolidated Wagon & Machine Co.; dir. U.P. R.R. Co., etc. Sr. editor "Juvenile Instructor," and the "Improvement Era" (monthly mag.), organ of the Young Men's Mutual Improvement assns. Address: Salt Lake City, Utah. Died Nov. 19, 1918.

SMITH, Joseph Rowe, brig. gen., U.S.A.; b. Madison Barracks, N.Y., Apr. 18, 1831; s. Gen. Joseph R. and Juliet Philipps (de Hart) S.; A.B., U. of Mich., 1848, A.M., 1851; M.D., U. of Buffalo, 1853; LL.D., U. of Mich., 1900; m. Claramond Colquhoun Cleemann, Dec. 17, 1857. Civ. engr., locating ry. bet. Watertown and Sacketts Harbor, 1847; laying out boundary between Creeks and Cherokees, 1850; laying out territorial rds. in Minn., 1851. Asst. surgeon U.S.A., Dec. 15, 1854; maj. surgeon, June 11, 1862; lt. col. surgeon, Jan. 9, 1885; col. surgeon, Feb. 9, 1890; retired, Apr. 18, 1895; advanced to rank of brig. gen. retired, by act of Apr. 23, 1904. In Tex. and on expdn. against hostile Indians, 1854-58; chief med. officer 6th column, Utah forces, 1858, then with Gen. Sumner pursuing Cheyennes; organized gen. hosps. in Washington and Georgetown, 1861, for reception of wounded from 1st Bull Run; acting surgeon gen. U.S.A., 1862-63; bvtd. lt. col., Mar. 13, 1865, "for superior ability and excellent management" of the affairs of his dept., and col., Nov. 22, 1866, for "meritorious services and devotion to the sick during the prevalence of cholera at Little Rock, Ark." Del. Internat. Med. Congress, Phila., 1876, Washington, 1887, Rome, 1894, Pan-Am. Med. Congress, Washington, 1893 (hon. pres. to represent U.S.A.); corporator New York Post-Grad. Med. Sch. and Hosp. Fellow Am. Acad. Medicine, Am. Statis. Assn.; mem. Am. Acad. Polit. and Social Science, Dept. Archæology U. of Pa. Contbr. of papers to Wood's Reference Hand-Book of Medical Sciences, on duties of military surgeons; also many other scientific and professional papers. Home: Philadelphia, Pa. Died 1911.

SMITH, Josiah Renick, univ. prof.; b. Columbus, O., Oct. 24, 1851; s. Josiah Dickey and Ann Eliza (Osborn) S.; B.A., Amherst, 1871, M.A., 1883; U. of Leipzig, 1881-83; m. C. Emily Moore, June 19, 1879. Asst. prof. ancient langs., Ohio Agrl. and Mech. Coll. (now Ohio State U.), 1876-81; resigned and went abroad for 2 yrs.; prof. Greek, Ohio State U., 1883—. Trustee Starling Med. Coll. Republican. Conglist. Editor: Xenophon's Memorabilia (Coll. Series of Greek Authors), 1903. Reviewer of books in The Dial, Chicago, 1895-1913; mus. critic Columbus Evening Dispatch, 1896-1906, Columbus Citizen, 1906-13; author of various essays and poems. Address: Columbus, O. Died 1914.

SMITH, Judson, clergyman; b. Middlefield, Hampshire County, Mass., June 28, 1837; s. Samuel and Lucina (Metcalf) S.; grad. Amherst Coll., 1859; Oberlin Theol. Sem., 1863; m. J. Augusta Bushnell, Aug. 1, 1865. Tutor Latin and Greek, Oberlin, 1862-64; instr. mathematics and physics, Williston Seminary, Mass., 1864-66; ordained Congl. minister, 1866; prof. Latin, Oberlin, 1866-70; prof. ecclesiastical history, Oberlin Theol. Sem., 1870-84; lecturer on modern history, Oberlin, 1875-84; corr. sec. Am. Bd. of Commrs. for Foreign Missions, 1884—. Trustee Oberlin Coll., Mt. Holyoke Coll., Williston Sem. Asso. editor Bibliotheca Sacra; visited missions of the board in Turkey in 1888, those in China in 1898; del. to World's Missionary Conf., London, 1888; del. and chmn. gen. com. Ecumenical Conf. on Foreign Missions, 1900. Author: Lectures in Church History and the History of Doctrine, 1881; Lectures in Modern History, 1881; etc. Lecturer on foreign missions, Hartford Theol. Sem. Residence: Roxbury, Mass. Died 1906.

SMITH, Julia Holmes, physician; b. Savannah, Ga., Dec. 23, 1839; d. Willis and Margaret Manning (Turner) H.; grad. Spingler Inst., N.Y., 1857; student Boston U. Sch. of Medicine, 1873-75; M.D., Chicago Homœ. Coll., 1877; m. Waldo Abbot, 1860 (died 1864); 1 son, Willis John; m. 2d, Sabin Smith, 1872; 1 dau., Helen Page (Mrs. Hyde W. Perce). Began practice at Chicago, 1877; prof. gynecology and dean Nat. Med. Coll. until retired, 1914. Officer Inst. of Homœopathy; supt. Dept. of Northwest, New Orleans Cotton Expn., 1885; v.p. Homœ. Congress, Chicago Expn., 1892-93; apptd. by Gov. Altgeld to fill unexpired term as first woman trustee of U. of Ill. Mem. Woman's Med. Assn. (an organizer; first pres.), Ill. Woman's Dem. League (pres. 1913). Home: Chicago, Ill. Deceased.

SMITH, Justin Harvey, author; b. Boscawen, N.H., Jan. 13, 1857; s. Rev. Ambrose and Cynthia Maria (Egerton) S.; A.B., Dartmouth, 1877, A.M., 1881, Litt.D., 1920; LL.D., Norwich, 1908; student, Union Theol. Sem., 1879-81; unmarried. Publishing business, 1881-90; mem. firm of Ginn & Co., in charge of editorial dept., 1890-98; prof. modern history, Dartmouth, 1899-1908; mem. visiting com. on Romance philology, Harvard, 1896-1906; mem. advisory com., Am. Hist. Assn., on pub. of Revol. records, 1914; chmn. Hist. MSS. Commn. of Am. Hist. Assn., 1917-23. Received (1920) from Columbia U. the Pulitzer Prize for best book on American history pub. in 1919, and (1923) the First Loubat Prize for "the best book" in English, pub. during the previous five years, on the history, geography, archæology, ethnology, philology or numismatics of N.A. Author: The Troubadours at Home (2 vols.), 1899; Arnold's March from Cambridge to Quebec, 1903; A Tale of Two Worlds and Five Centuries, 1903; Our Struggle for the Fourteenth Colony—Canada and the Am. Revolution (2 vols.), 1907; The Annexation of Texas, 1911; The War with Mexico (2 vols.), 1919. Editor: The Historie Booke, 1903; Letters of Santa Anna, 1919; also mag. writer. Address: New York, N.Y. Died Mar. 21, 1930.

SMITH, Kirby Flower, univ. prof.; b. Pawlet, Vt., Dec. 6, 1862; s. Henry H. and Julia M. (Flower) S.; A.B., U. of Vt., 1884, LL.D., 1910; Ph.D., Johns Hopkins, 1889; m. Charlotte, d. Edmund Law Rogers, June 8, 1893. Prof. Latin, Johns Hopkins U., 1889—. Editor: The Elegies of Tibullus, with intro. and commentary, 1913. Contbr. to philol. publs., especially Am. Jour. Philology. Acting dir., Sch. Classical Studies Am. Acad. in Rome, 1914-15. Address: Baltimore, Md. Died Dec. 6, 1918.

SMITH, Langdon, journalist; b. Ky., Jan. 4, 1858; common sch. edn. at Louisville, 1864-72; m. Marie Antoinette Wright, Feb. 12, 1894. During boyhood served in Comanche and Apache wars; later was corr. in Sioux war. Went to Cuba for New York Herald when war broke out in 1895; was at battle of Jobite, with Maceo; went through Cuba with insurrectos. When U.S. declared war went to Cuba as corr. New York Journal; was at bombardments before Havana; circumnavigated Cuba on dispatchboat "Premier," was at bombardment of Santiago; was on hill with marines at Guantanamo and at battle of El Caney and San Juan. Author: On the Pan Handle; also short stories. Address: New York, N.Y. Died 1908.

SMITH, Laura Rountree, author; b. Chicago, July 30, 1876; d. George P. and Laura G. (Rountree) S.; grad. Platteville (Wis.) Normal Sch., 1897. Teacher in 2d and 3d grades pub. schs., Platteville, 7 yrs. Author: Bunny Cotton Tail Series, 1905; Bear Books, 1908; Indian Reader, 1908; Language Reader, 1910; Roly-Poly Book, 1910; Little Eskimo, 1911; Circus Book, 1913; Sixty Musical Games, 1914; The Pixie in the House, 1915; The Pixie Out Doors, 1917; The Pixie in School; Three Little Kittens Who Lost Their Mittens; Twinkle Toes and His Magic Mittens; The Like to Do Stories; Puppet Plays for Special Days; New Common School Song Book; The Pixie on the Farm, 1921; The Rainbow Fairy, 1921; Community Plays for Various Days, 1921; also The Pixie, In Bunny Land, Healthy Bunny, Polite Bunny, Mother Bunny and Her Flowers, Father Bunny and His Birds, The Party Twins, Fifty Funny Animal Tales, Tale of Curly Tail, Gingerbread Boy, The Treasure Twins, The Runaway Bunny, The Cotton-Tail Primer The Cotton-Tail First Reader, The Tiddly Winks, Good Night Stories—all issued in 1922-23. Composer of words to cantata, "Mother Goose in Town." Contbr. to The Musician, Woman's Home Companion, Designer, etc. Home: Platteville, Wis. Died Feb. 22, 1924.

SMITH, Leon Perdue, educator; b. nr. White Plains, Ga., Dec. 24, 1869; s. Rufus Wright and Oreon (Mann) S.; A.B., Emory Coll., Ga., 1892; M.S. in chemistry and geology, U. of Chicago, 1915; m. Lewie Bigham, 1892 (died 1901); children—Robert Bigham, Leon Perdue; m. 2d, Linnie Malone, 1903; children—Rufus Eugene, Mary Elizabeth, Rosser Malone, Maidee. Dean La Grange (Ga.) Coll., 1903-12; prof. chemistry and geology, Wesleyan Coll., Macon, Ga., 1912—, v.p., 1918-31, dean, 1931—. Pres. Ga. State Assn. Colls., 1915-18, Southern Assn. Women's Colls., 1923. Fellow Am. Geog. Soc., A.A.A.S.; mem. Ga. Acad. Science (pres. 1931). Ind. Democrat; chmn. Conv. Hoover Democrats, Ga., 1928. Methodist. Writer on mineral subjects. Home: Macon, Ga. Died May 4, 1937.

SMITH, Leonidas D'Entrecasteaux, lawyer; b. Sparta, Tenn., Nov. 25, 1866; s. William Gooch and Amanda (Templeton) S.; ed. Doyle (Tenn.) Coll. and U. of Tenn.; m. Ella Wallace, Nov. 25, 1888; children—Keilah (Mrs. W. M. Neece), Ucal (dec.). Admitted to Tenn. bar, 1888, and began practice at Cookeville; in gen. practice at Knoxville, 1906-07. Spl. judge, Circuit Ct. of Tenn., 18 mos.; spl. justice Supreme Ct. of Tenn., 1925-27; atty. gen. and reporter, Tenn., 1926—. Democrat. Mem. Christian (Disciples) Ch. Mason, Odd Fellow. Author: Tenn. State Reports, Vols. 154-162, 1927-31. Address: Nashville, Tenn. Died Nov. 1932.

SMITH, Lyman Cornelius, capitalist; b. Torrington, Conn., Mar. 31, 1850; s. Lewis Stevens and Eliza Ann (Hurlbut) S.; ed. com. and state normal schs.; m. Flora Elizabeth (Bates) Burns, Feb. 13, 1877. Removed to New York, 1872, where he managed a live stock commn. house; engaged in lumber business, Syracuse, 1875; mfd. breech-loading firearms, 1877-90. Began as mfr. of typewriters, 1886, and in 1890, organized Smith Premier Typewriter Co., of which was pres.; sold out to Union Typewriter Co. and became v.p. and mem. exec. bd.; resigned, Feb. 10, 1903; in 1903, with brothers, organized L. C. Smith & Bros. Typewriter Co.; pres. U.S. Transportation Co., Am. Transportation Co. of the Great Lakes, Nat. Bank of Syracuse, L. C. Smith Transit Co., Rochester, Syracuse & Eastern R.R. Co.; treas. (with controlling interest), Toledo (O.) Shipbuilding Co.; chmn. mng. dirs. Halcomb Steel Co. In 1900 gave Syracuse U. the Lyman Cornelius Smith Coll. of Applied Science; v.p. bd. trustees Syracuse U. Chevalier Légion d'Honneur, France. Mason; Knight Templar. Address: Syracuse, N.Y. Died 1910.

SMITH, Lyndon Ambrose, lawyer; b. Boscawen, N.H., July 15, 1854; s. Ambrose and Cynthia M. (Egerton) S.; A.B., Dartmouth, 1880; LL.B., Georgetown U., D.C., 1882, LL.M., 1884; m. Dora Rogers, Feb. 3, 1896. Asst. to U.S. commr. edn., Bur. of Edn., Washington, 1880-85; admitted to bar, 1883; pros. atty., Chippewa County, Minn., 1889-90, 1903-09; lt. gov. of Minn., 1899-1903; asst. atty. gen. Minn., 1909-12; atty. gen. of Minn., Jan. 2, 1912—. Republican. Del. Universal Congress Lawyers and Jurists, St. Louis, 1904; pres. Assn. of Attys. Gen., 1917. Mason, Odd Fellow. Author: Recent School Law Decisions, 1883. Home: Montevideo, Minn. Died Mar. 5, 1918.

SMITH, Marcus Aurelius, U.S. senator; b. nr. Cynthiana, Ky., Jan. 24, 1852; ed. at Transylvania U., Lexington, Ky.; admitted to bar. Removed to Ariz., 1881; pros. atty., 1882; del. 50th to 53d (1887-95), 55th (1897-99), 57th (1901-03) and 59th and 60th (1905-09) Congresses from Ariz.; U.S. senator, terms 1912-15, 1915-21; mem. Internat. Joint Commn., 1921—. Democrat. Home: Tucson, Ariz. Died Apr. 7, 1924.

SMITH, Marion Couthouy, author; b. Phila., Pa.; d. Henry Pratt and Maria Couthouy (Williams) S. Author: Doctor Marks, Socialist, 1897; The Electric Spirit, and Other Poems, 1906; The Road of Life, and Other Poems, 1909; The Final Star, 1917; Sphinx of Flight, 1925. Contbr. to mags., chiefly of poems. Address: New York, N.Y. Died Nov. 19, 1931.

SMITH, Mary Elizabeth, deaconess, author; b. Dawson County, Ga., May 17, 1880; d. Wilbur Fisk and Permelia (Williams) S.; grad. Winthrop Normal and Industrial Coll., Rock Hill, S.C., 1900; grad. Scarritt Bible and Training Sch., Kansas City, Mo., 1907; unmarried. Teacher pub. schs., S.C., 1900-05; consecrated deaconess M.E. Ch., S., Houston, Tex., Apr. 1907; head res. Wesley House, Louisville, Ky., 1907-10; deaconess-asst. to Rev. James W. Lee, St. John's Ch., St. Louis, 1912-13. V.p. Workers' Conf. of Woman's Missionary Council, M.E. Ch., S.; editor Workers' Quarterly. Author: In Bethany House, 1912. Home: Belton, S.C. Died Mar. 31, 1915.

SMITH, Mary Prudence Wells, author; b. Attica, N.Y., July 23, 1840; d. Dr. Noah S. and Esther Nims (Coleman) Wells; grad. Greenfield (Mass.) High Sch., 1858, Miss Draper's Female Sem., Hartford, Conn., 1859; became asst. teacher Greenfield High Sch.; later asst. in Franklin Savings Instn., Greenfield, Mass., first woman employed in a savings bank in Mass.; m. Judge Fayette Smith, Apr. 14, 1875 (died 1903). Author: Jolly Good Series (8 vols.), 1875-95; Miss Ellis's Mission, 1886; The Young Puritan Series, 1897-1900; The Old Deerfield Series, 1904-09; Summer Vacation Series, 1914-17. Home: Greenfield, Mass. Died Dec. 17, 1930.

SMITH, Matthew F., clergyman; b. Falls Creek, Pa., Oct. 12, 1882; s. John Hunter and Mary (MacDonald) S.; Ph.B., Grove City (Pa.) Coll., 1906, A.M., 1908; B.D., Western Theol. Sem., Pittsburgh, 1911; D.D., Geneva Coll., Beaver Falls, Pa., 1916; m. Helen Elizabeth Bargar, Jan. 1, 1913. Ordained Presbyn. ministry, 1911; pastor Hookstown and Mill Creek, Pa., 1911-15, 1st Ch., Beaver Falls, 1915-21, 1st Ch., Indianapolis, Oct. 1, 1921—. Mem. Bd. Nat. Missions, Presbyn. Ch. U.S.A. Republican. Home: Indianapolis, Ind. Died Feb. 27, 1926.

SMITH, May Riley, author; b. Rochester, N.Y., May 27, 1842; d. Justin and Abbey Jane (Hagaman) Riley; ed. Brockport (N.Y.) Collegiate Inst. (non-grad.); m. Albert Smith, Mar. 31, 1869 (died 1919). Episcopalian. Author: (poems) The Gift of Gentians, 1882; The Inn of Rest, 1888; Sometime and Other Poems, 1892; Cradle and Arm Chair, 1893; also numerous booklets. Awarded prize, 1916, in competition for the best poem of the year. Home: New York, N.Y. Died Jan. 14, 1927.

SMITH, Milton H., railway pres.; b. Greene County, N.Y., Sept. 12, 1836. Began railway service as operator and clerk, superintendent's office, Mississippi Central R.R., Holly Springs, Miss.; with military rys. in Northern Ala. during war; freight agt. L.&N. R.R., Louisville, 1865-68; gen. freight agt. same, 1868-78; gen. freight agt. B.&O. R.R., 1878-81; gen. agt. Pa. R.R., 1881-82; 3d v.p. and traffic mgr., Jan. to July, 1882, 1st v.p., 1882-84, gen. mgr., 1883-84, pres., 1884-86, v.p., 1886-91, pres., Mar. 9, 1891—, L.&N. R.R. Address: Louisville, Ky. Died Feb. 22, 1921.

SMITH, Minna Caroline, author; b. Monterey, Calif.; daughter of Rev. W. N. and Jane (Letts) S.; sister of Gertrude S.; ed. Harvard Annex. Editor The American Baby Magazine, Chicago. Author: Mary Paget, a Romance of Old Bermuda, 1900; The Boys of Cary Farm; Red Top Ranch, 1907. Translator: Trilby, the Fairy of Argyle (from the French of Nodier); Saragossa (from the Spanish of Galdos), 1899; The Joy of Captain Ribot (from the Spanish of Valdés), 1900; José (Valdés), 1902. Address: Chicago, Ill. Died Feb. 16, 1929.

SMITH, (Edmund) Munroe, univ. prof.; b. Brooklyn, N.Y., Dec. 8, 1854; s. Dr. Horatio Southgate and Susan Dwight (Munroe) S.; A.B., Amherst, 1874; LL.B., Columbia, 1877; J.U.D., Univ. of Göttingen, Germany, 1880; LL.D., Columbia, 1904, Amherst, 1916; J.D., Louvain, 1909; m. Gertrude Huidekoper, Apr. 17, 1890; 1 dau., Gertrude Munroe (Mrs. L. Cushing Goodhue). Instr., 1880-83, adj. prof. history, 1883-91, prof. Roman law and comparative history, 1922-24, emeritus, 1924, Columbia. Lecturer jurisprudence, 1891-1922, Bryce prof. European legal Roman law, Georgetown Law School, Washington, 1901-23. Mem. Acad. Polit. Science; v.p. Internat. Acad. Comparative Law, The Hague; pres. Am. Polit. Science Assn., 1917. Editor Political Science Quarterly, 1886-1924. Author: Bismarck and Germany Unity, 1898; Out of Their Own Mouths, 1917; Militarism and Statecraft, 1918; also legal articles in Harper's Classical Dictionary, Lalor's Cyclo. of Political Science, the Universal Cyclo., Internat. Cyclo., etc. Address: New York, N.Y. Deceased.

SMITH, Nicholas, author; b. Blackburn, Eng., Oct. 31, 1836; s. William and Sarah (Bailey) S.; never attended sch.; went to Wis., 1844; worked in lead mines winters and on the farm summers, 1847-60; studied law; admitted to bar, 1862; m. Julia Clara, d. Dr. Moses Meeker, Aug. 14, 1862. Pvt. 33d Wis. Inf., Aug. 1862; 2d lt., Oct. 1862; 1st lt., May 1863; capt., Aug. 1863. Took part in Grant's and Sherman's expdn. through Central Miss., 1862-63; siege of Vicksburg and capture of Jackson, 1863; mil. comdr. ill-fated steamer John Warner on Red River expdn., spring of 1864; on expdn. against Marmaduke, fall of 1864; resigned Jan. 1865, on account of disability; began newspaper work on Waukesha (Wis.) Freeman, 1869; editor Janesville (Wis.) Daily Gazette, 1874-91, Fond du Lac Daily Commonwealth, 1895-99. Chmn. Rep. State Central Com., 1891-94; commd. col. on Gov. W. E. Smith's staff, 1880; mem. state bd. supervision of charitable, reformatory and penal instns., 1885-91. Author: Stories of Great National Songs, 1899; Hymns Historically Famous, 1901; Songs from the Hearts of Women, 1903; Our National Flag—In History and Incident; Masters of Old Age, 1905; Grant—The Man of Mystery. Spl. contbr. to History of Milwaukee, 1894. Address: Milwaukee, Wis. Died 1911.

SMITH, Nora Archibald, author; b. Phila., Pa., d. Robert N. and Helen E. (Dyer) Smith; family removed to Calif., 1873; A.B., Santa Barbara (Calif.) Coll., 1877; took various degrees in kindergarten training schs.; taught in Mex. and Ariz.; in 1880 joined her sister (Kate Douglas Wiggin) in kindergarten work and was for some yrs. supt. Silver St. Kindergartens, San Francisco. Author: The Message of Froebel, 1900; Three Little Marys, 1902; Nelson, the Adventurer, 1906; The Adventures of a Doll, 1907; The Doll's Calendar, 1909; The Home-Made Kindergarten, 1912; Old, Old Tales from the Old, Old Book, 1916; Plays and Pantomimes for Children, 1917; The Christmas Child, 1920; Action-Poems and Plays for Children, 1923; Boys and Girls of Bookland, 1923; Twilight Stories, 1925; Kate Douglas Wiggin as Her Sister Knew Her, 1925; A Truly Little Girl, 1927; Bee, of the Cactus Country, 1931; also (in collaboration with her sister Kate Douglas Wiggin) The Story Hour, 1891; Children's Rights, 1893; Republic of Childhood (3 vols.); Froebel's Gifts, 1896; Froebel's Occupations, 1896; Kindergarten Principles and Practice, 1897; Golden Numbers, 1902; The Posy Ring, 1903; The Fairy Ring, 1906; Pinafore Palace, 1907; Magic Casements, 1907; Tales of Laughter, 1908; Tales of Wonder, 1909; The Talking Beasts, 1911. Home: Hollis, York Co., Me. Died Feb. 1, 1934.

SMITH, Oberlin, engineer; b. Cincinnati, O., Mar. 22, 1840; s. George R. and Salome (Kemp) S.; ed. W. Jersey Acad., Bridgeton, N.J., 1859, Poly. Inst., Phila., etc.; studied engring.; m. Charlotte Hill, Dec. 25, 1876; children—Winifred Hill, Percival Hill. Started, 1863, business which became Ferracute Machine Co.; invented and designed its standard products. Awarded about 70 patents upon mech. inventions. N.J. commr. to Pan-Am. Expn., 1901. Author: Press Working of Metals, 1896; The Material, Why Not Immortal?, 1920. Contbr. to engring. jours. and procs. Took active interest in Anti-Slavery cause, later in Y.M.C.A. and woman suffrage. Home: Bridgeton, N.J. Died July 18, 1926.

SMITH, O(nnie) Warren, clergyman, author; b. Weyauwega, Wis., Oct. 2, 1872; s. Warren M. and Mary Jane (Sanders) S.; student Lawrence Coll., Appleton, Wis., 1893-95; m. Nellie Blanche Sanders, June 9, 1897; 1 dau., Mrs. Mary Lucile Haglund. Ordained M.E. ministry, 1895; joined Congl. Ch., 1911; pastor Durand, Wis., 1911-14, Washburn, 1914-18, Evansville, Wis., 1918-27, Oconomowoc, 1927—. Republican. Author: Trout Lore, 1917; Casting Tackle and Methods, 1920; The Pike Book, 1922; Told by the Campfire, 1922; Book of Live Bait Fishing, 1929; Amateur Fly-Tyer's Work Bench, 1929. Contbr. North American Sportsman's Bureau; also to various publs. on religious and outdoor topics; angling editor Outdoors (mag.). Lecturer. Home: Oconomowoc, Wis. Died Sept. 22, 1941.

SMITH, Orlando Jay, editor; b. nr. Terre Haute, Ind., June 14, 1842; s. Hiram S.; grad. Asbury (now DePauw) Univ., LL.D., DePauw; m. Evelyn V. Brady, Mar. 28, 1881. Served in armies of the Potomac, Ohio and Cumberland in 16th Ind. Vol. Inf. and 6th Ind. Cav., Apr. 21, 1861 to Sept. 1865, as pvt., sergt., lt., capt., maj.; wounded nr. Atlanta, Aug. 3, 1864. Editor Terre Haute Mail, Terre Haute Express, Chicago Express, pres. Am. Press Assn., 1882—. Author: A Short View of Great Questions, 1899; The Coming Democracy, 1900; Eternalism, 1902; Balance, 1904. Mem. Loyal Legion. Residence: Dobbs Ferry, N.Y. Office: New York, N.Y. Died 1908.

SMITH, Ormond Gerald, publisher; b. N.Y. City, 1860; s. Francis Shubael and Mary Jellett (Duff) S.; prep. edn., France; B.A., cum laude, Harvard, 1883; m. Grace Hewitt Pellett, Dec. 25, 1899 (now dec.); 1 son, Gerald Hewitt. Founder Ainslee's, Popular, People's, Smith's, Top Notch and Picture Play mags., and pub. books comprising 3,500 titles; pres. Street & Smith Corp., Ormorge Realty Co.; v.p. New York Eye & Ear Infirmary, Nassau Hosp., Mineola, N.Y. Pres. and chmn. exec. com. Museum of French Art, French Inst. in U.S., also curator of Library of the Inst.; asso. of council New York U. Comdr. Legion of Honor (France). Republican. Episcopalian. Home: New York, N.Y. Died Apr. 17, 1933.

SMITH, Orson, banker; b. Chicago, Dec. 14, 1841; s. Orson and Mary Ann S.; ed. pub. and pvt. schs., Chicago; m. Anna M. Rice, Dec. 14, 1871. Began business career at 13 as "bundle boy" in retail dry goods store of Potter Palmer; a year later became clerk, banking house of F. Granger Adams; cashier Corn Exchange Nat. Bank, 1870-81, and Corn Exchange Bank (state bank), 1881-84; v.p., 1884-98, pres., 1898-1916, then chmn. bd. Merchants Loan and Trust Co. Home: Chicago, Ill. Died Mar. 3, 1923.

SMITH, Otis David, educator; b. New Haven, Vt., 1831; s. Hon. Oliver and Adaline (Doud) S.; grad. Univ. of Vt., 1853, A.M., LL.D., 1890; m. Miss Mary A. Howell, 1866. Taught in Ala., 1854-72; Salem Acad., and Opelika High School, prof. mathematics, Ala. Poly. Inst., 1874—. Mem. of State bd. edn., Ala., 1872-76; pres. Ala. Ednl. Assn. Contributor to mags. and ednl. publs. Address: Auburn, Ala. Died 1905.

SMITH, Otterbein Oscar, clergyman; b. nr. Macomb, McDonough County, Ill., Mar. 6, 1858; s. Rev. Oscar F. and Esther A. (Lynn) S.; ed. pub. schs., Ill., and under tutelage; studied theology under pvt. tutors and at Chicago Theol. Sem.; D.D., Capital U., Okla., 1905; m. Emma V. Ginsberg, Mar.

11, 1879; children—Milo Oscar, Mrs. Edith Amelia Perdue, Mrs. Alma Jessis Harris, Mrs. Isabel Esther Lane. Ordained Congl. ministry, 1835; pastor Neponset, Ill., 1886-90, Wayne, 1891-93, 2d Ch., Moline, Ill., 1893-95, Traer, Ia., 1895-99; state supt. S.S. work, Ia., 1899-1904; pastor 1st Ch., Council Bluffs, 1905-11, 1st Ch., Pierre, S.D., 1912-16, Ainsworth, Neb., 1916-19, 1st Ch., Fremont, Neb., 1919-23, First Ch., Pueblo, Colo., 1923-30, First Ch., Eaton, Colo., 1930-31, Berkeley Community Congl. Ch., Denver, Dec. 1931—. Republican. Mason. Author: Child Life and Sex Hygiene, 1912. Chautauqua and lyceum lecturer. Contbr. on psychic topics. Home: Denver, Colo. Died Apr. 16, 1934.

SMITH, Preserved, prof. history; b. Cincinnati, O., July 22, 1880; s. Henry Preserved (D.D.) and Anna (Macneale) S.; prep. edn., Lawrenceville Sch., 1896-97; B.A., Amherst Coll., 1901, Litt.D., 1927; A.M., Columbia, 1902, Ph.D., 1907; Litt.D., Muhlenberg, 1922; m. Helen I. Kendall, Apr. 28, 1909 (died 1913); 1 daughter, Priscilla; m. 2d, Lucy H. Humphrey, June 20, 1918 (died 1939). Instr. in polit. science, Williams Coll., 1904-06; fellow in history, Amherst, 1907-14; lecturer history, Harvard, 1919-20; prof. history, Cornell U., 1922—. Author: Life and Letters of Martin Luther, 1911; The Age of the Reformation, 1920; Erasmus—A Study of His Life, Ideals, and Place in History, 1923; A Key to the Colloquies of Erasmus, 1927; A History of Modern Culture, Vol. 1, 1930, Vol. 2, 1934. Contbr. to Ency. Britannica, New Internat. Ency., and to many Am., English, German and French mags. and revs. Address: Ithaca, N.Y. Died May 15, 1941.

SMITH, Richard Root, surgeon; b. Grand Rapids, Mich., Dec. 10, 1869; s. J. Morgan and Cordelia (Root) S.; Phillips Acad., Andover, Mass., 1884-87; U. of Mich. Med. Dept., 1892; attended European clinics, 18 mos., 1895-97; m. Myra R. Wonderly, Apr. 27, 1898; children—Dorothy Wonderly (Mrs. Thomas F. McAllister), Beatrice Raiguel (Mrs. Frank A. Bedford, Jr.). Practiced at Grand Rapids, Mich., 1897—; specialist in gynecology; chmn. staff Blodgett Memorial and Butterworth hosps.; an organizer Grand Rapids Clinic. Organizer and comdr. Hosp. Unit Q, World War; in service 1917-May 1919, in France 1 yr. Regent U. of Mich., 1931-37. Founder and fellow Am. Coll. Surgeons (regent 1929-38); fellow Am. Gynecol. Soc. Republican. Conglist. Author of many articles on gynecol. and surg. subjects. Home: Grand Rapids, Mich. Died May 7, 1940.

SMITH, Robert A. C., corp. official; chmn. bd. White Rock Mineral Springs Co. (Wis.); also chmn. bd. New Niquero Sugar Co.; pres. Conn. Ry. & Lighting Co.; dir. Brothers Valley Coal Co., Conn. Light & Power Co., Mohawk Hudson Power Corp., Conn. Electric Service Co. and officer or dir. various other corps. Office: New York, N.Y. Died July 27, 1933.

SMITH, Robert Burns, governor; b. Hickman County, Ky., Dec. 29, 1854; s. Dewitt C. and Eliza B. (Hughs) S.; acad. edn. at Milburn, Ky., to 1876; m. Kate Crossland, Apr. 9, 1878. Taught sch. 1 yr.; admitted to bar, Oct. 11, 1877, at Mayfield, Ky. Removed to Mont., 1882, and settled at Dillon. Mem. Constl. Conv., 1884; U.S. atty., 1885-89; city atty. for Helena, Mont., 1890-91; defeated for Congress, 1894; gov. of Mont., 1896-1901. Democrat. Address: Big Fork, Mont. Died 1908.

SMITH, Robert Keating, clergyman; b. Brooklyn, N.Y., Aug. 2, 1865; s. George Robert Keating and Anna Amelia (Gooch) S.; M.E., Stevens Inst. Tech., 1889; B.A., Harvard, 1893; B.D., Episcopal Theol. Sch., 1895; m. Bertha Helena Wiles, June 17, 1896; children—Mabel Wiles, Helen Lord. Deacon, 1895, priest, 1896, P.E. Ch.; rector St. Paul's Ch., Kansas City, Mo., 1896-1901; asst. Grace Ch., Newton, Mass., 1901-06; rector Ch. of Atonement, Westfield, Mass., 1906-27; with Dept. of Foreign Born, Nat. Council P.E. Ch., New York, 1927—. Civilian chaplain, Camp Bartlett, Westfield, 1917. Visitor from P.E. Ch. to Czechoslovak Ch., 1920, 23, asst. chaplain Internat. Boy Scout Camp, London, July 1920. Dir. Westfield br. Mass. Soc. Prevention of Cruelty to Children. Republican. Mason. Collaborator with William F. Clapp of R. K. Smith and W. F. Clapp collection of N.E. mollusks in Agassiz Mus., Harvard. Author of pamphlets and articles on Czechoslovaks and Mediæval history of Bohemia. Home: Westfield, Mass. Died Oct. 2, 1931.

SMITH, Robert Seneca, religious educator; b. Clarendon, Vt., Nov. 18, 1880; s. Seneca Eugene and Martha Fuller (Everest) S.; A.B., Yale, 1903, M.A., 1905; B.D., 1906, Ph.D., 1927; D.D., Middlebury Coll., 1938; m. Emma Wyman Kingsley, July 18, 1906 (died 1925); 1 son, Kingsley. Gen. sec. Yale Univ. Christian Assn., 1904-06; ordained ministry, Congl. Church, 1906; asst. minister First Congl. Ch., Montclair, N.J., 1906-11; minister First Congl. Ch., Poughkeepsie, N.Y., 1911-17; prof. Smith Coll., Northampton, Mass., 1917-25; Horace Bushnell prof. of Christian Nurture, Yale Div. Sch., 1925—. Dean and chaplain Conn. Congl. Young People's Conf., 1933-37; dean New Haven Religious Leadership Training Sch. for Teachers, 1927-36. Served in Y.M.C.A. with A.E.F. in France, World War. Trustee Wheaton Coll., Norton, Mass.; mem. Program Com. for Home Div., Nat. Council of the Y.M.C.A. Dir. Bd. of Home Missions, Pilgrim, Press Div. and Commn. on Worship of Congl. Christian Chs.; chmn. Youth Com. of Conn. Council of Chs.; mem. Com. of Religious Edn., Conn. Congl. Conf. Editor: (with Dean Luther A. Weigle) The Old Testament Speaks, 1933; The Career and Significance of Jesus, 1933; Faiths Men Live By, 1934; New Testament History and Literature, 1937. Author: The Work and Teachings of the Earlier Prophets, 1907; Fundamentals for Daily Living, 1921; The Use of the Old Testament in Current Curricula, 1929; New Trails for the Christian Teacher, 1934; The Person I Hope to Become, 1935; The Art of Group Worship, 1938. Contbr. to Pilgrim High Road. Home: Hamden, Conn. Died Jan. 14, 1939.

SMITH, R(obert) Waverley, banker; b. Buckingham County, Va., Aug. 10, 1865; s. Robert Bolyn and Mary (Taylor) S.; B.A., U. of Tex., 1887; m. Etta Jane Sealy, Sept. 29, 1896. Admitted to Tex. bar, 1889; city atty., Galveston, 1893-97; pres. First National Bank, Galveston, Jan. 1, 1901—. Author of the commission feature of the original Galveston Commn. Charter, 1901; chmn. Galveston Deep Water Com.; regent U. of Tex.; trustee Rosenberg Library, Galveston. Democrat. Home: Galveston, Tex. Died July 12, 1930.

SMITH, Rodney, brig. gen. U.S.A.; b. in Vt., Jan. 3, 1829; s. Israel and Delia (Ferguson) S.; m. Julia Ellen Coates, Sept. 22, 1875. Apptd. from Ky., maj. p.m. U.S.A., Feb. 23, 1864; lt. col. deputy p.m. gen., Jan. 24, 1881; col. asst. p.m. gen., Dec. 8, 1886; retired by operation of law, Jan. 3, 1893; advanced to rank of brig. gen., retired, by act of Apr. 23, 1904. Served in Civil War in Army Potomac, and in Dept. of the South. Home: Orwell, Vt. Died Nov. 12, 1915.

SMITH, Roland Cotton, clergyman; b. N.Y. City, Mar. 24, 1860; s. John Cotton and Harriette (Appleton) S.; B.A., Amherst, 1882, M.A., 1883; grad. Episcopal Theol. Sch., Cambridge, Mass., 1885; m. Margaret Sigourney Otis, Nov. 13, 1885. Deacon, 1885, priest, 1886, P.E. Ch.; rector St. Peter's Ch., Beverly, Mass., 1885-88; asst., Trinity Ch., Boston, 1888-92; rector St. John's Ch., Northampton, 1893-1902, St. John's Ch., Washington, D.C., 1902. Address: Ipswich, Mass. Died Aug. 30, 1934.

SMITH, Roland Kidder, commr. Shipping Bd.; b. Staunton, Va., Feb. 22, 1870; s. Orlando and Louisa (Atkinson) S.; grad. St. James Mil. Acad., Macon, Mo., 1887; m. Mabel Louise Waggener, Oct. 1897; children—Emma Hetherington (Mrs. George Pope MacNichol, Jr.), Helen Atkinson (Mrs. Gordon B. Hurlbut), Roland K. Agt. and telegraph operator U.P. R.R. and Wabash R.R., 1888-89; contracting frt. agt., later gen. agt. C.,B.&Q. R.R., 1889-99, asst. supt., 1899-1902, supt. Mo.P. R.R., 1902-05; gen. mgr. Detroit, Toledo & Ironton R.R. and Ann Arbor R.R., 1905-06; gen. mgr. and v.p. Miss. Central R.R., 1907-18; gen. mgr. U.S. R.R. Adminstrn., 1918-19; v.p. Roper Lumber Co. and Norfolk Southern Land Co., 1919-22; dir. Industrial Development of the Port of New Orleans, 1923-25; commr. U.S. Shipping Bd., by apptmt. of President Coolidge, 1926-29, reapptd. by President Hoover for term, 1929-35. Democrat. Episcopalian. Home: Washington, D.C. Died Apr. 17, 1937.

SMITH, Roy Campbell, naval officer; b. Ft. Mason, Tex., July 16, 1858; s. Charles Henry and Maria McGregor (Campbell) S.; grad. U.S. Naval Acad., 1878; m. Margaret Aldrich Sampson, Oct. 11, 1887. Promoted ensign, Apr. 8, 1882; lt. jr. grade, May 12, 1889; lt. Feb. 22, 1894; lt. comdr., Mar. 3, 1901; comdr., Jan. 7, 1906; capt., Dec. 27, 1909. Duty at Naval Acad., 1885-88, Torpedo Sta., 1892-95; served on Indiana, at Battle of Santiago, July 3, 1898; at Harvard U., 1899-1900; on Massachusetts, 1901-03; naval attaché, Paris and St. Petersburg, 1903-06; comd. Chattanooga, 1906-08; at Naval War Coll., 1908-10; duty Navy Dept., Washington, D.C., 1910-12; comd. Arkansas, 1912-14; participated in occupation of Vera Cruz, Mexico, 1914; dir. target practice and engring. competitions, Navy Dept., 1914-15; supervisor New York Harbor, 1915-16; apptd. gov. Guam and comdt. Naval Sta., Guam, May 30, 1916. Mem. U.S. Naval Inst. (gold medal), Naval History Soc.; officer Legion of Honor. Santiago and Cuban campaign medals. Home: Richmond, Va. Died Apr. 10, 1940.

SMITH, Roy Leon, normal sch. prin.; b. Plymouth, N.Y., Sept. 28, 1879; s. Leeman W. B. and Libbie N. (Sisson) S.; grad. high sch., Norwich, N.Y., 1896; A.B., Syracuse U., 1904; spl. course, Teachers Coll. (Columbia); m. Ethel Lewis, June 28, 1905; children—Majel Helene, Hilton Albert, Myron Elwood. Prin. high sch., Freeport, N.Y., 1904-11; teacher North Adams State Normal Sch., 1912-21; instr. summer schs., Castleton, Vt., 1914-18, Mass. Agrl. Coll., Amherst, 1919-21; prin. State Normal Sch., North Adams, Mass., 1921—. Republican. Methodist. Home: North Adams, Mass. Died June 8, 1932.

SMITH, Ruel Perley, author; b. Bangor, Me., Dec. 16, 1869; s. Ruel and Maria (Wood) S.; ed. Bangor pub. schs., and Harvard Law Sch.; m. Miss Ellen M. Cyr, June 19, 1896. Author: The Rival Campers, 1905; The Rival Campers Afloat, 1906; The Rival Campers Ashore, 1907; Prisoners of Fortune, 1907; Jack Harvey's Adventures, 1908. Home: Brooklyn, N.Y. Died July 30, 1937.

SMITH, S. Jennie (Miss), author; b. New York; d. Joseph L. T. and Elizabeth Smith; ed. pub. schs. and normal coll., New York. Engaged in writing stories and sketches for periodicals, principally for young people, 1890—. Author: Madge, a Girl in Earnest, 1902. Address: Astoria, L.I., N.Y. Died 1904.

SMITH, S(amuel) Calvin, M.D.; b. Hollidaysburg, Pa., Feb. 28, 1881; s. Geo. W. (M.D.) and Eliza Blodgett (Calvin) S.; B.S., Bucknell U., 1901, M.S., 1905, Sc.D., 1928; M.D., Jefferson Med. Coll., 1905; m. Louise Voorhes Warriner, May 28, 1905. In gen. practice at Hollidaysburg, Pa., 1905-16; instr. in medicine, Jefferson Med. Coll., Phila., Pa., 1920-22; cons. cardiologist Misericordia Hosp., 1925-30, West Chester Hosp., 1925-30, Coatesville U.S. Vets. Hosp., 1931-32. Served as maj. M.C., U.S.A. in Am. camps and with A.E.F. in France, World War I. Fellow Am. Coll. of Phys.; mem. Am. Med. Assn. (mem. spl. com. for the presentation of Modern Methods of Heart Study, 1924-28). Republican. Episcopalian. Author: Heart Affections—Their Recognition and Treatment, 1920; Heart Records—Their Interpretation and Preparation, 1923; How Is Your Heart?, 1924, Eng. edit., 1925; That Heart of Yours, 1934. Contbr. articles to jours. Home: Philadelphia, Pa. Died July 31, 1939.

SMITH, Samuel Edwin, psychiatrist; b. Gosport, Ind., Aug. 31, 1861; s. John W. (M.D.) and Mary E. (Davis) S.; B.S., Ind. U., 1882, M.S., 1885; M.D., U. of Louisville, 1884; m. Martha June Rogers, May 6, 1891; children—Edwin Rogers, Samuel Rogers. Practiced at Gosport, 1884-88; asst. phys. Northern Ind. Hosp. for Insane, Logansport, 1888-91; med. supt. Eastern Ind. Hosp. for Insane, Richmond, 1891-1923. Planned and supervised constrn. Southeastern Ind. Hosp. for Insane at Madison, Ind.; pres. of commn. on location of Ind. State Penal Farm, 1913, and advisor to bd. trustees. Chmn. Joint Purchasing Com. for all Ind. pub. instns.; mem. Ind. Com. on Mental Defectives; Com. on Relocation of Ind. Reformatory; exec. Com. Riley Memorial Hosp. for Children; chmn. com. to investigate St. Elizabeth's Hosp., Washington, also of com. to recommend changes in laws of commitment of mental cases to Federal instns. and make St. Elizabeth's Hosp. a training school for psychiatrists. Alumni trustee Indiana U., 1916-25, and provost, 1923—. Mem. Am. Medico-Psychol. Assn. (pres. 1914-15), Nat. Conf. Charities and Correction, Ind. State Conf. Charities and Correction (pres. 1910). Democrat. Presbyn. Mason. Author of many published addresses and papers concerning treatment of insane and defective classes. Home: Indianapolis, Ind. Died May 29, 1928.

SMITH, Samuel George, clergyman, author; b. Birmingham, Eng., Mar. 7, 1852; s. Rev. William and Harriet (Johnson) S.; A.B., Cornell Coll., Ia., 1872, A.M., 1875; A.M., Ph.D., Syracuse U., 1882; D.D., Upper Ia. U., 1884; LL.D., Cornell Coll., 1898; m. Mariam Antoinette Barnard, Mar. 18, 1874 (died 1888); m. 2d, Sadie Nicols, May 15, 1890. Prin. Albion Sem., Ia., 1872-75; pastor Osage, Ia., 1875-77, Decorah, Ia., 1877-79, First Ch., St. Paul, 1879-82; presiding elder St. Paul dist., 1882-84; pastor First Ch., St. Paul, 1884-88, People's Ch., St. Paul, 1888—; head prof. dept. sociology and anthropology, U. of Minn., 1890. Mem. State Bd. Visitors Pub. Instns., 1907—; founder, 1895, and pres. Asso. Charities of St. Paul; mem. State Bd. Charities and Corrections, 1889-96, St. Paul Sch. Bd., 1890-93; regent U. of Minn., 1897-1902; mem. commn. to locate Hosp. for Insane, 1898; commr. to visit instns. in Europe, 1892; mem. State Bd. of Parole, 1910—; pres. Nat. Conf. Charities and Corrections; mem. Nat. Prison Assn., Social Science Assn. Author: Retribution and Other Addresses, 1900; For Eyes That Weep, 1900; The Industrial Conflict, 1907; Religion in the Making, 1909; Social Pathology, 1911; Democracy and the Church, 1912. Frequent contbr. to jours., mags., and revs. Address: St. Paul, Minn. Died Mar. 25, 1915.

SMITH, Samuel William, congressman; b. Tp. of Independence, Oakland County, Mich., Aug. 23, 1852; s. Nicholas B. and Mary (Phillips) S.; ed. at Clarkston and Detroit, Mich.; LL.B., U. of Mich., 1878; m. Alida De Land, Dec. 1880. Began practice of law at Pontiac, Mich., 1879. Pros. atty., Oakland County, 1880-84; elected mem. Mich. Senate, 1884; mem. 55th to 63d Congresses (1897-1915), 6th Mich. Dist.; resumed practice. Republican. Home: Detroit, Mich. Died June 19, 1931.

SMITH, Seth MacCuen, M.D., surgeon; b. Hollidaysburg, Blair County, Pa., Mar. 6, 1863; s. George Washington (M.D.) and Elizabeth (MacCuen) S.; Hollidaysburg Acad.; M.D., Jefferson Med. Coll., Phila., 1884; m. Virginia Allen, Oct. 24,

1889; children—George Allen, Elizabeth MacCuen (Mrs. Stuart L. Bullivant), Lewis MacCuen. Practiced at Phila., 1885—; prof. otology, Jefferson Med. Coll., 1904—; attending otologist, Jefferson Coll. Hosp.; surgeon in charge ear, nose and throat, Germantown Hosp.; attdg. otologist and laryngologist, Jewish Hosp.; cons. otologist Memorial and Oncologic hosp. Commd. maj. Med. R.C., U.S.A., 1917. Republican. Presbyn. Mason. Editor: Atlas and Epitome of Otology (Brühl-Politzer), 1902; also chapter on Diseases of Ear, in Modern Treatment by American and English Authorities (Hare), 1911, and chapter on Diseases of Middle Ear in Sajous' Analytic Cyclo. of Practical Medicine, 1914. Contbr. to med. jours. Home: Germantown, Philadelphia, Pa. Died Sept. 14, 1929.

SMITH, Seymour Wemyss, writer, editor; b. Cleveland, O., Jan. 18, 1896; s. Rev. Wemyss (M.A., B.A., Oxford) and Madeleine (Putney) S.; ed. priv. schs.; unmarried. Spl. feature writer N.Y. Sun and Herald, 1917-18; financial and feature editor, Hartford Courant, 1918-23; later editor The Financial Digest (New York and Hartford); pres. Financial Digest Co. Contbr. to newspapers and mags. on financial and business subjects, including feature articles N.Y. Herald, Boston Transcript, etc. Republican. Episcopalian. Address: Hartford, Conn. Deceased.

SMITH, Sidney, cartoonist; b. Bloomington, Ill., Feb. 13, 1877; s. T. H. (M.D.) and Frances A. (Shafer) S.; ed. pub. schs.; m. Gertrude C. Craddock (dec.); m. 2d, Mrs. Kathryn Imogene Eulette. Began as cartoonist, Bloomington Sunday Eye, 1895; successively with Indianapolis News, Indianapolis Press, Phila. Inquirer, Pittsburgh Post, Pittsburgh Press, Indianapolis Sentinel, Toledo News-Bee, Chicago Examiner; with Chicago Tribune, 1911—; creator of "The Gumps" and "Old Doc Yak." Address: Chicago, Ill. Died Oct. 20, 1935.

SMITH, Sidney Irving, biologist; b. Norway, Me., Feb. 18, 1843; s. Elliot and Lavinia H. (Barton) S.; Ph.B., Sheffield Scientific Sch. (Yale), 1867; A.M., Yale, 1887; m. Eugenia P. Barber, June 29, 1882. Asst. in zoölogy, 1867-75, prof. comparative anatomy, 1875-1906, prof. emeritus, 1906—, Sheffield Scientific Sch. (Yale). Had charge of deep water dredging in Lake Superior for U.S. Lake Survey, 1871; and for U.S. Coast Survey about St. George's banks, 1872; asso. with biol. work, U.S. Fish Commn., for many yrs. Mem. Nat. Acad. Sciences, 1884—. Author of numerous papers, especially in marine zoölogy. Blind for several years. Address: New Haven, Conn. Died May 17, 1926.

SMITH, Sidney Mason, merchant; b. Boston, 1842; s. Frederick and Frances Green (Shipley) S., both of old New England families; ed. Roxbury, Mass., Latin School; m. Elizabeth Eldredge Greene, 1868. Resident of San Francisco, 1858—. Pres. Cutting Packing Co.; pres. Pacific Sheet Metal Works; pres. Sons of Am. Revolution. Address: San Francisco, Calif. Died 1902.

SMITH, Stephen, surgeon; b. Onondaga County, N.Y., Feb. 19, 1823; s. Lewis and Chloe (Benson) S.; acad. edn.; M.D., Coll. Phys. and Surg. (Columbia), 1850; hon. A.M., Brown, 1876; LL.D., U. of Rochester, 1891; m. Lucy E., d. Judge E. D. Culver, June 1, 1858. Resident surgeon, 1850-52, attending surgeon, 1854 Bellevue Hosp.; prof. surgery, 1861-65, anatomy, 1865-74, Bellevue Hosp. Med. Coll.; prof. clin. surgery, med. dept., New York U., 1874; cons. surgeon Bellevue, St. Vincent and Columbus hosps. Joint editor, 1853-57, editor, 1857-60, New York Jour. of Medicine; editor New York Med. Times, 1860-64; investigated sanitary condition of New York, 1865, and reported to the legislature; U.S. commr. to 9th Internat. Sanitary Conv., Paris, 1894; founder and 1st pres. Am. Pub. Health Assn. Mem. city and nat. bds. of health, commr. in lunacy, and commr. State Bd. of Charities, N.Y. Author: Handbook of Surgical Operations; Principles of Operative Surgery; Doctor in Medicine; The City that Was; Who Is Insane?, 1916; etc. Address: New York, N.Y. Died Aug. 26, 1922.

SMITH, Stuart Robertson, lawyer; b. Tyler, Smith County, Tex., Oct. 6, 1867; s. Edward Willis and Jonnie (Robertson) S.; ed. common schs. of Tex.; m. Ida Jarvis, Dec. 18, 1901. Admitted to Tex. bar, 1890; dist. atty. 7th Jud. Dist. Tex., 1896-98; mem. firm Smith, Smith & Boyd. Del.-at-large Dem. Nat. Conv., 1916, 1932; del. Dem. Nat. Conv., 1920; chmn. Tex. Dem. State Conv., 1926. Baptist. Home: Beaumont, Tex. Died Sept. 14, 1937.

SMITH, Sylvester Clark, congressman; b. Henry County, Ia., Aug. 26, 1858; s. Edward and Celia W. (Shockley) S.; ed. Howe's Acad., Mt. Pleasant, Ia.; m. Maria J. Hart, May 7, 1882. Admitted to bar, 1885, and in practice at Bakersfield, Calif., 1885—; pres. Echo Pub. Co.; propr. Bakersfield Morning Echo, also editor, Aug. 6, 1886—. Mem. Calif. Senate, 1895-1903; mem. 59th to 62d Congresses (1905-13), 8th Calif. Dist. Republican. Address: Bakersfield, Calif. Died Jan. 26, 1913.

SMITH, T. Guilford, engineer; b. Phila., Aug. 27, 1839; s. Pemberton and Margaretta E. (Zell) S.; A.B., Central High Sch., Phila., 1858, A.M., 1863; C.E., Rensselaer Poly. Inst., 1861; LL.D., Hobart, 1899, Alfred, 1903; hon. Phi Beta Kappa, Hobart, 1894; regent U. State of N.Y., 1890— (life office); m. Mary Stewart Ives, July 14, 1864. Civil engr. Phila. & Reading R.R., 1861-65; gen. mgr. Phila. Sugar Refinery, 1866-69; sec. Union Iron Co., Buffalo, 1873-78; sales agt. Phila. & Reading Coal & Iron Co., 1878-92; sales agt. Carnegie Steel Co., 1889-1911. Pres. Buffalo Library and Buffalo Fine Arts Acad.; pres. Charity Organization Soc. of Buffalo, 1888—; pres. Buffalo Soc. Natural Sciences; dir. Am. Soc. C.E., 1894-96; del. 11th Internat. Congress Medicine and Surgery, Rome, 1894; chmn. fine arts com. Buffalo Expn., 1901. Regent U. State of N.Y., 1890—. Mem. Am. Acad. Polit. and Social Science. Home: Buffalo, N.Y. Died Feb. 20, 1912.

SMITH, Theobald, pathologist; b. Albany, N.Y., July 31, 1859; s. Philip and Theresa (Kexel) S.; Ph.B., Cornell, 1881; M.D., Albany Med. Coll., 1883; hon. A.M., Harvard, 1901; LL.D., U. of Chicago, 1907, Washington U., 1915; U. of Pa., 1930; Sc.D., Harvard, 1910, Yale, Princeton, 1917; Rutgers, 1930; hon. M.D., U. of Breslau, 1911; hon. Dr. Royal Vet. Medicine, Budapest; m. Lillian H. Egleston, May 17, 1888; children—Dorothea Egleston, Lilian Hillyer (Mrs. Robert F. Foerster), Philip Hillyer. Dir. pathol. lab., Bur. Animal Industry, Dept. Agr., 1884-95; dir. pathol. lab., Mass. State Bd. Health, 1895-1915. Prof. bacteriology, Columbian (now George Washington) U., 1886-95; prof. comparative pathology, Harvard, 1896-1915; dir. dept. of animal pathology, Rockefeller Inst. for Med. Research, 1915-29 (mem. bd. dirs., 1901—); Harvard exchange prof. to Berlin, 1911-12; pres. Internat. Union Against Tuberculosis, 1926, Congress of American Physicians and Surgeons, 1928; mem. bd. trustees Carnegie Instn., Washington. Fellow Am. Acad. Arts and Sciences; hon. fellow Soc. Tropical Medicine and Hygiene (London), Pathol. Soc. Gt. Britain and Ireland. Recipient of Mary Kingsley, Kober, Flattery, Trudeau, Sedgwick, Holland Soc. and Gerhard medals; Copley medal of Royal Soc. of Great Britain. Contbr. numerous med. jours. on the nature and causation of infectious and parasitic diseases. Home: Princeton, N.J. Died Dec. 10, 1934.

SMITH, Thomas Berry, coll. prof.; b. nr. Bowling Green, Mo., Dec. 7, 1850; s. William Hugh and Isabella (Fullerton) S.; student Pardee Coll., Mo., 1868-69; A.B., Pritchett Coll., Mo., 1873, A.M., 1879; grad. studies in chemistry, Sheffield Scientific Sch. (Yale), 1875-76, U. Chicago, summer, 1908, U. of Colo. summer, 1919; LL.D., Central Wesleyan Coll., Mo., 1914; m. Emma Marvin Newland, Dec. 27, 1877; children—Erle Verner (dec.), Beryl Dean (Mrs. H. M. Ivy), Walton Caples, Shirley Steele. Prof. chemistry and physics, Carleton Coll., Minn., 1879-80; prof. natural sciences, N.Mo. State Normal, 1877-78; same Pritchett Coll., 1882-86; prof. chemistry and physics, 1886-1915, prof. chemistry, 1915-26, emeritus; actg. pres., 1901-03, Central Coll. Vol. observer weather service, 1883-1918. Sec.-treas. Mo. Coll. Union, 1906-25. Mem. Mo. Library Commn., 1916-19. Methodist. Author: In Many Moods (poems), 1900; Three Weddings (poems), 1927; History of the Missouri College Union, 1907, 24; illustrated History of Central College, 1928. Wrote a 60,000 word history of Howard County, Mo., for a History of Howard and Chariton Counties, 1923. Home: Fayette, Mo. Died 1933.

SMITH, Thomas F., congressman; b. N.Y. City; s. Thomas F. and Mary A. S.; student Manhattan Coll.; LL.B., New York Law Sch.; m. Margaret Furlong, Aug. 7, 1895. Admitted to N.Y. bar; clk. City Court of N.Y., 1897-1917; sec. Dem. County Com. of County of N.Y., 22 yrs.; sec. Soc. of Tammany, 22 yrs.; mem. N.Y. State Constl. Conv., 1915; del. Dem. Nat. Conv., 1916, 20; elected Apr. 12, 1917, to 65th Congress (1917-19), 15th N.Y. Dist., for unexpired term of Michael F. Conry, deceased; reëlected to 66th Congress (1919-21); pub. adminstr. of New York, 1921—. Home: New York, N.Y. Died Apr. 11, 1923.

SMITH, Thomas Franklin, physician; b. New York, Apr. 26, 1833; s. John T. S. and Amelia (Franklin) S.; ed. high sch., New York; degree Doctor in Medicine, New York Med. Coll., 1860; m. Emma Louisa Clark, Aug. 1, 1854. Enlisted in 7th Regt., N.G. N.Y., 1857; transferred to staff of 8th Regt., 1860, and commd. surgeon's mate, with rank of 1st lt.; promoted to surgeon with rank of maj.; mustered with regt. into U.S. service, Apr. 1861, as chaplain, and served 90 days; reënlisted as acting asst. surgeon U.S.A., Dept. of Va., for 15 mos.; participated in 1st battle of Bull Run and several skirmishes; hon. mustered out; later practiced in New York. Mem. Am. Inst. Homœpathy (sr. mem. and treas. 23 yrs.). Second v.p. Jennie Clarkson Home for Children, Valhalla, N.Y.; mgr. for many yrs. of Assn. for Improving Condition of the Poor. Republican; cast first vote for John C. Fremont for President of U.S. Baptist; clk. Southern N.Y. Bapt. Assn. 22 yrs. Home: New York, N.Y. Died June 1916.

SMITH, Thomas Octavius, banker; b. Elyton, Ala., Aug. 21, 1859; s. Joseph Riley and Margarett Harvie (Jordan) S.; student U. of Ala., 1875-78; Washington and Lee U., 1878-79; C.E., Va. Mil. Inst., 1882; m. Cornelia Smith, 1886-93, cashier, 1893-99, 1st Nat. Bank, Birmingham; cashier, 1900-04, v.p., 1904-23, pres., Jan. 1923—, Birmingham Trust & Savings Co.; pres. J. R. Smith Realty Co., Inc. Maj. 1st Ala. U.S. Vols., Spanish-Am. War; col. 3d Ala. Regt., A.N.G., 1899-1901. Democrat. Episcopalian. Mason. Home: Birmingham, Ala. Died Sept. 18, 1925.

SMITH, Uriah, editor, author; b. West Wilton, N.H., May 2, 1832; s. Samuel and Rebecca (Spalding) S.; grad. Phillips Exeter Acad., 1851; m. Harriet Newell Stevens, June 7, 1857. Connected with literary dept. of Advent Review and Sabbath Herald, 1853; editor, 1855—. Ordained to ministry (Seventh Day Adventist), Aug. 17, 1874; attended camp meetings in all Northern States; invented automatic folding school seat. Author: Thoughts on Daniel and the Revelation, 1881; Our Country: the Marvel of Nations, 1887; Here and Hereafter, 1884; Looking Unto Jesus, or Christ in Type and Antitype, 1898; Spiritualism a Sign of the Times, 1896; Synopsis of the Present Truth, 1884; A Word for the Sabbath (a poem), 1875; Diagram of Parliamentary Rules, 1890; etc.; all published by Seventh Day Adventists' Pub. Co., Battle Creek. Address: Battle Creek, Mich. Died 1903.

SMITH, Walter George, lawyer; b. Logan County, O., Nov. 24, 1854; s. Gen. Thomas Kilby and Elizabeth B. (McCullough) S.; A.B., U. of Pa., 1873, A.M., 1876, LL.B., 1877; LL.D., Catholic U. of America, 1915; m. Elizabeth L. Drexel, Jan. 7, 1890 (died 1890). Admitted to bar, 1877; mgr. Beneficial Saving Fund of Phila.; dir. Phila. Contributionship. Trustee U. of Pa.; mgr. Drexel Inst.; pres. Fedn. of Catholic Socs. of Pa., Conf. of Commrs. Uniform State Laws; trustee Catholic U. of Am.; del. Divorce Congress, Pa. Mem. Am. Bar Assn. (pres. 1917). Author: Life and Letters of Thomas Kilby Smith, Brevet Major Gen. U.S.V., 1898. Mem. Am. Com. for Relief of Near East. Home: Philadelphia, Pa. Died Apr. 4, 1924.

SMITH, Walter Inglewood, judge; b. Council Bluffs, Ia., July 10, 1862; s. George F. and Sarah H. S.; pub. sch. edn.; m. Effie M. Moon, July 10, 1890. Admitted to bar, 1882, and practiced at Council Bluffs. Judge Dist. Ct., 15th Jud. Dist., 1890-1900; elected to 56th Congress, Nov. 1900, for unexpired term (1900-01) of Smith McPherson, resigned; reëlected 57th to 62d Congresses (1901-13), 9th Ia. Dist.; apptd. U.S. circuit judge, 8th Circuit, Jan. 31, 1911; resigned from 62d Congress, Mar. 15, 1911. Republican. Address: Council Bluffs, Ia. Died Jan. 27, 1922.

SMITH, Walter Lloyd, judge; b. Elmira, N.Y., Apr. 18, 1856; s. H. Boardman and Ellen H. S.; A.B., Princeton, 1877; m. Jessie Gonzales, July 19, 1893; children—Wilton Lloyd, Boardman Lloyd (dec.), Parker Lloyd. Admitted to bar, 1879, and practiced at Elmira. Judge Supreme Ct. of N.Y., 6th Dist., 1888-Oct. 1925 (resigned); presiding judge Appellate Div., 3d Dept., 1907-15; resigned and designated asso. justice 1st Dept.; later practiced law in N.Y. City. Republican. Home: New York, N.Y. Died Mar. 5, 1928.

SMITH, Walter McMynn, librarian; b. Janesville, Wis., Aug. 17, 1869; s. Osmore R. and Jane L. (Richardson) S.; A.B., U. of Wis., 1890; m. Marion Burr Jones, Aug. 20, 1907; children—Olive Hoyt, Janet MacDonald, Burr W. Librarian U. of Wis., 1890—. Mem. A.L.A., Am. Library Inst., Am. Hist. Assn., Wis. Acad. Sciences, Arts and Letters. Home: Madison, Wis. Died Apr. 20, 1938.

SMITH, Walter Robinson, sociologist; b. Excelsior Springs, Mo., Jan. 31, 1875; s. Thomas Henry and Fannie (King) S.; Ph.B., Missouri Valley Coll., Marshall, Mo., 1899; Ph.M., U. of Chicago, 1901, Ph.D., 1907; studied Harvard, 1902-03, Columbia, summer 1912; m. Grace Woodward, Dec. 20, 1913; children—Katherine W., Hugh Robinson. Prin. Eastwood Sch., Marshall, Mo., 1899-1900; fellow U. of Chicago, 1901-02; instr. history and polit. science, Washington U., St. Louis, 1903-07; prof. history and social science, Heidelberg Coll., Tiffin, O., 1907-09; prof. sociology and economics, Kan. State Teachers 1919—. Instr. summer schs., U. of Mo., 1903, Ind. U., 1918, Teachers Coll. (Columbia), 1921, 22, 23, Harvard, 1925, 26, U. of Calif., 1924, 29, U. of Wisconsin, 1931. Presbyn. Author: History of the Louisiana Territory, 1904; Introduction to Educational Sociology, 1917; Constructive School Discipline, 1924; Principles of Educational Sociology, 1927. Coauthor: A Survey of the Leavenworth Public Schools, 1914. Contbr. to mags. on hist., social. and ednl. subjects. Home: Lawrence, Kan. Died Jan. 7, 1937.

SMITH, Walter Tenney, importer; b. Pepperell, Mass., Apr. 2, 1870; s. Noah Payson and Caroline Parsons (Baker) S.; grad. high sch., Pepperell; student Harvard Univ., 2 yrs.; m. Minnie Lee Turrentine, June 23, 1898; children—Kenneth Baker, Dudley

Tenney. Asst. engr. Metropolitan Elevated Ry., Chicago, in charge constrn. downtown loop; in bldg. constrn. work, 1897-1913; v.p. George A. Fuller Co., builders, 1913-33; president Thompson & Smith, Inc., importers; v.p. George A. Fuller Co. of Can., Ltd. Served as capt. engrs., N.Y.N.G., 1917-19. Mem. Board of Adjustment, City of Montclair. Conglist. Mason. Address: Newark, N.J. Died Nov. 11, 1940.

SMITH, Wilbert L., banker, typewriter mfr.; b. Torrington, Conn., Feb. 29, 1852; s. Lewis Stevens and Eliza Ann (Hurlbut) S.; ed. pub. schs. and State Normal Sch., Cortland, N.Y.; m. Louise L. Hunt, Oct. 26, 1886; children—Wilbert A., Elwyn L. Began in gun mfg. plant of brother, L. C. Smith, becoming supt.; about 1885 began mfr. of Smith Premier Typewriter; in charge production Smith Premier Co.; dir. Union Typewriter Co. (successor to Smith Premier Co.), to 1903; one of organizers, 1903, L. C. Smith & Bros. Typewriter Co., v.p., until 1910, pres., 1910-24; chmn. bd. L. C. Smith & Corona Typewriters, Inc., 1926—; chmn. bd. Syracuse Trust Co. (mem. exec. bd.). Mem. war service com. for typewriter industry, World War I. Republican. Home: Syracuse, N.Y. Died Aug. 28, 1937.

SMITH, Wilbur Fisk, univ. pres.; b. Lovettsville, Loudoun County, Va., May 21, 1856; s. Bennett Holloway and Matilda Caroline (Janney) S.; prep. edn., high sch. and Loudoun Valley Acad.; Richmond Coll., 1876; B.L., U. of Md., 1890; spl. studies, U. of Va. and Johns Hopkins; Litt.D., St. John's Coll., Annapolis, Md., 1912; m. Margaret Pattison, Apr. 16, 1884; children—Wilbur Clarence, Margery Janney (Mrs. John McNabb), Harriet Pattison (Mrs. Harold C. Hamm), Everard Pattison, Robert Hopper, Caroline Cator (dec.). Began teaching, 1873; prin. English-German Sch. No. 5, Baltimore, 1883-94, prof. English, Baltimore City Coll., 1894-1911, head of English dept., 1906-11, principal, 1911-26; pres. U. of Baltimore, 1926-35, emeritus, 1935—. Grand sec. Grand Council Royal Arcanum of Md. over 20 yrs.; dir. sec. Royal Arcanum Club Bldg. Co. Democrat. Episcopalian. Home: Baltimore, Md. Died Aug. 9, 1940.

SMITH, Willard Adelbert, publisher; b. Kenosha, Wis., Sept. 20, 1849; s. William Harrison and Mehitable (Allen) S.; A.B., Shurtleff Coll., 1869, A.M., 1875, LL.D., 1906; LL.B., Washington U., 1871; m. Maria C. Dickinson, May 1, 1872. Publisher and editor of the Railway Review, 1873—. Chief of dept. of transportation, exhibits, Chicago Expn., 1893; dir. of transportation and civ. engring. Am. Commn. to Paris Expn., 1900; chief dept. transportation, St. Louis Expn., 1904; U.S. del. to Internat. Ry. Congress, Paris, 1900, Washington, 1905. Trustee U. of Chicago; patron and hon. curator Field Mus. of Natural History. Home: Kenilworth, Ill. Died Nov. 29, 1923.

SMITH, William, brig. gen. U.S.A.; b. Orwell, Vt., Mar. 26, 1831; s. Israel S. and Delia (Ferguson) S.; A.B., U. of Vt., 1854, A.M., 1856; m. Mary O. McAllister, Oct. 10, 1867. Additional p.m. vols., Aug. 29, 1861; bvtd. lt. col., Mar. 13, 1865; hon. mustered out, July 20, 1866; apptd. from Minn., maj. p.m. U.S.A., Jan. 17, 1867; lt. col. deputy p.m. gen., Sept. 6, 1888; brig. gen. p.m. gen., Mar. 10, 1890; retired by operation of law, Mar. 26, 1895. Home: Pelham Manor, N.Y. Died 1912.

SMITH, William Alden, senator; b. Dowagiac, Mich., May 12, 1859; s. George Richard and Leah Margaret S.; common sch. edn.; hon. A.M., Dartmouth, 1901; moved with parents to Grand Rapids, 1872; newsboy and messenger boy in Western Union Telegraph office, and apptd. page Mich. Ho. of Rep., 1879; m. Nana Osterhout, Oct. 21, 1886. Admitted to bar, 1883, and began practice at Grand Rapids; pres. Grand Rapids Herald. Mem. Mich. Rep. State Central Com., 1888-90-92; elected 54th to 60th Congresses (1895-1909), 5th Mich. Dist.; resigned from 60th Congress, Jan. 28, 1907; elected U.S. senator, Jan. 1907, to succeed Hon. R. A. Alger, for term beginning Mar. 4, 1907, and upon death of Senator Alger was elected to fill out his unexpired term, taking his seat, Feb. 11; reëlected to Senate, Jan. 16, 1913, for term expiring Mar. 3, 1919. Republican. Home: Grand Rapids, Mich. Died Oct. 11, 1932.

SMITH, William Alexander, banker; b. Pottstown, Pa., Sept. 9, 1820; s. Robert Hobart and Mary (Potts) S.; ed. Phila. and Princeton, N.J.; m. Clara Mary, d. Rev. Levi Bull, 1847; m. 2d, Margaret, d. George and Serena (Mason) Jones, 1863. Began in banking business, 1844; treas. New York Stock Exchange, 1864-66, pres., 1866-67; treas. Parochial Fund; v.p. St. Luke's Hosp.; pres. Sheltering Arms; treas. Gen. Clergy Relief Fund. Home: New York, N.Y. Died 1911.

SMITH, William Austin, clergyman, editor; b. St. Paul, Minn., Oct. 9, 1872; s. Addison Talcott and Theresa (Metzger) S.; A.B., Harvard, 1895; B.D., Seabury Div. School, 1898; D.D., Cambridge Theological School, 1921; m. Anne Breed, June 29, 1904. Deacon, 1898, priest, 1899, P.E. Ch.; curate St. John's Ch., Providence, R.I., 1899-1902; resided abroad, 1901-02; rector St. Paul's Ch., Milwaukee, 1902-09; abroad, 1909-10; rector Christ Ch., Springfield, Mass., 1900-15 (resigned); editor The Churchman, 1916—. Home: New York, N.Y. Died Sept. 27, 1922.

SMITH, William Benjamin, univ. prof.; b. Stanford, Ky., Oct. 26, 1850; s. Jeremiah and Angelina (Kenley) S.; A.M., Ky. U., 1871; Ph.D., U. of Gottingen, 1879; m. Kathleen Merrill, Oct. 25, 1882 (died 1899); children—Merrill Neville (dec.), Yeremya Kenley, Katharyn, William Benjamin. Taught and studied langs. and sciences, 1871-80; prof. mathematics, Central Coll., Mo., 1881-85; prof. physics, 1885-88, mathematics, 1888-93, U. of Mo.; prof. mathematics, 1893-1906, prof. philosophy, 1906-15, emeritus prof., Oct. 26, 1915—, Tulane U. Del. of U.S. Govt. to First Pan-Am. Scientific Congress, Santiago, Chile, 1908. Fellow A.A.A.S.; mem. advisory council Simplified Spelling Bd. Author: Coordinate Geometry, 1885; Introductory Modern Geometry, 1893; Infinitesimal Analysis, 1898; Clew to Trigonometry, 1889; The Color Line, 1905; Der vorchristliche Jesus, 1906; "The Merman and the Seraph," crowned in the Poet Lore competition, 1906; Ecce Deus, German edit., 1911, English edit., 1912; Push? or Pull?, 1912; Mors Mortis, 1915; also articles in the Hibbert Jour., Psyche, etc. Address: New Orleans, La. Died Aug. 6, 1934.

SMITH, William Clarke, teacher; b. Manchester, N.H., Feb. 22, 1857; s. Isaac William and Amanda White (Brown) S.; student Dartmouth, 1880; M.A., U. of Berlin, 1895; unmarried. Began teaching in U. of Wyo., 1887; master and part owner St. Luke's Sch., Wayne, Pa. Republican. Episcopalian. Author: About Us and the Deacon, 1911; Roger, 1911; The Vigil, 1912; The Manger, 1913; Songs from the Foot-hills, 1915. Home: Wayne, Pa. Died Jan. 5, 1942.

SMITH, William Farrar, mil. and civil engr.; b. St. Albans, Vt., Feb. 17, 1824; s. Ashbel and Sarah (Butler) S.; apptd. to West Point, 1841; grad. in topog. engrs., 1845; m. Sarah Ward, Apr. 24, 1861. Served on survey of Upper Lakes, 1845-46; dept. mathematics, West Point, 1847-48; surveys in Texas, 1849-50, and of Mexican boundary, 1850-51; of Florida ship canal, 1853, and other engr. duties, 1861. Served under Gen. Butler to June 20, 1861; col. 3d Vt. vols., July 23, 1861, in defense of Washington; brig. gen. U.S. vols., Aug. 13, 1861; comd. div. in Army of Potomac in siege of Yorktown, battles of Lee's Mills, Williamsburgh, Golding's farm, Malvern Hill, Crampton's Gap, Antietam, etc.; comd. 6th corps at Fredericksburg, 1862; 9th corps, Mar. 17, 1863; comd. div. of N.Y. and Pa. militia at Gettysburg; chief engr. of army of the Cumberland, Oct. 3, 1863; planned and executed capture of Brown's Ferry, Tenn., Oct. 27, 1863, opening shorter line of communication for supplies; chief engr. div. of Miss., Nov. 16, 1863; planned battle of Missionary Ridge. Threw a bridge 1,500 feet long across the Tennessee River for Sherman's army. In command 18th army corps, Apr. 1864; in battles of Drury's Bluff and Cold Harbor; assaulted and carried line of fortifications at Petersburg, June 15, 1864, etc. Resigned as maj. gen. vols., Nov. 4, 1865; resigned from army, Mar. 7, 1867. Pres. Internat. Ocean Telegraph Co., 1865-73; pres. New York Bd. of Police, 1877; civil engr., 1881—. Author: From Chattanooga to Petersburg, under Generals Grant and Butler. Address: Philadelphia, Pa. Died 1903.

SMITH, William Hawley, lecturer, author; b. Sunderland, Franklin County, Mass., Oct. 7, 1845; s. Brainerd and Nancy O. (Hawley) S.; grad. State Normal U., Normal, Ill., 1870; m. Ellen Hinsdale Galusha, July 19, 1870. Reared on farm; taught sch., 1870-74; county supt. schs., McLean County, Ill., 1874-82; editor, 1882-87; in mfg. business, 1887-93; on lecture platform, 1893-1910; first in combination with "Bill" Nye, and then alone. Author: The Evolution of Dodd, 1883; Walks and Talks, 1894; The New Hamlet, 1902; The Promoters, 1904; All the Children of All the People, 1912. Address: Peoria, Ill. Died May 9, 1922.

SMITH, William Henry, church official; b. Evergreen, Ala., June 18, 1859; s. Edward C. and Virginia A. (Clark) S.; prep. edn., Trussville (Ala.) Acad.; M.A., Howard Coll., Birmingham, Ala., 1884; grad. Southern Bapt. Theol. Sem., Louisville, Ky., 1887; m. Minnie Gregory, Oct. 26, 1887; children—Isla Virginia (dec.), Mary Delia, William Gregory. Ordained ministry Bapt. Ch., 1887; pastor successively 1st Ch., Huntsville, Florence and Anniston, Ala., and Columbus, Ga., until 1906; editorial sec. Foreign Mission Bd. Southern Bapt. Conv., 1906-16; ednl. sec. State Bd. Ala. Bapt. Conv., 1916-20; pres. Ednl. Bd. Southern Bapt. Conv., 1923—. Home: Birmingham, Ala. Died June 14, 1933.

SMITH, William Owen, lawyer; b. Koloa, Kauai, H.I., Aug. 4, 1848; s. James William and Melicent (Knapp) S.; prep. edn., Punahou Acad., Oahu; student Mass. Agrl. Coll., 1869-70; studied law in office of A. S. Hartwell, Honolulu; m. Mary A. Hobron, Mar. 23, 1876. Active in securing annexation of Hawaiian Islands to U.S., 1898; mem. Legislature of Hawaii intermittently for 19 yrs.; atty. gen. 1893-98; mem. law firm Smith, Warren, Stanley & Vitousek; chmn. bd. trustees Bishop Trust Co., Ltd.; pres. Hawaiian Securities Co.; v.p. Alexander & Baldwin, Ltd.; dir. Inter Island Steam Navigation Co., Maui Agrl. Co. Trustee Kamehameha Schs., B.P. Bishop Museum, Children's Hosp., Lunalilo Home. Republican. Conglist. Odd Fellow. Home: Honolulu, H. Ty. Deceased.

SMITH, William Robert, judge; b. in Smith County, Tex., Aug. 18, 1863; s. of Samuel Augustus and Melissa Caroline (Dobbs) S.; grad. Sam Houston Normal Inst., Huntsville, Tex., 1883; m. Frances Lipscomb Breedlove, Nov. 6, 1890. Admitted to bar, 1885; removed from Smith County to Colorado, Mitchell County, Tex., Feb. 1888; apptd. by Gov. Culberson, 1897, and elected, 1898 and 1900, judge 32d Jud. Dist. of Tex.; mem. 58th to 64th Congresses (1903-17), 16th Tex. Dist.; U.S. dist. judge, Apr. 1917—. Democrat. Address: El Paso, Tex. Died Aug. 16, 1924.

SMITH, William Ruthven, army officer; b. Nashville, Tenn., Apr. 2, 1868; s. Robert McPhail and Lititia Clark (Trimble) S.; student Vanderbilt U. 2 yrs.; grad. U.S. Mil. Acad., 1892, Sch. of Submarine Defense, Ft. Totten, N.Y., 1908; m. Mary Prince, d. Gen. George B. Davis, U.S.A., Dec. 4, 1901; children—Katharine Alexander, William Ruthven. Commd. additional 2d lt. 1st Arty., June 11, 1892; 2d lt. 1st Arty., Sept. 23, 1892; 1st lt., Mar. 2, 1899; capt. Arty. Corps, May 8, 1899; maj. Coast Arty. Corps, Mar. 31, 1909; lt. col., July 1, 1916; col., May 15, 1917; brig. gen. N.A., Aug. 5, 1917; maj. gen. N.A., June 26, 1918; hon. discharged temp. apptmts., July 15, 1919; Gen. Staff, Aug. 22, 1919; chief of staff Philippine Dept., rank brig. gen. U.S.A., Apr. 27, 1921; maj. gen., July 23, 1924. Instr. and asst. prof. mathematics, natural and exptl. philosophy, ordnance and gunnery, U.S. Mil. Acad., 11 yrs.; asst. to chief of Coast Arty., Washington, D.C., 4 yrs.; dir. Dept. of Electricity and Mine Defense, School of Mine Defense, Ft. Monroe, Va., 3 yrs.; in charge of building and placing first submarine net put down in U.S., Feb. 1917; assigned to Camp Sheridan, Ala., 1917; comd. 62d Arty. brigades, 37th Div. Ohio N.G. and 37th Div. N.G.; comdr. 36th Div. (Tex. and Okla. N.G.), A.E.F., Meuse-Argonne campaign; comdt. coast Arty. Sch., Fort Monroe, Va., 1923-24; comdg. gen. Hawaiian Div., Schofield Bks., 1925-27; dept. comdr. Honolulu, Aug. 1927-Jan. 1928; supt. U.S. Mil. Acad., West Point, 1928-Apr. 30, 1932 (retired); supt. Sewanee Mil. Acad., Aug. 1, 1932—. D.S.M. (U.S.); Comdr. Legion of Honor (France); Croix de Guerre (France). Episcopalian. Address: Sewanee, Tenn. Died July 15, 1941.

SMITH, William Sooy, civil engr.; b. Tarlton, O., July 22, 1830; s. Sooy and Ann (Hedges) S.; A.B., Ohio U., 1849, later A.M.; grad. U.S. Mil. Acad., 1853; m. Elizabeth Haven; m. 2d, Josephine Hartwell, 1884; father of Charles Sooysmith. Apptd. 2d lt. 3d Arty. U.S.A.; promoted 2d lt. 3d Arty. U.S.A., and stationed in N.M.; resigned; went to Chicago, 1854, entered engring. service of I.C. R.R. Co.; soon afterward apptd. asst. engr. to Col. Graham, U.S. engr. in charge of improvements of Lake Michigan harbors, but resigned because of dangerous illness; conducted select sch. at Buffalo, 1855-57; practiced as civ. engr., 1857-59; chief engr. of co. building iron bridge across Savannah River for Savannah & Charleston R.R. Co., 1860-61; served as lt. col., col. and brig gen. U.S.A., Apr. 1861-Sept. 1864, when resigned because totally disabled by inflammatory rheumatism. When sufficiently recovered resumed practice as civ. engr. at Chicago. Did much difficult work as engr. and contractor for U.S. Govt. and ry. cos., including reconstruction of Waugoshanee Light House at western entrance of Straits of Mackinac; built 1st all-steel ry. bridge in world (Glasgow, Mo.), and sub-structures of 6 other bridges, by pneumatic process, which developed and greatly improved; with son, Charles Sooysmith, introduced into this country freezing process for difficult subaqueous work, and sank 2 shafts through quick-sands and boulders, to depth of 100 feet, which could not have been put down by any other known method. Completely changed methods of constructing foundations for heavy buildings in Chicago, carrying the loads down through mud and soft earth to hard bottom, 50 feet or more, by means of piles cut off below water surface, and where these could not be driven without endangering foundations of adjacent buildings, by sinking columns of concrete to hard bottom and resting the bldgs. on them; aided in development of plans of high steel bldgs. in Chicago and throughout world; leader in urging Govt. to create bd. to test Am. metals and mem. of that bd. during the 3 yrs. of its existence. Invented the 1st pneumatic caisson ever built; designed new system of fireproof building. Address: Medford, Ore. Died Mar. 4, 1916.

SMITH, William Strother, naval officer; b. Richmond, Va., Sept. 15, 1857; s. Samuel Brown and Margaret (Strother) S.; grad. U.S. Naval Acad.,

1880; m. Irma St. Clair-Abrams, Dec. 2, 1891. Asst. engr., June 1), 1882; promoted through grades to rear adm., Mar. 20, 1918; retired, Sept. 15, 1921. Served on Columbia and Yankee, Spanish-Am. War, 1898; asst. insp. machinery, Newport News, Va., 1903-05; on West Virginia, 1905-06; duty Bur. Steam Engring., Navy Dept., 1906-09, Bd. of Inspection and Survey, 1909-12; engr. officer Navy Yard, Phila., 1912-15; detailed spl. duty Navy Dept., Dec. 7, 1915; served as mem. Submarine Bd., Commn. for Laws Relating to Safety of Life at Sea, and Bd. of Inspection and Survey on Ships. Episcopalian. Home: Jacksonville, Fla. Died Sept. 7, 1927.

SMITH, William Thayer, physician; b. New York, Mar. 30, 1839; s. Asa Dodge and Sarah Ann (Adams) S.; A.B., Yale, 1860, A.M., 1874; M.D., Dartmouth Med. Sch., 1878, med. dept. U. of New York, 1879; LL.D., Dartmouth, 1897; m. Susan W. Kellogg, Jan. 14, 1885 (died 1902). Prof. physiology, Dartmouth Med. Sch., 1885-1907; prof. emeritus of physiology, 1907—; prof. clin. surgery, 1907—; surgeon Mary Hitchcock Memorial Hosp. Republican. Congregationalist. Author: Elementary Physiology and Hygiene, 1884; Primer of Physiology and Hygiene, 1885. Address: Hanover, N.H. Died 1909.

SMITH, William Walker, lawyer; b. Covington, Ky., Nov. 21, 1874; s. William Walker and Emily Louise (Van Deventer) S.; prep. edn., Franklin Sch., Cincinnati, and New York Mil. Acad., Cornwall-on-Hudson; LL.B., Cincinnati Law Sch. (U. of Cincinnati), 1897; m. Blanche Crawford, d. Henry Pogue. Practiced law in Cincinnati, 1897-1910; mem. Ohio Ho. of Rep., 1900-04; apptd. after examination, 3d sec. of Embassy, Apr. 1, 1910, and assigned to Constantinople, Turkey; sec. of Legation, Berne, Switzerland, serving as 1st sec. and chargé d'affaires, 1912-13; consul-gen. and 1st sec. Legation, Santo Domingo, 1913-14; acting chief Western European Div., Dept. of State, 1914-16; 1st sec. Legation, Copenhagen, Denmark, 1916-18; assigned as 1st sec. Legation, Lima, Peru, 1918, and when legation was raised to an embassy served as sec. of embassy and chargé d'affaires; sec. of legation, Berne, 1920, chargé d'affaires, 1921; promoted to sec. of Embassy, Class I, Jan. 12, 1922; chargé d'affaires, Tegucigalpa, Honduras, 1922; assigned to Div. Mexican Affairs, Dept. of State, 1923; resigned July 1, 1924, and resumed practice of law at Washington, D.C.; admitted to practice before Supreme Ct. of D.C., Ct. of Appeals of D.C., Treasury Dept., Supreme Ct. of U.S., Gen. Accounting Office of U.S. and Ct. of Claims. Commd. maj. M.I. Res. Officers' Corps, U.S.A., 1925. Republican. Presbyterian. Address: Washington, D.C. Died Sept. 16, 1932.

SMITH, William Waugh, college chancellor; b. Warrenton, Va., Mar. 12, 1845; s. Prof. Richard M. and Ellen (Blackwell) S.; served in C.S.A., 1862-65; twice wounded; A.M., Randolph-Macon Coll., 1871; LL.D., Wesleyan, Conn., 1889; m. Marion Love Howison, Jan. 27, 1875. Asso. and later sr. prin. Bethel Acad., 1871-78; prof., Randolph-Macon Coll., 1878-86, pres., 1886-97; chancellor Randolph-Macon System of Colls. and Acads., 1897—. Raised large sums to build and endow the Va. instns. organized into the Randolph-Macon System. Mem. Am. Social Science Assn. Author: Outlines of Psychology, 1880; A Comparative Chart of Syntax of Latin, Greek, German, French and English, 1882; also numerous ednl. tracts, mag. articles, poems, etc. Address: Lynchburg, Va. Died Nov. 29, 1912.

SMITH, Wilmot M., jurist; b. Suffolk County, N.Y., Mar. 21, 1852; grad. Cornell, 1874; m. Lizzie L. Mott, Nov. 24, 1881. Dist. atty. Suffolk County, N.Y., 1884-90; county judge, same, 1891-95; justice Supreme Ct. of N.Y., 2d jud. dist., 1895—. Address: Patchogue, L.I., N.Y. Died 1906.

SMITH, Wilson George, composer, pianist; b. Elyria, Ohio, Aug. 19, 1855; s. George Troupe and Calista M. S.; grad. Cleveland pub. schs.; began mus. edn. in Cincinnati, 1875, under Otto Singer; studied in Berlin, 1880-82, under Kullak, Kiel, Scharwenka, Moszkowski and Oscar Raif; m. Mez Brett (artist and writer), Apr. 16, 1883. Engaged as teacher of piano, voice and composition, 1882—; also mus. littérateur, editor and critic; music critic, Cleveland Press, 1902—. Piano compositions (several hundred) include books of piano studies, transcriptions and editorial revision of classic and modern works; composer many popular songs. Home: Lakewood, O. Died Feb. 26, 1929.

SMITH, Winchell, playwright; b. Hartford, Conn., Apr. 5, 1871; s. William Brown (nephew of John Brown) and Virginia (Thrall) S.; ed. pub. and high schs., Hartford; hon. Litt.D., Trinity Coll., Conn., 1924; m. Grace Spencer, Dec. 20, 1895. Actor, 1892-1904; produced, with Arnold Daly, a number of plays of Bernard Shaw. Began writing plays, 1906; the first dramatization of Brewster's Millions; later The Fortune Hunter; The Boomerang (with Victor Mapes); Turn to the Right (with John E. Hazzard); "Lightnin'" (with Frank Bacon); Love Among the Lions; The Only Son; The Wheel; Officer 666 (with Augustin McCue); Thank You (with Tom Cushing); The Holy Terror (with George Abbott); The New Henrietta (with Victor Mapes). Home: Farmington, Conn. Died June 10, 1933.

SMITH, Zachariah Frederick, author; b. Henry County, Ky., Jan. 7, 1827; s. Zachariah and Mildred (Dupuy) S.; ed. Bacon Coll., Ky.; m. Sue Helm, Jan. 27, 1852; m. 2d, Anna A. Pittman, June 5, 1890. Engaged in farming; pres. Henry Coll., New Castle, Ky., during Civil War; supt. pub. instrn. of Ky., 1867-71, and author of post-bellum sch. system of Ky.; originator, and pres. Cumberland and Ohio R.R. Co., 1869-73; engaged in ry. constrn. in Tex.; 4 yrs. mgr. of a dept. for D. Appleton & Co., pubs., New York; one of founders and 12 yrs. pres. Ky. Christian Edn. Soc.; a curator of Ky. (now Transylvania) U., Lexington, 1858—. Author: History of Kentucky; Memoirs of the Mother of Henry Clay; School History of Kentucky, 1889; Battle of New Orleans; History of the Reformation of the 19th Century, Inaugurated, Advocated, and Directed by Barton W. Stone, of Kentucky, 1800 to 1832. Address: Louisville, Ky. Died 1911.

SMITH, Zemro Augustus, editorial writer Indianapolis Journal; b. Wiston, Me., Aug. 26, 1837; A.M., Waterville Coll., 1862; m. Jane Steele, Oct. 8, 1891. Capt. maj., lt. col., 1st Me. heavy arty., regt. losing most men of any in Union army; bvtd. col. U.S.V. Republican. Address: Indianapolis, Ind. Deceased.

SMITH, Zilpha Drew, social worker; b. Pembroke, Mass., 1852; d. Silvanus (ship-builder) and Judith Winsor (McLauthlin) Smith; grad. Girls' High and Normal Sch., Boston, 1868; unmarried. Began as telegraph operator, later in charge of dept. in a mercantile agency and of records in probate office; employed by Asso. Charities of Boston from its establishment, most of time as gen. sec., 1879-1904; chmn. com. on Organization of Charity, 1888, and on Needy Families in Their Homes, 1901 (both in Nat. Conf. Charities); asso. dir. Boston Sch. for Social Workers, 1904-16; pres. Mass. State Conf. Charities, 1909; trustee Esther M. Hawks Trust (educational). Unitarian. Served at various times as civ. service examiner for philanthropic or semi-philanthropic positions; regarded as one of the leading authorities in U.S. as to charitable work. Address: Boston, Mass. Died Oct. 12, 1926.

SMITHEE, James Newton, editor; b. Sharp County, Ark., Jan. 11, 1842; edn. in country printing office; part owner Prairie County Democrat, Brownsville, Ark., 1860-61; served in Confederate arty., pvt. and 1st lt.; m. Annie E. Cowgill, Jan. 1, 1867. Worked as printer in Memphis, 1865-66; became foreman, 1866, and later editor and propr. Arkansas Gazette; on staff Gov. Baxter in "gubernatorial war," 1874; commr. State lands of Ark., 3 terms, disposing of Gazette; founded and edited for several months the Arkansas Democrat; chmn. Dem. State Com., 1878-82; spl. agt. land office in Colo. and N. Mex., 1885-90; on editorial staff Rocky Mountain News, Denver, 1890-92; bought majority of stock of Arkansas Gazette, 1896, but retired, 1899, returning to Denver. Address: Denver, Colo. Died 1905.

SMITHER, Henry Carpenter, army officer; b. Ft. Sill, Okla., July 28, 1873; s. Robert Gano and Mary Virginia S.; grad. U.S. Mil. Acad., 1897; m. Helen Lytle, June 28, 1900; children—Bernice Lytle (Mrs. George W. Gering), Henrietta Carpenter (Mrs. Paul L. Armel), Henry Carpenter. Commissioned 2d lieut., 8th Cavalry, June 11, 1897; promoted through grades to maj., January 30, 1917; colonel Signal Corps (temp.), October 10, 1917; colonel U.S.A., July 1, 1920; brig. gen., June 18, 1925. Served in Cuba, Spanish-Am. War, later in Philippines; mem. Gen. Staff Corps, 1913-15; asst. chief of staff, chief of 4th Sect., Service of Supply, A.E.F., 1918-19; chief of staff, 3d Div., Sept. 1920-July 1921. Selected by Gen. Dawes and appointed by the President to assist in making up Budget of U.S., 1921; apptd. by exec. order of the President, July 27, 1921, chief coördinator; retired Jan. 1, 1929. Decorated D.S.M. (U.S.); Officer Legion of Honor (French); D.S.M. (Republic of Panama). Address: Washington, D.C. Died July 13, 1930.

SMITHERS, Ernest Leonard, ry. official; b. St. Albans, Eng., Nov. 18, 1867; s. Sidney J. and Louisa B (Faulconbridge) S.; ed. pvt. sch., Eng.; m. Edith A Williams, July 9, 1892; children—Henry L., Horace G. (dec.), Eric F., Charles H. (dec.), Edith M., Winnie. Came to U.S., 1884; began as jr. clk. St Louis & Cairo Ry., 1884; clk. freight office, C.,B.&Q R.R., at Chicago, 1885; clk. Cleveland, Akron & Columbus Ry., at Akron, O., 1886; sec. to pres. L.&N R.R., at New York, 1886-89, clk. treasurer's office, 1889-1901, transfer agt., 1901-02, asst. sec. and asst treas., 1902-16, v.p., Apr. 20, 1916-Jan. 1, 1937, continuing as dir., 1926—. Republican. Methodist Home: East Orange, N.J. Died June 4, 1940.

SMITHEY, Royall Bascom, coll. prof.; b. Amelia County, Va., Jan. 20, 1851; s. Royall B. and Mary Ann (Hubbard) S.; A.B., A.M., Randolph-Macon Coll., 1876, Litt.D., 1908; m. Annie Shackelford, July 15, 1896. Prof. mathematics, Randolph-Macon Coll 1878-1917, emeritus, 1917—. Democrat. Author: History of Virginia, 1898; Civil Government of Virginia, 1898. Home: Ashland, Va. Died July 18, 1925.

SMITHIES, Frank, M.D.; b. Elland, Yorkshire, Eng., Dec. 21, 1880; s. John and Alice (Tattersall) S.; grad. Calumet High Sch., Chicago, Ill.; M.D., U. of Mich., 1904; Sc.D., Washburn Coll.; studied U. of Berlin and Guy's Hosp. (London), 1906, dept. of arts, U. of Mich., 1909; m. Mary Louise Kellam, Sept. 25, 1909; children—John Tattersall, Thomas Holliday, Katherine Jameson. Clinic asst. Rush Med. Coll., Chicago, 1904-05; instr. medicine and demonstrator of clin. medicine, U. of Mich., 1906-10; asst. pathologist, Moabit Hosp., Berlin, 1906; gastroenterologist Mayo Clinic, Rochester, Minn., 1911-14; same, Augustana Hosp., Chicago, 1914-22, also asso. dir. labs.; asso. prof. medicine, U. of Ill., 1915-20, prof., 1920-25; attending physician Henrotin Memorial Hosp., 1921-34; chief of clinic in digestive diseases, Municipal Tuberculosis Sanitarium, Chicago, 1927-34; cons. physician C.,M.&St.P. R.R. and Beaumont Nursing Home. Fellow Am. Therapeutic Society (pres. 1933), American Soc. of Tropical Medicine (pres. 1932); mem. A.M.A., and of Councilors of Scientific Assembly of same (1929-35), Am. Coll. Physicians (pres. 1927-28), Ill. State and Chicago med. socs., Am. Gastro-Enterol. Assn. (pres. 1929). Episcopalian. Jerome Cochran Lecturer (Alabama), 1916; Bedford Lecturer (Pittsburgh), 1924. Chevalier Legion of Honour (France), 1932. Author: Cancer of the Stomach, 1916; also numerous monographs on med. topics. Editor of Am. Jour. of Digestive Diseases and Nutrition; asso. editor Am. Jour. Tropical Medicine (Baltimore). Home: Chicago, Ill. Died Feb. 9, 1937.

SMITHSON, Noble, lawyer; b. Nolensville Williamson County, Tenn., Dec. 7, 1841; s. John Greene and Ann Vaughn (Ladd) S.; largely self ed.; m. Alice Josephine Patterson, Apr. 1, 1865. Teacher in country sch. admitted to Tenn. bar, 1866; practiced, Pulaski Tenn., 1867-87, Birmingham, Ala., 1888-93, Knoxville, Tenn., 1893—; mem. bar Supreme Ct. of U.S., also of Tenn., Ala., Ill. and N.Y.; sec. and gen. counsel W. Lonsdale Land Co. Dist. atty. gen., Tenn., 1867-69; mem. Tenn. State Senate, 1873-74; spl. judge, 1875-77. Mem. M.E. Ch., S. Mason. Author: Judge Ladd (a novel), 1900; Treatise on Civil Procedure in Tennessee, 1903; Smithson's Theory of Special Creation, 1911. Home: Knoxville, Tenn. Deceased.

SMITHSON, William Walpole, M.D., surgeon; b. Thomastown, Miss., Dec. 20, 1874; s. Charles Taylor and Julia (Landrum) S.; Agrl. and Mech. Coll., Starkville, Miss.; M.D., Memphis Hosp. Med. Coll., 1900; m. Meta M. Moore, Sept. 20, 1900; 1 son, Claude Taylor (dec.). Began practice at Kosciusko, Miss., 1900; sec. State Bd. of Health, Miss., 1912-13; supt. Miss. Insane Hosp., 1913-17; supt. Jackson Sanatorium, also v.p., 1923—. Democrat. Methodist. Home: Jackson, Miss. Died Sept. 9, 1931.

SMOCK, John Conover, geologist; b. Holmdel, Monmouth County, N.J., Sept. 21, 1842; s. Isaac G. and Ellen (Conover) S.; A.B., Rutgers, 1862; studied Bergakademie, and U. of Berlin, 1869-70; Ph.D., Lafayette, 1882; LL.D., Rutgers, 1902; m. Katherine E. Beekman, Oct. 15, 1874 (died 1922). Tutor in chemistry, 1865-67, prof. elec. mining and metallurgy, 1867, also prof., 1871-85, Rutgers; asst. on geol. survey of N.J., 1864-85; asst. in charge N.Y. State Mus., 1885-90; state geologist of N.J., 1890-1901; mem. bd. mgrs. N.J. Geol. Survey, 1901-15. Fellow A.A.A.S. Home: Hudson, N.Y. Died Apr. 21, 1926.

SMOOT, Charles Head, mech. engr.; b. Ilion, N.Y., Dec. 6, 1878; s. William Sidney and Mary Bunker (Head) S.; ed. Harvard and U. of Calif.; m. Katherine Elizabeth Ryan, Oct. 12, 1910; children—Mary Katherine, Charles Head, William Sydney. Engaged as mech. engr. in Calif., 1900; engr. and dir. Rateau Steam Regenerator Co., 1908-22; same, Rateau, Battu, Smoot Co., 1911-23; pres. Smoot Engring. Corp., 1923—. Republican. Home: Maplewood, N.J. Died Jan. 6, 1933.

SMOOT, Reed, senator; b. Salt Lake City, Jan. 10, 1862; s. Abraham O. and Anne K.S.; grad. Brigham Young Acad., Provo, Utah, 1879; m. Alpha M. Eldredge, Sept. 17, 1884 (died 1928); children—Harold Reed, Chloe, Harlow Eldredge, Annie K., Zella Esther, Ernest Winder; m. 2d, Mrs. Alice Taylor Sheets, July 2, 1930. Pres. Hotel Utah, Home Fire Insurance Co., Smoot Investment Co., Provo, and dir. corps. in Salt Lake City; mem. exec. com. of the Utah-Idaho Sugar Co. Apptd. one of the Presidents Utah Stake of the Ch. of Jesus Christ of Latter Day Saints, Apr. 1895, apostle, 1900. U.S. senator 5 terms, 1903-33; served as chmn. finance com. of Senate and mem. World War Foreign Debt Commn. Mem. Rep. Nat. Com., 1912-16, 1916-20; chmn. Rep. Senatorial Campaign Com., 1919—; chmn. Resolutions Com. Rep. Nat. Conv., 1928. Home: Salt Lake City, Utah. Died Feb. 9, 1941.

SMOOT, Thomas Arthur, clergyman; b. Olin, N.C., Mar. 6, 1871; s. James Franklin and Virginia (Brittingham) S.; A.B., Trinity Coll., Durham, N.C., 1895; studied Vanderbilt U., 1897-98; Curry Sch. of Expression, Boston; D.D., Randolph-Macon, 1912; m. Leila Gilchrist McGirt, Aug. 17, 1898; children—Thomas Arthur, Edward Brittingham, Mary Lily. Head master Trinity (N.C.) High Sch., 1895-96; prof. physics and chemistry, Greensboro (N.C.) Female Coll., 1898-1900; ordained ministry M.E. Ch., S., 1900; pastor Fayetteville, Durham and Wilmington, N.C., until 1910, Norfolk, Va., 1910-14, Centenary Ch., Richmond, 1914-22, Main St. Ch., Danville, Va., 1922-29; again pastor Epworth Ch., Norfolk, Va., 1929—. Trustee Randolph-Macon Coll. Member hospital board, 1922-26, commn. on budget, 1926-30, M.E. Ch., S.; del. Fed. Council of Chs., Cleveland, 1919, Gen. Conf. M.E. Ch., S., 1922, 30, 34; mem. Gen. Board Finance, Gen. Conf. M.E. Ch., S.; pres. Board of Christian Education, Va. Conf. M.E. Church, S. Author: The Standard of Pitch in Religion, 1914; The Start and Finish of a Day, 1922; The Evolution of a Churchman, 1926. Home: Norfolk, Va. Died Aug. 29, 1937.

SMULSKI, John F., banker; b. Posen, Poland, Feb. 4, 1867; s. William and Euphemia (Balcer) S.; common sch. and coll. edn.; m. Harriet Mikitynski, June 7, 1899; children—Harriet, John J. Early engaged in newspaper and publishing business; admitted to the Ill. bar, 1890; mem. law firm David, Smulski and McGaffey, 1890-1905; organizer and pres. North-Western Trust & Savings Bank, 1906—; dir. Second North-Western State Bank, Fullerton State Bank, Marshall Square State Bank, Inland Trust & Savings Bank, Keystone Trust & Savings Bank, Brighton Park State Bank. Alderman, Chicago, 1898-1903; city atty., 1903-07; state treas. of Ill., 1907-09. V.p. and treas. Chicago Assn. Commerce, 1911-14; pres. Bd. of West Chicago Park Commrs., 1907-13, 1916-20. Decorated Chevalier Legion of Honor by French Govt.; Comdr. Polonia Restituta by the Polish Govt. Home: Chicago, Ill. Died Mar. 18, 1928.

SMYSER, Martin L., congressman, lawyer; b. in Wayne County, O., Apr. 3, 1851; s. Emanuel and Catharine (Albert) S.; ed. country schs. and grad. Wittenberg Coll., Springfield, O., A.B., 1870; m. Alice A. France, Feb. 1, 1881. Admitted to Ohio bar, 1872, and practiced in all courts of Ohio, 1872—; also admitted to the various Federal courts, including the Supreme Ct. Pros. atty., Wayne County, 1 term; judge Circuit Ct., Ohio, 5th circuit; mem. Congress, 1889-91, and 1905-07, 17th Ohio dist. Republican; alternate 1884, del. 1888, 1892, 1904, Nat. Rep. convs.; del. to nearly every Rep. State Conv. in Ohio, 1873—. Address: Wooster, O. Died 1908.

SMYSER, William Emory, coll. dean; b. Baltimore County, Md., Sept. 17, 1866; s. Rev. Martin L. and Lydia Ann (Hoffman) S.; B.A., Wesleyan U., Conn., 1889, M.A., 1892; Johns Hopkins U., 1890-91; Litt.D., U. of Chattanooga, 1916; LL.D. from Hamline U., 1927; m. Elisabeth Arbuckle Craig, June 24, 1890; children—William Craig, Dorothy Elizabeth, Hamilton Martin, Margaret Lydia. Teacher of Latin, Dickinson Sem., Pa., 1889-90; instr. English, Northwestern U., 1891-92; prof. English, DePauw U., 1892-1900; prof. English, 1900—, registrar 1904-20, and dean, 1917—, Ohio Wesleyan U., prof. English, Ohio State U., summer terms, 1909, 10, 11. Dir. (Ohio) Students' War Service Campaign, summer 1918; asst. ednl. dir., Sixth District, S.A.T.C., Oct.-Nov. 1918. Mem. Ohio Coll. Assn. (pres. 1924-25), Central Ohio Schoolmasters' Club (pres. 1925-26), N. Central Assn. (1st v.p. 1928-29). Methodist; mem. Senate of Bd. of Edn. M.E. Ch., 1928—. Author: Spiritual Truth in Poetry of Tennyson, 1906. Contbr. of chapter on Religion in the Denominational College, to The Effective College, 1927; also to mags. and ednl. publs.; lecturer before teachers' institutes and on lit. subjects. Home: Delaware, O. Died May 24, 1935.

SMYTH, Albert Henry, author; b. Phila., June 18, 1863; s. William Clarke and Adelaide (Suplee) S.; grad. Johns Hopkins, 1886; prof. English lang. and lit., Central High Sch., Phila., 1886—; unmarried. Mem. and curator Am. Philos. Soc.; del. Am. Philos. Soc. to 450th anniversary of founding of U. of Glasgow; visited England every yr., 1886—, and traveled much in Russia, Poland, Greece and Asia Minor. Author: American Literature, 1888; Philadelphia Magazines and Their Contributors, 1892; Bayard Taylor (in American Men of Letters Series), 1896; Shakespeare's Pericles and Apollonius of Tyre, 1898. Founder and editor Shakespeariana, 1883-84; Works and Correspondence of Benjamin Franklin, with Life, Notes, etc. (10 vols.), 1905-06. Editor: Burke's Letter to a Noble Lord, 1898; Pope's Homer's Iliad, 1899. Contbr. to mags. and newspapers of papers about Shakespeare's Country. Residence: Germantown, Philadelphia, Pa. Died 1907.

SMYTH, Charles Henry, Jr., geologist; b. Oswego, N.Y., Mar. 31, 1866; s. Charles Henry and Alice (DeWolf) S.; Ph.B., Columbia, 1888, Ph.D., 1890; U. of Heidelberg, 1890-91; m. Ruth A. Phelps, July 30, 1891; children—Charles Phelps, Henry DeWolf. Prof. geology and mineralogy, Hamilton Coll., 1891-1905; prof. geology, Princeton U., 1905-34, emeritus, 1934. Fellow Geol. Soc. of America, A.A.A.S. Author of many papers on pre-Cambrian geology, petrology, ore deposits, etc. Address: Princeton, N.J. Died Apr. 4, 1937.

SMYTH, Constantine Joseph, judge; b. County Cavin, Ireland, Dec. 4, 1859; s. Brian and Rose (Clark) S.; brought to America, 1870; Creighton U., Omaha, 1878-82, A.M., 1907, LL.D., 1918; m. Katherine F. Murphy, Jan. 8, 1889. Admitted to bar, 1885, and practiced at Omaha. Mem. Neb. Ho. of Rep., 1887, Omaha Sch. Bd., 1889-94; chmn. Dem. State Central Com., 1894-96; chmn. Neb. delegation to Dem. Nat. Conv., 1896, 1904, del., 1912; attorney gen. of Neb. 2 terms, 1897-1900; Dem. nominee for governor, 1898, 1902. Asso. dean and prof. Creighton U. Coll. of Law, 1905-10. Spl. asst. to atty. gen. of U.S., 1913-17; chief justice Ct. of Appeals of D.C., 1917—. Prof. Georgetown U. Coll. of Law. Catholic. Home: Washington, D.C. Died Apr. 14, 1924.

SMYTH, Egbert Coffin; educator; b. Brunswick, Me., Aug. 24, 1829; s. Prof. William and Harriet Porter (Coffin) S.; grad. Bowdoin, 1848, D.D., 1866, LL.D., 1902 (D.D., Harvard, 1886); grad. Bangor Theol. Sem., 1853; studied in Germany; m. Portland, Me., Elizabeth Bradford Dwight, Aug. 12, 1857. Prof. rhetoric, Bowdoin, 1854-56; prof. natural and revealed religion, 1856-63, prof. eccles. history, Andover Theol. Sem., 1863—. Corporate mem. A.B.C.F.M.; trustee Abbot Acad., Dummer Acad., Bowdoin Coll. A co-founder, 1884, and co-editor Andover Review. Author: Three Discourses on the Religious History of Bowdoin College, 1858; also addresses, and many papers in hist. and theol. publs. Translator of Uhlhorn's "Conflict of Christianity with Heathenism" (with C. J. H. Ropes), 1879; furnished introduction and appendix to Observations Concerning the Scripture Œconomia of the Trinity by Jonathan Edwards, 1880; Influence of Jonathan Edwards on the Spiritual Life of New England, 1901. Joint Author: Progressive Orthodoxy, 1886; The Divinity of Jesus Christ, 1893. Address: Andover, Mass. Died 1904.

SMYTH, Ellison Adger, biologist; b. Summerton, Clarendon County, S.C., Oct. 26, 1863; s. James Adger and Annie R. (Briggs) S.; A.B., Princeton, 1884, A.M., 1887; law dept., Columbia, 1884-85; U. of Va., 1887; LL.D., U. of Ala., 1906; m. Grace C. Allan, Dec. 29, 1897; children—Thomas, Amey Allan, Ellison A., Grace Allan, James Adger. Adj. prof. biology, U. of S.C., 1889-91; prof. biology, Va. Poly. Inst., 1891-1925 (retired), also dean of faculty, 1902-06. Democrat. Presbyn. (elder). Author of various papers on entomology in Entomol. News; bird notes in "The Auk"; biography and estimate of works of John Bennett, in Library of Southern Literature. Address: Salem, Va. Died Aug. 19, 1941.

SMYTH, Herbert Weir, Hellenist; b. Wilmington, Del., Aug. 8, 1857; s. Clement Biddle and Sarah (Sellers) S.; A.B., Swarthmore, 1876; A.B., Harvard, 1878; Ph.D., Göttingen, 1884; m. Eleanor Adt, Dec. 20, 1887; children—Raymond Weir (dec.), Gladys Weir, Mrs. Evelyn Weir Fuller, Eirene Weir. Prof. Greek, Bryn Mawr Coll., 1888-1901; prof. Greek, 1901-02, Eliot prof. Greek lit., 1902-25, Harvard, emeritus, 1925—. Prof. Greek lang. and lit., Am. Sch. Class. Studies, Athens, 1899-1900. Fellow Am. Acad. Arts and Sciences; mem. Am. Philos. Soc., Am. Philol. Assn. (editor Transactions and Proceedings, 1889-1904, sec. 1889-1904, pres. 1904-05); v.p. Egypt Exploration Soc. Author: The Sacred Literature of the Jains (transl.), 1890; Greek Dialects, 1894; Greek Melic Poetry, 1900; Greek Grammar for Schools, 1915; Greek Grammar for College, 1920; Æschylus, text and transl., 1923-25; Æschylean Tragedy, 1923; editor of Greek Series for Colleges and Schools (20 vols.). Home: Cambridge, Mass. Died July 16, 1937.

SMYTH, James Adger, merchant; b. Charleston, S.C., June 8, 1838; s. Rev. Thomas and Margaret M. (Adger) S.; brother of Augustine Thomas and Ellison Adger S.; A.B., Coll. of Charleston (1st honor), 1858; m. Annie R. Briggs, Mar. 14, 1860 (died 1901); m. 2d, Ella Calvert Campbell, Nov. 17, 1903; father of Ellison Adger S. Merchant, 1859—. Vol. C.S.A., Apr., 1861; mem. State and Co. Dem. Exec. coms., 1876; alderman, 1877-95; mayor of Charleston, 1895-1903; retired 1903. Pres. Cotton Exchange, 1889-94; pres. C. of C., 1903-10. Grand Master 3 yrs., Grand High Priest 2 yrs., Masons of S.C. Home: Charleston, S.C. Died Apr. 25, 1920.

SMYTH, Julian Kennedy, clergyman; b. in N.Y., 1856. Pastor Church of New Jerusalem (Swedenborgian), New York; pres. Gen. Conv. Ch. of the New Jerusalem. Author: Footprints of the Savior, 1886; Holy Names as Interpretations of the Story of the Manger and the Cross, 1891; Swedenborg, 1911; Religion and Life, 1911; The Heart of the War, 1914; Christian Certainties of Belief, 1916. Home: New York, N.Y. Died Apr. 5, 1921.

SMYTH, Newman, clergyman; b. Brunswick, Me., June 25, 1843; s. Prof. William and Harriet C. S.; A.B., Bowdoin, 1863, A.M., 1866; 1st lt. 16th Me. Vols., 1864-65; grad. Andover Theol. Sem., 1867; D.D., N.Y. U., 1881, Yale, 1895, Bowdoin, 1921; m. Anna M. Ayer, June 20, 1871. Ordained Congl. ministry, 1868; pastor Mission Chapel, Providence, R.I., 1867-70, First Congl. Ch., Bangor, Me., 1870-75, First Presbyn. Ch., Quincy, Ill., 1876-82, First Congl. Ch., New Haven, Conn., 1882-1907, pastor emeritus, 1908. Fellow of Yale, 1899—. Author: Personal Creeds, 1890; Christian Ethics, 1892; The Place of Death in Evolution, 1897; Through Science to Faith, 1902; Passing Protestantism and Coming Catholicism, 1908; Modern Belief in Immortality, 1910; Constructive Natural Theology, 1913; The Meaning of Personal Life, 1916; Approaches Toward Church Unity, 1919; Story of Church Unity, 1924. Home: New Haven, Conn. Died Jan. 6, 1925.

SMYTH, William Henry, engineer; b. Birkenhead, Cheshire, Eng., May 16, 1855; s. Henry and Ann Jane (Finglass) S.; ed. Yorkshire Coll. of Tech., Leeds, followed by apprenticeship with Kitson & Co., Leeds; draftsman with Asquith & Co., Leeds, 1874-76; came to U.S.; in gen. practice as cons. engr., 1879—; m. Helen Pauline Bradshaw, 1884. Inventor of many machines and devices, including a drag-saw, 1879; many machines for making, soldering, testing and heading cans, 1889-1903; mech. movement, 1890; pneumatic apparatus, 1896; hydraulic and chain bucket dredger, 1898; air compressor valve, 1899; art of utilizing heat energy, 1900; internally fired engine, 1900; ore roasting furnace, mech. stoker, valve, etc., 1901; printing press, 1902; deep well pump, 1903; also inventor of system of raising water by direct explosion on its surface, later universally known as the direct explosion pump; segmental cargo boat for war use, 1917; power drive-chain, 1920; roller-hinge for heavy-duty chain, 1921; track-layer chain, 1922; resilient-track tractor, 1922; high-speed tractor, 1922; track-layer track-assembly, 1923; two-point-support wheel-base track-layer, 1923; convertible tractor, 1924; combined track-layer and round-wheel tractor, 1925; friction-drive track-layer, 1928; military tractor, 1929; convertible noiseless track-layer tractor, 1932; convertible tractor, 1932; new system of highspeed, non-stop, railroad transportation, 1933. Life fellow Royal Econ. Soc. (London); fellow Am. Geog. Soc.; mem. Am. Acad. Polit. and Social Science. Author: Is the Inventive Faculty a Myth, 1895; Technocracy—National Industrial Management, 1917; Federation of Nations, 1922; The Story of the Stadium, 1923; Concerning Irascible Strong, 1926; Did Man and Woman Descend from Different Animals? A New Theory of the Origin of the Sexes, 1927; Coming Events, "Social Credit" Criticized, The Truth About Technocracy, 1933; National Master Code—Industrial Constitution for National Industrial Management, 1934; Women in Industry, 1934; Money and Currency, 1935; Problem of Crime, 1938; also many essays on economics and social science. Home: Berkeley, Calif. Died Feb. 18, 1940.

SMYTH, Winfield Scott, publisher; b. Cazenovia, N.Y., Nov. 22, 1872; s. Winfield Scott and Lavinia Espey (Line) S.; student Stanford, 1893-95, U. of Chicago, 1896; m. Joan Maude Slote, Nov. 25, 1898; children—Winfield Scott (dec.), Beatrice Slote (Mrs. Gerald Irving Carper), Lavinia Georgie (Mrs. Edmund Lee Gamble), John Scott. Foreign lang. agt. D. C. Heath & Co., pubs., Boston, Mass., 1896-98; asst. mgr. Chicago office same co., 1898-1910, treas., 1910-28, v.p., 1922-27, pres. 1927-37, hon. chmn., 1937—. Republican. Mason. Home: Newtonville, Mass. Died June 8, 1940.

SMYTHE, Augustine Thomas, lawyer; b. Charleston, S.C., Oct. 5, 1842; s. Rev. Thomas and Margaret M. (Adger) S.; brother of Ellison Adger and James Adger Smyth; ed. schs. of Charleston and S.C. Coll. until outbreak of Civil War; enlisted Apr. 10, 1861, as pvt. S.C. Coll. cadets, in state troops, and a year later was mustered into C.S.A., in Co. A, 25th S.C. Vols., serving to end of war; after war studied law in office of Simonton & Barker of Charleston; m. Louisa R., d. Col. D. J. McCord, 1865. Admitted to bar, 1866; mem. firm of Smythe, Lee & Frost; state senator, 1880-94. Democrat. Prominent in Masonry—Grand Master, Grand Lodge, and Grand High Priest, Grand Chapter of S.C. Address: Charleston, S.C. Deceased.

SMYTHE, George Franklin, clergyman, educator; b. Toledo, O., Oct. 21, 1852; s. Anson and Caroline Augusta (Fitch) S.; A.B., Western Reserve U., 1874, A.M., 1877; D.D., Kenyon, 1898; m. Emma C. Hall, Aug. 1, 1878 (died 1927); 1 son, Frank Nelson. Teacher high sch., Cleveland, 1877-80, Greylock Inst., Williamstown, Mass., 1880-84; deacon, 1885, priest, 1886, P.E. Ch.; minister in charge Christ Ch., Oberlin, O., 1885-90; rector St. Andrew's Ch., Elyria, 1887-90, St. Paul's Ch., Toledo, 1890-91, St. Paul's Ch., Mt. Vernon, 1892-98, Trinity Ch., Bridgewater, Mass., 1898-1900; prof. Latin, Kenyon Coll., 1900-03; rector Harcourt Parish, and chaplain same coll., 1902-15; prof. homiletics and religious edn., 1915-20, dean, 1918-20, Divinity Sch. of Kenyon Coll. Historiographer, P.E. Diocese of Ohio. Author: Kenyon College, Its First Century; The God of Israel; History of the Diocese of Ohio, 1927. Home: Gambier, O. Died Aug. 25, 1934.

SMYTHE, Sidney Thomas, educator; b. Fredericton, N.B., Can., May 18, 1862; s. Thomas Campbell and Elisabeth (Ross) S.; A.B., St. Stephen's Coll., N.Y., 1883, A.M., 1886; S.T.B., Nashotah Theol. Sem., 1885; S.T.D., Hobart, 1897; m. Jeannette D. Strotz, June 16, 1897. Deacon, 1885, priest, 1886, P.E. Ch.; head master, 1886-94, pres., 1894—, also prof. Greek lang. and lit., St. John's Mil. Acad.; lecturer on constl. law, 1907. Rector St. John's Ch., Delafield, Wis., 1886-87. Mem. Wis. Acad. Sciences, Arts and Letters. Mason. Author: Thoughts With My Pupils; also occasional sermons and addresses. Address: Delafield, Wis. Died Mar. 3, 1923.

SMYTHE, William E(llsworth), author, irrigationist; b. Worcester, Mass., Dec. 24, 1861; s. William Augustus Somerset and Abbie (Bailey) Smythe; educated at Worcester, Mass.; m. Harriet Bridge, Dec. 28, 1882 (died 1918). Editor Kearney (Nebraska) Enterprise, 1888-90, Omaha Bee, 1890-91; founded, 1891, and editor, 1891-96, the Irrigation Age; editor Western Empire. Founded Nat. Irrigation Congress, 1891 (sec. 1891-93, chairman 1893-95); established New Plymouth Colony, Ida., 1895; lectured extensively on irrigation and Western institutions; conducted popular campaign in California under auspices of the Water and Forest Assn. and Calif. Constructive League, in behalf of radical reform of water laws and adoption of Australian system of land settlement, 1901-02; Dem. candidate for Congress, 8th Calif. Dist., 1902. Established "Little Landers" of San Diego, 1909, "Little Landers" of Los Angeles, 1913, and (with Charles Weeks) Runnymede, Calif., 1916; founded Little Lands in America (mag.), 1916. Associated, 1919-21, with Sec. Lane and Judge Payne, Interior Dept. on reconstruction program looking to extension of reclamation movement to entire U.S.; with Col. William L. White, founded Am. Homelanders Soc. for popular edn. in higher rural life and establishment of garden communities around large cities. Author: The Conquest of Arid America, 1900; Constructive Democracy, 1905; History of San Diego, 1907; City Homes on Country Lanes (1st vol. of "Triology of the New Earth"), 1921. Contbr. to mags. on irrigation and other subjects. Address: Washington, D.C. Died Oct. 6, 1922.

SNEATH, E. Hershey, educator; b. Mountville, Pa., Aug. 7, 1857; s. Jacob and Elizabeth S.; A.B., Lebanon Valley Coll., Pa., 1881, A.M., 1885; B.D., Yale, 1884, Ph.D., 1889; LL.D., Lebanon Valley, 1903, Litt.D., 1933; m. Anna S. Camp, June 19, 1890; children—Herbert Camp, Katharine Williams, Richard Sheldon. Lecturer on history of philosophy, 1889-91, instr. philosophy, 1891-93, asst. prof., 1893-98, prof., 1898, prof. philosophy of religion, 1912, and prof. emeritus, 1923, Yale. Trustee of Conn. Industrial Sch. for Girls. Fellow A.A.A.S. Organized and edited The Modern Philosophers Series (6 vols.); The Ethical Series (3 vols.). Author: The Philosophy of Reid, 1892; The Ethics of Hobbes, 1898; The Mind of Tennyson, 1900; Philosophy in Poetry, 1904; Wordsworth—Poet of Nature and Man, 1912. Joint Author: (with Dean Hodges and E. L. Stevens) Golden Rule Series (6 books), 1913; (with Dean Hodges) Manual of Moral Instruction for School and Home, 1913; (with Dean Hodges and Prof. Tweedy) The King's Highway Series (8 books), 1917; Religious Training in the School and Home, 1917; Shall We Have a Creed?, 1925. Editor: Religion and the War, 1918. Organizer and editor of The Great Leaders' Series, Handbooks for Moral and Religious Education Series, Religious Science and Literature Series, compositive volume, At One with The Invisible (1921), composite vol., Religion and the Future Life (1922), Composite Volume, Evolution of Ethics as Revealer in the Great Religions, 1927; America's Greatest Sonneteer, 1928; (with W. Earhart, J. A. O'Shea and H. E. Cogswell) Songs of Purpose (3 books), 1929; (with E. L. Thomas) A Child's Garden of Song, 1929; (with others) Religion as a Power in Human Development, 1934; also Vocational Series, Christian Service Series. Home: New Haven, Conn. Died Dec. 20, 1935.

SNEDECOR, James George, clergyman; b. on plantation, Tchula, Miss., June 21, 1855; s. George Gayle and Harriet Augusta (Godden) S.; A.B., U. of Miss., 1873; post-grad. studies, Cornell, 1874-76; read law Washington U., St. Louis, 1877; LL.D., U. of Ala., 1906; m. Emily Alston Estes, Jan. 22, 1880. Practiced law at Memphis, 1877-81; ordained Presbyn. ministry, 1889; pastor, Dunedin, Fla., 1889-90, Vinehill, Ala., 1890-91, Avondale Ch., Birmingham, Ala., 1891-96, Woodlawn Ch., Birmingham, 1897-1903; sec. Exec. Com. of Home Missions, Presbyn. Ch. in U.S., 1903-14. Head of Stillman Inst. (theol. sch. for negroes), Tuscaloosa, Ala., 1914—. Trustee Thornwell Orphans College, S.C. Democrat. Address: Tuscaloosa, Alabama. Died Nov. 20, 1916.

SNEDEKER, Charles Dippolt; b. New Brunswick, N.J., July 17, 1861; s. Cornelius and Mary Catherine (Stonaker) S.; desc. Jan Snedeker, from Holland, 1642; ed. pub. schs. and New Jersey Business Coll.; m. Mary, d. John J. Davison, Jan. 23, 1894; 1 son, Charles D. (dec.). With Dahmer, Snedeker & Runyon, retail clothing, New Brunswick, 10 yrs.; sec. and treas. Perth Amboy Dry Dock Co., 1894-1928, pres., 1928—; pres. First National Co., Perth Amboy; v.p. First Nat. Bank, Perth Amboy, Perth Amboy Gas Light Co.; pres. Bd. Water Commrs., Perth Amboy, 10 yrs. Chmn. Postal Savings drive, World War I. Presbyn. Home: Perth Amboy, N.J. Died Nov. 27, 1935.

SNEED, Frank Woolford, clergyman; b. Sedalia, Mo.; s. John M. and Mary (Stewart) S.; A.B., Westminster Coll., Fulton, Mo., 1885; McCormick Theol. Sem., Chicago, 1885-88; m. Eulalie Hockaday, May 18, 1895. Ordained Presbyn. ministry, 1888; pastor Riverside, Ill., 1888-92, Columbia, Mo., 1892-95, 1st Ch., Minneapolis, Minn., 1895-97, then Washington and Compton Av. Ch., St. Louis, East Liberty Ch., Pittsburgh, and again Washington and Compton Av. Ch., Feb. 1, 1922—. Trustee Western Theol. Sem., Presbyn. Hosp. Democrat. Home: St. Louis, Mo. Died Mar. 11, 1923.

SNEED, John Louis Taylor, jurist; b. Raleigh, N.C., May 12, 1820; s. Maj. Junius and Julia Rowan (Taylor) S.; academic edn.; m. Mary Ashe Shepherd, Aug. 1848. Admitted to Tenn. bar, 1841; mem. Tenn. gen. assembly, 1845-46; officer in Mexican war, 1846-47; dist. atty. gen., 1851-54; atty. gen. of Tenn. and Supreme Court reporter, 1854-59; brig. gen. provisional army of Tenn., 1861; judge Supreme Court, 1870-78; judge Ct. of Arbitration, 1879; Dem. elector for State-at-large, 1880; judge Court of Referees, 1883-84; chancellor 11th Chancery Div. of Tenn., 1894-1900 (resigned Jan. 3, 1900, retiring to private life). Edited 5 vols. Sneed's Tenn. Reports. Pres. Memphis Law School, 1887-93. Address: Memphis, Tenn. Died 1901.

SNELLING, Charles Mercer, univ. pres.; b. Richmond, Va., Nov. 3, 1862; s. of Zacheus and Cleopatra (Perdue) S.; grad. Va. Mil. Inst., 1884; student of mathematics, univs. of Göttingen and Berlin, 1893-94; hon. A.M., U. of Ga., 1890; Sc.D., U. of Pittsburgh, 1911; m. Matilda Janet Morton, June 18, 1891; children—Wm. Morton (dec.), Margaret (dec.), Pinckney Welch, Chas. Mercer, Albert Minor, David Barrow, John Richards, Robert Edwin. Adj. prof. mathematics, Va. Mil. Inst., 1884-85; prof. mathematics, Ga. Mil. Acad., Savannah, Ga., 1885-86, South Ga. Coll., Thomasville, Ga., 1886-88; adj. prof. mathematics and comdt. of cadets, U. of Ga., 1888-1906; prof. mathematics and dean Franklin Coll., U. of Ga., 1906-09; pres. Franklin Coll. and dean U. of Ga., 1909—; acting chancellor U. of Ga., 1925-26, chancellor, 1926-32; chancellor Univ. System, 1932; chancellor emeritus Univ. System, 1933. Democrat. Baptist. Pres. Commn. of Bonded Debt of Athens, Ga.; dir. Nat. Bank of Athens. Pres. Mountain City (Ga.) Packing Co. Home: Athens, Ga. Died Sept. 19, 1939.

SNELLING, Rodman Paul, textile mfr.; b. Forest Hills (now part of Boston), Mass., Apr. 26, 1861; s. Samuel George and Eleanora Ellicott (Paul) S.; prep. edn., St. Paul's Sch., Concord, N.H.; A.B., Harvard, 1881; m. Eva Burnham de Treville, June 12, 1900; 1 dau., Ella de Treville. Began in iron mfg. business, 1881; became treas. Pettee Machine Shop Works (later Saco-Lowell Shops), 1882, later v.p.; pres. Indian Head Mills, Cordova, Ala.; dir. Arkwright Mutual Fire Ins. Co., Harmony Mills, Liberty Mut. Ins. Co., Nashua Mfg. Co., Paper Mill Mut. Ins. Co., Scott & Williams, Inc.; trustee Ludlow Mfg. Associates. Republican. Episcopalian. Home: Boston, Mass. Died Aug. 15, 1935.

SNEVE, Haldor, physician; b. Albert Lea, Minn., Oct. 27, 1865; s. Peter and Anna (Hammer) S.; prep. edn. Owatonna (now Pillsbury) Acad., Minn.; M.D., Med. Coll. of Ohio (now Ohio-Miami Med. Coll., U. of Cincinnati), 1887; post-grad. work in Europe, 1890-92; m. Katherine Stickney, May 1, 1897. Asst. surgeon, Nat. Home for Disabled Vol. Soldiers, Dayton, O., 1887-88; asst. supt., Dayton State Hosp., 1888-90; practiced in Minneapolis, Minn., 1892-98, specializing in nervous and mental diseases; chief surgeon, C.G.W. Ry., St. Paul, 1898-1910; clin. prof. mental and nervous diseases, U. of Minn., 1912—. Republican. Chmn. 3d Dist. Bd., 1917-18. Home: St. Paul, Minn. Died June 14, 1924.

SNIDER, Denton Jaques, author; b. Mt. Gilead, O., Jan. 9, 1841; s. John R. and Catherine S.; A.B., Oberlin Coll., 1862, Litt.D., 1899; married. Lecturer. Author: Commentaries on the Literary Bibles (9 vols.—3 on Shakespeare and 2 each on Goethe, Dante and Homer), 1877-93; Walk in Hellas, 1882; The Freeburgers (novel), 1889; World's Fair Studies, 1895; Commentaries on Froebel's Play-Songs, 1895; Psychology and the Psychosis, 1896; The Will and Its World, 1899; The Psychology of Froebel's Play-Gifts, 1900; The Life of Frederick Froebel; The Father of History; Herodotus; Social Institutions, 1901; The State, 1902. Also (verse); Delphic Days, 1878; Agamemnon's Daughter, 1885; Prorsus Retrorsus, 1890; Homer in Chios, 1891; Johnny Appleseed's Rhymes, 1894; (prose) Ancient European Philosophy, 1903; Modern European Philosophy, 1904; Feeling and Psychology, 1905; Architecture, 1905; A Tour in Europe, 1907; European History, 1908; Cosmos and Diacosmos, 1909; Biacosmos, 1911; Music and the Fine Arts, 1913; Goethe's Life Poem (as set forth in his life and works), 1915; Shakespeariad, 1916; (verse) The House of Dreams, 1918; The St. Louis Movement in Philosophy, Education, Literature and Psychology, 1920; The American Ten Years War (1855-65), 1920; also several books on Abraham Lincoln. The Shakespeariad, etc. Address: St. Louis, Mo. Died Nov. 25, 1925.

SNIFF, Littleton M., coll. pres.; b. in Hocking County, Ohio, Nov. 30, 1849; s. Isaiah and Elizabeth (Moore) S.; A.B., Ohio Northern U., Ada, Ohio, A.M., 1881; m. Elvira Vandervort, Aug. 25, 1872. Head dept. of mathematics, Ohio Northern U., 1879-83; pres. Tri-State Coll., 1885—. Prohibitionist. Mem. Christian (Disciples) Ch. Odd Fellow. Home: Angola, Ind. Died Sept. 14, 1922.

SNIFFEN, Culver Channing, army officer; b. N.Y. City, Jan. 1, 1844; s. John and Margaret Melissa (Thompson) S.; ed. Coll. Grammar Sch., Brooklyn; m. Rebecca Sarah Ruan, Sept. 3, 1873 (died 1907); m. 2d, Zenobia Blanche Richardson, June 26, 1909. Exec. clk., 1869, and asst. sec., 1873-77, to President Grant. Apptd. from N.Y., maj. p.-m. U.S.A., Mar. 3, 1877; lt. col. deputy p.-m.-gen., Mar. 31, 1899; col. asst. p.-m.-gen., May 3, 1901; brig. gen. p.-m.-gen. U.S.A., Sept. 11, 1906; retired Jan. 1, 1908. Chief p.-m. 5th Army Corps, Santiago, Cuba, and Montauk Point, L.I., Aug. 1-Sept. 8, 1898. Republican. Mason. Home: Washington, D.C. Died July 28, 1930.

SNIVELY, William Andrew, P.E. clergyman, retired; b. Greencastle, Pa., Dec. 6, 1833; s. Daniel and Mary Ann (Culbertson) S.; grad. Dickinson Coll., Pa., 1852, S.T.D., Columbia, 1875; m. Ella Pirtle, 1865. Ordered deacon, 1865; ordained priest, 1865; asst. St. Andrew's, Pittsburgh, 1865-67; rector of parishes in Cincinnati, O., Albany, N.Y., Brooklyn, N.Y., and New Orleans, La.; deputy to Gen. Conv. P.E. ch., 1871-92; pres. Standing Com. Diocese of La., 1889-92. Author: The Oberammergau Passion Play, 1881; Aesthetics in Worship, 1887; Parish Lectures on the Prayer Book, 1887; Testimonials to the Supernatural, 1888; Family Prayer for the Christian Year, 1888; Genealogical Memoranda; The Cathedral System in the American Church. Address: Louisville, Ky. Died 1901.

SNODDY, Elmer Ellsworth, prof. philosophy; b. Stilesville, Ind., May 13, 1863; s. James Henry and Charlotte (Drake) S.; A.B., Hiram (O.) Coll., 1896; grad. student U. of Chicago, 1897, 1901-02, U. of Mich., 1903, Yale, 1909-10, A.M., Yale, 1910; LL.D., Drake U., Des Moines, Ia., 1928; D.D., Transylvania U., 1934; m. Mina Bradley, Aug. 28, 1894; 1 son, Leland Bradley. Teacher pub. schs. of Ind. and S.Dak., 10 yrs.; prof. Greek, Hiram Coll., 1896-1910, prof. philosophy, 1910-14; prof. philosophy, Transylvania Coll., 1914—, also prof. doctrine, Coll. of the Bible. Ordained ministry Disciples of Christ, 1888. Democrat. Widely known speaker and writer in behalf of academic freedom in interpretation of science and the Bible. Home: Lexington, Ky. Died Apr. 20, 1936.

SNODGRASS, David La Fayette, judge; b. Sparta, Tenn., Apr. 6, 1851; s. Thomas and Eliza J. (Evans) S.; ed. U. of Tenn.; m. Blanche Fouche. Admitted to bar, 1872; mem. Tenn. Ho. of Rep., 1879-80; mem. of Ct. of Referees, 1883-85; asso. justice, 1886-94, chief justice, 1894-1902, Supreme Ct. of Tenn.; clerk U.S. Circuit Ct., Eastern Dist., Tenn., 1905-Jan. 1, 1912, when the office terminated by operation of law; resumed practice at Chattanooga. Home: Chattanooga, Tenn. Died Oct. 10, 1917.

SNODGRASS, George Merrill, coll. pres.; b. Boscobel, Wis., Jan. 4, 1879; s. Thomas J. and Jennie (Nuzum) S.; student Northwestern U., 1896-98; Ph.B., Hamline U., St. Paul, Minn., 1900; grad. study U. of Wis., summers 1923-26; m. Inez L. Toby, June 21, 1905; children—Kathrine G., Herbert M., George H. Teacher elementary sch., Wausau, Wis., 1901; teacher high sch., River Falls, 1901-04; supervising prin., Alma and Barron, Wis., 1904-10; supt. schs., Oconto and Neillsville, Wis., 1910-14; prin. Barron County Normal Sch., 1914-16; dir. teacher training, State Normal Sch., Superior, Wis., 1916-26; pres. Wis. State Teachers Coll., La. Crosse, 1926—. Republican. Methodist. Mason. Home: La Crosse, Wis. Died Jan. 12, 1939.

SNODGRASS, Robert, lawyer; b. in Dauphin County, Pa., Oct. 12, 1836; s. Benjamin and Ann (Wilson) S.; A.B., Lafayette Coll., Pa., 1857, A.M., 1860; m. Anna E. Peale, Pa., Dec. 25, 1866. Admitted to bar, 1863; prothonotary Supreme Ct. of Pa., Middle Dist., 1871-82; dep. atty. gen. of Pa., 1882-87; solicitor Northern Central Ry. Co., 1897—. Mem. State Bd. of Law Examiners; commr. for Promotion of Uniformity of Legislation in U.S. from Pa., 1909. Home: Harrisburg, Pa. Deceased.

SNOW, Albert Sydney, naval officer; b. Rockland, Me., Nov. 18, 1845; apptd. to U.S. Naval Acad. from Me., 1861, grad. 1865; m. Frances M. Keating, Mar. 13, 1873. Ensign, Dec. 1, 1866; promoted through grades to rear adm., Feb. 21, 1905; retired Nov. 18, 1907. Summer of 1864, on board the Marblehead in pursuit of Confederate steamers Florida and Tallahassee; on bd. Pensacola, 1866-69, Alaska, 1870-73; duty Torpedo Sta., Newport, 1873; on bd. Congress, 1874-76, receiving-ship, Wabash, 1877-78; duty Navy Yard, Boston, 1878-79, 1882-83; exec. officer Portsmouth, 1879-81; coast survey duty, 1883-87; spl. duty at Newport, R.I., 1887; mem. Bd. Inspection and Survey, 1888-90; comd. Essex, 1890-92; duty Naval Acad., 1893-94; light house insp. 3d dist., 1895-98; duty Navy Yard, Portsmouth, 1898; comd. Badger during Spanish-Am. War, 1898; comdt. Naval Sta., San Juan, P.R., 1898-99; comd. New York, 1899-1900; duty Navy Yard, New York, 1900-01; comd. receiving-ships Vermont, 1901, Columbia, 1901-03, Hancock, 1903-04; duty Navy Yard, Boston, 1904-05, comdt. 1905-07. Pres. Gen. Court Martial, Navy

Yard, Boston, 1918-19. Home: Brookline, Mass. Died July 14, 1932.

SNOW, Alpheus Henry, author; b. Claremont, N.H., Nov. 8, 1859; s. Alpheus Franklin and Sarah Maria (Dean) S.; Trinity Coll., Conn., 1876-77; A.B., Yale, 1879; LL.B., Harvard, 1883; m. Margaret Maynard Butler, June 29, 1887. Practiced law, Hartford, Conn., 1883-87, Indianapolis, 1887-95; lit. work at Washington, 1899—. Lecturer on Colonial govt., George Washington U., 1908, 09; U.S. del. Internat. Conf. on Social Ins., The Hague, 1910. Trustee George Washington U., 1910-11, and 1915-18. Mem. exec. council Am. Soc. Internat. Law; mem. Am. Bar Assn., Assn. Bar City of N.Y., Acad. Polit. Science, Am. Polit. Science Assn. Author: The Administration of Dependencies, 1902; The Question of Aborigines in the Law and Practice of Nations, 1919; articles in reviews and periodicals. Address: Washington, D.C. Died Aug. 19, 1920.

SNOW, Benjamin Warner, physicist; b. Henry, Ill., Aug. 15, 1860; s. Norman G. and Charlotte D. (Warner) S.; B.S., Cornell; 1885; U. of Göttingen, 1887; U. of Strassburg, 1888; U. of Berlin, 1890-92, Ph.D., 1892; m. Agnes Campbell Butler, Sept. 22, 1896 (dec.). Fellow in physics, Cornell U., 1885-86; instr. physics, Ohio State U., 1886-87, Cornell, 1888-90; prof. physics, Ind. U., 1892-93, U. of Wis., 1893-1926 (retired). Fellow A.A.A.S. (sec. Sect. B, 1894). Home: Madison, Wis. Deceased.

SNOW, Charles Armstrong, lawyer; b. Boston, Sept. 23, 1862; s. Franklin and Anna Elizabeth (Armstrong) S.; A.B., Harvard, 1882; student Harvard Law Sch.; m. Fannie Devens (Sherburne) Wallace, Jan. 28, 1899. Admitted to Suffolk bar, 1885; formerly mem. firm of Moody, Burdett, Wardell & Snow, of which Justice Moody of U.S. Supreme Ct. was sr. partner; counsel in the famous Peter Bent Brigham and Stephen Salisbury will cases, in the Copper Range litigation against Thomas W. Lawson and A. C. Burrage, and in cases in U.S. Sup. Ct. involving constitutionality of income tax, corp. excise and Mass. fgn. corp. tax laws. Dir. Tri-Mountain Mining Co., Mich. Smelting Co., Bohemia Mining Co. Pres. Columbus Av. Bd. Trade; mem. Nantucket Com. on Safety. Edited Mass. section Law of Municipal Franchises (2 vols.), 1892. Address: Boston, Mass. Died Sept. 1, 1920.

SNOW, Donald Francis, congressman; b. Bangor, Me., Sept. 6, 1877; s. James H. and Ellen (Dickey) S.; A.B., Bowdoin, 1901; LL.B., U. of Me., 1903; LL.M., 1904; m. Christine L. Pennell, Oct. 3, 1906; 1 son, William P. Began practice of law, Bangor, 1904; county atty., Penobscot County, Me., 1911-13; mem. 71st and 72d Congresses (1929-33), 4th Me. Dist. Republican. Conglist. Mason, K.P. Co-Author: (with John Clair Minot) Tales of Bowdoin, 1901. Home: Bangor, Me. Deceased.

SNOW, Elbridge Gerry, insurance pres.; b. Barkhampsted, Conn., Jan. 22, 1841; s. Elbridge Gerry and Eunice (Woodruff) S.; grad. Ft. Edward (N.Y.) Collegiate Inst., 1860; m. Frances J. Thompson, Sept. 5, 1865. Clerk, 1862, state agt. for Mass., 1872-85, sec., 1885-88, v.p., 1888-1903, pres., 1903—, Home Ins. Co., New York; also pres. Franklin Fire Ins. Co. of Phila., City of N.Y. Ins. Co.; dir. Am. Trust Co., N.Y. Life Ins. Co., Home Ins. Co., Am. Exchange Nat. Bank, Manhattan Ry. Co., Am. Exchange Nat. Bank. Episcopalian. Home: New York, N.Y. Died Nov. 7, 1925.

SNOW, Ernest Albert, judge; b. Hanover, Mich., 1875; s. Eugene A. S.; grad. high sch., Saginaw, Mich., 1893; LL.B., U. of Mich., 1896; m. Jennie J. Frazee, 1900. Admitted to Mich. bar, 1896 and began practice at Saginaw; practiced with father as mem. firm Snow & Snow; became justice Supreme Court of Mich. Home: Saginaw, Mich. Died Oct. 20, 1928.

SNOW, Francis Huntington, educator; b. Fitchburg, Mass., June 29, 1840; grad. Williams Coll., 1862, A.M., 1865, Ph.D., 1881; grad. Andover Theol. Sem., 1866; LL.D., Princeton, 1890; m. Jane Appleton Aiken, July 8, 1868. Mem. of 1st faculty of State U. of Kan., 1866-70, as prof. mathematics and natural science, prof. natural history, 1870-89, pres. of the faculties, 1889-90, chancellor, 1890-1901, prof. organic evolution, systematic entomology and meteorology same, 1901—. Kan. legislature, 1885, appropriated $50,000 for a bldg. at the univ. which was called Snow Hall of Natural History, to contain collections made by him. Prominent in ornithology, meteorology, and systematic and economic entomology, especially in artificial application of fungus diseases to the destruction of chinch bugs in the field. Has conducted 26 expdns. to Kan., Colo., N.Mex., Tex. and Ariz., making the Kan. Univ. collection of 22,000 species of insects, one of the largest in U.S. Fellow A.A.A.S. Address: Lawrence, Kan. Died 1908.

SNOW, Frederic (Elmer), lawyer; b. Auburn, Me., Sept. 12, 1864; s. Joseph Crocker and Lydia Jane (Howe) S.; A.B., Tufts, 1883; m. Lilian T. Townsend, Feb. 11, 1896; children—William Townsend, Kitchell (dec.), Crocker, Frederic Elmer. In practice of law at Boston, 1886—; mem. Gaston, Snow, Saltonstall & Hunt; dir. Boston Consol. Gas Co., Boston Wharf Co., Fisher Mfg. Co., Mystic Iron Works, N.E. Coal & Coke Co., N.E. Mfg. Co., Nat. Shawmut Bank, Winthrop Mills Co., Mass. Bonding and Insurance Co., Koppers Coal and Transportation Co., United Drug Co., Consolidated Investment Trust; trustee Boston Dwelling House Co., Eastern Gas and Fuel Associates, Mass. Gas Cos., Mystic Steamship Co., N.E. Fuel & Transportation Co. Republican. Universalist. Home: Boston, Mass. Died Mar. 5, 1935.

SNOW, Leslie Perkins, judge; b. Eaton, N.H., Oct. 19, 1862; s. Edwin and Helen M. (Perkins) S.; grad. Bridgton Acad., 1881; A.B., Dartmouth, 1886; LL.B., Columbian Law Sch. (now dept. George Washington U.), 1890; m. Susie E. Currier, Nov. 28, 1888 (died 1892); children—Conrad Edwin, Leslie Whitmore; m. 2d, Norma C. Currier, of Haverhill, N.H., June 27, 1895. Admitted to N.H. bar, 1890, and began practice at Rochester, N.H., as mem. firm Worcester, Gafney & Snow, later alone; mem. N.H. Ho. of Rep., 1887, 88; mem. N.H. Constl. Conv., 1918-20; pres. N.H. Senate, 1921; asso. justice Supreme Ct. of N.H., term 1921-32. Mem. firm E. Snow & Son, gen. store and mfg., 1881-1907; pres. Rochester Nat. Bank, 1902-16; pres. Rochester Trust Co., 1920—. Pres. Rochester Pub. Safety Commn., World War. Mem. N.H. Bankers' Assn. (pres. 1922-23), N.H. Bar Assn. (pres. 1919-20). Pres. Gafney Home for the Aged, 1917—. Republican. Conglist. Mason, Odd Fellow. Home: Rochester, N.H. Died Mar. 16, 1934.

SNOW, Lorenzo, pres. Mormon Ch., elected Sept. 13, 1898; b. Mantau, Portage County, O., Apr. 3, 1814; s. Oliver and Rosetta Leonora (Pettibone) S.; studied Ravenna, O., schools and Oberlin Coll.; convert to Mormonism, 1836; became missionary, 1837; went to England and later to various countries; returned and became capt. Nauvoo Legion, Mormon mil. co. Mem. Utah legislature (serving in each house), 1852-82; founded and named Brigham City, Utah. Ordained one of the Twelve Apostles, Feb. 12, 1849; pres. of the Twelve, Apr. 1889; pres. of the Temple, 1893-98. Author: The Italian Mission; The Only Way to Be Saved; The Voice of Joseph; The Palestine Tourists. Translated Book of Mormon into Italian. Address: Salt Lake City, Utah. Died 1901.

SNOW, Louis Franklin, prof. English; b. Providence, R.I., Apr. 19, 1862; s. George Washington and Lucinda Maria (LeValley) S.; Ph.B., Brown U., 1887; A.B., Harvard, 1889, A.M., 1890, Ph.D., Columbia, 1903; m. Susan, d. Thomas Oakes and Martha (Wilson) Conant, Oct. 24, 1894; children—Katherine (dec.), Robert Conant, infant dau. (dec.). Instr. elocution, 1890-92, dean Women's Coll., 1892-1900, Brown U.; sec.-treas. Examiner Co., New York, 1903-05; registrar, Teachers Coll. (Columbia U.), 1905-06; head dept. English, Normal Sch., Cortland, N.Y., 1908-09; dean Teachers Coll., and prof. edn., State U. of Ky., 1909-11; prof. philosophy and edn., Wells Coll., Aurora, N.Y., 1911-12; librarian, U. of Pittsburgh, 1912-14; asso. prof., chief of English dept., and librarian, 1914-15, and prof., 1915-19, U. of the Philippines (on leave for war work, Washington, 1919); dept. of English, State Normal Sch., Natchitoches, La., 1919, U. of Alabama, 1920; prof. English, U. of Chattanooga, 1921-31, also prof. English and public speaking, Chattanooga Coll. of Law, 1924—. Mason. Republican. Episcopalian. Author: The College Curriculum, 1907. Address: Chattanooga, Tenn. Died Dec. 28, 1934.

SNOW, Marshall Solomon, univ. dean; b. Hyannis, Mass., Aug. 17, 1842; s. Rev. Solomon P. and Maria J. (Pratt) S.; A.B., Harvard, 1865, A.M., 1868; LL.D., Washington U., 1905; m. Ellen Frances Jewell, July 9, 1867. Sub-master high sch., Worcester, Mass., 1865-66; prin. High Sch., Nashville, Tenn., 1866-67; prof. Latin, Univ. of Nashville, and prin. of Montgomery Bell Acad., 1867-70; prof. belles lettres, 1870-74, history, 1874-1912, registrar of coll., 1871-76, dean, 1876-12, prof. history emeritus, 1912, acting chancellor, 1887-91, and 1907-08, Washington U. Pres. Mo. Hist. Soc., 1894-1900; sec. Standing Com. P.E. Diocese of Mo. Author: The City Government of St. Louis; Higher Education in Mo.; also various mag. articles. Address: St. Louis, Mo. Died May 28, 1916.

SNOW, William Dunham, lawyer; b. Webster, Mass., Feb. 2, 1832; settled Rochester, N.Y.; published The Tribune there, 1852-54; later removed to Ark.; mem. Ark. Constitutional Conv., 1863; helped raise a brigade of Ark. troops for U.S.A., but declined commn. as brig. gen.; elected U.S. senator, 1865, under proclamation of President Johnson, but was not admitted to a seat; grad. Columbia Law Sch., 1876; established practice in New York. Invented a carburetor, gas-regulator, thermostatic apparatus, etc. Home: Hackensack, N.J. Died 1910.

SNOWDEN, A(rchibald) Loudon, diplomat; b. Cumberland County, Pa., Aug. 11, 1837; s. Dr. Isaac Wayne and Margery (Loudon) S.; A.B., Jefferson Coll., Pa., 1856; A.M., 1888, LL.D., Washington and Jefferson, 1902; read law under David Webster, Phila., and law dept. U. of Pa.; m. Elizabeth Robinson Smith, Feb. 16, 1864. Served as lt. col. in Pa. Vols.; participated in various battles during Civil War. Register, and later chief coiner, U.S. Mint, Phila.; postmaster, Phila., 1877-79; supt. U.S. Mint, Phila., 1879-85; twice declined directorship of all U.S. mints, tendered by President Hayes; minister resident and consul gen. to Greece, Roumania and Servia, 1889-91; minister to Spain, 1891-93. Commr. and pres. Fairmount Park, Phila.; orator and writer; authority on coins and coinage and author many papers on those and other subjects. Decorated with Grand Cordon of the Saviour (Greece), Grand Cordon of the Crown (Roumania), Grand Cordon of Isabella the Catholic (Spain). Home: Philadelphia, Pa. Died Sept. 9, 1912.

SNOWDEN, James Henry, theologian, author; b. Hookstown, Pa., Oct. 18, 1852; s. William and Violetta (Thayer) S.; A.B., Washington and Jefferson Coll., 1875; grad. Western Theol. Sem., Allegheny, Pa., 1878; D.D., Lafayette Coll., 1900; LL.D., Mo. Valley Coll., 1906; m. Mary A. Ross, Aug. 1, 1878; children—Grace, Roy Ross, Harold Winters. Ordained Presbyn. ministry, 1879; pastor Huron, O., 1879-83, Sharon, Pa., 1883-86, Second Ch., Washington, Pa., 1886-1911; prof. syst. theology, Western Theol. Sem., 1911-26; prof. apologetics, Western Theol. Sem., 1926-29; adj. prof. polit. economy and ethics, Washington and Jefferson Coll., 1893-98; editor-in-chief Presbyn. Banner, Pittsburgh, 1898-1917, 1926—; editor Presbyn. Mag., New York, 1921-26. Author: The Psychology of Religion, 1917; Can We Believe in Immortality?, 1918; The Coming of the Lord, 1919; Is the World Growing Better?, 1919; A Wonderful Night, 1919; The Personality of God, 1920; The Truth About Christian Science, 1920; A Wonderful Morning, 1921; The Attractions of the Ministry, 1921; The Meaning of Education, 1921; Snowden's Sunday School Lessons (15 ann. vols.), 1921-34; Immortality in the Light of Modern Thought, 1925 ($1,000 prize vol.); The Truth About Mormonism, 1926; Old Faith and New Knowledge, 1928; Jesus as Judged by His Enemies, 1922; The Making and Meaning of the New Testament, 1923; Outfitting the Teacher of Religion, 1929; What Do Present-Day Christians Believe?, 1930; The Discovery of God, 1932. Office: Pittsburgh, Pa. Died Dec. 19, 1936.

SNOWDEN, Robert Bogardus, capitalist; b. New York, N.Y., May 24, 1836; lineal descendant of Everardus Bogardus, one of 1st settlers at New Amsterdam; brought up in Nashville, Tenn.; academic edn.; with New Orleans grocery firm, 1856-58; in business in Nashville, 1858-61; served, adj. to col., in Confederate army, 1861-65, surrendered with Lee at Appomattox; m. Annie Brinkley, g.d. Judge John Overton, founder of Memphis, Tenn., May 1868. Importer in New York, 1865-70; in Memphis, 1870—; pres. George Peabody Real Estate and Improvement Co.; interested in many enterprises. Apptd. maj. gen. of militia, 1895. Address: Memphis, Tenn. Died 1909.

SNOWDEN, Thomas, naval officer; b. Peekskill, N.Y., Aug. 12, 1857; grad. U.S. Naval Acad., 1879; married; 1 son, Thomas. Ensign jr. grade, Mar. 3, 1883; promoted through grades to rear adm., July 1, 1917; retired Aug. 12, 1921. Served on Dolphin, Spanish-Am. War, 1898; navigation officer, Illinois, 1902-05; duty Office of Naval Intelligence, Navy Dept., 1905-06; Compass Office, Bur. of Equipment, 1906-08; comd. Mayflower, 1908-10; mem. Board Inspection and Survey of Ships, Navy Dept., 1910-11; comd. South Carolina, 1911-13; at Naval War Coll., Newport, R.I., 1913-14; comd. Navy Yard and Sta., Portsmouth, N.H., 1915; comd. Wyoming, 1915-16; apptd. hydrographer Navy Dept., June 21, 1916. Home: Washington, D.C. Died Jan. 27, 1930.

SNOWDEN, Yates, coll. prof.; b. Charleston, S.C., May 8, 1858; s. William S. (M.D.) and Mary A. (Yates) S.; grad. Coll. of Charleston, 1879, LL.D., 1910; admitted to bar, 1882; post-grad. work, Columbia U., 1904-05; m. Annie E. Warley, Oct. 25, 1894. On staff Charleston News and Courier, 1886-1904; prof. history, Univ. of S.C., Sept. 1905—. Democrat. Mason. Contbr. to hist., bibliog. and other periodicals. Address: Columbia, S.C. Died Feb. 22, 1933.

SNURE, John, newspaper man; b. Adamsville, Mich.; s. Samuel Edward and Eliza Jane (Johnson) S.; grad. Mich. State Normal Sch., Ypsilanti, 1891; m. Margaret B. Turner, 1905; children—Anne, John, Robert T. Reporter Twin City Journal, La Salle Co., Ill., 1892-96, Des Moines Leader, 1896, Des Moines Register and Leader, to 1903; Washington (D.C.) corr. various newspapers, 1903—; with Washington Bur. of New York Herald Tribune and Des Moines Register and Tribune. Served as corpl., Ia. Vol. Inf., Spanish-Am. War and Philippine Insurrection. Home: Silver Spring, Md. Deceased.

SNYDER, Albert Whitcomb, clergyman; b. Lisbon, N.Y., Apr. 8, 1842; s. John H. and Agnes (Ballentine) S.; ed. Racine (Wis.) Coll., and Kenyon Coll., Ohio; S.T.B., Nashotah Theol. Sem., Wis., 1866; m. Josephine M., d. Maj. Henry Smith, U.S.A., Jan. 6, 1875. Deacon, 1866, priest, 1867, P.E. Ch.; rector successively, Calvary Ch., Chicago, Rockford, Ill., Lehigh U., Pa., Wellsboro, Pa., and St. Paul's Ch., Woodside, N.Y., Apr. 1899—. Author: The Living Church, 1888; The Chief Things, 1888; Confirmation, 1888; The Chief Days, 1899; How Is a Man to Know What to Believe?; Church Doctrine for the People; etc. Editorial writer in religious and secular journals. Address: Elmhurst, N.Y. Died Feb. 3, 1914.

SNYDER, Edgar Callender, U.S. marshal of D.C.; b. Phila., Pa., Sept. 6, 1860; s. Amos and Mary (De Muth) S.; LL.B., U. of Pa., 1883; m. Emily Rose, June 21, 1887; children—Mrs. Dorothy De Muth Watson, Mrs. Margery Snyder. City editor Omaha (Neb.) Republican, 1884-85; later attached to staff Omaha Bee, and, 1895-1922, Washington corr. Omaha Bee; editor National Hotel and Travel Gazette. U.S. marshal for D.C., 1922-34. Mem. League of Republican State Clubs (pres.), Bar Assn. of D.C. Pres. 1st incorporated community center in U.S., The Wilson Normal School Community, Washington. Del. to Rep. Nat. Conv., Chicago, 1932, and mem. Com. on Resolutions; alternate to Rep. Nat. Conv., Kansas City, 1928. Mason (33°), K.P. (supreme rep., D.C.), Elk. Home: Washington, D.C. Died Apr. 2, 1940.

SNYDER, Edward, prof. of modern languages, and dean Coll. of Literature, U. of Ill., 1868-95, prof. emeritus, 1895—; b. Sokal, Austrian Poland, Oct. 7, 1835; ed. Bernardine Gymnasium, Lemberg, Poland; mil. edn. in Imperial Sch. of Infantry, Mauer, Austria; A.M., Norwich Univ.; m. Mary Stoddard Patchen, 1869. Served in Austrian army, 1849-59, 1st lt., 78th inf.; taught in cadet school there; served in U.S.A., 1862-65, in 7th and 178th N.Y. inf. vols., col. Ill. Nat. Guard, 1874-80; after 28 yrs. of service with univ. retired, as prof. emeritus of German language and literature. Gave $12,000 to Univ. of Ill., as a student aid fund, 1897. Home: Pacific Beach, Calif. Deceased.

SNYDER, Harry, chemist; b. Cherry Valley, N.Y., Jan. 26, 1867; s. David W. and Mary A. S.; B.S., Cornell, 1889 (spl. work in chemistry); m. Adelaide C. Craig, 1890. Prof. agrl. chemistry and soils, U. of Minn.; chemist Minn. Expt. Sta., 1891-1909; chemist, Russell Miller Milling Co., Minneapolis, 1909—. Collaborator in nutrition investigations, U.S. Dept. Agr., 1895-1905. Fellow A.A.A.S.; pres. Assn. Official Agricultural Chemists, 1908. Author: The Chemistry of Plant and Animal Life, 1903; Soils and Fertilizers, 1905; Dairy Chemistry, 1906; Human Foods and Their Nutritive Value, 1908; The Nomenclature of Wheat Flours, 1923; Bread (a selection of writings and lectures on soils, cereals, and nutrition), 1930. Contbr. many articles to scientific and gen. publs. Home: Minneapolis, Minn. Died Oct. 11, 1927.

SNYDER, Henry, school supt.; b. Easton, Pa., Jan. 30, 1858; s. Casper and Barbara (Dauberschmidt) S.; A.B., Lafayette Coll., Easton, Pa., 1878 (classical honor), A.M., 1888, Sc.D., 1907; m. Mary Collmar, July 24, 1883. Teacher elementary schs., Easton, 1878-79; prin. Easton High Sch., 1879-87; instr. Latin and Greek, 1887-91, prin. Grammar Sch. No. 2, 1891-92, supt. schs., 1893—, Jersey City, N.J. Mem. State Bd. Examiners, N.J.; trustee Free Pub. Library, Jersey City; exec. com. local Red Cross; mem. commn. which revised Teachers' Retirement Fund Law, 1906; mem. State Commn. Mil. Training in High Schs., N.J., 1916-17; pres. Dept. of Superintendence N.E.A., 1914-15, chmn. com. on mil. edn., 1916-17; apptd. state commr. edn., 1921, but declined. Lutheran. Mason. Author: (with Edward S. Ellis) School History of New Jersey, 1910; New Jersey Supplement of Brigham and McFarland's Geography, 1916. Home: Jersey City, N.J. Died July 27, 1923.

SNYDER, Henry Steinman, steel mfr.; b. Bethlehem, Pa., May 21, 1869; s. Mifflin H. and Angeline (Steinman) S.; ed. pub. schs.; m. Mary Taylor, Nov. 21, 1892. Began with Bethlehem Steel Co., 1886, serving as sec. and treas.; v.p. Bethlehem Steel Corp. from its organization, 1904, retired Aug. 1925. Trustee and treas. St. Luke's Hosp. Dir. Union Bank & Trust Co., Bethlehem, Pa.; Pres. Bach Choir. Republican. Presbyn. Home: Bethlehem, Pa. Died Oct. 1, 1941.

SNYDER, Homer P., congressman; b. Amsterdam, N.Y., Dec. 6, 1863; s. Edwin and Mary E. (Rivenburg) S.; ed. pub. schs.; m. Jessie Falla Breese, June 27, 1882. Employed in knitting mills until 1890; engaged in manufacture of knitting machinery, Little Falls, N.Y., 1890, under title of Snyder & Fisher; business incorporated 1898 as the Homer P. Snyder Mfg. Co., mfrs. of bicycles, of which became treasurer; v.p. Little Falls Nat. Bank; dir. Little Falls Hotel Co., Robbins Enterprises (Utica). Rep. candidate for Congress, 1912; mem. 64th to 68th Congresses (1915-25), 33d N.Y. Dist. Home: Little Falls, N.Y. Died Dec. 30, 1937.

SNYDER, Jefferson, lawyer; b. Berks County, Pa., Nov. 6, 1848; A.B., Lafayette Coll., Easton, Pa., 1872; m. Annie Lizzie Jaeger, Oct. 16, 1877. Admitted to Pa. Bar, 1875, practiced at Reading, 1877—. Home: Reading, Pa. Died June 29, 1926.

SNYDER, Jonathan Le Moyne, coll. president; b. Butler County, Pa., Oct. 29, 1859; s. Hiram and Eliza (Patton) S.; A.B., Westminster Coll., Pa., 1886, Ph.D., 1891; LL.D., Univ. of Michigan, 1908; Ag.D., Syracuse University, 1915; m. Clara Mifflin, June 15, 1892. Supt. schs., Butler County, Pa., 1887-88; prin. Fifth Ward schs., Allegheny, Pa., 1889-96, adding kindergarten and manual training depts.; pres. Mich. State Agrl. Coll., 1896-1915, and pres. emeritus, 1915. Home: East Lansing, Mich. Died Oct. 22, 1919.

SNYDER, Meredith Pinxton, merchant; b. Winston-Salem, N.C., 1859; s. Kehlin D. and Elizabeth (Hier) S.; ed. Yadkin (N.C.) Coll.; m. May Ross, 1888. Began in furniture store in Los Angeles, Calif., 1880; became clerk Coulter Dry Goods Company. Elected mem. Bd. Police Commrs., 1890, reelected, 1893; mem. City Council, 1894-96; mayor of Los Angeles, 4 terms between 1897 and 1921; mem. State Industrial Accident Commn., term 1931-35. Democrat. Mason, K.P. Address: Los Angeles, Calif. Died Apr. 8, 1937.

SNYDER, Monroe B(enjamin), astronomer; b. at Quakertown, Pa., Mar. 13, 1848; s. Amos Hinkle and Mary Ann (Plank) S.; prep. edn. Bucks County Normal and Classical Sch. and prep. dept. Pa. Coll.; Pa. Coll., 1866-68 and 1870; B.A., U. of Mich., 1872, M.A., 1875; m. Martha Julia Sheain, July 6, 1875 (died 1879); m. 2d, Susan Chaplin Berry, June 14, 1882. Instr. astronomy and mathematics, 1873-80, prof., 1880—, head of dept. of mathematics, 1896—, in charge obs., 1873-97, dir. Phila. Obs., 1897—, Central High Sch., Phila. Pres. bd. examiners elec. exhbn. Franklin Inst., 1884; mem. and sec. U.S. Elec. Commn., 1884; sec. Nat. Conf. Electricians, 1884. First to propose and plan Nat. Bur. of Standards in address, Sept. 10, 1884, before Nat. Conf. of Electricians, which, with the comments thereon by Sir William Thomson (Lord Kelvin), was reprinted for the 56th Congress, 1900, establishing the bureau. Planned Phila. Obs. equipment, 1897-1905, which was almost wholly destroyed by fire, Mar. 9, 1905, and was later partially restored. Fellow Royal Astron. Soc., A.A.A.S. Contbr. astron. articles on edn., and papers on astronomy in scientific jours. Announced, Jan. 20, 1905, discovery of the cosmic force, radioaction, due to the explosive transformation of the elements at critical physical conditions in the stars; discovered, 1909, stellar and terrestrial evidence of the serial explosive transformation of the atoms in the rare gas group; discovered, 1917, relation between atomic number and atomic mass of the elements which led by Aug. 3, 1918, to the complete, definitive proof that all atoms are explosive compounds of hydrogen, and to its expression in "The Fundamental Periodic Table of the Chemical Elements," which gives the true atomic number and true atomic mass of every known and unknown element and records the incidental discovery of the new rare gas, astron. Address: Philadelphia, Pa. Died 1932.

SNYDER, Reginald Clare, publisher; b. Findlay, O., Sept. 25, 1873; s. William Edward and Sarah Helen (DuDuit) S.; student St. Paul's Sch., Garden City, L.I., 1888-92, Harvard, 1892-94; m. Alice R. Mack, Oct. 20, 1897; 1 dau., Alice Davenport (Mrs. Dudley Allen White). Reporter Findlay (O.) Courier and Republican, 1894-99; purchased control Coshocton Daily Age, 1907; purchased, 1912, Evening Herald and Daily Reflector, Norwalk, O., merging them into Reflector-Herald, becoming owner and pub.; purchased and merged into one co., Sandusky (O.) Register and Star Jour., 1929; pres. Sandusky Newspapers, Inc., Associated Ohio Dailies; dir. Huron County Banking Co. V.p. Press Congress of The World; dir. Whittlesey Acad. Arts and Sciences (Norwalk, O.), Firelands Hist. Soc. (Norwalk). Republican. Episcopalian. Mason, Elk. Home: Norwalk, Ohio. Died Oct. 3, 1941.

SNYDER, Robert McClure, natural gas producer; b. Louisville, Ky., Jan. 17, 1876; s. Robert M. and Frances (Hord) S.; student U. of Mo. 3 yrs.; m. Mary Bowen, Apr. 10, 1906; children—Edward LeRoy, William Kenneth, Frederick Perry, Robert McClure, III. Producer of natural gas, 1902—; associated with father in organizing pipe-line system and connecting for the first time the gas fields of Southern Kan. and Okla. with Kansas City, Mo., and about 40 cities and towns in Kan. and Mo., effecting a reduction of about 75% in price of gas; pres. Snyder Estate Co.; v.p. Kan. Natural Gas Co.; with brothers joint owner of the Ha-Ha-Tonka Estate, Ozark Mountains of Mo. Trustee Fine Arts Inst., Kansas City, for 10 yrs. Mem. Christian (Disciples) Ch. Wrote: Hahatonka in the Ozarks, Historical and Bibliographical Notes, 1931. Owner extensive library on history and Western Americana. Home: Kansas City, Mo. Died Feb. 9, 1937.

SNYDER, Simon, brig. gen., U.S.A.; b. Selinsgrove, Pa., Feb. 9, 1839; s. Henry W. and Mary C. (Smith) S.; m. Mary T. Wardwell, Oct. 9, 1869. Apptd. from Pa. 2d lt. 5th U.S. Inf., Apr. 26, 1861; 1st lt., June 25, 1861; capt., July 1, 1863; maj. 11th Inf., Mar. 10, 1883; transferred to 5th Inf., May 17, 1883; lt. col. 10th Inf., Jan. 2, 1888; col. 19th Inf., Sept. 16, 1892; brig. gen. vols., May 4, 1898; hon. discharged from vols., May 12, 1899; brig. gen. U.S.A., Apr. 16, 1902; retired at own request after 40 yrs.' service, May 10, 1902. Bvtd. maj., Feb. 27, 1890, for action against Indians at Bear Paw Mountains, Mont., Sept. 30, 1877. Comd. 1st Brigade, 1st Div., 1st Army Corps, and en route to Province of Santa Clara, Cuba, Nov. 1898, to Jan. 1899; gov. Province of Santa Clara, Dec. 6, 1898-Jan. 25, 1899; later on spl. duty to Ponce, P.R.; on duty with regt. at Manila, P.I., Aug. 21-Sept. 15, 1899, comdg. U.S. troops and sub-dist. Cebu, P.I., Sept. 1899-Apr. 2, 1900; acting insp. gen. Dept. of the Lakes, 1900-01; en route to Philippines, Aug.-Oct. 1901; comd. regt., Oct.-Dec. 1901; comd. 5th Separate Brigade, Div. of the Philippines, Dec. 1901, to May 1902. Home: Reading, Pa. Died Apr. 12, 1912.

SNYDER, Valentine P., banker, pres. and dir. Nat. Bank of Commerce; dir. Equitable Life Assurance Soc. of U.S., Sixty Wall St., Union Nat. Bank (Newark); trustee Am. Surety Co. and many other corps. Address: New York, N.Y. Died Nov. 6, 1934.

SNYDER, Zachariah Xenophon, coll. pres.; b. at Reagantown, Westmoreland, Pa., Aug. 31, 1850; s. Daniel and Catharine S.; B.S., Waynesburg Coll., Pa., 1876, Ph.D., 1886; m. Maggie E. Smith, 1876. Prin. graded schs., Wisconisco, Pa.; prof. of higher mathematics and natural history, Waynesburg Coll., 1882-83; prin. graded schs., Greensburg, Pa., 1884-87; supt. city schs., Reading, Pa., 1887-89; pres. Indiana (Pa.) State Normal Sch., 1889-91, State Teachers Coll. of Colo., Greeley, 1891—. Address: Greeley, Colo. Died Nov. 11, 1915.

SOHN, Joseph, musician, author; b. New York City, March 22, 1867; s. Louis and Jeannette (Beringer) S.; ed. Coll. City of New York, and Neue Akademie der Tonkunst, Berlin, also pvt. pupil of Kullak and Scharwenka. Prof. in piano dept. Met. Coll. of Music; mem. academic faculty, Coll. City of New York, 1904-18; mus. critic New York American and Journal, The Forum. First appeared as pianist, with Philharmonic Club, at Steinway Hall, New York, at age of 16; devoted attention during later yrs. to pianoforte instruction, lecturing, and to a close psychol. analysis, with a view to publication in essay form, of the nature and works of classical and modern composers. Author: Haggard and Wagner, 1892 (an extract of this work subsequently incorporated as preface to an early Am. edit. of "Nada the Lily," by Sir H. Rider Haggard); Robert Schumann, a Lyrical Poet, 1896; Lessons of the Opera, 1903; Music in America and Abroad, 1904; Joseph Joachim, the Greatest Living Violinist, 1904; The Dawn of a New Musical Era in America, 1904; A Plea for Something Higher in Pianoforte Construction, 1906; Opera in New York, 1907; The Mission of Richard Wagner, 1910 (transl. into German and French); The Centenary of Wagner—Its Significance, 1913; The Centenary of Rubinstein—Reminiscences, 1929. Contbr. on music to Imperial, Funk & Wagnall's, New Internat., Collier's, Appleton's and White's encys. Frequent contbr. to North Am. Rev., Forum, Scribner's, and other mags. Address: New York, N.Y. Died Mar. 16, 1935.

SOKOLOW, Alexander Theodore, lawyer; b. N.Y. City, Oct. 6, 1891; s. Louis and Anna (Abrams) S.; grad. N.Y. Law Sch., 1911; m. Lillian Rosenthal (newspaperwoman), Aug. 6, 1918; 1 son, Norman Haskell. Admitted to Los Angeles (Calif.) bar, 1913, specialized in law relating to newspapers and other publs., 1913—; atty. sec. and dir., Los Angeles Examiner, 1912—; sec. and dir. Cosmopolitan Productions, Inc., Ltd.; v.p. and dir. McCloud River Land Co. Capt. Calif. Naval Militia. Republican. Reformed Jewish religion. Mason. Home: Los Angeles, Calif. Deceased.

SOLEY, James Russell, lawyer; b. Boston, Oct. 1, 1850; s. John J. S.; A.B., Harvard, 1870; LL.B., Columbian (now George Washington) U., 1890; m. Mary Woolsey Howland, Dec. 1, 1875. Prof. and head dept. history and law, U.S. Naval Acad., 1872-82; dept. of edn., Paris Expn., 1878; prof. U.S. Navy, 1876-90; asst. sec. of the navy, 1890-93; in practice at New York, 1893—. Counsel of Venezuela at Paris Arbitration, Venezuela-British Guiana Boundary, 1899; lecturer internat. law. Naval War Coll., Newport, R.I. Author: History of the Naval Academy, 1876; Foreign Systems of Naval Education, 1879; The Blockade and the Cruisers, 1883; Rescue of Greeley (with Winfield S. Schley), 1885; Boys of 1812, 1887; Sailor Boys of '61, 1888; Life of Admiral Porter, 1903. Home: New York, N.Y. Died 1911.

SOLLY, Samuel Edwin, physician; b. London, Eng., May 5, 1845; s. late Samuel and Jane S.; ed. Rugby School and St. Thomas Hosp. Med. Coll.; held various apptmts. at hosp.; m. Elizabeth, d. Thomas Mellor, 1876. Lived in London, 1867-74; in Colo., 1874—. Pres. Am. Climatol. Assn., Am. Laryngol., Rhinol. and Otol. Soc.; v.p. Internat. Tuberculosis Congress, 1901; dir. Nat. Assn. for the Study and Cure of Tuberculosis. Author: Handbook of Medical Climatology; Tubercular Laryngitis; Temperament; The Relation of Nasal Disease to Pulmonary Tuberculosis; The Influence of Altitude Upon the Blood; also numerous med. essays. Address: Colorado Springs, Colo. Died 1906.

SOMERNDIKE, John Mason, Sunday School official; b. Frankford, Phila., Pa., Oct. 29, 1877; s. John Mason and Isabella (Farr) S.; grad. Central High Sch., Phila., 1894; D.D., Coll. of Ozarks, Clarksville, Ark., 1931; and also from Waynesburg (Pa.) College; m. Lydia Moor, Nov. 8, 1900 (died 1907); m. 2d, Edna Smith, Nov. 4, 1908; children—Isabel M. (Mrs. Frederick O. Green), Jean S. (dec.), Vira Orswell, John Mason. Identified with S.S. missions of Presbyn. Ch.,

U.S.A., 1895—, apptd. dir., 1912; developed the missionary extension work of the Presbyn. Ch., U.S.A. Sec. Bd. Nat. Missions Presbyn. Ch. in U.S.A. in charge of S.S. Missions, Indian, and Alaska Work. Mem. exec. com. of Internat. Council of Religious Edn. Republican. Mason. Author: On the Firing Line, 1912; By-products of the Rural Sunday School, 1916; Sunday School Missionary Exercises, 1918; Sunday School Builders, 1922; The Sunday School in Town and Country, 1924; Manual of Week Day Bible Lessons, 1925. Home: South Orange, N.J. Died Mar. 14, 1939.

SOMERS, Orlando Allen, soldier; b. Middletown, Ind., Jan. 24, 1843; s. Valentine and Mary McClain (Williams) S.; ed. Howard Coll., Ind.; m. Mahala Ellen, d. William Burton Morris, Apr. 5, 1866; m. 2d, Emma, d. John Osborne Heaton, Mar. 24, 1887. Teacher and supt. schs., Howard County, Ind.; postmaster, Kokomo, 1879-85; county commr., 1892-95; mem. Ind. Ho. of Rep., 1898-1900; supervisor 12th Decennial Census, 11th Dist., Ind.; pub. instr. in highway constrn. and maintenance, conservation of soils, coöperative production, and sale of farm products, Purdue U. Pvt. 39th Regt. Ind. Vols. and 8th Regt. Ind. Vet. Cav., 1861-65; participated in battles of Shiloh, Stone's River, Chickamauga, and many minor engagements. Orator Soc. Army of the Cumberland, 1904, sec., 1905-13, pres., 1913-18 (only pvt. soldier that has held any office in this soc.); post comdr. G.A.R., at age of 24; comdr. Dept. of Ind., 1909-10; comdr. in chief G.A.R., 1917-18. Republican. Unitarian. Home: Kokomo, Ind. Died June 8, 1921.

SOMERVILLE, Henderson Middleton, judge; b. Madison County, Va., Mar. 23, 1837; s. James (M.D.) and Helen Glassell (Wallace) S.; A.B., U. of Ala., 1856, A.M., 1859; LL.B., Cumberland Law Sch., 1859; LL.D., Georgetown, Ky., Coll., 1886, Southwestern U., Tenn., 1887, U. of Ala., 1887; m. Cornelia Banks Harris, Mar. 1862; m. 2d, Mrs. Mary Wyman Saville, Aug. 29, 1881; father of Ormond Somerville. Editor Memphis (Tenn.) Appeal, 1859-62; instr. mathematics, 1862-65, founded law school, 1873, lecturer constl. and common and statute law, 1873-90, U. of Ala.; asso. justice Supreme Ct. of Ala., 1880-90; mem. Nat. Bd. Customs Appraisers, 1890—(pres.). Member Ala. Dem. State Exec. Com., 1872-80; trustee Ala. Insane Hosp., 1876-92; mem. State Commn. in Lunacy, 1876-93; trustee Peabody Edn. Fund, 1890—. Pres. N.Y. Medico-Legal Soc., 1892-93; mem. Am. Acad. Polit. and Social Science; pres. Alabama Soc. of N.Y., 1908—. Home: New York, N.Y. Died Sept. 15, 1915.

SOMERVILLE, James Alexander, ry. official; b. Carthage, Ill., Nov. 25, 1867; s. William and Charlotte (Alexander) S.; ed. pub. schs.; m. Mary Wilkinson, June 9, 1896; children—William W., Andrew W., James A. Began in local office of C.,B.&Q. R.R. Co. at Keokuk, Ia., 1887, and continued with same rd. successively as gen. agt. at Hannibal, Mo., 1897-99, local freight agt., St. Louis, 1899-1900, contracting freight agt., St. Joseph, 1900-02, chief clk. to gen. freight agt., St. Louis, 1902-03, gen. agt., Keokuk, 1903-05, supt. terminals, St. Louis, 1905-08; supt. M.P. R.R. Co., Kansas City, Mo., 1908-13; supt. transportation same rd., St. Louis, 1913-17, and gen. supt. transportation, Jan.-Mar. 1917; with Commn. on Car Service, U.S. R.R. Adminstrn., Mar.-Dec. 1917; asst. mgr. car service div. same, Washington, D.C., 1918-19; gen. supt. transportation, M.P. R.R. Co., St. Louis, Jan.-Apr. 1919; gen. mgr. under U.S. R.R. Adminstrn. of T.&P. Ry., T.M.T.,D.&P.S. R.R., W.,M.W.&N.W. Ry. Co., G.,T.&W. Ry., and Ft.W.Belt Ry. Co., 1919-20; gen. mgr. T.&P. Ry. Co., 1920-24; v.p. T.&P. Ry. Co. and subsidiaries. Republican. Episcopalian. Home: Dallas, Tex. Died July 7, 1939.

SOMERVILLE, Ormond, judge; b. Tuscaloosa, Ala., Nov. 26, 1868; s. Henderson Middleton and Cornelia Banks (Harris) S.; A.B., U. of Ala., 1887, A.M., LL.B., 1890; m. Kate Walter, Sept. 14, 1892 (died 1895); 1 dau., Cornelia Frederica (Mrs. Orion Perry); m. 2d, Bessie Randolph Edgar, Dec. 22, 1898; children—Elizabeth Fry (Mrs. John A. Woodbridge), Ormond. Practiced law, Tuscaloosa, 1890-96; county solicitor, Tuscaloosa County, 1891-92; prof. law, U. of Ala., Jan. 1896-Sept. 1909; asso. justice Supreme Court of Ala., terms 1911-17, 1917-23, 1923-29. Democrat. Southern Presbyn. Home: Montgomery, Ala. Died Sept. 8, 1928.

SOMMER, Charles G., composer, director; b. Cleveland, O., July 16, 1864; s. George and Mary Otillia (Haack) S.; ed. pub. and high schs. and Brooks Mil. Acad.; began mus. training at 5; studied Royal Conservatory of Music, Dresden, nearly 3 yrs.; further studies under German masters. Teachers, 1891—; dir. of many mus. organizations; dir. Canton Symphony Orchestra, 1904-10. Among compositions are symphonies, overtures, piano concertos, pieces for piano, violin and orchestra, choruses and songs; compositions published in Leipzig and U.S.; writer and lecturer on music; awarded first prize, 1893, by Am. Mus. Teachers' Nat. Assn., for symphonic poem, "Hero and Leander," receiving highest marking given up to that time. Studio: Cleveland, O. Died Feb. 12, 1925.

SOMMER, Ernst August, surgeon; b. 1870; M.D., Willamette U. Med. Dept., 1890. Practiced at Portland, Ore., 1894—; surgeon St. Vincent's Hosp.; chief surgeon Pacific Northwest Pub. Service Co.; asso. clin. prof. surgery, U. of Ore. Med. Sch. Fellow Am. Med. Assn., Am. Coll. Surgeons. Mem. bd. dirs. Gorgas Memorial Inst. Home: Portland, Ore. Died Mar. 1936.

SOMMER, Peter W., manufacturer; b. nr. Fairbury, Ill., Sept. 10, 1869; s. Peter and Mary (Breisacker) S.; ed. country dist. school; m. Elizabeth Getz, Nov. 5, 1893. With the Keystone Steel & Wire Co., 1889—, pres., 1905—. Republican. Mem. Apostolic Christian Ch. Home: Peoria, Ill. Died Apr. 7, 1924.

SOMMERVILLE, Charles William, clergyman, educator; b. White Post, Clarke County, Va., May 22, 1867; s. William (M.D.) and Maria Louisa (Aby) S.; prep. education, Front Royal High Sch.; A.B., 2d honor, Hampden-Sidney Coll., 1890, B.S., 1890, A.M., 1896; diploma, Union Theol. Sem. in Va., 1895; post-grad. study, Ky. Theol. Sem., Southern Baptist Theol. Sem., U. of Chicago; toured Europe, 1902, 06; m. Kate Nelson Gregory-Dabney, Aug. 4, 1892 (died 1936); 5 step-children. Began teaching, 1885; asst. prof. Latin and German, Hampden-Sidney Coll., 1891-96; licensed ministry Presbyn. Ch. in U.S., 1895; pastor successively Ch. of the Covenant, Baltimore, Md., St. Albans, W.Va., Crescent Hill (Louisville), Ky., until 1910; professor Hebrew and N.T. Greek, Southwestern Presbyterian U., 1910-15; pastor Westminster Ch., Memphis, Tennessee, 1915-25; prof. English Bible and religious edn., Queens (now Queens-Chicora) Coll., Charlotte, N.C., 1925—. Y.M.C.A. camp religious dir. U.S. Marines, Parris Island, S.C., July-Dec. 1918. Democrat. Author various pamphlets on religious subjects. Editor Covenant Chronicle, Baltimore, 1901-05, Crescent Hill Presbyterian, Louisville, 1907-10, Westminster Men and Women, Memphis, 1921-25. Home: Charlotte, N.C. Died May 7, 1938.

SOMMERVILLE, Maxwell, prof. glyptology, U. of Pa., 1894—; b. Phila., Pa., May 1, 1829; grad. Central High Sch., Phila., 1847. Publisher in Phila. from 1900; became wealthy and took up study of gem archæology; spent greater part of life in Europe and Asia, devoting more than 30 yrs. to his quest for rare gems, cameos, intaglios and specimens of lapidaries' art of hist. value. Gathered and arranged one of the most celebrated collections of gems in the world; exhibited in Metropolitan Museum of Art, New York, and in Archæol. Museum, U. of Pa. Created and installed Indian Hindoo Museum and erected a Buddhist temple, both in museum, U. of Pa. Author: Engraved Gems (edition de luxe); Siam on the Meinam from the Gulf to Ayuthia; Sands of Sahara, 1901 (written after recent expdn. in Africa). Engraved Gems, 1902; A Wanderer's Legend, 1902; Joliffe, 1903. Monographs: The Triumph of Constantine, 1896; Jupiter Ægiochus, 1898; Grand Cameo of France, 1900; Buddhist Temple, 1900. Address: Philadelphia, Pa. Died 1904.

SOMMERVILLE, Walter Byers, judge; b. New Orleans, La., Oct. 7, 1854; s. William Byers and Eleanor (Casey) S.; LL.B., U. of La. (Tulane U.), 1880; m. Fannie Palmer Caldwell, Nov. 15, 1906. Admitted to La. bar, 1880, to bar Supreme Ct. of U.S., 1891; practiced, New Orleans; apptd. judge Civil Dist. Ct. (state ct.), Aug. 1900, elected to same office, Nov. 1900, for term of 12 yrs.; elected asso. justice Supreme Ct. of La., Mar. 1911, reëlected, Nov. 26, 1912, term of 12 yrs. Democrat. Presbyn. Pres. bd. trustees, John M. Bonner Memorial Home; pres. advisory bd. King's Daughters and Sons of La. Home: New Orleans, La. Died Oct. 13, 1924.

SONIAT, Leonce Martin, sugar planter; b. Carrollton (now part of New Orleans), La., Aug. 22, 1841; s. Pierre (Soniat du Fossat) and Clorinde (Hardi de Boisblanc) S.; A.B., U. of La., 1858; grad. in Latin, U. of Va., 1860; m. Leona Saulet, Nov. 19, 1867. Pvt. 30th La. Vols., 1862-65; in gen. mdse. business, Pascagoula, Miss., 1866, later St. Charles Co., La.; moved to County of Iberville, 1875, and engaged as sugar planter and mcht. V.p. Bank of White Castle, La.; pres. Soniat & Deblieuse, sawmill, Opelousas, La. Protectionist. Roman Catholic. Address: White Castle, La. Died 1922.

SONNECK, Oscar George Theodore, musician, historian, librarian; b. Jersey City, N.J., Oct. 6, 1873; s. Georg S. and Julia (Meyne) S.; ed. Kieler Gelehrtenschule, Kiel, Germany, 1883-89; Kaiser Friedrich's Gymnasium, Frankfort-on-the-Main, 1889-93; U. of Heidelberg, 1893; U. of Munich, 1893-97; history of music under Sandberger, philosophy, etc., under Stumpf, Riehl, Lipps, composition under M. E. Sachs; Conservatory at Sondershausen, 1898, principally conducting; piano at Frankfort-on-the-Main under Kwast; instrumentation under Knorr; m. Marie Elisabeth Ames, Nov. 9, 1904. Chief of music div., Library of Congress, 1902-17; v.p. G. Schirmer, Inc., music publishers, New York. Editor Musical Quarterly, 1915—. U.S. delegate Internat. Mus. Congress, Rome and London, 1911, also to Beethoven Centenary, Vienna, 1927; sec. Beethoven Assn.; exec. mem. Soc. for Publication of Am. Music. Author: Protest gegen den Symbolismus in der Musik, 1897; Classification of Music and Literature of Music, 1904, rev. edit., 1917; Francis Hopkinson and James Lyon—Two Studies in Early American Music, 1905; Bibliography of Early Secular American Music, 1905; Early Concert Life in America, 1907; Catalogue of Dramatic Music in the Library of Congress, 1908, Orchestral Music, 1912, of Early Librettos (before 1800), 1914; Report on the "Star Spangled Banner," "America," "Hail, Columbia," "Yankee Doodle," 1909; The Star Spangled Banner, 1914; Early Opera in America, 1915; Catalogue of First Editions of S. C. Foster (with W. R. Whittlesey), 1915, of Edward MacDowell, 1917; Suum Cuique, Essays in Music, 1916; Miscellaneous Studies in the History of Music, 1921; Beethoven—Impressions of Contemporaries, 1926; Beethoven Letters in America, 1927; The Riddle of the Immortal Beloved, 1927; also numerous contbns. to musical periodicals (music) Cyklus für Baryton aus Eine Totenmesse, op. 9; Vermischte Lieder, op. 12; four songs to poems by Edgar Allan Poe, op. 16; six songs, op. 14-15; Pessimistische Lieder, op. 17; Kleiner Lieder Cyklus, op. 18; Studies in Song, op. 19; (poetry) Seufzer, 1895, and Eine Totenmesse, 1898 (both published at Frankfort). Pres. U.S. Sect. Internat. Soc. Contemp. Music, 1923-24. Address: New York, N.Y. Died Oct. 30, 1928.

SONNICHSEN, Albert, author; b. San Francisco, Calif., May 5, 1878; s. Nicholas and Bertha (Leichardt) S.; ed. pub. schs. Went to sea at 15; was before the mast 3 yrs., then q.m. U.S. transport steamer Zeleandia, to Manila, during Spanish-Am. War; captured as prisoner of war by Filipino insurgents and held 10 mos. Did first lit. work in prison; returned to United States, 1900; m. Gladys Brooks, 1919; children—Eric, Noel, Olive. On staff New York Tribune 6 mos., 1901-02; engaged in lit. work for McClure, Phillips & Co., 1903; went to Balkans as corr. for New York Evening Post, in Bulgaria, 1904-06, in field with Macedonian revolutionists in Turkey, 1906; returned to U.S. and investigated Slavic immigrants in Middle West for U.S. Immigration Commn., 1907-08; sec. of Coöperative League (soc. for production and distribution on Rochdale system), 1910-12; free lance lit. work and journalism, 1913—. Sec. Co-operative League of America, 1919-21, v.p., 1924-26; editor The Coöperative Consumer, 1914-17. Author: Ten Months a Captive Among Filipinos, 1901; Deep Sea Vagabonds, 1903; Confessions of a Macedonian Bandit, 1909; Consumers Coöperation, 1919. Home: Willimantic, Conn. Died Aug. 15, 1931.

SONNICHSEN, Yngvar, artist; b. Christiania, Norway, Mar. 9, 1875; s. Sönke Postimus and Inga Mathea (Gran) S.; grad. Polytechnic Sch., Christiania, 1894; student art, Royal Acad., Antwerp and Brussels, and Acad. Julian, Paris, 1895-99; m. Agnes Gunhilde Anderson, Aug. 28, 1908 (died 1913). Came to Can., 1904, to Seattle, Wash., 1908. Painter of portraits, landscapes and mural decorations. Exhibited annually in Norway, 1900-04; at Internat. Expn., St. John, N.B., 1906 (1st prize); Seattle Expn., 1909 (gold medal and silver medal); Island Club of Arts and Crafts, Victoria, B.C.; "one man" show, Art Assn., Seattle, etc. Prin. works: Portraits of Ole Bull, the violinist; Edvard Grieg, the Norwegian composer; Capt. Roald Amundsen, the Arctic explorer; mural decorations, Norway Hall, Seattle; landscapes of Southeastern Alaska; engaged by Civil Works Adminstrn. to paint landscapes for pub. schs. of Seattle, Dec. 1933-Mar. 1934. Mem. Norwegian Luth. Ch. Address: Seattle, Wash. Deceased.

SONNTAG, Marcus S(mith), banker; b. Evansville, Ind., Feb. 17, 1859; s. John Haviland and Ellen (Brennan) S.; ed. high sch., Evansville, Ind.; m. Genevieve M. Cook, Feb. 12, 1884; children—Marion (Mrs. George Albert Cunningham), Jeanie (Mrs. James Cutler Vickery). In ins. business, 1894-1904; pres. Union Investment Co., 1894-1904; became pres. Am. Trust & Savings Bank, 1904, liquidating agent, 1931. Pres. Evansville Development Co., Abstract & Title Guarantee Co.; sec. and treas. Ingleside Land Co.; dir. Sunbeam Electric Mfg. Co., Union Bldg. & Loan Assn.; dir. Old Nat. Bank, 1901—. Chmn. Liberty Loan campaign, Southern Ind., World War I. Pres. Ind. World War Memorial Commn. (monument erected at cost of $10,000,000); pres. Evansville Pub. Library, 1912-23; mem. Bd. of Edn. 9 yrs. Del. to Rep. Nat. Conv., 1908. Mem. Am. Bankers Assn. (v.p. 1912; mem. exec. com. 1924-26), Ind. Bankers Assn. (pres. 1913-14); mem. advisory com. Bankers Industrial Expn., New York. Trustee Y.M.C.A. Evansville (dir. 25 yrs.). Presbyn. Home: Evansville, Ind. Died Aug. 25, 1936.

SONNTAG, William Louis, artist; b. nr. Pittsburgh, Mar. 2, 1822; went to Cincinnati in boyhood; studied there, 1846-53; in Europe, 1853-54, 1855-57 and 1861; home in New York, 1854—; landscape painter; associate, 1860, acedemician, 1861, Nat. Acad. of Design; m. in Cincinnati, O., Oct. 31, 1851. Address: New York, N.Y. Died 1900.

SONSTEBY, John J., judge; b. Milwaukee, Wis., Jan. 15, 1879; s. Knudt J. and Christiana (Sorensen) S.; m. Alice R. Osland, May 28, 1913; children—Helene Alice (Mrs. Henry M. Sinclair), Mona Katherine. Began practice of law in Chicago, 1906; admitted to bar of N.S. Supreme Ct., in 1912; member Chicago Board of Education, 1906-09 and 1912-15; atty. for city treas., Chicago, 1916-18; elected chief

Justice Municipal Ct. of Chicago, Nov. 4, 1930, re-elected, 1936. Chmn. Bds. of Instruction, Northern Dist. Ill. during World War I; government appeal agt. and mem. legal advisory com. of Exemption Board No. 78, Selective Service. Democrat. Lutheran. Trustee John Marshal Law Sch., Norwegian Am. Hosp. Assn. Mason; mem. O.E.S., White Shrine, Maccabees, Royal League, National Union. Home: Chicago, Ill. Died Apr. 16, 1941.

SOOYSMITH, Charles, civil engr.; b. Buffalo, N.Y., July 20, 1856; s. William Sooy and Elizabeth (Haven) Smith; C.E., Rensselaer Poly. Inst., 1876; studied at Polytechnicum, Dresden, and other places in Europe, 1876-78; m. Pauline Olmstead, Dec. 17, 1887. Asst. supt. maintenance dept. A.,T.&S.F. R.R., 1879-80; pres. Sooysmith & Co., contracting engrs., 1884-1900, builders of many important subaqueous engring. works. Introduced into U.S. so-called freezing process for excavating, and took out many patents covering its application to building of subaqueous tunnels. Inaugurated pneumatic caisson method for foundations of large buildings; served as expert in connection with underground works, notably with Underground Rapid Transit R.R. in New York; mem. Met. Sewerage Commn. of New York. Home: New York, N.Y. Died June 1, 1916.

SOPER, Alexander Coburn, lumber mcht.; b. Rome, N.Y., June 6, 1846; s. Albert and Esther Barton (Farquharson) S.; A.B., Hamilton Coll., 1867, A.M., 1870, LL.D., 1920; m. Mary Eliza Pope, Apr. 20, 1871; children—Alexander C., Willard Pope (dec.), Edward H.; m. 2d, Grace C. Shinn, Feb. 26, 1925. Mem. Pond & Soper, Chicago, 1869, succeeded by Soper Lumber Co., 1883, became chmn. bd.; chmn. bd. Menominee Bay Shore Lumber Co.; dir. Safety Car Heating and Lighting Co., Safety Car Co., Standard Coupler Co. Trustee Hamilton Coll. Mem. Am. Acad. Polit. and Social Science. Republican. Presbyterian. Home: Lakewood, N.J. Died June 10, 1930.

SOPER, Erastus Burrows, lawyer, banker; b. Pitcher, N.Y., Sept. 15, 1841; s. Jacob and Celinda (Harvey) S.; A.B., Cornell Coll., Ia., 1868, A.M., 1871, LL.D., 1904; m. Lizzie A. Cory, Nov. 19, 1867. Pvt. Co. K, 1st Ia. Inf., Apr.-Aug. 1861; sergt. to capt. Co. D, 12th Ia. Inf., 1861-65; admitted to bar, 1870; located in practice at Estherville, Ia., 1871, and established office at Emmetsburg, 1876; pres. First Nat. Bank of Emmetsburg. Trustee Cornell Coll., 1877— (later pres. bd.); chmn. Ia. Shiloh Mil. Park Commn. Republican. Methodist; lay del. Gen. Conf. M.E. Ch., Los Angeles, 1904, Baltimore, 1908. Home: Emmetsburg, Ia. Died Mar. 31, 1917.

SOPER, Henry Marlin, elocutionist, educator; b. Alden, Ill., Mar. 17, 1850; s. Isaiah W. and Polly L. (Trowbridge) S.; acad. and normal univ. edn.; grad. Nat. Sch. of Elocution and Oratory, Phila., Master of Oratory, 1877; m. Dora Schoonmaker, July 6, 1880. Several yrs. prin. graded and high schs.; located in Chicago, 1877; founder and pres. Soper Sch. of Oratory. Prof. elocution and oratory, Lake Forest U., acad. and sem., 1879-83; also in Morgan Park Theol. Sem., and several pvt. instns. of Chicago. One of founders, 1892 (pres., 1899-1902), Nat. Assn. of Elocutionists. Editor: Scrap Book Recitations; Soper's Select Speaker. Contbr. Werner's Magazine, etc. Address: Chicago, Ill. Died 1911.

SOPER, John Harris, business man; b. Plymouth, Eng., Nov. 17, 1846; s. Thomas Harris and Mary (Kipling) S.; came to U.S. in childhood; ed. Normal Sch., Bloomington, Ill., 1857-61; m. Mary Wundenberg, Sept. 11, 1871; children—John Frederick (dec.), William Henry, Josephine Mary, Blanche Ethel, Ruth Constance. Was miner, prospector, farmer, and plantation mgr., 1863-84. Marshal Hawaiian Kingdom, 1884-86, 1888-90; comdr.-in-chief mil. forces, Provisional Govt. of Hawaii, Jan. 17, 1893; adj. gen., chief of staff, 1894-1907; retired Apr. 2, 1907, with rank of brig. gen. N.G. of Hawaii, by authority of the War Dept., Washington. Republican. Home: Honolulu, H.T. Deceased.

SORG, Paul John, tobacco mfr.; b. Wheeling, W.Va., Sept. 23, 1840; spent his early yrs. as a laborer and mechanic; with John Auer, established, 1864, a small tobacco factory, from which grew the Paul J. Sorg Tobacco Co., of which he became pres.; pres. Merchants' Nat. Bank of Middletown, 1872—. Mem. Congress, 1895-97. Democrat. Address: Middletown, O. Died 1902.

SORLIE, Arthur Gustav, governor; b. Albert Lea, Minn., Apr. 26, 1874; s. Iver and Mary (Olson) S.; ed. Albert Lea Luth. Acad. 3 yrs.; m. Jennie Odegard, Sept. 1, 1900 (now dec.); children—Arthur, Louise, Ruth; m. 2d, Grace Hilleboe, Mar. 24, 1919; children—Glenn, Evelyn. Clk. Buxton State Bank 3 yrs., then mgr. gen. store; salesman for Kellogg-Johnson Co., shoe mchts., St. Paul, 4 yrs.; propr. cracker factory, Grand Forks, N.D., 1903-07; organizer, 1907, and pres. A. G. Sorlie & Co., fuel, seed and feed, Grand Forks; pres. Sorlie Motor Co. (Larimore, N.D.), Webster-Sorline Co. (Fisher, Minn.), Jefferson Motor Co. (Albert Lea, Minn.); v.p. State Bank of Douglas, N.D.; gov. of N.D., 2 terms 1925-28 inclusive. Republican. Norwegian Lutheran. Mem. K.P., A.O.U.W., U.T.C. Home: Grand Forks, N.D. Died Aug. 28, 1928.

SOTHERAN, Charles, journalist, author, bibliographer; b. Newington, Surrey, Eng., July 8, 1847; s. Charles and Frances Elise (Hirst) S.; ed. in England in pvt. schs. and St. Marie's Coll., Rugby; m. Mrs. Alice (Hyneman) Rhine, Oct. 17, 1893. Came to U.S., 1874, and began reportorial work on New York World. Was literary editor New York Recorder and Star; editor New York Echo, Bibliopolist, and Manchester (Eng.) Diocesan Church Calendar, 1873-74; asst. editor Export and Finance, Sunnyside Press, Nym Crinkle's Feuilleton, Advocate, Dramatic World, and others. Spoke throughout New York under auspices Dem. Nat. and State Coms., 1896; delegate to State Conv. Bryan and Sewall clubs, Buffalo, 1896. A founder and 1st librarian Theosophical Soc., 1876; an incorporator People's Inst.; vice-ruler and a founder Thirteen Club; past delegate Dist. Assembly 49, Knights of Labor; trustee New York Press Club, 1876-77, 1896-1900; prominent Mason and Sheikh of Kaaba; asst. grand sec. gen. Supreme Council Ancient and Accepted Scottish Rite, 1900—; 94th degree Rite of Memphis; grand representative of Great Britain and Ireland to U.S. of Supreme Council, Swedenborgian rite. Author: Alessandro di Cagliostro, Impostor or Martyr?, 1875; Percy Bysshe Shelley as a Philosopher and Reformer, 1875; Horace Greeley and Other Pioneers of American Socialism, 1892; The Theatres of New York, 1893. Also numerous separate bibliographies, etc. Home: New York, N.Y. Died 1902.

SOTHERN, Edward Hugh, actor; b. New Orleans, Dec. 6, 1859; s. Edward A. S., famous comedian; acad. edn., Eng.; studied painting in Spain; m. Virginia Harned, Dec. 3, 1896; m. 2d, Julia Marlowe, Aug. 17, 1911. First appeared, 1879, in small part with his father, Abbey's Park Theatre, New York; later toured U.S. with John McCullough; toured Eng., 1882-83; leading comedian in McCullough's co., 1883; wrote and played in farce, "Whose Are They?" 1884; played leading parts in "A Scrap of Paper," "Met by Chance," "Peg Woffington," "The Love Chase," and "One of Our Girls," 1884-86. First took leading rôle, Lyceum Theatre, New York, May 23, 1887, as Jack Hammerton, in "The Highest Bidder," and starred with his own co. in "Lord Chumley," "The Maister of Woodbarrow," "The Prisoner of Zenda," "An Enemy to the King," "The Adventures of Lady Ursula," "The Song of the Sword," "A Shilling's Worth," 1898, "The Sunken Bell," 1899, "Hamlet," 1900, "Richard Lovelace," 1901, "If I Were King," 1902-03, "Macbeth," "Twelfth Night," "As You Like It," "John the Baptist," "Joan of Arc," "Proud Prince," "Lord Dundreary," "Don Quixote," "The Fool Hath Said," "Much Ado About Nothing," "Merchant of Venice," "Romeo and Juliet," "Taming of the Shrew," etc. Died Oct. 29, 1933.

SOUBY, A(rmand) Max, teacher; b. Kenedy, Karnes County, Tex.; Mar. 23, 1880; s. Armand Maxie and Emma Lowry (Rose) S.; B.A., Vanderbilt U., 1907; post-grad. work same univ., 1908; U. of Chicago, 1911; traveled in Mexico, summer 1909; m. Susie I. Smith, July 21, 1915. Cowboy, railroad clk. and gen. salesman, 1897-1902; prof. history and economics Middle Tenn. State Normal Sch., Murfreesboro, Tenn., 1911-17; lecturer on "Backgrounds of the War," Blue Ridge Training Sch. for Y.M.C.A. Secretaries, summers, 1917, 18; Y.M.C.A. ednl. dir., Camp Gordon, Ga., Sept. 1917-Jan. 1918; departmental ednl. dir. Y.M.C.A., Southeastern Dept., Jan. 1918-May 1919; alumni sec. and mem. faculty Vanderbilt U., also editor Vanderbilt Alumnus. Mem. Am. Acad. Polit. and Social Science. Democrat. Mason. Home: Nashville, Tenn. Died Mar. 1922.

SOUCHON, Edmond, surgeon; b. Opelousas, St. Landry Parish, La., Dec. 1, 1841; s. Dr. Eugene and Caroline (Petit) S.; early edn. in Martinsville, La., Mobile, Ala., and New Orleans; collegiate edn., Paris; M.D., U. of La., 1867; m. Corinne Lavie, Dec. 6, 1869. Visiting surgeon, 1867-1906, mem. bd. of adminstrs., 1880-82, Charity Hosp.; demonstrator of anatomy, 1874-76, prof. anatomy and clinical surgery, 1885-1907, Tulane U.; designed and superintended erection of Tulane Med. Coll. bldgs.; founder Souchon Mus. of Anatomy, at Tulane; pres. La. State Bd. of Health, 1898-1906. Fellow Am. Surg. Assn. Published several surg. articles in New Orleans Medical and Surgical Journal and other jours.; inventor Souchon's Anesthetizer used in face and mouth operations. Retired on Carnegie pension in 1907. Home: New Orleans, La. Died Aug. 5, 1924.

SOULE, Andrew MacNairn, coll. pres.; b. Hamilton, Ont., Can., July 8, 1872; s. John and Margaret (Shaw) S.; asso. Ont. Agrl. Coll., 1892, B.S.A., U. of Toronto, 1893; Sc.D., U. of Ga., 1910; LL.D., 1916, D.Agr., 1928; Doctor, honoris causa, U. of Chile; m. Olivia Canby Porter, Aug. 29, 1895; children—Edward Porter, Robt. Murray. Asst. in exptl. dept., Ont. Agrl. Coll., 1891-92; asst. to dir. Mo. Expt. Sta., 1894; asst. prof. agr. and asst. agriculturist, Tex. Agrl. and Mech. Coll. and Expt. Sta., 1894-99; vice dir. and agriculturist, Tenn. Expt. Sta., 1899-1903, dir., 1903-04; chmn. agr. faculty, U. of Tenn., 1899-1904; dean, College of Agr., Va. Poly. Inst., and dir. Va. Expt. Station, 1904-07; pres. Ga. State Coll. of Agr. and Mechanic Arts, Athens, Sept. 1907—, and organizer co-education in same, 1918. Trustee Ga. Expt. Sta., 1907—; organizer state extension work in Ga., 1908; mem. Ark. Survey, 1921; founder Camp Wilkins, 1924. Spl. collaborator Bur. Plant Industry, Dept. Agr., 1900-04; mem. Internat. Jury Awards, St. Louis Expn., 1904. Sec. Tenn. Farmers' Institute, 1900-04, Va. State Farmers' Institute, 1904-07; dir. Farmers' Insts. of Ga., 1907—; pres. Am. Assn. Farmers' Inst. Workers, 1913; chmn. sect. on extension work, Am. Assn. Agrl. Colls. and Expt. Stas., 1912 (v.p. 1920); pres. Southern Agrl. Workers, 1927, Assn. of Land-Grant Colls. and Univs., 1929—. Federal food adminstr. for Ga., 1917-19. U.S. del. 2d Am. Congress of Economic Expansion and Commercial Instruction, Rio de Janeiro, Brazil, 1922. Fellow Royal Soc. of Arts (London). Presbyn. (elder). Author of numerous bulls. on agrl. subjects. Home: Athens, Ga. Died Apr. 16, 1934.

SOULE, Charles Carroll, publisher; b. Boston, June 25, 1842; s. Richard and Harriet (Winsor) S.; A.B., Harvard, 1862; pvt. and lt. 44th, and capt. 55th Mass. Vol. Inf., 1862-65; m. Louise C. Farwell, Oct. 9, 1878. Pres. Boston Book Co., 1889—. Author: The Lawyers' Reference Manual of Law Books and Citations, 1883; Library Rooms and Buildings, 1902; Year-Book Bibliography, 1901. Advisor on library planning, 1908—. Home: Brookline, Mass. Died Jan. 7, 1913.

SOULÉ, George, coll. pres.; b. Barrington, N.Y., May 14, 1834; s. Ebenezer and Cornelia E. (Hogeboom) S.; grad. Sycamore Acad., Ill., 1853; studied law and the business sciences, St. Louis, Mo., 1854-56; m. Mary J. Reynolds, Sept. 6, 1860. Founded, 1856, and pres. Soulé Commercial Coll. and Lit. Inst., New Orleans. Lt. col. C.S.A.; expert accountant; lecturer on ednl. and social questions. Mason; Past Grand Comdr. K.T. of La.; mem. Encampment K.T. of the U.S.; Past Grand Dictator La. Knights of Honor. Author: Analytic and Philosophic Commercial and Exchange Calculator, 1872; Contractions in Numbers, 1873; Intermediate Philosophic Arithmetic, 1874, 1922; New Science and Practice of Accounts, 1923; Gems of Business Problems, 1885; Manual of Auditing, 1892; Partnership Settlements, 1893; Practical Mathematics, 1924. V.p. Am. Unitarian Assn. Hon. LL.D., Tulane, 1918. Home: New Orleans, La. Died Jan. 26, 1926.

SOUSA, John Philip, musician; b. Washington, D.C., Nov. 6, 1854; s. Antonio and Elizabeth (Trinkhaus) S.; married. Teacher of music at 15, conductor at 17; band leader U.S. Marine Corps, 1880-92; dir. Sousa's Band, 1892—; toured in Europe various times and made tours of the world. Decorated Victorian Order (Eng.); Palms of the Acad., and Officer Public Instrn. (France); Grand Diploma of Honor, Acad. of Hainut (Belgium). Composer (marches): Washington Post; Liberty Bell; Stars and Stripes Forever; etc.; also suites, etc. Author: The Fifth String, Pipetown Sandy, 1905; The Dwellers in the Western World; Through the Year with Sousa, 1910; Transit of Venus. Address: New York, N.Y. Died Mar. 6, 1932.

SOUTH, Jerry C., chief clk. Ho. of Rep.; b. in Arkansas, Mar. 24, 1867; s. Samuel and Malvery (Jett) S.; grad. Ky. Mil. Inst.; student U. of Louisville; B.L., Law Dept., U. of Va., 1888; m. Ellen Chappell Hargis, Dec. 7, 1897. Began practice in Ark., 1888; chief counsel in more than 30 murder trials; mem. Ark. Ho. of Rep. or Senate, 1891-1901; del. Dem. nat. convs., 1896, 1900, 04, 08, 12; chief clk. Ho. of Rep., Washington, D.C., 1911-13, 1913-15. Capt. Co. M, 2d Ark. Inf., Spanish-Am. War. Trustee U. of Ark. Mem. Christian (Disciples) Ch. Mason. Home: Mountain Home, Ark. Died Sept. 24, 1930.

SOUTH, John Glover, diplomatic service; b. Frankfort, Ky., Jan. 23, 1873; s. Samuel S.; student U. of Ark., 1890-93; M.D., U. of Louisville, 1897; m. Christine, d. late U.S. Senator William O. Bradley, 1904. Practiced medicine at Frankfort, 1897-1921; E.E. and M.P. to Panama, 1921-30, to Portugal, 1930-33. Pres. Ky. Med. Assn., 1918-20; pres. Ky. State Bd. of Health 14 yrs. Republican. Home: Frankfort, Ky. Died May 13, 1940.

SOUTHARD, Elmer Ernest, physician; b. Boston, Mass., July 28, 1876; s. Martin and Olive Wentworth (Knowles) S.; A.B., Harvard U., 1897, A.M., 1902, M.D., 1901; Senckenberg Inst., Frankfort, and U. of Heidelberg, 1902; Sc.D., George Washington U., 1917; m. Dr. Mabel Fletcher Austin, June 27, 1906. Interne and asst. in pathology, 1901-03, asst. visiting pathologist, 1904-05, Boston City Hosp.; instr. of neuropathology, 1904-05, asst. prof., 1906-09, Bullard prof., 1909—, Harvard Med. Sch.; asst. phys. and pathologist Danvers State Hosp., 1906-09; pathologist to Mass. Commn. on Mental Diseases, 1909—; dir. Boston Psychopathic Hosp., 1912—. Dir. Eugenics Record Office, Cold Springs Harbor, N.Y.; mem. bd. scientific dirs. Bedford Hills Lab. Bur. of Social Hygiene, New York. Asst. editor Journal Nervous and Mental Diseases, Psychiatric Bulletin, and of Jour. Clin. and Lab. Medicine. Mem. Am. Acad. Arts and

Sciences. Author: (with H. C. Solomon) Neurosyphilis. Home: Cambridge, Mass. Died Feb. 8, 1920.

SOUTHARD, George Franklin, oil refining; b. N.Y. City, Jan. 25, 1852; s. George Warren and Mary Cynthis (Holmes) S.; B.A., Kenyon Coll., 1873; m. Lilla Hughes, Oct. 17, 1878; children—George Lee, Harry Ellis. With Standard Oil Co. interests, 1879-1904, in various cities in U.S., as gen. mgr. in France and Portugal, spl. rep. in India and in Roumania; pres. Independence Gypsum Co., Okla., 1904-12, Dewar Coal Mining Co., 1913-18, Southard Oil Co., 1918-19 (retired); dir. Central Nat. Bank, Enid, Okla. Apptd. by gov. mem. Bd. Commrs. Garfield Co., Okla., 1920; mem. Soldiers' Memorial Commn.; mem. Okla. Ednl. Survey Commn., 1922; pres. Carnegie Library, Enid, 10 yrs. Awarded bronze medal by Govt. of France for improving petroleum interests. Elk. Republican. Episcopalian. Owner of valuable library of rare old books. Home: Enid, Okla. Died Oct. 2, 1930.

SOUTHARD, James Harding, congressman; b. on farm, Washington Twp., Lucas County, Ohio, Jan. 20, 1851; s. Samuel and Charlotte (Hitchcock) S.; B.S., Cornell U., 1874; m. Carrie T. Wales, Mar. 23, 1882. Admitted to bar, 1877, in practice at Toledo, 1877—. Asst. pros. atty., 1882, pros. atty., 1883-89, Lucas County, O.; mem. 54th to 59th Congresses (1895-1907), 9th Ohio Dist. Republican. Dean, Law Sch. of Toledo U., 1914-15. Home: Toledo, O. Died Feb. 20, 1918.

SOUTHARD, Louis Carver, lawyer; b. Portland, Me., Apr. 1, 1854; s. William Lewis and Lydia Carver (Dennis) S.; B.S., U. of Me., 1875, M.S., 1892; LL.D., 1904; law student Boston U., 1875-76; admitted to bar, 1877, of U.S. Circuit Ct., 1887, of Supreme Ct. U.S., 1889; m. Nellie Copeland, June 1, 1881. Editor Easton (Mass.) Journal, 1877-80; mem. Mass. Ho. of Rep., 1887, Senate, 1895, 96; mem. Rep. State Com., 1888-94; lecturer U. of Me. Law Sch., 1897—. State del. U.S. Centennial Conv., Phila., 1887; alternate del.-at-large Rep. Nat. Conv., 1896; del. Universal Congress Lawyers and Jurists, St. Louis, 1904. Unitarian. Mason; Deputy Grand Master of Mass. Treas., gen. mgr. Internat. Purchasing Co.; treas. Hudson Tannery Co.; pres. State Wharf & Storage Co.; trustee Dorchester Savings Bank, etc. Mem. Alumni Advisory Council U. of Me. (chmn. exec. com.); asso. legal adviser Selective Service Bd., Brookline, Mass., during war period. Home: Brookline, Mass. Died Sept. 29, 1922.

SOUTHER, Henry, consulting engr.; b. Boston, Mass., Sept. 11, 1865; s. Henry and Mary (Wheeler) S.; grad. Mass. Inst. Tech., 1887; m. Elizabeth Sherman, Mass., Sept. 11, 1888. Engr. with Pa. Steel Co., 1888-93, Pope Mfg. Co., Hartford, Conn., 1893-99; in con. practice, Phila., 1899—; pres. Henry Souther Engring. Co., metallurgists and engrs.; v.p. Standard Roller Bearing Co. and Ferro Machine & Foundry Co., Cleveland. Water commr., Hartford, Conn., 1899-1907. Republican. Address: Cleveland, O. Deceased.

SOUTHERLAND, William Henry Hudson, naval officer; b. New York, N.Y., July 10, 1852; s. William and Phoebe E. S.; grad. U.S. Naval Acad., 1872; m. Mary Rodman, Aug. 1, 1877; children—Harriet Rodman (Mrs. J. Butler Wright), Mary Rodman (Mrs. Louis Bacon). Ensign, 1872; promoted through grades to rear adm., May 4, 1910. Served in Spanish-Am. War on Cuban coast, in command U.S.S. Eagle; mem. Bd. of Inspection and Survey, 1906-07, Naval Examining and Retiring Bd., 1910. Comdg. 2d Div., Pacific Fleet, 1911-12; comdr.-in-chief Pacific Fleet, 1912-13, and in command of expeditionary landing force in Nicaragua, Aug.-Oct. 1912; mem. Gen. Bd., 1913-14; retired by operation of law, July 10, 1914. Author: (with Comdr. S. Schroeder, U.S.N.) Azimuth Tables (U.S. Hydrographic Office). Wrote: Nautical Monograph No. 4—The North Atlantic Cyclone of August 1883. Home: Washington, D.C. Died Jan. 30, 1933.

SOUTHGATE, James Haywood, banker; b. Norfolk, Va., July 12, 1859; removed to N.C., 1861; ed. acad. and at U. of N.C.; m. Kate S. Fuller, 1882 (died 1893). In banking and ins. business, 1882—. Mem. platform com. of Prohibition Party's Nat. Conv. at Cincinnati, 1892, Pittsburgh, 1896; candidate on Nat. Prohibition ticket for V.P. of U.S., 1896. Pres. trustees Trinity Coll., N.C. Address: Durham, N.C. Died Sept. 29, 1917.

SOUTHGATE, Thomas Somerville, business man; b. Richmond, Va., 1868; s. Thomas M. and Mary E. S.; ed. pub. schs.; married; children—Nettie Virginia, Herbert Somerville, Mary Portlock. Pres. T. S. Southgate & Co., wholesale provisions, Norfolk, Va., 1892—; pres. Southgate Terminal Corp., importers and exporters, 1915—; pres. Southgate Packing Co., 1914—; also pres. Southgate Export Coal Co., Southgate Produce Co., Southgate Molasses Co., Southgate Importing & Exporting Co.; mem. exec. bd. Nat. Bank of Commerce, Trust Co. of Norfolk; dir. industrial Finance Corporation, New York, also dir. Norfolk & Western Railway. Mem. City Council 8 yrs., pres. 4 yrs.; mem. Charter Revision Commn., Norfolk. Mem. Southern Commercial Congress (1st v.p.), etc. V.p. Am. Commn. to Europe, 1913, to study rural credits, out of which report grew the present Farm Loan Bank System. Democrat. Methodist; pres. Southern Laymen's Assn. Home: Norfolk, Va. Died Sept. 27, 1928.

SOUTHWICK, George N., congressman; b. Albany, N.Y., March 7, 1863; s. Henry C. and Margaret J. S.; A.B., Williams Coll., 1884; Albany Law Sch., 1884-85; unmarried. On staff Albany Morning Express, 1885, mng. editor, 1888-89; mng. editor Albany Evening Journal, 1889. Mem. 54th and 55th (1895-99), and 57th (1901-03) Congresses, 20th N.Y. Dist., and 58th to 61st Congresses (1903-11), 23d Dist.; chmn. Rep. State Conv., 1896. Contbr. on several occasions to North American Review and minor mags. Home: Albany, N.Y. Died Oct. 17, 1912.

SOUTHWICK, George Rinaldo, gynecologist, surgeon; b. Sangersfield, N.Y., Sept. 4, 1859; s. Rinaldo M. and Mary A. (Porter) S.; M.D., Boston U., 1881; studied Rotunda Hosp. (Dublin), 1881, Berlin, Vienna, 1881-82, 87, London, 1902, 03, 04; M.D., Harvard, 1898; m. May Leland, May 18, 1887. Asso. prof. obstetrics, 1888-98, prof. gynecology, 1898—, Boston U. Sch. of Medicine; cons. gynecologist Mass. Homœ. Hosp.; gynecologist and mem. consulting bd. Westborough State Hosp. for the Insane. Mem. Royal Coll. Surgeons (England); licentiate Royal College of Physicians (London); fellow Am. Coll. Surgeons; mem. Am. Inst. Homœopathy (pres. surg. and gynecol. sect. 1917-18), Mass. Homœ. Med. Soc. (pres. 1912-13), Mass. Surg. and Gynecol. Soc. (pres. 1890), Boston Homœ. Med. Soc. (pres. 1910-11). Republican. Mason, Elk. Author: Practical Gynecology, 1888. Home: Boston, Mass. Died Jan. 7, 1930.

SOUTHWICK, Henry Lawrence, coll. pres.; b. W. Roxbury, Mass., June 21, 1863; s. John and Mary Frances (Lawrence) S.; grad. Dorchester High Sch., 1880, Monroe Coll. of Oratory, Boston, 1887, O.M., 1889; spl. instrn. in lit., art and langs.; hon. Litt.D., Berea College, Berea, Ky., 1930; m. Jessie Eldridge, May 30, 1889. Mem. staff of Boston Herald, 1880-87; won Old South prize for hist. essay on "Policy of Massachusetts Colony Toward Quakers," etc. Had charge of dept. of oratory, Martha's Vineyard Summer Inst., 1888; master of elocution and oratory, William Penn Charter School, Phila., 1888-89; associated with Dr. C. W. Emerson, in Emerson Coll. of Oratory, Boston, of which was prof. literary interpretation, prin. of oratory and dramatic art until spring of 1897; traveled in Europe, portions of 1896 and 1897; pursued spl. dramatic studies as mem. Augustin Daly's Co., winter of 1897; master of English at William Penn Charter Sch., Phila., 1898-99; returned to Emerson Coll. of Oratory, 1900, and became dean and pres.; lecturer on literature, oratory, and dramatic art; conductor for parties of foreign travel and study. Connected with Martha's Vineyard Summer Inst., U. of Virginia, and Summer Sch. of South. Home: Boston, Mass. Died Dec. 30, 1932.

SOUTHWICK, John Leonard, newspaper editor; b. Bombay, N.Y., Apr. 24, 1858; s. William Dana and Sarah Brown (Thickins) S.; grad. Franklin Acad., Malone, N.Y., 1878; Ph.B., Cornell U., 1883; m. Minnie L. Rolfe, July 3, 1883; children—Mabel Louise, Ethel Pearl (wife of Dr. Oliver N. Eastman). A founder, 1880, Cornell Daily Sun, Ithaca, N.Y., editor in chief until 1884; with Burlington (Vt.) Free Press, 1884—, editor in chief, 1907—; v.p. Burlington Mutual Fire Ins. Co.; corporator Burlington Savings Bank, Winooski Savings Bank. Del. to Rep. Nat. Conv., 1912; presdl. elector, Vt., 1916. Dir. Mary Fletcher Hosp., Burlington Symphony Orchestra. Conglist. Home: Burlington, Vt. Died Nov. 22, 1932.

SOUTHWORTH, Emma Dorothy Eliza Nevitte, author; b. (Nevitte) Washington, Dec. 26, 1819; m. Frederick H. Southworth, 1840. Taught school, 1844-49; published her first novel, "Retribution," 1849. Author: The Irish Visitor; The Hidden Hand, and forty others prior to 1872, when a uniform edition of 42 stories was republished. Since then: Unknown; Gloria; Trail of the Serpent; Nearest and Dearest; An Exile's Bride; etc. Address: Washington, D.C. Died 1899.

SOUTHWORTH, Thomas Shepard, M.D.; b. West Springfield, Mass., June 7, 1861; s. Edward and Mary Woodbury (Shepard) S.; A.B., Yale, 1883; M.D., Coll. Phys. and Surg. (Columbia), 1887; m. Jean Ponton Hamilton, Apr. 29, 1903; 1 son, Hamilton. Practiced in N.Y. City, 1887-1921 (retired); specialized in treatment of diseases of children—cons. physician New York Nursery and Child's Hosp., New York City Children's Hosp. Contbr. about 50 med. papers, chiefly on pediatrics; also sect. on Infant Feeding, in Carr's Pediatrics. Address: New York, N.Y. Deceased.

SOWDON, Arthur John Clark, retired; b. Boston, Mar. 6, 1835; s. John, Jr., and Charlotte Harrison (Capen) Sowdon; Boston Latin Sch.; A.B., Harvard U., 1857, LL.B., 1861; unmarried. In real estate and mortgage business, Boston, 1863-72. Mem. Com. of 15 chosen at Faneuil Hall meeting, 1874, to resist inflation of currency and secure a fixed standard of value; mem. Mass. Ho. of Rep., 1879-80; active in polit. matters for many yrs.; supported Rep. bolt against James G. Blaine and high tariff, 1884; took stump for Grover Cleveland; acted with Dem. party in nat. matters in later yrs. Del. to 5 triennial convs. Episcopal Ch.; warden St. Paul's Ch.; mem. diocesan bd. missions and of standing com., 17 yrs.; pres. Ch. Assn. for 30 yrs. Mem. Am. Acad. Polit. and Social Science; gov. Mass. Soc. Colonial Wars, 1896-1905, gov. gen., 1905—. Chief marshal Harvard Alumni, 1871; chief marshal at Bishop Brooks' consecration, Oct. 14, 1891, and at his funeral, Jan. 26, 1893. Address: Boston, Mass. Died 1911.

SOWER, Charles Gilbert, Sr., publisher; b. Norristown, Pa., 1821; s. David and Cecelia (Chollet) S.; and great g.s. of Christopher Sower, bishop Ch. of the Brethren, and great-great g.s. Christopher Sower, 1st famous printer of Germantown; ed. Montgomery Acad.; learned printing in father's establishment; pres. Christopher Sower Co., publishers; m. Caroline A., d. of Nathan R. Potts, 1849. Collector of specimens of early printing and other rare books. Address: Philadelphia, Pa. Died 1902.

SPAETH, (Philip Friedrich) Adolph (Theodor), clergyman; b. Esslingen, Germany, Oct. 29, 1839; s. Dr. Ernst H. Ph. and Rose E. (Boley) S.; grad. U. of Tübingen, 1861; D.D., U. of Pa., 1875; LL.D., Muhlenberg Coll., Pa., 1895; tutor in family of Duke of Argyle, Scotland, 1863; m. Maria Dorothea, d. Rev. John Duncan, May 8, 1865; m. 2d, Harriet Reynolds, d. Charles Porterfield Krauth, D.D., LL.D., Oct. 12, 1880; father of J(ohn) Duncan E(rnst) S. Ordained Luth. ministry, 1861; pastor Zion's Ch., Phila., 1864-67, St. Johannis Ch., 1867—; prof. Luth. Theol. Sem., 1873—. Pres. Gen. Council Evang. Luth. Ch. in N. America, 1880-88; pres. Ministerium of Pa., 1892-95; pres. Gen. Conf. of Luth. Motherhouses of Deaconesses in U.S., 1896. Author: Liederlust; Saatkörner; Biography of Dr. W. J. Mann; Biography of Dr. Charles Porterfield Krauth; Commentary on the Gospel of St. John, 1896; etc. Editor of Jugendfreund, 1877; Kirchenbote, 1906; German Church Book and German Sunday School Book of the General Council. Co-editor of Documentary History, Ministerium of Pa. Contbr. to Luth. Ency., 1899; Herzog-Hauck, Protestant Real Ency., Vol. I, 1898, Vol. II, 1909; Mensel, Kirchl. Handlexicon. Also to Luth. Church Review. Composed a number of hymn tunes. Home: Philadelphia, Pa. Died 1910.

SPAETH, Reynold Albrecht, physiologist; b. Phila., Pa., Nov. 22, 1886; s. Adolph and Harriet Reynolds (Krauth) S.; B.S., Haverford, 1909; M.A., Harvard, 1911, Ph.D., 1913; student Smithsonian Table, Naples, 1914; m. Edith Eleanor Taussig, Aug. 18, 1913. Fellow, Harvard, 1909-13; Sheldon fellow, Kiel and Naples, 1913-14; instr. biology, Clark Coll., 1914-15; instr. biology, Yale, 1915-17, in embryology, 1918; asst. in Hygienic Lab., U.S.P.H.S., 1918; also in physiology, 1918-23, asso. prof., 1923—, Sch. of Hygiene and Pub. Health of Johns Hopkins U. Instr. embryology, Woods Hole, Mass., 1915-16, in physiology, 1920—; consultant in personnel and industrial hygiene. Awarded Walker prize, Boston Soc. Natural History, 1913. Fellow A.A.A.S. Home: Baltimore, Md. Died June 26, 1925.

SPAFFORD, Frederick Angier, physician; b. Ludlow, Vt., Oct. 13, 1855; s. Alvah Merrick and Mary Eliza (Angier) S.; student U. of Vt., 1877; M.D., Dartmouth, 1879; post-grad. work, New York Policlinic, U. of Edinburgh, Harvard Med. Sch., privat kliniks, Berlin; m. Harriet E. A. Davis, Sept. 4, 1881. Prof. anatomy, Leonard Med. Sch., Raleigh, N.C., 1880-84; moved to S.D., 1884; v.p. Territorial Bd. of Health, 1886-89; state regent of edn., 1897-1909 and 1919—; pres. Bd. of Edn., Flandreau, 1885-1915; phys. in charge U.S. Indian Sch., Flandreau, 1892—; supt. Bd. of Health, Moody Co., S.D., 25 yrs. Lecturer med. legal jurisprudence, Coll. of Law, U. of S.D. Fellow Am. Coll. Surgeons, A.M.A. Baptist. Mason; Past Grand Comdr. K.T. of S.D.; Odd Fellow, Elk. Home: Flandreau, S.D. Died Mar. 3, 1922.

SPAHR, Charles Barzillai, asso. editor The Outlook, 1886—; b. Columbus, O., July 20, 1860; s. Rev. B. N. S.; grad. Amherst, 1881; studied at Leipzig, 1884-85; Ph.D., Columbia School of Political Science; m. Jean Gurney Fine, July 5, 1892. Author: Present Distribution of Wealth, 1896; America's Working People, 1900; also essays on The Taxation of Labor, The Single Tax, and Giffen's Case Against Bimetallism for Political Science Quarterly. Residence: Kingsbridge, New York City. Died 1904.

SPAHR, George W., lawyer; b. Berks County, Pa., Mar. 21, 1839; s. Jacob and Maria S.; B.S., Northwestern Christian U. (now Butler Coll.), 1861; LL.B., Indianapolis Law Sch.; m. Lizz V. Root, 1868. Entered mil. service Aug. 14, 1861, as pvt. Co. F, 3d Ind. Cav., and served 3 yrs. and 3 mos. Nat. comdr. Union Vet. Legion, 1902-03. Republican. Residence: Indianapolis, Ind. Deceased.

SPAID, William Winfield, stock broker; b. Pleasant City, O., Jan. 7, 1880; s. Martin Luther and Elizabeth (Hill) S.; student Muskingum Coll., New Concord, O., 1898; LL.B., LL.M., Nat. Univ. Law Sch., Washington, D.C., 1906; m. Ada Bain, 1903; 1 son, William. Began as stenographer for W. B. Hibbs & Co., stock brokers, Washington, 1900, partner, 1912—; pres. Dupont Nat. Bank, 1918-22. Mem.

Am. Inst. Banking (chmn. ednl. com. 1911-12; pres. Washington Chapter 1914-15), D.C. Bankers Assn. (pres. 1928-29), Associated Stock Exchanges, Assn. of N.Y. Stock Exchange Firms (v.p.). Mem. of bar of D.C. Mem. N.Y. Stock Exchange, N.Y Curb Exchange, Boston Stock Exchange, Philadelphia Stock Exchange, Washington Stock Exchange, New York Cotton Exchange, Chicago Board of Trade. Presbyterian. Mason. Home: Washington, D.C. Died May 21, 1938.

SPALDING, Albert Goodwill, merchant; b. Byron, Ill., Sept. 2, 1850; s. James L. and Harriet I. (Goodwill) S.; ed. pub. schs. of Byron and Rockford, Ill., and in Rockford Commercial Coll.; m. Josephine Keith, 1875 (died 1899); m. 2d, Elizabeth Churchill Mayer, 1900. At 17 had attained much local prominence as an amateur baseball player; gained nat. fame as a pitcher; joined Boston Club, 1871, and until 1875 was its pitcher and capt.; joined Chicago Club, 1876, and remained with it as, consecutively, mgr., sec. and pres., until 1891. Established with brother and brother-in-law, in 1876, firm of A. G. Spalding & Bros., sporting goods, of which became pres.; later organized a mfg. branch as the Spalding Mfg. Co., becoming pres. Organized and managed world-tour of the Chicago and All-Am. baseball teams, 1888-89. Address: Point Loma, Calif. Died Sept. 9, 1915.

SPALDING, Burleigh Folsom, lawyer; b. Craftsbury, Vt., Dec. 3, 1853; s. Rev. Benjamin Pendell and Ann (Folsom) S.; Ph.B., Norwich U., Vt., 1877, A.M., 1897, LL.D., 1912; m. Alida Baker, Nov. 25, 1880; children—Deane Baker, Frances Folsom (Mrs. Ray H. Nelson), Roscoe Conkling, Burleigh Mason, Carlton Cutler. Admitted to the bar, Mar. 1880; practiced at Fargo, N.D., 1880—, except while on bench. Mem. Capitol Commn. of Dakota Territory, 1883-87; mem. of N.D. Constl. Conv., 1889; mem. Joint Commn. to divide property, instns. and archives of Dak. Ty. between states of N.D. and S.D., 1889. Chmn. Rep. State Central Com., 1892-94; chmn. Rep. Good Govt. League of N.D., 1905-07; mem. 56th and 58th Congresses (1899-1901, 1903-05); apptd. judge of Supreme Court of N.D., by Gov. John Burke, Feb. 1, 1907; elected to same office, Nov. 1908, chief justice, Oct. 1911-Jan. 1915. Chmn. Rep. State Com., 1920-28; mgr. presdl. campaign for Rep. ticket in N.D., 1920; mem. com. on Policies and Platform of Republican Party, 1920-24; chmn. N.D. delegation to Rep. Nat. Conv., 1924; alternate del. to Rep. Nat Conv., 1928, del. at large, 1932; state dir. George Washington Bicentennial, 1932. Pres. N.D Lay Electoral Conf. M.E. Ch., 1929, 31. Mason, Elk. Rep. campaign speaker, also speaker on constl and ednl. questions, and in opposition to socialism and communism. Home: Fargo, N.D. Died Mar. 17, 1934

SPALDING, Franklin Spencer, bishop; b. Erie, Pa., Mar. 13, 1865; s. Rt. Rev. John Franklin and Lavinia D. (Spencer) S.; A.B., Princeton U., 1887; B.D., Gen. Theol. Sem., 1891, S.T.D., 1905; unmarried. Deacon, 1891, priest, 1892, P.E. Ch.; in charge All Saints' Ch., Denver, 1891-92, Jarvis Hall and St. Luke's, Montclair, Colo., 1892-96; rector St. Paul's Ch., Erie, Pa., 1896-1904; consecrated, Dec. 14, 1904, bishop of Salt Lake, title changed, Oct. 1907, to Bishop of Utah. Address: Salt Lake City, Utah. Died Sept. 25, 1914.

SPALDING, Frederick Putnam, univ. prof.; b. Wysox, Pa., Apr. 7, 1857; s. Israel Putnam and Ruth E. (Cooley) S.; C.E., Lehigh U., 1880; m. Annie Packer Wilbur, Jan. 22, 1885. Several yrs. in practice as civ. engr. upon river improvements and municipal work; instr. Lehigh U., 1886-88; asst. prof. civ engineering, Cornell, 1891-98; prof. civ. engring., U of Mo., Sept. 1900—. Fellow A.A.A.S. Author: Notes on Hydraulic Cement, 1893; Text-Book on Hydraulic Cement, 1893; Text-Book on Roads and Pavements, 1894; Hydraulic Cement, Its Properties, Testing and Use, 1897; Masonry Structures, 1921. Address: Columbia, Mo Died Sept. 4, 1923.

SPALDING, George Burley, clergyman; b. Montpelier, Vt., Aug. 11, 1835; s. Dr James and Eliza (Reed) S.; A.B., U. of Vt., 1856; Union Theol. Sem., 1858-60; graduate Andover Theol. Sem., 1861; D.D., Dartmouth, 1878, U. Vt., 1904; LL.D., Syracuse U., 1904; m. Sarah Livingston, d. Rev. Dr. John W. Olmstead, Aug. 6, 1861. Ordained Congl. ministry, 1861; pastor Vergennes, Vt., 1861-64, Hartford, Conn., 1864-69 (successor of Dr. Horace Bushnell), Dover, N.H., 1869-83, Manchester, N.H., 1883-85, First Presbyn. Ch., Syracuse, N.Y., 1885-1910, pastor emeritus, 1910—. Editorial writer New York World, Times and The Watchman, Boston, 1869-74; editor New Hampshire Journal, 1881-85. Mem. N.H. Ho. of Rep., 1876-77; mem. State Constl. Conv., 1877. Trustee Hamilton Coll., Auburn Theol. Sem. Contbr mags. and periodicals. Address: Syracuse, N.Y. Died Mar 1914

SPALDING, J. Walter, sporting goods; b. Byron, Ill., July 28, 1856; s. James Lawrence and Harriet I. (Goodwill) S.; ed. pub. schs.; m. Marie Boardman, June 17, 1884. Organized the business of A. G. Spalding & Bros., with brother A. G. Spalding, 1876; chmn bd A. G Spalding & Bros. of N.J and A. G. Spalding & Bros., Ltd., of London. Home: Monmouth Beach, N.J. Died Sept. 11, 1931.

SPALDING, Jack Johnson, lawyer; b. Morganfield, Ky., Aug. 29, 1856; s. Ignatius A. and Susan Ann (Johnson) S.; student St. Louis (Mo.) U. and Seton Hall Coll., South Orange, N.J.; grad. Moore's Southern Business Coll., Atlanta, Ga.; m. Betty Hughes, Dec. 18, 1877; children—Hughes, Suzanne (Mrs. William H. Schroder), Jack. Admited to Ky. bar, 1878, and began practice at Morganfield; moved to Atlanta, 1882; mem. King & Spalding, 1885-1920, later Spalding, Sibley, Troutman & Brock; gen. counsel Trust Co. of Ga., Atlantic Ice & Coal Co.; dir Habersham Mills, Grantville Hosiery Mills. County atty., Union County, Ky., 1881; county commr., Fulton County, Ga., 1895-99. Del. Dem. Nat. Conv., 1900; del.-at-large, 1932 and 1936. Decorated Knight of St. Gregory by Pope Benedict, 1927; Laetare medal, U. of Notre Dame, 1928; Knight of Malta, 1931. Democrat. Catholic. Home: Atlanta, Ga. Died Dec. 8, 1938.

SPALDING, James Alfred, surgeon; b. Portsmouth, N.H., Aug. 20, 1846; s. Lyman Dyer and Susan Parker (Parrott) S.; A.B., Dartmouth, 1866; M.D., Harvard, 1870; m. Sarah Chase Shepley, Nov. 16, 1882. Practiced in Portland, 1873—; ophthal. and aural surgeon Me. Gen. Hosp., 1881-1914, later consultant. Fellow Am. Coll. Surgeons. Address: Portland, Me. Died Feb. 27, 1938.

SPALDING, James Field, educator; b. Enfield, Conn., Dec. 5, 1839; s. Asa Leffingwell (M.D.) and Mary (Dixon) S.; A.B., Williams Coll., 1862, A.M., 1865, S.T.D., 1887; m. Mary Harper, Apr. 28, 1864; father of Philip Leffingwell S. and Walter Raymond S. Tutor in Williams College, 1863-64; asso. prin. Round Hill Sch., Northampton, 1865-70; P.E. clergyman, 1869-91; withdrew from ministry and entered Catholic Ch., 1892; prof. English lit., Boston Coll., 1899-1903; lecturer in English lit. at many Catholic schs., colls. and theol. sems., 1896—. Author: The Teaching and Influence of Saint Augustine, 1886; The World's Unrest and Its Remedy, 1898. Contbr. to leading lit. rev. Address: Cambridge, Mass. Died Aug. 12, 1921.

SPALDING, Jesse, street ry. official; b. Bradford, County, Pa., Apr. 15, 1833; attended country schs.; m. Adelphia Moody. Engaged in lumbering on Susquehanna River until 1856, when he established lumber business in Chicago; established mill at Menekaunie, Wis., 1857, and later other mills on Cedar River; one of stock co. which built first planing mill in Chicago; in exclusively wholesale lumber business, 1882—. One of organizers and was 8 yrs. pres. Sturgeon Bay and Lake Mich. Canal and Harbor Co. Largely instrumental in building Camp Douglas during Civil war; collector customs, port of Chicago, 1883; govt. dir. Union Pacific R.R., 1889; was 3 yrs. mem. city council, Chicago; pres. Chicago Union Traction Co., 1899—. Republican. Home: Chicago, Ill. Died 1904

SPALDING, John Franklin, P.E. bishop of Colo.; b. Belgrade, Me., Aug. 25, 1828; grad. Bowdoin, 1853, D.D.; also D.D., Trinity; Gen. Theol. Sem., 1857; deacon, 1857; priest, 1858; several New England chs., 1857-62; rector St. James', Old Town, Me., St. George's, Lee, Mass., asst. Grace Ch., Providence, R.I.; rector St. Paul's, Erie, Pa., 1862-73; Bishop of Colo., 1873—. Author: A Manual for Mothers' Meetings; The Church and Its Apostolic Ministry, 1887; The Threefold Ministry of the Church of Christ; The Pastoral Office; The Best Mode of Working a Parish, 1889; Jesus Christ, the Proof of Christianity, 1890 Address: Denver, Colo. Died 1902.

SPALDING, John Lancaster, archbishop; b. Lebanon, Ky., June 2, 1840; A.B., St. Mary's, Md., 1859; S.T.D., U. of Louvain, Belgium, 1874; LL.D., Columbia, 1902. Ordained R.C. priesthood; sec. to bishop of Louisville, 1865; built St. Augustine's Ch. for Catholic negroes of Louisville, 1869; chancellor Diocese of Louisville, 1871; in New York, 1872-77; consecrated bishop of Peoria, May 1, 1877; resigned, 1908; created titular archbishop of Scyphopolis, May 1909. Apptd. by President, 1902, one of arbitrators in settlement of anthracite coal strike. Author: Life of Most Rev. M. J. Spalding, Archbishop; Essays and Reviews; Religious Mission of the Irish People; Lectures and Discourses, Education and the Higher Life; Things of the Mind; Means and Ends of Education; Thoughts and Theories of Life and Education; America, and Other Poems; The Poet's Praise; Songs; God and the Soul; Opportunity; Religion, Agnosticism and Education, 1902; Aphorisms and Reflections; Socialism and Labor, 1902; The Spalding Year Book, 1905; Religion and Art, and Other Essays, 1905. Address: Peoria, Ill. Died Aug. 25, 1916

SPALDING, Phebe Estelle, educator; b. Westfield, Vt., Mar. 13, 1859; d. Benjamin Pendell and Ann (Folsom) S.; Litt B., Carleton Coll., Minn., 1889, M.L., 1900; traveled and studied in England and on the continent, 1898-99, in Great Britain in 1914, and in Great Britain and Italy, 1921-22; Ph D., Boston U., 1908 Teacher pub schs. N.E., N.D and Minn. to 1885; instr English and history of art, 1889-90, pres. English literature and instr. in history of art, 1890-1927, Pomona College; professor emeritus, 1927—. Occasional lecturer on art and lit. topics. Congregationalist. Author: A Memory, 1903; Womanhood in Art, 1905; The Master Came (poem), 1906; The Tahquitch Maiden, 1911; Potestas et Opportunitas—An Ode of Today, 1913; English sketches, 1922-23; Through Nature to Eternity —A Shakespearean Meditation, 1933; Patron Saints of California, 1934. Home: Claremont, Calif. Died Mar 12, 1937

SPALDING, Philip Leffingwell, banking business; b Ithaca, N.Y., June 27, 1871; s. James Field and Mary (Harper) S.; A.B., Harvard, 1892, A.M., 1893, B.S., 1894; m. Katharine Hobart Ames, Oct. 10, 1900; children—Philip, Oakes Ames, Hobart Ames. Began in mechanical dept. Am. Bell Telephone Co., Boston, 1894; with Bell Telephone Co., Phila., 1895-1912; insp., chief engr., gen. supt., gen. mgr., 2d v.p. and dir. Bell Telephone Co. of Pa., Del. & Atlantic Telegraph & Telephone Co., Central Dist. Printing & Telegraph Co.; pres. N.E. Telephone and Telegraph Co., 1912-18, Providence Telephone Co., 1916-18; partner firm Estabrook & Co.; dir. N.E. Tel & Tel. Co., Am Dredging Company (Phila.), Yale and Towne Manufacturing Company, General Public Service Corp.; trustee Copley Square Trust. Dir. Mass. Soc. for Prevention of Cruelty to Children Unitarian. Home: Milton, Mass. Died Dec. 1, 1938.

SPALDING, Volney Morgan, botanist; b. E. Bloomfield, N.Y., Jan. 29, 1849; s. Frederick Austin and Almira (Shaw) S.; A.B., U. of Mich., 1873; Ph.D., U of Leipzig, 1894; m. Harriet Hubbard, Sept 7, 1876; m. 2d, Effie Almira Southworth, Jan. 1, 1896 Instr. zoölogy and botany, 1876-79, asst. prof botany, 1879-81, acting prof., 1881-86, prof., 1886-1904, U. of Mich.; engaged in research at the Desert Bot Lab. at Tucson, Ariz., of the Carnegie Instn., 1904-09. Member Mich. Acad. Sciences (pres. 1897-98). Author: Guide to the Study of Common Plants, and Introduction to Botany, 1895; Monograph on the White Pine, 1897; Biological Relations of Desert Shrubs, 1907; Distribution and Movements of Desert Plants, 1909; various papers in Annals of Botany, Science, American Naturalist, Therapeutic Gazette and other periodicals. Retired on Carnegie Foundation, Jan. 1, 1910. Address: Loma Linda Calif Died Nov. 12, 1918.

SPALDING, William Andrew, civil service officer; b. Ann Arbor, Mich., Oct. 3, 1852; s. Ephraim Hall and Jane (McCormick) S.; grad. commercial coll., Kansas City, Mo., 1868; U. of Mich., 1871-72; m. Mary Louise Dennison, Oct. 14, 1875. In various positions with Herald Express, and Times, Los Angeles, 1878-1903; state bldg. and loan commr., 1893-97; sec. Civ. Service Commn., Los Angeles, Apr. 1903-1911; chmn. Bd of Freeholders for revision of city Charter. Pres. Premier Ranch Co.; v.p. Spalding-Powell Co. (orange growing). Pres. Acad. of Sciences of Southern Calif. Unitarian. Author: The Orange—Its Culture in California, 1886; My Vagabonds (poems), 1892. Home: Los Angeles, Calif. Died Sept. 7, 1941.

SPAMER, Richard, music and drama critic; b. Cincinnati, O., Apr. 23, 1856; s. Hugo and Marie (Eckel) S.; ed. Cincinnati pub. and high schs.; m. Eliza Moën Fuller, Apr. 11, 1876; 1 son, Richard Fuller. Asst. librarian, Cincinnati Pub. Library, 1873-76; same position with St. Louis pub. schs., 1877-88; music and drama editor, St. Louis Star, 1889-1900; pub. St. Louis Dramatic News, 1905-09; music and drama editor, St. Louis Globe-Democrat, 1909-28; lecturer on Shakespeare, music and drama, at Lindenwood Coll. for Women, St. Charles, Mo. Home: St Louis, Mo. Died Aug. 24, 1938.

SPANGLER, Henry Wilson, engineer; b. at Carlisle, Pa., Jan. 18, 1858; s. John Kerr and Margaret Ann (Wilson) S.; grad. U.S. Naval Acad., 1878; hon. M.S., Univ. of Pa., 1896, Sc.D., 1906; m. Nannie Jane Foreman, Dec. 1, 1881. Engr. U.S.N., 1878-89 and 1898; asst. prof. mech. engring., 1881-84 and 1887-89, prof., 1889—. U. of Pa. Mem. advisory council Engring. Congress, Chicago Expn., 1893; mem. Jury of Awards, Buffalo Expn., 1901. Author: Valve Gears; Notes on Thermodynamics; Graphics. Co-Author: Elements of Steam Engineering. Address: Philadelphia, Pa. Died Mar. 18, 1912.

SPANGLER, Timon John, lawyer; b. Amboy, Ill., Mar. 28, 1869; s Elijah and Ellen (Farr) S.; LL.B., U. of Mich., 1893; m. Grace C. Carruthers, Dec. 27, 1899. Practiced at Mitchell, S.D., 1893—; dir. Mitchell Fruit & Grocery Co.; sec. Mitchell Power Co.; city atty. Mitchell, 1898-1900; county atty., Davison County, 1905-09. Republican. Episcopalian. Mason, Elk. Home: Mitchell, S.D. Died Nov. 23, 1926.

SPARKS, Arthur Watson, artist; b. Washington, D.C., Mar. 17, 1870; s. Frederick R. and Catherine (Hart) S.; studied at Julian Acad., and École des Beaux Arts, Paris, France, under Laurens, Cormon, Bougereau, Thaulow, Mucha, Ferrier and Courtois; m. Françoise C. Perrusset, July 6, 1910. Exhibited at Paris Salon, Carnegie Inst., Pa. Acad. Fine Arts, Nat. Acad. Design, Art Inst. Chicago, Corcoran Gallery, etc. Awarded bronze medal, San Francisco Expn., 1915; 2d prize, Associated Artists of Pittsburgh. Prin. works: The Steel Mills; Under the Birches; Grand View Arizona Canyon; Clemance and Cora; The Model at Rest; etc. Prof. painting, Carnegie Inst., Jan. 1909—. Home: Pittsburgh, Pa. Died Aug. 6, 1919.

SPARKS, Charles I., lawyer; b. Jackson Twp., Boone County, Ia., December 20, 1872; s. Alden B. and Jennie R. (Weston) S.; student Simpson Coll., Indianola, Ia., 1890-93; LL.B., State U. of Ia., 1896; m. Ida D. Roberts, Sept. 25, 1895; children—Catherine Gingles, Charles A., Clarence R. Admitted to Ia. bar, 1896, and practiced at Boone until 1906, at Goodland, Kan., 1907-15. County atty. Boone Co., 1899-1903; dist. judge 34th Kan. Dist., 1914-29; mem. 71st and 72d Congresses (1929-33), 6th Kan. Dist.; resumed practice as mem. firm Sparks & Sparks. Republican. Methodist. Mason. Home: Goodland, Kan. Died Apr. 10, 1937.

SPARKS, Edwin Erle, coll. pres.; b. Licking County, O., July 16, 1860; s. Erastus Felton and Jane Erle (Dodd) S.; A.B., Ohio State U., 1884, A.M., 1891; grad. student, Harvard, 1892; Ph.D., U. of Chicago, 1900; LL.D., Lehigh U., 1909; LL.D., Allegheny Coll., 1915; m. Katharine Cotton, Jan. 1, 1890. Asst. in history, Ohio State U., 1884-85; teacher pub. schs., Ohio, 1885-90; prin. prep. dept. and teacher history, Pa. State Coll., 1890-95; lecturer, 1895-96, instr. Am. history, 1896-97, asst. prof., 1897-1901, asso. prof., 1901-04; prof., 1904-08, curator Hist. Mus., 1905-08, dean Univ. Coll., 1905-07, U. of Chicago; pres. Pa. State Coll., 1908-20, pres. emeritus, 1920. Mem. Pa. State Bd. of Agr. Dir. Pa. State Chamber of Commerce. Author: Expansion of the American People, 1899; The Man Who Made the Nation, 1900; Formative Incidents in American Diplomacy, 1902; The United States of America (2 vols.), 1904; Foundations of National Development, 1907; The Lincoln-Douglas Debates of 1858, 1908; Worth-While Americans, 1922. Contbr. serials and essays on hist. and college administrative topics to periodicals and jours. Home: State College, Pa. Died June 15, 1924.

SPARKS, John, gov. of Nev., elected 2 terms, 1903-07, 1907-11. Democrat. Address: Carson City, Nev. Died 1908.

SPARKS, Will, landscape painter; b. St. Louis, Mo., Feb. 7, 1862; s. Sam and Julia Plauman Oge S.; ed. high sch., St. Louis; Washington U. Sch. of Art, 1883-86; Mo. Med. Coll., St. Louis, 1884-86; studied in Paris at École des Beaux Arts, Julian Acad., Colorossi Acad. and École de Medicine; m. Ethel Martin, 1916. Principal works: "Harbor of Bordeau," Bordeau, France; portrait, St. Louis Museum; "California Mission," Toledo (Ohio) Museum; oil painting "1906," acquired by the Palace of The Legion of Honor, San Francisco, 1934; also murals in various institutions. Member faculty U. of California, 1904-08. Address: San Francisco, Calif. Died Mar. 30, 1937.

SPARROW, Carroll Mason, physicist; b. Baltimore, Md., Jan. 10, 1880; s. Leonard Kip and Anne Elizabeth Temple (Magill) S.; A.B., Johns Hopkins, 1908, Ph.D., 1911; m. Lettice Latané, Dec. 14, 1912. With U.S. Coast and Geodetic Survey, 1901-07; adj. prof. physics, U. of Va., 1911-17, asso. prof., 1917-20, prof., 1920—. Served as capt. Air Service (science and research div.), U.S.A., July 31, 1918-Sept. 3, 1919. Fellow Am. Physical Soc., A.A.A.S. Democrat. Contbr. to scientific jours., mainly on spectroscopy. Asso. editor Physical Rev., 1920-23; asso. editor Virginia Quarterly Rev. Home: University, Va. Died Aug. 30, 1941.

SPARROW, William Warburton Knox, ry. official; b. Ireland, Dec. 30, 1870. Ry. service in Ireland and S. Africa until 1908; came to U.S., 1908; with Waddell & Harrington, cons. engrs., Kansas City, Mo., 1909-12; with H. Von Unwerth, same city, 1912-13; asst. chief engr. Mo. Pub. Service Commn., 1913-16; valuation engr. C.,B.&Q. R.R., Chicago, 1916-18; chief engr. C.,M.&St.P. R.R. during Federal control, 1918-20, asst. chief engr., Mar.-June 1920, then asst. to pres. same rd., in charge Federal valuation and settlement with U.S. R.R. Adminstrn.; placed in charge accounting dept. C.,M.&St.P. R.R., Nov. 1, 1920, elected v.p. Apr. 1, 1923, chief financial and accounting officer for receivers, 1925-28, v.p. C.,M.St.P.&P. R.R. Co., officers in charge of Finance Accounting and Real Estate for Trustees, Jan. 1, 1936—. Office: Chicago, Ill. Died Nov. 7, 1939.

SPAULDING, Edward Gleason, prof. philosophy; b. Burlington, Vt., Aug. 6, 1873; s. Americus V. and Mary A. (Rice) S.; B.S., U. of Vt., 1894; LL.D., 1921; A.M., Columbia, 1896; Ph.D. Univ. of Bonn, Germany, 1900; m. Olive Strong Miner, June 2, 1913. Instr. in philosophy, Coll. City of N.Y., 1900-05; asst. prof. philosophy, 1905-14, prof. philosophy, 1914—, Princeton. Lecturer in philosophy, Marine Biol. Lab., Woods Hole, Mass., 1907—. Served as 1st lt. Engr. Corps, U.S.A., in Chem. Warfare Service, June 5, 1918-Jan. 1, 1919. Lecturer, Brooklyn Inst. Arts and Sciences, 1918—, also at People's Institute, New York City; lecturer at summer sessions, Washington U., Harvard, U. of Chicago, U. of Calif., U. of Mich. Author: The New Rationalism, 1918; What Am I?, 1928; A World of Chance, 1936. Co-author: The New Realism, 1912; Roads to Knowledge, 1932. Contbr. philos. and scientific periodicals. Address: Princeton, N.J. Died Jan. 31, 1940.

SPAULDING, George Lawson, composer; b. Newburgh, N.Y., Dec. 26, 1864; s. William Douglas and Mary Victoria (Lee) S.; ed. pub. schs.; m. Jessica Moore, June 16, 1899. Mason. Republican. Presbyn. Composer: In Funland (operetta), 1904; Tunes and Rhymes for the Playground, 1906; Songs for Jack and Jill, 1907; Note-Speller, 1911; Musical Lays for Practice Days, 1918; Large Notes for Little Hands and Throats, 1919; (popular songs) My Mary Green; When You Know the Girl You Love Loves You; Take Back the Engagement Ring; Somebody Has My Heart; etc.; also numerous songs for children. Home: Roselle Park, N.J. Died June 1, 1921.

SPAULDING, Nathan Weston, saw mfr.; b. N. Anson, Me., Sept. 24, 1829; s. Walter and Lydia S.; ed. pub. schs., N. Anson, 1833-47, going to sch. part time and working the remainder as carpenter, millwright, and 1 yr. in saw factory; went to Calif., 1851; m. Mary Theresa Clinkinbeard, May 25, 1854. Was in mines in Calif.; constructed first quartz mill in Calif. —on Mokelumne river. Saw mfr., 1858—, first in Sacramento and in San Francisco, 1861—. Inventor of adjustable saw teeth, 1861; took out several patents on saws, saw teeth and machines; completed and copyrighted a scale for measurement of logs which is standard in several states. Asst. U.S. treas. at San Francisco, 1881-85; twice mayor of Oakland; trustee Leland Stanford Jr. U.; dir. Industrial Home for Adult Blind, Chabot Sheltering Home for Women; dir. State Bd. of Trade; a founder and dir. Mechanic's Inst. Mason. Home: Oakland, Calif. Deceased.

SPAULDING, Oliver Lyman, asst. sec. of Treasury; b. Jaffrey, N.H., Aug. 2, 1833; s. Lyman and Susan (Marshall) S.; A.B., Oberlin, 1855; m. Mary Cecilia Swegles, Aug. 12, 1862. Admitted to bar, 1858. Capt. Co. A, 23d Mich. Inf., Aug. 1, 1862; maj., Feb. 13, 1863; lt. col., Apr. 6, 1863; col., Apr. 16, 1864; bvtd. brig. gen. vols., June 25, 1865, "for faithful and meritorious services during the war"; mustered out, June 28, 1865. Regent U. of Mich., 1859-64; sec. of state, Mich., 1866-70; declined appmt. U.S. dist. judge, Utah Ty., 1871; mem. Mich. State Rep. Com., 1871-78; spl. agt. U.S. Treasury, 1875-81; mem. 47th Congress (1881-83), 6th Mich. Dist.; chmn. U.S. Govt. commn. sent to Sandwich Islands to investigate matters pertaining to Hawaiian reciprocity treaty, 1883; again spl. agt. U.S. Treasury, Jan.-Dec. 1885 and 1889-90; declined appmt. as circuit judge, 1889, tendered by gov. of Mich.; asst. sec. of the treasury, 1890-93 and 1897-1903. Pres. 1st Pan-Am. Customs Congress, 1903; del. Rep. Nat. Conv., 1896. Home: St. John's, Mich. Died July 30, 1922.

SPAULDING, William Stuart; b. Boston, Mass., Feb. 17, 1865; s. Mahlon D. and Emily (Smith) S.; A.B., Harvard, 1888; m. Katrina Fairlee, Sept. 14, 1909; children—Katrina, William S., Alice O. After leaving college became partner in firm Nash, Spaulding & Co.; trustee Suffolk Savings Bank for Seamen and Others. Republican. Home: Boston, Mass. Died Aug. 15, 1937.

SPEAKMAN, Harold, author, painter; b. Greenville, N.J., Nov. 30, 1888; s. William A. and Virginia B. (Dunham) S.; student Chicago Acad. Fine Arts, 1908-10, Munich, 1911-12, Paris, 1912-13; m. (Frances) Russell Lindsay, artist, July 3, 1925. Instr. Chicago Acad. Fine Arts, 1914, Brooklyn Sch. Allied Arts, 1916. Contbr. verse, decorations, Harper's, Everybody's Mag., Life, etc. Joined R.O.T.C., Plattsburg, N.Y., May 1917; commd. 2d lt. inf. and assigned to 332d Regt.; served on Italian front, Piave trenches, Battle of Vittorio Veneto; in Balkans, Montenegrin Revolution; hon. discharged as 1st lt., May 1919. Author: Songs of Hope, 1917; The Youngest Shepherd, 1917; From a Soldier's Heart, 1919; Beyond Shanghai, 1922; Hilltops in Galilee, 1923; This Above All (novel), 1924; Here's Ireland, 1925 (all vols. illustrated by self except the novel); Mostly Mississippi, 1927. Made thousand-mile journey on foot around Ireland, 1924; descended Mississippi River from headwaters to Gulf by canoe and house boat, 1926-27. Home: New York, N.Y. Died Sept. 24, 1928.

SPEAR, Albert Moore, judge; b. Madison, Me., Mar. 17, 1852; s. Andrew P. and Alice P. (Moore) S.; A.B., Bates Coll., 1875; LL.D., Bates Coll., LL.D., U. of Me.; m. Helen Frances Andrews, July 21, 1875. Taught sch. winters, 1868-75; prin. Anson Acad., N. Anson, Me., 1876-77; admitted to bar, 1878; practiced at Hallowell, 1879-85, Gardiner, 1885-1902. Mem. Me. Ho. of Rep., 1883-85, Senate, 1891-93 (pres. 1893); mayor of Gardiner, 1889-92; asso. justice Supreme Jud. Ct. of Me., 1902-09, reapptd., 1909, 17, 23. Republican. Grand comdr. Grand Commandery K.T. of Me., 1899; grand master, Grand Masonic Lodge of Me., 1922-23. Address: Augusta, Me. Died Jan. 31, 1929.

SPEAR, Ellis, solicitor of patents; b. Warren, Knox County, Me., Oct. 15, 1834; s. James Marston S.; A.B., Bowdoin, 1858, LL.D. Capt. 20th Me. Inf., Aug. 29, 1862; maj., Aug. 28, 1863; col., May 29, 1865; bvtd. lt. col. vols., Sept. 30, 1864, "for gallant and distinguished services at battle of Peebles' Farm, Va."; col. vols., Mar. 29, 1865, "for gallant and meritorious services at battle of Lewis' Farm, Va."; brig. gen. vols., Apr. 9, 1865, "for faithful and meritorious services during campaign ending in surrender of Army of Northern Va."; hon. mustered out, July 16, 1865. Asst. examiner ry. and civ. engring., 1865-68; examiner, 1868-72, examiner-in-chief, 1872-74, U.S. Patent Office; asst. commr. of patents, 1874-76; resigned. Engaged in pvt. business, 1876, until Jan. 1877, when was apptd. commr. patents, serving until Nov. 1878; atty. and solicitor of patents, 1878—. V.p. Washington Loan & Trust Co., Equitable Coöperative Bldg. Assn. Overseer Bowdoin Coll. Home: Washington, D.C. Died Apr. 3, 1917.

SPEAR, William Thomas, judge; b. Warren, O., June 3, 1834; s. Edward and Ann (Adgate) S.; pub. sch. edn.; LL.B., Harvard, 1859; m. Frances E. York, Sept. 28, 1864. In practice at Warren, O., until 1878. Pros. atty. Trumbull Co., O., 1873-77; judge Ct. of Common Pleas, 1878-85; justice Supreme Ct. of Ohio, 1885— (elected 5 times, chief justice, 1892-98 and 1904, 1911). Home: Warren, O. Died Dec. 8, 1913.

SPEARMAN, Frank Hamilton, author; b. Buffalo, N.Y., Sept. 6, 1859; s. Simon and Emmaline E. (Dunning) S.; ed. pub. and pvt. schs. and Lawrence Coll., Appleton, Wis.; LL.D., Notre Dame U., Ind., 1917, Santa Clara U., 1924; Litt.D., Loyola, 1931; awarded Laetare Medal, Notre Dame U., 1935; m. Eugenie A. Lonergan, June 5, 1884; children—Thomas Clark, Thomas L. (dec.), Eugene Lonergan, Elaine (dec.), Frank Hamilton, Arthur Dunning. Ind. Republican. K.C. Author: The Nerve of Foley, 1900; Held for Orders, 1901; Doctor Bryson, 1902; The Daughter of a Magnate, 1903; The Close of the Day, 1904; The Strategy of Great Railroads, 1904; Whispering Smith, 1906; Robert Kimberly, 1911; The Mountain Divide, 1912; Merrilie Dawes, 1913; Nan of Music Mountain, 1916; Laramie Holds the Range, 1921; The Marriage Verdict, 1923; Selwood of Sleepy Cat, 1924; Your Son's Education, 1925; Flambeau Jim, 1927; Spanish Lover, 1930; Hell's Desert, 1932; Gunlock Ranch, 1934; (photoplays) Whispering Smith, 1915; Midnight; Nan of Music Mountain, 1917 (starring Wallace Reid); The Love Special (from The Daughter of a Magnate), starring same, 1919; Whispering Smith, 1926 (starring H. B. Warner); The Runaway Express, 1926 (from the Nerve of Foley); The Yellow Mail, 1927 (from Held for Orders); (serials) The Girl and the Game, 1915; Whispering Smith Rides, 1925. Contbr. short stories to mags. and econ. articles to revs. Home: Hollywood, Calif. Died Dec. 29, 1937.

SPEARS, John Randolph, author, journalist; b. in Ohio, 1850; s. Richard C. and Louisa S.; m. Celestia C. Smiley; children—Raymond Smiley, Eldredge Anson, John Randolph (dec.). Frequent contributor to periodical literature. Author: The Gold Diggings of Cape Horn, 1895; The Port of Missing Ships, and Other Stories of the Sea, 1896; The History of Our Navy, 1897; Our Navy in the War with Spain, 1898; The Fugitive, 1899; History of the American Slave Trade, 1900; History of the Mississippi Valley Period of Foreign Control, 1903; Life of Anthony Wayne, 1903; David G. Farragut (Am. Crisis Biographies), 1905; A Short History of the American Navy, 1907; Story of New England Whalers, 1908; A History of the American Navy, 1909; The Story of the American Merchant Marine, 1910; Master Mariners, 1911; Captain Nathaniel Brown Palmer, 1921; Buying for the Long Pull, 1922; Biography of John Bloomfield Jervis, C.E., 1933. Home: Utica, N.Y. Died Jan. 25, 1936.

SPEARS, Samuel Tilden, lawyer; b. Wetzel County, W.Va., Oct. 7, 1877; s. Aaron N. and Rhoda E. (Keener) S.; normal course, Fairmont (W.Va.) Teachers Coll., 1897; student W.Va. U. 1 yr., LL.B., 1903; m. Stella Gail Ford, Sept. 24, 1900; 1 dau., Marjorie Gail (Mrs. John Card Mather). Admitted to W.Va. bar, 1903, and practiced at Elkins, 1903—; mem. firm Spears & Irons; pres. Spears Lumber Co., Kelly Foundry & Machine Co. Served as 1st lt. W.Va. N.G., 1905. Chmn. Selective Draft Bd., World War I. Trustee Wesleyan Coll. 12 yrs.; dir. Boys Industrial Sch.; del. Gen. Conf. M.E. Ch., 1916. Democrat. Mason; Past Grand Master Masons of W.Va.; Past Eminent Comdr. Pilgrim Comdry. K.T.; Past High Priest R.A.M. Author: Evolution—Bible and Science Reconciled, 1926. Home: Elkins, W.Va. Died Jan. 25, 1936.

SPEED, John Gilmer, author, journalist; b. in Ky., Sept. 21, 1853; s. Philip and Emma (Keats) S.; grad. U. of Louisville, 1869 (A.M., C.E.); practiced civ. engring.; engr. for several railroads; later city engr. Louisville; connected with U.S. Bd. Transportation at Centennial Expn., 1876. Joined staff New York World, 1877, mng. editor, 1879-83; traveled abroad, 1883-85 and 1885-88; sec. Am. Exbn., London, 1887; edited American Magazine, 1888-89; for 2 yrs. editor Leslie's Weekly. Edited Keats' Letters and Poems, and wrote a life of the poet, who was his great-uncle. Author: A Fall River Incident; The Gilmers in America; A Deal in Denver; The Horse in America, 1905; etc. Contributor to Century,

Harper's, Forum, North American Review, McClure's, Lippincott's, Ainslee's, Outlook, etc. Address: Mendham, N.J. Died 1909.

SPEER, Alfred Alten, banker; b. in Carroll County, Ind., Oct. 8, 1858; s. William Wesley and Nancy (Douglas) S.; ed. pub. schs., and Lincoln Coll. (now extinct), Greenwood, Mo.; m. Narcissa Mahon, Mar. 10, 1886; 1 son, Boyd Alten. Contractor on line of Missouri Pacific Railway to 1886; in mercantile business, 1886-1914; pres. The First National Bank of Jefferson City, Mo., 1916-31; dir. Bank of Chamois, Bank of Osage City, Bank of Bonnot's Mill. Twice mayor of Chamois; mem. Mo. Ho. of Rep., 5 terms (speaker 1909); apptd. mem. Mo. State Capital Comm., Oct. 6, 1911 (vice chmn. bd. until completion of Capitol); del.-at-large to Rep. Nat. Conv., Chicago, 1912; del.-at-large Mo. State Constl. Conv., 1922-23 (chmn. com. on state offices and salaries). Chmn. exec. com. Mo. School of Mines and Metallurgy; curator U. of Missouri. Mason. Mgr. 11th Dist. (Mo.) Liberty Loan campaigns during war period. Home: Jefferson City, Mo. Died Nov. 20, 1935.

SPEER, Emory, judge; b. Culloden, Ga., Sept. 3, 1848; s. Rev. Eustace W. and Anne E. S.; pvt. 5th Ky. Mounted Inf. (Orphan Brigade), C.S.A., 1864-65; A.B., U. of Ga., 1869; LL.D., Mercer U.; m. Sallie Dearing; m. 2d, Eleanora D. Morgan. Admitted to bar, 1869; solicitor-gen. of Ga., 1873-76; alumni trustee U. of Ga., 1877-86; mem. 46th Congress (1879-81), as Independent Democrat; disagreeing with his party, returned to 47th Congress (1881-83) as Independent, and affiliated with Republicans on protection and other issues; mem. Ways and Means Com.; mem. House conf. with Senate on tariff bill of 1883; U.S. atty., 1883-85; U.S. dist. judge Southern district of Ga., Feb. 18, 1885—. Presided on trial U.S. vs. Lancaster, Hall and others, conspiracy and murder, 1891; on trial U.S. vs. Greene and Gaynor, conspiracy and embezzlement, 1906; Jones vs. U.S., upholding the constitutionality of the U.S. Nat. Mil. Service Law, Aug. 1917. Dean law dept., Mercer U., and lecturer on constitution of United States, 1893—; lecturer Storrs Foundation, Yale, 1906. Delivered orations, Grant Birthday, Galena, Ill., 1898; Peace Jubilee, Chicago, 1898; Centenary, U. of Georgia, 1901; Robert E. Lee, Emory Coll., Oxford, Ga., 1896; Centenary Abraham Lincoln, New York, 1909; Appomattox Day, Hamilton Club, Chicago, 1910; Lincoln's Birthday, Republican Club, New York, "Fortify Panama Canal," 1911. Author: Removal of Causes from State to United States Courts, 1888; Lectures on the Constitution of the U.S., 1897; Lincoln, Lee, Grant, and other Biographical Addresses, 1910. Address: Macon, Ga. Died Dec. 13, 1918.

SPEER, Peter Moore, lawyer; b. Oil City, Pa., Dec. 29, 1862; s. Alexander and Grizelda (Hays) S.; A.B., Washington and Jefferson Coll., Washington, Pa., 1887, A.M., 1890; m. Isabella Paul, June 30, 1891; children—Paul, Katharine (Mrs. Thomas M. Brown). Admitted to bar, 1889, and began practice at Oil City; dist. atty. Venango Co., Pa., 1891-94; mem. Pa. Ho. of Rep., 1897; mem. 62d Congress (1911-13), 28th Pa. Dist.; v.p. and gen. counsel Standard Oil Co. of N.Y., 1920—. Republican. Mason, Elk. Home: New York, N.Y. Died Aug. 3, 1933.

SPEER, Robert Walter, mayor; b. Huntingdon County, Pa., Dec. 1, 1855; s. George W. and Jane Ann (Brewster) S.; ed. pub. sch., and at Dickinson Sem., Williamsport, Pa.; m. Kate A. Thrush, 1882. Settled in Denver, 1877; postmaster of Denver, 1885-89; pres. Fire and Police Bd., Denver, 1891-93, 1897-99; pres. Bd. Pub. Works, 1901-04; mayor of Denver, 1904-12. Democrat. Home: Denver, Colo. Died May 14, 1918.

SPEER, William, Presbyn. missionary; b. New Alexandria, Pa., Apr. 24, 1822; grad. Kenyon Coll., O., 1840; studied medicine under his father; licensed to preach, 1846; D.D., Centre Coll., Ky.; LL.D., Washington and Jefferson; m. Cornelia Brackenridge, 1846 (died 1847); m. 2d, Elizabeth B. Ewing, 1852. With two colleagues established, 1846, 1st mission Presbyn. Bd. Foreign Missions; returned to U.S.; went to Calif., 1852, as 1st missionary in their own tongue to Chinese there, established mission house and Chinese ch., edited 2 yrs. The Oriental (Chinese and English paper); secured repeal of acts of 1854-55, excluding Chinese from mines; established Chinese mission in Hawaii, 1856; in evangelistic work in Southern States, Wis. and Minn., 1858-65. Corr. sec. Presbyn. bd. edn., 1865-76; traveled in Europe, Japan and China. Author: China and the United States, 1870; The Great Revival of 1800, 1872, 1903; God's Rule for Christian Giving, 1875; A Permanent Manual of the Board of Education, 1874; also numerous pamphlets on the Chinese, articles in reviews and mags. and printed sermons. Address: Washington, Pa. Died 1904.

SPEER, William McMurtrie, newspaperman; b. Huntingdon, Pa., Feb. 5, 1865; s. Hon. Robert Milton and Martha Ellen (McMurtrie) S.; brother of Robert Elliott S.; A.B., Yale, 1884; law student, Yale, 1884; LL.B., Albany Law Sch., 1887; m. Margaret Howard Post, Apr. 26, 1899. On staff Huntingdon (Pa.) Monitor, New Haven (Conn.) Morning News, 1884, New York Sun, 1884-93, Albany Argus, 1893-96, New York World, 1904-10. Sec. New York Johnstown Flood Com., sec. to the mayor, sec. to New York World's Fair Com.; mem. New York Constl. Commn., 1894. Presbyn. Home: Piermont, N.Y. Died Apr. 2, 1923.

SPEERS, James M., merchant; b. Jordanstown, White Abbey, County Antrim, Ireland, Jan. 9, 1862; s. William and Mary (Milliken) S.; came to U.S., 1880; ed. pub. schs.; m. Nellie Carter, June 14, 1888 (died 1922); children—William E., Thomas Guthrie, Peter Carter, James M., Wallace C., Theodore C.; m. 2d, Nellie Carter Dodd, Feb. 15, 1924. With James McCutcheon & Co., linens, 1880—, pres., 1912-30, chmn. bd., 1930—; dir. Patriotic Ins. Co. of America, Sun Indemnity Co. of New York, Sun Underwriters Co. V.p. Presbyterian Bd. Foreign Missions; treas. Student Volunteer Movement, Agrl. Missions Foundation; trustee Forman Christian Coll., Lahore, India; trustee Mt. Holyoke Coll. Presbyn. Home: Montclair, N.J. Died July 24, 1941.

SPELLMEYER, Henry, M.E. bishop; b. New York, Nov. 25, 1847; s. Matthias Henry and Mary S.; grad. New York Univ., 1866, A.M., 1869; Union Theol. Sem., 1869; D.D., Syracuse Univ., 1882; m. Matilda M. W. Smith, Nov. 8, 1871. Pastor for 35 consecutive yrs. in Newark, N.J., and immediate vicinity; mem. Gen. Conf., 1896, 1900, 1904; chmn. com. on entertainment, 1900 and 1904; mem. book com., 1896-1900 and 1900-04; elected M.E. bishop, May 1904. Trustee Centenary Collegiate Inst., Hackettstown, N.J., Syracuse Univ., Drew Theol. Sem. Address: Cincinnati, O. Died 1910.

SPENCE, Clara B., educator; b. Albany County, N.Y., 1862; d. William Douglas and Anne (Stewart-Tallman) S.; A.B., Boston U., 1879; post-grad. study, London. Prin. The Spence Sch. for Girls, 1892—. Trustee Barnard Coll., League for Polit. Edn., New York. Presbyn. Fellow Met. Mus. of Art, New York; mem. Nat. Inst. Social Sciences. Officer French Acad., Legion of Honor (France), 1921. Address: New York, N.Y. Died Aug. 9, 1923.

SPENCE, John Fletcher, educator, chancellor emeritus; b. Greenfield, O., Feb. 3, 1828; s. Stephen and Matilda S., grad. Ohio Wesleyan, 1853, A.B., 1856, A.M., 1880; D.D., Mt. Union, 1880; LL.D., Scio Coll., 1888; m. E. E., d. Judge William Cary, Aug. 1865. Ordained M.E. ministry, 1858; officer U.S. Vols., 1862-65; pres. Knoxville Female Coll., Tenn., 1865-68; founded E. Tenn. Wesleyan U., 1868; founder, 1867, pres. and chancellor 19 yrs., Grant Memorial U.; founded, 1893, chancellor, 1893-1904, chancellor emeritus, 1904—, Am. U. of Harriman. Chaplain-in-chief G.A.R., 1908-09. Address: Knoxville, Tenn. Died Jan. 24, 1912.

SPENCE, William H., clergyman; b. Ont., Can., Apr. 4, 1875; s. John and Susan (McClennan) S.; student Collegiate Inst., Stratford, Ont., 1899-1900, Victoria Coll. Sem., Toronto, 1902-03; A.B., U. of Toronto, 1904; D.D., Morningside Coll., Sioux City, Ia., 1915; m. Hope E. Morris, Nov. 9, 1904; children—Eileen Elizabeth (Mrs. Paul DeBarr Cook, Jr.), John Hartzell, William Fraser. Came to U.S., 1904, naturalized citizen, 1910. Pastor M.E. Ch., Lake Mills, Ia., 1904-07, Clarion, Ia., 1907-09, Fort Dodge, Iowa, 1909-17, Omaha, Nebraska, 1917-18, Sioux City, Iowa, 1918-20, Denver, Colo., 1920-23, Burlington, Ia., 1923-29, Mason City, Ia., 1929—. Nat. campaign speaker during World War I. Dir. Clear Lake (Ia.) Inst. Mem. Gen. Conf. M.E. Ch., 1916, 28; rep. for Neb. and Ia. on gen. bd. Epworth League, 1916-22; dean of Okoboji Lake Inst., 1918-20. Trustee of Cornell Coll. Republican. Mason. Contbr. to ch. publs. Home: Mason City, Ia. Died Dec. 1, 1935.

SPENCER, Alfred, Jr., banker; b. Suffield, Conn., Oct. 29, 1851; s. Alfred and Frances C. (Reid) S.; ed. Conn. Lit. Instn. and Edward Place Sch., Stockbridge, Mass.; m. Ella Susan Nichols, Oct. 14, 1879; children—Alfred Francis, Herbert. Clk., later cashier, 1st Nat. Bank, Suffield, 1872-91; cashier Aetna Nat. Bank, Hartford, 1891-99, pres., 1899, and after consolidation of Aetna Nat. Bank with Hartford Nat. Bank, as the Hartford Aetna Nat. Bank, pres. of latter until consolidation with U.S. Security Trust Co., 1927, then chmn. exec. com.; pres. Alfred Spencer Co.; chmn. bd. Gray Telephone Pay Station Co.; v.p. Am. Surety Co.; trustee State Savings Bank. Republican. Baptist. Mason. Home: Hartford, Conn. Died Sept. 12, 1934.

SPENCER, Anna Garlin, educator, minister; b. Attleboro, Mass., Apr. 17, 1851; d. Francis W. and Nancy Mason (Carpenter) Garlin; edn. largely pvt.; D.D. from Meadville Theological Sch., 1929; m. Rev. William H. Spencer, August 1878; 1 dau., Lucy (Mrs. Charles Sarver). Newspaper work, Providence Journal, 1869-78; pub. speaker, 1870—; writer, teacher, and occasional preacher, associated with husband, Haverhill, Mass., Florence, Mass., and Troy, N.Y. Ordained and installed as minister of Bell St. Chapel, Providence, R.I., 1891; asso. leader, N.Y. Soc. for Ethical Culture, 1903-09; asso. dir. and staff lecturer, New York Sch. of Philanthropy, 1903-13; spl. lecturer on social service and social aspects of edn., U. of Wis., 1908-11; dir. Summer Sch. of Ethics, for Am. Ethical Union, 1908-11; dir. Inst. of Municipal and Social Service, Milwaukee, Wis., 1910-11; Hackley prof. sociology and ethics, Theol. Sch., Meadville, Pa., 1913-18; lecturer at U. of Chicago, 1918. Mem. bd. of judges Dept. of Liberal Arts, Chicago Expn.; speaker World's Parliament of Religions, 1893. Author: Biography of James Eddy, with Memorial Address; The Care of Dependent, Neglected and Wayward Children (Report of the Second Section International Congress of Charities, Corrections and Philanthropy), 1894; Order of Service for Public Worship, 1896; Bell St. Chapel Discourses; History of Bell St. Chapel Movement, 1889-1902; Woman's Share in Social Culture, 1913; The Family and Its Members, 1922. Mem. bds. of Free Religious Assn., Federation Religious Liberals, Woman's Council U.S.A.; mem. Am. Sociol. Soc., Am. Social Hygiene Assn., Am. Conf. Social Work, Nat. Inst. Social Sciences. Spl. lecturer in social science, Teachers Coll. (Columbia), 1920-28. Address: New York, N.Y. Died Feb. 12, 1931.

SPENCER, Bunyan, educator; b. nr. Coshocton, O., July 16, 1854; s. Joseph C. and Jane (Fitz) S.; A.B., Denison U., 1879, A.M., 1882; instr. Greek and Latin, Denison, 1879-82; B.D., Bapt. Union Theol. Sem., Chicago, 1885; D.D., Colgate, 1922; m. Emily J. Gear, Aug. 28, 1884; children—Gladys, William Gear, Cornelia (Mrs. William Lee Smith), Eudora (Mrs. S. M. Braswell), Emily (wife of Rev. Roy B. Deer), Herman Gear. Ordained Bapt. ministry, 1885; pastor Hamilton Sq. Ch., San Francisco, Calif., 1885-88, Emanuel Ch., San Jose, Calif., 1889-90; pres. Bapt. Pastors' Conf. of Calif., 1885-86; pres. Interdenominational S.S. Conv. of Calif., 1887-88; pres. Calif. Bapt. Conv., 1887-88, 1889-90; sec. trustees Calif. Coll., 1887-90; v.p. and prof. Greek, Calif. Coll., East Oakland, 1890-94; pastor Alexandria (O.) Bapt. Ch., 1894-1902; mem. faculty, Denison U., 1902-29, prof. philosophy, dean, 1925-29, acting pres., 1925-27, also trustee and sec. bd., 1900-02. Trustee Ohio Bapt. Edn. Soc., 1895-1925, treas., 1908-25, corr. sec., 1911-18; trustee Shepardson Coll., 1897-1902. Pres. Granville Pub. Library Assn., 1917-22; pres. Ohio Bapt. Edn. Soc., 1925-28, later trustee. Republican. Author: Science of Reasoning, 1908. Home: Granville, O. Died July 6, 1932.

SPENCER, Claudius Buchanan, editor; b. Fowlerville, Mich., Oct. 20, 1856; s. Henry Norman and Electa J. (Brown) S.; A.B., Northwestern U., 1881, A.M., 1887, D.D., 1931; D.D., Lawrence, 1897; Litt.D., U. of Denver, 1902; LL.D., Neb. Wesleyan U., 1905; L.H.D., Oklahoma City Coll., 1923; studied in British Museum, 1914; m. Mary L. Mitchell, Oct. 20, 1886; children—Helen Mitchell, Mrs. Marjorie Elizabeth Frank, Mrs. Mildred Isabel Roper. Entered M.E. Ministry, 1881; pastor on Lake Superior, 1881-83, Detroit, 1883-87, Owosso, Mich., 1887-90, Detroit, 1890-92, Denver, 1892-96; mem. Colo. Conf., 1892—; editor Rocky Mountain Christian Advocate, 1892-1900, and Central Christian Advocate, Kansas City, 1900-32. Prohibition nominee for gov. of Colo., 1896. Sec. of conf. which organized Epworth League, 1889; del. Inter-Ch. Conf. on Federation, 1905; mem. bd. mgrs. Freedmen's Aid and Southern Edn. Soc., 1906-08; mem. Gen. Conf., 1908, 12; mem. com. on Ecumenical Conference, Toronto, 1908-11; mem. Ecumenical Conferences, London, Eng., 1921, Atlanta, Ga., 1931; asso. sec. organization of Federal Council of Churches of Christ, 1908; del. to World's Missionary Conf., Edinburgh, 1910; incorporator and mem. exec. com. Temperance Soc. of M.E. Ch., 1912-16; del. Internat. Congress for Promotion Arbitration; mem. Ch. Conf. on Internat. Peace, Constance, 1914; mem. nat. exec. com. of Anti-Saloon League America, 1917-26; unofficial rep. of M.E. Ch. at orgn. of M.E. Ch. of Mexico, Mexico City, 1930. Author: Blue Flower of Methodism, 1903; Easter Reflections, 1909; The Layman, 1912; That They May Be One, 1915. Home: Kansas City, Mo. Died July 14, 1934.

SPENCER, Corwin H., capitalist; b. Morgan County, O., Dec. 13, 1851; s. David and Angeline (Israel) S.; ed. country schs., Malta (O.) High Sch., and business coll.; m. Mary E. Harlow. Taught schs. in country dists., 1870-72; clerk in gen. store, McConnellsville, O., 1872-74; bookkeeper, salesman and later partner in grain firm, and later head of C. H. Spencer Grain and Elevator Co.; turned attention especially to elec. ry. interests, and was v.p. United Rys. Co., and St. Louis Transfer Co.; sr. mem. C. H. Spencer & Son, brokers; v.p. Mercantile Trust Co. Mem. St. Louis Merchants' Exchange (pres. 1896); 1st v.p. La. Purchase Expn. Republican. Presbyn. Residence: St. Louis, Mo. Died 1906.

SPENCER, Edgar A., judge; b. Cherry Valley, N.Y., Nov. 23, 1847; s. William D. and Mahitable P. (Glazier) S.; ed. Cherry Valley Acad. and Cooperstown Sem., N.Y.; m. Frances B. Hosmer, Sept. 1879. Admitted to bar, 1875, and practiced at Gloversville; city atty., 1879-82; mem. N.Y. Constl. Conv., 1895; state city commn., 1895; justice

Supreme Ct. of N.Y., 4th Dist., 1901-15. Republican. Address: Gloversville, N.Y. Died 1911.

SPENCER, Francis Marion, educator; b. Cedarville, O., Feb. 24, 1842; s. James and Nancy (Guthrie) S.; A.B., Westminster Coll., 1868; grad. Xenia (O.) Theol. Sem., 1871; D.D., Muskingum Coll., 1886; m. Ella Anderson, Nov. 2, 1871. Ordained U.P. ministry, 1871; pastor Leavenworth, Kan., 1871-79; pres. Muskingum Coll., 1879-86; pastor Norwich, O., 1886-89; pres. Cooper Coll., Sterling, Kan., 1889-1909 (resigned); also teaching and preaching during same period; pres. emeritus and financial agt., Cooper Coll., July 1, 1909—. Prohibitionist. Address: Sterling, Kan. Died Feb. 7, 1930.

SPENCER, George Hazelton, clergyman; b. Newbury, Vt., Aug. 17, 1866; s. Hazelton A. and Lydia (Hutton) S.; prep. edn., Montpelier Sem., 1881-85; Boston U., 1886-92; D.D., Norwich U., 1920; m. Rosetta Munroe, June 7, 1892; children—Hazelton, Marian Louise, Dorothy (dec.), Margaret (Mrs. Oscar L. Marble), Charlotte (Mrs. Warren H. Bateman), Rhoda. Ordained M.E. Ch., 1890; pastor Methuen, Mass., 1890-93, Somersworth, N.H., 1894-97, Newton Center, Mass., 1898-1901, Saratoga St. Ch., Boston, 1902-04, Everett, 1905-10; supt. Cambridge dist., 1911, Worcester, 1912; pastor Upham Memorial Ch., Boston, 1913-16, Greenwood Memorial Ch., Boston, 1917-18; corr. sec. Mass. Bible Soc., 1919—. Mem. Gen. Conf. M.E. Ch., 1924, 28, 32; mem. World Service Commn. M.E. Ch. Trustee Wesley Foundation, Harvard, N.E. Deaconess Hosp., Mass. Bible Soc.; dir. Ministers' Mut. Life Ins. Co., Gen. Theol. Library. Mem. Nat. Assn. for Advancement of Colored People (v.p. Boston br.). Home: Cambridge, Mass. Died Feb. 9, 1936.

SPENCER, Guilford Lawson, chemist; b. Lafayette, Ind., Dec. 21, 1858; s. Israel and Helen Virginia (Shipley) S.; B.S., Purdue U., 1879 (D.Sc., 1893), M.S., U. of Mich., 1882; m. Emma Louise Fiske, Sept. 11, 1888. Chief chemist, Magnolia Plantation, 1884-93, Chaparra Sugar Co., 1903, Nicaragua Sugar Estates, Ltd., 1898-1905, Cuban-American Sugar Co., 1906—. Author: A Handbook for Cane-Sugar Manufacturers and Their Chemists, 1899 (Spanish edit. 1917); A Handbook for Beet Sugar Chemists, 1897. Home: Herricks, Me. Died Mar. 23, 1925.

SPENCER, Horatio Nelson, otologist; b. Port Gibson, Miss., July 17, 1842; s. Horatio Nelson and Sarah (Marshall) S.; A.B., U. of Ala., 1862; pvt. Cowan's battery, Loring's div., C.S.A., 1862-65; M.D., Coll. Phys. and Surg. (Columbia), 1869; U. of Berlin, 1869-70; A.M., Southwestern Presbyn. U., Tenn., 1880; LL.D., Westminster, Mo., 1897; m. Anna Kirtland, Sept. 28, 1868; m. 2d, Lilla P. Dwight, July 6, 1887. In practice at St. Louis, 1870—; prof. diseases of the ear, Washington U., 1881-1911. A founder, 1879, editor, 1879-83, American Journal Otology. Address: St. Louis, Mo. Died Aug. 7, 1915.

SPENCER, J. W. (Joseph William Winthrop), geologist; b. Dundas, Ont., Can., Mar. 26, 1851; s. Joseph and Eliza Eleanor (Coe) S.; B.A.Sc., McGill U., Montreal, 1874; A.M., Ph.D., Univ. of Göttingen, 1877; LL.D., from U. of Ala., 1913, from U. of Manitoba, 1919; m. Katherine Sinclair Thomson, 1896. Science master, Collegiate Inst., Hamilton, Ont., 1877-80; prof. geology and chemistry, King's Coll., 1880-82; prof. geology, U. of Mo., 1882-87; state geologist of Ga., 1888-93; geologist, W.I., 1894-1904; spl. commr. Geol. Survey Can., 1905-08. First to show the Great Lake basins due to stream (not glacial) erosion, and to discover buried channels between them; also to describe and name their four great glacial ancestors (Lakes Warren, Algonquin, Lundy, and Iroquois); by scientific measurements, was first to investigate physical changes and determine age of Niagara Falls (39,000 ± 4,000 yrs.); demonstrated present stability of lake region, after measuring late maximum deformation and its direction; correlating these earth movements with anomalies of gravity and submarine canyons off the coast, demonstrated recent great changes of level of land and sea. "Founder of the scientific history of the Great Lakes; discoverer of the evolution of the Falls of Niagara; founder of the science of submarine valleys"; founder Mus. Historic Geology, U. of Manitoba. Author reports on Georgia, Reconstruction of the Antillean Continent, Evolution of the Falls of Niagara, History of the Great Lakes, Age of the Shores of Lake Ontario and the Modern St. Lawrence River, and many papers in scientific jours. relating to above subjects. Fellow Geol. Soc. London, Geol. Soc. America, A.A.A.S. Address: Washington, D.C. Died Oct. 9, 1921.

SPENCER, James Clark, lawyer; b. Ft. Covington, Franklin County, N.Y., May 29, 1826; ed. there; admitted to bar, 1848; U.S. atty. for Northern dist. of N.Y. under President Buchanan; removed to New York, Jan. 1, 1865; elected judge of the Superior Ct. of New York, Nov. 1870; was aqueduct commr. and pres. of the commn. for 5 yrs.; later asst. corporation counsel, New York. For many years one of the reporters of the Supreme Ct. and (with Hon. Samuel Jones), edited and issued 35 vols. Superior Court Reports. Home: New York, N.Y. Died 1901.

SPENCER, John R., M.D., surgeon; b. Washington County, O., Aug. 27, 1854; s. Albaness and Perlina (Dye) S.; student Marietta Coll., 1877-78; M.D., Eclectic Med. Coll., Cincinnati, O., 1881; M.D., Cincinnati Med. Coll., 1896; m. Eliza Becker, Mar. 27, 1883. Began practice at Stanleyville, O., 1881; settled in Cincinnati, 1897; prof. obstetrics, Eclectic Med. Coll., 1910-23. Republican. Baptist. Mason, K.P. Home: Cincinnati, O. Deceased.

SPENCER, John Wesley, judge; b. Mt. Vernon, Ind., Mar. 7, 1864; s. Elijah M. and Mary (Morse) S.; ed. high sch. and Central Normal Sch., Danville, Ind.; m. Lillie L. Lichtenberger, Dec. 12, 1885; children—Alethea L., John W. Began practice in Evansville, Ind., 1885; mem. firm Spencer & Brill, later Spencer, Brill & Hatfield; pros. atty. 1st Ind. Jud. Circuit, 1891-95. Dem. nominee for Congress, 1902; judge Vandersburgh Circuit Ct., 1911; chief justice Supreme Ct. of Ind., 1912-19; later operating Spencer's Law Offices. Interested in farming, stock raising and banking. Presbyn. Mason, K.P. Home: Evansville, Ind. Died June 28, 1939.

SPENCER, Lorillard; b. New York, Feb. 14, 1860; s. Lorillard and Sarah J. (Griswold) S.; ed. in Europe, and Columbia Coll. Law Sch.; m. Caroline S. Berryman, g.d. Stephen Whitney, Oct. 3, 1882. Spent much time in foreign travel; commr. from R.I. to Chicago Expn. Republican. Proprietor and publisher The Illustrated American. Home: Newport, R.I. Died Mar. 14, 1912.

SPENCER, Lorillard, aircraft mfr.; b. N.Y. City, July 4, 1883; s. Lorillard and Caroline Suydam (Berryman) S.; prep. edn., St. Paul's Sch., Concord, N.H.; student Columbia; m. Mary R. Sands, Sept. 19, 1905 (divorced); 1 son, Lorillard; m. 2d, Katherine Emmons Force, Dec. 6, 1922; children—Katherine Talmage Lorillard, Stephen Wolcott, William H. Force. With Pedersen Manufacturing Co., 1907-10, Colo. Fruit Products Co., 1913-14; pres. Somma Shops, Inc., 1913-25; pres. Austral Window Co., 1913-29; pres. Panama Engring. Co., 1914-16; dir. Advocate Realty Co., 1916-17; pres. Wittemann Aircraft Corp., 1921-22; pres. Atlantic Aircraft Corp., 1923-28; pres. Sixty-Third Street Corp., Fokker Aircraft Corp. of America, 1927-28, Aviation Consolidated, Inc., Color Pictures, Inc.; dir. Austral Sales Corp. Member Squadron A, N.Y. Cavalry, 1909-12; 2d lieutenant C.A.C. N.Y.N.G., 1912, 1st lieutenant, 1913, capt. 1915; lt. col. inf., N.Y.N.G., 1916, maj., 1917; mil. sec. to gov. of N.Y., 1915-17; served as maj. inf., U.S.A., World War I; received citations for Distinguished Service Cross (U.S.), Croix de Guerre and Cross of Legion of Honor (France) for "extraordinary heroism in action in Champagne sector on Sept. 26, 1918." Mem. bd. mgrs. Am. Soc. for Prevention of Cruelty to Animals; mem. bd. govs. and hon. scout commr., Manhattan Council Boy Scouts of America (one of founders of movement in U.S.); trustee French Inst. in U.S. and Moro Ednl. Foundation. Republican. Episcopalian. Mason. Home: New York, N.Y. Died June 9, 1939.

SPENCER, Oliver Martin, lawyer; b. in Buchanan County, Mo., Aug. 23, 1849; s. Obadiah Martin and Nancy (Williams) S.; A.B., Christian U., Canton, Mo., 1873; Harvard Law Sch., 1874-75; m. Lillian Tootle, 1876 (died 1880); m. 2d, Katherine Turner, Mar. 5, 1895. Began practice at St. Joseph, Mo., 1875; elected pros. atty., 1880; judge Circuit Court, 1887-91 (resigned); gen. solicitor Mo. lines till 1917; gen. counsel, 1917—, C.B.&Q. R.R. Democrat. Address: Chicago, Ill. Died June 5, 1924.

SPENCER, Paul, elec. engr.; b. East Orange, N.J., Mar. 19, 1866; s. George Gilman and Caroline (Arnold) S.; A.B., Yale, 1887; M.E., Stevens Inst. Tech., 1891; m. Frances Margaret Durbin, Apr. 25, 1894; children—Frederick Gilman, Frances Margaret (Mrs. Archibald G. Roberson), Caroline (dec.). With Field Engring. Co. of New York, 1891-94, Stanley Elec. Mfg. Co., Pittsfield, Mass., 1894-97; gen. supt. People's Light & Power Co., Newark, N.J., 1897-1900; elec. engr. with United Gas Improvement Co., Phila., 1900—. Republican. Unitarian. Home: Philadelphia, Pa. Died Aug. 9, 1927.

SPENCER, Robert, landscape painter; b. Harvard, Neb., Dec. 1, 1879; s. Solomon Hoag and Francis (Strickler) S.; student Nat. Acad. Design, New York, 1899-1901; New York Sch. of Art, 1903-05; pupil of Chase, DuMond, Henri, Garber, Francis Jones and Louis Mora; m. Margaret A. Fulton, Feb. 27, 1914; children—Margaret Fulton, Ann Harrison. Exhibited at prin. exhbns. in U.S., Toronto, Can., London and Paris; represented in permanent collections of Nat. Acad. Design, Nat. Arts Club, Salmagundi Club, Met. Mus., New York; Boston Art Club; Detroit Mus. of Art; Art Inst. Chicago; Nat. Corcoran Gallery; Phillips Memorial Art Gallery, Washington; Carnegie Inst. and Pittsburgh Athletic Club; Union League Club, Chicago; Albright Art Gallery, Buffalo; Brooks Memorial Art Gallery, Memphis; Newark (N.J.) Mus. Association; Art Club, Phila.; Wilmington (Delaware) Society of Fine Arts; also in permanent collection of Brooklyn Museum. Awards: 2d Hallgarten prize, N.A.D., 1913; hon. mention Art Club of Phila., 1913; Jenny Sesnan gold medal, Pa. Acad. Fine Arts, 1914; George Inness gold medal, N.A.D., 1914; gold medal and $1,000 purchase prize, Boston Art Club, 1915; gold medal, Panama, P.I. Expn., 1915; Norman Wait Harris bronze medal and $300 prize, Art Inst. Chicago, 1919; 2d Altman prize, $500, Nat. Acad., 1920 and 1921; hon. mention, Carnegie Inst., Pittsburgh, 1920; Salmagundi Club purchase prize, 1921; Mrs. W. K. du Pont landscape prize, Wilmington Soc. Fine Arts, 1921; gold medal, Sesquicentennial Expn., Phila., 1926; 3d prize, Carnegie Inst. Internat. Exhbn., Pittsburgh 1926; Isidor gold medal, N.A.D., 1928; gold medal, Art Club of Phila., 1929. A.N.A., 1914, N.A., 1920. Mem. Allied Artists of America. Home: New Hope, Pa. Died July 10, 1931.

SPENCER, Samuel, ry. mgr.; b. Columbus, Ga., Mar. 2, 1847; s. Lambert and Vernona (Mitchell) S.; grad. U. of Ga., 1867, and U. of Va., 1869; m. Louisa Vivian, d. Hon. H. L. Benning, Feb. 1872. Pres. B.&O. R.R. Co., 1887-88; receiver Richmond & Danville R.R. Co., 1893-97; East Tenn., Va. & Ga. Ry. Co., 1893-96; rapid transit commr., New York, 1891-94; pres. and dir. Ala. Great Southern R.R. Co., Cincinnati, New Orleans and Texas Pacific Ry. Co., Ga. Southern & Florida Ry. Co., Mobile & Ohio R.R. Co., Southern Ry. Co., and dir. Central of Ga. Ry. Co.; Chicago, Milwaukee & St. Paul Ry. Co., Erie R.R. Co., N. Pacific Ry. Co. and other corporations. Home: Washington, D.C. Died 1906.

SPENCER, Sara Andrews, prin. Spencerian Business Coll.; b. (Andrews) Savona, Steuben County, N.Y., Oct. 21, 1837; grad. Normal School, St. Louis, 1856; m. Henry C. Spencer, 1864. Removed to Washington. With 72 other women attempted to register and vote, 1871, but was refused. Brought suit with result that the Supreme Court of D.C., 1871, and Supreme Court of U.S., 1874, decided that women were citizens but could not vote without local enabling legislation; defeated pending bills to license the "social evil" in Washington, 1872-74; secured passage of bill by D.C. legislature, 1873, for rescue of outcast girls; sec. Nat. Woman Suffrage Assn., 1874-81; pres. Woman Franchise Assn. of D.C., 1871-76; sec. Am. Red Cross D.C. Auxiliary Assn., 1887-92; mem. Acad. Sciences, Am. Social Science Assn., Nat. Geog. Soc., N.E.A., Nat. Conf. Charities and corrections; one of founders Nat. Homœ. Hosp. and trustee 14 yrs. Engrossed the Woman's Declaration of Rights, and with Susan B. Anthony and three other women presented it to the officers of the Centennial Celebration of the Declaration of Independence at Phila., July 4, 1876; first woman to address a nat. presdl. conv., Chicago, 1876, asked for a plank in Rep. platform pledging itself to prohibit disfranchisement on account of sex. Author: Problems on the Woman Question; Thirty Lessons in the English Language. Address: New York, N.Y. Died 1909.

SPENCER, Selden Palmer, senator; b. Erie, Pa., Sept. 16, 1862; s. Samuel Selden and Eliza Deborah (Palmer) S.; A.B., Yale, 1884; LL.B., Washington U., 1886, M.A., 1892, Ph.D., 1896; hon. M.D., Mo. Med. Coll., 1896; LL.D., Westminster, 1909; m. Susan M. Brookes, Dec. 8, 1886. In practice at St. Louis, 1886—. Mem. Mo. Ho. of Rep., 1895-96; judge 8th Jud. Circuit of Mo., 1897-1903; received 64 votes for U.S. senator from Republicans in Mo. legislature, 1905; elected, 1918, to U.S. Senate to fill unexpired term, ending Mar. 3, 1921, of William J. Stone, deceased; reëlected Nov. 1920, for term expiring March 1927. Mem. Am. Bar Assn. (exec. com. 1915-17), Mo. Bar Assn. (pres. 1898), N.E. Soc. (pres. 1905), S.R. (pres. St. Louis Chapter, 1915; pres. gen., 1922-25). Republican. Presbyn. Pres. Internat. Y.M.C.A. Conv., 1907. Chmn. Dist. Exemption Bd., 1917; capt. and adj. 1st Regt., Mo. Home Guard, St. Louis. Home: St. Louis, Mo. Died May 16, 1925.

SPENCER, Walker Brainerd, lawyer; b. Natchez, Miss., Mar. 13, 1868; s. William Brainerd and Henrietta (Elam) S.; A.B., Tulane U., 1888, LL.B., 1891; studied law, U. of Virginia; m. Annie Cooley Clark, Dec. 15, 1891. Mem. firm of Spencer, Phelps, Dunbar & Marks, counsel for Tex. Pacific Railway Co., United Fruit Co., Western Union Telegraph Co., Hibernia National Bank, etc. Chmn. com. of Citizens' League, 1896, that framed charter for City of New Orleans; author of banking, corporation and ins. laws of La.; active in municipal reform movements. Mem. bd. adminstrs. Tulane Ednl. Fund. Independent Democrat. Episcopalian. Home: New Orleans, La. Died Mar. 15, 1941.

SPENCER, William Vaughan, publisher; b. Versailles Pike, Lexington, Ky., Apr. 23, 1899; s. Joseph and Julia (Vaughan) S.; student U. of Louisville, 1919-20; Ph.B., Yale, 1926; student Harvard Law Sch., 1927-28; m. Evelyn Lucile McGowin, Nov. 6, 1937; 1 son, William Vaughan, 2d. Brought up on a farm; served in U.S. Army, 1918; salesman, 1920-21; mfr. of Cakes, Charleston, W.Va., 1921-34, pres. and pub. Kentucky Farmers Home Jour., 1934—. Mem. Assn. Am. Agrl. Editors (sec.-treas., 1938—). Chancery Club of Cambridge, Mass. Baptist. Mason. Home: Louisville, Ky. Died Oct. 16, 1940.

SPENS, Conrad E., ry. official; b. Princeton, Ill., Aug. 14, 1875; ed. pub. schs. and business coll.; m. Edna Louise Keeline, Oct. 23, 1909; children—Jean, Conrad Keeline, Gordon. Began as stenographer in local frt. office, C.,B.&Q. Ry. Co., at Chicago, Feb. 22, 1892, and continued with that rd. successively as corr. clk. gen. frt. office, chief clk. to asst. gen. frt. agt., and chief clk. to traffic mgr. until 1903, asst. gen. frt. agt., 1903-05; gen. frt. agt. Lines West of Mo. River, at Omaha, Neb., 1905-12; asst. frt. traffic mgr., Chicago, 1912-17; v.p. C.,B.&Q. Ry. in charge of traffic, 1917-29; exec. v.p. same rd., also Colo. & Southern Lines, Jan. 1, 1929—; apptd. dir. transportation, U.S. Food Adminstrn., Feb. 18, 1918; apptd. asst. dir. of traffic, U.S. Railroad Adminstrn., Feb. 10, 1919, also mgr. inland traffic for U.S. wheat dir., July 1, 1919. V.p. in charge of traffic C.,B.&Q. R.R., Mar. 1, 1920—. Federal fuel distributor, Sept. 22, 1922-Jan. 1, 1923; v.p. C.&S. Ry. Co., June 1, 1927—. Republican. Episcopalian. Home: Chicago, Ill. Died Aug. 14, 1931.

SPENZER, John George, chemist, M.D.; b. Cleveland, O., Sept. 6, 1864; s. Peter Ignatius and Mary Theresa (Molloy) S.; student Cleveland High Sch., 1879; M.D., Western Reserve U., 1884; grad. student Adelbert Coll. (Western Reserve U.), 1884-87; Ph.D., U. of Strassburg, 1893; m. Minnie Elizabeth Kittelberger, June 15, 1898; children—John Calvin, Caroline. Assistant in chemistry, medical dept., Western Reserve U., 1880-84; research chem. student, Columbus, O., 1888-91; engaged in research in med. chemistry and pharmacology, Strassburg, Alsace, Germany, 1893-94; practical sch. medicine, Paris, France, 1894, instr. pharmacology, Western Reserve Med. Sch., and prof. chemistry, Dental Sch., 1894-96; med. chem. research, U. of Berne, Switzerland, 1895; prof. gen. and med. chemistry and pharmacology, Cleveland Coll. Phys. and Surg. (med. dept. Ohio Wesleyan U.), 1896-1910; prof. chemistry, legal chemistry and medical jurisprudence, Western Reserve U., 1910-17. Fellow Chemical Soc., Eng.; mem. Berlin Chem. Soc., Philomatic Soc., Alsace-Lorraine; fellow A.A.A.S. Author: The Principles of Pharmacology, with Practical Exercises, 1899. Home: Cleveland, O. Died 1932.

SPERANZA, Gino, lawyer; b. Conn., Apr. 23, 1872; s. Prof. Carlo L. and Adele (Capelli) S.; B.S., Coll. City of New York, 1892, M.S., 1895; LL.B., New York Law Sch., 1894; m. Florence Colgate, July 16, 1909. Practiced, New York, 1895—; gen. legal adviser to Royal Consulate Gen. of Italy, in New York, for 15 yrs.; as mem. Law Com. of Prison Assn. of N.Y. assisted in drafting probation law of N.Y. State. Apptd. by Gov. Hughes as mem. State Immigration Commn.; spl. agt. Royal Italian Embassy to investigate labor camp troubles in West Va., 1906. Served as dir. Prison Assn. of N.Y. Soc. for Italian Immigrants; chmn. Com. on Crime and Immigration of Am. Inst. Criminal Law. Volunteered his services to U.S. Govt. and assigned as asst. to mil. attaché of Am. Embassy at Rome; later attaché of Embassy, in Polit. Intelligence Div.; spl. corr. in Italy for the Outlook and New York Evening Post; reached highest altitude of any Am. corr., climbing to Lobbia Alta, 11,397 ft. Author: Race or Nation, 1925. Contbr. to Atlantic Monthly, World's Work, Outlook, etc. Home: Irvington, N.Y. Died July 12, 1927.

SPERR, Frederick William, mining engr.; b. Jefferson, O., June 5, 1856; s. Michael and Christine (Benighoff) S.; ed. Madison Sem., O., 1873-75; Ohio State U., 1879-81 and 1882-83; m. Julia S. Loomis, Aug. 10, 1884; children—Frederick William, Julian Dana, Percy Loomis, Donald (dec.), Harold George, Raymond, Bertram (dec.). Spl. agt. 10th Census, on bldg. stone investigation, 1881-82; engineer for Mining Stock Trust Co., Ariz., 1883-84, and supt. its successor, the Garden Springs Mining Corp., 1885-88; asst. prof. mining engring., Ohio State U., 1888-94; prof. civ. and mining engring., Mich. Coll. of Mines, 1894-1926; mining research, Mich. Coll. of Mining and Tech., 1926—. Consulting engr. and mining expert, 1888—, in mining states of the West, also Mexico, Ont. and B.C. Republican. Baptist. Author: Notes on Mine Surveying, 1895; Notes on Mine Accounting, 1895; Notes on Mining Engineering, 1895; Classification of Methods of Mining, 1917; revisions of same, also contbr. on tech. and ednl. topics. Home: Houghton, Mich. Died Nov. 19, 1929.

SPERRY, Charles Stillman, rear admiral U.S.N.; b. Brooklyn, Sept. 3, 1847; s. Corydon Stillman and Catherine Elizabeth (Leavenworth) S.; grad. U.S. Naval Acad., 1866; LL.D., Yale, 1909; m. Edith, g.d. Gov. William L. Marcy, of N.Y., Jan. 11, 1877. Ensign, Mar. 12, 1868; master, Mar. 26, 1869; lt., Mar. 21, 1870; lt. comdr., Mar. 1, 1885; comdr., June 22, 1894; capt., July 1, 1900; rear admiral, May 26, 1906; retired, Sept. 3, 1909. Pres. U.S. Naval War Coll. and mem. Gen. Bd. U.S.N., 1903; mem. Nat. Coast Defense Bd., 1905; comd. Atlantic Battleship Fleet on cruise around the world, 1908-09. Del. Geneva Conf. for Revision of Geneva Conv. for Treatment of Sick and Wounded, June 1906; del. 2d Hague Conf., June, 1907. Home: Waterbury, Conn. Died 1911.

SPERRY, Earl Evelyn, prof. European History; b. Jordan, N.Y., Feb. 19, 1875; s. Dwight Andrew and Medora Evelyn (Barr) S.; Ph.B., Syracuse U., 1898, Ph.D., Columbia, 1903; unmarried. Prof. history, later European history and civic edn., Syracuse U., 1902-37, except 2 yrs. as mem. faculty U. of Chicago. Retired from the Univ. and from teaching, 1937. Episcopalian; pres. of P.E. Church League. Mason. Wrote: (brochures) History of Clerical Celibacy, 1903; The Tentacles of the German Octopus (Nat. Security League), 1917; Pan-Germanism (same), 1918; German Plots and Intrigues in the United States (Com. on Pub. Information), 1918. Asso. editor The Chronicle (Poughkeepsie). Home: Syracuse, N.Y. Died Oct. 7, 1939.

SPERRY, Elmer Ambrose, elec. engr.; b. Cortland, N.Y., Oct. 12, 1860; s. Stephen Decatur and Mary (Burst) S.; student State Normal and Training Sch., Cortland, N.Y., 1876-79; Cornell U., 1879-80; E.D., Stevens, 1921, Lehigh, 1927; Sc.D., Northwestern, 1925; m. Zula A., d. Edward Goodman, June 28, 1887; children—Mrs. Helen Marguerite Lea, Edward Goodman, Lawrence Burst (dec.), Elmer Ambrose. Founder, 1880, Sperry Electric Co., Chicago, mfrs. arc lamps, dynamos, etc.; founder Sperry Electric Ry. Co., mfrs. cars, Cleveland, O. (sold to Gen. Electric Co., New York, 1894); inventor of gyro-compass, aeroplane and ship stabilizers, highest intensity searchlight (1½ billion candle power), compound internal combustion engine, fire control apparatus, gyro track recorder, transverse fissure detector, and numerous special devices, principally for the U.S. Navy; pres. Sperry Gyroscope Co., Brooklyn, 1910-26, chmn. bd., 1926-29; pres. Sperry Development Co., Inc.; mfg. own inventions, 1910. Erected 350-foot electric beacon on Lake Michigan in 1883; also invented 1st electric chain mining machine, 1888; devised detinning and electrochem. processes and machinery for making fuse wires; designed electric automobile; held over 400 patents issued in U.S. and Europe. Member Naval Consulting Board, 1915— (chmn. coms. on aeronautics, mines and torpedoes, aids to navigation). Awards: First prize, Aero Club of France, 1914; Franklin medal, Philadelphia, 1914; grand prize for gyro-compass and gyroscopes, San Francisco Expn., 1915; Collier trophy, 1915, for drift set, 1916; Scientific Am. medal, Am. Mus. of Safety; also awarded John Fritz medal in 1927, Holley medal, 1927; Franklin Inst. medal, 1929; Am. Iron and Steel Inst. medal, 1930. Decorated by Czar Nicholas of Russia for navigation equipment; decorated by Emperor of Japan with Order of Rising Sun, and Order of Sacred Treasure. Mem. Am. Inst. E.E. (a founder), Am. Electrochem. Soc. (a founder), Nat. Acad. Science, Nat. Research Council (chmn. div. engring. and industrial research, 1928-30); chmn. Am. Com. World Engring. Congress, Tokyo, 1929. Author numerous papers and addresses. Died June 16, 1930.

SPERRY, Lyman Beecher, lecturer; b. Sherman, N.Y., Feb. 19, 1841; s. Henry W. and Harriet (Williams) S.; student Oberlin Coll., 1860-63 hon. A.M., 1883; in Union Army (civilian service), 1864-65; M.D., U. of Mich., 1867; practiced, 1867-68; traveled and studied, 1868-69; m. Rosalie Harris, of Bellevue, O., July 21, 1870. Prof. physical sciences, Ripon (Wis.) Coll., 1869-73; agt. of U.S. to Arickaree, Gros Ventre, and Mandan Indians, 1873-75; prof. geology, chemistry and physiology, Carleton Coll., Minn., 1875-84, non-resident lecturer on sanitary science, 1884-1904. Pub. lecturer on ednl. and gen. themes, 1886—. During summers 1894-1906 camped, climbed and explored in Mont. Rockies, particularly in the region since set apart by Congress and named "Glacier Nat. Park"; Sperry Glacier, Sperry Glacier Basin and Sperry Chalets named in his honor. Author: Concerning Narcotics; Confidential Talks with Young Men, 1892; Confidential Talks with Young Women, 1893; Husband and Wife, 1900; Physiology, Fear and Faith, 1902; also pamphlets and newspaper articles. Address: Los Angeles, Calif. Died July 1, 1923.

SPERRY, Nehemiah Day, congressman; b. Woodbridge, New Haven County, Conn., July 10, 1827; s. Enoch and Mary Atlanta S.; common sch. edn.; learned trade of house builder; began business on own account, 1847; m. Eliza H. Sperry, 1847; m. 2d, Minnie B. Newton, Dec. 3, 1874. Mem. Common Council, 1853, alderman, 1854, New Haven; sec. of state, Conn., 1855, 56; postmaster, New Haven, 1861-85, 1889-93; del. Rep. Nat. Conv., 1864; sec. Rep. Nat. Com., and Rep. Nat. Exec. Com., 1864; pres. Rep. State Conv., 1868; nominated for Congress 1884, but declined; mem. 54th to 61st Congresses (1895-1911), 2d Conn. Dist. Pres. New Haven Chamber of Commerce, 1896-97. Address: New Haven, Conn. Died 1911.

SPERRY, Watson Robertson, newspaperman; b. Saquoit, Oneida County, N.Y., June 25, 1842; s. Rev. Lyman and Amanda K. (Robertson) S.; entered printing office at 15; became editorial writer at 21 for Otsego Republican, Cooperstown, N.Y.; A.B., Yale, 1871; m. Anna Marie Lippold, Feb. 5, 1913. On staff, 1871, managing editor, 1875-81, New York Evening Post; propr. and editor Wilmington (Del.) News, 1882-1900; U.S. minister resident to Persia, 1892-93; editorial writer, 1901-09, foreign corr., 1909-11, editorial writer and stockholder, 1911-18, Hartford Courant. Address: Hartford, Conn. Died Feb. 13, 1926.

SPEYER, James, banker; b. N.Y. City, July 22, 1861; ed. at Frankfort-on-the-Main, Germany; LL.D., Lincoln Memorial U.; hon. mem. Univ. of Frankfort-on-the-Main; m. Mrs. John A. Lowery (nee Ellin L. Prince) d. late John Dyneley and Mary (Travers) Prince, Nov. 11, 1897 (died 1921). Entered family's banking house at Frankfort-on-the-Main at age 22; later transferred to Paris and London to enlarge banking experience before returning to New York to become partner of New York banking house of Speyer & Co. (founded 1837), sr. partner, 1899-1939 (co. discontinued business); officer or dir. many cos.; trustee Teachers College, 1900-32, to which in 1902, in Mrs. Speyer's and own name presented the Speyer Sch.; trustee, a founder in 1894 and pres., Provident Loan Soc. Hon. pres. Council of Univ. Settlement Soc.; a founder, 1913, Am. Soc. for Control of Cancer; hon. trustee Mt. Sinai Hosp.; hon. treas. New York Women's League for Animals, Inc.; trustee United Hosp. Fund of New York; trustee Am. Museum of Safety; mem. advisory bd. Salvation Army; founder, 1923, dir. and mem. adv. com. Moderation League; mem. and v.p. New York Division of Assn. Against Prohibition Amendment, 1922; delegate N.Y. State Conv. for Repeal 18th Amendment, 1933; trustee, 1923—, donor and chmn. finance com. Museum City of New York; an incorporator New York World's Fair, 1939, Inc.; mem. "Com. of Seventy," 1894; mem. New York Bd. of Edn., 1897; mem. Real Estate Bd., Chamber of Commerce State of N.Y.; hon. v.p. Pan-American Society, Inc. (awarded gold insignia 1940); dir. New York State Economic Council; mem. bd. govs. Hundred Year Assn. of New York (awarded gold medal 1938). Mem. Plattsburg Training Camp, 1915, Veteran Corps of Artillery Post, 1st Provisional Regt., N.Y.N.G. (hon.; awarded gold insignia, 1939); Legion of Honor, U.S. Flag Assn. (life mem. Order of the Flag); trustee Federal Hall Museum; trustee City History Club. Awarded German Red Eagle, II Class, Hungarian Order of Merit, II Class. Home: New York, N.Y. Died Nov. 1, 1941.

SPEYERS, Arthur Bayard, rear admiral U.S.N.; b. New York, Aug. 15, 1846; s. James and Fanny (Pigot) S.; grad. U.S. Naval Acad., 1868; unmarried. Midshipman U.S.N., 1868; promoted through the various grades to rear admiral and retired, Jan. 11, 1905. Comd. U.S.S. Cæsar in southern blockade of Cuba during Spanish-Am. War. Address: New York, N.Y. Died Nov. 19, 1918.

SPICER, Anne Higginson (Mrs. Vibe K.), author; b. Burlington, Ia.; d. Charles Maynard and Catherine (Nihen) Higginson; grad. Miss Kirkland's Sch., Chicago; studied drawing and perspective, Art Inst. Chicago; m. Vibe Kierulff Spicer, of Boston, Mass., Oct. 18, 1893. Exhibited woodcarving, pottery and metal work at Art Inst. Chicago, and at various arts and crafts exhibits; owner of notable garden at Kenilworth, Ill. Active in war work for Council of Defense, etc.; frequent contbr. to mags. in U.S. and Can., also to Chicago, N.Y. and Boston papers (under name of "Anchusa"); lecturer and reader. Republican. Episcopalian. Author: Songs of the Skokie, 1918; The Last Crusade, 1919; A Cookshire Lad, 1922. Home: Kenilworth, Ill. Died Sept. 9, 1935.

SPICER, Clarence Winfred, mech. engr.; b. West Hallock (now Edelstein), Ill., Nov. 30, 1875; s. John Green and Cornelia (Babcock) S.; student Alfred (N.Y.) U., 1891-94, D.Sc., 1935; student Cornell U., 1900-04; m. Anna Olive Burdick, Dec. 1, 1896; children—Harold Willis, Robert Thurston, John Reed, Wilfred Clarence. Inventor Spicer universal joint, 1902; owner and mfr. Spicer Universal Joints, 1904-05; pres. Spicer Universal Joint Mfg. Co., Plainfield, N.J., 1905-10; pres. Spicer Mfg. Co., Plainfield, 1910-14; pres. Spicer Mfg. Corp., 1914-15, v.p., 1915—, at Toledo, 1930—. Trustee Alfred U. Republican. Baptist. Contbr. articles to engring. jours. Home: Toledo, O. Died Nov. 21, 1939.

SPIEGEL, Frederick Siegfried, lawyer; b. Hovestadt, Prussia, Germany, Nov. 20, 1858; s. Simon and Rosalie (Hersberg) S.; Gymnasium, Paderborn, Germany; grad. Southern Inst., Gadsden, Ala., 1875; LL.B., Cincinnati Law Sch. (U. of Cincinnati), 1880; m. Minna Steinberg, Dec. 19, 1883. Chief of Ohio State Bur. Statistics, 1880-82; mem. Cincinnati Bd. of Edn., 1880-83; solicitor Hamilton County, O., 1890-96; judge Ct. of Common Pleas, 1st Dist., Ohio, 1896-1906; judge Superior Ct. of Cincinnati, 1908-14; mayor of Cincinnati, 1914-16; counsel Bd. of Rapid Transit Commrs., 1916—. Republican. Jewish religion. Mason, Elk. Home: Cincinnati, O. Died Jan. 24, 1925.

SPIEKER, Edward Henry, univ. prof.; b. Baltimore, Apr. 18, 1859; s. Herman Henry and Margaret Elizabeth (Dorges) S.; brother of George Frederick S.; grad. Baltimore City Coll., 1877; A.B., Johns Hopkins, 1879, Ph.D., 1882; m. Adelaide

Marie Maute, July 15, 1891. Fellow in Greek, 1880-82, instr. Greek and Latin, 1882-86, asso. in Greek and Latin, 1886-88, asso. prof., 1888-1915, collegiate professor of Greek, 1915—, Johns Hopkins. Author: Greek Prose Composition, 1904. Contbr. to philol. jours. Home: Baltimore, Md. Died Feb. 2, 1918.

SPIEKER, George Frederick, theologian; b. Howard County, Md., Nov. 17, 1844; s. Herman Henry and Margaret Elizabeth (Dorges) S.; brother of Edward Henry S.; student Baltimore City Coll., 1859-63, Luth. Theol. Sem., Gettysburg, 1863-65; grad. Luth. Theol. Sem., Philadelphia, 1867; D.D., Roanoke Coll., Va., 1887; LL.D., Thiel Coll., Pa., 1911; m. Hannah Hoch, Oct. 12, 1869. Ordained Luth. ministry, 1867. Acting prof. German lang. and lit., Pa. Coll., 1864-66; prof., Keystone Normal Sch., Kutztown, Pa., 1867-68; prof. Hebrew, Muhlenberg Coll., Pa., 1887-94. Pastor Kutztown, 1867-83, Allentown, 1883-94; prof. ch. history, O.T. theology and introduction, Luth. Theol. Sem., Phila., 1894—. Asso. editor Lutheran Church Review. Trustee Muhlenberg Coll. Author: Commentary on II Corinthians, 1897. Monographs: The Evangelical Lutheran Church; Questions on Luther's Small Catechism. Translator: Wildenhahn's Martin Luther. Co-translator: Hutter's Compend of Lutheran Theology. Address: Philadelphia, Pa. Died Sept. 7, 1913.

SPIERING, Theodore, violinist; b. St. Louis, Sept. 5, 1871; s. Ernst and Theresa (Bernays) S.; pub. sch. edn.; studied at Cincinnati Coll. of Music under Henry Schradieck, 1886-88, at Berlin, under Joseph Joachim, 1888-92; m. Frida, d. Wilhelm Mueller, Oct. 2, 1895. Organized, 1893, and leader of the Spiering Quartet, Chicago, 1893-1905; with Thomas Orchestra, 1892-96; dir. Spiering Violin School, 1899-1902; mus. dir. Chicago Mus. Coll., 1902-05; concertizing in Europe, 1905-09; concert master New York Philharmonic Soc., 1909-11, and conductor of final 17 symphony concerts in place of Gustav Mahler, season 1910-11; in Berlin, 1911-14, and mus. adviser of Neue Freie Volksbühne (people's free stage) and conductor of their symphony concerts; in New York, 1914—. Conducted 97 performances of Maeterlinck's Betrothal (music by Delamarter, staged by Winthrop Ames), New York, season 1918-19; Master Class Cornish School, Seattle, Aug. 1921; guest conductor, Berlin and Vienna, Sept. 1923. Mem. Internat. Jury Awards, St. Louis Expn., 1904; Officier d' Académie, France, 1905. Address: New York, N.Y. Died Aug. 11, 1925.

SPIES, Albert, engineer, editor; b. New York, July 20, 1862; s. Peter and Elise (Schuessler) S.; M.E., Stevens Inst. Tech., 1881; m. Gretchen Antonia Weisker, Dec. 23, 1895. In engring. practice and tech. journalism, 1881—; editor The Electrical Record, Jan. 1907—; dir. the Pulsometer Steam Pump Co., New York. Editor: The Life and Inventions of Edison; The Harnessing of Niagara, 1895; also many papers on tech. subjects. Home: Jersey City Heights, N.J. Died 1910.

SPILLER, William Gibson, neurologist; b. Baltimore, Sept. 13, 1863; s. Robert Miles and Anna Augusta (Maltby) S.; M.D., U. of Pa., 1892; Sc.D., U. of Pa., 1934; LL.D., Lafayette, 1934; m. Helen C. Newbold, Jan. 3, 1888; children—Helen Newbold (Mrs. Randolph G. Adams), Robert Ernest, William Raymond, Donald Percival. Asst. clin. prof. nervous diseases and asst. prof. neuropathology, U. of Pa., 1901-03, prof. neuropathology and asso. prof. neurology, 1903-15, prof. of neurology, 1915-32 (emeritus); prof. nervous diseases, Phila. Polyclinic; clin. prof., Woman's Med. Coll. of Pa., 1902-25; hon. consulting neurologist Phila. Gen. Hosp. Mem. Am. Neurol. Assn. (pres. 1905); Phila. Neurol. Soc. (pres.); fellow Coll. Physicians, Phila. Extensive contbr. on neurology. Home: Philadelphia, Pa. Died Mar. 18, 1940.

SPILLMAN, Ora Seldon, lawyer; b. nr. Grinnell, Ia., Mar. 10, 1881; s. James Alexander and Sarah Elizabeth (Vestal) S.; B.Did., Highland Park Coll. (now Des Moines U.), 1902; post-grad. work same coll., 1903-04; LL.B., U. of Neb., 1908; m. Florence Marjorie Parminter, Nov. 27, 1924 (county supt. schs., Pierce County, at time of marriage). Admitted to Neb. bar, 1908, and began practice at Pierce, 1909; county atty. Pierce County, 1912-14; Rep. nominee for Congress, 3d Neb. Dist., 1913; mem. Neb. Constl. Conv., 1920 (chmn. suffrage com.); elected atty. gen. of Neb. 1922, and reelected, 1924, and again in 1926, by two of the largest majorities ever received up to that time by a candidate for state office in Neb.; mem. of law firm of Spillman & Ptak, Norfolk. Secured seat for farmers in Omaha Grain Exchange; fought gasoline and power trusts and combines; won first victories, and obtained first decrees under discrimination sections of Neb. anti-trust laws against oil and power cos.; called first Nat. Conf. of Attys. Gen. in Chicago, 1923, and presided over same (26 states and U.S. Dept. of Justice represented); rep. of Neb. in action against "Pittsburgh Plus" system. Mem. Am. and Neb. State bar assns., Internat. Assn. Attys. Gen. (pres. 1928), Nat. Conf. Attys. Gen. (chmn. permanent exec. com.). Methodist. Mason. Am. Legion. Home: Norfolk, Neb. Died Mar. 24, 1941.

SPILLMAN, William Jasper, agricultural economist; b. Lawrence County, Mo., Oct. 23, 1863; s. Judge Nathan Cosby and Emily Paralee (Pruitt) S.; B.S., U. of Mo., 1886, M.S., 1889, D.Sc., 1910; m. Mattie Ramsay, May 20, 1889; 1 son, Ramsay. Scientific agriculturist, 1894—; with U.S. Dept. Agr., 1902—, chief, Office of Farm Management, 1905-18, cons. specialist same, 1921; asso. editor Farm Journal, 1918-21; cons. specialist, U.S. Dept. Agr., 1921—. Special studies in heredity of plants; independent discoverer of Mendel's Law of Recombination, 1901 (announced in Bull. 115, office of expt. stas.); discovered mathematical form of law of diminishing returns, 1920. Wrote Quantitative Studies on Distribution of Parental Characters in Hybrid Offspring, 1901; contbr. to scientific jours. Editor, heredity sect., American Naturalist, 1908-15. Fellow A.A.A.S. Author: Farm Grasses of the U.S.; Farm Science; Farm Management; Balancing the Farm Output. Joint Author: Law of Diminishing Returns; also numerous bulls. on agrl. subjects. Home: Washington, D.C. Died July 11, 1931.

SPILMAN, Edward Guthrie, lawyer; b. Warrenton, Va., Jan. 5, 1855; s. Edward M. and Eliza Comyn (Day) S.; grad. Culpeper Acad., Jeffersonton, Va., 1874; studied law in father's office, 1874-76; m. Christiana Morton Sloan, Oct. 24, 1884; 1 dau., Marie Morton (wife of H. S. Wygant, U.S.A.). Taught pvt. sch. while studying law; admitted to Va. bar, 1876; register of the U.S. Land Office, Devils Lake, N.D., 1888-91, at Kingfisher, Okla., 1893-97; in pvt. practice, 1897-1907; asst. atty. gen. of Okla., 1907-13. As register at Devils Lake presented data to members of Congress and initiated movement which resulted in passage, Mar. 2, 1889, of bill to repeal timber culture law and permitting commutation or purchase of these lands; among first to advocate law, which went into effect May 17, 1900, making Okla. lands free to homestead settlers. Del. Universal Congress Lawyers and Jurists, St. Louis, 1904. Compiler of a digest of the reports of Okla. Criminal Ct. of Appeals. State librarian of Okla., Apr. 1915. Mem. State Council Defense, Okla., during war period; v.p. for Okla. of Nat. Sesquicentennial Com. Episcopalian. Democrat. Home: Warrenton, Va. Died Sept. 3, 1930.

SPILMAN, Lewis Hopkins, lawyer; b. Covington, Ky., Mar. 8, 1860; s. Rev. Jonathan Edwards (D.D.) and Eliza (Taylor) S.; Central U., Richmond, Ky., 1875-76; read law under Judge Chancey S. Conger, Carmi, Ill.; m. Lillian Swepson Saunders, June 24, 1896; children—Lewis Saunders (dec.), Robert Redd, Lillian Saunders (Mrs. Frank Catlett Howard), Samuel Taylor, Martha Anderson (Mrs. Martin Ross Baker), Virginia Lee (Mrs. Ben A. Batson). Admitted to bar at Springfield, Ill., 1888; admitted to Tennessee bar, practiced alone at Knoxville, Tenn., except as mem. firm of Comfort & Spilman, 1890-1900, dissolved by death of partner; admitted to practice Supreme Court of U.S., 1896; frequently served as spl. judge Circuit and Chancery Courts. Pres. Knoxville Bd. of Edn. Democrat. Presbyn. Writer on nature topics; contbr. many stories to Forest and Stream over pseudonym "Lewis Hopkins." Home: Knoxville, Tenn. Died May 23, 1938.

SPILSBURY, Edmund Gybbon, engineer; b. London, Eng., 1845; grad. U. of Louvain, Belgium, 1862; married. Asst. engr. Eschweiler Co., Stolberg, large miners and smelters of lead and zinc ores, 1862; engaged in important works in Europe until 1870; in U.S., 1870—; mng. dir. Trenton Iron Co., 1888-97; head E. G. Spilsbury Engring. Co., New York. V.p., 1893, pres., 1896, Am. Inst. Mining Engrs. Author of numerous technical papers. Home: Brooklyn, N.Y. Died May 28, 1920.

SPINGARN, J(oel) E(lias), author, publicist; b. N.Y. City, May 17, 1875; s. Elias and Sarah (Barnett) S.; A.B., Columbia, 1895, Ph.D., 1899; Harvard, 1895-96, Phi Beta Kappa Poet, Columbia, 1901. Asst. and tutor comparative lit., 1899-1904, adj. prof., 1904-09, prof., 1909-11, Columbia. Owner Amenia (N.Y.) Times, 1911-26. Rep. cand. for Congress, 18th N.Y. District, 1908; del. Prog. Nat. Conv., Chicago, 1912, 1916. Maj. inf., U.S.A., 1917-19; with A.E.F., France, 1918-19; lt. col. O.R.C. One of founders and lit. adviser Harcourt, Brace & Co., pubs., 1919-32. Chmn. dirs. Nat. Assn. Adv. Colored People, 1913-19, treas., 1919-30, pres., 1930—; founded movement for rural coop. recreation, 1910-15; founded Spingarn medal, 1913. Hon. citizen U. of Munich, 1924. Mem. bd. mgrs. New York Bot. Garden; dir. Hort. Soc. of N.Y.; awarded Jackson Dawson Memorial Medal by Mass. Hort. Soc., 1937. Author: A History of Literary Criticism in the Renaissance, 1899 (Italian transl., 1905, with introduction by Benedetto Croce); The New Criticism, 1911; The New Hesperides and Other Poems, 1911; Creative Criticism, 1917; Poems, 1924; Poetry and Religion, 1924; Creative Criticism and Other Essays, 1931; Henry Winthrop Sargent and the Early History of Landscape Gardening and Ornamental Horticulture in Dutchess County, N.Y., 1937. Editor: Critical Essays of the Seventeenth Century (3 vols.), 1908-09; Temple's Essays, 1909; A Renaissance Courtesy Book, the Galateo of Della Casa, 1914; Goethe's Literary Essays, 1921; Criticism in America, 1924; European Library (25 vols.), 1920-25; Troutbeck Leaflets, 1924-31. Contbr. to Civilization in the U.S., Dictionary of American Biography, Cambridge History of English Literature, Taylor's Garden Dictionary, Markham's Clematis. Home: New York, N.Y. Died July 26, 1939.

SPINING, George Lawrence, clergyman; b. Dayton, O., May 15, 1840; s. George Burnett and Elizabeth Cassatt (Monfort) S.; ed. Highland (Kan.) U., hon. M.A., 1876, D.D., 1880; Hanover (Ind.) Coll.; grad. McCormick Theol. Sem., Chicago, 1869; m. Marion Agusta Parker, Apr. 20, 1869. Ordained Presbyn. ministry, 1869; pastor, Cleveland, 1880-85, San Francisco, 1885-87, Cincinnati, 1887-90, Phillips Memorial Ch., New York, 1890-93; pastor emeritus First Ch., S. Orange, N.J., 1906—. Served in Co. C, 7th Kan. Cav., Civil War; in Indian War, 1865, had charge of supply trains to Govt. forts on the plains and in Rocky Mountains. Widely known as "the friend of the American Indian." Home: Pasadena, Calif. Died Sept. 25, 1923.

SPINK, Mary Angela, M.D.; b. Washington, Ind., Nov. 18, 1863; d. Urban and Rosanna (Morgan) S.; St. Simon's Acad., Washington; M.D., Med. Coll. of Ind., 1887; post-grad. course in mental and nervous diseases, New York Post-Grad. Sch. Pathologist at Central Ind. Hosp. for Insane, 1886-87; with Dr. William Baldwin Fletcher, established the Dr. W. B. Fletcher's Sanatorium, Indianapolis, 1888; became supt. after Dr. Fletcher's death, 1907, and later pres. Mem. Ind. State Bd. Charities for 30 years. Home: Indianapolis, Ind. Deceased.

SPIRO, Charles, inventor; b. N.Y. City, Jan. 1, 1850; s. Joseph and Louise S.; LL.B., Washington U., 1874, New York U., 1875; m. Grace Smadbeck, June 9, 1880. Practiced law, 1875-84; designed a matrix-making machine, 1879; pub. new system of phonography, dispensing with shaded lines, 1880; patented the "Columbia" typewriter, 1885, with feature of variable spacing; later the "Bar-lock" typewriter, with writing constantly in view; other inventions, including the "Visigraph" typewriter; patented watch, telegraphic and automatic machinery for various purposes; pres. C. Spiro Mfg. Co. Author: Spiro's Simple, Swift Shorthand, 1880. Home: Dobbs Ferry, N.Y. Died Dec. 17, 1933.

SPITZER, Ceilan Milo, banker; b. Batavia, N.Y., Nov. 2, 1849; s. Aaron Bovee and Laura Maria (Perkins) S.; Oberlin (O.) Coll., 1868-69; m. Lillian Cortez, d. Alexander McDowell, Mar. 20, 1884. Entered banking business with his father, Seville, O., 1871; opened branch bank, Medina, O., 1877; organized German-Am. Bank, Cleveland, 1878; latter failed, 1880, and 10 yrs. later Mr. Spitzer paid its debts in full. Opened bank of Fremont, O., Aug. 1880; sold out in 1881; formed firm Spitzer, Wideman & Co., Toledo; Wideman retired, 1882, firm becoming Spitzer & Co. (later Spitzer, Rorick & Co.); opened branch at Boston, 1887; resided there, 1887-95; removed Boston office to New York, May 1, 1899; dir. 6 banks, including Ohio Savings Bank & Trust Co., and Security Trust Co., of Toledo, pres. Spitzer Bldg. Co.; elected pres. Ohio Centennial Co., Dec. 1898. Was q.m. gen. Ohio N.G.; brig. gen., 1900-04. Home: Toledo, O. Died Feb. 20, 1919.

SPITZKA, Edward Anthony, physician; b. New York, June 17, 1876; s. of Edward Charles and Catherine (Watzek) S.; ed. Coll. City of New York; M.D., Coll. Phys. and Surg. (Columbia), 1902; m. Alice Eberspacher, June 20, 1906. Demonstrator anatomy, 1904-06, prof. gen. anatomy, 1906-14, Jefferson Med. Coll.; dir. Daniel Baugh Inst. of Anatomy, Phila., 1911-14; pvt. practice, nervous and mental diseases, New York, 1914—. Performed autopsy and examined brain of Czolgosz, assassin of President McKinley, and attended many electrocutions, recording detailed observations upon electric death, anat. variations, etc., of criminals; studied brains of many eminent men and of various races; mem. Commn. on Resuscitation from Electric Shock. Fellow A.A.A.S.; mem. Com. on 1st Aid Treatment of Surg., Med. and Gas Poisoning Cases, Internat. Assn. Fire Engrs. Mem. Vets. 7th Regt. N.G.N.Y. Editor 18th Am. edition of Gray's Anatomy. Commd. capt., Med. R.C., June 1, 1917; assigned command of Field Hosp., Co. 341, 311th Sanitary Train, 86th Div., Camp Grant, Ill.; maj., Dec. 13, 1917; assigned as comdr. 311th Field Hosp. Sect.; lt. col. Med. Corps, Aug. 9, 1918; assigned as comdr. 311th Sanitary Train; overseas duty Sept. 16, 1918-Jan. 19, 1919; hon. discharged, Jan. 28, 1919; lt. col. Med. R.C., Nov. 7, 1919. Certified by U.S. Civil Service Commn. as spl. expert, med. referee, 1921; medical referee, neuro-psychiatric sect., U.S. Veterans' Bur., Washington, Mar. 1-Aug. 25, 1921; chief med. rating sect., U.S. Veterans' Bur., New York Office, Aug. 26, 1921—. Home: Mt. Vernon, N.Y. Died Sept. 5, 1922.

SPITZKA, Edward Charles, neurologist; b. New York, Nov. 10, 1852; s. Charles Anthony and Johanna (Tag) S.; ed. Coll. City of New York, 1870-73; M.D., Univ. Med. Coll. (New York U.), 1873; studied Leipzig and Vienna, 1873-76; m. Catherine

Watzek, June 30, 1875; father of Edward Anthony S. In practice as specialist in internal diseases, particularly of nervous system; med. expert in cases of insanity or injury to brain or spinal cord; notably in the trial of Guiteau, assassin of President Garfield, where he testified to the prisoner's insanity; prof. of med. jurisprudence and neurology, New York Post-Grad. Med. Coll., 1885-87; cons. neurologist Sydenham Hosp. Discoverer of the inter-optic lobes of the reptilian brain. Editor Am. Jour. of Neurology, 1881-84. V.p. sect. neurology, 9th Internat. Med. Congress, 1887, chmn. Sect. of Somatology, Med. Congress, St. Louis Expn., 1904; mem. Am. Neurol. Assn. (pres. 1890), N.Y. Neurol. Soc. (pres. 1883-84), Assn. Am. Anatomists. Author: Treatise on Insanity, 1883. Address: New York, N.Y. Died Jan. 13, 1914.

SPIVAK, Charles David, M.D.; b. Krementshug, Russia, Dec. 25, 1861; s. Samuel David and Deborah Adel (Dorfmann) S.; left Russia, 1882, on account of polit. views; avoided thereby exile to Siberia; day laborer (N.Y.), mill hand (Me.), farmer (N.J.), teacher and librarian (Phila.); M.D., Jefferson Med. Coll., 1890; U. of Berlin, 1891-92; m. Jennie Charsky, of Russia, 1893; children—David Hayem, Deena, Ruth. Chief of clinic, gastro-intestinal diseases, Phila. Policlinic, 1894-95; lecturer on diseases of the gastro-intestinal tract, 1896-1900, prof. anatomy, 1897-98, prof. clin. medicine, 1900-07, Denver Sch. of Medicine; sec. and gastro-enterologist to Sanatorium, Jewish Consumptives' Relief Soc., 1904—. Editor of Medical Libraries, 1898-1902, Denver Jewish News, 1915-18, The Sanatorium, 1907—. Joint author (with Yehoash) of Yiddish Dictionary. Contbr. of numerous articles on gastroenterology and history medicine to Jewish Ency., and Annals of Med. History; compiler and editor Medical Coloradoana, and a number of bibliographies on Jewish medicine; editor Longevity Almanac (Yiddish), 1921. Contbr. series (Yiddish) in the Daily Forward on hygiene and longevity from Jewish standpoint. Spl. commr. of joint distribution com. to study health and sanitation among the Jews of Europe, 1920; sec. of com. of Sanatorium Assn. to study the mortality of tuberculosis in Colo., 1921. Address: Denver, Colo. Deceased.

SPIVEY, Thomas Sawyer, author; b. Gallatin County, Ill., Feb. 27, 1856; s. Lindley Murray and Jane (Street) S.; A.B., Cumberland Presbyn. Coll., Ill., 1879; m. Dorothy H. Kleine, Feb. 27, 1917. Went to Cincinnati, 1879, and engaged in mfg.; pres. Victor Safe & Lock Co., 1885—; retired from active labors, 1897, and engaged in lit. and travel. Mem. Internat. Law Assn., Am. Acad. Polit. and Social Science, Science League America. Mason. Author: Lavius Egyptus (2 vols.), 1901; Jane and I, 1903; The Autobiography of a Johnny, 1904; The Hoosier Widow, 1908; Dr. Paul McKim, 1909; The Seven Sons of Ballyhack, 1912; The Caverns of Crail, 1912; The Pacific Ocean the End of Human Endeavor; Is This a Dying World? The Revelation; The Resurrection; Visible Evolution; Truth Series; Christianity and Mythology, 1927; Ecclesiastical Vocabulary, 1927; The Last of the Gnostic Masters, 1928; The Last Word, 1935; The Awakening, 1935. Contbr. to newspapers and mags. Home: Shawneetown, Ill. Died Nov. 7, 1938.

SPOFFORD, Ainsworth Rand, chief asst. librarian of Congress; b. Gilmanton, N.H., Sept. 12, 1825; s. Rev. L. A. and Grata (Rand) S.; classical edn. from pvt. tutors; LL.D., Amherst, 1882; m. Sarah P. Partridge, 1852 (dec.). Book-seller and publisher, Cincinnati; asso. editor Cincinnati Daily Commercial, 1859-61; first asst. librarian of Congress, 1861-64; librarian-in-chief, 1864-97; chief asst. librarian, 1897—. Editor: Catalogues of the Congressional Library; Annual American Almanac, 1878-89; edited, with others, Library of Choice Literature (10 vols.), Library of Historic Characters and Famous Events (10 vols.); Library of Wit and Humor (5 vols.). Author: Practical Manual of Parliamentary Rules, 1884; A Book for All Readers—an aid to collection, use and preservation of books, and the formation of libraries, 1905; numerous articles in revs. and cyclos., lectures, etc. Home: Washington, D.C. Died 1908.

SPOFFORD, Harriet Prescott, author; b. Calais, Me., Apr. 3, 1835; d. Joseph Newmarch and Sarah (Bridges) Prescott; grad. Putnam Free Sch., Newburyport, Mass., 1852; m. Richard S. Spofford, 1865. Author: Sir Rohan's Ghost; The Thief in the Night; The Marquis of Carabas: A Lost Jewel; Hester Stanley at St. Mark's; Hester Stanley's Friends; The Scarlet Poppy; Art Decoration Applied to Furniture; House and Hearth; The Servant Girl Question; Poems; Ballads about Authors; The Amber Gods; Azarian; New England Legends; A Master Spirit; An Inheritance; In Titian's Garden; Four Days of God, 1905; The Children of the Valley, 1901; The Great Procession, 1902; Old Madame; The Maid He Married; Priscilla's Love Story; Old Washington, 1906; The Fairy Changeling, 1910; The Making of a Fortune, 1911. Address: Newburyport, Mass. Died Aug. 15, 1921.

SPOONER, Florence Garrettson, reform worker; b. Baltimore; d. J. Aquilla and Eleanor Garrettson; ed. Morrison Acad.; m. Henry T. Spooner (dec.). Actively engaged as worker and writer in humane and reformatory lines; apptd. by Gov. Greenhalge mem. Com. of 12 from Mass. to Cotton States and Internat. Expn., Atlanta, Ga.; founder Anti-Death Penalty League; initiated movement that resulted in substitution of electric chair for scaffold, and abolition of dark cells in prisons of Mass.; pres. Mass. Prison Reform League. Awarded World's Gold Medal and Diploma by St. Louis, and Lewis and Clark expns. Address: Boston, Mass. Died May 7, 1935.

SPOONER, Henry Joshua, congressman; b. Providence, R.I., Aug. 6, 1839; s. Joshua and Ann Crawford (Noyes) S.; A.B., Brown U., 1860; LL.B., Albany Law Sch., 1861; m. Mary Slack Brown, Nov. 16, 1868. Served as 2d lt., 1st lt. and adj., 4th R.I. Inf., 1862-65; admitted to R.I. bar, 1865; justice Ct. of Magistrates, 1866-69; mem. R.I. Ho. of Rep., 1875-81, 1903 (speaker, 1879-81); mem. 47th to 52d Congresses (1881-91), 1st R.I. Dist.; during later yrs. of active practice mem. Spooner & Miller, and Spooner, Miller & Brown; dir. United Wire & Supply Co., Franklin Mut. Fire Ins. Co. Republican. Home: Providence, R.I. Died Feb. 9, 1918.

SPOONER, John Coit, senator; b. Lawrenceburg, Ind., Jan. 6, 1843; s. Judge Philip L. and Lydia (Coit) S.; removed to Madison, Wis., 1859; A.B., U. of Wis., 1864, hon. Ph.B., A.M., 1869, LL.D., 1895; LL.D., Yale, 1908, Columbia, 1909; m. Annie E. Main, Sept. 10, 1868. Served pvt. Co. A, 40th Wis. Inf.; capt. and bvt. maj. 50th Wis. Inf.; pvt. and mil. sec. to Gov. Lucius Fairchild, of Wis., 1866-67. Admitted to bar, 1867; asst. atty. gen. of Wis., and in gen. practice at Madison, 1867-70; practiced at Hudson, Wis., 1870-84; regent U. of Wis., 1882-85; mem. Wis. Assembly, 1872; U.S. senator, 1885-91, and 1897-1907, resigned, Mar. 3, to take effect May 1, 1907; in law practice at New York, 1907—. Chmn. Wis. delegation Rep. Nat. convs., 1888, 92; candidate for gov. of Wis., 1892; tendered portfolio of Sec. of the Interior by President McKinley, 1898, membership on British-Am. Joint High Commn., 1898, and portfolio of Atty. Gen. of U.S., 1901, but declined. Address: New York, N.Y. Died June 11, 1919.

SPOOR, John Alden, capitalist; b. Freehold, N.Y., Sept. 30, 1851; s. John and Amanda (Alden) S.; ed. Hudson River Inst., Claverack, N.Y.; m. Frances Samuel, Feb. 12, 1889. Gen. mgr. Wagner Palace Car Co., 1893-97; pres., 1899 and chmn. bd. Chicago Junction Ry. Co.; pres., 1899 and chmn. bd. Union Stock Yard & Transit Co., Chicago Junction Ry.; dir. Chicago Surface Lines, Chicago Junction Rys. and Union Stock Yards Co. of N.J., Pullman Co., First Nat. Bank, First Trust & Savings Bank, Nat. Safe Deposit Co., Stock Yards Nat. Bank (Chicago), Nat. Surety Co., Guaranty Trust Co. (New York), Montgomery Ward & Co. Trustee Newberry Library, St. Luke's Hosp. (pres.); trustee Children's Memorial Hosp., Chicago Hist. Soc. Republican. Episcopalian. Mem. Bd. of Trade, Chicago, Chicago Stock Exchange. Home: Chicago, Ill. Died Oct. 15, 1926.

SPRAGUE, Albert Arnold, merchant; b. Randolph, Vt., May 19, 1835; s. Ziba and Caroline M. (Arnold) S.; grad. Kimball Union Acad., 1854; A.B., Yale, 1859; m. Nancy A., d. of Ebenezer Atwood, Sept. 29, 1862. Went to Chicago, 1862, engaging in wholesale grocery trade; founder and pres. Sprague, Warner & Co.; dir. Chicago Telephone Co., Commonwealth Edison Co., Elgin Nat. Watch Co., Liverpool & London & Globe Ins. Co.; organizer and dir. Northern Trust Co., 1873-1912, Relief and Aid Soc. (pres. 1887-90); dir. Art Inst. of Chicago; trustee Presbyn. Hosp., and Rush Med. Coll. Republican. Home: Chicago, Ill. Died Jan. 10, 1915.

SPRAGUE, Augustus Brown Reed, soldier, banker; b. Ware, Mass., Mar. 7, 1827; s. Lee and Lucia (Snow) S. (Mayflower descendant in 7th generation); ed. pub. and pvt. schs.; m. Elizabeth Janes Rice, 1846; m. 2d, Mary Jennie Barbour, Oct. 23, 1890. Clerk in stores in Worcester, 1842-46; in mercantile business for himself, 1846-61; served in Civil War 3 yrs. and 9 mos. as capt., lt. col. and col., Mass. vols.; bvtd. brig. gen. "for gallant and meritorious service during the war." U.S. collector internal revenue, 8th Mass. Dist., 1867-72; sheriff Worcester County, 1871-90; mayor Worcester, 1896-97. Republican. Pres. Worcester Mechanics' Savings Bank, Jan. 1900—; pres. Worcester Electric Light Co., Sept. 1901—. Mem. G.A.R. (comdr. Dept. of Mass., 1868), Loyal Legion, etc. Address: Worcester, Mass. Died 1910.

SPRAGUE, Carleton, editor; b. Buffalo, N.Y., Dec. 24, 1858; s. Eben Carleton and Elizabeth H. (Williams) S.; grad. Phillips Acad., Exeter, N.H., 1877; A.B., Harvard, 1881; m. Alice Louise Brayley, Apr. 17, 1883. With the Buffalo Pitts Co., mfrs., as v.p., treas. and pres., 1882-1906, and chmn. board of trustees, 1907-14; engaged in editorial work N.Y. City; became asst. sec. Western Union Telegraph Co. Mem. board of directors and exec. com. and bldgs. and grounds and fine arts coms., Buffalo Expn., 1901; mem. bd. dirs. Buffalo Fine Arts Acad., 1898-1914 (v.p. 1903-04, pres. 1906-07); pres. Buffalo Soc. of Artists, 1909, 10, Buffalo Assn. for the Blind, 1907-13, Nicholas Sch.; trustee Charity Orgn. Soc., 1893-1915; mem. council U. of Buffalo, 1901-15. Republican. Unitarian. Author: The Mission of Beauty, 1905. Home: New York, N.Y. Died Nov. 19, 1916.

SPRAGUE, Charles Ezra, banker; b. Nassau, N.Y., Oct. 9, 1842; s. Ezra and Elisabeth B. (Edgerton) S.; A.B., Union Coll., 1860, A.M., 1884, Ph.D., 1893; Litt.D., Olivet (Mich.) College, 1910; m. Ray Ellison, Apr. 2, 1866. Served in Union Army, becoming bvt. col., N.Y. Vols.; wounded and disabled at battle of Gettysburg. Certified pub. accountant under law of 1896; pres. Bd. Examiners for Public Accountants, 1896-98; connected with Union Dime Savings Bank, New York, 1870—, pres. 1892—. Prof. of accountancy, New York U. (Sch. of Commerce, Accounts and Finance), 1900. Inventor of devices and systems for savings bank and other bookkeeping. Mem. Am. Bankers' Assn. (pres. Savings Banks Sect. 1904-05). Author: Hand-Book of Volapük, 1888; The Accountancy of Investment, 1904; Extended Bond Tables, 1905; The Philosophy of Accounts, 1907; also many articles on lang. and bookkeeping. First Am. advocate of Volapü. Home: New York, N.Y. Died Mar. 21, 1912.

SPRAGUE, Charles Franklin, congressman; b. Boston, June 10, 1857; grad. Harvard, 1879; studied law, Harvard Law School and Boston U.; admitted to Suffolk bar; mem. common council, Boston, 1889-90; mem. Mass. legislature, 1891, 1892; park commr. (latter part chmn. of bd.), Boston, 1893-94; mem. Mass. senate, 1895, 1896; mem. Congress from 11th Mass. dist., 1897-1901. Republican. Home: Brookline, Mass. Died 1902.

SPRAGUE, Charles James, bank officer; b. Boston, Jan. 16, 1823; s. Charles S. (the "Banker Poet"); ed. private schools; held several positions in Globe Bank, 1842-82, retiring as cashier. For 50 yrs. contributor of poems, literary and scientific papers and translations to various periodicals; several yrs. curator, dept. of botany, Boston Soc. Natural History; made notable collections of fungi and lichens, later in the soc.'s herbarium; published lists of New England fungi. Address: Boston, Mass. Died 1903.

SPRAGUE, Frank Julian, engineer, inventor; b. Milford, Conn., July 25, 1857; s. David Cummings and Frances Julia (King) S.; grad. U.S. Naval Acad., 1878; D.Eng., Stevens Inst., 1921; D.Sc., Columbia, 1922; LL.D., U. of Pa., 1924; m. Mary Keatinge, 1885; 1 son, Frank D'Esmonde; m. 2d, Harriet Chapman Jones, Oct. 11, 1899; children—Robert Chapman, Julian King, Frances Althea. Mem. of jury, Crystal Palace Expn., London, England, 1882, and had charge of tests of dynamo-electric machines, gas engines and electric lights, as reported to Navy Dept.; elec. studies and experiments at Stevens Inst., Brooklyn Navy Yard and U.S. Torpedo Sta., Newport; resigned, 1883, to devote attention to elec. work; asst. for a time to Thomas A. Edison; founded, 1884, Sprague Electric Ry. & Motor Co., which, using his constant speed elec. motor, was first to engage in gen. mfr. and introduction of industrial elec. motors (endorsed by Edison Electric Light Co. 1885); developed pilot control of indsl. and other motors; pioneer in ry. electrification; equipped first modern trolley ry. in U.S. at Richmond, Va., 1887, later in Florence, Italy, Halle, Germany, and more than 100 rys. in 2 yrs.; developed A.C. induction smelting furnace, also high speed and house automatic elec. elevators and installed Central London equipment; invented method of operating two elevators on same rails in a common shaft, and acceleration control of car safeties; invented multiple-unit system of elec. train control, now in general use, and also system of regeneration used on mountain elec. rys. and on high speed elec. elevators; promoted high tension, direct current elec. ry. system; developed system of automatic signal and brake train control to enforce obedience to signals; etc.; engaged for yrs. in promoting underground rapid transit; pres. Sprague Development Corp., Sprague Safety Control & Signal Corp.; cons. engr. Sprague, Westinghouse, Otis and Gen. Electric cos.; mem. Terminal Electrical Commn. N.Y.C. & H.R. R.R. As cons. engr. S.P. Co. made studies for electrification of Sierra Nevada sect. of that system; selected as mem. U.S. Naval Consulting Bd. by Am. Inst. E.E. and the Inventors' Guild, and engaged during World War I in development of fuses and air and depth bombs. Trustee Sch. Applied Design for Women. Fellow and past pres. Am. Inst. E.E., New York Elec. Soc., Am. Inst. Consulting Engrs., Inventors' Guild. Awarded gold medal, Paris Expn., 1889, for elec. ry. development; Elliott Cresson medal, Franklin Inst., 1904, for multi-unit system; grand prize for "invention and development in electric rys.," St. Louis Expn., 1904; Edison gold medal "for meritorious achievement in electrical science, engineering and art," 1910; Franklin medal, 1921, "for fundamental inventions and achievements in elec. engring." Author of various scientific papers on electricity. On 75th birthday was designated as

"Father of Electric Traction"; also, in 1934, a bronze portrait bust of him was presented to Am. Inst. E.E. Home: New York, N.Y. Died Oct. 25, 1934.

SPRAGUE, Franklin M(onroe), clergyman; b. East Douglass, Mass., Nov. 1, 1841; s. Edward Lee and Sarah Charlotte (Sessions) S.; matriculated in Yale, 1861, but left at end of 3 yrs. on account of ill health, A.M., 1901, as of 1867; m. Abbie R. Fellows, Oct. 31, 1866. Admitted to Mass. bar, and practiced law in Worcester, Mass., 1870-76; ordained Congl. ministry, 1875; pastor Leon and Sparta, Wis., 1876-78, Chelmsford and Carlyle, Mass., 1878-82, Springfield, 1882-90, Agawam, 1890-95, Tampa, Fla., 1897-1908. Lt. and capt., Co. G, 11th Regt. Conn. Vols., 1861-63 (resigned on account of ill health). Republican. Author: Eulogy on Rev. William L. Gaylord, 1883; Socialism from Genesis to Revelation, 1893; The Laws of Social Evolution, 1895; Made in Germany, 1915; The City Problem in Our Country, 1897; The Creed and Need of the New Congregationalism, 1920; The Bible Versus the Secretary, 1923. Home: Tampa, Fla. Died Dec. 30, 1926.

SPRAGUE, Henry Harrison, lawyer, author; b. Athol, Mass., Aug. 1, 1841; s. George and Nancy (Knight) S.; A.B., Harvard, 1864, A.M., 1867; studied law, Harvard Law Sch. and office of Henry W. Paine, Boston; m. Charlotte Sprague Ward, June 3, 1897. Admitted to Suffolk bar, Feb. 25, 1868. Mem. Boston Common Council, 1874-76; mem. Mass. Ho. of Rep., 1881-83, Senate, 1888-91 (pres. 1890-91); chmn. commn. to revise election laws of Mass.; chmn. Metropolitan Water Bd. from its establishment, 1895, until its consolidation with sewerage commn., 1901; then chmn. of Met. Water and Sewerage Bd. to Jan. 1914. Trustee Boston City Hosp. nearly 30 yrs.; trustee and v.p. Boston Lying-in Hosp.; sec. and trustee Mass. Charitable Fire Soc., 1883-1914; overseer Harvard Coll. 6 yrs.; one of trustees holding building of Women's Ednl. and Industrial Union; v.p. (formerly pres.) Boston Civ. Service Reform Assn.; sec., 1867-79, and v.p. 1879-1909, Boston Y.M.C.U. Author: Women Under the Law of Massachusetts, 1884, 1903; City Government in Boston, 1890; Water Supply and Work of Metropolitan Water Board for Paris Exposition, 1900; A Brief History of the Massachusetts Charitable Fire Society, 1893, Supplement, 1904; Story of a New England Town (Athol), 1904; The Founding of Charlestown by the Spragues, 1910. Home: Boston, Mass. Died July 28, 1920.

SPRAGUE, Homer Baxter, educator, lecturer, author; b. Sutton, Mass., Oct. 19, 1829; s. Jonathan and Mary Ann (Whipple) S.; descended in direct line from William (youngest son of Edward Sprague, of Upway, Dorsetshire, Eng.), who was joint founder of Charlestown, Mass. (1628-29) and of Hingham (1636); A.B., Yale (class valedictorian), 1852, A.M., 1855; student Yale Law Sch., 1853-54, also with Mayor Chapin, of Worcester, Mass.; admitted to bar, 1854; Ph.D., U. of New York, 1873; LL.D., Temple U., 1916; m. Antoinette E. Pardee, Dec. 28, 1854 (died 1913). Practiced law at Worcester, 1855-56; principal Worcester High School, 1856-59, practiced law at New Haven, Conn., 1859-61; mem. New Haven Board of Edn., 1860-61. Raised 2 mil. cos. for war, 1861; served as capt., maj., lt. col., 13th Conn. Inf., 1862-66; wounded in action, Irish Bend, La., Apr. 14, 1863; mem. of two "forlorn hopes"; bvtd. col. for conduct at Port Hudson; recd. commn. col. 11th C.D.A.; prisoner of war (battle of Winchester), Sept. 19, 1864-Feb. 1865; served on courts martial, mil. commns., ednl. supt., freedmens courts, etc., 1865-66; mustered out, Apr. 28, 1866. Prin. Conn. Normal Sch., 1866-67; mem. Conn. Ho. of Rep., 1868; secured abolition of the odious tuition "rate bills," thus making the pub. schs. free, the reopening of State Normal Sch., and the trebling of the annual appropriation for teachers' inst.; prof. rhetoric and Eng. lit., Cornell U., 1868-70; prin. Adelphi Acad., Brooklyn, 1870-75; headmaster Girls' High Sch., Boston, 1876-85; founder and 1st pres. Martha's Vineyard Summer Inst., 1879-82; pres. Mills Coll., Cal., 1885-86; pres. U. of N.D., 1887-91; univ. extension lecturer, 1892-96; prof. and lecturer, Drew Theol. Sem., 1896-1900; editor dept. rhetoric, Students' Journal, 1898-1903; strongly supported for U.S. senator, N.D., 1889. Pres. Am. Inst. Instrn., 1883-85 (dir.); councillor N.E.A., 1887-88; asso. founder and 1st pres. N.D. Teachers' Assn. Author: American Liberty, 1900; The Two Parties, 1900; The Assassination, 1901; Alleged Law Blunders in Shakespeare, 1902; The Nation's Honor Roll, 1902; Right and Wrong in Our Civil War, 1903; The People's Party, 1904; Recollections of Henry Ward Beecher, 1905; The True Macbeth, 1909; Appreciation of Daniel C. Gilman, 1910; War Pensions and Promises, 1910; Cæsar and Brutus, 1911; The Elevation of His Statanic Majesty, 1912; Metrical Version of the Book of Job, 1913; The European War—Its Cause and Cure, 1914; Lights and Shadows in Confederate Prisons, 1915; also many annotated masterpieces. Editor Yale Lit. and took 1st De Forest gold medal. Home: Newton, Mass. Died Mar. 23, 1918.

SPRAGUE, Hugh Almeron, newspaperman; b. Orfordville, Wis., Apr. 26, 1866; s. Edwin Ruthven and Julia Ann (Rice) S.; ed. high sch., Broadhead, Wis.; m. Elizabeth Quarles, Oct. 10, 1895; children—Floyd McEwen, Hugh Almeron (dec.), Katherine Elizabeth. Began as reporter St. Joseph (Mo.) News, 1891; editor and pub. St. Joseph Journal of Commerce, 1892-95; advertising mgr. St. Joseph News, later St. Joseph News-Press, 1895-1918, business mgr., 1918-27, pub., also v.p. The News Corp., 1927—; also pub. St. Joseph Gazette, 1928—; dir. Buchanan Hotel Co. Mem. Mo. Relief Commn. Ind. Republican. Mason, Elk. Home: St. Joseph, Mo. Died July 11, 1939.

SPRAGUE, Leslie Willis, lecturer; b. Erie County, N.Y., May 2, 1869; s. Eli W. and Adelia (Pray) S.; student Stanford U., U. of Chicago, and Columbia U.; B.D., St. Lawrence U., 1904; m. Lila A. Frost, July 10, 1889; children—Theodate Frost (dec.), Burwell Edna, Lewis Clarence. Ordained to ministry, 1890; Congl. pastorates, Brooklyn, N.Y., Chicago, Ill., Sioux Falls, S.D. Founder Brooklyn Soc. of Ethical Culture, 1905; staff lecturer Am. Soc. Extension of Univ. Teaching, 1904-07; extension lecturer, U. of Chicago, 1907-08; staff speaker U.S. Dept. of Labor, 1918-19; dir. Community Motion Picture Bur., 1919-20; staff speaker and campaign mgr., Am. City Bur., New York, Chicago and San Francisco, 1920-21; dir. benevolence finance campaigns with Ward, Wells, Dreshman and Gates, 1921-23; with Tamblyn & Brown, 1924—. Chautauqua lecturer. Home: Bayside, L.I., N.Y. Died Oct. 27, 1938.

SPRAGUE, Levi L., educator; b. Beekman, Dutchess County, N.Y., Dec. 23, 1844; s. Nelson L. and Laura A. (Spencer) S.; prep. edn. Wyoming Sem., Pa.; M.A., Allegheny Coll., Pa., 1879; D.D., Wesleyan U., Conn., 1886; LL.D., Rutherford Coll., N.C., 1899; L.H.D., Syracuse U., 1920; m. Jennie E. Russell, Dec. 22, 1869 (died 1921); children—Laura Jennie, E. Russell. Began teaching in Wyoming Sem., 1866, pres., Nov. 1882—. Trustee Wyoming Sem., Syracuse U. Mem. Wyo. Conf. M.E. Ch., 1874—; trustee Wyoming Conf.; del. 3 Gen. Confs., 1892, 1896, 1904. Mason. Republican. Author: Practical Bookkeeping, 1873; Practical Grammar, 1894. Home: Kingston, Pa. Died Mar. 6, 1936.

SPRAGUE, Robert James, educator; b. Frankfort, Me., Jan. 19, 1868; s. James Edwin and Cornelia C. (Anderson) S.; ed. Ohio Wesleyan U., 1892-93, 1894-95; A.B., Boston U., 1897, A.M., 1899, Ph.D., 1901; Harvard, 1899-1901, M.A., 1900; research work in Europe, 1898, 1903; m. Helen M. Guernsey, Sept. 15, 1900; children—Eleanor M., Richard G. (dec.), Frances G. (dec.), Robert G., Miriam G. Carnegie Instn. investigator of the history of banking in Ill., 1906; prof. economics and sociology, Knox Coll., 1901-06, U. of Me., 1906-11; head of div. of Humanities and prof. economics and sociology, Mass. Agrl. Coll., Amherst, 1911-20; dean Rollins Coll., Winter Park, Fla., 1920-26, prof. economics and sociology, 1926—. Fellow A.A.A.S. Mem. Nat. Eugenics Council. Conglist. Contbr. to periodicals on problems of Southern Negroes, taxation and development of crime in America, birth control, nat. eugenics. Home: Winter Park, Fla. Died Dec. 27, 1929.

SPRAGUE, William, senator; b. Cranston, R.I., Sept. 12, 1831; s. Amasa and Fanny (Morgan) S.; ed. Cranston, E. Greenwich and Scituate, R.I., and Irving Inst., Tarrytown, N.Y.; hon. A.M., Brown, 1861; m. Katharine, d. Hon. Salmon P. Chase, Nov. 12, 1863; m. 2d, Inez Weed. Entered his uncle's mercantile house, 1845, succeeding to management, 1856; elected gov., R.I., 1860, 1861, 1862; active in raising troops for Civil War; went to Washington with first troops from R.I., Apr. 18, 1861, and participated in 1st Battle of Bull Run, July 21, 1861; served throughout Peninsular campaign; commd. brig. gen. U.S.V. but declined; elected U.S. senator, May 28, 1862, resigning as gov., Mar. 3, 1863; reëlected U.S. senator, June 9, 1868, for term expiring Mar. 3, 1875. Trustee Brown U., 1866—. Address: Narragansett, Rhode Island. Died Sept. 11, 1915.

SPRAGUE, William Cyrus, author; b. Malta, O., Feb. 25, 1860; s. William P. (M.C.) and Martha A. (Roberts) S.; A.B., Denison U., 1881; LL.B., Cincinnati Law Sch., 1883; m. Caroline Ellis, June 24, 1885; m. 2d, Mabel Jones Bush, Feb. 1913. Practiced in Ohio, Minn. and Mich. 19 years. Pres. Sprague Publishing Co., Sprague Correspondence Sch. of Law, and Sprague Correspondence Sch. of Journalism (3 separate corps.). Editor National Bankruptcy News and Reports, 1901-01; mng. editor American Legal News, 1889-1908; mng. editor Law Students' Helper, How to Write, The Am. Boy (all monthlies), The Lawyer's Internat. Blue Book, and editor of the Consular News and Internat. Law Notes, 1911-13. Mem. Commercial Law League of America (pres. 1895-96, chmn. exec. com. 1896-1900), Ohio Soc. of Detroit (pres. 1904-05). Author: Sprague's Abridgment of Blackstone, 1893; After Dinner Speeches, 1895; Wit and Wisdom, 1896; Quiz Books in Law, 1896; Three Boys in the Mountains, 1902; Napoleon Bonaparte, 1904; Felice Constant, 1904; The Boy Courier of Napoleon, 1904; The Boy Pathfinder, 1905; Davy Crockett, 1915; The Commercial Lawyer and His Work, 1918; also many pamphlets on legal and miscellaneous subjects. Home: Chicago, Ill. Died Nov. 29, 1922.

SPRAGUE-SMITH, Charles, educator, lecturer; see Charles Smith.

SPRATT, Frederick, banker; b. Salisbury, Eng., Jan. 26, 1852; s. Nehemiah and Mary Ann (Fleming) S.; ed. St. John's Coll., Battersea, London, and Oxford U.; m. Fannie Foster Hall, 1895; children—Frederick Fleming Percy, Rosa Mary Frideswide, Horace Bright. Came to U.S., 1883; in banking business at Ripon, 1885—; became pres. First Nat. Bank, 1918, later chmn. bd. Pres. Ripon Pub. Library; trustee Ripon Coll. Episcopalian. Home: Ripon, Wis. Died Oct. 18, 1932.

SPRAY, Ruth Hinshaw, humanitarian; b. Mooresville, Ind., Feb. 16, 1848; d. Benjamin and Nancy (Carter) Hinshaw; student Simpson Coll., Indianola, Ia.; B.S., Earlham Coll., Ind., 1874; m. Samuel J. Spray, Dec. 28, 1880; 1 dau., Mary Elizabeth (Mrs. L. Oscar Moon). Teacher pub. schs., and later Raisin Valley Sem., Adrian, Mich., 1874-77, Penn Coll., Oskaloosa, Ia., 1877-80. Officer Colo. State Bur. of Child and Animal Protection, 1900—, working in the interest of neglected and dependent children; asso. mem. Nat. Child Labor Com.; worker in internat. peace cause, 1896—, also in behalf of entrance of U.S. into World Court. Mem. Soc. of Friends. Address: Denver, Colo. Died Feb. 1929.

SPRECKELS, Adolph Bernard, mfr.; b. San Francisco, Jan. 5, 1857; s. Claus and Anna C. S.; brother of John Diedrich S.; ed. San Francisco, and Hanover, Germany; m. Alma De Bretteville, May 11, 1908. V.p. J. D. Spreckels & Bros. Co., Spreckels Sugar Co., Oceanic Steamship Co., J. D. & A. B. Spreckels Securities Co. Park commr., San Francisco, 1900. Office: San Francisco, Calif. Died June 28, 1924.

SPRECKELS, Claus, sugar refiner; b. Lamstedt, Hanover, 1828; came to U.S., 1846; employed at Charleston, S.C., and New York; went to San Francisco, 1856; conducted a store, and later a brewery. Established Bay Sugar Refinery, 1863, procuring raw material from Hawaii; invented new refining processes; acquired sugar properties in Hawaii; built new refineries; owner of beet-sugar farm and factory at Watsonville, Calif.; large owner in Oceanic Steamship Co., plying between San Francisco and Honolulu. Address: San Francisco, Calif. Died 1908.

SPRECKELS, John Diedrich, capitalist; b. Charleston, S.C., Aug. 16, 1853; s. Claus and Anna C. S.; brother of Adolph Bernard S.; ed. Oakland Coll., Calif., and Poly. Sch., Hanover, Germany; m. Miss L. Siebein. Founded, 1880, J. D. Spreckels & Bros. Co., shipping and commn. mchts.; president Oceanic Steamship Co. (mail and passenger line to Hawaii), Western Sugar Refining Co., Spreckels Sugar Co., Coronado Beach Co., Hotel Del Coronado, Coronado Tent City, San Diego Electric Ry. Co., Coronado Water Co., San Diego & Coronado Ferry Co., San Diego & Coronado Transfer Co., United Light, Fuel & Power Co., San Diego & Ariz. Ry. Co., Pajaro Valley R.R., etc. Home: San Francisco, Calif. Died Aug. 8, 1921.

SPRING, Alfred, judge; b. Franklinville, N.Y., Feb. 19, 1851; s. Judge Samuel and Ellen (Hogg) S.; U. of Mich., 1870-72, LL.D., 1901; m. Anna Tarbell, May 9, 1877. Admitted to bar, 1875; supervisor of town, 1876; surrogate Cattaraugus County, N.Y., 1880-92; apptd. justice Supreme Ct. by Gov. Morton, Jan. 1895; elected for terms 1895-1909, 1910-21; judge Appellate Div., 1899—. Republican. Contributor to Am. Law Review, Outlook, etc. Home: Franklinville, N.Y. Died Oct. 22, 1912.

SPRING, George E., lawyer; b. Franklinville, N.Y., Oct. 27, 1859; s. Samuel Stowell and Ellen (Hogg) S.; grad. Ten Broeck Acad., 1880; m. Rena F. Allen, Jan. 10, 1884. Admitted to N.Y. bar, 1884; began practice at Franklinville with firm of Alfred & George E. Spring, continuing until Alfred Spring was apptd. justice Sup. Ct. of N.Y., 1895; practiced alone except for a few yrs. as Spring & Spring, 1895—; pres. Franklinville Canning Co.; v.p. Empire Mfg. Co. Mem. N.Y. State Commn. to Paris Expn., 1900. Pres. Franklinville Free Library. Mem. N.Y. State Senate, 1915-16. Republican. Presbyn. Address: Franklinville, N.Y. Deceased.

SPRING, La Verne Ward, chemist, metallurgist; b. Coldwater, Mich., Sept. 22, 1876; s. Emerson and Lucinda (Ward) S.; A.B., U. of Mich., 1901; m. Emelyn J. Atkinson, Aug. 1905; children—Robert Ward, Dorothy Jane. Chemist, Ill. Steel Co., South Chicago, Ill., 1899-1900, Wolverine Portland Cement Co., Coldwater, Mich., 1901; again with Ill. Steel Co., 1901-03; chemist, Crane Co., Chicago, 1903-15, and chief chemist and metallurgist. Author: Non-Technical Chats on Iron and Steel, 1917; also various articles on chem. and physical testing and metallurgy. Home: Chicago, Ill. Died Mar. 23, 1932.

SPRING, Leverett Wilson, college prof.; b. Grafton, Vt., Jan. 5, 1840; s. Edward and Martha (Atwood) S.; A.B., Williams, 1863; studied theology at Hartford Theol. Sem., and Andover Theol. Sem.,

D.D., U. of Kan., 1886; m. Elizabeth, d. Prof. William Thompson, Sept. 25, 1867. Ordained Congl. ministry, 1868; pastor Rollstone Ch., Fitchburg, Mass., 1868-75, Plymouth Ch., Lawrence, Kan., 1876-81; prof. English lit., U. of Kan., 1881-86, Williams Coll., 1886-1909, emeritus prof. English lang. and lit., 1909—. Author: Kansas (in the Commonwealths series), 1885; Mark Hopkins, Teacher, 1888; Williams College in History of Berkshire County, Mass., 1906; also mag. contributions. Editor: The Centennial Anniversary of Williams College, 1893; The Addresses of President Hopkins and the Rev. Thomas Robbins at the Semi-Centennial of Williams College, 1843, 1893; Induction of President Garfield, 1909. Address: Boston, Mass. Died Dec. 24, 1917.

SPRING-RICE, Sir Cecil Arthur, diplomat; b. London, Eng., Feb. 27, 1859; s. Hon. Charles and Elizabeth (Marshall) Spring-Rice; grad. Balliol Coll., Oxford, 1882; m. Florence, d. Rt. Hon. Sir Frank Lascelles, 1904. Clk. in War Office and Foreign Office; sec. in diplomatic service at Brussels, Washington, Tokio, Berlin and Constantinople; chargé d'affaires, Teheran, 1900; British commr. of Pub. Debt, Cairo, 1901; sec. of embassy, St. Petersburg, 1903-06; minister and consul-gen. to Persia, 1906-08; E.E. and M.P. to Sweden, 1908-13; ambassador E. & P. from Great Britain to U.S., May 6, 1913—. Decorated Order of 1st Class, Medjidie, 1st Class, Polar Star, Knight Grand Cross of the Victorian Order, Knight Commander of St. Michael and St. George. Died Feb. 14, 1918.

SPRINGER, Charles, cattleman; b. Louisa Co., Ia., Dec. 19, 1857; s. Francis and Nancy R. (Coleman) S.; ed. Bapt. Coll. (Burlington, Ia.) and State U. of Ia.; m. Mary Chase, 1899. Settled in Colfax Co., N.M., 1879; asso. with Henry Koehler, Jr., 1905, in organization of the St. Louis, Rocky Mountain & Pacific Co., which purchased and developed extensive coal mines and coking plants in Colfax Co. and built 120 miles of railroad; with brother, Frank Springer, built Eagle's Nest Dam, capacity 100,000 acre feet of water for irrigation; pres., treas. Cimarron Valley Land Co. (28,000 acres), Charles Springer Cattle Co., Charles Springer & Co.; chmn. bd., treas. St. Louis, Rocky Mountain & Pacific Co.; v.p., treas. S. M. Chase Cattle Co. Pres. N.M. Bd. Water Commrs. 3 terms; mem. N.M. Constl. Conv., 1911; pres. State Highway Commn., 1917-23. Pres. Dist. Bd. for N.M. under Selective Service Act, 1917-18; field sec. Council of Nat. Defense for N.M., 1917-18; chief exec. officer N.M. Council of Defense, 1917-19. Republican. Home: Cimarron, N.M. Died Feb. 12, 1932.

SPRINGER, Francis Edwin, clergyman, educator; b. New Sheffield, Pa., July 2, 1872; s. James H. and Mary Ann S.; A.B., Mt. Hope (O.) Coll., 1898, A.M., 1899; student McCormick Theol. Sem., 1898-99; grad. Western Theol. Sem., Pittsburgh, Pa., 1901; B.D., Princeton Theol. Sem., 1906; granted LL.D., by the College of Idaho in 1926; D.D., Coll. of Puget Sound, Tacoma, Wash.; m. Mary D. Scott, June 8, 1898; children—Edwin D., Mary E., Norine E. Ordained Presbyn. ministry, 1901; pastor Mineral Ridge, O., 1901-02, New Bedford, Pa., 1903-05, Caldwell, Ida., 1906—; prof. philosophy, Coll. of Ida., 1906—, also dean of edn. Major, chaplain 41st Div. N.G.; retired with rank of lt. col., 1936. Home: Caldwell, Ida. Died May 1940.

SPRINGER, Frank, paleontologist; b. Wapello, Ia., June 17, 1848; s. Francis and Nancy R. S.; ed. State U. of Ia.; m. Josephine M. Bishop, Oct. 10, 1876; children—Laura (Mrs. John J. K. Caskie), Helen (Mrs. John F. Fairbairn), Eva, Ada (Mrs. Warren B. Davis), Edward Thomas, Henry Strong (dec.), Lew Wallace. Admitted to the bar, 1869; also member bar of U.S. Supreme Court; mem. Legislative Council, N.M., 1901; pres. bd. trustees Maxwell Land Grant Co.; regent Museum of New Mexico. Author: Revision of the Palæocrinoidea, 1879-86 (Phila. Acad. Natural Science); North American Crinoidea Camerata, 1897; Uintacrinus, its Structure and Relations, 1901; Cleiocrinus, 1905; New American Fossil Crinoids, 1911; Scyphocrinus, 1917; Mysticocrinus, 1918; Pentacrinus from East Indies, 1918; Crinoidea Flexibilia, 1920; Dolatocrinus, 1921; Crinoids from Northern Canada, 1921; Balanocrinus from Mexico, 1922; Family Catillocrinidae, 1923; Tertiary Crinoid from West Indies, 1924; The genus Holopus, 1924; Pentacrinus in Alaska, 1925; Apiocrinus in America, 1925; Unusual Forms Fossil Crinoids, 1926. Home: East Las Vegas, N.M. Died Sept. 22, 1927.

SPRINGER, Franklin Wesley, electrical engr.; b. Anoka, Minn., Jan. 18, 1870; s. Wesley John and Mary Elizabeth (Norris) S.; B.E.E., U. of Minn., 1893, E.E., 1898; studied factories and engring. schs. abroad, 1900; engring. schs. of Berlin and Paris, 1910-11; m. Grace Hamilton Pierce, Dec. 31, 1912; 1 dau., Suzanne. Asst. prof. elec. engring., 1900-07, prof., 1907—, U. of Minn., also acting head of the dept., 1925-28. Has taken out several patents on elec. and automobile devices. Fellow Am. Inst. E.E. (v.p. 1921-22). Republican. Methodist. Home: Minneapolis, Minn. Died Jan. 23. 1933.

SPRINGER, Rebecca Ruter, author; b. Indianapolis, Ind., Nov. 8, 1832; d. Calvin W. and Harriet C. Ruter; ed. in private schools, New Albany, Ind., 1840-48; grad. Wesleyan Coll., Cincinnati, O., June, 1850; m. William McKendree Springer, Dec. 15, 1859. Author: Beechwood, 1873; Self, 1881; Songs by the Sea (poems), 1889; Intra Muros, 1898. Home: Washington, D.C. Died 1904.

SPRINGER, William McKendree, U.S. judge; b. Sulliman Co., Ind., May 30, 1836; s. Thomas B. S.; ed. public schools and Ill. Coll., Jacksonville, Ill.; grad. Ind. State Univ., 1858; (A.M., 1861; LL.D., Ill. Coll., 1886). Newspaper editor and corr., 1858-62; admitted to bar, 1859; m. Rebecca Ruter, Dec. 15, 1859. Mem. Ill. legislature, 1872; mem. Congress, 1875-95; chmn. Ways and Means, Territories, Banking and Currency and other important coms., and a Dem. leader in Congress. Author Springer Bill, organizing Territory of Okla. and creating judicial system for Indian Territory, and bill admitting Washington, Mont. and N. and S. Dak. as states into the Union. Apptd. U.S. judge, Northern dist. I.T., and chief justice U.S. Court of Appeals, I.T., 1895-99; resumed law practice in Washington, 1900. Home: Washington, D.C. Died 1903.

SPRINGS, Leroy, mfr., banker; b. Ft. Mill, York Co., S.C., Nov. 12, 1861; s. A. Baxter and Julia Blandia (Baxter) S.; student U. of N.C., 1878-80; m. Grace Allison, d. Samuel E. White, of Ft. Mill, Dec. 28, 1892; m. 2d, Lena, d. T. M. Jones, of Pulaski, Tenn., Nov. 29, 1913. Began as salesman for Springs & Burwell, wholesale grocers, Charlotte, N.C., 1880; founded Leroy Springs & Co., wholesale and retail mdse., Lancaster, S.C., 1884, now Lancaster Mercantile Co. of which was pres. 16 yrs.; organized Springs & Shannon (Camden, S.C.), 1885, Kershaw (S.C.) Mercantile & Banking Co., 1888, Springs Banking & Mercantile Co. (Heath Springs, S.C.), 1889, The Bank of Lancaster, 1889, Bank of Kershaw, 1904, also Lancaster Cotton Mills (largest in the South), 1896, Eureka Cotton Mills, 1899, Kershaw Cotton Mills, 1913; reorganized 2 mills of Ft. Mill (S.C.) Mfg. Co., 1904; now pres. 7 cotton mill companies; pres. Bank of Lancaster, Lancaster & Chester Ry., Lansford Water Power Co.; vice pres. Bank of Kershaw; trustee Mut. Life Ins. Co. of New York; an organizer and v.p., Columbia (S.C.) Nat. Bank. Col. on staff of Gov. John P. Richardson, 1886-90; chmn. bd. trustees Lancaster Graded Sch. One of the founders, and dir. Stone Mountain Confederate Monumental Assn. Presbyn. Home: Lancaster, S.C. Died Apr. 7, 1931.

SPROUL, Elliott Wilford, congressman; b. Apohaqui, Canada, Dec. 28, 1856; s. Elliott Burgoyne and Rebecca Jane (Earl) S.; ed. pub. schs.; m. Jessie M. Sibbet, June 2, 1881 (died Jan. 11, 1920). Came to U.S., 1878, naturalized citizen, 1886; began as building contr., Chicago, 1880, later pres. E. W. Sproul Co. until succeeded by son, 1913. Mem. City Council, Chicago, 1896; del. Rep. Nat. Conv., Chicago, 1920; mem. 67th to 71st Congresses (1921-31), 3d Ill. District. Mason, Odd Fellow. Home: Chicago, Ill. Died June 22, 1935.

SPROUL, William Cameron, governor; b. Octoraro, Pa., Sept. 16, 1870; s. William Hall and Deborah Dickinson (Slokom) S.; B.S., Swarthmore, 1891; LL.D., Franklin and Marshall, 1912, Gettysburg, 1918, U. of Pa., U. of Pittsburgh, Lafayette, Pa. Mil. Coll., Swarthmore, 1919, Allegheny and Grove City, 1920; m. Emeline Wallace Roach, Jan. 21, 1892; children—Dorothy (Mrs. Laurence P. Sharples), John Roach. Farmer, mfr., journalist; pres. Chester Daily Times, and Morning Republican, Chester; organizer and pres. Seaboard Steel Casting Co. (now owned by Am. Locomotive Co.), Chester; organizer and chmn. Gen. Refractories Co., with 15 plants in Pa., Ky. and Ill.; also Lebanon Iron Co., Lackawanna & Wyoming Valley R.R.; organized and developed numerous railroads, mining, traction and power enterprises in W.Va.; actively interested in many banks. Elected to Pa. Senate, 1896, and reëlected 5 times, continuous service of 22 yrs.; pres. pro tem. of Senate, 1903-05; elected gov. of Pa. by plurality of 245,000, term 1919-23. Received unanimous vote of State and other scattering votes through 7 ballots for nomination for pres. of U.S., at Rep. Nat. Conv., 1920. "Father of good roads in Pa." Trustee Swarthmore Coll., Mercersburg Acad. Mason, Elk. Mem. Friends Ch. Owns nearly 2,000 acres of orchards in Pa.; built and endowed Sproul Obs., at Swarthmore Coll.; restored at own expense ancient Chester Court House, oldest pub. bldg. in Pa. Lives at Lapidea Manor, historic home place, Nether Providence Twp., nr. Chester, Pa. Hunting Lodge, "Songbrook," Dingman's Ferry, Pa. Died Mar. 21, 1928.

SPROUL, William H., congressman; b. nr. Livingston, Tenn., Oct. 14, 1867; s. J. Q. A. and Lee Ann B. (Roberts) S.; moved with parents to Kansas in 1883; prep. edn., high sch. and normal sch.; student U. of Kansas; taught school 4 yrs.; LL.B., Univ. of Kan., 1894; m. Kathryn Maynard, Aug. 27, 1894; children—Mrs. Pauline Jolliffe, W. M., Lea (dec.). Began practice at Sedan, Kan., 1895; county atty., 1897-1901; has also engaged in agriculture, stock raising and in production of oil and gas; mem. 68th to 71st Congresses (1923-31), 3d Kan. Dist. Republican. Conglist. Home: Sedan, Kan. Died Dec. 27, 1932.

SPROULE, Charles H., editor; b. San Francisco, Aug. 31, 1853; ed. common school and Petaluma City Coll., Calif. Has for yrs. been editor and propr. Elko (Nev.) Free Press; State senator Nev. 2 terms; mem. bd. regents, State Univ., 1881-82; delegate to Rep. Nat. Conv., St. Louis, 1896; mem. for Nev. of Rep. Nat. Com., 1896-1900. Home: Elko, Nev. Died 1904.

SPROULE, William, railway pres.; b. Ireland, Nov. 25, 1858; m. Marie Baird Baldwin, Dec. 5, 1905. Began railroading as freight clk., S.P. Co., 1882; asst. gen. freight agt., 1887-97, gen. freight agt., 1897-98, Pacific System; gen. traffic mgr., 1898-1906, traffic mgr., dir. and mem. exec. com. Am. Smelting & Refining Co., 1906-10; pres. Wells Fargo & Co., 1910-11; pres. S.P. Co., 1911-18; pres. Asso. Oil Co., 1912-18; chmn. Western Dept., R.R. War Bd., Apr. 1, 1917-July 1, 1918; dist. dir. Central Western Region, U.S. R.R. Administration, July 1, 1918-Dec. 31, 1919; again dir. and pres. S.P. Co., 1920-28, retired, Dec. 31, 1928; pres. Central Pacific Ry. Co. and S.P. R.R. Co., 1929—. Class C dir. Federal Reserve Bank (12th Dist.), San Francisco, Jan. 1, 1921-Mar. 1933. Home: San Francisco, Calif. Died Jan. 1, 1935.

SPROULL, William Oliver, educator; b. Allegheny, Pa., May 8, 1848; s. Rev. Thomas and Magdalene (Wallace) S.; A.B., Washington and Jefferson Coll., 1869; univs. Berlin, Jena, and Leipzig, 1874-77, A.M., Ph.D., Leipzig, 1877; (LL.D., U. of Wooster, 1890; L.H.D., Miami, 1895); m. Clara J. Haslett, Apr. 3, 1879. Prin. of Newell Inst., Pittsburgh, 1873-74; instr. Zencker Inst., Jena, 1875-76; prof. Latin and Arabic, 1880-1900, dean, 1892-93, U. of Cincinnati; prof. Bay View Summer Sch., 1895-96; sec. Presbyn. Union of Pittsburgh; pres. Ins. Inspection & Appraisal Co. Author: An Extract from Ibn Kutaiba's Adab-al-Katib, or, The Writer's Guide, with translation and notes taken from an Arabic MS. found in the Imperial Court Library in Vienna, Leipzig, 1877. Home: Pittsburgh, Pa. Died 1911.

SPRUANCE, William Corbit, electrical engr.; b. Wilmington, Del., Sept. 26, 1873; s. William Corbit and Maria Louisa (Spotswood) S.; grad. Friends' Sch., Wilmington, 1890; Princeton Univ., 1894, E.E., 1895; m. Alice Moore Lea, May 4, 1907. Cons. practice until 1903; with duPont Co., 1903—, except mil. service; v.p. and dir. E. I. du Pont de Nemours & Co. Commd. maj. Ordnance R.C., U.S.A., Dec. 1917; lt. col. N.A., Jan. 1918; col. U.S.A., Oct. 1918; served as chief of explosives and loading div. Ordnance Dept.; mem. commodity sect. on explosives War Industries Bd. and com. on explosives investigation Nat. Research Council; hon. discharged, Feb. 1919. Awarded D.S.M. (U.S.), 1919. Republican. Presbyn. Home: Wilmington, Del. Died Jan. 9, 1935.

SPRUNT, Alexander, clergyman; b. Glasgow, Scotland, July 10, 1852; s. Alexander and Jane (Dalziel) S.; brought to U.S. in infancy; A.B., Davidson (N.C.) Coll., 1875, D.D., 1897; grad. Union Theol. Sem., in Va., 1878; m. Ellen Richardson Peck, Apr. 30, 1879. Ordained Presbyn. ministry, 1878; asst. to Rev. H. M. White, Winchester, Va., 1878-79; pastor Augusta, Va., 1879-85, 1st Ch., Henderson, N.C., 1885-91; supt. Home Missions Synod of N.C., 1891-92; pastor 1st Ch., Rock Hill, S.C., 1892-1901, 1st Ch., Charleston, S.C., 1901—. Moderator Gen. Assembly Presbyn. Ch. in U.S., 1923. Trustee Columbia Theol. Sem., Thornwell Orphanage (Clinton, S.C.). Home: Charleston, S.C. Died Dec. 15, 1937.

SPRY, William, governor; b. Windsor, Eng., Jan. 11, 1864; s. Philip and Sarah (Field) S.; came to America, 1875; common sch. edn.; m. Mary Alice Wrathall, July 10, 1890. Connected with Z.M.C.I. (gen. mdse. house), Salt Lake City, 1891-93; farming and stockraising, 1893-1904; pres., dir. Farmers & Stockgrowers' Bank, Salt Lake City, and dir. various other instns. County collector Tooele County, Utah, 1894-96; city councilman, Grantsville, 1896-1903; pres. State Bd. Land Commrs., 1905-06; U.S. marshal for Utah, 1906-08, resigned; gov. of Utah, terms 1909-13, 1913-17; commr. Gen. Land Office, 1921—. Republican. Mormon. Home: Salt Lake City, Utah. Died Apr. 21, 1929.

SPURGEON, William Porter, editor; b. Norwich, Eng., Nov. 29, 1867; s. Robert and Mary Elizabeth (Porter) S.; came to U.S.; 1881; ed. pub. and pvt. schs.; m. Mary J. Turner, Sept. 1, 1896 (died 1917). With New York Press, 1888-89; with Washington Post, 1894-1913, mng. editor same, 1907-13; editor Washington Herald, 1914-16; again mng. editor Washington Post, Jan. 1917—. Apptd. commr. to China and Japan for P.P. Internat. Expn., 1913. Republican. Episcopalian. Home: Washington, D.C. Died June 4, 1920.

SPURGIN, William Fletcher, army officer; b. Carlisle, Ky., Oct. 18, 1838; s. David McKendree and Amanda (Secrest) S.; ed. in Ky. and Asbury (now DePauw) Univ., to junior yr.; studied West Point, July 1, 1858, to Mar. 12, 1861 (A.M., DePauw); m. Martha L. Hair, Dec. 31, 1861, Martha L. Hair. In Civil war served 1st lt., and adj. 54th Ind. vols., June 10, 1862, to Sept. 26, 1862; capt. 15th U.S.

colored inf., 9th, Apr. 1864, 100th U.S. colored inf., June 9, 1864; hon. mustered out Dec. 26, 1864; bvtd. maj. vols. for spl. gallantry at Johnsonville, Tenn., Nov. 1864, and Nashville, Tenn., Dec. 16, 1864; 1st lt. 38th U.S. inf., July 28, 1866; capt. 21st inf., June 2, 1876; maj. 23d inf., Dec. 2, 1897; lt. col. 16th inf., May 4, 1899; col. 4th inf., Mar. 1, 1901; brig. gen., May 16, 1902; retired at own request, after 40 yrs. service, May 29, 1902. Took part in Nez Percé campaign, 1877, Bannock campaign, 1878; U.S. Mil. Acad., Sept. 2, 1881, to May 15, 1899; collector customs Philippine Islands, Sept. 1899, to Oct. 1900; comd. dept. Texas, Apr. 3, 1902, to retirement. Died 1904.

SQUIER, George Owen, army officer; b. Dryden, Mich., Mar. 21, 1865; s. Almon Justice and Emily (Gardner) S.; grad. U.S. Mil. Acad., 1887; fellow, Johns Hopkins, 1902-03 and 1903-04, Ph.D., 1903; hon. D.Sc. from Dartmouth College, 1922; unmarried. Apptd. 2d lieut. 3d Artillery, June 12, 1887; 1st lt., June 30, 1893; capt. signal officer vols., May 20, 1898; lt. col. signal officer vols., July 18, 1898; hon. disch. from vols., Dec. 7, 1898; 1st lt. signal corps U.S.A., Feb. 23, 1899; capt. signal officer vols., Apr. 17, 1899; hon. disch. from vols., June 30, 1901; capt., signal corps U.S.A., Feb. 2, 1901; maj., Mar. 2, 1903. Comd. U.S. Cable-ship Burnside, 1900-02, during laying of Philippine cable-telegraph system. U.S. mil. attaché at London, Eng., 1912; commd. lt. col. Signal Corps, Mar. 17, 1913; brig. gen., chief signal officer U.S.A., Feb. 14, 1917; maj. gen., Oct. 6, 1917; in charge of army air service, May 20, 1916-May 20, 1918. Mem. nat. council Boy Scouts of America. D.S.M. (U.S.); Knight Comdr. St. Michael and St. George (Great Britain); Commander Order of the Crown (Italy); Commander Legion of Honor (France). Elliott Cresson gold medal, Franklin medal. Researches: Electrochemical effects due to magnetization; the polarizing photochronograph; the sine wave systems of telegraphy and ocean cabling; the absorption of electro-magnetic waves by living vegetable organisms; multiplex telephony and telegraphy; tree telephony and telegraphy, multiplex telephony and telegraphy, over open circuit bare wires laid in the earth or sea. Inventor of the monophone for broadcasting over telephone wires and over power wires, also wired wireless, 1910; inventor of "Quickaid," a first aid kit for Army and Red Cross use. War Department rep. and technical adviser to Am. delegation at Internat. Conf. on Elec. Communications, Washington, 1920; rep. dept. of State at sessions of Provisional Tech. com. of Internat. Conf. on Elec. Communications, Paris, 1921; designated an expert asst. to Am. Commrs. at Conf. on Limitation of Armament, Washington, 1921; ex-officio mem., representing War Dept., of U.S. Nat. Com. Internat. Electrotech. Commn. Founder, 1918, of "A Country Club for Country People," Dryden, Mich. Died Mar. 24, 1934.

SQUIERS, Arnon Lyon, judge; b. Smyrna, N.Y., Oct. 6, 1869; s. James P. and Ellen W. (Lyon) S.; grad. Cazenovia (N.Y.) Sem., 1889; A.B., Columbia, 1893; LL.B., New York Law Sch., 1894; m. Gertrude Cooper, 1902. Asst. prof. mathematics, Columbia, 1893-95; instr. mathematics, Barnard Coll., 1894-95; admitted to N.Y. bar, 1895, and practiced in N.Y. City; mem. Bd. of Aldermen, N.Y. City, 1914-19; elected justice Supreme Court of N.Y., 2d Jud. Dist., Nov. 1919, for term ending 1933. Trustee Cazenovia Sem., 1902—. Republican. Conglist. Mason; Dist. Grand Master 1st Dist., Kings Co. Editor: One Hundred Per Cent America, 1918. Home: Brooklyn, N.Y. Died Oct. 28, 1921.

SQUIERS, Herbert Goldsmith, diplomat; b. Madoc, Can., Apr. 20, 1859; s. John T. and Elizabeth J. S.; Canandaigua Acad., Minn. Mil. Acad., Md. Agrl. Coll.; grad. U.S. Arty. Sch., 1880; (hon. A.M., St. John's Coll., N.Y., 1887, LL.D., 1906); m. Helen L., d. W. G. Fargo, Oct. 11, 1881 (died 1886); m. 2d, Harriet Bard, d. Dr. William P. Woodcock, Nov. 12, 1889. Second lt. 1st U.S. Inf., Oct. 12, 1877; transferred to 7th Cav., Aug. 31, 1880; mil. instr., St. John's Coll., 1885-90; 1st lt., 1st Cav., Dec. 17, 1890; transferred to 7th Cav., Feb. 27, 1891; resigned, Nov. 28, 1891. Second sec. U.S. Embassy, Berlin, Nov. 15, 1894; retired May 1897; apptd. sec. legation at Peking, Jan. 10, 1898; chief of staff to Sir Claude MacDonald, during siege of Peking, 1900-01, for which received thanks of British Govt.; E.E. and M.P. of U.S. to Cuba, May 1902-Nov. 1905, resigned; E.E. and M.P. to Panama, 1906-10. Died 1911.

SQUIRE, Andrew, lawyer; b. Mantua, O., Oct. 21, 1850; s. Andrew Jackson and Martha (Wilmot) S.; A.B., Hiram (O.) Coll., 1872; admitted to bar, 1873; m. Mrs. Eleanor Seymour Sea, d. Belden Seymour, of Cleveland, June 24, 1896. Mem. Squire, Sanders & Dempsey, 1890—; dir. Union Trust Co., Cleveland Quarries Co., Cleveland & Pittsburgh R.R. (pres.), Union Carbide & Carbon Corporation. Member board Hiram College and bd. of Western Reserve U.; dir. Case Library. Republican. Home: Cleveland, O. Died Jan. 5, 1934.

SQUIRE, Frances (Mrs. Frances Boardman Squire Potter), univ. prof.; b. Elmira, N.Y., Nov. 12, 1867; d. Dr. Truman H. and Grace (Smith) S.; A.B., Elmira (N.Y.) Coll., 1887, A.M., 1889; research work, Cambridge (Eng.) U., 1906; A.M., U. of Minn., 1909; m. W. Scott Potter, Dec. 10, 1891. Instr. Elmira Coll., 1890; instr. E. High Sch., Minneapolis, 1900; instr. old English, 1901-02, asst. prof. English lit., 1903-07, prof., 1907—, U. of Minn.; extension lecturer Coll. of Edn., U. of Minn., 1909. Corr. sec. Nat. Am. Woman Suffrage Assn., 1909; chmn. lit. and library extension dept. of Gen. Fedn. of Women's Clubs, 1910; gen. lecturer Nat. Woman's Trade Union League, 1910; editor dept. Life and Labor, 1910. Author: (play) Germelshausen (collaboration), 1904; The Ballingtons (novel), 1905; Jamieson (play), 1909. Contbr. to mags. under pen name Frances Boardman, later under Frances Squire. Home: Minneapolis, Minn. Died Mar. 25, 1914.

SQUIRE, Watson Carvosso, senator; b. Cape Vincent, N.Y., May 18, 1838; s. Rev. Orra and Erretta (Wheeler) S.; A.B., Wesleyan U., 1859; prin. Moravia, N.Y., Inst., 1859-61; LL.B., Cleveland (O.) Law Sch., 1862; LL.D., Wesleyan U., Conn., 1911. Pvt. and 1st lt., Co. F, 19th N.Y. Vols., 3 mos., 1861; raised, Oct. 1862, 7th Independent Co. of Ohio Sharpshooters, afterward known as "Gen. Sherman's Body Guard," comd. it in Army of the Cumberland; comd. battalion of sharpshooters Chickamauga campaign; judge advocate, dist. of Tenn., 1864-65; bvtd., July 1866, by President and U.S. Senate, lt. col. and col. "for gallant and meritorious services," mustered out, Aug. 1865; m. Ida, d. Philo Remington, Dec. 23, 1868; children—Philo Remington, Shirley, Aidine (Mrs. Arthur V. White), Marjorie (Mrs. John F. Jennings). Mgr. Remington Arms Co., New York, 1866-79; moved to Seattle, Wash., 1879, inaugurating extensive business enterprises there and a large dairy farm; pres. Union Trust Co., Squire Investment Co. Gov. of Washton Ty., 1884-87; pres. State Conv., 1889; elected U.S. senator, Nov. 21, 1889, under act of Congress admitting Wash Ty. to the Union, reëlected, 1891, for term, 1891-97. Republican. Died June 7, 1926.

SQUIRES, Vernon Purinton, prof. of English; b. Cortland, N.Y., Nov. 4, 1866; s. James Samuel and Libbie A. (Purinton) S.; grad. State Normal Sch., Cortland, 1885; B.A., Brown U., 1889; fellow U. of Chicago, 1893-97, M.A., 1895; Litt.D., Brown U., 1914; m. Ethel Claire Wood, July 9, 1902; children—James Duane, Alden Wood, Emily Ruth, Vernon Calvert, Donald Edgcomb, Ethel Hope. Instr. in science, Worcester Acad., Mass., 1889-90; prof. Greek and Latin, State Normal Sch., Oneonta, N.Y., 1890-93; prof. English U. of N.D., 1897-1901; prof. English and History, Kalamazoo Coll., Mich., 1901-02; prof. English, 1902—, dean Coll. Liberal Arts, 1914—, U. of North Dakota; visiting lecturer, U. of California at Los Angeles, 1926-27. Baptist. Alderman, Grand Forks, 1911-14. Mem. Lions Internat., S.A.R. Editor: Tennyson's In Memoriam, 1906. Author: North Dakota Syllabus of Bible Study. Lectures frequently at chautauquas and ednl. gatherings. Home: Grand Forks, N.D. Died Aug. 16, 1930.

ST. JOHN, Charles Edward, solar physicist; b. Allen, Mich., Mar. 15, 1857; s. Hiram A. and Lois A. (Bacon) S.; grad. classical course, Mich. Normal Coll., 1876; B.S., Mich. Agrl. Coll., 1887; studied U. of Mich., 1890-92; A.M., Harvard, 1893, Ph.D., 1896; U. of Berlin, 1894-95; hon. Pd.M., Mich. Normal Coll., 1906; hon. Sc.D., Oberlin College, 1931; unmarried. Teacher of physics, Michigan Normal College, 1885-92; instructor in physics, U. of Mich., 1896-97; asso. prof. physics and astronomy, 1897-99, prof., 1899-1908, dean Coll. of Arts and Sciences, 1907-08, Oberlin Coll.; astronomer, Mt. Wilson Observatory of Carnegie Instn., 1908—. Mem. internat. commns. on solar rotation and on standards of wavelength; pres. Internat. Commn. on Solar Physics. Author of Revision of Rowland's Preliminary Table of Solar Spectrum Wave-lengths. Home: Pasadena, Calif. Died Apr. 26, 1935.

ST. JOHN, Charles Elliott, clergyman; b. Prairie du Chien, Wis., Dec. 19, 1856; s. Thomas Elliott and Henrietta (Knox) S.; A.B., Harvard U., 1879, A.M., B.D., 1883; m. Martha E. Everett, June 26, 1888. Ordained Unitarian ministry, 1883; pastor Second Congl. (Unitarian) Church, Northampton, Mass., 1883-91, First Unitarian Ch., Pittsburgh, 1891-1900; sec. Am. Unitarian Assn., Boston, 1900-07; pastor First Unitarian Ch., Phila., Sept. 1907—. Trustee Meadville (Pa.) Theol. Sch. Author: The Religion of the Dawn, 1910. Died Feb. 25, 1916.

ST. JOHN, Cynthia Morgan; b. Ithaca, N.Y., Oct. 11, 1852; d. Edward Jay (M.D.) and Anne (Bruyn) Morgan; ed. pvt. schs. and Cornell U.; m. Henry Ancel St. John, June 25, 1883. Chiefly interested in works of William Wordsworth, English poet; has collected what is claimed to be the most complete Wordsworth library in the world. Conglist. Author: Wordsworth for the Young, 1891. Editor: Memorial Lines to Charles Lamb (by William Wordsworth), 1904. Home: Ithaca, N.Y. Died Aug. 1919.

ST. JOHN, Everitte, ry. official; b. in Conn., Feb. 4, 1844; began ry. service as ticket clerk, 1862, Quincy & Toledo R.R.; was with C.,R.I.&P. R.R., July 4, 1863, to Jan. 1, 1895, from ticket clerk to gen. mgr., Jan. 1, 1895, became v.p. Seaboard Air Line and a yr. later also gen. mgr., which position he continued to occupy until Jan. 11, 1901; and in connection was also pres. Chesterfield & Kershaw R.R. Corp.; v.p. and gen. mgr. Richmond, Petersburg & Carolina R.R., and of Ga. & Ala. R.R., 1900-01; also 1st v.p. Fla. Central & Peninsular R.R., 1900-01. Reorganized, 1891, and was permanent chmn., 1891-95, Gen. Mgrs.' Assn. of Chicago, and had charge of its operations in connection with suppression of the "Debs" strike of 1894; has also had official connection with various freight assns., and was chmn. of the Railroad Finance Com., World's Columbian Expn. Freemason. Episcopalian. Past pres. Sons of Conn., Chicago; mem. Chamber Commerce, Norfolk, Va. Home: Wellesley, Mass. Died 1908.

ST. JOHN, John Pierce, governor; b. Brookville, Ind., Feb. 25, 1833; s. Samuel and Sophia (Snell) S.; ed. in log schoolhouse in Ind.; served as capt. and lt. col. in Civil War; went to Kan. after the war; mem. Kan. Senate, 1872-73; gov. of Kan., 1879-83; candidate on Prohibition ticket for President of U.S., 1884; supported Bryan for President, 1900. Home: Olathe, Kan. Died Aug. 31, 1916.

ST. JOHN, Samuel Benedict, surgeon; b. Hudson, O., July 24, 1845; s. Samuel and Amelia Palmer (Curtis) S.; A.B., Yale, 1866; M.D., Coll. Phys. and Surg. (Columbia) 1870; studied univs. of Berlin and Vienna; m. Mary Harris Morgan, Oct. 10, 1882. Practiced in New York, 1874-78, then at Hartford. Surgeon Eye and Ear Infirmary, New York, 1877-88; ophthalmic and aural surgeon Hartford Hosp., 1888—; cons. surgeon St. Francis and Litchfield County hosps. Pres. Am. Ophthal. Society, 1908-09 (sec. 1888-1908). Dir. Hartford Public Library, 1890— (pres. 1892-93). Republican. Conglist. Home: Hartford, Conn. Died 1909.

STAAKE, William Heaton, judge; b. Brooklyn, Dec. 5, 1846; s. Frederick and Sopsia Smith (Heaton) S.; A.B., Central High Sch., Phila., 1865, A.M., 1870; LL.B., U. of Pa., 1868; m. Henrietta C. Wagner, June 9, 1870. Admitted to Pa. bar, Mar. 14, 1868; practiced at Phila.; judge Ct. of Common Pleas No. 5 for Co. of Phila., May 16, 1906—. Commr. from Pa., 1901—, chmn. commn. from Pa., and chmn. exec. com. Nat. Conf. of Commrs. on Uniform State Laws (pres. 1915-16); del. and sec. Nat. Divorce Congress; commr. to codify divorce laws of Pa.; sec. bd. having charge of Independence Hall and its hist. museums and collections; mem. Municipal Civ. Service Examining Bd. Dir. Mary J. Drexel Home and Phila. Mother House of Deaconesses (pres.), Maternity Hosp., Phila. (pres.); trustee Rush Hosp. for Consumptives; mem. advisory com. Phila. Home for Incurables; mem. bd. mgrs. Phila. House of Refuge. V.p. Evang. Luth. Ch. of the Holy Communion, Phila. (30 yrs. mem. of its ch. council); dir. Luth. Theol. Sem.; sec. Luth. Mission and Ch. Extension Soc., 1873-1911; treas. Gen. Council Evang. Luth. Ch. in N. America, 1876-1919, treas. trustees Gen. Council, 1876-1917 (also treas. Bd. Foreign Missions same, 1876-1901); dir. Pa. Bible Soc.; chmn. Bd. Law Examiners, Phila. County; chmn. Legal Com. Y.M.C.A., Phila. Republican. Author: Centennial History of the Magdalen Society of Philadelphia, 1900; Functions and Duties of Probation Officers. Sec. Central Com. on Selective Draft in Pa.; mem. Pa. War History Commn. Home: Philadelphia, Pa. Died July 30, 1924.

STABLER, John Gates, judge; b. nr. St. Matthews, S.C., Oct. 3, 1871; s. William David and Johanna Frances (Zeigler) S.; student Orangeburg (S.C.) Collegiate Institute; A.B., Wofford Coll., Spartanburg, S.C., 1905, LL.D. from the same college, 1934; LL.B., University of S.C., 1908; m. Hallie Murray, June 20, 1912. Teacher pub. schs., Orangeburg County, S.C., 1893-1900, Orangeburg Collegiate Inst., 1901, Wofford Fitting Sch., 1904-05, Carlisle Fitting Sch., 1905-06; admitted to S.C. bar, 1908, and began practice at St. Matthews; mem. S.C. Senate, 1921-26; elected asso. justice Supreme Court of S.C., Jan. 1926, to fill unexpired term, 1926, of T. B. Frazer, deceased, and later for full term expiring July 31, 1936; elected chief justice Mar. 1935, for term expiring July 31, 1944. Chmn. Calhoun County Legal Advisory Bd., World War, also mem. S.C. State Council of Defense and four-minute speaker. Democrat. Methodist. Home: St. Matthews, S.C. Died Jan. 3, 1940.

STABLER, Jordan Herbert, diplomat, financier; b. Baltimore, Md., Oct. 16, 1885; s. Jordan and Caroline (Semple) S.; A.B., Johns Hopkins, 1907; studied U. of Md., Sorbonne (Paris) and Collége de France; m. Elizabeth Huidekooper Wells, June 5, 1915; children—Warwick Brooke, Wells. Pvt. sec. to Am. minister at Brussels, Belgium, 1909; sec. Am. Legation, Quito, Ecuador, 1909-11, chargé d'affaires, Guatemala, 1911-12, sec. of legation, Stockholm, Sweden, 1912-13; asst. to chief Div. Latin-Am. Affairs, Dept. of State, 1913-14; 2d sec. of embassy, London, 1914-16; acting chief, 1916-17, chief of Div. Latin-Am. Affairs, 1917-19; adviser to Am. Commn. to Negotiate Peace, Paris, 1918; v.p. All America Cables, Inc., 1919-22; sec. gen., with rank of M.P.,

Conf. on Central Am. Affairs, 1922-23; sec. gen. Plebiscitary Commn., Tacna-Arica Arbitration, 1925-26; chief of Div. Latin Am. Affairs, Dept. State, 1926-27; rep. of Venezuela Gulf Oil Corp., Caracas, Venezuela, 1927—. Traveled to Ecuadorean headwaters of the Amazon, 1910, in Tunisia, 1912, Haiti, 1913, Ecuador, 1924, Venezuela and Colombia, 1928. Fellow Royal Geog. Soc. (London). Author: Bolivar—In Memoriam, 1930. Editor: Fragments from an XVIII Century Diary—The Travels and Adventures of Don Francisco de Miranda (1771-1789), 1931. Home: Caracas, Venezuela. Died Dec. 30, 1938.

STABLER, Laird Joseph, chemist; b. Bethany, O., Aug. 27, 1865; s. Daniel F. and Rachel A. (Le Sourd) S.; Ph.C., U. of Mich., 1885; B.S., Purdue U., 1890, M.S., 1892; Sc.D., U. of Southern Calif., 1916; m. Maude Jones, Aug. 27, 1890. Prof. industrial chemistry and dean Coll. of Pharmacy, U. of Southern Calif., 1894—. Dir. Bd. of Health, Los Angeles, 6 yrs.; trustee Pub. Library, 4 yrs. Republican. Methodist. Specialized in chemistry of petroleum oils. Died Nov. 26, 1939.

STACEY, Alfred Edwin, chair mfr.; b. Elbridge, N.Y., Jan. 20, 1846; s. Richard and Agnes (Pierce) S.; ed. pvt. and pub. schs. and Munroe Collegiate Inst., Elbridge, 1851-66; m. Ellen Gorham, June 1, 1871 (died 1881); children—Mabel Conelia (Mrs. Walter Bliss), Maud Ellen (Mrs. George H. Lamb); m. 2d, Jessie Rowe, Mar. 15, 1883; 1 son, Alfred Edwin. Began as salesman for A. Wood & Son, 1863; salesman at Skaneateles and Auburn, N.Y., 1866-69; bought business of A. Wood & Sons (dealing in gen. mdse.), 1869, conducting it until 1884; engaged in mfr. of chairs as Elbridge Chair Co., 1884—; bought farm, 1890, residing thereon; former post master, mayor and clerk of Elbridge, N.Y.; mem. N.Y. State Assembly, 1886-87; treas. Onondaga County, 1903-06; trustee Elbridge School. Enlisted in Co. L, 9th N.Y. Heavy Arty., Sept. 5, 1864; mem. 2d Brigade, 3d Div., 6th A.C. to end of Civil War; wounded twice at Cedar Creek; served on Richmond and Petersburg fronts and at Appomatox on surrender of Gen. Lee; chmn. Draft Bd., World War—only mem. G.A.R. so serving. Dept. comdr. N.Y. State G.A.R., 1920, also asst. adj. and q.m. gen.; comdr. in chief Nat. G.A.R., 1934-35. Odd Fellow. Home: Elbridge, N.Y. Died Mar. 10, 1940.

STACEY, John Franklin, artist; b. Biddeford, Me., Mar. 16, 1859; s. John and Agnes (Ricker), S.; grad. Mass. Normal Art Sch., Boston; student Julian Acad., Paris; m. Anna Lee Dey, Oct. 15, 1891. Awards: bronze medal, St. Louis Expn., 1904; bronze medal, Buenos Aires Expn., 1910 (picture purchased by Art Mus., Santiago, Chile); Grower prize, Art Inst. Chicago, 1911; Logan bronze medal, Chicago Artists' Expn., 1924; The L. S. Valentine Prize awarded 1937, Chicago Painters & Scupltors Exhbn.; landscape prize, Pasadena Soc. Artists, 1938. Pres. Chicago Soc. Artists, 1907-09; v.p. Soc. Chicago Painters and Sculptors. Home: Pasadena, Calif. Died Feb. 3, 1941.

STACKPOLE, Edward James, editor; b. McVeytown, Pa., Jan. 18, 1861; s. Edward H. H. and Margaret (Glasgow) S.; ed. pub. schs.; m. Kate Hummel, Oct. 10, 1889; children—Catherine Hummel (Mrs. Walter Bruce Caldwell), Margaret (Mrs. John C. Herman), Edward James, Albert Hummel. Began in employ of uncle, on McVeytown Journal; editor and part owner Orbisonia (Pa.) Dispatch, 1881-83; became asst. foreman and exchange editor Harrisburg Telegraph, 1883; Harrisburg corr. New York, Chicago, Phila. and Pittsburgh papers, 1884-1901; chief owner, editor in chief and pres. Harrisburg Telegraph, 1901—; dir. Harrisburg Trust Co. postmaster, Harrisburg, 1901-13; mem. Commn. on Amendment and Revision of State Constn., 1920; del. Rep. Nat. Conv., 1920. Served in N.G. Pa. 3 yrs.; chmn. 6th Pa. Dist. in United War Work campaign; member Com. National Defense for Pa., etc.; 1917-18. Pres. Harrisburg Board of Trade, 1903; pres. Chamber Commerce, 1920; pres. Associated Dailies of Pa. several yrs. Republican. Presbyn. Author: Tales of My Boyhood, 1922; Behind the Scenes With a Newspaper Man, 1927; Cruising the World Around, 1929; (booklet) South America and the Mediterranean Region; South Africa—Impressions of an American, 1933. Home: Harrisburg, Pa. Died Jan. 2, 1936.

STACKPOLE, Everett Schermerhorn, clergyman; b. Durham, Me., June 11, 1850; s. Samuel Owen and Eliza Swett (Macomber) S.; A.B., Bowdoin Coll., 1871, A.M., 1874 (D.D., 1888); S.T.B., Boston U. Sch. of Theology, 1878; m. Elizabeth Augusta Blake, Aug. 20, 1878. Ordained M.E. ministry, 1882; pastor, Kingsfield, Me., 1878-79. Lisbon, 1879-81, Deering, 1881-83, Westbrook, 1883-84, Bath, 1884-87, Portland, 1887-88; pres. Theol. Sch., Florence, Italy, 1888-92; pastor, Auburn, Me., 1894-98, Augusta, 1898-1900, Congl. Ch., Bradford, Mass., 1901—. Corporate mem. A.B.C.F.M. Mason. Author: The Italy Mission, 1894; The Evidences of Salavation, 1893; Prophecy, or Speaking for God, 1897; History and Genealogy of the Stackpole Family, 1898; History of Durham, Maine, 1899; Old Kittery and Her Families, 1903; Macomber Genealogy, 1908. Home: Bradford, Mass. Deceased.

STACKPOLE, Pierpont L(angley), lawyer; b. Brookline, Mass., Feb. 16, 1875; s. Stephen Henry and Julia Langley (Faunce) S.; prep. edn., Colgate Acad., Hamilton, N.Y.; student Colgate U., 1892-95; A.B., Harvard, 1897, LL.B., 1900; m. Mrs. Laura McGinley Knowles, May 10, 1922. Admitted to Mass. bar, 1900, and began practice at Boston; mem. Warner, Stackpole & Bradlee; director and mem. exec. com. Crompton & Knowles Loom Works. Served as lt. col. F.A., U.S.A.; with A.E.F., Sept. 1917-Sept. 1919; civilian aide to sec. of war, 1st Corps Area, 1922-29. Trustee South End House Assn., Children's Aid Assn., N.E. Conservatory of Music, Boston Symphony Orchestra. Awarded D.S.M. (U.S.); Officier Etoile Noir du Bénin (France); Officier Ordre de la Couronne (Belgium). Home: Boston, Mass. Died Dec. 26, 1936.

STACY, Thomas Hobbs, clergyman; b. North Berwick, Me., July 26, 1850; s. Daniel Lowe and Elizabeth Ann (Hobbs) S.; A.B., Bates Coll., 1876, B.D., 1879, D.D., 1906; m. Clara I. Farnham, Aug. 27, 1879 (dec.); 1 dau., Mrs. Anne Clarabelle Spooner; m. 2d, Leanora M. Harlow, Dec. 26, 1891; 1 dau., Mrs. Elizabeth Maie Jameson. Taught in Bates Coll. 3 yrs. and in Div. Sch. 1 yr.; ordained Free Baptist ministry, Sept. 17, 1879; pastor Fairport, N.Y., 1879-82, Lawrence, Mass., 1882-86, Auburn, Me., 1886-93, Saco, Me., 1893-1902, Concord, N.H., 1902-Oct. 1919; in charge ch. federation, Sandwich, N.H., 1920—. Ten times a mem. of Gen. Conf.; corr. sec. Free Bapt. Foreign Mission Soc., 1882-94; made tour of world as mission sec., 1890-91; mem. Gen. Conf. Bd., 1904—(exec com., 1905—, and recording sec. of both bodies); mem. com. of 12 on conference with other Christian people, 1905-10; now com. of 5, and sec. same; pres. Ministers' Conf. Me. Free Bapt. Assn., 1894-1902, York Co. Enforcement League, 1896-1902; editor Me. Dept., The International Evangel, St. Louis, 1897-99; trustee Bates Coll., New Hampton Lit. Instn.; pres. Council on Sacred Orders for Free Bapts. in N.H., 1902-16, N.H. S.S. Assn., 1903-04 (exec. com.); mem. bd. mgrs. Am. Bapt. Foreign Mission Soc., 1911—; mem. Federal Council Chs. of Christ in America; sec. N.H. Interdenominational Commn., Mar. 1906—. Author: In the Path of Light Around the World, 1895; Conditions of Spiritual Life, 1901; Life of O. R. Bacheler, M.D., D.D., Fifty-Three Years Missionary to India, 1904; Wayside Garniture, 1912; Historical Sketch, Bengal Mission, 1912. Home: Center Sandwich, N.H. Died May 14, 1927.

STADDEN, Corry Montague, lawyer, newspaper corr.; b. Utica, O., May 24, 1870; s. George W. and Orilla M. (Lusk) S.; ed. Newark, O.; LL.B., LL.M., George Washington U.; m. Mary Lillian Arnold, Oct. 14, 1903. Washington corr., May 1893—; sr. mem. Stadden & Stewart; counselor of legation of Nicaragua, 1901-10; spl. counsel for State of La. in land cases; del. for Nicaragua to Internat. Coffee Commn., 1902. Extensive writer on Isthmian Canal and other Nicaraguan topics. Home: Washington, D.C. Died Jan. 8, 1916.

STADELMAN, William Francis, clergyman; b. Woods Run, North Side Pittsburgh, Pa., Feb. 12, 1869; s. Sebastian and Rosalia (Ehinger) S.; B.S. and B.A., Duquesne U., Pittsburgh, 1892, M.A., 1905; studied philosophy and theology, Paris, 1893-98; traveled in Europe, 1922, 25. Ordained priest R.C. Ch., 1898; joined Congregation of the Holy Ghost (C.S.Sp.); teacher classics, French and German, Duquesne U., 1898-1903; chaplain and instr. ch. history and religion at Belmead and St. Francis Inst. Rock Castle, Va., 1903-14; dir. Apostolic Coll., Cornwells Heights, Pa., 1914-18; pastor St. Benedict's Ch., Pittsburgh, 1918-21; nat. dir. from 1921 of Holy Childhood Assn. for U.S. (internat. orgn. for ransom and edn. of abandoned pagan children and outcasts). Sec. Provincial Council Holy Ghost Fathers; mem. advisory bd. Catholic students Mission Crusade; mem. Exec. Council Holy Childhood, Paris; mem. Inst. des Missions, Fribourg, Switzerland. Made domestic prelate by Pope Pius XI, 1922. Author: Eucharistic Soul Elevations, 1906; Sparks of Truth, 1908; Cord of St. Francis, 1917; Glories of the Holy Ghost, 1919; Beginnings and Growth of St. Benedict's Church, 1920; St. Francis Xavier, Worker of Miracles, 1921; Association of the Holy Childhood (history of Am. branch), 1923. Home: Pittsburgh, Pa. Died Nov. 6, 1928.

STAFFORD, Charles Lewis, clergyman; b. Clark Co., O., Sept. 26, 1844; s. William H. and Mary Elizabeth S.; A.B., Ia. Wesleyan U., 1871, A.M., 1874; D.D., Upper Ia. U., 1889; LL.D., Ia. Wesleyan, 1905; m. Mary Jane Allen, July 4, 1871; children—Clarence Allen, Charles Ralph, Eva May (dec.), William Reuben (dec.). Ordained M.E. ministry, 1871; in active ministry as pastor and presiding elder in Ia. Conf., 1870-91; pres. Ia. Wesleyan U., 1891-99; sec. Ia. Conf., 1893-99. Del. Gen. confs., 4 times, and for 3 sessions one of the secs.; del. to Ecumenical Conf., London, 1901. Home: Muscatine, Ia. Died Sept. 15, 1930.

STAFFORD, Orin Fletcher, chemist; b. Hillsboro, O., Feb. 7, 1873; s. E. and Sarah (Kurtz) S.; A.B., U. of Kan., 1900, A.M., 1902; U. of Berlin, 1908-09; m. Mary E. Straub, Dec. 24, 1903; children—Howard Straub, Miriam, John Edward. Asst. prof. chemistry, U. of Ore., 1902-06, prof., 1906—, also head of dept. and later dean of science and of Lower Division. On leave of absence, 1918-22, to develop autogenous process for wood carbonization applicable to use of waste woods; consulting practice. Home: Eugene, Ore. Died Sept. 17, 1941.

STAGG, Charles Tracey, lawyer; b. Elmira, N.Y., Dec. 16, 1878; s. Charles Edward and Ella Campbell (Van Allen) S.; grad. Elmira (N.Y.) Acad., 1896; LL.B., Cornell U., 1902 (Boardman scholarship, 1901-02); m. Madeleine Estelle Goff, June 24, 1903; 1 son, Norman Goff. Admitted to N.Y. bar, 1902, U.S. Dist. Court, 1904; clerk to Hon. W. L. Smith, justice Supreme Court of N.Y., 1902-04; mem. Gibson & Stagg, Elmira, 1904-06, Newman & Stagg, Ithaca, 1906-09; instr., 1908-09, asst. prof., 1909-14, prof., 1914-21, Coll. of Law, Cornell U., also sec. of the coll. Counsel to the gov. of N.Y., 1921-22; deputy conservation commr. N.Y. State, 1922-24; adviser State Council of Parks, 1924; special dep. atty. gen., 1925; mem. Stagg & Heath, 1924-30, Stagg, Thaler & Stagg, 1930—; state senator, 41st New York Dist., 1935—. Pres. Village of Cayuga Heights, 1915-20; mem. and sec. local bd., Tompkins Co., N.Y., under Selective Service Law, 1917-19; chmn. Ithaca National Recovery Act Com., 1933. Republican. Presbyterian. Mason; Representative of Grand Lodge of Turkey; Grand High Priest Grand Chapter R.A. Masons, State of N.Y., 1922-23. Home: Cayuga Heights Village, Tompkins Co., N.Y. Died July 13, 1939.

STAGG, John Weldon, college pres.; b. Richmond, Va., Aug. 17, 1864; s. John Fox and Sarah Ann (Brazeal) S.; Westminster College, 1885; A.B. and B.D., Southwestern Presbyn. U., 1888; studied at Berlin, Germany, 1896-97; (D.D., Davidson Coll., N.C., 1896); m. Nellie Rice, June 4, 1891. Ordained Presbyn. ministry, 1888; pastor 2d Ch., Nashville, Tenn., 1888-91, 1st Ch., Bowling Green, Ky., 1891-96, 2d Ch., Charlotte, N.C., 1896-1903, 1st Ch., Birmingham, Ala., 1903-09; pres. Ala. Presbyn. Coll. for Men, Anniston, July 1909—. Trustee Gen. Assembly Presbyn. Ch. in U.S., 1897-1903. Democrat. Mason, Odd Fellow, K.P. Author: Calvin, Twisse and Edwards on Universal Salvation of Infants, 1902; The Race Problem in the South, 1904; Racial Ideals, 1905. Died Dec. 24, 1915.

STAHEL, Julius, soldier; b. Hungary, Nov. 5, 1825; s. Andreas and Barbara (Nag) S.; ed. Budapest; unmarried. Fought in struggle for Hungarian independence, under Louis Kossuth, 1848, and was wounded and decorated for gallantry; came to America, 1856; in newspaper work at New York, 1856-61; lt. col. 8th N.Y. Inf., Apr. 17, 1861; col., Aug. 27, 1861; brig. gen. vols., Nov. 12, 1861; maj. gen. vols., Mar. 14, 1863; resigned Feb. 8, 1865. Awarded medal of honor, Nov. 4, 1893, for leading his division after he was severely wounded, and turned the enemy's flank, at Piedmont, Va., June 5, 1864. Covered retreat of Union Army at head of his regt. at 1st battle of Bull Run; comd. advance column of Gen. Fremont's army in Shenandoah Valley; comd. brigade, 1st div., 2d battle of Bull Run; placed in command 11th Army Corps, Jan. 15, 1863; sent for by Pres. Lincoln and assigned to command in front of Washington, Mar. 13, 1863. Apptd. consul at Yokohama, Japan, and consul gen. at Shanghai, China, 1884; resigned, 1885, on account of ill health. Died Dec. 4, 1912.

STAHLMAN, Edward Bushrod, newspaper pub.; b. Mecklenburg, Germany, Sept. 2, 1843; s. Frederick and Christine (Lange) S.; ed. common schs., Germany; came to U.S., 1854; m. Mollie T. Claiborne, Oct. 4, 1866; m. 2d, Sarah Shelton, Aug. 23, 1920. Pres. City Council, Nashville, 1875-78; freight contracting agt., 1871-75, gen. agt., 1875-78, gen. freight agt., 1878-80, gen. traffic mgr., 1880-81, v.p., 1885-90, L.&N. R.R.; v.p. Louisville, New Albany & Chicago R.R., 1882-84; commr. Southern Ry. & Steamship Assn., Atlanta, Ga., 1891-95; pres. Nashville Banner Pub. Co., 1885—; pres. Mecklenburg Real Estate Co., owner Stahlman Bldg., Nashville. Represented rys. of the South, 1885-95, in matters of nat. legislation affecting ry. interests. Home: Nashville, Tenn. Died Aug. 12, 1930.

STAHR, John Summers, college prof.; b. Bucks Co., Pa., Dec. 2, 1841; s. John and Sarah (Summers) S.; A.B., Franklin and Marshall Coll., 1867, A.M., 1870, Ph.D., 1883; (D.D., Lafayette, 1891; LL.D., Pa. Coll., 1904); m. Francina E. Andrews, July 23, 1872. Tutor in German and history, 1867-68, asst. prof., 1868-71, prof. natural science and chemistry, 1871, financial agt., 1887-89; pres. pro tem, 1889, president, 1890-1909, prof. philosophy, 1909-15, and prof. emeritus, 1915—, Franklin and Marshall College. Studied theology privately; ordained to ministry, 1872. Mem. Internat. S.S. Lesson Com., 1890-1908; was consulting mem. on editorial staff Standard Dictionary; mem. 8th Council of Alliance of Reformed Chs., Liverpool, 1904, and 10th Council, Aberdeen, 1913. Home: Lancaster, Pa. Died Dec. 21, 1915.

STAKELY, Charles Averett, clergyman; b. Madisonville, Tenn.; A.M., Mercer U., Macon, Ga., 1884; D.D., Richmond (Va.) Coll., 1889; LL.D., Furman

U., Greenville, S.C., 1898, U. of Ala., 1924; m. Sarah Jessie Davis, 1882; children—Davis Fonville, Anne Kilpatrick (Mrs. Henry F. Martin), Frances Sloan (Mrs. James D. Wilcox), Mrs. Flora Cooledge, Charles Averett. Ordained Bapt. ministry, LaGrange, Ga., 1880; pastor, Elberton and Hartwell, Ga., 1881-82, Curtis Ch., Augusta, Ga., 1883, Citadel Sq. Ch., Charleston, S.C., 1883-87, First Ch., Washington, D.C., then First Ch., Montgomery, Ala., until 1929; pastor emeritus. Home: Montgomery, Ala. Died May 22, 1937.

STALEY, Augustus Eugene, mfr. corn products; b. Julian, N.C., Feb. 25, 1867; s. William and Mary Jane (Ledbetter) S.; ed. country sch.; LL.D., High Point Coll., High Point, N.C., 1939; m. Emma Louise Tressler, Dec. 14, 1898; children—Ione (Mrs. Harold Dunlap), Ruth (Mrs. Floyd Hunt), Augustus Eugene, Mary Louise, Andrew Rollin. Began in starch mfg. business, Baltimore, Md., 1898; bought Wellington Starch Works, Decatur, Ill., 1909; became chmn. bd. A. E. Staley Mfg. Co., Decatur and Baltimore; dir. Wabash Ry. Co. Democrat. Mason, Elk. Home: Decatur, Ill. Died Dec. 26, 1940.

STALEY, John Wilson, banker; b. Danville, Pa., Apr. 6, 1871; s. John and Mary Lewis (Wilson) S.; B.A., Albion (Mich.) Coll., 1892; m. Harriet Esther Bewick, Dec. 21, 1907; 1 dau., Elizabeth. Entered employ of First and Old Detroit Nat. Bank, 1892, and advanced to asst. cashier, 1908, v.p., 1912; 1st vice pres. Peoples State Bank, 1917-19, pres., 1919—; dir. Bankers Trust Co., New York. Executive mgr. Liberty Loan Committee of Detroit and Wayne Co. World War. Trustee Albion Coll., Grace Hosp. (Detroit), Detroit Y.W.C.A. Republican. Presbyn. Home: Grosse Pointe, Mich. Died Feb. 17, 1928.

STALKER, Arthur William, clergyman; b. Commerce, Mich., Nov. 6, 1860; s. Thomas and Catherine Mary (Harrison) S.; A.B., U. of Mich., 1884, A.M., 1909; D.D., Lawrence (Wis.) Coll., 1902; m. Mary M. Hendrickson, 1885. Ordained M.E. ministry, 1886; pastor Dixboro, Mich., 1884-87, Clinton, 1887-92, Preston M.E. Ch., Detroit, 1892-97, Sault Ste. Marie, 1897-1900, First Ch., Madison, Wis., 1900-05, First Ch., Ann Arbor, Mich., 1905—. Republican. Mem. of Gen. Conf. M.E. Ch., 1908, 12, 16. Exchange preacher in London, British Council Interchange of preachers, 1921. Home: Ann Arbor, Mich. Died Nov. 18, 1930.

STALL, Sylvanus, author; b. Elizaville, N.Y., Oct. 18, 1847; s. William I. and Caroline (Tinklepaugh) S.; A.B., Pa. Coll., Gettysburg, 1872 (D.D., 1893); studied theology there, Union Theol. Sem., 1872-73, Gen. Theol. Sem., 1873-74; m. Kate D., d. Hon. David A. Buehler, of Gettysburg, Pa., Sept. 2, 1874. Ordained Luth. ministry, 1874; pastor Cobleskill, N.Y., 1874-77, Martin's Creek, Pa., 1877-80, Lancaster, Pa., 1880-87, Baltimore, 1888-91; asso. editor Lutheran Observer, 1890-1901; propr. Vir Pub. Co., Phila., May 1897—. Statis. sec., 1887-93, Gen. Synod Luth. Ch., and edited and published, 1884-88, Stall's Luth. Year Book and Hist. Quarterly. Author: Pastor's Pocket Record, 1876; Hand-Book to Hymns, 1879; How to Pay Church Debts, 1880; Methods of Church Work, 1887; Five Minute Object Sermons, 1894; Talks to the King's Children, 1896; Bible Selections for Daily Devotion, 1896; What a Young Boy Ought to Know, 1897; What a Young Man Ought to Know, 1897; What a Young Husband Ought to Know, 1899; What a Man of Forty-five Ought to Know, 1901; Faces Toward the Light, 1903; The Social Peril, 1905; Parental Honesty, 1905; With the Children on Sundays, 1911. Home: Bala, Pa. Died Nov. 6, 1915.

STALLO, John Bernhard, diplomatist; b. Sierhausen, Oldenburg, Mar. 16, 1823; came to U.S., 1839; taught in Cincinnati and New York until 1847; studied law; practiced in Cincinnati; judge court of common pleas and district court, 1853-55; took part in Liberal Republican movement, 1872; minister to Italy, 1885-89; now lives in Italy. Author: Concepts and Theories of Modern Physics; General Principles of the Philosophy of Nature; Reden, Abhandlungen und Briefe. Home: Florence, Italy. Died 1900.

STALLWORTH, Nicholas Eugene, lawyer; b. Evergreen, Ala., Sept. 17, 1874; s. Nicholas and Sarah Eugenia (Hines) S.; prep. edn., Evergreen (Ala.) Acad.; A.B., U. of Ala., 1894, LL.B., 1895; m. Gelene Armor, Oct. 9, 1901; children—Gelene Armor (Mrs. Claude Mood Scarborough), Nicholas. Was admitted to Alabama bar, 1895, and began practice of law at Mobile; gen. adminstr. Mobile County, 1906-08; state's atty. Mobile County, 1908-09; spl. asst. to atty. gen. of U.S. at Mobile, 1924; U.S. atty., Southern Dist. of Ala., 1926-27; spl. counsel with state atty. gen. in defense of Ala. Unemployment Compensation Law from cts. of first instance through U.S. Supreme Ct., 1936-37. Democrat. Home: Mobile, Ala. Died Mar. 5, 1941.

STALNAKER, Frank D., banker; b. Sioux City, Ia., Dec. 31, 1862; s. Lemuel E. and Martha (Jameson) S.; ed. high schs., Dublin and Stockwell, Ind., and business coll., Indianapolis; m. Cecelia Mansur, Aug. 25, 1914; 1 dau., Marjory S. Alig. Identified with banking business at Indianapolis, 1883—; pres. Indiana Nat. Bank, 1912—; v.p. Coburn Warehouse Co.; dir.. mem. exec. com. Union Trust Co., State Life Ins. Co. Pres. Indianapolis Clearing House; mem. bd. govs. Indianapolis Bd. of Trade. Mem. Dramatic Art Assn., Indianapolis. Republican. Mason. Home: Indianapolis, Ind. Died Aug. 9, 1932.

STAMBAUGH, John, iron and steel mfr.; b. Girard, O., Feb. 15, 1862; s. John and Caroline (Hamilton) S.; prep. edn. Greylock Inst., South Williamstown, Mass.; Ph.B., Cornell U., 1884; m. Cora L. Bunts, Sept. 21, 1887; children—Caroline (Mrs. Irving T. Snyder), John. Chemist Youngstown Steel Co., 1885-87; gen. mgr. and pres. The William Tod Co., heavy machinery, 1887-1900; sec., treas. Youngstown Steel Co., 1900-12; treas. Brier Hill Steel Co., 1912-21; dir. Federal Reserve Bank of Cleveland, 1915—; dir. Youngstown Sheet & Tube Co., Stambaugh-Thompson Co., etc. Founder John Stambaugh Chair of History, Cornell U. Republican. Episcopalian. Home: Youngstown, O. Died Oct. 6, 1927.

STANARD, Edwin Obed, miller; b. Newport, N.H., Jan. 5, 1832; s. Obed and Elizabeth Ann (Webster) S.; family removed to what is now Southern Ia., 1836; grad. commercial coll., St. Louis, 1855; m. Esther Kauffman, June 19, 1856. In grain commn. business, St. Louis, 1857-66, milling, 1866—; pres. E. O. Stanard Milling Co., 1885—, Stanard-Tilton Milling Co. Lt. gov. of Mo., 1868-70; defeated for mayor of St. Louis, 1870; mem. 43d Congress (1873-75); mem. Indianapolis Monetary Conf., 1897-98. Pres. Merchants' Exchange, 1866. Home: St. Louis, Mo. Died Mar. 11, 1914.

STANARD, Mary Newton, author; b. Westmoreland Co., Va.; d. Rt. Rev. John Brockenbrough (D.D.) and Roberta Page (Williamson) Newton; grad. Leache-Wood Sch., Norfolk, Va.; m. William Glover Stanard, Apr. 17, 1900. Mem. Assn. for Preservation of Va. Antiquities (life), Va. Soc. Colonial Dames of America (v.p.). Episcopalian. Mem. Va. War History Commn. Author: The Story of Bacon's Rebellion, 1907; The Dreamer—a Romantic Rendering of the Life Story of Edgar Allan Poe, 1909, 25; John Marshall and His Home, 1913, 23; Colonial Virginia—Its People and Customs, 1917; Richmond—Its People and Its Story, 1923; John Brockenbrough Newton—a Biographical Sketch, 1924. Editor of Edgar Allan Poe Letters, 1925. Mem. exec. com. Edgar Allan Poe Shrine Assn. Home: Richmond, Va. Died June 5, 1929.

STANARD, William Glover, editor; b. Richmond, Va., Oct. 2, 1858; s. Capt. Robert C. (C.S.A.) and Virginia M. (Cowan) S.; student William and Mary Coll., and Richmond Coll., 1876-80; LL.D. William and Mary Coll., 1915; m. Mary Mann Page Newton, Apr. 17, 1900 (died 1929). Corr. sec. Va. Hist. Soc., and editor Virginia Magazine of History and Biography, Oct. 1898—. Author: Colonial Virginia Register, 1902; Some Emigrants to Virginia, 1911. Home: Richmond, Va. Died May 6, 1933.

STANCHFIELD, John Barry, lawyer; b. Elmira, N.Y., Mar. 13, 1855; s. John K. and Glovina S. S.; A.B., Amherst Coll., 1876; Harvard Law Sch., 1877-78; m. Clara, d. Henry C. Spaulding, of Elmira, Sept. 2, 1886. Admitted to bar, 1878; practiced at Elmira, 1878-1900; partner of U.S. Senator David Bennett Hill, Elmira, 1878-85; mem. Reynolds, Stanchfield & Collin, 1885-1905; in New York, 1900—. Dist. atty. Chemung Co., 1880-85; mayor of Elmira, N.Y., 1886-88; assemblyman, 1895-96 (Dem. minority leader, 1896); Dem. candidate for gov. of N.Y., 1900; Dem. nominee for U.S. senator, 1901. Home: New York, N.Y. Died June 25, 1921.

STANDISH, John Van Ness, educator; b. Woodstock, Vt., Feb. 26, 1825; s. John Winslow and Caroline Williams (Myrick) S.; A.B., Norwich U., 1847, A.M., 1855; (hon. Ph.D., Knox Coll., 1879; LL.D., St. Lawrence U., 1893, Norwich U., 1896, Knox College, Ill., 1912); m. Harriet Augusta Kendall, Mar. 24, 1859. Taught in public schs., Vermont and New Hampshire, and graded schs. Central N.Y. for several yrs.; conducted teachers' insts. and lectured in many cos. of Ill.; prof., Lombard U., 41 years, 6 of which was pres. and acting pres. Mem. com. for Promotion Univ. of U.S.; pres. Galesburg Park Commn. Has traveled extensively in Europe, Africa, Holy Land and N. America. Republican. With his wife, made a bequest to Knox Coll., of $100,000, 1908. Now city forester of Galesburg. Home: Galesburg, Ill. Died Jan. 6, 1919.

STANDISH, Myles, M.D.; b. Boston, Mass., Oct. 17, 1851; s. Francis and Caroline Amanda (Rogers) S.; grad. Roxbury Latin Sch., 1871; A.B., Bowdoin Coll., 1875, A.M., 1878; M.D., Harvard, 1879; U. of Berlin, 1880-81; Sc.D., Bowdoin, 1910; m. Louise Marston Farwell, Apr. 28, 1890; children—Barbara (Mrs. Bradley M. Patten), Lora (Mrs. William H. Weston, Jr.), Myles, Alexander. Interne Carney Hospital, 1879-80; house surgeon Mass. Charitable Eye and Ear Hosp., 1881-83; formerly asst. in ophthalmology Mass. Gen. Hosp.; asst. ophthalmic surgeon Boston City Hosp., ophthalmic surgeon Carney Hosp.; asst. ophthalmic surgeon, 1888-92, ophthalmic surgeon, 1892-1913, and consulting ophthalmic surgeon, 1913—, Mass. Charitable Eye and Ear Infirmary; formerly prof. ophthalmology, Dartmouth Coll. Med. Sch.; asst. in ophthalmology, 1892-1901, instr. 1901-04, asst. prof., 1904-09, Williams prof., 1909-14 (emeritus), Harvard Med. Sch.; cons. ophthalmic surgeon Carney Hosp. Appointed comdr. ambulance corps, M.V.M., 1889 (retired, 1901). Unitarian. Compiler and pub.: The Standishes of America, 1894. Home: Boston, Mass. Died June 26, 1928.

STANFORD, Jane Lathrop, (Mrs.), philanthropist; b. Albany, N.Y., Aug. 25, 1825; m. Leland Stanford. Social life began when Mr. Stanford was elected gov. of Calif., 1861. With husband established The Leland Stanford, Junior, Univ., opened Oct. 1891; built Children's Hosp., Albany, N.Y., $100,000, supported by endowment of $100,000 more; also gave $160,000 to kindergarten schools, San Francisco; from time of husband's death (he was then senator from Calif.), she devoted her attention to development of the university. Home: Palo Alto, Calif. Died 1905.

STANGE, Charles Henry, veterinarian; b. Cedar Co., Ia., May 21, 1880; s. Claus and Sophie (Richmann) S.; D.V.M., Ia. State Coll. Agr. and Mechanic Arts, 1907; post-grad. work in pathology and bacteriology, U. of Chicago, 1908; m. Harriet Beyer, Oct. 20, 1909; children—Robert B. (dec.), Elizabeth J., Jean. With U.S. Bur. Animal Industry, June-Sept. 1907; prof. vet. medicine, 1907-08, acting dean vet. div., 1908-09, dean vet. div., 1909—, Iowa State Coll. Agr. and Mechanic Arts, also prof. of veterinary hygiene, 1930—; organized the div., also organized State Biol. Lab. and established vet. research work in the college. Republican. Presbyterian. Mason. Rotarian. Organized Ia. for hog cholera control; conducted survey of veterinary colleges of U.S. for Bur. of Edn., Interior. Dept., Washington. Home: Ames, Ia. Died Apr. 26, 1936.

STANLEY, Albert Augustus, univ. prof.; b. Manville, R.I., May 25, 1851; s. Dr. George W. and Augusta A.S.; grad. in music Leipzig Conservatory; hon. A.M., U. of Mich., 1890, Mus.D., 1930; Mus.D., Northwestern U., 1916; m. Emma F. Bullock, Dec. 27, 1875; m. 2d, Dorothea Oestreicher, Dec. 1, 1921. Prof. music, U. of Mich., 1888-1921, emeritus prof. of music, 1921—; dir. Univ. Sch. of Music, same, 1903-21; comdr. Ann Arbor May Festival, 1892-1921. Sec., treas., twice pres. Music Teachers' Nat. Assn.; founder Coll. of Musicians; several yrs. hon. v.p. Manuscript Soc.; rep. Internat. Musik Gesellschaft (pres. Am. Sect. 1906-12); twice pres. Mich. Music Teachers' Assn.; v.p. Am. Mus. of Music. Composer songs, ch. music, etc.; Symphony, "The Soul's Awakening," "Chorus Triumphalis"; symphonic poem, "Attis," for orchestra; "Psalm of Victory," for tenor solo, chorus and orchestra, 1906; incidental music (Greek) to Percy Mackaye's tragedy of Sappho and Phaeon; music to "Alkestis"; "Laus Deo" for chorus, orchestra and organ; music to Iphigenia among the Taurians; Musical Settings of Greek Fragments, 1919; "Fair Land of Freedom," for solo, chorus, orchestra and organ, 1919; music to Cantica of the Menæchmi of Plautus, 1917; Catalogue of the Stearns Collection of Musical Instruments, 1919, 2d edit., 1921; Greek Themes (treatise); Musical Instruments in their Sociological Relations. Home: Ann Arbor, Mich. Died May 19, 1932.

STANLEY, Caroline Abbot, author; b. Callaway Co., Mo., Aug. 16, 1849; d. Rufus and Mary Rebecca (Hart) Abbot; grad. Kalamazoo (Mich.) Training Sch., 1879; m. Elisha Stanley, Oct. 31, 1871 (dec.). Critic-teacher, 1879-82, prin., 1882-96, Kalamazoo Training Sch.; gave up teaching for lit. work, 1896. Hon. mem. Ladies' Lit. Club of Salt Lake; hon. mem. D.A.R. Presbyn. Author: Authors' Birthdays, 1888; Order No. 11, 1904; A Modern Madonna, 1906; The Master of The Oaks, 1912; The First Church's Christmas Barrel, 1912; Their Christmas Golden Wedding, 1913; The Keeper of the Vineyard, 1913; Dr. Llewellyn and His Friends, 1914. Died Jan. 13, 1919.

STANLEY, David Sloane, brig. gen. U.S.A., retired June 1, 1892; b. at Chester, O., June 1, 1828; s. John B. and Sarah (Peterson) S.; ed. public schools, Canaan Acad. and West Point, graduating, 1852; m. Anna M. Wright (died 1895). Consecutively 2d lt. 2d dragoons, 1st lt. 1st cav., capt. 4th cav., maj. 5th cav. During war was brig. gen and maj. gen. vols.; comd. 4th corps, Army of the Cumberland, and took part in many battles, notably in the fights in and around Corinth and the battles of the Atlanta campaign and until he was severely wounded at Franklin in a desperate hand-to-hand conflict; was active in the engagements around Nashville. After war was col. 22d U.S. inf. and brig. gen. U.S.A. Died 1902.

STANLEY, Edwin James, clergyman; b. Buffalo, Mo., Feb. 19, 1848; s. Henry and Sally Ann (Campbell) S.; ed. by home study; m. Lulu Lee Brooke, Dec. 23, 1886. Joined Mo. Conf., M.E. Ch., S., 1869; pastor Irving Mission, Mont., 1869-70, Troy Circuit, 1870-71, Radersburg Circuit, 1871-72, Hamilton Circuit, 1872-83, Diamond City, 1873-74; presiding elder Virginia City Dist., and pastor Virginia City, 1874-75; pastor Virginia City and Silver Star, 1875-76, Silver Star, 1876-77; presiding elder Mont. Dist., 1877-78, Deer Lodge Dist., and pastor Silver Star and Butte City, 1878-79; served as presiding elder, various periods, and editor Montana Methodist several yrs. Charter mem. Denver Conf., 1874, Mont. Conf., Helena, Mont., 1878; A pioneer in securing organization of Gen. Bd. Ch. Extension M.E. Ch., S. Democrat. Author: Rambles in Wonderland, 1877; Life of L.B. Stateler, or Sixty Years on the Old Frontier, 1907; Patriotism and Religion, 1888. Home: Whitehall, Mont. Died Apr. 17, 1919.

STANLEY, Freelan O., inventor; b. Kingfield, Me., June 1, 1849; s. Solomon and Apphia (French) S.; ed. Hebron Acad. and Bowdoin Coll.; m. Flora Tileston, 1876. Inventor, 1883 (with twin brother Francis E. (deceased), of Stanley dry plate, which revolutionized photography, also of Stanley steam automobile, 1897; a builder of car that made fatest mile record (up to that time) in the world (28⅕ seconds) at Ormond Beach, 1906, and 2 miles in 59¾ seconds; a founder of Stanley Motor Co.; has developed plan for mfg. violins on a large scale, on scientific basis. Propr. Stanley Hotel, Estes Park, Colo. Writer and lecturer. Republican. Unitarian. Home: Newton, Mass. Died Oct. 2, 1940.

STANLEY, Sir Henry Morton, G. C. B., explorer; b. Denbigh, Wales, 1841; emigrated to U.S., 1857; was adopted by New Orleans mcht., a Mr. Stanley; m. July 12, 1890, Dorothy Tennant. Sent to Africa by New York Herald, 1870, and again in 1874; found Livingstone; discovered course of the Congo; returned to Africa for the King of the Belgians, 1879-84; his work resulted in the founding of the Congo Free State, 1887-89; commanded Emin Relief Expedition. Mem. British Parliament for N. Lambeth, as Liberal Unionist, 1895-1900. Made Grand Cross of the Bath, 1899. Author: How I Found Livingstone, 1872; My Kalulu, Prince, King and Slave, 1873; Coomassie and Magdala, 1874; Through the Dark Continent, 1878; The Congo and the Founding of Its Free State, 1885; In Darkest Africa, 1890; My Dark Companions, 1893; My Early Travels in America and Asia, 1894; Slavery and the Slave Trade, 1894; Through South Africa, 1898. Died 1904.

STANLEY, John Joseph, street ry. operator; b. Cleveland, O., Mar. 5, 1863; s. Joseph and Eliza (Bragg) S.; ed. pub. schs.; m. Rhoda Francis, Sept. 2, 1885; children—Rhoda (Mrs. F. R. Latta), Frances E., Laura (Mrs. R. C. Snell). Identified with Cleveland Street rys., 1885—; pres. The Cleveland Ry. Co.; Mutual Building & Investment Co.; v.p. Wade Park Manor Co. Presbyn. Mason. Home: Cleveland Heights, O. Died Oct. 4, 1926.

STANLEY, W. E., governor; b. in Ohio, 1848; spent his boyhood in Hardin, O.; moved to Jefferson Co., Kan., 1870, and to Wichita, 1872; m. Emma L. Hills, 1876. Admitted to bar, 1870; co. atty. Jefferson Co., 1871-72; co. atty. Sedgwick Co., Kan., 1874-80; declined appmt. to Supreme bench by Gov. Morrill; gov. of Kansas, 1899-1903. Republican; mem. Commn. to the Five Civilized Tribes, 1903-04. Home: Wichita, Kan. Died 1910.

STANLEY, William, electrical engr. inventor; b. Brooklyn, Nov. 22, 1858; s. William and Elizabeth A. (Parsons) S.; ed. Williston Sem., Easthampton, Mass., and short time at Yale, class of '81, self-ed. in elec. science; m. Lila C. Wetmore, Dec. 22, 1884. Chief engr. Westinghouse Electric Co., 1885-88, Stanley Elec. Mfg. Co., 1890-95, Stanley Instrument Co., 1898-1903. Inventor alternating-current system of long distance light and power transmission. Home: Great Barrington, Mass. Died May 14, 1916.

STANLEY-BROWN, Joseph, banker; b. Washington, Aug. 19, 1858; s. John Leopold and Elizabeth M. Stanley-Brown; grad. Yale, 1888, Ph.B., as of class of 1888, 1895; m. Mary, d. President James A. Garfield, June 14, 1888. Stenographer to late Maj. John Wesley Powell, on geol. survey of Rocky Mountains, 1877-79; pvt. sec. to President Garfield, 1880-81; member U.S. Geol. Survey, 1882-85, asst. geologist, 1888-89; expert Bering Sea Arbitration, 1891-93; supt. N. American Commercial Co., Alaska, 1894-99; asst. sec. U.P. and S.P. ry. systems, New York, 1899-1902; asst. to the pres. L.I. R.R. Co., 1902-04; mgr. railroad dept. Fisk & Robinson, bankers, New York, 1905—. Home: Cold Spring Harbor, L.I., N.Y. Died Nov. 2, 1941.

STANTON, Elizabeth Cady, reformer; b. at Johnstown, N.Y., Nov. 12, 1815; d. Daniel C. (judge New York Supreme Court) and Martha (Livingston) Cady, d. Col. Jas. Livingston, of Gen. Washington's staff; ed. Johnstown Acad. and Emma Willard's Sem., Troy, N.Y.; grad., 1832; m. 1840, Henry Brewster Stanton, anti-salvery orator, senator, lawyer (died 1887). First Woman's Rights conv. was called by her and was held at Seneca Falls, N.Y., July 1848. She then made the 1st demand for woman suffrage, carrying it after long debate and opposition; in 1840 advocated Married Woman's Property bill, following up the agitation until it passed in N.Y., 1848. For last quarter century has annually addressed com. of Congress in favor of a 16th amendment for women, to Constitution of U.S. She addressed the New York legislature on the rights of married women in 1854, and in advocacy of divorce for drunkenness, 1860, and has canvassed many States in favor of woman suffrage. Was pres., 1861, Woman's Loyal League; pres. Nat. Woman Suffrage Assn., 1865-93, now hon. pres.; was a candidate for Congress, 1868. With Susan B. Anthony and Parker Pillsbury, edited The Revolution. Resident of New York from 1890. In 1895 her 80th birthday was celebrated, under the auspices of the Nat. Council of Women, by 3,000 delegates from all women's socs., at Metropolitan Opera House. Author: The History of Woman suffrage (with Susan B. Anthony and Matilda Joslyn Gage), 1881; Eighty Years and More, 1895; The Woman's Bible, 1895; etc. Died 1902.

STANTON, Frank Lebby, author; b. Charleston, S.C., Feb. 22, 1857; s. Valentine and Catherine Rebecca S.; common sch. edn.; served apprenticeship as printer; married. Identified with Atlanta press for yrs.; verse-writer; on staff Atlanta Constitution; also gives pub. readings from his poems. Author: Songs of the Soil; Comes One With a Song, 1898; Songs from Dixie Land, 1900; Up from Georgia, 1902; Little Folks Down South, 1904. Home: Atlanta, Ga. Died Jan. 7, 1927.

STANTON, Horace Coffin, clergyman; b. Wolfboro, N.H., Apr. 1, 1849; s. Benjamin and Catharine Philbrook (Coffin) S.; father prof. in Union Coll., Schenectady, N.Y.; A.B., Union Coll., 1867; admitted to bar; grad. Princeton Theol. Sem., 1873 (prize for Hebrew scholarship); Ph.D., Boston U., 1884, S.T.D., 1902; D.D., Bates; unmarried. Ordained Presbyn. ministry, 1874; stated supply, Batchellerville, N.Y., 1873-76; Northville, 1874-75, 3d Ch., Albany, 1877-87, stated supply Central Ch., Denver, Colo., 1888-89, Bethany Ch., Albany, N.Y., 1889-90; acting pastor 2d Ch., Kansas City, Mo., 1890; stated supply 1st Ch., Oakland, Calif., 1890, Colorado Springs, Colo., 1890-91; pastor 1st Ch., Kansas City, 1891; ministry marked by repeated revivals. Republican. Author: The Starry Universe, the Christian's Future Empire, 1909; Telepathy of the Celestial World, 1913. Home: Philadelphia, Pa. Died Nov. 15, 1925.

STANTON, John, mining engr.; b. Bristol, Eng., Feb. 25, 1830; s. John and Joan (Locke) S.; came with parents to Pa., 1835; studied engring. took active management of his father's iron mines at Dover, N.J.; m. Elizabeth R. McMillan, Dec. 24, 1857. Engaged in copper mining, 1852-61, in Md., Va. and Tenn.; mines in Tenn. confiscated by Confederate govt.; later developed copper mines in Lake Superior region and in Ariz., in which he is still largely interested, being pres. and mgr. of several cos. One of founders and 1st pres. N.Y. Mining Stock Exchange. Home: New York, N.Y. Died 1906.

STANTON, John Gilman, M.D., surgeon; b. New Orleans, La., Dec. 25, 1848; s. John and Sophia (Cook) S.; A.B., Amherst, 1870; studied medicine in Göttingen, Berlin and Wurzburg, M.D., U. of Wurzburg; m. Elizabeth Savage Cooper, Oct. 1875; 1 dau., Alice Cooper (Mrs. Harrison F. Sheldon). Dispensary phys., Boston, 3 yrs.; surgeon to out-patients, Boston City Hosp., 1876-77; located in New London, Conn., 1877; surgeon Central Vt. Ry. Co.; actg. asst. surgeon Pub. Health & Marine Hosp. Service; surg. 3d Regt., Conn. N.G. Mem. State Council of Defense (med. sect.), 1917—. Pres. Lawrence and Memorial Asso. Hospitals; pres. New London Public Library. Active worker in ednl. lines; mem. Bd. of Edn., New London, about 20 yrs. (chmn. most of time); trustee New London Man. Train. School, and Savings Bank of New London. Democrat. Unitarian. Mason. Home: New London, Conn. Died Sept. 28, 1927.

STANTON, Jonathan Young, educator; b. West Lebanon, Me., June 16, 1834; s. James and Sabra (Wentworth) S.; A.B., Bowdoin Coll., 1856, A.M., 1859 (Litt.D., 1894); studied law in office of Hon. Daniel M. Christie, Dover, N.H., 1856-57; student Andover Theol. Sem., 1859-62; m. Harriet Cushman Woodman, Aug. 7, 1866. Teacher, New Hampton (N.H.) Lit. Instn., 1857-59; principal Derry (N.H.) Acad., 1862-64; prof. Greek, 1864-1906, emeritus, 1906, Bates Coll. Conglist. Home: Lewiston, Me. Died Feb. 17, 1918.

STANTON, Lucy M., portrait painter; b. Atlanta, Ga., May 22, 1875; d. William Lewis and Frances Louisa (Megee) S.; studied art, École Colarossi, École de la Grande Chaumière and with Lucien Simon, Emile Blanche, M. Koopman; water color with Ertz, miniature with Virginia Reynolds; A.M., Cox Coll., Atlanta, 1895. Exhibited Salon, Paris; Soc. Nat. des Beaux Arts. Represented with oil portrait of Gen. Howell Cobb in Congressional Hall, Washington; oil portrait of Chancellor Chas. M. Snelling, U. of Ga.; "Aunt Liza," Concord (Mass.) Art Assn.; "Uncle Ingraham," Lincoln Museum, Milton, Mass.; etc. Awarded Medal of Honor, Pa. Soc. Miniature Painters, 1917; 1st prize Atlanta Art Assn., 1917; Medal of Honor, Concord Art Assn., 1923; hon. mention, Nat. Acad. Women Painters and Sculptors, 1925. Formerly teacher Dana Hall, Wellesley, Mass., and Choate Sch., Boston; teacher art history, Milton Acad., 1920-26. Democrat. Self portrait (miniature) bought by Pa. Soc. Miniature Painters, 1929, to be hung in the New Museum Parkway, Phila. Home: Athens, Ga. Died Mar. 19, 1931.

STANTON, Oscar Fitzalan, rear admiral U.S.N.; b. Sag Harbor, N.Y., July 18, 1834; s. Joseph and Elizabeth (Cooper) S.; m. Caroline Eliza Gardiner, July 6, 1859. Apptd. midshipman U.S.N., Dec. 29, 1849; promoted through grades to commodore May 19, 1891; rear admiral, July 21, 1894. Served on St. Mary's, Pacific Squadron, 1860-62; exec. officer Tioga in James River and Potomac flotilla and West Indies Flying Squadron, 1862-63; comd. gunboat, West Gulf Blockading Squadron, 1863-64; present at battle of Mobile Bay; New York Navy Yard, 1864-65; on Powhatan and Tallapoosa, 1865; Naval Acad., 1865-67; comd. Tahoma, 1867; Purveyor, 1867-68; receiving-ship Vandalia, 1870-71; Monocacy and Yantic, Chinese and Japanese waters, 1872-74; Norfolk Navy Yard, 1874-77; Newport, R.I., Torpedo Sta., 1878; comd. training ship Constitution, 1879-81; was at Naval Asylum, Phila., 1881-84; comd. flagship Tennessee, N. Atlantic Sta., 1884-85; naval sta., New London, Conn., 1885-89; training sta., Newport, R.I., 1890-91; gov. Phila. Naval Home, 1891-93; comd. flagship Newark, S. Atlantic sta., 1893; comd. N. Atlantic Squadron and was on bd. Kearsarge when she was wrecked, Feb. 2, 1894; later comd. San Francisco; retired July 30, 1894. Home: New London, Conn. Died July 5, 1924.

STANTON, Robert Brewster, engineer; b. Woodville, Miss., Aug. 5, 1846; s. Robert Livingston (D.D.) and Anna Maria (Stone) S.; A.B., Miami U., 1871, A.M., 1878; (hon. A.M., U. of Wooster, 1885); m. Jean Oliver Moore, Dec. 1, 1881. Resident engr. Cincinnati Southern R.R., 1874-80; div. engr. U.P. Ry., 1880-84, and built noted "Georgetown Loop" ry., 1882-83; consulting civ. and mining engr., 1884—. Made ry. survey as chief engr. through Grand Cañon of the Colorado, 1889-90; engr. of various mines in U.S., Can., Mex., West and East Indies, Cuba; explorations for gold in island of Sumatra, Dutch East Indies, 1904. Author: The Cañons of the Colorado River of the West for Railway Purposes, 1892; The Great Land-Slides on the Canadian Pacific Ry. in British Columbia, 1898. Home: New York, N.Y. Died Feb. 23, 1922.

STANTON, Thaddeus H., brig. gen. U.S.A.; b. in Indiana; was private, 3d battalion, D.C. inf., April to July 1861; capt. 19th Iowa inf., Aug. to Dec. 1862; became additional paymaster, U.S.V., Dec. 18, 1862, to April 8, 1867. Apptd. maj. paymaster, U.S.A., Jan. 17, 1867; lt. col., dept. paymaster gen., March 15, 1890; col. asst. paymaster gen., Jan. 22, 1893; brig. gen. and paymaster gen., U.S.A., March 27, 1895. Brevets: lt. col. vols., March 13, 1865, for faithful and meritorious services during Civil war; lt. col., U.S.A., Feb. 27, 1890, for gallantry in action against Indians under Crazy Horse on Powder Horn River, March 17, 1876. Home: Washington, D.C. Died 1900.

STANTON, Theodore, author; b. Seneca Falls, N.Y., Feb. 10, 1851; s. Henry Brewster and Elizabeth (Cady) S.; student Coll. of the City of New York, 1866-68; A.B., Cornell U., 1874, and A.M., 1877; m. Marguerite Berry, of Paris, 1881. Berlin corr. of the New York Tribune, 1880-81; European agt., N. Am. Review, Harper & Brothers, D. Appleton & Co. and Henry Holt & Co., for many years. Member Internat. Jury, Paris Expn., 1889; Paris agt. N.Y. Associated Press, 1890-93; resident commr. in Paris, Chicago Expn., 1891-93. Author: Woman Question in Europe, 1884; Life of Rosa Bonheur, 1910; etc. Editor: Le Goff's Life of Thiers; Manual of American Literature (in Tauchnitz Edition); Life of Elizabeth Cady Stanton (with Mrs. Stanton Blatch), 1922; A Soldier of France to His Mother; A Soldier Unafraid; etc. Founder and editor for 10 years dept. of Am. lit., Mercure de France. Officier de l'Instruction Publique. Home: Paris, France. Died Mar. 1, 1925.

STANTON, William, brig. gen. U.S.A.; b. in N.Y., Oct. 13, 1843; s. Gen. Henry and Alexandrine (Macomb) S. Private, corporal and sergt. Co. G, 43d Ohio Inf., Sept. 3, 1862-Mar. 11, 1863; apptd. from Mich., 2d lt. 2d U.S. Arty., Sept. 3, 1867; grad. Arty. Sch., 1871; 1st lt., Nov. 16, 1874; transferred to 6th Cav., Feb. 9, 1877; capt., May 21, 1886; maj. 8th Cav., June 9, 1899; lt. col. 11th Cav., Sept. 13, 1902; col. 6th Cav., Mar. 18, 1905; brig. gen. and retired, Mar. 7, 1906. Present at siege of Santiago, Cuba, comdg. a cav. squadron, July 1-Aug. 6, 1898. Home: New York, N.Y. Died Apr. 7, 1927.

STANWOOD, Edward, editor; b. Augusta, Me., Sept. 16, 1841; s. Daniel Caldwell and Mary Augusta (Webster) S.; A.B., Bowdoin, 1861 (Litt.D., 1894); m. Eliza M. Topliff, Nov. 10, 1870. Asst. editor, 1867-82, editor, 1882-83, Boston Daily Advertiser; mng. editor Youth's Companion, 1887-1911. Spl. agt. 11th Census to collect statistics of cotton manufactures; 12th Census for textile manufacturers; spl. agt. census manufacturers, 1905. Trustee Bowdoin Coll.; member and recording secretary Mass. Hist. Society, 1905—; sec. Arkwright Club, 1891—. Author: History of Presidential Elections, 1884; History of the Presidency, 1898; History of the Class of 1861 of Bowdoin College, 1897; American Tariff Controversies, 1903; James Gillespie Blaine (Am. Statesmen, New Series), 1905; History of the Presidency (1897-1909). 1912. Home: Brookline, Mass. Died Oct. 11, 1923

STAPLES, Abram Penn, professor law; b. Stuart, Va., Aug. 14, 1858; s. Samuel Granville and Caroline Harris (De Jarnette) S.; student Va. Agrl. and Mech. Coll., 1874-75, Richmond (Va.) Coll., 1876-79, LL.B., 1879; m. Sallie Clement Hunt, Sept. 17, 1884. Practiced in Henry Co., Va., 1881-90, Roanoke, 1890-1904; prof. law, Washington and Lee U., 1904—. mem. Va. Senate, 1885, 1889; Dem. presdl. elector, 1896. Presbyn. Author: A Suit in Bankruptcy, 1909. Home: Lexington, Va. Died Sept. 1913.

STAPLES, Arthur Gray, editor; b. Bowdoinham, Me., July 4, 1861; s. Anthony and Mary Gray (Blake) S.; A.B., Bowdoin Coll., 1882, hon. A.M., Bowdoin, 1919, Litt.D., 1923; LL.D., Bates, 1921; m. Jane Lambert Dingley, Oct. 21, 1895; 1 dau., Mary Gray (Mrs. Ralph Churchill Harvey). City editor Bath Daily Times, 1882; city editor, 1883-93, mng. editor, 1893-1919, editor-in-chief, 1919—, Lewiston Journal; dir. and treas. Lewiston Journal Co. Mem. Maine (State) Development Commission, 1937-40; dir. New England Council, 1937. Del. to Rep. Nat. Conv., 1904, alternate, 1908, del., 1912-24; del. League of Rep. Clubs, Cincinnati, 1908. York and Scottish Rite Mason. Mem. Alumni Council Bowdoin Coll., 1917-18, now mem. Bd. Overseers; trustee Westbrook Jr. College, Monmouth Acad., Hebron Acad. Author: Familiar Essays; Just Talks on Common Themes, 1919; Jack in the Pulpit; Katahdin and the Allegash; The Inner Man, 1925; Just Betwen Friends, 1926. Editor the Fairfield Letters, 1921; The Passing Age, 1924. Home: Auburn, Me. Died Apr. 2, 1940.

STAPLES, Henry Franklin, M.D.; b. Berlin, Mass., Mar. 29, 1870; s. Charles Franklin and Frances Amanda (Gwinn) S.; B.S., Mass. Agrl. Coll., 1893; M.D., Cleveland U. of Medicine and Surgery (now dept. Ohio State U.), 1896; m. Emily S. Milburn, Sept. 29, 1896; 1 son, Milburn Dean (dec.). Practiced at Solon, O., 1896-1902, Cleveland, 1902—; prof. hygiene and sanitary science, Cleveland-Pulte Med. Coll., 1905-14. Mem. Am. Inst. Homœopathy (pres. Senate of Seniors 1932; trustee 1933—; v.p. 1934; hon. pres. 1936), Homœ. Med. Soc. of Ohio (pres. 1911; necrologist), Cleveland Homœ. Med. Soc. (pres. 1908). Baptist. Mason. Home: Cleveland, O. Died May 26, 1938.

STAPLETON, Ammon, clergyman; b. Earl, Pa., Jan. 15, 1850; s. William and Elisabeth S.; entered Union Army when only 14 yrs. of age; served under Sheridan; A.B., Central Pa. Coll., 1871 (hon. M.S., 1888, A.M., 1895; D.D., Ursinus Coll., 1907); m. Sarah E. Crandall, Mar. 11, 1875. Ordained Evang. ministry, 1875; presiding elder, 1895—; pastor St. Paul's Ch., York, Pa., 1907—. Author: Natural History of the Bible, 1885; Compend of Church History, 1896; Evangelical Annals, 1900; Memorials of the Huguenots in America, 1901; Flashlights on Evangelical History, 1908; Life and Times of Albright, 1911; The Henkel Memorial, 1912. Home: Williamsport, Pa. Died Sept. 18, 1916.

STAPLETON, Luke D., judge; b. Brooklyn, N.Y., Dec. 11, 1869; s. Thomas and Catharine (Quinn) S.; A.M., Manhattan Coll., New York, 1891; LL.B., New York U. Law Sch., 1891; (LL.D., Seton Hall Coll., N.J., 1908, Manhattan Coll., 1917, Coll. of the City of New York, 1918); m. Catharine F. Nowlen, Aug. 29, 1893. Asst. corp. counsel City of N.Y., 1898-1901; apptd. to Supreme Ct. of N.Y. by Gov. Hughes, Mar. 10, 1908, for unexpired term; nominated by Dem. and Rep. parties and elected justice Supreme Ct. of N.Y., for term 1909-Dec. 31, 1922; asso. justice Appellate Div., 1913-17; resigned, Dec. 30, 1917, and resumed practice. Mem. Dist. Bd. under the Selective Service Act, 1918. Democrat. Trustee Coll. of New Rochelle, N.Y. Catholic. Home: Brooklyn, N.Y. Died Feb. 12, 1923.

STARIHA, John, bishop; b. Semic, Krain, Austria, May 12, 1845. Ordained R.C. priest at Marquette, Mich., 1869; consecrated bishop of Lead, S.D., Oct. 28, 1902; resigned, Apr. 1909. Died Nov. 28, 1915.

STARIN, John Henry, steamboat propr.; b. Sammonsville, N.Y., Aug. 27, 1825; academic edn.; became drug clerk and, 1848-52, postmaster, Fultonville, N.Y.; mfd. medicines and toilet articles in New York; established a freight agency; secured, vessel by vessel, a large fleet of harbor and river tugs and vessels for freight and passengers. Now head Starin City River and Harbor Transportation Lines; owns shipyard, drydock and iron works on Staten Island. Mem. Congress, 1877-81. Republican. Vice pres. N.Y. Rapid Transit Commn. Has a home and 1,600-acre farm at Fultonville. Home: New York, N.Y. Died 1909.

STARK, Otto, artist; b. Indianapolis, Jan. 29, 1859; s. Gustav S. and Leona (Jonas) S.; ed. Cincinnati Art Sch., Art Students' League, New York, Acad. Julien, and under M. F. Carmon, Paris, France; m. Maria Nitschelm, of Paris, Dec. 15, 1886 (died 1892). Located in Indianapolis, Ind., 1895; was head of the art dept. of the Manual Training High School, and instr. in composition, John Herron Art Inst., Indianapolis, resigned. Exhibited twice in Paris Salon, at Internat. Expn. of Art and History, Rome, and in many exhbns. in U.S. Winner of Foulke prize, Richmond, Ind., 1908; 1st Holcombe prize, annual exhbn. of Ind. artists, 1915. Exhibited San Francisco Expn., 1915 (mem. advisory com.), San Diego Expn., 1916. First pres. Ind. Artists Club, 1916-17. Home: Indianapolis, Ind. Died Apr. 14, 1926.

STARKEY, Thomas Alfred, P.E. bishop of Newark, Jan. 8, 1880—; b. Philadelphia, 1819; ed. as civ. engr., but later studied theology; (D.D., Hobart, 1864); ordered deacon 1847; ordained priest, 1848; founder and 1st rector Ch. of the Holy Apostles, St. Clair, Pa.; rector Christ Ch., Troy; St. Paul's Albany; Trinity, Cleveland, O.; Epiphany, Washington; St. Paul's, Paterson, N.J. Died 1903.

STARKWEATHER, Chauncey Clark, lawyer, editor; b. Chicago, Nov. 7, 1851; s. Charles R. and Mary (Eager) S.; A.B., Yale, 1874; LL.B., Columbia, 1877; m. Isabella B. Anstey, Nov. 8, 1882. Admitted to bar, 1877; largely engaged in editorial work, translations and compiling for New York pubs.; contbr. of weekly poems to papers and mags. Mem. S.A.R. Home: New York, N.Y. Deceased.

STARLING, William, chief engr. Mississippi levee dist.; b. Columbus, O., Jan. 25, 1839; grad. New York Univ., 1856 (A.M., C.E.). Served in Union army in Civil war. Member Loyal Legion; Am. Soc. Civil Engrs.; Instn. of Civil Engrs. of Great Britain; etc. Prominent Mason—past grand high priest; past grand comdr. Knights Templar; present grand master Masons in Mississippi. Unmarried. Author: The Improvement of the Mississippi River; Some Notes on the Holland Dikes; The Discharge of the Mississippi River; The Floods of the Mississippi River; etc. Home: Greenville, Miss. Died 1900.

STARR, Eliza Allen, author, art teacher and lecturer; b. Deerfield, Mass., Aug. 29, 1824; d. Oliver and Lovina Allen S.; studied art in Boston, then taught art in Brooklyn, Phila. and Natchez, Miss. Established studio in Boston, 1854; removed to Chicago, 1856, where she has since remained, devoting her time to authorship, art teaching and delivering art lecture courses. Visited Italy, France and England, 1876. Received, 1885, Lætare medal, conferred by Notre Dame Univ., Ind.; received gold medal from World's Columbian Expn., as an art-teacher. In 1900 Pope Leo XIII sent her a cameo medallion as a mark of his approbation of her literary labors. Author: Poems, 1867; Patron Saints, 1871; Pilgrims and Shrines, 1878; Songs of a Lifetime, 1887; Isabella of Castile, 1889; What We See, 1891; Christmas-tide, 1891; Christian Art in Our Own Age, 1891; Three Keys to the Camera della Signatura of the Vatican, 1895; Seven Dolors of the Blessed Virgin Mary, 1898; The Three Archangels and Guardian Angels in Art, 1899. Home: Chicago, Ill. Died 1901.

STARR, Frederick, anthropologist; b. Auburn, N.Y., Sept. 2, 1858; s. Rev. Frederick and Helen Strachan (Mills) S.; B.S., Lafayette Coll., 1882, M.S., Ph.D., 1885, Sc.D., 1907; unmarried. Teacher of sciences, Wyman Inst., 1882-83; prof. sciences, State Normal Sch., Lock Haven, Pa., 1883-84; prof. biol. sciences, Coe Coll., 1884-85; in charge of ethnology, Am. Mus. Natural History, 1889-91; registrar, Chautauqua U., 1888-89; asst. prof. anthropology, 1892-95, asso. prof., 1895-1923, and curator anthropol. sect. Walker Mus., U. of Chicago. Has done field work in ethnography and phys. anthropology, especially in Mexico; went to Japan, 1904, on behalf of St. Louis Expn., to secure a group of the Ainu, the aboriginal population of Japan, for which was awarded a grand prize; led expdn. into Congo Free State, 1905-06, investigating conditions there, visiting 28 different tribes; field study in P.I., 1908; in Japan, 1909-10, 17; in Korea, 1911, 13 and 1915-16; in Liberia, 1912; lectures on anthropology and his various travels and investigations. Author: American Indians, 1899; Indians of Southern Mexico, 1899; The Ainu Group at St. Louis, 1904; Readings from Modern Mexican Authors, 1904; The Truth About the Congo, 1907; In Indian Mexico, 1908; Filipino Riddles, 1909; Japanese Proverbs and Pictures, 1910; Congo Natives, 1912; Liberia, 1913; Korean Buddhism, 1918; Fujiyama, the Sacred Mountain of Japan, 1924. Editor: The Anthropological Series; Central America (reader). Foreign recognition, museums medal, Holland, 1900; Officer Order Leopold II (Congo), 1907; Comdr., 1911; palms of Officer of Public Instruction (France), 1908; Chevalier Order Crown of Italy, 1911; Knight Comdr. Order of African Redemption (Liberia), 1915; 3d grade Order Sacred Treasure (Japan), 1921; Academico Correspondiente Nat. Acad. of Cuba, 1929. Home: Seattle, Wash. Died Aug. 14, 1933.

STARR, Louis, physician; b. Philadelphia, Pa., Apr. 25, 1849; s. Isaac and Lydia (Ducoing) S.; A.B., Haverford Coll., Pa., 1868; M.D., U. of Pa., 1871; (LL.D., Haverford, 1908); m. Mary Parrish, Sept. 16, 1882. Interne, 1871-73, asst. physician, 1873-74, visiting phys., 1875-84, Episcopal Hosp., Phila.; asst. phys. Children's Hosp., 1874; visiting phys. same, 1879; phys. Southern Home for Destitute Children, 1874-78; out-patient phys., Univ. Hosp., 1878-80; cons. pediatrist to Maternity Hosp., 1879—; instr. physiology and therapeutics, 1874-77, lecturer on symptomatology, 1877-79, on diseases of children, 1880-84, clin. prof. diseases of children, 1884-90, med. dept. U. of Pa. Fellow Coll. Physicians, Phila.; foundation mem. Pediatric Society. Asst. editor Pepper's System of Medicine, 1885; Am. editor Goodhart's Diseases of Children, 1885, 89; editor An American Text Book of the Diseases of Children, 1895, 99; editor of dept. of Diseases of Children, in the Am. Year Book of Medicine and Surgery. Author: Diseases of Digestive Organs in Infancy and Childhood, 1886, 91; Hygiene of the Nursery (7 edits., 1888-1906); Diets for Infants and Children in Health and in Disease, 1896; A Synopsis of the Physiological Action of Medicines, 1877, 80. Home: New York, N.Y. Died Sept. 12, 1925.

STARR, Merritt, lawyer; b. Ellington, N.Y.; s. James Comfort and Cynthia (MacKoon) S.; moved to Rock Island, Ill., in boyhood; A.B., Oberlin, 1875, A.M., 1878; A.B., Griswold Coll., 1876; A.B., and LL.B., Harvard, 1881; LL.D., Oberlin, 1925, Knox Coll., Galesburg, Ill., 1926; m. Leila Wheelock, Sept. 8, 1885; children—Winifred (Mrs. Fletcher Dobyns), Philip Comfort (lt. U.S.A., killed in action at Ypres, France), Dr. Merritt Paul, Beatrice (Mrs. Newton Jenkins). Practiced at Chicago, 1882—; member Peck (George R.), Miller (John S.) & Starr, 1893-1911, firm Miller, Starr, Brown, Packard & Peckham, 1915-22, Hopkins, Starr & Hopkins, 1922—. Active in organizing Civil Service League, drafting city, co. and state civ. service laws and promoting their passage, and in promoting passage of laws establishing municipal and juvenile courts. Professional work includes trusts, estates, legal adjustments involved in constrn. of pub. works, and growing out of interstate commerce and anti-trust laws; organization and reorganization of corporations; refunds of income and estate taxes and wrongful taxation, conducted mainly by conference and negotiation, without litigation. By appmt. of gov. became atty. for the state to maintain navigability and public right in Des Plaines River, established by the Supreme Court of U.S., Apr. 11, 1921. Village atty., Winnetka, Ill., 1894-95; New Trier Twp. Bd. of Edn., 1899-1907 (pres. 1900-02, 1903-05). Trustee Oberlin Coll., 1893-1924; trustee Nat. Kindergarten and Elementary Coll., 1922—, and pres. of its bd. trustees, 1926—; mem. exec. com. Civil Service Reform Assn., 1884-1914; dir. Chicago Law Inst., 1888-90, 1905-08 (pres. 1895-97); pres. Harvard Club of Chicago, 1906-07, Chicago Literary Club, 1910-11. Author: Starr's Reference Digest of Wisconsin Reports, 1882; Gould on Waters, 1883; Annotated Statutes of Illinois (8 vols.), 1883-96; vols. 1-17 (Ill. portions) of Northeastern Reporter, 1885-88; Competition: Legislative and Judicial Treatment of, 1907; Theodore Roosevelt, 1919; Lincoln's Lineage, 1920; Dante 600 Years After, 1921; Economic Equality and Some New Uses of National Power, 1922. Home: Winnetka, Ill. Died Aug. 2, 1931.

STARR, M(oses) Allen, neurologist; b. Brooklyn, N.Y., May 16, 1854; s. Egbert and C. Augusta (Allen) S.; A.B., Princeton, 1876, A.M., 1879, Ph.D., 1884; M.D., Coll. Phys. and Surg. (Columbia), 1880; LL.D., Princeton, 1899; Sc.D., Columbia, 1904; m. Alice Dunning, June 7, 1898; 1 dau., Katharine Eunice. Lecturer diseases of the mind and nervous system, 1887-89, prof., 1889-1900, prof. neurology, 1903-15, and emeritus professor, 1915—, Columbia U. U.S. delegate to Charcot Centennial, Paris, 1925. Fellow A.A.A.S., N.Y. Acad. sciences. Author: Familiar Forms of Nervous Diseases, 1893; Brain Surgery, 1895; Atlas of Nerve Cells, 1897; Nervous Diseases, Organic and Functional, 1913. Home: Mt. Kisco, N.Y. Died 1932.

STARRETT, Helen Ekin, educator, author; b. Allegheny Co., Pa., Sept. 19, 1840; d. Rev. John and Esther Fell (Lee) Ekin; ed. Pittsburgh High Sch.; m. Rev. William Aiken Starrett, Feb. 15, 1864. Founder Kenwood Inst., Chicago, 1884; prin. Starrett Sch. for Girls, 1893-1915 (prin. emeritus). Author: Future of Educated Women, 1880; Letters to a Daughter, 1882; Letters to Elder Daughters, 1883; Gyppie, an Obituary, 1884; After College, What? For Girls, 1885; Letters to a Little Girl, 1886; Crocus and Wintergreen, poems (with her sister, Frances Ekin Allison), 1906; The Future of Our Daughters, and Other Educational Essays, 1909; The Charm of Fine Manners; Three-Minute Chapel Talks for Girls, 1918; Highways and Byways of Literature, 1918; Little Book of Good Manners in Home and School, 1919. Home: Portland, Ore. Died Dec. 16, 1920.

STARRETT, Henry Prince, consular service; b. Boston, Mass., Dec. 14, 1885; s. Edmund J. and Letitia (Roberts) S.; student U. of Adelaide, 1919-20; m. Emma Virginia Ferguson, June 16, 1909; children—William Ferguson, Virginia Ferguson, Richard Ferguson. Stenographer, 1903-05; clerk in consulate, Santiago de Cuba, 1905-06, in engr. office, U.S. Army, Cuba, 1906, Santiago and Habana, 1906-07; dep. consul gen., Habana, 1907-13; consul, Cartagena, Colombia, 1913-14, Owen Sound, Ont., 1914-15, Ft. William and Port Arthur, Can., 1915-16, Mombasa, E. Africa, 1916-18, Adelaide, Australia, 1918-21, Batavia, Java, 1921-22, Sydney, Australia, 1922-23, Belfast, Ireland, 1923; consul general, Genoa, Italy, 1926-30; counselor of embassy, Lima, Peru, 1930—. Died Mar. 18, 1933.

STARRETT, Lewis Frederick, lawyer; b. Warren, Me., June 20, 1844; s. Marcus and Lovina (Lawrence) S.; Warren Acad.; admitted to bar, 1897; m. Mrs. Emma J. Bradford Ballou, June 5, 1889. Clerk of courts, Knox Co., Me., 1878-88, 1893-96; referee in bankruptcy for Knox Dist., 1898-1910. Democrat. Conglist. Author: Poems and Translations (from German verse), 1887; General Henry Knox—His Family, His Manor: His Manor House, and His Guests, 1902. Home: Rockland, Me. Deceased.

STARRETT, Theodore, constr. fireproof bldgs.; b. Lawrence, Kan., Jan. 21, 1865; s. William Aiken and Helen (Ekin) S.; ed. U. of Kan., Lake Forest U., class of 1884, but did not complete course (A.B., 1903). Became engr., 1886, for Burnham & Root, Chicago architects (who designed Chicago Expn.); builders and engineer, 1889—; built over 150 fireproof buildings, of which more than 100 are skyscrapers and monumental buildings, at Chicago, New York, Buffalo, Cleveland, Columbus, Boston, Princeton, Phila., Pittsburgh, Washington, Baltimore, San Francisco, Winnipeg, including the Washington Terminal, and the Pa. Sta. at Columbus; leader in the establishment of the constrn. co. idea; founder of the Thompson-Starrett Co. and pres., 8 yrs.; resigned to engage in constrn. work in individual capacity. Home: Prospect Plains, N.J. Died Oct. 9, 1917.

STARRETT, William Aiken, architect, engr.; b. Lawrence, Kan., June 14, 1877; s. William A. and Helen (Ekin) S.; ed. U. of Mich., 1893-95, B.S. in C.E., 1917; m. Eloise Gedney, June 14, 1900; children—Helen Ruth, David. A founder, 1901, and v.p. Thompson-Starrett Co., gen. contractors, New York, continuing until 1913; mem. Starrett & Van Vleck, Mar. 1913-Jan. 1, 1918. Mem. Plattsburg Training Camp, 1916; engr. corps training work, winter 1916-17; chmn. emergency constrn. com. of Council Nat. Defense, in charge govt. bldg. program, including constrn. cantonments, May 1, 1917; commd. capt., Engr. R.C., May 2, 1917, maj., June 13, 1917, col. Q.M.C., Mar. 18, 1918; hon. disch., Mar. 22, 1919. Col., U.S.A., R.C. V.p. George A. Fuller Co., gen. contractors, New York, 1919-21; with brothers, Paul and Ralph, founded Starrett Bros., Inc., Builders, New York, 1922, of which is v.p.; pres. The Starrett Corp. Introduced into Japan several modern steel frame buildings, 1919-21, specially designed to resist earthquake. Mayor of Madison, N.J., 1919-21. Author: Skyscrapers and the Men Who Build Them, 1929. Home: Madison, N.J. Died Mar. 26, 1932.

STARRING, Frederick A(ugustus), civil and mining engr., lawyer, soldier; b. Buffalo, N.Y., May 24, 1834; s. Capt. Sylvenus Seaman and Adeline (Williams) S.; ed. Buffalo, Paris, Heidelberg, Vienna and grad. Harvard, class of 1865-66; admitted to bar, 1859; m. Louise Perle Whitehouse, July 21, 1889. Engr. on Ill. Central, location surveys and boundary line surveys, Tex. & Ind. Ter., etc. Sec. Cairo & Fulton R.R. Co. of Ark. and Mo., 1859-61. Served Civil war, maj. 46th Ill. inf., maj., 2d Ill. light arty., col. 72d Ill. inf. (Chicago Bd. of Trade regt.); brig. gen. comdg. 1st, 2d and 3d brigades, Army of Tenn., and maj. gen. and provost marshal gen., dept. of the Gulf. U.S. diplomatic and consular agt. Europe and other foreign countries, 1869-83. Home: New York, N.Y. Died 1904.

STARRING, Mason Brayman, corp. pres.; b. Chicago, Ill., May 8, 1859; s. Henry Justin Dimick and Alida M. (Tower) S.; ed. common and high schs. of Chicago; m. Helen, d. of late Prof. David Swing, of Chicago, Oct. 27, 1886; children—David Swing, Mason Brayman. His father was a prominent railroad man and the inventor of the American system of baggage checking. Admitted to bar, 1894; asst. gen. counsel, 1894-98, gen. solicitor, 1898-1904, gen. mgr. and dir., 1904-06, v.p., 1906-07, Chicago City Ry Co.; pres. Northwestern Elevated R.R. and chmn. bd., 1907-11; pres. and chmn. bd. Chicago & Oak Park Elevated R.R. Co., from July 1911; also pres. and mng. dir. Chicago & Oak Park Elevated Ry. Co. of N.J.; chmn. bd. Lenal Corp.; pres. Calif. & Pittsburgh Utilities Corp., Calif. Corp., Carrabelle Corp., The Home Utilities Co., Permian Oil & Gas Co., Sandar Corp.; dir. and mem. exec. com. K.C. Southern Ry. Co. For many yrs. was active in control of corps., including rys., pub. utilities, oil and gas cos., etc.; resigned as pres. of 12 corps. and as dir. of 18. Mem. S.A.R. Home: Lake Geneva, Wis. Died Jan. 31, 1934.

START, Charles Monroe, judge; b. Bakersfield, Vt., Oct. 4, 1839; s. Simeon Gould and Mary Sophia (Barnes) S.; acad. edn., Bakersfield and Barre, Vt.; 1st lt. Co. I, 10th Vt. Inf., 1862; removed to Rochester, Minn., 1863; m. Clara Wilson, Aug. 10, 1865. Pros. atty., Olmstead Co., Minn., 1868-76; atty. gen. of Minn., 1880-81; judge 3d Jud. Dist., 1881-94; reëlected, 1894, for 6 yrs. but resigned, Jan., 1895, having been elected chief justice Supreme Ct. of Minn.; reëlected, 1900, 1906; retired Jan. 6, 1913. Home: St. Paul, Minn. Died Dec. 19, 1919.

START, Edwin Augustus, educator, editor; b. North Bridgewater, Mass., June 1, 1863; s. Rev. William Augustus and Philena Churchill (Stevens) S.; A.B., Tufts Coll., 1884; A.M., Harvard, 1893; m. Julia Edith Moor, Sept. 9, 1885 (died 1892); m. 2d, Caroline Mason Knowles, June 26, 1907. Journalist, 1885-92; head dept. history, Tufts Coll., 1892-1900; sec. Mass. Forestry Assn., 1900-09; farmer, Billerica, Mass., 1902-09; exec. sec. Am. Forestry Assn., Oct. 1909-Oct. 1911; editor American Forestry, 1909-11; dir. extension div., U. of Wash., 1912—. Editor dept. of modern history (Europe, Asia, Africa), New Internat. Ency. Pres. trustees University Unitarian Ch., Seattle; v.p. Pacific Unit. Conf. Sec. King Co. (Wash.) Council Defense, 1917-18; instr. (capt.) in mil. science, R.O.T.C. (U. of Wash. unit), 1917-18. Home: Seattle, Wash. Died Oct. 3, 1923.

START, Henry R., judge Supreme Court, Vt., 1890-1906; b. Bakersfield, Vt., Dec. 28, 1845; ed. Bakersfield and Barre Acad.; served in Civil war, Co. A, 3d Vt. inf.; practiced law and was State's atty.; State senator, 1880; mem. and speaker Vt. Ho. of Reps., 1890; presdl. elector, 1880. Republican. Home: Bakersfield, Vt. Deceased.

STATLER, Ellsworth Milton, hotel owner; b. Somerset Co., Pa., Oct. 26, 1863; s. William Jackson and Mary A. (McKinney) S.; ed. pub. schs.; m. Mary I. Manderbach, Apr. 16, 1895 (died 1925). Founded Statler's Restaurant, Buffalo, N.Y., 1896; built and operated hotel at Pan-Am. Expn., Buffalo, 1901, Inside Inn at St. Louis Expn., 1904; pres. and dir. Hotels Statler Co., Inc., owning and operating Hotels Statler in Buffalo, Cleveland, Detroit, St. Louis; also operating Hotel Pennsylvania, N.Y. City. Pres. New York Hotel Statler Co., Inc. Pres. Hotel Men's Mut. Benefit Assn. U.S. and Can.; mem. N.Y. State Hotel Assn., Buffalo Hotel Assn., etc. Republican. Presbyn. Mason. Home: New York, N.Y. Died Apr. 16, 1928.

STATTON, Arthur Biggs, bishop; b. Sycamore, Ill., Mar. 27, 1870; s. Isaac Kuykendall and Hester (Wallahan) S.; A.B., Western Coll., Toledo, Ia., 1890, A.M., 1893; D.D., Lebanon Valley Coll., Annville, Pa., 1907; m. Lola M. Brown, Aug. 8, 1893; children—Philo A., Madeline L. (Mrs. Edward Oswald, Jr.). Instr. in Latin, York (Neb.) Coll., 1890-94; ordained ministry U.B. Ch., 1896; pastor Olin Circuit, Ia., 1894-97, St. Paul Ch., Hagerstown, Md., 1897-1917; supt. Pa. Conf., 1917-25; bishop Southwest Area (Ia., Mo., Neb., Colo., Okla., N.M.), 1925—. Mason. Home: Kansas City, Mo. Died Dec. 8, 1937.

STAUFFER, David McNeely, engineer; b. Mount Joy, Pa., March 24, 1845; s. Jacob and Mary Anna (McNeely) S.; left Franklin and Marshall Coll. without graduating, for war (hon. Litt.D., 1903); m. Florence Scribner, Apr. 19, 1892. Served in U.S.N. in Civil War; comd. U.S.S. "Alexandria" in Mississippi River Fleet, 1865; civil engr. in railroad work, bridge and tunnel building, 1865-82; editor, and one of proprs. Engineering News, 1882-1906; retired. Mem. of Palisades Interstate Park Commn. under appmt. from govs. of New York and N.J. Author: Modern Tunnel Construction, 1906; American Engravers on Copper and Steel, 1907. Home: Yonkers, N.Y. Died Feb. 5, 1913.

STAUFFER, Vernon, educator; b. New London, O., Nov. 23, 1875; s. Michael W. and Rosilla Emily (Winbigler) S.; A.B., Hiram (O.) Coll., 1901; Union Theol. Sem., 1907 and 1911-13; A.M., Columbia, 1913, Ph.D., 1918; m. Laura Emma Hoffman, Dec. 25, 1905. Ordained Disciples of Christ ministry, 1904; pastor Richmond St. Ch., Cincinnati, O., 1901-04, Angola, Ind., 1904-11; dean and prof. N.T., Hiram Coll., 1913-21; dean and exec. head, Calif. Sch. of Christianity, Los Angeles, 1921-22; prof. N.T., Coll. of the Bible, Lexington, Ky., 1922—. Author: New England and the Bavarian Illuminati, 1918. Home: Lexington, Ky. Died July 15, 1925.

STAUNTON, Sidney Augustus, naval officer; b. Ellicottville, N.Y., June 7, 1850; s. Joseph Marshall and Mary Elizabeth (Wilber) S.; grad. U.S. Naval Acad., 1871; m. Emily Duncan Biddle, Sept. 23, 1886(died 1892). Ensign, July 1872; promoted through grades to rear adm., Feb. 20, 1910; retired June 7, 1912. Served on Iroquois, Congress, Wabash, Plymouth, Franklin, Powhatan, Marion, Trenton, Swatara, Pensacola, Chicago, Iowa, New York, Yankton, Rainbow, Helena, Colorado (in command of last 4) and various duties on shore, including service on Gen. Bd. of the Navy, and Joint Bd. of Army and Navy. On staff of Rear Admiral Sampson, comdr.-in-chief of Atlantic Fleet, during Spanish-Am. War; mentioned by that officer in dispatches and recommended for advancement. Comdr.-in-chief special service squadron sent to the Argentine Republic, Apr.-July 1910, to assist in the celebration of the first centennial of Argentine independence, and naval representative of the U.S. at that celebration. Comd. 5th div. Atlantic Fleet, July 1910-Aug. 1911; mem. spl. commn. sent by the President to Europe, May-June 1912, to encourage participation by foreign govts. in the Panama-Pacific Expn. Home: Washington, D.C. Died Jan. 11, 1939.

STAYTON, Joseph Markham, lawyer; b. Helena, Ark., Apr. 18, 1864; s. John William and Sarah Jane (Wickersham) S.; B.A. and M.A., Ark. Coll., Batesville, Ark., 1882; LL.B., Vanderbilt U., Nashville, Tenn., 1885; unmarried. Jr. mem. John W. and Joseph M. Stayton, Newport, Ark., 1885—; mem. Ark. Ho. of Rep., 1889; pros. atty., 3d Jud. Circuit, 2 terms, 1890-94; Dem. presdl. elector, Ark., 1897. Methodist. Mason. Home: Newport, Ark. Died May 22, 1923.

STEALEY, Orlando O., newspaper corr.; b. Jeffersonville, Ind., Jan. 4, 1842; s. John O. and Mary A. S.; common sch. edn.; m. Lollie Sherley, Dec. 8, 1874. Has been on Louisville Courier-Journal 40 yrs., from carrier boy to Washington corr., filling latter posion, 1881—; filled all chairs at home office except editor-in-chief. Author: Twenty Years in Press Gallery. Home: Washington, D.C. Died Dec. 29, 1928.

STEARLY, Wilson Reiff, bishop; b. Phila., Pa., May 8, 1869; s. Wilson and Mary (Reiff) S.; A.B., Phila. High Sch., 1886; studied Paris and Berlin, 1896-97; student Union Theol. Sem., 1887-89; D.D., Kenyon, 1915, Western Reserve, 1916; m. Helen B. Neuhauser, Feb. 12, 1895; children—Wilson Watters, Garrett Reiff, Helen George. Ordained Ref. Ch. ministry, 1889; pastor Hough Av. Ref. Ch., Cleveland, O., 1889-99; deacon and priest P.E. Ch., 1900; rector Emmanuel Ch., Cleveland, 1900-09, Ch. of Holy Apostles, Phila., 1909-12, St. Luke's Church, Montclair, N.J., 1912-15; successively bishop suffragan of Newark, 1915-17, bishop coadjutor, 1917-27; became bishop of Newark, Oct. 25, 1927; retired. Author: The Master of the Feast, 1912. Home: Montclair, N.J. Died Nov. 8, 1941.

STEARNS, Charles Cummings, college prof.; b. Lunenburg, Vt., Dec. 10, 1850; s. Josiah Milton and Freelove Phillips (McIntyre) S.; B.A., Yale, 1872, M.A., 1879; B.D., Union Theol. Sem., 1875; studied at Athens, Greece, 1875; U. of Berlin, 1893-94; m. Sophie D. P. Seymour, Sept. 20, 1875. Missionary teacher, Manisa, Turkey, 1875-77 inclusive; prof. Greek, Doane Coll., Neb., 1878-85 (absent on leave, 1881-85); head of Classical Sch. for Boys at Hartford, Conn., 1885-93, 1898-1906; asso. prof. and lecturer on archeology, Hartford, Theol. Sem., 1893-97 (absent on leave, 1893-94, in Europe); prof. Bibl. history and lit., Pomona Coll., 1906-23 (emeritus). Visited Palestine and Egypt, 1913. Conglist. Delivered Carew lectures Hartford Theol. Sem., 1892 and 1897; made a spl. study of Catacombs at Rome, and Early Christian art and epigraphy. Home: Claremont, Calif. Died May 25, 1924.

STEARNS, Frank Preston, author; b. Medford, Mass., Jan. 4, 1846; s. George Luther and Mary E. (Preston) S.; A.B., Harvard, 1867; studied art in Germany and Italy; studied lit. with David A. Wasson; m. Emilia Maciel, Sept. 28, 1898. Mem. Union Soc. of Civil War. Author: The Real and Ideal in Literature, 1892; Life of Tintoretto, 1894; The Mid-summer of Italian Art, 1895; Concord Sketches, 1895; Modern English Prose Writers, 1897; Life of Bismarck, 1899; Four Great Venetians, 1900; Napoleon and Machiavelli, 1903; True Republicanism, 1905; Cambridge Sketches, 1905; Life of Hawthorne, 1906; Life of Maj. George L. Stearns, 1907; Politics and Metaphysics, 1915. Died Jan. 1917.

STEARNS, Frank Waterman, dry goods mcht.; b. Boston, Mass., Nov. 8, 1856; s. Richard Hall and Louisa Maria (Waterman) S.; B.A., Amherst, 1878, LL.D., 1932; m. Emily Williston Clark, Feb. 26, 1880; children—Foster, Mrs. Emily W. Giese, Mrs. Louisa Prescott. Now chmn. bd. dirs. R. H. Stearns Company, established by father in 1847. Republican. Catholic. Home: Boston, Mass. Died Mar. 6, 1939.

STEARNS, Frederic Pike, engineer; b. Calais, Me., Nov. 11, 1851; s. William Henry Clark and Mary Hobbs (Hill) S.; prep. edn. Calais High Sch.; (hon. A.M., Harvard, 1905; D.Sc., U. of Pa., 1906); m. Addie C. Richardson, June 21, 1876. In city surveyor's office, Boston, 1869-72; investigation, constrn. and maintenance additional water supply for Boston, 1872-80; constrn. and maintenance Boston main drainage works, 1880-86; chief engr. Mass. State Bd. of Health, 1886-95; mem. bd. of sanitary engrs. to devise system of sewerage for D.C., 1889-90; chief engr. Mass. Met. Water Works, 1895-1907; consulting engr. Charles River Basin Commn., 1903-10, Bd. of Water Supply, New York, 1905-14; mem. board of cons. engrs. for Panama Canal, 1905-06; mem. bd. to devise system of sewage disposal for Baltimore, 1905-06; mem. bd. to examine and report on water supply for Los Angeles, 1906; mem. bd. consulting engrs. accompanying Sec. of War William H. Taft, to Panama, 1907 and 1909; mem. bd. to report on additional water supply for Baltimore, 1908-09; mem. bd. to report on water supply for Winnipeg, 1913; consulting engr. new water supply for Providence, 1914—. Fellow Am. Acad. Arts and Sciences. Home: Boston, Mass. Died Dec. 1919.

STEARNS, Frederick William, lawyer; b. Chicago, Ill., Dec. 6, 1867; s. John William and Florence Ella (Blood) S.; A.B., U. of Wis., 1889, LL.B., 1891; m. Emma V. Drinker, Aug. 26, 1903; m. 2d, Stella K. Wilhelm, June 11, 1918; children—Florence Katherine, John William. Admitted to Wis. bar, 1891; practiced at Seattle, Wash., 1891-93, Chicago, Ill., 1909-14, San Diego, Calif., 1893-1909, and 1915—; mem. Stearns, Luce & Forward; v.p. and gen. counsel Union Title Ins. Co., Union Trust Co.; dir. and gen.

counsel Qualitee Dairy Products Co.; v.p. San Diego Consolidated Gas & Electric Co. Republican. Home: San Diego, Calif. Died Oct. 1, 1936.

STEARNS, Henry Putnam, physician; b. Sutton, Mass., Apr. 18, 1828; s. Asa and Polly (Putnam) S.; grad. Yale, 1853, A.M., 1856, M.D., 1855; m. Annie Elizabeth Storer, Glasgow, Scotland, 1857. Surgeon of 1st Conn. regt. Apr. 1861, for 3 mos. service; afterward surgeon U.S. vols. 4 yrs., with positions of med. dir. and acting insp.; supt. and physician Hartford Retreat for Insane for over 30 yrs.; lecturer on insanity, Yale, 1877-97. Republican. Author: Medical Examinations in Life Insurance, 1868; Insanity, Its Causes and Prevention, 1883; Mental Diseases, 1893. Home: Hartford, Conn. Died 1905.

STEARNS, Robert Edwards Carter, biologist; b. Boston, Feb. 1, 1827; s. Charles and Sarah (Carter) S.; pub. sch. edn. Boston; m. Mary Ann Libby, Mar. 28, 1850 (died 1879). Business training in a Boston bank; investigated coal fields of Southern Ind., 1850; paymaster and resident clerk for several Boston copper mining cos. at Keeweenaw Point, Lake Superior, 1854; went to San Francisco, 1858; in printing and publishing business and on editorial staff "The Pacific;" deputy clerk Supreme Court, Calif., 1862-63; sec. Bd. State Harbor commrs., 1863-68; in east, 1868-70; made natural history collections in Fla., 1869; sec. Bd. Regents, Univ. of Calif., 1874-82; Ph.D. Univ. of Calif., 1881; adj. curator dept. mollusks, U.S. Nat. Mus., 1884; also paleontologist U.S. Geol. Survey until 1892; resigned; from 1892 hon. asso. zoölogy, U.S. Nat. Museum. Mem. numerous scientific societies. Home: Los Angeles, Calif. Died 1909.

STEARNS, Sarah Burger, reformer; b. New York, Nov. 30, 1836; grad. Normal, Ypsilanti, Mich.; m. O. P. Stearns, Feb. 18, 1863 (died 1896). In 1856 induced a class of young women to prepare with her for making application in 1858 for admission to Mich. Univ. Agitation continued, thus making Mich. the first State univ. to open its doors to women, 1869. Engaged in lit., philanthropic, woman suffrage, and other reform work. Home: Los Angeles, Calif. Deceased.

STEARNS, Theodore, composer; b. Berea, O., June 10, 1880; s. Charles Wesley and Lucy (Pease) S.; ed. Oberlin Conservatory of Music and at Wurzburg Royal Conservatory, Bavaria, M.A., 1898; m. Margaret L. Middleton, May 6, 1920; children—Irving, Charles, Pindar. Conducted Cleveland High Sch. Orchestra and played viola in Cleveland Philharmonic Orchestra; conducted opera and symphony in Wurzburg, also conducted for Victor Herbert, Fritz Kreisler and others; editor The Etude, 1899-1900; music critic Chicago Herald Examiner, 1922, New York Morning Telegraph, 1922-26 and 1927-28; for creative work, recipient of Guggenheim Foundation award, in Germany, 1927-28; radio program arrangements for Mittel-Europa Rundfunk and in U.S., 1929-31; prof. music and chmn. music dept. U. of Calif. at Los Angeles, 1932—. Composer: Atlantis (music drama, book and music), 1929; Endymion, opera, produced at Hofgeismar, Germany, 1896; Indian Suite, 1898; Snowbird, one-act lyric episode, produced at Chicago, 1923 and Dresden, Germany, 1928; Suite Caprese, 1927, prod. by Los Angeles Philharmonic Orchestra, 1932; In Death's Garden, symphonic poem for orchestra and solo soprano, 1930; orchestral and choral tone-poem Baal-Hamon, 1935; songs, etc. Author: Story of Music, 1931. Home: West Los Angeles, Calif. Died Nov. 2, 1935.

STEARNS, Wallace Nelson, coll. prof.; b. Chagrin Falls, O., Aug. 26, 1866; s. Rev. Horatio N. and Adaline (Munn) S.; grad. Canfield (O.) Normal Coll., 1886, A.B., 1889; A.B., Ohio Wesleyan U., 1891, A.M., 1894; A.B., Harvard, 1893, B.D., 1896, A.M., 1897; Ph.D., Boston U., 1899; studied Univ. of Chicago, summer, 1901, British Mus. and Bodleian Library, summer, 1911, Berlin, summer, 1912, U. of Illinois, summer, 1930; m. Addie G., d. Allen and Elizabeth Busey McClain, of Urbana, Ill., Dec. 31, 1913. Instr. Greek and ancient history, Ohio Wesleyan U., 1891-92, Summer Sch. same, 1893-95; instr. N.T. lit., Chautauqua, N.Y., 1895-97; clerk to com. on revision N.T., 1897-98; tutor N.T. Greek, Boston Univ., 1898-99; instr. Greek and ancient history, 1899-1901, adj. prof. Greek, 1901-02, Ohio Wesleyan Univ.; prof. ancient langs., Baldwin U., 1902-03; financial sec. Religious Edn. Assn., 1903-04; pvt. sec. to pres., and univ. examiner, Northwestern U., 1904-05; pvt. sec. to pres. U. of Ill., 1905-06; prof. Bibl. lit., Wesley Coll. and U. of North Dakota, 1906-12; prof. Bibl. lit. and ancient history, Fargo (N.D.) Coll., 1912-18; prof. Bibl. lit. and history, McKendree Coll., Lebanon, Ill., 1919-23; prof. Bibl. lit., Ill. Woman's Coll., 1923—. Area ednl. sec. A.E.F., Y.M.C.A., 1918; area supt. instrn., A.E.C., 1919. Dir. religious edn. N.D. (Internat. S.S. Assn.), 1910-16. Mem. Palestine Exploration Fund (hon. sec.), Egypt Exploration Soc. (v.p.), Morgan Co. Hist. Soc. (pres. 1928—). Mason. Author: A Manual of Patrology, 1899; Fragments of Græco-Jewish Writers, 1908; Primers of Hebrew History, 1909, of Hebrew Private Life, 1910; Hebrew and Greek Primers, 1914, also Primers of the Early Church, 1927; A Working Basis, 1914; Judas Maccabeus, 1917. Home: Jacksonville, Ill. Died Feb. 3, 1934.

STEARNS, William Guilford, M.D.; b. Lamartine, Wis., Feb. 11, 1865; s. William and Elsie (Randall) S.; ed. Oshkosh (Wis.) State Normal Sch. and Potsdam (N.Y.) State Normal and Training Sch.; M.D., Northwestern U. Med. Sch., 1893; m. Grace Whitney, June 24, 1897. Interne St. Luke's Hosp., 1893-94; asst. phys. Ill. Eastern Hosp. for the Insane, Kankakee, 1894-95, pathologist same, 1895-97, med. supt., 1897-99; med. supt. Oakwood and Lakeside sanatoria, Lake Geneva, Wis., 1900-04; prof. pathol. anatomy and gen. pathology, Northwestern Univ. Dental Sch., 1894-98; asst. prof. mental diseases and med. jurisprudence, Northwestern Univ. Med. Sch., 1898-1900; lecturer neurology, Coll. Phys. and Surg., 1900-02; prof. nervous and mental diseases, Chicago Clin. Sch., 1900-03; med. dir. North Shore Health Resort, Winnetka. Chmn. sect. on insanity, Nat. Conf. of Charities and Correction, 1898. Served with Med. Advisory Bd. No. 3E, Selective Service, 1917-19, consultant on neuro-psychiatry. Fellow Am. College Physicians, A.M.A., Chicago Acad. of Medicine. Home: Evanston, Ill. Died Jan. 11, 1937.

STEARNS, William Marion, M.D., surgeon; b. Dale, N.Y., June 20, 1856; s. George W. and Harriet N. (Chaffee) S.; ed. high sch.; grad. Chicago Homœ. Med. Coll., 1880; m. Fannie, d. Dr. William S. Foote, of Belvidere, Ill., June 1, 1887; children—Helen Frances (Mrs. J. W. McConnell), Eugene Marion, Clarence Foote. Served as house physician, State Penitentiary, Joliet, 3 yrs.; studied diseases of ear, nose and throat at Berlin and Vienna, 1883-85; clinical asst., eye and ear, 1885-90, prof. rhinology and laryngology, 1890-1905, dean, 1902-05, Chicago Homœ. Med. Coll.; prof. same, Hahnemann Med. Coll., 1905-11, and emeritus prof., 1911—. Has confined practice to diseases of the ear, nose and throat, 1883—. Fellow Am. Coll. Surgeons. Mason. Home: Evanston, Ill. Died Dec. 1, 1939.

STECHER, Henry William, banker; b. Huntington, Ind., July 29, 1856; s. Anton Daniel and Margaret (Lehman) S.; prep. edn. high sch., Sheboygan, Wis.; Ph.C., U. of Mich., 1878; m. Stella Grace Dean, 1885; children—Frederick William (dec.), Henry Dean; m. 2d, Margaret Dixon, Apr. 3, 1900; children—Helen Louise, Martha Dixon. Asst. prof. chemistry, U. of Mich., 1877-78; drug business, Cleveland, O., 1882-95; prof. pharmacy, Cleveland Sch. of Pharmacy, 1883-95, an organizer Pearl St. Savings Trust Co., 1889, sec. and treas., 1895-1907, pres., 1907-25, chmn. bd., 1925—; organized, 1902, and pres. Nat. Woolen Co.; pres. Cleveland Cooperage Co.; v.p. Cleveland Trust Co.; dir. and mem. executive com. Theurer Norton Provision Co., Lake Erie Provision Co. Republican. Episcopalian. Mason. Home: Lakewood, O. Deceased.

STEDMAN, Charles Manly, congressman; b. Pittsboro, N.C., Jan. 29, 1841; grad. U. of N.C., 1861; m. Catherine de Rosset, d. Joshua G. Wright of Wilmington, N.C., Jan. 8, 1866. Enlisted as pvt. Fayetteville (N.C.) Independent Light Inf. Co., 1st N.C. Inf.; lt., capt. and maj. 44th N.C. Inf. to end of war; served in Gen. R. E. Lee's army during entire war; thrice wounded. Admitted to bar and practiced at Wilmington, 1867-98, Greensboro, N.C., 1898—; sr. mem. Stedman & Cooke. Lieut. gov. N.C., 1885-89; candidate for Dem. nomination for gov., 1888; mem. 62d to 71st Congresses (1911-31), 5th N.C. Dist. Dir. (state appmt.) N.C. R.R. Co., 1909, pres., 1910; former trustee U. of N.C.; dir. Guilford (N.C.) Battle Ground Co. Home: Greensboro, N.C. Died Sept. 23, 1930.

STEDMAN, Edmund Clarence, poet, critic; b. Hartford, Conn., Oct. 8, 1833; s. Maj. Edmund Burke and Elizabeth C. (Dodge) S.; ed. Yale, class of 1853, A.M. (L.H.D., Columbia, LL.D., Yale). Editor Norwich (Conn.) Tribune, 1852-53; Winsted (Conn.) Herald, 1854-55; on staff New York Tribune, 1859-61; war corr. World, 1861-63; filled a position under U.S. Atty. Gen. Bates; mem. N.Y. Stock Exchange, 1869-1900. Delivered initatory course of lectures of Turnbull Chair of Poetry, Johns Hopkins, later repeated at Columbia and Univ. of Pa. Succeeded Mr. Lowell as pres. Am. Copyright League, 1891; pres. Nat. Inst. of Arts and Letters, 1904-05. Author: Poetical Works, 1875; Hawthorne, and Other Poems, 1877; Lyrics and Idyls, with Other Poems, 1879; Poems Now First Collected, 1894; Mater Coronata, 1900; also volumes of poems. Critical works: Victorian Poets, 1875; Poets of America, 1885; The Nature and Elements of Poetry, 1892. Editor Cameos from the Poems of Walter Savage Landor, (with T. B. Aldrich); Poems of Austin Dobson; A Library of American Literature (11 vols., with Ellen M. Hutchinson), 1888-89; The Works of Edgar Allan Poe (10 vols., with Prof. G. E. Woodbury), 1895; A Victorian Anthology, 1895; An American Anthology, 1900; History of N.Y. Stock Exchange, 1905. Home: New York, N.Y. Died 1908.

STEDMAN, Henry Rust, physician; b. Boston, Sept. 19, 1849; s. Charles Harrison (M.D.) and Lucy Rust (Ingalls) S.; A.B., Harvard U., 1871, M.D., 1875; m. Mabel Weiss, 1879. Medical house officer Boston City Hosp., 1872-73; surgical house officer Mass. Gen. Hosp., 1873-74; asst. phys. Edinburgh Royal Asylum and West Riding Asylum, Yorkshire, England, 1881; asst. physician and acting supt. Danvers State Hosp., 1879-84; supt. and resident phys. Bournewood Hosp. for mental diseases, Brookline, Mass., 1884-1918. Editor dept. "Insanity," Reference Handbook of the Medical Sciences. Home: Brookline, Mass. Died Feb. 20, 1926.

STEDMAN, Thomas Lathrop, M.D.; b. Cincinnati, Oct. 11, 1853; s. George Turner and Abigail (Porter) S.; A.B., Trinity Coll., Hartford, 1874, A.M., 1896; studied medicine, Jefferson Med. Coll., Phila., 1874-75; M.D., Coll. Phys. and Surg. (Columbia), 1877; m. Linda Edevene Wadman, June 1, 1893. House surgeon St. Luke's Hosp., New York, 1876-79, New York Orthopedic Hosp. and Dispensary, 1881-86. Editor Medical Record, New York. Author: A Chinese and English Phrase Book in the Canton Dialect (with K. P. Lee), 1888; Modern Greek Mastery, 1896; A Practical Medical Dictionary, 1911, 13th edit., 1935; The Nurse's Medical Lexicon, 1931; A Shorter Medical Dictionary, 1931. Editor: The Twentieth Century Practice of Medicine (21 vols.), 1895-1903; The Complete Pocket Guide to Europe (founded by Edmund Clarence Stedman), annual; Dunglison's Medical Dictionary, 23d edit., 1904; Reference Handbook of the Medical Sciences (8 vols.), 4th edit., 1923; Monographs for the General Practitioner, 1931. Home: New York, N.Y. Died May 26, 1938.

STEEDLY, Benjamin Broadus, surgeon; b. Barnwell Co., S.C., Dec. 24, 1874; s. William Broadus and Georgetta (Garris) S.; student, U. of Ga., 1890-92; M.S., Cornell U.; M.D., Coll. Phys. and Surg. (Columbia), 1901; studied New York Polyclinic, New York Post-Grad. Med. Sch., New York Lying-In Hosp., various European clinics; m. Florence Pittman, Sept. 1, 1897; children—Benjamin Broadus, Edith Florence. Practiced at Gaffney, S.C., 1902-08; house surgeon, Woman's Hosp., New York, 1908-09; formerly pres. Steedly Hosp. Co., Spartanburg Rotary Club; dir. Steiner Clinic for Cancer and Allied Diseases, Atlanta, Ga., 1924—; visiting surg. Spartanburg Gen. Hosp.; chief surg. to Chicks Springs (S.C.) Sanitarium and Wallace-Thompson Hosp., Union, S.C. Pres. Steedly Clinic, Spartanburg. Fellow A.C.S. Home: Spartanburg, S.C. Died Jan. 12, 1932.

STEEL, George Alexander; b. Stafford, O., Apr. 22, 1846; s. William (cousin of W. E. Gladstone) and Elizabeth (Lawrey) S.; common sch. edn.; went from Woodsfield, O., to Portland, Ore., 1863; m. Eva Pope, Feb. 18, 1869. Merchant, 1871-76; co. treas., 1870-72; spl. agt. P.O. Dept., 1877-79; deputy collector of customs, 1879-80; postmaster Portland, Ore., 1881-85, 1890-94; mem. Ore. Senate, 1886-90. In real estate and ins. business, 1885-89; pres. East Side Ry. Co., Portland; retired from active business. Several times chmn. Rep. State Com.; mem. Rep. Nat. Com. for Ore., 1896-1904; state treas. of Ore., 1907-11. Home: Portland, Ore. Deceased.

STEELE, Albert Wilbur, cartoonist; b. Malden, Ill., June 18, 1862; s. Henry D. and Louisa (Peabody) S.; ed. Denver pub. schs.; was surveyor for 5 yrs.; became cartoonist, 1890; m. Anne Crary, March 27, 1884. Cartoonist Rocky Mountain News, 1890-97, Denver Post, 1897—. Died Mar. 12, 1925.

STEELE, Charles, lawyer; b. Baltimore; s. I. Nevett and Rose L. (Nelson) S.; A.M., U. of Va., 1878; LL.B., Columbia, 1880; m. Miss N. G. French. Admitted to bar, 1880; in practice at New York, 1880—. Mem. firm of J. P. Morgan & Co. Home: New York, N.Y. Died Aug. 5, 1939.

STEELE, Daniel, clergyman, author; b. Windham, N.Y., Oct. 5, 1824; s. Perez and Clarissa (Brainerd) S.; A.B., Wesleyan U., 1848, A.M., 1851 (D.D., 1868); tutor Wesleyan, 1848-50; m. Harriett, d. Rev. Amos Binney, of Wilbraham, Mass., Aug. 8, 1850. Ordained M.E. ministry, 1850; pastor Fitchburg, 1850, Leominster, 1851-52, Lynn, 1854-55, Boston, 1856-57, Malden, 1858-59, Springfield, 1860-61; prof. Genesee Coll., Lima, N.Y., 1862-71; 1st pres. Syracuse U., 1872; pastor in Mass. at Boston, 1872, Auburndale, 1873-74, Lynn, 1875-78, Salem, 1878-79, Peabody, 1880-83, Reading, 1884-87, Boston, 1886-88; prof. N.T. Greek, 1884 and 1891, systematic theology, 1886-89, practical theology, 1892, Boston U. Author: Commentary on Joshua, 1873; Binney's Theological Compend Improved, 1874; Love Enthroned, 1875; Milestone Papers, 1878; Commentary on Leviticus and Numbers, 1891; Half Hours with St. Paul, 1895; Defense of Christian Perfection, 1896; Gospel of the Comforter, 1897; Jesus Exultant, 1899; A Substitute for Holiness, or Antinomianism Revived, 1899; Half Hours with St. John's Epistles, 1901; Steele's Answers, 1912. Home: Milton, Mass. Died Sept. 2, 1914.

STEELE, Daniel Atkinson King, surgeon; b. Delaware Co., O., Mar. 29, 1852; s. Rev. Daniel and Mary Leatham Orr (Anderson) S.; M.D., Chicago Med. Coll., 1873; (LL.D., U. of Ill., 1906); m. Alice L. Tomlinson, Sept. 7, 1876. One of founders, 1882, pres. and prof. principles and practice of surgery and clin. surgery, 1894-1917, Coll. Phys. and Surg.

(med. dept. U. of Ill.), Chicago; sr. dean and prof. surgery and head of dept., Coll. of Medicine of U. of Illinois, Chicago, to July 1917 (dean and prof. surgery emeritus); pres. and prof. University Hosp. from 1907; prof. clin. surgery, Post-Graduate Medical School, 1894; attending surgeon, Michael Reese and Univ. hosps. Commd. maj., Med. R.C., Apr. 1917; mem. Med. Exam. Bd., Chicago, for applicants for Med. R.C., 1917; apptd. chief surgeon U.S.A. Gen. Hosp. No. 9, Lakewood, N.J. Fellow Am. Coll. Surgeons (charter mem. and gov.). Home: Sarasota, Fla. Died July 19, 1931.

STEELE, David, Reformed Presbyn. clergyman; b. nr. Londonderry, Ireland, 1827; s. James S. (6th generation from Capt. John Steele, Lismahago, Scotland, who fought on the Covenanter's side at the battle of Drumclog, June 1, 1679) and Eleanor (Fulton) S., related to the inventor Fulton; grad. Miami Univ., 1857; A.M., 1859; (D.D., Rutgers, 1866; LL.D,. Miami, 1900); m. Elizabeth J. Dallas, 1864. Licensed to preach, 1860; ordained minister, 1861; since then pastor 4th Reformed Presbyn Ch., Phila.; prof. Hebrew, Greek and pastoral theology, 1863-75, of doctrinal theology, 1875—, Theol. Sem. of Reformed Presbyn. Ch. Moderator Gen. Synod R.P. Ch., 1868 and 1886; pres. bd. of foreign missions R.P. Ch.; mem. Presbyn. Alliance Councils, 1880, Phila., 1896, Glasgow, Scotland; visited Europe, 1873, 1884, 1892, 1896; apptd., 1896, to visit R.P. mission in Northern India. Author: The Times in Which We Live and the Ministry They Require, 1871; Endless Life the Inheritance of the Righteous, 1873; Elements of Ministerial Success, 1884; The Two Witnesses, 1887; A Nation in Tears, 1881; The House of God's Glory, 1893; The Wants of the Pulpit, 1894; Christ's Coronation, 1897; History of the Reformed Presbyterian Church in North American, 1898; Personal Religion, 1898; On Reading the Scriptures, 1901; Our Martyred Chief, 1901. Editor: The Reformed Presbyterian Advocate, 1867-77. Mem. exec. council Presbyn. Hist. Soc., Archæol. Soc. of Univ. of Pa.; life mem. Pa. Bible Soc. and Sabbath Assn. of Phila. Home: Philadelphia, Pa. Died 1906.

STEELE, Esther Baker, author; b. Lysander, N.Y., Aug. 4, 1835; d. Rev. Gardner and Esther (Scott) Baker; ed. Mexico Acad. and Falley Sem. Fulton, N.Y.; (hon. Litt.D., Syracuse U., 1892); m. Prof. Joel Dorman Steele, July 7, 1859 (died 1886). Author (in collaboration with her husband) of the Barnes' Brief Histories: United States, 1871; France, 1875; Centenary History of United States, 1875; Ancient Peoples, 1881; Mediæval and Modern Peoples, 1883; General History, 1883; Greece, with Selected Readings, 1884; Rome, with Selected Readings, 1885; Revised United States, 1885. Since her husband's death she has prepared new edits. of these joint works and also of her husband's science books, Hygienic Physiology, enlarged edition, 1888; General History, 1893. Home: Elmira, N.Y. Died Nov. 23, 1911.

STEELE, George Washington, congressman; b. Fayette Co., Ind., Dec. 13, 1839; s. Asbury and Mary Louisa S.; student Ohio Wesleyan U., 1 term, 1860; admitted to bar, 1861; m. Marietta E. Swayzee, Oct. 11, 1866. Enlisted in 8th Ind. Inf., Apr. 19, 1861, not mustered; state service, May 2, 1861; 1st lt. 12th Ind. Inf., July 20, 1861; hon. mustered out, May 19, 1862; 1st lt. 101st Ind. Inf., Sept. 2, 1862; capt., Sept. 6, 1862; maj., Jan. 27, 1863; lt. col., May 31, 1863; hon. mustered out of vol. service, June 24, 1865; 2d and 1st lt. 14th U.S. Inf., Feb. 23, 1866; resigned, Feb. 1, 1876. Pres. First Nat. Bank, Marion, Ind., 1890. Member 47th to 50th and 54th to 57th Congresses (1881-89, 1895-1903), 11th Ind. Dist.; 1st gov. of Okla. Ty., 20 mos., 1890, 91. Republican. Mem. bd. mgrs. Nat. Home Disabled Vol. Soldiers, 1890-1904; now gov. Nat. Soldiers' Home, Indiana. Died July 13, 1922.

STEELE, Harry Lee, army officer; b. Benton Co., Ark., June 28, 1874; s. John Bell and Mary (Van Winkle) S.; grad. Rogers (Ark.) Acad., 1894, Army War Coll., 1928; m. Cornelia Elizabeth Lundeen, Dec. 25, 1901; children—Lee, John Chandler, Lundeen Van Winkle, Ruth. Enlisted as pvt., Battery A, 5th Arty., U.S.A., Aug. 27, 1895, and promoted through grades to maj. gen., chief of coast arty., Feb. 9, 1935. Served in Q.M. Corps in P.I. and China, 1915-16, in Panama, 1919-22, Hawaii, 1931-34. Home: Washington, D.C. Died Mar. 31, 1938.

STEELE, Henry J., congressman; b. Easton, Pa., May 10, 1860; ed. pub. schs. and business coll.; (hon. A.M. and LL.D., Lafayette Coll.; LL.D., Muhlenberg). Admitted to Pa. bar, 1881; mem. 64th to 66th Congresses (1915-21), 26th Pa. Dist. Pres. Pa. Bar Assn., 1914. Home: Easton, Pa. Died Mar. 19, 1933.

STEELE, Henry Maynadier, civ. engr.; b. Baltimore, Md., Sept. 26, 1865; s. Isaac Nevett and Rosa (Nelson) S.; ed. pvt. sch., acad. and Mass. Inst. Technology; m. Margaret Hollins McKim, Feb. 6, 1894. Asst. engr. B.&O. R.R., 1886-87; prin. asst. engr. Erie R.R., 1887-92; southern agt. Hall Signal Co., Baltimore, 1893; cons. engr., Asheville, N.C., 1894-97; chief engr., Central of Ga. Ry., 1897-1906; chief civ. engr. J. G. White & Co., July 1906—. Home: Woodmere, L.I. Died 1909.

STEELE, Hiram Roswell, lawyer; b. Stanstead, Can., July 10, 1842; s. Sanford and Mary (Hinman) S.; acad. edn., St. Johnsbury, Vt.; capt. Co. K, 10th Vt. Inf., Aug. 12, 1862; bvtd. maj. vols., Dec. 19, 1865, "for faithful services in subsistence dept."; hon. mustered out, Jan. 4, 1866; m. Mary E. Porter, Sept. 19, 1877. Admitted to bar, 1868; judge Parish Court, La., 1868-72; judge Superior Criminal Court, New Orleans, 1875-76; dist. atty., La., 1872-75; asst. atty. gen. of La., 1875; mem. La. Constl. convs., 1868, 79; in law practice at New York, 1890—; senior, Steele, DeFriese & Steele; trustee New York Life Ins. Co., South Brooklyn Savings Instn. Dist. atty. Kings Co., 1899. Republican. Home: Brooklyn, N.Y. Deceased.

STEELE, James Dallas, clergyman; b. Philadelphia, Pa., Nov. 6, 1864; s. Rev. David (D.D., LL.D.) and Elizabeth J. (Dallas) S.; B.A., U. of Pa., 1884, LL.B., 1886, M.A., 1887, B.D., 1891; Ph.D., U. of Omaha, 1892; D.D., New York U., 1911; m. Emma Roberta Abbott, Dec. 8, 1898. Admitted to Pa. bar, 1886, N.Y. bar, 1893; instr. in Hebrew, U. of Pa., 1890-91; lecturer in Hebrew, Columbia, 1891-92; ordained ministry Ref. Presbyn. Ch. (Covenanters), 1891; pastor 1st R.P. Ch., New York, 1891-1906, 1st Presbyn. Ch., Passaic, N.J., 1906-21; stated clerk of the Presbytery of Jersey City, 1922—; lecturer Bloomfield (N.J.) Theol. Sem. Prof. O.T. lit. and ch. history, Ref. Presbyn. Theol. Sem., 1902-06. Spl. speaker for Y.M.C.A. in camps and cantonments, 1917-19. Republican. Home: Rutherford, N.J. Deceased.

STEELE, James King, author; b. Keokuk, Ia., June 30, 1875; s. Daniel and Anna (Wilson) S.; ed. high sch., Keokuk; m. Edith Shorb, July 19, 1904; 1 son, Shorb. Pub. and editor Del Monte (Calif.) Weekly, 1909-11, World Traveler, 1911-16; editor Pacific Golf and Motor, 1916-17; editor and pub. Japan, travel monthly, 1918-29; exec. sec. Philippine Tourist Assn., 1930-35; travel editor San Francisco Call-Bulletin, 1935-36; publicity mgr. in New York for Robert L. Ripley of Ripley's Believe It or Not, Inc., 1936-37; mng. dir. Nevada Unlimited, Reno, Nev., Aug. 1937—. Lt. comdr. U.S.N.R.F. Knight of Dragon of Annam; Officer of the Dragon of Camboge; Chevalier of the Million Elephants and White Parasol (Indo-China). Author: Wandering Feet, 1919; Strange Beds, 1921; Bits of Jade, 1923. Home: San Francisco, Calif. Died Dec. 25, 1937.

STEELE, John Nelson, lawyer; b. Baltimore, Md., Apr. 1853; s. Isaac Nevett and Rosa L. (Nelson) S.; LL.B., U. of Va., 1873, U. of Md., 1874; m. Mary Alricks Pegram, Mar. 1, 1880 (died 1903); m. 2d, Marion L. Grosvenor, Aug. 25, 1917. Practiced with father, in Baltimore, 1874-89; mem. Steele, Semmes & Carey, 1889-1904, Steele & Semmes, 1904-06; gen. counsel and dir. Copper River & Northwestern R.R. Co., Kennecott Copper Corp., Alaska Development & Mineral Co. Republican. Episcopalian. Home: Mamaroneck, N.Y., and Palm Beach, Fla. Died Mar. 7, 1933.

STEELE, Leslie J., congressman; b. DeKalb Co., Ga., Nov. 21, 1868; A.B., Emory Coll. (now Univ.), Atlanta, Ga., 1893; LL.B., U. of Ga., 1899; m. Ruby Sprayberry, Nov. 16, 1904. Admitted to Ga. bar, 1899; mayor of Decatur, 1915-20; mem. Ga. Ho. of Rep., 2 terms; mem. 70th Congress (1927-29), 5th Ga. Dist. Democrat. Home: Decatur, Ga. Died July 24, 1929.

STEELE, Robert Wilbur, judge; b. Lebanon, O., Nov. 14, 1857; s. Henry King and Mary Frances (Dunlavy) S.; grad. Denver High Sch., 1877; studied law dept. Columbian U., 1878-79; (A.M., Centre Coll.; LL.D., U. of Denver, 1907); m. Anna B. Truax, Feb. 28, 1884. Admitted Colo. bar, 1881; clerk Co. Ct., Arapahoe Co., Colo., 1881-85; dist. atty. 2d Jud. Dist., Colo., 1892-95; co. judge Arapahoe Co., 1895-1901; justice Supreme Ct. of Colo., 1901—, chief justice, 1907-11. Home: Denver, Colo. Died 1910.

STEELE, Rufus (Milas), author; b. Hope, Ark., Mar. 3, 1877; s. Rev. Columbus Oney and Sallie Elizabeth (Carruth) S.; B.Sc., Pacific Methodist Coll., Santa Rosa, Calif., 1896; m. Mira Mabel Walden, Jan. 1, 1901. Editor Redding (Calif.) Free Press, 1900-02; writer, 1902-04, Sunday editor, 1904-06, San Francisco Chronicle; Sunday editor San Francisco Call, Aug. 1, 1906-Dec. 15, 1912. Editor div. of films, U.S. Com. on Pub. Information, 1918-19; coach in magazine spl. article writing, U. of Miami, 1927; asso. prof. English same university, 1929-31; columnist for The Christian Science Monitor, Boston, Mass., writing daily front page feature, "The March of the Nations," Sept. 1, 1931—. Author: The City That Is, 1909; The Fall of Ug—A Masque of Fear, prod. in Bohemian Grove, Calif., Aug. 9, 1913, pub. 1913; Rule G, 1915; Aces for Industry, 1919; What's Right with the Movies, 1925; What's Right with Florida, 1925; Scar Neck, 1930. Author and producer numerous motion pictures. Lecturer on Latin-Am. relations, architecture and home-building, aviation and outdoor subjects. Home: Boston, Mass. Died Dec. 25, 1935.

STEELE, Theodore Clement, artist; b. Owen Co., Ind., Sept. 22, 1847; s. Samuel Hamilton and Harriet N. (Newall) S.; m. Mary E. Lakin, Feb. 14, 1870; m. 2d, Selma Neubacher, Aug. 7, 1907. Studied in Munich under Professors Bentzur and Loeffts, 1880-85; exhibited at Paris Expn., 1900; pictures in museums at St. Louis, Cincinnati, Indianapolis and Boston Art Club; Fine Arts Bldg. Prize ($500), Chicago, 1909. A.N.A., 1913; mem. Internat. Jury of Awards, St. Louis Expn., 1904. LL.D., Indiana U., 1916. Home: Bloomington, Ind. Died July 24, 1926.

STEELE, Thomas J., congressman; b. Rush County, Ind., Mar. 19, 1853; s. Ira C. S.; ed. pub. schs. of Ia. and Axline's Sem. (defunct); studied law in pvt. office at Sheldon, Ia.; m. Ella McCullough. In cattle commn. business at Sioux City, Ia., 1897—, operating largely in S.D. and Neb.; pres. Steele-Simon Commn. Co., T. J. Steele & Co., etc. Mem. 64th Congress (1915-17), 11th Ia. Dist. Democrat. Conglist. Mason. Home: Sioux City, Ia. Died Mar. 21, 1920.

STEELE, Thomas Sedgwick, artist, author; b. Hartford, Conn., June 11, 1845; s. Thomas S.; ed. Hartford High School; m. Annie E. Smith, Nov. 10, 1868; m. 2d, Sarah C. Goff, Oct. 26, 1876. Studied art with P. Marcius-Simons, Paris, France; admitted to Nat. Acad. of Design, 1877; artist in fish, game, fruit, flowers and still life; has traveled extensively in Egypt, Norway, Russia and Europe generally. Author: Canoe and Camera, 1880; Paddle and Portage, 1882; A Voyage to Viking Land, 1896; etc. Home: Hartford, Conn. Died 1903.

STEELL, Willis, playwright; b. Detroit, Mich.; s. William and Jessica (Tait) S.; A.B. from Albion (Mich.) College, 1885; m. Emily Higman, Nov. 27, 1898. Episcopalian. Author: Isidra, 1888; Mortal Lips; Mountain of Gold; Death of the Discoverer; In Seville; Vaudevilles, 1908; The Fifth Commandment, 1907; (plays) The Kindergarten (1900), A Juliet of the People (1901), Battle of the Strong (1901), Consuelo (1902), Firm of Cunningham (1905), Morning After the Play (1906), Brother Dave (1907), Girl of the Golden Horn (mus. comedy, with Reginald de Koven), 1909; The Prospector, prod., Pittsburgh, 1912; Lionnette, prod. Princess Theatre, New York, 1914; The Gift of the Madonna, prod. at Inceville, Calif., by New York Picture Co., 1914; also (books) The Prospector, 1912; We're Ready!, 1915; Art and the New Religion, 1916; Parerga, 1919; The Long Walk of Samba Diouf, 1923; Forgotten People, 1926; Benjamin Franklin of Paris, 1928. Died Jan. 31, 1941.

STEENERSON, Halvor, congressman; b. Dane Co., Wis., June 30, 1852; s. Steener and Birgith (Roholt) Knudson; high school edn., Rushford, Minn.; studied law in office and in Union Coll. of Law, Chicago; m. Maria C. Fjaagesund, Nov. 24, 1878. Admitted to bar, 1878; began practice in Minn., 1878; in practice at Crookston, Minn., Apr. 1880—; interested in farming. Co. atty. Polk Co., 1881-83; mem. Minn. Senate, 1883-85; city atty., and mem. bd. edn., Crookston, 1880-90; mem. 58th to 67th Congresses (1903-23), 9th Minn. Dist. Now sr. law firm Steenerson & Neils. Home: Crookston, Minn. Died Nov. 22, 1926.

STEENSTRA, Peter Henry, theologian; b. in Holland, Jan. 24, 1833; came to U.S., settling in St. Louis, Mo., in early boyhood; A.B., Shurtleff Coll., Ill., 1858 (D.D., 1882); m. Miss S. B. Learned, Nov. 4, 1858. Entered Bapt. ministry, 1858, but changed to that of P.E. Ch., 1864. Prof. O.T. lit. and interpretation, Episcopal Theol. Sch., Cambridge, Mass., 1867-1907, prof. emeritus, 1907. Edited and translated Lange's Commentaries on Judges and Ruth, 1872. Author: The Being of God as Unity and Trinity, 1891; also chapters on the Earlier History of Israel and on Hebrew Literature in vol. 2 of Prof. Wright's History of all Nations, 1905. Home: Robbinston, Me. Died 1911.

STEERE, Joseph Beal, scientist; b. Lenawee Co., Mich., Feb. 9, 1842; s. William Millhouse and Elizabeth (Beal) S.; A.B., Univ. of Mich., 1868, LL.B., 1870 (hon. Ph.D., 1875); m. Helen Buzzard, Sept. 30, 1879. Made a scientific trip around the world by way of Brazil, up the Amazon, across the Andes, China, etc., 1870-75; instr., and asst. prof. zoölogy, 1876-79, prof., 1879-93, U. of Mich.; engaged in farming and study, 1893—. Led party of students to Amazon, 1879, to Philippines, 1887-88; on 3d trip to Amazon, 1901, collecting specimens for Smithsonian Instn. and Buffalo Expn. Author: Fifty New Species of Philippine Birds. Home: Ann Arbor, Mich. Died Dec. 7, 1940.

STEERE, Joseph Hall, judge; b. Addison, Mich., May 19, 1852; s. Isaac and Elizabeth (Comstock) S.; A.B., also grad. in pedagogy, U. Mich., 1876, LL.D., 1921; unmarried. Admitted Mich. bar, 1878; pros. atty. Chippewa Co., Mich., 1879-81; circuit judge, 11th Jud. Circuit, Mich., 1881-Sept. 1, 1911; resigned to accept appmt. as justice Supreme Court of Mich. (chief justice, 1913 and 1921); elected, spring of 1910, as judge 11th Jud. Circuit, but declined, owing to accepting position on Supreme bench; retired after over 46 yrs. of continuous judicial service. Republican. Quaker by birthright. Trustee Sch. Bd. and Pub. Library, Sault Ste. Marie, Mich. Died Dec. 16, 1936.

STEFFENS, Cornelius M., coll. pres.; b. Veldhuizen, Germany, Sept. 28, 1866; s. Nicholas M.

(D.D.) and Jane (Sutherland) S.; pub. schs., German Valley, Ill., and New York; A.M., Hope Coll., Mich., 1892; grad. Western Theol. Sem., Holland, Mich., 1895; D.D., Lenox and Coe colls., 1907; m. Anna M. Meulendyke, Apr. 29, 1898; 1 son, Ralph Sutherland. Ordained, 1895; pastor Rochester, N.Y., 1895-98, Little Falls, N.J., 1898-1900; pres. U. of Dubuque, Ia., Feb. 2, 1902-Jan. 1, 1924, emeritus, 1925—. Came to America at age of 4; greatly interested and successful in Americanization of the fgn. speaking people of this country. Author: Adventures in Money Raising, 1930. Home: Chicago, Ill. Died Jan. 15, 1933.

STEFFENS, (Joseph) Lincoln, writer, lecturer; b. San Francisco, Apr. 6, 1866; s. Joseph and Elizabeth Louisa (Symes) S.; Ph.B., U. of Calif., 1889; student philosophy, etc., univs. of Berlin, Heidelberg, Leipzig, the Sorbonne, Paris, 1889-92; m. Josephine Bontecou, 1891 (dec.); m. 2d, Ella Winter, 1924; 1 son, Pete Stanley. Reporter and asst. city editor New York Evening Post, 1892-98; city editor New York Commercial Advertiser, 1898-1902; mng. editor McClure's Mag., 1902-06; asso. editor American and Everybody's mags., 1906-11. Author: The Shame of the Cities, 1904; The Struggle for Self-Government, 1906; Upbuilders, 1909; The Least of These, 1910; Moses in Red, 1926; The Autobiography of Lincoln Steffens, 1931; Boy on Horseback, 1935. Mem. Bullitt mission to Russia, 1919. Home: Carmel, Calif. Died Aug. 9, 1936.

STEGER, (Harry) Peyton, editor; b. Moscow, Tenn., Mar. 2, 1883; s. Thomas Peyton and Alice (Scales) S.; U. of Tex., B.A., 1902, M.A., 1904; Heidelberg and Bonn, Germany, 1905; Rhodes scholar, Balliol Coll., Oxford, Eng., 1905-06; m. Dorothy Jane McCormick, June 9, 1910. Editor "Short Stories" (mag.), 1908—; lit. adviser Doubleday, Page & Co., 1911—; lit. executor of O. Henry. Author: O. Henry, A Biographical Collection, 1912; Up From College, 1912. Home: Freeport, L.I., N.Y. Deceased.

STEHLE, Aurelius, clergyman, educator; b. Pittsburgh, Pa., Apr. 30, 1877; s. Richard and Rose (Niggel) S.; A.B., St. Vincent Coll., Pa., 1895; A.M., St. Vincent Sem., 1898; D.D., Rome, 1920; LL.D., Notre Dame U., Ind., 1925. Joined the Benedictine Fathers (O.S.B.), 1893; ordained priest Roman Catholic Church, under canonical age with special Papal dispensation, 1899; prof. Latin and Greek, St. Vincent Coll., later prefect of Sem., coadjutor abbot, 1918, archabbot (pres.) St. Vincent Archabbey, and pres. St. Vincent Coll. and Sem., Sept. 3, 1920—. Pres. Benedictine Soc. of Westmoreland Co., Pa.; chancellor Catholic U. of Peking, China. Republican. Author: Manual of Episcopal Ceremonies, 1914. Home: Latrobe, Pa. Died Feb. 11, 1930.

STEIGER, Ernst, publisher; b. Gastewitz, Saxony, Oct. 4, 1832; learned book-selling business; came to U.S., 1855; m. Bertha Krehbiel, May 11, 1867. Began book business for himself, 1864; pub. works of German-Americans and language textbooks. Author: Der Nachdruck in Nordamerika; Das Copyright-Law in den Vereinigten Staaten; Periodical Literature (a bibliography); Dreiundfünfzig Jahre Buchhändler in Deutschland und Amerika (an autobiography), 1901; Das Gespenst des Nachdrucks deutscher Bücher in Nordamerika, 1902; Urheberrecht und Nachdruck in Nordamerika, 1908; etc. Home: New York, N.Y. Died Aug. 2, 1917.

STEIGERS, William Corbet, soldier, newspaperman; b. St. Louis, Sept. 15, 1845. Served in 8th Mo. Regt., later sergt. U.S. Signal Corps, Civil War; discharged for physical disability after siege of Vicksburg. Joined St. Louis Dispatch, 1868, and in 1878, when the paper was consolidated with the Post as St. Louis Post-Dispatch, became adv. mgr.; business mgr. and v.p. same, 1898—. Died May 25, 1923.

STEIN, Evaleen, author, artist; b. Lafayette, Ind.; d. John Andrew and Virginia (Tomlinson) S.; ed. pub. schs., Lafayette; Art Inst. of Chicago. Decorative designer and illuminator; exhibited illuminated manuscripts at Arts and Crafts Soc., Chicago, Indianapolis, etc. Contbr. of verse to Indianapolis Journal, 1886-1900; represented in Stedman's Am. Anthology and other verse collections. Author: Gabriel and the Hour Book, 1906; A Little Shepherd of Provence, 1910; The Little Count of Normandy, or The Story of Raoul, 1912; The Christmas Porringer, 1914; Our Little Norman Cousin of Long Ago, 1915; Rosechen and the Wicked Magpie, 1917; Our Little Frankish Cousin of Long Ago, 1917; Child Songs of Cheer, 1918; Our Little Celtic Cousin of Long Ago, 1918; Our Little Crusader Cousin of Long Ago, 1921; When Fairies Were Friendly, 1922; Little Poems from Japanese Anthologies, rendered into English verse, 1922; Poems of Giovanni Pascoli, freely rendered into English verse, 1923. Home: Lafayette, Ind. Died Nov. 1923.

STEIN, John Philip, pastor St. Thomas Reformed Ch., Reading, 1892—; b. Annville, Pa., June 11, 1836; s. Daniel and Catherine (Forney) S.; grad. Franklin and Marshall, 1861 (A.M., 1871, D.D., 1899); grad. Theol. Sem., Mercersburg, Pa., 1863; Union Theol. Sem., New York, 1864; then entered ministry; stated clerk Eastern Synod from 1881 and of Gen. Synod "Reformed Ch. in the U.S.," 1896—; formerly mem. Bd. Visitors, Theol. Sem., Lancaster, Pa., until 1898. Home: Reading, Pa. Died 1909.

STEIN, Robert, arctic explorer; b. Rengersdorf, Silesia, Prussia, Jan. 9, 1857; s. Joseph and Francisca (Kasper) S.; ed. at Glatz, 1873-75; came to U.S., 1875, and engaged in teaching; M.D., Georgetown Coll., 1886; unmarried. Entered U.S. Geol. Survey, 1885, and became translator of German, French, Italian, Danish, Swedish, Russian, Dutch, Spanish, Portuguese and other langs. In 1893 he published plan for exploring Ellesmereland which attracted attention of Am. and European geographers; joined the 7th Peary expdn., 1897, landing with 3 Eskimo boatmen on western Greenland (lat. 74°-75°) to explore and map the coast, afterward returning on the same vessel. In 1899 he took passage on the Diana, with 2 companions, to carry out his plan for exploring Ellesmereland; landing at Cape Sabine, he spent 2 yrs. mainly in linguistic studies among the Eskimos, returning to the U.S. in Oct. 1901. Author of various articles on economic and social subjects and on Arctic work in the Nat. Geog. Magazine, and Arctic work in leading reviews. Advocating an internat. conf. of experts in phonetics to devise a universal alphabat to serve as a uniform notation of the sounds of speech in particular as a uniform key to pronunciation in dictionaries. Died 1917.

STEINER, Bernard Christian, librarian; b. Guilford, Conn., Aug. 13, 1867; s. Lewis Henry and Sarah Spencer (Smyth) S.; A.B., Yale, 1888, A.M., 1890; Ph.D., Johns Hopkins, 1891; LL.B., U. of Maryland, 1894; Litt.D., Dickinson College, Pa., 1923; m. Ethel Sımes Mulligan, Nov. 7, 1912. Instr. history, in charge of dept., Williams Coll., 1891-92; librarian, Enoch Pratt Free Library, Baltimore, 1892—. Instr. history, 1893, asso., 1894-1911, Johns Hopkins; dean and prof. constl. law, Baltimore U., 1897-1900; dean and prof. pub. law, Baltimore Law Sch., 1900-04. Author: Education in Connecticut, 1893; Education in Maryland, 1894; Citizenship and Suffrage in Maryland, 1895; Genealogy of Steiner Family, 1896; History of Guilford, Conn., 1898; Life of Sir Robert Eden, 1898; Institutions and Civil Government of Maryland, 1899; Life and Correspondence of James McHenry, 1907; Life of Reverdy Johnson, 1914; Life of Henry Winter Davis, 1916; Life of Henry Barnard, 1919; Life of Roger B. Taney, 1922. Editor Archives of Maryland, 1916—. Mem. Gen. Assembly Presbyn. Ch. U.S.A., 1920-21. Republican. Presbyn. Home: Baltimore, Md. Died Jan. 12, 1926.

STEINFELD, Albert, mcht.; b. at Hanover, Germany, Dec. 23, 1854; s. Levi and Lina S.; brought to U.S., 1863; ed. N.Y. City High Sch.; m. Bettina V. Donau, Feb. 15, 1883. Began in mercantile business in N.Y. City; went to Denver, Colo., 1870, to Tucson, Ariz., 1872; active in mercantile business, 1872—; now pres. Albert Steinfeld & Co. Mason. Home: Tucson, Ariz. Died Feb. 8, 1935.

STEINHART, Frank (Maximilian), pub. utility pres.; b. Munich, Germany, May 12, 1864; s. Simon and Regina (Levinger) S.; ed. pub. schs. and high sch., Munich, Germany; read law 4 yrs. and studied foreign langs.; m. Alice Florence Ledden, Feb. 8, 1890; children—Florence, Frank, Alice. Private, corporal and sergeant U.S.A., 1882-89; transferred to headquarters Div. of the Mo., Chicago, as clerk, serving as such and as asst. chief clerk under Gens. Schofield, Crook, Terry, Miles, Ruger, Merritt and Brooke; apptd. chief clerk, 1st Army Corps, May 1898, and accompanied Gen. Brooke to P.R.; apptd. chief clerk, Dept. P.R.; transferred to Cuba as chief clerk of mil. govt., serving under Gen. Wood until May 20, 1902; apptd. agt. War Dept., U.S.A., with residence in Cuba, and in charge of archives of mil. govt., 1902-03. Am. consul gen. at Havana, 1903-07. Republican. Pres., gen. mgr. Havana Electric Rys. Died Dec. 9, 1938.

STEINITZ, William, chess champion-author; b. Prague, Bohemia, May 14, 1836; ed. there and in Polytechnic Instn., Vienna; became locally known as chess expert in Vienna; won 1st prize in local tournament 1861; participated in London Chess Congress, 1862 (6th in prize list); played Prof. Anderson, 1866, winning world's championship, which he held against all comers until 1894 (about 18 years longer than any previous champion); tied for chief honors with Winower, the Russian, in Emperor's prize tournament, Vienna, 1783; defeated by Lasker for championship, 1894, and again in Moscow, 1897. First came to U.S. 1882; came to reside about a year later. Edited International Chess Magazine, 1885-91 (7 vols.); Book of Sixth American Chess Congress of 1889; Part I and portion of Part II, Modern Chess Instructor. Died 1900.

STEINMAN, Andrew Jackson, editor; b. Lancaster, Pa., Oct. 10, 1836; s. John Frederick and Mary Smith (Fahnestock) S.; A.B., Yale, 1856, A.M., 1859; m. Caroline Morgan Hale, Jan. 25, 1882. Admitted to bar, 1859; editor Lancaster Intelligencer, 1868—; owns large interests in iron mfg. as chmn. Penn Iron Co., Ltd., etc. Also engaged in law practice. Democrat. Home: Lancaster, Pa. Died Nov. 17, 1917.

STEINMETZ, Charles Proteus, electrician; b. Breslau, Germany, Apr. 9, 1865; s. Carl Heinrich and Caroline (Neubert) S.; ed. Breslau, Berlin, Zürich, Switzerland; spl. studies mathematics, elec. engring., chemistry; (hon. A.M., Harvard, 1902; Ph.D., Union U., N.Y., 1903). Consulting engr. Gen. Elec. Co., 1893—; prof. electrophysics, Union Univ., 1902—. Author: Theory and Calculation of Alternating-Current Phenomena, 1897, 5th edition, 1916; Theoretical Elements of Electrical Engineering, 4th edit., 1915; Theory and Calculation of Transient Electric Phenomena and Oscillations, 1909, 3d edit., 1919; General Lectures on Electrical Engineering, 5th edit., 1917; Radiation, Light and Illumination, 1909, 2d edit., 1911; Engineering Mathematics, 1910, 3d edit., 1917; Electric Discharges, Waves and Impulses, 1911; America and the New Epoch, 1916; Theory and Calculation of Electric Circuits, 1917; Theory and Calculation of Electrical Apparatus, 1917. Also sundry math. papers and investigations and numerous papers on theoretical, experimental investigations in elec. engring. Past pres. Am. Inst. Elec. Engrs. (1901-02), Illuminating Engring. Soc., Nat. Assn. Corp. Schs. Pres. Bd. of Edn., Schenectady, 1912—; pres. Common Council, 1916—. Home: Schenectady, N.Y. Died Oct. 26, 1923.

STEINMETZ, Joseph Allison, mechanical engr.; b. Phila., Pa., Mar. 22, 1870; s. John and Frances Morris (Janney) S.; prep. edn., Phila. Central High Sch.; student Lehigh U., 1900; m. Oma Frances Fields, 1903; children—Joseph Janney, Frances Margaret. Assisted Prof. Langley in producing spl. steel parts, early airplane engines, 1900; sr. mem. Janney-Steinmetz & Co., seamless steel containers, 1893—; president "Globar" Corp.; Phila. asso. Am. Car & Foundry Co.; designed and patented numerous devices for aerial and submarine warfare; engr. of land reclamation, Greenwich League Island Area, 1912-18; located Hog Island for war shipyard; founder and dir. Sch. of Aircraft Building, Phila., 1917-18. Mem. Submarine Defense Assn., New York, 1917-19, World War; spl. service overseas for War Industries Survey, 1918-19; mem. engring. div. Nat. Research Council, 1918; lt. col. U.S. ord. (Res.), 1919. Registered engr., Pa. Trustee Fairmount Park Art Assn. Member of numerous societies. Donor of annual medal for safety in aeronautics, by Soc. Engrs. of Phila. Home: Germantown, Pa. Died July 11, 1928.

STEINWAY, Charles Herman, piano mfr.; b. June 3, 1857; s. Charles G. and Sophie S.; ed. America and abroad; m. Marie A. Mertens, Oct. 10, 1885. Pres. and dir. Steinway & Sons; trustee Citizens Savings Bank, New York City. Chevalier of the Legion of Honor (France), Order of the Liakat (Turkey), Order of the Lion and the Sun (Persia). Home: New York, N.Y. Died Oct. 30, 1919.

STEIWER, Frederick, senator; b. Jefferson, Ore., Oct. 13, 1883; s. John F. and Ada (May) S.; B.S., Ore. State Agrl. Coll., 1902; B.A., U. of Ore., 1906; student Law Sch., same univ.; m. Frieda Roesch, Dec. 12, 1911; children—Elisabeth, Frederick Herbert. Admitted to Ore. bar, 1908, and began practice at Pendleton, 1909; continued professional career until 1926; now associated with Maguire, Shields and Morrison, Portland; actively identified with wheat growing. Deputy dist. atty., 1909-10, dist. atty., 1912-16; mem. Ore. State Senate, 1916-17; served as 1st lt. F.A., U.S.A., 1917-19; mem. U.S. Senate, 2 terms, 1927-39, resigned, Jan. 31, 1938. Delivered "keynote" address at Rep. Nat. Conv., 1936. Republican. Episcopalian. Mason, Elk. Rotarian. Home: Portland, Ore. Died Feb. 3, 1939.

STELLA, Antonio, M.D.; b. Muro Lucano, Italy, Aug. 18, 1868; s. Michele (lawyer) and Vincenza (Cerone) S.; B.S., M.A., Royal Lyceum, Naples; M.D., maxima cum laude, Royal U. of Naples, 1893; m. Emma Elvira Wessler, of Dresden, Germany, Jan. 21, 1899. Practiced at N.Y. City, 1894—; naturalized citizen of U.S., 1909; specializes in internal medicine; now consulting phys. Manhattan State Hosp., Italian Hosp.; visiting phys. Columbus Hosp.; examiner in lunacy, N.Y. State. V.p., trustee Italian Savings Bank. Del. of Italian Govt. to 6th Internat. Tuberculosis Congress, Washington, D.C., 1909; del. of U.S. Govt. to 7th Internat. Tuberculosis Congress, Rome, 1912; hon. commr. U.S. Govt. to Internat. Expn. Commerce and Labor, Turin, 1912. A founder and v.p. Caruso Am. Memorial Foundation. Decorated Chevalier of the Crown of Italy, 1910, Officer, 1914, Commendatore, 1916; Officer Order of SS. Maurice and Lazarus, 1923 (Italy). Author: Some Aspects of Italian Immigration to the United States, 1924. Republican. Catholic. Home: New York, N.Y. Died July 2, 1927.

STELLHORN, Frederick William, theologian; b. Hanover, Germany, Oct. 2, 1841; s. Johann Dietrich and Catharine Elizabeth (Wessling) S.; A.B., Concordia Coll., Ft. Wayne, Ind., 1862; (D.D., Muhlenberg Coll., Pa., 1896); m. Christiana Maria Buenger, Jan. 3, 1866 (died 1899); m. 2d, Mrs. Louise (Lang) Darst, July 10, 1901. Ordained Luth. ministry, 1865; pastor St. Louis, 1865-67, in DeKalb Co., Ind., 1867-69; prof. Northwestern U., Wis., 1869-74, Concordia Coll., Ft. Wayne, Ind., 1874-81; prof. theology and German, 1881—, pres., 1894-1900, dean

Theol. Sem., 1903—, Capital U. Except a brief intermission, has been editor Lutherische Kirchenzeitung, 1881-98; editor Theologische Zeitblaetter (combined with Columbus Theol. Mag., 1911), 1882—. Author: Kurzgefasstes Wörterbuch zum Griechischen Neuen Testament (2d edit., 1905); A Brief Commentary on the Four Gospels for Study and Devotion, 1891; Annotations on the Acts of the Apostles, 1896; The Error of Modern Missouri, 1897; Die Pastoralbriefe Pauli übersetzt und erklärt (2 vols.), 1899; The Epistle of St. Paul to the Romans Briefly Explained, 1899, 2d, enlarged edit., 1917; Schriftbeweis des Lutherischen Katechismus. Home: Columbus, O. Died Mar. 17, 1919.

STELLWAGEN, Edward James, banker; b. Washington, D.C., Oct. 18, 1854; s. Charles K. and Eliza (Tucker) S.; ed. Gonzaga Coll. and Emerson Inst., Washington, D.C.; LL.B., Columbian (now George Washington) U., 1875; m. Charlotte M. Fisher, Sept. 29, 1880. Identified with banking business at Washington, 1899—; pres. Union Trust Co. of D.C., 1900—; also officer or dir. of many corps. Republican. Episcopalian. Home: Washington, D.C. Died June 2, 1932.

STELWAGON, Henry Weightman, physician; b. Philadelphia, Dec. 3, 1853; s. Joseph and Margaretta W. (Duckett) S.; B.S., Andalusia Coll., Pa., 1872; M.D., Ph.D., U. of Pa., 1875; m. Elizabeth Bender, Easton, Pa., Oct. 9, 1884. Resident phys. Phila. (Blockley) Hosp., 1875-76; student hosps. Vienna and Berlin, 1876-78; phys.-in-charge Phila. Dispensary Skin Diseases, 1880-90; instr. dermatology, U. of Pa., 1885-90; asso. in professional partnership with Prof. Duhring, 1885-90; dermatologist to Phila. (Blockley) Hosp., 1888-1915 (and cons. dermatologist, 1916—), to Northern Dispensary, 1882-1900, and to Howard Hosp., 1885-1912, and cons. dermatologist, 1912—; clin. prof. dermatology, Woman's Med. Coll., Phila., 1888-1907; prof. dermatology, Jefferson Med. Coll., 1890—. Author: Essentials of Diseases of the Skin, 1890, 7th edit., 1909; Treatise on Diseases of the Skin, 1901, 8th edit., 1916. Translator and editor Mracek's Atlas of Skin Diseases, 1898. Home: Philadelphia, Pa. Died Oct. 18, 1919.

STELZLE, Charles, sociologist; b. New York, June 4, 1869; s. John and Dora S.; ed. pub. schs.; tech. instrn. in sch. of R. Hoe & Co., New York, 1885-90, and machinist with same company, 1885-93; private teacher and theol. instruction, 1890-1900; LL.D., Cumberland U., Tenn., 1933; m. Louise Rothmayer, Nov. 28, 1889; 1 son, Robert Clarence; m. 2d, Louise Ingersoll, Sept. 11, 1899; children—Hope Ingersoll, Frances (dec.). Ordained Presbyn. ministry, 1900; pastor Hope Chapel, Minneapolis, 1895-97, Hope Chapel, New York, 1897-99, Markham Memorial Ch., St. Louis, 1899-1903; supt. dept. church and labor, Presbyn. Ch. in U.S.A., 1903-13; established "Labor Sunday," 1904, and the exchange of delegates between central labor unions and ministerial associations; del. to ann. convs. Am. Fedn. Labor, 1905-15; field sec. Federal Council Chs. of Christ in America, 1916-18. Supt. dept. of immigration, 1908-10; organizer and supt. Labor Temple, New York, 1910-12; dean social service dept. of Men and Religion Forward Movement, 1912; supt. work among foreign-speaking people, auspices New York Presbytery, 1908-10; dir. dept. Christian sociology, Bible Teachers' Training Sch., New York, 1912, 13; investigated economic aspects of liquor problem in U.S. and European countries, with members of personal staff, 1914, 15; dir. relief and emergency measures, mayor's com. on unemployment, New York, winter of 1914-15; arbitrator of labor disputes in New York daily newspaper offices, 1913—; made social surveys of 200 leading Am. cities with staff of investigators; mgr. "Strengthen America Campaign." Editorial staff Newark News, 1913-14, Phila. North American, 1914-15; religious editor Newspaper Enterprise Assn., 1917, 18, 19; dir. publicity for Am. Red Cross, Washington, in its depts. for labor and chs., 1918; publicity dir. social and religious enterprises, 1920—; made study of economic conditions in Eng., Germany and League of Nations in Geneva, 1924. Publicity dir. World Alliance for Internat. Friendship; 10th anniversary celebration in U.S. of founding of League of Nations; Boy Scouts America $10,000,000 campaign; 5 yr. program for Am. Home Missions Council; exec. dir. Good Neighbor League, 1936-39, publicity counselor, 1939—. Author: The Workingman and Social Problems, 1903; Boys of the Street, 1904; Messages to Workingmen, 1906; Christianity's Storm Center, 1907; Letters from a Workingman, 1908; Principles of Successful Church Advertising, 1909; Church and Labor, 1910; American Social and Religious Conditions, 1912; Gospel of Labor, 1912; Why Prohibition?, 1918; A Son of the Bowery (autobiography), 1926. Home: New York, N.Y. Died Feb. 27, 1941.

STEMBEL, Roger Nelson, rear admiral U.S.N., retired; b. Middleton, Md., Dec. 27, 1810; entered navy, midshipman, Mar. 27, 1832; was in cruiser Porpoise, wrecked near Vera Cruz, 1833; on duty, naval school, New York, 1834-38; passed midshipman, June 23, 1838; lt., Oct. 23, 1843; on coast survey until 1847; then on various stations until beginning of Civil war; fitted out gunboats at Cincinnati and served in Mississippi River flotilla; commanded river gunboat Lexington; was in numerous engagements; commanded Cincinnati, which was sunk in aciton with rams at Fort Pillow, when he was seriously wounded; commd. capt. July 25, 1866, commodore July 13, 1870; retired Dec. 27, 1872; promoted rear admiral on retired list, June 5, 1874. Home: Washington, D.C. Died 1900.

STENGEL, Alfred, M.D.; b. Pittsburgh, Pa., Nov. 3, 1868; s. G.S.; M.D., U. of Pa., 1889; Sc.D., U. of Pittsburgh; LL.D., Lafayette College and Univ. of Pa.; married; 3 children. Phys. to University Hospital; emeritus prof. medicine, and vice-pres. Univ. of Pa. Fellow Coll. of Physicians, Phila. Author: A Text-Book of Pathology, 8 edits., 1898-1924. Wrote: Diseases of the Blood, Twentieth Century Practice of Medicine, Vol. VII; Diseases of the Spleen, same, Vol. IX. Editor: Am. edit. of Nothnagel's Cyclopedia of Medicine. Home: Philadelphia, Pa. Died Apr. 10, 1939.

STEPHENS, Alice Barber, illustrator; b. nr. Salem, N.J., 1858; d. Samuel C. and Mary (Owen) Barber; ed. pub. schs., Phila.; art edn., Phila. Sch. of Design for Women, Pa. Acad. Fine Arts and Acad. Julian, Paris; m. Charles H. Stephens, 1890; 1 son, D. Owen. Became wood-engraver for Scribner's Magazine and illustrator for Harper's, Century, and other mags.; also taught portrait and life classes Phila. Sch. of Design for Women. Home: Moylan, Pa. Died July 13, 1932.

STEPHENS, Ambrose E. B., congressman; b. Hamilton Co., O., June 3, 1862; s. S. Kyle and Minerva (Smith) S.; ed. Chickering Inst., Cincinnati, O.; married; children—James Kyle, Maude C., Mrs. Corrine Brunner, Mrs. Lucretia Montague. Admitted to Ohio bar and began practice at Cincinnati; clerk courts of Hamilton Co. 3 terms; mem. 66th to 69th Congresses (1919-27), 2d Ohio Dist. Served as capt. and q.m. 1st Inf., Ohio N.G., 1901-03; col. same regt., 1910-11. Republican. Home: North Bend, O. Died Feb. 12, 1927.

STEPHENS, Charles Asbury, author; b. Norway Lake, Me., Oct. 21, 1847; A.B., Bowdoin, 1869; M.D., Boston U., 1887. On staff Youth's Companion, 1870—. Author: Camping Out; Left on Labrador; Off to the Geysers; Lynx Hunting; Fox Hunting; On the Amazon; The Moose Hunters; The Knockabout Club, 3 vols.; also biol. works: Living Matter; Pluricellular Man; Long Life; Natural Salvation, 1905; Salvation by Science, 7th edit., 1913 (all pub. by The Laboratory, Norway Lake, Me.). Home: Norway Lake, Me. Died Sept. 22, 1931.

STEPHENS, Dan Voorhees, congressman; b. Bloomington, Ind., Nov. 4, 1868; s. Richard Lewis and Martha (Lamkins) S.; ed. Valparaiso U., 1886, 87; m. Hannah Boe, June 24, 1890; children—Edith (dec.), Estella (dec.). In bus., Fremont, Neb., 1889—; county supt. schs., Dodge Co., Neb., 1890-94; pres. Hammond & Stephens Co., ednl. pubs.; pres. Stephens Nat. Bank; v.p. Neb. State Building & Loan Assn., Crystal Refrigerator Co.; pres. Fremont State Co. Mem. State Bd. Edn., 1923-26; del. Dem. Nat. Conv., St. Louis, 1904, Denver, 1908 (chmn. delegation); del. at large and chmn. delegation, San Francisco, 1920, New York, 1924, del. at large Chicago, 1932; 4 times chmn. Congressional Com.; elected 62d Congress, Nov. 7, 1911; reëlected to 63d to 65th Congresses (1913-19), 3d Neb. Dist. Apptd. by President Roosevelt mem. Bd. Pub. Works for Neb. under NRA, 1933. Pres. Neb. Brown Swiss Cattle Breeders Assn.; mem. various breeders' assns. Author: Silas Cobb, 1902; Phelps and His Teachers, 1903; Cottonwood Yarns, 1935; Peter Stephens and Some of His Descendants (a family history), 1936. Home: Fremont, Neb. Died Jan. 13, 1939.

STEPHENS, David Stubert, univ. chancellor; b. Springfield, O., May 12, 1847; s. Oliver Perry and Mary Anna (Biddle) S.; student Wittenberg Coll., Springfield, O., to jr. yr.; A.B., Adrian (Mich.) Coll., 1868; U. of Edinburgh, 1869-70, passing exams. for degree of M.A. in philosophy; Harvard, 1873-74; (hon. A.M., Wittenberg, 1872; D.D., Western Md. Coll., 1885; LL.D., Adrian Coll., 1906); m. Marietta L. Gibson, Oct. 7, 1874. Was mem. 134th Ohio Inf., in Civil War; hon. disch., 1864. Ordained Meth. Protestant ministry, 1880; prof. logic and philosophy, 1874, pres., 1881-88, Adrian Coll.; chancellor Kansas City U., 1896—. Editor Methodist Recorder, Pittsburgh, 1888-96. Pres. Gen. Conf. M.P. Ch., 1900-04; rep. from M.P. Ch. to Ecumenical Conf., London, 1901. Has been active in movement for union of Congl., U.B. and M.P. chs.; permanent chmn. gen. council same, Feb. 1906—. Wrote: Wesley and Episcopacy, 1892. Home: Kansas City, Kan. Died Sept. 1, 1921.

STEPHENS, Edwin Lewis, coll. pres.; b. Natchitoches Parish, La., Nov. 27, 1872; s. Joseph Henry and Isabella Carolina (Whitfield) S.; A.B., La. State U. and Agrl. and Mech. Coll., Baton Rouge, La., 1892; Pd.M., New York U., 1897, Pd.D., 1899; m. Beverly Randolph, July 14, 1902; children—Beverly Randolph (Mrs. Frederick Hard), Caroline Parham, Margaret Fitz Randolph. Instr. Latin and science, Louisiana State Normal School, Natchitoches, 5 yrs.; teacher and conductor summer normal schs., 1895-99; Helen Gould scholar, New York U., 1896-97 and 1898-99; apptd. instructor physics and chemistry, Boys' High Sch., New Orleans, Oct. 1899; first pres. Southwestern La. Inst. of Liberal and Tech. Learning, Lafayette, 1900-38; editor La. Sch. Rev. 3 yrs.; prof. history of edn., Summer Sch. of the South (U. of Tenn.), 1909. Active in Red Cross, War Saving Stamp, and Salvation Army drives, and organized S.A.T.C. Unit in Southwestern Inst., World War. Mem. Commn. on Instns. of Higher Edn. of Southern Assn. of Colleges and Secondary Schools. Mason. Home: New Orleans, La. Died Nov. 5, 1938.

STEPHENS, Edwin William, journalist; b. Columbia, Mo., Jan. 21, 1849; s. James L. and Amelia (Hockaday) S.; A.B., U. of Mo., 1867, A.M., 1870, LL.D., 1905, William Jewell College, 1905; m. Laura Moss, Sept. 26, 1871; children—Hugh, James L., E. Sydney, Mrs. W. A. Gray. Editor and pub. Columbia (Mo.) Herald, 1870-1905; pres. E. W. Stephens Pub. Co., Columbia, Mo., 1905-15; pres. Tribune Printing Co., Jefferson City, Mo.; pres. Central Bapt. Pub. Co., St. Louis. Was pres. Nat. Editorial Assn., Mo. Press Assn., bd. curators U. of Mo., bd. curators Stephens Coll. (Columbia, Mo.), Bd. of Home and Foreign Missions of Baptists of Mo.; moderator Bapt. Gen. Assn., Mo.; commr. to build Lunatic Asylum No. 3; pres. Southern Bapt. Conv., and Gen. Bapt. Conv. of N. America; mem. exec. com. Bapt. World's Alliance. Pres. Y.M.C.A. of Mo. Chmn. commn. to build state capitol of Mo.; chmn. bd. mgrs. Mo. Baptist Sanitarium; 1st v.p. Northern Bapt. Conv. Chmn. Mo. Old Trails Highway Assn.; treas. Roger Williams Bapt. Ch. Memorial Fund, Bapt. World's Alliance; chmn. Boone Co. Red Cross. Author: Around the World. Home: Columbia, Mo. Died May 22, 1931.

STEPHENS, (George) Frank, sculptor, lecturer; b. Rahway, N.J., Dec. 28, 1859; s. Henry Louis (illustrator) and Charlotte Anne (Wevill) S.; ed. Rutgers Coll.; Pa. Acad. Fine Arts; m. Caroline Eakins (dec.); children—Margaret E. (dec.), Donald, Roger; m. 2d, Elenor Getty. After leaving art sch. worked several yrs. on sculpture of new City Hall, Phila.; since has been sec.-treas. Stephens, Cooper & Co., archtl. decorations, stone carving, etc.; joined with Ira C. Conkling in establishing Stephens-Conkling Terra Cotta Co. (now Conkling-Armstrong Co.); later treas. New York Architectural Terra Cotta Co. Has been instr. in modeling in several art schs.; instr. in Drexel Inst. Lecturer on economics, Henry George Lecture Assn.; also for University Extension and New York Bd. of Edn. Founder, with architect, Will Price, of the single tax village, "Arden." Mem. Henry George Foundation, Nat. Single Tax League (sec.), Peoples Council of America (exec. sec.). Fellowship of Pa. Acad. Fine Arts (Phila.). Home: Arden, Del. Died June 16, 1935.

STEPHENS, George Ware, economist; b. Wapello, Ia., Sept. 18, 1878; s. Nathaniel Ewing and Harriet (Dotson) S.; Ph.B., Ia. Wesleyan Coll., 1904; student Columbia; A.M., U. of Wis., 1907, Ph.D., 1911; (LL.D., U. of Me., 1919); m. Florence Currier, June 28, 1905; children—Helen Frances, Florence Marjorie, Alice Louise. Prof. economics, Ia. Wesleyan Coll., 1907-10; prof. economics and sociology, U. of Maine, 1911-19; prof. economics, Washington U., 1919—, dean of freshmen, 1926-29, dean of students, 1929—, dean of Coll. of Liberal Arts, 1939—. Home: Webster Groves, Mo. Died May 13, 1940.

STEPHENS, H(enry) Morse, univ. prof.; b. Edinburgh, Scotland, Oct. 3, 1857; s. John Edward and Emma (Morris) S.; ed. Haileybury Coll., Eng., 1871-76; B.A., Balliol Coll. (Oxford U.), 1880, M.A., 1892; (Litt.D., Harvard, 1909). Author and journalist, 1880-92; contbr. to the Academy, Daily Chronicle, Speaker, etc.; London corr. the Statesman, and Friend of India, Calcutta; editor of India (mag.); staff lecturer on Oxford U. Exten. System, 1890-94. Lecturer on Indian history, Cambridge, Eng., 1892-94; prof. modern European and English history, Cornell U., 1894-1902; delivered Lowell Inst. lectures, 1900, 05, 09; prof. history, 1902—, and dir. of univ. extension, 1902-09, U. of Calif. Pres. Am. Hist. Assn., 1915 (mem. council, 1895-99); one of editors Am. Hist. Review, 1895-1905; mem. Mass., Va., Wis., and Ore. hist. socs.; sec. Acad. Pacific Coast History, 1907. Author: History of the French Revolution, Vol. I, 1886; Vol. II, 1892; The Story of Portugal, 1891; Albuquerque (in Rulers of India series), 1892; Revolutionary Europe, 1789-1815, 1893; Syllabus of a Course of Lectures on Modern European History, 1600-1890, 1899; (with Prof. A. L. Lowell) Colonial Civil Service, 1900; St. Patrick at Tara (a forest play), 1909. Edited: (with Prof. G. B. Adams) of Select Documents of English Constitutional History, 1901; (with Prof. H. E. Bolton) The Pacific Ocean in History, 1915. Died Apr. 16, 1919.

STEPHENS, Herbert Taylor, theologian; b. Mechanicsburg, O., Sept. 10, 1864; s. Oliver Perry and Mary Anna (Biddle) S.; student Ohio State U., 1882-87; Ph.B., Adrian (Mich.) Coll., 1888 (first honor orator and class poet), A.B., 1889, D.D., 1911;

Western Theol. Sem., Pittsburgh, Pa., 1888-89; S.T.B., Boston U., 1891, grad. work, 1893-94; A.M., Harvard, 1893; fellow in ch. history, U. of Chicago, 1907-09; m. Emma West Johnston, Oct. 15, 1891 (died 1920); children—Brooks Palmer, Winifred Johnston, Dorothy, Lois Biddle, Herbert Roosevelt; m. 2d, Maude Mary Cockins, Dec. 25, 1924. Ordained M.P. Ch., 1891; pastor New Cumberland, W.Va., 1891-92, Congl. Ch., Plymouth, Mass., 1892, Waynesburg (Pa.) M.P. Ch., 1894-96; prof. hist. and systematic theology, 1896-1909, dean Coll. of Theology, 1909-20, Kansas City U.; prof. philosophy and Bibl. lit., Western Md. Coll., 1920—; also prof. N.T. Greek and exegesis, Westminster Theol. Sem., 1920—. Mem. Pittsburgh (Pa.) Conf. M.P. Ch. Chmn. Mich. Inter-Collegiate Prohibition Conv., Ann Arbor, 1887; 1st prize, Centennial Ode, Greene Co. (Pa.) Centennial, 1896. Home: Westminster, Md. Died Sept. 12, 1929.

STEPHENS, John Leonard, Masonic official; b. Kenton Co., Ky., Mar. 26, 1852; s. of Napoleon Bonaparte and Rebekah Patterson (Hughes) S.; ed. under pvt. tutelage; m. Mary Carr Cochran, Jan. 12, 1875. Bookkeeper German Nat. Bank, Covington, Ky., 1872-77; founder and pres. Am. Wire Nail Co., Covington, 1877-86; later in mfg. and electrical supply business until 1908. Removed to Dallas, Tex., 1900. Mason. Served as Past Deputy District Grand Master, Texas, 1916; Grand Rep. Grand Lodge P.I., 1916-31; gen. secretary all bodies Scottish Rite in Dallas, Tex.; elected Knight Comdr. Ct. of Honor, 1907; Insp. Gen. Hon., 1911; mem. Royal Order of Scotland, Red Cross of Constantine, Shrine. Sec. Dallas Scottish Rite Cathedral Assn. Democrat. Presbyn. Home: Dallas, Tex. Died Mar. 16, 1934.

STEPHENS, Kate, author; b. Moravia, N.Y., Feb. 27, 1853; d. Nelson Timothy and Elizabeth (Rathbone) S.; A.B., U. of Kan., 1875, A.M., 1878; grad. study in Cambridge, Mass., and in Germany. Asst. prof. Greek, 1878-79, prof., 1879-85, U. of Kansas. Wrote on women's status and education for Am. Supplement of Ency. Britannica, Forum, Atlantic Monthly, etc. Editor: Johnson's Life of Pope, 1897; Stories from Old Chronicles, 1909. Author: The Greek Spirit, 1914; The Mastering of Mexico, 1916; Workfellows in Social Progression, 1916; Life at Laurel Town; In Anglo-Saxon Kansas, 1920; Truths Back of the Uncle Jimmy Myth; His Secretary, 1927; A Curious History in Book Editing Inclosing Letters of the Senior Editor Charles Eliot Norton, 1927; Lies and Libels of Frank Harris, 1929. Editor and pub. The Love-Life of Byron Caldwell Smith, 1930; Commemoration of Nelson Timothy Stephens at The University of Kansas, 1933. Home: Lawrence, Kan. Died May 10, 1938.

STEPHENS, Lawrence Vest, governor; b. Boonville, Mo., Dec. 21, 1858; s. Joseph L. and Martha (Gibson) S.; acad. edn.; student Washington and Lee U., 1877; (LL.D., U. of Mo., 1898); m. Margaret Nelson, Oct 5, 1880. Learned printer's trade; formerly editor Boonville Advertiser; bookkeeper, cashier, v.p., and dir., 1880—, Central Nat. Bank, Boonville; apptd. govt. receiver Fifth Nat. Bank, St. Louis, 1887. State treas. of Mo., 1889-97; gov., 1897-1901. Democrat. Home: St. Louis, Mo. Died Jan. 10, 1923.

STEPHENS, Martin Bates, educationist; b. nr. Denton, Md., Oct. 5, 1862; s. William Barker and Sarah Ann (Wooters) S.; student Dickinson Coll., Carlisle, Pa., 1881-82, A.M., 1890; Ph.D., Washington Coll., Md., 1901; m. Nellie Rowena Johnson, Jan. 12, 1910. Teacher, later prin., Greensborough (Mo.) Acad., 1885-1900; state supt. pub. edn., Md., 1900-20. Democrat. Methodist. Mason. Home: Denton, Md. Died Aug. 24, 1923.

STEPHENS, Redmond Davis, lawyer; b. Marion, Ia., May 30, 1874; s. R. D. and Louisa (Brier) S.; A.B., Harvard, 1896; LL.B., Northwestern U., 1899; m. 2d, Edna Davis Moore, May 20, 1924. Began practice in Chicago, 1899; was mem. Scott, Bancroft, Martin & Stephens. Capt. U.S.A., Aug. 21, 1918-Mar. 10, 1919; mem. War Dept. Claims Bd., Mar. 11-June 30, 1919; asst. to dir. Bur. of the Budget, Washington, D.C., July 1, 1922-Dec. 31, 1925; resigned to practice law in San Francisco. Dir. Glenwood Manual Training Sch. Republican. Home: San Mateo, Calif. Died Feb. 18, 1931.

STEPHENS, Robert Neilson, author; b. New Bloomfield, Pa., July 22, 1867; s. James Andrew and Rebecca Neilson S.; ed. in his father's acad. at Huntingdon, Pa., and high school; m. Maud Helfenstein, Nov. 6, 1889. Worked as "printer's devil" on country newspaper; later clerk; sec. to mng. editor, Phila. Press, Dec. 1886; became dramatic editor of that paper; wrote short stories for mags.; became theatrical agt. and dramatist in New York, 1893, writing sensational plays, notably the Steve Brodie melodrama, On the Bowery. Later wrote An Enemy to the King, prod. by E. H. Sothern, Sept. 1896. Author: (novels) An Enemy to the King, 1897; The Continental Dragoon, 1898; The Road to Paris, 1898; A Gentleman Player, 1899; Philip Winwood, 1900; Captain Ravenshaw, 1901; The Mystery of Murray Davenport, 1903; The Bright Face of Danger, 1904; The Flight of Georgiana, 1905; Part author: Miss Elizabeth's Prisoner (dram. from The Continental Dragoon), prod. by Lewis Waller in London, 1904. From 1899 lived abroad, mostly in England. Died 1906.

STEPHENS, Ward, musician, composer; b. Louisville, Ky., Sept. 9, 1879; s. Joseph Harris and R. Isabella (Sodene) S.; moved with parents to Newark, N.J., in childhood; began piano studies at 7; student Rutgers Coll., New Brunswick, N.J., 1895-99; studied piano with David Lyon and William Sherwood, organ with Wenham Smith and S. P. Warren; later went to Europe and studied with various masters, including Brahms and Emil Sauer (Vienna), Scharwenka and Moszkowski (Berlin), Saint-Saëns, Massenet and de Pachmann (Paris); m. Ida May Pierpont, Sept. 11, 1904; 1 dau., Ruth Pierpont. Organist Calvary Presbyn. Ch., Newark, N.J., at age of 12; organist Plymouth Ch., Brooklyn, N.Y., at 16, later with Pierrepont St. Bapt. Ch., Brooklyn, 3 yrs.; début as pianist at Chickering Hall, New York, at 17; Paris début as pianist, playing Liszt's E flat Concerto, July 1896; toured European countries for 9 yrs.; returned to U.S., 1908; from then devoted attention largely to composition and coaching singers in repertoire work; accompanist for Mme. Yvette Guilbert during her tour of the U.S., 1915; toured U.S. with Suzanne Adams and Giuseppi Campanari (both of Met. Opera, New York), Franz Wilczek, violinist, Victor Herbert, cellist; accompanist for Sembrich, Alda, Melba, Kubelik, Chaminade, Kreisler, Schumann-Heink, Matzenauer and others. Organist 1st Ch. of Christ, Scientist, New York, 1910-21; apptd. asst. conductor of opera at Manhattan Opera House, New York; mus. dir. Mozart Festival and Ward-Stephens Male Chorus Club, Harrisburg. Republican. Composer of two symphonies, three light operas and several hundred songs, including Christ in Flanders, The Nightingale, Summertime, In the Dawn of an Indian Sky, The Cry of the Exile, etc. Died Sept. 11, 1940.

STEPHENSON, Edward Morris, religious educator; b. Carnforth, Eng., Nov. 25, 1853; s. Edward and Elizabeth (Preston) S.; brought to U.S., 1857; Valparaiso U., 1875-76; Th.B., Baptist Union Theol. Sem., U. of Chicago, 1888; studied medicine; D.D., U. of Denver, 1908; m. Mary Elizabeth Wilkinson, Sept. 29, 1880; children—Mary Lillian (Mrs. C. F. Kennedy), Ruth Evelyn (dec.), Elizabeth (Mrs. J. K. Bowman), Grace Marguerite (Mrs. L. L. Evans), Clarence Edward. Ordained Bapt. ministry, 1879, and pastor at Richmond, Cassopolis, Pentwater, South Haven, Ovid, and Jackson, Mich., until 1895, also sec. Mich. Bapt. Y.P. Union; originated Colportage Wagon Work as S.S. missionary in Mich., 1895-1900; dist. sec. Bapt. Publ. Soc., Chicago, 1900-03; spl. sec. Div. Sch., U. of Chicago, 1903-05; returned to missionary work, hdqrs. at Denver, Colo., 1906-11; dir. religious edn. Pa. hdqrs., 1911-20, also lecturer Crozer Theol. Sem. and Bapt. Inst. Christian Workers. Republican. Author: The Chord (hymn book), 1892; Child Study for Sunday School Teachers, 1907; The Story of a Sunday School, 1908; Handbook for Sunday School Workers, 1920; (with L. C. Barnes) Pioneers of Light, 1924; (with Daniel G. Stevens) First Hundred Years of the Am. Baptist Publication Society, 1925. Home: Camp Hill, Pa. Died Feb. 18, 1926.

STEPHENSON, Isaac, senator; b. Fredericton, N.B., June 18, 1829; s. Isaac and Elizabeth (Watson) S.; went, in 1840, to Bangor, Me., and a yr. later to Wis.; worked on farm; common sch. education. Bought a schooner, which he sailed between Milwaukee and Escanaba; invested his savings in timber lands; now pres. and controlling owner in the N. Ludington Co., The Stephenson Co., Stephenson Nat. Bank. Mem. Wis. Ho. of Rep., 1866, 68; mem. 48th to 50th Congresses (1883-89), 9th Wis. Dist.; elected U.S. senator, 1907, for unexpired term (1907-09), of Hon. John Coit Spooner, resigned; reelected for term, 1909-15. Republican. Home: Marinette, Wis. Died Mar. 15, 1918.

STEPHENSON, Nathaniel Wright, coll. prof.; b. Cincinnati, July 10, 1867; s. Reuben Henry and Louisa (Wright) S.; A.B., Ind. U., 1896; U. of Cincinnati, 1888-89; Harvard U., 1889-91; Litt.D., Dartmouth, 1923; LL.D., Coll. of Charleston, 1927; m. Martha Tucker Mazyck, 1909. Editorial writer and staff corr. Cincinnati Tribune, 1892-95; instr. English, Ind. U., 1895-97; lit. editor Cincinnati Commercial Tribune, 1898-1900; prof. history, College of Charleston, 1902-23; visiting prof. history, Yale U., 1920-21; visiting lecturer, Am. history, Columbia U., 1922-23; lecturer, Columbia U. Summer Sch., 1921, 22; editor, Chronicles of America, Photoplays, 1922-27; prof. history and biography, Scripps Coll., Claremont, Calif., 1927—. Author: An American History, 1913; The Spiritual Drama in the Life of Thackeray, 1913; Abraham Lincoln and the Union (Vol. 32, Chronicles of America), 1918; The Day of the Confederacy (Vol. 33, Chronicles of America), 1919; Texas and the Mexican War (Vol. 24, same), 1921; Lincoln, 1922; An Autobiography of Abraham Lincoln (compiled), 1926; Nelson W. Aldrich, 1930; Typical Americans and Their Problems, 1930; A History of the American People, 1934. Died Jan. 17, 1935.

STEPHENSON, Rome Charles, banker; b. Wabash, Ind., Feb. 19, 1865; s. Hugh McDonald and Maria Jane (Thompson) S.; ed. pub. schs.; studied law under George W. Holman, Rochester, Ind.; m. Ella Jane Maxwell, Oct. 16, 1889; children—Joseph Maxwell, Hugh Robert. Admitted to Ind. bar, 1887, and began practice at Rochester; mem. Holman & Stephenson until 1908; pres. Rochester Trust & Savings Co., 1906-08; v.p. St. Joseph County Savings Bank, South Bend, Ind., 1908—, now also exec. mgr.; pres. St. Joseph Loan & Trust Co., 1914—. Mem. Ind. State Senate, 1904-08. Republican. Presbyterian. Home: South Bend, Ind. Died Dec. 4, 1934.

STEPHENSON, William Worth, lawyer; b. Madison Co., Ky., Oct. 24, 1857; s. Dr. Andrew Tribble and Elizabeth Ann (Smith) S.; Ky. U., Lexington, 1876-78; A.B., Bethany (W.Va.) Coll., 1879, A.M., 1884; unmarried. Prin. Harrodsburg (Ky.) Acad., 1879-80; admitted to bar, 1881, and began practice at Harrodsburg. Mem. Ky. Ho. of Rep., 1889-93, Senate, 1894-98; served as spl. circuit judge by appointment. Mem. bd. commrs. Ky. Sch. for Deaf, Danville. Mem. Christian Ch. Mem. of various hist. societies. Mason. Home: Harrodsburg, Ky. Died 1914.

STERKI, Victor, zoölogist; b. Solothurn, Switzerland, Sept. 27, 1846; s. Anton and Magdalena (Müller) S.; acad. edn.; med. student, Berne and München, 1868-73; M.D., U. of Berne, 1873, post-grad. study, 1878; m. Mary Lanz, of Huttwyl, Switzerland, Feb. 2, 1875. Came to U.S., Sept. 13, 1883; spl. student of mollusca and protozoa; asst. curator of mollusca, Carnegie Mus., Pittsburgh, Apr. 1, 1910—. Home: New Philadelphia, O. Died Jan. 25, 1933.

STERLING, Edward Canfield, manufacturer; b. Chapinsville, Conn., Aug. 3, 1834; s. Frederick Augustine and Caroline Mary (Dutcher) S.; bro. of Theodore S.; ed. pub. schs.; m. Cordelia Seavey, Sept. 7, 1860. Worked in his father's saw-mill nr. Cleveland, O., 1850-56; afterward, with a brother, operated saw-mill at Oshkosh, Wis.; esteablished, 1860, a plant in Memphis, Tenn., to mfr. brick from dry clay under hydraulic pressure, but breaking out of the war caused the business to be suspended; later he started in same line at St. Louis; afterward consolidated his plant with others in the same line all over U.S. as the Hydraulic-Press Brick Co., of which he is president. Home: Redlands, Calif. Died 1911.

STERLING, George, author; b. Sag Harbor, N.Y., Dec. 1, 1869; s. George Ansel and Mary Parker (Havens) S.; ed. pvt. and pub. schs., St. Charles Coll., Ellicott City, Md.; m. Carrie Rand, Feb. 7, 1896 (dec.). Private sec. to Frank C. Havens, Oakland, 1898-1908. Author: The Testimony of the Suns and Other Poems, 1903; A Wine of Wizardry and Other Poems, 1908; The House of Orchids and Other Poems, 1911; Beyond the Breakers and Other Poems, 1914; Exposition Ode, 1915; Yosemite, 1915; The Caged Eagle and Other Poems, 1916; The Binding of the Beast and Other Poems, 1917; Lilith (dramatic poem), 1919; Rosamund (dramatic poem), 1920; Sails and Mirage and Other Poems, 1921; Selected Poems, 1923; Truth (dramatic poem), 1923. Died Nov. 18, 1926.

STERLING, Guy, civil engr.; b. Cleveland, May 1, 1860; s. Theodore and Charlotte (Higgins) S.; Kenyon Coll., Gambier, O., 1877-78; C.E., Cornell U., 1887; spl. work in elec. engring., Lewis Inst., Chicago, 1904; m. Harriot Brewer, Sept. 4, 1890. In wholesale and retail carpet business with Sterling & Co., Cleveland, 1878-83; asst. engr. maintenance of way, Denver, 1887-88, topog. engineer surveys in northeastern Calif., 1888-89, U.P. Ry.; topographer U.S. Geol. Survey, on Clear Lake, Calif., and Snake River (Ida.) irrigation surveys, 1889; asst. engr. in charge constrn. Phyllis Canal, Ida., 1890; asst. chief engr. Sunnyside Canal, nr. Yakima, Wash., 1890-91; chief engineer Cowiche and Wide Hollow irrigation dist. nr. Yakima, Wash., 1891-92; again asst. chief engr. Sunnyside Canal, 1892-94; constrn. pvt. irrigation projects nr. N. Yakima, 1894-95; chief engr. Priest Rapids Project, on Columbia River north of Pasco, Wash., 1895; in practice in Utah and other states, Aug. 1895—, principally hydraulic engring., examinations and reports for eastern investors, supervision of constrn., etc. Republican. Episcopalian. Chmn. com. on research and invention Utah Council Defense, 1917-18. Inventor and patentee of processes for extracting potash from mother liquor salts and from silicates including wyomingite. Home: Salt Lake City, Utah. Deceased.

STERLING, John A., congressman; b. LeRoy, Ill., Feb. 1, 1857; s. Charles and Anna S.; A.B., Ill. Wesleyan U., 1881, A.M., 1887; m. Clara M. Irons, May 20, 1886. Admitted to bar, 1884, and began practice at Bloomington; mem. Welty & Sterling, 1884—. State's atty. McLean Co., Ill., 1892-96; mem. Rep. State Central Com., 1896-98; mem. 58th to 62d Congresses (1903-13), and 64th and 65th

Congresses (1915-19), 17th Ill. Dist. Republican. Home: Bloomington, Ill. Died Oct. 17, 1913.

STERLING, John William, lawyer; b. May 1844; s. Capt. John William and Catherine Tomlinson (Plant) S.; A.B., Yale, 1864, A.M., 1869; LL.B., Columbia, 1867; (LL.D., Yale, 1893); unmarried. Dir. Nat. City Bank, Bond & Mortgage Guarantee Co., Duluth, South Shore & Atlantic Ry., Consolidated, New Amsterdam, Standard, Northern Union and Central Union gas cos., Northern Westchester Lighting Co., Peekskill Lighting & R.R. Co., etc.; trustee New York Trust Co. Mem. firm Shearman & Sterling. Home: New York, N.Y. Died July 5, 1918.

STERLING, Theodore, college dean; b. Falls Village, Conn., Feb. 8, 1827; s. Frederick Augustine and Caroline Mary (Dutcher) S.; brother of Edward Canfield S.; A.B., Hobart Coll., 1848, A.M., 1851; M.D., Western Reserve U., 1851; (LL.D., Hobart, 1881); m. Charlotte Maria Higgins, Oct. 18, 1854. Practiced medicine, 1851-59; prin. Cleveland Central High Sch., 1859-67; prof. mathematics, 1867-70 and 1896-1901, prof. natural philosophy and chemistry, 1870-96, pres., 1891-96, prof. emeritus and dean of coll. faculty. 1901—, Kenyon Coll.; was prof. chemistry, Columbus Med. Coll. 10 yrs. One of v.p.'s Evang. Alliance. Home: Gambier, O. Died July 23, 1912.

STERLING, Thomas, senator; b. nr. Amanda, O., Feb. 21, 1851; s. Charles and Anna (Kesler) S.; A.B., Ill. Wesleyan U., 1875, A.M., 1878; m. Anna Dunn, Oct. 17, 1877 (died 1881); children—Cloyd D., Geneva (dec.); m. 2d, Mrs. Emma R. Thayer, May 1, 1883 (died 1923); m. 3d, Mayme E. McCaslin, Mar. 11, 1925. Admitted to Illinois bar, 1878; city atty., Springfield, Ill., 1880-81; removed to Spink Co., S.D., 1882; district atty., Spink County, 1887-89; mem. S.D. Constl. Conv., 1883, 1889; mem. Senate 1st State Legislature, S.D., 1890 (chmn. judiciary com.); dean Coll. Law, U. of S.D., 1910-11; U.S. senator, 2 terms, 1913-25; mem. faculty Nat. Univ. Law Sch., Washington, D.C. Republican. Home: Washington, D.C. Deceased.

STERN, Jo. Lane, soldier, lawyer; b. Caroline Co., Va., Dec. 23. 1848; s. L. and Elizabeth (Hall) S.; prep. edn., Fontaine Hill Acad., Caroline Co., and Squire's Sch., Richmond, Va.; B.P., Washington Coll. (now Washington and Lee U.), 1869, LL.B. 1870; unmarried. Admitted to Va. bar, 1870, and began practice in Caroline County; settled in Richmond, 1871; partner with Hon. James Lyons (mem. Confederate States Congress), 1872-79; chmn. State Council of Defense, 1918-19; mem. War History Commn. of Va. Served in C.S.A. of Northern Va. 3 yrs.; paroled at Richmond, May 2, 1865. Enlisted in Va. N.G., 1871, and actively identified with that organization for 51 yrs.; promoted through grades to lt. col. 1st Inf.; insp. gen., 1884-1918; acting adj. gen. Spanish-Am. War; adj. gen. and draft executive, World War, rank of brig. gen., 1918-22; retired as maj. gen., Mar. 15, 1922. Democrat. Compiler of Roster of Commissioned Officers of Va. Vols., 1871-1920; Reports A.G.O. and Selective Draft, 1918-21. Adj. gen. Army of Northern Va., Dept. U.C.V. Home: Richmond, Va. Died May 3, 1932.

STERN, Louis, merchant; b. in Germany, Feb. 22, 1847; s. M.A. and Sophia S.; ed. Albany, N.Y.; m. Miss L. Strupp, July 30, 1879. President Stern Bros., dry goods; dir. Madison Safe Deposit Co., Lincoln Trust Co., Casein Co. of America; trustee Atlantic Mutual Ins. Co. of America; trustee Atlantic Mutual Ins. Co., Mut. Life Ins. Co., of N.Y.; pres. Library Sq. Realty Co. Rep. candidate for pres. Manhattan Borough, 1897; U.S. commr. Paris expn. 1900; chmn. exec. com. N.Y. State Commn. to St. Louis Expn., 1904. Pres. Hebrew Orphan Asylum. Home: New York, N.Y. Died June 21, 1922.

STERN, Simon Adler, banker, author; b. Philadelphia, Dec. 8, 1838; s. Julius and Henrietta S.; ed. Phila. Was treas. The Finance Co. of Pa. until Feb. 1903; retired. Author: Jottings of Travel in China and Japan, 1889. Translator: Heinrich Heine's Florentine Nights and Excerpts, 1873; and of Berthold Auerbach's On the Heights and Wolfried. Home: Philadelphia, Pa. Died 1904.

STERNBERG, George Miller, brigadier gen. U.S.A.; b. Hartwick Sem., Otsego Co., N.Y., June 8, 1838; s. Levi (D.D.) and Margaret Levering (Miller) S.; bro. of Charles Hazelius S.; M.D., Coll. Phys. and Surg. (Columbia), 1860; (LL.D., U. of Mich., 1894, Brown U., 1896); m. Martha L. Pattison, 1869. Apptd. asst. surgeon U.S.A., May 28, 1861; capt. asst. surgeon, May 28, 1866; maj. surgeon, Dec. 1, 1875; lt. col. deputy surgeon-gen., Jan. 12, 1891; brig. gen. surgeon gen., May 30, 1893; retired June 8, 1902. His service began in the army of the Potomac, and later was in Dept. of the Gulf; at end of Civil War was in charge of U.S. Gen. Hosp., Cleveland, O.; served through cholera and yellow fever epidemics; had command of med. service in war with Spain, 1898; was mem. and sec. Havana Yellow Fever Commn. Nat. Bd. of Health, 1879. Author: Photo-Micrographs, and How to Make Them, 1883; Bacteria; Malaria and Malarial Diseases, 1884; Man-

ual of Bacteriology, 1893; Text-Book of Bacteriology, 1895; Immunity, Protective Inoculations, and Serum-Therapy, 1897. Home: Washington, D.C. Died Nov. 3, 1915.

STERNBURG, Herman von Speck- (Baron), diplomat; b. Leeds, Eng., Aug. 21, 1852; s. Baron Alexander and Martha (Shaw) Speck-Sternburg; ed. Furstenschule St. Afra, Meissen, Saxony, and Mil. Acad., Potsdam, Prussia; spl. studies in internat. law, polit. economy, mil. and naval sciences; m. London, Lillian May Langham, of Louisville, Ky. Fought through Franco-German war in 2d Saxon Dragoons; in active mil. service until 1885; apptd., 1885, as mil. attaché German legation, Washington; reapptd., 1889, and transferred as maj. to gen. staff; joined diplomatic service, 1890, and transferred as 1st sec. legation to Peking, China; chargé d'affaires. Belgrade, Servia; 1st sec. German embassy at Washington, 1898; high commr. on Samoan Commn., 1898; consul gen. of Germany for British India and Ceylon, 1900; His Imperial German Majesty's minister plenipotentiary and envoy extraordinary to Washington, on spl. mission, 1903; ambassador of Germany to U.S., July 1903—. Decorations: Red Eagle (1st class); Order of Crown (1st class); Grand Cross Order of Albrecht (Saxony); war medal, in the Franco-German War. 1870-71; Cross of Military Merit (Saxony); Star of the Order of Francis-Joseph (Austria); Star of the Order of the Double Dragon (China); Star of the Takowo (Servia); Cross of the Order of St. Anne (Russia). Died 1908.

STERNE, Albert Eugene, M.D., surgeon; b. Cincinnati, April 28, 1866; s. Charles Falk and Eugenie (Fries) S.; A.B., Harvard, 1887; M.D., U. of Berlin, 1891; studied univs. of Strassburg, Paris, Vienna, London and Dublin; m. Laura Mercy Laughlin, Mar. 4. 1905 (died 1909); m. 2d, Stella Gallup Pickrell, Oct. 18, 1913; 1 dau., Genevieve Pickrell. Has practiced at Indianapolis, 1893—; prof. nervous and mental diseases, Sch. of Medicine, Ind. U. Republican. Home: Indianapolis, Ind. Died June 30, 1931.

STERNE, Niel Paul, lawyer; b. Albany, Ga., Dec. 25, 1883; s. Anselm and Henrietta (Smith) S.; LL.B., Yale, 1908; m. Leone Robinson, July 15, 1911; 1 dau., Adelaide Carleton. In practice of law at Anniston, Ala., 1908—; sr. mem. Knox, Acker, Sterne & Liles; dir. Protective Life Ins. Co., First Nat. Bank of Anniston. Argued constitutionality of federal Social Security statute, on behalf of taxpayers attacking the statute, in Supreme Court of U.S., Apr. 1937. Trustee Carnegie Library of Anniston, Anniston Community Chest; dir. Choccolocco Council Boy Scouts America. Democrat. Jewish religion. Home: Anniston, Ala. Died Feb. 13, 1939.

STERNE, Simon, lawyer; b. Philadelphia, July 23, 1839; s. Henry and Regina S.; ed. public schools, Phila., and short term at Univ. of Heidelberg; grad. law dept. Univ. of Pa., 1859; m. Mathilde Elsberg, 1870. Admitted N.Y. bar, 1860; represents many large corporate interests; makes specialty of R.R. and constl. law. Mem. Acad. Polit. Science; Washington Acad. Science; N.Y. Proportional Representation Soc. (pres.); Bar Assn., N.Y.; Law Inst., N.Y. Apptd. by Gov. Tilden. 1875, one of commrs. to devise plan for govt. of cities in N.Y.; by Gov. Morton, 1895, on commn. to recommend changes in methods of administration; by President Cleveland, 1896, to report as to relation of western European govts. to the rys. Lectured on polit. science. Cooper Inst., 1861-63 (Saturday evenings); editor Commercial Advertiser, 1867; sec. com. of 70 for overthrow of Tweed Ring, 1870. Author: Representative Government. 1871; Development of Political and Constitutional History of the United States, 1882, 1894; Report to President Cleveland on the Relation of the Government of the Nations of Western Europe to the Railways, 1887. Home: New York, N.Y. Died 1901.

STERRETT, James Macbridge, university prof.; b. Howard. Pa., Jan. 13. 1847; s. Robert and Sarah Elizabeth S.; A.B., U. of Rochester, 1867 (D.D., 1886); A.M., Harvard. 1870; B.D., Episcopal Theol. Sch., Cambridge, Mass., 1872; (Litt.D., George Washington U.); m. Adlumia Dent, Jan. 20, 1876. Deacon, 1872, priest. 1873, P.E. Ch.; asst. minister Lawrence, Mass., 1872-73; rector Wellsville, N.Y., 1873-77, Bedford, Pa., 1879-82; prof. ethics and apologetics, Seabury Div. Sch., Minn., 1882-92; prof. philosophy, George Washington Univ., 1892-1909; prof. emeritus on Carnegie foundation; asst. minister Ch. of the Epiphany. Washington, 1892-1911; rector All Souls' Ch., Washington, 1911-17, and asso. rector same from 1917. Pres. Soc. for Philosophical Inquiry, 1893—; Southern Soc. for Philosophy and Psychology, 1908. Author: Studies in Hegel's Philosophy of Religion, 1890; Reason and Authority in Religion, 1891; The Ethics of Hegel, 1893; The Freedom of Authority. 1905. Home: Washington, D.C. Died Mar. 15, 1923.

STERRETT, James Ralston, lawyer; b. Academia, Pa., Mar. 21, 1853; s. John Patterson and Annie (Kennedy) S.; A.B., Washington and Jefferson Coll., 1877; m. Emma W. McConnell, Oct. 20, 1887; chil-

dren—Elenor Slagel (Mrs. Oliver Ledlie Smith), Marian Kennedy (Mrs. Philip Sheridan Chess), James Ralston. Admitted to Pa. bar, 1880, and began practice at Pittsburgh; associated in practice with uncle. John M. Kennedy. 1891-1900; mem. Patterson & Sterrett, changed to Patterson, Sterrett & Acheson. 1913, Sterrett & Acheson, and, 1929—, Sterrett. Acheson & Jones. Trustee Shady Side Acad. Republican. Presbyterian. Home: Pittsburgh, Pa. Died Nov. 24, 1939.

STERRETT, John Robert Sitlington, univ. prof.; b. Rockbridge Baths. Va., Mar. 4. 1851; s. Robert Dunlap and Nancy Snyder (Sitlington) S.; ed. univs. of Va., Leipzig, Berlin. Athens, Munich, 1872-80; Ph.D., U. of Munich, Aug. 1880; (LL.D., Aberdeen, 1902); m. Josephine Moseley Quarrier, Mar. 1, 1892. Prof. Greek. Miami U. 1886, Univ. of Texas, 1888-92, Amherst Coll.. 1892-1901; head dept. of Greek, Cornell Univ., 1901—. Leader of various archeol. expdns. to Asia Minor; prof. Am. Sch. of Classical Studies. Athens, 1896-97 (mem. bd. mgrs.). Corr. mem. Imperial German Archeol. Inst. Joint editor Cornell Classical Studies; asso. editor Am. Jour. of Archeology. Author: Qua in re Hymni Homerici quinque majores inter se differant, 1881; Inscriptions of Sebaste; Inscriptions of Assos, 1885; Inscriptions of Tralles, 1885; Epigraphical Journey in Asia Minor, 1888; Wolfe Expedition to Asia Minor, 1888; Leaflets from the Notebook of a Traveling Archæologist, 1889; The Torch-Race, 1902; The Iliad of Homer, 1907; A Call of Contemporary Society for Research in Asia Minor and Syria, 1911. Organizer of Cornell Expdn. to Asia Minor and the Assyro-Babylonian Orient, Hittite Inscriptions, 1911. Editor and trans. of Strabo for the Loeb Classical Library (9 vols.). Home: Ithaca, N.Y. Died June 17, 1914.

STETSON, Augusta E.; b. Waldoboro, Me.; d. Peabody and Salome (Sprague) Simmons; ed. Damariscotta. Me., High Sch., Lincoln Acad.. Newcastle, Maine, Blish School of Oratory, Boston. Metaphysical Coll.. Boston; degree of Christian Science Doctor (C.S.D.), conferred by Rev. Mary Baker. Eddy; m. Capt. Frederick J. Stetson (dec.). Began to practice Christian Science healing, 1884. in Boston, and in 1885 preached on alternate Sundays in The Mother Ch.. Chickering Hall. Boston; sent to N.Y. City by Mrs. Eddy. 1886. and was among charter members who organized First Ch. of Christ, Scientist, N.Y. City. 1887; preached regularly in that church, and apptd. pastor. 1888; in 1895 title of pastor changed to first reader. which position she continued to fill until rotation in office was inaugurated. making it a term of three years, her total tenure of office as pastor and first reader being 17 consecutive years. Prin. N.Y. City Christian Science Inst., chartered in 1891; raised $1,250,000 to build First Ch. of Christ. Scientist, N.Y. City, and dedicated it, free of debt as soon as completed (1903). This entire amount was contributed by her and her students. Resigned from membership in First Ch. of Christ, Scientist, N.Y. City. 1909. Author: Reminiscences. Sermons, and Correspondence; Vital Issues in Christian Science. with Facsimile Letters of Mary Baker Eddy; My Spiritual Aeroplane; Poems, written on the Journey from Sense to Soul; Greetings and a Message to the Dear Children; Sermons Which Spiritually Interpret the Scriptures, and Other Writings on Christian Science. Home: New York, N.Y. Died Oct. 12, 1928.

STETSON, Caleb Rochford, clergyman; b. Boston, Mass., Apr. 16. 1871; s. George Rochford and Helen Sybil (Avery) S.; A.B.. Harvard, 1894; studied medicine Johns Hopkins, 1894-95; Va. Theol. Sem. 1895-96; grad. Gen. Theol. Sem., 1898; D.D., St. Stephen's, 1922; S.T.D. General Theol. Sem.. Columbia, and Hobart, 1922. U. of the South, 1927; m. Helen Richards. June 30. 1914. Deacon, 1898, priest. 1899, P.E. Church; priest in charge Cathedral Mission Chapel of the Good Shepherd. Washington, D.C., 1899-1907; vicar Trinity Ch.. New York, 1907-11; rector St. Mark's Ch.. Washington, D.C., 1911-21. Trinity Parish. New York, Dec. 1921—. Delegate to the General Conv. of P.E. Church 4 times between 1916 and 1928. Trustee Sailors' Snug Harbor, Leak and Watts Asylum, Gen. Theol. Sem.. New York Episcopal Pub. Sch., Columbia U. Cathedral of St. John the Divine. Am. Ch. Bldg. Fund, City Mission Soc.. Soc. Promoting Religion and Learning, St. Stephens Coll. Republican. Home: New York, N.Y. Died June 15, 1932.

STETSON, Charles Walter, artist; b. Tiverton Four Corners. R.I., Mar. 25. 1858; s. Rev. Joshua Augustus and Rebecca Louisa (Steere) S.; grad. Providence High Sch., 1876; m. Grace Ellery Channing, June 11. 1894. Began exhibiting in Providence, 1878, later exhbns. in Boston, at Pa. Acad. Fine Arts, Phila., Art Museum, Boston, Boston Art Club, and Water Color Soc., Art Instn. of Chicago, art museums at Cincinnati, Detroit, St. Louis, Worcester, Buffalo Expn., New Orleans, San Francisco, "New Gallery," London, and the Expn. of the Belle Arti e Cultori. Rome, 1905. Etchings in pvt. collections, Boston Mus., etc. Lived many yrs. in Southern Calif.; residing in Rome, Italy. Died 1911.

STETSON, Francis Lynde, lawyer; b. Keeseville, N.Y., Apr. 23, 1846; Lemuel (M.C. 1843-45) and Helen (Hascall) S.; A.B., Williams Coll., 1867, A.M., 1870; LL.B., Columbia, 1869; (LL.D., St. John's Coll., Md., and Colgate U.); m. Elizabeth Ruff, June 26, 1873. Admitted to bar, 1869, and began practice at New York; mem. Stetson, Jennings & Russell, 1894—. General counsel of the Internat. Mercantile Marine Co., N.P. Railway Co., Southern R.R. Co., U.S. Rubber Co. Dir. N.Y. Botanical Gardens; trustee Williams Coll. Home: New York, N.Y. Died Dec. 5, 1920.

STETSON, Isaiah Kidder, banker; b. Bangor, Me., Apr. 3, 1858; s. George and Adaline (Hamlin) S.; prep. edn., Phillips Acad., Andover, Mass.; A.B., Yale, 1879; m. Clara C. Sawyer, Nov. 30, 1882; children—Ruth Wolcott, Irving Gay. Spent 2 years in the office of father and then entered into partnership with brother Edward under title of E. & I. K. Stetson, shipbuilding, lumbering, and operators of ice plants; formerly chmn. bd. First Nat. Bank; mgr. Timberland Lands; mem. Me. Ho. of Rep., 1897, 99 (speaker), Senate, 1901, 03. Treas. U. of Me., 1898-1912. Republican. Unitarian. Mason. Home: Bangor, Me. Died July 14, 1940.

STETSON, John Batterson, mfr., philanthropist; b. Orange, N.J., May 5, 1830; learned hat trade; started for himself on a small scale and moved to Phila., 1865; from this grew the present John B. Stetson Co. (of which he is pres.), capital, $4,000,000; factories are the largest in the world. Connected with them are reading rooms, library, hall seating 2,000, dispensary and hosp. and Sunday-sch. for the employes' benefit. He built Elizabeth Hall and other bldgs. for Deland Univ., Deland, Fla., the name of the institution being changed to "John B. Stetson Univ." Prominent in Bapt. Ch. Home: Ashbourne, Pa. Died 1906.

STETSON, Paul Clifford, supt. schs.; b. Logansport, Ind., June 21, 1884; s. Herbert Lee and Mary (Clifford) S.; A.B., Kalamazoo (Mich.) Coll., 1907; A.B., Univ. of Chicago, 1907, A.M., 1917; LL.D., from Butler U., Indianapolis, 1932; m. Annie Louise Crosby, July 28, 1909. Prin. high sch., Bangor, Mich., 1907-08; prin. high sch., Big Rapids, 1908-09; supt. schs. Big Rapids, 1909-11; prin. high sch., Grand Rapids, 1911-18; supt. schs., Muskegon, Mich., 1918-21, Dayton, O., 1921-30, Indianapolis, 1930—; lecturer Western State Teachers Coll., Kalamazoo, 3 summers, U. of Chicago, 4 summers, U. of Michigan, 1 summer. Mem. staff, survey of N.Y. City schs., 1924, survey of W.Va. schs., 1928; mem. bd. trustees Franklin Coll., Ind., 1930—; mem. Ind. State Board of Edn., 1930-33. Life mem. N.E.A. (nat. commn. on reorganization of curriculum, dept. of superintendence, 1922—, and exec. com. same dept.; pres. dept. of superintendence 1933). Baptist. Home: Indianapolis, Ind. Died June 1, 1937.

STETSON, William Wallace, lecturer, writer; b. Greene, Me., June 17, 1849; s. Reuben and Christiana (Thompson) S.; bro. of Herbert Lee S.; (LL.D., Colby, 1902, Monmouth, 1907); m. Rebecca Jane Killough, July 4, 1871. Taught in common schs., Me., in common, normal and high sch., Ill.; supt. city schs., Rockford, Ill., 1880-85; supt. city schs., Auburn, Me., 1885-95; state supt. pub. schs. of Me., 1895-1907. Has delivered ednl. addresses before numerous nat. ednl. bodies, state teachers' assns., teachers' insts. Lectured before state summer schs. in Ill., N.H., La., Ia., Ind., N.C., and Mass., Yale U., Woman's Coll., Greensboro, N.C.; etc. Author: History and Civil Government of Maine, 1899. Home: Auburn, Me. Died 1910.

STETSON, Willis Kimball, librarian; b. Natick, Mass., May 8, 1858; s. Daniel Kimball and Mary Weeks (Sanborn) S.; A.B., Wesleyan U., Conn., 1881, A.M., 1884; m. Lillian Alla Minor, Nov. 25, 1886. Librarian Wesleyan U., and Russell Library, Middletown, 1881-87, Free Pub. Library, New Haven, 1887-1929 (advisory librarian). Home: New Haven, Conn. Died Jan. 9, 1942.

STETTINIUS, Edward R., banker; b. St. Louis, Mo., Feb. 15, 1865; s. Joseph S.; ed. St. Louis U.; m. Judith Carrington, Oct. 18, 1894. Removed from St. Louis to Chicago, 1892; treas. and later v.p. and gen. mgr. of the Stirling Co., machinery mfrs., 1892-1905; formed Stirling Consolidated Boiler Co., 1905, which was consolidated, 1906, with Babcock & Wilcox Co., of which he became v.p.; elected treas. Diamond Match Co., 1908, pres., 1909. Was retained, Jan. 1915, by J. P. Morgan & Co., to organize dept. for purchase of munitions, materials, etc., for British and French govts.; became mem. J. P. Morgan & Co., Jan. 1, 1916; apptd. surveyor gen. of supplies for War Dept., of U.S. Govt., Jan. 1918, mem. War Council, Mar. 1918, 2d asst. sec. of war, Apr. 6, 1918; representative of U.S. on Interallied Munitions Council, Paris, July 1918, and spl. rep. of the U.S. War Dept. in Europe, Aug. 1918-Jan. 1919, when resigned position with U.S. Govt. and resumed connection with J. P. Morgan & Co. Home: New York, N.Y. Died Sept. 3, 1925.

STEUART, George Hume, soldier; b. Baltimore, Aug. 24, 1828; grad. U.S. Mil. Acad., 1848; lt. 2d Dragoons, Nov. 1849; 1st lt., 1st cav., March 1855; capt., Dec. 1855. Resigned April 1861, and entered C.S.A.; lt. col. 1st Md. inf., June 1861, col., July 1861, brig. gen., March 1862; led cav. with Stonewall Jackson in advance upon Gen. Banks, and later in command of inf. brigade; wounded at Cross Keys, June 8, 1862; took part in attack on Culp's Hill, Gettysburg; defended the "bloody angle" at Battle of the Wilderness; taken prisoner, but exchanged some months later. Retired to private life after the war. Home: South River, Anne Arundel Co., Md. Died 1903.

STEUART, James Aloysius, physician; b. Baltimore, April 3, 1828; s. Richard Sprigg and Maria Louisa (de Bornabeau) S.; grad. St. Mary's Coll., Baltimore, 1847; A.M., 1849; grad. School of Medicine, Univ. of Md., 1850; m. Mix Baxter, 1851. Physician City Gen. Dispensary, 1850-56; asst. physician Md. Hosp. for Insane, 1854-61; health commr. and registrar of vital statistics and pres. city bd. of health, 1873-89; sec. State bd. of health, 1892-96; mem. Med.-Chirurg. Faculty of Md. Home: Baltimore, Md. Died 1903.

STEVENS, Albert Clark, financial editor; b. Buffalo, N.Y., Oct. 10, 1854; s. Albert G. and Sarah C. S.; student U. of Mich., 1872; m. Edith May Gardiner, Apr. 1903. Reporter Buffalo Express, 1874-75, Buffalo Courier, 1875-76; asso. editor, Courier, 1877; in hotel business, Parsons, Kan., 1877-80; editor Bradstreet's, 1880-98; editor New York Commercial, 1898-99; editor and mgr. Paterson Daily Guardian, 1899-1901; financial editor Newark (N.J.) Evening News; New York corr. various Am. and foreign economic, financial and other publications. Mason. Author: Cyclopædia of Fraternities, 1899. Home: East Orange, N.J. Died Aug. 1919.

STEVENS, Alviso Burdett, univ. prof.; b. Tyrone, Mich., June 15, 1853; s. Harvy Root and Hannah Ann (Gale) S.; Ph.C., U. of Mich., 1875; Ph.D., Berne, 1905; Sc.D., U. of Mich., 1926; m. Amoretta L. Search, Aug. 1, 1876 (died 1918); 1 son, Don Search. Instr. pharmacy, 1886-90, lecturer, 1890-92, asst. prof., 1892-1906, jr. prof., 1906-09, prof., 1910-19, actg. dean, 1912, dean, 1917-19, prof. emeritus of pharmacy, 1919—, Univ. of Mich. Mem. com. for revision U.S. Pharmacopœia, 8th and 9th revisions; com. for 3d and 4th revision Nat. Formulary. Author: Arithmetic of Pharmacy, 1907; Manual of Pharmacy and Dispensing, 1909. Home: Escondido, Calif. Died Jan. 25, 1940.

STEVENS, Benjamin Franklin, bibliographer; b. Barnet, Vt., Feb. 19, 1833; entered Univ. of Vt., 1853; did not finish course (hon. L.H.D.); went to London, 1860, to join his brother Henry (noted bibliographer, died, 1886) in bookselling business; became U.S. Despatch Agent in London, and purchasing agt. for Am. libraries; m. Charlotte Whittingham, artist, d. Charles Whittingham, printer, London, Jan. 28, 1865. Fellow Soc. of Antiquarians, Soc. of Arts of Zoöl. Soc. and Royal Hist. Soc.; mem. Société d'Histoire Diplomatique; corr. or hon. mem. of the Conn., Md., Minn., N.H. and Vt. Hist. socs., of the Am. Antiquarian Soc. and Am. Hist. Assn. With staff of assts., engaged over 30 yrs. making manuscript chronol. and alphabetical catalogue index of Am. papers in many archives in England, France, Holland and Spain from 1763 to 1784; has made facsimilies of 2,107 important hist. manuscripts in European archives relating to America, 1773-83, with descriptions, editorial notes, translations, etc. (25 foolscap vols., only 200 copies printed). Also facsimile, photographed from original in Foreign Office, Paris, of the MS. Codex Columbus "His Own Book of Privileges, 1502, with English translation, etc."; "The Campaign in Virginia, 1781," being the Clinton-Cornwallis Controversy (2 vols. royal 8vo.); Gen. Sir William Howe's Orderly Book from June 17, 1875, to May 26, 1876, with precis of the correspondence between the British Govt. and Gen. Howe (1 vol. royal 8vo.). Has calendared for Royal Commn. on Hist. Manuscripts, the Am. portion of Earl of Dartmouth's papers; calendaring Headquarters papers of the British commanders-in-chief of America: Gens. Sir William Howe, Sir Henry Clinton and Sir Guy Carleton—now preserved in the Royal Instn.; issued Jan. 1901, facsimile of the unpublished British Headquarters colored manuscript map of New York and environs (1782), 10 feet by 4 feet, which be discovered in the War Office, London. Home: Surbiton, Surrey, Eng. Died 1902.

STEVENS, Charles A(nthony), merchant; b. Colchester, Ill., Mar. 16, 1859; s. Socrates and Amanda Jane S.; ed. pub. schs.; m. Fannie E. Tompkins, Mar. 16, 1882; children—Elmer T., Alta C. (Mrs. Anson Cameron), Hazel M. (Mrs. James P. Loper). Entered retail mercantile business on own account, at Avon, Ill., at age of 20; settled in Chicago, 1890, and established retail dry goods business under title of Charles A. Stevens & Bros., of which is chmn. bd. Mem. Chicago Assn. Commerce, Field Museum. Home: Chicago, Ill. Died Dec. 24, 1932.

STEVENS, Charles Ellis, clergyman, author; b. Boston, July 5, 1853; ed. Univ. of Pa.; Yale, A.M., Ph.D.; grad. Berkeley Divinity School, 1875; (LL.D., Univ. of Wooster, 1888, D.C.L., King's Coll., Canada, 1888); m. Ella Montieth, d. Walter Montieth Aikman, F.S.A. Ordained in Episcopal Ch. and became archdeacon of Brooklyn; later rector Christ Ch., Phila. Special lecturer on constitutional law, Univ. of Wooster, Univ. of Pa., and other colls. Fellow Royal Geog. Soc. and mem. of other European and Am. learned socs. Has been made Knight Comdr. of the Order of Christ by the King of Portugal, Knight of the Order of Isabella of Castile by the Queen Regent of Spain, and officer of the Académie de France, in recognition of services to polit. science; historian gen. Soc. Colonial Wars; chaplain gen. Mil. Order Foreign Wars (comdr. Pa. commandery). Author: The City, 1885; Sources of the Constitution of the United States, 1894 (also pub. in England and translated into French, 1897); The Romance of Arenfels, and Other Tales of the Rhine, 1897; History of the House of Fitz Stephen, 1904. Home: Brooklyn, N.Y. Died 1906.

STEVENS, Daniel Gurden, clergyman, editor; b. Baltimore, Md., Sept. 17, 1869; s. Daniel Gurden and Katharine B. (Ford) S.; grad. Baltimore City Coll., 1888; A.B., Johns Hopkins, 1891, Ph.D., 1894; B.D., Crozer Theol. Sem., 1898, Th.M., 1901; m. Gertrude Castle Stifler, June 22, 1897; 1 dau., Gertrude. Ordained Bapt. ministry, 1896; pastor First Ch., Xenio, O., 1896-99, Lower Merion Ch., Bryn Mawr, Pa., 1899-1906, First Ch., Bordentown, N.J., 1907-13; book editor Am. Bapt. Publ. Soc., May 1, 1913—. Author: (with Edward Morris Stephenson) The First Hundred Years of The American Baptist Publication Society, 1925; (with Edward Bagby Pollard) Luther Rice. Home: Lansdowne, Pa. Died May 11, 1931.

STEVENS, Durham White, diplomatic adviser to Korean Govt.; b. Washington, Feb. 1, 1852; s. Ezra Lincoln and Catherine Seymour (Durham) S.; ed. Oberlin (O.) Prep. Sch. and Coll., A.B., 1871, Columbian Law Sch., Washington, 1871-73, leaving for Japan just before date of graduation; unmarried. Sec. U.S. legation at Tokio, 1873-83; resigned and became counsellor of Japanese legation at Washington, 1883; served in Foreign Office at Tokio, mostly as mem. Bureau du Protocol, of the Conf. for the Revision of Treaties between Japan and foreign powers, 1884-87; attached to embassy sent to Corea by Japan, 1884, to adjust difficulties which threatened war between Japan and China; returned to Japanese Legation at Washington, 1887; returned to Japan on official duty, 1893, 1900 and 1901; was in legation at Washington when Mexican treaty and treaty between U.S. and Japan were revised; Japanese agt. to Hawaii, 1900-01, to assist in settling pending questions; from Dec. 1904, diplomatic adviser to Korean Govt., under protocol concluded bet. Japanese and Korean Govts. Decorated by Emperor of Japan with 3d class Order of Rising Sun, 1884 (2d class, 1897), 2d class, Order of Sacred Treasure, 1894 (1st class, 1904). Republican. Died 1908.

STEVENS, E(dmund) Ray, judge; b. Town of Lake, Ill., June 20, 1869; s. George B. and Frances Ellen (Kellogg) S.; B.L., U. of Wis., 1893, LL.B., 1895, LL.D., 1923; m. Kate L. Sabin, June 23, 1898; children—Myron Ray, Henry Sabin. Admitted to Wis. bar, 1895, and began practice at Madison; mem. Wis. legislature, 1901; lecturer Law Sch., U. of Wis., 1900-04; judge 9th Jud. Circuit, Wis., 1903-25; justice Supreme Court of Wis., term 1926-36. Conglist. Mason. Widely quoted for decisions in Circuit Court, reviewing actions of state officers and state commissions of Wis.—the pioneer state in development of this new field of law. Home: Madison, Wis. Died Aug. 25, 1930.

STEVENS, Edward Lawrence, educator; b. Malone, N.Y., May 20, 1867; s. Clinton and Sabra (Lawrence) S.; A.B., Hamilton Coll., 1890, A.M., 1893; (L.H.D., St. Lawrence Univ., 1906); m. Carrie M. Hatch, 1894. Asso. supt. schs., 1898—, in charge high schs., 1904—, New York; mem. State Exam. Bd. Home: New York, N.Y. Died Apr. 3, 1914.

STEVENS, Edwin Augustus, engineer; b. Philadelphia, Mar. 14, 1858; s. Edwin Augustus (engr. and founder Stevens Inst. Tech.) and Martha Bayard (Dod) S.; A.B., Princeton, 1879; (D.Eng., Stevens Inst. Tech.); m. Emily Contee Lewis, Oct. 28, 1879. Pres. Hoboken Land Improvement Co.; trustee Stevens Inst.; has held various local offices; was col. 2d Regt., N.J. N.G.; pres. Dem. Soc. of State of N.J.; Dem. candidate for presdl. elector, 1888, 1892, 1904. Pres. N.J. Commrs. of the Palisades Interstate Park; state commr. pub. roads, 1911—. Designed the 1st screw ferryboat. Life mem. and v.p. Am. Soc. Mech. Engrs.; v.p. Soc. Naval Architects and Marine Engrs. Home: Bernardsville, N.J. Died Mar. 8, 1918.

STEVENS, Elbert Marcus, psychologist; b. Ringwood, Ill., Apr. 12, 1867; s. Marcus B. and May (Pierce) S.; A.B., U. of S.D., 1894, LL.D., 1917; studied U. of Chicago, Cornell U.; A.M., Yale, 1899; m. Mabel White, Dec. 23, 1897; children—Doris Amy, Margaret White, Evelyn White, Marion White, Rollin Elbert. Supt. schs., Centerville, S.D., 1894-97; instr. modern langs., S.D. Sch. of Mines, 1899-1906; prin. Avery Inst., Charleston, S.C., 1906-09;

pres. Straight Coll., New Orleans, 1909-16; acting prof. psychology and edn., and extension sec., Carleton Coll., Northfield, Minn., 1916-18; prof. philosophy U. of S.D., 1918—. Republican. Conglist. Mason, Woodman. Author: Psychology of Space Perception, 1915. Home: Vermillion, S.D. Died Jan. 28, 1937.

STEVENS, Eugene Morgan, banker; b. Preston, Minn., Feb. 1, 1871; s. Andrew J. and Clara Morgan (Bentley) S.; ed. pub. schs.; m. Mary Frances Rolfe, 1899; children—Eugene M., Charles Rolfe. With Winona (Minn.) Wagon Co., 1887-91; in employ F. H. Peavey & Co., grain merchants, Minneapolis, 1891-1901; with Eugene M. Stevens & Co., and Stevens, Chapman & Co., investment bankers, Minneapolis, 1901-17; v.p. Ill. Merchants Trust Co., Chicago, 1917-27, pres., 1927-29; pres. Continental Ill. Bank & Trust Co., 1929-30; chmn. bd., federal reserve agt. and Class C dir. Federal Reserve Bank of Chicago, 1931-36; vice chmn. Blythe & Co., 1936—. Formerly mem. Minn. N.G.; mem. exec. com. Liberty Loan campaigns of Chicago Federal Reserve Dist. Trustee Chicago Memorial Hosp., Am. Library Assn. of Chicago, Carleton Coll. (Northfield, Minn.), U. of Chicago; pres. John Crerar Library (Chicago). Republican. Methodist. Home: Evanston, Ill. Died Jan. 22, 1937.

STEVENS, Frank Lincoln, coll. prof.; b. nr. Syracuse, N.Y., Apr. 1, 1871; s. Henry Benjamin and Helen C. (Lincoln) S.; B.L., Hobart Coll., 1891; B.S., Rutgers Coll., 1893, M.S., 1897; post-grad. work, Ohio State U., 1894-96; fellow in botany, U. of Chicago, 1898-99, Ph.D., magna cum laude, 1900; traveling fellow, same, univs. Bonn and Halle, 1900-01; studied Naples Zoöl. Labs.; Sc.D., U. of San Marcos, Lima, Peru, 1925; LL.D. from U. of Glasgow, Scotland, 1928; m. Adeline T. Chapman, June 16, 1897. Student asst., Rutgers Coll. and N.J. Agrl. Expt. Sta., 1891-93; teacher science, Racine Coll., 1893-94; teacher chemistry and botany, high sch., Columbus, O., 1894-97; analyst Chicago Drainage Canal Investigation, 1899-1900; instr. biology, 1901-02, prof. botany and vegetable pathology, 1902-12, N.C. Coll. of Agr. and Mech. Arts; for years biologist and head dept. of plant diseases, N.C. Agrl. Expt. Sta.; dean Coll. Agr. and Mech. Arts, U. of P.R., 1912-14; prof. plant pathology, U. of Ill., Feb. 1914—; Bishop Museum fellow Yale Univ., 1921-22; prof. plant pathology, U. of Philippines, 1930-31. Mem. N.C. State Bd. of Examiners for certification of teachers. Lecturer at farmers' institutes. Episcopalian. Joint author: Agriculture for Beginners; The Hill Readers, 1906; Practical Arithmetic, 1909; Diseases of Economic Plants, 1910. Author: The Fungi That Cause Plant Disease; Plant Disease Fungi. Home: Urbana, Ill. Died Aug. 18, 1934.

STEVENS, Frank Walker, lawyer; b. Leon, N.Y., Dec. 16, 1847; s. Daniel S. and Catharine Elizabeth (Hurty) S.; ed. common schs., Randolph Acad., pvt. tutelage; Harvard Law Sch., 1870-71; m. Mary B. Miller, May 12, 1874; 1 dau., Margaret Katharine (Mrs. John R. Sackrider). Admitted to N.Y. bar, 1871; in gen. practice at Jamestown, N.Y., 1882-1907; chmn. Pub. Service Commn., 2d Dist. N.Y., July 1, 1907-May 2, 1913. Gen. valuation counsel for all N.Y. Central Lines, 1913-24; now cons. valuation counsel, same. Dist. atty., Cattaraugus Co., 1878-83; mem. Bd. of Edn., Jamestown, 1891-97, 1907; mem. Water Bd., Jamestown, 1903-07. Author: The Beginnings of the New York Central Railroad, 1926. Home: Jamestown, N.Y. Died Nov. 8, 1928.

STEVENS, Frederic William, judge; b. Hoboken, N.J., June 9, 1846; s. James Alexander and Julia (Beasley) S.; A.M., Columbia, 1864 (LL.D., 1908); m. Edith de Gueldry Twining, Sept. 9, 1903. Admitted as atty. N.J. bar, 1868, counselor, 1871; judge 2d Ct. of Newark, N.J., 1873-75; county counsel, Essex Co., 1889-92; apptd. vice chancellor, N.J., Apr. 14, 1896, reapptd. 1903, 1910 and 1917. An arbitrator, with Judge Dillon in settlement of back taxes of D.,L.&W. R.R. Co. Episcopalian. Democrat. Home: Morristown, N.J. Died Nov. 6, 1919.

STEVENS, Frederick Charles, public official; b. Attica, N.Y., July 5, 1856; s. Robert S. and Mary P. (Smith) S.; ed. Attica High Sch. and Cornell U.; m. Belle C. Sprowle, Jan. 12, 1879. Dir. First Nat. Bank (Parsons, Kan.). Trustee Cornell Univ. (New York). Mem. N.Y. Senate, 46th N.Y. Dist., 1903-04, 1905-06; chmn. of joint com. of Senate and House, 1905, which reported in favor of reduction in price of gas and electric light to consumers in New York; apptd. supt. pub. works by Gov. Hughes, 1907, and reapptd., 1909. Republican. Home: Attica, N.Y. Died Mar. 14, 1916.

STEVENS, Frederick Clement, congressman; b. Boston, Jan. 1, 1861; s. Dr. John and Cornelia O. S.; A.B., Bowdoin Coll., 1881; LL.B., State U. of Ia., 1884; m. Ellen J. Fargo, July 16, 1889. Practiced at St. Paul, 1884—; mem. Minn. Ho. of Rep., 1888-91; mem. 55th to 63d Congresses (1897-1915), 4th Minn. Dist. Republican. Home: St. Paul, Minn. Died July 1, 1923.

STEVENS, Frederick Waeir, lawyer; b. Clinton, Mich., May 24, 1865; s. Linus Felt and Mary E. (Waeir) S.; LL.B., U. of Mich., 1887, LL.D., 1923; m. Nellie M. Henshaw, Aug. 28, 1888. Admitted to Mich. bar, 1887; mem. Smith & Stevens, Grand Rapids, Mich., 1887-90; asst. U.S. dist. atty., Western Dist. of Mich., 1890-91; mem. Smiley, Smith & Stevens, Grand Rapids, 1891-97, Crane, Norris & Stevens, 1897-1900; gen. counsel Pere Marquette R.R. Co., Detroit, 1900-09; asso. with J. P. Morgan & Co., New York, 1909-15. Rep. in Peking of the Am. group in Chinese Consortium, 1920-23. Pres. Michigan Trust Co., Grand Rapids, 1923—; dir. Atlantic Coast Lumber Corp. Republican. Conglist. Home: Grand Rapids, Mich. Died Nov. 2, 1926.

STEVENS, George Barker, prof. systematic theology, Yale, 1895—; b. Spencer, N.Y., July 13, 1854; s. Thomas J. and Weltha B. S.; grad. Univ. of Rochester, 1877; (B.D., Yale, 1880, Ph.D., Syracuse, 1883; D.D., Univ. of Jena, 1886, Ill. Coll., 1902; LL.D., Univ. of Rochester, 1902); m. Kate A. Mattison, Nov. 23, 1880. Pastor in Buffalo, 1st Congl. Ch., and Watertown, N.Y., 1st Presbyn. Ch., 1880-85; student in Germany, 1885-86; prof. N.T. criticism and interpretation, Yale, 1886-95. Author: The Pauline Theology, 1892; The Johannine Theology, 1894; The Epistles of Paul in Modern English, 1898; The Theology of the New Testament, 1899; The Messages of Paul, 1900; The Messages of the Apostles, 1900; The Teaching of Jesus, 1901; etc. Home: New Haven, Conn. Died 1906.

STEVENS, George Thomas, physician; b. Essex Co., N.Y., July 25, 1832; s. Rev. Chauncey Coe and Lucinda (Hoadley) S.; ed. in N.Y. State; M.D., Castleton (Vt.) Med. Coll., 1857; (Ph.D., Union Coll., 1877); m. Harriet W. Wadhams, 1861. Commd. surgeon 77th N.Y. Vols., 1861; served in campaigns of Army of the Potomac, operating surgeon for his div. 2½ yrs., and for a time med. insp. 6th Army Corps; prof. physiology and diseases of the eye, Union U., 1870-5; in practice in New York, 1880—. Highest prize from Royal Acad. of Medicine of Belgium for treatise on Functional Diseases of the Nervous System, 1883. Author: A Treatise on the Motor Apparatus of the Eyes, 1905; A Series of Studies of Nervous Diseases, 1911. Home: New York, N.Y. Died Jan. 30, 1921.

STEVENS, George Walter, ry. pres.; b. Utica, O., June 29, 1851; s. James S. and Julia A. S.; pub. sch. edn.; m. Virginia Wilson, Dec. 27, 1881. Entered ry. service, 1864; held various positions on different rys., 1864-89; gen. supt., 1890-91, gen. mgr., 1891-1900, pres., Feb. 1, 1900—, Chesapeake & Ohio Ry.; pres. Hocking Valley R.R., Wellston & Jackson Belt Line. Home: Richmond, Va. Died Nov. 3, 1920.

STEVENS, George Washington, art dir.; b. Utica, N.Y., Jan. 16, 1866; s. George and Elizabeth S.; pupil of J. Francis Murphy; hon. M.A., Kenyon Coll., 1919; m. Nina de Garmo Spalding, June 12, 1902. On editorial staff Toledo Times, 1900-03; dir. Toledo Mus. of Art, Nov. 1903—. Pres. Am. Fedn. Photographic Soc., 1909-10; v.p. Faculty of Arts, London; mem. Nat. Inst. Social Sciences; hon. sec. Egypt Exploration Fund; pres. Assn. of Mus. Directors, 1919—. Author: The King and the Harper, and Other Poems, 1900; Things, 1903. Home: Toledo, O. Died Oct. 29, 1926.

STEVENS, Harry Clay, newspaper corr.; b. Washington, D.C., Aug. 4, 1866; s. Henry C. and Caroline (Rhodes) S.; ed. pub. schs.; m. Martha Jane Edmonston, Apr. 29, 1891. Washington corr. Minneapolis Journal, 1892—. Republican. Methodist. Mason. Home: Washington, D.C. Died May 10, 1936.

STEVENS, Hazard, lawyer; b. Newport, R.I., June 9 1842; s. Gen. Isaac Ingalls and Margaret L. S.; Phillips Acad., Andover, Chauncy Hall Sch., Boston, and Harvard Coll., freshman yr.; (hon. A.M., Harvard, 1900); unmarried. First lt. adj. 79th N.Y. Inf., Aug.-Sept. 12, 1861; capt. a.-a.-g. vols., Oct. 16, 1861; maj., Oct. 13, 1864; hon. mustered out, Sept. 30, 1865. Bvtd.: lt. col. vols., Aug. 1, 1864, "for gallantry and distinguished services in campaign before Richmond"; col. vols., Oct. 19, 1864, "for gallant and meritorious services in battles of Winchester, Fishers Hill and Cedar Creek, Va."; brig. gen. vols., Apr. 2, 1865, for same before Petersburg, Va.; awarded Congressional Medal of Honor, June 13, 1894 "for having led a party that captured Ft. Huger, Va., Apr. 19, 1863." Admitted to bar, 1870; pres. Olympia (Wash.) Light & Power Co. Collector internal revenue, Washington Ty., 1868-70; commr. on British claim on San Juan Archipelago, 1874-75; mem. Mass. Ho. of Rep., 1885-86. Gold Democrat. Made 1st ascent of Mount Tacoma or Rainier, State of Washington, Aug. 17, 1870. Sec. Am. Free Trade League, 1901-03. Independent candidate for Congress, 10th Congressional Dist., Mass., 1908. Author: Life of Isaac Ingalls Stevens, 1900. Established a dairy farm ("Cloverfields Farm") at Olympia, Wash. Home: Olympia, Wash. Died Oct. 11, 1918.

STEVENS, Hiram Fairchild, lawyer, educator; b. St. Albans, Vt., Sept. 11, 1852; s. Dr. Hiram Fairchild and Louise I.S.; ed. Univ. of Vt., class of '72, LL.D., 1902; grad. Columbia Law Sch., 1874; m. Laura A. Clary, Jan. 26, 1876. Served 5 yrs. Vt. Nat. Guard; admitted to Vt. bar, St. Albans, 1874; from Dec. 1879, in active practice at St. Paul; also practices in Supreme Court U.S.; senior mem. Stevens, O'Brien, Cole and Albrecht; v.p. and gen. counsel Canada Atlantic Transit Co.; counsel to numerous corps. Lecturer on law of real property, 1892-1900; pres. and dean, 1900—, St. Paul Coll. of Law; pres. St. Paul Bd. Park Commrs., 1886; mem. and chmn. judiciary coms. Minn. Ho. Reps. and Senate, 1889-99; chmn. Minn. Statute Revision Commn., 1901. Home: St. Paul, Minn. Died 1904.

STEVENS, Horace Jared, copper specialist; b. Conewango, N.Y., Jan. 5, 1866; s. David and Louise (Young) S.; ed. com. schs. and acad.; m. Nellie Shea, 1887. Country schoolmaster, 1882-83; carpenter, fireman, pumpman, engr., miner, surveyor's asst., timekeeper, etc., Beaufort mine, Mich., 1883-84; reporter Marquette Mining Journal, 1884-89; mgr. and owner Peninsular News Bureau, Ishpeming and Houghton, Mich., and from 1901 editor and pub. the Copper Handbook, an annual devoted to copper interests of the world; editor Michigan Mineral Statistics, 1900, 1901, pub. by State of Mich. Home: Houghton, Mich. Died Apr. 22, 1912.

STEVENS, Isaac Newton, lawyer; b. Newark, O., Nov. 1, 1858; s. Lewis Augustus and Sarah (Sperry) S.; grad. Newark High Sch.; taught school two terms, one in Ohio, one in Ill.; read law in office of Hedge & Blythe, Burlington, Ia.; m. Mrs. Helen M. Tonge, Nov. 17, 1884 (died 1909). Began practice in Denver, 1880; asst. U.S. atty., 1883-85 (state) dist. atty., 1888-92 (tried many noted cases, principal of which was that against Dr. T. Thatcher Graves, charged with poisoning Mrs. Josephine Barnaby, a rich widow of Providence, R.I.; crime committed by sending poisoned whisky through U.S. mails; all evidence circumstantial; Graves convicted, and later committed suicide in jail); co. atty., 1893-94; mem. Colo. World's Fair Commn., 1893; editor and propr. Colorado Springs Gazette, 1900-03, of Pueblo Chieftain, 1903-11; returned to practice in Denver; lacked 1 vote of election to U.S. Senate, 1895; chmn. Rep. City Com., Denver, 6 yrs.; sec. Rep. State Com., 2 yrs.; Prog. party candidate for U.S. Senate, 1912; city atty. of Denver, under new commn. form of govt., 1913-15; pres. Commonwealth Casualty Co. of Phila., 1915—. One of 3 men who introduced beet sugar industry into Colo. Conglist. Mason. Author: The Liberators, 1908; An American Suffragette, 1911; What Is Love?, 1917. For lit. purposes spent 4 yrs. in visiting and studying the people in all parts of the world. Home: Denver, Colo. Died Feb. 11, 1920.

STEVENS, James Franklin, physician; b. Van Buren, Ill., Aug. 19, 1859; s. Sylvester George and Mary M. (Green) S.; A.B., Classical Sem. (now extinct), Paw Paw, Ill., 1881; M.D., Northwestern U., 1884; M.A., U. of Neb., 1900; m. Lillian E. Carnahan, Mar. 1888. Began practice at Shabbona, Ill.; removed to Neb., 1892; lecturer principles of medicine, Lincoln Dental Coll., 1903-05; prof. internal medicine, 1905-09, dean, 1905-09, Neb. Coll. of Medicine (Neb. Wesleyan U.); lecturer Nurses Training Sch., Neb. Wesleyan Hosp., 1905-09; obstetrician and lecturer on obstetrics, St. Elizabeth Hospital, Lincoln; lecturer, 1909-17, adj. prof. in charge materia medica, 1909-14, prof. introductory medicine, 1914—, U. of Neb. Trustee Doane Coll. Republican. Conglist. Home: Lincoln, Neb. Died Feb. 23, 1921.

STEVENS, James Stacy, univ. dean; b. Lima, N.Y., Aug. 21, 1864; s. Henry Francis and Emeline (Haydock) S.; B.S., U. of Rochester, 1885, M.S., 1888, LL.D., 1907; M.S., Syracuse U., 1889; Litt.D., U. of Maine, 1922; m. Bertha E. Bowerman, August 21, 1890; children—Edwin Henry, Arthur James. Instr. science, Cook Acad., Montour Falls, N.Y., 1885-91; prof. physics, 1891—, dean College Arts and Sciences, 1905-32, acting head of dept. of English, 1917-19, U. of Maine (dean emeritus). Author: Outlines of General Physics, 1900; Outlines of Laboratory Physics, 1901; Theory of Measurements, 1915; A Dramatization of Job, 1917; A Chapel Service Book (with K. P. Harrington and A. W. Harris), 1919; The English Bible, 1921. Compiler: Quotations and References in Charles Dickens, 1929; Whittier's Use of the Bible. Home: Orono, Me. Died Mar. 30, 1940.

STEVENS, James William, insurance; b. Colchester, Ill., May 25, 1853; s. Socrates and Amanda Jane S.; ed. pub. schs., McDonough Co., Ill.; m. Jessie Louise Smith, Feb. 26, 1873; children—Raymond W., Ernest J.; m. 2d, Alice M. Bradley, Jan. 21, 1905. Began in gen. merchandise business at Colchester; removed to Chicago and engaged in dry goods business under style of Charles A. Stevens & Bros.; in 1893 took active part in organization of Illinois Life Insurance Co., of which is now chairman board; also chmn. bd. Hotel LaSalle Co., Stevens Hotel Co.; dir. Continental Ill. Bank and Trust Co., Stevens Brothers Corporation, Charles A. Stevens Bros. Mason. Republican. Mem. Christian (Disciples) Ch. Home: Chicago, Ill. Died May 14, 1936.

STEVENS, John Amos, consulting engr.; b. Galva, Ill., Sept. 16, 1868; s. George M. and Georgeanna (Ames) S.; direct desc. of John Alden of the Mayflower; student U. of Mich., 1891-92; m. Luella E. Holland, Oct. 6, 1896; children—Holland A., Richard A. Apprentice in shops of Mitts & Merrill, Saginaw, 3 yrs., later engr. on lake and ocean steamers; chief engr. Merrimac Mfg. Co., Lowell, 1896-1909; cons. practice, 1909—; treas. Stevens Products Co., Lowell. Mem. High Sch. Building Commn., Lowell; granted 13 patents on water tube boilers and 11 patents on shock absorbing devices; co-inventor Stevens-Pratt boiler. Chmn. com., apptd. 1911, by Am. Soc. Mech. Engrs., which prepared the standard boiler code; was mem. original Mass. Bd. of Boiler Rules; standardization engr. U.S. Shipping Bd. Emergency Fleet Corp., World War. Donor of John A. Stevens Trust Fund, Am. Soc. Mech. Engrs., for encouraging inventions in conservation of fuels and in generation of light, heat and power; presented with medal by Nat. Assn. Cotton Mfrs., 1917, for paper on "Evolution of the Steam Turbine in the Textile Industry." Home: Lowell, Mass. Died Nov. 18, 1929.

STEVENS, John Austin, author; b. New York, Jan. 21, 1827; s. John Austin and Abby (Weld) S.; A.B., Harvard, 1846; m. Margaret A. Morris (of the Morrisania family), June 5, 1855. Became mcht. in New York and, 1862-68, sec. N.Y. Chamber of Commerce; sec. Treasury Note Com.; later librarian New York Hist. Soc. Was founder, and for many yrs. editor, Magazine of American History; founded and was 1st pres. Soc. of S R.; founded the Loyal Nat. League. Author: The Expedition of a Lafayette Against Arnold, 1878; The French in Rhode Island, 1878-81; New York City in the Nineteenth Century, 1901; Life of Albert Gallatin (Am. Statesmen series), 1902; The Physical Evolution of New York City in a Hundred Years, 1807-1907, 1907; The Duke de Lauzan in France and America, 1907. Home: Newport, R.I. Died 1910.

STEVENS, John Calvin, architect; b. Boston, Oct. 8, 1855; s. Leander and Maria Jane Hancock (Wingate) S.; descended from Moses S., Wells, Me., 1700; grad. Portland High Sch., 1873; m. Martha Louise Waldron, Dec. 25, 1877; children—John Howard, Caroline Maria, Margaret Louise, Dorothy Wingate. Entered archtl. office of F. H. Fassett, 1873; mem. Fassett & Stevens, 1880-84, spending about 2 yrs. of that time in charge of Boston office; practiced with A. W. Cobb, 1885-91, with son, John H. Stevens, 1906—. Designed new surgery building at Me. Gen. Hosp.; Me. Med. Sch. Bldg.; Portland Athletic Club Bldg.; Me. State Sanatorium, Hebron, Me.; Eastern Me. Insane Hosp., and many pub. bldgs. and pvt. residences in Me. and other states. Trustee Me. Eye and Ear Infirmary; pres. Me. Charitable Mechanics' Assn., 1890-91. Republican. Fellow A.I.A., 1889 (pres. Maine chapter). Mason, Odd Fellow. Author: (with A. W. Cobb) Examples of Domestic Architecture, 1891. Home: Portland, Me. Died Jan. 25, 1940.

STEVENS, J(ohn) Franklin, consulting engr.; b. Philadelphia, Pa., Jan. 1, 1870; s. John Stewart and Sarah Franklin (Bacon) S.; B.Sc., U. of Pa., 1890, M.E., 1891; m. Jessie M. Speace, Nov. 28, 1902. Engr. and mem. John S. Stevens & Sons, 1891-93; sec. and treas. LaRoche Electric Works, 1893-95; pres. Keystone Elec. Instrument Co., 1894-1911; v.p. Am. Meter Co., 1896-1900; mem. Stewart & Stevens Iron Works, 1902-13; consulting practice, 1911—. Vice chmn. conservation bd. and dist. chmn. for Southeast Pa. of power and conservation divs. of Federal Fuel Administration, 1918-19. Frequent lecturer and contbr. to engring. jours. Fellow Am. Inst. E.E. (mgr. 1912-15, v.p. 1915-17, chmn. finance com., etc.). Holder of 6 patents on elec. measuring instruments; dir. Cambria Mining & Mfg. Co., 1920—. Traveled and studied engring. practice and econ. conditions in Orient and Africa, 1921-25. Home: Philadelphia, Pa. Died Dec. 1933.

STEVENS, Lillian M. N., temperance worker; b. Dover, Me., Mar. 1, 1844; d. Nathaniel and Nancy (Parsons) Ames; ed. Foxcroft Acad.; in early womanhood a teacher; (hon. A.M., Bates Coll., Me., 1911); m. Michael Stevens, merchant, 1867. Assisted, 1874, in organizing Maine W.C.T.U., becoming its treas., 1874-77 (pres.); v.p. Nat. W.C.T.U., 1894-98; after death of Miss Willard, 1898, became acting pres.; elected pres. on meeting of Nat. W.C.T.U. Conv., Nov. 1898, at St. Paul; reëlected each yr.; v.p.-at-large World's W.C.T.U. For yrs. Me. rep. in Nat. Conf. of Charities and Correction; a lady manager Chicago Expn., 1892-93. Home: Portland, Me. Died Apr. 6, 1914.

STEVENS, P. F., bishop in charge spl. missionary jurisdiction of the South, R.E. Ch. Home: Charleston, S.C. Died 1910.

STEVENS, Raymond William, life ins.; b. McDonough Co., Ill., Aug. 31, 1874; s. James William and Jessie Louise (Smith) S.; A.B., U. of Chicago, 1896; m. Anna H. Hull, June 7, 1899; children—Kathryn (Mrs. Webster N. Stafford), James W. II, Eleanor (Mrs. George Champion), Raymond W. Began as solicitor Ill. Life Ins. Co., 1896, v.p., 1900-24, pres., 1924—; v.p. Hotel La Salle Co., Stevens Hotel Co.; dir. Central Republic Bank & Trust Co. of Ill., Stevens Bros. Corp., Charles A. Stevens & Bros. Republican. Presbyn. Home: Highland Park, Ill. Died Mar. 23, 1933.

STEVENS, Thomas Holdup, 3d, rear admiral U.S.N.; b. Honolulu, H.I., July 12, 1848; s. Thomas Holdup, 2d, and Anna Maria (Christie) S.; grad. U.S. Naval Acad., 1868; m. Washington, Cara de la Montaigne, d. late A. Oakey Hall, Apr. 29, 1903. Entered U.S.N., Oct. 1, 1863; after 22 yrs.' sea service and 40 yrs.' service, was advanced to rank of rear admiral and retired at own request, Feb. 11, 1905 (third of same name to attain flag rank in U.S.N.). Served in Civil War and in P.I. during insurrection. Youngest original naval mem. Mil. Order Loyal Legion U.S.; mem. S.R., Mil. Order of the Carabao. Died Oct. 3, 1914.

STEVENS, Thomas Wood, author; b. Daysville, Ill., Jan. 26, 1880; s. William Gurney and Charlotte (Wood) S.; grad. Armour Scientific Acad., 1897; took 3 yrs.' course in mech. engring., Armour Inst. Tech., Chicago; m. Helen F. Bradshaw, 1904. Founded the Blue Sky Press, Chicago; became lit. critic to The Inland Printer, 1902; took charge dept. of illustration, Art Inst. of Chicago, 1903; lecturer art history, U. of Wis., 1912-13; head of sch. of drama, Carnegie Inst. of Tech., 1913—. Author: The Lesser Tragedy (prize story in Metropolitan Mag. literary competition), 1904; The Etching of Cities, 1913; Lettering, 1916. Co-author: (with Alden C. Noble) The Morning Road, 1902. Dramatic works: The Chaplet of Pan (with Wallace Rice), prod. by Donald Robertson, 1908; A Pageant of the Italian Renaissance, prod. and published, Chicago Art Inst., 1909; An Historical Pageant of Illinois, prod. and published, Northwestern U., 1909; Pageant of the Old Northwest, Milwaukee, 1911; Independence Day Pageant (with K. S. Goodman), Chicago, 1911; Masques of East and West (with same), Chicago, 1915; The Pageant of St. Louis, 1914; The Pageant of Newark, 1916; The Drawing of the Sword (Red Cross pageant), 1917; pageant-play, Joan of Arc, prod. with John Craig, with Am. troops at Domremy, France, Sept. 1918; Pageant of Victory and Peace, 1919. Home: Pittsburgh, Pa. Died Jan. 29, 1942.

STEVENS, Walter Barlow, writer; b. Meriden, Conn., July 25, 1848; s. Rev. Asahel Augustus and Mary Comstock (Bristol) S.; youth passed at Peoria, Ill.; A.B., U. of Mich., 1870, A.M., 1872; LL.D., Washington U., St. Louis, 1908; m. Sarah Rebecca (Thomson) Croft, Dec. 26, 1912. Connected with St. Louis newspapers, as reporter, city editor, and staff corr., after graduation from coll.; Wash. corr. St. Louis Globe-Democrat, 1884-1901; pres. Gridiron Club, Washington, 1895; traveled extensively and corresponded for Globe-Democrat through U.S., Can., Mex., Cuba, P.R., Jamaica, and Panama. Sec. La. Purchase Expn. Co. from organization, 1901; dir. of exploitation, and mem. Superior Jury of Awards, same, 1904; sec. City Plan Commn. of St. Louis, 1912-16; exec. sec. 4th American Peace Congress, 1913. Knight of Crown of Italy, 1904; 1st Grade, 3d Class, Order of Double Dragon, China, 1905; Chevalier Order of Leopold, Belgium, 1905; medal of honor, 1st Class, Philippine Govt., 1905; 4th Class, Order of Rising Sun, Japan, 1906; Officer's Cross, Order of Red Eagle, Germany, 1907; Officier de l'Instruction Publique, France, 1907. Conglist. Republican. Author: Through Texas, 1892; The Ozark Uplift, 1900; Introduction and Notes on Facsimiles of Poems and Letters of Robert Burns, 1907; The Building of St. Louis, 1908; St. Louis, the Fourth City, 1909; The Log of the Alton, 1909; One Huundred Years in a Week, 1910; The Brown-Reynolds Duel, 1911; History of St. Louis, 2 vols., 1911; Life of Samuel Morris Dodd, 1912; Book of the Fourth American Peace Congress, 1913; St. Louis Nights wi' Burns, 1913; Eleven Roads to Success, 1913; Missouri, the Center State, 2 vols., 1914; Grant in St. Louis, 1915; Halsey Cooley Ives, 1915; Lincoln and Missouri, 1916; Missouri Centennial, 1917; A Reporter's Lincoln, 1917; Missourians, One Hundred Years Ago, 1918; Ambassador Francis, 1919; The Missouri Tavern, 1921; Centennial History of Missouri, 2 vols., 1921; Robert H. Stockton, 1923; The New Journalism in Missouri, 1925; etc. Died Aug. 28, 1939.

STEVENS, Walter Le Conte, physicist; b. Gordon Co., Ga., June 17, 1847; s. Dr. Josiah P. and Anna (Le Conte) S.; A.B., U. of S.C., 1868; hon. Ph.D., U. of Ga., 1882; Strassburg, Berlin, Zürich, 1890-92; m. Virginia Lee Letcher, d. war gov. of Va., Aug. 29, 1900. Prof. chemistry, Oglethorpe Coll., Atlanta, Ga., 1870-72; instr. physical science, Chatham Acad., Savannah, Ga., 1873-76, Cooper Inst., New York, 1879-82; prof. mathematics and physics, Packer Collegiate Inst., Brooklyn, 1882-90; prof. physics, Rensselaer Poly. Inst., 1892-98, Washington and Lee U., 1898-1922; retired and made prof. emeritus, 1922. Fellow A.A.A.S., N.Y. Acad. Sciences, Brooklyn Inst. Arts and Sciences, Royal Micros. Soc., London. Author: Revision of Steele's Physics, 1886. Home: Lexington, Va. Died Dec. 29, 1927.

STEVENS, William Arnold, prof. New Testament Interpretation, Rochester Theol. Sem., 1877—; b. Granville, O., Feb. 5, 1839; s. Prof. John S., D.D.; grad. Denison Univ., O., 1862, A.M., 1865, D.D., 1882; studied Rochester Theol. Sem., Harvard Univ., Univ. of Leipzig, Univ. of Berlin (LL.D., Rochester Univ., 1882); m. Caroline A. Clarke. Prof. Greek lang. and lit., Denison Univ., 1868-77. Author: Select Orations of Lysias, 1876; Commentary on the Epistles to the Thessalonians, 1887; Outline Handbook of the Life of Christ (with Ernest D. Burton), 1892; Harmony of the Gospels for Historical Study (with Ernest D. Burton), 1894; Life of the Apostle Paul, 1894. Home: Rochester, N.Y. Died 1910.

STEVENSON, Adlai Ewing, Vice President of the U.S.; b. Christian Co., Ky., Oct. 23, 1835; s. John T. and Eliza (Ewing) S.; ed. Centre College, Ky.; (LL.D.); family removed to Bloomington, Ill., 1852; m. Letitia, d. Rev. Lewis W. Green, of Danville, Ky., Dec. 20, 1866 (died 1913). Admitted to bar, 1857; master in chancery, 1860-64; dist. atty., 1865-69; mem. 44th and 46th Congresses (1875-77, 1879-81); del. Dem. Nat. convs., 1884-92; 1st asst. postmaster-gen., 1885-89. Vice President of the U.S., 1893-97; Dem. nominee for Vice President, 1900, for gov. of Ill., 1908. Mem. commn. to Europe, 1897, to try to secure internat. bimetallism. Home: Bloomington, Ill. Died June 15, 1914.

STEVENSON, Andrew; b. Bayonne, N.J., June 28, 1879; s. Samuel Alexander and Margaret Emma (Beach) S., educated public schools and Ia. Business College, Des Moines; m. Genevieve Hardin, Oct. 4, 1905; children—Andrew, James, Ruth, John H. Began active career with Wabash R.R., Des Moines, 1890; with C.,B.&Q. R.R., Chicago, 1894-96, Chicago & E. Ill. R.R., 1896-98; chief rate clerk Western Passenger Assn., 1898-1905; Ill. mgr. Columbian Nat. Ins. Co., 1905-07; v.p. and gen. mgr. Ia. Light & Traction Co. and gen. mgr. Ia. Constrn. Co., 1907-14; mng. dir. Asso. Alaskan Properties; founder, 1st pres. and dir. banks of Alaska, Skagway, Wrangell, Anchorage, Cordova, Alaska; pres. Chicago, Springfield & St. Louis Ry., Jacksonville & Havana R.R.; co-founder, v.p., treas. Inland Fuel Co.; v.p. and gen. mgr. Nevada Manhattan Corp.; v.p. Mid Pacific Railroad, Vice pres. Nat. Transportation Inst., 1922-23; v.p. Am. Economic Inst., 1924. A founder of Young Men's Presbyterian Union, Chicago, Presbyn. Brotherhood of America. Author: Chicago Preëminently a Presbyterian City, 1907; A Short Life Well Lived, 1908; Faith of Our Fathers, 1924; An Educated Young Man and the Bible, 1925; Why I Am a Presbyterian, 1927. Originator of Stevenson plan for consolidation of railroads under transportation act. Home: Los Angeles, Calif. Died Nov. 29, 1933.

STEVENSON, Elliott Grasette, lawyer; b. Middlesex County, Can., May 18, 1856; s. William and Mary (McMurray) S.; removed to Mich. in early childhood; ed. pub. schs., Port Huron, and acad., London, Ont.; studied law in office of O'Brien & Atkinson, Port Huron; m. Emma A. Mitts, 1879. Admitted to bar, 1877, and practiced at Port Huron; removed to Detroit, 1887; mem. Stevenson, Carpenter, Butzel & Backus; v.p. Union Trust Co., Toronto; dir. 1st Nat. Bank, Detroit. Pros. atty. St. Clair Co., Mich., 2 terms, 1878-82; mayor of Port Huron, 1889-96; chmn. Dem. State Central Com., Mich., 1894-96. Mason. Home: Detroit, Mich. Died Mar. 7, 1925.

STEVENSON, Eugene, judge; b. Brooklyn, N.Y., June 28, 1849; s. Paul Eugene and Cornelia (Prime) S.; A.B., New York U., 1870, LL.B., 1870, LL.D., 1920; m. Helen, d. Rev. William H. Hornblower, D.D., June 11, 1884. Admitted to N.J. bar as atty., 1874, counsellor, 1877; prosecutor of pleas, Passaic Co., N.J., by appmt. of Gov. Ludlow, 1881-86; vice chancellor of N.J., 3 terms, 1901-22. Democrat. Presbyterian. Pres. N.J. State Bar Assn., 1900-01. Mem. Council of N.Y. Univ., 1904— (v.p. 1910—). Home: Paterson, N.J. Died May 22, 1928.

STEVENSON, Frank Herbert, clergyman; b. Grand Island, Neb., Apr. 15, 1883; s. Andrew Lloyd (M.D.) and Florence Adelaide (Israel) S.; student Pomona Coll., 1901-02; grad. Princeton Theol. Sem., 1911; D.D., Hanover (Ind.) Coll., 1920; m. Mary Shillito, Oct. 23, 1917; children—Frank Herbert, Mary Shillito. In telephone and electric light business on Pacific Coast, 1902-08, missionary to Ft. Peck Indian Reservation, La Plata, Mont., 1909; minister Free Ch., St. Andrews, Scotland, 1910; ordained ministry Presbyn. Ch. U.S.A., 1911; asso. minister First Ch., Pittsburgh, Pa., 1911-15; minister Ch. of the Covenant, Cincinnati, 1915-28; pres. bd. trustees Lane Theol. Sem., 1925-28; mem. bd. dirs. Princeton Theol. Sem., 1927-29; an organizer and mem. bd. of control Westminster Theol. Sem., Phila., 1929, and lecturer on pastoral theology same, 1929—, also pres. bd. trustees. Republican. Mason. Author: Tracts for the Times (sermons printed and circulated by Ch. of the Covenant). Home: Princeton, N.J. Died Aug. 2, 1934.

STEVENSON, Frederic Augustus, telephone official; b. N.Y. City, Apr. 27, 1867; s. John H. and Henrietta (Stavey) S.; B.A., Yale, 1888; m. Elisabeth Farrington, Dec. 20, 1893. Clerk Edison Machine Works,

Schenectady, N.Y., 1888-90; head accountant Edison Gen. Electric Co., N.Y. City, 1890-91; sec. Schenectady St. Ry. Co., 1891-93; dist. supt. Am. Telephone & Telegraph Co., Chicago, 1893-99; spl. agt. Am. Telephone & Telegraph Co., New York, 1899-1907; gen. supt. of plant, Am. T. and T. Co., N.Y. City, 1907-18, dir. long lines dept., 1919—, asst. v.p., 1927—; apptd. mem. operating bd. U.S. Telegraph and Telephone Administration, Dec. 1918. Republican. Episcopalian. Home: New York, N.Y. Died Dec. 17, 1937.

STEVENSON, Frederick, composer, theorist; b. Newark, Nottinghamshire, Eng., Sept. 16, 1845; s. John Webster and Anne (Fisher) S.; A.B., St. John's Coll., Hurstpierpoint, Sussex, Eng., 1866; studied harmony with Dr. Macfarren, Cambridge, counterpoint with Dr. Bridge, Westminster Abbey; m. Mary Jordan Ford, of London, Aug. 6, 1873. Professional work in London, 15 yrs.; precentor St. John's Cathedral, Denver, Colo., 1883; later organist and choirmaster, St. Mark's Ch., Denver, and dir. Denver Conservatory of Music; removed to Los Angeles, Calif., 1894; formerly organist and choirmaster St. John's Ch., Christ Church and Temple B'nai B'rith. Composer of nearly 100 solo, choral and instrumental works, of which the best known are: I Sought the Lord (anthem with alto solo); The Salutation of the Dawn (for contralto, cello and piano); Light (sacred song with original text); Easter Eve and Morn (cantata); Omnipotence (soprano solo and male chorus, piano and organ); Viennese Serenade; Idylle Mongolienne; An American Ace. Home: Los Angeles, Calif. Died Oct. 25, 1925.

STEVENSON, Frederick Boyd, editor and writer; b. Sandusky, O., Jan. 6, 1869; s. John Wesley and Caroline Converse (Mathews) S.; ed. pvt. and pub. schs.; studied law, but abandoned that profession for newspaper work; m. Anna, d. Col. Robert A. Constable, of Athens, O., Jan. 25, 1888. Had charge of state politics for Cleveland Herald before he reached his majority; afterward in Chicago, becoming city editor Daily News and Sunday editor Tribune; from 1900 in editorial, lit. and dramatic work in New York and Sunday editor Brooklyn Eagle, and writer of daily column, etc., until 1931. Was selected, Sept. 10, 1896, by City of Cleveland to write an epic poem on The Battle of Lake Erie, which he read on "Perry's Victory Day," on the centennial anniversary of the city. Author of "The Amalgamated Americans"; writer on economic and polit. subjects. Publicist and lecturer on nat., internat. and civic affairs. Home: Brooklyn, N.Y. Died Aug. 3, 1938.

STEVENSON, George, banker; b. Philadelphia, Pa., June 24, 1845; s. Hugh and Elizabeth (Cressman) S.; ed. grammar schs. and Central High Sch., Phila.; m. Mary Hughes Barnes, Dec. 19, 1867. Enlisted at 16, and served in Co. A, 109th Pa. Vols. Mem. Sailer & Stevenson, bankers, Phila., June 24, 1866-Jan. 1, 1911; retired; dir. of Minehill & Schuylkill Haven R.R. President bd. trustees General Assembly Presbyn. Ch. in U.S.A., 1909—; trustee Presbyn. Hospital in Phila., Phila. Stock Exchange. Lecturers on financial subjects at the Wharton Sch. Finance (U. of Pa.) and School Commerce of Central High School. Home: Philadelphia, Pa. Died Sept. 28, 1925.

STEVENSON, James Henry, Assyriologist; b. Peterborough, Ont., Can., Apr. 16, 1860; s. James and Hannah (Scarborough) S.; A.B., McGill U., 1889; grad. Wesleyan Theol. Coll., Montreal, 1891; Ph.D., U. of Chicago, 1897; studied Assyrian contract tablets, British Mus., 1896, 99, 1902; studied Berlin, 1899, 1900; (D.D., Wesleyan Theol. Coll., Montreal, 1910); m. Evelyn, d. Rev. Dr. A. Sutherland, of Toronto, Can., Feb. 5, 1891. Teacher pub. schs., Ontario, 1879-81; ordained Meth. Ch. of Can. ministry, 1889; pastor Islington, Toronto, 1890-91; prof. Hebrew, Vanderbilt U., 1893—; minister M.E. Ch., S.; mem. Gen. Conf. M.E. Ch., S., 1906. Author: Herodotus and the Empires of the East (Tolman and Stevenson), 1898; Babylonian and Assyrian Contracts, with Aramaic Reference Notes, 1902; Hymnology of the Assyrians and Babylonians. Home: Nashville, Tenn. Died Dec. 20, 1919.

STEVENSON, John James, geologist; b. New York, N.Y., Oct. 10, 1841; s. Rev. Andrew and Ann Mary (Willson) S.; A.B., New York U., 1863, A.M., 1866, Ph.D., 1867; (LL.D., Princeton, 1893, Washington and Jefferson, 1902); m. Mary A. Macgowan, Apr. 13, 1865 (died 1871); m. 2d, Mary C. Ewing, Jan. 1, 1879. Prof. chemistry and natural history, W.Va. U., 1869-71; prof. geology, 1871-82, chemistry and physics, 1882-89, geology and biology, 1889-94, geology, 1894-1909, emeritus prof., 1909, New York U. Aid on Ohio Geol. Survey, 1871-72, 74; geologist U.S. Geog. Survey, west of 100th Meridian, 1873, 74, 78, 79, 2d Geol. Survey of Pa., 1875-78, 1881-82. Corr. or hon. mem. geol. socs. of Russia, Hungary, Belgium, Vienna, Edinburgh, Liverpool, Australasia, acads. of Halle, Dresden, Moscow, Padua, Palermo, Pisa, London; del. Internat. Geol. Cong., 1903 (v.p. for U.S.). Author: Geology of a Portion of Colorado, 1875; Report on Greene and Washington Districts, Pa., 1876; Report on Fayette and Westmoreland Districts, Pa., 1877-78; Geological Examinations in Southern Colorado and Northern New Mexico, 1881; Geology of Bedford and Fulton Counties, Pa., 1882. Died Aug. 10, 1924.

STEVENSON, J(oseph) Ross, theologian; b. Ligonier, Pa., Mar. 1, 1866; s. Rev. Ross and Martha A. (Harbison) S.; A.B., Washington and Jefferson, 1886, A.M., 1889, D.D., 1897; grad. McCormick Theol. Sem., Chicago, 1889; U. of Berlin, 1889-90; LL.D., Ursinus, 1908, Lafayette, 1915; D.D., U. of Edinburgh, 1919, Presbyn. Coll., Halifax, 1920; m. Florence Day, May 16, 1899; children—William Edwards, Donald Day, Theodore Dwight. Ordained Presbyn. ministry, 1890; pastor Sedalia, Mo., 1890-94; adj. prof. eccles. history, 1894-97, prof., 1897-1902, McCormick Theol. Sem., Chicago; pastor Fifth Av. Ch., New York, 1902-09, Brown Memorial Ch., Baltimore, 1909-14; pres. Princeton Theol. Sem., 1914-36. Moderator Gen. Assembly Presbyn. Ch. U.S.A., 1915; pres. Internat. Med. Missionary Soc.; mem. Com. to Revise Confession of Faith; mem. Presbyn. Bd. Foreign Missions; chmn. Assembly's Dept. on Ch. Co-operation and Union; chmn. business com. and asso. vice chmn. continuation com. World Conf. of Faith and Order; mem. Am. sect. Universal Christian Council for Life and Work. In service of Y.M.C.A. and Army Ednl. Commn., overseas, 1918-19; rep. Presbyn. Ch. on counselling commn. of Y.M.C.A. Home: Princeton, N.J. Died Aug. 13, 1939.

STEVENSON, Katharine Adelia Lent, temperance advocate; b. Copake, N.Y., May 8, 1853; d. Marvin Richardson and Hannah Williams (Louzada) Lent; grad. Amenia (N.Y.) Sem., 1873, grad. Boston U. Sch. of Theology, 1881; m. James Stevenson, Feb. 14, 1883. Elected corr. sec. Mass. W.C.T.U., 1891; nat. editor books and leaflets, 1893; corr. sec. Nat. W.C.T.U., 1894; pres. Mass. W.C.T.U., 1898—; elected world's supt. and mem. exec. com., World's W.C.T.U., 1900; made tour of world as rep. of W.C.T.U., 1908-10, and delivered addresses in Japan, China, Australia, New Zealand, Ceylon, Burma, India, Egypt, Palestine, Greece and Italy; now v.p. Nat. W.C.T.U. Mem. exec. com. Prohibition Party of Mass.; mem. advisory bd. Frances E. Willard Settlement. Editor in chief Our Message. Methodist; preacher, 1890—. Author: A Brief History of the Women's Christian Temperance Union, 1906. Home: Newton, Mass. Died Mar. 28, 1919.

STEVENSON, Lewis Green, farmer; b. Chenoa, Ill., Aug. 15, 1868; s. Adlai E. (vice-pres. of U.S.) and Letitia (Green) S.; student Washington and Jefferson Coll., 1895-97; m. Helen L. Davis, Nov. 23, 1892. Newspaper corr. in Japan and China, 1893-94; pvt. sec. to father, 1894-97; mgr. Ariz. and N.M. gold and copper mines for Mrs. Phoebe A. Hearst, 1897-1903; chmn. Ill. Bd. of Pardons, 1913-14; sec. of State of Ill., 1914-17; spl. investigator for U.S. Navy, Washington, D.C., 1917-18; mgr. 49 farms in Ill., Ia. and Ind., comprising 10,500 acres. Home: Bloomington, Ill. Died Apr. 5, 1929.

STEVENSON, Mark Delimon, oculist; b. Trafalgar, Ont., Feb. 18, 1876; s. James Usher and Jane (Darling) S.; grad. Woodstock Collegiate Inst., 1894; M.D., Rush Med. Coll., Chicago, 1897; Royal Ophthalmic Hosp. (London), 1898-99 and 1901; unmarried. Ophthalmic surgeon, City Hosp., Akron; oculist Children's Home, etc. Inventor of instruments for eye surgery. Author: Photoscopy (Skiascopy or Retinoscopy), 1906. Editorial writer, Ophthalmology. Home: Akron, O. Died May 21, 1915.

STEVENSON, Matilda Coxe, ethnologist; b. San Augustine, Tex.; d. Alexander H. and Maria Matilda (Coxe) Evans; moved in infancy to Washington, D.C.; ed. Miss Anable's, Phila.; m. James Stevenson, ethnologist, Apr. 18, 1872 (died 1888). With husband 13 yrs. in explorations of Rocky Mountain region, receiving from him spl. instruction in ethnology; with expdn. under his charge, from Bur. of Ethnology, to Zuñi, N.M., 1879; assisted in collecting archaic implements, ceramics and ceremonial objects for U.S. Nat. Mus.; on staff Bur. Am. Ethnology, Smithsonian Instn., 1889—. Studied the Zuñi mythology, philosophy and sociology and made extensive vocabulary; explored cave, cliff and mesa ruins of N.Mex.; visited all Pueblo tribes of N.Mex., Tusayan and Navajo of Ariz., Mission Indians of Calif., etc.; was received with Mr. Stevenson in secret organizations of these peoples and studied their esoteric institutions; spent 1904-10 studying Taos and Tewa Indians, giving spl. attention to their philosophy, religion, symbolism and sociology, the Taos people, Zuñi medicinal and edible plants, preparation of cotton and wool for loom, etc. On jury for anthropology, Chicago Expn., 1893. Author: Zuñi and the Zuñians, 1881; Religious Life of the Zuñi Child, 1884; The Sia, Zuñi Scalp Ceremonials, 1890; Zuñi Ancestral Gods and Masks, 1898; The Zuñi Indians, Their Mythology, Esoteric Fraternities, and Ceremonies, 1903; etc. Died June 24, 1915.

STEVENSON, Paul Eve, author; b. New York, May 19, 1868; s. Vernon King S.; attended Columbia grammar school; spl. course Columbia Univ.; m. Maud Zeilin, Jan. 17, 1893. Author: A Deep Water Voyage, 1896; By Way of Cape Horn, 1898. Home: Garden City, L.I., N.Y. Died 1910.

STEVENSON, Richard Taylor, university prof.; b. Taylorsville, Ky., Sept. 24, 1853; s. Rev. Daniel and Sarah A. (Corwine) S.; student Ky. U., Lexington, 3 yrs.; A.B., Ohio Wesleyan, 1873, Ph.D., 1893; B.D., Boston U., 1877; U. of Berlin, 1907-08; (D.D., Wooster Coll., 1910; LL.D., Ohio Wesleyan U., 1913); m. Julia Tevis, Apr. 16, 1884. Ordained M.E. ministry, 1879, pastor Danville, Ky., 1879-81, Shelbyville, Ky., 1881-83, Sandusky, O., 1883-86, Wooster, O., 1886-90, Mansfield, O., 1890-93; prof. history, 1893—, v.p., 1909—, Ohio Wesleyan U. Mem. N. East Ohio Conf. M.E. Church, and of book com.; mem. General Conferences, 1912, 1916. Republican. Author: One Hundred Years of Methodism in Ohio, 1898; Missionary Interpretation of History, 1905; Growth of the Nation in "History of North America" (Vol. XII, 1809-1837), 1905; John Calvin, Statesman, 1907; Missions versus Militarism, 1916. Home: Delaware, Ohio. Died Aug. 19, 1919.

STEVENSON, Sara Yorke, archæologist; b. Paris, France, Feb. 19, 1847; d. Edward and Sarah (Hanna) Yorke; ed. in Paris to 1862; lived in Mexico; (Sc.D., U. of Pa.—the 1st hon. degree that instn. ever conferred on a woman); m. Cornelius Stevenson, June 30, 1870. Sec. Am. Exploration Soc., 1897, dept. archæology, U. of Pa., 1894 (pres. 1904); pres. Acorn Club, Phila., 1894, Depository and Phila. Exchange for Woman's Work, 1895; pres. Pa. branch Archæol. Inst. America, 1899-1903; trustee Phila. Museums, 1894-1901; mem. and v.p. jury for ethnology, Chicago Expn., 1893; asst. curator Pa. Museum, 1908—. Mem. Citizens' Advisory Com. (1st woman called by the mayor), 1897, to consult on municipal loan of $12,000,000; pres. Civic Club of Phila., 1894-1900, v.p., 1900-07, again pres., 1913, and honorary pres., 1914—; pres. Pa. Equal Suffrage Soc., 1909. Went to Rome, 1897, on spl. mission for dept. of archæology and palæontology, U. of Pa., and 1898 to Egypt for the Am. Exploration Soc. and the City of Phila. in connection with archæol. work in the Nile Valley. (First woman lecturer on Harvard calendar [Peabody Mus.], 1894.) Pres. Contemporary Club, 1913-14. V.chmn. emergency aid com. and chmn. French War Relief Com. of Phila., 1914—. Awarded academic palms by French Govt., as Officier d'Instruction Publique, 1916, for services. Author: Maximilian in Mexico. Lit. editor Public Ledger, 1908—. Chmn. women's com. of 100, United Rep. Campaign Com. for Mayor of Phila. (Moore), 1919. Home: Philadelphia, Pa. Died Nov. 14, 1921.

STEVENSON, Sarah Hackett, physician; b. Buffalo Grove, Ill., Feb. 2, 1843; d. Col. John Davis S.; grad. State Univ., Bloomington, Ill., 1863; studied at South Kensington Science Schools, London; grad. Woman's Med. Coll., 1873; delegate from Ill. Med. Soc. to Am. Med. Assn., 1876; 1st woman mem. of latter; one of promoters of Home for Incurables and Ill. Training School for Nurses; has been delegate to several nat. and internat. med. congresses. Prof. obstetrics Woman's Med. School, Northwestern Univ.; pres. Nat. Temperance Hosp.; founder Maternity Hosp. and Training School for Nursery Maids; 1st woman on Cook Co. Hosp. staff; attending physician to Mary Thompson's Hosp., 1874—; consultant Woman's Hosp.; etc. Author: Biology (2 vols.), 1874 A2; also medical papers. Home: Chicago, Ill. Died 1909.

STEVENSON, William Holmes, merchant; b. Pittsburgh, Jan. 19, 1857; s. George K. and Mary Dickson (Brown) S.; ed. pub. and high schs.; m. Fannie La Une Large, Apr. 7, 1881. Pres. George K. Stevenson Co., importing grocers (establ. 1826); v.p. Polar Water Co. Dir. Pittsburgh Free Dispensary. Mem. Pittsburgh Council, 1902-04, 1906-09 (elected both times on reform ticket); reform candidate for mayor, 1909; pres. Lake Erie & Ohio River Canal Bd. Mem. Carnegie Hero Fund Commn.; pres. Pittsburgh Chamber Commerce, 1913-15 (dir.); pres. Hist. Soc. Western Pa.; mem. Pa. Hist. Commn. (chmn. 1919-23); dir. Chamber Commerce U.S.A., 1914-16; pres. Presbyterian Union, 1907-09. Chmn. Council Nat. Defense and Pub. Safety for Allegheny Co., 1917-18. Home: Pittsburgh, Pa. Died Sept. 22, 1930.

STEVICK, David William, publisher, editor; b. Hutchinson, Kan., Feb. 7, 1887; s. William Henry and Jennie (Getter) S.; ed. pub. schs., Bloomington, Ill.; m. Helen Mary Taylor, Aug. 29, 1910; 1 dau., Marajen. Advertising mgr. Bloomington (Ill.) Bulletin, 1903-15; owner since 1915 of Champaign (Ill.) Daily News, now Champaign News-Gazette (purchased Champaign Gazette 1919); purchased 3 newspapers of Texarkana, Ark.-Tex., 1926, and merged same as Texarkana Gazette (morning) and Texarkana News (evening); pres. The Texarkana Gazette Co. Mem. Christian (Disciples) Ch. Mason. Author: You and I in Hawaii; You and I with the Fleet; You and I Tuna Fishing; and other travel books. Home: Texarkana, Tex.; also Los Angeles, Calif. Died Dec. 15, 1935.

STEWARD, Thomas Gifford, govt. officer; b. Cambridge, N.Y., Dec. 5, 1857; s. Rev. Lanson and Abby Jane (Smith) S.; grad. high sch., Huntington, L.I., N.Y., 1874; LL.B., Nat. U., 1883, LL.M., 1885, C.E., 1881; m. Grace Gould Garriott, Oct. 15, 1895. Clerk in mercantile house, Huntington, 1874-76; machinist, Plano, Ill., 1876-79; clerk Gen. Land Office, Washington, 1879-81; entered Patent Office, 1881; chmn. Bd. of Examiners-in-Chief, 1897—. Home: Washington, D.C. Died Feb. 1936.

STEWARDSON, Emlyn Lamar, architect; b. Philadelphia, Pa., Jan. 6, 1863; s. Thomas and Margaret

(Haines) S.; B.S., U. of Pa., 1884; m. Mary Brinton Mitchell, July 12, 1897; children—Rosamund, Margaret, John. Practices in Phila. Spent 6 mos. in France with Am. Red Cross, World War. Home: Philadelphia, Pa. Died Feb. 10, 1936.

STEWART, Alexander, lumberman; b. York Co., N.B., Can., Sept. 12, 1829; common sch. edn.; moved, 1849, to Wis., settling where city of Wausau is now located; engaged in lumber business. Del. Rep. Nat. Conv., 1884; mem. 54th to 56th Congresses (1895-1901), 9th Wis. Dist. Republican. Home: Wausau, Wis. Died May 24, 1912.

STEWART, Alexander Mair, contractor; b. Kingston, Ont., Can., Oct. 2, 1857; s. James and Martha (Lyall) S.; ed. pub. and high schs., St. Louis; m. Emily Elizabeth Peabody, d. of W. W. Peabody, pres. O.&M. and B.&O. Southwestern rys., Apr. 5, 1887. Began studying architecture, 1878, under father and later went into contracting business; jr. mem. James Stewart & Co., 1886; until retirement of James Stewart, 1892, when became sr. mem. firm (name unchanged) with hdqrs. in New York, 1903, now chmn. bd. Rebuilt the entire water front of Galveston after storm of 1899; did large work in England, including British Westinghouse Electric Works, Manchester; Midland Railway Co.'s Hotel, Manchester; Savoy Hotel, London; Naval Training School for Admiralty at Osborne, Isle of Wight; many skyscrapers, banks and monumental bldgs., including Interstate Commerce Bldg., Dept. of Labor Bldg. with Connecting Auditorium, largest building in Washington; Federal Court House, Federal Office Bldg., Vesey St., New York City; a banking bldg. in Tokio for the Mitsui Gomei Kaisha with largest banking room in the world (80 x 357 feet); the Union Terminal Station, Cincinnati, Ohio; hot and cold strip mills for Lackawanna Steel Co., Buffalo, N.Y., capitols at Salt Lake City and Boisé, Ida., Oklahoma City, and Jefferson Memorial at St. Louis, also dredging 65 miles of the New York Barge Canal, and at Toronto, Ont., reclaiming by dredging and filling a one thousand acre industrial territory adjoining the harbor, involving the removal of forty million yards of material, constrn. of over 12 miles of concrete sea walls and wharves; etc. During war built many govt. bldgs. in U.S. and France, also established a shipyard at Bordeaux; supplied and erected large tanks in many places in France for furnishing gasoline and oil for the U.S. forces, employing 6,500 men. Chmn. board James Stewart & Co., of N.J.; pres. Canadian Stewart Co., Ltd., The Inland Waterways Equipment & Dredging Co. (New York), The Stewart Realty Co., Stewart Land Co. of Pittsburgh; v.p. 49 E. 79th St. Corp. Awarded "Grand Commander of the Cross of Italy," 1926, by Italian Govt. for services rendered to them in U.S. Democrat. Presbyn. Home: New York, N.Y. Died Dec. 22, 1939.

STEWART, Alexander P., commr. Chickamauga Nat. Park, Sept. 1890—; b. Rogersville, Tenn., Oct. 2, 1821; s. William and Elizabeth (Decherd) S.; prep. edn. in Tenn.; grad. U.S. Mil. Acad., West Point, N.Y., June 1842 (LL.D., Cumberland Univ.); m. Harriet Byron Chase, Aug. 7, 1845 (died 1898). Apptd. 2d lt. 3d U.S. Arty., June 1842; an asst. to prof. mathematics, U.S. Mil. Acad., 1843; resigned, 1845; prof. mathematics and natural philosophy in Cumberland and Nashville univs., 1845-60; volunteered in State Army of Tenn.; apptd. by gov. maj. arty. corps; transferred to C.S.A., 1861 commd. brig. gen., Nov. 1861; maj. gen., 1863; lt. gen., 1864; in command Army of Tenn. at close of the war; chancellor Univ. of Miss., 1874-86; Southern mem. Chickamauga Park Commn., 1890—. Home: Biloxi, Miss. Died 1908.

STEWART, Allison Vance, publisher; b. McAlevys Fort, Pa., June 17, 1856; s. Robert V. and Jane (Angell) S.; pub. sch. and acad. edn.; m. Ida C. Garrett, Jan. 12, 1881. Manager of agencies, Warder, Bushnell & Glessner Co., Chicago, 1887-1901; engaged in publs. of Christian Science movement and in publishing works of Mary Baker Eddy. Dir. The First Ch. of Christ, Scientist, Boston; trustee under the will of Mary Baker Eddy. Independent Republican. Home: Brookline, Mass. Died Mar. 14, 1919.

STEWART, Alphonso Chase, lawyer; b. Lebanon, Tenn., Aug. 27, 1848; s. Gen. Alexander P. and Harriet Byron (Chase) S.; ed. in pvt. schs. of Tenn.; served in Stearns' 4th Tenn. Cav., C.S.A.; cadet on staff of Lt. Gen. Alex. P. Stewart; Ala. Mil. Corps Cadets; m. Elizabeth Smith, July 19, 1871. Admitted to bar, 1867; practiced in Tenn. and Miss. until 1873, then in St. Louis, Mo.; now mem. Stewart, Bryan & Williams; pres. Vinita Realty Co., Spring Avenue Realty Co., Champion Mfg. & Sales Co.; sec., treas. Southwestern Improvement Assn.; treas. Vaughn Rail Support Co. Pres. Bd. Police Commrs., St. Louis. Democrat. Presbyterian. Home: St. Louis, Mo. Died Apr. 1916.

STEWART, Charles Seaforth, col. U.S.A., retired, Sept. 16, 1886; b. at sea, April 11, 1823; s. Rev. Charles Samuel S. (chaplain U.S.N.) and Harriet Bradford (Tiffany) S.; m. Cecilia Sophia de Louville Tardy, April 15, 1857 (died 1886). Grad. West Point, 1846; asst. engr. fortifications New London and Boston Harbor, 1846-49; acting asst. prof. engineering, West Point, 1849-54; 1st lt. engrs., 1853; capt., 1860; maj., 1863; lt. col., 1867; col., 1882. Asst. engr., 1854-57; superintending engr. construction fortifications Boston Harbor, 1857-61; same, construction defenses Hampton Roads and Ft. Monroe, Va., 1861-64, in charge defenses, Delaware River and Bay, and of construction river and harbor work there, 1865-70. Bvtd. lt. col., Feb. 25, 1865, for long, faithful and efficient services; bvt. col., March 13, 1865, for gallant and meritorious services during the Rebellion—declined. Mem. bd. engrs. for fortifications on Pacific Coast, 1870-86; superintending engr. construction fortifications Fort Point, Point San José and Angel Island, San Francisco Harbor, 1870-86; Ft. San Diego, Calif., 1873-86; improvement San Diego Harbor, 1875-86; mem. various engring. bds., 1866-86; retired on own application having served 40 yrs. as commd. officer. Home: Cooperstown, N.Y. Died 1904.

STEWART, Charles West, librarian, historian; b. Champaign, Ill., Aug. 5, 1859; s. Hugh C. and Lavinia (Smith) S.; ed. U. of Illinois, 1875-77; U.S. Naval Acad., 1877-81, final graduation, 1883, after 2 yrs.' service afloat; m. Isabel M. Marble, Dec. 17, 1891 (died 1919); 1 son, Charles West (mem. Corps of Engineers, U.S. Army). U.S. asst. engineer with Mississippi River Commn., 1884-93; U.S. examiner in Patent Office, 1894-98; chief clk., Library and Naval War Records, 1898-1902; supt. Library and Naval War Records, 1902-20; again examiner in Patent Office, 1920-30. As representative of Navy Dept., selected site and design for Union Navy Memorial at Vicksburg Nat. Mil. Pk. Mem. U.S. Bd. on Geographic Names, 1907. Conglist. Mason. Author: Mississippi River St. Louis to the Sea, 1892; William Barker Cushing, 1912; John Paul Jones Commemoration, 1907; The Stars and Stripes from Washington to Wilson; The Stars and Stripes, a History of the United States Flag. Editor: Official Records Union and Confederate Navies, 1898-1920. Home: Washington, D.C. Died Oct. 3, 1929.

STEWART, David Denison, physician; b. Philadelphia, Oct. 10, 1858; s. Franklin and Amelia (Barron Jaques) S.; ed. pvt. schs. and tutors and grad. Jefferson Med. Coll. (1879), followed by hosp. and laboratory work; began practice in Phila. in 1885. Chief among the teaching and hosp. positions held at various times are: Physician to St. Christopher's Hosp. for Children, St. Mary's Hosp., Episcopal Hosp.; chief med. clinic, Jefferson Med. Coll.; lecturer on diseases of the nervous system, Jefferson Med. Coll.; demonstrator clin. med., Jefferson Med. Coll.; later lecturer on medicine, Jefferson Med. Coll.; prof. diseases stomach and intestines, Phila. Polyclinic. Published essays and research work on lead poisoning, diseases of the nervous system, diseases of the kidneys and on albumin testing; on the treatment of aneurism by electrolysis through wire; on diseases of the digestive system, etc. Contbr. to various Med. Works, Professional Jours., etc. Home: Philadelphia, Pa. Deceased.

STEWART, De Lisle, astronomer; b. Wabasha, Minn., Mar. 16, 1870; s. John and Malvina (Davis) S.; B.Litt., Carleton Coll., Northfield, Minn., 1891, Ph.D., 1895; m. Mary. E. Hannemann, March 16, 1896; children—Catharine (dec.), John De Lisle, Philip Bruce, Louis Hannemann, Mary Elizabeth (Mrs. William Girdner). Teacher district school, Fertile, Minnesota, 1891-92; assistant Goodsell Observatory R.R. Time Signals, 1893-95; assistant Arequipa br. Harvard Coll. Obs., 1896-1902; instr. in astronomy, U. of Cincinnati, 1903-08; asst. in Cincinnati Obs., same univ., 1903-10, also observer Internat. Latitude Service, 1905-10. Makes a specialty of astronomical photography. Fellow A.A.A.S.; organizer, 1911, and pres. Cincinnati Astron. Society. Devoted much time to preservation of H. H. Richardson's Romanesque arches of former Cincinnati Chamber of Commerce Bldg. and use in the building of a photographic observatory, construction of which began July 1935, under Louisa M. Colclesser bequest. Conglist. Author: Richardson, the Architect, 1914. Home: Cleves, Ohio. Died Feb. 8, 1941.

STEWART, Douglas; b. Pittsburgh, July 15, 1873; s. David Alexander and Nancy (Scott) S.; A.B., Yale, 1896; Sc.D., U. of Pittsburgh, 1924; m. Agnes C. Dickson, Apr. 22, 1902; children—Agnes C., Anne D. Traveled in various countries, 1896-98; asst. in administrative office, Carnegie Mus., 1898-1919, asst. dir., 1919, dir., 1922—. Asso. dir. Bur. of Prisoners Relief, Am. Red Cross, Washington, 1918-19. Republican. Episcopalian. Home: Pittsburgh, Pa. Died Apr. 21, 1926.

STEWART, Douglas Hunt, surgeon; b. Brooklyn, N.Y., Aug. 30, 1860; s. Samuel Brandt and Elizabeth Ball (Pond) S.; Coll. City of New York, 1877-79; M.D., Columbia, 1882; m. Annie MacCollum, Dec. 25, 1889; 1 son, Douglas MacC. Practiced at N.Y. City, 1882—. Head of Varicose Vein Clinic, Knickerbocker Hosp. Widely known for original methods in use of antiseptics, in wound healing, and in disease of veins. Fellow Am. Coll. Surgeons. Episcopalian. Mason. Home: New York, N.Y. Died Mar. 15, 1933.

STEWART, Edwin, paymaster gen. U.S.N.; b. New York, May 5, 1837; s. John and Mary (Aikman) S.; bro. of John Aikman S.; A.B., Williams, 1862, A.M., 1882 (LL.D., 1898); m. Laura S. Tufts, Aug. 24, 1865; 2d, Susan M. Estabrook May 17, 1877. Apptd. from N.Y., asst. p.-m., Sept. 9, 1861; p.-m., Apr. 14, 1862; war service in battles of Port Royal, Port Hudson and Mobile Bay; promoted pay-insp., Mar. 8, 1870; pay dir., Sept. 12, 1891; paymaster-gen., May 16, 1890; re-apptd., May 16, 1894; again re-apptd., May 16, 1898; rear adm., Mar. 3, 1899, and retired, May 5, 1899. Elected comdr. D.C. Commandery Loyal Legion, 1900, N.Y. Commandery, 1913-17; sr. v. comdr.-in-chief, 1912, 17; mem. Loyal Legion, Soc. Am. Wars. Home: South Orange, N.J. Died Feb. 28, 1933.

STEWART, Eliza Daniel ("Mother Stewart"), temperance evangelist; b. Piketown, O., April 25, 1816; d. James and Rebecca Daniel; edn. in seminaries, Ohio; became teacher, m. 1848, Hiram Stewart. Active in sanitary and relief work during Civil war; received name of "Mother Stewart" from Union soldiers; platform lecturer; leader and organizer of Women's Crusade against liquor saloons; introduced W.C.T.U. work into Great Britain and the South. Author: Memories of the Crusade, 1888; The Crusader in Great Britain, 1893. Home: Springfield, O. Died 1908.

STEWART, Ethelbert, statistician; b. Chicago, Ill., Apr. 22, 1857; s. Corydon Forbes and Mary A. (Johnston) S.; ed. pub. and high schs., Ill.; m. Lettie M. Cox, Dec. 27, 1879 (died 1917); children—Zelda Ermine, Elliott Walter, Ruby Gay, Estelle May, Margaret Winfield, H. D. Lloyd, Lettie Ethel. Editor various newspapers, until 1887; became connected with U.S. Bur. of Labor, 1887; apptd. spl. agt. Bur. of Labor, 1889; sent to Europe by Tariff Bd., 1911, to report on "Schedule K" (cost of prodn. of wool goods); chief statistician Children's Bur., 1912-13; same for Bur. of Labor Statistics, July 1913-June 30, 1918; apptd. mem. Meat Commn., Apr. 1918. Dir. of investigation and inspection service under Dept. of Labor, War Labor Emergency Adminstrn., July 1, 1918-June 30, 1919; sent to Eng. by Dept. of Labor on orgn. industrial conf. League of Nations, July 1919; U.S. commr. of labor statistics, 1920-32, retired. Visited prin. countries of S.A. with sec. of labor, studying immigration, labor conditions and legislation, 1924; apptd. rep. Dept. of Labor at Internat. Inst. of Statistics conv., Rome, Sept. 1925; Am. rep., 4th Internat. Conf. Labor Statisticians, Geneva, 1931, also Porto Rico labor Statisticians, Geneva, 1931, also Puerto Rico labor Congress, 14th Ill. Dist., 1888, Sec.-treas. Internat. Assn. Industrial Accident Bds. and Commns. Fellow Am. Statis Assn. Home: Washington, D.C. Died Oct. 13, 1936.

STEWART, Francis Torrens, surgeon; b. Philadelphia, Pa., Dec. 2, 1877; s. William Francis and Emily (Randal) S.; M.D., Jefferson Med. Coll., 1898; m. Matilda Keller, June 9, 1901. Prof. clin. surgery, Jefferson Med. Coll., 1910—; surgeon to Jefferson, Pa., and Germantown hosps. Republican. Presbyn. Author: Manual of Surgery, 1908. Home: Philadelphia, Pa. Died Feb. 4, 1920.

STEWART, George Black, theologian; b. Columbus, O., Feb. 28, 1854; s. Alexander Adams and Louisa Susannah (Black) S.; A.B., Princeton, 1876, A.M., 1879; attended McCormick Theol. Sem.; grad. Auburn Sem., 1879; D.D., Washington and Jefferson, 1887, LL.D., 1901; S.T.D., Hobart, 1912; m. Mary Adeline Thompson, June 18, 1879 (died 1903); m. 2d, Ella L. Hart, Dec. 7, 1914. Ordained Presbyn. ministry, 1879; pastor Calvary Ch., Auburn, 1878-84, Market Sq. Ch., Harrisburg, Pa., 1884-99; pres. and prof. practical theology, Auburn Theol. Sem., 1899-1926, now pres. emeritus and prof. practical theology. A founder, and for 5 years pres., Pa. Chautauqua; pres. Pa. Christian Endeavor Union, 2 yrs.; trustee Wilson Coll., 1884-1900, Princeton U., 1887—. Author: Centennial Memorial, English Presbyterian Congregation, Harrisburg, Pa., 1894; Life of Jesus for Juniors, 1896; A Study of the Life of Jesus, 1907; Efficiency Tests for Pastors and Churches, 1915. Home: Auburn, N.Y. Died June 23, 1932.

STEWART, George Craig, bishop; b. Saginaw, E.S., Mich., Aug. 18, 1879; s. George Forbes and Katharine (Craig) S.; grad. Evanston Acad., 1898; B.A., Northwestern Univ., 1902; grad. Western Theol. Sem., Chicago, 1903; post-grad. work, Northwestern, 1903-04; L.H.D., Kenyon Coll., 1915; D.D., Northwestern, 1917; S.T.D., Western Theol. Sem., 1930; (hon.) D.D. King's College, Halifax, N.S., 1937; m. Mary Gertrude Clyde, Mar. 31, 1902; children—Katharine Craig (dec.), John Clyde, George Craig, Jr. Ordained M.E. ministry, 1900; pastor Calumet Heights Ch., Chicago, 1897-1900, St. Stephen's Ch., Chicago, 1900-02; deacon and priest P.E. Ch., 1903; rector, Glencoe, 1903-04, St. Luke's Ch., Evanston, 1904-30; bishop of Chicago, 1930—. Sec. War Commn. P.E. Ch., 1918; chaplain, Evacuation Hosp. No. 6, A.E.F. Del. Gen. Conv. P.E. Ch., 6 times; spl. preacher Princeton, Chicago, Ia., Wis., Mich. univs.; lecturer homiletics, Western Theol. Sem. Trustee Northwestern U., Seabury-Western Theol. Sem. (Chicago); mem. Nat. Council, P.E. Ch., Commn. on World Conf. Faith and Order, Provisional Com. of World Council, Edinburgh Conf. Continuation Com., Boy Scouts Evanston Council (vice-pres.). Fellow Am. Ecclesiological Society. Democrat. Author: Why Baptize Babies?, 1911; The Colors of the Republic, 1915; Evolution a Witness to God, 1921; What Is My Life Work?, 1925; Spanish Summer, 1928; Six Altars, 1929; The Call of Christ, 1931; The Face of Christ, 1932; The Victory of Faith, 1935. Asso. editor Anglican Theol. Rev. Home: Evanston, Ill. Died May 2, 1940.

STEWART, George David, surgeon; b. Cumberland Co., N.S., Dec. 28, 1862; s. Daniel and Mary J. (McCallum) S.; ed. Teachers Coll. (Truro, N.S.), St. Francis Xavier Coll.; M.D., Bellevue Hosp. Med. Coll. (New York U.), 1889; m. Ida M. Robb, 1890. Interne Bellevue Hosp., 1890, later becoming prof. surgery, Bellevue Hosp. Med. Coll. Fellow Am. Coll. Surgeons (pres.). Home: New York, N.Y. Died Mar. 9, 1933.

STEWART, George H., judge; b. Connorsville, Ind., Feb. 26, 1858; s. Matthew R. and Nancy (Harlan) S.; B.S., Valparaiso (Ind.) Coll., 1879, LL.B., 1881; m. Agnes L. Sheetz, July 26, 1886. Pros. atty. Frontier Co., Neb., 1887-88; mem. Ida. Senate, 1903-04; dist. judge, 3d Jud. Dist. of Ida., 1897-1907; asso. justice Supreme Ct., 1907-13; chief justice, 1911-12. Republican. Trustee Albion State Normal Sch., 1903-05; mem. Bd. of Edn., Boise, 1895-1903. Author: Digest of Supreme Court Decisions, Idaho. Home: Boise, Ida. Died Sept. 24, 1914.

STEWART, George Neil, univ. prof.; b. London, Can., Apr. 18, 1860; s. James Innes and Catherine (Sutherland) S.; A.M., U. of Edinburgh, 1883, B.S., 1886, D.Sc., 1887, M.B., C.M., 1889, M.D., 1891, LL.D., 1920; D.P.H., U. of Cambridge, 1890; married. Demonstrator of physiology, Owens Coll., Manchester, Eng., 1887-89; George Henry Lewes student, U. of Cambridge, 1889-93; examiner in physiology, U. of Aberdeen, 1891-94; instr. Harvard Med. Sch., 1893-94; prof. physiology and histology, Western Reserve U., 1894-1903; prof. physiology, U. of Chicago, 1903-07; prof. exptl. medicine, Western Reserve U., 1907—. Author of many original papers, 1887—. Home: Cleveland, O. Died May 28, 1930.

STEWART, George Taylor, physician, surgeon; b. New Milford, Conn., Nov. 25, 1855; s. Thomas Elliott and Hariette Allen (Taylor) S.; attended Yale, 1873-74; A.B., Trinity Coll., Hartford, 1878, A.M., 1881; M.D., Hahnemann Med. Coll., Phila., 1882; M.D., Montreal Homœ. Coll. Phys. and Surg., 1896; m. May A. Fargo, June 15, 1887. Chief of staff, Metropolitan Hosp., 1890-1900; gen. supt. Bellevue and allied hosps., 1900-02; supt. Hosp. Dept. of Health, New York. Home: New York, N.Y. Died July 25, 1940.

STEWART, Gideon Tabor, lawyer; b. Johnstown, N.Y., Aug. 7, 1824; ed. Oberlin Coll.; admitted Ohio bar, 1846; Supreme Court U.S. bar, 1866; m. Abby N. Simmons, 1857. Auditor Huron Co., O., 1850-56; editor Dubuque, Ia., Times, 1861-65; Norwalk Reflector; Toledo Blade; Toledo Commercial; candidate (Prohibition ticket) V.P. U.S., 1876; 3 times for gov. Ohio, 9 times for judge Supreme Court, 3 times for judge circuit court; was Grand Worthy Patriarch, Sons of Temperance; 3 times Grand Worthy Chief Templar, Good Templars of Ohio; life mem. Bible Society. Pres. Huron County, O., Law Library Assn.; past pres. Fireland Hist. Soc., past pres. Whittlesey Acad. Arts and Sciences. Home: Pasadena, Calif. Died 1909.

STEWART, Graeme, merchant; b. Chicago, Ill., Aug. 30, 1853; ed. pub. schs., Dyrenfurth Handel Schule, and Chicago Univ. Began business life, 1869, as office boy in wholesale grocery house, which he afterward served as clerk and salesman; partner, 1880—, W. M. Hoyt Co., wholesale grocers. Mem. and pres. Bd. of Edn., Chicago, 1882-88. Mem. Nat. Rep. Com. for Ill., 1900—; Republican candidate for mayor of Chicago, 1903. Home: Chicago, Ill. Died 1905.

STEWART, Humphrey John, musician, composer; b. London, Eng., May 22, 1854; hon. Mus.Doc., U. of the Pacific, Calif., 1898. Organist chs. in San Francisco, 1886-1901; organist Trinity Ch., Boston, 1901-02, St. Dominic's Ch., San Francisco, 1902-14; official organist, Panama-Calif. Expn., San Diego, 1915. Solo organist, Buffalo Expn., 1901; teacher of music. One of founders of Am. Guild Organists (gold medal for composition, 1900). Composer: His Majesty, comic opera, 1890; The Conspirators, comic opera, 1900; The Nativity, oratorio, 1888; orchestral suite, "Montezuma," 1903; Mass in D minor, 1907; orchestral suite, "Scenes in California," 1906; Mass in G, 1911; King Hal, romantic opera, 1911; The Hound of Heaven (oratorio); Ballet Suite (for organ); Flag of the Brave (patriotic cantata); Scenes from Shakespeare's "The Tempest" (suite for organ); also numerous songs, pianoforte and violin pieces, part songs, ch. music, and Requiem Mass, dedicated to the Pope, 1919. Municipal organist, San Diego, Calif., 1915—. Presented with the official flag of the City of New York, June 1921, "for distinguished ability as a recital organist." Composed music for Bohemian Club Grove play, "St. John of Nepomuk," 1921. Decorated Comdr. Order of the Holy Sepulchre, by Pope Pius XI, 1930. Home: San Diego, Calif. Died Dec. 28, 1932.

STEWART, James Fleming, congressman; b. Paterson, N.J., June 15, 1851; ed. public and private schools, and at Univ. City of New York; grad. Law School of latter, 1870; practiced law, New York, 1870-75; then in Paterson; 3 times apptd. recorder (criminal magistrate) of Paterson. Mem. Congress, 1895-1903, 5th N.J. dist. Republican. Chmn. Com. on Expenditures of Navy Dept., 55th Congress. Home: Paterson, N.J. Died 1904.

STEWART, John, judge; b. Shippensburg, Pa., Nov. 4, 1839; s. Alexander (M.D.) and Elizabeth (Hamill) S.; A.B., Princeton, 1857 (LL.D., 1907); m. Jane Holmes Larmour, Sept. 7, 1862. Admitted to bar, 1860, and practiced at Chambersburg, Pa. Mem. Pa. Constl. Conv., 1872; mem. Pa. Senate, 1880-84; pres. judge 39th Jud. Dist. of Pa., 1888-1906; justice Supreme Ct. of Pa., 1906-27. Was adj. 126th Pa. Vols., Aug. 7, 1862-May 7, 1863. Home: Chambersburg, Pa. Deceased.

STEWART, John Aikman, banker; b. N.Y. City, Aug. 26, 1822; s. John and Mary (Aikman) S.; student Columbia, 1840, hon. A.M., 1899; m. Mary Olivia Capron, Nov. 25, 1890. On engr. constrn. corps N.Y., L.E.&W. R.R., 1840-42; clk. bd. of edn., New York, 1842-50; actuary U.S. Life Ins. Co., 1850-53; organized U.S. Trust Co., and was its sec., 1853-64, pres. 1865-1902, chmn. bd. trustees, 1902—. Asst. treas. U.S., 1864-65. Trustee Princeton U., 1868—. Home: New York, N.Y. Died Dec. 17, 1926.

STEWART, John Appleton, mfr.; b. Morrisville, N.Y., Nov. 8, 1865; s. James Steven and Emeline Elizabeth (Tucker) S.; ed. Cazenovia (N.Y.) Sem. and Ft. Edward Collegiate Inst.; LL.D., U. of Toronto, 1915; m. Alice Josephine Collins, Feb. 22, 1900 (died 1915); m. 2d, Ida Fassoli (b. Venice, Italy, g.d. of the painter). Dir. Am. Ammone Co., Nat. Art Film Assn. Pres. Rep. League of Clubs State of N.Y., Internat. League for Highway Improvement; a founder N.Y. State Sch. of Agr., at Morrisville, N.Y.; chmn. bd. governors Sulgrave Instn.; chmn. Inst. for Pictorial Edn.; v.p. Nat. Council Am. Patriots; exec. chmn. Am. Soc. (for nat. unity). Conglist. Mason. Home: Brooklyn, N.Y. Died Oct. 31, 1928.

STEWART, John Lammey, economist; b. Philadelphia, Pa., Nov. 18, 1867; s. John and Anne (Lammey) S.; grad. Central High Sch., Phila., 1887; A.B., U. of Pa., 1889; studied Wharton Sch. of Finance and Economy, same univ.; m. Mary Eno Mumford, June 18, 1895. Prof. economics and history, Lehigh U., 1898—; also dir. University Library and dir. Coll. of Business Administration. Mem. Pub. Service Commn. of Pa., 1923—. Republican. Episcopalian. Home: Bethlehem, Pa. Died Apr. 11, 1927.

STEWART, John Leighton, editor, publisher; b. Bakerstown, Pa., Aug. 12, 1876; s. William Grove and Mary Jane (Wright) S.; grad. Redstone Acad., Uniontown, Pa., 1895; A.B., Washington and Jefferson Coll., Washington, Pa., 1899; studied law Harvard, 1900-02; m. Margaretta Murdoch Donnan, Apr. 20, 1904; 1 daughter, Lucy Donnan (Mrs. Cecil P. Northrop). Has been editor, publisher and pres. Washington (Pa.) Observer and The Reporter (daily newspapers), 1912—; pres. The Tribune (Beaver Falls). Pres. Washington Sem., Washington Hosp., trustee Washington & Jefferson Coll. Republican. Presbyn. Home: Washington, Pa. Died May 31, 1940.

STEWART, John Minor, lawyer; b. Des Moines Co., Ia., Dec. 14, 1856; s. James Andrew and Lucinda (Cowles) S.; student Parsons Coll., Fairfield, Ia., 1 yr., Kirksville (Mo.) Normal Sch. 1 yr.; m. Alice W. Warner, 1881; children—Frantz E., Helen B. (Mrs. Earl B. Day), Marcia L. (Mrs. W. Mayo), Donald W.; m. 2d, Harriet Gilrye Muir, June 1, 1915. Admitted to Neb. bar, 1880, and began practice at Minden; moved to Lincoln, 1887. County atty. Kearny Co., Neb., 1881-85; mayor of Minden, 1883; asst. atty. gen. of Neb., 1887; city atty. Lincoln, 1907-11. Chmn. com. exec. dept., Neb. Constl. Conv., 1920. Home: Lincoln, Neb. Died Sept. 15, 1940.

STEWART, John Truesdale, civil engr.; b. Loda, Ill., Jan. 13, 1868; s. William R. and Nancy (Barr) S.; B.S., in C.E., U. of Ill., 1893, C.E., 1909; m. Ida Belle Wilson, Jan. 1, 1900. In pvt. practice to 1897; field asst., topographic corps, U.S. Geol. Survey, 1898-1903; drainage engr., U.S. Dept. Agr., 1904-08; prof. and chief div. of agrl. engring., U. of Minn., 1908-17. Cadet officer U. of Ill.; bvt. capt. Ill. N.G., 1893; organized and drilled company for Spanish-Am. War, 1898, but not called into service; maj., Engrs. U.S.R., on active duty, May 26, 1917; lt. col. engrs., Oct. 18, 1918; hon. disch., Oct. 13, 1919; lt. col. E.O.R.C., Jan. 31, 1920, col. Jan. 14, 1924. In charge of ednl. activities in schools and colleges for Portland Cement Assn., Jan. 1921-Mar. 1922; consulting engr., drainage and wet land development, Apr. 1922—. Presbyn. Senior author of Engineering on the Farm. Home: St. Paul, Minn. Died June 9, 1928.

STEWART, John Wolcott, governor; b. Middlebury, Vt., Nov. 24, 1825; s. Ira and Elizabeth (Hubbell) S.; A.B., Middlebury Coll., 1846, A.M., 1849 (LL.D., 1876); m. Emma Battell, Nov. 21, 1860. Admitted to bar, 1850, and practiced at Middlebury. Pros. atty., 1852-54; mem. Vt. Ho. of Rep., 1856-57, 1864-67, 1876 (speaker, 1865-67, 1876), Senate, 1861-62; gov. of Vt., 1870-72; mem. 48th to 51st Congresses (1883-91), 1st Vt. Dist.; apptd. U.S. senator to succeed Senator Redfield Proctor, deceased, and served Mar. 24 to Oct. 21, 1908. Republican. Home: Middlebury, Vt. Died Oct. 29, 1915.

STEWART, Joseph, exec. asst. to postmaster gen.; b. Humboldt, Kansas, Oct. 30, 1859; s. Watson and Elizabeth (Tipton) S.; pub. sch. and business coll. edn.; LL.B., Columbian (now George Washington) U., 1884, LL.M., 1885; m. Jessie Stewart Bailey, Apr. 9, 1887; children—Elmer, Phyllis Patrecia. In ins. and banking business, Humboldt, 1880-82; clerk in Postoffice Dept., Washington, 1882-87; practiced law at Kansas City, 1887-90; reëntered govt. service, 1891; apptd. asst. supt. ry. adjustments, P.O. Dept., July 1, 1902, also law clerk, July 1, 1905; apptd. supt. ry. adjustments, July 19, 1907, 2d asst. postmaster gen., Sept. 29, 1908, spl. asst. to the atty. general, Sept. 1, 1915, exec. asst. to postmaster gen., July 1924. Head U.S. delegation to Universal Postal Congress, Stockholm, Sweden, 1924, U.S. del. Congress Commn. of Study, Cortina, Italy, 1925. Head U.S. delegation, Pan.-Am. Postal Congress, Mexico, 1926. Republican. Unitarian. Author: The Esoteric Art of Living, 1900; Realization (3 vols.), 1901, 02, 03. Editor: Digest of Decisions of United States and Other Courts Affecting the Postoffice Dept. and Postal Service, 1905. Home: Washington, D.C. Died July 1, 1929.

STEWART, Joseph Spencer, univ. prof.; b. Oxford, Ga., Sept. 23, 1863; s. Joseph Spencer and Rebecca Hannah (Starr) S.; A.B., Emory Coll., 1883; M.A., U. of Ga., 1897, Ped.D., 1913; m. Selma Hahr, Aug. 19, 1890; children—Alice Hahr, Rebecca Starr, Joseph Spencer, Selma Hahr (dec.), Frederick Rhinhold, Franz von Scheele. Prin. Cherokee Inst., Cave Spring, Ga., 1883-89; pres. Harwood Sem., Marietta, Ga., 1889-91; organized, and supt. Marietta pub. sch. system, 1891-1907; pres. N.Ga. Agrl. Coll., 1897-1903; prof., secondary edn., U. of Ga., and state high sch. insp., 1903—. Apptd. by Gov. Terrell to plan curriculum of congressional dist. agrl. schs., 1897; secured constl. amendments making high schs. a part of ednl. system, 1910; organized state corn and cotton clubs for boys, 1905. State examiner for entrance to medical colls.; v.p. Southern Assn. Colls., 1921; mem. reviewing com. of N.E.A. com. on reorgn. of secondary edn., 1914-24; founder, and pres. Ga. High Sch. Assn.; mem. fraternal relations com. Southern and N. Central Assn., 1913-22; dir. U. Summer School, 1922—. Democrat. Methodist. Author: Georgia Oratory. Editor The High School Quarterly, 1912—. Home: Athens, Ga. Died Mar. 25, 1934.

STEWART, Lispenard, lawyer; b. in Westchester Co., N.Y., June 19, 1855; A.B., Yale, 1876; LL.B., Columbia, 1878. Trustee the Rhinelander estate, 1878—; treas. Rhinelander Real Estate Co. Dir. New York Zoöl. Soc.; trustee Fulton Trust Co., Roosevelt Hosp., 1909-19, New York Eye and Ear Hosp., 1879—. Mem. N.Y. Senate, 1889-90; presdl. elector, 1888; pres. State Commn. of Prisons, 1895-1903. Identified with charitable, philanthropic and ednl. work. Home: New York, N.Y. Died Oct. 15, 1927.

STEWART, Malcolm Montrose, foreign trade adviser; b. Charlotte, N.C., June 22, 1877; s. George and Annie Margaret (Riegler) S.; prep. edn., Univ. High Sch., Birmingham, Ala.; grad. Meth. Tr. Sch., Nashville, Tenn.; m. Viola Lester Taylor, Jan. 6, 1902. Journeyman printer until 1902; contracting business, 1902-09; ordained ministry M.E. Ch., S., holding pastorates in and nr. Nashville while attending sch., 1909-11; teacher of Biblical history, Payne Coll., Augusta, Ga., 1911-12; missionary, Isle of Pines, 1912-15; organizer, 1915, operator, 1915-17, Santa Fe Packing and Development Co.; mgr. Foreign and Domestic Commerce Dept. of Cincinnati Chamber Commerce, 1919—; sec.-treas. Cincinnati Sales Executives Council; sec. Cincinnati Foreign Trade Club. Pvt. Inf., Spanish-Am. War; pvt., sergt., lt. and capt. cav., Ala. N.G., 1899-1909; held unlimited commn. under Pres. Menocal for suppression of German espionage in Cuba, 1917; same, U.S. Dept. Justice, in charge Muscle Shoals dist., 1918. Democrat. Mason. Lecturer. Editor of Foreign Trade-Merchant Marine News. Home: Beaufort, Ladies Island, S.C. Died Feb. 27, 1937.

STEWART, Merch Bradt, army officer; b. Mitchell Sta., Va., June 24, 1875; s. James Robinson and Grace Alice (Bushong) S.; prep. edn. Glens Falls (N.Y.) Acad.; grad. U.S. Mil. Acad., 1896; m. Nan Wheelihan, Feb. 16, 1898; 1 son, Peter. Commd. add. 2d lt. inf., June 12, 1896; promoted through grades to brig. gen. Dec. 16, 1925; maj. gen., Oct. 2, 1927; retired, Oct. 3, 1927; col., later brig. gen. N.A., Aug. 15, 1917-Aug. 15, 1919. Active service in Spanish-Am. War, Philippine Insurrection and World War; mem. Gen. Staff 4 yrs.; mem. Inf. Equipment Bd., 1909-10, Inf. Drill Regulation Bd., 1911, Land Defense Bd., Panama Canal, 1915-16; comdt. cadets, U.S. Mil. Acad., 1923-26; supt. of same, 1926-27, retired. Awarded D.S.M. (U.S.); Officer Legion of Honor and Croix de Guerre, with Palm

(French). Presbyn. Author: The Nth Foot in War, 1898; Military Character, Habit, Deportment, Courtesy and Discipline, 1913; Physical Development of the Infantry Soldier, 1913. Co-author: Junior Military Manual, 1917; Thirty Minute Talks, 1920; The Drillmaster, 1921. Died July 3, 1934.

STEWART, Nathaniel Bacon, consul gen.; b. Taylor Co., Ga., Jan. 4, 1871; s. Bennett and Mary (Turner) S.; A.B., U. of Ga., 1893; student George Washington U. Law Sch.; m. Lucy Cobb Taylor, Oct. 25, 1911. Clerk U.S. Civ. Service, Navy Dept., Washington, 1893-97, War Dept., 1897-99; chief Div. of Accts., Engr. Dept., Havana, Cuba, 1899-1901; paymaster same dept., 1902; provincial treas. Philippine Islands, 1902-07; consul at Castellamare di Stabia, Italy, 1907-08, Madras, India, 1908-10, Durban, Natal, 1910-13, Milan, Italy, 1913-14; apptd. consul gen. at large, July 17, 1914; consul gen., Mexico City, 1920-21; chief of consular personnel, Dept. of State, 1921-23; consul gen. at Yokohama, Japan, Sept.-Dec. 1923, Tokyo, 1923-25; apptd. foreign service officer of Class one, July 1, 1924; consul gen. at Barcelona, Jan. 7, 1926—. Home: Americus, Ga. Died Apr. 17, 1931.

STEWART, Oliver Wayne, prohibitionist; b. Mercer Co., Ill., May 22, 1867; s. Charles and Eliza J. S.; A.B., Eureka Coll., 1890, LL.D., 1916; ordained Ch. of Christ ministry, 1887; m. Ella J. Seass, Aug. 20, 1890. Lecturer; always interested in temperance work; sec. of Dist. Lodge, I.O.G.T., 1887; candidate for Congress (Prohibition), 9th Ill. Dist., 1890; sec. Ill. Christian Endeavor Union, 1893-95; pres. same, 1895-97; mem. Ill. State Prohibition Com., 1894-1908; chmn. Ill. State Prohibition Conv., 1896, 1908, 16, Nat. Prohibition Conv., Pittsburgh, Pa., 1896; chmn. Ill. State Prohibition Com., 1896-1900; elected chmn. Nat. Prohibition Com., Dec. 1899, to fill vacancy; reelected nat. chmn. Nat. Prohibition Com., 1900 and 1904; resigned Jan. 1905; elected as Prohibitionist, 1902, as mem. Ill. Ho. of Rep., from 5th Dist., serving 1903; candidate for mayor of Chicago (prohibition), 1905. Pres. Prohibition Trust Fund Assn. of New York, 1900-12; chmn. Nat. Prohibitionist Extension Com., 1907-11; field sec. Nat. Temperance Soc. of New York, 1910-12. Mem. Flying Squadron of America, visiting 255 Am. cities, 1915-20; v.p., 1915-20, pres., Aug. 1, 1920 (succeeding J. Frank Hanly, deceased), of Flying Squadron Foundation, Inc., and editor Nat. Enquirer; engaged in nation-wide law enforcement campaign, 1921-29; v.p. United Com. for Prohibition Enforcement, 1924-25; attended Rep. and Dem. nat. convs., 1928, as mem. exec. com. of nat. orgn. for dry planks; a founder of Nat. Conf. of Prohibition Orgns. Supporting 18th Amendment, 1928, and represents Flying Squadron on same; an organizer, 1929, of Coöp. Com. for Prohibition Enforcement (exec. com.). Mem. Nat. Temperance Council, 1913—; chmn. Prohibition Nat. Campaign Com., 1916; mem. Nat. Legislative Conf., rep. Flying Squadron Foundation. A founder and v.chmn. Allied Forces for Prohibition, formed 1931; founder and editor of Allied News—organ of Allied Forces; mem. Nat. Bd. of Strategy, created to unite dry forces for campaign of 1932; in June 1932, reopened Flying Squadron headquarters in Indianapolis and renewed publication of Nat. Enquirer as part of campaign for orgn. of local socs. on behalf of nat. prohibition, conducting nationwide speaking campaign through 1933; led Flying Squadron Campaigners in nation-wide tour, 1934-35. Home: Chicago, Ill. Died Feb. 15, 1937.

STEWART, Robert, missionary; b. Sidney, O., Jan. 31, 1839; s. James Harris (M.D.) and Jane Abigail (Fuller) S.; A.B. (1st honors), Jefferson Coll., Pa., 1859; grad. U.P. Theol. Sem., Pa., 1865; (D.D., Washington and Jefferson, 1875; D.D., Westminster, 1875, LL.D., 1906); m. Eliza Frazier, d. Rev. J. B. Johnston, of St. Clairsville, O., Dec. 1, 1881. Ordained U.P. minister, 1866; stated supply Ashland and Savannah, O., 1865-66, Dayton, 1866-68; stated supply and pastor Davenport, N.Y., 1868-72; prof. Newburg (N.Y.) Theol. Sem., 1872-78; editor Evang. Repository and S.S. periodicals, 1879-80; mem. bd. dirs. of foreign missions, U.P. Ch., 1880-81; commr. to visit missions in Egypt and India, 1880, 81; theol. prof. and missionary in India, 1881—; prin. Theol. Sem., U.P. Synod of the Punjab. Republican. Author: Life and Work in India, 1896; Apostolic and Indian Missions Compared, 1903; Ancestors and Children of Col. Daniel Fisher and Sybil Draper, 1899; Col. George Steuart and Margaret Harris, their Ancestors and Descendants, 1907; Introduction to Books of the New Testament (Urdu tongue), 1909; Our Ecclesiastical and Missionary Blessings and Our Consequent Duty, 1913. Translator (into Urdu): Schaff's History of the Christian Church, several vols., 1892-1911. Home: Gujranwala, India. Died Oct. 23, 1915.

STEWART, Rowe, newspaper pub.; b. Phila., Pa., Nov. 5, 1876; s. Samuel Jackson and Mary Alice (Walton) S.; ed. Central High Sch. and Pierce Business Coll., Phila.; m. May Belle Diehl, Sept. 8, 1909; children—James Rowe, John Howard. Began as office boy, Phila. Record, 1895; with Phila. North American, 1904-09; adv. mgr. Phila. Evening Times, 1909; with Tracy, Parry & Stewart, adv. agts., 1910-13; adv. mgr. Phila. Record, 1913-23, gen. mgr. 1924; pres. Record Pub. Co., 1925-29; pres. Stewart-Jordan Co., advt. specialists, Phila. V.p. Chamber Commerce of Phila., Benjamin Franklin Memorial, Inc. Chmn. bd. Taxpayers Forum of Pa. Decorated Order of Social and Civic Merit (France). Democrat. Presbyn. Mason. Home: Philadelphia, Pa. Died May 12, 1940.

STEWART, Russell C., lawyer; b. Easton, Pa., Sept. 2, 1859; s. Charles and Anna E. (Chidsey) S.; A.B., Lafayette Coll., 1878, A.M., 1881; studied Columbia Law Sch.; (LL.D., Muhlenberg Coll., 1917, Lafayette, 1919); m. Mattie M. Seitz, Jan. 25, 1885. Admitted to bar, 1881; dist. atty., Northampton Co., Pa., 1886-89; Rep. candidate for Congress, 1900; judge 3d Jud. Dist. of Pa., Dec. 31, 1906—. Home: Easton, Pa. Died Feb. 5, 1942.

STEWART, Samuel Vernon, judge; b. Monroe County, O., Aug. 2, 1872; s. John W. and Maria A. (Carle) S.; Kan. State Normal Sch., Emporia, 2 yrs.; LL.B., Law Dept., U. of Kan., 1898; m. Stella Baker, Apr. 27, 1905. Began practice of law at Virginia City, Mont., July 1, 1898; city atty., Virginia City, 5 yrs.; co. atty., Madison Co., 2 terms, 4 yrs.; chmn. Dem. State Central Com., 1910-12; gov. of Mont., 2 terms, 1913-21; city atty., Helena, 1922-27; was mem. Stewart & Brown; asso. justice Supreme Court of Mont., term 1933-39. Mason, Elk, Eagle, Woodman. Home: Helena, Mont. Died Sept. 15, 1939.

STEWART, Thomas Jamison, soldier; b. Belfast, Ireland, Sept. 11, 1848; s. John and Eliza. S.; came to America with parents, 1849; ed. pub. schs., Norristown, Pa.; m. Mrs. A. R. Weaver, Nov. 28, 1901. Pvt. 138th Pa. Vols., Civil War; officer N. G. of Pa., 1868—; sec. internal affairs of Pa., 1886-95; adj. gen. of Pa., Jan. 1895—. Asst. adj. gen. G.A.R. of Pa., 1882-89; comdr. Pa. Dept. G.A.R., 1890; adj. gen. G.A.R., 1898-1900, comdr.-in-chief, 1902-03. Republican. Home: Harrisburg, Pa. Died Sept. 11, 1917.

STEWART, William Henry, chaplain U.S.N.; b. Andover, Mass., July 11, 1831; s. John and Dorcas (Baxter) S.; m. Roline Mayo, July 11, 1860; m. 2d, Azuba E. Tolles, Jan. 20, 1885. Apptd. chaplain U.S.N., Mar. 10, 1863; served at naval sta., Cairo, Ill., 1863-65, Naval Acad., 1866-67, and later on various vessels and at various stas.; retired, July 11, 1893; advanced to rank of rear adm., retired, June 29, 1906; for services during Civil War. Home: De Land, Fla. Died Mar. 31, 1913.

STEWART, William Lyman, oil producer; b. Titusville, Pa., 1868; s. Lyman and Sarah Adelaide (Burrows) S.; student U. of Calif.; m. Mrs. M. E. Arnold, 1894. Pres. Union Oil Co. of Calif., Los Angeles. Presbyterian. Died June 21, 1930.

STEWART, William Morris, U.S. senator, lawyer; b. Lyons, N.Y., Aug. 9, 1827; early childhood in Ohio; academic edn. Entered Yale Coll., but was attracted by gold discoveries to Calif., arriving in San Francisco, May 1850; m. Annie E., d. Gov. and Senator Foote, of Miss. Mined in Nevada Co., and accumulated some money; studied law; admitted to bar, 1852; dist. atty., 1852; atty. gen. of Calif., 1854; removed to Virginia City, Nev., 1860; practiced law; became interested in Comstock lode. Mem. Territorial council, 1861; mem. Constl. Conv., 1863; U.S. senator, 1863-75; resumed practice of law, 1875-87; U.S. senator again, 1887-1905. Home: Bullfrog, Nev. Died 1909.

STEWART, William Rhinelander, humanitarian; b. New York, Dec. 3, 1852; s. Lispenard and Mary Rogers (Rhinelander) S.; Anthon's and Charlier's schs., New York; LL.B., Columbia Sch. of Law, 1873; M.A., honoris causa, Columbia, 1913. Practiced law for several yrs. in office of Platt, Gerard & Buckley; retired from practice to devote attention as executor, trustee, or to works of philanthropy; pres. Rhinelander Real Estate Co., 1908—; trustee Greenwich Savings Bank, 1893—; dir. Corn Exchange Bank, 1897—. Apptd. by Gov. Cornell commr. for 1st Jud. Dist. on State Bd. of Charities, May 31, 1882, and has served continuously (pres. of bd. for 25 years). Organizer, 1900, of State Conf. Charities and Correction (pres. 1903); an organizer N.Y. City Conf. Charities and Correction, 1910; chmn. state commn. for establishment of Letchworth Village (farm colony for the feeble minded); identified with other charitable instns. Elected pres. 25th Nat. Conf. Charities and Correction, New York, 1898 (medal struck by Am. Numismatic Soc. and only copy in gold presented Mr. Stewart by Com. of One Hundred). Originator, 1889, and treas. of com. which erected Washington Arch, Washington Sq., New York, and transferred same to Mayor Strong at pub. ceremonies, May 4, 1895. Mem. Co. K, 7th Regt., N.G.N.Y., 1871-79; mem. Citizens' Com. of Seventy which elected Mayor Strong, 1894. Episcopalian; jr. warden Grace Ch. and treas., 1893-1913. Author: The Philanthropic Works of Josephine Shaw Lowell, 1911; Grace Church and Old New York, 1924. Home: New York, N.Y. Died Sept. 4, 1929.

STEWART, William Shaw, physician; b. Stewart's Sta., nr. Pittsburgh, Nov. 13, 1838; s. John and Margaret (Shaw) S.; g.s. Capt. John S., of Revolutionary army; grad. Jefferson Coll., Pa., 1860; Jefferson Med. Coll., 1863 (A.M., Washington and Jefferson Coll.); m. Delia Allman, Nov. 14, 1872. Served asst. surgeon, U.S.A., in Civil War, holding many responsible positions in med. service of army; was offered commn. as full surgeon to remain in army, but established practice in Phila. at close of war. One of founders, and was 10 yrs. dean and prof. obstetrics and clinical gynecology (prof. emeritus), Medico-Chirurgical Coll., Phila.; one of founders (1st v.p.) Am. Acad. Medicine; dir. pub. schs., 9 yrs. Republican. Presbyn. Home: Merion Sta., Pa. Died 1903.

STICKNEY, Albert, lawyer; b. Boston, Feb. 1, 1839; grad. Harvard, 1859; Harvard Law School, 1862. Served as lt. col., 47th Mass. vols., Civil war; aide on staff of Maj. Gen. Banks and insp. gen. on staff of Maj. Gen. Emory. Author: The Lawyer and His Clients; A True Republic; Democratic Government; a Study of Politics; The Political Problem; The Transvaal Outlook, 1900; Organized Democracy, 1906. Home: New York, N.Y. Died 1908.

STICKNEY, Alpheus Beede, ry. builder; b. Wilton, Me., June 27, 1840; s. Daniel and Ursula Maria (Beede) S.; ed. common schs. and acads., N.H. and Me.; m. Kate W. H. Hall, 1864; m. 2d, May Crosby, 1901. Taught sch.; admitted to bar, 1862; practiced law, 1862-69; from 1869 engaged in bldg. and operating rys. Organized, 1871, and built 1st sect. N. Wis. Ry., now part of Chicago, St. Paul, M. & O. system; supt. constrn. of abt. 500 miles G.N. and Canadian Pacific rys., 1879-81; organized and built 1st sec. Wis., Minn. & Pacific Ry., 1881; organized 1883, and began constrn. C.G.W. Ry., of which was pres., 1884-1909; receiver same rd., 1908-09; organized and built St. Paul Union Stockyards and packing houses, 1882. Home: St. Paul, Minn. Died Aug. 9, 1916.

STICKNEY, Amos, brig. gen. U.S.A.; b. St. Louis, Mo., Aug. 27, 1843; s. Benjamin and Sarah J. S.; grad. U.S. Mil. Acad., 1864; m. Virginia Fetter, July 10, 1866. Commd. 1st lt. engrs., June 13, 1864; capt., Mar. 7, 1867; maj., Jan. 2, 1881; lt. col., May 18, 1893; col., May 2, 1901; brig. gen. and retired by operation of law, Aug. 27, 1907. Bvtd. capt., Dec. 21, 1864, for campaign in Georgia, 1864; maj., Mar. 13, 1865, for campaign through Georgia and Carolinas. Engr. on staff comdg. gen., Dept. of the Mo., June-Aug. 1864, and on staff Gen. Cullum, at Nashville, Aug.-Sept. 1864; asst. engr., Oct. 1864-June 1865, and chief engr., June-July 1865, Army of the Tennessee, and engaged in various movements and operations of Ga. and Carolina campaigns; served on constrn. of forts until 1866; prof. engring., West Point, 1866-67; chiefly occupied with work of river and harbor improvement from 1868; pres. Mo. River Commn., 1896-1902, Miss. River Commn., 1901-03; chmn. of commn. to establish and mark the boundary line between the States of Ky. and Ind. under the orders of the U.S. Supreme Court. Home: New York, N.Y. Died Oct. 25, 1924.

STICKNEY, Herman Osman, naval officer; b. Pepperell, Mass., Dec. 10, 1867; s. Walter Brooks and Lydia Jane (Edwards) S.; grad. U.S. Naval Acad., 1888; m. Jennie Griffin Milhado, Oct. 16, 1895. Assistant engr., July 1, 1890; trans. to line and promoted through grades to rear adm., Dec. 22, 1919; retired, Dec. 27, 1921. Served on Iowa, Spanish-Am. War, 1898; on Princeton, Philippine Insurrection, 1899-1901; Navy Yard, Norfolk, Va., 1901-02; navigator Texas, 1902-05; at U.S. Naval Acad., 1905-06; duty Navy Yard, Norfolk, Va., 1906-07; exec. officer South Dakota, 1908-10; insp. in charge 4th Light House Dist., Phila., 1910-12; comd. Massachusetts, 1912; at U.S. Naval Acad., 1912-13; comd. Prairie, 1913-14; adminstr. of customs, Vera Cruz, Mexico, 1914; at Naval War Coll., Newport, R.I., 1915; comd. Vermont, 1915-18; Bd. of Inspection and Survey, Washington, 1918; sr. mem. Pacific Coast Bd. of Inspection, San Francisco, 1919; comdr. train, Pacific Fleet, July 1921; U.S. commr. to Sesquicentennial Expn., Phila., 1926-27, in charge all federal participation in that expn. Atty. at law; admitted to practice in Va., June 27, 1923. Home: Norfolk, Va. Died Sept. 13, 1936.

STICKNEY, Joseph L., journalist; b. "The Mines," nr. Marion, Ky., July 12, 1848; s. John Charles and Abby Anna (Clifford) S.; grad. U.S. Naval Acad., 1867; m. Edith Lucy Cooley, June 1900. Entered navy as midshipman, Sept. 25, 1862; in Civ. War, served as midshipman aboard Marion, Franklin with Admiral Farragut, Frolic, Guard, Ohio, Congress and Nantasket; resigned as lt., 1871. Began as reporter, 1873; corr. Chicago Tribune, Russo-Turkish War, 1877-78; editorial writer Phila. Record, 1881-82; mng. editor Milwaukee Sentinel, 1883-84; editor and propr. Detroit Post, 1884-85; foreign editor and editorial writer, New York Herald, 1887-98. Aide to Commodore Dewey at battle of Manila Bay, May 1, 1898, receiving personal mention in Commodore's official report of that battle; corr. in P.I. and in S. Africa, 1899-1900. Home: Chicago, Ill. Died 1907.

STICKNEY, William Wallace, governor; b. Plymouth, Vt., Mar. 21, 1853; s. John W. and Ann (Pinney) S.; grad. Phillips Acad., Exeter, N.H., 1877;

LL.D., Norwich U., 1902; m. Elizabeth Lincoln, May 4, 1881; m. 2d, Sarah E. Moore, June 1, 1905. Admitted to bar, 1878; practices in state and federal cts.; mem. Stickney, Sargent & Chase. Clerk Vt. Ho. of Rep., 1882-92; state's atty., 1882-84, 1890-92; speaker Vt. Ho. of Rep., 1892-96; gov. of Vt., 1900-02. Pres. Vt. Bar Assn., 1905; life pres. Vt. Hist. Soc.; v.p. N.E. Hist.-Geneal. Soc. Dir. Nat. Life Ins. Co. (Montpelier, Vt.), Vt. Mutual Fire Ins. Co. (Montpelier). Home: Tyson, Vt. Died Dec. 15, 1932.

STIEGLITZ, Julius (Oscar), chemist; b. Hoboken, N.J., May 26, 1867; s. Edward and Hedwig (Werner) S.; brother of Alfred S.; grad. Real-gymnasium, Karlsruhe, Germany, 1886; A.M., Ph.D., U. of Berlin, 1889; (hon. D.Sc., Clark University, 1909; Ch.D., University of Pittsburgh, 1916); m. Anna Stieffel, of Karlsruhe, Germany, Aug. 27, 1891 (died 1933); m. 2d, Mary M. Rising, Aug. 30, 1934. With U. of Chicago, 1892—, prof. chemistry, 1905-33, prof. emeritus; dir. analytical chemistry, 1909-15, dir. univ. labs., 1912-24, chmn. chemistry dept., 1915-33. Hitchcock lecturer, U. of Calif., 1909; Dohme lecturer, Johns Hopkins, 1924; Fenton lecturer, U. of Buffalo, 1933. Fellow Am. Acad. Arts and Sciences, Washington Acad. of Sciences, A.A.A.S. (v.p.). Member Internat. Commn. Annual Tables Constants, 1915-21. Mem. div. of chemistry, Nat. Research Council, 1917-19 (chmn. com. synthetic drugs, 1917-19; v. chmn. div. of chemistry, 1919-21); spl. expert Public Health Service, 1918—. Willard Gibbs medal, 1923. Home: Chicago, Ill. Died Jan. 10, 1937.

STIFLER, James Madison, prof. N.T. exegesis Crozer Theol. Sem.; b. nr. Altoona, Pa., Dec. 8, 1839; s. John H. S.; grad. Shurtleff Coll., Alton, Ill. (A.M., D.D.); spl. studies in divinity; ordained to Bapt. ministry; m. Jennie M. Carr, April 21, 1868. Author: An Introduction to the Study of The Acts of the Apostles, 1892; The Epistle to the Romans; A Commentary, Logical and Historical, 1898. Home: Chester, Pa. Died 1902.

STILES, Charles Wardell, zoölogist; b. Spring Valley, N.Y., May 15, 1867; s. Rev. Samuel Martin and Elizabeth (White) S.; ed. Wesleyan U., Conn., 1885-86; Collège de France, 1886-87; U. of Berlin, 1887-89, U. of Leipzig, 1889-90; Trieste Zoöl. Sta., 1891; Pasteur Inst. and Collège de France, 1891; A.M., Ph.D., Leipzig, 1890; hon. M.S., 1896, D.Sc., 1906, Wesleyan U.; LL.D., U. of N.C., 1912; hon. M.D., Richmond, Va., Coll., 1913; D.Sc., Yale, 1915; m. Virginia, d. of Hon. Lewis Baker, June 1897. Zoölogist, 1891-1902, consulting zoölogist, 1902-04, Bur. Animal Industry, U.S. Dept. Agr.; prof. of zoölogy, U.S.P.H.S., 1902-30; asst. surgeon general (res.), U.S.P.H.S., 1919-30, medical dir. same, 1930-31; prof. medical zoölogy, Georgetown U., 1892-1906; spl. lecturer on same, Army Med. Sch., 1894-1902, Johns Hopkins, 1897-1937, Navy Med. Sch., 1902—; hon. custodian helminthological collections, U.S. Nat. Mus., 1893-1931; sec. advisory com. Smithsonian Table at Naples Zoöl. Sta., 1894—. U.S. Govt. del. Internat. Zoöl. Congresses, Leyden, 1895, Cambridge, 1898, Berlin, 1901, Berne, 1904, Boston, 1907, Gratz, 1910, Monaco, 1913, Budapest, Hungary, 1927, Padua, 1930; sec., 1898-1936, Internat. Commn. on Zoöl. Nomenclature; sec., 1910-27, Internat. Commn. on Med. Zoölogy; detailed as agrl. and scientific attaché U.S. Embassy, Berlin, Germany, 1898-99; scientific sec. Rockefeller commn. for eradication of hookworm disease, 1909-14. Associate Smithsonian, 1931—; prof. zoölogy, Rollins College (winter faculty), 1931-38. Mem. many Am. and European scientific and medical societies; elected, 1892, successor to Joseph Leidy as foreign corr. Société de Biologie, France; elected 1896, fgn. corr. Académie de Médecine, France; 1899, corr. mem. Zoöl. Soc., London. Author: Trichinosis in Germany, 1901; Index Catalogue of Medical and Veterinary Zoölogy from 1902 (continuing publ.); The Cattle Ticks (Ixodoidea) of the United States, 1902; Emergency Report on Surra, 1902; Report on Hookworm Disease (Uncinariasis) in the United States, 1903; Illustrated Keys to Trematode and Cestode Parasites of Man; Trematoda, 1908; Taxonomic Value of Stigmal Plates in Ixodoidea, 1910; Watsonius Watsoni, 1910; Cestoda, 1912; Nematoda, 1920; Studies on Intestinal Parasites (especially Amœbæ) in Man, 1923; Key-Catalogue of the Protozoa Worms, Crustacea, Arachnoids, and Insects of Man, Primates, Chiroptera, Insectivora, Carnivora, 1925-32; Early History of the Hookworm Campaign in Our Own Southern U.S., 1939. Home: Washington, D.C. Died Jan. 24, 1941.

STILES, Meredith Newcomb, editor; b. New Bedford, Mass., Apr. 16, 1880; s. Rev. William Curtis and Mary Allen Arey (Newcomb) S.; A.B., Amherst, 1902; m. Katherine Elizabeth Toof, June 19, 1912; 1 son, Meredith N. Began as reporter New York Commercial Advertiser, 1902, later with New York World, New York Herald, New York Evening Sun and New York News Bur. until 1911; staff reporter, Asso. Press, 1911-16; city editor same in N.Y. City, 1916-19; chief of Asso. Press Bur., Buenos Aires, Argentina, 1919-25; in charge Latin-Am. service of Asso. Press, 1925-26; foreign news editor for Asso. Press, 1926-28; became associated with George Eastman, 1928; speaker and writer in promotion of calendar reform, and as asst to Nat. Com. on Calendar Simplification for U.S.; rep. of Nat. Com. on Calendar Simplification to League of Nations Preparatory Com. on Calendar Reform, Geneva, 1931; adviser, Internat. Conf. on Calendar Reform, Geneva, 1931; Am. sec. Internat. Fixed Calendar League, 1932-34; mem. Shaw Scientific Expdn. to British Columbia, 1907; Asso. Press staff corr., Argentina, Brazil, Chili conf. on Mexico, at Niagara Falls, 1914; with Hughes Mission to Brazil, 1922; at Pan-Am. Conf., Santiago, Chile, 1923. Conglist. Author: The World's Work and the Calendar. Home: Rochester, N.Y. Died June 26, 1937.

STILES, Percy Goldthwait, physiologist; b. Newtonville, Mass., July 1, 1875; s. Edmund Ely and Elmina Catherine (Kendall) S.; S.B., Mass. Inst. Tech., 1897; Ph.D., Johns Hopkins, 1902; m. Caroline Leonora Holden, Sept. 6, 1904. Instr. physiology, Bellevue Hosp. Med. Coll., New York, 1902-03; later instr. physiology, Mass. Inst. Tech., and instr. and prof., Simmons Coll., Boston; asst. prof. physiology, Harvard. Fellow Am. Acad. Arts and Sciences. Conglist. Author: Nutritional Physiology, 1912. Home: Newtonville, Mass. Died 1936.

STILES, Theodore Lamme, lawyer; b. in Clarke Co., O., July 12, 1848; s. Daniel J. and Maria S. (Lamme) S.; studied Ohio U., Athens; B.A., Amherst, 1871, Sch. of Law, Columbia, 1871-72; m. Mary Louise Duff Barbour, Nov. 24, 1887. Admitted to practice at Indianapolis, 1872; practiced at New York, 1872-78, at Tucson, Ariz., 1878-87; removed to Tacoma, Wash., 1887; mem. Wash. Constl. Conv., 1889; chmn. 1st Rep. State Conv. of Wash., Walla Walla, 1889; asso. justice Supreme Ct. of Wash., 1890-95; resumed practice, 1895; city atty., Tacoma, 1908-16. Home: Tacoma, Wash. Died Oct. 11, 1925.

STILES, William Curtis, clergyman; b. Stoneham, Me., June 14, 1851; s. William H. and Martha P. S.; took elective course Tufts Coll., B.D., Tufts Div. Sch., 1876; m. Mary A. A. Newcomb, Oct. 15, 1876. Ordained Universalist ministry, 1876; entered Congl. ministry, 1880; pastor Brooklyn, 1880-84, St. Louis, 1884-86, Pittsfield, N.H., 1887-90, Jackson, Mich., 1892-96, Stonington, Conn., 1897-1901. Editor on Standard Dictionary, 1890-93. Preaches at call. Prohibition Republican. Author: (stories) Literary Dozen, 1893; Matter of Business, 1898; Excuse Me, 1898; Double Jeopardy, 1899; Master's Mission, 1900; Out of Kishineff, 1903; The Upper Way, 1904; Union Prayer Meeting Helper (with collaborator), 1897, 98. Co-editor: Modern Sermons by World Scholars, 1909. Home: Brooklyn, N.Y. Died 1911.

STILL, Andrew Taylor, osteopath; b. Jonesboro, Va., Aug. 6, 1828; s. Abraham and Martha Poage (Moore) S.; ed. log sch. house, Jonesboro, Va., Holston Coll., Newmarket, Tenn., and pvt. schs.; m. Mary E. Turner, Nov. 15, 1860 (died 1910). Surgeon and maj. 21st Kan. Vols. in Civil War. Practicing osteopathy, June 22, 1874—; pres. Am. Sch. Osteopathy, Kirksville, Mo., 1892—. Republican. Author: Autobiography of A. T. Still, 1897 (rev. 1908); Philosophy of Osteopathy, 1899; Mechanical Principles, 1902; Practice and Research, 1910. Home: Kirksville, Mo. Died Dec. 12, 1917.

STILL, William, philanthropist; b. Shamony, N.J., Oct. 7, 1821; African descent; brought up on farm; located in Phila., 1844; clerk in office of Pa. Anti-Slavery Soc., 1847; m. Letitia George, 1847. Chmn. and corr. sec. Phila. branch "Underground Railroad," 1851-61; sheltered the wife, daughter and sons of John Brown while he was awaiting execution in Charleston, Va.; post-sutler, Camp William Penn for colored troops during Civil war; was mem. Freedmen's Aid Union and Commn.; v.p. and chmn. bd. of mgrs. Home for Aged and Infirm Colored Persons; and other charitable bodies. Author: The Underground Railroad; Voting and Laboring; Struggle for the Rights of the Colored People of Philadelphia. Home: Philadelphia, Pa. Died 1902.

STILLÉ, Alfred, M.D.; b. Philadelphia, Oct. 30, 1813; grad. Univ. of Pa., 1832; med. dept., 1836; (LL.D., Pa. Coll., 1876; Univ. of Pa., 1889). Resident physician Phila. Hosp., 1836; Pa. Hosp., 1840-41; visiting physician St. Joseph's Hosp., 1849-71; Phila. Hosp., 1865-72; prof. theory and practice of medicine Pa. Med. Coll., 1854-59; same chair Univ. of Pa., 1864-84 (prof. emeritus). Author: Elements of General Pathology; The Unity of Medicine; Humboldt's Life and Character; War as an Element of Civilization; Othello and Desdemona; The National Dispensatory (with John M. Maish); Therapeutics and Materia Medica; Epidemic Meningitis; Epidemic or Malignant Cholera. Home: Philadelphia, Pa. Died 1900.

STILLÉ, Charles Janeway, pres. Hist. Soc. of Pa.; b. Philadelphia, Sept. 23, 1819; grad. Yale, 1839, (LL.D., 1868); admitted to bar, but devoted his attention to literature; mem. exec. com. U.S. Sanitary Commn. during Civil war; prof. history, 1866, and provost, 1868-80, Univ. of Pa. Author: How a Free People Conduct a Long War; Northern Interests and Southern Independence; Memorial of the Great Fair for the U.S. Sanitary Commn.; History of the U.S. Sanitary Commn.; Studies in Mediæval History; Historical Development of American Civilization; Studies in Mediæval Civilization; Beaumarchais and the Lost Million; Life and Times of John Dickinson; General Anthony Wayne and the Pennsylvania Line. Home: Philadelphia, Pa. Died 1899.

STILLINGS, Charles Arthur, printer; b. Boston, Apr. 20, 1871; s. Ephraim Bailey and Celia Crowell (Kemp) S.; ed. Phillips Grammar Sch. and English High Sch., Boston; m. Caroline Spuck, June 30, 1914. Left high school in 14th year to enter father's printing office (E. B. Stillings & Co.), Boston, 1885, in which worked from printer's devil to gen. mgr., and 1902-03, as sales mgr. of successor, The Griffith-Stillings Press. Mgr. Printers' Bd. of Trade, Washington, Sept. 1, 1903-May 1, 1905; mgr. Printers' Bd. of Trade of New York, May 1-Nov. 1, 1905; public printer of U.S., 1905-08; pres. The Sanitary Shipping-Container Corp., Washington, D.C. Died June 23, 1917.

STILLINGS, Ephraim Bailey, printer; b. Somersworth, N.H., May 18, 1846; s. Rook and Mary (Hodsdon) S.; ed. high sch., Somersworth, N.H.; m. Celia Crowell Kemp; father of Charles Arthur S. Pvt. Co. B, 46th Mass. Inf., and Co. A, 2d Mass. Heavy Arty. in Civil War; in service 37 mos. to close of war; began in printing trade, Boston, 1868; formerly treas. Griffith-Stillings Press. Republican. Unitarian. Comdr. E. W. Kinsley Post No. 113 G.A.R., Boston 1904; elected jr. v.comdr.-in-chief G.A.R., 1905, to fill vacancy caused by death of W. W. Blackmar, term expiring 1905; adj. gen. G.A.R., 1910-11. Home: Somerville, Mass. Died Dec. 30, 1917.

STILLMAN, James, banker; b. Brownsville, Tex., June 9, 1850; s. Charles S.; youth spent Hartford, Conn., and in pvt. sch. at Ossining, N.Y.; m. Elizabeth Rumrill. Partner Smith, Woodward & Stillman, New York, 1871-73, and from 1873 in their successors, Woodward & Stillman, cotton commn. mchts.; pres. Nat. City Bank, 1891-1909, chmn. bd. dirs., 1909—; dir. C.&N.W. Ry. Co., Western Union Telegraph Co., U.S. Trust Co., N. British & Mercantile Ins. Co., Queen Ins. Co., etc. Home: New York, N.Y. Died Mar. 15, 1918.

STILLMAN, John Maxson, chemist; b. New York, Apr. 14, 1852; s. Dr. Jacob Davis Babcock and Caroline B. (Maxson) S.; Ph.B., U. of Calif., 1874, Ph.D., 1885 (LL.D., 1916); m. Emma Rodolph, June 1878. Asst. in chemistry, U. of Calif., 1873-75; student in chemistry, Strassburg and Würzburg, 1875-76; instr. organic and gen. chemistry, U. of Calif., 1876-82; chemist Boston and Am. Sugar Refining cos., 1882-91; prof. chemistry, 1891-1917, v.p., 1913-17, emeritus, 1917, Leland Stanford Jr. U. Asst. ednl. dir. S.A.T.C., 1918. Author: Paracelsus, as Physician, Chemist and Reformer, 1920. Died Dec. 13, 1923.

STILLMAN, Stanley, surgeon; b. Sacramento, Calif., Aug. 23, 1861; s. J. D. B. and Mary G. (Wells) S.; U. of Calif., class of 1882; M.D., Cooper Med. Coll., San Francisco, 1889; m. Josephine Welsh, Feb. 26, 1894; children—Elisabeth Lane, Stanley. Adj. prof. surgery, 1895-98, prof., 1898-1909, Cooper Med. Coll.; prof. surgery, Stanford Med. School, 1909-26 (emeritus). Asst. visiting surgeon, 1891-99, visiting surgeon, 1899-1909, City and Co. Hosp., San Francisco; visiting surgeon Lane Hosp., 1898—. Surgeon U.S. N.R.F., 1917; dir. Navy Base Hosp. No. 2; comdr. M.C. U.S.N.R.F., 1919. Fellow Am. Surg. Assn., Am. Coll. Surgeons. Home: San Francisco, Calif. Died Oct. 15, 1934.

STILLMAN, Thomas Bliss, chem. engr.; b. Plainfield, N.J., May 24, 1852; s. Dr. Charles H. and Mary Elizabeth (Starr) S.; B.S., Rutgers Coll., 1873, M.Sc., 1876; Ph.D., Stevens Inst. Tech., 1883; grad. Fresenius Lab., Weisbaden, Germany, 1877; m. Emma Louise Pomplitz, Nov. 3, 1881. Instr. analyt. chemistry, 1874-76, and 1881-86, prof. analyt. chemistry, 1886-1903, prof. engring. chemistry, 1903-09, Stevens Inst. Tech.; retired upon Carnegie Pension Fund, 1909. Apptd. state insp. of oils, N.J., 1884; examiner in chemistry Municipal Civil Service, N.Y., 1911—. City chemist, Jersey City, and Bayonne, N.J.; chemist to Medical Milk Commn., Newark. Editor The Stevens Institute Indicator, 1895. Author: Engineering Chemistry, 1897, 1901, 05, 10. Home: Hoboken, N.J. Died Aug. 10, 1915.

STILLMAN, William James, journalist; b. Schenectady, N.Y., June 1, 1828; grad. Union, 1848 (A.M., L.H.D.); editor Crayon, New York, 1855-57; U.S. Consul at Rome, 1861-65; at Crete, 1865-69; corr. London Times, 1876-98; retired on pension from the Times; m. Laura Mack (died 1869); m. 2d, Marie Spartali, 1871. Author: History of the Cretan Insurrection; Poetic Localities of Cambridge; The Uprising in Herzegovina; On the Track of Ulysses; Early Italian Painters; Apollo and Venus; Billy and Hans; The Old Rome and the New, and Other Studies; The Union of Italy; Francisco Criski, a Biography; Little Bertha; etc. Home: London, England. Died 1901.

STILLMAN, William Olin, physician, philanthropist; b. Normansville, N.Y., Sept. 9, 1856; s. Rev. Stephen Lewis and Lucretia (Miller) S.; M.D., Albany Med. Coll., 1878; studied univs. of Berlin, Vienna, Paris and hosps. of London, 1883-84; (hon. A.M., Union Coll., 1880); m. Frances M. Rice, Apr. 17, 1880. Phys. to Open Door Mission, and Hosp. for Incurables, 1887-88, Babies' Nursery, and Lathrop Memorial, 1888-92, Home for Christian Workers,

1892, etc.; lecturer on history of medicine, Albany Med. Coll., 1896-1914. Pres. and founder National Training Sch. for Certified Nurses, 1905. Pres. 1st Am. Internat. Humane Conf., Washington, 1910; pres. Am. Humane Assn., 1905—, N.Y. State Humane Edn. Com., 9 yrs., Mohawk and Hudson River Humane Soc., 1892—; v.p. N.Y. State Conv. Anticruelty Socs., 19 yrs., now pres.; officer N.Y. Conf. Charities and Corrections; awarded gold medal at St. Louis Expn., 1904, for philanthropic work; silver medal, Ohio Humane Soc.; gold medal, San Francisco Soc. Prevention Cruelty to Animals; promoter humane legislation. Founder Albany Hist. and Art Soc.; hon. mem. Finland, Italian, and Cologne (Germany) socs. prevention of cruelty to animals, Fed. Humane socs. of Pa., Mich. State Humane Assn., New York Horse Aid Soc.; hon. v.p. of Audubon Soc. State of N.Y.; pres. N.Y. State Hist. Society. Editor of the Nat. Humane Review. Pres. Internat. Fedn. of Socs. for Prevention of Cruelty to Animals, 1914—; founder, and dir. gen. Am. Red Star Animal Relief, 1916—. Author: The Mineral Springs of Saratoga, 1882. Home: Albany, N.Y. Died Mar. 15, 1924.

STILLWELL, Homer Allison, merchant; b. at Nineveh, Pa., Dec. 31, 1860; s. Addison and Rhoda (Thompson) S.; student U. of Ill., 1878-81; m. Ellen Hill, Mar. 1, 1886. Removed to Chicago in 1882, and entered employ of Butler Brothers, of which became gen. mgr., 1893, dir., 1902, v.p., 1907, pres., July 1914—; dir. Nat. City Bank, A.,T.&S.F. Ry., Merchants Loan & Trust Co. Pres. Chicago Assn. of Commerce, 1910. Republican. Presbyn. Home: Chicago, Ill. Died June 23, 1918.

STILLWELL, Lewis Buckley, electrical engr.; b. Scranton, Pa., Mar. 12, 1863; s. Richard and Margaret (Snyder) S.; student Wesleyan U., Conn., 1882-84; E.E., Lehigh U., 1885, M.S., 1907, D.Sc., 1914; Sc.D., Wesleyan, 1907; m. Mary Elizabeth Thurston, Apr. 19, 1892; 1 son, Richard. Asst. electrician, Westinghouse Elec. & Mfg. Co., 1886-90; chief elec. engr., same, 1890-97; elec. dir. Niagara Falls Power Co., 1897-1900; in practice as cons. elec. engr., New York, 1900—; cons. engr. Manhattan Elev. Ry. Co. (electrification of elevated lines in N.Y. City), 1899-1906; elec. dir. Rapid Transit Subway Constr. Co., 1900-09; cons. engr. Hudson Cos., 1905-13; mem. Erie R.R. elec. commn., 1906; cons. engr. United Rys. & Elec. Co. of Baltimore, 1906-20, Interborough Rapid Transit Co., 1909-20, N.Y.,N.H.&H. R.R. Co. (Hoosac Tunnel electrification), 1910-11, N.Y., Westchester & Boston Ry. Co., 1911-15, Lehigh Navigation Elec. Co., 1912-18; consulting engr. Holland Vehicular Tunnels, 1924-27; cons. engr. Port of New York Authority, 1927—. Life trustee, Princeton U., 1918—; mem. bd. dirs. Chamber of Commerce, U.S.A., 1921-23. Home: Princeton, N.J. Died Jan. 19, 1941.

STILLWELL, William Burney, lumberman; b. Rome, Ga., Mar. 11, 1851; s. Rev. Charles Harden and Mary Stewart (Marshall) S.; largely self-educated; m. Mary Riley Royall, Oct. 13, 1875 (dec.); children—William Horace, Edith (Mrs. W. F. Train, dec.), Herbert Landrum, Walter Brooks, Royall (dec.), Mary Royall (Mrs. J. T. Mann), Laleah Pratt (Mrs. F. B. Vincent). In lumber business, 1866—; became mem. D. C. Bacon & Co., 1876, and its successor, Stillwell, Millen & Co., 1887, Southern Pine Co. of Ga., 1895, now sec. and treas. latter. Prominent for many yrs. in lumber mfrs.' and dealers' and commercial orgns. of Ga. and the South; an organizer, later v.p., Nat. Lumber Mfrs.' Assn.; has frequently appeared before committees of Congress and state legislatures, in behalf of public improvements and lumber industry; a founder of Savannah Board of Trade (pres.); chmn. Savannah Harbor Commn.; dir. Southern Settlement and Development Orgn. of Baltimore; v.p. Ga. Land Owners' Assn. Baptist. Democrat. Home: Savannah, Ga. Died Nov. 8, 1927.

STILWELL, Arthur Edward; b. Rochester, N.Y., Oct. 21, 1859; s. Charles H. and Mary (Pierson) S.; ed. pub. schs.; m. Jennie A. Wood, 1879. Officer Travelers Ins. Co., Hartford, Conn., until 1887; built Kansas City Sub Belt R.R., Kansas City Southern Ry. (pres. of same at 32); built in all 7 railroads—2,500 miles; designed and built Port Arthur, Texas, and Port Arthur Ship Canal; founder, and pres. 4 yrs., Nat. Surety Co., pres. Am. Patents Development Co.; dir. Ft. Lee & Manhattan Realty Co. Author: The Great Plan (how to pay for the war), 1918 (trans. into French and Swedish); To All the World; The Light That Never Failed; Live and Grow Young, 1921; The Empire of the Soul. Home: New York, N.Y. Died Sept. 26, 1928.

STILWELL, Herbert Fenton, clergyman; b. Hunterdon Co., N.J., Sept. 1, 1856; s. Charles and Mary Catherine (Hunt) S.; A.B., Bucknell U., 1881 (Latin oration), A.M., 1889; grad. Crozer Theol. Sem., 1884; D.D., Macalester, 1902, Bucknell, 1902; LL.D., Denison, 1923; m. Mary Twining Scott, Sept. 11, 1884; children—Charles James, Clifford Scott. Chapel pastor, 1st Bapt. Ch., Phila., 1881-84; ordained Bapt. ministry, 1884; pastor Freehold, N.J., 1884-95, Calvary Ch., Minneapolis, Minn., 1895-98, 1st Ch., St. Paul, 1898-1903, 1st Ch., Cleveland, 1903-15; gen. supt. of evangelism, Am. Bapt. Home Mission Soc. 1915-26; prof. of evangelism Eastern Bapt. Theol. Sem., Phila., 1926—. Pres. bd. Denison U., Granville, O.; mem. Edn. Bd. of Northern Bapt. Conv.; trustee Ohio Bapt. Conv. (pres. 1909-13). Home: Cleveland, O. Died Nov. 26, 1935.

STIMPSON, William G., U.S. Pub. Health Service; b. Ilchester, Md., Apr. 24, 1865; s. William and Annie L. S.; M.D., George Washington U. Med. Sch., 1886; m. Grace Tozier, Dec. 3, 1895; children—Charlotte (Mrs. Louis Hasbrouck), Winnifred, Margaret (Mrs. John L. Evans). Commd. asst. surgeon U.S.P.H.S., Mar. 11, 1890; passed asst. surgeon, May 25, 1894; surgeon, June 2, 1906; sr. surgeon, Mar. 1, 1921; asst. surgeon gen. in charge Marine Hosp. Div. U.S.P.H.S., Washington, Nov. 7, 1913-Sept. 23, 1920; retired July 1, 1929. Fellow Am. Coll. Surgeons. Episcopalian. Home: Winter Park, Fla. Died Nov. 18, 1940.

STIMSON, Charles D., lumber mfr.; b. Mich., 1857; s. Thomas D. and Achsah (Spencer) S.; student Racine (Wis.) Coll.; m. Harriet Overton, 1882; children—Thomas Douglas, Mrs. Dorothy Bullitt. In lumber mfg. business, Seattle, Wash., 1889—; now pres. Stimson Mill Co., Metropolitan Building Co., South Seattle Land Co.; chmn. bd. trustees C. D. Stimson Co. Mgr. Northwestern Div. Am. Red Cross 2½ yrs. during World War, now chmn. advisory com. Mem. Chamber of Commerce, Seattle. Home: Seattle, Wash. Died Aug. 29, 1929.

STIMSON, Daniel MacMartin, surgeon, b. Edinburgh, N.Y., Jan. 2, 1844; s. Azariah E. and Margaret (MacMartin) S.; A.B., Union Coll., 1864, A.M., 1867; M.D., Coll. Phys. and Surg. (Columbia U.), 1868; Charity (now City) Hosp., New York; studied at Berlin, Vienna, and Paris; (LL.D., Union U., 1904); m. Edith Parker, Apr. 13, 1871. Formerly visiting surgeon St. Peter's Hosp., attending phys. Alms House and Lunatic Asylum (Albany, N.Y.), attending surgeon Presbyn. and Mt. Sinai hosps. (New York), cons. surgeon State Emigrants' Hosp., Sailors' Snug Harbor; now cons. surgeon Mt. Sinai Hosp., New York Skin and Cancer Hosp., New York Infirmary for Women and Children, Loomis Sanitarium, Northern Dispensary; formerly prof. anatomy, Women's Med. Coll., New York Infirmary, later prof. surgery, same. Trustee N.Y. Infirmary for Women and Children. Democrat. Presbyn. Home: New York, N.Y. Died Feb. 21, 1922.

STIMSON, Henry Albert, clergyman; b. N.Y. City, Sept. 28, 1842; s. Henry C. and Julia M. (Atterbury) Stimson; A.B., Yale, 1865, A.M., 1868; Union Theol. Sem., 1866-67; grad. Andover Theol. Sem., 1869; (D.D., Ripon, 1885, Yale, 1893); m. Alice, d. late Pres. S. C. Bartlett, of Dartmouth Coll., Apr. 19, 1877; children—Alice M., Julia C., Lucile H., Henry Bartlett, Philip Moen, Dorothy, Barbara B. Ordained Congl. ministry, 1870; pastor Plymouth Ch., Minneapolis, 1869-80, Union Ch., Worcester, Mass., 1880-86, Pilgrim Ch., St. Louis, 1886-93, Broadway, Tabernacle, New York, 1893-96, Manhattan Church, New York, 1896-1917, emeritus. Lecturer at Oberlin Theol. Sem., 1891, Andover Theol. Sem., 1900-02, Chicago Theol. Sem., 1902-03, Yale Div. Sch., 1904, 08. Rec. sec. A.B.C.F.M., 1880-1915; pres. Congl. Bd. Ministerial Relief to 1923; trustee Mt. Holyoke Coll., Hartford Theol. Sem. to 1919; pres. bd. of visitors Andover Theol. Sem. to 1912; v.p. Am. Tract Soc.; dir. Am. Bible Soc. Author: Religion and Business, 1894; Questions of Modern Inquiry, 1894; The Apostles' Creed, 1899; The Right Life, 1905; The New Things of God, 1908; Behind This World and Beyond, 1910; While the War Rages, 1914. Home: New York, N.Y. Died July 18, 1936.

STIMSON, John Ward artist; b. Paterson, N.J., Dec. 16, 1850; s. Henry C. and Julia M. (Atterbury) S.; A.B., Yale U., 1872; grad. École des Beaux Arts, Paris; married; 6 children. Was lecturer and art teacher, Princeton U.; dir. art schools, Met. Mus. of Art, New York, 5 yrs.; founder and 12 yrs. dir., Artist-Artisan Inst., New York, 1888; served as dir. Art and Science Instn., Trenton, N.J., and as instr. Art Students' League. Asso. editor The Arena. Author: The Law of Three Primaries; Principles of Vital Art Education; The Gate Beautiful; Wandering Chords; etc. Home: Corona, Calif. Died July 1930.

STIMSON, Lewis Atterbury, surgeon; b. Paterson, N.J., Aug. 1844; s. Henry C. and Julia M. (Atterbury) S.; brother of Henry Albert and John Ward S.; A.B., Yale, 1863; M.D., Bellevue Hosp. Med. Coll. (New York U.), 1874; (LL.D., Yale, 1900); served in Union Army in Civil War as capt. and a.-d.-c., 1864-65; traveled and studied abroad until 1873; m. Candace Wheeler, Nov. 1866; father of Henry Lewis S. Prof. of physiology, 1883-85, anatomy, 1885-89, surgery, 1889-98, New York U.; prof. surgery, Cornell U. Med. Coll., 1898—. Regent U. State of N.Y., 1893-1904. Author: Operative Surgery, 1900; Fractures and Dislocations (6th edit.), 1910. Home: New York, N.Y. Died Sept. 17, 1917.

STIMSON, Thomas Douglas, lumber mfr.; b. Muskegon, Mich., Mar. 23, 1884; s. Charles D. and Harriet (Overton) S.; prep. edn., Cascadilla Sch.; student Cornell U., 1904-05; m. Emma Baillargeon, June 24, 1914; children—Frances Ann, Thomas David, Emma Eleanor, Douglas Joseph. In U.S. Air Service World War, hon. discharged as ensign U.S. Naval Res. Flying Corps. Pres. C. D. Stimson Co., Olympic Development Co., Seattle, Wash.; treas. South Seattle Land Co. Died Apr. 26, 1931.

STINE, Milton Henry, clergyman; b. East Prospect, Pa., Sept. 4, 1853; s. Adam and Barbara (Schoenberger) S.; A.B., Pa. Coll., Gettysburg, 1877, A.M., 1880, Ph.D., 1896; grad. Luth. Theol. Seminary, Gettysburg, 1880; state teacher's certificate, Pa., 1894; D.D., Susquehanna University, 1909; Litt.D. from Gettysburg, 1931; m. Mary Atland, June 24, 1880; children—Charles M., Walter S. Ordained Luth. ministry, 1880; pastor Lebanon, Pa., 1883-92, Los Angeles, Calif., 1892-95, Harrisburg, Pa., 1895-1904, Lebanon, Pa., 1908-15, Wilmington, Del., 1915-21, Hollywood, Calif., 1921-26, Harrisburg, Pa., 1929—. Visited British Guiana as rep. of Bd. of Foreign Missions, 1914; one of first presidents of Calif. Synod of Luth. Ch.; dir. Theol. Sem., Gettysburg, 1912-18. Author: Seven Golden Candlesticks, 1906; Baron Stiegel, 1904; The Devil's Bride, 1909; The Fortunes of a Foundling, 1921; Autobiography of Mary Jane, 1923; Man in the Making, 1930; Ancient Cities and Civilizations Modernized, 1931. Home: Los Angeles, Calif. Died Mar. 27, 1940.

STINE, Wilbur Morris, author, educator; b. Tyrone, Pa., Nov. 3, 1863; s. Rev. John Sharp and Sarah (Riegel) S.; Ph.B., Dickinson Coll., Carlisle, Pa., 1886, Sc.M., 1889, Sc.D., 1893; grad. study, Ohio U., 1886-87, Ph.D., 1893; studied in Germany, 1889; m. Corinne Elizabeth, d. Charles William Super, June 7, 1893; m. 2d, Grovina R. Boyer, Jan. 29, 1907. Instr., later asso. professor and professor physics and engring., Ohio University, 1886-93; dir. elec. engring., Armour Inst. Tech., 1893-98; Williamson prof. engring., Swarthmore, 1898-1900; has devoted attention to authorship, 1909. Mem. jury elec. awards, Chicago Expn., 1893, Nat. Export Expn., Phila., 1899. Editor Electrical Engineering, 1893-94. Author: (in science) Photometrical Measurements, 1900; The Contributions of Lenz to Electromagnetism, 1905, 21; The Discovery of the X or Ionic Ray, and Contributions to Its Physics, 1930, 31, and more than 125 papers, monographs and contributions to physics, technology and edn. Began research in X-rays, Dec. 1891, and obtained a true sciagraph, Feb. 14, 1892, earliest date on record; announced discovery of the source of Roentgen rays, 1896, and first suggested remedial use of X-rays, especially for treatment of cancer, 1897. Author (lit.): Amos Meakin's Ghost. Home: Philadelphia, and Mechanicsburg, Pa. Died July 4, 1934.

STINESS, John Henry, judge; b. Providence, R.I., Aug. 9, 1840; s. Philip Bessom and Mary (Marsh) S.; entered Brown U., 1857 (A.M., by spl. vote, 1876, LL.D., 1893); m. Maria E. Williams, Nov. 19, 1868. Admitted to bar, 1865, and practiced at Providence; mem. R.I. Ho. of Rep., 1874-75; asso. justice, 1875-1900, chief justice, 1900-04, Supreme Ct. of R.I. Republican. Trustee Providence Pub. Library, 1882—; fellow Brown U., 1897—; mem. commn. on uniform legislation, 1896-1907; chmn. R.I. Commn. on Revision of the Jud. System; pres. R.I. Hist. Soc., 1896-1903. Mem. standing com. P.E. Diocese of R.I. Author: Two Centuries of Liquor Legislation in Rhode Island, 1882; History of Lotteries in Rhode Island, 1896; Civil Changes in the State, 1897. Home: Providence, R.I. Died Sept. 6, 1913.

STIRLING, Yates, naval officer; b. Baltimore, Md., May 6, 1843; s. Archibald and Elizabeth Ann (Walsh) S.; apptd. to U.S. Naval Acad. from Md., 1860, grad. 1863; m. Ellen Salisbury Haley, Aug. 29, 1867; children—Helen, Marie Yates (Mrs. J. Lee Tailer), Yates, Margaret Yates (Mrs. J. Pembroke Thom), Archibald, Alice, Walter (dec.). Ensign, May 28, 1863; promoted through grades to rear adm., June 8, 1902; retired May 6, 1905. Served on Shenandoah, N. Atlantic Blockading Squadron, 1863-65; participated in both attacks on Ft. Fisher; on bd. Mohongo, Pacific Squadron, 1865-67, Wampanoag, Jan.-Mar. 1868, Contoocook, 1868-69; duty Hydrographic Office, 1870; on bd. receiving ship Independence, 1871-72; exec. officer receiving ships New Hampshire, 1875, Worcester, 1876; torpedo duty, 1877; ordnance duty, Navy Yard, Washington, 1878, 1882-84; exec. officer Lackawanna, 1878-81; comd. Iroquois, 1884-86, receiving-ship Dale, 1887-89, Dolphin, 1890-91; light house insp. 5th dist., 1892-94; comd. Newark, 1895-96, Lancaster, 1896-97; mem. Lighthouse Bd., 1898-1900; comdt. Naval Sta., San Juan, P.R., 1900-02, Navy Yard, Puget Sound, 1902-03; comd. Philippine Squadron, Asiatic Fleet, 1902-03, Cruiser Squadron, Asiatic Fleet, 1904; comdr.-in-chief Asiatic Fleet, 1904-05. Home: Baltimore, Md. Died Mar. 5, 1929.

STITES, Fletcher Wilbur, lawyer; b. Cape May, N.J.; s. Edgar Page and Sarah Elizabeth (Edmunds) S.; grad. Taylor U., Upland, Ind., 1900; LL.B., U. of Pa., 1904, also LL.D.; m. Edith G. Austin, June 6, 1906; 1 son, Richard Lawrence. Admitted to Pa. bar, 1904; pres. Keystone Indemnity Exchange, 1926. Became mem. Pa. Ho. of Rep., 1917, Pa. State Senate, 1923. Chmn. Commn. to Investigate Prison System, 1917; Rep. presdl. elector for Pa., 1920. Methodist. Home: Narberth, Pa. Died June 26, 1933.

STITES, John, capitalist; b. Christian Co., Ky., Oct. 9, 1850; s. John and Elizabeth (Hunt) S.; studied law, U. of Louisville; m. Mildred Ann Chenoweth, Oct. 4, 1877; children—Mrs. Helen Gill, Mrs. Mildred Gant, John Hunt, Mrs. Elizabeth Hannah, Francis Bell, Mrs. Ann Lenore Karraker, James W. Practiced law at Louisville, 1873-87; Aug. 1, 1887, with Fidelity Trust Co., as v.p., pres., and chmn. bd. to Jan. 7, 1911; v.p., 1911-13, became pres., 1913, now chmn. bd., Louisville Trust Co.; pres. La Grange Land Co. Dir., treas. Presbyn. Theol. Sem. of Ky., Presbyn. Com. Relief and Edn.; pres. Internat. S.S. Assn., 1908-11. Gold Democrat. Home: Louisville, Ky. Died Dec. 1, 1938.

STITT, Edward Walmsley, educator; b. N.Y. City, Apr. 25, 1862; s. James Samuel and Sophia (Hardy) S.; B.Sc., Coll. City of New York, 1881, M.Sc., 1898; Pd.D., New York U., 1900; LL.D., Dickinson U., 1922; Ph.D., New York U., 1924; m. Jennie Amanda Britton, Nov. 26, 1890; children—Edward Walmsley, William Britton. Prin. pub. schs., N.Y. City, 1896-1903; dist. supt. schs., same, 1903-23, asso. supt. schs., 1923—. Chmn. sch. com., Victory Loan campaign, 1918. Trustee Leopold Schepp Foundation, New York City Mission Society. Baptist. Mason. Author: Memory Selections, Their Value and Importance, 1925. Joint author: Let's Act, 1925. Home: New York, N.Y. Died July 14, 1927.

STOCKARD, Charles Rupert, biologist, anatomist; b. Washington Co., Miss., Feb. 27, 1879; s. Dr. Richard Rupert and Ella Hyde (Fowlkes) S.; B.Sc., Miss. Agrl. and Mech. Coll., 1899, M.S., 1901; Ph.D., Columbia, 1906; M.D., U. of Würzburg, 1922; Sc.D., Univ. of Cincinnati, 1920; studied Carnegie Inst. Lab. for Tropical Biology, Dry Tortugas, Fla.; Naples Zoöl. Sta.; also visited chief zoöl. and anat. labs. of Europe; m. Mercedes Müller, of Munich, Germany, Aug. 14, 1912; children—Marie Louise, Richard Robert. Commandant and acting prof. mil. science and tactics, Miss. Agrl. and Mech. Coll., 1898-1900, Jefferson Mil. Coll., 1900-03; asst. in zoöl. dept., Columbia, 1905, 06; asst. in embryology and histology, 1906-08, instr. of comparative morphology, 1908-09, asst. prof. embryology and exptl. morphology, 1909-11, prof. anatomy, June 1911—, Cornell Med. Coll.; also investigator for Huntington Fund for Cancer Research, 1908—; pres. board Rockefeller Inst. Medical Research; DeLamar lecturer, Johns Hopkins, 1925, Harrington lecturer, U. of Buffalo, 1926, Beaumont Foundation lecturer, Detroit, 1927, Lane lecturer, Stanford, 1930, Potter Memorial lecturer, Jefferson Medical College, 1934; trustee Marine Biol. Lab., Woods Hole, Long Island Biol. Assn., Bermuda Sta. for Biol. Research. Mng. editor Am. Jour. of Anatomy; editor Jour. Experimental Zoölogy, Am. Anatomical Memoirs. Fellow A.A.A.S. (v.p. 1933), N.Y. Zoöl. Soc., N.Y. Acad. Medicine. Author: Origin of Blood, 1915; Hormones and Structural Development, 1927; The Physical Basis of Personality, 1931. Home: New York, N.Y. Died Apr. 7, 1939.

STOCKARD, Henry Jerome, educator; b. in Chatham Co., N.C., Sept. 15, 1858; s. James Gibbs and Mary (Johnson) S.; ed. Graham (now Elon) Coll. and U. of N.C.; A.M., Elon Coll., 1889; m. Sallie J. Holleman, Apr. 11, 1878 (died 1888); m. 2d, Margaret Lula Tate, Jan. 22, 1890. Taught in pub. schs., 1880-84; instr. and later prin. Graham High Sch., 1884-90, and part of same time co. supt. schs.; asso. in English, U. of N.C., 1890-96; prof. English and polit. science, Fredericksburg Coll., 1896-1900; prof. Latin, 1900-07, pres., May 1907-May 1912, Peace Inst., Raleigh, N.C. Presbyn. elder. Democrat. Author: Fugitive Lines (poems), 1897; A Study in Southern Poetry, 1911. Home: Raleigh, N.C. Died 1914.

STOCKARD, Virginia Alice Cottey, coll. pres.; b. nr. Edina, Mo., Mar. 27, 1848; d. Ira Day and Sarah Elizabeth (Eads) Cottey; mainly self-ed.; LL.D., Ia., Wesleyan Coll., Mt. Pleasant, 1930; m. Samuel M. Stockard, Mar. 6, 1890 (died 1896). Began teaching in rural schs., 1869; later teacher in Richmond Coll., Mo., and Central Coll., Lexington, Mo.; founder, 1884, and served as pres. Cottey Junior Coll. for Women (coll. now owned and controlled by P.E.O. Organization), pres. emeritus, trustee, and chmn. endowment com. Methodist. Home: Nevada, Mo. Died July 16, 1940.

STOCKBRIDGE, Frank Parker, author, journalist; b. Gardiner, Me., June 11, 1870; s. Rev. Winfield Scott and Emily (Parker) S.; grad. high sch., Washington, D.C., 1888; student med. dept., Nat. U. (now George Washington U.), 1888-91; m. 3d, Bertha Edson, d. Seth Harris Lay, of N.Y. City, Feb. 16, 1917; children (by 1st marriage)—Arthur William (dec.), Katherine Emily (dec.); (by 3d marriage) Janet Josephine Osteyee (adopted). Learned printer's trade; reporter, editorial writer, Buffalo Express, 1894-1901; editor and pub. official program, Pan-Am. Expn., 1901; founder and editor Am. Home Mag., 1901-02; reporter, staff corr., New York American, 1902-04; mng. editor History of Universal Expn., St. Louis, 1904-05; city editor New York Globe, 1905-07; reporter New York Herald, 1907-08; polit. editor Cincinnati Times-Star, 1908-11; with late Dr. Walter Hines Page launched campaign of publicity for nomination of Woodrow Wilson for pres. of U.S., Mar. 1911, conducting same until Nov. 1911; editor Town Development Mag., 1911-12; editor Popular Mechanics, 1913-15; pres. and mng. editor N.Y. Evening Mail, 1915-17; editor Old Colony Mag., 1919, 21; editor and pub. Co-operative Commonwealth, 1921-22; editor Am. Press and editor in chief Pubs. Autocaster Service, 1929-36. Director Library Information Service; vice chmn. freedom of the press com. of Thomas Jefferson Memorial Foundation. Democrat. Mason. Author: (with others) The School of Tomorrow, 1911; Yankee Ingenuity in the War, 1919; (with M. R. Trabue) Measure Your Mind, 1920; Florida in the Making (with John H. Perry), 1925; The New Capitalism, 1926; So This Is Florida, 1938; Hedging Against Inflation, 1939. Home: Stockbridge, Mass. Died Dec. 7, 1940.

STOCKBRIDGE, Henry, judge; b. Baltimore, Md., Sept. 18, 1856; s. Henry and Fanny E. (Montague) S.; A.B., Amherst, 1877; LL.B., U. of Md., 1878; LL.D., Amherst, and St. John's, Md., 1911; m. Helen M. Smith, Jan. 5, 1882. Began practice at Baltimore, 1878; examiner for equity courts of Baltimore, 1882-88; one of editors Baltimore American, 1887-89; mem. 51st Congress (1889-91), 4th Md. Dist.; commr. of immigration Port of Baltimore, 1891-95; asso. judge Supreme Bench of Baltimore, 1896-1911; apptd. judge Ct. of Appeals of Md., Apr. 13, 1911; elected to same office, Nov. 1911, for term, 1912-26. Republican. Presbyn. An incorporator Am. Nat. Red Cross; regent U. of Md.; pres. Enoch Pratt Free Library; Md. commr. on Uniform State Laws. Home: Baltimore, Md. Died Mar. 22, 1924.

STOCKBRIDGE, Horace Edward, agrl. chemist; b. Hadley, Mass., May 19, 1857; s. Levi and Joanna (Smith) S.; B.S., Mass. Agrl. Coll., 1878; student Boston U., and U. of Göttingen; Ph.D., Göttingen, 1884; m. Belle Lamar, Mar. 30, 1885; children—Basil Levi, Abigail Montague, Derry Lamar, John Sylvester. Asso. prof. chemistry, Mass. Agrl. Coll., 1884-85; prof. chemistry and geology, Imperial Coll. of Agr. and Engring., Japan, 1885-89; chief chemist Japenese Govt., 1887-89; dir. Ind. Expt. Sta., 1889; pres. N.D. Agrl. Coll., and dir. N.D. Expt. Sta., 1890-94; prof. agr., Fla. Agrl. Coll. and dir. State Agrl. Institutes of Florida, 1897-1906; editor Southern Ruralist, Atlanta, propr. Walnut Vale Farm. Mem. Nat. Bd. of Farm. Orgns., Am. Acad. Polit. and Social Science, pres. Farmers' Nat. Congress, 1916-17; mem. Nat. Agricultural War Conference. Writer of reports and mag. articles on agrl. and scientific subjects. Treas., Ga. State Rep. campaigns, 1920-24. Author: Rocks and Soils, 1888, 95, 1902; Land Teaching, 1910. Editor Southern Farm and Dairy. Address: Atlanta, Ga. Died Oct. 30, 1930.

STOCKER, Harry Emilius, clergyman; b. Nazareth, Pa., Mar. 19, 1876; s. Emilius Theodore and Angelica Margaret (Giersch) S.; ed. State Normal School, Stroudsburg, Pa.; A.B., Moravian Coll., Bethlehem, Pa., 1900, A.M., 1913, Ph.D., 1915; B.D., Moravian Theol. Sem., 1902; m. Alice Belle Stratton, Aug. 26, 1908; 1 son, Arthur Frederick. Teacher pub. schs., Pa., 1893-96; ordained ministry Moravian Ch., 1902; pastor Northfield, Minn., 1902-08, West Salem, Ill., 1908-11, South Bethlehem, Pa., 1911-19; teacher Moravian Coll., Bethlehem, 1918-19; pastor 1st Ch., N.Y. City, Apr. 1910—. Pres. Moravian Christian Endeavor Union, 1914-15; chmn. Moravian Country Ch. Commn.; mem. larger life com. Moravian Ch.; mem. administrative com. of Fed. Council of Chs.; exec. sec. Am. Soc. in Aid of Moravian Missions; sec. Italian com. Moravian Ch.; sec. Moravian City Union of N.Y. Republican. Author: History of the White River Indian Mission in Indiana, 1917; Moravian Customs and Other Matters of Interest, 1918; History of the Moravian Church in New York City, 1922; A Home Mission History of the Moravian Church, 1923; also brochures. Made transl. from the German of the Diary of the White River Indian Mission in Indiana for Ind. Hist. Soc., 1914-16. Home: New York, N.Y. Died Dec. 26, 1929.

STOCKHAM, Alice Bunker, author; b. Cardington, Ohio, Nov. 8, 1833, of Quaker parentage; d. Slocum and Matilde F. (Wood) Bunker; ed. Olivet (Mich.) Coll.; M.D., Eclectic Med. Coll., Cincinnati, 1854; M.D., Chicago Homœ. Coll., 1880; m. G. H. Stockham, Aug. 11, 1857. Practiced in Ind. and Chicago; established the Stockham Pub. Co., becoming pres., to publish her own works and other "advanced" books. A leader in introduction of "sloyd" into Chicago pub. schs.; active worker for social purity, woman suffrage and social reform. Established a sch. of philosophy at Williams Bay, Wis., 1900. Author: Tokology, a Book of Maternity, 1883; Koradine, 1893; Karezza, 1896; Tolstoi, a Man of Peace, 1900; The Lover's World, a Wheel of Life, 1903; also numerous pamphlets, etc. Address: Alhambra, Calif. Died Dec. 3, 1912.

STOCKHAM, Edward Villeroy, business man; b. Camden, N.J., Oct. 17, 1863; s. Charles and Mary Humes (Tomb) S.; grad. U.S. Mil. Acad., 1889; m. Marion, d. Gen. John F. Hartranft, Nov. 16, 1900. Commd. 2d lt., 17th Inf., U.S.A., 1889 (resigned); capt. and adj. 1st Regt., Pa. N.G. (resigned); capt. Co. B, 6th Regt. N.J. N.G. (resigned); offered services to Govt. at opening of Spanish-Am. War. V.p. J. H. Mathis Shipbuilding Co.; pres. Charles Stockham Lumber Co. (Camden, N.J.), Edward V. Stockham, Inc. (Perryman, Md.). Commd. capt., Q.M.C., Aug. 6, 1917, maj., June 1, 1918; comd: 306th Supply Train and 306th Ammunition Train, A.E.F.; discharged, July 1, 1919. Address: Perryman, Md. Deceased.

STOCKHAM, William Henry, mfr.; b. Lafayette, Ind., Sept. 15, 1861; s. Gabriel Henry and Alice (Bunker) S.; B.S., in Mech. Engring., U. of Ill., 1885; m. Kate F. Clark, Apr. 28, 1887. Supt. and sec. Ill. Malleable Iron Co., Chicago, 1887-92; pres. Stockham Mfg. Co., Chicago, 1896-1902; pres. Stockham Pipe & Fittings Co., Birmingham, Ala., 1903—; v.p. Junalusha Hotel Co., Lake Junalusha, N.C. Mem. exec. com. and chmn. bd. trustees Internat. S.S. Assn.; mem. exec. com. World's S.S. Assn.; v.p., gen. supt. and commr. The Southern Assembly; mem. exec. com. Ala. State Y.M.C.A.; pres. Birmingham S.S. Assn.; trustee Birmingham Southern Coll., Athens (Ala.) Coll. Home: Birmingham, Ala. Died Nov. 16, 1923.

STOCKING, Jay Thomas, clergyman; b. Lisbon, N.Y., Apr. 19, 1870; s. Myron T. and Elizabeth (Thompson) S.; A.B., Amherst, 1895, D.D., 1913; master of English, Lawrenceville (N.J.) Sch., 1895-98; B.D., Yale Div. Sch., 1901; studied U. of Berlin, 1902-03; m. Grace Cordelia Porter, Oct. 21, 1903; children—Harriet Porter, Elizabeth Porter, Alice Porter, Josephine Porter. Ordained Congl. ministry, 1901, asst. pastor Ch. of the Redeemer, New Haven, 1901-03; pastor 1st Ch., Bellows Falls, Vt., 1903-05, Central Ch., Newtonville, Mass., 1905-14; 1st Ch., Washington, D.C., 1914-15, Union Congl. Ch., Upper Montclair, N.J., 1915-27, Pilgrim Congl. Ch., St. Louis, Mo., 1927—. Pres. bd. trustees Congl. Conf. of Mo.; trustee Congl. Annuity Fund, Drury Coll., Oberlin Coll., Iberia Acad.; mem. exec. com. Fed. of Chs.; chmn. Congl. Commn. of Missions; mem. Bd. of Ministerial Relief; mem. commn. on internat. justice and good-will of Federal Council of Chs.; dir. Am. Peace Soc. Author: The Dearest Spot on Earth, 1908; The City That Never Was Reached, 1911; The Golden Goblet, 1914; Henry J. Patrick—An Appreciation; Mr. Friend o' Man, 1920; Query Queer, 1926; The Child in the Congregation, 1929. Home: St. Louis, Mo. Died Jan. 27, 1936.

STOCKING, William Alonzo, Jr., dairy husbandman; b. Simsbury, Conn., May 13, 1872; s. William A. and Serinda (Delanoy) S.; B.Agr., Conn. Agrl. Coll., 1895; B.S.A., Cornell U., 1898, M.S.A., 1904; m. Harriet M. Bliss, June 27, 1900. Asst. prof. dairy industry, 1906-09, prof., 1909—, Cornell U.; acting dir. N.Y. State Coll. of Agr., at Cornell U., 1913-14. Presbyn. Author: A Manual of Milk Products. Address: Ithaca, N.Y. Died Feb. 4, 1926.

STOCKTON, Charles G., M.D.; b. Madison, O., Aug. 27, 1853; s. Dr. Charles Lewis S.; ed. Westfield (N.Y.) Acad.; M.D., U. of Buffalo, 1878; ad eundem Niagara U.; m. Mary L. Taylor; children—Mrs. Harriet Sarah Kimball, Mary Louise (dec.), Lucy Witham, Mrs. Dorothy Taylor Sikes. Prof. materia medica and therapeutics, Niagara U., 1883-87; prof. medicine and clin. medicine med. dept. U. of Buffalo, 1887-1918, emeritus prof. medicine, 1918—; cons. phys. Buffalo Gen. Hosp., N.Y. State Hosp. for Crippled and Deformed Children, etc. Contbr. to Wilson's Am. Text Book of Applied Therapeutics, Loomis and Thompson's Am. System of Practical Medicine, Gould's Cyclo. of Medicine and Surgery, Personal Hygiene (Pyle), Nothnagle's Ency. of Practical Medicine (Am. edit.), Osler's Modern Medicine, Oxford System of Medicine, Nelson's Living Medicine. Author: Diseases of the Stomach. Home: Buffalo, N.Y. Died Jan. 6, 1931.

STOCKTON, Charles Herbert, rear admiral U.S.N.; b. at Phila., Oct. 13, 1845; s. Rev. William R. and Emma T. S.; apptd. to U.S. Naval Acad. from Pa., 1861, grad. 1865; LL.D., George Washington U., 1909; m. Cornelia Carter; m. 2d, Pauline Lentilhon King, Nov. 23, 1880. Ensign, Dec. 1, 1866; master, Mar. 12, 1868; lt., Mar. 26, 1869; lt. comdr., Nov. 15, 1881; comdr., Apr. 3, 1892; capt. July 8, 1899; rear admiral, Jan. 7, 1906. Summer of 1864, on board the Macedonian, in pursuit of Confederate steamers Florida and Tallahassee; served on Dacotah, Chattanooga and Mohican; service Navy Yard, Phila., 1869-70, 1873, 1874; Congress and Brooklyn, 1870-73; Dictator, 1873; Swatara, 1874-75; Hydrographic Office, 1875-76; Plymouth, 1876-79; Navy Yard, New York, 1879-80; Navy Yard, Washington, 1880-82; Iroquois, 1882-85; Bur. of Yards and Docks, 1885-89; comd. Thetis, 1889-91; Naval War Coll., 1891-94; spl. duty, 1894-95; comd. Yorktown, 1895-97; pres. Naval War Coll., 1898-1900; comd. Kentucky, 1901-03; naval attaché, Am. Embassy, London, 1903-06; pres. Bd. Inspection and Survey, 1906; pres. Naval Examining and Retiring Bds., 1906-07; comdg. Spl. Service Squadron, visiting Bordeaux, France, for the maritime expn., 1907; retired, Oct. 13, 1907. Pres. George Washington U., 1910-18. First U.S. del. to London

Naval Conf., 1908-09. Author of U.S. Naval War Code, and various works and papers on internat. law. Home: Washington, D.C. Died May 31, 1923.

STOCKTON, Francis Richard, author; b. Phila., Apr. 5, 1834; s. W. S. and Emily H. S.; grad. Phila. High School; journalist on Phila. and New York newspapers; began career as author (under name of Frank R. Stockton) by contributions to mags.; joined staff of Scribner's Monthly, and later was asst. editor St. Nicholas. Author (juvenile books): Roundabout Rambles; Tales Out of School; A Jolly Fellowship; Captain Chap; The Story of Viteau; Ting-A-Ling Stories; What Might Have Been Expected; The Floating Prince Kobel Land; The Bee Man of Orne; The Clocks of Rondaine; Personally Conducted; Stories of New Jersey; Buccaneers and Pirates of Our Coast. Novels and stories: The Lady or the Tiger; The Young Master of Hyson Hall; The Late Mrs. Null; The Great War Syndicate; The Hundredth Man; Stories of Three Burglars; A Chosen Few, Adventures of Captain Horn; Mrs. Cliff's Yacht; The Great Stone of Sardis; The Girl at Cobhurst; Rudder Grange; The Rudder Grangers Abroad; Pomona's Travels; The Casting Away of Mrs. Lecks and Mrs. Aleshine; Christmas Wreck and Other Stories; The Dusantes (sequel to Mrs. Lecks & Aleshine); Amos Kilbright; Ardis Claverden; The Merry Chanter; The House of Martha; The Watchmaker's Wife; A Story Teller's Pack; The Associate Hermits; The Vizier of the Two-Horned Alexander; Afield and Afloat; Bicycle of Cathay. Address: Charlestown, W.Va. Died 1902.

STOCKTON, Fred Everett, clergyman; b. Meadville, Pa., Apr. 26, 1877; s. Cyrus J. and Lucina A. (Bowles) S.; A.B., Allegheny Coll., Meadville, Pa., 1904, A.M., 1907; grad. Rochester Theol. Sem., 1907; D.D., Sioux Falls (S.D.) Coll., 1923; m. Lucy Evelyn Swisher, Aug. 23, 1905; children—Evelyn Strong, Virginia Helen, Richard Herbert (dec.), Faith Lucy, Delight, Mariam. Ordained Bapt. ministry, 1907; pastor Madison, S.D., later Watertown until 1919; missionary S.Dak. Bapt. Conv., 1919-20; gen. supt. N.Dak. Bapt. Conv., 1920. Editor N.Dak. Bapt. Bulletin. Mem. bd. dirs. Sioux Falls Coll., Northwestern Bapt. Hosp. Assn. Republican. Home: Fargo, N.D. Died Apr. 3, 1938.

STOCKTON, George, physician; b. Bainbridge, Ross County, Ohio, Apr. 17, 1854; s. Joseph Platler and Emma (Brown) S.; grad. Central High Sch., Columbus, 1872; studied Starling Med. Coll., Columbus; M.D., Bellevue Med. Coll. (New York U.), 1875; unmarried. Began practice at Chillicothe, O., 1875; asst. phys., 1880-1902, supt., 1902-December 15, 1909, Columbus State Hosp. Republican. Methodist. Contbr. to med. jours. Address: Columbus, O. Died Jan. 9, 1917.

STOCKTON, Howard, lawyer, financier; b. Phila., Pa., Feb. 15, 1842; s. Philip Augustus and Mary Ann (Remington) S.; silver medalist, Royal Saxon Poly. Inst., Dresden, 1862; m. Mary Mason, Jan. 6, 1870; 1 son, Philip S. Apptd. capt. U.S.V., June 9, 1862; 1st lt., 3d R.I. Cav., Mar. 17, 1864; 2d lt., Ordnance Corps U.S.A., May 23, 1864; bvtd. 1st lt., and capt., Sept. 14, 1866; 1st lt. Ordnance Corps U.S.A., May 13, 1867; resigned from army June 1, 1871. Lawyer at Boston, Sept. 20, 1871—. Treas. Cocheco Mfg. Co., 1876-87, Salmon Falls Mfg. Co., 1880-87; pres. Am. Bell Telephone Co., 1887-89; v.p. Old Colony R.R. Co.; dir. Merchants Nat. Bank, Boston Mfrs.' Mut. Fire Ins. Co.; treas. Merrimac Mfg. Co., 1889-1900, Essex Co., Boston, 1880—; actuary Mass. Hosp. Life Ins. Co. Pres. Boston Athenæum; trustee Mass. Inst. Tech.; del. to Diocesan convs., 1888-92; mem. Standing Com. Diocese of Mass., 1892. Home: Boston, Mass. Died Apr. 22, 1932.

STOCKTON, Joseph, soldier, transportation agt.; b. Pittsburgh, Pa., Aug. 10, 1833; ed. schs. of Pittsburgh; moved to Chicago, 1851; clerk in commn. house, then in Am. Transportation Co., and Ft. Wayne R.R., 1851-62. Enlisted, July 1862, in 1st Bd. of Trade regt. (72d Ill. inf.), serving as 1st lt. to lt. col.. 1862-65; wounded in battle of Franklin, Tenn., Nov. 30, 1864; bvtd. col. and brig. gen. for meritorious services. Agt. Empire Transportation Co., 1866—. Mem. Bd. Commrs. Lincoln Park, 1869-93, and leader in securing completion of Grant Memorial. Republican. Home: Chicago, Ill. Died 1907.

STOCKTON, Philip, financier; b. Brookline, Mass., March 20, 1874; s. Howard and Mary (Mason) S.; A.B., Harvard, 1896; B.S., Mass. Inst. Tech., 1899; m. Margaret Head, Feb. 3, 1906; children—Charles Head, Margaret (Mrs. Charles Francis Adams, Jr.). Civ. engr. Merrimac (cotton) Mfg. Co., Huntsville, Ala., 1900; treas. Lowell (Mass.) Bleachery, 1901; pres. Old Colony Trust Company, 1910-34; pres. First National Bank of Boston, 1920—; dir. Am. Tel. & Tel. Co., Submarine Signal Co., Fall River Gas Works Co., Ludlow Mfg. Associates, N.E. Mut. Ins. Co., Am. Sugar Refining Co., Guarantee Co. of N. America, Haverhill Gas Co., General Electric Co.; trustee Bankers' Electric Protective Assn., Boston Five Cents Savings Bank; dir. many other cos. Mem. corp. and chmn. finance com. Mass. Inst. Tech., 1936—. Home: Manchester, Mass. Died Feb. 11, 1940.

STOCKTON, Robert Henry, mfr.; b. Mt. Sterling, Ky., July 5, 1842; s. George Jouett and Gusta Ann (Somersall) S.; ed. common schs.; m. Bettie May Warder, Dec. 1867 (died 1904). Served 4 yrs. in C.S.A.; lt. Co. I, 2d Mo. Regt., Cockrell's Brigade. First sec. of Simmons Hardware Co., St. Louis, 10 yrs., v.p. 10 yrs.; pres. Majestic Mfg. Co., mfrs. of charcoal, iron and malleable iron ranges; dir. Miss. Valley Trust Co. Dir. La. Purchase Expn. (chmn. press and publicity com.), 1904; mem. bd. of Washington U. Mem. Christian (Disciples) Ch. Home: St. Louis, Mo. Died 1923.

STOCKTON, William Tennent, lawyer; b. Jacksonville, Fla., Dec. 2, 1887; s. John Noble Cumming and Fannie Gilchrist (Baker) S.; student Princeton, 1905-08, A.M., 1927; B.A., Oxford U. (Rhodes scholar), 1910, diploma econs., 1911; m. Nell Owens Waldo, Jan. 5, 1918; children—William Tennent, Albigence Lamar Waldo. Admitted to Florida bar, 1912; member Stockton, Ulmer & Murchison, 1925-33 and, 1935—; asso. gen. counsel Home Owners Loan Corp., Washington, D.C., 1933-35; pres. Ortega Company, 1930-33. Commissioned capt. F.A., U.S.A., 1917; in St. Mihiel and Argonne offensives; bravery citation, Nov. 1918. Trustee Bolles Sch., Jacksonville. Democrat. Episcopalian. Home: Jacksonville, Fla. Died Oct. 31, 1937.

STOCKWELL, Chester Twitchell, author; b. Royalston, Mass., Sept. 5, 1841; s. Emmons and Elvira (Wood) S.; common and high school edn. at Royalston and Winchendon, Mass., and bus. coll., Poughkeepsie, N.Y.; m. Sophia G., d. Capt. Jonas Pierce, 1866. In comml. pursuits, 1863-67; in newspaper work on Iowa State Register and others; studied medicine; in dental practice, Des Moines, Ia., 1872-75; later in Springfield, Mass.; edited New England Dental Jour., Springfield, and Archives of Dentistry, St. Louis. Author: The Evolution of Immortality, 1887; New Modes of Thought, 1901; also various articles in mags. Address: Stockbridge, Mass. Died 1911.

STOCKWELL, Frederick Emerson, ch. official; b. Providence, R.I., Jan. 23, 1868; s. Thomas Blanchard and Harriet Elizabeth (Davis) S.; grad. Classical High Sch., Providence, 1886; A.B., Brown U., 1890; B.D., Union Theol. Sem., 1898; A.M., Columbia, 1899; D.D., Miami U., 1915; m. Fay Mary MacCracken, Dec. 5, 1899; children—Catherine MacCracken (Mrs. Walter Herman Linder), Martha Munn (Mrs. Dwight Curtis Mumford), Frederica Mayhew, Eunice LeBaron. Teacher, Franklin Sch., Phila., Pa., 1890-92, Classical High Sch., Providence, 1892-94; ordained ministry Congl. Ch. in U.S.A., 1898; asst. pastor West End Presbyn. Ch., N.Y. City, 1898-99, pastor First Presbyn. Ch., Beverly, N.J., 1900-07, First Ch., Newburgh, N.Y., 1907-17, Third Ch., Trenton, N.J., 1917-19; gen. dir. dept. of colls., theol. sems. and training schs., Presbyn. Bd. Christian Edn. in U.S.A., 1919—. Mem. coll. bd., Presbyn. Ch. in U.S.A., 1912-18; mem. Presbyn. Bd. Ministerial Relief and Sustentation, 1918-19. Mem. Am. Council on Edn., 1931—. Republican. Home: Philadelphia, Pa. Died June 21, 1933.

STOCKWELL, John Nelson, astronomical mathematician; b. Northampton, Mass., Apr. 10, 1832; s. William and Clarissa (Whittemore) S.; ed. common schs., Brecksville, O.; hon. A.M., 1862, Ph.D., 1876, Western Reserve; m. Sarah Healy, Dec. 6, 1855. Known for original investigations in astronomy. Author: Memoir on the Secular Variations of the Planetary Orbits, in Smithsonian Contributions to Knowledge, 1872; Stock and Interest Tables, 1873; Theory of the Moon's Motion, 1881; Eclipse Cycles, 1901; Sheet Tax Tables, 1903; Theory of Planetary Perturbations, and the Cosmogony of Laplace, 1904; Ocean Tides, with elaborate tables for their computation, 1919. Contbr. Am. and foreign scientific jours. Fellow Am. Acad. Arts and Sciences, A.A.A.S. Address: Cleveland, O. Died May 18, 1920.

STOCKWELL, Thomas Blanchard, educator; b. Worcester, Mass., July 6, 1839; s. Amos W. and Susan LeB. S.; grad. Brown U., 1862, A.M., 1865; m. Harriet E. Davis, May 15, 1866. Teacher, 1862-75; commr. pub. schs., State of R.I., 1875—. Home: Providence, R.I. Died 1906.

STODDARD, Charles Augustus, clergyman; b. Boston, Mass., May 28, 1833; s. Charles and Mary (Noble) S.; A.B., Williams Coll., 1854, A.M., 1857; studied U. of Edinburgh and Free Ch. of Scotland Theol. Sem., 1855-56; grad. Union Theol. Sem., 1859; D.D., Williams, 1871; m. Mary, d. Dr. Samuel I. Prime, Nov. 16, 1859. Ordained Presbyn. ministry, 1859; pastor Washington Heights Ch., New York, 1859-83; asso. editor, 1869, part owner, The Observer, 1873, editor-in-chief after death of Dr. Prime, July 18, 1885, until 1902. Pres. New York Instn. for Instrn. Deaf and Dumb, Canton (China) Christian Coll. Am. Seamen's Friend Soc.; v.p. Am. Foreign Christian Union, Am. Tract Soc.; hon. sec. Evang. Alliance. Author: Across Russia from the Baltic to the Danube, 1891; Spanish Cities, with Glimpses of Gibraltar and Tangier, 1892; Beyond the Rockies, 1894; A Spring Journey in California, 1895; Cruising Among the Caribbees, 1895, 1903. Edited The Centennial Celebration of Williams College; many sermons and pamphlets. Home: New York, N.Y. Died June 5, 1920.

STODDARD, Charles Warren, author, educator; b. Rochester, N.Y., Aug. 7, 1843; s. Samuel Burr and Harriet Abigail (Freeman) S.; ed. common schs. N.Y. and Calif. and U. of Calif.; ill health prevented graduation; L.H.D., Catholic U. of Am.; Ph.D., Santa Clara Coll., Calif. Began as actor; 7 yrs. spl. traveling corr. San Francisco Chronicle, visiting nearly every part of the globe, including 5 yrs. in the South Seas. Prof. English lit., U. of Notre Dame, Ind., 1885-87; same, Catholic U. of America, 1889—. Author: Poems, 1867; South Sea Idyls, 1873; Marshallah, a Flight into Egypt, 1881, A2; The Lepers of Molokai, 1885; A Troubled Heart, 1885; Lazy Letters from Low Lattitudes, 1894, N1; The Wonder Worker of Padua, 1896; A Cruise Under the Crescent from Suez to San Marco, 1898, R1; Over the Rocky Mountains to Alaska, 1899; In the Footprints of the Padres, 1902, R10; Exits and Entrances, 1903, L9; For the Pleasure of His Company, 1903, R10; Father Damien—A Sketch, 1903, The Island of Tranquil Delights, 1904; The Confessions of a Reformed Poet, 1907; The Dream Lady, 1907. Address: Monterey, Calif. Died 1909.

STODDARD, Cora Frances, temperance worker; b. Irvington, Neb., Sept. 17, 1872; d. Emerson Hathaway and Julia Frances (Miller) Stoddard; B.A., Wellesley, 1896. Editor Scientific Temperance Jour. (quarterly), 1906—; a founder and exec. sec. Scientific Temperance Fedn.; sec. exec. com. Nat. Temperance Council; dir. Intercollegiate Prohibition Assn.; mem. exec. com. World League Against Alcoholism. Del. of U.S. Govt. to Internat. Congress on Alcoholism, London, 1909, Washington, 1920, Lausanne, Switzerland, 1921, Copenhagen, 1923; sec. United Com. on War Temperance Activities, 1917-20. Mem. Am. Acad. Polit. and Social Science. Republican. Conglist. Author: Handbook of Modern Facts about Alcohol, 1914 (Spanish edit., 1921); Wet and Dry Years in a Decade of Massachusetts Public Records, 1922; More Massachusetts Records and Prohibition, 1925; Science and Human Life in the Alcohol Problem, 1925; Fifteen Years of the Drink Question in Massachusetts (with Amy Woods), 1929; The Scientist Experiments with Alcohol (with Aubra D. Williams), 1935; (pamphlets) Alcohol's Ledger in Industry; Alcohol in Every Day Life; The World's New Day and Alcohol; Alcohol in Experience and Experiment; Some Practical Aspects of the Alcohol Question. Home: Seymour, Conn. Died May 13, 1936.

STODDARD, Elizabeth Drew Barstow, author; b. (Barstow) Mattapoisett, Mass., May 6, 1823; ed. Wheaton Female Sem., Mass.; m. Richard Henry Stoddard, 1852. Author: The Morgesons; Two Men; Temple House; Lolly Dinks' Doings (a juvenile book); Poems. Contribution to Harper's Atlantic and other mags. Address: New York, N.Y. Died 1902.

STODDARD, Enoch Vine, physician; b. New London, Conn., July 10, 1840; s. Enoch Vine and Mary S. (Allen) S.; grad. Trinity Coll., Hartford, 1860, A.M., 1863; studied med. dept. Yale Coll., 1861-62; grad. Albany Med. Coll., 1863; m. Caroline Sarah Butts, 1878. Surgeon 1st U.S. Chasseurs, 65th N.Y. vols., 1863-64; in practice at Rochester, 1864—. Health commr., Rochester; pres. State Bd. of Charities. Author: Bertrand Du Guesclin, His Life and Times, 1897. Address: Rochester, N.Y. Died 1908.

STODDARD, Francis Hovey, univ. prof.; b. Middlebury, Vt., Apr. 25, 1847; s. Solomon and Frances Elizabeth (Greenwood) S.; A.B., Amherst Coll., 1869, A.M., 1886; Ph.D., Western U. of Pa. (now U. of Pittsburgh), 1896; LL.D., New York U., 1914; student Oxford U., Eng., 1884-86; m. Lucy M. Smith, May 14, 1873; 1 dau., Lucy. Instr. U. of Calif., 1886-88; prof. English lang. and lit., 1888—, dean faculty of Coll. of Arts and Pure Science, 1911-14, prof. emeritus, 1914—, New York U. Author: The Modern Novel, 1883; The Ideal in Literature, 1884; Psycho-Biography, 1885; Women in the English Universities, 1886; The Cædmon Poems, 1887; Conditions of Labor in England, 1887; Miracle Plays and Mysteries, 1887; Tolstoi and Matthew Arnold; The Uses of Rhetoric; Inductive Work in College Classes, 1890; Literary Spirit in the Colleges, 1893; The Study of the English Language; Lord Byron (Introduction to Works), 1899; The Evolution of the English Novel, 1900; Life of Charles Butler, 1903. Editor: Poems of National Spirit, 1904. Home: New York, N.Y. Died Feb. 6, 1936.

STODDARD, John Lawson, lecturer; b. Brookline, Mass., Apr. 24, 1850; s. Lewis Tappan and Sarah (Lothrop) S.; A.B., Williams Coll., 1871; studied Yale Div. Sch.; m. Mary H. Brown, Dec. 24, 1877; m. 2d, Ida M. O'Donnell, Aug. 15, 1901. Extensive traveler; author and promoter of the Stoddard lectures in larger Am. cities for nearly 20 yrs.; retired from platform, 1897. Author: Red Letter Days Abroad, 1884; Glimpses of the World, 1892; Stoddard Lectures on Travel Abroad and in America (15 vols.), 1898-1909; The Stoddard Library, an Anthology, 1910; Poems, 1911; Rebuilding a Lost Faith, 1921; Two Arguments for Catholicism, 1927; Life of St. Paul, 1928; Life of Pope Gregory the Great, 1929; Evening of Life, 1929. Translation from the German, Christ and the Critics (2 vols.), 1923-24; translation from the French, The Theology of St. Paul, 2 vols., 1925,

26. Home: Merano, Alto Adige, Italy. Died June 4, 1931.

STODDARD, John Tappan, chemist; b. at Northampton, Mass., Oct. 20, 1852; s. William H. and Helen (Humphrey) S.; A.B., Amherst, 1874; student chemistry and physics, 1875-76; A.M., Ph.D., Göttingen, 1877; m. Mary Grover Leavitt, June 26, 1879; father of William Leavitt S. Asst. prin. Northampton High Sch., 1874-75; prof. physics and mathematics, 1878-81, chemistry and physics, 1881-97, chemistry, 1897—, Smith Coll. Author: Outline of Qualitative Analysis, 1883; Lecture Notes on General Chemistry (2 vols.), 1884, 1885; Quantitative Experiments in General Chemistry, 1908; Introduction to General Chemistry, 1910; The Science of Billiards, 1913; An Introduction to Organic Chemistry, 1914. Contbr. scientific articles and revs. to cyclos. and mags. Address: Northampton, Mass. Died Dec. 8, 1919.

STODDARD, Richard Henry, poet; b. Hingham, Mass., July 2, 1825; m. Elizabeth D. Barstow, 1852. Worked as iron moulder in youth; soon began to contribute to papers; held a position in custom house, 1853-70; confidential clerk to Gen. McClellan, 1870-73; city librarian, New York, 1874-75; literary reviewer N.Y. World, 1860-70; of N.Y. Mail and Express, 1880—. Author: Poems; Adventures in Fairy Land; Life of Humboldt; Songs and Summer; The King's Bell; The Book of the East; Abraham Lincoln, A Horatian Ode; Putman the Brave; A Century After; Life of Washington Irving; The Lion's Cub and Other Verse; Under the Evening Lamp; etc. Edited the Bric-a-Brac Series. Address: New York, N.Y. Died 1903.

STODDARD, William Osborn, author, journalist; b. Homer, N.Y., Sept. 24, 1835; s. Prentice S. and Sarah A. (Osborn) S.; A.B., U. of Rochester, 1858, A.M., 1861; m. Susan E. Cooper, 1873 (deceased); father of William Osborn Stoddard, Jr. Journalist and farmer Chicago, and Champaign, Ill., 1857-60; in U.S. Vols., 3 months in 1861; sec. to President Lincoln, 1861-64; U.S. marshal of Ark., 1864-66. Journalist and in business pursuits in New York, 1866—; also an inventor, with 9 patents; held office under New York city govt. Republican. Wrote first editorial upon nomination of Abraham Lincoln for President, Central Illinois Gazette, May 1859; first similar article naming him for President, McElrath's New York Century, letters, etc., May 1859. Author: Little Smoke, 1891; Table Talk of Lincoln, 1892; Men of Business, 1892; Battle of New York, 1892; The White Cave, 1893; Guert Ten Eyck, 1893; On the Old Frontier, 1893; Christ the Model Maker, 1894; The Partners, 1895; Chumley's Past, 1895; The Windfall, 1896; The Swordmaker's Son, 1896; Walled In, 1897; Lost Gold of the Montezumas, 1897; The Red Patriot, 1897; The Whistle Dispatch Boat, 1898; First Cruiser Out, 1898; Success Against Odds, 1898; With the Black Prince, 1898; The Young Financier, 1899; Running the Cuban Blockade, 1899; Lincoln at Work, 1899; Ulric the Jarl, 1899; Ned, Son of Webb, 1900; The Noank's Log, 1900; Montanye, 1901; Jack Morgan, 1901; Boys of Bunker Academy, 1902; Voyage of the Charlemagne, 1902; Errand Boy of Andrew Jackson, 1902; Ahead of the Army, 1902; The Spy of Yorktown, 1903; The Fight for the Valley, 1904; Long Bridge Boys, 1904; The Boy Lincoln, 1905; Dan Monroe, 1905; Two Cadets With Washington, 1906; In the Open, 1908. Address: Madison, N.J. Died Aug. 29, 1925.

STODDART, James Henry, actor; b. Barnsley, Yorkshire, England, Oct. 13, 1827 (son of actor of same name); reared and ed. Glasgow, Scotland; entered theatrical profession there; acted in most of prin. cities of England; came to U.S., 1854; joined company of the Elder Wallack; later with Lester Wallack, Laura Keene, Mrs. John Wood, Dion Boucicault, and 20 yrs. with A.M. Palmer at Union Sq. and Madison Sq. theatres. Address: Sewaren, N.J. Died 1907.

STODDART, Joseph Marshall, editor, pub.; b. Phila., Aug. 10, 1845; s. Joseph M. and Eliza (Fahnestock) S.; ed. pub. schs. and acads. Founded To-Day (weekly) and Stoddart's Review (monthly); mng. editor Lippincott's Mag., 1886-94; editor New Science Review, 1896; later editor The Era. Address: New York, N.Y. Died Feb. 25, 1921.

STOECKEL, Carl; b. New Haven, Conn., Dec. 7, 1858; s. Gustave Jacob and Matilda Bertha (Wehner) S.; ed. Thomas Sch. and Hopkins Grammar Sch., New Haven, and under pvt. tutors in America and Europe; hon. A.M., Yale, 1905; m. Ellen Battell Terry, May 6, 1895. Edited and printed for pvt. and gratuitous circulation, The Letters of John Sedgwick, Maj. Gen., U.S.A. (2 vols.), and erected battle monument to him at his birthplace, Cornwall Hollow, Conn.; purchased the birthplace and farm of John Brown, at Torrington, Conn., and presented it to the John Brown, Assn.; founded Litchfield County Univ. Club, 1896, composed of 200 graduates of colls.; founded, 1899, the Litchfield County Choral Union, 700 members, and built on his pvt. grounds, for annual concerts of same, the "Music Shed," at Norfolk, admission being by invitation; also established fund for yearly production of 2 compositions; provided a fund for ann. publ. of a book pertaining to Litchfield County, to be written by a member of the club, for free distribution. Trustee N.E. Conservatory of Music. Concerts in the "Music Shed" attracted some of the highest talent of America and Europe, and many remarkable compositions have been given initial performance there. Brought to U.S. the Anglo-African composer, S. Coleridge Taylor, the Finnish composer, Jean Sibelius to conduct original works in the "Shed," and the English composer, R. Vaughn Williams. Address: Norfolk, Conn. Died Nov. 1, 1925.

STOECKEL, Gustave Jacob, musician, educator; b. Maikammer, Germany, Nov. 9, 1819; grad. Kaiserslauten, Bavaria; Mus.D., Yale, 1864; teacher and organist in Germany; came to U.S., 1847, and in 1849 became instr. in music at Yale and organist in Coll. Chapel; Battell prof. music, Yale, and 1st head of the dept. of music, 1890-96, prof. emeritus, 1896—. Pub. collections of sacred music, a College Hymn Book used at Yale for male voices, as well as instrumental and vocal compositions of various kinds; composed several operas, selections from which have been performed by full orchestra. Address: Norfolk, Conn. Died 1907.

STOEK, Harry Harkness, mining engr.; b. Washington, D.C., Jan. 16, 1866; s. Jacob F. and Susan (Lear) S.; B.S., Lehigh U., 1887, E.M., 1888; m. Miriam Ricketts, Dec. 20, 1894. Asst. engr. Susquehanna Coal Co., Wilkes-Barre, 1888-90; instr. in mining, metallurgy and geology, Lehigh U., 1890-93; asst. prof. mining engring., Pa. State Coll., 1893-97; editor Mines and Minerals, Scranton, Pa., 1897-1909; prof. mining engring. and head of dept., U. of Ill., 1909—. Sec. Ill. Mine Rescue Commn.; mem. Ill. Mining Investigation Commn. Republican. Episcopalian. Author: The Anthracite Coal Field, 1900; Economic History of Anthracite; Subsidence in Mining; Education of Mine Employees; The Storage of Coal. Also various bulletins. Address: Urbana, Ill. Died Mar. 1, 1923.

STOETZER, Herman Goethe, clergyman; b. Tambach, Saxony, Germany, July 10, 1863; s. Martin and Louise (Koenig) S.; came to U.S. 1871; Fairmont (W.Va.) Normal Sch.; A.B., West Va. U., 1889; A.M., Princeton, 1892; grad. Princeton Theol. Sem., 1893; post-grad. work same, 1893-94; D.D., Waynesburg, 1910; m. Margaret A. Brown, 1894; 1 son, John James Brown. Ordained Presbyn. ministry, 1894; pastor Mooredale, Pa., 1894-99, 1st Ch., Fairmont, W.Va., 1900-25; pastor emeritus, 1925—. Moderator Synod of W.Va., 1910; commr. to Gen. Assembly, 1899, 1903, 10, 22. Rotarian. Mason. Home: Fairmont, W.Va. Died June 9, 1931.

STOKES, Anson Phelps, banker; b. New York, Feb. 22, 1838; s. James and Caroline (Phelps) S.; ed. by tutors and in pvt. schs., New York; m. Helen Louisa, d. Isaac Newton Phelps, Oct. 17, 1865; father of James Graham Phelps and Anson Phelps S., Jr. Partner in Phelps, Dodge & Co., mchts.; afterwards in Phelps, Stokes & Co., bankers; chmn. bd. dirs. The Woodbridge Co. and of The Haynes Co.; dir. U.S. Trust Co., Mechanics' Bank. Trustee or dir. in Aged and Infirm Clergy Fund, Am. Social Science Assn., Liverpool and London and Globe Ins. Co., Second Nat. Bank, etc. First pres. Reform Club; for 2 terms vice-comdr. New York Yacht Club 1863, went by steamer to Calif., 1863, and returned overland; made a number of cruises in his yachts Clytie, Mermaid and Sea Fox; pres. Nat. Assn. Anti-Imperialist Clubs, 1900. Democrat. Prominent in free-trade and civil service reform movements. Author: Joint-Metallism, 1894; Dangers of the Proposed National Paper-Money Trust (pamphlet), 1898; Cruising in the West Indies, 1902; Cruising in the Caribbean with a Camera, 1903. Home: New York, N.Y. Died June 28, 1913.

STOKES, Arthur Charles, surgeon; b. Bury, Quebec, Canada, Dec. 24, 1869; s. Charles Henry and Mary Ann (Chapman) S.; brought to U.S., 1882; B.Sc., Ia. State Coll. Agr. and Mechanic Arts, 1892; student medicine, U. of Ill., 1895-97; M.D., U. of Neb., 1899; post-grad. work univs. of Halle, Kiel and Berlin; m. Bertha Shackleford, Dec. 17, 1910. Began practice at Omaha, Neb., 1899; prof. clin. surgery U. of Neb. Coll. of Medicine, 1904-25, also regent of the univ., 1931—; med. dir. and mem. bd. Guarantee Mut. Life Ins. Co., World Accident Co. Organized and went to France with Base Hosp. No. 49 (U. of Neb.), 1917, continuing there until May 1919; col. Med. Res. Corps. Citation for war record: Victory medal. Chmn. Omaha Chapter Am. Red Cross, 1920-35. Fellow Am. Coll. Surgeons, 1908—. Republican. Episcopalian. Mason. Contbr. to med. jours. Home: Omaha, Neb. Died Jan. 24, 1940.

STOKES, Charles Francis, M.D., surgeon; b. N.Y. City, Feb. 20, 1863; s. Charles and Helen (Durham) S.; Adelphi Acad. and Poly. Inst. of Brooklyn; M.D., Coll. Phys. and Surg. (Columbia U.), 1884, Sc.D., 1911; LL.D., Jefferson Med. Coll., Phila., 1911; M.A., Harvard, 1912; m. Charlotte Bermingham, Apr. 18, 1892; 1 son, John Fraser. Entered U.S. Navy as asst. surgeon, Feb. 1, 1889; promoted surgeon, May 31, 1900, later med. insp. and med. dir.; retired Jan. 10, 1917. Surgeon gen. U.S.N. and chief Bur. Medicine and Surgery, with rank of rear admiral, Feb. 5, 1910-14. Later practiced in N.Y. City. Fellow Am. Coll. Surgeons (mem. original bd. of regents, 1913); pres. Am. Electrotherapeutic Assn. Home: New York, N.Y. Died Oct. 29, 1931.

STOKES, Frederick Abbot, publisher; b. Brooklyn, N.Y., Nov. 4, 1857; s. Frederick Abbot and Caroline Augusta (Allen) S.; B.A., Yale, 1879; m. Ellen R. Colby, May 10, 1883; children—Frederick Colby (dec.), Horace Winston, Frederick Brett. Established, 1881, house which later became Frederick A. Stokes Co., of which pres., 1890—. Pres. Am. Pubs.' Assn., 1911-14 (sec. 1903-07), MacDowell Club, 1913-16 (treas. 1906-08); chmn. Am. Pub. Copyright League; sec. Aldine Club, 1895-97; v.p. Nat. Assn. Book Pubs., 1928-30; hon. chmn. Children's Garden Bldg. Com., 1927—. Republican. Episcopalian. Author: College Tramps, 1880. Editor: The Poems of Sir John Suckling, 1886; The Pocket Magazine, 1898-1901. Contbr. to various periodicals. Chmn. Book Publishers' War Service Com., 1918-19. Home: New York, N.Y. Died Nov. 15, 1939.

STOKES, Henry Bolter, insurance; b. New York, Dec. 23, 1847; s. Henry and Mary A. S.; ed. Mt. Pleasant Acad. and Columbia Grammar Sch., New York; m. Sophia I. Lockwood, Oct. 7, 1874 (died 1884). Chmn. bd. of dirs. Manhattan Life Ins. Co.; 1st v.p. Manhattan Savings Instn.; dir. Citizens' Central Nat. Bank; special partner in Walter C. Stokes & Co. Home: Mamaroneck, N.Y. Died Jan. 2, 1914.

STOKES, Henry Warrington; b. Philadelphia, Pa., June 24, 1867; s. Francis and Katherine Wistar (Evans) S.; A.B., Haverford (Pa.) Coll., 1887; m. Helen B., d. Dr. James Tyson, May 20, 1905; 1 son, James Tyson. Treas. York Haven (Pa.) Co., 1889-1914, pres., 1914-29; dir. Provident Mut. Life Ins. Co. Mem. Am. Paper Pulp Assn. (pres. 1923-25), Wrapping Paper Manufacturers' Service Bur. (pres. 1918-28). Pres. Rush Hosp. for Consumptives; pres. bd. mgrs. Sleighton Farm Sch. for Girls, Darlington, Pa., and of Haverford (Pa.) Coll.; mem. bd. mgrs. Dunwoody Home for Convalescents, Newton Sq., Pa. Republican. Home: Media, Pa. Died Nov. 30, 1938.

STOKES, James William, congressman; b. Orangeburg County, S.C., Dec. 12, 1853; grad. Washington and Lee U., 1876; taught school 12 years and meanwhile grad., M.D., Vanderbilt U.; m. E. L. Landess, Dec. 29, 1881. Farmer, 1889; pres. State Farmers' Alliance 2 terms; mem. State senate, 1890; del. at large to Nat. Dem. Conv., 1892; presdl. elector same year; received certificate of election to Congress, 1894, but seat was declared vacant; reëlected, Nov. 1896, for short term, 54th Congress; mem. Congress, Dec. 1896—, from 7th S.C. dist. Democrat. Home: Orangeburg, S.C. Died 1901.

STOKES, John Patrick, lawyer; b. Pensacola, Fla., Nov. 30, 1886; s. John and Mary (Conlin) S.; ed. public schs. and business coll.; hon. LL.B., U. of Miami, Fla.; m. Bertha D. Hendrix, Aug. 18, 1906; children—John P., Thomas Jefferson. Began practice at Pensacola, 1904; moved to Miami, Fla., 1923; div. solicitor F.E.C. Ry. Co.; mem. firm Loftin, Stokes & Calkins. U.S. commr. and Circuit Ct. commr.; mem. Fla. Ho. of Rep., 1909, Senate, 1911-13, 1919-21, 23 (resigned); chmn. joint legislative com. that investigated convict abuses in Fla.; state's atty. 1st Fla. Circuit, 1913-17. Democrat. Elk. Author of Florida's Constl. amendment prohibiting levy of state income and inheritance taxes. Home: Miami, Fla. Died Apr. 10, 1939.

STOKES, Rose Pastor, social worker; b. Augustava, Suvolk, Russia, July 18, 1879; d. Jacob and Anna (Lewin) Wieslander; ed. Jewish Free Sch., London, 1887-89; lived at London, Eng., 1883-90; came to U.S., 1890; worked as cigar maker, Cleveland, 1890-1903; contbr., 1901-05, asst. editor, 1903-05, Jewish Daily News, NewYork; m. J. G. Phelps Stokes, July 18, 1905. Engaged in propaganda of socialism, Aug. 11, 1906; resigned from Socialist Party, 1917, and one of organizers and mem. exec. com. National Party. Lecturer, Intercollegiate Socialist Soc. Author: The Woman Who Wouldn't (play in three acts), 1916; Songs of Labor (translation). Home: New York, N.Y. Died June 20, 1933.

STOLL, Charles Augustus, coll. pres.; b. Brookfield, Wis., Oct. 28, 1872; s. Jacob and Margaret (Harbeck) S.; ed. Greenville Coll., Greenville, Ill., 1900-04; A.M., U. of Wis., 1909; student U. of Colo., 1923; m. Emma M. Baldwin, Aug. 26, 1903; 1 dau., Marion Joy. Ordained ministry of Free Methodist Ch., 1905; dean Central Acad. and Coll., McPherson, Kan., 1915-18, dean and acting pres., 1919, pres., 1921—. Edni. sec. Y.M.C.A. and lecturer during World War I. Free Methodist. Home: McPherson, Kan. Died Apr. 5, 1939.

STOLZ, Benjamin, lawyer; b. Syracuse, N.Y., Oct. 13, 1867; s. David and Regina (Strauss) S.; ed. grammar and high schs., Syracuse; studied law in office of Jenney, Brooks, Marshall & Ruger; LL.B., cum laude Columbia, 1889; m. Rose Landsberg, Dec. 26, 1898; children—Max Landsberg, Regina. Admitted to N.Y. bar, 1889, and began practice at Syracuse;

asso. in practice with Col. Edwin S. Jenney and William S. Jenney as Jenney, Jenney & Stolz; mem. firm McGowan & Stolz (later himself and son), 1896—. Chmn. Legal Advisory Bd. 4th Dist. Onondago Co., World War I. Organizer, 1918, pres. Fed. Jewish Charities of Syracuse; treas. United Jewish Charities, Hebrew Free Loan Assn., Flower Memorial Fund; dir. Syracuse Foundation, Jewish Orphan Assn. of Western N.Y.; pres. Jewish Communal Home; pres. Soc. of Concord (religious orgn.). Democrat. Home: Syracuse, N.Y. Died May 29, 1937.

STOLZ, Joseph, rabbi, b. Syracuse, N.Y., Nov. 3, 1861; s. David and Regina (Strauss) S.; B.L., U. of Cincinnati, 1883; grad. as rabbi, Hebrew Union Coll., Cincinnati, 1884, D.D., 1898, D.H.L., 1931; m. Blanche Rauh, June 24, 1890; children—Mrs. Edna Brody, Leon, Mrs. Regina S. Greenbaum. Ordained rabbi, 1884; rabbi B'nai Israel Temple, Little Rock, Ark., 1884-87, Zion Temple, Chicago, 1887-95, Isaiah Temple, Chicago, 1895-1927, rabbi emeritus, Temple Isaiah-Israel, 1927—. Mem. exec. com. Central Conf. Am. Rabbis (hon. pres.; pres., 1905-07); mem. Am. Jewish Com.; pres. Chicago Rabbinical Assn., 1920-25; exec. com. Chicago Fed. Synagogues; mem. exec. bd. Union of Am. Hebrew Congregations. Mem. Chicago Bd. Edn., 1899-1905; mem. Chicago Crime Commn. Author: Funeral Agenda of Jews, 1897. Address: Chicago, Ill. Died Feb. 6, 1941.

STONE, Alfred, architect; b. E. Machias, Me., July 29, 1834; s. Rev. Thomas Treadwell and Laura (Poor) S.; grad. high school, Salem, Mass., 1850; architectural edn. in offices in Boston; began practice there, 1856; in active practice in Providence, R.I., 1864—; m. Ellen M. Putnam, July 14, 1864. Designed R.I. State prison, Providence county court house, Providence public library, Y.M.C.A. bldg., schools, hosps., coll. bldgs., bus. blks., pvt. houses, etc. Pres. R.I. Chapter Am. Inst. Architects for many yrs.; sec. Am. Inst. Architects, 1893-99. Address: Providence, R.I. Died 1908.

STONE, Allison, newspaper pub.; b. Providence, R.I., July 17, 1873; s. Charles Morgan and Sarah Frances (Hart) S.; B.P., Brown U., 1896. Gen. mgr. Providence Journal Co., 1917—. Episcopalian. Home: Providence, R.I. Died Sept. 11, 1940.

STONE, Arthur John, silversmith; b. Sheffield, Eng., Sept. 26, 1847; s. Joseph and Ann (Mills) Stones; (final "s" was dropped on coming to America); ed. ch. schs. of Sheffield and at Sheffield Sch. of Art; m. Elizabeth Bent Eaton, 1896. Designer and chaser for James Dixon & Sons, Sheffield, 1874-84, and for W. B. Durgin, Concord, N.H., 1884-87; designer and head of hollow-ware dept., F. W. Smith & Co., Gardner, 1887-95; engaged in mfr. of silver toys with J. P. Howard, of Howard & Co., 5th Av., New York, 1895-96; an exponent of hand-wrought silver in the arts and crafts movement, 1901—; maker of the Pres. Eliot and Edwin Abbott loving cups; Sarah Wyman Whitman chalice, Trinity Ch., Boston; gold monstrance in Ch. of the Advent, Boston; communion plate and altar cross for St. Andrews Brotherhood, Ch. of St. James, Chicago; commemorative plate for Berkeley Coll., Yale U. Episcopalian. Republican. Mason. Home: Gardner, Mass. Died Feb. 6, 1938.

STONE, Carlos Huntington, educator; b. Mexico, N.Y., Oct. 23, 1857; s. Benjamin S. and Sarah (Chester) S.; A.B., Hamilton Coll., 1878, Ph.D., 1896; grad. Auburn Theol. Sem., 1883; m. Harriet E. Bristol, June 1883. Ordained Presbyn. ministry, 1883; pastor Fort Collins, Colo., 1883-86, Fulton, N.Y., 1886-87; headmaster the Stone Sch., 1887-1916; rep. of the Commn. for Relief in Belgium, 1916-17; dir. sec. Y.M.C.A., with A.E.F., Chaumont, France, 1918-19. Address: Brooklyn, N.Y. Died Feb. 2, 1934.

STONE, Charles Augustus, elec. engr., financier; b. Newton, Mass., Jan. 16, 1867; s. Charles H. and Mary Augusta (Green) S.; S.B., Mass. Inst. Tech., 1888; hon. A.M., Harvard, 1914; m. Mary A. Leonard, June 2, 1902; children—Charles Augustus, Margaret, Whitney, Janet Elizabeth. With Edwin S. Webster organized, 1889, firm of Stone & Webster, engrs. and mgrs. public service cos.; investigated and reported on operations of pub. utility cos.; soon assumed management of such cos. for pvt. owners; later undertook engring. work and constrn. of street rys., electric light and power plants, hydro-electric plants and gas and indsl. properties, among them the power sta. of Mississippi River Power Co., at Keokuk, Ia., and transmission line to St. Louis. Firm constructed cantonment at San Antonio, Tex., enlarge U.S. Arsenal at Rock Island, Ill., built ordnance base for A.E.F. in France, besides engaging in other war constrn. work. Pres. Am. Internat. Corp., 1916-23, and aided in revival of Pacific Mail Steamship service, acquisition and development of N.Y. Shipbuilding Co., constrn. of Hog Island Shipyard and building of ships for Emergency Fleet Corp., besides large engring. and constrn. developments in S. America and elsewhere. Chmn. bd. Stone & Webster, Inc.; dir. Fed. Res. Bank of N.Y., 1919-23; dir. Stone & Webster Engring. Co., Union Pacific R.R. Co., Stone & Webster and Blodget, Incorporated, Research Corp., Stone & Webster Service Corp. Mem. corp., Mass. Inst. Tech. Home: New York, N.Y. Died Feb. 25, 1941.

STONE, Charles Francis, judge; b. Cabot, Vt., May 21, 1843; s. Levi H. and Mary C. (Osgood) S.; A.B., Middlebury Coll., 1869; studied law with Hon. J. W. Stewart, Middlebury, and Judge Ellery A. Hibbard, Laconia; admitted to bar, 1872; m. Minnie A. Nichols, July 27, 1870 (died 1875); m. 2d, Mrs. Isabel S. Muncie, Sept. 12, 1896. Began practice at Laconia, 1872; chmn. Dem. State Com., 1882-90; mem. N.H. Ho. of Rep., 1883-84, 1887-88; candidate for Congress, 1892; naval officer port of Boston, 1894-98; Dem. candidate for gov. of N.H., 1898; received full party vote for U.S. Senate in Legislature of 1898-99; judge Superior Ct. of N.H., 1901—. Address: Laconia, N.H. Died July 25, 1910.

STONE, Charles Warren, congressman; b. Groton, Mass., June 29, 1843; s. Warren F. and Mary (Williams) S.; A.B., Williams Coll., 1863; m. Elizabeth Moorhead, Jan. 30, 1868. Admitted to bar, 1866; in practice at Warren, Pa.; also interested in lumbering, oil producing and farming. County supt. schs. Warren County, Pa., 1865; mem. Pa. Ho. of Rep., 1870-71, Senate, 1877-78; lt. gov. of Pa., 1879-83; sec. of the commonwealth, 1887-90; elected 51st Congress, 1890, for unexpired term (1890-91) of L. F. Watson, deceased; reëlected 52d to 55th Congresses (1891-99), 27th Pa. Dist. Republican. Mem. S.R., Am. Acad. Polit. and Social Science. Address: Warren, Pa. Died Aug. 15, 1912.

STONE, Charles Waterman, engr.; b. Providence, R.I., Dec. 24, 1874; s. Waterman and Emily Clark (Steere) S.; ed. U. of Kan., 3½ yrs.; m. Harriet Anna Westinghouse, Sept. 4, 1902. Began with Franklin Electric Co., Kansas City, Mo., 1894; with W. S. Hill Electric Co., New Bedford, Mass., 1896-98, and Hancock Equipment Co., Boston, 1899; with Gen. Electric Co., Schenectady, N.Y., Aug. 1, 1899—, first draughting dept., later cons. engr., in charge of cons. dept., later mgr. central sta. dept., then cons. engr.; pres. Pioneer Thresher Co., Inc. Fellow Am. Inst. E.E. Republican. Episcopalian. Contbr. numerous papers to engring. assns. and lectured at various times before Engrs. Sch., Washington, D.C., Columbia U., etc. Home: Schenectady, N.Y. Died Feb. 3, 1938.

STONE, Charles Wellington, educator; b. Templeton, Mass., Dec. 13, 1853; s. Leonard and Margaret (Wellington) S.; A.B., Harvard, 1874, A.M., 1881; m. Ellen Buckingham, Oct. 2, 1877 (died 1881); m. 2d, Alice Stone, Sept. 26, 1883; children—Alice Wellington (dec.), Elsa Wellington. Established sch. preparatory for Harvard, 1879, the sch. No. 38 of the "English" Report of the Harvard Overseers; sec. Handel and Haydn Soc., 1890-97; pres. Stone Family Assn. Received silver medal of Mass. Hort. Soc., 1888. Author: Needles of Pine, 1886; various textbooks in secondary edn. Wrote various pub. articles on ednl. and hist. subjects. Address: Boston, Mass. Died Jan. 22, 1927.

STONE, Ellen Maria, missionary teacher; b. Roxbury, Mass., July 24, 1846; d. Benjamin Franklin and Lucy Waterman (Barker) Stone; grad. grammar and high schs., Chelsea, Mass.; unmarried. Taught schs. in Chelsea, 1866-67; on editorial staff Boston Congregationalist, 1867-78; became missionary A.B.C. F.M., 1878, located at Samokov, Bulgaria; afterward located at Philippopolis, S. Bulgaria, and in 1898 removed to Salonica, Macedonia. Sept. 3, 1901, she and Mrs. Katerina S. Tsilka (wife of an Albanian Protestant preacher) were kidnapped by brigands on a mountain road between Bansko and Djumia, Macedonia, European Turkey. Brigands demanded ransom of $110,000; ransom of nearly $65,000 finally paid, which had been raised by pub. subscription in U.S. and captives released after nearly 6 mos. of captivity. Contributed story of captivity to McClure's Magazine, May-Oct. 1902; her mss. and illustrations of book on "American Mission Work in the Balkans," concluding with story of captivity, were destroyed in Chelsea fire, Apr. 12, 1908. Mem. Am. Bd. W.B.M., W.C.T.U. (nat. lecturer in Dept. of Cooperation with Missions), Internat. Missionary Union. Lecturer, contbr. articles to missionary publs., also raising money for missions in Bulgaria, Macedonia, and Albania; gave much time to forwarding bill introduced into Congress by State Dept. at Washington, Mar. 1908, recommending appropriation of $66,000 to reimburse givers to ransom (when dept. had abandoned efforts to gain satisfaction from Turkey). Home: Chelsea, Mass. Died Dec. 13, 1927.

STONE, Frederick, jurist; b. Charles County, Md., Feb. 7, 1820; grad. St. John's Coll., Md., 1839; admitted to bar, 1841, in Southern Md.; apptd., 1852, one of commrs. to simplify and abridge the rules of pleading and conveyancing in Md. Mem. Md. legislature, 1865 and 1871; mem. Congress, 1867-71; chief judge 7th judicial circuit, Md., 1881-90; retired on account of age. Married 2d, Mrs. Jennie Fergusson, June 15, 1870. Address: La Plata, Md. Died 1899.

STONE, George Edward, botanist; b. Leicester, Mass., Sept. 6, 1860; s. Samuel Lamb and Sophia S. (McCrea) S.; B.S., Mass. Agrl. Coll., 1886; Mass. Inst. Tech, 1885-88; Ph.D, Leipzig, 1893; m. Mary Edward, d. Prof. Henry James Clark, Jan. 26, 1899. Botanist from youth; prof. botany, Mass. Agrl. Coll., 1893-1916, and plant physiologist, Mass. Agrl. Expt. Sta., 1895-1916; botanist to Mass. Bd. Agr. Fellow A.A.A.S. Home: Amherst, Mass. Died May 28, 1941.

STONE, George Frederick, sec. Bd. of Trade; b. Newburyport, Mass., Apr. 24, 1836; son Jacob and Eliza (Atkins) S.; alumnus Chicago-Kent Coll. of Law; m. Julia S., d. Rev. Ephriam Spaulding, one of the first band of missionaries from the U.S. to the Sandwich Islands. Mem. firm of Stone, Denny & Co., commn. merchants, Boston; pres. Boston Commercial Exchange (later Boston Chamber of Commerce), 1871-73; sec. Bd. of Trade of the City of Chicago, 1884—. Consul for several years for Guatemala, Nicaragua and Honduras. Republican. Mason, Odd Fellow (Past Grand). Mem. bd. of mgrs. Nat. Bd. of Trade. Home: Evanston, Ill. Deceased.

STONE, George Hapgood, mining geologist; b. New York, Nov. 22, 1841; s. Rev. David and Louise (Ingalls) S.; A.B., Wesleyan U., 1868, A.M., 1871; m. Mary E. Clarke, June 18, 1871; m. 2d, Mary H. Hill, Nov. 20, 1876. Taught at Lima, 1869-72, Kent's Hill, Me., 1874-81; prof. geology, Colo. Coll., 1881-88; asst. geologist U.S. Geol. Survey. Author of monograph on glacial geology of Me. for U.S. Geol. Survey; and other geol. papers; also a work on monetary science, entitled "World Money," 1909. Inventor of a universal surveying instrument, and apparatus for the care of the helplessly ill. Address: Colorado Springs, Colo. Died Feb. 20, 1917.

STONE, George Whitefield; b. Moravia, N.Y., Feb. 29, 1840; s. Jacob Thompson and Mary (Bennett) S.; grad. Cortland Acad., Homer, N.Y., 1860; m. Catherine Cushing Graupner, Feb. 28, 1865; m. 2d, Jane E. Stikeman, Oct. 13, 1920. Enlisted in Union Army, Apr. 1861; commd. capt. 12th N.Y. Vols., May 1, 1861; apptd. actg. asst. p.m., U.S.N., Aug. 1861; detailed as judge advocate during last 2 yrs. of war. In merc. bus. till 1889; nat. bank examiner, 1889-95 (resigned); apptd. treas. Am. Unitarian Assn., 1895; ordained Unitarian ministry, 1898; field sec. Unitarian Ch. for Pacific Coast, 1898-1907 (resigned); mayor of Santa Cruz, Calif., July 1911-July 7, 1913. Apptd. by Gov. Johnson mem. State Bd. of Edn., Aug. 29, 1913, reapptd. term 1917-21. Contbg. editor Santa Cruz Sentinel. Mason. Home: Santa Cruz, Calif. Died Mar. 19, 1923.

STONE, Henry Lane, lawyer; b. Bath County, Ky., Jan. 17, 1842; s. Samuel and Sally (Lane) S.; ed. pub. schs. and acad., Bainbridge, Putnam County, Ind.; law sch., taught by Hons. Jonathan W. Gordon and John Coburn, Indianapolis, 1859-60 (one term); m. Pamela Lane Bourne, Feb. 21, 1866. Joined battalion of Maj. Robert G. Stoner, C.S.A., Oct. 7, 1862, which was consolidated with battalion of Maj. William C. P. Breckinridge, forming 9th Ky. Cav., in Gen. John H. Morgan's command; served as pvt., sergt. maj. and ordnance sergt. till surrender, May 1865; on Ind. and Ohio raid of Gen. Morgan, 1863; imprisoned in Camps Morton and Douglas 3 mos.; escaped from latter, Oct. 1863; recaptured in Ky. and imprisoned in jail at Mt. Sterling; escaped to Canada, returning through Fed. lines and rejoined regt. in Va., June 1864. Licensed to practice law by Circuit Ct. of Putnam County, Ind., May 1862; began practice at Owingsville, Ky., Jan. 1. 1866; county atty., Bath County, 1866-70; mem. Ky. Ho. of Rep., 1873-74; partner Hon. Newton P. Reid, as Reid & Stone, 1870-75; removed to Mt. Sterling, Ky., 1878, and formed partnership with Hon. Richard Reid, as Reid & Stone, continuing till 1883; removed to Louisville, 1885; mem. firm of Stone & Sudduth, 1889-99; city atty., Louisville, 2 terms, 1896-1904; gen. counsel Louisville & Nashville R.R. Co., 1905-Apr. 23, 1921. Dem. presdl. elector 9th Dist., Ky., 1872, 1876. Mem. of Christian (Disciples) Ch. Home: Louisville, Ky. Died May 31, 1922.

STONE, Horace Greeley, lawyer; b. Kalamazoo County, Mich., Feb. 23, 1852; s. Horace A. and Hannah M. (Robbins) S.; grad. Kalamazoo High Sch., 1868. Employed in wholesale notion house, Kalamazoo, 1868-77, meanwhile studying law in office of U.S. Senator J. C. Burrows; removed to Chicago, and engaged in various pursuits until admitted to bar, 1878; atty. Chicago & W.I. Ry., 1878-81; pres. 1st Nat. Bank, Grand Forks, N.D., 1881-83; asst. receiver Northwestern Mfg. & Car Co., 1884-87; atty. in many corp. causes, among them the suit between 3 rys. involving 600,000 acres of land in northern Minn.; suit involving control of Duluth, Messabe & Northern R.R. and iron mines; Russell Sage suit for land grant in Minnesota; attorney for A. H. Wilder et al., St. Paul, defendants in $3,000,000 stock and double-liability suits; iron ore washing patent cases involving $40,000,000; chief counsel for Captain Oberlin M. Carter, U.S. Army, in suits to recover $500,000 by U.S. Govt.; atty. Ward will case; Detroit and Pewabic Mining Co. cases in Upper Mich.; suits involving laws seeking to break up department stores;

foreclosure of "Alley L"; etc. Returned to Chicago, 1895; mem. Gurley, Stone & Wood, 1895-1906, practiced alone, 1906—. Inventor glass device preventing damage from freezing of water in engines, etc., method by which soft coal in two hours is divided into coke, by-products and gas worth over 3 times the value of the coal; methods of saving the iron ore and heat in blast furnace gas; also a spring tooth harrow, tractor wheel, auto spring wheel, concentrator for separating iron ore from sand, etc. Republican. Accompanied William H. Taft as his chief asst. throughout the entire presdl. campaign of 1908. Presbyn. Home: Chicago, Ill. Died Apr. 10, 1923.

STONE, James Samuel, clergyman; b. Shipston-on-Stour, Eng., Apr. 27, 1852; s. James Samuel and Anne (Print) S.; grad. Phila. Div. Sch., 1877; B.D., Episcopal Theol. Sch., Cambridge, Mass., 1880; D.D., Bishop's Coll., Lenoxville, Can., 1886; m. Lydia Anna, d. Isaac H. and Martha (Flavelle) Rocap; 1 dau., Violet Elfrida (Mrs. John W. Norton); m. 2d, Caroline, d. Lewis P. Worthington, Jan. 4, 1898. Deacon, 1876, priest, 1877, P.E. Ch.; rector St. Philip's, Toronto, 1879-82, St. Martin's, Montreal, 1882-86, Grace Church, Phila., 1886-95, St. James', Chicago, 1895-1923, emeritus. Deputy Gen. Conv. P.E. Ch., Diocese of Pa., 1892, and Diocese of Chicago, 1895, 98, 1904, 13. Author: Simple Sermons on Simple Subjects, 1879; The Heart of Merrie England, 1887; Readings in Church History, 1889; Necessity of Dogma in the Church, 1892; Woods and Dales of Derbyshire, 1894; Over the Hills to Broadway, 1894; From Frankfort to Munich, 1894; Three Hours' Service for Good Friday, 1903; The Prayer Before the Passion, 1911; The Passion of Christ, 1912; The Glory After the Passion, 1913; The Preparation for the Passion, 1915; The Tercentenary of William Shakespeare, 1916; The Taking of Jerusalem, 1918; Theodore Roosevelt—a Sermon Commemorative, 1919; Music in Worship and the Spirit of Chivalry, 1921; Quietness and Confidence, 1924; The Hope of the Ages, 1924. Home: Evanston, Ill. Died May 8, 1928.

STONE, John Charles, educator; b. Albion, Ill., Jan. 11, 1867; s. James Scott and Elizabeth S. (Hocking) S.; grad. Southern Collegiate Inst.; A.B., A.M., Ind. U., 1897; m. Gertrude L. Walser, Aug. 5, 1891; children—Gertrude Lucile, John Sydney. Teacher pub. schs. of Edwards County, Ill., 1885-94; head of mathematics and physics, Elgin (Ill.) High Sch., 1897-98, Lake Forest (Ill.) Acad., 1898-1900; asso. prof. mathematics, Mich. State Normal Coll., 1900-09; prof. of mathematics, State Teachers Coll., Montclair, N.J., 1909-34, prof. emeritus, 1935. Unitarian. Author: Method in Geometry, 1904; The Teaching of Arithmetic, 1905; The Modernization of Arithmetic, 1914; Method in Arithmetic, 1916; Junior High School Mathematics (3 bks.), 1919; How to Teach Primary Numbers, 1921; A Child's Book of Numbers, 1924; The Stone Arithmetics, 1925; The New Mathematics, 4 books, 1926; How to Teach Elementary Arithmetic, 1928; High School Arithmetic, 1928; First Year Algebra, 1928. Joint Author: (with G. A. Southworth) Southworth-Stone Arithmetics, 1904 (3 books); Primary Arithmetic, 1908; An Exercise Book in Arithmetic, 1909; (with James F. Millis) Essentials of Algebra, 1907; First Algebra, 1908; Secondary Arithmetic, 1908; Plane Geometry, 1910; Plane and Solid Geometry, 1911; Elementary Algebra, 1st Course, 1912; Elementary Algebra, 2d Course, 1913; Stone-Millis Arithmetics (3 books), 1912, revised, 1920; New Plane and Solid Geometry, 1916; Advanced Arithmetic, 1916; Elementary Algebra (with Howard F. Hart), 1924; Second Course in Algebra, 1926; Modern Plane Geometry (with Virgil S. Mallory), 1929; Manual on the Teaching of Algebra, 1929; Solid Geometry, 1930; A Second Course in Algebra, 1930; A Higher Arithmetic, 1931; (with C. N. Mills) The Unit Mastery Arithmetics (6 books), 1932; Unit Mastery Mathematics for Junior High School, 1933; Mathematics for Everyday Use (with V. S. Mallory), 1935; A First Course in Algebra (with V. S. Mallory), 1936. Spl. lecturer, extramural courses, New York U., 1920—; methods in mathematics, summer sessions, Sch. of Edn., Cleveland, O., 1918-23, Tulane U., 1924, State Teachers' Coll., Greeley, Colo., 1926. Address: St. Petersburg, Fla. Died May 21, 1940.

STONE, John Francis, lawyer; b. nr. Wabash, Ind., Feb. 12, 1860; grad. Butler U., Irvington, Ind., B.S., 1884, M.S., 1885, Ph.M., 1894; m. Fannie M. Phillips, Nov. 24, 1887. Lived Indianapolis, Ind., till 1888, teaching; admitted to practice law, 1887; removed Guthrie, Okla., 1889; asst. U.S. dist. atty. Okla., 1891-94; col. Okla. N.G., Mar. 1899; maj. comdg. Okla. batn. 1st Territorial U.S. vol. inf., July 16, 1898-Feb. 15, 1899. Address: Guthrie, Okla. Died 1900.

STONE, John Holden, lawyer; b. Boston, Mass., Aug. 22, 1881; s. Oscar Perry and Martha Alice (Rice) S.; grad. high sch., Malden, Mass., 1900; A.B., Harvard, 1904, LL.B., 1907; m. Louise Freeman, May 19, 1908; children—John Freeman, Paulina, Harriet. Admitted to Mass. bar, 1907, and began practice with Choate, Hall & Stewart at Boston; gen. practice, 1908-18; gen. counsel Atlantic Refining Co., Phila., and its subsidiaries; pres. Atlantic Co. City counsel, Everett, 1909; mem. Ho. of Reps., Mass., 1913. Served as maj. Judge Adv. General's Dept., U.S.A., in France and Belgium, 1918-19. Republican. Unitarian. Mason. Home: Wayne, Pa. Died Apr. 7, 1935.

STONE, John Marshall, gov.; b. Gibson, Tenn., Apr. 30, 1830; ed. in neighborhood schools; went to Miss., 1855; served capt. to col. 2d Miss. vols. in Confederate army; after war, station agt. at Iuka, of Memphis & Charleston R.R.; mayor of Iuka; treas. Tishomingo County, 1866-68, but removed by military authority; State senator, 1869-77; pres. pro tem. senate, 1876-77; acting gov., 1876-77; gov., 1878-81 and 1890-95. Democrat. Address: Iuka, Miss. Died 1900.

STONE, John Theodore, ins. pres.; b. Baltimore, Nov. 21, 1859; s. James Harvey and Harriet Newell (Fusselbaugh) S.; ed. pub. schs. and Baltimore City Coll. to 15; m. Clara May Brinton, Jan. 5, 1882. Began as clerk, with Harry Mudge & Co., 1874; asst. cashier Am. Nat. Bank, Baltimore, 1891-95; organizer, and sec. and treas. Am. Bonding & Trust Co., 1895-98; organizer Md. Casualty Co., and pres., 1898—; also pres. Md. Assurance Corp. Pres. Bd. Casualty and Surety Underwriters of U.S. Republican. Methodist. Home: Baltimore, Md. Died May 1920.

STONE, John Wesley, judge; b. Wadsworth, O., July 18, 1838; s. Rev. Chauncey and Sarah (Bird) S.; ed. pub. and pvt. schs.; m. Delia M. Grover, May 2, 1861 (died 1902). County Clerk, Allegan County, 1860-64; admitted to bar, 1862; pros. atty., Allegan County, 1864-70; judge Circuit Ct., 20th Circuit, Mich., 1873-75, resigned; removed to Grand Rapids, Mich., and resumed law practice; mem. 45th and 46th Congresses (1877-81), 5th Mich. Dist.; U.S. atty. Western Dist. of Mich., 1882-86; removed to Upper Peninsula; judge Circuit Ct., 25th Circuit of Mich., 1890-1909; asso. justice Supreme Ct. of Mich., 1890-1909; asso. justice Supreme Ct. of Mich., Jan. 1, 1910—. Republican. Episcopalian. Home: Marquette, Mich. Died Mar. 24, 1922.

STONE, Livingston, fish culturist; b. Cambridge, Mass., Oct. 21, 1835; s. Peter Robert Livingston and Lavinia (Winship) S.; A.B., Harvard, 1857, A.M., 1860; grad. Meadville (Pa.) Theol. Sem., 1860; m. Rebecca Saulsbury Cushing, Apr. 8, 1875. Pastor Unitarian chs., Billerica, Mass., Detroit and Phila., 1860-64, Charlestown, N.H., 1864-68; established trout breeding sta. at Charlestown, N.H., 1866 (2d attempt at practical fish culture in U.S.); apptd. dep. U.S. fish commr., 1872; established salmon hatching stas. for U.S. Govt. on McCloud River, Calif., 1872 and 1879, and on Columbia River, for cannerymen, 1877; in early 70s transported car load of live Atlantic fish and fish eggs across continent and deposited same in Pacific Ocean, this being first successful attempt of the kind ever made; accompanied Govt. expdn. to Alaska to investigate salmon fisheries, as a result of which Afognac Island was designated as a reservation for salmon culture by President Harrison; in charge Cape Vincent (N.Y.) Sta., 1897-1906; retired, 1906. Awarded 2 diplomas at Internat. Expn., Berlin, 1880; diploma Internat. Expn., London, 1883; hon. bronze medal Société d'Aclimatation, Paris, etc. Author: Domesticated Trout, 1872. Home: Edgewood Park, Pa. Died Dec. 24, 1912.

STONE, Melville Elijah, journalist; b. Hudson, Ill., Aug. 22, 1848; s. Rev. Elijah and Sophia (Creighton) S.; moved to Chicago, 1860; grad. high sch., 1867; A.M., Yale; LL.D., Ohio Wesleyan U., Columbia, Knox Coll., Middlebury Coll.; m. Martha McFarland, 1870; children—Herbert Stuart (dec.), Melville Edwin (dec.), Elizabeth Creighton. Reporter Chicago Tribune in 1864; conducted a foundry and machine shop, 1869-71; burned out in fire, 1871; editor of several Chicago dailies, 1871-74; established, with two partners the Chicago Daily News, 1st issue appearing Christmas Day, 1875; bought out his partners and sold that interest to Victor F. Lawson; in 1881 they started the Chicago Morning News, which became Chicago Record; sold out his entire interest to Mr. Lawson, 1888, and spent 3 yrs. in Europe; became president of Globe Nat. Bank, 1892, until its consolidation with Continental Nat. Bank, 1898; gen. mgr., 1893-1921, counselor, Apr. 27, 1921—, Asso. Press, New York. Address: New York, N.Y. Died Feb. 15, 1929.

STONE, Nat, mcht.; b. Sept. 22, 1866; s. Isaac and Anna S.; ed. pub. schs.; m. Minnie Salzenstein, Oct. 30, 1895; children—Medford W., Lester C. Began as newsboy, later clk., traveling salesman; in wholesale jewelry business, Chicago, 1899-1907; pres. Boston Store, Milwaukee, 1907—. Jewish religion. Home: Milwaukee, Wis. Died Jan. 20, 1931.

STONE, Ormond, astronomer; b. Pekin, Ill., Jan. 11, 1847; s. Rev. Elijah and Sophia (Creighton) S.; U. of Chicago, 1866-70, A.M., 1875; m. Catharine Flagler, May 31, 1871 (died 1914); m. 2d, Mary Florence Brennan, June 9, 1915. Asst. U.S. Naval Obs., Washington, 1870-75; dir. Cincinnati Obs., 1875-82; prof. astronomy, U. of Va., and dir. Leander McCormick Obs., 1882-1912; retired on the Carnegie Foundation. Made noteworthy observations of double and variable stars, nebulæ, satellites of Saturn, etc. Observed total eclipse of sun, Ia., 1869; in charge U.S. Naval Obs. eclipse expdn. to Colo., 1878, McCormick Obs. eclipse expdn. to S.C., 1900. Founder and editor Annals of Mathematics. Emeritus mem. A.A.A.S. (v.p. 1888); mem. Internat. Congress Arts and Sciences, St. Louis, 1904 (chmn. sect. astrometry); v.p. Va. State Teachers' Assn., 1902-12. Mem. and sec. Bd. Visitors to U.S.N. Obs., Washington, D.C., 1901-03. Contbr. to match. and astron. jours. Home: Clifton Station, Va. Died Jan. 17, 1933.

STONE, Rufus Barrett, lawyer; b. Groton, Mass., Nov. 24, 1847; s. Warren Fay and Mary (Williams) S.; grad. Lawrence (Mass.) Acad., 1867; spl. course, Williams Coll., 1867-68; m. Margaret Sarah Baldwin, Apr. 18, 1872. Engaged in U.S. Revenue Service, in Miss.; admitted to Miss. bar, 1872; chancellor 17th Dist. of Miss., 1874-76; removed to Bradford, Pa.; mem. law firm of Stone & Weil, later Stone, Brown & Sturgeon; operated extensively in oil and gas; pres. Central Oil Co., Muncie Mining Co.; v.p. McKean County Lumber Co., etc. A founder, later owner, Bradford Evening Star. Served as pvt. Co. B, 6th Mass. Vols. ("Bloody Sixth"), at close of Civil War; lt. col. Miss. Vol. Militia; hon. mem. "Bucktail" Rifle Regt., Pa. Vols.; pres. Carnegie Pub. Library (Bradford), Commonwealth Humane Soc., Bradford Hospital; trustee State Hosp. for Insane, Beacon Light Mission. Republican. Author: Arthur George Olmstead, 1919; McKean, The Governor's County, 1926; Sinnontouan in the War of the Revolution, 1927. Lecturer. Home: Bradford, Pa. Died Mar. 19, 1929.

STONE, Walter Robinson, mayor; b. Whitesville, Ind., Sept. 7, 1872; s. Horace G. and Ellen (Fennell) S.; student Amherst, 1891-95 (hon. M.A., 1917); m. Alice Meade Palmer, Mar. 11, 1897; children—Alice Manning (Mrs. Aubrey T. Northrop), Ellen Palmer (Mrs. Clarence C. Van Blarcum). Dry Goods business, Syracuse, N.Y., 1895-1920; mem. Stone, Seymour & Co., investment bankers, Syracuse, 1920-29; pres. Syracuse Savings & Loan Assn., 1929-35. Member Syracuse Park Commn., 1906-14 (pres., 1911-14); mayor of Syracuse, terms 1916-17, 1918-19; treas. The Manlius (N.Y.) Sch. Mem. Syracuse C. of C. (treas. 1909-14); pres. N.Y. State Mayor's Conf., 1919-20; chmn. Research Bur. N.Y. State Mayors' Conf., 1931—; dir. field service N.Y. State Mayors' Conf.; mem. exec. com. N.Y. State Waterways Assn. Mem. N.Y. State Tax Assn. (dir.), Nat. Inst. Social Sciences. Republican. Baptist. Home: Syracuse, N.Y. Died Feb. 1937.

STONE, Warren Sanford, labor leader and banker; b. at Ainsworth, Ia., Feb. 1, 1860; s. of John and Sarah (Stewart) S.; ed. at Washington Acad. and Western Coll.; m. Carrie E. Newell, Oct. 15, 1884. Spent entire railroad service with the Rock Island System, beginning as fireman, Sept. 27, 1879; promoted to engr., Apr. 12, 1884. Apptd. grand chief of the Internat. Brotherhood of Locomotive Engineers on the death of Grand Chief Arthur, Aug. 1903; elected at Los Angeles meeting, 1904; re-elected, June 1912, and June 1918, for term of 6 yrs. Pres. Brotherhood of Locomotive Engrs. Coöperative Nat. Bank of Cleveland (1st of kind in U.S.). Mem. Industrial Peace Com., which com. is the custodian of the Nobel Peace Prize. Home: Cleveland, O. Died June 12, 1925.

STONE, Wilbur Fisk, lawyer; b. Litchfield, Conn., Dec. 28, 1833; s. Homer Bishop and Lucy (Lindsey) S.; student Asbury (now DePauw) U., Ind., A.M., 1865; A.B., Ind. U., 1857, LL.B., 1858, A.M., 1860; m. Sarah J. Sadler, Feb. 1866. Editor-in-chief Daily Enquirer, Evansville, Ind., 1858-59; began practice of law, 1859; went to Omaha, Neb., 1859, and became editor of the Nebraskian, also asst. postmaster; crossed the plains to "Pikes Peak," spring of 1860; mem. 1st legislature of Colo. Ty., 1861, 1862, and 1864; asst. U.S. atty. for Colo., 1862-66; mem. Constl. Conv., 1876 (chmn. judiciary com.); asso. justice Supreme Ct. of Colo., 1877-86; judge of Criminal Ct., Denver, 1887-90; one of 5 judges of U.S. Ct. of Mexican and Spanish Land Grant Claims, 1891-1904 (until work of ct. was ended). Spent winter of 1892-93 in Spain on official business, examining Crown Grant title records of the Royal Archives of Madrid and Seville. First gen. atty. of D.&R.G. R.R., 1872-77; negotiated building of A.,T. &S.F. Ry. from Kan. to Pueblo, Colo. Mem. Colo. State Bar Assn. (pres. 1908-09), Denver Bar Assn. Trustee St. Luke's Hosp., Wolfe Hall (young ladies' sch.). Democrat. Episcopalian, and chancellor of the diocese. Author of many pub. addresses on legal, hist., polit. and lit. subjects; also a history chapter "Judiciary of Colorado," for history of the state, 1911; contbr. prose and verse. U.S. commr. Fed. Dist. Ct. of Colo., Jan. 1915—. Home: Denver, Colo. Died Dec. 27, 1920.

STONE, William Alexis, governor; b. Delmar Tp., Tioga County, Pa., Apr. 18, 1846; s. Israel and Amanda S.; attended State Normal Sch., Mansfield, Pa.; m. Ellen Stevens, Aug. 1870. Second lt. Co. A, 187th Pa. Vols., 1864-65; lt. col. Pa. N.G 1872-

74; admitted to bar, 1870; practiced at Wellsboro, Pa., 1870-77, Pittsburgh, 1877—. Dist. atty. Tioga County, 1864-67; U.S. dist. atty., Western Dist. of Pa., 1880-86; mem. 52d to 55th Congresses (1891-99), 23d Pa. Dist.; gov. of Pa., 1899-1903; later prothonotary of Supreme and Superior cts. of Pa. Republican. Address: Philadelphia, Pa. Died Mar. 1, 1920.

STONE, William Joel, senator; b. Madison County, Ky., May 7, 1848; ed. U. of Mo., LL.D., 1893; m. Sarah Louise Winston, Apr. 2, 1874. Admitted to bar, 1869; practiced at Jefferson City, Mo. Pros. atty. Vernon County, 1873-74; presdl. elector, 1876; mem. 49th to 51st Congresses (1885-91), 13th Mo. Dist.; gov. of Mo., 1893-97; mem. Dem. Nat. Com., 1896-1904 (vice chmn., 1900-04); U.S. senator for terms 1903-09, 1909-15, 1915-21. Chmn. Senate Com. on Foreign Relations, etc. Address: Jefferson City, Mo. Died Apr. 14, 1918.

STONE, William Leete, historical writer; b. New York, Apr. 4, 1835; s. Col. William L. and Susannah (Wayland) S.; A.M., Brown, 1858, LL.B.; admitted to bar, 1859; m. H. D. Gillette. Centennial historian for State of N.Y., making speech at Independence Hall, Phila., May 10, 1876. Hon. mem. Oneida, Chicago, Me., Vt., Buffalo, New Haven Colony, N.H., R.I., Wis., Trinity (Dallas, Tex.), and N.J. hist. socs., Am. Hist. Assn., etc.; corr. mem. N.Y., Wyo. and Kan. hist. socs., Am. Numismatic and Archæol. Soc., N.Y. Geneal. Soc., Lit. and Hist. Soc. of Quebec, Albany Inst.; life mem. N.Y. Inst. for Deaf and Dumb; mem. Royal Soc. of Copenhagen; sec. Saratoga Monument Assn. Author: The Life and Times of Sir William Johnson, Bart.; Revolutionary Letters; Pausch's Journal; Burgoyne's Campaign and St. Leger's Expedition; Life and Military Journals of Major-General Riedesel: Letters and Journals of Mrs. General Riedesel; History of New York City; Life and Writings of Colonel William L. Stone; Reminiscences of Saratoga and Ballston; The Saratoga Battle Grounds; Ballads of the Burgoyne Campaign; Sir John Johnson's Orderly Book; Historical Guide Book to Saratoga Springs and Vicinity; Third Supplement to Dowling's History of Romanism; The Starin Genealogy; The Stone Genealogy; History of Washington County, N.Y., and the Classic Ground of America; The Life of Governor George Clinton; Life of John Hay, late Secretary of State. Mr. Stone's bed-fellow at Brown; also about 90 sketches in Appleton's Gen. Cyclo. and Appleton's Biog. Cyclo. Address: Mt. Vernon, N.Y. Died 1908.

STONE, Winthrop Ellsworth, univ. pres.; b. Chesterfield, N.H., June 12, 1862; s. Frederick L. and Ann (Butler) S.; B.S., Mass. Agrl. Coll., 1882; B.S., Boston U., 1886; Ph.D., Göttingen, 1888; LL.D., Mich. Agrl. Coll., 1907. Asst. chemist, Mass. State Agrl. Expt. Sta., 1884-86; chemist, Tenn. Agrl. Expt. Sta., 1888-89; prof. chemistry, 1889-1900, v.p., 1892-1900, pres., 1900—, Purdue U. Mem. Ind. State Bd. of Edn., and numerous learned socs. Published numerous chem. researches upon the carbo-hydrates; also ednl. papers and reports. Address: Lafayette, Ind. Died July 16, 1921.

STONE, Witmer, naturalist; b. Phila., Pa., Sept. 22, 1866; s. Frederick D. and Anne E. (Witmer) S.; A.B., U. of Pa., 1887, A.M., 1891, Sc.D., 1913; m. Lillie M. Lafferty, Aug. 1, 1904. Asst. curator Acad. Natural Sciences, Phila., 1891-1908, curator, 1908-24, dir. of Museum, 1925-28, v.p., 1927, dir. emeritus, 1929—. Fellow Am. Ornithologists' Union (pres. 1920-23), A.A.A.S.; mem. Internat. Com. on Zoöl. Nomenclature. Author: Birds of Eastern Pennsylvania and New Jersey, 1894; American Animals (joint author), 1902; Mammals of New Jersey, 1908; Birds of New Jersey, 1909; Flora of Southern New Jersey, 1912; Report on Birds of Yucatan and Southern Mexico; The Molting of Birds; Birds and Mammals of the McIlhenny Alaskan Expedition; The Phylogenetic Value of Color Characters in Birds; Birds of the Princeton Patagonian Expdn.; and a number of other papers in Proc. Acad. Natural Sciences, on birds, mammals, reptiles; etc. Editor of the Auk, 1912-36. Address: Philadelphia, Pa. Died May 24, 1939.

STONEMAN, Frank B., editor; b. Indianapolis, Ind., June 26, 1857; s. Mark D. (M.D.) and Aletha (White) S.; ed. Carleton Coll., Northfield, Minn., and U. of Minn. (non-grad.); m. Lillian Trefethan, June 12, 1889 (died 1912); 1 dau., Marjory; m. 2d, Lillias E. Shine, Apr. 14, 1914. Admitted to Fla. bar, 1896; in newspaper business in Florida, 1901—. Dem. presdl. elector for Fla., 1904; judge Municipal Ct. of Miami 10 years. Episcopalian. Mason; Past Grand Comdr. K.T. of Fla.; Past Grand High Priest, R.A.M., Fla. Home: Miami, Fla. Died Feb. 1, 1941.

STONER, Mrs. Winifred Sackville, author, lecturer; m. Dr. James Buchanan Stoner, U.S. Public Health Service, 1900 (died 1925); 1 dau., Winifred Sackville (Countess de Bruché). Founder of Natural Education System, 1902; lecturer, and child-training expert; head of Mother Stoner, Inc., pubs.; served as dir. reconstruction schs. for soldiers, 1917-19. Dir. Internat. Assn. for Natural Edn.; pres. of U.S.A. Natural Edn. Forum; member Authors' League America, Authors Guild, League of Am. Pen Women, Soc. Arts and Sciences (New York), London Soc. of Authors, Playwrights and Composers, World League for Fostering Genius. Author: Natural Education, 1914; Manual of Natural Education (with daughter), 1916; Mother Stoner Song Book, 1917; Mother Stoner Nursery Rhymes, 1919; Arithmetic Through Play, 1919; Geography in Jingles; Memory Helpers; Games With Aims, 1921; Castles in Spain, 1923, 24; and many others. Collaborated with Dr. Francis Snow in transl. Edwin Markham's poems into Esperanto. Inventor of natural edn. toys, Geom. Kiddies, Lares and Penates. Composer music for songs in Mother Stoner Jinglelays (Winifred Sackville Stoner, Jr., author of the words), 1923; Mother Stoner's Rhythmic Band; Magic Sesame (musical comedy). Organizer Esperanto Chorus. An asst. editor World Book (home library), etc. Made tour of U.S. in behalf of League of Fostering Genius. Home: New York, N.Y. Died Nov. 11, 1931.

STOOKEY, Lyman Brumbaugh, physiologist, pathologist; b. Belleville, Ill., July 30, 1878; s. Dr. Lyman Polk and Louise (Brumbaugh) S.; A.B., Yale, 1900, Ph.D., 1902; U. of Strassburg, 1904-05; m. Margaret Powell, Dec. 31, 1903. Asso. in physiology, N.Y. State Path. Inst., 1902-04; prof. physiology, U. of Southern Calif., 1905—; pathologist to Clara Barton Hosp., 1906-18; med. adviser U.S. selective service, Los Angeles, World War I. Am. contbr. to Internat. Year Book of Chemical Physiology and Pathology, 1905—; published many researches in physiol. and pathol. chemistry in Am. and European jours. Fellow A.A.A.S., Am. Inst. Chemists, asso. fellow A.M.A. Democrat. Mason. Home: Los Angeles, Calif. Died Feb. 13, 1940.

STORER, Bellamy, lawyer; b. Cincinnati, Aug. 28, 1847; s. late Judge Bellamy and Elizabeth (Drinker) S.; A.B., Harvard, 1867, A.M., 1870; LL.B., Cincinnati Law Sch., 1869; m. Maria, d. Joseph Longworth, Mar. 20, 1886. Admitted to Ohio bar, 1869, and in practice at Cincinnati, 1869—. Mem. 52d and 53d Congresses (1891-95), 1st Ohio Dist.; U.S. minister to Belgium, 1897-99, to Spain, 1899-1902; Am. ambassador to Austria-Hungary, 1902-06. Republican. Address: Cincinnati, O. Died Nov. 12, 1922.

STORER, Francis Humphreys, chemist; b. Boston, Mar. 27, 1832; s. David Humphreys (M.D., LL.D.) and Abby Jane (Brewer) S.; brother of Horatio Robinson S.; student Lawrence Scientific Sch. (Harvard), 1850-51; asst. to Prof. Cooke, in chemistry, 1851-53; chemist, U.S. North Pacific exploring expdn., 1853; S.B., Harvard, 1855, A.M., 1870; studied abroad, 1855-57; m. Catharine A. Eliot, June 21, 1871. Practiced as chemist at Boston, 1857-65; prof. gen. and industrial chemistry, Mass. Inst. Tech., 1865-70; prof. agrl. chemistry, 1870-1907, dean Bussey Instn., 1871-1907, Harvard. Fellow Am. Acad. Arts and Sciences. Author: Dictionary of the Solubilities of Chemical Substances, 1864; Manual of Inorganic Chemistry, 1869; Manual of Qualitative Chemical Analysis, 1868 (both with Charles W. Eliot); Cyclopædia of Quantitative Chemical Analysis, Agriculture in Some of Its Relations with Chemistry, 1897; Elementary Manual of Chemistry (with W. B. Lindsay), 1894; Manual of Qualitative Analysis (with W. B. Lindsay), 1899; Bulletin of the Bussey Institution; Alloys of Copper and Zinc; Manufacture of Paraffin Oils; etc. Address: Boston, Mass. Died July 30, 1914.

STORER, Horatio Robinson, physician; b. Boston, Feb. 27, 1830; s. David Humphreys (M.D., LL.D.) and Abby Jane (Brewer) S.; brother of Francis Humphreys Storer; A.B., Harvard, 1850, A.M., M.D., 1853, LL.B., 1868; studied medicine, 1853-55, Paris, London, Edinburgh; LL.D., Fordham U., N.Y., 1912. Established practice at Boston, 1855; prof. obstetrics, and med. jurisprudence, Berkshire Med. Coll., 1865-69; later gave post-grad. lectures on gynecology and retired from active practice; cons. phys. Newport Hosp., and St. Joseph's Hosp., Providence, R.I. Devised a number of surg. and gynecol. instruments and methods. Life pres. Newport Med., and Natural History socs. and Gynecol. Soc. of Boston; fellow Am. Acad. Arts and Sciences; v.p. A.M.A., 1868, and gynecol. sect. 9th Internat. Med. Congress, 1887; pres. Am. Med. Editors' Assn., 1871; foreign asso. Royal Numismatic Soc., Belgium, Kon. Nederland. Genoot. Munt-en Penning, Amsterdam. Prominent as a numismatist; wrote many papers on medical medals and tokens, besides writing largely on med. subjects. Editor: Obstetric Memoirs and Contributions of Prof. (Sir) James Y. Simpson, of Edinburgh (with Dr. Sir William O. Priestley of London), 1855. Author: Criminal Abortion in America, 1859; Criminal Abortion, Its Nature, Its Evidence and Its Law (with F. F. Heard); Why Not?—a Book for Every Woman, 1865; Is It I?—a Book for Every Man, 1869; On Nurses and Nursing; On Insanity in Women. Gold medalist A.M.A., 1865, for essay on Physical Evils of Forced Abortions; gold Liberty Service medal, Nat. Inst. Social Sciences, 1918, for aiding in control of pestilence among soldiers and sailors of U.S. On his 91st birthday received loving cup from citizens of Newport, for aid to the public health for nearly 50 years. Home: Newport, R.I. Died Sept 18, 1922.

STORER, John Humphreys; b. Boston, Sept. 28, 1859; s. Horatio Robinson and Emily Elvira (Gilmore) S.; A.B., Harvard, 1882, LL.B., 1885; m. Edith, d. Robert Treat Paine, Nov. 18, 1885; children—Emily Lyman, John Humphreys, Edith, Robert Treat Paine, Theodore Lyman, Lydia Lyman. Interested principally in real estate and finance, and developing and building up suburbs in some 30 of the larger eastern cities; trustee Merchants Real Estate Trust (Boston). Mem. bd. of incorporators of the Am. Nat. Red Cross; trustee Robert Treat Paine Assn., Utica (Miss.) Inst. Mem. Am. Polit. and Social Science. Mem. Episcopal City Mission. Home: Waltham, Mass. Died Dec. 25, 1935.

STORER, Maria Longworth (Mrs. Bellamy Storer); b. Cincinnati, O., Mar. 20, 1849; d. Joseph and Annie (Reeves) Longworth; g.d. Nicholas Longworth, one of founders of Cincinnati; m. George Ward Nichols, 1868 (died 1895); m. 2d, Bellamy Storer, lawyer and diplomat, Mar. 20, 1896 (died 1922). Founder of Rookwood Pottery, 1880; did notable work as decorator in pottery and metal; awarded gold medal, Paris Expn., 1889 and 1900. Roman Catholic. Home: Cincinnati, O. Died May 3, 1932.

STOREY, Moorfield, lawyer; b. Roxbury, Mass., Mar. 19, 1845; s. Charles William and Elizabeth Eaton (Moorfield) S.; A.B., Harvard, 1866, A.M., 1869; Harvard Law Sch., 1866-67; m. Gertrude Cutts, Jan. 6, 1870. Admitted to bar, 1869, and in practice at Boston, 1869—; sr. mem. Storey, Thorndike, Palmer & Dodge. Pvt. sec. to Charles Sumner, 1867-69; editor Am. Law Review, 1873-79. Overseer Harvard Coll., 1877-88 and 1892-1910; pres. Am. Bar Assn., 1896; pres. Mass. Reform Club, 1898-1901; v.p. Nat. Civ. Service Reform League; pres. Mass. Civil Service Reform Assn.; pres. Anti-Imperialist League from 1905; pres. Bar Assn. of the City of Boston, 1909-13; pres. Mass. Bar Assn., 1913-14; pres. Nat. Assn. for Advancement of Colored People, 1910—; hon. pres. Indian Rights Assn. Fellow Am. Acad. Arts and Sciences. Author: Life of Charles Sumner (Statesman series), 1900; Ebenezer Rockwood Hoar, a Memoir (with E. W. Emerson), 1911; The Reform of Legal Procedure (Storr's lectures at Yale Law Sch.), 1911; Problems of To-Day (Godkin lectures at Harvard College, 1920); pamphlets; Politics as a Duty and as a Career, 1889; What Shall We Do with Our Dependencies?, 1903; The Democratic Party and Philippine Independence, 1915; The Negro Question, 1918; also various other pamphlets, addresses and articles. Home: Lincoln, Mass. Died Oct. 24, 1929.

STOREY, William Benson, ry. official; b. San Francisco, Nov. 17, 1857; s. William Bainbridge and Ellen (Dean) S.; Ph.B., U. of Calif., 1881, LL.D., 1924; m. Laura B. Roe (née Rice), May 21, 1913. Began ry. service on S.P., 1881, asst. engr., 1883-93; asst. engr. U.S. Debris Commn., 1894-95; chief engr. and gen. supt. San Francisco & San Joaquin Valley Ry., 1895-1900; chief engr. A.,T.&S.F. Ry., 1900-06; chief engr., A.,T.&S.F. Ry. System, 1906-09; v.p. A.,T.&S.F. Ry. Co., Oct. 1, 1909-18; federal mgr. A.,T.&S.F. Ry., 1918-20, pres., 1920-33 (retired), continuing as mem. bd. dirs. and exec. com. Home: Chicago, Ill. Died Oct. 24, 1940.

STORMS, Albert Boynton, clergyman; b. Lima, Washtenaw County, Mich., Apr. 1, 1860; s. Irving and Mary (Boynton) S.; A.B., U. of Mich., 1884, A.M., 1893; D.D., Lawrence U.; LL.D., Drake U., 1904; m. Lovie Laura Whitcomb, Jan. 2, 1883; children—Albert Claire (dec.), Lillian Boynton, Mary Laura, Florence M. Ordained M.E. ministry, 1884; pastor Franklin, Mich., 1884-87, Hudson, Mich., 1887-90, Detroit, 1890-98, Madison, Wis., 1898-1900, Des Moines, Ia., 1900-03; pres. Ia. State Coll. of Agr. and Mech. Arts, July 1903-Aug. 30, 1910; pastor Central Av. Ch., Indianapolis, 1910-15; supt. Indianapolis Dist. M.E. Ch., 1915-18; pres. Baldwin-Wallace Coll., Berea, O., 1918—. Author: Stopping at an Inn, 1900; The Cool of the Day, 1902; The Outlook, 1904; The Master-Secret, 1913. Contbr. to Methodist Review. Pres. Ch. Fedn. of Ind. Home: Berea, O. Died July 1, 1933.

STORROW, James Jackson, banker; b. Boston, Jan. 21, 1864; s. James J. and Annie M. (Perry) S.; A.B., Harvard, 1885, LL.B., 1888; m. Helen Osborne. Mem. firm Lee, Higginson & Co., bankers, 1900—; dir. U.S. Smelting, Refining & Mining Co., U.S. Mining Co., Centennial-Eureka Mining Co., Ry. & Light Securities Co., Columbia Rope Co., William Underwood Co., Essex Co., Nash Motors Co. (chmn. bd.). Home: Boston, Mass. Died Mar. 13, 1926.

STORRS, Caryl B., critic, author; b. Saginaw, Mich., Apr. 22, 1870; s. Lucius C. and Ellen (Buell) S.; prep. edn. Mich. Mil. Acad.; M.D., Mich. Coll. Medicine and Surgery, Detroit Mich., 1892; unmarried. Practiced medicine in Mich., 1892-1901; dramatic and musical critic Minneapolis Tribune, 1901—. Mem. Am. Red Cross Agrl. Unit to Serbia, Apr.-Oct. 1918. Republican. Mason, Elk. Author: Nature's Press Agent, 1910; "Visitin' 'Round in Minnesota," 1916. Home: Minneapolis, Minn. Died Jan 18, 1920.

STORRS, Richard Salter, clergyman; b. Braintree, Mass., Aug. 21, 1821; grad. Amherst, 1839, D.D., Union Coll., 1853, Harvard, 1859; LL.D., Princeton, 1874; L.H.D., Columbia, 1887. Taught in Monson Acad. and Williston Sem.; studied law under Rufus Choate, but abandoned it for theology. Grad. Andover Theol. Sem., 1845; ordained same year; pastor Harvard Congl. Ch., 1845-46; pastor Ch. of the Pilgrims, Brooklyn, 1846—; m. Mary Ewell Jenks, Oct. 1, 1845. Pres. Am. Bd. of Commrs. for Foreign Missions, 1887-97; one of the editors The Independent, 1848-61. Author: Report on the Revised Edition of the English Version of the Bible; The Constitution of the Human Soul; Conditions of Success in Preaching Without Notes; Early American Spirit, and the Genesis of It; Declaration of Independence, and the Effects of It; John Wycliffe and the First English Bible; Manliness in the Scholar; Recognition of the Supernatural; Bernard of Clairvaux; Divine Origin of Christianity; The Prospective Advance of Christian Missions; Forty Years of Pastoral Life; etc. Address: Brooklyn, N.Y. Died 1900.

STORY, George Henry, artist; b. New Haven, Conn., Jan. 22, 1835; served 3 yrs.' apprenticeship to wood-carver; studied under Charles Hine 3 yrs. and in Europe 1 yr. Went to Portland, Me.; received Me. state medal, 1859; studio in Washington 2 yrs.; spent a year in Cuba; moved to New York; paints portraits and genre pictures; medal, Centennial Expn., Phila.; curator dept. of paintings, Met. Mus. Art, New York, 1889-1906, acting dir., 1904-05, curator emeritus, 1906—; curator Wadsworth Athenæum, Hartford, Conn., 1899—. A.N.A., 1875. Works in Met. Mus., New York, Wadsworth Athenæum, etc.; portrait of Abraham Lincoln in Nat. Gallery, Washington, D.C. Pres. New York Artists Fund Soc. 9 yrs. Home: New York, N.Y. Died Nov. 24, 1922.

STORY, John Patten, major gen. U.S.A.; b. Waukesha, Wis., Aug. 25, 1841; s. John Patten and Elizabeth (Quarles) S.; grad. Carroll Coll., Waukesha, Wis., 1857, U.S. Mil. Acad., 1865; m. Caroline Sherman, Sept. 10, 1868. Apptd. 2d and 1st lt. 16th Inf., June 23, 1865; trans. to 34th Inf., Sept. 21, 1866; assigned to 2d Arty., Dec. 15, 1870; trans. to 4th Arty., Jan. 1, 1871; capt. 4th Arty., Sept. 14, 1883; maj. 7th Arty., Mar. 8, 1898; lt. col. arty. corps, May 8, 1901; col., Oct. 15, 1902; brig. gen. chief of arty. U.S.A., Jan. 22, 1904; maj. gen., June 17, 1905; retired at own request after 40 yrs.' service, June 19, 1905. Instr. in Arty. School, Ft. Monroe, Va., 1888-98; arty. insp., Atlantic coast, 1898-1902; comdt. Arty. Sch., 1902-04; gen. officer Gen. Staff U.S.A. and mem. Joint Army and Navy Bd., 1902-04; mem. Bd. Ordnance and Fortification, 1901-02, 1904-05; mem. Nat. Coast Defense Bd., 1905-07. Home: Pasadena, Calif. Died Mar. 25, 1915.

STORY, Julian, artist; b. Walton-on-Thames, Eng.; s. W. W. (poet and sculptor) S.; g.s. Justice Joseph Story of Supreme Ct. of U.S.; ed. Eton and Oxford, A.M., Oxford, 1879; pupil of Frank Duveneck, Boulanger and Lefebvre, Paris; m. 2d, Elaine Sartori, 1909. Awards: 3d class medal and honorable mention, Paris Salon, 1889; gold medal, Berlin, 1891; silver medal, Paris Expn., 1900; silver medal, Buffalo Expn., 1901, San Francisco Expn., 1915. Represented in City Art Mus., St. Louis, Telfair Acad., Savannah, Ga., Peabody Inst., Baltimore. Chevalier Légion d'Honneur, France, 1900. A.N.A. Address: Philadelphia, Pa. Died Feb. 24, 1919.

STORY, Nelson, Jr.; b. Bozeman, Mont., May 12, 1874; s. Nelson and Ellen (Trent) S.; ed. Shattuck Sch., Faribault, Minn., and at Ogden, Utah, and St. Louis, Mo.; m. Etha Lou Mayo, June 10, 1895 (dec.); children—Nelson, Mayo. Real estate business, Los Angeles, Calif., and Bozeman, farming in Mont.; pres. Story Motor Supply Co.; dir. Montana Flour Mills. Served as mem. City Council and mayor, Bozeman; mem. Mont. Ho. of Rep., 1908, 12; county commr. Gallatin County, Mont.; lt. gov. of Mont., 1920-24. Republican. Episcopalian. Mason, Elk. Home: Bozeman, Mont. Died Oct. 21, 1932.

STORY, William Edward, mathematician; b. Boston, Mass., Apr. 29, 1850; s. Isaac and Elizabeth Bowen (Woodberry) S.; A.B., Harvard, 1871; univs. of Berlin and Leipzig, 1871-75, Ph.D., Leipzig, 1875; m. Mary D. Harrison, June 20, 1878; 1 son, William Edward. Tutor mathematics, Harvard, 1875-76; asso., asst. prof., and asso. prof. mathematics, Johns Hopkins, 1876-89; prof. mathematics, Clark U., 1889-1921, emeritus, 1921. Editor in charge Am. Jour. Mathematics, 1878-82; editor Mathematical Review. Fellow Am. Acad. Arts and Sciences. Contbr. papers to Am. Jour. Mathematics, Proceedings London Math. Society, Mathematische Annalen, Proceedings Am. Acad., Transactions Am. Math. Soc., Math. Review; philos. mag. (London, Edinburgh and Dublin), Zeitschrift für Physikalische Chemie (Leipzig). Address: Worcester, Mass. Died Apr. 10, 1930.

STOTESBURY, Edward Townsend, banker; b. Phila., Pa., Feb. 26, 1849; LL.D., U. of Pa., Franklin & Marshall Coll. Became connected with Drexel & Co., bankers, Phila., 1866, partner, 1883; mem. firm J. P. Morgan & Co., Morgan & Cie. (Paris); chmn. exec. com. Reading Co.; pres. Beaver Coal Corp., Beaver Coal Co.; dir. Lehigh & Hudson River Ry. Co., Phila., Newton and New York R.R. Co., Phila. & Reading Terminal R.R. Co., New York & Long Branch R.R. Co., New York & Middle Coal Field R.R. & Coal Co., Highland Coal Co., Transportation Mutual Ins. Co., Wyoming Valley Water Supply Co., Second & Third St. Passenger Ry. Co., Nat. Storage Co. Pres. Commrs. of Fairmount Park (Phila.), Art Jury (Phila.); dir. Pa. Acad. Fine Arts; trustee U. of Pa., Pa. Mus. of Art, University Museum, Lankenau Hosp. Mem. and trustee Phila. Stock Exchange, Phila. Riders and Drivers Assn. (hon. pres.), Bryn Mawr Horse Show (hon. v.p.). Dir. Benjamin Franklin Memorial; mem. Pan-Am. Union, English-Speaking Union; treas. Phila. Council of Boy Scouts of Am.; trustee Grant Monument Assn.; mem. Colonial Soc. of Pa., Pa. Soc. Sons of Revolution, Adirondack Mountain Reserve (chmn. bd.), Pa. Soc. (N.Y.), Am. Soc. of Royal Italian Orders. Colonel Vet. Corps, First Reg. Inf., Nat. Guard Pa. Decorated Legion of Honor (France); Order of the Crown (Italy). Home: Philadelphia, Pa. Died May 16, 1938.

STOTSENBURG, Evan Brown, lawyer; b. New Albany, Ind., May 16, 1865; s. John H. and Jane F. (Miller) S.; student Kenyon Coll., Gambier, O., 1884-85; m. Zenobia Borden, June 1, 1892; children—Mary B., Jane M. Admitted to Ind. bar, 1886, practiced in New Albany; mem. Stotsenburg, Weathers, Minton & Phillips. Co. atty., Floyd Co., 1900-04; mem. Ind. Ho. of Rep., 1895, Senate, 1907-15 (pres. pro tem. 1911); apptd. atty-gen. Ind., Nov. 1915, unexpired term. Democrat. Mem. Ind. Commn. Panama P.I. Expn., 1915; mem. State Highway Commn. Indiana, 1933—. Represented State of Ind. in suit for injunction against submission of the so-called "Marshall" Constn., 1911; and in suit to test constitutionality of primary election law, 1915. Del. Conf. on Uniform State Laws, Salt Lake City, 1915. Episcopalian. Home: New Albany, Ind. Died July 31, 1937.

STOTT, Henry Gordon, engineer; b. Orkney Islands, Scotland, 1866; s. Rev. David and Elizabeth Jane (Dibblee) S.; ed. Watson Coll. Sch., Edinburgh; Coll. Science and Arts, Glasgow, and Glasgow and W. of Scotland Tech. Coll.; m. Anna Mitchell, July 23, 1894. Worked with electric light co. at Glasgow, 1884; asst. electrician to Anglo-Am. Telegraph & Cable Co., 1885-89; devoted much time to exptl. work; asst. engr. Brush Electric Engring. Co.'s light plant, Bournemouth, Eng., 1889-90; electric works at Madrid, Spain, 1890-91; engr. with Buffalo Gen. Electric Co., 1891-1901; supt. motive power Interborough Rapid Transit Co., New York, 1901—, and New York Rys. Co., 1912—. Wrote many engring. papers. Home: New Rochelle, N.Y. Died Jan. 15, 1917.

STOUGH, Henry Wellington, evangelist; b. Pulaski, Williams County, O., Aug. 15, 1870; s. William Edward and Frances Jane (Newman) S.; student Oberlin Coll., 1888-91; Moody Bible Inst., Chicago, 1892-93; Chicago Theol. Sem., 1893-96; D.D., Defiance Coll., 1911; m. Helen Amelia Russ, June 23, 1898; children—William Russ (dec.), Paul Pinney, Rachel Elizabeth (Mrs. B. O. Keefer), Henry W., Philip Newman, Harold Edward, Virginia Eloise. Gen. sec. Y.M.C.A., East Liverpool, O.; pastor 3d Ch., Oak Park, Ill., 1894-1901; ordained Congl. ministry, 1896; evangelist, 1901—, conducting services under title of "Stough Evangelistic Campaign"; sec. and treas. Interdenom. Evangelistic Assn., 1906-12; founder, 1926, and pres. Soc. of the Healing Christ; founder, 1930, and pres. Soc. of the Midnight Cry; nat. commr. and lecturer upon religious and economic subjects for the Anglo-Saxon Fedn. of America, 1932; founder, and nat. dir. America-Israel Movement, Knoxville, Tenn., 1934—. Prohibitionist. Author: Across the Deadline of Amusements, 1912; The Outlaw, 1913; Faith and Prayer in Their Conflict with Unbelief, 1913; Stubble or Silver, 1913; also Significance of the Great Seal of the United States, Forgiveness and Debts, and other brochures, 1935. Asso. editor America-Israel Message. Mem. evangelistic staff, War Council Y.M.C.A. Home: Knoxville, Tenn. Died Oct. 27, 1939.

STOUT, George Clymer, M.D.; b. Bethlehem, Pa., June 29, 1862; s. Dr. Abraham and Mary (Cortright) S.; grad. U.S. Naval Acad., 1883; M.D., U. of Pa., 1891; m. Anna Wetherell Addicks; children—Mrs. Mary Blabon, Rebecca (Mrs. Rebecca Hundt), Margaret (Mrs. Margaret Bodsius). Lt. U.S.N. in Spanish-Am. War; specialist in ear and throat diseases; late prof. otology, Phila. Polyclinic; chief dept. otology and laryngology, Presbyn. Hosp. Fellow Am. Coll. Surgeons. Contbr. to Woods' Reference Handbook of the Medical Sciences, 1902; to Taylor & Welles on Diseases of Children; also to med. jours. Home: Berwyn, Pa. Died Jan. 27, 1932.

STOUT, Henry Rice, physician; b. Westfield, N.Y., Mar. 17, 1843; s. Charles Brockden and Laura (Chapin) S.; ed. Kenyon Coll., Gambier, O.; left coll. at end of 3 yrs. to enter army; M.D., Hahnemann Med. Coll., Chicago, 1868; m. Mary Eddy, May 7, 1869 (died 1907). Pvt. Co. A, 131th Ill. Vol. Inf., 1864; practiced, Chicago, 1868-75, in Jacksonville, Fla., 1875—. Pres. Bd. Homœ. Med. Examiners State of Fla.; pres. Pub. Library Assn., Jacksonville, 1877—. Republican. Episcopalian. Mason. Author: Our Family Physician, 1870. Contbr. many articles to med. jours. and socs. Address: Jacksonville, Fla. Died Oct. 14, 1914.

STOUT, James Coffin, clergyman, educator; b. Irvington-on-Hudson, N.Y., Nov. 25, 1869; s. Thomas Hance and Sarah Lambdin (Coffin) S.; grad. Rutgers Prep. Sch., 1887; A.B., Rutgers Coll., 1891; grad. Princeton Theol. Sem., 1897, B.D., 1910; studied U. of Berlin, 1911-12; D.D., Coll. of Wooster, O., 1925; m. Phebe Elizabeth Van Antwerp, May 10, 1898. Ordained ministry Ref. Ch. in America, 1898; pastor Brighton Heights Ref. Ch., New Brighton, S.I., 1898-1902, Memorial Presbyn. Ch., St. Augustine, Fla., 1902-09; prof. ch. history, Bibl. Sem. in New York, 1912. Home: Bronxville, N.Y. Died Mar. 14, 1930.

STOUT, James Huff, lumberman. Lived in Wis. for many yrs., having large business and mfg. interests; mem. Wis. Senate. Gave liberally to cause of manual training, traveling libraries, the good roads movement, and various works of practical philanthropy; founder of Stout Inst., Menomonie, Wis. Address: Menomonie, Wis. Died 1910.

STOUT, Oscar Van Pelt, civil engr.; b. Jerseyville, Ill., Nov. 14, 1865; s. John P. and Jane (McIntyre) S.; B.C.E., 1888, C.E., 1897, U. of Neb., hon. D.Eng., 1932; m. Edith Forbes, Oct. 23, 1890; children—Richard Forbes, Donald John, Oscar Charles, Marian Edith (Mrs. J. J. Wikkerink), Harris Pinkerton, Burt Elihu. With engr. depts. U.P.,C.,B.& Q. and M.P. rys., 1886-90; city engr., Beatrice, Neb., 1890, 91; various grades from instr. to head prof. civ. engring., 1891-1920, also dean Coll. of Engring., 1912-20, U. of Neb.; in business, 1920-21; employed on coöperative irrigation investigations, U.S. Dept. Agr. and State of Calif., 1922—. Resident hydrographer, Neb. and adjoining states, U.S. Geol. Survey, 1894-1903; irrigation expert and engr. U.S. Dept. Agr., 1902-13; engr. Neb. State Bd. Agr.; irrigation engr., Neb. Agrl. Expt. Sta. Hon. mem. Am. Soc. Agrl. Engrs. (1st McCormick medalist 1932). Commd. maj. Engr. R.C., 1917; active service, Dec. 28, 1917-Feb. 1, 1919. Home: Berkeley, Calif. Died Aug. 4, 1935.

STOUT, Ralph Emerson, newspaperman; b. Adrian, Mich., July 11, 1866; s. Jared Comstock and Martha (Montgomery) S.; ed. U. of Kan., 1881-85; m. Mary McCabe, July 28, 1898. Reporter, 1886-89, city editor, 1889-1905, mng. editor, Kansas City Star, 1905—. Home: Kansas City, Mo. Died Oct. 10, 1926.

STOVALL, Pleasant Alexander, newspaper editor; b. Augusta, Ga., July 10, 1857; s. Bolling Anthony and Martha (Wilson) S.; B.S., U. of Ga., 1875, LL.D., 1922; m. Mary Ganahl, Jan. 7, 1885. Entered newspaper business in Athens, Ga., and later moved to Augusta, and was news editor, city editor, asso. editor Augusta Chronicle until 1891; founder, 1891, and owner Savannah Press; later editor Savannah Evening Press. Chmn. Ga. Bicentennial Commn., 1932. Mem. Georgia Ho. of Reps. 5 years; a.d.c. on staffs of two govs. of Ga.; trustee U. of Ga., later of pub. schs., Savannah; E.E. and M.P. to Switzerland, 1913-20; chmn. Ga. delegation to Dem. Nat. Conv., San Francisco, 1920; Ga. chmn. Woodrow Wilson Foundation, 1921, 22. Awarded gold medal by parliament of Belgium for work during World War I. Episcopalian. Mason. Author: Life of Robert Toombs, 1891. Home: Savannah, Ga. Died May 14, 1935.

STOVER, George Henry, roentgenologist; b. Ft. Collins, Colo., Mar. 8, 1871; s. William Charles and Jane McMaster (White) S.; U. of Denver, 1 yr.; M.D., Med. Dept. same, 1893; New York Post-grad. Med. Sch., 1896; Johns Hopkins Post-Grad. Sch., 1896; m. Anna Harp, June 6, 1899. Interne Arapahoe County Hosp., 1893; practiced at Eaton, Colo., 1893-96; removed to Denver, 1897, and began practice of roentgenology; asst. in medicine, U. of Denver Med. Dept., 1897; lecturer on electro-therapeutics and hematology,, 1898-1909, dean and prof. roentgenology, 1909, Denver and Gross Med. Coll.; prof. roentgenology, 1910—, U. of Colo. Med. Sch., formed by merger of State Med. Sch. and Denver and Gross Med. Coll. Mem. Pub. Health Com. of Denver C. of C., 1911. Mason. Author of numerous monographs on Roentgenology. Home: Denver, Colo. Died Mar. 25, 1915.

STOVER, Martin Luther, judge; b. Waterloo, N.Y., Oct. 19, 1845; s. Martin J. and Lydia (Hartman) S.; student Wittenberg Coll., Springfield, O., but before finishing his 1st yr., at age of 16, enlisted in the 86th Ohio Inf.; from 1863, served 17th Ohio Battery until close of war; resumed coll. studies, 1865, and after graduation taught sch. in Amsterdam, N.Y., and devoted spare time to study of law; m. Helen E. Shuler, 1874. Admitted to bar, 1870; practiced at Amsterdam until 1892, New York, 1906—. Mem. N.Y. Assembly, 1874; justice Supreme Ct. of N.Y., 1891-1905, Appellate Div., 1900-05; official referee of state courts. Home: Amsterdam, N.Y. Died June 7, 1921.

STOWE, Frederick Arthur, newspaper editor; b. Chicago, Ill., Aug. 29, 1870; s. George Edwin and Arabella (Edwards) S.; Ph.B., State U. of Ia., 1892; grad. study U. of Chicago and Northwestern U., 1892-94; m. Marion E. Hull, Sept. 11, 1902; children—Mary Wynne, Seymour Franklin. Began as reporter Chicago Tribune, 1894; polit. writer Chicago Chronicle, 1896-1907; asst. to pres. Chicago City Ry. Co., 1907-11; editor Peoria (Ill.) Transcript, 1911—, Peoria Journal, 1916—. Dir. Peoria Pub. Library. Republican. Conglist. Home: Peoria, Ill. Died May 3, 1938.

STOWELL, Calvin Llewellyn, financier; b. Ansonia, Pa., Aug. 28, 1854; s. Thomas Pollard and Henrietta (Fowler) S.; brother of Charles Frederick S.; ed. pvt. tutors; m. Grace L. Stowell, Apr. 28, 1908. Began business career in a bank; removed to Rochester, N.Y., 1875; became dir., gen. mgr., v.p. and pres. of numerous corps., including banks, ry., steamship and fire ins. cos. Mem. Am. Acad. Polit. and Social Science. Author: Christian Knighthood; Stories of Abraham Lincoln; Constantine the Great; Trips to the West Indies; Flotsam and Jetsam; Idiosyncrasies of Great Men; etc. Contbr. to scientific and lit. periodicals. Home: Rochester, N.Y. Deceased.

STOWELL, Charles Frederick, engineer; b. Owego, N.Y., Feb. 28, 1853; s. Thomas Pollard and Henrietta (Fowler) S.; student Rochester Free Acad.; C.E., Rensselaer Poly. Inst., Troy, N.Y., 1879; m. Emily A. Blossom, Oct. 10, 1882; children—Grace Elizabeth, Thomas Charles. Engaged in practice, 1879; bridge engr. to Bd. of R.R. Commrs., State of N.Y., 1883-91; bridge engr. to Bd. of R.R. Commrs., Vt., 1901-07; designing and cons. engr. on bridges. Democrat. Author: Report on Strains in Railroad Bridges, State of New York, 1891. Home: Albany, N.Y. Died Aug. 31, 1933.

STOWELL, Charles Henry, editor, author; b. Perry, N.Y., Oct. 27, 1850; s. David P. and Mary A. (Blanchard) S.; grad. Genesee Wesleyan Sem., 1868; M.D., U. of Mich., 1872; m. Louise Maria Reed, July 10, 1878. Instr. in physiol. lab., 1877-79, lecturer physiology and histology, 1879-80, asst. prof., 1880-81, asst. prof. histology and microscopy 1881-83, prof., 1883-89, U. of Mich.; med. writer and spl. practitioner, Washington, 1885-97; gen. mgr., treas. J. C. Ayer Co., Lowell, Mass., 1900-20. Editor 5 monthly jours: Trained Motherhood, Food, Practical Medicine, The Microscope, and Nat. Med. Review. Author: Primer of Health; A Healthy Body; The Essentials of Health; Laboratory Manual for Teaching Physiology; Students' Manual of Histology; Microscopical Diagnosis; Structure of Teeth; etc. Home: Lowell, Mass. Died 1932.

STOWELL, Frederick M(oody), mfr. underwear; b. Holden, Mass., Aug. 1, 1870; s. Frederick Manning and Lucy Ann (Hubbard) S.; ed. high sch., Newton, Mass.; m. Sara Morris, Dec. 12, 1893; children—Frederick Morris, Eleanor. Began as errand boy, Dana Hardware Co., Boston, Mass., 1885; with The Munsingwear Corp., Minneapolis, Minn., 1890—, pres., 1912—. Republican. Methodist. Home: Minneapolis, Minn. Died June 1932.

STOWELL, Thomas Blanchard, univ. prof.; b. Perry, Wyoming County, N.Y., Mar. 29, 1846; s. David Page and Mary Ann (Blanchard) S.; A.B., Genesee Coll., 1865, A.M., 1868; Ph.D., Syracuse U., 1881; LL.D., St. Lawrence U., 1909; m. Mary C., d. Rev. George H. Blakeslee, Aug. 3, 1869. Prin. acad., Addison, N.Y., 1865-66, Union Sch., Morrisville, N.Y., 1866-67; prof. mathematics, Genesee Wesleyan Sem., 1867-68; prin. Morris High Sch., Leavenworth, Kan., 1868-69; head dept. natural science, State Normal Sch., Cortland, N.Y., 1869-89; prin. State Normal and Training Sch., Potsdam, N.Y., 1889-1909; head dept. of edn., U. of Southern Calif., 1909-19; dean emeritus, Sch. of Education, same univ., 1919—. Fellow A.A.A.S. Republican. Methodist. Wrote numerous papers on the nervous system of the domestic cat; also, Outlines of Comparative Anatomy, Outlines of Pedagogical Psychology, History of Education, etc. Address: Los Angeles, Calif. Died 1927.

STOWELL, William Henry Harrison, paper mfr.; b. Windsor, Vt., July 26, 1840; s. Sylvester and Fanny Chandler (Bowen) S.; grad. English High Sch., Boston, 1858; m. Emma Clara, d. Gen. John T. Averill, Nov. 13, 1873 (died 1911). With C. O. Whitmore & Sons, ship owners, Boston, in East India trade, 1858-65; mem. West, Beardsley & Co., lumber, etc., Richmond, Va., 1865; a founder, sec. and treas., Fox River Pulp Co., Appleton, Wis., 1876, Atlas Paper Co., Appleton, 1878, Duluth Iron Steel Co., 1887; pres. Mfrs'. Bank, West Duluth, 1889-95; retired, 1896. Apptd. U.S. commr. for Va., 1865; collector internal revenue, 4th Dist. of Va., 1868; mem. 42d, 43d and 44th Congresses (1871-77), 4th Va. Dist.; chmn. Rep. State Com. of Va., 1872-73; del. at large and chmn. Va. delegation to Rep. Nat. Conv., Cincinnati, 1876. Episcopalian. Wrote: (brochures) Separation of Church and State (Paris, France), 1907; The Results of Our Mexican Policy, 1916; What America Thinks—a Reminiscence of Gen. Garibaldi, 1916; Letters and Talks with Sir Edward Carson, 1916; The Descendants of Samuel Hyde (N.E. Hist.-Geneal. Soc. Register), 1917; Stowell Genealogy. Home: Amherst, Mass. Died Apr. 27, 1922.

STRAHAN, Kay Cleaver, writer; b. LaGrande, Ore., Jan. 4, 1888; d. Alonzo and Laura Ann (Bryson) Cleaver; ed. Eugene (Ore.) High Sch., and Portland Business Coll.; m. William Nicholas Strahan, Nov. 30, 1910. Author: Peggy-Mary, 1915; Something That Begins with "T," 1918; Desert Moon, 1928; Footprints (awarded $2,500 Scotland Yard prize), 1928; Death Traps, 1930; October House, 1931; Oh, Happy Youth, 1931; The Meriwether Mystery, 1933; The Hobgoblin Murder, 1934; The Desert Lake Mystery, 1936. Home: Portland, Ore. Died Aug. 14, 1941.

STRAIGHT, Willard Dickerman, consul gen.; b. Oswego, N.Y., Jan. 31, 1880; s. Henry H. and Emma (Dickerman) S.; Bordentown, N.J., Military Institue, 1897; B. Arch., Cornell, 1901; m. Dorothy Payne, d. William C. Whitney, Sept. 7, 1911. In Chinese Imperial Maritime Customs Service, Nanking and Peking, 1902-04; corr. Reuter's Agency and Associated Press in Seoul, Tokio and Manchuria, 1904-05; Am. vice consul gen. and pvt. sec. to Am. minister, Seoul, 1905; pvt. sec. Am. minister, Havana, 1906; consul gen. at Mukden, 1906-08; acting chief Div. of Far Eastern Affairs, Dept. of State, Nov. 1908-June 1909; apptd. rep. in China for the American Group (J. P. Morgan & Co., Kuhn, Loeb & Co.; First Nat. Bank, Nat. City Bank), June 8, 1909. Commd. maj., adj. gen.'s dept. U.S.R., 1917. Fellow Royal Geog. Soc. (London). Trustee Cornell U. Home: Old Westbury, L.I. Died Nov. 28, 1918.

STRANG, Lewis Clinton, author; b. Westfield, Mass., Dec. 4, 1869; s. Clinton W. (D.D.S.) and Ella J. (Lewis) S.; A.B., Boston U., 1892; m. Martha W. Locke, Aug. 7, 1895. Became reporter for Boston Jour., fall of 1892, Sunday edition, 1893, asst. city editor and asst. in dramatic dept., 1894, dramatic editor and critic, fall of 1898; editorial writer Boston Jour. and Evening News, 1903; leading editorial writer and dramatic critic, Washington Times, 1904. Christian Science practitioner, 1904—. Author: Famous Actresses of the Day (1st series), 1899 (2d series), 1901; Famous Actors of the Day (1st series), 1899 (2d series), 1901; Prima Donnas and Soubrettes of Light Opera and Musical Comedy in America, 1900; Celebrated Comedians of Light Opera and Musical Comedy in America, 1900; Players and Plays of the Last Quarter Century (2 vols.), 1902. Home: East Weymouth, Mass. Died Jan. 14, 1935.

STRANGE, John, paper mfr.; b. Oakfield, Wis., June 27, 1852; s. Thomas and Martha (Dixon) S.; ed. pub. schs., and spl. studies, Beloit (Wis.) Coll.; m. Mary Margaret McGregor, July 11, 1876. Comml. and lumber bus., Wis. and Ia., 1875-86, paper bus., 1886—; pres. John Strange Paper Co., John Strange Pail Co., Stevens Point Pulp & Paper Co.; mem. Menasha Common Council, Menasha Sch. Bd., and register of deeds Winnebago County, Wis.; lt gov. of Wis., 1909-10; del. Progressive Party Nat. Conv., 1912, 16. Curator Wis. Hist. Soc. Mem. nat. and Wis. State bds. Anti-Saloon League America. Home: Neenah, Wis. Died May 28, 1923.

STRANGE, Robert, bishop; b. Wilmington, N.C., Dec. 6, 1857; s. Robert and Caroline (Wright) S.; A.B., U. of N.C., 1879; grad. Berkeley Div. Sch., Conn., 1883; D.D., U. of N.C., 1895; m. Elizabeth Stone Buford, Sept. 29, 1886. Deacon, 1884, priest, 1885, P.E. Ch.; missionary to colored people in Southern Va., 1883-85; rector Ch. of the Good Shepherd, Raleigh, N.C., 1885-87, St. James', Wilmington, 1887-1900, St. Paul's, Richmond, Va., 1900-04; elected, May 26, 1904, and consecrated, Nov. 1, 1904, bishop coadjutor of Diocese of East Carolina, bishop, Apr. 17, 1905. Deputy to Gen. Conv. P.E. Ch., from East Carolina, 1898, from Va., 1904. Address: Wilmington, N.C. Died Aug. 23, 1914.

STRANSKY, Josef, orchestral conductor; b. Humpolec, Czechoslovakia, Sept. 9, 1874; s. Hermann and Eleonore (Taus) S.; ed. gymnasium, Prague, and univs. of Prague, Vienna, Leipzig; studied music under Jadassohn, at Leipzig, and Fuchs and Bruckner, at Vienna; married. Conductor Royal Opera, Prague, Bohemia, 1898-1903, and Hamburg (Germany) Opera and Symphony Concerts, 1903-10; condr. Blüthner Orchestra, Berlin, and chief kapellmeister New Royal Opera, 1909-10; condr. Dresden Symphony Soc., and directed operatic performances and concerts in various cities of Europe; condr. Philharmonic Soc. of New York, 1911-23; became condr. State Symphony Orchestra of N.Y. and gen. mus. dir. New York Wagnerian Opera Co., 1923; retired from musical activities and partner Wildenstein and Co., New York and Paris. Composer of songs, an opera, suite for orchestra symphony, etc. Home: New York, N.Y. Died Mar. 6, 1936.

STRATEMEYER, Edward ("Capt. Ralph Bonehill" and "Arthur M. Winfield"), author; b. Elizabeth, N.J., Oct. 4, 1862; s. Henry J. and Anna (Seigel) S.; ed. high sch. and by pvt. tutor; m. Magdalene B. Van Camp, 1891; children—Mrs. Harriet Adams, Edna Camilla. Propr. Stratemeyer Syndicate. Editor of Good News, Bright Days and Young People of America. Author: Old Glory Series, 1898-1902; Soldiers of Fortune Series, 1900-04; Colonial Series, 1901-06; Mexican War Series, 1900-04; Pan-American Series, 1902-08; Dave Porter Series, 1905-19; Lakeport Series, 1904-09; American Boys Life of William McKinley, 1901; American Boys Life of Theodore Roosevelt, 1904; and 40 other vols.; also, under the noms de plume, Rover Boys' Series, 1899-1925; Flag of Freedom Series, 1899-1905; Frontier Series, 1903-07; Boy Hunters Series, 1906-11; Putnam Hall Series, 1905-12. Home: Newark, N.J. Died May 12, 1930.

STRATON, John Roach, clergyman; b. Evansville, Ind., Apr. 6, 1875; s. Henry Dundas Douglas and Julia Rebecca (Carter) S.; student Mercer U., Ga., 1895-98; Southern Bapt. Theol. Sem., Louisville, Ky., 1900-02; studied U. of Chicago, Boston Sch. of Oratory and Expression; D.D., Shurtleff Coll., 1906; m. Georgia Hillyer, Nov. 2, 1903; children—Hillyer Hawthorne, John Charles, Warren Badenock, Catherine Eager (dec.), George Douglas. Prof. oratory and interpretation of lit., Mercer U., 1899; ordained Bapt. ministry, 1900; mem. faculty, Baylor U., 1903-05; pastor 2d Ch., Chicago, 1905-07, 7th Immanuel Ch., Baltimore, Md., 1908-13, 1st Ch., Norfolk, Va., 1913-17, Calvary Ch., New York, 1918—. Trustee Anti-Saloon League America, Lord's Day Alliance U.S.A. Winner of intercollegiate oratorical championship of Ga. and of Southern interstate oratorical championship; winner of $1,000 prize by Commercial Club of Portland, Ore., for article on "Portland and the Northwest," and $500 prize by Anti-Saloon League for best essay on "The Mental, Moral, Physical and Economic Cost of the Liquor Traffic." Author: The Salvation of Society; The Menace of Immorality in Church and State, 1920; The Heavenly Home, 1920; The Gardens of Life, 1921; Church vs. Stage, 1921; Our Relapse into Paganism, 1921; Dance of Death, 1922; The Old Gospel at the Heart of the Metropolis, 1925; The Famous New York Fundamentalist-Modernist Debates, 1925; The Fakes and Fancies of the Evolutionists, 1925. Lecturer; syndicate writer. Home: New York, N.Y. Died Oct. 29, 1929.

STRATTON, Frederick Eugene, coll. prof.; b. Athol, Mass., July 5, 1847; s. Joseph and Alice Whitney (Mann) S.; A.B., Williams, 1871, A.M., 1874; Ph.D., Ill. Wesleyan U., Bloomington, 1891; student Harvard, U. of Chicago, U. of Calif. and U. of Wis.; m. Mary Tryphena Goddard, Mar. 14, 1874; 1 dau., Alice Belle (wife of Rev. H. E. Stocker). Teacher and prin. N.E. acads. and high schs. until 1883; prin. high sch., Davenport, Ia., 1883-92; prin. acad. connected with Carleton Coll., Northfield, Minn., 1892-1904, also instr. Greek; acting prof. Greek, Carleton Coll., 1904-06; apptd. prof. Greek, Fargo Coll., 1906, also served as dean, 1906-11, and librarian of the college. Instr. and dir. teachers' training schools in Ia. and Minn., 12 summers; mem. scientific expdn. sent from Williams Coll. to Central America, winter 1870-71. An organizer, dir. and sec. many yrs. Ia. State Teachers' Reading Circle, also mem. Ia. State Ednl. Council. Republican. Conglist. K.T. Author: The Game of the Greek Verb. Home: Fargo, N.D. Died June 4, 1928.

STRATTON, Frederick Smith, lawyer; b. Oakland, Calif., Jan. 22, 1859; s. James Thompson and Cornelia (Smith) S.; grad. high sch., Oakland, 1876; LL.B., Hastings Coll. of Law (U. of Calif.), 1881; m. Grace Gregory, June 18, 1890. In practice at San Francisco, 1881—; sr. mem. firm Stratton, Kaufman & Torchiana. Atty. for U.S. in Ala. Claims Commn. cases, French spoliation claims cases and Benson land fraud cases in Calif., 1883-90; atty. for Bd. of State Harbor Commn., 1884-94; mem. Calif. Senate, 1895-99; collector customs, port of San Francisco, Dec. 1, 1900-Aug. 18, 1913. Republican. Episcopalian. Home: Oakland, Calif. Died Nov. 30, 1915.

STRATTON, Samuel Wesley, physicist; b. Litchfield, Ill., July 18, 1861; s. Samuel and Mary B. (Webster) S.; B.S., U. of Ill., 1884, D.Eng., 1903; D.Sc., Western U. of Pa. (now U. of Pittsburgh), 1903, Cambridge, 1909, Yale, 1919; LL.D., Harvard, 1923; Ph.D., Rensselaer Poly. Inst., 1924; unmarried. Instr. mathematics, asst. prof., and prof. physics and elec. engring., U. of Ill., 1885-92; successively asst. prof., asso. prof. and prof. physics, U. of Chicago, 1892-1901; dir. Nat. Bur. of Standards, Washington, 1901-23; pres. Mass. Inst. of Tech., 1923—. Ensign, lt. jr. grade, lt., and lt. comdr. Ill. Naval Militia, 1895-1901; lt. U.S.N., during Spanish-Am. War, May-Nov. 1898; comdr. comdg. D.C. Naval Militia, 1904-12. Mem. Internat. Com. on Weights and Measures, Am. Inst. Elec. Engrs., Nat. Acad. Sciences, Nat. Advisory Com. for Aeronautics. Chevalier Legion of Honor, 1909, Officer, 1928. Home: Cambridge, Mass. Died Oct. 18, 1931.

STRATTON, William B., architect; b. Ithaca, N.Y., 1865; s. David and Lucretia H. (Buck) S.; B.S. in Architecture, Cornell, 1888; m. Mary Chase Perry, 1918. Engaged as architect in Detroit, Mich.,

1890—. Mem. Mich. Naval Militia during Spanish-Am. War. Fellow A.I.A. Home: Grosse Pointe Park, Mich. Deceased.

STRAUB, Oscar Itin, army officer; b. in Pa., Feb. 19, 1865; grad. U.S. Mil. Acad., 1887, Arty. Sch., 1892. Commd. add. 2d lt. 1st Arty., June 12, 1887; 2d lt., Aug. 11, 1887; 1st lt., 5th Arty., Jan. 3, 1894; capt. Arty. Corps, Feb. 12, 1901; maj., Jan. 25, 1907; lt. col. Coast Arty. Corps, July 28, 1911; col., Aug. 9, 1915. Participated in campaign in Puerto Rico, with Light Battery D, 5th Arty., July-Aug., 1898; in engagement at Harmigueros, Aug. 10, 1898; comd. 28th Battery, Field Arty., Ft. Snelling, Minn., 1904-07; duty at Ft. Howard, Md., 1917. Address: Washington, D.C. Died July 9, 1922.

STRAUGHN, William Ringgold, educator; b. Mardella Springs, Md., Apr. 23, 1882; s. Rev. John Lee and Roberta Elizabeth Alice (Acworth) S.; Baltimore City Coll., 1902; A.B., Johns Hopkins, 1905, post-grad. student, 1905-06; Ph.D., U. of Kansas City, 1908; m. Dorothy Lloyd, July 7, 1909; children—(John) Lloyd, William R., Robert A. Teacher, Baltimore City Coll., 1902-06; prof. of lit. and pedagogy, 1st Pa. State Normal Sch., Millersville, Pa., 1906-11; supt. schs., DuBois, Pa., 1911-14; pres. State Teachers Coll., Mansfield, Pa., Apr. 1, 1914—; president First Nat. Bank of Mansfield, Pa. Mem. Pa. State Council of Edn., 1926—. Mem. Am. Polit. Science Assn. Methodist. Mason. Lecturer on ednl. and lit. topics. Home: Mansfield, Pa. Died Aug. 21, 1936.

STRAUS, Adolph D., merchant; b. in Germany, May 13, 1839; s. Joseph and Barbara (Schwarz) S.; brought to America, 1848; ed. pub. schs., New Orleans, and Spring Hill Coll., Ala.; m. Emily Saarbach, Sept. 15, 1875. Served as capt., 3d Battalion La. regt. vols., 1861-65; went to Nicaragua, 1865, and became gen. in army of Nicaragua; returned to U.S., 1867; in newspaper work on New York Asso. Press, New York Times, and New Orleans Picayune, until 1875; founder, 1876. A. D. Straus & Co., New York; dir. Hanover Fire Ins. Co. Consul gen. of Nicaragua, at New York, 1889-12. Mugwump. Hebrew. Knight Isabel la Catholica, of Spain; awarded gold medal Histoire Internationale, Paris, France. Home: New York, N.Y. Died Apr. 30, 1925.

STRAUS, Herbert Nathan, merchant; b. N. Y. City, Nov. 2, 1881; s. Isidor and Ida (Blun) S.; grad. Dr. Sach's Collegiate Inst., 1899; A.B., Harvard, 1903; m. Therese Kuhn, July 15, 1907; children—Edward Kuhn, Oliver Herbert, John Wendell. Began with R. H. Macy & Co., N.Y. City, 1903, sec.-treas., 1919—, v.p., 1922—; dir. The La Salle & Koch Co., Toledo, O., Davison-Paxon Co., Atlanta, Ga. Served with Food Adminstrn. Bd. and War Trade Bd., Washington, D.C., World War I. Del. to Rep. Nat. Conv., 1928; treas. N.Y. State Rep. Com. and N.Y. Hoover-Curtis Committee, 1928. Member of visiting committee of Harvard Coll. Home: New York, N.Y. Died Apr. 6, 1933.

STRAUS, Isidor, merchant; b. Rhenish Bavaria, Feb. 6, 1845; s. Lazarus and Sara (Straus) S.; brother of Nathan and Oscar Solomon S.; came to U.S. with his parents, 1854; ed. Collinsworth Inst., Talbotton, Ga.; LL.D., Washington and Lee U., 1905; m. Ida Blun, 1871. Sent abroad, 1863, by Ga. Export & Import Co., of Columbus, Ga., as asst. to the agt. who was to purchase steamers and supplies for shipment to the Confed. States; in 1866 joined his father in forming firm of L. Straus & Sons, importers of pottery and glassware. With brother, Nathan, became partner in R. H. Macy & Co., dept. store, 1888; mem. firm Abraham & Straus, Brooklyn, dept. store, 1892; dir. various banks and financial instns. First pres. New York Crockery Bd. of Trade; New York City's representative on N.Y. and N.J. Bridge Commn. Connected with various tariff reform and sound money movements. At spl. election elected to 53d Congress (1893-95), where as bosom friend of William L. Wilson, was in constant consultation in formation of Wilson Tariff. Pres. Ednl. Alliance; v.p. J. Hood Wright Memorial Hosp.; mem. one of visiting coms. of Harvard U.; on bd. trustees many financial, charitable and philanthropic instns. Home: New York, N.Y. Died Apr. 15, 1912.

STRAUS, Jesse Isidor, ambassador; b. New York City, June 25, 1872; s. Isidor and Ida (Blun) S.; prep. edn., Sach's Prep. Sch., New York; B.A., Harvard, 1893; LL.D. from U. of Ga.; m. Irma S. Nathan, Nov. 20, 1895; children—Beatrice (wife of Dr. Robert L. Levy), Jack Isidor, Robert Kenneth. Began as clk. Hanover Nat. Bank, N.Y. City, then with Abraham & Straus, Brooklyn; connected with R. H. Macy & Co., 1896—, becoming pres. 1919. A.E. and P. to France, Mar. 16, 1933—. Mem. Am. Acad. Polit. and Social Science, Council on Foreign Relations, Foreign Policy Assn. Democrat. Jewish religion. Home: New York, N.Y. Died Oct. 4, 1936.

STRAUS, Nathan, merchant; b. Rhenish, Bavaria, Jan. 31, 1848; s. Lazarus and Sara (Straus) S.; came to the U.S., 1854, with family; settled in Talbotton, Ga., where attended sch.; afterward went to New York; grad. Packard's Business Coll.; m. Lina Gutherz, 1875 (died 1930); 2 sons, 1 dau. Joined father in L. Straus & Sons, 1866, importers pottery and glassware; mem. firm Abraham & Straus, dept. store, Brooklyn; retired, 1914, to devote time to philanthropic activities. Park commr., New York, 1889-93; mem. New York Forest Preserve Bd., 1893; Dem. nominee for mayor of New York, 1894 (declined); pres. Bd. of Health, New York, 1898. Originated in 1892 and maintained at his own expense until 1920, system of distribution of pasteurized milk in N.Y. City; gave installation for pasteurization of milk to various cities in U.S. and abroad; originated, winter of 1892-93, and maintained system of depots for distribution of coal, bread and groceries to poor of N.Y. City; during panic winter, 1893-94, maintained system of lodging houses for homeless where for five cents, 1,200 people were given shelter and breakfast daily; donated ice plant to Santiago, Cuba, 1898; founded, 1909, 1st tuberculosis preventorium for children, at Farmingdale, N.J.; U.S. del. to Internat. Health Congress, Berlin, 1911, Rome, 1912; established in Palestine the first health dept. and the first Pasteur Inst., 1912, and maintained soup kitchens where more than 200 people received a free meal daily, regardless of race, creed or color; conducted pasteurization campaign in Calif., winter 1913-14; contributed to war relief in helping to send relief ships and feeding war orphans; contributed toward sending the food-ship Vulcan to war sufferers in Palestine, 1915, and annually spent more than his income to relieve suffering in U.S. and abroad; sold his steam yacht, 1916, and gave proceeds for the feeding of war orphans; started free distribution of pasteurized milk to soldiers and sailors, June 1918; reëlected chmn. Am. Jewish Congress, 1920, 28; turned over Pasteurization Lab. and its equipment to New York Health Dept. to be used for preparing ready-to-drink modified pasteurized milk in nursing bottles, 1920; in vote taken by Jewish Tribune as to ten Jews who had served America best, led the poll; received largest number of votes and was presented with city flag at Silver Jubilee of Greater New York, 1923, for services rendered during preceding 25 yrs.; sent immediate relief for afflicted in earthquake, Palestine, 1927; in commemoration of eightieth birthday, 1928, sent funds for relief of unemployment to Palestine; erected two health and welfare centers for the benefit of people of all races and creeds in Palestine; one in Jerusalem dedicated with due ceremonies and accepted, 1929; prevailed on Dr. John Haynes Holmes of Community Ch., New York, to go to Palestine, 1929, and study conditions there and elsewhere in the Near East, to enable him to work towards peace among nations and unity among all races and creeds. Author of various addresses on pasteurized milk and various social problems; compiled an illustrated volume, "Disease in Milk: The Remedy Pasteurization, 1917. Home: Mamaroneck, N.Y. Died Jan. 11, 1931.

STRAUS, Oscar Solomon, ambassador; b. Dec. 23, 1850; s. Lazarus and Sara (Straus) S.; lived at Talbotton, Ga., and afterwards at Columbus, Ga., until 1865, when he removed to New York; A.B., Columbia, 1871, LL.B., 1873, A.M., 1874; Litt.D., Brown, 1896; LL.D., Washington and Lee, 1898, U. of Pa., 1900, Columbia, 1904; m. Sarah, d. Louis Lavanburg, Apr. 19, 1882. Practiced law at New York, 1873-81; mem. firm L. Straus & Sons, importers pottery and glassware, New York, 1881-1906. E.E. and M.P. to Turkey, 1887-89, 1898-1901; apptd. mem. Permanent Ct. of Arbitration at The Hague, 1902, to fill vacancy of ex-President Harrison; reapptd. by Presidents Roosevelt, Taft and Wilson; Sec. Dept. Commerce and Labor, in cabinet of President Roosevelt, Dec. 17, 1906-Mar. 4, 1909; A.E. and P. to Turkey, May 1909-Dec. 1910. Chmn. N.Y. Pub. Service Commn., 1st dist., 1915-18. Pres. N.Y. Bd. of Trade and Transportation, Nat. Primary League, Am. Social Science Assn.; v.p. Nat. Civic Federation, Internat. Law Assn. Author: The Origin of Republican Form of Government in the United States, 1886; Rogers Williams, the Pioneer of Religious Liberty, 1894; The Development of Religious Liberty in the United States, 1896; Reform in the Consular Service, 1897; United States Doctrine of Citizenship, 1901; Our Diplomacy with Reference to our Foreign Service, 1902; The American Spirit, 1913; Under Four Administrations, 1922. Chmn. arbitration com. to decide wage dispute bet. eastern rys. and their engrs., 1912; chmn. Paris Com. of League to Enforce Peace, 1919; mem. President Wilson's 2d Industrial Conf. Home: New York, N.Y. Died May 3, 1926.

STRAUS, Simon William, banker; b. Ligonier, Ind., Dec. 23, 1866; s. Frederick and Madlon (Goldsmith) S.; ed. pub. schs.; m. Hattie Klee, Apr. 25, 1893. Became connected with father's mortgage and loan business, 1884, admitted as partner, 1888, chmn. bd. S. W. Straus & Co., Inc., 1898—; chmn. bd. Franklin Trust & Savings Bank, Chicago, 1928—; pres. Straus Nat. Bank & Trust Co. of New York, Straus Nat. Bank & Trust Co. of Chicago. Pres. Am. Soc. for Thrift. Author: History of the Thrift Movement in America, 1920. Originator of the "Straus Plan" of financing loans on buildings and industrial plants. Office: New York, N.Y. Died Sept. 7, 1930.

STRAUSS, Albert, banker; b. N.Y. City, Aug. 26, 1864; s. Philipp and Anna F. (Rohman) S.; student Coll. City of New York, 1879-82; m. Lucretia Mott Lord, 1896. Entered banking business in New York, 1882; mem. J. & W. Seligman & Co., 1901-18, and Jan. 1, 1921—; vice gov. Federal Reserve Bd., 1918-20, resigned; dir. Cuba Cane Sugar Corp., Manati Sugar Co., Pierce Arrow Motor Car Co., Cuban Tobacco Co., Brooklyn Manhattan Transit Corp. Republican. Home: New York, N.Y. Died Mar. 28, 1929.

STRAUSS, Charles, lawyer; b. N.Y. City, Nov. 28, 1854; s. Isaac and Henrietta (Westheimer) S.; ed. Coll. City of New York, 1869-73; Columbia U. Law Sch., 1873-75; m. Pauline Loewenstein, Jan. 4, 1886; children—Eugene (dec.), Edith S. (Mrs. E. Howard Figg). Admitted to N.Y. bar, Dec. 31, 1875; mem. firm of Strauss, Reich & Boyer; pres. Eastchester Development Co., Seaman Realty Co.; dir. Underwood Elliott Fisher Co. (finance com.). Pres. Bd. of Water Supply, New York, 1911-18; commr. of edn., N.Y., 1890-98; mem. Court House Bd., N.Y., 1909-10. Trustee Coll. City of New York; v.p. Nat. Security League, N.Y. Law Inst.; dir. Flower Hosp. Democrat. Home: New York, N.Y. Died Apr. 11, 1934.

STRAUSS, Joseph Baermann, engineer; b. Cincinnati, O., Jan. 9, 1870; s. Raphael and Lena (Baermann) S.; ed. grammar and high schs., Cincinnati; C.E., U. of Cincinnati, 1892, D.Sc., 1930; m. May Van, June 9, 1895; children—Ralph V., Richard K. Draftsman N.J. Steel & Iron Co., Trenton, N.J., 1892-94; instr. Coll. of Engring., U. of Cincinnati, 1894-95; detailer, insp., estimator and designer Lassig Bridge & Iron Co., Chicago, 1895-97; designer and squad boss Sanitary Dist. of Chicago, 1897-99; prin. asst. engr. in charge of office of Ralph Modjeski, Chicago, 1899-1902; cons. engr. in pvt. practice, 1902-04; pres. and chief engr. The Strauss Engineering Corp., cons. engrs., 1904—. Made a specialty of original design and movable and long span bridge design; built nearly 500 bridges in U.S., Can. and abroad; originated the 5 types of the Strauss trunnion bascule bridge which became a world standard, and 2 types of Strauss lift bridge; designed and built the Aeroscope at the San Francisco Expn., and the portable searchlight outfits employed by the U.S. and Russian govts. during the World War I; invented and perfected the yielding barrier used in bridges and for grade crossing protection; designed and built a series of reinforced concrete freight cars as a war emergency measure; invented and built the bascule-door hangar and many other bridge and mechanical devices employed in the arts; apptd. chief engr., 1929, for the Golden Gate Bridge, at San Francisco, Calif., the longest single-span bridge in the world, main span 4,200 feet, total length 9,200 feet; co-designer of Montreal-South Shore Bridge for Harbour Commn., Montreal, 2 miles long; designer and engr. Columbia River Bridge at Longview, Wash., second longest cantilever built; designing engr. for the bascule span of the Arlington Memorial Bridge across Potomac River at Washington, D.C.; cons. engr. to Port of New York Authority on George Washington Memorial Bridge, second-longest single span in the world, across Hudson River, at 178th St., New York, also the 1,650-ft. Bayonne Arch. Originator of movement for better citizenship through medium of citizenship training; founder of Citizen-Training Corps. Address: San Francisco, Calif. Died May 16, 1938.

STRAUSS, Moses, editor; b. Keokuk, Ia., Nov. 9, 1872; s. Maurice and Bertha S.; grad. Hughes High Sch., Cincinnati, 1889; studied U. of Cincinnati Hebrew Union Coll. (non-grad.); m. Eleanor McGregor, Apr. 14, 1909; children—Hilda Bertha, Moses Gordon, Victor Maurice Bradford. Identified with newspaper business, 1899—; mng. editor Cincinnati Times-Star, 1923-37. Mem. Home Guards, World War I; member of Anti-Tuberculosis League. Republican. Mason, Elk; mem. B'nai B'rith. Author: What's the News?; Newspaper Practices in a Changing World. Home: Cincinnati, O. Died July 14, 1938.

STRAUSS, Nathan, dry goods mcht.; b. N.Y. City, July 17, 1868; s. Reuben and Caroline (Schlussel) S.; ed. pub. schs., N.Y. City; unmarried. With Fleischner Mayer & Co., wholesale dry goods, Portland, Ore., 1882—, mng. partner, 1913—; pres. Portland Remedial Loan Assn.; dir. Portland Br. of Fed. Res. Bank of San Francisco, Portland Industries Financing Service, Ore. Mutual Life Ins. Co., Salem Linen Mills. Pres. Federated Jewish Socs.; v.p. Pub. Welfare Bureau; treas. Doernbecker Children's Hospital Guild. Dir. Chamber of Commerce of U.S.A. Republican. Jewish religion. Home: Portland, Ore. Died Oct. 14, 1933.

STRAWBRIDGE, William Correy, patent lawyer; b. Chester County, Pa., June 24, 1848; s. James Alexander and Mary Niven (Hodgson) S.; grad. Rensselaer Poly. Inst., engr., 1870. Became asst. supt. Pa. Steel Works, Harrisburg. Studied law; admitted to Phila. bar, March 1873. Exclusively engaged in patent law practice, 1875—; counsel for U.S. in Bell Telephone case. Gen. counsel for many industrial cos., including leading interests relating to ship and engine bldg., car constrn and steel and iron mfr. Address: Philadelphia, Pa. Died 1908.

STRAYER, Louis William, newspaper man; b. Princeton, Ill., May 4, 1869; s. John William and Martha Jane (Mercer) S.; ed. high sch., Akron, O.; m. Minnie Watson Jones, Aug. 29, 1892 (died 1910). Began as reporter Akron Beacon, 1887; became reporter Pittsburgh Post, 1891, later with other newspapers in Pittsburgh; Washington corr. Pittsburgh Gazette-Times, 1902-08; in charge Washington bur. Pittsburgh Dispatch, 1908—. Reported important events throughout U.S. and Europe. Republican. Presbyn. Home: Washington, D.C. Died Jan. 28, 1922.

STRAYER, Paul Moore, clergyman; b. Baltimore, Dec. 30, 1871; s. Rev. Webster M. and Martha (Bevan) S.; ed. Baltimore City Coll., 1887-92; U. of Chicago, 1896-97; U. of Edinburgh, 1899-1900; B.D., Yale Div. Sch., 1903; D.D., U. of Rochester, 1915; m. Beulah Gilbert, 1899 (died 1903); 1 son, Paul Gilbert; m. 2d, Emily (Betts) Loomis, May 15, 1912. Ordained Presbyn. ministry, 1897; pastor 1st M.P. Ch., Pittsburgh, 1897-99, Crouch Hill Presbyn. Ch., London, Eng. (6 mos.), 1900, 1st Congl. Ch., South Norwalk, Conn., 1900-03, 3d Presbyn. Ch., Rochester, N.Y., 1903-25; pastor emeritus, 1925—. Founder of People's Sunday Evening Meetings, Rochester. Dir. Rochester Orphans' Home. Author: The Reconstruction of the Church with Regard to Its Message and Program, 1915. Dir. Internat. Reform Bur. Home: Rochester, N.Y. Died Apr. 3, 1929.

STREAMER, Volney, editor, librarian; b. Magnolia, Ill.; s. Jacob and Sarah Louisa (Clark) S.; ed. prep. course 1 yr., Ill. Wesleyan U.; unmarried. With publ. house A. C. McClurg & Co., Chicago, 1877-86; mem. Edwin Booth's theatrical co., 1886-87; librarian The Players, Dec. 1905—. Editor and Compiler: In Friendship's Name, 1887; What Makes a Friend, 1893; A Cluster of Gems, 1895; The World Awheel, 1896; Voices of Doubt and Trust, 1897. Address: New York, N.Y. Died Apr. 14, 1915.

STRECKER, Herman, sculptor, lepidopterist; b. Phila., March 24, 1836; s. Ferdinand H. and Anna (Kern) S.; ed. pub. schs.; removed to Reading, 1847, Ph.D., Franklin and Marshall Coll.; began granite and marble work when 12 yrs. old; acquired great skill as sculptor and designer; designed Soldiers' Monument at Reading and numerous other works; spent all spare time in study of zoölogy, mineralogy, archæology and botany; specially well known for his works on butterflies and his collection of over 370,000 of those insects. Author: Lepidoptera, Rhopaloceres and Heteroceres, Indigenous and Exotic, 1872-77; Butterflies and Moths of North America, 1878; etc. Address: Reading, Pa. Died 1901.

STRECKER, John Kern, curator; b. Waterloo, Ill., July 10, 1875; s. John Kern and Felicia (Agnew) S.; ed. pub. schs.; hon. M.S., Baylor U., 1925; m. Mary Robert Boyd, Oct. 27, 1915. Curator Mus. Baylor U., 1903—, head librarian, 1919—. Chmn. Dem. Exec. Com., 10th Supreme Jud. Dist., Tex.; chmn. McLennon County Dem. Exec. Com. 18 yrs.; head poultry dept., Tex. Cotton Palace Expn., 1911-30. Mem. A.A.A.S., Am. Soc. Mammalogists, Am. Soc. Ichthyologist and Herpetologists, Biol. Soc. Washington, Scientific Soc. San Antonio, Texas Folk-Lore Soc. (pres.), Texas Academy Science (pres.), Tex. Game and Fish Protective Assn. (pres.). Democrat Presbyn. Mason, Odd Fellow, Woodman of the World (formerly head consul, Tex.). Contbr. to Auk, Jour. of Mammalogy, etc. Editor of Contributions from Baylor U. Museum and Baylor U. Contributions to Folk-Lore. An authority on reptiles and amphibians of Tex. Home: Waco, Tex. Died Jan. 9, 1933.

STREET, Jacob Richard, coll. dean; b. Palmyra, Ont., Can., July 18, 1860; s. Joseph Lockwood and Hannah (Teeple) S.; A.B., Victoria U., Can., 1884; A.M., Toronto U., 1887; Ph.D., Clark U., Mass., 1898; m. Rose Northcott, Jan. 1, 1885. Master modern langs., Smithville (Ont.) High Sch., 1884-85, Walkerton High Sch., 1886-87; prin. Caledonia High Sch., 1887-95; prof. education, Mt. Holyoke Coll., 1898-1900; prof. edn., 1900-06, dean Teachers Coll., 1906-17, Syracuse U. Lit. editor Jour. of Pedagogy, 1903-04; lecturer for State Edn. Dept. at teachers' insts., N.Y., 1905—. Mem. Bd. Edn., Syracuse, 1906-10. Address: Syracuse, N.Y. Died June 11, 1920.

STREET, Robert Gould, lawyer; b. Greensboro, Ala., Dec. 12, 1843; s. John Vernon and Elizabeth (Torrence) S.; A.B., U. of Ala., 1861; m. Ethelveda Lauve, Dec. 24, 1868 (died 1880). Served as pvt. in 20th Ala. Regt. Infantry, later in 51st Regt. Cav., C.S.A., 1861-65. Admitted to Ala. bar, 1866; removed to Galveston, Tex., 1867; mem. Gould & Street, later Street & Kleburg. Mem. Tex. Senate, 18?9; judge Dist. Ct., Galveston, 1902—. Democrat. Contbr. to popular and professional jours. Author: Law of Personal Injuries. Editor 6th edit. Shearman and Redfield on Negligence, and 2d edit. Bishops Non-Contract Law. Address: Galveston, Tex. Deceased.

STREET, Thomas Atkins, judge, author; b. Marshall County, Ala., Mar. 14, 1872; s. Thomas Atkins and Julia Ann (Beard) S.; A.B., U. of Ala., 1892, A.M., 1893, LL.B., 1894; m. Lallie Abercrombie, Apr. 22, 1911; children—Lura Martin, Julia Alice. Admitted to bar, 1894; practiced law at Nashville, Tenn., 1894-1902; adj. prof. law, Vanderbilt U., 1900-02; on staff Edward Thompson Co., law pubs., Northport, N.Y., 1902-08; prof. equity, U. of Mo. Sch. of law, 1908-10. Draftsman, Internal Revenue Law of 1914 (P.I.); as mem. Code Com. (1910-17) was principal codifier of Administrative Code of Philippine Islands, 1916, and of revised Administrative Code, 1917. Asso. justice Supreme Court of P.I., July 1917—. Author: Foundations of Legal Liability (3 vols.), 1906; Federal Equity Practice (3 vols.), 1909. Address: Manila, P.I. Died Mar. 17, 1936.

STREET, Webster, judge; b. Salem, Ohio, June 8, 1846; s. Samuel and Sarah S.; ed. common schools and Antioch Coll.; grad. Salem High Sch., 1867. Admitted to Ohio bar, 1871; practiced law in Pittsburgh, Pa.; moved to Ariz., 1877, and engaged in practice; sec. and chmn. Rep. Central Com. of Ariz.; judge Territorial court, 1885-86; chief justice Supreme Ct., Ariz., Nov. 6, 1897-1902. Address: Phoenix, Ariz. Died 1909.

STREETER, Frank Sherwin, lawyer; b. E. Charleston, Vt., Aug. 5, 1853; s. Daniel and Julia (Wheeler) S.; A.B., Dartmouth, 1874, LL.D., 1913; m. Lillian Carpenter, Nov. 14, 1877. Admitted to bar, 1877; mem. N.H. Ho. of Rep., 1885; pres. N.H. Constl. Conv., 1902; pres. Rep. State Conv., 1892; del.-at-large Rep. Nat. Conv., 1896; mem. Rep. Nat. Com., 1904-08. Dir. Manchester Traction Co., etc. Mem. Am. Sect. Internat. Joint Commission (created by treaty with Great Britain for settlement of water boundary questions between U.S. and Can.), Mar. 16, 1911-Oct. 1, 1913. Trustee Dartmouth Coll., 1892—. Mem. N.H. Historical Society (president 1914-15), American Historical Assn., N.H. Bar Assn. (pres. 1903-04), Am. Bar Assn.; del. Universal Congress Lawyers and Jurists, St. Louis, 1904; mem. sub exec. com. for Celebration 100th Anniversary of Peace Among English-Speaking Peoples, 1913; mem. exec. com. League to Enforce Peace, 1915; chmn. N.H. Belgian Relief Com., 1915; exec. com. Nat. Security League; pres. New Hampshire Defense League, 1917. Chairman State Bd. of Edn., 1919-21. Unitarian. Home: Concord, N.H. Died Dec. 11, 1922.

STREETER, John Williams, physician; b. Ashtabula, O., Sept. 17, 1841; s. Sereno W. and Mary (Williams) S.; ed. Monroe (N.Y.) Acad.; served in 1st Mich. light arty., 1862-65, in campaigns of Army of the Cumberland; mustered out as 1st lt. arty.; studied medicine, U. of Mich., fall of 1865; grad. Hahnemann Med. Coll., Chicago, 1868; m. Mary Clark, Sept. 2, 1869. Prof. diseases of women, Chicago Homœ. Coll., 1877—; for 10 yrs. pres. homœ. staff Cook County Hosp.; established, 1888, Streeter Hosp. Mem. Loyal Legion; charter mem. Mil. Surgeons of U.S.A.; lt. col. and asst. surgeon gen. Ill. Nat. Guard. Address: Chicago, Ill. Died 1905.

STREETT, David, dean medical coll.; b. Harford County, Md., Oct. 17, 1855; s. Corbin Grafton and Ann S.; ed. Bethel Acad., Md.; M.D., Coll. Phys. and Surg., Baltimore, 1878; spl. student Johns Hopkins, 1889-91; hon. A.M., Loyola Coll., 1895; m. Sadie Fusselbaugh, Apr. 25, 1882. Resident phys. Maternité Hosp., Baltimore, 1878-79, City Hosp., 1879-80; phys.-in-chief Md. Gen. Hosp., 1885—; prof. principles and practice of medicine and clin. medicine, 1885—, dean, 1888—, Baltimore Med. Coll. Trustee Baltimore Med. Coll., Md. Gen. Hosp. Pres. Med. and Surg. Soc. of Baltimore, 1891-92, Baltimore Med. Assn., 1899; v.p. Med. and Chirurg. Faculty of Md., 1891-92, 1899-1900, Assn. Am. Med. Colls., 1899-1900, 1909. Mem. City Council of Baltimore, 1883-84, 1884-85. Author of pub. med. papers and addresses. Home: Baltimore, Md. Died July 30, 1915.

STREIGHTOFF, Frank Hatch, economist; b. Brooklyn, N.Y., Feb. 23, 1886; s. C. Frank and Jennie D. (Hatch) S.; A.B., Wesleyan U., at Middletown, Conn., 1909, A.M., 1910; Ph.D., Columbia, 1913; m. Frances Elizabeth Doan, June 10, 1915; 1 son, Frank Doan. Instr. in economics and head dept., De Pauw U., 1912-13, asst. prof., 1913-15, prof., 1915-18, registrar, 1916-18; prof. bus. adminstrn. and head of dept., Coll. of Emporia, Kan., Jan. 1919-June 1920; asso. prof. bus. adminstrn., Ind. Univ. Extension Div., 1920-24, prof. in charge commerce courses, Indianapolis, 1924—. Dir. Cost of Living Survey, N.Y. State, 1914; economist War Dept., Apr.-Aug. 1918. Sec. Com. on Lit. and Peace of Western Yearly Meeting of Friends; rep. Am. Friends Service Com. Author: Standard of Living, 1911; Distribution of Incomes, 1912; Cost of Living in New York State, 1914; Indiana (in collaboration), 1916; Elementary Accounting, 1928; Advanced Accounting, 1932. Address: Indianapolis, Ind. Died Jan. 13, 1935.

STRICKLAND, Frederic Hastings, lumberman; b. Bangor, Me., Sept. 9, 1856; s. William Hastings and Clara (Laighton) S.; ed. Highland Mil. Acad., Worcester, Mass.; m. Charlotte Coombs, Dec. 9, 1885; 1 dau., Eleanor. Began in lumber business at Bangor, 1877; dir. Penobscot Log Driving Co.; trustee Penobscot Savings Bank. Mem. Me. Ho. of Rep. 3 terms, 1907-11; mem. Pub. Safety Com., World War I. Lt. col. governor's staff, 1881-83; a.d.c., lt. col., later maj. brigade insp. Me. N.G. Pres. bd. trustees U. of Me.; hon. A.M., U. of Me., 1922. Democrat. Unitarian K.P. Home: Bangor, Me. Died Sept. 16, 1939.

STRICKLER, Givens Brown, theologian; b. Strickler's Springs, Rockbridge County, Va., April 25, 1840; s. Joseph and Mary Jane (Brown) S.; student Washington and Lee U., 1868, Union Theol. Sem., Va., 1868-70; D.D., Washington and Lee, 1878; LL.D., Davidson Coll., N.C., 1894; capt. Co. I, 4th Va. Regt., "Stonewall Brigade," C.S.A., 1861-65; m. Mary Frances Moore, Nov. 6, 1871 (died 1905). Ordained Presbyn. ministry, 1870; pastor Tinkling Spring Ch., Augusta County, Va., 1870-83, Central Ch., Atlanta, Ga., 1883-96; prof. systematic theology, Union Theol. Sem., 1896—. Address: Richmond, Va. Deceased.

STRIEBY, William, chemist; b. Mt. Vernon, Ohio, Aug. 12, 1852; s. Rev. Michael E. (D.D.) and Ellen Frances (Griswold) S.; A.B., New York U., 1875, A.M., 1877; E.M., Columbia Sch. of Mines, Columbia, 1878; D.Sc., Colo. Coll., 1913; m. Anna Breath, Aug. 22, 1879. Prin. Santa Fe (N.M.) Acad., 1878-80; prof. chemistry and metallurgy, 1880—, head prof., 1908—, acting pres., 1887-88, Colorado College. Mem. Am. Inst. Mining Engrs., 1877. Congregationalist. Wrote: The Origin and Use of Natural Gas at Manitou, Colo., 1894; The Story of the Prehistoric Lake at Florissant, Colo.; Ventilation Through Chimneys and Fireplaces, etc. Address: Colorado Springs, Colo. Died Oct. 8, 1920.

STRINGER, George Alfred, business man; b. Hartford, Conn.; s. George and Clarissa Alden (Ellsworth) S.; on maternal side direct descendant of John Alden of the Mayflower; ed. schs. and pvt. tutelage, Hartford, Conn., and Rochester, N.Y.; hon. A.M., Hobart, 1904; m. Eliza Coe, d. of Hon. Jesse Walker (wife died 1907). Jr. partner Rounds, Hall & Co., gen. ins. agts., Buffalo, to 1868; mem. firm of Stringer & Cady, 1868-94, later alone. Republican. Episcopalian. Author of several monographs on hist. and lit. subjects. Home: Buffalo, N.Y. Died Feb. 22, 1923.

STRINGFELLOW, Henry Martyn, horticulturist; b. Winchester, Va., Jan. 21, 1839; s. Horace and Harriet Louisa (Strother) S.; A.M., William and Mary Coll., Va., 1858; Theol. Sem., Alexandria, Va., 1859-61; m. Alice Johnston, Dec. 15, 1863. Voted against secession, 1861; enlisted in C.S.A. as pvt., June 1861; participated in campaign at Yorktown, Va., and around Richmond, 1862; went to Tex. with Gen. Magruder, fall of 1862; was in battle of Galveston, and capt. in ordnance dept. at close of war. Pioneer in discovering value of gulf coast of Tex. for raising fruit and vegetables; planted first pear orchard on coast, 1882; planted first Satsuma oranges in Tex., 1884; in nursery business until 1895, later devoting attention to experiments in horticulture; moved to Fayetteville, Ark., 1909, and set out the first English walnut grove of 500 trees, in the state. Democrat. Spiritualist. Author: The New Horticulture, 1896. Address: Fayetteville, Ark. Died June 17, 1912.

STRINGHAM, (Washington) Irving, educator; b. Yorkshire (later Delevan), N.Y., Dec. 10, 1847; s. Henry and Eliza (Tomlinson) S.; attended Washburn Coll., Topeka, Kan., 1866-73; grad. Harvard, 1877; in Paris, summer of that year; Ph.D., Johns Hopkins, 1880; m. Martha Sherman, d. Roger Sherman Day, June 28, 1888. In Europe, 1880-82, studying mathematics at Leipzig; in Spain, summer 1887; in Paris, academic year, 1899-1900; prof. mathematics, 1882—, dean, 1886—, U. of Calif. Author: Uniplanar Algebra, 1893. Editor and Author: American edition of Charles Smith's Elementary Algebra, 1894. Address: Berkeley, Calif. Died 1909.

STROBEL, Charles Louis, engineer; b. Cincinnati, O., Oct. 6, 1852; s. Carl and Ida Louise (Merker) S.; C.E., Royal Inst. Tech., Stuttgart, Germany, 1873; m. Henrietta Baxter, Dec. 2, 1890 (died 1905); children—Charles Louis, Marion (Mrs. James Herbert Mitchell); m. 2d, Mary Wilkins, July 30, 1910. Began as draftsman in r.r. office in Cincinnati, 1873; asst. engr. Cincinnati Southern Ry., 1874-78; chief engr. and v.p. Keystone Bridge Co., Pittsburgh, 1878-85, also cons. engr. to Carnegie, Phipps & Co., Ltd., and, as such, brought out and edited the co.'s handbook for engrs. and architects, designing new standard sections for steel beams and introducing Z-bar column. Rep. of Keystone Bridge Co. and Carnegie firms in Chicago, 1885-93, at the same time cons. engr., and taking a leading place in the development of skeleton steel constrn. for Chicago office bldgs.; designed large bridges over the Mo., Miss., Ohio and other rivers; in independent business as contracting engr., 1893—, incorporated, 1905, as Strobel Steel Constrn. Co.; retired 1926. Home: Chicago, Ill. Died Apr. 4, 1936.

STROBEL, Edward Henry, diplomatist; b. Charleston, S.C., Dec. 7, 1855; s. Maynard Davis and Caroline Lydia (Bullock) S.; A.B., Harvard, 1877; LL.B., Harvard Law Sch., 1882, LL.D., 1906; unmarried. Admitted to N.Y. bar, 1883; practiced New York, 1883-85; sec. U.S. legation, Madrid, 1885-90 (for about one-third of time chargé d'affaires); detailed by U.S. Govt. on spl. business to Morocco, 1888, 89; 3d asst. Sec. of State, U.S., April 1893 to April 1894; E.E. and M.P. to Ecuador, April 1894, transferred to Chile, Dec. 1894, resigned, 1897; apptd., Aug. 1897, arbitrator in Fréraut claim between France and Chile; apptd., 1899, counsel for Chile before U.S. and Chilean Claims Commn., Washington; Bemis prof. internat. law, Harvard Law Sch., 1898-1906; gen. advisor to Govt. of Siam, 1903—, being granted leave of absence by Harvard; apptd. mem. Hague Permanent Court of Arbitration, 1903. Officer Legion of Honor of France, 1898; Grand Cross Order of Elephant of Siam, 1905. Democrat. Fellow Am. Acad. Arts and Sciences. Author: The Spanish Revolution, 1898. Died 1908.

STROBRIDGE, Idah Meacham, writer; b. Contra Costa County, Calif., June 9, 1855; d. George W. and Phebe Amelia (Craiger) Meacham; ed. Mills Sem., Oakland, Calif.; became known as an elocutionist; m. Samuel Hooker Strobridge, Sept. 3, 1884 (died 1888). Founded the Artemisia Bookbindery, Los Angeles, 1901; highest award (silver medal) for fine handicraft book-binding, Calif. State Fair, 1908; gold medal, Seattle Expn., 1909. Author: In Miners' Mirage-Land, 1904; The Loom of the Desert, 1907; The Land of Purple Shadows, 1909. Contbr. to mags. Address: Los Angeles, Calif. Died Feb. 8, 1932.

STROCK, Daniel, M.D.; b. Flemington, N.J., Sept. 6, 1851; s. James Thomas and Kaziah Frances (Lamb) S.; ed. pub. schs.; M.D., Jefferson Med. Coll., Phila., 1877; m. Amelia F. Ritzel, Feb. 23, 1879 (died 1914). Practiced at Phila., 1877-80, Camden, N.J., 1880—; attending surgeon, Cooper Hosp., Camden, 1889-1912, later consulting surgeon. Lt. and asst. surgeon, later maj. and surgeon, 6th Regt. N.G.N.J.; maj. and surgeon 3d Regt., N.G.N.J.; lt. col. and surg. 2d brigade, N.G.N.J. to 1900. Methodist. Sec. bd. mgrs. Camden City Dispensary. Contbr. numerous articles on med. and scientific subjects. Chmn. Camden Co. Chapter Am. Red Cross. Mem. Camden Chapter Nat. Assn. Organists. Address: Camden, N.J. Died June 10, 1927.

STROMME, Peer, editor; b. Winchester, Wis., Sept. 15, 1856; s. Ole O. and Elen (Haugen) S.; A.B., Luther Coll., Decorah, Ia., 1876; grad. Concordia Theol. Sem., St. Louis, 1879; m. Laura Erickson, Nov. 12, 1879. County supt. schs., Norman County, Minn., 1881-86; prof. mathematics, St. Olaf Coll., Northfield, Minn., 1887-88; editor Norden, and Amerika, Norwegian papers published in Chicago, and Madison, Wis., 1888-98; asso. editor Minneapolis Times, 1898-1900; spl. corr. for newspaper syndicate in Russia and Norway, 1890, 1906; an editor of Eidsvold, a Norwegian mag., Grand Forks, N.D., 1909; toured the world as corr. for Norwegian papers, 1910-13; editor Normanden, 1911—. Speaker sent out by Nat. Dem. Com. in every campaign, 1888—. Lutheran. Author popular stories and mag. articles in Norwegian; also verse and stories in English. Lectured extensively in U.S. and Norway on Scandinavian lit. and kindred subjects. Address: Madison, Wis. Died Sept. 15, 1921.

STRONG, Augustus Hopkins, theologian; b. Rochester, N.Y., Aug. 3, 1836; s. Alvah and Catherine (Hopkins) S.; A.B., Yale, 1857; grad. Rochester Theol. Sem., 1859; in Europe, 1859-60; D.D., Brown U., 1870, Yale, 1890, Princeton, 1896; LL.D., Bucknell, 1891, Alfred, 1894; Litt.D., Rochester, 1912; m. Harriet Louise Savage, Nov. 6, 1861; m. 2d, Marguerite G. Jones, Jan. 1, 1915. Ordained to the Baptist ministry, 1861; pastor First Ch., Haverhill, Mass., 1861-65, First Ch., Cleveland, O., 1865-72; pres. and prof. systematic theology, Rochester Theol. Sem., 1872-1912, pres. emeritus, 1912—. Pres. Am. Bapt. Missionary Union, 1892-95; pres. Gen. Conv. Baptists of N. America, 1905-10. Author: Systematic Theology, 1886; Philosophy and Religion, 1888; The Great Poets and Their Theology, 1897; Christ in Creation and Ethical Monism, 1899; Miscellanies, Hist. and Theol., 1912; One Hundred Chapel-Talks to Theol. Students, 1913; Union with Christ, 1913; Popular Lectures on the Books of the New Testament, 1914; American Poets and Their Theology, 1917; A Tour of the Missions, 1918. Address: Rochester, N.Y. Died Nov. 29, 1921.

STRONG, Benjamin, banker; b. Fishkill-on-Hudson, N.Y., Dec. 22, 1872; s. Benjamin and Adeline Torrey (Schenck) S.; ed. pub. schs., Montclair, N.J.; LL.D., Princeton, 1918; m. Katherine Converse. Clerk with Cuyler, Morgan & Co., New York; later sec. Atlantic Trust Co., Metropolitan Trust Co.; pres. Bankers Trust Co.; gov. Fed. Res. Bank, New York, Oct. 1914—. Mem. Acad. Polit. Science. Chevalier Légion d'Honneur, 1919. Home: New York, N.Y. Died Oct. 16, 1928.

STRONG, Charles Augustus, psychologist; b. Haverhill, Mass., Nov. 28, 1862; s. Augustus Hopkins and Harriet Louise (Savage) S.; ed. Gütersloh Gymnasium, 1881-83; A.B., U. of Rochester, 1884, LL.D., 1919; A.B., Harvard, 1885; Rochester Theol. Sem., 1885-86; Berlin, 1886-87, Paris, Berlin and Freiburg, 1889-90; m. Bessie, d. John D. Rockefeller, Mar. 22, 1889 (died 1906). Instr. philosophy, Cornell, 1887-89; docent Clark U., 1890; asso. prof. psychology, U. of Chicago, 1892-95; lecturer psychology, 1895-1903, prof psychology, 1903-10, Columbia. Author: Why the Mind Has a Body, 1903; The Origin of Consciousness, 1918; The Wisdom of the Beasts, 1921; A Theory of Knowledge, 1923. Home: Fiesole, Italy. Died Jan. 23, 1940.

STRONG, Charles Hall, clergyman; b. New Orleans, La., Dec. 29, 1850; A.B., Yale, 1870, A.M., 1873; studied at Oxford, 1871-72; D.D., U. of Ga. Deacon, 1872, priest, 1875, P.E. Ch.; rector Grace Ch., Brooklyn, Christ Ch., Stratford, Conn., St. John's, Savannah, Ga. Author: Creed in Deed; A Fair Agnostic; Is Hell Endless?; In Paradise; Sermons, etc. Address: Savannah, Ga. Died Jan. 1915.

STRONG, Edward Trask, rear admiral U.S.N.; b. Ipswich, Mass., Feb. 10, 1840; s. Simeon E. S., M.D.; ed. Andover, Mass.; m. June 11, 1867. Entered navy, vol. officer, Nov. 24, 1862; served through remainder of Civil war; commissioned ensign in regular navy, March 12, 1868; master, Dec. 18, 1868; lt., March 21, 1870; lt. comdr., July 2, 1882; comdr., Jan. 9, 1893; capt., Oct. 10, 1899; retired with rank of rear admiral Nov. 21, 1900. Served at sea on the North Atlantic, Pacific, European and Asiatic stas. Address: Albany, N.Y. Died 1909.

STRONG, Elnathan Ellsworth, editorial sec.; b. Hardwick, Vt., May 2, 1832; s. Elnathan and Jane C. S.; A.B., Dartmouth, 1852, A.M., 1855, D.D., 1883; grad. Andover Theol. Sem., 1855; m. Elizabeth Gilman Mitchell, Dec. 16, 1856; father of William Ellsworth S. Ordained Congl. ministry, 1859; pastor S. Natick, Mass., 1859-65, Waltham, Mass., 1865-78; editorial sec. A.B.C.F.M., 1878—. Editor Missionary Herald, 1879—. Editor: Mission Stories of Many Lands, 1887; In Lands Afar, 1897. On deputation of Am. Bd. to Africa, 1903. Home: Auburndale, Mass. Died Apr. 2, 1914.

STRONG, Frank, univ. prof.; b. Venice, N.Y., Aug. 5, 1859; s. John Butler and Mary (Foote) S.; A.B., Yale, 1884, A.M., 1893, Ph.D., 1897; LL.D., Baker U., Kan. State Agrl. Coll., and U. of Ore., 1909; m. Mary Evelyn Ransom, June 24, 1890; children—Otis Ransom (dec.), John Butler (dec.), Mary Evelyn, Frank Ransom. Atty. at law, Kansas City, Mo., 1886-88; prin. St. Joseph High Sch., 1888-92; supt. schs., Lincoln, Neb., 1892-95; lecturer on history, Yale, 1897-99; pres. U. of Ore., 1899-1902; chancellor, 1902-20, prof. constl. law, 1920-34, U. of Kan. Chmn. Rhodes Scholarship for Kan., 1904-32. Author: Life of Benjamin Franklin (in courses of Univ. Assn., Chicago); A Forgotten Danger to the New England Colonies (ann. report Am. Hist. Assn. for 1898); Cromwell's West Indian Expedition, 1654-55, Am. Hist. Rev., 1899; Government of the American People, 1901. Contbr. to mags. Pres. Kan. State Teachers' Assn., 1910, Nat. Assn. of State Univs., 1915. Mem. Kan. State Council Defense; exec. com. Kan. Food Adminstrn.; war council Nat. Assn. State Univs. Pres. Kan. Tuberculosis Assn., 1920-34. Mem. Kan. State Board of Edn., 1902-20, Board of Edn. of Northern Bapt. Conv., 1915-17. Baptist. Mason. Died Aug. 6, 1934.

STRONG, Frederick Smith, army officer; b. Paw Paw, Mich., Nov. 12, 1855; s. Samuel Filer and Anna Maria (Fish) S.; grad. Kalamazoo (Mich.) High Sch., 1876, U.S. Mil. Acad., 1880, U.S. Arty. Sch., 1884; m. Alice Marion Johnston, Oct. 3, 1883; 1 son, Frederick Smith. Commd. 2d lt. 4th Arty., June 12, 1880; promoted through grades to brig. gen., May 4, 1915; maj. gen., Aug. 5, 1917. Served in Spanish-Am. War, 1898; comd. 40th Div., Aug. 25, 1917-Apr. 20, 1919; in France, Aug. 12, 1918-Mar. 3, 1919; retired from active service at own request, Aug. 17, 1919. Home: San Diego, Calif. Died Mar. 9, 1935.

STRONG, Henry A., capitalist; b. Rochester, N.Y.; s. Alvah and Catherine (Hopkins) S. Entered employ of uncle, Myron H. Strong, mfr. whips, etc., Rochester, becoming a partner in the firm; later mem. firm of Strong & Woodbury; became interested in kodak mfg. business with George Eastman, later pres. Eastman Kodak Co. Office: Rochester, N.Y. Died July 26, 1919.

STRONG, James George, congressman; b. Dwight, Ill., Apr. 23, 1870; s. James George and Rebecca M. (Witt) S.; prep. edn. schs., Ill. and Kan., and Episcopal Mission, Yankton (Dak.) Agency; student Baker U., Baldwin, Kan., 1887-89; read law at Blue Rapids, Kan.; m. Frances E. Coon, Dec. 18, 1894; children—George, Eugene, Erma Elizabeth (Mrs. Paul Haworth). Admitted to bar, Marshall County, Kan., 1895; organizer and pres. Blue Rapids Telephone Co.; organizer, mgr. and sec. Marshall County Power & Light Co. City atty. Blue Rapids, 15 yrs.; asst. atty. gen. Marshall County, Kan., 1911-12 (enforced prohibition); alternate del. Rep. Nat. Conv., 1912, del., 1928; atty. Marshall County, 1916-17; mem. 66th to 72d Congresses (1919-33), 5th Kan. Dist.; 1st asst. treas. Home Owners Loan Corp., Washington. Episcopalian. Odd Fellow, K.P., Elk; mem. Modern Woodmen of America. Home: Washington, D.C. Died Jan. 11, 1938.

STRONG, James Woodward, educator; b. Brownington, Vt., September 29, 1833; s. Elijah Gridley and Sarah Ashley (Partridge) S.; A.B., Beloit Coll., 1858, A.M., 1861, D.D., 1872; grad. Union Theol. Sem., New York, 1862; LL.D., Ill. Coll., 1896; m. Mary Davenport, Sept. 3, 1861 (died 1910). City clerk, 1854-55, city supt. schs., 1855-56, Beloit; ordained Congl. ministry, 1862; pastor, Broadhead, Wis., 1862-64, Faribault, Minn., 1865-70; 1st pres. Carleton Coll., 1870-1903, pres. emeritus, 1903—. Corporate mem. A.B.C.F.M., 1871—; pres. Minn. State Home Missionary Soc., 1872-1905; mem. almost every Nat. Congl. Council, 1865-1907; mem. Internat. Council, 1899, Ecumenical Missionary Conf., 1900. Address: Northfield, Minn. Died Feb. 24, 1913.

STRONG, Josiah, clergyman; b. Naperville, Du Page County, Ill., Jan. 19, 1847; s. Josiah and Elizabeth Clough (Webster) S.; removed to Hudson, O., 1852; A.B., Western Reserve Coll., 1869; Lane Theol. Sem., 1869-71; m. Alice Bisbee, Aug. 29, 1871. Ordained Congl. ministry, 1871; pastor Cheyenne, Wyo., 1871-73; instr. theology and chaplain, Western Reserve Coll., 1873-76; pastor Sandusky, O., 1876-81; sec. Home Missionary Soc. for Ohio, Ky., W.Va., and Western Pa., 1881-84; pastor Cincinnati, 1884-86; gen. sec. of Evangelical Alliance for U.S., 1886-98; organizer, and pres. League for Social Service, 1898-1902; pres. Am. Inst. for Social Service (League for Social Service reorganized), 1902—; pres. Social Center Assn. America, 1911. Pres. Am. Foreign and Christian Union, Chaplain Wyo. Ho. of Rep., 1871-72; trustee Oberlin Coll., 1881-87. Author: Our Country, 1885; The New Era, 1893; The Twentieth Century City, 1898; Religious Movements for Social Betterment, 1900; Expansion, 1900; The Times and Young Men, 1901; The Next Great Awakening, 1902; The Challenge of the City, 1907; My Religion in Every Day Life, 1910; Our World; The New World-Life, 1913; Our World; The New World Religion, 1915. Editor of Social Progress (a year book), 1904-06; editor Gospel of the Kingdom (mag.), 1908—. Home: New York, N.Y. Died Apr. 28, 1916.

STRONG, Lee A(bram), plant pest control; b. Russell, Ia., June 17, 1886; s. Hez G. and Julia B. (Ashby) S.; ed. public schools, Nehawka, Neb.; hon. D.Sc., Louisiana State U., 1938; m. Edith M. Colton, Mar. 2, 1921; children—Madeleine Virginia, Lee A., Helen Tesora. Hort. insp., Los Angeles County, Calif., 1910-12; plant quarantine insp., Calif. State Dept. Agr., July 1912-18; served with 537th Engrs., U.S.A., Mar. 1918-July 1919, 12 mos. in France; with Calif. State Dept. Agr., 1919-23; in charge port inspection work, Federal Hort. Bd., U.S. Dept. Agr., 1923-25; asst. dir. Calif. State Dept. Agr., 1925-29; chief of plant quarantine and control administrn. and chmn. plant quarantine bd., U.S. Dept. Agr., Dec. 1929-June 30, 1932; chief Bur. of Plant Quarantine to Sept. 30, 1933; chief Bur. of Entomology, 1933-34; chief Bur. Entomology and Plant Quarantine, July 1934—; chmn. Nat. Plant Bd., 1924-29. Republican. Mason. Home: Chevy Chase, Md. Died June 2, 1941.

STRONG, Nathan L., congressman; b. Summerville, Jefferson County, Pa., Nov. 12, 1859; ed. pub. schs. Telegraph operator, 1878-94; admitted to Pa. bar, 1891; dist. atty. Jefferson County, 1895-1900; pres. Mohawk Mining Co.; dir. Peoples Bank of Ford City; dir. Pittsburgh & Shawmut R.R., Brookville Title & Trust Co. Pres. Brookville Park Assn., Jefferson County Agrl. Assn.; mem. 65th to 73d Congresses (1917-35), 27th Pa. Dist. Republican. Home: Brookville, Pa. Died Dec. 14, 1939.

STRONG, Sydney Dix, clergyman, writer; b. Seville, O., Jan. 25, 1860; s. Lyman Whitney and Ruth Maria (Dix) S.; student Wooster (O.) Coll., 1877-78, Ohio Wesleyan U., 1878-79; A.B., Oberlin (O.) Coll., 1881, B.D., 1884, D.D., 1897; grad. study Yale Div. Sch., summer sch., Oxford (Eng.) Coll.; m. Ruth Tracy, Nov. 20, 1884; children—Anna Louise, Tracy, Mrs. Charles H. Niederhauser. Pastor First Congl. Ch., Mt. Vernon, O., 1887-92, Walnut Hills Congl. Ch., Cincinnati, O., 1892-97, Pilgrim Ch., Oak Park, Ill., 1897-1906, Bethlehem Bohemian Settlement, Chicago, 1907, Queen Anne Congl. Ch., Seattle, Wash., 1908-21, Australian Ch., Melbourne, Australia, 1922; asso. editor Unity, 1921—. Corr. Melbourne Age, 1922—. Organizer, with Rabbi Samuel Koch, Seattle, Central Social Agencies, 1910-16. Author: Child in the Midst, 1900; His Last Week, 1906; South African Sermons to Boys and Girls, 1906; The Master Man, 1910; Bible Hero Classics (20 vols.), 1910; A Seattle Pulpit (10 vols.), 1917-20; The World's Best Man, 1921; Roger Claps Memoirs, 1928; His Coming, 1929. Compiler (symposiums): We Believe in Immortality, 1929; We Believe in Prayer, 1930; What I Owe to my Father, 1931; How to Find God, 1931; The Rise of American Democracy, 1935; From Seville to Seattle (autobiography), 1937. Contbr. of travel letters to Unity; conductor of symposiums, New York Times, New York World. Asso. editor of Unity. Pres. "The Peacemaker." Address: Seattle, Wash. Died Dec. 30, 1938.

STRONG, Sylvester Emory, physician surgeon; b. Palenville, N.Y., Dec. 2, 1837; s. Sylvester Sanford (M.D.) and Emma Louise (Ireland) S.; A.B., Wesleyan U., 1860, A.M., 1863; M.D., Univ. Med. Coll. (New York U.), 1862; m. Anna A., d. Hon. James M. Ray, Mar. 3, 1863. Contract surgeon and acting med. dir. at Indianapolis, Civil War, 1862-63; pres. Dr. Strong's, The Saratoga Springs Sanitarium. Republican. Methodist. Address: Saratoga Springs, N.Y. Died Mar. 17, 1913.

STRONG, Theron George, lawyer; b. Palmyra, N.Y., Aug. 14, 1846; s. Theron Rudd and Cornelia (Barnes) S.; A.B., U. of Rochester, 1868; LL.B., Columbia, 1870; m. Martha Howard Prentice, June 4, 1878. Began practice in N.Y. City, 1870; extensive practice in cases on appeal, in state and fed. courts, and Supreme Ct. of U.S.; frequently served by appmt. of court on pub. commns., also as referee, and on coms. to pass upon character of applicants for admission to the bar; Rep. condidate for judge, 1884, 85; mem. Rep. County Com., New York County. Mem. Bd. of Trustees N.Y. Presbytery; elder and deacon Ch. of the Covenant; elder Brick Ch. Mem. bd. dirs. N.Y. Juvenile Asylum, Legal Aid Soc., N.Y. Bible Soc. Author: Landmarks of a Lawyer's Lifetime, 1914; Joseph H. Choate, New Englander, New Yorker, Lawyer, Ambassador, 1917. Home: New York, N.Y. Died Dec. 6, 1924.

STRONG, Walter Ansel, journalist, publisher; b. Chicago, Ill., Aug. 13, 1883; s. Albert Bliss (M.D.) and Idea C. (Cook) S.; grad. in engring., Lewis Inst., Chicago, 1901; B.S., Beloit Coll., 1905; LL.D., John Marshall Law Sch., Chicago, 1912; m. Josephine Haviland Webster, Apr. 14, 1913; children—Walter Ansel, Jonathan Webster, Robert Kitchell, Anne Haviland, David Seymour. Began newspaper work with Chicago Record, 1899; with Chicago Daily News, 1905—, successively audit clk., auditor, business mgr. and after decease of Victor F. Lawson in 1925, controlling owner and pres. The Chicago Daily News, Inc. and pub. Chicago Daily News; dir. Fansteel Products Co.; trustee Village of Winnetka; trustee Beloit Coll. Episcopalian. Home: Winnetka, Ill. Died May 10, 1931.

STRONG, William Barstow, railroad pres., retired; b. Brownington, Orleans County, Vt., May 16, 1837; s. Elijah Gridley and Sarah Ashley (Partridge) S.; brother of James Woodward S.; Beloit (Wis.) pub. schs.; grad. Bell's Business Coll., Chicago, 1855; m. Abby J. Moore, Oct. 2, 1859. Began as sta. agt. and telegraph operator, Milton, Wis., Mar. 22, 1855; later sta. agt. at White Water and Monroe; gen. western agt. Southwestern div. C.,M.&St.P. Ry., Janesville, Wis.; asst. supt. McGregor Western Ry., McGregor, Ia., 1865-67; gen. western agt. C.&N.-W. Ry., Council Bluffs, Ia., 1867-70; asst. gen. supt. C.,B.&Q. Ry. Co., Burlington, Ia., 1870-72; asst. gen. supt. consolidated B.&M. and C.,B.&Q. Ry. Co., Chicago, 1872-74; gen. supt. M.C. R.R., Chicago, 1874-75; gen. supt. C.,B.&Q. Ry. Co., 1875-77; v.p. and gen. mgr. A.,T.&S.F. Ry., Topeka, Kan., 1877-80, pres. at Boston, 1880-89; then retired. Republican. Conglist. Mason. Home: Los Angeles, Calif. Died Aug. 5, 1914.

STRONG, William Ellsworth, clergyman; b. S. Natick, Mass., Apr. 9, 1860; s. Elnathan Ellsworth Strong and Elizabeth Gilman (Mitchell) S.; A.B., Dartmouth, 1882, D.D., 1912; grad. Hartford Theol. Sem., 1885; m. Ellen Olmsted, June 28, 1887; children—Margaret (Mrs. Stuart M. Hill), Ellsworth Olmsted (dec.), Helen Webster (Mrs. Harold H. Lounsberry), Robert Chamberlain. Ordained Congl. ministry, 1885; pastor Washington Street Ch., Beverly, Mass., 1885-95, First Ch., Jackson, Mich., 1895-1901, First Ch., Amherst, Mass., 1901-06; editorial sec., 1907-21, corr. sec., 1921-30, A.B.C.F.M. Editor Missionary Herald, 1906-21. Trustee Hartford Theol. Sem., Jaffna Coll., Ceylon, Fukien Christian U., China. Author: The Story of the American Board, 1910. Home: Newtonville, Mass. Died Mar. 7, 1934.

STRONG, William L., merchant, mayor; b. on farm, Richland County, O., March 22, 1827; dry goods salesman, Wooster and Mansfield, O., 1843-53; same in New York, 1853-57; with Farnham, Dale & Co., commission dry goods, 1858-69; head of W. L. Strong & Co. in same line, 1869—. Prominent Republican; elected mayor of New York by a combination of Republicans and anti-Tammany Democrats. Last mayor of the old city—later Manhattan Borough of Greater N.Y. City. Home: New York, N.Y. Died 1900.

STROOCK, Solomon M., lawyer; b. New York, Sept. 22, 1873; s. Samuel and Mariana (Marcuse) S., B.S., Coll. City of N.Y., 1891; Sch. of Polit. Science (Columbia), 1891-92, M.A., 1892; LL.B., Columbia, 1894; D.H.L., Inst. Jewish Religion, 1931; D.H.L., Jewish Theol. Sem. of America, 1935; m. Hilda Weil, Mar. 6, 1904; children—Mrs. Minette Kuhn, Robert L. (dec.), Alan M. Practiced, New York, 1894—; mem. Platzek & Stroock, 1896-1907, later Stroock & Stroock. Mem. Draft Exemption Bd., 1917. Chmn. com. on character and fitness, Appellate Div. N.Y. Supreme Court, 1931—. Chmn. bd. regents Jewish Theol. Sem. Mem. Am. Acad. Polit. and Social Science. Am. Polit. Science Assn. Awarded Univ. Medal for Excellence, Columbia, 1931. Democrat. Author: Switzerland and American Jews, 1903. Home: New York, N.Y. Died Sept. 11, 1941.

STROTHER, (Edgar) French, administrative asst. to the President; writer; b. Marshall, Mo., Oct. 5, 1883; s. John Pryor and Mildred Elizabeth (Lewis) S.; ed. high sch., Fresno, Calif.; m. Grace Dudley Farley, May 18, 1906; children—Elizabeth Farley (dec.), E(dgar) French. Began as reporter Fresno Republican, 1902; staff World's Work, N.Y. City, 1904-07; asso. editor California Weekly, San Francisco, 1909-10; in office state supt. pub. instruction, Sacramento, 1911; again staff World's Work, 1912, mng. editor, 1913-23, asso. editor, 1923-26; administrative asst. to President Hoover, Mar. 1920-May 1931 and Feb. 1932—; helped organize White House Conf. on Child Health and Protection, President's Conf. on Homes and Home Bldg., Research Com. on Social Trends. Trustee fund for Walter Hines Page Sch. of Internat. Relations (Johns Hopkins U.). Democrat. Author: Fighting Germany's Spies, 1918; (with Henry Morgenthau) All in a Life-Time, 1922; (with same) I Was Sent to Athens, 1929; Maid of Athens, 1932; Four Years of Hoover; An Interpolation (N.Y. Times Feb. 26, 1933). Home: Garden City, L.I., N.Y. Died Mar. 13, 1933.

STROTHER, James French, congressman; b. Pearisburg, Giles County, Va., June 29, 1870; s. Philip W. and Nannie (Pendleton) S.; ed. Pearisburg (Va.) Acad.; Va. Agrl. and Mech. Coll. (later Va. Poly. Inst.); studied law at U. of Va., 1894; m. Lucile Surface Lucas, Dec. 31, 1924; 1 dau., Sue French. Settled at Welch, W.Va., 1895, and began law practice with father; apptd. judge Criminal Ct. of McDowell County, W.Va., Jan. 1, 1905, to fill vacancy caused by resignation of Judge L. L. Chambers, and elected three times, serving until 1924; mem. 69th and 70th Congresses (1925-29), 5th W.Va. Dist.; v.p. McDowell County Nat. Bank, Mohawk Coal & Coke Co.; sec. and treas. Mohawk Land Co. Republican. Episcopalian. Mason. Home: Welch, W.Va. Died Apr. 10, 1930.

STROUD, Morris Wistar, corp. exec.; b. Phila., Pa., May 14, 1860; s. William Daniel (M.D.) and Charlotte Wistar (Beesley) S.; ed. Friends Select Sch., Phila., William Penn Charter Sch.; m. Margaret Perkins Rutter, Jan. 19, 1887. Began in employ of Am. Gas Co., Phila., 1890, pres., 1900—; dir. Am. Gas & Electric Co., Phila. Electric Co., Huntington & Broad Top Mountain R.R. & Coal Co. Episcopalian. Home: Villanova, Pa. Died Jan. 7, 1941.

STROUT, Sewall Cushing, judge; b. Wales, Me., Feb. 17, 1827; s. Ebenezer and Hannah S.; acad. edn. at Portland, Me.; hon. A.M., Bowdoin, 1894; m. Octavia J. P. Shaw, Nov. 22, 1849. Admitted to bar, 1848; practiced at Portland, 1854-94; judge Supreme Jud. Ct. of Me., 1894-1908. Democrat. Address: Portland, Me. Died Aug. 10, 1914.

STROVER, Carl Bernhard Wittekind, lawyer, author; b. Wedigenstein, Prussia, Dec. 11, 1865; s. Bernhard and Caroline (Boedecker) S.; grad. Gymnasium, Minden, Prussia, 1884; studied agriculture, politics and economics, U. of Berlin, 1888-90; LL.B. and M.A., Univ. of Wis., 1894; m. Martha Gross, 1904; children—Dorothy and Warren (both adopted). Served in the Prussian Inf., 1887-91, commd., 1890, lt. 54th Prussian Inf.; came to U.S., 1891; naturalized citizen, 1896. Admitted to Wis. and Ill. bar, 1894, U.S. Supreme Ct., 1910; maj. Ill. vols. Spanish-Am. War, 1898. Author: The Hawaiian Problem, 1898; Monetary Reconstruction, 1922; Hard Times Can Be Ended, 1930; Monetary Progress, 1937. Home: Chicago, Ill. Died Apr. 19, 1941.

STRUDWICK, Edmund, life insurance; b. Hillsboro, N.C., Apr. 17, 1854; s. William Samuel and Caroline (Watters) S.; ed. pvt. schs.; m. Ann Collins Hughes, June 1890; children—Edmund, Jane Daves (Mrs. Edmund M. Preston). Began as cotton commn. mcht., Norfolk, Va.; founder and owner Old Dominion Guano Co., absorbed by Va. Carolina Chem. Co., of which became an executive; pres. Atlantic Life Ins. Co., 1905-27, chmn. bd., 1927—. Presbyn. Home: Richmond, Va. Died Mar. 5, 1928.

STRUTHERS, Joseph; b. New York, Nov. 13, 1865; s. Joseph and Anne E. (Galloway) S.; Coll. City of New York, 1880-81; Ph.B. in Chemistry, School of Mines (Columbia), 1885; Ph.D., Columbia, 1895; unmarried. On staff of instrs., Dept. of Metall., Columbia, 1895-1900, hon. lecturer in metall., 1900-02; organized and conducted first summer sch. in practical metall. of Columbia U., at Butte, Mont., 1896. Field asst. U.S. Geol. Survey, 1901, 1902. Spl. agt. U.S. Census, 1903; sec. Div. Mining Engring., St. Louis Expn., 1904; chmn. Jury Mines and Metallurgy Sect., Jamestown Expn., 1907; del. Am. Inst. Mining Engrs. to Governors' Conf. on Conservation of Nat. Resources, Washington, D.C., 1908. Asst. editor, 1903-06, asst. sec., editor and asst. treas., 1906-11, sec., editor and asst. treas., 1911-13, Am. Inst. Mining Engrs.; v.p. Johnson Electric Smelting Co., New York, 1914-15; treas. Federal Export Corp., Fed. Shipping Co., 1916; supervising engr. of tests, Ordnance Dept., U.S.A., N.Y. Dist., 1918-20. Sec., trustee Engrs. Club, New York, 1909—; treas., dir., United Engring. Soc., 1910—; treas. Engring. Foundation, 1916—; asst. treas. Mil. Engring. Com., New York, 1917. Author: Quiz Compend of Chemistry and Physics, 1890. Editor: Mineral Industry, Vols. VIII-XI, 1901-04; Bulletin Am. Inst. Mining Engrs., Nos. 1-75, 1905-13; Transactions Am. Inst. Mining Engrs., Vols. XXXVII-XLIII, 1907-13. Home: New York, N.Y. Died Feb. 18, 1923.

STRYKER, Melancthon Woolsey, coll. pres.; b. Vernon, N.Y., Jan. 7, 1851; s. Rev. Isaac Pierson and Alida Livingston (Woolsey) S.; A.B., Hamilton Coll., 1872; grad. Auburn Theol. Sem., 1876; D.D., Hamilton, 1889, L.H.D., 1919; D.D., Lafayette Coll., 1889, LL.D., 1892; LL.D., Wesleyan U., 1909; m. Clara Elisabeth Goss, Sept. 27, 1876; children—Goss Livingston, Mrs. Alida Root, Robert McBurney (dec.), Lloyd Paul, Mrs. Evelyn Scarritt, Mrs. Elisabeth W. Stevens. Ordained Presbyn. ministry, 1876; pastor Auburn, 1876-78. Ithaca, 1878-83, Second Congl. Ch., Holyoke, Mass., 1883-85, Fourth Presbyn. Ch., Chicago, 1885-92; pres. Hamilton Coll., 1892-1917. A student of hymnology; writer of hymns and poems. Author: (or editor) Song of Miriam, 1888; Church Song (hymnal), 1889; Dies Iræ, with versions, 1893, 1910-23; Hamilton, Lincoln and Addresses, 1895; Letter of James (polyglot), 1895; Lattermath (verse), 1896; Hymnal, 1897; Well by the Gate (sermons), 1903; Baccalaureate Sermons, 1905; Attempts in Verse, 1911; English Bible Versions and Origins, 1915; Complete versing of the Psalms of Israel, 1915; Faculæ Annorum (collected verse), 1917; Three Addresses on Lincoln, 1917; Vesper Bells (verse), 1919; Christian Praise (a hymnal), 1920; Lincoln's Land, and Other Verse, 1921; Ethics in Outline, 1923; Embers (collected verse), 1926. Home: Rome, Oneida County, N.Y. Died Dec. 6, 1929.

STRYKER, Samuel Stanhope, physician; b. Trenton, N.J., May 4, 1842; s. Samuel Stanhope Smith and Mary (Scudder) S.; A.B., Princeton, 1863, A.M., 1866; M.D., U. of Pa. Med. Dept., 1866; m. Grace Medora Bartlett, Apr. 11, 1877. In practice in Phila., 1866—. Trustee Lawrenceville Sch. Republican. Presbyterian. Home: Philadelphia, Pa. Died Oct. 25, 1929.

STRYKER, William Scudder, pres. N.J. Hist. Soc.; b. Trenton, N.J., June 6, 1838; grad. Princeton, 1858; studied law; assisted in organizing 14th N.J. vols.; in Feb. 1863, aide to Gen. Quincy A. Gillmore, with rank of maj.; took part in capture of Morris Island and in the night attack on Ft. Wagner; later sr. paymaster in charge of disbursements dist. of Columbus, O.; bvtd. lt. col.; resigned, June 30, 1866; later on mil. staff gov. N.J.; commissioned adj. gen., N.J., Apr. 12, 1867; admitted to bar, 1866. Pres. Trenton Banking Co. Pres. Trenton Saving Fund Soc.; pres. Trenton Battle Monument Assn.; pres. Soc. of the Cincinnati in the State of N.J. Author: Officers and Men of New Jersey in the Revolutionary War; Officers and Men of New Jersey in the Civil War; The Battles of Trenton and Princeton. Address: Trenton, N.J. Died 1900.

STUART, Alexander Tait, educator; b. Washington, D.C., Aug. 28, 1848; s. Donald and Mary (Tait) S.; Ph.B., Columbian (Now George Washington) U., 1869, A.M., 1904; m. Mary Ellen Burris, Dec. 24, 1875. Engaged in teaching, 1870-75; supervising prin., 1877-1900; supt. pub. schs., Washington, July 1900-July 1906, and Jan. 1908-July 1911; dir. intermediate instrn., 1911—. Methodist. Trustee George Washington U. Home: Washington, D.C. Died Sept. 5, 1924.

STUART, Ambrose Pascal Sevilon, educator; b. Sterling, Mass., Nov. 22, 1820; A.M., Brown, 1847; prof. Acadia Coll., 1847-49; prin. Elm St. Grammar School, Providence, R.I., 1849-51, prin. Holtem High Sch., Danvers, Mass., 1851-54; again prof. Acadia Coll., 1854-58; studied in German univs., 1858-61; prin. Worcester Acad., 1861-64; asst. instr. Lawrence Scientific Sch., 1864-68; prof. chemistry Univ. of Ill., 1868-74; retired 1875; m. Mrs. Martha E. Cushman, June 6, 1876. Residence: Lincoln, Neb. Died 1899.

STUART, Charles Macaulay, theologian; b. Glasgow, Scotland, Aug. 20, 1953; s. Lewis and Mary (Home) S.; A.B., Kalamazoo (Mich.) Coll., 1880, A.M., 1883; B.D., Garrett Bibl. Inst., 1883; A.M., Northwestern U., 1887; D.D., Garrett, 1885, Wesleyan, 1906; Litt.D., Syracuse, 1904, Ohio Wesleyan, 1909; LL.D., Neb. Wesleyan, 1909, and Northwestern University, 1912; L.H.D., Kalamazoo College, 1923; m. Emma Rachel Littlefield, Oct. 10, 1883. Ordained M.E. ministry, 1880; pastor River Forest, Ill., 1880-83, Fort St. Ch., Detroit, 1883-85; asso. editor Michigan Christian Advocate, 1885-86; asst. editor Northwestern Christian Advocate, 1886-96; prof. sacred rhetoric, Garrett Bibl. Inst., 1896-1909; editor Northwestern Christian Advocate, 1909-11; elected prof. Christian ethics and philosophy of religion, Wesleyan U., Conn., June 1911; pres. Garrett Bibl. Inst., Evanston, Ill., 1911-24, pres. emeritus and prof. homiletics, retired. Sec. joint hymnal commn. M.E. Ch. and M.E. Ch., S.; del. Gen. Conf., 1912, 20, 24. Author: Descriptive Text of Photogravures of the Holy Land, 1890; Life and Selected Writings of Francis Dana Hemenway (with C. F. Bradley and A. W. Patten), 1890; Gospel Singers and Their Songs (with F. D. Hemenway), 1891; Vision of Christ in the Poets,

1896; Story of the Masterpieces, 1897. Editor: Methodist Hymnal, 1905; In Memoriam, Charles J. Little, 1912; The Manifold Message of the Gospel, 1913; Literary and Biographical Studies of Charles J. Little, 1916. Mem. com. M.E. Ch. on Meth. Work in Europe; mem. com. Fed. Council on Relations with France and Belgium. Home: Evanston, Ill. Died Jan. 26, 1932.

STUART, Daniel Delehanty Vincent, rear admiral U.S.N.; b. Albany, N.Y., Sept. 15, 1847; s. John and Mary (Delehanty) S.; student Albany Acad., 1861-62; midshipman in active service during Civil War; grad. U.S. Naval Acad., 1869; m. Alicia A. Smith, Sept. 26, 1883; children—Daniel Delehanty Vincent, Bartlett Gregory (dec.). Promoted through the various grades to rear admiral, Sept. 3, 1900; retired by operation of law, Sept. 15, 1909. During Spanish-American War comd. Mangrove; during Philippine campaign comd. Isla de Luzon, Don Juan de Austria, and Yorktown. Medals for Civil War, Spanish campaign, Philippine campaign and for service while in command of Mangrove. Home: Washington, D.C. Died Apr. 13, 1932.

STUART, Duane Reed, univ. prof.; b. Oneida, Ill., Sept. 27, 1873; s. Reed and Helen (Soule) S.; A.B., U. of Mich., 1896, Ph.D., 1901; Am. Sch. Archæology, Athens, 1898-99; U. of Munich; m. Emilie Eugenie Meddaugh, June 25, 1898; children—Emilie Maynard (Mrs. Arthur Bliss Perry), Philip Meddaugh (dec.), Duane Reed, Douglas Edmunds, Alison Edmunds. Prof. Latin, Mich. State Normal Coll., 1899-1900; instr. in Latin, 1900-01, instr. in Greek, 1902-04, asst. prof., 1905, U. of Mich.; preceptor in classics, 1905-07, prof., 1907—, Princeton; Sather prof. classical lit., U. of Calif., 1924-25; visiting lecturer, Bryn Mawr Coll., 1927-28; visiting prof., Yale, 1931. Author: Epochs of Greek and Roman Biography, 1928. Editor: The Agricola of Tacitus, 1909; The Germania of Tacitus, 1916. Joint Collaborator: Greek Inscriptions of Southern Syria, 1911-15. Home: Princeton, N.J. Died Aug. 29, 1941.

STUART, Edwin Roy, army officer; b. Arnettsville, W.Va., Aug. 19, 1874; s. Samuel Calvin and Sarah Emeline (Cox) S.; grad. U.S. Mil. Acad., 1896; m. Emma Smith Jervey, Jan. 4, 1900. Commd. add. 2d lt. engr. corps, June 12, 1896; 2d lt., July 31, 1897; 1st lt., July 5, 1898; capt., Apr. 23, 1904; maj., Oct. 16, 1909; prof. drawing, U.S. Mil. Acad., rank of lt. col., Oct. 4, 1911. On duty U.S. Engr. Office, Charleston, S.C., 1896-97; student officer U.S. Engr. Sch., 1897-99; instr. Dept. of Engring., U.S. Mil. Acad., 1899-1903; adj. 1st Battalion Engrs., 1903-04; instr. Engring. Staff Coll., Ft. Leavenworth, Kan., 1904-07; in charge U.S. Engr. Office, Charleston, S.C., 1907-08; in charge mil. surveys of P.I., 1908-10; at Staff Coll., Ft. Leavenworth, 1910-11; assigned as prof. at U.S. Mil. Acad., 1911. A joint editor Internat. Mil. Digest. Author: Individual and Combined Military Sketching, 1907. Home: West Point, N.Y. Died Mar. 6, 1920.

STUART, Edwin Sydney, gov.; b. Phila., Pa., Dec. 28, 1853; s. Hugh and Anna (Newman) S.; ed. pub. schs., Phila.; LL.D., Lafayette, 1907, U. of Pa., 1908, U. of Pittsburgh, 1910; unmarried. Engaged in bookselling and publishing, 1863; Rep. presdl. elector, 1884, 1900; del. Rep. Nat. convs., 1888, 1896, 1908; mayor of Phila., 1891-95: pres. electoral coll. of Pa., 1901; gov. of Pa., 1907-11. Dir. Bell Telephone Co. of Pa., Diamond States Telephone Co. Home: Phila., Pa. Died Mar. 21, 1937.

STUART, Eleanor, see Eleanor Stuart Childs.

STUART, Francis Hart, physician; b. Longansport, Ind., July 29, 1846; s. Judge William Z. and Minerva Hart (Potter) S.; A.B., Dartmouth, 1871; student Coll. Phys. and Surg. (Columbia), 1871-72; M.D., L.I. College Hosp., 1873; hon. A.M., Hamilton, 1877; m. Rebecca Sabina Kemper, Feb. 9, 1875. Established practice in Brooklyn; adj. phys. St. Peter's Hosp., 1874-76; adj. surgeon and lecturer on obstetrics, L.I. Coll. Hosp., 1874-80; registrar vital statistics, Brooklyn Board of Health, 1874-78; obstetrician Brooklyn Hosp., 1894—. Contbr. to text-books and to med. and surg. papers, principally on obstetrics and gynecology. Translator Vierordt's Medical Diagnosis, 1st and 4th edits., 1891, 1898. Address: Brooklyn, N.Y. Died 1910.

STUART, Francis Lee, engr.; b. Camden, S.C., Dec. 3, 1866; s. Barnwell Rhett and Emma Croome (Lee) S.; ed. Emerson Inst., Washington; m. Anne Morson Rives, Mar. 18, 1901; children—Anne M., Emma L., Elizabeth S., Rives. Asst. engr. B.&O. R.R., 1892; div. engr. Nicaragua Canal Commn., 1898, Isthmian Canal Commn., 1900; dist. engr., 1901-03, engr. of surveys, 1903-04, B.&O. R.R.; chief engr. Erie R.R., 1905-11; chief engr., B.&O. R.R., 1911-15; pvt. practice cons. engr., 1915—. Chmn. terminal port facilities com., War Industries Bd., and mem. depot bd., War Dept., 1917; chmn. budget com. U.S. R.R. Admintsrn., 1918; cons. engr. Cunard project, N.Y. Harbor and Hydro-Electric Power Commn. project, Niagara Falls, 1920; engring. expert Port Development Commn., Baltimore, 1921; vice-chmn. tech. bd., N.Y. Port Authority, 1921; mem. Transit Advisory Bd., Phila., 1923; cons. engr. Greater Harbor Com. of 200, Los Angeles, Calif., 1924-25; mem. Chicago Bd. of Review, lake lowering controversy; mem. com. on Regulation of Gt. Lakes and com. on Lake to Gulf Transportation; mem. Giant Power Survey Bd. of Pa., 1924; cons. engr. Hudson River Bridge, New York; cons. engr. Com. of R.R. Executives, Port of New York. Home: Essex Fells, N.J. Died Jan. 15, 1935.

STUART, George Rutledge, clergyman; b. Talbott, Tenn., Dec. 14, 1857; s. Caswell Cobb and Mariah (Worley) S.; A.B., Emory and Henry Coll., Emory, Va., 1882, A.M., 1884, D.D., LL.D., Birmingham-Southern Coll., Ala., 1923; m. Zollie Sullins, Sept. 6, 1882; children—David Sullins, Mary, Margaret, Elizabeth, George Rutledge. Ordained ministry M.E. Ch., S., 1883; pastor Cleveland, Tenn., 1883-84; prof. English and natural science, Centenary Coll., Cleveland, Tenn., 1885-90; pastor Centenary Ch., Chattanooga, 1890-91; evangelist M.E. Ch., S., 1892-1907; platform lecturer, 1907-12; pastor Knoxville, 1912-16, First Ch., Birmingham, Ala., 1916—; dir. Southern Assembly, N.C. Widely known as evangelist and lecturer. Author: Book of Sermons, Stories and Parables, 1907; The Saloon under the Searchlight, 1908; What Every Methodist Should Know, 1923. Compiler: Sam Jones' Famous Sayings, 1908; also several song books. Home: Birmingham, Ala. Died May 11, 1926.

STUART, Henry Carter, governor; b. Wytheville, Va., Jan. 18, 1855; s. William Alexander and Mary Taylor (Carter) S.; A.B., Emory and Henry Coll., 1874; law course, U. of Va., 1874-75; LL.D., 1913 and 1915; m. Margaret Bruce Carter, Feb. 26, 1896. Began business 1875; pres., treas. The Stuart Land & Cattle Co. of Va.; pres. Buckhorn Coal Co.; pres. First Nat. Bank of Lebanon, Va., 1898-1905. Del. Dem. Nat. Conv., 1892; mem. Va. Constl. Conv., 1901-02, bd. of visitors, U. of Va., 1902, Va. State Corp. Commn., 1903-08; gov. of Va., 1914-18; del. at large Dem. Nat. Conv., 1916, 24. Chmn. Nat. Agrl. Adv. Com., 1917-18; mem. commn. apptd. by President Wilson to investigate large packers, 1918, also mem. price fixing com. of War Industries Bd., 1918; mem. of President's Industrial Conf., Dec. 1919. Apptd. mem. Inter-State Commerce Commn., 1920, but declined; dir. U.S. Chamber Commerce, 1929; pres. Va. Pay-As-You-Go Road Assn., 1923. Home: Elk Garden, Va. Died July 24, 1933.

STUART, James Edward, postoffice insp.; b. Forfar, Scotland, July 8, 1842; s. James and Helenor (Edwards) S.; removed to Oshkosh, Wis., with parents, 1851; ed. Arbroath, Scotland, and in Oshkosh pub. schs.; law student in office of Hon. Gabriel Bouck, Oshkosh, until war broke out; mustered in as pvt. Co. B, 21st Wis. Vols., Aug. 1862, becoming successively 1st sergt., 2d lt., and capt., then detailed as aide to Gen. Harrison C. Hobart, comndg. 1st Brigade, 1st Division, 14th Army Corps, until general muster-out at Washington, summer of 1865; m. Marie E., d. Hon. Peter Roberts, Oct. 3, 1870. After muster-out became postal clerk until 1868; chief clerk, ry. mail service of Ia., 1870-73; postoffice insp., in charge div. comprising Ill., Mich. and Wis., 1873—. Active in 2d Regt. I.N.G., 1885— of which was capt., maj. and col.; brig. gen. I.N.G., retired, July 1906, after 22 yrs.' service; enlisted with regt. for war with Spain and was sent to Jacksonville, Fla., and thence to Havana, Cuba; placed on detached service after war as chmn. military postal com. and established postal service in Puerto Rico. Mem. Union Vet. League, Loyal Legion and G.A.R. Home: Chicago, Ill. Died Mar. 8, 1931.

STUART, James Everett, painter; b. Me., Mar. 24, 1852; s. Daniel Soloman and Lydia H. (Philpot) S.; ed. pub. schs.; art studies San Francisco Sch. of Design; unmarried. Discovered a process of painting upon aluminum by which pigments could be made to attach themselves to and practically become a portion of the metal painted, which time does not deface. Began making sketches along the Sacramento and San Joaquin rivers in Calif., in 1861, before levees were built and scenery was most beautiful; spent summers of 1891 and 1907 in Alaska making sketches; developed sketches into pictures, showing the natural beauty of parts of Calif. in the earlier periods; made many sketches of Donner Lake, Lake Tahoe, the Yosemite, the high Sierras, valleys and meadows near to and including the coast, also of missions and adobe shacks in Calif. and Mexico; painted scenes along the streams that flow into Half Moon Bay 25 miles south of the Golden Gate, and many landscapes, ranging from Alaska to the Panama Canal and from Me. to Calif. Sold five paintings for $15,000 each (fine finish on aluminum) four of them being "Sunset Glows" on snow peaks and the fifth entitled "Raspberries." Represented in hdqrs. of Soc. of Liberal Arts Joslyn Memorial, Omaha, Neb.; Kalamazoo Art Assn.; Oakdale (Calif.) Pub. Library; Exposition Park Mus., Los Angeles, and Doheny Library, Univ. of Southern Calif.; Golden Gate Park Mus., San Francisco; State Library, Sacramento, Calif.; E. B. Crocker Art Gallery, Sacramento, Calif.; Municipal Art Commission, Los Angeles, Calif.; Northwestern Univ., Evanston, Ill.; Southwest Museum, Highland Park, Friday Morning Club, Los Angeles Art Assn., Los Angeles, Calif.; and in many pvt. collections in U.S. and Europe. Address: San Francisco, Calif. Died Jan. 2, 1941.

STUART, Milo H., school principal; b. Sheridan, Ind., Feb. 10, 1871; s. Elias and Adaline W. (Kendall) S.; A.B., Ind. U., 1898; studied U. of Chicago, 1 yr.; m. Ethel Symons, 1903; children—Riley Symons, Miriam Adaline. Teacher, prin. and supt. schs. until 1899; science teacher, Manual Training High Sch., Indianapolis, 1900-07, also dir. night schs., 3 yrs.; prin. Johnson High Sch., St. Paul, Minn., 1907-09; asst. prin. Manual Tr. High Sch., Indianapolis, 1909-10, prin., 1910-16; prin. Arsenal Tech. Schs., Indianapolis, 1912-30; asst. supt. schs., in charge secondary edn., Indianapolis, Ind., 1930—. Republican. Methodist. Mason. Kiwanian. Author: The Comprehensive High School. Contbr. 5 chapters to book, "Types of Schools for Boys." Joint Author: Guidance at Work. Home: Indianapolis, Ind. Died July 24, 1933.

STUART, Robert Young, forester; b. S. Middleton Tp., Cumberland County, Pa., Feb. 13, 1883; s. William Chalmers and Janet (Morris) S.; A.B., Dickinson Coll., 1903, A.M., 1906; M.F., Yale, 1906; m. Janet Mary Agnes Wilson, Dec. 9, 1907; children—Janet Crichton, Helen. Asst., U.S. Forest Service, Mont., Ida., Wyo., later chief of timber sale and planting, Missoula (Mont.) dist., 1906-12; forest insp., Washington, D.C., 1912-17; dep. commr. forestry, Pa., 1920-22, commr., 1922-23; sec. of forests and waters, Pa., 1923-27; chief of pub. relations, U.S. Forest Service, 1927-28; chief of U.S. Forest Service, May 1, 1928—. Served as capt., later maj., Forest Engrs., U.S.A., 1917-19; citation from Gen. Pershing for work with A.E.F. Mem. Tri-State Delaware River Treaty Commn., 1923-27; chmn. Pa. Sesquicentennial Commn.; 1926; mem. Nat. Capital Park and Planning Commn. Episcopalian. Mason. Home: Chevy Chase, Md. Died Oct. 23, 1933.

STUART, Ruth McEnery, author; b. Avoyelles Parish, La.; d. James and Mary Routh (Stirling) McEnery; ed. New Orleans until 1865; Litt.D., Tulane U., 1915; m. Alfred O. Stuart, a cotton planter, Aug. 6, 1879 (dec.). Author: A Golden Wedding and Other Tales, 1893; Carlotta's Intended, 1894; The Story of Babette, 1894; Solomon Crow's Christmas Pockets, and Others, 1896; In Simpkinsville, 1897; Moriah's Mourning, 1898; Sonny, 1896; Holly and Pizen, 1899; The Woman's Exchange, 1899; Napoleon Jackson, 1902; George Washington Jones, 1903; The River's Children, 1904; The Second Wooing of Salina Sue, 1905; Aunt Amity's Silver Wedding, 1908; Sonny's Father, 1910; The Haunted Photograph, 1911; Daddy Do-funny's Wisdom Jingles, 1913; The Cocoon, 1915. Home: New York, N.Y. Died May 4, 1917.

STUB, Hans Gerhard, theologian; b. Muskego, Wis., Feb. 23, 1849; s. Rev. H. A. and Ingeborg (Arentz) S.; student Gymnasium, Bergen, Norway, 1861-65; grad. Luther Coll., Decorah, Ia., 1866; grad. Concordia Coll., Ft. Wayne, Ind., 1869; grad. Concordia Theol. Sem., St. Louis, 1872; studied U. of Leipzig, 1881-82; D.D., Concordia Sem., 1903; Litt.D., Capital U., 1922; LL.D., Luther Coll., 1924; L.H.D., St. Olaf Coll., 1925; m. Didrikke Ottesen, Aug. 11, 1876 (died 1879); children—Jacob A. O., Hans A.; m. 2d, Valborg Hovind, July 31, 1884 (died 1901); 1 son, Ingolf Arentz; m. 3d, Anna Skabo, Aug. 8, 1906. Ordained minister, 1872; pastor, Minneapolis, 1872-78; prof. Luther Sem., Madison, Wis., 1878-88, later at Robbinsdale, nr. Minneapolis; pastor and prof. Luther Coll., Decorah, Ia., 1896-1900; prof. Luther Theol. Sem., St. Paul, Minn., 1900-16; pres. Synod Norwegian Luth. Ch. America, 1910-17; pres. three united Norwegian Luth. Ch. bodies, 1917-25, pres. emeritus, 1925—. Editor Theological Quarterly. Decorated Knight Order of St. Olaf, 1906, Comdr., 1912, Grand Cross, 1922. Author of numerous theol. treatises and monographs. Home: St. Paul, Minn. Died Aug. 1, 1931.

STUBBS, Henry Elbert, congressman; b. in Tex., Mar. 4, 1881; s. Henry Harrisson and Susie (Foreman) S.; student Phillips U., Enid, Okla., 1912-13; m. Ruby B. Hall, July 23, 1905; children—Elbert Roe, Andrea Audine (Mrs. Frank Faris). Ordained to ministry Christian Ch. Mem. 73d and 74th Congresses (1933-37), 10th Calif. Dist. Democrat. Mem. Christian Ch. Mason, Eagle, Red Man, I.O.O.F. Home: Santa Maria, Calif. Died Feb. 28, 1937.

STUBBS, Joseph Edward, university pres.; b. Ashland, O., Mar. 19, 1850; s. Joseph Deyarmon and Mary J. (Gray) S.; brother of John C. S.; B.A., Ohio Wesleyan U., 1873, M.A., 1876; grad. Drew Theol. Sem., 1875; U. of Berlin, 1890-91; D.D., German Wallace Coll., 1890; m. Ella A. Sprengle, July 10, 1873. Ordained M.E. ministry, 1874; pres. Baldwin U., Berea, O., 1886-94, U. of Nev., 1894—. Lay del. Gen. Conf., 1888; del. Ecumenical Conf., London, 1901. Pres. Ohio Coll. Assn., 1891-92; pres. Assn. of Am. Agrl. Coll. and Experiment Stas., 1899-1900; Oxford U., 1912-13; mem. permanent Am. Commn. for Study of Agrl. Finance, Production, Distribution, and Rural Life, 1913—. Address: Reno, Nev. Died May 27, 1914.

STUBBS, Walter Roscoe, gov.; b. Richmond, Wayne County, Ind., Nov. 7, 1858; s. John T. and Esther (Bailey) S.; moved with parents to Hesper, Douglas County, Kan., 1869; student U. of Kan.; m. Stella Hostettler, 1886. Began as r.r. contractor; later owner and operator cattle ranches in Kan., Tex., N.M. and Colo. Mem. Kan. Ho. of Rep., from Douglas County, 3 terms, 1903, 05, 07; chmn. Rep. State Com. of Kan., 1904-08; gov. Kan. 2 terms, 1909-13. Apptd. mem. U.S. Livestock Industry Com., 1917. Republican. Mem. Friends Ch. Mason. Home: Lawrence, Kan. Died Mar. 25, 1929.

STUBBS, William Carter, agriculturist; b. Gloucester County, Va., Dec. 7, 1846; s. Jefferson W. and Ann Walker Carter (Baytop) S.; student William and Mary Coll., 1860; A.B., Randolph-Macon Coll., 1862; grad. U. of Va., 1867; m. Elizabeth Saunders Blair, July 27, 1875. Served in C.S. cav. until surrender at Appomattox, 1865; prof. natural sciences, East Ala. Coll., 1869-72; prof. chemistry, Agrl. and Mech. Coll. of Ala., 1872-85; state chemist, Ala., 1882-85; dir. La. Expt. Sta. and prof. agr., La. State U., 1885-1905; state chemist of La., 1886—; dir. of the three expt. stas. in charge State Geol. Survey; state commr. St. Louis Expn., 1904, Jamestown Expn., 1907. Author: Sugar (2 vols.); The Descendants of Mordecai Cooke, of Mordecai's Mount, Va., 1650; Descendants of John Stubbs of Cappahosic, Va., 1652; A History of Two Virginia Families Transplanted from County Kent, Eng., Thos. Baytop of Tenterden, 1638, and John Catlett, of Sittingbourne, 1622; also many bulls. of Agrl. Expt. Sta. of La., etc. Address: New Orleans, La. Died July 7, 1924.

STUBENRAUCH, Arnold Valentine, pomologist; b. New Orleans, Apr. 27, 1871; s. Valentine and Henrietta (Weber) S.; B.S., U. of Calif., 1899; M.S., in agr., Cornell, 1901; m. Marie Elizabeth Meyer, Jan. 8, 1895. Instr. horticulture, U. of Ill., 1901-02; asst. prof. horticulture, U. of Calif., 1902-05; U.S. fruit transportation and storage investigations in Calif., 1906-10; in charge of fruit transportation and storage investigations, 1910; in charge of office of field investigations in pomology, 1910-12, pomologist and horticulturist in charge of Office of Hort. and Pomol. Investigations, 1912-14, U.S. Dept. of Agr.; prof. pomology, U. of Calif., 1914—. Fellow A.A.A.S. Author: A Country Reader (with H. B. M. Buchanan), 1905. Home: Berkeley, Calif. Died Feb. 12, 1917.

STUCK, Hudson, clergyman; b. in England, Nov. 11, 1863; s. James and Jane (Hudson) S.; came to America, 1885; grad. Theol. Dept., U. of South, Sewanee, Tenn., 1892, D.D., 1907; unmarried. Deacon and priest, P.E. Ch., 1892; rector Grace Ch., Cuero, Tex., 1892-94; dean St. Matthew's Cathedral, Dallas, 1894-1904; archdeacon of the Yukon, 1904—. Deputy Gen. Conv., P.E. Ch., 1898, 1901, 1913. Author: Ascent of Denali (Mt. McKinley), 1914; Ten Thousand Miles With a Dog Sled, 1914; Voyages on the Yukon and its Tributaries, 1917; A Winter Circuit of Our Arctic Coast, 1920. Awarded Back Grant of Royal Geog. Soc., London, 1919, "for travels in Alaska and Ascent of Mt. McKinley." Address: Fort Yukon, Alaska. Died Oct. 10, 1920.

STUCKENBERG, John Henry Wilburn, clergyman, author; b. Bramsche, Hanover, Germany, Jan. 6, 1835; s. Hermann R. and Anna Maria S.; A.M., Wittenberg Coll., O., 1860; studied divinity in same; divinity and philosophy in univs. of Halle, Göttingen, Berlin and Tübingen, Germany; D.D., Wooster Univ., 1875; LL.D., Pa. Coll., 1899; m. Mary Gingrich, Oct. 27, 1869. Pastor of chs. in Davenport, Ia., Erie, Pa., and Pittsburg, Pa.; chaplain 145th Pa. vols., Civil war; with regt., Fredericksburg, Chancellorsville, Gettysburg. Prof. theol. dept., Wittenberg Coll., 1873-80; pastor Am. Ch., Berlin, Germany, 1881-94. Author: History of the Augsburg Confession, 1868; Christian Sociology, 1880; The Final Science, 1885; Introduction to the Study of Philosophy, 1888; The Age and the Church, 1893; Tendencies in German Thought, 1896; The Social Problem, 1897; Introduction to the Study of Sociology, 1898. Wrote several pamphlets and numerous articles on theol., ednl., philos. and sociol. subjects in Am. and English mags. and journals; edited European dept. and social section in Homiletic Review, New York. Address: Cambridge, Mass. Died 1903.

STUCKSLAGER, Willard Coldren, banker; b. Lisbon, Ia., Oct. 24, 1869; s. Harrison and Mary (Coldren) S.; student Cornell Coll., Mt. Vernon, Ia., 1887-90, hon. M.A., 1903; studied U. of Chicago, 1892-93; m. Rowena Eloise Bronson, Nov. 9, 1893; children—Mary Coldren (Mrs. Harold Van Metre), Rowena Eloise (Mrs. Raymond B. McConlogue), Elizabeth (Mrs. Lanning Macfarland), Constance. Began in banking business at Lisbon, 1894; later pres. Stuckslager & Auracher Bank, Lisbon; also pres. Mt. Vernon (Ia.) Bank; mem. Ia. Ho. of Rep., 1900-04, Senate, 1904-13. Trustee and treas. Cornell Coll.; mem. State Bd. of Edn., Ia. Republican. Methodist. Home: Lisbon, Ia. Died Feb. 23, 1931.

STUDEBAKER, Clement, mfr.; b. Gettysburg, Pa., Mar. 12, 1831; s. John S., wagon maker; moved to Ashland, O., 1836; learned blacksmith trade with father; went to South Bend, Ind., 1850; taught school one winter; engaged in smithing and wagon business with brother Henry, 1852; business grew until one of the largest vehicle factories in the world; business was incorporated, 1868; pres. of co., 1868—. Del. to several Rep. Nat. Convs.; commr. to Paris Expn.; pres. Ind. Commn. to World's Columbian Expn.; mem. Pan-Am. Congress; pres. Chautauqua Assembly of N.Y. Address: South Bend, Ind. Died 1901.

STUDEBAKER, Clement, Jr., public utilities; b. South Bend, Ind., Aug. 11, 1871; s. Clement and Ann (Milburn) S.; ed. Northwestern U., Ill.; m. Alice Rhawn, Apr. 27, 1893; children—Clement III, Esther. Entered employ Studebaker Bros. Mfg. Co. at 20, becoming treas., 1901, and 2d v.p. and treas. The Studebaker Corp. upon its orgn., 1911, resigned 1914; later pres. North Am. Light and Power Co., Illinois Power and Light Corp., Ill. Traction Co., Ill. Traction, Inc.; chmn. bd. Ill. Terminal Co. Trustee DePauw U., Chautauqua Instn. Republican. Methodist. Home: Chicago, Ill. Died Dec. 3, 1932.

STUDEBAKER, John Mohler, mfr.; b. Gettysburg, Pa., Oct. 10, 1833; s. John and Rebecca (Mohler) S.; removed to Ashland County, O., 1835; ed. dist. sch.; m. Mary Jane Stull, Jan. 2, 1860. Removed with father's family to S. Bend, 1851; in spring of 1852 entered employ of John Cotton, wagonmaker, of S. Bend. Made woodwork of a wagon, in winter of 1852, for which his brothers, Henry and Clem, made ironwork; gave this wagon to a company organized to go to Calif. to pay for his share of the company's expenses; party disbanded at Hangtown, Calif., Aug. 31, 1853; worked for H. L. Hines, a blacksmith, and was later his partner; returned to S. Send, 1858; bought his brother Henry's interest in firm of Studebaker Bros., which then became C. & J. M. Studebaker (with brother Clem); they later admitted two other brothers, P. E. and Jacob F., building up Studebaker Bros. Mfg. Co., of which became pres., company operating largest vehicle works in the world. Address: South Bend, Ind. Died Mar. 16, 1917.

STUDER, Jacob Henry, author; b. Columbus, O., Feb. 26, 1840; s. George and Regina (Werst) S.; ed. pub. schs., Columbus, O. Worked in printing offices, Columbus, 1852-58; founder Bd. of Trade, Columbus, Nov. 1872; writer, 1870—; ornithologist; widower. Pres. Natural Science Assn. of America. Author: Columbus, Ohio—Its History, Resources and Progress, 1873; The Birds of North America, 1888; Ornithology, or the Science of Birds, 1888. Address: New York, N.Y. Died 1904.

STUMP, John Sutton, clergyman; b. Gilmer County, W.Va., Dec. 4, 1861; s. Bailey and Sallie (Sutton) S.; Glenville Normal Sch., W.Va., 1 term; grad. Crozer Theol. Sem., Chester, Pa., 1890; D.D., Denison, 1911; m. Lily R. Budwell, Mar. 2, 1892 (died 1925); children—Felix Budwell, Josephine Ragland (dec.), John Sutton. Ordained Bapt. ministry, 1891; missionary, Parkersburg, W.Va., 1890-91; pastor Buckhannon, 1892-93; organizer, incorporator, and corr. sec. W.Va. Bapt. Edn. Soc., 1891-94; supt. W.Va. Bapt. State Missions, 1896-1901; dist. sec. Am. Bapt. Home Mission Soc., 1901-09; joint dist. sec. same soc. and Am. Bapt. Foreign Mission Soc., 1909-20; asst. sec. Am. Bapt. Home Mission Soc., Mar. 1920-Nov. 1926; sec. Dept. Ch. Edifice Work Am. Bapt. Home Mission Soc., 1926-29; retired, 1931. Mem. bd. mgrs. Gen. Conv. Baptists of N.A., 1911 to dissolution. Democrat. Home: Clarksburg, W.Va. Died July 28, 1936.

STUMP, Joseph, theologian; b. Marietta, Pa., Oct. 6, 1866; s. Michael and Leah (Hoover) S.; A.B., Capital U., Columbus, O., 1884, A.M., 1887; grad. Luth. Theol. Sem., Phila., 1887; D.D., Muhlenberg Coll., Allentown, Pa., 1908; LL.D., Carthage (Ill.) Coll., 1925; L.H.D., Capital U., Columbus, O., 1925; m. Alice A. Cooper, June 18, 1891; children—Marian Alice, George Paul, Anna Lydia (dec.), Joseph Luther, Rose Margaret Leah, William Richard, Theodore Emanuel. Ordained Luth. ministry, 1887; pastor Great Bend, Pa., 1887-89, Ephrata, Pa., 1889-92, Grace Ch., Phillipsburg, N.J., 1892-1915; prof. systematic theology, Chicago Luth. Theol. Sem., Maywood, Ill., 1915-20; dean and prof. systematic theology, Chicago (Ill.) Luth. Div. Sch., 1920-21; pres. and prof. systematic theology, Northwestern Luth. Theol. Sem., 1921—. Author: Life of Philip Melanchthon, 1897, Bible Story, 1898; Bible Teachings, 1902; An Explanation of Luther's Small Catechism, 1907; Russellism, A Counterfeit Christianity, 1922; The Christian Life, A Handbook of Christian Ethics, 1930; The Christian Faith; A System of Christian Dogmatics, 1932. Joint Author: An Explanation of the Common Service, 1908. Translator and editor of Starck's Daily Handbook, 1904. Mem. Am. Acad. Polit. and Social Science. Home: Minneapolis, Minn. Died May 24, 1935.

STUNTZ, Homer Clyde, M.E. bishop; b. Albion, Erie County, Pa., Jan. 29, 1858; s. Edward W. and Isabel (Hilborn) S.; ed. State Normal, Edinboro, Pa., and acad. of Northwestern U.; took law course in Ia.; studied Garrett Bibl. Inst., class of 1884; S.T.B., Garrett, 1896; D.D., Upper Ia. U., 1896; m. Estelle Clark, May 26, 1885. Ordained M.E. ministry, 1884; missionary to India, 1886-95; supt. M.E. missions, P.I., 1901-07; field sec. Bd. of Foreign Missions M.E. Ch. for eastern div., Mar. 19, 1907-June 1908; asst. corr. sec. Bd. of Foreign Missions, 1908-12; elected bishop May 16, 1912. Nat. adminstr. Meth. war work, 1917—. Author: The Philippines and the Far East, 1904; South American Neighbors, 1915. Home: Omaha, Neb. Died June 3, 1924.

STUNTZ, Stephen Conrad, botanist; b. Clarno, Wis., Apr. 4, 1875; s. Albert Conrad and Lydia Ann (Sturtevant) S.; B.S., U. of Wis., 1899, grad. student, 1899-1902; m. Lena Grayson FitzHugh, June 4, 1907. Library asst., U. of Wis., 1895-1902; cataloguer and classifier, Library of Congress, 1902-08; bibliographer, Bur. of Soils, 1908-10; botanist, office of Foreign Seed and Plant Introduction, 1910—. Conducted geneal. and hist. research in State Hist. Soc. Library at Madison, 1897-1902. Presbyn. Author: The Second Mrs. Jim, 1904; Mrs. Jim and Mrs. Jimmie, 1905; The Soil of Our Hills, 1915. Writer under pseudonym Stephen Conrad. Home: Vienna, Va. Died Feb. 2, 1918.

STURANI, Giuseppe, conductor; b. Ancoma, Italy, Nov. 15, 1877; s. Count Carlo and Countess Margherita (Bianchetti) S.; ed. Conservatory of Music, Bologna; pupil of Prof. Martucci; awarded degree of Music Master, Conservatory of Bologna, 1899; m. Ada Parenzo, Sept. 15, 1921. Began as violinist, 1897; conductor of opera, 1904—; appeared in leading opera houses of Italy, including those of Naples, Palermo and Bologna, also in Barcelona and Lisbon, Buenos Aires, and Rio de Janeiro; came to U.S., 1907; with Hammerstein Opera Co., New York and Phila., until 1910; with Metropolitan Opera Co., 1913, and 1927—; with Chicago Opera Co., 1913-20; later gen. musical sec. and conductor, Metropolitan Opera Co. Home: New York, N.Y. Died Jan. 17, 1940.

STURGES, Dwight Case, etcher; b. Boston, Mass., Oct. 21, 1874; s. Perley Frank and Emma Maria (Healy) S.; ed. pub. schs.; art education, Cowles Art Sch., Boston, Mass.; m. Clara Blanche Vaughan, Mar. 19, 1900; children—Alton Vaughan, Dwight Richard, Natalie Clare (Mrs. Benjamin Butler). Began as sketch artist with Boston Globe, 1895; newspaper artist, 1895—, with various metropolitan dailies; with Christian Science Monitor, 1917—. Awarded Lamont prize, Chicago Soc. Etchers, 1915; silver medal, Panama Pacific Expn., 1915; Logan medal, Art Inst. Chicago, 1924; asso. members' prize, Chicago Soc. Etchers, 1925; Huntington prize, Print Makers Soc. Calif., 1927. Republican. Mason. Home: Boston, Mass. Died Sept. 7, 1940.

STURGIS, Clarence Eugene, editor; b. Lewiston, Me., Jan. 22, 1860; s. Albert H. and Ruth Ellen (Thomas) S.; ed. pub. schs., Nichols Latin Sch., under pvt. tutors, and business coll., Lewiston; m. Katherine I. Clark, Oct. 5, 1886. Compositor to city editor, Lewiston Evening Journal, 1876-85, except 1 yr. as accountant in wholesale grocery house; city editor Lewiston Daily News, 1885; editor, Standard, Jamaica, L.I., 1886; N.E. mgr. at Boston, Am. Press Assn., 1886-89; with Boston Herald in various editorial capacities, and mng. editor, 1889-1914; editorial staff, Denver (Colo.) Times, 1914-15, Kansas City Post, Apr. 1915, news editor and Sunday editor to Oct. 1921. Mem. Co. C, 1st Regt., Me. Vol. Militia, 1877-78. Republican. Christian Scientist. Mason. Home: Hanford, Calif. Died July 1, 1922.

STURGIS, Frank Knight, broker. Mem. firm of Strong, Sturgis & Co., and of New York Stock Exchange; pres. Madison Sq. Garden Co.; v.p. Standard Trust Co.; dir. various financial and other corps. Home: New York, N.Y. Died June 15, 1932.

STURGIS, Frederic Russell, physician; b. Manila, P.I., July 7, 1844; s. Henry P. and Mary Georgiana (Howard) S.; ed. in Eng. and U.S.; M.D., Harvard, 1867; m. Martha DeWolf Hazard, Apr. 6, 1870. Lecturer venereal diseases, 1874-80, prof. diseases of genito-urinary organs and venereal diseases, 1880-82, New York U.; visiting surgeon (Charity) City Hosp., 1873-93. Fellow N.Y. Acad. Medicine. Author: Human Cestoids, 1867; Syphilis in New-born Children, 1883; Early Manhood—Some of Its Dangers, 1886; Cystoid Diseases of the Testicle, 1899; Sexual Debility in Man, 1900; Student's Manual of Venereal Diseases, 1901; Notes and Reflections on the Causes which Induce Marital Infelicity due to the Relations of the Sexes, 1908; also various mag. articles. Am. editor: Diday on Hereditary Syphilis, with notes. Address: New York, N.Y. Died May 6, 1919.

STURGIS, Julian, author; b. Boston, Mass., Oct. 21, 1848; s. Russell S.; went to England when 7 months old; ed. Eton; M.A., Balliol Coll., Oxford; barrister at law; became British subject; traveled in Levant, 1878; visited Turkish and Russian armies before Constantinople; came to U.S., 1880, visiting Leadville. Author: John-a-Dreams; An Accomplished Gentleman; Dick's Wandering; John Maidment; Thraldom; My Friends and I; Comedy of a Country House; A Master of Fortune; After Twenty Years; The Folly of Pen Harrington; Little Comedies; Stephen Calinari; Count Julian, a Tragedy; A Book of Song; also several libretti, etc. Address: London, Eng. Died 1904.

STURGIS, Russell, merchant; b. Boston, Mass., Aug. 3, 1831; ed. Harvard; his father was a merchant in China trade, at Canton, and after graduation he went there; was U.S. consul at Canton, but returned to U.S. and engaged in business in Boston; capt. and maj. 45th Mass. regt., 1862-63; active in Y.M.C.A., 1858—, as pres. of the Boston Assn., chmn. State com. and member Internat. com. Address: Boston, Mass. Died 1899.

STURGIS, Russell, architect, author; b. Baltimore County, Md., Oct. 16, 1836; s. Russell and Margaret D. (Appleton) S.; A.B., Coll. City of New York, 1856, Ph.D., 1893; A.M., Yale, 1870; m. Sarah, d. D. N. Barney, May 26, 1864. Studied architecture in Europe; practiced until 1880; went to Europe to reside, because of failing health; active in management of art socs. in New York, and in writing and lecturing on art subjects, 1885—. Editor for decorative art of Century Dictionary, and for fine art in general of Webster's Internat. Dictionary, new edit. Johnson's (now Appleton's) Universal Cyclo., and Ency. Americana, 1904-05; also contbr. of art subjects to new internat. Ency.; editor Dictionary of Architecture and Building (3 vols.), 1901-02. Author: Manual of Jarves Collection of Early Italian Pictures, 1868; European Architecture, A Historical Study, 1896; Annotated Bibliography of Fine Art, 1897; How to Judge Architecture, 1903; The Appreciation of Sculpture, 1904; The Interdependence of the Arts of Design, being the Scammon Lectures for 1904, 1905; The Appreciation of Pictures, 1905; A Study of the Artist's Way of Working in the Various Handicrafts and Arts of Design (2 vols.), 1905; History of Architecture, vol. 1, 1906; also more than 500 monographs and articles in periodicals, dealing with fine and decorative art. Made complete revision of Lübke's History of Art (2 vols), 1904. Address: New York, N.Y. Died 1909.

STURGIS, Samuel Davis, army officer; b. St. Louis, Mo., Aug. 1, 1861; s. Samuel Davis and Jerusha (Wilcox) S.; student Washington U., St. Louis; grad. U.S. Mil. Acad., 1884; m. Bertha Bement, July 29, 1896; children—Samuel Davis, Elizabeth Tracy (Mrs. Hugh A. Murrill, Jr.), Robert Bement. Commd. 2d lt. 1st Arty., June 15, 1884; promoted through grades to brig. gen., July 1, 1917; maj. gen. N.A., Aug. 24, 1917; maj. gen. regular army, Oct. 7, 1921. Aide to Brig. and Maj. Gen. Wesley Merritt, 1891-96; asst. adj. gen. Dept. of Pacific and 8th Army Corps, 1898; participated in campaign against Manila, P.I., 1898; adj. gen. Dept. of Pinar del Rio, Cuba, Jan.-May 1899; asst. adj. gen. Philippine Div., 1899-1901; mem. Gen. Staff Corps, 1907-11; with 3d F.A., at Ft. Sam Houston, Tex., 1911-13; col. 1st Field Arty., in Hawaiian Islands, 1913-16; organized 7th Field Arty. at San Antonio, Tex., July 1916; comd. Camp Funston, Leon Springs, Kan., until Aug. 24, 1917; apptd. comdr. 87th Div., N.A., Camp Pike, Little Rock, Ark., Aug. 25, 1917; arrived in France, Sept. 11, 1918; detached service, with 1st and 42d divs. in Meuse-Argonne operations, Oct. 4-18, 1918; comd. 80th Div., Nov. 18, 1918-Apr. 12, 1919; comd. Camp Gordon, Atlanta, Apr. 30-July 2, 1919, Camp Pike, July 3-Nov. 10, 1919; comd. Camp Sherman, O., 1920-21; comd. Panama Canal Dept., 1921-24; comd. 3d Corps Area, 1924-25; retired from active service Aug. 1, 1925. Roman Catholic. Address: Washington, D.C. Died Mar. 6, 1933.

STURGISS, George Cookman, congressman; b. Poland, O., Aug. 16, 1842; s. Rev. Alfred G. and Sabra L. (Minor) S.; ed. Wayne Acad., O., and Monongalia Acad., Morgantown, Va. (now W.Va.); m. Sabra J. Vance, Sept. 22, 1863 (died 1903); m. 2d, C. C. Kent, Nov. 25, 1909. Admitted to bar, 1863, in practice at Morgantown, W.Va., 1863—; built Sabraton (later known as the Morgantown & Kingwood) Ry.; also interested in many other business enterprises. County supt. of schools, Monongalia County, W.Va., 1866-70; mem. W.Va. Ho. of Dels., 3 terms, 1870-72; pros. atty., 1873-80; Rep. candidate for gov. of W.Va., 1880; U.S. dist. atty., 1889-93; mem. 60th and 61st Congresses (1907-11), 2d W.Va. Dist.; judge 23d Jud. Circuit W.Va., term 1913-21. Lay del. Gen. Conf. M.E. Ch., 1896; sec. bd. regents State U. W.Va., 13 yrs., and pres. bd. 1897-1901; trustee Am. Univ. (Washington), W.Va. Coll. (Buchanan); mem. W.Va. State Bd. Trade (1st pres.), Morgantown Bd. Trade (pres.). Address: Morgantown, W.Va. Died Feb. 26, 1925.

STURM, Ernest, fire insurance; b. N.Y. City, Aug. 24, 1878; LL.B., New York U., 1903; m. Louise Elsie Foster, Sept. 2, 1908; children—Ruth Foster, Kenneth Ernest. With Continental Ins. Co., N.Y. City, 1892—, beginning as office boy, cashier local dept. of the co., 1905-10; gen. cashier same co., also Fidelity-Phenix Fire Ins. Co., 1910-11; financial sec. both companies, 1911-20, sec. and treas., 1920-23, v.p. and sec., 1923-24; chmn. bd., 1924—, Continental Ins. Co., Fidelity-Phenix Fire Ins. Co., Am. Eagle Fire Ins. Co., First Am. Fire Ins. Co., Niagara Fire Ins. Co., Maryland Ins. Co., Fidelity & Casualty Co.; mem. advisory com. Maiden Lane Br. of Chase Nat. Bank of New York; trustee Central Hanover Bank & Trust Co. Office: New York, N.Y. Died Dec. 22, 1936.

STURTEVANT, John Loomis, newspaper pub.; b. Delavan, Wis., Mar. 18, 1865; s. Charles Holmes and Amanda (Brown) S.; ed. high sch.; m. Nellie Terres Chesley, Nov. 27, 1890. Reporter, Pioneer Press, St. Paul, Minn., 1885-89; pub. Waupaca Post, 1889-1907, Wausau Daily Record-Herald, 1907—. V.p. Associated Press, 1919-20; pres. Wis. Daily League, 1918-20. Republican. Episcopalian. Mason. Elk. Author: The Sturtevant Family of Wisconsin, 1924. Home: Wausau, Wis. Died May 17, 1939.

STUTESMAN, James Flynn, lawyer; b. Peru, Ind., July 19, 1860; s. James Madison and Elizabeth (Shields) S.; A.B., Wabash Coll., 1884, A.M., 1895; m. Jessie Emilie Herron, June 30, 1910. Admitted to bar, 1893, and practiced at Peru, Ind.; E.E. and M.P. to Bolivia, 1908-10; resumed law practice at Washington, Oct. 1, 1910. U.S. commr. gen. to Central America and W.I. for Panama-Pacific Internat. Expn., 1913. Republican. Presbyn. Home: Crawfordsville, Ind. Died Dec. 15, 1917.

STUTSMAN, Jesse O(rila), prison mgr.; b. Phila., Ind., Feb. 19, 1871; s. Henry Clay and Victoria (Domanget) S.; A.B., De Pauw U., 1895; grad. study Johns Hopkins, 1907; m. Lyda Winslow, Aug. 19, 1891; children—Rachel V., Ruth A., Paul W. Ordained ministry M.E. Ch., 1896; pastor successively Goldsmith, Selma and La Fountain, Ind., 1906-10; gen. sec. Prisoners' Aid Assn. of Md., 1910-12; supt. research dept. Bd. Pub. Welfare, Kansas City, Mo., 1912-18, also supt. Kansas City Municipal Farm for Misdemeanants; with War Camp Community Service various mil. camps, 1918-20; supt. Detroit House of Correction, 1920-23; served as gen. supt. Rockview Penitentiary, Bellefonte, Pa., 1923-29; supt. U.S. Detention Hdqrs. and prin. Fed. Training Sch. for Prison Officers, N.Y. City, 1929—. Republican. Methodist. Mason. Kiwanian. Author: Curing the Criminal, 1926. Contbr. to Annals Am. Acad. Polit. and Social Science. Exponent of character analysis in study of criminals; lecturer on farm colonies for misdemeanants. Address: New York, N.Y. Died Apr. 25, 1933.

STUTZ, Harry C., mfr.; b. Ansonia, O., Sept. 12, 1876; s. Henry J. and Elizabeth S.; ed. pub. schs.; m. Clara M. Dietz, Oct. 25, 1898. Began with machine shop, Dayton, 1897; in charge Lindsey-Russell Axle Co., Indianapolis, Ind., 1903, later with G. & J. Tire Co. and sales engr. Schebler Carburetor Co.; designed the American car; engr. and factory mgr. Marion Motor Car Co., 1906-10; asso. with Henry Campbell in Stutz Auto Parts Co., and in 1911 the Ideal Motor Car Co. was organized to mfr. the Stutz Car, the two cos. consolidated in 1913 to form the Stutz Motor Car Co., of which was pres.; sold out, 1919, and asso. with Mr. Campbell in the H.C.S. Motor Car Co., of which is pres. Mason. Made a notable collection of guns. Home: Indianapolis, Ind. Died June 26, 1930.

SUDDUTH, William Xavier, physician; b. Springfield, Ill., Jan. 18, 1853; s. James McCreary and Amanda Elisabeth S.; Ph.B., Ill. Wesleyan U., 1873, A.M., 1889; D.D.S., Phila. Dental Coll., 1881; practiced dentistry, Bloomington, Ill., 2 yrs.; studied Coll. Phys. and Surg. New York, 1883-84; M.D., Medico-Chirurg. Coll., Phila., 1885; post-grad. studies univs. of Berlin, Heidelberg, and Vienna. Dir. Physiol. Lab. and lecturer Medico-Chirurg. Coll., 1884-90; prof. pathology and oral surgery, U. of Minn., 1890-95; later in spl. practice, nervous diseases, Chicago. Retired from practice and engaged in mfg. alfalfa products, ranching and farming. Lectured in univ. extension courses; prof. morbid psychology and psycho-therapeutics and dir. psychophysical lab. Post-Grad. Med. Sch., Chicago; well known as med. editor and writer. Home: Billings, Mont. Died Mar. 7, 1915.

SUDWORTH, George Bishop, dendrologist; b. Kingston, Wis., Aug. 31, 1864; s. Bishop Birch and Mary Elizabeth S.; A.B., U. of Mich., 1885; m. Frances Gertrude Kingsbury, Feb. 24, 1897. Instr. botany, Mich. Agrl. Coll., 1885-86; botanist in Div. of Forestry, U.S. Dept. of Agr., 1886-95; dendrologist, div. and bur. of forestry, 1895-1904; chief of dendrology, Forest Service, Dept. of Agr., 1904—. Author: Forest Flora of the Rocky Mountain Region; Forest Flora of Washington, D.C.; Forest and Ornamental Trees of Savannah (Ga.) City Park; Forest Flora of Tennessee; Nomenclature of Arborescent Flora of the United States; Trees of the United States Important in Forestry; Check List of North American Forest Trees with Geographical Distribution; Collecting Tree Seeds and Raising Forest Trees; Forest Resources of Western Colorado Timber Reserves; The Forest Nursery; The Forests of Allegany Co., Md.; Forest Resources of the Northern California Timber Reserves; Forest Conditions of the Sierra Timber Reserve; Forest Trees of the Pacific Slope; Forest Trees of the Rocky Mountain Region. Home: Washington, D.C. Died May 10, 1927.

SUFFREN, Charles Carroll, lawyer; b. Haverstraw, Rockland County, N.Y., Nov. 19, 1854; s. Andrew Edward and Mary Jane (Sloat) S.; paternal ancestors first arrived in America, 1713, maternal ancestors, 1660; Phillips Acad., Andover, Mass., 1871; Yale U., 1871-75 (non-grad.); LL.B., Yale, 1878; m. Martha Wentworth, June 3, 1880. Admitted to bar, 1878; practiced Haverstraw, 1878-89, New York, 1889-Jan. 1, 1898, when obliged on account of ill health to retire temporarily; with Lawyers Title Ins. Co., Brooklyn office, Nov. 1900-Nov. 1902; head of law dept. of The Title Ins. Co. of New York, Nov. 1, 1902-June 18, 1913; resumed law practice, firm of Suffren, Humphreys and Orr. Dir. Kings County Mortgage Co. Democrat. Episcopalian. Mem. Am. Bar Assn., Brooklyn Bar Assn., Brooklyn Inst. Arts and Sciences, Kings Co. Hist. Soc. Mason. Home: Brooklyn, N.Y. Died Dec. 17, 1917.

SUGDEN, Walter S(mith), Masonic official; b. Amsterdam, N.Y., Apr. 9, 1880; s. James Taylor and Elizabeth Lockheed (Smith) S.; A.B., Harvard, 1903; student Harvard Law Sch., 1903-06; m. Rachel E. Hutchison, Feb. 12, 1916 (now dec.); 1 dau., Elizabeth Jane; m. 2d, Katharyn Knott Donley, July 6, 1922. Admitted to W.Va. bar, 1910; practiced at Sistersville, 1910—; mem. firm Kimball & Sugden, 1912—; city atty. Sistersville, 1917-28; dir. 1st Tyler Bank & Trust Co., Petroleum Engr., Inc.; sec. and dir. Oil Review Pub. Co. Republican. Episcopalian (vestryman). Mason (32°, K.T., Shriner); Senior Grand Warden Grand Lodge of W.Va., 1936, trustee, 1932—; Imperial Potentate A.A.O.N.M.S., 1937. Home: Sistersville, W.Va. Died July 7, 1938.

SUKER, George Francis, M.D., ophthalmologist; b. Detroit, Mich., Oct. 12, 1869; s. Herman and Emilie (Toelle) S.; prep. edn., German-Am. Sem., Detroit; M.D., U. of Mich., 1892; married. Practiced at Chicago, 1901—; prof. ophthalmology, Post-Grad. Med. Sch.; ophthalmologist Post-Grad. Hosp.; attending ophthalmologist (chief of service) Cook County Hosp.; attending ophthalmologist Grant Hosp.; attending consultant ophthalmologist Edward Hines Jr. Hosp. (Vets. Bur.). Lt. col. Med. O.R.C. Fellow Am. Acad. Ophthalmology and Oto-Laryngology, A.M.A., Am. Coll. Surgeons. Home: Winnetka, Ill. Died July 2, 1933.

SULLIVAN, Corliss Esmonde, banker; b. Millersburg, O., Dec. 19, 1876; s. Jeremiah J. and Selina (Brown) S.; A.B., Yale, 1900; m. Mrs. Price McKinney, Dec. 26, 1936. Began business career in coal business, 1900; v.p. Glens Run Coal Co.; pres. Superior Savings & Trust Co., Cleveland, O., until consolidation with Central Nat. Bank & Trust Co., of which was pres.; became chmn. bd. Central Nat. Bank. Mem. federal advisory council of Nat. Fed. Res. Bd., 1921. Home: Gates Mills, O. Died Feb. 14, 1939.

SULLIVAN, Edward Dean, author; b. New Haven, Conn., Nov. 24, 1888; s. Michael F. and Mary Ellen (Murphy) S.; student New Haven pub. schs., 1894-1901, Hillhouse Prep. Sch., 1901-05; studied law under pvt. tutors; m. Margaret White Callahan, Apr. 18, 1910; 1 son, Edward White. Sporting editor New Haven Union, 1905-07, New Haven Register, 1907-09; with N.Y. Herald, 1910-19; sporting editor Chicago Herald Examiner, 1919-24; feature writer N.Y. Herald Tribune, 1929-30; feature editor Boston Evening American, 1933-34; asso. editor of The Bystander, 1933—; columnist for N.Y. Post, 1935. Democrat. Roman Catholic. Author: Rattling the Cup, 1928; Chicago Surrenders, 1929; I'll Tell My Big Brother, 1929; Sold Out!, 1929; Look at Chicago, 1930; Ex-It, 1931; Benedict Arnold, Military Racketeer, 1932; This Kidnapping Business, 1933; Romeo Reverse, 1934; The Fabulous Wilson Mizner, 1935. Contbr. to leading mags. Address: New Haven, Conn. Died Apr. 4, 1938.

SULLIVAN, Francis John (Francis "Fontenoy" Sullivan), lawyer; b. San Francisco, Calif., Jan. 21, 1854; s. John and Katherine (Farrelly) S.; father a pioneer of Calif., 1844; St. Ignatius Coll., San Francisco; Stonyhurst Coll., England; LL.B., Columbia Law Sch., New York, 1877; m. Alice Phelan, philanthropist, May 11, 1882 (died 1912). Mem. Calif. State Senate, 1882; candidate on Dem. ticket for Congress, 1884 and 1886 (elected, 1886, so found in Congressional election case of Sullivan vs. Felton); park commr., San Francisco, 1902; Dem. Presdl. elector, 1904. Anti-monopoly Democrat. Erected monument to Irish soldiers on battlefield of Fontenoy, 1900; orator at meeting of Irish people on the battlefield, 1905 and 1907, also on many other occasions in Calif. and elsewhere. Obtained from Esdaile family previously unpublished verses by Percy Bysshe Shelley, on "Robert Emmett's Grave." Author: Ireland, Creator of the Common Law. Home: San Francisco, Calif. Died Nov. 16, 1930.

SULLIVAN, Isaac Newton, judge; b. Delaware County, Ia., Nov. 3, 1848; s. Aaron and Jane (Lippincott) S.; ed. Adrian (Mich.) Coll., 1866-69; m. Miss Chastine Josephine Moore, Feb. 14, 1870; children—Willis Eugene, La Verne Latimer. Admitted to bar, 1875; practiced at Delhi until 1881; removed to Hailey, Ida., 1881; asso. justice Supreme Ct. of Ida., 1890-1917 (5 times chief justice); resumed law practice in firm Sullivan & Sullivan, Boise and Hailey, Ida., 1917. Republican. Home: Boise, Ida. Died Jan. 31, 1938.

SULLIVAN, James, educator; b. Baltimore, Md., Feb. 13, 1873; s. James and Martha Jennie (Meeker) S.; A.B., Harvard, 1894, A.M., 1895, Ph.D., 1898; LL.D., Syracuse, 1927; student École des Chartes, Paris, 1895-96, U. of Berlin, 1896-97; m. Amelia L. Owen, July 3, 1901; 1 dau., Martha. Asst. instr. history, 1894-95, traveling fellow, 1895-97, instr. history and govt., 1897-99, Harvard; instr. history, De Witt Clinton High Sch., New York, 1899-1902; prin. High

Sch. of Commerce Annex, 1902-03; lecturer on the teaching of history and civics, Columbia, 1905-06; head dept. history, High Sch. of Commerce, New York, 1902-07; prin. Boys' High Sch., Brooklyn, 1907-1916; state historian and dir. of archives and history, U. of the State of N.Y., 1916-23; asst. commr. for secondary edn. in N.Y. State, 1923-26; asst. commr. for higher and professional edn. in N.Y. State, 1926—. Lecturer on the teaching of civics and on modern history, Summer Sch. of Harvard, 1908-10; lecturer on modern English history, Summer Sch., Columbia U., 1911; lecturer on teaching of history and civics, New York U., 1908-15; lecturer Cornell U. Summer Sch., 1916-17, Johns Hopkins U. Summer Sch., 1922. Home dir. Y.M.C.A. Ednl. Commission for A.E.F., 1918-19. Author: An Elementary History of England, 1904; The Government of New York State, 1906; Community Civics for New York State, (with G. E. Turkington), 1925. Editor: Washington's and Webster's Addresses, 1908; American Democracy, Washington to Wilson, 1919; Sir William Johnson Papers, 1922; Albany Committee of Correspondence, 1775-1778, 1923; New York, A History of the Empire State, 1927; Primary Histories for Children, 1929. Editor Quarterly Jour. of N.Y. State Hist. Assn. Contbr. to hist. reviews, proc. of socs., Nelson's Ency. and Ency. Americana, on hist. subjects, Cyclo. of Edn., Cyclo. of Am. Government and Dictionary of Am. Biography. Home: Albany, N.Y. Died Oct. 8, 1931.

SULLIVAN, James Edward, athletic official, publisher; b. New York, N.Y., Nov. 1860; s. Daniel J. and Julia S.; ed. grammar sch., New York; m. Margaret Eugenie Byrne, 1882. Connected with pub. house of Frank Leslie, 1878-89; founded The Athletic News, one of the first athletic papers published in U.S. devoted wholly to track and field athletics; business mgr., editor and later owner of N.Y. Sporting Times; organizer and pres. Am. Sports Pub. Co., pub. of Spalding's Athletic Library; editor Spalding's Official Athletic Almanac. Began athletic career, 1877; won all-around championship of Pastime Athletic Club, 1880, 81; an organizer, sec., 1889-1906, pres., 1906, Amateur Athletic Union of U.S.; mem. bd. Pastime Athletic Club; officiated in Am. championship track and field games for 25 yrs.; asst. Am. dir. Olympic Games, Paris, 1900; dir. Buffalo Expn. athletic dept., 1901; chief dept. phys. culture St. Louis Expn., 1904; sec. Am. com. Olympic Games, at Athens, Greece, 1906; hon. dir. athletics Jamestown Expn., 1907; sec. Am. com. Olympic Games, London, 1908; an organizer Pub. Schs. Athletic League, and Outdoor Recreation League, New York. Olympic medal, St. Louis Expn., 1904; Golden Cross Knights of Royal Order of the Savior, Greece, 1906. Apptd. mem. Bd. Edn., and Playground Commn. of New York, 1909; mem. Spl. Investigation Commn., 1910. Home: New York, N.Y. Died Sept. 16, 1914.

SULLIVAN, James F., banker; b. Grange, nr. Mallow, Ireland, Aug. 20, 1846; s. John Curtin and Ellen Upton (Supple) S.; ed. pub. schs. and pvt. tutors; m. Lulue Romaine Nichols; children—Frances L., R. Livingston, Mrs. Elaine S. Hoffman. After leaving school was clerk in wholesale white goods and notion business in Phila.; with brother, Jeremiah J., in same line, in firm of Sullivan & Bro., 1886-1907. Active in many underwritings, passenger ry. consolidations and their development in Phila. and other cities; v.p. Midvale Steel Co., 1889-1915; pres. Market St. Nat. Bank of Phila.; dir. Frankford & Southwark Passenger Railroad Co., Green & Coates Passenger Railway Co., Real Estate Trust Co.; mgr. and dir. Lehigh Coal & Nav. Co.; dir. Lehigh & N.E. R.R. Co., Alliance Coal Mining Co., Cranberry Creek Coal Co., Panther Valley Water Co., Nesquehoning Valley R.R. Co. Mem. Acad. Natural Sciences. Trustee Catholic High Sch., Pa. Mus. and Sch. of Industrial Art; dir. Mercantile Library, Apprentices Library. Home: Radnor, Pa. Died Mar. 17, 1930.

SULLIVAN, James Mark, diplomatic service; b. Killarney, Ireland, Jan. 6, 1873; brought to U.S. when a child; LL.B., Yale, 1902. Practiced, Conn., 1902-06, New York, 1906-13; E.E. and M.P. to Dominican Republic, Aug. 12, 1913—. Died Aug. 1920.

SULLIVAN, Jeremiah Francis, judge; b. Litchfield County, Conn., Aug. 19, 1851; s. Michael and Margaret (Bohane) S.; B.A., St. Ignatius Coll., San Francisco, 1870, M.A., 1872, LL.D., 1905; m. Helen M. Bliss, Sept. 13, 1876 (died 1918); children—Harry F., Gertrude (Mrs. B. M. Breeden), Helen (wife of R. W. Schumann, U.S.N.), Jeremiah F., Marguerite (wife of Arvid R. Croonquist, U.S.A.). Began practice in San Francisco, 1874; mem. Bd. of Edn., San Francisco, 1877-79; judge Superior Ct., 1880-89; apptd. asso. justice Supreme Ct. of Calif., Nov. 19, 1927. Democrat. Catholic. Pres. Calif. State Bar Assn., 1923-24, Bar Assn., San Francisco, 1917, 24. Home: San Francisco, Calif. Died Jan. 23, 1928.

SULLIVAN, Louis Henry, architect; b. Boston, Mass., Sept. 3, 1856; s. Patrick and Andrienne S.; ed. pub. schs., Boston; spl. courses in Mass. Inst. Tech. and École des Beaux Arts, Paris, France; m. Margaret Hattabough, July 1, 1899. Practicing architecture, Chicago, 1880—; with late Daukmar Adler until 1895, alone, 1895—. Architect for Transportation Bldg., Chicago Expn., 1893, Auditorium (theatre, hotel and office bldg.), Carson, Pirie, Scott & Co. (dept. store), Stock Exchange Bldg. (Chicago), Condict Bldg. (New York), Prudential Bldg. (Buffalo), Terminal Sta. (New Orleans), Wainwright Bldg., Union Trust Bldg. (St. Louis), Grand Opera House Bldg. (Pueblo, Colo.), and many others. Fellow Am. Inst. Architects. Gold medal, Union Centrale des Arts Decoratifs, Paris, 1894. Contbr. of numerous monographs and articles to tech. publs. Address: Chicago, Ill. Died Apr. 14, 1924.

SULLIVAN, Margaret Frances, journalist; b. in Ireland; d. James and Susan (Gorman) Buchanan; m. Alexander Sullivan, 1874. Editorial writer on Chicago daily newspapers and for leading journals of New York and Boston; chief editorial writer Times-Herald, 1895; editorial writer and art critic, Chicago Chronicle, 1901. Contbr. to mags. Sent to Paris, 1889, as special cable corr. of the Asso. Press at Universal Exhibition. Author: Ireland of To-day; Mexico: Picturesque, Political and Progressive (with Mary E. Blake). Home: Chicago, Ill. Died 1903.

SULLIVAN, Michael Crowley, clergyman; b. Sandwich, Mass., May 6, 1865; s. Timothy and Bridget (Crowley) S.; A.B., St. Joseph's (now Columbia) Coll., Dubuque, Ia., 1886; S.T.B., Grand Sem., Montreal, Can., 1888. Ordained priest R.C. Ch., 1889; pastor St. John's Ch., Sioux City, Ia., 1890-91, Waverly, 1891-94; instr. history and mathematics, St. Joseph's Coll., Dubuque, Ia., 1894-1904; chancellor Archdiocese of Dubuque, 1912—, vicar gen., 1923—; made domestic prelate, Nov. 17, 1925. Home: Dubuque, Ia. Died Sept. 21, 1928.

SULLIVAN, Patrick, woolgrower and business man; formerly chmn. Rep. State Com., Wyo.; mem. Rep. Nat. Com. and long a leader in state affairs of Wyo.; apptd. mem. U.S. Senate, Dec. 1929, by Governor Emerson, to fill vacancy occasioned by death of Francis E. Warren. Home: Casper, Wyo. Died Apr. 8, 1935.

SULLIVAN, Patrick F., capitalist; b. County Cork, Ireland, Mar. 16, 1856. Pres. Bay State Ry. Co., Boston & Revere Electric Co., etc.; pres. Commercial Finance Corp., Mut. Finance Corp.; mem. exec. com. Liberty Mut. Co.; dir. Dorchester Mut. Fire Ins. Co., Everett Mills, Old Colony Trust Co., Union Nat. Bank (Lowell, Mass.); trustee Central Savings Bank (Lowell). Republican. Roman Catholic. Home: Lowell, Mass. Died Aug. 29, 1927.

SULLIVAN, Roger C., politician; b. Belvidere, Ill., Feb. 2, 1861; s. Eugene and Mary S.; ed. pub. schs.; m. Helen M. Quinlan, 1885. Pres. Ogden Gas Co., Chicago. Clerk of Probate Ct. of Cook County, Ill., 1890-94; mem. Cook County Dem. Com., 1890—; mem. Dem. Nat. Com., 1904-16. Catholic. Home: Chicago, Ill. Died April 14, 1920.

SULLIVAN, Thomas Crook, army officer; b. Montgomery County, O., Nov. 14, 1833; grad. West Point, 1856; 2d lt. 1st Arty., July 1, 1856; unmarried. 1st lt., Apr. 27, 1861; capt. commissary of subsistence, Aug. 3, 1861; lt. col. vols., Aug. 20, 1862-Jan. 27, 1863, and Mar. 21-Aug. 1, 1865; bvtd. maj. and lt. col., Mar. 13, 1865, for faithful and meritorious services during the war; maj., Apr. 14, 1875; lt. col. asst. commissary gen., July 14, 1890; col., Dec. 27, 1892; brig. gen. commissary gen. of subsistence, Jan. 18, 1897; retired Nov. 14, 1897. Home: Troy, O. Died 1908.

SULLIVAN, Thomas Russell, author; b. Boston, Nov. 21, 1849; s. Rev. Thomas Russell and Charlotte Caldwell (Blake) S.; ed. Boston Latin Sch. and pvt. schs.; m. Lucy Wadsworth, 1899. Lived in Europe, 1870-73; clerk and cashier Lee, Higginson & Co., bankers and brokers, Boston, 1873-88; engaged in lit. work exclusively, 1888—, spending several yrs. in Europe. Mem. Nat. Inst. Arts and Letters. Author: Roses of Shadow, 1885; Day and Night Stories (2 series), 1890, 1893; Tom Sylvester, 1893; Ars et Vita, 1898; The Courage of Conviction, 1902; Lands of Summer, 1908; The Heart of Us, 1912; Boston New and Old, 1912; The Hand of Petrarch, 1913; also several plays. Address: Boston, Mass. Died June 28, 1916.

SULLIVAN, William Cleary, lawyer; b. Washington, D.C., Sept. 25, 1880; s. George North and Kate (Cleary) S.; ed. parochial and pub. schs.; grad. Business High Sch., Washington, 1896; LL.B., Georgetown U. Sch. of Law, 1901; m. Ida Gabrielle Wagener, Nov. 27, 1917. Admitted to practice in Supreme Ct. of D.C., 1901, Ct. of Appeals, 1901, Supreme Ct. of U.S., 1904, also state and federal courts of Maryland, U.S. Treasury Dept., Bd. of Tax Appeals; asso. in practice with Joseph J. Darlington, Washington, 1901, until his death, 1920, succeeding him in practice. Mem. faculty Georgetown U. Sch. of Law, 1910-18, and 1921-32; engaged in gen. practice. Mem. American Bar Assn. (originator of resolution, 1922, for appointment of committee to devise means for more thorough examination into character of applicants for admission to the bar, and mem. com. apptd. for that purpose). Organizer and 1st pres. Catholic Amateur League of U.S. K.C. Home: Chevy Chase, Md. Died Oct. 5, 1935.

SULLIVAN, William Laurence, author, clergyman; b. East Braintree, Mass., Nov. 15, 1872; s. Patrick and Joanna (Desmon) S.; Ph.B., Boston Theol. Sem., 1896; S.T.B., Catholic U., 1899, S.T.L., 1900; D.D., Meadville Theol. Sch., 1917; m. Estelle Throckmorton, 1913. Ordained priest R.C. Ch., 1899; teacher of theology, Washington, 1900-07; joined Unitarian Ch., 1909; pastor Schenectady, N.Y., and N.Y. City; later mission preacher to Unit. Chs. in U.S. and Can.; pastor Ch. of the Messiah, St. Louis, Mo.; pastor Germantown (Pa.) Unitarian Ch. Republican. Author: Letters to Pius X, 1910; The Priest, 1912; From the Gospel to the Creeds, 1917. Address: Philadelphia, Pa. Died Oct. 5, 1935.

SULLOWAY, Alvah Woodbury, mfr.; b. Framingham, Mass., Dec. 25, 1838; s. Israel W. and Adeline (Richardson) S.; ed. Green Mountain Liberal Inst., S. Woodstock, Vt., Barre (Vt.) Acad., Canaan (N.H.) Union Acad.; m. Susan K. Daniell, June 5, 1866; children—Mrs. Alice Thompson, R. W., F. J. Gained practical knowledge of mill work in father's mill; began at 21 with Walter Aiken in mfr. of hosiery at Franklin, and 4 yrs. later became mem. of firm of Sulloway & Daniell; sole propr. of mill, 1869-88; business incorporated, 1888, as the Sulloway Mills (pres. and treas.); one of first to engage in mfr. of full-fashioned hosiery in U.S. after passage of Dingley tariff bill, 1897; identified with the Mayo Knitting Machine Co., 1888—, and organized the Mayo Knitting Machine & Needle Co., 1896; pres. Franklin Nat. Bank, 1879—. Mem. N.H. House of Rep., 1871, 72, 74, 75, Senate, 1891; state railroad commr., 1874-77; mem. N.H. Constl. Conv., 1876, 89; del. to every Dem. Nat. Conv., 1872-96, and mem. Dem. Nat. Com., 1876-96; resigned and retired from politics. Unitarian. Home: Franklin, N.H. Died Apr. 22, 1928.

SULLOWAY, Cyrus Adams, congressman; b. Grafton, N.H., June 8, 1839; s. Greeley and Betsey L. S.; acad. edn. Admitted to bar, 1863; in practice at Manchester, N.H., Jan. 1864—. Mem. N.H. Ho. of Rep., 1872-73, 1887-93; mem. 54th to 62d Congresses (1895-1913), and 64th Congress (1915-17), 1st N.H. Dist. Republican. Address: Manchester, N.H. Died Mar. 11, 1917.

SULLY, Alfred, railroad organizer; b. Ottawa, Can., May 2, 1841; ed. Buffalo, N.Y.; grad. Law School, Cincinnati Coll., 1862; unmarried. Practiced law, Davenport, Ia., 1862-72; banker, New York, 1872-76; in r.r. bus., 1876—; successively pres. Ohio Southern R.R. Co., Richmond & Danville; Richmond and West Point Terminal, and many other small roads; identified for some yrs. with the Phila. & Reading R.R. Co. and its reorganization. Address: Hackettstown, N.J. Died 1909.

SULLY, Daniel (Sullivan), actor; b. Newport, R.I., Nov. 6, 1855; s. Patrick C. and Catharine (McCarthy) Sullivan; ed. Newport, R.I., pub. schs.; m. Louise A. Fox, Feb. 1886. A dancer from boyhood; went on stage 1875, as specialty performer. Wrote and prod. The Corner Grocery, 1884; Daddy Nolan, 1885; Capital Prize, 1886; Con Conroy & Co.; O'Brien, The Contractor; Uncle Bob; prod. The Parish Priest, 1899; Old Mill Stream, 1903; The Chief Justice, 1903; Our Pastor, 1904. Address: Woodstock, N.Y. Died 1910.

SULLY, Daniel J., broker; b. Providence, R.I., Mar. 9, 1861; ed. public schs., Providence, Russell Acad., New Haven, Conn., 1 yr., and Episcopal Acad., Cheshire, Conn.; m. Emma Frances, d. Col. David M. Thompson, 1885. Clerk in Providence and Boston several yrs.; later in business in Providence and New York; inaugurated a "corner" in cotton, 1903 and 1904, in New York; failed Mar. 18, 1904. Mem. N.Y. Stock Exchange, N.Y. Coffee Exchange, N.Y. Cotton Exchange, Liverpool Cotton Assn., New Orleans Cotton Exchange, Chicago Bd. Trade. Dir. Merchants' Trust Co., U.S. Title Guaranty & Indemnity Co. Home: New York, N.Y. Died Sept. 19, 1930.

SULLY, John Murchison, mining engr.; b. Dedham, Mass., July 5, 1868; s. John and Agnes Eliza (Murchison) S.; B.S., Mass. Inst. Tech., 1888; m. Beulah K. Lilly, 1892; children—Kenneth M., Gertrude Agnes, Ruth; m. 2d, Marjorie L. Bloom, Dec. 10, 1924; children—James Allan, John Murchison. With Boston & Mont. Consol. Silver & Gold Mining Co., 1888; asst. supt. Bergen Pt. Chem. Works, Bayonne, N.J., 1888-90; with Nier & Hartford, engrs., Chattanooga, 1890-92, Hebert & Co., Chattanooga, 1892-93; engr. and supt., Chickamauga Coal & Iron Co., 1894-1900; in charge mines, at Joplin, Mo., 1900-01, Hites Cove Mining Co., Mariposa, Calif., 1901-02; exam. mines, Calif. and Mex., 1902-03; asst. supt. Woodstock Iron Co., Anniston, Ala., 1903-04; with Hermosa Copper Co., Hanover, N.M., 1904; made examination and report on properties of Santa Rita (N.M.) Mining Co., 1905-06; examining Mexican properties, 1906-08; cons. engr. and engr. in charge Santa Rita (N.M.) Mining Co., 1908-09; with Chino Copper Co., 1909-24; gen. mgr. same and Ray Consolidated Copper Co., 1924-26; gen. mgr. Chino Mines, N.M. Div., and Nev. Consol. Copper Co.; v.p. and mng. dir. Gallup (N.M.) American Coal Co. Mem. N.M. Council of Defense, World War I. Regent N.M. State Sch. of Mines. Republican. Conglist. Mason, K.P., Elk. Home: Santa Rita, N.M. Died July 15, 1933.

SULZBACHER, Louis, judge; b. Kirchheimbolanden, Bavaria, May 10, 1842; s. Prof. Jacob and Regine (Schwarz) S.; academic and legal edn., Frankfort-on-

Main; m. Pauline Flersheim, Dec. 5, 1869. Admitted to bar, 1870; practiced in N.M., 1870-96; justice Supreme Ct. of Puerto Rico, 1900-04; U.S. dist. judge, Western Dist. of Ind. Ty., 1904-07. Republican. Address: Kansas City, Mo. Died Jan. 17, 1915.

SULZBERGER, Cyrus L., merchant; b. Phila., Pa., July 11, 1858; s. Leopold and Sophia (Lindauer) S.; ed. Central High Sch., Phila.; m. Rachel Hays, May 13, 1884; children—Leopold (dec.), Arthur H., David H. Bookkeeper in Phila. until 1877; then in New York as bookkeeper for N. Erlanger, Blumgart & Co.; admitted as partner in 1891, became pres. upon incorporation, 1902, chmn. bd., 1929—. Anti-Tammany candidate for pres. Borough of Manhattan, 1903. Apptd. by Gov. Hughes mem. State Commn. on Congestion of Population and by Gov. Sulzer (reapptd. by Gov. Glynn) mem. bd. mgrs. Reformatory for Misdemeanants. Trustee of Jewish Agrl. Aid Soc. (pres.); dir. and chmn. Indsl. Removal Office; pres. United Hebrew Charities; chmn. exec. com. Bur. Jewish Social Research; dir. Jewish Publ. Soc. America; mem. exec. com. Am. Jewish Com.; trustee and asso. treas. Fedn. of Jewish Philanthropic Instns.; sec. Am. Jewish Relief Com. (exec. com. joint distribution com.); exec. com. (pres.) New York City Conf. Charities and Correction; pres., mem. exec. com. Nat. Conf. Jewish Social Service; mem. Am. advisory council Hebrew Univ. of Jerusalem. Independent Democrat. Home: New York, N.Y. Died Apr. 30, 1932.

SULZBERGER, Mayer, judge; b. Heidelsheim, Baden, June 22, 1843; s. Abraham and Sophia S.; A.B., Central High Sch., Phila., 1859, A.M., 1864; LL.D., Jefferson Med. Coll., 1896, and Temple U., Phila., 1916; L.H.D., Jewish Theol. Seminary of America, 1913; unmarried. Admitted to bar, 1865; practiced at Phila., 1865-95; judge Ct. of Common Pleas, 1895-1916, presiding judge, 1902-16. Editor of The Occident, a monthly mag. for Jewish knowledge, 1868-69. Author: Am ha-Aretz (the Ancient Hebrew Parliament), 1909; The Polity of the Ancient Hebrews, 1912; The Ancient Hebrew Law of Homicide, 1915. Home: Philadelphia, Pa. Died Apr. 20, 1923.

SULZER, Charles August; b. Roselle, Union County, N.J., Feb. 24, 1879; s. Thomas and Lydia (Jelleme) S.; ed. Pingry Sch., Elizabeth, N.J., Berkeley Acad., N.Y. City; student U.S. Mil. Acad., 1899-1901; m. Gertrude Harrison, Oct. 11, 1905. Served with 4th N.J. Vols., Spanish-Am. War; went to Alaska, 1902, and engaged in mining and merchandising; mem. from 1st Jud. Div., Senate of Alaska Ty., 1914; del. to Congress from Alaska, 1917-19. Democrat. Mason, Elk. Home: Sulzer, Alaska. Died Apr. 16, 1919.

SULZER, William, governor; b. Elizabeth, N.J., Mar. 18, 1863; s. Thomas and Lydia S.; ed. pub. schs. and Columbia Coll. Law Sch.; m. Clara Rodelheim, Jan. 7, 1908. Admitted to N.Y. bar, 1884, in practice, 1884—. Mem. N.Y. Assembly, 1890-94 (speaker 1893, minority leader 1894); mem. 54th to 57th Congresses (1895-1903), 11th N.Y. Dist., and 58th to 62d Congresses (1903-13), 10th Dist.; elected gov. of N.Y., Nov. 5, 1912, for term Jan. 1, 1913-Dec. 31, 1914; impeached as governor and removed from office, Oct. 18, 1913; elected to N.Y. Assembly, Nov. 4, 1913, on Independent ticket. Nominated for President, 1916, by American Party (declined). Presbyn. Mason. Address: New York, N.Y. Died Nov. 6, 1941.

SUMMERBELL, Carlyle, clergyman, educator; b. Springboro, Pa., Nov. 24, 1873; s. Joseph James, D.D., and Martha Alice (Bell) S.; prep. edn., Central High Sch. (Phila.), and Bucknell Acad., Lewisburg, Pa.; A.B., cum laude, Bucknell Coll., 1897, A.M., 1899; student Meadville Theol. Sem., and Div. Sch. U. of Chicago; D.D., Palmer Coll., Albany, Mo., 1906; m. Susannah Emeline Kerr, Jan. 6, 1898; children—Faith (Mrs. John T. Blake), Robert Kerr, Marie (Mrs. Kent L. Pellett). Ordained ministry Christian Ch., 1897; entered ministry Unitarian Ch., 1923; pastorates in Ohio, Ia., Mass. and N.H.; minister Roslindale Ch., Boston, 1926-31, First Unitarian Ch., Tampa, Fla., 1931—; pres. Palmer Coll., 1899-1906. Served as chaplain 133d and 318th Field Arty., A.E.F., World War I, major, chaplain, U.S.A. (Aux. Res.). Mason, Odd Fellow. Editor: Modern Words of Religion, 1915; Public Activities of J. J. Summerbell, 1916. Widely known as debater on religious questions. Dir. of Forum for all Religious radio program. Home: Tampa, Fla. Died May 21, 1935.

SUMMERBELL, Martyn, educator; b. Naples, N.Y., Dec. 20, 1847; s. Rev. Benjamin Ferris and Elizabeth (Martin) S.; A.B., Coll. City of New York, 1871, A.M., 1874; Ph.D., New York U., 1889; D.D., Union Christian Coll., Ind., 1889; LL.D., Elon Coll., N.C., 1909; m. Elizabeth P. Corwith, May 28, 1872; children—Ray, Flora, Grace, Ferris, Laura Frances (dec.), Edith, Sidney Frank. Ordained minister of the Christians, 1867; pastor Ch. Evangel., Brooklyn, 1866-80, Fall River, Mass., 1880-86, St. Paul's Evang. Ch., New York, 1886-88, Main St. Free Bapt. Ch., Lewiston, Me., 1888-98; pres. Palmer Inst. (Starkey Sem.), Lakemont, N.Y., 1898-1935. V.p. Defiance (Ohio) Coll., 1912-31. Sec. N.Y. State Fedn. of Chs. and Christian Workers; mem. Internat. Christian Endeavor; pres. Francis Asbury Palmer Fund, N.Y., May 1903—; a sec. Inter-Ch. Conf. on Fedn., 1905, Federal Council Chs. of Christ in America, 1908. Non-resident prof. ch. history, Elon Coll., N.C., 1911—. Trustee Aged Christian Ministers' Home, Lakemont, 1908—, treas., 1926-35, pres., 1931. Editor Writings of Austin Craig, 1911. Author: Special Services for Ministers, 1885; (with others) People's Bible History, 1895; Religion in College Life, 1913; Faith for the College Man, 1915; Christian Home Training, 1916; Christ in Word and Work, 1920; Rebirth of Europe, 1922; Our Friends in Other Folds, 1929. Contbr. to religious press and lecturer on hist. subjects. Mason. Home: Lakemont, N.Y. Died Sept. 12, 1939.

SUMMERS, Alex, statistician; b. Knox County, Tenn., Apr. 10, 1856; s. George Washington and Mary Ann (Johnson) S.; B.Sc., U. of Tenn., 1876, M.A., 1893; post-grad. work in polit. science, George Washington U., 1895-97; m. Katherine Judson Smith, July 10, 1881 (died 1901); 1 son, Norman. Teacher in country schs., Tenn., 1876-78; reporter, Evening Post, Atlanta, Ga., 1878-80; mem. Bean, Summers & Wallace, pubs. Knoxville Daily Tribune, later pres. Tribune Pub. Co. and editor Tribune, 1880-92; chief of Statis. Div., U.S. Bur. of Edn., Apr. 1894-Mar. 1917; collector and compiler of statistics, div. of rural edn., same bur., 1921-26. Officer N.G.D.C., 1898—; maj. comdg. Divisional Machine Gun Bn., 41st Div. A.E.F., in France and Belgium, 1917-19. Democrat. Baptist. Contbr. to jours. Home: Washington, D.C. Died Jan. 31, 1933.

SUMMERS, James Colling ("Blue Peter"), writer; b. Southgate, Eng., Feb. 19, 1854; s. Rev. James (prof. Chinese, Brit. Mus.) and Jane (Frankland) S.; ed. English schs. and King's College, London, England; m. Emily Simms, 1881. Served in the British merchant service, 1864-72; mate, master, and pilot U.S. steamers, 1872-81; in N.Y. naval militia, 1890-98; commd. ensign U.S.N., 1898; promoted lt. 1899, during Spanish-Am. War; at age of 62, commd., Feb. 9, 1917, lt. jr. grade U.S.N. (Fleet Reserve Class 1), for duty German-Am. War, in 3d Naval Dist., New York; promoted lt., Dec. 1, 1917. Yachting editor New York Tribune, 1899-1917. Drafted, 1897, bill introduced in Congress by Congressman Adolph Meyer, asking for 6 coast defense monitors for use of naval militia. Mem. The Old Guard (New York), Naval and Mil. Order Spanish-Am. War, Vets. Fgn. Wars, U.S. Revolver Assn., Masonic Vets., United Spanish War Vets. Editor "Who Won?" (ann. official yacht record), 1885-96. Editor and pub. Burgee and Pennant (illustrated yachting weekly), 1893-95; also Yachting (monthly mag.), 1895-98. Contbr. to mags. Home: Brooklyn, N.Y. Died Feb. 2, 1929.

SUMMERS, John Edward army officer; b. in Va., Jan. 24, 1822. Apptd. from Va., asst. surgeon U.S.A., Dec. 13, 1847; capt. asst. surgeon, Dec. 13, 1852; maj. surgeon, May 21, 1861; lt. col. med. insp. vols., Feb. 27, 1863; hon. mustered out of vol. service, Oct. 31, 1863; lt. col. surgeon, Mar. 17, 1880; col. surgeon, Jan. 9, 1885; retired by operation of law, Jan. 24, 1886; advanced to rank of brig. gen. retired, by act of Apr. 23, 1904. During Civil War was at Gen. Hosp., Alexandria, Va., 1862-63; hosp. at Memphis, Tenn., 1863; med. dir. Dept. of Tenn. to Oct. 1866, and with Grant's Army in field until Oct. 1865; med. dir. Dept. Dakota to Sept. 1870; post-surgeon to Fortress Monroe, Va., 1870-74; med. dir. Dept. of the Platte, Omaha, Neb., 1874-86. Address: Washington, D. C. Deceased.

SUMMERS, John Edward, surgeon; b. Fort Kearney, Neb., Jan. 2, 1858; s. Gen. John Edward (U.S.A. Med. Corps) and Caroline Jane (Stuart) S.; student U.S. Military Acad., 3 years; M.D., Coll. Phys. and Surg. (Columbia), 1881; studied Vienna, Austria, 2 yrs.; m. Laura M. Hoagland, Apr. 24, 1895. Visiting surgeon, Clarkson Memorial Hosp.; chief of staff and visiting surgeon, Douglas County Hosp.; prof. clin. surgery, U. of Neb., Med. Dept. Acting asst. surgeon, U.S.A., 1881-83; surgeon gen. Neb. N.G., on staff Gov. J. E. Boyd; col. on staff Gov. A. J. Shallenberger. Mem. Bd. Omaha Pub. Library. Fellow A.M.A., Am. Surg. Assn. (v.p. 1916). Democrat. Episcopalian. Author: Modern Treatment of Wounds, 1899; also numerous articles on surg. subjects in trans. of various socs. Contbr. to Binnie's Treatise on Regional Surgery, 1918. Home: Omaha, Neb. Died Feb. 7, 1935.

SUMMERS, John William, congressman; b. Valeene, Orange County, Ind., Apr. 29, 1870; s. James Monroe and Sarah (Tower) S.; grad. Southern Ind. Normal College, 1889; M.D., Ky. Sch. Medicine, 1892; post-grad. work, Louisville Med. Coll., New York, London, Berlin and U. of Vienna; m. Jennie B. Burks, 1897; children—A. Burks, Paul D., Hope, Jean. Began medical practice at Mattoon, Ill.; moved to Walla Walla, Wash., 1908, and engaged in med. practice and as wheat grower and orchardist. Mem. Wash. Ho. of Rep., 1917; mem. 66th to 72d Congresses (1919-33), 4th Washington District. Republican. Mem. Christian Ch. Mem. Co. A, Wash. N.G.; lieut. col. R.C., U.S.A. (med. sect.). Mason, K.P. Home: Walla Walla, Wash. Died Sept. 25, 1937.

SUMMERS, Leland Laflin, consulting engr.; b. Cleves, O., Mar. 6, 1871; s. Charles H. and Emma (Porter) S.; grad. high sch., Highland Park, Ill.; m. Eve H. Brodlique, Apr. 4, 1899; children—Lesley E. (dec.), Llewelyn L. B. Asst. engr. Western Union Telegraph Co., 1889-92; electrician Postal Telegraph Cable Co., Western Div., 1892-94; cons. practice, Chicago, 1894-1914; tech. advisor on munitions purchases, to J. P. Morgan & Co., 1915-17; advisor munitions to U.S. Govt., 1917-18; head of firm L. L. Summers & Co. Mem. War Industries Bd., Washington, D.C., 1917-18; tech. advisor same, and chmn. War Industries Bd. in Europe; tech. advisor Am. Commn. to Negotiate Peace, Paris, France, 1917-18; Am. mem. Inter-Allied Munitions Council, Paris. Decorated Officier Légion d'Honneur (French); Officer Crown of Italy; Commander Order of the Crown (Belgian); D.S.M. Home: Whitestone, N.Y. Died Mar. 10, 1927.

SUMMERS, Maddin, consular service; b. Nashville, Tenn., Feb. 1, 1877; ed. Vanderbilt and Columbian univs. Began as clk. in bank, Nashville; apptd. consular clk., July 27, 1899; vice and deputy consul gen. at Barcelona, 1900-01; detailed to legation at Madrid; duty with 2d Pan-Am. Congress, Mexico City, Nov. 1901; apptd. asst. sec. Am. delegation, Nov. 20, 1901; spl. duty in Spain obtaining evidence for Spanish Treaty Claims Commn., 1902-04; vice consul, Madrid, 1904-05; retired as vice consul Jan. 1905, reappointed Feb. 1905; consular asst., 1908-10; detailed for spl. work on Alsop claim, 1910; chargé d'affaires ad interim, La Paz, Bolivia, 1911; consul at Belgrade, 1911-13, Santos, 1913-15, Sao Paulo, Mar. 2, 1915—. Died May 4, 1918.

SUMMERS, Walter G., educator; b. New York, N.Y., Mar. 23, 1889; s. John A. and Mary E. (McKenna) S.; student St. Francis Xavier Coll., 1903-07; A.B., Woodstock Coll., 1914; Ph.D., Georgetown U., 1919, Gregorian U., Rome, Italy, 1923. Mem. Soc. of Jesus. Prof. of physics, Georgetown U., 1914-19; regent Georgetown Med. and Dental Sch., 1923-30; prof. of physiology, Georgetown U., 1923-30; prof. and head dept. of psychology, Fordham U. Grad. Sch., 1931—; cons. psychologist N.Y. State Police. Dir. Ground Sch. of Aviation, U.S.N., 1917-19. Catholic. Contbr. to ednl. and psychology jours. Inventor of a lie detecting device called the "pathometer." Address: New York, N.Y. Died Sept. 24, 1938.

SUMMERVILLE, Amelia Shaw, actress; b. Kildare, Ireland; d. Thomas Serby and Susan (Wilson) Shaw (Summerville an assumed name); ed. pub. sch., Toronto, Can.; m. Fred Runnells; m. 2d, Max Eugene Stepan. First appearance on stage with Holman's English Opera Co., Toronto, at age of 8; later acted and created many parts under management successively of Charles Frohman, Augustus Pitou, Barton & Collier, William Brady, Fred Whitney, Edward Rice, and in stock co. of New York Theatre, Sire Bros., mgrs. Married when quite young; divorced in New York, with full custody of two children. Among notable parts created by her are: Baby Malone in Irish opera, Brian Boru; Rosetta, the Mountain Maid, in Adonis; Trilby and Mme. Sans Géne, in burlesque of The Merry World; The Widow in Cumberland '61; Polly Piston, in Jane; Kitty Marshall, in the Cotton King. Also played and sang all the contralto rôles in Gilbert & Sullivan's operas; ballet dancer with Howard Langrische, of Caril's Black Crook Co., 3 yrs. Season 1905, Garrick Theatre, Chicago, with Shubert Bros., playing Mrs. Shimmering Black in The Earl and the Girl; 1907, played with Twenty Days in the Shade Co., Savoy Theatre, New York; 1909, with Al Woods Co., New York Theatre; 1910, created the part of Teriffa, the lion tamer in He Came from Milwaukee, Casino Theatre, New York; played Mrs. William Smith in "When Dreams Come True," Garrick Theatre, Chicago, 1913. Starred in motion pictures, Frohman Amusement Corp., 1915. Author: Why Be Fat, 1916. Address: New York, N.Y. Died Jan. 21, 1934.

SUMNER, Charles Allen, lawyer; b. Great Barrington, Mass., Aug. 2, 1835; s. Increase and Pluma Barston S.; academic edn. (A.M., Trinity Coll., Hartford). Became shorthand reporter and lawyer; q.m. U.S. vols., and later commissioned col. 1st Nevada inf. vols.; mem. and pres. pro tem. Nevada senate; congressman-at-large from Calif., 1883-85. Edited several daily papers, including the Sacramento Sentinel, San Francisco Mirror, and Gold Hill (Nev.) News; mng. editor San Francisco Herald. Lecturer on Scenes and Incidents in Foreign Lands, Cremation; etc. Author: A Government Postal Telegraph, 1870; Compilation of Speeches in Congress and Elsewhere, on a Genuine Postal Telegraph, 1870; Poems, 1877; Shorthand and Reporting, 1882; Golden Gate Sketches, 1884; Notes of Travel in Sweden, 1885; Cremation, 1900; etc. Residence: Oakland, Calif. Died 1903.

SUMNER, Charles Ralsey, M.D.; b. Gilbertville, Otsego County, N.Y., Mar. 12, 1852; s. Dr. Charles and Mary J. (White) S.; A.B., U. of Rochester, 1874, A.M., 1877; M.D., New York Homœ. Med. Coll.,

1877; m. Julia L. Parsons, Oct. 11, 1877 (now dec.); children—Louise (dec.), Marjorie (dec.), Cyril, Grace (dec.), Estelle. Health commr. City of Rochester, 1894-1900. Pres. Rochester Acad. Science; pres. staff Rochester Homœ. Hosp. Presbyn. Republican. Commr. Mt. Hope Cemetery. Mem. Dist. Exemption Bd., 1917. Address: Rochester, N.Y. Died Jan. 27, 1928.

SUMNER, Edwin Vose, brig. gen. U.S.A.; b. Carlisle, Pa., Aug. 16, 1835; s. Maj. Gen. Edwin Vose and Hannah W. (Forster) S.; brother of Samuel Storrow S.; m. Margaret, d. Gen. John Forster, July 18, 1866. Apptd. from N.Y., 2d lt. 1st U.S. Cav., Aug. 5, 1861; 1st lt., Nov. 12, 1861; maj. a.d.c. vols., May 19, 1863; hon. mustered out of vol. service, Aug. 15, 1863; capt. U.S.A., Sept. 23, 1863; col. 1st N.Y. Mounted Rifles, Sept. 8, 1864; bvtd. gen. vols., Mar. 28, 1865; hon. mustered out of vol. service, Nov. 29, 1865; maj. 5th U.S. Cav., Mar. 4, 1879; lt. col. 8th Cav., Apr. 15, 1890; col. 7th Cav., Nov. 10, 1894; brig. gen. vols., May 27, 1898; hon. discharged from vols., Feb. 24, 1899; brig. gen. U.S.A., Mar. 27, 1899; retired at own request, over 30 yrs.' service, Mar. 30, 1899. Participated in Modoc, Nez Perces and Bannock wars, campaign in southeast Nev., Sioux campaign, 1890-91. Home: Syracuse, N.Y. Died Aug. 24, 1912.

SUMNER, Frederick Azel, clergyman, educator; b. Eastford, Conn., Mar. 26, 1864; s. Azel Cunningham and Sarah Jane (Hanks) S.; B.A., Oberlin, 1891; grad. Hartford Theol. Sem., 1894; M.A., Yale, 1908; m. Mary E. Buchanan, July 27, 1898. Ordained Congl. ministry, 1894; pastor Glenwood (Minn.) Union Ch., 1894-97, Little Falls, Minn., 1897-1902, Pilgrim Ch., Minneapolis, 1902-07, 1st Ch., Milford, Conn., 1907-16; pres. Talladega Coll. (colored), 1916—. Republican. Home: Talladega, Ala. Died Dec. 26, 1933.

SUMNER, George Watson, rear admiral U.S.N.; b. Constantine, Mich., Dec. 31, 1841; s. Dr. Watson and Hester Ann (Welling) S.; apptd. to U.S. Naval Acad. from Ky., Sept. 20, 1858, grad. 1861; m. Maudthilde Willis, Feb. 20, 1886. Lt., Aug. 1, 1862; lt. comdr., July 25, 1866; comdr., June 13, 1876; capt., Oct. 2, 1891; rear admiral, Mar. 3, 1899. Served on Colo., W. Gulf Blockading Squadron, 1861; Mortar Flotilla, 1862; participated in bombardments of Fts. Jackson and St. Philip; engagements with Vicksburg batteries, 1862; West Gulf Blockading Squadron, 1863-64; Pensacola, 1864; Naval Acad., May-July, 1864; Massasoit, N. Atlantic Blockading Squadron, 1864-65; comd. Massasoit, Jan. 1865, during the engagement with the Confederate ironclads and batteries at Dutch Gap, James River, Va.; De Soto, Atlantic, 1866-67; Franklin, European Squadron, 1868-71; Hydrographic Office, 1872-77; comd. Monocacy, 1877-80; spl. duty, Washington, 1880-81; Bur. of Ordnance, 1881-86; Naval War Coll., 1887; Torpedo duty, and at Naval War Coll., 1888; comd. Galena, 1888-90; equipment officer, Navy Yard, New York, 1891-93; comd. Baltimore, Feb.-May 1893; gen. insp. of Columbia, 1893; comd. Columbia, 1894-95; comd. Monadnock, 1896-97; capt. of yard, Navy Yard, New York, 1897-99; commandant Naval Sta., Port Royal, 1899-1901, Navy Yard, Phila., 1901-02; comdr.-in-chief S. Atlantic Squadron, 1902-03; retired, Dec. 31, 1903. Home: Patchogue, N.Y. Died Feb. 20, 1924.

SUMNER, Guilford Herman, physician; b. Marengo, McHenry County, Ill., Nov. 11, 1857; s. George Halda and Sarah (Phillips) S.; B.S., Valparaiso (Ind.) U., 1892; M.D., Med. Dept., Iowa State U., 1896; spl. instruction in pathology and bacteriology, same, 1896; life diploma to teach in Ia. schs.; m. Isabel Crinklaw, Apr. 4, 1878 (died 1912). Taught sch., Delaware County, Ia., for a number of yrs.; practiced medicine, Waterloo, Ia., 1896-1910; sec. Ia. State Bd. of Health and Med. Examiners, Jan. 1, 1910—; health officer, Waterloo, Ia., 1901-09. Baptist. Mason. Home: Des Moines, Ia. Deceased.

SUMNER, John Osborne, prof. history; b. Boston, Mass., Nov. 23, 1863; s. Austin and Catharine Osborne (Sargent) S.; A.B., Harvard, 1887; post-grad. work at Berlin, Germany, and in Italy; m. Mary Shreve Hutchinson, May 24, 1900 (died 1915); children—Roger, Robert Emlen, John Osborne; m. 2d, Margaret Paulding, June 8, 1921. Became instr. history, 1894, prof. history, Mass. Inst. Tech., 1907-33 (resigned). Courses dealt with history of civilization and of art and were primarily intended for students in dept. of architecture. Fellow Am. Acad. Arts and Sciences. Address: Boston, Mass. Died Feb. 20, 1938.

SUMNER, Samuel Storrow, army officer; b. Carlisle, Pa., Feb. 6, 1842; s. Maj. Gen. Edwin Vose and Hannah W. (Forster) S.; ed. at army posts, pvt. sch., Syracuse, N.Y., and Walnut Hill, Geneva, N.Y.; m. Frederica N. Bennett. Apptd. from N.Y., 2d lt. 2d (later 5th) Cav., June 11, 1861; promoted through grades to brig. gen. vols., May 4, 1898; maj. gen., Sept. 7, 1898; brig. gen. regular army, Feb. 4, 1901; maj. gen., July 26, 1903; retired, Feb. 6, 1906. Bvtd. 1st lt., June 1, 1862, for battle of Fair Oaks, Va.; capt., Sept. 17, 1862, for Antietam; maj., Mar. 13, 1865, for campaign against Vicksburg; lt. col., Feb. 27, 1890, for action against Indians at Summit Springs, Colo., July 11, 1869. Comd. cav. brigade and div. in Cuban campaign, 1898; mil. attaché Am. Embassy, London, 1899-1900; comd. brigade in China during uprising, 1900; comd. dist. Southern Luzon, 1901-02, dist. Northern Luzon, 1902; comd. Dept. Mindanao, P.I., 1902-03; comd. Dept. of the Mo., 1903-04, Southwestern Div., 1904-05, Div. of the Pacific, 1905-06. Silver star citation, Battle of San Juan, Cuba, July 1, 1898. Home: Brookline, Mass. Died July 26, 1937.

SUMNER, Walter Taylor, bishop; b. Manchester, N.H., Dec. 5, 1873; s. Charles Davenport and Rintha (Thompson) S.; B.S., Dartmouth, 1898; grad. Western Theol. Sem., Chicago, 1904; D.D., Northwestern, 1912, Dartmouth, 1913, and Western Theological Sem., 1915; hon. Phi Beta Kappa, Dartmouth Coll., 1933; m. Myrtle Mitchell, Jan. 1, 1918; children—Elizabeth Ann, Mary Jane. Deacon, 1903, priest, 1904, P.E. Ch.; sec. to bishop of Chicago; 1903-06; pastor St. George's Ch., Chicago, 1904-06; dean, Cathedral SS. Peter and Paul and supt. City Missions of the Episcopal Ch., Chicago, 1906-15; consecrated bishop of Oregon, Jan. 6, 1915. Mem. Chicago Bd. of Edn., 1909-15; chmn. Chicago Municipal Vice Commn., 1st v.p. and exec. com. Juvenile Protective Assn. and chmn. gen. advisory and west side advisory coms. United Charities; pres. Wendell Phillips Social Settlement (for colored persons), Men's Inst. Chicago; also sec. Ch. Assn. in the Interests of Labor; trustee Ch. Home for Aged Persons; chmn. Diocesan Social Service Commn., Tribune Lodging House for Unemployed Men, both of Chicago; mem. joint com. on Payment of Prisoners, Loan Sharks, Child Labor and as mem. advisory com. Citizens' Health Assn., Chicago Children's Benefit League, Ill. Industrial Home for Girls; state rep. Internat. Prison Congress; mem. advisory council Boy Scouts America, and mem. advisory bd. and chaplain, Three Arts Club of Chicago; etc. Chaplain 1st Ill. Cav., I.N.G., until 1915. Mem. bd. of dirs. Ore. Social Hygiene Soc., Pub. Welfare Soc. Ore. Tuberculosis Assn.; mem. Honor Court of Boy Scouts; chaplain Police Reserves; pres. Good Samaritan Hosp., St. Helen's Hall. Address: Portland, Ala. Died Sept. 4, 1935.

SUMNER, William Graham, univ. prof.; b. Paterson, N.J., Oct. 30, 1840; s. Thomas and Sarah (Graham) S.; grad. Yale, 1863; studied in Univs. of Göttingen, Germany, and Oxford, Eng.; LL.D., U. of E. Tenn.; m. Jeannie Whittemore Elliott, Apr. 17, 1871. Tutor Yale, 1866-1909; took orders in P.E. Church, and was asst. Calvary Ch., New York, and rector Ch. of the Redeemer, Morristown, N.J., until 1872; prof. polit. and social science, Yale, 1872—. Especially prominent as a free trader and advocate of the gold standard. Author: A History of American Currency, 1874; What Social Classes Owe to Each Other, 1882; Collected Essays in Political and Social Sciences, 1883; Protectionism, 1885; Lives of Andrew Jackson; Alexander Hamilton and Robert Morris, 1891; The Financier and Finances of the Revolution, 1892; A History of Banking in the U.S., 1896; Folkways, 1907. Address: New Haven, Conn. Died 1910.

SUNDAY, William Ashley, evangelist; b. Ames, Ia., Nov. 19, 1863; s. William and Mary Jane (Cory) S.; ed. high sch., Nevada, Ia.; student Northwestern; D.D., Westminster Coll., 1912; m. Helen A. Thompson, Sept. 5, 1888; children—Helen Edith (Mrs. M. P. Haines, dec.), George Marquis, William Ashley (dec.), Paul Thompson. Professional baseball player, 1883-90, in the Chicago, Pittsburgh and Phila. teams of the Nat. League. Asst. sec. Y.M. C.A., Chicago, 1891-95; evangelist, 1896—; received from 1,000 to 5,000 converts per month, 1904-07, and later engaged continuously in evangelistic services, in principal cities of U.S. Ordained Presbyn. ministry by Chicago Presbytery, Apr. 15, 1903; elected Apr. 1918 by Chicago Presbytery, as del. to Gen. Assembly Presbyn. Ch. U.S.A., Columbus, O., May 1918. Prohibitionist. Said to have preached to more people (estimated at 80,000,000) than any other man in the history of Christianity, and credited with being greatest single influence in arousing sentiment which resulted in the overthrow of the saloon in U.S. Address: Winona Lake, Ind. Died Nov. 6, 1935.

SUNDERLAND, Eliza Read, writer, lecturer; b. Huntsville, Ill., 1839; d. Amasa and Jane (Henderson) Read; grad. Mt. Holyoke (Mass.) Sem., 1865; Ph.B., U. of Mich., 1889, Ph.B., 1892; m. Jabez Thomas Sunderland, Dec. 7, 1871. Prin. high sch., Aurora, Ill., 1866-71; teacher high schs., Chicago, and Ann Arbor, Mich., 1877-98; asso. editor Ill. Social Science Jour., Chicago, 1878; pres. Women's Western Unitarian Conf., 1882-87; dir. Nat. Soc. Advancement of Women, 1885-95; prominent speaker at the World's Parliament of Religions, and also Woman's Congress, Chicago, 1893; mem. Sch. Bd., Hartford, Conn., 1907—; preached (not ordained) and lectured extensively. Author: Stories from Genesis, 1890; Heroes and Heroines, 1895; Centennial Memorial to James Martineau, 1905; also various addresses and articles in mags. and newspapers. Unitarian. Address: Hartford, Conn. Died 1910.

SUNDERLAND, Jabez Thomas, clergyman; b. Yorkshire, Eng., Feb. 11, 1842; s. Thomas and Sarah (Broadhead) S.; A.B., U. of Chicago, 1867, A.M., 1869; B.D., Bapt. Union Theol. Seminary, Ill., 1870; D.D., Tufts Coll., Mass., 1914; m. Eliza J. Read, Dec. 7, 1871; children—Gertrude, Edson R., Florence. Ordained Baptist ministry, 1870; pastor Milwaukee, Wis., 1871-72, Northfield Mass. (Unitarian ch.), 1872-76, Chicago, 1876-78, Ann Arbor, Mich., 1878-98, Oakland, Calif., 1898-99, London, Eng., 1900-01, Toronto, Can., 1901-07, Hartford, Conn., 1907-11, Ottawa, Can., 1912-13, Poughkeepsie, N.Y., 1911-27. General sec. Western Unitarian Conf. and western agt. Am. Unitarian Assn., 1885-86. Went to India, 1895-96, on commn. from British Unitarian Assn., to study and report upon the ednl., social, and religious conditions of the Indian people; non-resident lecturer on sociology and the religion of India in theol. schs., at Meadville, Pa., and Canton, N.Y.; Billings lecturer of Am. Unitarian Assn. to Japan, China, P.I., Ceylon and India, 1913-14. Pres. All-India Theistic Conf., 1913-14. Editor of the Unitarian Monthly, 1886-95. Pres. India Home Rule League of America, and editor of Young India (monthly, New York), 1919-20. Author: A Rational Faith, 1878; What Is the Bible?, 1878; The Liberal Ministry, 1889; Home Travel in Bible Lands, 1894; The Origin and Growth of the Bible, 1894; A College Town Pulpit, 1895; Liberal Religion in India, 1896; A Pacific Coast Pulpit, 1898; Travel and Life in Palestine, 1900; James Martineau, 1905; The Causes of Famine in India, 1906; The Bible and Bible Country, 1900; Oh, to Be Rich and Young, 1910; The Orient and Liberal Religion, 1914; Rising Japan, 1917; Channing, 1920; Because Men Are Not Stones, 1923; India, America and World-Brotherhood, 1924 (published in Madras, India); Evolution and Religion, 1925; India in Bondage, 1928, also French and Japanese edits., 1933; The Truth About India, 1930; Eminent Americans Whom India Should Know, 1933. Address: Ann Arbor, Mich. Died Aug. 13, 1936.

SUNDT, Edwin Einar, clergyman; b. Helsingfors, Finland, Dec. 16, 1892; s. Anders and Hanna (Johanson) S.; Diploma, Crozer Theol. Sem., 1924, B.D., 1929, Th.M., 1930; U. of Pa., 1923-24; B.R.E., Hartford Sch. of Religious Edn., 1929; m. Alice Hazel Gautreaux, Dec. 16, 1914; children—Dorothy Hazel, Valery Edwin, Rosa-Ann; m. 2d, Alice Hazel Amidon, Feb. 25, 1933. Arrived U.S., 1911. Clerk dry goods store, 1911-16, shoe business, 1916-21; ordained ministry Bapt. Ch., 1924; pastor Federated Chs. of Willington, 1924-29; nat. dir. of town and country work, Am. Bapt. Home Mission Soc., 1929-33; pastor Pleasant View Ch., Pawtucket, 1933—; lecturer Crozer Theol. Sem., 1930-32, Colgate Rochester Div. Sch., 1933. Republican. Baptist. Mason. Author: (with A. J. William Myers) The Country Church as it Is, 1930; The Country Church and our Generation, 1932; A History of the Baptist Church, 1932; Immigrants in Rural Areas, 1933; etc. Contbr. to various religious journals and publs. Home: Pawtucket, R.I. Deceased.

SUPER, Charles William, author. educator; b. Pottsville, Pa., Sept. 12, 1842; s. Henry and Mary (Diener) S.; A.B., Dickinson Coll., 1866; studied Tübingen, Germany, 1869-71; Ph.D., Ill. Wesleyan, 1874; A.M., Syracuse U., 1883; LL.D., Dickinson, 1894; m. Mary Louise Clewell, Dec. 24, 1867 (died 1913); children—Corinne Elizabeth (Mrs. W. M. Stine), Frank Henry, Ralph Clewell, Frederic Paul (dec.). Prof. langs., Cincinnati Wesleyan Coll., 1872-78; studied law, 1878-79; prof. Greek, 1882-1907, acting pres., 1883-84, pres., 1884-1901, Ohio U.; resigned, 1907, to devote attention to business and lit. work. Joint editor The Journal of Pedagogy, 1887-93. Made school inspection tour, England, France, Germany, Switzerland, 1882; again in Europe, 1896, 1903. Author: Weil's Order of Words in the Ancient Languages Compared with that of Modern Languages, 1887; A History of the German Language, 1893; Between Heathenism and Christianity, 1899; Wisdom and Will in Education, 1902; A Liberal Education, 1907; Plutarch on Education, 1907; German Idealism and Prussian Militarism (translated into the Czecho-Slovak lang.), 1916; Pan-Prussianism, 1918; Prohibition and Democracy, 1921; A Pioneer College and Background (Dickinson), 1923; A Pioneer College and Its Background (Ohio U.), 1924. Contbr. to about 20 ednl., philos. and hist. periodicals in English and German. Methodist. Home: Athens, O. Died Oct. 9, 1939.

SURETTE, Thomas Whitney; b. Concord, Mass., Sept. 7, 1861; s. Louis A. and Frances J. (Shattuck) S.; ed. pub. and pvt. schs., Concord, Mass.; spl. student Harvard, class of '94; m. Ada Elizabeth Miles, June 20, 1899. Lecturer on music, Graduate Sch. of Edn., Harvard; apptd. staff lecturer on music, Oxford U., 1907; dir. of music, Cleveland Mus. of Art; dir. of music Bryn Mawr (Pa.) Coll., 1921. Founder and dir. Concord (Mass.) Summer Sch. of Music. Composer: (operetta) Priscilla, or, The Pilgrim's Proxy; Dramatic Ballad for soli, chorus and orchestra, The Eve of St. Agnes, etc. Author: The Appreciation of Music (with D. G. Mason); The Development of Symphonic Music; Music and Life. Co-Author: The Significance of the Fine Arts; The Effective College, 1927. Contbr. to reviews and mags. on musical topics. Address: Concord, Mass. Died May 19, 1941.

SUTER, Charles Russell, brig. gen. U.S.A.; b. New York, May 5, 1842; s. Alexander F. S. (U.S.A.).

Grad. U.S. Mil. Acad., 1862; 2d lt., June 17, 1862, 1st lt., Mar. 3, 1863, corps of engrs. (bvt. capt., July 18, 1863, "for gallant and meritorious services during siege of Morris Island, S.C."); capt. corps of engrs., June 17, 1864 (bvt. maj., Mar. 13, 1865, "for faithful and meritorious services during war"); maj., Oct. 10, 1871; lt. col., Jan. 10, 1887; col., Oct. 12, 1895, corps of engrs.; brig. gen. and retired by operation of law, May 5, 1906. After Civil War engaged as asst. engr. on survey of upper Miss. River, 1873-76, and on various engring. works, river commns., engr. bds.; in charge fortifications and river and harbor works in vicinity of Boston; later at New York. Address: Brookline, Mass. Died Aug. 7, 1920.

SUTHERLAND, Evelyn Greenleaf, newspaper and mag. writer, playwright; b. Cambridge, Mass.; d. James and Rachel (Arnold) Baker; ed. private schs., Boston and Geneva, Switzerland; m. John Preston Sutherland, M.D., Mar. 10, 1879. For many yrs. dramatic editor and editorial writer, Boston Commonwealth; on dramatic staff Boston Transcript, 1888-96; dramatic critic, Boston Journal, 1897-98. Author: Po' White Trash, and Other One-Act Dramas, 1899; In Office Hours, and Other Vaudeville Sketches, Boston, 1899; also many one-act plays in professional use. Also (with Gen. Charles King) four-act army drama, "Ft. Frayne." Adapter (with author) of Booth Tarkington's Monsieur Beaucaire. Co-author: (with Beulah Marie Dix) The Breed of the Treshams; Boy O'Carroll; The Road to Yesterday; Young Fernald. Contbr. tales, poems, essays to McClure's, Puck, Life, Smart Set, Criterion, etc. Won prize in McClure short story competition, 1894, with army story, Dikkon's Dog. Address: Boston, Mass. Died 1908.

SUTHERLAND, John Preston, dean med. sch.; b. Charlestown, Mass., Feb. 9, 1854; s. John and Mary (Ross) S.; pub. sch. edn., Boston; M.D., Boston U., 1879; m. Evelyn Greenleaf Baker, Mar. 10, 1879. Prof. anatomy, 1888-1908, prof. theory and practice, 1908—, and dean Med. School, 1900—. Boston U. Editor New England Medical Gazette, 1883-97, 1906-09; mem. med. bd. and trustee Mass. Homœ. Hosp.; mem. cons. bd. Westborough Insane Hosp., Worcester Homœ. Hosp. Author: Hints on Urinary Analysis, 1895. Home: Boston, Mass. Died Feb. 21, 1941.

SUTHERLAND, William A., lawyer; b. Hopewell, N.Y., May 30, 1849; s. Rev. Andrew and Mary (McLean) S.; ed. Genesee Wesleyan Sem., 1865-69, and Genesee Coll., Lima, N.Y., 1869-70; m. Inez L. Jackson, Mar. 6, 1878 (died 1905); m. 2d, Clara E. Bowen, Oct. 9, 1906. Grand master of Masons, N.Y., 1897-99; pres. Rochester Bar Assn., 1898; mem. Rep. Nat. Com., 1892-96; del. Rep. Nat. Conv., 1896; del. to every Rep. State Conv. for yrs.; counsel for Rep. party in senatorial election cases, 1891, reapportionment cases, 1892; asso. counsel to Lexow Com., 1894; Rep. nominee for atty. gen., N.Y., 1891; corp. counsel, Rochester, 1902-03; counsel to spl. tax commn., 1906; campaign speaker, platform orator. Author: Addresses, 1899 (N.Y. Grand Lodge). Residence: Rochester, N.Y. Died 1908.

SUTHERLAND, William James, normal sch. pres.; b. Cherry Valley, Ill., Apr. 14, 1865; s. James and Frances (Dunwell) S.; grad. State Normal U., Normal, Ill., 1892; Ph.B., U. of Wis., 1901, M.A., 1909; m. Vinnie M. Robbins, July 18, 1894. Supt. schs., at Oregon and Charleston, Ill., 1892-1900; prof. geography and geology, State Normal Sch., Macomb, Ill., 1902-08; prin. City Normal Sch., St. Paul, Minn., 1908-09; pres. State Normal Sch., Platteville, Wis., Sept. 1909—. Republican. Conglist. K.T. Author: The Teaching of Geography, 1909; Geography of Indiana, 1910; Geography of Kansas, 1910; Practical Exercises in Geography (with Chester M. Sanford), 1915. Contbg. editor to Journal of Geography; lecturer on ednl. subjects. Home: Platteville, Wis. Died Dec. 9, 1915.

SUTRO, Florence Clinton, founder and 1st pres. Nat. Federation Musical Clubs and Societies (incorporated in Ill., Jan. 1898); b. in England, May 1, 1865; d. Hon. Harry W. and Frances (Greenwood) Clinton; pvt. edn.; grad. Grand Conservatory of Music, New York (Mus. Doc., same—first woman in U.S. to receive this title); 1st woman law student in a univ. in New York (valedictorian); spl. courses in art, Columbia; m. Theodore Sutro, Oct. 1, 1884. Society leader and musician; officer Coll. Women's Club; mem. Sorosis; life mem. Vassar Aid Soc.; hon. pres. Grand Conservatory Alumnæ; mem. Portia Club, Soc. of Am. Authors, Drawing Room Club, Press Club, Women's Legal Ednl. Soc., Patria, Soc. for Prevention Cruelty to Children, Soc. for Improving Condition of Poor, Riding Club, Women's Auxiliary to Guild for Crippled Children; pres. Hosp. for Crippled Children; del. from St. Michael's Episcopal Ch. in Diocesan Com. for Extension of the Cathedral and Pro-Cathedral Work; received gold medal and award of honor for work in behalf of women in music, and silver medal and award of honor for work for women in study of legal jurisprudence from Atlanta Expn., Ga. Especially prominent in organizations and as writer for promotion of advance of women as composers and musicians; patron Am. Sch. of Opera, and People's Symphony Concerts. Composed national anthem, "America." Author: Women in Music, 1899; (compiler) Milestones on Life's Pathway, 1905. Address: New York, N.Y. Died 1906.

SUTRO, Oscar, lawyer; b. Victoria, Can., June 18, 1874; s. Emil and Adelaide (Zadig) S.; brought by parents to U.S., 1875; B.L., U. of Calif., 1894, M.L., 1896; m. Mary Ellen O'Sullivan, Aug. 4, 1904; children—Mary Ann (Mrs. Balfour Bowen), Barbara, Oscar. Law clk. Pierson & Mitchell, San Francisco, 1895-1901; mem. Calif. Assembly, 1901; mem. Pillsbury & Sutro, Manila, P.I., 1901-04, Pillsbury, Madison & Sutro, San Francisco, 1904—; dir. Standard Oil Co. of Calif., 1926—; also v.p. and counsel, 1930—; trustee Calamba Sugar Estate; v.p. Pampanga Sugar Mills. Republican. Home: Piedmont, Calif. Died June 9, 1935.

SUTRO, Richard, banker; b. N.Y. City, Dec. 24, 1863; s. Bernhard and Pauline (Josephthal) S.; ed. Coll. City of N.Y., 1883; m. Ella H., d. Richard R. Hunt, Jan. 8, 1889; children—Mrs. May Rothschild, Mrs. Edith H. S. Ward. Chmn. finance com., mem. exec. com., dir. Conn. Electric Service Co., Conn. Light & Power Co.; chmn. Conn. Electric Syndicate; dir. N.Y., Westchester & Boston R.R. Co., Pierce Oil Corp., Pierce Petroleum Corp., Pittsburgh & W.Va. Ry. Co., Southern Agrl. Chem. Co., Tenn. Copper Co., Tenn. Copper & Chem. Corp., West Side Belt R.R.; mem. spl. com. D.&R.G. Western R.R. Home: Port Chester, N.Y. Died Aug. 3, 1930.

SUTRO, Theodore, lawyer; b. Aachen (Aix la-Chapelle), Prussia, Mar. 14, 1845; s. Emanuel and Rosa (Warendorff) S.; brought to U.S., 1850; A.B., Harvard, 1871; LL.B., Columbia, 1874; m. Florence Edith Clinton, Oct. 1, 1884 (died 1906). Admitted to bar, 1874, and began practice in N.Y. City; in 1887 saved the interests of the Sutro Tunnel Co. (owning and operating the Sutro Tunnel in Nev.) and organized its successor, the Comstock Tunnel Co., of which was 1st pres., and managed its affairs until 1894; commr. of taxes, New York, 1895-98, sr. member law firm Sutro & Wright, 1902-23; later advisory counsel of firm Lorenz & Lorenz. Mem. commn. in celebration of the 300th anniversary of Henry Hudson's discovery of the Hudson River in 1609; etc. Active as a leader for N.Y. State to purchase homestead and farm of Gen. Nicholas Herkimer, hero of the Revolutionary War, and later pres. of this Homestead Assn. Author: The Sutro Tunnel Co. and the Sutro Tunnel, 1887; Thirteen Chapters of American History represented by the Edward Moran Series of Thirteen Historical Marine Paintings, 1905. Pub. poems and letters to his wife, compiled by her under title: "Milestones on Life's Pathway." Writer on taxation, corp. law, med. jurisprudence, and mining, also gen. lit. and poetry; pub. speaker, in English or German langs. Prominent in German-Am. matters; pres. and editor Deutsches Journal and pres. German Publ. Soc. Collector of paintings, specially of members of the Moran family artists; loaned to Met. Mus. of Art, 1904-06, and to the Nat. Mus. (Smithsonian Instn.), the 13 famous Am. hist. marine paintings by Edward Moran. Home: New York, N.Y. Died Aug. 28, 1927.

SUTTON, (Eli) Ransome, writer; b. Greeley, Kan., Aug. 25, 1869; s. Ottawa and Elizabeth (Poplin) S.; grad. Kan. State Normal Sch., 1888; LL.B., U. of Mich., 1891, M.L. and B.S., 1892; m. Grace Louise Williams, July 1, 1896; children—Dorothy Hathaway (Mrs. Edward Clarke Ingraham), Anita Elizabeth (Mrs. Edward Hillebrandt Whitehouse). Practiced law in Detroit, 1892-1903; at request of the mayor of Detroit, visited the delta of the Orinoco River in S. America and reported location of a large deposit of asphalt; reported the last third of the Boer War in S.Africa for an American newspaper syndicate; with Los Angeles Times, 1920—, writer and editor science page (weekly); dir. A. B. Williams Co., Sodus, N.Y. Regent U. of Mich., 1898-1900. Republican. Author: The Passing of the Fourteen, 1916; Traction Development, 1906; Highlands of the Tropics (Mexico), 1905. Contbr. scientific articles and fiction. Address: Los Angeles, Calif. Died Oct. 14, 1934.

SUTTON, Rhoades Stansbury, physician, surgeon; b. Indiana, Pa., July 8, 1841; s. James and Sarah (Stansbury) S.; grad. Washington and Jefferson Coll., 1862, A.M., 1865; med. dept., U. of Pa., 1865; LL.D., U. of Wooster, O., 1886; m. Josephine, d. Hon. James McCullough, Apr. 17, 1867. In practice, 1865—. Fellow Am., Brit., and Internat. Gynecol. socs.; prof.-elect of operative surgery, Baltimore, 1880, and of gynecology, Cleveland, 1886; pres. Am. Acad. Medicine, Miss. Valley Med. Soc., and Pittsburg Gynecol. Soc. Maj. chief surgeon in Spanish-Am. War. Contbr. to the Am. System of Gynecology (1st edit.); to New York Med. Journal, Internat. Jour. of Surgery; Med. Review of Reviews; Med. News; the Med. and Surg. Reporter; Am. Gynecol. and Obstet. Journal, and Journal of the Am. Med. Assn. Residence: Pittsburgh, Pa. Died 1906.

SUTTON, W(illiam) Henry, lawyer; b. Haddonfield, N.J., Sept. 11, 1835; s. Rev. Henry and Anne (Craig) S.; B.A., Wesleyan U., Conn., 1857, M.A., 1860; studied law, Albany Law Sch., 1860-61, and with Hon. William M. Meredith, Phila., 1861-63; LL.D., Southern Temperance U., 1900; D.C.L., Dickinson Coll., 1908; m. Hannah C. Anderson, June 25, 1872 (direct descendant of Major Patrick Anderson, who was with Col. Anthony Wayne's regt.). Teacher in Asylum for the Deaf Mutes, Hartford, Conn., 1857-60; admitted to Pa. bar, 1863, in practice in Phila., N.J., and surrounding country, 1863—. Auditor and mem. Sch. Bd., Lower Merion, 1880-83; mem. Pa. State Senate, 1882-86. Mem. M.E. Social Union of Phila., Pub. Edn. Assn., Am. Acad. Polit. and Social Science. Author of various S.S. publs. and articles on Masonic history. Home: Haverford, Pa. Died Mar. 14, 1913.

SUYDAM, John Howard, clergyman; b. Brooklyn, Oct. 1, 1832 (descendant Sarah Rapalje, first white child born in New Netherlands); grad. Erasmus Hall, Flatbush, Rutgers Coll., A.M., D.D.; Theol. Sem., New Brunswick, N.J.; m. Sarah Augusta Van Arsdale; m. 2d, Mary Frances Ludwig. Successively pastor Ref. Ch., Fishkill Landing, N.Y., Phila., Jersey City, N.J., Rhinebeck, N.Y.; retired from active ministry, Nov. 1, 1903. Pres. Rutgers Coll. Alumni; pres. Gen. Synod Reformed Ch., 1885. Author: The Cruger Family; Cruel Jim; The Wreckmaster; Hendryck Rycken, the Progenitor of the Suydam Family in America. Address: Philadelphia, Pa. Died 1909.

SUZZALLO, Henry, educator; b. San José, Calif., Aug. 22, 1875; s. Peter and Anne (Suzzallo) S.; A.B. from Stanford, 1899; A.M., Columbia, 1902, Ph.D., 1905; LL.D., U. of Calif., 1918, U. of British Columbia, 1925, U. of Ala., 1929, Columbia, 1929, U. of Colo., 1930; Sc.D., U. of Southern Calif., 1930; m. Edith Moore, Feb. 8, 1912. Asst. instr. and asst. prof. edn., Stanford, 1902-07; fellow and lecturer in edn., 1903-05, adj. prof. elementary edn., 1907-09, prof. philosophy of edn. (ednl. sociology), 1909-15, Columbia; pres. U. of Wash., 1915-26; visiting Carnegie prof. internat. relations in Europe, 1927-28; specialist in higher edn., Carnegie Foundation, 1927-30, pres., 1930—. Mem. com. on higher edn., North Central Assn., 1929—; dir. President's nat. advisory com. on edn. Chmn. Wash. State Council Defense, 1917-19; umpire Nat. War Labor Bd., July 13, 1918; adviser, War Labor Policy Bd., Oct. 1918. Trustee Carnegie Foundation for Adv. of Teaching, 1919 (chmn. bd., 1926—), Carnegie Corp. of N.Y., Nat. Council Edn., 1926—, Stevens Inst. Tech., 1927—. Mem. at large Nat. Research Council, div. states relations, 1919-23; mem. advisory council Inst. Internat. Edn.; elector Hall of Fame, 1920—; mem. Bd. of Visitors U.S. Naval Acad., 1924; mem. policy advisory bd. U. of Denver, U. of Wyo., Colo. Coll.; mem. ednl. research com. of Commonwealth Fund, 1925-27; chmn. com. of selection, Rhodes Scholarship Trust, 1915-26; mem. ednl. com. nat. council Boy Scouts of America. Republican. Fellow A.A.A.S.; honorary member National Assn. State Univs. (pres. 1921-22), Nat. Inst. Social Sciences; mem. Am. Acad. Political and Social Science (editorial council of Annals), Am. Fed. of Arts (dir.). Editor: Riverside Educational Monographs, 1909—. Lecturer, author, contbr. to edn. mags. Address: New York, N.Y. Died Sept. 25, 1933.

SVERDRUP, Georg, Lutheran clergyman, educator; b. Balestrand, Norway, Dec. 16, 1848; s. Rev. H. U. and K. M. (Suur) S.; early edn. private; grad. Nissen's Latin School, Sept. 1865; grad. Divinity School of Christiania U., Norway, Dec. 1871; m. Kathrine E. Heiberg, 1874; m. 2d, Elise S. Heiberg, 1890. Came to U.S., 1874; pres. Augsburg Sem. (Lutheran), and sec. Luth. Bd. of Missions, 1876—. Address: Minneapolis, Minn. Died 1907.

SVERDRUP, George, educator; b. Minneapolis, Minn., Aug. 3, 1879; s. Georg and Katharine (Heiberg) S.; A.B., Augsburg Coll., Minneapolis, Minn., 1898; studied U. of Minn., 1899-1901, Yale, 1901-02, 1903-05, M.A., 1902; Thayer fellow, Am. Sch. Archæology, Jerusalem, 1905-06; studied at univ. of Leipzig and Berlin, 1908-09, Christiania, Norway, 1914-15; L.H.D. from Upsala Coll., 1929; m. Hjalma Stenvig, Aug. 17, 1909; children—Katharine Anna, Valborg Elise, Ruth Audrey (dec.), George Marshall. Instr. Gerard Inst., Sidon, Syria, 1905, Syrian Protestant Coll., Beirut, 1906-07; Am. v. and dep. consul gen., Beirut, 1907; prof. of mathematics, Augsburg Coll., Minneapolis, Minn., 1907-08, prof. O.T., Augsburg Sem., 1908—, pres., 1911—. Mem. bd. trustees Luth. Bd. Missions, Norwegian Luth. Deaconess Inst., Folkebladet Pub. Co., 1911-23. Home: Minneapolis, Minn. Died Nov. 11, 1937.

SWAIM, Joseph Skinner, editor; b. Worcester, Mass., May 2, 1851; s. Rev. Samuel B. and Aurora (Skinner) S.; A.B., Harvard, 1873; in Europe and the Near East, 1873-74; grad. Newton Theol. Instn., 1877; m. Caroline Tiffany Dyer, Nov. 14, 1877. Ordained Bapt. ministry, Oct. 1877; pastor, Claremont, N.H., 1877-83, Providence, R.I., 1883-87, Binghamton, N.Y., 1887-90, New Bedford, Mass., 1890-1904; editor The Watchman, Boston, 1904-13. Trustee Newton Theol. Instn., 1895-1912; pres. N.E. Bapt. Library Assn., Boston Bapt. City Mission Soc., Civic Soc. Home: Cambridge, Mass. Died Dec. 6, 1918.

SWAIN, George Fillmore, civil engr.; b. San Francisco, Mar. 2, 1857; s. Robert Bunker and Clara Ann (Fillmore) S.; B.S., Mass. Inst. Tech., 1877; Royal Poly. Sch., Berlin, 1877-80; LL.D., New York U., 1907, U. of Calif., 1918; m. Katharine Kendrick Wheeler, July 7, 1891 (died 1901); 1 dau., Barbara; m. 2d, Mary Hayden Lord, Jan. 23, 1904 (died 1914); 1 dau., Clara; m. 3d, Mary Augusta Rand, Aug. 21, 1914; step-daughter, Alice Rand. Hydraulic expert 10th U.S. Census, 1880-84; Hayward prof. civ. engring., Mass. Inst. Tech., 1887-1909; prof. civ. engring., Harvard Engring. Sch., 1909-29 (emeritus). Cons. engineer Mass. R.R. Commn., 1887-1914; mem. 1894-1918, chmn, 1913-18, Boston Transit Commn. Mem. of many commns., and engr. for many structures and other works; made appraisal of assets and liabilities of N.Y.,N.H.&H. R.R. for state commn., 1910; also valuations of N.Y. Central, Chicago elevated, Canadian railroads and other rys. Mem. delegation of Am. engrs. to France, 1918, and mem. Franco-Am. Engring. Commn., 1919. Fellow Am. Acad. Arts and Sciences. Author: Notes on Hydraulics, 1885, 90; Conservation of Water by Storage, 1915; How to Study, 1917; The Young Man and Civil Engineering, 1922; Strength of Materials, 1924; Fundamental Properties of Materials, 1924; Stresses, Graphical Statics and Masonry, 1927; also articles on hydraulic and structural subjects. First recipient of Lamme medal, 1928. Home: Brookline, Mass. Died July 1, 1931.

SWAIN, Henry Huntington, educator; b. Providence, R.I., Mar. 29, 1863; s. Leonard and Julia Maria (Allen) S.; B.A., Beloit Coll., 1884; student U. of Chicago, 1895; Ph.D., U. of Wis., 1897; m. Mira L. Olmsted, July 31, 1889; children—Joseph Ward, Albert Free, George (dec.). Headmaster, Markham Acad., Milwaukee, 1887; prof. history and economics, Yankton Coll., 1887-95; prof. economics, Mont. State Normal Coll., 1898-1912, pres., 1901-12; asst. state supt. pub. instrn., Mont., 1913-17; exec. sec. U. of Mont., 1917—, acting chancellor, 1922-23. Founder and for 4 yrs. editor of The Inter-Mountain Educator. Twice apptd. by gov. to represent Mont. at Internat. Tax Conf., once at Nat. Conf. on Trusts and Monopolies; chmn. Merit System Council, State Dept. Pub. Welfare. Episcopalian. Mason (33°). Author: Economic Aspects of Railroad Receiverships, 1898; Civics for Montana Students, 1907. Contbr. numerous articles to mags. Home: Helena, Mont. Died Jan. 13, 1941.

SWAIN, Henry Lawrence, M.D.; b. Nantucket, Mass., May 3, 1864; s. George Hussey and Henrietta (Weeks) S.; M.D., Yale U., 1884; studied abroad 2 yrs.; m. Etta Viola Winchell, Dec. 24, 1890 (died 1926); 1 dau., Josephine Ethel; m. 2d, Jane Elizabeth Schmitt, Oct. 15, 1931. Practiced at New Haven, 1886—; laryngologist New Haven Dispensary, 1887—, New Haven Hosp., 1893—; lecturer on diseases of ear and throat, 1886-95, clin. prof., 1895—, Yale Med. Sch. Fellow Am. Laryngol. Assn. (sec. 1895-1900; pres.); hon. fellow New York Laryngol. Assn. Republican. Methodist. Home: New Haven, Conn. Died Jan. 1940.

SWAIN, Joseph, coll. pres.; b. Pendleton, Ind., June 16, 1857; s. Woolston and Mary A. S.; B.L., Ind. U., 1883, M.S., 1885; LL.D., Wabash coll., 1893, Lafayette, 1911, U. of Pa., 1912, Ind. U., 1920, Swarthmore, 1921; m. Frances M. Morgan, Sept. 22, 1885. Instr. mathematics and biology, 1883-85, asso. prof. mathematics, 1885-86, prof., 1886-91, Ind. U.; prof. mathematics, Leland Stanford Jr. U., 1891-93; pres. Ind. U., 1893-1902; pres. Swarthmore coll., 1902-21, emeritus pres., 1921. Mem. World's Peace Foundation. Pres. N.E.A., 1913-14. Home: Wallingford, Pa. Died May 19, 1927.

SWALLOW, George Clinton, geologist; b. Buckfield, Me., Nov. 9, 1817; grad. Bowdoin Coll., 1843; A.M., M.D., Mo. Med. Coll.; LL.D., U. of Bo.; lecturer on botany, Bowdoin, 1843; prin. Hampden (Mo.) Acad., 1848; prof. geology and chemistry U. of Mo., 1852; State geologist, Mo., 1852; led movement for agrl. dept. in U. of Mo., established 1859, and taught its first class; prof. geology and dean Agrl. Coll., U. of Mo., 1870; now retired. Was State geologist of Kan., 1865. In 1858 announced discovery of permian rocks in Kansas (the first in America); helped build first silver furnace at Argenta, Mont., and first silver mill at Philipsburg, Mont.; apptd. inspector of mines by Gov. Lesley of Mont. Died 1900.

SWALLOW, Silas C., editor; b. Plains, Pa., Mar. 5, 1839; s. George and Sarah S.; ed. Wyoming Sem., Kingston, Pa.; D.D., Taylor U., Ft. Wayne, Ind.; m. Louisa Robbins, Jan. 30, 1866. Editor Pennsylvania Methodist; supt. Methodist book rooms; published exposé of Pa. politicians, 1897; was tried and acquitted. Editor of Church Forum for several years. Prohibition candidate for state treas., 1897, for gov. of Pa., 1898, 1902, for Pres. of U.S., 1904. Author: Camp Meetings and the Sabbath; "III Score & X," or Selections, Collections and Recollections of Seventy Busy Years. Home: Harrisburg, Pa. Died Aug. 13, 1930.

SWALM, Albert Winfield, Am. consul; b. Womelsdorf, Pa., Nov. 30, 1845; s. John E. and Elizabeth (Christ) S.; ed. Iowa pub. schs.; m. Pauline Given, Oct. 1, 1872. Served as pvt. 33d and 34th Ia. Inf. regts. in Civil War. Pub. newspapers in Ia., including Daily Herald and Weekly Herald, Oskaloosa, 1870-97; pres. Ia. State Press Assn., 1885-88; regent State U. of Ia., 1885-97; postmaster, Oskaloosa, 1888-92; Am. consul at Montevideo, Uruguay, 1897-1903, at Southampton, Eng., 1903—; later consul, Hamilton, Bermuda. Comd. 3d Ia. N.G., 5 yrs. Mason. Home: Des Moines, Ia. Died Aug. 24, 1922.

SWAN, Gustaf Nilsson; b. Råfstad, nr. Rimforsa, Sweden, May 16, 1856; s. Christopher and Anna Lovisa (Persson) S.; came to U.S., 1870; Augustana Coll., Ill., 1877-79, hon. A.M., 1900, L.H.D., 1917; m. Caroline S. Samuelsson, June 12, 1884 (died 1888). Sec. and mgr. Sioux City (Ia.) Plow Co., 1880-87; asst. cashier and cashier, Merchants Nat. Bank, Sioux City, 1890-1910; pres. Larson-Swan Dry Goods Co., 1908-13. Vice consul of Sweden for State of Ia., 1899-1928. Dir. Augustana Coll. and Theol. Sem., 1893-1912. Republican. Lutheran. Author: Holmes och Zetterstrand, 1912; Svenskarna i Sioux City (The Swedes in Sioux City), 1912; Gamla Svenska Biblar i Amerika (Old Swedish Bibles in America), 1918. Translated "In the Coils" by Graham, into Swedish, 1885. Knight Royal Swedish Order of Vasa, 1st Class, 1918; Knight Royal Swedish Order of the North Star, 1928. Mem. bd. dirs. Augustana Book Concern, Rock Island, Ill., 1917-26. Home: Sioux City, Ia. Died June 30, 1938.

SWAN, Henry Harrison, judge; b. Detroit, Oct. 2, 1840; s. Joseph G. and Mary C. (Ling) S.; student U. of Mich., 1858-61, LL.D., 1902; m. Jennie E. Clark, Apr. 30, 1873. Engaged in steamboating in San Joaquin and Sacramento rivers, Calif., in earlier years; admitted to Calif. bar, 1867, Mich. bar, 1867; asst. U.S. district atty., Detroit, 1870-77; U.S. dist. judge, Eastern Dist. of Mich., 1891—. Republican. Non-resident lecturer, law faculty of U. of Mich., 1893-1909. Home: Grosse Pointe, Detroit, Mich. Died June 12, 1916.

SWAN, John Nesbit, chemist; b. New Jefferson, O., Oct. 14, 1862; s. Thomas and Jane (Hadden) S.; A.B., Westminister Coll., Pa., 1886; Ph.D., Johns Hopkins U., 1893; m. Jane Duffield, Mar. 19, 1890; children—Stewart Duffield, Thomas Hadden, William Orr. Teacher in Burlington, Ia., 1886-87; in Tarkio Coll., 1887-88, Westminster Coll., 1889-91, Monmouth Coll., 1893-1915 (acting pres. 1902-03); head of dept. of chemistry, U. of Miss., 1915—. Fellow by courtesy, Johns Hopkins, 1930-31; research asso., Westminster Coll., Pa., 1931-32. Chmn. North Miss. Development Assn. Home: University, Miss. Died June 8, 1937.

SWANK, James Moore, vice pres. and gen. mgr. Am. Iron & Steel Assn.; b. Westmoreland Co., Pa., July 12, 1832; s. George W. and Nancy (Moore) S.; ed. Elders Ridge Acad., and freshman class Jefferson Coll., Pa.; hon. Ph.D., Washington and Jefferson Coll., Pa., 1900; LL.D., Temple U., Phila., 1909; married. Clerked in store; taught sch.; edited and published weekly campaign Whig newspaper at Johnstown, Pa., 1852; founded, 1853, and was 11 yrs. editor and pub. Johnstown Tribune; chief clerk U.S. Dept. of Agr., 1871-72; sec., 1873-85, Am. Iron & Steel Assn., v.p. and gen. mgr. same, 1885—, and editor of its publs., 1873—. Active advocate of protective policy. Author: History of the Department of Agriculture, 1872; Iron Making and Coal Mining in Pennsylvania, 1878; History of the Manufacture of Iron in All Ages (1st edit.), 1884, (2d edit.), 1892; Notes and Comments on Industrial, Economic, Political, and Historical Subjects, 1897; Progressive Pennsylvania, 1908; Cambria County Pioneers, 1910. Has written and compiled about 100 tariff tracts. Home: Philadelphia, Pa. Died June 21, 1914.

SWANSON, Claude Augustus, secretary of the Navy; b. Swansonville, Va., Mar. 31, 1862; s. John M. S.; A.B., Randolph-Macon Coll., 1885; LL.B., U. of Va., 1886; engaged in practice at Chatham, Va. Mem. 53d to 58th Congresses (1893-1905), 5th Va. Dist.; reëlected to 59th Congress, but resigned; gov. of Va., 1906-10; apptd. U.S. senator, Aug. 1, 1910, for unexpired term (1910-11) of John W. Daniel, deceased; reapptd., Mar. 4, 1911, until meeting of Gen. Assembly, which elected him for unexpired term ending Mar. 3, 1917; reëlected, 3 terms, 1917-35; resigned to become secretary of Navy, Mar. 4, 1933. Am. del. to Disarmament Conf., Geneva, Switzerland, 1932. Democrat. Died July 7, 1939.

SWARTHOUT, Elvin, lawyer; b. Ovid, Mich., Oct. 5, 1864; grad. high sch., Ovid, 1879; Ph.B., Albion (Mich.) Coll., 1885; Ph.M. and LL.B., U. of Mich., 1887; m. Elizabeth Master, July 20, 1887; children—Donald G., Dorothy F., Marian E., Anthony M. Admitted to Mich. bar, 1886, and began practice at Grand Rapids, 1887; law clk. Fletcher & Wanty, 1887; mem. firm Fallass & Swarthout, 1888-95; in partnership with Byron M. Cutcheon, 1895-97, with Sheridan F. Master, 1912-17, practised alone, 1917—. Mem. City Council, Grand Rapids, 5 terms; mem. Bd. of Edn., 1899-1902, mayor Grand Rapids, 1924-30. Trustee M. J. Clark Memorial Home (sec.), First M.E. Ch. Pres. Grand Rapids Area Council Boy Scouts America. Republican. Mason. Home: Grand Rapids, Mich. Died Feb. 1, 1935.

SWARTS, Gardner Taber, dermatologist; b. Providence, R.I., Dec. 13, 1857; s. Gardner Taber and Harriet A. (Wood) S.; Providence pub. schs.; M.D., Harvard U., 1879; m. Fannie May Stinson, Sept. 15, 1879. Surgeon, 1894, later consulting surgeon dept. of skin diseases, R.I. Hosp., Providence City Hosp., and Memorial Hosp., Pawtucket, R.I. Sec. R.I. State Bd. of Health and state registrar of vital statistics of R.I., 1894-1917. Republican. Home: Providence, R.I. Died May 12, 1925.

SWARTWOUT, Richard Henry, stock broker; b. Morristown, N.J., Oct. 16, 1874; s. William Henry and Meriam (Evans) S.; ed. pub. sch.; m. Ethel Rogers, Oct. 9, 1909; 1 dau., Ethel Victoria. Identified with stock brokerage business N.Y. City, 1893—; mem. Swartwout & Appenzellar, 1898-1927; chmn. bd. Intertype Corp., Dictaphone Corp.; dir. Norfolk Southern R.R. Served as maj. U.S. Army, World War. Presbyn. Office: 40 Wall St., New York, N.Y. Died July 21, 1938.

SWARTZ, Edward James, journalist, dramatic author; b. Buffalo, N.Y., Apr. 19, 1848; s. Jacob, inventor, and Harriet Newell S.; ed. public schools; joined local staff Evening Telegraph, Phila., 1866, city editor, 1871-97, mng. editor, 1897—. Dramatic author, produced plays: A Square Man, 1882; Dad's Girl, 1883; Princess Chuck, 1884; The Governess, 1888; Our Angel, 1889; The Kaffir Diamond, 1890; The Envoy, 1891; Bossett's Fairy, 1893; The Clipper, 1894; The Syndicate, 1894; m. Ella Carlisle, d. late Edwin Miller, mcht., Phila., Sept. 3, 1895. Died 1910.

SWARTZ, Samuel Jackson, mayor of Columbus, O., elected Apr. 3, 1899; b. North Berne, O., Feb. 8, 1859; s. Eli B. and Lizzie (Jackson) S.; grad. Wesleyan U., 1881; studied law; admitted to bar, 1888; m. Daisy E. Hanna, Mar. 10, 1888. Apptd. judge city court by Gov. Bushnell, Jan. 1897; elected same position, Apr. 1898; alternate to Nat. Rep. Conv., Philadelphia, 1900; interested in various business and public enterprises in Columbus and Ohio. Mng. editor, 1889-90, of The League Gazette, pub. by the Republican League of Clubs. Interested in promoting various forms of outdoor sports; contbr. to publications on hunting and fishing. Died 1905.

SWASEY, Ambrose, mfr.; b. Exeter, N.H., Dec. 19, 1846; s. Nathaniel and Abigail Chesley (Peavey) S.; ed. Exeter, N.H.; Dr. Engring., Case Sch. Applied Science, Cleveland, 1905; Sc.D., Denison U., 1910, U. of Pa., 1924, Brown U., 1931; LL.D., U. of Calif., 1924, U. of Rochester, 1925, U. of New Hampshire, 1930; m. Lavinia D., d. David and Sarah Ann (Dearborn) Marston, of Hampton, N.H., Oct. 24, 1871. In 1880 entered into partnership with W. R. Warner in firm of Warner & Swasey (inc. as The Warner & Swasey Co., 1900), mfrs. of machine tools and astronomical instruments. The 36-inch Lick telescope, 26-inch telescope of Naval Obs., Washington, and 40-inch Yerkes telescope, as well as exceptionally accurate dividing engine, are some of the firm's achievements; 72-inch reflecting telescope for Canadian Govt., was completed 1916; 60-inch, for the Argentine Nat. Obs., completed in 1922, and 69-inch telescope for Ohio Wesleyan U., completed in 1923. Invented Swasey range and position finder, adopted by U.S. Govt. Dir. Cleveland Trust Co. Trustee Denison U., Adelbert College, Western Reserve U., Case School of Applied Science. Officer Legion of Honor, France, 1921; founder Engineering Foundation, 1914. Awarded the John Fritz gold medal, 1924; Cleveland medal for public service, 1930; Franklin gold medal, 1932; Am. Soc. M.E. medal, 1933; Washington award, 1935. Wrote: A New Process for Generating and Cutting the Teeth of Spur Wheels, and Some Refinements of Mechanical Science, Trans. Am. Soc. M.E., vols. XII and XXVI. Home: Cleveland, O. Died June 15, 1937.

SWAYNE, Alfred Harris, corp. official; b. Washington, D.C., Apr. 5, 1870; s. Wager and Ellen (Harris) S.; grad. St. Paul's Sch., Concord, N.H.; B.A., Yale, 1892; LL.B., New York Law Sch., 1894; unmarried. Admitted to N.Y. bar, 1894, and began practice with firm of Davies, Stone & Auerbach, counsel for Mutual Life Ins. Co. and other corps.; tour of world, 1895, 96; entered law firm of father, Swayne & Swayne; went to Cuba, 1899, as legal adviser North Am. Trust Co. which had contract to act as fiscal agt. for U.S. Govt.; assisted in establishing a banking system in Cuba; returned to New York, 1899, and was made sec. original Bankers Trust Co., and treas. Atlantic Trust Co., with which Bankers Trust Co. consolidated; associated with Moore & Schley, members N.Y. Stock Exchange; mem. New York Stock Exchange firm of Tailer & Robinson, 1901; became v.p. Gen. Motors Acceptance Corp., 1919, chmn. bd., 1921—, also v.p. General Motors Corp., North River Savings Bank; dir. E. W. Bliss Co. (New York), Irving Trust, Lehigh Valley R.R., Long Island R.R., St. Louis, Southwestern Ry. Co., C. Tennant Sons & Co. Dollar a year man, 1917; participated in Liberty Loan and Federal Reserve activities. Vice pres. and dir. Automobile Mfrs.

Assn. Homes: New York City, and Shinnecock Hills, L.I., N.Y. Died Apr. 16, 1937.

SWAYNE, Charles, U.S. dist. judge for Northern dist. Fla., 1889—; b. Guyencourt, Del., Aug. 10, 1842; s. Henry and Ann (Parry) S.; ed. public schools and acad.; taught high school, 1864-70; grad. law dept. U. of Pa., June 1871; admitted to Phila. bar, 1871; m. Lydia C. Gawthrop, July 17, 1867. Removed to Fla., Mar. 1885; defeated as Rep. candidate for Supreme Court, 1888; was very extensively endorsed for Supreme Court justice in autumn of 1897 after death of Justice Field of Calif. Home: Pensacola, Fla. Died 1907.

SWAYNE, Wager, lawyer; b. Columbus, O., Nov. 10, 1834; s. Noah H. S. (asso. justice Supreme Court U.S.); grad. Yale, 1856; Cincinnati Law School, 1859; began practice at Columbus; m. Ellen Harris, Dec. 22, 1868. Apptd. maj., Aug. 13, 1861; lt. col., Dec. 14, 1861; col., Oct. 18, 1862, of 43d Ohio vols.; served through Atlanta campaign and lost a leg at Salkahatchie, S.C.; bvtd. brig. gen. U.S. vols., Feb. 5, 1865, becoming full brig. gen., March 8, 1865, and maj. gen., June 20, 1865; mil. administration in Ala., 1865-68; was made col. 45th regt. inf., July 28, 1866, and bvt. brig. gen. and maj. gen. U.S.A. for gallant and meritorious services during war; retired July 1, 1870. Practiced law in Toledo, O., until 1880; then in New York, where he was for yrs. gen. counsel Western Union Telegraph Co., the Wabash Ry. Co., the Associated Press, and other corporations. Was also pres. Ohio Soc. of New York, New York Commandery Loyal Legion, Am. Ch. Missionary Soc. Died 1902.

SWAYZE, Francis Joseph, judge; b. Newton, N.J., May 15, 1861; s. Jacob Lowrance and Joanna (Hill) S.; early edn. at Newton, N.J.; A.B., Harvard, 1879, A.M., 1880; student Harvard Law Sch; LL.D., Rutgers, 1911, Harvard, 1916; m. Louise Barrett, Oct. 13, 1887. Admitted to N.J. bar as atty., 1882, as counsellor, 1885; practiced law, Newton, N.J., 1882-92, and at Newark, N.J., 1892-1900; judge Circuit Court, 1900-03; justice Supreme Court of N.J., terms 1903-10, 1910-17, 1917-24. Del. Rep. Nat. Conv., 1892. Overseer Harvard Coll., 1909-15 and 1917-23. Pres. Harvard Alumni Assn., 1915-16, N.J. Hist. Soc., 1912-22; trustee Washington Assn. of N.J. Home: Newark, N.J. Died Sept. 25, 1932.

SWAYZE, George Banghart Henry, physician; b. Hope, N.J., Feb. 3, 1833; s. Robert B. and Sarah C. (McMurtrie) S.; ed. common schs. and sem.; M.D., Jefferson Med. Coll., Phila., 1859; m. Margaret A. Simington, Nov. 8, 1860; m. 2d, Mary Ford, Feb. 3, 1876. Asst. surgeon 178th Regt. Pa. Inf., Civil War; practiced in Phila., 1871—; one of founders, 1881 and first dean Medico-Chirurg. Coll. Republican. Presbyn. Author: Yarb and Cretine, 1907. Extensive contbr. to med. mags. Deceased.

SWEARINGEN, Embry L., banker; b. Bullitt County, Ky., Jan. 27, 1863; s. George W. and Mary (Embry) S.; prep. edn., Rugby Sch., Louisville, Ky.; student U. of Va.; m. Lalla Robinson, 1887; children—Amelia (dec.), Lalla Robinson (Mrs. Ralph C. Gifford), George W.; m. 2d, Ada Badger, June 1902. Began in banking business, 1892; chmn. bd. 1st Nat. Bank, Louisville. Home: Louisville, Ky. Deceased.

SWEARINGEN, Henry Chapman, clergyman; b. Hookstown, Pa., Apr. 28, 1869; s. William and Nancy Isabelle (Shannon) VanS.; Westminster Coll., 1891; grad. Allegheny Theol. Sem., 1894; D.D., Westminster Coll., 1902; LL.D., Jamestown Coll., 1918, James Millikin, and Dubuque, 1922, Carroll Coll., 1927; m. Belle Haney Comin, Aug. 8, 1894; children—Isabelle Comin, Henry Chapman (dec.). Ordained U.P. ministry, 1894; pastor Espyville, Pa., 1894-95, 3d Ch., Allegheny, Pa., 1895-1902, 1st Presbyn. Ch., Lincoln, Neb., 1902-07, House of Hope Presbyn. Ch., St. Paul, 1907—. Fraternal del. to Gen. Synod Ref. Ch. of U.S., 1899, to M.E. Gen. Conf., 1912; moderator Synod of Minn., 1912-13; mem. exec. commn., 1918-23, general council, 1923—, member dept. ch. coöperation and union, 1922—, Presbyn. Ch. in U.S.A.; moderator Gen. Assembly Presbyn. Ch. in U.S.A., 1921; exec. com. Presbyn. Alliance, 1921—, Federal Council of Churches, 1922—; del. Pan-Presbyn. Council, 1925, 29; del. Universal Conf. on Life and Work, 1925; chmn. Gen. Assembly's Spl. Commn., 1925. Trustee Macalester Coll. (pres. pro tem. 1923), Presbyn. Theol. Sem., Chicago; pres. Presbyn. Home Mission Council, 1915-16; mem. Minn. State Bd. of Parole, 1915—. Home: St. Paul, Minn. Died June 2, 1932.

SWEATT, William R.; b. Mitchell, Ia.; s. Charles and Cornelia (Lyons) S.; ed. pub. schs.; m. Jessie W. Wilson, 1888; children—Harold W., Charles B., Virginia W., Bernice W. Sec. and treas. Electric Thermostat Co. (now Minneapolis Honeywell Regulator Co.), 1893-96, pres., 1896-1927, chmn. bd., 1927—. Republican. Episcopalian. Home: Palm Beach, Fla. Deceased.

SWEENEY, Bo, asst. sec. of the Interior; b. Henry County, Mo., Sept. 20, 1863; s. Joshua and Martha (Weldon) S.; LL.B., Cumberland U. Law Sch., Lebanon, Tenn., 1888; m. Lillian E. Reeves, July 1, 1897. Admitted to Colo. bar, 1888, and practiced in Trinidad; mem. Colo. Ho. of Rep., 1893, 94, 97 (Dem. nominee for speaker, 1897); del. at large Dem. Nat. Conv., Chicago, 1896; removed to Seattle, Wash., 1897; Dem. nominee for corp. counsel, 1902, for justice Supreme Ct. of Wash., 1906; asst. sec. of the Interior, Washington, July 1, 1914—. Home: Seattle, Wash. Died July 16, 1917.

SWEENEY, Zachary Taylor, clergyman, lecturer; b. Liberty, Ky., Feb. 10, 1849; s. G. E. and Talitha (Campbell) S.; grad. Scottville (Ill.) Sem.; 1 yr. at Eureka Coll., Ill., and 3 yrs., De Pauw U.; LL.D., Butler U.; m. Linnie Irwin, Mar. 10, 1875; children—Nettie S., Joseph T. (dec.), Elsie I. Sch. teacher, 1866; in ministry Christian (Disciples) Ch., 1869—; minister Paris, Ill., 1869-71, Columbus, Ind., 1871-96; pastor emeritus. Exclusively engaged as lyceum lecturer by Redpath Bur., 1897—. U.S. consul gen. at Constantinople, 1889-93; Imperial Ottoman commr. to Chicago Expn., 1893. Dir. Indianapolis, Columbus & Southern R.R.; now commr. of fisheries and game for Ind. Was chancellor Butler U.; mem. advisory com. World's Congress of Religions, 1893. Decorated Turkish Order of the Osmanieh. Pres. Am. Christian Missionary Soc. Pres. Commn. on Foreign Relations. Author: Under Ten Flags, 1888; Pulpit Diagrams, 1899; Bible Readings (2 vols.); Querish Drawer; The Spirit and the World; also biennial reports as commr. fisheries, etc., 1899, 1901, 03, 05, 07. Contbr. to popular and scientific mags. Chmn. commn. on foreign relations Am. Christian Missionary Soc. Home: Columbus, Ind. Died Feb. 4, 1926.

SWEENIE, Denis J., chief of Chicago fire dept. from 1879, resigned June, 1901; b. Glasgow, Scotland, July 29, 1834; came to Chicago, 1849; engaged as mfr. of leather hose, fire hats, etc.; mem. volunteer fire dept., 1850-58; becoming asst. and later chief engr.; organized paid dept., 1858; became foreman; distinguished himself in fire of 1871; 1st asst. fire marshal, 1873-79. Home: Chicago, Ill. Died 1903.

SWEET, Alexander Edwin, journalist, asso. editor Tammany Times and editor N.Y. Sunday Star; b. St. John, N.B., March 28, 1841; went to Texas in boyhood; early edn. in San Antonio schools; grad. College Hill, Poughkeepsie, N.Y., 1859; grad. Karlsruhe, Germany, 1861; m. Marie Zittel, Carlsruhe, Baden, Germany, May 5, 1862; served, 1862-65, in 33d Texas cav., Confederate army; after war practised law; then entered newspaper work on San Antonio Express; his humerous sketches in that paper and later in the Galveston News attracted wide attention. Founded 1881, and until 1895 edited Texas Siftings. Author: Through Texas on a Mustang (with J. Armoy Knox); Three Dozen Good Stories from Texas Siftings. Died 1901.

SWEET, Edwin Forrest, asst. sec. of commerce; b. Dansville, New York, Nov. 21, 1847; s. of Sidney and Hannah (Redmond) S.; A.B., Yale, 1871; LL.B., U. of Mich., 1874; m. Sophia Fuller, Apr. 26, 1876; children—Carroll Fuller, George Philo (dec.), Sidney Edward, Cornelia Van Renssalaer (Mrs. D. C. Stanwood), Sophia Fuller. Practiced law, Grand Rapids, 1876-1904, when retired. Member Bd. Edn., 1899-1906; mayor of Grand Rapids, 1904-06; mem. 62d Congress (1911-13), 5th Mich. Dist.; asst. sec. of commerce, 1913-21. Mem. Bd. Edn., Grand Rapids, 1923—; mem. City Commn., Grand Rapids, 1926—. Democrat. Episcopalian. Home: Ojai, Calif. Deceased.

SWEET, Elnathan, civil engr.; b. Cheshire, Mass., Nov. 20, 1837; grad. Scientific course, Union Coll., 1859; engaged in practice and made specialty of bridges; div. engr., N.Y. State canals, 1876-80; State engr., 1884-87; author numerous reports and tech. papers; mem. Am. Soc. Civil Engrs., 1878—. Albany, N.Y. Died 1903.

SWEET, Frank Herbert, author; b. W. Greenwich, R.I., Aug. 1, 1856; s. Amos R. and Sarah A. (Coggswell) S.; pub. sch. edn.; m. Myrtle Palmer, Sept. 20, 1886; children—Frank Palmer, Amos Alexander Roberts. Author: Ingathering (poems), 1901; Minister's Family, 1902; A Mountain Hero, 1902; Rufe and Ruth, 1902; Going Into Business, 1903; Hobby Camp, 1905; Judy, Heroine, 1906; Judy, Pioneer Girl, 1907; Young Switch Tender, 1907; Three Boys and Their Ambition, 1907; Craig Cameron, 1907; Blue and Gray, 1907; Grandfather Tales, 1907; Grandmother Tales, 1907; Illustrious Boys of Many Lands, 1908; Illustrious Girls of Many Lands, 1908; Bunny Cottontail, 1908; Holiday Book of Dialogues, 1908; Cadet Rat, 1910; The Lost Airship, 1910; Puss in Boots, 1912; Mother Goose's House Party, 1913; Short Stories, 1915; Buzzard's Den, 1916; Bill Wittles, Optimist, 1920; In the Midst of the Deep Woods, 1925. Home: Waynesboro, Va. Died Feb. 3, 1930.

SWEET, John Edson, manufacturer; b. Pompey, N.Y., Oct. 21, 1832; s. Horace and Candace (Avery) S.; ed. dist. schs.; farmer boy, then carpenter's apprentice, 1850; builder and architect in the South until 1861; m. Caroline V. Hawthorne, Nov. 24, 1870; 2d, Irene A. Clark, May 9, 1889. Inventor and mech. draughtsman until 1873; prof. practical mechanics, Cornell, 1873-79; pres. Straight Line Engine Co., 1880—. Pres. Am. Soc. Mech. Engrs., 1883-84; expert for govt. and one of the jurors Chicago Expn., 1893, on machine tools; first pres. Engine Builders' Assn. of the U.S., 1899-1901; pres. Syracuse Metal Trades Assn., 1906-07, John Fritz Medal Assn., 1906; Recipient 10th John Fritz medal, 1914. Author: Things That Are Usually Wrong, 1906. Home: Syracuse, N.Y. Died May 8, 1916.

SWEET, Louis Dennison, agriculturist; b. Barry, Ill., May 4, 1863; s. John L. and Ella (Peck) S.; ed. pub. schs.; m. Jennie Mulliken, Aug. 27, 1889; 1 son, Stuart Louis. Cowboy, South Park, Colo., 1880-84; ry. operator agt., 1885-87; county treas., Pitkin County, Colo., 1888-94; gen. mgr. Ry. Supply Co., Denver, Colo., 1894-1900; v.p. Manifold Co., N.Y. City, 1900-04; farming in Colo., 1904—. Mem. com. which organized Colo. for war work, 1917; with U.S. Food Administration, Washington, 1917-Nov. 11, 1918, U.S. Dept. Agr. until Nov. 1919; mem. War Finance Agency for Colo. Pres. Potato Assn. America, 1914-18; pres. Colo. State Forestry Assn., Denver Civic and Commercial Assn.; mem. exec. com. Agr. and Live Stock Bur. Republican. Conglist. Mason. Home: Denver, Colo. Deceased.

SWEET, Owen Jay, brigadier gen. U.S.A.; b. Kent, Conn., Sept. 4, 1845; s. James S. and Aurilla (Duncan) S.; ed. Binghamton, N.Y.; m. Mary E. Bolt, 1873. Apptd. 2d lt. 137th N.Y. Inf., Sept. 6, 1862; served in 3d Brigade, 2d Div., 12th Army Corps, Army of Potomac, serving in many skirmishes, and battles of Fredericksburg, Chancellorsville and Gettysburg; capt. May 21, 1863; served in Army of the Cumberland, 20th Army Corps, taking part in all its battles up to and including the capture of Atlanta, then in Army of Ga., taking part in Sherman's March to the Sea, and the fighting in front of and capture of Savannah, where was the first officer to enter enemy's fortifications; afterwards in Sherman's campaign through the Carolinas; bvtd. maj., Mar. 13, 1865, "for gallant and meritorious services during the war"; mustered out of vol. service, Bladensburg, Md., June 9, 1865. Apptd. 2d lt. 40th Inf., May 27, 1867; 1st lt. 25th Inf., Aug. 19, 1873; promoted through grades to brig. gen. and retired, Sept. 4, 1909. Served through several campaigns against Indians, and in the Philippines, 1899-1901, and 1903-04; comd. 3d mil. dist., comprising the Sulu Archipelago; comd. Ft. Snelling, Minn., 1904-06; comdg. regt. and sta., Matanzas, Cuba, 1906-09. Died Jan. 6, 1928.

SWEET, Thaddeus C., congressman; b. Phoenix, N.Y., Nov. 16, 1872; s. Anthony Wayne and Sarah Elizabeth (Campbell) S.; g.g.f. was a mem. Washington's staff, Revolutionary War; ed. high sch.; m. Lena May McCarthy, Dec. 5, 1894. Clk., traveling salesman; an organizer, 1895, and pres. Sweet Bros. Paper Mfg. Co.; pres. Hydro-Asphalt Products Co.; chmn. bd. Oswego County Trust Co.; mem. N.Y. Ho. of Rep., 1909-20 (speaker of House, 1914-20); formerly Rep. County committeeman, later mem. exec. com. Rep. State Com.; mem. 68th and 69th Congresses (1923-27), 32d N.Y. Dist. Baptist. Mason (K.T., Shriner), Odd Fellow, Elk. Led in successful movement to deny Am. Socialists seats in N.Y. legislature, 1920. Home: Phoenix, N.Y. Died May 1, 1928.

SWEET, Timothy Bailey, capitalist; b. Farmington, Me., Apr. 11, 1841; s. Lorella and Mary (Bailey) S.; ed. pub. schs. and Farmington Acad.; m. Annie Brown, Apr. 29, 1873. Engaged in ins., banking and bonds, 1868-72; located in Topeka, Kan., 1872; pres. Kansas Loan & Trust Co., 1873-93, Trust Co. of America, 1893-98; pres. Kaw Milling Co. Methodist. Mem. Am. S.S. Union for Kan. (v.p.), Am. Bible Soc. (life); trustee Washburn Coll., Christ's Hosp. Home: Topeka, Kan. Died Apr. 3, 1918.

SWEET, William Merrick, ophthalmologist; b. Phila., Pa., June 4, 1860; M.D., Jefferson Med. Coll., 1886. Clin. prof. ophthalmology, Jefferson Med. Coll., 1913-24; consulting surgeon, Wills Hosp., Philadelphia. Mem. A.M.A., Med. Soc. State of Pa., Am. Acad. Ophthalmology and Oto-Laryngology, Am. Ophthal. Soc. (pres. 1922), Am. Roentgen Ray Soc. (hon.). Died Dec. 24, 1926.

SWEETLAND, Cornelius Sowle, banker; b. Johnston, R.I., July 15, 1845; s. Cornelius Sowle and Louisa (Cheney) S.; A.B., Brown U., 1866, A.M., 1869; m. Mary H. Anthony, Sept. 1869. Was president Providence Banking Co.; treas. United Traction & Electric Co.; treas. and mgr. Alfred Anthony Estate Co.; pres. Rumford Chem. Works. Trustee, 1892—, treas., 1900—, Brown U. Republican. Episcopalian. Mem. R.I. Sch. of Design. Home: Providence, R.I. Died May 30, 1923.

SWEETLAND, William Howard, judge; b. Pawtucket, R.I., Dec. 19, 1856; s. William and Nancy Greene (Howard) S.; A.B., Brown U., 1878, A.M., 1881; LL.D., R.I. State Coll., 1922, Brown U., 1924; m. Florence Gardiner Reynolds, June 11, 1889; children—Reynolds, John, William Howard. Admitted to bar, 1881; practiced at Providence; clerk R.I. Ho. of Rep., 1887-88; clerk 6th Dist. Ct., 1889-95; judge same, 1895-1905; presiding justice Superior Court of R.I., 1905-09, justice Supreme Court of R.I., 1909—, and chief justice of R.I., 1920-29 (retired). Home: Providence, R.I. Died Jan. 18, 1932.

SWEETS, David Matthis, clergyman, editor; b. Elizabethtown, Ky., Jan. 31, 1868; s. Michael and Sarah Kate (Matthis) S.; student Central U. of Ky., 1882-83, 1884-88; grad. Union Theol. Sem., Va., 1891; D.D., Presbyn. Coll. of S.C., 1908; LL.D., Austin Coll., Sherman, Tex., 1924; m. Bessie Breck McDowell, Mar. 10, 1892; children—Eunice Lees, William McDowell. Adj. prof. Latin and Greek, Central U. of Ky., 1887-89; ordained Presbyn. ministry, 1891; pastor Morganfield, Ky., 1891-94, Portland Av. Ch., Louisville, 1894-99, 1st Ch., Shelbyville, 1899-1909; editor Christian Observer, 1909—. Stated clk. Louisville Presbytery, 1895-1917, Synod of Ky., 1913-17. Trustee Gen. Assembly Presbyn. Ch. in U.S., also of Centre Coll., Ky. Democrat. Mason. Home: Louisville, Ky. Died June 3, 1932.

SWEETSER, Delight; b. Hartford City, Ind., Jan. 21, 1873, d. James Vermilyea and Emma (Harter) S.; ed. in Ind.; student at Wellesley Coll.; studied drawing and music in Boston; lived in Europe several yrs., studied languages; m. Francis Fleury Prentiss, Jan. 3, 1900. Wrote for Chicago and Indianapolis newspapers; made translations from French; wrote for Chicago Interior; in 1897 made a journey around the world. Author: One Way Round the World, 1898. Various translations published. Died 1903.

SWEETSER, Edwin Chapin, clergyman; b. Wakefield, Mass., Mar. 16, 1847; s. Paul Hart and Louisa (Foster) S.; A.B., Tufts Coll., 1866; student Canton Theol. Sch., 1866-68; S.T.D., Tufts, 1882; m. Mary T. Pulsifer, June 27, 1882; children—Sidney Pulsifer, Edith, Marion, Norman. Ordained Universalist ministry, 1869; pastor Syracuse, N.Y., 1868-69, 3d Ch., New York, 1869-79, Church of the Messiah, Phila., 1879-1920, became pastor emeritus, Mar. 1, 1920. Pres. Universalist Gen. Conv., 1886, 87, trustee, 1887-1903; preached the opening sermon at the session of the Gen. Conv., 1911. One of speakers at World's Parliament of Religions, Chicago, 1893. Prohibitionist. Author: The Image of God, 1923. Home: Philadelphia, Pa. Died Oct. 22, 1929.

SWEETSER, Kate Dickinson, author; b. N.Y. City; d. Charles H. (founder and editor New York Mail) and Mary N. S.; ed. pvt. schs. Author: Ten Boys from Dickens, 1901; Ten Girls from Dickens, 1902; Micky of Alley, 1903; Teddy Baird's Luck, 1904; Boys and Girls from George Eliot, 1906; Boys and Girls from Thackeray, 1907; Ten Boys from History, 1910; Ten Girls from History, 1912; Book of Indian Braves, 1913; Ten Great Adventurers, 1915; Ten American Girls from History, 1917; uniform edit., The Sweetser Juveniles, 1923; Peggy's Prize Cruise, 1925; Famous Girls of the White House, 1930; Great American Girls, 1931. Died Mar. 22, 1939.

SWENEY, Joseph Henry, congressman; b. Russell, Pa., Oct. 2, 1845; s. Hugh and Esther A. (Phillis) S.; ed. State U. of Ia., LL.B., same; unmarried. Pvt., corpl. and sergt. Co. K. 27th Ia. Inf., 1862-65; served in Ia. N.G., 12 yrs., retiring as brig. gen. insp. gen. Admitted to bar; elected to Ia. Senate, 1883, 1887 (unanimously elected pres. pro tem., 1886); mem. 51st Congress (1889-91). In 1874, with his bro. Charles, founded Sweney Bros. Bank of Osage; later the Mitchell Co. Savings Bank; in law practice at Osage, Ia. Trustee for 30 yrs., and part of time pres., Cedar Valley Seminary, Osage. Republican. Congregationalist. Mason (K.T.). Died Nov. 1918.

SWENGEL, Uriah Frantz, bishop; b. nr. Middleburg, Pa., Oct. 28, 1846; s. John and Sarah (Frantz) S.; grad. Union Sem. (later Central Pa. Coll.), New Berlin, Pa., now Albright Coll., Myerstown, Pa.; A.M., Central Pa. Coll., 1898; D.D., Richmond Coll., Ind., 1899; m. 3d, Bertha Luella Buck, Mar. 15, 1898. Enlisted in Co. I, 184th Regt., Pa. Vols., Aug. 27, 1864; participated in Battle of Hatcher's Run and was with Union Army in the closing months of the war and present at the surrender of Gen. Lee, at Appomattox, Va., Apr. 9, 1865; hon. discharged June 10, 1865. Admitted to ministry Evangelical Assn., 1867; ordained at Baltimore, Md., 1869; pastor various counties, Pa., 1868-79; presiding elder Juniata dist., Pa., 1880-84; editor S.S. lit. United Evang. Ch., Cleveland, 1884-87; pastor Baltimore, 1887-90, York, Pa., 1891-93, Baltimore, 1894-97, York, 1898; presiding elder York dist., 1899-1902, Lewisburg dist., 1903-06; pastor Lewistown, Pa., 1907-10; bishop United Evang. Ch., and pres. Bd. of Bishops, 1910-18; pres. Bd. of Missions and pastor Mt. Holly Springs, Pa., 1919—. Chmn. Commn. on Ch. Union United Evang. Ch., 1910-18; exec. com. Federal Council Churches of Christ in America. Trustee Albright Coll., United Soc. Christian Endeavor, Am. Anti-Saloon League for Pa. Pres. United Evang. Ch. Hist. Soc. Author: Modes and Methods of Sunday School Work, 1885; Manual of the United Evangelical Church. Died Mar. 8, 1921.

SWENK, Myron Harmon, univ. prof.; b. Polo, Ill., Aug. 8, 1883; s. Howard and Susanna (Harmon) S.; A.B., U. of Neb., 1907, A.M., 1908, grad. student, 1909-16; m. Jane Chandler Bishop, Apr. 24, 1918. Lab. asst. in entomology, U. of Neb., 1904-07, adj. prof., 1907-10, asst. prof., 1910-11, asso. prof., 1911-14, prof. of economic entomology, 1914-19, prof. and chmn. dept. of entomology, 1919—; asst. entomologist, Neb. Expt. Sta., 1907-13, asso. entomologist, 1913-19, entomologist, 1919—; asst. state entomologist, Neb., 1908-19; state entomologist, 1919-28. Mem. or officer various ornithol. socs. Republican. Mason. Author: Birds of Nebraska (with L. Bruner, R. H. Wolcott), 1904; Mammals of Nebraska, 1908. Editor: Proceedings of Neb. Ornithologists Union, 1908-15; Nebraska Bird Review, 1933—; Mo. Valley Fauna, 1939—; author of Agrl. Expt. Sta. bulletins. Home: Lincoln, Neb. Died July 17, 1941.

ington, Mass. Died July 21, 1930.

SWENSON, David Ferdinand, prof. philosophy; b. Sweden, Oct. 29, 1876; s. Gustaf F. and Augusta Maria (Johanson) S.; brought to U.S., 1882; B.S., U. of Minn., 1898; studied Columbia; m. Lillian B. Marvin, Aug. 22, 1912. With U. of Minn., 1901—, successively instr., asst. prof., asso. prof., and 1917—, prof. philosophy; visiting prof. philosophy, Coll. City of New York, 1921-22. Served 3 terms as mem. Bd. of Edn., Minneapolis. Conglist. Contbr. to Jour. of Philosophy, Philos. Rev. Home: Minneapolis, Minn. Died Feb. 11, 1940.

SWENSSON, Carl Aaron, founder, 1881, and pres. Bethany Coll., 1889—; b. Sugar Grove, Pa., June 25, 1857; s. Rev. Jonas and Maria (Blixt) S.; grad. Augustana Coll., Rock Island, Ill., 1877; A.M., 1889; Ph.D., 1893, Royal Univ. of Upsala, Sweden; grad. in theology Augustana Sem., 1879, D.D., Augustana Coll. and Sem., and Thiel Coll., Pa., 1900. Knight Royal Order of the North Star, Sweden, 1901. Pastor Bethany Luth. Ch., 1879—. Sec. Gen. Council Luth. Ch. of North America, 1885; pres. same, 1893-94; mem. Kan. legislature, 1889-90; delegate-at-large to Rep. Nat. Conv., St. Louis, 1896. Author and compiler of hymn books and books of devotion in Swedish; also books of travel in Swedish and English. Home: Lindsborg, Kan. Died 1904.

SWERDFEGER, Elbert Byron, otolaryngologist; b. on farm, nr. Sabetha, Kan., June 25, 1876; s. Philip and Christeen (Jacobs) S.; prep. edn., State Normal Sch., Peru, Neb., and high school, Sabetha; M.D., Denver Coll. of Phys. and Surg., 1904; m. Isabelle Dye, July 8, 1903; children—Mark Daniel, Elmer Philip, Marychristabel (dec.), Margaret Virginia. Practiced at Denver, 1904—. Mem. staffs Presbyn., Denver Gen., Colo. Gen., Children's and St. Luke's hosps.; phys. to Belle Lennox Nursery; asso. prof. otolaryngology, Colorado U. Medical Coll. Fellow Am. Coll. Surgeons, Am. Acad. Ophthalmology and Otolaryngology. Commd. capt. M.C., "YD," 26th Div., 1917. Conglist. Home: Denver, Colo. Died Feb. 10, 1937.

SWETLAND, Roger Williams, educator; b. Harrison Valley, Pa., Sept. 28, 1861; s. Austin Aaron and Susan Agnes (Thomas) S.; B.E., Lockhaven (Pa.) State Normal Sch., 1882; A.B., U. of Rochester, 1894, hon. A.M., 1908, LL.D., 1916; m. Carrie Belle Thomas, May 31, 1885; children—Mark Wallace, Lois May (dec.), Ruth Katherine. Principal Troupsburg (N.Y.) Union Sch., 1883-85, Woodhull (N.Y.) Acad. and Union Sch., 1887-90, Cook Acad., Montour Falls, N.Y., 1894-98, Peddie School, Hightstown, N.J., 1898—. Mem. bd. mgrs. Am. S.S. Union, Am. Bapt. Pub. Soc.; mem. Bd. Edn. of Northern Bapt. Conv.; trustee Internat. Bapt. Sem. Republican. Baptist. Home: Hightstown, N.J. Died Sept. 1934.

SWETT, John, educator, author; b. Pittsfield, N.H., July 31, 1830; s. Eben and Lucretia (French) S.; ed. Pittsfield Acad., 1843-47; Pembroke, N.H., Acad., 1848-50; Merrimack Normal Inst., Reed's Ferry, N.H., 1851; hon. A.M., Coll. of Calif., 1866, Dartmouth, 1866; m. Mary Louise Tracy, May 8, 1862. Taught winter term of dist. schs., 1847-51; prin. grammar school, San Francisco, 1853-62; state supt. of schs., Calif., 1863-68; deputy supt. schs., San Francisco, 1870-73; prin. Girls' High and Normal Sch., 1876-89; city supt. schs., San Francisco, 1891-94; fruit grower and farmer, 1895—. Republican. Editor-in-chief Calif. State Educational Journal, 1864-68. Author: History of the Public School System of California, 1876; Methods of Teaching, 1880; American Public Schools, 1900; School Elocution, 1886. Joint Author: (Elementary school books, with William Swinton) Swinton's Word-Book and Word Primer, 1872; Swinton's Grammar, Language Lessons and Language Primer, 1873-74; Swinton's Geography, 1875. Home: Martinez, Calif. Died Aug. 22, 1913.

SWETT, Louis William, entomologist; b. Riverside, Calif., Oct. 2, 1880; s. Lewis Girdler and Anna Jones (Norcross) S.; student Harvard, 1900-02; m. Alice Fairall Trochu, Oct. 2, 1911; 1 dau., Sylvia. Propr. The Modern Shop, dry goods, Lexington. Specialist in butterflies and moths; regarded as authority on geometrid moths of U.S.; donated his collection of butterflies and moths (the largest pvt. collection then in U.S.) to Agassiz Mus., Harvard, 1912. Asso. editor The Lepidopterist. Home: Lexington, 1925—. Lecturer in psychology and edn., sum-

SWETT, Sophia Miriam, author; b. Brewer, Me.; d. of Nathaniel and Susan (Brastow) S.; ed. pub. and pvt. schs., Boston. At one time asso. editor Wide Awake; writer of short stories and juvenile books. Author: Captain Polly, 1889; Flying Hill Farm, 1891; Mate of the Mary Ann, 1894; The Ponkaty Branch Road, 1896; Captain Thistletop, 1896; Tom Pickering of Scutney, 1897; Bilberry Boys and Girls, 1898; Pennyroyal and Mint, 1898; The Lollipops' Vacation, 1898; Stories of Maine, 1899; The Littlest One of the Browns, 1900; The Boy from Beaver Hollow, 1900; A Cape Cod Boy, 1900; The Young Ship Builder, 1902; Sarah the Less, 1902; The Wonder Ship, 1902; Long Tom and How They Got Him, 1904; The Lion Tamer's Little Girl, 1904; Peaseblossom's Lion, 1904; The Yellow-capped Monkey, 1904; Mary Augusta's Price, 1904; Sonny Boy, 1904; Princess Wisla, 1908; Six Little Pennypackers, 1911. Home: Arlington Heights, Mass. Died Nov. 12, 1912.

SWETT,* Susan Hartley, author; b. Brewer, Me.; d. Nathaniel and Susan (Brastow) S.; sister of Sophia Miriam Swett. Published many poems in Harper's, St. Nicholas, The Cosmopolitan, Youth's Companion. Author: Field Clover and Beach Grass (collection of stories), 1898. Home: Arlington Heights, Mass. Died 1907.

SWEZEY, Goodwin Deloss, astronomer; b. Rockford, Ill., Jan. 10, 1851; s. Lewis Samuel and Sarah (Cook) S.; A.B., Beloit (Wis.) Coll., 1873, A.M., 1876; Yale Div. Sch., 1873-74, 1875-76; B.D., Andover (Mass.) Theol. Sem., 1880; studied summer schs. of U. of Ill. and Ind. U.; m. Mary Frances Hill, Aug. 7, 1884 (died 1891); children—Mrs. Minnie Elmendorf, Emma Josephine, Marien Francis. Instr. natural sciences, Beloit Coll., 1874-75, 1876-79; prof., Doane College, Crete, Neb. 1886-94; meteorologist, Neb. State Bd. Agr., 1891-1900; prof. astron. and meteorology, U. of Neb., 1896—. Dir. Neb. Weather Service, 1884-96; meteorologist, U.S. Expt. Sta., Lincoln, 1894-1906. Author: New Elementary Agriculture (with others), 1903; Practical Exercises in Astronomy, 1904; Boys' Book of Astronomy, 1929. Home: Lincoln, Neb. Died July 10, 1934.

SWIFT, Carl Brown, clergyman, educator; b. Billings, Mo., May 30, 1888; s. William H. and Lucinda Frances (Turner) S.; student Marionville (Mo.) Coll., 1906-10; A.B., Culver-Stockton Coll., Canton, Mo., 1915, D.D., 1924; B.D., Yale Div. Sch., 1918; m. Dorothy Pearl Wallace, Sept. 8, 1912; children—Milton Wallace, Bertha Karleen, Helen Rosemary. Ordained ministry Disciples of Christ, 1918; pastor Uhrichsville, O., 1918-20, Joplin, Mo., 1920; prof. English Bible, Drury Sch. of the Bible, 1921—, also dean. Republican. Mason, K.P. Author of 6 handbooks (S.S. lessons) for Disciples of Christ. Home: Springfield, Mo. Died Oct. 26, 1930.

SWIFT, Clarence Franklin, clergyman; b. Oberlin, O., July 27, 1861; s. Henry O. and Angelina R. S.; A.B., Oberlin Coll., 1883; student Oberlin Theol. Sem., 1883-84; grad. Union Theol. Sem., 1886; D.D., Knox Coll., Galesburg, Ill., 1900; m. Janet Huntington McKelvey, July 27, 1886. Ordained Congl. ministry, 1886; pastor Smyrna, N.Y., 1886-88, Saratoga Springs, 1888-94, Plymouth Ch., Lansing, Mich., 1894-99, Park Av. Ch., Minneapolis, Minn., 1899-1902, Central Ch., Fall River, Mass., 1902—. Pres. Congl. Edn. Soc., 1913—. Republican. Died Mar. 25, 1918.

SWIFT, Eben, army officer; b. Ft. Chadbourne, Tex., May 11, 1854; s. Ebenezer (surgeon U.S.A.) and Sarah Edwards (Capers) S.; student Racine Coll. (Wis.), Washington U., Dickinson Coll., Carlisle, Pa.; grad. U.S. Mil. Acad., 1876; m. Susanne Palmer Swift, May 17, 1880; children—Eben, Innis Palmer, Wesley Merritt, Mrs. Clara Humphrey, Mrs. Katharine McKinney. Commd. 2d lt. 14th Inf., 1876; promoted through grades to brig. gen. regular army, Sept. 30, 1916; served as maj. gen. N.A., 1917-18; retired, May 11, 1918; promoted to rank of major general, retired. Served in Indian campaigns, Wyoming, Mont., Neb., Idaho, Colo., against Sioux, Cheyenne, Bannock and Ute Indians; later a.d.c. to Gen. Wesley Merritt; served in Cuba and Puerto Rico; asst. instr. Inf. and Cav. Sch.; asst. comdt. at Gen. Service and Staff Coll.; dir. Army War Coll.; in campaign against Moros in Philippines; chief of staff Western Dept.; comdt. Army Service Schs.; comdr. 2d Cav. Brigade in Mexico; comdr. cav. div. at El Paso, Tex., 1916; assigned as comdr. Camp Gordon, Atlanta, Ga., 1917; organized and comd. 82d Div. till Dec. 1918; with A.E.F. in France till Feb. 1918; chief Am. mil. mission and comdr. U.S. forces in Italy, Feb.-Aug. 1918. Died Apr. 25, 1938.

SWIFT, Edgar James, psychologist; b. Ravenna, O., July 24, 1860; s. Charles Edgar and Emily (Folger) S.; grad. Phillips Exeter Acad., 1882; A.B., Amherst, 1886; studied univs. of Leipzig and Berlin, 1889-92; Ph.D., Clark U., 1903; m. Claire Martha Coburn, Dec. 22, 1906. Science teacher, Lake Forest, Ill., Acad., 1887-89; teacher psychology, Stevens Point Normal Sch., 1895-1900; prof. psychology and edn., Washington U., 1903-25, head dept. of psychol-

mer session, Peabody Coll. for Teachers, Nashville, Tenn., 1914, U. of Wyoming, 1915, U. of Chicago, 1916, Kansas Agricultural Coll., 1917, U. of Calif., 1921; spl. lecturer applied psychology, Post Grad. Sch., U.S. Naval Acad., 1920-27, Naval War Coll., 1921-24. Author: Mind in the Making, 1908; Youth and the Race, 1912; Learning by Doing, 1914; Psychology and the Day's Work, 1918; Business Power Through Psychology, 1925; Psychology of Youth, 1927; How to Influence Men, 1927; The Psychology of Childhood, 1930; The Jungle of the Mind, 1931; also articles in scientific jours. Home: St. Louis, Mo. Died Aug. 30, 1932.

SWIFT, Edward Foster, capitalist; s. Gustavus Franklin and Ann Maria (Higgins) S.; m. Hortense Newcomer; children—Annie May (Mrs. Huntington B. Henry), Theodore Philip, Edward Foster. Pres. Compania Swift Internacional, S.A., Swift Refrigerator Transportation Co.; v.p., Swift & Co., Libby, McNeill & Libby, Ft. Worth Stock Yards Co.; dir. Swift & Co., Ltd. (London), Swift Refrigerator Transportation Co., Ft. Worth Stock Yards Co., Lake Shore Trust & Savings Bank, Continental Ill. Bank & Trust Co., Continental Chicago Corp., Chicago Corp. Home: Chicago and Lake Forest, Ill. Died May 28, 1932.

SWIFT, Ernest John, vice chmn. Central Com. Am. Red Cross; b. Santa Cruz, Calif., Jan. 8, 1883; s. Elias John and Libby Ann (Wilson) S.; ed. Stanford U., 1904-08; m. Helen Griffin, of Washington, D.C., Oct. 6, 1927. Newspaper work San José, San Francisco, Honolulu, 1908-14; ins. exec. San Francisco and New York, 1914-18; enlisted with American Red Cross for service overseas, assigned to 2d Div., U.S. Army, 1918; dep. commissioner American Red Cross in Montenegro, 1919-20; asst. to European commr. Am. Red Cross, Paris, 1920-23; asst. to v. chmn. in charge insular and foreign operations, Washington, D.C., 1923-31; sec. gen. League of Red Cross Socs., Paris, 1932-36; vice chmn. Central Com. Am. Red Cross, 1935—. Mem. Am. Red Cross China Famine Investigation Commn., 1929; dir. Am. Red Cross Hurricane Relief, Dominican Republic, 1930; dir. Am. Red Cross Earthquake Relief Nicaragua, 1931; mem. governing body Nansen Internat. Office for Refugees League of Nations, 1932-36; rep. League of Red Cross Socs. on exec. com. Internat. Relief Union, 1932-36; v.p. 15th Internat. Red Cross Conf., Tokyo, 1934; chmn. Am. delegation Internat. Air Ambulance Congress, Brussels, 1935; sec. gen. Third Pan-Am. Red Cross Conf., Rio de Janeiro, 1935; mem. U.S. govt. delegation to 16th Internat. Red Cross Conf., London, 1938. Chmn. Am. Red Cross del. to investigate European war relief needs, 1939. Decorated Legion of Honor (France); Order of Crown of Italy; Order of Sacred Treasure (Japan); Orders of White Eagle and St. Sava (Jugoslavia); Order of Merit (Germany); Medal of Honor (Ecuador); Order Three Stars (Latvia); also decorations from Bulgaria, China, Costa Rica, Cuba, Spain, Estonia, Hungary, Latvia, Norway, Poland, Uruguay, Venezuela. Mem. Kappa Sigma. Home: Washington, D.C. Died Oct. 19, 1941.

SWIFT, George Wilkins, surgeon; b. Whidby Island, Wash., Aug. 31, 1882; s. James Henry and Emily C. (Wilson) S.; Ph.G., U. of Wash., 1901; M.D., Northwestern U., 1907; studied U. of Vienna, 1909-10; m. Florence Hilda Shirecker, June 29, 1910. Interne Ill. Eye, Ear, Nose and Throat Infirmary, 1907-08; asst. eye surgeon same, 1908-09, also clin. asst. Rush Med. Coll.; settled in Seattle, 1910, and specialized in ophthalmology and later neuro-surgery; pres. Neuro Surgical Clinic, 1928—; chief dept. neuro-surgery, King County Hosp. (Harborview), Children's Orthopedic Hosp.; formerly chief dept. neuro-surgery Seattle City Hosp. A leader in development and equipment of Harborview Hosp., Seattle; founder and former pres. Public Health League of Wash. Served as lt., later capt., U.S. Army, 1917-18. Trustee Gorgas Memorial. Fellow Am. Coll. Surgeons. Republican. Congregationalist. Mason. Contbr. to History of American Medicine, also to med. jours.; asso. editor Western Jour. of Surgery and Am. Jour. Surgery. Home: Seattle, Wash. Died Dec. 18, 1938.

SWIFT, Gustavus Franklin, packer, merchant; b. Cape Cod, Mass., June 24, 1839; engaged in packing business and inaugurated business of shipping fresh meats; pres. Swift & Co., one of the largest Am. packing firms. Home: Chicago, Ill. Died 1903.

SWIFT, James Carroll, live stock commn. merchant; b. Winsted, Conn., Feb. 7, 1869; s. John Henry and Nora (Carroll) S.; LL.B., Cornell U., 1893; m. Laura Laing, Nov. 1898; children—Mary Laing, John Carroll, Nora Carroll (Mrs. Wendel Baker), Laura Laing. Admitted to bar, 1893, and in practice 1893-99; in business, 1899—; pres. Swift and Henry Live Stock Commn. Co., Kansas City, and St. Joseph, Mo.; pres. Am. Royal Live Stock Show, Kansas City. Mem. Kansas City Chamber of Commerce. Trustee U. of Kan., Sunset Hill Sch. for Girls. Republican. Catholic. Home: Kansas City, Mo. Died Feb. 2, 1938.

SWIFT, Lewis, astronomer; b. at Clarkson, N.Y., Feb. 29, 1820; s. Gen. Lewis and Anna (Forbs) S.; ed. Clarkson Acad.; hon. Ph.D., U. of Rochester, 1880; twice married. About 1854 took up study of astronomy, and made a 3-in. refractor, which was accidentally broken; bought a 4½-in. refractor with which he discovered numerous comets; became dir. Warner Obs., Rochester, N.Y., 1882; subsequently of Lowe Obs. Discovered many comets and nebulæ, and received medals and prizes from leading Am. and foreign socs. Before the completion of the Warner Obs. the people of Rochester presented Dr. Swift with a 16-in. refractor costing $11,000, with which he discovered 900 nebulæ there and over 300 at Echo Mountain, Calif., and in both places a dozen comets. In 1878, during the total solar eclipse, at Denver, discovered two intra-Mercurial planets; received 3 gold, 1 silver, and 4 bronze medals and $1,150 cash for astron. discoveries. Fellow Royal Astron. Soc. of England, 1879. Author: Simple Lessons in Astronomy, 1888. Died Jan. 5, 1913.

SWIFT, Lindsay, editor; b. Boston, July 29, 1856; s. John Lindsay and Sarah Edes (Allen) S.; A.B., Harvard, 1877; m. Katherine Agnes Jackson, July 19, 1881. Editor Boston Public Library. Pres. N.E. & Clifton Copper Co., of Ariz., 1903-06. Author: Massachusetts Election Sermons, 1897; The Great Debate between Hayne and Webster, 1898; Brook Farm (Nat. Studies in Am. Letters Series); Literary Landmarks of Boston, 1903; Benjamin Franklin (Beacon Biographies) 1910; William Lloyd Garrison (Am. Crisis Biographies), 1911. Edited several works on Am. history. Home: West Roxbury, Mass. Died Sept. 11, 1921.

SWIFT, Louis Franklin, packer; b. Sagamore, Cape Cod, Mass., Sept. 27, 1861; s. Gustavus F. and Ann M. (Higgins) S.; m. Ida May Butler, Sept. 9, 1880. Pres. Swift & Co., packers, Chicago, 1903-31, chmn. bd., 1931-32. Mem. Soc. Mayflower Descendants. Home: Lake Forest, Ill. Died May 12, 1937.

SWIFT, Oscar William, congressman; b. at Paines Hollow, N.Y., Apr. 11, 1869; student U. of Mich., 1888-90; LL.B., New York Law Sch., 1896; married. Admitted to N.Y. bar, 1897; mem. law firm of Watson, Kristeller & Swift. Mem. 64th and 65th Congresses (1915-19), 9th N.Y. Dist. Republican. Home: Brooklyn, N.Y. Died June 30, 1940.

SWIFT, Polemus Hamilton, clergyman; b. Palmyra, Wis., Oct. 24, 1853; s. Nathaniel and Lydia (Hamilton) S.; A.B., Northwestern U., 1881, D.D., 1896; grad. Garrett Bibl. Inst., 1883; A.M., Ph.D., Syracuse U., 1888; m. Olive Lois Boynton, Nov. 20, 1883; children—Marian Ella (dec.), George Hamilton (dec.), Mildred Eloise (Mrs. Richard H. Manny), Rosamond Boynton (dec.). Ordained M E ministry, 1882; pastor Centenary Ch., Chicago, 1883-84, Court St. Ch., Rockford, Ill., 1885-90, Oakland (Chicago), 1890-95, Englewood (Chicago), 1895-1900, Wesley (Chicago), 1900-04, Austin (Chicago), 1904-09, Madison Av. Church, Baltimore, Apr. 1909-15, River Forest, Ill., 1915-18; dist. supt. Chicago Southern Dist., 1918-23; chmn. finance com. Rock River Conf. Commn., 1923-25. Trustee Garrett Bibl Inst., 1899-1905; del. Gen. Conf., M.E. Ch., 1896, 1900, 04, 08, 20; del. Ecumenical Conf., London, 1901. Author: Star in the West, 1898; Magnetism of the Cross, 1904; Gospel Cheer Messages, 1908. Died Apr. 14, 1935.

SWIFT, Samuel, music and art critic; b. Newark, N.J., Jan. 19, 1873; s. Joseph and Gertrude Horton (Dorr) S.; B.S., U of Pa., 1894; Phila. Mus. Acad., 1890-93; m. at Phila., Ellen Mary Faulkner, of Leicestershire, Eng., June 8, 1896. Organist in various chs., Wilmington, Del., 1891-94; mus. critic New York Evening Mail (The Mail and Express), 1894-1907; art critic, same, 1896-1907; also did miscellaneous editorial work: London and Paris corr same, 1900; asst. music critic New York Tribune, 1907-09, New York Sun, 1909-10; art critic, New York Sun, 1912-13; frequent contbr. to mags. on music and art topics. One of founders New Music Soc. of America (sec. 1906). Sec. treas. Wm. J. Smith Co., N E. Paper Box Machine Co., New Haven, Conn., 1907-10; sec. treas. Alvord & Swift, Inc., New York, 1911—. Independent Republican. Home: New York, N.Y. Died July 21, 1914.

SWIFT, William, rear admiral U.S.N.; b. Windham, Conn., Mar. 17, 1848; s. William and Harriet Gray (Byrne) S.; grad. U.S. Naval Acad., 1867; m. Grace Virginia, d. Commodore George M. Ransom, of Richfield Springs, N.Y., Sept. 18, 1872. On flagship Susquehanna, home sta., 1867; became ensign, 1868; promoted through grades to rear admiral, Jan. 3, 1908. Ordnance duty, Washington Navy Yard, 1886-90; cruiser New York and battleship Indiana, 1894-97; ordnance officer, Navy Yard, New York, 1897-1900; comdg. Prairie, Concord, Yorktown, 1900-02; mem. Gen. Bd., and Army and Navy Joint Board, 1902-06; commandant Navy Yard, Boston, 1907-09; aid for material, Navy Dept., 1909-10; retired, Mar. 17, 1910. Home: Richfield Springs, N.Y. Died May 30, 1919.

SWIGART, Edmund Kearsley, mfr.; b. Bucyrus, O., Apr. 16, 1867; s. Joseph R. and Augusta M. (Sweeney) S.; ed. pub. schs.; m. Henrietta M. Meyers, June 3, 1891; 1 son, Harry M. U.S. mail service, 1885-91; with Bucyrus Co., 1891—, successively accountant, sec. and treas., and sr. v.p., 1911—; chmn. bd. Oilgear Co. Republican. Presbyn. Home: Milwaukee, Wis. Died July 7, 1934.

SWIGER, Wilbur Moore, editor; b. Bridgeport, W.Va., July 30, 1890; s. George Washington and Mary Catherine (Moore) S.; grad. Clarksburg (W.Va.) High Sch., 1911; student U. of Wis. Sch. of Journalism, 1913; unmarried. Began as reporter for Clarksburg Daily News, 1909; later reporter and city editor Clarksburg Telegram; then night news editor, Bluefield Daily Telegraph; feature writer Clarksburg Telegram, 1928, editor-in-chief, 1934—. Served in U.S. Marine Corps, 1918-19, World War. Mem. Am. Legion (vice comdr. local post, 1920). Republican. Methodist. Mason. Author of series of travel articles on W.Va. scenery. Home: Clarksburg, W.Va. Died Apr. 12, 1939.

SWINBURNE, William Thomas, rear admiral U.S.N.; b. Newport, R.I., Aug. 24, 1847; s. Daniel Thomas and Harriet (Knowles) S. Grad. U.S. Naval Acad., 1866; after graduation on bd. Saco, West Indian Squadron, 1866-67; Kearsarge, S. Pacific Squadron, 1868-70; promoted ensign, 1868; master, 1869; lt., 1870; Michigan, 1870-72; flagship Lancaster, S. Atlantic, 1872-74; torpedo sch., 1875; Hartford, 1875-77; Trenton, China sta., 1883-86; Naval Acad., 1886-90; promoted lt. comdr., 1887; exec. officer Boston, 1890-93; comd. battalion landed in Honolulu, Jan. 16-Apr. 1, 1893; head dept. seamanship, Naval Acad., 1893-97; promoted comdr., 1896; comd. Helena, 1897-99; served in N. Atlantic Fleet during Spanish-Am. War; captured Spanish steamer Miguel Jovar, Apr. 23, 1898; with convoy to Santiago-Cienfuegas blockade, June 1898; engagement of Tunas, July 1 and 2, 1898, Manzanilla, destruction Spanish gunboats and transports, July 18, 1898; joined fleet at Manila under Admiral Dewey, Feb. 1899; convoyed 23d Inf. to Jolo, June 1899; senior officer in command of vessels assisting Gen. Lawton in his campaign, Paranaque and Bacoor (Manila Bay), June 10-13, 1899; Portsmouth Navy Yard, Oct. 1899-1902; promoted capt., Mar. 1901; comd. Texas, 1902-04; mem. General Bd., Washington, 1904-06; rear admiral, July 22, 1906; comdr.-in-chief Pacific Squadron, 1906-09; War Coll., June 10-Oct. 1, 1909; retired, Aug. 24, 1909; m. Katherine Elsie Vincent, Nov. 27, 1875 (died 1904); m. 2d, Mrs. Sophie Cook Poe, Sept. 7, 1905. Home: New York, N.Y. Died Mar. 3, 1928.

SWINDALL, Charles, judge; b. College Mound, Tex., Feb. 13, 1876; s. Jonathan Ward and Mary E. (Standley) S.; grad. high sch., Terrell, Tex., 1895; student Vanderbilt, 1895-96; LL.B., Cumberland U., Lebanon, Tenn., 1897; m. Emma Eulala Endres, Jan 31, 1911. Admitted to Okla. Ty. bar, 1897, and began practice at Grand; county atty. of Day (now Ellis) Co., 1898-1900; mem. 66th Congress (3d session 1920-21, unexpired term of Dick T. Morgan, dec.), 8th Okla. Dist.; judge Dist. Court of Okla., 20th Dist., 1924-29; became justice Supreme Court of Okla., 1929. Died June 14, 1939.

SWING, Albert Temple, theologian; b. Bethel, O., Jan. 18, 1849; s. George W. and Rosannah (West) S.; A.B., Oberlin Coll., 1874, A.M., 1894, D.D., 1901; D.B., Yale, 1877; U. of Berlin, 1890-91, U. of Halle-Wittenberg, 1891-92; m. Alice Edwards, d. Prof. Hiram Mead, of Oberlin, O., Aug. 1, 1882. Ordained Congl. ministry, 1878; pastor Fremont, Neb., 1878-86, Cortland, N.Y., 1886-87, Detroit, 1887-90; historical travel, 1892-93, 1905-06; prof. church history, 1893-1916, and became emeritus professor 1916, Oberlin Theol. Sem. Author: Theology of Albrecht Ritschl, 1901; Outline of the Doctrinal Development in the Western Church, 1904; Life of James Harris Fairchild, 1907; Pre-Reformers and the Reformation, 1910. Visited univs. in Germany, Scotland and Eng., 1913-14. Home: Coconut Grove, Fla. Died Sept. 21, 1925.

SWINTON, John, editor, author; b. near Edinburgh, Scotland, Dec. 12, 1829; s. William and Jane S.; earlier edn. there; afterward at Easthampton Sem., Mass.; later entered New York Med. Coll., class of 1859, but was not graduated; chief of editorial staff New York Times, 1860-70; later editorial writer, chief of staff, and again editorial writer, New York Sun, 1875-97; propr. and editor John Swinton's Paper (weekly), 1883-87. Author: John Swinton's Travels, 1880; Striking for Life, 1894. Wrote for newspapers and magazines. Home: Brooklyn, N.Y. Died 1901.

SWISHER, Charles Clinton, univ. prof.; b. Muncy, Pa.; s. Charles and Lucinda (Clinton) S.; Bloomsburg Acad.; A.B., Yale, 1876; Berlin, Heidelberg, and Paris, 1876-79; LL.B., Columbia, 1881; LL.D., Univ. of Guadalajara, 1890; Ph.D., Cornell U., 1895; LL.D., Mt. St. Mary's Coll., Emmitsburg, Md., 1905; unmarried. Planted coffee and cocoa in Mexico and S.A., 1883-96; commd. by President Diaz, of Mexico, to study the condition of coffee production in other countries and possibilities of the eucalyptus for Mexican planting; also traveled extensively in Europe, Asia, Africa, Australasia, and S.A. After an attack of yellow fever, returned to U.S., 1892, and resumed under Dr. Moses Coit Tyler of Cornell, the study of history which he had begun under Dr. Leopold

Ranke, in 1878; prof. history, Columbian (now George Washington) U., 1896-99; prof. comparative politics, Sch. of Jurisprudence and Diplomacy, George Washington U., 1899-1927 (emeritus). Author: History of the Work of the Religious Orders in Mexico, 1888; The Eucalyptus, Native and Transplanted, 1889; The Cultivation of Coffee and Cocoa in the Islands of Java and Sumatra, 1890. After retirement travelled in N. Africa, visiting Fez, Timbucktu, Khartum and Zanzibar. Home: Washington, D.C. Died Feb. 3, 1940.

SWITZER, George Washington, clergyman; b. Tippecanoe County, Ind., Nov. 2, 1854; s. Peter and Catharine (Shambaugh) S.; A.B., Asbury (now DePauw) U., Greencastle, Ind., 1881, A.M., 1884, D.D., 1900; m. Lida Westfall, Sept. 20, 1881. Ordained M.E. ministry, 1880; pastor Plainfield, Ind., 1881-84, Shawnee Mound, 1884-87, Crawfordsville, 1887-92, Brazil, 1892-95, West Lafayette, 1895-1901, La Porte, 1901-03; presiding elder, Lafayette Dist., 1903-09; spl. appmts., 1910-11; pastor Stidham Memorial Ch., nr. Lafayette, 1912-17, Epworth Memorial, South Bend, 1918, Epworth Memorial Ch., Cleveland, O., 1919; asst. pastor Epworth-Euclid Ch., Cleveland, 1920-22; asst. pastor Epworth M.E. Ch., South Bend, Ind.; pres. Golden Jubilee Camp Meeting, Battle Ground, Ind., 1923; pres. Battle Ground Assembly, 1925-26, pres. emeritus, 1928—. Trustee, De Pauw U., 1924, mem. exec. com. Republican. Sr. mem. northwest Ind. Conf. M.E. Ch. Lectures on "Fifty Years in the Ministry"; "The Man Behind Ben Hur," with personal recollections of Gen. Lew Wallace. Mason. Lectured on "Humanics," Nov. 9, 1939. Home: St. Joseph, Mich. Died July 9, 1940.

SWITZER, Maurice, author; b. New Orleans, La., Oct. 16, 1870; s. Henry and Matilda (Steinhardt) S.; ed. pub. schs.; m. Sophie Cohn, Jan. 27, 1898. Began as ad. mgr. Havana-Am. Co., New York, 1901; ad. mgr. Wilson Distilling Co., 10 yrs.; with Leslie-Judge Co., New York, 1914-15; vice-pres. Kelly-Springfield Tire Co. Author: Wild and Tame Advertising, 1914; Who Pays the Advertising Bills, 1915; Letters of a Self-Made Failure, 1915; Satire and Song (verse), 1917; Cashing in on What You've Got, 1918; Trying It on the Dog, 1921. Home: New York, N.Y. Died Apr. 1929.

SWOOPE, William Irvin, congressman; b. Clearfield, Pa., Oct. 3, 1862; s. H. Bucher and Susanna Patton (Irvin) S.; grad. Hill Sch., Pottstown, Pa., 1882; Phillips Andover Acad.; LL.B., Harvard, 1886; m. Elizabeth Hartswick, Oct. 4, 1899. Began practice at Clearfield, 1886; dist. atty. Clearfield County, 1901-07; speaker for Rep. Nat. Com. in all presdl. campaigns, 1900-20; dep. atty. gen. of Pa., 1919-23; mem. 68th and 69th Congresses (1923-27), 23d Pa. Dist. Presbyn. Home: Clearfield, Pa. Died Oct. 9, 1930.

SWORD, James Brade, artist; b. Phila., Oct. 11, 1839; s. John D. and Mary (Parry) S.; A.B., Central High Sch., Phila., 1856; m. Matilda Wagner Shuster, Feb. 11, 1869. Landscape and portrait painter. Gold medal, oil painting, Am. Art Soc., 1903, and gold medal, water color, 1903; awarded prize, New Orleans Expn. Commd. by Congress, 1911, to paint portrait of Former Speaker J. W. Jones, for Ho. of Rep. Pres. Phila. Soc. Artists, Artists' Fund Soc.; founder and hon. mem. Art Club Phila. Home: Philadelphia, Pa. Died Dec. 1, 1915.

SWORDS, Henry Cotheal, banker; b. Oct. 31, 1854; s. James Richard and Ann Maria (Cotheal) S.; m. Elizabeth Clarkson. Pres. and trustee Fulton Trust Co.; trustee Bank of New York & Trust Co. Home: New York, N.Y. Died Feb. 6, 1924.

SYDENSTRICKER, Edgar, sanitarian; b. Shanghai, China, July 15, 1881; s. Rev. Absolom (D.D.) and Caroline (Stulting) S.; came to U.S., 1896; M.A., Washington and Lee U., 1902; post-grad. work, Washington & Lee U., U. of Chicago and Johns Hopkins U.; m. Alice May Ringer, Sept. 21, 1908 (divorced 1932); children—Rhoda Virginia, Charles Edgar; m. 2d, Phyllis Perrott, Oct. 5, 1932. Fellow in polit. economy, U. of Chicago, 1907-08; teacher, high schs., Va., 1902-05; editorial and spl. writer various newspapers and mags., 1904-08; spl. investigator in charge industrial community studies U.S. Immigration Commn., and U.S. Commn. on Industrial Relations, 1908-15; apptd. 1st pub. health statistician U.S. Public Health Service, 1915; granted leave of absence, 1923-24, to serve as chief of service of epidemiol. intelligence and public health statistics, League of Nations, Geneva, in initiating the statis. work of the League's Internat. health orgn.; statistical consultant to N.Y. State Charities Aid Assn., 1926—, and U.S.P.H.S., 1928—; dir. of research, Milbank Memorial Fund, 1928—. Lecturer vital statistics, George Washington U., 1921-23, on social research, Columbia, N.Y. City, 1929—, on population problems, Nanking U., China, 1930. Fellow Am. Statis. Assn., Am. Public Health Assn., Royal Statis. Soc. (Gt. Britain), A.A.A.S. Democrat. Presbyn. Author: Collective Bargaining in Anthracite Industry; Conditions of Labor in U.S.; Brief History of Taxation in Virginia; Health and Environment. Died Mar. 19, 1936.

SYKES, Frederick Henry, college pres.; b. Queensville, Ont., Oct. 21, 1863; s. James and Sarah (Earp) S.; A.B., U. of Toronto, 1885, A.M., 1886; student, scholar and fellow Johns Hopkins, 1891-95, Ph.D., 1894; mem. Exeter Coll., Oxford, Eng., 1899; m. Louise Lavell Ryckman, of Brockville, Ont., 1899. Teacher in secondary schs. of Ontario, 1885-91; lecturer Ont. Sch. of Pedagogy, 1892-93; examiner in English, edn. dept. of Ont. and U. of Toronto, 1893-97; prof. English and history, Western Univ., London, Ont., 1895-97; staff lecturer, English lit., Am. Soc. for Extension Univ. Teaching, 1897-1903; prof. English lit. and dir. extension teaching, Columbia, 1903-10; dir. tech. edn. (schs. of indsl. and household arts) and prof. English, Teachers Coll. (Columbia), 1910-13; pres. Conn. Coll. for Women, New London, 1913—. Lecturer, Johns Hopkins, 1900-02, U. of Chicago, 1902, Brooklyn Inst., 1900-02, 1906-10. Author: French Elements in Middle English, 1899; Elementary English Composition, 1901, 1904; Syllabus of Lectures on Shakespeare, 1903; Syllabus of Lectures on the History of English Literature in the Nineteenth Century, 1904; Composition for Grammar Schools, 1898; Ontario Public School Composition, 1910. Died Oct. 13, 1917.

SYKES, Jerome H., comic opera comedian; b. Washington; s. Henry S.; ed. Baltimore; made début as actor Mar. 9, 1884; married. In 1898 played Foxy Quiller in The Highwayman; starred 1900 in Chris and the Wonderful Lamp; in 1901 in Foxy Quiller, and in 1903 in The Billionaire, in Klaw & Erlanger Opera Co. Died 1903.

SYKES, Mabel, author; b. Chicago, Ill., Feb. 6, 1868; d. James W. and Sarah Jane (Clark) S.; grad. West Div. High Sch., Chicago, 1886; B.S., Wellesley, 1891; grad. work U. of Chicago, 1896-1901. Teacher, Natick, Mass., 1891-92, Alma Coll., St. Thomas, Ont., Can., 1892-95, Bowen High Sch., Chicago, 1895—. Presbyn. Republican. Author: Source Book of Problems in Geometry, 1912; also (with Clarence E. Comstock) Plane Geometry, 1918, Solid Geometry, 1922, Beginner's Algebra, 1922, Second Course in Algebra, 1923; CBA Hurdle Tests for Elementary Algebra. Home: Chicago, Ill. Died Feb. 6, 1938.

SYLE, Louis du Pont, educator, journalist, author; b. Shanghai, China, Aug. 2, 1857; s. Edward William and Jane Mary Winter (Davis) S.; grad. Yale, 1879, A.M., 1888; m. Edith Wilkinson, June 17, 1882. U.S. consul in Madeira, 1882-84; asst. prof. English, Univ. of Calif., 1892-1902; dramatic critic San Francisco Examiner, 1898-1900, San Francisco Call, 1900-01. Author: From Milton to Tennyson, 1894; Four English Poems, 1896; Essays in Dramatic Criticism, 1898. Plays: Angelica's Choice (comedy); Lord Ogleby; The Chaplain's Revenge; Love and Law (from French of Sandeau and Regnier); Francine's Love Problem (from French of Dumas fils); Mrs. Moneyton's Prince (comedy—with Edward Elsner); In Southern El Dorado (dramatic sketch); Villiers (romantic opera—music by N. Clifford Page). Editor: Burke on Conciliation (critical edit.); Scott's Lady of the Lake; DeFoe's Plague Year. Died 1903.

SYLVESTER, Frederick Oakes, artist; b. Brockton, Mass., Oct. 8, 1869; s. Charles Fred and Mary Louise (Kilburn) S.; grad. Durfee High Sch., Fall River, Mass., 1888; Mass. Normal Art Sch., Boston, 1888-92; m. Florence Gerry, Dec. 25, 1892. Prof. of art, Newcomb Coll., New Orleans, 1892; teacher of drawing and painting, Central High Sch., St. Louis, 1892-1913. Represented in permanent collection of City Art Mus., St. Louis; mural decorations, Noonday Club, Central High Sch. (St. Louis), High Sch., Decatur, Ill. Bronze medal, St. Louis Expn., 1904; silver medal, Portland Expn., 1905; Fine Arts Bldg. prize, Soc. Western Artists, 1906. Christian Scientist. Author: Verses, 1900; The Great River (containing half tones of 24 oil paintings by author), 1911. Home: St. Louis, Mo. Died Mar. 2, 1915.

SYMMES, Edwin Joseph, architect; b. Livermore, Calif., Feb. 14, 1883; s. Charles Henry and Sarah Elizabeth (Johnson) S.; prep. edn., pub. schs., Livermore and Oakland, Calif., Oakland Evening High Sch.; student Calif. Sch. of Mech. Arts, San Francisco, 1 yr.; B.S., U. of Calif., 1909; m. Minnehaha Harris, July 9, 1913; children—Robert Edward, Barbara Eleanor. Began as draftsman, Bliss & Faville, architects, San Francisco, 1909; with William C. Hays, architect, 1912; in practice for self, 1913—; supervising architect of concessions, Panama Pacific Expn., 1913-15; moved to Bakersfield, Calif., 1927; partner firm Symmes & Cullimore, 1927-30; in practice alone, 1930—. Prin. works: Glacier Point Hotel; bldgs. at Neptune Beach Park and Fernside Park (both in Alameda, Calif.); Alameda Masonic Temple; many high sch. and grammar sch. bldgs.; Christian Science Ch., Bakersfield; libraries, Oildale and Tehachapi; etc. Mem. bd. mgrs. Yosemite Nat. Park Co., 1920-23; mem. Alameda City Planning Commn., 1927; pres. Bakersfield Community Theater, 1930-32. Mem. S. J. Council, State Chamber of Commerce. Awarded silver and bronze medals, Panama Pacific Expn., 1915. Republican. Mason, Moose, Eagle. Home: Bakersfield, Calif. Died Sept. 10, 1935.

SYMMES, Frank Jameson, businessman; b. Kingston, Mass., June 7, 1847; s. William and Caroline Hannah (Jameson) S.; ed. Partridge Acad., Duxbury, Mass., 1860-64, Lawrence Scientific Sch., Harvard, 1864-66, S.B., 1900, as of class of 1867; U.S. Naval Acad., engr. class, 1866-68 (spl. grad. with first engr. class, made up of grads. of scientific schs.); m. Anna A. Day, Mar. 30, 1871. Served on Dacotah, S. Pacific Squadron, Aug. 1868-July 1869, Pensacola, Saginaw, Resaca and flagship Saranac, 1870-71; resigned from Navy, July 1871, as 2d asst. engr. Salesman, 1871-76, pres., 1886-1903, then v.p. Thomas Day Co., gas fixtures, San Francisco; pres. Central Trust Co. of Calif., 1903-07; treas. Pacific Meter Co., 1902—. Apptd. receiver Citizens' State Bank, Feb. 18, 1908, Calif. Safe Deposit & Trust Co., Mar. 24, 1910—. Mem. Bd. Edn., San Francisco, 1894-95; mem. Bd. Visitors U.S. Naval Acad., 1899; chmn. com. San Francisco exhibit, St. Louis Expn., 1904. Pres. Mchts. Assn., 1901-08; pres. State Conf. and v.p. (1904-06) Nat. Conf. Charities and Correction; v.p. Calif. Sch. Mech. Arts; mem. exec. com. Pub. Health Commission, 1903-06; trustee and moderator of bd. First Unitarian Soc., 1901-06. Republican. Home: Berkeley, Calif. Deceased.

SYMMONDS, Charles Jacobs, army officer; b. Holland, Mich., Oct. 6, 1866; s. Robert and Phillis Wey (Jacobs) S.; grad. U.S. Mil. Acad., 1890; m. George Crook, d. Brig. Gen. Earl D. Thomas, U.S.A., Fort McIntosh, Texas, Feb. 21, 1894; children—Robert Earl (killed in action, World War), Katharine Godfrey, Phillis Wey. Commissioned 2d lt. 18th Inf., June 12, 1890; promoted through grades to brig. gen. Nov. 3, 1923; served as capt. a.q.m., vols., Spanish-Am. War, 1898; comdr. Intermediate Depot, Gièvres, France, the principal storage depot of A.E.F. during World War; retired, Oct. 31, 1930. Awarded D.S.M. "for exceptionally meritorious and distinguished service" at Gièvres; Officer Legion of Honor (France); Officer Polonia Restituta (Poland). Home: Chevy Chase, Md. Died July 16, 1941.

SYMONDS, Brandreth, physician; b. Ossining, N.Y., Mar. 4, 1863; s. Col. Henry C. and Beatrice (Brandreth) S.; A.B., Hobart Coll., 1881, A.M., 1884, LL.D., 1921; M.D., Coll. Phys. and Surg., 1884; house phys., Bellevue Hosp., 1886; m. Caroline B. Bachelder, Dec. 31, 1889 (died 1902); m. 2d, Florence Bacon, June 11, 1904. Has been connected with Mut. Life Ins. Co. of New York, 1888—, passing through grades of med. examiner and asst. med. dir., med. dir., 1903-07, chief med. dir., 1907—. Lecturer on life ins., Coll. Phys. and Surg. (Columbia U.), 1907-11. Sec. Assn. of Life Ins. Med. Dirs. America, 1900-07, v.p., 1910, pres., 1911; fellow N.Y. Acad. Medicine. Episcopalian. Author: Manual of Chemistry, 1889; Life Insurance Examinations, 1904. Home: St. George, S.I., N.Y. Died Aug. 10, 1924.

SYMONDS, Frederick Martin, rear admiral U.S.N.; b. Watertown, N.Y., May 16, 1846; s. Charles F. and Louise S.; apptd. to U.S. Naval Acad. from N.Y., 1862, grad. 1867; m. Annie C. Parker, 1871. Ensign, Dec. 18, 1868; master, Mar. 21, 1870; lt., Mar. 21, 1871; lt. comdr., July 31, 1899; comdr., June 19, 1897; capt., Mar. 16, 1902; retired with rank rear admiral, Dec. 1, 1902. Summer of 1863, was in active service on board Macedonian in pursuit of Confed. steamer Tacony; served on Piscataqua and Delaware, 1867-70; torpedo duty, 1871; on bd. Tuscarora, 1872-75; Minnesota, 1875-78; Jamestown, 1879-81; New Hampshire, 1882-85; Mohican, 1885-88; Michigan, 1889-92; insp. ordnance, Mare Island, Calif., 1893-96; comd. Pinta, 1896-97, Marietta, 1897-99; insp. 9th light house dist., 1899-1902; duty in connection with steamboat inspection service, 1904-05. Home: Galesville, Wis. Died Mar. 14, 1926.

SYMONDS, Joseph White, lawyer; b. Raymond, Me., Sept. 2, 1840; s. Joseph and Isabella (Jordan) S.; A.B., Bowdoin Coll., 1860, A.M., 1863; admitted to bar, 1863; (LL.D., Bowdoin, 1894); m. Mary Campbell Stuart, May 1884. Judge Supreme Jud. Ct. of Me., 1878-84; resumed practice at Portland; city solicitor, 1868-72; sr. mem. Symonds, Snow, Cook & Hutchinson, 1893—. Republican. Home: Portland, Me. Died Sept. 28, 1918.

SYMONS, (George) Gardner, artist; b. Chicago, 1865; studied Art Inst. Chicago, at Paris, Munich and London. Principal works: "The Winter Sun," Art Institute, Chicago; "Snow Clouds," Corcoran Gallery, Washington; "Sorrow," Cincinnati Mus.; "The Opalescent River," Met. Mus., New York. Awarded Carnegie prize, Nat. Acad. Design, 1910; Evans prize, Salmagundi Club, 1910; bronze medal, Buenos Aires Expn., 1910; Nat. Arts Club prize and gold medal, 1912; 3d Corcoran medal, 1912; Saltus gold medal, 1913; Dallas (Tex.) medal, 1914. N.A., 1911. Home: New York, N.Y. Died Jan. 12, 1930.

SYMONS, Thomas William, colonel U.S.A.; b. Keesville, N.Y., Feb. 7, 1849; s. Thomas and Syrena (Eaton) S.; grad. U.S. Mil. Acad., 1874; m. Letitia V. Robinson, Oct. 12, 1884. In service on civ. and mil. engring. works in Washington, D.C., Ore., Calif., Nev., Wash., Ida., Mont., and the Great Lakes until retired from mil. service, 1898, to devote attention to work of bldg. the New York state canals. Built the largest breakwater in the world, at Buffalo, N.Y.; had charge of U.S. light houses from Detroit, Mich., to Ogdensburg, N.Y.; was supt. pub. bldgs. and grounds and mil. aide to the President; mem. Canal Advisory Bd. and consulting engr. on canals State of N.Y. Author: The Columbia River, 1882; A Ship Canal from the Great Lakes to the Sea (engring. report), 1897. Home: Washington, D.C. Died Nov. 22, 1920.

SYNNOTT, Joseph J., pres. of Seton Hall Coll., 1896—; b. Long Island, N.Y., Feb. 6, 1863; common school edn. at Montclair, N.J.; grad. St. Francis Xavier's Coll., New York, 1882 (D.D., Innsbruch Univ., A.M., Yale); studied theology; ordained to R.C. priesthood. Home: South Orange, N.J. Died 1899.

SYNNOTT, Thomas Whitney; b. Glassboro, N.J., 1845; s. Myles and Harriet Heston (Whitney) Synnott; educated West Jersey Acad.; LL.D., Maryville (Tenn.) Coll., 1926, Coll. of the Ozarks, 1931; m. Mary D. Eldridge, 1872. In glass mfg. business, 1865-92; retired to devote attention to benevolent work; dir. in numerous corps. Trustee Princeton Theol. Sem. Mem. Gen. Assembly's Com. on Evangelistic Work; pres. Presbyn. Bd. of Trustees, Bd. of Publ. and S.S. Work, Bd. of Aid for Colls., v.p. Bd. of Christian Edn. Presbyn. Ch. in U.S.A.; pres. Lord's Day Alliance of N.J.; v.p. Lord's Day Alliance United States. Home: Wenonah, N.J. Died Mar. 19, 1941.

SZINNYEY, Stephen Ivor, journalist, dramatist; b. Ungvar, Hungary, June 30, 1863; s. Hermanus and Regina (Grossè) S.; ed. high sch. and univ., Budapest; Dr. Juris, U. of Budapest, 1887; unmarried. Came to U.S., 1891; was editor Troy (N.Y.) Free Press, Albany (N.Y.) Sunday Journal, Albany Herold until 1893; pub. and propr. Stevens Point (Wis.) Post, 1895; connected with Hearst publs., San Francisco and New York, 1896-1909. Served as lt. in Reserve of Austro-Hungarian Army. Became naturalized citizen of U.S., 1900. Mason (Shriner). Author: (play) The Son of the People (prod. New Theatre, now Century Theatre, New York, Feb. 28, 1910); Neutrality (book under pen name S. Ivor Stephen), 1916. Home: New York, N.Y. Died 1919.

SZUMOWSKA, Antoinette, pianist; b. Lublin, Poland, Feb. 22, 1872; d. Alexander and Wanda (Roszkowska) Szumowski; grad. Conservatory of Music, Warsaw; studied with Paderewski in Paris, also theory and composition at Paris Conservatory; m. Joseph Adamowski, of Warsaw, Sept. 1, 1896; children—Helenka, Tadeusz. First appeared in concert at Warsaw, at age of 18; recital at Salle Érard, Paris, 1891; played in London, Chapel's Popular Concerts, with symphony orchestra under Henschel and Sir Henry J. Wood; gave concerts in London and Paris; came to U.S., 1894; played with Boston Symphony Orchestra and other principal orchestras and musical orgns. in U.S.; mem. Adamowski Trio; mem. faculty N.E. Conservatory of Music, Boston, 1920—. Founder and pres. Soc. of Friends of Poland, World War. Catholic. Home: Cambridge, Mass. Died Aug. 16, 1938.

T

TABB, John Banister, R.C. priest, poet; b. Amelia Co., Va., Mar. 22, 1845; s. Thomas Yelverton and Marianna Bertrand (Archer) T.; ed. by pvt. tutors. Clerk in C.S.N., 1861-65; prisoner of war, 1864-65; studied music at Baltimore; taught St. Paul's Sch., Baltimore and Racine Coll., Mich.; became R.C., 1872; student St. Charles' Coll., Md., 1872-74, and instr. English there, 1875, 1878-82 and from 1886; ordained R.C. priest, 1884. Author: Poems; Lyrics; An Octave to Mary; Rules of English Grammar; Poems Grave and Gay, 1899; Two Lyrics, 1900; Quips and Quiddits, 1907. Home: Ellicott City, Md. Died 1909.

TABER, Henry, prof. mathematics; b. Staten Island, N.Y., June 10, 1860; s. Charles C. and Cornelia F. (Martin) T.; Ph.B., Yale, 1882; Ph.D., Johns Hopkins, 1888; m. Fanny Lawrence, Jan. 28, 1886; children—Mrs. Dorothea Stafford, Frances, Carlotta L. Asst. in mathematics, Johns Hopkins, 1888-89; docent, 1889-92, asst. prof. mathematics, 1892-1903, prof., 1903-21, prof. emeritus, 1921, Clark U. Fellow Am. Acad. Arts and Sciences. Democrat. Episcopalian. Home: Stowe, Vt. Died Jan. 6, 1936.

TABER, William Ira, banker; b. Middleville, N.Y., May 29, 1865; s. Philip and Esther (Sanderson) T.; ed. pub. schs.; m. Jennie Stuart Earl, Dec. 12, 1900 (dec.); children—Samuel Earl, Ira De Witt; m. 2d, Bessie Woodworth Organ, Oct. 5, 1919 (dec.); m. 3d, Emma B. Elwood, Feb. 12, 1927. Began with Herkimer Bank, 1883, asst. cashier, 1885-92, cashier, 1892-1906; pres. Citizens Trust Co., Utica, N.Y., 1906-28, chmn. bd., 1928—. chmn. bd. Consol. Water Co., Citizens Utica Corp., Citizens Safe Deposit Co. Pres. Masonic Hall and Asylum Fund; mem. advisory bd. Faxton Hosp. Mem. Trust Cos. Assn. State of N.Y. (v.p.), Mohawk Valley Engrs., Utica Chamber Commerce (pres.). Episcopalian. Mason. Home: Utica, N.Y. Died Sept. 10, 1931.

TADD, J. Liberty, educator; b. in England, 1854; ed. Pa. Acad. of Fine Arts; (Pd.D.); m. Phila., 1880. Owner and dir. Adirondack Summer Art Sch., Saranac Lake, N.Y.; dir. Pub. Industrial Art Sch., Phila., 1884—; has lectured in U.S., Eng., and Can. on edn. and art; Cantor lecturer, Royal Arts Soc., London, 1901. Author: New Methods in Education, 1900. Home: Philadelphia, Pa. Died June 9, 1917.

TAFEL, Gustav, lawyer; b. Munich, Germany, Oct. 13, 1830; early edn. at Ulm, Germany; grad. Latin Acad., Schorndorf, Germany, 1847; m. Therese Dorn, Jan. 19, 1870. Arrived in Cincinnati, Sept. 20, 1847; learned printing trade; engaged in journalistic work; admitted to bar 1858; in 1848 one of founders of first German Gymnastic Assn. ("Turners") in America. Enlisted private 9th Ohio inf., April 1861; served until July 1865, when mustered out as col. 106th regt. Ohio vol. inf.; elected to legislature, 1865. Mayor Cincinnati, 1897-99. Home: Cincinnati, O. Died 1908.

TAFT, Charles Phelps, editor; b. Cincinnati, Dec. 21, 1843; s. Alphonso (Atty. Gen., 1876-77) and Fannie (Phelps) T.; half brother of President William Howard, Henry Watters and Horace Dutton T.; A.B., Yale, 1864, A.M., 1867; J.U.D., Heidelberg, 1887; also studied at Berlin and Paris; LL.D., U. of Cincinnati, 1923; m. Annie, d. David Sinton, of Cincinnati, Dec. 4, 1873; children—Jane Ellison (Mrs. Albert S. Ingalls), David Sinton (dec.), Anna Louise (Mrs. William T. Semple), Charles Howard. Admitted to bar, 1866; practiced at Cincinnati, 1869-79; purchased controlling interest in Cincinnati Times, 1879, which he consolidated with the Star, 1880, as the Times-Star, of which he became editor. Mem. Ohio Ho. of Rep., 1871; mem. 54th Congress (1895-97), 1st Ohio Dist.; pres. Bd. Sinking Fund Trustees, Cincinnati, 1898-1908; presdl. elector-at-large from Ohio, 1904; pres. Ohio electoral coll., Jan. 1905 Home: Cincinnati, O. Died Dec. 31, 1929.

TAFT, George Wheaton, theologian; b. Salem, Mich., July 17, 1865; s. Rev. Howard Bailey and Harriett C. (Cole) T.; B.S., Kalamazoo (Mich.) Coll., 1886 (D.D., 1915); grad. Rochester Theol. Sem., 1889; attended lectures Colgate U., Hamilton, N.Y., 1898-1902; m. Mary A. Boyden, June 26, 1889 (died 1890); children—Howard Boyden, Stanley Cole; m. 2d, Jessie D. Humpstone, Nov. 14, 1892; children—Robert Wheaton, Gordon Dunmore, Kendall Benard, Henry Humpstone (dec.). Ordained Bapt. ministry, 1889; Am. Bapt. Missionary Union missionary to Tokyo, Japan, 1889; prof. ch. history, Japan Bapt. Theol. Sem., 1893-96; missionary, Kobe, Japan, 1896-97; field worker Bapt. Foreign Missionary Soc., 1897-1902; pastor Pittsburgh, Pa., Norman, Okla., and Hastings, Neb., 1902-13; pres. Grand Island (Neb.) Coll., 1913-16; dean and prof. church history and homiletics, Northern Bapt. Theol. Sem., Chicago, Dec. 1916, pres. 1918-36, pres. emeritus, 1936—. Member board dirs. Winona Assembly and Bible Conf., 1917-26, advisory com., 1926—; v.p. Ill. Bapt. State Conv., 1921-22; v.p. Theol. Faculties Union of Chicago, 1925-26, pres. 1926-27. Organizer and first pres. Bapt. Orphanage and Home Soc. of W.Pa., 1909-10; mem. and officer many local, state and nat. coms. and bds.; mem. adv. committee Columbiana-on-Lake George Conf., 1927—. Editor: Uhlhorn's Conflicts of Heathenism with Christianity (Japanese edit.), 1895). Home: Winona Lake, Ind. Died Jan. 21, 1939.

TAFT, Lorado, sculptor; b. Elmwood, Ill., Apr. 29, 1860; s. Prof. Don Carlos and Mary Lucy (Foster) T.; B.L., U. of Ill., 1879, M.L., 1880; studied École des Beaux Arts, 1880-83; L.H.D., Northwestern U., 1913; Litt.D., U. of Colo., 1927; LL.D., U. of Ill., 1929; m. Carrie L. Scales, Oct. 4, 1890 (died 1892); m. 2d, Ada Bartlett, Feb. 11, 1896; children—Mary, Emily, Jessie Louise. Instr., Art Inst. Chicago, 1886-1907, and lecturer at the same instn., 1886-1929; lecturer on art, univ. extension dept., Univ. of Chicago, 1892-1902; professorial lecturer, same, 1909—; non-resident prof. of art, Univ. of Ill., 1919—. Prin. works: Solitude of the Soul, Art Inst. Chicago; Blackhawk, Oregon, Ill.; Columbus Memorial Fountain, Washington, D.C.; Ferguson Fountain of the Great Lakes, Chicago; Thatcher Memorial Fountain, Denver; The Fountain of Time, Chicago; Lincoln, Urbana, Ill.; The Pioneers, Elmwood, Ill.; Alma Mater, Univ. of Ill.; The Crusader (Victor Lawson Memorial), Graceland Cemetery, Chicago; two groups, The Patriots, and The Pioneers, New State Capitol, Baton Rouge, Louisiana. Awarded Designer's medal, Chicago Expn., 1893; silver medal, Buffalo Expn., 1901; gold medal, St. Louis Expn., 1904; commendatore from the Italian government, 1933. A.N.A., 1909, N.A., 1911; mem. Am. Acad. Arts and Letters; hon. mem. A.I.A. Apptd. mem. Bd. of Art Advisers of Ill., 1917 and 1929; mem. Nat. Commn. of Fine Arts, Washington, D.C., 1925-28. Author: The History of American Sculpture, 1903; Recent Tendencies in Sculpture, 1921. Home: Chicago, Ill. Died Oct. 30, 1936.

TAFT, Robert Wendell, cotton mfr., banker; b. Providence, R.I., Nov. 21, 1868; s. Royal C. and Mary Frances (Armington) T.; Ph.B., Brown U., 1891; m. Alice A. Grinnell, Jan. 11, 1893. Engaged as cotton mfr., 1891—; director Coventry Co., Merchants National Bank; trustee Providence Instn. for Savings, 1894—; dir. numerous ins. companies. A. d. c. with rank of col. on governor's staff, 1895-97; asst. adj. gen. of R.I., 1897-1901. Republican. Home: Providence, R.I. Died Feb. 11, 1934.

TAFT, Royal Chapin, governor; b. Northbridge, Mass., Feb. 14, 1823; s. Orsmus and Margaret (Smith) T.; ed. Worcester Acad.; (hon. A.M., Brown, 1891); m. Mary Frances Aimington, Oct. 31, 1850. Engaged in mfg. cotton and woolen goods, 1849, with Royal Chapin, Providence, R.I., as Royal Chapin & Co.; afterward acquired large interests in other mills; trustee Providence Instn. for Savings. Mem. Providence City Council, 1855-56; mem. R.I. Ho. of Rep., 1880-84; commr. from R.I. to Centennial Expn. in 1876; gov. of R.I., 1888; served 1 yr., declined renomination. Republican. Was lt. and captain R.I. Horse Guards several yrs. Home: Providence, R.I. Died June 4, 1912.

TAFT, Russell Smith, judge Supreme Court Vt., 1880—; apptd. chief judge, Jan. 19, 1899; b. Williston, Vt., Jan. 28, 1835; s. Elijah and Orinda (Kimball) T.; ed. in common schools, Williston Acad., and Newbury, Vt., Sem.; (A.M., Univ. of Vt., 1877; LL.D., 1899). Admitted to bar, 1856; selectman of town, 1861-64; alderman City of Burlington, 1865-69; State's atty. Chittenden Co., 1862-65; senator from same, 1865-67; city atty. Burlington, 1871-73; register of probate in dist. of Chittenden, 1863-80; lt. gov., Vt., 1872-74; member legislature, 1880. Republican. Married, Jane Marlette, June 27, 1876. Home: Burlington, Vt. Died 1902.

TAFT, William Howard, twenty-seventh President of the United States; b. Cincinnati, Sept. 15, 1857; s. Alphonso (Atty. Gen., 1876-77) and Louisa Maria (Torrey) T.; grad. Woodward High Sch., Cincinnati, 1874; B.A., Yale, 1878 (2d in class of 121, salutatorian and class orator); LL.B., Cincinnati Law Sch., 1880, dividing 1st prize; LL.D., Yale, 1893, U. of Pa., 1902, Harvard, 1905, Miami U., 1905, State U. of Ia., 1907, Wesleyan, 1909, Princeton, 1912, McGill U., 1913, Cambridge, 1922, Aberdeen, 1922; U. of Cincinnati, 1925; D.C.L., Hamilton, 1913; Oxford, 1922; hon. bencher, Middle Temple, 1922; m. Helen, d. John W. Herron, Cincinnati, June 19, 1886. Admitted to Ohio bar, 1880; law reporter Cincinnati Times, and later of Cincinnati Commercial, 1880; asst. pros. atty. Hamilton Co., O., 1881, 82, 83; practiced law at Cincinnati, 1883-87; asst. county solicitor Hamilton Co., 1885-87; judge Superior Ct., Cincinnati, 1887-90; solicitor gen. of U.S., 1890-92; U.S. circuit judge, 6th Circuit, 1892-1900; prof. and dean law dept., U. of Cincinnati, 1896-1900; pres. U.S. Philippine Commn., Mar. 12, 1900-July 4, 1901; first civil gov. of P.I., July 4, 1901-Feb. 1, 1904; sent to Rome by President Roosevelt, 1902, to confer with Pope Leo XIII concerning purchase of agrl. lands of religious orders in the P.I.; twice declined apptmt. from President Roosevelt as asso. justice Supreme Ct. of U.S., 1903; Sec. of War in cabinet of President Roosevelt, Feb. 1, 1904-June 30, 1908; sent to Cuba by President Roosevelt to adjust insurrection there, 1906, and acted short time as provisional gov.; in Mar. and Apr. 1907, visited Panama, Cuba and P.R., by direction of the President, to take up various matters and familiarize himself with conditions; later he visited Japan and P.I., returning to America via Russia. Nominated for President by Rep. Nat. Conv., Chicago, June 1908, and elected Nov. 3, 1908, for term, Mar. 4, 1909-Mar. 4, 1913; received 321 electoral votes against 162 for William Jennings Bryan, the Dem. candidate; renominated for the Presidency June 1912, by Rep. Nat. Conv., Chicago; defeated in Nov. election following by Woodrow Wilson, Dem. candidate. Kent prof. of law, Yale, 1913-21; apptd. and confirmed by the Senate Chief Justice of the U.S., June 30, 1921. Apptd. mem. Nat. War Labor Conf. Bd., Apr. 1918, and co-chmn. same until bd. dissolved Aug. 1919. Pres. Am. Nat. Red Cross, 1906-13, Am. Bar Assn., 1913, Am. Acad. Jurisprudence, 1914; pres. League to Enforce Peace, engaged in promotion and ratification of Treaty of Peace and League of Nations; chancellor Smithsonian Instn., 1923. Author: Four Aspects of Civic Duty, 1906; vol., 1913, containing 8 Yale lectures and 2 addresses before Am. Bar Assn., on Popular Government; The Anti-Trust Act and the Supreme Court, 1914; The United States and Peace, 1914; Our Chief Magistrate and His Powers, 1916; Taft Papers on League of Nations, 1920. Home: Washington, D.C. Died Mar. 8, 1930.

TAG, Casimir, banker; b. New York, N.Y., Mar. 10, 1847; s. Charles F. and Caroline H. (von Rippon) T.; ed. Dr. Rudolf Dulon's pvt. sch., New York; m. Hannah M. Ockershausen, Dec. 14, 1871. In mercantile business as mem. Charles F. Tag & Son, 1870-93; engaged in banking business, 1898; has been interested in many corporations, etc. Home: Brooklyn, N.Y. Died Sept. 21, 1913.

TAGG, Francis Thomas, editor, clergyman; b. Union Mills, Md., June 2, 1845; s. William and Mary Ann (Stonesifer) T.; ed. pub. and pvt. schs. and Carroll Acad., Union Mills; (D.D., Adrian Coll., Mich., 1893; A.M., Western Md. Coll., 1915); m. Anna Jane Dever, March 9, 1875. Teacher and prin. Carroll Acad., 1863-

70; ordained M.P. ministry, 1870; pastor Queen Anne's Circuit, 1870-74, Norfolk, Va., 1874-75, Salisbury, Md., 1875-77, Baltimore, 1877-79, Easton, Md., 1879-82, Washington, 1883-84; missionary sec. M.P. Ch., 1884-92, organized work in Japan and put mission bd. on substantial basis; editor Methodist Protestant, 1892—. Pres. Gen. Conf. M.P. Ch., 1904; del. World's S.S. Conv., Toronto, 1879, World's Missionary Congress, London, 1888, New York, 1900, Ecumenical Conf., of Methodism, London, 1901, Ch. Fedn. Conf., New York, 1905, Fed. Council of Chs. of Christ in America, Phila., 1907, and all gen. confs. M.P. Ch., 1884—. Independent Republican. Home: Baltimore, Md. Died June 18, 1923.

TAGGART, David Arthur, lawyer; b. Goffstown, N.H., Jan. 30, 1858; A.B., Harvard, 1878; m. Elbra, d. Dr. A. B. Story, Nov. 11, 1884. Admitted to bar, Sept. 1, 1881, and began practice at Manchester, N.H. Mem. N.H. Ho. of Rep., 1883; pres. N.H. Senate, 1889; Rep. nominee for Congress, 1890. Home: Manchester, N.H. Deceased.

TAGGART, (William) Rush, lawyer; b. Smithville, O., Sept. 4, 1849; s. William Wirt and Margaret Jane T.; A.B., U. of Wooster, 1871, A.M., 1874; LL.B., U. of Mich., 1875; (LL.D., Wooster, 1900); m. Margaret Waterworth, Sept. 13, 1877. Practiced in New York, largely for corps., including Pennsylvania Co., Western Union Telegraph Co., Wabash R.R. Co., C.,H.&D. R.R. Co., Tex. & Pacific Ry. Co.; now v.p. and general counsel Western Union Telegraph Co.; dir. Am. Telegraph & Cable Co., etc.; pres. Mt. Hope Cemetery Assn. Home: New York, N.Y. Died Sept. 28, 1922.

TAGGART, Thomas, hotel propr.; b. Co. Monyhan, Ireland, Nov. 17, 1856; s. Thomas and Martha (Kingsbury) T.; located at Xenia, O., 1861; removed to Garrett, Ind., 1871, and to Indianapolis, 1877; m. Eva D. Bryant, June 16, 1877. Pres. French Lick Springs Hotel Co. In Dem. politics, 1886—; elected auditor Marion Co., 1886; reëlected 1890; chmn. Dem. State Com., 1892-94; dist. chmn. 7th Congressional Dist., 12 yrs.; mayor of Indianapolis, 3 terms, 1895-1901; mem. Dem. Nat. Com. from Ind., 1900-16 (chmn. 1904-08); apptd. U.S. senator, Mar. 20, 1916, to fill vacancy caused by death of Benjamin F. Shively. Chmn. bd. Fletcher-Am. Nat. Bank, Indianapolis. Home: French Lick, Ind. Died Mar. 6, 1929.

TAGGART, Walter Thomas, prof. chemistry; b. Phila., Pa., Apr. 15, 1872; s. Joseph and Sarah (Miller) T.; prep. edn., Rugby Acad., Phila.; B.S. in Chemistry, U. of Pa., 1896, Ph.D., 1903; studied U. of Berlin, 1903, U. of Göttingen, 1903-05; m. Inez Marquez Forbes, June 9, 1916. Began teaching at U. of Pa., 1896, asst. prof. chemistry, 1905, prof., 1913; Blanchard prof. same, 1920, dir. John Harrison Lab., U. of Pa., 1920-27. Chem. Expert Ordnance Dept., U.S.A., Nitrate Div., 1918; chmn. U.S. Assay Commn., 1926-27. Mem. Chem. Div. Nat. Research Council, 1921-23, and 1927—. Translator: (with Edgar F. Smith) Richter's Inorganic Chemistry, 1900. Home: Philadelphia, Pa. Died June 9, 1937.

TAGUE, Peter F., postmaster; b. Boston, Mass., June 4, 1871; grad. Frothingham and English high schs.; m. Josephine T. Fitzgerald, Jan. 31, 1900. Mfg. chemist; mem. Boston Common Council, 1894, 95, 96; mem. Mass. Ho. of Rep., 1897, 98, 1913, 14, Senate, 1899, 1900; mem. 64th to 68th Congresses (1915-25), 10th Mass. Dist.; chmn. Bd. of Election Commissioners, City of Boston; postmaster of Boston, Oct. 1935—. Democrat. Home: Charleston, Boston, Mass. Died Sept. 17, 1941.

TAINTER, Charles Sumner, inventor; b. Watertown, Mass., Apr. 25, 1854; s. George and Abigail (Sanger) T.; pub. sch. edn.; m. Lila R. Munro, June 22, 1886; m. 2d, Laura Fontaine Onderdonk, Apr. 7, 1928. Inventor of the graphophone, also of the dictaphone; associate inventor of the radiophone, an instrument for transmitting sounds to a distance through the agency of light; member of the U.S. expedition sent to the South Pacific to observe transit of Venus, 1874. Awarded gold medal at Electrical Exhbn., Paris, 1881, for inventions in connection with the radiophone; Officier de l'Instruction Publique, France, for invention of graphophone, 1889; John Scott medal, 1900, by City of Phila., for the invention of the graphophone; gold medal, 1915, at Panama P.I. Expn. for work in connection development of the talking machine. Home: San Diego, Calif. Died Apr. 20, 1940.

TAINTOR, Henry Fox, mfr.; b. Buffalo, N.Y., June 30, 1833; ed. Homer, N.Y., Acad.; m. Frances L. Noyes, May 27, 1869. Engaged in railroad enterprises, Milwaukee, 1856-62; removed to New York; became associated with Samuel J. Tilden in financial management of Western railroads; leader in the overthrow of the "Tweed ring," 1871-79; pres. H. F. Taintor Mfg. Co., and Am. Whiting and Putty Mfg. Co. Home: New York, N.Y. Died 1909.

TAINTOR, Jesse Fox, college prof.; b. Milwaukee, Wis., Aug. 21, 1851; s. William and Mary Jane (Barrows) T.; prep. edn. Ripon (Wis.) Coll. Acad.; A.B., Ripon Coll., 1873; grad. Andover Theol. Sem., 1878; studied U. of Chicago, 1903; m. Sarah E. Buckley, Aug. 15, 1883. Ordained Congl. ministry, 1878; pastor Decorah, Ia., 1878-80, Dewitt, Ia., 1880-84, Fergus Falls, Minn., 1884-86, Rochester, Minn., 1886-1903, Elkhorn, Wis., 1904-05; prof. English lit., Ripon Coll., Sept. 1905—. Home: Ripon, Wis. Died Mar. 2, 1935.

TAIT, Arthur Fitzwilliam, artist; b. nr. Liverpool, Eng., Aug. 5, 1819; ed. at country school, Lancaster, Eng. In art is entirely self-taught, having gone to work in Agnew's picture store, Manchester, Eng., at 12; saw there the best pictures of the time; devoted every spare moment to studying from casts in the Manchester Royal Instn.; came to U.S., 1850; settled in New York; Nat. Academician, 1858—. Home: Yonkers, N.Y. Died 1905.

TAIT, John Robinson, landscape painter; b. Cincinnati, Jan. 14, 1834; s. George and Eliza Dickey (Morrison) T.; studied Woodward Coll., Cincinnati, 1845-50; grad. Bethany Coll., Va., 1852; studied art and painted in Florence, Italy, 1853-56; in Düsseldorf, 1859-71; Munich, 1873-76; m. Anna Dolores Tiernan, Dec. 26, 1872. Author: European Life, Legend and Landscape, 1859; Dolce far Niente (poems), 1859. Was for several yrs. art critic New York Mail and Express. Home: Baltimore, Md. Died 1909.

TAKAMINE, Jokichi, chemist; b. Takaoka, Japan, Nov. 3, 1854; s. Dr. Seichi and Yuki T.; grad. in chem. engring., Engring. Coll., Imperial U. of Tokyo, 1879; Japanese Govt. student, U. of Glasgow and Andersonian U., Glasgow, 3 yrs., 1879-81; (Dr. Chem. Engring., Imperial U. of Japan, 1899, Dr. Pharm., 1906); m. Caroline Hitch, 1885. Head chemist Imperial Dept. Agr. and Commerce, Tokyo, 1881-84; Imperial Japanese commr. to Cotton Centennial Expn., New Orleans, 1884-85; organized and erected 1st superphosphate works at Tokyo, 1887; came to America, 1890, and applied new process of conversion and fermentation to practical use resulting in production of diastatic enzyme ("Takadiastase"), now largely used as a starch digestant; established research lab. in New York and originated a process for isolating the active principle of the suprarenal glands, the product being known as ("adrenalin"); cons. chemist. Decorated by Emperor of Japan with 4th Order of the Rising Sun, 1915; apptd. by Emperor mem. Royal Acad. Sciences, Japan, 1913. Home: Passaic, N.J. Died July 22, 1922.

TALBERT, Joseph Truitt, banker; b. Hardy, Miss., Aug. 15, 1866; s. James Benjamin and Margaret E. (Gattis) T.; student U. of Miss., 1881-84; m. Mrs. M. T. Gibson, Mar. 8, 1917. Assistant cashier San Angelo (Texas) National Bank, 1887-89; asst. cashier, 1889-90, v.p., 1890-94, Farmers & Mechanics Nat. Bank, Ft. Worth; nat. bank examiner, in West and Southwest, also in Wis., Minn. and Chicago, 1894-97; v.p. Commercial Nat. Bank (now Continental & Commercial Nat. Bank), Chicago, 1897-1909; v.p. Nat. City Bank, New York, 1909—. Mem. currency commn. Am. Bankers' Assn., 1906—. Republican. Protestant. Mason. Home: New York, N.Y. Died May 8, 1920.

TALBOT, Ethelbert, bishop; b. Fayette, Mo., Oct. 9, 1848; s. John A. and Alice (Daly) T.; A.B., Dartmouth, 1870, D.D., 1888; grad. Gen. Theol. Sem., 1873, S.T.D., 1887; LL.D., U. of Mo., 1887; married; 1 dau., Anne Harvey (Mrs. Francis Donaldson). Deacon and priest, P.E. Ch., 1873; rector St. James', Macon, Mo., and of St. James Mil. Acad., 1873-87; consecrated missionary bishop of Wyo. and Ida., May 27, 1887; transferred to See of Central Pa. (later changed to See of Bethlehem, Pa.), Feb. 2, 1898. Author: My People of the Plains; A Bishop Among His Flock; Tim—an Autobiography of a Dog; A Bishop's Message. Home: Bethlehem, Pa. Died Feb. 27, 1928.

TALBOT, Eugene Solomon, dentist; b. Sharon, Mass., Mar. 8, 1847; s. Solomon and Emily (Hawes) T.; Stoughtonham Inst., Sharron; D.D.S., Pa. Dental College, 1871; M.D., Rush Med. Coll., Chicago, 1880; (LL.D., Kenyon Coll., 1902; M.S., Whitman Coll., 1903; Sc.D., Univ. of Pennsylvania, 1915); m. Flora Estey, Sept. 20, 1876. Prof. stomatology, Ill. Med. College. Hon. pres. dental sect., 10th Internat. Med. Congress, Berlin, 1890; hon. pres. dental sect., 12th Internat. Med. Congress, Moscow, 1897; hon. mem. foreign societies. Home: Chicago, Ill. Died Dec. 20, 1924.

TALBOT, Henry Paul, chemist; b. Boston, May 15, 1864; s. Zephaniah and Eliza Frances T.; B.S., Mass. Inst. Tech., 1885; Ph.D., Leipzig, 1890; Sc.D., Dartmouth, 1921; m. Frances E. Dukehart, June 17, 1891; 1 son, Paul Dukehart (dec.). Asst., 1885-87, instr. 1887-88 and 1890-92, asst. prof., 1892-95, asso. prof., 1895-98, prof. analyt. chemistry, 1898-1902, prof. inorganic chemistry, in charge dept. chemistry and chemical engring., 1902-20, in charge dept. chemistry, 1920-22, chmn. faculty, 1919-21, chmn. administrative com., 1920-23, dean students, 1921—, Mass. Inst. Tech. Lecturer Wellesley Coll., 1892-94. Mem. Advisory Bd. U.S. Bur. Mines (gas defense), 1917. Fellow Am. Acad. Arts and Sciences, A.A.A.S. Author: Introductory Course of Quantitative Chemical Analysis, 1897; Bibliography of the Analytical Chemistry of Manganese, 1902; The Electrolytic Dissociation Theory (with A. A. Blanchard), 1905. Home: West Newton, Mass. Died June 18, 1927.

TALBOT, Howard, composer, conductor; b. Yonkers, N.Y., Mar. 9, 1865; s. Alexander and Margaret Freeman (Young) Munkittrick; dropped surname and adopted Christian name; taken to England at 4 yrs. of age; ed. for practice of medicine at King's Coll., London; studied Royal Coll. of Music; studied composition under Sir Hubert Parry; m. Dorothy Maud, d. Arthur E. Cross, organist at Sandringham Ch. to King Edward; children—Dorothy Betty, Joy, Mary Alexandra, Agnes. Gained public notice by cantata, performed at Oxford, 1892; has served as conductor at various theatres, London. Composer: (comic opera) Wapping Old Stairs, 1894; Monte Carlo, 1896; A Chinese Honeymoon, 1899; Kitty Grey (part composer), 1900; Little Maids (part composer), 1902; The White Chrysanthemum, 1905; The Girl Behind the Counter, 1906; The Belle of Brittany, 1908; also part composer, The Arcadians, 1909; The Mousme, 1911; The Pearl Girl, 1913; The Light Blues, and My Lady Frayle, both 1915; Mr. Manhattan, 1916; High Jinks, 1916; The Boy, 1917; Who's Hooper, 1919. Holds the record for the 2 longest runs in musical comedy—A Chinese Honeymoon, 1,075 consecutive performances, and The Arcadians, 829 consecutive performances; My Nieces, 1921. Home: Reigate, Surrey, Eng. Died Sept. 12, 1928.

TALBOT, Israel Tisdale, M.D., dean faculty and prof. surgery Boston Univ. Sch. of Medicine; grad. Homœ. Med. Coll., Philadelphia, 1853; Harvard, 1854; pres. Internat. Congress of Homœopathists, 1891; dir. med. bd., Mass. Homœ. Hosp.; pres. Mass. Homœ. Med. Soc. and Am. Inst. Homœopathy; hon. member Brit. Homœ. Soc. and of Académie de Medicine Homœopathique de France. Home: Boston, Mass. Died 1899.

TALBOT, John William, supreme pres. Order of Owls; b. South Bend, Ind., Dec. 12, 1863; s. Peter William and Johanna Mary (Talbot) T.; read law in office of Warren Woodbury, Detroit, Mich.; m. Minnie E. O'Brien, Sept. 24, 1894. Admitted to Mich. bar, 1892; practiced at South Bend, Ind., 1893—. Founder, 1904, and supreme pres. Order of Owls (500,000 members in 14 countries); dir. Co-operative Investment Co.; sec., treas., dir. Mishawaka Realty Co. Trustee Owl Hosp., South Bend. Sec. Am. Game Bird Soc. Democrat. Rationalist. Author: Jim Connors, 1915; Game Laws and Game, 1917; Old Maid Ryan, 1920. Home: South Bend, Ind. Died Dec. 14, 1937.

TALBOTT, Henry James, clergyman; b. Greencastle, Ind., Jan. 8, 1847; s. Henry S. and Martha L. (Harter) T.; A.B., Ind. Asbury U. (now De Pauw U.), 1873 (D.D., 1894, Denver U., 1914); m. Anna Elva Irvine, Sept. 23, 1875. Ordained M.E. ministry, 1873; pastor New Albany Circuit, John Street Ch., New Albany, Elizabeth Circuit, Corydon Circuit, each 1 yr., Martinsville, 1877-86, Meridian St. Ch., Indianapolis, 1880-83; presiding elder Rockfort Dist., 1884-86; pastor Centenary Ch., New Albany, 1886-89; presiding elder Indianapolis Dist., 1889-90 and 1895-98; pastor Trinity Ch., New Albany, 1890-95; presiding elder Indianapolis Dist., 1895-98, Evansville Dist., 1898-1900; trans. to Ore., 1901; supt. missions of M.E. Ch. in Utah, 1904-14; pres. Kimball Coll. of Theology, Salem, Ore., 1914—. Served in 4th Ind. Cav., 1862-65, part of time as dispatch carrier. Mem. Gen. Conf. M.E. Ch., 1888, 96, 1900, Ecumenical Conf., 1891. Trustee De Pauw Coll. for Young Ladies, 3 yrs., De Pauw U., 12 yrs. Republican. Home: Salem, Ore. Died Oct. 19, 1921.

TALBOTT, J(oshua) Fred(erick) C., congressman; b. nr. Lutherville, Md., July 29, 1843; s. Edward C. and T. Ellen T.; pub. sch. edn.; began study of law, 1862; served in C.S.A., as pvt. 2d Md. Cav., 1864-65; admitted to bar, 1866; m. Laura B. Cockey, Feb. 3, 1869 (dec.). Pros. atty. Baltimore Co., 1871-75; del. Dem. Nat. Conv., 1876, 96, 1904, del.-at-large, 1908, 12, 16; mem. Dem. Nat. Com., 1907—, mem. 46th to 48th Congresses (1879-85), 2d Md. Dist.; ins. commr. of Md., 1889-93; mem. 43d Congress (1893-95) and 58th to 65th Congresses (1903-19), 2d Md. Dist. Home: Lutherville, Md. Died Oct. 5, 1918.

TALCOTT, Charles Andrew, congressman; b. June 10, 1857; A.B., Princeton, 1879, A.M., 1882. In practice of law at Utica, N.Y. Corp. counsel, Utica, 1886; mem. Bd. Police and Fire Commrs., 1888-92; trustee pub. library, 1893-1901; mayor, 1902-06; mem. 62d Congress (1911-13), 27th N.Y. Dist., and 63d Congress (1913-15), 33d Dist. Democrat. Home: Utica, N.Y. Died Feb. 28, 1920.

TALCOTT, Edward N. Kirk, civil and mech. engr.; b. Cuba, N.Y., June 10, 1840; s. William H. and Harriet N. T.; grad. Univ. City of New York, 1859. Private 7th N.Y. Nat. Guard, 1861-62; in 1st regt. N.Y. engrs., U.S. vols., 1862-65 (2d lit., 1st lt., capt.). Asst. Thomas Iron Works, Pa., 1865-66; supt. other large iron mfg. enterprises, 1866-76; supt. Ill. Mil. Acad., 1876-90; consulting civ. and mech. engr.; m. Antoinette M. Watkins; May 23, 1867; m. 2d, Lillian Baird, Nov. 26, 1884. Home: Goshen, N.Y. Died 1901.

TALIAFERRO, Thomas Hardy, educator; b. Jacksonville, Fla., Mar. 22, 1871; s. Warner Throckmorton and Fannie Johnston (Hardy) T.; C.E., Va. Mil.

Inst., 1880; Ph.D., Johns Hopkins, 1896; m. Janie Gambrill Smith, June 30, 1897; 1 dau., Frances Warner Throckmorton (dec.). Asst. prof. Va. Mil. Inst., 1890-91; instr. Mo. Mil. Acad., 1891-92; instr. Pa. State Coll., 1896-1901, acting prof. mil. science and tactics, 1899-1900; pres. Fla. Agrl. Coll. and U. of Fla., 1901-04; also dir. Fla. Agrl. Expt. Sta., 1901-04; hon. fellow in mathematics and economics, Johns Hopkins, 1904-05; asst. statis. editor Bur. of Census, 1905-07; prof. civil engring., 1907-20, prof. mathematics, 1920—, dean of faculty, 1937—, dean College Arts and Sciences, 1927-37, dean College Engineering, 1916-20, U. of Maryland. First Jackson Hope medallist, Va. Mil. Inst. Episcopalian. Mason. Home: Washington, D.C. Died Sept. 25, 1941.

TALIAFERRO, Thomas Seddon, Jr., lawyer; b. Gloucester Co., Va., July 1, 1866; s. Thomas Seddon and Harriotte Hopkins (Lee) T.; ed. Episcopal High Sch. of Va. and Gloucester (Va.) Acad.; m. Lucy Ramsay, Apr. 15, 1896; children—William Ramsay, Thomas Seddon III, Arthur-Lee, Beverly Wellford, Edward Ludwell, Lucy Ramsay, Harriotte Lee. Admitted to Wyo. bar, 1900, and began practice at Rock Springs; chmn. bd. State Bank of Green River (Wyo.); pres. 1st Nat. Bank of Green River, Green River Mercantile Co.; mgr. Green River Livestock Co., Big Sandy Livestock Co.; sec. Rock Spring Grazing Assn. Capt., Wyo. N.G., 1894-1900. Pres. Sweetwater Co. (Wyo.) Pub. Library; chancellor, Episcopal Diocese of Wyo. Democrat. Mason. Home: Rock Springs, Wyo. Died Aug. 17, 1940.

TALLICHET, Jules Henri, lawyer; b. Nashville, Tenn., Apr. 20, 1877; s. Henri René Lucien and Virginia (McAlester) T.; LL.B., U. of Tex., 1900, LL.M., 1901; m. Agnes Estelle Montelin, Sept. 22, 1904; children—Virginia, Mary Estelle, Emily McAlester, Jules Henri. Admitted to Tex. bar, 1900, and began practice at Austin; moved to Houston, Tex., 1909; mem. Baker, Botts, Andrews & Wharton; atty. S.P. Tex. Lines, 1909-12, gen. atty., 1912-27, gen. counsel, 1927—; gen. counsel and dir. Tex. & New Orleans R.R. Co. and other S.P. Lines in Tex. Democrat. Episcopalian. Mason. Home: Houston, Tex. Died Nov. 24, 1937.

TALLMADGE, Thomas Eddy, architect; b. Washington, D.C., Apr. 24, 1876; s. Lewis Cass and Lida M. (Eddy) T.; B.S., Mass. Inst. Tech., 1898; hon. M.A., Northwestern U., 1927; unmarried. Architect of many bldgs., chiefly ecclesiastical; formerly lecturer on archtl. history, Art Inst. Chicago, prof. archtl. history, Armour Inst. Tech.; pres. Summer Sch. of Painting, Saugatuck, Mich. Architect in chief of Victory Loan decorations, Chicago, 1918. Chmn. board of art advisers, State of Ill.; mem. Architectural Commn. for Restoration of Williamsburg, Va.; collaborator at large U.S. project, Historic Am. Bldg. Survey; asso. archt. Julia Lathrop Homes, Federal Housing Project, Chicago. Fellow A.I.A.; mem. Art Inst. Chicago (gov. mem.), Republican. Methodist. Author: The Story of Architecture in America, 1927; The Story of England's Architecture, 1934. Co-editor: Significance of the Fine Arts, 1921. Home: Evanston, Ill. Died Jan. 1, 1940.

TALLY, Robert Emmet, mine mgr.; b. Virginia City, Nev., Nov. 5, 1877; s. T. J. and Jane B. (Rogers) T.; student University of Nev., 1894-99, receiving degrees B.S. and M.E.; m. Emma Eulalie Charlebois, Apr. 10, 1912. Engaged in mining, metallurgy and engring, 1898—. Chancellor bd. of regents, U. of Arizona. Republican. Mason, Elk. Home: Prescott, Ariz. Died Dec. 1936.

TALMAGE, James Edward, geologist, theologian; b. Hungerford, Berkshire, Eng., Sept. 21, 1862; s. James J. and Susannah (Preater) T.; emigrated, 1876, family having embraced faith of Latter-Day Saints; Brigham Young Acad., Provo, Utah, 1876-82; Lehigh U., 1882-83; Johns Hopkins, 1883-84; B.S., Lehigh, 1891; Ph.D., Ill. Wesleyan U., 1896; hon. D.Sc. and Didactics, Ch. of Jesus Christ of Latter-Day Saints, 1890; hon. D.Sc., Lehigh, 1912; LL.D., Brigham Young U. and U. of Utah, 1922; m. Mary May Booth, June 14, 1888; children—Sterling Booth, Paul Booth, Zella (dec.), Elsie, James Karl, Lucile, Helen May, John Russell. Prof. chemistry and geology, Brigham Young Acad., 1884-88; pres. Latter-Day Saints Coll., Salt Lake City, 1888-93; pres. U. of Utah, 1894-97; resigned presidency, 1897, retaining chair of geology; resigned professorship, July 1907. Ordained one of twelve apostles Ch. of Jesus Christ of Latter-Day Saints, Dec. 1911. Del. from Royal Soc. of Edinburgh to Internat. Geol. Congress, St. Petersburg, 1897. Author: First Book of Nature, 1888; Domestic Science, 1891; The Articles of Faith, 1899; The Book of Mormon, an Account of Its Origin, etc., 1899; Tables for Blowpipe Determination of Minerals, 1899; The Great Salt Lake, Present and Past, 1900; The Story of Mormonism, 1907; The Great Apostasy, 1909; The House of the Lord, 1912; The Philosophy of Mormonism, 1914; Jesus the Christ, 1915; The Vitality of Mormonism, 1919. Home: Salt Lake City, Utah. Died July 27, 1933.

TALMAGE, T(homas) DeWitt, Presbyn. clergyman, lecturer; b. Bound Brook, N.J., Jan. 7, 1832; ed. Univ. City of New York, but was not graduated (A.M., 1862); grad. New Brunswick, N.J., Theol. Sem., 1856 (D.D., Univ. of Tenn., 1884); ordained, 1856, pastor Reformed Dutch Ch., Belleville, N.J.; pastor at Syracuse, N.Y., 1859-62; Phila., 1862-69; Central Ch., Brooklyn, 1869-94; then in Washington; has edited the Christian at Work, Advance, Frank Leslie's Sunday magazine; now editor The Christian Herald. Author: Crumbs Swept Up; Around the Teatable; Mask Torn Off; The Marriage Ring; Woman: Her Powers and Privileges; From Manager to Throne; Sports that Kill; The Earth Girdled; The Pathway of Life; Old Wells Dug Out; Every-Day Religion; Sundown; Fishing Too Near Shore. His sermons have been published weekly for 29 yrs., without the exception of a week, and now through syndicates are published in numerous papers of the U.S. and fgn. countries. Home: Washington, D.C. Died 1902.

TALMAN, Charles Fitzhugh, meteorologist, writer; b. Detroit, Aug. 31, 1874; s. late Robert Fitzhugh and Jessica (Mack) T.; ed. Detroit pub. schs., Kalamazoo (Mich.) Coll. and pvt. tutors; m. Grace F., d. Lt. Comdr. B. L. Edes, U.S.N., Nov. 16, 1909; children—Constance Elizabeth Marjorie (wife of Mario Rodriguez), Benjamin Long Edes. With U.S. Weather Bur., Oct. 1896—; in charge meteorol. stas. in S. America and W.I., 1898-99; librarian, 1908-35, meteorol. consultant, July 1, 1935—, jr. prof. meteorology, 1912-14, prof. meteorology, 1914-22, meteorologist, 1922—, U.S. Weather Bureau. Fellow Am. Meteorol. Soc., A.A.A.S. Specialist in meteorology for Standard Dictionary, 1910-11; writer for Science Service, 1921—. Author: Meteorology, the Science of the Atmosphere, 1922 (republished as Our Weather, 1925); The Realm of the Air, 1931, republished as A Book about the Weather, 1935. Home: Washington, D.C. Died July 24, 1936.

TANNAHILL, Samuel O., mem. Democratic Nat. Com.; b. Elden, Ia., Aug. 10, 1868; s. John L. and Elmira F. (Jones) T.; student Emporia (Kan.) State Normal Sch., 1885-86; LL.B., Valparaiso (Ind.) Coll., 1904; m. Josephine Krier, May 6, 1925. School teacher, 1886-89; admitted to Ida. bar, 1905, and began practice at Lewiston City Council, 1897-1905; pros. atty. Lewis Co., Ida., 1913-18; mem. Dem. Nat. Committee, 1932—. Democrat. Presbyn. Home: Lewiston, Ida. Died Dec. 30, 1935.

TANNER, Benjamin Tucker, bishop; b. Pittsburgh, Pa., Dec. 25, 1835; s. Hugh S. and Isabel H. T.; ed. Avery Coll., Allegheny, and Western Theol. Sem.; was not grad.; (hon. A.M., Avery, 1870; D.D., LL.D., Wilberforce); m. Sarah Elizabeth Miller, Aug. 19, 1858; father of Henry Ossawa T. Ordained A.M.E. ministry; elected bishop, 1888. Editor Christian Recorder (organ of A.M.E. Ch.) 16 yrs.; founder, and 4 yrs. editor, A.M.E. Church Review. Author: Outlines of African Methodist Episcopalian Church History; The Dispensations in the History of the Church; The Negro in Holy Writ; A Hint to Ministers. Especially of the African Methodist Episcopal Church. Del. 3d Ecumenical Meth. Conf., Sept. 1901, London, Eng.; read paper before that body on "The Elements of Pulpit Effectiveness." Home: Philadelphia, Pa. Died Jan. 15, 1923.

TANNER, Edwin Platt, coll. prof.; b. Paterson, N.J., Dec. 12, 1874; s. Robert James and Emma C. (King) T.; A.B., Columbia, 1897, A.M., 1898, Ph.D., 1908; unmarried. Fellow in Am. history, Columbia, 1898-1900; instr. history, high sch., Stillwater, Minn., 1900-01, Syracuse U., 1901-03, Adelphi Coll., Brooklyn, 1903-07; asst. prof. Am. history, Ohio State U., 1908-09; asso. prof. Am. history, 1909-15, prof., 1915—. Syracuse U. Democrat. Episcopalian. Author: The Province of New Jersey, 1908; (with William H. Mace) Story of Old Europe and Young America, 1915; Yesterday's Children, 1927. Home: Syracuse, N.Y. Died July 1936.

TANNER, Henry Ossawa, artist; b. Pittsburgh, Pa., June 21, 1859; s. Benjamin Tucker and Sarah Elizabeth (Miller) T.; studied Pa. Acad. Fine Arts under Thomas Eakins; pupil of Jean Paul Laurens and Benjamin Constant, Paris; m. Jessie Macaulay Olssen, Dec. 14, 1899 (dec.). Specialty: religious subjects. Hon. mention, Salon, 1896; 3d class medal, 1897; 2d class medal, 1907; Walter Lippincott prize, Phila., 1900; Harris prize, Chicago; 2d medal, Paris Expn., 1900; 2d medal, Buffalo Expn., 1901; 2d medal, St. Louis Expn., 1904; gold medal, San Francisco, 1915. Represented in the Luxembourg, the Wilstach Collection, Carnegie Inst., Pa. Acad. Fine Arts, Phila., Chicago Art Inst., Los Angeles Art Gallery, Des Moines Art Gallery; painting Destruction of Sodom and Gomorrah in Met. Mus., New York. Knight Legion of Honor. N.A., 1927. Served with Am. Red Cross in France 18 mos., World War. Studio: Paris, France. Died May 25, 1937.

TANNER, James, public official; b. Richmondville, N.Y., Apr. 4, 1844; s. Josiah and Elizabeth (Earl) T.; ed. in dist. sch.; pvt. and corporal 87th N.Y. Vols.; lost both legs at 2d battle of Bull Run; under doorkeeper and clerk of com. N.Y. Assembly; clerk in War Dept.; returned to N.Y., 1866; m. Mero L. White, Nov. 17, 1866 (dec.). Studied law; received appmt. N.Y. Custom House; deputy collector under Gen. Arthur; tax collector, Brooklyn, 1877-85; lecturer; campaign speaker; U.S. commr. of pensions, 1889 (resigned); prosecuting claims against govt., 1889-1904; apptd. register of wills, D.C., Apr. 1, 1904. Dept. comdr. G.A.R., N.Y., 1876; comdr.-in-chief G.A.R., 1905-06. Home: Washington, D.C. Died Oct. 2, 1927.

TANNER, John Henry, univ. prof.; b. Ft. Plain, N.Y., Mar. 1, 1861; s. Charles F. and Minnie E (Lenz) T.; B.S., Cornell U., 1891; Ph.D., N.H. Coll., 1901; studied Göttingen, 1894-96; m. Clara M. Williams, June 20, 1893. Instr. mathematics, 1891-94, asst. prof., 1894-1904, prof., 1904-26, sec. faculty arts and scs., 1897-1903, Cornell U. (emeritus). Author: Analytic Geometry (Tanner and Allen), 1898; An Elementary Algebra, 1903; Key to Elementary Algebra, 1905; High School Algebra, 1907; Brief Course in Analytic Geometry, 1911. Editor: Plane and Solid Geometry (Hart and Feldman), 1909. Home: Ithaca, N.Y. Died Mar. 11, 1940.

TANNER, John Riley, governor of Ill.; b. Warrick Co., Ind., April 4, 1844; private 98th Ill. and 61st Ill. regts., 1863-65; farmer in Clay Co., 1865—; sheriff, 1870-72; clerk circuit court, 1871-75; State senator, 1881-83; U.S. marshal, southern dist. Ill., 1883-84; State treas., 1887-89; railroad commr., 1891-93; asst. U.S. Treas., Chicago, 1892-93; chmn. Rep. State com. of Ill., 1894-95; elected gov. for term 1897-1901; m. Cora E. English, Dec. 30, 1896. Home: Springfield, Ill. Died 1901.

TANNER, Zera Luther, comdr. U.S.N., retired; b. Warsaw, N.Y., Dec. 5, 1835; s. Zera and Ruth Emeline T.; common school edn.; followed the sea in merchant marine, 1855-62; in vol. navy, 1862-67; after that in regular navy, through grades to comdr., retiring by reason of age, Dec. 5, 1897; cruised in all parts of the world. On leave of absence, 1874-78, comdg. Pacific Mail Steamers Colon and City of Peking; engaged in scientific deep-sea explorations, 1879-94. During Spanish war, 1898, on duty at Navy Dept., Washington, San Francisco and Honolulu; m. Helen Benedict, Nov. 11, 1884. Home: Warsaw, N.Y. Died 1906.

TANNRATH, John Joseph, clergyman; b. St. Louis, Mo., Apr. 26, 1864; s. Capt. Benjamin and Caroline (Hunt) T.; ed. St. Louis U.; St. Joseph's Coll., Teutopolis, Ill., and St. Meinrad's Sem., Ind. Ordained priest R.C. Ch., 1888; asst. pastor St. Charles, Mo., 1888, St. Liberius Ch., 1889, St. Mary's Ch., 1890-93, St. John's Ch., 1893-96 (all of St. Louis); asst. chancellor, St. Louis, 1896-98; pastor St. Agnes Ch., St. Louis, 1898-1915, Ch. of St. Louis of France (Old Cathedral), 1915-22, St. Louis Cathedral, Dec. 8, 1922—. Chancellor St. Louis (Mo.) Diocese, 1910—. Apptd. domestic prelate, Apr. 1916. Republican. Died June 1929.

TAPLIN, Frank E., coal producer; b. Cleveland, O., Oct. 28, 1875; s. Charles Grandy and Frances (Smith) T.; ed. Central High Sch., Cleveland; m. Edith Smith, Feb. 1, 1912; children—Frank E., Clara Louise, Thomas Ely. Began with Standard Oil Co., Cleveland, 1892; salesman Pittsburgh Coal Co., 1898-1901; sales mgr. Youghigheny & Ohio Coal Co., 1901-12; organizer, 1912, pres. until 1926, Cleveland & Western Coal Co.; organizer, 1926, and from then pres. North Am. Coal Corp.; pres. Pittsburgh, W.Va. R.R. Founder Cleveland Inst. Music. Republican. Baptist. Mason. Home: Cleveland, O. Died June 7, 1938.

TAPPAN, Benjamin, naval officer; b. New Orleans, La., Apr. 12, 1856. Apptd. U.S. Naval Acad. from Ark., Sept. 22, 1871, grad. 1876; midshipman, June 21, 1876; promoted through grades to capt., Oct. 30, 1908. Served on Tennessee, 1876-78; Franklin, 1879; Constellation, 1879-81; New Hampshire, 1882-84; Saratoga, 1884-87; Bur. of Navigation, Navy Dept., 1888-91; Newark, 1891-93; Miantonomoh, 1893-94; equipment duty, Navy Yard, New York, 1895-96; Amphitrite, 1896-97; Raleigh, 1897-98; was advanced 5 numbers in rank for eminent and conspicuous conduct in the battle of Manila Bay, May 1, 1898; comd. Callao, 1898-99; charge branch hydrographic office, Baltimore, 1900-01; staff Iowa, 1901-02, New York, 1902; Naval War Coll., 1903; comd. Petrel, 1903-04; Navy Yard, New York, 1904-05; comd. Newport, 1905-06, Tacoma, 1906-09, Indiana, 1909-10; capt. of yard, Navy Yard, Mare Island, Calif., 1910-11; supervisor naval auxiliaries, 1911; comdt. naval sta., Olongapo and Cavite, P.I., Mar. 15, 1913-16; retired with rank of rear admiral, Apr. 26, 1916. Took part in many engagements during insurrection in Philippines; specially commended in dispatches by Rear Admiral Watson for part taken by Callao at capture of Dagupan, Lingayen Gulf, Luzon, in coöperation with forces under Maj. Gen. Wheaton. Active duty World War, as comdt. Naval Sta., Phila., and comdt. 8th Naval Dist., New Orleans; retired Oct. 1, 1919. Died Dec. 18, 1919.

TAPPAN, David Stanton, clergyman; b. Steubenville, O., Apr. 2, 1845; s. Dr. Benjamin and Oella (Stanton) T. (sister Edwin M. Stanton, War Sec. under Lincoln); A.B. (head of class), Miami U., 1864, A.M., 1886; grad. Western Theol. Sem., Allegheny, Pa., 1867; (hon. A.M., Wooster, 1878, LL.D., 1899; D.D., Lenox, 1887); m. Anna Grand Girard,

Aug. 12, 1869. Prin. Slate Lick Acad., Pa., 1865, Callensburg (Pa.) Acad., 1866. Ordained Presbyn. ministry, 1868; pastor Chariton, Ia., 1868-71, Mt. Pleasant, Ia., 1871-90, Portsmouth, O., 1890-99; pres. Miami U., 1899-1902; pastor Circleville, O., 1902-13. Trustee Parsons Coll., 1887-90, U. of Wooster, 1896-99; moderator Synod of Ohio, 1898; del. Pan-Presbyn. Council, New York, 1909. Author: History of Presbyterianism in Iowa, 1887; Miscellaneous Sermons, 1899. Home: Los Angeles, Calif. Died Mar. 20, 1922.

TAPPAN, Eva March, author; b. Blackstone, Mass., Dec. 26, 1854; d. Rev. Edmund March and Lucretia (Logée) T.; A.B., Vassar Coll., 1875; A.M., U. of Pa., 1895, fellow, 1895-96, Ph.D., 1896. Author: Charles Lamb, the Man and the Author, 1896; In the Days of Alfred the Great, 1900; In the Days of William the Conqueror, 1901; In the Days of Queen Elizabeth, 1902; Old Ballads in Prose, 1901; England's Story, 1901; Our Country's Story, 1902; The Christ Story, 1903; In the Days of Queen Victoria, 1903; Robin Hood, His Book, 1903; A Short History of England's Literature, 1905; The Golden Goose and Other Fairy Tales (from the Swedish), 1905; A Short History of America's Literature, 1906; A Short History of England's and America's Literature, 1906; American Hero Stories, 1906; America's Literature, with Selections from Colonial and Revolutionary Writers, 1907; Letters from Colonial Children, 1908; The Story of the Greek People, 1908; The Chaucer Story Book, 1908; Dixie Kitten, 1910; A Friend in the Library (12 vols.), 1910; The Story of the Roman People, 1910 (also pub. in Holland as De Geschiedenis van het Romeinsche Volk); An Old, Old Storybook, 1910; Old-World Hero Stories, 1911; When Knights Were Bold, 1912; The House with the Silver Door, 1913; The Farmer and His Friends; Diggers in the Earth; Makers of Many Things; Travelers and Traveling; The Little Book of the Flag, 1917; Our European Ancestors, 1918; The Little Book of the War, 1918; Food Saving and Sharing (for U.S. Food Administration), 1918; The Little Book of Our Country (for Y.M.C.A.), 1919; Hero Stories of France, 1920; Heroes of Progress, 1921; Story of Our Constitution, 1922; Ella, a Little Schoolgirl of the 'Sixties, 1923; American History Stories for Very Young Readers, 1924; Barry, the Dog Hero of the St. Bernard Pass (in A Book of Good Dogs), 1924; Stories of America for Very Young Readers, 1926; The Prince from Nowhere, 1928. Editor: Selections from Emerson, 1898; The Children's Hour (10 vols.), 1907, 5 vols., 1916; The World's Story (14 vols.), 1914; The Words of a Man, 1915; Andrew Carnegie's Own Story for Boys and Girls, 1923; American History Stories for Very Young Readers, 1924; The Little Lady in Green, 1925. Asst. editor U.S. Food Administration, 1918. Republican. Episcopalian. Home: Worcester, Mass. Died Jan. 29, 1930.

TAPPEN, Frederick D., pres. Gallatin Nat. Bank; b. New York, N.Y., Jan. 29, 1829; s. late Col. Charles B. T.; grad. New York Univ., 1849; m. Sarah A. B. Little; entered Nat. Bank of New York (now Gallatin Nat. Bank), 1850; cashier same, 1857; pres., 1868—. Has been pres. Clearing House Assn.; now v.p. and trustee Metropolitan Trust Co. and Bank for Savings; dir. Astor Nat. Bank, Bank of New Amsterdam, Mobile & Ohio R.R. Co., etc.; trustee Royal Ins. Co. of England. Home: New York, N.Y. Died 1902.

TAPPER, Bertha Feiring, musician; b. Christiania, Norway, Jan. 25, 1859; d. Lars Olsen and Berthe (Iversen) Feiring; studied music under John Svendsen and Agathe Backer-Gröndahl Christiania; grad. Leipzig Conservatory of Music, Germany, 1878; studied under Theodor Leschetizky, Vienna; came to America, 1881; m. Thomas Tapper, Sept. 22, 1895. Grad. teacher, N.E. Conservatory of Music, Boston, 1889-97; instr., Inst. of Musical Art, New York, 1905-10. Editor: Grieg's Piano Works, Vol. I, 1908, Vol. II, 1909. Home: New York, N.Y. Died Sept. 2, 1915.

TARBELL, Edmund C., painter; b. W. Groton, Mass., Apr. 26, 1862; s. Edmund Whitney and Mary (Fernald) T.; pupil of the Museum of Fine Arts, Boston; under Boulanger and Lefebre, Paris; D.Litt., Dartmouth College in 1929; m. Emeline Arnold Souther, Nov. 7, 1888; children—Josephine, Mercie, Mary, Edmund Arnold. Instr. drawing and painting, Boston Art Mus., from 1889. Mem. Jury of Award, St. Louis Expn. Awards: Clarke prize, Nat. Acad. Design, 1892; Shaw fund ($1,500), Soc. Am. Artists, 1893; medal, Chicago Expn., 1893; 1st Hallgarten prize, Nat. Acad. Design, 1894; Walter Lippincott prize, and Temple gold medal, Pa. Acad. Fine Arts, 1895; gold medal, Art Club, Phila., 1895; 2d W. S. Elkins prize ($2,500), Pa. Acad., 1896; hon. mention, Nashville Expn., 1897; 1st prize Worcester Mus., 1900; three medals, Boston Charitable Mechanics' Assn.; bronze medal, Paris Expn., 1900; bronze, silver, and gold medals, Carnegie Inst., Pittsburgh; Harris prize, Art Inst. of Chicago; Pa. Acad. Medal of Honor, 1908; gold medal, Nat. Acad. Design, 1908; Richard Greenough Memorial prize, Newport Art Assn., 1935. Rep. in exhbns. Cincinnati Art Mus., Pa. Acad. Worcester Art Mus., St. Louis Mus., Corcoran Gallery, Washington, Boston Art Mus., R.I. Sch. of Design, Buffalo Albright Art Gallery. A.N.A., 1902, N.A., 1906; 1st pres. Guild of Boston Artists. Mem. Internat. Jury of Awards, Panama P.I. Expn., 1915, also of Jury of Awards, Sesquicentennial Expn., Phila., 1926. Mem. Am. Acad. Arts and Sciences. Former chmn. council and of faculty Sch. of Museum of Fine Arts, Boston. Popular prize, Carnegie Inst., 1928. Home: Newcastle, N.H. Died Aug. 1, 1938.

TARBELL, Frank Bigelow, archeologist; b. Groton, Mass., Jan. 1, 1853; s. John and Sarah (Fosdick) T.; A.B., Yale, 1873, Ph.D., 1879; unmarried. Tutor Greek, 1876-82, asst. prof. Greek and instr. logic, 1882-87, Yale; annual dir. Am. Sch. of Classical Studies, Athens, 1888-89; instr. Greek, Harvard, 1889-92; sec. Am. Sch. Classical Studies, Athens, 1892-93; asso. prof. Greek, 1892-94, prof. classical archæology, 1894-1918, U. of Chicago. Author: The Philippics of Demosthenes, 1880; A History of Greek Art, 1896; Catalogue of Bronzes, etc., in Field Mus. of Natural History, 1909. Died Dec. 4, 1920.

TARBELL, Gage E., capitalist; b. Smithville, N.Y., Sept. 20, 1856; ed. Clinton Liberal Inst. Taught sch. for 1 yr.; admitted to bar and practiced, 1880-84; mgr. Southern N.Y. dept. Equitable Life Assurance Soc., 1884-88; gen. agt. same, for Wis., at Milwaukee, 1888-89; partner in Northwestern dept., same, at Chicago, 1889-91; resident sec. of soc. with sole charge of its affairs in Ill. and Wis., 1891-93; 3d v.p., 1893-99, 2d v.p., May 1899-Mar. 1907, Equitable Life Assurance Soc., now dir.; v.p. Westchester-Biltmore Corp. Home: New York, N.Y. Died Sept. 5, 1936.

TARBELL, Horace Sumner, educator; b. Chelsea, Vt., Aug. 19, 1838; s. Rev. Sumner T.; grad. Wesleyan Univ., 1859; (LL.D., Brown Univ., 1896); m. Martha Treat, Dec. 29, 1859. Supt. public schools E. Saginaw, Mich., 1870-76; supt. public instruction, Mich., 1877-78; supt. public schools, Indianapolis, Ind., 1878-84; supt. pub. schs., Providence, 1884-1902. Contbr. monographs and spl. articles to ednl. jours. Mem. Nat. Council Edn. (pres. 1896). Author: Tarbell's Lessons in Language and Grammar, Book I, Book II; Werner's Introductory Geography; Werner's Grammar School Geography; Tarbell's Introductory Geography; Tarbell's Complete Geography; Essentials of English Composition, 1902. Home: East Orange, N.J. Died 1904.

TARKINGTON, Grayson Emery, M.D.; b. Oakland, La., Dec. 25, 1894; s. Addison Richardson and Vinila (Chandler) T.; grad. Hot Springs (Ark.) High Sch., 1912; M.D., U. of Md., 1917; m. Delia Moss Lock, Dec. 24, 1918; m. 2d, Sally Jane Baker, Oct. 19, 1933. Began practice at Hot Springs, 1919; member exec. bd., dir. out-patient dept. and visiting phys. Leo N. Levi Memorial Hosp.; chief of syphilis staff, U.S.P.H.S. Clinic; mem. house staff St. Joseph's Infirmary, Presbyn. and St. Joseph sanatoriums; dist. chmn. Am. Cancer Control Com.; sec. Hot Springs Bd. of Health, etc. Served as 1st lt. Med. R.C., U.S.A., Aug. 15, 1917-Jan. 31, 1919. Asso. editor Am. Jour. Syphilis. Democrat. Presbyn. Mason. Home: Albuquerque, N.M. Died Jan. 12, 1933.

TARKINGTON, John Stevenson, lawyer; b. Centreville, Ind., June 24, 1832; s. Rev. Joseph and Maria (Slauson) T.; A.B., Asbury (now De Pauw) U., Greencastle, Ind., 1852, A.M., 1855; m. Elizabeth Booth, Nov. 19, 1857 (died 1909); m. 2d, Linda H. Schulz, Sept. 10, 1910; father of (Newton) Booth T. In law practice at Indianapolis, 1855—; mem. Ind. Ho. of Rep., 1863; capt. Co. A, 132d Ind. Inf., 1864; judge 7th Jud. Circuit, Ind., 1870-72. Republican. Methodist. Author: The Hermit of Capri, 1910; Auto-Orphan, 1913. Home: Indianapolis, Ind. Died Jan. 30, 1923.

TARPEY, Michael Francis; b. in Ireland, 1848; s. Patrick and Bridget (Grady) T.; brought to Calif., 1855; ed. St. Ignatius Coll., San Francisco; m. Emma Maude Bainbridge, Nov. 24, 1878; children—Arthur Bainbridge, Dollie Bainbridge (dec.). Began in mining business, White Pine Co., Nev., 1868; sec. and gen. mgr. Meadow Valley Mining Co. 5 yrs.; operated smelting and reduction plant, Melrose, Calif.; was long the owner of stock farm in Stanislaus Co., extensive vineyards in Fresno Co., and interests in Mexico. Served as pres. Fresno Irrigation Dist. Mem. Dem. Nat. Com. 24 yrs., and Dem. State Com. many yrs.; Dem. nominee for lt. gov. Calif., 1886. Died Nov. 24, 1925.

TARR, Ralph Stockman, university prof.; b. Gloucester, Mass., Jan. 15, 1864; s. Silas Stockman and Abigal (Saunders) T.; S.B., Lawrence Sci. Sch. (Harvard), 1891; m. Kate Story, Mar. 28, 1892. Asst. U.S. Fish Commn. and Smithsonian Instn., 1882-83; asst. geologist, Tex. Geol. Survey, 1889; asst., U.S. Geol. Survey, 1888 and 1891; asst. in geology, Harvard, 1890-91; asst. prof. geology, 1892-97, prof. dynamic geology and physical geography, 1897-1906, prof. physical geography, 1906—, Cornell U.; spl. field asst. U.S. Geol. Survey, 1903-06. Author: Economic Geology of United States, 1893; Elementary Physical Geography, 1895; Elementary Geology, 1897; First Book of Physical Geography, 1897; Tarr and McMurry Geographies, 1900, 1902; Physical Geography of New York State, 1902; New Physical Geography, 1904. Home: Ithaca, N.Y. Died Mar. 21, 1912.

TARR, William Arthur, geologist; b. New Cambria, Mo., Mar. 29, 1881; s. John W. and Ida Elizabeth (Hill) T.; B.S., Oklahoma A. and M. College, 1904, hon. D.Sc., 1927; B.S. in Mining Engring., U. of Arizona, 1908; Ph.D., Univ. of Chicago, 1916; m. Coralynn Gertrude Neumann, Apr. 30, 1905. Instr. in geology and mining, U. of Ariz., 1908-09; research asst., U. of Chicago, 1909-11; instr. geology and mineralogy, 1911-13, asst. prof., 1913-17, asso. prof., 1917-19, prof., 1919—, U. of Missouri. Democrat. Conglist. Author: Introductory Economic Geology, 1930; Introduction to Geology, 1935. Home: Columbia, Mo. Died July 28, 1939.

TARRANT, Warren Downes, judge; b. Durand, Wis., Dec. 10, 1867; s. George and Clara (Runey) T.; grad. Durand High Sch., 1883; B.Litt., U. of Wis., 1890, LL.B., 1892; unmarried. Mem. Tarrant & Kronshage, Milwaukee, 1892-97, Tarrant, Kronshage & McGovern, 1897-1902; apptd. judge 2d Jud. Circuit, Wis., Jan. 15, 1902; elected for unexpired term of Judge Eugene L. Elliott, deceased, Apr. 1, 1902, re-elected without opposition, Apr. 1905, again Apr. 1911, for full terms 6 yrs.; presided over Branch No. 2, Milwaukee Circuit Ct.; was 2d in seniority of Milwaukee circuit judges. Republican. Spl. lecturer Marquette U. Law Sch., Law Sch. U. of Wis.; pres. Milwaukee Lecture Service League, 1910-11. Mason. Home: Milwaukee, Wis. Died May 14, 1912.

TARVER, William Allen, lawyer; b. nr. Summit, Miss., May 30, 1883; s. William Allen and Julia Elizabeth (Muse) T.; B.S., Southwestern U., Georgetown, Tex., 1906, LL.D., 1932; m. Esther Mae Woods, June 30, 1908; children—Laura Elizabeth (Mrs. George Jonte), Esther Mae (Mrs. Girard Kinney), William Allen, Martha Ann; m. 2d, Sara Garrett; 1 son, William Allen. Admitted to Texas bar, 1907; member Treadwell & Tarver, Corsicana, 1907-12; prosecuting atty. Navarro Co., 1919-23; mem. Davis, Jester and Tarver, Corsicana, 1924-29; apptd. life ins. commr. and chmn. Bd. Ins. Commrs. of Texas, 1929-33; examiner with Reconstruction Finance Corp., Washington, D.C., 1933; apptd. chief counsel prohibition unit, Dept. of Justice, June 20, 1933; rep. of Dept. of Justice on Fed. Alcohol Control Administration and chief counsel alcoholic beverage unit, Div. of Investigation of Department of Justice, 1933-34, bond and spirits div., 1934—; apptd. spl. asst. to atty. gen. of U.S., Tex., 1939. Member Texas House of Rep., 1907-15. Elected pres. Nat. Ins. Commrs. Conv., 1932. Pres. Boy Scout Council Navarro Co., 1923-28; trustee Southwestern U., 1924-33, vice chmn. bd., 1929-33. Mem. Com. on Legal Edn., D.C., 1939. Mason, Woodman, Odd Fellow. Edited and compiled Digest State Insurance Laws of Texas, 1930 and 1932. Home: Corsicana, Tex. Died May 15, 1940.

TASSIN, Algernon de Vivier, author; b. Ft. Halleck, Nev., Dec. 11, 1869; s. Augustus Gabriel de Vivier and Mary McLeod (Tilley) T.; A.B., Harvard, 1892, A.M., 1893; m. Miriam Coulter Taylor, Nov. 4, 1918. Followed the stage, 1894-1905; with Columbia U., 1905—, now asso. prof. English. Decoration Officer Legion of Honor, France, because of father's service in Franco-Prussian War. Democrat. Author: Rust, 1911; The Magazine in America, 1916; The Craft of the Tortoise, 1919; The Rainbow String, 1921; The Oral Study of Literature, 1923; A Child's Story of American Literature (with Arthur Bartlett Maurice), 1923. Died Nov. 3, 1941.

TASSIN, Wirt, chemist, metallurgist; b. Ft. Whipple, Va., Aug. 11, 1869; s. Col. A. G. and Mary (Tilley) T.; grad. Cornell and Harvard; m. Mary Scott Moran, Aug. 15, 1895. Engaged in applied chemistry, then became spl. agt. U.S. Geol. Survey at Chicago Expn.; chemist and asst. curator, div. of mineralogy, U.S. Nat. Mus., 1893-1909; consulting metallurgist and chem. engr., May 1909—. Home: Washington, D.C. Died Nov. 2, 1915.

TATE, Hugh McCall, former Interstate Commerce commr.; b. Morristown, Tenn., Sept. 15, 1882; s. Edward Oscar and Carrie (Tate) T.; A.B., U. of Tenn., 1902, LL.B., 1903; m. Clara Hill, Oct. 22, 1910; children—Edward Oscar, Hugh M. and Clara (twins), Emily Y., Samuel David, William Knox. Admitted to Tenn. bar, 1903, and began practice at Morristown in firm of McCanless & Tate; served as city atty. Morristown, county atty. Hamblen Co. and chmn. Rep. Exec. Com. Hamblen Co.; settled in Knoxville, Tenn., 1909; mem. Lucky, Fowler, Andrews & Tate, 1909-10, Green, Webb & Tate, 1910-18, Cates, Smith, Tate & Long, 1920-30; elected judge 11th Chancery Div. of Tenn., 1918, for term of 8 yrs. (resigned 1920); mem. Interstate Commerce Commission, 1930-37. Pres. Tenn. Volunteer State Soc., 1934. Presbyn. Mason. Home: Knoxville, Tenn. Died May 29, 1938.

TATE, Sam, marble mfr.; b. Cartersville, Ga., June 13, 1860; s. Stephen Clayton and Eliza Dora (Buffington) T.; ed. North Ga. Agrl. Coll.; LL.D., Univ. of Georgia, 1931; unmarried. Mcht. until 1905; controlling owner and chmn. bd. Ga. Marble Co., producers and mfrs. Ga. marble, Tate, Ga., 1905—; dir. Bank of Canton (Ga.), dir. Canton Cotton Mills. Member staff four govs. of Georgia for 13 years; chmn. State Highway Board of Georgia. Trustee Emory U., Wesleyan Coll., Young Harris (Ga.) Coll., 7th Dist. Agrl.

and Mech. Coll., Tate High Sch. (pres. bd.), Ga. State Vocational Bd. Democrat. Methodist. Mason. Home: Tate, Ga. Died Oct. 11, 1938.

TATE, William Knox, educator; b. nr. Tate Springs, Tenn., Sept. 8, 1870; s. William C. and Mary Rebecca (Lowe) T.; U. of Ark.; A.B., Peabody Coll. for Teachers, Nashville, Tenn., 1892; A.M., U. of Nashville, 1900; m. Lizzie J. Harris, Sept. 9, 1896. Teacher, Siloam Springs, Ark., 1888-90; teacher and prin. High Sch., Tyler, Tex., 1892-98; prin. Memminger Normal Sch., Charleston, S.C., 1898-1910; asst. supt. schs., Charleston, 1908-10; state supervisor country schs. for S.C., 1910-14; prof. elementary edn., U. of S.C., 1910-14, Winthrop Normal Coll., 1910-14; prof. rural edn. and treas., George Peabody Coll. for Teachers, Nashville, 1914—. Mem. of faculty Summer Sch. of South, 1901-13; spl. rep. of U.S. Bur. Edn. to study Swiss sch. system, 1912. Democrat. Mason. Author: Teachers' Manual for Elementary Schools of South Carolina, 1911; Some Suggestive Features of the Swiss School System, 1913. Home: Nashville, Tenn. Died Feb. 7, 1917.

TATLOCK, John, astronomer; b. Williamstown, Mass., Mar. 12, 1860; s. Rev. John (D.D.) and Lucy Beman (Whitman) T.; B.A., Williams, 1882, M.A., 1885; m. Kate Chamberlin, Mar. 2, 1886. Asso. astronomer, U. of Wis., 1883-84; prof. astronomy, Beloit Coll., Wis., 1884-85; asst. actuary Mut. Life Ins. Co. of New York, 1889-1905; pres. Washington Life Ins. Co., 1905-08; pres. Westchester Av. Bank, New York, 1910-17. Fellow Royal Astron. Soc., London, New York Acad. Sciences (treas.); asso. Inst. of Actuaries, London. Presbyn. Home: New York, N.Y. Died Jan. 3, 1926.

TATNALL, Henry, ry. official; b. Wilmington, Del., Apr. 30, 1855; s. William and Rachel Burgess (Moon) T.; ed. pvt. schs.; m. Lola De Haven Robinson, 1881; children—Emmett R., Mrs. Rachel T. Earnshaw, H. Chace. Began with Girard Trust Co., Phila., 1879, treas., 1881-85, v.p., 1885-1900, resigned, 1900, to become pres. Franklin Nat. Bank; apptd. one of receivers of Asphalt Co. of America, 1901; elected 6th v.p. and treas., Pa. R.R., 1904; advanced through various steps to v.p. in charge of finance, May 8, 1912; retired May 1, 1925; mem. advisory board Guarantee Co. of N. America, Phila., Del. R.R., Guarantee Co. of N. America (Montreal, Can.). Republican. Home: Bryn Mawr, Pa. Died Mar. 1, 1939.

TATSCH, J(acob) Hugo, Masonic author; b. Milwaukee, Wis., Jan. 29, 1888; s. Jacob and Louise Hedwig (Hartmann) T.; student George Washington U., 1923-24; grad. Army Finance Sch., Washington, D.C., 1924; student Coe Coll., Cedar Rapids, Ia., 1925-27; grad. Command and Gen. Staff Sch., U.S.A., 1929; D.Litt., Theosophical U., Pt. Loma, Calif., 1929; M.A., Atlantic U., Virginia Beach, Va., 1933; m. Harriett Hughes, Oct. 3, 1928. With Old National Bank, Spokane, Wash., 1905-19; in foreign depts., Chem. Nat. Bank, N.Y. City, and 1st Nat. Bank, Boston, Mass., 1919; asst. cashier Union Bank & Trust Co., Los Angeles, Calif., 1921-22; asst. sec. and asst. editor Nat. Masonic Research Soc., Cedar Rapids, 1923; with Masonic Service Assn. of U.S., Washington, D.C., 1923-24; curator Ia. Masonic Library, Cedar Rapids, and asso. editor Grand Lodge Bulletin (Iowa), 1925-29; v.p. Macoy Pub. Co., New York, 1927-34; pres. Glastonbury Press, Brookline, Mass.; sec., treas. Ednl. Research Associates, Inc., Washington, D.C.; acting librarian, curator, Library Grand Lodge A.F.&A.M., Mass. and Supreme Council, 33°, N.M.J., Boston. Capt. N.G., Washington; 1917-18; spl. agt. Mil. Intelligence Div., U.S.A., 1918; capt. finance dept. O.R.C., 1924; maj., 1929, lt. col., 1935; Ia. member 7th Corps Area Advisory Board, U.S.A., 1927-28. Fellow Nat. Masonic Research Soc. Mason, mem. various Am. and foreign Masonic socs.; awarded European decorations and diploma for Masonic bibliog. and ednl. services. Author: Short Readings in Masonic History, 1926 (Spanish and Russian translations); High Lights of Crescent History, 1926; (with Winward Prescott) Masonic Bookplates, 1928; Freemasonry in the Thirteen Colonies, 1929; A Reader's Guide to Masonic Literature, 1929; The Facts About George Washington as a Freemason, 1931; Lodge Officers' Speech Book, 1934; Books on Freemasonry, 1935; (with Harry Smith) Moses Michael Hays; John James Joseph Gourgas, 1938; (with M. A. Davis) List of Masonic Subject Headings, 1937. Home: Brookline, Mass. Died July 17, 1939.

TAUBENHAUS, Jacob Joseph, plant pathologist; b. Saffed, Palestine, Oct. 20, 1884; s. Meyer and Bet Sheba T.; grad. Nat. Farm Sch., Doylestown, Pa., 1904; B.S. Cornell U., 1908, M.S., 1909; Ph.D., U. of Pa., 1913; m. Esther Hirchenson, 1910; children—Leon Yahir, Ruth Ziporah. Asso. plant pathologist Delaware Coll., Newark, 1909-16; chief of div. of plant pathology and physiology, Tex. Agrl. Expt. Sta., 1916—; in charge cotton root rot investigations in Texas. Russell lecturer, Mass. Hort. Soc., 1916. Mason. Author: Culture and Diseases of Sweet Pea, 1917; Diseases of Truck Crops, 1918; Diseases of Greenhouse Crops, 1920; Diseases of the Sweet Potato, 1923; Culture and Diseases of the Onion in America, 1924. Home: College Station, Tex. Died 1937.

TAUSSIG, Edward David, rear adm. U.S.N.; b. St. Louis, Nov. 20, 1847; s. Charles and Anna (Abeles) T.; grad. U.S. Naval Acad., 1867; m. Ellen Knefler, Nov. 9, 1873. Ensign, Dec., 1868; promoted through grades to rear adm., May 15, 1908. Commended to dept. by Comdr. Gillis for services during the earthquake at Arica, Aug. 13, 1868. Served on the European and Pacific stations and in the coast survey; comd. the Bennington, Aug., 1898-Aug. 1899; took possession of Wake Island for the U.S. and took charge of Guam on Feb. 1, 1899; served in the Philippines and during the summer of 1900 in North China; comd. Yorktown, June 1900, to June 1901; at Navy Yard, Washington, Nov. 1901, to Jan. 1902, Navy Yard, Boston, to May 1902; comd. Enterprise, May 1902, to Oct. 27, 1902, Navy Yard, Pensacola, Jan.-Oct. 1903; comd. Independence, Oct. 1903-Oct. 1904; comdg. battleship Massachusetts, Nov. 1, 1904; transferred to battleship Indiana, Jan. 6, 1906, Navy Yard, New York, Mar. 15, 1907; comdt. Navy Yard, Norfolk, Va., Dec. 1907; retired, Nov. 20, 1909. Home: Jamestown, R.I. Died Jan. 29, 1921.

TAUSSIG, Frank William, economist; b. St. Louis, Mo., Dec. 28, 1859; s. William and Adele (Wuerpel) T.; A.B., Harvard, 1879, Ph.D. and A.M., 1883, LL.B., 1886, Litt.D., 1916; Litt.D., Brown U., 1914, from U. of Cambridge, England, 1933; LL.D., Northwestern University, 1920, and from U. of Michigan, 1927; hon. Ph.D., U. of Bonn, Germany, 1928; m. Edith Thomas Guild, June 29, 1888; children—William Guild, Mrs. Mary Guild Henderson, Catharine C., Helen B.; m. 2d, Laura Fisher, 1918. Instr. polit. economy, 1882-86, asst. prof., 1886-92, prof., 1892-1901, Henry Lee prof., 1901-35 (emeritus), Harvard U.; chmn. U.S. Tariff Commn., 1917-19. Fellow Am. Acad. of Arts and Sciences. Author: Tariff History of United States, 1888; Silver Situation in United States, 1892; Wages and Capital, 1896; Principles of Economics, 1911, 4th edit., 1939; Some Phases of the Tariff Question, 1915; Inventors and Money-Makers, 1915; Free Trade, the Tariff and Reciprocity, 1919; International Trade, 1927; Social Origins of American Business Leaders, 1932. Editor of Quarterly Journal of Economics, 1896-1937. Home: Cambridge, Mass. Died Nov. 11, 1940.

TAUSSIG, Rudolph Julius, merchant (retired); b. New York, Feb. 1, 1861; s. Gabriel and Clara (Fried) T.; student Coll. City of New York class of '78; m. Emma M. Henicke, Feb. 22, 1891. In San Francisco, 1876—. Pres., now trustee, Mechanics Inst.; regent U. of California; chmn. com. Wilmerding School of Industrial Arts; pres. bd. trustees Calif. Sch. of Mech. Arts. Republican. Pres. Pacific Coast Hist. Assn.; mem. Calif. Acad. Science (treas.). Collector of books on early Spanish-Am. history, and author hist. papers. Sec., dir. Panama- Pacific Internat. Expn. Co., Mar. 1910—. Home: San Francisco, Calif. Died Jan. 24, 1922.

TAUSSIG, William, pres. St. Louis Bridge Co.; b. Prague, Bohemia, Feb. 28, 1826; s. John L. and Charlotte (Bondy) T.; grad. U. of Prague, 1844; M.D., St. Louis Sch. of Medicine, 1850; LL.D., Washington U., 1905; m. Adele Wuerpel, May 3, 1857; father of Frank William T. In practice, 1850-64; mayor of Carondelet, 1852; mem. 1859-65, presiding justice, 1863-65, St. Louis Co. Ct.; pres. Traders' Bank, 1866-69, dir. and gen. mgr. St. Louis (Eads) Bridge, 1867-96; pres. Terminal R.R. Assn., 1889-96, retiring from that position, 1896, but continues St. Louis Bridge Co. Mem. from 1899—, Bd. of Edn. (pres., 1903-04); pres. Self-Culture Hall Assn., 1895—; pres. Tenement House Assn. of St. Louis, 1905—; mem. Ethical Soc. of St. Louis. Home: St. Louis, Mo. Died July 10, 1913.

TAVENNER, Clyde Howard, congressman; b. Cordova, Ill., Feb. 4, 1882; s. John E. and Lucinda (Vanderburgh) T.; ed. country schs.; m. Isabel E. Martin, July 11, 1912; children—Isabel Lucinda, Elsa Mildred, Clyde H. At 13 began working in country newspaper office; later became writer for city dailies; began, 1908, to write daily signed article and for 10 years syndicated a daily Washington letter to 100 daily papers, weekly letter to 2,600 weekly papers; went abroad, 1909, and wrote series of letters on tariff systems of England, France, Germany, and Italy. Dir. of publicity for Dem. Nat. Congressional Com., Campaigns of 1910, 12; mem. 63d and 64th Congresses (1913-17), 14th Ill. Dist. Democrat. Visited Siberia, Japan, and Philippines, 1919, and wrote series of articles favoring Philippine independence. Founded The Philippine Republic, monthly mag., 1923. Died Feb. 7, 1942.

TAWNEY, James A., congressman; b. nr. Gettysburg, Pa., Jan. 3, 1855; s. John E. and Sarah (Boblitz) T.; common sch. edn.; learned blacksmithing and machinist trade; went to Winona, Minn., 1877; worked at machinist's trade until Jan. 1881; m. Emma B. Newell, Dec. 19, 1883. Admitted to bar, 1882, and since in practice at Winona. Mem. Minn. Senate, 1890-92; mem. 53d to 61st Congresses (1893-1911), 1st Minn. Dist. Republican. Apptd. by President Taft mem. Internat. Joint Commn. (created by treaty with Great Britain for settlement of internat. disputes between U.S. and Can.), Mar. 9, 1911, and was chmn. U.S. Sect. same. Home: Winona, Minn. Died June 12, 1919.

TAYLER, Benjamin Walter Rogers, clergyman; b. British Guiana, S.A., Mar. 13, 1859; s. Rev. Joseph and Mary Sophia (Buttersworth) T.; ed. King's Coll. U., N.S., 1884; D.D., Union U., 1907; D.C.L., King's, 1918; m. Louisa J. Ritchie, Nov. 2, 1886. Ordained Episcopal ministry, 1888; rector St. George's Ch., Schenectady, N.Y., 1906—. Author: Lays of a College Bohemian, 1884; Alexandra and Other Poems, 1911; The Old Faith in a New Setting, 1911. Home: Schenectady, N.Y. Died Apr. 10, 1924.

TAYLER, Robert Walker, judge; b. Youngstown, O., Nov. 26, 1852; s. Robert W. (1st comptroller of the Treasury) and Louisa Maria (Woodbridge) T.; A.B., Western Reserve Coll., 1872; LL.D., Oberlin, 1908; supt. schs., Lisbon O., 1873-75; editor the Buckeye State, 1875-76; m. Helen Vance, May 18, 1876. Admitted to bar, 1877; pros. atty. Columbiana Co., 1880-86; mem. 54th to 57th Congresses (1895-1903), 18th Ohio Dist.; nominated for 58th Congress but declined; U.S. dist. judge Northern Dist. of Ohio, Jan. 1905—. Republican. Home: Cleveland, O. Died 1910.

TAYLOR, Albert Pierce, writer; b. St. Louis, Mo., Dec. 18, 1872; s. George Archibald Albert and Melissa (Pierce) T.; ed. pub. schs., Leadville, Colo., and St. Mark's Episcopal High Sch., Salt Lake City; m. Ella De Mund, Oct. 19, 1896; 1 dau., Mary Isabel (Mrs. Wesley Peck); m. 2d, Emma Ahuena Davison, 1902. With U.P. Ry., Salt Lake City, 1891-93; surveying Utah-Calif. railroad route through Nev., 1893; asst. sec. Nat. Silver Party Conv., St. Louis, 1896, and same Nat. Silver Party hdqrs., Washington, D.C., 1896; with Cubans in Cuban Insurrection, 1896-97; secretary Hawaiian Annexation Commn., Washington, 1897-98; with secretarial force U.S. Commission to Hawaii, 1898; with American forces, Philippine Insurrection, 1899; dep. clk. Circuit Courts Republic of Hawaii; editorial staff Honolulu Advertiser most of time, 1899-1924; chief of detectives, Honolulu, 1906-08; rep. of Hawaii at San Francisco Expn., 1913-15; sec. Hawaii Tourist Bur., 1915-17; librarian Archives of Hawaii, 1924—. Mem. Capt. Jas. Cook Commn., 1927-28. Mem. Hawaiian Hist. Soc.; hon. mem. art, hist. and scientific assns. of Vancouver, B.C. Republican. Episcopalian. Author: Under Hawaiian Skies, 1922, 26; Rulers of Hawaii and Iolani Palace, 1927; Capt. Cook Sesquicentennial, Hawaii, 1928. Home: Honolulu, T.H. Died Jan. 12, 1931.

TAYLOR, Albert Reynolds, univ. pres.; b. Magnolia, Ill., Oct. 16, 1846; s. John and Mary Ann (Mills) T.; student Ill. State Normal U.; Ph.B., Lincoln U., 1872, Ph.D., 1882; LL.D., Cumberland University, 1906; L.H.D. from Millikin U. in 1925; m. Frances Minerva Dent, Oct. 16, 1873; children—Mrs. Jessie Minerva Newman, Mrs. Kittie Mary Cronkhite. Prof. natural sciences, Lincoln Univ., 1872-82; pres. State Normal Sch. of Kan., 1882-1901; pres. James Millikin U., Decatur, Ill., 1901-13; acting pres .of same, 1915-19, 1924, and president emeritus, 1919—. Lecturer before chautauquas, etc. Pres. Nat. Council Edn., 1899; life dir. N.E.A. Republican. Presbyn. Author: The Study of the Child, 1898, also pub. in Spanish and Japanese; Apple Blossoms (joint author), 1899; Among Ourselves, 1900; The Government of the State and Nation (joint author), 1901; Quarter-Centennial History of the James Millikin University, 1922; Life Story of James Millikin, 1926. Home: Decatur, Ill. Died Aug. 12, 1929.

TAYLOR, Alfred Alexander, governor; b. Happy Valley, Tenn., Aug. 6, 1848; s. Nathaniel Green and Emma (Haynes) T.; ed. Edge Hill Sch. (Princeton, N.J.), Pennington (N.J.) Sem., Kelsey's Sch. (Clinton, N.Y.); m. Jennie Anderson, June 22, 1881; children—John Anderson, Nathaniel G., Ben H., David H., J. Blaine, Alfred A., Robert L., Mary E., Ann Katherine, Frank J. Admitted to Tenn. bar, 1870; mem. Tenn. Ho. of Rep., 1875-76; Rep. candidate for gov. against brother Robert L. 1886 (defeated); mem. 51st-53d Congresses (1889-95); elected Gov. of Tenn., 1920, for term expiring Jan. 1923. Methodist. Mason, Elk. Home: Milligan College, Tenn. Died Nov. 24, 1931.

TAYLOR, Alva Edwards, judge; b. Rock Island, Ill., Mar. 28, 1859; s. Rodolphus B. and Sarah M. (Edwards) T.; LL.B., Chicago-Kent Coll. of Law, 1895; LL.M., Chicago Law Sch., 1897; D.C.L., Ill. Coll. of Law, 1898 (LL.D., 1899); m. Eugenie J. Cowles, Mar. 28, 1882. Admitted to Ia. bar, 1881, and practiced at Cherokee; removed to Dakota Ty., 1882, and practiced at Huron; removed to Chicago, 1892, and became atty. for N. Am. Loan & Trust Co.; was prof. and lecturer, Ill. Coll. of Law, and lecturer, Chicago Law Sch.; returned to Huron, S.D., 1899; partner of John L. Pyle (atty.-gen. S.D.), then of Coe I. Crawford (later mem. U.S. Senate), and of A. B. Fairbank, of Sioux Falls; asst. atty. gen. S.D., 1899-1903; judge of 9th Jud. Circuit, S.D., 1908-38. Liberal Republican. Trustee Huron Coll. Mason. Home: Huron, S.D. Died Mar. 7, 1941.

TAYLOR, Asher Clayton, brig. gen. U.S.A.; b. Fredonia, N.Y., Feb. 21, 1842; s. Joel and Almira (Parrish) T.; ed. Hillsdale Coll., Mich., 1865-66, Ripon Coll., Wis., 1866-67; m. Mary J. Branigan, Oct. 30, 1872. Corporal and sergt. Co. D and sergt. maj. 3d Wis. Inf., Apr. 25, 1861-Oct. 28, 1864; 1st lt. and adj. 3d Wis. Vet. Inf., Oct. 29, 1864; hon. mus. lt. 15th U.S. Inf., Oct. 16, 1867; 1st lt., Aug. 25, 1868; assigned to 2d Arty., Jan. 1, 1871; grad. Arty. Sch., 1876; capt., Jan. 20, 1889; maj. 4th Arty., June 18, 1900; lt. col. arty. corps, Feb. 21, 1902; col., Aug. 10, 1903; brig. gen., Jan. 21, 1904; retired at own request after 40 yrs. service, Jan. 22, 1904. Participated with regt. in capture of the secession legislature of Maryland, Sept. 17, 1861, thereby saving the state to the Union; served in Army of the Potomac, 1861-63, Army of Cumberland, 1863-64; participated in campaigns to Atlanta, Savannah, and from Savannah to Washington, under Gen. Sherman; battles of Winchester, Va., Cedar Mountain, Antietam, Chancellorsville, Gettysburg, Resaca, Dallas, Kenesaw Mountain, Peach Tree Creek; siege and capture of Atlanta, of Savannah, battles of Averysboro, N.C., Bentonville; in campaign from Goldsboro, N.C., to Raleigh, N.C., etc. On reconstruction duty in Ala. and Tex., 1867-69; at Sitka, Alaska, 1871-72; with army of occupation at Havana, 1899-1900, comdg. guard in charge of governor's palace, Jan.-May 1899. Distinguished marksman U.S.A., 1886—. Republican. Home: Cottonwood, Calif. Died Jan. 20, 1922.

TAYLOR, Barnard Cook, theologian; b. Holmdel, N.J., May 20, 1850; s. James C. and Sarah (Duell) T.; A.B., Brown U., 1874, A.M., 1877; grad. Crozer Theol. Sem., 1877; D.D., Richmond Coll., 1889; m. Martha R. Parmelee, June 20, 1877 (died 1905); children—Mabel (dec.), H. Weston, Edward Miller, Albert Parmelee. Ordained Bapt. ministry, 1883; instr. Hebrew, 1877-80, asso. prof. Bibl. interpretation, 1880-83, prof. O.T. lit. and exegesis, Crozer Theol. Sem., 1883-1920; resigned; prof. O.T. interpretation, Eastern Bapt. Theol. Sem., 1925—. Author: Outline Analysis of the Books of the Bible, 1892; Historical Books of Old Testament, 1895; Death of Christ as Taught in O.T., 1923; Prophecy and the Prophets, 1923; Miscellaneous Notes on O.T. Topics, 1929. Home: Philadelphia, Pa. Died Sept. 24, 1937.

TAYLOR, Bert Leston, author; b. Goshen, Mass., Nov. 13, 1866; s. A. O. and Katherine (White) T.; ed. Coll. City of New York; m. Emma Bonner, Nov. 16, 1895. Conducts column "A Line o' Type or Two" in The Chicago Daily Tribune. Author: The Well in the Wood, 1904; The Charlatans, 1906; A Line-o'-Verse or Two, 1911; The Pipesmoke Carry, 1912; Motley Measures, 1913; also booklets The Bilioustine and The Book Booster, 1901. Home: Glencoe, Ill. Died Mar. 19, 1921.

TAYLOR, Charles Elisha, educator; b. Richmond, Va., Oct. 28, 1842; s. Rev. James Barnett and Mary (Williams) T.; A.B., U. of Va., 1870; (D.D., Richmond Coll., 1884; Litt.D., U. of N.C., 1889; LL.D., Mercer, 1898); m. Mary Hinton Prichard, Sept. 11, 1873. Prof. Latin, 1870-84, pres., 1884-1905, Wake Forest (N.C.) College. Author: Gilbert Stone (poem), 1891; How Far a State May Educate, 1894; The Story of Yates, 1898. Died Nov. 5, 1916.

TAYLOR, Charles Fayette, M.D.; retired; b. Williston, Vt., April 25, 1827; grad. Univ. of Vt., M.D., 1856; practiced in New York; m. Martha Skinner, June 6, 1850 (died 1852); m. 2d, Mary S. Skinner. Prominent specialist in treatment of deformities and diseases of the bones and joints, and as an inventor of many appliances for treatment of cripples. Author: Theory and Practice of the Movement Cure; Spinal Irritation; Sensation and Pain; Mechanical Treatment of Angular Curvature of the Spine; Treatment of Disease of the Hip Joint; Infantile Paralysis. Home: Redlands, Calif. Died 1899.

TAYLOR, Charles Fremont, editor; b. Attica, Ind., July 3, 1856; s. Jackson and Amanda (Bartlette) T.; pub. sch. edn.; taught sch.; M.D., Central Coll. Phys. and Surg., Indianapolis, 1880; m. Estelle Foreman, Dec. 1892 (died 1894); m. 2d, Mrs. Amelia Cameron, Dec. 1898. Practiced in Ind., 1880-83; editor The Medical World, Phila., 1883—; editor and pub. Equity (quarterly), dealing with improved methods of government. Author: A Conclusive Peace; etc. Home: Philadelphia, Pa. Died Nov. 4, 1919.

TAYLOR, Charles Henry, journalist; b. Boston, Mass., July 14, 1846; ed. Boston pub. schs.; (hon. A.M., Dartmouth, 1896); m. Georgiana O. Davis, Feb. 7, 1866. Began career as printer and reporter on Boston Daily Traveller; pvt. sec. to gov. of Mass., 1869-71; mem. Mass. Ho. of Rep., 1872, clerk, same, 1873; editor and mgr. Boston Daily Globe, 1873—. Served during Civil War in 38th Mass. Regt.; wounded at Port Hudson, La., June 13, 1863; lt. col. on staff of Gov. Claflin, 1869-71; brig. gen. on Gov. Russell's staff, 1891-93. Home: Boston, Mass. Died June 22, 1921.

TAYLOR, Charles Henry, journalist; b. Charlestown, Mass., Oct. 2, 1867; s. Charles Henry and Georgiana O. (Davis) T.; grad. Boston Latin Sch., 1886; student Harvard Univ., 1886-89; LL.D., College of William and Mary, 1933; hon. A.M., Harvard, 1937; m. Marguerite Falck, Dec. 2, 1890. Manager and treasurer Boston Globe, 1893-1937, resigned. Pres. Am. Newspaper Pubs. Assn., 1901-04; pres. Business Hist. Soc., 1925-35, Boston Society of Natural History, 1927-35; chmn. bd. Mass. State Library, 1927-36. Mem. council Am. Antiquarian Soc., 1929—; pres. Industrial Sch. for Crippled and Deformed Children (Boston), 1933-40. Fellow Am. Acad. Arts and Sciences (dir. Bostonian Soc., 1906—); life mem. Confederate Memorial Lit. Soc., Va. Hist. Society. Home: Boston, Mass. Died Aug. 18, 1941.

TAYLOR, Charles Jay, artist; b. New York, N.Y., Aug. 11, 1855; s. Charles John and Elizabeth (MacDonald) T.; New York pub. schs.; LL.B., Columbia, 1874; studied art, Nat. Acad. Design, Art Students' League, and London and Paris; hon. A.M., Middlebury (Vt.) Coll., 1911; m. Mary Adelaide Levison, Feb. 23, 1876; children—Adelaide, Virginia. Has exhibited at Nat. Acad. Design, Soc. Am. Artists, Pa. Acad. Fine Arts, Art Inst. Chicago, Salon, Paris, World's Fair, Chicago, Paris Expn., 1900; hon. mention Pan-American Expn., 1901; medal, Carnegie Inst., Pittsburgh, 1907. Mem. Am. Fedn. Arts, Nat. Geog. Soc., Pittsburgh Artists' Assn., Pittsburgh Archtl. Club. Prof. of fine arts, Carnegie Tech. Schools, Pittsburgh, Sept. 1, 1911; now head of dept. painting and illustration, Coll. Fine Arts, Carnegie Inst. Tech., Pittsburgh. Has illustrated: The Tailor-Made Girl, 1884; Short Sixes (H. C. Bunner), 1894; More Short Sixes (same), 1895; Made in France (same), 1896; The Suburban Sage (same), 1897; In the Four Hundred (C. J. Taylor), 1897; Short Rations (Williston Fish), 1898; England (C. J. Taylor), 1899; Poems with Music (Bunner), 1898; Partners of Providence (C. D. Stewart), 1907; etc. Has drawn for Life, Puck, Judge, London Punch and other periodicals. Mem. Internat. Jury Award in Fine Arts, Panama-P.I. Expn., 1915 (medal for distinguished services in art, 1919); medal, Dept. of Fine Arts, Sesquicentennial, Phila., 1926. Home: Pittsburgh, Pa. Died Jan. 19, 1929.

TAYLOR, Charles Lewis, trustee; b. Philadelphia, Pa., Apr. 3, 1857; s. John D. and Sarah Potts (Rutter) T.; E.M., Lehigh U., Pa., 1876 (D.Eng., 1919); m. Lillian, d. late Robert Pitcairn, Oct. 31, 1883. Asst. chemist and later asst. supt. blast furnaces, Cambria Iron Co., Johnstown, Pa., 1876-80; chemist, 1880-82, supt., 1882-86, Pittsburgh Bessemer Steel Co. (Homestead Steel Works); gen. mgr. Hartman Steel Co., Pittsburgh, 1887-90; asst. sec. Carnegie, Phipps & Co., Ltd., 1890-93; asst. to the pres., Carnegie Steel Co., Ltd., 1893-1901; chmn. Carnegie Relief Fund, 1901-10; v.-chmn. U.S. Steel and Carnegie Pension Fund, 1911—; pres. Carnegie Hero Fund Commn., 1904—; pres. Kingsley House Assn., 1913—; v.p. Western Pa. Inst. for Blind, 1907; trustee Carnegie Peace Fund, 1910—, also Carnegie Library, Carnegie Inst. and Carnegie Inst. Tech., Pittsburgh, Lehigh U., S. Bethlehem, 1904—, Estate of Asa Packer. Home: Pittsburgh, Pa. Died Feb. 3, 1922.

TAYLOR, David Watson, naval constructor; b. Louisa Co., Va., Mar. 4, 1864; s. Henry and Mary Minor (Watson) T.; Randolph-Macon Coll., Va., 1877-81; grad. U.S. Naval Acad., 1885, head of class and excelled highest record ever made there up to that time; sent to Greenwich in 1885, received highest honors of Royal Coll., 1888, again making the highest record of any student there up to that time; hon. D.Engring., Stevens Inst., Hoboken, N.J., 1907; D.Sc., George Washington U., 1915; LL.D., Randolph-Macon Coll., 1922, U. of Glasgow, Scotland, 1924; m. Imogene Maury Morris, Oct. 26, 1892; children—Dorothy Watson, May Coleman, David Watson, Imogene Morris. Capt. U.S.N., Mar. 4, 1901; promoted to rank of rear admiral, 1917. Awarded gold medal by British Instn. Naval Architects, for best original paper on Ship-Shaped Stream Forms (first American so honored). In 1899 constructed (and had charge of) first experimental tank ever built in U.S. Retained by British Govt. as expert in suit growing out of Hawke-Olympic collision, 1911. Chief constructor U.S.N. and chief of Bur. of Constrn. and Repair, Navy Dept., 1914-22; retired, Jan. 15, 1923; awarded D.S.M. (U.S.); Comdr. Legion of Honor (France). Vice chmn. Nat. Advisory Com. for Aeronautics; mem. Soc. Naval Architects and Marine Engrs. (pres. 1925-27), (British) Instn. of Naval Architects (hon. v.p. 1931). John Fritz Medalist, 1931; gold medalist (British) North East Coast Instn. of Engrs. and Shipbuilders, 1931. Awarded 1st David Watson Taylor Gold Medal (established in his honor) by Soc. Naval Architects and Marine Engrs., 1936; new U.S. David Watson Taylor Model Basin named in his honor, 1937. Author: Resistance of Ships and Screw Propulsion, 1893; Speed and Power of Ships, 1910. Home: Waldrop, Va. Died July 28, 1940.

TAYLOR, Edward Ballinger, ry. official; b. Riverton, N.J., Feb. 6, 1850; s. John Gardiner and Rebecca Haines (Ballinger) T.; A.B., Haverford, 1869; B.C.E., Poly. Coll. of Pa., 1870, M.C.E., 1873; m. Marianna Satterthwaite, Oct. 24, 1872. Rodman and clerk, 1870-71, supervisor, 1871-72, asst. engr., 1872-76, supt. Lewiston div., 1876-79, W. Pa. div., 1879-81, Pa. R.R.; supt. Pittsburgh, Cincinnati & St. Louis Ry., 1881-88; gen. supt. Northwestern System, Pa. Lines, 1888-90; gen. supt. transportation all Pa. Lines W. of Pittsburgh, 1890-1902; v.p. and comptroller Penna. R.R. Western Lines; retired Mar. 1, 1920. Pres. Bd. Water Commrs., Sewickley Borough, 1895—. Home: Sewickley, Pa. Died Nov. 8, 1922.

TAYLOR, Edward Livingston, lawyer; b. Columbus, O., Mar. 20, 1839; s. David and Margaret (Livingston) T.; A.B., Miami U., Ohio, 1860; m. Katherine Noble Myers, July 14, 1864 (died 1894); father of Edward Livingston T., Jr. Capt. Co. D, 95th Ohio Inf., Civil War; admitted to bar, 1862; began practice, 1864; in partnership with brother, Henry C., as Taylor & Taylor, until 1891; son Edward, Jr., entered firm and it became Taylor, Taylor & Taylor; retired from practice, 1908. Trustee Miami U., 18 yrs. Hon. mem. Ohio Archæol. and Hist. Soc. Republican. Unitarian. Home: Columbus, Ohio. Died 1910.

TAYLOR, Edward Randolph, chemist; b. Brasher Falls, N.Y., July 1, 1844; s. Thomas R. and Julia E. (Taft) T.; B.S., Lawrence Scientific School (Harvard), 1868; m. Mrs. Carrie A. Williams, Oct. 8, 1873. Prof. chemistry and toxicology, Homœ. Hosp. Coll., Cleveland, 1869-73; chemist, Cleveland Rolling Mill Co., 1869-76; pres. Taylor Chem. Co., Penn Yan, N.Y., founded, 1876. Trustee Keuka Coll., Keuka Park, N.Y. Republican. Presbyn. Awarded Elliott Cresson gold medal, Franklin Inst., 1907. Del. Internat. Congress Applied Chemistry, Berlin, 1903, Rome, 1906, London, 1909. Home: Penn Yan, N.Y. Died May 28, 1917.

TAYLOR, Edward Robeson, lawyer; b. Springfield, Ill., Sept. 24, 1838; s. Henry West and Mary (Thaw) T.; ed. Kemper Sch., Boonville, Mo.; M.D., Toland Med. Coll. (now med. dept., U. of Calif.), 1865; m. Agnes Stanford, Apr. 20, 1870; m. 2d, Eunice Jeffers, Feb. 8, 1908. Went to Calif., Jan. 1862; admitted to Calif. bar, 1872, Supreme Ct. U.S., 1879; pvt. sec. to gov. of Calif., 1867-71; dean Hastings Coll. of Law (Univ. of Calif.), 1899-1919. Mem. Bd. Freeholders, 1886-87, and of 5th Bd. of Freeholders in 1898, to frame existing charter for San Francisco; apptd. mayor of San Francisco, July 1907, and elected mayor, Nov. 1907, for term which expired Jan. 8, 1910. Democrat. Was v.p. and pres. Cooper Med. Coll. 30 yrs. and until its incorporation by Stanford U.; pres. San Francisco Law Library; trustee San Francisco Public Library, 1886-1921. Author: Selected Poems, 1907; Lavender and Other Verse, 1910; Into the Light, 1912; In the Court of the Ages (poems); To Arms (war poems); Chants with the Soul, 1920. Decorated with Cross of Legion of Honor, France, 1920. Home: San Francisco, Calif. Died July 5, 1923.

TAYLOR, Edward Thomas, congressman; b. Metamora, Ill., June 19, 1858; s. Henry R. and Anna (Evans) T.; grad. Leavenworth (Kan.) High Sch., 1881; prin. Leadville (Colo.) High Sch., 1881-82; LL.B., U. of Mich., 1884; hon. LL.D., Western State Coll. of Colo., 1935; returned to Leadville and began practice of law; m. Etta Tabor Durfee, Oct. 19, 1892; children—Edward T., Jr., Mrs. Irving M. Baker, Joseph E. Co. supt. schs., Lake Co., Colo., 1884-85; deputy dist. atty., 1885-86; in practice at Glenwood Springs, Colo., 1887—; dist. atty., 9th Jud. Dist., Colo., 1887-89; mem. Colo. Senate, 3 terms, 1896-1908 (pres. pro tem term, and author of 40 gen. statutes and 5 constl. amendments, adopted by vote of the people of Colo.); served 5 terms as city atty., Glenwood Springs, and 2 terms as co. atty., Garfield Co., Colo.; mem. 61st to 63d Congresses (1909-15), Colo. at large and 64th to 76th Congresses (1915-41), 4th Colo. Dist.; chmn. Dem. caucus, 74th Congress and majority leader, 1935. One of only 6 out of 8,124 members of Congress elected 16 consecutive times. Home: Glenwood Springs, Colo. Died Sept. 3, 1941.

TAYLOR, Ezra B., congressman; b. Nelson, O., July 9, 1823; s. Elisha and Thirza (Couch) T.; acad. edn.; m. Harriet M. Frazier, Nov. 9, 1849. Admitted to bar, 1845; was pros. atty. Portage Co.; judge Ct. of Common Pleas, 1877-80; elected to 46th Congress, Nov. 30, 1880, for unexpired term (1880-81) of James A. Garfield, elected President; reëlected 47th to 52d Congresses (1881-93), 19th Ohio Dist. Republican. Home: Warren, O. Died 1912.

TAYLOR, Francis Matthew Sill, clergyman; b. Erie, Pa., Mar. 19, 1851; s. Matthew and Sarah H. (Sill) T.; student Cornell U., 1868; A.B., Princeton, 1872, A.M., 1875; grad. Gen. Theol. Sem., 1875; (D.D., Western Theol. Sem., 1905); m. Adele C. Seymour, Apr. 20, 1876. Deacon, 1875, priest, 1876, P.E. Ch.; in charge St. Thomas Ch., Pittsburgh, 1875-78, Ch. of the Holy Spirit, Rondout, N.Y., 1878-81; dean St. Paul's Cathedral, Indianapolis, 1881-83; rector St. Paul's Ch., Alton, Ill., and archdeacon Diocese of Springfield, Ill., 1883-89; rector Grace Ch., Paducah, Ky., 1889-90, Ch. of the Ascension, Mt. Vernon, N.Y., 1890-1907 (rector emeritus); rector St. Paul's Ch., E. St. Louis, Oct. 18, 1908-13; archdeacon, Diocese of Erie, Pa., 1913—. Republican. Author: An American Hierarchy, 1896; America's Mission, 1900; Dionysius the Areopagite, 1901. Died June 1, 1915.

TAYLOR, Frank, brigadier gen. U.S.A.; b. Calais, France, Apr. 29, 1842; ed. in France and England. Served as pvt. and sergt. gen. service, Oct. 24, 1860-Apr. 1, 1863; apptd. from Iowa, 2d lt. 2d U.S. Inf.,

Oct. 29, 1867; assigned to 14th Inf., July 31, 1869; 1st lt., Feb. 25, 1876; capt., Mar. 23, 1892; transferred to 8th Inf., Apr. 17, 1900; maj. 15th Inf., Oct. 9, 1900; lt. col. 19th Inf., Aug. 13, 1903; brig. gen., Apr. 9, 1905; retired at own request, Apr. 10, 1905. Served in Civil War, Indian campaigns, and in P.I. Home: Seattle, Wash. Died May 20, 1920.

TAYLOR, Frank Mansfield; b. New York, N.Y., Apr. 5, 1850; s. H. Augustus and Catherine A. (Osborn) T.; A.B., Amherst, 1871; m. Lida Ross Eshleman, Nov. 29, 1876 (died 1924); children—Harry Augustus (dec.), David Paul; m. 2d, Genevieve Folsom Hallett, Nov. 21, 1928. Manager mining companies Georgetown and Leadville, Colo., 1875-82; mining engr., New York and London, 1883-88; in Aspen, Colo., 1889-99; located in Denver, 1899; engaged extensively in planning, building and managing works for sampling, concentrating and milling precious metal; mem. Taylor & Brunton, 1880—; pres. Taylor & Brunton ore sampling cos., 1889-1911; retired. Pres. Colo. Mus. Natural History, 1916—. Mem. Denver Bd. of Edn., 1917-29, pres. 1926-29; v.p., chmn. bd. mgrs. St. Luke's Hosp., Denver, 1922—. Episcopalian. Home: Denver, Colo. Died Feb. 22, 1930.

TAYLOR, F(rank) Walter, artist; b. Philadelphia, Pa., Mar. 8, 1874; s. Frank Hamilton and Margaret (Johnston) T.; Friends Sch., Phila.; Pa. Acad. Fine Arts, 1896 (awarded traveling scholarship); studied independently in Paris; m. Elsie Carleton Megary, Apr. 19, 1917. Established studio in Phila., 1898. Mem. The Fellowship of Pa. Acad. Fine Arts, Soc. of Illustrators. Illustrator various books and short stories. Medal of honor, Panama P.I. Expn., 1915. Home: Philadelphia, Pa. Died July 27, 1921.

TAYLOR, Frederick Eugene, clergyman; b. Newark, N.J., Sept. 8, 1867; s. Charles and Catherine (Holmes) T.; ed. corr. course, U. of Chicago and under pvt. tutors; grad. Colgate U. Div. Sch., 1899; D.D., Franklin (Ind.) Coll., and Denison U.; D.D., Colgate, 1924; m. Hattie Hedden, Oct. 1, 1889. Began in wholesale saddlery business, New York, later traveling salesman; sec. Dover (N.J.) Y.M.C.A., 1891-92; asso. pastor Peddie Memorial Bapt. Ch., Newark, N.J., 1892-94, 2d Ch., St. Louis, Mo., 1894-96; ordained Bapt. ministry, 1895; pastor Central Church, Brooklyn, N.Y., 1899-1903; evangelistic work, 1903-06; pastor 1st Ch., Indianapolis, Ind., 1906—. Dir. camp religious work, Camp Green, N.C., summer and fall of 1917; dir. religious work Central Mil. Dept., in charge 25 camps and forts, 1918. Pres. Northern Bapt. Conv., 1921-22; mem. bd. Am. Bapt. Foreign Mission Soc., bd. of Missionary Coöperation, Ind. Bapt. State Conv., and Franklin Coll. Author: The Evangelistic Church, 1928. Home: Indianapolis, Ind. Died Apr. 28, 1932.

TAYLOR, Frederick William, P.E. clergyman; b. Toledo, O., Jan. 11, 1853; s. Alfred Taylor, M.D. (surgeon maj. 2d O.V.C., Civil war), and Helen Augusta Mills (Leonard) T.; grad. Western Reserve Coll., Hudson, O., 1873; A.M., in course 1875; grad. B.D., Gen. Theol. Sem., New York, 1876 (D.D., Nashotah Theol. Sem., causa honoris, 1890); m. Cora L. Kingsley, Aug. 11, 1874 (died 1894). Ordered deacon, July 5, 1876; ordained priest in Ch. of Transfiguration, New York, Sept. 30, 1877; rector Holy Trinity, Danville, Ill., 1878-86, St. Paul's Pro-Cathedral, Springfield, Ill., 1886—; archdeacon of Springfield; mem. com. on canons; instr. church polity and canon law, Western Theol. Sem., Chicago; chaplain State senate, Ill., 38th Gen. Assembly; local sec. Egyptian Exploration Fund; mem. Asso. Alumni Gen. Theol. Sem., pres. standing com., Diocese of Springfield. Author: The Confession of Our Christian Faith, commonly called the Creed of St. Athanasius, with brief notes, 1883, p. 12. Wrote: The Church of England During the Reign of King Edward VI, Am. Church Review, April 1886; St. Patrick, the Apostle of Ireland, Church Eclectic, March 1899, and many others. Home: Springfield, Ill. Died 1903.

TAYLOR, Frederick Winslow, engineer; b. Germantown, Phila., Pa., Mar. 20, 1856; s. Franklin and Emily (Winslow) T.; prepared for Harvard at Phillips Exeter Acad., 1874; left because of impaired eyesight; M.E., Stevens Inst. Tech., 1883; (Sc.D., U. of Pa., 1906; LL.D., Hobart Coll., 1912); m. Louise M. Spooner, May 3, 1884. Entered employ Midvale Steel Co., Phila., 1878, and was successively gang boss, asst. foreman, foreman of machine shop, master mechanic, chief draftsman, and chief engr. to 1889; left 1889 to begin work of organizing management of mfg. establishments of various kinds, in shop, office, accounting and sales dept.; has organized many kinds, including the Bethlehem Steel Co., Cramp's Shipbuilding Co., Midvale Steel Co. Inventor of Taylor-White process of treating modern high-speed tools, for which received personal gold medal from Paris Expn., 1900, and Elliot Cresson gold medal of Franklin Inst. Has received about 100 patents for various inventions. Unitarian. Author: Concrete, Plain and Reinforced (with S. E. Thompson), 1905; Art of Cutting Metals, 1906; Concrete Costs (with S. E. Thompson), 1911; The Principles of Scientific Management, 1911; Shop Management, 1911. Won double championship of U.S., at Newport, 1881, in lawn tennis. Home: Philadelphia, Pa. Died Mar. 21, 1915.

TAYLOR, George Boardman, Baptist clergyman; b. Richmond, Va., Dec. 27, 1832; s. Rev. Dr. James Barnett and Mary (Williams) T.; grad. Richmond Coll. and Univ. of Va. (D.D., Richmond Coll. and old Univ. of Chicago). He was the first pastor of Franklin Sq. Ch., Baltimore; later at Staunton, Va., and for 2 terms chaplain Va. State Univ. From 1873, under appointment of foreign mission board, Richmond, Va., in charge of their mission in Italy; m. Susan Braxton, 1858 (died 1884). Since 1901 prof. systematic theology, Bapt. Theol. Sch., Rome. Author: "Oakland" series juvenile stories, 1859-65; Coster Grew; Roger Bernard, the Pastor's Son; Walter Ennis, a Tale of the Early Virginia Baptist, 1866-70; Baptists—Who They Are and What They Have Done (4 vols.), 1872-73; Italy and the Italians, 1898. Home: Rome, Italy. Died 1907.

TAYLOR, Graham, sociologist; b. Schenectady, N.Y., May 2, 1851; s. Rev. William James Romeyn and Katharine (Cowenhoven) T.; A.B., Rutgers Coll., 1870, A.M., 1873; grad. Ref. Theol. Sem., New Brunswick, N.J., 1873; (D.D., Rutgers, 1888; LL.D., Ill. Coll., 1897, Rutgers, 1916, Knox, 1921); m. Leah Demarest, 1873 (died 1918); children—Helen Demarest (Mrs. George Wallace Carr), Graham Romeyn, Lea Demarest, Katharine; m. 2d, Mrs. Isabella Bishop McClintock, Nov. 1921 (died 1926). Ordained (Dutch) Reformed ministry, 1873; pastor Reformed Church, Hopewell, Dutchess County, N.Y., 1873-80, Fourth Congl. Church, Hartford, Conn., 1880-92; prof. practical theology, Hartford Theol. Sem., 1888-92; prof. social economics, Chicago Theol. Sem., 1892—. Founder and resident warden, Chicago Commons Social Settlement, 1894—. Pres. Chicago Sch. of Civics and Philanthropy, 1903-20; asso. editor The Survey. Editorial contbr. Chicago Daily News. Author: Religion in Social Action, 1913; Pioneering on Social Frontiers, 1930; Chicago Commons Through Forty Years, 1936. Chmn. Selective Service Local Bd., Div. 39, Chicago, 1917-19, and Bureau for Soldiers, Sailors and Marines, 1919. Home: Chicago, Ill. Died Sept. 26, 1938.

TAYLOR, Hannis, lawyer; b. New Bern, N.C., Sept. 12, 1851; s. Richard N. and Susan (Stevenson) T.; ed. U. of N.C.; (LL.D., Dublin U., 1900, Edinburgh U., 1904, and from eight American universities; m. Leonora Le Baron, May 8, 1878. Admitted to bar, 1870; practiced at Mobile, 1870-92; U.S. minister to Spain, 1893-97; spl. counsel for U.S. Govt. before Spanish Treaty Claims Commn., 1902; counsel for U.S. before Alaska Boundary Commn., 1903; now in gen. practice at Washington. Honored by Inst. of France, 1909. Author: The Origin and Growth of the English Constitution; International Public Law, 1902; Jurisdiction and Procedure of the Supreme Court of the U.S.; The Science of Jurisprudence, 1908; The Origin and Growth of the American Constitution; Cicero—A Sketch of His Life and Works, 1916; Due Process of Law, 1916. Home: Washington, D.C. Died Dec. 26, 1922.

TAYLOR, Harry, army officer; b. Tilton, N.H., June 26, 1862; s. John Franklin and Lydia T.; grad. U.S. Mil. Acad., 1884, Engr. Sch. of Application, 1887; m. Adele Austin Yates, Oct. 30, 1901. Commd. 2d lt. engrs., June 15, 1884; promoted through grades to maj. gen., June 19, 1924. Engr. duties on Columbia River, and river and harbor works in Ore. and Wash., 1891-96, in charge defense works, Puget Sound, Wash., 1896-1900; in Philippines, 1903; comd. 3d Batln. Engrs., in P.I., 1904; engr. officer Dept. of Luzon, 1903-04; fortification constrn., 1904-05; in charge defenses of eastern entrance L.I. Sound and various improvements, 1906-11; asst. to chief of engrs., War Dept., 1911-16; in charge river and harbor works New York Harbor, Hudson River and Lake Champlain, dept. engr. Eastern Dept., Governors Island, 1916-17; chief engr. A.E.F. in France, May 1917-Sept. 1918; apptd. asst. chief of engrs. U.S.A., Sept. 1918, and chief of engrs., June 1924; retired 1926. Awarded D.S.M. (U.S.); Comdr. Legion of Honor (French). Episcopalian. Home: Washington, D.C. Died Jan. 28, 1930.

TAYLOR, Harry G., ry. executive; b. Wilber, Neb., June 30, 1880; s. Charles William and Emma Jane T.; ed. pub. schs., Wesleyan Univ., Salina, Kan., York (Neb.) Coll., until 1900; m. Jessie L. Hart, Apr. 22, 1913; children—Bruce Winslow and Stanley Hart (twins). Began as pub. country weekly newspaper, at Almena, Kan., 1899; purchased weekly Nonpareil, Central City, Neb., Jan. 1903, and continued as publisher until 1913; mem. Neb. Ho. of Rep., 1911; mem. State Ry. Commn., Neb., 1913-27; mgr. pub. relations, Am. Ry. Assn., Washington, D.C., 1927-32; commr. Western Railroads and chmn. Western Assn. of Ry. Executives, Chicago, Dec. 1, 1932—. Republican. Methodist. Home: Evanston, Ill. Died Aug. 10, 1938.

TAYLOR, Henry A. Coit, financier; A.B., Columbia, 1861, A.M., 1864. Mem. bd. mgrs. D.,L.&W. R.R.; dir. Cayuga & Susquehanna R.R., Met. Opera & Real Estate Co. (v.p.), Nat. City Bank of New York, N.Y. Life Ins. & Trust Co., Newport (R.I.) Trust Co., Lackawanna & Western Ry. Co. Home: New York, N.Y. Died May 28, 1921.

TAYLOR, Henry Clay, rear admiral U.S.N.; b. Washington, Mar. 4, 1845; apptd. from Ohio, Sept. 20, 1860; Naval Acad., 1863; promoted ensign May 28, 1863; served in Civil war on board the Shenandoah in the actions off Wilmington, 1863, and spring of 1864; then in Iroquois to relieve the Kearsarge in the English Channel; thence searching for Confederate cruisers in E. Indies. Promoted master, Nov. 10, 1865; lt., Nov. 10, 1866; lt. comdr., Mar. 12, 1868; comdr., Dec. 16, 1879; capt., Apr. 16, 1894; served on many duties and stas.; was pres. Naval War Coll. Newport, R.I., Nov. 1893, to Dec. 1896; later comd. battleship Indiana, in which he served in operations against Spain, 1898, including the destruction of Cervera's fleet; confirmed by Senate as Chief Bureau of Navigation, Apr. 26, 1902. Died 1904.

TAYLOR, Henry Fitch, artist; b. Cincinnati, O., Sept. 5, 1853; s. Sylvester and Emily Frances (Smith) T.; ed. pub. schs., Cincinnati; studied art, Academie Julien, Paris; m. Clara Sidney, d. late Bishop Potter, of New York, Mar. 20, 1913. Has exhibited at London, Paris, Rome, New York, Phila., Chicago, San Francisco. Democrat. Mental Scientist. Inventor of The Taylor System of Organized Color (a device for indicating harmonious color relations). Home: Cornish, N.H. Died Sept. 10, 1925.

TAYLOR, H(enry) Genet, physician; b. nr. Troy, N.Y., July 6, 1837; s. Dr. Othniel H. and Eveline C. T.; descendant on mother's side of "Citizen Genet," the 1st ambassador of France to U.S.; ed. Camden, N.J., city schools and P.E. Acad., Phila.; M.D., U. of Pa., 1860; (hon. A.M., Rutgers, 1889); practices in Camden, N.J.; m. Helen Cooper, Oct. 23, 1879. Served, 1861-64, asst. surgeon 8th N.J. Vols. and surgeon of Artillery Brigade, 3d Corps, Army of Potomac; later, asst. surgeon bd. of enrollment, 1st Congressional Dist., N.J.; surgeon 6th Regt. N.J. N.G., 1869-82; brigade surgeon during strike of 1887. Holds several hosp. appmts.; mem. bd. mgrs. and med. dir. Cooper Hosp., chmn. and sec. attending staff. Home: Camden, N.J. Died Jan. 14, 1916.

TAYLOR, Henry Kirby, prof. education; b. Vanceburg, Ky., Aug. 10, 1858; s. Peter and Sarah Ellen T.; A.B., Ky. Wesleyan Coll., Winchester, 1879, A.M., 1880, LL.D., 1927; m. Sallie Brinkley Sandifer, Sept. 2, 1880; children—Walter B., Lucile P. (Mrs. Victor Ivan), Emma Lee (Mrs. Joseph J. Codbey), Henry Kirby, John Carter, Hattie Mae (Mrs. Lloyd C. Clark). Teacher of science, Wesleyan Coll., 1879-81; prin. Riverside Sem., 1882-83; pres. Logan Coll. for Women, Russellville, Ky., 1883-89; prin. Louisville Training Sch. for Boys, 1889-1906; pres. Ky. Wesleyan Coll., 1906-09, N.W. Mo. Teachers Coll., 1909-13; prin. Arlington (Tex.) Training Sch., 1913-16; prof. edn., Tex. Woman's Coll., Ft. Worth, 1916-22; prof. edn. and dir. extension sch., Southern Meth. Univ., 1922—. Mem. M.E. Ch., S. Died Jan. 21, 1934.

TAYLOR, Henry Ling, surgeon; b. New York, Mar. 17, 1857; s. Dr. Charles Fayette and Mary S. (Skinner) T.; Ph.B., Sheffield Scientific Sch. (Yale), 1877; M.D., Coll. Phys. and Surg. (Columbia), 1881; m. Daisy Louise Brodt, Dec. 30, 1890. Prof. orthopedic surgery, Post-Grad. Med. Sch. and Hosp., New York, 1902-17; surgeon Southampton (N.Y.) Fresh Air Home; cons. orthopedic surgeon Mountainside Hosp., Montclair, N.J.; attending surgeon Hosp. for Ruptured and Crippled. Pres. Am. Orthopedic Assn., 1908. Author: Orthopedic Surgery for Practitioners, 1909. Home: Montclair, N.J. Died June 9, 1923.

TAYLOR, Henry Longstreet, M.D.; b. Cincinnati, O., Aug. 19, 1857; s. David H. and Laura (Carroll) T.; A.B., Haverford (Pa.) Coll., 1878, A.M., 1885, LL.D., 1928; M.D., Med. Coll. Ohio, 1882; student U. of Berlin, 1878-79, 1884, U. of Strassburg, 1882 and 1884, U. of Vienna, 1882, 83, U. of London, 1884; m. Ethelberta Geer, Sept. 8, 1910; children—Henry Longstreet, Laura Carroll. Began practice at Cincinnati, 1882; asst. prof. surgery, Med. Coll. of Ohio, 1884-89; moved to St. Paul, 1893; asso. prof. medicine, U. of Minn. Grad. Sch., 1920—; builder, 1905, now pres. Pokegama (Minn.) Sanatorium, for care and treatment of tuberculosis; mem. staff Children's, St. Luke's, Miller, St. Paul and Bethesda hosps. Mem. Med. R.C., World War. Chmn. State Tuberculosis Commn., Minn., 1901-18; med. dir. Ramsey County Preventorium. Republican. Unitarian. Home: St. Paul, Minn. Died Jan. 2, 1932.

TAYLOR, Henry Osborn, author; b. New York, Dec. 5, 1856; s. Henry Augustus and Catharine A. (Osborn) T.; A.B., Harvard, 1878, D.Litt., 1912; LL.B., Columbia U., 1881; hon. Litt.D. from same university, 1926; L.H.D., Wesleyan U., Conn., 1921; m. Julia Isham, Oct. 21, 1905. Author: Treatise on Law of Private Corporations, 5th edit., 1902; Ancient Ideals, a Study of Intellectual and Spiritual Growth from Early Times to the Establishment of Christianity, 2 vols., 2d edit., 1913; The Classical Heritage of the Middle Ages, 4th edit., 1925; The Mediæval Mind, 2 vols., 5th edit., 1938; Deliverance—The Freeing of the Spirit in the Ancient World, 1915 (revised and reissued as Prophets, Poets and Philosophers of the Ancient World, 1919); Thought and Expression in Sixteenth Century, 2 vols., 2d edit., 1930; Greek Biology and Medicine, 1922; Freedom of Mind in History, 1922, 2d edit., 1924; Human Values and Verities, 1928; Fact—the Romance of Mind, 1932; A

Layman's View of History, 1935; A Historian's Creed, 1939. Lowell lecturer, 1917; West lecturer, Leland Stanford, 1920. Home: New York, N.Y. Died Apr. 13, 1941.

TAYLOR, Herbert Worthington, congressman; b. Belleville, N.J., Feb. 19, 1869; s. James C. and Mary E. (Worthington) T.; LL.B., New York U., 1891; m. Florence Watson, Oct. 21, 1895; children—Herbert Watson, Mrs. Dorothy W. Luehs, Florence Bradley, Charles Meredith, Alice Gregory. Admitted to bar N.Y., 1891, N.J., 1897; mem. Common Council, Newark, N.J., 1899-1903; mem. N.J. Assembly, 1904, 05; chmn. Essex Co. (N.J.) Rep. Com., 1913-17; county counsel Essex Co., 1916-18; co. atty., 1918-21; mem. 67th and 69th Congresses (1921-23, 1925-27), 8th N.J. Dist. Republican. Episcopalian. Mason, mem. Modern Woodmen of America, Jr. Order Am. Mechanics, Royal Arcanum, Elks. Home: Newark, N.J. Died Oct. 15, 1931.

TAYLOR, Howard, lawyer; b. New York, Nov. 23, 1865; s. Henry Augustus and Catherine Augusta (Osborn) T.; A.B., Harvard, 1886. Admitted to the bar in 1888, from the office of the late Judge Hornblower, and with him as jr. partner until 1899; become head of law firm which is now Taylor, Jackson, Brophy & Nash. Episcopalian. Democrat. Home: New York, N.Y. Died Nov. 26, 1920.

TAYLOR, Howard Emerson, business mgr. Berea Coll.; b. nr. Philadelphia, Pa., June 8, 1869; s. George and Martha F. (Trumbower) T.; ed. Doylestown Sem., Bucks Co., Pa.; m. Laura Beans, Oct. 5, 1899. Teacher rural sch., Pa., 1883-88; with Mitchell Fletcher & Co., importers, Phila., 1888-98; mem. Hanscom Bros., wholesale grocers, Phila., 1898-1909; retired from business; business mgr. Berea Coll., 1909—. Served as organist Temple Ch., Phila., 1895-1909; organist Union Ch., Berea, 1909—; dir. personnel, Army Y.M.C.A., A.E.F., 1918-19; mem. state bd. Y.M.C.A., Ky., 1915—. Put Berea Coll., with holding of over $15,000,000, on firm business basis. Republican. Presbyn. Kiwanian. Home: Berea, Ky. Died Oct. 30, 1934.

TAYLOR, Isaac Montrose, physician, alienist; b. New Bern, N.C., Oct. 29, 1857; s. Dr. Alexander and Sarah A. (Cole) T.; Ph.B., U. of N.C., 1879; M.D., Coll. Phys. and Surg. (Columbia), 1882; m. Susan M. Evans, Jan. 23, 1889. In pvt. practice, 1882-86; asst. phys., State Hosp., Morganton, N.C., 1886-1901; supt. and resident phys., Broadoaks Sanatorium, Morganton, 1901—. Mem. local health bds.; pres. Bd. of Med. Examiners State of N.C., 1915-16. Episcopalian. Mason. Home: Morganton, N.C. Died Nov. 26, 1921.

TAYLOR, Isaac Stockton, architect; b. Nashville, Tenn., Dec. 1850. Employed 1868-74, office of George I. Barnett, architect; partner with him (Barnett & Taylor), 1874-79, firm being architects who built The Southern Hotel. In practice alone, 1879—; architect of Liggett & Myers blk., Drummond Tobacco factory, Liggett & Myers tobacco factories (largest in world); Rialto, Columbia, Mercantile Club, Globe-Democrat, Republic, Mercantile Trust, Nat. Bank of Commerce, Planters Hotel, Municipal Courts Bldg., Jefferson Memorial Bldg., Library Bldg., and other bldgs., St. Louis, and many in Ill. and Texas. Dir. of Works for La. Purchase Expn. Home: St. Louis, Mo. Died Oct. 28, 1917.

TAYLOR, J. Will, compressman; b. Union Co., Tenn., Aug. 28, 1880; s. James W. and Sarah Elizabeth (Rogers) T.; student Holbrook Normal Coll. (Fountain City), Am. Temperance U. (Harriman), Cumberland U. (Lebanon), all of Tenn.; LL.B., Lebanon Law Sch. Began practice at La Follette, Tenn., 1902; postmaster, La Follette, 1904-09; mayor of La Follette, 2 terms, 1910-12; ins. commr. of Tenn., 1913-14; chmn. Rep. State Exec. Com., Tenn., 1917-18; mem. 66th to 75th Congresses (1919-39), 2d Tenn. Dist. Member Rep. Nat. Com. Methodist. Mason. Home: La Follette, Tenn. Died Nov. 14, 1939.

TAYLOR, James Anderson, author; b. Westfield, N.C., June 1, 1876; s. Augustin John and Virginia Elizabeth (Stone) T.; ed. pub. and pvt. schs.; D.D.S., Georgetown U., 1914; m. Orller Blizzard, Oct. 3, 1897 (divorced 1921); children—Frank E., Hester (dec.); m. 2d, Louise Ellen Ellis, Sept. 9, 1922; 1 dau., Helen Louise. With Treasury Dept., Washington, D.C., 1904-10, Dept. Agr., 1910-14; prof. dental jurisprudence, ethics, economics and history, Dental Dept. Georgetown U., 1919, 24. Republican. Baptist. Mason, Woodman. Author: History of Dentistry, 1922. Home: Winston-Salem, N.C. Deceased.

TAYLOR, James Monroe, educator; b. Brooklyn, N.Y., Aug. 5, 1848; s. Rev. Elisha E. L. and Mary Jane (Perkins) T.; A.B., U. of Rochester, 1868; grad. Rochester Theol. Sem., 1871 (D.D., Rochester, 1886, Yale, 1901; LL.D., Rutgers, 1894, Smith, 1913); m. Kate Huntington, Sept. 10, 1873. Ordained Bapt. ministry, 1871; in Europe, 1871-72; pastor South Norwalk, Conn., 1873-82, Providence, R.I., 1882-86 prof. ethics and pres., Vassar Coll., to Feb. 1914. Trustee Carnegie Foundation Advancement of Teaching, 1910-14. Author: Psychology, 1893; New World and Old Gospel, 1900; Practical or Ideal, 1901; Before Vassar Opened, 1914; Vassar (with G. H. Haight), 1915. Died Dec. 19, 1916.

TAYLOR, James Morford, univ. prof.; b. Holmdel, N.J., Sept. 15, 1843; s. James J. and Lucy (Morford) T.; A.B., Colgate U., 1867, A.M., 1869, D.Sc., 1919, 2 yrs. in div. sch. same; LL.D., William Jewell, 1891; m. Mary Paddock, Aug. 3, 1871; children—James P., Mrs. Florence T. Morris, Henry W., Mrs. Mary T. Goodhue. Professor of mathematics, Colgate University, 1869-Sept. 1920. Author: Elements of the Differential and Integral Calculus, 1884, enlarged edit., 1898; College Algebra, 1889; Academic Algebra, 1893; Elements of Algebra, 1900; Plane Trigonometry, 1904; Plane and Spherical Trigonometry, 1905; Five-place Logarithmic and Trigonometric Tables, 1905. Home: Hamilton, N.Y., and Hanover, N.H. Died July 31, 1930.

TAYLOR, James W., physician; b. Lexington, N.C., 1833; s. William and Mary (Colley) T.; ed. in Coweta Co., Ga.; M.D., Atlanta Med. Coll., 1858; m. Miss Wilson, 1854 (died 1892). Served in C.S.A. as 1st lt.; mem. Ga. Assembly, 1877, 1896, 1897, Senate, 1907-08; local surgeon Central R.R. of Ga. Prominent in Masonic order; Grand High Priest of Grand Chapter of Ga., 1886-95; Grand Master of Masons, 1897-98; now Gen. Grand High Priest of Gen. Grand Chapter, Royal Arch Masons. Home: Luthersville, Ga. Died Dec. 16, 1925.

TAYLOR, J(ohn) Madison, M.D.; b. Lancaster Co., Pa., July 4, 1855; s. William Johnson and Mary (Bearden) T.; A.B., Princeton, 1876, A.M., 1879; M.D., U. of Pa., 1878; m. Emily Heyward Drayton, Oct. 15, 1879; children—Edith Moore (Mrs. Mansfield Patterson), Mable Heyward (Princess Hohenlohe Schillingfürst), Percival Drayton. Assistant to Dr. S. Weir Mitchell, 16 yrs.; in ranch life with Theodore Roosevelt, 1886. Prof. physical therapeutics, Temple U., 1910—. Fellow Am. Acad. Medicine, Coll. Physicians Phila., Am. Therapeutic Soc., Am. Clin. and Climatol. Soc. Author: "Ourselves," A Personal and Family History Record; Diseases of Children (text-book, Taylor and Wells), 1898. Home: Philadelphia, Pa. Died Oct. 3, 1931.

TAYLOR, John Metcalf, insurance pres.; b. Cortland, N.Y., Feb. 18, 1845; s. Charles Culver and Jane Maria (Gifford) T.; A.B., Williams, 1867, A.M., 1888; m. Edith Emerson, Oct. 4, 1871. Admitted to bar at Pittsfield, Mass., 1870; practiced, 1870-72; asst. sec., Conn. Mut. Life Ins. Co., 1872-78, sec., 1878-84, v.p., 1884-1905, pres., 1905—; v.p. Conn. Trust & Safe Deposit Co.; trustee Soc. for Savings. Pres. Loomis Inst.; an incorporator Hartford Retreat. Episcopalian. Independent Republican. Author: Maximilian and Carlotta: A Story of Imperialism, 1894; Roger Ludlow—the Colonial Law-maker, 1900; Witchcraft Delusion in Colonial Connecticut, 1647-97, 1908. Home: Hartford, Conn. Died Nov. 1918.

TAYLOR, John Phelps, clergyman; b. Andover, Mass., Apr. 6, 1841; s. Rev. Prof. John Lord (D.D.) and Caroline Lord (Phelps) T.; descendant on maternal side of William Phelps, of E. Windsor, Thomas Lord, Hartford, Conn., John Phillips, sec. of John Milton, and of Peter Bulkeley, 1st minister of Concord, Mass.; grad. Phillips Acad., Andover, 1858; A.B., Yale, 1862, A.M., 1865; studied Paris, Bonn and Venice, 1863-65; grad. Andover Theol. Sem., 1868; studied with Prof. David Gordon Lyon, Harvard, winters of 1884, 1885, with Prof. Paul Haupt, Johns Hopkins, 1886, 1887, with Prof. Richard James Horatio Gottheil, Columbia, 1888-89, etc.; (D.D., Middlebury Coll., Vt., 1897); m. Antoinette Hall (mem. D.A.R. and desc. of founder of Milford, Conn.), Oct. 14, 1868. Teacher Latin and Greek, Phillips Acad., 1866-67; ordained Congl. ministry, 1868; pastor South Ch., Middletown, Conn., 1868-74, Newport, R.I., 1874-76, Second Ch., New London, Conn., 1877-83; prof. bibl. theology and history, and Oriental archeology, Andover Theol. Sem., 1883-99; lecturer on Egyptology, Peabody Inst., Baltimore, 1885. Trustee Abbott Acad., Andover, 1892—; contbg. editor on archeology, Andover Review, 1884-93; mem. Com. of 15 at 250th anniversary of incorporation of Town of Andover. Republican. Conglist. Home: Andover, Mass. Died Sept. 13, 1915.

TAYLOR, John Yeatman, medical dir. U.S.N.; b. E. Nottingham, Pa., Jan. 21, 1829; s. Job and Susanna (Yeatman) T.; acad. edn.; M.D., Jefferson Med. Coll., Phila., 1852; m. Sabella Barr Bryson, Feb. 6, 1878; father of C. Bryson T. Apptd. asst. surgeon U.S.N., Sept. 26, 1853; passed asst. surgeon, Sept. 26, 1858; surgeon, Aug. 1, 1861; med. insp., June 29, 1872; med. dir., Apr. 20, 1879; retired, Jan. 10, 1891; advanced to rank of rear adm., retired, June 29, 1906, for services during Civil War. Fleet surgeon S. Atlantic sta., 1877-79; in charge Naval Hosp., Washington, 1879-83; Norfolk, Va., 1883-86, New York, 1886-88. Home: Washington, D.C. Died 1911.

TAYLOR, Joseph Judson, clergyman; b. Henry Co., Va., Nov. 1, 1855; s. Rev. Daniel Gray and Martha (King) T.; A.M., U. of Richmond, Va., 1880; Southern Bapt. Theol. Sem., 1880-81; D.D., Howard Coll., 1889; LL.D., Union U., Tenn., 1904; m. Anna Hinton, 1882. Ordained Bapt. ministry, 1876; pastor Calvary Church, Lexington, Ky., 1881-87, First Church, Mobile, Ala., 1887-99, Freemason St. Church, Norfolk, Va., 1899-1903; pres. Georgetown (Ky.) Coll., 1903-07; pastor First Ch., Knoxville, Tenn., 1907-15, First Church, Savannah, Ga., 1915-18. Vice pres. Home Mission Bd., Southern Bapt. Conv., 1884-87. Author: The Ordinances, 1889; A Country Preacher, 1894; Christian Science Cult, 1903; Commentary on Mark, 1911; The Sabbatic Question, 1913; The God of War, 1920; Radiant Hopefulness, 1922. Home: Lexington, Ky. Deceased.

TAYLOR, Joseph Russell, univ. prof.; b. Circleville, O., July 10, 1868; s. Thomas Russell and Mary Elizabeth (Shoemaker) T.; A.B., Ohio State U., 1887; A.M., Columbia, 1897; m. Esther Stafford, June 23, 1897. Asst. in drawing, 1889-94, in rhetoric, 1894-97, asst. prof., 1897-99, asst. prof. English lit., 1899-1901, asso. prof., 1901-04, asso. prof. English, 1904-08, prof., 1908—, Ohio State U. Author: The Overture (poems), 1903; Composition in Narration, 1909; Wintergreen (poems), 1911; What You Will (poems), 1921; Our Dancing Days (poems), 1922. Represented in Stedman and Hutchinson's Library of Am. Literature, and in Columbia Verse. Home: Columbus, O. Died Mar. 30, 1933.

TAYLOR, Joseph S., educator; b. Passer, Pa., Nov. 15, 1856; s. Thomas and Mary (Schimmel) T.; grad. State Teachers Coll., Millersville, 1878; Doctor Pedagogy, New York U., 1892, Ph.D., 1924; studied Clark U.; m. Katharine Moore Johnson, 1884; children—Deems, Katharine Ralston. Grade teacher public schools, N.Y. City, 13 years; school principal, 1898-1902, district supt., 1902-27 (retired). Lecturer on teaching and sch. supervision New York U. 14 yrs., Coll. City of New York 3 yrs., Hunter Coll., 4 yrs., Brooklyn Inst. 1 yr. Mem. Dutch Ref. Ch. Author: Art of Class Management and Discipline, 1908; Graded Movement Writing for Beginners (with Margaret M. Hughes), 1910; Word Study in the Elementary School, 1910; Principles and Methods of Teaching Reading, 1913; A Handbook of Vocational Education, 1914; Every Child's Language Book, 1925; Supervision and Teaching of Handwriting, 1926. Home: New York, N.Y. Died July 3, 1932.

TAYLOR, Julian Daniel, coll. prof.; b. Winslow, Me., Jan. 29, 1846; s. Daniel and Mehitable (Hayden) T.; A.B., Colby Coll., 1868, A.M., 1871, LL.D., 1900; m. Mary Keely Boutelle, Sept. 12, 1892. Tutor Colby Coll., 1868-73, prof. Latin, 1873-1918, Taylor prof. Latin, 1918—. V.p. Ticonic Nat. Bank. Home: Waterville, Me. Died Oct. 13, 1932.

TAYLOR, Katharine Haviland, author; b. Mankato, Minn.; d. Arthur Russell and Emma Louisa (Haviland) T.; ed. at home and abroad by father. Mem. Authors' League America. Episcopalian. Author: Natalie Page, 1921; Real Stuff, 1921; A Modern Trio in an Old Town, 1922; Tony from America, 1924; Stanley John's Wife, 1926; The Secret of the Little Gods, 1927; The Youngest One, 1928; Pablito, 1929; When Men a Wooing Go, 1930; The Nine Hundred Block, 1932; Night Club Daughter, 1933; Boulevard, 1934; New Ground, 1935; Daughter of Divorce, 1939; Back Roads, 1939; also (plays) Keeping Him Home, 1927; The Taming of the Crew, 1928; A Mother's Influence, 1929; Mix Well and Stir, 1930; The Family Failing, 1931; Rest and Quiet, 1932; Who Can Cook?, 1934; The Failure (filmed as One Man's Journey and played by Lionel Barrymore and May Robson; also filmed, 1939, as A Man to Remember, featuring Anne Shirley and Edward Ellis). Home: York, Pa. Died Nov. 29, 1941.

TAYLOR, Lewis Harvie, surgeon; b. Chula, Va., July 26, 1875; s. Armistead Green and Pattie Hardaway (Harvie) T.; M.D., Columbian U., 1903; unmarried. Med. interne, Govt. Hosp. for Insane, 1903-04; resident phys., George Washington U. Hosp., 1904-07; attending surgeon same, 1907-10; asst. prof. surgery, George Washington Sch. of Medicine, 1906-10; cons. surgeon, Govt. Hosp. for Insane, and mem. bd. visitors, 1921-33; attending surgeon, Casualty Hosp., 1916-20; pres. Sibley Memorial Hosp., Washington, D.C., 1936—. Lt., M.C.U.S. N.R.F. Episcopalian. Mason. Home: Washington, D.C. Died Mar. 30, 1940.

TAYLOR, Marion Sayle ("The Voice of Experience"), author, lecturer; b. Louisville, Ky., Aug. 16, 1889; s. Rev. Francis W. and Addie (Macklin) T.; student William Jewell College, 1903-06, LL.D., 1935; A.B., Pacific Univ., 1911, D.Humanities, 1935; post-grad. work Ore. Agrl. Coll. and U. of Ore. Began as pipe organist, 1904, but hands were crushed in an accident; supt. schs. North Bend, Ore., 3 yrs.; Chautauqua lecturer, 4 yrs.; now broadcasting daily under title "Voice of Experience" over Nat. Broadcasting network, Mutual Broadcasting System and coast to coast Canadian network; pres. Voice of Experience, Inc., Voice of Experience Service Plan (ins.); v.p. Rex Film Corp.; co-producer and narrator of more than 25 motion picture featurettes released by Columbia Pictures Corp., 1935-36; founder, 1937, the Voice of Experience Foundation at Babies Hospital of Columbia Presbyterian group of hosps., N.Y. City. Author: The Male Motor, 1927; Voice of Experience,

1933; Notebook of Intimate Problems, 1934; Stranger than Fiction, 1934; Life Must Go On, 1934; Making Molehills of Mountains, 1935; A Million Private Lives, 1935; Black Sheep, 1941. Daily columnist Paul Block Syndicate and other independent papers, also London Daily Star and associated syndicate. Home: Beverly Hills, Calif. Died Feb. 1, 1942.

TAYLOR, Mary Imlay, author; b. Washington, D.C.; d. George and Eleanor (Imlay) T.; ed. pvt. tutors; unmarried. Author: Who Pays?, 1918; A Candle in the Wind, 1919; The Wild Fawn, 1919; Mr. Battle Pays the Bills, 1927; Love Bridge, 1925; Man Who Awoke, 1927; Mark Turns West; also photoplays, The Ploughshare; Friend Wilson's Daughter; The McCues; The Purchased Bride; etc. Home: New York, N.Y. Died Aug. 28, 1938.

TAYLOR, Moses, capitalist; b. New York, N.Y., Jan. 30, 1871; s. H. A. C. and Charlotte T. (Fearing) T.; A.B., Yale, 1893; m. Edith Bishop, Aug. 19, 1896. Mem. Kean, Taylor & Co.; chmn. bd. Lackawanna Steel Co.; v.p. Westchester & Bronx Title & Mtg. Guar. Co., Lake Champlain & Moriah R.R. Co., South Buffalo Ry. Co., Tilly Foster Iron Mines; trustee Consolidated Gas Co. of N.Y.; pres. N.Y. & Queens Gas Co. Home: New York, N.Y. Died May 26, 1928.

TAYLOR, Nelson, publisher; b. Stockton, Calif., June 9, 1854; s. Nelson and Mary Ann (Bruen) T.; grad. Phillips Exeter Acad., 1871; A.B., Harvard, 1875; spent a yr. in Europe in study of langs., and travel; m. Aliette de Carrière, of Kischineff, Russia, July 26, 1906. Admitted to bar, 1878; practiced at S. Norwalk, Conn., where was mayor, 1885; organized, 1885, Baker & Taylor, book pubs., which became, 1886, The Baker & Taylor Co., of which is pres. and treas.; also pres. and treas. The Fairfield Co., The Stuyvesant Co. Cleveland Democrat. Home: South Norwalk, Conn., and New York, N.Y. Died June 26, 1912.

TAYLOR, Richard V., mayor of Mobile; b. New Bern, N.C., August 11, 1859; s. Richard N. and Susan (Stevenson) T.; ed. Barton Acad., Mobile, Ala., 9 mos., 1871-72; m. Helen Buck, Aug. 10, 1882; children—Adrian S., Richard V., William B., Helen (Mrs. Lloyd Abbot). Began in accounting dept., Mobile & Ohio R.R., Oct. 1, 1877; advanced to v.p. and gen. mgr. same rd., Oct. 1904; federal mgr. small group of Southern rys., during govt. control; mayor of Mobile and mem. city administration, commn. form of govt., 1921-26, reëlected member commission for term, 1931-37; mem. Interstate Commerce Commn., by apptmt. of President Coolidge, 1926-30; again mayor of Mobile, 1933-37; elected commr. of Mobile for term 1937-43. Democrat. Baptist. Home: Mobile, Ala. Died Dec. 22, 1939.

TAYLOR, Robert Howard, clergyman; b. Phila., Pa., Sept. 18, 1860; s. John Kinsey and Jeanie (Cosh) T.; student Wabash Coll., Ind., 1889-91; grad. Princeton Theol. Sem., 1894; m. Annie Lee Moore, Feb. 10, 1897; children—Robert Harper, Theodore Howard. Gen. sec. Y.M.C.A., Phila., 1885-88, Trenton, N.J., 1888-89; ordained Presbyn. ministry, 1894; pastor 2d Ch., Baltimore, 1894-1901; evangelist, 1901-02; pastor 1st Ch., Canonsburg, Pa., 1902-06; 1st Ch., Oxford, Pa., 1906-12; gen. sec. Internat. Council Brotherhood of Andrew and Philip, Phila., 1912-16, Family Altar League, Chicago, 1916-19; welfare service counselor, 1920-26; evangelist, 1926—. Republican. Home: Chicago, Ill. Died Jan. 20, 1936.

TAYLOR, Robert Longley, college prof.; b. New Rochelle, N.Y., Nov. 21, 1861; s. James Henry and Frances Caroline (Hitchings) T.; A.B., Hamilton Coll., 1882; Ph.D., Yale, 1900; m. Grace Lawrence, Apr. 11, 1906. Instr. English, U. of Kan., 1882-83; tutor, Robert Coll., Constantinople, Turkey, 1883-87; teacher French and German, Hill Sch., Pottstown, Pa., 1887-94; instr. French, Yale, 1894-1900; asst. prof. French, Dartmouth, 1900-12; prof. Romance langs., Williams, 1912—. Republican. Author: Alliteration in Italian, 1900. Editor: La Bibliothèque de Mon Oncle, 1898; L'Abbé Daniel, 1906. Home: Williamstown, Mass. Died May 27, 1923.

TAYLOR, Robert Love, senator; b. Happy Valley, Tenn., July 31, 1850; s. Nathaniel G. (M.C., commr. of Indian affairs) and Emily (Haynes) T.; acad. edn., Pennington, N.J.; m. Sarah L. Baird, 1878. Admitted to bar, 1878, and practiced at Nashville. Mem. 46th Congress (1879-81), 1st Tenn. Dist.; presdl. elector-at-large, 1884, 1892; pension agt. at Knoxville, 1885-87; gov. of Tenn. 3 terms, 1887-91 and 1897-99; U.S. senator, 1907-13. Democrat. Editor-in-chief of Bob Taylor's Magazine, 1905-06; editor The Taylor-Trotwood Magazine, 1906—. Home: Nashville, Tenn. Died Mar. 31, 1912.

TAYLOR, Robert Stewart, lawyer; b. Ross Co., O., May 22, 1838; s. Rev. Isaac N. and Margaretta Smith (Stewart) T.; moved with family to Ind. in childhood; acad. edn.; m. Fanny Wright, June 30, 1858; father of Frank Bursley T. Admitted to bar, 1860; practiced at Fort Wayne; now sr. mem. Taylor & Hulse. Prosecuting atty., 1867-68; judge Common Pleas Ct., 1869-70; mem. Ind. Ho. of Rep., 1871-72; mem. Miss. River Commn., 1881-1914; mem. Monetary Commn. apptd. by exec. com. Indianapolis Monetary Conf., 1897. Republican. Home: Fort Wayne, Ind. Died Jan. 28, 1918.

TAYLOR, R(obert) Tunstall, surgeon; b. Norfolk, Va., Jan. 16, 1867; s. Robertson and Baynham (Tunstall) T.; A.B., Johns Hopkins, 1889; M.D., U. of Va., 1891; m. Florence Templeman, Oct. 6, 1891. Began practice at Baltimore, 1891; prof. orthopedic surgery, U. of Md., 1900—; also prof. same, Coll. Phys. and Surg., Baltimore; surgeon-in-chief James-Lawrence Kernan Hosp. and Industrial Sch. for Crippled Children (founder); orthopædic surgeon to University, Women's, St. Agnes' and St. Joseph's hosps.; surgeon to Mercy and West Baltimore Gen. hosps.; consultant to State Industrial Accident Commn., Md. Casualty Co., Emergency Hosp. of Annapolis, Waynesboro Hosp., Crisfield Aid Hosp.; also consultant U.S. Pub. Health Service and U.S. Veterans' Bur. Lt. col., M.C., on staff of Generals Gorgas and Ireland, and chief of orthopædic service, Ft. McHenry, 1917-19; now col. M.R.C. Author: The Spine, 1907; The Surgery of the Spine and Extremities, 1923. Episcopalian. Home: Baltimore, Md. Died Feb. 21, 1929.

TAYLOR, Samuel Mac, consul gen.; b. Champaign Co., O., July 24, 1856; s. John and Miriam (Daniel) T.; A.B., Ohio Weslayan U., 1882; LL.B., Cincinnati Law Sch., 1884; m. Myrta B. Bradrick, Oct. 16, 1884. Practiced law at Urbana, O., from 1884. Mem. Gen. Assembly, 1887-93; sec. of state of Ohio, 1893-97; consul at Glasgow, Scotland, 1897-1906; consul gen. at Callao, Peru, June 22, 1906-10; consul at Nottingham, Eng., May 3, 1910-13, at Birmingham, Mar. 2, 1915—. Republican. Home: Urbana, O. Died Dec. 7, 1916.

TAYLOR, Samuel Mitchell, congressman; b. Ittawamba Co., Miss., May 25, 1852; ed. pub. and pvt. schs.; m. Mary Bell, 1879. Began practice of law, Tupelo, Miss., 1876; elected mem. Miss. Ho. of Rep., 1879; removed to Pine Bluff, Ark., 1887; pros. atty., 11th Jud. Dist., Ark., 3 terms, 1889-95; chmn. Dem. State Conv., Ark., 1910-12; mem. 63d to 66th Congresses (1913-21), 6th Ark. Dist. Home: Pine Bluff, Ark. Died Sept. 13, 1921.

TAYLOR, Walter Herron, banker; b. Norfolk, Va., June 13, 1838; s. Walter Herron and Cornelia (Wickham) T.; ed. Norfolk Acad., and Va. Mil. Inst.; m. Elizabeth Selden, d. John L. Saunders, U.S.N., of Norfolk, Apr. 3, 1865. Bank officer, 1856-61; served in C.S.A., 1861-65, on staff Gen. Robert E. Lee, part of time as his a.d.c., and part of time as adj. gen. Army of Northern Va.; present at all gen. engagements of the army under Gen. Lee. Mem. Va. Senate, 1869-73; pres. Marine Bank of Norfolk, 1877—. Author: Four Years with General Lee, 1877; General Lee, 1861-1865, 1906. Home: Norfolk, Va. Died Mar. 1, 1916.

TAYLOR, William, M.E. missionary bishop for Africa, May 1884—; b. Rockbridge Co., Va., May 2, 1821; brought up as farmer and tanner; entered Methodist ministry, 1842; missionary in Calif., 1849-56; 5 yrs. in Canada and New England; went to Europe, 1862; conducted missionary services in Australia, Tasmania and New Zealand 3 yrs.; visited S. Africa and converted many Kaffirs to Christianity; spent a yr. in evangelistic work in Great Britain; organized many self-supporting chs. in India, 1872-76, and in S. America, 1876-84; afterward in Africa establishing mission stas. on the Congo and elsewhere. Author: Seven Years' Street Preaching in San Francisco; California Life Illustrated; The Model Preacher; Reconciliation: or, How to Be Saved; Infancy and Manhood of Christian Life; Christian Adventures in South Africa; Four Years' Campaign in India; Pauline Methods of Missionary Work; The Flaming Torch in Darkest Africa; Story of My Life; etc. Home: New York, N.Y. Died 1902.

TAYLOR, William Alexander, author; b. Perry Co., O., Apr. 25, 1837; s. Thomas and Mary (Owens) T.; pub. school edn.; m. Jane Allen Tarrier, Nov. 10, 1870. In newspaper work, 1865-1910; for 25 years on staff Cincinnati Enquirer. Dem. candidate for sec. of state, Ohio, 1892, for lt. gov., 1893, defeated by a small majority. Author: Eighteen Presidents and Contemporaneous Rulers, 1876; Primary Tariff Lessons, 1878; The Peril of the Republic, 1885; Roses and Rue, 1892; Ohio Statesmen, 1900; Ohio in Congress, 1901; Intermere, 1902; The Evolution of the Statesman, 1905. Prin. author, The Book of Ohio, 1902; Twilight of Dawn, 1903; The Next Morning Philosopher, 1903; Evolution of the Statesman, 1905; Ohio and Its People—A History of the State of Ohio (4 vols.), 1910. Apptd. commr. of soldiers' claims for State of Ohio, Apr. 1910. Home: Columbus, Ohio. Died 1912.

TAYLOR, William Dana, engineer; b. Montgomery, Ala., Jan. 22, 1859; s. William Thomas and Mary (Hubbard) T.; B.E., Ala. Poly. Inst., 1881, C.E., 1885; grad. student in mathematics, Johns Hopkins; summer work, Cornell U., 1894, U. of Chicago, 1896; m. Annie L. MacIntyre, Feb. 1897. Civil engr. on Mexican Central R.R., 1882-83; taught in acads. at Eclectic and Evergreen, Ala., 1883-84 and 1885-86; chief engr. rys. in Ala., 1886-91; prof. engring., La. State U., 1891-98; apptd., July 1898, capt. 3d U.S.V. engrs.; became chief engr. St. Louis, Peoria & Northern R.R., Nov. 1898, and in 1902, chief engr. Knoxville, LaFollette & Jellico R.R., of Louisville & Nashville System; prof. ry. engring., U. of Wis., 1901-06; expert engr. to Wis. State Bd. of Assessment, 1903-06; chief engr. C.&A. R.R., Feb. 1, 1906—, Toledo, St. Louis & Western Ry., Oct. 1907—, Minneapolis & St. Louis, and Ia. Central rys., Oct. 1909—. Presbyn. Republican. Home: Chicago, Ill. Died 1911.

TAYLOR, William George Langworthy, university prof.; b. New York, May 13, 1859; s. Dr. George H. and Sarah E. (Langworthy) T.; A.B., Harvard, 1880; Columbia U. Law Sch., 1880-81; LL.B., Harvard, 1883; studied in Europe, 1886-90, École des Sciences Politiques and Collège de France, Paris, 1886-88, U. of Leipzig, 1888-90; (LL.D., U. of Nebraska, 1915); m. Frances Chamberlain Brown (A.B., A.M., Smith Coll), June 21, 1894. Prof. economics, 1893-1911, prof. emeritus, Sept. 1, 1911—, U. of Nebraska Abroad, 1910-13. Author: Exercises in Economics, 1900; The Credit System, 1913. Home: Lincoln, Neb. Died July 5, 1941.

TAYLOR, William H., capitalist; b. Paterson, N.J., Sept. 30, 1859; s. William H. and Katharine G. (Deeths) T.; ed. Dickinson Sem., Williamsport, Pa.; m. Nellie G. Barker, June 17, 1886. Entered father's store, Allentown, Pa., 1872, and succeeded to business as W. H. Taylor & Co., 1880; established branch at Scranton, 1884, Hazleton, 1889; organized St. Clair Coal Co., anthracite coal operators, 1895; became pres. Goodwin Car & Mfg. Co., Chicago and New York, 1903; also pres. St. Clair Coal Co., Schuylkill Supply Co., Wm. H. Taylor Finance Corp. Republican. Christian Scientist. Mason. Home: New York, N.Y. Died Feb. 28, 1928.

TAYLOR, William Henry, judge; b. Wheelock, Vt., July 18, 1863; s. Benjamin F. and Amanda M. (Stetson) T.; B.S., Dartmouth, 1886; studied law in office of Ide & Stafford, St. Johnsbury, Vt.; m. Nettie I. Clark, July 27, 1887. Prin. Hardwick Acad., 1886-89; supervisor pub. schs., Caledonia Co., Vt., 1889-91; admitted to Vt. bar, 1892, and practiced in Hardwick; mem. Taylor & Dutton. State's atty., Caledonia Co., 1894-98; mem. Vt. Ho. of Rep., 1900, Senate, 1906; judge Superior Ct., Vt., 1906-13; apptd. justice Supreme Ct. of Vt., Oct. 1, 1913, and elected for terms 1915-25. Republican. Methodist. Mason. Home: Hardwick, Vt. Died Mar. 28, 1926.

TAYLOR, William Johnson, surgeon; b. on Winchester Farm, Worcester Co., Md., Oct. 13, 1861; s. William Johnson and Mary E. (Beardon) T.; prep. edn. Prep. Dept., East Tenn. U., Knoxville, Tenn.; M.D., U. of Pa., 1882; m. Emily Buckley Newbold, Apr. 29, 1891. Formerly resident phys. Pa. Hosp., attending surgeon St. Mary's Hosp. and prof. orthopedic surgery, Phila. Polyclinic; now attending surgeon Phila. Orthopedic Hosp. and Infirmary for Nervous Diseases, and St. Agnes Hosp.; cons. surgeon to West Phila. Hosp. for Women, and to Woman's Hosp. Pres. Coll. of Physicians of Phila.; mem. bd. dirs. Library Co. of Phila. Fellow Am. Surg. Assn., Phila. Acad. Surgery. Lt. col., M.C. U.S.A. Home: Philadelphia, Pa. Died Jan. 1936.

TAYLOR, William Ladd, artist, illustrator; b. Grafton, Mass., Dec. 10, 1854; s. William H. and Anna Maria (Darling) T.; ed. Worcester, Mass.; art schs., Boston and New York, and under Boulanger and Le Fèbvre, Paris, 1884-85; since then painter and illustrator in U.S.; m. Mary Alice Fitz, 1888. Recent works: Selections from Longfellow's poems; series of pictures illustrating The 19th Century in New England; series of pictures of the Pioneer West; A New Longfellow Series, 1904; The Psalms Series, 1906; Old Songs Series, 1908-09; Our Home and Country, a book of pictures of Am. life, 1908; Pictures from American Literature, 1910; Pictures from the Old Testament, 1913; Pictures from the Bible, 1925. Home: Wellesley, Mass. Died Dec. 26, 1926.

TAYLOR, William Rivers, clergyman; b. Philadelphia, Sept. 28, 1856; s. Rev. William James Romeyn and Maria Louise (Cowenhoven) T.; A.B., Rutgers Coll., 1876, A.M., 1879; grad. New Brunswick Theol. Sem., 1879; D.D., U. Rochester and Rutgers; m. Annie Brown, d. James Spear, of Phila., Jan. 24, 1888; children—Louise van Campen (Mrs. Wellington Hay), Anne (Mrs. John C. Case), William James Romeyn, James Spear. Ordained Reformed Ch. ministry, 1879; pastor Franklin Park, N.J., 1879-84, First Ch., Phila., 1884-88, Brick Presbyn. Ch., Rochester, N.Y., 1888-1923, emeritus, 1923—. Chairman Gen. Assembly's com. on young people; mem. com. on preparation of Book of Common Worship; Exec. Commission and of Exec. Council Presbyn. Gen. Assembly. Republican. Home: Philadelphia, Pa. Died June 1, 1941.

TAYLOR, William Sylvester, lawyer; b. Butler Co., Ky., Oct. 10, 1853; s. Sylvester T.; ed. common schs. of Butler Co.; m. Sarah B. Tanner, Feb. 10, 1878. Clerk Butler Co. (Ky.) Ct., 1882-86; judge Butler Co., 1886-94; atty. gen. of Ky., 1895-99; elected gov. of Ky. and, in 1900, removed from that office by Ky. Gen. Assembly. Republican. Home: Indianapolis, Ind. Died Aug. 2, 1928.

TAYLOR, William Watts, mfr.; b. Opelousas, La., Mar. 19, 1847; s. Reuben Miles Whitney and Frances

Anne (Menefee) T.; Kenyon Coll., 1860-62; Harvard, class of 1868 (hon. M.A., 1904); unmarried. Mem. Taylor Bros., commn. mchts., Cincinnati, 1870-83; pres. The Rookwood Pottery Co., 1883—. Pres. Municipal Art Soc. Cincinnati; a v.p. Nat. Arts Club; trustee Cincinnati Mus. Assn. (art mus.). Episcopalian. Chevalier Legion of Honor, France. Home: Cincinnati, O. Died Nov. 12, 1913.

TEAD, Edward Sampson, clergyman, ednl. sec.; b. Boston, Sept. 14, 1852; s. Edward Long and Lucretia Hovey (Cleasby) T.; A.B., Amherst, 1875; Yale Div. Sch., 1876; grad. Andover Theol. Sem., 1878; m. Louisa M. Graves, July 2, 1878 (died 1887); m. 2d, Louise Moore Ordway, Oct. 3, 1889. Ordained Congl. ministry, 1878; pastor Cumberland Mills, Me., 1878-84, Somerville, Mass., 1884-1901; sec. Congl. Edn. Society, July 1901—. Republican. Trinitarian Conglist. Home: Atlantic, Mass. Died Sept. 8, 1919.

TEAL, Joseph Nathan, lawyer; b. Eugene, Ore., Sept. 24, 1858; s. Joseph and Mary Elizabeth (Coleman) T.; ed. Portland (Ore.) Acad. and St. Augustine Coll., Benicia, Calif.; m. Bessie Meldrum Thompson, Oct. 24, 1894; 1 dau., Ruth (Mrs. Carleton W. Betts). Admitted to Ore. bar, 1884, and began practice in Portland; atty. for Portland Traffic and Transportation Assn., Willamette Valley Lumber Mfr.'s Assn. and West Coast Lumber Mfg. Assn.; dir. Security Savings & Trust Co., Oregon Life Insurance Co. Democrat. Episcopalian. Mason. Home: Portland, Ore. Died May 25, 1929.

TEASDALE, Sara, author; b. St. Louis, Mo., Aug. 8, 1884; d. John Warren and Mary Elizabeth (Willard) T.; ed. pvt. schs., St. Louis; m. Ernst B. Filsinger, Dec. 19, 1914 (divorced 1929). Author: Sonnets to Duse, and Other Poems, 1907; Helen of Troy and Other Poems, 1911; Rivers to the Sea, 1915; Love Songs, 1917; Flame and Shadow, 1920; Dark of the Moon, 1926; Stars Tonight, 1930. Editor of The Answering Voice—One Hundred Love Lyrics by Women, 1917, 2d edit. (with 50 additional poems), 1928; Rainbow Gold, Poems Old and New, Selected for Boys and Girls, 1922. Died Jan. 29, 1933.

TEASDALE, William Bernard, lawyer; b. Potosi, Mo., Apr. 12, 1856; s. John and Catherine (Mundy) T.; ed. pub. schs., Potosi, Mo., St. Louis Univ., St. Louis Law Sch., LL.B., 1877; m. Lydia Guinotte, Dec. 26, 1883. Admitted to bar, 1877; asst. pros. atty., 1881-82; justice of peace, 1882-86; State senator, 1888-92; judge Circuit Court, Mar. 1901—, Kansas City. Pres. Kansas City Bar Assn., Mo. State Bar Assn. Democrat. Chmn. Dem. City Com., Kansas City, Dem. Co. Com., Jackson Co., Mo.; mem. Dem. State Com., Mo. Catholic. Home: Kansas City, Kan. Died 1907.

TEDROW, Harry B., lawyer; b. Woodburn, Ia., May 6, 1875; s. Joseph Leech and Hester Ann (Proudfoot) T.; grad. Hastings (Neb.) High Sch., 1892; U. of Denver, 1897-98 (left univ. to enlist n Spanish-Am. War); m. Camilia Roberts, Apr. 22, 1903. Admitted to Colo. bar, 1899; practiced in Cripple Creek, 1901, then in Denver and Boulder; mem. Tedrow & Fitzgerald, 1912—. Mem. Colo. State Bd. of Pardons, 1909-15; co. atty. Boulder Co., 1913-14; U.S. dist. atty. for Colo., June 26, 1914—. Democrat. Mem. Troop B, 2d U.S. Vol. Cav., Spanish-Am. War; col. Colo. N.G., 1901-02. Home: Boulder, Colo. Died Jan. 1, 1921.

TEEL, Warren Floyd, educator; b. Martins Creek, Pa., Apr. 11, 1868; s. Amos and Anna (McFall) T.; Ph.B., Northwestern Coll., Naperville, Ill., 1900; student, Cornell U., 1903, Harvard U., 1904; A.M., U. of Pa., 1914; D.D., Franklin and Marshall College, 1914; LL.D., Lebanon Valley College, 1931; m. Bessie J. Dubs, Aug. 15, 1906; children—Floyd Russell, Paul Dubs, Helen Anna. Pres. Albright Coll. (formerly Schuylkill Coll.), Reading, Pa., 1901—. Pres. Young People's Alliance, 1903-07; mem. Evang. Church; del. Gen. Conf. same, 7 times to 1930. Author: Educational Addresses. Lecturer on Lincoln. Home: Reading, Pa. Died July 12, 1932.

TEELE, Ray Palmer, economist, b. Fillmore Co., Minn., Oct. 22, 1868; s. Edwin and Sarah (Dearborn) T.; A.B., U. of Neb., 1897, A.M., 1899; m. Mary D. Hazard, 1897; children—Edwin Norman (dec.), Ray Palmer. Economist U.S. Dept. Agr., 1899-1919 and 1921—. Spl. agt. in charge of irrigation, U.S. Bur. Census, 1910-12 and 1919-21. Author: Irrigation in the United States, 1915; Economics of Land Reclamation in the United States, 1927; also govt. reports on irrigation and drainage. Home: Silver Springs, Md. Died Aug. 27, 1927.

TEEPLE, John Edgar, cons. chemist; b. Kempton, Ill., Jan. 4, 1874; s. William Harvey and Abby M. (Hinckley) T.; B.S., Valparaiso (Ind.) U., 1893, A.B., 1894; B.S., Cornell U., 1899, Ph.D., 1903; m. Lina Pease, Aug. 17, 1897; children—John Hazen, Charlotte Marion, Granger Odell. Instr. in chemistry and physics, Fremont (Neb.) Coll., 1894-98; instr. in organic and physiol. chemistry, Cornell U., 1899-1904; dir. Industrial Labs., N.Y. City, 1904-08; cons. chemist and chem. engr., N.Y. City, 1908—; interim prof. chemistry and chem. engring., Columbia, 1917; cons. chem. engr. Am. Potash & Chem. Corp., Darco Corp. Asso. editor Chem. Markets. Awarded Perkin medal, 1927. Author: The Industrial Development of Searles Lake Brines, 1929; Maya Astronomy, 1930. Home: Montclair, N.J. Died Mar. 1931.

TEFFT, Lyman Beecher, college pres.; b. Exeter, R.I., July 15, 1833; s. of Jonathan and Mary (Gates) T.; A.M., Brown U., 1858 (D.D., 1893); grad. Rochester Theol. Sem., 1860; m. Susan M. Ham, Dec. 16, 1860 (died 1870); m. 2d, Emma Thurber Brown, May 13, 1873 (died 1894). Ordained Bapt. ministry, 1862; pastor, Prescott, Wis., 1862-63, Winona, Minn., 1863-66, Norwich, Conn., 1866-69, Mankato, Minn., 1869-71, Colchester, Conn., 1871-74; instr. and acting prin., Nashville Normal and Theol. Inst., 1874-83; pres. Hartshorn Memorial College, Richmond, Va., 1883-1912. Author: Curiosities of Heat, 1870; Institutes of Moral Philosophy, 1899. Home: Meshanticut Park, R.I. Died Nov. 29, 1926.

TEFFT, William Wolcott, cons. engineer; b. Milbank, S.D., Feb. 28, 1882; s. Levant C. and Ada M. (Wolcott) T.; B.S. in C.E., U. of Mich., 1907, Dr. Engring., 1930; m. Ethel L. Foote, Oct. 8, 1910; children—Richard F. (dec.), Robert F. Asst., civ. engring. dept., U. of Mich., 1907; in charge field surveys, later resident engr., Cooke Dam, Au Sable River, Mich., Kalamazoo Steam Plant, and Grand Rapids, Mich., for Commonwealth Power Co., 1908-11; mem. Fargo Engring. Co., 1911-19, in charge report and economics dept., 1915-19; with Hodenpyl, Hardy & Co., Jackson, Mich., Feb. 1919 to 1928; cons. civil and hydraulic engr., Consumers Power Co., 1919-24, v.p., 1922—; v.p., chief engr. Commonwealth Power Corp., 1924-28; chief engr. Central Ill. Light Co., Southern Ind. Gas & Electric Co., Ohio Edison Co., Ill. Power Co., Ill. Electric Power Co., Northern Ohio Power & Light Co., Tenn. Electric Power Co., 1924-28; cons. engr., 1928—; pres. Gen. Power Corp.; v.p. Fargo Engring. Co. Mem. Am. com., World Power Conf. Pres. bd. trustees Albion (Mich.) Coll.; pres. Methodist Foundation of Mich., 1931; chmn. finance com. Mich. George Washington Bicentennial Commn., 1932. Republican. Methodist. Elk. Home: Jackson, Mich. Died June 24, 1932.

TEIGAN, Henry George, congressman; b. Forest City, Ia., Aug. 7, 1881; s. Anders Olson and Brita (Monson) T.; A.B., Valparaiso (Ind.) U., 1908, A.M., 1912; m. Ethel L. Herbert-Reamer, Mar. 29, 1911; children—Gladys Fern (Mrs. Reuben F. Grandquist), Maybelle Ann (Battner). Teacher in rural schools, Iowa, 1900-04, at Des Lacs, N.D., 1909-10, at Logan, N.D., 1912-13; N.D. state sec. Socialist Party, 1913-16; sec. Nat. Nonpartisan League, 1916-23; sec. to U.S. Senator Magnus Johnson, 1923-25; editor Farmer-Labor Advocate and Minn. Leader, 1923-33; state senator, Minn., 1933-35; editor Minn. Leader, 1935-37; mem. 75th Congress (1937-39), 3d Minn. Dist. Mem. Farmer-Labor Party. Eagle, Son of Norway. Home: Minneapolis, Minn. Died Mar. 12, 1941.

TELFORD, Robert Lee, clergyman; b. Rome, Ga., May 23, 1863; s. William Brazleton and Susan Felicia (Eddins) T.; grad. Hampden-Sydney (Va.) Coll., D.D., 1894; grad. Union Theol. Sem., Hampden-Sydney, Va. (now at Richmond), 1890; m. Anna Boone Brown, Oct. 20, 1890; children—Brownie Eddins, Anna Boone, Josephine Lindsley, Robert Lee, Bess Brown (dec.), Rachel Couch, John Brown, William Brazleton, Margaret Moore. Ordained ministry Presbyterian Church in the U.S., 1890—; pastor Old Stone Church, Lewisburg, W.Va., 1890-92; pres. Lewisburg Seminary (now Greenbrier Coll. for Women), 1892-1910; raised $100,000 for new building for the Sem.; pastor First Ch., Richmond, Ky., 1914—. Moderator Synod of Ky., 1922; pres. bd. trustees Sayre Coll., Lexington, Ky. Pres. Health and Welfare League of Madison Co., Ky., 1920—. Presented with silver loving cup by City of Richmond for work as chmn. United War Work Campaign of Madison County. Democrat. Mason. Home: Richmond, Ky. Died Mar. 28, 1934.

TELLER, Henry Moore, senator; b. Granger, N.Y., May 23, 1830; s. John and Charlotte T.; ed. Alfred U. (LL.D., 1886); m. Harriett M. Bruce, June 7, 1862. Taught sch. several yrs.; admitted to bar, Binghamton, N.Y., 1856; practiced in Ill., 1858-61, when he removed to Colo., and resumed practice of law; maj. gen. Colo. militia, 1862-64. U.S. senator from Dec. 4, 1876, until Apr. 17, 1882; sec. of the interior in cabinet of President Arthur, Apr. 1882-Mar. 1885; again U.S. senator from Colo. 4 terms, 1885-1909; reëlected, 1891, as Republican, but withdrew from Rep. Nat. Conv., 1896, because of financial plank in platform; reëlected, 1897, as Independent Silver Republican. Home: Central City, Colo. Died Feb. 23, 1914.

TELLER, James Harvey, judge; b. Granger, N.Y., June 14, 1850; s. John and Charlotte Chapin (Moore) T.; student Cornell U., 1871; A.B., Oberlin Coll., 1874, LL.D., 1919; m. Frances L. Wheelock, May 3, 1875. Began practice at Cleveland, O., 1876; organized, 1880, and became pres. Leslie Sewing Machine Co. (now Standard Sewing Machine Co.); mem. Sioux Indian Commn., Dak. Ty., 1882-83; sec. Dak. Ty., 1883-86; practiced in Chicago, 1890-1902; removed to Denver, Colo., 1902; apptd. judge Dist. Court City and County of Denver, Dec. 1, 1911; elected for term of 6 yrs., Nov. 1912, on Dem., Rep., Prog., Proh. and Citizens' tickets; elected asso. justice Supreme Court of Colo., Nov. 1914, term 1915-25; resumed practice. Democrat. Conglist. Author: The Battle of the Standards, 1896. Home: Denver, Colo. Died Jan. 29, 1937.

TELLER, John Du Bois, lawyer; b. Sandy Hill, N.Y., May 11, 1845; s. Benjamin F. and Elizabeth (Du Bois) T.; A.B., Williams College, 1867; (LL.D., George Washington Univ., 1919); admitted to bar, 1870; unmarried. Recorder City of Auburn, 1877-80; surrogate Cayuga Co., 1884-89; nominee for justice Supreme Ct., 1887, for judge Ct. of Appeals, 1895, for state senator, 1898. Democrat. Trustee Cayuga Co. Nat. Bank. Home: Auburn, N.Y. Died Jan. 19, 1922.

TELLER, Philip Shepheard, commr. U.S. Shipping Bd.; b. San Francisco, Jan. 14, 1861; s. John de Peyster and Sarah Jane (Shepherd) T.; ed. pub. and high schs.; m. Annie Cora Newman, Sept. 18, 1886 (died 1922); 1 dau., Alice Teller (Mrs. L. R. Weinmann). Served as shipping clk., salesman and traveling man; organized Norton, Teller & Co., wholesale grocery and provisions, 1888; retired 1924; became commr. U.S. Shipping Bd., Jan. 14, 1926; dir. Bank of Alameda. Chmn. Rep. State Central Com., Calif., 1909. Mem. exec. com. Boy Scouts of America, San Francisco Council; v.p. Panama-Pacific Preservation League; pres. Masonic Hall Assn., Alameda, Calif. Episcopalian. Mason. Home: Alameda, Calif. Died Aug. 8, 1930.

TEMPLE, Edward Arthur, bishop; b. Walkerton, Va., Sept. 5, 1867; s. John and Mathilda (Wright) T.; ed. Va. Poly. Inst. and Va. Theol. Sem.; (D.D., U. of the South, 1913, Episcopal Theol. Sem. of Va., 1913); m. Mary Craik Davis, Nov. 9, 1909. Deacon, 1895, priest, 1896, P.E. Ch.; rector Calvary Ch., Front Royal, Va., 1895-1903, St. Paul's, Waco, Tex., 1903-10; consecrated missionary bishop of N. Tex., Dec. 15, 1910. Home: Amarillo, Tex. Died Jan. 10, 1924.

TEMPLE, Edward Lowe, author; b. Ft. Winnebago, Wis., May 12, 1844; s. Charles T.; ed. schs. in Wis. and Vt. and Rutland (Vt.) Acad. and High Sch.; hon. A.M., U. of Vt., 1886, Middlebury Coll., 1887; m. Lucy Graves, Sept. 29, 1869; children—Grenville, Arthur Winthrop, Edith Graves, Edward Clarence. Town and city supt. schs., Rutland, 1887-98; co. examiner of teachers for Rutland Co., 1890-94; treas. Marble Savings Bank, Rutland, 1883-1903; treas. Diocese of Vt. (P.E.), 1881-1903; deputy from Diocese of Vt. to Triennial Gen. convs. of P.E. Ch., 1886-1901. Pres. Vt. State Assn. of D.C., 1907. Author: The Church in the Prayer Book (liturgical), 1893; Old World Memories (travel in Europe), 2 vols., 1898; Shakespeare—the Man and His Art, a Study, 1913; One Hundred Years of Church Life, 1894; The Twentieth Century Outlook Upon Holy Scripture, 1913; Old Rutland (Vt.), 1923. Home: Wellesley, Mass. Died Oct. 9, 1928.

TEMPLE, Jackson, justice Supreme Court Calif., 1894—; b. Heath, Franklin Co., Mass., Aug. 11, 1827; s. David and Rosamond (Nims) T.; grad. Williams, 1851; studied law; removed to Calif. and engaged in practice; was dist. judge; also judge Superior Court, Sonoma Co.; decided the débris suits which prevented injury to farming lands by hydraulic mining. Home: Santa Rosa, Calif. Died 1902.

TEMPLE, Oliver Perry, lawyer; b. Green Co., Tenn., Jan. 27, 1820; s. James and Mary (Craig) T.; grad. Washington Coll., Tenn., 1844; m. Scotia C. Hume, Sept. 9, 1851; admitted to bar, 1846; candidate for Congress, 1847; moved to Knoxville, 1848; apptd. by President Fillmore, 1850, mem. of commn. to visit Indian tribes of N.M., Ariz. and Calif.; one of Bell-Everett presdl. electors for Tenn., 1860; made first Union speech delivered in the State after the election of President Lincoln; one of Union leaders in E. Tenn.; one of chancellors of Tenn., 1866-78; retired from bar, 1881; postmaster, Knoxville, 1881-85; retired from all active duties. Visitor to West Point under apptmt. of President Grant, 1874; trustee Univ. of Tenn., 40 yrs. Author: The Covenanter, The Cavalier and the Puritan, 1897; East Tennessee and the Civil War, 1899; Union Leaders of East Tennessee, 1903. Home: Knoxville, Tenn. Died 1907.

TEMPLE, William Chase, businessman; b. Starke, Fla., Dec. 28, 1862; s. William Clemmons and Mattie Josephine (Chase) T.; B.S., Harkness Acad., Del., 1879; m. Carrie Lee Wood, Apr. 13, 1884. Began active career in fruit business, Fla.; went to Chicago, 1884, to New York, 1885, to Pittsburgh, 1889, in various lines of promotion business; became dir. of more than 20 corps.; organized and operated, 1895-1905, the Cahall Sales Dept., marketing total production of steam boilers of the Altman & Taylor Machinery Co. Retired from business at Pittsburgh, 1905, and thereafter devoted attention to organization and development of citrus growing industry in Fla. Pres. Wilcardo Fruit Company. Owned and operated the Pittsburgh Nat. League Baseball Club, 1892-93, and gave the Nat. League trophy known as the "Temple Cup," 1894. Organized, 1914, and 1st pres. Gasparilla Carnival Assn. of Tampa, Fla.; mayor of Winter Park, Fla., 1915. Home: Pittsburgh, Pa., and Winter Park, Fla. Died Jan. 9, 1917.

TEMPLETON, Fay, actress; b. Little Rock, Ark.; d. John and Alice (Vane) T. (both actors); pub. sch. edn., Key West, Fla.; m. at 15, William West; 2d, Howell Osborne (died 1895); 3d, William Patterson, 1906. Made first appearance on stage at age of 4 yrs. in her father's co., and from then followed profession continuously, appearing in many comic operas; 4 seasons with Webber & Fields; played in her own co., 1903-04; later starred in comic operas. Died Oct. 3, 1939.

TEMPLETON, Howard, lawyer; b. Franklin Co., Tex., June 25, 1861; s. Gordon S. and Margaret C. (Ward) T.; ed. high sch., Honey Grove, Tex.; m. Mary Blackwell, July 11, 1886; children—Ruth (Mrs. Horace Walling), Clive, Jean (Mrs. T. D. Rife), Mary (Mrs. S. A. Wells), Lloyd. Admitted to Tex. bar, 1882, and began practice at Cooper; moved to Sulphur Springs, Tex., 1885, San Antonio, Tex., 1910; mem. Templeton, Brooks, Napier & Brown. Dist. atty., 8th Jud. Dist., 1891-92; judge, Dist. Court, Tex., 1896-1900, Court of Civil Appeals, Dallas Dist., 1900-03. Presdl. elector, Tex., 1888; mem. Dem. State Exec. Com., Tex., 1905-06; chmn. Dem. State Conv., 1906. K.P. Home: San Antonio, Tex. Died June 25, 1937.

TEN EYCK, William Hoffman, clergyman Reformed (Dutch) Ch. in America; b. Schenectady, N.Y., May 19, 1818; s. Dr. Harman Hoffman and Maria (Beekman) T.; grad. Rutgers Coll., class of 1845 (D.D., same, 1870); m. Anna M., d. Nicholas A. Vedder, May 16, 1849. Stated clerk of North Classis, L.I., 1864-1905; permanent clerk Gen. Synod Reformed Ch. in America, 1871-1907; mem. bd. edn., Reformed Ch. in America, 1859-1907; corr. delegate to Gen. Synod (German) Reformed Ch. in U.S., 1871; several of his addresses have been published, and a Pamphlet on Scriptural Temperance. Home: Astoria, L.I., N.Y. Died 1908.

TENNANT, John Hunter, editor; b. Albany, N.Y., Jan. 28, 1869; s. Andrew and Mary T.; grad. pub. schs., Albany; m. Gertrude Ruth Snyder, July 25, 1923; 1 dau., Jean Hunter. Washington and Albany corr. New York World; mng. editor first tabloid newspaper, New York Daily Continent, 1891; formerly mng. editor New York World; mng. editor New York Evening World, 1904-31; deputy commr. City Planning of New York. V.p. Nat. Child Welfare Com. and identified with playground and pub. recreational life of New York. Home: New York, N.Y. Died June 1, 1933.

TENNENT, David Hilt, biologist; b. Janesville, Wis., May 28, 1873; s. Thomas and Mary (Hilt) T.; B.S., Olivet (Mich.) Coll., 1900; Ph.D., Johns Hopkins, 1904; m. Esther Margaret Maddux, Apr. 8, 1909; 1 son, David Maddux. Acting prof. biology and physics, Randolph-Macon Coll., Va., 1903; lecturer in biology, 1904-05, asso., 1905-06, asso. prof., 1906-12, prof., 1912-38, research prof., 1938—, Bryn Mawr Coll. Dir. instrn. in dept. of embryology, Marine Biol. Lab., Woods Hole, Mass., 1920-22; visiting prof. biology, Keio Univ., Tokyo, 1930-31; exec. officer Tortugas Marine Biol. Lab. Carnegie Instn. of Washington, 1937-40. Investigations in marine biology at Marine Biol. Lab., Woods Hole, Mass., Cold Spring Harbor, L.I., Bur. Fisheries Lab., Beaufort, N.C., Hopkins Marine Sta., Pacific Grove, Calif., Carnegie Inst. Washington, at Dry Tortugas, Fla., Jamaica, Naples Sta., Torres Strait, Australia, Japan. Home: Bryn Mawr, Pa. Died Jan. 14, 1941.

TENNEY, Charles Daniel, diplomatic service; b. Boston, June 29, 1857; s. Daniel and Mary Adams (Parker) T.; A.B., Dartmouth, 1878, A.M., 1879, LL.D., 1900; student, Oberlin (O.) Theol. Sem., 1879-82; m. Anne Runcie Jerrell, Mar. 29, 1882. Prin. Anglo-Chinese Sch., Tientsin, China, 1886-95; pres. Imperial Chinese U., Tientsin, China, 1895-1906; Chinese sec., Tientsin provisional govt., 1900-02; supt. high and middle schs. in Chihli Province, China, 1902-06; dir. Chinese govt. students in America, 1906-08; Chinese sec. at Am. Legation, Peking, Mar. 11, 1908-Mar. 31, 1912; Am. consul, Nanking, China, Apr. 1, 1912-Sept. 6, 1913. Chinese sec. of Legation, Peking, May 1, 1914; sec. of Legation Class 1 and counselor of Legation, July 21, 1919; chargé d'affaires, Sept. 15, 1919-July 1, 1920; returned to U.S. on leave, Oct. 1920; retired Mar. 1, 1921. Am. vice consul and interpreter, Tientsin, Mar. 6, 1894-June 30, 1896; del. Joint Internat. Opium Commn., Shanghai, China, 1909. Decorated, Chinese Double Dragon, 3d Class No. 1, 1895, 2d class No. 3, 1903; bvt. Mandarin, 2d class, 1902; decorated by Chinese Republic "Chiaho," 2d class, 1921. Trustee Peking Meth. U. Republican. Conglist. Author: Tenney's English Lessons, 1890; Tenney's English Grammar, 1892; Geography of Asia, 1898. Home: Palo Alto, Calif. Died Mar. 14, 1930.

TENNEY, Edward Davies, merchant; b. Plainfield, N.Y., Jan. 26, 1859; s. Lucien Pomeroy and Mary Elizabeth (Davies) T.; ed. pub. schs.; m. Rose Williams Makee, of Hawaii, Mar. 5, 1889 (died 1926); children—Wilhelmina, Vernon Edward. Began in mercantile business at Honolulu, 1880; chmn. bd. Castle & Cooke, Ltd., Bank of Hawaii, Ltd., Hawaiian Trust Co., Ltd., Matson Navigation Co., Oceanic & Oriental Navigation Co.; pres. Ewa Plantation Co., Waialua Agrl. Co., Ltd., Kohala Sugar Co., Territorial Hotels, Ltd., Oceanic Steamship Co. Republican. Episcopalian. Mason. Home: Honolulu, Hawaii. Deceased.

TENNEY, Edward Payson, author; b. Concord, N.H., Sept. 29, 1835; s. Rev. A. P. and Mary T.; ed. Pembroke Acad., 1851-54; Dartmouth Coll., 1854-55; grad. Bangor Theol. Sem., 1858; post-grad. studies Andover Theol. Sem., 1860; 9 yrs.' course of topical studies in the libraries of Boston; (hon. A.M., Dartmouth, 1878); m. Sarah J. Holden, Dec. 1, 1860; 2d, Ellen Weeks, Dec. 8, 1862. Ordained Congl. ministry; pastor in Eastern Mass., 18 yrs.; brief editorial service on The Pacific, San Francisco, and the Congl. Review, Boston; pres. Colo. Coll., 1876-84. Author: The Silent House, 1876; Coronation, 1877; Agamenticus, 1878; The New West, 1878; Colorado and the New West, 1880; Constance of Acadia; The Triumphs of the Cross, 1895; Our Elder Brother, 1897; The Dream of My Youth, 1901; Contrasts in Social Progress, 1907 (new rev. edit., 1910); Looking Forward Into the Past, 1910; The Twentieth Century Imitation of Christ, 1916. Also Chinese transl. of Social Progress, 1910. Home: Lynn, Mass. Died July 24, 1916.

TENNEY, Horace Kent, lawyer; b. Portage, Wis., Sept. 11, 1859; s. Henry W. and Hannah (Cadle) T.; student U. of Vt.; LL.B., U. of Wis., 1881, also LL.D.; m. Eleanor Favill, Nov. 25, 1887; children—Elizabeth (Mrs. F. G. Cheney), Henry F., Horace Kent. Practiced at Chicago, 1881—; mem. Tenney, Harding, Sherman & Rogers; prof. law, U. of Chicago, 1903-11. Republican. Home: Winnetka, Ill. Died Oct. 29, 1932.

TENNEY, Ulysses Dow, portrait painter; b. Hanover, N.H., Apr. 8, 1826; s. John and Tryphene (Dow) T.; ed. Hanover and Lebanon schs.; m. Hannah W. Dow, Dec. 9, 1853 (dec.). Studio in Manchester, 1849-63, New Haven, Conn., 1866-78, in N.H., 1878—. Has painted portraits of Pres. Franklin Pierce, Prof. Benjamin Silliman, Sr., 13 govs. N.H., Sec. Long and other secs. navy, coll. presidents and many N.E. notables. Home: Branford, Conn. Died 1908.

TENNEY, William Lawrence, clergyman; b. Boston, Sept. 9, 1862; s. Rev. Daniel and Mary Adams (Parker) T.; A.B., Oberlin, 1885; B.D., Oberlin Theol. Sem., 1888; studied Harvard Grad Sch., 1888; (D.D., Knox, 1903, Oberlin, 1908); m. Elizabeth Moore Colby, June 25, 1907. Ordained Congl. ministry, 1889; pastor Madison Av. Ch., Cleveland, 1889-92, Winthrop Ch., Holbrook, Mass., 1892-95, 1st Ch., North Adams, 1895-1903; western sec. Am. Missionary Assn., Chicago, 1903-13; asst. pastor Plymouth Ch., Brooklyn, 1913—. Mason. Home: Brooklyn, N.Y. Died Nov. 17, 1917.

TENNY, Charles Buckley, missionary; b. Hilton, N.Y., Sept. 10, 1871; s. Delos Perkins and Fanny Elizabeth (Lee) T.; grad. Brockport State Normal Sch., 1891; B.A., U. of Rochester, 1897, D.D., 1917; grad. Rochester Theol. Sem., 1900; Turner fellow, Newton Theol. Instn., with work at Harvard, 1911-12; m. Grace E. Webb, May 11, 1905 (died 1910); children—Ruth Hana, Paul Webb (dec.); m. 2d, Elizabeth Wilson, d. Rev. James H. Pettee, June 16, 1915; 1 son, Francis Briggs. Ordained Bapt. ministry, 1900; missionary A.B.F.M.S., in Japan, 1900—; prof. N.T. lang. and lit., Japan Bapt. Theol. Sem., 1910—; pres. same, 1913-17; exec. sec. Japan Mission A.B.F.M.S., 1917-27; sec. Tokyo Christian Ednl. Assn., 1925; founder and chmn. bd., pres. 1926-32, pres. emeritus, 1932—, Kanto Gakuin (Mabie Memorial), Bapt. sch. for men and boys (including acad., coll. and theol. depts.), Yokohama. Lectured in U.S., 1924-25, in interest of better Am.-Japanese relations. Home: Rochester, N.Y. Died 1936.

TERBELL, Joseph Bodine, mfr.; b. Corning, N.Y., Feb. 12, 1863; s. William and Celina (Robinson) T.; A.B., Hamilton Coll., 1884; m. Gladys Green, Apr. 1903; children—Joseph Bodine, Thomas Green. Officer Fall Brook Ry., 1884-97; pres. Corning Brake Shoe Co., 1897-1902; v.p. Am. Brake Shoe & Foundry Co., 1902-19, pres., 1919—, also chmn. bd., 1922—; chmn. bd. Am. Forge Co., Southern Wheel Co., Am. Malleables Co., Manganese Steel Rail Co., Nat. Bearing Metals Corp., Racor Pacific Frog & Switch Co. Republican. Episcopalian. Home: New York, N.Y. Died Apr. 5, 1931.

TERHUNE, Edward Payson, clergyman; b. New Brunswick, N.J., Nov. 22, 1830; s. John and Esther T.; grad. Rutgers Coll., 1850 (D.D., 1869); grad. New Brunswick Theol. Sem., 1854; m. Mary Virginia Hawes, 1856. Ordained in Presbyn. Ch., West Hanover, Va., 1855; pastor Presbyn. Ch., Charlotte Court House, Va., 1859, First Reformed Ch., Newark, N.J., 1859-76; chaplain Am. Ch., Rome, Italy, 1876-77 (also chaplain Am. Ch. in Paris); pastor First Congl. Ch., Springfield, Mass., 1879-84; First Ref. Ch., Williamsburg, L.I., 1884-91; Puritan Congl. Ch., Brooklyn, 1891-95. Home: Pompton, N.J. Died 1907.

TERHUNE, Mary Virginia, see "Marion Harland."

TERHUNE, William Lewis, publisher; b. Newark, N.J., Oct. 30, 1850; s. Daniel Johnson and Maria Louisa (Wood) T.; ed. pvt. schs., Newark, 1859-67; m. Nellie E. Littlefield, Jan. 7, 1873 (died 1927); children—Everitt B., Mrs. Inez M. Carpenter, Mrs. Lillian T. Jordan; m. 2d, Isabelle M. McClure, Dec. 14, 1931. Founder and pres. First Nat. Amateur Press Assn., 1869; mgr. Merry's Museum Youth's Magazine, 1870; pub. N.H. Independent, 1872; editor Auburn (Me.) Herald, 1877; writer Boston Globe, 1878; founded, 1882, and pub. Boot and Shoe Recorder; pub. The Apparel Retailer and The Southern Retailer; retired, 1909. Baptist. Mason. Pres. Fossil Club of New York, 1913-14. Home: Brookline, Mass. Died Feb. 23, 1936.

TERRAL, Samuel Heidelberg, judge of Supreme Court Miss., May 10, 1897—; b. Jasper Co., Miss., Feb. 4, 1835; academical edn.; grad. Univ. of Miss., 1857; admitted to bar and engaged in practice; dist. atty., 1872-79; circuit judge, 1882-97. Home: Quitman, Miss. Died 1903.

TERRELL, Alexander Watkins, diplomat; b. Patrick County, Va., Nov. 3, 1827; s. Christopher Joseph and Susan (Kennerly) T.; ed. U. of Mo.; married 3 times. Admitted to bar, 1849; began practice at St. Joseph, Mo.; removed to Tex.; judge Dist. Ct., 1857-62; col. of cav., C.S.A.; mem. Tex. Ho. of Rep., 4 yrs., Senate, 10 yrs.; U.S. minister to Turkey, 1893-97. Portrait hung in Tex. Ho. of Rep., 1903, in recognition of prominence as legislator. Home: Austin, Tex. Died Sept. 9, 1912.

TERRELL, Edwin Holland, lawyer, diplomat; b. Brookville, Ind., Nov. 21, 1848; s. Rev. Williamson and Martha (Jarrell) T.; A.B. (valedictorian), DePauw, 1871, A.M., 1874; LL.B., Harvard, 1873; studied in Europe, 1873-74; (LL.D., DePauw, 1892), practiced law, Indianapolis, 1874-77; removed to San Antonio, Tex., 1877; m. Mary Maverick, Aug. 17, 1874 (died 1891); 2d, Lois Lasater, Feb. 7, 1895. Mem. Rep. State Exec. com., Tex., 1894-1900, Am. minister to Belgium, 1889-93; plenipotentiary to Slave Trade Conf., Brussels, 1889-90; to Customs-Tariff Conf., 1890; conducted negotiations for U.S., with the six powers holding possessions in Congo Basin and secured from them "Protocol of Dec. 22, 1890," granting U.S. and its citizens full commercial provileges, etc., in entire Congo Basin; mem. Commission Technique to revise Berlin treaty of 1885 under "General Act of Brussels," 1891; plenipotentiary to negotiate commercial treaty with Congo Free State, 1891; commr. to and v.p. Internat. Monetary Conf., Brussels, 1892; has negotiated or assisted in drafting in conf., three treaties subsequently ratified by President and Senate. Grand Officer Order of Leopold, 1893. From 1901, pres. bd. trustees, Carnegie Library, San Antonio. Mason. Home: San Antonio, Tex. Died 1910.

TERRELL, Frederick, banker; b. Lafayette, Ind., Mar. 31, 1856; s. Gen. Charles Milton and Sarah (Speake) T.; desc. William Tyrrell, from Eng. to Hanover Co., Va., abt. middle of 17th century; student Earlham College, Ind.; A.B., De Pauw, 1876; M.D., Harvard U., 1881; m. Marion Clement, Sept. 6, 1882 (died 1924); 1 dau., Sarah (Mrs. Albert G. Engelke). Began practice at San Antonio, 1881; acting asst. surgeon U.S.A., 1881; U.S. pension exam. surgeon, 1886; alderman and mayor of San Antonio, 1903; pres. Pub. Sch. Bd., San Antonio, 1907-09; chmn. Selective Service Bd., Bexar Co., Tex., 1917-18; pres. Carnegie Library. Formerly pres. Old City Nat. Bank; active in merger, State Nat. Bank and Central Trust Co., forming City-Central Bank & Trust Co., of which was chmn. board. Chmn. bd. trustees Firemen's and Policemen's Pension Bd. Home: San Antonio, Tex. Died Mar. 11, 1940.

TERRELL, Glanville, univ. prof.; b. Jerdone Castle, Va., Oct. 20, 1859; s. Oliver Hazard Perry and Mary Jerdone (Coleman) T.; reared in Orange Co., Va.; A.B., Stanford, 1894; A.M., Harvard, 1898, Ph.D., 1900; unmarried. Teacher in pub. schs. of Orange Co., Va., 1877-80; prin. high sch., Halifax, Va., 1881-85; practiced law, Halifax, 1885-88; teacher Latin and Greek, Bardstown (Ky.) Inst., 1888-89; prin. high sch., Nipomo, Calif., 1890-93, Palo Alto, 1894-96, San Luis Obispo, 1896-97; prof. Greek and German, 1900-04, prof. Greek and Latin, 1904-09, Georgetown (Ky.) Coll.; prof. Greek, 1909-18, prof. philosophy, 1918-29, State U. of Ky.; retired as emeritus professor of philosophy. Teacher Harvard Summer School, 1904; acting prof. Greek, Brown U., 1912-13. Pres. Maury Birthplace Assn., 1932-33. Democrat. Baptist. Home: Louisa, Va. Died Oct. 4, 1936.

TERRELL, J. O., lawyer, banker; b. Kaufman Co., Tex., Apr. 6, 1856; s. Jonathan W. and Amelia (Love) T.; ed. Trinity U., Tex., 1873-75; m. Mattie Simpson, Dec 12, 1877. Admitted to Tex. bar, 1877; practiced Terrell, Tex., until 1895, then at San Antonio; mem. Terrell & Terrell; organized 1910, and from then pres. Central Trust Co., San Antonio; senior mem. J. O. Terrell & Sons, stock breeders (a breeder of Jersey cattle for many yrs. and at one time owned largest held in the world). Mem. Tex.

Senate from Dallas dist., 1885-89; Rep. nominee (by unanimous vote) for governor of Tex., 1910. Home: San Antonio, Tex. Died June 1923.

TERRELL, Joseph Meriwether, governor; b. Greenville, Ga., June 6, 1861; s. Joel E. G. and Sarah R. (Anthony) T.; common sch. edn.; admitted to bar, 1882; m. Jessie Lee Spivey, Oct. 19, 1886. Mem. Ga. Ho. of Rep., 1884, 1886, Senate, 1890-92; atty. gen. of Ga., 1892-1902 (resigned); gov. of Ga., 1902-07; apptd. U.S. senator, Nov. 17, 1910, by Gov. Joseph M. Brown, to fill vacancy occasioned by death of Senator Clay, and held until July 12, 1911, when Legislature elected his successor; resumed law practice at Atlanta, Ga. Democrat. Home: Atlanta, Ga. Died Nov. 17, 1912.

TERRES, John B., consul; b. Charlotte, N.C., Sept. 25, 1847; M.D., Richmond Med. Coll., 1866. Apptd. v. consul gen. at Port au Prince, July 20, 1880; resigned, 1885, reappointed Oct. 1, same yr.; consul, Port au Prince, May 5, 1904—. Died Nov. 1, 1920.

TERRETT, William Rogers, prof. Am. history Hamilton Coll., 1889—; b. New York, July 19, 1849; s. Rev. John Cotton and Eliza Reed (Rogers) T.; grad. Williams Coll., 1871, A.M., 1874 (D.D.); grad. Princeton Theol. Sem., 1874; m. Eleanor Merrill, Nov. 20, 1878. Filled Presbyn. and Congl. pastorates until 1889. Home: Clinton, N.Y. Died 1902.

TERRY, Benjamin Stites, univ. prof.; b. at St. Paul, Apr. 9, 1857; s. John Carlos and Emily (Wakefield) T.; A.B., Colgate U., 1878, A.M., 1881; Ph.D., U. of Freiburg, 1892; LL.D., Colgate, 1903; div. studies, Hamilton Theol. Sem., 1878-79, 1880-81, Rochester Theol. Sem., 1879-80; m. Mary, d. Rev. George C. Baldwin, of Troy, N.Y., June 1, 1881. Ordained Bapt. ministry, Aug. 31, 1881; pastor Perry, N.Y., 1881-83, Fairport, N.Y., 1883-85; prof. history, Colgate U., 1885-92; student Freiburg and Göttingen, 1891-92; prof. English history, 1892 (emeritus prof.), U. of Chicago. Author: History of England from Earliest Times to Death of Victoria, 1901; A History of England for Schools, 1903; Die Heimstaettengesetz-Bewegung, 1905. Home: Chicago, Ill. Died Oct. 31, 1931.

TERRY, Charles Appleton, lawyer; b. S. Weymouth, Mass., Mar. 2, 1858; s. Rev. James Pease and Catharine A. (Matson) T.; A.B., Amherst, 1879; LL.B., Columbia, 1883; m. Marie E. Cady, June 22, 1886; children—Charles Francis (dec.), Catharine Louise (wife of William Neely Ross, D.D.), Matson Cady. Admitted to New York bar, 1883; pres. Stalwart Realty Co.; hon. v.p. Westinghouse Elec. & Mfg. Co. Republican. Presbyterian. Home: New York, N.Y. Died Feb. 18, 1939.

TERRY, Charles Thaddeus, lawyer; b. Albany, N.Y., Sept. 16, 1867; s. Griffith P. and Eleanor (Lasher) T.; A.B., Williams Coll. (valedictorian—awarded 13 out of 14 prizes open to his class), 1889; LL.B., Columbia, 1893; 2 yrs. at Summer Sch. of Law, New York Law Sch.; student history, economics and lit., U. of Berlin, 1890; m. Katherine Lansing Hendrick, June 22, 1898. Admitted to bar, 1893; prize lecturer on equity and code pleading and practice, 1893-95, lecturer, 1896-1901, prof. law, 1901—, Columbia. Commr. of State of N.Y. to Nat. Conf. of Commrs. of the States of the Union on Uniform State Laws, 1905 (pres. nat. conf.); chmn. N.Y. State Bd. Commrs. on Uniform State Laws, 1905—; mem. N.Y. State exec. com. and chmn. com. on uniform state laws of Nat. Civic Fedn.; chmn. directors N.Y. Civic League. Trustee Williams College and Brick Presbyn. Ch. Author: Corporation Minute Book, 1910; Terry on Uniform State Laws in the U.S., 1920. Home: New York, N.Y. Died Feb. 19, 1923.

TERRY, Ellen, actress; b. Feb. 27, 1848; first appearance Apr. 1856, at Princess Theatre, London, under Charles Kean's management; in 1867 first acted with Henry Irving in The Taming of the Shrew, at Queen's Theatre, then acted at Haymarket Theatre; retired for 7 yrs.; reappeared at Queen's Theatre in The Wandering Heir; played Olivia, amongst others, at Court Theatre (John Hare's management) and Portia, amongst others, at Prince of Wales Theatre (Bancroft's management); played Ophelia, Dec. 30, 1878, for first time at Lyceum with Henry Irving; visited America with him, 1883, and many times subsequently; remained at Lyceum until its dissolution in 1901; produced Ibsen's The Vikings, 1903, and Shakespearean plays with her own co. at Imperial Theatre; in 1905 played at Duke of York's Theatre in J. M. Barrie's Alice-Sit-by-the-Fire; played at Court Theatre, Lady Cicely Waynflete in Bernard Shaw's Captain Brassbound's Conversion, 1906; celebrated her stage jubilee, Apr. 28, 1906; played in America, spring of 1907; m. George Frederick Watts, painter; m. 2d, Charles Wardell, actor, 1868; m. 3d, Pittsburgh, James Carew, actor, Mar. 22, 1907. Visited Australia, New Zealand and America on a Shakespearean lecture tour, 1914-15. Died July 21, 1928.

TERRY, George S., assistant treas. of U.S.; b. Hudson, N.Y.; A.B., Williams Coll. Began active career in dry goods house, New York, and became mem. William I. Peake & Co. and successors, Peake, Opdyke & Co. and Opdyke, Terry & Steele; sec. of Dock Bd. under Mayor Strong; sec. Park Bd. under Mayor Low; asst. treas. Rep. Nat. Com., 1904; apptd. asst. treas. of U.S., at New York. Died 1911.

TERRY, John Taylor, financier; b. Hartford, Conn., Sept. 9, 1822; s. Roderick and Harriet (Taylor) T.; ed. schs. of Hartford and acads. at Westfield, Mass., and Ellington, Conn.; became clerk, 1841, and partner, 1844, in banking, importing and mercantile house of E. D. Morgan (afterward gov. of N.Y.); succeeded to the business of E. D. Morgan & Co., 1883; m. Elizabeth Roe Peet, July 22, 1846. Dir. Am. Exchange Nat. Bank, Met. Trust Co., Commercial Union Assurance Co., Ltd., of London, Commercial Union Fire Ins. Co. of New York, etc. Trustee Presbyn. Hosp. Home: Irvington, N.Y. Died May 3, 1913.

TERRY, John Wharton, lawyer; b. Brazoria, Tex., Apr. 8, 1860; s. Clinton and Arie G. T.; ed. pub. schs., Brazoria and Columbia, Tex.; studied law in office, Stockton, Calif.; m. Anna Davis, July 28, 1888; 1 dau., Rebecca S. (Mrs. Newton H. White, Jr.). Admitted to Texas bar, 1881. Democrat. Home: Galveston, Tex. Died Aug. 25, 1936.

TERRY, Marshall Orlando, physician; b. Watervliet Center, N.Y., June 21, 1848; s. William Henry and Sally (Burke) T.; scientific edn.; grad. Cleveland Homœ. Hosp. Coll., 1872; 2 yrs. in New York at Ophthalmic and Aural Inst., Manhattan Eye and Ear Infirmary and New York Eye and Ear Infirmary; special instrn. under Heitzmann in microscopy, at Bellevue in physical diagnosis and surgery; also in England; m. Mrs. A. M. McGregor, 1905 (died 1912); m. 2d, Mrs. A. R. Merritt. Practiced, 1872—. Apptd. by Gov. Cornell surgeon with rank of maj. N.G.N.Y., 1880; apptd. by Gov. Morton surgeon gen., rank of brig. gen., Jan. 1, 1895, reapptd. by Gov. Black, Jan. 1, 1897; apptd. by President Cleveland U.S. pension exam. surgeon and was pres. bd. 4 yrs.; declined position of chief surgeon of div. during Spanish-Am. War, offered by President McKinley, because of duties as surgeon gen. N.Y. Surgeon-in-chief Utica Homœ. Hosp., 1895-1905; formerly mem. surg. staff Gen. Hosp., and surgeon-in-chief Commercial Travelers' Mut. Accident Assn. America. Invented Terry stretcher and field case, adopted by State of N.Y., as were ambulance and regimental chest; discovered spread of typhoid due largely to flies. Decorated by Oneida Co. War Com. "in recognition of patriotic services during war between U.S. and Spain." Hon. mem. Coronado (Calif.) Camp No. 59, United Spanish War Vets. Hon. pres. bd. trustees Am. Legion Post 6, San Diego, Calif.; member Association Army of U.S. Republican. Episcopalian. Author: The Soldier's Medical Friend (for gift to allied troops). Home: Coronado, Calif. Died Oct. 11, 1933.

TERRY, Milton Spenser, theologian; b. Coeymans, N.Y., Feb. 22, 1840; s. John and Elisabeth (McLowen) T.; ed. Charlotteville Sem., Troy U., and Yale Div. Sch.; (hon. A.M., Wesleyan, Conn., 1870, D.D., 1880; LL.D., Northwestern, 1895); m. Frances O. Atchinson, May 15, 1864. Ordained M.E. ministry, 1864; pastor chs. in N.Y., 1863-84; prof. Christian doctrine, Garrett Bibl. Inst. (Northwestern U.), 1885—. Author: Biblical Hermeneutics, 1883; The New Apologetic, 1897; Biblical Apocalyptics, 1898; Moses and the Prophets, 1901; The New and Living Way, 1902; The Mediation of Jesus Christ, 1903; Primer of Christian Doctrine, 1906; Biblical Dogmatics 1907; The Shinto Cult, 1910. Home: Evanston, Ill. Died July 13, 1914.

TERRY, Nathaniel Matson, physicist; b. Lyme, Conn., Apr. 6, 1844; s. Rev. James Pease and Catharine A. (Matson) T.; A.B., Amherst, 1867, A.M., 1870; Ph.D., U. of Göttingen, 1871; hon. A.M., Yale, 1873; LL.D., Amherst, 1917; m. Frances A. Griswold, Nov. 6, 1878 (died 1915); children—Frances Griswold (wife of A. K. Atkins, U.S.N.), Nathaniel Matson, Louisa Mather. Prof. physics, U.S. Naval Acad., 1872-1917, head of dept. of physics and chemistry, 1886-1913. Commd. prof. mathematics U.S.N., 1913, and ordered to duty in connection with post-grad. course at U.S. Naval Acad.; retired with rank of commodore, U.S.N., 1917. Mem. bd. control Naval Inst., 22 years; trans. to retired list U.S. naval officers, 1917. Mem. exec. com. Navy Athletic Assn., 10 yrs.; hon. mem. U.S. Naval Acad. Graduates' Assn.; pres. First Ecclesiastical Soc. of Old Lyme. Home: Lyme, Conn. Died Oct. 12, 1938.

TERRY, Roderick, clergyman; b. Brooklyn, Apr. 1, 1849; s. John T. and Elizabeth R. (Peet) T.; A.B., Yale, 1870; Andover Theol. Sem., 1870-72; grad. Union Theol. Sem., 1875; (D.D., Princeton, 1881); m. Linda Marquand, Sept. 22, 1875; 1 son, Roderick. Ordained to Presbyn. ministry, Nov. 11, 1875; pastor, Peekskill, N.Y. 1875-79, South Ref. Ch., New York, 1881-1905; lit. work, Newport, R.I., 1906—. Chaplain 12th Inf. N.G.S.N.Y., 1890-1900. Trustee Rutgers Coll., 1882-1905; mem. Council New York U., and Bellevue Hosp. Med. Coll., 1883-98. Home: Newport, R.I. Died Dec. 28, 1933.

TERRY, Silas Wright, rear admiral U.S.N.; b. Wallonia, Ky., Dec. 28, 1842; s. Abner R. and Eleanor (Dyer) T.; apptd. to U.S. Naval Acad. from Ky., Sept. 28, 1858, grad. 1861; m. Louisa G. Mason, Oct. 14, 1873. Promoted ensign, Sept. 16, 1862; advanced through grades to rear admiral, Mar. 29, 1900. Served on Dale, Atlantic coast, 1861-62; Wabash and Alabama, 1862; N. Atlantic Blockading Squadron, 1862-63; Miss. Squadron, 1863-64; N. Atlantic Blockading Squadron, 1864-65; participated in battles with Fts. Fisher and Anderson, and other engagements on coast of N.C.; on Ticonderoga, 1865-68; receiving-ship at New York, 1869; Naval Acad., 1869-71; Severn, 1871; Worcester, 1871-73; Naval Observatory, 1873-74; light house insp. 5th dist., 1877-80; comd. Marion, 1881-82; Navy Yard, League Island, 1883-84; comd. Portsmouth, 1884-86, Jamestown, 1886; Navy Yard, Washington, 1887-89; mem. Naval Examining and Retiring Bds., 1887-93; comd. Newark, 1893-95, receiving-ship, Franklin, 1895-98, Iowa, 1898-99; comdt., Navy Yard, Washington, 1900-03, Naval sta., Honolulu, 1903-04; retired, Dec. 28, 1904. During Civil War was engaged in blockading service on Atlantic Coast, 1861-62; in Mississippi Squadron and on Red River expdn., 1863-64; advanced 5 numbers in his grade for gallant conduct on latter; was present during naval operations and serving on staff of Admiral Porter, against Fts. Fisher and Anderson, and capture of Wilmington, Feb. 1865; later on James River; was present at fall of Richmond, accompanied President Lincoln when he entered Richmond. In Jan. 1882, while comdg. the Marion, rescued crew of bark Trinity, which had been wrecked, Oct. 1880, on Heard Island, Indian Ocean, lat. 53 deg. 30 min. S., long. 73 deg. 30 min. E.; in Feb. 1881, while at Cape Town, hauled English ship Poonah off the beach, saving her from total loss, for which he received the thanks of the Govt. of Cape Colony and of the English Govt. Home: Washington, D.C. Died 1911.

TERRY, Theodore Brainard, agriculturist; b. at Lafayette, N.Y., Jan. 2, 1843; s. Rev. Parshall and Fannie Buel (Howell) T.; ed. Painesville (O.) Acad., and Western Reserve Coll., Hudson, O.; m. Eleanor M. Tillotson, Mar. 1, 1865. Bought a poor farm in 1870, made a success of it and for 27 yrs. has been in demand as lecturer at farmers' insts., and writer; has worked in 17 states. Pres. Hudson Telephone Co. Author: A B C of Potato Culture; A B C of Strawberry Culture; Our Farming; How to Keep Well and Live Long, 1909. Associate editor Practical Farmer, Phila. Home: Hudson, O. Died Jan. 1, 1916.

TETLOW, John, educator; b. Providence, Apr. 1, 1843; s. John and Mary A. (Buckley) T.; A.B., Brown U., 1864, A.M., 1879 (D.Sc., 1892); m. Elizabeth I. Harrington, 1870; 2d, Elizabeth P. Howard, 1880. Head master Boston Girls' High and Latin schs., 1885-1907 (emeritus Latin Sch.). With William C. Collar and R. G. Huling, organized N.E. Assn. of Colls. and Prep. Schs., 1885 (pres., 1893); pres. Mass. Classical and High Sch. Teachers' Assn., 1886-87; mem. and sec. Nat. Com. of Ten on Secondary Sch. Studies, 1892-93; pres. Mass. Sch. Masters' Club, 1902-03; pres. Headmasters' Assn. of U.S., 1904-05. Author: Inductive Latin Lessons, 1884. Edited series of School Classics, 1893-1901. Home: Brookline, Mass. Died Dec. 9, 1911.

TETRAZZINI, Luisa, operatic soprano; b. Florence, Italy, 1874; studied music under Signor Ceccherini, at Liceo Musicale, Milan; m. Senor Bazelli. Début as Inez in Meyerbeer's "L'Africaine," at Teator Verdi, Florence; later sang in Teator Argentine, Rome, and made tour of leading cities of S. America; after returning to Europe filled engagements in Lisbon, Madrid, St. Petersburg, Moscow, and won brilliant triumphs in Italy; went to Mexico City and to Tivoli Opera House, San Francisco; New York début as Violetta in "La Traviata" at Metropolitan Opera House, Jan. 15, 1908, before a great audience; repertoire includes 33 operas, mostly Italian; leading successes in "Rigoletto," "La Lonnambula," "Lucia di Lammermoor," "Lakme," "The Cobbler and the Fairy," etc.; with Chicago Grand Opera Co., season of 1913-14. Lives in Italy. Died Apr. 28, 1940.

TEUSLER, Rudolf Bolling, physician; b. Rome, Ga., Feb. 25, 1876; s. Rudolf and Mary Jefferson (Bolling) T.; M.D., Med. Coll. of Va., 1894; m. Mary Stuart Woodward, July 21, 1898; children—Mary Stuart, Virginia Bolling, Mildred Minor, Rudolf Bolling. Began practice at Richmond, Va., 1894; asst. prof. pathology and bacteriology, Med. Coll. Va., 1896-1900; dir. St. Luke's Internat. Hosp., Tokyo, Japan, 1900—; mem. Associated Press staff in Japan, 1903-04; physician to British Embassy, Tokyo, 1909-12; mem. Am. Embassy staff, Am. Episcopal Mission; mem. com. to provide post-grad. med. training in U.S. for Japanese students. Capt. asst. surgeon 1st Regt. Inf. Va., 1895-98; commr. Am. Red Cross to Siberia, rank of col., 1918-21. Decorated Order Saint Vladimir (Russian); War Medal (Czechoslovakian); Order Rising Sun (5th class, Japan). Democrat. Episcopalian. Dir. St. Barnabas' Hosp., Osaka, 1925—. Died Aug. 10, 1934.

TEWKSBURY, H(arold) Josiah Royal, newspaper editor; b. East Dover, Me., Aug. 7, 1886; s. Samuel

Staples and Emma Ann (Royal) T.; LL.B., Hamilton Coll. of Law, 1905; m. Ethel Harriett Blake, Aug. 7, 1912; children—Blake, Grayson. Reporter Lewiston (Me.) Daily Sun, 1905-06, Lewiston Morning News, 1906-07, Kennebec Jour., Augusta, Me., 1907-09; on editorial staff Lewiston Daily Sun, 1909-18, Portland Evening Express, 1918-29; editor Portland Sunday Telegram, 1929—; dir. Pine State Bldg. & Loan Assn., Portland. Chmn. bd. trustees cemeteries and parks, City of Westbrook; mem. bd. dirs. Western Me. Council of Camp Fire Girls. Republican. Conglist. Mason. Mem. editorial bd. Christian-Pilgrim. Home: Westbrook, Me. Died Oct. 6, 1937.

THACH, Charles Coleman, college pres.; b. Athens, Ala., Mar. 15, 1860; s. Robert H. and Elizabeth Lockhart (Coleman) T.; B.E., Ala. Poly. Inst., 1877; student Johns Hopkins, 1880-81; (hon. A.M., U. of Ala., 1887, LL.D., 1901); m. Ellen Stanford Smith, Nov. 11, 1885. Prof. modern langs., Austin Coll., Tex., 1881-82; prof. English, 1885-1902, pres., June 9, 1902—, Ala. Poly. Inst. Mem. The Ala. History Commn., 1898-1900; supt. Library, Ala. Poly. Inst., 1886-1901; mem. Ala. Rhodes Scholarship Commn. Pres. Ala. Ednl. Assn., 1915; pres. Ala. S.S. Assn. Mem. Ala. br. Council of Nat. Defense. Home: Auburn, Ala. Died Oct. 3, 1921.

THACHER, Arthur, mining engr.; b. Newtonville, Mass., May 8, 1857; s. Thomas and Catherine (Worcester) T.; E.M., C.E., Columbia, 1877; m. Carrie Greene, June 19, 1890; children—Theodora, Arthur Worcester. Has engaged in mining in Mex., Ariz., Colo. and Ida.; adj. prof. metallurgy, Washington U., 1891; pres. and gen. mgr. Central Lead Co., 1892-1905; consulting engr. Am. Smelting Securities Co., 1906; Western mgr. of mines N.J. Zinc Co., 1906—. Home: St. Louis, Mo. Died July 2, 1934.

THACHER, Edwin, engineer; b. DeKalb, N.Y., Oct. 12, 1839; s. Seymour and Elizabeth (Smith) T.; C.E., Rensselaer Poly. Inst., 1863; m. Anna E. Bartholomew, Apr. 22, 1872. Chief engr. Keystone Bridge Co., 1881-87; cons. engr. for bridges and bridge contractor; mem. Concrete-Steel Engring. Co. Inventor and patentee Thacher's cylindrical slide rule, improved duplex slide rule, steel bridge trusses, combination bridge trusses, system of concrete-steel arches, steel super-structure for concrete-steel bridges, bar for reënforcing concrete, and system for concrete-steel floors. Home: New York, N.Y. Died Sept. 21, 1920.

THACHER, John Boyd; b. Ballston, N.Y., Sept. 11, 1847; grad. Williams Coll., 1869 (A.M.); m. Emma Treadwell, Sept. 11, 1872. Mem. N.Y. senate, 1884-85; introduced measures which later resulted in the reforms of the tenement houses; introduced the resolution, 1885, calling on New York mems. of Congress to vote for placing Gen. Grant on the retired list, which (coming from a Democrat) gave that movement its final successful impetus. Mayor of Albany, 1886, 1887, also in 1896 and 1897; apptd., 1890, by President Harrison, mem. World's Columbian Expn., and became chmn. of its Bureau of Awards. Author: The Continent of America, Its Discovery and Its Baptism, 1896; Charlecote—Or, the Trial of William Shakespeare, 1896; Little Speeches (discourses on pub. questions); The Cabotian Discovery; Awards; Christopher Columbus, His Life, His Work, His Remains, 3 vols., 1903-04; Outlines of the French Revolution Told in Autographs, 1905. Home: Albany, N.Y. Died 1909.

THACHER, John Seymour, physician; b. New Haven, Conn., June 10, 1856; s. Thomas Anthony and Elizabeth (Day) T.; brother of Thomas T.; A.B., Yale, 1877; M.D., Coll. Phys. and Surg. (Columbia), 1880; m. Frances Lake, Nov. 25, 1902. Demonstrator pathology, 1896-97, pathol. anatomy, 1897-1903, prof. clin. medicine, 1903—, Columbia; attending phys. Presbyn. Hospital, 1903-14, Roosevelt Hosp., 1907—. Home: New York, N.Y. Died 1922.

THACHER, Sherman Day, teacher; b. New Haven, Conn., Nov. 6, 1861; s. Thomas Anthony and Elizabeth Baldwin (Sherman) T.; B.A., Yale, 1883, LL.B., cum laude, 1886, hon. M.A., 1923; m. Eliza Seely Blake, June 24, 1896; children—Elizabeth, George Blake, Anson Stiles, Helen Sherman, Harriet Janet, Sherman Day. Founder, 1889, and headmaster Thacher Sch., Ojai, Calif. Chmn. Co. Exemption Draft Bd., during war period; chmn. exec. com. Ojai Valley Men's League; dir. Ojai Civic Assn. Died Aug. 5, 1931.

THACHER, Thomas, lawyer; b. New Haven, Conn., May 3, 1850; s. Thomas Anthony and Elizabeth (Day) T.; bro. of John Seymour T.; A.B., Yale, 1871, A.M., 1874; LL.B., Columbia, 1875; (LL.D., Yale, 1903); m. Sarah McC. Green, New York, Dec. 1, 1880. In practice at New York, 1875—. Mem. Simpson, Thacher & Bartlett; lecturer on corps., Yale Law Sch., 1889—. Home: Tenafly, N.J. Died July 30, 1919.

THACKARA, A(lexander) Montgomery, consul gen.; b. Philadelphia, Sept. 24, 1848; s. Benjamin and Mary E. T.; prep. edn., Phila. pub. schs.; grad. U.S. Naval Acad., 1869; served in U.S.N., 1869-82; m. Eleanor, d. General W. Tecumseh Sherman, May 5, 1880. Engaged in business, Phila., 1882-97; consul at Havre, France, 1897-1905; consul gen. at Berlin, Oct. 1, 1905-Sept. 1913, at Paris, Sept. 1913—. Home: Philadelphia, Pa. Died Jan. 19, 1937.

THAELER, Arthur David, clergyman; b. on Island of St. Christopher, B.W.I., Oct. 21, 1871; s. Rev. Samuel L. and Marie Louise (Gruhl) T.; grad. Nazareth Hall Mil. Acad., Nazareth, Pa., 1886; A.B., Moravian Coll., Pa., 1890, B.D., 1892, D.D., 1917; m. Ruth Caroline, d. Abraham S. Schropp, of Bethlehem, Oct. 30, 1894. Ordained Moravian ministry, 1892; pastor Calvary Ch., Winston-Salem, N.C., 1892-1901, Bethlehem, Pa., 1901-18; prin. Nazareth Hall Mil. Acad., 1918-29; pastor First Ch., N.Y. City, 1930—. Trustee Moravian Coll. and Theol. Sem. Home: Arlington, N.J. Died July 20, 1932.

THAMES, Travis Butler, clergyman; b. in Monroe Co., Ala., 1856; s. Cornelius Ellis and Mary E. (McCollum) T.; B.S., Howard Coll., 1876; grad. Southern Bapt. Theol. Sem., Louisville, Ky., 1881; (D.D., Richmond Coll., 1892); m. Sallie Long, Dec. 1882. Ordained Bapt. ministry; pastor Shelbyville, Ky., 1879-84, La Salle Ch., Chicago, 1884-89, Danville, Va., Elizabeth, N.J., Newnan, Ga. First pres. Bapt. Edn. Bd. Trustee Roanoke Coll., Danville, Va. Democrat. Mason. Author: Colonial Virginia, 1906. Home: Newnan, Ga. Died Feb. 26, 1914.

THARET, Octave. See Alice French.

THATCHER, Joseph Addison, banker; b. Shelbyville, Ky., July 31, 1838; s. John Pemberton and Patsy (Hickman) T.; ed. pub. schs., and Jones Commercial Coll., St. Louis, Mo.; m. Frances Kirtley, 1865. Began in banking business at Central City, Colo., 1863; organizer Denver Nat. Bank, 1884, and its pres. for 30 yrs. (chmn. bd.). Democrat. Episcopalian. Home: Denver, Colo. Died Oct. 25, 1918.

THATCHER, Mahlon Daniel, banker; b. New Buffalo, Pa., Dec. 6, 1839; s. Henry and Lydia Ann (Albert) T.; acad. edn., Juniata Co., Pa.; m. Luna Ada Jordan, Aug. 1, 1876. Merchant at Pueblo, 1865-71, banker, 1871—; pres. First Nat. banks, Pueblo, Trinidad, Florence, Colo., Montrose (Colo.) Nat. Bank, Bent Co. Bank (Las Animas, Colo.), Internat. Trust Co. (Denver); v.p. First Nat. Bank (Denver); dir. Am. Smelting & Refining Co. Mayor of Pueblo, 1877. Republican. Trustee Colo. Coll. Mason. Home: Pueblo, Colo. Died Feb. 22, 1916.

THATCHER, Moses, banker, mfr., stockraiser; b. Sangamon Co., Ill., Feb. 2, 1842; s. Hezekiah and Alley (Kitchen) T., of Va.; Mormons; family followed Saints to Utah, 1847; went to Calif., 1849; returned to Utah, 1858; became Mormon missionary at 15; m. 1861, Lettie Farr. Went to England, 1865; supt. Sunday schools, 1865; pres., 1877, Cache Stake of Zion; apostle, 1879-96; deposed for refusal to recognize church control in civil affairs. Mem. Territorial legislative council, 1872-82, Utah constl. convs., 1872 and 1894; v.p. Deseret Nat. Bank, Deseret Savings Bank. Was candidate for U.S. senator from Utah before State legislature of 1896; defeated by church influence because of his contention for complete separation of Church and State, he having drafted that requirement of Utah State constitution; in vindication, majority of Utah legislature, 1898, tendered him U.S. senatorship, but he declined. Is stocking with cattle a 50,000-acre ranch which he owns in Chihuahua, Mex. Pres. Thacher Bros. Banking Co., Logan, Utah, Jan. 9, 1903—; dir. Utah Mexican Rubber Co., owning 75,000 acres land in Tabasco, Mexico; pres. Utah Farmers' Loan Assn.; pres. and gen. mgr. Thatcher Milling & Elevator Co. Democrat. Home: Logan, Utah. Died 1909.

THATCHER, Roscoe Wilfred, college president; b. Chatham Centre, O., Oct. 5, 1872; s. Charles Phelps and Lida Elizabeth (Packard) T.; B.Sc., U. of Neb., 1898, M.A., 1901, D.Agr., 1920; LL.D., Hobart Coll., 1925; ScD., Catholic University of Chile, 1930; m. Nellie Elizabeth Fulmer, Aug. 25, 1896; children—Harold Glenn (dec.), Lida Marguerite, Dorothy Grace (dec.). Asst. chemist Neb. Agrl. Expt. Sta., 1899-1901; asst. chemist, 1901, chemist, 1903, dir., 1907-13, Wash. Agrl. Expt. Sta.; prof. agrl. chemistry, Wash. State Coll., 1907-13; prof. plant chemistry, 1913-17, dean dept. of agr., 1917-21, U. of Minn., also asst. dir. Minn. Agrl. Expt. Sta., 1916-17, dir., 1917-21; dir. N.Y. Agrl. Expt. Sta., 1921-23; dir. expt. stations, N.Y. State Coll. Agr., 1923-27; pres. Mass. State Coll., 1927—. Apptd. by President Coolidge, mem. President's Agrl. Commn., 1924. Republican. Conglist. Mason (K.T.). Editor Jour. Am. Soc. Agronomy, 1922-27. Author: Chemistry of Plant Life, 1921. Home: Hillside, Amherst, Mass. Died Dec. 6, 1933.

THAW, Mary Copley; b. Appleby Manor, Pa.; d. Josiah and Margaret Copley; m. William Thaw (dir. Pa. R.R. and v.p. and dir. in other rys. and large owner in Red Star and Am. Steamship Lines), who died 1889. Mr. Thaw was a liberal patron of art, science and edn. Mrs. Thaw has founded, in his memory, fellowships for scientific research in Harvard and Princeton univs. Home: Pittsburgh, Pa. Died June 9, 1929.

THAXTER, Roland, botanist; b. Newton, Mass., Aug. 28, 1858; s. Levi L. and Celia (Laighton) T.; A.B., Harvard, 1882, Ph.D., and A.M., 1888; m. Mabel Gray Freeman, June 8, 1887; children—Charles Eliot (dec.), Katharine, Elizabeth, Edmund Lincoln. Asst. in biology, Harvard, 1886-88; mycologist, Conn. Agrl. Expt. Sta., 1888-1891; asst. prof. cryptogamic botany, 1891-1901, prof., 1901-19, prof. emeritus, 1919—, Harvard. Fellow Am. Acad. Arts and Sciences, A.A.A.S. Contbr. scientific publs. Home: Kittery Point, Me. Died 1932.

THAYER, Abbott Handerson, artist; b. Boston, Aug. 12, 1849; s. William Henry (M.D.) and Ellen (Handerson) T.; g.s. Gideon F. T., founder Chauncy Hall Sch., Boston; ed. Chauncy Hall Sch., 1863-66; École des Beaux Arts, Paris, mainly under Gérôme, 1875-79; m. Kate Bloede, June 5, 1875; m. 2d, Emeline B. Beach, Sept. 3, 1891. Painted animals from childhood; at 16 decided to make painting his profession; painted portraits and occasional landscapes, 1879-91, after that chiefly ideal figure pictures, including one mural decoration; was discoverer of the law of the protective coloration of the animal kingdom, first made pub. 1896, in article reprinted in Smithsonian report, 1897. N.A., 1901; mem. Am. Acad. Arts and Letters, L'Insigne Reale Accademia Romana delle Belle Arti Denominata di San Luca; was pres. Soc. Am. Artists, 2 yrs. Joint author with his son of Concealing Coloration in the Animal Kingdom, 1909. Home: Monadnock, N.H. Died May 29, 1921.

THAYER, Addison Sanford, physician; b. Medway, Mass., Aug. 5, 1858; s. Addison Parsons and Lydia Sanford (Partridge) T.; A.B., Harvard, 1881; M.D., Bowdoin Med. Sch., 1886, Harvard Med. Sch., 1888; studied in Germany, and in New York, Phila., and Baltimore; hon. Sc.D., Bowdoin College, 1921; m. Ida Lawrence Greene, Oct. 8, 1891. Teacher high sch., Portland, 1881-85; house officer Me. Gen. Hosp., 1886-87, McLean Hosp., Mass., 1887-88; practiced in Portland, 1888—; prof. medicine and dean, 1912-21, Bowdoin Med. Sch.; visiting phys. Me. Gen. Hosp., 1894— (pres. staff, 1911—). Pres. Me. Med. Assn., 1921. Home: Portland, Me. Died Dec. 14, 1923.

THAYER, Amos Madden, U.S. circuit judge, 8th circuit, Aug. 9, 1894—; b. Mina, N.Y., Oct. 10, 1841; s. Ichabod and Fidelia (La Due) T.; grad. Hamilton Coll., Clinton, N.Y., 1862 (LL.D., 1892). Served in Civil war 3 yrs. as 1st lt. U.S. Signal Corps; settled in St. Louis, Feb. 1866; admitted to bar, 1868; circuit judge, St. Louis, 1876-86; U.S. dist. judge, Eastern dist. Mo., from Feb. 24, 1887, until 1894; m. Sidney Hunton Brother, Dec. 22, 1880. Home: St. Louis, Mo. Died 1905.

THAYER, Benjamin Bowditch, mining engr.; b. San Francisco, Calif., Oct. 20, 1862; s. Benjamin Bowditch and Lucy W. (Phipps) T.; Ph.B., Lawrence Scientific Sch. (Harvard), 1885; m. Marie C. Renouard, Jan. 29, 1890. Began in employ Anaconda Copper Mining Co., 1885, of which was pres., 1908, until its absorption, 1915, by the Amalgamated Copper Co.; pres. Raritan Copper Works, Anaconda Sales Co., Electrolytic Zinc Process Co., Santiago Mining Co.; v.p. Anaconda Copper Mining Co., Internat. Smelting Co., Potrerillos Ry. Co., Andes Copper Mining Co., Chile Copper Co., Chile Exploration Co. Mem. Naval Cons. Board, 1915 (chmn.). Republican. Home: New York, N.Y. Died Feb. 22, 1933.

THAYER, Charles Paine, physician; b. West Randolph, Vt., Jan. 22, 1843; s. Samuel White and Sarah L. (Pratt) T.; served in Civil War, 1861-65; M.D., U. of Vt., 1865 (hon. A.M.). Has served as health officer and city phys. Burlington, Vt.; surgeon N.P. R.R.; prof. anatomy and sec. faculty Tufts Coll. Med. Sch., 1893-1909; retired from active practice. Compiler Medical Directory of Vermont. Home: Philadelphia, Pa. Deceased.

THAYER, Emma Homan, author, artist; b. New York, Feb. 13, 1842; d. George W. and Emma Homan; ed. Rutgers Coll., N.Y.; studied art in Nat. Acad. Design, New York; one of original mems. Art League of New York; exhibited many figure paintings at Nat. Acad.; m. George A. Graves (died 4 yrs. later); 2d, Elmer A. Thayer, 1877. Moved to Colo., 1882; made paintings of the flora of that region. Author: Wild Flowers of Colorado, 1885; Wild Flowers of Pacific Coast, 1887; The English American, 1889; Petronilla, the Sister, 1898; A Legend of Glenwood Springs, 1900; Dorothy Scudder's Science, 1901. Home: Denver, Colo. Died 1908.

THAYER, Ernest Lawrence; b. Lawrence, Mass., Aug. 14, 1863; s. Edward Davis and Ellen (Darling) T.; A.B., Harvard, 1885; m. Rosalind Buel Hammett, Sept. 9, 1913. Journalist with Hearst Newspapers, 1886-88; editor in chief of the Harvard Lampoon until 1885; wrote a number of ballads for San Francisco Examiner, 1887-88, for the New York Journal, 1896-97; author of famous poem, "Casey at the Bat," June 1888. Home: Santa Barbara, Calif. Died Aug. 21, 1940.

THAYER, Eugene Van Rensselaer, banker; b. Boston, Mass., Sept. 27, 1881; s. Eugene Van Rensselaer and Susan (Spring) T.; A.B., Harvard, 1904; m. Gladys Brooks, Sept. 3, 1903; m. 2d, Mrs. Elizabeth Harding Prince, June 30, 1923. Brokerage business, Boston, 1904-12; pres. Merchants' Nat. Bank, 1912-17; pres. Chase Nat. Bank, New York, 1918-21; was chmn. bd. Bankers & Shippers Ins. Co. (dir.); chmn.

exec. com. Central Trust Co. of Ill. (Chicago), 1929-31; partner firm Herrick, Berg & Co., brokers; dir. many companies; apptd. co-receiver Miss. Valley Utilities Investment Co., 1932. Episcopalian. Home: New York, N.Y. Died Jan. 1, 1937.

THAYER, Ezra Ripley, lawyer; b. Milton, Mass., Feb. 21, 1866; s. James Bradley and Sophia B. (Ripley) T.; bro. of William Sydney T.; A.B., Harvard, 1888, A.M., 1891, LL.B., 1891; (LL.D., Brown, 1912); m. Ethel Randolph Clark, June 23, 1898. Admitted to bar at Boston, 1891; mem. Brandeis, Dunbar & Nutter, 1896-1900, of Storey, Thorndike, Palmer & Thayer, 1900-10; Dane prof. law and dean, Law Sch. of Harvard U., Apr. 1910—. Home: Boston, Mass. Died Sept. 1915.

THAYER, George Augustine, clergyman; b. Randolph, Mass., Dec. 6, 1839; s. Elihu and Elizabeth (Tirrell) T.; grad. Harvard Div. Sch., 1869; (S.T.D., Antioch, O., 1886); m. Katherine T. Hathaway, Dec. 22, 1880. Served in 2d Mass. Inf., Army of the Potomac, and Army of the Cumberland, 1862-65. Ordained Unitarian ministry, 1869; pastor Boston, 1869-82, 1st Congl. Ch. (Unitarian), Cincinnati, 1882-1916 (pastor emeritus). Mem. Boston Sch. Bd., 1873-82. Home: Cincinnati, O. Died Oct. 4, 1925.

THAYER, Harry Bates, retired corp. officer; b. Northfield, Vt., Aug. 17, 1858; s. James Carey Barrell and Martha Jane (Pratt) T.; A.B., Dartmouth College, 1879, A.M., same college, 1915, LL.D., 1929; m. Carrie M. Ransom, Apr. 26, 1887; children—Dorothy (Mrs. F. C. Noble), Ruth (Mrs. W. W. Weeks), John Alden. Clerk, 1881-83, mgr., 1883-1902, v.p., 1902-08, v.p. and gen. mgr., Mar.-Oct. 1908, pres., 1908-19, chmn. bd., 1919-Dec. 6, 1921, dir., 1902-21, Western Electric Co.; v.p., 1909-15, and again, 1918-19, dir., 1914-15, pres., dir. and mem. exec. com., 1919-25, chmn. bd., Jan. 20, 1925-Aug. 17, 1928, Am. Telephone and Telegraph Co. Trustee Dartmouth Coll. Home: New Canaan, Conn. Died Sept. 3, 1936.

THAYER, Harry Irving, congressman; b. Pembroke, Mass., Sept. 16, 1869; s. Wendell Phillips and Amelia (Josselyn) T.; descendant of John Alden and Myles Standish of the Mayflower; ed. pub. schs., Hanover, Mass.; m. Emma Bates, Dec. 31, 1891; children—Lloyd J., Raymond H., W. Phillips. Began mfr. of leather in Boston as Thayer, Foss & Co., 1894; incorporated, 1905, as the Thayer-Foss Co., of which is pres. and treas.; dir. Wakefield Trust Co. Dir. N.E. Shoe and Leather Assn. Republican. Conglist. Mason, Odd Fellow. Home: Wakefield, Mass. Died Mar. 10, 1926.

THAYER, James Bradley, prof. of law, Harvard, 1874—; b. Haverhill, Mass., Jan. 15, 1831; s. Abijah Wyman and Susan (Bradley) T.; grad. Harvard, 1852; grad. Harvard Law School, 1856; (LL.D., Harvard, 1894, Iowa State Univ., 1891); admitted to bar (Boston), 1856, and practiced there till 1874; master in chancery, 1864; m. Sophia Bradford, d. Rev. Samuel Ripley, of Concord, Mass., April 24, 1861. Author: A Western Journey with Mr. Emerson, 1884; The Origin and Scope of the American Doctrine of Constitutional Law, 1893; The Teaching of English Law in Universities; Cases on Evidence, 1892; Cases on Constitutional Law, 1895; The Development of Trial by Jury, 1896; A Preliminary Treatise on Evidence at the Common Law, 1898. Home: Cambridge, Mass. Died 1902.

THAYER, John Adams, publisher; b. Boston, Feb. 20, 1861; s. John Adams and Arvilla (Skinner) T.; ed. pub. and high schs., Cambridge, Mass.; m. Marie E. Dickie, June 22, 1893. Printer and typefounder; adv. mgr. Ladies' Home Journal, 1892-98; adv. dir. The Delineator, 1889-1903; in April 1903, joined in organizing The Ridgway-Thayer Co., publishers of Everybody's Mag.; retired 1906; resided in Paris, 1906-11; publisher and owner, Smart Set Mag., 1911-14; dir. gen. of Philippine Publicity in U.S., 1915; exec. officer Periodical Publishers' Assn. America, 1917-20; treas. Borden Bookstack Co., 1927; cons. typographer and printing engr., 1928—. Mem. or chmn. Westport Bd. of Finance, 1917-27. Author: Astir, a Publisher's Life Story, French edition, Les Étapes du Succès. Home: Westport, Conn. Died Feb. 21, 1936.

THAYER, John Alden, congressman; b. Worcester, Mass., Dec. 22, 1857; s. Eli T. (mem. Congress, 1857-61) and Caroline Maria (Capron) T.; A.B., Harvard, 1879; LL.B., Columbia, 1889; m. Maude Albee, June 20, 1906. In law practice at Worcester, 1890—; mem. Thayer & Perry, 1897-1915. Clerk, Central Dist. Ct., Worcester, 1892-96; Dem. nominee for atty. gen. of Mass., 1906; mem. 62d Congress (1911-13), 3d Mass. Dist.; postmaster of Worcester, Apr. 1, 1915—. Democrat. Episcopalian. Home: Worcester, Mass. Died July 31, 1917.

THAYER, John Borland, ry. official; b. Philadelphia, Apr. 21, 1862; ed. U. of Pa. Clerk in auditor's office, Empire Fast Freight Line, 1881-83; clerk gen. freight dept., soliciting agt., Pa. R.R., 1883-89; div. freight agt., Northern Central Ry. and Baltimore & Potomac R.R. at Baltimore, 1892-94; asst. gen. freight agt. and gen. freight agt., 1894-1903, 5th v.p., 1903-05, 4th v.p., 1905-09, 3d v.p., Mar. 24, 1909—, Pa. R.R. Home: Haverford, Pa. Died Apr. 15, 1912.

THAYER, John Eliot, ornithologist; b. Boston, Mass., Apr. 3, 1862; s. Nathaniel and Cornelia (Van Rensselaer) T.; (mother a dau. of Stephen Van Rensselaer, of Albany, the last Patroon); A.B., Harvard, 1885, hon. A.M., 1910; m. Evelyn Duncan Forbes, June 22, 1886; children—John E., Evelyn, Nora Forbes, Natalie, Duncan Forbes. Trustee of the Clinton Savings Bank. Chmn. selectmen Town of Lancaster; mem. staff of Gov. William E. Russell, 3 yrs. Mem. board Am. Unitarian Assn. He built a museum in town of Lancaster, which is open to the public and has one of the most complete collections of N.Am. birds in the world. Fellow Am. Acad. Arts and Sciences. Home: Lancaster, Mass. Died July 22, 1933.

THAYER, John M., judge; b. Thompson, Conn., Mar. 15, 1847; s. Charles D. and Lucy E. (Nichols) T.; A.B., Yale, 1869; unmarried. Read law with Judge James A. Hovey, Norwich, Conn., and was his law partner at Norwich, 1872-76; partner of brother, Charles F. T., 1881-89; judge City Ct. of Norwich, 1875-77; state's atty., New London Co., 1883-89; judge of Superior Ct. of Conn., 1889-1907; asso. judge Supreme Ct. of Errors of Conn., 1907—. Democrat. Episcopalian. Home: Norwich, Conn. Died Jan. 13, 1924.

THAYER, John Milton, lawyer; b. Bellingham, Mass., Jan. 24, 1820; s. Elias and Ruth T.; grad. Brown Univ.; studied law; admitted to Neb. bar; m. Mary Torrey Allen, 1843. Lived some time in Washington, in Neb., 1854—; brig. gen. and maj. gen. Territorial forces operating against Indians, 1855-61; captured Pawnees and placed them on reservation, 1859; col. and brig. gen. U.S. vols., 1861-65; assisted Gen. Sherman in operations against Vicksburg; U.S. senator, 1867-71; gov. Wyoming Ty., 1875-79; dept. comdr. G.A.R., Neb., 1886; gov. Neb., 1887-93. Home: Lincoln, Neb. Died 1906.

THAYER, Joseph Henry, prof. of New Testament criticism and interpretation Divinity School, Harvard, 1884—; from 1901 emeritus; b. Boston, Mass., Nov. 7, 1828; s. Joseph Helyer and Martha Stevens (Greenough) T.; grad. Harvard, 1850; (D.D., Yale, 1873; Harvard, 1884; Princeton, 1896; Litt.D., Dublin, 1892); Andover Theol. Sem., 1857; pastor Salem, Mass., 1859-64; prof. sacred literature Andover Theol. Sem., 1864-82. Author: A Greek-English Lexicon of the New Testament; trans. Winer's N.T. Grammar (Andover, 1869); trans. of Buttmann's N.T. Grammar (ib., 1873); Biog. Sketch of Ezra Abbot, 1884; editor of Abbot's Critical Essays, 1888; Notes on Scrivener's Plain Introduction, etc., 1885; etc. Home: Cambridge, Mass. Died 1901.

THAYER, Lucius Harrison, clergyman; b. Westfield, Mass., Nov. 28, 1857; s. Lucius Fowler and Martha Ann (Harrison) T.; A.B., Amherst, 1882; B.D., Yale Div. Sch., 1888; Dwight fellow, Yale, 1889; D.D., Dartmouth, 1909; m. Helen Chadwick Rand, June 29, 1892; children—Dorothy Goldthwait (Mrs. Theodore A. Greene), Lucius Ellsworth, Sherman Rand. Ordained Congl. ministry, 1891; pastor North Ch., Portsmouth, N.H., 1890-1928 (emeritus). Pres. N.H. Congl. Conf. Progressive Republican. Home: Dublin, N.H., and Newton, Mass. Died Sept. 20, 1931.

THAYER, Martin Russell, jurist; b. Petersburg, Va., Jan. 27, 1819; ed. partly at Mt. Pleasant Classical Inst. and partly at Amherst Coll.; grad. Univ. of Pa., 1840 (A.M., LL.D.); admitted to bar, Phila., Sept. 1842; apptd. by gov. to revise revenue laws of Pa., 1862; mem. Congress, 1863-67 (chmn. Com. on Private Land Claims; mem. Bankrupt Law and other coms., 38th and 39th Congresses); judge dist. court, Phila., 1867; apptd. pres. judge court of common pleas, 1874; resigned, Oct. 1896, after about 30 yrs. on the bench; for over 30 yrs. deputy to Episcopal diocesan conv. of Pa. Author: The Duties of Citizenship; The Great Victory (of the Civil war), Its Cost and Its Value; The Law Considered as a Progressive Science; The Philippines: What Is Demanded of the United States by the Obligations of Duty and National Honor. Home: Philadelphia, Pa. Died 1906.

THAYER, Nathaniel, capitalist; A.B., Harvard, 1871. Pres. Eastern Ky. Ry. Co., Hamilton Woolen Co., St. Mary's Mineral Land Co.; v.p. Champion Copper Co., Chicago Junction Rys. & Union Stock Yards Co.; dir. U.S. Steel Corp., N.Y.,N.H.&H. R.R., St.L.&S.F. R.R. Co., Old Colony R.R. Co., Am. Bell Telephone Co., etc.; trustee of Suffolk Savings Bank for Seamen and Others, Cushing Real Estate Trust, Municipal Real Estate Trust. Trustee of Mass. Gen. Hosp., McLean Hosp., Convalescent Home in Waverly; mem. corp. Mass. Inst. Tech. Home: Boston, Mass. Died 1911.

THAYER, Rufus Hildreth, judge; b. Plymouth, Mich., June 29, 1849; s. Rufus and Hersilora Eliza (Utley) T.; A.B., U. of Mich., 1870, A.M., 1874 (LL.D., 1911); LL.B., Law Dept. George Washington U., 1874; m. Harriet Isabella, d. William Barnes, of Albany, N.Y., and g.d. of Thurlow Weed, Jan. 12, 1905. Admitted to bar, Supreme Ct., D.C., 1874; chief law clerk supervising architect's office, Treasury Dept., Washington, 1875-85; in practice at Washington, 1885-1909; judge U.S. Ct. for China, Jan. 1, 1909-Dec. 31, 1913. Republican. Member bar of U.S. Supreme Ct., U.S. Ct. of Claims, Supreme Ct. and Ct. of Appeals, D.C. Judge advocate gen. D. of C. N.G., 1894-1902; mem. sch. board, Washington, D.C., 1894-98; trustee Pub. Library, 1903-09, Girls Reform Sch., 1906-09. Home: Albany, N.Y. Died July 12, 1917.

THAYER, Samuel Richard, lawyer; b. Richmond, N.Y., Dec. 12, 1837; s. George and Phebe (Wood) T.; grad. Union Coll., 1860, LL.D., 1892; studied law; admitted to bar, 1864; unmarried. U.S. minister to Netherlands, 1889-93. Republican. Died 1909.

THAYER, Stephen Henry, banker, author; b. New Ipswich, N.H., Dec. 16, 1839; s. Stephen and Joanna (Pond) T.; ed. Appleton Acad., New Ipswich, N.H.; m. Emma F. Halsted, Nov. 25, 1863. Engaged in banking, and mem. New York Stock Exchange. Financial editor Christian Union and Outlook, 1883-94. Author: Songs of Sleepy Hollow, 1886; Songs from Edgewood, 1902; Daughters of the Revolution (novel), 1900. Died Dec. 16, 1919.

THAYER, Theodora W., artist; b. Milton, Mass., 1868; d. James Bradley and Sophia Bradford T.; pupil of Joseph De Camp. Mem. Soc. of Am. Miniature Painters. Exhibits annually at Phila. Acad. Fine Arts and Soc. Am. Artists; exhibited at Paris Expn., 1900; received gold medal, La. Purchase Expn., St. Louis, 1904. Home: Cambridge, Mass. Died 1905.

THAYER, Walter Nelson, Jr., M.D.; b. Troy, N.Y., July 5, 1875; s. Walter Nelson and Adelaide (Briggs) T.; student Troy Acad., 1893-95, U. of Vt., 1895; M.D., New York U. Med. Sch., 1897; m. Adelaide H. McDonell, June 20, 1899; children—Harold (dec.), Harry M., Walter Nelson III. Physician Conn. State Prison, 1898-1900; in pvt. practice, 1900-04; asst. physician Clinton Prison, Dannemora, N.Y., 1904-13; physician Eastern N.Y. Reformatory, Napanoch, N.Y., 1913-20, supt., 1920-21; supt. Instn. for Defective Delinquents, 1921-29; supt. of prisons, State of Md., 1929-30; commr. of correction, State of N.Y., 1930—, and mem. of cabinets of Gov. Roosevelt and Gov. Lehman. Methodist. Mason. Home: Napanoch, N.Y. Died Jan. 6, 1936.

THAYER, William Armour, organist; b. Brooklyn, N.Y., Oct. 5, 1874; s. Joseph S. and Jane H. (Brown) T.; grad. Adelphi Acad., Brooklyn, 1892; pupil of John Hyatt Brewer (organ), Dudley Buck (theory), John Dennis Mehan (voice); m. Leah Hutchinson, Oct. 19, 1897. Began playing organ at 16; dir. Coral Soc. concerts, 1898-99; organist, St. James' P.E. Ch., Brooklyn, 1893-1914, St. Mark's M.E. Ch., Flatbush, 1914-20, Emmanuel Bapt. Ch., Brooklyn, 1920—. Prof. music, Adelphi Coll., 1907—; conductor Apollo Club, Brooklyn, 1928—. Republican. Episcopalian. Home: Brooklyn, N.Y. Died Dec. 9, 1933.

THAYER, William Roscoe, author; b. Boston, Mass., Jan. 16, 1859; s. Frederick W. and Maria (Phelps) T.; fitted for coll. under tutor in Europe; A.B., Harvard, 1881, A.M., 1886; (LL.D., Western Reserve, 1913; Litt.D., Harvard Univ., 1913, Brown Univ., 1913; L.H.D., Williams College, 1913, Yale Univ., 1914); m. Elizabeth H. Ware, 1893. Asst. editor Phila. Evening Bulletin, 1882-85; editor Harvard Graduates' Mag., 1892-1915. Overseer, Harvard U., 1913-19, 1920—. Del. Harvard Coll. and Am. Hist. Assn. to Internat. Hist. Congress, Rome, 1903, and to Italian Hist. Congress, Milan, 1906. Knight of Order of Crown of Italy, 1902; Knight Order of Saints Maurizio and Lazzaro, Italy, 1917. Fellow Am. Acad. Arts and Letters, Am. Acad. Arts and Sciences; mem. numerous hist. societies. Author: Confessions of Hermes, 1884; Hesper, 1888; The Best Elizabethan Plays, 1890; The Dawn of Italian Independence, 1893; Poems, New and Old, 1894; History and Customs of Harvard University, 1898; Throne-Makers, 1899; A Short History of Venice, 1905; Italica, 1908; Life and Times of Cavour, 2 vols., 1911; Life and Letters of John Hay, 2 vols., 1915; Germany vs. Civilization, 1916; Letters of John Holmes (edited), 1917; Theodore Roosevelt—An Intimate Biography, 1919; Out of Their Own Mouths (introduction), 1917; Collapse of Superman, 1917. Awarded gold medal for biography, Nat. Inst. Arts and Letters, 1918; foreign fellow, Royal Acad. of the Lincei, Rome, Brit. Royal Hist. Society. Home: Cambridge, Mass. Died Sept. 7, 1923.

THAYER, William Sydney, M.D.; b. Milton, Mass., June 23, 1864; s. James B. and Sophia B. (Ripley) T.; A.B., Harvard, 1885 (Phi Beta Kappa; pres. 1929), M.D., 1889; LL.D., Washington Coll., Chestertown, Md., 1907, Edinburgh U., 1927, McGill U., 1929; hon. Dr. U. of Paris, 1928; Sc.D. from U. of Chicago; m. Susan Chisolm, d. late Benjamin Huger Read, of Charleston, S.C., Sept. 3, 1901. Visiting phys. Johns Hopkins Hosp.; prof. emeritus of medicine, Johns Hopkins U. (Phi Beta Kappa). Mem. Bd. Overseers, Harvard, two terms; mem. Bd. Trustees, Carnegie Inst. of Washington, 1929. Fellow Am. Acad. Arts and Sciences; mem. numerous Am. and fgn. societies. Maj. and dep. commr. Am. Red Cross Mission to Russia, June 1917-Jan. 1918; maj., col. and brig. gen. Med. Corps, U.S.A., and chief consultant med. services, A.E.F., in France, Mar. 1918-Jan. 1919; became brig. gen. Medical Sect. O.R.C., U.S.A.; brig. gen. Auxiliary, U.S.A., 1929. Awarded distinction badge, Red Cross of Russia, 1918; D.S.M. (U.S.), 1919; Comdr. Legion of Honor, France, 1928; Bright medalist, Guy's Hosp., London, 1927. Author: Lectures on the Malarial Fevers, 1897; (with Dr. Hewetson) The Malarial Fevers of Baltimore (Johns Hopkins Hosp. Reports), 1895; Studies on Bacterial Endocarditis (pub. by same), 1925; America—1917, and Other Verse, 1926. Home: Baltimore, Md. Died Dec. 10, 1932.

THAYER, William Wallace, lawyer, governor; b. Lima, N.Y., July 15, 1827; admitted to N.Y. bar, 1851; practiced Tonawanda, N.Y., 1851-62; moved to Lewiston, Idaho (then in Oregon), 1862; was member legislature; dist. atty., 3d judicial dist., 1866-67; removed to Portland; gov., 1878-82; judge supreme court, 1884-90; m. Semanth Vincent, Nov. 11, 1852. Home: Portland, Ore. Died 1899.

THAYER, William Wentworth, lawyer, banker; b. Concord, N.H., Apr. 15, 1884; s. William Fiske and Sarah Clarke (Wentworth) T.; B.A., Harvard, 1905, LL.B., 1910; Rhodes scholar from N.H., 1905-07, B.A., Oxford, 1908, M.A., 1913; unmarried. Began practice at Concord, 1910; v.p. First Nat. Bank; treas. and trustee Union Trust Co. Pros. atty. Merrimack Co., N.H., 1917-18; mem. N.H. Ho. of Rep., 1921, 23. Govt. appeal agent Selective Service Law, 1917-18; rep.; U.S. War Trade Bd. at London and Paris, 1918-19; attached to Am. Commn. to Negotiate Peace (on blockade questions), 1919. Republican. Conglist. K.P., Grange. Home: Concord, N.H. Died June 15, 1926.

THELBERG, Elizabeth Burr, M.D.; b. Bangor, Me., Oct. 29, 1860; d. Joseph J. and Sarah Buck (Morrill) Burr; M.D., Woman's Med. Coll. of the New York Infirmary, 1884; m. Dr. John Thelberg, Dec. 25, 1883; 1 dau., Elizabeth Burr (Mrs. Richard Selden Spencer). Asst. prof. eye and ear and children's diseases, Woman's Med. Coll., 1885-86; resident phys. Infant Asylum and Nursery and Children's Hosp., New York, 1886-87; prof. physiology and hygiene and resident phys., Vassar Coll., 1887—. Died Apr. 22, 1935.

THEOBALD, Samuel, ophthalmologist, otologist; b. Baltimore, Nov. 12, 1846; s. Elisha Warfield and Sarah Frances (Smith) T.; M.D., U. of Md., 1867; studied ophthalmology under Arlt and Jaeger, in Vienna, and at Royal London Ophthalmic Hosp., and otology under Politzer, in Vienna, 1870-71; m. Caroline Dexter DeWolf, Apr. 30, 1867. Began practice in Baltimore, 1867; clin. prof. ophthalmology and otology, 1894-1912, clin. prof. ophthalmology, 1912-25, prof. emeritus of ophthalmology, Jan. 1, 1925—, Johns Hopkins; ophthalmic surgeon, Johns Hopkins Hosp., 1889-1925, visiting ophthalmologist; ophthalmic surgeon, Baltimore Eye, Ear and Throat Charity Hosp., 1882—; consulting ophthalmic and aural surgeon, S. Baltimore Gen. Hosp. Author: Prevalent Diseases of the Eye, 1906. Died Dec. 20, 1930.

THERIAT, Charles James, artist; b. New York, Jan. 4, 1860; s. Edward Louis and Anna Thorn (Allen) T.: student Jules Lefèbvre and Boulanger in Paris. Hon. mention, Paris Expn., 1889; Salon, 1896, and Expn., 1900, bronze medal, Buffalo Expn., 1901. Mem. Paris Soc. Am. Painters. With Am. Red Cross, Oct. 1917-July 1919; chief of Am. Line of Communication Canteens for the French. Knight of the Legion of Honor and Médaille de la Reconnaissance Française. Home: Paris, France. Died Apr. 17, 1937.

THIEME, Hugo Paul, prof. French; b. Fort Wayne, Ind., Feb. 12, 1870; s. Frederick John and Clara Hanna T.; student Concordia Coll., Ft. Wayne, until 1890; A.B., Johns Hopkins, 1893, Ph.D., 1897; studied in Paris and Berlin, 1894-95; m. Evaleth Mabel Thurston, Sept. 6, 1899; children—Florence Léonie, Elliott. Asst. in French lit., Johns Hopkins, 1895-97; actg. head modern lang. dept., Earlham Coll., Richmond, Ind., 1897-98; instr. French, 1898-1902, asst. prof., 1902-08, jr. prof., 1908-14, prof., 1914—, U. of Mich., also chmn. dept. of Romance languages. Decorated Chevalier de la Légion d'Honneur (France), Prix de la Langue Française, 1929 (Académie Française). Republican. Conglist. Author: La Littérature Française au XIXe Siècle (Paris, France), 1897; The Technique of the French Alexandrine, 1899; Women of Modern France, 1907; Guide Bibliographique de la Littérature Française de 1800-1905 (Paris), 1907; A French Grammar (with J. R. Effinger), 1908; Essai sur l'Histoire du Vers Française, Paris, 1916; La Civilisation Française, Paris, 1924; Essais sur la Civilisation Française, Paris, 1933; Bibliographie de la Littérature Française de 1800 à 1930, 3 vols., Paris, 1933. Crowned by the Académie Française. Translator: (with A. McLaughlin) Giraud's The French Miracle and French Civilization, 1917. Editor: Malot's Sans Famille, 1902; Balzac's Cousin Pons, 1909. American corr. of La Revue d'Histoire littéraire de la France. Home: Ann Arbor, Mich. Died June 2, 1940.

THIESSEN, John Peter, farmer, banker; b. Southern Russia, June 25, 1852; s. Peter and Margaretha (Van Riesen) T.; ed. country sch., Schoenau, Russia; m. Aganetha Heidebracht, Dec. 6, 1871. Left Russia for American, 1874, with colony of 175 persons, being one of com. of 3 selected as leaders of the party; located with colony on open plain in Neb. and has been for many yrs. a leader among Russian-Am. citizens of Neb. Engaged in farming, also for many yrs. in various lines of business; pres. Mut. Fire Ins. Co.; v.p. State Bank of Jansen; treas., mgr. Farmers' Coöperative Telephone Co. Pres. Jefferson Co. Agrl. Soc., 1911—; twice apptd. by gov. of Neb. del. to Nat. Live Stock Conv. Postmaster, Jansen, Neb., 4 yrs.; sch. dir., 20 yrs.; mem. Neb. Ho. of Rep., 2 terms, 1907-11. Republican. Mennonite. Home: Jansen, Neb. Died Oct. 19, 1920.

THILLY, Frank, univ. prof.; b. Cincinnati, O., Aug. 18, 1865; s. Pierre and Mary (Barth) T.; A.B., U. of Cincinnati, 1887; U. of Berlin, 1887-89, U. of Heidelberg, 1889-91; A.M., Ph.D., Heidelberg, 1891; fellow philosophy, 1891-92, instr. logic and history of philosophy, 1892-93, Sage Sch. of Philosophy, Cornell U.; LL.D., U. of Mo., 1909, U. of Cincinnati, 1913; m. Jessie, d. Prof. G. H. Matthews, of Columbia, Me., Mar. 23, 1895; children—Gertrude, Margaret, Frank (dec.). Prof. philosophy, U. of Mo., 1893-1904; prof. psychology, Princeton, 1904-06; prof. philosophy, 1906—, dean Coll. of Arts and Sciences, 1915-21, Cornell U. First mng. editor School Review, 1892-93; editor, University of Missouri Studies, 1901-04, Internat. Jour. of Ethics, 1909-14; asso. editor Kant-Studien and of Philosophical Review. Author Leibniz's Controversy with Locke, Heidelberg, 1891; An Introduction to Ethics, 1900 (transl. into German); History of Philosophy, 1914 (transl. into Japanese and Chinese). Translator: Paulsen's Introduction to Philosophy, 1895; (with W. W. Elwang) Paulsen's German Universities, 1906. Editor and translator: Weber's History of Philosophy, 1896; Paulsen's System of Ethics, 1899. Died Dec. 28, 1934.

THIRKIELD, Wilbur Patterson, bishop; b. Franklin, O., Sept. 25, 1854; s. E. B. T.; A.B., Ohio Wesleyan, 1876, A.M., 1879, D.D., 1889, LL.D., 1906; S.T.B., Boston Univ., 1881; D.D., Emory Univ., 1889; m. Mary Haven, Oct. 27, 1881; children—Gilbert Haven, Pearl (Mrs. Geo. Alexander Wood), Wilbur (dec.), Helen (Mrs. O. W. E. Cook), Norman (dec.). Entered M.E. ministry, 1878; 1st pres. Gammon Theol. Sem., Atlanta, Ga., 1883-1900; secured endowment and equipment of $600,000; elected gen. sec. Epworth League, Nov. 28, 1899; gen. sec. Freedmen's Aid and Southern Edn. Soc. of M.E. Ch., 1900-06; pres. Howard U., Washington, 1906-12; elected bishop M.E. Ch., May 1912; retired 1928. Chmn. Commn. on Worship and Music, apptd. by Gen. Conf. M.E. Ch. Pres. bd. trustees Gammon Theol. Sem. and Bennett Coll. for Women; mem. bd. trustees Meharry Med. Coll., Clark U., Howard U. (hon.). Mason. Author: The Personality and Message of the Preacher; The Higher Education of the Negro; Service and Prayers for Church and Home; The Negro and Organic Union of Methodism; The English Speaking Peoples—Will They Fail in Their Mission to the World?, 1926; Book of Common Worship for the Several Communions of the Church of Christ. Editor and compiler: Hymns of Faith and Life. Home: New York, N.Y. Deceased.

THISTLEWOOD, Napoleon B., congressman; b. Kent Co., Del., Mar. 30, 1837; s. Benjamin and Eliza T.; ed. pub. schs., Del.; removed to Ill., 1858; m. Sarah E. Taylor, Sept. 6, 1866. Enlisted in Union Army as pvt., 1862; commd. capt. Co. C, 98th Ill. Inf., Sept. 24, 1864; served in Wilder's brigade, Army of Cumberland; participated in batles of Stone River, Tullahoma, Chickamauga, Mission Ridge, etc., and Atlanta campaign; wounded, Selma, Ala., Apr. 2, 1865. Mayor of Cairo, Ill., 1879-83, 1897-1901; elected to 60th Congress to fill unexpired term of George W. Smith, deceased; reëlected 61st and 62d Congresses (1909-13), 25th Ill. Dist.; defeated for reëlection, 1912. Republican. Comdr. Dept. Ill. G.A.R., 1901. Home: Cairo, Ill. Died Sept. 16, 1915.

THOBURN, Crawford Rockwell, chancellor Consolidated Univ., Portland, Ore., 1898—; b. Nynee Tal, India, Oct. 4, 1862 (son J. M. Thoburn, D.D., LL.D., missionary bishop for India, M.E. church). Grad. Allegheny Coll., 1885, A.M. (D.D., Univ. of The Pacific). Became M.E. minister; missionary to India, 1885-87; invalid, 1887-89; prof. history Southern Kansas Coll., 1889-90; pastor Trinity Ch., New Whatcom, Wash., 1890-92; chancellor Puget Sound Univ., Tacoma, Wash., 1892-98; m. Adelaide S. Bennett, April 3, 1889. Home: Portland, Ore. Died 1900.

THOBURN, James Matthew, clergyman; b. St. Clairsville, Ohio, June 23, 1856; s. David and Elizabeth (Murdick) T.; B.A. from Allegheny Coll. in 1881, M.A., 1883 (D.D., 1893); m. Emma Frances Merchant, June 14, 1882. Ordained M.E. ministry, 1884; pastor Warren, Pa., 1880-83, Dunkirk, N.Y., 1883-84, Calcutta, India, 1884-88, Oil City, Pa., 1888-93, Duluth, Minn., 1893-95, Detroit, Mich., 1895-1900, N.S. Calvary Ch., Pittsburgh, Pa., 1900-10; dist. supt. Allegheny Dist., 1910-16; pastor Uniontown, Pa., 1916-21; pres. Beaver Coll. for Women, 1921-23; pastor Trinity Ch., Pittsburgh, 1923-25, Mary S. Brown Memorial Ch., Pittsburgh, 1925-32, Smithfield Street Ch., Pittsburgh, 1932—. Home: Pittsburgh, Pa. Died Aug. 16, 1937.

THOBURN, James Mills, bishop; b. St. Clairsville, O., Mar. 7, 1836; s. Matthew and Jane Lyle (Crawford) T.; A.B., Allegheny Coll., Pa., 1857; widower. M.E. missionary in India, 1859-1908, stationed successively at Nynee Tal, Pauri, Moradabad, Lucknow, Calcutta and Bombay, and presiding elder Indian Conf.; in U.S., 1886-88; missionary bishop in India and Malaysia, 1888-1908; retired May 1908. Author: My Missionary Apprenticeship; Missionary Sermons; India and Malaysia; Light in the East; The Deaconess and Her Vocation; Christless Nations; The Church of Pentecost, 1901; Life of Isabella Thoburn, 1903; The Christian Conquest of India. Died Nov. 28, 1922.

THOBURN, Joseph Bradfield, writer; b. Bellaire, O., Aug. 8, 1866; s. Maj. Thomas Crawford and Mary Eleanor (Crozer) T.; parents migrated to Kan. frontier, 1871; B.S., Kansas State College, 1893; D.Litt., U. of Oklahoma City, 1931; m. Rachel Caroline Conwell, June 6, 1894 (died 1931); children—Mary Eleanor, Jeanne Isabel (Mrs. A. V. Wyss). Learned the printer's trade; moved to Oklahoma City, Okla., 1899; sec. Okla. Ter. Bd. of Agr., 1902-05; directorate Okla. Hist. Soc., 1903-17, research asst., 1917-19, sec., 1919-26, curator and research dir., 1926-31, mem. directorate, 1932-37, curator, 1938; newspaper writer until 1907; instr. in history, U. of Okla., 1913-17; from 1907 he devoted attention mainly to research and writing along lines of local and Midland history. Extensive archæol. investigations in Okla., including systematic excavation of mounds, burial grounds, cave-dwellings, etc.; secured proof that numerous "natural mounds," so called, west of Miss. River and south of Mo. River were of Caddoan domiciliary origin. Methodist. Mason. Author: History of Oklahoma, 1916; Oklahoma—A History of the State and Its People (with Muriel H. Wright), 1929. Published hypothesis of tropical and subtropical civilizations and cultures and of subsequent migrations thereof, northward and eastward into the present U.S., 1938. Died Mar. 2, 1941.

THOM, Alfred Pembroke, lawyer; b. "Elkington," Northampton Co., Va., Dec. 15, 1854; s. William Alexander and Anne (Parker) T.; ed. pvt. schs., Richmond (Va.) Coll., 1 yr., U. of Va., 3 yrs. in acad. dept. and 1 yr. law dept.; LL.D., Washington and Lee Univ., 1913; m. Mrs. Virginia W. (Tunstall) Baylor, Sept. 20, 1881; 1 son, Alfred Pembroke; m. 2d, Mrs. Jessie Gertrude (Griffin) Respess, March 29, 1916. Was admitted to the bar, 1876, and practiced law at Norfolk, Va., 1878-1905; receiver, 1891-94, gen. counsel, 1894-99, Atlantic & Danville Ry. Co.; counsel in charge Atlantic & Danville Ry. lines, 1899-1902, counsel in Va., 1902-05, and gen. counsel at Washington, 1905-17, Southern Ry. Co.; gen. counsel Assn. of Ry. Executives, 1917-32, and Am. Ry. Assn., 1922-33, when became asso. gen. counsel. Mem. Va. Constl. Conv., 1901-02. Democrat. Episcopalian. Home: Washington, D.C. Died Feb. 15, 1935.

THOM, Burton Peter, M.D., author; b. Baltimore, Md., Sept. 22, 1874; s. Peter F. and Josephine M. (Clark) T.; prep. edn., pub. schs. and Friends Academy, Baltimore, Md.; M.D., Baltimore Medical College, 1897; M.A., New York U., 1931; m. Edith Eleanore Menke, Nov. 17, 1906. Gen. practice, N.Y. City, 1903—; consulting physician to hosps. of Dept. of Correction, N.Y. City. Republican. Protestant. Author: Syphilis, A Textbook, 1922; Hygeia, or Disease and Evolution, 1926; Dust to Life, 1929. Home: Lido Beach, L.I. Died May 3, 1933.

THOM, DeCourcy Wright, farmer, businessman; b. Baltimore, Md., Oct. 14, 1858; s. Joseph Pembroke and Ella L. (Wright) T.; U. of Va., 1876-80, grad. internat. and constl. law, etc., 1880; course in rhetoric, English lit., psychology, logic and metaphysics, U. of Edinburgh, 1880; m. Mary Pleasants Gordon, Oct. 29, 1885 (died 1892); children—Anne Gordon, Mary Gordon; m. 2d, Mrs. Mary Washington Stewart, d. H. Irvine Keyser, of Baltimore, June 14, 1910; children—Elizabeth Keyser, W. H. DeCourcy Wright. Banker and a stock broker, 1882-92; abandoned active business and moved to country residence, "Blakeford," in Queen Anne's Co., Md. Established cement branch of Security Cement & Lime Co.; v.p. Industrial Corp. of Baltimore City; dir., charter mem. Continental Am. Life Ins. Co. Mem. Md. Development Commn., Md. State Forestry Bd., Md.-Yorktown Sesqui-centennial Com.; chmn. Md.-George Washington Bi-centennial Commn.; member exec. com. Friends of Johns Hopkins U. Library. Was private 5th Maryland Regiment; originator, 1909, and pres. Anti-Wilson Ballot Law Assn. of Queen Anne's County; originator, 1909, and pres. Just Representation League of Md., gaining for Baltimore 2 more senators and 12 more delegates in Md. legislature; originated the idea and was active in securing the heroic bronze statue of Cecilius Calvert, Baltimore. Mem. advisory bd. Allegheny Forestry District (Md., Del., N.J., Pa.); pres. James Lawrence Kernan Hosp. and Industrial Sch. for Crippled and Deformed Children; pres. Prisoners' Aid Assn.; vice chmn. Navy Recruiting League. Democrat. Episcopalian. Author: A Brief History of Panics in the United States, 1893, 4th edit., 1916; Mid-Summer Motoring in Europe, 1916. Home: Baltimore, Md., and Queen Anne's County, Md. Died Aug. 6, 1932.

THOM, William Taylor; b. Fauquier County, Va., Apr. 27, 1849; s. John Catesby and Ada Matilda (Downman) T.; B.A., Washington Coll. (Washington and Lee U.), 1869, M.A., 1870, Litt.D., 1889; studied univs. of Berlin, Paris, and Heidelberg, 1872-75; Ph.D., Johns Hopkins, 1899; m. Emma Augusta Mertins, July 12, 1882 (died 1883); 1 dau., Emma Mertins; m. 2d, Elizabeth Porter Miller, Oct. 23, 1888 (died 1991); children—Mrs. Julia Downman Eves, William Taylor, Benjamin Miller (dec.), Lucy Lewis McReynolds, Elizabeth Thom Pearson. Asst. prof. English, Richmond (Va.) Coll., 1870-82; teacher in pvt. schs.; admitted to Va. bar, 1878; prof. English and history, Hollins (Va.) Inst., 1879-90; lecturer and teacher, pvt. schs., 1893-96; mem. editorial staff, U.S. Geol. Survey, 1902-22 (retired). Democrat. Episcopalian. Author: Shakespeare and Chaucer Examinations, 1887; The Struggle for Religious Freedom in Virginia, 1900; A Notable Beta of Yesterday (James M. M. Ambler of Jeannette Expedition). Asst. editor 2d edit. Recollections and Letters of General R. E. Lee. Home: Princeton, N.J. Died July 2, 1930.

THOMAN, Leroy Delano, lawyer; b. Salem, O., July 31, 1851; s. Jacob Somers and Mary (Sonnedecker) T.; ed. pub. schs. Ohio and Ind., and 2 yrs. at acad. S. Whitley, Ind.; m. Mary Cartwright, Mar. 29, 1876 (died 1876); m. 2d, Florence Smith, Feb. 25, 1892. Teacher 5 yrs.; admitted to bar, Aug. 1872; pros. atty. 1 yr.; judge for 6 yrs.; U.S. Civil Service Commr., 1883-86. Democrat. Home: Evanston, Ill. Died 1909.

THOMAS, Albert D., lawyer; b. Williamsport, Ind., Jan. 17, 1841; s. Horatio J. and Rebecca (Dewey) T.; B.S., M.S., Wabash Coll., Ind., 1864, A.M., 1868, LL.D., 1910; student law dept. U. of Mich., 1865-66; m. Ruth Vance, July 1878 (died 1888); 1 dau., Helen Louise (Mrs. Will H. Hays). Began practice at Crawfordsville, 1867; judge Court of Common Pleas, 1873; judge Circuit Court, 1873-79. Dir. Farmers-Merchants & Clements Trust Co. Pres. State Bd. of Pardons, Ind., 1909—; pres. bd. trustees Wabash Coll., 1916—. Republican. Presbyn. Home: Crawfordsville, Ind. Died Nov. 13, 1925.

THOMAS, Allen Clapp, college prof.; b. Baltimore, Md., Dec. 26, 1846; s. Richard H. (M.D.) and Phebe (Clapp) T.; A.B., Haverford Coll., 1865, A.M., 1882; m. Rebecca Hill Marble, Aug. 20, 1872 (died 1905). Shipping mcht., 1869-78; prof. history, 1878-1912, and librarian, 1878-1915, Haverford Coll. (emeritus). Minister Society of Friends (Quakers); presiding clerk Baltimore Yearly Meeting of Friends, 1897—. Editor Bulletin of Friends' Hist. Society of Phila., 1907—. Author: A History of the United States for Schools and Academies, 1894 (transl. into Yiddish, 1911); Family of Love or Familists, 1893; William Penn, 1895, 1896; An Elementary History of the United States, 1900; History of the Society of Friends in America (with Dr. Richard Henry Thomas), 4th edit., 1905; A History of England, 1913; A History of Pennsylvania, 1913. Died Dec. 16, 1920.

THOMAS, Arthur Lloyd, governor; b. Chicago, Ill., Aug. 22, 1851; s. Henry J. and Eleanor T.; common sch. edn. at Pittsburgh, Pa.; unmarried. Sec. of Utah Ty., 1879-87; supervisor census of Utah, 1880; spl. agt. of Govt. to collect ch. and sch. statistics, 1881; mem. commn. to compile and codify laws of Utah, 1884; mem. Utah commn., 1886-89; gov. of Utah, 1889-93; signed the 1st pub. free-sch. law for Utah; during his term the practice of plural marriages was formally renounced by the Mormon Ch. Called the 1st great Nat. Irrigation Congress at Salt Lake City, 1890, and the 1st Internat. Irrigation Congress at Los Angeles, Calif., 1891; postmaster Salt Lake City, Feb. 1, 1898-Mar. 31, 1914; now v.p. Herald-Republican Pub. Co., Salt Lake City; pres. Thomas Ins. & Investment Co. Republican. Mem. commn. to visit U.S. Mint at Phila., 1920. Home: Salt Lake City, Utah. Died Sept. 15, 1924.

THOMAS, Augustus, playwright; b. St. Louis, Mo., Jan. 8, 1857; s. Dr. Elihu Baldwin and Imogene (Garrettson) T.; ed. St. Louis pub. schs.; M.A., Williams, 1914; Litt.D., Columbia, 1921; LL.D., U. of Mo., 1923; m. Lisle Colby, Aug. 16, 1890; children—Luke Garrettson, Glory (Mrs. William Elliott, Jr.). Studied law 2 yrs. with John Colby (father of wife). Page boy 41st Congress; 6 yrs. in practical railroading, freight dept.; spl. writer and illustrator on St. Louis, Kansas City and New York newspapers; was editor and propr. of Kansas City Mirror. Has been candidate for the legislature. Democrat. Mem. Am. Acad. Arts and Letters, Nat. Inst. Arts and Letters (pres. 1914-16; gold medal for life work in drama); pres. Soc. Am. Dramatists, 1906-11; mem. Producing Manager's Assn. (exec. chmn., 1922-25). Decorated Chevalier de la Légion d'Honneur (France). Author: (dramas) Alabama; In Mizzoura; Arizona; also plays (printed for copyright purposes only): The Burglar; Colorado; Man of the World; After Thoughts; The Meddler; The Man Upstairs; Oliver Goldsmith; On the Quiet; A Proper Impropriety; That Overcoat; The Capitol; New Blood; The Hoosier Doctor; The Earl of Pawtucket; The Other Girl; Mrs. Leffingwell's Boots; The Education of Mr. Pipp; Jim De Lancey; The Embassy Ball; The Witching Hour; The Harvest Moon; As a Man Thinks; Indian Summer; Rio Grande; The Copperhead; Palmy Days; Nemesis; Still Waters; Song of the Dragon. Home: Nyack, N.Y. Died Aug. 16, 1934.

THOMAS, Augustus Orloff, educator; b. Mercer County, Ill., Feb. 21, 1863; s. William Lee and Mary Elizabeth (Cox) T.; B.Sc., Western Normal Coll., 1891; Ph.B., Amity Coll., Iowa, 1894, Ph.D., 1896; B.Ed., Neb. State Teachers Coll., Peru, 1908; LL.D., Bates, 1925, also fellow Ednl. Inst. of Scotland, 1925; m. Ellamay Colvin, June 14, 1894; children—Paul Augustus, Katheryn Colvin. Prin. schs., Cambridge, Neb., 1891-93; supt. schs., St. Paul, Neb., 1893-96, Minden, 1896-1901, Kearney, 1901-05; organizer and pres. State Normal Sch., Kearney, 1905-13; state supt. pub. instruction, Neb., 1915-16; state supt. pub. schs. of Me., July 1, 1917-29. Lecturer on ednl. topics. Republican. Member Disciples of Christ. Mason. Author: Thomas' Rural Arithmetic, 1916. Revised the J. Sterling Morton History of Nebraska (two vols.). Chmn. World Conf. on Edn., San Francisco, 1923; pres. World Federation of Edn. Assns., 1923-27, sec.-gen., 1931—. Home: Washington, D.C. Died Jan. 30, 1935.

THOMAS, Benjamin Franklin, physicist; b. Palmyra, O., Oct. 14, 1850; s. David D. and Eleanor (Evans) T.; B.S., Ripon Coll., 1874, M.S., 1877; Ph.D., Stevens Inst., Hoboken, N.J., 1880; grad. student Stevens Inst., and Mass. Inst. Tech., 1878-79; research asst. (with Prof. A. M. Mayer) Stevens Inst., 1879-80; m. Caroline P. Smith, Apr. 13, 1881. Farmer (in charge instrn. of Indians in outdoor work), Ft. Berthold (Dak.) Indian Reservation, 1875-76; instr. physics and mathematics, Carleton Coll., Northfield, Minn., 1876-79; prof. physics, U. of Mo., 1880-85; prof. physics, Ohio State U., 1885—; ex-officio state sealer of weights and measures, 1890—. Mem. bd. examiners Phila. Elec. Expn., 1884, jury of awards, Dept. Electricity, Chicago Expn., 1893; has made investigations in rapidly varying phenomena in elec. circuits, and in photometry (papers, A.A.A.S., and Am. Inst. Elec. Engrs.). Episcopalian. Republican. Home: Columbus, O. Died 1911.

THOMAS, Bryan M., supt. city schools, Feb. 1, 1891—; b. Milledgeville, Ga., 1836; s. John S. T.; ed. Oglethorpe Coll., 1851-54; grad. U.S. Mil. Acad., West Point, 1858; m. Mary Withers, Nov. 14, 1864. Three yrs. in U.S.A., 4 yrs. in C.S.A., passing through various grades from 1st lt. to brig. gen.; engaged in farming and teaching after Civil war. Democrat. Home: Dalton, Ga. Died 1905.

THOMAS, Calvin, college prof.; b. near Lapeer, Mich., Oct. 28, 1854; s. Stephen V. and Caroline L. (Lord) T.; A.B., U. of Mich., 1874, A.M., 1877 (LL.D., 1904); m. Mary Eleanor Allen, June 16, 1884. Teacher Latin and Greek, high sch., Grand Rapids, Mich., 1874-77; student of philology, Leipzig, 1877-78; instr. German, 1878-81, asst. prof., 1881-86, prof. Germanic langs. and lits., 1886-96, U. of Mich.; prof. Germanic langs. and lits., Columbia U., 1896—. Author: A Practical German Grammar, 1895; Life and Works of Schiller, 1901; German Literature (a history), 1909; Goethe, 1917. Editor: (English intro. and notes) Goethe's "Torquato Tasso," 1888; Goethe's "Faust," First Part, 1892, Second Part, 1897; Goethe's "Hermann und Dorothea," 1891; An Anthology of German Literature, 1909. Home: New York, N.Y. Died Nov. 4, 1919.

THOMAS, Carl Clapp, engineer; b. Detroit, Mich., July 14, 1872; s. George Roscoe and Caroline Melissa (Clapp) T.; Leland Stanford Jr. U., 1891-94; M.E., Sibley Coll. (Cornell U.), 1895; m. Katharine L. Nash, July 14, 1899; children—Dorothy Grace (dec.), Alfred Randall, Roscoe. Draftsman, asst. engr., chief engr. Globe Iron Works Co., Cleveland, 1895-99; chief draftsman marine dept. Md. Steel Co., 1899-1901; prof. marine engring. and naval architecture, New York U., 1901-03; asst. prof. mech. engring., U. of Calif., 1903-04; prof. marine engring., Cornell, 1904-08; prof. steam engring., U. of Wis., 1908-13; prof. mech. engring., Johns Hopkins, 1913-20; western rep. and vice pres. Dwight P. Robinson & Co., Inc., 1920—; city director of Pasadena, Calif., 1921-24; associate in engineering research, Calif. Institute Tech. Member Nat. Guard of Calif., 1889-92. Mgr. machinery fabrication of Am. Internat. Shipbuilding Corp., Phila. (on leave from Johns Hopkins), 1917-19. Author: Steam Turbines, 1906. Inventor of the Thomas electric gas meters, steam calorimeters and separators. Home: Pasadena, Calif. Died June 5, 1938.

THOMAS, Charles Mitchell, naval officer; b. Phila., Oct. 1, 1846; s. Joseph T. and Belinda J. T.; apptd. to U.S. Naval Acad. from Pa., 1861, grad. 1865; m. Ruth, d. Rear Admiral Edward Simpson, U.S.N., Nov. 3, 1874. Promoted ensign, Dec. 1, 1866; advanced through grade to rear adm., Jan. 12, 1905. Served on Shenandoah, 1865-69; Navy Yard, League Island, 1869; on Supply, 1869-70; Guerriere, 1870-71; receiving-ship Potomac, 1872; Ajax and Terror, 1872-73; at Torpedo Sta., Newport, 1873-74; on Dictator, 1874-75; at Navy Yard, Phila., 1875; Centennial Expn., 1875-77; on receiving-ship St. Louis, 1877-78; Constitution, 1878-80; at Naval Acad., 1880-84; exec. officer Hartford, 1884-87; coast survey steamer Patterson, 1887-89; hydrographic insp. coast survey, 1889-91; Bureau of Navigation, 1891-93; comd. Bennington, 1893-95; Naval Home, Phila., 1895-97; Naval War Coll., Newport, 1897; Naval Acad., 1897-98; light-house insp. 5th dist., 1898-99; comd. Lancaster, 1899, Brooklyn, 1900-01, Oregon, 1901-02, receiving-ship Franklin, 1902-04; comdt. Naval Training Sta., Newport, R.I., and 2d naval dist., 1904-05; supt. naval training service, 1905-07; comdg. 2d div. Atlantic Fleet, Jan.-Aug. 1907; comdg. 2d Squadron, Atlantic Fleet, 1907—. Home: Newport, R.I. Died 1908.

THOMAS, Charles Monroe, ophthalmologist; b. Watertown, N.Y., May 3, 1849; A.B., Central High Sch., Phila., 1868, A.M., 1874; M.D., Hahnemann Medical Coll., Phila., 1871; studied surgery in Europe, 1872-74; m. Marion Elmslie Turnbull, Apr. 18, 1876. Demonstrator of surgery, 1875-78, prof. operative surgery, ophthalmology and otology, 1878-91, dean, 1903-06; Hahnemann Med. Coll.; from 1891 devoted himself exclusively to diseases of eye and ear; retired from practice Mar. 1910. Home: West Chester, Pa. Died Jan. 14, 1916.

THOMAS, Charles Preston, surgeon; b. Lincoln, Mo., Nov. 12, 1864; s. Ely C. and Eleanor (Wainright) T.; attended State Normal Sch., Warrensburg, Mo., 1883; M.D., U. of Ore., 1888; m. Elsie A. Beckon, Nov. 6, 1901. Practiced gen. medicine, Wilbur, Fairhaven and Everett, Wash., 1890-96, surgery, Spokane, Wash., 1896-1910, Los Angeles, Calif., 1910—; has performed hundreds of major operations. Pres. First Nat. Bank in Santa Monica, Calif. Republican. Home: Santa Monica, Calif. Died Feb. 22, 1927.

THOMAS, Charles Spalding senator; b. Darien, Ga., Dec. 6, 1849; s. William B. and Caroline B. (Wheeler) T.; went to Mich. in boyhood; LL.B., U. of Mich., 1871; LL.D. from same university in 1916; m. Emma Fletcher, Dec. 29, 1873; children—Mrs. Helen T. Malburn (dec.), Edith Marie, Charles Sewell, Hubert Fletcher, George Kenneth. Practiced law at Denver, 1871-79, Leadville, 1879-85, Denver, 1885—; sr. mem. Thomas, Bryant & Lee, 1890-1903, later Thomas, Bryant & Malburn, and mem. Thomas & Thomas, 1924—. Member Dem. Nat. Com., 1884-96; gov. of Colorado, 1899-1901; temporary chmn. Dem. Nat. Conv., Kansas City, 1900; elected U.S. senator, Jan. 14, 1913, for unexpired term (1913-15), of Charles J. Hughes, deceased; reëlected for term 1915-21. Spl. counsel to the Korean Commn. at Washington, for securing the independence of Korea; spl. counsel U.S. Dept. of Justice, 1922-23. Home: Denver, Colo. Died June 24, 1934.

THOMAS, Chauncey, naval officer; b. Barryville, N.Y., Apr. 27, 1850; s. Chauncey and Margaret (Bross) T.; apptd. to U.S. Naval Acad. from Pa., 1867, and grad. 3d in class, 1871; m. Carrie Ella Flagg, Sept. 12, 1876. Promoted ensign, 1872; advanced through grades to rear adm., Mar. 10, 1910. Served on various ships and at various stations; in Nautical Almanac Office, Washington, 1878-81, 1885-86; aide to Admiral David D. Porter, 1886-91; at Hydrographic Office, Washington, 1894-96, 1900-01; exec. officer Yorktown, during Philippine insurrection, participating in several engagements; exec. officer battleship Oregon and comd. monitor Monadnock, 1899; comd. Albatross, 1901, and made scientific cruise, of 5 mos., in and about H.I.; comd. Bennington, 1902-03; comd. Maryland, at Woosung, China, 1907-08, leading U.S.N. in small arms target practice, and took battleship trophy for excellence in record target practice, 1908; insp. 3d light house dist., June 25, 1908-Jan. 26, 1910; pres. Bd. Inspection and Survey for Ships, Feb. 1-Oct. 20, 1910; comdr. 2d div. U.S. Pacific Fleet, Nov. 1, 1910-Jan. 16, 1911; then made comdr.-in-chief U.S. Pacific Fleet, flagship California; relieved Mar. 9, 1912, at Honolulu, T.H., transferred flag to U.S.S. West Virginia for passage to Navy Yard, Puget Sound; retired from active service by operation of law, Apr. 27, 1912. Mem. court martial and court of inquiry U.S.N., 1917. Mem. Calif State Council Defense, 1917. Home: Pacific Grove, Calif. Died May 9, 1919.

THOMAS, Cullen Fleming, lawyer; b. Rutherford, Tenn., June 16, 1868; s. Charles Crawford and Elizabeth (Cowan) T.; attended U.S. Naval Acad., 1885-88; LL.B. first honors, U. of Tex., 1891; LL.D., Howard Payne Coll., Brownwood, Tex., 1921; m. Maude Moore, Dec. 10, 1895; 1 dau., Margaret Elizabeth (Mrs. William A. Powe); m. 2d, Olga Sheppard, June 9, 1913; children—Cullen Sheppard, Elizabeth Cowan, Barbara Sheppard. Admitted to Tex. bar, 1891; practiced in Waco, 1892-1909; moved to

Dallas; mem. Cockrell, Gray & Thomas, 1909-13; mem. Thomas, Frank, Milam & Touchstone, 1913-27; dir. Republic Life Ins. Co. Member Texas House of Representatives, 1894-96; dist. atty., Waco, 1896-1902; chmn. Dem. State Conv., 1912; presidential elector, 1916. Declined to consider seat on Railroad Commn., 1922; delined judgeship Court of Civil Appeals, 1923. Vice chmn. Oil States Advisory Com.; pres. Tex. Centennial Commn. (to celebrate in 1936, 100 yrs. Tex. independence), 1933-35; apptd. U.S. commr. gen. for Texas Centennial Exposition by Pres. Roosevelt, Aug. 1935; selected by New York World's Fair of 1939 mem. of Nat. Adv. Com. for Texas. Trustee Baylor U., Waco. Democrat. Baptist. K.P. Home: Dallas, Tex. Died Dec. 8, 1938.

THOMAS, Cyrus, ethnologist; b. Kingsport, Tenn., July 27, 1825; s. Stephen and Maria (Rogan) T.; ed. village schs. and acad.; admitted to bar, 1851, and practiced until 1865; m. Dorothy Logan, sister of Gen. John A. Logan, of Murphysboro, Ill., June 13, 1850; m. 2d, Miss L. V. Davis, Apr. 20, 1865. County clerk Jackson Co., Ill., 1850-53; minister Evang. Luth. Ch., 1865-69; asst. on U.S. Geol. and Geog. surveys of Territories, under Ferdinand V. Hayden, 1869-73; prof. natural sciences, Southern Ill. Normal U., 1873-75; state entomologist of Ill., 1874-76; mem. U.S. Entomol. Commn., 1876-77; archeologist U.S. Bur. of Ethnology, 1882—. Author: Synopsis of the Acrididæ of North America; Noxious and Beneficial Insects of Illinois (5 vols. reports as state entomologist); Aid to the Study of Maya Codices; The Cherokees and Shawnees in Pre-Columbian Times; Mound Explorations of Bureau of American Ethnology; Prehistoric Works East of the Rocky Mountains; Introduction to American Archæology; Numeral Systems of the Mexican and Central American Tribes; The Mayan Calendar Systems; Indians of North America in Historic Times; Prehistoric North America; Languages of Mexico and Central America. Died 1910.

THOMAS, Douglas, banker; b. De La Brooke, Md., June 4, 1879; s. James (M.D.) and Ann Elizabeth (Nelson) T.; prep. edn., Charlotte Hall Mil. Acad., St. Mary's Co., Md.; student U. of Md.; m. Catherine Bowie Clagett, Oct. 19, 1905; children—Catherine Bowie Clagett (dec.), Douglas II. With Mercantile Trust & Deposit Co., Baltimore, became mem. exec. staff, serving until 1923; pres. Century Trust Co., 1923-29; was exec. v.p. Baltimore Trust Co., into which Century Trust Co. merged, 1929. Lt. and bn. adj. Md. N.G. 13 yrs. Democrat. Episcopalian. Mason. Home: Baltimore, Md. Died Sept. 13, 1933.

THOMAS, Douglas Hamilton, banker; b. Baltimore, Md., Jan. 1, 1847; s. John Hanson and Annie Campbell (Gordon) T.; ed. Univ. of Md.; m. Alice Lee Whitridge, Jan. 25, 1870. Cashier Marine Bank, Baltimore, 1878-80; cashier, 1880-86, pres., 1886-1913, Merchants' Nat. Bank; pres. Merchants-Mechanics Nat. Bank, Baltimore, 1913-16, and of its successor Merchants Mechanics First Nat. Bank, Oct. 1916—. Finance commr., Baltimore, 1886-92; commr. pub. parks, 1890-1901; mem. paving commn., 1914—. Md. commr., Centennial Expn., 1876, Jamestown Expn., 1907. Capt. and maj. 5th Regt. Md. N.G., 1870-77. Home: Baltimore, Md. Died Mar. 12, 1919.

THOMAS, Douglas Hamilton, Jr., architect; b. Baltimore, Md., Mar. 5, 1872; s. Douglas H. and Alice Lee (Whitridge) T.; A.B., Johns Hopkins, 1893; studied architecture, Mass. Inst. Tech., 1895, Paris, France, 1897-98; m. Bessie Chadwick, Jan. 5, 1901. Began practice, 1889; mem. Parker & Thomas, Baltimore and Boston, 1900-07, Parker, Thomas & Rice, 1907—. Prin. works: Hotel Belvedere, Baltimore & Ohio R.R. Co.'s office bldg., Savings Bank of Baltimore, Johns Hopkins Univ. group plan; Harvard Club bldg. (Boston), U.S. Postoffice and court houses, Huntington, W.Va., and Marblehead, Mass. Fellow Am. Inst. Architects, etc. Home: Ruxton, Md. Died June 11, 1915.

THOMAS, Earl Denison, brig. gen. U.S.A.; b. McHenry, Ill., Jan. 4, 1847; s. Edwin E. and Naomi (Patterson) T.; ed. Todd's Acad., Woodstock, Ill., 1859-61; grad. U.S. Mil. Acad., 1869; m. Clara M. Church, 1869. Pvt. and corporal Co. H, and sergt. maj. 8th Ill. Cav., Apr. 1, 1862-Apr. 23, 1865; commd. 2d lt. 5th U.S. Cav., June 15, 1869; 1st lt., Mar. 1, 1872; capt., Apr. 1, 1885; maj. insp. gen. vols., May 12, 1898; maj. 8th U.S. Cav., Feb. 14, 1899; hon. disch. from vol. service, Mar. 7, 1899; transferred to 5th U.S. Cav., May 23, 1899; insp. gen., Feb. 28, 1901; lt. col. 13th Cav., Nov. 16, 1901; col. 7th Cav., Apr. 19, 1903; transferred to 11th Cav., Apr. 21, 1903; brig. gen. U.S.A., Apr. 18, 1907. Bvtd. 1st lt., Feb. 27, 1890, "for gallant services in action against Indians nr. Ft. McPherson, Neb., June 8, 1870"; capt. for same in action against Indians at the Caves, Ariz., Dec. 28, 1872, and campaign against Indians in Ariz., 1874. Served at various frontier posts and in Indian country, 1870-98, in Spanish-Am. War, P.R., P.I. and Cuba; second intervention of Cuba, 1906, in comd. 11th U.S. Cav. hdqrs. Pinar del Rio, Cuba; in charge of the Province of Pinar del Rio, 1906-07; in comd. of Dept. of Colorado, 1907-11; in charge of operations on the border of Ariz. and N.M. in Mexican troubles, 1910; retired Jan. 4, 1911. Home: Laurel, Md. Died Feb. 17, 1921.

THOMAS, Eben Briggs, railway pres. Was several yrs. mgr. of C.,C.,C.&I. Ry. until 1885; 2d v.p. and gen. mgr. Richmond & Danville and Ga. Pacific; 2d v.p., 1888-90, 1st v.p., 1890-94, pres., 1894-95, N.Y.,L.E.&W.; also gen. mgr., 1890-91, 1st v.p., 1891-94, Chicago & Erie R.R.; one of receivers N.Y.,L.E.&W., 1894-95, until it was reorganized as the Erie R.R., of which was pres., 1895-1901, and chmn. of bd., 1901-03. Pres. L.V. R.R. Co., Dec. 1902-Feb. 1917, then chmn. bd. and exec. com.; dir. Lehigh Valley Coal Co, Lehigh & Hudson River R.R. Co., etc. Home: Morristown, N.J. Died Sept. 4, 1919.

THOMAS, Edith Matilda, author; b. Chatham, O., Aug. 12, 1854; d. Frederick J. and Jane Louisa (Sturges) T.; ed. Geneva, O., Normal Inst.; from 1888 in New York. Author: Lyrics and Sonnets, 1887; In Sunshine Land, 1895; In the Young World, 1895; A Winter Swallow, with Other Verse, 1896; The Dancers, 1903; Cassia and Other Verse, 1905; The Children of Christmas (verse), 1908; The Guest at the Gate (verse), 1909; The White Messenger, 1915; The Flower from the Ashes, 1915. Died Sept. 13, 1925.

THOMAS, Flavel Shurtleff, physician, author; b. Hanson, Mass., Sept. 7, 1852; s. Isaac and Abby (Shurtleff) T.; ed. Phillips Acad., Andover, Mass.; M.D., Harvard, 1874; Cornell U.; M.A., Shurtleff Coll., 1876; Boston U., Ill. Wesleyan U., Mass. Inst., Tech.; V.S., Montreal Veterinary Coll., 1879; B.Sc., Syracuse U., 1885, M.Sc., 1886; D.V.Sc., McGill U., 1890; (LL.D., Shurtleff, 1892; diploma, Dec. 1, 1907, as one of Authors' League of Am. Health League of the A.A.A.S.); m. Caroline Moore Smith, July 9, 1879. Has devoted much time to zoölogy, comparative medicine, preventive medicine and univ. edn., administration, and degrees; town phys., sch. phys., insp. of animals, phys. to Gordon Rest, and to Maquan Sanatorium. One of editors of Standard Dictionary of the English Language. Author: A Dictionary of University Degrees; also of the work on univ. degrees and education in the Standard Dictionary. Mason. Home: South Hanson, Mass. Died Nov. 26, 1922.

THOMAS, Frank Morehead, clergyman; b. Bowling Green, Ky., July 3, 1868; s. Richard Curd (M.D.) and Elizabeth (Wright) T.; A.B., Ogden Coll., Bowling Green, Ky., 1886, A.M., 1892; B.D., Vanderbilt U., Nashville, Tenn., 1893; (D.D., Ky. Wesleyan Coll., Winchester, Ky., 1906); m. Stella F. Phillips, Jan. 18, 1900. Ordained ministry M.E. Ch., S., 1893; pastor Louisville, 1893-97, Henderson, Ky., 1899-1903, Louisville, 1903-04, Owensboro, 1904-08, Morganfield, 1908-10; presiding elder, Louisville Dist., 1910-14; pastor Fourth Avenue Church, Louisville, 1914-18; became book editor M.E. Ch., S.; editor Meth. Quarterly Rev. Fraternal messenger M.E. Ch., S., to Gen. Conf. M.E. Ch., 1912; sec. Meth. Joint Commn.; sec. Federal Council of Methodism; exec. com. Federal Council Chs. of Christ in America; mem. Ecumenical Conf. of Methodism at Toronto, 1911; pres. Louisville Conf. Bd. of Edn. Chaplain 3d Ky. Inf., 1894-1916; served in Spanish-Am. War, in Cuba. Author: The Apostolic Church, 1906; A Short Guide to Bookdom, 1903; The Coming Presence, 1913. Home: Nashville, Tenn. Died May 9, 1921.

THOMAS, George Herbert, clergyman; b. Providence, R.I., Mar. 29, 1872; s. Charles Lloyd and Sarah Sophia (Barstow) T.; B.A., Yale, 1895, M.A., 1896; B.D., Episcopal Theol. Sem., Cambridge, Mass.; D.D., Western Sem., Evanston, Ill.; m. Margaret Codrington Foster, Feb. 8, 1899; children—Margaret Codrington (Mrs. John Alden), Arthur Abbot, Allen Foster. Ordained deacon, 1898, priest, 1899, P.E. Ch.; curate St. Mark's Ch., Minneapolis, Minn., 1900; missionary-in-charge All Saints Ch., Minneapolis, 1900-05, rector, 1905-07; rector Christ Ch., Fitchburg, Mass., 1907-15, St. Paul's Ch., Chicago, 1915—; dean Chicago Deanery South, 1931—; elected and declined missionary bishop of Wyoming, 1929. Elected dep. to Gen. Conv. P.E. Ch., 7 times. Republican. Home: Chicago, Ill. Died Feb. 5, 1935.

THOMAS, Henry M., neurologist; b. Baltimore, Md., May 25, 1861; s. Dr. James Carey and Mary (Whitall) T.; brother of M. Carey T.; Haverford Coll., 1878-79; Johns Hopkins, 1879-82; M.D., U. of Md., 1885; studied abroad, 1886; (hon. A.M., Johns Hopkins, 1902); m. Josephine Gibson Carey, Oct. 10, 1889. Clin. prof. neurology, Johns Hopkins, 1896—; neurologist Johns Hopkins Hosp. and Dispensary, 1896—. Home: Baltimore, Md. Died June 21, 1925.

THOMAS, Hiram Washington, clergyman; b. Hampshire Co., Va., April 29, 1832; s. Joseph and Margaret (McDonald) T.; ed. in common schools, Preston Co., Va., Cooperstown Sem., Pa., and Berlin; studied under private tutors (D.D., Ind. Asbury Univ., 1870); m. Emeline C. Merrick, Mar. 19, 1855 (died 1896); m. 2d, Vandelia Varnum, Aug. 16, 1899. Entered ministry of Evangelical Assn., 1852; of M.E. Ch., 1856; went to Chicago, 1869; tried for heresy and expelled from Methodist Ch., 1881; pastor of The People's Ch., McVicker's Theatre, Chicago, 1880-1901; emeritus and in the ministry at large, and chaplain 1st Regt., I.N.G., from 1881. Long popular as a pulpit orator; pres. Congress of Religion. Author: Origin and Destiny of Man; Life and Sermons; The People's Pulpit; etc. Home: Chicago, Ill. Died 1909.

THOMAS, James Augustus, merchant; b. Lawsonville, N.C., Mar. 6, 1862; s. Henry Evans and Cornelia Caroline (Jones) T.; grad. Eastman Nat. Business Coll., Poughkeepsie, N.Y., 1881; m. Dorothy Quincy Hancock Read, Nov. 21, 1922; children—James Augustus, Eleanor Lansing. Dir. British-Am. Tobacco Co., Ltd., British Cigarette Co. (chmn.), Mustard & Co., Ltd., 1905-22; retired, 1922. Introduced western ways into many countries in the Orient; pioneer in introduction of Am. cigarettes, 1888-1923, into Australia, Tasmania, New Zealand, India, Japan, China and other countries of the Far East; organized Chinese-Am. Bnk of Commerce and established two schs. for Chinese; in China during Boxer Rebellion, 1900, Russo-Japanese War, 1904-05, Chinese rebellion of 1911. Life mem. Chinese Red Cross. Decorated by Dalai Lama, 1905; Crystal Button Mandarin, Empress of China, 1905; 6th and 3d classes Order of the Golden Harvest; Order of the Jade, Red Cravat with White and Blue Borders, China, 1937. Treas. China Famine Relief (U.S.A.); chmn. China Child Welfare Assn., The Duke Memorial; mem. Ch. Com. for China Relief; trustee Shanghai Am. School, Am. Hosp. of Istanbul; dir. China Soc. of America; mem. bd. govs. White Plains (N.Y.) Hosp.; charter associate Federal Council of Chs. of Christ in America; trustee Duke University; member advisory com. on foreign participation New York World's Fair, 1939. Presbyterian. Mason. Author: A Pioneer Tobacco Merchant in the Orient, 1928; Trailing Trade a Million Miles, 1931. Home: White Plains, N.Y. Died Sept. 10, 1940.

THOMAS, Jesse Burgess, theologian; b. Edwardsville, Ill., July 29, 1832; s. Jesse Burgess and Adeline C. (Smith) T.; A.B., Kenyon Coll., Ohio, 1850; (D.D., U. of Chicago, 1866; LL.D., Georgetown Coll., Ky., 1898); admitted to bar, 1852; m. Abbie A., d. Dr. T. Eastman, of Ottawa Co., Mich., May 30, 1855. Practiced law in Chicago, 1857-62; pastor Waukegan, Ill., 1862-64, First Bapt. Ch., Brooklyn, 1864-69 and 1874-88, First Ch., San Francisco, 1869, Michigan Av. Ch., Chicago, 1869-74; prof. ch. history, Newton Theol. Instn., 1888-1905 (emeritus). Author: The Old Bible and the New Science, 1877; The Mould of Doctrine, 1883; Significance of the Historical Element in Scripture; Some Parables of Nature, 1911. Home: Newark, N.J. Died June 7, 1915.

THOMAS, Jessie Beattie, (Mrs.), composer, author; b. Red Bud, Ill.; d. Dr. Andrew B. Beattie; grad. Visitation Acad., St. Louis (A.B., A.M.); m. John R. Thomas. Author and composer of The Golden Rod (National flower song); Memorare; Egyptian Lullaby; I'll Be Your Sweetheart; Speak Your Heart. Home: Muskogee, Ind. Ty. Deceased.

THOMAS, John Hampden, clergyman, educator; b. Hamilton, O., May 5, 1848; s. Thomas E. T., D.D.; ed. Dayton (O.) high school; attended Yale, 1864-65; Theol. Sem., Xenia, O., 1884-85; (A.M., Hanover Coll., 1890; A.M., Yale, 1898; D.D., Miami Univ., 1900); ordained to Presbyn. ministry, 1885; m. Linda S. Rogers, Jan. 17, 1878. Formerly pres. Oxford, O., Coll.; lecturer at Chautauqua assemblies, etc., on History of Christianity and other topics. Home: Oxford, O. Died 1904.

THOMAS, John Jenks, neurologist; b. Columbus, O., Sept. 6, 1861; s. Alfred and Martha A. (Hoge) T.; A.B., Williams, 1886; M.D. and A.M., Harvard, 1890; studied univs. of Heidelberg, Berlin and Vienna; m. Frances Pickering, d. Rear Admiral John G. Walker, Oct. 21, 1899; children—John G. W., Henry Pickering, Alfred Rebecca Pickering. Dist. phys. and phys. to Boston Dispensary, 1892-97; asst. phys. for nervous system, Boston City Hosp., 1893-1906, phys. same, 1906-25, and consulting physician to same from 1925; asst. neurologist, Children's Hosp., 1893-1913, neurologist, 1913-19, and consulting neurologist to same, 1919—; pathologist, Boston Insane Hosp., 1898-1903; instr. in neurology, 1902-06, asst. prof., 1906-12, prof., 1912-16, prof. emeritus, 1916—, Tufts Coll. Med. Sch.; asso. in neurology, Harvard Grad. Sch. of Medicine; consulting neurologist to Quincy City, Infants' hosps. Served with Harvard Unit at English Base Hosp., 1915, as lt. col. comdg. med. div.; maj. Med. Corps, A.E.F., 1918-19; with Base Hosp. 7, and as consultant in neuro-psychiatry. Joint author: Modern Treatment of Nervous and Mental Diseases; Cerebral Paralyses of Children, in Nelson's Loose Leaf Medicine; "Malingering," in Peterson, Haynes and Webster's Legal Medicine and Psychology. Home: Boston, Mass. Died July 17, 1935.

THOMAS, John Lloyd, humanitarian; b. Witton Park, Eng., Apr. 22, 1857; s. Rev. Isaac and Mary (Hopkins) T.; ed. Darlington, Eng., and Utica, N.Y.; m. Mary A. Brant, Apr. 15, 1880. Removed to New York, 1888, and was editor and writer for a number of papers until 1896; mgr. Mills Hotels and Model Dwellings, 1897—. Pres. Queensboro Development Corp.; treas. Protective Land Corp.; editor of Brotherhood (monthly mag.). Editor The Constitution, New York, 1890-96; has lectured on sociol. questions in U.S., Can. and Great Britain. Sec. Nat. Prohibition Party and Nat. Constitutional League for several yrs.; traveled in Europe studying subjects of model dwellings and similar movements for benefit of working men. Lecturer. Member board mgrs. and exec. com. N.Y. Home for Incurables; trustee N.Y. State Masonic Home. Home: New York, N.Y. Died Feb. 6, 1925.

THOMAS, John Robert, congressman; b. Mt. Vernon, Ill., Oct. 11, 1846; s. Maj. William A. and Caroline (Neely) T.; ed. Hunter Coll. Inst., Princeton, Indiana; (LL.D., McKendree Coll., Ill., 1895); served in Civil War, rising from pvt. to capt.; m. Lottie Culver, Dec. 28, 1870 (died 1880). Admitted to bar, 1869; city atty., Metropolis, Ill., 2 terms, 1869, 1870; state's atty., 1871-74; mem. 46th to 50th Congresses (1879-89); served on various important coms., including com. on Naval Affairs; has been called "father of the modern Am. Navy"; judge U.S. courts, Ind. Ty., 1897-1901; resumed practice, 1901; elected 1st mem. Congress from Ind. Ty. under Sequoyah Constn., 1905; nominated for judge Supreme Ct. by 1st Rep. State Conv. of Okla. (declined); mem. State Code Commn. of Okla., 1909-10. Was Grand Master Masonic Grand Lodge, Ill., and held other Masonic offices; mem. G.A.R. Home: Muskogee, Okla. Died Jan. 19, 1914.

THOMAS, John Rochester, architect; b. Rochester, N.Y., June 18, 1848; s. John Williams and Elizabeth Rodda T.; ed. under Dr. Anderson of Univ. of Rochester; studied architecture and engaged in practice. Architect and sole commr. for erection of State Reformatory, Elmira; architect 8th Regt. Armory, Madison Av., New York; received 1st prize among over 100 competitors in New York City Hall competition; architect of New York Hall of Records, also of several hundred chs., etc. Home: New York, N.Y. Died 1901.

THOMAS, John Wilson, Jr., ry. official; b. Murfreesboro, Tenn., Aug. 24, 1856; s. J. W. and Elizabeth T.; ed. Vanderbilt U., Nashville, Tenn., 1875-77; m. Dillie Duncan, Feb. 3, 1879. Began as locomotive engr., Nashville, Chattanooga & St. Louis Ry., 1878, and has continued with same rd. as follows: trainmaster 1881-84; engr., conductor, etc., 1884-86; sec. to pres., also purchasing agt., 1886-89; asst. gen. mgr. and purchasing agt., 1889-99; gen. mgr., 1899-1906; pres. and gen. mgr., same rd., Feb. 28, 1906—. Home: Nashville, Tenn. Died Dec. 14, 1913.

THOMAS, Kirby, mining engineer; b. Wisconsin; ed. U. of Wisconsin; married. Iron and copper explorations, Lake Superior region and Can., prior to 1906; examination and valuation mining properties in western states, 1906-09; in Mexico, 1909-10; asso. editor Engineering and Mining Journal, New York, 1910-11. Extensive work in Brazil and Mexico, 1915-17; consulting practice. Home: New York, N.Y. Died June 22, 1931.

THOMAS, Lot, congressman; b. on farm, Fayette Co., Pa., Oct. 17, 1843; attended dist. school in winter until 1864, Vermillion Inst., Hayesville, O., 1864-68; went to Iowa; taught school 2 winter terms and meantime read law; entered law dept. Iowa State Univ., Jan. 1870, and remained 2 terms; admitted to bar; established practice in Buena Vista Co., Ia.; judge dist. court from Jan. 1, 1885, until he resigned, Aug. 16, 1898 to accept Rep. nomination for Congress. Mem. Congress, 1899-1905, 11th Iowa dist.; m. Miss Barton, Aug. 19, 1873. Home: Storm Lake, Ia. Died 1905.

THOMAS, M. Carey (Miss), educator; b. Baltimore, Jan. 2, 1857; d. Dr. James Carey and Mary (Whitall) T.; A.B., Cornell (Phi Beta Kappa), 1877; studied Johns Hopkins, 1877-78, U. of Leipzig, 1879-82, U. of Zurich, 2d semester, 1882, College de France and Sorbonne, 1882-83; Ph.D., summa cum laude, U. of Zurich, 1882; LL.D., Western U. of Pa., 1896, Brown, 1914, Swarthmore and Johns Hopkins, 1922; L.H.D., Goucher, 1916. Apptd. dean, and prof. English and organizer Bryn Mawr Coll., 1884-85, dean and prof. English, 1885-94, pres. 1894-1922, now pres. emeritus. As dean (first use of "dean" in U.S. as coll. executive), organized in 1885 the undergrad. group system of studies in operation at Bryn Mawr for 37 years, and the first grad. sch. connected with any woman's coll., with resident scholarships and fellowships, and founded 8 European fellowships for study at Bryn Mawr, the first of such fellowships awarded by any grad. sch. in U.S. Coöperated with late Mary Elizabeth Garrett in founding the Bryn Mawr Sch. for Girls at Baltimore, Md., 1885, and served as treas. of corp., 1890-1915, chmn. bd., 1915-27; also coöperated with her in opening to women the med. dept. of Johns Hopkins, 1893, and has served as chmn. woman's advisory com. of the Med. Sch., 1915—; founded, in 1910, first purely grad. sch. of social economy and social research in connection with any Am. coll. or univ.; first sch. on college campus for workers in industry opened in 1922, for summer session of 8 weeks and is still in operation, first chmn. bd. of mgrs., same, 1920-22, and life mem. of bd., 1922—. Worker for woman suffrage, 1906, until it was accomplished, 1918; pres. Nat. Coll. Equal Suffrage League, 1906-13, a founder of Assn. to Promote Scientific Research by Women, 1900, also of Internat. Fedn. of University Women, serving as chmn. com. on club houses of the Federation and as mem. com. to organize Reid Hall, Paris. Author: The Higher Education of Women, 1900 (gold medals, Paris Expn., 1900, St. Louis Expn., 1904); Should the Higher Education of Women Differ from That of Men?, 1901; also The College (Ednl. Rev.), 1905; Statistical Study of Coeducation in the United States (Ency. Americana). Home: Haverford, Pa. Died Dec. 2, 1935.

THOMAS, Martin Henry, supt. of schs.; b. Hanover, Pa., Oct. 5, 1865; s. John and Lovina (Mummert) T.; A.M., Gettysburg (Pa.) Coll., 1921; B.S., Lebanon Valley Coll., Annville, Pa., 1929; m. Mary Emma Fisher, Aug. 11, 1908. Teacher rural schs. of Pa., 1890-1900; teacher, Harrisburg City Schs., 1900-02, teaching prin., 1902-14, supervisor, 1914-19, asst. dist. supt., 1919-30, supt. schs., 1930—. Mem. Chamber of Commerce. Republican. Lutheran. Mason. Home: Harrisburg, Pa. Died 1935.

THOMAS, Mason Blanchard, college dean; b. New Woodstock, N.Y., Dec. 16, 1866; s. Mansier C. and Ester A. (Blanchard) T.; B.S., Cornell U., 1890, fellow, 1891-92; (hon. Ph.D., Wabash Coll., 1907); m. Annie M. Davidson, June 21, 1893. Prof. botany, 1891—, dean, 1907—, Wabash Coll., Crawfordsville, Ind. Trustee Ind. Boys' Sch. Republican. Presbyn. Author: Manual of Plant Histology (with W. R. Dudley), 1894; Syllabus for Elementary Botany, 1909. Died Mar. 6, 1912.

THOMAS, Nathaniel Seymour, bishop; b. Faribault, Minn., June 20, 1867; s. Rt. Rev. Elisha Smith and Georgine Mary (Brown) T.; A.B., U. of Minn., 1890; B.D., Kan. Theol. Sch., 1891; spl. student Fitzwilliam Hall, Cambridge, Eng., 1891; D.D., Phila. Div. Sch., 1909; LL.D., Colorado Coll.; m. Edith Ellsworth, d. Col. Edward Prince, of Quincy, Ill., June 4, 1896. Deacon, 1891, priest, 1893, P.E. Ch.; rector Grace Ch., Ottawa, Kan., 1891-92; prof. of ethics and chaplain, Bethany Coll., Topeka, Kan., 1892-93; prof. N.T., Kan. Theol. Sch., 1893-95; rector St. Paul's Ch., Leavenworth, Kan., and chaplain U.S. Penitentiary, 1895-97; rector of St. Matthew's Ch., Wheeling, W.Va., 1897-99, Holy Apostles, Phila., 1899-1909; elected to the bishopric of Salina, 1902, declined, of Del., declined; consecrated bishop of Wyo., May 6, 1909; resigned bishopric of Wyo., 1927. Lecturer on pastoral care, Phila. Div. Sch., 1902-05, 1927, 29, 30; served as bishop in charge American Ch. in Europe, Paris; rector Bethesda by the Sea, Palm Beach, Fla. Mem. Peace Centenary Commn.; pres. Wyo. State S.S. Assn. Home: Palm Beach, Fla. Died Mar. 31, 1937.

THOMAS, Ralph W(ilmer), lawyer; b. Cornwallis, Nova Scotia, June 11, 1862; s. David Samuel and Martha A. (Rogers) T.; A.B., Colgate U., 1883, A.M., 1891; grad. student in English, Columbia; admitted to bar, Albany, N.Y., 1885; m. Effie Southwick, Sept. 23, 1891. Teacher of English, Albany Acad. for Boys, 1883-87; chief examiner regent's office, U. of State of N.Y., 1887-92; prof. rhetoric and pub. speaking, 1892-1909, prof. rhetoric, 1909-11, Colgate U. Lecturer on English, State Dept. of Edn. teachers' insts., Sept., 1908-10; commr. N.Y. State Bd. of Charities, 1903-10; mem. N.Y. State Advisory Bd. on Agrl. Edn., 1911-15; N.Y. State tax commr., 1915-19; editor and propr. The Suffolk Times. Member Board of Edn., Hamilton, N.Y. Elected to N.Y. Senate, May, 1910; reëlected for full terms, Nov. 1910 and 1912. Republican. Baptist. Author: A Manual of Debate, 1909; The Income Tax, 1913. Home: Greensport, N.Y. Died Mar. 20, 1920.

THOMAS, Reuen, clergyman, author; b. Penns, nr. Birmingham, Eng., June 14, 1840; s. William and Ann (Cotton) T.; ed. High Sch., Sutton-Coldfield, Eng., and University Coll., London; A.M., Ph.D., Germany; (D.D., Bowdoin Coll.); widower. In Congl. ministry from 1862; pastor Harvard Ch., Brookline, Mass. Author: Divine Sovereignty, 1885; Through Death to Life, 1888; Leaders of Thought in Christian Church, 1892; The Kinship of Souls, 1899. Died 1907.

THOMAS, Richard Curd Pope, judge; b. Bowling Green, Ky., Mar. 22, 1872; s. Richard Curd (M.D.) and Elizabeth (Wright) T.; A.B., Ogden Coll., Bowling Green, Ky., 1890; m. Margaret Hogle, Sept. 6, 1930. Admitted to Ky. bar, 1897; city atty. Bowling Green, 1906-10; mem. first Workmen's Compensation Bd. of Ky., 1916-20, chmn. 2 yrs.; judge Warren County (Ky.) Ct., 1930-33; dist. judge, Dist. of Canal Zone, one term beginning 1933. Del. Dem. Nat. Conv., Houston, 1928, Chicago, 1932. Regent and trustee Ogden Coll., 1922—. Democrat. Methodist. Elk. Home: Bowling Green, Ky. Died Nov. 11, 1939.

THOMAS, Richard Henry, physician; b. Baltimore, Jan. 26, 1854; s. Dr. Richard H. and Phebe Clapp T.; grad. Haverford Coll., 1872, U. of Md. Sch. of Medicine, 1875, post-graduate studies in London and Vienna; m. Anna Lloyd Braithwaite, Mar. 28, 1878. Minister in Soc. of Friends (orthodox); traveled in Great Britain, Ireland and Continental Europe in that capacity; about 10 yrs. prof. diseases of throat and chest in Woman's Med. Coll., Baltimore, and for several yrs. dean of the coll.; resigned professorship on account of other duties in 1893; again prof. diseases of the nose, throat and chest in the same coll. in 1900. Author: Echoes and Pictures, poems (London, 1895); "Penelve, or Among the Quakers," a story, 1898; History of the Society of Friends in America (with Prof. A. C. Thomas, of Haverford Coll.), 1894; also various med. pamphlets. Mem. Med. and Chirug. Faculty of Md.; pres. Peace Assn. of Friends in America. Address: Baltimore, Md. Died 1904.

THOMAS, Robert Young, Jr., congressman; b. Logan County, Ky.; A.B., A.M., Bethel Coll., Russellville, Ky.; married. In law practice at Central City, Ky.; mem. Ky. Ho. of Reps., 1886; state's atty., 7th Jud. Dist. of Ky., 1904-09; mem. 61st to 68th Congresses (1909-25), 3d Ky. Dist. Democrat. Home: Central City, Ky. Died Sept. 3, 1925.

THOMAS, Rolla L., M.D.; b. Harrison, O., Aug. 17, 1857; s. Milton L. and Susan J. (Rybolt) T.; A.B., Ind. Asbury (now DePauw) U., 1878, A.M., 1881; M.D., Eclectic Med. Coll., Cincinnati, O., 1880; m. Sallie B. Cook, July 1, 1880. Practiced at Harrison, 1881-87; moved to Cincinnati, 1887; mem. staff, Seton Hosp.; prof. practice of medicine, Eclectic Med. Coll., 1887—, dean, 1906—, also trustee. Republican. Methodist. Author: Eclectic Practice of Medicine, 1906, 4th edit., rev., 1922. Home: Cincinnati, O. Died Dec. 28, 1932.

THOMAS, Samuel, capitalist; b. at South Point, O., Oct. 27, 1840; ed. Marietta, O.; clerk with Keystone Iron Co. until 1861; in Union army, 1861-65, pvt. to bvt. brig. gen.; after the war asst. commr. for Miss. and later asst. adj. Freedmen's Bur. until 1867; then in coal and iron interests in Hocking Valley; acquired large ry. interests; became pres. E. Tenn., Va., and Ga. and other Southern roads; pres. Louisville, New Albany & Chicago; pres. Duluth, South Shore & Atlantic; contractor for building the Croton Aquedust, New York. Home: New York, N.Y. Died 1903.

THOMAS, Seth Edward, Jr., pres. Seth Thomas Clock Co.; b. N.Y. City, July 2, 1876; s. Seth Edward and Sarah A. (Gross) T.; prep. edn., Cutler Sch., New York and under tutors; Ph.B., Yale, 1899; m. Josephine van Beuren Reynolds, Feb. 20, 1908; children—Emily Augusta, Josephine Reynolds. Began with Seth Thomas Clock Co., New York, 1899, pres. 1915—; v.p. Spingler van Beuren Estates; dir. First Nat. Bank of Morristown, N.J. Mem. N.Y.N.G., 1899-1910. Pres. Morristown Memorial Hosp.; dir. N.Y. Assn. for the Blind. Republican. Home: New Vernon, N.J. Died June 7, 1932.

THOMAS, T. Rowland, banker; b. Della Brooke, Md., Mar. 7, 1874; s. James (M.D.) and Nannie (Nelson) Thomas; ed. Charlotte Hall Sch.; m. Mary L. Thomas, 1902. Began with Stein Bros., bankers, Baltimore; later with Nat. Howard Bank, and Nat. Mechanics Bank; cashier Third Nat. Bank, 1908-10; v.p., 1910-11, and pres., 1911—, of Nat. Bank of Baltimore, into which the Third Nat. Bank was merged. Democrat. Episcopalian. Mason. Address: Baltimore, Md. Died Oct. 27, 1923.

THOMAS, Theodore, orchestra leader; b. Esens, Hanover, Germany, Oct. 11, 1835; s. August and Sophia T.; ed. in music by his father and other New York musicians; Mus.D., Yale; made début as violinist in Germany at 10; came to U.S., 1845; played for some yrs. as solo violinist in New York and during a 2-yrs.' tour in the South; returned to New York; played in concerts and opera—1st as violinist and afterwards as orchestra condr.; in connection with other musicians gave annual series of chamber concerts; inaugurated orchestral concerts, 1864; founded Thomas Orchestra, 1867, and maintained it until 1888; elected condr. Brooklyn Philharmonic Soc., 1862, and of N.Y. Philharmonic Soc., 1877, holding these positions almost continuously until 1891, when he moved to Chicago; condr. Chicago Orchestra, 1891—; dir. Cincinnati Coll. of Music, 1878-80; condr. Cincinnati biennial musical festivals, 1873-98, condr. Am. Opera Co., 1885-87; musical dir. World's Columbian Expn., 1893; m. Minna L. Rhodes, 1864; m. 2d, Rose Fay, 1890. Home: Chicago, Ill. Died 1905.

THOMAS, Theodore Gaillard, physician; b. Edisto Island, nr. Charleston, S.C., Nov. 21, 1831; s. Rev. Edward T. (4th generation from Rev. Samuel T., sent by Ch. of Eng. to S.C., 1700) and Jane Marshall (Gaillard) T. (4th generation from Theodore Gaillard, Huguenot refugee to S.C. on revocation of Edict of Nantes). Grad. Med. Coll. of Charleston, 1852; resident physician Bellevue and Ward's Island hosps., New York, and Rotunda Hosp., Dublin, Ireland. Prof. obstetrics and gynecology, Coll. Phys. & Surg., New York; cons. surgeon to several New York hosps. and mem. many med. socs. in U.S. and abroad. Author: Diseases of Women, 1868, translated into French, German, Italian, Spanish and Chinese; assisted in preparing A Century of American Medicine, 1876; large contbr. to med. journals. Address: New York, N.Y. Died 1903.

THOMAS, Washington Butcher, capitalist; b. Pittston, Me., Aug. 14, 1857; s. Joseph B. and Martha T. (Seran) T.; A.B., Harvard, 1879; m. Caroline Wadleigh, Aug. 20, 1883. Entered Standard Sugar Refinery, Boston, upon leaving college,

1879; pres. Am. Sugar Refining Co., 1908-11, chmn. bd. dirs., 1911; also dir. Pacific Coast Co. Pres. Nat. Golf Assn., 1899-1900. Home: Boston, Mass. Died May 29, 1929.

THOMAS, William, lawyer; b. Worcester, Mass., Sept. 5, 1853; s. Benjamin Franklin and Mary Ann (Park) T.; A.B., Harvard, 1873, LL.B., 1876; m. Emma Gay, Mar. 1875; children—Molly McMullin, Helen Kimble, Benjamin F., Gertrude Boequeraz. Practiced in San Francisco, 1877—; mem. Thomas, Beedy, Presley & Paramore; an organizer, pres. 2 yrs., Calif. Fruit Canners' Assn.; an organizer Calif. Title Ins. and Trust Co., and chmn. of its legal staff for many yrs.; went to Europe, 1906, representing 60 law firms in collection of ins. from cos. seeking to evade claims and secured $7,000,000 for San Francisco claimants. Overseer Harvard, 1916-22. Republican. Unitarian. Address: San Francisco, Calif. Deceased.

THOMAS, William David, congressman; b. Middle Granville, N.Y., Mar. 22, 1880; s. David D. and Mary (McKenzie) T.; Ph.G., Union Coll., Schenectady, 1904; m. Carolyn G. Haffner, July 24, 1907; 1 dau., Lillian H. Pharmacist at Hoosick Falls, N.Y., 1905—; town clk., 1917-25; mem. N.Y. Ho. of Reps., 1925-27; treas. Rensselaer County, 1927-33; mem. 73d and 74th Congresses (1933-37), 29th N.Y. Dist. Co. Republican chmn., 1927—. Presbyn. Mason, K.P., Elk. Home: Hoosick Falls, N.Y. Died May 17, 1936.

THOMAS, William Henry Griffith, clergyman; b. Oswestry, England, Jan. 2, 1861; s. William and Annie Nightingale (Griffith) T.; Associate (A.K.C.), King's Coll., London, 1885; B.A., Oxford, 1895, M.A., 1898, B.D., 1902, D.D., 1906; m. Alice Monk, 1898. Ordained ministry Ch. of Eng., 1885; curate St. Peter's, Clerkenwell, 1885-88, St. Aldate, Oxford, 1888-96; vicar St. Paul, Portman Sq., 1896-1905; prin. Wycliffe Hall, Oxford, 1905-10; prof. O.T. lit., Wycliffe Coll., Toronto, Can., 1910-19; also prof. systematic theology, 1915-19; teacher of Bible in confs. and Bible schs. in U.S. Author: Methods of Bible Study, 1903; The Apostle Peter, 1905; Christianity is Christ, 1909; The Catholic Faith, 1911; The Work of the Ministry, 1912; The Book of Genesis, 3 vols., 1913; The Epistle to the Romans, 1913; The Holy Spirit of God, 1913; The Prayers of St. Paul, 1914; Life Abiding and Abounding, 1914; The Acts of the Apostles, 1915; Grace and Power, 1916; Strongholds of Truth, 1916; The Christian Life and How to Live It, 1919; Evolution and the Supernatural, 1922; Let Us Go On, 1923; Christ Pre-Eminent, 1923; The Apostle John, 1923. Contbr. leading article, weekly, on Internat. S.S. Lessons, to S.S. Times. Fellow of King's Coll., London, 1923. Home: Germantown, Pa. Died Jan. 2, 1924.

THOMAS, William Sturgis, physician; b. Poughkeepsie, N.Y., Oct. 16, 1871; s. Henry Livingston and Alice R. (Phinney) T.; M.D., George Washington U., 1892; m. Emma Rheinfrank, Apr. 25, 1905; children—Catherine Livingston (Mrs. Arthur Thomas Jersild), William Stephen. Interne St. Luke's Lying-In; chief of surgical clinic St. Luke's Hosp., 1908-11, examining physician, attending physician and dir. Allergy Clinic, 1921—, also mem hosp. bd.; cons. physician New York Home for Convalescents. Served as asst. surgeon U.S. Navy, Spanish-Am. War, med. officer, World War I. Decorated Chevalier Legion of Honor of France. Mem. corp. N.Y. Bot. Garden; mem. advisory com. New York World's Fair, 1939. Republican. Episcopalian. Author: Testbook on Asthma, 1928; Field Book of Common Mushrooms, 1928; Members of the Society of the Cincinnati, 1929; History of the Society of the Cincinnati, 1935. Contbr. articles to Jour. of A.M.A., Jour. of Allergy, etc., also to outdoor mags. Home: New York, N.Y. Died Dec. 21, 1941.

THOMAS, William Widgery, diplomat; b. Portland, Me., Aug. 26, 1839; s. William Widgery and Elizabeth White (Goddard) T.; A.B., Bowdoin, 1860, A.M., 1866; LL.D., Bethany, 1901, Bowdoin, 1913; read law; m. Dagmar Törnebladh, Swedish noblewoman, Oct. 11, 1887 (died 1912); children—William Widgery (dec.), Oscar Percival, Wolfgang Ragner (adopted); m. 2d, Mrs. Aina Törnebladh, Swedish noblewoman, June 2, 1915. Began diplomatic career in 1862, as U.S. bearer of dispatches; carried a treaty to Turkey; became vice consul gen. at Constantinople, later acting consul, Galatz, Moldavia; war consul at Gothenburg, Sweden, until 1865 (resigned); received for services as consul "special thanks of Dept. of State." Completed legal studies at Harvard, and admitted to Me. bar, 1866; practiced at Portland; commr. public lands, Maine, 1869; commr. of immigration for Me., 1870-73; visited Sweden, 1870, bringing back 51 Swedish colonists and settling them in Northern Me., founding flourishing colony of New Sweden (2,000 Swedish-Am. inhabitants, 1920). Mem. Me. Ho. of Reps., 1873-75 (speaker of House, 1874-75), Senate, 1879; pres. Me. Rep. Conv., 1875; del. Rep. Nat. Conv., 1880. Minister resident of U.S. to Sweden and Norway, 1883-85; Am. E.E. and M.P., Sweden and Norway, 1889-94, and 1897-1905. First minister to hoist Am. flag in Stockholm. In behalf of America, on board U.S. Warship, Baltimore, Stockholm harbor, 1890, delivered to King and people of Sweden body of great Swedish-Am., John Ericsson; delivered oration in Swedish, unveiling Ericsson monument, Stockholm, 1901; three times secured good offices King Oscar in settlement of controversies between U.S., Gt. Britain and Germany; procured official participation of Sweden in La. Purchase Expn., 1904, after Swedish Govt. had twice declined. On resigning post, 1905, Sec. of State Hay wrote: "You have had the longest, the most distinguished and the most useful term of service (in Sweden and Norway) that any American has ever had." Author: Sweden and the Swedes (2 vols.), 1891. Translator: The Last Athenian (from the Swedish), 1869. Home: Portland, Me. Died Apr. 25, 1927.

THOMPSON, Albert Clifton, judge; b. Brookville, Pa., Jan. 23, 1842; s. Judge John J. Y. and Agnes (Kennedy) T.; ed. Jefferson Coll., Pa.; LL.D., Washington and Jefferson Coll., Pa.; served pvt., to capt., Union Army, 1861-65. Admitted to bar, 1864; settled at Portsmouth, O., 1865; probate judge Scioto County, 1869-72; judge common pleas, 2d subdiv., 7th jud. dist., Ohio, 1882-85; mem. Congress, 1885-91. Republican. Chmn. Ohio Tax Commn., 1893; chmn. Commn. to Revise and Codify Penal Laws of U.S., 1897; judge U.S. Dist. Ct., southern dist. Ohio, commd. Sept. 16, 1898. Home: Cincinnati, O. Died 1910.

THOMPSON, Alfred Clark, normal sch. prin.; b. Norwich, Conn., Mar. 25, 1867; s. Charles and Prudence Stanton (James) T.; A.B., Yale, 1892; post-grad. work, Clark U. and Ludwig-Maximilian U.; Pd.D., N.Y. State Coll. for Teachers, 1913; m. Lina M. Cook, June 30, 1896; 1 dau., Miriam C. (Mrs. Robert F. Winne). Prin. Hopkins Acad., Hadley, Mass., 1892-95, Rutland (Vt.) High Sch., 1895-97; supt. schs., Palmer, Mass., 1897-1902, Wakefield, Mass., 1902-05, Auburn, N.Y., 1905-10; prin. State Normal Sch., Brockport, N.Y., Sept. 1, 1910—. Mem. N.Y. State Regents Joint Legislative Com. Took course in mil. science at Yale; sergt. Co. I, 2d Regt., M.V.M., 1893-95. Mem. bd. trustees, Brockport, 12 yrs.; chmn. Bd. of Sch. Directors, Monroe County, N.Y.; chmn. bd. of mgrs. Monroe County Traveling Library. Republican. Presbyn.; chmn. bd. trustees First Presbyn. Ch. Mason. Home: Brockport, N.Y. Died Feb. 17, 1937.

THOMPSON, Almon Harris, geographer; b. Stoddard, N.H., Sept. 24, 1839; s. Lucas and Mary (Sawyer) T.; ed. Southboro, Mass., 1848-56, and Wheaton, Ill., Coll., 1857-61 (scientific course); m. Ellen L. Powell, July 8, 1862. Soldier Civil war, 1st lt. 139th Ill. vol. inf.; supt. schools, Lacon, Ill., 1865-67, Bloomington, Ill., 1867-68; acting curator Ill. Natural History Soc., 1869-70; topographic engr., 1870—. Engaged in exploration Colo. River of the West, in charge of geog. work, with Maj. J. W. Powell, 1870-78; geographer U.S. Geol. Survey, 1882—; in charge geog. work of U.S. Geol. Survey, west of Mississippi River, 1884-95; field and office work, U.S. Geol. Survey, 1896-1903; in charge exhibits U.S. Geol. Survey, La. Purchase Expn., 1904. Address: Washington, D.C. Died 1906.

THOMPSON, Arthur Webster, capitalist; b. Erie, Pa., May 8, 1875; s. Sheldon E. and Laverne B. (Webster) T.; C.E., Allegheny Coll., 1897; LL.D., St. John's, Md., and U. of Pittsburgh, 1921; D.Sc., U. of Pa., 1927; m. Marion Dinwiddie Gordon, June 29, 1905; children—Gordon, Arthur Hugh, Rolland Dinwiddie. Draftsman with Wilkins & Davison, Pittsburgh, later instrumentman P.&L.E. R.R. and chief of party on surveys of B.&O. R.R.; with B.&O. R.R., 1900-18, successively as asst. div. engr., div. engr., supt., chief engr. m. of w., chief engr., gen. mgr., 3d v.p., in charge of operations, v.p. in charge of operations, traffic, engring. and comml. development; apptd. fed. mgr. by U.S. R.R. Adminstrn., June 1, 1918, for B.&O. R.R., Western Md. Ry., Cumberland & Pa. R.R., Cumberland Valley R.R., Coal & Coke Ry., Staten Island Lines in N.Y., Wheeling Terminal Ry.; elected pres. Phila. Co. and its affiliated cos., including the Duquesne Light Co. and Pittsburgh Rys. Co., of Pittsburgh, Feb. 1, 1919; pres. United Gas Improvement Co., Phila., 1926-29; dir. Am. Surety Co. (New York), Consol. Gas, Electric Light & Power Co. of Baltimore, Girard Trust Co. (Phila.), Pa. R.R. Co., Phila. Nat. Bank, Guarantee Co. of N. America (Phila.), McKinney Mfg. Co., and Union Trust Co. (Pittsburgh), Hookless Fastener Co. (Meadville, Pa.). Chmn. bd. trustees Allegheny Coll. Mem. Am. Acad. Polit. and Social Science. Episcopalian. Home: Philadelphia, Pa. Died Nov. 9, 1930.

THOMPSON, Augustus Charles, pastor Eliot Congl. Ch., Roxbury, Mass., July 27, 1842—; b. Goshen, Conn., April 30, 1812; s. Augustus and Kezia (Hopkins) T.; student Yale, 1835; was not graduated because of feeble health; hon. M.A., 1841; D.D., Amherst, 1860; grad. Hartford Theol. Sem., 1838; studied, Univ. of Berlin, 1838-39, with Rev. Rufus Anderson, D.D.; pastor Eliot Congl. Ch., Roxbury, Mass., July 27, 1842—; deputy to missions of Am. Bd. in India, 1854-55; del. to Mildmay Missionary Conf., 1878, London Missionary Conf., 1888. Author: Better Land, 1855; Morning Hours in Patmos, 1860; The Mercy Seat, 1863; Seeds and Sheaves, 1869; Moravian Missions, 1882; Foreign Missions, 1889; Protestant Missions, 1894; Eliot Memorial, 1900; sermons, addresses, etc. Address: Boston, Mass. Died 1901.

THOMPSON, Basil, editor, insurance; b. New Orleans, La., June 21, 1892; s. Thomas Payne and Ida (Zorn) T.; A.B., Loyola U., 1910; law student Tulane, 1910-11, Washington and Lee U., 1911-12; A.M., from Loyola, 1917; m. Rebekah Brown, July 28, 1914; agt. for Equitable Life Assurance Soc., 1913—, at Chicago 1914-16, New Orleans, 1916—; co-founder, 1920, and co-editor, with Julius Weis Friend, of Double Dealer (mag.). Served in Field Arty., World War I. Author: Auguries, 1918; Estrays (co-author), 1918; Louisiana in These United States, 1923. Contbr. to Nation, Bookman, Century, New Republic, Forum, etc. Home: New Orleans, La. Died Apr. 6, 1924.

THOMPSON, Beach, capitalist; b. Brooklyn, N.Y., Dec. 5, 1865; s. Samuel and Emma R. (Hubbard) T.; B.S., Univ. of Mich., 1889; M.A., Leland Stanford Jr. U., 1892; m. Augusta Veeder, Feb. 25, 1896. Instr. English, Leland Stanford Jr. U., 1891-92; pres. San Domingo Gold Mining Co., 1896-1905; engaged in development of hydro-electric enterprises in Calif., 1899—. Pres. Tuolumne Water Power Co., 1905-10; v.p. Metropolitan Light & Power Co., 1905-10; pres. Poulsen Wireless Corp., Federal Telegraph Co.; dir. Sierra & San Francisco Power Co. Del. Rep. Nat. Conv., Chicago, 1908. Home: Menlo Park, Calif. Deceased.

THOMPSON, Charles Edwin, mfr. steel products; b. McIndoe Falls, Vt., July 16, 1870; s. Thomas and Mary Ann (Young) T.; ed. Boston Prep. ch.; m. Maora H. Hubbard, Jan. 3, 1900 (dec.); m. 2d, Alberta Brown, 1919; 1 son, Edwin Groot. Insp. and branch mgr. Cleveland Telephone Co., 1892-98; mgr. Dallas (Tex.) exchange, 1898-1900; returned to Cleveland, 1900, and became asso. with Cleveland Cap Screw Co.; apptd. gen. mgr. same co., 1905, and name changed to Electric Welding Products Co., later to Steel Products Co. which absorbed Mich. Welding Co. of Detroit and Metals Welding Co. of Cleveland, name changed to Thompson Products Co., of which became pres.; pres. Ross Mfg. Co.; dir. Union Trust Co., Toledo Steel Products Co., Electric Ry. Improvement Co. Hon. corp. 22d Batt., Alpine Chasseurs. Republican. Episcopalian. Home: Cleveland, O. Died Oct. 4, 1933.

THOMPSON, Charles James, congressman; b. Wapakoneta, O., Jan. 24, 1862; s. Thomas James and Emily (Sallads) T.; student Ohio Wesleyan U., 1881-82; m. 2d, Katharien A. Howe, Jan. 6, 1925; children (by 1st marriage)—Lewis B., Frederick S., Samuel C., Charles J. Learned printer's trade; newspaper owner; mem. Rep. State Central Com., 1893-94, postmaster Defiance, O., 1898-1915; mem. 66th to 71st Congresses (1919-31), 5th Ohio Dist. Mason, K.P., Elk. Home: Defiance, O. Died Mar. 27, 1932.

THOMPSON, Charles Lemuel, clergyman; b. Allentown, Pa., Aug. 18, 1839; s. Aaron and Julia (Shearer) T.; A.B., Carroll Coll., 1858; theol. course Princeton and McCormick Theol. sems.; D.D., Monmouth, Ill., 1876, Princeton, 1911; LL.D., Carroll Coll., 1907. Ordained Presbyn. ministry, 1861; pastor Juneau, Wis., 1861-62, Janesville, Wis., 1862-67, First Ch., Cincinnati, 1867-72, Fifth Ch., Chicago, 1872-78, Third Ch., Pittsburgh, 1879-82, Second Ch., Kansas City, 1882-88, Madison Av. Ch., New York, 1888-98; sec. Presbyn. Bd. of Home Missions, Mar. 1898—; chmn. Home Missions Council, 1908—. Moderator Gen. Assembly Presbyn. Ch. U.S.A., Phila., 1888. Editor Our Monthly, 1870-71, the Interior, 1875-78. Mem. Ch. Peace League of America. Author: History of American Revivals, 1877; Etchings in Verse, 1889; The Story of the Presbyterian Church, 1903; Religious Foundations of America, 1917; The Soul of America, 1919. Home: New York, N.Y. Died Apr. 14, 1924.

THOMPSON, Charles Thaddeus, newspaperman; b. Detroit, Mich.; s. Jonathan and Harriett (Brewster) T.; student U. of Mich., 1877-79, LL.B., 1880; m. Flora McDonald. Chief of Associated Press Bur. at Paris, for southwestern Europe, 1902-06, London, 1906-07; supt. Eastern div., Asso. Press, comprising Eastern and N.E. States, 1907-12; supt. Washington bur. Asso. Press, 1912-15; supt. fgn. service during war, 1915-19; supt. fgn. service Asso. Press, 1919—. "Academic Palms," from French Govt., 1899; Chevalier of the Legion of Honor, 1905. Home: New York, N.Y. Died Apr. 18, 1925.

THOMPSON, Charles William, miner, mfr.; b. Mt. Pleasant, Ia., June 8, 1851; s. Gen. William and Lucille (Wilcox) T.; ed. Kenyon Coll. and U.S. Mil. Acad.; m. Heppie T. Lambert, 1875. Civil engr. Southern Pacific Ry. on construction of div. from El Paso, Tex., W. to Pacific Coast; next operated coal mines in N. Dak. until 1890; in mining business in Wash., 1890—; pres. Wash. Coöperative Mining Syndicate operating coal mines, mfg. coke, and also owning valuable copper, gold and silver properties in Pierce County, Wash.; pres. Montezuma Mining Co., dir. Tacoma Co. Steel Corp. Col. in Nat. Guard Dak. on staff Gov. Church; served in Indian wars in N.Dak., and was one of the first who went into the Black Hills country of S.Dak., 1876. Home: Tacoma, Wash. Deceased.

THOMPSON, Charles Winston, congressman 5th Ala. dist., 1901-05; b. Macon County, Ala., Dec. 31, 1860; s. William P. and Mary W. T.; high school edn., Tuskegee, Ala., grad. Bryant and Stratton Bus. Coll., Louisville, Ky., 1879; m. Estelle Alley, 1880. County supt. of edn. of Macon County, 1885-89; lt. col. on staff Gov. Johnston, 1896-1901. Organizer and pres. the Bank of Tuskegee, 1891—; chmn. Dem. Exec. Com. of Macon Co., Ala., 1894-99; State senator 26th dist., Ala., 1897-1901. Address: Tuskegee, Ala. Died 1904.

THOMPSON, Cyrus, M.D.; b. Richlands, Onslow County, N.C., Feb. 8, 1855; s. Franklin and Leah (Brown) T.; student Randolph-Macon Coll., Ashland, Va., 1872-76; U. of Va., 1876-77; M.D., U. of La., 1878; m. Florence Garland Kent, Dec. 5, 1882; children—Florence Kent, Cyrus, Virginia Garland, Charles Edward (dec.), Gertrude, Lorimer Wilder, Marguerite, Franklin, Horace Kent, Minnette Gordon. Began practice, Richlands, N.C., 1878; moved to Jacksonville, 1881; county supt. health, 1907-13; mem. State Bd. of Health, 1913—. Mem. N.C. Ho. of Reps., 1883, Senate, 1885; sec. of state, N.C., 1897-1901; received Populist vote of N.C. for U.S. senator, 1897, Rep. and Prog. vote for same, 1913; declined nomination for gov., 1912. Republican. Methodist. Home: Jacksonville, N.C. Died Nov. 20, 1930.

THOMPSON, Daniel Varney, headmaster; b. Augusta, Me., May 10, 1867; s. William Ladd (M.D.) and Sarah Bickford (Varney) T.; A.B., Amherst, 1889, A.M., 1893; L.H.D., 1924; m. Grace B. Randall, Sept. 5, 1893; children—William Ladd, Randall, Daniel Varney. Master Newark Acad., 1889-96; head dept. of English, Sachs Sch., New York, 1896-1903, Lawrenceville Sch., 1904-20; headmaster Roxbury Latin Sch., 1921—. Field dir. Am. Red Cross, 1918-20. Mem. Headmasters' Assn., Country Day Headmasters' Association, N.E. Association Colleges and Secondary Schs. Conglist. Editor: Burke's Speech on Conciliation; Macbeth; Book of British Verse. Home: West Roxbury, Mass. Died Aug. 20, 1932.

THOMPSON, David Alphæus, church official; b. Ramsey County, Minn., Mar. 13, 1872; s. Socrates Atlas and Angeline (Fish) T.; B.A., Macalester Coll., 1900, D.D., 1924; M.A., Princeton, 1902; B.D., Princeton Theol. Sem., 1903; m. Edna Flanders, May 26, 1903; children—Genevieve Grace (Mrs. Joseph Melville Dyer), David Egbert. Ordained ministry Presbyn. Ch., 1903; pastor Sellwood Ch., Portland, Ore., 1903-11, First Ch., Olympia, 1911-16, Mizpah Ch., Portland, 1916-22; synodical exec. Presbyn. Ch., Ore., 1922—; stated clk. Synod of Ore., 1923—; pres. Home Missions Council, Ore.; chaplain part-time sessions, State Senate and House, Washington, 1913-15. Y.M.C.A. sec., A.E.F., in Bordeaux, France, 1917-19. Pres. Ore. Christian Endeavor Union, 1906; world v.p. Christian Endeavor, 1912; moderator Presbytery of Portland, 1906, 21; trustee Albany Coll., 1924—; trustee San Francisco Theol. Sem., 1926—; trustee Friendly House, Portland. Republican. Editor: The Oregon Trail (quarterly mag.). Home: Portland, Ore. Died Jan. 1935.

THOMPSON, David Decamp, journalist; b. Cincinnati, O., Apr. 29, 1852; s. R. P. and Mary L. (Carr) T.; alumnus Ohio Wesleyan U., 1876, A.M., Northwestern U., 1901; LL.D., McKendree Coll., 1903; m. Alia L. Grosh, 1876. Layman Methodist Episcopal Ch. Asst. editor, 1892-1901, editor, 1901—, Northwestern Christian Advocate. Author: Abraham Lincoln, the First American, 1896; John Wesley as Social Reformer, 1898. Home: Evanston, Ill. Died 1908.

THOMPSON, David P., contractor, banker; b. Harrison County, O., Nov. 8, 1834; m. Mary R. Meldrum, 1861. Worked on ry. surveys; later, blacksmith's apprentice; started for Ore. overland in Jan. 1853, driving sheep from Ill. for his board on the way; compassman on U.S. survey work; mem. Ore. vols., 1855-56, capt. 1st Ore. cav., 1861-63; saw service against Indians. Resumed surveying, 1864, and built the 1st ry. in Ore.; became pres. Ore. Woolen Mills, 1866; gov. Idaho, 1874-76; engaged as contractor; as pres. Ore. Constrn. Co., built a large part of lines of the Oregon Ry. and Navigation Co., Northern Pacific and Southern Pacific rys. Pres. Portland Savings Bank, 1880-86; Commercial Nat. Bank, 1886-92; State senator; twice mayor Portland, 1880-82; U.S. minister to Turkey, 1892-93; mem. State bd. equalization, 1897-98. Republican. Address: Portland, Ore. Died 1901.

THOMPSON, Denman, actor; b. Girard, Pa., 1833; reared in N.H.; early professional life a dancer, Irish character actor and general utility man; took up comedy and starred in "Joshua Whitcomb," a play of his own, afterward remodeled as "The Old Homestead." Address: West Swanzey, N.H. Died 1911.

THOMPSON, Dwinel French, coll. prof.; b. Bangor, Me., Jan. 1, 1846; s. Joel Dwinel and Harriet Newell (French) T.; Bowdoin, 1863-65; B.S., Dartmouth, 1869, M.S., 1914; m. Mary Lena Saxton, Jan. 1, 1880. Tutor, Dartmouth, 1869-72; prof. descriptive geometry, stereotomy and drawing, Rensselaer Poly. Inst., 1872-1916, emeritus prof., 1916—. Edited and illustrated a book on Free-Hand Drawing by Prof. Woodman, 1870; revised and enlarged Mahan's Industrial Drawing, 1873. Pres. Deborah Powers Old Ladies' Home. Address: Troy, N.Y. Died Apr. 19, 1919.

THOMPSON, Eben Francis, lawyer; b. Worcester, Mass., Jan. 29, 1859; s. Francis Henry and Fannie H. (Thomas) T.; pvt. instrs. and Harvard Law Sch.; widower; children—Rev. Harold H. R., Mary Frothingham (Mrs. James Howe Colton). Admitted to bar, 1884, practiced in Worcester, 1884—. Editor: The Student's Kent, 1886; Shakespearean Essays and Other Books. Translator: The Quatrains of Omar Khayyam, 1906; FitzGerald's Rubaiyat with Persian Text, 1907; The Definitive Edition of The Rose Garden of Omar Khayyam (weighs but 1¼ grains), 1932 (smallest printed book in the world). Address: Sutton, Mass. Died Dec. 2, 1939.

THOMPSON, Edward Herbert, archæologist; b. Worcester County, Mass., Sept. 28, 1860; s. Josiah A. and Mary E. (Thayer) T.; grad. Worcester Tech. Inst., 1879. Am. consul to Yucatan, 1885-1909; devoted many yrs. to research and exploration of ruins of the Maya civilization; spent 14 mos. collecting material, under auspices of the Peabody Museum, for exhibition at the World's Fair, Chicago, 1893; discovered the long sought "Hidden City" buried in the interior of Yucatan; purchased plantations of Chichen and tracts adjoining, rebuilt the plantation house, later center of a colony of scientists, and instituted many modern improvements; uncovered the "Maya Venus," the mausoleum of the high priest, the Temple of the Painted Columns, and the ancient city, Old Chichen, also the "Chichen Tablet," and successfully explored the "Sacred Well" of Chichen Itza, recovering many objects of great archæol. interest; became writer and lecturer. Author: Children of the Cave, 1929; People of the Serpent, 1932; also various reports of the Peabody Mus., Field Mus., etc. Address: West Falmouth, Mass. Died May 11, 1935.

THOMPSON, Fayette Lathrop, general sec.; b. Fenton, Genesee County, Mich., Feb. 12, 1862; s. Lafayette and Mary Lathrop (Chipman) T.; Northwestern U.; 4 yrs. elective work Garrett Bibl. Inst., Evanston, Ill.; D.D., Cornell Coll., Ia., 1904; m. Georgena D. Peabody, June 8, 1890. Ordained M.E. ministry, 1880; pastor Lansing, Mich., 1895-99, Jackson, 1899-1901, Davenport, Ia., 1901-04, Minneapolis, 1904-07, St. Louis, 1907-10; gen. sec. Methodist Brotherhood, Apr. 1910—; also asso. campaign leader Men and Religion Forward Movement. Mem. London Soc. Bibl. Archæology, British Sch. of Archæology in Egypt; asso. Victoria Inst. Author of various brochures, pamphlets and articles on religious subjects. Address: New York, N.Y. Died Apr. 26, 1912.

THOMPSON, Frank Dutton, judge; b. Irasburg, Vt., Apr. 9, 1876; s. Laforrest H. and Eliza (Dutton) T.; grad. St. Johnsbury (Vt.) Acad., 1894; student U. of Vt., 1894-95; LL.B., Boston U. Sch. of Law, 1899; m. Mabel A. Miles, Oct. 31, 1900. Admitted to Vt. bar, 1899; mem. firm Porter & Thompson, St. Johnsbury, 1899-1906; in practice at Barton, 1906; judge Superior Ct., 1923-29; justice Supreme Ct. of Vt., 1929-37. Congregationalist. Mason. Home: St. Petersburg, Fla. Died June 12, 1940.

THOMPSON, Frank Forrester, prof. elec. engring.; b. Milroy, Pa., Nov. 16, 1870; s. Samuel Thomas, D.D., and Clara Ashmead (Barr) T.; A.B., Princeton, 1894, A.M., 1895, E.E., 1897; instr. physics, Union Coll., 1897-98; instr. elec. engring., Pa. State Coll., 1898-1901; instr. physics and mathematics, 1903-06, asso. prof., 1906-08, prof. elec. engring., 1908—, Rutgers U. Presbyn. Home: New Brunswick, N.J. Died Sept. 4, 1927.

THOMPSON, Frank M., lawyer; b. Paris, Henry County, Tenn., Dec. 22, 1860; s. Samuel W. and Ellen (Bunch) T.; common sch. edn.; m. Mary E. Sidebottom, Dec. 29, 1887 (died 1917); 1 son, Neal L.; m. 2d, Nettie Florine Gaines, Nov. 28, 1918. Admitted to Tenn. bar, 1881; practiced at Paris, 1881-90; removed to Chattanooga, 1890. Railroad commr. of Tenn., 1897-99; chmn. Dem. State Exec. Com., Tenn., 1902-06; elected atty. gen. and reporter of Tenn., Sept. 17, 1913, by Supreme Ct. to succeed Charles T. Cates (resigned), reëlected Sept. 2, 1918, for term of 8 yrs.; mem. firm Thompson, Cornelius & Swiggart. Mem. Christian (Disciples) Ch. Home: Nashville, Tenn. Died July 20, 1926.

THOMPSON, Frank Victor, educator; b. Batesville, Ark., July 28, 1874; s. Edward Williams and Marie Louise (LeProhon) T.; A.B., Ph.B., St. Anselm's Coll., Manchester, N.H., 1895, Ph.D., 1906; A.M., Harvard, 1907; m. Blanche Pitman Wingate, June 17, 1903. Prin. North Walpole Grammar Sch., 1895-97; instr. Lawrence High Sch., 1897-98; prin. Wetherbee Grammar Sch., Lawrence, 1898-1901; jr. master South Boston High Sch., 1901-06; head master High Sch. of Commerce, Boston, 1906-10; asst. supt. schs., Boston, 1910, supt., 1918—. Sergt. Co. H, 1st N.H. Vols., Spanish-Am. War; mem. secondary sch. sect. of com. on edn. Advisory Commn. of Council Nat. Defense; mem. Mass. Com. on Pub. Safety; pres. Harvard Teachers' Assn., 1916. Home: Boston, Mass. Died Oct. 23, 1921.

THOMPSON, Frederic Diodati, Count, author; b. New York, Dec. 17, 1850; s. David and Sarah (Diodati) T.; ed. pvt. schs.; grad. law dept. Columbia; admitted to N.Y. bar and bar Supreme Ct. U.S.; unmarried. Turkish commr. to World's Columbian Expn., 1893; created Roman count, 1902. Chevalier Order St. Maurice and St. Lazarus; Chevalier Order Holy Sepulchre Jerusalem; Grand Officer Order of the Osmanie, and of Order of the Medjidie, Turkey. Author: In the Track of the Sun. Contbr. to newspapers and mags. Address: New York, N.Y. Died 1906.

THOMPSON, Frederic Lincoln, prof. history; b. Augusta, Me., Apr. 12, 1869; s. William Ladd and Sarah Bickford (Varney) T.; A.B., Amherst, 1892; studied U. of Paris, 1903-05; A.M., Harvard, 1907; m. Marietta Brown, Sept. 1897. Prof. history, Amherst, 1907—. Fellow Am. Geog. Soc.; mem. Am. Hist. Assn., Am. Polit. Science Assn. Congregationalist. Officier de l'Instruction Publique de la République Française, 1919. Home: Amherst, Mass. Died Nov. 19, 1935.

THOMPSON, Frederick Henry, physician; b. New Salem, Mass., Aug. 5, 1844; s. Clark and Nancy (Kendall) T.; grad. Phillips Exeter Acad., 1861; enlisted in 10th Mass. Vols., Aug. 1862; student Harvard, 1862, Amherst, 1864; M.D., Harvard, 1870; surg. interne, Mass. Gen. Hosp., 1869-70; m. Harriet Fiske Howes, June 1, 1870. Practiced at Lancaster, Mass., 1870-74, at Fitchburg, 1874—. Phys. State Industrial Sch. for Girls, 1874; maj. surgeon 10th Regt. Mass. V.M., 1876-78; mem. sch. com., 1875-81; city phys., 1878; mem. Board of Health, 1910-16 (chmn. Feb. 1911-Feb. 1916), Fitchburg; med. dir. Mass. Mut. Aid Soc., 1882-84; mem. U.S. Pension Examining Bd., 1884-87; visited Europe, 1886, 1901, 1905; trustee, 1891—, surgeon, 1895, Burbank Hosp., Fitchburg, later cons. surgeon; med. examiner for the 3d Worcester Dist. of Mass., 1898-1905; med. examiner for 3d Dist., Worcester County, 1908-15. Trustee Pub. Library, Fitchburg, 1882— (with exception of 1 yr.). Republican. Unitarian. Commd. capt. and surgeon on med. staff State Guard of Mass., Aug. 1, 1917. Chmn. Med. Advisory Bd., Selective Service, Dist. 14, Mass., 1918; mem. Med. R.C., U.S.A. Address: Fitchburg, Mass. Died Dec. 14, 1939.

THOMPSON, George, editor; b. Devonshire, Eng., 1840; s. George and Sophia T.; acad. edn. Oxford; m. Abigail I. Wheeler, May 20, 1885. Owner and pub. of St. Paul Dispatch and St. Paul Pioneer Press, of which became editor-in-chief. Home: St. Paul, Minn. Died Jan. 7, 1917.

THOMPSON, George, lawyer; b. nr. Winchester, Tenn., Nov. 10, 1857; s. Burwell J. and Betty Ann (Wilkinson) T.; grad. Carrick Acad., Winchester, Tenn., 1877; m. Anna Bland Baker, Nov. 27, 1885. Began practice at Winchester, 1880; moved to Ft. Worth, Tex., 1887; apptd. atty. T.&P. Ry. Co., 1887; gen. atty. for Tex. & Ark., same co., 1914; gen. solicitor same co. under federal control, also of Internat. Gt. Northern and other lines, World War I, gen. solicitor T.&P. Lines for Tex. and Ark., Mar. 1, 1920—; also gen. solicitor Weatherford, Mineral Wells & Northern Ry.; dir. Continental Nat. Bank, Continental Bank & Trust Co.; mem. law firm Thompson, Barwise & Wharton, gen. attys. Ft. Worth & Denver City Ry. Democrat. Presbyn. Mason, K.P. Home: Ft. Worth, Tex. Died Jan. 10, 1925.

THOMPSON, George B., clergyman; b. Aurora, Ind., Sept. 24, 1862; s. John and Catherine (Costello) T.; Battle Creek (Mich.) Coll., 1885-86; m. Delia A. Hicks, Sept. 29, 1891 (died 1914); m. 2d, Stella M. Slaten, 1915. Ordained to the ministry Seventh Day Adventist Ch., 1893; missionary in Africa, 1893-96; in gen. charge work of the ch. in W.Va., 1897-98, N.Y., 1898-1903; sec. S.S. work for the world, 1904-12; gen. sec. Seventh Day Adventist ch. work in North America, 1912-18, field sec. for the World, 1918-26; also asso. editor Review and Herald. Traveled and preached in India, Egypt, Great Britain, Scandinavia, and other countries of Europe and Far East. Author: Ministry of the Spirit, 1915; Soul Winning, 1916; In His Name, 1918. Home: Washington, D.C. Died June 21, 1930.

THOMPSON, George Wallace, judge; b. St. Mary's, Ont., Can., Aug. 9, 1850; s. Robert and Theresa (Lee) T.; B.A., Toronto (Ont.) U., 1874; m. Hettie Linsley, Sept. 11, 1884. Admitted to Ia. bar, 1875, and practiced in Osceola; removed to Galesburg, Ill., 1877; mem. Bd. of Aldermen, 1880-84; judge Circuit Ct., 9th Circuit, Ill., 1897—; judge Appellate Ct., 2d Ill. Dist., 1906-12, 3d Dist., 1912—. Dir. Galesburg Nat. Bank. Republican. Baptist. Mason. Address: Galesburg, Ill. Died Feb. 6, 1921.

THOMPSON, Gilbert, topographer U.S. Geological Survey; b. Blackstone, Mass., Mar. 21, 1839; s. William Venner and Harriet (Gilbert) T.; ed. common sch.; m. Mary Frances Reed McNeil, Sept. 23, 1869. Printer by trade; soldier, U.S. engr. battalion, Nov. 22, 1861, to Nov. 21, 1864; asst. engr. headquarters Army of Potomac, 1864-65 on Western explorations and surveys, etc., 1866—; comd. engr. battalion, D.C. militia, 1890-98; historian Veteran U.S. Engrs. Assn. Address: Washington, D.C. Died 1909.

THOMPSON, Harry Arthur, editor; b. Phila., Pa., Sept. 5, 1867; s. James Daniel and Sue (Wharton) T.; A.B., Wesleyan U., Conn., 1893; m. Louise Tackaberry, Nov. 7, 1899; children—Elizabeth Wharton (dec.), John Cranwill, Lewis Gordon, James Daniel.

Master of Choristers' Sch., Grace Ch., New York, 1894-95; in book pub. bus., New York, 1895-1903; asso. editor The Saturday Evening Post, 1903-06, art editor, 1906-12; editor The Country Gentleman, 1912-17; dir. bur. of publicity Am. Red Cross, Pa. Div., 1917—. Address: Greenwich, Conn. Died June 13, 1936.

THOMPSON, Heber Samuel, engr.; b. Pottsville, Pa., Aug. 14, 1840; s. Samuel and Elizabeth (Cunningham) T.; A.B., Yale, 1861, A.M., 1871; studied mining engring. in pvt. offices; m. Sarah E. Beck, Jan. 23, 1866. Enlisted, pvt., Apr. 16, 1861, "First Defenders," 1st troops of war of secession to enter Washington (Apr. 18, 1861); later served, 1861-65; lt. and capt. 7th Pa. Cav.; engr. and agt. Girard Estate, Mar. 16, 1874—. Pres. bd. trustees State Hosp. for Injured, anthracite coal region, Pa., Ashland, Pa. ("Miners' Hosp."); apptd. under act of assembly, by gov. of Pa., on "Coal Waste Commn."—pub. report, 1893. Address: Pottsville, Pa. Died 1911.

THOMPSON, Helen Elizabeth, teacher; b. Brattleboro, Vt., Apr. 2, 1857; d. Charles Frederick and Elizabeth (McCune) T.; A.B., Vassar Coll., 1878; L.H.D., Smith Coll., Northampton, Mass., 1929. Teacher French and German, The Mary A. Burnham School, 1879—; also teacher of Italian; became head of the family, 1887, head mistress, 1910, head of the sch., 1916, and prin., 1921, prin. emeritus, 1921—. Republican. Conglist. Address: Northampton, Mass. Died Jan. 18, 1936.

THOMPSON, Henry Adams, clergyman; b. Stormstown, Center County, Pa., Mar. 23, 1837; s. John and Lydia (Blake) T.; A.B., Jefferson Coll., Canonsburg, Pa., 1858; student Western Theol. Sem., Allegheny City, Pa.; D.D., Jefferson, 1873; LL.D., Westfield Coll., Ill., 1886; m. Harriet E. Copeland, Aug. 7, 1862. Taught select sch., Marion and Noblesville, Ind., 1861; prof. mathematics, Western Coll., Ia., 1861-62; same, Otterbein U., O., 1862-67; supt. pub. schs., Troy, O., 1867-71; prof. mathematics, Westfield Coll., 1871-72; pres. Otterbein U., 1872-86; candidate for Congress, Prohibition ticket, 1874, for lt. gov. of Ohio, 1875, for gov. 1877; chmn. Nat. Prohibition Conv., 1876; nominated for v.p. on ticket with Neal Dow, 1880; del. Methodist Ecumenical Conf., London, 1881; commr. dept. science and edn. at Ohio Centennial Expn., Columbus, 1889; asso. editor S.S. literature, 1893-97, editor-in-chief S.S. lit. U.B. Ch., 1897-1901; editor United Brethren Quarterly Rev., 1901-09; frequent contbr. to Telescope, jour. of U.B. Ch. Prohibition candidate for gov. of Ohio, 1911. Author: Schools of the Prophets; Power of the Invisible; Our Bishops: Biography of Bishop J. Wearer; Bible Study and Devotion, 1905; Women of the Bible, 1914. Address: Dayton, O. Died July 8, 1920.

THOMPSON, Henry Burling, cotton mfr.; b. Darby, Pa., Aug. 6, 1857; s. Lucius Peters and Caroline Jones (Burling) T.; B.S., Princeton, 1877; m. Mary Wilson, Apr. 14, 1891; children—Mrs. Mary Reath, Mrs. Katharine Wood, Henry Burling, Mrs. Elinor Donaldson, James H. W. Began mfg. under Thomas Dolan, E. Phila., 1877-79; with Pacific Mills, Lawrence, 1880-81; treas. Joseph Bancroft & Sons Co., 1889-1911; pres. United States Finishing Co., 1913-33; chmn. bd. The W. S. Finishing Co., 1933—. Dep. chmn. bd. and class C dir. Fed. Res. Bank, Phila., 1916-24. Chmn. Del. Rep. State Com., 1898-1902; mem. Rep. Nat. Com., 1898; jury commr. Newcastle County, Del., 1908. Life trustee Princeton U.; pres. bd. trustees U. of Delaware. Episcopalian. Home: Greenville P.O., Del. Died Nov. 20, 1935.

THOMPSON, Henry Dallas, univ. prof.; b. Metuchen, N.J., Aug. 24, 1864; s. John B. and Hannah G. (Reeve) T.; A.B., Princeton, 1885, fellow in mathematics, 1885-86; A.M., 1888, D.Sc., 1889; fellow Johns Hopkins, 1886-87; Ph.D., Göttingen, 1892; m. Genevieve Lemoine, Dec. 28, 1908. Tutor in mathematics, 1888-91, asst. prof., 1891-94, prof., 1894—, Princeton. Elected to N.J. Assembly, 1906, 07, 08. In New Zealand, Australia, China, Japan, P.I., 1915-16, studying govtl. and ednl. methods, and in India, China, Japan, 1921-22. Sec. N.J. Mil. Camp, summer 1917. Rep. presdl. elector, 1920. Fellow A.A.A.S. Author: Translation of Euclid (with Henry Burchard Fine), 1890; Elementary Solid Geometry and Mensuration, 1896; Coördinate Geometry (with H. B. Fine), 1907; also various scientific articles in tech. jours. Home: Princeton, N.J. Died Aug. 30, 1927.

THOMPSON, Holland, coll. prof., author; b. Randolph County, N.C., July 30, 1873; s. D. Matt and Mary Elizabeth (Rice) T.; Ph.B., U. of N.C., 1895; LL.D., U. of N.C., 1935; A.M., Columbia, 1900, Ph.D., 1906; m. Isobel Graham Aitkin, July 19, 1905; 1 son, Laurence. Prin., Concord (N.C.) High Sch., 1895-99; fellow Columbia, 1899-1900; tutor history, 1901-02, instr., 1902-06, asst. prof., 1906, prof. Coll. City of N.Y., 1920—; lecturer in history, Columbia, 1923-24; visiting prof. history, U. of N.C., summer 1935. Mem. Acad. Polit. Science, Am. Hist. Assn., Nat. Inst. Social Sciences, Am. Assn. Univ. Profs. (charter member). Independent Democrat. Editor in chief: The Book of Knowledge, 20 vols., 1910-11, frequent revisions. Editor: The People and the Trusts, 1912; The World War, 1920; Lands and Peoples, 1929-30. Author: From Cotton Field to Cotton Mill, 1906; History of Our Land, 1911; Prisons of the Civil War, 1911; The United States, 1915; The New South, 1919, and The Age of Invention, 1921 (in Chronicles of America). Contbr. New Internat. and Nelson's encys., Ency. Britannica, Dictionary of Am. Biography, Dictionary of Am. History, also to hist. and econ. jours. Awarded gold medal, Sesquicentennial Expn., Phila., 1926. Home: New York, N.Y. Died Oct. 21, 1940.

THOMPSON, Hugh Miller, P.E. bishop of Miss.; b. County Londonderry, Ireland, June 6, 1830; s. John and Annie (Miller) T.; academic edn., Cleveland, O.; grad. Nashotah Theol. Sem., Wis., 1852, S.T.D., Hobart Coll., 1863; D.D., U. of the South; LL.D., U. of Ala. Ordered deacon, 1852; ordained priest, 1856; prof. church history Nashotah Theol. Sem., 1860-70. Editor Am. Churchman, Chicago, 1860-70; Church Jour., New York, 1870-77. Asso. rector St. Paul's Milwaukee, 1866-70; rector St. James' Chicago, 1870-71; Christ Ch., New York, 1871-75; Trinity, New Orleans, 1876-83; consecrated, 1883, coadjutor bishop, becoming bishop, 1887. Author: Unity and Its Restoration, 1859; Sin and Penalty, 1862; First Principles, 1863; Copy, 1871; Kingdom of God, 1872; Absolution, 1872; The World and the Logos, 1886; The World and the Kingdom, 1888; The World and the Man, 1890; The World and the Wrestlers, 1895; More Copy, 1897; lectures, sermons, pamphlets. Address: Jackson, Miss. Died 1902.

THOMPSON, Hugh Smith, gov.; b. Charleston, S.C., Jan. 24, 1836; s. Henry Tazewell and Agnes (Smith) T.; grad. S.C. Mil. Acad., 1856; m. Miss Clarkson, 1858. Lt. and prof. French Arsenal Acad., Columbia, S.C., 1858-60; capt. battalion of State cadets of S.C., C.S.A., 1861-65; prin. Columbia Male Acad., 1866-76; State supt. edn., 1876-82; gov., 1882-86; asst. sec. treasury, U.S., 1886-89; U.S. civil service commr., 1889-92; comptroller New York Life Ins. Co., 1892. Democrat. Home: New York, N.Y. Died 1904.

THOMPSON, Ira Francis, judge; b. Crawford County, Wis., June 20, 1885; s. Josiah and Zylphia (Alderman) T.; student pub. schs., Wis., 1891-1900; grad. high sch., Eureka, Calif., 1904; student U. of Calif., 1904-09; m. Hilda Manning, June 1, 1910; children—Cora Elisabeth, John Francis. Admitted to Calif. bar, 1909; practiced in Oakland 1 yr., in Los Angeles, 1910-23; judge of Superior Ct., 1923-26; justice of Dist. Ct. of Appeals, 1926-32; asso. justice Supreme Ct. of Calif., 1932—; lecturer in law, U. of Southern Calif.; 1926-32. Four-Minute Man and sec. Legal Advisory Bd., 17th Calif. Dist., World War I. Republican. Mason, K.P., Elk. Home: Los Angeles, Calif. Died Aug. 4, 1937.

THOMPSON, James Edwin, surgeon; b. Northwich, Cheshire, Eng., May 21, 1863; s. John and Mary (Molyneux) T.; Owens Coll., Manchester, Eng., 1879-86; M.B., U. of London, 1887, B.S., 1888; F.R.C.S., Eng., 1888; m. Eleanor Waters Roeck, May 16, 1896; children—Kate Waters, John, Mary Molyneux, Eleanor Roeck, James Edwin, Rhoda, Frederick Roeck, Edward Randall. Resident surgeon, Manchester Royal Infirmary, 1890-91; prof. surgery, U. of Tex., 1891—; surgeon to John Sealy Hosp., 1891—. Maj. Med. R.C. Fellow Am. Surg. Assn., Southern Surg. Assn., Am. Coll. Surgeons, Tex. Surg. Soc. Democrat. Episcopalian. Extensive contbr. to med. jours. and trans. surg. societies. Home: Galveston, Tex. Died Apr. 9, 1927.

THOMPSON, James Westfall, univ. prof.; b. Pella, Ia., June 3, 1869; s. Rev. Abraham and Anna (Westfall) T.; A.B., Rutgers, 1892, Litt.D., 1922; Ph.D., U. Chicago, 1895; research Paris and other foreign archives, 1903, 07, 09, 13; m. Martha Landers, Aug. 15, 1911. Asst. in history, 1895-97, asso., 1897-99, instr. Europe history, 1899-1904, asst. prof., 1904-08, asso. prof., July 1, 1908-13, prof. mediæval history, 1913-32, U. of Chicago; Sidney Hellman Ehrman prof. European history, U. of Calif., 1932-39; prof. emeritus, July 1, 1939—. Pres. Social Science Research Conf. of Pacific Coast, 1935-36. Fellow Mediæval Acad. of America. Author: The Wars of Religion in France—the Huguenots, Catherine de Medici and Philip II, 1559-1576, 1909; The Frankfort Book Fair, 1911; The Last Pagan, 1916; The Lost Oracles, 1921; Feudal Germany, 1929; Economic and Social History of the Middle Ages, 1929; Economic and Social History of the Later Middle Ages, 1931; The Middle Ages (2 vols.), 1931; The Living Past, 1931; The Medieval Library, 1939; Literacy of Laity in Middle Ages, 1939; also articles in periodicals. Home: Berkeley, Calif. Died Sept. 30, 1941.

THOMPSON, John Cameron, lawyer; b. Princeton, Wis., Apr. 28, 1872; s. John Cowen and Catherine Maria (Cameron) T.; prep. edn., Ripon (Wis.) Prep. Sch.; student Ripon Coll.; LL.B., U. of Wis., 1893; m. Mabel Adeline Gile, June 28, 1899; children—John Cameron, Robert Reese, Barbara Gile (Mrs. John Day Buckstaff). Admitted to Wis. bar, 1893, and began practice at Oshkosh; mem. firm Thompson, Gruenewald & Frye; dir. First Nat. Bank, First Trust Co., First Investment Co., Campbell & Cameron Co., W. J. Campbell Lumber Co., Percey Fur House, Algoma Park Co., Island Point, Inc. (all of Oshkosh, Wis.), North Continent Utilities Co. (Chicago), Sawyer Co. and Wis. Delaware Co. (Wilmington, Del.), Sawyer Cattle Co. (San Angelo, Tex.), Green Bay & Miss. Canal Co. (Appleton, Wis.), Northeastern Wis. Investment Co. Trustee Ripon Coll., Elizabeth Batchelder Davis Orphans Home. Republican. Mason. Elk, K.P. Home: Oshkosh, Wis. Died Dec. 26, 1934.

THOMPSON, J(ohn) Milton, brig. gen. U.S.A.; b. Lebanon, N.H., Aug. 1, 1842; s. Ira W. and Cynthia Wheeler (Spalding) T.; ed. pub. and pvt. schs.; hon. A.M., Dartmouth College, 1907; m. Mary Elizabeth Walcott, Mar. 5, 1871; m. 2d, Carrie Alice Ellis, Nov. 21, 1914. Enlisted pvt. 7th N.H. Inf., Nov. 7, 1861; apptd. 2d lt. 33d U.S.C. Inf., Jan. 15, 1863, 1st lt., Jan. 27, 1863, capt., Nov. 7, 1863, until end of Civil War; apptd. 2d lt. 38th U.S. Inf., July 28, 1866, 1st lt., Nov. 4, 1867; capt. 24th Inf., Dec. 23, 1878, maj., Apr. 26, 1898 (col. 42d U.S. Vol. Inf., Aug. 17, 1898); lt. col. 14th Inf., Oct. 19, 1899; col. 23d Inf., Apr. 22, 1901; brig. gen. U.S.A., Aug. 9, 1903, and retired. Bvtd. 1st lt., Mar. 2, 1867, "for gallant and meritorious service at James Island, S.C." Address: Washington, D.C. Died Apr. 6, 1922.

THOMPSON, John Q., lawyer; b. Rossville, Ill., Jan. 12, 1862; s. Lewis M. and Judith A. T.; common school edn., LL.B., U. of Mich., 1882. Began law practice, Danville, Ill., 1882; State's atty., Vermilion County, Ill., 1888-90; judge Vermilion County, 1890-97 (resigned); asst. atty. gen. of U.S., 1897—. Home: Washington, D.C. Died Feb. 26, 1913.

THOMPSON, John R., restaurateur; b. Vermillion County, Ill., Nov. 13, 1865; s. John R. and Elizabeth (Wright) T.; ed. Normal Sch., Danville, Ill., 2 yrs.; m. Rose Holloway, Aug. 5, 1891; children—John R., Ruth E., Florence H. Began in merc. bus., Fithian, Ill., 1887; moved to Chicago, 1891, entered restaurant business; later inc. John R. Thompson Co., operating 109 restaurants (1925). Owner of live stock farm at Fithian, Vermilion County, Ill. Treas. Cook County, Ill., 1906-10. Home: Lake Forest, Ill. Died June 17, 1927.

THOMPSON, John Taliaferro, army officer, mech. engr., inventor; b. Newport, Ky., Dec. 31, 1860; s. Lt. Col. James and Julia Maria (Taliaferro) T.; student Ind. U., 1876-77; grad. U.S. Mil. Acad., 1882; torpedo course, U.S. Engrs.' Sch., 1884; grad. U.S. Arty. Sch., 1890; LL.D., Ind. U., 1922; m. Juliet Estelle, d. Judge M. B. and Almira Lewis Hagans, July 27, 1882; 1 son, Lt. Col. Marcellus Hagans. Commd. 2d lt. arty., June 13, 1882; promoted through grades to col., Oct. 30, 1913; retired, Nov. 2, 1914; brig. gen. ordnance, O.R.C., Army of U.S., 1924. Served various garrisons, Naval Gun Factory, Nat. Armory, etc.; lt. col. U.S. Vols., Tampa, Fla., 1898, and in Cuba; connected with development of service small arms; charged by War Dept. with preparation of war plans of Ordnance Dept., 1908-14, lecturer Army War Coll, 1908-14—; cons. engr., New York, 1914-17; in charge design and mfr. of all small arms and cartridge for U.S., Apr. 16, 1917-18. Brig. gen. (temp.), Aug. 1918; advisory engr. to chief of ordnance; dir. of ordnance training; dir. of arsenals. Awarded D.S.M., 1919, "For exceptionally meritorious and conspicuous service," as chief of small arms div.; later pres. John T. Thompson Corp., New York. Episcopalian. Writer of various tech. pamphlets and articles. Inventor of firearms, machinery and airplane devices. Home: Great Neck, L.I., N.Y. Died June 21, 1940.

THOMPSON, Joseph B., congressman; b. Grayson County, Tex., Apr. 29, 1871; s. James M. and Caroline T.; A.B., Savoy Coll., Fannin County, Tex., 1890; m. Mary Miller, Sept. 5, 1894. Admitted to Tex. bar, 1892; began to practice, Ardmore, Ind. Ty.; U.S. commr., Purcell, Ind. Ty., 1893-97; located in Pauls Valley, Okla.; mem. Dem. Territorial Exec. Com., 1896-1904; del. Dem. Nat. Conv., Kansas City, Mo., 1900, St. Louis, 1904, Denver, 1908; chmn. Dem. State Com. to prepare constn for State of Okla., 1906-10; mem. Okla. Senate, 1911-Mar. 17, 1913 (resigned); mem. 63d Congress (1913-15), Okla. at large, and 64th and 65th Congresses (1915-19), 5th Dist. Methodist. Mason. Home: Pauls Valley, Okla. Died Sept. 18, 1918.

THOMPSON, Josiah Van Kirk, banker; b. Fayette County, Pa., Feb. 15, 1854; s. Jasper Markle and Eliza (Caruthers) T.; B.S., Washington and Jefferson Coll., 1871; m. Mary Anderson, Dec. 11, 1879 (died 1896); m. 2d, Mrs. B. A. Gardner Hawes, Aug. 11, 1903. Entered First Nat. Bank, Uniontown, Pa., 1871, cashier, 1877, pres., 1889—; large coal operator for many yrs. Republican. Presbyn. Home: Uniontown, Pa. Died Sept. 27, 1933.

THOMPSON, Laforrest Holman, jurist; b. Bakersfield, Vt., Jan. 6, 1848; ed. common schools, Lamoille County Grammar School, Johnson, Vt., and Kimball Union Acad., Meriden, N.H.; A.M., U. of Vt.; m. Mary Eliza Dutton (died 1881); m. 2d, Helen C. Kinney. Admitted to bar, March 1, 1871; established practice Irasburgh, Vt., 1871; member Vt. legislature, 1880-81, 1882-83, and 1890; State senator and pres. senate, 1884-85; in 1890 elected sixth asso. judge of supreme court, and reëlected biennially, 1890—, becoming 5th asso. judge. Address: Irasburgh, Vt. Died 1900.

THOMPSON, Maurice, author; b. Fairfield, Ind., Sept. 9, 1844, reared in Ga.; ed. by pvt. tutors on plantation in Ga. for civil engr.; carefully trained in Greek, Latin and French; served in Confed. army; after war chief engr. of a railroad in Ind.; later practiced law, Crawfordsville, Ind.; mem. Ind. legislature, 1878; del. to Dem. Nat. Conv., St. Louis, 1888; State geologist of Ind., 1885-89; m. Alice, eldest dau. Hon. John Lee, 1868. Explored, 1867, Lake Okeechobee, Fla., making a list of its birds, animals and plants; also made ornithol. explorations of the Okefinokee Swamp, the Terre aux Bœufs and islands of Southern La., the wilds of Northern Mich., and the hill country of Ala., Miss. and Ga. For years a literary editor on staff of N.Y. Independent. Author: Poems; A Tallahassee Girl; Stories of the Cherokee Hills; Ethics of Literary Art; Toxophilus in Arcadia; His Second Campaign; At Love's Extremes; A Fortnight of Folly; The Ocala Boy; King of Honey Island; Hoosier Mosaics; The Witchery of Archery; Songs of Fair Weather; Byways and Bird Notes; Sylvan Secrets; The Story of Louisiana; Lincoln's Grave (poem); etc. Home: Crawfordsville, Ind. Died 1901.

THOMPSON, Melville Withington, financial accountant, lawyer; b. Washington, D.C., Oct. 22, 1871; s. Niles Hibbard and Lucy (Withington) T.; m. Mary L. Glass, 1925. Mem. Thompson & Black, accountants and tax consultants, N.Y. City; pres. Thompson & Black, Incorporated, oil producers, Tulsa, Oklahoma. Commd. lt. col. U.S.A., Aug. 15, 1917; pres. War Credits Bd. of War Dept.; hon. discharged, Nov. 29, 1918; (civilian) gov. War Credits Bd. from Nov. 1918. Awarded D.S.M. Home: Mt. Kisco, N.Y. Died July 15, 1936.

THOMPSON, Richard Wigginton, sec. navy; b. Culpeper County, Va., June 9, 1809; went to Ky., 1831, becoming clerk in Louisville store; moved to Lawrence County, Ind.; admitted to bar, 1834; member Ind. legislature, 1834-36, senate, 1836-38; short time pres. senate and acting lt. gov.; presdl. elector on Harrison and Tyler ticket, 1840; member Congress, 1841-43 and 1847-49; presdl. elector, 1864; del. Nat. Rep. convs. 1868 and 1876; judge 5th Ind. circuit, 1867-69; sec. navy in Hayes cabinet, 1877-81; became chmn. Am. com., Panama Canal Co., 1881. Author: The Papacy and the Civil Power; Footprints of the Jesuits; History of the Tariff; Personal Recollections of Sixteen Presidents. Address: Terre Haute, Ind. Died 1900.

THOMPSON, Robert Andrew, cons. engr.; b. New Waverly, Walker County, Tex., July 11, 1869; s. Andrew Jackson and Mary (Gillespie) T.; B.S. in C.E., U. of Tex., 1892, M.A., 1893, C.E., 1900; m. Evelyne Dickson, Cleburne, Tex., Dec. 21, 1897; children—Frances, Robert, Elizabeth, Eleanor, Evelyne, Frederick, Lucy. Instr. civ. engring., U. of Tex., 1893-94 and 1897-98; chief engr. R.R. Commn. of Tex., 1898-1908; chief engr. Wichita Falls & Northwestern R.R., 1908-11; chief engr. R.R. Commn. of Calif., 1911-13; mem. engring. bd. (R.R. valuation) Interstate Commerce Commn., 1913-21; chief engr. and gen. mgr. Wichita County (Tex.) Water Im. Dist. No. 1, 1921-23; chief engr. (with J. C. Nagle) on constrn. Garza Dam for Dallas, Tex., 1923-27; mem. firm Thompson & Butler, cons. engrs., San Francisco, 1925-26; chief engr. Tex. Highway Dept., Austin, Tex., 1927-28; cons. highway engr. Dallas Chamber Commerce, 1928-33, and 1934-38; cons. engr. Brown County (Tex.) Water Improvement Dist. Reservoir Dam, 1930-33; state engr. for Tex., Fed. Emergency Adminstrn. of Public Works, 1933-34. Democrat. Presbyn. Address: Ft. Worth, Tex. Died May 30, 1941.

THOMPSON, Robert Ellis, educator; b. nr. Lurgan, Ireland, April 5, 1844; s. Samuel and Catherine (Ellis) T.; A.B., U. of Pa., 1865, A.M., 1868; Ph.D., Hamilton Coll., 1870; S.T.D., U. of Pa., 1887; LL.D., Muhlenberg College, 1909; m. Mary E. Neely, 1874 (died 1894); m. 2d, Catherine Neely, 1910. Licensed to preach by Reformed Presbytery of Phila., 1867; ordained, 1874; prof. Latin and mathematics, 1868-71, social science, 1871-81, history and English lit., 1881-92, U. of Pa.; prin. Central High Sch., Phila., 1894-1921. Lecturer on protective tariffs, Harvard, 1885, Yale, 1886-87; Stone lecturer Princeton Theol. Sem., 1891. Editor Penn Monthly, 1870-81; editor The American, 1881-92; on staff of the Irish World, 1884—, and Sunday School Times, 1892—. Author: Social Science and National Economy, 1875; Elements of Political Economy, 1881; Protection to Home Industry (Harvard lectures), 1885; De Civitate Dei—The Divine Order of Human Society (Princeton Stone lectures), 1891; History of the Presbyterian Churches of America, 1895; Political Economy for High Schools, 1895; The National Hymn-Book of the American Churches, 1893; The Hand of God in American History, 1902; The Historic Episcopate, 1910; Nature, the Mirror of Grace, 1907; The Apostles as Every Day Men, 1912; The History of the Dwelling-House and Its Future, 1914. Editor: The Ency. Americana, supplement to Ency. Britannica, Vols. I and II (Stoddard edit.), 1884-85; The Latin Hymn-Writers and Their Hymns, by Samuel W. Duffield, 1889; The Life of George Hay Stuart, written by himself, 1890. Employed by alumni of Central H.S. to write a history of the school, also continued as prin. emeritus to teach ethics and polit. economy, at request of alumni, although retired legally. Address: Philadelphia, Pa. Died Oct. 19, 1924.

THOMPSON, Robert Harvey, lawyer; b. Copiah County, Miss., August 25, 1847; s. John H. and Margaret Ann (Watson) T.; A.B., U. of Miss., 1869; studied law, U. of Miss., 1869-70, LL.D., 1893; m. Mary Louise Coleman, 1871 (died 1874); m. 2d, Mrs. Frances Patterson Myers, 1876 (died 1916). Served as pvt., C.S.A. at 16; began practicing law, Brookhaven, 1871; state senator, 1876-80; mem. Constl. Conv., 1890; atty. I.C. R.R., 1878-97 (resigned); gen. atty. Ala. & Vicksburg Ry. Co., 1897, until it became part of I.C. System, 1912, and continued as atty. for that ry.; sr. mem. firm of R. H. & J. H. Thompson. New Capitol commr., 1900-01. Chmn. Code Commn., which prepared the Annotated Code of Miss., 1892; trustee U. of Miss., 1889-1906. Democrat. Wrote: Mississippi Tax Titles (Proc. Miss. Bar Assn.), 1886; Suffrage in Mississippi (Proc. Miss. Hist. Soc.), 1899; Constitution of Mississippi, 1923. Joint author of McWillie and Thompson's Digest of Mississippi Supreme Court Reports, 1911. Home: Jackson, Miss. Died May 30, 1935.

THOMPSON, Robert John, author; b. La Porte City, Ia., Oct. 15, 1865; s. Francis M. and Eliza H. T.; ed. La Porte City High Sch.; pvt. instrn. in law and philosophy; m. Martha Leimer, June 27, 1885; m. 2d, Muriel Stevenson, 1913; children—R. P., Madeleine M., Robert J., Cyril Sherman. School teacher, 1883-85; in U.S. ry. postal service, 1885-91; later on editorial staff Chicago Times; inventor automatic recording safe, and pres. Automatic Recording Safe Co., Chicago. Originator and dir. Lafayette Monument project; diplomatic envoy of President McKinley to President Loubet, 1900; sec. and dir. Lafayette Monument Commn. Apptd. consul to Cienfuegos, Cuba, 1905 (did not serve); Am. consul at Hanover, Germany, 1906-12, Sheffield, Eng., 1912-13, Aix-la-Chapelle, Germany, 1913-15 (resigned). Officier de la Légion d'Honneur (France). Author: (and compiler) The Proofs of Life After Death—A Twentieth Century Symposium; A Square Deal for Every Man (collation of quotations from addresses and messages of Theodore Roosevelt); England and Germany in the War. Adequate Brevity—Philosophy of Coolidge; contbr. to mags. Address: Chicago, Ill. Died Aug. 23, 1931.

THOMPSON, Robert Means; b. Corsica, Pa., Mar. 2, 1849; s. Judge John J. Y. and Agnes McClure (Kennedy) T, and g.s. and g.g.s. of ministers of Presbyn. Ch.; grad. U.S. Naval Acad., 1868; ensign, 1869, master, 1871, resigned, Oct. 1871; admitted to bar, 1872; LL.B., Harvard, 1874; LL.D., George Washington U., and Washington and Jefferson Coll., 1921; m. Sarah, d. William Channing Gibbs, Apr. 30, 1873. Practiced in Boston; mem. Boston Common Council, 1876, 77, 78; identified with mining and smelting interests; became resident of N.J.; col. and a.d.c. on staff of the gov. of N.J. Am. organizer of Navy Athletic Assn. and donor of Thompson cup, played for in football contests between U.S. Mil. and Naval acads.; organizer and pres. New York Naval Acad. Alumni Assn. and trustee Naval Acad. Alumni Assn. at Annapolis; pres. emeritus Navy League; chmn. Am. Olympic Com. at games held in Stockholm, 1912, and in Paris, 1924; 1st pres., and pres. emeritus, Am. Olympic Assn.; served as pres. Soc. Naval Architects and Marine Engrs., Pa. Soc. of New York; mem. Loyal Legion from its orgn. and was mem. of council N.Y. Comdry. and comdr. Washington Commandery, later comdr. in chief of the Loyal Legion. Visited Japan on invitation of Japanese Govt. and was awarded by the Emperor, Order of Rising Sun, 2d Class; also awarded Order of Gustavus Vasa (Sweden); Cross of Comdr. Legion of Honor (France). Office: New York, N.Y. Died Sept. 5, 1930.

THOMPSON, Slason, journalist; b. Fredericton, N.B., Jan. 5, 1849; s. George and Charity Sobieski (Slason) T.; ed. U. of N.B.; m. Julia D. Watson, 1887; children—Julia (Mrs. Le Baron Turner), Barbara (Mrs. John C. Mechem), Margaret. Admitted to bar, N.B., 1870, Calif., 1874; entered journalism, San Francisco Morning Call, 1876; reporter N.Y. Tribune, 1878, 79; western agt. N.Y. Asso. Press, Chicago, 1880; one of founders Chicago Herald, 1881; one of founders America; held editorial positions with Chicago Record, Evening Journal, Post; chief editorial writer of the Times-Herald and Record-Herald, 1898-1903, Railway News Bur., 1903—. Author: Eugene Field (biography), 1902; Cost, Capitalization and Estimated Value of American Railways, 1907; Railway Statistics of the United States, annually, 1905—; A Short History of American Railways, 1925; Life of Eugene Field, 1927; Way Back When, 1930; (plays) M'liss, 1878; Sharps and Flats, 1880. Compiler: The Humbler Poets, 1886; Sharps and Flats, 1900; The Railway Library, annually, 1909-15. Home: Lake Forest, Ill. Died Dec. 22, 1935.

THOMPSON, Theodore Strong, pay dir. U.S.N.; b. Northampton, Mass., April 23, 1842; s. Augustus C. and Sarah Elizabeth (Strong) T.; ed. Williams Coll. Served 9 mos. in U.S. Vols. Civil War; apptd. acting asst. p.m. U.S.N., Oct. 9, 1863; hon. discharged, Aug. 31, 1865; apptd. asst. p.m., July 23, 1866; passed asst. p.m., Feb. 1, 1868; p.m., Jan. 25, 1878; pay insp., July 10, 1898; pay dir., Sept. 21, 1901; retired, Dec. 26, 1903, with rank of rear admiral for services during Civil War. Home: Brookline, Mass. Died July 27, 1915.

THOMPSON, Thomas Clarkson, mayor; b. Columbia, S.C., Sept. 21, 1860; s. Hugh Smith and Elizabeth Anderson (Clarkson) T.; ed. Columbia Male Acad.; LL.D., U. of Chattanooga, 1913; m. Clara Mabelle Berry, June 15, 1887 (died 1912); children—Thomas Clarkson, Hugh Smith, Benjamin Berry; m. 2d, Anna May Signaigo, June 1, 1915; children—Elizabeth Clarkson, Catherine Clarkson, Waddy, Emily Clarkson. Began at 15, in cotton export business, Charleston, S.C.; connected with S. M. Inman Company, cotton shippers, at Atlanta, Ga., 1880-90; in Boston, representing large cotton interests, 1890-93, Chattanooga, 1893—; also mgr. Nat. Life Ins. Co. of Vt., for Tenn., 1898—. Served as officer S.C. and Tenn. N.G. Elected mayor of Chattanooga, 1909; legislature changed form of govt. to commn. plan, Jan. 1911; again elected mayor for term, 1911-15. Civilian aid to adj. gen. U.S.A., World War I. Awarded Kiwanis Cup, 1933, for being most useful citizen of Chattanooga. Trustee Children's Hosp. (Chattanooga), Hosp. for Crippled Adults (Memphis), Children's Home Soc. (Nashville), U. of Chattanooga. Episcopalian. Democrat. Home: Chattanooga, Tenn. Died Mar. 21, 1938.

THOMPSON, Thomas Payne, underwriter; b. Montgomery, Ala., Nov. 11, 1860; s. William Dunbar and Mary L. (Joyner) T.; ed. common schs. until 14; m. Julia Elder, Oct. 1887 (died 1888); m. 2d, Ida M., d. Dr. A. U. Zorn, Apr. 21, 1890. Traveling salesman, from New Orleans, 1880-91; with Equitable Life Assurance Soc., 1891—, asso. gen. agt. for La. and Miss., 1911—; pres. Bienville Realty Co., Greater New Orleans Bldg. & Loan Co.; v.p. Panama Planting Co.; dir. Canal-Commercial Bank, Mut. Homestead Assn., Title & Mortgage Guaranty Co. On staff of Governor J. Y. Sanders, of La., with rank of col., 1910-12; pres. 14th Ward Health Assn., to repel yellow fever, 1905; led successful campaign against race-track gambling, 1908; originator of movement, in 1907, to hold internat. expn. at New Orleans, commemorating opening of Panama Canal; chmn. exec. com. World's Panama Expn.; pres. Judah Touro Fund, Shakespeare Home for Aged, La. State Mus. History and Commerce, Life Underwriters' Assn. of La., Marquette Soc. for Higher Edn.; v.p. State Bd. Charities and Corrections, Prison Reform Soc. Democrat. Knights of Columbus (Past Master 4° for La., Miss., Ala.). Author: Bibliography, A List of Louisiana Writers, 1904; Project for World's Exposition at New Orleans, 1910; also Logical Point Pamphlets (series, Nos. 1-21), 1910, articles in cyclos., mags. and newspapers. Editor: Bibliography of Louisiana; collected Americana relating to La. and Miss. Valley. Home: New Orleans, La. Died Nov. 5, 1924.

THOMPSON, Vance (Charles), author, playwright; b. Apr. 17, 1863; s. Rev. Charles L. and Mary B. T.; grad. Princeton, 1883; Ph.D., U. of Jena, Sachsen-Weimar, Germany; m. Lilian Spencer, actress, playwright, July 27, 1890. Founder and editor M'lle New York (fortnightly rev.). Author: (dramas) In Old Japan; The Dresden Shepherdess; The Japanese Doll; The Peace Girl; Florianne's Dream (musical pantomime, collaboration with Ethelbert Nevin); Jane Shore (tragic drama, collaboration with Eugene Morin); (books) French Portraits, 1900; Diplomatic Mysteries, 1905; Killing the Mandarin; Life and Letters of Ethelbert Nevin, 1913; The Night Watchman and Other Poems, 1914; Eat and Grow Thin, 1914; The Ego Book, 1914; The Carnival of Destiny, 1916; Take It from Me, 1916; Drink, 1917; Woman, 1917; The Pointed Tower, 1922; The Green Ray, 1923; Louisa, 1924. Lit. editor-in-chief The Outline of Christianity, 1924. Attaché Am. Embassy, Rome, 1919. Home: Los Angeles, Calif. Died June 5, 1925.

THOMPSON, Waddy, author; b. Columbia, S.C., Aug. 13, 1867; s. Hugh Smith and Elizabeth Anderson (Clarkson) T.; A.B., U. of S.C., 1887; m. Pauline Spain, Oct. 30, 1895. In journalism, 1887-95; in life ins. and pub. business, 1895—. Democrat. Episcopalian. Author: A History of the United States, 1904; A Primary History of the United States, 1910; A History of the People of the United States, 1919; The First Book in United States History, 1921; History of American Progress (with Fremont P. Wirth), 1933. Home: Atlanta, Ga. Died Mar. 19, 1939.

THOMPSON, Wallace, author, editor; b. Topeka, Kan., Aug. 2, 1883; s. Alton Howard and Fannie (Geiger) T.; B.Sc., Washburn Coll., Topeka, Kan., 1903, Litt.D., 1927; m. Mrs. Nancy Clark Dixon Coffin, Oct. 24, 1927. Asst. editor Modern Mexico (mag.), New York, 1903-04; news editor Mexican Herald, Mexico City, Mex., 1904-10; polit. corr. Kansas City Journal, 1910-11; Paris corr. various papers, 1911-13; mng. editor Town and Country, New York, 1914-15, Popular Science Monthly, 1915-16; mem. Doheny Research Foundation, Mex., 1917; service War and State depts., 1918; U.S. vice consul, Monterey,

Mexico, 1918-19; editor in chief Ingenieria Internacional, New York, 1927—; NRA corr. for "Business Week," in Washington, 1933-34. Capt., M.I., Res. Fellow Royal Geog. Soc. Author: The People of Mexico, 1921; Trading with Mexico, 1921; The Mexican Mind, 1922; Rainbow Countries of Central America, 1926; Greater America, 1932. Address: New York, N.Y. Deceased.

THOMPSON, Will L., song writer; b. Beaver County, Pa., Nov. 7, 1847; s. Josiah T.; ed. public sch., East Liverpool, O.; musical edn. Boston Music Sch. and Boston Conservatory of Music, 1870-75; grad. Leipzig Conservatory; m. Elizabeth Johnston, Apr. 23, 1891. Song writer, 1870—. Author: Thompson's Class and Concert, 1890; Thompson's Popular Anthems, 1895, 2d vol., 1901; also about 100 popular songs, such as "Gathering Shells on the Sea Shore," "Drifting with the Tide," "Come Where the Lilies Bloom," "Moonlight Will Come Again." Contbr. to almost every hymnal and gospel song collection published in America. His "Softly and Tenderly, Jesus Is Calling" has been published in hymnals throughout the world; compiled and published New Century Hymnal, 1905, vol. 2, 1906. Address: East Liverpool, O. Died 1909.

THOMPSON, William Bess, cotton factor; b. Kosciusko, Attala County, Miss., Sept. 17, 1865; s. William B. and Mary Phalbe (White) T.; grad. U. of the South, Tenn., 1886; Johns Hopkins, 1886-87; LL.B., Columbia, 1889; unmarried. Practiced law at Dallas, Tex., 1889-96; called to New Orleans, 1896, on account of death of father, who was at head of a large cotton factorage business; later head of W. B. Thompson & Co. Mem. New Orleans Cotton Exchange (pres. 1908-11, unanimously elected 4 times); pres. World's Cotton Conf., 1919; chmn. La. div. Am. Cotton Assn., 1919—. Chmn. La. State Bd. of Arbitration and Conciliation, 1908; pres. pro tem., New Orleans Pub. Belt Railroad Commn., 1909-12; commr. of pub. utilities, City of New Orleans, 1912-16; pres. Bd. of Port Commrs., Dec. 1916-Oct. 1919. Home: New Orleans, La. Died Aug. 11, 1928.

THOMPSON, William Boyce; b. Virginia City, Mont., May 13, 1869; s. William and Anna M. (Boyce) T.; ed. Phillips Exeter Acad. and Columbia Univ. Sch. of Mines; LL.D., U. of Pittsburgh, 1921, U. of Ky., 1923; D.Sc., U. of Ariz., 1929; m. Gertrude Hickman, Feb. 6, 1895; 1 dau., Margaret (Mrs. Boyce Thompson Schulz). Dir. Federal Res. Bank of New York from organization until Dec. 1919; dir. Met. Life Ins. Co. Rep. presdl. elector, 1912; del. Rep. Nat. Conv., 1916, 1920. Pres., founder and endower Boyce Thompson Inst. for Plant Research. Hon. pres. Roosevelt Memorial Assn.; trustee Phillips Exeter Acad. Head of Am. Red Cross Mission to Russia, 1917; envoy extraordinary of the U.S. to first Centennial of the Proclamation of Independence of Republic of Peru, July 1921; mem. advisory com. to Am. delegation in Conference on the Limitation of Armament, 1921. Awarded George Robert White medal of honor by Mass. Hort. Soc., 1928. Died June 27, 1930.

THOMPSON, William Gilman, M.D.; b. N.Y. City, Dec. 25, 1856; s. Rev. Joseph Parrish and Elizabeth Coit (Gilman) T.; Ph.B., Sheffield Scientific Sch. (Yale), 1877; M.D., Coll. Phys. and Surg. (Columbia), 1881; m. Harriet Howard Pomeroy, Aug. 11, 1887. Held various chairs in New York U. Med. Coll., 1887-98; prof. medicine emeritus, Cornell U. Med. Coll.; cons. phys. Bellevue Hosp., Reconstruction Hosp. Author: A Text-Book of Practical Medicine, 1902; Practical Dietetics, 1909; The Occupational Diseases, 1915; etc. Editor The American System of Medicine, 1897. Address: New York, N.Y. Died Oct. 27, 1927.

THOMPSON, William Goodrich, lawyer; b. Peacham, Vt., Nov. 16, 1864; s. Charles Oliver and Maria (Goodrich) T.; A.B., Harvard Coll., 1888, A.M., 1891; LL.B., Harvard Law Sch., 1891; m. Mary Hinckley Huntington, Sept. 5, 1896; children—Miriam Phillips, Katharine, William Huntington, Charles Goodrich, Margaret Wendell. Practiced, Boston, 1891—; asst. U.S. atty., Dist. of Mass., 1893-95; mem. firm Thompson, Spring & Mears, 1925—. Lecturer on brief making, Harvard Law Sch., 1912, 14, on practice, 1915, on brief making and preparation of cases, 8 periods, 1916-31, inclusive, on brief making and practice 1934. Episcopalian. Contbr. Harvard Law Review. Home: Chestnut Hill, Mass. Died Sept. 12, 1935.

THOMPSON, William Henry, senator; b. Perrysville, O., Dec. 14, 1853; s. Eli and Eliza (Kirby) T.; ed. pub. schs. and spl. pvt. instrn.; Upper Ia. U., Fayette, Iowa, 1872-75; LL.B., State U. of Ia., 1877; m. Nettie I. Hutchison, Sept. 7, 1879. Began practice at Brush Creek (now Arlington), Ia.; settled at Grand Island, Neb., 1881. An organizer and dir. State Bank of Grand Island. City atty., Grand Island, Neb., 1885-86, and 1891-92; county atty., Hall County, Neb., 1887-88. Dem. candidate for Congress, 1890; del. at large Dem. Nat. Conv., five times, beginning 1892. Mem. bd. trustees Grand Island Coll. (Baptist), 1893-1913; mayor, Grand Island, Neb., 1895-98; mem. Dem. Nat. Com., 1896-1900, 1920-24. Dem. candidate for U.S. Senate, 1901; Dem. candidate for gov. of Neb., 1902. Mem. capitol commn. for erection new state capitol; judge Supreme Ct. of Neb., by appointment, Apr. 1924-Jan. 1925, and by election, Jan. 1925, term 6 yrs.; apptd. U.S. senator, May 24, 1933, to fill vacancy caused by death of Hon. Robert B. Howell. 1st v.p. Bryan Memorial Assn., 1925. Presbyterian. Home: Grand Island, Neb. Died June 6, 1937.

THOMPSON, William Howard, senator; b. Crawfordsville, Ind., Oct. 14, 1871; s. John Franklin and Dora Emma (McGriff) T.; moved to Kan. with parents, 1880; grad. Seneca (Kan.) Normal Sch., 1886; studied law under father; m. Bertha Felt, Aug. 29, 1894. Admitted to Kan. bar, 1894; clk. Kan. Ct. of Appeals, 1897-1901; judge 32d Jud. Dist., Kan., 2 terms, 1906-13; U.S. senator, 1913-19. Del.-at-large Dem. Nat. Conv., 1916 (platform com.). Mem. law firm Thompson & Thompson; settled in Tulsa, Okla., 1923. Mason. Home: Tulsa, Okla. Died Feb. 8, 1928.

THOMPSON, William Oxley, univ. pres.; b. Cambridge, O., Nov. 5, 1855; s. David Glenn and Agnes Miranda (Oxley) T.; A.B., Muskingum Coll., 1878, A.M., 1881; grad. Western Theol. Sem., Allegheny City, Pa., 1882; D.D., Muskingum Coll., 1891, Princeton, 1928; LL.D., Western U. of Pa. (now U. of Pittsburgh), 1897, Oberlin, 1908, U. of Vt., 1911, U. of Mich., 1915, Miami U., 1922, Ohio Wesleyan U., 1924, Heidelberg U., 1925, Wilberforce, 1925, Western Reserve, 1925, Occidental Coll., 1927, Ohio State U., 1929, Ore. State Agrl. Coll., 1931; m. Estelle Godfrey Clark, June 28, 1894. Ordained Presbyn. ministry, 1882; missionary and pastor, Odebolt, Ia., 1882-85; pres. Longmont (Colo.) Coll., 1885-91, and pastor there, 1885-91; pres. Miami U., 1891-99; pres. Ohio State U., 1899-1925, pres. emeritus, Nov. 5, 1925. Chmn. Agrl. Commn. to Eng. and France, 1918; chmn. commn. to settle anthracite coal controversy, 1920. Home: Columbus, O. Died Dec. 9, 1933.

THOMPSON, William Townsend, lawyer; b. Fennimore, Wis., May 23, 1860; s. James and Charlotte (Hall) T.; ed. at Simpson Coll., Indianola, Ia.; m. Florence Busselle, Apr. 1885; 3 daughters. Admitted to Ia. bar, 1884; practiced at Indianola, 1884-85, Central City, Neb., 1885-1904; county atty., Merrick County, Neb., 1888-90; mem. Neb. Ho. of Reps., 1899-1903; deputy atty. gen. Neb., 1905-07, atty. gen., 1907-10 (resigned); solicitor of U.S. Treasury, 1910-14; mem. Supreme Ct. Commn. of Neb., 1925-29, reappointed, 1931. Republican. While atty. gen. Neb. successfully prosecuted Neb. Retail Lumber Dealers' Assn. to enforce anti-trust law, and various express cos. to enforce express rate reduction; mgr. for state constl. prohibition in Neb., 1916, which carried. Presbyn. Home: Lincoln, Neb. Deceased.

THOMSEN, Mark Lawrence, lawyer; b. Denmark, Oct. 16, 1872; s. Thomas Nielsen and Maren (Christensen) T.; brought by parents to U.S., 1886; grad. Oberlin (O.) Acad., 1895; A.B., Oberlin Coll., 1898; LL.B., Western Reserve U., 1902; m. Mary Louise Hamlen, June 29, 1909 (died 1925); children—Wells Hamlen, Elinor Louise, Mark Lawrence. Teacher of English and history, high sch., Clarinda, Ia., 1898-99; instr. in English, Adelbert Coll., Cleveland, 1900-01; admitted to Ohio bar, 1902, and began practice at Cleveland; mem. firm Snyder, Henry, Thomsen, Ford and Seagrave, 1918—; pres. Miner-Mayfield Co.; v.p., counsel of the Cleveland Worm and Gear Co.; treas., counsel The Speeday Co. Vice consul for Denmark, State of O., 1905-14. City solicitor Newburgh, O., 1902-13, Idlewood, 1913-24; mem. Cleveland Bd. of Edn., 1915-19 (pres., 1917-19); pres. Ohio Assn. Bd. of Edn. Presidents, 1917-19. Trustee Oberlin Coll. Republican. Conglist. Rewrote tax laws of Ohio as related to the pub. sch. system. Home: Cleveland, O. Died May 27, 1934.

THOMSON, Alexander, paper mfr.; b. Cincinnati, O., Nov. 24, 1879; s. Peter Gibson and Laura (Gamble) T.; student Ohio Mil. Inst., 1896-1900; hon. B.Sc., Hampden Sydney Coll., Va., 1930; LL.D., Beaver Coll., Jenkintown, Pa.; m. Mary Moore Dabney, May 9, 1906; children—Alexander, Mary Moore (dec.), Charles Dabney, Lewis Clark, Chilton. Apprentice Champion Coated Paper Co., 1896, progressing through various positions, pres., 1932—; chmn. bd. Champion Paper & Fibre Co. Trustee Beaver Coll., Jenkintown, Pa. Republican. Presbyn. Mason. Home: Cincinnati, O. Died June 27, 1939.

THOMSON, Charles Goff, author; b. Little Falls, N.Y., Feb. 9, 1883; s. William Philander and Henrietta (Nellis) T.; D.V.M., Cornell, 1907; m. Hazel Gibbs, Apr. 30, 1912; children—Peter, Robert Dade. Dir. Alabang Serum Lab., P.I., 1908-10; in charge mil. and civilian forces operating against rinderpest in Philippines, 1910-13; asst. dir. prisons for Philippine Govt., 1914-17. Capt. Remount Div., comdg. remount depots at Camp Gordon and Camp Dix, 1917; lt. col. and comdr. all troops at Lux, France, Aug. 1918-May 1919. Became supt. Yosemite Nat. Park, Calif. Author: Terry—A Tale of the Hill People, 1921; Time Is a Gentleman, 1929. Contbr. to mags. Home: Yosemite National Park, Calif. Died Mar. 23, 1937.

THOMSON, Edgar Steiner, ophthalmologist; b. Mt. Savage, Md., Dec. 18, 1871; s. Alexander and Eliza S. (Slack) T.; M.D., U. of Pa., 1893; m. Mrs. Martha M. Shellman-Freeman, Feb. 20, 1899. Practiced at N.Y. City, 1895—. Surgeon and dir. Manhattan Eye, Ear and Throat Hosp.; cons. ophthalmologist to Babies', Perth Amboy and Ossining hosps. Home: New York, N.Y. Died Jan. 1931.

THOMSON, Edward, lecturer; b. Delaware, O., June 5, 1848; s. Edward (bishop M.E. Ch.) and Maria Louisa (Bartley) T.; A.B., Ohio Wesleyan U., 1869, A.M., 1872; S.T.B., Northwestern U., 1881; Ph.D., Cornell, 1882; course in law, Chicago Law Sch.; course in medicine, U. of Mich.; LL.D., M.E. Coll. of Neb. (now Neb. Wesleyan U.); m. Ella Macy, Sept. 6, 1870 (died 1887); m. 2d, Ella M. Tarr, Ph.D., preceptress U. of Southern Calif., July 6, 1888 (died 1913). Prof. chemistry, Baldwin U., 1872-75; prin. Neb. Conf. Sem., York, 1879-82; pres. York Coll., 1882-86; v.p. U. of Southern Calif., 1886-88; engaged in lecturing for Sunday League of America, 1889-1906; pres. Arlington Heights Coll., Ft. Worth, Tex., 1906-June 1912; nat. sec. Sunday League of America. Attended summer lectures, Oxford, England, 1910. Author: Life of Bishop Thomson, 1883; Pneuma-Therapy, 1890; American Law in Its Relation to Religion, 1891, and other works. Charter mem. North East Ohio Conf. M.E. Ch., 1912. Home: St. Louis, Mo. Deceased.

THOMSON, Elihu, electrician; b. Manchester, Eng., Mar. 29, 1853; s. Daniel and Mary A. (Rhodes) T.; A.B., Central High Sch., Phila., 1870, A.M., 1875; hon. A.M., Yale, 1890; Ph.D., Tufts, 1894; Sc.D., Harvard, 1909; LL.D., U. of Pa., 1924; D.Sc., Victoria Univ., Manchester, England, 1924; m. Mary L. Peck, May 1, 1884 (died 1916); children—Stuart (dec.), Roland D., Malcolm, Donald T.; m. 2d, Clarissa Hovey, 1923. Prof. chemistry and mechanics, Central High Sch., Phila., 1870-80; 1880—, electrician for Thomson-Houston and General Electric cos., which operate under his inventions, more than 700 patents having been obtained; inventor of electric welding, which bears his name, and many other important inventions in electric lighting, power; dir. Thomson Lab. of Gen. Electric Co., Lynn, Mass. Pres. Internat. Elec. Congress and chamber of official delegates thereto, St. Louis, 1904; pres. Internat. Electrotech. Commn., 1908-11. Fellow Am. Acad. Arts and Sciences (v.p.); mem. Nat. Acad. Sciences. Awarded Grand Prix in Paris, 1889 and 1900, for elec. inventions; decorated, 1889, by French Govt., Chevalier and Officer Legion of Honor, for elec. research and inventions; grand prize, St. Louis, 1904, for elec. work; Rumford medal, 1902; awarded 1st Edison medal, Am. Inst. E.E., 1910; Elliott Cresson medal, John Fritz medal, and Hughes medal of Royal Soc., London, 1916; Kelvin medal, 1924; the Franklin medal, by the Franklin Inst., 1925; Faraday medal, by Instn. of Elec. Engrs., Gt. Britain, 1927; also twice awarded the John Scott Legacy medal and premium, by City of Phila., and medals, Trans. Miss. Expn., Omaha, and Columbian Expn., Chicago; also Grashof Medal awarded by the Verein Deutscher Ingenieure of Germany, Mar. 29, 1935. Trustee and pres. Peabody Mus., Salem, Mass.; mem. Corp. Mass. Inst. Tech. and its acting pres., 1920-22; v.p. Am. Philos. Soc. Mem. Nat. Research Council. Contbr. to tech. jours. Home: Swampscott, Mass. Died Mar. 13, 1937.

THOMSON, Henry Czar Merwin, mfr.; b. New Haven, Conn., Apr. 20, 1863; s. Giles Griswold and Mary Josephine (Lum) T.; grad. Hopkins Grammar Sch., New Haven, Conn., 1879; A.B., Yale, 1883; m. Alice Maria Hoggson, Sept. 16, 1891; 1 dau., Dorothy. Began with P. & F. Corbin, New Britain, Conn., 1884, mgr. Chicago warehouse, 1888-1901; treas. Hoggson Bros., New York, 1901-13; pres. Am. Hardware Corp., New Britain, Conn., 1913-24; dir. New Britain Nat. Bank until Dec. 1924 (resigned). Republican. Conglist. Home: New Britain, Conn. Died June 18, 1926.

THOMSON, James William, chief engr. U.S.N.; b. Wilmington, Del., Nov. 10, 1836; s. James William and Sarah (Peters) T.; acad. edn.; m. Laura N. Troth, Oct. 7, 1862. Apptd. 3d asst. engr. U.S.N., June 26, 1856; 1st asst. engr., Aug. 2, 1859; chief engr., Feb. 2, 1862; retired, June 26, 1896; advanced to rank of rear admiral retired, June 29, 1906, for services during Civil War. Served on various vessels and at various stations during Civil and Spanish wars; mem. bd. Naval Acad., Oct.-Nov. 1875, bd. of inspection, Nov. 5, 1875-Aug. 1, 1876, bd. of examiners, May 12-May 31, 1881, examining bd., Phila., 1885-87. Home: Moorestown, N.J. Died Mar. 17, 1914.

THOMSON, James William, educator; b. Abbeville, S.C., July 28, 1863; s. Thomas and Margaret (Gomilion) T.; A.B., Erskine Coll., Due West, S.C., 1881; LL.D., Erskine, 1919; Litt.D., Presbyn. Coll. of S.C., 1924; m. Sarah A. Perrin, Dec. 8, 1885 (died 1901); children—Mary Livingston (Mrs. S. Reid Spencer), James William, Emma Cothran (Mrs. Lacy McLean), Thomas (dec.), Wardlaw Perrin, Margaret, John Livingston (dec.). Admitted to bar, 1884; head of pvt. sch., 1886-92; supt. schs., Rock Hill, S.C., 1892-98; prof. edn., ethics and Bible, Winthrop Coll., 1898—. Mem. State Bd. Edn. Democrat. Presbyn. Kiwanian. Home: Rock Hill, S.C. Died May 10, 1938.

THOMSON, John, librarian; b. in England; ed. at London; hon. A.M., U. of Pa., 1909; Litt.D., Ursinus Coll., 1913. Pvt. librarian to Clarence H. Clark, of Phila., 8 yrs., to Jay Gould, of Irvington-on-Hudson, 3 yrs.; librarian Free Library of Phila., 1894—. Mem. Bd. of Pa. Library Commn. Mem. Council A.L.A.; pres. emeritus Keystone State Library Assn., and Pa. Library Club. Author: Hither and Thither, 1906; also Descriptive Catalogue of the Library of C. H. Clark (2 vols.); Catalogue of the Irvington Library of Jay Gould; Descriptive Catalogue of the Works of Sir Walter Scott, and of Library of Old Authors, printed for the Free Library. Home: Philadelphia, Pa. Died Feb. 20, 1916.

THOMSON, Peter Gibson, paper mfr.; b. Cincinnati, O., Dec. 16, 1851; s. Alexander and Mary Ann (Edwards) T.; ed. pub. schs. of Cincinnati; m. Kate P. Woolley, Ohio, Mar. 20, 1920; children—(by previous marriage) Peter G., Alexander, Mary Bell (Mrs. Walter D. Randall), Hope T. (Mrs. Reuben B. Robertson), Logan G. Bookseller, 1867-80; paper mfr., 1893—; pres. Champion Coated Paper Co., Champion Fibre Co.; dir. First Nat. Bank. V.p. Cincinnati Gymnasium; trustee Cincinnati Art Mus. Republican. Presbyn. Died July 10, 1931.

THOMSON, Thaddeus Austin, diplomatic service; b. Burleson County, Tex., Jan. 17, 1853; s. Thomas Coke and Mary Jane T.; ed. Salado College and Tex. Mil. Inst.; m. Annie Eloise, d. of Thomas J. H. and Ann H. Anderson, June 14, 1883; children—Eloise, Thaddeus Austin, Eleanor Lee, Mary Jane. Planter and ranchman; admitted to Tex. bar, July 11, 1881; del. Dem. Nat. Conv., Baltimore, 1912; E.E. and M.P. to Colombia, June 10, 1913-16. Signed treaty bet. U.S. and Rep. of Colombia, Apr. 6, 1914, known as the Thomson-Urrutia treaty. Life mem. Navy League U.S. Methodist. Home: Austin, Tex. Died Jan. 18, 1927.

THOMSON, W. H. Seward, judge; b. Beaver County, Pa., Nov. 16, 1856; s. Alexandre R. and Hannah (Charles) T.; student Marshall Coll., Huntington, W.Va., 1871-73; Washington and Jefferson Coll., Pa., 1875-77; LL.D., same, also Muskingum Coll., 1915; m. Mary E. Imbrie, May 12, 1887. Admitted to W.Va. bar, 1880, Pa. bar, 1881; practiced in Beaver, Pa., 1881-94; removed to Pittsburgh, and formed partnership with Frank Thomson as Thomson & Thomson, 1894; U.S. dist. judge, Western Dist. Pa., by appmt. of President Wilson, July 30, 1914—. Democrat. Home: Pittsburgh, Pa. Deceased.

THOMSON, William, physician, surgeon; b. Chambersburg, Pa., Jan. 28, 1833; ed. Chambersburg Acad. and by pvt. tutors; grad. Jefferson Med. Coll., 1855; practiced at Merion, nr. Phila., 1855-61; entered regular army, 1861, as asst. surgeon; served at hdqrs. Army of Potomac, 1862; surgeon in charge Douglass Hosp., 1863; became med. insp., Dept. of Washington, 1864; received 2 bvts.; was sent to La. after the war; passed 2d exam. but resigned from the army, Feb. 25, 1866; practicing at Phila., 1866—. As an army surgeon introduced local application of carbolic acid as disinfectant in treatment of wounds; also introduced several reforms in med. and surg. field service. Specialist in ophthalmic surgery; filled many professional and hosp. positions and wrote much on his specialty. 25 yrs. teacher (later emeritus prof. ophthalmology), Jefferson Med. Coll.; cons. surgeon of Wills Eye Hosp. With Dr. W. F. Norris made 1st successful photographic negatives with microscope, in 1864, at Douglass Hosp. Address: Philadelphia, Pa. Died 1907.

THOMSON, William Hanna, physician; A.B., Wabash Coll., 1850, A.M., 1857; M.D., Albany Med. Coll., 1859; hon. A.M., Yale, 1861; LL.D., New York U., 1885. Engaged in practice in New York, 1859—. Asst. phys. Quarantine Hosp., New York, 1859; U.S. med. insp., 1861-65; phys. to Charity Hosp., 1868—; phys. to Charity and Roosevelt hosps. Address: New York, N.Y. Died Jan. 18, 1918.

THOMSON, William Judah, naval officer; b. Washington, Apr. 27, 1841; s. William and Mary (Delano) T.; ed. Baltimore schs.; m. Maud Spurgeon, Apr. 25, 1898. Apptd. acting asst. p.m. U.S.N., Mar. 29, 1865; asst. p.m., July 23, 1866; passed asst. p.m., Mar. 20, 1868; p.m., Feb. 16, 1878; pay insp., Apr. 9, 1899; pay dir., Mar. 9, 1902; retired, Jan. 10, 1903, with rank of rear admiral for services during Civil War. Home: Seattle, Wash. Died 1909.

THORINGTON, William Sewell, lawyer; b. Montgomery, Ala., July 30, 1847; s. Jack and Mary Lord (Parker) T.; ed. U. of Ala., LL.D., 1906; m. Wilella Chilton, Oct. 24, 1867. Served as 1st lt. and adj. Ala. Corps of Cadets, 1864-65; admitted to bar, 1867; mem. firm of Morgan, Bragg & Thorington, 1871-74 (John T. Morgan, afterwards U.S. senator; Walter L. Bragg, afterwards Interstate Commerce commr.), Bragg & Thorington, 1871-83; alone, 1883—. Judge advocate gen. on staff of Gov. E. A. O'Neal, 1882-86; city atty., Montgomery, 1891; judge City Ct. of Montgomery, 1892; apptd. asso. justice Supreme Ct. of Ala., Apr. 1892; retired, Dec. 1892; nominated as del. to Constl. Conv., 1901, under first legislative call; declined renomination under second call; dean law dept. U. of Ala., 1897—. Apptd., August 1909, spl. master by U.S. Circuit Ct. for Middle Dist. of Ala., in the Railroad Rate Cases between the state and railroad cos. Mem. bd. of trustees U. of Ala. 18 yrs. (resigned 1897). Apptd. by gov. del. to Southern Commercial Congress, Mobile, Ala., 1913. Author of City Code of Montgomery; spl. reporter (by request of Ct.) of 2 vols. (C and CVII) Reports of Supreme Ct. of Ala. Address: Montgomery, Ala. Died Jan. 24, 1915.

THORNBURG, Zenas Charles, educator; b. Redfield, Ia., July 14, 1872; s. Thomas A. and Jennie (Vestal) T.; Highland Park (Ia.) Normal Sch.; A.B., Highland Park Coll., 1908; m. Laura Loehle, Sept. 30, 1903. County supt. schs., Polk County, Ia., 5 yrs., 1898-1903; asst. supt. schs., Des Moines, 1908-13, supt. 1913-21; dir. Inst. Des Moines U., Ia. Republican. Methodist. Mason. Home: Des Moines, Ia. Died May 3, 1925.

THORNBURGH, George, editor, auditor; b. Havana, Ill., Jan. 25, 1847; s. Eli and Elizabeth (Thoman) T.; ed. Hillhouse Inst., Smithville, Ark.; pvt. C.S.A., 1865; student Cumberland Law Sch., Lebanon, Tenn., 1868; m. Margaret C. Self, Sept. 30, 1868 (died 1900); m. 2d, Lucy B. (Gibson) Green, Mar. 17, 1903. Editor Masonic Trowell, 1867-1919; business mgr. Ark. Methodist, 1889-1903. Mem. Ark. Ho. of Reps., 1871, 73, 81, 85 (speaker 1881); dir. Ark. Bldg. & Loan Assn. Sunday sch. supt. 40 yrs.; pres. Ark S.S. Assn. 4 terms; pres. Ark. Anti-Saloon League 13 yrs.; pres. Ark. Meth. Orphanage 15 yrs.; supt. Ark. School for the Blind, Jan. 1, 1919—. Pres. Ark. Press Assn. Col. Ark. Militia, 1871. Del. Gen. Conf. M.E. Ch., S., 3 times. Mason (33°); served as Grand Master, Grand High Priest and Grand Comdr. Author: Masonic Monitor, 1903; History of Freemasonry, 1914. Address: Little Rock, Ark. Died Mar. 9, 1923.

THORNDIKE, Ashley Horace, univ. prof.; b. Houlton, Me., Dec. 26, 1871; s. Edward R. and Abby B. (Ladd) T.; A.B., Wesleyan U., 1893, L.H.D., 1909; A.M., Harvard, 1896, Ph.D., 1898; m. Annette Marian Lowell, June 21, 1899; children—Marian Lowell, Edward (dec.), Eleanor (dec.), Ashley. Prin. Smith Acad., Hatfield, Mass., 1893-95; instr. Boston U., 1895-98; instr. and asso. prof. Western Reserve U., 1898-1902; prof. English lit., Northwestern U., 1902-06; prof. English, Columbia, 1900—. Mem. Modern Lang. Assn. America, Nat. Inst. Arts and Letters. Author: Influence of Beaumont and Fletcher on Shakespeare, 1901; Elements of Rhetoric and Composition, 1905; Tragedy, 1908; Everyday English, 1913; Facts About Shakespeare, 1915; Shakespeare's Theater, 1916; Literature in a Changing Age, 1920; A History of English Literature, 1920; English Comedy, 1929; The Outlook for Literature, 1931. Editor: Tudor Shakespeare; Library World's Best Literature; Longmans' English Classics; Everyday Classics; Modern Eloquence; Modern Readers' Series; etc. Contbr. to periodicals. Home: New York, N.Y. Died Apr. 17, 1933.

THORNDIKE, Paul, surgeon; b. Beverly, Mass., Mar. 2, 1863; s. William and Martha (Abbott) T.; A.B., Harvard, 1884; M.D., 1888; m. Rachel Ewing, d. Gen. William T. Sherman, U.S.A., Dec. 30, 1892 (dec.); children—William Tecumseh, Martha, Anna. House officer Boston City, Boston Lying-in hosps.; practiced in Boston, 1888—; asst. clin. surgery, 1894-96, asst. genito-urinary and clin. surgery, 1896-99, asst. prof. genito-urinary surgery, 1909, clin. prof., Harvard, later emeritus; retired from active practice, Apr. 15, 1938. Republican. Home: Brookline, Mass. Died May 27, 1939.

THORNDIKE, Townsend William, M.D.; b. Boston, May 12, 1872; s. William Henry (M.D.) and Sarah Wayland (Smith) T.; Harvard, 1894-95, M.D., Harvard Med. Sch., 1902; m. Mary Elizabeth Cayford, Jan. 26, 1907; children—Sarah Herbert, William, Charles. Specialist in skin diseases; visiting dermatologist to Boston City Hosp.; prof. diseases of the skin and syphilis, Tufts Med. Sch. Fellow Mass. Med. Soc. Home: Cambridge, Mass. Died Apr. 5, 1929.

THORNE, Charles Embree, agriculturist; b. Greene County, O., Oct. 4, 1846; s. Elijah and Mary (Charles) T.; ed. Mich. Agrl. Coll., summer, 1866; Antioch Coll., 1868-69, 1869-70; hon. M. Agr., Ohio State U., 1890; hon. D.Sc., Coll. of Wooster, 1926; m. Viola J. Hine, May 10, 1871 (died 1924); children—Bertram Hine (dec.), Mrs. Bessie Mary Brooks, Charles Brooks. Raised on farm, Greene County; farm mgr. Ohio State U., 1877-81; asso. editor Farm and Fireside, Springfield, O., 1882-88; dir. 1887-1921; chief in soil fertility, 1888-1925, cons. chief, 1925—. Ohio Agrl. Expt. Sta. Pres. Am. Soc. Agronomy, 1914-15 (fellow 1925); pres. Assn. Am. Agrl. Colls. and Expt. Stas., 1915-16, Soc. Promotion Agrl. Science, 1915-16; pres. Wayne Bldg. & Loan Co., 1905—. Author: Farm Manures, 1913; Maintenance of Soil Fertility, 1931. Home: Wooster, O. Died Feb. 29, 1936.

THORNE, Chester, financier; b. N.Y. City, Nov. 11, 1863; s. Edwin and Charlotte T.; Ph.B., Yale, 1884; m. Anna Hoxie, Nov. 10, 1886. In engring. dept. Mo.P. Ry., 1884-86, traffic dept., 1887-88; moved to Tacoma, Wash., 1890; pres. Nat. Bank of Commerce, 1893-1913; chmn. bd. Nat. Bank of Tacoma, 1913—; v.p. Pac.S.S. Co. Home: Tacoma, Wash. Died Oct. 16, 1927.

THORNE, Clifford, lawyer; b. Brooklyn Ia., Jan. 20, 1878; s. William George and Rachel Mary (Young) T.; A.M., LL.B., State U. of Ia., 1899; Ph.D., Yale, 1901; LL.D., Ia. Wesleyan Coll., Mt. Pleasant, 1912; m. Ruth Latta, Feb. 14, 1918. Began practice of law in Washington, Ia., 1901; acted as spl. counsel for shippers, cities and states in various cases before Interstate Commerce Commn., U.S. Supreme Ct. and before coms. of Congress; mem. Bd. of R.R. Commrs., Ia., 1910-17 (chmn. bd. 1912-17); resigned Jan. 1917, and practiced at Chicago, 1917—. Pres. Nat. Assn. Ry. Commrs., 1914-15; mem. Am. Acad. Polit. and Social Science. Republican. Methodist. Mason; K.P. Author of law in Ia. creating office of commerce counsel as an advocate for the public in cases brought before state and interstate commerce commns. (first law of the kind in U.S.); author of Ia. law against unfair competition in prices of commodities for the purpose of destroying competition. Contbr. to various mags. on pub. regulation, and on jurisprudence. Home: Evanston, Ill. Died Nov. 12, 1923.

THORNE, Edwin, corp. officer; b. Millbrook, N.Y., Aug. 3, 1861; s. Samuel and Phebe (Van Schoonhoven) T.; prep. edn., Hopkins Grammar Sch., New Haven, Conn.; Ph.B., Sheffield Scientific Sch. (Yale), 1882; m. Phebe Ketchum, Jan. 21, 1886; children—Landon Ketchum, Phebe Van Schoonhoven (Mrs. John Tucker), Francis Burritt, Ann Augusta (Mrs. Robert Richard Titus). Trustee Mutual Life Ins. Co., Central Hanover Bank & Trust Co. V.p. New York Soc. for Prevention of Cruelty to Children. Republican. Presbyn. Home: West Islip (Babylon P.O.), L.I., N.Y. Died Sept. 29, 1935.

THORNE, Samuel, capitalist; b. Dutchess County, N.Y., Sept. 6, 1835; s. Jonathan T.; m. Phebe, d. William Van Schoonhoven, 1860. Began career as farmer, importer and breeder of improved stock at Thorndale, N.Y.; moved to New York, 1868, and joined brothers in the business of tanning and selling leather; retired, 1872. Dir. Bank of America, Central Trust Co., N.Y. Life Ins. & Trust Co., N.Y. Dock Co., Northern Securities Co., 6th Av. R.R. Co., G.N. Ry., C.B.&Q. R.R. Co., C.&S. Ry. Co. Mgr. New York Zoöl. Soc., New York Bot. Garden. Address: New York, N.Y. Died July 4, 1915.

THORNE, William Van Schoonhoven, ry. dir.; b. Millbrook, N.Y., Mar. 22, 1865; s. Samuel and Phebe Smith (Van Schoonhoven) T.; Ph.B., Sheffield Scientific Sch. (Yale), 1885; m. Julia Therese Keyser, Nov. 16, 1905. With G.N. Ry. as asst. engr., clerk to gen. supt., chief clerk to gen. mgr., asst. purchasing agent, supt. St. Cloud Shops, asst. supt. Breckinridge div. and supt. Eastern Ry. of Minn. div., 1886-95, resigned; v.p. and gen. mgr. Pa. Coal Co. and v.p. Erie & Wyoming Valley R.R., with hdqrs. in New York, and later pres. Delaware Valley & Kingston Ry., to 1900, when these 3 properties were sold to the Erie R.R.; spent 18 mos. traveling in Europe; asst. to E. H. Harriman, of S.P. and U.P. rys., 1902-03; dir. of purchases U.P. Ry., Ore. Short Line, Ore.-Wash. R.R. & Navigation Co., S.P. Co. and Chicago & Alton Ry., 1903-13; v.p. U.P., Ore. Short Line and Ore.-Wash. R.R. & Nav. Co., Feb. 1913-July 1, 1914; dir. U.P., Ore. Short Line, Ore.-Wash. R.R. & N. Co., Wells Fargo & Co. Express, Railroad Securities Co., Hanover Nat. Bank (New York), Morristown Trust Co. (Morristown, N.J.). Treas. and mem. bd. mgrs. Presbyn. Hosp., New York; trustee Soc. for Relief of Half Orphan and Destitute Children; mem. bd. mgrs. Manhattan Maternity Hosp. and Dispensary and Woman's Hosp. Home: New York, N.Y. Died Feb. 6, 1920.

THORNTON, Gustavus Brown, physician, sanitarian; b. Bowling Green, Va., Feb. 22, 1835; s. James Bankhead and Mariana T. Thornton; ed. Richmond Coll., 1852-56; M.D., U. Med. Coll. (New York U.), 1860. Asst. surgeon C.S.A., 1861-62; chief surgeon of div., Army of the Tenn., 1862-65; asst. phys., 1866-68, phys.-in-charge, 1868-79, Memphis City Hosp. (covering yellow fever epidemics, 1873 and 1878); pres. Memphis bd. of health, 1879-89 and 1893-98, and founder of the new City Hosp., 1897, and had charge of the famous sanitary reformation of Memphis; reapptd., 1893; local surgeon I.C. R.R. Co., Southern R.R. Co., Union R.R. Co. (Belt Line), etc. Pres. Med. Soc. of Tenn., 1881-82; officer Am. Pub. Health Assn.; pres. Assn. of Med. Officers of the Army and Navy of the Confederacy, 1910. Author: Yellow Fever, Pathology and Treatment, 1878; Six Years' Sanitation in Memphis; and essays and official reports. Address: Memphis, Tenn. Died May 13, 1914.

THORNTON, Sir Henry Worth, ry. mgr.; b. Logansport, Ind., Nov. 6, 1871; s. Henry Clay and Millamenta Comegys (Worth) T.; grad. St. Paul's Sch., Concord, N.H., 1890; B.S., U. of Pa., 1894, D.Sc., 1923; m. Virginia Dike Blair, June 20, 1901; children—Anna Blair, James Worth; m. 2d, Martha Watriss, Sept. 11, 1926. Began, 1894, as draughtsman in office of chief engr. of Southwest System of Pa. Lines West of Pittsburgh; asst. engr. of constrn., Cleveland & Marietta R.R. (a subsidiary of the Pa. R.R.), 1895-96, and later in field work of Southwest System, supervisor yards at Columbus, O., asst. engr. Cincinnati div. and asst. engr. in spl. work; engr. maintenance of way, Erie & Ashtabula div. Northwest System of Pa. R.R., 1899-1901; supt. Cleveland, Akron & Columbus R.R., 1901-02, Erie & Ashtabula div., 1902-11; asst. gen. supt. L.I. R.R., Feb.-Nov. 1911, gen. supt. 1911-14; apptd. gen. mgr. Gt. Eastern Ry., Eng., 1914. Served on exec. com. of Gen. Mgrs. which, under direction of the Govt., controlled and worked the English railways upon the outbreak of war in 1914; dep. dir. of inland water transportation with rank of col. in Royal Engrs., 1916; asst. dir. gen. of movements of rys. in France, 1917; apptd. dep. dir. gen., same, with rank of brig. gen., Dec. 1917; insp. gen. of transportation with rank of maj. gen., 1918; served on commn. to investigate operations and financial condition of the Metropolitan Water Bd. of City of London, 1920; apptd. chmn. and pres. Canadian National Rys., Oct. 1922. Naturalized British subject, 1919; Knight Comdr. Order British Empire, 1919; Companion Legion of Honor (French); Officer Order of Leopold (Belgian); D.S.M. (U.S.). Address: Montreal, Quebec. Died Mar. 14, 1933.

THORNTON, James Brown, physician; b. Gilmanton, N.H., Oct. 5, 1861; s. James Brown and Catherine Mary (Stoughton) T.; student Bowdoin Coll., 1881-82; M.D., Med. Sch. of Me. (Bowdoin Coll.), 1885; m. Alice M. Tibbetts, 1892 (died 1897); m. 2d, Catherine Ruth Curane, 1899. In practice, Boston, 1890—; official phys. to 12 Boston theatres; U.S. pension examining surgeon. Republican. Conglist. Fellow Mass. Med. Soc.; fellow A.M.A. Companion Mass. Commandery Loyal Legion. Address: Boston, Mass. Deceased.

THORNTON, John Randolph, senator; b. Iberville Parish, La., Aug. 25, 1846; ed. La. State U. until 1863; served as pvt. C.S.A. until close of war. Admitted to bar, 1877, and in practice in Rapides Parish, La., 1877—. Judge of parish, 1878-80; mem. La. Constl. Conv., 1898; mem. bd. supervisors La. State U.; apptd. U.S. senator, Aug. 27, 1910, elected, Dec. 7, 1910, to fill unexpired term (1910-15), of Samuel D. McEnery, deceased. Democrat. Address: Rapides, La. Died Dec. 30, 1917.

THORNTON, Leila Cameron Austell; b. Atlanta, Ga., July 28, 1861; d. Gen. Alfred and Francina (Cameron) Austell; grad. Mme. Lefebvre's Sch., Baltimore, and Mrs. Sylvanus Reed's Sch., New York; m. Albert E. Thornton, Dec. 21, 1881 (died 1907); children—Alfred Austell (dec.), Albert Edward, Jane Thornton (Mrs. Alfred Kennedy). Treas. Woman's Dept. Cotton States and Internat. Expn., 1895; v.p. U.S. Good Roads Assn., 1922-27; pres. Woman's Commn. Bankhead Nat. Highway Assn., 1921-27; mem. advisory bd. Salvation Army, Southeastern Div., 1923-26, World Council Y.W.C.A., 1922-25; v.p. Ga. Forestry Assn., 1922-26; pres. Atlanta Fedn. Women's Clubs, 1920-22; v.p. Atlanta Art Assn., 1918-25; pres. 19th Century History Class; chmn. good roads, Ga. Fedn. Women's Clubs; mem. Ga. com. for purchase of Monticello as nat. shrine. Served as chmn. nursing service Atlanta Chapter Am. Red Cross during World War I. Pres. Woman's Auxiliary, 1st Presbyn. Ch., Atlanta, Ga., 1915-19. Apptd. by Gov. Hardwick del. to Southern Illiteracy Conf., Montgomery, Ala., 1922. Democrat. Presbyn. Address: Atlanta, Ga. Died May 1931.

THORNTON, William Mynn, univ. prof.; b. Cumberland County, Va., Oct. 28, 1851; s. John Thruston (col. C.S.A.) and Martha Jane (Riddle) T.; A.B., Hampden-Sydney Coll., 1868; grad. U. of Va., 1870; spl. engring. studies at U. of Va., 1871-73; LL.D., Hampden-Sydney; m. Eleanor Rosalie Harrison, Dec. 22, 1874 (died 1920); children—John Thruston, Eliza Carter, Eleanor Rosalie, Janet, William Mynn, Edward; m. 2d, Gertrude Waller Massie, July 30, 1921. Prof. Davidson Coll., N.C., 1874-75; adj. prof. applied mathematics and civ. engring., U. of Va., 1875-85, prof., 1885-1931 (emeritus), also chmn. faculty, 1888-96, dean dept. engring., 1904-25. U.S. commr. to Internat. Expn., Paris, 1900; mem. Jury of Awards, civil engring., St. Louis Expn., 1904. Editor for several yrs. of Annals of Mathematics. Home: University, Va. Died Sept. 12, 1935.

THORNTON, William Taylor, governor; b. Henry County, Mo., Feb. 9, 1843; ed. pvt. sch.; LL.B., Ky. U., Louisville, 1868. Served in C.S.A., 1861-65, except over a yr. as prisoner of war at Alton, Ill. After war practiced law at Clinton, Mo.; mem. of town council 2 terms; mem. Mo. Legislature, 1876. Removed to Santa Fé, N.M., 1877; mem. Territorial Council, 1880; 1st mayor of Santa Fé, 1891; gov. of N.M., 1893-97. Democrat. Interested in mining enterprises in Mexico and N.M. Address: Santa Fé, N.M. Died Mar. 16, 1916.

THORNTON, William Wheeler, lawyer; b. nr. Logansport, Ind., June 27, 1851; s. John A. and Ellen (Thomas) T.; ed. high sch. and Smithson Coll., Logansport, Ind.; LL.B., U. of Mich., 1876; m. Mary F. Groves, Jan. 25, 1882 (died 1905); m. 2d, Irene Bleckledge, June 20, 1911. Deputy atty. gen. Ind., 1880-82; judge Superior Ct. of Marion County, Ind., 1914-22. Republican. Author: Statutory Construction (Indiana), 1887; Indiana Practice Code, Annotated, 1888; Lost Wills, 1890; Indiana Municipal Law, 1890; Railroad Fences, 1892; Gifts and Advancements, 1893; Indiana Practice Forms, 1893; Decedents' Estates, 1895; Revised Statutes of Indiana, 1897; Indiana Township Guide, 1898; Building Associations, 1898; Government of Indiana, 1898; Oil and Gas, 1904; Indiana Negligence, 1908; Federal Employes' Safety Appliance Acts, 1909; Intoxicating Liquors, 1910; Pure Food and Drugs Act; The Sherman Anti-Trust Act; Indiana Instructions to Jurors, 1914; Indiana County Officeers, 1925; Combinations in Restraint of Trade, 1928. Home: Indianapolis, Ind. Died Jan. 21, 1932.

THORP, Frank, brig. gen. U.S.A.; b. in Me., Mar. 29, 1842. Second lt. 28th Me. Inf., Oct. 14, 1862; hon. mustered out, Aug. 31, 1863; 2d lt. 1st Me. Light Arty., Dec. 30, 1863; hon. mustered out, June 21, 1865; apptd. from Me., 2d lt. 5th U.S. Arty., May 11, 1866; 1st lt., June 6, 1867; grad. Arty. Sch., 1875; capt., Apr. 24, 1891; maj., Jan. 25, 1901; lt. col. Arty. Corps, Sept. 20, 1902; col., Jan. 21, 1904; brig. gen. and retired at own request, over 40 yrs.' service, Feb. 9, 1906. Address: Washington, D.C. Died Aug. 8, 1924.

THORPE, Ervin Llewellyn, clergyman; b. Malden, Bureau County, Ill., Sept. 2, 1856; s. Eli O. and Ardelia E. T.; A.B., Baker U., Kan. 1877, D.D., 1896; A.M., 1880; LL.B., Ia. State U., 1879, B.D., 1884; A.M., Ph.D., Syracuse U., 1885; M.L., Yale, 1887, B.D., 1888; D.C.L., U. of Chicago, 1890; m. Margaret Elizabeth Esdon, Sept. 13, 1882. Ordained M.E. ministry; pastor, Garrison, Ia., 1879-80, Centre Point, Ia., 1880-81, Nashua, Ia., 1881-83; v.p. and prof. elocution and belles-lettres, Upper Ia. U., Fayette, 1883-85; pastor, West Haven, N.Y., 1888-89, Bay Shore, N.Y., 1890, First Ch., Hartford, Conn., 1891-95, Bridgeport, Conn., 1896-97, First Ch., Topeka, Kan., 1898, Brooklyn, N.Y., 1899-1901, 27th St. Ch., New York, 1902-06, Riverhead, N.Y., 1907-08; became pastor S. Second St. Ch., Brooklyn, 1909; then pastor St. Andrew's Ch., New Haven, Conn. Republican. Mason, Odd Fellow. Home: Brooklyn, N.Y. Died Sept. 5, 1919.

THORPE, Francis Newton, univ. prof.; b. Swampscott, Mass., Apr. 16, 1857; s. Judah Welles and Rosanna (Porter) T.; Lake Shore Sem. (now St. Mary's Coll.), 1871-75; Ph.D., Syracuse U., 1883; admitted to bar, 1885; law student, U. of Pa., 1885-86; LL.D., Syracuse, 1907; m. Marion Haywood Shreve, June 4, 1895; 1 dau., Marion Edgerton. Fellow and prof. Am. constl. history, U. of Pa., 1885-98; prof. polit. science and constl. law, U. of Pittsburgh, 1910—. Author: The Government of the People of the United States, 1889; Franklin and the University of Pennsylvania, 1893; The Story of the Constitution, 1891; The Government of the State of Pennsylvania, 1894; The Constitution of the United States with Bibliography, 1894; A Constitutional History of the American People, 1776-1850 (2 vols.), 1898; The Constitutional History of the United States, 1765-1895 (3 vols.), 1901; A History of the United States for Schools, 1901; A (Social and Industrial) History of the American People, 1901; The Life of William Pepper, M.D., LL.D., 1903; The Spoils of Empire—A Romance of the Old World and the New, 1903; Short Constitutional History of the United States, 1904; The Divining Rod, 1905. Editor: History of North America, Vols. IX, XV, XVI, XVIII, XIX, XX, 1906-07; The History of the Civil War—National View, 1906; The Federal and State Constitutions, Colonial Charters, and other Organic Laws of the States, Territories, and Colonies Now or Heretofore Forming the United States of America (7 vols.), 1909; The Statesmanship of Andrew Jackson, 1909; An American Fruit Farm, 1915; The Essentials of American Constitutional Law, 1917; Essentials of American Government, 1922. Mem. Constl. Commn. of Pa., 1920. Address: Pittsburgh, Pa. Died May 8, 1926.

THORPE, George Cyrus, lawyer, officer U.S.M.C.; b. Northfield, Minn., Jan. 17, 1875; s. George Carleton and Adelaide (Carpenter) T.; B.S. and LL.B., New York U., 1910; grad. Naval War Coll., 1915; A.M., Brown U., 1916; grad. Gen. Staff Coll., 1921; m. Cora Wells, Apr. 8, 1908; children—Amy Elizabeth (Mrs. Arthur J. Pack), Jane Wells, George Wells. Commd. 2d lieutenant U.S. Marine Corps, 1898, and advanced through grades to col. (temp.), July 1918; col. (permanent), Mar. 9, 1919. Served on U.S.S. Yale, Santiago Campaign, Spanish-Am. War, 1898, and in 1st P.R. Expdn.; Philippine Insurrection, 1899-1901; fleet marine officer, European Fleet, 1892-93; with Am. expdn. to Syria, 1903; comd. marines in expdn. through Abyssinia to make treaty with Menelik; with Army of Cuban Pacification, 1906-08; comd. Naval Prison, Portsmouth, 1911-14; chief of staff 2d Brig. Marines, 1917-18; with Naval War Coll., 1919-20; Gen. Staff Coll., 1920-21; comdg. Marine Barracks, Pearl Harbor, T.H., Aug. 1921; retired. Lawyer; mem. bars of Mass., N.H. and D.C. Bvtd. captain "for distinguished service and gallant conduct," at Novelta, P.I., Oct. 1899. Decorated with star of Ethiopia, by Menelik. Mason. Author: Pure Logistics, 1917; Recruit Manual, 1918; Preparation of International Claims, 1924; Federal Departmental Organization and Practice, 1925; Prohibition, National and State, 1925. Co-author: Hughes Federal Practice, 1931; Thorpe and Ellis' Federal Securities Act Manual, 1933. Home: Washington, D.C. Died July 28, 1936.

THORPE, Rose Hartwick, author; b. Mishawaka, Ind., July 18, 1850; d. William and Mary Hartwick; grad. High Sch., Litchfield, Mich., 1868; hon. A.M., Hillsdale Coll., 1883; m. E. Carson Thorpe, Sept. 11, 1871 (died 1916); children—Lulo May (Mrs. E. Y. Barnes), Lillie Maude (dec.). Well known for poem "Curfew Must Not Ring To-night." Author: Fred's Dark Days, 1881; The Fenton Family, 1884; Nina Bruce, 1886; The Chester Girls, 1887; The Year's Best Days, 1889; verse: Temperance Poems, 1887; Ringing Ballads, 1887; Curfew Must Not Ring To-night (illustrated booklet), 1882; The Yule Log, 1881; Sweet Song Stories, 1898; White Lady of La Jolla, 1904; Poetical Works of Rose Hartwick Thorpe, 1912; From California, 1914; (booklet) In Sunset Land, 1927. Address: San Diego, Calif. Died July 19, 1939.

THORSON, Thomas, banker; b. nr. Stavanger, Norway, Nov. 14, 1848; s. Svend Thorson Wagle and Malene (Espeland); brought to America, 1854; ed. pub. schs. and business coll., McGregor, Ia.; m. Jessie Hunt, July 12, 1882. Opened first mdse. store in Lynn County, Ia., 1871; in real estate business 30 yrs.; pres. 1st Nat. Bank, Canton, S.D.; pres. Bradstad Concrete Machinery Co.; v.p. Canton Co-operative Telephone Co.; treas. Bergstrom Plow Co. First county recorder of Lyon County, Ia., and county auditor, 1874-75; mem. provisional state legislature of S.D., 1885; mayor of Canton 2 terms; sec. of state of S.D., 1893-96 inclusive; mem. Rep. Nat. Com., 1908-16. Lutheran. Mason. Address: Canton, S.D. Died Aug. 30, 1915.

THRASHER, Allen Benton, M.D., surgeon; b. Fayette County, Ind., July 6, 1851; s. Woodson W. and Barbara (Daubenspeck) T.; A.B., Butler Coll., 1873, A.M., 1875; M.D., Med. Coll. of Ohio, 1881; m. Edith Williams, July 3, 1888. Interne Cincinnati Hosp., 1880-81; practiced in Cincinnati, 1881—; laryngologist Good Samaritan Hosp., Christ Hosp.; trustee Cincinnati Hosp., 1901-06. Fellow Am. College Surgeons, Am. Laryngol. Assn., Am. Laryngol., Rhinol. and Otol. Soc. Mason. Republican. Home: Cincinnati, O. Died July 31, 1927.

THRASHER, Max Bennett, journalist; b. Westmoreland, N.H., April 11, 1860; s. John R. T.; ed. pub. schs. Coventry, Vt., and St. Johnsbury, Vt., Acad.; unmarried. Postmaster, Newport, Vt., 1886-91; in gen. literary work, 1892-93; abroad, 1894; on staff Boston Journal, 1895-97; asst. supt. Farm School, Thompson's Island, Boston, 1898-99; in gen. literary work, 1899. Author: Tuskegee: Iits Story and Its Work, 1901. Wrote: Tuskegee Institute and Its Work, Popular Science Monthly, Sept. 1899: Tuskegee Institute and the Negro Conference, Chautauquan, Aug. 1900. Address: New York, N.Y. Died 1903.

THROCKMORTON, Archibald Hall, law educator; b. Loudoun County, Va., Mar. 28, 1876; s. Mason and Annie Humphrey T.; A.B., Roanoke Coll., 1896; A.M., Princeton, 1897; LL.B., Washington and Lee U., 1900; LL.D., Centre Coll., Danville, Ky., 1926; m. Julia Elizabeth Painter, June 29, 1899. Practiced law, Leesburg, Va., 1900-02; dean Law Sch. Central U. of Ky., 1902-11; prof. Law Sch., Ind. U., 1911-14, Western Reserve U., 1914—. Mem. Bd. of Health, Cleveland Heights, also Cuyahoga County; mem. Charter commn. Cleveland Heights, 1921. Democrat. Presbyn. Author: Cases on Contracts, 1913; Cases on Evidence, 1913; Cases on Equity Jurisprudence, 1923; Cases on Code Pleading, 1926; Cases on Torts, 1932. Editor: Clark on Contracts, 1914; Eaton on Equity, 1923; Throckmorton's Cooley on Torts, 1930. Evans's Cases on Constitutional Law, 1933. Co-editor: Clark on Contracts, 1930; Cases on Contracts, 1930; Hepburn's Cases on Torts, 1935. Editor in chief Throckmorton's Ohio General Code, 1921. Home: Cleveland, Ohio. Died May 20, 1938.

THROGMORTON, William P., editor, clergyman; b. Henry County, Tenn., Sept. 19, 1849; s. Lewis W. and Margaret J. (Morton) T.; ed. pub. schs.; D.D., Ewing Coll., 1890, LL.D., 1920; m. Eliza C. Baker, Sept. 24, 1868 (died 1921); m. 2d, Kathrine Edwards, June 28, 1922. Teacher pub. schs., 1866-77; ordained ministry Bapt. Ch., 1871; pastor successively Benton and Mt. Vernon, Ill., Louisiana, Mo., Ft. Smith, Ark., Du Quoin, Ill., 1st Ch., Marion, and Third Ch., Marion, 1925—; erected 4 chs.; editor denom. papers, 1877—; editor Ill. Baptist, 1905—. Trustee Ewing (Ill.) Coll., Southwestern Bapt. Theol. Sem., Ft. Worth, Tex. Republican. Prohibitionist. Mason, Odd Fellow. Home: Marion, Ill. Died Dec. 1929.

THRUSTON, Gates Phillips, soldier, author; b. Dayton, O., June 11, 1835; s. Hon. R. A. and Marianna (Phillips) T.; A.B. (valedictorian), Miami U., 1855, A.M., 1858, L.H.D., 1899; LL.B., Cincinnati Law Sch., 1859; m. Ida Hamilton, Dec. 21, 1865 (died 1893; m. 2d, Fanny Dorman, Sept. 1894. Capt. 1st Ohio Inf., Aug. 24, 1861; maj. asst. adj. vols., Sept. 4, 1863; lt. col., Nov. 1, 1863; bvtd. lt. col. vols., Mar. 13, 1865, "for faithful and meritorious services during the war"; col. and brig. gen. vols., Mar. 13, 1865, for same and particularly "for gallant and meritorious services at battles of Stone River and Chickamauga"; a.a.g. and chief on staff, 20th Army Corps, at Chickamauga; later judge advocate, Army of the Cumberland; hon. mustered out, Dec. 19, 1865. Settled at Nashville, 1865; chief dept. history and antiquities, Tenn. Centennial Expn. Fellow A.A.A.S.; v.p. Tenn. Hist. Soc.; pres. Soc. Army of the Cumberland, 1906—. Author: Antiquities of Tennessee and Adjacent States, 1890. Contbr. to mags. on antiquarian and mil. subjects. Address: Nashville, Tenn. Deceased.

THULSTRUP, Thure de, artist; b. Sweden, 1848; s. Magnus and Hedwig (Akrell) T.; father was minister of war of Sweden; grad. Nat. Mil. Acad., Stockholm; officer in French Army, serving in Algeria, etc.; studied drawing at Paris; went to Canada as topog. engr.; later in Boston; m. Lucie Bavoillot, June 3, 1879. First illustrations for N.Y. Graphic; on staff Graphic, Leslie's Weekly, Harper's Weekly many yrs.; self-taught in painting. Mem. Soc. Illustrators, Am. Water Color Soc., John Ericsson Soc. Swedish Engrs. Knight of Order of Vasa, Sweden. Died June 9, 1930.

THUM, Patty Prather, painter; b. Louisville, Ky.; d. Mandeville (M.D.) and Louisiana (Miller) Thum; grad. Vassar Coll.; studied painting with Henry Van Ingen at Vassar, later at Art Students' League, New York, and with William M. Chase, New York. Hon. mention for book illustrations, Chicago Expn., 1893. Pictures in Louisville Pub. Library and in many pvt. collections. Mem. Louisville Art Assn., Am. Federation of Arts. Episcopalian. Contbr. to art mags. and newspapers on art topics. Art dir. of Ky. State Fair, 1921. Home: Louisville, Ky. Died Sept. 28, 1926.

THURBER, Charles Herbert, editor; b. nr. Owego, N.Y., Mar. 24, 1864; s. John A. and Sarah M. (Aber) T.; Ph.B., Cornell, 1886; traveled and studied abroad part of 1887-89; A.M., Haverford Coll., 1890; student Royal Polytechnicum, Dresden, Saxony, 1890-91; student Clark Univ., 1899-1900, Ph.D., 1900; m. Anna E. Billings, June 25, 1891; 1 dau., Gertrude Ruth (Mrs. W. M. Tanner). Registrar and sec. Cornell, 1886-88; spl. agt. U.S. Bur. Edn., abroad, 1890-91; instr., Cornell U., 1891-93; prof. Colgate U., 1893-95; asso. prof., U. of Chicago, 1895-1900; editor Ginn & Co., pubs., 1900, and mem. firm, 1904-32. Asst. editor-in-chief Johnson's Universal Cyclo., 1892-94; editor School Review, 1892-1901. Mem. of bd. of trustees Clark Univ. Author: The Principles of School Organization, 1901; Fritz Reuter, 1914. Home: Framingham Centre, Mass. Died Dec. 8, 1938.

THURBER, Edward Gerrish, clergyman; b. Monroe, Mich., May 28, 1836; s. Hon. Jefferson G. and Mary Bartlett (Gerrish) T.; A.B., U. of Mich., 1857, A.M., 1860; Union Theol. Sem., 1859-61; grad. Andover Theol. Sem., 1862; S.T.D., Hamilton, 1882; m. Sarah Augusta Wood, Sept. 5, 1865. Ordained Congl. ministry, 1862; pastor, Congl. Ch., Walpole, Mass., 1862-70, Park Central Presbyn. Ch., Syracuse, N.Y., 1870-89, Am. Ch., Paris, France, 1889-1904; in New York, 1904—. Republican. Address: New York, N.Y. Died Nov. 7, 1913.

THURBER, Francis Beatty, merchant lawyer; b. Delhi, N.Y., Nov. 13, 1842; s. Abner Gilman and Lucy (Dunham) T.; ed. Delaware Acad., Delhi, 1851-54, and Union Hall Acad., 1855-56; studied law, Univ. Law Sch., New York, 1896-98; m. Jeannette Meyer, 1869. In warehouse business, New York, 1856-64; wholesale grocer, 1864-93; later lawyer; admitted to bar, 1899, at age of 57 (oldest law student in State of N.Y.). Organized N.Y. State Anti-Monopoly League, which created the N.Y. State R.R. Commn., and assisted in creating Inter-State Commerce Commn. Pres. U.S. Export Assn., v.p. Nat. Bd. Trade, v.p. Irrigation Assn. Author: Coffee from Plantation to Cup, 1878. Contbr. to leading reviews. Home: New York, N.Y. Died 1907.

THURBER, Howard Ford, telephone official; b. Brooklyn, N.Y., Aug. 6, 1869; s. Abner D. and Annie M. (Ford) T.; Poly. Inst. of Brooklyn; M.E., Cornell, 1890; unmarried. Began as engring. asst. Met. Telephone & Telegraph Co., New York, 1890, asst. chief engr., 1893, gen. supt., 1894-1906; gen. mgr. New York Telephone Co., 1906-08, v.p., gen. mgr., 1908-12; v.p. Eastern Group Bell Telephone Cos., 1912-19; pres. New York Telephone Co., 1919-24, chmn. bd., 1924; chmn. bd. Empire City Subway Co.; dir. Bell Telephone Co. of Pa. and asso. cos. Home: New York, N.Y. Died Apr. 21, 1928.

THURSTON, Charles Rawson, newspaper man; b. Newport, R.I., June 17, 1860; s. Parker Hall and Louisa Maria (Rawson) T.; grad. Rogers High Sch., Newport, 1878; A.B., Brown U., 1882, A.M., 1885; m. Mary A. Anthony, 1891. Began in gen. newspaper work, Newport, 1882; Newport corr. Providence (R.I.) Jour. and Asso. Press, 1885-91; news editor Providence Jour., 1891-1906; news editor and city editor Providence Tribune, 1906-19; editor Pawtucket Times, 1919-27; lecturer in journalism, univ. extension, Brown U., 1921—; editorial writer Newport News and Woonsocket Call; asso. editor Diocesan Record of R.I. Republican. Episcopalian. Mason. Royal Arcanum. Home: Pawtucket, R.I. Died Feb. 9, 1929.

THURSTON, Howard, magician; b. Columbus, O., July 20, 1869; s. William H. and Margaret (Cloude) T.; ed. Moody and Sankey Sch., Northfield, Mass.; m. 2d, Nina L. Fielding, 1 dau., Jane Thurston. Magician since boyhood; made tour of the world, 1904-07, performing before many rulers and notables; in America starred jointly with Kellar, 1907-08; later toured alone throughout U.S. Democrat. Mason, Elk. Author: My Life of Magic, 1929; also The Demon (mystery drama) and various brochures on magic. Address: Whitestone, N.Y. Died Apr. 13, 1936.

THURSTON, Ida Treadwell. Author: A Bachelor Maid and Her Brother, 1898; Bishop's Shadow, 1899; Boys of the Central; The Captain of the Cadets, 1899; Don Malcolm; A Frontier Hero, 1898; A Genuine Lady; Kent Fielding's Ventures; Next-Door Neighbors; Ruth Prentice; A Village Contest, 1899; Citizen Dan of the Junior Republic, 1901; The Big Brother of Sabin Street, 1909; The Scout Master of Troop 5, 1912; The Torch Bearer, 1913; Just Girls, 1915; Billy Burns of Troop 5, 1916. Address: Washington, D.C. Died June 3, 1918.

THURSTON, John Mellen, senator; b. Montpelier, Vt., Aug. 21, 1847; s. Daniel Sylvester and Ruth (Mellen) T.; removed to Wis., 1854; ed. at pub. schs. and Wayland U., Beaver Dam, Wis., supporting himself by farm work, driving teams and other manual labor; admitted to bar, May 21, 1869; following Oct. located in Omaha; m. Martha Poland, Dec. 25, 1872 (died 1898); m. 2d, Lola, d. Maj. William J. Purman, Nov., 1899. Mem. city council, 1872-74; city atty., 1874-77; mem. Neb. Legislature, 1875-77; presdl. elector, 1880; asst. atty., 1877-88, and, 1888—, gen. counsel U.P. Ry. Co.; Rep. caucus nominee for U.S. senator, 1893; U.S. senator from Neb., 1895-1901. Pres. Rep. League of U.S., 1889-91; chmn. Rep. nat. convs., 1888 and 1896; apptd., 1901, U.S. commr., St. Louis Expn. Later mem. law firm Thurston, Crow & Morrison. Address: Omaha, Neb. Died Aug. 9, 1916.

THURSTON, Lorrin Andrews, lawyer; b. Honolulu, Hawaii, July 31, 1858; s. Asa G. and Sarah (Andrews) T.; student Oahu Coll., 1873-76, Columbia Law Sch., New York, 1880-81; m. Harriet Potter, Apr. 5, 1894; children—Robert Shipman, Margaret Carter, Lorrin Potter. Admitted to bar, Honolulu, 1878. Mem. House of Reps., Hawaii, 1886; minister interior, Kingdom of Hawaii, 1887-90; ex-officio mem. Legislature, 1887, 1888, 1890; mem. Bd. of Health, 1887-90; pres. Bd. of Immigration, 1890; elected mem. House of Nobles, 1892; mem. Com. of Safety in connection with overthrow of Hawaiian monarchy, 1893; mem. advisory council, Provisional Govt. of Hawaii, 1893; spl. commr. to U.S. to negotiate annexation to U.S., 1893; minister of Provisional Govt. of Hawaii to U.S., 1893; minister Republic of Hawaii to U.S., 1894, to Portugal, 1894; spl. commr. to U.S. to negotiate treaty of annexation, 1897. Pres. Advertiser Pub. Co., Olaa Sugar Co.; v.p. Honolulu Rapid Transit Co. Trustee Oahu Coll.; pres. Hawaiian Volcano Research Assn.; pres. Pan-Pacific Press Conf. Republican. Compiler: Fundamental law of Hawaii, 1904. Home: Honolulu, T.H. Died May 11, 1931.

THURSTON, Robert Henry, univ. prof., engr., author; b. Providence, R.I., Oct. 25, 1839; s. Robert L. and Harriet (Taylor) T.; grad. Brown U., C.E. and Ph.B., 1859, A.M., 1869; LL.D., 1889; Dr.Engring., Stevens Inst. Tech., 1885; trained in his father's shops until 1861; in U.S.N., 1861-72, asst. engr. and engr. in charge of vessels; at U.S. Naval Acad., Annapolis, acting asst. prof. natural philosophy, 1865-71; prof. mech. engring., Stevens Inst. of Tech., 1871-85; dir. Sibley Coll., Cornell U. and prof. mech. engring., 1885—; m. Susan Taylor Gladding, Oct. 1865 (died 1878); m. 2d, Leonora Boughton, Aug. 4, 1880. First pres. (two terms, 1880-83) Am. Soc. Mech. Engrs.; 3 times v.p. A.A.A.S., 1877-78 and 1884; v.p. Am. Inst. Mining Engrs., 1878-79; inventor of testing machines, engine governors and other devices; U.S. commr. to Vienna Expn., 1873, Paris, 1889; served on many U.S. and State commns. Author: Friction and Lubrication; Materials of Engineering, 3 vols., 1884; Manual of the Steam-Engine, 2 vols., 1890, 1901; Materials of Construction, 1884; Stationary Steam Engines, 1885; Friction and Lost Work in Machinery and Mill Work, 1885; Manual of the Steam Boiler, 1888; Handbook of Engine and Boiler Trials, 1889; Motive Power of Heat (from French of Carnot), 1890; Heat as a Form of Energy, 1890; Life of Robert Fulton, 1891; History of the Steam Engine, 1878, 1901. Also about 300 professional and scientific papers. Is an editor of Science and of Johnson's and Appleton's Cyclopædias. Address: Ithaca, N.Y. Died 1903.

THURSTON, Theodore Payne, bishop; b. Delavan, Ill.; s. Benjamin Easton and Mary Ann (Siddall) T.; A.B., Trinity Coll., Hartford, 1891, S.T.B., 1894, D.D., 1911; Episcopal Theol. Sch., Cambridge, 1891-94; m. Jane Mitchell, Sept. 21, 1904 (died 1905); m. 2d, Mrs. Daisy Carroll Speer, June 8, 1920. Deacon, 1894, priest, 1895, P.E. Ch.; rector St. Paul's Owatonna, Minn., 1894-97, Winona, Minn., 1897-1903. Minneapolis, 1903-11; consecrated bishop of Eastern Okla., Jan. 25, 1911, bishop of Okla., 1919-26 (resigned). Charter mem. trustees Shattuck Sch., Faribault, Minn.; trustee U. of the South, Sewanee, Tenn. Mason. Home: San Diego, Calif. Died Jan. 28, 1941.

THWAITES, Reuben Gold, historian; b. Dorchester, Mass., May 15, 1853; s. William George and Sarah (Bibbs) T.; ed. common and high schs. there, followed by self-instruction in collegiate course; post-grad. work at Yale, 1874-75; LL.D., U. of Wis., 1904; m. Jessie Inwood Turville, 1882. Mng. editor Wis. State Jour., Madison, 1876-86; sec. and supt. State Hist. Soc. of Wis., 1886. Pres. A.L.A., 1900, later mem. exec. council; chmn. Am. Hist. Manuscript Commn., 1900; vice chmn. Wis. Free Library Commn.; sec. and editor Wis. History Commn., lecturer on American history, U. of Wis. Author: Down Historic Waterways, 1888; The Story of Wisconsin, 1890; The Colonies, 1492-1750, 1891; Our Cycling Tour in England, 1892; On the Storied Ohio, 1897; Stories of the Badger State, 1900; History of the University of Wisconsin, 1900; Father Marquette, 1902; Daniel Boone, 1902; Brief History of Rocky Mountain Exploration, 1904; France in America, 1905; Wisconsin (Am. Commonwealth series), 1909; School History of U.S., 1912; also numerous monographs on the history of New France and the Middle West. Editor: Wisconsin Historical Collections (Vols. II-XIX), 1888-1911; Chronicles of Border Warfare, 1895; The University of Wisconsin, 1900; The Jesuit Relations (73 vols.), 1896-1901; new edition of Kinzie's "Wau Bun," 1901; Hennepin's "New Discovery," 1903; Original Journals of Lewis and Clark, 1905; Early Western Travels, 1748-1846 (33 vols.), 1904-07; Lahontan's New Voyages to North America, 1905; Documentary History of Dunmore's War, 1905; Revolution on the Upper Ohio, 1908; Frontier Defenses on the Upper Ohio, 1911. Address: Madison, Wis. Died Oct. 22, 1913.

THWING, Charles Franklin, univ. pres.; b. New Sharon, Me., Nov. 9, 1853; s. Joseph P. and Hannah M. (Hopkins) T.; A.B., Harvard, 1876; grad. Andover Theol. Sem., 1879; S.T.D., Chicago Theol. Sem., 1889; LL.D., Marietta, 1894, Ill. Coll., 1894, Waynesburg, 1901, Washington and Jefferson, 1902, Kenyon, 1910; Litt.D., U. of Pa., 1917; L.H.D. from Western Reserve U., 1926; m. Carrie F. Butler, Sept. 18, 1879 (died 1898); children—Mary Butler (Mrs. J. M. Shallenberger), Francis Wendell Butler-Thwing, Apphia (Mrs. Roy K. Hack); m. 2d, Mary Gardiner Dunning, Dec. 22, 1906 (died 1931). Ordained in Congl. ministry, 1879; pastor North Ave. Ch., Cambridge, Mass., 1879-86, Plymouth Ch., Minneapolis, 1886-90; pres. Western Reserve U. and Adelbert Coll., 1890-1921, pres. emeritus, 1921. Sec. bd. trustees Carnegie Foundation for the Advancement of Teaching, 1905-21; elector, Hall of Fame; pres. United Chapters, Phi Beta Kappa, 1922-28, also life senator; v.p. Cleveland br. English-Speaking Union. Trustee Cleveland Clinic, Hiram House Social Settlement, Anatolia Coll., Greece, Foreign Language Information Service. Awarded medal for Pub. Service by Cleveland Chamber Commerce, 1925. Mem. Soc. Arts and Sciences, Am. Hist. Assn., Am. Acad. of Arts and Sciences. Author: The American College, 1914; Education According to Some Modern Masters, 1916; The Ministry, 1916; The Training of Men for the World's Future, 1916; The College Gateway, 1919; The American Colleges and Universities in the Great War, 1920; Higher Education in Australia and New Zealand, 1922; Human Australasia, 1923; What Education Has the Most Worth?, 1924; The College President, 1925; Guides, Philosophers, and Friends—Studies of College Men, 1927; The American and the German University, 1928; Education and Religion, 1929; American Society—Interpretations of Educational and Other Forces, 1931; Friends of Men, being a second series of Guides, Philosophers, and Friends, 1933; The American College and University —A Human Fellowship, 1935; also annual reports of Western Reserve U. and Adelbert Coll. Address: Cleveland, O. Died Aug. 29, 1937.

THWING, Eugene, editor, pub.; b. Quincy, Mass., Jan. 17, 1866; s. Edward Payson (D.D., M.D., Ph.D.) and Susan Maria (Waite) T.; brother of Edward Waite T.; ed. pub. schs. and Adelphi Coll., Brooklyn; m. Mary Eva Steinmetz, June 26, 1890. Connected with Funk & Wagnalls Co., pubs., 1882-1908; editor and pub. The Circle and Success Magazine, 1908-15; organizer, 1913, and pres. and treas. The Purity Products Co. Lecturer West Side Y.M.C.A., New York, 1915-18; mem. bd. of instrn. for drafted men, 1918; connected with The Literary Digest, 1918—. First pres. bd. trustees Ridgewood Pub. Library. Methodist. Mason. Founder of The House of Good Will, Inc.,

1923, internat. fraternal order for world peace. Contbr. spl. war service articles in over 100 dailies and weeklies in U.S. and Can. during the war. Author: The Red-Keggers, 1903; The Man from Red-Keg, 1905; Thwing's Business Letters, 1911; Life and Meaning of Theodore Roosevelt, 1919; Twelve Practical Guides to Health, 1926; Unto the Least, 1927. Compiler: The World's Best 100 Detective Stories, 10 vols. (anthology), 1929; The Literary Digest Political Cyclo., 1932; New Mental Efficiency Manual, 1934. Editor in chief The American States, 50 vols. in preparation. Organizer, 1931, and exec. sec. Nat. Bd. of Health Counsel. Home: Ridgewood, N.J. Died May 29, 1936.

TIBBETTS, Frederick Horace, civ. and cons. engr.; b. Oshkosh, Wis., Apr. 28, 1882; s. Horace Albert and Amanda (Arnold) T.; grad. Commercial Dept., U. of Pacific, 1901, B.S., Coll. of Liberal Arts, 1903, M.S., 1905; B.S., U. of Calif., 1904, M.S., 1906; m. Flora Macdonald; 1 son, Reginald. Began practice civ. engring., San Francisco, Calif., 1905; asst. instr. later asst. prof. civ. engring., U. of Calif., 1906-11; mem. Haviland & Tibbetts, civ. engrs., later Haviland, Dozier & Tibbetts Constrn. Co., 1909-17; civ. and cons. engr., San Francisco, 1917—; chief engr. Nev. Irrigation Dist., Sacramento River West Side Levee Dist., Linden Irrigation Dist., Knights Landing Drainage Dist., Anchorage Light & Power Co., Reclamation dists. 108 and 2047; cons. engr. Pershing County and Roosevelt water conservation dists. of Nev. and Ariz., Santa Clara Valley Water Conservation District. Republican. Methodist. Mason. Home: Berkeley, Calif. Died Aug. 2, 1938.

TIBBITS, Charles Edward Dudley, trustee; b. Hoosac, Rensselaer County, N.Y., Aug. 18, 1834; s. George Mortimer and Sarah (Bleecker) T.; pvt. schs. and Rensselaer Poly. Inst., Troy, N.Y.; m. Mary Elizabeth Knox, June 8, 1865 (died 1875). Many yrs. a dir., and pres., 1892-95, Walter A. Wood Mowing & Reaping Machine Co., Hoosick Falls, N.Y.; dir. United Nat. Bank of Troy, 1878—. Trustee of estates, Troy Orphan Asylum, Troy Pub. Library. Chmn. Com. of 100 in charge of celebration of 100th anniversary of Troy, 1889. A founder and v.p. Nat. Municipal League; a v.p. Am. Rights League. Episcopalian. Home: Troy, N.Y. Died Aug. 19, 1924.

TIBBLES, Thomas Henry, newspaperman; b. Washington County, O., May 22, 1838; s. William and Martha (Cooley) T.; ed. Mt. Union Coll., Alliance, O.; m. Amelia Owen, 1861 (died 1879); m. 2d, Susette LaFlesche, 1882 (died 1903); m. 3d, Ida B. Riddle, Feb. 24, 1907. Mem. John Brown's Co. in Kan., 1856; guide and scout on plains; in secret service and newspaper corr. during Civil War; on staff Omaha Bee, 1873-74, Omaha Herald and World-Herald, 1876-79; Washington corr. Nonconformist, 1893-94; founded The Independent at Lincoln, Neb., 1895; lecturer and Indian reformer; candidate for V.P. on People's ticket, 1904; editor The Investigator, 1905-10; editorial and feature writer, Omaha World-Herald, 1910—. Author: Hidden Power, 1880; Ponca Chiefs, 1881; The American Peasant, 1890. Home: Omaha, Neb. Died May 14, 1928.

TICHBORNE, Josephine Caroline Sawyer, author; b. Watertown, N.Y., Sept. 5, 1878; d. Hon. A. H. (LL.D.) and Frances C. (Fox) Sawyer; ed. Irving Sch., Watertown, to 1895, Pelham Hall, Pelham Manor, N.Y., 1895-97; m. Walter Francis Carson Tichborne, April 18, 1906. Author: Every Inch a King, 1901; All's Fair in Love, 1904. Address: Poughkeepsie, N.Y. Died Jan. 31, 1924.

TICKNOR, Caroline, author; b. Boston, Mass.; d. Benjamin H. and Caroline (Cushman) Ticknor; g.d. William D. T., founder of pub. house of Ticknor & Fields. Writer of stories, plays, etc. Author: (or editor) A Hypocritical Romance, 1896; Miss Belladonna, 1897; a Poet in Exile, 1910; Hawthorne and His Publisher, 1913; Dr. Holmes' Boston, 1915; Poe's Helen, 1916; Glimpses of Authors, 1922. One of the editors of Internat. Library of Famous Literature (20 volumes), 1898; Masterpieces of the World's Literature (20 vols.), 1899; Library of Oratory (15 vols.), 1902; Vocations (10 vols.), 1911; New England Aviators (2 vols.), 1919; Classic Concord, 1926; May Alcott, 1928; Book of Famous Horses, 1929. Home: Jamaica Plain, Mass. Died May 11, 1937.

TICKNOR, Howard Malcom, educator, lecturer, journalist; b. Boston, Mass., July 4, 1836; s. William Davis and Emeline Staniford (Holt) T.; M.A., Harvard, 1856; studied vocal music and languages in Italy, 1868-78; m. Helen Frances Adams, Feb. 2, 1864. Mem. of the publishing firm of Ticknor & Fields, 1864 et seq.; asst. editor (with Lowell) Atlantic Monthly; editor Our Young Folks, from inception to 1869; during Italian residence, 1868-78, in consular service, generally as vice consul, at Naples, Venice, Rome; fgn. corr. for Am. and London jours.; instr. elocution, Harvard and Brown univs. and in important schs., St. Paul's, etc., 1878-87; mus. and dramatic critic Boston Daily Advertiser, Globe, Herald, Jour., etc., 1878-1904. Republican. Home: Franklin, Mass. Died 1905.

TIDBALL, John Caldwell, army officer; b. Ohio County, Va. (now W.Va.), Jan. 25, 1825; s. William and Maria (Caldwell) T.; grad. West Point, 1848; m.

Mary Langdon Dana, d. of Gen. N. J. T. Dana, U.S.A. Bvtd. 2d lt. 3d arty., July 1, 1848; promoted 2d lt. 2d arty., Feb. 14, 1849; 1st lt., Mar. 31, 1853; capt., May 14, 1861. Bvts. for gallant and meritorious services: Bvtd. maj., June 27, 1862 (for Gaines' Mill); bvtd. lt. colonel, Sept. 17, 1862 (for Antietam); bvtd. brig. gen. U.S.V., Aug. 1, 1864 (gallant and distinguished services in the battles of the Po, Spottsylvania C.H., and operations before Richmond); bvtd. col. and brig. gen. U.S.A., Mar. 13, 1865 (Ft. Steadman, Va.); bvtd. maj. gen. U.A.V. (Fts. Steadman and Sedgwick, Va.). Served in regular arty. in Civil war until Aug. 28, 1863, then col. 4th N.Y. vol. arty. until mustered out of vol. service Sept. 30, 1865; participated in many battles; maj. 2d arty., Feb. 5, 1867; col. staff aide-de-camp to gen.-in-chief, Jan. 1, 1881, to Feb. 8, 1884; lt. col. 3d arty., June 30, 1882; transferred to 1st arty. Nov. 10, 1882, to 3d arty. Jan. 25, 1884, col. Mar. 22, 1885; in command Arty. Sch. for Practice and Post of Ft. Monroe, Va., Nov. 7, 1883, to Nov. 4, 1888; retired Jan. 25, 1889. Author: A Manual of Heavy Artillery Service, 1880. Address: Montclair, N.J. Died 1906.

TIEDEMAN, Christopher Gustavus, lawyer, author; b. Charleston, S.C., July 16, 1857; s. Otto and Caroline Amelia T.; grad. Coll. of Charleston, 1876; A.M., Columbia Law School, 1879; LL.M., 1892, LL.D., 1895, New York U.; m. Helen Bruce Seymour, 1885. Prof. law 10 yrs., U. of Mo.; 6 yrs. in New York U.; dean Buffalo Law Sch., May 1902—. Mem. Am. Acad. Polit. and Social Science. Author: The Law of Real Property, 1883, 1892; Limitations of Police Power, 1886; Commercial Paper, 1889; Unwritten Constitution of the United States, 1890; Sales of Personal Property, 1891; Municipal Corporations, 1893; Cases of Real Property, 1897; Bills and Notes, 1898; State and Federal Control of Persons and Property, 1900. Home: Buffalo, N.Y. Died 1903.

TIEKEN, Theodore, M.D.; b. Oldenburg, Germany, Sept. 11, 1866; s. Frederick and Katherine (Sievers) T.; ed. pub. schs., Ill.; M.D., Coll. Phys. and Surg. (U. of Ill.), Chicago, 1899; B.S., U. of Chicago, 1917; m Bessie Chapman, September 11, 1901 (died 1930); children—Helen, Robert Theodore. Prof. of therapeutics, Rush Medical College, 1908—; later clin. prof. medicine U. of Chicago, and head Dept. of Materia Medica, Therapeutics and Toxicology; attending phys. Cook County Hosp.; attending phys. Presbyn. Hosp.; cons. phys. Norwegian Am., Garfield and J. B. Murphy hosps. Fellow Inst. of Medicine, Chicago (gov.). Home: Chicago, Ill. Died Oct. 15, 1932.

TIEMANN, Daniel Fawcett, paint and color mfr.; b. New York, Jan. 9, 1805; pvt. edn.; m. Martha W. Clowes, niece of Peter Cooper, Aug. 30, 1826. Clerk in wholesale drug house, 1818-24; entered father's paint bus. as employe, 1824; became partner, 1827; succeeded to bus. on father's death, 1848. Asst. alderman and later alderman, 1839; again asst. alderman, 1849, alderman, 1850-55; gov. of Almshouse, 1854-57; mayor of New York, 1858-60; State senator, 1871. Home: New York, N.Y. Died 1899.

TIERNAN, Charles Bernard, lawyer; b. Baltimore, Sept. 4, 1840; s. Charles and Gay Robertson (Bernard) T.; ed. St. Mary's and Loyola colls., A.B., 1860, A.M., 1861; post-grad. course in modern lit., Johns Hopkins; studied law under Seven Teackle Wallis; unmarried. Admitted to bar, 1862. Counsel for Hibernian Soc., Clan Robertson, Scotland, Soc. of Colonial Wars, S.A.R.; pres. Cathedral branch St. Vincent de Paul Soc., Cathedral branch Young Catholic Friends Soc.; supt. Cathedral S.S.—400 girls and boys; trustee of the Cathedral; v.p. Alumni Assn. of Loyola Coll. Mem. 53d Regt. Md. N.G., Apr. 19, 1861, at beginning of war; ordnance sergt. 7th Regt. in riots of 1877. Democrat. Author: Tiernan Family in Maryland, 1898; Tiernan and Other Families, 1901. Address: Baltimore, Md. Deceased.

TIERNEY, Michael, R.C. bishop; b. Ballylooby, County, Tipperary, Ireland, Sept. 29, 1839; grad. St. Joseph's Sem., Troy, N.Y. Ordained priest, May 26, 1866; consecrated bishop of Hartford, Feb. 22, 1894. Address: Hartford, Conn. Died 1908.

TIERNEY, Richard Henry, editor; b. N.Y. City, Sept. 2, 1870; B.A., St. Francis Xavier Coll., N.Y. City, 1892; M.A., Woodstock Coll.; Ph.D., Fordham U.; entered Soc. of Jesus (Jesuits), 1892; studied Frederick, Md., 1892-96; Woodstock (Md.) Coll., 1896-99 and 1903-07; in Austria, 1907-08. Prof. Latin and Greek, Gonzaga Coll., Washington, D.C., 1899-1901, Holy Cross Coll., Worcester, Mass., 1901-03; prof. philosophy and pedagogy, Woodstock Coll., 1909-14; editor of America (nat. Catholic weekly) and Catholic Mind, 1914-25. Author: Teacher and Teacher, 1914. Contbr. to Am. Catholic Quarterly, Am. Ecclesiastical Rev., etc. Lecturer on psychology of edn. Address: New York, N.Y. Died Feb. 11, 1928.

TIERNON, John Luke, army officer; b. Madison, Ind., Jan. 18, 1841; s. Anthony and Katherine (Sendelbach) T.; ed. St. Mary's Sem., Mo., m. Harriet Virginia Pickett, Feb. 1, 1865. Apptd. from Mo., 2d lt. 3d Arty., Feb. 19, 1862; 1st lt., Jan. 20,

1864; grad. Arty. Sch., 1869; capt., July 2, 1877; maj. 1st arty., Sept. 1, 1896; lt. col. 5th Arty., July 15, 1900; col. arty. corps, Aug. 22, 1901; brig. gen., Aug. 11, 1903; retired at own request after 40 yrs.' service, Aug. 12, 1903. Address: Buffalo, N.Y. Died 1910.

TIFFANY, Charles Comfort, P.E. clergyman; b. Baltimore, 1829; s. Comfort and Laura (Burr) T.; A.M., 1853, Dickinson Coll., D.D., 1883; Andover Theol. Sem., univs. of Halle, Heidelberg and Berlin; D.D., St. Stephen's, 1893, D.D., Yale, 1897; m. Julia H. Wheeler, Apr. 27, 1882. Ordained Episcopal minister, 1866; rector St. James', Fordham, N.Y., 1867-71; asst. on the Green Foundation Trinity Ch., Boston, 1871-74; rector Ch. of the Atonement, New York, 1874-80; Zion Ch., New York, 1880-90; archdeacon of New York, 1893—. Author: Expression in Church Architecture; Modern Atheism; History of the Protestant Episcopal Church, 1895; The Prayer Book and the Christian Life, 1897. Died 1907.

TIFFANY, Charles Lewis, jeweler; b. Killingly, Conn., Feb. 15, 1812; s. Comfort T., a pioneer in the cotton goods industry; ed. in local schools; in business at Killingly until 1837; in that yr., with J. B. Young, started Tiffany & Young, a stationery store, with a stock also of Chinese and Japanese goods, pottery, fans, canes, etc.; later added French jewelry; afterward manufactured jewelry, silverware and other artistic merchandise, and became extensive dealers in gems and precious stones; after various changes firm became Tiffany & Co., with branch houses in London and Paris; m. Harriet O., d. Judge Young, Nov. 30, 1841 (celebrated golden wedding in 1891). Chevalier Nat. Legion of Honor of France; received from Emperor of Russia the honor of Præmia Digno. Home: New York, N.Y. Died 1902.

TIFFANY, Flavel Benjamin, ophthalmologist; b. Oneida County, N.Y., Apr. 28, 1846; s. Ambrose Benjamin and Electa (Sheperd) T.; U. of Minn., 1869-72; M.D., Med. Dept., U. of Mich., 1874; post-grad. work, Berlin, Vienna, Leipzig, 1877-78 and later; made trip around world, 1912-13, visiting all the prin. eye clinics; hon. A.M., Bethany Coll., Lindsborg, Kan., 1900; m. Olive E. Fairbanks, June 2, 1879 (died 1910); m. 2d, Zoe Clark, Sept. 12, 1912. Practiced, East St. Louis, Ill., and Medford, Minn., 1874-76, Kansas City, Mo., 1878—; retired and engaged in lit. work and farming; charter mem., 1879, later pres. Univ. Med. Coll., Kansas City; oculist for M.,K.&T. and C.,B.&Q. rys.; originator of several operations on the eye. Mem. 2d Battery Light Arty., Minn., 1864-65. Fellow A.M.A. Home: Kansas City, Mo. Died Jan. 4, 1918.

TIFFANY, Francis, Unitarian clergyman; b. in Md., 1827; ordained Unitarian minister, 1852; pastor West Newton, Mass., 1865-82. Author: Life of Dorothea Lynde Dix; Bird Bolts; Life of Charles Francis Barnard; This Goodly Frame, the Earth (travels). Address: Cambridge, Mass. Died 1908.

TIFFANY, Louis Comfort, artist; b. N.Y. City, Feb. 18, 1848; s. Charles Lewis T., the well known jeweler, and Harriet Olivia (Young) T.; studied art under George Inness and Samuel Coleman, New York and Léon Bailly, Paris; hon. A.M., Yale, 1903; m. Mary Woodbridge Goddard, May 15, 1872 (died 1884); m. 2d, Louise Wakeman, d. Rev. J. H. Mason Knox, Nov. 9, 1886. His paintings in oil and water colors include many Oriental scenes. Did much decorative work; pres. and art dir. Tiffany Studios; v.p. and dir. Tiffany & Co.; v.p. and dir. Tiffany & Company Safe Deposit Co. Discovered new formulas for making decorative glass known as "Tiffany Favrile glass." Gold medal and decoration Chevalier of Legion of Honor, Paris, 1900. Awarded 54 medals, Chicago Expn., 1893; grand prix, Paris Expn., 1900, St. Petersburg, 1901; gold medal, Buffalo Expn., 1901, Dresden Expn., 1901; grand prix and spl. diploma, Turin Expn., 1902; gold medal, St. Louis Expn., 1904, Jamestown Expn., 1907; grand prize, Seattle Expn., 1909; gold medal, Panama P.I. Expn., 1915; gold medal, Sesquicentennial Expn., Phila., 1926. A.N.A., 1871, N.A., 1880; mem. Am. Water Color Soc., New York Soc. Fine Arts, Architectural League, Imperial Soc. Fine Arts, Tokio, Japan, Société Nationale des Beaux Arts, Paris. In 1918 established the Louis Comfort Tiffany Foundation for art students at Oyster Bay, N.Y., and deeded to it his entire collection of paintings, glass and other art objects, with Laurelton Hall, his country home, the picture gallery and museum, and the Tiffany Chapel, and over 60 acres of land, together with a million dollar fund, income from which to be used for the maintenance and operation of the Foundation. Address: New York, N.Y. Died Jan. 17, 1933.

TIFFANY, Louis McLane, surgeon; b. Baltimore, Oct. 10, 1844; s. Henry and Sally (McLane) T.; A.B., U. of Cambridge, Eng., 1866, A.M.; M.D., U. of Md., 1868; m. Evelyn May Bayly, Jan. 1879. Began practice of surgery at Baltimore, 1868; demonstrator of anatomy, 1869-74, prof. operative surgery, 1874-80, prof. surgery, 1880-1902, U. of Md.; cons. surgeon Johns Hopkins, St. Joseph hosps.; Church Home and other instns.; surgeon-in-chief B.&O.

R.R. 15 years; retired, 1903. Address: Baltimore, Md. Died Oct. 23, 1916.

TIFFANY, Ross Kerr, cons. engr.; b. Union, Ia., June 11, 1879; s. Walter John and Harriet Emily (Kerr) T.; B.C.E., Cornell Coll., Mt. Vernon, Ia., 1901, C.E., 1905; m. Ella Eichar, July 3, 1903; children—Ross K., June. Maintenance engr., later chief engr. and mgr. for pvt. corp., Yakima Project, Wash., 1901-10; supt. and project mgr. Yakima Project, U.S. Reclamation Service, 1910-20; mgr. Spokane Valley Irrigation System, and cons. engr. on irrigation and drainage, 1920-25; state hydraulic engr., Wash., 1925-29; cons. engr. on hydroelectric power and irrigation. Mem. U.S. Com. on Conservation and Adminstrn. of Pub. Domain, 1929-30; exec. officer Wash. State Planning Council, 1934—. Conglist. Mason. Home: Olympia, Wash. Died June 1, 1939.

TIFFT, Henry Neville, lawyer; b. Geneva, N.Y., Sept. 6, 1854; s. Jonathan Neville and Martha Elizabeth (Fish) T.; B.S., Coll. City of N.Y., 1873, M.S., 1876; LL.B., Columbia, 1876; m. Gertrude Havens, Nov. 20, 1883. Teacher in pub. schs., New York, 1875-79; admitted to bar, 1876; began practice, 1879; asst. U.S. dist. atty. under Elihu Root, Gov. Dorsheimer, and Stephen H. Walker, 1883-86. School insp. 21st dist., and chmn. local sch. bd., 14th dist., New York, under Mayors Strong, Van Wyck, and Low; apptd. mem. Bd. of Edn., May 1903; elected pres. Bd. Edn., City of New York, Nov. 23, 1904, to fill unexpired term; reëlected for full term, Feb. 6, 1905. Dir. and sec. bd. trustees N.Y. Juvenile Asylum, 1891—; trustee and treas. bd. Madison Sq. Ch. House; elder and clerk of session 1st Presbyn. Ch.; mem. bd. management and exec. com. West Side Branch, Y.M.C.A. Presbyn. Independent Republican. Home: New York, N.Y. Died Mar. 11, 1925.

TIGERT, John James, M.E. Ch., South, clergyman, editor; b. Louisville, Ky., Nov. 25, 1856; s. John James and Mary (Van Veghten) T.; grad. Vanderbilt U., 1877, S.T.B.; D.D., Emory and Henry; LL.D., U. of Mo.; m. Amelia McTyeire, Aug. 28, 1878. Tutor and prof. moral philosophy, Vanderbilt, 1881-90; pastor, Kansas City, Mo., 1890-94; book editor, M.E. Ch., South, and editor Meth. Quarterly Rev., 1894—; asst. sec. Gen. Confs., 1882, 1890, 1894, sec., 1898, 1902, M.E. Ch., South. Author: Constitutional History of American Episcopal Methodism, 1894; The Journal of Thomas Coke, 1896; The Making of Methodism, 1898; Theism—a Survey of the Paths that Lead to God, 1901; The Doctrines of the Methodist Episcopal Church in America, 2 vols., 1902; also numerous contbns. to Am. and English reviews. Editor: Summer's Systematic Theology, 2 vols., 1886; McTyeire's Passing Through the Gates, 1889; Banks, Manual of Christian Doctrine, 1897. Address: Nashville, Tenn. Died 1906.

TIGHE, Ambrose, lawyer; b. Brooklyn, May 8, 1859; s. James M. and Kate M. T.; A.B., Yale, 1879; A.M., 1891; Douglas fellow, 1880-81, tutor in Roman history and law, 1881-85, Yale; m. Harriet F. Gotzian, June 14, 1893; children—Laurence G., Mrs. Katharine Fessenden, Richard L., Caroline. Admitted to bar, 1885; in practice at St. Paul, 1886—; pres. Minnesota Water Works Co., 1890; pres. Duluth, Red Wing & Southern Ry. Co., 1901; v.p. and counsel Security Trust Co., 1904, and pres. C. Gotzian & Co., shoe mfrs., St. Paul, 1909. Mem. St. Paul Charter Commn., 1899; mem. Minn. Ho. of Reps., 1903, 1907; spl. asst. atty. gen. of Minn. and counsel for Minn. Commn. of Pub. Safety, 1917-19. Home: St. Paul, Minn. Died Nov. 11, 1928.

TIGHT, William George, educator; b. Granville, O., Mar. 12, 1865; s. George H. and Thalia Ann (French) T.; grad. Denison U., B.S., 1886, M.S., 1887; Ph.D., U. of Chicago, 1901; m. Arabella Guy. Prof. geology, Denison U., 14 yrs.; later pres. and prof. geology, U. of N.M. Mem. (past pres.) Ohio State Acad. Science; 10 yrs. permanent sec. Denison Scientific Assn.; fellow A.A.A.S., Geol. Soc. of America (pres. Cordilleran Section, 1905). Contbr. to bulls. of survey and author of professional paper No. 13; Brief Geological History of New Mexico, in Anderson's History; New Mexico supplement to Frye's geography. Address: Albuquerque, N.Mex. Died 1910.

TIHEN, John Henry, bishop; b. Oldenburg, Franklin County, Ind., July 14, 1861; s. Herman B. and Angela (Bruns) T.; ed. St. Benedict's Coll., Atchison, Kan., St. Francis' Sem., Milwaukee, and Catholic U. of America, Washington. Ordained R.C. priest, 1886; asst. pastor St. John's Ch., St. Louis, to Feb. 1, 1889; pastor St. Aloysius' Pro-Cathedral, Wichita, Kan., and chancellor, Diocese of Wichita, 1889-1911; consecrated bishop of Lincoln, Neb., July 6, 1911; apptd. bishop of Denver, Sept. 18, 1917; resigned, 1931; made titular bishop of Bosana. Address: Wichita, Kan. Died Jan. 14, 1940.

TILDEN, Douglas, sculptor; b. Chico, Butte County, Calif., May 1, 1860; s. Dr. W. P. Tilden, of Md., and Mrs. C. M. Tilden-Brown, of San Francisco; lost hearing, result of scarlet fever, at 5; ed. State Instn. for the Deaf, Berkeley, Calif.; grad. same, 1879, teacher same, 1879-87; entered U. of Calif., 1879, but did not take up course; sculptor, 1887—; student Nat. Acad. Design, New York, 1887-88, pupil of Ward, Flagg and Mowbray; pupil of Choppin, Paris; m. Elizabeth Delano Cole, June 12, 1896 (divorced); children—Gladys, Willoughby Lee. Prof. sculpture, Mark Hopkins Art Inst., U. of Calif., 1894-1900. Apptd. by Mayor Phelan hon. mem. com. on artistic improvement of San Francisco; on jury on sculpture, Chicago Expn., 1893. Started and was v.p. 1st Internat. Congress of the Deaf, during World's Fair, Paris, 1889; mem. com. on programme, 2d Internat. Congress, under auspices World's Columbian Expn., 1893; mem. com. on programme 3d Internat. Congress, Paris, France, 1900. Notable works: Baseball Player (Golden Gate Park, San Francisco), Paris Salon, 1889; Tired Boxer (Olympic Club, San Francisco); Indian Bear Hunt, Paris Salon, 1892, Chicago Expn., 1893; Football Players (U. of Calif.), Paris Salon, 1893. Monuments: Commemorating Admission of Calif. to Union; to the Mechanics of San Francisco; to the Calif. Vols. of the Spanish-Am. War, and Ore. Vols. of same (Portland), etc.; to Junipero Serra, San Francisco; to Senator Stephen M. White, Los Angeles, etc. Hon. mention, Paris Salon, 1890; medal, Paris Expn., 1900; commemorative gold medal, St. Louis Expn., 1904 (mem. jury on sculpture); gold medal, Seattle Expn. Studio: Berkeley, Calif. Died Aug. 4, 1935.

TILDEN, Edward, packer, banker; b. Utica, N.Y., June 17, 1858; s. I. D. and Margaret (Averill) T.; pub. sch. edn. Delavan, Wis.; m. Annie Evenhuis, Feb. 20, 1883. Asst. cashier Drovers' Nat. Bank, Union Stock Yards, Chicago, then treas. Libby, McNeill & Libby, packers, to 1897, pres. and treas., 1897—; v.p. and dir. Drovers Deposit Nat. Bank, Nat. Packing Co., Anglo-Am. Provision Co.; treas. and dir. Sioux City Stock Yards; dir. St. Louis Stock Yards, Drovers Trust & Savings Bank, C.&A. R.R. Co., etc. Mem. Chicago Bd. of Edn. Democrat. Methodist. Home: Chicago, Ill. Died Feb. 5, 1915.

TILDEN, George Thomas, architect; b. Concord, N.H., Mar. 19, 1845; s. Rev. William Philips (Unitarian minister) and Mary Jacobs (Foster) T.; ed. Phillips Exeter Acad., N.H.; lectures, Mass. Inst. Tech.; in architectural offices of William R. Ware (later Ware & Van Brunt), Boston; left office of William Ralph Emerson, 1869, to go abroad for a yr.; studied in atelier under Emil Vaudremer, Paris; m. Alice O. Butler, Oct. 5, 1871. Asso. in practice with Arthur Rotch, as Rotch & Tilden, 1880-94, practiced alone, 1894—. Designed and erected many ch., library and sch. bldgs., and pvt. residences in Me., Boston, Washington, Charleston, S.C., etc. Fellow A.I.A. Address: Milton, Mass. Died July 10, 1919.

TILDEN, Joseph Mayo, coll. pres.; b. Worcester, Mass., Mar. 12, 1873; s. Charles Houghton and Ann Maria (Mayo) T.; B.S., Worcester Poly. Inst., 1895; grad. Mass. State Normal Sch., 1897; A.M., New York U., 1906; LL.D., Northern Ill. U., 1916; L.H.D., St. Lawrence U., 1918; m. Gertrude Estelle Bennett, July 28, 1897; children—Sidney Edward, Donald Mayo and Dorothy Mary (twins). Instr. Harvard Coll., Agrl. Dept., 1895-98; instr., asst. to prin., Erasmus Hall High Sch., Brooklyn, N.Y., 1898-1910; lecturer on architecture, N.Y. City pub. lecture system, 7 yrs.; adv. and sales mgr. Am. Sanitary Works, New York, 1910-15; pres. Lombard Coll., Galesburg, Ill., June 1, 1916—. Republican. Universalist. Home: Galesburg, Ill. Died Feb. 23, 1928.

TILDEN, William Tatem, merchant; b. St. George, New Castle County, Del., Mar. 9, 1855; s. Edwin Marmaduke (M.D.) and Williamina (Tatem) T.; A.B., Central High Sch., Phila., 1872; m. Selina Hey, Nov. 6, 1879. Hair and wool merchant, 1880—; dir. Union Nat. Bank, Fire Assn. of Phila.; for 10 yrs. or more in polit. reform movements and chmn. exec. com. Business Men's League of Pa. Mem. Bd. Pub. Edn., Phila. Home: Germantown, Pa. Died July 29, 1915.

TILESTON, Mary Wilder, author; b. Salem, Mass., Aug. 20, 1843; d. Caleb and Mary Wilder (White) Foote; m. John Boies Tileston, Sept. 25, 1865 (died 1898); children—Mary Wilder, Margaret Harding, Roger, Amelia Peabody, Wilder, Edith, Eleanor Boies. Author: (or compiler) Heroic Ballads, 1883; Daily Strength for Daily Needs, 1884; Sugar and Spice, collection of nursery rhymes, 1885; Tender and True, 1892; Selections from Isaac Penington, 1892; Prayers, Ancient and Modern, 1897; Joy and Strength for the Pilgrim's Day, 1901; Memorials of Mary Wilder White, 1903; Children's Treasure Trove of Pearls, 1908; The Child's Harvest of Verse, 1910; Caleb and Mary Wilder Foote, 1918; Amelia Peabody Tileston and Her Canteens for the Serbs, 1920. Home: Brookline, Mass. Died July 3, 1934.

TILFORD, Frank, financier; b. New York, July 22, 1852; s. John M. T.; grad. Mt. Washington Collegiate Inst. At early age entered business with his father in firm of Park & Tilford, of which became pres., 1906; v.p. Bank of New Amsterdam, 1889-96, pres. 1896-1901; pres. Tailfer Co.; dir. Park & Tilford, Mi Favorita Cigar Co., Telegrapho Cigar Co., Inc., Manhattan Eye, Ear and Throat Hosp. Rep. presdl. elector, 1900. Address: New York, N.Y. Died Mar. 6, 1924.

TILFORD, Joseph Green, brig. gen. U.S.A.; b. Georgetown, Ky., Nov. 26, 1829; s. Col. Alexander and Agnes T.; grad. U.S. Mil. Acad., 1851; m. Cornelia Van Ness Dean, 1864. Bvt. 2d lt. Mounted Rifles, July 1, 1851; 2d lt., Jan. 27, 1853; 1st lt., June 14, 1858; capt. 3d Cav., July 31, 1861; maj. 7th Cav., Nov. 14, 1867; lt. col., Sept. 22, 1883; col. 9th Cav., Apr. 11, 1889; retired at own request after 40 yrs.' service, July 1, 1891; advanced to rank of brig. gen. retired, under act of Apr. 23, 1904. Bvtd. maj., Feb. 21, 1862, for battle of Valverde, N.M.; lt. col., Mar. 13, 1865, for services during the war. Participated in defense of Ft. Craig, 1862, battle of Valverde, Feb. 21, 1862, skirmish before Albuquerque, actions at Peralta, Apr. 1862, Parugo, May-July 1862, and other operations in N.M.; served with Sherman's expdn. to Chattanooga, Oct.-Nov. 1863; engaged in actions of Cherokee, Ala., Oct. 24, 1863, Tuscumbia, Oct. 27, 1863, Lookout Mountain and Missionary Ridge, Nov. 23-25, 1863, etc. Home: St. Louis, Mo. Died 1911.

TILLETT, Charles Walter, lawyer; b. Warren County, N.C., Sept. 27, 1857; s. Rev. John and Eliza (Wyche) T.; grad. Webb Sch., Bellbuckle, Tenn.; A.B., Randolph-Macon Coll., Va., 1880; m. Carrie Patterson, Feb. 18, 1885; children—Duncan Patterson, Charles Walter, John, William Smith, Laura Elizabeth (Mrs. Osborne Bethea). Admitted to N.C. bar, 1882, and began practice in Richmond County; moved to Charlotte, 1887; later member firm Tillett, Tillett & Kennedy. Democrat. Methodist. Wrote: "A Column of Comment by a Near Iconoclast"; "Ginger and Pepper," in opposition to anti-evolution act before N.C. legislature; "Al Smith and Fair Play," a plea for religious tolerance. Home: Charlotte, N.C. Died July 1936.

TILLETT, Wilbur Fisk, theologian; b. Henderson, N.C., Aug. 25, 1854; s. Rev. John and Elizabeth (Wyche) T.; A.B., Randolph-Macon Coll., 1877; A.M., Princeton, 1879; grad. Princeton Theol. Sem., 1880; D.D., Randolph-Macon, 1886, Wesleyan, 1909; LL.D., Southwestern, 1903; S.T.D., Northwestern, 1907; m. Kate O. Schoolfield, Nov. 15, 1888 (died 1889); m. 2d, Laura E. McLoud, Jan. 25, 1894 (died 1935). Ordained Methodist Episcopal ministry, 1883; pastor Danville, Va., 1880-82; chaplain and tutor in theology, 1882-83, adj. prof. systematic theology, 1883-84, prof., 1884-1919, prof. Christian doctrine, 1919-36, dean theol. faculty and vice-chancellor, 1886-1919, dean emeritus, 1919—, Vanderbilt U. Author: Our Hymns and Their Authors, 1889; Discussions in Theology, 1890; Personal Salvation—Studies in Christian Doctrine Pertaining to the Spiritual Life, 1902; The Doctrines of Methodism, 1903; A Statement of the Faith of Worldwide Methodism, 1906; (with C. S. Nutter) Hymns and Hymn Writers of the Church, 1911; The Hand of God in American History, 1923; The Paths That Lead to God, 1924; Providence, Prayer and Power, 1926; also papers in mags. and revs. Mem. Gen. Conf. M.E. Ch., S., 4 times. Three times apptd. mem. commns. to make the authorized hymnals of Methodist Ch. (1886, 1904, 1930); chmn. com. on selection of new hymns (1930-32) for joint hymnal of the M.E. Ch., M.E. Ch., S., and M.P. Ch. Address: Nashville, Tenn. Died June 4, 1936.

TILLEY, Benjamin Franklin, officer U.S.N.; b. Bristol, R.I., Mar. 29, 1848; s. Benjamin Rogers and Susan W. (Easterbrookes) T.; ed. pub. schs., Bristol, R.I.; grad. U.S. Naval Acad., 1867 (No. 1 of class); m. Emily Edelin Williamson, June 6, 1878. Served as midshipman on Franklin, flagship, European fleet, 1867-68, steamer Frolic, 1868-69; promoted ensign, 1868, master, 1870; commd lt., 1871, lt. comdr., Sept. 1887, comdr., Sept. 1896, capt., Sept. 1, 1901. Comd. U.S.S. Newport, 1897-98, during Spanish-Am. War; captured a number of prizes and was on blockade duty off Havana and other ports; comdt. Navy Yard, Norfolk, Va., 1898-99; comdg. Abarenda, and comdt. Naval Sta., Tutuila, Samoa, 1899-1901; 1st naval gov. of Samoa; capt. Navy Yard, Mare Island, 1902; later comdg. battleship Iowa, N. Atlantic squadron. Address: Washington, D.C. Died 1907.

TILLINGHAST, Benjamin Franklin, journalist; b. East Greenwich, R.I., July 4, 1849; s. Samuel R. and Julia A. (Searle) T.; ed. pub. schs. of Providence, R.I., prep. depts. Beloit Coll. and Monmouth Coll., grad. Monmouth Coll., B.S., 1870; m. Nellie Nourse, Sept. 25, 1878. Editor Coll. Courier at Monmouth Coll., 1868-70; editor Moline (Ill.) Rev., 1872; city editor, Davenport (Ia.) Gazette, 1878; asso. editor, 1882-94, editor, 1904—, Davenport (Ia.) Democrat. Sec. of organization sending relief to Russia, 1892. Independent in politics. U.S. del to Internat. Conf. of Red Cross, St. Petersburg, Russia, 1902. Author: Rock Island Arsenal, in Peace and War, 1898. Address: Davenport, Ia. Died Jan. 11, 1937.

TILLINGHAST, Caleb Benjamin, librarian, educator; b. W. Greenwich, R.I., Apr. 3, 1843; s. Pardon and Eunice (Tillinghast) T.; ed. common and pvt. schs. Windham County, Conn., hon. A.M., Harvard, 1897; Litt.D., Tufts, 1905; m. Mrs. Martha A. Wonson, 1886—. Teacher and officer of schs. in Windham County, Conn.; on staff, and city editor, Boston Jour., 1870-79; acting librarian of Mass. State Library, 1879—; state librarian, 1883—. Mem. and chmn. Mass. Free Public Library Commn. V.p. and chmn. com. on publication N.E. Historic Geneal. Soc.; treas.

Mass. Bd. of Edn., 1879—, and twice acting sec. Home: Boston, Mass. died 1909.

TILLINGHAST, Mary Elizabeth, artist; b. New York, N.Y.; d. Philip and Julia Anna (Cozzens-Titus) Tillinghast; ed. by pvt. tutors; studied art in Paris with Carolus Duran and Henner; in New York with John LaFarge; unmarried. Artist in stained glass, 1882—. Gold medal, Chicago Expn., 1893; gold medal, cotton States Expn., 1895; bronze medal, same. Executed mosaic glass windows for Mrs. Russell Sage in honor of Miss Helen Gould in Home of the Friendless; for the Misses Smith, an astron. and classic window, "Urania," in new Allegheny Obs.; "Revocation of the Edict of Nantes," in window N.Y. Hist. Soc. bldg.; mural decorations, Café of Savoy Hotel, New York; also all memorial windows in churches at Terre Haute (M.E.) and Washington, D.C. (Luth.), and large window, "Faith, Hope and Charity," at Attleboro, Mass. Address: New York, N.Y. Deceased.

TILLINGHAST, Pardon E., jurist; b. West Greenwich, R.I., Dec. 10, 1836; reared on farm; ed. pub. schs. W. Greenwich and Killingly, Conn., and in several acads.; hon. M.A., Brown U.; taught in dist. and grammar schs., 1854-62; in 1862 pvt. 12th R.I. vols., serving in 9th army corps; promoted to q.m. sergt. and acting q.m. Admitted to bar, 1867; practiced in Pawtucket, R.I.; town solicitor, Pawtucket, 1872-81; asso. justice Supreme Ct. of R.I., 1881—; several times mem. gen. assembly; served in R.I. Militia for yrs., becoming judge advocate gen. of R.I., with rank of brig. gen. Judge court of common pleas, 1881-91; in appellate div., 1891—. Address: Providence, R.I. Died 1905.

TILLMAN, Benjamin Ryan, senator; b. Edgefield County, S.C., Aug. 11, 1847; s. Benjamin R. T., a planter; acad. edn.; joined C.S.A., July 1864, but was stricken with severe illness which caused the loss of his left eye and kept him an invalid for 2 yrs., so that he saw no mil. service; m. Sallie Starke, 1868. Followed farming as sole pursuit until 1886, when he became prominent in an agitation for indsl. and tech. edn. and other reforms. Elected gov. of S.C. in 1890 and 1892, and U.S. senator for 4 terms, 1895-1919; Founded Clemson Agrl. and Mech. Coll. at Calhoun's old home, Fort Hill, and also Winthrop Normal and Industrial Coll. at Rock Hill; the first for boys, the last for girls; they are the two largest schs. of the kind in the South; author of the dispensary system of selling liquor under state control; central figure in the S.C. Constl.Conv., 1895, which instituted ednl. qualification for suffrage; one of the leaders in securing the insertion of advanced positions in Dem. platform of 1896. Prominent in Dem. Nat. convs. of 1900 and 1904, and in latter was active in work of harmonizing contending factions of Democracy. Member Dem. Nat. Com., 1912—. Home: Trenton, S.C. Died July 3, 1918.

TILLMAN, George N., lawyer; b. Bedford County, Tenn., Jan. 23, 1851; s. Lewis and Mary Catherine (Davidson) T.; brother of James Davidson, Samuel Escue and Abram Martin T.; A.B., Bethany Coll., W.Va.; LL.B., Nat. Law Sch., Washington. In practice at Nashville, Tenn.; v.p. Merchants' Bank, Nashville; gen. counsel Nashville & Decatur R.R. Co.; asst. U.S. atty. for Middle Tenn., 1877-82; U.S. marshal for Middle Tenn., 1882-86; mem. Tenn. Ho. of Reps., 1873-74; Rep. candidate for gov., 1896 and 1908, for U.S. senator, 1899. Trustee U. of Nashville; trustee and treas. Fanning Orphan Sch.; elder Christian Ch. Address: Nashville, Tenn. Died May 15, 1923.

TILLMAN, John Newton, congressman; b. Springfield, Mo., Dec. 13, 1859; s. Newton J. and Mary (Mullins) T.; A.B., U. of Ark., 1880; LL.D., U. of Miss., 1906; LL.D., U. of Vt., 1911; admitted to bar, 1883; m. Tempy Walker, Mar. 4, 1885. Circuit clerk, Washington County, Ark., 1884-88; mem. Ark. Senate, 1888-92; pros. atty. 4th Jud. Dist., Ark., 1892-98; judge, same, 1900-05; pres. U. of Ark., 1905-12; mem. 64th to 70th Congresses (1915-29), 3d Ark Dist. Democrat. Home: Fayetteville, Ark. Died Mar. 9, 1929.

TILLMAN, John Plummer, lawyer; b. Perry County, Ala., Jan. 25, 1849; s. John Miller and Mary Elizabeth (Plummer) T.; Howard Coll., Marion, Ala., 1865-68; U. of Ky., 1868-70 (non-grad.); studied law in office of Edmund W. Pettus and Nathaniel H. R. Dawson, Selma, Ala.; m. Sallie B. Hurt, Jan. 13, 1876 (died 1890); m. 2d, Annie Simms Chew, Nov. 9, 1892. Admitted to Ala. bar, 1871; practiced at Selma until 1883; spl. reporter Ala. Supreme Ct. Montgomery, Ala., 1883-84; removed to Birmingham, 1884; became mem. Tillman, Bradley & Morrow; firm attys. for L.&N. R.R. Co., Seaboard Air Line Ry., Birmingham Ry., Light & Power Co., Birmingham Trust & Savings Co., Am. Radiator Co., Standard Oil Co. of Ala., etc. City atty., Selma, 1872-73; mem. City Council, 1878-79; one of code commrs. of Code of Ala., 1886. Democrat. Mem. M.E. Ch., S. Reporter of the 69th, 71st, 73d and 75th Ala. Reports; also with John W. Sheppard, 68th Ala. Report; sole commr. for printing Code of Ala., 1886. Home: Birmingham, Ala. Died Mar. 24, 1923.

TILLSON, George William, engineer; b. Thomaston, Me., Dec. 18, 1852; s. Perez and Harrriet (Collins) T.; C.E., Bowdoin College, 1877, Sc.D., 1910; m. Mary E. Abbott, Oct. 5, 1887; 1 dau., Madalene Abbott. Asst. engr. in charge sewer costrn., Memphis, Tenn., 1880; made plans and constructed sewer system, Kalamazoo, Mich., 1880-81; in charge paving and sewer constrn., Omaha, Neb., 1881-87; city engr., 1887-92; asst. engr. in charge pavements, 1895-1902, Brooklyn; chief engr. Bur. of Highways, Borough of Brooklyn, 1902-07; chief engr. Bur. of Highways, Borough of Manhattan, New York City, 1907-11; cons. engr. Dept. of Pub. Works, Borough of Brooklyn, N.Y., May 1, 1911-July 1918; actg. commr. of pub. works, Borough of Brooklyn, 1913-14; pres. bd. dirs. La Grange Pub. Library, 1936—. Mem. Commn. of engrs. of Am. Soc. C.E., to visit France, 1918, to confer with a French congress for reconstruction work after the war. Author: Street Pavements and Paving Materials, 1900. Also 4 sections of American Highway Engineers' Pocket Book. Contbr. several papers on paving subjects to Proceedings Am. Soc. Municipal Improvements, and to engineering periodicals. Home: La Grange, Ill. Died May 13, 1940.

TILLSON, John Charles Fremont, army officer; b. New York, N.Y., May 26, 1856; grad. U.S. Mil. Acad., 1878; Army War Coll., 1910. Commd. add. 2d lt. 5th Inf., June 14, 1878; 2d lt., June 21, 1878; 1st lt., Mar. 24, 1883; capt. 14th Inf., Mar. 18, 1897; maj. 4th Inf., Mar. 12, 1902; lt. col. 18th Inf., Dec. 7, 1908; col. of inf., Nov. 27, 1911; assigned to 8th Inf., Mar. 28, 1912; trans. to 15th Inf., July 1, 1913. Prof. mil. science and tactics, North Ga. Agrl. Coll., Dahlonega, Ga., 1897-98; comd. Co. F, 14th Inf., China Relief Expdn., 1900; participated in capture of Peking and attack on Forbidden City; provost marshal, Am. Dist., Chinese City, until withdrawal of forces, May 1901; in charge Officers' Sch., Ft. Thomas, Ky., 1905-06; in Philippine Islands, 1908; duty Ft. Jay, N.Y., 1917. Address: Washington, D.C. Died Dec. 15, 1941.

TILNEY, Albert Arthur, banker; b. Brooklyn, N.Y., Feb. 11, 1868; s. Joseph and Janet (Fingland) T.; ed. Poly. Inst. of Brooklyn and pvt. sch.; A.B., Yale, 1890; m. Augusta M. Murray, Nov. 28, 1894; 1 dau., Bertha. With Pa. R.R. Co., N.Y. City, 1890-92; with Harvey Fisk & Sons, 1892-1915; rep. of firm in Boston, 1894-1907, admitted as partner, 1901; retired from firm Jan. 1, 1915; with Bankers Trust Co., Aug. 1, 1915—, asst. to pres. until 1916, v.p., 1916-23, later chmn. bd.; dir. Lehigh Power Securities Corp., Power Securities Corp., Nat. Power & Light Co., Electric Power & Light Corp., Elec. Securities Corp., Babcock & Wilcox Co., Newark Factory Sites, Am. Gas and Electric Co., Internat. Agrl. Corp., South Puerto Rico Sugar Co., Central Romana, Inc. Republican. Presbyn. Home: Plainfield, N.J. Died Aug. 27, 1937.

TILNEY, Frederick, neurologist; b. Brooklyn, N.Y., June 4, 1875; s. Thomas J. and Katharine (Hutchinson) T.; A.B., Yale, 1897; M.D., Long Island Coll. Hosp., 1903; Ph.D., Columbia, 1912; m. Camilla Hurley, June 15, 1903. Practiced in N.Y. City, 1905—; prof. neurology, Coll. Phys. and Surg. (Columbia), 1914—; med. dir. New York Neurol. Inst.; attending neurologist and consultant to Roosevelt, Presbyn., Brooklyn, Methodist Episcopal, Kings County, Coney Island and Greenwich hosps. Mem. bd. visitors N.Y. State Training Sch. for Boys (Warwick). Fellow Am. Philos. Soc., N.Y. Zoöl. Soc., N.Y. Acad. Science. Republican. Home: New York, N.Y. Died Aug. 7, 1938.

TILROE, William Edwin, prof. theology; b. Niles, Mich., Dec. 26, 1861; s. William and Mary Ann (Dunning) T.; B.D., Garrett Bibl. Inst. (Northwestern), 1891, D.D., 1902; m. Alice C. Gould, Apr. 21, 1885 (died 1939); children—Welcome Agnes, Carlyle. Licensed minister M.E. Ch., 1882; pastor in Ill. until 1910; supt. Chicago Dist., 1902-08; pastor Grace Ch., Los Angeles, Calif., 1910-15, University Ch., 1915-19, Lake Av. Ch., Pasadena, 1919-21; prof. practical theology, Maclay Sch. of Religion (U. of Southern Calif.), 1915-23; prof. hist. theology, same sch., 1921-28 (retired). Engaged in lit. work. Republican. Author: Sent Forth, 1923; Proverbs in Rhyme, 1940. Home: Los Angeles, Calif. Died June 3, 1940.

TILTON, Dwight, see Wilder Dwight Quint.

TILTON, Edward Lippincott, architect, archæologist; b. New York, Oct. 19, 1861; s. Benjamin W. and Mary (Baker) T.; Chappaqua Mountain Inst.; École des Beaux Arts, Paris, 1887-90; m. Mary Eastman Bigelow, June 5, 1901. In practice as architect, 1891—; also archæologist; in Greece, 1895-96, for Archæol. Inst. America, to restore site of Hera (Argive Heræum). Fellow Am. Inst. of Architects. Awarded gold medal, Paris Expn., 1900; gold medal, Am. Inst. Architects, 1925; medals—Buffalo Expn., 1901, St. Louis Expn., 1904. Wrote chapters: "Greece, Architecture of," in Dictionary of Architecture (Russell Sturgis), 1901; "Architecture of the Argive Heræum," in The Argive Heræum, 1902. Home: Scarsdale, N.Y. Died Jan. 5, 1933.

TILTON, George Henry, author; b. Nashua, N.H., Jan. 31, 1845; s. William Wells and Sarah Ann (Morrill) T.; A.B., Amherst, 1870 (Phi Beta Kappa), A.M., 1873; grad. Andover Theol. Sem., 1873; m. Ella Minerva Mann, June 6, 1876. Ordained Congl. ministry, 1874; pastor Attleboro Falls, Mass., 1874-75, Wolfboro, N.H., 1876-77, Rehoboth, Mass., 1878-91, Lancaster, N.H., 1891-96, Woburn, Mass., 1896-1915. Republican. Author: A Memorial of Marshall Henshaw, 1901; History of Rehoboth, Mass., 1918: The Fern Lover's Companion, 1923. Home: Melrose, Mass. Jan. 8, 1926.

TILTON, Howard Winslow, editor The Daily Nonpareil, Council Bluffs, Ia.; b. Frankfort, Me., June 9, 1849; s. Rev. H. C. T.; ed. at Evansville, Wis., and Northwestern U., A.M., Lawrence U., Appleton, Wis.; editor, 1875—. Author: Lay Sermons, 1899. Address: Council Bluffs, Ia. Died 1902.

TILTON, McLane, Jr., banker, lawyer; b. Annapolis, Md., Sept. 6, 1874; s. McLane and Ann Maine (Wells) T.; U. of Va., 1894-97; B.L., U. of Mich., 1900; m. Gertrude Lee Scoville, Jan. 9, 1899. Organizer, 1902, and pres. 1st Nat. Bank, Pell City, Ala.; also 1st Nat. Bank, Lincoln, Ala., 1909—; southern rep. Chemical Nat. Bank of New York. Ordinary seaman U.S.S. Yosemite in Spanish-Am. War. Independent Democrat. Home: Charlottesville, Va. Died Dec. 1937.

TILTON, Ralph, art editor Saturday Evening Post; b. Brooklyn, N.Y., June 20, 1869; attended Brooklyn Poly. Inst.; m. Gracia Lunt, Jan. 5, 1897. Adv. mgr. Ladies' Home Journal, became art editor of Saturday Evening Post. Home: Philadelphia, Pa. Died 1907.

TILTON, Theodore, journalist, author; b. New York, Oct. 2, 1835; s. Silas and Eusebia T.; early edn. pub. sch., New York; grad. Coll. City of New York, 1855; m. Elizabeth Richards (dec.). Editor The Independent, New York, 1856-70, The Golden Age, 1871-74, Brooklyn Union, 1874-76; Lyceum lecturer, 1865-84. Lived in Paris, 1888—. Author: A Career Unique, a Memorial to Frederick Douglass, 1895; Complete Poetical Works, 1897; Our American Don Quixote (a ballad on Ponce de Leon), 1898; Confessions of a Pyramid, and Other Poems, 1905; The Fading of the Mayflower (poem), 1906. Address: Paris, France. Died 1907.

TIMBERLAKE, Charles B., congressman; b. Wilmington, O., Sept. 25, 1854; s. Alfred and Phoebe (Doan) T.; student Earlham Coll., 1871-74; m. Marguerite E. Fall, 1882; children—Mrs. Lucile Stover; m. 2d, M. Catherine Ballard; m. 3d, Mrs. Roberta E. Elliott, Dec. 23, 1930. Moved to Colo., 1887, and engaged in farming and stock raising. County supt. schs., Phillips County, 1889-95; county clk., 1895-97; receiver U.S. Land Office, at Sterling, 1897-1914; mem. 64th to 72d Congresses (1915-33), 2d Colo. Dist. Mem. Rep. State Com., Colo., 1892-1910. Quaker. Mason, Odd, Fellow, K.P., Elk. Home: Sterling, Colo. Died May 31, 1941.

TIMBY, Theodore Ruggles, inventor, author; b. Dover, Dutchess County, N.Y., Apr. 5, 1819; s. George W. and Sarah Johnson T., of Pittsfield, Mass.; ed. pub. schs.; hon. degrees: A.M., Madison U., 1867; S.D., U. of Troy, O., 1882; LL.D., Iowa Wesleyan U., 1891; m. Charlotte M. Ware, 1844. Invented floating dry-dock, 1836; invented, 1841, the revolving turret used on the Monitor, and battleships; invented practical method of raising sunken vessels, 1841, the Am. turbine waterwheel or motor, 1844, and in 1857, the first commercially portable 33-inch mercurial barometer. From 1861 to 1891, invented and patented, at home and abroad, a system of coast defenses known as follows: The sighting and firing of heavy guns by electricity; the tower and shield; the cordon across the channel; the planetary and subterranean systems, with 15 other modifications of the turret system; invented and patented improvements in pneumatic and hydraulic power; also a new prin. in Turbine water-wheels or motors. In 1890 the N.Y. legislature, by unanimous concurrent resolution, and the judges of N.Y. Supreme Ct. and Ct. of Appeals, by petition, asked Congress to give him nat. recognition. Author: Beyond; Stellar Worlds; Lighted Lore for Gentle Folk. Address: Brooklyn, N.Y. Died 1909.

TIMLIN, William Henry, lawyer; b. Mequon, Wis., May 28, 1852; s. Edward and Hannah (McConville) T.; m. Celia L. Arpin, June 5, 1880. Began law practice at Kewaunee, 1877; justice Supreme Ct. of Wis., 1906-17. Home: Milwaukee, Wis. Died Aug. 21, 1916.

TIMLOW, Elizabeth Weston, educator; b. Rhinebeck, N.Y., June 24, 1861; d. Rev. Heman R. and Martha Fay (Bigelow) Timlow; ed. pvt. schs. and spl. coll. courses at Wellesley and Cornell. Prin., Cloverside, boarding sch. for girls, Washington, D.C., 1894-1918. Author: Cricket books—What Came to Winifred; Dorothy Dot; April Fool Twins; A Nest of Girls; The Heart of Monadnock. Contbr. to mags. Lecturer on applied psychology. Home: Fitzwilliam, N.H. Died Jan. 17, 1931.

TIMS, John Chapel, clergyman; b. Kosciusko, Miss., Aug. 23, 1870; s. William Chapel and Elizabeth (Thompson) T.; A.B., Southwestern U., Memphis, Tenn., 1896; studied Union Theol. Sem., Va., 1896-98; D.D., Rollins Coll., 1910; m. Elizabeth Pasco, Nov. 20, 1901. Ordained ministry Presbyn. Ch., U.S.A., 1898; asst. pastor First Ch., Macon, Ga., 1898-99; pastor First Ch., Lake City, Fla., 1899-1901, Moultrie, Ga., 1901-07, First Ch., Tampa, Fla., 1907—. With Y.M.C.A. at Camp Wheeler, Macon, Ga., World War I. Mason, Knight of Constantine. Democrat. Home: Tampa, Fla. Died Sept. 1933.

TINCKER, Mary Agnes, author; b. Ellsworth, Me.; d. Richard and Mehitabel (Jellison) Tincker; ed. Ellsworth and in acad. at Bluehill, Me.; began teaching in pub. sch. at age of 13, later teaching a parochial Catholic sch., and writing a little, anonymously, from her 15th yr.; soon gave up teaching, devoting her attention solely to writing. During part of the Civil war was a vol. nurse in Washington. Made her home in Italy, 1873-87, visiting Spain, France and England during that period. Author: The House of Yorke; A Winged Word; Grapes and Thorns; Six Sunny Months; Signor Monaldini's Niece; By the Tiber; The Jewel in the Lotus, Aurora, 1882; Two Coronets, 1887; San Salvador, 1889; Autumn Leaves, 1898. Mem. Soc. of the Arcadia, Rome, Italy, Soc. Am. Authors, Am. Polit. and Social Science. Address: Boston, Mass. Died 1907.

TINGLEY, Katherine, theosophist; b. Newburyport, Mass., July 6, 1852; d. James P. and Susan Westcott, desc. of early Colonial ancestry; ed. pub. sch. and under pvt. tutelage; m. P. B. Tingley, inventor, 1889. Leader and official head (for life) of the Universal Brotherhood and Theosophical Soc. throughout the world, Feb. 18, 1898—; also "outer head" of Inner Sch. of Theosophy, successor to H. P. Blavatsky and W. Q. Judge. Conducted two theosophical crusades around the world, 1896-97 and 1904; established relief work for Indian famine sufferers; founded Internat. Brotherhood League, 1897; Summer Home for Children, Spring Valley, N.J., 1897; home for orphan children, Point Loma, Calif., 1898; Sch. of Antiquity (inc.), and Raja Yoga acads., Point Loma and San Diego; 3 acads. for boys and girls in Cuba. Organized relief corps in New York and established emergency hosp. at Montauk Point, L.I., for sick and wounded soldiers returning from Spanish-Am. War, later carrying on same work in Cuba, U.S. Govt. through President McKinley furnishing transportation and permission to establish hosps. in Manila and Cuba. Founded Parliament of Peace and Universal Brotherhood, 1913; founded Theosophical Univ., Point Loma, 1919; established branch hdqrs. of Universal Brotherhood and Theosophical Soc. at Los Angeles, 1921. Owner of Isis Theatre, San Diego, Calif.; owner of ednl. sites, San Juan Hill, Cuba, Visingsoe, Sweden, and at Fleet, Hampshire, Eng. Established summer sch. for children at Visingsoe, 1924; established 7 new theos. centres in Europe, 1925. Editor of Theosophical Path, pub. at Point Loma, Calif.; theosophical mags. in Holland, Germany and Sweden also published under her direction; founded The New Way, 1911, for free distribution to prisoners. Author: Theosophy and Some of the Vital Problems of the Day; Marriage and the Home; Theosophy, the Path of the Mystic; The Wine of Life; The Gods Await; The Travail of the Soul. Received Medal of Honor of German Red Cross, 1925. Home: Point Loma, Calif. Died July 11, 1929.

TINGLEY, Richard Hoadley, writer; b. Windham, Conn., July 4, 1856; s. George Curtis and Georgiana Harriet Matilda (Sage) T.; Ph.B., Brown U., 1876; m. Bertha Franklin Tingley, Apr. 1887; children—Mary Antoinette (Mrs. C. W. Anderson, Jr.), Maurice, Pauline Evelyn. Civ. engr., Providence, R.I., and New York, for many yrs.; lit. research and spl. article writer, 1912—, contbg. regularly to many mags. Republican. Episcopalian. Author: Trade Acceptances, 1916; Banka Tin, 1922 (pub. by Dutch East India Govt.). Home: Port Chester, N.Y. Died Dec. 13, 1935.

TINKHAM, Henry Crain, surgeon; b. Brownington, Vt., Dec. 7, 1856; s. Samuel Stone and Clarissa (Richmond) T.; ed. Derby (Vt.) Acad.; M.D., U. of Vt., 1883; m. Clara E. Day, Oct. 17, 1886. Practiced at Burlington, Vt., 1883—; prof. clin. surgery, and dean Med. Dept., U. of Vt. Republican. Congregationalist. Address: Burlington, Vt. Died Dec. 6, 1925.

TINKHAM, Herbert Linwood, shoe mfr.; b. Middleboro, Mass., Mar. 13, 1869; s. Charles C. and Abigail (Ashley) T.; ed. pub. schs., Middleboro, Mass.; m. Kathryn W. Stetson, Apr. 11, 1900; 1 son, Herbert Linwood. With W. L. Douglas Shoe Co., 1889—, pres., 1924—; dir. Shawmut Nat. Bank (Boston), Home Nat. Bank (Brockton). Pres. Brockton Hosp. Republican. Mason. Home: Brockton, Mass. Died May 24, 1941.

TINNEY, Frank, actor; b. Phila., Pa., Mar. 29, 1878; s. Hugh Frank and Mary (Carroll) T.; ed. pub. schs.; m. Edna Davenport. Made first appearance on stage in "black face," in Vaudeville, Phila., at age of 4; début in "The Follies of 1910," at Winter Garden, New York, May 1910; 1st appearance in London, Eng., in "black face," 1913, scoring a great success; toured U.S. in "The Follies of 1913"; served in U.S. Army, latter part of World War I; played in "Some Time," "Tickle Me," etc. Home: Baldwin, L.I., N.Y. Died Nov. 27, 1940.

TINNON, Robert McCracken, clergyman; b. Giles County, Tenn., Feb. 6, 1840; s. Robert and Elisabeth (Abernathy) T.; grad. Giles Coll., Pulaski, Tenn., 1859; admitted to Tenn. bar, Mar. 1861; served C.S.A., 1861-65; wounded 3 times; mustered out with rank of maj.; D.D., Trinity U., Tex., 1887; m. Sarah J. Preston, Apr. 27, 1865. Ordained Cumberland Presbyn. ministry, 1873; pastor Huntsville, Ala., 1875-77, Nashville, Tenn., 1877-84, Fort Worth, Tex., 1884-92, Lincoln, Ill., 1892-1902, First Ch., Denver, 1902-05, First Ch., Nashville, Tenn., 1905-08, First Presbyn. Ch., Herington, Kan., Oct. 1, 1908—. Mem. bd. of publ. Cumberland Presbyn. Ch.; mem. Assembly's bd. missions, 1894-98; pres. Ch. Extension Assn. of Ill., 1894-98; v.p. Coll. Commn. of Ill., Ind., and Ia., of C.P. Ch.; moderator Gen. Assembly C.P. Ch., 1904-05, and mem. Com. on Union of C.P. Ch. and Presbyn. Ch. U.S.A., 1904-05. Contbr. for over 20 yrs. to periodical lit. of ch. Address: Herington, Kan. Died Apr. 30, 1917.

TINSLEY, Richard Parran; b. York County, Va., Aug. 10, 1867; s. Alexander (M.D.) and Mary Dare (Parran) T.; B.C.S., N.Y.U. Sch. of Commerce, Accounts and Finance, 1902; m. Lucie Marshall Morris, June 10, 1896. Began with Standard Oil interests, 1892; v.p. Waters-Pierce Oil Co., St. Louis, 1905-08; foreign travel for Standard Oil Co., 1908-11; treas. Standard Oil Co. of New York, 1911-15, and 1921—; sec. and treas. Socony-Vacuum Corp.; sec., treas., later v.p. and sec., Am. Internat. Corp., 1915-21. Home: New York, N.Y. Died Nov. 21, 1936.

TIPPLE, Ezra Squier, clergyman; b. Camden, N.Y., Jan. 23, 1861; s. Martin and Sarah E. (Squier) T.; A.B., Syracuse U., 1884, A.M., 1885, Ph.D., 1886; B.D., Drew Theol. Sem., 1887; D.D., Syracuse U., 1899, LL.D., 1913; L.H.D., Allegheny Coll., 1933; m. Edna E. White, June 24, 1897. Entered ministry of M.E. Ch., 1887; pastor of St. Luke's Ch., New York, 1887-92, Grace Ch., 1892-97, St. James' Ch., 1897-1901; exec. sec. Met. Thank-Offering Commn. M.E. Ch., New York, 1901-04; pastor Grace Ch., New York, 1904-05; prof. practical theology, Drew Theol. Sem., 1905-29, pres., 1912-28; pres. Drew U., 1928-29, hon. pres., 1929-33, pres. emeritus, 1933—. Mem. bd. mgrs. Missionary Soc. M.E. Ch., 1895—; rec. sec. Bd. of Edn. M.E. Ch., 1904-24; sec. book com., exec. com. Meth. Book Concern, New York; chmn. com. on revisions Am. Bible Soc.; pres. Meth. Historical Soc., New York. Speaker Y.M.C.A., France and Eng., 1918. Author: Heart of Asbury's Journal, 1905; The Minister of God, 1906; Drew Sermons—first series, 1906, second series, 1907; Drew Sermons on the Golden Texts, 1908, 1909, 1910; Life of Freeborn Garrettson, 1910; Some Famous Country Parishes, 1911; Life of Francis Asbury, 1916; Drew Theological Seminary, 1867-1917—A Review of the First Half Century, 1917; The Wendels, 1936. Home: New York, N.Y. Died Oct. 17, 1936.

TIRRELL, Charles Quincy, congressman; b. Sharon, Mass., Dec. 10, 1844; s. Dr. Norton Quincy and Susan J. T.; A.B., Dartmouth, 1866; m. Mary E. Hollis, Feb. 13, 1873. Prin. Peacham (Vt.) Acad., 1867-68, St. Johnsbury (Vt.) High Sch., 1868-69; admitted to bar, 1870, in practice at Boston, 1870—. Mem. Mass. Ho. of Reps., 1872, Senate, 1881, 1882; presdl. elector, 1888; mem. 57th to 61st Congresses (1901-11), 4th Mass. Dist. Republican. Home: Natick, Mass. Died 1910.

TISDALL, Fitz Gerald, coll. prof.; b. New York, Mar. 15, 1840; s. Fitz Gerald and Elizabeth A. (Clute) T.; A.B., Coll. City of New York, 1859, A.M., 1862; hon. Ph.D., New York U., 1874; m. Florence V. Rodrigue, Dec. 23, 1885. Tutor in N.Y. Free Acad., 1860-79; prof. Greek lang. and lit., Coll. City of New York, 1879—. Dir. Cooper Union Schs. Science and Art, 1870-79; lecturer. Trustee pub. sch. fund, Woodbridge, N.J., 1892-98; justice of peace, Woodbridge, 1892-94; visited Europe, 1882, 1885, 1888. Author: Heroic Hexameter, 1889. Home: New York, N.Y. Died Nov. 11, 1915.

TISINGER, Benjamin Louis, judge; b. Talbot County, Ga., Jan. 21, 1866; s. James Stinson and Mary Ann (Powell) T.; student U. of Ga., 1882-85; m. Lillian Eades, June 10, 1914. Began practice at Thomaston, Ga., 1886; mem. Ga. Ho. of Reps., 1898-1902, Senate 1902-05; removed to Magnum, Okla., 1908, and asso. in practice with T. P. Clay, later judge Dist. Ct. of Okla., 18th Dist.; mayor of Magnum, 1911-12; asso. justice Supreme Ct. of Okla., Mar. 5, 1918-Jan. 13, 1919; resumed practice at Oklahoma City. Asst. U.S. atty. for Western Dist. of Okla., 1920-21. Democrat. Mem. M.E. Ch., S. Mason, Elk. Home: Oklahoma City, Okla. Died July 6, 1925.

TISON, Alexander, lawyer; b. St. Louis County, Mo., Dec. 23, 1857; s. Hippolyte and Hannah E. (Doyle) T.; A.B., Olivet (Mich.) Coll., 1878, A.M., 1881; A.M., LL.B., Harvard, 1886; m. Annie H. Stevens, Nov. 21, 1894; children—Paul, Claire, Alexander. Admitted to Mich. bar, 1885, N.Y. bar, 1887; practiced at New York, 1887-89; prof. English and Am. law, Imperial U., Tokyo, 1889-94. Practiced, New York, 1894-1936. Decorated Order Sacred Treasure, 4th, 3d and 2d class, and Order Rising Sun, 4th class (Japan). Home: Darien, Conn. Died July 16, 1938.

TITCHENER, Edward Bradford, psychologist; b. Chichester, Eng., Jan. 11, 1867; s. John and Alice Field (Habin) T.; B.A., Brasenose Coll., Oxford U., 1890; Ph.D., Leipzig, 1892; M.A., Oxford, 1895; D.Sc., Oxford, 1906; LL.D., U. of Wis., 1904; D.Litt., Clark, 1909; D.Sc., Harvard, 1909; m. Sophie Kellogg Bedlow, June 19, 1894; children—Margaret Seymour, John Bradford, Frances Haliburton, Alice McLellan. Sr. scholar of Brasenose Coll. (in classics and philosophy) and sr. Hulmean exhibitioner, 1885-89; research student in physiology, Oxford, 1889-90; extension lecturer in biology, Oxford, 1892; asst. prof. psychology, 1892-95, Sage prof., 1895-1910; prof. in charge of music, 1896-98, Sage prof. psychology, Grad. Sch., 1910—, Cornell U. Lecturer Columbia U., 1907-08, U. of Ill., 1909, Lowell Inst., 1911. Am. editor of Mind (a quarterly review of philosophy and psychology), 1894-1920; asso. editor, 1895-1921, editor, 1921-25, Am. Jour. Psychology. Fellow Zoöl. Soc. London, A.A.A.S., Royal Soc. Medicine; mem. Aristotelian Soc. London, Am. Philos. Soc.; mem. internat. com. 3d, 4th and 5th congresses of Psychology, v.p. 6th Congress; foreign mem. Polish Acad. Arts and Science. Author: An Outline of Psychology, 1896; A Primer of Psychology, 1898; Experimental Psychology, 1901-05; Elementary Psychology of Feeling and Attention, 1908; Experimental Psychology of the Thought-Processes, 1909; Textbook of Psychology, 1910; A Beginner's Psychology, 1915. Translator of several psychol. works. Home: Ithaca, N.Y. Died Aug. 3, 1927.

TITCOMB, John Wheelock, fish culturist; b. Farmington, N.H., Feb. 24, 1860; s. George Alfred and Mary Elizabeth Lemist (Lancaster) T.; grad. Phillips Exeter Acad., 1880; passed examination for Harvard with honors; m. Martha Ross, Dec. 22, 1896; children—Elizabeth, Jonathan Ross. In employ of Howe Scale Co., 1880-93, asst. supt., 1888-93; chmn. Vt. Fish and Game Commn., 1891-1902; chief of Div. of Fish Culture, U.S. Bur. of Fisheries, 1902-09; state fish and game commr. of Vt., 1910-16, also pvt. sec. to Theodore N. Vail; state fish culturist, New York, 1916-21; supt. Conn. State Bd. of Fisheries and Game, 1922—. Employed by Argentine Govt., 1903-04, to explore waters of the country; built first hatchery in S.A., and introduced several species of salmonidæ, trout, etc. Republican. Conglist. Mason. Home: Bloomfield, Conn. Died Jan. 26, 1932.

TITCOMB, Mary Lemist, librarian; b. Farmington, N.H., 1857; d. George Alfred and Mary Elizabeth (Lemist) T.; Robinson Sem., Exeter, N.H. Librarian, Washington Co. (Md.) Free Library (first county library with rural book delivery), 1901—. Sec. Washington County Museum of Fine Arts. Episcopalian. Home: Hagerstown, Md. Died June 5, 1932.

TITHERINGTON, Richard Handfield, editor; b. Chester, Eng., Oct. 2, 1861; s. William and Eliza (Fluitt) T.; ed. Winchester Coll. and Magdalen Coll., Oxford, Eng.; came to U.S., 1884; m. Harriet E. Bishop, 1886 (died 1902); 1 dau., Grace (Mrs. Myron E. Fuller); m. 2d, Kate Gregory Lane, June 1, 1904; children—Richard Handfield, William Kent, John Bisbrowne. Engaged in teaching, 1884-86; with pub. house of Frank A. Munsey, Sept. 1886—; mng. editor Munsey's Magazine, 1891-1913 and 1914-25; trustee of the Frank A. Munsey Estate and sec. Frank A. Munsey Co.; v.p. New York Sun. Author: History of the War with Spain, 1900. Home: New York, N.Y. Died Dec. 5, 1935.

TITSWORTH, Alfred Alexander, coll. prof.; b. Plainfield, N.J., Dec. 4, 1852; s. Isaac Dunham and Hannah Ann (Sheppard) T.; B.S., Rutgers Coll., 1877, M.S., 1880, C.E., 1880, D.Sc., 1907; m. Georgiana Alberti, Sept. 11, 1878; children—Waldo Alberti, Ernest Shipley (dec.), Mrs. Elmina DeWitt. Prof. graphics and mathematics, 1886-1903, civ. engring. and graphic, 1903-09, civ. engring., 1909-21, and dean of engring., 1915-20, Rutgers Coll.; prof. mathematics, Rutgers Coll., and N.J. Coll. for Women, 1921—. Engaged on the Geodetic Survey of N.J. (U.S. Coast and Geodetic Survey) part of each yr., 1875-96. Chmn. of commn. to resurvey and mark boundary line bet. Morris and Somerset counties, N.J., 1894, and bet. Hunterdon and Morris counties, N.J., 1896; pres. Advisory Sewage Disposal Commn., 1910—, and mem. Advisory Water Commn., 1911—, of New Brunswick, N.J. Author: Elements of Mechanical Drawing, 1906. Home: New Brunswick, N.J. Died Aug. 15, 1936.

TITSWORTH, Judson, clergyman; b. Shiloh, N.J., Oct. 23, 1845; s. Isaac Dunham and Hannah Ann (Sheppard) T.; brother of Alfred Alexander T.; A.B., Amherst, 1870; B.D., Union Theol. Sem., 1873; D.D., Beloit, 1885, Amherst, 1908; m. Julia Ellen Van Duzer, Sept. 23, 1873. Ordained Congl. ministry, 1873; pastor First Ch., Westfield, Mass., 1873-78, Chelsea, Mass., 1878-83, and Plymouth Ch., Milwaukee, 1883-1909, emeritus, 1909—; chaplain Nat. Home for Disabled Vol. Soldiers, Milwaukee, 1909. Trustee Beloit (Wis.) College, Milwaukee-Downer College,

Rochester (Wis.) Acad. Author: The Moral Evolution, 1899. Home: Milwaukee, Wis. Died Apr. 9, 1919.

TITSWORTH, Paul Emerson, coll. pres.; b. Ashaway, R.I., May 31, 1881; s. Wardner Carpenter and Isabelle (Glaspey) T.; Ph.B., Alfred (N.Y.) Coll., 1904; studied Berlin and Dresden, summer 1902, Ohio State U., 1903-04, U. of Marburg, 1913; Ph.D., U. of Wis., 1911; m. Vida Rose Stillman, Sept. 15, 1904; children—Elizabeth Rose, Eleanor, Katharine Stillman. Instr. modern langs., 1904-07, prof., 1909-19, prof. English, 1919-23, dean, 1920-23, Alfred (N.Y.) Coll.; pres. Washington Coll., Chestertown, Md., 1923—. Pres. Village of Alfred, 1917. Gov. 34th Dist. Rotary Internat. Seventh Day Baptist. Author: A Bibliography for High School Teachers of Modern Languages, 1902. Co-translator: (from the French) Emancipation of Medieval Towns, 1906. Home: Chestertown, Md. Died Dec. 10, 1933.

TITTMANN, Otto Hilgard, geodesist; b. Belleville, Ill., Aug. 20, 1850; s. Edward and Rosa (Hilgard) T.; ed. pub. schools, St. Louis, 1859-66; D.Sc., Stevens Inst. and Washington U., 1915; LL.D., George Washington U., 1915; m. Kate Trowbridge Wilkins, 1880; 1 son, Charles Trowbridge. With Coast and Geodetic Survey, 1867—; asst. astronomer Transit of Venus Expdn. to Japan, 1874; in charge various surveying expdns. E. and W. coast of U.S.; in charge of weights and measures, 1889-93; sent to Paris, 1890, to bring to U.S. the Nat. standard metre and to inspect weights and measures offices, London, Paris and Berlin; U.S. del. to Internat. Geodetic Conf., Berlin, 1895. Mem. Permanent Commn. Internat. Geodetic Assn., 1900; asst. in charge U.S. Coast and Geod. Survey Office, 1895-99, asst. supt., 1899-1900, supt., 1900-Mar. 1915. Apptd. to represent U.S. in demarkation of boundary between Alaska and Canada under modus vivendi of Oct. 1899; U.S. commr. Alaska Boundary, 1904, and of Northern Boundaries, excepting Great Lakes, under Treaty of 1908, resigned 1915. Fellow Philos. Soc. Washington (pres. 1899); mem. Am. Philos. Soc.; pres. Nat. Geog. Soc., 1915-19, Washington Acad. Sciences, 1913. Contbr. to publs. of Survey, also geod. and meteorological articles in various jours. Home: Leesburg, Va. Died Aug. 21, 1938.

TITUS, Bennett Eaton, editor; b. Moriah Center, Essex County, N.Y., Dec. 9, 1859; s. Edwin Bristol and Lucy Maria (Eaton) T.; ed. Troy Conf. Acad., Poultney, Vt., and Sherman Collegiate Inst., Moriah, N.Y.; m. Lucy Estelle, d. late Judge Riford, June 29, 1881. Began religious journalism upon Southwestern Christian Advocate, New Orleans, 1889-90; with Northern Christian Advocate, 1890—, as bus. mgr., mng. editor, and editor, 1900—, apptd. by Gen. Conf. of that yr., to which he was 1st lay del. from Central N.Y. Conf. Proposed and has been active in forwarding the project of a Sch. of Journalism as a dept. of Syracuse U. Home: Danvers, Mass. Died Nov. 29, 1913.

TITUS, Robert Cyrus, judge; b. Eden, Erie County, N.Y., Oct. 24, 1839; s. James B. and Esther (Yeomans) T.; acad. edn., Oberlin, O., 1859-61; m. Arvilla R. Clark, Aug. 22, 1867. Admitted to bar, 1865, and practiced at Buffalo, N.Y. Dist. atty. Erie County, 1878-80; mem. N.Y. Senate, 1882-85; elected judge Superior Ct. of Buffalo, 1885, for 14 yrs., ending Dec. 31, 1899; transferred to Supreme Ct., 1896, term expired 1899. Candidate, 1896, for judge Ct. of Appeals; candidate in Dem. State Conv. for gov. N.Y., 1898. Address: Buffalo, N.Y. Died 1918.

TIVNAN, Edward P., clergyman, educator; b. Salem, Mass., Mar. 10, 1882; s. Patrick and Mary (Kenny) T.; student Boston Coll.; A.B., Woodstock (Md.) Coll., 1910, A.M., 1912; Ph.D., Georgetown U., 1917. Joined Soc. of Jesus (Jesuits), 1899; ordained R.C. priest, 1914; prof. chemistry, Boston Coll. and Fordham; pres. Fordham U., 1919-24; pres. Weston Coll., 1924-31; treas. Soc. of Jesus of N.E.; dir. Retreats for Layman. Address: Cohasset, Mass. Died Mar. 31, 1937.

TJADER, Richard, author, lecturer; b. Karlskrona, Sweden, Apr. 21, 1869; s. Karl Jacob and Thecla Maria (Slöör) T.; ed. high schs., Stockholm and Upsala, Sweden, and coll. at Berlin, 1890-91; came to U.S., Nov. 11, 1898; m. Margaret B. Thorne, Sept. 19, 1899. Led expdn. into East Africa, 1906, for Am. Mus. Natural History, securing new species of antelopes, a waterbuck and a bushbock (both named after him), and numerous specimens of other animals. Pres. of the Marine Efficiency Co. Author: Heils and Lobgesänge (German), 1892; Bibelns Triumf (Swedish), 1897; The Big Game of Africa, 1910. Inventor of Tjader Interdeck-Davitt, device for lowering of lifeboats from between decks of vessels. Home: Rowayton, Conn. Died Dec. 27, 1916.

TOD, J(ohn) Kennedy, financier; b. Glasgow, Scotland, Sept. 1852; s. Andrew and Mary (Kennedy) T.; ed. in Scotland, and at Williston, Mass.; m. Maria Howard Potter, Nov. 15, 1882. Came to U.S. 1st in 1868, but returned to Glasgow and engaged in iron trade; came to U.S. 1879 and entered firm of J. S. Kennedy & Co., then largely interested in the G.N. Ry. Co. and in financing constrn. of Canadian Pacific Ry.; on retirement of John S. Kennedy, firm was reorganized as J. Kennedy Tod & Co. Actively interested in the reorganization of Am. Cotton Oil Co., Minneapolis & St. Louis Ry. Co., C.&S. Ry. Co., S.L.&S.F. R.R., Phila. & Reading Ry. Co., Norfolk & Western Ry. Co.; U.S. trustee Caledonian and Norwich Union ins. cos.; dir. in many ry. and industrial cos.; trustee Children's Aid Soc. Independent in politics; treas. Citizens' Union (anti-Tammany movement) 3 times; mem. com. of 70. Chevalier de la Légion d'Honneur (France). Address: New York, N.Y. Died June 2, 1925.

TODD, Albert May, chemist, polit. economist; b. farm nr. Nottawa, St. Joseph County, Mich., June 3, 1850; s. Alfred and Mary Ann (Hovey) T.; grad. high sch., Sturgis, Mich.; student Northwestern U.; traveled in foreign countries studying their institutions and govts.; m. Augusta M. Allman, Jan. 23, 1878; children—William Alfred, Albert John, Ethel May (Mrs. Edwin Le Grand Woodhams), Paul Harold, Allman. Organizer A. M. Todd & Co., 1889, retiring 1929 as pres. Todd Foundation, "for enlargement of happiness of mankind." Prohibition nominee for governor of Mich., 1894; mem. Congress, 1897-99. Pres. Pub. Ownership League of America from its foundation, 1916-22; mem. Am. Acad. Polit. and Social Science, Am. Proportional Representation League, Mich. Acad. of Science, Arts and Letters, Coöperative League America, Am. Civil Liberties Union, League for Industrial Democracy, Nat. Child Labor Com. Actively interested in progressive government; spent 14 months (1912-13) in foreign countries studying applied democracy—chiefly pub. ownership of pub. utilities, and coöperation; advocate of pub. ownership. Founded three art museums and library of 10,000 rare books and illuminated MSS. Author: Municipal Ownership in Europe and America, 1918; The Relation of Public Ownership to Social Justice and Democracy, 1920. Home: Kalamazoo, Mich. Died Oct. 1931.

TODD, Chapman Coleman, rear admiral U.S.N.; b. Frankfort, Ky., Apr. 5, 1848; s. Harry Innes and Jane (Davidson) T.; grad. U.S. Naval Acad., 1866; m. Eliza James, Oct. 1872. Cruised in the Pacific Ocean, 1866-67. Promoted ensign, Apr. 1868; master, Mar. 26, 1869; lt., March 25, 1870; lt. comdr., Nov. 1886; comdr., May 1895; capt., Feb. 11, 1901; rear admiral and retired, Oct. 31, 1902, after 41 yrs.' service. Comd. Wilmington, May 1897, to Aug. 1899, and served as hydrographer from Jan. 22, 1900, until November 1901; comdr. flagship Brooklyn, Asiatic sta., until Sept. 1902. Advanced "for eminent and conspicuous conduct in battle" during war with Spain. Address: Washington, D.C. Died Apr. 28, 1929.

TODD, David, astronomer; b. Lake Ridge, N.Y., Mar. 19, 1855; s. Sereno Edwards and Rhoda (Peck) T.; A.B., Amherst, 1875, A.M., 1878; Ph.D., Washington and Jefferson Coll., 1888; m. Mabel Loomis, Mar. 5, 1879; 1 dau., Millicent (wife of Dr. W. V. Bingham). Asst. U.S. Transit of Venus Commn., 1875-78; chief U.S. Naval Observatory eclipse parties in Tex., 1878; chief asst. on U.S. Nautical Almanac, 1878-81; prof. astronomy and nav. and dir. of obs., Amherst Coll., 1881-1920; prof. emeritus (Carnegie Foundation), 1920. Astronomer in charge Lick Obs. observations, transit of Venus, 1882; prof. astronomy and higher mathematics, Smith Coll., 1882-87; astronomer in charge Am. eclipse expdn. to Japan, 1887; chief U.S. scientific expdn. to W. Africa, 1889-90; chief Amherst eclipse expdn. to Japan, 1896, to Tripoli, Barbary, 1900, to Dutch E. Indies, 1901, Tripoli, 1905, Russia, 1914, Florida, 1918, South America, 1919, and in 1925 (Mitchel Field, L.I.) securing, in coöperation with U.S. Army Air Service, first photograph of the solar corona from an aeroplane; chief of the Lowell Mars expedition to the Andes, 1907. Fellow A.A.A.S., Astron. Soc. America, Royal Soc. Arts, London. Imperial Saki cup from Mikado of Japan for services to Japanese education. Author: A New Astronomy, 1897; Stars and Telescopes, 1899; Népszerü Csilla gászat (Popular Astronomy in Hungarian, Budapest), 1901; Lessons in Astronomy, 1902; Astronomy To-Day, 1924; also articles in mags. and revs. Editor: Columbian Knowledge Series (3 vols.), 1893-95. Designed and erected new observatories at Smith Coll., Northampton, 1886-87, and at Amherst Col., 1903-05. Address: New York, N.Y. Died June 1, 1939.

TODD, Earle Marion, clergyman; b. Vernon, Jennings County, Ind., Oct. 17, 1863; s. Marion David and Myra Ellen (Knapp) T.; ed. Butler Coll., Indianapolis, until middle sr. yr., 1885; A.B., Garfield U., Wichita, Kan., 1888; D.D., Christian U., Canton, Mo., 1916; unmarried. Ordained ministry Disciples of Christ, 1888; pastor McPherson, Kan., 1889-91, University Ch. of Christ, Des Moines, Ia., 1891-93, Chester, Eng., 1893-98, West London Tabernacle, London, 1898-1905, North Tonawanda, N.Y., 1905-07; spl. mission, Manchester, N.H., 1907-08; pastor West Jefferson St. Ch., Ft. Wayne, Ind., 1909-13, Canton, Mo., 1913-14; pres. Christian U., later Culver-Stockton Coll., 1914-17; dir. social service and pastor Community Ch., Leeland, Tex., 1917-20. Pres. Rio Grande Valley Citrus Growers Assn., Mercedes, Tex. Home: Harlingen, Texas. Died Jan. 13, 1940.

TODD, Frank Chisholm, surgeon; b. Minneapolis, Oct. 15, 1869; s. Shubael Downs and Anna (Whicher) T.; A.B., D.D.S., U. of Minn., 1891, M.D., 1892; post-grad. work in New York, London, Paris, Berlin and Vienna; m. Mabel Odell, Oct. 15, 1894. Practiced in Minneapolis, 1895—; prof. and chief of dept. eye, ear, nose and throat diseases, U. of Minn. Sch. of Medicine and Surgery, 1899—; surgeon to U. of Minn. Hosp., Hill Crest Surg. Hosp., C.,M.& St.P. Ry. Co. Fellow Am. Coll. Surgeons. Author of various monographs on med. and surg. subjects; collaborator Am. Ency. Ophthalmology. Maj., Med. R.C., 1917, and in active service at Base Hosp., Camp Dodge, Des Moines, Ia. Home: Minneapolis, Minn. Died July 4, 1918.

TODD, George Walter, mfr.; b. Pultneyville, N.Y., Feb. 29, 1860; s. Asahel and Sarah M. (McLouth) T.; ed. pub. sch.; m. Grace Ledyard, July 21, 1885; children—Walter Ledyard, Donald Scott, George Libanus. Mfg. business, Rochester, N.Y., 1899—; chmn. bd. Stromberg-Carlson Telephone Mfg. Co.; dir. Eastman Kodak Co., Lincoln Alliance Bank. Mem. bd. dirs. Highland Hosp. Republican. Universalist. Mason. Home: Rochester, N.Y. Died Mar. 19, 1938.

TODD, Harry L., postmaster; b. California, Mo., Nov. 3, 1868; s. James R. (M.D.) and Louisa S. (Anderson) T.; ed. high sch., Gridley, Calif., and extension course, U. of Calif.; m. Mary A. Layson, July 14, 1896; 2 children (died in infancy). Advanced from clerk to dept. mgr., Anglo London, Paris Nat. Bank, San Francisco, Calif., 1900-27; dir. Rubber Corp. America, State Capital Co., Calif. Mut. Savings & Loan Assn. Became postmaster, San Francisco, 1927. Dir. Parnassus Hall Assn. Republican. Methodist. Mason. Lecturer on patriotic topics. Home: San Francisco, Calif. Died Jan. 3, 1938.

TODD, Henry Alfred, philologist; b. Woodstock, Ill., Mar. 13, 1854; s. Rev. Richard Kimball (founder of Todd Sem.) and Martha (Clover) T.; A.B., Princeton, 1876, fellow and tutor, 1876-80; studied at Paris, Berlin, Rome, Madrid, 1880-83; Ph.D., John Hopkins, 1885; m. Miriam, d. John S. Gilman, July 30, 1891. Instr. and asso. Johns Hopkins, 1883-91; prof. Romance langs., Leland Stanford Jr. U., 1891-93; prof. Romance philology, Columbia, 1893—. Mem. Congress of Arts and Sciences, St. Louis Expn., 1904; v.p. French Inst. in the U.S.; chmn. trustees French Union; mem. mission de rapprochement in France, 1919. Author of works on philology. Co-editor Romanic Review. Home: New York, N.Y. Died Jan. 1925.

TODD, Henry Davis, naval officer; b. Cambridge, Mass., Aug. 25, 1838; s. John N. Todd (formerly of the Navy); ed. Nyack, N.Y., Acad.; apptd. U.S. Naval Acad., 1853; grad. 1857; m. Flora Johnson, Sept. 28, 1865. Promoted to passed midshipman, June 25, 1860, master, Oct. 24, 1860; lt., April 3, 1861; lt. comdr., Jan. 3, 1863; apptd. prof. mathematics, Sept. 16, 1877. At beginning of Civil war was on Cumberland at burning of Norfolk navy yard, and afterward took part in 11 engagements, heavy batteries and sharp shooters, slightly wounded in gunboat night attack, Appomattox River, 1862; flag lt. with Admiral Wilkes, 1862-63, and on Sacramento during rest of war. Instr. mathematics, Naval Acad., 1865-66, head of dept. physics and chemistry same, 1879-86; on duty at Nautical Almanac Office, 1886-1900, dir., 1899-1900; retired from active service, Aug. 25, 1900, at age limit. Address: Washington, D.C. Deceased.

TODD, H(enry) Stanley, portrait painter; b. St. Louis, Mo., June 7, 1871; s. Washington and Mary Low (Davis) T.; student Washington U., 1886-88; studied art, St. Louis Sch. of Fine Arts, 1887-91, Julian Acad., Paris, 1892-96; pupil of Benjamin Constant and Jean P. Laurens; m. Jean Benton Doty, Apr. 9, 1898 (died 1930); m. 2d, Virginia Cabanne Little, May 9, 1931. Studied steam engring. and was pres. Universal Turbine Co., 1915-19. Portrait painter, 1894—; painted portraits of Theodore Roosevelt, William McKinley and Lincoln for Union League Club (Brooklyn), Frances E. Willard, Cardinal Newman, Oscar Johnson of St. Louis (donor of Oscar Johnson Inst. for Research), Mary Baker Eddy, and many others; "Nazarene or Christ Triumphant" painted in 1932, exhibited in 38 chs., Hall of Religion at Century of Progress Expn. and in many cities: "Immortality" exhibited at Rockefeller Center (N.Y. City), San Diego Fair, and Los Angeles. Awarded medals, Buffalo and St. Louis expns. On staff European Relief Council under Herbert Hoover, 1920-21. Hon. mem. Clergy Assn. and Rotary Club for painting "Nazarene." Enlisted in U.S. Army, May 1917, and assigned to Intelligence Div. of Gen. Staff, rank of capt., after armistice joined staff of Col. Robert E. Olds (in France), commr. for Europe of Am. Red Cross and appointed dep. commr. for France and Belgium, later commr. for both these countries; later col. U.S.A. Awarded Silver War Cross (France), 1919, and Chevalier Legion of Honor, 1924. Republican. Mason. Home: New York, N.Y. Died Apr. 2, 1941.

TODD, James Edward, geologist; b. Clarksfield, O., Feb. 11, 1846; s. Rev. John and Martha (Atkins) T.; A.B. Oberlin, 1867, A.M., 1870; Union

Theo. Sem., 1867-69; Oberlin Theol. Sem., 1869-70; studied at Sheffield Scientific Sch., Yale, 1870-71; Harvard Summer Sch. of Geology, 1875; m. Lillie J. Carpenter, June 15, 1876. Pvt. Co. K, 150th Ohio Inf., 100 days, 1864; on U.S. Fish Commn., 1871-73; prof. natural science, Tabor Coll., 1871-92; adj. prof. natural science, Beloit (Wis.) Coll., 1881-83; prof. geology and mineralogy, 1892-1903, acting pres., 1897-98, U. of S.D.; asst. prof. geology and mineralogy, U. of Kan., 1907—. Asst. geologist and spl. asst. U.S. Geol. Survey, 1881-1909, on Mo. Geol. Survey, 1891-92, Minn. Geol. Survey, 1892-93; state geologist of S.D., 1893-1903. Fellow A.A.A.S., Geol. Soc. America. Conglist. Progressive. Author of papers and pamphlets on geol. subjects. Address: Lawrence, Kan. Died 1922.

TODD, Luther Edward, clergyman; b. New Franklin, Howard County, Mo., Sept. 16, 1874; s. Theodore Hyatt and Cordelia B. (Summers) T.; Ph.B., Central Coll., Fayette, Mo., 1897, A.B., 1899, D.D., 1912; student Vanderbilt U., 1898-99; m. Margaret Lee Wheeler, Sept. 17, 1901; children—Mary Elizabeth, Virginia Lee, Helen Wheeler, Robert Luther. Ordained ministry M.E. Ch., S., 1899; pastor Hundley Ch., St. Joseph, 1899-1902, 1st Ch., St. Louis, 1902-05, Lafayette Park Ch., St. Louis, 1905-08, Centenary Ch., 1908-12, Wagner Pl. Ch., 1912-15; presiding elder St. Louis Dist., 1915-18; sec. Gen. Bd. of Finance of the M.E. Ch., S., 1918—. Mason. Author: Evangelism Exemplified—or Pulpit and Pew in United Action, 1914; The One-to-Win-One Helper, 1915; The Child Church Member, 1917; various pamphlets, etc., on evangelism, The Call of the Forgotten Man, and numerous pamphlets concerning superannuated preachers. Home: St. Louis, Mo. Died Nov. 25, 1937.

TODD, Mabel Loomis, author; b. Cambridge, Mass.; d. Eben Jenks and Mary Alden (Wilder) Loomis; pvt. sch. edn., Washington and Boston; m. David Todd, Mar. 5, 1879; 1 dau. Millicent (Mrs. Walter Van Dyke Bingham). Accompanied husband to Japan to observe total eclipses of sun, 1887 and 1896, to Tripoli, Barbary, for the eclipses of 1900 and 1905; around the world, 1901, for eclipse in Dutch E. Indies, and to Chile, 1907, for opposition of Mars and to Russia for eclipse of 1914. Founder, Mary Mattoon Chapter D.A.R. (hon. regent), Amherst Hist. Soc. (hon. pres.); dir. Mass. State Fedn. Woman's Clubs 3 years. Author: Footprints, 1883; Total Eclipses of the Sun, 1894; Corona and Coronet, 1898; A Cycle of Sunsets, 1909; Tripoli the Mysterious, 1912. Editor: Poems of Emily Dickinson, 1890-96; Letters of Emily Dickinson, 1894; A Cycle of Sonnets, 1896; Steele's Popular Astronomy, 1899. Contbr. to mags. on astronomy, travel, the Ainu aborigines of Japan, and other topics. Home: Coconut Grove, Fla. Died Oct. 14, 1932.

TODD, Percy R., ry. official; b. Toronto, Ont., Dec. 4, 1859; ed. Collegiate Inst., Ottawa, Ont. Began ry. service as telegraph operator in 1874; Canadian agent Ogdensburg & Lake Champlain R.R., 1878-82; gen. traveling agent Nat. Despatch Line, at Chicago, 1882-85; comml. agt. N.Y., West Shore & Buffalo R.R., at Albany, 1885; chief clerk gen. freight dept. same, at New York, 1885-86; gen. freight and pass. agt. Canada Atlantic R.R., at Ottawa, 1886-89; gen. frt. agt., 1889-92, gen. traffic mgr., 1892-1901, West Short R.R.; 2d v.p., 1901-03, 1st v.p.; dir., 1903-07, N.Y.,N.H.&H. R.R.; v.p. Bangor & Aroostook R.R., 1907-13, pres., 1913—. Home: Bangor, Me. Died Oct. 23, 1935.

TODD, Robert I., street ry. official; b. Lakewood, N.J., Nov. 29, 1869; s. Francis M. and Mary C. (Titus) T.; E.E., Johns Hopkins, 1893; m. Charlotte L. Vinal, Apr. 17, 1901; 1 son, Robert William, Supt. and elec. engr. Eckington & Soldiers Home Ry. Co., Washington, D.C., 1893-99; chief engr. Am. Air Power Co., New York, 1899-1900; master mechanic, Consol. Street Rys., Pittsburgh, Pa., 1900-01; v.p., gen. mgr. Cincinnati Traction Co., 1901-02; with United Gas & Improvement Co., Phila., 1902-03; gen. mgr. Rhode Island Co., Providence, 1903-06; became v.p., gen. mgr., 1906, of Indianapolis Traction & Terminal Co., later Indianapolis Street Ry. Co., and pres. and gen. mgr.; also pres., gen. mgr. Terre Haute, Indianapolis & Eastern Traction Co.; pres. Broad Ripple Traction Co., Terre Haute Traction & Light Co., Indianapolis & Northwestern Traction Co., Indianapolis & Eastern Ry. Co., Indianapolis & Greenland Rapid Transit Co., Arcade Realty Co., United Tractions Coal Co., Indiana Motor Transit Co., etc. Republican. Presbyn. Mason. Home: Indianapolis, Ind. Died July 12, 1928.

TODD, T(homas) Wingate, anatomist; b. Sheffield, Eng., Jan. 15, 1885; s. James and Katharine (Wingate) T.; M.B., and Ch.B., Manchester U. and London Hosp., 1907; m. Eleanor Pearson, Nov. 9, 1912; children—Arthur Wingate, Donald Pearson, Eleanor Margaret. Jr. and sr. demonstrator anatomy, Manchester U., 1907-08; house surgeon Royal Infirmary, 1909; lecturer on anatomy and clin. anatomy, U. of Manchester, 1910; prof. anatomy, Western Reserve U., 1912—. Dir. Hamann Mus. Comparative Anthropology and Anatomy; chmn. Brush Foundation; dir. research, Development Health Inquiry of the Asso. Foundations, Cleveland. Fellow of the Royal College of Surgeons (England), 1911; mem. Am. Assn. Anatomists, Soc. Anatomists Great Britain and Ireland, Am. Anthropol. Assn.; fellow Galton Soc. Home: Cleveland Heights, O. Died Dec. 28, 1938.

TODD, William Henry, shipbuilder; b. Wilmington, Del., Nov. 27, 1867; s. James and Sarah E. (Moody) T.; ed. pub. schs.; m. Mary E. Babcock. Pres. Todd Shipyards Corp., Robins Dry Dock & Repair Co., Tietjen & Lang Dry Dock Co., Todd Engring. Dry Dock & Repair Corp. (New Orleans), Todd Shipbuilding & Dry Dock Co. (Mobile, Ala.), Todd Dry Dock, Inc., Seattle, Todd Dry Dock Constrn. Corp. (Tacoma, Wash.), Erie Basin Towing & Hoisting Co. (chmn. bd.). Republican. Episcopalian. Mason (33°). Home: Brooklyn, N.Y. Died May 15, 1932.

TOLBERT, Benjamin Arthur, educator; b. Greenwood, S.C., Feb. 22, 1882; s. Elias Lake and Agnes (Ross) T.; student Wofford Coll., Spartanburg, S.C., 1897-1900; B.A.E., U. of Fla., 1927; m. Kate Jennings, Aug. 7, 1906 (died 1931); children—Robert Jennings (deceased), Kate Jennings; m. 2d, Heloise Bowyer Handley, Dec. 21, 1935. Teacher pub. schs. Barnwell County, S.C., 1901-04; supt. schs., Columbia, Miss., 1905-09; supt. Lamar County Agrl. High Sch., Purvis, Miss., 1909-14, Wilkinson County Agrl. High Sch., Woodville, 1914-17; prin. Carolina Mil. Acad., Hendersonville, N.C., 1919-21; prof. edn., U. of Fla., 1926-28, dean of students, 1929—. Maj. Coast Arty. Corps, U.S.A., 1917-19; served at Ft. Monroe and with Training Instruction Br., Gen. Staff, Washington, D.C. Democrat. Methodist. Scottish Rite Mason. Home: Gainesville, Fla. Died July 13, 1937.

TOLFREE, James Edward, pay dir. U.S.N.; b. Ithaca, N.Y., Aug. 29, 1837; s. John Edward and Caroline Rebecca (Cole) T.; ed. Ithaca Acad. and in France and Italy under pvt. tutors; m. Caroline Overman, Oct. 9, 1872. Apptd. acting asst. p.m. in the vol. navy from N.Y., Sept. 13, 1862; apptd. asst. p.m. in regular service, Mar. 3, 1865; promoted p.m., Jan. 22, 1866; pay insp., Aug. 10, 1886; pay dir., Feb. 12, 1898; retired as pay dir. with rank of rear admiral, Aug. 29, 1899. Served during the Civil War on Vanderbilt, 1862-67; Savannah, 1868; Richmond, 1869-71; Vermont, 1872-75; in 1875, was advanced 10 numbers in rank "for eminent and conspicuous conduct in battle" during the Civil War; on Colorado, 1875-77; on Trenton and fleet p.m., 1877; naval storekeeper, Ville Franche, 1877-78; navy yard, Washington, 1879; Shenandoah, 1879-82; receiving-ship Colorado, 1882-85; Trenton, Omaha, and Brooklyn, as fleet p.m., Asiatic Fleet, 1885-89; Navy Yard, New York, 1889-90; Minnesota, 1891-92; Navy Yard, Norfolk, 1892-93; Navy Yard, New York, 1894-96; in charge navy pay office, New York, 1896-99. Home: New York, N.Y. Died Jan. 10, 1920.

TOLL, Roger Wolcott, supt. Yellowstone Nat. Park; b. Denver, Colo., Oct. 17, 1883; s. Charles H. and Katharine E. (Wolcott) T.; grad. Manual Training High Sch., Denver, 1901; student Denver U., 1901-02; C.E., Columbia, 1906; m. Marguerite Cass, Sept. 21 1910; children—Donald Alan, Natalie, Roger W. With engring. dept. Mass. State Bd. of Health, 190?; with U.S. Coast and Geodetic Survey, Alaska, 19?3; in engring. dept., later chief engr. Denver Tramway Co., 1908-16; supt. Mt. Rainier Nat. Park, 1919-20; supt. Rocky Mountain Nat. Park, 1921-29; supt. Yellowstone Nat. Park, Feb. 1, 1929—. Served as capt. and maj. Ordnance Dept., U.S.A., World War I. Republican. Protestant. Author: Mountaineering in the Rocky Mountain National Park, 1919; The Mountain Peaks of Colorado, 1923. Climbed all of the fifty mountain peaks in Rocky Mountain Nat. Park; made first ascent, with 3 other persons, of Mt. Rainier, by the Kautz Glacier route, June 1920. Died Feb. 1936.

TOLL, William Edward, bishop; B.D., Nashotah House, Wis., 1871. Deacon, 1871, priest, 1872, P.E. Ch.; asst., Grace Ch., Chicago, 1871-72; rector St. James', Cleveland, 1872-74, St. Peter's, Sycamore, Ill., 1874-81, Christ Ch., Waukegan, Ill., 1881-1907; archdeacon, Diocese of Chicago, 1907-11; consecrated 1st suffragan bishop, Diocese of Chicago, Dec. 27, 1911. Home: Chicago, Ill. Died June 27, 1915.

TOLLES, Sheldon Hitchcock, lawyer; b. Burton, O., Oct. 1, 1858; s. Henry S. and Cynthia H. Tolles; A.B., Western Reserve U., 1878; m. Jessie Russell King, Apr. 13, 1887; children—Sheldon H., King. Practiced at Cleveland, O., 1880—. Republican. Home: Cleveland, O. Died July 14, 1926.

TOLMAN, Albert Harris, univ. prof.; b. Lanesboro, Mass., June 17, 1856; s. Albert and Jane A. (Tower) T.; A.B., Williams, 1877; prin. high sch., Chicopee Falls, Mass., 1879-82; Johns Hopkins U., 1882-84; Ph.D., U. of Strassburg, 1889; L.H.D., Williams Coll., 1916; m. Isabel Stevens, Aug. 29, 1889; 1 son, Joshua Stevens. Prof. English, Ripon (Wis.) Coll., 1884-93; asst. prof. English lit., 1893-1907, asso. prof., 1907-14, professor of English lit., 1914-25, emeritus, 1925, U. of Chicago, also asst. examiner and dean in colleges, 1895-1900. Editor: Julius Cæsar, and Introduction to Shakespeare, 1901. Author: The Views About Hamlet, and Other Essays, 1904; Questions on Shakespeare (2 vols.), 1910; Questions on Shakespeare, Select Comedies (7 pamphlets), 1912; Falstaff and other Shakespearean Topics, 1925. Home: Chicago, Ill. Died Dec. 25, 1928.

TOLMAN, Herbert Cushing, univ. dean; b. S. Scituate, Mass., Nov. 4, 1865; s. James and Mary T. (Briggs) T.; A.B., Yale, 1888, Ph.D., 1890; student U. of Berlin, 1896; U. of Munich, 1905; D.D., Peabody Coll., 1901; S.T.D., Hobart, 1913; LL.D., U. of Nashville, Tenn., 1914, and U. of Louisville, Ky., 1917; m. Mary Wells, Aug. 26, 1891. Asst. Indo-European langs., Yale, 1891; instr. Latin, 1891-92, asst. prof. Sanskrit, 1892-93, U. of Wis.; prof. Sanskrit and acting prof. Greek, U. of N.C., 1893-94; prof. Greek, 1894—, dean of Coll. of Arts and Science, 1914—, Vanderbilt U. Declined presidency of Hobart Coll., 1913. Hon. canon All Saints Cathedral, Milwaukee, 1904. Mem. Internat. Congress Arts and Sciences, St. Louis Expn., 1904, Archæol. Congress, Athens, Greece, 1905. Lecturer, Archæol. Inst. America, 1912. In charge, summers, of Holy Trinity Church, New York, American Ch., Munich, Christ Ch., Lucerne, and spl. preacher at Old Trinity, New York, on several occasions. Author: Harper and Tolman's Cæsar's Gallic War, 1891; Tolman's Persian Inscriptions, 1892; Kerr and Tolman's Greek Gospel of Matthew, 1892; Harper and Tolman's Text Edition of Cæsar, 1893; Harrington and Tolman's Greek and Roman Mythology, 1897; Tolman and Stevenson's Herodotus and the Empires of the East, 1899; Art of Translating, 1900; Urbs Beata, 1902; Mycenæan Troy (with G. C. Scoggin), 1904; Via Crucis, 1907; Ancient Persian Lexicon and Texts, 1909; Ancient Persian Language and Cuneiform Supplement, 1910; Christi Imago, 1915. Editor Vanderbilt Oriental Series (9 vols. completed); asso. editor World's Progress (10 vols.); co-editor Studies in Philology and History. Writer of various monographs on Oriental, philol. and archæol. topics in revs. and soc. proceedings. Address: Nashville, Tenn. Died Nov. 24, 1923.

TOLMAN, Warren W., judge; b. Kendall County, Ill., Dec. 8, 1861; s. Charles Warren and Sarah (Haigh) T.; LL.B., Northwestern U., 1888; m. Maud Ingersoll, Apr. 30, 1889; children—Leland I., Mrs. R. J. Raymond. Began practice at Chicago, 1888; moved to Spokane, Wash., 1892; mem. Wash. Senate, 1901-05; mem. Bd. of Edn., Spokane, 1903-06; chmn. Dist. Appeal Bd., Selective Service, July 1917-May 1918; asso. justice Supreme Ct. of Wash., from May 11, 1918 to Sept. 20, 1937 (retired before end of term on account of health); chief justice, 1925-26, 1931-32. Democrat. Mason. Home: Spokane, Wash. Died May 15, 1940.

TOLTZ, Max, cons. engr.; b. Koeslin, Germany, Sept. 2, 1857; s. Hermann and Malvine (Beilfuss) T.; C.E., Royal Acad. Science and Engring., Berlin, Germany, 1887; D.Eng., Ramsey Inst. Tech., 1924; m. L. Elizabeth Argue, 1919. Came to U.S., 1882, naturalized, 1892. Began as draftsman, G.N. Ry., 1882, successively asst. engr., bridge engr., acting chief engr. and mech. engr. in charge motive power dept. until 1904; cons. engr. C.P. Ry., Butte, Anaconda & Pacific Ry., N.P. R.R., Erie R.R., G.N. Ry., 1904-07; cons. engr. in pvt. practice, 1907—. Mem. Minn. N.G. 23 yrs., advancing to maj., engrs.; supervising engr. constrn. div., U.S.A., 1917-18. Republican. Home: St. Paul, Minn. Died Jan. 12, 1932.

TOMKINS, Calvin, manufacturer; b. East Orange, N.J., Jan. 26, 1858; s. Walter and Emma Augusta (Baldwin) T.; A.B., Cornell U., 1879; m. Kittie Neeley, Dec. 4, 1889. Pres. Newark Plaster Co., Tomkins Cove Stone Co., Albert Mfg. Co. (Can.), Bonner Brick Co.—mng. dir. in New York and gen. sales agt. of cos. named. Commr. of docks and ferries of City of New York, Jan. 1910-Apr. 1913. Mem. inland waterways com. of U.S. R.R. Adminstrn., 1918. Democrat. Pres. Municipal Art Soc., N.Y., 1906-07. Author of numerous pamphlets and articles relating to physical development of New York. Home: Tomkins Cove-on-Hudson, N.Y. Died Mar. 13, 1921.

TOMKINS, Floyd Williams, clergyman; b. N.Y. City, Feb. 7, 1850; s. Floyd Williams and Eliza (Dunham) T.; Charlier French Inst., New York; A.B., Harvard, 1872; B.D., Gen. Theol. Sem., New York, 1875; S.T.D., U. of Pa., 1901; LL.D., Temple Coll., 1903; D.D., U. of the South, Sewanee, Tenn., 1911; m. Ann Maria Grant Cutter, 1875; children—Sarah Graham, Ann Gibson, Floyd W., Jeannette. Deacon, 1875, priest, 1876, P.E. Ch.; missionary in Colo., Wyo. and Middle West, 1875-83; rector St. James' Ch., Keene, N.H., 1883-84; minister in charge Calvary Chapel, New York, 1884-88; rector Christ Ch., Hartford, Conn., 1888-91, St. James', Chicago, 1891-94, Grace Ch., Providence, R.I., 1894-99, Ch. of the Holy Trinity, Phila., 1899—. Preacher at Harvard, 1902-05; chaplain 1st Regt. N.G. Pa. Mem. Civic Service Reform Assn., Pa. Prison Soc. Trustee Divinity Sch. of P.E. Church, Phila. Republican. Author: The Christian Life, 1896; Following Christ, 1900; My Best Friend, 1901; Beacons on Life's Voyage, 1904; Helps Toward Nobler Living, 1908; The Faith and Life of a Christian, 1909; Prayers for the Quiet Hour, 1910; Sunshine on Life's Way, 1912. Address: Phila., Pa. Died Mar. 24, 1932.

TOMLINSON, Arthur Hibbs, head master; b. Makefield, Bucks County, Pa., Jan. 20, 1856; s. Robert

Knowles and Mary Eliza (Hibbs) T.; M.E., State Normal Sch., West Chester, Pa., 1877, B.Sc., 1883; post-grad. work, U. of Mich., 1 yr.; m. Emma Taylor Pyle, Aug. 4, 1886. Teacher pub. schs., 1874-76; prin. Friends' School, Calvert, Md., 1877-81; Friends' School, Oxford, Pa., 1881-83, Friends' Acad., Locust Valley, N.Y., 1884-87, Friends' Sch., Jenkinton, Pa., 1887-92; owner and head master Swarthmore (Pa.) Prep. Sch., 1892—. Pres. Swarthmore Nat. Bank, 1904-11. Mem. Hicksite Friends; treas. exec. com. Friends' Nat. Peace Conf. Address: Swarthmore, Pa. Died Jan. 14, 1920.

TOMLINSON, Everett Titsworth, author; b. Shiloh, N.J., May 23, 1859; s. Rev. George E. and Amanda P. (Titsworth) T.; student Williams Coll., class of 1879, A.M., 1883; hon. A.M., Colgate, 1879, Ph.D., 1888; Litt.D., Bucknell, 1906; m. Anna M. Greene; children—Mrs. Ruth Allen, Everett T., Paul Greene. Prin. high sch., Auburn, N.Y., 1881-83; head master prep. dept. Rutgers Coll., 1883-88. Author: The Search for Andrew Field, 1894; The Boy Soldiers of 1812, 1895; The Colonial Boys, 1895; The Boy Officers of 1812, 1896; Three Young Continentals, 1896; Tecumseh's Young Braves, 1897; Washington's Young Aide, 1897; Boys with Old Hickory, 1898; Two Young Patriots, 1898; Boys of Old Monmouth, 1898; Camping on the St. Lawrence, 1899; A Jersey Boy in the Revolution, 1899; In the Hands of the Redcoats, 1901; The House Boat on the St. Lawrence, 1901; Young Folks' History of the American Revolution, 1902; Under Colonial Colors, 1902; A Lieutenant Under Washington, 1903; The Rider of the Black Horse, 1904; The Red Chief, 1905; Soldier of the Wilderness, 1905; Winning His Degree, 1905; Four Boys in the Yellowstone, 1906; Marching Against the Iroquois, 1906; The Camp-Fire of Mad Anthony, 1907; The Fruit of the Desert, 1907; Four Boys in the Land of Cotton, 1907; Mad Anthony's Young Scout, 1908; Four Boys on the Mississippi, 1908; Light Horse Harry's Legion, 1910; The Champion of the Regiment, 1911; The Young Minute-Man of 1812, 1912; The Young Sharpshooter, 1913; Scouting with Daniel Boone, 1914; Places Young Americans Want to Know, 1915; The Story of General Pershing, 1917; Young People's History of the American Revolution, 1921; Days and Deeds of '76, 1927. Home: Elizabeth, N.J. Died Oct. 30, 1931.

TOMLINSON, George Ashley, capitalist; b. Lapeer, Mich., Jan. 26, 1869; s. Samuel James and Abigail (Gage) T.; ed. high sch., Detroit; m. Laura I. Davidson, 1902. Spent 2 yrs. in Wyo. as a cowboy, and was captured and tortured by Indians; engaged in newspaper work in Detroit, and on the New York Sun, later mng. editor Detroit Times; moved to Duluth, Minn., 1893, identified with shipping interests there, 1893—; pres. Duluth, Superior, Globe and Inter Ocean steamship cos.; apptd. gen. mgr. N.Y. canal sect. U.S. Railroad Adminstrn., also gen. mgr. N.Y. and N.J. canals, July 15, 1918. Republican. Home: Duluth, Minn. Died Jan. 25, 1942.

TOMLINSON, Vincent Eaton, clergyman; b. Perry, Wyoming County, N.Y., Mar. 20, 1862; s. DeWitt Clinton and Emmeline C. (Eaton) T.; B.S., Buchtel Coll., Akron, O., 1880; B.D., Tufts Div. Sch., 1884; D.D., Tufts Coll., 1903; m. Clarissa A. Hindley, Sept. 27, 1887; 1 dau., Ruth. Ordained Universalist ministry, 1884; pastor Valley Falls, 1883-87, Ballou Ch., Providence, R.I., 1887-90, 1st Ch., Hudson, N.Y., 1890-95, St. Paul's Ch., Little Falls, N.Y., 1895-1900, 1st Ch., Worcester, Mass., 1900—. Pres. Mass. Universalist Conv., 1912-13, trustee, 1902—. Chaplain Little Falls Light Inf., 1895-1900; mem. Worcester Sch. Com., 1903-12 (chmn. 1909-12); pres. bd. mgrs. Worcester Fresh Air Fund. Trustee Universalist Pub. House, Boston; trustee Universalist Gen. Conv., 1917-25; mem. Nat. Bd. of Lectureship, Universalist Ch. Mem. Bd. of Aldermen, Worcester, 1916-17 (pres. 1917); mem. Pub. Library Bd., 1918-23 (pres. 1923); pres. Pub. Edn. Assn., Worcester, 1914-17; mem. exec. com. Worcester Welfare Fedn.; life trustee Tufts Coll. Chaplain of Grand Lodge of Masons of Mass., 1927. Republican. Mason. Address: Worcester, Mass. Died June 16, 1938.

TOMPERS, George Urban, mfr.; b. Providence, R.I., Oct. 26, 1877; s. Nicholas Max and Flora (Olney) T.; ed. pub. schs., Providence and Pawtucket, R.I.; m. Lucie Margaret Hartt, Dec. 1900; 1 dau., Jaqueline. Pres. F. Ad. Richter & Co., Riedel & Co., Loujac Corp. Baptist. Home: Garden City, N.Y. Died Dec. 15, 1936.

TOMPERT, Russell Howard, banking; b. Dayton, O., Aug. 5, 1892; s. William and Minnie T.; ed. Steele High Sch., Dayton, 1906-10, Miami Jacobs Business Coll., 1911-12; m. Florence E. Zwick, Nov. 5, 1913; children—James Russell, Robert Samuel. With The Winters Nat. Bank & Trust Co., 1910—, pres., 1929—; pres. The Winters Nat. Co.; treas. and dir. Van Cleve Hotel Co., Dayton Airport Co. Trustee Montgomery Co. Children's Home. Baptist. Mason. Address: Dayton, O. Died Dec. 8, 1934.

TOMPKINS, Arnold, educator; b. Paris, Ill., 1849; s. Henry and Delilah T.; grad. Ind. State Normal Sch., 1880; Ind. U., 1889, A.M., 1891; 2 yrs. post-grad. work, U. of Chicago, Ph.D., Ohio State U.; m. Jennie Snyder, 1875. Teacher, 1870—; supt. pub. schs., 1875-85; prof. in normal schs., 1885-93; prof. pedagogy, U. of Ill., 1895-99; pres. Ill. State Normal Sch., 1899-1900; prin. Chicago Normal Sch, 1900—. Lecturer on ednl. topics. Author: Science of Discourse, 1889; Philosophy of Teaching, 1892; Philosophy of School Management, 1895; Literary Interpretations, 1896. Address: Chicago, Ill. Died 1905.

TOMPKINS, Arthur Sidney, judge; b. Schoharie County, N.Y., Aug. 26, 1865; s. Sidney B. and Mary H. (Yocum) T.; pub. sch. edn.; m. Jeanie C. Logan, May 18, 1889; children—Marjorie J., Arthur S. Admitted to bar, 1886; practiced at Nyack, N.Y.; elected police justice, Nyack, 1887; mem. N.Y. Assembly, 1889, county judge, Rockland County, 1893-99; mem. 56th and 57th Congresses (1899-1903); justice Supreme Ct. of N.Y., 1906-35; apptd. to Appellate Div., 2d Dept., Jan. 1930; retired by legal age limit and resumed practice of law with firm Greenbaum, Wolff & Ernst, N.Y. City and White Plains, N.Y. Pres. State Firemen's Home, Hudson, N.Y. Republican. Baptist. Mason (Past Master, Past Dist. Dep. Grand Master, Grand Master, State of New York, May 1922-23); P.G.M. Odd Fellows, State of N.Y.; mem. Grand Forum B.P.O.E. Home: Nyack, N.Y. Died Jan. 20, 1938.

TOMPKINS, Charles Henry, brig. gen., U.S.A.; b. Ft. Monroe, Va., Sept. 12, 1830; s. Daniel D. and Mary (Pierce) T.; cadet U.S. Mil. Acad., 1847-49; m. Augusta Root Hobbie, Dec. 17, 1862. Served pvt., corpl., and sergt. Co. F, 1st Dragoons, Jan. 21, 1856-Jan. 10, 1861; 2d lt. 2d Cav., Mar. 23, 1861; 1st lt., Apr. 30, 1861; capt. a.q.m., Nov. 13, 1861; col. 1st Vt. Cav., Apr. 24, 1862; resigned, Sept. 9, 1862; lt. col. q.m. vols., July 1, 1865; col. q.m. vols., June 13, 1866; lt. col. deputy q.m. gen. U.S.A., July 29, 1866; col. a.q.m. gen., Jan. 24, 1881; retired by operation of law, Sept. 12, 1894; advanced to rank of brig. gen. retired, by act of Apr. 23, 1904. Bvtd.: maj., Mar. 13, 1865, "for gallant conduct at battle of Fairfax C.H., Va., May 31, 1861"; lt. col., Mar. 13, 1865, "for meritorious services in campaigns of Gens. Banks and McDowell, 1862, 1863"; col., Mar. 13, 1865, for same in q.m. dept., 1863-65; brig. gen., Mar. 13, 1865, "for faithful and meritorious services during the war"; awarded Congressional Medal of Honor, Nov. 13, 1893, "for distinguished gallantry in action at Fairfax C.H., Va., June 1, 1861." Home: Washington, D.C. Died Jan. 18, 1915.

TOMPKINS, Daniel A., engineer; b. Edgefield County, S.C., Oct. 12, 1852; s. DeWitt Clinton and Hannah Virginia (Smyly) T.; S.C. Coll.; C.E. Rensselaer Poly. Inst., 1873; unmarried. Learned machinist's trade in Bessemer steel works of John A. Griswold & Co., Troy, N.Y., and 10 yrs. with Bethlehem Iron Works, Pa., under John Fritz, as machinist, draftsman, head draftsman and asst. to master machinist; master machinist Crystal Plate Glass Works and Crystal Ry. Co., Crystal City, Mo., 1880-82, building large addition to plant; at Charlotte, N.C., 1882—, as contracting engr., constructing many cottonsed oil mills and refineries, cotton mills, elec. light works, acid phosphate works, etc.; pres. D. A. Tompkins Co., mfrs., engrs. and contractors; pres. High Shoals and Atherton cotton mills, etc. Pres. Underwriters Fire Ins. Co. of Greensboro, N.C.; dir. Equitable Assurance Soc. of the U.S. Mem. U.S. Industrial Commn. Author: Cotton Mill, Processes and Calculations; Cotton Mill Commercial Features; Cotton and Cotton Oil; American Commerce, Its Expansion; Cotton Values in Textile Fabrics; History of Mecklenburg County, North Carolina; and many pamphlets. Address: Charlotte, N.C. Died Oct. 18, 1914.

TOMPKINS, Frank Hector, artist; b. Hector, N.Y., May 13, 1847; s. Moses (M.D.) and Mary Ann (Smith) T.; ed. pub. schs.; student Cincinnati Acad. of Design; Art Students' League, New York; Royal Acad. of Arts, Munich, Germany, 1882-87. Studio at Paris, France, 1898-1900. Gold medal, Mass. Charitable Mechanics' Assn.; tech. medal first class, Munich Royal Acad. Represented in permanent collection of the Pa. Acad. Fine Arts, Boston Mus. Fine Arts. Address: Boston, Mass. Died July 11, 1922.

TONDORF, Francis Anthony, seismologist; b. Boston, Mass., July 17, 1870; s. Joseph and Louise (Musler) T.; A.B., Woodstock (Md.) Coll., 1895; Ph.D., Georgetown U., 1914; unmarried. Asst. Georgetown U. Obs., later chief Georgetown U., Seismol. Obs. Fellow A.A.A.S., Royal Astronomical Soc. Catholic. Author various brochures, and articles in scientific jours. Known for researches in epicentres and microseisms. Address: Washington, D.C. Died Nov. 29, 1929.

TONER, Edward C., publisher; b. Shelby Co., Ind., Nov. 11, 1871; s. James E. and Sophia (Sala) T.; A.B., Ind. U., 1895; m. Harriet Williams, Aug. 17, 1904; children—Williams McCulloch, Jane. Reporter on Anderson Herald, 1895-1904, owner and pub., 1904—; in dry goods business, Martinsville, Ind. Del. Rep. Nat. Conv., 1912; candidate of Progressive Party for Congress, 1912; chmn. Progressive State Com., 1914; del. at large Rep. Nat. Conv., 1916; candidate for Rep. nomination for gov. of Ind., 1919, 24. Mason, Elk, Moose. Methodist. Home: Anderson, Ind. Died Jan. 10, 1927.

TONGUE, Thomas H., congressman; b. Lincolnshire, Eng., June 13, 1844; s. Anthony and Rebecca T.; removed with parents to Washington County, Ore., Nov. 1859; grad. Pacific U., 1868; studied law; admitted to bar, Sept. 1870; practiced at Hillsboro, Ore., 1870—; also identified with farming and livestock interests; State senator, 1888-92; permanent chmn. State Rep. conv., 1890 and 1894; pres. State organization of Rep. Clubs, 1892-94; del. to (and Ore. v.p. of) Nat. Rep. Conv., 1892; mem. State and chmn. congressional Rep. coms.; mem. Congress from 1st Ore. dist., 1897-1903. Home: Hillsboro, Ore. Died 1903.

TOOKER, Lewis Frank, author; b. Port Jefferson, N.Y., Dec. 18, 1855; s. Lewis H. and Mary (Rowland) T.; A.B., Yale, 1877, hon. A.M., 1907; m. Violette Swezey, Nov. 15, 1883. Deputy clerk Suffolk County, N.Y., 1882-85; on editorial staff Century Magazine, July 1885, later asso. editor. Mem. Nat. Inst. of Arts and Letters. Author: The Call of the Sea, 1902; Under Rocking Skies, 1905; Life of Paul Jones, 1915; The Middle Passage, 1920. Contbr. to many mags. Home: Riverside, Conn. Died Sept. 17, 1925.

TOOLE, Joseph Kemp, governor; b. Savannah, Mo., May 12, 1851; s. Edwin and Lucinda S. T.; acad. edn.; removed to Mont., 1870; m. Lily, d. Gen. William Starke Rosecrans, May 7, 1890; children—Rosecrans (dec.), Warren, Joseph Porter. Admitted to bar, 1872 and engaged in practice at Helena, Mont. Dist. atty. 3d Jud. Dist., 1872-76; mem. Territorial Legislature; mem. Mont. Constl. Conv., 1884; del. to 49th and 50th Congresses (1885-89); 1st gov. of Mont., 1889-93; reëlected for 2 terms, 1901-09. Democrat. Home: Helena, Mont. Died Mar. 11, 1929.

TOOMBS, Percy Walthall, M.D., prof. obstetrics; b. Greenville, Miss., Aug. 5, 1880; s. Reuben Sanders and Fannie (Ray) T.; A.B., Georgetown (Ky.) Coll., 1901, LL.D., 1926; M.D., Tulane U., 1905; m. Amy Randolph Morton, Feb. 15, 1915; 1 son, William Percy. Began practice at Greenville, 1905; dist. surgeon for Yazoo & Miss. Valley R.R. and Southern R.R., 1905-07; moved to Memphis, Tenn., 1907; prof. physiology, Coll. Physicians and Surgeons, Memphis (now Coll. of Medicine, U. of Tenn.), 1907-09; dist. surgeon I.C. R.R., 1908-16; prof. obstetrics, Med. Coll., U. of Tenn., 1909—; obstetrician in chief, Bapt. Memorial and Memphis General hosps. Fellow A.C.S., A.M.A., Am. Assns. Obstetricians, Gynecologists and Abdominal Surgeons (v.p. 1929-30), Southern Med. Assn.; hon. fellow Kansas City Southwest Clinical Soc. Democrat. Episcopalian. Mason. Contbr. to Memphis Med. Monthly, Am. Jour. Obstetrics and Gynecology, Southern Med. Jour., etc. Home: Memphis, Tenn. Died Jan. 3, 1933.

TOOMEY, De Lally Prescott, editor; b. Homer, Claiborne Parish, La., Dec. 5, 1868; s. De Lally Pendelton and Sarah Ann (Prescott) T.; ed. principally by parents at home; m. Mary Carter, Feb. 14, 1895. Connected with Dallas News, 1889—, began as mailing clk.; studied newspaper illustration in New York and returned to Dallas as staff artist and writer; successively asst. city editor, staff corr., Sunday editor, and mng. editor, 1901—. Independent Democrat. Mem. publicity com. Fed. Food Adminstrn. Home: Dallas, Tex. Died Oct. 13, 1918.

TOON, Thomas Fentress, farmer; b. Columbus County, N.C., June 10, 1840; s. Anthony Fentress and Mary (McMillan) T.; grad. Wake Forest Coll., N.C., 1861; enlisted in C.S.A., May 20, 1861, as pvt. Co. K, 20th N.C. regt.; promoted 1st lt., June 17, 1861; capt., July 1861; col. 20th regt., N.C. troops, Feb. 26, 1863; brig. gen., May 31, 1864; assigned to command of Johnston's brigade, June 4, 1864; took part in the prominent battles of Civil war; wounded 5 times; m. Carrie E. Smith, Jan. 24, 1866; m. 2d, Rebecca Cobb Ward, Oct. 29, 1891. Elected to N.C. legislature, 1881, to N.C. senate, 1883; State supt. public instruction, N.C., 1900. Address: Lumberton, N.C. Died 1902.

TOPAKYAN, Haigazoun Hohannes, merchant, consul gen.; b. Constantinople, Turkey, Nov. 5, 1864; s Hohannes H. and Diroohi H. (Keshkekian) T.; ed. pub. schs. and Am. Coll., Turkey; m. Rosie Yeretzian, Aug. 26, 1891. Engaged in dry goods business in Turkey with father at 18; came to U.S., 1887, importer Persian rugs and carpets, 1887—; apptd. by Persian Govt. imperial commr. and dir. gen. of its exhibits, World's Columbian Expn., 1892; built Persian and Ottoman pavilion at own expense and was awarded 48 diplomas and 48 medals, also receiving personal thanks and diploma from President Cleveland; presented to the U.S., 1907, a $50,000 Persian rug (now hangs in White House), 6½ ft. in length and 4 ft. wide, and set with rubies, pearls, turquoises, etc.; presented a 2d rug in 1910, during President Taft's adminstrn.; presented to the Field Mus., Chicago, a large Persian antique carpet; consul gen., Persia, at New York, 1908—. Baptist. Decorated Imperial Order of the Lion and Rising Sun, Persia; the Medjidie, Turkey; Buste del Libertad, Venezuela. Col. Albany (N.Y.) Burgesses Corps, 1909; v.p. Internat. Peace Forum, 1911. Persian commr. gen. Panama P.I. Expn., 1915, and received from Persian Govt.

a gold decoration (1st class) and Grand Cordon. Home: Morris Plains, N.J. Died Oct. 13, 1926.

TOPE, Homer W., temperance worker; b. Dell Roy, Carroll County, Ohio, May 28, 1859; s. Gabriel and Elizabeth (McHugh) T.; Mt. Union Coll., O.; Oberlin Coll., O.; Capital U., Columbus, O.; A.B., Harlem Springs Coll., Carroll County, O., 1885, A.M., 1888; grad. Mt. Airy Theol. Sem., Phila., 1888; D.D., Carthage Coll., Ill.; taught sch. 7 yrs. and read law 2 yrs.; m. Alice Mackaman, 1881. Ordained Luth. ministry, 1888; pastor Grace Ch., Youngstown, O., 1888-97, Grace Ch., Chicago, 1897-99, Freeport, Ill., 1900; supt. Anti-Saloon League, 1900—, at Poughkeepsie, Rochester, Albany and Syracuse, N.Y., Springfield, Mass., Boston, Pittsburgh, and at Phila., 1907—; state supt. Pa. Anti-Saloon League, 1920—. Mem. Com. on Moral and Social Welfare of United Luth. Ch. in America. Republican. Mason. Author: Gustavus Adolphus, 1905. Lecturer. Home: Philadelphia, Pa. Died June 4, 1936.

TOPLITZKY, Joe, realtor; b. New Haven, Conn., Dec. 25, 1888; s. Meyer and Ida T.; ed. pub. schs.; m. Elsie B. Crossley, July 10, 1912; children—Beth, Elsie. In real estate and ins. business as Joe Toplitzky Co., Los Angeles, 1913—; officer or dir. many corps. Home: Los Angeles, Calif. Died Sept. 2, 1935.

TOPPAN, Robert Noxon, author, lawyer; b. Phila., Pa., Oct. 17, 1836; s. Charles and Laura Ann (Noxon) T.; grad. Harvard, 1858; Columbia Law School, 1861; mem. Am. Hist. Soc.; corr. sec. Prince Soc., Boston; served on internat. coinage com., Am. Social Science Assn.; del. to Internat. Congress, 1878, for unification of weights, measures and money. Author: Historical Summary of Metallic Money; also numerous pamphlets on monetary science; Biographical Sketches of Old Newbury; translated Jouffroy's "Ethics." Address: Cambridge, Mass. Died 1901.

TOPPING, John Alexander, financier; b. St. Clairsville, O., June 10, 1860; s. Henry and Mary (Tallman) T.; ed. pub. and high schs., Kansas City, Mo.; m. Minnie C. Junkins, Jan. 18, 1883 (dec.); m. 2d, Mrs. Louise Johnston Manning, Apr. 28, 1914. Entered iron business, 1878, as payroll clerk Aetna Iron & Nail Co. and became pres., 1898; 1st v.p. Am. Sheet Steel Co., 1900-03, resigned; reorganized the La Belle Iron Works, Wheeling, W.Va., 1904; pres. Am. Sheet & Tin Plate Co., 1904-06; pres. and later chmn. Republic Iron & Steel Co. and the Tenn. Coal, Iron & R.R. Co., 1906-07; chmn. Republic Iron & Steel Co., 1906-30. Home: Greenwich, Conn. Died Aug. 24, 1934.

TORBERT, John Bryant, topographic and geologic draftsman; b. Washington, D.C., May 8, 1867; s. John Peyton and Elizabeth (Bryant) T.; high sch. edn., Washington; LL.B., Columbian (now George Washington) U., 1888, LL.M., 1889; m. Florence Kalbfus, Nov. 19, 1890; children—Florence, John Peyton, Mrs. Elizabeth Bryant Mertz, Helen May (dec.). Admitted to bar, 1889; draftsman U.S. Geol. Survey, 1886-93, in topographer's office, Post-Office Dept., 1893-1908, U.S. Geol. Survey, 1908—. Identified with 8th Internat. Geog. Congress, Washington, D.C., 1904. Hist. cartographer, Jamestown Expn., 1907. Scientific illustrator U.S. Geol. Survey. Contbr. articles, maps and drawings to mags. and scientific publs., besides illustrating the works of others. Diploma of Highest Excellence, Turin Expn., 1911. Mem. D.C. Liberty Loan Com.; four-minute man; dist. food administrator, 1917-19. Address: Cleveland Park, D.C. Deceased.

TORCHIANA, Henry Albert van Coenen, consul gen.; b. Java, Dutch East Indies, December 25, 1867; s. William George and Elizabeth Johanna (Coenen) T.; grad. Amsterdam (Netherlands) Coll. of Commerce, 1887; Litt.D. from U. of Southern Calif., 1930; LL.D., Hope Coll., Holland, Mich., 1933; m. Catherine Geloudemans. Came to U.S., 1890, naturalized citizen, 1895. Hort. commr. and entomologist, Merced, Calif., 1894-96; admitted to Calif. bar, 1900, and began practice in Santa Cruz County; moved to San Francisco, 1910; mem. firm Stratton, Kaufman and Torchiana, 1910-16; consul gen. of Netherlands, for the Pacific Coast and Intermountain states, 1913—. Resident commr. gen. of the Panama Pacific Internat. Expn., 1914, dean of foreign commrs., 1915; controller of Netherlands nav. on Pacific Ocean, 1916-19. Founder, 1912, and hon. pres., 1912-38, Holland-Am. Chamber of Commerce for Pacific Coast States. Decorated Knight Comdr. Sacred Treasure of Japan; Knight Comdr. St. George (Greece); Comdr. Order Oranje-Nassau (Netherlands); Knight Lion of Netherlands; Knight Comdr. Gold Rice of China. Republican. Dutch Reformed Ch. Author: Holland, Birthplace of American Liberty, 1915; Tropical Holland, Java and Other Islands, 1921; California Gringos, 1930; The Story of the Mission of Santa Cruz, 1933. Home: Santa Cruz, Calif. Died Mar. 1, 1940.

TORCHIO, Philip, electrical engineer; born Vercana (Como), Italy, Aug. 2, 1868; s. Filippo and Luisa (Prandi) T.; B.A., U. of Pavia, 1890; M.E. and E.E., Royal Polytechnic, Milan, 1893; m. Angela de Nova, 1893; children—Anna Luisa, T. Desmond, Philip, Brady, Angela. Draftsman and chief draftsman, Sprague Electric Elevator Co., New York, 1893-95; with New York Edison Co., Inc., as engr. of economics, 1895-1901, engr. of distribution, 1901-05, chief elec. engr., 1905-24, v.p., 1924-31, sr. v.p., 1931-36, and with merged company, The Consol. Edison Co., as v.p. till 1938; cons. engr., 1905-28; dir. N.Y. & Queens Electric Light & Power Co. and other allied companies, 1931-38; retired, 1938; chmn. bd., pres. and dir. Bank of Naples Trust Co. of N.Y. Important work in development of electricity in steam and hydraulic stations and unification of systems of transmission and distribution over large territories; originated improvements in apparatus, cables, storage batteries, and electric control. Mayor of Bronxville, 1929-31. Mem. New York City Mayor's Defense Com., 1941. Past pres. N.Y. Elec. Soc.; fellow Am. Inst. E.E. Presented numerous papers and results of original researches before tech. socs. and internat. congresses at St. Louis, Turin and Pan-American Congress, Washington; also lectured at Columbia, Yale, Johns Hopkins. Grand Officer Crown of Italy. Awarded Edison medal by Am. Inst. Elec. Engrs., 1939. Home: Bronxville, N.Y. Died Jan. 14, 1942.

TOREK, Franz, surgeon; b. Breslau, Germany, Apr. 14, 1861; s. Albert and Anna (Wiesner) T.; came with parents to U.S., 1872; A.B., Coll. City of New York, 1880, A.M., 1887; M.D., Coll. Phys. and Surg., Columbia, 1887; m. Minnie Volkening, Apr. 29, 1896; children—Gretchen (Mrs. Edwin Stein), Paul. Teacher pub. sch., New York, 1880-84; began practice at N.Y. City, 1887; surgeon New York Skin and Cancer Hosp. (now Stuyvesant Sq. Hosp.), 1889-1928, cons. surgeon, 1928—; surgeon German Hosp. of New York (now Lenox Hill Hosp.), 1904-26, cons. surgeon, 1926—; instr. in surgery, New York Post-Grad. Med. Sch., 1891-99, adj. prof. surgery, 1899-1915. Contbr. chapter on surgery of the esophagus to Nelson's Surgery; chapter on thoracic surgery, Johnson's Operative Therapeusis; article on esophagectomy in Cyclo. of Medicine. Home: Montclair, N.J. Died Sept. 19, 1938.

TORNEY, George Henry, surgeon gen. U.S.A.; b. Baltimore, Md., June 1, 1850; s. John P. and Mary M. (Peacock) T.; student Carroll Coll., New Windsor, Md., 1862-67; M.D., U. of Va., 1870; m. Mary A. Johnston, Jan. 22, 1872. Apptd. asst. surgeon U.S.N., Nov. 1, 1871; passed asst. surgeon, Nov. 1, 1874; resigned from navy, June 30, 1875; apptd. 1st lt. asst. surgeon U.S.A., July 1, 1875; promoted capt. asst. surgeon, July 1, 1880; maj. surgeon, June 6, 1894; lt. col. deputy surgeon gen., Aug. 8, 1903; col. Med. Corps, Apr. 23, 1908; surgeon gen. U.S.A., Jan. 14, 1909—. Republican. Catholic. Died Dec. 27, 1913.

TORRANCE, David, jurist; b. Scotland, Mar. 3, 1840; s. Walter and Annie T.; ed. Norwich, Conn.; married. Admitted to bar, New Haven, Conn., 1868; served in Union army during Civil war, June 1862 to Oct. 1865. Asso. justice Supreme Court of Errors, Conn., 1890 to 1901; chief justice, 1901—. Died 1906.

TORRANCE, Francis J., mfr.; b. Allegheny City, Pa., June 27, 1859; s. Francis and Jane (Waddell) T.; ed. Western U. of Pa.; m. Marrie R. Dibert, Nov. 6, 1884. Began, 1875, as clk. Standard Mfg. Co., of which father was pres.; became 1st v.p. its successor, the Standard Sanitary Mfg. Co., mfrs. plumbing supplies. Del. Rep. Nat. Conv., 1892, del.-at-large, 1900; commr. of pub. charities, State of Pa., 1894—; active worker for many yrs. in prison reform and philanthropy. Trustee Bucknell U., Western Pa. Classical and Scientific Inst. Baptist. Home: Pittsburgh, Pa. Died Jan. 8, 1919.

TORRENS, William Erskine, export mcht.; b. New York, N.Y., July 15, 1870; s. William D. and Isabella Gordon (Erskine) T.; ed. New York city schs., 1876-82; then under tutors, 1882-84; studied mfg. economy in various mills in N.E., and Pa., 1884; studied mill finance and mfg. methods at Phila., 1885; also edited dept. on above subjects in various trade papers. Principal Torrens-van Daell Co., export commn. mchts., and partner foreign dept., C. H. Tenney & Co. Apptd. 1896, foreign commr. to S. America for the Nat. Assn. of Mfrs. of U.S.; spl. foreign commr., same, 1897-99; visited every country in the world, studying possibilities of introduction of Am. manufactured goods. Secured concessions from Venezuelan, Argentine, Brazilian, Cape Colony, Chinese, Japanese govts. for the establishment of sample warehouses in the interests of the Nat. Assn. of Mfrs., U.S.A. Author: Commercial Traveling in South America, 1897; Commercial Traveling in South Africa, 1898; Commercial Traveling in the East, 1899, all published by Nat. Assn. of Mfrs. of U.S.A., Phila.; also series of articles in American Trade, and other trade jours. on the trade possibilities in various foreign countries. Pres., treas. importing and exporting concern of Wm. E. Torrens & Co., New York. Homes: N.Y. City and Bayshore, L.I., N.Y. Died June 20, 1914.

TORREY, Bradford, author; b. Weymouth, Mass., Oct. 9, 1843; s. Samuel and Sophronia (Dyer) T.; ed. pub. schs.; unmarried. Author: Birds in the Bush, 1885; A Rambler's Lease, 1889; The Foot-Path Way, 1892; A Florida Sketch-Book, 1894; Spring Notes from Tennessee, 1896; A World of Green Hills, 1898; Every-Day Birds, 1900; Footing It in Franconia, 1900; The Clerk of the Woods, 1903; Nature's Invitations, 1904; Friends on the Shelf, 1906. Editor: Thoreau's Journal. An editor, Youth's Companion, 1886-1901. Home: Santa Barbara, Calif. Died Oct. 7, 1912.

TORREY, Elbridge, business man; b. Weymouth, Mass., Sept. 17, 1837; s. Joseph and Harriet (Wade) T.; grad. Bridgewater (Mass.) State Normal School; studied and traveled in Europe; m. Alice White Shaw, Oct. 14, 1862. Entered mercantile business, 1862; became mem. firm of Fowle, Torrey & Co., importers of carpets, 1869, succeeded by Torrey, Bright & Capen, 1875; pres. Torrey, Bright & Capen Co., 1895-1909; retired 1909. Corporate mem. A.B.C.F.M., 1876— (mem. prudential com. 17 yrs.); mem. of delegation of 3 that visited chs. and missionary stations in Turkey; elected trustee Bradford Acad., 1880, Hartford Theol. Sem., 1889 (pres. bd.), Mt. Holyoke Coll., 1899; pres. bd. trustees Central Turkey Coll., Cullis' Consumptives' Home; v.p. Congl. Ch. Bldg. Soc.; trustee Mt. Pleasant Home; dir. Mass. Soc. for Prevention of Cruelty to Animals; mem. council Home for Aged Couples. Home: Dorchester, Mass. Died Jan. 2, 1914.

TORREY, Herbert Gray, U.S. assayer; b. New York, N.Y., 1841; s. Prof. John and Eliza (Shaw) T.; B.A., Coll. City of New York, 1860; m. M. Louise Snow, 1868. U.S. assayer, 1860—, first as asst. to his father, and after death of latter in 1873, as assayer-in-chief; also chemist, govt. expert in textile fabrics, and examiner of mines. Presbyn. Home: Stirling, N.J. Died Aug. 29, 1915.

TORREY, Raymond Hezekiah, conservationist; b. Georgetown, Mass., July 15, 1880; s. Grafton Francis and Leonora Margaret (Warren) T.; grad. high sch., Georgetown, 1898; m. Elizabeth R. Bastible, Apr. 18, 1909; children—Raymond Francis, Leonora Warren (Mrs. George Millet). Reporter Georgetown Advocate, 1896-99, Springfield (Mass.) Union, 1899-1903; reporter, re-write man, copy reader, night mgr., N.Y. City News Assn., 1903-11; with N.Y. American, 1911-13 and 1916-19, N.Y. Tribune, 1913-16, N.Y. Evening Post (editor rotogravure sect.), 1919-24; sec. N.Y. State Council of Parks, 1924; field sec. Nat. Conf. on State Parks, 1925-27; sec. Am. Scenic and Hist. Preservation Soc., 1927—; sec. Assn. for Protection of Adirondacks, 1929—. Mem. bd. mgrs. N.Y. Bot. Garden. Chmn. field com. Torrey Bot. Club, 1927—. Republican. Protestant. Author: New York Walk Book (with Frank Place and R. L. Dickinson), 1923; New York Walk Book (with same), 1934; State Parks and Recreational Uses of State Forests in U.S., 1926. Conducted "Long Brown Path" column, N.Y. Post, 1919. Editor: Guide to the Appalachian Trail from the Housatonic River to the Susquehanna River, 1934. Contbr. numerous articles on bot. subjects. Locates roadside markers for Hist. Preservation Soc., coöperating with State Education Dept.; directed trail-making as chmn. N.Y.-N.J. Trail Conf. Home: Hollis, L.I., N.Y. Deceased.

TORREY, Reuben Archer, evangelist; b. Hoboken, N.J., Jan. 28, 1856; s. Reuben Slayton and Elizabeth A. (Swift) T.; A.B., Yale, 1875, B.D., 1878; student Leipzig and Erlangen, 1882-83; m. Clara B. Smith, Oct. 22, 1879; children—Edith Clare, Mrs. Blanche Wiggs, Reuben Archer, Elizabeth (dec.), Mrs. Margaret Parker (dec.). Ordained Congl. ministry, 1878; was for some yrs. supt. city missions in Minneapolis; became associated with the work of the late Dwight L. Moody, and was supt. of the Moody Bible Inst., 1889-1908. On tour 1902-03 visited and preached in England, Scotland, Ireland, Germany, France, Australia, New Zealand, Tasmania, China, Japan, nd India; returned to Britain, 1903-05, holding meetings in prin. English and Scotch cities, including 5 mos. in Royal Albert Hall, London; held meetings in leading Canadian and American cities, 1906-11; revisited England, Scotland and Ireland, 1911, Japan and China, 1919, China and Korea, 1921. Dean Bible Institute, Los Angeles, 1912-24, and pastor Church of the Open Door, Los Angeles, 1915-24; held meetings in many states, 1924-28; special lecturer at Moody Bible Inst., Chicago, 1927—. Author: How to Work for Christ, 1901; How to Promote and Conduct a Successful Revival; Real Salvation and Whole Hearted Service, 1905; Lessons in the Life and Teachings of Our Lord, 1907; The Person and Work of the Holy Spirit, 1910; The Voice of God in the Present Hour, 1917; The Fundamental Doctrines of the Christian Faith, 1919; The Real Christ, 1920; The Importance and Value of Proper Bible Study, 1921; The Gospel for Today, 1922; Is the Bible the Inerrant Word of God?, 1922; The God of the Bible, 1923; How to Be Saved and How to Be Lost, 1923; The Christ of the Bible, 1923; Soul Winning Sermons, 1924; The Power of Prayer and Prayer of Power, 1924; How to Get the Gold Out of the Word of God, 1925; Lectures on First Epistle of John, 1928; many other publications. Works have been translated into numerous languages. Died Oct. 26, 1928.

TORREYSON, Burr Walter, coll. pres.; b. Hillsboro, Va., Dec. 10, 1855; s. James William and Sarah Ann (Stone) T.; ed. Nat. Normal Sch., Lebanon, O., and summer study various state instns.; LL.D., U. of Ark.; m. Alice Bulgin, June 30, 1898; 1 dau., Elizabeth. Teacher common schs., Va. and Mo. until 1888; prin. high sch., Mexico, Mo., 1888-93, Ft. Smith, Ark., 1893-1903; supt. schs., Ft.

Smith, 1903-05, Little Rock, 1905-09; prof. edn., U. of Ark., 1909-17; pres. Ark. State Teachers' Coll., Conway, 1917-31, pres. emeritus. Democrat. Presbyn. Elk. Rotarian. Home: Conway, Ark. Died May 29, 1932.

TORRISON, Oscar M., judge; b. Manitowoc, Wis. Aug. 29, 1861; s. Osuld and Martha (Findal) T., grad. high sch., Manitowoc, 1878; A.B., Luther Coll. Decorah, Ia., 1881; LL.B., State U. of Ia., 1882; LL.B., Columbia, 1884; m. Ida Michelson, Feb. 27. 1889; children—Margaret, Osuld, Helen. Practiced at Elbow Lake, Minn., 1886-90, and was pres. of the village 3 terms; removed to Chicago, 1890, and practiced until 1906; judge Municipal Court of Chicago, 1906-14; judge Circuit Court, 1915-27; in gen. practice of law. Presided at trials of South Water St. Condemnation and Improvement (costing $22,000,000); Michigan Av. Trust Co. receivership; City of Chicago vs. Peoples Gas Co. ($10,000,000 Gas Case). Republican. Mem. Bd. of Edn., Chicago, 1896-97. Served several years as dir. Chicago Bd. of Charities and pres. of its northwest dist. Lutheran. Home: Evanston, Ill. Died June 10, 1931.

TOTTEN, Charles Adiel Lewis, inventor, author; b. New London, Conn., Feb. 3, 1851; s. Gen. James and Julia H. (Thatcher) T.; grad. Trinity Coll., Hartford, 1869, A.M., 1885; grad. West Point, 1873; m. Eda, d. Maj. Lewis Smith, U.S.A.; m. 2d, Mary, d. Matthew Bunker, of Garden City, L.I. Commissioned 2d lt., 4th Arty., 1873; 1st lt., Nov. 1, 1874; prof. mil. science and tactics Mass. Agrl. Coll., 1875-78; afterward served in west, including Bannock War, 1878, and Chiricahua campaign; prof. mil. science and tactics, Cathedral Sch., St. Paul, N.Y., 1883-86, and at Yale, 1889-92; resigned to devote attention to Biblical investigations. Publisher of Our Race (devoted to his theories of the Second Advent, and the identity of the Anglo-Saxon race with the ten lost tribes of Israel). Inventor and patentee of "Strategos" (military game), and other inventions. Author: Important Questions in Metrology, 1887; Strategos, 1881; Lost Israel Found in the Anglo-Saxons, 1890; Joshua's Long Day and the Dial of Ahaz, 1891; The Kings Daughters, 1891; The Coming Crusade, 1897; some 300 books and brochures; all published by Our Race Pub. Co., New Haven. Home: Milford, Conn. Died 1908.

TOTTEN, George Oakley, Jr., architect; b. New York; s. George Oakley and Mary Elizabeth (Styles) T.; Newark Tech. Sch.; Ph.B., Columbia, 1891, A.M., 1892, McKim traveling fellowship, 1893; pupil, Atelier Daumet-Esquie, Paris, 1893-95, École des Arts Decoratif, Paris; m. Mrs. Vichen von Post, sculptor, of Stockholm, Sweden, Aug. 22, 1921; children—George Oakley, Gilbert von Post. Served as chief designer in Office of Supervising Architect, Washington, D.C., 1895-97; began practice independently, 1898; architect of pub. bldgs., legation bldgs., many large pvt. city and country houses, Washington and elsewhere; architect Waterbury, Conn., post office; designing architect Newark post office and court house. U.S. del. Internat. Congress of Architects, Brussels, 1897, Paris, 1900, Spain, 1904, London, 1906, Vienna, 1908, Rome, 1911, Budapest, 1931; served as sec. and v.p. of said congresses. Mem. A.I.A., Archæol. Inst. America, Maya Soc. Maj. of engrs., World War. Author: Maya Architecture. Home: Washington, D.C. Died Feb. 1, 1939.

TOULMIN, Harry Theophilus, judge; b. Mobile County, Ala., Mar. 4, 1838; s. Theophilus Lindsay and Amante E. (Juzan) T.; student U. of Ala., and U. of Va.; m. Mary Montague Henshaw, May 4, 1869. Pvt. to col. C.S.A., 1861-65. Presdl. elector, 1868; mem. Ala. Assembly, 1870-72; judge 6th Jud. Circuit, 1874-82; U.S. district judge, Southern Dist. of Ala., 1886—. Democrat. Died Nov. 12, 1916.

TOUMEY, James William, forester; b. Lawrence, Mich., Apr. 17, 1865; s. Dennis and Mary (Buckley) T.; B.S., Mich. Agrl. Coll., 1889, M.S., 1895; spl. student, Harvard, 1893; hon. M.A., Yale U., 1907; hon. Sc.D., Syracuse, 1920; hon. F.D., Michigan State Coll., 1927; m. Constantia Hayes Blake, June 17, 1897; 1 son, James William; m. 2d, Nannie Byrne Trowbridge, Sept. 1908. Asst., dept. botany, Mich. Agrl. Coll., 1890-91; prof. biology, U. of Ariz., 1891-98; dir. Ariz. Agrl. Expt. Sta., 1897-98; supt. of tree planting, Div. of Forestry, U.S. Dept. of Agr., 1898-1900; asst. prof. forestry, 1900-03, prof. forestry, 1903-09, prof. silviculture, 1909, dean Sch. Forestry, 1910-22, prof. silviculture, 1922—, Yale. Author: Seeding and Planting in the Practice of Forestry; Foundations of Silviculture upon an Ecological Basis; bulls. and articles on bot. and forestry subjects. Home: New Haven, Conn. Died May 6, 1932.

TOURGÉE, Albion Winegar, jurist, author, U.S. consul gen. Halifax, N.S.; b. Williamsfield, O., May 2, 1838; grad. Rochester U., 1862; A.M., LL.D.; Ph.D., U. of Copenhagen, 1883; admitted to Ohio bar, 1864; m. Emma L. Kilbourne, May 14, 1863. Officer Union army; twice wounded, 6 months prisoner of war, Libby prison. Lived in N.C. 1865-81; mem. N.C. constitutional convs., 1868, 1874; judge superior court, 1868-75; N.C. mem. commn. for code revision; U.S. consul to Bordeaux, 1897-1903; became consul gen., Halifax, N.S., July 1903. Editor The

Continent, literary weekly, 1881-84; contbr. to newspapers and mags.; lecturer. Author: (novels) A Royal Gentleman, Figs and Thistles, A Fool's Errand, Bricks Without Straw, Hot Plowshares, Black Ice, Button's Inn, With Gauge and Swallow, Pactolus Prime, Murvale Eastman, John Eax, The Hip-Roof House, A Son of Old Harry, Out of the Sunset Sea, The Man Who Outlived Himself, The Story of a Thousand (historical), An Outing with the Queen of Hearts, An Appeal to Cæsar, Letters to a King (essays), War of the Standards (finance), The Code with Notes, N.C.; Digest of Cited Cases, N.C. Wrote: The Twentieth Century Peacemaker, Contemporary Rev., London, June 1899. Home: Mayville, N.Y. Died 1905.

TOURSCHER, Francis Edward, prof. Latin; b. Dushore, Pa., May 10, 1870; ed. Villanova Coll.; S.T.D., by examination, in Dublin, Ireland, 1908. With Villanova (Pa.) Coll., 1898—, prof. Latin, 1898-1903, prof. evidences of religion and ch. history, 1906-21, prof. patristic Latin, 1921—, trustee, 1905—, librarian, 1925—, sec., 1924—. Mem. Order of St. Augustine, Am. Cath. Hist. Soc. (mem. bd. mgrs.; chmn. com. on hist. research). Author: The Hogan Schism of 1820-29, 1930. Translator and editor numerous works of St. Augustine, including, De Beata Vita, 1922, De Immortalitate Animae, 1922, De Magistro, 1924, De Quanitate Animae, 1924; War and Peace in St. Augustine's De Civitate Dei (pamphlet), 1934; De Immortalitate Animae—De Beata Vita and De Libero Arbitrio, 1937; also translated and edited Diary of Rt. Rev. Francis Patrick Kenrick, 1916, The Kenrick-Frenaye Correspondence, 1920, Old St. Augustine's In Philadelphia, with some Records of the Austin Friars in U.S.A., 1937. Died Jan. 30, 1939.

TOURTELLOTTE, Edward Everett, coll. pres.; b. Stillwater, Okla., Dec. 26, 1893; s. Lee and Mary Anna (Reed) T.; B.S., M.S., Okla. Agrl. and Mech. Coll., 1914; M.S., Ph.D., Okla. Sch. of Mines and Metallurgy, 1926; m. Beatrice Roll, Apr. 4, 1920; children—Dorothy Marie, Betty Louise, Mary Anna, Edward Everett, Richard Lee, James Roll. Instr. science, high sch., Plymouth, Wis., 1914-16, Denison, Ia., 1916-17; head dept. of agr., Central State Teachers' Coll., Okla., 1919-21; state inspector of high schs., Okla., 1921-24; pres. Eastern Okla. Coll., 1924—. Home: Wilburton, Okla. Deceased.

TOUSEY, William George, coll. prof.; b. Portage, N.Y., Sept. 22, 1842; s. George and Laura (Utter) T.; A.B., Tufts Coll., 1869, A.M., 1871, S.T.B. 1871 (S.T.D., 1900); m. Katherine Hall, Nov. 23, 1874; children—Coleman, Ruth, Maud. Prof. logic and ethics, Tufts Coll., Mass., 1871—. Author of treatise, Human Destiny, as Conditioned by Free Will; and miscellaneous papers. Pres. trustees Pub. Library, Somerville, Mass. Served in U.S. Navy in Civil War, on barque Roebuck, gunboat Huntsville, and frigate St. Lawrence. Deceased.

TOUTON, Frank Charles, educator; b. Ft. Atkinson, Wis., July 25, 1880; s. Lou and Kathryn (Zimmerman) T.; Ph.B., Lawrence Coll., Appleton, Wis., 1901; A.M., Columbia U., 1917, Ph.D., 1919; m. Edith Cammack, Apr. 3, 1912; children—Harriette Louise, Mary Frances. Principal of State Graded School, Wisconsin, 1901-02; instr. in high sch. mathematics, Galesburg, Ill., 1902-04, and Central High Sch., Kansas City, Mo., 1904-11; prin. Central High Sch. and Jr. College, St. Joseph, Mo., 1911-16; research scholar, 1917-18, research fellow, 1918-19, Teachers' Coll., Columbia U.; state high sch. supervisor in Wis., 1919-21; lecturer in edn., U. of Calif., 1921-22; prof. sch. adminstrn., Ohio State U., summer 1919; lecturer U. of Calif., summers 1921-23, Cornell Univ., summer 1927; with U. of Southern Calif., Los Angeles, 1922—, vice pres., dir. of educational program of Univ., dean Coll. of Letters, Arts and Sciences, and prof. psychol. and ednl. research. Formerly vice chmn. Ednl. Commn., Calif. Taxpayers' Assn. Officier de l'Instruction publique de France, 1935. Democrat. Methodist. Author: Solving Geometric Originals, also of an annotated bibliography, "Professional Literature in Secondary Schools." Co-author of Hawkes, Luby and Touton's First and Second courses in algebra, with three revisions, plane and solid geometries, with revisions; also co-author of Miner, Elwell and Touton's Business Arithmetic and Essentials of Business Arithmetic, Touton and Struthers' Junior High School Procedure and von KleinSmid and Touton's Effective Study Procedures. Died June 1, 1936.

TOWER, Charlemagne, diplomat; b. Phila, Apr. 17, 1848; s. Charlemagne and Amelia (Bartle) T.; A.B., Harvard, 1872; studied in Europe, 1872-76; LL.D., Lafayette, 1894, Glasgow, 1901, U. of Chicago, 1904, St. Andrew's, Scotland, 1906, Hamilton, 1909; m. Helen, d. G. Frank Smith, of Oakland, Calif., Feb. 8, 1888. Admitted to bar, 1878; practiced at Phila., 1878-82; lived at Duluth, Minn., 1882-87; pres. Duluth & Iron Range R.R., and mng. dir. Minn. Iron Co.; returned to Phila., 1887; has large interests; officer and dir. in several corps. E.E. and M.P. to Austria-Hungary, 1897-99; ambassador extraordinary and plenipotentiary to Russia, 1899-1902, to Germany, 1902-08. Republican. Grand Officer Legion of Honor, France; Grand Cordon

Order St. Alexander Newski, Russia. Trustee U. of Pa., 1894-99, Hamilton Coll., Colgate U.; mem. Bd. of City Trusts, Phila. Pres. Hist. Soc. of Pa., 1917. Author: The Marquis de La Fayette in the American Revolution (2 vols.), 1895; Essays Political and Historical, 1914. Died Feb. 24, 1923.

TOWER, George Edward, naval officer; b. Ashtabula, O., Apr. 11, 1836; s. Reuben and Clarissa W. (Sheffer) T.; ed. Ashtabula Acad.; m. Phebe Wetherex, Mar. 5, 1863 (died 1895); m. 2d, Jennie MacIntire, Oct. 19, 1897. Began as engr. on Lake Erie, 1856; apptd. 3d asst. engr. U.S.N., Jan. 1862; promoted 2d asst. engr., Oct. 1, 1863; 1st asst. engr., Jan. 1868; comd. chief engr., June 1887; retired, Feb. 1897. Was in N. and S. Atlantic squadrons during Civil War; prin. engagements, at Yorktown and West Point, Va.; with Admiral Farragut at Battle of Mobile Bay and bombardment of Ft. Morgan, and with Admiral Porter in both attacks on Ft. Fisher; served in Spanish-Am. War, May 11-Dec. 22, 1898. Republican. Presbyterian. Died June 9, 1914.

TOWER, George Warren, Jr., geologist; b. Cambridge, Mass., Oct. 27, 1871; s. George W. and Abby A.T.; A.B., Harvard, 1894, A.M., 1895; m. Clara Burchard, Jan. 5, 1898; children—William Burchard, George Warren, Elizabeth A., Jessica C. U.S. geologist 4 yrs.; wrote reports on mining dists. of Butte, Mont., Tintic, Utah, Rico, Colo., and Black Hills, S.D.; geologist and consulting engr.; consulting mining engring. Staff of Guggenheim Bros., 1918-37; gen. consultation work in mining and geology, 1937-38. Home: Denver, Colo. Died Sept. 13, 1939.

TOWER, Ralph Winfred, curator; b. Amherst, Mass., May 24, 1870; s. Francis Emory and Ella Sophia(Shepardson) T.; student Colby U., 1888-90; Brown U. 1890-93, and 1894-95, A.B., 1892, A.M., 1893, Ph.D., 1903; student U. of Leipzig, 1893-94, med. dept. Harvard U. (John Ware Memorial Fellowship), 1900-01; m. Bessie Belle West, 1893. Demonstrator of anatomy, 1894-95, instr. chem. physiology, 1895-98, asst. prof., 1898-1901, asso. prof., 1901-03, Brown U. Curator of physiology, 1903-12. Curator anatomy and physiology, 1912-21, curator comparative physiology, 1921—, Am. Museum Natural History, Librarian, 1904—, recording secretary and editor, 1917—, New York Acad. of Sciences; also librarian N.Y. Micros. Soc. and Linnæan Soc. of N.Y.; asst. Biol. Lab., U.S. Fish Commn., Woods Hole, Mass., 1898-1903; expert spl. agent U.S. Census of Fisheries, 1908. Pres. trustees Rochelle Public Library. Fellow A.A.A.S., New York Academy of Sciences; corr. mem. Sociedad Cubana de Historia Natural. Author: Laboratory Guide to the Dissection of the Cat (with Frederic Poole Gorham), 1895; Laboratory Course in Chemical Physiology, 1897; also numerous scientific papers. Hon. curator Natural History Libraries, Columbia U., 1913—. Home: Rochelle Park, New Rochelle, N.Y. Died Jan. 26, 1926.

TOWERS, Walter Kellogg, editor, author; b. Chicago, Ill., Aug. 8, 1888; s. Josiah M. and Clara Belle (Kellogg) T.; grad. Lewis Inst., Chicago, 1905; A.B., U. of Mich., 1910, J.D., 1912; m. Berenice L. Jones, Oct. 15, 1912; children—Whitney Kellogg, Jacqueline. Business staff, The Engineer, Chicago, 1905, athletic editor, 1910-11, editor, 1911-12, University of Michigan Daily, Ann Arbor; asst. editor, 1912-15, mng. editor, 1915-17, The American Boy; editor Milestones, Detroit, 1917-18; publicity dir. A.E.F., Y.M.C.A., Paris, 1918-19; sales promotion and export mgr. Reo Motor Car Co., Lansing, Mich., 1919-21; advertising mgr. Paige-Detroit Motor Car Co., Detroit, Mich., 1921-27. Prog. Republican. Methodist. Author: Letters from Brother Bill, Varsity Sub, 1915; Masters of Space, 1916; From Beacon Fire to Radio, 1925. Home: Detroit, Mich. Died Feb. 17, 1931.

TOWN, David Edward, newspaper mgr.; b. Cleveland, O., Mar. 3, 1871; s. David and Eleanor (Madden) T.; ed. pub. schs. and business coll., Springfield, Ohio; m. Camma Hood, Oct. 16, 1902; children—Eleanor Frances, Camma Edda. Began in newspaper business, Chicago, 1900; apptd. business mgr. Chicago Evening Post, 1903; gen. mgr., 1914-21, of Shaffer group of newspapers, including Chicago Evening Post, Rocky Mountain News, Denver Times, Louisville Herald, Indianapolis Star, Muncie Star, Terre Haute Star; dir. Associated Press, 1915-22; pres. Watab Paper Co., 1920—; mem. exec. com. Hearst Corps., 1924—. Home: New York, N.Y. Died May 27, 1933.

TOWNE, Charles Arnette, senator; b. Oakland County, Mich., Nov. 21, 1858; s. Charles Judson and Laura Anne (Fargo) T.; ed. common schs. and U. of Mich.; m. Maude Irene Wiley, Apr. 20, 1887. Admitted to bar in Mich., 1886; removed to Duluth, Minn., 1890; mem. Congress, 1895-97; notable as orator and advocate of bimetallism; left Rep. Nat. Conv., 1896, because of gold-standard plank; Nat. chmn. Silver Rep. Party, 1897-1901; voted for by Minn. Legislature, 1899, as Fusion candidate for U.S. senator; nominated for Vice President by Nat. Conv. People's Party Sioux Falls, S. Dak., 1900, and by Silver Rep. Nat. Conv., Kansas City, 1900; declined both nominations. Apptd. by Gov. Lind, Dec. 5, 1900, as U.S. senator to fill vacancy until action by Legislature, and served two months. Elected to Congress from 14th N.Y. Dist. as a Democrat, 1904; mem. law firm of Towne & Spellman. Home: New York, N.Y. Died Oct. 22, 1928.

TOWNE, Edward Owings, writer, playwright; b. Pella, Ia., Feb. 19, 1859; s. Rev. Edward Owings and Mary Virginia (Shull) T.; ed. Ia. Central U.; m. Sara Johnston Cooper, 1887 (died 1935); 1 son, Fennimore Cooper (dec.). Admitted to bar, 1888; practiced at Chicago, 10 yrs. mainly as a trial lawyer; became widely known in the Eugene V. Debs conspiracy case, and others; became a writer and playwright, and produced his own comedy "Other People's Money," etc.; removed to New York, 1902; pres. New Era Book Corp.; dir. and atty. Studdabud Creations, Inc., Eldorado Press, Inc. Lecturer and recitalist. Author of several brochures, plays. Home: Glenwood-on-Hudson, Yonkers, N.Y. Deceased.

TOWNE, Henry Robinson, manufacturer, engr.; b. Phila., Aug. 28, 1844; s. John Henry and Maria (Tevis) T.; student U. of Pa., 1861-62; hon. A.M., 1887; m. Cora E. White, 1868 (died 1917). Began active career in 1862, as draughtsman, Port Richmond Iron Works, owned by the firm of I. P. Morris, Towne & Co., for nearly 2 yrs., and in 1863 was put in charge of Govt. work in the shops for repairs of gunboat Massachusetts; in 1864-66 was in charge of erecting engines in monitors Monadnock and Agamenticus and similar work, until war closed. After war became spl. student of engring. with Robert Briggs, and took spl. course in physics at the Sorbonne, Paris; afterward connected with shops of William Sellers & Co., Phila. Became associated, in summer 1868, with Linus Yale in mfr. of locks and after Mr. Yale's death, Dec. 1868, became pres. Yale & Towne Mfg. Co., Stamford, Conn., until 1915; later chmn. bd.; chmn. bd. Morris Plan Co. N.Y. Life mem. Am. Soc. M.E. (v.p. 1884-86, pres. 1888-89); pres. Merchants' Assn. of New York, 1908-13. Author: Towne on Cranes, 1883; Locks and Builders' Hardware, 1905. Home: New York, N.Y. Died Oct. 15, 1924.

TOWNE, Salem B., clergyman; b. Paoli, Ind., Aug. 19, 1847; s. Rufus R. (M.D.) and Frances A. (Kirkwood) T.; A.B., Ind. Asbury (now DePauw) U., 1866, A.M., 1869; M.D., Chicago Med. Coll. (now Northwestern U. Med. Sch.), 1868; M.D., Bellevue Hosp. Med. Coll. (New York U.), 1871; S.T.D., DePauw, 1891; m. Laura Tevis Lockwood, June 21, 1871; children—Elinor K., Mary R., Elizabeth P., Salem L., Lockwood J., Laura F. Instr. mathematics, Hamline U., Minn., 1868; phys. and druggist, Frankfort, Ind., 1871-74; entered ministry M.E. Ch., Northwest Ind. Conf., 1875; pastor in Ind., at Argos, 1875, Dayton and Rossville, 1876-79, South Bend, 1880-82, Crawfordsville, 1883-84, Terre Haute, 1885-89, Greencastle, 1890-93, South Bend, 1894-96; presiding elder, Greencastle Dist., 1897-1903; asst. to pres. and financial sec. and treas. DePauw U., 1904-29, treas. emeritus, 1920—. Mem. Gen. Conf. M.E. Ch., 1892, 1900. Home: Greencastle, Ind. Died Dec. 5, 1933.

TOWNE, Walter James, ry. official; b. Leavenworth, Kan., Nov. 28, 1867; s. Isaac N. and Katherine (O'Brien) T.; C.E., Rensselaer Poly. Inst., Troy, N.Y., 1895; m. Ethel White, Jan. 1902. Rodman, instrumentman and asst. engr., A.,T.&S.F. Ry., 1886-91; asst. engr. on N.Y. State Canal, 1896-99; asst. engr. at Boone, Ia., 1899-1900, at Kaukauna, Wis., 1900-01, at Escanaba, Mich., 1901-02, div. engr. at Baraboo, Wis., 1902-04, at Chicago, 1904-06, engr. maintenance of way, 1906-12, gen. supt., 1912-14, asst. gen. mgr., 1914-20, chief engr., 1920—, C.&N.W. Ry. Republican. Home: Oak Park, Ill. Died Nov. 23, 1930.

TOWNER, Daniel Brink, composer; b. Rome, Pa., Mar. 5, 1850; s. John Griffin and Julia (Forbes) T.; ed. Rome (Pa.) Acad.; studied music with his father, and later under George F. Root, at the National Normal Inst.; studied voice under John Howard, F. W. Root and others; Bachelor of Music, Harriman Univ., 1898; m. Mary E. McGonigle, Dec. 26, 1870. Began as music teacher and chorus leader at Binghamton, N.Y., 1873; went to Cincinnati, 1882; joined Dwight L. Moody as soloist and musical dir., 1884; organized music course, 1893, and dir. same, Moody Bible Inst. of Chicago, 1893—; also music dir. Moody Ch. Editor (music books): Tone Temple, 1882; Temperance Evangel, 1883; Model Singer, 1883; Sons of Free Grace, 1883; Hymns New and Old, 1886 (revised, 1889); Towner's Male Chorus, 1893; Treble Clef Choir, 1894; One Hundred Hymns for Male Voices, 1898; Gospel Pilot Hymnal, 1899; Hymns of Faith and Praise, 1901; Gospel Hymn Book, 1903; Revival Hymns, 1905; Songs of Praise, 1906; Famous Hymns, 1907; Ideal Song and Hymn Book, 1909; Gospel Songs, 1910; Hymns Tried and True, 1911; Song for Men, 1912; The Voice of Thanksgiving, 1913; World Wide Sacred Praises, 1914; Select Revival Hymns, 1915; Tabernacle Hymns, 1916; Towners Male Quartettes, 1918. Home: Chicago, Ill. Died Oct. 13, 1919.

TOWNER, Horace Mann, lawyer; b. Belvidere, Ill., Oct. 23, 1855; s. John Loop and Keziah (Brownell) T.; student U. of Chicago, Union Coll. of Law, Chicago; LL.B., State U. of Ia.; m. Harriet Elizabeth Cole, Oct. 26, 1887; children—Leta E., Horace Cole, Constance M. Admitted to bar, 1877; practiced law, Corning, until 1890; judge 3d Jud. Dist., Ia., 1890-1910; mem. 62d to 67th Congresses (1911-23), 8th Ia., Dist.; reëlected to 68th Congress (1923-25), and after serving 1 month on the new term resigned to become gov. of Puerto Rico, 1923, continuing until 1929; resumed practice of law at Corning, also engaged in lit. work. Republican (chmn. state conv., del. to nat. convs.). Lecturer on constl. law, State U. of Ia. Home: Corning, Ia. Died Nov. 23, 1937.

TOWNES, John Charles, lawyer; b. Tuscumbia, Ala., Jan. 30, 1852; s. Eggleston D. and Martha Cousins (Betts) T.; student Baylor U., Tex., 1867-69; LL.D., 1898; m. Kate R. Wildbahn, Dec. 28, 1871. Admitted to bar, 1873; practiced at Austin, Tex., 1873-77; removed to San Saba County, 1877; judge 33d Jud. Dist. of Tex., 1882-85; resigned and resumed practice at Georgetown, Tex.; judge 26th Jud. Dist., Mar.-Aug. 1888; resigned and entered practice at Austin with S. R. Fisher, 1888; prof. law U. of Tex. Democrat. Baptist. Author: Townes' Texas Pleading, 1901; Studies in American Elementary Law, 1903; General Principles of the Law of Torts, 1907; Civil Government in the United States and in Texas, 1908; Law Books and How to Use Them, 1909; Pleading in the District and County Courts of Texas, 1913. Home: Austin, Tex. Died Dec. 18, 1923.

TOWNLEY, Calvert, electrical engr.; b. Cincinnati, Oct. 18, 1864; s. John Ackerman and Carrie A. (Calvert) T.; Ph.B., Sheffield Scientific Sch., 1886, M.E., 1888; m. Edith W. Case, Sept. 18, 1889; children—Clifford Calvert, Donald Case; m. 2d, Mabel McCormaick Steele, Dec. 30, 1911. Connected with Westinghouse Electric & Mfg. Co., 1887-1904 and 1911—; was v.p. of about 30 utility corps. controlled by N.Y.,N.H.&H. R.R. Co., 1904-11, also consulting elec. engr. for electrification out of New York; asst. to pres. Westinghouse Elec. & Mfg. Co. until 1932, retired. Fellow Am. Inst. E.E. (past pres.). Republican. Conglist. Home: New York, N.Y. Deceased.

TOWNSEND, Charles Elroy, senator; b. Concord, Mich., Aug. 15, 1856; s. James W. and Eunice S. (Parmeter) T.; grad. Jackson High Sch., 1877; U. of Mich., 1877-78; m. Rena Paddock, Sept. 1, 1880 (died 1920); m. 2d, Nannette B. Loomis, Mar. 16, 1921. Admitted to the bar, 1895, and practiced at Jackson, Mich. Register of deeds, Jackson County, 1886-97; del. to Rep. Nat. Conv., 1888; mem. Rep. State Central Com., 1898-1902; mem. 58th to 61st Congresses (1903-11), 2d Mich. Dist.; reëlected to 62d Congress; nominated in primary election, Sept. 7, 1910, and elected by Legislature, Jan. 18, 1911, U.S. senator, terms 1911-17, 1917-23; mem. Internat. Joint Commn., Mar. 1923—. Home: Jackson, Mich. Died Aug. 3, 1924.

TOWNSEND, Charles Orrin, pathologist; b. Washtenaw County, Mich., Jan. 16, 1863; s. Orrin Russell and Phebe Ellen (DeMill) T.; grad. Mich. State Normal Sch., 1884; B.S., U. of Mich., 1888, M.S., 1891; Ph.D., U. of Leipzig, 1897, specializing in botany and plant physiology; m. Mary Louise Taylor, Mich., Feb. 3, 1891; 1 dau., Martha Ellenor. Prof. natural science, St. John's Coll., Annapolis, Md., 1888-91, Wesleyan Coll., Macon, Ga., 1891-95; instr. botany, Barnard Coll., New York, 1897-98; prof. botany Md. Agrl. Coll. and state plant pathologist for Md., 1898-1901; in charge of sugar beet investigations, 1901-09, sugar plant investigations, 1909-10, collaborator, 1910-12, U.S. Dept. of Agr.; consulting agrlist., U.S. Sugar & Land Co., Garden City, Kan., 1910-12; plant pathologist, 1912-14, pathologist in charge of sugar beet investigation, 1914-17, of sugar plant investigations, 1917-23, U.S. Dept. of Agr.; spl. expert sugar div., 1923-25, chief, 1925-34, U.S. Tariff Commn.; retired. Author of bulls. relating to diseases and production of sugar beets and other plants. Home: Woodside, L.I., N.Y. Died June 2, 1937.

TOWNSEND, Charles Wendell, ornithologist, author; b. Boston, Nov. 10, 1859; s. Thomas Davis and Frances Barnard (Smith) T.; A.B., Harvard, 1881, M.D., 1885; m. Gertrude Flint, Sept. 28, 1891 (died 1917); children—Gertrude, Margaret (Mrs. Hale Sutherland), Frances (Mrs. Wendell Taber), Charles; m. 2d, Sarah G. Flint, July 2, 1919 (died 1924). Visiting phys. Sea Shore Home, Boston, Mass., 1887-90; asst. in obstetrics, Harvard Med. Sch., 1887-97; phys. to out-patients dept. Children's Hosp., 1887-1903, Boston Lying-in Hosp., 1887-98, Mass. Gen. Hosp., 1891-1909; visiting phys., Floating Hosp., 1907-09. Author: The Birds of Essex County, Mass., 1905; Along the Labrador Coast, 1907; Birds of Labrador (joint author), 1907; A Labrador Spring, 1910; Captain Cartwright and His Labrador Journal, 1911; Sand Dunes and Salt Marshes, 1913; In Audubon's Labrador, 1918; Supplement to Birds of Essex Co., 1920; Beach Grass, 1923; From Panama to Patagonia, 1931; also chapter on birds in Grenfell's book on Labrador. Home: Ipswich, Mass. Died Apr. 3, 1934.

TOWNSEND, Curtis McDonald, army officer; b. Brooklyn, Mar. 22, 1856; s. M. L. and A. S. (McDonald) T.; A.B., Coll. City of New York, 1875; grad. U.S. Mil. Acad., 1879; 2d lt., Corps of Engineers United States Army, June 30, 1879; 1st lt., June 15, 1882; capt., Oct. 5, 1889; maj., Jan. 29, 1900; lt. col., Jan. 11, 1907; col., 1909. Has been connected with river and harbor improvements on the east shore of Lake Michigan, on the Mississippi near Rock Island; chief engr. officer Philippine div., in charge of harbor improvements, P.I.; in charge of improvement of harbors of Ohio on Lake Erie; in charge of improvement of waterways connecting the Great Lakes; comd. 12th (Ry.) Engrs., serving with 3d Brit. Army in operations around Cambrai; afterwards engr. purchasing agt. A.E.F.; organized Batn. of Cement Engrs. and operated French cement factories; pres. Miss. River Commn. and div. engr. Western Div.; retired, Feb. 15, 1920, after more than 40 yrs.' service. Awarded French Legion of Honor. Reassigned to duty, Jan. 1, 1924, in charge improvement of mouth of the Miss. River and div. engr. South Western Div., relieved, Oct. 1, 1926. Author: Hydraulic Principles Governing River and Harbor Construction. Died May 26, 1941.

TOWNSEND, Edwin Franklin, army officer; b. New York, July 14, 1833; s. Edwin and Ann Eliza T.; grad. U.S. Mil. Acad., 1854; m. Mary Jane Wadhams, Feb. 8, 1858; 2d, Katherine Claire Durant, Apr. 19, 1899. Bvtd. 2d lt. 3d U.S. Arty., July 1, 1854; commd. 2d lt., Jan. 31, 1855; resigned, Mar. 11, 1856; commd. 1st lt., 14th U.S. Inf., May 14, 1861; capt. 16th Inf., May 14, 1861; transferred to 25th Inf., Sept. 21, 1866; maj. 27th Inf., June 22, 1868; transferred to 9th Inf., Mar. 15, 1869; lt. col. 11th Inf., Mar. 20, 1879; col. 12th Inf., Oct. 13, 1886; retired at own request, Oct. 1, 1895, over 62 yrs. of age; advanced to rank of brig. gen. retired, by act of Apr. 23, 1904. Bvtd. maj., Apr. 7, 1862, for gallant and meritorious conduct in battle of Shiloh; lt. col., Mar. 13, 1865, for continued and faithful service in ordnance dept. In Civil War served in Dept. of the Cumberland, 1861-62; in Tenn. and Miss. campaigns comdg. battalion (Army of the Ohio), engaged in march to Nashville, Pittsburg Landing, battle of Shiloh, siege of Corinth, etc., and in command ordnance depot at Nashville, Tenn., 1862-65; afterward on various duties in South and on frontier until retired. Home: Washington, D.C. Died 1909.

TOWNSEND, George Alfred ("Gath"), journalist, author; b. Georgetown, Del., Jan. 30, 1841; s. Rev. Stephen and Mary (Milbourne) T.; A.B., Central High Sch., Phila., 1860; m. Dec. 1865. Entered journalism, 1860, on Phila. Inquirer; later on Phila. Press. In 1861 local agent New York Herald in Phila.; war corr. Herald, 1862; later in year went to England, wrote for English and Am. periodicals and lectured on the war; war corr. New York World, 1864-65, and, his letters being signed, made reputation as a descriptive writer; described Austro-Prussian war, 1866, for World; after 1867 for 40 yrs. wrote a daily letter of two to four columns for the Chicago Tribune, Cincinnati Enquirer and many other papers, under pen-name "Gath." Owned an estate on the battlefield of Crampton's Gap, South Mountain, Md., where a village has grown up, which he called "Gapland." Author: The Bohemians (play), 1862; Campaigns of a Non-Combatant, 1865; Life of Garibaldi, 1867; Real Life of Abraham Lincoln, 1867; The New World Compared with the Old, 1868; Poems, 1870; Lost Abroad, 1870; Washington Outside and Inside, 1871; Mormon Trials at Salt Lake, 1872; Washington Rebuilded, 1873; Tales of the Chesapeake, 1880; Bohemian Days, 1881; Poetical Addresses, 1883; The Entailed Hat, 1884; President Cromwell (drama), 1885, Katy of Catoctin, 1886; Life of Levi P. Morton, 1888; Tales of Gapland; Mrs. Reynolds and Hamilton, 1887; Columbus in Love, 1892; Poems of Men and Events, 1900. Home: "Gapland," Md. Died Apr. 15, 1914.

TOWNSEND, George Washington, publisher, author; b. West Chester, Pa., Feb. 1, 1839; s. Solomon and Hester A. (Huston) T.; ed. public and classical schools, Phila.; admitted to Phila. bar, 1874; unmarried. Merchant, 1856-69; lawyer, 1874; real estate mgr.; champion badge winner as wing shot; mem. Am. Soc. Am. Authors. Claimed to have solved the problem "how to educate," as author of the "Wherewithal Method," and made an argument before congressional com. in its favor. Author: Wherewithal, or New Discoveries in Cause and Effect; Fifteen Minutes' Sunday Work; Jacob's Ladder. Home: Philadelphia, Pa. Died 1905.

TOWNSEND, Henry C., gen. passenger and ticket agt. Mo. Pacific Ry.; b. Pittsburgh, Pa., Aug. 11, 1849. Entered ry. service, 1863, and was clerk, auditor's office, Bellefontaine R.R., 1863-64; clerk, freight office, Phila., Wilmington & Baltimore R.R., 1864-65; advertising clerk, gen. passenger dept., Pa. R.R., 1865-71; gen. passenger and ticket agt., Toledo, Peoria & Warsaw Ry., 1871-77; same, Wabash Ry., Toledo; same, Wabash, St. Louis & Pacific

Ry., St. Louis, 1879-83; gen. passenger agt. Mo. Pacific Ry. lines and Wabash, St. Louis & Pacific Ry., 1883-84; same Mo. Pacific Ry., 1884—. Pres. Am. Assn. Gen. Passenger and Ticket Agts. Deceased.

TOWNSEND, Horace, author; b. Claughton, Cheshire, Eng., Feb. 3, 1859; s. Jackson and Pauline (Yaniewicz) T.; ed. Birkenhead Sch., Eng.; studied architecture under Charles Barry, pres. Royal Inst. Brit. Architects; came to U.S., 1880; m. Mary Ella Worth, July 16, 1883. Mem. staff New York Tribune, 1882-90; London corr. New York Herald and Phila. Ledger, 1890-1900; devoted to lit., 1890—, and regarded as an authority on works of art. Author: A Little Girl in Grey, 1898; A Handful of Silver, 1902; Old Wedgwood, 1907; Old English Potteries and Porcelains, 1914; (plays) Myles Aroon (joint author); Mavourneen (joint author), prod. by W. Scanlan and Chauncey Olcott, 1887-88; Child of Naples, prod. by Alexander Salvini, 1889. Editor: Some Letters of R. L. Stevenson, 1902. Home: New York, N.Y. Died May 9, 1922.

TOWNSEND, Hosea, jurist; b. Greenwich, O., June 16, 1840; enlisted as pvt. in 2d Ohio cav., 1861; promoted to 2d lt.; resigned, 1863, on account of disability; admitted to the bar at Cleveland, O.; practiced law, Memphis, Tenn.; elected to Tenn. State legislature, 1869; removed to Colorado, 1879; elected to 51st and 52d Congresses; apptd. judge U.S. Court for the Southern dist. of Ind. Ty., 1897; reapptd. 1902, 1906. Home: Ardmore, Okla. Died 1909.

TOWNSEND, James Bliss, editor; b. New York, Sept. 30, 1855; s. Dwight and Emily (Hodges) T.; A.B., Princeton, 1878, A.M., 1883 (on thesis "Art Progress in America"); m. Eugénie Gibert, Mar. 1, 1886. Began journalism as Princeton Coll. corr. New York Tribune, 1875; mem. city staff New York Tribune, 1878; editor Art Interchange, 1879; art editor New York World, 1881-87; mgr. and sec. Press News Assn. and writer on art topics, 1887-95; art critic New York Times, 1894-1900; art writer and on editorial staff New York Herald, 1902-07. Founder, 1904, owner and editor American Art News (weekly jour.). Dir. S.I. Beach Land Improvement Co. Sec. 25th assembly dist. Rep. organization, 1888-92; Rep. candidate for Congress, 13th N.Y. Dist., 1896; N.Y. commr. Charleston Expn., 1901-02; art dir. Charleston Expn., 1901-02. Episcopalian. Republican; stumped N.Y. State in campaigns of 1892, 1896. Traveling representative in Europe, American Embassy Assn., 1909. Exec. mem. Am. Rights and Anti-Disloyalty leagues. Author: Random Fancies, Sonnets and Translations, 1901. Home: New York, N.Y. Died Mar. 10, 1921.

TOWNSEND, James Mulford, retired; b. Jan. 20, 1825; s. Hon. William Kneeland and Eliza Ann (Mulford) T.; was 3 yrs. clerk in New York importing house, 5 yrs. in business in New Haven; then sec. and treas. and later pres. City Savings Bank of New Haven; m. Maria Theresa Clark, 1847 (died 1884). Was pres. and dir. in banking, railroad, ins. and many other corporations; v.p. Joseph Parker & Son Co., mfrs. blotting paper; large oil interests in Pa.; was pioneer in development of petroleum in Pa.; was capt. New Haven Grays; partially equipped New Haven Grays and Townsend Rifles for service in Civil War; sec. Nat. Whig Conv., 1852, which nominated Fillmore for President; mem. Conn. senate, 1864; refused renomination; also refused nomination for lt. gov. of Conn., 1866; mem. New Haven bd. edn.; built and was pioneer pres. electric road in Conn. (New Haven to Morris Cove); was chief of staff of the "Ancient and Honorable 2d Conn. Governor's Foot Guards" (organized 1775 with Benedict Arnold as capt.). Home: New Haven, Conn. Died 1901.

TOWNSEND, James Mulford, lawyer; b. New Haven, Conn., Aug. 26, 1852; s. James Mulford and Maria Theresa (Clark) T.; A.B., Yale, 1874; LL.B., Columbia, 1876; m. Harriet Bailey Campbell, Nov. 15, 1882. In practice at New York, 1876—; sr. mem. Townsend & Button; gen. counsel DuPont Powder Co., and other corps. Lecturer on transfer of monetary securities, Yale Law Sch., 1887—. Trustee New York Law Sch. Home: New York, N.Y. Died Oct. 31, 1913.

TOWNSEND, Joseph Hendley, physician; b. New Haven, Conn., Jan. 18, 1862; s. John and Harriet E. (Sears) T.; B.A., Yale, 1885; M.D., Yale Med. Sch., 1887; m. Bertha Goodyear, Apr. 28, 1896. Mem. house staff New Haven Hosp., 18 mos., 1887-89; practiced New Haven, 1889—; mem. New Haven Bd. of Health, 1895-1900; apptd. mem. State Bd. of Health, 1901, sec. and exec. officer, 1906—. Mem. Conn. N.G., 1891—, chief surgeon State Brigade, with rank of maj. Lecturer on hygiene in Med. Dept., Yale U. Republican. Conglist. Home: New Haven, Conn. Died Jan. 7, 1916.

TOWNSEND, Julius Curtis, naval officer; b. Athens, Mo., Feb. 22, 1881; s. James William and Harriet Morrison (Curtis) T.; grad. U.S. Naval Acad., 1902; m. Martha B. Gaither, Jan. 14, 1909; children—Harriet Gaither (dec.), Martha Gaither. Commd. ensign, U.S. Navy, 1904, and advanced through the grades to rear adm., 1936; comdr. U.S. Naval Aviation Base, Aghada, Eng., World War; comdr. Cruisers Battle Force, U.S. Fleet, 1936—. Decorated Congl. medal of honor, Navy Cross. Mem. Mil. Order of the Caribou. Episcopalian. Died Dec. 28, 1939.

TOWNSEND, Luther Tracy, clergyman; b. Orono, Me., Sept. 27, 1838; s. Luther K. and Mary True (Call) T.; early life in N.H.; worked on railroad as fireman; A.B., Dartmouth, 1859, D.D., 1871; grad. Andover Theol. Sem., 1862; hon. A.M., Wesleyan, 1866; served, 1862-63, pvt. and adj. 16th N.H. Regt., 19th Army Corps.; m. Laura C. Huckins, Sept. 27, 1865. Entered M.E. ministry, 1864; prof. Hebrew, Chaldee and N.T. Greek, 1868-70, prof. hist. theology, 1872, and practical theology and sacred rhetoric, 1872-93. emeritus prof. same, 1893, Boston U. Devoted time to literature, 1893—. Filled leading Congl. pulpits in N.E. and M.E. appmts. in Northern and Middle Southern states. Del. to the Methodist Ecumenical Council, London, 1881, World's Parliament of Religions, Chicago, 1893; dean Chautauqua Sch. of Theology, 1882-85; asso. editor Bible Champion, Reading, Pa. Author: Credo, 1869; Sword and Garment, 1871; Godman, 1872; Lost Forever, 1873; Arena and Throne, 1874; Supernatural Factor in Revivals, 1877; Intermediate World, 1878; Fate of Republics, 1880; Art of Speech (2 vols.), 1880, 1881; Mosaic Record and Modern Science, 1881; Collapse of Evolution, 1905, 1922; God and the Nation, 1905; Bible Studies; Rules of Interpretation and Current Difficulties and Objections, 1913; The Stars Are Not Inhabited, 1914; God and War, 1915; Hell and Demons—Are They Myths or Realities?, 1921; Riddle of Spiritism, 1921; many other publications. Home: Brookline, Mass. Deceased.

TOWNSEND, Marion Ernest, educator; b. Hammondsport, N.Y., May 16, 1889; s. (Rev.) Colwell and Levia Jane (Davis) T.; A.B., Colgate, 1912, A.M., 1922; A.M., Columbia, 1927, Ph.D., 1932; m. Blanche Buckbee, June 26, 1912; 1 dau., Agatha. Began as teacher in rural sch., 1907; prin. pub. sch., Lyndonville, N.Y., 1912-16; supervising prin., Brocton, N.Y., 1916-18; supt. schs., Walden, N.Y., 1918-21, Boonton, N.J., 1921-23, Millville, N.J., 1923-26; asst. supt. schs., Trenton, N.J., 1926-28; asst. commr. of edn., State of N.J., 1928-29; pres. N.J. State Teachers Coll., Newark, 1929—. Pres. Interstate Conf. on Teacher Training, N.J. Council on Adult Edn.; mem. exec. com. N.J. Mental Hygiene Assn.; mem. Nat. Advisory Bd. on Mental Hygiene in Edn.; mem. many ednl. assns. Republican. Unitarian. Mason. Author: Administration of Student Personnel Services in Teacher Training Institutions, 1932. Lecturer on mental hygiene and occupations. Home: Glen Ridge, N.J. Died Dec. 21, 1939.

TOWNSEND, Martin Ingham, congressman, lawyer; b. Hancock, Mass., Feb. 6, 1810; s. Nathaniel and Cynthia T.; bred a farmer; grad. Williams Coll., 1833; A.M., 1836; LL.D., 1866; m. Louisa B. Kellogg, 1836 (died 1890). Settled in Troy, 1833; practiced law from 1836 until retired, Jan. 1901; dist. atty., Rensselaer County, 1842-45; mem. constitutional conv. for State at large, 1867-68; mem. Congress, 1875-79; U.S. Atty. northern dist. of N.Y., 1879-87; mem. State constitutional commn., 1890. Regent Univ. of State of N.Y., 1873—. Died 1903.

TOWNSEND, Mary Ashley, author; b. (Van Voorhees) N.Y., 1836; married. Author: Xariffa's Poems; Down the Bayou and Other Poems; Distaff and Spindle; The Captain's Story (a poem); The Brother Clerks. Died 1901.

TOWNSEND, Randolph W., lawyer; b. Hancock, Mass., May 4, 1812; grad. Williams, 1835; studied law in Saratoga County; practiced in New York, 1838—; m. Mrs. Jane A. Norton (née Warren), May 1886. Was mem. bd. of edn.; mem. various clubs; a mgr. Presbyn. Hosp.; trustee University Pl. Presbyn. Church. Home: New York, N.Y. Deceased.

TOWNSEND, Robert Donaldson, editor; b. Brooklyn, N.Y., Mar. 15, 1854; adopted s. of Amos and Melissa H. Townsend, of New Haven, Conn.; B.A., Yale, 1875, LL.B., 1878; m. Elizabeth Gaston, June 11, 1890. Mem. Conn. bar; engaged in reference book and editorial work in N.Y. City; mem. editorial staff The Christian Union, later The Outlook, 1885—, mng. editor, 1897-1923; dir. Outlook Co., 1926-28. Pres. Cranford (N.J.) Free Pub. Library. Home: Cranford, N.J. Died Mar. 29, 1933.

TOWNSEND, Theodore Irving, M.D.; b. Staten Island, N.Y., Nov. 20, 1869; s. Charles Higbee and Ellen Louise Payson (Wyer) T.; ed. Trinity Sch., Staten Island; Brooklyn Collegiate and Poly. Inst., 1883-85; M.D., Coll. Phys. and Surg. (Columbia), 1891; m. Katharine, d. Francis M. Burdick, of New York, Oct. 14, 1908; children—Katharine B., Charles B., Sarah Louise. Pvt. practice in New York, 1891-96; phys. J. Hood Wright Memorial Hosp., New York, 1891-92; asst. surgeon Harlem Eye, Ear, Nose and Throat Infirmary, 1893-95; examining phys., Barnard Sch., 1894-96; med. sanitary insp. New York Health Dept., 1894-96; phys. Manhattan State Hosp., Ward's Island, 1896-1900, King's Park State Hosp., 1900-02, Utica State Hosp., 1902-06; 1st asst. phys. Dannemora State Hosp., 1906-09, Bloomingdale Hosp., White Plains, N.Y., 1909-11, Binghamton State Hosp., 1911-21; sr. asst. phys. Willard State Hosp., 1921-24; neuro-psychiatrist to Binghamton City Hosp., Lourdes Hosp., Ideal Hosp. (Endicott), Susquehanna Valley Home. Republican. Presbyterian. Capt. M.C.U.S.A., Aug. 16, 1918-Apr. 25, 1919. Wrote monograph "The Ganser Symptom and Symptom-Complex." Home: Binghamton, N.Y. Died June 22, 1932.

TOWNSEND, William Hay, judge; b. Barnwell, S.C., Jan. 9, 1868; s. William Hutson and Harriet Ford (Hay) T.; ed. pvt. schs.; unmarried. Admitted to S.C. bar, 1889, and began practice at Beaufort; solicitor, 2d Circuit, S.C., 1899-1901; code commr., S.C., 1901-03; asst. atty. gen. of S.C., 1903-05; reporter, Superior Court, S.C., 1914-18; judge, Circuit Court, S.C., 1918—. Democrat. Presbyn. Home: Columbia, S.C. Died Aug. 15, 1934.

TOWNSEND, William Kneeland, U.S. circuit judge; b. New Haven, Conn., June 12, 1849; s. James M. T.; grad. Yale, 1871; (LL.B., 1874; D.C.L., 1880); m. Mary Leavenworth Trowbridge, July 1, 1874. Admitted to bar, 1874; engaged in practice in New Haven; served as corp. counsel there; judge U.S. Dist. Court, dist. of Conn., from Mar. 28, 1892; promoted, 1902, judge U.S. Circuit Court, 2d circuit. Is prof. law of contracts, Yale Univ. Author: New Connecticut Civil Officer; History of American Law of Patents, Trademarks, Copyrights and Admiralty. Home: New Haven, Conn. Died 1907.

TOWNSEND, William Warren, surgeon; b. Elizabeth, N.J., Apr. 8, 1870; s. Louis and Caroline (McKinley) T.; M.D., U. of Vt., 1893; m. Agnes L. Graves, 1894; children—Wm. Graves, Guy Ballard. Practiced at Burlington, Vt., 1896—; prof. genito-urinary diseases, U. of Vt. Coll. of Medicine; attending genito-urinary surgeon, Mary Fletcher Hosp. (Burlington), Fanny Allen Hosp. (Winooski, Vt.); cons. genito-urinary surgeon, Rutland City, and Proctor (Vt.) hosps., etc.; attending urologist Bishop De Goesbriand Hosp., Burlington, Vt. Genito-urinary consultant to Ports of Embarkation World War; lt. col. Med. O.R.C. Fellow Am. Coll. Surgeons. Republican. Episcopalian. Home: Burlington, Vt. Died Feb. 20, 1928.

TOWNSEND, Wisner Robinson, orthopedic surgeon; b. Staten Island, N.Y., Aug. 5, 1857; s. Wisner Helme and Emily (Kyle) T.; A.B., Columbia, 1877, A.M., 1880; M.D., Coll. of Phys. and Surg. (Columbia), 1880; m. Elizabeth Walker, Apr. 27, 1893. Practiced in New York, 1880—; asso. surgeon Hosp. for Ruptured and Crippled; cons. orthopedic surgeon to French Hosp. and S. R. Smith Infirmary and Hosp. Home: New York, N.Y. Died Mar. 12, 1916.

TOWNSLEY, Clarence Page, army officer; b. DeKalb, N.Y., Sept. 24, 1855; s. Hon. Elias Page and Louisa Ellen (Thompson) T.; grad. State Normal Sch., Potsdam, N.Y., 1872; C.E., Union Coll., 1876, hon. Sc.D., 1913; grad. U.S. Mil. Acad., 1881, Arty. Sch., Ft. Monroe, Va., 1884, Torpedo Sch., Willetts Point, N.Y., 1885; m. Marian Howland, Jan. 7, 1891; children—Marian Page, Helen Howland, Clarence Page. Cadet U.S. Mil. Acad. from Ia., 1877; commd. 2d lt. arty., 1881; promoted through grades to brig. gen., July 1, 1916; maj. gen., N.A., Aug. 5, 1917. Maj. and chief ordnance officer vols., 1898-99; during Spanish-American War on staff of chief of arty. and chief ordnance officer, Dept. of Havana, Cuba, on staff of Gen. Ludlow; comdt. Coast Arty. Sch., Ft. Monroe, Feb. 1909-Sept. 1911, and comdg. 2d Provisional Regt. Coast Arty. in Tex., Mar.-July 1911; supt. U.S. Mil. Acad., Aug. 31, 1912-July 1, 1916; apptd. comdr. 30th Div., N.G., Oct. 13, 1917; retired as brig. gen. U.S.A., Nov. 29, 1918. Episcopalian. Home: Washington, D.C. Died Dec. 28, 1926.

TOWSE, J(ohn) Ranken, dramatic critic; b. Streatham, Surrey, Eng.; Apr. 2, 1845; ed. Highgate Sch. and Cambridge U., Eng.; came to U.S., 1869. On staff, 1870—, dramatic critic, 1874—, New York Evening Post. Author: Sixty Years in the Theatre, 1916. Home: New York, N.Y. Died Apr. 12, 1933.

TOY, Crawford Howell, university prof.; b. Norfolk, Va., Mar. 23, 1836; s. Thomas Dallam and Amelia (Rogers) T.; A.M., U. of Va., 1856; U. of Berlin, 1866-68; (LL.D., U. of N.C., 1889, Harvard, 1904); m. Nancy, d. of Rev. R. M. Saunders, of Norfolk, Va., 1888. Prof. Hebrew, Southern Bapt. Theol. Sem., Greenville, S.C., and Louisville, Ky., 1869-79; Hancock prof. Hebrew and other Oriental langs., Harvard, 1880-1909 (emeritus); also Dexter lecturer on bibl. lit. until 1903. Author: The Religion of Israel, 1882; Quotations in the New Testament, 1884; Judaism and Christianity, 1890; Hebrew Text and English Translation of Ezekiel, 1899; Commentary on Proverbs, 1899; Introduction to the History of Religions, 1913; etc. Died May 12, 1919.

TRABUE, Edmund Francis, lawyer; b. "Wehawken," Franklin Co., Ky., Mar. 25, 1855; s. S. F. J. (lawyer) and Alice Elizabeth (Berry) T.; A.B., Ky. Eclectic Inst., Frankfort, Ky., 1874; B.L., U. of Louisville, 1875; attended Prof. John B. Minor's summer law course, U. of Virginia, 1878; m. Caroline Bullitt Cochran, Oct. 1, 1883; 1 dau., Lucinda (wife of Dr. J. Rowan Morrison). Admitted to Ky. bar, 1875, and began practice at Louisville; mem. Trabue, Doolan, Helm & Helm. Mem. commn. U.S. Circuit Court Appeals, 6th Circuit, to revise Federal Equity Rules, 1911; apptd. Oct. 1930, by U.S. Supreme Court, spl. master in equity suit between Vt. and N.H. to report findings of fact and law and recommend decree in the settlement of boundary between the states; apptd. spl. master in r.r. bankruptcy, U.S. Circuit Court, 1933. Home: Louisville, Ky. Died Mar. 3, 1936.

TRABUE, Isaac Hodgen, lawyer, orange grower; b. Russell Co., Ky., Mar. 25, 1829; s. Rev. Chasteen and Elizabeth T. (Huguenot ancestry); ed. at Western Mil. Inst., Georgetown, Ky.; grad. law dept. Transylvania Univ., Lexington, Ky., 1854; m. Virginia Taylor, 1865. Was aid to Gov. Magoffin, 1859; raised co. of Union soldiers June 1861; served in Civil war, capt. to col.; was large slave-holder—set male slaves to work in commissary dept. and women as nurses in hosps., leaving children on farm nr. Louisville. Rep. candidate for Congress 1st Ky. dist., 1872; elector State at large on Greenback (Peter Cooper) ticket, 1876, on Gen. Benj. F. Butler ticket, 1884; Greenback candidate for treas. Ky., 1877; for atty.-gen., 1879; well known amateur chess player, beating Zuckertort, then world's champion, 1883; edited the chess column in Sunday Argus, Louisville, 3 yrs. Took leading part in causing the people of Fla. to vote against removal of the capitol from Tallahassee, in 1900 election. Founded town of Trabue, now Punta Gorda, Fla. Freethinker. Socialist. Author: Hobson Blowing Up the Merrimac in Santiago Bay (drama); Black Wench (novel), 1904; Rules and Directions to Play Four-handed Trabue, American Chess, 1904. Home: Punta Gorda, Fla. Died 1907.

TRACEWELL, Robert J., comptroller of the treasury; b. Warren Co., Va., May 7, 1852; s. W. N. and L. V. T.; A.B., Hanover (Ind.) Coll., 1874, A.M., 1883 (LL.D.); m. Grace G. Bean, 1878. Admitted to ar, 1875; practiced at Corydon, 1876-94; mem. 54th Congress (1895-97), 3d Ind. Dist.; comptroller of the treasury, July 26, 1897-May 15, 1913; judge of Vanderburgh Superior Court, Dec. 1, 1918-22. Republican. Home: Evansville, Ind. Died July 29, 1922.

TRACEY, Charles, mfr.; b. Albany, N.Y., 1847; s. John and Maria (McCarthy) T.; ed. Albany Acad., afterward studied abroad; m. Hermine Duchesnay, June 14, 1883. Enlisted in Papal Zouaves and served two terms; returned to United States; is pres. and treas. Columbia Distilling Co., with distillery at Waterloo, N.Y. Was a.d.c. of Gov. Tilden, 1875; apptd. by Gov. Robinson, commissary gen., 1877, and by Govs. Cleveland, Hill, Flower and Morton mgr. State House of Refuge; mem. Congress, 1887-95. One of the leading Dem. opponents of free silver; active in Gold Democratic movement; chmn. Nat. Com. (Gold) Dem. party, 1900—. Home: Albany, N.Y. Died 1905.

TRACEY, James Francis, lawyer; b. Albany, N.Y., May 30, 1854; s. John and Maria (McCarthy) T.; A.B., Georgetown U., 1874 (LL.D., 1910); LL.B., Albany Law Sch., 1875; m. Lucianne Bossé, of Quebec, Can., May 10, 1893. Practiced at Albany, 1875—; mem. Tracey Cooper & Savage. Lecturer on law of corps., Albany Law Sch., 1890-1905; apptd. asso. justice Supreme Ct. of P.I., July 1, 1905; resigned Feb. 1, 1909. Name sent by President Roosevelt to U.S. Senate, Jan. 1908, as Philippine commr. and sec. finance and justice, but appointment declined. Independent Democrat. Regent Georgetown U. Home: Albany, N.Y. Died Sept. 19, 1925.

TRACY, Benjamin Franklin, secretary of the navy; b. Owego, N.Y., Apr. 26, 1830; s. Benjamin T.; ed. Owego Acad.; m. Delinda E. Catlin, 1851. Admitted to bar, 1851; dist. atty. Tioga Co., 1853-59; one of organizers of Rep. party in N.Y.; mem. N.Y. Assembly, 1862. In July and Aug. 1862, raised 109th and 137th N.Y. Vols.; was made col. 109th, Aug. 28, 1862; col. 127th U.S. C.T., Sept. 10, 1864; comdr. mil. post at Elmira, N.Y., 1864-65; received Congressional Medal of Honor, June 21, 1895, "for gallantry in battle of the Wilderness"; bvtd. brig. gen., Mar. 14, 1865, "for gallant and meritorious services during the war"; hon. disch. June 13, 1865. U.S. dist. atty. Eastern Dist. N.Y., 1866-73; judge N.Y. Ct. of Appeals, 1881-82; sec. of the navy in cabinet of President Harrison, 1889-93; resumed law practice in New York, 1893; pres. of commn. which drafted new charter for Greater New York; defeated as Rep. candidate for mayor of Greater New York, 1897. Home: New York, N.Y. Died Aug. 6, 1915.

TRACY, Charles Chapin, educator; b. E. Smithfield, Pa., Oct. 31, 1838; s. Orramel and Cynthia (Kellogg) T.; A.B., Williams, 1864 (D.D., 1894); grad. Union Theol. Sem., 1867; m. Myra A. Park, Aug. 14, 1867. Ordained Presbyn. ministry, 1867; missionary of A.B.C.F.M., Marsovan, Turkey, 1868—; pres. Anatolia Coll., Marsovan, 1886-1913. Author: Letters to Families, 1872 (pub. by Am. Bd. Commrs. Foreign Missions, Constantinople); Myra; or, a Child's Story of Missionary life, 1876; Talks on the Verandah, in a Faraway Land, 1893; Notes on Hebrews. Died Apr. 19, 1917.

TRACY, Clarissa Tucker, instr. botany and mathematics Ripon Coll., 1859—; b. Jackson, Pa., Nov. 12, 1818; d. Stephen and Lucy (Harris) Tucker; ed. common schools, and Troy Female Sem.; taught schools near her birthplace until 1839; at Honesdale, Pa., 1839-44; m. Horace Tracy, 1844 (died 1848). Resumed teaching at Honesdale, and later at Neenah, Wis.; took position in Brockway (now Ripon) Coll., Wis., 1859. Author: Manual of the Flora of Ripon and Vicinity. Home: Ripon, Wis. Died 1905.

TRACY, Evarts, architect; b. New York, May 23, 1868; s. J. Evarts and Martha Sherman (Green) T.; B.A., Yale, 1890; École des Beaux Arts, Paris, France, 1892-94; m. Caroline Fredericka Streuli, June 1894. With McKim, Mead & White, architects, New York, 1890-95; practiced alone, 1895-1901; mem. Tracy & Swartwout, 1901—. Architect Yale Club bldg., New York; Minneapolis Club bldg.; Denver Cathedral; U.S. Post Office and Court House, Denver; Nat. Met. Bank bldg., National Armory, Washington, D.C., Mo. State Capitol, etc. Major Engrs. R.C. U.S.A., in charge of camouflage work in France, 1917; camouflage officer 1st Army; in 3 maj. engagements, twice cited; duty 2 mos. coast defenses, Panama Canal Zone. Author tech. mil. manuals of instrn. camouflage for U.S.A.; returned to civil life, Aug. 1919. Died Feb. 2, 1922.

TRACY, Frank Basil, editor; b. Brighton, Ia., Oct. 18, 1866; s. Basil and Martha Ann (Fleak) T.; A.B., U. of Ia., 1888; m. Wegia Hope Hall, May 18, 1891. In newspaper business in Ia., Omaha and N.D., 1888-97; on staff of Boston Transcript, Mar. 1897—, editor-in-chief, Oct. 24, 1910—. Episcopalian. Republican. Editor: Hon. Charles Denby's "China and Her People," 1905. Author: The Tercentenary History of Canada (3 vols.), 1908. Home: Wollaston, Mass. Died 1912.

TRACY, Frank W., pres. 1st Nat. Bank of Springfield, Ill., 1879—; b. at Baltimore, Md., July 21, 1833; grad. Baltimore City Coll., 1852; m. Miss S. E. Jones, Oct. 23, 1855. Became teller 1st Nat. Bank, Springfield, Ill., 1863; passed through all grades to pres., 1879; pres. Ohio and Mississippi R.R. from 1892 until it was consolidated with the Baltimore & Ohio system; mem. and has been v.p. and pres. Ill. State Bankers' Assn. One of founders Am. Bankers' Assn. Several terms mem. of exec. council, and now chmn. of its com. on uniform laws. Home: Springfield, Ill. Died 1903.

TRACY, James Madison, musician, composer; b. Bath, N.H., Jan. 27, 1837; s. Luther and Mary Clough Roe (Dimond) T.; ed. high sch., Concord, N.H.; studied music with Carl Hauser, L. H. Southard, of Boston, at Leipzig Conservatory, 1858-60, and pupil of Liszt, at Weimar, 1860-61; hon. A.M., Dartmouth, 1871; m. Cateau Stegeman, pianist. Teacher of piano, theory and harmony, Boston Music Sch. and Boston Conservatory, 1868-84; successively with Livingston Park Sem., Mrs. Eaton's Select Sch. for Girls, Miss Tracy's Boarding Sch. for Young Ladies (Rochester, N.Y.), Highland Park Normal College (Des Moines), Des Moines Conservatory of Music, etc.; founder, 1900, and dir. Liszt Sch. of Music, Denver, Colo. Author: Three Years of Student Life in Germany, 1872; James M. Tracy's Theory and Rudimental Harmony, 1878; also (musical novels) Manton Lee, 1890; George Monroe, 1894. Compiler: Boston Conservatory Method; Student's Modern Method; Technical Concert Studies; Art of Technical Perfection. Editor of various piano works. Specializes in coaching for concert stage. Home: Denver, Colo. Died Sept. 3, 1928.

TRACY, Roger Sherman, M.D.; b. Windsor, Vt., Dec. 9, 1841; s. Ebenezer Carter and Martha S. (Evarts) T.; A.B., Yale, 1862; M.D., Coll. Phys. and Surg. (Columbia), 1868; interne Bellevue Hosp., New York, 1867-69; studied Berlin, Germany, 1869-70. Sanitary insp., chief sanitary insp., deputy register and registrar of records, New York Health Dept., 1870-1901. Author: Handbook of Sanitary Information for Householders, 1884; Outlines of Anatomy, 1889; Essentials of Anatomy, Physiology and Hygiene, 1889; The White Man's Burden (under pseudonym T. Shirby Hodge), 1915. Home: Ballardvale, Mass. Died Mar. 6, 1926.

TRACY, Samuel Mills, botanist; b. Hartford, Vt., Apr. 30, 1847; s. Samuel and Emeline (Newton) T.; B.S., Mich. State Agrl. Coll., 1868, M.S., 1871; spl. work in botany, Harvard, 1885; m. Martha A. Terry, July 23, 1874 (died 1904). Prof. botany and horticulture, U. of Mo., 1877-87; dir. Miss. Agrl. Expt. Sta., 1887-97; special agent, 1897-1914 and agronomist, 1914—. U.S. Dept. Agriculture. Pvt. Co. A, 41st Regt. Wis. Vols., Civil War. Episcopalian. Pres. State Hort. Soc. of Mo., 1886; pres. Soc. for Promotion Agrl. Science, 1910-11. Author: Flora of Missouri, 1886; Flora of the Southern United States, 1899. Home: Laurel, Miss. Died Sept. 5, 1920.

TRACY, William W., horticulturist; b. Hudson, O., May 21, 1845; B.S., Mich. State Agrl. Coll., East Lansing, Mich., 1867, M.S., 1870 (hon. Sc.D., 1907). Prof. horticulture, Mich. State Agrl. Coll., 1870-72; supt. testing gardens, U.S. Dept. Agr., 1902—. Home: Washington, D.C. Died Mar. 1, 1932.

TRAEGER, William Isham, congressman; b. Porterville, Calif., Feb. 26, 1880; s. Augustus and Martha Ellen (Dunn) T.; student Stanford U., 1899-1902, U. of Southern Calif., 1911-13; m. Alice Collier, 1902; 1 dau., Laura (Mrs. Horace Martin); m. 2d, Ruth Lorraine McAllister, Apr. 8, 1912; 1 dau., Frances. Dep. U.S. marshal, Southern Dist. Calif., 1903-06; dep. sheriff Los Angeles County, 1907-10, sheriff, 1921-32; dep. clk. Calif. State Supreme Court, 1911-21; mem. 73d Congress (1933-35), 15th Calif. Dist. Corpl. U.S.A., Spanish-Am. War, 1898; pvt. U.S.A., World War. Republican. Mason, Elk, Moose, Eagle, I.O.O.F. Home: Los Angeles, Calif. Died Jan. 21, 1935.

TRAFTON, Mark, retired clergyman-author; b. Bangor, Me., Aug. 1, 1810; ed. in school there and in Kent's Hill Academy, Me.; m. Eliza Young, June 29, 1835 (died 1882). Became prominent Methodist clergyman of New England; also temperance and anti-slavery advocate. Had churches in Boston and suburbs; Providence, R.I.; Springfield, Mass.; New Bedford, Mass., and Albany, N.Y. Member Congress, 1855-57, from Mass.; delegate to Peace Congress, Frankfort, Germany, 1850. Author: Safe Investment; Baptism: Its Subjects and Mode; Rambles in Europe; Scenes in My Life; The Birch Canoe (poem); etc. Home: Somerville, Mass. Died 1901.

TRAFTON, William Henry, statistician; b. Brooklyn, Aug. 7, 1857; s. William H. and Catherine Elizabeth (Miller) T.; ed. Mil. Acad., Jamaica, N.Y., and pvt. tutor; m. Kiersted, Jan. 22, 1881. Statistician and corr., 1876—; has been commercial editor New York Produce Exchange Reporter; also of The World, Commercial, Mail and Express, and Evening Post (New York). Home: New York, N.Y. Died Nov. 15, 1926.

TRAIN, Charles J., officer U.S.N.; b. in Mass.; apptd. to navy from Mass., Nov. 26, 1861; Naval Acad., 1861-64; promoted master, Dec. 1, 1866; lt., Mar. 12, 1868; lt. comdr., June 30, 1869; comdr., Jan. 1886; capt., Nov. 22, 1898; served on many stas. and duties; was naval officer of Atlanta Expn., 1894-96; comd. U.S.S. Prairie, auxiliary cruiser in N. Atlantic patrol squadron, March to Nov. 1898; was comdr. Puritan; later Massachusetts; pres. Bd. of Inspection and Survey, 1901-04; promoted rear admiral, Sept. 12, 1904, and served on Asiatic Station. Died 1906.

TRAIN, Ethel Kissam, author; b. New York, Dec. 29, 1875; d. Benjamin P. and Lucy Hartwell (Warren) Kissam; m. Arthur Train, Apr. 20, 1897. Author: Son, 1911; Bringing Out Barbara, 1917. Home: New York, N.Y. Died May 15, 1923.

TRAIN, George Francis, author; b. in Boston, Mar. 24, 1829; s. Oliver and Maria (Pickering) T.; orphaned, New Orleans, 1833, father, mother and three sisters dying of yellow fever; went North alone, at 4, to grandmother at Waltham, Mass.; attended village sch.; successively farmer boy, grocer boy, shipping clerk, partner at 20; established branch firm in Liverpool, 1850; m. Wilhelmina Wilkinson, d. Col. G. T. M. Davis, Oct. 5, 1851 (died 1879). Established Train & Co., shipping agts., Melbourne, Australia, 1853; started 1st clippers to Calif. (1849). Promoted bldg. Atlantic and Great Western R.R., 400 miles (1858); 1st st. rys. in Europe (1860-62), Asia and Australia; Union Pacific Ry. (1864-69); built Train Villa, Newport, 1868; made independent race for President U.S., 1872; organized the French Commune at Marseilles, Oct. 1870; lived "Mills Palace," 1898—. Made 4 trips around world, last 3 in 80, 67½ and 60 days (holding record). Author: An American Merchant in Europe, Asia and Australia; Young America Abroad, 1857; Young America in Wall Street, 1858; Spread-Eagleism, 1858; Downfall of England, 1862; Irish Independence, 1861; Championship of Women, 1867; My Life in Many States and in Foreign Lands, 1902. Died 1904.

TRAMMELL, Leander Newton, member, Oct. 15, 1881—, and chmn., 1888—, R.R. commn. of Ga.; b. Nacoochee Valley, Ga., June 5, 1830; brought up on farm; ed. country school; attended law school, Lebanon, Tenn.; admitted to bar; m. Zenobia J. Barclay, Apr. 2, 1856. Represented Catoosa Co. in legislature, 1861-63; capt. quartermaster, Confederate army; member Ga. constl. conv., 1867, 1868 and 1877; State senator and pres. senate; pres. State Dem. conv., 1881; chairman State Democratic exec. com., 1881-82; elector on Tilden ticket, 1876. Home: Marietta, Ga. Died 1900.

TRAMMELL, Park, senator; b. Macon Co., Ala., Apr. 9, 1876; s. John W. and Ida E. (Park) T.; parents moved to Fla. in his infancy; ed. pub. schs. of Polk Co., Fla., to 15; studied law, Vanderbilt U., and LL.B., Cumberland U., Lebanon, Tenn., 1899; m. Virginia Darby, Nov. 21, 1900 (died 1922). Began as clk. in store, Tampa, Fla., later bookkeeper; admitted to Fla. bar, 1899; practiced, Lakeland and Tampa. Mayor of Lakeland, 1900, 02; mem Fla. Ho. of Rep., 1903-04, State Senate, 7th Dist. 1905-09; atty. gen. of Fla., 1909-13; gov. of Fla., 1913-17;

U.S. senator for 3 terms, 1917-35. Democrat. Baptist. Home: Lakeland, Fla. Died May 8, 1936.

TRAPHAGEN, Frank Weiss, chemist, metallurgist; b. Eaton, O., July 20, 1861; s. Henry Laurens and Martha M. (Weiss) T.; Ph.B., Sch. of Mines (Columbia), 1882, Ph.D., 1883; m. Hattie M. Van Horn, Apr. 25, 1883; children—Gertrude Lucienne (Mrs. Floyd M. Belleau), Elizabeth Lynde (Mrs. Robert P. Shollenberger). Instr. chemistry and physics, Staunton (Va.) Mil. Acad., 1884; prof. chemistry, Coll. of Mont. and Mont. Sch. of Mines, Deer Lodge, Mont., 1887-93; assayer and metallurgist, Champion Mining Co., 1888-92; in charge of Mont. Mining Exhibit, Chicago Expn., 1893; prof. chemistry, Mont. State Coll., and chemist Mont. Expt. Sta., Bozeman Mont., 1893-1903; prof. metallurgy and assaying, Colo. Sch. of Mines, 1903-16; pres. and gen. mgr. Colo. Metal Mining & Reduction Co., Georgetown 1916-17; prof. metallurgy, S.D. Sch. of Mines, Rapid City, 1917-21; metallurgist and mgr. White Hills Mining Co., 1922-24; research chemist Standard Metal & Chemical Corp., Denver, Colo., 1925, mgr. and tech. director, 1926-28; vice-pres. Sewage Treatment Corp. of Chicago. First pres. Western Assn. Tech. Chemists and Metallurgists. Cons. metallurgist, 1927—. Home: Loudonville, N.Y. Died Jan. 21, 1941.

TRASK, John Ellingwood Donnell, art inst. dir.; b. Brooklyn, N.Y., Feb. 18, 1871; s. Gustavus D. S. and Ella Frances (Donnell) T.; grad. St. Austin's Sch., New Brighton, S.I., N.Y., 1888; m. Alice Nicholson Coates, May 29, 1900. Newspaper and mag. work, 1888-96; asst. mgr., 1896-1905, mgr. and sec., 1905-12, Pa. Acad. Fine Arts; U.S. commr. gen. Exposicion Internacional de Arte del Centenario, Buenos Aires, 1910, and Exposicion Internacional de Bellas Artes, Santiago, Chile, 1910; chief Dept. of Fine Arts, San Francisco Expn., 1915; dir. of Fine Arts, San Diego Expn., 1916; dir. Milwaukee (Wis.) Art Institute, 1924—. Died Apr. 16, 1926.

TRASK, Kate Nichols ("Katrina Trask"), author; b. Brooklyn; d. George L. and Christina (Cole) Nichols; m. Spencer Trask, Nov. 12, 1874 (died 1909). Author: Under King Constantine, 5th edit.; Sonnets and Lyrics, 1894, 1903; John Leighton, Jr., 1898; Lessons in Love, 1900; Free, Not Bound, 1903; Night and Morning, 1906; Mors et Victoria, 1906; King Alfred's Jewell, 1908, 3d edit., 1909 (last two pub. anonymously); In the Vanguard (drama), 1913; The Mighty and the Lowly, 1915; Without the Walls, 1919. Home: Saratoga Springs, N.Y. Died Jan. 8, 1922.

TRASK, Spencer, banker; b. New York, Sept. 18, 1844; grad. Princeton, 1866 (A.M.); m. Kate Nichols, Nov. 12, 1874. On graduation entered Wall St. banking business; interested in Edison electric enterprises from earliest days as pres. and dir., etc.; dir. several railroads which are more or less controlled by him and his firm, and also in different financial instns. Trustee Teachers Coll., Gen. Theol. Sem. Author: Bowling Green, 1898. Homes: Saratoga, N.Y., and Tuxedo, N.Y. Died 1909.

TRASK, William Blake, hist. writer; b. Dorchester, Mass., Nov. 25, 1812; ed. common schools; apprenticed at cabinet making; (A.M., Dartmouth Coll., 1888); m. Rebecca, d. Richard and Mary Clap, of Dorchester, Nov. 25, 1844. Mem. Dorchester Antiquarian and Hist. Soc., and of New England Historic Geneal. Soc.—was its historiographer, 1861-68; corr. mem. of similar assns. in U.S. Editor, compiler and asst. in hist., geneal. and biog. writings. Home: Dorchester, Mass. Died 1906.

TRAUBEL, Horace, author; b. Camden, N.J., Dec. 19, 1858; s. Maurice and Katharine (Grunder) T.; ed. pub. schs., Camden; m. Anne Montgomerie, May 28, 1891. Literary executor Walt Whitman (with Thomas B. Harned). Editor of The Conservator, Phila.; editor of The Dollar or the Man, a compilation of cartoons of Homer Davenport, 1900. Founder The Contemporary Club, Phila., 1886; sec. Walt Whitman Fellowship (internat.). Author: Chants Communal, 1905; With Walt Whitman in Camden—a Diary, Vol. I, 1905, Vol. II, 1908, Vol. III, 1914; Optimos (poems), 1910; Collects, 1914. Home: Camden, N.J. Died Sept. 7, 1919.

TRAUTWINE, John Cresson, Jr., engineer; b. Philadelphia, Mar. 17, 1850; s. John Cresson and Eliza (Ritter) T.; ed. pvt. schs., Phila., 1855-65; studied civ. engring. with father; m. Lucy L. Smith, May 23, 1872. Chief Bur. of Water, Phila., 1895-99. Advocated waste-restriction by use of water-meters and purification by means of filters. Life mem. Franklin Inst., Phila.; mem. and past pres. Engrs. Club, Philadelphia. Editor and propr. from 1888 of father's Civil Engineer's Pocket Book, 1872. Home: Philadelphia, Pa. Died July 4, 1924.

TRAWICK, Henry, clergyman; b. Marvyn, Ala., Oct. 13, 1868; s. Moses Taylor and Annie (Buchanan) T.; A.B., Southern U., Greensboro, Ala., 1891; theol. studies, Vanderbilt U., Nashville; m. Ethel Mae Philips, Apr. 12, 1894. Ordained M.E. Ch., S., ministry, 1888; pastor, Marianna, Fla., 1893-94, Demopolis, Ala., 1895-96, Greenville, Ala., 1897-98, Marion, Ala., 1899-1900, Tuskegee, Ala., 1901-02, Troy, Ala., 1903; editor Ala. Christian Advocate, 1904-05; pastor Perry St. Ch., Montgomery, Ala., 1906, Greensboro, Ala., 1907-08; presiding elder Montgomery Dist., 1909; pastor Court St. Ch., Montgomery, 1910-11; agt. Superannuate Homes, 1912-13. Mem. Gen. Bd. Ch. Extension M.E. Ch., S. Mason. Author: Modern Revivalism, 1898. Home: Opelika, Ala. Died Dec. 14, 1913.

TRAYLOR, Melvin Alvah, banker; b. Breeding, Ky., Oct. 21, 1878; s. James Milton and Kitty Frances (Harvey) T.; educated public schools, Adair County, Kentucky; studied law nights; m. Dorothy Arnold Yerby, June 8, 1906; children—Nancy, Frances, Melvin Alvah. Went to Texas, 1898; admitted to Texas bar, 1901; city clk., Hillsboro, 1901; asst. county atty., Hill Co., Tex., 1904-05; cashier bank of Malone, Tex., 1905-08; became cashier Citizens Nat. Bank of Ballinger, Tex., 1907, later v.p., and when that bank and First Nat. Bank consolidated, was elected pres. First Nat. Bank; v.p. Stock Yards Nat. Bank, East St. Louis, Ill., 1911-14; v.p. Live Stock Exchange Nat. Bank, Chicago, 1914, pres., 1916; also pres. Chicago Cattle Loan Co., 1914-19; pres. First Trust & Savings Bank (now First-Union Trust & Savings Bank), Chicago, Jan. 1, 1919—; v.p. First Nat. Bank, Chicago, Jan. 1, 1919, pres. Jan. 13, 1925—. Mem. com. for organization of International Bank, 1929—. Pres. Shedd Aquarium Soc. (Chicago). Trustee Northwestern U., Newberry Library, Berea (Ky.) Coll. Pres. U.S. Golf Assn., 1928. Democrat. Mason. Home: Chicago, Ill. Died Feb. 14, 1934.

TREANOR, John, corp. official; b. Fall River Mills, Calif., July 31, 1883; s. James Henry and Mary (Harrington) T.; ed. pub. schs.; m. Catherine Elizabeth Coghill, Nov. 26, 1907; children—Thomas Coghill, John Stanly, Mary Elnore. Stenographer, 1898-1900; salesman various cos., 1900-08; sales mgr. Riverside Cement Co., 1908-12, v.p. and gen. mgr., 1912-28, pres., 1928—; pres. San Diego Co. Water Co., San Diego Water Supply Co., Carneros Ranch and Vineyard Co. Served on various commns. promoting water and park development, 1920—. Trustee Pomona Coll., Claremont Colleges, Southwest Museum. Republican. Home: Los Angeles, Calif. Died Oct. 20, 1936.

TREANOR, Walter Emanuel, judge; b. Loogootee, Ind., Nov. 17, 1883; s. James Donnelly and Gertrude (Sommers) T.; A.B., Indiana Univ., 1912, LL.B., 1922, J.D., 1923, LL.D., 1939; S.J.D., Harvard Univ., 1927; m. Elma Frank, Apr. 16, 1906 (died 1914); m. 2d, Aline Elizabeth Jean, Dec. 9, 1916; 1 dau., Rosemary. Began as pub. sch. teacher, 1902; teacher Latin and history, Petersburg (Ind.) High Sch., 1903-11, prin., 1912-15; supt. Petersburg pub. schs., 1915-17; prof. of law Indiana U. Law Sch., 1922-30; judge Ind. Supreme Court, term 1930-36; became judge U.S. Circuit Court of Appeals, 7th Dist. Served as 2d lt. U.S.A., World War. Democrat. Home: Bloomington, Ind. Died Apr. 27, 1941.

TREAT, Charles Gould, army officer; b. Me., Dec. 30, 1859; grad. U.S. Mil. Acad., 1882, Arty. Sch., 1888; Army War Coll., 1911; married; children—Joseph B., Margaret, Katherine, Godfrey Macdonald (stepson). Commd. 2d lt. 5th Arty., June 13, 1882; 1st lt., Apr. 15, 1889; capt. a.a.g. vols., May 12, 1898; maj. vols., Jan. 10, 1899; hon. discharged vols., May 12, 1899; capt. 7th Arty., Mar. 2, 1899; promoted through grades to brig. gen., Oct. 18, 1916; maj. gen., Aug. 5, 1917. Sr. instr. F.A., U.S.M.A., 1900-01, comdt. cadets same, 1901-05. Apptd. comdr. Camp Sheridan, Montgomery, Ala., Aug. 1917; assigned to Western Dept., San Francisco, Calif., Apr. 1918. Chief of Am. Mil. Mission to Italy, June 1918-May 1919; comdg. Base Sect. 8, and A.E.F. in Italy; Camp Sherman, O., 1919; assigned to duty, Philippine Islands, 1920; retired, Apr. 27, 1922. Died Oct. 11, 1941.

TREAT, Charles Henry, treasurer of the U.S.; b. Frankfort, Me., July 15, 1841; s. Henry and Abigail (Treat) T.; student E. Me. Conf. Sem., Bucksport, Me., Bates Coll., Lewiston, Me.; B.S., Dartmouth, 1865; m. Frances Emily Huxford. On leaving coll. entered father's firm, which owned 28 vessels, and was engaged in export and import trade with W. I. and S. A.; stumped states of Me., N.J. and N.Y., 1876, for Hayes and Wheeler; removed to Del., 1877, and engaged in mfg. bus. Del.-at-large Rep. Nat. Conv., 1888, and solidified delegation for Benjamin Harrison for President; seconded nomination of Levi P. Morton for Vice President in same conv.; nominated for Congress; conducted Rep. campaign in Del., 1888, resulting in Rep. majority in Legislature for first time in history of state and election of first Rep. senator from Del.; was leading candidate for U.S. senator, but defeated by 2 votes; afterward removed to New York; from 1892 active in the local politics of New York and has taken prominent part in the polit. work of the Rep. Club of City of New York. Collector of Internal Revenue for 2d (Wall St.) Dist. of N.Y., 1897-1905; treas. of U.S., 1905-09. Shortly after war with Spain, in association with New York capitalists, organized Manila Navigation Co., of which is pres.; also pres. Fentress Coal & Coke Co., Knoxville Power Co., Am. Petroleum & Separating Co. Trustee Grant Monument Assn. of New York. Episcopalian. Republican. Home: East Orange, N.J. Died 1910.

TREAT, Charles Payson, ry. contractor; b. Tallmadge, O., Feb. 17, 1847; s. Garry and Mary (Woodruff) T.; A.B., Oberlin Coll., 1870; m. Sara Hale Wellington, Jan. 1, 1883. Railroad builder, 1879—; built about 1,500 miles of ry. in various parts of U.S. and Canada. Was one of the promoters of Nicaragua Canal; began its actual constrn., and built ry. across the swamps at Greytown, Nicaragua, in 1890; resided Paris, London, and Leipzig, 1894-1902. Pvt. in Co. B, 46th Ia. Vol. Inf., 1864. Home: Palo Alto, Calif. Died Jan. 27, 1926.

TREAT, John Harvey, historiographer; b. Pittsfield, N.H., July 23, 1839; s. James Augustus and Dorothy Wentworth (Harvey) T.; grad. Harvard, 1862 (A.M.). Entered business with father at Lawrence; but retired in 1892. Presented, 1888, large entomol. collection and large and valuable library to Harvard. In June, 1900, gave portion of Count Riant Library to Harvard, and, 1901, gave fund to purchase all books illustrating history of the Roman catacombs. In 1888 presented to the New England Historic Geneal. Soc. a collection of ancient Greek, Roman and Hebrew coins. In 1902 erected large brass in Parish Ch. at Pitminster, Somerset, Eng., in memory of Hon. Richard Treat, the emigrant, and of his son, Robert Treat, for 30 yrs. deputy gov. and gov. colony of Conn., who were baptized there. Author: Notes on the Rubrics; The Catholic Faith; The Treat Genealogy Truro Baptisms; Ancestry of Col. John Harvey, 1907; The Catacombs of Rome; History of the Tombs of the Apostles Peter and Paul; etc. Home: Lawrence, Mass. Died 1908.

TREAT, Mary, naturalist; b. (Davis) Tompkins Co., N.Y., Sept. 7, 1830; d. of Methodist minister; ed. in common schs.; m. Dr. Joseph Treat, 1863. Author: Home Studies in Nature; Chapters on Ants; Insects Injurious to Vegetation; My Garden Pets; Through a Microscope (with Samuel Wells); also wrote on flora of N.J. for "Garden and Forest." Home: Vineland, N.J. Deceased.

TREAT, Robert Byron, merchant; b. Centreville, R.I., Feb. 11, 1868; s. Franklin and Elizabeth (Lapham) T.; grad. English and Classical High Sch., Providence, 1886; m. Mary G. Turner, June 1, 1892 (died 1922); children—Robert, Mrs. Hazel Roemer. Began in cotton mfg., 1899 (sold mill, 1903); converter of cotton cloth at Phenix, R.I., 1904-20; pres. and treas. Warwick and Coventry Water Co. Republican presdl. elector, 1900; mem. R.I. State Senate, 1901-02; pres. R.I. Commn. to La. Purchase Expn., 1903-04; mem. State Bd. of Public Roads, 1901-14 (chmn. 1913-14); chmn. Draft Registration Bd., div. 2, and mem. Dist. Appeal Bd., under Selective Service Act, 1917-19. Methodist. Pres. corp. East Greenwich (R.I.) Acad., 1895-1905. Home: Providence, R.I. Died Apr. 9, 1926.

TREDWELL, Daniel M., lawyer; b. Hempstead, L.I., July 26, 1826; s. Daniel and Susan (Ellsworth) T.; grad. Hempstead Acad.; studied law in office of Smith & Lowery, 1850, Columbia Law Sch., 1851; m. Sarah A. Eldert, 1848. Connected with office of clerk of Supreme Ct. of N.Y., 1852-94. Mem. various hist. societies. Author: Literature of the Civil War; Sketch of the Life of Apollonius of Tyana; Lace as a Fine Art; Nomads of the Sea; Reminiscences of Long Island; Legends and Traditions of Flatbush and Flatlands; Indians of Long Island; Booksellers of Old Brooklyn. Died Nov. 10, 1921.

TREE, Herbert Beerbohm, English actor; b. London, Dec. 17, 1853 (name is "Beerbohm," "Tree" being stage name); m. Maud Holt, actress. Début, 1878; mgr. Haymarket Theatre, London, 1887-96; now mgr. Her Majesty's Theatre; prominent as tragedian; has made starring tours in U.S. Author of lectures on The Imaginative Faculty, and on Hamlet from an Actor's Prompt Book; etc. Died July 2, 1917.

TREE, Lambert, diplomat, publicist; b. Washington, D.C., Nov. 29, 1832; s. Lambert and Laura M. (Burrows) T.; LL.B., U. of Va., 1855; admitted to Washington bar, 1855; moved to Chicago, 1855; m. a d. H. H. Magie, a Chicago pioneer, 1859. Pres. Chicago Law Inst., 1864; circuit judge, 1870-74; Dem. candidate for U.S. senator, 1885; defeated by John A. Logan by one vote; U.S. minister to Belgium, 1885-88; U.S. minister to Russia, 1888-89; apptd. by President Harrison as Dem. mem. of the monetary commn. held in Washington, Jan. 1891; life trustee Newberry Library. Pres. Ill. State Hist. Library Bd., 1892-96; 2d v.p. Chicago Hist. Soc. Incorporator of Nat. Am. Red Cross and v.p. Ill. branch; officer of Legion of Honor, France; grand officer Belgian Nat. Order of Leopold; mem. S.A.R. Presented to city of Chicago bronze statue of La Salle, 1889, and bronze statue of Sioux warrior on horseback, 1894, entitled "A Signal of Peace," both now in Lincoln Park. Home: Chicago, Ill. Died 1910.

TREGOE, James Harry, economist; b. Baltimore, Md., Aug. 24, 1865; s. George Washington and Rebecca Dyott (Kinnamon) T.; ed. high sch.; LL.B.,

U. of Md., 1905; m. Hester Anne Little, 1895 (dec.); children—Benjamin Bainbridge, Hester Anne Little; m. 2d, Eva May Peters, 1913. In business since 15; investment banking, 1905-12; exec. head Nat. Assn. Credit Men, 1912-27, pres., 1902-04; dir. Tregoe Economic Organization, 1927—. Prof. of finance, U. of Southern Calif., 1927—. Served as pres. Municipal League (Baltimore), Travelers and Merchants Assn. of Baltimore, Baltimore Y.M.C.A.; dir. Merchants and Mfrs.' Assn. Pres. Md. Prisoners' Aid Assn.; mem. bd. Federated Charities of Baltimore; mem. advisory bd. Pub. Athletic League. Republican. Presbyn. Author: (with John Whyte) Effective Collection Letters, 1924; Through the Year with Tregoe, 1927; Credit and Its Management, 1931. Lecturer. Home: Beverly Hills, Calif. Died Oct. 4, 1935.

TREMAIN, Henry Edwin, soldier, lawyer; b. New York, Nov. 14, 1840; s. Edwin Ruthven and Mary (Briggs) T.; A.B., Coll. City of New York, 1860; LL.B., Columbia, 1867; m. Sarah Brownson Goodrich, June 1, 1869. Pvt. 7th Regt. N.Y. State Militia Apr. 19, 1861; 1st lt. 73d N.Y. Inf., Aug. 14, 1861; capt., Nov. 1, 1862; maj. a.d.c. U.S.V., Apr. 25, 1863. Bvtd.: lt. col., vols., Mar. 13, 1865, "for gallant and meritorious services"; col. vols., June 12, 1865, for same during the war; brig. gen. vols., Nov. 30, 1865, "for faithful and meritorious services"; awarded Congressional Medal of Honor, June 30, 1892, "for distinguished conduct" at battle of Resaca, Ga., May 15, 1864. First asst. U.S. atty., New York, 1873-77; active in Rep. campaigns; col. veterans of 7th Regt., N.G.S. N.Y., 1887-89; pres. Republican Club of City of New York, 1901, 1906. Author: Last Hours of Sheridan's Cavalry, 1904; Two Days of War, 1905; Sectionalism Unmasked, 1907. Also "Fifty Papers," writings and addresses on mil., polit. and legal subjects, and in favor of a protective tariff, municipal ownership, etc. Died 1910.

TREMAINE, Henry Barnes, musical instrument mfr.; b. Brooklyn, N.Y., July 20, 1866; s. William Burton and Emeline Cornelia (Dodge) T.; grad. high sch., N.Y. City, 1881; m. Maud Aline Cooke, Apr. 2, 1890; children—Dorothy, Henry Cooke, Ruth Burrows. Chmn. bd. Aeolian Co., Weber Piano Co.; dir. Kempton Cadillac Corp. Decorated Order of Leopold, Knight (first class) Order Philip the Magnanimous (Belgium), 1922; Order St. Gregory the Great (papal), 1923; Cavalier Order Crown of Italy, 1926; Officer Legion of Honor, 1927. Republican. Home: Pelham Manor, N.Y. Died May 13, 1932.

TREMAN, Charles Edward, banker, merchant; b. Ithaca, N.Y., Oct. 11, 1868; s. Elias and Elizabeth (Lovejoy) T.; B.L., Cornell U., 1889; m. Mary A. Bott, Dec. 5, 1900; children—Arthur B., Elizabeth L., Charles E. Entered business, Aug. 1889, with Treman, King & Co. and became mem. firm, 1892; pres. and dir. same; pres. Ithaca Trust Co., 1919—; dir. Tompkins Co. Nat. Bank. Trustee Cornell U., 1902—. Presbyn. Mem. Dem. State Exec. Committee. N.Y. State supt. pub. works, 1911; mem. N.Y. State Highway Commn., 1911; chmn. N.Y. State Commn. on Barge Canal Operation, 1912; federal food administrator for N.Y. State outside Greater New York, 1918-19. Home: Ithaca, N.Y. Died Oct. 16, 1930.

TREMAN, Robert Henry, banker; b. Ithaca, N.Y., Mar. 31, 1858; s. Elias and Elizabeth (Lovejoy) T.; grad. Cornell U., 1878; m. Laura Hosie, June 25, 1885. Chmn. bd. Ithaca, Treman, King & Co., wholesale hardware; pres. Tompkins County Nat. Bank, 1902-32, Ithaca Trust Co., 1932-35, and pres. of consolidation of the two banks under title of Tompkins County Trust Co., June 1935—; dir. Federal Reserve Bank of New York, 1914-29, dep. gov., 1916-19; mem. Federal Reserve Advisory Council, 1931-33; pres. Ithaca (N.Y.) Trust Co., 1932-35; v.p. N.Y. State Park Council, 1934—. Mem. Creek and Park Commn., 1907, 08, 09; mem. bd. Pub. Works, 1909; trustee Letchworth Park Com., 1920-29; chmn. Stewart Park Commn.; chmn. N.Y. State Finger Lakes Park Commn.; mem. N.Y. State Council of Parks. Democrat. Presbyn. Trustee Cornell U., Old Ladies' Home. Author: Trade Acceptances, 1917. Home: Ithaca, N.Y. Died Jan. 4, 1937.

TRENCHARD, Thomas Whitaker, judge; b. Centreton, N.J., Dec. 13, 1863; s. William B. and Marie G. T.; grad. S. Jersey Inst., 1882; m. Harriet M. Manning, Nov. 17, 1891. Admitted to bar, 1886, counsellor, 1893; practiced at Bridgeton, N.J.; apptd. law judge of Cumberland Co. by Gov. Voorhees, 1899, reappointed by Gov. Murphy, 1904; city solicitor Bridgeton, 1892-99; mem. Ho. of Assembly, 1889; Rep. presdl. elector, 1896; apptd. justice of Supreme Ct. to fill vacancy, June 8, 1906; apptd. for full term, Jan. 15, 1907; term expires, 1914. Home: Bridgeton, N.J. Died 1911.

TRENHOLM, William Lee, pres. North American Trust Co., 1898—; b. Charleston, S.C., Feb. 3, 1836; grad. South Carolina Coll., 1855; m. Kate Louise Macbeth, Jan. 22, 1856; U.S. Civil Service Commr., 1885-86; U.S. Comptroller Currency, 1886-89; pres. Am. Surety Co., 1889-98. Author: The People's Money. Home: New York, N.Y. Died 1901.

TRENHOLME, Norman Maclaren, professor history; b. Montreal, Can., Sept. 29, 1874; s. of Hon. Norman William and Lucy Wilkes (Hedge) T.; father was justice Court of King's Bench, Quebec, Can.; A.B., McGill U., 1895 (1st rank honors in English and history); A.M., Harvard, 1897 (highest honors in history), Ph.D., 1899; research study and travel in Europe, 1899-1900; m. Ida Ethel Hurst, of Montreal, Dec. 18, 1901 (died 1917); 2d, Anna Louise Irby, Aug. 9, 1923. Asst. in modern history, 1898-99, Harris fellow in history, 1899-1900, Harvard; prof. history and English, Western U., London, Ont., 1900-01; instr. in charge of history and polit. science, Pa. State Coll., 1901-02; asst. prof. of history, in charge of dept., 1902-05, prof. history and chmn. of dept., 1905-16, 1919-24, chmn. of junior college com., 1921—, Univ. of Missouri. Episcopalian. Author: The Right of Sanctuary in England (U. of Mo. Studies), 1903; Syllabus for the History of Western Europe, 1907; Outline of English History, 1909; Syllabus of the Background and Issues of the World War, 1918. Home: Columbia, Mo. Died June 11, 1925.

TRENT, Richard Henderson, pres. and mgr. First Federal Savs. & Loan Assn. of Hawaii; b. Somerville, Tenn., Sept. 14, 1867; s. William Clough and Mary Virgin (Bonner) T.; ed. pub. schs.; m. Marcia Potter Ireland, Sept. 16, 1919 (dec.); 1 dau., Mary Belle. Served as printer's apprentice, Somerville Falcon, 1880-81, S.C. Toof & Co., Memphis, Tenn., 1882-83; mgr. and pub. Clarksdale (Miss.) Banner, 1884-85; bookkeeper and cashier various mercantile establishments, Memphis, 1886-94; partner Joy, Trent & Co., merchandise brokers, Memphis, 1894-1900; bookkeeper, J. R. Newberry & Co., grocers, Los Angeles, Calif., 1900; treas. Henry Waterhouse Trust Co., Honolulu, T.H., 1901-04; pres. and mgr. Trent Trust Co., Honolulu, 1904-31; pres., mgr. First Sav. & Loan Assn., 1934—; sec. and mgr. Mutual Bldg. and Loan Society of Hawaii, 1904-37; pres. Realty Auction Co.; dir. Bank of Hawaii. Treas. of Honolulu (city and county), 1905-10; mem. territorial pub. lands bd., 1910-14; spl. rep. in Hawaii, U.S. alien property custodian, 1918-23; mem. Honolulu City Planning Commn., 1929-30. Mem. bd. of regents, U. of Hawaii, 1920-22; trustee Kamehameha Schs., Honolulu, B. P. Bishop Mus.; pres. Honolulu Y.M.C.A., 1912-19; pres. Honolulu Stock Exchange, 1913-14. Trustee First M.E. Ch. of Honolulu. Democrat. Mason. Home: Honolulu, Hawaii, U.S.A. Died Apr. 11, 1939.

TRENT, William Peterfield, univ. prof.; b. Richmond, Va., Nov. 10, 1862; s. Dr. Peterfield and Lucy Carter (Burwell) T.; A.M., U. of Va., 1884; post-grad. in history, Johns Hopkins, 1887-88; LL.D., Wake Forest, 1899; D.C.L., U. of the South, 1905; m. Alice Lyman, Dec. 8, 1896 (died 1921); children—Lucia, William Peterfield. Taught school at Richmond, Va., and read law, 1885-87; prof. of English, 1888-1900, and dean academic dept., 1894-1900, U. of the South; prof. English lit., Columbia U., 1900-29, emeritus. Editor of many literary works. Author: Life of William Gilmore Simms, 1892; Southern Statesmen of the Old Régime, 1897; Robert E. Lee, 1899; Verses, 1899; John Milton, a Short Study of His Life and Works, 1899; Authority of Criticism, 1899; War and Civilization, 1901; The Progress of the United States in the Century, 1901; A History of American Literature, 1607-1865, 1903; (with C. K. Adams) History of the United States for Schools, 1903; A Brief History of American Literature, 1904; Greatness in Literature, and Other Papers, 1905; Longfellow and Other Essays, 1910; (with W. T. Brewster and C. L. Hanson) An Introduction to the English Classics, 1911; (with John Erskine) Great American Writers, 1912; Defoe—How to Know Him, 1916; Verse Jottings, 1924. Co-editor of Columbia University edition of Complete Writings of John Milton, 1931. Episcopalian. Died Dec. 6, 1939.

TRESSLER, Victor George Augustine, theologian; b. Somerfield, Pa., Apr. 10, 1865; s. Rev. John William and Carrie (Augustine) T.; Pa. State Coll., Bellefonte, Pa., 1880-82; A.B., summa cum laude, Pennsylvania Coll., Gettysburg, 1886, A.M., 1889; student of law, Chicago, 1887-88; B.D., McCormick Theol. Sem., 1891; corr. student Hebrew, U. of Chicago, 1895; U. of Leipzig, 1897-1900, Ph.D., magna cum laude, 1900; U. of Berlin, 1900, U. of Paris, 1901; (D.D., Susquehanna U., 1905); m. Mary Baugher Gotwald, 1906. Ordained Luth. ministry, 1892; pastor Grace Luth. Ch., San José, Calif., 1891-98; lecturer history, San José Acad., 1896-98; dean and prof. philosophy, Ansgar Coll., Hutchinson, Minn., 1901-02; prof. Greek, Wittenberg Coll., 1903-05, N.T. philology and criticism, Hamma Divinity Sch., Springfield, O., 1905—. Pres. Gen. Synod Evang. Luth. Ch. U.S.A., 1917—. Democrat. Mason. Home: Springfield, O. Died Sept. 1923.

TRETTIEN, Augustus William, psychologist; b. Appleton, Wis., Sept. 3, 1867; s. Frederick and Caroline (Slater) T.; grad. State Normal Sch., Oshkosh, Wis., 1894; B.L., U. of Wis., 1899; Ph.D., Clark U., 1904; m. Mary E. Goodell, June 26, 1895; children—Helen, Marion. Teacher dist. schs., 1888-90; prin. schs., Appleton, 1894-97; prof. edn., State Normal Sch., Oshkosh, 1900-03; dir. Sch. of Observation, same, 1904-07; prof. philosophy and edn., Carroll Coll., Waukesha, Wis., Feb.-Sept. 1907; prof. psychology and edn., U. of S.D., 1907-11; asso. prof. edn. and dir. Training Sch., U. of Kan., 1911-14; prof. philosophy and edn., Drury Coll., Springfield, Mo., 1914-15; prof. psychology and dir. psychol. clinic, Toledo U., 1915-32, dean Coll. of Edn., 1916-19; dir. Trettien Psychol. Clinic Laboratory, 1932—. Lecturer on edn., State U. of Ia., summer 1908, U. of Mo., summers 1910-15; lecturer on psychology, Kan. State Normal Coll., Emporia, Kan., summer 1911; lecturer on psychology, U. of Wash., summers 1913, 14. Expert consulting psychologist in business and court relations and psychol. and psychopathic problems. Presbyn. Republican. Mason. Author: Trent-Chasing a Career; The Psychology of the Human Emotions; etc. Home: Toledo, O. Died July 1, 1936.

TREVER, Albert Augustus, historian; b. Chilton Twp., Calumet Co., Wis., Oct. 31, 1874; s. Joseph Sanderson and Maria (Dale) T.; A.B., Lawrence Coll., Appleton, Wis., 1896; S.T.B., Boston U., 1900; Jacob Sleeper fellow, univs. of Halle and Berlin, 1902, 03; A.M., U. of Chicago, 1910, Ph.D., 1913; m. Elizabeth Ella French, Sept. 11, 1901; children—Karl LeClerc, Helen Frances, Ruth French. Instr. Hebrew and Bibl. lit., De Pauw U., 1900-02; prof. Greek lang. and lit., 1905-16, prof. ancient and medieval history, 1916—, Lawrence Coll. Acting prof. ancient history, Cornell, 1923-24. Methodist. Author: History of Greek Economic Thought, 1915; History of Ancient Civilization, Vol. I (The Ancient Near East and Greece), 1936; The Roman World, Vol. II, 1939. Lecturer on social and internat. problems; lecturer in history on James Boring Mediterranean Cruise, summer of 1933. Home: Appleton, Wis. Died Apr. 25, 1940.

TREVER, George Henry, theologian; b. Newcastle, Eng., Oct. 13, 1856; s. Joseph Sanderson and Maria (Dale) T.; A.B., Lawrence U., Appleton, Wis., 1881, A.M., 1884, D.D., 1893; B.D., Boston U., 1883, Ph.D., 1884; post-grad. work, Oxford U., 1 yr., U. of Berlin, 1 yr.; m. Ada S. Peabody, June 30, 1881 (died 1913); m. 2d, Frances B. Graff, Jan. 2, 1915. Ordained M.E. ministry, 1880; pastor in Wis., at Sheboygan Falls, 1883-84, Waupun, 1884-87, Beloit, 1887-88, Janesville, 1888-89, Fond du Lac, 1889-91 and 1893-95, Washington Av. Ch., Milwaukee, 1895-1901, Whitewater, 1901-04; prof. Greek and Hebrew exegesis, 1904-13, N.T. exegesis and Christian doctrine, 1913—, Gammon Theol. Sem., Atlanta, Ga., pres., 1925-May 1929. Trustee Lawrence Coll., 1889-92. Delegate General Conf. M.E. Church, 1896, 1904, 12, 20, reserve del., 1900. Prohibition Party candidate for lt. gov. of Wis., 1904. Author: Studies in Comparative Theology, 1896. Home: South Atlanta, Ga. Deceased.

TREVOR, Joseph Ellis, univ. prof.; b. Lockport, N.Y., Oct. 11, 1864; s. James Breading and Martha (Ellis) Trevor; student Cornell U., 1888-90; U. of Leipzig, 1890-92, Ph.D., 1892; m. Mary Tuft Guild, June 17, 1890; children—Karl Robert, Margaret, Barbara, Bertram. Asst. prof. gen. and physical chemistry, 1892-1900, prof. physical chemistry, 1900-08, prof. thermodynamics, 1906-34, prof. emeritus, 1934—, Cornell University. Editor of the Journal of Physical Chemistry, 1896-1909. Author: The General Theory of Thermodynamics, 1927. Died May 4, 1941.

TREVOY, William Vivian, educator; b. Gloucester, Mass., Jan. 25, 1880; s. Edward and Alexina (Grant) T.; B.A., Amherst, 1902, M.A., 1905; studied Columbia and Union Theol. Sem., 1906-07; unmarried. Teacher Storm King Sch., 1902-11; social work, 1911-28, as headworker in settlements, organizer and dir. community centers and community service consultant; dir. Beacon Sch., Wellesley Hills, Mass., 1929—. Trustee Deerfield (Mass.) Acad.; served as trustee or dir. at Brooklyn, N.Y., of Lincoln Colored Settlement, Flatbush Boy's Club, Jewish Welfare League, People's Inst., United Neighborhood Guild, and Little Italy Neighborhood House. Died July 3, 1938.

TREWIN, James Henry, lawyer; b. Bloomingdale, Ill., Nov. 29, 1858; s. Henry and Mary Ann T.; ed. Bradford Acad., Cedar Valley Sem. and Lenox Coll., Ia.; m. Martha E. Rector, Apr. 14, 1883 (died 1911); 1 son, Harold Rector; m. 2d, Nellie S. Hatton, Apr. 17, 1915. Taught sch., 1874-80; admitted to Ia. bar, 1883; practiced at Earlville, Ia., 1883-89, Lansing, 1889-1900, then at Cedar Rapids; mem. Trewin, Simmons & Trewin, 1916—. Owns farms in Ia. and takes great interest in agr. Mem. Ia. Ho. of Rep., 1894-96, Senate, 1896-1904; mem. Ia. Commn. St. Louis Expn., 1904; mem. State Bd. of Edn., 1909-14 (pres. 1909-13); chmn. commn. to codify laws, 1919-21; state dir. of campaign of edn. in principles of Am. govt. Mem. U.S. Commn. on Uniform Legislation. Republican. Presbyn. Mason. Home: Cedar Rapids, Ia. Died Mar. 21, 1927.

TREXLER, Harry C., businessman; b. Easton, Pa., Apr. 17, 1854; s. Edwin W. and Matilda (Sourpeck)

T.; ed. pub. schs. of Allentown and Tremont Sem., Norristown, Pa.; m. Mary M. Mosser, Jan. 22, 1885. In lumber business at Allentown, 1878—; pres. Trexler Lbr. Co. (Allentown); chmn. bd. Lehigh Portland Cement Co., Bell Telephone Co. of Pa.; dir. L.V.R.R. Co., Lehigh Valley Transit Co., Pa. Power & Light Co., etc.; also extensively interested in farming, horticulture, trout breeding and game propagation. Trustee Allentown State Hosp., Sacred Heart Hosp. (Allentown), St. Luke's Hosp. and Lehigh U. (Bethlehem), Franklin and Marshall Coll. (Lancaster) Muhlenberg College (Allentown). Served in Pa. N.G. 25 yrs., retired with rank of brig. gen., Apr. 22, 1918. Republican. Mason. Home: Allentown, Pa. Died Nov. 17, 1933.

TRIBBLE, Samuel Joel, congressman; b. in Franklin Co., Ga., 1868; student lit. dept., and grad. law dept., U. of Ga., 1891; m. Minnie B. McEntire. Admitted to bar, 1891, and began practice at Athens, Ga. Solicitor, City Ct., Athens, 5 yrs.; solicitor gen. Western Circuit, Ga., 4 yrs.; mem. 62d to 64th Congresses (1911-17), 8th Ga. Dist. Democrat. Home: Athens, Ga. Died Dec. 8, 1916.

TRIBUS, Louis Lincoln, civil and sanitary engr.; b. Northampton, Mass., May 26, 1865; s. Louis and Harriet Jeannette (Kingsley) T.; B.S. and C.E., New York U., 1885, M.S., 1888; m. Letitia Hall McCampbell, Oct. 3, 1899; children—Lucien Hall, Theron Kingsley. With Samuel R. Bullock & Co., water works constructors, 1885-87; with Charles B. Brush, consulting engr., 1887-93; instr. and asst. prof. engring., New York U., 1887-90; in pvt. practice, 1894—; mem. Tribus & Massa; in charge of pub. improvements, Borough of Richmond, City of New York, 1902-13. Engr. mem. and sec. N.Y. Bay Pollution Commn., 1903-06. Republican. Home: Richmond, New York, N.Y. Died Nov. 9, 1930.

TRICKETT, William, dean law school; b. Leicester, Eng., Jan. 9, 1840; s. John and Mary T.; A.B., Dickinson Coll., 1868, A.M., 1871, D.C.L., 1925; A.M., Central High School, Phila., 1860; LL.D., DePauw U., 1890; admitted to bar, 1876. Principal Dickinson Grammar School, 1868-69; adjunct prof. philosophy, 1869-71, prof. modern langs., 1874-75, prof. law and dean Law Sch., 1890—, Dickinson Coll. Del. Pa. Constl. Conv.; Dem. candidate for judge Superior Court of Pa., 1898. Author: Law of Liens in Pennsylvania (3 vols.), 1882, 1891; Law of Limitations in Pennsylvania, 1884; Law of Assignments in Pennsylvania, 1884; Law of Boroughs in Pennsylvania (2 vols.), 1893, 1898; Law of Streets and Roads in Pennsylvania, 1894; Law of Guardians in Pennsylvania, 1900; Law of Partition in Pennsylvania, 1900; Law of Witnesses in Pennsylvania, 1901; Law of Landlord and Tenant, 1904; Law of Crimes in Pennsylvania, 1907. Home: Carlisle, Pa. Died Aug. 1, 1928.

TRIEBER, Jacob, judge; b. Raschkow, Germany, Oct. 6, 1853; s. Morris and Blume (Brodeck) T.; ed. schools in Germany and in St. Louis; admitted to bar, Helena, Ark., May 1876, U.S. Supreme Court, 1883; m. Ida Schradzki, Jan. 10, 1882; children—Harry Marshall, Mrs. Bess S. Newton. Nominated for U.S. senator, Ark. Rep. caucus, 1891; U.S. atty. Eastern Dist. Ark., 1897-1900; U.S. dist. judge Eastern Dist. of Ark., 1900—. Was Grand Master Masons of Grand Lodge of Ark., 1906-07. Home: Little Rock, Ark. Died Sept. 17, 1927.

TRIGGS, Filoyd Willding, cartoonist, writer; b. Winnebago, Ill., Mar. 1, 1872; s. Rev. Matthew and Martha Jane T.; ed. U. of Minn., and Art Inst. of Chicago; m. Effie Gertrude Overly, July 31, 1903. Cartoonist Chicago Daily News, until 1903, New York Press, until 1912; now connected with The Christian Science Monitor, Boston. Home: Darien, Conn. Died Sept. 23, 1919.

TRILLEY, Joseph, rear admiral U.S.N.; b. in Ireland, Sept. 25, 1838; s. Samuel and Ann T.; ed. Phila., and Baltimore; studied engring. Md. Inst. Sch. of Design; m. Blanche Haynes, Apr. 25, 1868. Apptd. 3d asst. engr. U.S.N., Aug. 11, 1860; 2d asst. engr., July 1862; 1st asst. engr., July 1864; chief engr., Feb. 1871; capt. in the line, Mar. 1899; rear admiral, Sept. 25, 1899, and retired same date. During Civil War took part in engagements at Fort Sumter, burning of Norfolk Navy Yard, Acquia Creek, Hatteras Inlet, Hilton Head, Fernandina, Port Hudson, Donaldsonville, Mobile Bay and several other minor engagements. Served on the West Indian, European (and, as fleet engr.) on the China and Pacific stas.; also as chief engr. of the Portsmouth and Mare Island Navy Yards. Died 1911.

TRIMBLE, Harvey Marion, comdr.-in-chief G.A.R.; b. nr. Wilmington, Clinton Co., O., Jan. 27, 1842; removed to Princeton, Ill., with family, 1843; s. of Mathew and Lydia (Thatcher) T.; ed. common schs. and partial course Eureka Coll., Ill.; quit coll. to enter army; studied law alone; m. Margaret S. Dakin, Oct. 9, 1866. Deputy clerk Circuit Ct. of Bureau Co., Ill., 1865-67; admitted to Ill. bar, 1867; practiced successively in firms of Paddock & Trimble, Henderson & Trimble, Henderson, Trimble & Butler, H. M. Trimble, Henderson, Trimble & Colton, and H. M. & Cairo A. Trimble. Master in chancery Circuit Ct. of Bureau Co., 1868-77; county judge of Bureau Co., 1877-90, 1894-97; circuit judge 13th Jud. Circuit, 1897-1903. Mem. Bd. Edn. Princeton, 1878-97, Princeton High Sch. Bd., 1881-86; an organizer, and mem. 1st bd. dirs., 1886-88, Pub. Library, Princeton. Enlisted in Co. K, 93d Regt., Ill. Vol. Inf., Aug. 21, 1862; elected sergt. maj., Sept. 8, 1862; promoted 1st lt. and adj. of regt., Apr. 13, 1864; served as a.-a.-g. of 2 brigades, Mar. 28, May 31, 1865; mustered out of service June 23, 1865; was with regt. on every march (except 10 miles) and in every battle; captured and held prisoner by Confederates 14 days. Comdr. Ferris Post G.A.R., Princeton, 1897-98; comdr. Dept. of Ill., 1902-03; elected comdr.-in-chief G.A.R., Aug. 25, 1911. Republican. Mem. Christian (Disciples) Ch. Mason. Author: History of the Ninety-Third Regiment Illinois Volunteer Infantry, 1898. Home: Princeton, Ill. Died Jan. 10, 1918.

TRIMBLE, Richard, steel mfr.; born N.Y. City, Mar. 26, 1858; s. Merritt and Mary S. (Underhill) T.; A.B., Harvard, 1880; m. Cora Randolph. In cattle business in Wyo. several yrs.; sec. and treas. U.S. Steel Corp.; treas. and dir. Minn. Steel Co.; dir. Elgin, Joliet & Eastern Ry. Co., Lake Superior Consolidated Iron Mines, Nat. Tube Co., Tenn. Coal, Iron & R.R. Co., Union Steel Co. Served as ensign on monitor Puritan, Spanish-Am. War, 1898. Home: New York, N.Y. Died Feb. 18, 1924.

TRINKLE, Elbert Lee, governor; b. Wytheville, Va., Mar. 12, 1876; s. Elbert S. and Letitia M. (Sexton) T.; A.B., B.Sc., Hampden-Sydney Coll., 1896, LL.D., 1936; B.L., U. of Va., 1898; LL.D., Williams and Mary Coll., 1937; m. Helen Ball Sexton, Feb. 21, 1910. Began practice at Wytheville, 1898; pres. Shenandoah Life Ins. Co., Roanoke, Va. Mem. Va. Senate, 1914-20; gov. of Va., term 1922-26. Pres. Va. State Bd. of Edn. Democrat. Presbyn. Mason. Home: Roanoke, Va. Died Nov. 25, 1939.

TRIPLETT, Norman, educator; b. Perry, Ill., Oct. 1, 1861; s. Milton and Anna Beatty (Meredith) T.; A.B., Ill. Coll., Jacksonville, Ill., 1889; A.M., Ind. U., 1898; Ph.D., Clark U., 1900; m. Laura D. Wickard, July 3, 1902; 1 dau., Dorothy. Supt. schs., New Berlin, Ill., 1889-91; teacher science, high scho., Quincy, Ill., 1894-97; instr. pedagogy, Mt. Holyoke (Mass.) Coll., 1900-01; prof. philosophy and psychology, Kan. State Normal Sch., Emporia, Kan., 1901-31, also dean, 1913-31, and dir. summer sch., 1914-31. Democrat. Mason. Home: Emporia, Kan. Died 1934.

TRIPP, Bartlett, jurist; b. Harmony, Me., July 15, 1842; s. William and Naamah (Bartlett) T.; student Waterville Coll. (now Colby U.), 1857-60; LL.B., Albany Law Sch., 1867; (LL.D., U. of S.D., 1893, Colby, 1898, Yankton Coll., 1906); m. Ellen M. Jennings, Sept. 1863; 2d, Mrs. Maria Janet (Davis) Washburn, Nov. 1887. Practiced law, Augusta, Me., 1867-69, Yankton, from 1869. Pres. Yankton Sch. Bd., 1875-85; one of the incorporators of Yankton Coll., 1881; on 1st bd. of regents U. of S.D.; mem. commn. for codifying laws of Dak. Ty., 1877, and state of S.D., 1902; Dem. nominee for del. in Congress, 1878; pres. 1st Constl. Conv., 1883; chief justice Supreme Ct. of Dak. Ty., 1885-89; U.S. minister to Austria, 1893-97; mem. and chmn. Samoan Commn. to settle questions between England, Germany and America, 1899; lecturer on constl. law, U. of S.D., 1902—. Home: Yankton, S.D. Died 1911.

TRIPP, Guy Eastman, chmn. bd. Westinghouse Electric & Mfg. Co.; b. Wells, Me., Apr. 22, 1865; s. Alonzo K. and Abbie F. (Yeaton) T.; ed. South Berwick (Me.) Acad. Dir. Am. Internat. Corp., Am. Sugar Refining Co., Am. Surety Co., Brazilian Securities Corp., Bryant Electric Co., Canadian Westinghouse Co., Ltd., Chase Nat. Bank, Compania Westinghouse Electric Internat. Electric Ry. Equipment Securities Corp., N.E. Westinghouse Co., Radio Corp. of America, Westinghouse Acceptance Corp., Westinghouse Commercial Investment Co., Westinghouse Electric & Mfg. Co., Westinghouse Electric Products Co., Westinghouse Electric Internat. Co., Westinghouse Lamp Co., Westinghouse Gear & Dynamometer Co. Apptd. chief production div. of Ordnance Dept., Washington, Jan. 1918; resigned as asst. to chief of ordnance, U.S.A., Nov. 21, 1918. Awarded D.S.M., 1919, "for exceptionally meritorious service to U.S. Govt." Homes: Greenwich, Conn., and New York, N.Y. Died June 14, 1927.

TRIPPE, Andrew Cross, lawyer; b. Baltimore, Nov. 29, 1839; s. Joseph Everitt and Sarah Patterson (Cross) T.; A.B., Lafayette Coll., 1857, A.M., 1860; m. Caroline Augusta McConky, Nov. 7, 1872. Admitted to bar, 1861; entered C.S.A., 1862, as pvt. of inf.; served in the Valley of Va.; commd. lt. arty. and ordnance officer Md. Line, June 1863; wounded at Gettysburg and disabled from active service. Maj. gen. comdg. Md. div. U.C.V.; was col. and a.-d.-c. to Govs. Robert M. McLane and Henry Lloyd of Md. Home: Baltimore, Md. Died July 16, 1918.

TRIPPE, James McConky, lawyer; b. at Baltimore, Mar. 4, 1874; s. Andrew Cross and Caroline Augusta (McConky) T.; Shakespearean and Peabody scholar Baltimore City Coll., 1893; A.B., Johns Hopkins, 1896; LL.B., U. of Md., 1898; m. Mary Hanson Kirby, Dec. 24, 1906. Admitted to Md. bar, 1898, and practiced in Baltimore. Speaker Md. House of Delegates, 1912-14; Dem. presdl. elector, 4th Md. Dist., 1913; pres. Dem. State Senatorial Conv., 1914; mem. Joint Fisheries Commn. of Md. and Va., 1914-16; chmn. exec. com. Md. Commn. to Panama P.I. Expn., 1915; judge of Appeal Tax Court, Baltimore, 1915-20 (pres. judge, 1918-20). Trustee Md. Agrl. Coll., 1912-15; mem. bd. visitors, St. John's Coll., Annapolis, 1912-15. Mem. com. on laws of Supreme Council Royal Arcanum, 1921, exec. com., 1931—. Home: Baltimore, Md. Died July 10, 1936.

TRIPPET, Oscar A., judge; b. Princeton, Ind., Mar. 6, 1856; s. Caleb and Mary M. (Fentress) T.; State Normal Sch., Ind.; U. of Va.; m. Cora Wilson Larimore, Nov. 5, 1902. Began practice, Princeton, Ind., 1879; moved to Calif., 1887; judge U.S. Dist. Ct., Southern District of Calif., Mar. 1, 1915. Democrat. Mem. Christian (Disciples) Ch. Home: Los Angeles, Calif. Died July 15, 1923.

TRISCOTT, Samuel Peter Rolt, artist; b. Gosport, Eng., Jan. 4, 1846; s. Capt. Triscott, R.N.; gen. edn. pvt. sch.; ed. as civ. engr. and studied art in England; came to U.S., 1871; engaged as artist, 1871—. Represented in permanent exhibit of Boston Museum Fine Arts. Address: Monhegan, Me. Died Apr. 16, 1925.

TROEGER, John Winthrop, educator; b. Oswego, Ill., Aug. 20, 1849; s. George A. and Catherine B. (Opel) T.; B.S., Northwestern Coll., Naperville, Ill., 1875; m. Elizabeth Rassweiler, June 15, 1876. Taught dist. sch., Clayton County, Ia., 1869, La Salle County, Ill., 1874-76; prin. Paw Paw, Ill., Classical Sem., 1876-80; supt. schs., Blue Island, Ill., 1881-85, Hinsdale, Ill., 1885-86; prin. Irving Grammar Sch., Chicago, 1893—. Author: Troeger's Science Book, 1892; Hand Book of Geography, 1893; Key to New Model Arithmetic, 1893; Harold's Discoveries, 1897; Harold's Rambles, 1899; Harold's Quests, 1899; Harold's Explorations, 1900; Harold's Discussions, 1902. Editor Herds and Flocks, jour. devoted to thoroughbred stock, 1888-89. Address: La Grange, Ill. Died Dec. 17, 1936.

TROLAND, Leonard Thompson, research engr.; b. Norwich, Conn., Apr. 26, 1889; s. Edwin and Adelaide Elizabeth (O'Brien) T.; B.S., Mass. Inst. Tech., 1912; A.M., Harvard, 1914, Ph.D., 1915; Bowdoin prize in chemistry, 1914; Sheldon traveling fellow, 1915-16; m. Florence Rogers Crockford, 1924. Research in physiol. optics, Nela Research Lab., Gen. Electric Co., Cleveland, 1915-16; with Harvard, 1916—, asst. prof. psychology, 1922-29; lecturer on psychology, 1929—. Engr. with Kalmus, Comstock & Westcott, Inc., 1918-25; research for Technicolor Motion Picture Corp., manufacturers colored motion pictures, 1918-25, dir. of research and process control, 1925—; co-inventor, and responsible for development of manufacturing methods of Technicolor process for motion pictures in natural colors. Employed by U.S.N. during World War I, in development of submarine listening devices; mem. sub. com. of Nat. Research Council on vision and aviation psychology, during the war, also com. on physiol. optics. Fellow Am. Physical Soc., Acoustical Soc. America. Methodist. Author: (with Daniel F. Comstock) The Nature of Matter and Electricity, 1917; The Present Status of Visual Science, 1922; The Mystery of Mind, 1925; The Fundamentals of Human Motivation, 1928; The Principles of Psychophysiology (4 vols.), 1929-32; also numerous tech. papers. Home: Cambridge, Mass. Died May 27, 1932.

TROOP, J(ared) G(rassie) Carter, educator; b. Bridgetown, N.S., Can., Mar. 20, 1869; s. William Henry and Georgiana (Coster) T.; A.B., Trinity Coll. (U. of Toronto), 1892, A.M., 1893; 3 yrs.' post-grad. work in Toronto; m. Minnie Plenderleath Temple, Oct. 7, 1896; children—Eric, Constance, Marjorie. Editor of The Week (lit. and polit. jour. established by Goldwin Smith, 1882), 1894-97; instr. English, 1898-99, asst. prof., 1899-1904, asso. prof. Eng. lit., 1904-13, U. of Chicago; prof. English lit., Trinity Coll., U. of Toronto, Can., 1913-18. Sent by Dominion Govt. to Australia, 1893, to report on possibilities of trade development between that country and Can.; delivered many pub. addresses in Australian cities; lectured in nearly every state in the Union and province in Can., and traveled extensively in Europe and the East. Mem. exec. convocation Trinity Coll., 1894-97. Chief work delivering public addresses on lit. subjects, Univ. Extension in U.S. Pub. lecturer for the N.Y. Bd. of Edn.; his Sunday afternoon lectures on the more important books of the day attracted wide attention. Contbr. English and Am. revs. and mags., etc. Mem. Society of Arts and Sciences (New York). Republican. Episcopalian. Address: New York, N.Y. Deceased.

TROTTER, Alfred Williams, engr.; b. N.Y. City, July 10, 1856; s. Jonathan Thompson and Esther Melvina (Williams) T.; B.S. and C.E., New York U., 1875; m. Gertrude Evelyn Kilpatrick, d. Galvin Gay Watson, June 24, 1905. Professional work in connection with Met. Elevated Ry., New York, N.Y., West Shore & Buffalo, South Pa. R.R., Genesee & Wyoming

Valley R.R., etc., also gas and mining cos. Promotor, and chief engr. and dir. of Retsof Mining Co., opening and operating, 1883-93, the salt deposits in Western N.Y.; pres. Port Dixie Ry. & Terminal Co., Shallow Water Boat Co.; v.p. Transit Development Co. Vet. 7th Regt., N.Y.N.G., in which served 12 yrs. Fellow New York Acad. Sciences. Home: New York, N.Y. Deceased.

TROTTER, Frank Butler, coll. prof.; b. Washington County, O., Feb. 27, 1863; s. James and Elizabeth (Stock) T.; A.B., Roanoke Coll., Va., 1890 (highest grade in class), A.M., 1895, L.H.D., 1935; LL.D., W.Va. Wesleyan Coll., 1914; Harvard Grad. Sch., 1891-92; m. Lillian List Steele, Aug. 22, 1895; 1 son, Lorentz Steele. Teacher in pub. schs., 4 yrs., and pvt. schs. 2 yrs., W.Va.; prof. Latin and modern langs., 1890-1907, v.p., 1894, acting pres., 1898, W.Va. Conf. Sem. (W.Va. Wesleyan Coll., 1902—); prof. Latin, 1907—, dean Coll. Arts and Sciences, 1911-16, acting pres., 1914-16, pres., 1916-28, prof. Latin, 1928—; West Virginia U. Republican. Methodist; del. Gen. Conf. M.E., Ch., 1900, 12, 16, 20. Home: Morgantown, W.Va. Died Mar. 7, 1940.

TROTTER, Melvin E. (Mel. Trotter), evangelist; b. Orangeville, Ill., May 16, 1870; s. William and Emily J. (Lorch) T.; ed. pub. schs.; D.D., Bob Jones Coll., Cleveland, Tenn., 1935; m. Lottie M. Fisher, Apr. 23, 1891 (dec.). Began evangelistic work at Pacific Garden Mission, Chicago, 1897; founded more than 67 city missions in U.S. Ordained ministry Presbyn. Ch. U.S.A., 1905. Republican. Author: Jimmie Moore of Bucktown, 1910; The Double Cure, 1920. Home: Grand Rapids, Mich. Died Sept. 11, 1940.

TROTTER, Spencer, coll. prof.; b. Phila., Feb. 8, 1860; s. Newbold H. and Annie M. (Dawson) T.; ed. Friends' Select Sch., Phila.; M.D., U. of Pa., 1883; m. Laura Lee, 1889; 1 son, Spencer Lee. Teacher, 1888—; prof. biology and geology, Swarthmore Coll. Mem. Acad. Natural Sciences, Phila.; fellow Royal Geog. Soc. Author: Lessons in the New Geography, 1895; The Geography of Commerce (Macmillan's Commercial Series), 1903; also articles on ornithology, geography, Americana, etc., in Scientific Monthly and other publs. Home: West Chester, Pa. Died 1931.

TROTZ, J(ohan) O(tto) Emmanuel, engr.; b. Hammersta, Sweden, Mar. 6, 1860; s. Sir Carl Otto and Lady Ebba Maria Augusta (née Baroness Löwen) T.; grad. in mining and metallurgy, Royal High Sch. of Mines, 1883; in research work for Assn. Swedish Iron Masters, 1884; came to U.S., 1887; m. Selma P. Ahlström, June 7, 1890. Chemist, insp. of material, gen. supt. and metall. engr., attached to office of pres. of U.S. Steel Corp., 1887-1904; cons. and expert engr., and designer and supt. of erection of steel plant and rolling mills of John A. Roebling's Sons Co., Trenton, N.J., 1904-08; pres. and gen. mgr. Kockums Jernverks Aktb., Sweden, 1910—; dir. Aktb. Svenska Handelsbanken, etc. Knight Order of Vasa, by King Oscar of Sweden, 1907. Address: Svanevik, nr. Ronneby, Sweden. Died July 18, 1925.

TROUBETZKOY, Prince Pierre, portrait painter; b. Milan, Italy, Apr. 19, 1864; s. Prince Pierre and Ada (Winans) T.; ed. Collegio Calchi Taeggi, Milan; m. Amélie Rives, Feb. 1896. Came to U.S., 1896. Painted portraits of Gladstone, in the National Gallery, Edinburgh, and in National Portrait Gallery, London; Marquis of Dufferin and Ava, in Town Hall, Dover, Eng.; Dr. Philip Bruce, for U. of Va.; Archer Huntington, in Instituto de Valencia de Don Juan, Madrid, etc. Home: Cobham, Va. Died Aug. 25, 1936.

TROUP, Alexander, editor; b. Halifax, N.S., Mar. 31, 1840; came to U.S., 1856; ed. public schools; printer by trade; worked in Boston, Springfield and New York; founder, editor and mgr. New Haven Union, 1871—; mem. New Haven tax commn., 1880; mem. Conn. legislature, 1883-85; collector internal revenue for Conn. and R.I., 1885-89; chmn. Dem. State Com., 1896-98; Conn. mem. Dem. Nat. Com., 1896-1900; dir. public works, New Haven, July 1, 1899-Sept. 30, 1900 (resigned). Home: New Haven, Conn. Died 1908.

TROUT, Ethel Wendell, author; b. Phila., Pa., Aug. 14, 1878; d. S. Edgar and Frances Sherburne (Wendell) T.; grad. high sch., Wilkes-Barre, Pa., 1896; A.B., Bryn Mawr, 1901, post-grad. work, 1901-02, U. of Pa., 1925-26. With Presbyn. Bd. of Publication, later Bd. of Christian Edn., 1907-27; asst. editor for the Children's Div., 1925-26; writer of Westminster Jr. Uniform Quarterly, 1921-28. Republican. Episcopalian. Author: Jesus the Light of the World, 1922; Stories of the Beginnings, 1923; The Rise and Fall of the Hebrew Nation, 1924—all in series, Westminster Textbooks of Religious Edn.; Bible Girls, 1929. Home: Atlantic City, N.J. Died Jan. 16, 1935.

TROWBRIDGE, Alvah, banker; b. Putnam County, N.Y., 1835; s. William Crane and Mary Elizabeth (Hobby) T.; ed. common sch. and local acad.; m. Ada Greene Smith, 1859. Began banking in 1853 and was clerk and officer in country bank till 1880; with Nat. Bank of N. America, 1880-99; pres. N. Am. Trust Co., 1899-1900; pres. 9th Nat. Bank of New York until its consolidation with Citizens' Nat. Bank. Mem. exec. com. Am. Bankers' Assn., 1896-99, pres. 1900-01. Presbyn. Republican. Home: Hackensack, N.J. Died 1907.

TROWBRIDGE, Augustus, physicist; b. New York, Jan. 2, 1870; s. George Alfred and Cornelia Polhemus (Robertson) T.; Phillips Acad., 1886-87; Columbia U., 1890-93, D.Sc., 1929; A.M., Ph.D., U. of Berlin, 1898; m. Sarah Esther Fulton, Sept. 20, 1893. Instr. physics, U. of Mich., 1898-1900; asst. prof. physics, 1900-03, prof. 1903-06, U. of Wis.; later prof. physics, Princeton; dean of Grad. Sch. Princeton, 1928—. Mem. Internat. Congress Applied Chemistry, Berlin, 1903; sec. Physics Sect., Internat. Congress Arts and Sciences, St. Louis, 1904. Trustee Princeton U. Press. Commd. maj., Engr. R.C., 1917; intelligence dept., attached to Gen. Pershing's staff at hdqrs. A.E.F. in France; lt. col., 1918; discharged, 1919. D.S.M. and D.S.O.; Officer Legion of Honor (France); Knight of Order of St. Olav (Norway). Republican. Member National Acad. Sciences (chmn. div. physics, 1921); chmn. div. physical sciences and mem. research fellowship bd., Nat. Research Council, 1920-21, and mem. research fellowship bd. in physics and chemistry, 1920-25; European dir. for Science Internat. Edn. Bd.; fellow A.A.A.S. Address: Princeton, N.J. Died Mar. 14, 1934.

TROWBRIDGE, Charles Christopher, physicist; b. Astoria, L.I., N.Y., Apr. 26, 1870; s. Gen. William Petit and Lucy (Parkman) T.; B.S., Trinity Coll., Conn., 1892, M.S., 1903, Sc.D., 1908; unmarried. Asst. in physics, 1892-96, tutor, 1896-1903, instr., 1903-13, asst. prof., 1913—, Columbia. Fellow A.A.A.S. Contbr. to scientific jours. Home: New York, N.Y. Died June 3, 1918.

TROWBRIDGE, Edward Dwight, engr., author; b. of Am. missionary parentage, Marash, Turkey, Oct. 1, 1870; s. Rev. Tillman C. (D.D., LL.D.) and Margaret (Riggs) T.; student U. of Mich., 1887-88; m. Flora Lindsay, Nov. 9, 1897. With Am. Telephone & Telegraph Co., at Detroit and Cleveland, 1892-99; supt. Erie Telegraph & Telephone Co., 1899-1901; gen. mgr. Mich. Telephone Co., Detroit, 1901-05; connected with Pearson Engring. Corp., London, Eng., successively as asst. gen. mgr. Rio Janeiro Tramway, Light & Power Co., 1906-09, gen. mgr. Mexican Light & Power Co., 1910-11, and as v.p. Ebro Irrigation & Power Co., 1911-15; pres. The Apartments Co. of Detroit. Served during war period on Draft Bd. and on Civil Bd. for Examinations for Commns. in N.A. Republican. Episcopalian. Author: Mexico Today and Tomorrow, 1919. Home: Detroit, Mich. Died Nov. 24, 1929.

TROWBRIDGE, John, physicist; b. Boston, 1843; s. John Howe and Adeline T.; S.B., Lawrence Scientific Sch. (Harvard), 1865, S.D., 1873; m. Mary Louise Thayer, 1875. Tutor Harvard, 1866-69; asst. prof. physics, Mass. Inst. Tech., 1869-70; asst. prof. physics, 1870-80, prof., 1880-88, Rumford prof. applied science, 1888—, dir. Jefferson Physical Lab., 1884—, Harvard. Asso. editor Am. Jour. of Science. Mem. Internat. Congress of Electricians, Paris, 1883; del. U.S. Congress of Electricians, Phila., 1884. Mem. Nat. Acad. Sciences, Am. Acad. Arts and Sciences (pres.). Author: The New Physics, 1884; The Electrical Boy, 1891; Three Boys on an Electrical Boat, 1894; What Is Electricity?, 1896; The Resolute Mr. Pansy, 1897; Philip's Experiments in Electrical Science, 1898. Address: Cambridge, Mass. Died Feb. 18, 1923.

TROWBRIDGE, John Townsend, author; b. Ogden, Monroe County, N.Y., Sept. 18, 1827; s. Windsor Stone and Rebecca (Willey) T.; attended common sch., and went to classical sch. at Lockport winter of 1844-45; chiefly self-taught; hon. A.M., Dartmouth, 1884; m. Cornelia Warren, 1860; m. 2d, Ada Newton, 1873. Lived on farm until 17 yrs. of age; taught sch. in Ill. and in Lockport, N.Y. Went to New York City, 1847, and began to write for the press; went to Boston, 1848; active as editor and contbr. to mags. and jours, 1848—. Author: The Pocket Rifle, 1881; A Home Idyl, and Other Poems, 1881; The Jolly Rover, 1882; Tinkham Brothers' Tide Mill, 1882; Phil and His Friends, 1883; Farnell's Folly, 1884; The Little Master, 1886; His One Fault, 1886; Peter Budstone, 1887; A Start in Life, 1888; Biding His Time, 1888; The Lost Earl and Other Poems, 1888; Adventures of David Vane and David Crane, 1889; The Kelp Gatherers, 1890; The Scarlet Tanager, 1891; The Fortunes of Toby Trafford, 1892; Woodie Thorpe's Pilgrimage, 1893; The Satinwood Box, 1894; The Lottery Ticket, 1895; The Prize Cup, 1896; Two Biddicut Boys and Their Adventures with a Wonderful Trick Dog, 1898; My Own Story, with Recollections of Noted Persons, 1903; Poetical Works, 1903; A Pair of Madcaps, 1909. Address: Arlington, Mass. Died Feb. 12, 1916.

TROWBRIDGE, Mary Elizabeth Day, writer; b. Sturgis, Mich.; d. Rev. Gershom Buckley and Elizabeth (Benjamin) Day; ed. Kalamazoo Coll.; Conservatory of Music, New York, 1869; m. Rev. Luther H. Trowbridge (died 1904). Founder (with husband), 1870, and asso. editor Michigan Christian Herald until 1902. Trustee Kalamazoo Coll., Hartshorn Memorial Coll. (Richmond, Va.), Northwestern Free Dispensary, New York. Baptist. Pres. Woman's Auxiliary (philanthropic orgn.), New York, Daughters of Mich. in New York. Author: Vacation Notes, 1892; Pioneer Days, 1894; The Way of Life, 1895; This Do in Remembrance of Me, 1896; History of Baptists in Michigan, 1907. Address: New York, N.Y. Died Oct. 1, 1918.

TROWBRIDGE, Perry Fox, dir. N.D. Agrl. Expt. Sta.; b. Three Rivers, Mich., Apr. 25, 1866; s. George Martin and Lesbia (Fox) T.; grad. Mich. State Normal Coll., 1889, B.Pd., 1892, M.Pd., 1908; Ph.B., U. of Mich., 1892, A.M., 1905; grad. study German Sugar Tech. School and U. of Marburg, Germany, 1898-99; Ph.D., U. of Ill., 1906; m. Grace Hall, Sept. 4, 1894; children—Hugh Merton, Eleanor (Mrs. J. C. Stewart), Vernor Hall, Neva (Mrs. Lawrence E. Souers), Marion. Inst., Kalamazoo (Mich.) Coll., 1889-92, 94, Mich. State Normal Coll., 1892-93; asst. and instr., U. of Mich., 1892-1902; agriculturist and chemist, beet sugar factories, Mich. and Calif., 1902-04; asst. prof., later prof. agrl. chemistry, U. of Mo., also Mo. state chemist, 1907-18; dir. N.D. Agrl. Expt. Station and prof. expt. sta. methods, 1918-34, dir. emeritus, 1934—. Republican. Baptist. Contbr. to Jour. Am. Chem. Soc., Jour. Assn. Official Agrl. Chemists, Jour. Am. Soc. Animal Production, etc. Home: Fargo, N.D. Died May 15, 1937.

TROWBRIDGE, S(amuel) Breck Parkman, architect; b. New York, May 20, 1862; s. Gen. William P. and Lucy (Parkman) T.; B.A., Trinity, 1883, M.A., 1891; Ph.B., Columbia U. Sch. of Architecture, 1886; Sch. of Classical Studies, Athens, Greece, and École des Beaux Arts, Paris (atelier, Daumet-Girault); (Sc.D., Trinity Coll., 1910); m. Sophia Pennington Tailer, Jan. 26, 1896. After graduation from Sch. of Architecture, 1886, sent out by Archæol. Inst. to superintend erection of bldg. of Am. Sch. of Classical Studies, Athens, Greece; after study in Paris, returned to New York and was 4 yrs. in office of George B. Post; mem. firm Trowbridge & Livingston. Served as mem. Troop A, also as 1st lt. 12th Inf., N.G.N.Y. Apptd. by Pres. Roosevelt chmn. Nat. Council Fine Arts; incorporator, v.p. and trustee Am. Acad. in Rome; fellow A.I.A.; mem. Nat. Inst. Arts and Letters. Chevalier Legion of Honor, France; Officier Knights of the Royal Order of the Redeemer, Greece; Grand Comdr. Knights of Royal Order of St. Sava, Serbia; decorated Servian Red Cross; Comdr. Royal Order Crown of Roumania, 1919. Episcopalian. Home: New York, N.Y. Died Jan. 29, 1925.

TROY, Alexander, lawyer; b. Bladen County, N.C., Mar. 14, 1853; s. Alexander James and Maria Jane (Smith) T.; acad. edn. Whiteville, N.C., and Montgomery, Ala.; admitted to bar, 1875, and in practice at Montgomery, 1876—; m. Alice B. Watts, Dec. 26, 1876. Alderman Montgomery City Council, 1891-93; sec. and treas. and editor ann. proc. (46 vols.) Ala. State Bar Assn., Jan. 15, 1879-May 1924. Home: Montgomery, Ala. Deceased.

TRUAX, Charles Henry, jurist; b. Durhamville, Oneida County, N.Y., Oct. 31, 1846; s. Henry P. T., and descended from Philippe du Trieux, a Walloon, who came to the Island of Manhattan about 1623; student Hamilton Coll., 1867, A.M., LL.D.; m. Nancy C. Stone, Feb. 9, 1871; m. 2d, Caroline Sanders, Mar. 4, 1896. Judge of Superior Ct. City of New York, 1880-94; justice Supreme Ct., State of N.Y., Jan. 1896; mem. Constitutional Conv., State of N.Y., 1894. Democrat. Home: New York, N.Y. Died 1910.

TRUAX, Charles Vilas, congressman; b. Wyandot County, O., Feb. 1, 1887; s. John and Ada (Boley) T.; ed. pub. schs.; m. Helen Roberts, Mar. 20, 1913; children—Dorothea Vivian, John Charles, Charles Vilas. Engaged in farming, 1904—; editor and field rep. Swine World, 1917-21; one of organizers first Nat. Swine Show, Omaha, 1917; dir. of agr., State of Ohio, 1923-29. Nominated for U.S. Senate, 1928; mem. 73d Congress (1933-35), Ohio at large. Mem. bd. control, Ohio Agrl. Expt. Sta., 1923-29; vice chmn. Conv. of 22, sponsoring McNary-Haugen Bill, 1925-29; chmn. Lake Erie Conservation Council, 1926-29; exec. sec. Internat. European Corn Borer Orgn., 1929; mem. Ohio State Bd. for Vocational Training. Democrat. Methodist. Mason, Elk. Home: Bucyrus, Ohio. Died Aug. 9, 1935.

TRUAX, Chauncey Shaffer, lawyer; b. Durhamville, N.Y., Mar. 11, 1854; s. Henry Philip and Sarah A. (Shaffer) T.; grad. Hamilton Coll., 1875, LL.D., 1901, grad. Columbia Law Sch., 1877; m. Alice M. Hawley, Sept. 30, 1886. Admitted to bar, 1877; instr. internat. and comml. law, Robert Coll., Constantinople, Turkey, 1877-79; in practice in New York, 1879—; del. to N.Y. Constitutional Conv., 1894. Democrat. Mem. com. of 100; trustee Hamilton Coll., 1899—. Home: New York, N.Y. Deceased.

TRUDE, Alfred Samuel, lawyer; b. on Atlantic Ocean, Apr. 21, 1847; s. Samuel and Sally T.; parents English; childhood in Lockport, N.Y.; studied Union Coll. of Law, Chicago; m. Algenia D. Pearson,

Apr. 7, 1868. Admitted to bar, 1871; especially noted as a criminal lawyer; also counsel for many corps.; prosecuted P. E. J. Prendergast, who was convicted and hanged for murder of Carter H. Harrison; also tried large number of celebrated will cases, among which were the Wilbur F. Storey will contest and the Henrietta Snell will contest. Many years in politics. Democrat. Home: Chicago, Ill. Died Dec. 12, 1933.

TRUDEAU, Edward Livingston, physician; b. New York, Oct. 5, 1848; s. Dr. James and Cephise (Berger) T.; M.D., Coll. Phys. and Surg. (Columbia), 1871; hon. M.S., Columbia, 1899; LL.D., McGill U., Can., 1904; LL.D., U. of Pa., 1913; m. Charlotte G. Beare, June 29, 1871. Began practice in New York, 1872, but ill health forced him to go to the Adirondack Mountains, where became resident; founded, 1884, Adirondack Cottage Sanitarium for treatment of incipient consumption in working men and women, first of its kind in America; founded, 1894, Saranac Lab. for the study of tuberculosis, first research lab. for the purpose in America. Address: Saranac Lake, N.Y. Died Nov. 15, 1915.

TRUE, Alfred Charles, specialist states relations work; b. Middletown, Conn., June 5, 1853; s. Rev. Charles Kittredge and Elizabeth Bassett (Hyde) T.; A.B., Wesleyan U., Conn., 1873, A.M., 1876, hon. Sc.D., 1906; Harvard, 1882-84; Ph.D., Erskine Coll., S.C., 1886; m. Emma Fortune, Nov. 23, 1875; children—Elizabeth Fortune (Mrs. James Herbert Twamley), Henry Hyde. Prin. high sch., Essex, N.Y., 1873-74; instr. State Normal Sch., Westfield, Mass., 1875-82; instr. Wesleyan U., 1884-88; editor, 1889-90, vice-dir., 1891-92, dir. 1893-1915, Office of Expt. Stas., Dept. of Agr. Editor-in-chief "Experiment Station Record" and "Experiment Station Work"; had general supervision of expenditures of agrl. expt. stas. in all states and tys., agrl. investigations in Alaska, Puerto Rico, Hawaii, and Guam, investigations on agrl. edn., food and nutrition of man, and irrigation and drainage investigations throughout U.S.; dir. states relations service, Dept. of Agr., 1915-23; counselor to sec. of agr., on states relations, July 1, 1923—. Dean Grad. Sch. of Agr., of Ohio State U., 1902, U. of Ill., 1906, Cornell U., 1908, Iowa State Coll., 1910, Mich. Agrl. Coll., 1912, U. of Mo., 1914, Mass. Agrl. Coll., 1916. Agrl. editor New Internat. Ency. and Year-Book. Fellow A.A.A.S. Author of monographs on agrl. expt. stas. in U.S. and agrl. edn. Advisory mem. of exec. com. Am. Farm Bur. Fedn. Trustee Am. Univ. Home: Washington, D.C. Died Apr. 23, 1929.

TRUE, Frederick William, zoölogist; b. Middletown, Conn., July 8, 1858; s. Rev. Charles Kittredge and Elizabeth Bassett (Hyde) T.; brother of Alfred Charles T.; B.S., New York U., 1878, M.S., 1881, LL.D., 1897; m. Louise E., d. D. Webster Prentiss, M.D., Feb. 16, 1887. Joined Govt. service, 1878; expert spl. agt. 10th census (on Fisheries), 1879; custodian of collections of U.S. Fish Commn. at Berlin Fisheries Exhbn., 1880; librarian, 1881-83, curator of mammals, 1883-92, exec. curator, 1892-99, head curator dept. biology, 1897-1911, U.S. Nat. Mus.; asst. sec., Smithsonian Instn., in charge of library and exchanges, June 1911—. Rep. of Smithsonian Instn. and Nat. Mus. at expns., at Nashville, 1897, Omaha, 1898, Buffalo, 1901, St. Louis, 1904, and Portland (Ore.), 1905, and at Internat. Fisheries Congress, 1908; U.S. delegate 7th Internat. Zoöl. Congress, 1907. Fellow A.A.A.S. Made a spl. study of whales. Author: Review of the Family Delphinidæ (or the dolphins), 1889; The Whalebone Whales of the Western North Atlantic (Smithsonian Contbns. to Knowledge, Vol. 33), 1904; An Account of the Beaked Whales of the Family Ziphiidæ (Bull. U.S. Nat. Mus., No. 73), 1910; also numerous short papers on cetaceans and other mammals. Home: Washington, D.C. Died June 25, 1914.

TRUE, Gordon Haines, animal husbandman; b. Baraboo, Wis., Dec. 14, 1868; s. John Mathias and Mary Anne (Beede) T.; B.S., U. of Wis., 1894; m. Elizabeth Spayd Stubbs, Oct. 3, 1904; children—Elizabeth Ella, Gordon Haines, Eunice Miriam. Instr. in dairy husbandry, Mich. Agrl. Coll., 1894-98; prof. animal husbandry, U. of Ariz., 1898-1902; prof. agr. and animal husbandry, 1902-13, dir. Agrl. Expt. Sta., 1912-13, U. of Nev.; prof. animal husbandry, U. of Calif., July 1, 1913—. Mem. Nev. State Bd. Agr., 1912-13; state quarantine officer, Nev., 1913. Republican. Conglist. Fellow A.A.A.S. Mason. Chmn. live stock commn. U.S. Food Adminstrn. for Calif., 1918; sec. and mgr. Calif. Internat. Live Stock Show, 1919. Home: Berkeley, Calif. Died June 4, 1928.

TRUE, John Preston, author; b. Bethel, Me., Feb. 13, 1859; s. Dr. Nathaniel Tuckerman and Susannah (Webber) T.; ed. Exeter (N.H.) Acad., and Roxbury Latin Sch., Boston; m. Lilian Sarah Crawford, July 22, 1885. With ednl. dept. Houghton, Mifflin & Co., pubs., 1879-1919. Author: Their Club and Ours, 1883; Shoulder Arms, 1889; The Iron Star (illustrated by Mrs. True), 1899; Scouting for Washington, 1900; Morgan's Men, 1901; On Guard Against Tory and Tarleton, 1902; Scouting for Light Horse Harry, 1911 (3 last illustrated by Mrs. True). Sec.-treas. Nat. Archery Assn., 1918; sec.-treas. Newton (Mass.) Archers, 1916-22. Home: Waban, Mass. Died Jan. 4, 1933.

TRUE, Rodney Howard, botanist, physiologist; b. Greenfield, Wis., Oct. 14, 1866; s. John M. and Mary Annie (Beede) T.; B.S., U. of Wis., 1890, univ. fellow in botany, 1890-92, M.S., 1892; student botany under Pfeffer, at Liepzig, 1893-95, Ph.D., 1895; m. Katharine McAssey, July 1, 1896 (dec.); 1 son, Rodney Philip; m. 2d, Martha A. Griffith, Dec. 22, 1927. Taught common schs. in Wis. 2 yrs.; prin. Wis. Acad., Madison, 1892-93; instr. pharmacognosy, 1895-96, asst. prof. pharmacognosy, 1896-99, U. of Wis.; lectured at Harvard, winter, 1899-1900, and asst. Radcliffe Coll.; lecturer in botany, Harvard, 1900-01; plant physiologist, U.S. Dept. Agr., 1901-20, in charge physiol. investigations; prof. botany and dir. Botanic Garden, U. of Pa., 1920-37, emeritus prof. of botany, 1937—; dir. Morris Arboretum, U. of Pa., 1933—. Mem. gen. com. for revision of 9th U.S. Pharmacopœia; adv. council of Allegheny Forest Expt. Sta., 1934—, chmn., 1936—. Fellow A.A.A.S. (sec. com. one hundred on scientific research, 1925, mem. council, 1926). Episcopalian. Contbr. of papers on original research to Annals of Botany, Botanisches Centralblatt, and other scientific jours. and govt. bulls. Home: Philadelphia, Pa. Died Apr. 8, 1940.

TRUE, Theodore Edmond, brig. gen. U.S.A.; b. Coles County, Ill., Dec. 24, 1842; s. Edmond White and Mary Blackburn (Jones) T.; ed. schs. and acads. in Ill.; grad. U.S. Inf. and Cav. Sch., Ft. Leavenworth, Kan., 1883; m. Cynthia L. Bowman, Nov. 29, 1864. Corporal Co. B, 7th Ill., Inf., Apr. 25, 1861; sergt. Co. D, 41st Ill. Inf., July 30, 1861; promoted 2d lt. 41st Ill. Inf., "for meritorious services" at battle of Ft. Donelson, Tenn., where was twice wounded, Feb. 15, 1862; capt. 6th U.S.C. Arty., Nov. 28, 1863; 2d lt. 4th U.S. Inf., July 24, 1866; 1st lt. 4th U.S. Inf., Feb. 26, 1876; capt. a.q.m. U.S.A., Oct. 23, 1889; maj. q.m., Nov. 13, 1898; lt. col. deputy q.m. gen. U.S.A., Feb. 24, 1903; brig. gen. U.S.A., Jan. 23, 1904, and retired. Participated in battles of Civil War, including capture of Ft. Henry, Tenn., battles of Ft. Donelson, Tenn., Big Hatchie River, Tenn., attack on transport fleet near Island 82, Mississippi River, Siege of Vicksburg, Defense of Vidalia, La., etc., and skirmishes with hostile Indians in Wyo. in 1869, 70. Baptist. Republican. Home: Los Angeles, Calif. Died Aug. 30, 1925.

TRUEBLOOD, Benjamin Franklin, publicist; b. Salem, Ind., Nov. 25, 1847; s. Joshua A. and Esther (Parker) T.; A.B., Earlham Coll., 1869, A.M., 1875; LL.D., State U. of Ia., 1890; studied theology; m. Sarah H. Terrell, July 17, 1872. Minister Soc. of Friends; pres. Wilmington, O., Coll., 1874-79, Penn Coll., Oskaloosa, Ia., 1879-90; resided in France, 1890-91; gen. sec., 1892-1915, hon. sec. Am. Peace Soc., 1915—; at The Hague, 1899, during Peace Conf.; made many trips abroad in interests of internat. arbitration and peace movement; lecturer and writer on internat. subjects. Editor "Advocate of Peace," 1892-1915. Author: The Federation of the World, 1898; translated Kant's Zum Ewigen Frieden, 1897. Retired May 7, 1915. Home: Newton Highlands, Mass. Died Oct. 26, 1916.

TRUESDALE, William Haynes, ry. official; b. nr. Youngstown, O., Dec. 1, 1851; s. Calvin and Charlotte T.; common sch. edn., Rock Island, Ill.; m. Annie Topping, Oct. 2, 1878; children—Mrs. Marie Bissell, Calvin, Melville D. Entered ry. service, 1869; held various positions, 1869-83; asst. to pres. Minneapolis & St. Louis Ry., 1883; v.p., 1883-87, pres., 1887-94, receiver, 1888-94, same ry.; 3d v.p. and gen. mgr., 1894-97, 2d v.p. and gen. mgr., 1897-98, 1st v.p. and gen. mgr., 1898-99, C.,R.I.&P. Ry.; pres. and mem. exec. com. D.,L.&W. R.R. Co., Mar. 1, 1899-July 1, 1925, later chmn. bd. mgrs.; v.p. Chester R.R. Co., Mut. Life Ins. Co. of N.Y.; dir. Western Union Telegraph Co., etc. Home: Greenwich, Conn. Died June 2, 1935.

TRUESDELL, Hobart George, educator; b. Mt. Upton, N.Y., Oct. 30, 1882; s. Harvey A. and Anna (Babcock) T.; hon. A.M., Wesleyan U., Conn., 1913; Pd.D., Temple U., Phila., 1920; Litt.D., Colgate, 1923; m. Alice H. Wheeler, June 8, 1911 (died 1921); m. 2d, Julia Newton Brooks, Aug. 18, 1923. Head master Worrall Hall Mil. Acad., Peekskill, N.Y., 1908-09; head dept. of history, Mercersburg (Pa.) Acad., 1909-11; instr., 1911-12, head master, 1912—, Suffield School (formerly Conn. Lit. Instn.). Baptist. Home: Suffield, Conn. Died June 5, 1924.

TRUETTE, Everett Ellsworth, organist; b. Rockland, Mass., Mar. 14, 1861; s. Joseph and Catherine Pierce (Holbrook) T.; grad. Phillips Acad., Andover, Mass., 1878; studied N.E. Conservatory of Music; Mus.B., Boston U., 1883; studied with Haupt (Berlin), Guilmant (Paris), Best (Liverpool and London); m. Fannie Elizabeth Sherman, Jan. 1, 1886; children—Morton Sherman (dec.), Arthur Pierce (dec.), Ethel (Mrs. Harry L. Foster). Organist and choirmaster, Eliot Congl. Ch., Newton, Mass., 1897—; widely known as concert organist and teacher. A founder Am. Guild of Organists (dean of the New England Chapter, 1918-19). Conglist. Mason. Composer of numerous anthems and organ pieces; editor books of organ music and a treatise, Organ Registration. Home: Brookline, Mass. Died Dec. 16, 1933.

TRUITT, Warren, judge; b. Fayette, Ill.; s. Samuel and Cynthia (Carr) T.; A.B., McKendree Coll., Lebanon, Ill., 1878; m. Kathryn Mayer, Feb. 28, 1888. Admitted to bar, 1878, and practiced in Ore., Ida. and Wash., except when holding pub. office. Mem. Ore. Ho. of Rep., 1882; register U.S. Land Office, 1889-92; U.S. dist. judge, Alaska, 1892-96; mem. U.S. Assay Commn., 1905; mem. Ida. Senate, 1906-08; del.-at-large from Ida. Rep. Nat. Conv., Chicago, 1908; justice Supreme Ct. of Ida., 1914-15; U.S. Commr.; city atty., Moscow; pres. Ida. State Bar Commn. Methodist. Mason. Home: Moscow, Ida. Died Oct. 29, 1935.

TRUMAN, Benjamin Cummings, soldier, author; b. Providence, R.I., Oct. 25, 1835; s. Henry Hammond and Susan (Cummings) T.; ed. pub. and pvt. schs., Providence and Boston; taught sch., Canterbury, N.H., at age of 17; learned to set type at 18; compositor and proofreader New York Times, 1854-60; reporter Phila. Press, 1861; m. Augusta Mallard, 1869. Went to Nashville, Tenn., as capt. and on staff of Andrew Johnson (then mil. gov. of Tenn.) in Mar. 1862; served in Army of the Cumberland as staff officer, and corr. New York Times. After death of Lincoln was 18 months on President Johnson's staff; went to Calif. as spl. agt. P.O. Dept., 1866-69 and 1877-78; census marshal of Southern Calif., 1870; later spl. agt. Treasury Dept.; went to China, Japan, Hawaii and Alaska for Govt., and 4 times to Europe; also traveled in Egypt, Algiers, Morocco and Palestine, as corr. San Francisco Chronicle; asst. chief floriculture, World's Columbian Expn.; one of Calif. commrs. to Paris Expn., 1900; also Yosemite Valley commr. Author: See How It Sparkles; The South During the War; Semi-Tropical California; Occidental Sketches; Summer and Winter Resorts of California; From the Crescent City to the Golden Gate; Homes and Happiness in the Golden State; The Field of Honor; History of World's Fair in Chicago; Campaigning in Tennessee; Vasquez, the Bandit; Tourists' California Guide; The Missions of California; Pictorial Southern California; Pictorial Los Angeles; Divorced on the Desert. Home: Los Angeles, Calif. Died July 18, 1916.

TRUMAN, James, dentist; b. Abington, Pa., Nov. 22, 1826; s. George and Catharine Truman; ed. in pub. and pvt. schs.; D.D.S., Pa. Coll. Dental Surgery, 1854; LL.D., U. of Pa., 1904; m. Mary A. McClintock, Jan. 13, 1852; m. 2d, Mrs. Julia A. Tay, Dec. 4, 1884. Demonstrator and prof. operative dentistry, Pa. Coll. Dental Surgery, 1864-76; prof. dentistry, 1882-1909, prof. emeritus, 1909—, dean Dental Sch., 1883-95, U. of Pa. Editor, Dental Times, 1865 69, Internat. Dental Jour., 1890-1905. Contbr. dental and med. jours. Address: Philadelphia, Pa. Died Nov. 26, 1914.

TRUMBULL, Charles Gallaudet, editor; b. Hartford, Conn., Feb. 20, 1872; s. H. Clay and Alice Cogswell (Gallaudet) T.; grad. Hamilton Sch., Philadelphia; A.B., Yale, 1893; Litt.D., Wheaton Coll., 1928; m. Aline van Orden, Nov. 18, 1897. With The Sunday School Times, 1893—, editor, 1903—; also v.p., sec., dir. The Sunday School Times Co.; for many years staff writer Toronto Globe; every week writer Phila. Evening Pub. Ledger, Sioux Falls (S.D.) Daily Argus-Leader, Long Beach (Calif.) Morning Sun, Bradenton (Fla.) Herald, Augusta (Georgia) Chronicle, Johnson City (Tennessee) Times, Companion of first class Military Order Loyal Legion; member Victoria Inst., Eng., Palestine Exploration Fund, Eng., Archæol. Inst. America. Presbyn. Treas. Belgian Gospel Mission; dir. Pioneer Mission Agency, Keswick Colony of Mercy, Victorious Life Testimony; v.p. World's Christian Fundamentals Assn., Am. Tract Soc. Author: A Pilgrimage to Jerusalem, 1904; Taking Men Alive, 1907; Men Who Dared, 1907; Genesis and Yourself, 1912, 26; Anthony Comstock, Fighter, 1913; What Is the Gospel?, 1918; Life Story of C. I. Scofield, 1920; Prophecy's Light on Today, 1937. Home: Philadelphia, Pa. Died Jan. 13, 1941.

TRUMBULL, Frank, railway pres.; b. Arcadia, Mo., Nov. 7, 1858. Held various positions on M.,K.&T. and M.P. rys., 1874-82; freight auditor M.P. Ry., 1882-86; auditor Tex. & Pacific Ry., 1886-88; engaged in wholesale coal business in Colo., 1888-93; receiver and gen. mgr. U.P., Denver & Gulf Ry., 1893-99, Denver, Leadville & Gunnison Ry., 1894-99; pres. Colo. Midland Ry., 1890-1909; pres. C.&S. Ry. and subsidiary lines, 1899-1909; chmn. bd. C.&O. Ry. Co., Feb. 23, 1909—; also chmn. bd. M.,K.&T. Ry. Co., and Hocking Valley Ry. Co.; dir. Nat. City Bank (New York). Trustee Tuskegee Normal and Industrial Inst. Address: New York, N.Y. Died July 12, 1920.

TRUMBULL, Gurdon, artist, ornithologist; b. Stonington, Conn., May 5, 1841; s. Gurdon and Sarah A. (Swan) T.; studied in Hartford and New York; made many notable paintings of fish; of recent years devoted to study of birds. Author: Names and Portraits of Birds Which Interest Gunners, with descriptions, 1888. Wrote notable paper on The American Woodcock (Philohela minor) in Forest and Stream, Dec. 11, 1890, containing 1st record of a bird's power to curve the upper mandible. Address: Hartford, Conn. Died 1903.

TRUMBULL, Henry Clay, author, clergyman; b. Stonington, Conn., June 8, 1830; s. Gurdon and Sarah Ann (Swan) T.; ed. Stonington Acad. and Williston Sem.; A.M., Yale; D.D., Lafayette and U. of New York; m. Alice Cogswell Gallaudet, 1854 (died 1891). Moved to Hartford, 1851; in railroad bus. until 1858; missionary Conn. State Sunday Sch. Assn., 1858-62; ordained Congl. minister; chaplain 10th Conn. regt., 1862-65; was in several Confederate prisons. New England sec. of Am. Sunday School Union, 1865-75; editor The Sunday Sch. Times, 1875—. Author: Friendship the Master Passion, 1891; A Lie Justifiable, 1893; Studies in Oriental Social Life, 1894; Prayer: Its Nature and Scope, 1896; In Tribulation, 1896; Teachers' Meetings, 1896; War Memories of an Army Chaplain, 1898; The Covenant of Salt, 1899; Illustrative Answers to Prayer, 1900; Individual Work for Individuals, 1901; Old Time Student Volunteers, 1902. Home: Philadelphia, Pa. Died 1903.

TRUMBULL, Jonathan, writer; b. Norwich, Conn., Jan. 23, 1844; s. Daniel L. and Alexandrine N. (Wilson) T.; ed. Norwich Free Acad.; m. Harriet Roosevelt Richards, Dec. 17, 1868. Treas. Wm. W. Backus Hosp.; fellow Norwich Free Acad.; dir. Eliza Huntington Memorial Home; corporator Dime Savings Bank. Wrote: The Lebanon War Office, The Defamation of Revolutionary Patriots—A Vindication of General Israel Putnam, both in Year Book of Conn. Soc. S.A.R., 1895-96; Joseph Trumbull, First Commissary General of the Continental Army, New London Co. Hist. Soc. Publ., V. II, Pt. 3; The Share of Connecticut in the Revolution, American Monthly Magazine, Aug. 1897; The Jaques of the Modern Stage, Shakespeareana; Shylock, same; Walt Whitman's View of Shakespeare, Poet-Lore, Vol. III; also Connecticut in the Revolution (in Vol. 2 of Conn. as a Colony and State). Address: Norwich, Conn. Died May 21, 1919.

TRUSCOTT, Frederick Wilson, univ. prof.; b. New Harmony, Ind., Aug. 12, 1870; s. Thomas J. and Catharine (Wilson) T.; A.B., Ind. U., 1891, A.M., 1892; A.M., Harvard, 1894, Ph.D., 1896; student Germanic philology and German lit., U. of Berlin, 1896-98, 1900-01; m. Georgia Phillips Craig, Sept. 7, 1904; children—Frederick Wilson, Thomas Craig. Instr. German, Ind. U., 1891-93; prof. Germanic langs., W.Va. U., 1897-1923; prof. German, Wilson Coll., Chambersburg, Pa., 1924-32; prof. German, Washington Coll., Chestertown, Maryland, 1932-33; county supervisor ednl. projects for State Emergency Relief Bd., 1934-35. Joint Translator: Laplace's Philosophical Essay on Probabilities, 1902. Editor: Wildenbruch's "Kinderthraenen" (with notes and vocabulary), 1905. Joint Author: Elementary German Composition, 1914. Author: German in the High Schools of West Virginia in 1911-12, 1912. First lt. and capt., Mil. Int. Div., Gen. Staff, U.S.A., July 2, 1918-Aug. 30, 1919; capt. O.R.C., Nov. 30, 1919. Episcopalian. Mason. Address: Shippensburg, Pa. Died May 30, 1937.

TRUSDELL, Charles Gregory; b. Montgomery, N.Y., May 1, 1826; ed. common sch. and acad.; m. Sarah J. Raymond, Dec. 22, 1846. Became Meth. minister, 1857, in Iowa; presiding elder Iowa City dist., 1865; later pastor Grant Place M.E. Ch., Chicago, until the great fire, 1871, when he was apptd. gen. supt. Chicago Relief and Aid Soc., and as such distributed nearly $5,000,000 contributed from all parts of the world for the sufferers. The organization continued for the relief of the poor of Chicago, Mr. Trusdell acting as supt., 1871—. Sent in resignation when, in 1885, was apptd. presiding elder, Chicago dist., M.E. Church, but it was not accepted. Home: Lake Bluff, Ill. Died 1903.

TRYON, Dwight William, landscape painter; b. Hartford, Conn., Aug. 13, 1849; s. Anson and Delia O. (Roberts) T.; studied art in Paris under J. de la Chevreuse, C. Daubigny and A. Guillemet, and at École des Beaux Arts. Hon. A.M., Smith Coll., 1923. Took medal, Boston, 1882; gold medal, Am. Art Assn., New York, 1886, 1887; Hollgarten prize, Nat. Acad. Design, 1887; Webb prize, Soc. Am. Artists, 1889; Ellsworth prize, Chicago, 1889; Palmer prize, Inter-State Expn., Chicago; first-class gold medal, Munich Internat. Expn.; 13 medals. Chicago Expn., 1893; 1st prize,. Cleveland Exhbn., 1895; 1st prize, Nashville, Centennial Expn., 1897; 1st prize, gold medal and $1,500, Carnegie Inst., 1898; Chronological medal, Carnegie Inst., Pittsburgh, 1901; gold medal, Buffalo Expn., 1901; gold medal, St. Louis Expn., 1904. N.A., 1891; mem. Nat. Inst. Arts and Letters. Address: New York, N.Y. Died July 1, 1925.

TRYON, Frederick Gale, mineral economist; b. Minneapolis, Minn., Mar. 23, 1892; s. Charles John and Isabel (Gale) T.; A.B., U. of Minn., 1914, Shevlin fellow, 1915, A.M., 1916; m. Ruth Wilson, Aug. 16, 1919; children—John Griggs, Richard Gale, Joseph Lee. Geologist, Empire Gas & Fuel Co., 1916. asst. geologist U.S. Geol. Survey, 1917; attached to com. on coal production, Council Nat. Defense; in charge statistics of mineral raw materials for War Industries Bd.; capt. U.S.A., in statistics br., Gen. Staff, Washington, D.C., and G.H.Q., France, 1917-18; maj. Spl. Res., U.S.A. Am. sec. raw materials sect., Supreme Econ. Council, Am. Peace Commn., Paris, Jan.-May 1919; in charge coal statistics, U.S. Geol. Survey, 1919-24; same, Bur. Mines, 1925-34, chief Coal Economics Div., 1934-37; statistician Nat. Bituminous Coal Commn., 1937—; lecturer U. of Penna., 1924-25, Robert Brookings Grad. Sch. of Economics, 1925-27; on leave Brookings Instn., 1926, 31, 33. Mem. President Harding's fuel distribution com. during 1922 coal strike; statis. adviser U.S. Coal Commn., 1922-23; mem. staff President's Research Com. on Social Trends, 1931, and study of population redistribution, 1935. Fellow American Statis. Assn. Author of official repts. and tech. papers on economics of coal, fuels and power, and collaborator in group studies: Boycotts and Peace, 1932; Recent Social Trends, 1932; America's Capacity to Produce, 1934; Migration and Economic Opportunity, 1936; Technological Trends, 1937. Editor and author (with others): What the Coal Commission Found, 1925; Mineral Economics (Brookings lecturers), 1932. Home: Washington, D.C. Died Feb. 15, 1940.

TRYON, James Rufus, medical dir. U.S.N.; b. Coxsackie, N.Y., Sept. 24, 1837; A.B., Union Coll., 1858, Ph.D., 1891, LL.D., 1895; unmarried. Entered U.S.N. as asst. surgeon, 1863; passed through all grades; apptd. surgeon gen. U.S.N., May 1893; retired as rear adm., Sept. 24, 1899. Address: Coxsackie, New York. Died Mar. 21, 1912.

TUBBS, Frank Dean, coll. prof.; b. Mexico, N.Y., Apr. 9, 1864; s. Lewis and Cynthia (Waters) T.; A.B., Ohio Wesleyan U., 1888, A.M., 1893, S.T.D., 1898; m. Lottie I. Kerr, Aug. 2, 1888 (died 1897); children—Arthur Dean (dec.), Margaret Thurston, Agnes Randall (dec.); m. 2d, Euphemia Fowler, Sept. 7, 1898; children—Alice Evangeline, Katharine Sybil. Prof. natural history, Mexican Methodist Coll., Puebla, Mex., 1889-94; pres. South Am. Sch. of Theology, Mercedes, Argentine Republic, 1894-97; prof. biology and geology, 1899-1901, acting pres., 1899-1900, Kan. Wesleyan U.; prof. science, 1902-07, prin., 1903-07, Marion (O.) High Sch.; prof. geology and astronomy, Bates Coll., 1907-29 (emeritus). Lecturer on science, Bangor Theol. Sem., 1910-12. Fellow A.A.A.S. Unitarian. Author and translator of works in Spanish; lecturer and writer on science and current problems. Home: Kingston, N.Y. Died Feb. 23, 1939.

TUCK, Edward, banker; b. Exeter, N.H., 1842; s. Amos T.; A.B., Dartmouth, 1862, LL.D., 1903; m. Julia Stell (Officier Légion d'Honneur 1921), 1872. Endowed Dartmouth Coll. Founded Amos Tuck Sch. of Adminstrn. and Finance. Erected building for and endowed New Hampshire Hist. Soc., Concord. Founded and Endowed Hôpital Stell and School of Domestic Economy, Rueil-Malmaison; donated Domain of Bois-Préau and Napoleonic relics to Malmaison; donated collection of works of art to City of Paris (Petit Palais), 1930; restored at La Turbie, France, Trophée des Alpes, Roman monument erected B.C. 5. Awarded Grand Croix de la Légion d'Honneur, Lauréat Académie Française; made Citoyen de Paris, 1932. Writer on money, in defense of bimetallism, and advocacy of resumption of specie payments. Home: Paris, France. Died Apr. 30, 1938.

TUCK, Henry, ins. exec.; b. Barnstable, Mass., May 9, 1842; grad. Harvard, 1863, A.M., 1866; Harvard Med. Sch., 1867; m. Emma R. Beers, (dec.), Nov. 26, 1873. m. 2d, Elenore Hammond, Sept. 23, 1903. V.p. N.Y. Life Ins. Co., 1885—. Home: New York, N.Y. Died 1904.

TUCK, Somerville Pinkney, judge; b. Annapolis, Md., Sept. 24, 1848; s. Judge William Hallam and Margaret Sprigg Bowie (Chew) T.; attended St. John's Coll., Annapolis, A.M., 1889, LL.D., 1894; grad. U. of Va., 1869; m. Emily Rosalie Snowden, only d. Charles Marshall, May 14, 1885. Admitted to bar, Md., 1871, N.Y., 1872. Supreme Ct. U.S., 1885; practiced in New York City, 1872-94; nominated by President Cleveland and apptd. by Khedive of Egypt, Judge Internat. Ct. of First Instance, Mansourah, Egypt, Feb. 1894; trans. to Cairo, Dec. 1897; a presiding justice, same, 8 yrs.; promoted judge Internat. Ct. Appeals, Alexandria, Egypt, Nov. 1908; mem. Internat. Commn. and Nov. 11, 1911, of the Legislative Assembly created by Khedivial decree; retired on reaching age limit, Nov. 1, 1920. Democrat. Episcopalian. One of commrs. in New York of Ct. of Ala. Claims, 1882-85; special agt. Dept. State to make search in Eng., Europe, and W.I. for evidence relating to French spoliation claims, 1885-88 (3 reps. printed by Congress); U.S. asst. commr. gen. to Paris Expn., 1889, and mem. Internat. Jury Awards and of superior jury and commn. of 25 which revised the 30,000 awards; mem. jury for comml. and tech. edn., Paris Expn., 1900, and del. Supreme Jury. Officer Legion of Honor, France, 1889, Commandeur, 1900; Officier Pub. Instrn., France, 1894; Order of the Nile, 2d class (Egypt). Del. from Egyptian Govt. Universal Congress Lawyers and Jurists, St. Louis Expn., 1904. Address: Menton, France. Died Apr. 14, 1923.

TUCKER, Beverley Dandridge, bishop; b. Richmond, Va., Nov. 9, 1846; s. Nathaniel Beverley and Jane Shelton (Ellis) T.; ed. in Eng. and Switzerland and at U. of Toronto; grad. Alexandria (Va.) Theol. Sem., 1873; D.D., Roanoke Coll.; LL.D., William and Mary Coll.; m. Anna Maria Washington, July 22, 1873. Deacon, 1873, priest, 1875, P.E. Ch.; rector Richmond County, Va., 1873-82, St. Paul's Ch. Norfolk, 1882-1906; consecrated bishop coadjutor of Southern Va., Oct. 3, 1906. Served in Va. Arty., C.S.A. Author of Confederate memorial verses and essays; My Three Loves (poems), 1910. Address: Norfolk, Va. Died Jan. 17, 1930.

TUCKER, Gardiner Chylson, clergyman; b. Boston, Mass., Oct. 1, 1851; s. Rev. Levi (D.D., LL.D.) and Jeanette (Lee) T.; ed. Shurtleff Coll., Upper Alton, Ill., 1862-65; D.D., U. of the South, 1931; m. Melville Leigh Eckford, Dec. 13, 1873; children—Gardiner Leigh, Melville Louise (dec.), Ernest Eckford, Royal Kenneth, Joseph Louis (dec.), Irene Robert (Mrs. C. C. Cole), Irwin St. John, Melville Jeanette (Mrs. J. M. Nester), Edith Marguerite Loraine (Mrs. H. L. Gordon), Cyril Theodore. Ordained ministry Bapt. Ch., 1876, changed to P.E. Ch., 1881; rector Christ Ch., Collinsville, Ill., 1881-82, St. James Ch., St. Louis, 1882-85, St. John's Ch., Mobile, Ala., 1885—. Chaplain 1st Regt., Ala. N.G., 1886-98. Ind. Democrat. Mason, Odd Fellow, K.P. Historiographer Province of Sewanee and Diocese of Ala. Home: Mobile, Ala. Died Nov. 10, 1941.

TUCKER, George Fox, lawyer; b. New Bedford, Mass., Jan. 19, 1852; A.B., Brown U., 1873, Ph.D., 1891; LL.B., Boston U., 1875. Practiced at Boston, 1882—; reporter decisions Supreme Jud. Ct. of Mass., 1892-1900; mem. Mass. Ho. of Reps., 1890-93. Author: Manual Relating to the Preparation of Wills, 1884; The Monroe Doctrine, 1885; Manual Relating to the Formation and Management of Mercantile and Manufacturing Corporations, 1888, 1905; Manual Relating to the Constitution, 1894; Notes on U.S. Revised Statutes (with J. M. Gould), 1889; The Federal Penal Code Annotated (with Charles W. Blood), 1910; A Quaker Home (novel), 1891; Mildred Marvel (novel), 1899; International Law (with George Grafton Wilson), 1901. Home: Boston, Mass. Feb. 14, 1929.

TUCKER, Gilbert Milligan, author; b. Albany, N.Y., Aug. 26, 1847; s. Luther and Margaret Lucinda Smith (Burr) T.; A.B., Williams, 1867, A.M., 1870; m. Sara Edwards Miller, June 7, 1877; children—Margaret Cleveland, Gilbert Milligan. Editor from 1867, editor-in-chief, 1897-1911, The Country Gentleman. Author: Our Common Speech, 1895; History of American Agricultural Periodicals, 1909; A Layman's Apology, 1913; American English, 1921; also addresses and articles in reviews. Home: Albany, N.Y. Died Jan. 13, 1932.

TUCKER, Henry St. George, congressman; b. Winchester, Va., Apr. 5, 1853; s. John Randolph (M.C.) and Laura (Powell) T.; A.M., Washington and Lee U., 1875, B.L., 1876; LL.D., U. of Miss., 1899, Columbian, 1903; m. Henrietta Preston Johnston, Oct. 25, 1877 (died 1900); children—John Randolph, Rosa Johnston (Mrs. Silas B. Mason), Albert Sidney Johnston, Laura Powell (wife of Prof. Forest Fletcher), Henry St. George, Henrietta Preston (wife of Dr. T. Preston White); m. 2d, Martha Sharpe, Jan. 13, 1903 (died 1928); m. 3d, Mary Jane Williams, June 26, 1929. Admitted to bar, 1876, and practiced at Staunton, Va. Mem. 51st to 54th Congresses (1889-97); prof. constl. and internat. law and equity, 1897-1902, dean Law Sch., 1899-1902, Washington and Lee U.; dean schs. of Jurisprudence and Law, and Politics and Diplomacy, Columbian (now George Washington) U., 1903-05. Democrat. Pres. Am. Bar Assn., 1904-05; pres. Jamestown Expn. Co., 1905-07. Editor: Tucker on the Constitution, 1899. Author: Limitations on the Treaty-Making Power—Under the Constitution of the United States, 1915; Woman Suffrage by Constitutional Amendment, 1916. Elected to 67th Congress, Mar. 21, 1922, to fill vacancy occasioned by decease of Henry D. Flood, and reëlected 68th to 72d Congresses (1923-33), 10th Va. Dist. Home: Lexington, Va. Died July 23, 1932.

TUCKER, John Francis, lawyer, author; b. N.Y. City, Feb. 25, 1871; s. Francis J. and Mary O'Neill (Bateman) T.; LL.B., New York U. Law Sch., 1893, LL.M., 1894; post-grad. work U. of Pa. Admitted to N.Y. bar, 1894; candidate for assembly on fusion ticket, 1903; asso. with Austin Abbott in editorial work; editor Univ. Law Rev., 1895-98. Fellow Royal Soc. Arts; gov. Soc. Arts and Sciences. Author: Story of Washington Square, 1895; The Power Political, 1899; Collected Short Stories, 1905; also (play) Husbands by Purchase, prod. Criterion Theatre, London, 1899. Home: Harmon-on-Hudson, N.Y. Died Feb. 28, 1921.

TUCKER, W(alter) Leon, editor, evangelist; b. Pleasanton, Linn County, Kan., 1871; s. Edgar Marion and Sarah Adeline (Tansey) T.; ed. high sch. (Pleasanton), Bible Training Sch. (Kansas City, Mo.), Moody Bible Inst. (Chicago); m. Olive B. Hulsizer, Dec. 31, 1896; 1 dau., Evangeline Standard. Ordained Bapt. ministry, 1900; pastor successively at Belton (Mo.), Benton Boul. Ch. (Kansas City, Mo.), First Ch. (Riverside, Calif.), Calvary Ch. (Los Angeles) until 1915; evangelist and Bible lecturer in

U.S., Can., Gt. Britain and Europe, 1915—; mem. faculty Los Angeles Bible Inst., 1910-13; editor Wonderful Word Magazine. Mason. Author: Life of Paul Rader, 1918; The Dragon and the Lamb; also various Bible studies, including The University Bible Course. Address: Harrisburg, Pa. Died June 7, 1934.

TUCKER, William Jewett, educator; b. Griswold, Conn., July 13, 1839; s. Henry and Sarah (Lester) T.; A.B., Dartmouth, 1861; grad. Andover Theol. Sem., 1866; D.D., Dartmouth, 1875, U. of Vt., 1904; LL.D., Williams, 1893, Yale, 1895, Wesleyan, 1903, Columbia, 1906; m. Charlotte H. Rogers, June 22, 1870 (died 1882); children—Alice Lester (wife of Prof. Frank H. Dixon), Margaret (wife of Judge Nelson P. Brown); m. 2d, Charlotte B. Cheever, June 23, 1887; 1 dau., Elizabeth Washburn (wife of Professor Franc W. Cushwa). Ordained in Congl. ministry, 1867; pastor Franklin St. Ch., Manchester, N.H., 1867-75, Madison Sq. Presbyn. Ch., New York, 1875-79; prof. sacred rhetoric and lecturer on pastoral theology, Andover Theol. Sem., 1879-93; pres. Dartmouth Coll., 1893-1909, pres. emeritus, 1909—. Asso. editor Andover Rev., 1884-93; founder Andover House (later South End House), Boston (social settlement); lecturer, Lowell Inst., 1894, Union Theol. Sem., 1897; Lyman Beecher lecturer Yale Div. Sch., 1897-98; univ. preacher, Harvard, 1899-1901. Fellow A.A.A.S. Author: From Liberty to Unity, 1892; The Making and the Unmaking of the Preacher, 1899; Public-Mindedness, 1910; Personal Power, 1910; The Function of the Church in Modern Society, 1911; The New Reservation of Time, 1916; My Generation, An Autobiographical Interpretation, 1919. Contbr. to Atlantic Monthly, Educational Review. Home: Hanover, N.H. Died Sept. 29, 1926.

TUCKER, Willis Gaylord, chemist; b. Albany, N.Y., Oct. 31, 1849; s. Luther and Margaret Lucinda Smith (Burr) T.; brother of Gilbert Milligan T.; ed. Albany Acad.; M.D., Albany Med. Coll., 1870; hon. Ph.D., Union, 1882; Ph.G., Albany Coll. of Pharmacy, 1882; m. May Newman, Sept. 17, 1879. Prof. chemistry and toxicology, 1876-1915, registrar, 1882-1914, and dean faculty, 1914-15, Albany Med. Coll.; prof. chemistry, 1881-1918, dean faculty, 1883-1918, hon. dean, 1918—, Albany Coll. of Pharmacy. Fellow A.A.A.S. Home: Albany, N.Y. Died 1922.

TUCKERMAN, Alfred, bibliographer; b. New York, Jan. 15, 1848; s. Lucius and Elizabeth Wolcott (Gibbs) T.; A.B., Harvard, 1870; Ph.D., Leipzig, 1874; m. Clara L. Fargis, Dec. 10, 1879. Asst. Astor Library, New York, 1876-80. Fellow A.A.A.S., N.Y. Acad. Sciences; orig. life mem., founder Nat. Hist. Soc. Pub. in miscellaneous collections of Smithsonian Instn.: Index to the Literature of the Spectroscope, 1861-1887, 1888; same, continued to 1900, 1902; Index to the Literature of Thermodynamics, 1890; Bibliography of the Chemical Influence of Light, 1891. Home: Newport, R.I. Died May 25, 1925.

TUCKERMAN, Bayard, author; b. New York, July 2, 1855; s. Lucius and Elizabeth Wolcott (Gibbs) T.; A.B., Harvard, 1878; studied at Paris, 1878; m. Annie, d. Rev. Cotton Smith, D.D., Sept. 26, 1882. Lecturer on English lit., Princeton, 1898-1907. Author: History of English Prose Fiction, 1882; Life of General LaFayette, 1889; Diary of Philip Home, 1889; Peter Stuyvesant, 1893; William Jay, and the Abolition of Slavery, 1893; Philip Schuyler, Major-General in the American Revolution, 1903; Notes on the Tuckerman Family of Massachusetts, 1914; The Cotton Smith Family of Sharon, Conn., 1915. Home: Ipswich, Mass. Died Oct. 20, 1923.

TUCKERMAN, Frederick, anatomist; b. Greenfield, Mass., May 7, 1857; s. Frederick G. and Hannah L. (Jones) T.; B.S., Mass. Agrl. Coll. and Boston U., 1878; M.D., Harvard, 1882; student London and Berlin, 1882-83, Berlin, London and Heidelberg, 1892-94; A.M., Ph.D., Heidelberg, 1894; m. Alice G. Cooper, Sept. 6, 1881; children—Margaret, Frederica. Lecturer anatomy and physiology, Mass. Agrl. Coll., 1883-86; fellow Clark U., Worcester, 1889-90. Fellow A.A.A.S. Edited Diaries and Letters of Samuel Cooper, 1901-03; (with others) Life of Charles Anthony Goessmann, 1917. Author: Amherst Academy, a New England School of the Past, 1929; also various papers on vertebrate anatomy and embryology. Address: Amherst, Mass. Died 1929.

TUFTS, Bowen, banking; b. Lexington, Mass., June 17, 1884; s. Albert N. and Mary Tufts (Locke) T.; ed. grammar and high schs. of Somerville, Mass.; m. Octavia E. Williams, Sept. 23, 1907; children—Mary Octavia, Bowen Charlton, David Albert, Jeanne Elizabeth. Began with Jose Parker & Co., bankers, 1899, mgr., 1904; mem. firm of C. D. Parker & Co., 1910-12; v.p., mgr. C. D. Parker & Co., Inc., 1912—; dir., v.p. and trustee Mass. Utilities Associates, Nat. Service Cos., Mass. Cities Realty Co.; dir. New Ocean House, Inc. Republican. Unitarian. Home: Winchester, Mass. Died Apr. 7, 1935.

TUFTS, James Arthur, educator; b. Alstead, N.H., Apr. 26, 1855; s. Timothy and Sophia Philette (Kingsbury) T.; grad. Phillips Exeter Acad., 1874; A.B., Harvard, 1878; hon. A.M., Dartmouth, 1917; LL.D., U. of N.H., 1920; Litt.D., Boston U., 1928; m. Effie Locke, Dec. 21, 1878; children—Effie Miriam (dec.), Irving Elting, Theodora, Delmont Locke, James Arthur, Helen; m. 2d, Ruth B. Kilbourn, May 8, 1936. Prof. English, Phillips Exeter Acad., and sec. of faculty, 1878-1928 (emeritus). Mem. advisory council, Coll. of Practical Arts and Letters, Boston U. Mem. N.H. Ho. of Reps., 1905, 07 and 33 (chmn. com. on edn., first two sessions); mem. N.H. Senate, 1919-22 (chmn. com. on edn., both sessions; pres. of Senate, 1921-22). Trustee Robinson Sem., Exeter Pub. Library, Kensington Social Library; overseer Stoneleigh Coll. Progressive. Unitarian. Pres. Merrill Inst.; hon. v.p. Am. Unitarian Assn. Home: Exeter, N.H. Died Nov. 21, 1938.

TUHOLSKE, Herman, surgeon; b. Meseritz, Prussia, Mar. 27, 1848; s. Newman and Johanna (Arnfield) T.; ed. gymnasium, Meseritz, in Prussia, in Berlin, Vienna and London Med. univs.; M.D., Mo. Med. Coll., 1870; LL.D., Westminster Coll.; m. Sophie Epstein, June 24, 1874. Practiced at St. Louis, 1870—; phys.-in-chief St. Louis City Dispensary, 1870-75; demonstrator anatomy, 1873-81, prof. surgery till 1899, Mo. Med. Coll.; surgeon 1st Regt. Mo. N.G., 1895-99; surgeon in chief Jewish Hospital, 1902—; consulting surgeon St. John's Hosp.; prof. of surgery, Washington U., 1899-1909. Fellow Am. Coll. Surgeons; v.p. St. Louis Soc. Relief and Prevention Tuberculosis; mem. Nat. Assn. for Study and Prevention of Tuberculosis; founder mem. Internat. Gynecol. Assn. Home: St. Louis, Mo. Died 1922.

TULEY, Henry Enos, physician; b. Louisville, Ky., Jan. 11, 1870; s. Enos S. and Mary Eliza (Speed) T.; grad. pub. schs., 1888; M.D., U. of Louisville, 1890; N.Y. Polyclinic, 1891; Ky. Sch. of Medicine, Louisville, 1893; m. Ethel Brown Engelbach, June 26, 1894. Resident phys. N.Y. Infant Asylum, 1891-92; same, Sloane Maternity Hosp., New York, 1892; dean and prof. pediatrics emeritus, Med. Dept. of U. of Louisville, and supt. Louisville City Hosp. Pres. staff Masonic Widows and Orphans' Home. Sec., pres. Miss. Valley Med. Assn.; F.A.C.P.; mem. Congress on Internal Medicine; charter mem. and pres. Nat. Milk Commn. Author: Obstetrical Nursing, 1902; Pediatrics, 1904; Diseases of Children, 1909. Address: Louisville, Ky. Died Oct. 22, 1923.

TULEY, Murray F., jurist; b. Louisville, Ky., March 4, 1827; removed to Chicago, 1843; admitted to Ill. bar, 1847; served in Mexican war in 5th Ill. regt., 1847-48; practiced at Santa Fe, N.Mex., 1848-54; was 2 yrs. atty. gen. N.Mex., and 1 term mem. legislature; practiced law in Chicago, 1854-79; corp. counsel, 1869-73; circuit judge Cook County, Ill., 1879—. Democrat. Address: Chicago, Ill. Died 1905.

TULLY, William John, lawyer; b. Corning, N.Y., Oct. 1, 1870; s. Joseph J. and Sarah (Byers) T.; grad. Corning Free Acad., 1888; student Poly. Inst., Brooklyn, and Columbia U.; LL.B., New York Law Sch., 1892; LL.D., Alfred U., 1909; m. Clara Mabel Houghton, Oct. 5, 1898; children—Mrs. Reeve Hoover, Alice Bigelow. Practiced at Corning, 1893-1908, N.Y. City, 1908—; mem. N.Y. Senate, 1904-08 (resigned); mem. spl. legislative com. which investigated management of life ins. cos., 1905-06; atty. for Assn. Life Ins. Presidents, 1908-09; gen. solicitor Metropolitan Life Ins. Co., 1909-27, retired. Republican. Episcopalian. Home: Locust Valley, L.I., N.Y. Died Aug. 1930.

TUNNELL, Ebe Walter, governor; b. Blackwater, Del., Dec. 31, 1844; s. Nathaniel and Maria (Walter) T.; ed. pub. and pvt. schs., Lewes, Del.; unmarried. Merc. bus., Blackwater, 1862-98; also drugs and hardware, Lewes, 1871-1903; pres. Farmers Bank of Del., Georgetown, 1882—. Mem. Del. Ho. of Reps., 1871; clerk of ct., 1884-89; candidate for gov., Del., 1894; elected gov., term 1897-1901. Democrat. Presbyn. Home: Lewes, Del. Died Dec. 13, 1917.

TUNSTALL, Richard Baylor, lawyer; b. Norfolk, Va., July 1, 1848; s. Robert Baylor and Elizabeth Walke (Williamson) T.; brother of Robert Williamson T.; Norfolk Acad., William R. Galt's Sch., Va. Mil. Inst. (1864-65); M.A., U. of Va., 1868; taught Norwood Sch., Nelson Co., Va., 1 yr.; B.L., U. of Va., 1870; m. Isabel M. Heiser, Dec. 18, 1878 (died 1905). In May 1864, with cadets of Va. Mil. Inst., was in battle of New Market, under Gen. Breckenridge, C.S.A. Practiced law, Norfolk, Va., 1870-71, New York, 1871-83; again in Norfolk, 1883-1907 (retired). Dir. Norfolk Ry. & Light Co. Del. Universal Congress Lawyers and Jurists, St. Louis, 1904. Democrat; elector on Palmer and Buckner ticket, 1896. Episcopalian; chancellor Diocese of Southern Va., 1912-13. Address: Norfolk, Va. Died Oct. 11, 1919.

TUNSTALL, Robert Williamson, educator; b. Norfolk, Va., Dec. 18, 1851; s. Robert Baylor and Elizabeth Walke (Williamson) T.; brother of Richard Baylor T.; B.A., U. of Va., 1874; m. Isabel McRoberts, Sept. 3, 1901. Pvt. sec. to late Andrew Reid of Baltimore, 1874-78; taught in various schs. in South, 1878-82; prin. Norfolk, Va., Acad., 1882-1900; prof., 1900—, asst. to dir., 1905-16, Jacob Tome Inst. Episcopalian. Democrat. Editor: Cicero's Orations (for sch. use). Author: The Latin Ladder. Address: Port Deposit, Md. Died Nov. 1917.

TUPPER, Claude A., cons. engr.; b. Chicago, Ill., May 26, 1877; s. Charles A. and Louise V. (Aikens) Tupper; spl. courses in engring., U. of Wis.; m. Caroline A. Davis, June 3, 1905; children—Preston E. (dec.), Leslie C., Ellis C., Jane Elizabeth. Field engring. and mil. campaigns various countries, particularly of the Orient, until 1905; with Allis-Chalmers Mfg. Co., Milwaukee, 1905-12; sec. Penton Pub. Co., Cleveland, O., 1912-14; pres. Internat. Trade Press, Inc., Chicago, 1914-30; cons. engr., 1930—. Republican. Baptist. Home: Oak Park, Ill. Died Apr. 8, 1937.

TUPPER, Henry Allen, Bapt. clergyman; b. Charleston, S.C., Feb. 29, 1828; grad. Madison U., N.Y., 1848; Theol. Sem., same, 1850; D.D., 1870; ordained, 1850; pastor Granitesville, S.C., 1850-53; Washington, Ga., 1853-72, except the war period, when was chaplain 9th Ga. regt., C.S.A.; corr. sec. foreign missionary bd. Southern Bapt. Conv. about 20 yrs. from 1872. Author: Foreign Missions of the Southern Baptist Convention; Truth in Romance; American Baptist Missions in Africa. Address: Brooklyn, N.Y. Died 1902.

TUPPER, Henry Allen, clergyman; b. Washington, Ga., June 22, 1856; s. Henry Allen and Nannie (Boyce) T.; student Charleston (S.C.) Coll., Richmond (Va.) Coll., and U. of Va.; grad. Southern Bapt. Theol. Sem., 1879; D.D., 1890; LL.D., 1906, Georgetown Coll., Ky.; m. Marie Louise Pender, 1879; children—Allene, Katherine (Mrs. Clifton Brown), Tristram. Ordained Bapt. ministry, 1879; pastor Harrodsburg, Ky., Broadway Bapt. Ch., Louisville, Ky., Seventh Bapt. Ch., Baltimore, Calvary Bapt. Ch., Brooklyn, 1899-1919, 1st Bapt. Ch., Washington, 1919—. Held special missions among soldiers at Jacksonville, Miami and Key West, during Spanish-Am. War. Pres. New York Bapt. Ministers' Conf., New York Foreigners' Mission; trustee Garden Cities Assn. of America, Bur. Missions of America, Samaritan Hosp., etc. Apptd., Aug. 1912, spl. peace commr. of Internat. Peace Forum, and during his 14 trips to Mexico had fruitful conferences with the leaders of fed. and constitutionalist parties. Author: Armenia—Its Present Crisis and Past History, 1897; Around the World with Eyes Wide Open, 1898; Columbia's War for Cuba, 1898; Uncle Allen's Party in Palestine, 1899; A Ray for Each Day from the Sun of Righteousness, 1905; Democracy: The Hope of Humanity, 1919. Editor and contbr. to System Bible, 1921. Address: Baltimore, Md. Deceased.

TUPPER, Kerr Boyce, clergyman; b. Washington, Ga., Feb. 2, 1854; s. Rev. Henry Allen and Nancy (Boyce) T.; A.B., Mercer U., 1871; hon. A.M., 1874, LL.D., 1898; B.D., Southern Bapt. Sem., 1875; D.D., Pella (Ia.) U., 1888; m. Lucilla Houston Sloan, Nov. 20, 1875; children—Kerr Boyce (dec.), May Belle (Mrs. Warner Marshall), Frank Boyce. Ordained ministry Bapt. Ch., 1875; pastor First Ch., Charlottesville, Va., 1875-78, First Ch., Paducah, Ky., 1878-81, First Ch., Marquette, Mich., 1881-84, Fountain St. Ch., Grand Rapids, Mich., 1884-89, First Ch., Denver, 1889-95, First Ch., Phila., 1895-1905. Madison Av. Ch., N.Y. City, 1905-08; prof. of theology and lecturer on pub. speaking, Mercer U., 1935—; preached and lectured in univs. of Ga., Va., Rochester, Colo., Stanford, and others. Mem. Bd. of Home and Fgn. Missions and Publ. and Edn. Socs. at Phila. and N.Y. City. Republican. Mason. Author: Robertson's Living Thoughts, 1881; Treatise on Baptism, 1891; Seven Great Lights, 1894; Gladstone and Other Addresses, 1898; monograph of George Dana Boardman, 1898; The English Bible as a Classic. Awarded Algernon Sydney Sullivan Medallion, Mercer U., 1939. Home: Macon, Ga. Deceased.

TURCHIN, John Basil, soldier farmer; b. in Province of Don, Russia, Jan. 30, 1822; his name being Ivan Vasilevitch Turchininoff, which he anglicized as above. Served in Hungarian campaign and Crimean war in Russian army, reaching rank of col. Came to U.S., 1856; engr. with Ill. Central R.R.; served in Union army in Civil war as col. 19th Ill.; later brig. gen. After war solicitor of patents in Chicago; in 1873 established Polish colony of Radom in Washington County, Ill., where he lived on a farm. Author: The Campaign and Battle of Chickamauga. Address: Radom, Ill. Died 1901.

TURCK, Fenton Benedict, physician; b. Milwaukee, Aug. 25, 1857; s. J. Byron and Sarah A. (Ashby) T.; prep. edn. Markham Acad., Milwaukee; M.D., Chicago Med. Coll. (Med. Dept. Northwestern U.), 1891; m. Avis L. Paine, June 10, 1897; children—Katherine Paine, Fenton Benedict. House surgeon, Alexian Bros. Hosp., Chicago, 1891-92; prof. internal medicine, Post-Grad. Med. Sch., 1893; lecturer Jefferson Med. Coll., Phila., 1896, Coll. Phys. and Surg., Chicago, 1901-02, U. of Rome, Italy, 1906. Admitted Feb. 21, 1913, to practice in N.Y. without examination by Bd. of Regents Univ. State of N.Y., "because of having attained a position of eminence and authority in his profession"; dir. Research Lab. Turck Foundation. Capt. Reserve M.C., U.S.A. Fellow New York Acad. Medicine. Del. Internat. Med

Congress 5 times between 1894 and 1913. Devised instruments, including gyromele for exploration and scientific research in the alimentary tract, 1893; original research on gastritis, peptic ulcer, traumatic shock, etc.; studies in immunity on the shock phenomena and related living processes; investigations on Cytost-Anticytost reaction in cell division, regeneration and metabolism in plants and animals. Author of "Experimental Studies in Biology," and numerous original scientific publs. Home: New York, N.Y. Died Nov. 16, 1932.

TURINI, Giovanni, sculptor; b. nr. Verona, Italy, May 23, 1841; studied sculpture at Milan and Rome; later prof. at Milan; volunteer in 4th regt. Garibaldi's army, 1866; came to New York, 1867, and had studio there, 1867—. Among his works are group, "Angelica and Medoro;" bust of Leo XIII (in the Vatican, Rome); statue of Garibaldi (Washington Sq., New York); colossal bust of Mazzini and equestrian statue of General Bolivar in Central Park, New York; m. Margaret Thurston, 1882. Address: New York, N.Y. Died 1899.

TURK, Morris Howland, clergyman; b. Greenwood, Ind., June 2, 1867; s. Francis Scott and Sarah Tamma (Howland) T.; A.B., DePauw U., Greencastle, Ind., 1890, A.M., 1893; Ph.D., Boston U., 1902; D.D., Washburn Coll., Topeka, Kan., 1917; m. Olive Hays, Oct. 17, 1891. Ordained ministry Congl. Ch., 1898; pastor Wenham, Mass., 1898-1904, Natick, 1904-12; jr. pastor 1st Ch., Los Angeles, Calif., 1913-15; pastor Westminster Ch., Kansas City, Mo., 1915-20, Williston Ch., Portland, Me., 1921-34; author, preacher and lecturer, 1934—. Chaplain 7th Regt., Mo. N.G., 1918. Chmn. Nat. Council Commn. on Interchurch Relations; del. to World Conf. on Faith and Order, Lausanne, Switzerland, 1927, Edinburgh, 1937; mem. continuation com., World Conf.; mem. Internat. Congl. Council, Bournemouth, Eng., 1930; mem. Fed. Councils Commn. for Study of Christian Unity, 1937—. Republican. Mason. Author: They Live—and Are Not Far Away, 1923; The Shepherd of Jerusalem, 1929; In the Shadow of the Sphinx, 1933. Spl. writer for Pilgrim Press, 1934—. Address: Portland, Me. Died Mar. 2, 1939.

TURKLE, Alonzo John, clergyman; b. Fairview, O., Aug. 1, 1859; s. Francis and Mary Elizabeth (Nace) T.; A.B., Wittenberg Coll., Springfield, O., 1883, A.M., 1886, D.D., 1903; B.D., Yale, 1886; m. Amelia Manss, Nov. 25, 1886; children—Ruth (Mrs. Willard H. Buente), Lois (Mrs. William F. Trimble), Grace (Mrs. John P. Frazier), Dorothy (Mrs. Arthur MacFadden). Ordained ministry United Luth. Ch., in America, 1886; pastor St. Paul's Ch., Hillsboro, Ill., 1886-90, Kountze Memorial Ch., Omaha, Neb., 1890-99, Trinity Ch., Pittsburgh, Pa., Feb. 1899—. Pres. Bd. Edn. United Luth. Church in America. Republican. Home: Pittsburgh, Pa. Died Oct. 14, 1937.

TURLEY, Thomas Battle, senator; b. Memphis, Tenn., Apr. 5, 1845; served through war as pvt. in C.S.A.; LL.B., U. of Va., 1867; practiced law in Memphis, 1867—; m. Irene Rayner, 1871. Apptd. U.S. senator, July 29, 1897, and later selected by legislature to succeed Isham G. Harris; term expired 1901. Democrat. Address: Memphis, Tenn. Died 1910.

TURNBULL, Charles Smith, ophthalmologist; b. Phila., Nov. 10, 1847; s. Dr. Laurence and Louisa Paleska (Smith) T.; A.B., Central High Sch., Phila., 1868, A.M., 1869; Ph.D., U. of Pa., 1871, M.D., 1873; studied at Vienna, 1874-75; m. Elizabeth Claxton, Oct. 18, 1877. Surgeon U.S. Geol. Survey in Wyo. and Mont., 1872, and Yellowstone Park, 1871-72; resident surgeon N.Y. Ophthalmic and Aural Inst., 1873-75; chief aural dept. Jefferson Med. Coll., 10 yrs.; ophthalmic and aural surgeon to leading Phila. hosps.; oculist to German Hosp. Served as vol. 119th Pa. Vols. at close of Civil War; also in N.G. Pa.; maj. surgeon, 1st Regiment (active), also surg. maj. vet. corps 1st Regt. N.G. of Pa.; received spl. mention from regimental and div. headquarters for services as brigade surgeon at time of Pittsburgh riots, 1877. Fellow Am. Acad. Medicine. Address: Philadelphia, Pa. Died Feb. 21, 1918.

TURNBULL, Edwin Litchfield, composer; b. Baltimore, Md., Nov. 14, 1872; s. Lawrence and Francese Hubbard (Litchfield) T.; A.B., Johns Hopkins, 1893; studied music, Baltimore, 1887-90, in London, Florence, Munich, 1893-94; m. Rebecca Trueheart, 1923. In real estate bus., Baltimore, 1895-1920; organized, 1890, and conducted Beethoven Terrace Amateur Orchestra of 25 members, giving concerts in Baltimore and elsewhere; condr. of professional orchestra and band concerts and condr. of orchestra at Johns Hopkins pub. exercises, 1895-1915. Founder, 1919, and pres. Johns Hopkins Musical Assn., giving free symphony concerts with amateur orchestra of 100 pieces. Composer of songs for solo voice; hymns for mixed voices; compositions for male voices; arrangements, transcriptions and compositions for orchestra, etc. Address: Baltimore, Md. Died Sept. 22, 1927.

TURNBULL, Francese Hubbard Litchfield, author; b. in N.Y.; d. Edwin C. and Grace Hill (Hubbard) Litchfield; ed. at home and abroad, chiefly under pvt. tutors; m. Lawrence Turnbull, Jan. 24, 1871. A founder, 1890, pres. 7 yrs., Woman's Literary Club of Baltimore; with husband, founded, 1890, Percy Turnbull Memorial Lectureship of Poetry in Johns Hopkins U., in memory of a deceased son. Author: The Catholic Man (of which the prin. character is a study of Sidney Lanier, the poet), 1890; Val-Maria—a Romance of the Time of Napoleon, 1893; The Golden Book of Venice—A Historical Romance of the Sixteenth Century, 1900; The Royal Pawn of Venice—A Romance of Cyprus, 1911. Address: Baltimore, Md. Died Feb. 28, 1927.

TURNBULL, Laurence, M.D.; b. Shotts, Lanarkshire, Scotland, Sept. 10, 1821; m. Louise Paleske Smith, dau. late Col. Charles Somers Smith, 1846. Grad. Philadelphia Coll. Pharmacy, 1842; took charge of a dept. in chemistry, making several important discoveries in pharm. chemistry; grad. Jefferson Med. Coll., 1845, from office Prof. John K. Mitchell. Lecturer on chemistry applied to the arts, Franklin Inst., 1848-50; prof. eye and ear dept., Howard Hosp., 1857-87; vol. surgeon during Civil war; pres. sub-sect. otology, Brit. Med. Assn.; chairman sect. otology Am. Med. Assn. (New York meeting); invited to take part in Internat. Congress of Otology, London, Aug. 1899. Author: The Electro-Magnetic Telegraph; Imperfect Hearing and Hygiene of the Ear; Nature and Treatment of Nervous Deafness; Clinical Manual of Diseases of the Ear; A Manual of Anæsthetic Agents and Their Employment in the Treatment of Disease. Address: Philadelphia, Pa. Died 1900.

TURNBULL, Walter Mason, religious educator; b. Peterboro, Ont., Can., Oct. 10, 1881; s. John C. and Charlotte (Finlay) T.; A.B., McMaster U., Toronto, 1913; Teachers' Coll. (Columbia), 1914; D.D., Wheaton Coll., 1915; m. Cora M. Rudy, Dec. 28, 1916; m. 2d, Victoria Alexandrina Fleming, July 25, 1929. Ordained as missionary, 1903; missionary to India, 1903-09; city mission, Vancouver, 1910-14; prin. Wilson Memorial Academy, 1914-15; dean Missionary Training Inst., Nyack, N.Y., 1915—. Y.M.C.A. dir. at Camp Merritt, World War I. Mem. bd. mgrs. Christian and Missionary Alliance (ednl. sec. 1917-26, vice pres., 1926—). Editor Alliance Weekly, 1925—. Home: Nyack, N.Y. Died May 12, 1930.

TURNER, Archelaus Ewing, coll. pres.; b. Greenville, Ill., Apr. 27, 1861; s. Rev. William and Julia (Scott) T.; A.B., Lincoln (Ill.) Coll., 1881, A.M., 1884; m. Nettie I. Harry, June 23, 1887. Pres. Lincoln Coll., 1888-1900, Waynesburg (Pa.) Coll., 1900-04, Trinity U., Tex., 1904-07, Hastings (Neb.) Coll., 1907-12; asso. dir. Chautauqua Assn. of Pa., 1912-19; pres. Lincoln (Ill.) Coll., 1919—. Pres. Ill. Christian Endeavor Union, 1898-99. Home: Lincoln, Ill. Died June 23, 1938.

TURNER, Arthur Henry, organist, conductor; b. Meriden, Conn., Feb. 6, 1873; s. Henry Kitson and Ellen (Fletcher) T.; ed. pub. schs.; m. Elizabeth Ankar, Jan. 1, 1896; children—Clarence R., Mabel A., Mrs. Eleanore La Zazzera. Municipal organist, Springfield, Mass. 1918—; organizer, 1922, and dir. Springfield Symphony Orchestra; dir. Turner Sch. Music, Jr. Symphony Ensemble, MacDowell Male Choir, St. Cecilia Female Choir; organist and choirmaster Old First Ch. Home-Studio: Springfield, Mass. Died Mar. 29, 1938.

TURNER, Charles Edward, mayor; b. Richardson, Tex., Sept. 13, 1886; s. John Edward and Mary Elizabeth (Heffington) T.; grad. Oak Cliff High Sch., Dallas, 1904; m. Valine Leachman Oct. 28, 1920; 1 dau., Betty. In cattle business 1905-06; in wholesale drug bus., Dallas, 1911-14, real estate bus., 1914-17; pres. firm Chas. E. Turner & Co., Inc., 1919—; city plan commr., Dallas, 1925-29; mayor of Dallas, 1932-35; pres. Crown Hill Co.; dir. finance and comptroller Tex. Centennial Central Expn.; dir. Dallas Office & Club Bldg. Co.; mem. Advisory Bd. Rivers and Harbors Congress. Served as lt., later capt. inf., U.S.A., in France, World War I. Dir. Dallas Real Estate Bd. Democrat. Baptist. Scottish Rite Mason (33°). Home: Dallas, Tex. Died Mar. 5, 1936.

TURNER, Charles Willard, univ. prof.; b. Boston, Feb. 23, 1844; s. Roswell Willard and Mary (Howard) T.; A.B., Amherst, 1865, A.M., 1892; m. Kate Hamilton Hill, Oct. 1, 1866. Admitted to bar, 1867; practiced law, 1867-92; asso. prof. law, 1892-1905, lecturer on history, 1893-95, acting prof. history, 1895-97, acting prof. constl. history, 1897-1905, prof. law and constl. history, 1905—, and dean College of Law, July 1915—, U. of Tenn. Author: Syllabi of Work in Evidence, Insurance and Domestic Relations, 1900. Address: Knoxville, Tenn. Died May 14, 1922.

TURNER, Charles Yardley, mural painter; b. Baltimore, Nov. 25, 1850; s. John C. and Hannah (Bartlett) T.; grad. Art Sch. of Md. Inst., 1870; student Nat. Acad. Design; student, founder, pres., Art Students' League, New York; student in Paris with Jean Paul Laurens, M. Munkacsy and L. Bonnât; unmarried. Prof. drawing and painting, Art Students' League, 1881-84; asst. dir. of color and decorations Chicago Expn., 1893; dir. of color Buffalo Expn., 1901. Dir. Md. Inst., Baltimore. N.A., 1886 (v.p. N.A.D., 1903, 04). Address: Baltimore, Md. Died Dec. 31, 1918.

TURNER, Clarence W., congressman; b. nr. Clydeton, Tenn.; B.S., Nat. Normal U., Lebanon, O.; A.B. and LL.B., Northern Ind. Normal Coll.; m. Mrs. Nell Rust Cowen, Dec. 18, 1919. Owner and editor Waverly (Tenn.) Sentinel; chmn. Dem. Exec. Com. of Humphreys County; elected to Tenn. State Senate, 1900, 09, 11; city atty. and mayor of Waverly; elected, 1922, mem. 67th Congress to fill unexpired term; mem. 73d to 75th Congresses (1933-39), 6th Tenn. Dist. Presbyn. Mason. Home: Waverly, Tenn. Died Mar. 24, 1939.

TURNER, Douglas Kellogg, Presbyn. clergyman; b. Stockbridge, Mass., Dec. 17, 1823; descendant Elder William Brewster (Mayflower 1620); grad. Yale, 1843; studied theology at Andover Theol. Sem. and Yale Divinity Sch.; licensed to preach by Hampden East Congl. Assn., 1846; m. Rachel H. Darrah, May 14, 1856; m. 2d, Rebecca Darrah, May 28, 1868. Ordained pastor of Neshaminy Presbyn. Ch., April 18, 1848, to April 20, 1873; supplied Presbyn. chs. of Plumsteadville and Carversville, Pa., 1884; corr. sec. and librarian Presbyn. Hist. Soc., Phila., 1883-93; trustee Bucks County Hist. Soc.; mem. Pa. Hist. Soc.; mem. Council Presbyn. Hist. Soc., Phila. Author: History of Neshaminy Presbyterian Church; also 20 published historical essays. Address: Hartsville, Bucks County, Pa. Died 1902.

TURNER, Edward Raymond, univ. prof.; b. Baltimore, May 28, 1881; s. Charles and Rosalind (Flynn) T.; A.B., St. John's Coll., Md., 1904; Ph.D., Johns Hopkins, 1910; m. Eleanor Howard Bowie, Sept. 1, 1917; children—Eleanor Bowie, Charles Edward, Raymond. Asso. in history, Bryn Mawr Coll., 1910-11; prof. European history, U. of Mich., 1911-24; prof. English history, Yale, 1924-25; prof. European history, Johns Hopkins, 1925—. Episcopalian. Mem. Am. Hist. Assn. (Justin Winsor prize, 1910). Author: The Negro in Pennsylvania, 1910; The New Market Campaign, 1912; Ireland and England, 1919; Europe, 1789-1920, 1920; Europe since 1870, 1921; Europe, 1450-1789, 1923; Europe since 1789, 1924; The Privy Council of England in the 17th and 18th Centuries (2 vols.), 1927, 28; various articles in Am. Hist. Rev. and English Hist. Rev. Lecturer Schouler foundation, Johns Hopkins U., 1923. Home: Baltimore, Md. Died Dec. 31, 1929.

TURNER, Fennell Parrish, missionary sec.; b. Danielsville, Dickinson County, Tenn., Feb. 25, 1867; s. Rev. William Allen and Mary Jane (Pickett) T.; B.A., Vanderbilt U., 1891; L.H.D. from Hope Coll., Holland, Mich.; student Theological Sch., Vanderbilt, 1891-92; m. Rose Vaughan, Nov. 3, 1897. Prin. Dixon Acad., Shelbyville, Tenn., 1888-90; asst. editor and bus. mgr. Tennessee Methodist, 1891-95; state Y.M.C.A. sec. of North Carolina, 1895-97; gen. sec. Student Vol. Movement for Foreign Missions, 1897-1919; mem. and sec. Bd. of Missionary Preparation, 1912-28; sec. Com. of Reference and Council, 1918-28; sec. Foreign Missions Conf. of N.A., 1919-28. Mem. Gen. Com. World's Student Christian Fedn., 1912-19; mem. Bd. Am. Christian Lit. Soc. for Moslems; mem. Editorial Council Missionary Rev. of the World. Del. World's Missionary Conf., Edinburgh, 1910, Internat. Missionary Conf., Crans, Switzerland, 1920, Lake Mohawk, N.Y., 1921, Oxford, Eng., 1923, Jerusalem, 1928; mem. Internat. Missionary Council, 1920-28; exec. com. World Alliance for Promoting Internat. Friendship Through the Chs.; administrative com. Fed. Council of Chs.; mem. Commn. on Internat. Justice and Goodwill, 1919-28; del. Congress on Christian Work in Latin America, Panama, 1916, Montevideo, 1925. Havana, 1929; sec. Foreign Missions Conv., Washington, D.C., 1925; sec. Missionary Edn. and Foreign Extension of Gen. S.S. Bd., M.E. Ch., S., 1928-30; mem. Laymen's Foreign Missions Inquiry, in India, China and Japan, 1930-31. Methodist. Editor: Call, Qualification and Preparation of Missionary Candidates; Twenty-five Years of the Student Volunteer Movement; Students and the Present Missionary Crisis; Students and the World-Wide Expansion of Christianity; The Candidate and the Candidate Department of a Foreign Mission Board; also various repts. on missionary topics. Address: New York, N.Y. Deceased.

TURNER, Frederick Jackson, univ. prof.; b. Portage, Wis., Nov. 14, 1861; s. Andrew Jackson and Mary (Hanford) T.; A.B., U. of Wis., 1884, A.M., 1888, Litt.D., 1921; Ph.D., Johns Hopkins, 1890; LL.D., U. of Ill., 1908; Litt.D., Harvard, 1909; Ph.D., Royal Frederic U., Christiania, 1911; m. Caroline Mae Sherwood, 1889; children—Dorothy Kinsley (Mrs. John S. Main), Jackson Allen (dec.), Mae Sherwood (dec.). Tutor rhetoric and oratory, 1885-88, asst. prof. Am. history, 1889-91, prof. history, 1891-92, prof. Am. history, 1892-1910, U. of Wis.; prof. history, Harvard, 1910-24, emeritus; research asso. Henry E. Huntington Library, 1927-30. Mem. bd. editors, Am. Hist. Rev., 1910-15; mem. nat. bd. for Hist. Service, 1917; research asso., dept. history, Carnegie Instn., 1916-17. Pres. Am. Hist. Assn., 1910-11, Colonial Soc. of Mass., 1914-16; fellow Am. Acad. Arts and Sciences. Author: Rise of the New West, 1906; Frontier in American History, 1920. Also monographs and articles. Address: San Marino, Calif. Died Mar. 14, 1932.

TURNER, George, senator; b. Edina, Mo., Feb. 25, 1850; s. Granville D. and Maria (Taylor) T.; common sch. edn.; m. Bertha C. Dreher, June 4, 1878. U.S. marshal for southern and middle dists. of Ala., 1876-80; asso. justice Supreme Ct., Wash., 1884-88; mem. Constl. Conv. of Wash. Rep. in politics prior to campaign of 1896. Elected U.S. senator by a state orgn. called the People's Party, composed of a fusion of Silver Republicans, Democrates and Populists, for term 1897-1903. On conclusion of service in the Senate, apptd. mem. Alaska Boundary Tribunal, London, 1903, which settled the Alaska boundary dispute, pending between U.S. and Great Britain; one of counsel for U.S. in the North Eastern Fisheries Arbitration between U.S. and Great Britain, argument held at The Hague, spring of 1910; mem. Internat. Joint Commn., U.S. and Can., under treaty of Jan. 11, 1909, 1913-14. Home: Spokane, Wash. Died Jan. 26, 1932.

TURNER, Henry McNeal, bishop; b. Newberry C.H., S.C., Feb. 1, 1834; s. Hardy and Sarah (Greer) T.; learned to read and write by his own perseverance; at 15 yrs., employed in law office, Abbeyville C.H., and young lawyers in office often assisted him with his studies; learned to read accurately and studied geography, arithmetic, history, astronomy, hygiene and anatomy. United with M.E. Ch., S., 1848; licensed to preach, 1853; traveled and preached among the colored people in S.C., Ga., Ala., and other Southern states. Transferred membership to A.M.E. Ch., 1858; shortly after, joined Mo. Annual Conf.; became itinerant minister; transferred to Baltimore Annual Conf. by Bishop D. A. Payne, D.D.; remained 4 yrs., meantime studying Latin, Greek, Hebrew and divinity at Trinity Coll.; LL.D., U. of Pa., 1872; D.D., Wilberforce, 1873; D.C.L.; m. Eliza Ann Peacher, Aug. 31, 1856; m. 2d, Mrs. Martha De Witt, Aug. 1893; m. 3d, Harriet A., widow of Bishop A. W. Wayman, Aug. 16, 1900; m. 4th, Laura Pearle Lemon, Dec. 3, 1907. Pastor Israel Ch., Washington, 1863; commd. chaplain U.S.C.T. by President Lincoln (1st colored chaplain ever commd.); mustered out Sept. 1865; commd. by President Johnson chaplain in regular army, detailed as officer Freedmen's Bur. in Ga.; resigned commn.; resumed ministry; organized sch. for colored children; elected mem. Constl. Conv., Ga., 1867; mem. Ga. Legislature, 1868 and 1870; postmaster Macon, later insp. of customs, then U.S. secret detective. Elected by Gen. Conf. A.M.E. Ch., 1876, mgr. of its publs. at Phila.; elected bishop by Gen. Conf. at St. Louis, 1880; one of principal agitators of return of his race to Africa; organized 4 annual confs. in Africa, 1 in Sierra Leone, 1 in Liberia, 1 in Prætoria, Transvaal, and 1 in Queenstown, S. Africa; later presiding bishop in Can. and Mich. Author: Methodist Polity; Hymn Book of A.M.E. Church; also a catechism, various sermons, lectures, etc. Address: Atlanta, Ga. Died May 8, 1915.

TURNER, Henry Ward, geologist, mining engr.; b. Silver Lake, Susquehanna County, Pa., Aug. 22, 1857; s. Edwin Morgan and Martha L. (Ellis) T.; student Cornell U., 1874-76 and 1882; Leipzig, 1879-80; B.S., Columbian (now George Washington) U., 1895; m. Caroline Wadsworth, Apr. 18, 1892. Mem. U.S. Geol. Survey, 1882-1900; pvt. practice, 1901—. Author: The Origin of Yosemite Valley, 1900; several geol. folios of Calif., papers on geology of Calif. and other regions in annual reports geol. survey and in geol. and mining jours. Address: Ross, Calif. Died Nov. 25, 1937.

TURNER, Herbert Beach, lawyer; b. Cheshire, Conn., 1835; s. Rev. Dr. Samuel Hulbeart and Mary Cather (Beach) T.; grad. Columbia, 1855; studied law, Albany Law Sch.; admitted to bar; m. Sarah Kirkland Floyd, 1863. Mem. law firm, Turner, McClure & Rolston; dir. Lawyers Mortgage Ins. Co., Lawyers Title Ins. Co. Interested in movements for reform of nat. and municipal politics. Home: New York, N.Y. Died 1903.

TURNER, James H., educator; b. Franklin County, Va., Oct. 23, 1841; s. John T. B. and Jane (Wright) T.; A.B., Roanoke Coll., 1867, A.M., 1870, D.D., 1902; studied div. pvtly.; m. Josephine M. L. Glossbrenner, Oct. 23, 1867. Pvt. and lt. C.S.A., 1861-65; served under Stuart, Hampton, Fitzhugh Lee, W. H. E. Lee, and comd. his co. in all important engagements from Gettysburg to end of war. Entered ministry of English Luth. Ch. (Gen. Synod of U.S.), 1869; taught in pvt. acads., Blountville, Tenn., and Fairmount, Md.; pastor Blacksburg, Va., 1872-76, Burkittsville, Md., 1876-80; pres. Md. Coll. for Women, 1880-1908. Address: Lutherville, Md. Died June 25, 1930.

TURNER, James Patrick, Roman Catholic prelate; b. Phila., Pa.; s. William and Elizabeth (Dempsey) T.; ed. St. Philip's Sch., Phila., and St. Charles' Sem., Overbrook; D.D., Spring Hill Jesuit Coll., Mobile, Ala., 1905. Priest R.C. Ch., June 11, 1885; missionary in Phila., Colo. and Calif., 1885-86; sec. to Bishop Machebeuf of Denver, 1886; sec. to Archbishop Ryan, Phila., 1899, and chancellor of the Archdiocese, 1901-10; vicar-gen., 1902-10; domestic prelate, July 29, 1905; prothonotary apostolic, Nov. 12, 1906; rector Ch. of Nativity, Phila., 1911—; spiritual dir. Holy Name Union of Phila. Mng. editor, Am. Catholic Quarterly Rev., 1898—; supervising editor Quarterly Annals Tabernacle Soc., 1893—. Mem. bd. dirs. Rush Hosp. for Consumptives, etc. Address: Philadelphia, Pa. Died May 31, 1929.

TURNER, Joseph Augustine, agriculturist; b. Hollins, Va., Nov. 21, 1875; s. Joseph Augustine and Leila Virginia (Cocke) T.; ed. Richmond (Va.) Coll., 1892-94, U. of Va., 1894-97, Eastman Business Coll., summer 1899; m. Mary VanFossen Masters, Feb. 16, 1904; children—Mary VanFossen, Joseph Augustine, Susanna Pleasants. Teacher Alleghany Inst., 1897-98; with Hollins Coll., 1898—; gen. mgr. and mem. bd. of govs., 1901-32, bus. mgr. and sec. Hollins Coll. Corp., 1932—. Mem. bd. visitors Virginia Agrl. and Mech. Coll. and Poly. Inst., 1912-19. Awarded certificate Va. Agrl. and Mech. Coll. and Poly. Inst. "for promoting development of agriculture." Democrat. Baptist. Contbr. to farm jours. Speaker on education, agriculture, Va. history, etc. Died Oct. 21, 1937.

TURNER, Laura Lemon; b. McDonough, Ga., Aug. 4, 1880; d. George and Louise Lemon; A.B., Morris Brown Coll., 1898; m. Bishop Henry M. Turner, of A.M.E. Ch., Dec. 3, 1907. Lecturer and missionary worker; editor Woman's Missionary Recorder; pres. Woman's Home and Foreign Missionary Soc. of A.M.E. Ch. Address: Atlanta, Ga. Died Nov. 11, 1915.

TURNER, Martin Luther, banker; b. Greene County, Mo., Oct. 1, 1863; s. John N. and Harriet (Nichols) T.; ed. pub. schs., Webster County, Mo., 1876-81; m. Hallie Switzler, Nov. 4, 1883. Lived on farm until 1876; in grocery store, 1876-77; in grain trade, 1878-83; in banking business, 1887-89; handled municipal bonds in Colo., 1890; handled state, county and city bonds in Northwest, 1891, living at Spokane, Wash.; located at Guthrie, Okla., 1891; pres. and half owner Capitol Nat. Bank, Guthrie, 1892-95; treas. Okla. Ty., 1894-98; established Jan. 1, 1899, and pres., Western Nat. Bank, Okla. City On Aug. 22, 1904, purchased $3,000,000 Philippine 4 per cent bonds in competition with Wall St. and other eastern financiers. Receiver Kansas City, Mexico & Orient Railway, 1912-15. Home: Oklahoma City, Okla. Died Feb. 16, 1921.

TURNER, Ross Sterling, artist; b. Westport, Essex County, N.Y., June 29, 1847; s. David and Eliza Jane (Cameron) T.; academic edn. Williamsport, Pa.; engaged as artist, 1873—; studied in Europe, mostly in Germany (Munich) and Italy, 1876, 80, 82; m. Miss E. Louise Blaney, 1884. Pictures in oil and water colors; A Small Court, Mexico; El Jardin Modesto; A Painted Ship (ancient marine); The Flying Dutchman (ancient marine); A Bermuda Wedding (pastel). Prof. Normal Art Sch., Boston, Oct. 1, 1909—. Author: Water Colors; Art for the Eye—School Room Decorations, etc. Published reproduction of the Golden Galleon picture, Century Magazine, March 1899. Address: Salem, Mass. Died Feb. 12, 1915.

TURNER, Walter Victor, engineer, inventor; b. Epping Forest, Essex County, Eng., Apr. 3, 1866; s. George and Beatrice (Brandon) T.; ed. Textile Tech. Sch., Wakefield, Yorkshire, Eng.; m. Beatrice Woolford, Nov. 1887. Came to U.S., 1888; sec. and mgr. Lake Ranch Cattle Co., Raton, N.M., 1893; with A.,T.&S.F. R.R., 1897, and same yr. developed first patent; with Westinghouse Air Brake Co., 1903—, apptd. mech. engr., 1907, chief engr., 1910, asst. mgr., 1915, mgr. of engring., 1916. His elec., mech. and pneumatic inventions covered by over 400 U.S. patents, and in use on most of rys. of world and in many large indsl. plants; awarded Longstreth medal, 1911, Elliott Cresson medal, 1912; testimonial as the leading air brake expert, by Air Brake Assn., Richmond, Va., 1912. Fellow Royal Soc. of Arts (Eng.). Republican. Methodist. Author: Train Control—Its Development and Effect on Transportation Capacity (2 vols.), 1918. Home: Wilkinsburg, Pa. Died Jan. 9, 1919.

TURNER, Wilfred Dent, lawyer; b. Turnersburg, Iredell County, N.C., Jan. 30, 1855; s. Wilfred and Dorcas (Tomlinson) T.; A.B., Trinity Coll., N.C., 1876, A.M., 1879; m. Ida L. Lanier, Jan. 30, 1878 (died 1894); children—Mrs. Mabel M. Calvert, Laura L., Mrs. Edna E. Robertson, Wilfred Jackson; m. 2d, Julie H. MacCall, June 9, 1897 (died 1925); children—Dent, Dorcas Tomlinson; m. 3d, Mrs. Sarah F. Goff, Dec. 7, 1927. Admitted to N.C. bar, 1877, and practiced at Statesville, 1877—; sr. mem. firm Turner, Moss & Winberry, 1931—; pres. Imperial Furniture Mfg. Co. Mem. of N.C. Senate 4 terms; lt. gov. of N.C., 1901-05; as pres. of Senate presided over court of impeachment of Chief Justice Furches and Asso. Justice Douglass of Supreme Ct. of N.C., 1901. Mem. Am. and N.C. bar assns. Democrat. Methodist. Home: Statesville, N.C. Died Nov. 8, 1933.

TURNER, William, bishop; b. Kilmallock, Ireland, Apr. 8, 1871; s. Patrick and Bridget (Carey) T.; A.B., Royal U., Ireland, 1888, 1st honors in philosophy; S.T.D., Am. Coll., Rome, 1893; studied Institut Catholique, Paris, 1893-94. Ordained priest R.C. Ch., 1893; prof. philosophy St. Paul (Minn.) Sem., 1894-1906; prof. philosophy, Catholic U. of America, 1906-19. Consecrated bishop of Buffalo, 1919. Librarian Catholic U. and editor Catholic U. Bulletin. Lecturer Brooklyn Inst. Arts and Sciences, 1911, 12, 13; lecturer Trinity Coll., Washington, and various Catholic summer schools. Democrat. Author: History of Philosophy, 1903; Lessons in Logic, 1911. Editor Am. Eccles. Rev., 1914-19; asso. editor Catholic Hist. Rev. K. of C. Address: Buffalo, N.Y. Died July 10, 1936.

TURNER, William Henry, commodore U.S.N.; b. Cincinnati, O., Jan. 28, 1848; s. Samuel and Rachel Sparks (Wiltsee) T.; unmarried. Grad. U.S. Naval Acad., 1869; commd. ensign, July 12, 1870; master, Apr. 12, 1872; lt., May 13, 1875; lt. comdr., May 16, 1897; comdr., Mar. 29, 1900; capt., May 6, 1905; commodore and retired, June 30, 1906. Served in N. and S. Atlantic squadrons, European, Asiatic, and N. and S. Pacific squadrons and several spl. cruises; served on shore duty at New York, Norfolk and Portsmouth navy yards; stationed at Washington, and U.S. Naval Acad. Home: Cincinnati, O. Died June 25, 1926.

TURNEY, Daniel Braxton, clergyman; b. Shawneetown, Ill., Apr. 17, 1848; s. L. Jay S. and Elizabeth (Parrish) T.; ed. pub. schs., and Willamette U., Salem, Ore.; A.M., D.D., LL.D.; m. Emma Virginia Oglesby, Apr. 14, 1875. Entered M.P. ministry, 1873; in active pastoral work, 1873—. Ministerial mem. 3 Gen. Confs. and pres. of his annual conf. several times. Research in polemics, polemic of M.P. Ch., having participated in fully 200 joint discussions. Nominee of United Christians for President U.S., 1908, renominated for 1912. Author: The Mode of Baptism According to the Scriptures, 1887; also various theol. and polemical articles and tracts. Pres. Union of Am. Pacificators. Address: Decatur, Ill. Died Jan. 17, 1926.

TURNEY, Peter, lawyer, gov.; b. Jasper, Marion County, Tenn., Sept. 22, 1827; s. Hopkins L. T. (U.S. Senator from Tenn.); ed. pub. and pvt. schs.; admitted to bar, 1848; practiced at Winchester, Tenn.; defeated for atty. gen., 1854; alternate elector, Breckinridge and Lane ticket, 1860; col. Turney's 1st Tenn. regt.; recommended for promotion, but failed to get it because of unfriendliness of Jefferson Davis; judge Supreme Ct. Tenn., 1870-93 (chief justice, Sept. 1886, to Jan. 1893); defeated for U.S. senator, 1876; gov. Tenn., 1893-97. Address: Winchester, Tenn. Died 1903.

TURNEY, William Ward, lawyer, banker; b. Marshall, Tex., July 11, 1861; s. Albert Gallatin and Salina (Ward) T.; ed. Sam Houston Normal Sch., Huntsville, Tex.; m. Iva Guthrie, Dec. 15, 1892. Admitted to Tex. bar, 1887; mem. Jones, Turney, Hardie, Grambling & Howell, El Paso, Tex.; gen. counsel A.T.&S.F. Ry. Co., El Paso Union Passenger Depot Co., Mexico Northwestern Ry. Co. Extensively identified with live stock business. County attorney, Brewster County, Tex., 1887-88; mem. Tex. Ho. of Rep., 1892-96, Senate, 1896-1902. Home: El Paso, Tex. Died Mar. 23, 1939.

TURNLEY, Parmenas Taylor, soldier, author; b. Dandridge, Tenn., Sept. 6, 1821; s. John Cunnyngham and Mahala (Taylor) T.; grad. West Point, 1846; joined Gen. Zachary Taylor's army, then on Rio Grande, beginning war against Mexico; served through Mexican war, and until 1852, locating and building mil. stas., along Rio Grande and Marking boundary line bet. Mexico and U.S.; on various duties and details until 1857; on Gen. Albert Sidney Johnston's Utah Expdn., 1857-61; had charge of bldg. mil. post 40 miles from Salt Lake; at work establishing army depots at Annapolis, Md., St. Louis, Cairo, Ill., Columbus, Ky., Memphis, Tenn., 1861-62. Disabled by chronic gastritis and retired by President Lincoln from service, Sept. 17, 1863, "for long and faithful service and disease contracted in line of duty." Resident of Highland Park, Ill., 1881—, alderman and mayor. Author: Turnley's Narrative from Diary, 1893; "The Turnley's," 1905. Address: Highland Park, Ill. Died 1911.

TURPIE, David, lawyer; b. Hamilton County, O., July 8, 1829; grad. Kenyon Coll., 1848; admitted to bar, Logansport, Ind., 1849; apptd. judge ct. of common pleas, 1854, and judge of circuit ct., 1856, resigned; in 1853 and 1858 mem. Ind. legislature; U.S. senator, 1863, from Jan. to Mar., to fill unexpired term; later mem. and speaker Ind. Ho. of Reps. Commr. to revise the laws of Ind., 1878-81; U.S. Atty. for Ind., 1886-87; U.S. senator, 1887-99. Address: Indianapolis, Ind. Died 1909.

TURRILL, Charles Beebe; b. nr. Folsom, Sacramento Co., Calif., Mar. 26, 1854; s. Madison Hollister and Laura (Vary) T.; ed. Lincoln Grammar Sch., San Francisco, Boys' High Sch. and pvt. schs.; unmarried. In various lines of business until 1878; gen. mgr. San Diego C. of C., 1887-88; sec. Calif. State Viticultural Commn., 1889; resource, indsl. and hist. photography, 1900-16. Commr. of Calif., New Orleans Expn., 1884-85 and 1885-86. Republican. Founder the Charles B. Turrill Hist. Library, containing over 15,000 vols., chiefly California, and about 15,000 hist. pictures relating to Calif. Devoted attention largely to Calif. hist. research; contbr. of many articles to mags. and newspapers. Chmn. War History Com. of San Francisco. Home: San Francisco, Calif. Died May 11, 1927.

TUSKA, Gustave Robisher, cons. engr.; b. N.Y. City, July 15, 1869; s. Adolph and Elsie (Robisher) T.; B.Sc., Coll. City of N.Y., 1888, M.Sc., 1891; C.E., Sch. of Mines (Columbia), 1891; m. Isabel Pappenheim, Nov. 24, 1902. Asst. engr. Link Engring. Co., 1891-92; bridge engr., L.I. R.R. Co., 1892-93; lecturer on bridge design and masonry constrn., Columbia, 1893-97; resident engr., Knoxville, Cumberland Gap and Louisville R.R. Co., 1894-95; engr. to Health Dept., N.Y. City, 1894-96; resident engr. Central N.Y. and Western R.R., 1896; chief engr. Panama R.R. and superintending engr. Panama S.S. Co., 1896-99; pres. and chief engr. Am. Process Co., in charge constrn. plants handling waste products, 1899-1925; pres. and chief engr. Atlantic Constrn. Co., 1899-1907; lecturer on municipal engring., Columbia, 1915-17. Consultant on municipal engring. work, City of New York, St. Louis, Chicago, Buffalo, Washington, D.C., and water power plants, railroads and piers, N.H., Va., N.Y., etc.; pres. Internat. Engineering Corp., 1923—. Maj. engrs. U.S.A., Sept. 24, 1917-July 28, 1919, at Camp Lee and Camp Humphrey's, Va., on staff of chief of engrs. U.S.A., and at office of Dir. Gen. Mil. Rys., Washington; lt. col. engrs., Res., U.S.A., 1923. Mem. steel com. War Industries Bd., Washington, 1918; mem. Mexican Com., U.S. Govt., 1919; del. 2d Pan-Am. Congress, Washington, 1920, to 3d Pan-Am. Congress, 1927. Fellow A.A.A.S.; mem. Nat. Inst. Social Sciences, Am. Acad. Polit. and Social Science; trustee Allied Patriotic Socs. Home: New York, N.Y. Died May 28, 1931.

TUSTIN, Ernest Leigh, lawyer; b. Lewisburg, Pa., Dec. 20, 1862; s. Francis Wayland and Maria M. (Probasco) T.; A.B., Bucknell U., 1884, LL.D.; read law at Sunbury, Pa.; admitted to bar, 1886; post-grad. law course, U. of Pa.; m. Ella Mae Woodruff, June 4, 1889. In practice at Phila., 1887—; mem. law firm Tustin & Wesley, 1899—; v.p. Wm. H. Hoskins Co. Mem. Pa. Senate, 1905-12. Recorder City of Phila. and pres. Playgrounds Assn.; trustee Bucknell U., Hahnemann Med. Coll., Crozer Theol. Sem., Bd. Trade, Am. Bapt. Publ. Soc., Pa. Bapt. Edn. Soc., Child Fedn. Home: Overbrook, Phila. Died Dec. 19, 1921.

TUTHILL, Richard Stanley, judge; b. Vergennes, Jackson County, Ill., Nov. 10, 1841; s. Daniel Braley and Sally (Strong) T.; A.B., Middlebury Coll., Vt., 1863, A.M., 1868; LL.D., Ill. Coll., 1901, St. Ignatius Coll., Chicago, 1898, Middlebury, Vt., 1909; entered army 1863, served as scout attached to command Gen. John A. Logan, later 2d and 1st lt. Battery H, 1st Mich. Light Arty., 3d Div., 17th Army Corps, Army of Tenn.; resigned, May 29, 1865, at close of war; m. Jane Frances Smith, Aug. 24, 1868 (died 1872); m. 2d, Harriet, d. Edward McKey, Jan. 2, 1877 (died 1909); m. 3d, Susan Payne Trimble, Sept. 1911. Admitted to the bar, 1866; practiced at Nashville, Tenn., 1866-73; state's atty. Nashville Circuit, 1867-71; located at Chicago, 1873; city atty., 1875-79; U.S. dist. atty., 1884-86; judge Circuit Ct., Cook County, Ill., 1887—. Republican. Under juvenile ct. law of 1899 was chosen by brother judges to organize and hold juvenile ct., in addition to other duties; held this ct. for 6 yrs. This was the original "Juvenile Court," which has extended throughout the U.S. and the world. Organizer and mem. bd. of trustees (state) St. Charles (Ill.) Sch. for Boys, until change of law; pres. Chicago Law Sch. One of 306 who in Rep. Nat. Conv. of 1880 voted to the last for Gen. Grant. Mason. Episcopalian. Home: Evanston, Ill. Died Apr. 10, 1920.

TUTHILL, Theodore Robinson, judge; b. Moravia, N.Y., July 19, 1868; s. Tyrus Truman and Harriet (Robinson) T.; attended Union High Sch., Moravia; law dept. Cornell U., 1888-90; m. Edith, d. Clinton F. Paige, Mar. 18, 1909. Began practice at Oswego, N.Y., 1891; moved to Binghamton, 1898; elected justice Supreme Ct. of N.Y., 6th Dist., Nov. 1919, for term ending Dec. 31, 1933. An organizer, sec. and counsel Peoples Trust Co., Binghamton, until 1920, later dir. Republican. Episcopalian. Mason. Home: Binghamton, N.Y. Died Dec. 14, 1922.

TUTT, John Calhoun, writer; b. Warrenton, Va., Mar. 31, 1851; s. James M. and Ann (Kemper) T.; removed with parents to Mo., 1859; ed. pvt. and pub. schs. and acads.; m. Augusta Maynard, Dec. 25, 1878. First employed in printing office, Edina, Mo.; worked on Commercial, Louisville, Ky., and later became reporter and mng. editor of Evening Ledger; employed on newspapers of St. Joseph, Mo., and Indianapolis, 1874-88; lectured on religious and biog. topics, 1875; wrote regularly for Chicago Sunday Times and occasionally for Chicago Tribune, 1888-92, also proof reader Chicago Herald; professional reader Shakespeare's tragedies, specializing Othello and Hamlet, 1893-94; began writing for Phila. Times, 1895; writer of Sunday polit. articles for St. Louis Globe-Democrat, 1896-1914; editorial writer N.Y. American, 1914; later with Indianapolis Star. Republican. Methodist. Home: Indianapolis, Ind. Died Oct. 13, 1917.

TUTTLE, Albert Henry, biologist; b. Cuyahoga Falls, O., Nov. 19, 1844; s. Henry Blakeslee and Emeline (Reed) T.; B.Sc., State Coll. of Pa., 1868, M.Sc., 1872, hon. A.M., 1918; m. Kate Austin Seeley, Aug. 7, 1873; children—William Buckhout, Clara Mary (Mrs. W. Ramsey Probasco), Anna Seeley (Mrs. W. Harry Heck, dec.). Prof. natural sciences, State Normal Sch., Platteville, Wis., 1868-70; instr. microscopy, Harvard, 1870-72; commr. from Ohio to Vienna Expn., 1873; prof. zoölogy and comparative anatomy, Ohio State U., 1874-88; prof. biology, U. of Va., 1888-1913; retired upon Carnegie Foundation. Fellow A.A.A.S. (v.p. sect. microscopy, 1882), Royal Micros. Soc., London. Author occasional papers on scientific and ednl. subjects. Address: University, Va. Deceased.

TUTTLE, Alexander Harrison, clergyman; b. Bordentown, N.J., Feb. 28, 1844; s. Rev. James M. and Margaret (Dickerson) T.; A.B., Wesleyan U., 1866, A.M., 1869; B.D., Drew Theol. Sem., 1874; Ph.D., Grant Memorial U., 1886; D.D., Syracuse, 1886; S.T.D., Wesleyan, 1907; m. Charlotte T. Gamewell, May 23, 1872. Ordained M.E. ministry, 1869; stated supply Green Village, N.J., 1866-68; pastor Hackensack, N.J., 1869-71, Jersey City, 1872-74, Union St. Ch., Newark, 1875-77, Hackettstown, N.J., 1878-80, Elizabeth, N.J., 1881-82, Plainfield, N.J., 1883-85, First Ch., Wilkes-Barré, Pa., 1886-88, Mt. Vernon Pl. Ch., Baltimore, 1889-92, Roseville Ch., Newark, N.J., 1893-96, St. Luke's, Newark, 1897-99, East Orange, N.J., 1900, Summit, N.J., 1901-14. Author: The Jew, 1899; Analysis of Romans, 1892; The Young Man, 1901; The Living Word, 1904; Safe and Sure, 1906; Life of Mary Porter Gamewell, Missionary in China, 1907; Letters from Palestine and Egypt; Nathan Bangs, 1909; The Exodus, 1911; Egypt to Canaan, 1912; also articles in Methodist Rev. and Biblical Rev., New York. Home: East Orange, N.J. Died Dec. 4, 1932.

TUTTLE, Bloodgood, architect; b. N.Y. City, Jan. 23, 1889; s. Wylie Fay and Marion (Bloodgood) T.; prep. edn., Chicago (Ill.) Manual Training High Sch.; study Art Inst. Chicago and Ecole des Beaux Arts, Paris; m. Elizabeth Whittaker, Sept. 8, 1907; children—Marion Elizabeth, Arthur Bloodgood; m. 2d, Jessica Marie Blackwell, Oct. 8, 1919. Began practice at New York, 1914. Prin. works: Gates of Heaven Cemetery, St. Patrick's Cathedral, N.Y. City; Midland County (Mich.) Court House; Kroger Bldg., Cleveland, O.; Alberly Manor and Luedeking Estate, Cincinnati, O. Episcopalian. Mason. Lecturer on archæol. modelling, Beaux Arts Inst. Design. Home: Cleveland, O. Deceased.

TUTTLE, Charles Augustus, economist; b. Hadley, Mass.; s. Worster Henry and Margaret Elizabeth (Helmsing) T.; A.B., Amherst, 1883, A.M., 1886; Ph.D., U. of Heidelberg, 1886; LL.D., Wabash, 1913; A.M., ad eundem, Wesleyan U., Conn., 1915; m. Affa Sophia, d. of David Worthington Miner, M.D., Jan. 6, 1891; children—Miner Worthington, Elizabeth Mary Affa. Prin. high sch., Ware, Mass., 1883-84; instr. polit. economy, 1886-92, asso. prof. polit. economy and internat. law, 1892-93, Amherst; prof. history and sociology, 1893-98, polit. economy and polit. science, 1898-1913, Wabash Coll.; prof. and head dept. of economics and social science, Wesleyan U., Conn., 1913-28, emeritus, 1928—. Prof. economics and social science, Ind. U., summers, 1911-13, 1915. On editorial staff for econ. terms, Standard Dictionary; wrote Outline of Course in Economic Theory, 1894; Principles of Economics, 1919; also A Functional Theory of Economic Profit, 1927 (in vol. of economic essays published under auspices of Am. Economic Assn. in honor of the 80th birthday of John Bates Clark). Home: Middletown, Conn. Died June 19, 1935.

TUTTLE, Daniel Sylvester, bishop; b. Windham, Greene County, N.Y., Jan. 26, 1837; s. Daniel B. and Abigail C. (Stimson) T.; A.B., Columbia, 1857, A.M., 1860; grad. Gen. Theol. Sem., 1862; D.D., Columbia U., 1867; D.D., U. of the South, 1887; LL.D., Washington U., 1890; m. Harriet Minerva Foote, Sept. 12, 1865; father of George Marvine T. Deacon, 1862, priest, 1863, P.E. Church; asst. and rector Morris, N.Y., 1862-67; consecrated missionary bishop of Mont., Utah and Ida., May 1, 1867; translated to the Diocese of Mo., 1886, presiding bishop, 1903—. Address: St. Louis, Mo. Died Apr. 17, 1923.

TUTTLE, David Kitchell, chemist; b. at Whippany, Morris County, N.Y., Sept. 10, 1835; s. Silas and Lorania (Baker) T.; student New York U., 1851-53; B.S. summa cum laude, Lawrence Scientific Sch. (Harvard), 1855; Ph.D., Georgia Augusta U., Göttingen, 1857 (hon. diploma Jubilee 50th yr.); m. Ellen White Humes, April 7, 1864 (dec.). Asst. prof. chemistry, U. of Va., 1857-61; in pvt. business as tech. chemist, 1861-86; melter and refiner Carson City Mint., 1886-88, Phila. Mint, 1888—. Mem. Am. Acad. Polit. and Social Science. Author: Qualitative Analysis (Tuttle and Chandler). Contbr. to tech. jours. and reports. Home: Philadelphia, Pa. Died Apr. 8, 1915.

TUTTLE, George Marvine, M.D.; b. Morris, N.Y., Sept. 21, 1866; s. Daniel Sylvester and Harriet Minerva (Foote) T.; A.B., Columbia, 1888; M.D., Coll. Phys. and Surg. (Columbia), 1891; m. Grace Dean Wallace, Sept. 26, 1899. Resident phys. St. Luke's Hosp., 1891-93, Nursery and Child's Hosp., 1894, New York; removed to St. Louis, 1894; prof. clin. pediatrics, med. dept. Washington U., 1908—; on med. staff St. Luke's Hosp. and St. Louis Children's Hosp. Republican. Author: Manual of Diseases of Children, 1906. Address: St. Louis, Mo. Died Sept. 2, 1926.

TUTTLE, George Montgomery, physician; b. Rochester, N.Y., Oct. 2, 1856; s. Rev. James H. and Harriet M. T.; A.B., Yale, 1877; M.D., Coll. Phys. and Surg. (Columbia), 1880; m. Mrs. T. Story Kirkbride, Jr., Apr. 5, 1906. Phys.-in-chief N.Y. State Emigrant Hosp., 1881-83; attending phys. Bellevue Hosp., 1885-89; lecturer on gynecology, 1884-85, prof., 1885-1903, Columbia; attending gynecologist Roosevelt Hosp., 1888—. Contbr. to Am. Text-Book of Gynecology, New York Med. Record, New York Med. Jour. Address: New York, N.Y. Died Oct. 29, 1912.

TUTTLE, George Thomas, M.D.; b. Northwood, N.H., Mar. 18, 1850; s. Thomas and Olive Furber (Garland) T.; A.B., Dartmouth, 1872; M.D., Harvard, 1878. Began practice at Boston, 1878; 2d asst. phys., 1879-80, 1st asst. phys., 1880-1904, med. supt., 1904-Apr. 15, 1919, McLean Hosp. Republican. Home: Milton, Mass. Deceased.

TUTTLE, Hiram Americus, governor; b. Barnstead, N.H., 1837; s. George T.; moved with parents to Pittsfield, N.H., when 9 yrs. of age; attended public schs. and Pittsfield Acad. until 17; became clerk in clothing store, soon going into same business for himself, which he still conducts; m. Mary C., d. John L. French, 1859. Town clerk, Pittsfield, 1860; mem. N.H. Ho. of Reps., 1873-74; mem. gov.'s staff, 1875-76; mem. exec. council, 1879-83; gov. N.H., 1891-93. Dir. N.H. Fire Ins. Co., Concord and Montreal R.R.; dir. and pres. Suncook Valley R.R.; pres. Pittsfield Savings Bank; pres. Manchester Savings Bank. Address; Pittsfield, N.H. Died 1911.

TUTTLE, Hudson, author; b. Berlin Heights, O., Oct. 4, 1836; s. Nathan and Maria Leland (Munroe) T.; self ed.; m. Emma Rood, 1857. Connected, as editor or contbr., with reform and spiritualistic jours.; lecturer. Author: Arcana of Nature; Origin and Antiquity of Man; The Career of the God Idea; The Career of the Christ Idea; The Career of Religious Ideas; Origin of Man; Studies in Psychic Science; Religion of Man; Philosophy of Spirit; Secrets of the Convent; Heresy; Life in Two Spheres; Arcana of Spiritualism; What Is Spiritualism? Mediumship and Its Law; The Evolution of the God, and Christ Ideas, 1907; Protista—The Kingdom of the Unseen (with wife); Stories from Beyond the Borderland, 1910. Apptd., 1903, editor-at-large for Nat. Spiritual Assn. Address: Berlin Heights, O. Died 1910.

TUTTLE, James Patterson, lawyer; b. New Boston, N.H., July 17, 1856; s. James Moore and Rachel Patterson (McNeil) T.; ed. Francestown (N.H.) Acad., Cushing Acad. (Ashburnham, Mass.); student Boston U. Law Sch., 1884-85; m. Elizabeth J. Bunton, Jan. 1, 1887. Supt. schs., New Boston, 1881-83; admitted to N.H. bar, 1885, and began practice at Manchester; mem. N.H. Ho. of Reps., 1887; solicitor Hillsborough Co., N.H., 1893-1903; apptd. atty. gen. of N.H., 1912, reapptd., 1917, for term ending 1922. Republican. Presbyn. Mason, Odd Fellow. Home: Manchester, N.H. Died Feb. 11, 1935.

TUTTLE, Joseph Farrand, coll. pres.; b. Bloomfield, N.J., March 12, 1818; grad. Marietta Coll., 1841; Lane Theol. Sem., Cincinnati, 1844; m. Susan Caroline, d. Rev. Barnabas Kings, D.D., Oct. 1, 1845. Pastor Presbyn. churches at Delaware, O., 1845-47; Rockaway, N.J., 1847-62; pres. Wabash Coll. from 1862 for about 30 years; then pres. emeritus. Author: The Way Lost and Found; Life of William Tuttle; Annals of Morris County, N.J.; also baccalaureate address as pres. of Wabash Coll. Address: Crawfordsville, Ind. Died 1901.

TUTTLE, Lucius, ry. official; b. Hartford, Conn., Mar. 11, 1846; s. George and Mary Loomis T.; ed. Hartford Pub. High Sch.; m. Estelle Hazen Martin, Oct. 14, 1875. Entered ry. service, 1865; held various positions, 1865-89; commr. Trunk Line Assn., 1889-90; gen. mgr., 1890-92, v.p., 1892-93, N.Y.,N.H. &H. R.R.; pres. Boston & Me. Ry., 1893-1910, chmn. of bd., 1910-13; also pres. Maine Central Ry., 1896-1910. Home: Boston, Mass. Died Nov. 30, 1914.

TUTTLE, Mary McArthur Thompson, artist, author; b. Hillsboro, Highland County O., Nov. 5, 1849; d. of James H. and Eliza Jane (Trimble) Thompson; grad. Hillsboro Coll., 1868; grad. Sch. of Design, McMickin U. (now Art Acad. of Cincinnati); studied art, foreign langs. and lit. in Europe, 1874-75; m. Prof. Herbert Tuttle, L.H.D., July 5, 1875 (died 1894). Lived in Berlin, Germany, 1875-79; at Cornell U., Ithaca, N.Y., 1881-94. Portrait and lanscape painter, and lecturer on "Color" before schs., colls. and lit. clubs, 1895—. Painted portrait of her mother which was in W.C.T.U. exhibit, St. Louis Expn., 1904, and in Tremont Temple, Boston, at World's W.C.T.U.; portraits of Prof. Tuttle in Hist. Seminary Room, Cornell U., and Billings Library, U. of Vt. Author: Chronological Chart of the Schools of Painting; Family Records in Hillsboro Crusade Sketches; The Mother of an Emperor; Types of Men and Women, 1908; Follow the Gleam, 1911. Edited autobiography of her grandfather, Gov. Allen Trimble, 1909; International Ties, 1915. Address: Hillsboro, O. Died Sept. 1, 1916.

TUTTLE, William Edgar, Jr., congressman; b. Horseheads, N.Y., Dec. 10, 1870; s. William E. and Frances M. (Bonham) T.; grad. Elmira (N.Y.) Free Acad., 1887; Cornell U., 1887-89; unmarried. In lumber business, Westfield, N.J., 1897—; sr. mem. firm Tuttle Bros.; dir. Peoples Nat. Bank. Del. Dem. Nat. Conv., 1908, 16; mem. 62d and 63d Congresses (1911-15), 5th N.J. Dist. U.S. commr. to Panama Expn., 1916. Pres. Dept. of Conservation and Development of N.J., 1919. Commr. Banking and Ins. of N.J., 1921—. Conglist. Home: Westfield, N.J. Died Feb. 11, 1923.

TUTWILER, Julia Strudwick, coll. pres.; b. Tuscaloosa, Ala.; d. Dr. Henry and Julia (Ashe) Tutwiler; student Vassar Coll., and at Berlin and Paris; unmarried. Long engaged in ednl. work; pres. Ala. Normal Coll., Livingston, Ala. As result of her efforts U. of Ala. was opened to the girls of the state; the trustees named the Woman's Annex for Miss Tutwiler. Labored long for prison reform in Ala., having on several occasions induced the legislature to pass laws ameliorating the convict-lease system. Contbr. to various periodicals; author of numerous songs, including "Alabama," "The Dixie Now," and "The Southern Yankee Doodle," which are used in the pub. schs. of Ala., and "Duty," a song used for the Lee Centennial. Address: Birmingham, Ala. Died Mar. 24, 1916.

TUTWILER, Thomas Henry, pres. Memphis Street Ry. Company; b. Fluvanna County, Va., Sept. 22, 1866; s. Thomas H. and Caroline (Sloan) T.; ed. pub. schs.; studied civ. engring., under pvt. tutors; m. Mary E. Goodloe, Dec. 19, 1894. Began in employ of Ga. Pacific R.R. (now Southern Ry.); in charge of constrn. Sunflower River Bridge, in Miss., 1889; with L.,N.O.&T. R.R. (now Yazoo & Miss. Valley R.R.) in charge constrn., in Miss., 1890-92, and built Minter City branch of Yazoo & Miss. Valley R.R.; with New Orleans City R.R. system, 1892-1901; engr. Birmingham (Ala.) street ry. system, 1901-02; engr. at Kansas City, Mo., converting cable system of surface transportation to electric ry. system, 1902; in charge rehabilitating Nashville street rys., 1903-04; elected v.p. and gen. mgr. Memphis St. Ry. Co., 1905, pres. and gen. mgr., 1906-30, pres. Memphis Power & Light Co., 1923-30. Home: Memphis, Tenn. Died Sept. 1938.

TWATCHMAN, John Henry, artist; b. Cincinnati, Aug. 4, 1853; pupil Cincinnati School of Design, 1873-74, and Frank Duveneck, 1874-75; acad. in Munich, under Ludwig Löfftz, 1875-78, and a year under Duveneck in Venice; École Julien, Paris, under Boulanger and Lefebvre. Webb prize Soc. Am. Artists, 1888; medal Columbian Expn.; Temple gold medal, Pa. Acad. Fine Arts, 1895; honorable mention Carnegie Inst., 1899. Address: Greenwich, Conn. Died 1902.

TWEED, Charles Harrison, lawyer; b. Calais, Me., Sept. 26, 1844; s. Hon. Harrison and Huldah Ann (Pond) T.; A.B., Harvard, 1865, A.M., 1868; studied law under Edmund H. Bennett and in law dept., Harvard; m. Helen Minerva, d. Hon. William M. Evarts, Oct. 27, 1881. Admitted to bar; entered office of Evarts, Southmayd & Choate; partner in firm, 1874-83; withdrew to become gen. counsel for the Central Pacific, the Chesapeake & Ohio, and asso. ry. corps.; when Southern Pacific Co. was organized, became its gen. counsel; co-partner in banking house of Speyer & Co., Jan. 1, 1903-Jan. 1, 1907; retired. Home: New York, N.Y. Died Oct. 11, 1917.

TWEEDELL, Edward David; b. Phila., Pa., Sept. 16, 1879; s. William B. and Margaret (Collier) T.; Ph.B., Brown U., 1901; N.Y. State Library Sch., Albany, N.Y., 2 yrs.; m. Lida Bothwell, June 8, 1910. Auditor, Providence Pub. Library, 1903-07; with John Crerar Library, Chicago, 1907—, becoming asst. librarian. Home: Hinsdale, Ill. Died Mar. 30, 1928.

TWEEDY, Frank, topographical engr.; b. N.Y. City, June 12, 1854; s. Oliver Burr and Maria (Lord) T.; C.E., Union Coll., Schenectady, N.Y., 1875; m. Emma Adelaide Hydn, Dec. 20, 1888. Engr. on N.Y. State Adirondack survey, 1875-79; sanitary engr. under late George E. Waring, Jr., Newport, R.I., 1880-81; asst. topographer on Northern Transcontinental Survey, 1882-83; topographer, 1884-1915, then topog. engr., U.S. Geol. Survey; retired from govt. service. Author: Flora of the Yellowstone; also short stories. Home: Washington, D.C. Died 1937.

TWICHELL, Joseph Hopkins, clergyman; b. Southington, Conn., May 27, 1838; s. Edward and Selina D. (Carter) T.; A.B., Yale, 1859, A.M., 1886; Union Theol. Sem., 1859-61; Andover Theol. Sem., 1864-65. Ordained Congl. ministry, 1863; chaplain 71st N.Y. Vols., 1861-64; pastor Asylum Hill Ch., Hartford, many years. Fellow, Yale, 1874—. Author: Life of John Winthrop; Some Old Puritan Love Letters (correspondence of John and Margaret Winthrop); etc. Home: Hartford, Conn. Died Dec. 20, 1918.

TWINING, Kinsley, editor; b. West Point, N.Y., July 18, 1832; grad. Yale, 1853, D.D.; L.H.D., Hamilton; m. Mary Ellen Gridley, Aug. 25, 1870. One of the founders Reform Club, New York. In active Congregational ministry, 1857-76; literary editor The Independent, 1880-98; literary editor The Evangelist, New York, 1898—. Home: Morristown, N.J. Died 1901.

TWINING, Nathan Crook, naval officer; b. Boscobel, Wis., Jan. 17, 1869; s. Nathan Crook and Mary Jane (Rennie) T.; grad. U.S. Naval Acad., 1889; m. Caroline Salisbury Baker, Apr. 5, 1899. Commd. ensign U.S.N., July 1, 1891; lt. jr. grade, Aug. 2, 1898; lt., Mar. 3, 1899; lt. comdr., July 1, 1905; comdr., July 1, 1910; capt. July 29, 1915; rear admiral (temp.), Apr. 14, 1920; rear admiral, permanent rank, June 3, 1921. Chief Bur. of Ordnance, with rank of rear admiral, June 7, 1911-Oct. 6, 1913, resigned; comdg. U.S.S. Tacoma, Oct. 18, 1913; attending Naval War Coll., July 26, 1915-Apr. 2, 1917; comdg. Squadron Two, Patrol Force, Atlantic Fleet, April 5, 1917-July 15, 1917; chief of staff to vice admiral comdg. U.S. naval forces in European waters, Aug. 1, 1917-Dec. 20, 1918; comd. U.S.S. Texas, Dec. 31, 1918-July 15, 1919; chief of staff to admiral comdg. Pacific Fleet, July 16, 1919-July 5, 1921; naval attaché, Am. Embassy, London, Aug. 27, 1921-Jan. 31, 1922. Retired Jan. 4, 1923, for physical disability incurred in service. Officer Legion of Honor; Officer Order of Leopold; Companion of the Bath. Mem. U.S. Naval Inst. Episcopalian. Home: Newport, R.I. Died July 4, 1924.

TWITCHELL, Herbert Kenaston, banker; b. Weybridge, Vt., Nov. 26, 1865; s. Ira J. and Sarah (Samson) T.; ed. Beeman Acad., New Haven, Vt.; m. Mary Adelaide Edwards, Sept. 7, 1893. Began as asst. teller, Chase Nat. Bank, New York, 1889; asst. cashier, Chemical Nat. Bank, 1907-11, v.p., 1911-17, pres., 1917-20, chmn. bd., 1920-23; pres. Bank for Suffolk County; pres. and trustee Seamen's Bank for Savings, 1923—; dir. J. E. Curran Corp., Bankers Trust Co., United Combustion Engrs., Gen. Heating Corp. Commr. Port of Authority of New York. Trustee Middlebury (Vt.) Coll., Adelphi Coll. Republican. Presbyn. Home: Brooklyn, N.Y. Died July 11, 1928.

TWITCHELL, La Fayette, lawyer; b. Hardin County, Ill., Dec. 22, 1859; s. La Fayette and Harriett A. (Steele) T.; ed. pub. schs. Elizabethtown, Ill.; legal edn., Bloomington (Ill.) Law Sch., 1879-80; m. Mary H. Ledbetter, Nov. 27, 1882 (died 1918); children—Edna (Mrs. William J. Poland), Goudy Ledbetter (dec.), Austin (dec.), Blanche (dec.). Employed in office of Clerk of Circuit Ct. and recorder, Elizabethtown, 1873-76; mgr. gen. mdse. store, 1877-78; in law office, 1880-81; admitted to Ill. bar, 1880, Colo. bar, 1883, bar of U.S. Supreme Ct., 1916; practiced in Elizabethtown, 1881-82, and 1886-89, Gunnison, Colo., 1883-85, Montrose, 1890-94, Denver, 1895—; sr. partner Twitchell, Clark & Burkhardt; mayor of Montrose, 1893-94; county atty. Denver County, 1897-98. Republican. Odd Fellow. Home: Denver, Colo. Died May 29, 1936.

TWITCHELL, Ralph Emerson, lawyer; b. Ann Arbor, Mich., Nov. 29, 1859; s. Daniel Sawin and Delia (Scott) T.; student U. of Kan.; LL.B., U. of Mich., 1882; m. Margaret Olivia Collins, Dec. 9, 1885 (died 1899). Asst. solicitor for N.M. of A.,T.&S.F. Ry. Co.; dist. atty. N.M., 1889-92. Actively identified with reclamation and conservation, 1889—; 1st v.p. Nat. Irrigation Congress; chmn. Rep. Territorial Com., 1902-03; receiver N.M. Central Railway Co., 1918-19. Pres. N.M. Bar Assn., 1888-89; v.p., dir. N.M. Hist. Soc.; mem. State Bd. of Hist. Service, 1918-20; regent N.M. State Mus.; mem. mng. com. Archæol. Inst. America; chmn. N.M. Bd. Expn. Mgrs. Panama-Calif. Expn. Editor Old Santa Fé, hist. quarterly. Author: Military Occupation of New Mexico, 1846-51, 1909; Leading Facts of New Mexican History (2 vols.), 1910; Spanish Archives of New Mexico (2 vols., complied by authority of state under statutory enactment), 1914. Fellow Am. Geog. Soc. Spl. asst. atty. gen. in charge of Pueblo Indian litigation in the Southwest. Home: Santa Fe, N.M. Died Aug. 26, 1925.

TWOMBLY, Alexander Stevenson, clergyman, author; b. Boston, Mar. 14, 1832; s. Alexander Hamilton and Mary (Perley) T.; ed. Boston Latin Sch.; grad. Yale, 1854, A.M., 1857, S.T.D., 1883; grad. Andover Theol. Sem., 1858; studied in Heidelberg, 1856; m. Abby Quincy Bancroft, Dec. 23, 1858. Ordained Congl. ministry, 1858, pastor Cherry Valley, N.Y., 1858-62, Albany, N.Y., 1862-67; Stamford, Conn., 1867-72; Boston, 1872-91. On Christian Commn., Army of Potomac, 1864; literary editor Silver, Burdett & Co., publishers, 1896-98; spent winter and spring in Hawaiian Islands, 1894. Pres. Asso. Charities, Newton, Mass. Author: Marry Maple Leaves, 1872; The Choir Boy of York Cathedral, 1890; Masterpieces of Michelangelo and Milton, 1896; Life of Dr. John Lord, 1896; Hawaii and Its People, 1900; Kelea, the Surf Rider, 1900. Edited: The Silver Series of English Classics (10 vols.), 1897. Contributor to mags., revs. and newspapers. Address: Newton, Mass. Died 1907.

TWOMBLY, Hamilton McKown, capitalist; grad. Harvard, 1871; m. Florence Adele, d. William H. Vanderbilt, 1877. Dir. C.&N.W., C.,C.,C.&St.L., Del., Lackawanna & Western, L.S.&M.S., N.Y.C.& H.R., N.Y., Chicago & St. L., Pittsburgh & Lake Erie, Buffalo, Erie Basin, Columbus, Hope & Greensburg, N.J. Shore Line, N.Y. Central, Niagara River, N.Y. Junction, West Shore R.R., Chesapeake & Ohio Ry. Co., C.,St.P., M.&O. Ry. Co., Erie R.R., L.E.& W. R.R. Co., Lehigh Valley R.R. Co., M.C. R.R. Co., N.Y.,N.H.&H.R.R. Co., Central R.R. of N.J., Phila & Reading Coal & Iron Co., and officer or dir. in more than 30 other corps. Home: New York, N.Y. Died 1910.

TYE, John L(ewis), lawyer; b. McDonough, Ga., Mar. 4, 1859; s. Lewis M. (M.D.) and Mary Ann (Crockett) T.; A.B., U. of Ga., 1876; LL.B., Columbian (now George Washington) U., 1880; m. Carrie Wilson, June 8, 1883; children—Myrtle, Benjamin W., Ethel (Mrs. John M. Gilchrist), Carolyn (wife of I. A. Ferguson, M.D.), Carroll, William W., John L. Admitted to Ga. bar, 1880, practiced at Atlanta, 1880—; sr. mem. firm Tye, Thomson & Tye; div. counsel Nashville, Chattanooga & St. Louis Ry.; dist. atty. L.&N. R.R.; dir. Ga. Savings Bank & Trust Co., Ga. Marble Co. Democrat. Presbyn. Home: Atlanta, Ga. Died Jan. 10, 1935.

TYLER, Bayard Henry, artist; b. Oneida, N.Y., Apr. 22, 1855; s. Henry H. and Elizabeth (Stevens) T.; ed. Whitestown Sem. and Syracuse U.; grad. Nat. Acad. Design, New York, 1882; pupil of Theo. Kaufmann and William M. Chase; m. Charlotte E. Wiltsie, 1883; children—Mary Spofford, Myra J. Represented in Corcoran Gallery, Washington, D.C.; Albright Memorial Library, Scranton, Pa.; state collection, Albany, N.Y.; etc. Painted portraits of President Roosevelt, Admiral W. H. Brownson, Augustus Van Wyck (justice Supreme Court), Bishop James E. Freeman, Alexander S. Cochran, etc. Awarded medal N.Y. Water Color Club; hon. mention Washington Soc. Artists, 1913; first purchase prize, Yonkers Art Assn., 1927. Republican. Presbyn. Home: Yonkers, N.Y. Died June 6, 1931.

TYLER, Charles Mellen, clergyman; b. Limington, Me., Jan. 8, 1832; s. Daniel and Lavinia (Small) T.; A.B., Yale, 1855, A.M., 1890, D.D., 1892; Union Theol. Sem., 1855-56; m. Ellen A. Davis, 1857; m. 2d, Kate E. Stark (prof. music, Syracuse U.), 1892. Ordained Congl. ministry, 1857; pastor Galesburg, Ill., 1857-58, Natick, Mass., 1858-67, South Ch., Chicago, 1867-72, First Ch., Ithaca, N.Y., 1872-91; Sage prof. history and philosophy of religion and Christian ethics, 1891-1903, emeritus prof., 1903, Cornell. Mem. Mass. Ho. of Reps., 1861-62; city librarian Ithaca, and trustee of Cornell U., 1886-92, and, 1907—. Capt. U.S. vols., 1864-65; served through Wilderness and Spottsylvania battles, and about Petersburg. Author: Life of Lt. George Wolcott, U.S.V.; Bases of Religious Belief, Historic and Ideal, 1892. Also of last chapter of Prof. Pfleiderer's Geschichte der Religious Philosophie (Berlin), and various articles in papers and mags. Address: Scranton, Pa. Died May 16, 1918.

TYLER, D(avid) Gardiner, judge; b. East Hampton, L.I., N.Y., July 12, 1846; s. John Tyler (10th President U.S.) and Julia (Gardiner) T.; student, Washington Coll. (now Washington and Lee U.), 1862-63; served in coll. co. in C.S.A., 1863-64, in 1st Va. Arty., 1864-65; student Carlsruhe, Baden, Germany, 1865-67; grad. law sch., Washington Coll., 1869; m. Mary Morris Jones, June 6, 1894. Dem. presdl. elector, 1888; mem. Va. Senate, 1891-92 and 1900-04; mem. 53d and 54th Congresses (1893-97), 2d Va. Dist.; judge, 14th Jud. Circuit, Va., terms 1904-20. Dir. Eastern State Hosp., Williamsburg, Va., 1884-86; visitor William and Mary Coll., Va., 1876-1904. Episcopalian. Home: Holdcroft, Va. Died Sept. 5, 1927.

TYLER, Harry Walter, coll. prof.; b. Ipswich, Mass., Apr. 16, 1863; s. David M. and Harriet (Willcomb) T.; B.S., Mass. Inst. Tech., 1884; U. of Göttingen, 1887-88; Ph.D., U. of Erlangen, 1889; m. Alice I. Brown, June 20, 1887; children—Margaret, Elizabeth, Catherine, Frances Genevieve. Asst. mathematics, 1884-86, instr., 1886-87, asst. prof., 1890-91, asso. prof., 1892, prof., 1893-1930, head of dept., 1901-30, sec., 1889-90 and 1891-1906, Mass. Inst. Tech. Fellow Am. Acad. Arts and Sciences (corr. sec. 1915-24), A.A.A.S. Author: Entertainments in Chemistry, 1886; Short History of Science (with W. T. Sedgwick); also math. monographs and articles in tech. and ednl. jours. and revs. Home: Newton Center, Mass. Died 1938.

TYLER, Henry Mather, coll. dean; b. Amherst, Mass., Nov. 18, 1843; s. William Seymour and Amelia Ogden (Whiting) T.; A.B., Amherst, 1865, A.M., 1868, D.D., 1902; L.H.D. Smith Coll., 1926; m. Mary Frances Disbrow, July 30, 1872 (died 1918); children—Harry D., Marjorie Edwards, Donald Whiting. Teacher Williston Sem., Easthampton, Mass., 1865-66; studied and traveled in Europe, 1866-68; Walker instr. Latin, Amherst, 1868-69; prof. Greek and German, Knox Coll., Ill., 1869-72; ordained Congl. ministry, 1872; pastor Fitchburg, Mass., 1872-77; prof. Greek, Jan. 1, 1877-1912, dean faculty, 1900-12, Smith Coll. Pres., dir. Northampton St. Ry.; v.p. Northampton Inst. for Savings. Pres. bd. Williston Acad.; mem. mng. com. Am. Sch. Classical Studies, Athens, Greece, Archæol. Inst. America. Republican. Edited (with intro. and notes) Selections from Greek Lyric Poets, 1879, 1905; reëdited and revised W. S. Tyler's editions of the Germania and Agricola of Tacitus, 1878, and Plato's Apology and Crito, 1887. Wrote: A Greek Play and Its Presentation, 1891. Home: Northampton, Mass. Died Nov. 3, 1931.

TYLER, James Gale, marine artist; b. Oswego, N.Y., Feb. 15, 1855; s. Major R. D. S. and Mary J. (Hubbell) T.; ed. pub. schs., Oswego, N.Y., until 1870; studied for marine artist with A. Cary Smith, naval architect, who was in 1871 marine artist; m. Ida M. Jourdan, 1885. Contributed illustrations and marine art studies to L. Prang, the Harper's, Century, Truth and other mags. Home: Pelham Manor, N.Y. Died Jan. 29, 1931.

TYLER, James Hoge, governor; b. Caroline County, Va., Aug. 11, 1846; s. George and Eliza (Hoge) T.; ed. Minor's Academic Sch., Albemarle County, Va.; served as pvt. in C.S.A.; m. Sue M. Hammet, Nov. 16, 1868. Mem. Va. Senate, 1877; lt. gov. of Va., 1889, gov., 1898-1902. Democrat. Farmer; pres. Va. State Farmers' Inst.; pres. S.W. Va. Live Stock Assn. Address: East Radford, Va. Died Jan. 3, 1925.

TYLER, James M., judge; b. Wilmington, Vt., Apr. 27, 1835; s. Ephraim and Mary (Bissell) T.; ed. Brattleboro (Vt.) Acad.; LL.B., Albany Law Sch., 1860; hon. A.M.; Middlebury, 1879; LL.D., U. of Vt., 1891; m. Ellen E. Richardson, Dec. 11, 1861 (died 1871); m. 2d, Jane P. Miles, Sept. 1, 1875. Mem. Vt. Gen. Assembly, 1863-64, 1865; state's atty., Windham County, 1867-68; mem. 46th and 47th Congresses (1879-83), 2d Vt. Dist.; judge Supreme Ct. of Vt., 1887-1908. Chmn. trustees Brattleboro Retreat. Pres. Vt. Nat. Bank, Feb. 1917—. Republican. Home: Brattleboro, Vt. Died Oct. 13, 1926.

TYLER, John Mason, biologist; b. Amherst, Mass., May 18, 1851; s. Prof. William Seymour and Amelia Ogden (Whiting) T.; A.B., Amherst, 1873, A.M., 1876; Union Theol. Sem., 1874-76; univs. of Göttingen and Leipzig, 1876-79; hon. Ph.D., Colgate, 1888; m. Elizabeth Smith, July 12, 1883; children—Mason Whiting (dec.), Elizabeth Stearns (dec.). Instr. biology, 1879-81, zoölogy and botany, 1881-82, Stone prof. biology, 1882, emeritus, 1917, Amherst Coll. Author: Whence and Whither of Man, 1897; Growth and Education, 1907; Man in the Light of Evolution, 1908; New Stone Age, 1921; Coming of Man, 1923. Home: Amherst, Mass. Died Apr. 12, 1929.

TYLER, John Poyntz, bishop; b. Hanover County, Va., June 15, 1862; s. Wat Henry (M.D.) and Jane (Blake) T.; g. nephew of John Tyler, 10th pres. of U.S.; grad. Theol. Sem. in Va., 1888, D.D., 1914; m. Ada Rodrick, 1890; children—Mary, Jane, Blake, Ada Rodrick, Wat Henry, John Poyntz. Deacon, 1888, priest, 1889, P.E. Ch.; in charge Westover Parish, Charles City County, Va., 1888-91; rector Christ's Ch., Millwood, Va., 1892-95, St. Paul's Ch., Greenville, O., 1895-96, Ch. of Advent, Phila., 1896-1904; archdeacon of Va., 1904-07; rector St. John's Ch., Hagerstown, Md., 1907-13, and archdeacon of Cumberland; elected archdeacon Diocese of Ala. and Diocese of Southern Va.; elected bishop of Missionary Dist. of N.Dak., Oct. 1913, consecrated Jan. 6, 1914. Home: Fargo, N.D. Died July 13, 1931.

TYLER, Lyon Gardiner, educator, author; b. Charles City County, Va., Aug. 1853; s. John T. (10th Pres. U.S.); A.B., U. of Va., 1874, A.M., 1875; LL.D., Trinity Coll., Conn., 1895, U. of Pittsburgh, 1911, Brown U., 1914, William and Mary Coll., 1919; m. Annie B., d. St. George Tucker, Nov. 14, 1878; children—Julia (wife of Dr. J. S. Wilson), Elizabeth (wife of Alfred H. Miles, U.S.N.), John; m. 2d, Sue Ruffin, d. John A. Ruffin, of Charles City County, Va., Sept. 12, 1923; children—Lyon Gardiner, Harrison Ruffin. Prof. belles-lettres, William and Mary Coll., 1877-78; prin. high sch., Memphis, Tenn., 1878-82; practiced law at Richmond, Va., 1882-88; a founder of and teacher Richmond Mechanics Night Sch., 1883-88; pres. Coll. of William and Mary, Williamsburg, Va., 1888-1919; resigned, 1919, and made pres. emeritus. Mem. Va. Ho. of Delegates, 1887; mem. State Bd. of Edn., 1903-07; mem. State Library Bd., 1915— (later chairman bd.). Author: The Letters and Times of the Tylers, 1884; Parties and Patronage in the United States, 1891; Cradle of the Republic, 1900; England in America, 1904; Williamsburg, the Old Colonial Capital, 1907; also addresses and pamphlets. Editor and propr. William and Mary Coll. Quarterly Historical Magazine, founded in 1892, also of Tyler's Quarterly Hist. and Geneal. Mag., founded, 1919. Editor: Narratives of Early Virginia (1606-1625), 1907; Men of Mark in Virginia (5 vols.); Biographical Dictionary of Virginia (5 vols.), 1915. Home: Holdcroft, Charles City County, Va. Died Feb. 12, 1935.

TYLER, Mason Whiting, lawyer; b. Amherst, Mass., June 17, 1840; s. Prof. William S. and Amelia Ogden (Whiting) T.; grad. Amherst, 1862; served 2d lt. to col. 37th Mass. vols., 1862-65; studied Columbian Coll. Law Sch., 1865-66; m. Eliza M. Schroeder, Dec. 29, 1869. Admitted to bar, Oct. 1866; student and clerk in office of Evarts, Southmayd and Choate, 1866-69; mem. law firm Tremain & Tyler, 1869-94, Tyler & Durand, 1894-1902; law firm of Tyler & Tyler, 1902—. Pres. bd. directors Plainfield Public Library; mem. bd. trustees Amherst Coll. Home: Plainfield, N.J. Died 1907.

TYLER, Morris Franklin, treas. Yale Univ. from 1899 to 1904; b. New Haven, Conn., Aug. 12, 1848; s. Morris Tyler; ed. New Haven public and Hillhouse high schools; grad. Yale, 1870; law dept. Yale, 1873, A.M., 1873; m. Delia T. Audubon, Nov. 5, 1873. Address: New Haven, Conn. Died 1907.

TYLER, Moses Coit, educator; b. Griswold, Conn., Aug. 2, 1835; grad. Yale, 1857; (A.M., 1863; L.H.D., Columbia, 1888; LL.D., Wooster U., 1875); studied theology at Yale and at Andover Theol. Sem.; m. Jeannette Hull Gilbert, 1859. Pastor Congl. Ch., Poughkeepsie, N.Y., 1860-62; prof. English lang. and lit., U. of Mich., 1867-81, prof. Am. history, Cornell U., 1881—. Became an Episcopalian; ordered deacon, 1881; ordained priest, 1883. Literary editor The Christian Union, 1873-74. Author: History of American Literature During the Colonial Period, 1606-1765; The Literary History of the American Revolution; The Brawnville Papers; Life of Patrick Henry; Three Men of Letters; Manual of English Literature; Glimpses of England. Address: Ithaca, N.Y. Died 1900.

TYLER, William Trevor, ry. official; b. Janesville, Wis., July 29, 1871; s. William and Annie (Johnson) T.; Gale U., Galesville, Wis., 1886, 87; m. Alice M. Ermatinger, Feb. 4, 1890. Began as messenger, Wis. Central Ry., 1883, later with Milwaukee, Lake Shore & Western and N.P. rys.; yardmaster, agt., trainmaster and supt., G.N. Ry., 1890-1900; supt. and gen. supt. Mo.P. Ry., 1900-06; gen. supt. and gen. mgr. St.L.&S. R.R., 1906-14; supt. N.P. Ry., 1915-16; gen. mgr. St.L.S.W. Ry., 1917; sr. asst. dir. operation, later dir. operation, U.S.R.R. Adminstrn., Jan. 15, 1918-Feb. 29, 1920; v.p. N.P. Ry. in charge operation and maintenance, Mar. 1, 1920—. Mason. Home: St. Paul, Minn. Died Apr. 6, 1924.

TYNAN, Joseph James, ship builder; b. Sion Mills, County Tyrone, Ireland, Oct. 8, 1871; s. Robert and Elizabeth T.; ed. Spring Garden Inst., Philadelphia, Pa., and Internat. Corr. Sch.; m. Margaret McGinty, Apr. 1902; children—Margot (Mrs. J. Curtis Taylor), Joseph J.; m. 2d, Ruth Williams, Nov. 30, 1922; 1 dau., Ruth Patsy. Came to U.S., 1890, naturalized, 1896. With Bethlehem Shipbuilding Corp., San Francisco, Calif., 1906—, v.p., 1909—. Builder of Columbia River-Longview Bridge; built 10 submarines for Brit. Admiralty in Can. (built in 5 mos.), S.S. Invincible (built in 29 working days); awarded gold medal by Dir. Gen. Chas. M. Schwab of Emergency Fleet Corp. for mcht. vessels delivered during World War I. Mem. Bd. of Police Commrs., San Francisco, 1930; mem. Bd. of Harbor Commrs., San Francisco, 1931—. Republican. Catholic. Elk. Inventor of number of pneumatic tools and appliances. Home: San Francisco, Calif. Died June 5, 1933.

TYNDALL, Charles Herbert, clergyman; b. Alton, N.Y., July 31, 1857; s. M. P. and Emeline (York) T.; grad. State Normal Coll., Albany, 1880, Boys' Acad., Albany, 1881; sr. yr. in Williams Coll., class of 1882; grad. Auburn Theol. Sem., 1885; A.M., New York U., 1893, Ph.D., 1895; U. of Berlin, 1895-96; S.T.D., Harriman U., 1901, D.D., 1902; m. Jessie Van Auken, May 23, 1885; children—Gertrude V. (Mrs. E. W. K. Mould), Helen J. (Mrs. R. E. Haas), Dorothy Y. (Mrs. F. H. Wheeler). Ordained Presbyn. ministry, 1885; pastor Escanaba, Mich., 1885-89, Broome St. Tabernacle, New York, 1889-95, Reformed Ch., Mt. Vernon, N.Y., 1897-1921, emeritus. Lectured before Liverpool C. of C. and elsewhere in Eng., 1904, on wireless telegraphy, before Elec. Club of St. Louis Expn., 1904, and elsewhere in U.S. and Can. V.p. dir. and prof. of science and the Bible and of object lesson teaching in Fla. Fundamental Bible Inst. at Temple Terrace, Tampa, Fla., 1932—. Author: Object Sermons in Outline, 1891; Quickening, Filling and Enduring of the Holy Spirit, 1893; Object Lessons for Children, 1896; Electricity and Its Similitudes, 1902; Simon Tsara, 1909; Through Science to God, 1926; Nature and Religion, a Handbook of Religious Education, 1930. Home: Mt. Vernon, N.Y. Died Feb. 22, 1935.

TYNE, Thomas James, lawyer; b. Nashville, Tenn., Nov. 29, 1868; s. James William and Catherine (Healy) T.; LL.B., Vanderbilt U., 1891; m. Jane Ratterman, June 7, 1898; children—Thomas James, Elleanore, William John, George Henry, Catherine Jane. Admitted to Tenn. bar, 1891, practiced in Nashville, 1891; mem. Tyne, Peebles, Henry & Tyne; mem. Tenn. Ho. of Reps., 1892-93; gen. counsel Nat. Life and Accident Ins. Co., 1903—, also v.p.; resident counsel Du Pont Engr. Co.; spl. asst. to U.S. atty. gen. in Old Hickory Powder Plant cases; dir. Am. Nat. Bank. Democrat. Catholic. K.C. Home: Nashville, Tenn. Died Nov. 1, 1936.

TYNER, Charles L., fire ins. official; mem. bd. dirs. Home Ins. Co., N.Y. City, City of New York Ins. Co., Franklin Fire Ins. Co. of Phila., Corn Exchange Bank of New York, Title Guarantee & Trust Co. of New York, New Brunswick (N.J.) Fire Ins. Co., etc. Address: New York, N.Y. Died Aug. 15, 1939.

TYNER, James Noble, lawyer; b. Brookville, Ind., Jan. 17, 1826; academic edn.; admitted to bar; mem. Congress from Ind., 1869-75; 2d asst. and 1st asst. Postmaster Gen., and Postmaster Gen., 1875-82; asst. atty. gen. for P.O. Dept., 1889-93, reapptd., May 1897; resigned May 1903. Del. from U.S. to International Postal Congresses at Paris, 1878, and Washington, 1897. Address: Washington, D.C. Died 1904.

TYRRELL, Henry, newspaperman; b. Feb. 3, 1865; A.B., Cornell U., 1890; m. Nellie Kerslake, Apr. 26, 1906 (died 1915). On staff New York Sunday World, 1903-31. Author: Lee of Virginia (serially in Pall Mall Magazine, London), 1897; Shenandoah (novel, based upon the drama by Bronson Howard), 1912. Contbr. of verse and art revs. to mags. and newspapers. Home: Arrochar, S.I., N.Y. Died Jan. 13, 1933.

TYSON, James, physician; b. Phila., Oct. 26, 1841; s. Henry and Gertrude (Haviland) T.; A.B., Haverford Coll., 1860, A.M., 1864; M.D., U. of Pa., 1863; LL.D., Haverford Coll., 1908, U. of Pennsylvania, 1912; m. Frances Bosdevex, Dec. 5, 1865. Professor pathology and morbid anatomy, 1876-89, dean med. faculty, 1888-92, prof. practice of medicine, 1899-1910, prof. emeritus, 1910—, U. of Pa. Pres. Assn. Am. Physicians, 1907-08; fellow Coll. Physicians, Phila., pres., 1907-10. Author: Introduction to Normal Histology, 1873; The Cell Doctrine—Its History and Present State, 1878; Practical Examination of Urine, 1902; Physical Diagnosis, 1913; Text-Book of Practice of Medicine, 1909; Bright's Disease and Diabetes, 1904; also numerous papers on med. subjects. Address: Philadelphia, Pa. Died Feb. 26, 1919.

TYSON, John Russell, congressman; b. Lowndes County, Ala., Nov. 28, 1856; s. John A. and Matilda (Warren) T.; A.B., Howard Coll., Ala., 1877; LL.B., Washington and Lee U., 1879; m. Mary Dossie Jordan, 1879. Mem. Ala. Ho. of Reps., 1880-82; settled at Montgomery, 1884; judge 2d Jud. Circuit, Ala., 1892-98; asso. justice Supreme Ct. of Ala., 1898-1906, chief justice, 1906-09; mem. 67th Congress (1921-23), 2d Ala. Dist. Democrat. Baptist. Home: Montgomery, Ala. Died Mar. 27, 1923.

TYSON, Lawrence Davis, senator; b. Greenville, N.C., July 4, 1861; s. Richard Lawrence and Margaret Louise (Turnage) T.; grad. U.S. Mil. Acad., 1883; LL.B., U. of Tenn.; m. Bettie Humes McGhee, Feb. 10, 1886. 2d lt. 9th U.S. Inf., June 13, 1883; 1st lt., Oct. 15, 1889; prof. mil. science and tactics, U. of Tenn., 1891-95; admitted to bar, 1895; resigned from U.S.A., Apr. 15, 1896. Pres. Poplar Creek Coal & Iron Co., Lenoir City Co., E. Tenn. Coal & Iron Co.; v.p. Coal Creek Mining & Mfg. Co.; pres. and pub. Knoxville Sentinel Co. Apptd. by President McKinley col. 6th U.S. Vol. Inf., May 20, 1898; served in P.R., during Spanish-Am. War; mustered out Mar. 15, 1899; brig. gen. and insp. gen. on staff gov. of Tenn., 1902-06. Mem. Tenn. Ho. of Reps., 1903 (speaker of House); del. at large Dem. Nat. Conv., 1908; candidate for U.S. Senate before Gen. Assembly of Tenn., 1913, receiving 62 votes, 67 being necessary to elect; elected U.S. Senator for term, 1925-31. Commd. brig. gen. N.A., Aug. 5, 1917 and apptd. comdr. 59th Brigade, 30th Div.; comdr. brigade with British at Ypres and Lys Canal sector, later at breaking of Hindenburg line at Bellicourt and Nauroy in the Somme sector; discharged, Apr. 15, 1919. Awarded D.S.M. "for extraordinary conduct during the war." Episcopalian. Home: Knoxville, Tenn. Died Aug. 24, 1929.

TYSON, Stuart Lawrence, clergyman; b. Penllyn, Pa., Nov. 12, 1873; s. Herbert Benezet and Mary (Stuart) T.; grad. Nashotah House, Wis., 1895; M.A., 2d highest honors, St. John's Coll., Oxford U., England, 1903, post-graduate, 1903-07, D.D. in course, 1923; m. Katharine Emily Rosengarten, Apr. 25, 1895 (died 1915); children—Stephen (dec.), Katharine E., Paul L., Edmund H., Philip, Hugh, John, James, Elizabeth, Mark, Mary, Cyril, Hope; m. 2d, Margaretta Wentz, Apr. 18, 1927. Deacon, 1895, priest, 1897, P.E. Ch.; spl. preacher, Oxford, Eng., 1899-1903; asst. St. Paul's Ch., Oxford, 1904-07; tutor, Oxford, 1903-05; prof. N.T., Western Theol. Sem., Chicago, 1907-08; prof. N.T. and liturgics, U. of the South, 1908-13, chaplain of the univ., 1910; lecturer and spl. preacher, Cathedral of St. John the Divine, New York, hon. vicar, 1919-23; lecturer, Tyson Lectureship Foundation, New York. Received into Congl. ministry, 1925. Trustee Emerald Hodgson Hosp., Sewanee, Tenn. Republican. Author: The Eucharist in St. Paul, 1923. Home: Pelham Manor, N.Y. Died Sept. 16, 1932.

U

UDDEN, Johan August, geologist; b. Lekasa, Sweden, Mar. 19, 1859; s. Andrew Larson and Inga Lena (Andersdotter) U.; immigrated to Carver, Minn.,

1861; A.B., Augustana Coll., Rock Island, Ill., 1881, hon. Ph.D., 1900, LL.D., 1929; Sc.D., Bethany Coll., Lindsborg, Kan., 1921, Tex. Christian U., 1923; m. Johanna Kristina Davis, 1882; children—Antonia Thilda, Jon Andreas, Anton David, Svante Mauritz. Taught at Bethany Coll., Lindsborg, Kan., 1881-88; studied U. of Minn. part of 1886; Oscar II prof. geology and natural history, Augustana Coll., 1888-1911; geologist, Bureau of Econ. Geol. and Technology, 1911-15, dir. 1915—, U. of Tex. Spl. asst. Ia. Geol. Survey, 1899-1903; asst. geologist, U. of Tex. Mineral Survey, 1903-04; geologist, Ill. Geol. Survey, 1906-11; spl. agt. U.S. Geol. Survey, 1908-14. Knighted by King of Sweden, 1911 (Riddare af nordstjerneorden). Fellow Geol. Soc. America, A.A. A.S., Am. Inst. Mining and Metall. Engrs.; member American Association of Petroleum Geologists; del. 12th Internat. Geol. Congress, Toronto, 1913. Author: The Mechanical Composition of Wind Deposits; An Old Indian Village, 1900; The Mechanical Composition of Clastic Sediments; The Texas Meteor of October 1, 1917; Aids to the Identification of Geological Formations; and many other papers on geol. subjects. First to discover potash in the Permian of Tex. and first suggested the likelihood of finding petroleum on the State Univ. lands in W. Tex. Home: Austin, Tex. Died Jan. 5, 1932.

UELAND, Andreas, lawyer; b. Norway, Feb. 21, 1853; s. Ole Gabriel and Ane (Ollestad) U.; father a leader in Norwegian Storting (parliament) many yrs.; came to U.S., 1871; ed. pub. schs., bus. coll., and under pvt. tutor, Minneapolis; studied law in an office; m. Clara Hampson, June 19, 1885; children—Anne (wife of Dr. Kenneth Taylor), Elsa, Brenda, Sigurd, Arnulf, Rolf, Torvald. Practiced in Minneapolis, 1877—; mem. Ueland & Ueland; partner of Gov. John Lind, 1901-14; counsel Swedish-Am. Nat. Bank; dir. and counsel Midland Nat. Bank & Trust Co., 1909—; gen. counsel Fed. Res. Bank of Minneapolis, Red Lake & Manitoba Ry. Co. Democrat. Author: Recollections of an Immigrant, 1929; A Minor Melting Pot, 1931. Home: Minneapolis, Minn. Died July 30, 1933.

UFER, Walter, artist; b. Louisville, Ky., July 22, 1876; s. Peter and Alvina (Mauseer) U.; grad. pub. schools, Louisville, 1891; apprenticed to lithographer, Louisville, 1892; student Royal Applied Art Schs. (Dresden), 1895-96, Royal Acad. (Dresden), 1897-98, Art Inst. Chicago; student J. Francis Smith Art Sch. (Chicago), 1901-03 (gold medal, 1903), teacher same, 1904-05; m. Mary Monrad Frederiksen, May 5, 1905. With adv. dept. Armour & Co., Chicago, 1905-11; studied with Prof. Walter Thor, Munich, 1911-12; painted in Paris, Italy and N. Africa, 1913; exhibits at leading art exhbns. of the country. Awarded Martin B. Cahn prize, Chicago, 1916; first Logan medal, Chicago, 1917; Thomas B. Clarke prize, Nat. Acad. Design, 1918; hors concours, Ill. painters, Peoria, 1918; exhibited with first 100 Am. artists, Luxembourg, Paris, 1919; 3d class medal and $500, internat. exhbn., Carnegie Inst., Pittsburgh, 1920; 1st Altman prize, Nat. Acad., 1921; gold medal, Arts Club, Phila., 1922; hon. mention, Conn. Art Assn., 1922; Temple Fund gold medal, Pa. Acad. Fine Arts, 1923; 1st prize, Ky. artists, Nashville, Tenn., 1925; 2d Altman prize, Nat. Acad., 1926, also Isidor medal, Nat. Acad., 1926. A.N.A., 1920, N.A., 1926; hon. asso. mem. Boston Art Club, Modern Soc. Artists (Los Angeles); fellow Royal Soc. Arts (London), 1922. Address: Taos, N.Mex. Died Aug. 2, 1936.

UFFORD, Walter Shepard, social worker; b. Cambridge, Mass., Feb. 26, 1859; s. Hezekiah Gold and Mary Caroline (Shepard) U.; A.B., Amherst, 1882, A.M., 1885; Yale Divinity Sch., 1886-88, Andover Theol. Sem., 1889-91; Ph.D., Columbia, 1897; m. Elizabeth Brown, 1913. Teacher Cheltenham Mil. Acad. (nr. Phila.), 1882-86, acting prin., 1888-89; ordained Congl. ministry, 1891; pastor Trinity Ch., Bronx Borough, N.Y., 1891-94; sometime resident Toynbee Hall, Whitechapel, London, and Univ. Settlement, New York; mgr. press bur. Citizens' Union, in municipal campaign in New York, 1897; sec. Citizen's Com. of 100 to arrange for quarter-centennial celebration Nat. Conf. Charities and Correction, New York, 1898; supt. inspection N.Y. State Bd. of Charities, 1899-1902; gen. sec. Baltimore Federated Charities, 1902-07; gen. sec. Asso. Charities, Washington, 1909-34; mem. Commn. on Pub. Welfare Legislation for D.C., 1924-26. Home: Washington, D.C. Deceased.

UHL, Willis Lemon, prof. education; b. Angola, Ind., Apr. 22, 1885; s. William Wesley and Mary Elizabeth (Hall) U.; B.A., Northwestern U., 1911; Ph.D., U. of Chicago, 1921; m. Alta Vaughan Williamson, 1906; children—Katharine and Jeannette. Prof. edn., Northwestern U., 1916-20, U. of Wis., 1920-28; prof. of education and dean coll. of edn., U. of Wash., 1928—; acting asso. prof. edn., Yale, 1925. Conglist. Author: Scientific Determination of the Content of the Elementary School Course in Reading (Univ. of Wis.), 1921; The Materials of Reading—Their Selection and Organization, 1924; Principles of Secondary Education, 1925; Secondary School Curricula, 1927. Co-author: The Pathway to Reading (series), 1925-28; The Supervision of Secondary Subjects, 1929; Psychological Principles of Education, 1933. Editor Century Studies in Education; asso. editor Jour. Ednl. Research, Jr.-Sr. High Sch. Clearing House. Home: Seattle, Wash. Died Feb. 28, 1940.

UHLER, Philip Reese, scientist; b. Baltimore, June 3, 1835; s. George Washington and Anne Maria (Reese) U.; ed. at D. Jones' Latin School and under pvt. tutors; LL.D., New York U., 1900; m. Sophia Werdebaugh, 1869 (died 1883); m. 2d, Pearl Daniels, Apr. 29, 1886. Spent nearly 3 yrs. at Harvard as librarian and asst. to Prof. Louis Agassiz, in his mus. of comparative zoölogy; explored parts of Island of Hayti for him; became connected with Peabody Library, Baltimore, 1862, later librarian, devising new methods adopted in its catalogue. Pres. Md. Acad. Sciences; asso. in natural sciences, Johns Hopkins U.; fellow A.A.A.S. Author of numerous papers on geology, entomology, archæology and libraries. Home: Baltimore, Md. Died Oct. 21, 1913.

UHLMANN, Fred, grain and elevator business; b. Fürth, Bavaria, Germany, May 19, 1864; s. Sigmund and Emma (Rosenfeld) U.; ed. in Germany; m. Hattie Abt, May 9, 1893; children—Alice (Mrs. Jack A. Benjamin), Richard. Came to U.S., 1888. Entered grain and elevator business, 1901; sec. J. Rosenbaum Grain Co. until 1921; pres. Uhlmann Grain Co., 1923—. Asso. Northwestern U. Mem. Chicago Bd. of Trade. Republican. Jewish religion. Home: Chicago, Ill. Died Oct. 10, 1938.

ULKE, Henry, portrait painter; b. Frankenstein, Silesia, Prussia, Jan. 29, 1821; studied in Breslau, and, 1842-46, under Prof. Wach, Berlin; engaged in fresco paintings at Royal Museum, Berlin, 1846-48. Became involved in Revolution of 1848; emigrated to U.S., 1851; settled in Washington, 1857. Painted portraits of U.S. Grant, James G. Blaine, John Sherman, S. P. Chase, Charles Sumner, Sec. Stanton, Gen. Rawlins, Sec. Carlisle, Gen. Francis P. Blair, Attorney Gen. Garland, Gen. Spinner, John Wanamaker, Carl Schurz, R. G. Ingersoll, W. W. Corcoran, Profs. Henry, Baird, Simon Newcomb and Bell, Lord Elgin, Sir F. Bruce, Earl Gray, etc., for different depts. U.S. Govt. Also known as musical critic and entomologist. Address: Washington, D.C. Died 1910.

ULMANN, Doris, art photography; b. N.Y. City; d. Bernhard and Gertrude (Maas) Ulmann; ed. pub. sch. and normal dept. of Sch. of Ethical Culture, New York. Engaged in art photography, N.Y. City, 1918. Mem. Pictorial Photographers of America, Am. Woman's Assn. Her portraits of eminent men have been published under following titles: Portraits, College of Physicians and Surgeons, 1920; Portraits, Medical Faculty Johns Hopkins, 1922; A Portrait Gallery of American Editors, 1925; Roll Jordan Roll, with text by Julia Peterkin. Contbr. pictures and portraits to Theatre Art Monthly, Bookman, Spur, Vanity Fair, etc. Exhibited at Delphic Studios, New York, 1933. Home: New York, N.Y. Died Aug. 28, 1934.

ULRICH, Barry Stribling, lawyer; b. Chicago, Ill., July 6, 1888; s. Augustus Louis and Louisa (Stribling) U.; A.B., Harvard, 1910, LL.B., 1913; m. Evelyn Wells, June 22, 1918; children—Priscilla Louise, Barry Wells. Began practice at Honolulu, T.H., 1913; asso. with Pillsbury, Madison & Sutro, San Francisco, 1914-16, alone, 1916-17; mem. Thompson, Cathcart & Ulrich, Honolulu, 1919-23, again in San Francisco, 1923-25; practiced alone; spl. prosecutor for Ty. of Hawaii in case against Grace Fortescue, Massie, et al., 1932. Enlisted in 144th F.A. ("California Grizzlies") summer of 1917; lt. U.S.A., at Camp Zachary Taylor, Louisville, Ky., until close of war. Republican. Presbyn. Mason. Home: Honolulu, T.H. Deceased.

ULRICH, Charles Frederic, artist; b. New York, Oct. 18, 1858; studied art at Cooper Inst., National Acad. Design, and in Munich; bronze medal at Munich Acad., 1879; followed his profession in New York, 1879-84; asso. Nat. Acad. Design, 1883—; Clarke prize from the acad., 1884; same year went to Venice; resided there several years. Died 1908.

UMBSTAETTER, Herman Daniel, editor, publisher; b. Parma, Ohio, Feb. 26, 1851; s. Charles and Helene (Hege) U.; ed. pub. schs., Cleveland; m. Nelly Littlehale, artist, Oct. 25, 1893. In newspaper office, Cleveland, 1868-72; went to New York, 1872, and later to Baltimore where engaged in pub. and advertising business, 1873-87; removed to Boston; founded, 1895, The Black Cat, of which became editor and publisher. Author of short stories, The Red-Hot Dollar, When the Cuckoo Called, Asleep at Lone Mountain, Her Eyes, Your Honor, etc. Home: Boston, Mass. Died Nov. 25, 1913.

UNDERHILL, Edwin Stewart, congressman; b. Bath, N.Y., Oct. 7, 1861; s. Anthony L. and Charlotte (McBeth) U.; A.B., Yale, 1881; m. Minerva Elizabeth Allen, Oct. 9, 1884 (died 1921); children—William Allen, Edwin Stewart; m. 2d, Mary A. Allen, Feb. 4, 1925. Asso. with his father in publishing and editing Steuben Farmers' Advocate and other newspapers until latter's death, 1902; pub. the Advocate and Corning (N.Y.) Evening Leader, 1902—; v.p. Farmers and Merchants Trust Co. (Bath). Chmn. Dem. Co. Com., 1884-94; mem. 62d Congress (1911-13), 33d N.Y. Dist., and 63d Congress (1913-15), 37th Dist. Mem. Bd. of Edn.; pres. Davenport Library, Bath, N.Y. Pres. N.Y. State Press Assn., 1902, N.Y. State Associated Dailies, 1907. Apptd. food adminstr. Steuben County, N.Y., Jan. 1918; chmn. Bath Chapter Am. Red Cross, July 1917-19, 1921-27. U.S. del. Interparliamentary Union, Stockholm, Sweden, 1914. Episcopalian. Mason, Elk, Rotarian. Home: Bath, N.Y. Died Feb. 7, 1929.

UNDERHILL, Frank Pell, pharmacology; b. Brooklyn, N.Y., Dec. 21, 1877; s. David Bonnett and Emma (Housie) U.; Ph.B., Yale, 1900, Ph.D., 1903; studied Harvard, 1913; m. Lavina Reed Chasmar, Sep. 2, 1903. Asst. in physiol. chemistry, 1900-03, instr., 1903-07, asst. prof., 1907-12, prof. pathol. chemistry, 1912-18, prof. experimental medicine, prof. experimental medicine, 1918-21, prof. pharmacology and toxicology, 1921—, Yale. In charge U.S. Gas investigation at New Haven; chmn. com. on biol. chemistry, Nat. Research Council; Goldsmith lecturer, New York Pathol. Soc., 1913; Harvey Soc. lecturer, 1919. Asso. editor Chem. Abstracts. Lt. col., Chem. Warfare Service; comdg. officer New Haven Sta.; U.S. rep. to Interallied Gas Warfare Conf., Paris, France, Oct. 1918, and v.p. of the conf.; duty with Chem. Warfare Service, A.E.F., 1918. Republican. Methodist. Author: The Physiology of Amino Acids, 1915; The Lethal War Gases, 1919; Manual of Biochemical Methods, 1921; Toxicology—or the Effects of Poisons, 1924, 28. Contbr. on physiol. and pathol. chemistry in Reference Handbook of Med. Sciences, article, "Toxicology," in Nelson's Loose Leaf Medicine, also many papers in jours. Home: New Haven, Conn. Died June 28, 1932.

UNDERHILL, John Quincy, congressman; b. New Rochelle, N.Y., Feb. 19, 1848; s. Geo. W. L. and Julia H. U.; attended Coll. City of New York; m. Minnie B. Price, 1872. V.P. and treas. Westchester Fire Ins. Co. of N.Y.; employed by company 30 yrs.; sec. 20 yrs. Pres. village of New Rochelle, 4 yrs.; trustee 6 yrs.; mem. bd. edn. 3 yrs.; commr. sewers 11 yrs.; mem. 56th Congress, 16th N.Y. dist. Democrat. Home: New Rochelle, N.Y. Died 1907.

UNDERWOOD, Benjamin Franklin, author; b. New York, July 6, 1839; s. Raymond C. and Harriet E. (Booth) U.; ed. Westerly (R.I.) Acad.; m. Sara A. Francis, Sept. 6, 1862. Pvt. 15th Mass. Vols.; wounded and captured at Ball's Bluff, Va., Oct. 21, 1861; exchanged, 1862; became 1st lt. and adj., R.I. Heavy Arty.; war corr. Newport (R.I.) News; lecturer 30 yrs.; especially widely known, 1870-85, as a rep. of liberal religious thought, meeting in pub. debate, before audiences of from 1,000 to 3,000, leading clergymen, and, in 1873, in Boston, before the Evang. Alliance (composed of 400 orthodox clergymen), opened a discussion on Evolution and Evang. Theology, in which Profs. P. A. Chadbourne and Asa Gray were the other disputants. Bus. mgr. and co-editor Boston Index (organ of Free Religious Assn.), 1880-86, Open Court, Chicago, 1887. Editor Illustrated Graphic News, Chicago, 1888, Philosophic Jour. (organ Psychical Science Congress), 1893-95; chmn. Congress of Evolutionists; sec. Psychical Science Congress, Chicago Expn., 1893; editorial writer Quincy Jour., 1897—. Hon. member 19th Century Club (New York); mem. Am. Free Trade League. Author: Influence of Christianity on Civilization, 1871; Essays and Lectures, 1874; Letters of Junius, 1876; Spencer's Synthetic Philosophy, 1891; and many mag. articles. Address: Quincy, Ill. Died Nov. 10, 1914.

UNDERWOOD, Clarence F., artist.; b. Jamestown, N.Y., 1871; s. Frederick E. and Sophia U.; ed. Allegheny Coll., Meadville, Pa.; studied at Art Students' League, New York, and Julian Acad., Paris, under Constant and Jean Paul Laurens, and Bonguereau; m. Katherine Spotswood Whitehead, Feb. 23, 1905. Illustrator for mags. Creator of "Palm Olive Girl." Address: New York, N.Y. Died June 11, 1929.

UNDERWOOD, Horace Grant, missionary; b. London, Eng., July 19, 1859; s. John and Elizabeth (Mair) U.; A.B., New York U., 1881, A.M., 1884; Rutgers Coll., 1882-84; grad. New Brunswick (N.J.) Theol. Sem., 1884; hon. degrees D.D., 1890, and LL.D., 1912, New York U.; m. Lillias Stirling Horton, Mar. 13, 1889. Ordained Ref. Dutch ministry, 1884; pastor, Pompton, N.J., 1884; missionary, Seoul, Korea, 1885—. Teacher chemistry and physics, Royal Korean Med. Coll., 1887-89; chmn. bd. Bible translators, 1887-1911; treas., 1885-89, chmn., 1888-90, Korean Presbyn. Mission; corr. sec. Korean Tract Soc., 1889; chmn. Korean Ednl. Fedns.; pres. Korean Religious Tract Soc.; prof. theology, Korean Theol. Sem., 1907—; prin. John D. Wells Training Sch., Seoul. Foreign mission lecturer, Princeton Theol. Sem., 1908; lecturer, Deem's Philos. Foundation (New York U.), 1909. Author: English-Korean Dictionary, 1889; Korean Grammar, 1889; The Call of Korea, 1908; Religions of Eastern Asia, 1910; Introduction to the Korean Spoken Language, 1915. Address: Seoul, Korea. Died Oct. 12, 1916.

UNDERWOOD, John Cox, engr.; b. Georgetown, D.C., Sept. 12, 1840; s. Judge Joseph Rogers (of

Ky.) and Elizabeth Threlkeld (Cox) U.; C.E., Rensselaer Poly. Inst., Troy, N.Y., 1862; hon. A.M., Center Coll., Ky., 1876; m. Drue A. Duncan, May 16, 1867. Officer in C.S.A., Civil War, reaching rank of lt. col.; prisoner in Fort Warren nearly a year; mayor of Bowling Green, Ky., 1870-72; city, county and cons. state engr., 1866-75; lt. gov. of Ky., 1875-79. Conservative Democrat. Grand Sire and Generalissimo, I.O.O.F. of World, 1888-90; lt. gen. Patriarchs Militant, 1885-93; maj. gen. United Confederate Vets., and erected monument over Confederate dead at Chicago, 1891-95. Chronol. and geneal. historian. Address: Covington, Ky. Died Oct. 26, 1913.

UNDERWOOD, Lineas Dott, patent lawyer; b. Amsterdam, O., Oct. 22, 1872; s. Phillip G. and Elizabeth (Armstrong) U.; student Ada (O.) Normal Sch., 1891, Bryant and Stratton Inst., Indianapolis, 1893; B.S., George Washington U., 1899, M.P.L., 1903; m. Margaret Lasky, June 1, 1899; 1 son, Richard L.; m. 2d, Blossom Fisher, Jan. 11, 1926. Teacher pub. schs., Lima, O., 1890-92; teacher Elwood (Ind.) Bus. Coll., 1893; examiner, U.S. Patent Office, Washington, D.C., 1897-1907, prin. examiner, 1908-17, law examiner, 1918-21; in practice of patent law, 1922—; pres. Card Digests Co. Republican. Mason. Author: Underwood's Adjudicated Patents, 3 vols., 1907, 17, 22; Underwood's Patent Digest and Underwood's Trade-Mark and Copyright Digest (cards). Home: Washington, D.C. Died Jan. 19, 1933.

UNDERWOOD, Loring, landscape architect; b. Belmont, Mass., Feb. 15, 1874; s. William James and Esther Crafts (Mead) U.; A.B., Harvard, 1897; student Bussey Inst., Harvard, 1898-99; studied landscape architecture under Edward Andre, Paris, 1899-1900; m. Emily Walton, Oct. 14, 1897; children—Lorna, Nina W. (Mrs. D. H. McAlpin, III), Esther Mead. Practiced landscape architecture, 1900—. Pres. Boston Soc. Landscape Architects. Unitarian. Author: The Garden and Its Accessories, 1906; The Underwood Garden Diary. Lecturer on village improvement work and Old New England Gardens. Home: Belmont, Mass. Deceased.

UNDERWOOD, Lucien Marcus, botanist; b. New Woodstock, N.Y., Oct. 26, 1853; s. John Lincklaen and Jane H. (Smith) U.; lived on farm in boyhood; grad. Syracuse U., 1877, Ph.D.; m. Marie Antoinette Spurr, Aug. 10, 1881. Taught in various colls. in Ill., 1879-83; Syracuse U., 1883-91; De Pauw U., Ind., 1891-95, Ala. Polytechnic Inst., 1895-96, prof. botany, Columbia, 1896—. Author: Descriptive Catalogue of North American Hepaticæ, 1884; Moulds, Mildews and Mushrooms, 1899; Our Native Ferns and Their Allies, 1900; Our Native Ferns and How to Study Them, 1901. Address: New York, N.Y. Died 1907.

UNDERWOOD, Oscar W., senator; b. Louisville, Ky., May 6, 1862; s. Eugene and Frederica Virginia U.; ed. Rugby Sch., Louisville, and U. of Va.; m. Eugenia Massie, Oct. 8, 1885 (died Jan. 31, 1900); children—John Lewis, Oscar W.; m. 2d, Bertha Woodward, Sept. 10, 1904. Admitted to bar, 1884, in practice at Birmingham, 1884—. Chmn. Dem. Exec. Com., 9th Dist., Ala., 1892; chmn. Dem. Campaign Com. that adopted present constn. of Ala.; mem. 54th to 63d Congresses (1895-1915), 9th Ala. Dist. Leader of the House and chmn. Ways and Means Com., 62d and 63d Congresses; U.S. senator, terms 1915-27; elected Dem. leader of the Senate, Apr. 1920. Commr. plenipotentiary for U.S., Internat. Conf. Limitation of Armament, Washington, 1921; apptd. mem. Internat. (Peace) Commn. between U.S. and France, Sept. 12, 1927. Home: Birmingham, Ala. Died Jan. 25, 1929.

UNDERWOOD, Sara A. (Francis), author; b. (Francis) Penrith, Eng., July 21, 1838; ed. pub. schs.; m. Benjamin Franklin Underwood, Sept. 6, 1862. Asso. editor with her husband on free-thought journals, 1881-87 and 1893-94; treas. for Mass. Nat. Woman Suffrage Assn., 1884-86; mem. of and speaker at Com. Psychical Science Congress, World's Columbian Expn., 1893; speaker and writer on Woman's Advancement, and contbr. essays, stories and poems to mags. Author: Heroines of Free Thought, 1876; Automatic Writing, 1895. Address: Quincy, Ill. Died 1911.

UNDERWOOD, William Jackson, ry. official; b. Milwaukee, Apr. 19, 1852; s. Enoch D. and Harriet (Denny) U.; pub. sch. edn., Milwaukee; m. Evelyn E. Browne, Oct. 1884. Brakeman and Conductor, 1872-84, div. supt., 1884-94, asst. gen. supt., 1894-1900, gen. supt., Feb.-Dec. 1900, asst. gen. mgr., 1900-1905, gen. mgr., Dec. 1, 1905—. C.,M.& St.P. Ry. Home: Wauwatosa, Wis. Died Jan. 3, 1917.

UNDERWOOD, William Lyman, naturalist, lecturer; b. Belmont, Mass., Mar. 4, 1864; s. William James and Esther Crafts (Mead) U.; pub. sch. edn.; m. Ida Cushing, Nov. 16, 1887 (died 1922); 1 son, William James; m. 2d, Elizabeth Farley Kelly, Sept. 8, 1923. Left sch., 1880, to enter father's business, William Underwood Co., mfrs. canned goods, established 1822, of which became dir. Began lecturing in Boston and vicinity, 1896; lecturer in biol. dept. Mass. Inst. Tech., 1900—; writer and lecturer on bacteriology as applied to canned and preserving industries, mosquitoes and their extermination, the Gypsy and Brown Tail Moth problems; also on wild life in field and forest. Fellow A.A.A.S., Am. Acad. Arts and Sciences. Unitarian. Author: Wild Brother; Wilderness Adventures. Home: Belmont, Mass. Died Jan. 28, 1929.

UNSELD, Benjamin Carl, composer, teacher; b. Shepherdstown, W.Va., Oct. 18, 1843; s. John George and Susan (Eaty) U.; gen. edn. in schs. of native place; took up serious study of music at 21; 1st teacher Dr. Eben Tourjée; also studied under Dr. William Mason, James G. Webb, Theodore F. Sewart; m. Sally Helen Rickard, Sept. 6, 1887. Prin. Va. Normal Music Sch., established 1874, virtually the progenitor of the system of normal music schs.; asso. for many yrs. with Theodore F. Sewart in compilation of Tonic Solfa publs. Edited, alone or in association with others, over 20 musical works, including Temple Star, Tonic Solfa, Music Reader, Tonic Solfa School Series, Choral Standard, Progress in Song, Practical Voice Culture, etc. Became prin. Vaughan Normal Sch. of Music; editor Musical Visitor. Address: Lawrenceburg, Tenn. Deceased.

UNTERMYER, Samuel, lawyer; b. Lynchburg, Va., June 6, 1858; s. Isadore and Therese U.; father a Va. planter who served in Confederate Army; student Coll. City of New York; LL.B., Columbia, 1878; m. Minnie Carl, Aug. 9, 1880 (died 1924); children—Alvin, Irwin, Irene (Mrs. Stanley L. Richter). Admitted to bar, 1879, in practice in New York, 1879—; became mem. Guggenheimer & Untermyer, later sr. counsel; at age of 21 had argued many cases. Defended Asa Bird Gardiner against attempt to remove him from office as dist. atty. of New York County; as counsel for dist. atty. Thomas T. Crain of New York County, 1931, successfully defended him against removal charges, preferred by Gov. Franklin D. Roosevelt and heard before Commr. Samuel Seabury; represented the Wertheimers, English art dealers, in their controversy against the Count and Countess de Castellaine, and secured to creditors of Castellaine Estate payment in full of their claims, amounting to 20,000,000 francs for art treasures purchased for their Paris palace "Petit Trianon"; organizer and counsel various syndicates of investors in Gt. Britain, 1888-93, for purchase from American owners of flour mills, breweries, steel works, etc., involving more than $80,000,000; represented Mr. and Mrs. Charles W. Morse, in the Dodge-Morse controversy, in which Mrs. Morse was restored to her marital rights; counsel for James Hazen Hyde, in the struggle of James W. Alexander to oust Mr. Hyde from control of Equitable Life Ins. Soc., resulting in investigations of life ins. cos. and passage of reform laws in many states; represented H. Clay Pierce in preventing the Standard Oil Co., after its dissolution, from dominating the Waters-Pierce Oil Co.; carried through the merger of the Utah Copper Co. with the Boston Consol. and Nev. Con. cos., representing a market value of $100,000,000, for which was paid a lawyer's fee of $775,000, approved by the court; counsel for Joint Legislative (N.Y.) Com. on Housing (Lockwood Com.) in investigation, prosecution and conviction of Robert Brindell, controller of building trades, labor leaders, profiteering mfrs. and dealers, conspiring with labor unions to maintain high prices in building materials; lifelong champion of organized labor, representing them nationally and locally, also prosecuted many cases against labor unions, arbitrator in disputes, etc.; spl. atty. gen. in prosecution disclosed by Lockwood Com., securing convictions with prison sentences or fines, of over 300 persons and corps. for violation of anti-trust laws; participated in formulation of Fed. Res. Law; counsel for Rogers-Rockefeller-Lewisohn interests in contest with F. Augustus Heinze over Montana copper mines; counsel for Rogers and Rockefeller in controversy with Thomas W. Lawson over publication of "Frenzied Finance"; counsel various committees for reorganization of r.r. and indsl. cos.; rep. William Randolph Hearst before Supreme Ct. of U.S. in suit by Asso. Press against him in which the principle was involved of a property right in news; rep. Edward S. Stokes in controversy with John W. Mackay over ownership of Postal Telegraph Co. Counsel for sec. of Treasury and comptroller, U.S., in suit of the Riggs Nat. Bank of Washington, D.C., charging conspiracy to wreck the bank, the court deciding there was no conspiracy; secured divorce for Geraldine Farrar in suit against Lou Telegen; rep. Alexander Cochran in divorce from Ganna Walska in France; counsel for Com. on Banking and Currency of the Ho. of Reps., Washington, D.C., in "Pujo Money Trust Investigation," resulting in enactment of remedial laws; chmn. bd. at Washington that formulated Income Tax and Excess Profit laws, during World War I; spl. adviser to Govt. on interpretation of income tax and war emergency tax laws, also acted with Govt. in connection with preparation of proclamation for taking over the railroads; counsel in various internat. controversies, including one between Turkish princes and British interests over Mosul Oil Fields; another between Munsey, Sabin and Replogel (Am. syndicate) and the Archduke Frederick, involving return of confiscated properties of the Archduke in 9 European countries and whether these properties were subject to confiscation under the treaties; another suit involving claims of Austrian and German noblemen to properties confiscated by the Czechoslovakian Govt.; counsel, 1924, before U.S. Senate Com. on Campaign Contbns., when investigations were held on charges of Senator La Follette of the use of vast sums of money in Coolidge campaign. Advocate of Govt. ownership of pub. utilities, nat. corp. law, enactment to place N.Y. Stock Exchange under fed. or state regulation, etc.; acted for Gov. Smith in water-power controversy over the St. Lawrence water-power, resulting in defeat of grant of water-power rights of N.Y. state to pvt. interests; counsel for Herman Bernstein in first suit brought against Henry Ford because of articles against Jewish people pub. in Dearborn Independent and later in vols. under title of "The International Jew," resulting in securing retraction of all charges against Jews in the Dearborn Independent, in Ford's agreement "to gather in and destroy all copies of The International Jew," and his apology and retraction of charges against the Jewish people; defended Helen Elwood Stokes against suit of W. E. D. Stokes for divorce, resulting in verdict in her favor and establishment of trust fund of $100,000 for her and her children, also acted for children in contesting Stokes' will, recovering about $2,000,000 to be held for them; counsel in proceedings of Georgia Timken Fry Estate for the removal of Fifth Av. Bank and its counsel, as trustees for that estate, claims amounting to about $12,000,000, for alleged gross negligence and misconduct. Spl. counsel for Transit Commn. in formulating Unification Plan for rapid transit lines and for Commn. and City of New York in suits by and against the Interboro Rapid Transit Co. for maintenance of five cent fare; spl. counsel for Bd. of Estimate in transit matters, and financial adviser to City of New York, 1933, in formulating plan and rehabilitating its finances; counsel for Fox Film Co. and William Fox in successfully resisting receivership for Fox and bringing about pvt. sale of Fox interests, and friendly reorganization, involving $200,0000,000 in properties, for which service, extending over 3 mos., was paid fee of $1,000,000; one of arbitrators between Warner Bros. Pictures and Am. Tel. & Tel. Co.; counsel for bondholders committees of Kreuger & Toll and Internat. Match Co., in internat. failures of Ivar Kreuger. Mem. U.S. Sect. Internat. High Commn., 1916—; pres. Non-Sectarian Anti-Nazi League to Champion Human Rights, engaged in counteracting Nazi propaganda in U.S. and in internat. movement for counter-boycott of German-made goods; spl. counsel for Interborough and Manhattan Rys. in negotiation and proceedings for unification of Subway lines of N.Y. City. Served as pres. bd. mgrs. State Industrial Farm Colony; pres. bd. trustees Andrew Freedman Home. Del. Dem. Nat. convs., 1904, 08, 12, 16, 32, 36; delegate-at-large from N.Y., 1920; delegate-at-large to N.Y. State Constl. Conf., 1938. Home: Yonkers, N.Y. Died Mar. 16, 1940.

UPDEGRAFF, Milton, astronomer; b. Decorah, Ia., Feb. 20, 1861; s. William B. and Lydia Maria (Shear) U.; B.S. and B.C.E., U. of Wis., 1884, M.S., 1886; m. Alice M. Lamb, Sept. 8, 1887; children—Helen, Mabel, Ruth. Aid, U.S. Coast and Geod. Survey, 1882-83; asst. astronomer in Washburn Obs., U. of Wis., 1884-87; astronomo segundo Observatorio Nacional, Cordoba, Argentine Republic, 1887-90; prof. astronomy, U. of Mo., 1890-99; prof. mathematics, U.S.N., June 1899—; astronomer U.S. Naval Obs., Washington, 1899-1902; instr. U.S. Naval Acad., 1902-07; dir. Nautical Almanac, Washington, 1907-10; also in charge 6-inch Transit Circle U.S. Naval Obs., 1908-10. In charge U.S. Naval Obs. eclipse party at Barnesville and Griffin, Ga., May 1900; in charge geod. and other scientific work, Survey of Am. Samoa, 1913-14; on court martial and other duty, Navy Yard, Mare Island, Calif., 1915-17; in charge of meteorol. observations at Whipple Barracks, Prescott, Ariz., 1918-20. Placed on retired list U.S.N. with rank of comdr., July 1920. Fellow A.A.A.S. Elector New York U. Hall of Fame, 1925, 30, 35. Home: Prescott, Ariz. Died Sept. 12, 1938.

UPDEGRAFF, Thomas, congressman; b. Tioga County, Pa., Apr. 3, 1834; s. William and Rachel (Smith) U.; acad. edn.; m. Laura A. Platt, June 1, 1858 (died 1865); m. 2d, Florence E. H. Haight, Oct. 2, 1867 (died 1902). Clerk dist. ct., Clayton County, Ia., 1856-60; admitted to bar, 1861; practiced at McGregor, Ia., 1860—. Mem. Ia. Ho. of Reps., 1878; mem. bd. edn. and city solicitor, McGregor, 1870-92; mem. 46th and 47th Congresses (1879-83) and 53d to 55th Congresses (1903-09), 4th Ia. Dist.; del. Rep. Nat. Conv., 1888, and mem. notification com. Address: McGregor, Ia. Died 1910.

UPDYKE, Frank Arthur, coll. prof.; b. Daggett, Tioga County, Pa., Oct. 25, 1866; s. Edward and Emma (Hogaboom) U.; grad. Wayland Acad., Beaver Dam, Wis., 1887; A.B., Brown U., 1893, A.M., 1896, Ph.D., 1907; grad. study, U. of Chicago, Brown U., U. of Geneva, Switzerland; m. Cornelia Parish, June

4, 1894. Asst. prof. polit. science, 1907-11, prof., 1911—, Dartmouth. Albert Shaw lecturer on Am. diplomatic history, Johns Hopkins, 1914. Mem. N.H. Constl. Conv., 1912. Mem. Am. Polit. Science Assn. Author: The Diplomacy of the War of 1812. Contbr. to Am. Polit. Science Rev., Annals of Am. Acad., etc. Home: Hanover, N.H. Died Sept. 20, 1918.

UPHAM, Francis Bourne, clergyman; b. Bristol, R.I., Nov. 21, 1862; s. Samuel Foster and Lucy Graves (Smith) U.; A.B., Wesleyan U., Conn., 1885. A.M., 1888; B.D., Drew Theol. Sem., 1888; D.D., Syracuse U., 1903, Wesleyan U., 1935; m. Fannie E. Williamson, Apr. 28, 1891; children—Fannie Williamson, Francis Bourne, S. Foster, Lucy Norman, Philips Webb. Ordained M.E. ministry, 1888; pastor Francis Ch., Brooklyn, 1888-91, Carroll Park, Brooklyn, 1891-93, Bushwick Av. Ch., Brooklyn, 1893-97, Ridgefield, Conn., 1897-99, Mamaroneck, N.Y., 1899-1904, 1st Ch., Bridgeport, Conn., 1904-07, Sands St. Memorial Ch., Brooklyn, 1907-10, S. Norwalk, Conn., 1910-11; supt. Brooklyn N. Dist., 1911-17; pastor Sumner Av. Church, Brooklyn, 1917-19; sec. Endowment Fund, N.Y. East Conf., 1920-21; pastor "Old John St. Ch.," New York, 1922-34. Retired May 1935. Trustee Drew Theol. Univ. Republican. Author: Simon Peter, Fisherman, 1903; Life of Thomas Coke, 1909; Simon Peter, Shepherd, 1909. Home: Mamaroneck, N.Y. Died Mar. 19, 1941.

UPHAM, Frank Brooks, rear admiral; b. Ariz., Sept. 7, 1872; grad. U.S. Naval Acad., 1893. Promoted through grades in U.S.N. to rear adm., June 2, 1927; comdr. Control Force, 1928-30; chief Bur. of Navigation, 1930-33; admiral, comdr. in chief, Asiatic Fleet, 1933-36; chmn. Gen. Bd., Navy Dept., 1936; retired as rear admiral. Awarded Navy Cross; Letter of Commendation War Dept. Address: Washington, D.C. Died Sept. 15, 1939.

UPHAM, Frederic William, businessman; b. Racine, Wis., Jan. 29, 1861; s. Calvin H. and Amanda E. (Gibbs) U.; A.B., Ripon (Wis.) Coll.; m. Helen Hall. With Upham Mfg. Co., Marshfield, Wis., 1880-94; removed to Chicago, 1894, and entered lumber business; pres. Consumers Co.; dir. Peabody Coal Co. Del. Rep. Nat. Conv., 1892, 1912, 16, 20 (chairman com. on arrangements, 1908, 12, 16, 20); western treas. Rep. Nat. Com. campaigns 1908, 16. Treasurer Rep. Nat. Com., Feb. 1918—. Elected alderman of the 22d Ward, Chicago, 1898 (resigned); mem. Cook County Bd. of Rev., 1899-1913. Mem. Ill. State Council of Defense during World War I. Pres. Ill. Mfrs.' Assn., 1908-09, later dir. Home: Chicago, Ill. Died Feb. 15, 1925.

UPHAM, Samuel Foster, M.E. clergyman; b. Duxbury, Mass., May 19, 1834; s. Frederick and Deborah (Bourne) U.; grad. Wesleyan U. (Conn.), 1856, A.M.; D.D., Mt. Union, O., Coll., 1872; LL.D., Hamline U., 1888, Wesleyan, 1898; m. Lucy Graves Smith, Apr. 15, 1857. Joined Providence conf., M.E. Ch., 1856; transferred to New England conf., 1862; mem. Christian Commn., 1862; chaplain Mass. legislature, 1865; mem. gen. conf., M.E. Ch., 1880-88-92-96-1900; mem. gen. missionary com. M.E. Ch., 1882-1902; trustee Wesleyan U., 1871—; Wilbraham Acad. (Mass.), 1880—; sec. com. on constitutional law, M.E. Ch., 1896-1900. Pastor chs. at Taunton, Mass.; Pawtucket, R.I.; New Bedford, Mass.; Bristol, R.I.; Lowell, Mass., Boston, 3 chs.; elected, 1880, and began duties March 13, 1881, as prof. practical theology, Drew Theol. Sem.; mem. Methodist Centennial Conf., Baltimore, 1884. Chmn. Hymnal Com., M.E. Ch., 1900. Address: Madison, N.J. Died 1904.

UPHAM, Warren, geologist, archæologist; b. Amherst, N.H., Mar. 8, 1850; s. Jacob and Sarah (Hayward) U.; A.B., Dartmouth, 1871, A.M., 1894, D.Sc., 1906; m. Addie M. Bixby, Oct. 22, 1885; 1 dau., Pearl (dec.). Asst. geol. survey of N.H., 1875-78; on geol. survey of Minn., 1879-85; on U.S. Geol. Survey, 1885-95; sec. and librarian of Minn. Hist. Soc., St. Paul, 1895-1914, and archæologist, 1914—. Fellow A.A.A.S. Author: The Glacial Lake Agassiz, 1895; Greenland Icefields and Life in the North Atlantic, with a New Discussion of the Causes of the Ice Age (with Prof. G. F. Wright), 1896; Minnesota in Three Centuries, Vol. I, 1908; Catalogue of the Flora of Minnesota, 1884; Minnesota Geographic Names, 1920; Congregational Work of Minnesota, 1832-1920; Stages of the Ice Age, 1922; Chapters of Minnesota and Its People, 1924; also many geol. reports and papers in scientific and hist. mags., chiefly relating to glacial subjects and Minn. history. Editor: Minn. Hist. Soc. Collections, vols. 8-17, 1898-1920, contributing papers on Groseilliers and Radisson, the First White Men in Minnesota, and the Progress of Discovery of the Mississippi River. Address: St. Paul, Minn. Died Jan. 29, 1934.

UPHAM, William H., governor; b. Westminster, Mass., May 3, 1841; s. Alvin U.; uncle of Frederic William U.; ed. common schs.; removed to Niles, Mich., 1852, to Racine, Wis., 1853; entered 2d Wis. Inf., 1861; shot through the lungs at Bull Run, July 21, 1861, and reported dead; prisoner of war 6 mos.; apptd. to U.S. Mil. Acad. by President Lincoln; grad. 1866; lt. U.S.A., until 1869, resigned; m. Mary C. Kelley, Dec. 17, 1869. Engaged in lumber, furniture mfg. and banking at Marshfield, Wis., 1878—; pres. Upham Mfg. Co. Gov. of Wis., 1895-97. Republican. Mem. G.A.R. (maj. on staff dept. comdr., 1891-92; comdr. Dept. of Wis., 1893-94). Mem. bd. visitors, Annapolis, by apptmt. of Pres. Arthur, bd. of visitors, West Point, by Pres. McKinley. Address: Marshfield, Wis. Died July 2, 1924.

UPJOHN, Richard Mitchell, architect; b. Shaftesbury, Eng., Mar. 7, 1828; s. Richard U., architect; came to New York, 1829; attended sch. until 1846; entered father's office 1846; took charge of his father's business, 1850-51; studied abroad, 1851-52; partner with his father, 1853-71; alone, 1871—. Among his independent designs and works are the Capitol of Conn., Hartford; Hobart Coll. Library, Geneva, N.Y.; Cathedral, Fond du Lac, Wis.; entrance to Greenwood Cemetery, New York; Central Congl. Ch., Back Bay, Boston; St. Paul's and St. George's, Brooklyn; Trinity Ch., East New York; St. Chrysostom's Trinity Parish Sch., Middle Dist. Sch., Hartford; Park Ch., Hartford, and a vast number of buildings throughout U.S. Mem. Am. Inst. Architects from its founding (pres. New York Chapter). Address: Brooklyn, N.Y. Died 1903.

UPSHUR, John Henry, rear admiral U.S.N.; b. Northampton County, Va., Dec. 5, 1823; s. John Nottingham and Elizabeth (Parker) U.; student William and Mary Coll.; grad. U.S. Naval Acad., 1848, having previously served on various naval vessels in the Mediterranean, Brazil, and Gulf of Mexico; present at siege and capture of Vera Cruze; promoted master, 1855; lt., Sept. 1855; served with Perry expdn. in opening Japan to Commerce; flag lt. of African Squadron, 1857-59; instr. at Naval Acad. when Civil War began; served 2 yrs. in N. Atlantic Squadron during war; present at capture of Fort Hatteras and Port Royal, S.C., and in minor actions and expdns. on the coast; commd. lt. comdr., July 16, 1862; comd. flagship in N. Atlantic Fleet, 1864; present in actions with and final capture of Fort Fisher, Jan. 1865; commd. comdr., July 25, 1866; capt., Jan. 31, 1872; commodore, July 1880; rear admiral, Oct. 1884. Comd. flagship, Pacific Squadron, 1872-73, flagship S. Atlantic Squadron, 1875-76, Navy Yard, New York, 1882-84; ordered to command naval forces in Pacific when promoted rear admiral; in May 1885, retired at own application, after 44 yrs.' service. Address: Washington, D.C. Died May 30, 1917.

UPSHUR, John Nottingham, physician; b. Norfolk, Va., Feb. 14, 1848; s. George Littleton and Sarah Andrews (Parker) U.; prep. edn. Norfolk Mil. Acad., Va. Mil. Inst.; student U. of Va.; M.D., Med. Coll. of Va., 1868; m. Lucy T. Whittle, Nov. 19, 1873 (died 1876); m. 2d, Elizabeth S. Peterkin, Dec. 11, 1879. Mem. New Market Corps, Va. Mil. Inst.; seriously wounded at Battle of New Market, May 15, 1864; practiced in Richmond, Va., 1869—; prof. materia medica and therapeutics, 1884-94, clin. lecturer, diseases of women and children, 1884-92, prof. practice of medicine, 1894-99, Med. Coll. of Va. Delivered address, representing New Market Corps, at unveiling of memorial statue, "Virginia Mourning Her Dead," 1903; mem. bd. visitors, Va. Mil. Inst., 1903-06. Hon. fellow State Med. Soc. of Va. (pres.), Richmond Acad. Medicine and Surgery (pres.). Democrat. Episcopalian. Mason. Author: Disorders of Menstruation, 1886. Home: Richmond, Va. Died Dec. 10, 1924.

UPSON, Andrew Seth, mfr.; b. Burlington, Conn., June 16, 1835; s. Seth and Martha (Brooks) U.; ed. pub. and pvt. schs.; m. Chloe A. Moses, Oct. 2, 1859. Began at 18 in factory of Dwight Langdon, Farmington (Unionville), Conn., and became traveling salesman; succeeded to bus., 1860, and became mem. firm of Upson & Dunham, inc., 1866 as The Union Nut Co., chartered, 1883, as The Upson Nut Co., factories at Farmington, Conn., and Cleveland, O.; pres. Upson Nut Co., Union Nut & Bolt Co. (Unionville, Conn.), Union Rolling Mill Co. (Cleveland); v.p. State Banking & Trust Co.; dir. Union Nat. Bank, Western Reserve Ins. Co., Bankers Surety Co. (all of Cleveland), Aetna Nut Co. (Southington, Conn.); mem. advisory bd. Citizens' Savings & Trust Co., Cleveland. Mem. Conn. Ho. of Reps., 1872-73, Senate, 1879-82; del. Rep. Nat. Conv., 1880. Congregationalist. Home: Unionville, Conn. Died 1911.

UPSON, Anson Judd, educator; b. Phila., Nov. 7, 1823; s. Dana Judd and Mary F. (Clarke) U.; grad. Hamilton Coll., 1843, A.M., 1846; D.D., 1870; LL.D., Union Coll., 1880; L.H.D., Colgate U., 1895. Studied law at Utica; tutor 1845-49, prof. rhetoric and moral philosophy 1849-53, prof. rhetoric 1853-70, Hamilton Coll. Ordained Presbyn. clergyman, 1868; pastor Second Presbyn. Ch., Albany, N.Y., 1870-80; prof. sacred rhetoric, Auburn Theol. Sem., 1880-87; prof. emeritus, 1887. Regent, 1874—, vice-chancellor, 1890-92, chancellor, 1892—, U. of State of N.Y. Author numerous literary and hist. lectures, sermons, addresses and articles. Address: Glens Falls, N.Y. Died 1902.

UPTON, Daniel, normal sch. prin.; b. Lawrence, Mich., Jan. 25, 1864; s. John B. and Julia A. (Sherman) U.; M.E., Cornell U., 1890; B.S., Olivet (Mich.) Coll., 1891; Pd.D., N.Y. State Normal Coll.; m. Sara C. Chatham, Dec. 18, 1894. In charge of trade schs., N.Y. State Reformatory, Elmira, 1890-92; supervisor industrial edn. pub. schs. and prin. Tech. High Sch., Buffalo, 1893-1909; prin. Buffalo State Normal Sch., 1909—. Republican. Presbyn. Address: Buffalo, N.Y. Died July 18, 1919.

UPTON, George Putnam, journalist, author; b. Boston, Oct. 25, 1834; s. Daniel P. and Lydia N. U.; Roxbury (Mass.) Latin School; A.M., Brown U., 1854; m. Georgiana S. Wood, Sept. 22, 1880. On staff Native Citizen, Chicago, 1855-56; city editor Evening Jour., 1856-62; city editor and war corr., 1862-63, musical critic, 1863-81, asso. editor, 1872-1905, editorial writer, 1870—, Chicago Tribune. Author: Letters of Peregrine Pickle, 1869; Woman in Music, 1880; Standard Operas, 1886; Standard Oratorios, 1887; Standard Cantatas, 1888; Standard Symphonies, 1889; Musical Pastels, 1902; Standard Light Operas, 1902; Life Stories for Young People (36 vols.), 1904-12; Life of Theodore Thomas, 1905; Life of Remenyf, 1906; Standard Concert Guide, 1908; Standard Concert Repertory, 1909; In Music Land, 1913; The Song, 1914. Translator: Max Müller's "Memories"; Nohl's lives of Haydn, Beethoven, Wagner and Liszt; Storm's "Immensee." Address: Chicago, Ill. Died May 19, 1919.

UPTON, Jacob Kendrick, Life-Saving Service, U.S. Treasury Dept.; b. Wilmot, N.H., Oct. 9, 1837; s. Daniel and Asenath (Teel) U.; ed. New London, N.H., Literary and Scientific Instn., A.B., Columbian Univ.; LL.B., Columbian Law Sch., 1866; m. Mrs. Mary de Hass Hoblitzell, 1884. Served in U.S. Treasury; chief clerk 2 yrs.; asst. sec. under Secs. Sherman, Windom and Folger; financial statistician 11th census; trans., 1895, from Census Office to Life-Saving Service, U.S. Treasury Dept. Author: Money in Politics, 1885; A Coin Catechism (exposition of the money question from the gold standard side), 1895; annually prepares the article on "The Finances of the United States" for Appleton's Annual Cyclo. Residence: Gaithersburg, Md. Died 1902.

UPTON, La Roy Sunderland, army officer; b. Decatur, Mich., Oct. 8, 1869; s. Capt. John B. and Julia (Sherman) U.; grad. U.S. Mil. Acad., 1891; honor grad. Army Sch. of the Line, 1914; grad. Army Staff Coll., 1915; m. Agnes Millar, Sept. 4, 1902. Commd. 2d lt., June 12, 1891; promoted through grades to brig. gen. Nov. 5, 1923. Duty various posts in N.Y., 1892-98; recruiting service, Mich., 1898; with regt. at Montauk Pt., L.I., N.Y., 1898; collector customs, Tunas de Zaza and Manzanila, Cuba, 1899-1902; in Philippines, 1908; p.m. N.Y. City, 1911-12; duty Panama Canal, 1912-13, 1915-16, Fort Leavenworth, Kan., 1913-15, Eagle Pass, Tex., 1916-17; arrived in France, June 26, 1917; returned to U.S. May 14, 1919. Awarded D.S.C. "for extraordinary heroism" in action nr. Soissons, France, July 18-19, 1918; D.S.M. "for exceptionally meritorious and distinguished services" in trench sector South of Verdun, and in operations before Chateau Thierry; Croix de Guerre with three palms, on citations dated Oct. 25, 1918, and Mar. 28, 1919, Apr. 25, 1919; Italian War Cross for Merit "for gallantry shown and merit acquired for common cause" June 8, 1919; Companion of St. Michael and St. George, "in recognition of meritorious service rendered the Allied cause"; Officer Legion of Honor (French), May 5, 1919; La Solidaridad medal, 2d class, Panama, "in recognition of meritorious services rendered the Allied cause," 1919. Address: Washington, D.C. Died Mar. 1, 1927.

UPTON, Winslow, astronomer; b. Salem, Mass., Oct. 12, 1853; s. James and Sarah Sophia (Ropes) U.; A.B., Brown, 1875; A.M., U. of Cincinnati, for grad. course in astronomy, 1877; Sc.D. Brown, 1906; m. Cornelia A., d. Wm. H. Babcock, Feb. 8, 1882. Asst. Harvard Obs., 1877-79; asst. engr. U.S. Lake Survey, 1879-80; computer U.S. Naval Obs., 1880-81; computer and asst. prof. U.S. Signal Service, 1881-83; prof. astronomy, 1883—, dean, 1900-01, Brown U. Mem. U.S. Eclipse expdns., 1878, 1883, and of 4 pvt. eclipse expdns., 1887, 1889, 1900, 1905; dir. Ladd Obs., 1891—; absent on leave from Brown, attached to Southern Sta. of Harvard Obs. at Arequipa, Peru, 1896-97. Author: Star Atlas (for schools) 1896; etc. Address: Providence, R.I. Died Jan. 8, 1914.

URBAN, Joseph, architect, artist; b. Vienna, Austria, 1872; s. Joseph and Helen (Weber) U.; grad. Art Acad., and Polytechnicum, Vienna; pupil of Baron Carl Hasenauer; m. Mary Porter Beegle, Jan. 23, 1919. Came to U.S., 1911, naturalized citizen, 1917. Gen. production mgr. Internat. Film Studio, New York. Architect for County Esterhazy (Hungary), interior Municipal Bldg., (Vienna), "Czar Bridge," over Neva River (Russia), palace of Khedive of Egypt. Operatic and stage work in Royal theatres (Vienna), Opera Astroc (Paris), Covent Garden (London), for Boston Opera Co., Met. Opera Co. (New York). Practiced architecture in N.Y. City and Palm Beach, Fla., in addition to interior and stage art. Awarded Grand Prix, Paris, Venice, St. Louis Expn. (for decoration of room used for Austrian art exhbn.); govt. medals, Germany, Austria, etc. Home: Yonkers, N.Y. Died July 10, 1933.

URMY, Clarence, author; b. San Francisco, July 10, 1858; s. William S.U.; ed. Nana Coll. Organist and choir-master; writes songs and verses characteristically Californian. Author: A Rosary of Rhyme, 1884; A Vintage of Verse, 1897. Contbr. Harper's, Lippincott's, Century, etc. Address: San José, Calif. Deceased.

USHER, Edward Preston, author; b. Lynn, Mass., Nov. 19, 1851; s. Roland Green and Caroline M. (Mudge) U.; A.B., Harvard, 1873, A.M., 1875, LL.B., 1880; m. Adela L. Payson, June 25, 1879. Lawyer; also pres. Grafton & Upton R.R., 1887-1911. Author: Sales of Personal Property, 1886; Protestantism, a Study in the Direction of Religious Truth, 1896; A Genealogy of the Usher Family, 1630-1895, 1895; A Translation of Juvenal into English Verse, 1876; The Church's Attitude Towards Truth, 1907; The Greek Gospel, an Interpretation of the Coming Faith, 1909. Home: Grafton, Mass. Died Dec. 26, 1923.

USHER, Nathaniel Reilly, naval officer; b. Vincennes, Ind., Apr. 7, 1855; s. Nathaniel and Pamela (Woolverton) U.; grad. U.S. Naval Acad., 1875; m. Anne Usher, July 29, 1891. Ensign, July 18, 1876; promoted through grades to rear adm., Sept. 14, 1911. Comd. Ericsson during Spanish-Am. War; with Gen. Bd., Navy Dept., 1903-04; Bur. of Navigation, 1904-06; comd. St. Louis, 1906-08; asst. to Bur. of Navigation, 1908-09; comd. Michigan, 1910-11; pres. Naval Examining and Retiring Boards, Washington, 1911-12; comd. 4th div., Atlantic Fleet, 1912, 2d div., 1912-13, 3d div., 1913; commandant Navy Yard, Norfolk, Va., 1913-14, Navy Yard, New York, 1914-18; apptd. comdt. 3d Naval Dist., 1914; retired Apr. 7, 1919. Home: Potsdam, N.Y. Died Jan. 8, 1931.

USSHER, Brandram Boileau, bishop, physician; b. Dublin, Ireland, Aug. 6, 1845; s. Capt. Richard Beverly (of H. M. 86th Regt.) and Henrietta (Boileau) U.; diploma Royal Dublin Soc. at 17; studied medicine at U. of Mich., 1865, 66; received degree Doctor of Eclectic Medicine after exam. by Bd. Nat. Med. Assn., Chicago session, 1870, 71; M.D., Univ. Medical Coll., Kansas City (allopathic), 1894; grad. English course, Harvard Summer Sch., 1899; m. E. L. Thompson, July 16, 1867; m. 2d, Mary Reed Whitney, widow of F. W. Pelton, Aug. 6, 1897. Began course of divinity under direction of Bishop Whitehouse of Ill., 1871; left P.E. Ch. for R.E. Ch., 1874; ordained deacon by Bishop Cheney in Chicago; presbyter in Ottawa, Can., by Bishop Cheney, 1876; pastor, Toronto and Montreal; consecrated bishop Reformed Ch. of Eng., June 19, 1882, and elected bishop of Canada; resigned, 1891, and filled pastorates at Kansas City, Mo., and Peoria, Ill., until 1898, when retired; pastor emeritus, Emmanuel Union Ch., Lakeview, N.C. Lecturer Emerson Coll. of Oratory. A founder, mem. exec. bd., and pres., 1909, Victorian Club, Boston; mem. council Actors' Ch. Alliance. Lecturer Jamaican Inst., Jamaica, and commr. from that island to the Pan-Am. Expn., Buffalo, 1901. Removed to Calif., Sept. 1921. Home: Santa Monica, Calif. Died Feb. 16, 1925.

UTLEY, Henry Munson, librarian; b. Plymouth, Mich., Aug. 5, 1836; s. Hiram and Jane (Sands) U.; A.B., U. of Mich., 1861, A.M., 1870; m. Kate Lilly Burr, Mar. 1864. On staff Detroit Free Press, 1861-66; city editor Detroit Post and its successor the Post-Tribune, 1866-81; sec. Detroit Bd. Edn., 1881-85; city librarian, Detroit, 1885-1913, emeritus, 1913—. Republican. Presbyn. Pres. A.L.A., 1895. Author: Wildcat Banking in Michigan, 1875; The First President of Michigan University, 1882; History of Michigan as Province and State, 1906. Home: Detroit, Mich. Died Feb. 16, 1917.

UTLEY, Samuel, judge; b. Chesterfield, Mass., Sept. 29, 1843; s. Thomas Knowlton and Thedocia (Knox) U.; prep. edn. Williston Sem., Easthampton, Mass., 1858-60, Wesleyan Acad., Wilbraham, Mass., 1862-64; LL.B., Harvard U. Law Sch., 1867; m. Julia M. Martin, Dec. 8, 1875 (died 1922). Admitted to Mass. bar, 1867; practiced at Worcester; justice Central District Ct., Worcester, Sept. 13, 1882—. Mem. Am. Antiquarian Soc., and of its council, also its biographer (retired 1925). Home: Worcester, Mass. Deceased.

UTTER, George Herbert, congressman; b. Plainfield, N.J., July 24, 1854; s. George Benjamin and Mary Starr (Maxson) U.; A.B., Amherst Coll., 1877; LL.D., Alfred (N.Y.) U., 1906; m. Elizabeth L. Brown, May 19, 1880. Learned printing trade as a boy; continuously engaged as printer and newspaper publisher at Westerly, R.I., 1877—. Personal aide on staff of Gov. A. O. Bourn of R.I., 1883-85; mem. R.I. Gen. Assembly, 1885-89 (speaker 1888-89), Senate, 1889-91; sec. of state of R.I., 1891-94, lt. gov., 1904, gov., 1905-06; mem. 62d Congress (1911-13), 2d R.I. Dist. Republican. Seventh-Day Baptist. Address: Westerly, R.I. Died Nov. 3, 1912.

UTTER, Rebecca Palfrey, author; b. Barnstable, Mass., May 1844; d. Rev. Cazneau Palfrey; grad. Belfast, Me., high sch., 1862; m. Rev. David Utter (Unitarian), Sept. 1872. Author: The King's Daughter, and Other Poems, 1888; also contributions to papers and mags. Address: Denver, Colo. Died 1905.

UTTER, Robert Palfrey, prof. English; b. Olympia, Wash., Nov. 23, 1875; s. David and Rebecca Salisbury (Palfrey) U.; A.B., Harvard, 1898, Ph.D., 1906; m. Madeleine Bôcher, May 18, 1907; children—Robert Palfrey, Cicily Anne. Editorial staff, Youth's Companion, 1898; with New York Evening Post, 1899; instr, English, Harvard, 1902-06; instr. English, Amherst, 1906-09, asso. prof., 1909-19; asso. prof. English, U. of Calif., 1920-23, prof., 1923—. Chmn. Dept. of English, A.E.F. Univ., Beaune, Cote d'Or, France, 1919. Unitarian. Author: A Guide to Good English, 1914; Everyday Words and Their Uses, 1916; Everyday Pronunciation, 1918; Pearls and Pepper, 1924. Home: Berkeley, Calif. Died Feb. 17, 1936.

V

VAIL, Charles Delamater, coll. prof.; b. Goshen, N.Y., Feb. 1, 1837; s. Jacob Arnot and Halia Ann (Smith) V.; A.B., Hobart Coll., 1859, A.M., 1862, L.H.D., 1904; m. Mary Louise Clarke, Dec. 27, 1867 (died 1874); m. 2d, Mrs. Helen (Hall) Houghton, Apr. 8, 1901. Prin. Manlius (N.Y.) Acad., 1859-60, Seneca Falls Acad., 1860-62; read law and variously engaged, 1862-65; asstd. in raising 126th N.Y. Vols. for Civ. War; classical instr., 1865-66; founder and prin. Geneva Grammar Sch., 1866-70; v.-prin. Geneva Classical and Union Sch., 1870-72; Horace White prof. rhetoric and elocution and of English lang. and lit., 1872-88, instr. elocution, 1888-1902, registrar, 1872-1903, librarian, 1872-1909, emeritus prof. English and librarian emeritus, 1909, Hobart Coll. V.p. Geneva Cutlery Co. Trustee Am. Scenic and Historic Preservation Soc.; mem. Letchworth Park Com.; mem. Civ. Service Reform Assn., Am. Civic Assn., Simplified Spelling Bd. (advisory council). Episcopalian. Writer and authority on local history; lecturer. Home: Geneva, N.Y. Died July 25, 1921.

VAIL, Charles Henry, clergyman; b. Tully, N.Y., Apr. 28, 1866; s. Frank A. and Tasy Lovisa (Palmer) V.; St. Lawrence U., 1889-92, B.D., 1893, D.D., 1918; m. Mary C. Ellis, Aug. 16, 1888 (died 1890); m. 2d, Nina Bedell, of Geneva, N.Y., July 7, 1892. Ordained Universalist ministry, 1893; pastor All Souls' Ch., Albany, N.Y., 1893-94, First Ch., Jersey City, N.J., 1894-1901, Richfield Springs, N.Y., 1902-05, Pullman Memorial Ch., Albian, N.Y., 1906-15, Ch. of Good Tidings, Brooklyn, N.Y., 1915-21, St. Paul's Universalist Ch., St. Paul, Minn., 1921-23, First Universalist Church, Auburn, N.Y., 1923—. Author: Modern Socialism, 1897; National Ownership of Railways, 1897; Scientific Socialism, 1899; The Industrial Evolution, 1899; Mission of the Working Class, 1900; The Socialist Movement, 1901; The Trust Question, 1901; Socialism and the Negro Problem, 1903; Ancient Mysteries and Modern Masonry, 1909; The World's Saviors, 1913; Militant and Triumphant Socialism, 1913. Address: Auburn, N.Y. Died June 15, 1924.

VAIL, Derrick T., Sr., ophthalmologist; b. Franklin, O., Oct. 2, 1864; s. Derrick G. and Elizabeth (Lane) V.; M.D., Miami Medical Coll., Ohio, 1890; m. Dellah Harris, Apr. 14, 1891. Practiced in Cincinnati, 1890—; emeritus prof. ophthalmology, Med. Coll. U. of Cincinnati; cons. ophthalmologist, Cincinnati Gen. Hosp. Founder fellow Am. Coll. Surg., Oxford (Eng.) Ophthal. Congress. Presbyn. Contbr. sect. Pupil in Health and Disease, in Wood's Am. Ency. Ophthalmology, Vol. XIV; writer of many articles in ophthalmol. jours. Discoverer (with Dr. William B. Wherry) of Tularemia-Conjunctivitis in Man. Author of chapter on Intracapsular Extraction of Cataract, in James Moores Ball's 5th edit. Modern Ophthalmology, 1926. Address: Cincinnati, O. Died Oct. 29, 1930.

VAIL, Henry Hobart, publisher, editor; b. Pomfret, Vt., May 27, 1839; s. Joshua and Harriet (Warren) V.; A.B., Middlebury Coll., 1860, LL.D., 1896; m. Minerva Elizabeth Hewitt, Oct. 10, 1867 (died 1895). Taught sch., Dayton, O., 1861; sergt. Co. C, 131st Ohio Inf., summer of 1864 (100 days' men); entered service of Sargeant, Wilson, Hinkle & Co., ednl. pubs., Cincinnati, 1866; admitted partner in successors, Wilson, Hinkle, & Co., 1874; remained partner with successors, Van Antwerp, Bragg & Co., whose business was bought by Am. Book Co., 1890; removed to New York; dir. and editor-in-chief, 1890-1907, v.p., 1904-11, Am. Book Co. In 1877 planned and directed preparation of Ray's New Arithmetics, and in 1878 directed and edited preparation of McGuffey's Revised Readers; also many other sch. books. Retired from business, 1911. Episcopalian. Home: Woodstock, Vt. Died Sept. 2, 1925.

VAIL, Theodore Newton, capitalist; b. Carroll County, O., July 16, 1845; s. Davis and Phoebe (Quinby) V.; ed. Morristown (N.J.) Acad.; studied medicine 2 yrs. with uncle; LL.D., Dartmouth, Middlebury Coll., Princeton, Harvard; D.Sc., U. of Vermont; m. Mabel Rutledge Sanderson, 1907. Asst. supt., 1873, asst. gen. supt., 1874, gen. supt., 1875-78, ry. mail service, Washington; in telephone business, 1878-87; traveled for health, 1887-93; Vt. farmer, 1893-96; in elec. enterprises in Argentine, S.A., 1896—; introduced Am. electric system street rys. in Buenos Aires and installed telephone systems in prin. cities; pres. Am. Telegraph & Telephone Co., 1907—; also pres. or dir. many corps. in U.S. and London. Mem. Am. Acad. Polit. and Social Science (Phila.), Acad. Polit. Science in City of New York, New York Academy Sciences, Nat. Inst. Social Sciences. Home: Lyndonville, Vt. Died Apr. 25, 1920.

VAILE, Anna Louise Wolcott (Mrs. J. F. Vaile), educator; b. Providence, R.I., May 25, 1868; d. Samuel (D.D.) and Harriet Amanda (Pope) Wolcott; ed. Wellesley Coll.; m. Joel Frederick Vaile, Jan. 4, 1913 (died 1916). Prin. Wolfe Hall, Denver, 1892-98; founder, 1898, Wolcott Sch. for Girls; founder, 1920, Wolcott Conservatory (later Denver Coll. of Music); regent U. of Colo., 1910-16; apptd. by Will H. Hays as mem. bd., Harding presdl. campaign. Dir. from Colo. of Nat. Bd. of Gen. Federation Women's Clubs. Home: Denver, Colo. Died Aug. 17, 1928.

VAILE, Joel Frederick, lawyer; b. Centerville, Wayne County, Ind., Mar. 14, 1848; s. Rawson and Ann Eliza (Pope) V.; A.B., Oberlin Coll., 1872; m. Charlotte M. White, Aug. 10, 1875 (died 1902); m. 2d, Anna Louise Wolcott, Jan. 4, 1913. Admitted to bar, 1875; pros. atty., 36th Jud. Dist., Ind., 1878; del. from Ind. to Rep. Nat. Conv., Chicago, 1880; removed to Denver, 1882; became gen. counsel for D.&R.G. R.R. Co.; sr. mem. law firm Vaile, McAllister & Vaile. Home: Denver, Colo. Died 1916.

VAILE, William Newell, congressman; b. Kokomo, Ind., June 22, 1876; s. Joel Frederick and Charlotte Marion (White) V.; A.B., Yale, 1898; spl. student law dept. U. of Colo., 1899, Harvard, 1899-1901; m. 2d, Kate Rothwell Varrell, June 14, 1915; 1 son, Joel Frederick. Began practice at Denver, 1901; mem. firm Vaile, McAlister & Vaile, 1908-16; Rep. candidate for Congress, 1916; mem. 66th to 69th Congresses (1919-27), 1st Colo. Dist.; mem. coms. on Public Lands, Immigration, Naturalization, and Expenditures of the Treasury Dept. Served as pvt. Battery A, 1st Conn. F.A., U.S. Vols., Spanish-Am. War, 1898; 2d lt. Co. A, 1st Separate Batn. of Inf., Colo. N.G., Mexican border service, 1916. Republican. Conglist. Mason (32°, K.T., Shriner; Grand Master Colo. Masons, 1924-25). Author: The Mystery of the Golconda (novel), 1925; also articles and stories in mags. Home: Denver, Colo. Died July 2, 1927.

VALENTINE, Edward Virginius, sculptor; b. Richmond, Va., Nov. 12, 1838; s. Mann S. and Elizabeth V.; ed. in pvt. schs. and by pvt. tutors; anat. studies at Med. Coll. of Va., afterward studied drawing under Couture, and later entered Jouffroy's students' atelier in Paris; in Florence under Bonaiuti, and in Berlin under Kiss; pupil Royal Acad. Arts, Berlin; LL.D., Washington and Lee University, 1922. Pres. Valentine Mus.; pres. Richmond Art Club; pres. Va. Hist. Soc. Prominent works: Recumbent figure Gen. Robert E. Lee, Memorial Chapel, Washington and Lee U., Lexington, Va.; bronze figure of Gen. Thomas J. (Stonewall) Jackson, same town; bronze figure Vice President Breckinridge, Lexington, Ky.; bronze figure Gen. W. T. Wickham, Monroe Park, Richmond, Va.; marble statue Thomas Jefferson, Jefferson Hotel, Richmond, Va.; classic group of Andromache and Astyanax; marble figure, The Blind Girl; ideal figure Judas and Grief; bronze busts of Commodore Mathew F. Maury, John V. Minor, U. of Va., Prof. J. Randolph Tucker, of Washington and Lee U., Henry Timrod, Gen. John S. Mosby, Gen. Albert Sidney Johnston, Col. Wm. Preston Johnston, William Wirt Henry; heroic bronze statues of Jefferson Davis and allegorical female figures, symbolical of the South, for Richmond, Va.; bronze statue of Gen. Hugh Mercer for U.S. Govt.; statue of R. E. Lee for Statuary Hall, Washington; statue of John James Audubon, for New Orleans; busts of Edwin Booth, Gen. Joseph E. Johnstone, Gen. George Pickett, and many others. Among earlier works were the small figure, "The Nation's Ward," and the bust "Uncl Henry." Mem. Va. Art Commn. Home: Richmond, Va. Died Oct. 19, 1930.

VALENTINE, John J., express co. exec.; b. Bowling Green, Ky., Nov. 12, 1840; s. William Crenshaw and Eliza Yates (Cunningham) V.; common school edn. Began business life 1854 with druggist and agt. for express line in Bowling Green; entered employ of Adams Express Co., remaining until 1861; removed to Calif., became agt. Wells, Fargo & Co. at Strawberry Valley, later at Virginia City, Neb., afterward supt. Pacific Div. Wells, Fargo express; gen. supt. New York, 1869-70; headquarters removed, 1870, to San Francisco; dir. and v.p. 1882; gen. mgr., 1884; pres., 1892—. His annually published summary of the American output of gold and silver is recognized as authoritative. Address: San Francisco, Calif. Died 1901.

VALENTINE, Lila Meade (Mrs. Benjamin B. Valentine); b. Richmond, Va., Feb. 4, 1865; d. Richard H. and Kate (Fontaine) Meade; ed. pvt. schs., Richmond; m. Benjamin B. Valentine, Oct. 28, 1886. Organizer and pres., 1910-20, Equal Suffrage League of Va.; organizer Visiting Nurse Assn., Richmond; officer Daughters of the King, Woman's Auxiliary to Bd. of Missions; mem. bd. Sheltering Arms Free Hosp., etc. Mem. Va. Hist. Soc., Assn. for Preservation Va. Antiquities, Huguenot Soc. Episcopalian. Home: Richmond, Va. Died July 11, 1921.

VALENTINE, Milton, theologian, clergyman; s. Jacob and Rebecca V.; b. nr. Uniontown, Md., Jan. 1, 1825; grad. Pa. Coll., Gettysburg, 1850; D.D., 1866; LL.D., Wittenberg Coll., O., 1886; m. Margaret G. Galt, Dec. 18, 1855. Ordained Luth. minister, Oct. 1852; preached at Winchester, Va., 1852-53; Greensburg, Pa., 1853-54; prin. Emaus Inst., Middletown, Pa., 1854-59; pastor St. Matthew's Ch., Reading, Pa., 1859-66; prof. eccles. history, Luth. Theol. Sem., 1866-68; pres. Pa. Coll., 1868-84; prof. of systematic theology and chmn. of faculty, Luth. Theol. Sem., Gettysburg, 1884-1903; emeritus. Joint editor Luth. Quarterly, 1871-76, 1880-85, and 1898—. Author: Natural Theology, or Rational Theism, 1885; Theoretical Ethics, 1897; Christian Truth and Life, 1898; also numerous pamphlets, and contbns. to reviews and others jours. Address: Gettysburg, Pa. Died 1906.

VALENTINE, Patrick Anderson, capitalist; b. Forres, Scotland, Dec. 13, 1861; s. John Ross and Johanna G. V.; ed. Victoria Coll., Channel Islands; m. May Lester Armour, Mar. 6, 1902. Long asso. as employe and partner with late Philip D. Armour. Chmn. bd. Central Leather Co.; dir. Nat. City Bank of New York, Susquehanna & N.Y. R.R., Tionesta Valley Ry., U.S. Leather Co., Union Tanning Co., U.S. Realty & Improvement Co. Home: New York, N.Y. Died Aug. 21, 1916.

VALENTINE, Robert Grosvenor, industrial counselor; b. West Newton, Mass., Nov. 29, 1872; s. of Charles Theodore and Charlotte Grosvenor (Light) V.; A.B., Harvard, 1896; m. Sophia French, Dec. 31, 1904. Asst. in English, Mass. Inst. Tech., 1896-99; with Nat. City Bank, New York, 1899-1901, part of time in accounting dept. U.P. Ry., at Omaha, Neb.; instr. English, Mass. Inst. of Tech., 1901-02; with Farmers Loan & Trust Co., New York, 1902-04; pvt. sec. to commr. Francis E. Leupp, of the Indian Service, 1905-08; supervisor of Indian Schs., 1908; apptd. asst. commr. Indian Affairs, Dec. 1, 1908, commr. June 15, 1909-Sept. 12, 1912; chmn. 1st Mass. Minimum Wage Bd., 1913; investigator and consultant in labor problems, Boston, Dec. 1912—. Home: South Braintree, Mass. Died Sept. 15, 1916.

VALENTINO, Rudolph (Rodolpho Alfonzo Raffaelo Pierre Filibert Guglielmi Di Valentina d'Antonguolla), actor; b. Castellaneta, Italy, May 6, 1895; s. Giovanni and Maria (Barbin) Guglielmi; ed. Dante Alighieri Coll. and Royal Acad. Agr.; m. Jean Acker; m. 2d, Winifred Hudnut (Natacha Rambova), Mar. 15, 1923. Came to U.S., 1913; began as a dancer; joined musical comedy co., later stranded in San Francisco; entered motion pictures at Los Angeles, taking small parts; scored triumph as Julio in "The Four Horsemen"; other plays—"The Conquering Power"; "Camille"; "The Sheik"; "Moran of the Lady Letty"; "Beyond the Rocks"; "The Young Rajah"; "Blood and Sand"; "Monsieur Beaucaire"; "The Sainted Devil." Home: Hollywood, Calif. Died Aug. 23, 1926.

VALLENTINE, Benjamin Benton ("Fitznoodle"), author, dramatist; b. London, Eng., Sept. 7, 1843; s. Benjamin V., mcht.; ed. King Edward VI's Sch., Birmingham; studied for bar; unmarried. Shipping, trading and mercantile pursuits in Australia a number of yrs. A founder of Puck, and its editor, 1877-84; came to U.S., 1871; matriculated in law dept. New York U.; mng. editor Irving Bacheller's newspaper syndicate, 1886-88; on editorial staff and dramatic critic N.Y. Herald, 1891-98. In N.Y. American wrote Lord Fitznoodle editorial interviews illustrated by Opper, 1902-03. Civil service employee, Dept. of Finance, City of New York, 1908—. Wrote signed dramatic biographies for Universal Ency. Author: Fitznoodle Papers; Fitznoodle in America; etc.; (plays) Fitznoodle; A Southern Romance; In Paradise; Fitz in New York; The Locksmith of Paris; The King of the World; etc. Translator of Zola's drama, Renee, under the title of Madam Saccard; Daudet's Sappho; etc. Contbr. to mags. Home: New York, N.Y. Died Mar. 30, 1926.

VALLIANT, Leroy Branch, judge; b. Moulton, Ala., June 14, 1838; s. Denton Hurlock and Narcissa (Kilpatrick) V.; A.B., U. of Miss., 1856, LL.D., 1898; LL.B., Cumberland U., 1858; m. Theodosia T. Worthington, 1862. Capt. Co. I, 22d Miss. Regt., C.S.A.; moved from Miss. to St. Louis, 1874; judge Circuit Ct., City of St. Louis, 1886-98; asso. justice Supreme Ct. of Mo., 1898—, becoming chief justice. Democrat. Grand Master of Masons of Mo., 1904-05. Address: St. Louis, Mo. Died Mar. 3, 1913.

VALUE, Beverly Reid, civil engr.; b. Montgomery, Ala., Apr. 7, 1863; s. Jesse Reine and Edith (Bailey) V.; E.M., Sch. of Mines (Columbia), 1884; m. Rebecca Roe Morris, Oct. 1886. Exec. engr., New Croton Dam, N.Y., during constrn., 1886-91; div. engr. Rapid Transit Commn. during constrn. of subways, 1900-03; chief engr. Elec. Development Co. during constrn. large hydro-electric plant, Niagara River, 1903-06; constrn. engr. McCall's Ferry Power Co., during constrn. large hydro-electric plant, Susquehanna River, 1906-08; v.p., dir. Interlake Engring. Co., Kerbaugh-Empire Co., Empire Engring. Co., Geo. W. Rogers & Co.; v.p. Bellwood Engring. Co. Episcopalian. Home: New York, N.Y. Died June 10, 1920.

VAN ALLEN, Daniel D., educator; b. Richford, N.Y., Jan. 7, 1834; s. John and Mary (MacAllester) V.; 7th in descent from Petrus van Haelen, burgess of New Amsterdam and Beverwyck; B.A., Alfred (N.Y.) U., 1859, M.A., 1862; M.A., Syracuse U., 1891, ad eundem; m. Frances Jane Holland, June 2, 1868 (died 1905); father of William Harman V. Prof. French and German, Dansville (N.Y.) Sem.; prin. Wellsboro (Pa.) Acad., Rogersville Sem., N.Y., and of high schs., Port Byron and Holland Patent, N.Y., Macedon Acad., high schs. Weedsport and Ellington, N.Y., Lawrenceville (N.Y.) Acad., high schs. Massena, Bainbridge and Crown Point, N.Y., until 1888; prin. and supt. schs., Camden, N.Y., 1888-97; retired, 1897. Republican. Mason. Address: Boston, Mass. Died May 26, 1913.

VAN ALSTYNE, Thomas Jefferson, lawyer; b. Richmondville, Schoharie County, N.Y., July 25, 1827; s. Dr. Thomas B. and Eliza (Gile) V.; A.M., Hamilton Coll., 1848; studied law; admitted to bar and practiced at Albany; judge Albany County, 1871-83; mem. 48th Congress, 1883-85; served on Coms. of Claims, Dept. of Justice, and spl. com. to investigate methods of administration, etc., of the marshal of the southern dist. of Ohio; mayor of Albany, N.Y., 1898-99. Democrat. Residence: Albany, N.Y. Died 1903.

VAN AMBURGH, Fred D., editor, pub.; b. Newburgh, N.Y., Apr. 5, 1866; s. John and Lucy (Early) V.; ed. high sch., business coll., and under pvt. tutors; m. Carrie Seeber, Dec. 24, 1887. Founder and pub. Chenango Forks (N.Y.) Herald, 1888-93, later one of owners Evening Herald, Binghamton, N.Y., and Binghamton Saturday Post; real estate, ins. and mining business, Colo., 1896-1902; broker in Wall St., N.Y. City, several yrs.; editor and pub. Silent Partner Magazine, 1913—. Republican. Mason. Author: The Silent Partner Scrap Book, 1915; By the Side of the Road, 1916; The Buck Up Book, 1918; Just Common Sense, 1920; The Mental Spark Plug 1923; Your Mother and My Mother, 1926; The Thought Arouser, 1929. Home: Binghamton, N.Y. Died Oct. 23, 1934.

VAN AMRINGE, John Howard, educator; b. Phila., Apr. 3, 1835; s. William Frederick and Susan Budd (Sterling) V.; A.B., Columbia, 1860, A.M., 1863, hon. Ph.D., U. State of N.Y., 1877; L.H.D., Columbia, 1890; LL.D., Union, 1895, Columbia, 1910; m. Cornelia Bucknor, June 20, 1865. Tutor mathematics, 1860-63, adj. prof., 1863-65, prof., 1865-1910, emeritus prof., 1910—, head dept. mathematics, 1892-1910, dean Sch. of Arts, 1894-96, dean Columbia Coll., 1896-1910, pres. pro tem., 1899, Columbia U. Fellow A.A.A.S.; mem. Am. Math. Soc., N.Y. Math. Soc. (pres., 1888-90). Trustee New York P.E. Pub. Sch., Soc. for Promoting Religion and Learning in the State of N.Y., N.Y. Bible and Common Prayer Book Society. Vestryman Trinity Parish, New York. Editor Davies' series math. works. Writer of pamphlets and articles on life ins., vital statistics, etc.; also of History of Columbia College and University, and numerous articles and addresses relating thereto and to alumni of Columbia. Address: New York, N.Y. Died Sept. 10, 1915.

VAN ANTWERP, William Clarkson, author; b. Omaha, Neb., July 13, 1867; s. William Henry and Charlotte Augusta (Jones) V.; grad. U.S. Naval Acad., 1888; unmarried. In banking business, 1890—; mem. firm of Van Antwerp, Bishop Co. Episcopalian. Author: The Stock Exchange From Within, 1913. Home: New York, N.Y. Died Feb. 17, 1938.

VAN BAUN, William Weed, physician; b. Phila., Pa., Aug. 20, 1858; s. St. John Divine and Harriet Finch (Weed) V.; M.D., Hahnemann Med. Coll. and Hosp., Phila., 1880; post-grad. course, U. of Vienna, 1888; unmarried. Practiced at Vicksburg, Miss., 1880-81, Phila., 1881—; phys. to Hahnemann Hosp., 1890—, trustee 15 yrs.; cons. phys. St. Luke's Hosp., West Phila. Homœ. Hosp., Woman's Southern Homœ. Hosp.; prof. pediatrics, 1904-12, prof. dietetics, 1912—, Hahnemann Med. Coll. Mem. Am. Inst. Homœopathy (pres. 1916-17), Pa. Homœ. Med. Soc. (pres. 1896), Phila. County Homœ. Med. Soc. (pres. 1892-93), Germantown Homœ. Med. Soc. (pres. 1915-16), Am. Acad. Polit. and Social Science; founder Alumni Assn. of Hahnemann Med. Col. (pres. 1898). Editor Hahnemannian Monthly, 1888-1901. Lived in Calif., 1920-21, regained health and resumed practice in Phila., 1922. Republican. Episcopalian. Mason. Home: Philadelphia, Pa. Died Oct. 6, 1930.

VAN BENSCHOTEN, James Cooke, univ. prof.; b. Dec. 15, 1827, La Grange, N.Y.; studied Genesee Coll., Lima, N.Y., 1850-54; A.B., Hamilton, 1856; A.M., Madison (now Colgate) U., 1857; LL.D., Rochester U., 1875; teacher ancient languages, Oxford Collegiate Inst., N.Y., 1855-56; prin. same, 1857-58; teacher ancient languages Susquehanna Sem., Binghamton, N.Y., 1856-57; studied univs. of Berlin, Bonn, Göttingen and Athens, and traveled in Europe, 1858-61; prin. high school, Lyons, N.Y., 1861-62; teacher ancient languages Oneida (now Central N.Y.) Conf. Sem., Cazenovia, N.Y., 1862-63; prof. Greek lang. and lit., Wesleyan U., 1863—; also 1863-73 instr. modern languages; dir. Am. School of Classical Studies, Athens, 1884-85. Address: Middletown, Conn. Died 1902.

VAN BENSCHOTEN, William Henry, lawyer; b. Addison, N.Y., Jan. 15, 1872; s. Henry and Mary (Northrop) V.; A.B., Syracuse U., 1894, A.M., 1895; LL.B., Albany Law Sch., 1895; m. Harriet E. Paddock, Sept. 21, 1898; children—Katharine, William H. Record clk. N.Y. State Constl. Conv., 1894; chief clk. in office of atty.-gen. of N.Y., 1896-97; admitted to bar, 1896; practiced with Bowers & Sands, New York; partner same, 1910-17; became mem. Bowers & Gerard, Dec. 1, 1917, and Duer, Strong & Whitehead, May 15, 1918. Of plaintiff's counsel in libel suit of Theodore Roosevelt vs. George A. Newett, 1913, and one of defendant's counsel in libel suit of William Barnes vs. Theodore Roosevelt, 1915. Chmn. Commn. on West Side Improvement N.Y. City, apptd. by Gov. Whitman, 1917; trustee Syracuse U., Drew Theol. Sem., etc. Lay del. Gen. Conf. M.E. Ch., 1920-24, Meth. Ecumenical Conf., London, 1921. Republican. Home: New York, N.Y. Died Aug. 11, 1928.

VAN BEUREN, Amedee J., motion picture exec.; b. N.Y. City, July 10, 1880; s. Alfred Vignot and Marietta (Ferguson) Van B.; ed. pub. and pvt. schs. and business coll.; m. Ethel Virginia Anderson, May 25, 1929. Pres. Van Beuren Corp., producers "Bring 'em Back Alive," "Wild Cargo," "Fang and Claw" (Frank Buck features), and the following short subj. series: "Struggle to Live," "Rainbow Parade Color Cartoons," "Dumbell Letters," "Sports with Bill Corum," "World on Parade," "Easy Aces." Pres. Colorado Springs Theatre Corp., The Kerneb Corp. Democrat. Home: Carmel, N.Y. Died Nov. 12, 1938.

VAN BOSKERCK, Robert Ward, artist; b. Hoboken, N.J., Jan. 15, 1855; s. Lucas J. and Katherine Zabriskie (Anderson) V.; grad. Sch. of Mines (Columbia), 1877; pupil in art of A. H. Wyant; unmarried. First exhibit at Nat. Acad. Design, 1880; silver medal, Buffalo Expn., 1901, St. Louis Expn., 1904. Represented in Union League and Lotos clubs (New York), Hamilton Club (Brooklyn), Ellicott Club (Buffalo), Layton Art Gallery (Milwaukee), Mappin Art Gallery (Sheffield, Eng.), etc., A.N.A., 1897, N.A., 1907. Address: New York, N.Y. Died **1932.**

VAN BRUNT, Charles H., justice of Supreme Court, N.Y., 1883—; b. Fort Hamilton, N.Y., Dec. 26, 1835; s. Albert N. Van Brunt; grad. U. of City of New York, 1856, LL.D.; m. Jennie E. Bull, Dec. 20, 1874. Admitted to bar, Nov. 1858; practiced New York; judge ct. of common pleas, city and county of New York, 1869-83; apptd. presiding justice general term 1st dept., 1886; presiding justice of appellate div., 1st dept., 1895. Address: New York, N.Y. Died 1905.

VAN BRUNT, Henry, architect; b. Boston, Sept. 5, 1832; s. Commodore Gershom Jacques, U.S.N., and Elizabeth Bradlee (Price) Van B.; grad. Harvard, 1854; served on admiral's staff, N. Atlantic squadron, U.S.N., 2 yrs., during Civil War; m. Alice S. Osborn, 1869. Practiced in Boston about 20 yrs.; removed to Kansas City, 1887. Architect of numerous buildings connected with Harvard, and of pub. libraries and other pub. bldgs. throughout U.S., bus. blocks, pvt. houses, railroad bldgs., churches, etc.; also of Electricity Bldg. in Court of Honor, World's Columbian Expn., Chicago; mem. firm Van Brunt & Howe; elected, 1898, pres. Am. Inst. of Architects. Author: Greek Lines and Other Architectural Essays, 1893; also numerous professional papers. Translated Viollet le Duc's "Discourses on Architecture." Home: Kansas City, Mo. Died 1903.

VAN BUREN, Albert Alexander, mcht. and mfr.; b. Watertown, N.Y., Dec. 18, 1852; s. James S. and Harriet (Stebbins) V.; ed. pub. schs., Cincinnati; m. Alicia Keisker, June 3, 1885. Began in piano business July 1871, with firm of D. H. Baldwin & Co., later became a partner until July 1903, when he retired. Long interested in art and gave part of time to study and painting of marines; exhibited two marines in Ky. Bldg., La. Purchase Expn., 1904. Home: Brookline, Mass. Died 1910.

VAN BUREN, Alicia Keisker, author; b. Louisville, Ky., Mar. 5, 1860; d. Henry William and Alicia (Bourke) Keisker; ed. pub. and pvt. schs., Louisville; m. Albert Alexander Van Buren, June 3, 1885 (died 1910). Author: Book of Songs, 1896; Five Songs, 1900; String Quartette, 1901; Group of Songs, 1902; As Thought Is Led (poems), 1904; Six Songs, 1909; Fireflies (poems), 1913. Address: Louisville, Ky. Died Apr. 11, 1922.

VAN BUREN, James Heartt, bishop; b. Watertown,, N.Y., July 7, 1850; s. James Saurin and Harriet Adelia (Stebbins) V.; brother of Albert Alexander V.; A.B., Yale, 1873; grad. Berkeley Div. Sch., 1876, D.D., 1902; m. Annie M. Smith, Apr. 11, 1877. Deacon, 1876, priest, 1877, P.E. Ch.; rector Milford, Conn., 1876-78, Seymour, Conn., 1878-81, Englewood, N.J., 1881-84, Newburyport, Mass., 1884-90, St. Stephen's, Lynn, Mass., 1890-1901; consecrated bishop of Puerto Rico, June 24, 1902. Address: Rio Piedras, P.R. Died July 10, 1917.

VANCE, Arthur Turner, editor; b. Scranton, Pa., Oct. 10, 1872; s. Jules C. and Marietta (Southworth) V.; ed. pub. and high schs., Binghamton, N.Y. Began newspaper work on Binghamton Leader; became editor of Home Magazine, 1896; later asso. editor New England Magazine; editor-in-chief Woman's Home Companion, 1900-07; later editor-in-chief Pictorial Review. Author: The Real David Harum, 1900. Contbr. to periodicals. Address: New York, N.Y. Died Sept. 8, 1930.

VANCE, Hiram Albert, educator; b. W. Frankfort, N.Y., July 23, 1860; s. William Matthew and Sarah Amanda V.; ed. Whitestown Sem., N.Y., and Troy Conf. Acad., Poultney, Vt.; grad. Hamilton Coll., 1888; Jena, Germany, Ph.D., 1893; m. Juliette Myrick, Sept. 12, 1894. Instr. history and asst. librarian Hamilton Coll., 1888-89; prof. English, U. of Nashville, and Peabody Coll. for Teachers, 1889—; acting prof. English philology, Vanderbilt U., 1904-05. Student in Germany on leave of absence, 1891-93. Author: Der Sermo in Festis Sanctae Mariae Virginis mit Rücksicht auf das Altenglische, 1894. Editor: Stevenson's Treasure Island (for use in secondary schs.), 1903. Address: Nashville, Tenn. Died 1906.

VANCE, James Isaac, clergyman, author; b. Arcadia, Tenn., Sept. 25, 1862; s. Charles Robertson and Margaret (Newland) V.; A.B., King Coll., Tenn., 1883, A.M., 1886; grad. Union Theol. Sem., Va., 1886; D.D., King Coll., 1896, Hampden-Sydney Coll., 1896; LL.D., King Coll., 1913, Austin Coll., 1916, U. of Ala., 1935; m. Mamie Stiles Currell, Dec. 22, 1886; children—Margaret, Currell, Agnes Wilkie, Ruth Armstrong, James Isaac (dec.), Charles Robertson. Ordained ministry Presbyn. Ch. in U.S., 1886; pastor Wytheville, Va., 1886-87, Alexandria, 1887-91, Norfolk, Va., 1891-94, First Ch., Nashville, Tenn., 1894-1900, North Ref. Ch., Newark, N.J., 1900-10, 1st Ch. Nashville, 1910—. Platform speaker. Chmn. exec. com. foreign missions Presbyn. Ch. Served as moderator Presbyn. Ch. in U.S.; chmn. Protestant Relief in Europe. Trustee Southwestern Coll. Author: Young Man Four-Square, 1894; Church Portals, 1895; College of Apostles, 1896; Predestination (pamphlet), 1898; Royal Manhood, 1899; Rise of a Soul, 1902; Simplicity in Life, 1903; A Young Man's Make-up, 1904; The Eternal in Man, 1907; Tendency, 1910; Life's Terminals, 1917; The Life of Service, 1918; The Silver on the Iron Cross, 1919; The Breaking of the Bread, 1921; Being a Preacher, 1923; God's Open, 1924; Forbid Him Not, 1925; Love Trails of the Long Ago, 1927; This Dreamer, 1928; The Field Is the World, 1930; Sermons in Argot, 1931; Worship God, 1932; Let Not Your Heart Be Troubled, 1934; Thus Pray Ye, 1935. Home: Nashville, Tenn. Died Nov. 24, 1939.

VANCE, Jessica Smith, educator; b. in Calif.; d. Thomas and Sophia Jane (Smith) V.; Ph.B., Coll. of the Pacific; A.M., Stanford, 1896. Instr. in philology at Stanford; prof. of lit. and philol., U. of Southern Calif., 1900-04; prin. Westlake Sch. for Girls, 1904—; dir. Holmby Coll., 1924—. Mem. Headmistresses' Assn. of Pacific Coast (pres. 1925-27), Headmistresses' Assn. of Atlantic Coast (asso.), Nat. Assn. Principles of Girls' Schools. Democrat. Episcopalian. Home: Los Angeles, Calif. Died Mar. 3, 1939.

VANCE, Louis Joseph, author; b. Washington, D.C., Sept. 19, 1879; s. Wilson and Lillie (Beall) V.; ed. prep. dept. Brooklyn Polytechnic Institute; m. Nance Elizabeth Hodges, 1898. Author: Terence O'Rourke, Gentleman Adventurer, 1905; The Brass Bowl, 1907; The Fortune Hunter, 1910; The Destroying Angel, 1912; The Lone Wolf, 1914; The Dark Mirror, 1919; Alias the Lone Wolf, 1921; Linda Lee, Inc., 1922; Baroque, 1923; The Lone Wolf Returns, 1923; Mrs. Paramor, 1924; The Road to En-Dor, 1925; White Fire, 1925; The Dead Ride Hard, 1926; They Call It Love, 1927; The Woman in the Shadow, 1930; Speaking of Women, 1930; The Trembling Flame, 1931; The Lone Wolf's Son, 1931, and many others. Home: New York, N.Y. Died Dec. 16, 1933.

VANCE, Selby Frame, theologian; b. Oneida, Ill., Nov. 17, 1864; s. Samuel Elbridge and Kate (Frame) V.; A.B., Lake Forest (Ill.) Univ., 1885, A.M., 1888; Princeton Theol. Sem., 1888-90; grad. McCormick Theol. Sem., Chicago, 1891; U. of Berlin, 1893-95; D.D., Parsons Coll., Ia., 1902; LL.D., Cumberland U., Tenn., 1916; m. Agnes Smith, Sept. 23, 1891; 1 son, Rev. Walker Frame; m. 2d, Jeannie Putnam, Sept. 1, 1909; children—Douglas Selby, Elbridge Putnam. Ordained Presbyn. ministry, 1891; pastor Girard, Kan., 1891-93; prof. Greek Parsons Coll., 1895-1900; prof. English Bible, U. of Wooster, Ohio, 1900-05; prof. ch. history, 1905-10, English Bible, 1910-21, Lane Theol. Sem.; prof. N.T. lit. and exegesis, Western Theol. Sem., 1921-35 (emeritus). Republican. Home: Ben Avon, Pittsburgh, Pa. Died Sept. 27, 1937.

VANCE, William Reynolds, prof. law; b. Middletown, Ky., May 9, 1870; s. Robert G. and Fannie (Stowe) V.; A.B., Washington and Lee U., 1892, A.M., 1893, Ph.D., 1895, LL.B., 1897; hon. A.M., Yale, 1910; LL.D., Washington and Lee, 1915; m. Anne Wilmer Hume, Sept. 24, 1902; children—Frances Stowe, Thomas Hume, Anne Gregory. Instr. English, 1891-95, prof. law, 1897-1903, dean law dept., 1901-03, Washington and Lee U.; prof. law, 1903-10, dean law dept., 1905-10, George Washington U.; Lines prof. of law, Yale, 1910-12; dean Law Sch., U. of Minn., 1912-20; Foster prof. law, Yale, 1920-38, emeritus; prof. law, U. of Chicago Law Sch., 3 summers, Cornell U., summers 1924, 26, U. of Calif., summers 1913, 28, U. of N.C., summer 1930. Gen. counsel, Bur. of War Risk Ins., 1918-19. Sec. Assn. Am. Law Schs., 1905-10, pres., 1910-11. Author: Slavery in Kentucky, 1895; Vance on Insurance, 1904, 2d edit., 1930; Early History of Insurance Law (in selected essays in Anglo-American Legal History), 1909; Cases on Insurance, 1914, 2d edit., 1931. Gen. editor American Case Book Series, 1912-35. Home: New Haven, Conn. Died Oct. 23, 1940.

VANCE, Wilson, editor; b. Findlay, O., Dec. 20, 1845; s. Joseph Colville and Melinda Bromwell (Baldwin) V.; ed. common schs., Harvard Law Sch., 1866-67; m. Rachel E. Johnston, Sept. 5, 1867 (died 1873); m. 2d, Lillie Bell Beall, May 31, 1877. Enlisted as pvt. 21st Ohio Inf., 1861; commd. 2d lt. after battle of Stone River, Tenn., Dec. 31, 1862-Jan. 2, 1863; in same battle won Congressional Medal of Honor; comd. his co. in battle of Chickamauga, Sept. 20, 1863; mustered out Mar. 26, 1866. Managing editor Ohio State Journal, 1870, Indianapolis Journal, 1873, New York Morning Advertiser, 1892-94; Washington corr. Ohio State Journal, Cincinnati Commercial, Chicago Tribune, St. Louis Republic, Phila. Times, St. Paul Pioneer Press, etc., at various times, 1870-81; mgr. The C. W. Post Press, Ltd.; editor The Square Deal, 1904—. Republican. Episcopalian. Author: Princes' Favors, 1879; Little Amy's Christmas, 1879; God's War, 1899; Big John Baldwin, 1909. Home: Brooklyn, N.Y. Deceased.

VAN CLEAVE, James Wallace, manufacturer; b. Marion Co., Ky., July 15, 1849; s. Henry Mason and Eliza Jane (Burks) V.; ed. Springfield (Ky.) Acad.; served in C.S.A. under Gen John H. Morgan, 1862-63; m. Katie L. Jefferson, Mar. 22, 1871. Began stove mfg. business, 1867; pres. The Bucks Stove & Range Co. Pres. Nat. Assn. of Mfrs., Citizens' Industrial Assn. of St. Louis; chmn. Nat. Council for Industrial Defense. Republican. Presbyn. Home: St. Louis, Mo. Died 1910.

VAN CLEEF, Mynderse, lawyer, banker; b. Seneca Falls, N.Y., Aug. 29, 1853; s. Alexander M. and Jane E. V.; B.S., Cornell U., 1874; Columbia Law Sch.; m. Elizabeth L. Treman, Dec. 21, 1882; children—Eugenia, Mrs. Jeannette Booth. Practiced at Ithaca, 1876—; atty. Cornell U. and various banking instns.; chmn. bd. dirs. Ithaca Trust Co.; pres. Ithaca Security Co.; dir. Tompkins Co. Nat. Bank; trustee Ithaca Savings Bank, Cornell U. (chmn. com. on administration), Cornell Library Assn. (city), Memorial Hosp. Assn., Presbyn. Ch. Republican. Home: Ithaca, N.Y. Died Mar. 6, 1935.

VAN COTT, Cornelius, postmaster New York; b. New York, Feb. 12, 1838; common school edn.; as boy ran hand printing press for Am. Tract Soc.; at 15 apprenticed to carriage-making, which he followed; dir. and later v.p. Etna Fire Ins. Co.; was insp. customs house; deputy collector internal revenue, 1869; active in campaign which overthrew Tweed ring; pres. bd. fire commrs., New York, 1873-77, 1881-85; State senator, 1888-89; postmaster, New York, 1889-93, and 1897—. Died 1904.

VANDEGRIFT, Margaret. See Margaret T. Janvier.

VANDEMAN, Esther Boise, archeology; b. S. Salem, O., Oct. 1, 1862; d. Joseph and Martha (Millspaugh) Van D.; A.B., Univ. of Mich., 1891, A.M., 1892; fellow Bryn Mawr, 1892-93; fellow U. of Chicago, 1896-98; Ph.D., Univ. of Chicago, 1898; grad. study, Am. Sch. in Rome, 1901-03. Instr. in Latin, Wellesley, 1893-95; asso. prof. Latin, Holyoke (Mass.) Coll., 1898-1901; asso. prof. Latin and archeology, Goucher Coll., Baltimore, Md., 1903-06; Carnegie fellow, Classical Sch. in Rome, 1906-10; asso., Carnegie Instn., Washington, D.C., 1910-25; Carnegie research prof. in Roman archeology, U. of Mich., 1925-30; retired staff mem. Carnegie Instn., 1930. Guest member Am. Acad. in Rome. Presbyn. Author: The Atrium Vestae, 1909; The Building of the Roman Aqueducts, 1933. Home: Rome, Italy. Died May 3, 1937.

VAN DEMAN, Henry Elias, pomologist; b. Ross Co., O., Nov. 3, 1845; s. Joseph and Elizabeth Sylvia (Case) V.; ed. pub. schs. and S. Salem Acad.; pvt. 1st Ohio vols., 1863-65; m. Anna McCormick, Dec. 28, 1876. Prof. botany and practical horticulture, Kan. State Agrl. Coll., 1878-79; chief and founder div. of pomology, U.S. Dept. Agr., 1886-93. Associate editor of Green's Fruit Grower, Rochester, New York, and Southern Fruit Grower, Chattanooga, Tenn. Pres. Am. Nut and Fruit Co. Author: Tropical and Semi-Tropical Fruits in America, 1887. Home: Washington, D.C. Died Apr. 28, 1915.

VANDERBILT, Alfred Gwynne, capitalist; b. New York, Oct. 20, 1877; s. Cornelius and Alice Claypoole (Gwynne) V.; g.s. William Henry V.; brother of Cornelius, III and Reginald Claypoole V.; A.B., Yale, 1899; m. Elsie French, Jan. 11, 1901; m. 2d, Margaret (Emerson) McKim, Dec. 17, 1911. Has traveled extensively abroad. Pres. National Horse Show Assn. of America; dir. Internat. Horse Show Assn. of London. Mem. numerous clubs in New York and elsewhere. Home: Newport, R.I. Died May 7, 1915.

VANDERBILT, Cornelius, capitalist; eldest son of late William H. Vanderbilt, and grandson of Cornelius ("Commodore") Vanderbilt; b. on his father's farm, Staten Island, N.Y., Nov. 27, 1843; academic edn. followed by training in bank and railroad offices; from 1867 official in various railways; m. Alice Gwynne. Headed directorate of New York Central & Hudson River, N.Y. & Harlem, Michigan Central and other roads until, because of failing health, his place as chairman of these boards was taken by Chauncey M. Depew as representative of the large Vanderbilt interests. Home: New York, N.Y. Died 1899.

VANDERBILT, Frederick William, capitalist; b. 1856; s. William Henry and Maria Louisa (Kissam) V.; Ph.B., Yale, 1876; m. Mrs. Alfred Torrence (née Anthony), 1880. Obtained business training in offices of his father's railroad system, going through every dept. in railroad service. Owns steam yacht, the Warrior; has large estate at Hyde Park on the Hudson. Dir. many ry. and other corporations. Home: New York, N.Y. Died June 29, 1938.

VANDERBILT, George Washington, capitalist; b. New Dorp, S.I., N.Y., Nov. 14, 1862; s. William Henry and Maria Louisa (Kissam) V.; brother of William Kissam and Frederick William V.; ed. private tutors and at best schools; traveled extensively and studied; m. Edith Stuyvesant Dresser, 1898. Gave to New York the 13th St. branch of the Free Circulating Library, which he founded, provided with suitable bldgs. and appmts.; presented New York Coll. for the Training of Teachers, its site on Morningside Heights, adjoining site selected for Columbia Coll.; presented Am. Fine Arts Soc. of New York the room in their bldg. known as the Vanderbilt Gallery. Mem. Century Assn. and leading clubs, S.A.R., etc. Purchased 100,000 acres of mountain land on the French Broad River, nr. Asheville, N.C., and laid it out in a vast park; erected mansion and stables; stocked this estate and spends much of his time superintending its improvements. Home: Biltmore, N.C. Died Mar. 6, 1914.

VANDERBILT, Reginald Claypoole, investor; b. New York, Dec. 19, 1880; s. Cornelius and Alice Claypoole (Gwynne) V.; brother of Cornelius, III and Alfred Gwynne V.; B.A., Yale U., 1902; m. Cathleen Gebhard Neilson, Apr. 14, 1903; m. 2d, Gloria M. Morgan, Mar. 6, 1923. Dir. Raquette Lake Ry., Raquette Lake Transportation Co., Fulton Chain Ry., Fulton Navigation Co. Pres. Assn. of American Horse Shows, Inc., and pres. Am. Hackney Horse Soc.; dir. Nat. Horse Show Assn. America, Ltd. Home: Newport, R.I. Died Sept. 4, 1925.

VANDERBILT, William Kissam, capitalist; b. Staten Island, Dec. 12, 1849; s. William Henry and Maria Louisa (Kissam) V.; acad. edn., studied several yrs. Geneva, Switzerland; m. 1st, Alva Smith; m. 2d, Mrs. A. H. Rutherfurd, Apr. 25, 1903. Was in the office of C. C. Clarke, treas. Hudson River R.R.; learned bookkeeping; 2d v.p. N.Y.C.&H.R. R.R., 1877-83; chmn. bd. of dirs. L.S.&M.S. Ry. for many yrs.; now dir. N.Y. Central R.R., M.C. R.R. Co., L.E.&W. R.R. Co., C.&N.W. Ry. Co., C.,St.P.,M.& O. Ry. Co., C.,C.,C.&St.L. Ry. Co., N.Y. & Harlem R.R. Co. (pres.), P.&L.E. R.R. Co., West Shore R.R. Co., and officer or dir. in numerous other corps.; also dir. Met. Opera Co., Met. Opera & Real Estate Co.; founder, and pres. The New Theatre. Mem. Colonia and Defender syndicates; united with his brothers in founding the Vanderbilt Clinic. Home: New York, N.Y. Died July 22, 1920.

VANDERLIP, Frank Arthur, banker; b. Aurora, Ill., Nov. 17, 1864; student U. of Illinois and U. of Chicago; hon. A.M., U. of Ill., 1905; LL.D., Colgate, 1911, Princeton Univ., 1919, Brown Univ.; m. Narcissa Cox, 1903; children—Narcissa, Charlotte D., Frank A., Virginia J., Kelvin, John M. Reporter, 1889, later financial editor, Chicago Tribune; asso. editor Economist, Chicago, 1894-97; pvt. sec. to Sec. of the Treasury Lyman Judson Gage, Mar. 4-June 1, 1897; asst. sec. of the treasury, 1897-1901; vice pres., 1901-09, pres., 1909-19, National City Bank, New York; now pres. Palos Verdes Corp.; has resigned from numerous directorates. Chmn. War Savings Com., by apptmt. of sec. of Treasury, to conduct sale of War Savings Certificates, Sept. 1917-Sept. 1918. Trustee Carnegie Foundation, New York U., Mass. Inst. Tech., Scarborough Sch. (chmn. bd.). Former pres. N.Y. Clearing House Assn.; exec. committee of the Chamber of Commerce State of New York. Author: Chicago Street Railways; The American Commercial Invasion of Europe; Business and Education, 1907; Political Problems of Europe; What Happened to Europe, 1920; What Next in Europe, 1922; Tomorrow's Money, 1934; From Farm Boy to Financier, 1935. Decorated Chevalier Legion of Honor (French); Order of Danilo I of Montenegro; Royal Order of George I of Greece; Commdr. Order of Leopold of Belgium. Home: Scarborough, N.Y. Died June 29, 1937.

VAN DERLIP, John Russell, lawyer; b. Dansville, N.Y., Jan. 25, 1860; s. John Adams and Anna (Day)

Van D.; grad. Dansville Sem., 1877; m. Ethel Morrison, Jan. 18, 1898 (died 1921). Admitted to N.Y. bar, 1881, and began practice at Dansville; moved to Minneapolis, 1883; mem. Wilson & Van Derlip, 1888-1902. Van Derlip & Lum, 1906-16; chmn. bd. The Munsingwear Corp., Munsingwear, Inc., Wayne Knitting Mills, Vassar Swiss Underwear Co. Active in creation of Minneapolis Inst. of Arts (mus.), pres. and trustee from foundation, 1915; also pres. and trustee Minneapolis Foundation, Minneapolis Sch. of Art; dir. Minneapolis Orchestral Assn.; trustee St. Mary's Hall, Faribault, Minn. Episcopalian. Home: Minneapolis, Minn. Died Mar. 23, 1935.

VANDER MEULEN, John Marinus, clergyman; b. Milwaukee, Wis., Apr. 12, 1870; s. John and Mary (Van Boven) V.; A.B., Hope Coll., Holland, Mich., 1891, A.M., 1896, D.D., 1909; Princeton Theol. Sem., 1893-95; grad. McCormick Theol. Sem., 1896; Columbia, 1909-12; m. Mary M. Veneklasen, June 15, 1905; 1 son, John Marion. Ordained Presbyn. ministry, 1896; pastor 2d Ref. Ch., Kalamazoo, Mich., 1896-99, 1st Ref. Ch., Grand Rapids, 1899-1901; supt. home mission, Okla., 1901-03; prof. psychology and pedagogy, Hope Coll., 1903-09, also pastor Hope Ch., 1907-09; pastor Hamilton Grange Ref. Ch., N.Y. City, 1909-12, 2d Presbyn. Ch. (U.S.), Louisville, Ky., 1912-17; 1st Presbyn. Ch., Oak Park, Ill., 1917-20; pres. Louisville Presbyn. Theol. Sem., 1920-30, prof. systematic theology, 1930—. Home: Louisville, Ky. Died June 7, 1936.

VANDERPOEL, Emily C. Noyes, author, painter; b. New York; d. William Curtis and Julia F. (Tallmadge) Noyes; ed. pvt. schs. New York; pupil of R. Swain Gifford and William Sartain; m. John A. Vanderpoel; 1 son, Floyd Lewis. Author: Color Problems, 1903; Chronicles of a Pioneer School, 1903; American Lace and Lacemakers, 1923; More Chronicles of a Pioneer School, 1927. Painting, "Ypres," by her, displayed in Nat. Mus., Washington, D.C., with army relics of the World War. Home: New York, N.Y. Died Feb. 20, 1939.

VANDERPOEL, John Henry, artist; b. Haarlemmer-Meer, Holland, 1857; s. John and Mary (Van Nes) V.; ed. pub. schs. Chicago; studied drawing and painting in Paris under Boulanger and Lefebvre; m. Jessie Humphreys, 1890. Now instr. drawing and painting and lecturer, Art Inst. of Chicago. Author: The Human Figure, 1907. Home: Chicago, Ill. Died 1911.

VAN DER STUCKEN, Frank V., music dir., composer; b. Fredericksburg, Tex., Oct. 15, 1858; s. J. Frank and Sophia (Schoenewolf) V.; lived in Europe, 1866-84; studied Conservatory of Music, Antwerp, under Peter Benoit; m. Mary Vollmer, of Hildesheim, Germany, 1880; children—Grety Lundin, Frank R., Isa Bobrik, Dirk H. Kapellmeister, Stadt Theatre, Breslau, Germany, 1881-82; conducted concert of his own compositions under protection of Franz Liszt, Weimar, Nov. 1883; became leader Arion Singing Soc., New York, 1884, and took it on concert tour in Europe, 1892; conducted Novelty Concerts, Steinway Hall, 1885-86, Symphonic Concerts, Chickering Hall, 1887-88; first concert of Am. compositions, 1885, New York, Am. Concert, Paris Expn., 1889; conductor Symphony Concerts, Cincinnati, 1895-1907; dean Coll. of Music of Cincinnati, 1897-1901 (hon. dean). Successor to Theodore Thomas as mus. dir. of Cincinnati May Festivals, 1906-12; conducted Wagner and Gluck festivals in Antwerp, 1920-21, Isaye concerts, Brussels, 1921-23; Cincinnati May Festival, 1923-25 and 1927. Decorated Order of Leopold and Officier de l'Ordre de la Couronne, by King of Belgium. Composer of songs, choruses, symphonic prologues, Pax Triumphans, etc. Died Aug. 16, 1929.

VANDER VEER, Albert, surgeon; b. Root, N.Y., July 10, 1841; s. Abram H. and Sarah (Martin) V.; ed. pub. schs., Free Sch. and Canajoharie Acad.; student Albany Med. Coll.; M.D., Nat. Med. Coll. (now med. dept. George Washington U.), 1863; hon. M.D., Albany Med. Coll., 1869; A.M., Williams 1882; Ph.D., Union, and Hamilton, 1883; LL.D., George Washington, 1904; m. Margaret E. Snow, June 5, 1867; children—Charles Anson (dec.), Margaret Snow (dec.), Edgar Albert, James Newell, Albert, Garrett (dec.). Surgeon 66th New York Volunteers, in the Civil War; surgeon 1st Division Hospital, 2d Army Corps, Army of the Potomac, 1864-65; prof. general and spl. anatomy, 1869-82, didactic clin., abdominal surgery, 1882-1902, prof. surgery, 1902-14, emeritus prof. surgery, 1914 (resigning as same June, 1915), dean, 1896-1905, Albany Medical College; sr. cons. surgeon, Albany Hospital. Formerly attending and consulting surgeon St. Peter's Hospital, also consulting surgeon South End Dispensary. Regent, 1895-1927, vice chancellor, 1915-21, chancellor, 1921-22, University State of New York; v.p. Albany Inst. and Hist. and Art Soc.; gov. Albany Hosp. Fellow Am. Coll. Surgeons, Brit. Gynecol. Assn.; trustee Assn. for Protection Adirondacks. Republican. Presbyterian. Home: Albany, N.Y. Died Dec. 19, 1929.

VAN DERVOORT, William H., mfr.; b. Ypsilanti, Mich., Feb. 28, 1869; s. Thomas S. and Euphrasia S. (Westfall) V.; student Mich. State Normal Sch.,

Ypsilanti; B.S. in Mech. Engring., Mich. Agrl. Coll., Lansing, Mich., 1899; M.E., Cornell U., 1893; m. Mary S. Smith, Nov. 9, 1892. Asst. prof. mech. engring., U. of Ill., 1893-99; organizer, 1900, and from then pres. and gen. mgr., The Root & Van Dervoort Engring. Co., East Moline, Ill.; organized Moline Automobile Co., 1906, and pres. and gen. mgr. same until its consolidation with The Root & Van Dervoort Engring. Co. in 1916; pres. and gen. mgr. R. & V.-Wagner Ordnance Co. Mem. Munitions Standardizations Bd., apptd. by sec. of war; mem. Nat. War Labor Bd., apptd. by Pres. Wilson; mem. Nat. Industrial Conf. Bd., and sent to Europe, 1919, to study industrial relations. Republican. Conglist. Author: Modern Machine Shop Practice, 1903. Home: Moline, Ill. Died Feb. 25, 1921.

VANDER VRIES, John Nicholas; b. Kalamazoo, Mich., May 23, 1876; s. Edward and Hattie (Hulst) V.; A.B., Hope Coll., Holland, Mich., 1896, A.M., 1897; Ph.D., Clark U., 1901; (LL.D., Hope, 1922); m. Bernice May Taber, June 9, 1910; 1 son, John N. Asst. prof. mathematics, 1901-06, asso. prof., 1906-11, prof., 1911-18, U. of Kan.; sec. central dist., 1917-23, mgr. north central div., 1923—, Chamber Commerce of U.S.A.; sec.-treas. Nat. Inst. for Commercial and Trade Orgn. Executives, 1924—. Mem. exec. com. Nat. Anti-Hoarding Campaign, 1932. Home: Winnetka, Ill. Died Feb. 14, 1936.

VAN DEVANTER, Willis, jurist; b. Marion, Ind., Apr. 17, 1859; s. Isaac and Violetta Maria (Spencer) V.; Ind. Asbury (now DePauw) U., 1875-78; LL.B., Cincinnati Law Sch., 1881; LL.D., DePauw U., 1911, U. of Cincinnati and Yale, 1927, U. of Wyoming, 1933, College of Charleston, S.C., 1935; m. Dollie, d. Winslow Paige and Rachel Ann (Dorman) Burhans, of Ionia, Mich., Oct. 10, 1883 (died 1934). Practiced law at Marion, Ind., 1881-84; then at Cheyenne, Wyo.; commr. to revise Wyoming Statutes, 1886; city atty., 1887-88; mem. Territorial Legislature (chmn. judiciary com.), 1888; chief justice Supreme Court of Wyo., 1889-90; chmn. Rep. State Com., 1892-94; mem. Rep. Nat. Com., 1896-1900; asst. atty. gen. of U.S. (assigned to Dept. Interior), 1897-1903; U.S. circuit judge, 8th Jud. Circuit, 1903-10; asso. justice Supreme Court of U.S., Dec. 16, 1910-June 2, 1937; mem. Internat. Comn. which arbitrated and determined Canadian Claims for sinking vessel "I'm Alone" by U.S. Coast Guard, 1934-35. Prof. equity pleading and practice, 1898-1903, equity jurisprudence, 1902-03, Columbian (now George Washington) U. Home: Washington, D.C. Died Feb. 8, 1941.

VAN DE VEN, Cornelius, bishop; b. Oirschot, Holland, June 16, 1865; s. Peter and Jane Mary (Roche) V.; ed. theol. sem. Bois-le-Duc, Holland; ordained R.C. priest, 1890, in Cathedral of Bois-le-Duc; came to U.S., fall of 1890; joined Archdiocese of New Orleans; successively asst. at New Iberia, pastor at Jennings, Lake Charles and Baton Rouge, La.; apptd., Aug. 10, 1904, to succeed late Bishop Durier as bishop of Natchitoches, La.; bishop of Alexandria, 1910—. Wrote pamphlet: To Whom Shall We Go?, 1897. Died May 8, 1932.

VAN DE VYVER, Augustine, bishop; b. Haesdnock, Belgium, Dec. 1, 1844. Ordained R.C. priest, Brussels, Belgium, July 24, 1870; consecrated bishop of Richmond, Oct. 20, 1889. Home: Richmond, Va. Died 1911.

VANDEWATER, George Roe, clergyman; b. Flushing, L.I., N.Y., Apr. 25, 1854; s. John Titus and Ellen Bernetta (Fowler) V.; A.B., Cornell U., 1874; grad. Gen. Theol. Sem., 1879; (D.D., Nashotah, 1886); m. Cornelia Townsend Youngs, 1879. Deacon, 1876, priest, 1879, P.E. Ch.; rector Oyster Bay, L.I., 1878-80, St. Luke's, Brooklyn, 1880; organized ch. and congregation of St. Bartholomew; active in mission revival of 1885, and in organizing the Parochial Mission Soc., of which became gen. sec. and later gen missionary; rector St. Andrew's Ch., Harlem, 1888-1920; rector Church of the Beloved Disciple, New York, 1920—. Chaplain Columbia U., 1892-1905; chaplain 71st N.Y. Vols., and with 5th A.C. in its campaign in Cuba. Trustee New York City Missions Society. Mason; Past Grand Chaplain Grand Lodge of Masons. State of New York. Author: History of the Christian Church (2 vols.), 1904; New York Forces in War with Spain (history of 71st Regt., U.S. Vols.), 1904; Life and Times of St. Paul (lectures); Masonic Teaching Bible Truth. Compiler and editor Manual of Church Missions: Manual of Church Prayer. Traveler and lecturer on "Dolomites" and "South America" (illustrated). Home: New York, N.Y. Died Mar. 15, 1925.

VAN DINE, S. S., author. See Willard Huntington Wright.

VANDIVER, Almuth Cunningham, lawyer; b. Gadsden, Ala., June 21, 1879; s. Wellington and Florence (Cunningham) V.; B.Sc., Ala. Poly. Inst., Auburn, Ala., 1898; LL.B., New York U. Law Sch., 1904; m. Eleanor M. S. Williams, Nov. 30, 1912; children—Almuth II, Wellington II. Dept. asst. dist. atty. New York Co., under William Travers Jerome, 1905-08; associated with Gov. Charles S. Whitman as Whitman & Vandiver, 1908-10; mem. O'Gorman, Battle & Vandiver, 1913-23, Battle, Van-

diver, Levy & Van Tine, 1923-27. Capt. 14th Inf. N.Y.G., 1918; maj. ord. dept. N.Y.G., 1918; maj. judge adv. Army of U.S., 1918-19; maj. judge adv. gen's. dept., N.Y.G., 1919-22; maj. J.A.G. (Res.), 61st Cav. Div., Army of U.S. Grand Officer Order of St. Sepulchre (Orthodox). Past sr. v. comdr. in chief Mil. Order World War. Home: New York, N.Y. Died June 21, 1931.

VANDIVER, Willard Duncan, congressman; b. Hardy Co., Va. (now W.Va.), Mar. 30, 1854; s. Rev. L. H. and Mary Ann (Vance) V.; moved to Missouri, 1856; grad. Central Coll., Fayette, Mo., 1877; m. Alice L., d. Rev. J. H. Headlee, June 1880. Prof. natural science, 1877-80, pres., 1880-89, Bellevue Inst.; prof. natural science, 1889-93, pres., 1893-97, State Normal School, Cape Girardeau, Mo. Mem. 55th to 58th Congresses (1897-1905), 14th Mo. Dist. Democrat; chmn. of com. that managed campaign of Joseph W. Folk for gov. of Mo., 1904; ins. commr. State of Mo., 1905. V.p. Central States Life Ins. Co., St. Louis, 1911—; asst. U.S. treas., at St. Louis, by apptmt. of Pres. Wilson, 1913-20. Pres. Mo. Soc. S.A.R., Boone County Hist. Society. Home: Columbia, Mo. Died May 30, 1932.

VAN DOREN, Ray Newton, lawyer; b. Oshkosh, Wis., Jan. 11, 1878; s. Jacob H. and Anna (Cook) V.; grad. high sch., Birnamwood, Wis., 1895; LL.B., U. of Wis., 1898; m. Grace A. Roberts, Sept. 11, 1901; children—Donald Wayne, Helen Grace, Gerald Ray, James Roberts. Admitted to Wis. bar, 1898, and practiced at New London until 1909, Merrill, 1909-16, Milwaukee, with Flanders, Bottum, Fawsett & Bottum, 1916-17; Wis. atty. C.&N.W. Ry. Co., 1917-21; asst. gen. solicitor same co., at Chicago, 1921-24, gen. solicitor, 1924-25, v.p. and gen. counsel, July 1, 1925—. Served under U.S.R.R. Administration, World War, as Neb. atty. C.&N.W. Ry. Co., at Omaha, gen. atty. same rd., at St. Paul, and again as Wis. atty., at Milwaukee. City atty. New London 5 yrs. Republican. Presbyn. Mason, K.P. Home: Evanston, Ill. Died Jan 12, 1933.

VAN DRESSER, Marcia, opera singer; b. Memphis, Tenn.; d. Alfred Philip and Elida (Huntington) V.; ed. Miss Higbee's Sch. for Girls, Memphis. Began with the "Bostonians," 1898, as understudy to Jessie Bartlett Davis, taking part of Alan-a-Dale, in "Robin Hood"; joined Alice Nielsen in her first starring tour in "The Singing Girl," playing New York engagement of 6 weeks; was understudy to Ada Rehan and Blanche Bates, in "The Great Ruby," taking place of the latter after 2 nights, to end of New York engagement; appeared as the Princess of Eboli, in Viola Allen's production of "In the Palace of the King"; leading lady with Otis Skinner, in revival of "Francesca da Rimini." Returned to opera, 1903, singing small rôles at Met. Opera House, New York; studied 3 yrs. in Munich, Germany; début as Elizabeth in "Tannhäuser," at Royal Opera House, Dresden, 1907; sang leading soprano rôles in Dessau, Anhalt (2 winters), and Frankfort-on-the-Main, 3 yrs., until breaking out of the war; sang in concert in U.S., winter of 1914-15; joined Chicago Grand Opera Co., and made début as Elizabeth, in "Tannhäuser," Nov. 25, 1915; mem. Met. Opera Co., New York, season 1917-18. Died July 11, 1937.

VAN DUZER, Henry Sayre, lawyer; b. N.Y. City, Feb. 26, 1853; s. Selah Reeve and Catherine Mathews (Sayre) V.; prep. edn., Phillips Acad., Andover, Mass.; A.B., Harvard, 1875; LL.B., Columbia, 1877; unmarried. Admitted to N.Y. bar, 1877, and began practice in N.Y. City; formerly mem. Van Duzer & Taylor. Maj. and judge advocate 1st Brigade, N.Y.N.G., 1879-98. Mem. bd. dirs. Nat. Kindergarten Assn.; pres. Holland Soc., New York. Republican. Protestant. Home: New York, N.Y. Died Mar. 1, 1928.

VAN DUZER, Lewis Sayre, officer U.S.N.; b. Elmira, N.Y., June 29, 1861; s. William Henry and Susan Rachel (Sayre) V.; entered U.S. Naval Acad., 1876, grad. 1880; m. Alice Louise Averill, Dec. 19, 1883 (died 1925). m. 2d, Clara L. Van Order, Nov. 2, 1927. Promoted through the various grades to capt., Mar. 3, 1911. Officer U.S.S. Iowa, and present at battle of Santiago and destruction of Cervera's fleet, 1898; also at attack on fortifications of San Juan, P.R., etc.; served in the Philippines throughout the Philippine Insurrection; went to China at beginning of Boxer rebellion, June 1900; instr. in ordnance, U.S. Naval Acad., 1900-02; commanded U.S.S. Cleveland, 1908-09; comdt. Olongapo Navy Yard, 1909-10; capt. of the yard, Navy Yard, New York, 1910-13; in command of U.S.S. Utah, 1913-14; retired at his own request, Apr. 1914. Served in the cruiser and transport service at New York, 1918. Received medal for services in West Indies, Spanish-Am. War, also medals for Santiago, Philippine Insurrection, Boxer campaign. Nautical and naval editor New Internat. Ency., 1900-31, Nelson's Ency., 1906-17. Home: Horseheads, Chemung County, N.Y. Died Mar. 28, 1936.

VAN DYCK, Francis Cuyler, physicist; b. Coxsackie, N.Y., June 3, 1844; s. Jacob Cuyler and Mary Frances (Bogardus) V.; freshman yr., Williams Coll., 1861; A.B., Rutgers, 1865, A.M., 1868; Ph.D., Union College, N.Y., 1888; (hon. Sc.D., Rutgers Coll., 1910, and LL.D., same 1915); m. Rebecca Jane Van Bergen, Dec. 27, 1871 (died 1879); m. 2d, Sarah Mercereau Van Nuis, Sept. 15, 1897. Tutor, 1866-70, prof. chemistry, 1870-78, physics, 1878-1917, dean, 1901-13, Rutgers Coll. Retired on Carnegie Foundation as prof. emeritus, June 1917. Home: New Brunswick, N.J. Died Apr. 12, 1927.

VAN DYKE, Carl Chester, congressman; b. Alexandria, Minn., Feb. 18, 1881; s. Chester B. and Bertha (Solum) V.; ed. grammar and high schs., Alexandria; m. Myrtle Lampman. Served as pvt. Co. B, 15th Regt. Minn. Vols., Spanish-Am. War. Taught sch.; entered U.S. Govt. service, 1901, as ry. mail clerk; studied law; represented ry. mail clerks at Washington, 1911-14; mem. 64th and 65th Congresses (1915-19), 4th Minn. Dist. Democrat. Episcopalian. Home: St. Paul, Minn. Died May 20, 1919.

VAN DYKE, Henry, author; b. Germantown, Pa., Nov. 10, 1852; s. Rev. Henry Jackson and Henrietta (Ashmead) V.; grad. Poly. Inst. of Brooklyn, 1869; Princeton, 1873, A.M., 1876; grad. Princeton Theol. Sem., 1877 (D.D., Princeton, 1884, Harvard, 1894, Yale, 1896; LL.D., Union, 1898, Penna., 1906, Geneva, Switzerland, 1909; D.C.L., Oxford, 1917); m. Ellen Reid, Dec. 13, 1881; children—Brooke, Tertius, Elaine, Paula, Katrina. Ordained Presbyn. ministry, 1879; pastor United Congl. Ch., Newport, R.I., 1879-82, Brick Presbyn. Ch., New York, 1883-1900, 02, 11; prof. English literature, Princeton, 1900-23; U.S. minister to Netherlands and Luxemburg, 1913-17 (resigned). Am. lecturer at U. of Paris, 1908-09. Moderator Gen. Assembly Presbyn. Ch. in U.S.A., 1902-03. Comdr. Legion of Honor, 1918. President National Inst. of Arts and Letters; mem. Am. Acad. of Arts and Letters; hon. fellow Royal Soc. Literature, 1910; corr. mem. Soc. Gens de Lettres, 1916. Author: The Reality of Religion, 1884; The Story of the Psalms, 1887; The National Sin of Literary Piracy, 1888; The Poetry of Tennyson, 1889; Sermons to Young Men, 1893; The Christ Child in Art, 1894; Little Rivers, 1895; The Other Wise Man, 1896; The Gospel for an Age of Doubt, 1896; The First Christmas Tree, 1897; The Builders, and Other Poems, 1897; Ships and Havens, 1897; The Lost World, 1898; The Gospel for a World of Sin, 1899; Fisherman's Luck, 1899; The Toiling of Felix, 1900; The Poetry of the Psalms, 1900; The Ruling Passion, 1901; The Blue Flower, 1902; The Open Door, 1903; Music, and Other Poems, 1904; The School of Life, 1905; Essays in Application, 1905; The Spirit of Christmas, 1905; Americanism of Washington, 1906; Days Off, 1907; The House of Rimmon, 1908; Out-of-Doors in the Holy Land, 1908; Le Génie de l'Amérique, 1909 (Paris); The White Bees, and Other Poems, 1909; The Spirit of America, 1910; Collected Poems, The Sad Shepherd, The Mansion, 1911; The Unknown Quantity, 1912; The Lost Boy, The Grand Canyon, and Other Poems, 1914; Fighting for Peace, 1917; The Red Flower, 1917; The Valley of Vision, 1919; Golden Stars, 1919; Camp Fires and Guide Posts, 1921; Companionable Books, 1922; Six Days of the Week, 1924; Half-Told Tales, 1925; The Golden Key, 1926; Chosen Poems, 1927; Even Unto Bethlehem, 1928; The Man Behind the Book, 1929; Travel Diary of an Angler, 1929; Gratitude, 1930. Editor: The Gateway Series of English Texts, Select Poems of Tennyson; Little Masterpieces of English Poetry (6 vols.). Home: Princeton, N.J. Died Apr. 10, 1933.

VAN DYKE, J. W., oil official; chmn. bd. Atlantic Refining Co.; pres. Atlantic Oil Producing Co., Atlantic Oil Shipping Co., Keystone Pipe Line Co., Atlantic Pipeline Co., Atlantic Refining Co. of Brazil, of Spain, Atlantic West African Co., Colombian Atlantic Refining Co., Venezuelan Atlantic Refining Co., Buffalo Pipe Line Co.; dir. First Nat. Bank of Phila., Monroe Coal Mining Co., First Trust Co.; Cambrian & Ind. R.R. Home: Philadelphia, Pa. Died Sept. 13, 1939.

VAN DYKE, John Charles, univ. prof.; b. New Brunswick, N.J., Apr. 21, 1856; s. Judge John and Mary Dix (Strong) V.; ed. pvtly.; studied at Columbia; studied art in Europe many yrs.; L.H.D., Rutgers, 1889, LL.D., from same, 1925; unmarried. Admitted to bar, 1877; librarian Sage Library, New Brunswick, 1878—; prof. history of art, Rutgers, 1889—. Lecturer Columbia, Harvard and Princeton. Mem. N.J. State Bd. of Education. Mem. Am. Acad. Arts and Letters. Author: How to Judge of a Picture, 1888; Art for Art's Sake, 1893; History of Painting, 1894; Nature for Its Own Sake, 1898; The Desert, 1901; The Meaning of Pictures, 1903; The Opal Sea, 1906; Studies in Pictures, 1907; The Money God, 1908; What Is Art?, 1910; The Mountain, 1916; American Art and Its Tradition, 1919; Grand Canyon of the Colorado, 1920; The Open Spaces, 1922; Rembrandt and His School, 1923; The Meadows, 1926; The Rembrandt Drawings and Etchings, 1927; In Java, 1929; In Egypt, 1931; In the West Indies, 1932. Editor: College Histories of Art; History of American Art; Autobiography of Andrew Carnegie, 1921. Edited The Studio, 1883-84, Art Review, 1887-88. Home: New Brunswick, N.J. Died Dec. 5, 1932.

VAN DYKE, Joseph Smith, clergyman; b. Bound Brook, N.J., Nov. 2, 1832; s. Benjamin and Elcy

(Smith) V.; A.B., Princeton, 1857; grad. Princeton Theol. Sem., 1861; (D.D., Princeton, 1884;) m. Sarah J. Swing, May 7, 1861. Ordained Presbyterian ministry, Oct. 3, 1860; pastor Bloomsbury, N.J., 1861-69, Cranbury, N.J., 1869-97, Glassboro, N.J., 1897-1900. Author: From Gloom to Gladness, 1880; Theism, Evolution, 1886; Be of Good Cheer, 1911. Home: Hightstown, N.J. Died Nov. 1, 1915.

VAN DYKE, Paul, univ. prof.; b. Brooklyn, N.Y., Mar. 25, 1859; s. Rev. Henry Jackson and Henrietta (Ashmead) V.; brother of Henry V.; A.B., Princeton, 1881, A.M., 1884; grad. Princeton Theol. Sem., 1884; Univ. of Berlin, 1884-85; D.D., Williams, 1898; L.H.D., Marquette; Docteur es Lettres, Toulouse; unmarried. Ordained Presbyn. ministry, 1887; pastor North Ch., Geneva, N.Y., 1887-89; instr. ch. history, Princeton Theol. Sem., 1889-92; pastor Edwards Congl. Ch., Northampton, Mass., 1892-98; prof. modern European history, Princeton, 1898—. Sec. Am. Univ. Union, Paris, and lecturer Y.M.C.A., July 1917-July 1919; Louis Liard lecturer, Sorbonne, Paris; twice Harvard lecturer to provincial univs. of France. Author: The Age of the Renaissance, 1897; Renaissance Portraits, 1905; Catherine de Medicis, 2 vols.; Ignatius Loyola, 1926; The Story of France, 1928; George Washington, the Son of His Country, 1931. Officer Legion of Honor; mem. Le Cercle Artistique et Littéraire, Le Cercle Interallié, Club de la Renaissance Française; dir. Am. Univ. Union, Paris, 1921-23 and 1928-29. Home: Princeton, N.J. Died Aug. 30, 1933.

VAN DYKE, Walter, asso. justice Supreme Court, Calif. for term Jan. 1, 1899, to Dec. 31, 1910; b. Tyre, N.Y., Oct. 3, 1823; ed. dist. sch.; select sch. Earlville, N.Y., and Liberal Inst., Clinton, N.Y.; studied law, Cleveland, O., 1846-48; m. Rowena Cooper, Sept. 1, 1854. Admitted to bar of the Supreme Court, Ohio, 1848; began to practice in Cleveland; went to Calif., starting in spring of 1849, crossing plains as one of party of 14 young men; arrived in Los Angeles, Jan. 1850, and in San Francisco a few weeks later; went to mines for few months, later settled at Trinidad, and on organization of Klamath Co., in 1851, was elected dist. atty.; elected mem. legislative assembly, 1852; removed to Humboldt Co. on its organization, 1853; elected dist. atty. there, 1854; practiced law and for some yrs. edited Humboldt Times; elected to State senate, 1861; removed to San Francisco, 1863; practiced there until 1884; U.S. atty. of Calif., 1874-77; practiced at Los Angeles, 1885-88; judge Superior Court of Los Angeles Co., 1888-98; elected to present position, 1898. Home: San Francisco, Calif. Died 1905.

VAN DYKE, William Duncan, insurance official; b. Milwaukee, Wis., Aug. 15, 1856; s. John H. and Mary McEldery (Douglass) V.; B.A., Princeton, 1878; m. Gertrude H. Goodrich, Aug. 5, 1885; children—Mary Douglass, Mrs. Gertrude Baird (dec.), Mrs. Nancy Scribner, William D. Admitted to bar, 1880; mem. Van Dyke & Van Dyke, 1880-1909. Trustee and mem. exec. and finance coms., 1904-09, v.p., 1909-19, and pres., Jan. 29, 1919—. Northwestern Mutual Life Ins. Co. Sec. and treas. Pewabic Co., Mineral Mining Co., Van Dyke Land and Investment Co., Milwaukee. Republican. Presbyn. Home: Milwaukee, Wis. Died June 7, 1932.

VAN DYNE, Frederick, lawyer; b. Palmyra, N.Y., Nov. 24, 1861; s. Charles H. and Carrie Esther (Brown) V.; ed. Palmyra High Sch.; LL.B., Georgetown U., 1890, LL.M., 1891; m. Clara M. Hutchins, Apr. 15, 1885. Read law in Palmyra office, 1881-83; admitted to bar of D.C., 1891; clerk Law Bur., Dept. of State, 1891-1900; asst. solicitor (specially created position), 1900-07, State Dept.; consul at Kingston, Jamaica, Apr. 1, 1907-July 1, 1910; asst. solicitor, Dept. of State, July 1, 1910-13; consul at Lyon, France, Nov. 24, 1913—. Lecturer on citizenship, Georgetown U. Law Sch., 1907-09. Author: Citizenship of the United States, 1904; Van Dyne on Naturalization, 1907; Our Foreign Service, 1909; The A B C of American Diplomacy. Home: Chevy Chase, Md. Died Apr. 21, 1915.

VAN ELTEN, (Hendrik Dirk) Kruseman, artist; b. Alkmaar, Holland, Nov. 14, 1829; s. Daniel Nicholas V.; ed. Alkmaar; began art study at same place and finished at Haarlem; had a studio at Amsterdam; gold medal, Internat. Exbn., Amsterdam, 1860; became mem. Royal Acads., Amsterdam and Rotterdam; from 1865 has lived in New York; asso., 1871, and from 1885 academician, Nat. Acad. Design; commr. of fine arts for Netherlands Govt. at Centennial Exbn. at Phila.; decorated by king with order of Netherlands Lion; hon. mem. of several British Art assns.; specialties: landscapes in oil and water colors; also etchings. Died 1904.

VAN EPS, Frank Stanley, clergyman; b. Hoffmans, nr. Schenectady, N.Y., July 4, 1859; s. Peter V. and Mary A. (Davenport) V.; A.B., Drury Coll., Springfield, Mo., 1883; m. Frances Marion Bosworth, Nov. 3, 1883 (died 1904); m. 2d, Jeanette E. Condé, Apr. 12, 1911. Ordained Congl. ministry, 1884; pastor Alexandria, S.D., 1884-85, Frankfort, S.D., 1885-86, Dodge Centre, Minn., 1886-88, Western Springs, Ill., 1888-91; asst. pastor Pilgrim Congl. Ch., New York, 1905-06; pastor Presbyn. Ch., Passaic, N.J., 1906-10; organizer, and pastor Christ Congl. Ch., Woodhaven,

N.Y. City, 1910-Aug. 31, 1915. Mem. and speaker for New York Peace Soc.; charter mem. League to Enforce Peace; sec.-treas. Congl. Ministers' Meeting of N.Y. and Vicinity, 1915-19, mem. exec. com. of same, 1919—. Engaged in preaching, lecturing and in lit. and hist. studies and productions. Republican. Home: Woodhaven, L.I., and N.Y. City. Died July 15, 1921.

VAN FLEET, Vernon W., lawyer; b. Bristol, Ind., Sept. 9, 1866; s. Judge John M. (legal text-book author) and Ellen C. (Wick) V.; student Hillsdale Coll., 1886-90 (Phi Delta Theta); m. Helen M. Cummins, Aug. 21, 1895; children—Stephen C., Francis M. Admitted to bar of Ind., 1891; practiced with father, 1892-1907; mem. Ind. Ho. of Rep. 1901-03; judge Superior Court, 1907-15; moved to South Bend, 1910; practiced law in South Bend, 1915-21; mem. Rep. State Central Com., 1918-20; spl. asst. to Atty. Gen. of U.S., 1921-22; mem. Federal Trade Commn., Washington, term 1922-29 (chmn. 1924-25); resigned July 31, 1926. Home: Washington, D.C. Deceased.

VAN FLEET, Walter, horticulturist; b. Piermont, N.Y., June 18, 1857; s. Solomon and Elvira (Du Bois) V.; common and pvt. schs.; M.D., Hahnemann Med. Coll., Phila., 1880; post-grad. work, Jefferson Med. Coll., Phila., 1887; m. Sarah C. Heilman, Aug. 7, 1883. Practiced medicine, central Pa., 1880-92; hort. editor Rural New Yorker, New York, 1890-1910, and v.p. Rural Pub. Co., 1902-10; expert plant breeder and physiologist, Bur. of Plant Industry, U.S. Dept. of Agr., 1910—; in charge U.S. Plant Introduction Garden, Chico, Calif., 1910-11. Has devoted large part of time to plant breeding, 1872—; widely recognized as leader in development of gladioli, garden roses and chestnuts. Author: Bird Portraits, 1888; The Gladiolus (with M. Crawford), 1911; (brochures) Vegetable Breeding, 1907, Breeding Hardy Roses, 1907, Hybridizing Gladiolus Species, 1909. Awarded George Robert White medal of honor for eminent services in horticulture, 1918, by Mass. Hort. Soc. Home: Glendale, Md. Died Jan. 22, 1922.

VAN FLEET, William Cary, judge; b. Maumee City, O., Mar. 24, 1852; s. Cornelius and Julia Anna (Runyon) V.; ed. pub. and pvt. schs.; m. Mary Isabella Carey, Apr. 12, 1877 (died 1878); m. 2d, Elizabeth Eldridge Crocker, Jan. 19, 1887. Admitted to the bar, 1873; asst. dist. atty., Sacramento Co., 1878-79; mem. Calif. Ho. of Rep., 1881-82; state prison dir., 1883-84; judge Superior Ct., 1884-92 (resigned Nov. 1892); justice Supreme Ct., of Calif., 1894-99; U.S. dist. judge, Northern Dist. of Calif., Apr. 2, 1907—. Mem. Calif. Code Commn., 1899-1903; mem. Rep. Nat. Com., 1900-04. Trustee Calif. State Library, 1899-1912; life mem. board of trustees Hastings College of Law. Mem. vestry St. Luke's (Episcopal) Parish, San Francisco. Home: San Francisco, Calif. Died Sept. 3, 1923.

VAN HAMM, Caleb Marsh, editor; b. Cincinnati, Mar. 11, 1861; s. Washington and Rebecca (Baldridge) V.; ed. Chickering Inst., Cincinnati, 1872-77; LL.B., U. of Cincinnati, 1882; m. Amy M. Perkins, Oct. 25, 1893. Engaged in practice of law, Cincinnati, 1882-83; city editor and later mng. editor Cincinnati News-Journal, 1883-85; edited weekly called "Sam," 1885; again practiced law until 1892, when went to New York; city editor Journal, 1894, Recorder, 1895; with World, 1895-1910, mng. editor morning edit., 1903-10; mng. editor New York American, Jan. 1, 1910—. Home: New York, N.Y. Died Dec. 27, 1919.

VAN HARLINGEN, Arthur, M.D.; b. Philadelphia, Oct. 25, 1845; s. John Martin and Isabel (Campbell) V.; Ph.B., Sheffield Scientific Sch. (Yale), 1864; M.D., Univ. of Pa., 1867; m. Bessie Butler Whitney, Aug. 31, 1882; 1 son, John Martin. Resident phys., Phila. and Pa. hosps., 1867-69, then in practice at Phila.; specialist in skin diseases. Chief of skin clinic, U. of Pa., 1871-83; prof. dermatology, Phila. Polyclinic, and clin. lecturer in Jefferson Med. Coll., Phila., 1883-95; emeritus prof. dermatology, Phila. Polyclinic, and dermatologist Children's Hosp., 1895-1912. Fellow Coll. Physicians, Phila.; sometime pres. Am. Dermatol. Assn. Episcopalian. Author: Handbook of the Diagnosis and Treatment of Skin Diseases (4 edits.), 1884; Handbook of Local Therapeutics (in collaboration), 1893. Home: Bryn Mawr, Pa. Died Sept. 23, 1936.

VAN HISE, Charles Richard, university pres.; b. Fulton, Wis., May 29, 1857; s. William Henry and Mary (Goodrich) V.; B.M.E., U. of Wis., 1879, B.S., 1880, M.S., 1882, Ph.D., 1892; (LL.D., U. of Chicago, 1903, Yale, 1904, Harvard, 1908, Williams, 1908, Dartmouth, 1909); m. Alice Bushnell Ring, Dec. 22, 1881. Instr. metallurgy, 1879-83, asst. prof., 1883-86, prof. same, 1886-88, prof. mineralogy, 1888-90, prof. archæan and applied geology, 1890-92, prof. geology, 1892-1903, pres., 1903—, U. of Wisconsin. Non-resident prof. structural geology, U. of Chicago, 1892-1903; mem. geologic br. U.S. Geol. Survey, 1883—; geologist in charge of Div. of Pre-Cambrian and Metamorphic Geology, same, 1900-08, and cons. geologist, same, 1909-15; cons. geologist, Wis. Geol. and Natural History Survey, 1897-1903; mem. Nat. Conservation Commn., 1909; chmn. Wis. State Conservation Commn., 1908-15; chmn. Bd. of Arbitration in Controversy between Eastern Railroads and Brotherhood of Locomotive Engrs., 1912; trustee Carnegie Foundation for Advancement of Teaching, 1909—. Author: The Conservation of the Natural Resources of the United States, 1910; Concentration and Control—A Solution of the Trust Problem in the United States, 1912. Joint author: Penokee Iron Bearing Series of Michigan and Wisconsin; The Marquette Iron Bearing District of Michigan; The Menomonee Iron Bearing District of Michigan; Geology of the Lake Superior Region. Home: Madison, Wis. Died Nov. 19, 1918.

VAN HOOK, Weller, surgeon; b. Greenville, Ind., May 16, 1862; s. William Russell and Tillie (Weller) V.; A.B., U. of Mich., 1884; M.D., Coll. Phys. and Surg., Chicago, 1885; studied univs. of Berlin and Vienna, 1894-95; m. Anna Charles Whaley, June 16, 1892. Has held chairs of surgery in Coll. Phys. and Surg. and Chicago Post-Grad. Med. Sch.; formerly head prof. surgery, Northwestern U. Med. Sch. Surgeon to Wesley Hospital, Chicago, Ill. Died June 30, 1933.

VAN HOOSE, Azor Warner, college pres.; b. Griffin, Ga., Oct. 31, 1860; s. Azor and Missouri Frances (Daniel) V.; A.B., U. of Georgia, 1882; (LL.D., Mercer U., Ga., 1911); m. Lucy E. Rucker, Aug. 11, 1887. Prof. math. science, South Ga. Coll., Thomasville, 1882-83; prof. mathematics and Latin, Howard Coll., Marion, Ala., 1883-84; adjunct prof. same, U. of Georgia, 1884-85; asso. pres. and later pres., 1886-1909, Brenau Coll., Gainesville, Ga.; pres. Shorter Coll., Rome, Ga., 1910—. Democrat. Baptist. Mason. Home: Rome, Ga. Died Dec. 11, 1921.

VAN HORN, Frank Robertson, geologist, mineralogist; b. Johnsonburg, N.J., Feb. 1872; s. George W. and Ellen J. (Robertson) V.; State Model Sch., Trenton, 1886-88; B.S., Rutgers, 1892, M.S., 1893, D.Sc., 1919; U. of Heidelberg, 1893-97, Ph.D., 1897; m. Myra Van Horn, June 8, 1898; children—Kent R., Hilda L. Instr. in mineralogy, Rutgers, 1892-93; instr. in geology and mineralogy, 1897-99, asst. prof., 1899-1902, prof., 1902—, Case Sch. Applied Science, Cleveland. Fellow Geol. Soc. America (librarian 1913-18), Mineral Soc. America (sec. 1923—), A.A.A.S. Progressive. Presbyn. Author: Lecture Notes on Systematic Zoölogy, 1902; Lecture Notes on General and Special Mineralogy, 1903; Geology and Mineral Resources of the Cleveland District, Ohio, 1931. Home: Cleveland Heights, O. Died Aug. 1, 1933.

VAN HORN, Peter Harry, pres. Nat. Fedn. of Textiles; b. Logan, O., Oct. 1, 1893; s. Jesse and Belle (Tedrow) V.; student Ohio State U., 1912-14, Univ. of Calif., 1915-17; m. Helen Genevieve Prosser, Sept. 20, 1920; 1 son, Peter Van Horn II. Began with Nat. City Bank, N.Y. City, 1919; v.p. Allen Archer Co., Los Angeles, 1920-21; pres. K. W. Kays Co., Los Angeles, Jan.-Oct. 1921; gen. mgr. Columbus Better Business Bur., 1926-34; pres. Nat. Assn. Better Business Bureaus, 1933-34, Nat. Fedn. of Textiles, Mar. 1934—. Served as lt. U.S. Army and as pilot Air Corps, World War, June 1917-March 1919; consultant, staff of NRA, Washington, D.C., 10 weeks, 1935. Protestant. Home: New York, N.Y. Died Dec. 18, 1936.

VAN HORN, Robert Osborn, army officer; b. Whipple Barracks, Ariz., Aug. 15, 1876; s. Col. James Hatch and Margaret (Wilson) Van H.; B.S. in Engring., U. of Mich., 1897; grad. Army Sch. of the Line, 1911, Army Staff Coll., 1912; m. Lucretia Blow Le Bourgeois, Oct. 19, 1908; children—Margaret Elizabeth (dec.), Lucretia. Pvt. 12th Inf., 1897; commd. 2d lt. inf., 1899; promoted through grades to brig. gen., Dec. 1, 1933; civil gov. Cotabato Dist., Moro Province, P.I., 1903-05; aide to President Theodore Roosevelt, 1907-08; comdg. 9th Inf., A.E.F. Awarded D.S.M., Silver Star medal with cluster. Died June 26, 1941.

VAN HORN, Robert Thompson, journalist; b. E. Mahoning, Pa., May 19, 1824; went to school winters until 15, then was apprenticed to printing trade; m. Adela H. Cooley, Dec. 2, 1848. Editor Kansas City Journal, 1855-96, except during war interval; lt. col. 25th Mo. Inf. during Civil War; took part in battle and siege of Lexington, Mo., Sept. 1861, battle of Shiloh, and other engagements. Mem. Mo. Senate, 3 yrs.; mem. Congress, 1865-71, 1881-83, 1895-97. Home: Kansas City, Mo. Died Jan. 3, 1916.

VAN HORNE, David, theologian; b. Glen, N.Y., Dec. 11, 1837; s. Cornelius C. and Hannah (Van Horne) V.; A.B., Union Coll., 1864; grad. New Brunswick (N.J.) Theol. Sem., 1867; D.D., Heidelberg, 1877; LL.D., Ursinus Coll., 1898; m. Mary G. Van Horne, Sept. 18, 1867. Ordained Reformed (Dutch) Ch. ministry, 1867; pastor Greenwich, N.Y., 1867-68, Dayton, O., 1868-75, First Ref. Ch., Phila., 1875-88; pres. and prof. systematic theology, Heidelberg Theol. Sem., Tiffin, Ohio (now Central Theol. Sem. of Reformed Ch., Dayton, Ohio), 1888-1916, emeritus prof. and hon. pres. same. Author: A History of the Reformed Church in Philadelphia, 1876; Shorter Heidelberg Catechism, 1881; Zwingle, the Mountain Boy of Wildhaus, 1884, Tent and Saddle Life in the Holy Land, 1885; Religion and Revelation, 1892; The Church and the Future Life, 1904. Home: Amsterdam, N.Y. Died Apr. 12, 1930.

VAN HORNE, Sir William Cornelius, railway pres.; b. Will Co., Ill., Feb. 3, 1843; s. C. C. and Mary Minier (Richards) V.; ed. com. schs.; m. Lucy Adaline, d. Erastus Hurd, 1867. Telegraph operator I.C. R.R., 1857; various capacities, M.C. R.R., 1858-64; train dispatcher, supt. telegraph, and div. supt. C.&A. R.R., 1864-72; gen. supt. St. Louis, Kansas City & Northern Ry., 1872-74; gen. mgr. Southern Minn. Ry., 1874-77, continuing as pres. to 1879; gen. supt. C.&A. Ry., 1877-79, C.,M.&St.P., 1880-81; gen. mgr., 1882-84, v.p. and gen. mgr., 1884-88, pres., 1888-99, chmn. bd. 1899-1910, Canadian Pacific Ry. Co. Pres. Cuba Co. Hon. K.C.M.G. Home: Montreal, Canada. Died Sept. 11, 1915.

VAN HORNE, William McCadden, brig. gen. U.S. Army; b. Ohio, Aug. 22, 1842. Enlisted as pvt. Co. E, 2d Ohio Inf., Aug. 14, 1861; discharged, Oct. 10, 1864; commd. 2d lt. 184th Ohio Inf., Jan. 4, 1865; transferred to 195th Ohio Inf., Mar. 17, 1865; capt., Mar. 17, 1865; hon. mustered out, Dec. 18, 1865; apptd. from Ohio, 2d lt. 17th U.S. Inf., Feb. 23, 1866; 1st lt., Feb. 23, 1866; capt., Dec. 31, 1872; maj. 22d Inf., May 23, 1896; transferred to 8th Inf., Oct. 24, 1898; lt. col. 18th Inf., Nov. 1, 1898; col. 29th Inf., Feb. 2, 1901; retired on account of disability incurred in line of duty, Oct. 16, 1901; advanced to rank of brig. gen. retired, by act of Apr. 23, 1904. Home: Chicago, Ill. Died Jan. 19, 1923.

VAN IDERSTINE, Robert, fire insurance; b. Brooklyn, N.Y., Mar. 5, 1873; s. Frederick A. and Adeline Castle (Pratt) Van I.; grad. Poly. Inst., Brooklyn, 1890; LL.B., Columbia, 1894; m. 2d, Katherine Kent, Oct. 23, 1924; children—(by former marriage)—Robert, Elizabeth. Practiced law in N.Y. City, 1894-1916; last law firm, Van Iderstine, Duncan & Barker; sec. Dept. of Water Supply, Gas & Electricity, of City of New York and subsequently as dep. commr. of dept., for the Borough of Brooklyn; chmn. bd. Am. Equitable Assurance Co.; v.p. Corroon & Reynolds Corp. Chmn. New York Child Welfare Com. Republican. Mason. Home: New York, N.Y. Died Aug. 7, 1933.

VAN INGEN, Gilbert, geologist, paleontologist; b. Poughkeepsie, N.Y., July 30, 1869; s. Henry and Josephine (Koelman) V.; student Cornell U., 1886-88, Yale, 1892-93; m. Harriet Galusha, Sept. 3, 1903. Asst. geologist, U.S. Geol. Survey, 1889-91; asst. paleontologist, Cornell U., 1891-92; at Columbia, 1893-95, curator geology, 1895-1901; spl. asst. paleontologist, N.Y. State, 1901-03; asst. geologist and curator invertebrate paleontology, 1903-08, asst. prof. geology, 1908-19, associate prof. of geology, 1919—, Princeton University. Dir. Princeton geol. expdns. to Newfoundland, 1912, 13, 14. Pres. Acad. Bd. U.S. School of Mil. Aeronautics at Princeton U., 1917-Feb. 1919. Fellow N.Y. Acad. Sciences, Geol. Soc. of America, Paleontological Society of America. Editor depts. geology and paleontology, New Internat. Ency., 1901-02. Home: Princeton, N.J. Died July 7, 1925.

VAN KIRK, Charles Clark, judge; b. Greenwich, N.Y., Sept. 21, 1862; s. Norman and Kate (Conant) V.; A.B., Colgate U., 1884, LL.D., 1916; m. Nancy Thompson, Oct. 28, 1903. Admitted to bar, 1888; mem. Gibson & Van Kirk, Greenwich, 1888-96, Rowe & Van Kirk, Port Henry, N.Y., 1896-97, Patterson, Bulkley & Van Kirk, Albany, 1897-1906; justice Supreme Court N.Y., 4th Dist., terms 1906-33, designated to Appellate Div., 3d Dept., Jan. 1921, presiding justice, Jan. 1928-32; became official referee N.Y. Supreme Ct. Republican. Baptist. Dir. First Nat. Bank. Home: Greenwich, N.Y. Died Apr. 18, 1937.

VAN LAER, Alexander Theabald, artist, lecturer; b. Auburn, N.Y., Feb. 9, 1857; s. Peter C. and Mina (Verbeek) V.; ed. high sch., Auburn, 1873-76; studied art at Nat. Acad. Design, New York, and Art Students' League, with R. Swain Gifford, and with George Poggenbeek, of Holland; m. Stella Stickney, 1886. Has exhibited at the leading Am. exhbns.; bronze medal, Charleston Expn. Has lectured on art history at Chautauqua, N.Y., 7 yrs.; in free lecture courses of New York 24 yrs.; at Brooklyn Inst. and before schs. and colls. and in leading cities. Mem. Jury of Selection and of Internat. Jury of Awards, St. Louis Expn., 1904. A.N.A., 1902, N.A., 1909. Home: Litchfield, Conn. Died Mar. 12, 1920.

VAN LENNEP, William Bird, surgeon; b. Constantinople, Turkey, Dec. 5, 1853; s. Rev. Henry J. (missionary) and Emily Bird V.; A.B., Princeton, 1876, A.M., 1880; M.D., Hahnemann Med. Coll., Phila., 1880; studied in Europe, 1882-84; m. Clara R. Hart, Apr. 1886. Prof. surgery, Hahnemann Med. Coll. and Hosp., 1884—, also sr. surgeon; cons. surgeon, Children's Homœ. Hosp., West. Phila. Gen. Homœ. Hosp. and Dispensary, West Jersey Homœ. Hosp. (Camden, N.J.), J. Lewis Crozer Home for Incurables and Homœ. Hosp. (Chester, Pa.), Abington Memorial Hosp. Fellow Am. Coll. Surgeons. Home: Philadelphia, Pa. Died Jan. 9, 1919.

VAN LOAN, Charles Emmet, author; b. San Jose, Calif., June 29, 1876; s. Richard and Emma J. (Blodgett) V.; ed. pub. schs. of Calif.; m. Emma C. Lenz, Nov. 20, 1902. Engaged in mercantile business until 1903; newspaper writer, Los Angeles and N.Y. City, 1904-10; contbr. to mags., 1910—. Author: The Big League, 1911; The Lucky Seventh, 1913; The Ten Thousand Dollar Arm, 1912; Inside the Ropes, 1913; Buck Parvin and the Movies, 1915; Old Man Curry, 1916. Home: Los Angeles, Calif. Died Feb. 2, 1919.

VAN METER, John Blackford, clergyman, educator; b. Phila., Pa., Sept. 6, 1842; s. Thomas Hurley and Johnetta (Blackford) V.; grad. Male Central High Sch. (now Baltimore City Coll.), 1859; hon. A.M., Dickinson, 1868, D.D., 1872; LL.D., Goucher, 1914; m. Lucinda Cassell, Dec. 19, 1866 (died 1907); children—Johnetta, Lydia. Admitted on trial M.E. ministry, 1864; ordained deacon, 1866, elder, 1868; pastor Md. and N.J., 1864-88, except 1872-81, as chaplain U.S. Navy (resigned); prof. philosophy, Goucher Coll., 1888-1914, dean 1892-1910, acting pres., 1911-13; retired on Carnegie Foundation, Aug. 31, 1914; dean emeritus, Goucher Coll., also trustee. Home: Baltimore, Md. Died Apr. 9, 1930.

VANN, Irving Goodwin, judge; b. Ulysses, N.Y., Jan. 3, 1842; s. Samuel R. and Catherine (Goodwin) V.; A.B., Yale, 1863, A.M., 1870; LL.B., Albany Law Sch., 1865; LL.D., Hamilton, 1882, Syracuse U., 1897, Yale, 1898; m. Florence, d. Henry A. Dillaye, of Syracuse, N.Y., Oct. 11, 1870. Began practice at Syracuse, 1865; mayor of Syracuse, 1879; justice Supreme Ct. of N.Y., 1882-96; apptd. by gov., 1896, judge Ct. of Appeals, elected to same, 1896, for term of 14 yrs.; reëlected, 1910 (retired on account of age, Jan. 1, 1913). Republican. Lecturer in Cornell, Syracuse, and Albany law schs. Home: Syracuse, N.Y. Died Mar. 22, 1921.

VAN NAME, Addison, librarian; b. Chenango, N.Y., Nov. 15, 1835; s. Cornelius and Theodosia (Ogden) V.; A.B., Yale, 1858, A.M., 1861; m. Julia Gibbs, Aug. 19, 1867. Librarian, Yale U., 1865-1905. Home: New Haven, Conn. Died Sept. 29, 1922.

VAN NESS, Thomas, clergyman; b. Baltimore, Md., June 29, 1859; s. William W. (M.D.) and Mary R. (Saladin) V.; A.B., Central High Sch., Phila., 1879; studied Harvard, until June 1883; m. Addie Sewall, July 5, 1886; children—Cornelius W., Ann E. Ordained Unitarian ministry, 1884; pastor at Denver, 1885, San Francisco, 1889-93, then pastor old historic North Ch., Boston (2d Ch.); resigned, 1928, to travel and lecture in Europe; now engaged in lit. work. Author: The Coming Religion; My Visit to Count Tolstoi (booklet); Count Tolstoi at Jasnai Polyania; The Coming Age; Twenty Years of Life, 1912; The Religion of New England, 1926. V.p. Japan Soc., Boston. Lecturer. Home: Baltimore, Md. Died Mar. 14, 1931.

VAN NOPPEN, Leonard Charles, author; b. Holland, Jan. 9, 1868; brought to U.S. at 6; A.B., Guilford (N.C.) Coll., 1890, U. of N.C., 1892; A.M., Haverford Coll., 1893; studied law, U. of N.C., 1894, admitted to N.C. bar; studied Dutch lit. at U. of Utrecht; attended lectures at Leyden; returned to U.S., 1898; m. Adah Maude Stanton Becker, Sept. 28, 1902. Has delivered courses of lectures on Dutch lit. at Columbia, Princeton, Johns Hopkins, Lowell Inst., etc.; Queen Wilhelmina lecturer at Columbia; "lit. ambassador" to Am. univs. by appmt. of Dutch univs. Hon. men. Soc. of Netherlands Lit. (Leyden). Enlisted in U.S.N.R.F., Jan. 24, 1918; apptd. lt. and served during the war as asst. naval attaché at The Hague, and later for 8 mos. in London. Author: The Challenge (war poems), 1918; a symphonic epic of evolution, entitled Armageddon. Translator of Vondel's Samson and of Vondel's Adam in Banishment, 1916; also "Lucifer," the masterpiece of the Dutch Shakespeare, Vondel, into English verse. Home: Greensboro, N.C. Died July 21, 1935.

VAN NORDEN, Charles, clergyman; b. New York, Oct. 10, 1843; s. Thomas L. and Margaret H. (Warner) V.; bro. of Warner V.; A.B., Hamilton Coll., 1863; grad. Union Theol. Sem., 1866; (D.D., N.Y. U., 1887; LL.D., Hamilton, 1892); m. Annie H. Mygatt, Oct. 15, 1873 (died 1896); m. 2d, Ruth Spilman, Aug. 2, 1902. Ordained Congl. ministry, 1866; pastor New Orleans, La., 1866-67, Beverly, Mass., 1868-73, St. Albans, Vt., 1873-83, North St. Ch., Springfield, Mass., 1883-86; stated supply Chicopee Centre, Mass., 1887; pres. Elmira (N.Y.) Coll., 1890-93; mgr. Central Calif. Electric Co., 1895-1905. Author: The Outermost Rim and Beyond, 1882; The Psychic Factor, 1894; Jesus, an Unfinished Portrait, 1906; Yoland of Idle Isle (a romance), 1907. Home: East Auburn, Calif. Died May 1913.

VAN NORDEN, Warner, capitalist; b. New York, N.Y., July 2, 1841; s. Thomas L. and Margaret H. V.; brother of Charles V.; New York U.; m. Martha A. Philips, May 30, 1867 (dec.); father of Warner Montague V. Pres. Nat. Bank of North America, 1891-1902; retired. Dir. Standard Milling Co., Fifth Av. Estates, The London & Edinburg Co. Mem. Chamber Commerce; pres. Holland Soc.; pres. bd. trustees of Presbytery; v.p. Bd. Foreign Missions, etc., Presbyn. Ch.; mem. bd. mgrs. Am. Tract Society. Home: New York, N.Y. Died Jan. 1, 1914.

VAN NORMAN, Amélie Veiller, educator; b. Paris, France; pvt.edn.; m. D. C. Van Norman, D.D., LL.D., 1875 (who founded, 1857, the Van Norman Inst.). Pres. Van Norman Ednl. Inst. Co. First pres. and hon. pres. Jeanne d'Arc Suffrage League; hon. pres.

Van Norman Alumnæ Assn.; mem. Anthrop. Soc. of London; asso. mem. New York City Fedn. of Women's Clubs; officer in Le Lycéum, Société des Femmes de France à New York. Home: Mt. Vernon, N.Y. Died Nov. 7, 1920.

VAN NORMAN, Hubert Everett, dairy husbandman; b. Tilsonburg, Ont., Can., Jan. 30, 1872; s. George Tillson and Julia Bright (Everett) V.; brought to U.S., 1880; B.S., Mich. Agrl. Coll., 1897; LL.D., Syracuse, 1923; m. Maud Rodden Carrigan, Aug. 28, 1915. Manager dairy farm, 1897-98; supt. univ. farm, Purdue U., 1898-1902; chief of dairy dept. Purdue U., 1902-05; prof. dairy husbandry, Pa. State Coll., 1905-13; prof. dairy management, U. of Calif., 1913-24, also vice dir. Agrl. Expt. Sta., and dean Univ. Farm Sch. to July 1921 (leave of absence, organizing World's Dairy Congress, 1923). Sec. Ind. Dairy Assn., 1898-1905; sec. Pa. Dairy Union, 1906-13; pres. Nat. Dairy Show, 1910-24, World's Dairy Congress Assn., 1921-23; pres. Am. Dry Milk Institute, 1925-29; director research, The Borden Co., 1929-33. Pres. Century Dairy Exhibit, Inc., 1932-34; director development and education for Chicago Mercantile Exchange, 1935-36, consultant, 1936—. Presbyn. Author: First Lesson in Dairying, 1908. Home: Chicago, Ill. Died July 28, 1938.

VAN ORSDEL, Josiah Alexander, judge; b. New Bedford, Pa., Nov. 17, 1860; s. Ralph and Margaret (Randolph) V.; Grove City (Pa.) Normal Acad. (now coll.); A.B., Westminster Coll., New Wilmington, Pa., 1885; LL.D., 1912; studied law with Dana & Long, New Castle, Pa.; LL.D., Grove City Coll., Pa., 1906; m. Kate Barnum, July 28, 1891. Admitted to bar, 1890; located at Cheyenne, Wyo., 1891; elected co. and pros. atty., Laramie Co., Wyo., 1892; mem. Ho. Rep., Wyo., 1894; apptd. by gov. chmn. commn. to revise, compile and codify laws of Wyo., 1895; atty. gen. of Wyo., 1898-1905; asso. justice Supreme Court of Wyo., Apr. 15, 1905-Feb. 1, 1906; asst. atty. gen. of U.S., Feb. 1, 1906-Nov. 1907; justice U.S. Court of Appeals of D.C., 1907—. Republican. Presbyterian. Mem. S.A.R. (pres. gen.). Home: Washington, D.C. Died Aug. 7, 1937.

VAN PATTEN, William James, manufacturer; b. Wauwatosa, Wis.; s. William Henry and Mary (Vanderpool) V.; ed. pub. sch. of Vt.; (hon. A.M., U. of Vt.); m. Harriet P. Lemon, June 9, 1874. Treas. Wells & Richardson Co., Burlington, 1872-1910; pres. Malted Cereals Co., 1899—, Burlington Bldg. & Loan Assn., 1894-1912. Mayor of Burlington, 1894-96; chmn. bd. Park Commrs. 12 yrs.; state senator, 1906. Republican. Conglist. Pres. Mary Fletcher Hosp., N.E. Kurn Hattin Homes. Vt. Conf. Social Work; pres. United Soc. Christian Endeavor 4 yrs. Home: Burlington, Vt. Died Feb. 13, 1920.

VAN PETTEN, John B., educator; b. in Sterling, N.Y., June 19, 1827; s. Peter and Lydia (Bullock) V.; grad. Wesleyan Univ., Conn., 1850; completed conf. course in divinity, 1856 (Ph.D., Syracuse Univ., 1888); m. Mary B. Mason, Aug. 10, 1850. Prin. Fairfield (N.Y.) Sem., 1855-61 and 1866-69. Was clergyman, M.E. Ch. chaplain 34th N.Y. inf., June 15, 1861, to Sept. 22, 1862; lt. col. 160th N.Y. inf., Sept. 25, 1862, to Jan. 20th, 1865; in permanent command of regt. over 2 yrs.; comd. 2d brigade of 1st div., 19th corps, at Pt. Hudson, June 14, 1863; severely wounded at battle of Opequan, Sept. 19, 1864; complimented in gen. orders by Gen. Sheridan for conspicuous gallantry; col. 193d N.Y. inf. and bvt. brig. gen. U.S.V., comdg. dist. of Cumberland in W.Va., June 1865, to Jan. 1866; State senator, 1868-69. Prin. Sedalia, Mo., Sem., 1877-82; prof. Latin and history, Claverack Coll., N.Y., 1885-1900. Home: Oswego, N.Y. Died 1908.

VAN RENSSELAER, Howard, physician; b. Albany, N.Y., June 26, 1858; s. Bayard and Laura (Reynolds) V.; student Albany Normal Sch. and St. Paul's Sch., Concord, N.H.; Ph.B., Yale, 1881; M.D., Coll. of Phys. and Surg. (Columbia), 1884; interne New York Hosp., 18 months; studied in hosps. all over Europe, 1887-89; engaged in practice at Albany; unmarried. Apptd. visiting phys. St. Peter's Hosp., 1889, and in dispensary of Child's Hosp.; instr. diseases of the chest, 1889, lecturer on materia medica, 1890, asso. prof. materia medica, 1892, prof. materia medica and therapeutics, and asso. prof. medicine, 1904—, Albany Med. Coll.; attending phys. Albany Hosp., St. Peter's Hosp., Hosp. for Incurables, Child's Hosp., Home for Friendless; med. dir. tuberculosis dept. Albany Hosp. Pres. Boys' Club, Charity Orgn. Society. Formerly editor Albany Medical Annals, and writer on med. and sanitary subjects. Served in M.C. U.S.A. nearly 2 yrs., retiring Apr. 1918, as major. Home: Albany, N.Y., and Newton Hook, N.Y. Died Mar. 31, 1925.

VAN RENSSELAER, M. King (Mrs.), author; b. New York, May 25, 1848; d. Archibald Gracie and Elizabeth Denning (Duer) King; ed. by governess and tutors; m. John King Van Rensselaer, Oct. 4, 1871. Author: Crochet Lace, 1882; The Devil's Picture Books, 1887; Van Rensselaers of the Manor, 1889; The Goede Vrouw of Mana-ha-ta, 1899; New Yorkers of the 19th Century, 1899; History of Newport, 1905; Nonsuch Euchre and Other Games, 1907; Prophetical, Educational and Playing Cards, 1913. Editor: A Girl's Life 80 Years Ago; Our Social Ladder. Home: New York, N.Y. Died May 11, 1925.

VAN RENSSELAER, Mariana Griswold, art critic, author; b. New York; d. George and Lydia (Alley) Griswold; Litt.D., Columbia University, 1910; m. Schuyler Van Rensselaer, 1873 (died 1934). Pres. Public Education Assn. of New York; hon. mem. Am. Inst. Architects, Am. Soc. Landscape Architects, 1925. Author: Henry Hobson Richardson and His Works, 1888; English Cathedrals, 1893; Six Portraits; Art Out of Doors, 1893, 2d edit. 1925; One Man Who Was Content, 1896; Niagara, A Description, 1901; History of the City of New York in the Seventeenth Century, 1909; Poems, 1910; Many Children, 1921. Pres. Am. Fund for French Wounded. Awarded gold medal, Am. Acad. Arts and Letters, "for distinction in literature," 1923. Elected fellow N.Y. State Hist. Assn., 1933. Home: New York, N.Y. Died Jan. 20, 1934.

VAN RENSSELAER, Martha, home economist; b. Randolph, N.Y.; d. Henry Killian and Arvilla A. (Owen) V.; grad. Chamberlain Inst., Randolph, N.Y., 1884; A.B., Cornell U., 1909; unmarried. Teacher pub. schs., 1884-94; sch. commr. of Cattaraugus Co., N.Y., 1894-1900; instr. teachers' insts., N.Y. State, 1896-1903; extension leader, N.Y. State Coll. of Agr. (Cornell U.), 1900—; prof. home economics, and dir. of Home Economics Coll. of Cornell U., 1911—. Elected by com. apptd. by Nat. League of Women Voters, one of the 12 greatest women in the U.S., 1923. Compiler Manual of Home Making (Van Rensselaer, Rose and Canon). Home making editor The Delineator, 1920-26. Mem. exec. staff U.S. Food Administration, 1918-19. Chevalier Order of the Crown (Belgium). Home: Ithaca, N.Y. Died May 26, 1932.

VAN RENSSELAER, Maunsell, P.E. clergyman; b. Albany, N.Y., April 15, 1819; grad. Union, 1838 (A.M., 1841; LL.D., 1870; D.D., Hobart, 1859); Gen. Theol. Sem., 1841. Deacon, 1841; priest, 1843; rector St. Paul's Whitehall, N.Y., 1841-45; Grace Ch., Albany, 1846-47; St. John's, Mt. Morris, N.Y., 1847-53; St. Paul's, Oxford, N.Y., 1853-54; St. Paul's, Rochester, N.Y., 1854-59; Emmanuel Ch., Geneva, Switzerland, 1877-78. Pres. De Veaux Coll., New York, 1859-69; prof. ethics, 1870-72, and pres., 1872-76, Hobart Coll.; became chaplain House of the Holy Comforter, New York, 1882. Author: Sister Louise, the Story of Her Life Work; Annals of the Van Rensselaers in the United States; etc. Home: New York, N.Y. Died 1900.

VAN REYPEN, William Knickerbocker, medical dir. U.S.N.; b. Bergen, N.J., Nov. 14, 1840; s. Cornelius C. and Christina Cantine (Van Alen) V.; A.B., New York U., 1858, A.M., 1863; M.D., Univ. Med. Coll. (New York U.), 1862; m. Nellie C. Wells, Sept. 21, 1876. Apptd. from N.J., asst. surgeon U.S.N., Dec. 26, 1861; passed asst. surgeon, May 26, 1865; surgeon, May 12, 1868; med. insp., Aug. 16, 1887; med. dir., Mar. 30, 1895. Served at the naval hosp., New York, 1862; on St. Lawrence, East Gulf Blockading Squadron, 1863-64; naval hosp., Chelsea, Mass., 1865, 1869-70; Lenapee, 1865-67; Ticonderoga and Frolic, 1867-69; naval hosps., Norfolk, 1870-71, Annapolis, 1871-72, New York, 1874-77; on Iroquois, 1872-74; Alaska, 1878-80; at Navy Yard, Norfolk, 1880; naval hospital, Brooklyn, 1881-83; Powhatan, 1883-84; asst. chief Bur. of Medicine and Surgery, 1884-92; fleet surgeon Pacific Fleet, 1892-94; mem. Bd. of Inspection and Survey, 1894-97; during Spanish-Am. War designed and fitted out the ambulance ship Solace, the first ever used in naval warfare; surgeon-gen. U.S.N., and chief of Bur. of Medicine and Surgery, with rank of commodore, 1897-99, with rank of rear adm., 1899-1902; retired on own application after 40 yrs.' service, with the rank of sr. rear adm., Jan. 25, 1902. Del. representing U.S.N. at 12th Internat. Med. Congress, Moscow, 1897; del. Red Cross Conf., St. Petersburg, 1902; pres. Am. Nat. Red Cross, 1904-05 (chmn. Central Com., 1905—). Home: Washington, D.C. Died Dec. 22, 1924.

VAN RIPER, John Crowell, banker; b. Cass Co., Mich., Feb. 22, 1863; s. George and Parthania (Crowell) V.; ed. pub. schools; m. Anna Moore Prather, May 25, 1886. Organized Peoples Bank, Sedalia, Mo., 1891; admitted to bar, 1898; sold out interests in bank and moved to Lincoln, Neb., 1900, to St. Louis, 1901; purchased control of First Nat. Bank of East St. Louis, Ill.; organized Ill. State Trust Co., of which was pres. until 1908; pres. Title Guaranty Trust Co. and Am. Trust Co., St. Louis, 1909-19; removed to Denver, Jan. 1920. Republican. Episcopalian. Home: Denver, Colo. Died Apr. 13, 1926.

VAN ROOSBROECK, Gustave Leopold, prof. Romance langs.; b. Antwerp, Belgium, Apr. 6, 1888; s. Leopold François and Maria (De Volders) V.; U. of Brussels; M.A., U. of Minn., 1916, Ph.D., 1919; came to U.S., 1916; naturalized citizen, 1921; m. Marie de Graef, of Antwerp, May 10, 1912; 1 son, Willy. Instr. Romance langs., U. of Minn., 1916-19, asst. prof., 1919—. Spl. instr., U. of Ill., summer 1922, Johns Hopkins, summer 1923-25; lecturer graduate school of New York U.; asst. prof. graduate school Columbia University. Decorated Knight Order of Crown of Belgium and Knight Order of Leopold (Belgium). Writer on lit. subjects. Compiler: Anthology of Modern French Poetry, 1927. Gen. Sec. Romanic Review; editor Publs. of Inst. of French Studies, Columbia U.; pres. Belgian Inst. in the U.S. Home: New York, N.Y. Died July 12, 1936.

VAN ROYEN, Jan Herman, diplomat; b. Zwolle, Netherlands, Mar. 28, 1871; s. Jan Herman and Anna Aleida (van Engelen) V.; graduate high sch., Zwolle; LL.D. and Dr. Polit. Science, U. of Groningen; m. Albertina Winthrop, May 17, 1904; children—Jan Herman, Robert Dudley. Apptd. attaché, 1897; sec. of Legation, 1899; sent to Berlin, 1900, U.S., 1901, Constantinople, 1904; councillor of Legation to London, 1906; apptd. minister to Japan, 1908, Madrid, 1914, Rome, 1919; E.E. and M.P., Washington, D.C., 1927—. Sec. to Peace Conf., The Hague, 1907. Decorated Knight Grand Cross, Order of Rising Sun (Japan), Dannebrog (Denmark), Isabella la Catolica (Spain), Crown of Italy, Grand Officer of the Medjidie (Turkey); Comdr. Order St. Anna (Russia), Pole Star (Sweden), Iron Crown (Austria); Grand Officer Order of Orange Nassau; Officer Legion of Honor (France), Crown of Prussia; Knight Order of the Netherlands Lion. Protestant. Author: The Consular Jurisdiction in Japan, 1895. Home: Washington, D.C. Died Aug. 31, 1933.

VAN SANT, Samuel Rinnah, governor; b. Rock Island, Ill., May 11, 1844; s. John W. and Lydia (Anderson) V.; ed. Rock Island grammar and high schs.; pvt. and corporal Co. A, 9th Ill. Cav., 3 yrs. in Civil War; student Knox Coll., 2 yrs.; LL.D., Cornell, Ia., 1904, Augustana, Ill., 1905; m. Ruth Hall, Dec. 7, 1868 (died 1928). Engaged in steamboat business after leaving coll. Elected to Minn. Ho. of Rep., 1892, 94, speaker of House, 1895; gov. of Minn., 2 terms, 1901-05. Republican. Comdr. Minn. dept. G.A.R., 1894; comdr. in chief G.A.R., 1909-10. Mem. S.A.R. Home: Minneapolis, Minn. Died Oct. 3, 1936.

VAN SANTVOORD, Alfred, pres. and prin. owner of Hudson River Day Line of Steamboats between New York and Albany; b. Utica, N.Y.; s. Abraham and Sarah Van S.; common school edn.; early took to business, first assisting his father, who was one of the early transportation men of the Hudson River trade. Besides large interests in passenger service, built numerous large freight-towing boats, and chartered a number of boats to Govt. during Civil War. His long connection with water transportation earned him popular title of "Commodore"; m. Anna Townsend, Jan. 23, 1852 (died 1890). Enthusiastic yachtsman and owner of fine steam yacht "Clermont"; mem. New York, Seawanhaka, Atlantic and Am. Yacht clubs. Dir. Chicago, Milwaukee & St. Paul Ry., Delaware & Hudson R.R. and United Railways of N.J. Home: New York, N.Y. Died 1901.

VAN SANTVOORD, Seymour, lawyer; b. Troy, N.Y., Dec. 17, 1858; s. George and Elizabeth (Van Schaack) V.; A.B., Union Coll., 1878; LL.B., Albany Law Sch., 1880; m. Caroline Hart Shields, Jan. 4, 1888; children—George, John Griswold, Richard Staats, Alexander Seymour, Mrs. Edith Campbell, Mrs. Virginia Bowen, Mrs. Agnes Rice. Admitted to bar, 1880, and began practice at Troy; pres. Security Trust Co. Security Safe Deposit Co. Pres. N.Y. State Trust Companies' Assn. Democrat. Mem. Dutch Reformed Ch. Mem. N.G.N.Y., 1882-87. Alternate del.-at-large, Dem. Nat. Conv., 1904; counsel to gov. of N.Y., 1912; chmn. Pub. Service Commn., 2d Dist. N.Y., 1914-18. Democrat presdl. elector, 1932. Trustee of Emma Willard School, Russell Sage Coll., Troy Orphan Asylum, Samaritan Hosp. (Troy), Albany Law Sch. Author: The House of Cæsar, 1904; The Roman Forum, 1906; Octavia, a Tale of Ancient Rome, 1923; St. Francis, The Christian Exemplar, 1927; Random Addresses, 1930. Home: Troy, N.Y., and Bennington, Vt. Died Nov. 14, 1938.

VAN SCOY, Thomas, pres. Montana Wesleyan Univ., 1898—; b. in Indiana, Feb. 13, 1848; grad. Northwestern Univ., 1875 (A.M.); Garrett Biblical Inst., B.D. (D.D., Univ. of the Pacific); pres. Willamette Univ., 1880-91; dean and acting pres. Portland Univ., 1891-98. Home: Helena, Mont. Died 1901.

VAN SICKLE, Frederick Levi, M.D.; b. Clarks Green, Pa., Sept. 12, 1862; s. Lewis and Dorcas A. (Gardner) V.; ed. high sch., Binghamton, N.Y.; M.D., Jefferson Med. Coll., Phila., 1886; m. Cora R. Hull, Sept. 25, 1888 (died 1895); m. 2d, Christine L. Macmillan, Oct. 25, 1905. Practiced at Olyphant, 1888-1920; first health officer Blakely Borough, Pa., 1890; med. dir. Mid-Valley Hosp., Peckville, Pa.; cons. surgeon to relief dept. of Pa. R.R. Fellow A.M.A., Med. Soc. State of Pa. (pres. 1918-19), Am. Acad. Medicine (pres.). Republican. Baptist. Mason. Former exec. sec. and editor Atlantic Med. Jour. (now Pa. Med. Jour.). Home: Harrisburg, Pa. Died Oct. 9, 1938.

VAN SICKLE, James Hixon, educator; b. S. Livonia, N.Y., Oct. 24, 1852; s. John Landis and Alexina (Curtis) V.; grad. N.Y. State Normal Coll., Albany, 1873; student Williams Coll., 1876-77; A.B., U. of Colorado, 1896, A.M., 1898; (hon. Pd.D., Albany, 1905; A.M., Williams, 1913); m. Caroline E. Valentine, Aug. 1, 1883. Teacher in village schs., New Providence, N.J., Caledonia, N.Y., Cook Acad. Havana, N.Y.; prin. city sch., Denver; supt. north side schools, Denver, 1890-1900, supt. pub. instrn., Baltimore, 1900-11; supt. schools, Springfield, Mass., Sept. 1, 1911-Sept. 1, 1923; retired. Editor Riverside Readers, Pilot Arithmetics. Lecturer on sch. administration, U. of Chicago, summer quarters, 1902, 04, 05, 06, Yale, 1907, Cornell, 1908, Summer Sch. of the South, U. of Tenn., 1909-11, Harvard, 1914-15. Dir. school surveys in Conn., Mass., Pa. Presbyn. Home: Dade City, Fla. Died Feb. 12, 1926.

VAN SICLEN, Matthew, mining engr.; b. N.Y. City, Nov. 8, 1880; s. George West and Sarah Jane (Gregory) Van S.; grad. Cornwall Heights Sch., Cornwall-on-Hudson, N.Y., 1898; B.A., Amherst, 1902, M.A., 1905; E.M., Sch. of Mines (Columbia), 1906; m. Alice V. Petar, May 4, 1936. Surveyor Tenn. Copper Co., 1905; with various mines in Chihuahua, Zacatecas, Durango, Hidalgo, Sonora, Mexico, 1907-12, advancing to gen. supt.; supt. of exploration (oil shale), at Rosevale, N.B., 1913; leaser in Northwest Ark., 1914; operator zinc and lead mines, Webb City, Mo., 1915-17; lt. Air Service, U.S. Army, 1917-18; Pa. anthracite, 1919; examining engr., War Minerals Relief Commn., 1919-21; asst. chief mining engr., U.S. Bur. Mines, Washington, D.C., 1921-24; engr. in charge Div. of Mining Research, same, 1924-26; del. U.S. Govt. to XIVth Internat. Geol. Congress, Madrid, Spain, 1926; inspected metal and coal mines and mining methods in Europe, 1926; cons. mining engr., 1927-33, 1935-37; mining engr. to Turkish Govt., 1933-35; chief engr., coal economics div., U.S. Bur. Mines, 1937—. Episcopalian. Home: Arlington, Va. Died Mar. 3, 1941.

VAN SLYKE, Clarence Allan, headmaster; b. Centralia, N.Y., Dec. 24, 1880; s. Henry V. and Eleanor I. Van S.; A.B., Allegheny Coll., Meadville, Pa.; m. Elsie M. Giles, Aug. 29, 1906; children—Verna May, Elda Irene, Robert Evan. Prin. high sch., Stockton, N.Y., 1906-07; instr. Nat. Prep. Acad., Highland Falls, N.Y., 1907-08, asst. headmaster, 1908-16; headmaster Nat. Prep. Acad., Cornwall-on-Hudson, 1916—. Mem. Dem. Co. Com., Chautauqua Co., N.Y., 1902-05. Methodist. Mason, Odd Fellow. Author: Important Facts of Ancient and Mediæval History, 1910. Home: Cornwall-on-Hudson, N.Y. Died June 24, 1932.

VAN SLYKE, Lucius Lincoln, chemist; b. Centerville, N.Y., Jan. 6, 1859; s. William J. and Katherine (Keller) V.; A.B., U. of Mich., 1879, A.M., 1881, Ph.D., 1882; student and fellow by courtesy in chem. lab., Johns Hopkins, 1889-90; m. Lucy W., d. Rev. R. H. Dexter, June 15, 1882 (died 1885); children—Donald Dexter, Carl Osborne (dec.); m. 2d, Julia Hanford, d. Dr. Francis Upson, Apr. 5, 1888 (died 1924); 1 son, Lawrence Prescott; m. 3d, Mrs. Hedwig Sheul, June 2, 1926. Asst. chem. lab., U. of Mich., 1882-85; prof. chemistry, Oahu Coll., Honolulu, and govt. chemist, H.I., 1885-88; lecturer on gen. chemistry, U. of Mich., 1888-89; chief research chemist, New York Agrl. Experiment Station, 1890-1929, also prof. dairy chemistry, N.Y. State Coll. Agr., Cornell Univ., 1920-29 (emeritus). Fellow A.A.A.S.; pres. Assn. Official Agrl. Chemists, 1900, N.Y. State Dairymen's Assn., 1897. Author: Modern Methods of Testing Milk and Milk Products, 1906; Science and Practice of Cheese Making (with C. A. Publow); Fertilizers and Crops, 1911; Cheese (with W. V. Price), 1927. Home: Geneva, N.Y. Died Sept. 30, 1931.

VAN SWERINGEN, Mantis James; b. Wooster, O., July 8, 1881; s. James Tower and Jennie (Curtis) Van S.; ed. pub. schs.; unmarried. An associate with brother, Oris P., in real estate business, at Cleveland, 1907—; partner, firm O. P. & M. J. Van Sweringen; chmn. bd. N.Y.,C.&St.L. R.R. Co. and actively identified with various ry. mergers having Cleveland as hdqrs. Republican. Protestant. Home: Shaker Heights, Cleveland, O. Died Dec. 12, 1935.

VAN SWERINGEN, Oris Paxton; b. Wooster, O., Apr. 24, 1879; s. James Tower and Jennie (Curtis) V.; ed. public schools; unmarried. Partner in firm of O. P. & M. J. Van Sweringen, Cleveland; became chmn. of bd. Mo. Pacific R.R., 1930. Apptd. mem. City Plan Commn., Cleveland, 1916, chmn., 1919-21 (resigned); trustee Cleveland Mus. Natural History. Republican. Home: Shaker Heights, Cleveland, O. Died Nov. 23, 1936.

VAN SYCKEL, Bennet, judge; b. Hunterdon Co., N.J., Apr. 17, 1830; s. Aaron and Mary (Bird) V.; A.B., Princeton, 1846 (LL.D.). Admitted to bar, and began practice at Flemington, N.J., 1851; justice Supreme Ct. of N.J., 1869-1904; resigned. Home: Trenton, N.J. Died Dec. 19, 1921.

VANT, Irving Artemus, banker; b. Milford, Mass., Feb. 13, 1871; s. Dexter Parkhurst and Emma J. (Gould) V.; ed. pub. schs., Chicago; m. Dollie A. Turner, Dec. 23, 1891. With financial dept. Swift & Co., Chicago, 1892-1905, asst. treas., 1901-05; traveled widely, 1905-07; pres. Denver (Colo.) Stockyards Bank, 1907; pres. St. Joseph (Mo.) Stockyards Bank, 1908—; sec. and treas. St. Joseph Stockyards Co.; treas. Union Terminal R.R. Co., St. Joseph Belt Ry., Grain Belt Mills, Terminal Warehouse Company. Mem. Ill. N.G. 6 yrs. Presbyn. K.T. Home: St. Joseph, Mo. Died Apr. 26, 1934.

VAN TUYL, George Casey, Jr., banker; b. Albany, N.Y., Apr. 3, 1872; s. George C. and Angeline E. (Hawley) V.; grad. Albany High Sch., 1888; unmarried. Sec. and treas. Albany Trust Co., 1900-06, v.p., 1906-08, pres., 1908-11, later v.p.; supt. of banks, State of N.Y., 1911-14; pres. Bankers Loan & Investment Co., New York, v.p. Howard Beach, Inc.; dir. Ala., Tenn. & Northern Ry. Co., The Bank of U.S., "Cartier," Inc., Acme Syndicate, Ltd., Colonial Bank, First Nat. Security Co. of N.Mex., Watrona Oil Co.; trustee Central Savings Bank, Altantic Mut. Ins. Co. Died Feb. 9, 1938.

VAN TYNE, Claude Halstead, historian; b. Tecumseh, Mich., Oct. 16, 1869; s. Lawrence M. and Helen (Rosacrans) V.; A.B., Univ. of Mich., 1896; studied at Heidelberg, Leipzig and Paris, 1897, 98; Ph.D., U. of Pa., 1900; m. Belle Joslyn, June 19, 1896; children—Evelyn, Josselyn, David, Claude H. Sr. fellow in history, U. of Pa., 1900-03; asst. prof. Am. history, 1903-06, prof., 1906, and head of dept. of history, 1911—, U. of Mich. Author: The Loyalists in the American Revolution, 1902; Guide to the Archives of the Government of the United States in Washington (with W. G. Leland), 1904; The American Revolution, 1905; (with Prof. A. C. McLaughlin) School History of the United States, 1911; Causes of the War of Independence, 1921; India in Ferment, 1923; England and America, Rivals in the American Revolution, 1927. Editor: The Letters of Daniel Webster, 1902. Lecturer, 1913-14, in the French provincial univs. on the Fondation Harvard pour les relations avec les Universités Françaises; held the Sir George Watson chair of Am. history, literature, and institutions in the British Universities, 1927. Pres. Mich. Hist. Commn. Asso. editor Am. Hist. Review, 1915-22. Home: Ann Arbor, Mich. Died Mar. 21, 1930.

VAN VALKENBURGH, Charles M., banker; b. Lockport, N.Y., May 22, 1854; s. Daniel A. and Lucinda S. (Bruce) Van V.; prep. edn., high sch., Lockport; student Deveaux Coll., Niagara Falls, N.Y., 1868-72; m. Carrie L. Doolittle, Aug. 8, 1878; children—Roy D., Marion B. (Mrs. Frank M. Hardiman). Connected with Niagara County Nat. Bank & Trust Co. from 1879; dir. over 50 yrs., pres. 19 yrs., chmn. bd. from 1919; dir. The Upson Company. City fire commr. of Lockport. Trustee Wyndham Lawn Home for Children. Republican. Episcopalian; vestryman over 50 years. Home: Lockport, N.Y. Died Feb. 19, 1931.

VAN VECHTEN, Ralph, banker; b. Mattawan, Mich., Aug. 29, 1862; s. Charles D. and Ada A. (Fitch) V.; ed. pub. schs. Cedar Rapids, Ia., and Minneapolis, Minn.; m. Fannie Brownell Maynard, Oct. 19, 1887; 1 dau., Duane. Newspaper work, Cedar Rapids, 1878-80; bank clerk, 1880, becoming cashier Cedar Rapids Nat. Bank, 1887, pres., 1910, and chmn. bd., 1921; 2d v.p., 1905-09, v.p., 1909-10, Commercial Nat. Bank of Chicago, and v.p. of its successor, Continental & Commercial Nat. Bank, 1910—; v.p. Continental & Commercial Safe Deposit Co.; dir. Continental & Commercial Trust and Savings Bank. Mem. Chicago Bd. of Trade. Ind. Republican. Home: Chicago, Ill. Died June 28, 1927.

VAN VLECK, John Monroe, mathematician, astronomer; b. Stone Ridge, N.Y., March 4, 1833; s. Peter and Ann (Hasbrouck) V.; A.B., Wesleyan Univ., 1850; (LL.D., Northwestern Univ., 1876, Wesleyan, 1900); m. Ellen Maria Burr, May 2, 1854 (died 1899); father of Edward Burr V. Teacher Greenwich (R.I.) Acad., 1850; asst. in Nautical Almanac Office, Cambridge, Mass., 1851-53; adj. prof. mathematics, 1853-57, prof. mathematics and astronomy, 1858-1904 (emeritus), v.p., 1890-1903, acting pres., 1872-73, 1887-89, 1896-97, Wesleyan Univ. Mem. U.S. solar eclipse expdn. at Mt. Pleasant, Ia., 1869; del. Meth. Ecumenical Confs., London, 1881, Washington, 1891, London, 1901. Prepared astron. tables in Am. Ephemeris and Nautical Almanac, 1855-96. Home: Middletown, Conn. Died Nov. 4, 1912.

VAN VOAST, James, brig. gen. U.S.A.; b. Schenectady, N.Y., Sept. 1827; s. John G. and Maria (Teller) V.; student Union Coll., 1846-48, A.M., 1852; grad. U.S. Mil. Acad., 1852; m. Helen Pierce Hoar, 1855; m. 2d, Virginia M. Harris, 1870. Bvtd. 2d lt. 3d Artillery, July 1, 1852; promoted 2d lt., Aug. 22, 1853; advanced through grades to col. 9th Inf., Feb. 20, 1882; retired from active service, Apr. 2, 1883, for disability incurred in line of duty; advanced to rank of brig. gen. retired, by act of Apr. 23, 1904. Early service largely on frontier, among Indians. Was stationed at San Francisco, 1861-64, as mil. provost marshal; then served with regt. on Pacific Coast; after war in various duties and stations until retired. Home: Cincinnati, O. Died July 16, 1915.

VAN VOORHIS, John, lawyer; b. Decatur, N.Y., Oct. 22, 1826; s. John Van V. (a descendant of Dutch settlers of New York, 1660); ed. Genessee Wesleyan Sem., Lima, N.Y., East Mendon, N.Y., Acad.; studied law at Rochester; admitted to bar, 1852; m. Frances Aristine, d. Deacon Martin Galusha (and g.d. Jonas Galusha, who was 9 times gov. of Vt.), Jan. 28, 1858. Mem. bd. edn., Rochester, 1857, city atty., 1859; delegate Rep. Nat. Conv., Baltimore, 1864; mem. Congress, 1879-83, 1893-95. Republican. Home: Rochester, N.Y. Died 1905.

VAN VORHIS, Flavius Josephus, lawyer; b. Pike Twp., Marion Co., Ind., Dec. 31, 1840; s. Isaac and Sarah (Cotton) V.; studied at Northwestern Christian U. (now Butler U.); M.D., Rush Medical Coll., Chicago, 1866; M.D., Bellevue Hosp. Medical Coll. (New York U.), 1871; LL.B., Central Law School, Indianapolis, 1880; m. Emma Burton, Jan. 6, 1864. Private, and later asst. surgeon, 86th Ind. Vols., 1861-65; practiced medicine, Indianapolis, 1866-78, law, 1880—. Mem. Ind. Senate, 1881, 1883; drafted and secured passage in 1881 of law creating first State Bd. of Health in Ind., therefore known as "Father of Health Legislation in Indiana." Was engaged in the successful litigation to compel proper appraisement of railroad property in Ind.; campaign speaker. Republican until 1896; was chmn. Silver Rep. State Com. of Ind. 8 yrs. Author: The Currency Trust Conspiracy, 1911. Home: Indianapolis, Ind. Deceased.

VAN VORST, Bessie, author; b. New York, N.Y., 1873; d. John, Jr., and Lydia (Matteson) McGinnis; ed. Miss Brackett's School, and the Brearley Sch., New York; m. John Van Vorst, 1899. Began corresponding for the New York Evening Post, 1898; contbr. to Harper's Magazine, Century Magazine, Revue des Deux Mondes, Saturday Evening Post, Ladies' Home Journal; novels published in Journal des Debats, Paris, in Corriere dela Sera, Milan, and Churchman, New York. Episcopalian. Author: Bagsby's Daughter (with Marie Van Vorst), 1901; The Woman Who Toils (with same), 1903; The Issues of Life, 1904; Letters to Women in Love, 1906; The Children Who Toil, 1907; The Cry of the Children, 1908. Died May 19, 1928.

VAN VORST, Marie (Mrs. Gaetano Cagiati), author; b. New York, N.Y., Nov. 23, 1867; d. Hon. Hooper C. (judge Supreme Court) and Josephine (Treat) V.; ed. by private tutors; m. Gaetano Cagiati, of Rome, Italy, Oct. 1916; adopted son, Frederick John. Contributor of verse and fiction to mags., New York Sun, Evening Post, etc.; 1st contbn. was verse in Scribner's Magazine, printed 1893. Sent by Harper & Bros. to write the "Rivers of the Old World," Tiber, 1907, Nile, 1908, Danube, and Seine, 1909. Author: Bagsby's Daughter (with sister, Bessie Van Vorst), 1901; The Woman Who Toils (with same), 1903; Amanda of the Mill, 1905; In Ambush, 1909; First Love, 1910; His Love Story, 1913; Store-Tremaine, 1918; Fairfax and His Pride, 1920; Traditions, 1921; Queen of Karmania, 1922; Sunrise, 1924; Good Night Ladies (story of New York in 1861); Gardenia, 1932; St. Peter Burnes Oates, 1932; St. Mary Magdelen di Pazzi (London), 1932. Began to paint, 1922; exhibited, Sterner Galleries, New York, 1923, Bernheim, Paris, 1924. Died Dec. 16, 1936.

van WAGENEN, Anthony, lawyer; b. Brighton, Ia., Dec. 28, 1852; s. I. W. and Elizabeth (Moreland) V.; Canisius College, Buffalo, N.Y., 1873-75; LL.B., State U. of Iowa, 1876; m. Gertrude Louis, June 27, 1887. Began practice, Washington, Ia., 1876; city atty., Washington, 1879-80; judge 4th Jud. Dist of Ia., 1892-95; U.S. dist. atty. Northern Dist. of Ia., May 6, 1913-21; moved to Casa Grande, Ariz., 1921. Chief atty. for co. and sch. dists., in Lyon Co. bond cases, involving about $600,000 county and sch. bonds, claimed void because issued in excess of constl. limit of indebtedness; cases decided 1891 to 1895, invalidating bonds; drew up act, adopted by Ariz. legislature, under which electric power from Roosevelt Dam may be utilized for pumping water for irrigation, also organized dist., and $500,000 bond issue was unanimously voted. Republican. Catholic. Author: Government Ownership of Railways, 1907; also booklet, "Exit Depression," 1934, and first sequel to same 1935, second sequel, 1936. Home: Casa Grande, Ariz. Died Sept. 8, 1937.

VAN WAGENEN, James Hubert, civil engr.; b. Adams Co., Ia., Nov. 8, 1881; s. Isaac and Margaret (McClintic) V.; Knox Coll., Galesburg, Ill., 1901-03; B.S. in C.E., U. of Mo., 1908; m. Lois Jean Andrews, Dec. 27, 1914; children—Elisabeth, Marcia Anne. Appraisal and valuation engr. with Interstate Telegraph & Telephone Co., in Ill., 1908; pvt. engring. practice in Ia., 1908-09; topographic engr. with U.S. Geol. Survey in N.D., 1909; asst. engr. Ill. Highway Commn., 1909-10; with Internat. Boundary Commn., May 1910—; engr. in charge field parties, Mont., N.D. and Minn. until 1915; chief engr. U.S. Sect. of Commn., 1915—, in charge work of commn. on line between Alaska and Can. and U.S. and Can.; apptd. U.S. commr. on Internat. Boundary Commn. U.S.—Alaska and Can., May 3, 1929. Mem. Bd. Surveys and Maps of Fed. Govt., apptd. chmn. 1921, of com. Am. Engring. Council to investigate devices for stabilizing business as part of the work of the "Conference on Unemployment" called by President Harding, Sept. 1921. Inventor of radio and automotive devices. Mem. Iowa N.G., 1900-06. Home: Washington, D.C. Died May 17, 1935.

VAN WESTRUM, Adriaan Schade, editor; b. Amsterdam, Netherlands, June 14, 1865; s. Anthony William and Philippine Christine (Londonck) V.; ed. at Amsterdam; came to U.S., 1885; naturalized, 1902;

m. Antonie Gertrude Behaghel, of Freiburg, Germany, May 26, 1885. Asst. editor and editor, Book Chat, New York, 1887-94; asst. editor The Critic, 1895-98 asst. lit. editor, 1899-1903, lit. editor, 1904-06, New York Mail and Express; lit. editor New York Commercial, 1907; editor Internat. Trade Bulletin, 1908. on editorial staff New York Tribune, May 1910—. dramatic editor, Tribune, Feb.-Oct. 1913, lit. editor, Mar. 1913—. Author: The Cousins of the King, 1893, Margaret's Misadventure, 1898; The Devil (from Molnar's play), 1908. Home: New York, N.Y. Died 1917

VAN WINKLE, Edgar Beach, engineer; b. New York, N.Y., Mar. 4, 1842; s. Edgar Simeon and Hannah (Beach) V.; A.B., Union College, 1860, C.E., 1861; m. Elizabeth, d. Judge William Mitchell, June 7, 1876 (died 1894); m. 2d, Mary Flower, d. William Speiden, of New York, June 3, 1899. Employed on Croton water works extension, 1861-62; pvt. and 1st lt., 1862, capt., 1865, U.S.V.; served on staffs of Gens. Viele, Gilmore and Hatch in Civil War. Elected Companion (1st class) Mil. Order Loyal Legion, 1866, recorder N.Y. Commandery, same, 1886; mem. Commandery-in-Chief, same. Col. and division engr., 1st Div. N.G.S.N.Y., 1876-83. As civil engr. employed on sewerage system, New York; also by Erie R.R., Shepaug Valley R.R.; chief engr. Dept. Public Parks, New York, 1878-84. Home: New York, and Litchfield, Conn. Died Apr. 27, 1920.

VAN WINKLE, Walling Wallenson, lawyer; b. Lodi, N.J., Nov. 19, 1845; s. Adolphus Walling and Petrina Van W.; ed. New York U.; office course in law; m. Hannah Cook, Oct. 26, 1868. Practiced in Parkersburg, 1866—; mem. Van Winkle & Ambler, 1875—, principally identified with organization and management of corps.; pres. 1st Nat. Bank, Peerless Milling Co.; dist. counsel B.&O. R.R.; dir. Parkersburg Industrial Co., Ohio River Bridge & Ferry Co., Shaffer Oil & Refining Co. (Chicago), Kanawha Traction & Electric Co. (Chicago), etc. Republican. Mem. Dutch Ref. Ch. Mason. Home: Parkersburg, W.Va. Died Apr. 15, 1921.

VAN WYCK, Augustus, lawyer; b. New York, Oct. 14, 1850; s. Hon. William and Lydia A. (Maverick) V.; prep. edn., Phillips Exeter Acad., N.H.; A.B., U. of N.C., 1864, A.M.; m. Leila G. Wilkins. Judge Superior City Ct. of Brooklyn, 1884-96; justice Supreme Ct. of N.Y., 1896-98; member State Dem. Com. of N.Y., many yrs.; del. numerous Dem. nat., city and dist. convs.; pres. Kings County Gen. Com., 1882; Dem. candidate for gov. of N.Y. against Theodore Roosevelt, 1898. Grand master Zeta Psi Fraternity of North America, 1882; pres. N.Y. Assn. of Zeta Psi, 1913; pres. Holland Soc. New York, 1892, 1919-20; pres. U. of N.C. Alumni Assn. of New York, 1900-13; trustee and pres. N.E. Soc., Brooklyn. Mem. standing com. Episcopal Ch. Diocese of L.I. Died June 8, 1922.

VAN WYCK, Robert Anderson, mayor; b. New York, July 20, 1849; s. William and Lydia A. (Maverick) V.; brother Augustus V.; LL B. (at head of class), Columbia, 1872. Judge City Court of New York, 1889-97; elected 1st mayor of Greater New York as Democrat, defeating Seth Low and Gen. B. F. Tracy, and served from Jan. 1898, to Jan. 1902. A founder of and first pres. Holland Society. Died Nov. 14, 1918.

VAN ZANDT, Clarence Duncan, mayor; b. Rochester, N.Y., Mar. 21, 1853; s. John Jacob and Mary Ann Harris V.; ed. pub. and pvt. schs.; m. Mary Emily White, Nov. 30, 1881 (dec.); children—Marie (Mrs. C. C. Keehn), Marjorie (dec.), Howard (dec.), Harold (dec.). Began with Paine Drug Co., Rochester, 1868, pres. and treas., 1910—. Mayor of Rochester, Jan. 1, 1922—. Mem. 54th Regt. N.G.N.Y., 1870-76. Republican. Presbyn. Mason. Home: Rochester, N.Y. Died June 17, 1926.

VAN ZANDT, Clarence Elmer, mfr.; b. Eagle Mills, N.Y., Nov. 7, 1861; s. Peter H. and Mary (Stafford) V.; grad. State Normal Coll., Albany, N.Y., 1880; m. Carrie D. Abbott, June 15, 1886. Pres. Van Zandt's, Inc., mfrs. collars and cuffs; vice pres. Albia Box Co. Mem. bd. Samaritan Hosp. Mem. Ch. of Christ. Mason. Home: Troy, N.Y. Died Nov. 22, 1936.

VAN ZANDT, Khleber Miller; b. Franklin Co., Tenn., Nov. 7, 1836; s. Isaac and Frances Cooke (Lipscomb) V.; m. 3d, Octavia Pendleton, Oct. 8, 1885. Began in banking business in Fort Worth, Tex., 1874; pres. Fort Worth Nat. Bank, 1884—; mem. Tex. Ho. of Rep., 1873. Served as 2d lt., maj., C.S.A., 1861-65; past gen. comdr. Confed. Vets. of U.S. Democrat. Men. Christian (Disciples) Ch. Home: Fort Worth, Tex. Died Mar. 19, 1930.

VAN ZANDT Marie (Mme. Petrovich Tscherinoff), prima donna; b. New York, 1858; d. of Mme. Van Z., a singer; g.d. Signor Blitz, musician; musical edn. in Europe; m. Prof. Petrovich Tscherinoff, of Moscow, Russia, May 1898. Début as Zerlina in Don Giovanni, Turin, 1882; later appeared in Paris in Lakme at Opera Comique; was the protégée of Mrs. John W. Mackay; sang at all European capitals in grand opera. First appearance in U.S. at Metropolitan Opera House, New York, 1891. Retired from stage and living abroad. Died Nov. 27, 1918.

VAN ZANDT, Richard Lipscomb, banker; Fort Worth, Tex., Dec. 1, 1871; s. Khleber Miller and Martha Virginia (Peete) V.; B.C.E., Agrl. and Mech. Coll. of Tex., 1890; post-grad. course in civ. engrng., Rensselaer Poly. Inst., Troy, N.Y.; m. Annabel Cooper, Oct. 26, 1898 (died Nov. 29, 1918); m. 2d, Hazel Rando, Apr. 8, 1922; 1 dau., Barbara Jean. With Fort Worth Nat. Bank, 1891-1901, Treas. Dept. of P.I., 1901-03; national bank examiner, 1905-14; governor. Federal Reserve Bank, Dallas, 1915-22; pres. Live Stock Nat. Bank, Omaha, Neb., 1923-27; receiver First Nat. Bank, St. Augustine, Fla., 1929; receiver Texas Nat. Bank, Fort Worth, Tex., 1930-36. Mason. Died Apr. 30, 1940.

VAN ZILE, Edward Sims, author; b. Troy, N.Y., May 2, 1863; s. Oscar Edward and Sarah M. (Perry) V.; A.B., Trinity Coll., Conn., 1884, A.M., 1887, L.H.D., 1903; m. Mary Morgan Bulkeley, Dec. 8, 1886. Editorial writer, Troy Times, 1884-86, New York World, 1886-90; later mgr. Literary Bur., United Press, and editor Current Literature. Author: Wanted—A Sensation, 1886; The Last of the Van Slacks, 1889; A Magnetic Man, 1890; Don Miguel, 1891; The Manhattaners, 1895; Kings in Adversity, 1897; The Dreamers, and Other Poems, 1897; With Sword and Crucifix, 1899; Defending the Bank, 1903; A Duke and His Double, 1903; Perkins, the Faker, 1905; Into the Sunset, 1914; The Game of Empires, 1915; Songs of World War, 1919; That Marvel—the Movie, 1923; also novelettes in Lippincott's Mag. and Smart Set. Corr. Wheeler Syndicate on French front, 1917; toured middle west speaking for Nat. Security League, 1918; asso. publicity writer Leonard Wood campaign, later editorial writer Rep. hdqrs., Harding campaign, 1920. Decorated Palmes d'Officier de l'Instruction, by French Govt., 1922. Home: New York, N.Y. Died May 29, 1931.

VAN ZILE, Philip Taylor, judge; b. Osceola, Pa., July 20, 1843; s. David M. and Elvira C. (Cook) V.; Ph.B., Alfred U., 1863; LL.B., Univ. of Mich., 1867; LL.D., Alfred U., 1893; m. Lizzie A. Jones, Dec. 28, 1865. Served in Battery E, 1st Ohio Arty. in Civil War. Began law practice at Charlotte, Mich., 1867; pros. atty. Eaton Co., Mich., 1868-72; judge of probate Eaton Co., 1872-75; circuit judge 5th Circuit of Mich., 1875-78; U.S. dist. atty. for Utah, 1878-84; in practice at Detroit, 1890—; sr. mem. Van Zile & Brownson, 1905-10; prosecuting atty. Wayne Co., Mich., 1909-10; circuit judge, 3d Jud. Circuit, Mich., 1911—. Dean of faculty, Detroit Coll. of Law, 1891—. Republican. Mason; Grand Comdr. K.T., Mich., 1900. Author: Bailments and Carriers; Equity Pleading and Practice, 1903. Home: Detroit, Mich. Died Oct. 28, 1917.

VARDAMAN, James Kimble, U.S. senator; b. Jackson Co., Tex., July 26, 1861; s. W. S. and Mary (Fox) V.; ed. pub. schs., Yalobusha Co., Miss.; read law, Carrollton, Miss.; m. Mrs. Anna E. Robinson, d. Dr. A.A. Burleson, May 31, 1883; children—Mrs. Alethe Fairley, Jim Money, James Kimball, Mrs. Minnie Ratliff. Admitted to bar, 1882, and began practice at Winona; editor Winona Advance, 1883, Greenwood (Miss.) Enterprise, 1890-96; established The Commonwealth, Greenwood, 1896; became editor The Issue, at Jackson, 1908. Mem. Miss. Ho. of Rep., 1890-96 (speaker, 1894); presdl. elector, 1892, 96 (pres. electoral coll.); capt. and maj. 5th U.S. Vol. Inf., 1898-99; candidate for gov., 1895, 99; elected gov., term 1904-08; candidate for U.S. senator, 1907; elected U.S. senator in 1911, for term 1913-19. Democrat. Methodist. Mason, K.P. Died June 25, 1930.

VARE, William Scott; b. Phila., Pa., Dec. 24, 1867; s. Augustus and Abigail (Stites) V.; pub. sch. edn.; m. Ida Morris, July 29, 1897; children—Beatrice, Mildred. Entered mercantile life at 15; mem. Select Council, Phila., 1898-1901; recorder of deeds, Phila., 3 terms, 1902-12; elected to 62d Congress to fill unexpired term of Gen. Henry H. Bingham; reelected 63d to 69th Congresses (1913-27), 1st Pa. Dist.; elected to U.S. Senate in 1926, term 1927-33, but rejected by Senate, 1930, because of excessive campaign expenditures. Mem. Rep. Nat. Com., 1934—. Methodist. Mason. Home: Philadelphia, Pa. Died Aug. 8, 1934.

VARIAN, Charles Stetson, lawyer; b. Dayton, O., Sept. 10, 1846; s. Miles Beach and Charlotte (Bartlett) V.; ed. acads., Springfield and Urbana, O., and Urbana U. (non-grad.); m. Florence L. Guthrie, July 29, 1871. Went from Cincinnati to San Francisco via Nicaragua, 1866; to Virginia City, Nev., 1867; co. treas., Humbolt Co., Nev., 1868-69, also deputy internal revenue assessor and collector; co. clk., 1870-72; admitted to bar, 1872; mem State Senate, Nev., 1872-73, 1874-75; U.S. atty., Nev., 1876-83; mem. Nev. Ho. of Rep., from Washoe Co., 1883 (speaker of House); asst. U.S. atty., Utah, 1884-87; U.S. atty., Utah, 1889-1903; mem. Utah Ho. of Rep., 1894; mem. Constl Conv., Utah, 1895; chmn. Police and Fire Commn., Salt Lake City, 1896; corp. counsel, Salt Lake City, 1912—; mem. State Prison Bd. of Corrections, 1917. Democrat from 1896. Mason. Home: Salt Lake City, Utah. Died Mar. 25, 1922.

VARIAN, George Edmund, artist; b. Liverpool, Eng., Oct. 16, 1865; s. Thomas J. and Laura (Melladew) V.; ed. Pub. Sch. No. 10, Brooklyn; art studies at Brooklyn Art Guild and Art Students' League, New York; m. Margaret Liseum Holland, Mar. 9, 1906. Illustrator for various mags. and books. Commissioned by McClure's to visit Mont Pelée at time of destruction of St. Pierre, and in company with George Kennan and Prof. Angelo Heilprin was first to reach the crater at top of the mountain; witnessed three eruptions of the mountain and was almost destroyed by one; accompanied Ray Stannard Baker to Europe and made illustrations for his book, "Seen in Germany"; also illustrated George Kennan's, "The Tragedy of Pelée." Exhibited at Paris Salon, 1907. Republican. Died Apr. 12, 1923.

VARIELL, Arthur Davis, physician; b. Gardiner, Me., Aug. 26, 1868; s. John Smith and Julietta (Hammond) V.; prep. edn., Me. Wesleyan Sem., Kent's Hill, 1885-87; student Portland Acad. Medicine, 1888-90; M.D., Bowdoin Med. Sch., 1894; m. Julia Curtiss, Oct. 3, 1897 (died 1909); children—Doris (Mrs. Howard Hart), Curtiss Arthur (dec.); m. 2d, Katharine B. Schley, Nov. 13, 1913; 1 son, Montfort Schley. Practiced medicine and surgery at Watertown and Waterbury, Conn., 1896-1916; sec. and half owner The Waterbury Steel Ball Co., 1916-23; vice pres. and half owner The Waterbury Lock & Specialty Co., 1923-28 (sold both interests). Served as pres. Bd. of Health, Waterbury, 2 yrs., and mem. staff Waterbury Hosp.; commr. of Canadian Govt. for State of Florida, 1932. Knighted by Patriarch of Syria; Knight of Honor of Order San Juan Bautista (Malta) of Spain; awarded Cross of Dedicacao (Portugal); Comdr. Order of the Black Eagle (Prince William of Wied); Diplome de Croix d'Honneur de l'Education Sociale (France); Knight of Honor of Imperial Constantinian Order of Saint George; Chevalier de la Grand Prix Humanitaire de Belgique. Hon. mem. Société de l'Education de France, Imperial Geog. Soc. of Iran (Persia), Société d'Education et d'Encouragement (France), etc. Colonel on Governor's staff, Kentucky. Republican. Episcopalian. Home: Kennebunk, Me. Died Apr. 16, 1940.

VARLEY, John Philip. See Langdon Elwyn Mitchell.

VARNUM, James M., lawyer; b. New York, June 29, 1848; s. Joseph B. V.; grad. Yale, 1868, LL.B., Columbia, 1871; m. Mary W. Dickey, June 14, 1899. Has practiced law, 1871—; mem. Assembly, 1879-80; Rep. candidate for atty. gen. N.Y., 1889; permanent chmn. Rep. State Conv., 1891; Rep. and Anti-Tammany Dem. candidate for judge Superior Court, 1890; senior a.d.c. to Gov. Cornell, 1880-83, with rank of col.; apptd. by Gov. Morton, 1895, paymaster gen. N.Y. with rang of brig. gen.; apptd. by Gov. Roosevelt, 1899, surrogate Co. of New York; v.p. Soc. of the Cincinnati in R.I.; chevalier Legion of Honor of France; gov. Soc. of Colonial Wars, N.Y. Home: New York, N.Y. Died 1907.

VASEY, Frank Thomas, supt. schs.; b. Taylorville, Ill., Oct. 26, 1876; s. Dowsland and Elizabeth (Hadley) V.; A.B., U. of Neb., 1904; A.M., State U. of Ia., 1918; m. Mable Walker Gibbs, June 4, 1912; children—Robert Hamilton, Virginia Walker. Teacher rural schs., 1902-06; prin. high sch., Pawnee City, Neb., 1904-06; supt. schs. Tarkio, 1906-10, Albia, Ia., 1910-13, Charles City, Ia., 1913-18, Mason City, Ia., 1918-30, Springfield, Ill., 1930—. Conglist. Rotarian. Home: Springfield Ill. Died Apr. 1, 1936.

VAUCLAIN, Samuel Matthews, chmn. bd. Baldwin Locomotive Works; b. Phila., Pa., May 18, 1856; s. Andrew C. and Mary A. (Campbell) V.; ed. pub. schs., Altoona, Pa.; Sc.D., U. of Pa., 1906, Worcester Poly. Inst., 1931; LL D., Villanova Coll.; m. Annie Kearney, Apr. 17, 1879; children—Samuel Matthews (dec.), Mary (Mrs. Franklin Abbott), Jacques L., Anne, Charles Parry, Constance Marshall (Mrs. William H. Hamilton, dec.). With Pa. R.R. System, 1872-83; with The Baldwin Locomotive Works, 1883—, v.p., 1911-19, pres., 1919-29, chmn. bd., 1929—; chmn. bd. Standard Steel Works Co., Baldwin-Southwark Corp., The Whitcomb Locomotive Co., Federal Steel Foundry Co., Baldwin-Southwark Corp., I. P. Morris & De La Vergne, Inc., De La Vergne Engine Co., Mfrs. Mutual Fire Ins. Co. Chmn. locomotive and car com., Council Nat. Defense, and chmn. spl. advisory com. on plants and munitions, War Industries Bd., World War. Chmn. Municipal Gas Commn., Phila.; mgr. Northern Liberties Hosp.; president and trustee Bryn Mawr Hospital. Mem. John Scott Medal Fund Committee; mem. numerous societies. Awarded D.S.M. (U.S.), 1919; Il Cancelliere Order Crown of Italy, 1920; Order of Polonia Restituta, 1923; Chevalier Legion of Honor (France), 1919; John Scott medal, 1891, 1931. Republican. Episcopalian. Home: Rosemont, Pa. Died Feb. 4, 1940.

VAUGHAN, Alfred Jefferson, maj. gen. and State comdr. United Confederate Veterans for Tenn.; b. Dinwiddie Co., Va., May 10, 1830; grad. Va. Mil. Inst., 1851; practiced as civil engr.; made survey of Hannibal & St. Joseph R.R.; later U.S. surveyor for dist. of Calif.; settled in Miss.; m. Martha J. Hardaway, 1856. Settled on farm in Miss.; served, capt. to brig. gen., in Confederate army; lost leg at Chickamauga; farmed in Miss. until 1872; as gen. agt. of Nat. Grange organized State Granges of Miss., Ark.

and Tenn.; was master State Grange of Miss.; established in mercantile business in Memphis, 1873; clerk criminal court Shelby Co., 1878-86. Democrat. Home: Memphis, Tenn. Died 1899.

VAUGHAN, Charles Parker, manufacturer; b. New Portland, Me., Feb. 17, 1867; s. Joseph Warren and Martha (Cutts) V.; grad. pub. schs., 1882; student Phillips Acad., Andover, Mass., 1884-87; Sc.D., Bucknell U., 1915; m. Fannie Winthrop Thomas, Dec. 27, 1898; children—Catherine Nelson (Mrs. Harry H., Hellerman, Jr.), Barbara Thomas (Mrs. William D. Watson, Jr.). Entered father's business, Vaughan Machine Co., 1887, continued in it until 1901; asso. with Dungan, Hood & Co., tanners of leather, 1902—, pres., 1906—; dir. Corn Exchange Nat. Bank & Trust Co., Fidelity Mutual Life Ins. Co. Apptd. dep. U.S. consul gen., Frankfurt, Germany, 1898. With Mass. Vol. Militia, 1901-11, retired with rank of capt. Chmn. bd. trustees Bucknell U.; v.p. and dir. Phila. Chamber of Commerce. Republican. Presbyn. Mason. Home: Philadelphia, Pa. Died Mar. 20, 1936.

VAUGHAN, Elmer E., surgeon; b. Woodbury, Vt., Aug. 18, 1865; s. Isaac Chace and Lucinda Thare (Blake) V.; ed. Lamoille Central Acad., Hyde Park, Vt.; Boston City Hosp. Training Sch.; M.D., Hahnemann Med. Coll., Chicago, 1889; post-grad. work, Rush Med. Coll., 1898, 99; m. Lydia Eldora Beecher, Dec. 25, 1890. Practiced, Chicago, 1889—; pres. bd. of dirs., Chicago Union Hosp.; pres. Chicago Union Hosp. Training Sch. for Nurses. Republican. Home: Chicago, Ill. Died Apr. 30, 1926.

VAUGHAN, Horace Worth, judge; b. Marion Co., Tex., Dec. 2, 1867; s. George T. and Tippah (Lary) V.; common sch. edn.; studied law under father; m. Pearl Lockett, Nov. 21, 1888. Admitted to Tex. bar, 1885; city atty., Texarkana, 1890-97; co. atty., Bowie Co., 1898-1906; dist. atty., 1906-10; mem. Tex. State Senate, 1910-13; mem. 63d Congress (1913-15), 1st Tex.; asst. U.S. atty. for Hawaii, Oct.-Dec. 1915, and U.S. atty., Dec. 1915-Apr. 1916; U.S. dist. judge, Dist. of Hawaii, Apr. 4, 1916—. Democrat. Methodist. Mason. Died Nov. 10, 1922.

VAUGHAN, John Colin, surgeon; b. in cabin of ship, Calais, Me., July 29, 1875; s. Capt. John A. and Ann (Larner) V.; lived at sea until 15, ed. pub. schs. and business coll.; M.D., Coll. Phys. and Surg. (Columbia), 1907; m. Mrs. Agnes Luidlan Roesler, May 29, 1912 (died 1919); m. 2d, Jane Copas, Oct. 1, 1921. Chief of Vanderbilt Clinic, 1910-17, also inst. surgery, Coll. Phys. and Surg.; asso. in anatomy same coll., 1910-21; asst. surgeon, 1915-17, and asst. pathologist, 1916-17, Presbyn. Hosp.; asst. visiting surgeon, acting dir., Bellevue Hosp., 1917-19; visiting surgeon Sing Sing Prison, 1914-22; visiting surgeon and dir. Volunteer Hosp., 1914-20, Beekman Street Hosp., 1920-22; asst. visiting surgeon Welfare Hosp.; cons. surgeon Manhattan Eye and Ear Hosp. Head of Exemption Bd., World War, also instr. Med. R.C., Bellevue Hosp., and in traumatic surgery, Coll. Phys. and Surg. Chmn. Am. Birth Control Soc.; med. dir. Workers Health Bur. Fellow Am. Coll. Surgeons. Democrat. Baptist. Author: Text Book on Minor Surgery, 1922. Engaged in Polar exploration 6 yrs. Home: New York, N.Y. Died Jan. 12, 1940.

VAUGHAN, John Gaines, clergyman, educator; b. Arcadia, Tenn., Mar. 5, 1858; s. Kenley Green and Rachel Anderson (Butler) V.; A.B., Syracuse U., 1882; B.D., Drew Theol. Sem., 1883; Ph.D., East Tenn. U. (now Chattanooga U.), 1885; (D.D., Am. U. of Harriman, Tenn., 1898); worked way through colls.; m. Mary A. Shober, Mar. 19, 1884 (died 1913); m. 2d, Annabelle Ambrose, June 30, 1915. Ordained M.E. ministry, 1882; pastor Ames Ch., New Orleans, La., 1883-84, Springboro, O., 1885-86, St. Paul Ch., Dayton, O., 1887-92, Grace Ch., Urbana, 1893-99, St. Paul Ch., Dayton, 1899-1905; sec. Bd. of Missions M.E. Ch., Special Funds, 1905-09; prof. comparative religion and missions, Lawrence Coll., Appleton, Wis., 1909—; secured the endowment for his chair. Author: Gem Encyclopedia of Illustration, 1889; The Wonderful Book (Bible), 1906; Diamond Dust in Dew Drops, 1913; Religion a Comparative Study, 1919. Lecturer. Home: Appleton, Wis. Died May 11, 1921.

VAUGHAN, John Henry, educator; b. Dobson, N.C., Aug. 13, 1880; s. John Martin and Sarah Diana (Holyfield) V.; A.B., U. of N.C., 1904, A.M., 1905; studied U. of Tenn., 1907, U. of Calif., 1918; m. Cora Lee Spainhower, July 5, 1905. Prin. high sch., Roswell, N.M., 1906-07; prof. history and English, N.M. Normal U., 1907-09; prof. history, 1909-13, prof. history and economics, 1913—, dean Sch. of Gen. Science, 1917—, N.M. Agrl. and Mech. Coll. Democrat. Presbyn. Odd Fellow. Author: History and Government of New Mexico, 1921. Home: State College, N.M. Deceased.

VAUGHAN, Lawrence J., clergyman, lecturer; b. Newark, N.J., 1864; s. James and Ann (Hogan) V.; student St. Benedict's Coll., Newark, St. Lawrence Coll., Wis., St. Vincent's, Mo., Kendrick Sem., St. Louis. St. John's Univ., Minn.; adopted theatrical profession, but later studied for priesthood; ordained priest R.C. Ch., at Collegeville, Minn., 1899. Founder of St. Joseph's R.C. Student Fund (for edn. of poor boys), also of Altoona Inst., sch. for boys and girls. Lecturing, 1903—. Also poet and author of plays: Disowned, Alice and Alexander, Prince Carl, Nance of Old Thunder. Home: Janesville, Wis. Died 1909.

VAUGHAN, Victor Clarence, scientist; b. Mt. Airy, Mo., Oct. 27, 1851; s. John and Adeline (Dameron) V.; B.S., Mt. Pleasant Coll., Mo., 1872; M.S., U. of Mich., 1875, Ph.D., 1876, M.D., 1878, LL.D., 1900; hon. Sc.D., U. of Western Pa., 1897; LL.D., Central Coll., 1910; Jefferson Med. Coll., Phila., 1915, U. of Mo., 1923; m. Dora Catherine Taylor, August 21, 1877; children—Victor C. (dec.), John Walter, Herbert Hunter, Henry Frieze, Warren Taylor. Assistant in chem. lab., 1875-83, lecturer med. chemistry, 1879-80, asst. prof., 1880-83, prof. physiol. and pathol. chemistry and asso. prof. therapeutics and materia medica, 1883-87, prof. hygiene and physiol. chemistry, and dir. Hygienic Lab., 1887-1909, dean dept. medicine and surgery, 1891-1921, U. of Mich. in Santiago campaign, 1898, as maj. and surgeon 63d Mich. Vol. Inf.; apptd. div. surgeon, 1898; recommended by President for bvt. of lt. col.; col., M.C. U.S.A., in charge of communicable diseases, 1917-18. Chmn. div. of med. sciences, Nat. Research Council; member Typhoid Commn. Awarded D.S.M. Pres. Assn. Am. Physicians, 1908-09; pres. A.M.A., 1914-15. Knight Legion of Honor, France, 1923. Author: Osteology and Myology of the Domestic Fowl, 1876; Text-book of Physiological Chemistry (3 edits.), 1879-83; Ptomaines and Leucomaines and Cellular Toxins (with Dr. Novy); Protein Split Products (with Victor C. Vaughan, Jr., and J. Walter Vaughan), 1913; (with Henry F. Vaughan and George T. Palmer) Epidemiology and Public Health, 3 vols.; A Doctor's Memories. Mng. editor Jour. Lab. and Clin. Medicine, 1915-23. Home: Detroit, Mich. Died Nov. 21, 1929.

VAUGHN, Francis Arthur, consulting engr.; b. Prairie du Chien, Wis., Dec. 6, 1871; s. Orion Squiers and Margaret (Howell) V.; B.S. in E.E., U. of Wis., 1895; m. Lucile K. Phillips, Jan. 11, 1897; children—Shirley Louise, Janice Margaret. With Milwaukee Electric Ry. & Light Co., 1896-1910; mem. Vaughn & Meyer, 1910-13 and 1916-21; pres. F. A. Vaughn, Inc., 1921-24. Firm consulting engr. State Bd. of Control of Wis., 1910-16, of Minn., 1916-20; consulting engr. City and Co. of Milwaukee on st. lighting, 1913 and 1921, 22; radio mgr., Radiocast Sta., WSOE, Milwaukee; vice-pres. Sch. Engring. and pres. Coll. Elec. Engring., Milwaukee. Lecturer U. of Pa., 1916. Fellow Am. Inst. E.E.; mem. numerous professional societies. Republican. Editor: Electrical Meterman's Handbook, 1912. Home: Milwaukee, Wis. Died Jan. 23, 1934.

VAUGHN, William James, university prof.; b. Wilcox Co., Ala., Feb. 15, 1834; s. John Pulliam and Rebecca (Richards) V.; A.B., U. of Ala., 1857, A.M., 1860; (LL.D., U. of Miss., 1883); m. Abbie Scott, Aug. 17, 1865. Tutor mathematics, 1857-60, instr. Latin and Greek, 1860-63, prof. mathematics, 1863-65, U. of Ala.; prin. Tuscaloosa (Ala.) Female College, 1865-66, Centenary Female Inst., Summerfield, Ala., 1867-71; prof. physics and astronomy, U. of Ala., 1871-73; pres. Tenn. Female Coll., Franklin, 1873-78; prof. mathematics, 1878-82, founded Sch. of Engring., 1881-82, U. of Ala.; prof. mathematics, 1882-95, mathematics and astronomy, 1895—, chief librarian, 1886—, Vanderbilt Univ. Home: Nashville, Tenn. Deceased.

VAUX, George, Jr., lawyer; b. Phila., Pa., Dec. 18, 1863; s. George and Sarah (Morris) V.; B.S., Haverford Coll., 1884; LL.B., U. of Pa., 1888; admitted to bar; m. Mary W. James, Apr. 2, 1907; children—George, III, Henry James. Largely engaged in reformatory and penological work, including Phila. House of Refuge; insp. State Penitentiary, Eastern Dist. of Pa., 1898-1905; mem. U.S. Bd. Indian Commrs., 1906— (chmn.). Wrote contbns. to Proc. Acad. Natural Sciences of Phila., 1899, and subsequently including original researches on glaciers of British Columbia. Mem. bd. mgrs. Wistar Inst., Haverford Coll., Carson Coll. Home: Bryn Mawr, Pa. Died Oct. 24, 1927.

VAWTER, Charles Erastus, supt. Miller Manual Labor School, Albemarle, Va., June 20, 1878—; b. Monroe Co., W.Va., June 9, 1841; s. John H. V. (who was 24 yrs. mem. Va. legislature); entered Emory and Henry Coll., 1858, left in junior yr., serving in Confederate army, 1861-65, in Stonewall Brigade, became capt.; prisoner at Ft. Delaware, Mar.-June 1865; re-entered Emory and Henry Coll.; grad., 1866; spl. course mathematics, Univ. of Va.; m. Virginia, d. Prof. Edmund Longley, July 24, 1866. Prof. mathematics Emory and Henry Coll., 1868-78; mem. bd. visitors, Va. Polytechnic Inst., Blacksburg, Va., 1886-1903; supt. Sunday Sch. Work, Albemarle Co., Va.; rector bd. visitors Va. Colored Normal and Industrial Inst., Petersburg, Va. Died 1905.

VAWTER, John William, illustrator; b. Boone Co., Va., Apr. 13, 1871; s. Dr. Louis A. and Emma Mary (Dameron) V.; educated in the public schools, Greenfield, Indiana; m. Mary Howey Murray, Nov. 19, 1902 (divorced 1919); m. 2d, Ola Lackey Genolin, Sept. 2, 1923. First professional work as artist on Indianapolis Sentinel, 1891; in 1897 wrote and illustrated series of comic verses for Cincinnati Commercial Gazette; in 1899, collaborated with sister, Clara Vawter, in producing child's book "Of Such Is the Kingdom" (title later changed to The Rabbit's Ransom). Has made occasional illustrations for Indianapolis News, Judge, Life and Success, New York. Now devoting time to landscape paintings in oil. Presbyn. Democrat. Illustrator: The Rabbit's Ransom, Bob Burdette's Smiles, E. O. Laughlin's Johnnie, Nesbit's Trail to Boyland, Bartlett's Tales of Kankakee Land, complete series of Riley's books, and several other books and poems. Awarded prizes, Chicago Salon, 1925, 26, etc. Home: Nashville, Ind. Died Feb. 11, 1941.

VAWTER, Keith, Chautauqua mgr.; b. Indianola, Ia., Apr. 1872; s. John Beverly and Flora (Keith) V.; student Drake U., 1895; LL.D., Culver-Stockton Coll., Canton, Mo., 1931; m. Cora E. Kiser, Aug. 1899. Mem. Vawter & Son, booksellers, Des Moines, Ia., 1896-99; established Standard Lecture Bur., Des Moines, 1899; became connected with Redpath Lyceum Bur., Chicago, 1902; organized Redpath Chautauquas, Chicago, 1903; organized Chautauqua circuit, 1904, Redpath-Vawter System, Redpath Chautauquas of N.Y. and N.E., 1913; now sec. and treas. Redpath Chautauqua of N.Y. and N.E.; sec. Redpath Lyceum Bur., Sunnyside Farms Co.; pres. Center Point Walker Bank & Trust Co. Pres. bd. trustees Drake U., 1918-19. Dir. Speakers Bur. for 3d and 4th Liberty Loans, Ia. Republican. Mem. Disciples of Christ Ch. Mason. Died Feb. 5, 1937.

VAYHINGER, Monroe, univ. pres.; b. Delaware, Ind., May 28, 1855; s. Gustavus and Margerethe (Schweklin) V.; A.B., Moores Hill Coll., 1883, A.M., 1886; B.D., Garrett Bibl. Inst., Evanston, Ill., 1903; studied U. of Chicago, 1898 99; D.D., Taylor Univ., 1908, LL.D., 1937; D.D., Moores Hill College, 1908; m. Culla F. Johnson, Mar. 28, 1889; children—Harold Dale (dec.), Paul Johnson, Lois Miriam Browning. Began teaching in pub. schs. at 16; prof. mathematics and English Bible, Moores Hill Coll., 1883-90, prof. philosophy and English Bible, 1894-1904, vice pres., 1896-1904; ordained M.E. ministry, 1885; pastor Madison, Ind., 1904-06, Hartsville, 1906-08; pres. Taylor U., 1908-21; teacher of Bible, Missionary Bands Bible Sch., Indianapolis, Ind. Republican. Mem. Ind. Conf. M.E. Ch., Ind. Coll. Assn., Ind. Teachers' Assn. Editor Taylor Univ. Register, 1908-12. Evangelist. Home: Upland, Ind. Died Nov. 1, 1938.

VEATCH, Arthur Clifford, geologist; b. Evansville, Ind., Oct. 26, 1878; s. Harry and Mary Kate (Babcock) V.; Ind. U., 1896-97, Cornell U., 1898 and 1900-01, U. of Wis., 1905; m. Caroline Hornbrook Evans, Apr. 16, 1902. Asst. geologist, La. Geol. Survey, 1898-1900; asst. in charge areal and stratigraphic geology, Cornell Sch. of Field Geology, 1900-01; petroleum geologist, Beaumont, Tex., 1901-02; prof. geology, La. State U., and geologist La. Geol. Survey, 1902; asst. in charge underground water investigations, La., Ark. and L.I., 1902 04; asst. geologist, 1904-06, geologist, 1906-10, U.S. Geol. Survey; chief geologist Gen. Asphalt Co., Trinidad and Venezuela, 1910-11; scientific adviser U.S. Dept. Justice, 1912, 1930-31; in charge oil exploration, fgn. dept., S. Pearson & Son, Ltd., London, 1913-19; cons. petroleum technologist, U.S. Bur. Mines, 1919—; in charge exploration dept. Sinclair Consol. Oil Corp., 1919-28; cons. petroleum geologist, 1928—. Investigated mining laws of Australia and New Zealand, as spl. commr., apptd. by President Roosevelt, 1907-08; organizer and chmn. oil, coal, mineral and water power bds., U.S. Geol. Survey, 1908-10. Mem. numerous professional societies. Republican. Presbyterian. Author: Quito to Bogota, 1917; Evolution of the Congo Basin, 1935. Home: Port Washington, L.I. Died Dec. 25, 1938.

VEATCH, Byron Elbert, author; b. nr. Springfield, Ill., Aug. 1, 1858; s. Dr. William H. and Elizabeth Harney (Sweet) V.; ed. pub. schs.; m. Fanny Elizabeth Roworth, Jan. 24, 1882; 1 dau., Marie. Spent early life in Ariz. and Colo., in cattle and in mercantile business at Pueblo, Colo., until 1884; now v.p., treas. Bell Lock Co., Chicago. Republican. Mason. Author: Men Who Dared, 1909; (booklets) Next Christmas, 1913; The Two Samurai, 1913; My River, 1923. Home: Chicago, Ill. Died Jan. 23, 1930.

VEAZIE, George Augustus, composer; b. Boston, Dec. 18, 1835; s. George A. and Hannah K. V.; ed. Eliot Sch., Boston; studies in music, practice and composition begun at about 15 yrs. of age; m. Anna K. Wellman, Jan. 10, 1858; m. 2d, Elizabeth F. Stearns, Sept. 10, 1895; m. 3d, R. Grace Leger, Sept. 30, 1899. In sch. music work was for yrs. associated with Luther Whiting Mason; sec. Nat. Summer Music Sch. several yrs.; supervisor music Chelsea pub. schs., 1869-1903; mem. faculty N.E. Conservatory of Music, 1888-1902. Composed several light operas, 1864-80; author of various sch. music books, 1886-1906. Home: Chelsea, Mass. Died Nov. 20, 1915.

VEBLEN, Andrew Anderson, retired college prof.; b. Ozaukee County, Wis., Sept. 24, 1848; s. Thomas Anderson and Kari (Bunde) V.; A.B., Carleton Coll., Minn., 1877, A.M., 1880; Johns Hopkins, 1881-83; m. Kirsti Hougen, July 11, 1877 (died 1908); children—Oswald, Agnes E. and Anne, Gertrude Ingeborg, Signy Arndora, Harold, Thorkel Alfred, Hilda Ingeleiv, Elling Haldor; m. 2d, Mrs. Elizabeth A. Ringstad, 1912 (died 1925). Prof. English and other branches, Luther Coll., Decorah, Ia., 1877-81; instr. and asst. prof. of mathematics, 1883-86, asst. prof. and prof. of physics, 1886-1905, State U. of Iowa; retired, 1905. Chief organizer, 1901, and pres. Valdris Samband (soc. of natives of Valdris, Norway, and their descendants, hon. pres., 1920—); pres. Council of Bygdelags (sister societies of Valdris Samband), 1916-20. Decorated Knight Order of St. Olaf by King of Norway, 1925. Editor Samband (monthly), 1910-17. Translator Vogt's Bible History, 1878. Author: The Valdris Book, 1920; Veblen Genealogy, 1925. Editor: Vang's Valdris-Rispo, 1930. Home: Los Angeles, Calif. Died 1932.

VEBLEN, Thorstein B., teacher, author; A.B., Carleton Coll., 1880; grad. student Johns Hopkins; Ph.D., Yale, 1884; fellow in economics and finance, Cornell, 1891-92; fellow U. of Chicago, 1892-93. Reader in polit. economy, 1893-94, asso., 1894-96, instr., 1896-1900, asst. prof, 1900-06, U. of Chicago; asso. prof. economics, Leland Stanford Jr. U., 1906-09; lecturer in economics, U. of Mo., 1911-18; teacher, New School for Social Research, New York, 1918—. Mng. editor Journal of Political Economy, 1896-1905. Author: The Theory of the Leisure Class, 1899; The Theory of Business Enterprise, 1904; The Instinct of Workmanship, 1914; Imperial Germany and the Industrial Revolution, 1915; An Inquiry Into the Nature of Peace and the Terms of Its Perpetuation, 1917; The Higher Learning in America, 1918; The Vested Interests, 1919; The Place of Science in Modern Civilization and Other Papers, 1920; The Engineers and the Price System, 1921; Absentee Ownership and Business Enterprise in Recent Times, 1923; translator: The Laxdæla Saga, 1925. Home: Palo Alto, Calif. Died Aug. 3, 1929.

VECKI, Victor G., surgeon; b. Zagreb, Jugoslavia, Dec. 8, 1857; s. John and Katharina Vecki de Gjurkovecki; ed. Zagreb, 1863-75, Imperial and Royal U. of Vienna, 1875-81, also M.D., 1881; m. 2d, Bessie Gallagher; children (by 1st wife)—Victor G. (D.D.S.), Marion (attorney), Morrell (M.D.). Has served as captain-surgeon Austro-Hungarian Army, Royal Croatian sanitary councillor. Author: Pathologie und Therapy der maennlichen Impotenz, 2d edit., 1897; Warum Tolstoy Aertze hasst und Liebe verachtet?, 1892 (confiscated by censor in Vienna); Pathology and Treatment of Sexual Impotence, 6th edit., 1919; Prevention of Sexual Diseases, 1910; Alcohol and Prohibition in Their Relation to Civilization and the Art of Living, 1923; Threatening Shadows (novel), 1931; Prevention of Premature Senility, 1931, 2d edit., 1937. Home: San Francisco, Calif. Died Nov. 16, 1938.

VEDDER, Charles Stuart, clergyman; b. Schenectady, N.Y., Oct. 7, 1826; s. Albert A. and Susan (Fulton) V.; A.B., Union Coll., 1851; D.D., New York U., 1876; D.D., 1876, LL.D., 1888, Charleston Coll.; L.H.D., Union Coll., Schenectady, N.Y., 1911; m. Helen A. Scovel, June 7, 1854. Ordained Presbyn. ministry, 1861; pastor Summerville, S.C., 1861-66, Huguenot Ch., Charleston, S.C., 1866-1914. Pres. Howard Assn., Training Sch. for Nurses, Ministerial Union. Home: Charleston, S.C. Died 1917.

VEDDER, Commodore Perry, lawyer; b. Ellicottville, N.Y., Feb. 23, 1838; drove team and worked on canal; ed. Springville Acad. Served, pvt. to lt. col., N.Y. vols.; captured at Chancellorsville; spent 2 weeks in Libby Prison and paroled; served with Sherman from Chattanooga to Atlanta, and from Atlanta to the sea and until close of war. Admitted to bar, 1866; register in bankruptcy, 1867-75; mem. N.Y. Assembly, 1872-75, Senate, 1875-77, 1884-91; state assessor, 1880-83; author of N.Y. laws taxing gifts, legacies and collateral inheritances, also of a bill taxing corps. for privilege of organization, etc. Del.-at-large N.Y. Constl. Conv., 1894; U.S. internal revenue assessor, 2 yrs. Pres. Va. Copper Co. of London, Eng., Elko Paint Co. of N.Y. and N.J., Ice Lines, Bank of Ellicottville, Bank of Norwood, Brigantine Transportation Co., Brooklyn Dock and Terminal Co. Home: Ellicottville, N.Y. Died 1910.

VEDDER, Elihu, painter, modeler; b. New York, Feb. 26, 1836; ed. Brinkerhoff Sch., Brooklyn; painted with Mattison at Sherburne, N.Y., and in atelier of Picot, Paris, 1856; worked in Italy, 1857-61; returned to U.S. until 1865, then, after one winter in Paris, went, in Jan., 1867, to Rome, where he established residence, making frequent visits to the U.S.; m. Caroline E. B. Rosekrans, July 13, 1869 (died 1909). His subjects principally imaginative; in 1884 he illustrated the Rubaiyat of Omar Khayyam; 5 decorative panels and the mosaic Minerva in the Congressional Library at Washington; panel in Bowdoin Coll. N.A., 1865; mem. Am. Acad. Arts and Letters. Author: The Digressions of V., 1910; Miscellaneous Moods (verse), 1914. Died Jan. 29, 1923.

VEDDER, Henry Clay, prof. ch. history; b. DeRuyter, N.Y., Feb. 26, 1853; s. Meander W. and Harriet (Cook) V.; A.B., U. of Rochester, 1873, A.M., 1876, D.D., 1897; grad. Rochester Theol. Sem., 1876; m. Minnie M. Lingham, Sept. 11, 1877; children—Edward Bright, Henry Rossiter (dec.). On editorial staff The Examiner, Bapt. newspaper, New York, 1876-92, editor, 1892-94; also editor Baptist Quarterly Rev., 1885-92; prof. ch. history, Crozer Theol. Sem., Dec. 1, 1894, until retired, 1926; editorial staff Chester Times, 1929—. Author: A History of the Baptists of the Middle States, 1898; The Baptists (vol. in the Story of the Churches series), 1903; Balthazar Hübmaier (in the "Heroes of the Reformation" series), 1906; Christian Epoch Makers (lectures on the history of missions), 1907; Our New Testament—Where Did We Get It?, 1908; Church History Handbooks (vols. I-IV), 1909; Socialism and the Ethics of Jesus, 1912; The Reformation in Germany, 1913; The Gospel of Jesus and the Problems of Democracy, 1914; The Johannine Writings and the Johannine Problem, 1917; The Fundamentals of Christianity, 1921; A Short History of Baptist Missions, 1927; also many articles in magazines, newspapers, encyclopædias. Home: Chester, Pa. Died Oct. 13, 1935.

VEDITZ, Charles William Augustus, economist; b. at Phila., Nov. 18, 1872; s. William and Augusta (Tramm) V.; Ph.B., U. of Pa., 1891; U. of Halle, 1891-93, Ph.D., and A.M.; U. of Berlin, 1893-94, U. of Leipzig, 1894-95, and U. of Paris, 1896-99, LL.B.; studies in economics, pub. law, sociology, history, Paris Sch. of Anthropology, 1896-98, Sch. of Polit. Science, 1898-99, Sorbonne, 1897-98, École des Hautes Études, 1896-97, Collège des Sciences Sociales, 1898-1900, Paris Sch. of Law, 1897-1900; m. Mildred Rita Onslow, 1901; children—Jean Robert, Ivy Constance, William Paul Carroll. Prof. economics, Bates College, 1901-05; same chair, George Washington U., 1905-09, and acting dean dept. of polit. sciences, 1908-09 and 1912-13, prof. sociology, 1910-13; spl. agt. U.S. Bur. of Corps., 1909; agent Bur. of Labor to investigate child labor in Europe, 1909; prof. sociology, U. of Mich., 1908; lecturer on economics, Yale, 1909-10; chief examiner, U.S. Tariff Bd., 1910-12; sec. Bd. of Arbitration which settled controversy between Am. Brotherhood Locomotive Engrs. and 52 railroads in U.S. (compiled and edited final report and award); tariff expert to Senate Com. on Finance, 1913; spl. agt. U.S. Dept. Commerce, 1914; commercial attaché of U.S. at Paris, Madrid and Berne, Sept. 1914-18; served for U.S. on inter-allied economic conferences; satistician U.S. Housing Corp., 1918; foreign trade expert, Bur. Applied Economics, Washington, D.C., foreign trade adviser, with Metal Export Co., New York, 1919, in Norway, Sweden and Germany, 1920; research economist, Nat. Industrial Conf. Bd., New York, 1920; lit. work, Washington, D.C., and corr. for Paris journal, "Le Soir," 1921—; asso. Internat. Inst. Sociology; founded Am. Sociol. Soc., 1905, and sec. 5 yrs. Author: The Philadelphia Gas Works, 1891; The Recent Development of American Pottery, 1891; Thuenen's Wertlehre (in Germany), 1896; Gide's Political Economy (Am. edit.), 1903; The American Revolution, 1904; Child Labor Laws in Europe (U.S. Bur. of Labor), 1910; The Pittsburgh Smoke Investigation, 1912; also contbr. articles on criminology, penology, etc., in Internat. Cyclo.; prepared for Bur. of Foreign and Domestic Commerce, repts. on hardware trade in France, Spain, Portugal and Italy, 1914, 15. Deceased.

VEEDER, Albert Henry, lawyer; b. Fonda, N.Y., Apr. 1, 1844; s. Henry and Rachel (Lansing) V.; A.B., Union Coll., 1865, A.M., 1868; m. Helen L., d. Rev. Isaac G. Duryea, Aug. 15, 1866 (died 1912). Supt. schs., Galva, Ill., 1866-68, admitted to bar 1868; practiced at Galva, 1868-74; in Chicago, 1874—. Gen. counsel for Swift & Co., St. Louis Nat. Stock Yards Co., St. Joseph (Mo.) Stock Yards Co., Libby, McNeil & Libby, and others. Home: Chicago, Ill. Died July 13, 1941.

VEEDER, Major Albert, physician; b. Ashtabula, O., Nov. 10, 1848; s. Gerrit and Martha (Williams) V.; A.B., Union Coll., N.Y., 1870, later A.M.; M.D., U. of Buffalo, 1883; m. Mary E. Wood, Sept. 5, 1871. Prin. Ives Sem., Antwerp, N.Y., 1875-78; practiced medicine, Lyons, N.Y., 1883—. Fellow A.A.A.S.; mem. Internat. Conf. of Charities and Corrections. Published many papers on public water supply, garbage disposal, the relative importance of flies and water supply in spreading disease; made study of the relation of pack ice in the great lakes of N. America to the glacial period; made extended investigation of electro-magnetic phenomena of solar origin, especially with reference to the causation of the aurora, and the production of certain weather conditions. Home: Lyons, N.Y. Died Nov. 16, 1915.

VELARDE, Hernán, diplomat; b. Lima, Peru, Sept. 30, 1863; s. Manuel and Angela Diez (Canseco) V.; ed. Scientific Inst., Lima; Naval Prep. Sch.; Dr. Laws, Philosophy and Letters, U. of San Marcos, Lima; m. Isabel Bergmann, Sept. 30, 1889. Served as sec. of Legation and chargé d' affaires, Brazil; under sec. Foreign Affairs; successively minister to Brazil, Colombia, and Argentina; A.E. and P. from Peru to U.S., Mar. 1924—. Participated in war with Chili, 1879-83; minister of the Interior and atty. gen. Superior Ct. of Lima; prof. æsthetics and history of art, U. of San Marcos; negotiated and signed 17 internat. treaties. Mem. Jurisprudence of Colombia, Coll. of Lawyers of Lima and of Brazil, Hist. Inst. Argentina, etc. Comdr. Order of Isabella the Catholic; grand officer Order of the Liberators, etc. Catholic. Died Nov. 12, 1935.

VELTIN, Louise de Launay, educator; b. Paris, France; d. Capt. Christian (U.S.A.) and Henriette (de Launay) Veltin; came to American at 7 yrs. of age; ed. Sacré Cœuer, and by pvt. tutors, Paris and New York. Owner and prin. The Veltin Sch., New York, 1886-1924, retired. Decorated Officier d'Académie, 1902; Médaille de la Reconnaissance Française. Died Jan. 7, 1934.

VELVIN, Ellen, author; b. Southampton, Eng.; d. John Frederick (A.M., M.D.) and Elizabeth Mary (Addington) Velvin; ed. at home. Editor Franco-English Review, 2 yrs., Children's Magazine, 2 yrs. Fellow Royal Zoöl. Society (London); mem. Inst. of Journalists (London). Author: Tales Told at the Zoo; More Tales Told at the Zoo; Jack's Visit; A Terrible Feud; Our Holiday in London; Rataplan, A Rogue Elephant; Wild Creatures Afield, 1904; Behind the Scenes with Wild Animals, 1906; Wild Animal Celebrities; From Jungle to Zoo, 1915; Portraits at the Zoo, 1915. Deceased.

VENABLE, Charles Scott, educator; b. Prince Edward County, Va., April 19, 1827; grad. Hampden-Sidney, 1842; U. of Va., 1848, LL.D., 1868; studied Berlin, 1852, and Bonn, 1854; prof. mathematics Hampden-Sidney Coll., 1848-56; prof. physics and chemistry, U. of Ga., 1856; of mathematics and astronomy, U. of S.C., 1858-61; capt. engrs., 1861-62; lt. col. and aide-de-camp to Gen. Robert E. Lee, 1862-65, in Army of Northern Va.; prof. mathematics U. of Va., 1865; chmn. of faculty, 1870-73, and again in 1887. Home: Charlottesville, Va. Died 1900.

VENABLE, Francis Preston, prof. chemistry; b. Prince Edward County, Va., Nov. 17, 1856; s. Charles Scott and Margaret Cantey (McDowell) V.; grad. U. of Va., 1879; studied at Bonn, 1879-80; A.M., Ph.D., Göttingen, 1881; Berlin, 1889; Sc.D., Lafayette, 1904; LL.D., U. of Pa., U. of Ala., U. of S.C., Jefferson Med. Coll.; m. Sally Charlton Manning, Nov. 3, 1884; children—Louise M., Cantey McD., Charles S., John M., Frances P. Prof. chemistry, 1880-1900, pres., 1900-14, prof. chemistry, 1914-30, U. of N.C. Mem. advisory bds. of Bur. of Mines, 1917-23, and of Chem. Warfare Service, 1918. Pres. Southern Ednl. Assn., 1903, Am. Chem. Soc., 1905, Southern Assn. of Sch. and Colls., 1909; fellow Chem. Soc., London, A.A.A.S. Author: Manual of Qualitative Analysis, 1883; Short History of Chemistry, 1894; Development of Periodic Law, 1896; Inorganic Chemistry According to the Periodic Law (with James Lewis Howe), 1898; Study of the Atom, 1904; Radioactivity, 1917; Zirconium and Its Compounds, 1921. Home: Chapel Hill, N.C. Died Mar. 17, 1934.

VENABLE, Joseph Glass, clergyman; b. Christiansburg, Ky., Sept. 17, 1877; s. Joseph Glass and Susan McCurdy (Hann) V.; A.B., Central U., Richmond, Ky., 1899; B.D., Presbyn. Theol. Sem. of Ky., 1905; D.D., Davidson, 1918; m. Mary Irvine Bird, Oct. 19, 1905; children—Elizabeth Bird, Joseph Glass, William Bird, Robert Hann. Ordained ministry Presbyn. Ch. in U.S., 1905; pastor successively Memorial and Mt. Olive chs., Saline County, Mo., First Ch., Moultrie, Ga., Riverside Ch., Jacksonville, Fla., and First Ch., Norfolk, Va., until 1924, First Ch., Chattanooga, Tenn., 1924—. Served with Y.M.C.A. in France, 1918. Mem. bd. dirs. Assembly Training Sch., Richmond, Va. Mason. Home: Chattanooga, Tenn. Died July 13, 1928.

VENABLE, Richard Morton, lawyer; b. Charlotte County, Va., Feb. 8, 1839; s. Richard N. and Magdalen (McCampbell) V.; A.B., Hampden-Sidney Coll., 1857, LL.D., 1888; U. of Va., 1859-60; LL.B., Washington and Lee U., 1868; unmarried. Entered C.S.A. as pvt., Apr. 21, 1861; became maj. of arty. and engrs. serving in Army of Northern Va. and Trans-Mississippi Dept. Prof. engring., U. of La., 1865; prof. mathematics, Washington and Lee U., 1867; in law practice Baltimore, 1869—; mem. Baltimore City Council, 1899-1903; pres. Bd. Park Commrs., Baltimore, Prof. law, U. of Md., 1870-1905. Trustee Johns Hopkins U.; v.p. Johns Hopkins Hosp. Home: Baltimore, Md. Died 1910.

VENABLE, William Henry, educator, author; b. Warren County, O., Apr. 29, 1836; s. William and Hannah (Baird) V.; grad. South-Western State Normad Sch., Lebanon, O., 1860; A.M., DePauw U., 1864; LL.D., Ohio U., 1886; D.Litt., U. of Cincinnati, 1917; m. Mary Ann Vater, Dec. 30, 1861; father of William Mayo and Emerson V. Prof. natural sciences, 1862-81, prin. and propr., 1881-86, Chickering Inst., Cincinnati. Organizer and first pres. Cincinnati Soc. for Polit. Edn., 1880; first pres. Teachers' Club of Cincinnati, 1891; pres. Western Assn. of Writers, 1895. Author: Beginnings of Literary Culture in the Ohio Valley, 1891; John Hancock, Educator, 1892; Let Him First Be a Man, and Other Essays, 1894; The Last Flight (verse), 1894; Tales from Ohio History, 1896; Santa Claus and the Black Cat, 1898; A Dream of Empire, 1901; Tom Tad, 1902; Ohio Literary Men and Women, 1903; Saga of the Oak, and Other Poems, 1904; Cincinnati—A Civic Ode, 1907; Floridian Sonnets, 1909; A Buckeye Boyhood, 1911; History of Christ Church, Cincinnati, 1917. Editor: Poems of William Haines Lytle (with memoir), 1894; Selections from the Poems of Robert Burns, 1898; Selections from the Poems of Lord Byron, 1898; Selections from the Poems of William Wordsworth, 1898. Home: Cincinnati, O. Died July 6, 1920.

VENNEMA, Ame, coll. pres.; b. Holland, Mich., May 25, 1857; s. Ame and Elizabeth (Van Der Haar) V.; grad. Hope Coll. Prep. Sch., 1872; A.B., Hope, 1879, A.M., 1882; D.D., 1904, Rutgers, 1916; grad. New Brunswick Theol. Sem., 1882; m. Henrietta Le-Febre, June 7, 1882. Ordained Reformed Ch. ministry, 1882; pastor New Paltz, N.Y., 1882-86, Second Ch., Kalamazoo, Mich., 1886-90, Second Ch., Rochester, N.Y., 1890-92, Port Jervis, N.Y. 1892-95, First Ch., Passaic, N.J., 1895-1911; pres. Hope Coll., Sept. 20, 1911-18; minister Reformed Ch., Mahwah, N.J., 1918-20. Mem. Bd. of Foreign, Missions Reformed Ch. in America. Republican. Home: Passaic, N.J. Died Apr. 26, 1925.

VENTH, Carl, musician; b. Cologne, Germany, Feb. 16, 1860; s. Carl and Frederika (von Turkowitz) V.; ed. Cologne Conservatory, Brussels Conservatory; last pupil of Henry Wieniawski; studied composition with Hiller, Jensen and Dupont; Mus.D. honoris causa, N.Y. College of Music, 1932; m. Cathinka Finch Myhr, of Christiania, Norway, July 1899. Came to America, 1880; concert master Metropolitan Opera House, New York, 1884; admitted to citizenship, 1885; organized Venth Coll. of Music, Brooklyn, 1888; condr. Brooklyn Symphony Orchestra 3 yrs.; dir. violin dept. Kidd-Key Conservatory, Sherman, Tex., 1908-11; condr. Sherman Musical Festival, 1910; condr. Dallas Symphony Orchestra, 1911-13; settled at Ft. Worth, 1913; became dean fine arts, Westmoorland Coll., San Antonio, Tex.; condr. Ft. Worth Symphony Orchestra; choir master First Meth. Ch., Ft. Worth. Div. band supt. Camp Bowie, Tex., 1918, also trained bands at Camp Travis. Mem. Evang. Ref. Ch. Composer: (operas) The Monk of Iona; The Fisherman; La Vida de la Mision (for the Texas Centennial); (comic opera) Fair Betty; (cantatas) The Rescurrection; Myth Voices; From Olden Times; The Quest of Beauty; awarded prize, Nat. Fed. Music Clubs, for "Pan in America," 1923. Died Jan. 29, 1938.

VERBECK, Guido Fridolin, educator; b. Aurora, N.Y., May 2, 1887; s. William and Katherin (Jordan) V.; grad. St. John's School, Manlius, N.Y., 1905; student Cornell U., 1906-09; Sc.D., Colgate U., 1934; m. Muriel Halcomb, June 1, 1911; children—Guido F., Samuel Sumner, Edith, Nan. Instr. St. John's Sch. (title changed to Manlius Sch., 1925), 1910-12, comdt., 1912-30, supt., 1930, later headmaster, also v.p. and trustee. Served as lt. col. 106th F.A., World War I; col. 368th F.A., Res. Awarded two silver star citations and Conspicuous Service Cross (U.S.). Pres. Assn. of Mil. Colleges and Schools of U.S. Republican. Episcopalian. Mason. Home: Manlius, N.Y. Died July 27, 1940.

VER BECK, Hanna. See Hanna Rion.

VERBECK, William, educator; b. Nagasaki, Japan, Jan. 18, 1861; s. Guido Fridolin (D.D.) and Maria (Manion) V.; hon. A.M., Syracuse U., 1897; lived in Japan until 17; m. Katherine Jordan, July 28, 1886; children—Guido Fridolin, Karl, William Jordan. Served lt., capt. and maj., Calif. N.G., and lt., capt. and maj., N.G.N.Y.; col. on dept. staff Govs. Morton and Black; bvtd. col., July 3, 1905; aide to Gov. Hughes, 1909. Pres. and head master, The Manlius (Military) Sch., Manlius, N.Y., 1888—. Adj. gen. State of N.Y., June 1, 1910-Dec. 31, 1912; apptd. maj. gen., Dec. 27, 1912. Pres. Assn. Mil. Schs. and Colls. of the U.S., 1918-20; mem. Nat. Inst. Social Sciences. Nat. scout commr., Boy Scouts of America, 1910-11. Decorated Comdr. Order of Crown (Italy). Republican. Episcopalian. Home: Manlius, N.Y. Died Aug. 24, 1930.

VER BECK, William Francis (Frank Ver Beck), author, illustrator; b. Belmont County, O., June 1, 1858; s. Bentley Benedict and Sarah Elizabeth (Knapp) Ver B.; ed. academy, Ohio. Specialist in representation of comic animals. Author: (and illustrator) The Dumpies and the Arkansas Bear (with Albert Bigelow Paine), 1896; The Three Bears, 1899; Acrobatic Animals, 1899; Beasts and Birds, 1900; Handbook of Golf for Bears, 1900; Book of Bears, 1906; Short Little Tales from Bruintown, 1915; Ver Beck's Bears in Mother Gooseland, 1915; The Little Lost Bear, 1915; Timothy Tuttle's Great Day, 1917; The Donkey Child, 1918; The Elephant Child, 1920; The Little Cat Who Journeyed to St. Ives, 1921; The Little Lost Lamb, 1922; The Little Bear Who Ran Away from Bruintown, 1923; Little Black Sambo and the Baby Elephant, 1925; The Arkansaw Bear Complete (with Albert Bigelow Paine), 1929; Little Black Sambo and the Monkey People, 1929. Home: Mansfield, O. Died July 13, 1933.

VERBRUGGHEN, Henri, violinist, conductor; b. Brussels, Belgium, Aug. 1, 1873; s. Henri and Elisa (Derode) V.; ed. in Belgium; studied music at Brussels Conservatoire under Hubay and Ysaye (first prize with distinction); m. Alice Gordon Beaumont, of London, Sept. 21, 1898; children—Adrien H. P. E., Sylvia Rosa (dec.), Philippe A. W. C., Marcel E., Gabrielle E. T., Victor P. First appeared as violinist at age of 8; taken to England by Ysaye at 15; played under Lamoureux, Sir George Henschel, Sir Frederic Cowen, Sir Henry J. Wood, etc.; condr. of Colwyn Bay Orchestra and Choir 3 yrs.; succeeded Dr. Coward as condr. of Glasgow Choral Union; chief of staff Athenæum Sch. of Music, Glasgow, 10 yrs., also Royal Coll. of Music, Dublin, 1 yr.; founder and dir. New South Wales State Conservatorium of Music, Sydney, Australia, 8 yrs.; founder and condr. New South Wales State Orchestra, and select choir 7 yrs.; directed concerts in Brussels, Berlin, Munich, Petrograd, Glasgow, Edinburgh, London, etc.; condr. Bach, Beethoven, Brahms festivals, Queens Hall, London, 1914, 15; head of Verbrugghen String Quartet, performing complete cycle of Beethoven quartets in cities of Britain, Australia and America. Guest condr. in Minneapolis Symphony Orchestra, season 1922-23, and permanent conductor, 1923—; also founded Minneapolis Symphony Chorus; chmn. music dept. and prof. chamber music and appreciation, Carleton Coll., Northfield, Minn. Home: Minneapolis, Minn. Died Nov. 12, 1934.

VERDAGUER, Peter, Roman Catholic bishop of Laredo; consecrated 1890. Home: Brownsville, Tex. Died 1911.

VERHAGEN, Aloysius Alphonsus, clergyman; b. Beek en Donk, Holland, Aug. 11, 1869; s. Gysbertus E. and Henrica (van de Rydt) V.; ed. U. of Louvain, 1888-92. Came to U.S., 1892, naturalized citizen, 1897. Ordained priest R.C. Ch., 1892; asst. pastor Our Lady of Lourdes' Cathedral, 1892-99, pastor, 1901—; pastor St. Patrick's Ch., Colfax, Wash., 1899-1901. Apptd. Domestic Prelate of Papal Household (Right Rev. Monsignor), Apr. 3, 1931. Home: Walla Walla, Wash. Died May 1, 1938.

VERMILION, Charles William, judge; b. Centerville, Ia., Nov. 6, 1866; s. William F. and Mary A. C. (Kemper) V.; student De Pauw U., 1883-86; LL.B., U. of Mich., 1889; m. Clare Eloise Biddle, June 2, 1897; 1 dau., Dane Eloise (Mrs. E. L. Simmons). Admitted to Ia. bar, 1889, and began practice at Centerville; county atty. Appanoose County, Ia., 1892-96; judge Dist. Ct. 2d Dist. of Ia., 1902-24; justice Supreme Ct. of Ia., 1924—. Republican. Presbyn. Home: Centerville, Ia. Died Sept. 2, 1927.

VERMILYE, Mrs. Kate Jordan (Kate Jordan), author; b. Dublin, Ireland; brought to America in childhood; ed. at home and in pub. and pvt. schs.; m. Frederic M. Vermilye, 1897. First story pub. at age of 12; contbr. many short stories to mags., also writer plays. Mem. Soc. of Am. Dramatists. Author: A Circle in the Land, 1905; Time the Comedian, 1909; The Creeping Tides, 1913; Secret Strings (play), 1914; Against the Winds, 1919; The Next Corner, 1921; Trouble-the-House, 1921. Died June 20, 1926.

VERNON, Leroy Tudor, newspaper corr.; b. Wilmington, O., Feb. 11, 1878; s. James Mercer and Helena Bertha (Tudor) V.; A.B., U. of Chicago, 1900; m. Georgia Mary Wheeler, Dec. 22, 1904. City editor Everett (Wash.) Times, 1898-99; reporter Chicago Inter-Ocean, 1898-1901; polit. editor, June 1902, legislative corr., Dec. 1902-May 1903, Washington corr., 1903-34, polit. editor, 1934—, Chicago Daily News. Publicity dir. Nat. Taft Bur., 1912; eastern publicity dir. Frank O. Lowden presdl. campaign, 1920. Mem. bd. visitors U.S. Naval Academy, 1930. Episcopalian. Home: Chicago, Ill. Died Jan. 3, 1938.

VERNON, Samuel Milton, clergyman; b. nr. Crawfordsville, Ind., Nov. 27, 1841; s. Joseph Bowers and Mariah (Monroe) V.; grad. Ia. Wesleyan U., Mt. Pleasant, Ia., 1867; grad. Drew Theol. Sem., 1869; A.M., De Pauw U., Greencastle, Ind., 1869; D.D., Allegheny Coll., 1875; m. Harriet Jane Kelly, 1862 (died 1894); m. 2d, Mrs. Annie Townsend, May 2, 1898. Ordained M.E. ministry, 1862; pastor Des Moines, Ia., 1864-65; pres. Simpson Coll., Indianola, Ia., 1866-68; pastor N.Y. City, 1869-72, Christ Ch., Emory and North Av., Pittsburgh, 1872-79, Roberts Park Ch., Indianapolis, 1879-83; successively pastor following chs., in Phila., 1883—, Trinity, Seventh St., Lancaster, Wharton St., Thirteenth St., 1st Ch., Germantown, St. Stephen's, West York St., Wissahickon, Christ Ch., and Central Ch., Roxborough, 1910—; prof. Christian ethics and Bibl. theology, Temple U., 1906—. Trustee Drew Theol. Sem., 1876-80, M.E. Hosp., Phila., 1899—; mem. Ch. Extension Bd., 1884-1908; corr. sec. Evangelical Alliance of Pa., 1906-15; mem. Gen. Conf. M.E. Ch., 1912. Mason. Author: Aumsements in the Light of History, Reason and Revelation, 1882; Probation and Punishment, 1886; Prohibition, 1887; Lux Vitæ, 1900; The Making of the Bible, 1916; also many articles in ch. papers. Traveled extensively in Europe, Egypt and Palestine. Home: Philadelphia, Pa. Died May 27, 1920.

VERRILL, Addison Emery, zoölogist, geologist; b. Greenwood, Me., Feb. 9, 1839; s. George Washington and Lucy (Hilborn) V.; B.S., Harvard, 1862; hon. A.M., Yale, 1867; m. Flora L., d. Elliot Smith, of Norway, Me., June 15, 1865; children—George Elliot, Evalina Flora (dec.), Alpheus Hyatt, Edith Barton, Clarence Sidney (dec.), Lucy Lavinia. Asst. in Museum Comparative Zoölogy, 1860-64, prof. zoölogy, 1864-1907, emeritus prof. 1907, curator Zoöl. Mus., 1865-1910, instr. geology, Sheffield Scientific School, 1870-94, Yale. Curator Boston Soc. Natural History, 1864-74; prof. comparative anatomy and entomology, U. of Wis., 1868-70; asso. editor Am. Jour. of Science, 1869-1920; asst. in charge of scientific explorations by the U.S. Fish Commn., 1871-87. Mem. Nat. Acad. Sciences; pres. Conn. Acad. Arts and Sciences; fellow Am. Acad. Arts and Sciences. Made valuable original investigations in relation to the invertebrata of the entire Atlantic and Pacific coasts of N. America, and especially of the deep-sea fauna, and on the marine faunæ of Bermuda, W. Indies, Brazil, H.I. and Panama; wrote over 350 papers on zoöl. and geol. subjects. Contributed all the zoöl. matter to Webster's Internat. Dictionary, 1890, and Supplement, 1900. Author: Report upon the Invertebrate Animals of Vineyard Sound and Adjacent Waters, 1873; The Bermuda Islands, 1903; Zoölogy of the Bermuda Islands, Vol. I, 1903; Geology and Paleontology of the Bermudas, 1905; Coral Reefs of the Bermudas, 1907; Monograph of the Shallow Water Starfishes of the North Pacific Coast, 1914; Report on West Indian Starfishes, 1915; Reports on Alcyonaria and Actinaria of Canadian Arctic Expedition, 1921; Crustacea of Bermuda, 3 parts, 1923; Alcyonaria of the Blake Expedition, 1925. Died Dec. 10, 1926.

VERRILL, Charles Henry, economist; b. Auburn, Me., Apr. 25, 1866; s. Alden Jackson and Ann (Parker) V.; A.B., Bowdoin, 1887, A.M., 1891; LL.B., Georgetown U., 1890, LL.M., 1891; m. Mrs. E. L. Richards, 1894; m. 2d, Mrs. W. A. Martindale, 1923. With U.S. Dept. of Labor, later Bur. Labor Statistics, 1888-1917; chief editor Bur. Labor Statistics many yrs.; chief statistician U.S. Employees' Compensation Commn., 1917; commr. same, Aug. 27, 1918—. Mem. Govt. Bd. Pan-Am. Expn., Buffalo, N.Y., 1901; rep. of U.S. Govt. at Internat. Conf. for Labor Legislation, at Lucerne, Switzerland, 1908, Zürich, 1912, Internat. Conf. on Unemployment, Zürich, 1912. Fellow Am. Statis. Assn. (v.p., 1916, 17). Republican. Unitarian. Home: Chevy Chase, Md. Died Jan. 19, 1928.

VERY, Frank Washington, astronomer; b. Salem, Mass., Feb. 12, 1852; s. Washington and Martha Needham (Leach) V.; S.B. (in chemistry), Mass. Inst. Tech., 1873; m. Portia Mary Vickers, Apr. 11, 1893; children—Alice Needham (Mrs. Edmund R. Brown), Marjorie Vickers, Arthur Oldfield, Eleonora Virginia, Ronald Winthrop. Instr., physical lab., Mass. Inst. Tech., 1877; astronomer at Allegheny (Pa.) Obs., 1878-95; adj. prof. astronomy and instr. in geology, Western U. of Pa., 1890-95; acting dir. Ladd Obs. and prof. astronomy, Brown U., 1896-97, completing, at own expense, research on Atmospheric Radiation, published as bull. "G" by U.S. Weather Bur., 1900; spl. agt. U.S. Weather Bur., 1900; dir. Westwood Astrophys. Obs., 1906—. For 10 yrs. Prof. Langley's prin. asst.; made many original investigations. Swedenborgian. Fellow A.A.A.S.; mem. Am. Astron. Soc.; hon. mem. Acad. Arts and Sciences, Utrecht, Holland. Frequent contbr. to leading scientific mags. and to publs. of the New Ch. Demonstrated that the solar constant exceeds 3.5 c.g. min.; proof of light absorption by a medium filling all space, and theory of origin of matter; proof that the white nebulæ are galaxies; confirmation of author's previous announcement of existence of water vapor and oxygen in the atmosphere of Mars, showing amount of oxygen to be about half of that in the earth's atmosphere; also zonal distribution of water vapor on Mars, etc. Invented instrument for making accurate quantitative measurements of intensities of Fraunhofer lines in the solar spectrum. Home: Westwood, Mass. Died Nov. 24, 1927.

VERY, Lydia Louisa Anna, author; b. Salem, Mass., Nov. 2, 1823; d. Captain Jones and Lydia Very, sister Rev. Jones V., poet; ed. General H. K. Oliver's Classical Sch.; taught in Salem pub. sch. and in a pvt. sch. 34 yrs. Unmarried. Published yrs. ago a booklet Red Riding Hood, cut in the outline shape of Red Riding Hood, the first book cut out in any but rectangular shape either in U.S. or Europe. Devoted much independent effort in behalf of dumb animals. Author: Poems and Prose Writings; Sayings and Doings Among Insects and Flowers; Sylph, the Organ-Grinder's Daughter; A Strange Disclosure; A Strange Recluse; An Old-Fashioned Garden. Home: Salem, Mass. Died 1901.

VERY, Samuel Williams, rear admiral U.S.N.; b. Liverpool, Eng., Apr. 23, 1846; s. Samuel (Jr.) and Sarah Williams (McKey) V.; pvt. and pub. schs.; U.S. Naval Acad., Newport, R.I., and Annapolis, Md., 1863-66; m. Martha Bourne Simonds, June 14, 1883. Ensign, Mar. 12, 1868; master, Mar. 26, 1869; lt., Mar. 21, 1870; lt. comdr., Mar. 4, 1886; comdr., Mar. 5, 1895; capt., Feb. 19, 1901; rear admiral, July 22, 1906. Served in numerous vessels of the Navy and at several naval stas., besides engaging in magnetic investigations on part of Coast Survey, 1880-81, and having charge of Transit of Venus Expdn. to Patagonia, 1882-83; comd. steamers Saturn and Cassius, 1898, in operations around Cuba, and the gunboat Castine, 1899-1900, in Philippine and Chinese waters; while comdg. Castine conquered and received surrender of Zamboanga, Mindanao, P.I., with results that were highly commended in report of Rear Admiral J. C. Watson; comd. U.S.S. San Francisco,

Mediterranean and Asiatic stas., Nov. 1903-Dec. 31, 1904; comdt. of Naval Sta., Hawaii, July 26, 1906-Apr. 23, 1908; retired Apr. 23, 1908. Home: Chestnut Hill, Mass. Died Jan. 3, 1919.

VEST, George Graham, U.S. senator; b. Frankfort, Ky., Dec. 6, 1830; grad. Center Coll., Ky., 1848; law dept. of Transylvania U., Ky., 1853; removed to Mo., 1853; established law practice; presdl. elector on Dem. ticket, 1860; mem. Mo. Ho. of Reps., 1860-61; mem. Confederate Congress (in house 2 yrs., senate 1 yr.); U.S. senator, 1879-1903. Democrat. Home: Kansas City, Mo. Died 1904.

VESTAL, Albert Henry, congressman; b. Frankton, Ind., Jan. 18, 1875; s. William H. and Mary E. (Jackson) V.; student Ind. State Normal Sch., Terre Haute, Ind.; A.B., Valparaiso (Ind.) U., 1896; m. Hulda M. Malone, Jan. 8, 1903. Admitted to Ind. bar, 1896, and began practice at Anderson; pros. atty. 50th Jud. Dist. of Ind., 3 terms, 1901-07; mem. 65th to 71st Congresses (1917-31), 8th Ind. Dist. Republican. Presbyn. Mason, K.P. Home: Anderson, Ind. Died Apr. 1, 1932.

VESTIN, John, R.C. bishop; b. Carniolia, Austria, July 17, 1844; ed. there and grad. Theol. Sem. of St. Francis, Milwaukee, Wis., 1866 (D.D.); ordained priest, Aug. 31, 1866, at Milwaukee; pastor at Houghton, Mich., 1866-71, and at Negaunee, Mich., 1871-79; consecrated, Sept. 14, 1879, bishop of Sault Sainte Marie and Marquette (Mich.). Died 1889.

VIBBERT, William H., clergyman; b. New Haven, Conn., Oct. 1, 1839; s. Rev. W. E. and Mary E. (Cooke) V.; A.B., Trinity Coll., 1858; studied Berkeley Div. Sch., Middletown, Conn.; S.T.D., Racine Coll., Wis., 1883; widower. Deacon, 1862, priest, 1863, P.E. Ch.; prof. Hebrew, Berkeley Div. Sch., 1863-73; rector Christ Ch., Middle Haddam, Conn., 1863-73, St. Luke's Ch., Germantown, Phila., 1873-83, St. James' Ch., Chicago, 1883-90, St. Peter's Ch., Phila., 1890-91; vicar Trinity Chapel, New York, 1891-1910, vicar emeritus, 1910—. Pres. House of Holy Comforter, New York P.E. Public Schs. (Trinity and St. Agatha's), Home for Old Men and Aged Couples, St. Luke's Home, House of Mercy, Trinity Chapel Home; v.p. N.Y. Bible and Prayer Book Soc.; trustee Trinity Coll., Society Promotion of Religion and Learning, Soc. Increase of Ministry, Church Congress, Clergyman's Retiring Fund Soc. Author: A Guide to Reading the Hebrew Text, 1872. Died Aug. 27, 1918.

VICK, Walker Whiting, receiver-gen.; b. Wilmington, N.C., Aug. 16, 1878; s. Capt. Samuel W. and Katherine (Rothwell) V.; m. Sadie Averill Plunkitt, Oct. 15, 1902. Engaged 18 yrs. in mining, smelting and indsl. enterprises; traveled extensively in Mexico, S.A. and Southern Spain; writer, and contbr. to newspapers; active in campaign resulting in locating Panama-Pacific Internat. Expn. at San Francisco; mgr. general hdqrs. Woodrow Wilson, at New York, pre-convention campaign, 1912; asst. sec. Dem. Nat. Com., 1912-16, and organized hdqrs. for 1912 campaign; sec. Wilson Inaugural Com., 1913; gen. receiver Dominican customs by appmt. Pres. Wilson, June 1913-Oct. 1914; visited Hayti and made report on conditions, 1913, which later resulted in Am. occupation and treaty control. Del. Dem. Nat. Conv., 1916. Publicity and investigation work, Washington and New York, 1921—. Served in U.S.N., Spanish-American War; pres. United Spanish War Veterans' Encampment Commn., 1912. Presbyn. Home: Rutherford, N.J. Died May 12, 1926.

VICKERS, Alonzo Knox, judge; b. on farm, Massac County, Ill., Sept. 25, 1853; s. James I. and Celia (Smith) V.; ed. grammar and high schs., Ill.; admitted to Ill. bar, 1882; m. Leora E. Armstrong, Nov. 18, 1880. Mem. Ill. Ho. of Reps., 1886; judge Circuit Ct., 1st Jud. Circuit, Ill., 1891-1906; judge Supreme Ct. of Ill., 1906—. Republican. Methodist. Home: East St. Louis, Ill. Died Jan. 21, 1915.

VICKERY, Herman Frank, physician; b. Rochester, N.Y., Aug. 20, 1856; s. John and Martha Bond (Perkins) V.; A.B., Harvard U., 1878, M.D., 1882; post-grad. study U. of Leipzig, 1 winter, Vienna Gen. Hosp., 1 summer; m. Abby Williams Davis, Sept. 28, 1886 (died 1911); m. 2d, Annie Louise (Bigelow), widow of Dr. James Sullivan Howe, Aug. 14, 1915. In practice at Boston, 1883-1917, retired; asst., 1884-90, instr. clin. medicine, 1890-1914, Harvard; phys. to out-patients, 1889-98, visiting phys., 1898-1915, cons. phys., 1915-17, Mass. Gen. Hosp. Pres. Boylston Med. Soc., 1887-88, Boston Soc. Med. Improvement (pres. 1914-15); pres. Suffolk Dist. Med. Soc., 1917. First lt. and asst. surgeon, 1st Regt., M.V.M., 1884-86. Episcopalian. Independent Republican. Asso. editor Sajous' Annual and Cyclo. of the Med. Sciences; joint translator Strümpell's Text-book of Medicine. Home: Brookline, Mass. Died Feb. 24, 1940.

VICTOR, Orville James, author; b. Sandusky, O., Oct. 23, 1827; grad. at sem. and Theol. Inst., Norwalk, O., 1847; m. Metta Victoria Fuller, authoress, July 1856. Contbr. to several mags., 1847-51; asso. editor Sandusky Daily Register, 1851-56; editor Cosmopolitan Art Jour., 1856-61; also U.S. Jour., 1858-60, in New York; for yrs. past representative of Associated Publishers, New York, to oppose legislation aimed at 2d class matter in U.S. mails. Edited The Biographical Library; the American Battles series, Library of Standard Romance, American Tales series, Speakers and Dialogues series, Hand Book series; etc., of the Beadle & Adams Publications, 1862-1870; Beadle's Mag. of To-day, 1865-66; Western World, an Illuminated Weekly, 1869; Saturday Journal, 1872-1880; The Fireside Library and Waverly Library, 1882-88; Banner Weekly, 1885-93. Author: History of the Southern Rebellion (4 vols.); Incidents and Anecdotes of the War; History of American Conspiracies; biographies of John Paul Jones, Israel Putnam, Anthony Wayne, Ethan Allen, Winfield Scott, Garibaldi for Dime Biographical Library and "Great Americans" Series. Home: Hohokus, N.J. Died 1910.

VIELÉ, Charles Delavan, brig. gen. U.S.A.; b. Albany, N.Y., Feb. 7, 1841; s. Rufus King and Phebe A. (Gregory) V.; ed. pvt. schs., Albany, N.Y.; m. Nannie D. Minor, Jan. 10, 1872. Apptd. 2d lt. 1st U.S. Inf., Oct. 24, 1861; 1st lt., Apr. 6, 1862; bvtd. capt., July 4, 1863, "for gallant and meritorious service during siege of Vicksburg"; assigned to 10th U.S. Cav., Dec. 31, 1870; maj. 1st U.S. Cav., Aug. 20, 1889; lt. col., Nov. 21, 1897; brig. gen. U.S.V., Sept. 21, 1898; col. 4th U.S. Cav., Sept. 14, 1899; retired from active service, Jan. 23, 1900, for disability in line of duty; brig. gen. U.S.A., retired, Apr. 23, 1904. Served with Regular Div., 5th Corps, Army of Potomac, until June 1862; with Gen. Grant in campaign resulting in capture of Vicksburg, July 4, 1863; participated in Red River campaign, 1864, on staff Gen. Dudley, comdg. 4th brigade of cav.; served in Ind. Ty., Ariz., Tex., Mont., 1871-95, participating in numerous Indian campaigns and scouting parties; on duty at Ft. Riley, Kan., and Ft. Sheridan, Ill., 1895-98; comd. 1st U.S. Cav. during Spanish War, taking part in battle of San Juan and siege of Santiago de Cuba; comd. Ft. Riley, Kan., 1998-99, Ft. Robinson, Neb., Jan.-Sept. 1899, when was ordered to Manila, P.I., where stationed until retired. Republican. Died Oct. 6, 1916.

VIELÉ, Egbert Ludovickus, soldier, engr., author; b. Waterford, N.Y., June 17, 1825; grad. West Point, 1847; served in Mexican war; also in Indian campaigns on Western frontier; resigned as lt., Oct. 26, 1850. Settled in practice in New York as civil engr.; State engr. of N.J., 1854-56; apptd. chief engr., 1856, of Central Park, New York, and prepared original plan which was adopted for the park; engr. Prospect Park, Brooklyn, 1860, but resigned on 1st call for vols., 1861, and comd. force that opened Potomac River to Washington; capt. engrs. 7th N.Y. regt.; commd. brig. gen. vols., Aug. 17, 1861. 2d in command of Port Royal expdn.; comd. at capture of Ft. Pulaski; planned and executed march on Norfolk, Va., mil. gov. Norfolk, May to Oct. 1863; resigned and resumed practice; engr. of many pub. works; commr. of parks, 1883, and pres. dept. parks, 1884; mem. Congress, 1885-87. Democrat. V.p. Am. Geog. Soc.; appeared before Com. of British House of Lords on subject of municipal adminstrn., 1896. Author: Handbook for Active Service; Topographical Atlas of City of New York; etc. Died 1902.

VIELÉ, Egbert Ludovicus (Francis Vielé-Griffin), French poet; b. Norfolk, Va., May 26, 1863; s. Gen. Egbert L. (U.S.V., and distinguished engr.) and Teresa (Griffin) V.; ed. in French univ., Collège Stanislas, and École de Droit, Paris; m. Marie Louise Brocklé de Grangeneuve, Apr. 16, 1885. Chevalier de la Légion d'Honneur, 1897. Contbr. Echo de Paris, Mercure de France, Nouvelle Revue Française, Revue de Paris, and various other publications. Author: Cueille d'Avril, 1866; Les Cygnes, 1887; Ancaeus, 1888; Joies, 1889; Nouveaux Cygnes, 1890; La Chevauchée d'Yeldis, 1893; Swanhilde, 1893; Laus Veneris (transl.), 1895; Poèmes et Poésies, 1895; la Clarté de Vie, 1897; Phocas le Jardinier, 1899; La Partenza, 1899; L'Amour Sacré, 1903; Plus Loin, 1906; Threne pour le Président Lincoln, 1908; Sapho, 1911; La lumière de Grèce, 1912. Promoted Officier de la Légion d'Honneur, Jan. 1913. Died Nov. 12, 1937.

VIELÉ, Herman Knickerbocker, author; b. New York, Jan. 31, 1856; s. Egbert L. and Teresa (Griffin) V.; studied engring. in father's office; practiced as civ. engr., notably on extension of City of Washington; m. Mary Wharton, 1887. As artist exhibited in New York and other Am. cities. Mem. Artists' Fund Soc. Author: The Inn of the Silver Moon, 1900; The Last of the Knickerbockers, 1901; Myra of the Pines, 1902; Random Verse, 1903; The House of Silence (play, prod. 1906). Contbr. stories, sketches and poetry to mags. Died 1908.

VIETOR, George Frederick, capitalist; b. New York, Oct. 13, 1839; s. Frederick and Marie (Hötterott) V.; m. Annie M. Achelis, Aug. 3, 1869. Mem. firm of Frederick Victor and Achelis, commn. mchts. (founded 1839), 1865—, head of firm, 1872—; trustee Am. Surety Co., Franklin Trust Co., German Savings Bank, Munich Reinsurance Co., N.Y. Reciprocal Underwriters, U.S. Trust Co., Washington Trust Co.; dir. Equitable Life Assurance Soc. of U.S., Credit Clearing House, Jefferson, Mount Morris, Nat. Park, Plaza and Yorkville banks, Kingsbridge Real Estate Co., etc.; pres. Poidebard Silk Mfg. Co., Hoboken, N.J.; treas. Griswold Worsted Co., Darby, Pa. Republican. Dir. German Hosp. Home: New York, N.Y. Died 1910.

VIGNAUD, (Jean) Henry, diplomatic service; b. New Orleans, Nov. 27, 1830, of old Creole family; s. Lucian and Clemence (Godefroy) V.; taught in pub. schs., 1852-56; at same time wrote for Le Courrier and other New Orleans papers; m. Louise Comte, of Paris, 1879. Editor L'Union de Lafourche, Thibodeaux, La., 1857-60, and of a weekly review, La Renaissance Lousianaise, 1860-61. Capt. 6th La. Regt., C.S.A., 1861-62; captured in New Orleans; sec. Confederate Diplomatic Commn., Paris, 1863; sec. Roumanian Legation at Paris, 1869; connected with Ala. Claims Commn., 1872, at Geneva; U.S. del. Internat. Diplomatic Metric Conf., 1873; 2d sec., 1875-82, 1st sec., 1882-1909, Am. Legation and Embassy at Paris; later hon. counselor; several times acted as chargé d'affaires. Pres. Société des Americanistes, Paris. Author: La Lettre et la Carte de Toscanelli sur la Route des Indes, 1901; Toscanelli and Columbus—The Letter and Chart of Toscanelli on the Route to the Indies by Way of the West, 1902; Letters to Sir Clements R. Markham and C. Raymond Beazley, 1903; The Real Birth Date of Columbus: 1451, 1903; La Maison d'Albe et les archives Colombiennes, 1904; Études critiques sur la vie de Colomb, 1905; Hist. critique de la grande entreprise de 1492, 2 vols., 1911; Americ Vespuce, 1911; Les expeditions des Scandinaves en Amerique, 1911; The Columbian Travelers, 1920; Le Vrai Colomb, 1921. Died Sept. 18, 1922.

VILAS, Charles Harrison, surgeon; b. Chelsea, Vt., July 22, 1846; s. Hon. Levi B. and Esther Green (Smilie) V.; Ph.B., U. of Wis., 1865, A.M., 1868; M.D., Hahnemann Med. Coll., Chicago, 1873. Emeritus pres. Hahnemann Med. Coll., Chicago, with which was connected, 1876—. For many years almost constantly traveled and visited the main hosps. and disease centers in Europe and the Far East. Del. to various foreign med. congresses in London, Paris, Moscow, etc. Mem. Wis. State Bd. Edn.; pres. and chmn. exec. com. regents U. of Wis.; mem. Wis. Branch Nat. Research Council. Author of the Vilas genealogy, and several med. works and numerous monographs on ophthal. and other subjects. Built and presented to First Unit. Soc., Madison, of which is a mem., its Parish House (1910) with complete furnishings, and (1915) its Parsonage; to the Madison Zoöl. and Aquarium Soc. its main bldg. (1917); the site and group of bldgs. of the Madison Anti-Tuberculosis Assn. (1917); furnished throughout the Y.M.C.A. building, and the dormitories of the Y.W.C.A. building, Madison, Wis., and presented to the latter Esther Vilas Memorial Hall. Wis. State committeeman of Gen. Med. Bd. of Council Nat. Defense, 1917-18. Mem. Dane County Humane Soc., Miss. Valley Anti-Tuberculosis Assn., Wis. Acad. Sciences, Arts and Letters, Wis. Archæol. Soc., etc. Home: Madison, Wis. Died Nov. 22, 1920.

VILAS, William Freeman, U.S. senator, lawyer; b. Chelsea, Vt., July 9, 1840; s. Hon. Levi B. and Esther G. (Smilie) V.; family settled at Madison, June 1851; grad. U. of Wis., 1858; Albany Law Sch., 1860; established practice. In July 1862, recruited Co. A, 23d Wis. vols.; took part in Vicksburg campaign; promoted to lt. col., comdg. his regt. during siege of Vicksburg and 2 months afterward; resigned commn. Aug. 1863; resumed practice; law prof., 1868-85, and 1881-85 and 1897-1905, regent, U. of Wis.; trustee Soldiers' Orphans' Home; mem. commn. to revise statutes of Wis., 1875-78; mem. Dem. Nat. Com., 1876-86; mem. Wis. legislature, 1885; permanent chmn. Nat. Dem. Conv., 1884; Postmaster Gen. U.S., 1885-88; Sec. of the Interior, Jan. 1888 to March 1889; U.S. senator, 1891-97; mem. commn. which built State Hist. Library, 1897-1903; joined the Nat. (gold standard) Dem. party 1896; chmn. Com. on Resolutions, Indianapolis Conv., 1896. Mem. commn. to build Wis. capitol, 1906—. Edited (with Ed. E. Bryant), Vols. 1, 2, 4, 6 to 20 Wis. Supreme Ct. Reports. Home: Madison, Wis. Died 1908.

VILLAMOR, Ignacio, judge; b. Bangued, Abra, P.I., Feb. 1, 1863; s. Florencio and Wencesla (Borbon) V.; A.B., San Juan de Letram Coll., Manila, 1885, M.A., 1887; LL.B., U. of St. Thomas, Manila, 1893, LL.M., 1894; m. Maria F. de Villamor, May 31, 1893. Apptd. pros. atty. Pangasinan Province, P.I., 1901; judge 6th Jud. Dist., P.I., 1902-07; atty. gen. P.I., 1907-13; exec. sec. (sec. of state), 1913-14; pres. U. of Philippines, 1914-18; dir. Philippine Census, 1918; asso. justice Supreme Ct. of P.I., 1920—. Admitted to practice in Supreme Ct. of U.S., 1911. Author: Criminality in the Philippines, 1909; Commentaries on the Election Law, 1909; Election Frauds and Their Remedies, 1912; Prontuario de Practica Administration Municipal y Provincial, 1914; Locust vs. Agriculture, 1914; Japan's Educational Development, 1916. Home: Manila, P.I. Died May 24, 1933.

VILLERS, Thomas Jefferson, clergyman; b. Centerville, Va., May 23, 1861; s. William Villers and Catherine (Dodd) V.; B.A., U. of Rochester, 1885, M.A., 1891, D.D., 1903; grad. Rochester Theol. Sem., 1888; LL.D., Denison, 1919; m. Rose Stanley Merriam, Oct. 25, 1888 (died 1907); 1 dau., Eleanor Rosella; m. 2d, Evelyn M. Prichard, Aug. 8, 1918. Ordained Bapt. ministry, 1888; pastor Gloucester, Mass., 1888-93, First Ch., Syracuse, N.Y., 1893-98, First Ch., Indianapolis, 1898-1906, Peddie Memorial Ch., Newark, N.J., 1906-13, 1st Ch., Detroit, 1913-22, 1st Ch. (White Temple) Portland, Ore., 1922-32. Pres. Am. Bapt. Foreign Mission Soc., 1918-20. Pres. Ind. Bapt. Conv. 5 yrs.; trustee Rochester Theol. Sem. 27 yrs.; bd. mgrs. Am. Bapt. Home Mission Soc. 9 yrs.; chmn. Commn. on Evangelism of Northern Bapt. Conv.; chmn. commn. on standardizing the Bapt. Ministry; v.p. Northern Bapt. Conv., 1916-17; dir. religious work of Y.M.C.A. at Camp MacArthur, Waco, Tex., 1917; pres. Detroit Bapt. Union, 1915. V.p. New York Baptist Union for Ministerial Edn.; mem. exec. com. Linfield Coll.; pres. Portland Council of Chs., 1923-25; hon. v.p. Bapt. Edn. Soc. of State of N.Y.; mem. exec. com. Ore. Bapt. State Conv. Preacher Northern Bapt. Convention Sermon, Detroit, 1928. Author: The Hurry Call of Jesus, 1928; The Christ I Know, 1932; also monographs, Our Baptist Heritage and A Century of Service. Home: Detroit, Mich. Deceased.

VINCENT, Bird J., congressman; b. nr. Clarkston, Mich., Mar. 6, 1880; s. Hermon H. and Elizabeth S. (Bird) V.; Ferris Inst., Big Rapids, Mich.; LL.B., U. of Mich., 1905; m. L. Maud Hinds, Aug. 24, 1907; 1 dau., Helen Louise. Began practice at Saginaw, 1905; asst. pros. atty., Saginaw County, 1909-14, pros. atty., 1915-17; city atty., Saginaw, 1919-23; mem. 68th to 71st Congresses (1923-31), 8th Mich. Dist. Republican. Served 21 mos. in U.S.A., World War I; in France 10 mos. as 1st lt. 6th Train Hdqrs. and 302d Train Hdqrs. Conglist. Mason, Elk. Home: Saginaw, Mich. Died July 18, 1931.

VINCENT, Boyd, bishop; b. Erie, Pa., May 18, 1845; s. B. B. and Sarah A. (Strong) V.; A.B., Yale, 1867, A.M., 1873; S.T.D., Berkeley Div. Sch. and D.D., Trinity, Conn., 1889; D.D., Yale, 1913; LL.D., Kenyon Coll., 1920; unmarried. Deacon, 1871, priest, 1872, P.E. Ch.; asst. St. Paul's Church, Erie, 1871-72; rector Cross and Crown Ch., Erie, 1872-74, Calvary Ch., Pittsburgh, 1874-89; consecrated coadjutor bishop of Southern Ohio, 1889, bishop of Southern Ohio, 1904; retired, Oct. 2, 1929. Pres. judge Ct. of Review, 5th Dept., P.E. Ch., 1904; pres. Missionary Council, 5th Dept., 1907; chmn. Ho. of Bishops, 1910-16. Author: God and Prayer, 1897; Our Family of Vincents, 1924; The Pastoral Epistles for Today, 1930; Recollections, 1933. Home: Cincinnati, O. Died Jan. 14, 1935.

VINCENT, Clarence Cornelius, prof. horticulture; b. Middleton, Ore., May 3, 1884; s. Thomas T. and Alice (Countryman) V.; B.S. in Agr., Ore. Agrl. Coll., Corvallis, 1907, M.S., 1909; M.S., Cornell U., 1910; Ph.D., Mass. Agrl. Coll., Amherst, Mass., 1929; m. Odalite Alice Horning, 1909; children—Robert Clarence, Elizabeth Alice, Wilbur Dale. Asst. horticulturist Ore. Agrl. Coll., 1907-09, U. of Ida., 1910-11; asso. prof. horticulture, Clemson (S.C.) Coll., 1911-12; asso. prof. horticulture, U. of Ida., 1912-14, prof., 1914—, also horticulturist Expt. Sta. Author numerous bulletins on hort. subjects; contbg. editor Idaho Farmer. Home: Moscow, Ida. Died Aug. 1934.

VINCENT, Clive Belden, mfr. metal goods; b. Oriskany, N.Y., Mar. 27, 1863; s. John Taber and Corsina Bonaparte (Dean) V.; grad. Phelps (N.Y.) Union and Classical Sch., 1883; m. Jennie Elizabeth Hotchkiss, Jan. 30, 1901. Began with The Torrington Co., mfrs. vacuum cleaners, needles, bicycle spokes, etc., chmn. bd. and treas., 1924—; sec. and treas. The Torrington Co. (Me.); dir. Brooks Bank & Trust Co., The Torrington Mfg. Co., The Hotchkiss Bros. Co., The Dayton Mfg. Co. Republican. Mason. Home: Torrington, Conn. Died 1936.

VINCENT, Frank, traveler, author; b. Brooklyn, Apr. 2, 1848; s. Frank and Harriet (Barns) V.; ed. Yale, hon. A.M., 1875; m. Harriet Stillman Vincent, June 3, 1909. Made systematic tour of entire world, civilized and uncivilized, covering 355,000 miles in 15 yrs., including explorations in Indo-China, Lapland, Brazil and Congo Free State; presented valuable collection of Indo-Chinese antiquities and art and indsl. objects to Met. Mus. of Art, New York. Hon. mem. 26 scientific and lit. socs. in U.S., and abroad; received 9 decorations from foreign sovereigns and govts. Author: The Land of the White Elephant, 1874; Through and Through the Tropics, 1876; Norsk, Lapp and Finn, 1881; Around and About South America, 1890; In and Out of Central America, 1890; The Lady of Cawnpore (in collaboration), 1891; Actual Africa, 1895. Editor: The Plant World, 1896; The Animal World, 1897; etc. Died June 19, 1916.

VINCENT, George Edgar, educator; b. Rockford, Ill., Mar. 21, 1864; s. John Heyl and Elizabeth (Dusenbury) V.; A.B., Yale, 1885; Ph.D., U. of Chicago, 1896, LL.D., 1911, Yale, 1911, U. of Mich., 1913, U. of Minn., 1930; m. Louise Palmer, Jan. 8, 1890. Editorial work, 1885-86; in Europe and Orient, 1886-87; lit. editor Chautauqua Press, 1886; vice-prin. Chautauqua System, 1888-98; prin. of instrn., 1898; pres. Chautauqua Instn., 1907-15, and hon. pres. 1915-37. Fellow in sociology, 1892-94, asst., 1894-95, instr., 1895-96, asst. prof., 1896-1900, asso. prof., 1900-04, prof., 1904-11, dean Jr. Colls., 1900-07, dean faculties of arts, lit. and science, 1907-11, U. of Chicago; pres. U. of Minn., 1911-17 (resigned); pres. Rockefeller Foundation, New York, 1917-29 (retired); mem. Gen. Edn. Bd., 1914-29; lecturer Scandinavian univs., 1933. Mem. Am.-Scandinavian Foundation, Commn. for Relief in Belgium, Ednl. Foundation; chmn. hosp. survey com. of United Hosp. Fund, N.Y. City, 1935. Mem. U.S. delegation to Pan-Am. Conf., Santiago, Chile, 1923. Author: Social Mind and Education, 1896; An Introduction to the Study of Society (with Albion Woodbury Small), 1895. Home: Greenwich, Conn. Died Feb. 1, 1941.

VINCENT, Harry Aiken, artist; b. Chicago, Ill., Feb. 14, 1864; s. Aiken and Sarah V.; m. Mildred Deltz, Sept. 30, 1916. Exhibited at Nat. Acad. Design, New York, Art Inst. Chicago, Carnegie Inst., Pittsburgh, Pa. Acad. Fine Arts; etc. A.N.A., 1919. Home: Rockport, Mass. Died Sept. 27, 1931.

VINCENT, Henry Bethuel, musical dir.; b. Denver, Colo.; s. Bethuel T. and M. Ella (Masters) Vincent; student Overlin (Ohio) Coll., 1889-90, 1892-93; Bordentown (N.J.) Inst.; studied music with Paur, Sherwood, Behrend, etc., London and Paris. Dir. Vincent Studio, Erie, Pa., 1900-29; dir. Erie Choral Soc. and Conneaut Choral Soc., 1914-18; organist and choirmaster successively 1st Presbyn. Ch., St. Patrick's Ch., Simpson Ch., Jewish Temple to 1932; condr. Erie Symphony Orchestra; gen. dir. Erie Playhouse, 1916—. Official organist Chautauqua Instn., 1904-23. Conductor, Fed. Music Project Orchestra, 1936-37. Lecturer before many schs., univs. and clubs. Commodore Erie Yacht Club, 1923-24 and 1927-29. Composer: (oratorio) The Prodigal Son, 1902; (Oriental song cycle) The Garden of Kama, 1905; (operettas) Indian Days, and Savageland; (opera) Esperanza, prod., Washington, D.C., 1906; over 100 songs, anthems and pieces for piano, organ and orchestra. Home: Erie, Pa. Died Jan. 7, 1941.

VINCENT, John Heyl, bishop; b. Tuscaloosa, Ala., Feb. 23, 1832; s. John Himrod and Mary (Raser) V.; early life spent at Lewisburg and Milton, Pa.; began to preach at 18; studied Wesleyan Inst., Newark, N.J.; hon. A.B., Mt. Union Coll., Ohio, 1875; S.T.D., Ohio Wesleyan, 1870, Harvard, 1896; LL.D., Washington and Jefferson, 1885; m. Elizabeth Dusenbury, Nov. 10, 1858 (dec.); father of George Edgar V. Traveled as jr. preacher on Luzerne circuit (Baltimore Conf. M.E. Ch.), 1851, cn Newark (N.J.) City Mission, 1852, N. Belleville, N.J., 1853-54, Irvington, 1855-56; transferred to Rock River Conf. and stationed at Joliet, Ill., 1857-58, Mount Morris, 1859, Galena, 1860-61, Rockford, 1862-65 (this includes 1 yr. spent on a trip to Europe and Palestine), Trinity Ch., Chicago, 1865. Established Sunday School Quarterly, 1865, Sunday School Teacher, 1866; corr. sec. S.S. Union and editor Sunday school publications, 1868-84; one of founders, 1874, Chautauqua Assembly; founder, 1878, Chautauqua Lit. and Scientific Circle, and chancellor, 1878—. Preacher, Harvard, Yale, Cornell, Wellesley and other colls.; resident bishop in charge of European work of M.E. Ch., 1900; retired from active episcopate, May 1904. Author: The Modern Sunday School; Studies in Young Life; Little Footprints in Bible Lands; The Church School and Sunday School Institutes; Earthly Footsteps of the Man of Galilee; Better Not; The Chautauqua Movement; To Old Bethlehem; Our Own Church; Outline History of England; Outline History of Greece; The Church at Home; Family Worship for Every Day in the Year, 1905; etc. Died May 9, 1920.

VINCENT, John Martin, univ. prof.; b. Elyria, O., Oct. 11, 1857; s. John M. and Phebe (Martin) V.; A.B., Oberlin (extra ordinem), 1883, A.M., 1888, student in Berlin and Leipzig, 1881-83; Ph.D., Johns Hopkins, 1890; LL.D., Ill. Coll., 1904, Oberlin, 1908, Docteur en Droit, Geneva, 1909; m. Ada J. Smith, Nov. 8, 1880. Instr., 1889-92, asso., 1892-95, asso. prof., 1895-1905, prof. European history, 1905-25, Johns Hopkins, prof. emeritus, 1925—. Editor, Johns Hopkins University Studies in Historical and Political Science. Author: State and Federal Government in Switzerland, 1891; Government in Switzerland, 1900; Historical Research, 1911, Aids to Historical Research, 1934; Costume and Conduct in The Laws of Basel, Bern and Zurich, 1370-1800, 1935. Editor: Evolution in Science and Revolution in Religion (by W. D. Ball), 1893; Borgeaud's Adoption and Amendment of Constitutions in Europe and America, 1895. Home: Pasadena, Calif. Died Sept. 22, 1939.

VINCENT, Leon Henry, author; b. Chicago, Jan. 1, 1859; s. Rev. B. T. Vincent; A.B., Syracuse U., 1882, Litt.D., 1901; in Europe, 1884-85; m. Jessie Van Vleck Thomas, Aug. 21, 1890. Lecturer on literary subjects, 1885—. Author: A Few Words on Robert Browning, 1891; The Bibliotaph and Other People, 1898; Hôtel de Rambouillet and the Précieuses, 1900; The French Academy, 1901; Corneille, 1901; Molière, 1902; American Literary Masters, 1906; Dewitt Miller, a Biographical Sketch, 1912; Dandies and Men of Letters, 1913; A Memoir of John Heyl Vincent, 1925. Died Feb. 10, 1941.

VINCENT, Marvin Richardson, theologian; b. Poughkeepsie, N.Y., Sept. 11, 1834; s. Leonard M. V.; A.B., Columbia, 1854, A.M., 1857; D.D., Union, 1865; m. Hulda F. Seagrave, 1858. Asso. in management of Columbia Grammar Sch., 1854-58; prof. langs., Meth. University, Troy, 1858-60; entered M.E. ministry, 1859; in 1863 changed to Presbyn. Ch.; pastor First Ch., Troy, N.Y., 1863-73, Ch. of the Covenant, New York, 1873-88; prof. N.T. exegesis and criticism, Union Theol. Sem., 1888, emeritus. Trustee Columbia, 1889-1913, New York Coll. of Dentistry, 1908. Author: Translation of Bengel's Gnomon of the New Testament, 1860-62; Amusement a Force in Christian Training, 1867; The Two Prodigals, 1876; The Law of Sowing and Reaping, 1877; Gates into the Psalm Country, 1878; Not Discerning the Lord's Body, 1879; Why Should I Join the Church?, 1879; Christ at the Door, 1879; Faith and Character, 1880; Ministers' Handbook, 1882; In the Shadow of the Pyrenees, 1883; God and Bread, 1884; The Expositor in the Pulpit, 1884; Christ as a Teacher, 1886; The Covenant of Peace, 1887; Word Studies in the New Testament, 1877, 1900; Students' New Testament Handbook, 1893; That Monster, the Higher Critic, 1894; Biblical Inspiration and Christ, 1894; The Age of Hildebrand, 1896; Critical Commentary on Philippians and Philemon (Internat. Commentary), 1897; A History of the Textual Criticism of the New Testament, 1899; The Gospel of Luke (Temple Bible); The Inferno of Dante, Translation and Commentary (1st part of Translation of the Divine Comedy of Dante). Died Aug. 18, 1922.

VINCENT, Thomas MacCurdy, army officer; b. nr. Cadiz, O., Nov. 15, 1832; s. Thomas Carleton and Jane (MacCurdy) V.; ed. high sch., Cadiz, O.; grad. U.S. Mil. Acad., 1853; m. Laura Louise Lancaster, Aug. 15, 1857. Bvt. 2d lt. 2d Arty., July 1, 1853, 2d lt., Oct. 8, 1853; promoted through grades to col. asst. adj. gen., Aug. 2, 1890; retired by operation of law, Nov. 15, 1896; advanced to rank of brig. gen. retired, by act of Apr. 23, 1904. Bvtd. lt. col. and col., Sept. 24, 1864, and brig. gen., Mar. 13, 1865, for faithful and meritorious services during the war. At various times acting adj. gen. U.S.A. Pres. Ft. Stevens Lincoln Nat. Mil. Park Assn. During Civil War in charge of organization and miscellaneous bus. of vol. armies, and their disbanding as planned by him, subsequently closing certain War Dept. bureaus, with financial responsibility of $33,000,000. Made official tours observation and inspection to main parts of U.S. and adjoining foreign territory. Author: Staff Organization; Military Power of the United States During the War of the Rebellion; Lincoln and Stanton; Lincoln; Florida Indians in Day of De Soto and Florida Seminole Wars; Battle of Bull Run, July 21, 1861; official reports on Army and Staff Organization, and many other official reports, 1853-96. Died 1909.

VINCENT, Walter B., lawyer; b. Mystic, Conn., Aug. 6, 1845; s. Ezra and Ann Maria (Denison) V.; grad. Peekskill (N.Y.) Mil. Acad., 1864; studied law with Thurston & Ripley, Providence, R.I.; grad. Albany Law Sch., 1866; m. Mary E. Wingate, Dec. 16, 1869 (died 1910); 1 dau., Edith (Mrs. Edward H. Weeks). Admitted to N.Y. bar, 1866, R.I. bar, 1867; practiced, Providence; clk. R.I. Senate, 4 yrs.; mem. R.I. Ho. of Reps., 3 terms; justice Supreme Ct. of R.I., Mar. 1912-Jan. 20, 1925; retired. Mason. Home: Providence, R.I. Died Nov. 14, 1931.

VINCENT, William David, banker; b. Macon, Mo., Dec. 3, 1866; s. Joseph and Augusta (McLaughlin) V.; ed. pub. schs.; m. Mary Allen Speidel, Sept. 14, 1898 (died 1907); children—Mrs. Josephine Cowin, Allen Leffingwell; m. 2d, Neen McVey, Sept. 20, 1910. Began in employ First Nat. Bank, Macon, Mo., Apr. 25, 1885, asst. cashier, 1886-91; an organizer Old Nat. Bank, Spokane, Wash., 1891, asst. cashier, 1894, cashier, 1895, v.p., 1915, pres., Jan. 1920—. Mem. Am. Bankers Assn. (pres. clearing house sect., 1916-17). Trustee Spokane Pub. Library (pres. 1919). Republican. Episcopalian. Mason, Elk. Made notable collection of books, autographed by authors, and books pertaining to history of the Northwest. Home: Spokane, Wash. Died Mar. 1, 1935.

VINING, Edward Payson, ry. official; b. Belchertown, Mass., Jan. 14, 1847; s. George Whitefield and Emily (Holland) V.; ed. Buffalo (N.Y.) High Sch.; hon. A.M., Yale U., 1886; LL.D., William Jewell Coll., 1908; m. Annabel Bodwell, May 22, 1867; m. 2d, Agnes E. Brooks, Nov. 14, 1895. Served in U.S.N., Aug. 1864-Oct. 1865; cashier Burlington & Mo. River R.R., 1865-66; gen. freight agt. Grand Rapids & Indiana R.R., 1867-70; gen. freight traffic mgr. U.P. R.R., 1871-83; commr. Western Trunk Line Assn., 1884-87; gen. traffic mgr. N.Y.&N.E.

R.R., 1888-89; asst. gen. mgr. St.L.&S.F. R.R., 1890; commr. Transcontinental Assn., 1891-93; gen. mgr. Market St. Ry. Co., San Francisco, 1894-1902; v.p. White River R.R. Co., 1907; retired from active business. Baptist. Fellow A.A.A.S. Author: The Mystery of Hamlet, 1881; An Inglorious Columbus, 1885; The Necessity for a Classification of Freight, 1886; Israel, or Jacob's New Name, 1908. Translator: The Epistle to the Hebrews. Edited and wrote introduction to "Hamlet," Vol. XI of The Bankside Shakespeare, pub. 1890, by the Shakespeare Soc. of New York, etc. Devoted his time principally during later years to a study of the prime meaning of the Hebrew and Greek words in the original text of the Bible, articles in relation thereto appearing in Watchword and Truth (mag.). Home: Brookline, Mass. Died Dec. 31, 1920.

VINJE, Aad John, judge; b. Voss, Norway, Nov. 10, 1857; s. John and Ingeborg (Klove) V.; came to U.S., 1869; B.S., U. of Wis., 1884, LL.B., 1887, LL.D., 1924; m. Alice Idell Miller, June 5, 1886; children—Arthur Miller, David Ray (dec.), Janet, Ethel. Asst. state librarian of Wis., 1884-89; asst. Supreme Ct. reporter, 1889-91; practiced at Superior, Wis., 1891-95; judge 11th Jud. Circuit, Wis., 1895-1910; apptd., Sept. 10, 1910, elected, Apr. 1911, 21, justice Supreme Ct., Wis.. terms 1912-22, 1922-32; chief justice, Feb. 11, 1922—. Republican. Unitarian. Home: Madison, Wis. Died Mar. 23, 1929.

VINSON, Taylor, lawyer; b. Wayne County, W.Va., Dec. 22, 1857; s. Samuel S. and Mary (Damron) V.; B.S., Bethany Coll., W.Va., 1878; studied law, U. of Va. and Boston U.; m. Mary Chaffin, June 1901. Practiced Huntington, W.Va., 1886—. Republican. Mem. Christian (Disciples) Church. Drafted pub. service commn. bill of W.Va. Home: Huntington, W.Va. Died Jan. 31, 1929.

VINTON, Alexander Hamilton, bishop; b. Brooklyn, Mar. 30, 1852; s. Gen. David Hammond (U.S.A.) and Eliza A. (Arnold) V.; A.B., St. Stephen's Coll., 1873, D.D., 1890, LL.D., 1902; S.T.B., Gen. Theol. Sem., 1876, D.D., 1902; grad. studies, U. of Leipzig; D.D., Williams Coll., 1909; unmarried. Deacon, 1877, priest, 1878, P.E. Ch.; in charge Ch. Holy Communion, Norwood, N.J., 1878, Ch. Holy Comforter Memorial, Phila., 1879-84; rector All Saints', Worcester, Mass., 1884-1902; elected 1st bishop Diocese of Western Mass., Jan. 1902. V.p. Ch. Congress; trustee Gen. Theol. Sem., Smith Coll.; examining chaplain, conv. preacher and mem. standing com. Diocese of Mass.; del. Gen. Convs., 1898, 1901. Died 1911.

VINTON, Arthur Dudley, lawyer; b. Brooklyn, Dec. 23, 1852; s. Francis and Elizabeth Mason (Perry) V.; ed. Rectory Sch., Hamden, Conn.; Brooklyn Poly. Inst.; grad. Columbia Law Sch., LL.B., 1873; unmarried. In law office Evarts, Southmayd & Choate, 1873-79; in partnership with Perry Belmont and George Griswold Frelinghuysen in firm of Vinton, Belmont & Frelinghuysen, New York. Invented automatic ry. signal patented 1898. Later mng. editor N. Am. Review, afterward resuming law practice. Author: The Pomfret Mystery, 1886; The Unpardonable Sin, 1888; Looking Further Backward, 1898. Died 1906.

VINTON, Frederic Porter, painter; b. Bangor, Me., Jan. 29, 1846; s. William Henry and Sarah Ward (Goodhue) V.; went to Chicago in childhood; ed. pub. schs.; clerk and bookkeeper business houses and banks, Boston, 1862-75, meanwhile studying art at Lowell Inst. and art anatomy under Dr. William Rimmer; studied under Léon Bonnât, 1875, and Jean Paul Laurens, 1877-78, Paris; Royal Acad., Munich; opened studio, Boston, 1878; m. Annie M., d. George Pierce, June 27, 1883. Painted portraits of leading Americans, several of which are in pub. collections. Exhibited Paris Salon, 1878, 1890 (hon. mention); gold medal, Chicago Expn., 1893; silver medal, Paris Expn., 1900; gold medal, Buffalo Expn., 1901; gold medal, St. Louis Expn., 1904. A.N.A., 1888, N.A., 1891; mem. Nat. Inst. Arts and Letters. Died 1911.

VIRGIL, Antha Minerva, musical dir.; b. Elmira, N.Y.; d. Urie and Minerva Ruth (Cole) Patchen; grad. Burlington (Ia.) high sch.; m. Almon Kincaid Virgil, 1878. Brought practice instruments into use for piano students in America; mfr. full size and portable practice keyboard; introduced the Metronome for all tech. practice; organized, 1891, and dir. the Virgil Piano Sch. and Sch. of Pub. Performance. Author: The Virgil Method of Piano Instruction, Vols. I and II, 1931; Harmony and Harmony Playing; 3 Sets of Studies—Melodious, Progressive and Artistic; Instructive Talks with Pianoforte Students; also 250 piano pieces, grades 1 to 6, inclusive. Home: Bergenfield, N.J. Died Feb. 4, 1939.

VISSCHER, William Lightfoot, author; b. Owingsville, Ky., Nov. 25, 1842; s. Frederick and Betty Walker (Lightfoot) V.; ed. Bath Sem., Owingsville, Ky.; LL.B., U. of Louisville, 1868; admitted to bar, 1868, but never practiced; m. Emma Mason, Mar. 16, 1876 (died 1896). Served 4 yrs. as a soldier in Civil War. Long engaged in newspaper work; wrote over 1,000 poems, pub. in many newspapers and mags. On lecture platform for several seasons; later acting in drama. Author: (novels) Carlisle of Colorado; Way Out Yonder; Thou Art Peter; Fetch Over the Canoe; Ten Wise Men and Some More; Amos Hudson's Motto; The Pony Express; How They Came to Be Statues (verse); Black Mammy; Harp of the South; Blue Grass Ballads; Chicago, an Epic; Poems of the South; Stars of Our Country; Portraits and Pen-Pictures; etc. Home: Chicago, Ill. Died Feb. 10, 1924.

VITALE, Ferruccio, landscape architect; b. Florence, Italy, Feb. 5, 1875; s. Lazzaro and Countess Giuseppina (Barbaro) V.; ed. Royal Mil. Acad. of Modena; m. Rosamond Flower Rothery, May 29, 1910; children—Giuseppina Barbaro (dec.), Rosamond Rothery, Lidia Giuliana. Came to U.S., 1898, naturalized citizen, 1921. Mil. attaché to Italian Embassy, Washington, D.C., 1898-99; mil. observer with Army of Philippines, 1898; began practice at New York, 1904; designer of Meridian Hill Park, Washington, D.C.; town plan of Scarsdale and Pleasantville, N.Y.; many pvt. estates. Appointed mem. Commn. of Fine Arts by Pres. Coolidge, Sept. 24, 1927, for term 1927-31. Trustee Am. Acad., Rome, Foundation for Architecture and Landscape Architecture, Lake Forest, Ill. Fellow Am. Soc. Landscape Architects (past pres. New York chapter). Winner of gold medal, Archtl. League of New York, 1920. Decorated Chevalier of the Crown (Italian). Home: New York, N.Y. Died Feb. 26, 1933.

VITS, George, mfr. aluminum goods; b. Manitowoc, Wis., Nov. 3, 1878; s. Henry and Mary (Hockemeyer) V.; ed. pub. schs.; m. Olive Proell, Aug. 20, 1903; children—George, Kathryn. Began with Aluminum Goods Mfg. Co., Manitowoc, 1889, pres., 1911—; pres. Handwear Mfg. Co., Hotel Manitowoc; v.p. 1st Nat. Bank of Manitowoc; dir. Northwestern Casualty and Surety Co. Mem. Rep. Nat. Com., 1928; referee of fed. patronage in Wis., 1928. Chmn. advisory bd. Holy Family Hosp.; mem. advisory com. Marquette U., Memorial Union finance com. U. of Wis.; mem. Central Sch. Bd., 1912-21; pres. Manitowoc Council Boy Scouts of America. Home: Manitowoc, Wis. Died Nov. 15, 1933.

VITTUM, Edmund March, clergyman; b. Sandwich, N.H., Oct. 24, 1855; s. Stephen and Ruth (Tappan) V.; A.B., Dartmouth, 1878, A.M., 1888; B.D., Yale, 1884; D.D, Ia. (now Grinnell) Coll., 1898; m. Annie Griswold, May 16, 1889 (died 1903). Prin. Orleans Liberal Inst., 1873-74; prof. mathematics, Robert Coll., Constantinople, 1878-81; ordained Congl. ministry, 1884; pastor Guilford, Conn., 1884-88, Cedar Rapids, Ia., 1888-91, Grinnell, Ia., 1891-1907; pres. Fargo (N.D.) Coll., 1907-09; prof. English lit., Ga. Normal Coll., Milledgeville, 1910-17; pastor Grinnell, Ia., 1917-19, Muscatine, Ia., 1919-25, retired. Republican. Author: Church Festivals in a Meetinghouse, 1888; Faith on the Frontier, 1890; Head of the Firm, 1891; A Modern Dreamer, 1919; The Vittum Folks, 1921. Home: Grinnell, Ia. Deceased.

VIVIAN, Harold Acton, newspaperman; b. nr. Kandy, Ceylon, Dec. 16, 1877; s. Rev. Arthur H. B. and Constance Irene (Silk) V.; ed. by father, and pvt. tutors, and Los Angeles High Sch.; m. Gertrude R. Spellan, writer, June 25, 1900. Arrived in New York from London, Nov. 1884, going to San Francisco and thence to San Diego, 1888; asst. librarian, San Francisco Chronicle, 1893-95; writer on San Francisco Sporting World, 1895-97, on San Francisco Call, 1899-1902, N.Y. American, 1902-03, N.Y. Evening Mail (Mail and Express), 1903-06, N.Y. Times, 1906-09, N.Y. World, 1909-20; sec. Com. on Am. Ideals, Chamber Commerce U.S.A., 1920-22; with N.Y. Herald, 1922-26, N.Y. Times, 1926-27; sec. comptroller, State of N.Y., 1928. Author: The Theatrical Primer, 1904. Home: Albany, N.Y. Died Oct. 15, 1929.

VIVIAN, Thomas Jondrie, editor; b. Cornwall, Eng., Aug. 3, 1858; s. Capt. James and Marie (Jondrie) V.; ed. Lycée National, Nantes, Brittany (Croix de la Mérite); m. Enocora Wadsworth, Aug. 3, 1882. Lecturer on langs. and lit., U. of Calif., Teachers' Inst., Los Angeles, Columbia Coll., New York, Fifth Av. Acad., New York; in editorial work, 1886—. Author: Seven Smiles and a Few Fibs; With Dewey at Manila; The Fall of Santiago; Everything About Our New Possessions; Luther Strong; The Fairy Spinning Wheel (transl. from Les Contes du Rouet, by Catulli Mendes). Home: New York, N.Y. Died Dec. 14, 1925.

VIZETELLY, Frank (Francis) Horace, lexicographer, editor, author; b. London, England, April 2, 1864; naturalized Am. citizen, 1926; s. of Henry Richard and Elizabeth Anne (Ansell) V.; ed. Lycée Baudard, Nogent-sur-Marne, France; Arnold Coll., Eastbourne, Sussex, Eng.; LL.D., St. John's Annapolis; Dept. of Philosophy, U. of Md.; m. Bertha M. Krehbiel, June 6, 1894. Mem. Vizetelly & Co., pubs., London; asso. editor Standard Dictionary, 1891-1903, mng. editor, 1903-13, editor, 1914—, new edit., 1937-38; asso. editor Standard Dictionary abridgements, Students Edit., 1897, Comprehensive, 1898, Concise, 1901; office editor of more than 250 miscellaneous publications on English, pub. speaking, mental efficiency, psychoanalysis, medicine, history, travel, etc.; asso. editor in compilation of Merck's Index of Chemicals and Drugs, 1895, 1906; revising editor Columbian Cyclo. (40 volumes), 1897, Cyclo. of Classified Dates, 1899; one of editors of Hoyt's Cyclo. of Practical Quotations, the New Schaff-Herzog Ency. of Religious Knowledge (12 vols.), 1905-12, and other reference books; mem. Funk & Wagnalls Co.'s editorial staff, 1891—; mgr. editorial dept., and corr. and rec. sec. Jewish Ency. Editorial Bd. and contbr. to same, 1899-1905; editor of "The Lexicographer's Easy Chair," of the Literary Digest to 1937; office editor of the Literary Digest Hist. of the World War (10 vols.), by F. W. Halsey, 1919. Only civilian permitted to visit Boer detention camps in Bermuda (1901). Radiologist from WOR (Newark, N.J.), 1924-26, KDKA (Pittsburgh), 1926, WNYC (New York), 1926-29, KMOX (St. Louis), Nat. Broadcasting Co.'s network through WJZ and WEAF, 1929-30, through WABC, 1930-31; dean of Columbia Broadcasting System Pronunciation Sch., 1930-31. Transatlantic unrelayed record (KDKA, Pittsburgh) to Cleator Moor, near Whitehaven, Cumberland, Eng., Nov. 17-18, 1926. Knight of Order of Francis-Joseph of Austria-Hungary, 1894. Fellow Am. Geog. Soc. Author: The Preparation of Manuscripts for the Printer, 1905; Desk-Book of Errors in English, 1906; The Development of the Dictionary of the English Language, 1915; Dictionary of Simplified Spelling, 1915; Essentials of English Speech and Literature, 1915; Desk-Book of 25,000 Words Frequently Mispronounced, 1917, The Soldier's Service Dictionary, 1917; Words We Misspell in Business, 1921; Mend Your Speech, 1921; Who? When? Where? What?, 1921-30; Punctuation and Capitalization—How to Make Use of Them, 1921; S.O.S.—Slips of Speech, 1921; Idioms and Idiomatic Phrases, 1921; 2,000 Simple Words Every One Should Know, 1923; How to Use English, 1932; How to Speak English Effectively, 1933; Our Color-Box of Speech, 1933. Editor: Mental Efficiency Series (10 vols.), 1916; A Practical Standard Dictionary, 1922; Conjunctions—Their Use and Abuse, 1924; Prepositions—How to Use Them, 1924; The New Comprehensive Standard Dictionary, 1937; Comprehensive School Dictionary, 1937; A Desk Standard Dictionary, 1929; Funk & Wagnalls New Standard Ency. of Universal Knowledge (25 vols.), 1931; The New International Year Book, 1932—; New Standard Ency. Year Book, 1932—. Home: New York, N.Y. Died Dec. 21, 1938.

VOGEL, Augustus Hugo, mfr.; b. Milwaukee, Wis., Dec. 16, 1862; s. Frederick and Auguste (Herpich) V.; A.B., Harvard, 1886; m. Anita Hansen, Feb. 16, 1892; six children. With Merchants Exchange Bank, Milwaukee, 1886-88; sec., gen. mgr. Pfister & Vogel Leather Co., 1888-1906, v.p., 1907—; mem. bd. dirs. Fed. Res. Bank, Chicago, 1914—; pres. Savings & Investment Assn.; v.p. Western Leather Co. (Milwaukee), Eagle Tanning Works (Chicago), Ottawa Leather Co. (Grand Haven, Mich.). Pres. Milwaukee Univ. Sch.; v.p. Milwaukee-Downer Coll.; trustee Milwaukee Citizens' Bur. of Municipal Efficiency; pres. Voters' League, 1906-08; chmn. bd. of Milwaukee Community Fund. Republican. Episcopalian. Mem. Shoe and Leather Committee of Council of National Defense, 1917; regional dir. War Industries Bd., 1918. Home: Milwaukee, Wis. Died Feb. 18, 1930.

VOGEL, Frank, educator; b. Boston, Mass., 1863; s. George and Caroline (Becker) V.; A.B., cum laude, Harvard, 1887; post-grad. study, 1887-92, A.M., 1892; studied U. of Heidelberg, Germany, 1893-94; m. Lucia L. Chafee, Aug. 17, 1893; children—Frank Chafee, Bertha Charlotte, Ruth Maria. Teacher Mitchell's Mil. Boys' Sch., Billerica, Mass., 1887-88; instr. in modern langs., 1888-92, asst. prof., 1892-99, asso. prof., 1899-1904, prof., 1904-09, head of modern lang. dept., 1909-1932, Mass. Inst. Tech.; instr. Simmons Coll., 1902-03. Mem. Boston Sch. Com., 1901-04. Trustee under will of Henry O. Peabody for an industrial sch. or coll. for girls. Mem. Rep. State Com. of Mass., 1910-17; alternate del. Rep. Nat. Conv., Chicago, 1912. Mason. Author: Peter Schlemihl's Wundersame Geschichte; Hauff's Lichtenstein, Storm, Geschichten aus der Tonne; and many articles in mags. Home: Jamaica Plain, Mass. Died June 9, 1932.

VOGEL, Fred, Jr., corp. official; pres. Pfister & Vogel Leather Co., Milwaukee; also pres. Trufir Corp., Vogel Real Estate Co., Western Leather Co., North Fork Lumber Co., Firnat Corp.; trustee Northwestern Mut. Life Ins. Co.; dir. Allis-Chalmers Mfg. Co., Am. Hair & Felt Co., First Wis. Nat. Bank, Milwaukee Electric Ry. & Light Co., and many other corps. Home: Milwaukee, Wis. Died Jan. 3, 1936.

VOGELGESANG, Carl Theodore, naval officer; b. N. Branch, Calaveras County, Calif., Jan. 11, 1869; s. Henry John and Anna (Vennigerholz) V.; grad. U.S. Naval Acad., 1890; m. Zenaide Stevens Shepard, Dec. 27, 1899; children—Shepard, Zenaide. Ensign, July 1, 1892; lt. jr. grade, Mar. 3, 1899; promoted through grades to rear admiral, Oct. 15, 1922. Served on Bancroft, Spanish-Am. War, 1898; duty with Bur. Nav., Navy Dept., 1904-06; navigator Louisiana, 1906-07; comdr. Mayflower, 1907-08; navigator Wisconsin, 1908-09, at Naval War Coll., Newport, R.I., 1909-12; exec. officer, Wyoming, 1912-14; comdr. Des Moines, 1914; at Naval War Coll., 1914-17; apptd. chief of staff, Asiatic Fleet, Apr. 14, 1917; chief of naval commn. to Brazil, Jan.-Nov. 1918; comdg. U.S.S. Idaho, Jan. 7, 1919-June 1920; chief of staff U.S. Fleet, July 1, 1920-July 1, 1921; comdt. Navy Yard, New York, and 3d Naval Dist., July 1, 1921-Nov. 27, 1922; chief of U.S. Naval Mission to Brazil, Nov. 27, 1922; comd. midshipman cruise, June 6-Aug. 30, 1925; comdr. Scouting Fleet, 1926. Died Feb. 16, 1927.

VOGELSANG, Alexander Theodore, lawyer; first asst. sec. Dept. Interior; b. Calaveras County, Calif., July 19, 1861; s. John Henry and Anna Margaret (Vennigerholz) V.; LL.B., Hastings Coll. of Law (U. of Calif.), 1886; m. Frances Johnson, Jan. 11, 1899. Mem. Vogelsang & Brown, San Francisco, 1891, and Vogelsang, Brown, Cram and Feely, Washington, D.C., 1921—. Pres. Bd. Fish and Game Commrs., Calif., 1896-1901; chmn. Pub. Utilities Com., Bd. of Supervisors, City and County of San Francisco, 1912-16; solicitor Dept. of Interior, Washington, Feb.-Sept. 1916, 1st asst. sec., 1916-21. Democrat. Mason. Home: San Francisco, Calif. Died Sept. 15, 1930.

VOIGT, Andrew George, clergyman; b. Phila., Pa., Jan. 22, 1859; s. Andrew G. and Anna C. (Dehnhart) V.; A.B., U. of Pa., 1880; student Luth. Theol. Sem., Mt. Airy, Pa., 1880-82, U. of Erlangen, Germany, 1882-83; D.D., Roanoke Coll., 1895; m. Clara M. Eisenhardt, Jan. 10, 1884. Ordained Luth. ministry, 1883; pastor Mt. Holly, N.J., 1883-85, Wilmington, N.C., 1898-1903; prof. theology, 1885-89 and 1891-98, Newberry (S.C.) Coll.; prof. Thiel Coll., Greenville, Pa., 1889-91; prof. theology and dean, Luth. Theol. Sem., Columbia, S.C., 1903—. Pres. United Synod Evang. Luth. Ch., S., 1906-10. Contbr. to Luth. Commentary N.T., Luth. Cyclo., Luth Periodicals. Author: Why We Are Lutherans, 1896; Biblical Dogmatics, 1917. Home: Columbia, S.C. Died Jan. 2, 1933.

VOIGT, Edward, judge; b. Bremen, Germany, Dec. 1, 1873; s. Charles and Helen (Helmers) V.; brought to Milwaukee, Wis., at 11; LL.B., U. of Wis., 1899; m. Hattie Wellhausen, Oct. 10, 1910; 1 dau., Carol M. Admitted to Wis. bar, 1899, and practiced at Sheboygan, 1899—; dist. atty., Sheboygan County, 3 terms, 1905-11; city atty., Sheboygan, 2 terms, 1913-17; mem. 65th to 69th Congresses (1917-27), 2d Wis. Dist.; judge 4th Jud. Dist. of Wis., term 1929-35. Republican. Lutheran. Home: Sheboygan, Wis. Aug. 26, 1934.

VOISLAWSKY, Antonie Phineas, M.D.; b. New York, N.Y., June 5, 1872; s. Silas P. and Antonia (Scharles) V.; B.S., New York U., 1894; M.D., Dartmouth, 1897; m. Margaret Rutgers Van Rensselaer, June 4, 1902; children—Van Rensselaer, Elizabeth Van Rensselaer (Mrs. Joseph Van Buren Wittman). Ear, nose and throat specialist, 1898—; cons. otologist, rhinologist and laryngologist Harlem Eye and Ear Infirmary, Manhattan Maternity, Northern Westchester, Staten Island and St. Lukes Hosp.; cons. laryngologist Hosp. for Ruptured and Crippled, Orphans' Home and Asylum of P.E. Ch., St. Luke's Home for Aged Women; cons. rhinologist and laryngologist Fifth Av. Hosp. Fellow Am. Laryngol., Rhinol., Otol. Soc. (mem. council 1929-31), Am. Coll. Surgeons. Served on med. advisory bd., Secret Service, 1917-18. Received New York U. Alumni award, 1932. Republican. Mem. Dutch Reformed Ch. Home: New York, N.Y. Died Feb. 22, 1939.

VOLDENG, Mathew Nelson, M.D., surgeon; b. on farm nr. Decorah, Ia., Jan. 21, 1863; s. Nels Lars and Anna Mathia (Christian) V.; entered Luther Coll., Decorah, at age of 14, receiving A.B., 1883; M.D., Coll. Phys. and Surg., Chicago (now the Med. Dept. U. of Ill.), 1887; post-grad. work, Berlin, Paris and London, 1895-96; LL.D., Buena Vista Coll., Ia., 1914; m. Sadie Weir Rosemond, Sept. 19, 1895; children—Weir N., Karl E. Asst. phys. Independence State Hosp., Ia., 1888-95; prof. pathology, 1897-98, prof. neurology and psychiatry, 1899-1902, Med. Dept., Drake U., Des Moines; supt. and med. dir. Cherokee (Ia.) State Hosp., 1902-15; supt. and med. dir. State Hosp. and Colony for Epileptics, Woodward, Ia., Mar. 1, 1915—. Trustee and mem. exec. com. Buena Vista Coll., Storm Lake, Ia. Republican. Presbyn. Mason. Extensively engaged in Red Cross and Vol. Med. Corps work, World War I. Mem. State Bd. of Eugenics. Home: Woodward, Ia. Died Oct. 21, 1934.

VOLK, Douglas, artist; b. Pittsfield, Mass., Feb. 23, 1856; s. Leonard W. and Emily C. (Barlow) V.; art education at Rome, Italy, and with Gerôme, 1873-78, at Paris; exhibited at Paris Salon, 1875-78; m. Marion B. Larrabee, June 25, 1881 (dec.); children—Leo (dec.), Wendell D., Marion (Mrs. E. R. Bridge), Gerome D. Instr. Cooper Inst., New York, 1879-84, 1908-12; instr. Art Students' League, New York, 1893-98; organized Minneapolis Sch. Fine Arts, 1886-93; instr. portrait class, Cooper Union, 1906-12; instr., Nat. Acad. of Design, New York, 1910-17. Medal, Chicago Expn., 1893; Shaw prize, Soc. Am. Artists, 1899; 1st prize, Colonial Exhbn., Boston, 1899; silver medal, Buffalo Expn., 1901; Carnegie prize, Soc. Am. Artists, 1903; silver medals, St. Louis Expn., 1904; gold medal, Carolina Art Expn., 1907; Proctor portrait prize, 1910; Saltus gold medal, 1911, and Maynard portrait prize, Nat. Acad. of Design; gold medal, San Francisco Expn., 1915; gold medal, Nat. Arts Club, 1915; Beck gold medal, Pa. Acad. Fine Arts, 1916. Represented in Carnegie Mus., Pittsburgh; Corcoran Gallery, Washington; Pittsfield Mus.; Minn. Capitol; Nat. Mus., Washington; Montclair (N.J.) Art Mus.; Met. Mus. of Art, New York; Nat. Arts Club; Rochester (N.Y.) Memorial Art Gallery; Muskegon (Mich.) Art Mus.; Omaha Art Mus.; Portland (Me.) Art Soc.; Brooklyn Museum of Art; war portraits of King Albert, General Pershing and Lloyd George, in Nat. Gallery, Washington, 1921; portrait of Lincoln in Albright Gallery, Buffalo; portraits of Gen. Foster and Gen. Granger, West Point, N.Y., A.N.A., 1898, N.A., 1899; mem. Am. Fedn. Arts, Archtl. League New York, Nat. Soc. Portrait Painters, Internat. Soc. des Beaux Arts et des Lettres, Nat. Inst. of Arts and Letters, Soc. Mural Painters. Officer of the Order of Leopold II, 1921. Asso. chmn. div. of pictorial publicity Com. on Pub. Information, 1918-19. Died Feb. 7, 1935.

VOLKERT, Edward Charles, artist; b. Cincinnati, O., Sept. 19, 1871; s. Philip and Catherine (Dair) V.; ed. Woodward High Sch., Mechanics' Inst., Art Acad., all of Cincinnati; winner of scholarship, Duveneck class, Cincinnati, 1900, in Art Students' League, New York. Specialized in cattle and landscape, in oil and water color. Exhibited at Paris; Corcoran Gallery, Nat. Acad. Design, Phila. Acad. Fine Arts, Art Inst. Chicago, Boston, Milwaukee, Cleveland; Cincinnati Art Mus., 1915; etc. Awarded Hudnut prize, N.Y. Water Color Club, 1920; Cooper prize, Conn. Acad. of Fine Arts, 1925, Gedney Bunce prize, 1929; Mr. and Mrs. Burton Mansfield prize, New Haven Paint and Clay Club, 1930; Goodman prize Lyme, for best group of paintings, 1932. Mem. Am. Water Color Soc., New York Water Color Club, Am. Federation Arts, Conn. Acad. Fine Arts. A.N.A., 1921. Home: Lyme, Conn. Died Mar. 4, 1935.

VOLLMER, John Phillip, capitalist; b. Birkenfeld, Würtemberg, Germany, Jan. 25, 1847; s. Otto Phillip and Elizabeth (Fix) V.; removed to Ind. in boyhood; ed. Northwestern Christian (now Butler) U. and Prof. Richter's Sch. of Tech., Indianapolis; m. Sallie Elizabeth Barber, Sept. 27, 1870. Engaged in banking, merchandising, milling, mfg., farming (owning about 300 farms), etc.; mem. firms of John P. Vollmer & Co., E. Baumeister & Co., Vollmer & Scott. Pres. First Nat. Bank, Lewiston, Ida., First Nat. Bank, Genesee, Ida., Vollmer-Clearwater Co., First Bank, Asotin, Wash., Sweetwater Ditch Co., Lewiston Milling Co., Bank & Trust Co., Vollmar, Ida.; propr. Asotin (Wash.) Flouring Mills Co.; First Nat. Bank, Grangeville, Ida.; interested in Cash Hardware Co., Lewiston, Scott Mercantile Co., Vollmer, Ida.; pres. Kendrick Warehouse & Milling Co.; v.p., dir. Nez Perce & Eastern R.R. Co. of Ida. Built first telegraph line in northern Ida., 1876; built and operated first practical Bell Telephone line on Pacific Coast, 1878. Republican. Mem. of Telephone Pioneers of America. Assisted Mark Twain by furnishing material for "Innocents Abroad," "Life on the Mississippi," and "Captain Stormfield," while en route with him from New York to San Francisco via the Isthmus of Panama, in March and April 1868. Home: Lewiston, Ida. Died May 7, 1917.

VOLLMER, Philip, theologian; b. Frankenthal, Germany, Nov. 28, 1860; s. Jacob and Catharine (Braun) V.; came to America, 1878; grad. Bloomfield (N.J.) Coll., 1881, and Presbyn. Sem., 1884; student Union Theol. Sem., New York, 1885; Ph.D., U. of Pa., 1893; summer semester U. of Heidelberg, Germany, 1895, U. of Strassburg, 1906; D.D., Ursinus Coll., Collegeville, Pa., 1901; m. Mathilde Wilhelmina Osann, June 29, 1885; children—Beatrice (Mrs. E. I. Powell), Rev. Philip, Prof. Clement, Paula (dec.), Thekla (Mrs. M. H. Day). Ordained ministry of Presbyn. Ch., Oct. 28, 1884; founder, and pastor, Presbyn. Ch. of Peace, Brooklyn, 1884-89; pastor St. Paul's Ref. Ch., Phila., 1889-1905; prof. theology, Ursinus Sch. of Theology, Phila., 1898-1907, Central Theol. Sem., Dayton, O., 1907-23, Eden Theol. Sem., St. Louis, Jan. 1923-25; exec. sec. Commn. on Christianity and Social Problems, 1925—. Instructor Bloomfield Coll., 1881-86; pres. German Ref. Synod of the East, 1901, German Ref. Classis, 1902; pres. bd. trustees German Synod of the East, 1898-1902; pres. Gen. Synod Bd. of Ministerial Relief. Dir. Ursinus Coll.; trustee Central Theol. Sem. Lecturer on religion, travel and sociol. topics; editor Friedenstaube, 1885-1905; dept. editor Reformed Church Messenger, 1893-1911; editor of Reformed Witness, 1905-07. Independent in politics. Author: Evangelischer Liederschatz, 1896; John Calvin, 1908; Modern Student's Life of Christ, 1911; Shorter Heidelberg Catechism, 1894; Der Heidelberger Katechismus, 1893; Life of Gustavus Adolphus, 1897; The Reformation, a Liberating Force, 1917; Outline Studies in the History and Literature of the Apostolic Church; New Testament Sociology, 1923; The New Testament Writings, 1924; Christian Family Altar, 1925. Home: Palmyra, N.J. Died Dec. 10, 1929.

VOLLRATH, Edward, army officer; b. Bucyrus, O., June 28, 1858; s. Charles and Eva Elizabeth (Hocker) V.; A.B., Princeton, 1883, A.M., 1886; m. Millie Wise, June 27, 1888 (died 1910); children—Jeanne Elizabeth, Mrs. Edna Grace Willaman, Charles Victor, Carol Pamilla, Edward Wise. Admitted to Ohio bar, 1885, and practiced at Bucyrus; judge Ct. of Appeals of Ohio, 1904-05. Enlisted as pvt. Co. A, 8th Ohio Inf., Apr. 30, 1884; sergt. maj., June 20, 1884; capt. Co. A, June 30, 1886; maj. 8th Ohio Inf., July 5, 1892; lt. col., Aug. 14, 1899; col., Dec. 22, 1899; brig. gen. N.A., Aug. 5, 1917. Served as maj. 8th Ohio Inf., with 5th Army Corps, at Santiago de Cuba, Spanish-Am. War, 1898; col. same regt. Mexican border service, June 19, 1916-Mar. 22, 1917; responded with regt. to President's call, July 15, 1917; successively apptd. comdr. 66th Depot Brigade, Aug. 1917, 66th Arty. Brigade, 41st Div., Sept. 1917; comd. 82d Inf. Brig. and 41st Div., A.E.F., in France, Dec. 15, 1917-Feb. 11, 1919. Hon. discharged, Mar. 1, 1919, and resumed practice of law at Bucyrus, O. Republican. Evang. Lutheran. K.P. Home: Bucyrus, O. Died Jan. 21, 1931.

VOLPE, Arnold, conductor; b. Kovno, Russia, July 9, 1869; s. Lewis and Ella (Gabrilowitsch) V.; studied violin at Warsaw Mus. Inst. under Prof. Isidor Lotto, 1884-87, and at Imperial Conservatory, St. Petersburg, under Prof. Leopold Auer, 1887-91; B.A., with highest honors, same, 1891; studied theory and composition, Imperial Conservatory, under Prof. Nicolas Soloview, 1893-97; m. Marie Michelson, Apr. 15, 1902. Came to America, 1898; mus. dir. Young Men's Symphony Orchestra, New York, 1902—; founder and conductor Volpe Symphony Soc. of New York, 1904—; dir. orchestra Brooklyn Inst. Arts and Sciences, 1910—; condr. Municipal Orchestral Concerts, New York, 1910-13; founder and condr. Stadium Symphony Orchestra, New York, 1918—. Vol. Russian Army, 1892-93. Composer of songs and instrumental music. Home: New York, N.Y. Died Feb. 2, 1940.

von ENDE, Carl Leopold, chemist; b. Burlington, Ia., July 2, 1870; s. Charles Ende (b. Carl Conrad von Ende) and Thusnelda (Leopold) E.; B.S. State U. of Ia., 1893, M.S., 1894; Ph.D., U. of Göttingen, Germany, 1899; m. Alice Ankeney, July 28, 1904; children—Eunice Ankeney, Carl Ankeney. Demonstrator in chemistry, State U. of Ia., 1894-95; science teacher, high sch., Burlington, Ia., 1895-96; instr. in chemistry, 1896-97, 1899-1905, asst. prof., 1905-07, State U. of Ia.; research asso., Research Lab. Physical Chemistry, Mass. Inst. Tech., 1907-08; prof. chemistry and head of dept., U. of Ida., 1908—; sabbatical leave at Univ. Coll. of Wales, Aberystwyth, 1928. Fellow A.A.A.S. Democrat. Translator: Dolezalek's Theory of the Lead Accumulator, 1904; Abegg's Electrolytic Dissociation Theory, 1907. Contbr. articles describing results of researches in physical and inorganic chemistry. Home: Moscow, Ida. Died Oct. 9, 1934.

VON HOLST, Hermann Eduard, educator; b. Fellin, Livonia, June 19, 1841; ed. there and at U. of Dorpat; Ph.D., U. of Heidelberg, 1865; m. Annie Isabelle Hatt, Apr. 23, 1872. Prof. history U. of Strassburg, 1872-74; prof. history U. of Freiburg, 1874-92; head prof. history, U. of Chicago, 1892-1900; corr. mem. of Prussian Akademie der Wissenschaften. For 10 yrs. mem. First Chamber of the Baden Landtag and 4 yrs. v.p. of same. Author: Constitutional History of the United States; Constitutional Law of the United States; John C. Calhoun; Life of John Brown; The French Revolution Tested by Mirabeau's Career; etc. Home: Freiburg, Germany. Died 1904.

VON KELER, Theodore M(aximilian) R., editor; b. Tiegenhof, Germany, July 26, 1877; s. Eugene R. and Maria Von K.; grad. Realgymnasium, Koenigsberg, Prussia; studied chemistry in Stuttgart Poly. High Sch.; m. Mildred Belle Keyler, July 12, 1911 (died 1921); 1 dau., Thelma Ortrude; m. 2d, Helen Dorothy Ashby, July 19, 1924. Came to U.S., 1904, naturalized citizen, 1914. Went to China as analyzing chemist sugar refinery, 1898; abandoned chemistry to take up writing; free-lance writer until 1909; asst. editor Motor World, 1909-12; asso. editor Automobile Topics, New York, 1912-15; editor Sugar, New York, 1917-21; asst. editor Liberty mag, Apr. 1924—; spl. writer for Scientific Am. on automobiles and internal combustion engines for many yrs. Republican. Lutheran. Author: Confessions of a Courier, 1913; Mystery of the Iron Mask, 1921; Essence of the Koran, 1922; The King Enjoys Himself, 1922; Thou Shalt Not Kill, 1926; also a series of opera books dealing with 30 famous operas, 1923-24. Home: Chicago, Ill. Deceased.

von MACH, Edmund (Robert Otto), author; b. Gaffert, Pomerania, Germany, Aug. 1, 1870; s. Edmund von and Melanie von (Otto) M.; came to America, 1891; A.B., Harvard, 1895, A.M., 1896, Ph.D., 1900; m. Mary Ware Peirce, June 23, 1903. Instr. fine arts, Harvard, 1899-1903; instr. history of art, Wellesley, 1899-1902; lecturer in history of art, Bradford Acad., Cambridge, Mass., 1902-15. Non-resident lecturer on art, Vassar Coll. Gave up academic career for study of law and entered law office of Hon. James A. Beha, New York, 1923. Served in German Army, 1889-91. Author: Greek Sculpture, Its Spirit and Principles, 1903; Handbook of Greek and Roman Sculpture, 1904; Outlines of the History of Painting, 1905; The Art of Painting in the Nineteenth Century, 1907; What Germany Wants, 1914; Germany's Point of View, 1915; Why Europe Is at War, 1915; Sir Edward's Evidence, 1915. Translator: German World Policies, by Paul Rohrbach, 1915. Contbd. The German Viewpoint to the Wednesday editions of Boston Evening Transcript, Oct. 14, 1914-May 5, 1915; regular contbr. to Viereck's American Monthly. Editor: Official Diplomatic Documents Relating to the Outbreak of the European War, 1916. Am. editor Allgemeines Lexikon der Bildenden Künstler. Home: West Brooksville, Me. Died July 1927.

von MOSCHZISKER, Robert, lawyer; b. Phila., Mar. 6, 1870; s. Frank A. and Clara (Harrison) von M.; ed. pub. schs. and pvtly.; LL.D., Lafayette Coll., Dickinson Coll., Pa. Mil. Coll., Temple U., U. of Pa., 1922, Juniata Coll., 1928; at 13 entered office of Edward Shippen and later studied law under him; admitted to bar, 1896; m. Anne Macbeth, June 29, 1912; children—Kate, Bertha, Michael. Practiced with Edward Shippen, 1896-1902; asst. dist. atty., Phila. Dist., Pa., 1902-03; judge Ct. of Common Pleas, No. 3, Phila. County, 1903-10; justice Supreme Ct. of Pa., 1910-21, chief justice, 1921-30; later in practice with law firm Ballard, Spahr, Andrews & Ingersoll, Phila. Trustee U. of Pa. Republican. Mason. Author: Trial by Jury; Judicial Review of Legislation; Legal Essays. Home: Philadelphia, Pa. Died Nov. 21, 1939.

VONNOH, Robert, painter; b. Hartford, Conn., Sept. 17, 1858; s. of William and Frederika V.; ed. Boston pub. schs.; in Mass. Normal Art Sch., Boston, 1875-79; instr. painting and drawing same, 1879-81; also instr. Roxbury Evening Drawing Sch., and Thayer Acad., S. Braintree, Mass.; studied Académie Julian, Paris, 1881-83; m. Grace D. Farrell, July 7, 1886 (dec.); m. 2d, Bessie O. Potter, Sept. 17, 1899. Instr. painting, Cowles Art Sch., 1884-85; prin. E. Boston Evening Drawing Sch., 1883-85; prin. instr. portrait and figure painting, Mus. of Fine Arts, Boston, 1885-87; abroad, 1887-91; prin. instr. portrait and figure painting, Pa. Acad. Fine Arts, Phila., 1891-96. Exhibitor Paris Salon, London, and Munich exhbns., Paris expns., 1889, 1900, Chicago Expn., 1893, Stockholm, 1896, Buffalo Expn., 1901, St. Louis Expn., 1904, Georges Petit, Paris, and exhbns. New York, Phila., Pittsburgh, Boston, Chicago, etc. Abroad, 1907-11. Mem. Nat. Jury for Am. Sect., Paris, 1900; Internat. juries, Carnegie expns., Pittsburgh; Internat. Jury of Awards, St. Louis Expn.; exec. com. Louis Comfort Tiffany Foundation. Received Thomas R. Proctor portrait prize, Nat. Acad. Design; gold medal, Charleston Expn.; gold medal, Panama P.I. Expn.; medals at Boston, Buffalo, Chicago, Paris, etc. Represented in Pa. Acad. Fine Arts, Mass. Hist. Soc. (Boston), The White House, Washington, Am. Philos. Soc., Metropolitan Mus., Brooklyn Mus., Youngstown, Ohio, Museum, etc. Chmn. of jury, Pa. Acad. Fine Arts; mem. jury, Nat. Acad. Design. N.A., 1906. Instr. composition class, Pa. Acad. Fine Arts, 1918-19, instr. painting life figure, 1919-20. Home: Lyme, Conn. Died Dec. 28, 1933.

VON RUCK, Karl, physician; b. Stuttgart, Germany, July 10, 1849; s. George and Clara von R.; B.S., Stuttgart, 1867; M.D., U. of Tübingen, 1877; M.D., U. of Mich., 1879; studied U. of Berlin, 1882; m. Delia Moore, Dec. 25, 1872. Founder, and med. dir. Winyah Sanatorium, Asheville, N.C., 1888-1910; cons. phys., 1910—; founder Von Ruck Research Lab. for Tuberculosis, Asheville, 1895, and in charge, 1895— (this laboratory for original investigations only). Discoverer of vaccine for the prevention and cure of tuberculosis. Contbr. to Am. and European jours. and revs. on subject of tuberculosis. Author: Studies in Prophylactic and Therapeutic Immunization against Tuberculosis (with his son), 1916. Home: Asheville, N.C. Died Nov. 6, 1922.

VON SALTZA, Charles Frederick, artist, portrait painter; b. Sorby, Sweden, Oct. 29, 1858; s. C. A. P. von S.; ed. Stockholm, Sweden; studied Royal Acad. Fine Arts, Stockholm; Royal Acad., Brussels; also under private teachers in Paris; m. Henrietta Stoopendaal, 1883. Instr. in painting and drawing, St. Louis School of Fine Arts, 1892-98; instr. in painting, Chicago Fine Arts Inst., 1898-99; instr. Teachers' Coll., Columbia U., 1899-1901; exhibited in Paris; Internat. Exhbn., Berlin, 1896; World's Fair, Chicago; Stockholm Internat. Exhbn., 1897; Nat. Acad. of Design, New York; Soc. of Am. Artists, N.Y.; Art Inst., Chicago. Home: New York, N.Y. Died 1905.

von STRUVE, Henry Clay, consular service; b. Marble Falls, Tex., July 30, 1874; s. Amand and Christiane (Fissler) von S.; LL.B., U. of Tex., 1894, LL.M., 1896; m. Cora Louise Fox, Dec. 27, 1897 (died 1925); children—Amand William, Henry Clay, Louise Cora. Admitted to Tex. bar, 1894; teacher of German and Latin, high sch., Brenham, Tex., 1897-98; prin. grammar sch., Herman, Mo., 1899-1900; practiced law, San Antonio, Tex., 1901-02, Gonzales, 1902-06; served as city atty., Gonzales; in banking business, Gonzales and Plainview, 1906-14; U.S. consul at Curaçao, Dutch West Indies, 1914, Erfurt, Germany, 1916; in office Foreign Trade Advisers, Dept. of State, 1917; consul at Havana, Cuba, 1918, La Guaira, Venezuela, 1919, Antilla, Cuba, 1920, Mexicali, Mexico, 1922, Stavanger, Norway, 1925, Göteborg, Sweden, 1926, Caracas, Venezuela, July 1930—. Mason. Died Nov. 5, 1933.

VOORHEES, Clark Greenwood, artist; b. New York, May 29, 1871; Ph.B., Yale, 1891; A.M., Columbia, 1894; studied art at Acad. Julian, Paris; m. Maud C. Folsom, Aug. 20, 1904. Exhibited Nat. Acad. Design, New York, Carnegie Inst., Pittsburgh, Pa. Acad. Fine Arts, Art Inst. of Chicago, etc. Awarded Hallgarten prize, Nat. Acad., 1905; bronze medal, St. Louis Expn., 1904; Eaton purchase prize, Lyme Art Assn., 1923. Served 6 yrs. in 7th Regt. N.G.S.N.Y. Capt. Co. F, 3d Regt., Conn. Home Guard. Studio: Lyme, Conn. Died July 18, 1938.

VOORHEES, Edward Burnett, agrl. chemist; b. Mine Brook, Somerset County, N.J., June 22, 1856; s. John and Sarah (Dilley) V.; A.B., Rutgers Coll., 1881, A.M., 1884; D.Sc., U. of Vt., 1900; m. Anna E. Amerman, Oct. 18, 1883. Asst. to prof. chemistry, Wesleyan U., 1881-82; asst. chemist, 1882-88, chemist, 1888-93, dir., 1893, N.J. Agrl. Expt. Sta.; dir. N.J. Agrl. College Expt. Sta., 1896. Prof. agr., Rutgers Coll., 1890—; supt. N.J. Agrl. Coll. Farm, 1896—; agt. U.S. Dept. Agr. for irrigation in N.J., 1896—; pres. bd. dirs. N.J. Weather Bur., 1893; v.p., 1893-1901, pres., 1901—, N.J. State Bd. Agr. Received Nichols Research Medal for best paper containing results of chem. research reported to Am. Chem. Soc. Jour. in 1902—for paper on Dentrification. Mem. Ref. Ch. in America. Republican. Author: First Principles of Agriculture, 1895; Fertilizers, 1898; Forage Crops, 1907; also many bulls. and mag. articles on agrl. topics. Lecturer before farmers' insts., bds. of agr., dairy and breeders' assns., and hort. socs. in all Eastern States. Home: New Brunswick, N.J. Died 1911.

VOORHEES, Foster MacGowan, governor; b. Clinton, N.J., Nov. 5, 1856; s. Nathaniel W. and Naomi (Leigh) V.; A.B., Rutgers, 1876, A.M., 1879, LL.D., 1899, Princeton, 1901; unmarried. Admitted to bar, 1880, in practice at Elizabeth, N.J., 1880—. Mem. bd. edn., Elizabeth, 1884-87; mem. N.J. Assembly, 1888-90, Senate, 1894-98 (pres. 1898), and acting gov. vice U.S. Atty. Gen. Griggs, resigned; gov. of N.J., 1899-1901. Republican. Home: Elizabeth, N.J. Died June 14, 1927.

VOORHEES, Samuel Stockton, chemical engr.; b. Springfield, O., Jan. 15, 1867; s. John Hunn and Elizabeth Aston (Warder) V.; student scientific course, Lehigh U., Pa., class of 1888 (non-grad.); spl. course in chemistry, Columbian (now George Washington U.), Washington, D.C.; m. Laura Toucey Kase, July 10, 1895. Asst. chemist Cambria Iron Co. and Pa. R.R., Altoona, Pa., 1887-96; chemist in charge for Southern Ry., Washington, 1896-99, N.Y.C.&H.R. R.R., 1899-1901; engr. of tests, U.S. supervising architect's office, 1901-08; engr. of tests, U.S. Geol. Survey, technol. work, 1908-10; engr. chemist U.S. Bur. Standards, July 1910—. Episcopalian. Author various repts. of tech. committees of scientific socs. Home: Washington, D.C. Died Sept. 23, 1921.

VOORHEES, Stephen Hegeman, banker; b. Griggstown, N.J., Aug. 3, 1864; s. Alfred I. and Emily (Suydam) V.; ed. pub. schs., Griggstown, and Normal and Model Sch., Trenton, N.J.; m. Helen Walton Gray, Oct. 31, 1893; children—Ruth Suydam (Mrs. Edward Le Roy Voorhees), Helen (Mrs. L. Josselyn Young). Began in employ Mercantile Nat. Bank, New York, 1884; with Chase Nat. Bank, 1889-99; organizer, and agt. Royal Bank of Can., at N.Y. City, 1899-1915; v.p. Nat. City Bank, 1915-24 (retired). Pres. Bd. of Health, Plainfield, N.J. Mem. Acad. Polit. Science. Republican. Presbyn. Home: Plainfield, N.J. Died Feb. 11, 1940.

VOORHEES, Theodore, ry. official; b. New York, June 4, 1847; s. B. F. and Margaret E. (Sinclair) V.; student Columbia Coll.; C.E., Rensselaer Poly. Inst., 1869; m. Mary E. Chittenden, Feb. 4, 1894. In ry. service, July 15, 1869—; engring. dept., 4 yrs., supt., 2 yrs., Syracuse, Binghamton & New York R.R. (D.,L.&W. R.R.); with transportation dept. Delaware & Hudson Canal Co., Albany, 1874-75; supt. Saratoga & Champlain Div., Northern R.R. dept., same, 1875-85; asst. gen. supt., 1885-90, gen. supt., 1890-93, N.Y.C.&H.R. R.R.; also gen. supt. Rome, Watertown & Ogdensburg R.R., 1890-93; 1st v.p. Phila. & Reading R.R., Feb. 1, 1893—. Trustee Rensselaer Poly. Inst. Home: Elkins Park, Pa. Died Mar. 12, 1916.

VOORHEES, Willard Penfield, judge; b. New Brunswick, N.J., July 28, 1851; s. Abraham and Jane (Jarvis) V.; A.B., Rutgers Coll., 1871, A.M., 1874, LL.D., 1910; m. Sarah Rutgers Neilson, Mar. 15, 1877. Began practice as atty., 1874, as counsellor, 1878; apptd. justice Supreme Ct. of N.J., Jan. 1908; term expiring 1915. Dir. New Brunswick Trust Co.; trustee F. E. Parker Memorial Home, Rutgers Coll. Republican. Presbyterian. Home: New Brunswick, N.J. Died May 31, 1914.

VOORSANGER, Jacob, rabbi; b. Amsterdam, Holland, Nov. 13, 1852; s. Wolf and Alicia (Pekel) V.; ed. Amsterdam; student theol. sem. and U. of Amsterdam; grad. rabbi, 1873, D.D., Hebrew Union Coll., Cincinnati; m. Eva Cooper, Aug. 24, 1873. Rabbi at Phila., 1873-76, Providence, 1876-78, Houston, Tex., 1878-86, San Francisco, 1886—. Prof. Semitic langs. and lits., U. of Calif., 1895—; v.p. Calif. Red Cross Soc.; mem. Hebrew Veterans of Spanish-Am. War. Author: Life and Works of Moses Mendelssohn; The Chronicles of Emmanuel, 1900. Editor Emanuel, San Francisco. Cons. editor and contbr. Jewish Ency. Home: San Francisco, Calif. Died 1908.

VOPICKA, Charles J.; b. Bohemia, Nov. 3, 1857; s. Joseph and Barbara V.; ed. high sch. and business coll.; m. Victoria Kubin, Feb. 3, 1883. Came to U.S., 1880; settled in Chicago, 1881; engaged in real estate and banking business until 1899; an organizer, and pres. of Atlas Brewing Co. West Park Commr., Chicago, 1894-97; mem. Sch. Bd., 1901-02; mem. Bd. of Local Improvements, Chicago, 1902-04; Dem. candidate for Congress, 5th Dist. Ill., 1904; mem. Charter Conv., Chicago, 1906; E.E. and M.P. to Roumania, Servia and Bulgaria, 1913-20; mem. Chicago Bd. of Edn., 1927-30. Author: Secrets of the Balkans. Home: Chicago, Ill. Died Sept. 4, 1935.

VORSE, Albert White, editor; b. Littleton, Mass., Aug. 18, 1866; s. Rev. Albert Buel and Harriet Ellen V.; A.B., Harvard, 1889; m. Mary Marvin Heaton, Oct. 18, 1898. With Children's Aid Soc., and People's Entertainment Soc., Boston, 1889-90; with Car Record Office, Pa. R.R., Phila., 1890-91; on staff Philadelphia Press, 1891-93; summer of 1892, corr. of the Press with the Peary Relief Expdn. to Greenland; music critic N.Y. Mail and Express, winter, 1893-94; lit. editor Boston Commonwealth, 1894-96; dramatic editor Illustrated Am., New York, Sept.-Dec. 1897; lit. adviser to G. P. Putnam's Sons, Jan. 1899-Mar. 1900; asso. editor Criterion, 1900-01; asst. mng. editor New Internat. Ency., 1901-03. Author: Laughter of the Sphinx. 1900; also chapters on Japan under the Constitution in "Japan," Stories of the Nations Series, 1906. Home: Provincetown, Mass. Died 1910.

VORYS, Arthur Isaiah, lawyer; b. Lancaster, O., Nov. 25, 1856; s. Isaiah and Emily (Webb) V.; ed. Lancaster High Sch. and Ohio State U., 1 yr.; admitted to bar, 1880; m. Jeanny M. McNeill, Feb. 5, 1891; children—Webb Isaiah, John Martin, Arthur McNeill, Hermann. City solicitor Lancaster, 1884-88; supt. of ins. of Ohio, 1900-07 (resigned); mem. Rep. Nat. Com., 1908-12; mem. law firm of Vorys, Sater, Seymour & Pease, Apr. 1909—; dir. Western and Southern Life Ins. Co. (Cincinnati), Ohio Farmers Ins. Co. Mem. Am. Bar Assn. (chmn. com. on ins. law in preparation of model ins. code), World's Ins. Congress (permanent chmn., San Francisco, 1915). Methodist. Home: Columbus, O. Died Jan. 26, 1933.

VOSBURGH, George Bedell, clergyman; b. Stockport, N.Y., Nov. 18, 1849; s. Bartholomew C. and Ann Eliza (Bedell) V.; grad. Albany (N.Y.) State Normal Coll., 1870; A.B., Collegiate U., Hamilton, N.Y., 1873, B.D., 1874; M.A., U. of Chicago, 1883, Ph.D., 1884; D.D., Shurtleff, 1892; m. Florence L. Learned, Aug. 1881 (died 1927); children—Edna H. (wife of Bernard Lentz, U.S.A.), Paul L. Ordained Bapt. ministry, 1874; pastor Cooperstown, N.Y., 1874-77, Jersey City, N.J., 1877-79, Millard Av. Ch., Chicago, 1879-83, First Ch., Decatur, Ill., 1883-90, First Ch., Elgin, Ill., 1890-93, Stoughton St. Ch., Boston, 1893-97, First Ch., Denver, 1897-1911. Pres. Colo. Bapt. State Conv., 4 yrs.; pres. Bapt. Pastors' confs., in Chicago, Boston and Denver; lecturer on art before coll. and lit. socs.; traveled extensively in Mexico, Europe, Egypt and Syria; around the world, 1911-12; spent 9 summers in Europe, engaged largely in research work; held lectureship, "Civilization in the 20th Century," for 14 yrs. (1914-28), U. of Denver. Chaplain Colo. Soc. S.R., 1898—; mem. Nat. Inst. Social Sciences. Mason. Home: Denver, Colo. Died Feb. 27, 1940.

VOSE, William Preston, army officer; b. Orrington, Me., July 19, 1839; s. William and Mary Wooderson (Phillips) V.; grad. U.S. Mil. Acad., 1864; m. Bettiea May Williams, Oct. 22, 1874. Apptd. 2d lt., 2d Arty. U.S.A., June 13, 1864; promoted 1st lt., 8th Arty., Mar. 8, 1865, capt., Oct. 2, 1883, maj., 6th Arty., Mar. 8, 1898, lt. col. Arty. Corps, May 8, 1901, col., Dec. 20, 1902, brig. gen. U.S.A., Apr. 23, 1904. Upon graduation was ordered to Army of the Potomac; assigned to Light Battery B, 4th Arty., of Arty. Brigade, 5th Army Corps; took part in all engagements of that army, including different attacks on Petersburg, Weldon R. R., Hatcher's Run, Peebles Farm, Weldon raid, Grovelly Run, Five Forks, Sailor's Creek and Appomattox; comd. battery during Appomattox Campaign until after gen. review of army at Washington. Served in nearly every State and Ty. of U.S., Hawaii, and nearly 3 yrs., 1898-1901, in P.I.; retired for age, 1903. Mem. Assn. Graduates Mil. Acad.; companion Loyal Legion. Died 1906.

VOSS, Ernst Karl Johann Heinrich, univ. prof.; b. Buetzow, Mecklenburg, Germany, Oct. 13, 1860; s. Heinrich and Dorothea (Amerpohl) V.; ed. Realgymnasium, Buetzow, and univs. of Rostock, Marburg and Leipzig; Ph.D., Leipzig; came to U.S., 1889; m. Auri Vail Hedrick, Oct. 26, 1904. Prof. German philology, U. of Mich., 1891-96, U. of Wis., 1896-1931; abroad on leave of absence, 1893-95, 1902-03, 1908-09, 2d semester, 1912-13, 2d semester, 1924-25. Mem. Modern Lang. Assn. America, Wis. Academy Sciences, Arts and Letters, Linguistic Society America. Democrat. Author: Vier Jahrzehnte im Amerika (Stuttgart), 1929. Editor Sixteenth Century Reprints. Contbr. to mags. Home: Madison, Wis. Died July 22, 1937.

VOTAW, Albert Hiatt; b. Richmond, Ind., Feb. 19, 1850; s. Isaac and Anna Maria (Hiatt) V.; A.B., Earlham Coll., Richmond, Ind., 1874; m. Phebe Nicholson, 1891; 1 son, Ernest Nicholson. Instr. Latin, Westtown Sch., Pa., 1877-1902; sec. Pa. Prison Soc. (oldest organization of the kind in existence, founded 1787), 1908-29. Mem. Am. Prison Assn., American Acad. Polit. and Social Science. Quaker. Republican. Author: Prison Efficiency, 1916; Review of the County Prisons of Pennsylvania, 1920. Editor The Prison Journal. Home: Lansdowne, Pa. Died Feb. 21, 1931.

VOTEY, Edwin Scott, mfr.; b. Ovid, N.Y., June 8, 1856; s. Charles A. and Fanny (Anderson) V.; ed. common schs.; m. Annie M. Gray, 1878; children —Fannie (Mrs. J. M. Rogers), Edwina (Mrs. J. E. W. Tracy), Charles H. Began with the Aeolian Co., mfrs. pianos, organs and phonographs, 1898, became v.p.; v.p. Aeolian Weber Piano and Pianola Co.; dir. First Nat. Bank (Summit, N.J.), Nat. Lock Washer Co., State Title & Mortgage Co., and 14 other corps.; inventor of pianola. Republican. Baptist. Home: Summit, N.J. Died 1931.

VOTEY, Josiah William, civil engr.; b. Ovid, N.Y., July 23, 1860; s. Charles Augustus and Fanny Graves (Anderson) V.; grad. Vermont Acad., 1881; C.E. U. of Vt., 1884, D.Sc., 1911; also D.Sc., U. of Me., 1922; m. Emma Luella Lane, Mar. 25, 1886; children—Florence, Ruth, Dorothy, Constance. Instr. civ. engrings., 1884-89, asst. prof., 1889-90, asso. prof., 1890-93, prof., 1893—, dean Coll. Engring., 1901—, U. of Vt. Cons. civ. and sanitary engr.; city engr., Burlington, 1887; mem. Vt. State Highway Commn., 1892-96; mem. Bd. of St. Commrs., Burlington, 1902-05; mem. Bd. Water Commrs., Burlington, 1908-09; sanitary engr., Vt. Bd. of Health, 1908—. Fellow A.A.A.S. Home: Burlington, Vt. Died Sept. 16, 1931.

VREELAND, Edward Butterfield, congressman; b. Cuba, N.Y., 1857; s. Simon V.; acad. edn.; m. Myra S. Price, of Friendship, N.Y. Supt. schs., Salamanca, N.Y., 1877-82; admitted to bar, 1881; practiced at Salamanca; pres. Salamanca Nat. Bank, 1891—. Elected 56th to 62d Congresses (1899-1913), 37th N.Y. Dist. Home: Salamanca, N.Y. Died May 8, 1936.

VREELAND, Walter J., lawyer; b. Wyckoff, N.J., Sept. 20, 1880; s. Lewis and M. Louise (Quakenbush) V.; LL.B., New York U., 1903; m. Fannie M. Sutherland, Apr. 10, 1907; children—Olga M., Walter J. Began practice at N.Y. City, 1903; pres. Great Neck Shores Corp., South 11th Street Warehouse Corp.; sec. and dir. New Niquero Sugar Co., The Cuban American Sugar Co.; sec. Nat. Sugar Refining Co. of N.J. Republican. Presbyn. Home: Brooklyn, N.Y. Died Jan. 16, 1939.

VROOM, Garret Dorset Wall, judge; b. Trenton, N.J., Dec. 17, 1843; s. Gov. Peter Dumont V.; bro. of Peter Dumont V.; A.B., Rutgers, 1862, LL.D., 1902; m. Charlotte Dickinson, June 8, 1871. Admitted to bar, 1865; city solicitor Trenton, 1866-70, 1873-76; prosecutor of pleas Mercer County, N.J., 1870-73; reporter Supreme Ct. of N.J., 1873; mayor of Trenton, 1881-84; later pres. bd. pub. works; tendered seat on Supreme Ct. bench, 1900, but declined; judge Ct. of Errors and Appeals, N.J., 1901-07, 1907-13. Democrat. Mem. Nat. Commn. for Promotion of Uniform Legislation; pres. Trenton Battle Monument Assn.; pres. bd. mgrs. N.J. State Hosp.; pres. Trenton Savings Fund Soc. Author: Revised Statutes, N.J., (with J. H. Stewart), 1877; General Statutes, N.J., 3 vols. (with Judge W. M. Lanning), 1895; N.J. Law Reports, vols. 36-70. Home: Trenton, N.J. Died Mar. 4, 1914.

VROOM, Peter Dumont, brig. gen. U.S.A.; b. Trenton, N.J., Apr. 18, 1842; s. Gov. Peter D. and Matilda (Wall) V.; C.E., Rensselaer Poly. Inst., 1862. First lt. adj. 1st N.J. Inf., Aug. 13, 1862; resigned, Sept. 19, 1863; maj. 2d N.J. Cav., Sept. 25, 1863; bvtd. col., Mar. 13, 1865; hon. mustered out, Oct. 24, 1865; apptd. from N.J. 2d lt. 3d U.S. Cav., Feb. 23, 1866; 1st lt., July 28, 1866; capt., May 17, 1876; maj. insp. gen., Dec. 10, 1888; lt. col. insp. gen., Jan. 2, 1895; col. insp. gen., Dec. 19, 1899;

brig. gen. insp. gen., Apr. 11, 1903; retired at own request after 40 yrs.' service, Apr. 12, 1903. Home: Trenton, N.J. Died Mar. 19, 1926.

VROOMAN, John Wright, banker; b. Herkimer County, New York, Mar. 28, 1844 (ancestors Holland Dutch, conspicuous in early Am. history and in Am. Revolution); ed. common schs. and acad.; hon. A.M., Hamilton Coll., N.Y.; LL.D., Philomath Coll., Oregon. Volunteer in U.S. Navy during Civil War, taking part in both attacks on Ft. Fisher; admitted to N.Y. bar after war and practiced, Herkimer, N.Y.; chief clerk surrogate's ct., Herkimer County, 1868-78; deputy clerk N.Y. Assembly, 1876-77; sec. N.Y. Senate, 1878-88; mem. Rep. State Com. and sec., 1880-88; Rep. nominee for lt. gov., 1891; presdl. elector, 1892. Banker at Herkimer, prior to 1890; then in business at New York, until retired. Grand Master of Masons, N.Y., 1889-91; trustee and pres. Holland Soc. of New York; pres. Life Underwriters' Assn. of New York; mgr. and life mem. M.E. Hosp., Brooklyn; life mem. New York Kindergarten Assn., Am. Tract Soc.; exec. mem. Am. Flag Assn.; mem. Internat. Com. Y.M.C.A.; hon. v.p. Boy Scouts America; officer Stony Wold Sanatorium; trustee Hudson-Fulton Commn.; trustee Herkimer Hosp. Actively interested in church, S.S., Y.M.C.A., patriotic and philanthropic work; mem. G.A.R. and on staff of dept. comdr.; pres. Gen. Herkimer Monument Commn.; mem. Nat. War Work Council of Y.M.C.A.; trustee Herkimer Free Library, M.E. Church; chmn. adv. bd. Centenary Cadets U.S. Mason (33°); hon. mem. many Masonic and patriotic orgns. Home: Herkimer, N.Y. Died Nov. 24, 1929.

W

WACHENHEIMER, J., banker; b. New York, N.Y., s. Abraham and Fanny (Levy) W.; ed. pub. schs., N.Y. City; m. Susie E. Hood. Began as clk. ins. office, later in banking business; vice pres. Commercial Merchants Nat. Bank & Trust Co. to 1922, pres., 1922—. Republican. Hebrew religion. Mason. Home: Peoria, Ill. Died June 23, 1934.

WACHTER, Frank C., congressman, 3d Md. dist., 1899-1907; b. Baltimore, Sept. 16, 1861; ed. private schools; learned trade of cloth cutter; later engaged in present business of examining, adjusting, sponging and refinishing woolens, cloths, etc. Mem. jail bd., Baltimore, 1896-98; Rep. caucus nominee for police commr. of Baltimore City in legislature of 1898. Home: Baltimore, Md. Died 1910.

WACKER, Charles Henry, chmn. Chicago Plan Commn.; b. Chicago, Aug. 29, 1856; s. Frederick and Catharine (Hummel) W.; ed. pub. schs., and at Lake Forest (Ill.) Acad. and Stuttgart, Germany; LL.D., U. of Chicago, 1925; m. Ottilie M. Glade, 1887 (died 1904); children—Frederick G., Charles H., Rosalie (Mrs. Earle J. Zimmerman); m. 2d, Ella Todtmann, Mar. 19, 1919. Traveled in United States, Europe and Africa, 1876-79; joined his father, 1880, in establishing the malting firm of F. Wacker & Son, which later became Wacker & Birk Brewing & Malting Co., of which was pres., 1884-1901; pres. Chicago Heights Land Assn.; dir. Illinois Merchants Trust Co. Was dir. and mem. com. on ways and means, World's Columbian Expn.; was for yrs. pres. Chicago Relief and Aid Soc. and United Charities of Chicago; governing mem. Art Inst. of Chicago; chmn. Chicago Plan Commn.; former sec. Chicago Zoning Commission; member Forest Preserve Commn. of Cook Co.; served as mem. State Council Defense; dir. and exec. com. Chicago Chapter Am. Red Cross. Hon. mem. A.I.A.; fellow Am. Geog. Soc.; hon. pres. Chicago Singverein; dir. Civic Music Assn. Awarded medal of honor, Soc. des Architects Français, 1921. Home: Chicago, Ill. Died Oct. 31, 1929.

WACKERNAGEL, William, coll. prof.; b. Basel, Switzerland, Sept. 25, 1838; s. Wilhelm W. (Ph.D., LL.D.) and Louise (Bluntschly) W.; ed. in Basel; hon. A.M., Muhlenberg Coll., 1881, LL.D., 1918; D.D., U. of Pa., 1883. Missionary in Holy Land, 1859-70; asst. editor, Der Pilger, Reading, Pa., 1870-76; ordained Luth. ministry, 1876; pastor Mauch Chunk, Pa., 1876-81; prof. modern langs. and lit., 1881-1921, prof. emeritus, June 1921, acting pres., 1903-04, Muhlenberg Coll., Allentown, Pa. Pastor St. Stephen's, Allentown, 1897-99; editor Der Jugend Freund; editor German S.S. lessons. German sec. Ministerium of Pa., 1882-87. Compiler: Die Liedergeschichten. Author: Dr. Martin Luther; Hans Egede. Home: Allentown, Pa. Died May 31, 1926.

WADDEL, (Mary) Louise Forsslund, author; b. Sayville, L.I., N.Y., Mar. 13, 1873; d. Andrew D. and Ann Eliza (Brown) Forsslund (or Foster); ed. pub. and high schs., Sayville, Packer Collegiate Inst., Brooklyn, and pvt. tutoring in literature and English; m. Charles Carey Waddel. Author: The Story of Sarah, 1901; The Ship of Dreams, 1902. Home: Sayville, L.I. N.Y. Died 1910.

WADDELL, Alfred Moore, congressman; b. Hillsboro, N.C., Sept. 16, 1834; s. Hon. Hugh and Susan H. (Moore) W.; U. of N.C., 1851-53, A.M., 1856 (LL.D., 1876); m. Julia Savage, 1857; m. 2d, Ellen Savage, 1878; m. 3d, Gabrielle De Rosset, 1896. Ad-

mitted to bar, 1854; in practice at Wilmington, N.C., 1856—; clerk court of equity, 1858-61; del. Conservative Conv., 1860, which nominated Bell and Everett; editor Wilmington (N.C.) Daily Herald, 1860-61; lt. col. 3d N.C. Cav., C.S.A., 1862-64; mem. 42d to 45th Congresses (1871-79), 3d, later 6th, N.C. Dist.; editor Charlotte Journal-Observer, 1881-82; presdl. elector-at-large, 1888; mayor of Wilmington, 1898-1905. Author: A Colonial Officer and His Times, 1891; Some Memories of My Life, 1908; History of New Hanover County, 1909. Home: Wilmington, N.C. Died 1912.

WADDELL, Charles Carey, author; b. Chillicothe, O., Mar. 3, 1868; s. William and Jane (McCoy) W.; A.B., Marietta (O.) Coll., 1889; m. (Mary) Louise Forrslund, Aug. 16, 1906 (died 1910); one son Forrslund (dec.); m. 2d, Stella Harrington, June 4, 1911; children—William C., Nancy. Reporter and city editor Chillicothe Daily News, 1890-93; mayor of Chillicothe, 1893-97; bought Chillicothe Daily News and was its editor and propr. until sold, Feb. 1900; mgr. dept. foreign credits, Exporters' Assn. of America, New York, 1900-01; engaged in writing fiction, 1901—. Contbd. 643 serial stories and novelettes to mags., 1903-28, besides many short stories and two dramatic sketches, both produced. Author: The Van Suyden Sapphires, 1905; Girl of the Guard Line, 1915; Breaking Into Print, 1919. Home: New York, N.Y. Deceased.

WADDELL, John Alexander Low, cons. engineer; b. Port Hope, Can., Jan. 15, 1854; s. Robert Needham and Angeline Esther (Jones) W.; prep. edn., Trinity Coll. Sch., Port Hope; C.E., Rensselaer Poly. Inst., 1875; B.Applied Science (ad eundem gradum), and M.Engring., McGill U., 1882, D.Sc., 1904; LL.D., Univ. of Mo., 1904; D.E., U. of Neb., 1911; Kogakuhakushi (D.Eng.), Imperial U. of Japan, 1915; D.Litt, University of Puerto Rico, 1934; m. Ada Everett, July 13, 1882 (died 1934); children—Needham Everett (dec.), Leonard, Ethel. Engring. work, C.P. Ry., 1876-77; asst. prof. rational and tech. mechanics, Rensselaer Poly. Inst., 1878-80; chief engr. Raymond & Campbell, bridge builders, Council Bluffs, Ia., 1881-82; prof. civ. engring., Imperial U. of Japan, 1882-86; cons. bridge engr., Kansas City and New York, 1887—; mem. Waddell & Hardesty. Knight Comdr. Order of the Rising Sun (Japan), 1888; Knight First Class Order of Société de Bienfaisance of Grand Duchess Olga of Russia (for services as prin. engr. Trans-Alaska-Siberian Ry. project); 2d Class Order of Sacred Treasure of Japan; 2d Class Order of Chia Ho (China); Cavaliere of Crown of Italy; awarded 1st Clausen gold medal, Am. Assn. Engrs., 1931. Engr. bridges in U.S.A., Canada, Mexico, Cuba, Japan, China, New Zealand, Russia, also bridges for over 25 important cities of U.S. and Can. and for numerous ry. bridges in U.S., Can. and Mexico; mainly occupied in the engring. of toll highway bridges, city bridges, and movable bridges; originator, 1889, of modern vertical-lift-bridge, of which has designed and engineered more than 100 moving spans. Retained by Chinese Govt. (Peking), 1921, as mem. jury of award in competition for new Yellow River bridge for Peking-Hankow Ry. and also to estimate upon some $20,000,000 worth of bridges; cons. engr. and tech. adviser to Ministry of Railways, Nat. Govt. of China (Nanking), 1929, hon. tech. adviser in U.S., 1929—. Author: Specifications for Steel Bridges, 1900; Engineering Specifications and Contracts, 1907; Nickel Steel for Bridges (Norman medal, 1909, of Am. Soc. C.E.); The Possibilities in Bridge Construction by the Use of High Alloy Steels (Norman medal, 1915); Alloy Steels for Bridge-Work; Bridge Engineering (2 vols.), 1916; Economics of Steel Arch Bridges (Norman medal, 1918); Economics of Bridgework, 1921; Principal Professional Papers (22 papers, edited by John L. Harrington), 1905; Memoirs and Addresses of Two Decades (75 papers, edited by Frank W. Skinner), 1928. Joint editor, with John L. Harrington, of Addresses to Engineering Students, 1911. Apptd. by Am. Assn. Engrs. mem. com. of 3 to compile book on Vocational Guidance in Engring. Lines. Home: New York, N.Y. Died Mar. 3, 1938.

WADDELL, Joseph Addison; b. Staunton, Va., Mar. 19, 1823; s. Addison (M.D.) and Kitty (Boys) W.; g.s. of Rev. Dr. James W., usually known as the "blind preacher," and Commodore Nathan Boys, of Phila.; ed. Washington Coll., Lexington, Va., and Univ. of Va.; studied law in law sch. of Judge L. P. Thompson; (LL.D., Washington and Lee U.); m. Virginia McClung; m. 2d, Laleah Dunwoody. Admitted to Va. bar; part owner and editor Staunton Spectator; commr. in chancery and clerk Supreme Ct. of Appeals, at Staunton, for many yrs.; retired. Was mem. Va. Ho. of Delegates and of State Senate (pres.); was also mem. State Constl. Conv. Democrat. Presbyn. Trustee of Mary Baldwin Sem., Staunton. Author: Annals of Augusta County, Va., 2d edit., 1902. Home: Staunton, Va. Died Feb. 17, 1914.

WADDILL, Edmund, Jr., judge; b. Charles City Co., Va., May 22, 1855; s. Edmund and Mary Louisa (Redwood) W.; admitted to Va. bar, 1877; m. Alma C. Mitchell, Dec. 19, 1878; children—Juliette (Mrs. Arthur M. Cannon), Mary Lamb (Mrs. Richard Furnival), Edmund C., Nannie Garland (Mrs. Menalaus

Lankford), Mitchell. County Judge Henrico Co., Va., 1880-83; U.S. atty. Eastern Dist., Va., 1883-85; mem. Ho. of Rep., 1885-89; Rep. nominee for Congress, 3d Va. Dist., 1886; mem. 51st Congress (1889-91), 3d Va. Dist.; U.S. dist. judge, Eastern Dist. of Va., 1898-1921; U.S. circuit judge, 4th Jud. Circuit, June 8, 1921-25; senior circuit judge, June 1925—. Home: Richmond, Va. Died Apr. 9, 1931.

WADE, Festus John, banker; b. Limerick, Ireland, Oct. 14, 1859; s. Thomas and Catherine (McDonough) W.; was brought to America in 1860; ed. pub. schs. of St. Louis to 10; Bryant & Stratton Business Coll., 4 yrs.; m. Kate V. Kennedy, Aug. 28, 1883. Sec. St. Louis Fair Ground Assn., 1883-88; pres. Anderson-Wade Realty Co., 1888-99; pres. Mercantile Trust Co., Nov. 16, 1899—; dir. Big Four Railroad, St.L. &S.F. R.R., Met. Life Ins. Co., C.&A. R.R. Treas. St. Louis Chap. A.R.C. Apptd. Mar. 1918, mem. advisory com. Div. of Finance and Purchases, under Ry. Administration. Democrat. Catholic. Home: St. Louis, Mo. Died Sept. 28, 1927.

WADE, Frank Edward, mfr.; b. Malta Bend, Mo., Oct. 6, 1873; s. William H. and Mary (Knott) W.; A.B., Yale, 1896; student law dept. Washington U.; LL.B., Syracuse U., 1898; m. Margaret Silsbee, June 4, 1904; children—Anna S., William, Margaret. Mem. law firm of McKenzie & Wade, Syracuse, N.Y., 1899-1909; engaged in mfg., 1909—; dir. Bankers' Commercial Securities Co., Syracuse Trust Co. Sergt. 203d Regt. N.Y. Vol. Inf., Spanish-Am. War. Originator of the "War Chest" system, June 1917, under which local war subscriptions were to be called for only once in a yr. and distributed by a central com.; system adopted by over 500 cities and communities in U.S. Chmn. Onondaga Co. (N.Y.) Defense Com., 1917-19; pres. Syracuse War Chest Assn., 1917-19; v.p. Nat. Investigation Bur., 1918-19. Republican. Home: Syracuse, N.Y. Died Mar. 3, 1930.

WADE, James Franklin, major gen. U.S.A.; b. Jefferson, O., Apr. 14, 1843; s. Benjamin F. (U.S. senator from Ohio) and Caroline M. (Rosecrans) W.; ed. common schools; m. Clara Lyon, May 27, 1866. Appointed from Ohio, 1st lt. 6th U.S. Cavalry, May 14, 1861; lt. col. 6th U.S. Colored Cav., May 1, 1864; col., Sept. 19, 1864; bvtd. brig. gen., Feb. 13, 1865; hon. mustered out of vol. service, Apr. 15, 1866; capt. U.S.A., May 1, 1866; maj. 9th Cav., July 28, 1866; lt. col. 10th Cav., Mar. 20, 1879; col. 5th Cav., Apr. 21, 1887; brig. gen., May 26, 1897; maj. gen. vols., May 4, 1898; hon. discharged from vol. service, June 12, 1899; maj. gen. U.S.A., Apr. 13, 1903; retired by operation of law, Apr. 14, 1907. Bvtd.: capt., June 9, 1863, "for gallant and meritorious services in battle of Beverly Ford, Va."; maj., Dec. 19, 1864, for same in action at Marion, East Tenn.; lt. col. and col., Mar. 13, 1865, for same during the war; brig. gen. vols., Feb. 13, 1865, "for gallant services in campaign in southwestern Va." Head of Cuban Evacuation Commn., 1898; served in P.I., 1901-04; comd. Div. of Philippines, 1903-04; comd. Atlantic Div., 1904-07. Home: Jefferson, O. Died Aug. 23, 1921.

WADE, Martin Joseph, judge; b. Burlington, Vt., Oct. 20, 1861; s. Michael and Mary (Breen) W.; ed. St. Joseph's Coll., Dubuque; LL.B., State U. of Ia., 1886; m. Mary Gertrude McGovern, Apr. 4, 1888; children—Julia R., Eleanor M. Practiced law at Iowa City, 1886-93; judge 8th Jud. Dist., Ia., 1893-1902; mem. 58th Congress (1903-05), 2d Ia. Dist.; mem. Wade, Dutcher & Davis, Iowa City, to 1915; judge U.S. Dist. Court, Southern Dist. of Ia., 1915—. Was mem. Dem. Nat. Com. Lecturer on law, 1891-1903, prof. med. jurisprudence, 1895-1905, State U. of Iowa. Author: (with W. F. Russell), The Short Constitution, 1921; Lessons in Citizenship; The Constitution and You; Down with the Constitution. Home: Iowa City, Ia. Died Apr. 16, 1931.

WADE, Mary Hazelton, author; b. Charlestown, Mass., Mar. 23, 1860; d. Charles Henry and Caroline Cecilia Blanchard; grad. Malden (Mass.) grammar and high schs., followed by study with private tutors; m. Malden, Louis Francis Wade, Nov. 14, 1882 (dec.); 1 son, David. Began as teacher, 1877; mem. Malden sch. bd., 1891-92. Author: Little Japanese Cousin, 1901; Little Brown Cousin, 1901; Little Indian Cousin, 1901; Little Russian Cousin, 1901; Little Eskimo Cousin, 1902; Little African Cousin, 1902; Little Philippine Cousin, 1902; Little Hawaiian Cousin, 1902; Little Cuban Cousin, 1902; Little Porto Rican Cousin, 1902; Little Italian Cousin, 1903; Little Swiss Cousin, 1903; Little Siamese Cousin, 1903; Little Norwegian Cousin, 1903; Little German Cousin, 1904; Little Turkish Cousin, 1904; Little Jewish Cousin, 1904; Little Irish Cousin, 1904; Ten Little Indians, 1904; Little Armenian Cousin, 1905; The Coming of the White Men, 1905; Ten Big Indians, 1905; Old Colony Days, 1905; Indian Fairy Stories, 1906; Building the Nation, 1907; Ten Indian Hunters, 1907; New Little Americans, 1908; Little Folks of North America, 1909; The Wonder Workers, 1912; White Bird, the Little Indian, 1912; Dolls of Many Lands, 1913; The Light Bringers, 1914; Pilgrims of To-day, 1916; Swift Fawn, 1916; Timid Hare, 1916; Twin Travelers in South America, 1918; Leaders to Liberty, 1919; Twin Travelers in the Holy Land, 1919; Twin Travelers in India, 1920; Real Americans, 1922; Twin Travelers in China and Japan, 1922; Trail Blazers, 1924; Master Builders, 1925; Adventurers All, 1927; The Boy Who Found Out (Story of Henry Fabre), 1928; The Boy Who Dared (Story of William Penn), 1929; The Boy Who Loved Freedom, 1930; The Boy Who Loved the Sea, 1931. New Pioneers, 1931. Died Mar. 5, 1936.

WADHAMS, Albion Varette, rear adm. U.S.N.; b. Wadhams Mills, N.Y., June 8, 1847; s. William Luman and Emeline Lorette (Cole) W.; apptd. from N.Y., and grad. U.S. Naval Acad., 1868; m. Caroline E. Henderson, Feb. 28, 1870; children—William Henderson, Albion James, Mae Elizabeth (dec.). Ensign, Apr. 19, 1869; master, July 12, 1870; lt. Mar. 25, 1873; lt. comdr., July 21, 1894; comdr., Mar. 3, 1899; capt., Dec. 27, 1903; retired as commodore, June 30, 1907; promoted to rear adm. on the retired list, May 9, 1925, to date from June 30, 1907. Served successively on the Pacific, Atlantic, China stas. in the Tuscarora, Albany, Alaska; at torpedo sta., on bd. Powhatan, and Alert. 1868-75; Naval Acad., 1875-78; coast survey, 1878-79; Nipsic, European sta., 1880-83; Navy Yard, Washington, 1884-86; Essex China sta.; Brooklyn, Monocacy, Marion, 1886-89; insp. 2d light house dist. and mem. Bd. Inspection, 1889-92; exec. officer Mohican, 1893-95, Boston and Monterey, 1895-96; insp. 8th light house dist., 1897-99; during Spanish-Am. War was in charge 8th Coast Defense Dist.; comd. Monongahela, Oct., 1899-Dec. 1900; insp. merchant ships and at Navy Yard, New York, 1901; comd. St. Mary's, 1901-02; in charge recruiting sta. and branch hydrographic office, Chicago, 1902-03; comd. Prairie, 1903-05; capt. Navy Yard, Norfolk, 1905-07; apptd. 1907 by Gov. Charles E. Hughes mem. of Bd. of Pardons and Parole for State Prisons; apptd. by Gov. Sulzer, 1913, commr. on new prisons. Called to active duty, 1917, and assigned as rep. of Navy Dept. at Am. Red Cross hdqrs., Washington, to Oct. 30, 1919; comd. Naval Prison, Portsmouth, N.H., Mar. 7, 1920-July 6, 1921; duty at Navy Yard, Portsmouth, to Aug. 1, 1921, relieved from active duty; 20 yrs. of sea service: 3 yrs. active service after retirement. Home: Wadhams, N.Y. Died Jan. 14, 1927.

WADHAMS, Frederick Eugene, lawyer; b. Wadhams, N.Y., Sept. 27, 1848; s. William Luman and Emeline Lorette (Cole) W.; father went to Calif., via Isthmus of Panama, 1849, returned to Wadhams, 1851, and again visited Calif. same year; studied at Cornell, 1869-71; LL.B., Albany Law Sch. (Union U.), 1876; m. Emma Louise Jones, Oct. 9, 1878. Admitted to N.Y. bar, 1876; began practice at Albany; secretary N.Y. State Bar Assn., 1899-1922; treas. Am. Bar Assn., 1902—. Secretary board of statutory consolidation appointed to consolidate and revise the laws of State of N.Y. Mem. S.R., Soc. War 1812. Editor: Consolidated Laws of the State of New York, 1909; Historical Record of General Statutes of the State of New York; also Annual Reports of Proceedings of New York State Bar Assn., 1899-1919. Apptd. by gov. of N.Y., June 1913, commr. for the preparation of an index to the session laws and statutes of the state. Trustee Memorial Hosp., Albany. Episcopalian, vestryman St. Peter's Ch., Albany. Mason. Democrat. Home: Albany, N.Y. Died Sept. 5, 1926.

WADHAMS, Robert Pelton, surgeon; b. Goshen, Conn., Jan. 10, 1879; s. John Hodges and Mary G. (Pelton) W.; Ph.B., Yale, 1902; M.D., New York U. and Bellevue Hosp. Med. Coll., 1906; unmarried. Practiced as gen. surgeon, New York, 1908—; teacher Bellevue Hosp. Med. Coll., 1910—, becoming prof. clin. surgery. Served as lt. col. Med. Corps, U.S. Army, World War. Republican. Conglist. Home: New York, N.Y. Died Dec. 16, 1940.

WADLEIGH, George Henry, rear adm. U.S.N.; b. Dover, N.H., Sept. 28, 1842; s. George and Sarah (Gilman) W., apptd. to U.S. Naval Academy from N.H., 1860, grad. 1863; m. Clara Robinson, Oct. 12, 1869. Ensign, May 28, 1863; promoted through grades to rear adm., Feb. 9, 1902. Served on Lackawanna, W. Gulf Blockading Squadron, 1863-65; present at attack on Fort Powell, Mar. 2, 1864, battle of Mobile Bay, Aug. 5, 1864, surrender of Ft. Morgan, Aug. 23, 1864; served on Richmond, Mar.-July 1865; Ticonderoga, European sta., 1865-69; Naval Acad., 1869-70; torpedo sta., 1870; exec. officer Shawmut, 1871-73, Canonicus, 1873-74, Ohio, 1874, St. Mary's, 1874-76, Pensacola, 1876-78, Navy Yard Portsmouth, 1878-81; comd. Alliance, 1881-82, on spl. Arctic cruise in search of Jeannette and reached latitude 80° 10'; light house insp. 2d dist., 1883-86; Navy Yard, Boston, 1887-89; comd. Mich., 1889-99; Navy Yard, Boston, 1892-94; comd. receiving ship Richmond, 1894; comd. Minneapolis, cruising off coast of Asia Minor to protect Am. missionaries, 1895-97; Navy Yard, Boston, 1897-98; comd. Phila., June-Oct., 1898, receiving ship Wabash, 1898-1902; comdt. Navy Yard, League Island, 1902; pres. Bd. of Inspection and Survey, 1902; retired, June 7, 1902. Home: Dover, N.H. Died July 11, 1927.

WADLIN, Horace Greeley, writer; b. Wakefield, Mass., Oct. 2, 1851; s. Daniel H. and Lucy E. (Brown) W.; ed. in schs. and by pvt. instrn.; (Litt.D., Tufts, 1905); studied architecture at Salem, and Boston; m. Ella Frances Butterfield, Sept. 8, 1875. Began practice as architect, Boston, 1875; became, 1879, spl. agt. and later in charge spl. lines of statis. work, Mass. Bur. of Statistics of Labor, and 1888, upon resignation of Col. Carroll D. Wright, became chief of bur. and relinquished professional practice; resigned, 1903; librarian Boston Public Library, Feb. 1903-June 1917 (librarian emeritus). Mem. Mass. House of Rep., 1884-88; supervisor U.S. Census, 1890, 1900; dir. Mass. decennial census, 1895; lecturer upon social science, history and art. Editor: Reports on the Statistics of Labor of Massachusetts, 1888-1901 (14 vols.); Annual Statistics of Manufacturers of Massachusetts, 1886-1901 (16 vols.); The Decennial Census of Massachusetts for 1895 (7 vols.); History of Boston Public Library, 1911. Home: Reading, Mass. Died Nov. 4, 1925.

WADSWORTH, Charles, Jr., clergyman; b. Philadelphia, Mar. 21, 1860; s. Charles Wadsworth (D.D.) and Jane (Locke) W.; B.A., U. of Pa., 1880, M.A., 1883; B.D., Yale, 1884; (D.D., Lafayette, 1895); m. Agnes E. Wood, June 17, 1890. Ordained Presbyn. ministry, 1886; pastor Plymouth Congl. Ch., Worcester, Mass., 1887-89, N. Broad St. Presbyn. Ch., Phila., 1899-1907; pres. Presbyn. Bd. Edn., 1908-21. Gov. gen. Order of Founders and Patriots of America; chaplain 2d Regt. Inf. N.G.P., 1906-10; chaplain (Gen.) Soc. of the Cincinnati, Pa. Soc. War of 1812, Pa. Soc. Order of Founders and Patriots of America. Trustee Presbyn. Hosp., Phila.; pres. bd. advisers Presbyn. Home for Widows and Single Women. Republican. Home: Philadelphia, Pa. Died Mar. 18, 1925.

WADSWORTH, Frank Lawton Olcott, engineer, inventor; b. Wellington, Ohio, 1867; s. Francis Sage W.; grad. E.M. (mining engr.), Ohio State U., 1888, B.Sc., 1889, M.E. (mech. engr.), 1889; Clark U., 1889-92; m. Laura Poole, Sept. 1893; m. 2d, Mildred Schinneller, July 1914. Del. from Smithsonian Instn. to Internat. Bur. Weights and Meas., Paris, to assist in establishing absolute length of standard meter, 1892; sr. asst. in charge Astrophysical Obs., Washington, 1892-94; asst. prof. physics, U. of Chicago, 1894-96; asst. prof. astrophysics, 1896-97, asso. prof., 1897-98, Yerkes Obs.; dir. Allegheny Obs., 1900-04; spl. engr. and expert work, Pittsburgh and Washington, 1898-99; consulting expert to the John A. Brashear Co., 1901-04; gen. mgr. Pressed Prism Plate Glass Co., 1904-05; chief engr. Am. Window Glass Co., 1905-08; consulting engr., 1908—. Pres. Miller Non-Corrosive Metal Co., 1909—; dir. Pressed Prism Plate Glass Co., 1904-13. Pres. bd. visitors Ohio State U. Asst. editor Astrophys. Jour.; asso. editor Harper & Bros. Scientific Memoirs. Has served on numerous public service coms. and commns., and has published over 100 papers and reports in scientific publs., and soc. proceedings. Patentee of over 250 inventions relating to manufacture of glass, steel, electric lights, railway appliances, machine tools, engrng. instruments, wire working machinery, appliances, tires, etc. Originator and designer vertical tower telescope, curved plate camera, fixed deviation spectroscope, polar reflecting heliostat, precision interferometers, and other novel forms of physical and astrophysical instruments; author of the hexaplex system of golf course design, and papers on economic subjects. Has testified as tech. expert in upwards of 200 patent suits in U.S. and Canadian courts. Home: Pittsburgh, Pa. Died Apr. 11, 1936.

WADSWORTH, Hiram Warren; b. Barre, Mass., Dec. 8, 1862; s. Joseph Dennis and Ann Jane (Rice) W.; prep. edn., Barre Acad., 1875-81; A.B., cum laude, Harvard, 1885; m. Ella Frances Hilton, June 8, 1887; children—Katharine (Mrs. Roland Benjamin Ahlswede), Mary Manter, Joseph Hilton, Suzanne (Mrs. Frederick Graham Runyon). Began with Wadsworth, Howland & Co., paint and varnish mfrs., Boston, Mass., 1885, sec., 1890-94; moved to Pasadena, Calif., because of health, 1896; mfr. paints and varnishes, 1896-1913. Mem. bd. dirs. of Pasadena, 1921-27, chmn. bd. (legal mayor), 1921-25; mem. City Pasadena Planning Commn., 1923-27; pres. Colo. River Aqueduct Assn. (sponsors of plan to bring to Southern Calif. water supply adequate for all time, 250 miles from Colo. River), 1924-29. Trustee Calif. Inst. Technology (vice pres.). Awarded Arthur Noble civic medal, Pasadena, 1928. Republican. Unitarian (pres. Union Liberal Church of Pasadena 1924-27). Mason. Home: Pasadena, Calif. Died Apr. 1939

WADSWORTH, James Wolcott, congressman; b. Philadelphia, Oct. 12, 1846; s. Gen. James Samuel and Mary (Wharton) W.; prepared at Hopkins Grammar Sch., New Haven, Conn., to enter Yale, but entered Union Army, 1864; (hon. A.M., Yale, 1898); capt. a.d.c. vols., Jan. 24, 1865; brvt. maj. vols., Apr. 1, 1865, "for gallant and meritorious services at battle of Five Forks, Va."; hon. mustered out, June 26, 1865; m. Louise, d. William R. Travers, of New York, Sept. 14, 1876. Supervisor town of Geneseo, N.Y., 1875-77; mem. N.Y. Assembly, 1878-79; comptroller of N.Y., 1880-81; mem. 47th and 48th Congresses (1881-85), and 52d to 59th Congresses (1891-1907). Second v.p. bd. mgrs. Nat. Home for Disabled Vol. Soldiers. Republican. Home: Geneseo, N.Y. Died Dec. 24, 1926.

WADSWORTH, Marshman Edward, geologist; b. Livermore Falls, Me., May 6, 1847; s. Joseph and Nancy F. (Eaton) W.; A.B., Bowdoin Coll., 1869, A.M., 1872; A.B., Harvard U., 1874, A.M., Ph.D., 1879; U. of Heidelberg, 1884-85; M.D., Nat. Med. Coll., 1894; (E.M., Pa. State Coll., 1917; Sc.D., U. of Pittsburgh, 1919). Principal and supt. schools in Maine, N.H., Minn. and Wis., 1863-73; prof. chemistry, Boston Dental Coll., 1873-74; instr. mathematics and mineralogy, Harvard, 1874-77; asst. in geology, Mus. Comparative Zoölogy, Harvard, 1877-87; prof. mineralogy and geology, Colby, 1885-87; asst. geologist, Minn. Geol. Survey, 1886-87; dir., prof. mining geology and petrography, 1887-97, pres., 1897-99, Mich. Coll. of Mines; state geologist of Mich., 1888-93; geologist and mining expert, Keweenawan Assn., 1898-1903; prof. mining and geology, and dean Sch. of Mines and Metallurgy, 1901-08, Pa. State Coll.; dean Sch. of Mines and prof. mining geol., 1907-12, emeritus dean and prof., and curator of mineral, and petrographical collections, 1912—, U. of Pittsburgh. Geologist Pa. State Bd. Agr., 1902-05. A pioneer in microscopic petrography (taught 1st course in U.S.), in meteorites, pre-cambrian geol., etc. Mason. Author: Geology of the Iron and Copper Districts of Lake Superior, 1880; Lithological Studies, 1884; Report of the Mich. Geol. Survey, 1893; The Azoic System (with the late Josiah Dwight Whitney), 1884; Crystallography, 1909; Michigan College of Mines in the Nineteenth Century, 1916. Home: Pittsburgh, Pa. Died Apr. 21, 1921.

WADSWORTH, Oliver Fairfield, ophthalmologist; b. Boston, Apr. 26, 1838; s. Alexander and Mary Elizabeth Hubbard (Fairfield) W.; A.B., Harvard U., 1860, A.M., 1863, M.D., 1865; studied in Germany, Austria, and Switzerland; m. Mary Chapman Goodwin, Apr. 16, 1867. Asst. surgeon 5th Mass. Cav., Apr.-Nov. 1865; clin. instr. ophthalmoscopy, 1881-91, prof. ophthalmology, 1891-98, Williams prof., 1898-1903, Harvard; ophthalmic surgeon Boston City Hosp., 1870—, to out-patients Mass. Gen. Hosp., 1873-1900; ophthalmic surgeon, 1892-1905, cons. surgeon, 1905—, Mass. Charitable Eye and Ear Infirmary; mem. bd. of consultation Mass. Gen. Hosp. Fellow Am. Acad. Arts and Sciences; asso. fellow Coll. Physicians of Phila. Home: Boston, Mass. Died Nov. 1911.

WADSWORTH, William Austin, farmer; b. Boston, Dec. 8, 1847; s. William Wolcott and Emmeline (Austin) W.; A.B., Harvard, 1870 (honors in chemistry); U. of Berlin, 1871-72; m. Elizabeth Greene Perkins, Sept. 4, 1901. Inherited large landed estate from grandfather. Member Independent Corps Cadets, 2d Regt., Mass. Vol. Militia; maj. and q.m. 8th Army Corps, Spanish-Am. War, 1898, at Manila and San Francisco, on staffs of Generals Merritt and Otis. Pres. N.Y. State Forest, Fish and Game Commn., N.Y. State Agrl. Soc.; trustee State Normal Sch.; pres. Village of Geneseo, Board Supervisors Livingston Co., Good Roads Assn., N.Y. Farmers Assn., Geneseo Pub. Library, Livingston Co. Agrl. Soc.; etc. Republican. Unitarian. Home: Geneseo, N.Y. Died May 2, 1918.

WAGER, Charles Henry Adams, coll. prof.; b. Cohoes, N.Y., Dec. 20, 1869; s. George H. and Lydia L. (Frink) W.; A.B., Colgate U., 1892; Ph.D., Yale Univ., 1895; Litt.D., Colgate Univ., 1910; L.H.D., Oberlin College, 1935; m. Annie Applegate, Aug. 18, 1896. Instr. Latin, Colgate, 1892-93; prof. English, Centre Coll., Ky., 1895-97, Kenyon Coll., Ohio, 1897-1900, Oberlin (O.) College, 1900-35 (emeritus). Registrar, 1903-05, advisory officer, 1905-11, Oberlin College. Author: To Whom It May Concern, 1st and 2d Series (essays), 1936, 37. Editor: Seege of Trove, 1899. Home: Oberlin, O. Died July 1, 1939.

WAGGENER, Balie Peyton, lawyer; b. in Platte Co., Mo., July 18, 1847; s. Peyton Randolph and Briseis (Willis) W.; ed. pub. schs.; m. Emma L. Hetherington, May 27, 1869. Entered law office of Otis & Glick, Atchison, 1866; admitted to practice, June 10, 1867; now mem. Waggener & Challiss. Gen. atty. M.P. Ry. Co., for Kan. and Neb., 1876-1910; gen. solicitor same, for Kan., Neb. and Colo., May 1, 1910—. Pres. Exchange Nat. Bank of Atchison, Feb. 1892—. Mem. Atchison City Council, 1869, candidate for atty.-gen. of Kan., 1872; city atty., 1873; mayor Atchison, 1889-91 and 1895-97; mem. Kan. Ho. of Rep., 1903-04, Senate, 1905-09. Mason. Baptist. Home: Atchison, Kan. Died Apr. 28, 1918.

WAGGONER, Alvin, lawyer; b. Cole's Station, Ill., Nov. 23, 1879; s. George D. and Ada (Feree) W.; grad. Eastern Ill. State Normal Sch., Charleston, Ill., 1904; studied U. of Ind. Biol. Sta., Warsaw, Ind.; LL.B., U. of Mich., 1906; m. Harriet E. Brown, June 18, 1908; children—George Fiske (dec.), Ruth Elizabeth. Admitted to S.D. bar, 1907, and began practice at Philip as mem. Philip & Waggoner; state's atty. Stanley Co., S.Dak., 1911-13; Rep. presdl. elector, 1916; official messenger bearing returns to Washington, 1917. Mem. Bd. of Regents of Edn. of S.D., 1921—, pres., 1929-32; v.p. Assn. Governing Bds. of State Univs. and Allied Instns., 1924, pres., 1925; mem. advisory com. Nat. Survey of Secondary Edn., 1930-32; chmn. Rhodes Scholarship Selection Com. of S.Dak., also chmn. Dist. Com., 1932—; chmn. S.D. Social Security Commn., 1937—. Unitarian. Mason, Odd Fellow, Woodman. Editor of S.D. Bar Jour., 1931—. Home: Philip, S.D. Died June 16, 1939.

WAGNALLS, Adam Willis, publisher; b. Lithopolis, O., Sept. 24, 1843; s. Christopher C. and Elizabeth (Schneider) W.; A.B., Wittenberg College, 1866 (Litt.D.; also LL.D., 1915); m. Anna Willis, June 4, 1868. Organizer, 1867, and pastor First English Lutheran Church, Kansas City, 1867-69; city clerk, Atchison, Kan., 1871-73; in publishing business at New York, 1876—; one of original founders and pres. Funk & Wagnalls Co.; prin. work the Funk & Wagnalls Standard Dictionary, and The Literary Digest. Home: Summit, N.J. Died Sept. 3, 1924.

WAGNER, Arthur Lockwood, col. U.S.A.; b. Ottawa, Ill., Mar. 16, 1853; s. Joseph H. and Matilda (Hapeman) W.; grad. West Point, 1875; 2d lt. 6th U.S. inf., June 16, 1875; 1st lt., Oct. 18, 1882; capt., Apr. 2, 1892; maj. and asst. adj. gen., Nov. 18, 1896; lt. col. and asst. adj. gen., Feb. 25, 1898; m. Annie B., d. Andrew Howard, of Pittsburgh, Sept. 5, 1883. Served in Dak., Mont., Colo. and Utah, Sioux campaigns, 1876-77; Ute campaigns, 1880-81; prof. military science and tactics at E. Fla. Sem., Gainesville, Fla., 1882-85, Ft. Douglas, Utah, 1885-86; instr. art of war. U.S. Inf. and Cav. School, Fort Leavenworth, Kan., Nov. 1886, to Apr. 1897; in charge mil. information div., War Dept., Washington, Apr. 1897, to May 1898; on staff Maj. Gen. Miles in war with Spain; detached for duty on staff Maj. Gen. Lawton in campaign in Cuba until surrender of Santiago; with Gen. Miles in Puerto Rico; adj. gen. Dept. Dak., St. Paul, Minn., Jan. to Nov., 1899; adj. gen. 1st div. 8th army corps, Philippine Islands, Dec. 22, 1899, to Apr. 7, 1900, on staff Maj. Gen. Bates in campaign in Province of Cavite; adj. gen. dept. Southern Luzon, Apr. 7, 1900, to Nov. 30, 1901; adj. gen. dept. North Philippines, Nov. 30, 1901, to Mar. 25, 1902; adj. gen. dept. of the Lakes, Chicago, May 7, 1902—. Author: The Campaign of Königgrätz, 1889; Organization and Tactics, 1895; The Service of Security and Information, 1893; A Catechism of Outpost Duty, 1896. Received gold medal of Mil. Service Instn. of U.S. (1884) for essay on "The Military Necessities of the United States and the Best Provisions for Meeting Them." Died 1905.

WAGNER, Charles Gray, physician; b. Minden, N.Y., Oct. 10, 1856; s. Edward and Alida E. W.; B.S., Cornell U., 1880; M.D., Coll. Phys. and Surg. (Columbia), 1882; m. Mrs. Elizabeth Bennett, Nov. 2, 1903. House phys. and surgeon, Presbyn. Hosp., N.Y. City, 1882-84; asst. phys., Utica State Hosp., 1884-92; med. supt. Binghamton (N.Y.) State Hosp., 1892—. Lecturer on insanity, Sage Sch. of Philosophy (Cornell U.), 1896-1900 inclusive; expert witness in many important trials. Asso. editor Am. Jour. Insanity, 1884-92. Trustee Cornell U., 1896-1906. Republican. Episcopalian. Died Nov. 6, 1923.

WAGNER, Frank Caspar, engineer; b. Ann Arbor, Mich., Oct. 5, 1864; s. William and Priscilla (Meller) W.; A.M., U. of Mich., 1884, B.S., 1885; D.Sc., Rose Polytechnic Inst., 1924; Dr.Engring., Univ. of Mich., 1927; m. Mabel E. Peck, June 16, 1892; children—Helen Ward (Mrs. J. L. McCloud), Frank Caspar, Priscilla Meller (Mrs. Fred B. Johnson), Willys Peck, Barbara, Constance (dec.). Engring. work with Thomson-Houston Electric Co., 1886-89; asst. prof. mech. engring., U. of Mich., 1890-96; asso. prof. steam engring., 1896-1904, prof. steam and elec. engring., 1904-20, prof. mech. engring., 1920-23, pres., 1923—, Rose Poly. Institute. Administrative engr. for Ind. of U.S. Fuel Administration, 1918. Author: Notes on Applied Electricity, 1903. Home: Terre Haute, Ind. Died Nov. 21, 1928.

WAGNER, Harr, writer, pub.; b. on farm in Pa., Mar. 20, 1857; grad. Wittenberg Coll., Springfield, O., 1881; m. Mrs. Madge Morris, Mar. 30, 1887; children—Morris, Pearl Johnson (step-dau.). Owner and editor The Golden Era, San Francisco, Calif., 1881-90; builder of San Diego (Calif.) Coll. of Letters, 1888; supt. schs., San Diego Co., 1891-95; editor Jour. Edn., State of Calif., 1898-1912; organizer, 1916, Harr Wagner Pub. Co. (successor to Whittaker & Ray-Wiggin Co., pubs. Western Books by Western Authors); one of owners and builders of Montara, Calif. Republican. Lutheran. Author: The Street and the Flower (novel), 1883; Pacific History Stories, 1895; California History (with Mark Keppel), 1824; A Man Unafraid (with Herbert Bashford), 1928; Joaquin Miller and His Other Self, 1929. Home: San Francisco, Calif. Died June 20, 1936.

WAGNER, Hugh Kiernan, lawyer; b. St. Louis, Mo., Sept. 29, 1870; s. Hugh K. and Mary Ann (Elliot) W.; ed. grammar and high schs., St. Louis; m. Annette Elliott Hill, June 7, 1893; children—Elliott Goodwyn (dec.), Paul Brookes. Admitted to bar, 1897; in practice, St. Louis, 1892—. Spl. counsel for city of St. Louis to revise city ordinances and prepare annotated "Revised Code of St. Louis, 1914." Lecturer, Benton Coll. Law, 1901-11, City Coll. of Law and Finance, 1911—. Counsel and director Industrial Aid for the Blind, Inc. Mem. 50th Mo. General Assembly. Mem. bd. of freeholders St. Louis County and City (1925-26) to extend limits of St. Louis City. Author: The Relations of Session and Trustees, 1906; Mechanical Equivalents, 1910; Damages, Profits, and Accounting in Patent, Copyright, Trade-Mark, and Unfair Competition Cases. Home: St. Louis, Mo. Deceased.

WAGNER, Louis, banker, soldier; b. Giessen, Hesse-Darmstadt, Germany, Aug. 4, 1838; s. Ludwig and Christina (Berg) W.; came to Phila. with family, 1849; ed. Zane St. Grammar Sch., Phila.; learned lithograph business; m. Hattie Slocum, Aug. 4, 1859. Entered Union Army, Aug. 1861; 1st lt. Co. D, 88th Pa. Vols.; promoted capt., 1862, col., 1863, bvtd. brig. gen., 1865; badly wounded at 2d Bull Run, Aug. 1862; wound broke out anew at Chancellorsville, and he was sent home; placed in charge Camp William Penn for organization of colored troops, and sent to the front over 14,000 men. Began in ins. business, 1866; pres. Third Nat. Bank, Phila., July 19, 1891—; dir. United Firemen's Ins. Co.; trustee N.Y. Life Ins. Co. Mem. council from 22d ward, 1867-73, 1876-78, was 3 times its pres.; mem. bd. edn., 1873-76; recorder of deeds, 1878-82; mem. bd. Guardians of the Poor, 1882; dir. pub. works, 1887-91; pres. bd. dirs. of City Trusts, 1891; chmn. Sinking Fund Commn., City of Phila. Mason. Comdr. in chief G.A.R., 1880-81; treas. bd. trustees Soldiers' and Sailors' Home, Erie, Pa.; chmn. 50th anniversary Battle of Gettysburg Commn., created by act of Legislature of Pa. Home: Germantown, Phila., Pa. Died Jan. 15, 1914.

WAGNER, Samuel, lawyer (retired); b. Philadelphia, Pa., Dec. 28, 1842; s. Samuel and Emilie Obrié (Duval) W.; A.B., U. of Pa., 1861, student Law Sch., same, 1864, A.M., 1864; m. Anne Leonard, d. Edward Seymour Harlan, and g.d. Dr. Richard Harlan, distinguished scientist, Sept. 5, 1893; children—Emilie Obrié (Mrs. Donald Galbraith Baird), Samuel. Master in mathematics, Episcopal Acad., 1861-63; served in 1st Regt., Pa. Militia, 1862-63. Admitted to Phila. bar, 1865, to Supreme Court of Pa., 1868, to Supreme Court United States, 1881; chief of editorial staff Penn Monthly, 1881-83; pres. Wagner Free Inst. of Science, 1884-1921, pres. emeritus. Trustee Free Library of Phila.; one of founders of Pa. Mus. and Sch. of Industrial Art, Pa. Civil Service Reform Assn., Medical Jurisprudence Soc., Am. Soc. for Extension of Univ. Teaching, and Free and Open Church Assn. Home: Philadelphia, Pa. Died May 17, 1937.

WAGNER, Samuel Tobias, civil engr.; b. Philadelphia, Pa., Aug. 30, 1861; s. John and Sarah A. (Wood) W.; B.Sc., U. of Pa., 1881 (sr. civ. engr. prize), C.E., 1884; m. Mary Clara Reeves Scull, Nov. 13, 1888; children—Mary, John Jr., William Worrell, Thomas Rowan. With Phoenix Iron Co., Phoenixville, Pa., as draftsman, insp., asst. master mechanic and supt. of shops, 1881-93; asst. engr. in charge of Pa. Av. Subway and Tunnel, Bur. of Surveys, Phila., 1894-1900; asst. engr. in charge of improvement and filtration of water supply, same, 1900-02; asst. engr. in charge of abolishment of grade-crossings, Phila. & Reading R.R. Co., 1902-15, chief engr., April 15, 1915-Jan. 1, 1927; cons. engineer, 1927—. Trustee Wagner Free Inst. of Science, and prof. engring., same, 1892—(pres. bd.); mem. Pa. State Bd. for Registration Professional Engrs. Republican. Episcopalian. Home: Germantown, Phila., Pa. Died Aug. 7, 1931.

WAGSTAFF, Alfred, lawyer; b. New York, N.Y., March 1844; s. Alfred and Sarah Platt (Du Bois) W.; LL.B., 1866; m. Mary A. Barnard, Mar. 1880. Capt., maj. and col. 16th Regt. N.G.S.N.Y., 1863-64; lt. col. 15th Regt. N.G.S.N.Y. in service of U.S., July 1864; maj 91st N.Y. Vet. Vols., 1864-July 1865; chief of staff 3d Div. 5th Army Corps, July 1865; col. and a.d.c. on staff of gov., 1867-69. Admitted to bar, 1866; mem. N.Y. Assembly, 1867-74, Senate, 1876-80; pres. New York & Brooklyn Bridge Co.; clk. Ct. of Common Pleas, N.Y., 1892-95; clk. appellate div. Supreme Ct. 1st dept., 1896—. Pres. Am. Society Prevention Cruelty to Animals, 1906—; pres. N.Y. Assn. Protection of Game; trustee Samaritan Home for the Aged. Democrat. Episcopalian. Home: New York, N.Y. Died Oct. 2, 1921.

WAHL, George Moritz, college prof.; b. Unkersdorf, Bezirk Dresden, Germany, May 31, 1851; s. Rev. Gustav Moritz and Emma Wilhelmine (Osterloh) W.; student univs. of Halle, Leipzig, and Berlin, Germany; A.M., Rutgers College, 1882 (L.H.D., same, 1890; A.M., Williams, 1896); m. Mary Warren Hardenbergh, Oct. 17, 1882. Master of German and Latin, Thayer Acad., S. Braintree, Mass., 1879-92; asst. prof. modern langs., 1892-94, prof. German language and literature, 1894-1917 (emeritus), Williams Coll. Editor: Revised Edition Otto's German Grammar, 1890. Contbr. to mags.; also Goethe Jahrbuch and Euphorion. Home: Williamstown, Mass. Died Dec. 23, 1923.

WAHL, Lutz, army officer; b. Wisconsin, Nov. 2, 1869; grad. U.S. Mil. Acad., 1891; grad. Army War Coll., 1916; grad. Gen. Staff Sch., 1921. Commd. 2d lt. inf., June 12, 1891; promoted through grades to brig. gen. asst. to the adj. gen., May 16, 1924, with rank for 4 yrs., now maj. gen.; served as brig. gen. N.A., Apr. 12, 1918-Oct. 31, 1919. Died Dec. 30, 1928.

WAHL, William Henry, scientific journalist, metall. and electro-chemist; b. Philadelphia, Pa., Dec. 14, 1848; s. John H. and Caroline R. W.; ed. public schools, Philadelphia and Dickinson Coll., A.B., 1867;

Ph.D., Univ. Heidelberg, Germany, 1869; special courses in chemistry, geology, mineralogy; m. Julia Lowther, Seafield, Co. Mayo, Ireland, Sept. 9, 1874. Resident Sec. Franklin Inst., 1870-74, and from 1882; instr. science Episcopal Acad., Phila., 1871-73; prof. physics and physical geography Central High School, 1873-74. Editor Polytechnic Review, Phila., 1876-78; asso. editor Engineering and Mining Journal, New York, 1878-80; editor Manufacturer and Builder, New York, 1880-95; editor Journal Franklin Institute, 1870-74 and from 1882. Author: Techno-chemical Receipt Book (with Wm. T. Brannt), 1885; Handbook of Assaying (Wedding) translated, with additions, from German; Iconographic Encyclopædia, Vol. V, Constructive Arts, Phila., 1893; Historical Sketch of the Franklin Institute, 1894. Home: Philadelphia, Pa. Died 1909.

WAID, Dan Everett, architect; b. Gouverneur, N.Y., Mar. 31, 1864; s. Andrew Jackson and Jane Josephine (Keyes) W.; B.S., Monmouth (Ill.) Coll., 1887, LL.D., 1923; archtl. dept., Columbia U.; m. Eva Clark, Dec. 31, 1891 (dec.); m. 2d, Mrs. Phyllis Fellowes Colmore, Feb. 2, 1934. Associated with Jenney & Mundie, architects, 1888-94; in practice in Chicago, 1894-98, then in New York. Fellow Am. Inst. Architects (pres. and treas.); mem. New York Chapter A.I.A. (pres.). Deputy director of production of housing for Emergency Fleet Corporation during the World War. Mem. Art Commn. Associates (N.Y.). Awarded medal New York Chapter A.I.A., 1929, "for distinguished work." Home: New York, N.Y. Died Oct. 31, 1939.

WAIDNER, Charles William, physicist; b. Baltimore, Md., Mar. 6, 1873; E.E., Johns Hopkins, 1892, A.B., 1896, Ph.D., 1898. Asst. in physics, Johns Hopkins, 1898-99; instr physics, Williams Coll., 1899-1901; ab. asst., 1901-04, asso. physicist, 1904-10, physicist, 1910—, Bur. Standards, Washington, D.C. Died Mar. 11, 1922.

WAINWRIGHT, Marie, actress; b. Philadelphia, Pa.; d. Commodore J. M. (U.S.N.) and Maria (Page) W.; ed. in France; m. Franklyn Roberts, June 3, 1899; m. 2d, Winston H. Slaughter. Became member Boston Musical Company, 1884; supported as leading woman, Booth and Salvini in their notable starring tour together, 1888; became leading woman for Lawrence Barrett in "Francesca da Rimini"; later made Shakespearean productions; starred with Louis James 3 yrs.; recent yrs. supported William Gillette and Frances Starr. Home: New York, N.Y. Died Aug. 17, 1923.

WAINWRIGHT, Richard, rear admiral U.S.N.; b. Washington, D.C., Dec. 17, 1849; s. Comdr. Richard (U.S.N.) and Sallie Franklin (Bache) W.; brother of Dallas Bache W.; apptd. to U.S. Naval Acad. by the President, at large, 1864; grad., 1868; LL.B., Columbian (now George Washington) U., 1884 (LL.D., 1900); m. Evelyn Wotherspoon, Sept. 11, 1873. Promoted ensign, Apr. 19, 1865; master, July 12, 1870; lt., Sept. 25, 1873; lt. comdr., Sept. 16, 1894; comdr., Mar. 3, 1899; capt., Aug. 10, 1903; rear admiral, July 11, 1908. Served on Jamestown and Colorado; at Hydrographic Office; coast survey on Asiatic Sta., and Richmond, 1868-30; Bur. of Navigation, 1880-84; Tennessee, 1884-86; Galena, 1886-87; Naval Acad., 1887-90; Alert, 1890-93; Hydrographic Office, 1893-96; chief, Intelligence Office, 1896-97; exec. officer Maine, Nov. 17, 1897, until she was blown up in Havana harbor, Feb. 15, 1898; comd. Gloucester during Spanish War and took part in the destruction of Admiral Cervera's squadron off Santiago, Cuba, July 3, 1898; was advanced 10 numbers in rank "for eminent and conspicuous conduct in this battle," presented with a silver loving cup by citizens of Gloucester, Mass., and a sword by citizens of Washington; comd. ships at Naval Acad., 1899-1900; supt. Naval Acad., 1900-02; comd. Newark, 1902-04; mem. Gen. Bd., 1904-07; comdg. Louisiana, 1907-08, 2d div. Atlantic Fleet, 1908-09, 3d div., 1909-10; aid for operations to Sec. of the Navy, 1910; retired by operation of law, Dec. 17, 1911. Died Mar. 6, 1926.

WAIT, Charles Edmund, chemist; b. Little Rock, Ark., Nov. 3, 1849; s. William B. and Martha L. (Reardon) W.; C.E., M.E., B.S., U. of Va., 1874; Ph.D., U. of Mo., 1888. Dir. Sch. of Mines of Mo., 1877-88; prof. chemistry, U. of Tenn., 1888—. Fellow Chem. Soc. of London, A.A.A.S. Author of bulletins on nutrition and numerous chem. papers. Home: Knoxville, Tenn. Died 1923.

WAIT, Henry Heileman, engineer, inventor; b. Chicago, Ill., Oct. 27, 1869; s. Horatio Loomis and Chara Conant (Long) W.; grad. Chicago Manual Training Sch., 1886; B.S. in E.E., Mass. Inst. Tech., 1891; m. Edna, d. Edward A. and Kate Davidson Kimball, May 24, 1913; children—Edward Kimball, Horatio Henry, Nathaniel Sears. In employ of Economic Elec. Mfg. Co., Boston, 1891-92; with Western Electric Co., Chicago, 1892-1905; pres. Rateau Turbine Co. Specially active in evolution and improvement of dynamos, both of bipolar and multipolar types, including type L, Western Electric multipolar direct-current generators; patentee of a varipolar motor or dynamo and a semi-automatic machine for winding small armatures, spools, etc., as well as for improvements on arc lamps; inventor and patentee Wait turbo-generator; designer and builder Wait "Bulldog" steam turbines, Wait "Bulldog" dynamos. Lieut. Illinois Naval Reserves. Republican. Home: Chesterton, Ind. Died Nov. 16, 1931.

WAIT, Horatio Loomis, lawyer; b. New York, N.Y., Aug. 8, 1836; s. Joseph and Harriet Heileman (Whitney) W.; ed. Trinity Sch. and Columbia Grammar Sch., New York; came to Chicago, 1856; m. Chara Conant Long, May 7, 1860; father of Henry Heileman W. Enlisted in Co. D, 60th Ill. Inf., 1861, but later became p.-m. with rank of master, U.S.N.; served under Admirals Dupont and Farragut in blockading Savannah, Pensacola and Mobile, and on Admiral Dahlgren's flagship, at bombardment of Ft. Sumter and siege of Charleston; on U.S.S. Ino after war, European Squadron; promoted to p.-m. with rank of lt. comdr., 1865, and on various duties until 1870, resigned. Returned to Chicago, and admitted to bar, 1870; master in chancery of Circuit Ct. of Cook Co., 1876—. Assisted in organization of Ill. Naval Reserves, 1893; one of founders of the Charity Organization Soc. Episcopalian; for some yrs. supt. Tyng Mission S.S. Home: Chicago, Ill. Died 1916.

WAIT, John Cassan, lawyer, civ. engr.; b. Norwich, N.Y., June 4, 1860; s. Andrew Marcellus and Ambrosia Jane (Sergent) W.; ed. common schs. and Norwich Acad. to 1878; apprentice in planing mill, 1878; received, 1878, competitive state scholarship to Cornell U.; C.E., Cornell, 1882, Master C.E., 1891; M.S., Norwich U., 1887; LL.B., Harvard U., 1891; m. Ginevra Caroline Westlake, June 1886; children—Luella Ambrosia (dec.), Annar Marie, Justin Federal, Constance Elaine. Instr. and asst. prof. in Harvard, 1887-94; engr. in charge N.Y. State canals, $9,000,000 improvement, 1896-97; asst. corp. counsel, City of New York, 1900-04. Independent Democrat. Asso. editor Railroad Gazette, 1894-95. Capt. arty., Vt. N.G., 1886-87. Author: Engineering and Architectural Jurisprundence, 1897; Law of Operations Preliminary to Construction in Engineering and Architecture, 1900; Law of Contracts, 1901; Descendants of Thomas Wait of Portsmouth, R.I., 1904; Genealogical and Biographical History of the Wait(e) families of New England. Pioneer as author and in practice of engring. and architectural jurisprudence, representing large constrn. and mfg. interests. Home: New York, N.Y. Deceased.

WAIT, Lucien Augustus, university prof.; b. Highgate, Vt., Feb. 8, 1846; s. Norval Douglas and Marion Sarah W.; A.B., Harvard, 1870; m. Anna J. Dolloff, Aug. 12, 1873; m. 2d, Mrs. Adaline E. Prentiss, June 7, 1906. U.S. consul at Athens and Piræus, Greece, 1873-74; asst. prof. mathematics, 1870-77, asso. prof., 1877-90, prof., 1890-95, head math. dept., 1895-1910, prof. emeritus, Cornell Univ. Founder and pres. bd. trustees and life treas. Cascadilla School (resigned, June 1910). Died Sept. 6, 1913.

WAIT, William B., educator, inventor; b. Amsterdam, N.Y., Mar. 25, 1839; s. Christopher B. and Betsey Grinnell (Bell) W.; grad. Albany Normal Coll., 1859; admitted N.Y. bar, 1862; m. Phebe J. Babcock, 1863. Prin. N.Y. Instn. for Blind, 1863-1905, emeritus prin., 1905—. Inventor Kleidograph, machine for writing New York Point system, Stereograph, machine for embossing same on metal plates for printing; power presses, for printing on both sides of the leaf from embossed plates, and improved method of binding embossed books. Trustee Am. Coll. of Musicians, Soc. for Providing Evang. Religious Lit. for the Blind. Author: The New York Tangible Point System of Literature, 1866; The New York Tangible Point System of Music for the Blind, 1872; Normal Course of Piano Technic, 1887; Harmonic Notation, 1888. Home: New York, N.Y. Died Oct. 25, 1916.

WAIT, William Cushing, judge; b. Charlestown, Mass., Dec. 18, 1860; s. Elijah Smith and Eliza Ann (Hadley) W.; A.B., summa cum laude, Harvard, 1882, A.M., 1885, LL.B., 1885; m. Edith Foote Wright, Jan. 1, 1889; 1 son, Richard. Began practice, Boston, 1885; became partner with Samuel J. Elder, 1890, later firm of Elder, Wait & Whitman; judge Superior Court, 1902-23; asso. justice Supreme Judicial Court of Mass., Dec. 26, 1923—. Alderman, 1893, mem. Sch. Com., 1895-1920, commr. Sinking Fund, 1896-1924, Medford, Mass.; mem. Commn. on Law's Delays, Commonwealth of Mass., 1909. Fellow Am. Acad. Arts and Sciences, Am. Geog. Society. Democrat. Unitarian. Home: Medford, Mass. Died Jan. 28, 1935.

WAIT, William Henry, university prof.; b. McConnell, Ill., Dec. 30, 1854; s. Nelson and Mary Catherine (Root) W.; A.B., Northwestern U., 1879, A.M., 1882; Ph.D., Allegheny Coll., Meadville, Pa., 1888; studied philology, univs. of Berlin and Bonn, 1893-94; m. Clara W. Hadley, Sept. 6, 1888. Instr. Latin, Greek and German, high sch., Peoria, Ill., 1880-83; prof. Latin and German, 1883-88, Latin and modern langs., 1888-90, acting pres., 1887-88, v.p. and dean, 1888-90, Ill. Wesleyan U.; classical instr., high sch., Peoria, 1890-95; with U. of Mich., 1895—, successively instr. Greek and Sanskrit, until 1897, Greek, Latin and Sanskrit, 1897-1901, German, 1901-04, asst. prof. modern langs., Coll. of Engring., U. of Mich., 1904-07, and in charge modern lang. work, same, 1904-12, jr. prof. modern langs., Coll. of Engring., 1907-15, asso. prof., 1915-24, prof., 1924—. Republican. Episcopalian. Editor: Select Orations of Lysias, 1898; German Science Reader, 1907. Home: Ann Arbor, Mich. Died Feb. 28, 1939.

WAITE, Byron Sylvester, U.S. gen. appraiser; b. Penfield, N.Y., Sept. 27, 1852; s. Elihu and Elizabeth (Tarbell) W.; desc. of Benjamin Waite, Hatfield, Mass., 1670; A.B., U. of Mich., 1880; m. Ismene Cramer, Jan. 20, 1881. Admitted to Mich. bar, 1879; mem. Mich. Ho. of Rep. from Menominee, sessions 1889, 95; asst. pros. atty. Wayne Co., Mich., 1895-98; judge Circuit Court, 3d Circuit, Wayne Co., 1898-1900; mem. Bd. U.S. Gen. Appraisers (Customs Court), 1902—. Mem. Mich. N.G. 5 yrs. Mem. S.A.R. Republican. Mason, Elk. Home: Yonkers, N.Y. Died Dec. 31, 1930.

WAITE, Charles Burlingame, author; b. Wayne Co., N.Y., Jan. 29, 1824; s. Daniel D. and Lucy (Clapp) W. (A.M., Knox Coll., Galesburg, Ill., 1854). Admitted to bar, 1847; practiced in Chicago until 1862; asso. justice Supreme Court, Utah, 1862-65; dist. atty. Idaho, 1865-66; then became engaged in literary pursuits in Chicago; m. Catharine Van Valkenburg, 1854. Author: History of the Christian Religion to the Year A. D. 200, 1881; A Conspiracy Against the Republic, 1899; Herbert Spencer and His Critics, 1900; Jesus the Essene. Home, Chicago, Ill. Died 1909.

WAITE, Davis Hanson, gov. Colo.; b. Jamestown, N.Y., April 9, 1825; s. Joseph and Olive (Davis) W.; ed. in village school and Jamestown Acad.; studied law; mcht. in Wis., 1850-57; m. Frances E. Russell, Sept. 15, 1851; m. 2d, Mrs. Celia O. Maltby, Jan. 8, 1855. Mem. Wis. legislature, 1857; Republican; taught high school at Houston, Mo., 1859-60; returned to N.Y., 1861; edited Chautauqua (N.Y.) Democrat (Republican organ), and later propr. Jamestown (N.Y.) Journal until 1876; conducted ranch and practiced law, Larned, Kan., 1876-79; mem. Kan. legislature, 1879; practiced law, Leadville, Colo., 1879-81; practiced law and edited Union Era, reform paper, Aspen, Colo., 1881-91; delegate to St. Louis Conf., 1892, which organized People's Party; gov. Colo., 1893-94; defeated for re-election. Populist. Home: Aspen, Colo. Died 1901.

WAITE, George Thomas, exec. sec. Baptist Board of Missions and Education; b. Caroline County, Va., Sept. 22, 1883; s. Henry Willis and Virginia (Faulkner) W.; A.B., U. of Richmond, 1907, A.M., 1908, D.D., 1925; Th.M., Southern Bapt. Theol. Sem., 1911; m. Evelyn Lois Gardner, Oct. 12, 1911; m. 2d, Mildred Marie Davis, Dec. 31, 1914; children—Elizabeth Boone, George Thomas. Ordained to ministry Bapt. Ch., 1909; pastor Herndon, Va., 1911-13, Siloam Ch., Marion, Ala., 1913-17, Barton Heights Ch., Richmond, Va., 1917-28; pres. Baptist Ministers' Conf. of Richmond, 1920-21; pres. Ministerial Union of Richmond; mem. Bapt. Board of Missions and Edn., 1926-28, exec. sec., 1928—; mem. exec. bd. Baptist Council of Richmond, 1918-28; mem. Bapt. Foreign Mission Board, 1925-28; v.p. Baptist General Assn. of Va., 1927; moderator Dover Baptist Assn., 1925-26. Trustee University of Richmond. Mason. Baptist. Home: Richmond, Va. Deceased.

WAITE, Henry Randall, editor; b. in Copenhagen, N.Y., Dec. 16, 1846; s. Rev. Hiram H. and S. Maria (Randall) W.; grad. Hamilton Coll., 1868; studied theology Union Theol. Sem. N.Y., followed by 3 yrs.' gen. studies in Europe (Ph.D., Univ. of Syracuse); m. Caroline A. Huntoon, Feb. 16, 1876. Founder and pastor Am. Union Ch., Rome, Italy, 1871-74. Congl. clergyman. Organized Italian Sunday Sch. Union and Italian Y.M.C.A., Rome, Italy, and undenominational ch. among soldiers of the Italian Army. Mem. bd. mgrs. Italian Bible Soc., 1872-73. Editor Utica Morning Herald, 1869, New Haven Evening Jour., 1876, International Rev., New York, 1878. Founded, 1885, and from then pres. Am. Inst. Civics; editor of its publs., including Civics, the Citizen, and The Common Good. Sec. Inter-State Commn. on Federal Aid to Education, 1882; expert statistician, 10th U.S. census, in charge inquiries relating to schs., colls., libraries, museums, religious orgns., and illiteracy. Republican. Founder Patria Club, New York; gov. N.J. Soc. Order Founders and Patriots, 1902-03. Author: The Mormon Problem, 1886; Dangerous Elements in the Suffrage. Home: East Orange, N.J. Died 1909.

WAITE, Herbert Harold, bacteriology; b. Leverett, Mass., July 4, 1868; A.B., Amherst, 1892, A.M., 1903; M.D., U. of Mich., 1901; m. Constance Elizabeth Webber, June 20, 1901 (died 1906); children—Wallace Leonard, Alice Webber; m. 2d, Mary Henderson Ames, April 8, 1908 (died 1911); children—Constance Elizabeth, Herbert Ames. Instr. in bacteriology, U. of Mich., 1896-1901; asst. prof. bacteriology and pathology, 1902-05, asso. prof., 1905-07, prof., 1907—, U. of Neb. Contract surgeon, U.S.A., Oct. 12, 1918-Jan. 9, 1919; maj. Med. Res. Corps, U.S.A. Delegate from Neb. to 15th Internat. Congress of Hygiene and Demography. Author: Disease Prevention, 1920. Home: Lincoln, Neb. Deceased.

WAITE, John Leman, editor; b. Ravenna, O., Aug. 29, 1840; s. John and Martha Amelia (Clark) W.; ed. Ravenna, 1848-59, and at Chicago Acad. and Business Coll.; m. Letitia Caroline Williams, Sept. 21, 1864. In telegraph service as operator and supt. telegraph, 1858-69; became city editor Burlington Hawk-Eye, 1869, mng. editor, editor and publ., 1885-1917, now editor in chief. Postmaster of Burlington, apptd. by President Arthur, 1882-86; apptd. postmaster by President McKinley, 1898, and by President Roosevelt, 1902 and 1906. Republican. Pres. Nat. Assn. of Postmasters of First Class Offices, 1907-08. Chmn. bd. Merchants Nat. Bank. Home: Burlington, Ia. Died Mar. 21, 1924.

WAKE, Charles Staniland, anthropologist; b. Kingston-upon-Hull, Eng., Mar. 22, 1835; ed. Hull Coll., Eng. With Field Mus. of Natural History, Chicago, 1895—. Dir. Anthrop. Inst. of Great Britain and Ireland; mem. gen. com. British Assn. Advancement of Science; corr. mem. Brooklyn Ethical Soc.; asso. Soc. for Psychical Research, Eng. Author: Chapters on Man, 1862; The Evolution of Morality (2 vols.), 1878; The Origin and Significance of the Great Pyramid, 1882; Serpent Worship, and Other Essays, 1888; The Development of Marriage and Kinship, 1889; Vortex Philosophy, or The Geometry of Science, 1907; also System of Color and Musical-Tone Relations. Editor of Memoirs of the Congress of Anthropology, Chicago, 1893-94. Home: Chicago, Ill. Died 1910.

WAKEFIELD, Edmund Burritt, college prof.; b. Greensburg, O., Aug. 27, 1846; s. Edwin and Mary Payne (Churchill) W.; A.B., Hiram Coll., 1870, A.M., 1873; Bethany Coll., 1868-69; m. Martha A. Sheldon, Aug. 23, 1870. Enlisted as pvt. Co. G, 177th Ohio Inf., Aug. 3, 1864; in active service with 23d Army Corps in Tenn. and N.C. till close of war. Prof. natural science, Hiram Coll., 1871-74; mem. U.S. Geol. Survey of Yellowstone, under Dr. F. V. Hayden, 1872; pastor Christian Ch., N. Bloomfield, O., 1874-83, Warren, O., 1883-90; prof., 1890-1902, acting pres., 1903, prof. Bibl. lit. and theology till 1912, Hiram Coll.; retired upon Carnegie Foundation, 1912. Republican. Author: Standard Sunday School Commentary (5 vols.), 1893-97. Home: Hiram, O. Died June 25, 1921.

WAKELEY, Arthur Cooper, judge; b. Whitewater, Wis., Mar. 19, 1855; s. Eleazer and Sabina S. (Comstock) W.; B.Litt., Cornell U., 1878; student law dept. Columbia, 1880-81; attended lectures, Oxford U., Eng., 1921; m. Fanny Dalrymple Wall, Oct. 15, 1890. Began practice at Omaha, Neb., 1881; mem. Bd. of Edn., Omaha, 1915-17; judge Dist. Court, 4th Jud. Dist. of Neb., for terms 1916-28; lecturer on civil law, Creighton U. Democrat. Christian Scientist. Elk (Exalted Ruler Omaha Lodge, 1908). Editor History of Douglas County, 1917. Represented Cornell U. in Intercollegiate Oratorical Contest, N.Y. City, 1878. Home: Omaha, Neb. Died Mar. 23, 1928.

WAKEMAN, Keith (Miss), actress; b. in Calif., Apr. 9, 1874; d. Capt. Edgar and Mary (Lincoln) W.; ed. State Normal Sch., San José, Calif. Began on stage in America, 1892; went to London, Eng., 1894, and continued 12 yrs. as star and leading woman, touring America with E. S. Willard; playing in U.S. in Shakespearean and modern rôles, 1907—; leading woman Ben Greet Co., 1909; leading woman with Robert B. Mantell in Shakespearean rôles. Author: The Sixth Sense, 1910. Died Oct. 17, 1933.

WAKEMAN, Thaddeus Burr, author; b. Greenfield Hill, Conn., Dec. 23, 1834; grad. Princeton, 1854; admitted to bar, 1856; m. Emily F. Ludlam, 1859 (died 1904). Was pres. Liberal U., Kansas City, but suspended univ. work, 1904, because of illness, and removed to Conn., where is engaged in lit. work. Author: An Epitome of Positive Philosophy and Religion; The Religion of Humanity; Liberty and Purity; The Age of Revision; Evolution or Creation. First suggested the "New Era" of "Science and Man," dating from 1600, A.D., the time of acceptance of Copernican Astronomy, the burning of Bruno, settlement of America, etc. Has made transl. of Goethe's religious and other poems, and lectures on these and scientific subjects. Sr. del. 1st Monist Congress, Hamburg, Germany, 1911. Home: Cos Cob, Conn. Died April 23, 1913.

WAKEMAN, Wilbur Fisk, publisher; b. Harvard, Ill., Apr. 3, 1857; s. Thaddeus Burr and Hannah (Bennett) W.; ed. Northwestern U.; m. Helen Edith Ainsworth, June 4, 1898. Reporter Chicago Inter-Ocean, and later with circulation dept. Phila. Press; mgr. Alta-California, 1885-86; circulation mgr. Kansas City Times, 1887-88; pub. American Economist, New York, 1889-1926. Pub. and distributor campaign lit. Rep. Nat. and Congressional coms., campaigns of 1892, 96, 98, 1900, 02, 04; U.S. appraiser port of New York, 1897-1901; sec. and treas. Am. Protective Tariff League, 1889-1926. Mem. S.R. Presbyn. Home: Staten Island, N.Y. Died Feb. 13, 1931.

WALBRIDGE, Cyrus Packard, merchant; b. Madrid, N.Y., July 20, 1849; s. Orlo Judson and Maria Althea (Packard) W.; ed. pub. schs. of DeKalb Co., Ill., and Stanton, Minn., to 1868, Carleton Coll., Minn., to 1871; LL.B., U. of Mich., 1874; m. Lizzie Merrell, Oct. 9, 1879. Practiced law at Minneapolis, 1874-76, St. Louis, 1876-85; house atty. for J. S. Merrell, wholesale druggist, St. Louis, 1879-85, becoming pres. of the J. S. Merrell Drug Co., 1885. Mem. St. Louis Ho. of Dels., 1881-83; pres. City Council, 1889-93, mayor of St. Louis, 1893-97; endorsed by Rep. State Conv., 1904, for Vice-President of U.S.; Rep. nominee for gov. of Mo., 1904. V.p. La. Purchase Expn. Co., 1904. Mem. Mo. Waterways Commn., 1908—; chmn. City Plan Commission. Trustee First Congl. Ch. Mason, K.P., Royal Arcanam. Died May 1, 1921.

WALBRIDGE, George Hicks, exec. engineer; b. Bennington, Vt., Aug. 22, 1869; s. James Hicks and Delia M. (Perry) W.; M.E., Cornell, 1890; m. Mary Gilley Taylor, Oct. 17, 1900; 1 dau., Elizabeth Stebbins. V.p. J. G. White & Co., engrs., 1890-1902; gen. engring. practice, 1902-07; pres. Colo. Power Co., in charge constrn. and management hydro-electric plants, 1907-11; with Bonbright & Co., investment bankers, 1911-20, v.p. from 1914; asso. with L. P. Hammond, management, pub. utilities and industrials, 1920-24; chmn. bd. Royalties Management Corp. Republican. Home: New York, N.Y. Died Aug. 5, 1936.

WALCOTT, Charles Doolittle, scientist; b. New York Mills, N.Y., Mar. 31, 1850; s. Charles D. and Mary (Lane) W.; ed. pub. schs., Utica, N.Y.; LL.D., Hamilton, 1898, U. Chicago, 1901, Johns Hopkins, 1902, U. of Pa., 1903, Yale, 1910, St. Andrews, 1911, Pittsburgh, 1912; Sc.D., U. of Cambridge, Eng., 1909, Harvard, 1913; Ph.D., Royal Fredericks U., Christiania, 1911; m. Helena B. Stevens, June 22, 1888 (died 1911); children—Charles D. (dec.), Helen B. (Mrs. Cole B. Younger), Sidney S., Stuart B. (dec.); m. 2d, Mary Morris Vaux, June 30, 1914. Early showed a predilection for geologic research; became asst. in N.Y. State Survey, 1876; asst. geologist U.S. Geol. Survey, 1879, the Cambrian rocks and faunas of the U.S. being his especial subjects of inquiry; presented his Cambrian researches before Internat. Geol. Congress, London, 1888. Paleontologist in charge invertebrate paleontology, 1888-93, geologist in general charge geology and paleontology, 1893-94, and dir., 1894-1907, U.S. Geol. Survey; hon. curator dept. paleontology, 1892-97, and 1898—; at head of Nat. Mus., Jan. 1897-July 1898, with title of acting asst. sec. Smithsonian Instn., and from Jan. 1907, sec. same; sec. Carnegie Instn., Washington, 1902-05, also vice chmn. bd. trustees and, 1917-22, chmn. exec. com. of same; dir. U.S. Reclamation Service, 1905-07; dir. Research Corporation, N.Y. City. Fellow Christiania Scientific Soc., Am. Acad. Arts and Sciences, Geol. Soc. America (pres. 1901), Geol. Soc. London (Bigsby medal, and Wollaston medal, 1918), Imperial Soc. Naturalists (Moscow), Royal Geog. Soc. (London), Acad. Science Inst. Bologna; Gaudry medal, Soc. Géol., France; foreign asso. French Acad. Sciences; Hayden medal, Acad. Natural Sciences Phila.; Mary Clark Thompson medal, Nat. Acad. Sciences, 1921; pres. Washington Soc. Archæol. Inst. America, 1915-18; mem. Royal Swedish Acad. Sciences, 1920, Trail Riders Canadian Rockies (pres. 1924—). Chairman Nat. Advisory Com. for Aeronautics, apptd. by Pres. Wilson; vice chmn. Nat. Research Council (chmn. govt. relations com.). Author: The Trilobite: Paleontology of the Eureka District; The Cambrian Faunas of North America; The Fauna of the Lower Cambrian or Olenellus Zone; Pre-Cambrian Fossiliferous Formations; Correlation Papers; Cambrian Geology and Paleontology; Cambrian Brachiopoda; The Cambrian Faunas of China; The Cambrian and Its Problems in the Cordilleran Region; Pre-Cambrian Algonkian Algal Flora; Discovery of Algonkian Bacteria; Evidences of Primitive Life; Appendages of Trilobites. Home: Washington, D.C. Died Feb. 9, 1927.

WALCOTT, Earle Ashley, author; b. Magnolia, Ill., Nov. 19, 1859; s. John and Rebecca Josephine (Butterfield) W.; prep. edn. Santa Barbara (Calif.) Coll., 1874-76; B.Litt., U. of California, 1883; m. Frances Van Reynegom, April 1915; children—Ashley V. R., Francis John. Editor The Occident (college weekly), 1882; editor Lodi Valley Review, 1884-85, San Franciscan, 1885-86; on staff San Francisco Chronicle, 1886; editorial writer San Francisco Post, 1886-89; editor Weekly Examiner, and editorial writer Daily Examiner, 1889-1909; exec. sec. Commonwealth Club San Francisco, Aug. 1, 1909—. Temporary chmn. and sec. San Francisco Charter Revision Convention, 1910; mem. commn. for location and constrn. of Calif. State Reformatory, term 1911-15; pres. San Francisco Civil Service Commn., 1912-14, 1919-21, 1924—; three times reapptd. commr., term ends 1931; mem. mayor's advisory conf. on charter amendments, 1912; sec. Exposition Preservation League, 1919—; pres. St. Francis Homes Assn., 1922-26; first v.p. Nat. Assembly Civil Service Commn., 1925-26, pres., 1926-27; mem. State Constl. Commn., 1930. Author: Blindfolded, 1906; The Apple of Discord, 1907; The Open Door, 1910; Influence of Immigration on Population, 1922. Editor of Trans. Commonwealth Club of Calif., vols. III to XXIV. Home: San Francisco, Calif. Died Jan. 1, 1931.

WALCOTT, Henry Pickering, M.D.; b. Salem, Mass., Dec. 23, 1838; s. Samuel Baker and Martha (Pickman) W.; A.B., Harvard U., 1858; studied medicine Harvard, and Bowdoin Coll., M.D., Bowdoin, 1861; studied 2 yrs. in Vienna and Berlin; LL.D., Yale, 1907, Harvard, 1927. Practiced at Cambridge, 1867-81; chmn. Mass. State Bd. of Health; also chmn. Metropolitan Water and Sewerage Bd. Prominent in movements to promote public health. Republican. President Mass. Med. Society, Am. Pub. Health Assn., Mass. Hort. Soc.; pres. Am. Acad. Arts and Sciences; hon. fellow Royal Sanitary Inst. of Great Britain; mem. Bd. of Pres. and Fellows of Harvard U., 1890-1927; overseer of the coll., 1887-90; acting pres. Harvard Coll., 1900, 05; chmn. trustees of Mass. Gen. Hosp.; trustee Carnegie Instn. of Washington; pres. 15th Internat. Congress on Hygiene and Demography, Washington, 1912. Home: Cambridge, Mass. Died 1932.

WALCUTT, Charles C., Jr., army officer; b. in Ohio, June 20, 1861; grad. U.S. Mil. Acad., July 1, 1886, Inf. and Cav. Sch., 1893; Army War Coll., 1912. Commd. 2d lt. 8th Cav., July 1, 1886; 1st lt. 3d Cav., Aug. 16, 1892; trans. to 8th Cav., Dec. 5, 1892; capt. a.q.m. vols., May 12, 1898; vacated Sept. 18, 1899; maj. 44th Vol. Inf., Aug. 17, 1899; hon. disch. vols., June 30, 1901; capt. 2d Cav. U.S.A., Feb. 2, 1901; q.m., Oct. 29, 1901; assigned to 5th Cav., Nov. 3, 1905; maj., Mar. 3, 1911; col., July 1, 1916; brig. gen. N.A., June 26, 1918. Ordered to Manila, P.I., 1898; depot q.m., Manila, 1899-1901; duty at Washington, D.C., 1901-02; constructing q.m. Whipple Barracks, Ariz., 1902; detailed as col., Bur. Insular Affairs, Washington, D.C., 1912, serving as asst. chief, later acting chief and chief of same. Died June 20, 1925.

WALD, Gustavus Henry, dean law dept. Univ. of Cincinnati; b. Cincinnati, O., March 30, 1853; s. Henry and Betty (Mayer) W.; grad. Yale, 1873; Harvard Law School, 1875 (LL.D., Univ. of Cincinnati, 1898); has practiced at Cincinnati, 1875—; Dem. nominee for judge Supreme Court, Ohio, 1891; prof. law dept. Univ. of Cincinnati. Editor Wald's Pollock's "Principles of Contract," 1881. Unmarried. Home: Cincinnati, O. Died 1902.

WALD, Lillian D., social worker, publicist; b. Ohio, 1867; d. Max and Minnie Wald; ed. pvt. schs., New York Hosp. Training Sch. for Nurses, Woman's Med. Coll.; LL.D., Mt. Holyoke Coll., 1912, Smith College, 1930. Founder, 1893, president, and organizer public health nursing, Henry Street Settlement (formerly Nurses' Settlement); originator first city sch. nursing work in the world, N.Y. City, 1902; originator of idea of Federal Children's Bur., established by Congress, 1908, also plan for town and country nursing, Am. Red Cross; lecturer, Teachers Coll., New York Sch. of Social Work. Mem. Joint Bd. Sanitary Control, and chmn. com. on home nursing, Council Nat. Defense, World War. Mem. Mayor's Pushcart Commn., 1906, N.Y. State Commn. of Immigration, 1909; mem. 1st Welfare Council, New York; mem. White House Conf. on Child Health and Protection, 1909, 30; mem. N.Y. City Loose Milk Commn., 1931; mem. U.S. Commn. on Cooperation in Pan-Am. Child Welfare Work; mem. exec. com. Welfare Council of New York (mem. exec. com. coördinating com. on unemployment 1930-31); trustee Nat. Child Labor Com.; mem. exec. com. N.Y. Child Labor Committee. Vice-pres. Bellevue-Yorkville Health Demonstration; mem. advisory bd. City Housing Corp., Milbank Memorial Fund. Mem. advisory council Am. Sch. of Nursing, Inst. Internat. Edn.; pres. Social Halls Assn.; v.p. Am. Russian Inst. Del. for Federal Children's Bur. to Internat. Conf., Cannes, France, 1919; Am. del. to Women's Internat. Conf., Zurich, 1919; mem. women's aux. com. of U.S., 2d Pan-Am. Scientific Congress; chmn. Am. Union Against Militarism. Awarded gold medal, Nat. Inst. Social Sciences, 1912; gold medal, Rotary Club, 1923; "Better Times" medal for distinguished social service, 1926; Abraham Lincoln High School award as "citizen rendering greatest service to City of New York," 1936; citation from Mayor La Guardia for distinguished service to the City of New York, 1937. Author: The House on Henry Street, 1915; Windows on Henry Street, 1934. Established Lillian D. Wald playground, 1937. Home: New York, N.Y. Died Sept. 1, 1940.

WALDECK, Carl Gustav, painter; b. St. Charles, Mo., Mar. 13, 1866; s. John and Katherine (Ludwig) W.; ed. pub. schs., St. Louis; student St. Louis Sch. of Fine Arts, and later at Académie Julian, Paris, under Jean Paul Laurens and Benjamin Constant; m. Ruby Beatrice Weedell, Dec. 30, 1920; children—Beatrice Ann, Carl Robert. Established studio in St. Louis, 1887; now figure and landscape painter; made 1st exhibition at Photographers' Assn. America, Washington, 1890, and awarded 1st prize for black-and-white drawings; bronze medal, St. Louis Expn., 1904; silver medal, Portland (Ore.) Expn., 1905; gold medal, Mo. State Expn., 1913; Brown prize, St. Louis Artists' Guild, 1914; Fine Arts prize, Soc. of Western Artists, Indianapolis, 1914; 1st prize, St. Louis Artists' League, 1915; 1st prize for best group of paintings, St. Louis Artists' Guild, 1923. Officier d'Académie, Paris, France, 1904. Home: Kirkwood, Mo. Died Feb. 17, 1931.

WALDEN, Freeman, clergyman; b. Floyd Co., Ind., Mar. 18, 1839; s. Joseph and Rhoda (Sparks) W.;

ed. pub. schs. and acad. in Ia.; m. Mary O. Berry, Aug. 20, 1862 (died 1891); m. 2d, Mrs. Anna E. Van Voorhis, Nov. 9, 1892. Minister Christian (Disciples) Ch., 1860—; not now in regular pastorate. Student and expert in horticulture and lecturer, Agrl. Coll., Pullman, Wash., and farmers' insts.; conducts 100 acre orchard; hort. editor The Ranch. Home: Seattle, Wash. Deceased.

WALDEN, John Morgan, bishop; b. Lebanon, Ohio, Feb. 11, 1831; s. Jesse and Matilda (Morgan) W.; A.B., Farmers' (now Belmont) College, near Cincinnati, 1852, A.M., 1860 (D.D., 1865; LL.D., McKendree Coll., 1879; D.D., Victoria Coll., British Columbia, 1911); m. Martha Young, July 3, 1859. Taught sch. over 4 yrs.; connected with press 4 yrs., part of time editor and pub. independent paper in Ill.; afterwards of a free-state paper in Kan.; mem. Kan. "Topeka Legislature," 1857; mem. Kan. Constl. Conv., 1858. Entered M.E. ministry, Cincinnati Conf., 1858; pastor Northbend Circuit, 1 yr., Lynchburg Circuit, 1 yr., York St. Ch., Cincinnati, 2 yrs., City Mission, 2 yrs.; lt. col., Union Army, 1862; editor Daily Advocate, 1864; corr. sec. Freedmen's Aid Commn. (undenominational), 1863-66; corr. secretary Meth. Freedmen's Aid Soc., 1866-68; one of publishing agts. Western Meth. Book Concern, 1868-84; elected bishop, 1884. Pres. Freedmen's Aid Soc., 1884—; mem. Ecumenical Conf., London, 1881, Washington, 1891, Toronto, 1911; mem. of Gen. Conf., 1868, 72, 76, 80, 84. Has made episcopal visits in every state and to the Meth. missions in Europe, Asia, S. America, and Mexico. Mem. G.A.R. Died Jan. 21, 1914.

WALDEN, Lionel, painter; b. Norwich, Conn., May 22, 1861; s. Treadwell and Elizabeth Leighton (Law) W.; studied with Carolus Duran, Paris. Second-class medal Crystal Palace, London; hon. mention, Salon, Paris; silver medal, Paris Expn., 1900; third class medal, Salon, 1903; represented in Luxembourg Gallery, Paris, Memorial Mus., Phila., and Cardiff, Wales, Cooke Gallery, Honolulu, Corcoran Gallery, Washington, D.C. Awarded silver medal, St. Louis Exposition, 1904; silver medal, Panama P.I. Expn., 1915. Chevalier, Legion of Honor, of France, 1910. Died July 12, 1933.

WALDEN, Treadwell, clergyman, author; b. Walden, N.Y. (a town founded by his father), Apr. 25, 1830; s. Jacob T. and Beulah Hoffman (Willett) W.; ed. pvt. schs., N.Y. City, at Coll. of St. James, Md., and St. Paul's Coll., L.I.; grad. Gen. Theol. Sem., New York, 1853; m. Elizabeth Leighton Law, 1858 (died 1883); m. 2d, Grace Gordon, 1885; father of Lionel W. Deacon, 1854, priest, 1856, P.E. Ch.; asst., and in charge Trinity Ch., Newark, N.J., 1854-56; rector Christ Ch., Norwich, Conn., 1857-63, St. Clement's, Phila., 1863-68, St. Paul's Cathedral, Indianapolis, 1869-72, St. Paul's, Boston, 1873-76, St. Paul's, Minneapolis, 1882-85. Lived in London, Eng., 1886-89, writing the "Story of England in Westminster Hall"; preached in Westminster Abbey, the Royal Chapel, Savoy, St. Margaret's, Westminster, and other English chs.; apptd. on 2 spl. commns. by U.S. Sanitary Commn., 1864, to investigate treatment of prisoners of war, both North and South; wrote the official account and edited vol. of testimony. Author: Lays of a Lifetime, 1856; The Sunday School Prayer Book, 1860; Narrative of Privations and Sufferings of U.S. Officers and Soldiers in Confederate Prisons, 1864; Our English Bible and Its Ancestors, 1870; An Undeveloped Chapter in the Life of Christ, 1882; The Great Meaning of Metanoia, in Two Essays, 1896. Home: Boston, Mass. Died May 21, 1918.

WALDO, Clarence Abiathar, univ. prof.; b. Hammond, N.Y., Jan. 21, 1852; s. Orange Gersham and Barbara Ellen (Zoller) W.; A.B., Wesleyan, Conn., 1875, A.M., 1878; univs. of Leipzig and Munich, 1882-83; Ph.D., Syracuse U., 1894; m. Abby Wright, d. late Levi W. Allen, of South Hadley, Mass., Aug. 2, 1881; children—Alice Goddard, Clarence A. (dec.). Instr. mathematics and registrar, Wesleyan Univ., 1877-81; prof. mathematics, 1883-91, acting pres., 1885-86, 1888-89, Rose Poly. Inst., Terre Haute, Ind.; prof. mathematics, DePauw U., 1891-95; head prof. mathematics, Purdue U., 1895-1908; Thayer prof. mathematics and applied mechanics, at Washington U., St. Louis, 1908-17, prof. emeritus, 1917—. Lit. work, 1917—. Author: Manual of Descriptive Geometry, 1888. Editor Proceedings Ind. Acad. of Science, 1896, 97, 98, Proc. Soc. Promotion Engring. Edn., 1901-03. Volunteer worker on 4 exemption bds. of Greater New York, 1917-18; vol. city surveyor for League of Chs., Sept. 1918-Apr. 1919; war emergency substitute office sec. of Meth. Bd. of Edn. Carnegie Foundation visitor to colleges in N.E., Sept. 1919-Jan. 1920. Home: New York, N.Y. Died Oct. 1, 1926.

WALDO, Dwight Bryant, educator; b. Arcade, N.Y., June 13, 1864; s. Simeon Smith and Martha Ann (Bryant) W.; high sch., Plainwell, Mich., 1875-79; Mich. Agrl. Coll., 1881-83; Ph.B., Albion (Mich.) Coll., 1887, A.M., 1890; Harvard, 1889-90; (LL.D., Kalamazoo College, 1912); m. Lilian Trudgeon, Sept. 14, 1904. Prof. history, Beloit (Wis.) Coll., 1890-92; prof. history and economics, Albion Coll., 1892-99; first prin. State Normal Sch., Marquette, Mich., 1899-1904; pres. Western State Teachers Coll., Kalamazoo, July 1, 1904-Sept. 1, 1936 (emeritus). Republican. Presbyterian. Apptd. mem. advisory com. on Federal Pub. Schs., Oct. 1918; mem. bd. of consultants Nat. Survey Education of Teachers. Home: Kalamazoo, Mich. Died Oct. 29, 1939.

WALDO, Frank, meteorologist, engineer; b. Cincinnati, Nov. 4, 1857; s. Frederic Augustus and Frances (Leonard) W.; brother of Leonard W.; B.S., Marietta Coll., 1878, Ph.D., 1889; Harvard U., 1880-84; m. Sarah M. Jaques, Sept. 13, 1881. Asst. in Harvard Obs., 1878-81; computer and prof. U.S. Signal Service, 1881-87; instr. astronomy, Harvard Annex (now Radcliffe Coll.), 1880-81; in U.S. Govt. service, in Europe, 1882-83; instr. meteorology, Corcoran Sch. of Science, Columbian U., 1884-85. Spl. agt. U.S. Weather Bur., 1890. Cattle ranching, 1896-1902; editorial work, 1902-07; expert in industrial edn. Mass. Commn. on Industrial Edn., Mass. State Bd. of Edn., 1907-11; improvement and building engring., 1914—; served as prof. of meteorology U.S.N., aviation detachment, Mass. Inst. Tech., 1917-18. Mem. staff Nat. Industrial Conf. Board. Author: Modern Meteorology, London, 1893; Elementary Meteorology, for Schools and Colleges, 1896. Coeditor: Blinds' George Eliot, 1904. Home: Belmont, Mass. Died May 7, 1920.

WALDO, Leonard, metallurgical and elec. engr.; b. Cincinnati, May 4, 1853; s. Dr. Frederic Augustus and Frances (Leonard) W.; brother of Frank W.; B.S., Marietta College, 1872, A.M., 1877; studied Columbia School of Mines; Sc.D., Harvard, 1879; (hon. A.M., Yale, 1880); m. Dora Fullerton, 1875 (dec.); m. 2d, Ada Louise Purdy, 1887. Asst. astronomer U.S. Transit of Venus expdn. to Tasmania, 1874; asst. in Harvard Obs., 1875-80; astronomer in charge horological bur., Yale Obs., 1879-88. Consultant for U.S. Steel Corp., etc., in steel research; consulting engr. War Dept. in production of shells and illuminants in World War. Inventor of magnesium production process. Mem. fatigue of metals com. of Nat. Research Council; medallist Royal Soc. Arts; sometime chmn. library bd. United Engring. Soc. Home: Plainfield, N.J. Died Jan. 25, 1929.

WALDO, Rhinelander, police commr.; b. New York, May 24, 1877; s. Francis W. and Gertrude (Rhinelander) W.; ed. Berkeley Sch., New York, and Sch. of Mines, Columbia U., 1899; m. Virginia Otis Heckscher, Apr. 20, 1910. Apptd. 2d lt. 17th U.S. Inf., Apr. 10, 1899; 1st lt., Feb. 2, 1901; capt. Philippine Scouts, Feb. 28, 1905; resigned Sept. 10, 1905; apptd. 1st deputy police commr. of New York, Jan. 23, 1906; fire commr., Jan. 1, 1910-May 1911; police commr., May 23, 1911-Dec. 31, 1913. Sent to Europe in 1906 by the City of New York to study police methods there; instituted finger print system and organized traffic squad upon its present basis; organized police of Catskill Aqueduct, 1907; organized the fire coll., the first of its kind, and inaugurated the motor fire apparatus service. Commd. maj., Inf. O.R.C., Sept. 22, 1916; maj. 301st Inf., N.A., Sept. 2, 1917; lt. col., U.S.A., Nov. 8, 1918; hon. discharged, July 10, 1919. Col. Inf., O.R.C., Jan. 8, 1923. Home: Garrison, N.Y. Died Aug. 13, 1927.

WALDOW, William F., congressman; b. Buffalo, N.Y., Aug. 26, 1872; s. Gustav R. and Caroline W.; ed. pub. schs.; m. Maud E. Lacey, Mar. 14, 1893. General contracting business; mem. Bd. of Aldermen, Buffalo, 1912-13; mem. Rep. State Com., 4th Assembly Dist., N.Y., 1916-18; mem. 65th Congress (1917-19), 42d N.Y. Dist. Republican. Protestant. Home: Buffalo, N.Y. Died Apr. 16, 1930.

WALDRON, James Albert, editor, writer; b. Sherburne, N.Y., Sept. 25, 1852; s. Ebenezer B. and Lavinia R. (Benton) W.; ed. pub. schs.; m. Mary Jane Deuel; children—LaMonte, George Albert, Mrs. Olive Warner. Polit. reporter Albany Argus, 1879-82; mng. editor Albany Evening Journal, 1883-89, New York Dramatic Mirror, 1891-1910; became editor of Judge, 1912, his short stories and social satires being features of that publn. Mem. Am. Press Humorists (pres. 1917-18). Developed, 1888-89, an analysis of the work of Shakespeare as a language creator, based on the hist. values of the Murray dictionary and the kindred relations of Shakespeare's contemporaries; this work was endorsed as a "discovery" by the late William J. Rolfe and other Shakespearean scholars. Author of a comedy, "Cupid & Co.," prod. 1909. Has done much fugitive lit. work. Home: Brooklyn, N.Y. Died June 2, 1931.

WALDRON, John William, sugar mfr.; b. Bidford, Eng., Aug. 2, 1873; s. George and Louise Elizabeth (Squire) W.; student Stratford Coll., Eng.; m. Else Grace Sophia Schaefer, Jan. 4, 1910; children—Dorothy Mary K. (wife of Guy C. Hitchcock, U.S.N.), Frederick August Schaefer, Else Elizabeth. With Empire Tobacco Co., Montreal, Can., 1896-97; settled in Hawaii in 1897; with F. A. Schaefer & Co., Ltd., 1899—, pres., 1917—; pres. Honokaa Sugar Co., Hawaiian Irrigation Co.; dir. Inter-Island Steam Navigation Co., Ltd., Sugar Factors Co., Ltd., Honolulu Iron Works, Olaa Sugar Co., Ltd.; sec.-treas., dir. August Dreer, Ltd.; trustee Calif. and Hawaiian Sugar Refining Corp., Ltd. Naturalized citizen of U.S., 1906. Chilean consul for Hawaii. Trustee Hawaiian Sugar Planters' Assn. Fellow Am. Geog. Soc., Royal Geog. Soc. (Eng.), Royal Statis. Soc., Chartered Inst. of Secretaries. Democrat. Mem. Ch. of England. Mason. Home: Honolulu, T.H. Died 1935.

WALDSTEIN, Louis, physician; b. New York, Apr. 15, 1853; s. Henry and Sophie W.; bro. of Martin E. and Charles W.; student Coll. Phys. and Surg. (Columbia); M.D., U. of Heidelberg, 1878; studied univs. of Zürich, Vienna, London and Paris. Asst. Pathol. Inst., Heidelberg, 1878-80; practiced, New York, 1880-98; in London, 1898—. Author: The Sub-Conscious Self in Its Relation to Education and Health, 1897; also numerous med. and scientific memoirs and articles. Home: London, Eng. Died Apr. 12, 1915.

WALES, George C(anning), artist; b. Boston, Mass., Dec. 23, 1868; s. Nathaniel and Susan E. (Stratton) W.; grad. English High Sch., Boston, 1885; student Mass. Inst. Tech., 1885-88; m. Marie Ames Sweet, Apr. 25, 1906. Draftsman, Peabody & Stearns, architects, Boston, 1888-91; mem. Wales & Holt, architects, Boston, 1893-1906; in practice alone, 1906-24; etcher and lithographer (specializing on old square-rigged ship), 1917. Represented by prints in Library of Congress, U.S. Nat. Mus., Brit. Mus., Victoria and Albert Mus., New York Pub. Library, Boston Mus. of Fine Arts, etc. Republican. Unitarian. Author: Etchings and Lithographs of American Ships, 1927. Home: Brookline, Mass. Died Mar. 21, 1940.

WALES, George Russell, lawyer; b. Middlebury, Vt., Nov. 22, 1862; s. Russell and Lucy Ann (Sumner) W.; A.B., Middlebury (Vt.) Coll., 1887, A.M., 1890, LL.D., 1925; LL.B., Nat. U. Law Sch., Washington, D.C., 1892, LL.M., 1915; LL.D., Columbus Univ., Washington, D.C., 1929; m. Josephine Brooks Abell, Oct. 12, 1907; children—George Herrick, Robert Corning. Formerly prin. Bristol (Vt.) graded sch.; mem. bar Supreme Ct. and Ct. of Appeals, D.C., and Supreme Court of U.S.; with U.S. Civ. Service Commn., 1892—, chief examiner, 1908-19, and commr., Mar. 1919—. Republican. Episcopalian. Home: Washington, D.C. Died Sept. 16, 1933.

WALES, Philip Skinner, M.D., medical dir. U.S.N.; b. Annapolis, Md., Feb. 27, 1837; ed. Univ. of Md. and in its med. dept.; also M.D. Univ. of Pa.; settled in Baltimore and later in Washington. Entered navy as asst. surgeon, Aug. 7, 1856; commissioned surgeon, Oct. 12, 1861; served in U.S.S. Fort Jackson of North Atlantic and Western Gulf squadrons, 1862-65. Member Bd. of Examiners, 1873-74; medical inspector, 1873-80; surgeon gen. of navy and chief of bureau of medicine and surgery, 1880-84; assisted in attendance on President Garfield after he had been shot. Author: Mechanical Therapeutics. Died 1906.

WALES, Salem Howe, journalist, v.p. New East River Bridge Commn., 1895—; b. Wales, Mass., Oct. 4, 1825; s. Capt. Oliver W.; ed. there and Attica, N.Y., Acad.; clerk in importing house, New York, 1846; mng. editor Scientific American, 1848-71; N.Y. commr. to Paris Expn., 1855; on exec. com. Christian Commn. during Civil war; pres. dept. of parks, New York, 1873; Rep. candidate for mayor New York, 1874; pres. dept. of docks, 1874-76; park commr., 1880-85; trustee Metropolitan Museum of Art; dir. Nat. Bank of N. America. Died 1902.

WALGREEN, Charles Rudolph, pres. Walgreen Co.; b. Knox Co., Ill., Oct. 9, 1873; s. Charles and Ellen (Olson) W.; ed. pub. schs. and Dixon (Ill.) Business Coll.; m. Myrtle R. Norton, Aug. 18, 1902; children—Charles R., Mrs. Justin W. Dart. Began as apprentice in drug store, Dixon; registered pharmacist; entered retail drug business in Chicago, 1902; founder, 1909, and pres. Walgreen Co., operating 504 drug stores (1937) in 31 states; dir. Dixon Nat. Bank. Served as pvt. Co. L, 1st Ill. Vols., Spanish-Am. War. Mem. Commn. of Fort Dixon Memorial to Abraham Lincoln, Gorgas Memorial Inst. (donor Walgreen essay prize). Founder mem. "Chicago World's Fair 1933." Established "Walgreen Foundation for study of American Institutions" at Univ. of Chicago, 1937. Mason. Home: Chicago, and Dixon, Ill. Died Dec. 11, 1939.

WALK, James Wilson, physician; b. near Chambersburg, Pa., Mar. 14, 1853; s. Rev. Frederick and Mary Harris (Brown) W.; A.B., Lafayette Coll., 1875; M.D., U. of Pa., 1878; unmarried. Devoted much attention to charities, and published a monthly jour. as exponent of organized charity; gen. sec. Phila. Soc. for Organizing Charity, 1882-99; member Pa. Ho. of Rep., 1887-91; dir. Phila. City Charities and Correction, 1892-97, Bur. of Health, 1897-99; now practicing medicine. Home: Philadelphia, Pa. Died Jan. 19, 1918.

WALKE, Frank Hicks, M.D., surgeon; b. Longview, Tex., Dec. 18, 1886; s. Calvert McArthur and Clara (Hicks) W.; grad. West Tex. Mil. Acad., San Antonio, Tex., 1906; student U. of Tex., 1906-08; M.D., U. of Md., 1912; m. Helen B. Larrimore, June 12, 1913 (divorced 1929); 1 son, Frank Hicks; m. 2d, Mrs. Nellie Webb Bubb, Apr. 30, 1935; 1 son, David. Resident phys., St. Joseph's Hosp., Baltimore, 1912; practiced at Shreveport, La., 1913—; asst. chief surgeon, Shreveport Charity Hosp. 4 yrs.;

mem. staff Highland Sanitarium, The Pines Sanitarium, Schumpert Memorial Hosp., Tri-State Sanitarium; surgeon Standard Oil Co. of La.; div. surgeon K.C.S. Ry., S.P. Ry.; med. examiner 13 life ins. cos.; phys. in chief Home for Aged (Shreveport). Parish health officer, Caddo Parish, La., 1916-20; federal jail physician, 1931-38; mem. Caddo Parish Sch. Bd., 1933—; mem. Com. of Nat. Reemployment Service for Caddo Parish; sec. Nat. Reëmployment Service, 1934—; pres. Community Concert Assn., 1935-39. Mem. Med. Advisory Bd. of La., World War. Democrat. Mem. bd. trustees Dodd College. Presbyn.; pres. Laymen of Red River Presbytery of La., 1934. Mason. Specializes in industrial surgery and restoration of function to injured limbs, etc. Home: Shreveport, La. Died Dec. 21. 1939.

WALKE, Willoughby, officer U.S.A.; b. Norfolk, Va., Jan. 28, 1859; s. Richard and Mary Diana (Talbot) W.; grad. U. of Va., 1879, U.S. Mil. Acad., 1883, Arty. Sch., 1888; m. Julia Armstead Sharp, Nov. 28, 1883. Promoted 2d lt. 2d Arty., June 13, 1883; 1st lt. 5th Arty., Apr. 24, 1891; transferred to 7th Arty., Mar. 8, 1898; maj. 3d U.S. Vol. Engrs., June 28, 1898-May 29, 1899; capt. 2d Arty., Aug. 28, 1899; maj. Arty. Corps, Oct. 1, 1906; lt. col., Coast Arty. Corps, Mar. 3, 1911; col., Aug. 3, 1912. Served in southern camps and in army of occupation at Matanzas, Cuba; comdr. Middle Atlantic Coast Arty. Dist., Sept. 1, 1917-Feb. 1919. Fellow Royal Chem. Soc. Author: Essentials of Chemistry; Lectures on Explosives, 1894; Gunpowder and High Explosives; Comparative Strength of High Explosives. Died Dec. 16, 1928.

WALKER, Albert Henry, lawyer; b. Fairfax, Vt., Nov. 25, 1844; s. Sawyer and Melinda (Gile) W.; desc. of 5 earlier generations of N.E. men and women; LL.B., Northwestern U., 1877; m. Esther Sayles, a descendant of Roger Williams, Sept. 16, 1874. Lawyer, 1877—; mem. Conn. Legislature, 1891, 92. Lecturer on patent law, Cornell U., 1889-1905, Univ. of Mich., 1896—. Polit. orator during many yrs. Has conducted hundreds of litigations throughout the U.S. Author: Walker on Patents, 1883, 4th edit., 1904; History of the Sherman Law, 1910; Christ's Christianity, 1911; Administration of William H. Taft, 1912; Analysis of the Income Tax Law, 1913. Home: New York, N.Y. Died Aug. 31, 1915.

WALKER, Albert Perry, headmaster; b. Alton Bay, N.H., June 9, 1862; s. Charles Dean and Hannah Perkins (Sawyer) Perry; parents died in 1867 and in 1868 respectively; was adopted by Albert D. Walker and name changed to Walker; A.B., Wesleyan U., Conn., 1884, A.M., 1887; m. Mary E. Frisbie, July 2, 1885. Was pvt. tutor in music, Latin and Greek; teacher Mitchell's Boys' Sch., Billerica, Mass., 1884-86; prin. Grafton (Mass.) High Sch., 1886-87; jr. master (teaching English and history), 1887-98, full master, 1898-1904, English High Sch., Boston; master in Boston Normal Sch., teaching history, 1904-07; headmaster The Girls' High Sch., Boston, Sept. 1, 1907—. Organist of chs. in Middletown, Conn., 1880-84, Grafton, Mass., 1886, Newton, Mass., 1888—; organist Ch. of the New Jerusalem, Newtonville, Mass., 1888-1906. Editor: Selections from Paradise Lost, 1898; Macaulay's Essay on Milton, 1899, and on Addison, 1899; Milton's Minor Poems, 1900; Selections from Milton's Poems, 1900; Macaulay's Life of Johnson, 1903; Essentials of English History, 1905. Home: Newtonville, Mass. Died 1911.

WALKER, Aldace F., chmn. of the bd. Atchison, Topeka & Santa Fé Ry.; b. W. Rutland, Vt., May 11, 1842; grad. Middlebury Coll., 1862; served lt. to lt. col. 11th Vt. vols., 1862-64; studied at Columbia Law School; practiced law in New York, 1867-73; after that at Rutland, Vt.; State senator, Vt., 1882; member Interstate Commerce Commn., 1887-89; chmn. Interstate Commerce Railway Assn., and its successor, the Western Traffic Assn., Chicago, 1889-92; chmn. Joint Committee (composed of presidents and vice presidents of the railroads, members of the Trunk Line and Central Traffic assns.), 1892-93; practiced law, 1893-94; receiver Atchison, Topeka & Santa Fé R.R., 1894-96; became head of reorganized company. Died 1901.

WALKER, Asa, rear adm. U.S.N.; b. Portsmouth, N.H., Nov. 13, 1845; s. Asa T. and Louisa W.; grad. U.S. Naval Acad., 1866; m. Miss A. W. Grant, June 11, 1890. Ensign, Mar. 12, 1868; promoted through grades to rear adm., Jan. 7, 1906. Has served on various stas., and 1873-76, 1879-83, 1886-90 and 1893-97 at the Naval Acad.; took command U.S.S. Concord, May 23, 1897, participating in battle of Manila Bay, May 1, 1898; advanced 9 numbers "for eminent and conspicuous conduct in battle," June 10, 1898; on duty at the Naval War Coll., Newport, R.I., 1899-1900; mem. Naval Examining Bd., 1900-01; comdg. U.S.S. San Francisco, Jan. 2, 1902-Nov. 21, 1903; mem. Gen. Bd., Jan.-Oct. 1904; commanded U.S.R.S. Wabash, 1904-05; apptd. supt. Naval Obs., Washington, Feb. 28, 1906. Retired, Nov. 13, 1907. Died Mar. 7, 1916.

WALKER, Bryant, lawyer; b. Detroit, July 3, 1856, s. Edward Carey and Lucy (Bryant) W.; B.A., U. of Mich., 1876, LL.B., 1879, Sc.D., 1912; m. Mary W. Maguire, June 10, 1890. Studied law in office of Walker & Kent, 1876; admitted to Mich. bar, 1878; partner of E. C. Walker (father), as Walker & Walker, 1880, until death of sr. mem., 1894; member Walker & Spalding, May 1896-1931. President Detroit Museum of Art, 1910-13; hon. curator of Conchology Museum of U. of Mich.; trustee Harper Hospital; served as trustee Detroit Med. Coll., and mem. Non-Game License Commn. of Mich., to 1925; dir. Detroit Zoöl. Soc. (pres. 1912); mem. Wayne Co. Library Commn., 1921-31; mem. City Plan Commn. of Detroit, 1922-27. Republican. Presbyn. Home: Detroit, Mich. Died May 26, 1936.

WALKER, Charles Abbot, clergyman; b. Phoenixville, Pa., Feb. 21, 1868; s. Jacob Garrett and Rebecca Longstreth (Rhoades) W.; A.B., Bucknell U., Lewisburg, Pa., 1889, A.M., 1892, D.D., 1920; grad. Crozer Theol. Sem., 1892; m. Minnie Maude Garrison, Nov. 23, 1892; 1 dau., Margaret Garrison (Mrs. J. Le Roy Good). Ordained Bapt. ministry, 1892; pastor, Bellwood, Pa., 1892-1901, Malvern, Pa., 1901-10, Clarion, Pa., 1910-13, Olivet Bapt. Ch., West Chester, Pa., 1913-22, Dover, Del., 1922—. Moderator Centre Bapt. Assn., 1899-1901; rec. sec. State Mission Bd., 1901—; clerk N. Phila. Bapt. Assn., 1904-10; rec. sec. Crozer Alumni Soc., 1901—, Pa. Bapt. Gen. Conv., 1907-22, Am. Bapt. Foreign Mission Soc., 1910-11; statistical sec. Northern Bapt. Conv., 1917—. Republican. Editor Am. Baptist Year Book, 1915—. Home: Dover, Del. Died Dec. 30, 1930.

WALKER, C(harles) Howard, architect; b. Boston, Mass., Jan. 9, 1857; s. George Samuel and Mary Lowe (Damrell) W.; ed. pub. schs.; studied in architect's office; went to New York, 1879; on archeol. expdn. to Asia Minor, 1881; traveled, 1882-83; hon. degree Dr. Fine Arts, U. of Pa., 1921; m. Mary Louisa Huckins, June 3, 1885; children—Harold Damrell, Katharine Marie (Mrs. Henry S. Hubbell). Has practiced in Boston, 1884—; mem. firm Walker & Kimball, 1889-1900 (firm were architects-in-chief Omaha Exposition, 1898); became mem. Walker & Walker. Lecturer Museum of Fine Arts, Boston, Mass. Inst. Tech.; Lowell Inst. lecturer, 1894; mem. Boston Art Commn., 1898-99; mem. Bd. Architects, St. Louis Expn., 1904, and designer of the plan of the Exposition; director Sch. of Fine Arts, Boston, 1913—. Lecturer fine arts, 1913-14, history of architecture, 1917—, Harvard Univ.; lecturer philosophy of architecture, 1922, European civilization and art, 1923—, Mass. Inst. Tech. Mem. Nat. Fine Arts Commn., 1909; pres. Met. Improvement League, Boston, 1902-12. A.N.A., 1921; mem. Am. Acad. Arts and Sciences, 1921, Nat. Inst. Arts and Letters, 1927; fellow A.I.A. Editor Architectural Review; writer on decoration and architecture. Home: Boston, Mass. Died Apr. 12, 1936.

WALKER, Charles Jabez, banking; b. Cass Co., Mich., Nov. 8, 1869; s. William Delmar and Elathe (Estherbrooks) W.; ed. pvt. sch. of N.Y. and pvt. study of law; m. Carrie Della Ziegler, June 23, 1895; children—Charles Ziegler, Gustavus Arthur, Marian Elathe (Mrs. Winchell Fansher Boice). Began in real estate and loan business, 1895; organized Farmers and Merchants Bank, Long Beach, Calif., 1907, pres. 1907-37, chmn. of bd., 1937—; dir. Long Beach Cemetery Assn. Installed Citizens Water Co.; one of the organizers Long Beach Y.M.C.A., pres. for many years, now hon. pres. Mayor, Long Beach, 1900-04. Republican. Methodist (chmn. bd. trustees many years). Home: Long Beach, Calif. Died May 13, 1938.

WALKER, Charles Thomas, clergyman; b. Hephzibah, Ga., Feb. 5, 1858; s. Thomas and Hannah W.; father died before son was born, and mother died when he was 8; ed. Augusta (Ga.) Inst. (colored), later Atlanta Bapt. Coll., now Morehouse Coll.; (D.D., State U. of Ky., 1891; D.D., Atlanta Bapt. Coll., 1903; LL.D., Lynchburg [Va.] U. and Theol. Sem.); m. Violet Franklin, June 28, 1879. Entered ministry Missionary Bapt. Ch. at 18; pastor in Ga. until 1899; pastor Mt. Olivet Ch., N.Y. City, 1899-1903; founder Colored Y.M.C.A., N.Y. City; founder, 1886, and from then pastor Bapt. Institutional Ch., Augusta (largest Negro ch. in U.S., built at cost of $100,000). Del. World Bapt. Alliance, London, Eng., 1905, later del. same, at Phila.; moderator Walker Bapt. Assn. 17 yrs.; v.p. Nat. Bapt. Conv., U.S.A.; v.p.-at-large Missionary Bapt. Conv. of Ga.; etc. Chaplain, rank of capt., 9th Immune Regt., Spanish-Am. War, 1898; served at Santiago, Cuba. Mason, Odd Fellow, K.P. Author: The Colored Man Abroad, or What I Saw in Europe and the Holy Land. Speaker at mass meeting of 12,000 people, at Chicago, Feb. 1918, on "The Nation's Call to Service and the Black Man's Answer"; addressed 8,000 delegates of Walker Bapt. Assn., at the Armory, Newark, N.J., Sept. 14, 1919, on "The Duty of the Negro During the Reconstruction Period." Home: Augusta, Ga. Died July 29, 1921.

WALKER, Cornelius, P.E. clergyman; b. Richmond, Va., June 12, 1819; s. William Woodson and Mary (Bosher) W.; ed. Episcopal High School, Fairfax Co.; ordered deacon, P.E. Ch., July 12, 1845; ordained priest, Sept. 23, 1846; minister in Amherst Co., Va., 1845-47; m. Margaret J. Fisher, Dec. 1847. Asst. St. Paul's Ch., Richmond, 1847-48; rector, Winchester, Va., 1848-60; Christ Ch., Alexandria, 1860-61; Emmanuel Ch., Henrico Co., Va., 1862-66; prof. church history, 1866-76, then prof. systematic divinity and homiletics, and later dean Va. Theol. Sem.; retired at close of session 1898. Author: Sorrowing Not Without Hope, 1887; Outlines of Theology, 1894; Lectures of Christian Ethics, 1896. Died 1907.

WALKER, Dugald Stewart, author, artist; b. Richmond, Va.; ed. at home and pvt. schs.; student New York Sch. of Art, Art Students' League. Author: (with Helen MacKay) Stories for Pictures, 1912; Dream Boats, 1918; The Dust of Seven Days, 1924. Illustrated books by same author: Fairy Tales from Hans Andersen, 1914; The Gentlest Giant, 1915; The Boy Who Knew What the Birds Said, 1918; The Girl Who Sat by the Ashes, 1919; Children Who Followed the Piper, 1924; The Boy Apprenticed to the Enchanter, 1920; The Six Who Were Left in a Shoe, 1923. Illustrated: Rainbow Gold (by Sara Teasdale), 1924; The Wishing Fairy's Animal Friends (by Mrs. Phoenix Ingram), 1921; etc. Prod. The Winged Soul (Wellesley Coll.), 1925. Died Feb. 26, 1937.

WALKER, Edwin, lawyer; b. Genesee Co., N.Y., April 15, 1832; s. Obediah and Phoebe (Cushman) W.; acad. edn. Admitted to bar, 1854; practiced at Logansport, Ind., 1854-65, Chicago, 1865—. General solicitor Cincinnati, Richmond & Logansport R.R. Co., 1860-65, and its successor, Chicago & Great Eastern Ry., 1870-83; Ill. counsel C.,M.&St.P. R.R. Co., 1870-96; spl. counsel for U.S. in Debs conspiracy strike, 1894; solicitor gen. Chicago Expn., 1893. Republican. Episcopalian. Home: Chicago, Ill. Died 1910.

WALKER, Edwin Robert, judge; b. Rochester, N.Y., Sept. 13, 1862; s. Walter (M.D.); ed. Model Sch., Trenton, N.J.; studied law in offices of Col. S. Meredith Dickinson and Judge Garret D. W. Vroom. Admitted to N.J. bar, 1886; counsel, Bd. of Chosen Freeholders of County of Mercer, 1891-92; counsel City of Trenton, 1892-93; apptd. vice chancellor of N.J., by Chancellor Magie, 1907, for term of 7 yrs.; apptd. chancellor by Gov. Wilson, Mar. 18, 1912, to succeed Mahlon Pitney. Democrat. Home: Trenton, N.J. Died Oct. 14, 1932.

WALKER, Emory Judson, physician; b. Brooklyn, Mich., Nov. 2, 1844; s. Amos and Mary (Bliss) W.; Kalamazoo (Mich.) Coll.; M.D., Hahnemann Med. Coll., Chicago, 1868; m. Martha Pittman, Feb. 23, 1869. Practiced, Pontiac, 1868-75, New Haven, Conn., 1875—; dir. and sec. Grace Hosp. from its orgn., also obstetrician, same, 1903—, and mem. bd. phys. and surg. Baptist. Mason. Home: New Haven, Conn. Died Sept. 11, 1918.

WALKER, Faye, Presbyterian clergyman; pres. Oxford Coll. from 1883 to 1900; b. Murdock, O., July 22, 1848; s. A. J. and Leah W.; grad. Miami Univ., 1868, and McCormick Theol. Sem., 1870 (A.M., Miami Univ.; D.D., Centre Coll., Danville, Ky.). Pastor Presbyn. chs., Dwight and Taylorville, Ill.; Indianapolis, Ind., and College Hill, O.; pres. Oxford Coll., 1883-1900; became pastor Hebron Memorial Presbyn. Ch., Phila.; traveled extensively in Europe; orator and lecturer. Died 1903.

WALKER, Ferdinand Graham, artist; b. Mitchell, Ind., Feb. 16, 1859; s. Rev. Francis and Mary E. (Graham) W.; ed. pub. schs.; studied art, École des Beaux Arts, Paris, and Académie Colarossi; pupil of Merson Dagnan Bouveret, Puvis de Chavannes, Blanche and Leroi; m. Mary E. Watkin, 1884; 1 son, Stanley Ward. Exhibited in Paris, London and cities of U.S. Work in permanent collections of Mich. Agrl. Coll.; Greenbrier (W.Va.) Coll.; Evansville (Ind.) Coll.; Univ. of Ky., Lexington, Ky.; Univ. of Louisville; State Hist. Soc., Frankfort, Ky.; Jefferson Davis Memorial, Fairview, Ky., etc.; portraits and landscapes in pub. libraries, Lexington and Louisville, Ky., and New Albany, Ind.; mural decoration, St. Peter's Evang. Ch., Louisville. Republican. Mason. Home: New Albany, Ind. Died June 11, 1927.

WALKER, Frank Banghart, surgeon; b. Hunter's Creek, Mich., Apr. 25, 1867; s. Roger Thomas and Harriet Lucinda (Banghart) W.; Ph.B., U. of Mich., 1890; M.D., Detroit Coll. of Medicine, 1892; m. Hattie Belle Venning, Sept. 4, 1894 (died 1902); m. 2d, Kate Huntington Jacobs, June 26, 1905. Practiced in Detroit, 1892—; emeritus prof. surgery, Detroit Coll. Medicine and Surgery; surgeon to Providence and Woman's hosps. Commd. lt. col. Med. R.C.; chief surg. sect., Detroit Coll. Medicine and Surgery, Base Hosp. No. 36, in active service in France, Nov. 1917-Jan. 1919. Editor of Physician and Surgeon, Ann Arbor and Detroit, Mich., 1889-1903. Fellow Am. Coll. Surgeons, A.M.A. Mason. Home: Detroit, Mich. Died Apr. 11, 1927.

WALKER, Gayle Courtney, prof. journalism; b. Bison, Okla. Ter., Dec. 19, 1903; s. Isaac Simeon and Margaret Orabel (Smith) W.; A.B., U. of Neb., 1924, A.M., 1930; student U. of Mo., summer 1924; m. Wilma Fae O'Connell, June 12, 1926 (divorced). Instr. in journalism, U. of Neb., 1924-30, asso. prof., 1930-32, prof., 1932—, acting dir. Sch. of Journalism,

1926-30, dir., 1930—. Nat. editor the Pyramid of Sigma Tau, 1927-31; associate editor U. of Neb. Prairie Schooner; editorial advisor to Neb. State Dental Assn., 1931—. Vice-pres. Am. Assn. of Schs. and Depts. of Journalism, 1929. National editor Am. Interprofessional Inst., 1936—(nat. dir. 1935-36). Democrat. Presbyn. Mason. Home: Lincoln, Neb. Died Oct. 10, 1941.

WALKER, George, surgeon; b. Yorkville, S.C., July 27, 1869; s. William Millen and Mary Ellen (Hudson) W.; S.C. Coll., Columbia, S.C., 1885, 87; M.D., Med. Dept. U. of Md., 1889; hon. LL.D., U. of S.C., 1921; surg. interne, Johns Hopkins Hosp., 1895, 96; in exptl. labs., univs. of Breslau and Leipzig, 1½ yrs., 1897-98; Berlin, 5 mos., 1907; unmarried. Practiced Yorkville, S.C., 1889-95, Baltimore, 1898—; apptd. asst. in outpatient surg. dept., 1898-1900, chief of clinic, 1900-02, instr. in surgery, 1902-05, asso. in surgery, 1905—, Johns Hopkins Univ.; visiting surgeon Union Protestant Infirmary and Ch. Home and Infirmary. Chmn. Md. State-wide Vice Commn., 1913—; dir. Social Service Corp. of Baltimore. Fellow Am. Coll. Surgeons. Democrat. Methodist. Commd. maj., Med. R.C., June 1917; went to France with Johns Hopkins Unit and remained with it 4 mos.; detached and sent to ocean ports to look after the prevention of venereal diseases in the Am. Army; apptd. urologist in chief to Am. Army with headquarters in chief surgeon's office, Tours, France, Dec. 26, 1918; promoted lt. col., Oct. 12, 1918, col., Feb. 27, 1919; returned to U.S., Sept. 20, 1919, and resumed practice. Citation in France, 1919; D.S.M. (U.S.), 1922. Author: Traffic in Babies, 1919; Venereal Disease in the American Expeditionary Forces, 1922. Died Mar. 31, 1937.

WALKER, George Leon, Congl. clergyman; b. Rutland, Vt., April 30, 1830; ed. public schools, Brattleboro, Vt., academic edn. by private study; post-graduate student Andover Theol. Sem., 1858 (D.D., Yale, 1870); m. Maria Williston, Sept. 16, 1858; m. 2d, Amelia R. Larned, Sept. 15, 1870. Pastor Portland, Me., 1858-66, New Haven, Conn., 1868-73, Hartford, Conn., 1879—. Member Bd. of Visitors Andover Theol. Sem., 1888-96; fellow Yale Univ., 1887—. Author: History of the First Church in Hartford; Thomas Hooker; Some Aspects of the Religious Life of New England. Home: Hartford, Conn. Died 1900.

WALKER, Harry Wilson, author; b. St. Louis, Mo., July 12, 1859; s. Ralph and Frances (Wilson) W.; student Drury Coll., Springfield, Mo., 1876-78, also under pvt. tutor; m. Nellie Gatchel, Aug. 10, 1883 (died 1903); m. 2d, Estelle Edelin, Oct. 20, 1904. Began on staff Post-Dispatch, St. Louis, 1879; with Chicago Herald, 1883-84, New York World and New York Herald, 1884-94; London corr. New York Commercial Advertiser, 1894-95; editor The New Yorker, 1900-04; Washington corr. until 1913; spl. agt. Dept. of State, 1914. Author: Trail of the Tammany Tiger, 1914; Ancestors of Woodrow Wilson, 1914; Story of Colonel House, 1918. Mem. personal staff of the chmn. of the War Industries Bd., 1918. Home: Washington, D.C. Died Sept. 30, 1926.

WALKER, Henry Hammersley, clergyman; b. Flint, Mich., Aug. 26, 1871; s. Henry Clark and Anne Jane (Hammersley) W.; A.B., U. of Mich., 1893; B.D., Andover Theol. Sem., 1896 (2 yrs. fellowship for foreign study); Ph.D., U. of Halle, Germany, 1898; m. Nellie F. Reed, July 16, 1896; children—Helen Frances, Florence Hammersley, Margaret. Ordained Congl. ministry, 1898; pastor, Boulder, Colo., 1898-1910; prof. ecclesiastical history, Chicago Theol. Sem., 1910—. Home: Chicago, Ill. Died Sept. 1, 1927.

WALKER, Henry Oliver, artist; b. Boston, May 14, 1843; s. Thomas Oliver and Sarah Lucy W.; studied art in Paris under Bonnât, 1879-82; established studio in New York; m. Laura Margaret, d. John P. Marquand, of New York, Apr. 19, 1888; children—John Marquand, Oliver. Painted pictures, mostly compositions of figures; painted decorative picture in Library of Congress, Washington, Appellate Court House, New York, Mass. State House, Boston, Minn. Capitol, St. Paul, Court House, Newark, N.J. N.A., 1902. Home: Belmont, Mass. Died Jan. 14, 1929.

WALKER, Horatio, artist; b. at Listowel, Ont., Can., 1858; studied miniature painting under J. A. Fraser, Toronto, and in New York. Awards: Evans prize, Am. Water Color Soc., 1888; gold medal, competitive exhbn., Am. Art Galleries; 3d class medal, Paris Expn., 1889; medal and diploma, Chicago Expn., 1893; exhibited Paris Expn., 1900. N.A., 1891. Home: Quebec, Can. Died Sept. 27, 1938.

WALKER, Ivan N., comdr.-in-chief G.A.R.; b. Rush Co., Ind., 1839; s. James and Jane W.; served, 1861-65, capt. to col., 73d Ind. vols., except nearly a year, 1863-64, in Libby prison, escaping through the tunnel, Feb. 1864; bvtd. brig. gen. U.S.V. Mem. G.A.R., 1867—; asst. adj. gen., 1887-91; dept. comdr., 1891-92, Ind. Dept. G.A.R.; comdr.-in-chief, 1895-96; State tax commr. Ind.; pres. bd. control State Soldiers and Sailors Monument. Home: Indianapolis, Ind. Died 1905.

WALKER, Jacob Garrett, clergyman; b. Philadelphia, Dec. 28, 1840; s. Charles B. and Mary W. (Morison) W.; A.B., Bucknell Univ., 1862, A.M., 1865 (D.D., 1883); m. Rebecca Longstreth Rhoades, Apr. 9, 1867; father of Charles Abbott W. Ordained Bapt. ministry, 1865; pastor, Pughtown, Pa., 1865-68, Conshohocken, 1868-72; Mantua Bapt. Ch., Phila., 1872—. Clerk of Phila. Bapt. Assn., 1877—; editor Am. Baptist Year Book; rec. sec. Am. Bapt. Publ. Soc. Comdr. George G. Meade Post No. 1, G.A.R. Home: Philadelphia, Pa. Died July 16, 1915.

WALKER, James Alexander, congressman, lawyer; b. Augusta Co., Va., Aug. 27, 1832; s. Alexander W.; ed. Va. Mil. Inst.; studied law at Univ. of Va., 1854-55; admitted to bar, 1850; engaged in practice. Served, capt. to brig. gen., in C.S.A.; was severely wounded at Spotsylvania Court House; commonwealth's atty., Pulaski Co., 1860; mem. Va. House of Delegates, 1871-72; lt. gov., Va., 1877; mem. Congress, 1895-99; chmn. Com. on Elections No. 3, in 55th Congress. Republican. Home: Wytheville, Va. Died 1901.

WALKER, James Baynes, physician; b. Whitpain, Pa., Dec. 15, 1846; s. Thomas Robinson and Mary (Baynes) W.; ed. Friends' Central Sch., Phila.; M.D., U. of Pa., 1872, Ph.D., 1874; m. Martha M. Abraham, Oct. 2, 1873. Taught sch. 5 yrs.; lecturer on physiology and hygiene Friends' Central Sch. 18 yrs.; interne, 1872-73, visiting phys., 1876-93, Phila. Hosp.; visiting phys. Woman's Hosp., 1879-90; prof. practice of medicine, Woman's Med. Coll. of Pa., 1879-90; mem. Pa. State Bd. Med. Examiners. Pres. Northern Med. Assn. of Phila.; sec., 1883-95, pres., 1896, Am. Climatol. Assn.; mem. various med. societies. Home: Philadelphia, Pa. Died 1910.

WALKER, John Brisben, editor; b. on Monongahela River, Pa., Sept. 10, 1847; ed. Georgetown Coll., U.S. Mil. Acad.; resigned cadetship to enter Chinese mil. service in which remained, 1868-70; m. Ethel Richmond. Mfr. in W.Va., 1870-73; Rep. candidate for 43d Congress, 1872; mng. editor Washington Chronicle, 1876-79; alfalfa farmer in Colo., 1878-89; founded Cosmopolitan Magazine, 1889; organized the Mobile Co. of America, 1899, and built factory at Philipse Manor, N.Y.; retired. Chmn. Nat. Conv. Friends of Peace and Justice, at Chicago, 1915. Home: Mount Morrison, Colo. Died July 7, 1931.

WALKER, John Grimes, rear admiral U.S.N., retired; b. Hillsborough, N.H., Mar. 20, 1835; s. Alden and Susan (Grimes) W.; apptd. to navy from Iowa, Oct. 5, 1850; grad. U.S. Naval Acad., 1856; promoted master, Jan. 22, 1858; lt., Jan. 23, 1858. In blockading service and Mississippi squadron during Civil war; became lt. comdr., July 16, 1862, comdr., July 25, 1866; capt., June 25, 1877; commodore, Feb. 1889; rear admiral, Jan. 1894; retired at age limit, 1897; m. Rebecca W. Pickering, Sept. 12, 1866. During Civil war participated in the capture of New Orleans; was in operations against Vicksburg, summer of 1862, including passage of batteries both ways; comd. iron-clad Baron de Kalb in Mississippi squadron in several engagements; comd. naval battery, 15th army corps, in siege of Vicksburg; later comd. gunboat in N. Atlantic squadron at capture of Wilmington, N.C., etc. Specially promoted, 1866, for war service; sec. to Light-House Bd., 1873-78; chief Bur. of Navigation, Navy Dept., 1881-89. Comd. squadron of evolution, 1889-93, during which time comd. the European Sta., the S. Atlantic Sta. and the N. Atlantic Sta. In 1894 ordered to command Pacific Sta., being particularly charged with maintenance of peace and good order in Hawaiian Islands. Later chmn. of Light-House Bd., 1895-96, and 1896-97 was chmn. of commn. for location of deep water harbor on coast of Southern Calif. Pres. Nicaragua Canal Commn., 1897-99; pres. Isthmian Canal Commn., 1899—. Died 1907.

WALKER, John Yates Gholson, financier; b. of Am. parents, Liverpool, Eng., Apr. 11, 1871; ed. pub. schs.; m. Elizabeth B. Almy, Feb. 19, 1919; children—Kenneth Stewart, Elizabeth Lee, Mabel B., John Yates Gholson, William Magruder. Partner Walker Brothers, brokers, New York City; dir. Continental Realty Investment Co.; mem. U.S. bd. finance Caledonian Instn.; chmn. finance com. North British & Mercantile Ins. Co.; 1st v.p., trustee Bank for Savings in City of New York, Central Hanover Bank and Trust Co.; dir. Commonwealth Ins. Co., Mercantile Ins. Co. of America, U.S. Guarantee Co., Caledonian-Am. Ins. Co. Home: West Orange, N.J. Died Feb. 17, 1940.

WALKER, Joseph Henry, congressman, capitalist; b. Boston, Dec. 21, 1829; s. Joseph W.; removed first to Hopkinton and then to Worcester; attended public schools and acad. (LL.D., Tufts Coll.); worked in father's boot and shoe factory; became partner in Joseph Walker & Co., Worcester, boot and shoe mfrs., 1850, until 1862, when he formed the firm of J. H. and G. M. Walker; in 1868 began mfg. leather in Chicago, that firm finally becoming Walker, Oakley & Co.; and dir. of 2 banks in Worcester for years. Several yrs. mem. and pres. common council; mem. Mass. legislature, 1879, 1880, 1887; mem. Congress, 1889-99. Republican; chmn. Com. on Banking and Currency, 54th and 55th Congresses. Trustee Brown Univ., Newton Theol. Sem., etc. Author: Money, Trade and Banking; writer on economic questions. Home: Worcester, Mass. Died 1907.

WALKER, Lapsley Greene, editor Chattanooga Times; b. Rogersville, Tenn., July 20, 1854; prep. edn., McMinn Acad., Rogersville; A.B., Princeton, 1876; m. Adele Branham, Sept. 12, 1883. Began as editor weekly newspaper, Rogersville, 1870; admitted to Tenn. bar and practiced at Rogersville until 1882; telegraph editor Chattanooga (Tenn.) Times, 1883-85, mng. editor, 1885-1903, with short interval as chmn. Chattanooga Bd. Pub. Works, became editor in chief, 1903. Chmn. bd. Hamilton County Industrial Sch. Democrat. Presbyn. Mason; Past Grand Commander Tenn. K.T., K.P. Home: Chattanooga, Tenn. Died July 12, 1939.

WALKER, Mary E., physician; b. Oswego, N.Y., Nov. 26, 1832; d. Alvah and Vesta (Whitcomb) W.; ed. under parents (both teachers); M.D., Syracuse Med. Coll., 1855. Began practice in Columbus, O.; later settled in Rome, N.Y.; asst. surgeon, U.S. Army, Civil War, rank of 1st lt. (first woman commissioned to serve on surg. staff of any army in time of war). Awarded Congressional Medal of Honor "for bravery and valuable services in the field." Advocate of equal suffrage, dress reform, etc. Spiritualist. Home: Washington, D.C. Died Feb. 21, 1919.

WALKER, Myron Hamilton, lawyer; b. Westboro, Mass., Jan. 17, 1855; s. Silas, Jr., and Louisa (Everett) W.; LL.B., U. of Michigan, 1878; m. Nettie E. Stevens, Aug. 18, 1888 (died Aug. 28, 1920); children—Marjorie Louisa, Richard Everett (dec.). Admitted to Michigan bar, 1878, and practiced in Grand Rapids; mem. Walker & Fitz-Gerald; Prohibition candidate for pros. atty. Kent Co., 1884, and later for atty. gen. Mich.; mem. of Congress and justice of Supreme Court, Mich.; Dem. candidate for Congress, 1902, and for regent U. of Mich., 1911; mem. commn. to frame revised charter for Grand Rapids under Home Rule Act, 1911-12; mem. State Commission to inquire into minimum wage for women, 1913-15; U.S. atty. Western Dist. of Mich., 1914-22; resumed practice. Del. Dem. Nat. Conv., 1925. Del. Northern Bapt. Conv., 1927. World War veteran. Home: Grand Rapids, Mich. Died Sept. 10, 1928.

WALKER, Nathan Wilson, univ. prof.; b. Currituck Co., N.C., Mar. 7, 1875; s. William Henry and Anthea Ellen (Walker) W.; A.B., U. of N.C., 1903; Ed.M., Harvard, 1921; m. Eva Pritchard, Dec. 29, 1903; children—Eva (deceased), Mildred, Katherine, Thomas Henry, Nathan Wilson, John Anthony. Supt. pub. schs., Ashboro, N.C., 1903-05; prof. edn., U. of N.C., 1905—, and actg. dean Sch. of Education, of same, 1921—. State high sch. insp., N.C., 1907-19; mem. State Bd. of Examiners (ednl.), 1907-17; sec. Commn. on Accredited Schs. of Southern States, 1912-16 (chmn. 1924); pres. Assn. Colls. and Secondary Schs. of Southern States, 1925-26; mem. N.E.A. com. of 100 on rural teaching problems, 1923—; dir. University of N.C. Summer School, 1908—. Pres. N.C. State Teachers' Assembly, 1918-19; mem. bd. trustees, N.C. Coll. for Negroes, 1925—. Editor The High School Journal. Democrat. Mem. M.E. Church, South. Home: Chapel Hill, N.C. Died Feb. 13, 1936.

WALKER, Newton Farmer, educator; b. Spartanburg Co., S.C., Jan. 12, 1845; s. Newton Pinckney and Martha Louisa (Hughston) W.; ed. St. John's Classical and Mil. Sch., Spartanburg, S.C.; LL.D., U. of S.C., 1909; hon. degree Dr. of Philanthropy and Charity, conferred by concurrent resolution of Gen. Assembly of S.C., 1912 (the only degree, it is claimed, that up to that time had ever been conferred by a state legislature); Dr. Humane Letters, Gallaudet Coll., Washington, D.C., 1924; m. Virginia E. Eppes, Jan. 22, 1867; children—Horace Eppes, Albert Hayne, Newton Pinckney (dec.), William Laurens, Mrs. Virginia Eppes Hitch. Enlisted in Co. K (Spartan Rifles), 5th Regt., S.C.V., Aug. 1861; hon. discharged Apr. 1862; supt. S.C. Sch. for the Deaf and Blind, Cedar Spring, 1866—. Pres. Am. Conv. of Instrs. of the Deaf, 1923-25. Extensively engaged in farming. Life trustee Converse Coll., Spartanburg. Formerly chmn. Dem. Com., Spartanburg Co. Elder in Presbyn. Ch. Mason; Past Eminent Grand Comdr. K.T. of S.C. Home: Cedar Spring, S.C. Died Feb. 4, 1927.

WALKER, Perley F., mech. engr.; b. Embden, Me., Apr. 28, 1875; s. Cephas and Martha Ann (Washburn) W.; B.M.E., U. of Me., 1896, M.E., 1900; M.M.E., Cornell U., 1901; m. Charlotte Edith Crowell, Dec. 22, 1902. Instr. mech. engring., U. of Me., 1896-1900; draftsman in estimating and design, Newport News (Va.) Shipbuilding Co., 1901-02; prof. mech. engring., U. of Me., 1902-05; prof. mech. engring., 1905—, dean Sch. of Engring., and prof. industrial engring., 1913—, U. of Kan.; consulting engr. petroleum and power engring. lines, reporting on industrial development possibilities. Entered mil. service, May 14, 1917; commd. maj. 314th Engrs., Aug. 15, 1917; lt. col. 109th Engrs., Oct. 9, 1917; col. engrs., and apptd. comdr. 219th Regt., Aug. 9, 1918; hon. discharged, Feb. 21, 1919; col. engr. sect. O.R.C., Aug. 13, 1919; comdr. 314th Engr. Reserves. Republican. Conglist. Author: Management Engineering, 1923. Coauthor of Industrial Coal, on results of coal storage investigation, 1924. Home: Lawrence, Kan. Died Oct. 16, 1927.

WALKER, Platt Dickinson, judge; b. Wilmington, N.C., Oct. 25, 1849; s. Thomas D. and Mary Vance (Dickinson) W.; student U. of N.C., 1865-67; LL.B., U. of Va., 1869; (LL.D., Davidson, 1903, U. of N.C., 1908); m. Nettie Settle Covington, June 5, 1878. Admitted to N.C. bar and practiced at Rockingham. Mem. N.C. Ho. of Rep., 1874-75; moved to Charlotte, N.C., 1876; asso. justice Supreme Ct. of N.C., terms 1902-10, 1910-18, 1918-27. Democrat. Trustee U. of N.C.; first pres. N.C. Bar Assn., 1899. Episcopalian. Home: Charlotte, N.C. Died May 22, 1923.

WALKER, Reuben Eugene, judge; b. Lowell, Mass., Feb. 15, 1851; s. Abiel and Mary (Powers) W.; A.B., Brown Univ., 1875; (LL.D., Dartmouth College, June 1916); m. Mary E. Brown, June 18, 1875. Admitted to bar, 1878, and practiced at Concord, N.H. Co. solicitor Merrimack Co., 1889-91; mem. N.H. Ho. of Rep., 1895; mem. N.H. Constl. Conv., 1902; asso. justice Supreme Ct. of N.H., April 1, 1901—. Republican. Home: Concord, N.H. Died Jan. 1, 1922.

WALKER, Richard Wilde, judge; b. Florence, Ala., Mar. 11, 1857; s. Richard Wilde and Mary A. (Simpson) W.; student Washington and Lee U., 1873-74; grad. Princeton, 1877; studied Columbia Law Sch., New York; m. Shelby White, June 22, 1886. Admitted to Ala. bar, 1878; justice Supreme Court of Ala., 1891-92; mem. Ala. Constl. Conv., 1901; mem. Ala. Ho. of Rep., 1903; presiding judge Court of Appeals of Ala., 1911-14; U.S. circuit judge, 5th Circuit, Oct. 5, 1914—. Democrat. Home: Huntsville, Ala. Died Apr. 10, 1936.

WALKER, Robert Franklin, judge; b. Florence, Mo., Nov. 29, 1850; s. Belford Stephenson and Abigail Lewis (Evans) W.; A.B., U. of Mo., 1873, LL.B., 1875, LL.D., 1926; m. Nannie A. Wright, Sept. 20, 1877 (died 1892); children—Mrs. Katharine Smith, Leland Ross; m. 2d, Geneva C. Percy, Sept. 28, 1896 (died 1929). Admitted to Missouri bar, 1876, to Supreme Court of United States, 1894; practiced in Morgan Co. until 1885; pros. atty., Morgan Co., 1877-85; asst. atty. gen. of Mo., 1885-89, atty. gen., 1893-97; in practice at St. Louis, 1897-1913; judge Supreme Court of Mo., Jan. 1, 1913-Dec. 31, 1932 (chief justice, 1927). Democrat. Mem. Revising Commn. Mo. Statutes, 1889 (chmn. of like commn., 1909). Home: Jefferson City, Mo. Deceased.

WALKER, Roberts, ry. official, lawyer; b. Rutland, Vt., Aug. 24, 1874; s. Aldace Freeman and Katharine (Shaw) W.; A.B., Amherst, 1896; A.M., Columbia, 1899; LL.B., Columbia Law Sch., 1899; m. Edna Morse, June 16, 1904; children—Katharine, Mary Manning, Diantha, Rhoda, Challis. Admitted to N.Y. bar, 1898; with Seward, Guthrie & Steele (later Guthrie, Cravath & Henderson), 1899-1904; asst. to gen. counsel Rock Island and Frisco rys., 1904-09; gen. counsel, chmn. exec. com. Rock Island Lines, and pres. Rock Island Co., Jan. 1910-May 1, 1912; mem. White & Case, May 1, 1912—; dir., 1914, and pres., 1918, v.p., 1920-22, C.&A. R.R. Co. Member Dist. Bd. New York, during war. Republican. Conglist. Home: Scarsdale, N.Y. Died Dec. 22, 1926.

WALKER, Ryan, cartoonist; b. Springfield, Ky., Dec. 26, 1870; s. Edwin Ruthwin and Dulcenia Clay (Ryan) W.; ed. pub. schs., Kansas City; pupil, Art Students' League, New York; m. Maud Helena Davis (writer), Oct. 22, 1899 (died 1925); m. 2d, Edith Lovejoy, 1927 (died 1928); m. 3d, Marjorie E. Smith, writer. Cartoonist, Kansas City Times, 1895-98, St. Louis Republic, 1898-1901, Boston Globe, 1901-02; free lance, contbg. to Life, Bookman, Judge, Times, Mail, etc., New York, 1902-04; cartoonist, Internat. Syndicate, Baltimore, 1904-11; cartoonist for New York Call, 1916-21; art dir. and rotogravure editor New York Evening Graphic, 1924-29. Cartoonist, originator of Henry Dubb Cartoons, 1912-17, "Bill Worker" series of cartoons, Daily Worker, 1930-31. Died June 21, 1932.

WALKER, Stuart, theatrical producer, playwright; b. Augusta, Ky.; s. Cliff Stuart and Tillie Taliaferro (Armstrong) W.; B.A., U. of Cincinnati; student Am. Acad. Dramatic Arts, New York. Play reader, actor, stage mgr. with David Belasco, 1909-14; stage dir. with Jessie Bonstelle, 1914; independent producer, July 1915—; originator of Portmanteau Theatre; dir. Repertory Co., in Indianapolis, 1917-23, 1926-28; dir. Repertory Co. in Cincinnati, 1922-29; dir. Cincinnati Stuart Walker Repertory Co., 1929-31; dir. for Paramount-Publix Corp., 1931-34; directed—Tonight Is Ours, The Eagle and the Hawk, Evenings for Sale; dir. for Universal, 1934-35; directed—Great Expectations, Mystery of Edwin Drood, Werewolf of London; producer, Paramount, 1936—. Author: Portmanteau Plays (The Trimplet, Nevertheless, The Medicine Show, Six Who Pass While the Lentils Boil), 1917; More Portmanteau Plays (The Lady of the Weeping Willow Tree, The Very Naked Boy, Jonathan Makes a Wish), 1919; Portmanteau Adaptations (Grammer Gurton's Needle, The Birthday of the Infanta, Nellijumbo, Sir David Wears a Crown), 1921; Five Flights Up, prod. 1922; The King's Great Aunt Sits on the Floor, 1923; The Demi-Reps (with Gladys Unger), 1936. Home: Beverly Hills, Calif. Died Mar. 13, 1941.

WALKER, Stuart Wilson, lawyer; b. Martinsburg, W.Va., Nov. 5, 1862; s. James H. and Mary E. (Kilmer) W.; ed. pub. schs. and Berkeley Acad., Martinsburg, and Washington and Lee U.; m. Annette M. Thayer, Oct. 4, 1893. Admitted to W.Va. bar, 1884, and practiced in Martinsburg; member Faulkner & Walker, later Faulkner, Walker & Woods. Mem. W.Va. Ho. of Rep., 1892-93; asst. U.S. atty. Northern Dist. of W.Va., 1893-95; U.S. atty. same dist., 1896-97, and Jan. 6, 1914—. Chairman Dem. State Com., campaign of 1912. Presbyn. Mason. Home: Martinsburg, W.Va. Died May 23, 1923.

WALKER, Thomas Barlow, lumberman; b. Xenia, O., Feb. 1, 1840; s. Platt Bayless and Anstis Keziah (Barlow) W.; ed. Baldwin U., Berea, O., now Baldwin-Wallace Coll. (LL.D.); m. Harriet G. Hulet; children—Gilbert Marshall, Julia (Mrs. Ernest F. Smith), Leon Barlow (dec.), Fletcher Loring, Willis Jay, Clinton Llewellyn, Archie Dean. Taught school, and later became a traveling salesman. Went to Minneapolis, 1862; was engaged on government surveys and later on survey for St. Paul & Duluth R.R. Large operator in Minn. timber lands and lumbering operations in the pine timber of Minn.; has extensive interests in Calif. white and sugar pine. Projector and builder of St. Louis Park, suburb, and the trolley line to it. Owned extensive property in Minneapolis; built central city market and the wholesale commn. district which placed Minneapolis in the front rank as a wholesale and retail market. Originator and builder Minneapolis Pub. Library; pres. library bd., annually elected for 34 yrs.; was responsible for the building up of Acad. of Science and its museum of science and art; presented to the city important collections of art, including over 500 oil paintings, 300 miniatures, and over 7,000 art objects, consisting of pottery, porcelain, jades, ancient glass, necklaces, crystals, etc., mostly from the tombs, ruins and temples of Syria, Egypt, Greece, Persia and Babylonia. Advocate of practical methods of conserving the forests for perpetual use. Home: Minneapolis, Minn. Died Aug. 28, 1928.

WALKER, William David, bishop; b. New York, N.Y., June 29, 1839; s. James and Mary (Lahey) W.; A.B., Columbia, 1859, A.M., 1863; grad. Gen. Theol. Sem., 1862; (D.D., Racine, 1884, Oxford, Eng., 1894; S.T.D., Columbia, 1884; LL.D., Griswold, 1886, Trinity Coll., Dublin, 1894; D.C.L., King's Coll., N.S., 1892); m. Bertha B. Bach, Mar. 4, 1905. Deacon, 1862, priest, 1863, P.E. Church; vicar Calvary Chapel, New York, 1862-83; missionary bishop N.D., 1883-96; transferred to Western N.Y., 1896; apptd. by President mem. U.S. Bd. Indian Commrs., 1887; select preacher of U. of Cambridge, Eng. Home: Buffalo, N.Y. Died May 2, 1917.

WALKER, William Henry, cartoonist, painter; b. Pittston, Pa., Feb. 13, 1871; s. Rev. Ira T. and Orcelia A. (Barnes) W.; Ky. University, 1888-89; B.S., U. of Rochester, 1891; studied Art Students' League, New York, 1891-93; m. Adelaide Miller, June 27, 1900; children—Robert Miller, William Henry, II. Has contributed social and polit. cartoons to leading periodicals; regular contbr. to Life, 1898-1924. Work principally landscape and portraits, 1923—. Pres. trustees Flushing Hosp. and Dispensary, 1915—. Home: Flushing, L.I., N.Y. Died Jan. 18, 1938.

WALKER, William Hultz, chemical engr.; b. Pittsburgh, Pa., Apr. 7, 1869; s. David H. and Anna (Blair) W.; B.S., Pa. State Coll., 1890; A.M., Ph.D., U. of Göttingen, 1892; Sc.D., U. of Pittsburgh, 1915; m. Isabelle Luther, Sept. 15, 1896. Prof. industrial chemistry, now chem. engring., Mass. Inst. Tech., 1894-1921; lecturer on industrial chemistry, Harvard, 1905-08; cons. chem. engr., 1900—; mem. Little & Walker, 1900-05; dir. research lab. applied chemistry, Chem. Products Co. Professional work has been principally in the production of art glass, the mfr. of sterling silver, the chemistry of cellulose and its industrial applications and uses, the cause and prevention of the corrosion of iron and steel, and the technology of petroleum. Has invented and introduced numerous industrial processes of value. Commd. lt. col. N.A., 1917; chief of chem. service sect.; promoted col. U.S.A., in charge Gas Offense Div. Chem. Warfare Service; comdr. officer Edgewood Arsenal. Fellow Am. Acad. Arts and Sciences, Am. Iron and Steel Inst., Am. Electrochem. Soc. (pres. 1910-11), Am. Chem. Soc. (pres. Eastern Sect. 1904), Am. Soc. for Testing Materials, Soc. Chem. Industry (London). Awarded Nichols medal, 1908. Presbyn. Awarded D.S.M., 1919. Home: Pasadena, Calif. Died July 9, 1934.

WALKER, William Kemble, neurologist; b. Phoenixville, Pa., Apr. 3, 1867; s. Thomas P. and Charlotte (Emma) W.; M.D., U. of Pa., 1891; m. Mrs. Jean McLean Swain, Nov. 9, 1927. Practiced at Pittsburgh, Pa., 1896-1927 (retired); prof. psychiatry, U. of Pittsburgh, 1909-27; cons. neurologist Western Pa. Hosp. Republican. Presbyn. Home: Phoenixville, Pa. Died April 24, 1937.

WALKER, Williston, university prof.; b. Portland, Me., July 1, 1860; s. Rev. George Leon and Maria (Williston) W.; A.B., Amherst, 1883; grad. Hartford Theol. Sem., 1886; Ph.D., Leipzig, 1888; (D.D., Western Reserve U., 1894, Amherst, 1895, Yale, 1901, U. of Geneva, Switzerland, 1909, Harvard, 1912; L.H.D., Marietta, 1910); m. Alice Mather, June 1, 1886. Asso. in history, Bryn Mawr Coll., 1888-89; asso. prof. ch. history, 1889-92, prof. Germanic and western ch. history, 1892-1901, Hartford Theol. Sem.; prof. ecclesiastical history, Yale, Oct. 1, 1901—. Trustee, 1896—, sec. of bd., 1899—, Amherst. Pres. N.H. Colony Hist. Soc., 1903-13. Fellow Acad. Arts and Sciences. Author: A History of the Congregational Churches in the United States, 1894; The Reformation, 1900; Ten New England Leaders, 1901; John Calvin, 1906; French Trans-Geneva, 1909; Great Men of the Christian Church, 1908; History of the Christian Church, 1918. Home: New Haven, Conn. Died Mar. 9, 1922.

WALL, Edward Clarence; b. Milwaukee, Wis., Aug. 11, 1843; s. Caleb and Julia Maria W.; ed. Racine and Beloit colls.; twice married. Entered his father's store; succeeded to business, 1868. Alderman, 1874-76; mem. Wis. Assembly, 1878, 79; collector internal revenue, 1885-89; mem. Dem. State Com., 1878-85, chmn., 1890-95; mem. Dem. Nat. Com., 1892-1900; was given unanimous vote of Wis. delegation as presdl. nominee at Dem. Nat. Conv., St. Louis, 1904. Pres. Milwaukee Chamber of Commerce three terms. Home: Milwaukee, Wis. Died Apr. 25, 1915.

WALL, Edward John, author; b. Eng., Dec. 24, 1860; s. Edward John and Eliza (Matthews) W.; ed. Euston Coll., London; m. Francis Emilie Walker, of London, 1886; children—Edward George (dec.), Phyllis May. Came to U.S., 1910. Editor Amateur Photographer, 1892-96, Photographic News, 1896-1900; prof. photography, Syracuse U., 1913-17; asso. editor American Photography, 1922—. Fellow Chem. Soc. (London), Royal Photographic Society. Republican. Episcopalian. Author: Dictionary of Photography, 1889; Carbon Printing, 1894; Photo-Lithography, 1895; The New Light and New Photography, 1896; Everyone's Guide to Photography, 1896; Natural-Color Photography, 1906; Practical Color Photography, 1922; Photographic Facts and Formulas, 1924; History of Three-Color Photography, 1925. Home: Wollaston, Mass. Died Oct. 13, 1928.

WALL, Garrett Buckner, ry. official; b. Kenton Co., Ky., Apr. 6, 1870; s. Garrett S. and Elizabeth Etheline (Buckner) W.; ed. Washington and Lee U. and U.S. Naval Acad.; m. Louise de Montmollin, Apr. 20, 1897; children—Mrs. Martha Lafferty, Garrett B. Began as clk. in gen. office of C.&O. Ry., at Cincinnati, 1889; chief clk. to supt. at Lexington and Ashland, Ky., 1892-95; chief clk. to gen. mgr., at Richmond, Va., 1895-1900, asst. to pres., 1900-17, asst. to federal mgr., 1918-20, v.p., 1920—, all C.&O. Ry.; v.p. Hocking Valley Ry., C.&O. Ry. Co. of Ind., C.&O. Northern; dir. White Sulphur Springs Co., Covington & Cincinnati Bridge Co., Merchants Nat. Bank (Richmond, Va.). Democrat. Episcopalian. Home: Richmond, Va. Died Jan. 26, 1928.

WALL, William Guy, consulting engr.; b. Baltimore, Md., Aug. 7, 1876; s. William Edward and Mary Catherine (Dade) W.; grad. in Civ. Engring., Va. Mil. Inst., 1894; B.S., Mass. Inst. Tech., 1896; m. Minnie Tyndall, 1909 (died 1931); m. 2d, Helen Wessel, 1934. Practiced at Indianapolis, 1900—; founder, v.p. and chief engr. Nat. Motor Car Co.; cons. engr. for several prominent automobile companies. Maj. and lt. col., U.S.A., World War; col. Res. Secretary, Am. Legion Endowment Fund Corp. Democrat. Episcopalian. Home: Indianapolis, Ind. Died Jan. 16, 1941.

WALLACE, Alexander Gilfillan, clergyman; b. Bridgeville, Pa., Mar. 2, 1829; s. William and Elizabeth (Gilfillan) W.; A.B., Jefferson Coll., 1847; grad. Allegheny Theological Sem.; (D.D., Erskine Coll., 1876; LL.D., Westminster Coll., Pa., 1901); m. Isabella S. West, Nov. 2, 1854. Ordained U.P. ministry, 1854; pastor Bethel, Westmoreland Co., Pa., 1854-68, New Brighton, 1868-84, Sewickley, 1886-88; clerk U.P. Gen. Assembly, 1868—; corr. sec. Bd. Ch. Extension of U.P. Ch., 1870—; editor Evangelical Repository, 1886-90; prof. pro tem. Allegheny Theol. Sem., 1885-87, dir., 1868—; editorial writer and asso. (sr.) editor The United Presbyterian, 1868—; mem. Presbyn. Alliance Commn., 1892—, chmn., 1909, 1910; Council Reformed Chs. in America. Author: Scotch and Scotch-Irish in Colonial America, 1909. Contbr. to ch. mags., etc. Home: Sewickley, Pa. Died Aug. 19, 1913.

WALLACE, Austin Edward, ry. official; b. Nashua, N.H., Mar. 2, 1879; A.B., Harvard, 1902. Began at Larimore, N.D., as clk. and timekeeper G.N. Ry., Nov. 1902; yard clk., timekeeper and chief clk. C.,R.I. &P. Ry., 1904-07; spl. insp., asst. extra gang foreman, asst. roadmaster, asst. trainmaster and trainmaster, C.,B.&Q. R.R., 1907-11; spl. insp. same rd., Feb.-Sept. 1911, and on staff 2d v.p. and asst. supt., 1911-12; supt. C.,R.I.&P. Ry., 1912-18; gen. supt. Erie R.R., at Chicago, Jan.-June 1918; asst. gen. supt. same rd., at Youngstown, O., 1918-20, and mgr. at Chicago, 1920-22; gen. mgr. M.,St.P.&S.S.M. Ry., 1922-25, v.p. and gen. mgr., Aug. 1, 1925—. Home: Minneapolis, Minn. Died June 1936.

WALLACE, Charles William, univ. prof.; b. Hopkins, Mo., Feb. 6, 1865; s. Judge Thomas Dickey and Olive (McEwen) W.; B.S., Western Normal Coll., Shenandoah, Ia., 1885; A.B., U. of Neb., 1898; U.

of Neb. Grad. Sch., 1900-02, U. of Chicago, summers, 1902, 03, 04; refused Am. vice consulship at Mannheim, 1904, for spl. study German univs., 1904-06; Ph.D., U. of Freiburg, 1906; m. Hulda Alfreda Berggren, June 14, 1893. Teacher country sch. at 17; prof. Latin and English, Western Normal Coll., Shenandoah, Ia., and at Lincoln, Neb., 1886-94; at Fremont (Neb.) Normal Sch., 1894-95; asst. in Latin, U. of Neb., 1896-97; founder Prep. Sch. to U. of Neb., 1897 (now Lincoln Acad.), prin. and dir. same, 1897-1900; asst. instr. English lit., 1901-03, instr., 1903-04, adj. prof., 1904-05, asst. prof., 1905-07, asso. prof., 1907-10, prof. English dramatic lit., 1910—, Univ. of Nebraska. Spl. research in Shakespeare and Tudor-Stuart drama (1485-1700) in European archives, summers 1904-09, and continuously during extended leave of absence on behalf of U. of Neb., 1909-16. Regarded as "the first living authority" on Shakespeare. A founder and fellow Soc. of Genealogists (London). Author: (or editor) Lyrics for Leisure Moments, 1892; The Children of the Chapel at Blackfriars, 1597-1603, 1908; Three London Theatres of Shakespeare's Time, 1909; Shakespeare and His London Associates (documents), 1910; The Evolution of the English Drama up to Shakespeare, 1912; The First London Theatre, 1913; also articles containing new Shakespeare discoveries, notably: New Shakespeare Documents, 1905; Shakespeare in London, 1909; Shakespeare as a Man Among Men (presenting his signed deposition), 1910; On Shakespeare, the Globe and Blackfriars (documents), 1910; On Ben Jonson and the Swan Theatre, 1911; A London Pageant of Shakespeare's Time, 1913; New Light on Shakespeare (documents), 1914; The Poet and Other William Shakespeare (documents), 1915; etc. Lectured on Shakespeare before univs. throughout America, 1916-17. Hon. v.p. Shakespeare Birthday Com. of N.Y. Amassed fortune in Tex. oil fields, 1918-19, while on leave of absence from U. of Neb., to secure money necessary to complete Shakespearean research; enlarged scope of investigation, converting increased oil and banking interests into fund for establishment of Foundation for Research. Home: Wichita Falls, Tex. Died Aug. 1932.

WALLACE, Dillon, author; b. Craigsville, N.Y., June 24, 1863; s. Dillon and Rachel Ann (Ferguson) W.; ed. pub. schs. at Ridgebury, N.Y.; mainly self ed.; LL.B., New York Law Sch., 1896; m. Jennie E. Currie, Apr. 7, 1897 (died 1900); m. 2d, Leila G. Hinman, June 17, 1917; children—Leila Ann, Dillon. Admitted to bar, 1897; retired from practice, Mar. 1918. Mem. Leonidas Hubbard, Jr., exploring expedition to Labrador, 1903; conducted expeditions to Labrador, 1905 and in 1913; research work in Mexico, 1907-08. Chief of Leek-Wallace Camp for boys, in Wyoming. Author: The Lure of the Labrador Wild, 1905; The Long Labrador Trail; Ungava Bog, 1907; Packing and Portaging, 1912; The Wilderness Castaways, 1913; The Gaunt Gray Wolf, 1914; The Fur Trail Adventurers, 1915; Bobby of the Labrador, 1916; The Arctic Stowaway, 1917; Grit A'Plenty, 1918; John Adney, Ambulance Driver, 1919; The Ragged Inlet Guards, 1920; Troop One of the Labrador, 1920; The Young Arctic Traders, 1921; Story of Grenfell of the Labrador, 1922; The Testing of Jim MacLean, 1924; The Way to Burning Mountain, 1926; Left on The Labrador, 1927; With Dog and Canoe, 1928; Kidnapped by Air, 1929; The Lost Mine, 1930; The Crew of the Pioneer, 1931; The Fur Traders of Kettle Harbor, 1931; Buddies of the Sea, 1932; The Camper's Handbook, 1936. Home: Beacon, N.Y. Died Sept. 28, 1939.

WALLACE, Henry, editor; b. West Newton, Pa., Mar. 19, 1836; s. John and Martha (Ross) W.; Geneva Coll., Northwood, O. (now Beaver Falls, Pa.), 1855-56-57; Jefferson Coll., Cannonsburg, Pa., 1857-58-59, A.B., 1859; Allegheny Theol. Sem., 1860-61; Monmouth Theol. Sem., 1862-63; m. Nannie Cantwell, Sept. 10, 1863 (died 1909). Pastor U.P. Ch., Rock Island, Ill., and Davenport, Ia., 1863-71, Morning Sun, Ia., 1871-76; stated supply, Wintereset, Ia., 1878-80; editor Wintereset Chronicle, 1880-81, Madisonian, 1881-83, Iowa Homestead, 1883-95, Wallace's Farmer, 1895—; pres. Wallace Pub. Co., Capital City Printing Plate Co. Republican. Engaged largely in farming, 1872-92; mem. Roosevelt's Country Life Commn., 1908; pres. 3d Nat. Conservation Congress, 1910-11. Author: Plymouth Brethren, 1878; Clover Culture, 1892; Uncle Henry's Letter to the Farm Boy, 1897; Clover Farming, 1898; Trusts and How to Deal with Them, 1899; Skim-Milk Calf, 1900; Letters to the Farm Folk, 1915. Trustee Christian U. of Cairo, 1914. Home: Des Moines. Deceased.

WALLACE, Henry Cantwell, sec. of agriculture; b. Rock Island, Ill., May 11, 1866; s. Henry and Nannie (Cantwell) W.; B.S.A., Ia. State Coll. Agr. and Mechanic Arts, 1892; m. Carrie May Brodhead, Nov. 24, 1887. Farmer and breeder pure bred live stock, Adair Co., Ia., 1887-91; prof. dairying, Ia. State Coll., 1893-95; editor Creamery Gazette, and Farm and Dairy, 1893-95; mgr. and asso. editor Wallace's Farmer, 1895-1916, editor same 1916-21; pres. and treas. Wallace's Pub. Co., Capital City Printing Plate Co.; dir. Central State Bank. Secretary of agr. in cabinets of Presidents Harding and Coolidge, Mar. 4, 1921—. Mem. U.S. Live Stock Industry Commn. (exec. com.) during the war; sec. Corn Belt Meat Producers' Assn. 14 yrs.; mem. National War Work Council Y.M.C.A.; chmn. Iowa War Work Council Y.M.C.A.; chmn. state exec. com. Ia. Y.M.C.A., 1914-20; mem. Internat. Com. Y.M.C.A.; mem. exec. com. Roosevelt Memorial Assn.; mem. Rock Creek Park Commn., Nat. Forest Reservation Commn., Federal Bd. for Vocational Edn., Federal Power Commn., War Finance Corp. United Presbyn. Mason. Home: Des Moines, Ia. Died Oct. 25, 1924.

WALLACE, Hugh Campbell; b. Lexington, Mo., Feb. 10, 1863; s. Thomas Bates and Lucy (Briscoe) W.; desc. Peter Wallace, from Scotland to Va., 1706; ed. pub. and pvt. schs., Lexington, and under pvt. tutors; m. Mildred, d. late Chief Justice Melville W. Fuller, of Supreme Court of U.S., Jan. 5, 1891; 1 son, Melville Weston Fuller. Receiver of pub. moneys for Utah, by appmt. of Pres. Cleveland, 1885-87 (resigned); elected mem. Dem. Nat. Com., 1892, reelected, 1896 (resigned), again elected, 1916, for term 1916-20; took a prominent part in nat. campaigns of 1892, 1912, 16; A. E. and P. to France, Feb. 1919-July 1921. Awarded Grand Cross Legion of Honor (France). Home: Tacoma, Wash. Died Jan. 1, 1931.

WALLACE, James, educator; b. nr. Wooster, O., Mar. 12, 1849; s. Benjamin and Janet (Bruce) W.; A.B., Coll. of Wooster, 1874, Ph.D., 1887, LL.D., 1899; m. Janet M., d. Rev. T. K. Davis, of Wooster, Sept. 28, 1878; children—Benjamin Bruce, Helen Margaret, Robert Sinclair, De Witt, Miriam Winifred. Instr., Coll. of Wooster, 1875-78; studied and traveled in Greece, 1878-79; asso. prof. Greek, 1879-80, prof., 1880-87, Coll. of Wooster; prof. Greek and Old English, 1887-90, dean of faculty, 1891-94, pres., 1896-1906, Macalester Coll., St. Paul; on leave of absence in N.Y., Greece, and Italy, 1907-09; head of Bibl. Dept. Macalester Coll., 1909-32; D.D., and made pres. emeritus, at "Wallace Commencement," June 1923. Presbyn. Author: Wallace-Bruce Family History, 1929. Editor: Harper-Wallace Anabasis, 1892; Fundamentals of Christian Statesmanship. Has written and spoken much in defense of the League of Nations and World Court; licensed to preach. Home: St. Paul, Minn. Died Aug. 23, 1939.

WALLACE, John Findley, civil engr.; b. Fall River, Mass., Sept. 10, 1852; s. David A. and Martha (Findley) W.; student monmouth (Ill.) Coll.; C.E., U. of Wooster, 1882; (LL.D., Monmouth Coll., 1904; Sc.D., Armour Inst., Chicago); m. Sarah E. Ulmer. Assistant U.S. engineer on upper Mississippi River and improvements of Rock Island Rapids, 1871-76; co. surveyor and city engr., 1876-78; chief engr. and supt. Peoria & Farmington R.R., 1878-81, Central Ia. Ry., in Ill., 1881-83; constrn. engr. and master of transportation Central Ia. Ry., 1883-86; bridge engr. A.,T.&S.F. R.R., 1886-89; resident engr. Chicago, Madison & Northern R.R., 1889-91; with I.C. R.R., 1891-1904, as engr. of constrn., 1891-92, chief engr., 1892-97, asst. to 2d v.p., 1897-1900, asst. gen. mgr., 1900-01, gen. mgr., 1901-04; 1st Am. chief engr. Panama Canal, 1904; Isthmian Canal commr. and v.p. and gen. mgr. Panama R.R. & Steamship Co., 1905; pres. and chmn. bd. dirs. Westinghouse, Church, Kerr & Company, 1906-17. Designed and constructed World's Fair terminals, Chicago, 1892; also new pass. terminals for C.&N.W. R.R., Chicago; conducted extensive surveys and examinations and created the initial orgn. for Panama Canal, etc.; chmn. Chicago Ry. Terminal Commn.; adviser and consultant to large corps. Independent. Presbyn. Home: New York, N.Y. Died July 3, 1921.

WALLACE, John J., clergyman, editor; b. Tuscarawas Co., O., Nov. 16, 1857; s. Robert and Mary (Houk) W.; Scio Coll., O., 1873-78; B.A., Mt. Union Coll., Alliance, O., 1886, D.D., 1896; B.D., Drew Theol. Sem., 1887; m. Celia A. Collamore, Oct. 3, 1883; children—Walter Bruce, Ione Wolcott. Began ministry M.E. Ch. in E. Ohio Conf., 1881; pastor Newton Falls, 1881-83, Highlandtown, 1883-86, Mentor, 1886-91, West Farmington, 1891-92, Harlem Springs, 1892-95, Alliance, 1895-98, New Phila., 1898-1901, Alliance, 1901-02; presiding elder Cambridge Dist., 1902-07; pastor Barnesville, 1907-08; editor Pittsburgh Christian Advocate, 1908-28. Mem. General Conf. 7 times; trustee Mt. Union Coll.; mem. Joint Commn. on Unification M.E. Ch. and M.E. Ch., S.; del. Ecumenical Meth. Conf., London, 1921. Independent Republican. Home: Pittsburgh, Pa. Died Apr. 13, 1933.

WALLACE, J(ohn) Sherman, clergyman, editor; b. Linn Co., Ore., Feb. 23, 1877; s. Pharaoh Lindsay and Ava Elizabeth (McBee) W.; A.B., McMinnville (now Linfield) Coll., 1901, D.D., 1930; B.D., Rochester Theol. Sem., 1904; U. of Wash., 1904-06, M.A., 1906; m. Grace Michael, July 24, 1901; children—Sherman LeRoy, Theodore Barton. Ordained Bapt. ministry, 1904; pastor South Tacoma Ch., 1904-05, 6th Av. Ch., 1905-09, Tacoma, Wash.; prof. Bible and pub. speaking McMinnville Coll., 1909-17. Acting pastor 1st Ch., Carleton, Ore., 1910-13, 1st Ch., McMinnville, 1914-15, 1st Ch., Amity, Ore., 1915-17; pastor Immanuel Bapt. Ch., Salt Lake City, Utah, 1918-21, 1st Bapt. Ch., Madison, Wis., 1921-23; editor young people's S.S. publications, Am. Bapt. Publ. Soc., 1923—. Pres. Ore. B.Y.P.U., 1911-12; bd. mgrs. Wis. Bapt. Conv., 1921-23; pres. Alumni Rochester Theol. Sem., 1924-25. Author: What of the Church?, 1911; The Real Imitation of Christ, 1912; True Wealth, or What Is He Worth?, 1913; The Life of the Christian (4 parts), 1924; The World a Field for Christian Service (4 parts), 1925; A Quiet Talk with God Each Day, yearly, 1927—; The Bible in the Church School (2 vols), 1929; Worship in the Church School, 1930. Writer of Young People's Class, and Young People's Teacher, quarterlies, Am. Bapt. Publ. Society, 1918-23. Chautauqua and lyceum lecturer. Home: Haddonfield, N.J. Died May 24, 1934.

WALLACE, Joseph, lawyer, author; b. in Carroll Co., Ky., Sept. 30, 1834; ed. Jefferson Co., Ind., and 1852-53, at Franklin Coll. (hon. A.M., June 1894); m. Mary E. Hoagland, Jan. 14, 1864. Studied law; admitted to Ill. bar, 1858; practiced in Springfield; has held various local offices. Author: Biography of Col. Edward D. Baker, 1871; (joint author) Springfield City Code, 1884; History of Illinois and Louisiana Under the French Rule, 1893. Home: Springfield, Ill. Died 1904.

WALLACE, Lewis ("Lew Wallace"), lawyer, soldier, diplomat, author; b. Brookville, Ind., April 10, 1827; s. Gov. David W.; self-educated; began study of law; served in Mexican war, 2d lt. Co. H, 1st Ind. inf.; resumed study of law; located in Covington, and later in Crawfordsville, Ind.; m. Susan Arnold Elston, 1852. At beginning of Civil War apptd. adj. gen. of Ind.; soon after col. 11th Ind. vols.; served in W.Va.; became brig. gen. vols., Sept. 3, 1861; comd. div. at Donelson; maj. gen., March 21, 1862; comd. a div. at Shiloh; prepared defenses of Cincinnati in 1863 and saved city from capture by Gen. Edmund Kirby Smith; later comd. Middle dept. and 8th army corps; intercepted march of Gen. Jubal A. Early on Washington; fought battle of Monocracy, and saved Washington from capture, July 9, 1864; was second mem. of the court that tried the assassins of President Lincoln, and pres. of court which tried and convicted Henry Wirz, comdt. of Andersonville prison; mustered out, 1865. Gov. New Mexico, 1878-81; U.S. minister to Turkey, 1881-85. Author: Ben Hur, a Tale of the Christ, 1880; Life of General Benjamin Harrison, 1888; The Fair God, 1873; The Boyhood of Christ, 1889; The Prince of India, 1893; The Wooing of Malkatoon, 1898. Home: Crawfordsville, Ind. Died 1905.

WALLACE, Robert Moore, judge; b. Henniker, N.H., May 2, 1847; s. Jonas and Mary (Darling) W.; A.B., Dartmouth, 1867; m. Ella M. Hutchinson, Aug. 25, 1874. Admitted to bar, 1872; established practice at Milford, N.H. Mem. N.H. Ho. of Rep., 1877, 78; pros. officer for Hillsborough Co., 1883-93; justice Supreme Ct. of N.H., 1893-1901; chief justice Superior Ct. of N.H., April 1901—. Home: Milford, N.H. Died 1913.

WALLACE, Rothvin, writer; b. Christiana, Pa., Feb. 23, 1882; s. Truman and Sarah Elizabeth (Baldwin) W.; ed. Rugby Acad., Wilmington, Del.; m. Alice Richards Horine, Dec. 18, 1916. Newspaper work, Washington, D.C., Phila. and New York; with New York World, 1911—; Contbr. numerous short stories to mags. Home: Oceanport, N.J. Deceased.

WALLACE, Rush Richard, commodore U.S.N.; b. Pond Spring, Tenn., Nov. 7, 1835; apptd. to U.S. Naval Acad. from Tenn., 1852; promoted passed midshipman, Apr. 29, 1859; advanced through grades to commodore, Nov. 11, 1894; retired, Nov. 7, 1897. Served on bd. St. Lawrence, Brazilian Squadron, 1856-59; Crusader, 1859-61; Constellation, Mediterranean Squadron, 1861-63; Shenandoah, N. Atlantic Blockading Squadron, 1863-64; participated in both attacks on Ft. Fisher; Fort Jackson, W. Gulf Blockading Squadron, 1864-65; Naval Acad., 1865-67; Guerriere, S. Atlantic Squadron, 1868; Richmond, European Fleet, 1869; comd. store-ship Idaho, 1870-71; Ashuelot, 1872-73; insp. ordnance, Navy Yard, Norfolk, 1873-74; light house insp. 15th dist., 1875-79; Torpedo Sta., Newport, 1881; spl. duty Navy Dept., 1881-82; comd. Vandalia, 1882-84; capt. of yard, Navy Yard, Washington, 1884-87; comdt. Navy Yard, Washington, 1887; mem. Naval Examining Board, 1887-91; comd. receiving-ship Franklin, 1892-93, Miantonomoh, 1893-94, Naval Sta., Newport, 1894-97; spl. duty and member Lighthouse Bd., 1898; mem. Board on Awards, 1902-05. Home: Washington, D.C. Died June 12, 1914.

WALLACE, Susan (Arnold) Elston, author; b. Crawfordsville, Ind., Dec. 25, 1830; d. Maj. J. C. Elston; grad. Poughkeepsie, N.Y., 1849; m. Gen. Lewis Wallace, 1852. Author: The Storied Sea, 1884; Ginevra, 1887; The Repose in Egypt, 1888; The Land of the Pueblas, 1888; Along the Bosphorus 1898; The City of the King, 1904. Home: Crawfordsville, Ind. Died 1907.

WALLACE, William, Jr., lawyer; b. Syracuse, N.Y., Jan. 28, 1864; s. William and Helen (Carpenter) W.; ed. high schs., Syracuse, and Brookline, Mass.; studied law with Hon. Joseph K. Toole, 3 times gov. of Mont.; m. Elizabeth Flowerree, Dec. 4, 1889.

Admitted to Mont. bar, 1883, and began practice at Helena, Mont., Washington, D.C., and N.Y. City. Atty. Lewis and Clarke Co., 1884-86; mem. Mont. Ho. of Rep., 1889-91; div. counsel N.P. Ry., 1896-1911; asst. atty. gen. of U.S., 1913-Jan. 10, 1917. Democrat. Home: New York, N.Y. Died Oct. 25, 1939.

WALLACE, William Henry; b. Port Hope, Mich., Sept. 17, 1861; s. Robert and Margaret (Deegan) W.; ed. high sch., Port Austin, Mich., and Goldsmith's Bus. U., Detroit, Mich.; m. Elizabeth Harding, Sept. 17, 1882 (died 1893), 5 children; m. 2d, Margaret McIntyre, Apr. 1, 1894; 2 children. Mgr. Wallace Stone Co., Bay Port, Mich., 1894-1900; gen. mgr. Sebewaing (Mich.) Sugar Co., 1902-06; gen. mgr. Mich. Sugar Co., Saginaw, 1906-24, became pres., 1924; also officer or dir. other companies. Mem. Mich. State Bd. Agr., 1901-22, Pub. Domain Commn., 1920-22; chmn. Conservation Commn., Mich., 1922-26. Republican. Presbyn. Mason, Elk. Home: Saginaw, Mich. Died 1933.

WALLACE, William James, judge; b. Syracuse, N.Y., Apr. 14, 1837; s. E. Fuller and Lydia W. W.; student Hamilton Coll., and LL.B., same; (LL.D., Hamilton, 1875, Syracuse Univ., 1882); m. Alice Heyward Wheelwright, Apr. 1878. Admitted to bar, 1858; mayor of Syracuse, 1873-74; U.S. dist. judge, Northern Dist. of N.Y., 1874-82; U.S. circuit judge, 2d Jud. Circuit, 1882-1907. Republican. Home: Albany, N.Y. Died Mar. 11, 1917.

WALLACE, William Miller, brig. gen. U.S.A.; b. Prairie du Chien, Wis., Jan. 9, 1844; s. Lt. Col. George Weed (U.S.A.) and Susan H. (Salter) W.; ed. Bowens and Loomis schools, Washington, and Georgetown, D.C., and Churchill's Mil. School, Sing Sing, N.Y.; m. Alice Knight, Jan. 18, 1871. First lt. N.Y. Arty., Mar. 29, 1864; hon. mustered out, May 6, 1864; apptd. from N.Y., 2d lt. 8th U.S. Inf., Oct. 2, 1866; 1st lt., Sept. 25, 1867; assigned to 6th Cav., Dec. 15, 1870; capt., May 17, 1876; maj. 2d Cav., Nov. 10, 1894; lt. col., Oct. 18, 1899; col. 15th Cav., Mar. 1, 1901; brig. gen. and retired at own request, over 40 yrs.' service, Oct. 2, 1906. Died Nov. 5, 1924.

WALLEN, Theodore Clifford, newspaperman; b. New Britain, Conn., Nov. 27, 1894; s. August Edward and Ellen (Nordstrom) W.; ed. high sch., New Britain, and Trinity Coll., Hartford, Conn.; m. Gladys Elizabeth Thomas, Aug. 26, 1918; children—Virginia Hope, June Elizabeth. Reporter New Britain Herald, 1913; successively reporter, asst. city editor, political editor and editorial writer, asst. mng. editor Hartford Courant, 1915-27; political writer New York Herald Tribune, 1927-29, chief Washington corr., 1929—. Served in U.S. Navy, 1917-18. Republican. Conglist. Home: Washington, D.C. Died Jan. 19, 1936.

WALLER, Claude, lawyer; b. Union Co., Ky., Aug. 14, 1864; s. William and Elizabeth (Muir) W.; B.S., Vanderbilt U., 1884, B.E., 1886, M.S., 1888, LL.B., 1890; m. Martha Armistead Nelson, Dec. 19, 1894. Began practice, Nashville, 1890; city atty., 1893-95; judge Circuit Ct., 1895-97 (resigned); asst. dist. atty. for Tenn., L.&N. R.R., 1897-99; gen. counsel Nashville, Chattanooga & St. Louis Ry., Jan. 1, 1899—. Trustee and sec. bd. of trust Vanderbilt U. Democrat. Home: Nashville, Tenn. Died Dec. 7, 1918.

WALLER, David Jewett, Jr., normal sch. prin.; b. Bloomsburg, Pa., June 17, 1846; s. Rev. David Jewett and Julia (Ellmaker) W.; A.B., Lafayette Coll., 1870; student Princeton Theol. Sem., 1871-72; grad. Union Theol. Sem., New York, 1874; (Ph.D., Lafayette; D.D., Ursinus Coll., 1892); m. Anna, d. of M. S. Appelman, of Bloomsburg, Pa., May 14, 1874. Ordained Presbyn. ministry, 1874; pastor Logan Square Ch., Phila., 1874-76, Orangeville, Pa., 1876-77; prin. State Normal School of Bloomsburg, 1877-90; supt. public instrn., Pa., 1890-93; prin. Indiana Normal Sch. of Pa., 1893-1906; prin. State Normal Sch., Bloomsburg, Pa., 1906-20 (resigned). Presdl. elector, 1908. Trustee Lafayette Coll., 1891-1919. Home: Bloomsburg, Pa. Died June 28, 1941.

WALLER, Elwyn, chemist; b. New York, N.Y., Mar. 22, 1846; s. Joseph Fernando and Martha (Brookes) W.; brother of Frank W.; A.B., Harvard, 1867, A.M., 1870; E.M., Columbia Sch. of Mines, 1870, Ph.D., 1875; m. Ella White, July 15, 1880 (died 1887); m. 2d, Margaret V. Dorsey, Dec. 2, 1888 (died 1906); m. 3d, Frances Dorsey, Nov. 28, 1907 (died 1908). Asst. instr., 1871-77, instr., 1877-85, prof. analytical chemistry, 1885-93, Columbia Sch. Mines. Mineralogist San Domingo Expdn., Jan. to Apr. 1871; health inspector and chemist, New York Health Dept., 1872-85. Edited, completed and revised Quantitative Analysis, by F. A. Cairns, 1880, 1896. Home: Morristown, N.J. Died July 6, 1919.

WALLER, Frank, artist; b. New York, N.Y., June 12, 1842; s. Joseph Fernando and Martha (Brookes) W.; brother of Elwyn W.; ed. Free Acad., New York; m. Almira S., d. Hon. E. W. B. Canning, June 6, 1883; m. 2d, Elizabeth Vandever, d. Stanton Dorsey, Dec. 28, 1896. Formerly engaged as architect; artist-painter, 1903—. Fellow Acad. Design, New York; has been pres. Art Students' League of New York, which he incorporated; was hon. sec. Egypt Exploration Fund Soc., and of Ur Exploration Soc.; hon. life fellow Met. Mus. of Art. Wrote: Report on Art Schools, 1879; also first report Art Students' League, 1886. Home: Morristown, N.J. Died Mar. 9, 1923.

WALLER, Lewis, actor; b. Bilbao, Spain, 1860; s. William James and Carlotta (Vyse) W.; ed. Kings Coll., London, and Saxe-Meiningen, Germany. Début as Hon. Claude Lorrimer, in "Uncle Dick's Darling," at Tool's Theatre, London, Mar. 26, 1883; played many parts with great success in leading theatres of England, also mgr. various theatres in London; Am. début was made as creator of Boris Androvsky, in "The Garden of Allah," Century Theatre, New York, Oct. 21, 1911; later produced "A Butterfly on the Wheel" under own management at Daly's Theatre, New York, and toured with same, 1912-13; made successful tour in Can., 1913. Home: London, Eng. Deceased.

WALLER, Littleton Waller Tazewell, officer U.S. M.C.; b. York Co., Va., Sept. 26, 1856. Apptd. 2d lt. U.S.M.C., June 16, 1880; promoted through grades to brig. gen., Aug. 29, 1916; major gen., Aug. 29, 1918. Participated in naval battle at Santiago, Cuba, July 3, 1898; in charge recruiting, Pa., Del. and western N.J., 1902-03; comd. Provisional Regt. Marines, Isthmus of Panama, 1904; comd. expeditionary forces for service in Cuba, 1906; comd. Provisional Brigade of Marines, in Cuba, 1911; duty Marine Barracks, Mare Island, Calif., 1911-14, Phila., 1914; comd. 1st Brig. of Marines for service in Mexico, 1914; comd. marine expeditionary forces ashore in Haiti, 1915-16; apptd. comdr. Advanced Base Force, Phila., Jan. 8, 1917. Bvtd. lt. col., Mar. 28, 1901, "for distinguished conduct and pub. service," in presence of enemy nr. Tientsin, China, and advanced 2 numbers in grade "for eminent and conspicuous conduct" in Battle of Tientsin. Retired June 1920. Home: Philadelphia, Pa. Died July 13, 1926.

WALLER, Mary Ella. Author: The Little Citizen, 1902; The Daughter of the Rich, 1905; Sanna—of the Island Town, 1905; (poem) Our Benny, 1909; My Ragpicker, 1911; A Year Out of Life, 1911; The Cry in the Wilderness, 1912; Flamsted Quarries, 1913; From an Island Outpost, 1914; Through the Gates of the Netherlands, 1914; The Woodcarver of Lympus, 1914; Out of the Silences, 1918. Died June 14, 1938.

WALLER, Osmar Lysander, civil engr., educator; b. Lykens, O., Nov. 30, 1857; s. Stephen and Martha (McKinley) W.; Ph.B., Hillsdale (Mich.) Coll., 1883, Ph.M., 1887, D.Sc., 1931; student law U. of Mich., 1883-84, 1886-87; LL.D., State College of Washington, 1929; m. Mary Belle Brown, Aug. 14, 1885; children—Florence M., Gladys, Anna McKinley. Supt. schs., Dexter, Mich., 1884-86, 1887-90; admitted to Mich. bar, 1886; supt. schs., Colfax, Wash., 1890-93; prof. mathematics and civ. engring., 1893-1930, vice-pres., 1909-30, State College of Washington (v.p. emeritus). Expert in irrigation, U.S. Dept. Agr., 1900-04, in charge field work during summers; consulting engr., State Bd. of Land Commrs. of Ida., on constrn. work of South Side Twin Falls Land & Water Co., 1907-08, also on Marysville Project, 1908; del. to Conf. of Governors, Washington, D.C., 1908; chmn. commn. to recommend to Wash. legislature changes in water laws, 1910; expert for Twin Falls (Ida.) Land & Water Co., 1912; cons. engr. U.S. Dept. of Interior for the Columbia Basin Irrigation Project, 1924-25. Mem. Bd. of Edn., Pullman, 1897-1903. Author various bulls. on irrigation and irrigation laws. Sec. Columbia Basin Survey Commn. Home: Pullman, Wash. Died Aug. 3, 1935.

WALLER, Peter August, mfr.; b. Ockelbo, Sweden, Jan. 15, 1868; s. Hans Johan and Karin (Pers-Dotter) W.; ed. pub. schs.; m. Carrie Cordelia Peterson, Nov. 7, 1889; children—Ruby Leora (dec.), Olga Louise (Mrs. Emerit Anson), Ellis Julian, Harold Everett. Came to U.S., 1885; mechanic and clk., 1885-93; with Boss Mfg. Co., mfrs. gloves, Kewanee, 1893, v.p., 1912—; pres. Kewanee Real Estate & Improvement Co.; elected pres. Boss Mfg. Co., 1924; dir. Union State Sav. Bank & Trust Co. Mem. Ill. Centennial Commn., 1915-17; candidate for U.S. Senate, 1920, for lt. gov. of Ill., 1928. Chmn. war service com. Cotton Glove Industry, World War. Pres. Kewanee Pub. Hosp. Assn. Lutheran. Mason. Home: Kewanee, Ill. Died Mar. 1, 1932.

WALLER, Rose (Rev. Mother), coll. pres.; b. St. Louis, Mo.; grad. Ursuline Convent, Arcadia, Mo. Mem. Sisters of St. Joseph (religious order); head of violin dept., Nazareth Acad., Concordia, Kan., 1890-1918; sec. to the Nazareth Convent Corp.; mother gen. and pres. Marymount Coll., Salina, Kan., 1922—. Died Mar. 20, 1941.

WALLER, Thomas McDonald, governor; b. New York, N.Y., 1840; s. Thomas C. and Mary Armstrong; orphaned at 9, and adopted by Robert K. Waller, of New London, Conn., whose name he assumed; pub. sch. edn., New London; (hon. A.M., Yale, 1883); m. Charlotte Bishop. Admited to bar, 1861 and practiced at New London. Mem. Conn. Gen. Assembly, 1867, 68, 72, 76 (speaker 1876); sec. of state of Conn., 1870; mayor of New London, 6 yrs.; state's atty. New London Co., 1876-83; gov. of Conn., 1882-84; reëlected gov. by popular vote but not having a constl. majority the legislature chose Henry B. Harrison, Rep. nominee; consul gen. at London, 1885-89. Democrat. Commr. Chicago Expn., 1893; pres. Dem. State Conv., Conn., 1906. Home: New London, Conn. Died Jan. 25, 1924.

WALLIN, Alfred, judge; b. Otsego Co., N.Y., Feb. 12, 1836; s. Charles C. and Dorothy (Strongatharm) W.; ed. Elgin, Ill., Acad.; attended one course law lectures, U. of Mich., 1860; m. Ellen Gray Keyes, Jan. 1, 1868. Admitted to bar, 1862; co. atty., Nicollet Co., Minn., 1868; elected judge Supreme Ct., of N.D., 1889; retired as chief justice, Jan. 1, 1903. Republican. Retired from practice. Home: Los Angeles, Calif. Died Jan. 1923.

WALLING, Emory A., judge; b. Erie Co., Pa., June 11, 1854; s. Thomas and Laura Ann (Eliott) W.; ed. State Normal Sch. (Edinboro, Pa.), Lake Shore Sem. (North East, Pa.); LL.D., Allegheny Coll., Meadville, Pa., 1920; m. Grace E. Marshall, 1880; children—William B., Ralph G., Laura C. (Mrs. H. L. Sawdey), Marion E. (Mrs. W. L. Crawford), Marietta M. (Mrs. L. S. Mosher). Admitted to Pa. bar, 1878, and practiced at Erie; dist. atty., Erie Co., Pa., 1881-84; mem. Pa. Senate, 1884-88; president judge, 6th Jud. Dist. of Pa., 1897-1916; mem. Supreme Court of Pa., Jan. 1916—. Republican. Methodist. Mason, Odd Fellow, K.P., Elk. Home: Erie, Pa. Died Dec. 29, 1931.

WALLING, William English, author; b. Louisville, Ky., Mar. 14, 1877; s. Willoughby and Rosalind (English) W.; B.S., U. of Chicago, 1897, grad. work in economics and sociology, 1899-1900; m. Anna Strunsky, June 1906; children—Rosalind English (dec.), Rosamond English, Anna Strunsky, Georgia, William Hayden English. Factory insp., Ill., 1900-01; resident at Univ. Settlement, New York, 1902-05. One of founders Intercollegiate Socialist Soc. (now League for Industrial Democracy), the Women's Trade Union League, Nat. Assn. for Advancement of Colored People (dir.). Progressive Dem. candidate for Congress, 4th Conn. Dist., 1924; exec. dir. Labor Chest for Relief and Liberation of Workers of Europe. Author: The Larger Aspect of Socialism, 1913; Progressivism and After, 1914; Socialists and the War, 1915; The Socialism of To-Day, 1916; Whitman and Traubel, 1916; State Socialism Pro and Con (with Harry Laidler), 1917; Sovietism, 1920; Out of Their Own Mouths (with Samuel Gompers), 1921; American Labor and American Democracy, 1927 (German, French and British edits., 1929); The Mexican Question Under Calles and Obregon, 1927; Our Next Step—A National Economic Policy (with Matthew Woll), 1933. Home: New York, N.Y. Died Sept. 12, 1936.

WALLING, Willoughby George, banker; b. Louisville, Ky., May 23, 1878; s. Willoughby and Rosalind (English) W.; Ph.B., U. of Chicago, 1899, Harvard Law Sch., 1899-1901; m. Frederika C. Haskell, Dec. 25, 1902; children—Willoughby Haskell, William English, Frederika Christina, Thompson Cheves. Pres. Personal Loan and Savings Bank; dir. Continental Ill. Nat. Bank & Trust Co., Stevens Hotel, Middlewest Corp. Mem. advisory bd. Reconstruction Finance Corp. Formerly lt. Illinois Naval Reserve. Member Chicago Harbor Commn., 1905; nat. chmn. Am. Red Cross Influenza Com., 1918-19; v. chmn. Nat. Am. Red Cross, 1919-20, mem. bd. of incorp.; chmn. delegation to League of Red Cross Socs., 1920. Pres. Chicago Council Social Agencies, 1920-27; vice chmn. Chicago Housing Commn.; chmn. Ill. Bd. of Pub. Welfare Commrs., 1928—; mem. Nat. Exec. Board Izaak Walton League; pres. North Shore Country Day Sch.; chmn. bd. Cook County Sch. of Nursing. Home: Hubbard Woods, Ill. Died Feb. 23, 1938.

WALLINGFORD, John Duvall, judge; b. Greensburg, Ind., Sept. 19, 1869; s. John Nicholas and Alice (Foster) W.; student Ind. U., 1889-91; A.B., Stanford U., 1892; m. Jean Lucas, Apr. 10, 1901. Newspaper editor, Alexandria, Ind., 1893-97; city clk., Alexandria, 1894-97; practiced at Greensburg, Ind., 1897-99, also city atty. one term; moved to Des Moines, Ia., 1899; judge Polk Dist. Court, Des Moines, 1920-22 (resigned); judge U.S. Dist. Court, Canal Zone, by apptmt. of President Harding, Sept. 1922—. Republican. Mason. Died Sept. 20, 1924.

WALLIS, Jenny, author. See Mary J. Whitney Morrison.

WALLS, William L., lawyer; b. Buffalo, N.Y., Sept. 26, 1868; s. William L. and Charlotts A. (Cooper) W.; student St. Joseph's Coll., Buffalo, and Columbia U.; m. Elyse Millstead, Feb. 13, 1920. Admitted to N.Y. bar and practiced at Buffalo; moved to Wyo.; co. atty., Park Co., Wyo., 1911-13; mem. Rep. State Central Com., 1913-19; atty. gen. of Wyo., Jan. 1919-23. Episcopalian. Mason. Home: Cheyenne, Wyo. Died Dec. 18, 1935.

WALSH, Blanche, actress; b. New York, Jan. 4, 1873; d. Thomas P. and Armenia (Savorie) W.; m. Alfred Hickman, 1896; m. 2d, W. M. Travers, actor, Nov. 15, 1906. Dramatic début as Olivia in "Twelfth Night," with Marie Wainwright, Chicago, Sept. 1889; remained with that co. until 1892, then in Charles Frohman's Co., playing various rôles; played title rôle in "Trilby," 1896; 1903 created part of Maslova in Tolstoi's "Resurrection," scoring artistic triumph of her career. Home: Great Neck, L.I. Died Oct. 31, 1915.

WALSH, Frank P(atrick), lawyer; b. St. Louis, July 20, 1864; s. James and Sarah (Delany) W.; ed. St. Patrick's Acad., St. Louis; m. Katharine M. O'Flaherty, Oct. 21, 1891; children—Marie, Louise, Cecelia, Frank P. (dec.), John, Jerome, Virginia, James. Admitted to Mo. bar, 1889; mem. Kansas City Tenement Commn., 1906-08; atty. Kansas City Bd. of Public Welfare, 1908-14; pres. Kansas City Bd. of Civil Service, 1911-13; chmn. Federal Commn. on Industrial Relations, 1913-15; editor and publisher Kansas City Post, 1915-16; in charge case of employes, in stock yards arbitration, Chicago, Feb. 1918; was joint chmn. (with Ex-Pres. Taft), War Labor Conf. Bd., 1918; mem. Nat. War Labor Bd., Apr. 1918, as a representative of the people, resigned Dec. 1918; admitted to N.Y. bar, 1919; dir. Brooklyn-Manhattan Transit Corp.; apptd. by Gov. Franklin D. Roosevelt, mem. N.Y. Commn. on Revision of Pub. Utility Laws, June 1929, also chmn. Power Authority of State of N.Y., May 1931—. Democrat. Catholic. Pres. Soc. of Medical Jurisprudence, 1933-35, chmn. bd. of trustees, 1935—; trustee St. Patrick's Cathedral, N.Y. City. Home: New York, N.Y. Died May 2, 1939.

WALSH, George Ethelbert, author; b. Brooklyn, N.Y., Mar. 12, 1865; s. George Elbert and Melissa (Walters) W.; ed. Long Island High School and Friends' Coll., L.I., N.Y.; m. Anne Vandervoort, d. Rev. William Henry Gleason, D.D., of New York, Dec. 20, 1891; children—Harold Vandervoort, Helen Gladwin. Joined staff of New York Tribune, 1890, spl. New York corr. for Atlanta Constitution and Phila. Times, 2 yrs.; started first tech. newspaper syndicate, 1893. Free lance in lit. for a number of yrs., contbg. to N.Am. Review, Cosmopolitan, Lippincott's, also 500 serials and 1,000 short stories. Progressive. Presbyn. Author: Polly Comes to Woodbine, 1915; Twilight Animal Stories 10 vols.; Bumper the White Rabbit, 1917; Buster the Bear, 1917; White Tail the Deer, 1917; Their Adventures, 1917; Boy Vigilantes of Belgium, 1919; Sandy the Crane, Pintail the Wild Duck, Scarlet the Ibis, 1920; Scavengers of the Sea, 1923; also The House that Silas Built, The Man-Faced Orchid, Strange Cargo of Southern Belle, The House Under the Snow, The Hound of Lost Swamp, etc. Died Feb. 4, 1941.

WALSH, Henry Collins, editor; b. Florence, Italy, Nov. 23, 1863; s. Robert W.; lived in Italy until 9 yrs. old; A.M., Georgetown U., D.C., 1888. Entered newspaper work on staff Phila. Times; later editor The Mansfield (Pa.) Advertiser; mng. editor Catholic World Magazine; on staff Internat. Encyclopedia. Founded, with W. S. Walsh, American Notes and Queries, Phila., lit. editor Lippincott's Magazine, 3 yrs.; traveled extensively in Arctic regions and Central America. Was war corr. New York Herald and Harper's Weekly during Spanish-Am. War; co-editor Smart Set magazine, 1902-06; editor Travel Mag., 1907-10; staff Am. Press Assn., 1911-18, and asso. editor of The National Marine, 1919-21; v.p. Nomad Pub. Co., 1924—. Organizer Arctic Club of America and Explorers' Club; pres. Nomad Travel Club, and pres. Adventurers Club. Author: By the Potomac, and Other Poems, 1889; The Last Cruise of the Miranda, a Record of Arctic Adventure, 1896; The White World (in collaboration with other members Arctic Club), 1903. Died Apr. 29, 1927.

WALSH, James Anthony, clergyman; b. Cambridge, Mass., Feb. 24, 1867; s. James and Hannah (Shea) W., student Boston Coll., 1881-85; Harvard, 1885-86; St. John's Ecclesiastical Sem., Brighton, Mass., 1886-92. Ordained Roman Catholic ministry, 1892; on duty at St. Patrick's Ch., Boston, 1892-1903; archdiocesan dir., Soc. for Propagation of the Faith, 1903-11; began publication of The Field Afar, 1907 (monthly, still in existence); made 1st president of Catholic Foreign Mission Soc. of America, 1911, now superior-gen.; consecrated titular bishop, June 29, 1933. Author: Choral Sodality Hand-Book, 1900; A Modern Martyr, 1907; Thoughts from Modern Martyrs, 1908; Stories from the Field Afar, 1913; Field Afar Tales, 1915; Observations in the Orient, 1919; In the Homes of Martyrs, 1922. Home: "Maryknoll," Ossining, N.Y. Died Apr. 14, 1936.

WALSH, John Henry, asso. superintendent schs.; b. Brooklyn, Mar. 17, 1853; s. Thomas and Mary (Ryan) W.; A.B., Georgetown Coll., 1873, A.M., 1889, Ph.D., 1912; LL.B., Columbia U., 1880; School of Pedagogy, New York U., 1888-90; m. Elizabeth McGee, Feb. 8, 1884. Prof. mathematics, Loyola College, Baltimore, 1875-76, St. Francis College, Brooklyn, 1876-78, Georgetown Coll., 1878-79; prin. Pub. Sch. No. 27, Brooklyn, 1885-89; asst. supt. schs., 1889-1901, supt. pub. instrn., 1901, Brooklyn; transferred by city charter, 1902, asso. supt. schs., New York; retired, 1923. Author (series of arithmetics): Elementary, Intermediate, Higher (three books), 1894; Primary, Grammar School (two books), 1895; New Primary, New Grammar Sch. (2 books), 1903; Arithmetic for Upper Grades, 1908; A Graded Mental Arithmetic, 1909; Methods in Arithmetic, 1910; Introductory Algebra, 1911; Walsh-Suzzalo Arithmetics, 10 books, 1913-15; Business Arithmetic, 1919. Democrat. Home: Brooklyn, N.Y. Died Dec. 13, 1924.

WALSH, Julius Sylvester, financier; b. St. Louis, Mo., Dec. 1, 1842; s. Edward and Isabelle (de Mun) W.; A.B., St. Joseph's Coll., Bardstown, Ky., 1861; LL.B., Columbia U. Sch. of Law, 1864; A.M., St. Louis U., 1865 (LL.D., 1904); m. Josephine Dickson, Jan. 11, 1870. Admitted to N.Y. bar, 1864; engaged in business, St. Louis, 1864; elected pres. Citizens Ry. Co., 1870, Union Ry. Co., 1873; 1st pres. of South Pass Jetty Co. (to provide open mouth to Miss. River), 1875; pres. St. Louis Bridge Co., 1875-90; became pres. Peoples Ry. Co., and Tower Grove & Lafayette Ry. Co., 1877; built Northern Central Ry., 1885; was made v.p. St. Louis Terminal Assn., 1895, pres., 1896, and chmn. bd., 1903; organized, 1890, and pres. Miss. Valley Trust Co. (chmn. bd.); pres. Miss. Glass Co., Union Electric Light & Power Co. Home: St. Louis, Mo. Died Mar. 21, 1923.

WALSH, Louis Sebastian, bishop; b. Salem, Mass., Jan. 22, 1858; s. Patrick and Hanorah W.; grad. Salem (Mass.) High Sch., 1876; studied Holy Cross Coll., Worcester, Mass., 1 yr., Montreal Sem., 2 yrs., St. Sulpice Theol. Sem., Paris, 3 yrs., Papal Sem. and Minerva U., Rome, 1 yr. (Licentiate in Canon Law and Theology, Rome, 1883.) Ordained R.C. priest, St. John Lateran, Rome, Dec. 23, 1882; asst. priest St. Joseph's Ch., Boston, 1882-83; prof. ch. history, canon law and liturgy and dir. St. John's Seminary, Brighton, Mass., 1884-97; mem. diocesan bd. of examiners, 1888-1906; supervisor Catholic schs., Archdiocese of Boston, 1897-1906; consecrated bishop of Portland (Me.), Oct. 18, 1906. One of founders N.E. Catholic Hist. Soc., Catholic Ednl. Assn. of America (pres. sch. dept.). Died May 12, 1924.

WALSH, Raymond Arnold, lawyer; b. St. Louis, June 17, 1889; s. John F. and Josephine B. (Cussen) W.; A.B., Christian Brothers Coll., St. Louis, 1907; Ph.B., Am. Coll., Rome, 1909; studied Benton Coll. of Law, St. Louis; m. Mary Pauline Moore, Jan. 1, 1912; children—Raymond Arnold, William Lindsay. Reporter, later editor and mng. editor, St. Louis Globe Democrat, Republic Times, 1911-18; European corr. Peace Conf. with President Wilson, 1918-19; judge St. Louis County Court, 1920-21; practice of law at St. Louis, 1921-24, partner Hawes & Walsh, Washington, D.C., 1924—; gen. counsel and code advisor for cordage, cotton garment and other industries of U.S. Democrat. Catholic. Home: Mt. Vernon View, Va. Died June 1939.

WALSH, Robert Douglas, army officer; b. in Calif., Oct. 14, 1860; grad. U.S. Mil. Acad., 1883; Army War Coll., 1912. Commd. 2d lt. 22d Inf., June 13, 1883; promoted through grades to col. 8th Cav., July 1, 1916; brig. gen. N.G., Aug. 5, 1917. Duty at Ft. Bowie, Ariz., Ft. Walla Walla, Jefferson Barracks, Mo., Boisé Barracks, Vancouver Barracks; in Philippine Islands, 1899-1902; at Ft. Leavenworth, Kan., 1908; apptd. comdr. 178th Inf. Brigade, Camp Beauregard, Alexandria, La., Aug. 25, 1917; comdg. gen. Base No. 1, St. Nazaire, France, Dec. 1, 1917-July 28, 1919; dep. dir. gen. transportation, to Nov. 7, 1918; comdg. gen. Base No. 2, Bordeaux, France, to Mar. 31, 1919; comdr. 164th Inf. Brigade to May 31, 1919; retired at his own request, after 41 yrs.' service, June 30, 1919. Awarded D.S.M.; Comdr. Legion of Honor, France. Bvtd. 1st lt., Feb. 27, 1890, "for gallant service in action against Indians" in Terrace Mountains, Mexico, Sept. 22, 1885, and Patagonia Mountains, Ariz., June 6, 1886. Died Aug. 15, 1928.

WALSH, Thomas, critic, poet; b. Brooklyn, N.Y., Oct. 14, 1875; s. Michael Kavanagh and Catherine (Farrell) W.; Georgetown U., 1889-92, Ph.D.; Columbia, 1892-95; Litt.D., Georgetown; LL.D., Notre Dame U., 1917. Author of class poem, "Columbus," Georgetown U., 1892; alumni ode, "The Crusaders," Georgetown U., 1901; poem read before Soc. Army of Potomac on battlefield of Antietam, Sept. 16, 1910; ode read at dedication of monument to Martyrs of the Prison Ships, Brooklyn, Nov. 14, 1908; ode for dedication of John Carroll monument, Georgetown, May 3, 1912. Staff contbr. Warner's Library of the World's Best Literature, Internat. Ency., Catholic Ency.; asso. editor The Commonweal. Hon. medal, Soc. Army of Potomac, Grand Cross of Isabel Catolica. Author: The Prison Ships, 1909; The Pilgrim Kings, 1915; Eleven Poems of Rubén Darío, 1916; Gardens Overseas and Other Poems, 1917; Hispanic Anthology, 1919; Don Folquet, 1920; The Catholic Anthology, 1927. Home: Brooklyn, N.Y. Deceased.

WALSH, Thomas F., mine owner and mining engr.; b. County of Tipperary, Ireland, 1851; ed. in public schools; learned millwright's trade; emigrated to U.S. at age of 19, and settled in Colo.; m. Carrie B. Reed, 1879. Engaged in mining business, made close study of geology, mineralogy, metallurgy, the deposition of ore bodies and the development and treatment of ores, and was instrumental in introducing new methods of treatment. Developed, equipped and is large owner in the Camp Bird mines, Ouray, Colo. One of Nat. Commrs. to Paris Expn., 1900. Home: Washington, D.C. Died 1910.

WALSH, Thomas James, senator; b. Two Rivers, Wis., June 12, 1859; s. Felix and Bridget (Comer) W.; ed. pub. schs.; LL.B., U. of Wis., 1884, LL.D., 1931; LL.D., Loyola Univ., 1928; m. Elinor C. McClements, Aug. 15, 1889 (died 1917). Taught school, becoming prin. of High Sch., Sturgeon Bay, Wis.; began practice of law with bro. Henry C., at Redfield, S.D., 1884; moved to Helena, Mont., 1890; mem. law firm of Walsh, Nolan & Scallon, 1907-25, Walsh, Scallon & Wine, 1925-29, Walsh & Scallon, 1929—. Dem. candidate for Congress, 1906; del. Dem. nat. convs. 6 times to 1928 (sub-com. on platform at each except last); candidate for U.S. Senate, 1910; U.S. Senator 4 terms, 1913-37; chmn. Dem. Nat. Conv., 1924, 32. Catholic. Home: Helena, Mont. Died Mar. 2, 1933.

WALSH, William Henry, M.D., consulting expert on hospital planning and organization; b. Philadelphia, Pa., Mar. 8, 1882; s. William M. and Mary A. (Hartigan) W.; ed. Girard College, Phila.; M.D., Medico-Chirurg. Coll. (U. of Pa.), 1909; m. Eugenia McIntosh, 1911; 1 dau., Yvonne; m. 2d, Irene Schulz, 1923; 1 son, William Frederic. In Hosp. Corps, U.S.A., Philippine Insurrection, 1899-1900; chief sanitary insp., Insular Bur. of Health of P.I., 1900-04, a. a. surgeon U.S.P.H.S., 1909-11; surgeon (R) U.S.P.H.S. in charge Markleton (Pa.) Hosp. for Tuberculosis, 1920; supt. Phila. Hosp. for Contagious Diseases, 1912-14; chief resident phys., Phila. Gen. Hosp., 1914; medical dir. Phila. Children's Hosp., 1914-16; exec. sec. Am. Hosp. Assn., 1916-18, also 1924-28; sec. Hosp. Board, U.S.P.H.S. Washington, D.C., 1919-20; med. dir. for Tropical Oil Co. in Colombia, S.A., Laurentide Paper & Power Co. in Quebec, Standard Fruit & S.S. Co. in Honduras, C.A. Served as consultant, administrator or in a clinical or advisory capacity in relation to hospitals for U.S. Government, state, county, and municipal govts. in the U.S., Canada, Central and South America, and Mexico; consultant, Chicago Health Department. Captain and major staff of Surgeon Gen. U.S. Army, Washington, 1917; lt. col. commanding Base Hosp. 58, Camp Grant, Ill. and Remoucourt, France, 1918; lt. col. med. Res. Corps. Fellow A.M.A., Am. Coll. of Physicians, Am. Assn. Industrial Physicians & Surgeons. Author: Synopsis for the Guidance of Hospital Inspectors, U.S.P.H.S. and Veterans Bureau, 1919. Home: Evanston, Ill. Died Mar. 28, 1941.

WALSTON, Charles (formerly Waldstein), author; b. New York, Mar. 30, 1856; s. Henry and Sophie Waldstein; student Columbia, 1871-73; univs. of Heidelberg and Leipzig, 1873-76; Ph.D., Heidelberg, 1875; hon. A.M., U. of Cambridge, Eng., 1882, Litt.D., 1887; A.M., Columbia, 1884, L.H.D., 1887; Litt.D., Trinity Coll., Dublin; m. Florence, widow of Theo. Seligman, New York, May 17, 1909; children—Evelyn Sophie Alexandra, Henry David Leonard George (dec.). Lecturer on classical archæology, 1880, reader, 1882, dir. Fitzwilliam Mus., 1883-89, U. of Cambridge; fellow, 1894—, and lecturer, King's Coll., Cambridge, and Slade prof. fine arts, 1895-1901, and 1904-11. Mem. standing com. of advice on art to Bd. Edn., 1889-95; dir. and prof., 1895-97, Am. Sch. of Classical Studies, Athens, Greece. V.p. English-Speaking Union; hon. asso. Royal Inst. Brit. Architects. Knighted, 1913; Knight Comdr. of the Order of the Redeemer (Greece); Knight of the Dannebrog. High sheriff, Cambs. and Hunts, 1922-23. Author: Excavations at the Heraion of Argos, 1889-1902; Essays on the Art of Phidias, 1885; The Expansion of Western Ideals and the World's Peace, 1899; The Argive Heræum, 1902; Art in the Nineteenth Century, 1903; Herculaneum, Past, Present and Future (with L. Shoobridge), 1908; Greek Sculpture in Its Relation to Modern Art, 1913; Aristodemocracy, etc., 1916; What Germany Is Fighting For, 1917; Patriotism National and International, 1917; The Next War; Wilsonism and Anti-Wilsonism, 1918; Truth—An Essay on Moral Reconstruction, 1919; The English-Speaking Brotherhood and the League of Nations, 1919; Eugenics, Civics and Ethics, 1922; Harmonism and Conscious Evolution, 1922; Alcamenes and the Establishment of the Classical Type in Greek Art, 1926; Notes on Greek Sculpture, 1927. Died Mar. 21, 1927.

WALTER, Alfred, ry. official; b. Brooklyn, Oct. 2, 1851; entered ry. service, 1872; held various positions, 1872-89; gen. supt. B.&O. lines east of Ohio River, 1889-92; gen. mgr. Erie div., N.Y., Lake Erie & Western Ry., 1892-94; pres. Del., Susquehanna & Schuylkill Ry., 1894-97; pres. Lehigh Valley Ry., Phila., 1897—. Died 1907.

WALTER, Ellery, writer, lecturer; b. Phila., Pa., June 16, 1906; s. John Alfred and Margaret Ellery (Hickman) W.; ed. U. of Washington, Seattle, 1924-26; student polit. economy, U. of Berlin, on fellowship of Carl Schurz Memorial Foundation, 1932-33; m. Elizabeth Adams Jenks, June 15, 1932. Thrown on own resources at 14; worked in electrical factory (Chicago), press room (Detroit News), on farm (Miss.), ranch (Tex.), oil fields (Mexico), as auto salesman (Ariz.), in logging camps (Wash. and British Columbia), fish cannery (Alaska), as seaman (Seattle-Orient run), newspaper reporter (Australia), courier (Europe); traveled around world, paying expenses by working, 1926-28; in Europe, 1929-30; interviewed Hindenburg, Mussolini, Pope Pius XI, and others; taught at Cranbrook (Mich.) Sch. for Boys, 1930-31; spl. corr. New York Herald Tribune in Soviet Union, 1931, for New York Herald Tribune and Nat. Broadcasting Co. in Far East, 1933-34. Episcopalian. Author: The World on One Leg, 1928; High Hats and Low Bows, 1931; Russia's Decisive Year, 1932; Manchurian Empire, 1934. Died Apr. 2, 1935.

WALTER, Eugene, playwright; b. Cleveland, O., Nov. 27, 1874; s. George Andrew and Jane (King) W.; pub. sch. edn.; m. Charlotte Walker, Dec. 1, 1908. Polit. or general news reporter Cleveland Plain Dealer, Cleveland Press, Detroit News, New York Sun, Globe, Cincinnati Post, Seattle Star, at various times, and business mgr. of theatrical and amusement enterprises, ranging from minstrels and circuses to symphony orchestras and grand opera cos. Mem. 1st Vol. Cav., Spanish-Am. War, Apr.-Oct. 1898. Author: The Undertow, 1906; The Real Issue, 1908; The Wolf, 1908; Paid in Full, 1908; (plays, prod. in N.Y.) Sergeant James, 1901; The Flag Station, 1905; Paid in Full, 1907; The Wolf, 1908; The Easiest Way, 1908; Inside the Circle, 1908; Just a Wife, 1910; Boots and Saddles, 1910; Fine Feathers, 1911; The Trail of the Lonesome Pine, 1911; also Just a Woman, 1916; Little Shepherd of Kingdom Come, 1916; The Knife, 1917; The Assassin, 1917; Friendship, 1917; The Challenge, 1919; The Man's Name (with Marjorie Chase), Under Northern Stars, 1921; The Toy Girl, 1921; Thieves in Clover; The Man Who Met God; Going Through; also a series of 10 lectures on the practical aspect of writing plays, pub. under title of How to Write a Play. Home: New York, N.Y. Died Sept. 26, 1941.

WALTER, George William, organist; b. New York, Dec. 16, 1851; musical edn. under John K. Paine and Samuel P. Warren; (Mus. Doc. Columbia U., 1882). Established in Washington, D.C., 1869, as organist; noted for registration and extemporaneous work; expert in organ construction. Deceased.

WALTER, Howard Arnold, missionary; b. New Britain, Conn., Aug. 19, 1883; s. of Henry Stanley and Martha (Arnold) W.; B.A., Princeton, 1905, M.A., 1909; B.D., Hartford Theol. Sem., 1909, fellow, 1909-10; studied at Glasgow, Edinburgh, U. of Marburg, and Kennedy Sch. of Missions, Hartford, Conn.; m. Marguerite Bearns Darlington, Nov. 21, 1910. Ordained Congl. ministry, 1910; teacher of English, Waseda U., Tokyo, Japan, 1906-09; asst. pastor Asylum Hill Ch. Hartford, Conn., 1910-12; sec. Internat. Com. Y.M.C.A., 1912—; nat. lit. sec. India Y.M.C.A., 1912—; sec. Missionaries to Moslems League for India and the Far East, 1914-16. Mason. Author: My Creed and Other Poems, 1912; Handbook of Work with Student Enquirers in India, 1915; The Ahmediya Movement (Religious Life of India Series), 1918; The Fact and Meaning of Islam, 1918. Compiler: Selections from the Confessions of Saint Augustine (Inner Shrine Series), 1918. Died Nov. 11, 1918.

WALTER, Raymond F(owler), civil and irrigation engr.; b. Chicago, Ill., Oct. 31, 1873; s. John Huffman and Susie (Garlock) W.; B.S. in Engring., Colorado State Coll., 1893, M.S. in Civ. and Irrigation Engring., 1929; m. Lillian Leon Phillips, Nov. 26, 1896; children—Dorothy Lillian (Mrs. George Harger), Donald Scott. Project engr., in charge constrn. Belle Fourche (S.D.) irrigation project, 1903-08; supervising engr., in charge constrn., Bur. Reclamation, U.S. Dept. Interior, on projects in Colo., Wyo., Neb., Kan., Okla., S.D., 1908-15, chief engr. for same bur., all Western States, 1924—; also chief engr. Boulder Dam and Boulder Canyon Project, 1929—, Grand Coulee Dam and Columbia Basin project and 20 other reclamation and power projects, 1933—. Presbyn. Mason, K.P. Home: Denver, Colo. Died June 30, 1940.

WALTER, Robert, physician; b. Acton, Can., Feb. 14, 1841; s. George and Elizabeth (Vodden) W.; ed. common schools, Acton and Hullett, Canada; M.D., Hahnemann Med. Coll., Phila., 1888; graduate Hygeio-Therapeutic Coll., New York, 1873; m. Eunice Clapp Lippincott, July 4, 1872. Prop. Walter Sanitarium, Walter's Park, Pa., 1876—. Author: Vital Science, 1899; The Exact Science of Human Health, 1903. Home: Walter's Park, Pa. Died Oct. 26, 1921.

WALTERS, Alexander, bishop; b. Bardstown, Ky., Aug. 1, 1858; s. Henry and Harriett W.; ed. common schs. and by pvt. tutors in theology; (A.M., 1900, D.D., 1891, Livingston Coll.); m. Katie Knox, Aug. 28, 1877. Licensed as local preacher A.M.E. Zion Ch., 1877; pastor successively in Ky., Calif., Tenn. and New York; bishop, 1892—. Elected 7 times pres. Afro-Am. Council; del. Gen. Conf., 1884, 88, 92, and Ecumenical Confs., 1884, 91, 1901 (London, Eng.); trustee Nat. Christian Endeavor Society, 1893-1907; lecturer on Negro question. Pres. A.M.E. Zion Ch. Industrial & Development Corp., New York. Deceased.

WALTERS, Anderson Howel, congressman; m. Jessie Octavia Woodruff. Editor and pub. Johnstown (Pa.) Tribune; mem. 63d Congress (1913-15), 66th, 67th and 69th Congresses (1919-23 and 1925-27), Pa. at large. Republican. Home: Johnstown, Pa. Died Dec. 7, 1927.

WALTERS, Henry, capitalist; b. Baltimore, Sept. 26, 1848; s. William T. and Ellen (Harper) W.; prep. edn. Loyola Coll., Baltimore, Georgetown U., and in Paris; student Lawrence Scientific Sch. (Harvard), 1869-73; m. Mrs. Sarah Wharton (Green) Jones, Apr. 11, 1922. Began ry. service in engring. corps Valley R.R. in Va., and later in operating supt.'s office Pittsburgh & Connellsville R.R.; entered service of the Atlantic Coast Line, of which his father was one of the organizers; advanced to gen. mgr.; greatly improved the property and finally merged with it the Plant System of Fla., and purchased control of the L.&N. System; largest stockholder in A.C.L. R.R., and chmn. bd. of A.C.L. and L.&N. rys.; head of W. T. Walters & Co.; chmn. bd. Safe Deposit & Trust Co., Baltimore. Mem. staff of U.S. dir. gen. of railroads, representing railroad interests, Jan. 1918-20. Extensive art collector; yachtsman (owner of the yacht Narada; mem. syndicates to build Am. cup defender). Builder of number of public baths in Baltimore. Trustee Metropolitan Mus. Art (v.p.), New York Pub. Library. Decorated Officer Legion of Honor (France). Home: Baltimore, Md. Died Nov. 30, 1931.

WALTERS, Henry C., lawyer; b. British Columbia, Can., Aug. 24, 1870; s. John and Margaret (MacDonald) W.; came to U.S., 1892; LL.B., U. of Mich., 1894; m. Charlotte G. Smith, Mar. 7, 1908. Admitted to Mich. bar, 1894; and began practice at Detroit; gen. practice with specialty in corporate and ins. law. Democrat. Presbyn. Died Nov. 30, 1931.

WALTERS, Theodore Augustus, asst. sec. of Interior; b. Garber, Ia., Aug. 21, 1876; s. Isaac N. and Elizabeth (Purman) W.; B.S., Upper Ia. U., 1900; student State U. of Ia., 1902-03; m. Minerva Ginter, June 15, 1905; children—John G., Ione, Lois. School teacher, 1900-04; supt. city schools, Brookings, S.D., 1904-06; admitted to Ida. bar, 1906, practicing in Caldwell; mem. Jackson & Walters, 1906-16, in own name, 1920-33. Mem. State Board Edn., 1914-17; atty. gen. of Ida., 1917-20; Dem. candidate for gov., 1920; chmn. State Bd. of Edn. to 1933, resigned; first asst. sec. U.S. Dept. of Interior, 1933—. Chmn. Dem. State Central Com. for Ida., 1928-33. Democrat. Methodist. Mason. Elk. Home: Caldwell, Ida. Died Nov. 27, 1937.

WALTON, Charles Edgar, surgeon; b. Cincinnati, May 30, 1849; s. Joshua P. and Elizabeth A. (Swain) W.; A.B., Marietta (O.) Coll., 1871, A.M., 1873; M.D., Pulte Med. Coll., 1874 (LL.D., Marietta, 1903); m. Jean G. Mitchell, Jan. 1, 1878. Practiced in Hamilton, O., 1875-89, Cincinnati, 1889—. Prof. surgery and gynecology, 1891—, registrar, 1889—, dean, 1904—, Pulte Med. Coll. Pres. Am. Inst. Homœopathy, 1900, Homœopathic Soc. State of Ohio, 1889. Home: Cincinnati, O. Died Aug. 26, 1926.

WALTON, Clifford Stevens, lawyer; b. Chardon, O., Mar. 2, 1861; s. Andrew J. and Caroline (Griswold) W., of English descent (Maperton House); ed. U.S. Mil. Acad., U. of Madrid, Spain; LL.M., Nat. Law U., Washington, 1889; m. Washington, Anne G. Veazey, d. Judge W. G. Veazey, of Vt., Apr. 9, 1890. Served as atty. for or against U.S. on several internat. law commns., including controversies between U.S. and Chile, Peru, Salvador, etc. Was maj. U.S.V., 1898-99, on staffs of Maj. Gens. Brooke and Ludlow, in P.R. and Cuba; consul gen. of Paraguay. Republican. Author: The Civil Law in Spain and Spanish America, 1900; Leyes Comerciales y Marítimas de la America Latina, 1907. Home: Washington, D.C. Died May 15, 1912.

WALTON, George Augustus, educator; b. S. Reading (now Wakefield), Mass., Feb. 18, 1822; s. James and Elizabeth (Bryant) W.; ed. pub. and pvt. schs., S. Reading Acad., Lexington Acad., 1838, Reading Acad., 1839-44, Bridgewater Normal Sch., grad., 1844, A.M., Williams Coll., 1869; m. Electa Nobles Lincoln, Aug. 27, 1850. Teacher Duxbury, Edgartown, Barnstable and W. Newton, Mass., 1843-47, Lawrence, Mass., 1848-68; book and inst. work, 1868-71; agt. Mass. State Bd. Edn., 1871-96. Under acts of Mass. legislature investigated and reported sch. attendance and truancy; also revised sch. attendance laws. Was Alderman, City of Lawrence, Mass. Mem. Am. Inst. Instrn., 1846— (formerly treas. and pres.); inst. conductor in Mass., N.Y., Va.; mem. Mass. Teachers' Assn., 1845—, N.E.A. Unitarian. Republican. Author: Mental Arithmetic, 1884; New Franklin Arithmetics with Key, 1895; Walton and Holmes 4 book series arithmetics, 1907-08. Home: West Newton, Mass. Died 1908.

WALTON, George Lincoln, neurologist; b. Lawrence, Mass., Mar. 16, 1854; s. George Augustus and Electa Nobles (Lincoln) W.; A.B., Harvard, 1875, M.D., 1880. In practice at Boston, 1883-1916; honorary physician Mass. General Hosp. Author: Why Worry?, 1908; Those Nerves, 1909; Practical Guide to the Wild Flowers and Fruits, 1909; The Flower-Finder, 1914; Peg Along, 1915; Oscar Montague—Paranoiac, 1919. Home: Boston, Mass. Died Jan 17, 1941.

WALTON, Lee Barker, prof. biology; b. Bear Lake, Pa., Nov. 12, 1871; s. Byron and Emma Theresa (Barker) W.; Ph.B., Cornell U., 1897, Ph.D., 1902; studied U. of Bonn, Germany, 1897-99; A.M., Brown U., 1901; m. Caroline Louise Graham, Mar. 1, 1898; children—Harold Graham, Robert Barker (dec.), Margaret Bai (Mrs. George P. Faust), Graham, Roger Lee. Was Goldwin Smith fellow, at Cornell U., Ithaca; prof. biology, Kenyon Coll., Gambier, O., 1902—. Republican. Episcopalian. Home: Gambier, O. Died May 15, 1937.

WALTON, Lucius Leedom, pharmacist; b. Clinton, N.J., July 8, 1865; s. Thomas Cooper and Jane Eliza (Fly) W.; grad. Clinton (N.J.) Classical Inst. and Dickinson Sem., Williamsport, Pa.; Ph G., Phila. Coll. Pharmacy, 1888, Pharm.M., honoris causa, 1912; Pharm.D., honoris causa, U. of Pittsburgh, 1912; m. Cora Olive Brooks, Nov. 1890; children—Beatrice Brooks (Mrs. Louis Saulbach), Brooks Lamar, Caroline Scott (Mrs. J. Lowell Budinger). Mem. L. L. Walton & Co., druggists, Williamsport, 1892—. Mem. Pa. State Bd. Pharmacy, 1906— (sec. 1909-26; pres., 1931—). Methodist. Home: Williamsport, Pa. Died Dec. 26, 1935.

WALTON, Mason Augustus, author; b. Oldtown, Me., July 31, 1838; s. Samuel and Sarah (Brown) W.; grad. Hampden (Me.) Acad., 1859; m. Olive Bradford, 1870 (died 1877). Until 1877, engaged for most part in hunting, lumbering, teaching and farming; lectured in Me. for Greenback party, 1878; in 1879 managed and edited The Greenbacker, 6 months' campaign paper, and in 1880 The Bangor Record, another 6 months' paper; lectured in Mass. in interest of B. F. Butler and in N.H. for Greenback party, 1879; removed to Gloucester, Mass., 1884, and for health lived in woods. Lecturer upon "The Intelligence of Animal Life," 1896—. Freethinker. Republican Greenbacker. Author: A Hermit's Wild Friends. Home: Gloucester, Mass. Died 1917.

WALTON, Thomas Cameron, naval officer; b. Cumberland, Eng., May 31, 1838; s. Thomas and Ann (Watson) W.; came to America, 1847; ed. Toronto Acad. and McGill Univ., Canada, 1860; M.D., Univ. of New York, 1862; m. Kate Lane Lynch, Feb. 1871. Apptd. asst. surgeon U.S.N., Oct. 5, 1861; advanced through the various grades and retired May 31, 1900, with rank of rear admiral. Served during Civ. War and Spanish-Am. War and at all the important naval stas.; senior med. officer at Naval Acad. and in Naval Laboratory, 1883-1900. Episcopalian. Home: Annapolis, Md. Died 1909.

WALTON, William, painter; b. Philadelphia, Nov. 10, 1843; s. Edward Hicks and Anne Mifflin (Townsend) W.; ed. pub. and high sch.; studied drawing at Pa. Acad. Fine Arts, Nat. Acad. of Design, New York, and under Carolus Duran, Paris, 1877-88; unmarried. Began by drawing on wood in Phila. and New York; figure and landscape painter; writer on art. Died Nov. 13, 1915.

WALTON, William Bell, congressman; b. Altoona, Pa., Jan. 23, 1871; s. Louis and Adessa (Bell) W.; ed. South Jersey Inst., Bridgeton, N.J.; m. Leoline Ashenfelter, Jan. 5, 1893; children—Eda Lou, Mrs. Leona Neblett, William B.; m. 2d, Frances Hoffman, Dec. 31, 1927. Began law practice in New Mexico, 1893; former owner of the Silver City (N.M.) Independent. Member House of Representatives, New Mexico Ty., 1901-02; mem. N.M. Constl. Conv., 1910; mem. 1st State Senate of N.M., 1912-16; mem. 65th Congress (1917-19), N.M. at-large; nominated U.S. Senator, 1918 (defeated); dist. attorney 6th Judicial Dist., N.M., 1925-32. Democrat. Mason. Grand Master of Masons in N.M., 1912. Home: Silver City, N.M. Died Apr. 14, 1939.

WALTZ, Elizabeth Cherry, journalist, author; b. Columbus, O., Dec. 10, 1866; d. Maj. John Nichols and Anne (Page) Cherry; grad. Columbus High Sch.; m. Frederick Hastings Waltz, July 4, 1898. Constantly in newspaper and mag. work from 1895, on Cincinnati Tribune, 1895-97, Springfield Republic-Times, 1898; Louisville Courier-Journal, 1899—, lit editor. Author: Pa Gladden, 1903. Home: Meadowbrook, Ky. Died 1903.

WALWORTH, Clarence Alphonsus, R.C. priest-author; b. Plattsburg, N.Y., May 30, 1820; son of Reuben Hyde Walworth (1788-1867), last of the chancellors of New York; grad. Union Coll., 1838 (LL.D.); studied law; admitted to bar, 1841; practiced at Rochester, 1841-42; studied theology 3 years at General Theol. Sem. (P.E.), New York; became Roman Catholic; went to Belgium; spent 3 years with Redemptionists and at Coll. of Wittenberg; ordained priest; returned to U.S., 1850; traveling missionary, 1850-64; one of five founders order of Paulists in U.S.; from 1865 rector St. Mary's Ch., Albany, N.Y.; prominent temperance advocate. Author: The Gentle Skeptic; The Doctrine of Hell; Andiatorocté and Other Poems. Died 1900.

WALWORTH, Ellen Hardin; b. Jacksonville, Ill., Oct. 20, 1832; d. of Gen. John J. Hardin, U.S.V.

(killed at Buena Vista, 1847) and Sarah Ellen (Smith) Hardin; ed. Jacksonville Acad. and by pvt. tutors; m. M. T. Walworth, 1852 (died 1873). Grad. woman's law class, U. of New York. Founder (one of three) Nat. Soc. D.A.R., 1890; trustee 18 yrs. of Saratoga Monument Assn.; pres. Shakespeare Club, Saratoga, 1875-85; pres. and founder Art and Science Field Club, Saratoga, 1880-85; founder and pres. Post Parliament, New York; one of first three women nominated and elected to sch. bd. under N.Y. law admitting women as trustees; director-gen. Woman's Nat. War Relief Assn., 1898; was at field hosp., Fortress Monroe, to meet first wounded brought from Santiago with supplies, nurses, etc. Was at Montauk, Aug. 12, and remained in field hosp. until it closed. Author: Battles of Saratoga; Parliamentary Rules, 1897. Home: Saratoga Springs, N.Y. Died June 23, 1915.

WAMBAUGH, Eugene, lawyer; b. nr. Brookville, O., Feb. 29, 1856; s. Rev. A. B. and Sarah (Sells) W.; A.B., Harvard, 1876, A.M., 1877, LL.B., 1880; LL.D., State U. of Iowa, 1892, Western Reserve U., 1908, Dartmouth Coll., 1908; m. Anna S. Hemphill, Apr. 7, 1881 (died 1938); children—Sarah, Miles. Admitted to Ohio bar, 1880; practiced at Cincinnati, 1880-89; prof. law, State U. of Ia., 1889-92, Harvard, 1892-1925, prof. law emeritus. Mem. bd. editors Am. Polit. Science Review, 1906-13; special atty. U.S. Bur. of Corps., 1908-12; spl. counsel U.S. State Dept., for war problems, 1914; U.S. mem. permanent internat. commn. under treaty with Peru, 1915—. Commd. maj., Judge Advocate's Section, O.R.C., U.S.A., Nov. 8, 1916; called to service and assigned to Northeastern Department, Boston, Mass., July 3, 1917; office of the judge advocate gen., Washington, Sept. 13, 1917 (chief of constl. and internat. law div.); lt. col. N.A., Feb. 13, 1918; col., July 19, 1918; hon. discharged, July 11, 1919. Del. Pan-Am. Scientific Congress, 1915-16 (chmn. subsect. on jurisprudence). Hon. prof. law, Western Reserve U., 1909—; lecturer, U. of Wis., 1909, Harvard Sch. of Pub. Health, 1913-25, Yale, 1921, U. of Cambridge (for bd. of history), 1923, U. of Oxford (for faculty of law), 1923. Counsel of Peruvian Government on Tacna-Arica plebiscite (at Arica and Washington), 1925-26; member Petersburg National Military Park Commn., Department of the Interior, 1934-37. Fellow Am. Acad. of Arts and Sciences. Author: The Study of Cases, 1892, 94; Cases for Analysis, 1894; Cases on Agency, 1896, 1925; Cases on Insurance, 1902; Littleton's Tenures, 1903; Cases on Constitutional Law, 1915; Guide to Articles of War, 1917. Home: Cambridge, Mass. Died Aug. 6, 1940.

WANAMAKER, John, merchant; b. Philadelphia, July 11, 1838; s. Nelson and Elizabeth D. (Kochersperger) W.; ed. public schs.; LL.D., Howard U., Ursinus Coll., U. of Pa.; m. Mary B. Brown. Errand-boy in book-store at 14; went to Indiana, but returned, 1856; retail clothing salesman, 1856-58; established, 1861, with Nathan Brown, clothing house of Wanamaker & Brown, Phila.; established, 1876, department store in Phila., and a similar business in New York in 1896 (successor of A. T. Stewart). Was an organizer, and dir. Merchants Bank. Active in politics as Republican of independent proclivities and an opponent of the "machine" in politics; declined Rep. nomination for 48th Congress, also independent candidacy for mayor, Phila., 1886; presdl. elector, 1888; mem. Rep. Nat. Exec. Com., 1889-93; Postmaster Gen. of U.S., 1889-93, in cabinet of President Harrison. Long active in religious work; founded, 1858, and from then supt. Bethany S.S. (Presbyn.), probably the largest in the U.S.; elected 1st salaried sec. in America of Y.M.C.A., 1858; one of founders Christian Commn. during Civil War; pres. Y.M.C.A. of Phila., 1870-83; mem. bd. finance Centennial Expn., 1876; helped found Presbyn. Hosp., of which was trustee, and with Mrs. Wanamaker built the children's ward; mgr. Univ. Hosp. some yrs.; founded Wanamaker Inst. of Industries, Bethany Dispensary, and First Penny Savings Bank of which became pres.; he erected Y.M.C.A. and coll. bldgs. in India, China, Japan, Korea and many chs. and other instns. Received decoration officer Legion of Honor, French Govt., 1912. Sent 2 relief ships to Belgium, 1914. Home: Philadelphia, Pa. Died Dec. 12, 1922.

WANAMAKER, (Lewis) Rodman, merchant; b. Phila., Pa.; s. John and Mary B. (Brown) W.; A.B., Princeton, 1886, A.M., 1902. Pres. John Wanamaker New York, and John Wanamaker Philadelphia; was resident mgr. for the stores, in Paris, France, for 10 yrs.; trustee Mut. Life Ins. Co. of New York; mem. bd. mgrs. Lehigh Coal & Navigation Co.; executor Estate of John Wanamaker, Estate of Thomas B. Wanamaker (including Phila. Record); apptd. executor Estate of James Gordon Bennett, 1918; pres. First Penny Savings Bank, Phila. Consul Gen. for Paraguay, and consul for Uruguay and Dominican Republic, at Phila. Sent 3 expdns. to the West to study Indian life, results of which have been deposited with U.S. Govt. at Washington, D.C.; presented art collection to Princeton U.; built airship "America," wrecked in storm, 1914, and built second "America" which became property of British Govt. after opening of World War. Apptd. spl. dep. police commr. in charge Police Reserves, N.Y. City; pres. bd. of Deputy Commrs. and Spl. Dep. Police Commrs., N.Y. City Police Dept.; chmn. Mayor's Com. to Welcome Homecoming Troops; chmn. Mayor's Com. on Permanent Memorial for N.Y. City; chmn. Mayor's Com. on Pub. Welfare; chmn. Mayor's Com. on Receptions to Distinguished Guests; chmn. New York Silver Jubilee, 1923; apptd. mem. Governor's staff, title of col., 1918. Decorated Comdr. Royal Victorian Order (British); Grand Officer Order Leopold II (Belgian); Comdr. Legion of Honor (French); Comdr. Order of St. Sava (Serbia); Comdr. Order of the Liberator (Venezuela); Officier Order of the Crown (Italian). Pres. bd. trustees Wanamaker Inst. of Industries, Phila.; mem. museum com. Phila. Mus. and Sch. Industrial Art. Died Mar. 9, 1928.

WANAMAKER, Thomas B., businessman; b. Philadelphia, Mar. 27, 1861; s. John and Mary (Brown) W.; A.B., Princeton, 1883, A.M.; m. Mary Lowber Welsh, Apr. 27, 1887. Dir. The Investment Co. of Phila.; consul of Santo Domingo at Philadelphia. Home: Philadelphia, Pa. Died 1908.

WANTY, George Proctor, U.S. dist. judge Western dist. Mich., March 16, 1900; b. Ann Arbor, Mich., March 12, 1856; s. Samuel and Elizabeth (Proctor) W.; ed. common and academic schools Ann Arbor; grad. Univ. Mich., law dept., LL.B., 1878; admitted Grand Rapids bar, 1878; m. Emma Nichols, June 22, 1886. Home: Grand Rapids, Mich. Died 1906.

WAPLES, Rufus, lawyer, author; b. Millsboro, Del., Aug. 11, 1825; s. Robert and descendant Peter Waples, who settled in Del. about 1690; ed. common school and Milton Acad., Del.; grad. Univ. of La., law dept., 1852; m. Margaret J. Aisworth, July 15, 1858. Admitted to bar, 1852, began practice in New Orleans, 1853, with brother, Stephen H. Waples; with James B. Eustis (late U.S. senator) established firm of Waples & Eustis, 1855; apptd. U.S. atty. for Eastern dist. of La., 1863, by Pres. Lincoln; served through Lincoln's and part of Johnson's administrations; admitted to bar U.S. Supreme Court, 1866; city atty. New Orleans for spl. cases, 1870-72; for several yrs. dir. public schools and trustee Straight Univ., New Orleans; moved to Ann Arbor, Mich., 1878 Independent Republican. Author: A Handbook of Parliamentary Practice, 1883. Home: Ann Arbor, Mich. Died 1902.

WAPPAT, Blanche King Smith, librarian; b. Pittsburgh, Pa., Sept. 19, 1889; d. James Alexander and Sue (Thompson) Smith; diploma, Carnegie Library Sch., Carnegie Inst., Pittsburgh, 1919; m. Fred William Wappat, Aug. 2, 1911. Library asst., Carnegie Library, Pittsburgh, 1910-13, Cleveland Pub. Library, 1910; librarian Sch. of Applied Design, Pittsburgh, 1913-19; librarian Carnegie Inst. Tech., 1920-29; spl. lecturer, Carnegie Library Sch., 1930-31. Episcopalian. Originator of spl. methods and details of administration for art libraries. Sec. 1st organized meeting of art reference librarians, A.L.A. Conf., 1924. Compiler: Bibliography of Mosaics, 1919. Home: Pittsburgh, Pa. Died Apr. 18, 1939.

WARBURG, Felix M., banker; b. Hamburg, Germany, Jan. 14, 1871; s. Moritz and Charlotte Esther (Oppenheim) W.; ed. pub. and high schs. of Hamburg; came to America, 1894; naturalized citizen, 1900; m. Frieda, d. Jacob H. Schiff, of New York, 1895; children—Mrs. Carola Rothschild, Frederick M., Gerald F., Paul F. S., Edward M. M. Mem. banking firm of Kuhn, Loeb & Company, New York, 1896—; director Staten Island Rapid Transit Ry. Co. Chmn. Fedn. for Support of Jewish Philanthropic Soc. of N.Y. City, Am. Jewish Joint Distribution Com.; pres. New York Foundation; v.p. Charity Orgn. Soc., Jewish Welfare Bd.; mem. Am. Assn. Adult Edn. (mem. council of 100); dir. Solomon and Betty Loeb Home for Convalescents, Henry Street Settlement, Inst. Musical Art (pres. and treas.), Jewish Theol. Sem.; trustee Teachers College. Home: New York, N.Y. Died Oct. 20, 1937.

WARBURG, Paul Moritz, banker; b. Hamburg, Germany, Aug. 10, 1868; s. Moritz and Charlotte Esther (Oppenheim) W.; ed. in Germany; m. Nina J. Loeb, 1894. Formerly mem. Kuhn, Loeb & Co., bankers, New York; resigned all directorships, trusteeships, etc., on apptmt. by Pres. Wilson as mem. Federal Reserve Bd. for term 1914-18. Apptd. mem. U.S. Sect. Internat. High Commn., 1917. Now chmn. bd. Internat. Acceptance Bank, New York, also chmn. bd. The Manhattan Co.; dir. B.&O. R.R., Western Union Telegraph Co., U.P. R.R. Co., Am. I.G. Chemical Corp., Agfa Ansco Corp., etc. Dir. Julliard Sch. of Music. Trustee Nat. Child Labor Com., Tuskegee Coll., Inst. of Economics (Washington, D.C.); treas. Inst. Musical Arts. Home: New York, N.Y. Died Jan. 24, 1932.

WARD, Aaron, rear admiral U.S.N.; b. Philadelphia, Oct. 10, 1851; s. Gen. Ward Benjamin and Emily (Ward) Burnett; ed. Cannstatt, Germany, and Lycee Bonaparte, Paris; grad. U.S. Naval Acad., 1871; m. Annie Cairns Willis, Apr. 20, 1876. Served on California, Pacific Sta., 1871-73; Brooklyn in W.I., 1874; Franklin, European Sta., 1875-76; Naval Acad., 1876-79; Constitution, training squadron, 1879-82; Hartford and Monongahela, Pacific Sta., 1885-88; naval attaché, Paris, Berlin, St. Petersburg, 1889-92; served on New York, in W.I. and Brazil, 1893-94; San Francisco, in Mediterranean, 1894-96; comd. Wasp during Spanish-Am. War, and advanced in grade for eminent and conspicuous service in battle; comd. Panther, in W.I., 1898-99; as comdr. and capt. served on Asiatic Sta. as chief-of-staff, also comd. Yorktown, Don Juan de Austria and Pennsylvania, 1901-08; supervisor New York Harbor, 1908-09; aid to Sec. of the Navy, head of Inspection Dept., 1909-11; rear admiral, 1910; 2d in command Atlantic Fleet, flagship Minnesota and Florida, 1911-12; retired Oct. 10, 1913. Episcopalian. Officer Legion of Honor, France. Editor: Luce's Seamanship, revised edit., 1884. Home: Roslyn, L.I., N.Y. Died July 5, 1918.

WARD, Albert Norman, clergyman, educator; b. Harford Co., Md., Nov. 27, 1871; s. John T. and Elizabeth (Mellor) W.; student Md. State Normal Sch., 1889-90; A.B., Western Md. Coll., 1895; A.M., George Washington U., 1902; D.D., Adrian, and Otterbein, 1920; LL.D., Kansas City Univ., 1921; LL.D. from George Washington U., 1932; m. Ethel Blanche Murchison, June 28, 1905; 1 son, Albert Norman. Ordained ministry M.P. Ch., 1897; pastor Christ Ch., Baltimore, Md., 1895, Mt. Royal Av. Ch., Baltimore, 1896-99, N. Carolina Av. Ch., Washington, D.C., 1899-1905, Seattle, Wash., 1905-10, Denton, Md., 1901-13; v.p. Western Md. Coll., 1913-17; pastor Salisbury, Md., 1917-19; chancellor Kansas City U., 1919-20; pres. Western Md. Coll., 1920—. Pres. Summer Conf., same, 1912-19; chmn. Liberal Arts Coll. Movement, 1929-31. Home: Westminster, Md. Died Sept. 22, 1935.

WARD, Anna Lydia, author; b. Bloomfield, N.J.; d. Israel Currie and Almeda (Hanks) W.; sister of Richard Halsted Ward; ed. Ripley Female Coll., Poultney, Vt.; removed to Waterbury, Conn., 1887. In 1886 (with Miss Florentine H Hayden) visited Labrador and reached points further north than any which, up to that date, had been attained by an Am. woman; made ethnol. study of the Eskimo of northern Labrador, and their mode of life; embodied results in illustrated lecture. Expert indexer; hon. corr. mem. Inst. of Jamaica, Kingston, B.W.I.; prominent in women's club work; pres., 1896-1921, The Waterbury (Conn.) Inst. of Craft and Industry, Inc.; apptd. by gov., commr. (1907-15) to appoint a woman factory inspector for Conn. Author: Dictionary of Quotations from the Poets, 1883; Quotations from American Authors (in Familiar Quotations), 1884; Waterbury (Conn.) Illustrated, 1889; Dictionary of Quotations in Prose, 1889. Home: Waterbury, Conn. Died Feb. 2, 1933.

WARD, Cabot, lawyer; b. N.Y. City, Mar. 17, 1876; s. Thomas Wrenn and Sophia (Howard) W.; A.B., Harvard, 1898; Harvard Law Sch., 1901. Admitted to N.Y. bar, 1901; admitted to bar of United States Supreme Court, 1910; began practice in New York; apptd. auditor-gen. of Puerto Rico, 1905; chmn. Franchise and Pub. Service Commn. of P.R., 1907; apptd. sec. of State of P.R., 1908; elected pres. of Exec. Council (Senate) of P.R., 1909; apptd. acting governor of P.R., 1909. Mem. U.S. delegation to 4th Pan-Am. Congress, Buenos Aires, July 1910; mem. U.S. commn. to Chile; etc. Pres. Park Bd. and commr. of parks, N.Y. City, 1914-17. Capt. 9th Coast Arty., N.Y., 1916-17; mem. mil. commn. studying anti-aircraft defense of cities in war zone and on French and Brit. fronts, Aug. and Sept. 1917; commd. maj. Aviation Sect. Signal Corps U.S.A., Oct. 1917; apptd. asst. chief of staff and chief of intelligence sect., line of communications, A.E.F., Dec. 24, 1917; promoted lt. col. Gen. Staff, G2, S.O.S., Mar. 1, 1918; lt. col. O.R.C. Dir. Am. Library of Paris, Franco-Am. Soc., Franco-Am. Welfare, France Amerique; comdr. Dept. Continental Europe Am. Legion; v.p. Interallied Vets.' Federation F.I.D.A.C.; chmn. Am. Legion Delegation to Interallied Com., Brussels, 1922; etc. Awarded D.S.M. (U.S.); Comdr. Legion of Honor (French); D.S.O. (British); Comdr. Order White Eagle (Serbian). Home: Nice, France. Died May 13, 1936.

WARD, Catharine Weed Barnes, journalist, author; b. Albany, N.Y., Jan. 10, 1851; d. William and Emily P. (Weed) Barnes; sister of Thurlow Weed and William Barnes, Jr.; m. H(enry) Snowden Ward, July 1893 (died 1911). Amateur photographer and magazine writer; has illustrated many books and magazines. One of the judges in Liberal Arts Department, Chicago Expn., 1893; resigned position on Am. Amateur Photographer, 1895. Author: (with husband), Shakespeare's Town and Times; The Real Dickens Land; The Canterbury Pilgrimages; and Shakespearean Guide to Stratford-on-Avon. Died July 31, 1913.

WARD, Charles Augustus; b. Marietta, O., July 27, 1870; s. Augustus T. and Katherine Louise (Wakefield) W.; B.A., Marietta Coll., 1890; m. Annie Reppert, Apr. 16, 1901; 1 son, Kenneth Reppert. In real estate and ins. business Superior, Wis., 1890-92; editor Inland Ocean, Superior, 1892-1900, hotel and mercantile business, Marietta, O., 1900-16; pres.

Washington County Savings Loan & Building Co., 1906-16; postmaster, Marietta, 1912-16; pres. Dayton (O.) Gas Co., 1916-24; with industrial relations dept. of Pure Oil Co., 1919—; pres. Beagle Drug Co. (Marietta); dir. treas. Stacey Engring. Co., dir. Lynbrook Realty Co. (both Columbus). Editor Pure Oil News. Trustee Marietta Coll. Republican. Conglist. Mason. Home: Columbus, O. Died Jan. 4, 1939.

WARD, Charles Sumner, financial specialist; b. Danville, Vt., Nov. 3, 1858; s. Thomas and Ruth (Weeks) W.; grad. St. Johnsbury (Vt.) Acad., 1877; B.A., Dartmouth, 1881, M.A., 1912; m. Bettie E. Randall, May 25, 1882; children—Lena, Alice, Ruth. Gen. sec. Y.M.C.A., New Britain, Conn., 1884-90, Grand Rapids, Mich., 1890-97; sec. Internat. Com. Y.M.C.A., 1897-1919. Developed plan for financing assn. bldgs. by which more than $100,000,000 was raised; also assisted in London, Eng., Edinburgh, Scotland, etc. As sec. finance com. of Am. Red Cross directed the 1917 campaign which produced over $100,000,000 in one week; mem. com. of U.S. Food Administration to enroll 10,000,000 families for food conservation, and dir. of nat. and local campaigns which have secured vast sums for philanthropic work. Senior partner Ward, Wells, Dreshman & Gates, which has conducted campaigns securing $500,000,000 for philanthropy and education in the 9 yrs. following the close of the World War. Republican. Conglist.; mem. exec. com. Nat. Council Congl. Chs. Home: Flushing, L.I. Died July 28, 1929.

WARD, David, capitalist; b. Keene, N.Y., Sept. 15, 1822; academic edn.; grad., M.D., Univ. of Mich.; m. Elizabeth Perkins, Dec. 1850. School teacher 3 years; land and timber inspector over 10 years; dealer in lands and lumberman many years, making large fortune thereby; holdings in land so extensive that he built a standard-gauge railroad, 150 miles long, through his own valuable timber lands; large owner of coal and timber lands; he confined his attention to individual operations in lands and lumber. Home: Detroit, Mich. Died 1900.

WARD, Edgar Melville, painter; b. Urbana, O., Feb. 24, 1839; s. John A. and Eleanor (Macbeth) W.; brother of John Quincy Adams W.; A.B., Miami U., 1858, A.M., 1861; studied art at Nat. Acad., New York, 1870-71, École des Beaux Arts, Paris, France, 1872-78. Now prof. in Nat. Acad. Design. Well known as genre painter; has exhibited at Nat. Acad., the Centennial and subsequent exbns., the Paris salons, etc. N.A., 1883. Home: New York, N.Y. Died May 15, 1915.

WARD, Elizabeth Stuart Phelps, author; b. Boston, Aug. 31, 1844; d. Rev. Austin and Elizabeth Stuart Phelps; m. Herbert Dickinson Ward, Oct. 20, 1888. Began to write for press when 13 yrs. old; lectured before Boston U., 1876. Author: The Gipsy Series (4 vols.); The Gates Ajar, 1868; The Silent Partner, 1871; Doctor Zay, 1882; Beyond the Gates, 1883; The Madonna of the Tubs, 1886; Jack the Fisherman, 1887; Come Forth (with husband), 1890; The Master of the Magicians (with same), 1890; A Singular Life, 1894; The Supply at St. Agatha's, 1896; The Story of Jesus Christ, 1897; Within the Gates, 1901; Successors to Mary the First, 1901; Avery, 1902; Trixy, 1904; The Man in the Case, 1906; Walled In, 1907; Though Life Us Do Part, 1908; Jonathan and David, 1909; The Oath of Allegiance, 1909. Home: Newton Centre, Mass. Died 1911.

WARD, Florence Elizabeth; b. Mauston, Wis.; d. Lemuel J. and Elizabeth (Herrington) W.; grad. Nat. Kindergarten Coll., Chicago, 1903; prof. edn., and in charge of kindergarten training dept., Iowa State Teachers Coll., 1906-14; prof. vocational edn., State Coll. of Wash., 1914-15; was placed in charge of extension work in agriculture and home economics of 12 eastern states, Office of Coöperative Extension Work, U.S. Dept. of Agr.; made trip to Europe under auspices of Nat. Civic League, 1908, to study problems of women; trip to England, Italy and Germany, 1913, to study methods of child care and training. Counselor home demonstration com. of Gen. Fedn. of Women's Clubs. Author: The Montessori Method and the American School. Lecturer. Home: Alexandria, Va. Died Feb. 1934.

WARD, Florence Nightingale Ferguson, surgeon; b. San Francisco, July 10, 1860; d. James P. and Anna J. Ferguson; grad. Normal Coll., San Francisco, 1879; M.D., Hahnemann Med. Coll. of the Pacific, 1887; post-grad. studies, New York Policline, 1887-88; hosps. of Germany and France, 1892; m. James William Ward, July 10, 1895. In practice at San Francisco, 1888—, specializing in gynecology and obstetrics. Fellow Am. Coll. Surgeons. Home: San Francisco, Calif. Died Dec. 16, 1919.

WARD, Frank Gibson, dean theol. sem.; b. Grafton, Vt., Nov. 9, 1869; s. Earl Johnson and Julia Eliza (Batchelder) W.; A.B., U. of Vt., 1891; B.D., Chicago Theol. Sem., 1894; A.M. and Ph.D., U. of Halle, 1898; D.D., Beloit Coll., 1924; m. Jessie Middlekauff, Aug. 10, 1899. Ordained Congl. ministry, 1894; pastor 1st Ch., Emporia, Kan., 1899-1905, Plymouth Ch., Lansing, Mich., 1905-10; prof. religious edn., 1910—, dean, 1912—, Chicago Theol. Sem. Home: Chicago, Ill. Died Oct. 17, 1930.

WARD, Franklin Wilmer, soldier; b. Phila., Pa., Dec. 4, 1870; s. Thomas P. and Sarah Elizabeth (Reeves-Stoy) W.; grad. Horace Binney Sch., Phila.; m. Mabel Loretta Downs, Jan. 9, 1898; 1 son, John Franklin. Enlisted as pvt. N.G. Pa., 1888; commd. 2d lt. N.G.N.Y., 1898; with 6th div. Mexican Border, 1916; chief of staff, adj. 27th Div., World War I, 1917-19; promoted col., comdg. 27th Trains and Mil. Police; comd. 106th U.S. Inf. at battles, St. Souplet, Arbre Guernon, St. Maurice River, France; assigned to War Dept. Gen. Staff, Washington, 1920-22; apptd. The Adj. Gen. of N.Y., 1926; maj. gen., 1930. Decorated with D.S.M. and Silver Star medal (U.S.); Officer Legion of Honor (France); Cross of War with Palm (Belgium); Grand Officer Order of Crown (Roumania); Comdr. Order of Polish Restitution; Conspicuous Service Medal of State of N.Y. Mem. United Spanish War Veterans, Mil. Order World War, Am. Legion, N.Y. Soc. Mil. and Naval Officers of World War, S.R., S.C.V. Co-author: The Service of Coast Artillery (with Gen. Frank T. Hines), 1910. Author: Between the Big Parades, 1932. Home: Albany, N.Y. Died Mar. 17, 1938.

WARD, Frederick King, brig. gen. U.S.A.; b. Newark, O., Mar. 19, 1847; s. Pruden Alling and Julia Bunnell (Ward) W.; grad. U.S. Mil. Acad., 1870; m. Lizzie Bell Dunn, June 26, 1873. Commd. 2d lt. 1st Cav., June 15, 1870; 1st lt., Nov. 11, 1875; capt., Feb. 11, 1887; maj. 10th Cav., July 11, 1899; transferred to 1st Cav., Aug. 2, 1899; lt. col. 14th Cav., Jan. 24, 1903; transferred to 1st Cav., Apr. 24, 1903; detailed insp. gen., Nov. 30, 1904; col. 2d Cav., June 23, 1905; detailed insp. gen., Oct. 1, 1906; assigned to 7th Cav., May 3, 1907; brig. gen. U.S.A., Feb. 11, 1910; retired by operation of law, Mar. 19, 1911. Home: Seattle, Wash. Died Oct. 25, 1933.

WARD, Geneviève (Lucy Geneviève Teresa, Comtesse de Guerbel), tragédienne; b New York, Mar. 27, 1838; d. Samuel and Lucy (Leigh) Ward; ed. in America, France and Italy; m. Comte Constantine de Guerbel, Russian officer, Nov. 10, 1856. Made début as operatic singer at La Scala, Milan, under name of "Madame Guerrabela," 1856; sang in "Messiah," Exter Hall, London, 1862; in winter of 1862 overwork in Cuba ruined her voice for singing. Taught vocal music in New York and prepared for dramatic stage. Made début as tragédienne, Theatre Royal, Manchester, Eng., 1873, as Lady Macbeth; afterward added many rôles, notably Stephanie in "Forget-Me-Not," first prod., Aug. 22, 1879, which she played over 2,000 times in every English-speaking country; played Lady Macbeth in French at Porte St. Martin, Paris, 1877; played several star engagements in U.S.; last appearances with Henry Irving, 1893-97. Played "Blind Queen" in Virgin Goddess at Adelphi Ttheatre, Nov. 1906, and "Volumnia" in Coriolanus at Shakespeare Festival, at Stratford-on-Avon, Apr. 1907. Address: London, Eng. Died Aug. 18, 1922.

WARD, George Clinton, engr.; b. White Plains, N.Y., Jan. 9, 1863; s. James and Elizabeth (Ennis) W.; grad. Phillips Acad., Andover, Mass., 1882; D.Eng., U. of Southern Calif., 1927; Sc.D., Oberlin, 1928; m. Katherine L. Schweinsberg, Sept. 15, 1886; 1 dau., Louise Whipple (Mrs. E. Frank Watkins). Began with engr. corps on construction New York, West Shore & Buffalo R.R., 1882; preliminary surveys, location and constrn. as asst. and chief engr. on various railroads, 1884-1902; in charge water works properties in Ohio, 1902-05; v.p. and gen. mgr. Huntington Land & Improvement Co., 1905-12; v.p. Pacific Light & Power Corp., 1912-17; v.p. Southern Calif. Edison Co., 1917—, later exec. v.p. Home: South Pasadena, Calif. Died Sept. 11, 1933.

WARD, George Gray, capitalist; b. Hertfordshire, Eng., Dec. 30, 1844; ed. pvtly. at Cambridge, Eng. Associated with late John W. Mackay in organizing the Atlantic and Pacific submarine cables of the Commercial Cable Co.; v.p. and gen. mgr. Commercial Co., Commercial Pacific Cable Co.; v.p. Postal Telegraph-Cable Co., The Mackay Cos.; pres. U.S. & Hayti Cable Co. Decorated by Emperor of Germany with decoration of Royal Prussian Crown, 1900, in connection with laying submarine cable between U.S. and Germany, and by Emperor of Japan with insignia of Comdr. of the Rising Sun, 1906, on completion of cable between U.S. and Japan. Home: New York. Died June 15, 1922.

WARD, George Morgan, coll. pres.; b. Lowell, Mass., May 23, 1859; s. Sullivan L. and Mary (Morgan) W.; student at Harvard, 2 yrs., class of 1881; A.B., Dartmouth, 1882, A.M., 1884, D.D., 1900; LL.B., Boston U., 1886; Johns Hopkins, 1894-95; B.D., Andover Theol. Sem., 1896; LL.D., Rollins Coll., 1903, same degree from U. of Fla.; m. Emma Merriam Sprague, June 15, 1896. Admitted to Mass. bar; sec. Internat. Soc. of Christian Endeavor, 1885-89; in business, Lowell, 1890-93; ordained Congl. ministry, 1896; pres. Rollins Coll., Winter Park, Fla., 1895-1903, Wells Coll., Aurora, N.Y., 1903-12, Rollins Coll., 1916-20. Pastor in charge Royal Poinciana Chapel, Palm Beach, Fla., winters, 1900—. V.p. Am. Humane Soc. Home: Billerica Centre, Mass. Died Dec. 28, 1930.

WARD, Hamilton, lawyer; b. Washington, D.C., Jan. 20, 1871; s. Hamilton and Mary Adelia (Chamberlain) W.; ed. under pvt. tutors and in father's law office; m. Grace E. Marsh, Feb. 18, 1903; children—Hamilton, John Chamberlain, Mary, Grace, Peter, Brewster. Admitted to N.Y. bar, 1892, and practiced at Buffalo until 1928; atty. gen. of N.Y., 1928-30; mem. Ward, Flynn, Spring & Tillou. Capt., N.Y. Vol. Inf., Spanish-Am. War. Asst. dist. atty., Erie County, N.Y., 1893-98; supervisor Erie County, 1901-05; commr. Allegany State Park, 1921-29, Erie County Parks, 1924-28 and, 1931—. Republican. Episcopalian. Author: Life and Speeches of Hamilton Ward, 1900; Holland Land Co. Titles, 1902; The History of a Remarkable Lawsuit, 1922. Home: Buffalo, N.Y. Died Oct. 8, 1932.

WARD, Henry Augustus, naturalist; b. Rochester, N.Y., Mar. 9, 1834; s. Henry Meigs and Eliza (Chapin) W.; ed. Middlebury Acad.; also, 1851-52, at Williams Coll., A.M., Williams; LL.D., Rochester U. Asst. to Prof. Louis Agassiz, Harvard Scientific Sch., 1854; studied at Paris, and traveled through Europe and the Orient, 1855-59; m. Phoebe A. Howell, Nov. 1860 (died 1890); m. 2d, Mrs. Lydia Avery Coonley, Mar. 18, 1897. Prof. natural sciences, Rochester U., 1860-65; mgr., gold mines in Mont. and in S.C., 1866-69; traveled, 1870-1900, in all countries, making large and valuable cabinets of mineralogy and geology (known as "Ward Cabinets") which are distributed to univs., coils., etc., throughout U.S. Founded at Rochester Ward's Natural Science Establishment, where cabinets are compiled; acting naturalist of U.S. Expdn. to Santo Domingo, 1871. Fellow A.A.A.S. Author: Notices of the Megatherium Cuvieri; Description of the Most Celebrated Fossil Animals in Royal Museums of Europe. Home: Chicago, Ill. Died 1906.

WARD, Henry Clay, brig. gen. U.S.A.; b. Worcester, Mass., Sept. 10, 1843; s. Artemus, 2d, and Huldah (Reed) W.; ed. pub. schs., Worcester, and army service schs.; m. Susie M. Denny, Feb. 12, 1867; m. 2d, Frances Crutcher, Dec. 6, 1876. Sergt. maj. 15th Mass. Inf., 1861; 2d lt., Apr. 9, 1863; hon. mustered out, Sept. 4, 1863; 1st lt. 57th Mass. Inf., Mar. 9, 1864; capt., July 31, 1864, until mustered out of vol. service, July 30, 1865. In regular army, 2d lt. and 1st lt. 11th Inf., Feb. 23, 1866; promoted through grades to brig. gen., Oct. 30, 1905, and retired. Served throughout Civil War in Army of Potomac, in battles of Ball's Bluff, siege of Yorktown, Fair Oaks, battles before Richmond, Va., June 1862; Seven Days' battles, and battle of the Wilderness; wounded at Antietam; participated battles of Fredericksburg, campaign under Gen. Grant from Rapidan to Petersburg; Spottsylvania (wounded); siege of Petersburg, Yellow Tavern, Va., Ft. Stedman, Va., where was taken prisoner; confined in Libby Prison, Mar. 25, 1865, until capture of Richmond, Va., then joined regt. until surrender of Lee's army. Bvtd. capt. U.S.A., "for bravery at battle of Ft. Stedman, Mar. 24, 1865." Served in Indian campaigns, 1880, and later, and in Philippines; with N.G. Tenn., 1892-96, and elected brig. gen. comdg., 1895. Mason. Episcopalian. Home: Wellesley Hills, Mass. Died Nov. 16, 1925.

WARD, Henry Galbraith, judge; b. New York, Apr. 19, 1851; s. Rev. Henry Dana and Charlotte (Galbraith) W.; B.A. and M.A., U. of Pa., 1870, LL.D., 1917; admitted to bar, 1873; m. Mabel Marquand, Aug. 13, 1891. U.S. circuit judge, 2d Circuit, 1907-25 (resigned). Home: New York, N.Y. Died Aug. 24, 1933.

WARD, Henshaw, author; b. Norfolk, Neb., Nov. 5, 1872; s. Thomas Walter and Clarinda Maria (Clary) W.; B.A., Pomona (Calif.) Coll., 1896; M.A., Yale, 1899; m. Florence Humphreys Jones, July 9, 1926. Teacher of English, Thacher Sch., Ojai, Calif., 1898-1903, Taft Sch., Watertown, Conn., 1903-22; teacher summer session, U. of Ia., 1920, 21, U. of Calif., 1924. Author: (under name Henshaw Ward) Evolution for John Doe, 1925; The Circus of the Intellect (Thobbing), 1926; Exploring the Universe, 1927; Charles Darwin: the Man and His Warfare, 1927; Builders of Delusion, 1931; (under name of C. H. Ward) What Is English?, 1916; Sentence and Theme, 1917; Junior Grammar, 1919; Theme-Building, 1920; Junior Highway to English, 1922; Exploring Nature, 1923; English Evidence, 1925; The M.O.S. series (5 books), 1929; Writing Craft, 1931; Grammar for Composition, 1933. Home: New Haven, Conn. Died Oct. 8, 1935.

WARD, Herbert Dickinson, author; b. Waltham, Mass., June 30, 1861; s. William Hayes and Ellen M. (Dickinson) W.; A.B., Amherst, 1884, A.M., 1887; m. Elizabeth Stuart Phelps, Oct. 30, 1888; m. 2d, Edna J. Jeffress, December 27, 1916. Editorial writer for daily and monthly publications. Author: The New Senior at Andover; The Master of the Magicians; The Captain of the Kittiwink; The Republic Without a President, and Other Short Stories; The White Crown; The Burglar Who Moved Paradise; A Lost Hero (with wife), 1889; Come

Forth (with same), 1890; The Master of the Magicians (with same), 1890; The Light of the World, 1901; A Dash to the Pole; Love Letters of an American Girl. Address: South Berwick, Me. Died June 18, 1932.

WARD, James William, surgeon; b. Minneapolis, Mar. 14, 1861; s. William Emerson and Elvira Jane (Canney) W.; grad. high sch., San Jose, Calif., 1878; M.D., New York Homœ. Med. Coll. and Flower Hosp., 1883; M.A., Hahnemann Med. Coll., Philadelphia. Med. staff Wards Island Homœ. Hosp. and res. phys. Hahnemann Hosp., New York, 1883-85; instr. physiology, 1885-86, dean and prof. abdominal surgery and gynecol., 1898-1918, Hahnemann Med. Coll. of the Pacific, San Francisco; served as gynecologist to Fabiola Hosp., Oakland, and as pres. Health Dept. of San Francisco, 1902-07; pres. Health Advisory Bd.; chmn. bd. Nursery for Homeless Children; abdominal surgeon, San Francisco and Hahnemann hosps. Founder Southern Homœ. Dispensary, 1890, Homœ. Sanatorium, 1896; founder Hahnemann Hosp., 1905. Pres. Am. Inst. Homœopathy, 1909-10 (trustee 6 yrs.); fellow Am. Coll. Surgeons, 1922. Mason. Office: San Francisco, Calif. Died July 1939.

WARD, John Chamberlain, bishop; b. Elmira, N.Y., Aug. 27, 1873; s. Hamilton and Mary Adelia (Chamberlain) W.; A.B., Harvard, 1896; B.D., Gen. Theol. Sem., 1899, S.T.D., 1923; D.D., Kenyon, 1924; unmarried. Deacon, 1899, priest, 1900, P.E. Ch.; rector St. Stephen's Ch., Buffalo, 1899-1902, Grace Ch., Buffalo, 1902-21; consecrated bishop of Erie, Pa., Sept. 22, 1921. Chaplain 74th Inf., N.G.N.Y., on Mexican border, 1916; chaplain same, local guard duty and Wadsworth, S.C., 1917; chaplain 105th Machine Gun Batn., 107th Inf., and 108th Inf., 27th Div., A.E.F., 1918, serving 9 mos., overseas; wounded in action; hon. discharged Mar. 1918, rank of capt. D.S.C. (U.S.); M.C. (British). Republican. Home: Erie, Pa. Died Apr. 20, 1929.

WARD, John Elliott, lawyer; b. Sunbury, Ga., Oct. 2, 1814; entered Amherst, 1831, but withdrew before completing course; admitted to bar, 1835; attended lectures at Harvard Law Sch.; solicitor-gen. Eastern dist. of Ga., 1836-38; U.S. dist. atty. for Ga., 1838; mem. Ga. legislature, 1839, 1845, and (speaker) 1853; mayor of Savannah, 1854; pres. Nat. Dem. Conv., Cincinnati, 1856; pres. Ga. senate and acting lt. gov., 1857; resigned, 1858; U.S. minister to China, 1858-61. Lawyer in New York, 1866—. Home: New York, N.Y. Died 1902.

WARD, John Henry Hobart, deputy co. clerk New York County; b. New York, June 17, 1823; ed. Collegiate Sch. of Trinity Ch.; in Mexican war as sergt. maj. 7th U.S. inf., from Corpus Christi to Cerro Gordo; asst. commissary gen. State of N.Y., 1850, commissary gen., 1850-59; col. 38th N.Y. vols., 1860; brig. gen. vols., Oct. 2, 1862; comd. 2d brigade, 1st div., 3d corps; comd. 1st div., 3d corps, at Gettysburg, Manassas Gap and Kelly's Ford, Army of Potomac. Mem. Supreme Council 33° Masonry. Home: New York, N.Y. Died 1903.

WARD, John Quincy Adams, sculptor; b. Urbana, O., June 29, 1830; s. John A. and Eleanor Macbeth W.; studied under and assisted Henry K. Browne, 1850-57; in Washington, 1857-58; later visited Indian country; had studio in New York, 1861—. Asso., 1862, academician, 1863—, Nat. Acad. Design (v.p., 1870-71, and pres., 1872); pres. Nat. Sculpture Soc. from its incorporation, 1896; v.p. Fine Arts Federation; trustee Metropolitan Museum; v.p. Century Club, and many other art socs. Among his principal statues are The Indian Hunter, Seventh Regt. Citizen Soldier, Shakespeare, and The Pilgrim (all in Central Park, New York); The Freedman, The Good Samaritan (in Boston); statues of Washington (Wall Street), Henry Ward Beecher (in City Hall, Brooklyn), Commodore Perry (Newport, R.I.), Israel Putnam (Hartford, Conn.), Gen. George H. Thomas (Washington), etc.; Crowning Group of Victory on the Naval Arch (for Dewey Reception) in New York; equestrian statues of Sheridan and Hancock; Pediment for Stock Exchange Bldg., New York City. Home: New York, N.Y. Died 1910.

WARD, John Wesley, physician; b. Salem, N.J., Feb. 12, 1840; s. Samuel Vance and Esther (Griffith) W.; acad. edn. Fairfield, N.Y.; M.D., U. of Pa., 1866; hon. A.M., Amherst, 1874; m. Horacana B Sager, Mar. 5, 1873. Apptd. 2d asst. phys., May 1866, sr. asst. phys., Feb. 1870, med. supt., Apr. 1876—, N.J. State Hosp. Address: Pennington, N.J. Died Aug. 23, 1916.

WARD, Julia Elizabeth, teacher; b. Plymouth, N.H., June 3, 1832; d. George Whitfield and Jemima Smith (Emerson) Ward; Mt. Holyoke Sem. (now Coll.), grad. 1857; D.Litt., Mt. Holyoke Coll., 1901; unmarried. Teacher, 1857-67, asso. prin., 1867-72, prin or pres., 1872-83, Mt. Holyoke Sem.; later pvt. teacher English lit. Congregationalist. Home: Lowell, Mass. Died Aug. 14, 1921.

WARD, Leslie Dodd, insurance official; b. Madison, N.J., July 1, 1845; s. Moses D. and Louise (Sayre) W.; ed. Newark (N.J.) Acad.; M.D., Coll. Phys. and Surg. (Columbia), 1868; m. Minnie Perry, Mar. 5, 1874. Connected with the Prudential Ins. Co. from its orgn., v.p., 1884—. Home: Madson, N.J. Died 1910.

WARD, Lester Frank, geologist; b. Joliet, Ill., June 18, 1841; A.B., Columbian (now George Washington) U., 1869, LL.B., 1871, A.M., 1873, LL.D., 1897. Served in Civil War; in U.S. Treasury Dept., 1865-72; asst. geologist, 1881-88, geologist, 1888, U.S. Geol. Survey. Specially known for researches in paleobotany; later extensive contbr. to the literature of sociology. Mem. Am. Acad. Polit. and Social Science; fellow A.A.A.S. Author: Guide to the Flora of Washington and Vicinity, 1881; Dynamic Sociology, 1883; Sketch of Paleobotany, 1885; Synopsis of the Flora of the Laramie Group, 1886; Types of the Laramie Flora, 1887; Geographical Distribution of Fossil Plants, 1888; Psychic Factors of Civilization; Psychological Basis of Social Economics; Political Ethics of Spencer; Principles of Sociology; Outlines of Sociology, 1898; Sociology and Economics, 1899; Pure Sociology, 1903; Text-book of Sociology (with James Quayle Dealey), 1905. Home: Providence, R.I. Died April 18, 1913.

WARD, Lydia Avery Coonley, author; b. Lynchburg, Va.; d. Benjamin F. and Susan (Look) Avery; ed. Louisville, Utica, and Phila.; lived in Louisville; m. John C. Coonley, 1867 (died 1882); m. 2d, Henry Augustus Ward, 1897 (died 1906). Lived in St. Louis, 1867-68, Louisville, 1868-73, Chicago, 1873—. Author: Under the Pines, and Other Verses, 1895; Our Flag, cantata (music by Dr. George F. Root), 1896; Singing Verses for Children, 1897; Magic Hour (cantata); Love Songs, 1898; Christmas in Other Lands; Washington and Lincoln; The Melody of Life, 1921; The Melody of Love, 1921; The Melody of Childhood, 1921. Contbr. to newspapers and mags. Founder of summer sch. at Wyoming, N.Y. Home: Wyoming, N.Y. Died Feb. 26, 1924.

WARD, May Alden, author; b. in Ohio, Mar. 1, 1853; d. Prince W. and Rebecca (Neal) Alden; direct descendant of John Alden and Priscilla Mullins, of Plymouth Colony; M.L.A., Ohio Wesleyan U., 1872, Phi Beta Kappa; honorary A.M., 1912; studied in Germany, 1874-75; m. William Godman Ward, May 3, 1873. Pres. Mass. State Fedn. of Women's Clubs, 1901-04, 1907-08; v.p. Gen. Fedn. of Women's Clubs, 1904-08; pres. N.E. Woman's Club; commr. of Mass. to St. Louis and Portland expns. Editor Fedn. Bulletin (nat. official publn. of Gen. Fedn. of Women's Clubs), 1903-10. Author: Life of Dante, 1887; Petrarch, a Sketch of His Life and Works, 1891; Old Colony Days, 1896; Prophets of the Nineteenth Century, 1900. Home: Boston, Mass. Died Jan. 15, 1918.

WARD, (A.) Montgomery, merchant; b. Chatham, N.J., 1844; s. Sylvester A. and Julia L. M. (Greene) W.; g.g.s. Capt. Israel Montgomery Ward, of Revolutionary fame; self-ed. and self-made; m. Elizabeth J. Cobb, 1872. Founded firm of Montgomery Ward & Co., 1872, pres., 1872—. Home: Chicago, Ill. Died Dec. 7, 1913.

WARD, Perley Erik, publisher; b. Chicago, Ill., Oct. 4, 1880; s. Cyrus Joseph and Rebecca Isadore (Steele) W.; ed. grammar schs., Chicago; m. Susanna Lewis Knight, Feb. 1, 1910; children—Susanne, Elizabeth, Robert Erik, Evelyn. Began with Constrn. News (mag.), Chicago, 1894; with the Rams Horn, 1897-1900, Orange Judd Co. and Phelps Pub. Co., 1900-18; asst. treas. Good Housekeeping Co., Springfield, Mass., 1913-18; asst. to pres. F. M. Lupton Co., pubs., N.Y. City, 1919-20; with Farm Journal, 1920—, pres., 1927-35, later dir. circulation. Dir Nat. Pubs. Assn., Agrl. Pubs. Assn. (pres. and dir.). Republican. Presbyn. Mason. Home: Wyncote, Pa. Died Jan. 22, 1939.

WARD, Reginald Henshaw, investment securities; b. Newton, Mass., Apr. 22, 1862; s. Andrew Henshaw and Anna Harriet Walcott (Field) W.; ed. pub. and pvt. schs.; m. Edyth Ward Newcomb (cousin), Nov. 1889 (died 1906). Mem. firm Clark, Ward & Co., bankers and brokers, Boston and New York, 1885-1901; in business at London and Paris, 1897-1915; pres. Henshaw, Ward & Co., Inc., New York; pres. Foreign & Domestic Acceptance Corp. of Mass., offices New York and Boston. Consul gen. for Rumania, at London, 1901-06; sec. Nicaragua Legation, Portugal, 1906-13; chargé d'affaires at The Hague, 1912-13; apptd. minister to Austria by Nicaragua, 1907. Apptd. mem. Com. to Rehabilitate Russia, June 1921. Decorated Grand Cross of Villa Vicosa, Grand Comdr. Christ (Portugese); Grand Comdr. Carlos III (Spanish); Grand Comdr. St. Sava (Serbian); Grand Officer Crown of Rumania (Rumanian); Hereditary Count, by Papal decree, Leo XIII, 1901; Grand Comdr. Sun and Lion (Persia); Grand Placque Red Cross of Spain; coronation medal Alphonso XIII, Spain, and King Carlos of Roumania; Grand Cross Order of Merit of Red Cross of Cuba. Fellow Royal Geog Soc. Republican. Episcopalian. Home: New York, N.Y. Died Nov 20, 1925.

WARD, Richard Halsted, biologist, microscopist; b. Bloomfield, N.J., June 17, 1837; s. Israel Currie and Almeda (Hanks) W.; A.B., Williams, 1858, A.M., 1861; M.D., College Phys. and Surg. (Columbia), 1862; m. Charlotte Allen Baldwin, June 10, 1862; father of Henry Baldwin W. Acting asst. surgeon in Civil War; practicing medicine at Troy, N.Y., 1863—. Instr. botany, 1867, prof. and lecturer on histology and microscopy, 1869-92, Rensselaer Poly. Inst.; gov., 1st v.p. and chmn. med. bd. Marshall Infirmary and Sanitarium, 1868—. Distinguished for original research in econ. botany and microscopy; witness as microscopist in murder and forgery trials, etc. Mem. for U.S. of hon. com. of patrons Internat. Expn. of Microscopy, Antwerp, 1891; del. at several meetings of Internat. Med. Congress and Brit. Assn. Adv. Sci. Fellow Royal Micros. Soc., A.A.A.S., Am. Acad. Medicine; pres. Nat. Micros. Congress, Indianapolis, 1878, Am. Micros. Soc. 1879 (hon. mem. 1896), Am. Postal Micros. Club, 1895, Troy Scientific Assn., 1870; hon. mem. Société Belge de Microscopie. Writer of numerous monographs and contributions on micros. subjects. Address: Troy, N.Y. Died Oct. 28, 1917.

WARD, Robert De Courcy, climatologist; b. Boston, Nov. 29, 1867; s. Henry Veazey and Anna Saltonstall (Merrill) W.; A.B., Harvard, 1889, A.M., 1893; m. Emma Lane, Apr. 28, 1897; children—Henry DeCourcy, Robert Saltonstall, Anna Saltonstall Magruder, Emma Lane. Asst. in physical geography, 1890-94, asst. in meteorology, 1894-95, instr., 1895-96, instr. climatology, 1896-1900, asst. prof., 1900-10, prof., 1910—, Harvard; exchange prof., Western colleges, 1927. Editor Am. Meteorol. Jour., 1892-96, contbg. editor Geog. Review. Member Shaler Memorial Expdn. to Brazil, 1908. Fellow Am. Acad. Arts and Sciences, Royal Meteorol. Soc., London, Assn. Am. Geographers (pres. 1917), Am. Meteorol. Soc. (pres. 1920, 21), Am. Assn. Advancement of Science; mem. Harvard Travellers Club (gold medalist, 1926); one of founders, 1894, Immigration Restriction League. Episcopalian. Author: Practical Exercises in Elementary Meteorology, 1899; Climate Considered Especially in Relation to Man, 1908; The Climates of the United States, 1925. Translator: Hann's Handbuch der Klimatologie, Vol. I. 1903. Contbr. to scientific jours., and to 11th, 12th and 13th editions Ency. Britannica. Home: Cambridge, Mass. Died Nov. 12, 1931.

WARD, Samuel Baldwin, physician; b. New York, June 8, 1842; s. Lebbeus Baldwin and Abby Dwight (Partridge) W.; brother of Willard Parker W.; A.B., Columbia, 1861, A.M., 1864; M.D., Georgetown U., 1864; hon. Ph.D., Union, 1882; m. Nina A. Wheeler, Oct. 10, 1871 (died 1883); m. 2d, Grace Fitz-Randolph Schenck, widow Erastus Corning, 3d, Apr. 29, 1897. Curator Med. Mus., Columbia, 1867-69; prof. anatomy, 1867-70, surgery, 1870-76, Woman's Med. Coll. of New York Infirmary; prof. surg. pathology, 1876-84, theory and practice of medicine, 1884—, dean, 1903—, Albany Med. Coll. Pres. bd. trustees Dudley Obs. Home: Albany, N.Y. Died June 3, 1915.

WARD, Seth, bishop M.E. Ch., S.; b. Leon County, Tex., Nov. 15, 1858; s. Samuel Goode and Sarah Ann (Wyche) W.; ed. pub. schs., Tex.; D.D., Southwestern U., Tex., 1900; ordained clergyman, M.E. Ch., S., 1881; m. Margaret E. South, Jan. 5, 1886. Pastor at Kosse, Calvert, Galveston, Huntsville, and Shearn Memorial Ch., Houston; asst. missionary sec., M.E. Ch., S., 1902-06; elected bishop, May 1906. Home: Houston, Tex. Died 1909.

WARD, Thomas, brig. gen. U.S.A.; b. West Point, N.Y., Mar. 18, 1839; s. Bryan and Eliza W.; grad. U.S. Mil. Acad., 1863; hon. A.M., Union Coll., 1878; m. Katharine L. Mott, Apr. 20, 1870; father of Philip R., colonel F.A.; and of Thomas, Jr., midshipman U.S.N., killed Apr. 13, 1904, aboard battleship Missouri; and of John M., 1st lieutenant A.E.F. Commd. 2d lieut., 1st U.S. Arty., June 11, 1863; 1st lt., July 18, 1864; capt., Nov. 1, 1876; maj. a.a.g., June 28, 1884; lt. col. a.a.g., Aug. 31, 1893; col. a.a.g., Sept. 11, 1897; brig. gen., July 22, 1902; retired at own request after over 40 yrs.' service, July 22, 1902. Bvtd.: 1st lt., June 3, 1864, "for gallant and meritorious services in battle of Cold Harbor, Va."; capt., Mar. 13, 1865, for same during the war. Prof. mil. science and tactics, Union Coll., 1873-77; pres. Bd. of Visitors to U.S. Mil. Acad., 1907. Home: Rochester, N.Y. Died Mar. 25, 1926.

WARD, Willard Parker, mining engr.; b. New York, Oct. 12, 1845; s. Lebbeus B. and Abby Dwight (Partridge) W.; A.B., Columbia, 1865, A.M., 1871; studied in mining schs., Clausthal, and Berlin, 1865-69; Ph.D., N.Y. U., 1875; m. Ruby, d. John Erskine, U.S. judge, Dist. of Ga., Oct. 23, 1872. Engaged in professional work, 1869—; 1st maker of ferromanganese in U.S. (1874). Engaged in gold and silver-mining in Far West, 1883—. Home: Savannah, Ga. Died Jan. 17, 1928.

WARD, William Breining, wholesale baker; b. Pittsburgh, Pa., Feb. 9, 1884; s. Robert Boyd and Mary Catherine (Breining) W.; student Allegheny Coll., Meadville, Pa., 1900-02; Wharton Sch., U. of Pa., 1903-05; m. Ethel Haney, Nov. 29, 1911; children—William B., Jack Boyd, Jane Elizabeth, Robert Theodore, Ethel Susanne. Began with the

Ward-Mackey Co., bakers, Pittsburgh, 1906; business rep. Ward-Corby Co., Boston, Providence and other cities, 1907-08; elected, 1908, treas. and dir. Ward Bread Co., later the Ward Baking Co., of which was mgr. plant in Bronx Borough, N.Y. City; resigned 1912 and incorporated the Ward Bros. Co., Rochester, N.Y., organizing cos. in Ohio, Ind. and Ill.; organized United Bakeries Corp. (capital $10,000,000) in 1921, acquiring many cos. and plants in Middle West and South; purchased, 1924, outstanding stock of Ward Baking Co., of which became pres. and resigned as chmn. bd. United Bakeries Corp.; later chmn. bd. Ward Backing Corp. Trustee Robert Boyd Ward Home for Children, Pittsburgh; trustee Syracuse U. Republican. Methodist. Mason. Home: New Rochelle, N.Y. Died Feb. 6, 1929.

WARD, William G., coll. prof.; b. Sandusky, O., Nov. 5, 1848; s. Hibbard Porter and Ann M. (Burdett) W.; A.B., Ohio Wesleyan U., 1872, A.M., 1875; B.D., Drew Theol. Sem., 1873; U. of Halle, 1873-74; later at Berlin; m. May Alden, May 3, 1873. Prin. Vermilion Inst., Hayesville, O., 1875-76; prof. history and polit. science, Baldwin U., Ohio, 1887-90; pres. Spokane (Wash.) Coll., 1890-92; prof. English lit. and head of dept. of English, Syracuse U., 1893-98, Emerson Coll. of Oratory, Boston, 1898—. Author: Tennyson's Debt to Environment, 1898; The Poetry of Robert Browning, 1898; Art for Schools, 1899; Studies in Literature, 1901. Died Nov. 3, 1923.

WARD, William Hayes, editor; b. Abington, Mass., June 25, 1835; s. Rev. James Wilson and Hetta Lord (Hayes) W.; brother of Susan Hayes W.; A.B., Amherst, 1856, A.M., 1859; Union Theol. Sem., 1856-57; grad. Andover Theol. Sem., 1859; D.D., Rutgers, 1873, New York U., 1873; LL.D., Amherst, 1885; m. Ellen M. Dickinson, 1859 (died 1874); father of Herbert Dickinson W. Ordained Congl. ministry, 1860; pastor Oskaloosa, Kan., 1859-60, teacher Utica (N.Y.) Free Acad., 1863-65; prof. Latin and sciences, Ripon (Wis.) Coll., 1865-67; asso. editor, 1868-70, superintending editor, 1870-96, editor-in-chief, 1896-1913, hon. editor, 1913—, The Independent, New York. Lecturer on Assyriology, Yale, 1878-79; dir. Wolfe expdn. to Babylonia, 1884-85. Trustee Amherst, 1891—. Pres. Am. Oriental Soc., 1890-94, 1909-10. Author: World's Christmas Hymn, 1883; Report of the Wolfe Expedition to Babylonia, 1885; Biography of Sidney Lanier, 1885; Cylinders and Other Oriental Seals in the Library of J. Pierpont Morgan, 1909; The Seal Cylinders of Western Asia, 1909; What I Believe and Why; also various notes on Oriental antiquities, etc. Home: South Berwick, Me. Died Aug. 28, 1916.

WARDALL, Ruth Aimee, home economist; b. Tolono, Ill.; d. Xenophon Leonidas and Emma A. (Sawyer) Wardall; student Knox Coll., Galesburg, Ill., 1895-97; A.B., U. of Ill., 1903, A.M., 1907. Teacher of Latin, Batavia (Ill.) High Sch., 1897-99; head home economics dept., S.D. State Coll., Brookings, S.D., 1903-06, Ohio State U., 1907-13, State U. of Ia., 1913-21, U. of Ill., 1921—. Presbyn. Author: A Study of Foods, 1914; Economics of the Family (joint author), 1923. Home: Urbana, Ill. Died July 15, 1936.

WARDE, Frederick, actor; b. Wardington, Oxfordshire, Eng., Feb. 23, 1851; s. Thomas and Anne (Barkham) W.; ed. City of London Sch.; studied law, then went upon stage; Litt.D., U. of Southern Calif., 1927; m. Annie Edmondson, 1871; children—Arthur Frederick, Annie Emelia, Ernest Charles (dec.), May. First appearance in minor part in Macbeth, Lyceum Theatre, Sunderland, Eng., 1867, then in successive seasons at Theatre Royal, Glasgow, Amphitheatre, Leeds and Princess Theatre, Manchester. Came to U.S., 1874; leading man in Booth's Theatre, New York, 3 yrs.; supported Edwin Booth and John McCullough; starred in all the greater tragedies, part of the time with Louis James, Sept. 1, 1881—. Lecturer on Shakespeare and kindred subjects. Author: Shakespeare's Fools; Fifty Years of Make-Believe, 1920; Shakespearean Studies Simplified, 1925. Home: Brooklyn, N.Y. Died Feb. 7, 1935.

WARDER, George Woodward, lawyer, author; b. Richmond, Mo., May 20, 1848; s. Luther Fairfax and Ellen K. (Woodward) W.; ed. at Chillicothe, Mo., and, 1865, U. of Mo.; m. Virginia D. McWilliams (died 1887). Admitted to Missouri bar, 1866; large investor in Kansas City real estate; built many houses, 3 hotels and Warder Grand Opera House; mayor, Kansas City, 1886. Literary and scientific lecturer. Author: Poetic Fragments, 1873; Eden Dell, or Love's Wanderings (poems), 1878; Utopian Dreams and Lotus Leaves (poems), 1885 (London); After Which, All Things (novel), 1895; The New Cosmogony, 1898; Invisible Light, or Electric Theory of Creation, 1899; The Conflict Between Man and Mammon, 1896; The Cities of the Sun, 1901; The Stairway to the Stars, 1902; The Universe a Vast Electric Organization, 1903; Life In Celestial Sun Worlds, 1905. Home: Kansas City, Mo. Deceased.

WARDER, John Haines; b. Cincinnati, Jan. 21, 1846; s. Dr. John A. and Elizabeth Bowne (Haines) W.; B.M.E., Polytechnic Coll. of Pa., Phila., 1867; m. Louise Hagen, Sept. 2, 1880. Engring. business Calif. and Ga., later with various rys.; civ. engr., Chicago, 1898-1900; sec. and librarian Western Soc. Engrs., Chicago, Jan. 1901—. also editor Jour. Western Soc. Engrs. Died Aug. 31, 1915.

WARDER, Robert Bowne, chemist; b. Cincinnati, March 28, 1848; s. John A. and Elizabeth Bowne W.; grad. Earlham Coll., Richmond, Ind., 1866, A.M., 1873; grad. Lawrence Scientific Sch., Harvard, B.S. (in chemistry), 1874; also studied in Germany, 1874-75; prof U. of Cincinnati, 1875-79, Haverford Coll., 1879-80, Purdue U., Ind. (and State chemist), 1883-87; prof. physics and chemistry, Harvard U., 1887—; m. Gulielma M. Dorland, Mar. 25, 1884. Fellow A.A.A.S. (v.p. for chemistry, 1890). Author of various papers on physical chemistry. Died 1905.

WARDMAN, Ervin, journalist; b. Salt Lake City, Utah, Dec. 25, 1865; s. George and Mary Virginia (Ervin) W.; A.B., Harvard, 1888; m. Caroline Klink Eyre, May 14, 1902; m. 2d, Violet Boyer, Feb. 8, 1910. On editorial staff New York Tribune, 1888-95; mng. editor, 1895-96, editor-in-chief, 1896-1916, New York Press; v.p. New York Press Co., Ltd.; pub The Sun, New York, July 1, 1916—, and New York Herald, Jan. 1920—; v.p. New York Herald Co., Sun Printing & Pub. Assn., Sun-Herald Corp. Member Troop A, U.S.V., Spanish-Am. War; apptd. 1st lt. 202d N.Y. Inf., a.-d.-c. to Maj. Gen. John R. Brooke, U.S.A., in Puerto Rico campaign. Republican. Episcopalian. Home: New Rochelle, N.Y. Died Jan. 13, 1923.

WARDROP, Robert, banker; b. Allegheny, Pa., July 17, 1850; s. James and Elizabeth (Thompson) W.; ed. Western U. (now U. of Pittsburgh); m. Agnes D. Miller, Oct. 11, 1877. In employ Ira B McVay & Co., bankers, 1869-73; paying teller Tradesman's Nat. Bank, 1874-77; treas. Pa. Lead Co., 1877-91; v.p. and cashier Tradesman's Nat. Bank, 1891-99; same, Peoples Nat. Bank of Pittsburgh, 1899-1903, pres., 1903-21, and after merger of People's Nat. Bank with First Nat. Bank, 1921, chmn. bd. of latter; dir. Fed. Res. Bank (Cleveland), Peoples-Pittsburgh Trust Co. Home: Sewickley, Pa. Died Sept. 28, 1937.

WARDWELL, William Thomas, capitalist; b. Bristol, R.I., Feb. 1, 1827; s. William Taylor and Mary (Hawes) W.; m. Eliza W. Lanterman, 1852; m. 2d, Martha W. Ruff, Dec. 1889. Treas. Standard Oil Co.; trustee Colonial Trust Co.; trustee Greenwich Savings Bank. Pres. and treas. N.Y. Red Cross Hosp. Prominent in Prohibition party; candidate for mayor New York, 1886, for gov. N.Y., 1900. Home: New York, N.Y. Died 1911.

WARE, Arthur, architect; b. New York, N.Y., Aug. 2, 1876; s. James Edward and Edith Cordelia (Backus) W.; student Wyoming Sem., Kingston, Pa., 1890-92, Dr. Chapins Sch., New York, 1892-94; B.S., Sch. of Architecture, Columbia, 1898; student Ecole de Beaux Arts, Paris, France, 1901-05; m. Florence Cobb Peterson, May 11, 1909; children—Arthur, Wilson Peterson. Architect with James E. Ware & Sons, New York, 1898-1918; mem. firm F.B.&A. Ware, 1918—; patron Atelier Ware, New York, 1912-20; asso. prof. of architecture, Columbia, 1914-22. Served in Co. B, 7th Regt., N.Y., 1899-1909. Awarded Columbia traveling scholarship, 1902. Mem. Soc. of Beaux Arts Architects (pres. 1931-33). Republican. Episcopalian. Mason, Elk. Home: Briarcliff Manor, N.Y. Died Feb. 19, 1939.

WARE, Edward Twichell, univ. pres.; b. Atlanta, Ga., Mar. 24, 1874; s. Edmund Asa (founder and 1st pres. Atlanta U.) and Sarah Jane (Twichell) W.; grad. Hartford (Conn.) High Sch., 1893; A.B., Yale, 1897; grad. Union Theol. Sem., 1901; m. Alice Holdship, June 30, 1905; children—Alexander Holdship, Henry Holdship. Chaplain, 1901-07, pres., 1907-22, pres. emeritus, and trustee, Atlanta U. Conglist. Home: Montclair, N.J. Died May 19, 1927.

WARE, Eugene F. ("Ironquill"), lawyer; b. Hartford, Conn., May 29, 1841; s. Hiram B. and Amanda Melvina (Holbrook) W.; ed. pub. schs., Burlington, Ia.; served through Civil War in Co. E, 1st Ia. Inf., and Co. L, 4th Ia. Cav., and mustered out as Capt Co. F, 7th Ia. Cav.; admitted to bar, Fort Scott, Kan., June 18, 1871, and to Supreme Ct. of U.S.; m. Jeannette P. Huntington, Oct. 22, 1874. Mem Kan. Senate, 1879-84; del. 2 Rep. Nat. convs.; U.S. pension commr., May 10, 1902-Jan. 1, 1905; mem. law firm Ware, Nelson & Ware, Kansas City, Kan Republican. Author: The Rise and Fall of the Saloon, 1900; The Lyon Campaign and History of First Iowa Infantry, 1907; The Indian Campaign of 1864, 1908, Rhymes of Ironquill, 1908; Ithuriel, 1909; From Court to Court, 1909. Translator: Coronado's March (from French of Ternaux-Compans, of Castaneda's account, 1596), 1895; Roman Water Law (from Latin of Justinian), 1905. Contbr. to legal and lit. publs. Home: Kansas City, Kan. Died 1911.

WARE, Helen (Helen Remer), actress; b. San Francisco, Calif., Oct. 15, 1877; d. John August and Elinor (Ware) Remer; ed. New York Normal Coll. Début with Maude Adams in "The Little Minister," 1899-1900; appeared in "An American Gentleman," "Under Two Flags," "Quo Vadis," etc.; played Celia in "The Kreutzer Sonata," 1906-07; rôle of Emma Brooks, in "Paid in Full," "The Third Degree," seasons 1908-09, Hudson Theatre, New York; appeared in "The Price," at Hudson Theatre, New York, 1911; with "The Escape," 1913; starred in "Within the Law," Eltinge Theatre, New York, 1913-14; in all star cast, "The Celebrated Case," Empire Theatre, New York, 1915; all star Red Cross tour, in "Out There," 1917, co-star with Lou Tellegen, 1919; played in "The Wandering Jew," "The Wasp," "The Fascinating Devil," "Thou Desperate Pilot" (1927), etc.; also appeared in vaudeville and motion pictures. Died Jan. 25, 1939.

WARE, Lewis Sharpe, engr., editor; b. Phila., June 18, 1851; s. Lewis S. and Elizabeth W. (Roberts) W.; Hill Sch., Pottstown, Pa.; grad. École Centrale, Paris, 1875; unmarried. A leader in establishing sugar-beet industry in U.S.; sent several tons of beet seed to U.S., 1874; which was gratuitously distributed among farmers east and west; investigated world's sugar production, visiting all sugar producing countries; wrote articles protesting against expensive and futile sorghum experiments of U.S. Dept. Agr., and in favor of the sugar beet. Sent to Paris Expn., 1889; apptd. by U.S. Govt., 1900, mem. Internat. Jury, Paris Expn., to represent cane and beet sugar industries of U.S., Cuba and Hawaii; U.S. commr. gen. Internat. Expn., Liege, Belgium, 1905. Chevalier Mérite Agricole, 1893, Officier, 1904; Chevalier de la Légion d'Honneur, 1901, Officier, 1906; Officer Ordre de Leopold; Commandeur Etoile Noire; Commandeur of Cambodge; Officier de l'Instruction Publique; Grand Officier Nichan Iftikhar. Editor The Sugar Beet (monthly jour.); contbr. to many jours. on sugar question; presented exhaustive paper on The Sugar Beet Industry at Nat. Tariff Conv., New York, 1881. Author: The Sugar Beet, 1880; Study of the Various Sources of Sugar, 1881; Production, Requirements and Selection of Sugar Beet Seed, 1896; Sugar Beet Seed, 1898; Cattle Feeding with Sugar Beets, Sugar, Molasses, etc., 1902; Beet Sugar, Manufacturing and Refining (2 vols.), 1907. Died Nov. 20, 1918.

WARE, William Robert, architect; b. Cambridge, Mass., May 27, 1832; s. Rev. Henry, Jr. and Mary Lovell (Pickard) W.; A.B., Harvard, 1852, B.S., 1856, LL.D., 1896; unmarried. Practiced architecture at Boston, 1860-81; prof. architecture, Mass. Inst. Tech., 1865-81, Columbia, 1881-1903, prof. emeritus, 1903—. Fellow Am. Acad. Arts and Sciences. Author: Modern Perspective, 1882; The American Vignola, 1903. Address: Milton, Mass. Died June 9, 1915.

WARFIELD, Benjamin Breckinridge, theologian; b. Lexington, Ky., Nov. 5, 1851; s. William and Mary Cabell (Breckinridge) W.; brother of Ethelbert Dudley W.; A.B., Princeton U., 1871, A.M., 1874; grad. Princeton Theol. Sem., 1876; U. of Leipzig, 1876-77; D.D., 1880, LL.D., 1892, Princeton; LL.D., Davidson College, N.C., 1892; Litt.D., Lafayette Coll., Pa., 1911; and S.T.D., Univ. of Utrecht, 1913; m. Annie Pearce Kinkead, Aug. 3, 1876. Ordained to Presbyterian ministry, 1879; instr. N.T. lang. and lit., 1878-79, prof., 1879-87, Western Theol. Sem.; prof. didactic and polemical theology, Princeton Theol. Sem., 1887—. Editor The Presbyterian and Reformed Rev. (quarterly), 1890-1902. Author: The Gospel of the Incarnation, 1893; Two Studies in the History of Doctrine, 1893; The Right of Systematic Theology, 1897; The Significance of the Westminster Standards, 1898; Acts and Pastoral Epistles, 1902; The Power of God, Unto Salvation (sermons), 1903; The Lord of Glory, 1907; Calvin as a Theologian and Calvinism Today, 1909; Hymns and Religious Verses, 1910; How Shall We Baptize?, 1911; The Saviour of the World (sermons), 1914; The Plan of Salvation, 1915; Faith and Life, 1916; Counterfeit Miracles, 1918; Calvin als Theoloog en de stand van het Calvinisme in onzen Tijd, 1919; also numerous articles to encys., revs. and newspapers. Lecturer on Smyth Foundation, Columbia (S.C.) Theol. Sem., 1917-18. Home: Princeton, N.J. Died Feb. 17, 1921.

WARFIELD, Edwin, governor; b. Howard County, Md., May 7, 1848; s. Albert G. and Margaret (Gassaway Watkins) W.; ed. pub. schs. Howard County and St. Timothy's Hall, Catonsville, Md.; m. Emma Nicodemus. Founder and pres. Fidelity and Deposit Co. of Md. and Fidelity Trust Co., Baltimore. State senator, and register of wills of Howard County; pres. of senate, 1886; surveyor port of Baltimore under President Cleveland, 1886-90; del. Dem. Nat. Conv., 1896; gov. Md., 1904-08. Pres. gen. Nat. Soc. S.A.R.; mem. advisory com. Mt. Vernon Assn. Died Mar. 31, 1920.

WARFIELD, Ethelbert Dudley, coll. pres.; b. Lexington, Ky., Mar. 16, 1861; s. William and Mary Cabell (Breckinridge) W.; A.B., Princeton, 1882, A.M., 1885; U. of Oxford, Eng., 1882-83; LL.B., Columbia, 1885; LL.D., Princeton, 1891, Miami U., 1891, U. of Pa., 1910; D.D., Washington and Jefferson, 1902; Litt.D., Lafayette, 1915; m. Sarah Lacy Brookes, Jan. 28, 1886; m. 2d, Eleanor F. Tilton, Aug. 28, 1890; children—William, Mary C., Eleanor F., Ethelbert D., Ruth B., Benjamin B., Robert B.

Practiced law at Lexington, Ky., 1886-88; pres. and prof. history, Miami U., 1888-91; pres. and prof. history, Lafayette Coll., 1891-1914; pres. Wilson Coll., Chambersburg, Pa., 1915—. Ordained Presbyn. ministry, 1899; chaplain gen. S.A.R., 1900-02, Moderator Synod of Pa., 1906-07; mem. board dirs. Princeton Theol. Sem., 1894-1929 (pres. bd. 1904-15). Trustee Lafayette Coll., Wilson Coll. Chmn. Franklin County Chapter, Am. Red Cross, 1918-21. Pres. Kittochtinny Hist. Soc., 1920-25. Author: The Kentucky Resolutions of 1798, an Historical Study, 1887; At the Evening Hour, 1898; Memoir of Joseph Cabell Breckinridge, U.S.N., 1898. Died July 6, 1936.

WARFIELD, George Alfred, univ. prof.; b. Ellison, Ill., Nov. 24, 1871; s. John Hollister and Bathania (Brent) W.; A.B., Neb. Wesleyan U., 1896; LL.B., U. of Neb., 1898; A.M., U. of Ore., 1899; post-grad. work, univs. of Calif. and Wis.; grad. St. Louis Sch. of Social Economy (Washington U.), 1913; Ph.D., U. of Denver, 1915; m. Sarah Newman Hall, June 30, 1903. Prof. Greek and Latin, Willamette U., Salem, Ore., 1902-03; prof. history and economics, Puget Sound U., Tacoma, Wash., 1903-06; prof. polit. and social science, Dak. Wesleyan U., Mitchell, S.D., 1906-11; prof. economics and sociology, 1911-21, prof. economics, 1911—, dean Sch. Commerce, Accounts and Finance, 1913-36, dean emeritus, 1936—, U. of Denver. Admitted to Nebraska bar, 1898. Methodist. Author: Outdoor Relief in Missouri (Russell Sage Foundation), 1915. Home: Denver, Colo. Died Sept. 15, 1939.

WARFIELD, R(ichard) Emory, fire ins.; b. Manor Glen, Md., Aug. 11, 1855; ed. pvt. schs. Clerk, later sec. Fireman's Ins. Co., Baltimore, Md., 1871-82; mgr. for Md. and Del. of Continental Ins. Co. of New York, 1882-85; in charge Baltimore dept., comprising Md., Va., W.Va., N.C. and D.C., of Royal Ins. Co. of Liverpool, Eng., 1885-96; asst. mgr., later mgr. consolidated Baltimore and Phila. depts. same co., 1896-1905; pres. Hanover Fire Ins. Co., 1906—. Pres. N.Y. Fire Ins. Exchange, 1911-13; pres. N.Y. Bd. Fire Underwriters, 1917-19, and treas., 1921-23. Home: New York, N.Y. Died Feb. 26, 1924.

WARFIELD, Ridgely Brown, surgeon; b. Howard County, Md., June 15, 1864; s. Milton Welsh (M.D.) and Mary Elizabeth (Dawley) W.; M.D., U. of Md. Sch. of Medicine, 1884; unmarried. Prof. principles and practice of surgery, Baltimore Med. Coll., 1907-12; prof. surgery, U. of Md., 1912—; chief surgeon, Md. Gen. Hosp.; surgeon, U. of Md. Hosp., and Church Home and Infirmary. Fellow Am. Coll. Surgeons. Home: Baltimore, Md. Died Feb. 4, 1920.

WARFIELD, S(olomon) Davies, banker; b. Baltimore County, Md.; s. Henry Mactier and Anna (Emory) W. Began in office of George C. Frick & Co., later clk. with D. J. Foley Bro. & Co., sugar importers; organized Warfield Mfg. Co.; organizer, 1898, and pres. Continental Trust Co.; mem. orgn. com. that consolidated and built ry. properties constituting present S.A.L. Ry. Co., later pres. and chmn. bd.; organized the group and purchased the Consol. Gas Co., now Consol. Gas, Electric Light & Power Co.; pioneer in development of Susquehanna River for electric power purposes; conducted negotiations leading to electric current from river being brought to Baltimore; mem. reorgn. coms. of Mo.P. Ry., Western Md. R.R., C.,R.I.&P. Ry., etc.; also pres. Baltimore Steam Packet Co.; dir. Richmond, Fredericksburg & Potomac R.R. Co., Consol. Gas, Electric Light & Power Co. (exec. com.), N.Y. Life Ins. Co. (exec. com.), Consolidation Coal Co., Maryland Casualty Co., Hanover Fire Ins. Co. (New York). Organizer, first pres., later chmn. exec. com., Nat. Assn. Owners of R.R. Securities, and pres. Nat. Ry. Service Corp. Postmaster of Baltimore, 1894-1905, under Cleveland, McKinley and Roosevelt. Mem. Am. Acad. Polit. and Social Science, Acad. Polit. Science, Nat. Inst. Social Sciences. Dir. Atlanta (Ga.) Musical Festival Assn. Home: Baltimore, Md. Died Oct. 24, 1927.

WARING, Thomas Richard, newspaper editor; b. Charleston, S.C., Dec. 7, 1871; s. Edward Perry and Anna Thomasine (Waties) W.; grad. Porter Acad., Charleston, 1887; B.L., Hobart Coll., Geneva, N.Y., 1890; LL.D., Coll. of Charleston, 1927; m. Laura Campbell Witte, Nov. 23, 1898; children—Charles Witte, Rosamond (Mrs. Harry Van Brun Salmons), Thomas Richard, Jr. Editor of Charleston Evening Post, 1897—; v.p. News and Courier Co.; sec. and treas. Evening Post Pub. Co. Del. Dem. Nat. Conv., 1908; mem. Charleston City Art Commn. Democrat. Episcopalian. Mason. Home: Charleston, S.C. Died May 31, 1935.

WARMAN, Cy, author, journalist; b. Greenup, Ill., June 22, 1855; s. John and Nancy (Askew) W.; ed. common schs.; m. Ida Blanch Hays, 1879 (died 1887); m. 2d, Myrtle Marie Jones (original of the song "Sweet Marie," of which he is author), May 17, 1892. Farmer and wheat broker, Pocahontas, Ill.; went to Colo., 1880; worked in shops D.&R.G. R.R.; locomotive fireman and engr.; editor Western Railway, Denver, 1888, Creede (Colo.) Chronicle, 1892; introduced to notice as "the Poet of the Rockies" by New York Sun, Sept. 4, 1892; went to New York, 1893; rode locomotive New York to Chicago and wrote his first r.r. story, "A Thousand Miles in a Night," McClure's Mag.; traveled 2 yrs., Europe and Orient; spent 2 yrs. in Washington. Author: Tales of an Engineer, 1895; The Express Messenger, 1897; Frontier Stories, 1898; The Story of the Railroad, 1898; The White Mail, 1899; Snow on the Headlight, 1899; Short Rails, 1900; The Last Spike, 1906; Weiga of Temagami, 1908. Contbr. verse and short stories to mags. Home: London, Ont., Can. Died Apr. 7, 1914.

WARMAN, Edward B., lecturer, author; b. Scotts Mountain, Warren County, N.J., Apr. 29, 1847; s. Caleb and Margaret (Rush) W.; ed. pub. schs., Dayton, O.; A.M., Boston U. Sch. of Oratory, 1878; m. Flora A. Martinstein, Oct. 19, 1890. Pvt. 11th Ohio Vol. Inf. during Civil War. Author, lecturer and syndicate writer on physical education and constructive psychology. Author: How to Read and Recite, 1889; Practical Orthoëpy, 1889; Gestures and Attitudes, 1891; The Voice, 1892; Health Series (10 booklets), 1889-1909; Don'ts, for the Speaker and Writer, 1909; Psychic Science Made Plain (2 vols.), 1910. Home: Los Angeles, Calif. Died Nov. 26, 1931.

WARMAN, Philip Creveling, editor, bibliographer; b. on farm, Warren County, N.J., July 27, 1859; s. Thomas and Mary Ann (Creveling) W.; ed. pub. sch., Broadway, N.J., and Centenary Collegiate Inst., Hackettstown, N.J.; grad. Sch. of Law, Georgetown U., 1880; LL.M., Sch. of Law, Columbian U., 1881; m. Mary Elizabeth Rymond, Dec. 29, 1880. Teacher in pub. schs., Warren County, N.J., 1875-78; local editor The Washington Star, Washington, N.J., 1878; read law in office of Oscar Jeffery, Washington, N.J., 1878-79; sec. to Maj. J. W. Powell, dir. U.S. Geol. Survey, 1882-94, and most of same period also asso. with J. C. Pilling in bibliographic work on Indian langs. for Bur. of Ethnology; editor U.S. Geol. Survey, 1894—. Author of Bulls. U.S. Geol. Survey, No. 100 (1893), No. 177 (1901), No. 215 (1903). Died 1908.

WARMOTH, Henry Clay, governor; b. McLeansboro, Ill., May 9, 1842; s. Isaac Saunders and Eleanor (Lane) W.; ed. pub. and pvt. schs., Fairfield and Salem, Ill.; admitted to bar, Lebanon, Mo., 1861; m. Sally, d. James M. Durand, May 30, 1877. Apptd. dist. atty. 18th Jud. Dist., Mo., 1862; resigned to become lt. col. 32d Mo. Inf.; wounded in battles Chickasaw Bayou and Arkansas Post; assigned to staff Maj. Gen. John A. McClernand; served during campaign below and around Vicksburg, including assault of May 19-22, 1863; later on staff Maj. Gen. E. O. C. Ord, 13th Army Corps; comd. his regt. during campaigns against Gens. Forrest and Stephen D. Lee; joined Grant's army in attack on Missionary Ridge and Lookout Mountain, his regt. leading in assault and capture of Rossville Gap; again on staff Gen. McClernand, 1864; served in Gen. Banks' Tex. campaign; assigned as judge mil. court, Dept. of Gulf, with jurisdiction over mil., civil and criminal cases, serving till end of war. Del. Phila. Conv., 1866; one of co. which followed President Johnson on his "swing around the circle" through Eastern and Northern States; elected gov. of La., 1868; Gen. Grant made him mil. gov. until new constitution of state was accepted by Congress; after that was inaugurated and served until 1873; became sugar planter Plaquemines Parish, La.; mem. La. Legislature, 1876-77; del. La. Constl. Conv., 1879; collector customs, port of New Orleans, 1889-93; del. Rep. Nat. convs., 1896, 1900; built, 1890, and pres. New Orleans, Fort Jackson & Grand Isle R.R. Died Sept. 30, 1932.

WARNE, Francis Wesley, bishop; b. Erin, Ont., Can., Dec. 30, 1854; s. Francis and Agnes (McCutcheon) W.; ed George Town Acad. and Albert Coll., Belleville, Ont.; grad. Garrett Bibl. Inst., Evanston, Ill., 1884; D.D., Northwestern U., 1900, Toronto U., 1924; m. Marguerite E. Jefferis, May 15, 1879; 1 dau., Edith Mary. Ordained ministry M.E. Ch., 1874; missionary to Brit. N. America, 1878-81; went to Calcutta, India, as a missionary, 1887; pastor Thoburn Ch. and presiding elder Calcutta dist., 1887-1900; elected missionary bishop to India, 1900, retired, 1928. Visited Malaysia, China, Corea, Japan, and Honolulu, 1915; officially visited the P.I. 5 times; visited Mesopotamia, Bagdad, Babylon, Mosul, and Ninevah, 1920. Gen. supt. M.E. Ch., 1920-28. Held conference officially in Japan, Corea, and China, 1924. Author: The Bible Sabbath; The Lord's Supper; A Covenant Keeping God; The Life of Mrs. Parker; The Story of Lizzie Johnson; Twenty Years a Shut-In; The Sinless Incarnation; The Lord's Supper: Ideals That Have Helped Me. Deceased.

WARNER, Adoniram Judson, congressman; b. Wales, N.Y., Jan. 13, 1834; s. Levi and Hepsibah (Dickinson) W.; ed. Beloit, Wis., and New York Central Coll.; m. Susan E. Butts, Apr. 5, 1856. Prin. Lewiston Acad., and supt. public schs. of Mifflin County; served for a time on Roger's geol. survey of Pa.; prin. Mercer Union (Pa.) schs., 1856-61; capt. 10th Pa. Reserves, July 21, 1861; lt. col. May 14, 1862; served throughout the Peninsular campaign under McClellan; last field officer to leave Harrison's landing, subsequently ordered by Burnside to conduct detachments of troops arriving at Fredericksburg too late to cross to Bull Run, to Alexandria, by river, thence to join main army. Joined own command and participated in battles of South Mountain and Antietam under Hooker, Reynolds and Meade; severely wounded at Antietam; recommended for promotion to brig. gen.; col., Apr. 25, 1863; rejoined regt. and, with wound unhealed and unable to walk without supports, went through the battle of Gettysburg; heard Lincoln's Gettysburg speech and served as pallbearer at his funeral services, held in Indianapolis; col. Vet. Reserve Corps, Nov. 15, 1863; sent to Indianapolis; resigned Nov. 17, 1865; bvtd. brig. gen., Mar. 13, 1865. Began building steam and electric rys. opening coal and iron mines and developing water power for generating electricity. Mem. 46th (1879-81) and 48th and 49th (1883-87) Congresses; pres. Bimetallic Union from its organization. Author: Appreciation of Money, 1877; Source of Value in Money, 1882; also numerous pamphlets and monographs on various subjects. Died 1910.

WARNER, Amos Griswold, univ. prof.; b. Elkader, Ia., Dec. 21, 1861; grad. U. of Neb., 1885; Ph.D., Johns Hopkins, 1888; m. Cora E. Fisher, Sept. 5, 1888. Gen. agt. Charity Organization Soc., Baltimore, 1887-89; lectured on economics U. of Neb., 1889-91; supt. charities, Dist. Columbia, 1891-93; prof. applied economics, Stanford, 1893—. Author: American Charities. Died 1900.

WARNER, Anna Bartlett ("Amy Lothrop"), author; b. in N.Y.; d. Henry W. and Anna M. (Bartlett) Warner; sister of late Susan Warner (penname "Elizabeth Wetherell," b. 1819, died 1885). Ed. at home. Author: Say and Seal (with her sister); Wych Hazel (with same); Gold of Chickaree (with same); Dollars and Cents; My Brother's Keeper; Patience; Ellen Montgomery's Bookshelf (except half of one volume); Sunday All the Week; Star Out of Jacob; Melody 23d Psalm; The Fourth Watch; The Other Shore; What Aileth Thee? Little Nurse of Cape Cod; The Light of the Morning; Three Little Spades; Blue Flag and Cloth of Gold; Yours and Mine; Tired Church Members; The Shoes of Peace; Up and Down the House; Cross Corners; Pond Lily Stories; Books of Blessing (half by sister); Miss Muff; Fresh Air Jack's Four Lessons; West Point Colors, 1904; Stories of Blackberry Hollow; Stories of Vinegar Hill; Robinson Crusoe's Farmyard; Wayfaring Hymns; Hymns of the Church Militant (a compilation); Susan Warner, "Elizabeth Wetherell"; etc. Died Jan. 22, 1915.

WARNER, Anne, see Anne Warner French.

WARNER, Beverley Ellison, clergyman; b. Jersey City, N.J., Oct. 14, 1855; s. James and Anna (Carscallen) W.; student Princeton, 1872-75, Trinity Coll., Conn., 1875-76; grad. Berkeley Div. Sch., 1879; hon. A.M., Trinity, 1886; D.D., U. of the South, 1896; LL.D., Tulane U., 1905; m. Alice M. Stoughton, June 1880. Deacon, 1879, priest, 1880, P.E. Ch.; rector S. Manchester, Conn., 1879-80, Stafford Springs, Conn., 1880-81, South Manchester, 1881-84, Stratford, Conn., 1884-86, Bridgeport, Conn., 1886-93, Trinity Ch., New Orleans, 1893—. Deputy Gen. convs., 1892, 1898, 1904; pres. standing com., Diocese of La. Lecturer and writer on lit. and sociol. topics; adminstr. of Tulane U., 1897. Author: Troubled Waters (novel), 1885; English History in Shakespeare's Plays, 1894; The Facts and the Faith, 1897; The Young Man in Modern Life, 1902; The Young Woman in Modern Life, 1905; Famous Introductions to Shakespeare's Plays, 1906. Home: New Orleans, La. Died 1910.

WARNER, Brainard Henry, realtor; b. Great Bend, Pa., May 20, 1847; s. Henry and Julia T. W.; LL.B., Columbian (now George Washington) U., 1870; LL.D., Erskine College, S.C.; m. Miss M. H. Phillips, June 2, 1887. Enlisted 1st as vol. nurse, Apr. 1863, and later in gen. service U.S.A.; detailed in War Dept., Aug. 1863; promoted and afterward held civilian appmt. until 1866; in Treasury Dept., 1886-87; collector internal revenue, Lancaster, Pa., 1867-68; in real estate bus. at Washington, 1869—. Founder B. H. Warner Co. (pres.), Rudolph & West Co., Columbia Nat. Bank, Washington Loan & Trust Co. (pres.); an organizer Columbia Fire Ins. Co., Columbia Title Co.; pres. The Andyke Co., New Century Apartment House Co.; erected over 1,000 houses in and near Washington; founded, 1890, Town of Kensington, Md. Rep. candidate for Congress, 6th Dist., Md., 1908. Pres. Nat. Com. to Secure Memorial to Heroes of Revolutionary War. Deceased.

WARNER, Charles Dudley, author; b. Plainfield, Mass., Sept. 12, 1829; grad. Hamilton Coll., 1851; law dept. U. of Pa., 1856, A.M., L.H.D., D.C.L.; practiced law, Chicago, 1856-60; removed to Hartford, Conn.; became editor Hartford Press, 1861, and of the Courant upon its consolidation with the Press, 1867; contributed an editorial dept. to Harper's Monthly Magazine, 1884—. Occasional lecturer on ednl. and literary topics; interested in prison reform; chmn. Sculpture Commn., State of Conn.; mem. Park Commn., City of Hartford; m. Susan, dau. of William Eliot Lee, 1856. Literary work began in college, with contbns. to the Knickerbocker and Putnam's Magazine. Author: A Book of Eloquence; My Summer in a Garden; Saunterings; Backlog Studies; The Gilded Age (with Samuel L. Clemens); Baddeck, and That Sort of Thing; Mummies and Moslems (reissued as My Winter on the Nile); In the Levant; Being a Boy; In the Wilderness; The American Newspaper; Studies of Irving (with William C. Bryant and George P. Putnam); Life of Washington Irving; Captain John Smith, Sometime Governor of Virginia and Admiral of New England; A Roundabout Journey; Papers on Penology (with others); On Horseback, a Tour in Virginia, North Carolina and Tennessee, with Notes of Travel in Mexico and California; A Little Journey in the World (novel); Their Pilgrimage; Our Italy—Southern California; As We Were Saying; Washington Irving; The Work of Washington Irving; As We Go; The Golden House, a Novel; The Relation of Literature to Life; The People for Whom Shakespeare Wrote; That Fortune (a novel). Edited: American Men of Letters; A Library of the World's Best Literature. Home: Hartford, Conn. Died 1900.

WARNER, Charles Mortimer, capitalist, mfr.; b. Van Buren, N.Y., Apr. 8, 1846; ed. pub. sch., Jordan, N.Y.; m. Alice Emerich, 1875 (died 1893). At 18 engaged in grocery business for himself at Peru, N.Y., but returned to Jordan, 1866, and engaged in milling, and later in coal and lumber bus.; in 1879 started malting bus. in Syracuse; pres. Warner-Quinlan Asphalt Co., Warner Sugar Refining Co.; dir. The Cuba Co., Corn Products Refining Co. Died Dec. 1, 1923.

WARNER, DeVer Howard, corset mfr., b. McGrawville, N.Y., Nov. 20, 1868; s. Ira DeVer and Lucetta M. (Greenman) W.; ed. Park Av. Inst., Bridgeport, Conn.; m. Maude Cady, May 13, 1888 (dec.); children—DeVer Cady, Margaret Lucetta (Mrs. John Field), Bradford Greenman; m. 2d, Flora Martin, Nov. 1931. Chmn. bd. The Warner Brothers Co., also of D. M. Read Co., Bridgeport Hydraulic Co., Bridgeport Gas Light Co.; v.p. Fairfield Trust Co.; dir. Bridgeport Trust Co., Investors Mortgage & Guaranty Co., Bridgeport Housing Co. Pres. Mountain Grove Cemetery Assn.; dir. Bridgeport Hosp. Republican. Presbyn. Home: Fairfield, Conn. Died Sept. 23, 1934.

WARNER, Donald Ticknor, judge; b. Salisbury, Conn., Dec. 15, 1850; s. Donald J. and Lois Ticknor (Ball) W.; Salisbury Acad. (Trinity Coll.), Hartford; hon. M.A., Trinity, 1892; m. Harriet E. Wells, Oct. 4, 1882; children—Donald Judson, Elizabeth Harrison (Mrs. Irving Kent Fulton), Lois Caroline, Mary Virginia, Philip Wells, Jeannette de Forest (Mrs. Howard Brett Smithers). Admitted to bar, 1873, in partnership with Donald J. Warner until 1881; practiced alone, 1881-91; mem. firm Warner & Landon, Salisbury, Conn., 1891-1917. Postmaster of Salisbury, 1874-85; judge of Probate Ct., dist. of Salisbury, 1885-1917; mem. Conn. Senate, 1895-99 (chmn. judiciary com., 1895, 1897); mem. Constl. Conv., 1902, and chmn. Statutory Revision Com., revision of 1902; state's atty., Litchfield County, 1896-1917; apptd. judge Superior Ct. of Conn., Mar. 15, 1917; state referee, 1920—. Republican. Episcopalian. Trustee Scoville Memorial Library, Salisbury. Home: Salisbury, Conn. Died Nov. 24, 1929.

WARNER, Ernest Noble, lawyer; b. Windsor, Wis., July 23, 1868; s. Clement Edson (col. 36th Wis. Vol. Inf.) and Eliza Irene (Noble) W.; desc. Andrew Warner, Cambridge, Mass., 1632; B.L., U. of Wis., 1889, LL.B., 1892; m. Lillian Dale Baker, July 5, 1894 (died 1924); children—John Clement, Elizabeth Dale, Ernest Noble. Practiced in Madison, 1892—; chmn. bd. N.W. Securities Co.; dir. The State Bank of Wis., and Madison Trust Co. Law examiner in office of atty. gen. of Wis., 1899-1903; mem. Wis. Ho. of Rep., 1905-07; author Wis. Civil Service Act. Leader in Wis. rural social movement for better country living. Pres. Wis. Country Life Conf. Assn.; mem. School Bd. of Madison, Madison City Planning Commn.; chmn. State Tornado Relief Com., 1924. Moderator Madison Dist. Congl. Conv., 1917, Wis. Congl. Conf., 1923-24; del. Nat. Congl. Council, 1917-29. Republican. Died July 9, 1930.

WARNER, Ezra Joseph, wholesale grocer; b. Middlebury, Vt., Mar. 8, 1841; s. Joseph and Jane (Meech) W.; A.B., Middlebury Coll., 1861; m. Jane Remsen, Nov. 25, 1861. In 1863, became asso. in wholesale grocery business with A. A. Sprague as Sprague & Warner, later joined by O. S. A. Sprague, as Sprague, Warner & Co. Local dir. 15 yrs. Liverpool & London & Globe Ins. Co., and chmn. bd. Donor of Warner Science Hall to Middlebury Coll., 1900. Trustee Lake Forest U.; governing mem. Art Inst. of Chicago. Home: Lake Forest, Ill. Died 1910.

WARNER, Ezra Joseph, pres. Sprague, Warner & Co.; b. Lake Forest, Ill., Mar. 10, 1877; s. Ezra Joseph and Jane Elizabeth (Remsen) W.; grad. Lake Forest Acad., 1895; B.A., Yale, 1899; m. Marion Aline Hall, Nov. 26, 1902; children—Marion (Mrs. Thomas C Dennehy, Jr.), Jane (Mrs. Edison Dick), Ezra Joseph. Identified, 1899—, with Sprague, Warner & Co., importers, mfrs. and distributors of food products at wholesale, of which was sec. and dir., then chmn. bd., and pres. and treas., 1918—; dir. Northern Trust Co. Trustee Chicago Bur. Pub. Efficiency, Y.M.C.A. of Chicago, Chicago Zoöl. Soc. (v.p.), Chicago Sunday Evening Club, Orchestral Assn. Chicago (v.p.); dir. Hosp. Assn. Lake Forest. Mem. advisory council Employers' Assn. of Chicago. Presbyn. Home: Lake Forest, Ill. Died May 9, 1933.

WARNER, Fred Maltby, governor; b. Hickling, Nottinghamshire, Eng., July 21, 1865; parents came to U.S. when he was 3 mos. old; a few mos. later mother died and he was adopted by Hon. P. D. and Rhoda E. Warner, of Farmington, Mich.; grad. Farmington High Sch. at 14; attended Mich. State Agrl. Coll. 1 term; m. Martha M. Davis, Sept. 19, 1888. Established large cheese factory at Farmington, 1889, and others at surrounding points; pres. Farmington State Savings Bank; v.p. Detroit United Bank. Mem. Mich. Senate, 1895-98; mem. village council, Farmington, 9 yrs., and 7 times pres. of village; sec. of state of Michigan, 1900, reëlected, 1902; gov. of Mich., 1904-08, 1908-10. Republican. Home: Farmington, Mich. Died Apr. 17, 1923.

WARNER, Horace Everett, author; b. Lake County, O., Jan. 10, 1839; s. Albert and Lucina (Snow) W.; A.B., Beloit (Wis.) Coll., 1867; m. Anna J. Riggs, Oct. 14, 1870. Served as pvt. Co. E, 22d Wis. Inf., Civil War, and lost an arm at battle of Resaca, Ga.; practiced law at Vinton, Ia., 1873-85; in U.S. civ. service, 1887-1904. Congregationalist. Author: The Ethics of Force, 1905; The Cricket's Song, and Other Melodies, 1907. Died Oct. 29, 1930.

WARNER, J. Foster, architect; b. Rochester, N.Y., May 5, 1859; s. Andrew J. and Kate (Foster) W.; ed. pub. schs., Rochester; studied architecture under father; m. Mary L. Adams, Apr. 18, 1883; children—Andrew J., John A. In practice at Rochester, 1884—; dir. Rochester Telephone Corp., Stromberg-Carlson Telephone Mfg. Co., Union Trust Co. (Rochester), Wayne Co. Trust Co. (Palmyra, N.Y.); chmn. City Planning Bd., Rochester. Fellow A.I.A.; mem. S.A.R.; del. Internat. Congress of Architects, London, 1906. Home: Rochester, N.Y. Died Apr. 1937.

WARNER, John DeWitt, congressman; b. Schuyler Co., N.Y., Oct. 30, 1851; s. Daniel DeWitt and Charlotte Gordon (Coon) W.; Ph.B., Cornell U., 1872; LL.B., Albany Law Sch., 1876; m. Lilian Augusta Hudson, June 14, 1877. Editor of the Ithaca Daily Leader, 1871; tariff editor N.Y. Weekly World, 1892. Admitted to bar, 1876; in practice at New York, 1876—; mem. 52d and 53d Congresses (1891-95), Democrat. Pres. Art Commn. City of New York, 1902-05; alumni trustee Cornell, 1882-87, 1893-98, 1903-08. Pres. Am. Free Trade League, 1905-09. Author of numerous pub. articles and addresses on miscellaneous topics. Of counsel Mut. Life Policyholders, 1906, and for commn. to revise N.Y. banking law, 1913. Home: New York, N.Y. Died May 27, 1925.

WARNER, Joseph Bangs, lawyer; b. Boston, Aug. 5, 1848; s. Caleb Henry and Elizabeth (Bangs) W.; A.B., Harvard, 1869, A.M., 1872, LL.B., 1873; m. Margaret Woodbury Storer, Sept. 20, 1876. In practice at Boston, 1873-1916; mem. firm Warner, Warner & Stackpole; retired from practice, 1916. Trustee Radcliffe Coll., Simmons Coll. Republican. Home: Boston, Mass. Died Jan. 1, 1923.

WARNER, Lucien Calvin, capitalist; b. Cuyler, N.Y., Oct. 26, 1841; s. Alonzo Franklin and Lydia Ann (Converse) W.; sergt. Co. K, 150th Ohio Inf., 1864; A.B., Oberlin, 1865, A.M., 1870; M.D., Univ. Med. Coll. (New York U.), 1867; LL.D., Oberlin College, 1900, and New York University, 1917; m. Keren S. Osborne, Apr. 12, 1868. Practiced medicine at McGrawville and New York, 1867-74; chmn. bd. Warner Bros. Co., and Warner Chem. Co.; dir. Home Ins. Co., etc. Interested in benevolent and philanthropic work. Trustee Oberlin Coll. (to which he gave building for conservatory of music and building for gymnasium); chmn. Internat. Com. Y.M.C.A., 1895-1910; pres. Congl. Ch. Bldg. Soc., 1897-1915; exec. com. Am. Missionary Assn.; pres. bd. trustees Talladega (Ala.) Coll. Died July 30, 1925.

WARNER, Southard Parker, consul; b. Washington, D.C., Oct. 29, 1881; A.B., Dartmouth, 1903. Apptd. consular agt. at Gera, Germany, Apr. 4, 1904; consul at Leipzig, 1904-09, Harbin, Aug. 22, 1912—. Died May 9, 1914.

WARNER, Vespasian, commr. of pensions; b. Mt. Pleasant (now Farmer City), Ill., Apr. 23, 1842; s. John and Cynthia A. W.; student Lombard U., 1859-60; pvt. to sergt. Co. E, 20th Ill Inf., to June 23, 1861; 2d lt., Feb. 4, 1862; capt., Feb. 10, 1865; bvtd. maj. vols., Mar. 13, 1865, "for meritorious services"; hon. mustered out, July 13, 1866; LL.B., Harvard, 1868; m. Winifred Moore (died 1894); m. 2d, Minnie Bishop, 1897. In practice of law at Clinton, 1868—. Col. and judge advo. gen. Ill. N.G., 1883-92; presdl. elector, 1888; mem. 54th to 58th Congresses (1895-1905); U.S. commr. of pensions, 1905-09 (resigned). Pres. the John Warner Bank, Clinton, Ill. Republican. Address: Clinton, Ill. Died Mar. 31, 1925.

WARNER, Willard, senator; b. Granville, O., Sept. 4, 1826; s. Willard and Eliva (Williams) W.; grad. Marietta Coll., 1845, LL.D. Served in army, 1861-65, as maj. and lt. col. 76th Ohio vol. inf.; col. 180th O. vol. inf., and insp. gen. on staff Gen. Wm. T. Sherman; bvtd. brig. gen. and maj. gen.; went to Ala., 1865, and to live in 1867; removed to Chattanooga, 1890. Mem. Ohio senate, 1866-67; mem. Ala. legislature, 1868; elected to U.S. Senate from Ala., 1868; collector port of Mobile, Ala., 1871-72; apptd. and confirmed gov. of New Mexico, 1872, but declined; mem. Tenn. legislature, 1897-98; mfr. of pig iron in Ala., 1873-90; built two blast furnaces at Nashville, Tenn., 1887-88, and one at Tecumseh, Ala., 1873-74; and Richmond Spinning Mill, Chattanooga, Tenn., in 1899; pres. Chattanooga Coffin & Casket Co.; dir. Chattanooga Savings Bank, Richmond Spinning Co. and Chattanooga Wagon Co.; 1st v.p. Chattanooga Mfrs.' Assn. Del. Rep. Nat. convs., 1860, 68, 76, 80 and 88. Home: Chattanooga, Tenn. Died 1906.

WARNER, William, senator; b. Lafayette County, Wis., June 11, 1840; s. Joseph and Mary (Dorking) W.; ed. Lawrence U., Wis., and U. of Mich.; LL.D., U. of Mich., 1905; served, 1862-65, in 33d and 44th Wis. regts., reaching rank of maj.; m. Sophia Bromley, Aug. 1866. In law practice at Kansas City, Mo., 1865—. City atty., 1867; circuit atty., 1869; mayor, 1871; Rep. presdl. elector, 1872; U.S. dist. atty., Western Dist. of Mo., 1882-84, 98, 1902-05; candidate for U.S. senator, 1885; mem. 49th and 50th Congresses (1885-89); candidate for gov., 1892; del. to Rep. Nat. convs., 1872, 84, 88, 92, 96; U.S. senator, Mo., 1905-11. Chmn. com. to notify Mr. Taft of his nomination, 1908. First dept. comdr. of Mo. and nat. comdr.-in-chief, 1888-89, G.A.R. Home: Kansas City, Mo. Died Oct. 4, 1916.

WARNER, Worcester Reed, mfr.; b. Cummington, Mass., May 16, 1846; s. Franklin J. and Vesta Wales (Reed) W.; ed. dist. sch., Cummington; D.Mech.Sc., Western U. of Pa., 1897; D.Eng., Case Sch. Applied Sci., 1925; m. Cornelia F. Blakemore, June 26, 1890; 1 dau., Helen B. Learned machinist's trade at Boston and at Exeter, N.H.; with Pratt & Whitney Co., Hartford, Conn., 1870-80, at same time pursued studies in astronomy and other scientific branches, and experimented in telescope building as a recreation; in 1881, with Ambrose Swasey, established firm of Warner & Swasey, Inc., as The Warner & Swasey Co., 1900, mfrs. machine tools and instruments of precision, including rangefinders, gun-sights, astron. telescopes, etc., for the govt. Designed and constructed 36-inch Lick telescope, 40-inch Yerkes telescope, 72-inch telescope for Dominion of Can. Dir. Guardian Trust Co., Cleveland Soc. for Savings. Trustee Western Reserve U., Case Sch. of Applied Science. Fellow Royal Astron. Soc., A.A.A.S. Republican. Home: Tarrytown, N.Y. Died June 25, 1929.

WARREN, Arthur, author; b. (Dorchester) Boston, Mass., May 18, 1860; s. Capt. M. H. and Ann M. Warren; m. Abbie N., d. James Gunnison, Jan. 13, 1887. Newspaper writer and corr., London, Eng., 1878-82; spl. writer and dramatic critic, Boston, 1883-88; London corr. Boston Herald, 1888-97, editorial writer and spl. corr., 1897-1907, editor, 1907-09; dramatic critic N.Y. Tribune, 1909-12. Author: The Charles Whittinghams, Printers, 1896; London Days, 1920. Contbr. to mags. Died Apr. 16, 1924.

WARREN, Benjamin S., sanitarian; b. Clayton, Ala., Nov. 9, 1871; s. Monroe (M.D.) and Mary Frances (Lawson) W.; prep. edn., Clayton (Ala.) Male Acad.; student Atlanta Med. Coll., 1889-90; M.D., Tulane, 1891; post-grad. work Polyclinic Sch., New York, 1893; m. Lee Ella Underwood, July 18, 1894; children—Monroe, R. Bates, Lee Ella, Hugh, Benj. S., Ruth. Practiced at Clayton, 1894-99; apptd. asst. surgeon U.S.P.H.S., June 22, 1900; passed asst. surgeon, July 11, 1905; surgeon, Dec. 1, 1912; asst. surgeon gen., Feb. 1, 1918; med. dir. Dist. No. 2, July 15, 1922; med. dir., July 1930. Prof. of hygiene, med. dept. of St. Louis U., 1909-11; sanitary adviser U.S. Commn. on Industrial Relations, 1913-15; med. dir. U.S. Employees Compensation Commn., 1917. Took active part in health legislation enacted by Congress, 1902, 12, 22; investigated health ins. systems and formulated a plan for coördinating such systems with existing health agencies. Democrat. Mason. Author of various Govt. bulls. and articles relating to open air schs., health ins., relation of wages to public health, etc. Home: Chevy Chase, Md. Died May 19, 1935.

WARREN, Charles Beecher, lawyer, ambassador; b. Bay City, Mich., April 10, 1870; s. Robert L. and Caroline (Beecher) W.; Ph.B., U. of Mich., 1891, hon. A.M., 1916; LL.B., Detroit Coll. of Law, 1893; LL.D., Albion Coll., 1924; m. Helen Wetmore, Dec. 2, 1902; children—Wetmore (dec.), Charles B., Robert, John Buel. Engaged in practice at Detroit, 1893—; asso. with Don M. Dickinson in firm of Dickinson, Warren & Warren until 1900; mem. of law firm of Warren, Hill, Hamblen, Essery and Lewis; dir. and gen. counsel, Nat. Bank of Commerce, Detroit; asso. counsel for U.S. before Joint High Commn. to determine Behring Sea claims, 1896; counsel for U.S. in N. Atlantic Coast Fisheries Arbitration with Great Britain, before The Hague Tribunal, 1910. Del. at large Rep. Nat. Conv., 1908; mem. Rep. Nat. Com. and Exec. Com., 1912-20; ambassador to Japan, June 1921-Mar. 1923 (resigned); head of High Commn. to Mexico that negotiated terms for resumption of diplomatic relations, May-Sept. 1923; ambassador to Mexico, Feb.-Aug. 1924 (resigned); del. at large Rep.

Nat. Conv., 1924 (chmn. com. on platform and resolutions). Commd. maj., R.C., Apr. 1917; lt. col. N.A., Feb. 1918; col. N.A., July 1918; hon. discharged Feb. 1919. Awarded D.S.M. Episcopalian. Named atty. gen. by President Coolidge but due to polit. controversy between President and Senate confirmation declined by that body; offer by President of recess appmt. was declined. Home: Grosse Pointe Farms, Mich. Died Feb. 3, 1936.

WARREN, Charles Howard, underwriter; b. Carlton, N.Y., Oct. 21, 1856; entered ry. service 1876 as clerk, C.&N.W. Ry., held various positions, 1876-88; comptroller St. Paul, Minneapolis & Manitoba Ry. and its successor, the G.N. Ry., 1888-94; gen. mgr. same road and allied lines, 1894-96; gen. mgr. Mont. Central Ry., 1894-96; asst. to pres. Central R.R. of N.J., 1897-99, 1st v.p., 1899-1902; 1st v.p. C.,R.I.&P. Ry., 1902-04; treas. Mut. Life Ins. Co. Died Nov. 29, 1935

WARREN, Edward K., mfr.; b. Ludlow, Vt., Apr 7, 1847; s. Rev. Waters and Caroline C. (Parsons) W.; ed. pub. schs., E. Berkshire, Vt., and Three Oaks, Mich.; m. Sarah E. Steavens, Nov. 3, 1867 (died 1879); m. 2d, Mary L. Chamberlain, Feb. 18, 1880. Engaged in business at Three Oaks, 1868-84; in 1883 invented "Featherbone," a substitute for whalebone, and in 1884 organized the Warren Featherbone Co., becoming pres.; also pres. E. K. Warren & Co., bankers. Owner of ranches, and breeder of cattle, in Tex., Mex., and N.M. Long interested in S.S. work; pres World's S.S. Conv. held in City of Jerusalem, Apr 17-19, 1904; as chmn. World's S.S. Exec. Com. promoted and carried through cruise to Jerusalem and Holy Land, chartered ship and carried 800 dels. of N. America, which was joined by English ship carrying 500 dels.; elected chmn. of World's S.S. Assn Exec. Com., Washington, 1910; spl. rep. of the Samaritan Nation to the World's S.S. Conv., Zürich, 1913, and chmn. same; pres. Internat. S.S. Assn., 1915; v.p. Moody Bible Inst. Progressive. Congregationalist. Established the Edward K. Warren Foundation for preservation of a primeval forest, and sand dunes on shore of Lake Mich., and the Chamberlain Memorial Mus. of local pioneer history at Three Oaks, Mich. Home: Three Oaks, Mich. Died Jan. 6, 1919

WARREN, Edward Leroy, clergyman, librarian; b Louisville, Ky., July 20, 1852; s. Levi L. and Mary Ann (Wood) W.; B.A., Centre Coll., Ky., 1873, M.A., 1883, D.D., 1888; B.A., Princeton, 1874; Danville (Ky.) Theol. Sem., Princeton Theol. Sem., Free Coll Theol. Sem of Edinburgh; m. Elizabeth J. Crawford, Oct. 28, 1884 (died 1925). Ordained ministry Presbyn. Ch. U.S.A., 1877; pastor Olivet Ch., Louisville, Ky., 1878-88, Clifton, Cincinnati, 1888-93, Immanuel Ch., Louisville, 1896-1901; librarian Presbyn. Theol. Sem., Louisville, 1901-25 Stated clerk Synod of Ky., 1884-89, and 1899-26; permanent clk. Gen. Assembly Presbyn. Ch. U.S.A., 1916-21. Sec. exec. com. Synodical Missions, 1896-1923; mem. bd. of trustees Centre Coll., Danville, Ky., 1886-91, and 1896—; pres. bd dirs. Danville Theol. Sem. at time of consolidation with Louisville Theol. Sem., 1901. Author: History of the Presbyterian Church in Louisville, Ky., 1896. Home: Louisville, Ky. Died Aug. 13, 1931.

WARREN, Edwin Walpole, clergyman; b. London, Eng., Nov. 28, 1839; s. Samuel and Eliza (Ballenger) W.; grad. Magdalen Coll., Cambridge, Eng., B.A., 1861, M.A., 1870; D.D., St. Stephen's Coll., Annandale, N.Y., 1890; m. Agnes Sarah Kennedy, June 21 1865 (died 1891); m. 2d, Lilla Warne (Browning) Kunhardt, May 1, 1895. Ordained in Ch. of Eng. 1864; came to U.S. and entered Episcopal ministry, naturalized Am. citizen, 1889; rector St. James and Holy Trinity chs., New York. Pres. Peabody Hosp. St. George's Soc.; British schs. and univs. Died 1903

WARREN, Fiske, paper mfr.; b. Waltham, Mass., July 3, 1862; s. Samuel Dennis and Susan Cornelia (Clarke) W.; B.A., Harvard, 1884; studied law at U of Oxford, Eng., 1906-07; m. Gretchen Osgood, May 14, 1891; children—Rachel (Mrs. Warren Lothrop), Marjorie (Mrs. William Whitman, 3d), Hamilton. In paper mfg. business, 1884—; partner firm of S. D. Warren & Co., Boston, 1889-1918; pres. S. D. Warren Co., 1918-24; treas. Cumberland Mfg. Co., installation of plants for filtration of water supplies, 1888-98 Operated electric road carriage in Waltham, 1891, 1st in Mass. and possibly 1st in U.S. Won amateur tennis championship of the U.S. in court of Boston Athletic Assn., 1893. Tours of the world, 1897, 1901, 05, 07, 31. Founded single-taxing community of Tahanto, in Harvard, Mass., 1909, that of Halidon, in Westbrook, Me., 1911, that of Sant Jordi in Santa Coloma, Republic of Andorra, 1918; and that of Shakerton, in Ayer, Mass., 1921; introduced the Raiffeisen system of coöperative credit in Arden, Del., 1911, the first in U.S.; founded Georgian Trust for promotion of single-tax, 1920. Writer of occasional articles, principally on single-tax and on Philippine question. Mem. exec. com. Anti-Imperialistic League, 1901-18; dir. Am. Peace Soc., 1903-11. Home: Boston, Mass. Died Feb. 1, 1938.

WARREN, Francis Emroy, senator; b. Hinsdale, Mass., June 20, 1844; s. Joseph S. and Cynthia Estella (Abbott) W.; acad. edn. in Mass.; pvt. and noncommd. officer 49th Mass. Vols., 1862-63; received Congressional Medal of Honor "for gallantry on battlefield at siege of Port Hudson"; later capt. Mass. Militia; m Helen M. Smith, Jan. 26, 1871 (died 1902); m. 2d, Clara Le Baron Morgan, June 28, 1911 Engaged as farmer and stockraiser in Mass.; moved to Wyo., then part of Ty. of Dak., 1868; became interested in real estate, mercantile, live stock and lighting business in Cheyenne; mem. territorial Senate, 1873-74 (pres.) and 1884-85; mem. City Council, Cheyenne, 1873-74, and again, 1883-85; mayor of Cheyenne, 1885; apptd. territorial treas 1876, 79, 82, 84; del. Rep. Nat. Conv., Chicago, 1888; chmn. Wyo. delegation to Rep. Nat. Conv., Phila., 1900, Chicago, 1904, 08, 12; chmn. Rep. Territorial Central Com., and Rep. State Central Com. of Wyo., 1896; apptd. gov. of Wyo. by President Arthur, Feb. 1885, and removed by President Cleveland, Nov. 1886; again apptd. gov. by President Harrison, Mar. 1889, and served until the territory was admitted as a state into the Union. Elected first gov. of Wyo., 1890; elected as a Republican to U.S. Senate, Nov. 18, 1890, and served until Mar. 4, 1893; resumed stock raising, farming, merchandising, etc.; again elected to Senate, 1894, and regularly reëlected to 1931. Home: Cheyenne, Wyo. Died Nov. 24, 1929.

WARREN, Frederick Morris, univ. prof.; b. Durham, Me., June 9, 1859; s. John Quincy and Ellen Maria (Cary) W.; B.A., Amherst, 1880; the Sorbonne, Paris, 1884-86; Ph.D., Johns Hopkins, 1887; L.H.D., Amherst, 1901; A.M., Yale, 1907; m. Estelle Ward Carey, June 8, 1892; children—Martha Stockbridge, James Carey. Instr. modern langs., Western Reserve Coll., 1881-83; instr. and asso. in modern langs., Johns Hopkins, 1886-91; prof. Romance langs., Adelbert Coll. (Western Reserve U.), 1891-1901; Street prof. modern langs., Yale, 1900-26; lecturer French lit., Johns Hopkins, 1896-1917 Author: A Primer of French Literature, 1889; A History of the Novel Previous to the Seventeenth Century, 1895; Ten Frenchmen of the Nineteenth Century, 1904 Asso. editor: Studies in Honor of A. Marshall Elliott, 2 vols., 1911 Editor of various French texts and asso editor Modern Philology; contbr. on French lit. to Modern Language Notes, Am. Jour. of Philology, etc. Died Dec. 7, 1931.

WARREN, George Frederick, prof. farm management; b. Harvard, Neb., Feb. 16, 1874; s. George Frederick and Julia Colista (Stanley) W.; B.Sc., U. of Neb., 1897; B.S.A., Cornell U., 1903, M.S.A., 1904, Ph.D., 1905; m. Mary Whitson, June 21, 1906; children—Stanley Whitson, Jean, Richard, George Frederick, Martha, Mary. Horticulturist N.J. Expt. Sta., 1905-06; asst. prof. agronomy, 1906-07, asst. prof. farm crops, 1907-09, prof. farm crops and farm management, 1909-11, prof. farm management, 1911-20, prof. agrl. economics and farm management, 1920—, Cornell U. Fellow Am. Statis. Assn., A.A.A.S. Author: Elements of Agriculture, 1909; Laboratory Exercises in Farm Management, 1910; An Agricultural Survey, Townships of Ithaca, Dryden, Danby, and Lansing, Tompkins County, New York, 1911; Farm Management, 1913. Co-Author: Dairy Farming, 1916; The Agricultural Situation, 1924; Inter-relationships of Supply and Price, 1928; The Physical Volume of Production in the United States, 1932; Wholesale Prices for 213 Years, 1720 to 1932, 1932; Prices, 1933; Gold and Prices, 1935. Died May 24, 1938.

WARREN, George Washington, dentist; b. Ocean County, N.J., Jan. 7, 1863; s. Daniel Appleton (M.D.) and Sarah J. (Bryan) W.; educated country schs. and Peddie Inst., Hightstown, N.J.; D.D.S. Pa. Coll. Dental Surgery, Phila., 1887; m. Helen W. Collins, Nov. 29, 1888; children—Harold Collins George Peirce. For 10 years chief of clin. staff prof operative dentistry and oral pathology, 1898-1909 Pa. Coll. Dental Surgery. Author: Dental Pathology and Dental Medicine; Dental Prosthesis and Metal lurgy. Edited two edits. Richardson's Mechanical Dentistry; asst. editor Internat. Dental Journal 1883-1901. Home: Swarthmore, Pa. Died May 29 1934.

WARREN, George William, prof music, Columbia Coll.; b. Albany, N.Y., Aug. 17, 1828; displayed musical talent in youth, but engaged in business in Albany; continued musical studies, became organist St. Peter's Ch., also St. Paul's Ch., Albany, until 1860; organist Ch. of the Holy Trinity, Brooklyn 1860-70; after that of St. Thomas's Ch., New York Composed much church music and pieces for the piano. Home: New York, N.Y. Died 1902.

WARREN, Harold Broadfield, artist; b. Manchester, Eng., Oct. 16, 1859; s. Samuel Mills and Sarah Anne (Broadfield) W.; ed. Owens Coll. (Manchester U.); student art dept. Boston Mus. of Fine Arts and under Profs. Charles H. Moore and Charles Eliot Norton, of Harvard, also pvtly. in Eng. and Italy m. Gertrude Reed, June 12, 1889; 1 son, Langford W. Came to U.S., 1876. Mem. faculty of architecture, Harvard, 1912-30. Exhibited water colors and oil pictures, Am. Soc. Artists, Boston Art Club Grosvenor Gallery (London), Royal Acad., Boston Mus., Portland (Ore.) Mus.; etc. Works on permanent exhbn. in Boston Mus.; pictures of the Parthenon, Cleveland Art Mus. Home: Cambridge, Mass. Died Nov. 23, 1934.

WARREN, Harry Marsh, clergyman; b. Hudson, N.H., Apr. 19, 1867; s. William and Eliza Ann (Brown) W.; student, Pinkerton Acad., Derry, N.H., 1878-80, Colgate U., 1884-89; Union Theol. Sem., 1889-91; spl. courses, Columbia, Oxford (Eng.), Heidelberg (Germany); D.D., Harriman (Tenn.) U.; Ph.D., Temple U., Phila.; m. Adelaide E. Butler, Oct. 11, 1893; children—Donald Butler (dec.), Beatrice Adelaide (wife of Prof. H. A. Lorenz), Harry Marsh. Ordained to ministry Baptist Ch., 1891; pastor Nepperhan Av. Ch., Yonkers, N.Y., First Ch., Salem, Mass., Central Park Ch., N.Y. City, 1895-1903; founded Nat. Save-a-Life League, for prevention suicide, pres., 1906—. Pres. The Christian League, Wayside Evangelism; v.p. Fla. Bible Inst.; sec. Churches of Christ in Poland; dir. New York Sch. Theology, Native Preachers Co., Nat. Com. Mental Hygiene; mem. Ministers Council of Northern Bapt. Conv. Republican. Mason. Contbr. articles to jours. Home: Chappaqua, N.Y. Died Dec. 21, 1940.

WARREN, Henry Pitt, head master; b. Windham, Me., Mar. 21, 1846; s. Rev. William and Mary Hubbard (Lamson) W.; grad. Phillips Acad., Andover, Mass., 1865; Amherst, 1 yr.; A.B., Yale, 1870; L.H.D., Rutgers, 1892, Williams, 1908; m. Annie L. Lyman, Aug. 18, 1879. Prin., grammar sch., New Bedford, Mass., 1870-72, high sch., Dover, N.H., 1872-75, N.H. State Normal Sch., Plymouth, 1879-83; English master, Lawrenceville (N.J.), Sch., 1883-87; head master, The Albany (N.Y.) Acad., 1886—. Republican. Presbyn. Trustee Albany Inst., Art and Hist. Soc. Author: History of Waterford, Oxford County, Maine, 1879; Stories from English History, 1899. Home: Albany, N.Y. Died May 27, 1919.

WARREN, Henry White, bishop; b. Williamsburg, Mass., Jan. 4, 1831; s. Mather and Anne Miller (Fairfield) W.; brother of William Fairfield W.; A.B., Wesleyan U., Conn., 1853, A.M., 1858; D.D., Dickinson, 1874; LL.D., Ohio Wesleyan, 1892; m. Diantha A. Kilgore, Apr. 1855 (died 1867); m. 2d, Mrs. Elizabeth Iliff, Dec. 27, 1883. Taught natural science, Amenia Sem., 1851, ancient langs., Wilbraham, 1853-55; ordained M.E. ministry, 1855; pastor Worcester, Mass., 1855-57, Boston, 1857-61, Lynn, 1861-63, Westfield, 1863-65, Cambridge, 1865-68, Charlestown, 1868-71, Phila., 1871-74, Brooklyn, 1874-77, Phila., 1877-80, elected bishop, 1880. Mem. Mass. Ho. of Rep., 1863. Author: Sights and Insights, 1874; The Lesser Hymnal, 1877; Studies of the Stars, 1878; Recreations in Astronomy, 1879; The Bible in the World's Education, 1892; Among the Forces, 1898; also hundreds of review and newspaper articles. Editor of The Study, 1896-1900. Died July 22, 1912.

WARREN, Herbert Langford, architect; b. Manchester, Eng., Mar. 29, 1857; s. Samuel Mills and Sarah Anne (Broadfield) W.; studied Owens Coll., Manchester, 1871-75, Mass. Inst. Tech., 1877-79; office study, with the late H. H. Richardson, architect, Brookline, Mass., 1879-84; spl. student Harvard, 1883-84; traveling student in Europe, 1884-85; hon. A.M., Harvard, 1902; m. Catharine Clark Reed, Nov. 8, 1887. On staff Sanitary Engineer, New York, 1886-87. Began practice Boston, 1885; mem. firm Warren & Smith. Instr. architecture, 1893-94, asst. prof., 1894-99, prof. 1899—, Harvard. Pres. Nat. League Handicraft Socs., 1907-11, Soc. of Arts and Crafts, Boston; fellow A.I.A. (dir. 1893-96), Boston Soc. of Architects (sec. 1891-95), Am. Acad. of Arts of Sciences, Archæol. Inst. America. Home: Cambridge, Mass. Died June 27, 1917.

WARREN, Howard Crosby, psychologist; b. Montclair, N.J., June 12, 1867; s. Dorman Theodore and Harriet (Crosby) W.; A.B., Princeton, 1889, A.M., 1891; Ph.D., Johns Hopkins, 1917; student univs. of Leipzig, Berlin, Munich, 1891-93; m. Catherine Campbell, Apr. 5, 1905. Instr. logic, 1890-91, demonstrator psychology, 1893-96, asst. prof., 1896-1902, prof. exptl. psychology, 1902-14, head of psychol. lab., 1904-24, and Stuart prof. psychology, 1914—, Princeton. Compiler, Psychol. Index, 1894-1907 and 1910-14; asso. editor Am. Naturalist, 1896-97; asso. editor, 1900-04, co-editor, 1904-10, Psychol. Rev.; sr. editor Psychol. Rev. Publs., 1910—; pres. Psychol. Rev. Co., 1911-25. Contbr. Johnson's Cyclo., Baldwin's Dictionary of Philosophy and Psychology. Translator: Tarde's Social Laws, 1899. Author: Human Psychology, 1919; History of the Association Psychology, 1921; Elements of Human Psychology, 1922. Fellow A.A.A.S. Home: Princeton, N.J. Died Jan. 4, 1934.

WARREN, J(ohn) Collins, surgeon; b. Boston, May 4, 1842; s. Jonathan Mason and Annie (Crowninshield) W.; A.B., Harvard, 1863, M.D., 1866; LL.D., Jefferson Medical Coll., 1895, Harvard, 1906, McGill, 1911; m. Amy Shaw, May 27, 1873. Instr. surgery, 1871-82, asst. prof., 1882-87, asso. prof., 1887-93, prof., 1893-99, Moseley prof. surgery, 1899-1907, prof. emeritus, 1907—, Harvard. Overseer of Harvard, 1908-14. Hon. fellow Royal Coll. Surgeons, Eng., Royal Coll. Surgeons, Edinburgh; fellow Am. Acad. Arts and Sciences; pres. Am. Surg. Assn., 1896. Editor Boston Med. and Surg. Jour., 1873-81. Republican. Author: Healing of Arteries in Man and Animals After Ligature, 1886; Surgical Pathology and Therapeutics, 1895. Editor and part author: International Text-Book of Surgery (2 vols.), by Am. and British authors, 1900. Died Nov. 2, 1927.

WARREN, Joseph Weatherhead, physician; b. Springfield, Massachusetts, June 24, 1849; s. Daniel D. and Louisa Maria (Weatherhead) W.; A.B., Harvard, 1871; univs. of Berlin, 1871-72, Leipzig, 1872-73, Bonn, 1873-80; licensed to practice in German Empire, 1879; M.D., U. of Bonn, 1880; unmarried. Practiced at Bonn, 1880-81; asst. phys. in pvt. hosp. for mental diseases; demonstrator and instr., Harvard Med. Sch., 1881-91; prof. physiology, Bryn Mawr Coll., 1891-1913; asst. to the commr. of health of Pa., 1913—. Fellow A.A.A.S., Coll. Physicians of Phila. Died Dec. 20, 1916.

WARREN, Maude Lavinia (Radford), author; b. Wolfe Island, Can.; d. Maj. Isaac Henry and Anna Radford; Ph.B., Ph.M., U. of Chicago; m. Prof. Joseph Parker Warren, Nov. 27, 1907 (died 1909). Author: King Arthur and His Knights, 1907; The Land of the Living (novel), 1908; Peter Peter, 1909; The Main Road, 1913; Barbara's Marriages, 1915; Robin Hood, 1915; Little Pioneers, 1916; The White Flame of France, 1918; The House of Youth, 1923; Mother Hubbard's Wonderful Cupboard, 1923; Adventures in the Old Woman's Shoe, 1924; Tommy Tucker's Stories, 1924; Carnival Colors, 1925; Never Give All, 1927. Contbr. short stories to mags. War corr., 1916-19; spl. corr. for Saturday Evening Post in Near East, 1919-20; field worker, Y.M.C.A., 1918-19; created hon. maj., 117th Field Signal Corps, Rainbow Div., for service under fire. First white woman to cross Great Bear Lake, North West Territory, Canada, 1930. Died July 6, 1934.

WARREN, Minton, univ. prof.; b. Providence, R.I., Jan. 29, 1850; s. Samuel S. and Ann E. W.; grad. Tufts, 1870; Ph.D., Strassburg, 1879; LL.D., Tufts, 1899, Columbia, 1900, U. of Wis., 1902; m. Salomé A. Machado, Dec. 29, 1885. Dir. Am. Sch. Classical Studies, Rome, 1896-97; pres. Am. Philol. Assn. 1897-98; prof. Latin Johns Hopkins, until 1899; prof. Latin, Harvard, 1899—. Died 1907.

WARREN, Richard Henry, composer, organist, conductor; b. Albany, N.Y., Sept. 17, 1859; s. George William W. (Mus. Doc.) and Mary Elizabeth (Pease) W.; pupil of his father and of P.S Schnecker, George Wiegand, John White, and others; studied in Europe, 1880, 1886; m. Helen Corbin Hurd. Organist and dir. music at New York in Ch. of St. John the Evangelist, 1877-79, Reformed Episcopal Ch., 1879-80, All Souls' (Anthon Memorial) Ch., 1880-86, St. Bartholomew's Ch., 1886-1905. Ch. of the Ascension, 1907—; also condr. Ch. Choral Soc. and various smaller organizations. Compositions: Many services and anthems for the church; operettas, "Ingala," 1880; "All on a Summer's Day," 1882; "Magnolia," 1896; romantic opera, "Phyllis," 1897 (prod. at Waldorf-Astoria Theatre, May 7-21, 1900); string quartette, "Ticonderoga"; cantata for chorus, baritone solo and orchestra; songs, etc. Died Dec. 3, 1933.

WARREN, Samuel Dennis, mfr.; b. Boston, Mass. Jan. 25, 1852; s. Samuel Dennis and Susan Cornelia (Clarke) W.; A.B., Harvard U., 1875, LL.B., 1877, A.M., 1878; m. Mabel, d. Hon. Thomas F. Bayard, Jan. 25, 1883. Admitted to Suffolk bar, Feb. 17, 1879, and to practice in U.S. Circuit Ct., Aug. 17, 1879; practiced law, firm of Warren & Brandeis, Boston, 1878-89; partner in S. D. Warren & Co., mfrs., Jan. 1, 1889—, and part owner in Cumberland Mills, Portland, Me., Copsecook Mill, Gardiner, Me., and Forest Paper Co., Yarmouth, Me. Pres. trustees Mus. Fine Arts, 1901-07; chmn. Bd. of Art Commrs., Boston, 1898—; trustee Mass. Gen. Hosp., 1896-1902. Independent Democrat. Home: Boston, Mass. Died 1910.

WARREN, Samuel Edward, educator; b. West Newton, Mass., Oct. 29, 1831; s. Samuel and Anne Catharine (Reed) W., 8th in descent from John Warren, one of original settlers of Watertown, Mass. (1630); grad. Rensselaer Poly. Inst., 1851; m. Margaret Miller, Nov. 18, 1884. Asst., 1851-54, prof. descriptive geometry and drawing, 1854-72, Rensselaer; same chair, 1872-75, Mass. Inst. Tech.; lecturer, 1872-75, Mass. Normal Art Sch.; engaged in private instruction, literary work, etc., 1875—; fellow A.A.A.S.; frequent press contbr. consulting investor, etc. Author: General Problems in Descriptive Geometry, 1860; Elementary Projection Drawing, 1861; Elementary Linear Perspective, 1863; Drafting Instruments and Operations, 1864; Plane Problems in Elementary Geometry, 1866; General Problems in Shades and Shadows, 1867; Higher General Problems in the Linear Perspectives of Form, Shadow and Reflection, 1868; Elements of Machine Construction and Drawing, 2 vols., 1870; Elementary Free-hand Geometrical Drawing, 1873; Problems, Theorems and Examples in Descriptive Geometry, 1874; Problems in Stone Cutting, 1875; Elements of Descriptive Geometry, Shadows and Perspective, 1877; A Primary Geometry, 1877; The Sunday Question, 1890; Descriptive Geometry, 1904. Died 1909.

WARREN, Samuel Prowse, organist; b. Montreal, Can., Feb. 18, 1841; s. Samuel Russel W.; studied music in Berlin, 1861-64. Returned to Montreal,

1864-65, thence to New York; organist at All Souls' (Unitarian) Ch., 1866-68, Grace (Episcopal) Church, 1868-74, Holy Trinity (Episcopal) Ch., 1874-76, returning to Grace Ch., where he remained until 1894; First Presbyn. Ch. (Munn Av.), E. Orange, N.J., 1895—. Conductor New York Vocal Union, 1880-88. Compositions (sacred and secular): Anthems, partsongs, organ and piano solos and transcriptions, etc. Died Oct. 7, 1915.

WARREN, Willard Clinton, publisher; b. New Canaan, Conn., Jan. 9, 1866; s. James Daskam and Mary Elizabeth (Smith) W.; ed. pub. schs.; m. Lillie K. Faulkner, Oct. 14, 1891; children—Keith Faulkner, Mrs. Margaret Moore Cross. Began in pub. business at New Haven, Conn., 1884; pres. of corps. owning The Bankers Mag., The House Furnishing Rev., Internat. Banking Directory, Banker and Tradesman, Banking Law Jour., Commercial Record, Am. Shoemaking, Fibre and Fabric, Record and Guide, Business Law Jour., New England Grocer. Republican. Episcopalian. Died Mar. 8, 1928.

WARREN, William C., editor; b. Buffalo, N.Y., Aug. 4, 1859; s. James D. and Mary (Mills) W.; Ph.B., Yale, 1880; m. Clara S. Wright, Apr. 2, 1891; children—William C., Charlotte L., John D. Began newspaper work on Buffalo Commercial, 1880, of which was editor and pub., 1894-1918, retired. Dir. Buffalo, Niagara & Eastern Power Co. Del. Rep. Nat. Convs., 1900, 04. Home: Buffalo, N.Y. Died Nov. 27, 1935.

WARREN, William Fairfield, educator; b. Williamsburg, Mass., Mar. 13, 1833; s. Mather and Anne M. (Fairfield) W.; A.B., Wesleyan U., Conn., 1853, LL.D., 1874; Andover Theol. Sem., 1854-56, U. of Berlin, 1856-57, U. of Halle, 1857-58; S.T.D., Ohio Wesleyan, 1862; LL.D., Boston U., 1923; m. Harriet Cornelia Merrick, Apr. 14, 1861; children—Mary Christine (Mrs. H. M. Ayars), William Marshall, Anna Merrick (Mrs. Geo. A. Dunn), Winifred (Mrs. Geo. Arthur Wilson). Ordained M E. ministry, 1855; prof. systematic theology in Mission Inst., Bremen, Germany (which later became Martin Inst., Frankfort), 1860-66; acting pres. Boston Theol. Sem., 1866-73; pres. Boston U., 1873-1903, prof. comparative theology and philosophy of religion, 1873—, dean Sch. of Theology, 1903-11; pres. emeritus Boston Univ., 1923—. Author: The True Key to Ancient Cosmology, 1882; Paradise Found—The Cradle of the Human Race at the North Pole, 1885; The Quest of the Perfect Religion, 1886 (also editions in Japanese, Chinese, Spanish and German); In the Footsteps of Arminius, 1888; The Story of Gottlieb, 1890 (transls. in Arabic and German); Constitutional Law Questions in the Methodist Episcopal Church, 1894; The Religions of the World and World-Religion, 1900; The Earliest Cosmologies—the Universe in the Thought of the Ancient Babylonians, Egyptians, Greeks, etc., 1909 (transl. into German by Dr. Archenhold, dir. of Berlin-Treptow Sternwarte, 1922); The Universe as Pictured in Milton's Paradise Lost, 1915; etc. Editorial contbr. to Deutsche Literaturzeitung, Leipzig, Babylonian and Oriental Record, London, Jour. Am. Oriental Soc., Jour. Royal Asiatic Soc., and other learned periodicals. Home: Brookline, Mass. Died Dec. 6, 1929.

WARREN, Winslow, lawyer; b. Plymouth, Mass., Mar. 20, 1838; s. Winslow and Margaret (Bartlett) W.; ed. Plymouth pub. schs.; A.B., Harvard, 1858, LL.B., 1861; m. Mary Lincoln Tinkham, Jan. 3, 1867; children—Charles, Margaret, Mary L. Hussey, Winslow. Admitted to bar and engaged in practice at Boston, 1861; asso. counsel the Boston & Providence R R.; later chiefly engaged in trustee work, sitting as auditor or referee, and advisory corp. work. Collector port of Boston, 1894-98; U.S. commr., 1861 69. Democrat. Pres. of the Dedham Water Co.; dir. Columbian Nat. Life Ins. Co., Boston Storage Co. Mem. Soc. of the Cincinnati (pres. gen.), Mass. Soc. of the Cincinnati (pres.); v.p. Bunker Hill Monument Assn. Overseer, Harvard, 1898-1910. Home: Dedham, Mass. Died Apr. 4, 1930.

WARRINER, Edward Augustus, P.E. clergyman, author; b. Agawam, Mass., Feb. 19, 1829; s. Ruel and Anna C. W.; reared on farm; A M., Union Coll. (N.Y.), 1855; m. Louisa Voorhis, 1865; m. 2d, Esther Bolles, 1881. After graduation was teacher; studied law; practiced Springfield, Mass., 3 yrs.; studied theology; made deacon, 1867, priest 1868; pastor St. Paul's Ch., Montrose, Pa., 1867—. Author: Victor La Tourette, a Theological Novel, 1875; Kear (a poem in 7 cantos), 1882; I Am That I Am, The Idea of God, 1887; The Gate Called Beautiful—An Institute of Christian Sociology, 1898. Died 1908.

WARRING, Charles Bartlett, educator; b. Charlton, N.Y., Jan. 15, 1825; s. Jeremiah and Sarah (Bartlett) W.; grad. Union Coll., N.Y., 1845; Ph D., New York U.; m. Catharine A. Lent, 1849. Prof. Latin and Greek, 1846-47, mathematics and science, 1848-52, prin., 1857-62, Collegiate Sch., Poughkeepsie, N.Y. Established Mil. Inst., Poughkeepsie, 1863, retired, 1891; specialist on the Hebrew and the present cosmogony. Contbr. to mags. on scientific and theologico-scientific subjects; mem. Victoria Inst., London, and New York Acad. of Sciences. Author: The Mosaic Account of Creation, the Miracle of To-day, 1877; Genesis I. and Modern Science, 1892; Gyroscopic Bodies. Died 1907.

WARRINGTON, Albert Powell, theosophist; b. Berlin, Md., Aug. 27, 1866; s. William and Emily Ann (Powell) W.; ed. high sch.; studied law under Prof. John B. Minor, of U. of Va.; m. Elizabeth Neely, Apr. 27, 1892 (dec.); 1 dau., Mary Neely; m. 2d, Mrs. Mary Corbin Balguy, Jan. 20, 1923 (divorced); m. 3d, Mrs. Betty Stoner Robertson, Dec. 31, 1930. Entered ry. service as a youth and became traffic mgr.; admitted to bar, 1892, and practiced at Norfolk, Va., until 1911 (retired from active business for theosophical work). Democrat. Fellow and gen. councillor Theosophical Soc. of Adyar, Madras, India (v.p. and pres. pro tem). Nat. pres. Am. Theosophical Soc., v.p. Krotona Inst. Theosophy. Author of article, "Theosophy and Occultism," in Ency. Americana. Editor, The Messenger, The Am. Theosophist, The Theosophist (Adyar). Contbr. chapter on theosophy in Braden's Varieties of Am. Religion, also articles to mags. Home: Ojai, Calif. Died June 16, 1939.

WARRINGTON, George Howard, lawyer; b. Cincinnati, O., Oct. 21, 1872; s. John Wesley and Caroline Virginia (Warrington) W.; A B., Yale, 1895; studied univs. of Göttingen and Berlin, Germany, 1895-96; LL.B., U. of Cincinnati, 1899; m. Elsie Holmes, Jan. 11, 1908 (died 1938); children—Rachel Gaff Leonard, Caroline Virginia Mackoy, John Wesley, Elsie Holmes Bailey. Admitted to Ohio bar, 1899, and began practice at Cincinnati; mem. firm Paxton, Warrington & Seasongood until 1917; with U S. Food Adminstrn., Washington, D.C., Sept. 1917-July 1919, also mem. War Trade Bd. last 6 mos.; spl practice, 1919—; dir. Niles-Bement-Pond Co. (New York), Cincinnati St. Ry. Co., Cincinnati Equitable Ins. Co. Chmn. City Survey Com. which made study of governmental conditions in Cincinnati and Hamilton Co., 1924, and pub. report under title of "Government of Cincinnati and Hamilton County"; chmn. bd. dirs. U. of Cincinnati, 1931—; trustee Am. Schs. Oriental Research, Cincinnati Art Museum, Cincinnati Conservatory of Music, Union Bethel; v.p. Cincinnati Inst. Fine Arts.; pres. Widows and Old Men's Home. Republican. Protestant. Home: Cincinnati, O. Died Nov. 30, 1940.

WARRINGTON, John W., judge; b. Clark County, O., July 22, 1846; s. Rev. Charles B. and Mary Davison W.; ed. pub. schs. and pvt. tutors; LL B , Cincinnati Law Sch., 1869; served Union Army, 1862-65; m. June 29, 1871; wife died Nov. 2, 1888; again married Aug. 2, 1892. Asst. city solicitor, 1869-73, city solicitor, 1873-75, Cincinnati; mem. law firm of Paxton & Warrington. Rep. presdl elector, 1876; U.S. circuit judge, 6th Jud. Circuit, Mar. 1909—, and presiding judge of Circuit Ct. of Appeals for the Circuit, Oct. 1, 1911—. Prof. equity jurisprudence and trusts Cincinnati Law Sch., 1901-04. Home: Cincinnati, O Died May 26, 1921.

WARTHIN, Aldred Scott, pathologist; b. Greensburg, Ind., Oct. 21, 1866; s. Edward Mason and Eliza Margaret (Weist) W.; A.B., Indiana U., 1888, LL.D., 1928; A.M., U. of Mich., 1890, M.D., 1891, Ph.D., 1893; music diploma (teacher), Cincinnati Conservatory of Music, 1887; post-grad. work in medicine, Vienna and Freiburg; m. Dr. Katharine Angell, June 27, 1900; children—Margaret, Aldred Scott, Virginia, Thomas Angell. Asst. in internal medicine, 1891-92, demonstrator internal medicine, 1892-95, demonstrator pathology, 1896, instr., 1897, asst. prof., 1899, junior prof., 1902, prof. and dir. pathol. lab., 1903—, med. dept. U. of Mich. Pres. Am. Assn. Pathologists and Bacteriologists, 1908; pres. Internat. Assn. Med. Museums, 1910-13, mem. council for U.S., 1914-17, v.p. Am. Sect., 1914, editor of Bulletin, 1913-19, Annals of Clinical Medicine, 1924—; mem. Assn. Am Physicians (council 1921-28; v.p., 1926-27; pres. 1927-28), Society Exptl. Medicine and Biology, Am. Assn. for Cancer Research (pres. 1927-28), Internat. Med. Hist. Soc. (vice-pres., 1929-30), Am. Heart Assn., Chicago Medical Hist. Soc., Assn. Exptl. Pathology (v.p. 1922-23, pres. 1924, del. to Nat. Research Council 1925-28); pres. Mich. Assn. Prevention and Relief of Tuberculosis, 1908-09, Michigan Social Hygiene Assn. 1917-18; sec. Ann Arbor Anti-Tuberculosis Assn. Author: Practical Pathology, 1896, 1911. Editor and translator of 10th edit. Ziegler's General Pathology, 1903; editor dept. Pathology, 2d and 3d edits., Wood's Reference Hand-Book of the Medical Sciences; Textbook of General Pathology, 1914; Medical Aspects of Mustard Gas Poisoning, 1919; Old Age—The Major Involution, 1929; The Creed of a Biologist, 1930. Wrote over 1,000 articles in medical journals and textbooks; contbns. from the Pathological Laboratory of U. of Mich., 14 vols., 1896-1927. Most important researches on anatomy and pathology of the hæmolymph glands, and the pathology of diseases of the blood and blood-forming organs, cardiac syphilis, latent syphilis, tuberculosis, and toxic action of mustard gas, fat embolism, action of X-rays, heart in diphtheria, thymus, heredity in cancer, pathology of goiter. Russell lecturer at U of Mich., 1929. Home: Ann Arbor, Mich Died May 23, 1931.

WARWICK, Charles Franklin, lawyer; b. Phila., Feb. 14, 1852; s. Edward and Anne (Minshall) W.; ed. Zane Street Grammar Sch., Penn Charter Sch.; LL.B., U. of Pa.; m. Ella Kate Gresemer, 1873. Asst. dist. atty. of Phila. Co., 1881-84; city solicitor of Phila., 1884-95; mayor of Phila., 1895-99. Republican. Author: Mirabeau and the French Revolution, 1905, Danton and the French Revolution, 1908; Robespierre and the French Revolution, 1909; Napoleon and the End of the French Revolution, 1910. Home: Philadelphia, Pa. Died Apr. 4, 1913.

WARWICK, Walter Winter, govt. service; b. Lucasville, O., Mar. 1, 1868; s. Newton Reed and Adelaide (Brown) W.; Hughes High Sch., Cincinnati; LL.B., Law Sch. Cincinnati Coll., 1890; LL.M., George Washington U.; m. Minnie Elsie McCormick, June 23, 1906; 1 son, Newton Beverly. Practiced in Cincinnati, 1890-93; sec. to William Howard Taft, then judge U.S. Circuit Ct., 1892-93; chief law clerk U.S. Treasury, Washington, 1893-98; in practice at Cincinnati, firm of Warwick & Warwick, 1898-1904; with Panama Canal Commn. in Washington, 1904-08, then at Panama as auditor and as asso. justice Supreme Ct. of Canal Zone, to 1911; mem. President's Commn. on Economy and Efficiency, Apr. 1911-May 1913; asst. comptroller of the treasury, 1913-15; comptroller of the treasury, 1915-21; asst. to dir. of the budget, 1922-23; fiscal agt. of Panama Govt., 1923-25; in practice in Washington, 1926—; chief counsel U.S. Employees' Compensation Commn., 1927—. Colonel finance dept. O.R.C., U.S.A., 1926. Democrat. Presbyterian. Mem. Am. Acad. Polit. and Social Science. Mason. Died Apr. 19, 1932.

WARWICK, William Edmund, petroleum oil mfr.; b. Oshkosh, Wis., Jan. 13, 1862; s. William P. and Mary E. (Palmer) W.; B.M.E., Ia. State Coll. Agr. and Mech. Arts, 1888; m. Ella V. Fredenburg, Oct. 23, 1902. Began as worker in mills of Oshkosh; moved to Chicago, 1888; with Standard Oil Co. (Ind.), 1889—, v.p. and gen. mgr., 1919—; pres. La. Coast Land Co.; v.p. First Nat. Bank of Whiting; mayor of Whiting, 1903-07. Democrat. Christian Scientist. Home: Chicago, Ill. Died Dec. 3, 1936.

WASHBURN, Albert Henry, diplomat; b. Middleborough, Mass., 1866; s. Edward and Ann Elizabeth (White) W.; Ph.B., Cornell U., 1889; LL.D., Dartmouth, 1924; pvt. sec. to Hon. Andrew D. White during coll. course; attended law schs. Georgetown U., and U. of Va.; LL.B., Georgetown, 1895; m. Florence B. Lincoln, Jan. 11, 1906. U.S. consul at Magdeburg, Germany, 1890-93; pvt. sec. to Senator Henry Cabot Lodge, 1893-96; asst. U.S. atty. for dist. of Mass., 1897-1901; spl. U.S. Treasury counsel in customs cases, 1901-04; resigned to enter pvt. practice, 1904. Alternate del. Rep. Nat. Conv., 1896; del. Mass. Constl. Conv., 1917-19; permanent mem. U.S. Legal Advisory Bd., Commonwealth of Mass., 1917-19; presdl. elector, Mass., 1921; pres. Assn. of the Customs Bar, 1917-22; prof. polit. science and internat. law, Dartmouth, 1919—; E.E. and M.P. to Austria, Feb. 1922—. Second U.S. del. on commn. of jurists to consider amendment of the laws of war pursuant to a resolution of the Washington Conf. on Limitation of Armament, sitting at The Hague Dec. 1922-Mar. 1923; pres. mixed commn. to adjust differences arising out of provisional comml. agreements between Austria and Jugoslavia, 1923-24. Chevalier, 1st class, Royal Order of Saint Olav, Norway, 1913. Home: Middleborough, Mass. Died Apr. 2, 1930.

WASHBURN, Charles Grenfill, congressman; b. Worcester, Mass., Jan. 28, 1857; s. Charles Francis and Mary Elizabeth (Whiton) W.; grad. Worcester Poly. Inst., 1875; A.B., Harvard, 1880; admitted to Suffolk bar, 1887; m. Caroline Vinton, d. Horatio N. Slater, Apr. 25, 1889; children—Slater, Esther Vinton (Mrs. Albert H. Crosby). Mem. Mass. Ho. of Rep., 1897-98, Senate, 1899-1900; mem. commn. to revise corpn. laws of Mass., 1902; del. Rep. Nat. Convs., 1904, 1916, mem. com. to notify Theodore Roosevelt of his nomination; elected 59th Congress, Dec. 18, 1906, for unexpired term (1906-07), of Rockwood Hoar, deceased; reëlected to 60th and 61st Congresses (1907-11), 3d Mass. Dist. Dir. Fed. Res. Bank of Boston. Del. Rep. Nat. Conv., 1916, Mass. Constl. Conv., 1917. Home: Worcester, Mass. Died May 25, 1928.

WASHBURN, Claude Carlos, author; b. Mankato, Minn., Oct. 3, 1883; s. Jed L. and Alma (Pattee) W.; A.B., Harvard, 1905; m. Ive Sinclair Gowen, 1911; 1 son, John Larry. Lived principally in Europe, 1905—. Attached to Am. Embassy, Rome, for 16 mos. during war period; resigned, Mar. 1, 1919. Author: Pages from the Book of Paris, 1910; Gerald Northrop, 1914; Order, 1920; The Lonely Warrior, 1922; The Prince and the Princess, 1925; The Green Arch, 1925. Occasional contbr. to mags. Home: Duluth, Minn. Died Aug. 10, 1926.

WASHBURN, Edward Wight, chemist; b. Beatrice, Neb., May 10, 1881; s. William Gilmor and Flora Ella (Wight) W.; U. of Neb., 1899-1901; B.S., Mass. Inst. Tech., 1905, Ph.D., 1908; m. Sophie Wilhelmina de Veer, June 10, 1910; children—William de Veer, Janet, Roger D., Barbara. Research asso. in phys. chemistry, Mass. Inst. Tech., 1906-08; asso. in chemistry, 1908-10, asst. prof., 1910-13, prof. phys. chemistry, 1913-16, prof. ceramic chemistry and head of dept. of ceramic engring., 1916-22, U. of Ill.; editor Internat. Critical Tables (phys. chem. and engring. constants), 1922-30; chief chemist U.S. Bur. Standards, 1926—. Vice-chmn. and actg. chmn., 1918-19, chmn., 1922-23, div. chemistry Nat. Research Council; del. Internat. Chem. Union, London, 1919, Lyons, 1922, Cambridge, 1923, and Internat. Research Council, Brussels, 1919 and 1922; Am. commr. Internat. commn. annual tables phys. and chem. constants, 1921-29; chmn. Internat. Commn. on Physico-Chemical Standards; mem. Internat. Com. Thermochemistry, 1929—. Fellow A.A.A.S. (chmn. Sect. C 1923-24), Royal Soc. Arts, Am. Ceramic Soc. (editor Jour. 1920-22). Author: Introduction to the Principles of Physical Chemistry, 1915 (French translation by Noyes and Weiss, Payot et Cie, Paris, 1925), etc. Died Feb. 6, 1934.

WASHBURN, Francis, clergyman; b. New York, July 9, 1843; s. Rev. Jacob Cheeseman (M.E.) and Margaret (Youry) W.; ed. by pvt. study; m. Elizabeth Floy Davis, Aug. 1869; father of Margaret Floy W. Licensed to preach, 1874; sec. New York Dist. Conf. M.E. Ch., 4 yrs.; corr. sec. Nat. Local Preachers' Assn., 1 yr.; deacon, 1878, priest, 1880, P.E. Ch., rector St. Andrew's, Walden, N.Y., 1879-80, Holy Spirit, Rondout, N.Y., 1882-92. Author: Soul Thirst, 1879; Thoughts on the Lord's Prayer, 1883; Meditations on Charity, 1887; An Imperilled Faith, 1899, etc. Contbr. verse and prose to religious and secular jours. Address: Newburgh, N.Y. Died Dec. 5, 1914.

WASHBURN, Frank Sherman, engr.; b. Centralia, Ill., Dec. 8, 1860; s. Elmer and Elizabeth Jane (Knight) W.; C.E., Cornell, 1883; post-grad. work in history and polit. science, 1885; m. Irene May Russell, Dec. 3, 1890. Engr. of bridges, C.&N.W. R.R., 1885-88; supt. and mgr. Union Stock Yard & Transit Co., Chicago, 1889; contracting and cons. engr. at N.Y. City, 1890-1900; Southern enterprises, 1900-1910; pres. Am. Cyanamid Co., chemicals (New York), Air Nitrates Corp. (New York), Goodham Mfg. Co. (Chicago). In charge engring., constrn. and operation of 3 govt. plants for converting air into nitrates, during World War I. Presbyn. Home: Rye, N.Y. Died Oct. 9, 1922.

WASHBURN, Frederic Leonard, biologist; b. Brookline, Mass., Apr. 12, 1860; s. Nehemiah and Martha (Parmelee) W.; A.B., Harvard U., 1882, grad. student, 1888-89, A.M., 1895, Johns Hopkins, 1886-87; m. Frances L. Wilcox, Dec. 27, 1887; children—Martha Wilcox (Mrs. C. D. Allin), Alice Julia (Mrs. Phillips Byfield). Instr. zoölogy, U. of Mich., 1887-88; prof. zoölogy, Ore. Agrl. Coll. and entomologist to Expt. Sta., 1889-95; prof. biology, U. of Ore., 1895-1902; state biologist Ore., 1899-1902; prof. entomology, 1902-18, prof. economic vertebrate zoölogy, 1918—, U. of Minn.; State entomologist of Minn., 1902-18. Home: Minneapolis, Minn. Died Oct. 15, 1927.

WASHBURN, George, clergyman; b. Middleboro, Mass., Mar. 1, 1833; s. Philander and Elisabeth (Homes) W.; A.B., Amherst, 1855; Andover Theol. Sem., 1857-58; D.D., Amherst, 1874; LL.D., U. of Mich., 1900, Princeton, 1900, and Amherst, 1900, U. of Pa., 1906; m. Henrietta Loraine Hamlin, Apr. 15, 1859; father of George Hamlin W. Ordained Congl. ministry, 1863; missionary A.B.C.F.M. at Constantinople, 1858-62 and 1863-68; prof. philosophy, 1869-1908, acting pres., 1870-78, pres., 1878-1903, Robert Coll.; resigned Sept. 20, 1903; left Constantinople, 1908. Lecturer Lowell Inst., Boston, 1909. Received Order of St. Alexander from Prince Alexander of Bulgaria, and Order of Civil Merit from King Ferdinand. Spoke on Mohammedanism at World's Parliament of Religions, Chicago, 1893; recognized authority upon questions connected with politics of South Eastern Europe. Author: Fifty Years in Constantinople. For 20 yrs. regular contbr. to the Contemporary Rev., London, and other English and Am. periodicals. Died Feb. 15, 1915.

WASHBURN, George Hamlin, M.D.; b. Constantinople, Turkey, May 22, 1860; s. George and Henrietta Loraine (Hamlin) W.; resided abroad most of time until 1876; prep. dept. Robert Coll., Constantinople; A.B., Amherst Coll., 1882; M.D., Harvard, 1886; m. Anna M. Hoyt, Sept. 22, 1887 (dec.); children—Mrs. Anna Loraine Hall, George Edward, Arthur Hoyt, Alfred Hamlin. Began practice at Boston, 1886; prof. emeritus obstetrics, Tufts Coll. Med. Sch.; visiting gynecologist St. Elizabeth's Hosp.; cons. surgeon Free Hosp. for Women. Republican. Conglist. Med. dir. Am. Com. for Relief in Near East. Home: Boston, Mass. Died Mar. 28, 1933.

WASHBURN, Henry Stevenson; b. Providence, R.I., June 10, 1813; s. Kimball and Mary (Stevenson) W.; ed. Worcester Acad. and short time in Brown Univ.; m. Maria C. Loring, Nov. 27, 1837. Early in life mfr. of wire, Worcester, Mass.; later pres. Union Mutual Life Ins. Co.; investigated life and accident ins. in Great Britain, France and Germany, 1876-78, and published extensive articles on subject. Mem. Mass. Ho. of Reps., 1871-72; Mass. senate, 1873-74 (chmn. Com. on Edn., 1874); mem. Boston grammar sch. bd., 8 yrs. Author: The Mystery of Life, 1862; The Vacant Chair, and Other Poems, 1895. Died 1903.

WASHBURN, Jed L., lawyer; b. Montgomery County, Ind., Dec. 26, 1856; s. Christopher C. and Julia A. (Showen) W.; resided in Minn., June 1857—; acad. edn., but mainly self-ed.; m. Alma J. Pattee, June 1882; children—Claude C. (dec.), Genevieve, Abbott McC., Mildred (Mrs. C. R. McLean), Hope, John Lawrence. Admitted to Minn. bar, May 1880; practiced at Mankato, 1880-90, later at Duluth; chmn. board Northern Nat. Bank; pres. and dir. several industrial and financial corps. Mem. Bd. Edn., Duluth, 1900-07; mem. State Normal Sch. Bd. and resident dir. State Normal Sch., Duluth, 1903-20. Pres. Minn. State Bar Assn., 1907-08. Served on various public bds. and commns. Published pamphlets on American constitutional and governmental subjects. Home: Duluth, Minn. Died Aug. 27, 1931.

WASHBURN, John, miller; b. Hallowell, Me., Aug. 1, 1858; s. Algernon S. and Anna Sarah (Moore) W.; ed. pvt. schs. and Bowdoin Coll.; m. Elizabeth Pope Harding, July 28, 1884. Removed to Minneapolis, Minn., 1880, and entered employ of Washburn Mills, advancing to position of buyer of wheat; became mem. Washburn-Crosby Co., and pres.; dir. First and Security Nat. Bank, Minneapolis, Minneapolis Trust Co., C.G.W. Ry. Co., Brown Grain Co., Barnum Grain Co., and pres. several milling and elevator corps. Republican. Universalist. Home: Minneapolis, Minn. Died Sept. 25, 1919.

WASHBURN, John Henry, fire underwriter; b. Amherst, Mass., Oct. 27, 1828; s. Rev. Royal and Harriet (Parsons) W.; Amherst Coll., 1849, A.B., 1865; read law Rutland, Vt., and Granville, N.Y.; m. Jane Ives, Oct. 17, 1853 (died 1898). Entered service of Home Ins. Co., 1859, asst. sec., 1865, sec., 1867, v.p., 1884, pres., 1901-04 (resigned). Mem. Soc. Colonial Wars, S.R., Founders and Patriots, Mayflowers Descendants, Descendants Colonial Governors. Died 1909.

WASHBURN, John Hosea, agriculturist; b. Bridgewater, Mass., June 5, 1859; s. Hosea and Wealthy (Packard) W.; B.S., Mass. Agrl. Coll., 1878; post-grad. in chemistry, Brown U., 1880-81, Mass. Agrl. Coll., 1881-83, U. of Göttingen, 1885, 1887-89, A.M., Ph.D., 1889; m. Martha W. Merrow, May 26, 1887. Teacher in common and high schs., 1878-81; prof. chemistry, Storrs (Conn.) Agrl. Sch., 1883-87; pres. and prof. agrl. chemistry, R.I. Coll. of Agr. and Mech. Arts, 1889-1902; dir. Nat. Farm Sch., Bucks County, Pa., 1892-Mar. 1, 1917. Republican. Mem. New Church (Swedenborgian). Died Aug. 3, 1932.

WASHBURN, Louis Cope, clergyman; b. Pottsville, Pa., Jan. 25, 1860; s. Daniel and Sarah Stratton (Carpenter) W.; student St. Stephen's Coll., Annandale, N.Y.; B.A., Trinity Coll., Conn., 1881, M.A., 1884; Berkeley Div. Sch., Middletown, Conn.; S.T.D., Hobart, 1894; U. of Pa., 1920; m. Henrietta Saltonstall Mumford, Apr. 8, 1890 (died 1922); children—Henrietta Mumford, Helen Carpenter, Louis Mumford. Deacon, 1884, priest, 1885, P.E. Ch.; rector St. Peter's Ch., Hazleton, Pa., 1884-88, St. Paul's Ch., Rochester, N.Y., 1888-95; archdeacon of Rochester, 1895-1904; rector Christ Ch., Phila., 1907-37; retired Feb. 5, 1937. Dep. to Gen. Conv. P.E. Ch., 1904, 13; established numerous chs. and religious enterprises; adminstr. various philanthropies; dir. Neighborhood House, Phila., 1911-37; mgr. Episcopal Hosp., Standing Commission of Diocese of Pennsylvania, etc.; chairman War Commn. Diocese of Pa., 1917-18. Democrat. Author: Soldiers' and Sailors' Manual, 1917; Christ Church, 1925; also essays, sermons and pamphlets. Home: Philadelphia, Pa. Died June 15, 1938.

WASHBURN, Margaret Floy, coll. prof.; b. New York, July 25, 1871; d. Rev. Francis and Elizabeth Floy (Davis) Washburn; A.B., Vassar Coll., 1891, A.M., 1893; Ph.D., Cornell U., 1894. Prof. psychology and ethics, Wells Coll., 1894-1900; warden Sage Coll. of Cornell U., 1900-02; asst. prof. psychology, U. of Cincinnati, 1902-03; asso. prof. philosophy, 1903-08, prof. psychology, 1908-37; prof. emeritus, 1937—, Vassar Coll. Author: The Animal Mind, 1908; Movement and Mental Imagery, 1916. Translator: Ethical Systems (Wilhelm Wundt); Principles of Morality (by same), 1901. Co-editor Am. Jour. Psychology. Contbr. to Psychol. Review, Jour. of Comparative Psychology, etc. Died Oct. 29, 1939.

WASHBURN, William Drew, senator; b. Livermore, Me., Jan. 14, 1831; s. Israel and Martha B. W.; A.B., Bowdoin Coll., 1854, LL.D., 1901; removed to Minn. and engaged in law practice, 1857; m. Elizabeth M. Muzzy, Apr. 19, 1859; father of Stanley and Cadwallader W. Became largely interested in flour mfg. and lumber enterprises; for years interested in the Washburn & Crosby flouring mills; stockholder and dir. in the Pillsbury-Washburn Co.; originator and promoter, and pres. for many years, Minneapolis & St. Louis R.R.; also projector and builder Minneapolis, St. Paul & Sault Ste. Marie R.R., pres. until 1889. Mem. Minn. Ho. of Rep., 1869, 1871; surveyor gen. of Minn., 1861-65; mem. 46th to 48th Congresses (1879-85); U.S. senator, 1889-95. Republican. Pres. Universalist Nat. Conv. Home: Fair Oaks, Minn. Died July 29, 1912.

WASHBURN, William Ives, lawyer, fire insurance; A.B., Amherst, 1876, A.M., 1878; LL.B., Columbia, 1878. Chmn. exec. com. and gen. counsel The Home Ins. Co., New York; also chmn. exec. com. and gen. counsel City of New York Ins. Co., chmn. exec. com. Franklin Fire Ins. Co. of Phila., Harmonia Fire Ins.

Co. of Buffalo, New Brunswick Fire Ins. Co., Carolina Ins. Co. of Wilmington, N.C.; dir. Lawyers Title & Guaranty Co., and officer or dir. various other corps. Died July 30, 1933.

WASHBURN, William Sherman, banker; b. Alpine, New York, Dec. 8, 1860; s. Henry and Charlotte (Smith) Washburn; graduate N.Y. State Normal Sch., 1884; prin. Kingsboro (N.Y.) Union Sch., 1884-87; LL.B., 1890, LL.M., 1891, M.D., 1894, Columbian U.; m. Lillian M. Graves, Sept. 25, 1895. Prof. Columbian U., 1895-1900; examiner U.S. Civ. Service Commn., 1890-1900; chmn. Philippine Civ. Service Bd., 1901-05; dir. of civ. service, P.I., 1905-09; U.S. Civil Service commr., 1909-13. Bank and corp. dir. Trustee George Washington U. Dep. gov. gen. Soc. Mayflower Descendants; fellow Am. Geog. Soc.; mem. A.A.A.S., Acad. Polit. Science. Author of papers on civ. service, edn., and health and climatic conditions in the Philippines. Died June 28, 1923.

WASHBURN, William Tucker, author; b. Boston, Aug. 15, 1841; s. William Rounseville and Susan (Tucker) W.; A.B., Harvard, 1862, A.M., 1866; law student, Harvard, 1863-64; m. Mary R. Doughty, Sept. 6, 1881. Admitted to bar, 1865, in practice at New York, 1865—. Author: Fair Harvard, 1869; The Unknown City, 1880; Spring and Summer (verse), 1890; The Deuce of Hearts, 1901; The First Stone, 1904; Poems, 1905. Home: New York, N.Y. Died Oct. 22, 1916.

WASHINGER, William Henry, bishop; b. Greythorne, Cumberland County, Pa., Sept. 9, 1862; s. Jacob and Sarah (Warner) W.; B.A., Lebanon Valley Coll., Annville, Pa., 1891, M.A., 1895, D.D., 1905; m. Romaine Elizabeth Funkhouser, Sept. 8, 1885. Pastor Harrisburg, Pa., 1890-94; ordained ministry U.B. Ch., 1894; pastor Chambersburg, Pa., 1894-1902; supt. Pa. Conf. U.B. Ch., 1902-17; bishop Pacific Dist. U.B. Ch., 1917. Built chs. at Harrisburg and Chambersburg. Trustee Lebanon Valley Coll., Quincy (Pa.) Orphanage and Home; dir. Col. R. M. Baker Home for Retired Ministers. Wrote booklet, "City Evangelization," 1906. Lecturer on social, economic, edni. and religious problems; etc. A v.p. Fed. Council Churches of Christ in America; mem. Ednl. Administration, Mission, and Evangelistic bds. of U.B. Ch. Home: Portland, Ore. Died May 1928.

WASHINGTON, Booker Taliaferro, educator; b. nr. Hale's Ford, Va., about 1859; of African descent; grad. Hampton Inst., Va., 1875; hon. A.M., Harvard U., 1896; LL.D., Dartmouth, 1901; m. Maggie J. Murray, Oct. 12, 1893. Teacher at Hampton Inst. until elected by state authorities as head of Tuskegee Inst., which he organized and of which was prin., 1884—. Writer and speaker on racial and ednl. subjects. Author: Sowing and Reaping, 1900; Up from Slavery, 1901; Future of the American Negro, 1899; Character Building, 1902; Story of My Life and Work, 1903; Working with Hands, 1904; Tuskegee and Its People, 1905; Putting the Most Into Life, 1906; Life of Frederick Douglass, 1907; The Negro in Business, 1907; The Story of the Negro, 1909; My Larger Education, 1911; The Man Farthest Down, 1912. Died Nov. 14, 1915.

WASHINGTON, Henry Stephens, petrologist; b. Newark, N.J., Jan. 15, 1867; s. George and Eleanor P. (Stephens) W.; A.B., Yale, 1886; A.M., 1888; Ph.D., Leipzieg, 1893; post-grad. studies, Yale, Leipzig, and Am. Sch. Classical Studies (Athens); m. Martha Rose Beckwith, Oct. 25, 1893. Asst. in physics, Yale, 1886-88; excavations in Greece, 1889-94; asst. in mineralogy, Yale, 1895-96; geol., volc., petrol. investigations in Greece, Asia Minor, Italy, Spain, Brazil, Hawaiian Islands, and U.S., and chem. study of igneous rocks and minerals; cons. mining geologist, 1906-12; bd. mgrs. Geol. Survey N.J., 1909-14; with Geophysical Lab., Carnegie Instn. of Washington, 1912—. Chem. asso. and scientific attaché Am. Embassy, Rome, 1918-19; vice chmn. sect. volcanology, Internat. Geophys. Union; chmn. Am. Geophys. Union, 1927-29. Decorated Cavalier Order Crown of Italy. Author: Chemical Analyses of Igneous Rocks, 1903, 1917; Manual of the Chemical Analysis of Igneous Rocks, 1904; The Roman Comagmatic Region, 1906. Joint Author: Quantitative Classification of Igneous Rocks, 1903. Contbr. of articles on petrol., mineral. and archæol. subjects in scientific jours., 1887—. Died Jan. 7, 1934.

WASHINGTON, Lawrence, librarian; b. Mt. Vernon, Fairfax County, Va., Jan. 14, 1854; s. John Augustine and Eleanor Love (Selden) W.; ed. Va. Mil. Inst., Lexington, Va., 1869-71; m. Fannie Lackland, June 14, 1876. Civ. engr., 1871-76; farming, 1876-97; reference librarian, Library of Congress, 1897—. Democrat. Episcopalian. Mason. Home: Washington, D.C. Died Jan. 28, 1920.

WASHINGTON, W(illiam) Lanier; b. Montgomery, Ala., Mar. 30, 1865; s. Maj. James Barroll and Jane Bretney (Lanier) W.; descendant of two brothers of Gen. George Washington—(1) Augustine Washington, whose only son, Col. William Augustine Washington, married his first counsin, Jane Washington, the eldest child of (2) Col. John Augustine Washington; ed. Burlington Coll. and U. of Pittsburgh; m. May Bruce Brennan, June 6, 1906; m. 3d, Augusta A. Koblank, New York. In railway business, 1886-1890; pres. Laurel Land Co., Pittsburgh, 1891-99; pres. and gen. mgr. Elliott-Washington Steel Co., 1893-98; chmn. and mng. dir. Pittsburgh Sheet Steel Mfg. Co., 1898-1901; pres. United Oil Cloth Co., Trenton, N.J., 1905-06; dir. Tokstad-Burger Co., 1912-19, etc. Settled in N.Y. City, 1899. Chief of adminstrn. and sec. gen. 1st Aviation Corps, Provisional Vols., U.S.A., 1913-17. Mem. bd. govs. Sulgrave Instn. Mem. Soc. of the Cincinnati (hereditary representative of Gen. Washington). Republican. Episcopalian. Mason. Author of numerous papers on George Washington. Home: New York, N.Y. Died Sept. 11, 1933.

WASON, Charles William, elec. engr.; b. Cleveland, Apr. 20, 1854; mech. engring. course, Cornell U., 1872-76; m. Jettie Morrill, 1882; m. 2d, Margaret Wright; m. 3d, Mabel Breckenridge. Established as elec. engr. in Cleveland, becoming distinguished as expert on application of electricity to propulsion; largely interested in street ry. co.'s stocks. Home: Cleveland, Ohio. Died Apr. 15, 1918.

WASON, Edward H., congressman; b. New Boston, N.H., Sept. 2, 1865; grad. N.H. Coll. Agr. and Mechanic Arts, 1886; LL.B., Boston U. Sch. of Law, 1890; married; 1 son. Sergt. at arms, asst. clk. and clk. N.H. Senate; mem. and pres. City Council, and mem. Bd. of Aldermen, Nashua; mem. N.H. Ho. of Rep., 1899,1909, 13; mem. N.H. Constl. Conv., 1902-12; solicitor County of Hillsboro, 1903-07; mem. 64th to 72d Congresses (1915-33), 2d N.H. District. Republican. Home: Nashua, N.H. Died Feb. 6, 1941.

WASON, Leonard Chase, engineer; b. Brookline, Mass., Aug. 5, 1868; s. Elbridge and Mary I. (Chase) W.; B.S. (in elec. engring.), Mass. Inst. Tech., 1891; m. Harriet C. Willis, Oct. 8, 1896; children—Elbridge, Alfred Boyd, Raymond, Lawrence Willis; m. 2d, Annie B. Redlon, June 24, 1916. Pres., 1895—. Aberthaw Co., specializing in reinforced concrete, and built numerous bridges, mills, residences, the Harvard Stadium, and the largest concrete standpipe for water in the world; dir. Fed. Mutual Liability Ins. Co., Fed. Mutual Fire Ins. Co.; mem. advisory bd. Lumbermen's Mut. Casualty Co. of Chicago. Pres. Am. Concrete Inst. Republican. Author: Engineer's Handbook of Reinforced Concrete, 1905. Awarded Phebe Hobson Fowler prize, Am. Soc. C.E., 1929, "for meritorious achievement in engineering." Home: Brookline, Mass. Died Apr. 30, 1937.

WASTE, William Harrison, judge; b. Chico, Calif., Oct. 31, 1868; s. John Jackson and Mary Catherine (McIntosh) W.; Ph.B., U. of Calif., 1891, LL.B., 1894; m. Mary J. Ewing, Sept. 16, 1896 (died 1927); children—William Ewing, Mrs. Eugenia McIntosh Ward; m. 2d, Lucile M. Scoonover, April 16, 1932. Began practice at Oakland, Calif., 1894; served as mem. Calif. legislature, 1903, 05; judge Superior Ct., Alameda County, 1905-18; presiding justice Dist. Ct. of Appeal, 1919-21; asso. justice Supreme Ct. of Calif., 1921-26, chief justice, 1926—. Trustee Coll. of the Pacific, Pacific Sch. of Religion. Republican. Methodist. Mason. Home: Berkeley, Calif. Died June 6, 1940.

WATERBURY, Frank C., mfg. chemist; b. Freeport, Ill., Apr. 16, 1866; s. Stephen (M.D.) and Lydia (Overman) W.; ed. pub. schs.; m. Coral P. Chaffin, July 12, 1892; children—Carl Chaffin, Chloris P. (Mrs. M. T. Straight). Pres. Waterbury Chem. Co., 1900—; also pres. same, New York, New Orleans and Toronto; pres. Waterbury, Inc., Suburban Investment Co., W. Grand Av. Investment Co., West Park Investment Co. V.p. Des Moines Sch. Pharmacy. Republican. Unitarian. Mason. Died Dec. 7, 1930.

WATERBURY, John Isaac, banker; b. Stamford, Conn., 1850; B.S., Coll. City of New York, 1870; m. Miss Moller, 1881; children—Ethel H. (Mrs. Duncan Campbell), Florence, Gladys F. Dir. Am. Telephone & Telegraph Co., Audit Co. of New York, C.,I.&L. Ry. Co., L.&N. R.R. Co., Pacific Coast Co., Telautograph Corp., Tex. & Pacific Ry. Co., U.S. Guarantee Co. V.p. Chamber Commerce State of N.Y., 1912-16; del. of Chamber Commerce of New York to London Chamber Commerce, 1901; U.S. del. Internat. Preliminary Conf. on Wireless Telegraphy at Berlin, 1903, Internat. Conf. on Wireless Telegraphy, Berlin, 1906, London, 1912; mem. of Com. of Trust Co. Presidents, 1907; mem. Am. Chamber Commerce in London, Am.-Belgian Chamber Commerce, Met. Mus. of Art, Am. Mus. Natural History, Am. Numismatic Soc. (trustee), Royal Soc. Arts, London, Japan Soc., French Inst. in U.S. (trustee), Am. Acad. Polit. and Social Science, Acad. Polit. Science, N.Y. Acad. Sciences. Home: Morristown, N.J. Died Mar. 4, 1929.

WATERHOUSE, Frank, ship owner; b. Cheshire, Eng., Aug. 8, 1867; s. Joseph and Mary Elizabeth (Horsfield) W.; ed. pvt. schs., Eng.; m. Lucy Dyer Hayden, 1893. Came to U.S. at 15; settled in Puget Sound country, 1892; became sec. Pacific Nav. Co., 1895, later gen. mgr.; resigned, 1897, to organize Frank Waterhouse & Co., Ltd., of Eng., for Alaska trade; pres. Frank Waterhouse, Inc., Frank Waterhouse & Co., of Can., Ltd., Seattle Taxicab Co., Yellow Cab Co., Gray Line Tours, Inc. Pioneer in building up shipping industry on Pacific Coast. Home: Seattle, Wash. Deceased.

WATERHOUSE, Richard Green, bishop; b. nr. Spring City, Rhea County, Tenn., Dec. 24, 1855; s. Franklin and Lorinda Rachel Sims (Thompson) W.; A.B., Emory and Henry Coll., Emory, Va., 1885; D.D., W.Va. U., 1891; m. Carrie Steele, Feb. 3, 1887 (died 1891); m. 2d, Mrs. M. R. Carriger, Oct. 10, 1894. Ordained M.E. Ch., S., ministry, 1880 and 1885; pastor, Jonesboro, Tenn., 1880-81; city missionary, Knoxville, 1885, and pastor Church St. Ch., Knoxville, 1886-90; presiding elder, Radford Dist., Va., 1890-92; prof. English, 1892-93, pres., 1893-1910, Emory and Henry Coll.; elected bishop, May 18, 1910. Mem. 5 Gen. Confs. M.E. Ch., S.; mem. Bd. Edn., 1902-10; trustee Emory and Henry Coll., and Martha Washington Coll., Abingdon, Va. Died Dec. 9, 1922.

WATERLOO, Stanley, author; b. St. Clair County, Mich., May 21, 1846; s. Charles H. and Mary Jane W.; ed. pub. sch. and U. of Mich., class of '69, hon. A.M., 1898; m. Anna C. Kitton, 1874. Reporter on Chicago papers, 1870-71; one of owners St. Louis Journal, 1872; later editor on St. Louis Republic, Chronicle and Globe-Democrat; started St. Paul Day, 1884; editorial writer Chicago Tribune; later editor-in-chief Chicago Mail, and afterward editor Washington Critic and Capital. Author: A Man and a Woman; An Odd Situation; The Story of Ab; Honest Money; Armagedon; The Wolf's Long Howl; The Launching of a Man; The Seekers; The Story of a Strange Career, 1902; These Are My Jewels, 1902; The Cassowary, 1906. Died Oct. 11, 1913.

WATERMAN, Arba Nelson, judge; b. Greensboro, Vt., Feb. 5, 1836; s. Loring F. and Mary (Stevens) W.; A.B., Norwich U., 1856; student Albany Law Sch., 1860-61; LL.D., U. of Vt., 1892; m. Eloise Hall, Dec. 16, 1862. Lt. col. 100th Ill. Vols. in Civil War; wounded at battle of Chickamauga; horse killed under him in battle. Admitted to bar, Supreme Ct. of N.Y., 1861, and practiced at Chicago; judge Circuit Ct. Cook County, Ill., 1887-1903; assigned as judge Appellate Ct., 1st Dist. of Ill. Dean John Marshall Law Sch., 1902—. Author: A Century of Caste, 1901; A Consideration of the Influences that Have Made Chicago, and the Prospect as to Its Future. Home: Chicago, Ill. Died Mar. 16, 1917.

WATERMAN, Charles M., judge; b. Frankfort, Ky., Jan. 5, 1847; s. Joseph A. and Sarah A. (McGhee) W.; acad. edn.; m. Anna Lowry, Oct. 25, 1878. Admitted to bar, 1871, and practiced at Davenport. Member 17th Gen. Assembly; district judge 7th Jud. Dist. of Iowa, 11 yrs.; judge Supreme Ct. of Iowa, 4½ yrs., to 1902; resigned; mem. firm of Lane & Waterman. Republican. Address: Davenport, Ia. Died Jan. 28, 1924.

WATERMAN, Charles Winfield, senator; b. Waitsfield, Vt., Nov. 2, 1861; s. John and Mary A. (Leach) W.; A.B., U. of Vt., 1885, LL.D., 1922; LL.B., U. of Mich., 1889; m. Anna R. Cook, June 18, 1890. Admitted to bar, 1889, and settled at Denver; mem. law firm Wolcott, Vaile & Waterman, 1902-08; counsel Great Western Sugar Co., 1908-23; also represented as counsel C.,B.&Q. R.R. Co., C.,R.I.&P. R.R. Co., D.&R.G. Ry., Gt. Western Ry. Co. and many other corps.; retired from practice; U.S. Senator, term 1927-33. Republican. Conglist. Home: Denver, Colo. Died Aug. 27, 1932.

WATERMAN, Lewis Anthony, lawyer; b. Providence, R.I., Mar. 24, 1871; s. Franklin Alonzo and Hannah (Eddy) W.; A.B., Brown U., 1894; student Boston U. Sch. of Law, 1894-95; m. Katharine Minerva Utter, Aug. 24, 1896. Admitted to R.I. bar, 1896, and practiced in Providence, 1896—; sr. mem. firm Waterman & Greenlaw. Mem. R.I. Ho. of Rep., 1907, 08; Dem. candidate for gov., 1910, 11. Mem. Am. Bar Assn., Am. Acad. Polit. and Social Science. Republican. Baptist. Scottish Rite Mason. Home: Providence, R.I. Died Jan. 12, 1923.

WATERMAN, Lucius, clergyman; b. Providence, R.I., Mar. 29, 1851; s. Henry (D.D.) and Eliza Greene (Harris) W.; B.A., Trinity Coll., 1871, M.A., 1874, D.D., 1892; student Berkeley Div. Sch., 1873-76; m. Abby J. Cate, Sept. 18, 1884. Deacon, 1876, priest, 1877. P.E. Ch.; asst. Trinity Ch., New Haven, Conn., 1876; rector St. Mary's Ch., E. Providence, R.I., 1877; asst. Christ Ch., Detroit, 1878; rector Trinity Ch., Tilton, N.H., 1878-83; prof. ch. history, Seabury Div. Sch., Faribault, Minn., 1883-85; officiating in Duchess County, N.Y., 1885-88; missionary Littleton, N.H., 1888-93, Laconia, N.H., 1893-98; rector Trinity Ch., Claremont, N.H., 1899-1902, St. Luke's, Charlestown, N.H., 1902-04, St. Thomas' Ch., Hanover, N.H., 1904-19. Cleveland Democrat. Author: The Post Apostolic Age (Vol. II in series Ten Epochs of Ch. History), 1898; Tables of Episcopal Descent, 1903; God's Balance of Faith and Freedom (Page lectures for 1910); The Primitive Tradition of the Eucharistic Body and Blood (Paddock Lectures for 1919); also occasional published sermons. Died July 26, 1923.

WATERS, Clara Erskine Clement, author; b. (Erskine) St. Louis, Mo., Aug. 28, 1834; m. James

Hazen Clement, 1852 (dec.); m. 2d, Edwin Forbes Waters. Descriptive and critical lecturer upon art, travel, etc. Author: Handbook of Legendary and Mythological Art; Painters, Sculptors, Architects, Engravers and Their Works; Artists of the XIXth Century (with Laurence Hutton); History of Egypt; Life of Charlotte Cushman; Eleanor Maitland (novel); Stories of Art and Artists; History of Painting, of Sculpture and of Architecture, for Beginners and Students; Venice, the Queen of the Adriatic; Naples, the City of Parthenope; Constantinople, the City of the Sultans; Rome, the Eternal City; Angels in Art; Saints in Art; Heroines of the Bible in Art; Women in the Fine Arts, 1904. Address: Newburyport, Mass. Died Feb. 20, 1916.

WATERS, Dudley E., banker; b. Grand Rapids, Mich., Nov. 27, 1862; s. Daniel Howard and Mary (Leffingwell) W.; pub. sch. edn.; m. Florence Hills, Jan. 14, 1892; children—Mary Hills (dec.), Dudley Hills. Entered banking business, 1901; chmn. bd. Grand Rapids Nat. Bank; receiver Pere Marquette R.R. Co., 1912-16; pres. Hackley-Phelps-Bonnell Co. (Wis.), Grand Rapids Industrial Land Assn., Grand Rapids Nat. Co., Klingman's Furniture Co., Furniture Exhbn. Bldg. Co.; v.p. Mich. Bell Telephone Co., Hayes Body Corp., Union Joint Stock Land Bank (Detroit), Grand Rapids Creamery Co., Furniture Mart of Grand Rapids; dir. in 21 corps. Pres. Grand Rapids Clearing House Assn.; dir. Grand Rapids Art Assn.; mem. Bd. Pub. Works, Grand Rapids, 1895-1901 (pres.); trustee Kent Scientific Inst. Democrat. Home: Grand Rapids, Mich. Died Jan. 19, 1931.

WATERS, Francis E., financier, lumberman; b. Snow Hill, Md., May 4, 1856; s. Richard T. and Hester A. (Hopkins) W.; father a leading lumberman; moved with family to Baltimore, Md., 1865; ed. pub. and pvt. schs.; m. Fannie Scott, Jan. 3, 1877; children—Jennie Scott (wife of Dr. Ronald T. Abercrombie), Mary Hester (Mrs. Joshua Marsh Matthews). Became mem. R. T. Waters & Son, 1874, owning extensive forests and mills in states of Va. and N.C.; pres. Surry (Va.) Lumber Co.; dir. Mercantile Trust & Deposit Co. (exec. com.), Phila., Baltimore & Washington R.R. Co., Savings Bank of Baltimore, Merchants & Miners Transportation Co. Mem. bd. dirs. Md. Penitentiary 20 yrs. and pres. of bd.; commr. from Md. to St. Louis Expn., 1904; mem. com. of 12 apptd. to remap and reconstruct City of Baltimore after the great fire; pres. Lumber Exchange, Baltimore, 1885, Bd. of Trade, 1907; chmn. Md. Council of Defense, 1917-20. Trustee Samuel Ready Sch., Crippled Children's Hospital Sch. Mem. Atlantic Waterways Commn. Col. on staff of Gov. Jackson; brig. gen. staff of Gov. Smith. Democrat. Presbyn. (mem. board of trustees Brown Memorial Church). Home: Baltimore, Md. Died Jan. 1936.

WATERS, Henry Jackson, coll. pres., editor; b. Center, Ralls County, Mo., Nov. 23, 1865; s. George Washington and Lavinia Jane (Smith) W.; B.S.A., U. of Mo., 1886; grad. student, same, 1886-87, and summer session, 1900; univs. of Leipzig and Zürich, 1904-05; LL.D., N.H. Agrl. Coll., 1913, Univ. of Mo., 1916; m. Margaret Watson, June 3, 1897. Asst. sec. Mo. State Bd. Agr., 1886-88; asst. in agr., Mo. Agrl. Expt. Sta., 1886-91; prof. agr., Pa. State Coll., and agriculturist to Expt. Sta., 1892-95; dir. Mo. State agrl. exhibit at St. Louis Expn., 1904; dean Coll. of Agr., dir. Expt. Sta., and prof. agr., U. of Mo., 1895-1909; mem. exec. com., 1895-1909, pres., 1908-09, Mo. State Bd. Agr.; pres. Kan. State Agrl. Coll., Manhattan, 1909-17; mng. editor Kansas City Weekly Star, Jan. 1, 1918—. Commr. of U.S. and Philippine Govt. to P.I. to report on agrl. and ednl. development of the islands; mem. Kan. State Bd. of Edn., 1909, Kan. State Sch. Book Commn., 1913-18; chmn. State Council Defense, 1917-18; fed. food adminstr., Sept.-Dec. 1917. Democrat. Episcopalian. Author: The Essentials of Agriculture, 1915; The Development of the Philippine Islands (War Dept., U.S. and Philippine Govt.), 1915; Laboratory Manual of Agriculture (with J. D. Elliff), 1918; Elementary Agriculture, 1923. Home: Kansas City, Mo. Died Oct. 26, 1925.

WATERS, John H., banker, corp. official; pres. and chmn. bd. Nat. Radiator Corp., Johnstown, Pa.; also pres. U.S. Nat. Bank, U.S. Trust Co., U.S. Savings & Trust of Conemaugh, Century Stove & Mfg. Co. Died Aug. 14, 1933.

WATERS, N. McGee, clergyman; b. Independence, W.Va., Nov. 2, 1866; s. William and Mary (McGee) W.; A.B., U. of W.Va., 1886 (Henshaw gold medal for oratory); S.T.B., Boston U., 1891; D.D., Syracuse, 1901; m. Katherine B. Pierce, Aug. 26, 1892. Ordained to ministry, 1891; pastor St. Luke's Ch., Dubuque, Ia., 1891-95, Emmanuel Ch., Evanston, Ill., 1895-99, 1st Congl. Ch., Binghamton, N.Y., 1899-1903, Tompkins Av. Congl. Ch., Brooklyn, 1903—. Corporate mem. A.B.C.F.M.; dir. Ch. Extension Soc. of N.Y., State Missionary Soc. N.Y. Author: The Religious Life, 1904; A Young Man's Religion, 1907; Heroes in Common Life, 1908. Widely known as platform lecturer and after-dinner speaker. Home: Brooklyn, N.Y. Died May 12, 1916.

WATERS, Robert, author; b. Thurso, Scotland, May 9, 1835; s. William and Alexandrina (Sutherland) W.; came to America in 8th yr.; m. Helen, d. of Edmund Ferrett, 1875. Worked in printing offices, Montreal and New York; meanwhile studied English branches, French and German; went to London, 1861, France, 1862, Germany, 1863; taught English and German in St. Quentin, Picardy, 1862-63; English in Commercial Sch., Offenbach-on-the-Main, Hesse-Darmstadt, 1863-67; taught in German-Am. schs., New York, 1867-68; prof. lang. and lit., Hoboken Acad., 1868-83; prin., and supt. West Hoboken pub. schs., 1883-1908 (resigned). Author: Intellectual Pursuits; Life of William Cobbett; Cobbett's English Grammar; Shakespeare as Portrayed by Himself; John Selden and His Table-Talk; Flashes of Wit and Humor; Career and Conversation of John Swinton; Culture by Conversation; Reminiscences of the Hoboken Academy, 1904; Culture by Self-Help. Translator: Magical Experiments, or Science in Play. Died Nov. 28, 1910.

WATERS, Russell Judson, congressman; b. Halifax, Vt., June 6, 1843; grad. Franklin Inst.; m. Mary Adelaide Ballard, Nov. 26, 1869. Learned machinist's trade; taught sch.; prof. Latin and mathematics, Franklin Inst.; admitted to bar, 1868; practiced at Chicago until 1886; went to Calif.; founded Redlands, San Bernardino County, Calif.; city atty., Redlands, 1 yr.; identified with numerous corps. at Redlands; moved to Los Angeles, 1894; mem. bd. park commrs., 1897; member 56th Congress (1899-1901). Republican. Pres. Citizens' Bank, Broadway Trust Co. (Los Angeles), First Nat. Bank (Alhambra, Calif.), Home Savings Bank, Los Angeles, Columbia Commercial Co., Los Angeles, California Cattle Co., San Jacinto Valley (Calif.) Water Co. Author: Lyric Echoes (poems); El Estranjero (novel). Died 1911.

WATERS, Thomas Franklin, clergyman; b. Salem, Mass., Apr. 12, 1851; s. Thomas S. and Mary A. (Cook) W.; A.B., Harvard, 1872, hon. A.M., 1909; grad. Andover Theol. Sem., 1875; m. Adaline M. Orswell, Mar. 26, 1879. Ordained Congl. ministry, Oct. 26, 1876; pastor, Edgartown, Mass., 1875-78, South Ch., Ipswich, Mass., 1879-1909, pastor emeritus, 1909. Fellow Am. Acad. Arts and Sciences. Author: Sketch of the Life of John Winthrop, the Younger, 1900; Ipswich in the Massachusetts Bay Colony, 1905; Augustine Heard and His Friends, 1916. Pres. Ipswich Hist. Soc. and compiler of its publs. Home: Ipswich, Mass. Died Nov. 23, 1919.

WATERS, William Everett, univ. prof.; b. Winthrop, Me., Dec. 20, 1856; s. Jabez M. and Martha Ellen (Webb) W.; A.B., Yale, 1878, Ph.D., 1887; m. Alma F. Oyler, June 28, 1888. Classical asst., Hughes High Sch., Cincinnati, 1880-83; tutor in classics, Yale, 1883-87; prof. Greek and comparative philology, U. of Cincinnati, 1890-94; prof. same, and pres. Wells Coll., 1894-1900; asso. prof. Greek, 1901-02, prof. Greek lang. and lit., 1902-23, New York U. Asst. sec. Coll. Entrance Exam. Bd., 1901-02. Author: (with William R. Harper) Inductive Greek Method, 1888; Town Life in Ancient Italy, 1902; Cena Trimalchionis of Petronius, 1902. Home: New York, N.Y. Died Aug. 3, 1924.

WATERS, William Otis, clergyman; b. North Norwich, N.Y., Sept. 4, 1861; s. Charles Sayres and Mary Jeanette (Lyon) W.; B.A., Hobart Coll., Geneva, N.Y., 1884, M.A., 1896, D.D., 1909; m. Anna Bianchi Freeman, Oct. 18, 1886. Deacon, 1890, priest, 1891, P.E. Ch.; asst. St. Andrew's Ch., Ann Arbor, Mich., 1890-91; rector St. Andrew's Ch., Detroit, 1891-1903, Grace Ch., Chicago, Feb. 15, 1903—. Dep. to Gen. Conv. P.E. Ch., 1901, 07, 13. Trustee St. Luke's Hosp., Nashotah Theol. Sem., Wis. Mem. Soc. Mayflower Descendants (gov. Ill. Soc. 1914-16, 1918-19). Pres. trustees Nat. Kindergarten Coll. Home: Chicago, Ill. Died Aug. 20, 1925.

WATHEN, John Roach, surgeon; b. Louisville, Ky., June 27, 1872; s. William H. (M.D., LL.D.) and Kate P. (Roach) W.; grad. Louisville Male High Sch., 1891; B.A., Yale, 1895; M.D., U. of Louisville, 1898; married. In practice of medicine, Louisville, 1898—; prof. surgery, U. of Louisville; surgeon to St. Anthony's, Louisville City hosps. Home: Louisville, Ky. Died 1935.

WATKINS, Aaron Sherman, clergyman; b. Rushsylvania, Ohio, Nov. 29, 1863; s. William White and Rebecca J. (Elliott) W.; B.S., Ohio Northern U., Ada, 1886, M.S., 1907, L.H.D., 1923; admitted to bar, after 4 yrs.' study in law office, 1889; LL.D., Taylor U., Upland, Ind., 1902; D.D., Asbury Coll., 1930; m. Emma L. Davis, Nov. 8, 1890; 1 son, Willard Merrill. Teacher in pub. schs., 1880-83, 1890-93; entered M.E. ministry, 1893, ordained, 1895; pastor at Continental, Ottawa, Edgerton, Delta, and N. Baltimore, O., 1893-1905; prof. lit. and philosophy, 1905-09, v.p., 1907-09, Ohio Northern U.; pres. Asbury Coll., Wilmore, Ky., 1909-10; lecturer, 1910-15; pastor Van Wert, O., 1915-16, Columbus Grove, O., 1916-18; pastor Germantown, O., and prof. English, Miami Mil. Inst., 1918-20; pastor Linwood, Cincinnati, 1920-23, Winton Pl. Ch., Cincinnati, 1923-27, Waynesville, O., 1927-28, Wesley Ch., Lima, O., 1928-32, Cairo, Ohio, 1932-35. Prohibition candidate for gov. of Ohio, 1905, 08, 32, for V.P. of U.S., 1908 and 1912, for Pres. of U.S., 1920. Trustee Ohio Northern U., 1914-19; del. Gen. Conf., 1924. Author: Principles of English Grammar. Home: Rushsylvania, O. Died Feb. 10, 1941.

WATKINS, Albert, historical writer; b. Worcester, Eng., Nov. 16, 1848; s. James and Mary Ann (Crockett) W.; removed to Wis., 1849; Ph.B., U. of Wis., 1871, LL.B., 1872; m. Margaret Anna Baker, Dec. 31, 1875. Supt. of schs., Iowa County, Wis., 1874-77; editor and part propr. Iowa County Democrat, Mineral Point, Wis., 1874-77, Sioux City Tribune, 1877-80, Daily State Democrat, Lincoln, Neb., 1882-86; postmaster Lincoln, 1885-90; opposed free silver from 1891. Historian Neb. State Hist. Soc. Author: History of Nebraska (3 vols.). Contbr. to newspapers and mags. on polit. and econ. topics. Home: Lincoln, Neb. Died Nov. 19, 1923.

WATKINS, Alexander Farrar, clergyman; b. Natchez, Miss., Dec. 18, 1856; s. William Hamilton (A.M., D.D.) and Elizabeth (Jones) W.; A.B., Vanderbilt U., 1883; D.D., Centenary Coll., Jackson, La., 1899; m. Lula Gaulding, June 30, 1892; children—James Gaulding (Capt. U.S.A.), Alexander Farrar, Elizabeth Holmes, Olive Andrews (dec.), Benjamin Drake (dec.), Lucie, Frances. Ordained ministry M.E. Ch. S., 1883; pastor Jackson, Miss., 1884, Martin circuit, 1885, Brookhaven, 1886-89; field agt. Millsaps Coll., Jackson, 1890-92; pastor 1st Ch., Jackson, 1893-96, Crawford St. Ch., Vicksburg, 1897-1900; pres. Whitworth Female Coll., Brookhaven, 1900-02; field agt. Connectional Superannuate Endowment Fund, 1903-04; presiding elder Jackson Dist., 1905-08; pastor 1st Ch., Hattiesburg, 1909-12; pres. Millsaps Coll., 1912-24; pres. bd. trustees, 1925—; later pastor Meridian, Miss. Trustee M.E. Ch., S., 1906-18; mem. gen. bd. missions, 1906-26; del. Gen. M.E. Conf., 1894-1922; sec. Gen. Conf., M.E. Ch., S., 1906—; del. Inter-Ch. Conf. Federation, New York, 1908, Ecumenical Conf., Toronto, 1911; mem. Joint Commn. on Unification M.E. Chs. of U.S.; mem. Joint Commn. (M.E. Ch. and M.E. Ch., S.) for exchange of territory and removal of causes of friction, 1918—, and mem. Joint Commn. on Edn. Dir. Miss. Orphans' Home. Democrat. Home: Meridian, Miss. Died July 26, 1929.

WATKINS, Charles W., insurance; b. East Salem, Washington County, N.Y.; s. Henry K. and Zina M. (Hanks) W.; attended common schs. and acad., Cambridge, N.Y.; moved to Allegan County, Mich., 1856; worked on farm; m. Mary Jane Gray, Sept. 19, 1867 (died 1895). Enlisted Co. B, 6th Mich. cav., Aug. 1862; promoted lt. 10th Mich. cav., 1864; bvtd. capt. for gallant service at Abbott's Creek, N.C., Apr. 1865; mem. Mich. legislature, 1871-73; moved to Grand Rapids, 1873; collector Internal Revenue 2½ yrs. under President Arthur; defeated for Congress, 1890, and for mayor Grand Rapids, 1894; v.p. Peninsular Trust Co., Grand Rapids; mem. Insular Commn., Jan.-Aug. 1899; commn. visited Puerto Rico, Feb. 1899. Home: Grand Rapids, Mich. Died 1906.

WATKINS, David Ogden, lawyer; b. Woodbury, N.J., June 8, 1862; s. William and Hannah W.; ed. pub. schs.; m. Mrs. Lidie M. Andrews. Admitted to bar, 1893; mayor of Woodbury, 1886-90, councilman, 1892-98 (pres. City Council, 1895-97); solicitor City of Woodbury, and counsel to Bd. Freeholders Gloucester County, N.J.; mem. N.J. Ho. Assembly, 1897-99 (speaker, 1898, 1899); acting gov. of N.J., Oct. 18, 1898-Jan. 16, 1899; U.S. atty. Dist. of N.J., 1900-03, resigned; commr. banking and ins., N.J., 2 terms, 1903-09; mem. Rep. State Com., 1904-08. Pres. Woodbury Trust Co. and Farmers & Mechanics Nat. Bank, Woodbury. Home: Woodbury, N.J. Died June 20, 1938.

WATKINS, Jabez Bunting, banker, land owner; b. nr. Punxsutawney, Pa., June 25, 1845; s. James and Barbara (Sprankle) W.; Dayton (Pa.) Acad., 1864-66; LL.B., U. of Mich., 1869; m. Elizabeth Josephine Miller, Nov. 10, 1909. Practiced law at Champaign, Ill., 1870-73; developed large business in examination of real estate titles and real estate loans. Removed to Lawrence, Kan., 1873, enlarged business, incorporating it in 1883, as J. B. Watkins Land Mortgage Co., starting branches in New York, 1876, London, 1878, Dallas, Tex., 1881; beginning with 1872, invested $12,000,000 in land mortgages; bought 1,500,000 acres of land in southwest La., 1883, from state and U.S. govts., on which, in 1890, he built, owned and operated 100 miles of ry., Lake Charles to Alexandria, La. Established Watkins Banking Co., Lake Charles, La., 1884; pres. Watkins Nat. Bank, Watkins Land Mortgage Co., Gulf Land Co.; pres. St. Louis, Watkins & Gulf R.R. Democrat. Baptist. Author: The True Money System for the United States, 1896. Home: Lawrence, Kan. Died Feb. 4, 1921.

WATKINS, John Elfreth, curator; b. Ben Lomond, Va., May 17, 1852; s. Dr. Francis B. and Mary (Elfreth) W.; grad. Lafayette Coll., C.E., 1871, M.Sc., 1874; Doctor of Engring., Stevens Inst. Tech., 1900. Mining engr., Delaware & Hudson Canal Co., 1871-72; asst. engr. of constrn., Pa. R.R. Co., 1872-73; lost a leg, disabling him from field work, Mar. 1873. Chief clerk, Amboy Div., Pa. R.R. Co. and Camden & Atlantic R.R., 1874-86; curator U.S. Nat. Museum, 1887-92; spl. agt. in charge Pa. R.R. exhibit, World's Columbian Expn., 1893; dir. industrial arts, Field Columbian Mus., Chicago, 1894; supt. and curator technol. collections, U.S. Nat. Mus., 1895—. Author: History of Pennsylvania Railroad, 1846-96; The Evolution of the Railway Passenger Car, 1888; also numerous papers on the evolution of railways and telegraph and other hist. and engring. subjects. Home: Washington, D.C. Died 1903.

WATKINS, John Thomas, congressman; b. Minden, La., Jan. 15, 1854; s. Judge J. D. and M. Flora (Morrow) W.; ed. Cumberland U., Lebanon, Tenn., 3 yrs.; studied law at Minden, La.; admitted to bar, 1878; m. Lizzie R. Murrell, Jan. 15, 1879. Judge Dist. Ct., La., 1892-1904; mem. 59th to 66th Congresses (1905-21), 4th La. District. Democrat. Home: Minden, La. Deceased.

WATKINS, Thomas James, gynecologist; b. Utica, N.Y., July 6, 1863; s. Robert and Eleanor (Williams) W.; prep. edn., Holland Patent (N.Y.) Acad. and Adams (N.Y.) Collegiate Inst.; student Med. Dept., U. of Mich., 1880-83; M.D., Belleuve Hosp. Med. Coll. (New York U.), 1886; m. Catherine Carman, May 4, 1892. Interne St. Peter's Hosp., Brooklyn, 1886-88, Woman's Hosp. of N.Y. State, 1888-89; asst. gynecologist, 1890-96, asst. prof. gynecology, 1896, clin. prof., 1900, prof., 1916—, Northwestern U. Med. Sch.; attending gynecologist St. Luke's Hosp., 1894—, Wesley Hosp., 1896-1914, Mercy Hosp., 1900-09. Apptd. 1st lt. U.S.A. Med. Reserve Corps, Feb. 1911. Home: Flossmoor, Ill. Died Apr. 1, 1925.

WATKINS, William Woodbury, physician; b. Warner, N.H., Aug. 3, 1846; s. Jason D. and Phebe W.; ed. Penacook, N.H., until 1860; grad. St. Louis (Mo.) Med. Coll., 1872; m. Caroline A. Woodhouse, Jan. 1873. Prof. in Coll. Phys. & Surg., St. Louis, Mo., 1886; sec. bd. of regents U. of Idaho, 1893-94; mem. bd. visitors to Naval Acad., Annapolis, Md., 1900; ry. surgeon for Northern Pacific R.R. and Ore. Ry. & Nav. Co. Republican. Pres. Idaho State Med. Soc., v.p. Idaho State Bd. of Med. Examiners. Frequent contributor to med. jours. of U.S. Died 1900.

WATMOUGH, James Horatio, officer U.S.N.; b. Whitemarsh, Pa., July 30, 1822; s. John Godard and Ellen (Coxe) W.; ed. U. of Pa.; m. Emmeline Sheaff, Oct. 19, 1848 (died 1904); m. 2d, Annie Bowie Harris, July 15, 1907. Acting midshipman U.S.N., 1843-44; p.m., Dec. 12, 1844; served in Mexican War; at capture of Calif.; bombardment and capture of Guaymas; commandant Santa Clara and Don José; fleet p.m. S. Atlantic Squadron, 1864-65, serving in actions on Stone River, and on James and John islands; later gen. pay insp. and 1873-77, p.m. gen.; retired July 30, 1884; advanced to rank of rear admiral, June 1906. Died Jan. 18, 1917.

WATRES, Louis Arthur, lawyer, banker; b. Mt. Vernon, Pa.; s. Lewis S. and Harriet G. W.; pub. sch. edn.; LL.D., Lafayette Coll., 1925, Washington and Lee, 1932. Admitted to Pa. bar, 1878; county solicitor Lackawanna County, 1881-90; mem. Pa. Senate, 1883-91; lt. gov. Pa., 1891-95; v.p. Pa. World's Fair Commn., 1893. Chmn. of the bd. Scranton Lackawanna Trust Co.; pres. Scranton Republican Pub. Co., Mansfield Water Co.; dir. First Nat. Bank; trustee Am. Surety Co. of New York. Served N.G. of Pa., 1877-91; inspector rifle practice with rank of col., on staff Gov. Beaver, 1887-91; judge adv. Pa. Div., N.G. Pa., 1894-98; col. 11th Regt. Provisional Guard, N.G. Pa.; after muster out of 11th Regt. on return from field, served as col. 13th Regt., N.G. Pa.; mem. State Armory Bd., Pa. Council of Safety and Defense. Pres. Scranton Chamber Commerce 8 yrs. Grand Master of Masons in Pa., 1916-17; pres. George Washington Masonic Nat. Memorial Assn. Home: Scranton, Pa. Died June 28, 1937.

WATROUS, Charles Leach, nurseryman; b. Freetown, N.Y., Jan. 13, 1837; s. Joseph and Lydia (Emerson) Leach W.; B.S., U. of Mich., 1862, LL.B., 1865; capt. 76th N.Y. Inf., 1862; m. Sophia Glover, Dec. 25, 1865. Moved to Ia.; mem. Ia. Ho. of Rep., 1883-85. Pres. Am. Assn. of Nurserymen, 1886-87, Am. Pomol. Soc., 1897, 99, 1901; pres. Ia. State Agrl. and Industrial League. Contbr. Bailey's Ency. of Horticulture. Died Feb. 9, 1916.

WATROUS, Elizabeth Snowden Nichols, artist; b. New York, N.Y., Nov. 1858; d. William Snowden and Elizabeth (Erickson) Nichols; Comstock Sch., New York; studied art with Henner and Carolus Duran; m. Harry Willson Watrous, Apr. 27, 1887. In art work, New York, 1885—. Author: "Ti" (Ticonderoga); "It." Home: New York, N.Y. Died Oct. 4, 1921.

WATROUS, George Ansel, educator; b. Binghamton, N.Y., Feb. 26, 1872; s. Charles O. and Angie (Kipp) W.; grad. Hamilton Coll., 1894, A.M., 1897; m. Grace Clarke, d. Cory D. Hayes, July 6, 1898. Teacher, 1894—; prof. English Utica Free Acad. Democrat. Editor (with intros. and notes): Selections from Dryden, Burns, Wordsworth and Browning, 1897; Three Narrative Poems, 1898; Pope, Gray and Goldsmith, 1899; Macaulay's Literary Essays, 1899; Macaulay's Historical Essays, 1900; Locke's Conduct of the Understanding, 1900. Author: First Year English, 1901; Second Year English, 1902; Third Year English, 1903; Elizabethan Drama, 1903. Deceased.

WATROUS, George Dutton, lawyer; b. New Haven, Conn., Sept. 18, 1858; s. George Henry and Harriet Joy (Dutton) W.; A.B., Yale, 1879, LL.B., 1883, M.L., 1884, D.C.L., 1890; m. Bertha Agnes Downer, June 7, 1888; children—Wheeler de Forest (dec.), Mrs. Charlotte Root Lyttle, George D., Jr., Mrs. Katherine Eliot Miller, Charles Ansel, Frederick Williams. Instr. law of contracts and torts, 1889-92, asst. prof. law, 1892-95, prof., 1895-1920, Yale Sch. of Law; mem. law firm Watrous, Hewitt, Gumbart & Corbin, 1933—; v.p. New Haven Gas Light Co.; v.p. Nat. Savings Bank. Pres. State Bar Assn. Conn., 1908-10, New Haven Co. Bar Assn., 1909-12; mem. Am. Acad. Polit. and Social Science; mem. bd. trustees Sheffield Scientific Sch., 1924—. Home: New Haven, Conn. Died Nov. 14, 1940.

WATROUS, Harry Willson, painter; b. San Francisco, Calif., Sept. 17, 1857; s. Charles and Ruth (Willson) W.; ed. pvt. schs., New York; art edn. at Atelier Bonnât and Academie Julian, Paris; m. Elizabeth, d. W. S. Nichols, 1887. Well known as genre painter with a splty. of small figures, very highly finished; Clark prize, Nat. Acad. Design, 1894; spl. gold medal, St. Louis Expn.; Altman $1000 prize, Nat. Acad. Design, 1929; Nat. Arts Club medal, 1931; Carnegie prize, Nat. Academy of Design, 1931, Saltus medal, 1934; Lippincott prize, Pa. Academy, 1935. Chmn. exec. com. on Art for N.Y. to St. Louis Expn.; sec. Nat. Acad. Design, 1898-1920, pres., 1933; mem. Art Commn. Associates, City of N.Y. A.N.A., 1894, N.A., 1895; pres. Nat. Acad. Assn., Sch. Art League. Home: New York, N.Y. Died May 9, 1940.

WATSON, Alfred Augustin, P.E. bishop; b. New York, N.Y., Aug. 21, 1818; s. Jesse and Hannah Maria W.; graduated U. of New York, 1837, A.M.; D.D., U. of N.C., and U. of the South; studied law in office of Judge Kent; licensed to practice in Supreme Ct., State of N.Y., 1841. Ordained deacon, 1844; priest, 1845; bishop of East Carolina, 1884; chaplain in N.C. State troops, C.S. army, during war. Died 1905.

WATSON, Amelia Montague, artist; b. East Windsor Hill, Conn., Mar. 2, 1856; d. Reed and Sarah (Bolles) W.; ed. pvt. schs.; unmarried. Exhibited at N.Y. Water Color Club, Am. Water Color Soc., Boston Art Club; teacher painting Martha's Vineyard Summer Inst. for many yrs.; distinctively a painter New England, Canadian and Southern scenery. Illus. Thoreau's "Cape Cod," 1896; made cover and frontispiece in colors for Margaret Warner Morley's "The Carolina Mountains," 1913, and for John Muir's "A Thousand Milke Walk to the Gulf," 1916; furnished portrait frontispiece and picture of Chicera Wood for "Chronicles of Chicera Wood," by Mrs. Elizabeth W. A. Pringle, 1921. Home: East Windsor Hill, Conn. Died Jan. 20, 1934.

WATSON, Andrew, missionary; b. Oliverburn, Perthshire, Scotland, Feb. 15, 1834; s. Andrew and Catherine (Roger) W.; A.B., Carroll Coll., Wis., 1857; Princeton Theol. Sem., 1858-59; Allegheny Theol. Sem., 1860-61; Jefferson Med. Coll., Phila.; D.D., Franklin Coll., Ohio, 1875; LL.D., Westminster Coll., Pa., 1911; m. Margaret MacVickar, July 10, 1861. Ordained U.P. ministry, May 15, 1861; missionary to Egypt, 1861—; prof. of systematic theology, Theol. Sem., Cairo, 1870—; del. to World's Missionary Conf., Edinburgh, 1910; mem. commn. for surveying missionary conditions in Egyptian Sudan, 1889; moderator Gen. Assembly U.P. Ch., Buffalo, 1890. Author: The American Mission in Egypt, 1897. Died Dec. 9, 1916.

WATSON, Benjamin Frank, lawyer; b. Warner, N.H., April 30, 1826; admitted to Mass. bar, 1850, and later to bar of Supreme Court of U.S.; counsel in leading case against the U.S. for the burning of Columbia, S.C., by Gen. Sherman, and as counsel for the owner, successfully presented the petition, under the Fugitive Slave Law, for the return to slavery of "The Slave Betty," before Chief Justice Lemuel Shaw at Boston, with John A. Andrew as counsel opposing. Editor and propr. Lawrence (Mass.) Sentinel, postmaster, city solicitor, and delegate to famous Democratic conventions (1860) at Charleston, S.C., and Baltimore. As major of 6th Mass. regt. offered the resolution passed by its col. and officers, tendering the regt., through Gov. Andrew, to President-elect Lincoln for service in case of need, thus distinguishing the regt. as the first to volunteer, as it was also the first in the field, in the Civil War, and the first to shed its blood and to force a way for the loyal troops through Baltimore to Washington; and as major, in command of one of the detachments of the regt. in Baltimore, April 19, 1861, ordered the shedding of the first blood in that war; elected lt. col. of 6th Mass. regt., and took command of it upon promotion of the col.; promoted to be bvtd. col. U.S.V.; declined command of another regt., and was apptd. and served as paymaster until became disabled in the service and retired from the army about Oct. 1864. Pres. Mass. Minute Men of 1861; apptd. by survivors of old 6th regt. to write the History of the Baltimore Campaign. In active practice of law in New York, 1867-1900, then retired. From that time devoted attention to benevolent work among working boys and young men. Pres. Church Temperance Legion. Died 1905.

WATSON, Charles Henry, clergyman; b. New York, N.Y., Jan. 1, 1847; s. Henry and Anne (Dixon) W.; A.B., Colgate U., 1873, A.M., 1876, D.D., 1897; grad. Hamilton Theol. Sem., 1875; m. Ada Bardeen, June 19, 1877; 1 son, Wayne (dec.). Ordained Bapt. ministry, 1875; pastor West Ch., Oswego, N.Y., 1875-81, 1st Ch., Arlington, Mass., 1881-1909. Univ. preacher or orator at Cornell, Colgate and Shaw univs., Colby and Acadia colls., and lecturer and baccalaureate preacher at Newton Theol. Instn., and pres. trustees, 1908-20. Author: The Mission of Unitarianism, 1885; Boston Letters, 1899; The Protestant Emphasis Upon the Minister's Personality, 1899; Eastern Notes, 1908. Librarian N.E. Bapt. Library, Boston, 1913—. Home: Belmont, Mass. Died Aug. 14, 1931.

WATSON, Clarence Wayland, senator; b. Fairmont, W.Va., May 8, 1864; s. James Otis and Matilda (Lamb) W.; ed. pub. schs., Marion County, W.Va.; m. Minnie Lee Owings, Oct. 10, 1894. Engaged in coal mining in W.Va. from early life; organized several cos. which later consolidated as Consolidation Coal Co., mines in W.Va., Md., Pa., Ky., of which was pres. until 1911, and 1919-28 (chmn. bd. 1911-18); pres. Elk Horn Coal Corp.; dir. Beaver Creek Consol. Coal Co.; Nat. Coal Assn. Del. to Dem. Nat. Convn., 1908, 20; elected U.S. senator from W.Va., Jan. 25, 1911, for unexpired term (1911-13) of Stephen B. Elkins, deceased. Commd. lt. col., Ordnance Dept., U.S.A., Mar. 25, 1918; hon. discharged, Jan. 23, 1919. Episcopalian. Mason. Home: Fairmont, W.Va. Died May 23, 1940.

WATSON, David Emmett, lawyer; b. Eminence, Ind., Feb. 4, 1870; s. John and Isabelle (Brasier) W.; LL.B., De Pauw, 1892; m. M. Effie Foster, Sept. 25, 1893 (died 1925). Practiced in Putnam County, Ind., 1892-96, in Martinsville, 1896-1912; judge pro tem Owen Circuit Ct., 1901-02; settled in Indianapolis, 1912; trial lawyer Indianapolis Street Ry. Co. and Terre Haute, Indianapolis & Eastern Traction Co., also corp. counsel both cos., 1912-29; v.p. and gen. counsel Indianapolis Rys., Inc., successor to Indianapolis St. Ry. Co.; v.p. Traction Terminal Corp., Peoples Motor Coach Co. Democrat. Mason. Deceased.

WATSON, David Thompson, lawyer; b. Washington, Pa., Jan. 2, 1844; s. James and Maria (Morgan) W.; A.B., Washington (now Washington and Jefferson) Coll., 1864; LL.B., Harvard, 1866; LL.D., U. of Pa., 1905; m. Margaret H. Walker, 1889. In practice at Pittsburgh, 1868—; sr. mem. Watson & Freeman; U.S. counsel before Alaska Boundary Commn., 1903; also counsel for govt. in "merger" cases. Home: Allegheny, Pa. Died Feb. 25, 1916.

WATSON, Ebbie Julian, state commr. S.C., b. Ridge Spring, S.C., June 29, 1869; s. Tilman and Helen O'Neall (Mauldin) W.; A.B., U. of S.C., 1889; m. Margaret Smith Miller, Dec. 17, 1896. City editor Evening Record, Columbia, S.C., 1889-91, Columbia State, 1891-1903, news editor, 1903-04; sec. Chamber of Commerce, Columbia, 1902-04; state commr. of agr., commerce and immigration (now agr., commerce and industries), S.C., Mar. 15, 1904—. Went to Europe, Aug. 1906, and established offices on behalf of state of S.C. in several foreign countries, to secure desirable immigrants for agrl. work; first to examine prospective immigrants in their own homes in Europe; landed at Charleston, S.C., Nov. 4, 1906, with shipload of 500 immigrants whose passage had been prepaid by the state; brought a second shipload, Feb. 1907, and established movement of new class of immigration to the South through port of Charleston. Pres. Southern States Assn. of Commrs. of Agr. 1906-07; v.p. and mem. exec. com. Interstate Sugar Growers' Assn.; v.p. Southern Industrial Parliament; v.p. Nat. Irrigation Congress, 1909; mem. dept. of immigration Nat. Civic Federation, S.C. Agrl. Soc. (hon.); v.p. Nat. Conservation Congress, 1910-11; pres. Southern Cotton Congress, 1911-16, Nat. Drainage Congress, 1914-16 (v.p. 1911-14); v.p. U.S. Good Roads Assn., 1912-14; pres. Ga.-Carolina Good Roads Congress, 1913; dir. Quebec & Miami Highway Assn., 1912-14; pres. Nat. Economic Research Soc., 1913; mem. Am. Acad. Polit. and Social Science, etc.; hon. mem. Pendleton Farmers' Soc. (1815), 1915. Democrat. Wrote about 65 reports, pamphlets, bulls., etc., upon resources of S.C. and agrl. and indsl. and economic subjects. Wrote Handbook of South Carolina, 1907-08. Raised $50,000,000 loan to resist attack on price of cotton, winter of 1911, and conducted a successful fight. Died Oct. 27, 1917.

WATSON, Edward Minor, judge; b. Holly Springs, Miss., Dec. 20, 1874; s. Edward Minor and Lillie Perrin (Moore) W.; student Miss. Agrl. and Mech. Coll., 1890-91; LL.B., U. of Miss., 1897; m. Louisa Emily Bradley, June 1, 1905. Began practice at Oxford, Miss., 1897; removed to Honolulu, H.T., 1901; mem. commn. to draft county act, providing county system of govt. for Hawaii, 1904; del. to Dem. Nat. Conv., 1908, 12; justice Supreme Ct., of Hawaii, 1914-16; resigned to resume practice; judge First Circuit Ct., Ty. of Hawaii, Div. of Domestic Relations, 1928-35, of U.S. Dist. Ct., July 1935—. Home: Honolulu, T.H. Deceased.

WATSON, Edward Willard, physician, author; b. Newport, R.I., Jan. 2, 1843; s. Rev. Benjamin and Lucy (Willard) W.; M.D., U. of Pa., 1865; m.

Georgiana Lester French; m. 2d, Delia Arthur Knipe, d. T. S. Arthur, 1900. Practicing physician; also employed in med. journalistic work. Author (verse): To-day and Yesterday, 1898; Songs of Flying Hours, 1900; Old Lamps and New, 1905; If Love Were King, 1915. Home: Philadelphia, Pa. Died Nov. 20, 1925.

WATSON, Emory Olin, clergyman; b. Newberry County, S.C., Aug. 5, 1865; s. Rev. John Emory and Lavinia N. (Ritchie) W.; ed. chiefly under father, a classical scholar; grad. Leesville (S.C.) Coll., 1885; D.D., U. of S.C., 1898; m. Mattie West, Mar. 10, 1885. Ordained ministry M.E. Ch., S., 1887; pastor various chs. in S.C. till 1899, and Bethel Ch., Charleston, S.C., 1900-03, Central Ch., Spartanburg, 1904-05; presiding elder Marion Dist., S.C., 1896-99; pastor Washington St. Ch., Columbia, 1910-12; founder and pres. Horry (S.C.) Indsl. Sch., 1913-14; pastor Bamberg, 1915-17; sec. War Work Commn., M.E. Ch., S., Washington, D.C., 1918-22; sec. of Washington office and Gen. Com. Army and Navy Chaplains, Fed. Council Chs. of Christ in America, 1919-25; gen. sec. Am. Friends of Greece, May 1, 1925-Nov. 1, 1926; editor Southern Christian Advocate, 1926-33. Decorated Silver Cross Order of the Savior (Greece). Democrat. Mason, K.P. Author of numerous brochures and articles. Editor Year Book of the Churches, 1922-23. Died Oct. 30, 1935.

WATSON, Eugene Winslow, rear adm. U.S.N.; b. Northampton, Mass., Feb. 17, 1843; s. Adolphus Eugene and Elisa Hovey (Mellen) W.; ed. P.E. Acad., Phila.; m. Virginia Cruse, Apr. 14, 1869. Apptd. master's mate on board the Lancaster, May 2, 1859, served on that vessel until Oct. 1861, Rhode Island, 1862-63; promoted acting ensign, Sept. 18, 1863; commd. ensign in regular service, Mar. 12, 1868; master, Dec. 18, 1868; lt., Mar. 21, 1870; lt. comdr., Nov. 1883; comdr., Apr. 27, 1893; capt., Nov. 22, 1899; retired with the rank of rear adm., after 40 yrs.' service, June 2, 1902. Died Dec. 11, 1914.

WATSON, Frank Rushmore, architect; b. Frankford, Phila., Pa., Feb. 28, 1859; s. Samuel and Anna (Brous) W.; B.A., Central High Sch., Phila., 1877, M.A., 1887, Dr. of Fine Arts, Muhlenberg Coll., 1931; m. Fannie Foulkroud, 1890 (died 1896); m. 2d, Rebecca S. Collins, Feb. 1, 1900; 1 dau., Margaret Anna. Practiced at Phila., 1883—; asso. with Samuel Huckel, Jr., 1902-17; practiced alone, 1917-22; mem. firm of Frank R. Watson, Edkins & Thompson, 1922-35; mem. firm Frank R. Watson and William Heyl Thompson, 1935—. Architect many churches, including Episcopal Cathedral, Diocese of Pennsylvania, etc. Hon. associate of American Guild of Organists; fellow A.I.A.; del. by apptmt. of U.S. Govt. and A.I.A. to Pan-Am. Congress of Architects at Santiago, Chile, 1923, Buenos Aires, 1927. Republican. Episcopalian. Home: Chestnut Hill, Pa. Died Oct. 29, 1940.

WATSON, George D., evangelist; b. Accomac County, Va., Mar. 26, 1845; s. James H. and Emaline (Scorboro) W.; ed. Bible Inst., Concord, N.H.; D.D., De Pauw U., 1876; m. Eva M. Watson, Oct. 7, 1869. Ordained ministry Wesleyan Meth. Ch., 1866; served as evangelist in Eng., West Indies, Can., New Zealand, Australia, Japan and Korea. Republican. Author: Love Abounding, 1892; Soul Food, 1906; Our Own God, 1911; Saints, 1913; God's Eagles, 1919; God's First Words, 1919; Coals of Fire; Heavenly Life; Steps to the Throne; White Robes; etc. Served as pvt. 42d Regt. Va. Vol. Inf., C.S.A., 1861-65. Home: Los Angeles, Calif. Deceased.

WATSON, Henry Chapman, commercial and financial journalist; b. Portchester, N.Y., Dec. 6, 1870; s. William Walpole and Jane (Bircham) W.; orphaned before he was 12 yrs. old and thrown on his own resources; early became asso. with newspaper work; m. Gwendolen Reid, May 10, 1901. Writer leading articles each week in Dun's Review while editor, and "Money and Business" editorial in each Monday's New York Tribune; compiler of Dun's Index Number, measuring the cost of living, for which a silver medal was awarded in Dept. of Sociology at St. Louis Expn., 1904, and Dun's Analysis of Commercial Failures—both accepted as the standard records on these subject. Prepared many statistics of Govt. Contbr. to mags. on economic conditions. Mem. Nat. Civic Federation. Chmn. finance com. Englewood City Council, and leader in Colby movement for reform of Republican politics in N.J. Home: Englewood, N.J. Died 1909.

WATSON, Henry David, editor, farmer; b. Amherst, Mass., Oct. 14, 1846; s. Oliver and Sarah W.; m. Harriet Cummings, Nov. 9, 1869. Left farm at the age of 20 to become traveling salesman; later mgr. subscription book dept. of D. Appleton & Co., pubs., and partner, A. J. Johnson, pub. Johnston Ency.; founder and pub. Good Cheer, The Housewife, and Country Home, Greenfield, Mass. Removed to the West, 1888, on account of failing health, and settled at Kearney, Neb.; developed Watson's ranch of about 8,000 acres; discovered that alfalfa would grow without irrigation and at one time had 2,500 acres in alfalfa; thanked by joint assembly of Nebraska Legislature for his enterprise in alfalfa, which plant at that time was yielding a revenue to Neb. of $40,000,000; his success in developing the dairy industry in Western Neb. necessitated the building of a dairy barn which held 320 cows—the largest barn of its kind in the world. Home: Kearney, Neb. Deceased.

WATSON, H(enry) Sumner, artist, educator; b. Bordentown, N.J., Aug. 1, 1868; s. Henry and Lyde Virginia (Eddy) W.; ed. Pa. Acad. Fine Arts, Phila., and Julian Acad., Paris, France; m. Anna Wood Mickle, Nov. 19, 1899. Began as illustrator Outing Mag., 1893, specializing in outdoor pictures and hunting scenes. Contbd. outdoor articles and stories to mags. Well known as a conservationist of forests, fish and game. Home: Jackson Heights, L.I., N.Y. Died Nov. 15, 1933.

WATSON, Henry Winfield, congressman; b. Bucks County, Pa., June 24, 1856; s. Mitchel and Anna (Bacon) W.; ed. pvt. schs.; m. Annie Masden Vaughan, Sept. 7, 1897. Admitted to Pa. bar, 1881, and practiced in Phila.; dir. Phila. Co. for Guaranteeing Mortgages. Mem. 64th to 72d Congresses (1915-33), 9th Pa. Dist. Republican. Home: Langhorne, Pa. Died Aug. 27, 1933.

WATSON, Irving Allison, physician; b. Salisbury, N.H., Sept. 6, 1849; s. Porter B. and Luvia E. (Ladd) W.; ed. common schs., Newbury (Vt.) Sem., and Collegiate Inst.; studied medicine, attended lectures Dartmouth Med. Coll. and U. of Vt.; U. of Vt., 1871; hon. A.M., Dartmouth, 1885. Practiced Graveton, N.H., 1871-81, at Concord, 1881—; m. Lena A. Farr, 1872. Several yrs. supt. schs. at Groveton; mem. N.H. Ho. of Rep., 1879-81; sec. N.H. State Bd. of Health, Sept. 1881—; sec. N.H. Commrs. of Lunacy; registrar vital statistics of N.H.; pres. State Bd. Cattle Commrs., 1891—. Sec. Am. Public Health Assn., 1883-97; pres. N.H. Med. Soc., 1903; pres. Internat. Conf. State and Provincial Bds. of Health, 1903; asst. sec. gen. first Pan-Am. Med. Congress. Compiled and edited: Physicians and Surgeons of America: New Hampshire Registration Reports, 1881—; Reports State Board of Health, 1882—; Reports American Public Health Association, 1883-97; Reports of New Hampshire Commissioners of Lunacy. Author of many papers on med. and sanitary subjects. Died Apr. 3, 1918.

WATSON, James, editor; b. Edinburgh, Scotland, Feb. 24, 1845; s. James and Agnes (Robertson) W.; ed. pvt. schs. and Jedburgh Acad.; m. Anna M. Ivens, Nov. 16, 1881. Sporting reporter of Spirit of the Times and N.Y. Sportsman, 1872-76; asst. editor and editor of sporting papers in Eng., 1876-80; afterwards on staff N.Y. Sportsman, 1 yr.; asso. sporting editor N.Y. Herald, 2 yrs.; sporting editor Phila. Press, 9 yrs., N.Y. Mail and Express, 3 yrs.; founded Field and Fancy as a kennel paper; contbr. to mags. on kennel subjects. Organizer, 1872, and 1st sec. Amateur Rowing Assn.; founder and life mem. Am. Spaniel Club, Collie Club of America; an organizer Am. Kennel Club. Author: The Dog Book, 1905-06. Deceased.

WATSON, James D., ry. official; b. Port Huron, Mich., June 30, 1870; s. William J. and Isabell (Taylor) W.; ed. pub. schs., Little Rock, Ark.; m. Ida Gordon Harrell, June 20, 1894; children—Lillian Arline, Cedric, Melvin. Began as messenger St. Louis, Iron Mountain & Southern Ry., at Little Rock, 1880, and advanced through various positions in machinery, car, store, operating and traffic depts.; contracting agt. and traveling freight agt., St. Louis Southwestern Ry., 1895-1901, continuing as div. freight agt., at Little Rock, 1901-04, chief clk. in gen. freight office, 1904-06, asst. gen. freight agt., at St. Louis, 1906-13; v.chmn. Southern Tariff Com., 1913-14; asst. freight traffic mgr. St.L.S.W. Ry., 1914-17, and asst. to pres. same rd. and St.L.S.W. Ry. of Tex., 1917-18; asst. div. of traffic, U.S.R.R. Adminstrn., 1918-20; apptd. gen. traffic mgr., St.L.S.W. Ry., Jan. 15, 1920; later asst. to pres. same rd. Republican. Presbyterian. Mason. Home: St. Louis, Mo. Died July 20, 1932.

WATSON, James Madison, author; b. Onondaga Hill, N.Y., Feb. 8, 1827; academic edn., supplemented by self-instruction; studied law; admitted to bar, Sept. 6, 1853, at Albany; became connected with publishing house of A. S. Barnes & Co.; author of many of their school-books. Author: Word Builder, or National First Reader, and six other readers and two spellers in the National Series; also Watson's Independent Series of Readers and Spellers; Handbook of Gymnastics; Manual of Calisthenics; and many anonymous works. Died 1900.

WATSON, John Crittenden, rear admiral U.S.N.; b. Frankfort, Ky., Aug. 24, 1842; s. Dr. Edward Howe and Sarah Lee (Crittenden) W.; apptd. to U.S. Naval Acad. from Ky., 1856, grad. 1860; m. his cousin, Elizabeth Anderson Thornton, May 29, 1873. Promoted midshipman, June 15, 1860; master, Aug. 31, 1861; lt., July 16, 1862; lt. comdr., July 25, 1866; comdr., Jan. 23, 1874; capt., Mar. 6, 1887; commodore, Nov. 7, 1897; rear admiral, Mar. 3, 1899; retired, Aug. 24, 1904. Served in Susquehanna, 1860-61; Richmond, 1861; Sabine, 1861; Hartford, W. Gulf Blockading Squadron, 1862-64; participated in bombardment and passage of Fts. Jackson and St. Philip, and Chalmette batteries, Apr. 1862; passage of Vicksburg batteries, June, July 1862; passage Port Hudson, Mar. 14, 1863; passage of Grand Gulf, Mar. 19 and 30, 1863; battle of Mobile Bay, Aug. 5, 1864; served in Colorado, Franklin and Canandaigua, European Squadron, 1865-69; Navy Yard, New York, 1869; spl. duty, Phila., 1869-70; Alaska, 1870-71; comdg. stationary store-ship Idaho, in harbor of Yokohama, 1871-73; on duty Navy Yard, New York, 1873-74, 1883-86, Navy Yard, Mare Island, 1874; aid to comdt., Navy Yard, Mare Island, 1874-77; comdg. Wyoming, 1878-80; torpedo instrn., 1880; light house insp. 11th dist., 1880-83; comdg. Iroquois, 1886-87; pres. Bd. of Inspection, San Francisco, 1888-90; capt. of yard, Navy Yard, Mare Island, 1890-92; comdg. San Francisco, 1892-94; mem. Naval Retiring Bd., 1894-95; gov. Naval Home, Phila., 1895-98; comdg. a div. of N. Atlantic Fleet, May-Sept., 1898, during war with Spain; comdr.-in-chief Eastern Squadron, July 1898, to threaten coast of Spain and reinforce Dewey's fleet; comdt. Navy Yard, Mare Island, 1898-99; commander-in-chief Asiatic Fleet, June 1899-Apr. 1900; pres. Naval Examining Bd., 1900-02; naval rep. to the coronation of King Edward VII, of England, 1902; pres. Naval Examining and Retiring Bds., 1902-04; spl. duty in Europe studying conditions for physical and moral betterment of enlisted personnel. Sr. v.comdr.-in-chief Loyal Legion, 1907-09. Mem. nat. council Boy Scouts of America. Home: Washington, D.C. Died Dec. 16, 1923.

WATSON, John Henry, judge; b. Jamaica, Vt., May 12, 1851; s. Asahel and Adelpha (Jackson) W.; acad. edn.; LL.D.; m. Clara L. Hammond, Mar. 25, 1879; children—John Henry, Hugh Hammond. Admitted to bar, 1877; practiced at Bradford, Vt., 1877-99. State's atty. Orange County, Vt., 1886-88; mem. Vt. Senate, 1892-94; asso. judge Supreme Ct. of Vt., Jan. 19, 1899-Feb. 1917; chief justice, 1917—. Republican. Home: Montpelier, Vt. Died Dec. 7, 1929.

WATSON, John Jay, corp. officer; b. Jamestown, R.I., Nov. 12, 1874; s. John Jay and Gertrude T. (Stanhope) W.; grad. Rogers High Sch., Newport, R.I., and Bryant and Stratton Bus. Coll., Providence, R.I.; m. Eliza J. Ralph, Nov. 14, 1900. Began in banking bus. with Industrial Trust Co., Providence; treas. Joseph Banigan Rubber Co., 1899-1910; moved to N.Y. City, 1901; treas. U.S. Rubber Co., 1901-10; pres. Gen. Rubber Co. and Rubber Goods Mfg. Co., 1908-10; mem. Watson & Pressprich, 1910-13; treas. Internat. Agrl. Corp., mfrs. fertilizers, 1913—, also v.p., 1914-23, pres., 1923—; pres., chmn. bd. dirs. Lee Rubber & Tire Corp.; mem. bd. of dirs. Am. Eagle Fire Ins. Co., Fidelity-Phenix Fire Ins. Co., Prairie Pebble Phosphate Co., Florida Mining Co., Phosphate Recovery Co. Mem. R.I. Ho. of Rep., 1899-1904; mem. R.I. State Bd. Charities and Corrections, 1899-1904. Mem. Chamber Commerce of U.S. Mem. Squadron "A," N.G.N.Y. Mem. Legion of Honor (French). Alternate del. Rep. Nat. Conv., 1904. Moderator town of Jamestown, R.I., 1897-98. President Nat. Fertilizer Assn. (2 yrs.). Episcopalian. St. John's Lodge No. 1 F.&A.M. and St. John's Commandery No. 1, K.T., Providence, R.I. Died Mar. 30, 1939.

WATSON, John Jordan Crittenden, consul; b. Frankfort, Ky., Feb. 18, 1878; s. Rear Adm. John Crittenden (U.S.N.) and Elizabeth Anderson (Thornton) W.; ed. high sch.; student law dept., U. of Pa., 1 yr.; LL.B., Centre Coll., Ky., 1899; m. Mary Gertrude Seeley, Oct. 3, 1917; children—John Crittenden, Joan Archibald. Practiced law at Louisville, Ky., 1899-1907; ins. solicitor, 1907-09; with Cumberland Telephone Co., 1909-12; real estate business, 1912-13; apptd. consul at Roubaix, France, Apr. 24, 1914; St. Pierre de Miquelon, France, 1915-16, Yarmouth, N.S., 1916-20, Barbados, B.W.I., 1920-26; Swansea, Wales, 1926-29, Dundee, Scotland, Jan. 1, 1929—. Democrat. Presbyn. Mason. Home: Louisville, Ky. Died Sept. 9, 1932.

WATSON, Joseph Franklin; b. Westfield, Mass., Aug. 31, 1849; s. Joseph Hanscom and Maria (Howe) W.; ed. common schs. and acad., Westfield; m. Mary Whalley, Nov. 17, 1880. Began as bookkeeper, Westfield, 1866; moved to Portland, Ore., 1871; with Ladd & Tilton's Bank, until 1879; v.p. Smith & Watson Iron Works; became sec. and gen. supt. Ore. Iron & Steel Co., 1890; pres. Merchants Nat. Bank, Portland, 1895-1911 (resigned), also during same period assisted in organizing, and officer, Merchants Savings & Trust Co. (Portland), 1st Nat. Bank (Elgin), 1st Nat. Bank (Condon), Grants Pass Banking & Trust Co., Linnton Savings Bank (v.p.); 2d v.p. Columbia River Shipbuilding Corp. Served as drummer boy, 46th Mass. Inf., 1 mo., Civil War. Mem. City Council, Portland, 2 terms. Republican. Episcopalian. Home: Portland, Ore. Died Dec. 23, 1922.

WATSON, Robert, clergyman; b. Aberdeen, Scotland, May 6, 1865; s. Robert and Catherine (Thomson) W.; came to Canada, 1873; B.A., U. of New Brunswick, 1893; M.A., Princeton, 1895; grad. Princeton Theol. Sem., 1896; Ph.D., Gale Coll., 1901; D.D., Cedarville, 1905, LL.D., 1923; D.D., Washington and Jefferson, 1915; m. Georgia Maud Belyea, July 23, 1896; children—Paul Belyea, Knox Belyea, Grace Navarre, Ruth Navarre, Robert (deceased), Mary Stewart, Robert Wycliffe. Ordained Presbyn. ministry, 1896; pastor Oxford, Pa., 1896-1905, Second Ch.

Cincinnati, 1905-08, Ch. of the Covenant, Cincinnati, 1908-15, Second Ch., New York, 1915-23, First Ch., Boston, 1923-29. Instr. pastoral theology, Lane Theol. Sem., 1905-09; prof. polity, Boston U., 1923—; prof. New Testament and sociology, Gordon Coll., 1923-29; gen. sec. Lord's Day League N.E., 1929—. Trustee Lincoln U., Pa.; dir. Am. Tract Soc., 1917—, Lord's Day Alliance of America, 1917-23 (v.p. N.E. Alliance, 1923-30; pres. New York Alliance, 1922-29). Commr. to seven Gen. Assemblies; del. Pan-Presbyn. Council, Aberdeen, Scotland, 1913, Cardiff, Wales, 1925, Belfast, Ireland, 1933; host of Pan-Presbyterian Council, Boston, 1929; fraternal del. Presbyn. Synod of Ohio to Synod of Ohio Ref. Ch., 1913; del. World's Christian Citizenship Conf., Portland, Ore., 1913; moderator Synod of New England, 1924-25. Mem. exec. commn. Presbyn. Ch., U.S.A.; mem. Gen. Assembly Judicial Commn., 1924-27 and 1930—. Hon. pres. Cincinnati Vigilance Soc.; chaplain St. Andrew's Soc. of New York, 1915-20, New York Scottish Regt. with rank of major, 1917-20, Scots Charitable Soc. of Boston, 1924—, Canadian Club of Boston, 1924-26, St. John's Lodge No. 1, 1926—. Pres. Presbyn. and Reformed Ministers' Assn. of New York and Vicinity, 1918-20, hon. pres. Union Club, Cincinnati. Spl. preacher and educational lecturer for Y.M.C.A., 1917-19; pres. and special lecturer Internat. Reform Bur., 1920-23; pres. Internat. Reform Fedn., 1923—; dir. Protestant Protective Unity League, 1919-23; dir. Motion Picture Theatre Assn. of the World, 1921—. Vice pres. Boston Sch. of Expression, 1925-26, pres., 1927-30. Pres. Mass. Fedn. of Chs., 1926-28; v.p. Greater Boston Fedn. of Chs., 1924—; pres. Press Radio Bur., 1924—. Member Am. Acad. Polit. and Social Science, Inter-Church Clergy Club. Republican. Mason. Home: Newton Center, Mass. Died Apr. 25, 1936.

WATSON, Thomas Augustus, electrician; b. Salem, Mass., Jan. 18, 1854; s. Thomas R. and Mary (Phipps) W.; ed. pub. schs., Salem and spl. course, geology, Mass. Inst. Tech.; hon., A.M., Union Coll., 1919; D.Eng., Stevens Inst. Tech., 1921; D.Sc., U. of N.H., 1929; m. Elizabeth S. Kimball, Sept. 5, 1882. Mfr. elec. apparatus, 1871-74; asso. with Prof. Alexander Graham Bell in experiments in the electric telephone, 1874-78; supt. Bell Telephone Co., 1878-81; mem. shipbuilding firm of F. O. Wellington & Co., 1884-1900; pres. Fore River Ship & Engine Co., 1900-03; retired from active business, 1903. Mem. sch. com., Braintree, Mass., 1891-1908 (chmn. 1891-98). Fellow Am. Inst. Elec. Engrs. Home: Boston, Mass. Died Dec. 13, 1934.

WATSON, Thomas E., U.S. senator; b. Columbia County, Ga., Sept. 5, 1856; s. John S. and Ann Eliza (Maddox) W.; studied 2 yrs. in Mercer Coll.; taught sch.; admitted to bar, 1875; practiced in Thomson, Ga. Mem. Ga. Ho. of Rep., 1882-83; Dem. elector at-large, 1888; mem. 52d Congress (1891-93), as Populist; candidate and claimed election (on honest count) at elections in 1892 and 1894, but opponent received certificate; resumed practice of law, 1895. While in Congress secured first appropriation for free delivery of mails in rural districts that Congress ever passed. Nominated for v.p. at St. Louis Populist conv. which endorsed Bryan for President, 1896; for some time conducted Populist paper at Atlanta. Nominated for President by People's Party, 1904, and made active campaign to revive the party; began pub. of Tom Watson's Mag., in New York, 1905; pub. Watson's Jeffersonian Magazine and The Weekly Jeffersonian, 1906—. U.S. senator from Georgia, for term 1921-27. Author: The Story of France, 1898; Life of Thomas Jefferson, 1900; Life of Napoleon, 1902; Bethany, a Study and Story of the Old South, 1904; Life and Times of Andrew Jackson, 1907; Handbook of Politics and Economics, 1908; Life and Speeches of Thomas E. Watson, 1908; The Methods of Foreign Missions Exposed, 1909; The Roman Catholic Hierarchy, 1910; Socialists and Socialism, 1909. Organized Jeffersonian Pub. Co., 1911. Prosecuted in U.S. Court for publ. of 3 chapters in The Roman Catholic Hierarchy; bill quashed by Judge Rufus E. Foster, 1914; 2d indictment procured, based on publ. same chapters; Judge William W. Lamdin overruled motion to quash; case tried and jury voted 10 to 2 for acquittal; tried again, Nov. 1916, and acquitted. In 1917 opposed conscripting soldiers for service abroad, and mails were closed to Watson's Mag. and Jeffersonian Weekly; later pub. The Sentinel; pres. McDuffie Bank. Died Sept. 26, 1922.

WATSON, Thomas Leonard, geologist; b. Chatham, Va., Sept. 5, 1871; s. Fletcher B. and Pattie Booker (Tredway) W.; B.Sc., Va. Agrl. and Mech. Coll. (now Va. Poly. Inst.), 1890, M.Sc., 1893; grad. student U. of Va., 1891; Ph.D., Cornell U., 1897; m. Adelaide Stephenson, Feb. 8, 1899. Instr. geology and mineralogy, Va. Agrl. and Mech. Coll., 1892-95; asst. chemist, Va. Expt. Sta., 1890-95; mem. Cornell U. party of geologists on 6th Peary Arctic expdn. to N. Greenland, 1896; pvt. research worker on rock decay, U.S. Nat. Mus., 1897-98; asst. state geologist of Ga., 1898-1901; prof. geology, Denison U., 1901-04; geologist, Ga. Geol. Survey, 1902, N.C. Geol. Survey, 1903; field asst., U.S. Geol. Survey, 1903-08; prof. geology, Va. Poly. Inst., 1904-07; prof. economic geology, 1907—, head prof. schools of geology, 1910—, U. of Va. State geologist and dir. Va. Geol. Survey, 1908—. Mem. sub-com. of Nat. Research Council; asso. mem. from Am. Inst. Mining Engrs. of War Minerals Com.; mem. Com. of 100 on Scientific Research; mem. exec. com. Nat. Conservation Congress. Fellow Geol. Soc. America (councilor, 1915-17), A.A.A.S., Mineral. Soc. America (councilor 1922—; chmn. com. on nomenclature and classification of minerals), Soc. Econ. Geologists. Co-author of Ries and Watson's Engineering Geology; Elements of Engineering Geology; contbr. numerous articles and books on theoretic and economic geology in various geol. publs. and reports of state and federal surveys. Died Nov. 10, 1924.

WATSON, Walter Allen, congressman; b. Nottoway County, Va., Nov. 25, 1867; s. Meredith and Josephine L. (Robertson) W.; A.B., Hampden-Sidney Coll., 1887; law student U. of Va., 1888-89; m. Constance R. Tinsley, Jan. 18, 1905. Admitted to Va. bar, 1893; practiced in Nottoway and adjoining counties, Va.; mem. Va. State Senate, 1891-95; sec. Dem. State Com., 1892; atty. for commonwealth, Nottoway County, 1895-1904; mem. State Constl. Conv., 1901-02; mem. Dem. State Exec. Com., 1901-02; circuit judge, 4th Jud. Circuit, Va., 1904-12; mem. 63d to 65th Congresses (1913-19), 4th Va. District. Democrat. Presbyn. Trustee Hampden-Sidney Coll., 1913—. Died Dec. 24, 1919.

WATSON, William, sec. Am. Acad. Arts and Sciences, 1884—; b. Nantucket, Mass., Jan. 19, 1834; s. William and Mary (Macy) W.; S.B., engring. (Boyden prize in mathematics), Harvard, 1857, S.B., mathematics, 1858; instr. differential and integral calculus, scientific sch., Harvard, 1857-59; Ph.D., U. of Jena, 1862; partial course École Nationale des Ponts et Chaussées, Paris, France; m. Margaret, d. Augustus H. Fiske, 1873. Univ. lecturer, Harvard, 1863-64; collected, 1860-63, information in Europe on tech. edn., which was made basis of scheme of organization, 1864, of Mass. Inst. Tech., in which was prof. mech. engring. and descriptive geometry, 1865-73. U.S. commr. to Vienna Expn., 1873; mem. Internat. Jury, Paris Expn., 1878; hon. pres. Paris Congress Architects and v.p. Internat. Congress of Hygiene, 1878; hon. pres. engring. sect. French Assn. Adv. Science, 1878, 81, 83, 89; v.p. International Congress of Construction, 1889; sec. World's Columbian Water Commerce Congress, 1893. Fellow Am. Acad. Arts and Sciences, A.A.A.S. Author: Technical Education, 1872; Descriptive Geometry, 1873; Civil Engineering, Architecture and Public Works at the Vienna International Exhibition, 1875; On the Protection of Life from Casualties in the Use of Machinery, 1880; Courses in Shades and Shadows, 1889; The Civil Engineering, Architecture and Public Works at the Paris Exposition of 1889, 1891; The International Water Transportation Congress, Chicago, 1893, 1894; also many tech. papers. Died Sept. 30, 1915.

WATSON, William Henry, physician; b. Providence, R.I., Nov. 8, 1829; only s. Hon. William Robinson and Mary Ann (Earle) W.; A.B., Brown, 1852; M.D., Homœ. Med. Coll. of Pa., 1854; studied at U. of Pa., and Pa. Hosp., Phila.; hon. A.M., Brown, 1855; hon. M.D. from Bd. Regents, U. State of N.Y., 1878; LL.D., Hobart Coll., 1901, "in recognition of long and faithful service in the development of the higher educational system of the State, especially those parts of it pertaining to the study of medicine"; m. Sarah T. Carlile, May 1, 1854 (died 1881); m. 2d, Mrs. Julia M. Williams, Dec. 16, 1891. Regent U. State of N.Y., 1881-1904. Inspired and procured passage of act fixing ednl. qualifications essential in beginning study of medicine; influential in extending term of study for practice of medicine from 3 yrs. to 4; decisively influential in determining basis of admission to practice in the three legalized branches of the med. profession through jurisdiction of independent court appointed by state. A founder and trustee Middletown State Hosp.; U.S. pension examining surgeon, 1875-81; surgeon gen. State of N.Y., with rank of brig. gen., 1880. Examiner in diagnosis and pathology in 1st N.Y. Bd. of State Med. Examiners apptd. under act of 1872. Mem. Advisory Bd. on Tuberculosis, N.Y. State Dept. Health. Sr. warden Grace Ch., Utica, Del. General Conv., P.E. Ch., 1889, 1904, 07; representative of U. of State of N.Y. at "Abel Fest" of Royal U. of Christiania, and at tercentenary of Bodleian Library, Oxford, 1902. Author of Medical Education and Medical Licensing (address at 23d Convocation U. State of N.Y.), 1885; Memorial Address on U.S. Senator Francis Kernan; also various addresses on med. subjects. Died Jan. 1913.

WATSON, William Richard, librarian; b. Cottage Grove, Minn., July 23, 1867; s. Robert and Mehitabel Winkley (Furber) W.; B.S., Carleton Coll., Minn., 1890; N.Y. State Library Sch., Albany, N.Y., 1893-95; m. Bessie Lawrence Barnes, June 1, 1901. Asst. librarian Carnegie Library, Pittsburgh, 1895-1904, Calif. State Library, Sacramento, 1904-07; librarian Public Library, San Francisco, 1907-12; dir. of library extension div., N.Y. State Edn. Dept., Jan. 1913—. Home: Albany, N.Y. Died Jan. 6, 1926.

WATT, James Robert; b. Meriden, Conn., Mar. 3, 1869; s. James and Alice (Hardy) W.; grad. high sch., Maynard, Mass., 1884; m. Louise Allemeyer, Nov. 23, 1892; children—Gladys Louise (dec.), James Robert. Began 1888, in employ of Berlin Bridge Co., later absorbed by Am. Bridge Company; dir. First Trust Co., Morris Plan Co., West End Savings & Loan Assn. Alderman, Albany, 1910-13; pres. Common Council, 1914-17; mayor of Albany, 1918-21. Sec. bd. of trustees Shriners Hospitals for Crippled Children (15 hospitals in U.S. and Canada). Republican. Episcopalian. Mason, Elk. Home: Albany, N.Y. Died Sept. 20, 1941.

WATT, Richard Morgan, naval officer; b. York, Pa., June 18, 1872; s. Andrew and Susan (Bahn) W.; grad. U.S. Naval Acad., 1891; B.S., U. of Glasgow, Scotland, 1893, D.Sc., 1911; m. Bessie Davis, Oct. 16, 1894; 1 son, Richard Morgan. Commd. in U.S. Navy, July 1, 1893; promoted through grades to rear adm., Feb. 1, 1934. Asst. to supt. of constrn. for U.S. Navy at Cramp's Shipyard, Phila., 1893-96; asst. to naval constructor, New York Navy Yard, 1896-1901; supt. constrn. Fore River Shipyard, Quincy, Mass., 1901-07; head dept. of constrn. and repair, Norfolk Navy Yard, 1907-10, mgr. indsl. dept., 1907-10 and 1915-21; chief constructor and chief Bur. of Constrn. and Repair, Navy Dept. (Washington, D.C.), 1910-14; mem. Claims Commn. U.S. Shipping Bd., 1921-23; mgr. indsl. dept. Phila. Navy Yard, 1924-30; insp. of material for U.S. Navy, Phila. Dist., 1930—. Awarded Navy Cross (U.S.). Presbyn. Home: Merion, Pa. Died May 15, 1938.

WATT, Rolla Vernon, ins. mgr.; b. Camden, O., Feb. 19, 1857; s. James Alexander and Elizabeth (McCabe) W.; ed. Eaton (Preble Co.) High Sch.; m. Jessie Shirlaw Mackay, Sept. 20, 1883. Clerk bookstore, 1876-82; in fire ins. office of Smith & Snow, San Francisco, 1882-87; mgr. Pacific Coast dept. Am., Central, Amazon, Pacific, Liberty and Delaware Ins. cos., 1887-94; mgr. Pacific Coast dept. Royal Ins. Co., 1894—, Queens Ins. Co., New York, 1896—, Royal Indemnity Co., 1911—, Newark Fire Ins. Co., 1918—; also pres. Fairfax Villa Co.; dir. Urban Realty Co., Royal Indemnity Co. Republican. Mem. Bd. of Fire Commrs., San Francisco, 1900-04. An organizer and mem. exec. com. Lincoln-Roosevelt League. Methodist; pres. bd. Central M.E. Ch.; pres. bd. Coll. of the Pacific; pres. bd. Y.M.C.A. 15 yrs.; trustee University Mound Old Ladies' Home; dir. Travelers' Aid Soc. Home: San Francisco, Calif. Died May 15, 1926.

WATTERS, Henry Eugene, clergyman, educator; b. Graves County, Ky., Sept. 14, 1876; s. Theodore Madison and Josephine (Ransom) W.; B.S., Southern Normal U., 1899; A.B., Union U., 1903; post-grad. work Brown U.; D.D., Hall-Moody Inst., 1906; A.M., Union, 1916, and LL.D., 1921; grad. work Southern Baptist Theol. Sem., 1935; m. Annette Routon, Aug. 28, 1899; m. 2d, Ethel Reed, July 22, 1931. Teacher and prin. pub. schs.; ordained Bapt. ministry, 1899; pastor of chs. several yrs.; pres. Hall-Moody Inst., Martin, Tenn., 1903-15; pres. Coll. of Marshall, Tex., 1916-18; pres. Union U., 1918-31; pres. Georgetown (Ky.) Coll., 1931-34; pres. Jonesboro (Ark.) Baptist Coll., 1935—. Mem. Commn. on Standardization, American Research Soc. Democrat. Mason, K.P., D.O.O.K. Author: Physics Simplified, 1905; The Bible of Superhuman Origin, 1906; Life Planning, 1935; Vocational Self-Guidance, 1935; Youth Makes the Choice, 1937. Died Apr. 15, 1938.

WATTERS, Philip Melancthon, clergyman, educator; b. Brooklyn, N.Y., Sept. 3, 1860; s. Philip and Eliza J. (Simonson) W.; A.B., Amherst, 1882 (Phi Beta Kappa); B.D., Union Theol. Sem., 1885; D.D., Wesleyan U., Conn., 1900; m. Hyla Ada Stowell, Sept. 3, 1885; children—Florence Ada, Philip Sidney, Hyla Stowell. Ordained M.E. ministry, 1887; pastor Central Valley, N.Y., 1885-87, Warwick, 1888-89, Dobb's Ferry, 1890-94, Washington St. Ch., Poughkeepsie, N.Y., 1895-96, Grace Ch., N.Y. City, 1897-1900, St. James Ch., Kingston, 1901-04; supt. N.Y. Dist., 1905-10; pastor Washington Sq. Ch., N.Y. City, 1911-13; pres. Gammon Theol. Sem., Atlanta, Ga., 1914-26 (retired). Republican. Mason. Author: Peter Cartwright, 1910. Home: New York, N.Y. Died Mar. 29, 1926.

WATTERS, Thomas, clergyman; b. Rauross, Ireland, Sept. 13, 1860; s. John W. and Elizabeth (Devor) W.; A.B., New York U., 1884; grad. Union Theol. Sem., 1888; D.D., Cedarville (O.) Coll., 1899; m. Margaret E. Downs, Oct. 24, 1899. Ordained Reformed Presbyn. ministry, 1889; pastor First Ch., Brooklyn, 1889-92, First Ch., Pittsburgh, 1892-1906, Tabernacle Presbyn. Ch., Pittsburgh, 1906-22. Moderator Gen. Synod Reformed Presbyn. Ch., 1894; mem. bd. of supts. Reformed Presbyn. Theol. Sem., Phila., 1891-1901; trustee Reformed Presbyn. Theol. Sem., Phila., 1904-06; sec. bd. trustees Cedarville Coll., 1898-1906. Pres. Bd. of Temperance and Moral Welfare, Presbyn. Ch., 1913; mem. Bd. of Christian Edn., 1923; pres. Pittsburgh Florence Crittenton Home, 1923. Home: Williamsport, Pa. Died Dec. 12, 1940.

WATTERSON, Henry, journalist; b. Washington, Feb. 16, 1840; s. Hon. Harvey Magee and Talitha (Black) W.; owing to defect of vision was mainly ed. by pvt. tutors; D.C.L., U. of the South, 1891; LL.D., Brown U., 1906; LL.D., U. of Ky., 1915); Staff officer C.S.A., during Civil War, 1861-65, and chief of scouts in Gen. Johnston's Army, 1864; m.

Rebecca, d. Hon. Andrew Ewing, Dec. 20, 1865. Reporter and editorial writer Washington States, 1858-61; editor Democratic Rev., 1860-61, Chattanooga Rebel, 1862-63, Republican Banner, Nashville, 1865-68; removed to Louisville, 1868, to assume management of the Journal, which, with W. N. Haldeman, he consolidated with the Courier and the Democrat, 1868, under name of Courier-Journal, of which was editor until Apr. 1919. Mem. 44th Congress, Aug. 12, 1876-Mar. 3, 1877, to fill an unexpired term; declined reëlection; del.-at-large Dem. nat. convs., 1876 (temporary chmn.), 1880 (chmn. platform com.), 1884, 1888 (chmn. platform com.), 1892. V.p. gen. Inter-State Perry Memorial Commn., 1910; juror Hall of Fame, U. of New York, 1914. Distinguished as journalist, orator and writer. Author: History of the Spanish-American War, 1899; History of the Manhattan Club; The Compromises of Life, Lectures and Addresses, 1902; Marse Henry, Looking Backward Sketches, 1919. Editor: Oddities of Southern Life and Character, 1882. Home: Jeffersontown, Ky. Died Dec. 22, 1921.

WATTIS, Edmund Orson, ry. contractor; b. Uintah, Utah, Mar. 6, 1855; s. Edmund and Mary Jane (Corey) W.; ed. pub. schs.; m. Martha Ann Bybee, June 25, 1879; children— Leland Ray, Mattie C. (Mrs. Wm. Henry Harris), Edmund Earl (dec.), Ethel Marie (Mrs. Wm. Rice Kimball), Marguerite E. (Mrs. Emil Joseph Hanke), Edna Orson (wife of Ezekiel Ricker Dumke, M.D.), Paul Lyman, Ruth. In railroad constrn. work from early youth; a dir. and in charge constrn. work Utah Constrn. Co., 1911—, v.p., 1911—, also chmn. bd.; an organizer, 1931, later pres. Six Companies, Inc., builders of Hoover Dam; pres. Lake View Mining Co.; v.p. Utah Rapid Transit Co.; dir. Lion Coal Co. Prin. works: W.P. R.R. from Salt Lake City to Oroville, Calif.; U.P. from Salt Lake City to Calif. state line; 100-mile extension of S.P. R.R. of Mexico; new constrn. and re-location for U.P. R.R., S.P. Co., D.&R.G. R.R., involving building over 200 tunnels; also builder of many concrete and earth dams for power and irrigation purposes, including O'Shaughnessy Dam, for water and power supply of San Francisco and Am. Falls Dam, Ida., for U.S. Dept. Interior, 2 of largest dams in world. Republican. Mason. Home: Ogden, Utah. Feb. 3, 1934.

WATTLES, Gurdon Wallace, banker; b. Richford, N.Y., May 12, 1855; s. James and Betsy Ann (Whiting) W.; Ia. State Coll., Ames, leaving coll. jr. yr. on account of illness; hon. M.Ph., same, 1906; m. Jennie Leete, Oct. 20, 1881; m. 2d, Julia Vance, June 1918. Admitted to Iowa bar, 1880; commenced banking as cashier, Farmers Bank, Carroll, Ia., 1882; pres. First Nat. Bank, Carroll, 1886-92; v.p., 1892-1901, pres., 1901-06; Union Nat. Bank, Omaha; became v.p. U.S. Nat. Bank, Omaha, 1906, and chmn. bd., 1916; western mgr. of Rochester (N.H.) Loan & Banking Co., 1886-1922; pres. Omaha & Council Bluffs St. Ry. Co., 1906-20; dir. C.G.W. Ry. Co.; pres. Keller-Wattles Co., Los Angeles, Calif., 1922—; chmn. bd. Municipal Bond Co. County supt. schs., Carroll County, Ia., 1879-81; pres. Omaha Expn., 1898; pres. Neb. State Commn. to St. Louis Expn., 1904; del. Rep. Nat. Conv., 1904; pres. Omaha Grain Exchange, 1904-09: pres. Ak-Sar-Ben, Omaha, 1905, 06, 07; trustee Bellevue Coll., 1909—; fed. food adminstr. for Nebraska, 1917-20. Republican. Episcopalian. Wrote: "A Crime Against Labor," 1909, a brief history of the Omaha street car strike; Autobiography and Genealogy, 1922. Home: Hollywood, Calif. Died Jan. 31, 1932.

WATTS, Edward Seabrook, lawyer; b. Montgomery, Ala., June 5, 1882; s. Thomas Henry and Johness Beale (Eddins) W.; LL.B., U. of Ala., Law Dept., 1904; post-grad. course Columbia Law Sch., 1904-05; m. Virginia Tyson Norwood, Nov. 4, 1908. Admitted to bar, 1904; mem. firm Watts & Son., 1905, Watts & Letcher, 1907. Troy, Watts & Letcher, 1909-10; mem. Chilton & Watts, comml. and corp. law; atty. for plaintiff in case of Bailey vs. State of Ala., in which question of constitutionality of Ala. labor contract law was raised; act declared by U.S. Supreme Ct., Jan. 3, 1911. to be unconstitutional; county atty., Montgomery County, 1908-11 (resigned); elected city atty., Montgomery, 1913; Dem. presdl. elector, 2d Congressional Dist., Ala., 1912. Mem. Alabama Epileptic Commn. to locate and erect bldgs. for epileptic colony. Baptist. Home: Montgomery, Ala. Died Oct. 7, 1916.

WATTS, Ethelbert, consul gen.; b. Phila., Feb. 25, 1845; s. Henry Miller (minister to Austria) and Anna Maria W.; ed. pvt. schs., Phila., and Paris, France, U. of Pa. and 3 yrs. at coll. in Freiberg, Saxony; m. Emily, d. Dr. William Pepper, 1867; m. 2d, Katharine L., d. William H. Gregg, Nov. 11, 1894. Enlisted pvt. 32d Pa. Vols. at 17, serving for 3 mos., when Lee made his raid into Pa. Engaged in iron business in Marietta and Phila., later sec. nad treas. Investment Co. of Phila. In U.S. consular service, 1896—; consul at Horgen, Switzerland, 1896-97; vice and dep. consul gen. at Cairo, Egypt, 1897-99; consul at Kingston, Jamaica, 1899-1901, at Prague, Bohemia, 1901-03; consul gen. at St. Petersburg, 1903-07, at Brussels, Belgium, Apr. 25, 1907-17. As vice consul gen. was in charge Am. agency in Cairo in 1898, when Spanish fleet under Admiral Camera entered harbor of Port Said and attempted to get coal to enable him to hurry to Manila to attack Admiral Dewey, it was prevented by his vigorous action, so that, after some delay, fleet was ordered back to Spain. Awarded by Khedive of Egypt decoration of Order of the Osmanieh. Order of Rising Sun (Japan) for services to Japanese subjects in Russia during the Russo-Japanese War. Republican. Episcopalian. Home: Philadelphia, Pa. Deceased.

WATTS, George Washington, mfr.; b. Cumberland, Md., Aug. 18, 1851; s. Gerrard S. and Ann E. W.; ed. pub. schs., Baltimore, 1859-68, and took civ. engring. course, U. of Va., 1868-71; m. Miss L. V. Beall, Oct. 19, 1875. Traveling salesman for tobacco commn. house of G. S. Watts & Co., Baltimore, 1871-78; removed to Durham, N.C., and aided in organizing firm of W. Duke, Sons & Co., becoming partner; firm joined Am. Tobacco Co., 1890; pres. Pearl Cotton Mills; v.p. Erwin Cotton Mills; dir. Seaboard Air Line Ry., Republic Iron & Steel Co., Va.-Carolina Chem. Co., Southern Cotton Oil Co., etc. Active in philanthropic enterprises and charitable orgns. Died Mar. 7, 1921.

WATTS, Legh Richmond, judge; b. Portsmouth, Va., Dec. 12, 1843; s. Dr. Edward M. and Ann Eliza (Maupin) W.; ed. private schs. and acads.; served in C.S.A., in Ga., N. and S.C.; studied U. of Va., 1865-66, 1866-67, LL.B., 1867; m. Mattie Peters, Nov. 26, 1868. Elected judge by Gen. Assembly of Va., 1870, and served until Feb. 1880; apptd. counsel Seaboard & Roanoke R.R., 1884; soon after apptd. gen. counsel S.A.L. system, gen. counsel present system, 1900-17, and consulting counsel, Aug. 1917—; mem. law firm Watts & Hatton; pres. The Bank of Portsmouth to 1919 and chmn. bd. reorganized nat. bank. Mem. bd. visitors, U. of Va., 8 yrs.; dir. Eastern Lunatic Asylum, Williamsburg, Va.; presdl. elector, Hancock ticket, 1880; chmn. Legal Advisory Bd., 1918; chmn. Portsmouth Chapter Am. Red Cross, 1918. Independent Democrat. Dep. Gen. Conv. P.E. Ch., 1913, 16, 19. Supreme Regent Royal Arcanum, 1889-91; mem. Stonewall Camp U.C.V. (comdr. 4 terms); pres. Va. State Bar Assn., 1915. Home: Portsmouth, Va. Died 1920.

WATTS, Richard Cannon, judge; b. Laurens, S.C., Mar. 15, 1853; s. John and Elizabeth C. (Cannon) W.; ed. U. of Va., 1871-72; m. Alliene Cash, Nov. 3, 1881 (died 1894); m. 2d, Lottie H., d. Chief Justice and Caroline McIver, Apr. 16, 1896 (died 1921). Read law with Colonel B. W. Ball; admitted to practice at Laurens, S.C., 1873, before 21, by special act of legislature; partner Hon. Y. J. Pope, of Newberry, S.C., 1874-80, B. W. Ball, 1880-92; mem. S.C. Ho. of Rep., 1890-94; judge Fourth Jud. Circuit, S.C., 1894-1912; became asso. justice Supreme Ct. of S.C., Jan. 10, 1912, elected chief justice, Jan. 12, 1927. A.d.c. on staff of Gov. Hampton, 1877-79; chief of staff to Gov. W. D. Simpson, 1879-80. Mason. Democrat. Episcopalian. Home: Laurens, S.C. Died Oct. 13, 1930.

WATTS, Ridley, corp. exec.; b. Newport, R.I., Apr. 5, 1872; s. William and Mary (Bigelow) W.; ed. pub. schs.; m. Gertrude Hoy, May 24, 1900; children—Ridley Watts, Erwin Hoy, John, Philip Howell, Florence Von Epps. Dir. Chemical Nat. Bank, Morristown Trust Co., Morristown Securities Corp., Continental Ins. Co., New York Life Ins. Co., Victor-Monaghan Co. (Greenville, S.C.), Wallace Mfg. Co. (Jonesville, S.C.), Norris (S.C.) Cotton Mills Co., Marion (N.C.) Mfg. Co., Industrial Cotton Mills Co. (Rock Hill, S.C.). Mem. bd. dirs. Morristown Memorial Hosp., N.J. State Hosp. Home: Morristown, N.J. Died Dec. 31, 1937.

WAUGH, Frederick Judd, artist; b. Bordentown, N.J., Sept. 13, 1861; s. Samuel Bell (portrait painter) and Mary Eliza (Young) W. (miniature painter); art edn. Pa. Acad. Fine Arts, Phila., and Acad. Julian, Paris; m. Clara Eugenie Bunn, 1892; children—Gwenyth, Coulton. Resided at various places in Europe, 1892-1907; illustrated for Graphic and London papers; exhibited at The Salon, Paris, previous to 1892, later in Royal Acad. (London); permanently represented by pictures at Bristol Acad. (Eng.), Walker Art Gallery (Liverpool), Durban Art Gallery (Natal, S. Africa), Nat. Gallery (Washington, D.C.), Met. Mus. (New York), Brooklyn (N.Y.) Inst., Art Club (Phila.), Masonic Temple (Phila.), Art Institute, Chicago, Dallas and Austin (Tex.), Delgado Art Mus., New Orleans, Pa. Acad. Fine Arts, Phila., Montclair Art Mus., Mus. of Art, Toledo, Lotos Club, Nat. Arts Club, City Art Museum (St. Louis), also in many pvt. collections in Eng. and U.S.; rep. by 3 murals of Niagara Falls, one on the S.S. Greater Detroit, and the other on the Greater Buffalo, also a mural of old Buffalo Harbor, on boat of the Detroit & Cleveland Nav. Co. N.A., 1909; mem. Bristol Acad. Fine Arts, Royal West of England Acad. Episcopalian. Author: (and illustrator) The Clan of Munes, 1916. Awarded Palmer Memorial marine prize of $1,000, Nat. Acad. Design, 1929; popular prize of $200, Carnegie Instn., 4 consecutive years, 1934-37. Home: Provincetown, Mass. Died Sept. 11, 1940.

WAUGH, Ida, artist; b. Phila.; d. Samuel Bell and Mary Z. (Mendenhall) Waugh; pupil Pa. Acad. Fine Arts, Phila., and in Paris at l'Académie Julién and l'Académie Délécluse, 1888 and 1891-92; unmarried. Principal painting, "Hagar and Ishmael" (property of Pa. Acad. Fine Arts), 1888; received the Norman W. Dodge prize, Nat. Acad. Design, for portrait of Dr. Paul J. Sartain, 1896; exhibited in Paris Salon, World's Fair (Chicago), 1893, New York, Phila., California, Cincinnati and other places. Mem. Pa. Acad. Fine Arts. Died Jan. 25, 1919.

WAUGH, William Francis, physician; b. Greenville, Pa., May 11, 1849; s. William and Annie Darlington (Lasher) W.; A.B., Westminster (Pa.) Coll., 1868, A.M., 1871; M.D., Jefferson Med. Coll., Phila., 1871; m. Kate Lasher, Oct. 25, 1873; m. 2d, Helen Nauman, Apr. 5, 1898; m. 3d, Alevia Harriman, Jan. 4, 1916. Resident physician, dept. of insane, West Pa. Hosp., Dixmont, Pa., 1871-72; asst. surgeon, U.S.N., 1873-76; prof. principles and practice of medicine, Medico-Chirurg. Coll. of Phila., 1880-90, Ill. Med. Coll., 1894-1904; dean and head dept. of therapeutics, Bennett Med. Coll. (Loyola U.), Chicago, 1909-13. V.p. and dir. Abbott Alkaloidal Co., Chicago, 1897-1908. Editor: The Med. World, Phila., 1881-82, Med. Times, Phila., 1882-86, Med. Times and Register, Phila., 1886-93, Dietetic Gazette, New York, 1887-88, Alkaloidal Clinic, Chicago, 1894, Am. Jour. Clin. Medicine, Chicago, 1911, Chicago Med. Times, 1910-11. Bronze medal, Misericordia Hosp., Rio de Janeiro, Brazil, 1875; gold medal and hon. diploma, Academia Fisico-Chemica, Italiana, Palermo, 1909. Mason. Author: Treatment of the Sick, 1898; The Houseboat Book, 1908. Died Sept. 5, 1918.

WAUL, Thomas Neville, soldier, lawyer; b. in Sumter Dist., S.C., Jan. 5, 1813; s. Thomas and Anna (Mulcahy) W.; ed. at Charleston, S.C., 1825-28; S.C. Coll., Columbia, 1829-32; studied law in office of Sargent S. Prentiss, Vicksburg, Miss., 1834-35; m. Mary America Simmons, Nov. 25, 1837. Licensed to practice law in Miss., 1834; apptd. dist. atty. River Dist., Miss.; practiced law at Grenada, Miss., 1836-50; removed 1850 to Gonzales County, Tex.; Dem. candidate for Congress Western dist., Tex., 1859—defeated; elected from Tex. elector at large on Breckinridge ticket, 1860; mem. provisional Congress Confederate States, 1861-62 organized Waul's (Tex.) Legion (2,000 troops) for C.S.A., became its col. and with it served through war; comd. defenses of Yazoo and Tallahatchie Rivers, Miss., at Fort Pemberton; at siege of Vicksburg; promoted brig. gen.; comd. brigade under Kirby Smith in Trans-Miss. Dept., leading it at battles of Mansfield and Pleasant Hill, La.; comd. div. at battle of Saline, where he was severely wounded. Elected to reconstruction Conv. of Tex., 1865; established practice in Galveston; abandoned practice, 1896, retiring to farm in country. Home: Neyland, Hunt County, Tex. Died 1903.

WAY, John, life ins.; b. Bedford County, Pa., Oct. 21, 1871; s. Samuel and Jane (Wilson) W.; ed. pub. schs., Bedford, and Westtown Boarding Sch., Chester County, Pa.; m. Lydia Annette Greene, May 18, 1897; 1 dau., Mary French. Began, 1893, with Provident Life and Trust Co., now Provident Mut. Life Ins. Co., of which v.p., 1916—; dir. Lumbermen's Ins. Co., Central Nat. Bank of Phila.; mgr. Mine Hill & Schuylkill Haven R.R. Co. Mem. bd. mgrs. Pa. Hosp.; treas. Overseers of Pub. Sch., founded 1697 by Charter of William Penn in Town and County of Pa. Mem. bd. dirs. Assn. for Promoting Coll. Edn. of Women; treas. Mission Bd. of Phila. Yearly Meeting of Friends. Mem. Friends' Ch. Home: Lansdowne, Pa. Died Feb. 20, 1929.

WAY, Joseph Howell, physician; b. Waco, Tex., Nov. 22, 1865; s. Charles Burr and Martha Julia (Howell) W.; of Puritan ancestry; 9th generation from Jehue Burr, original settler, Fairfield, Conn., 1632; 10th generation, from Henry Way, Dorchester, Mass., 1630; preliminary edn. under father; Med. Coll. of Va., 1884; M.D., Vanderbilt U., 1886; licensed to practice, 1885, at age of 19, after passing exam. in class of 53, before State Bd. of N.C., making highest grade of class; m. Marietta Welch, July 3, 1888; children—Hilda, Joseph Howell. In practice at Waynesville, 1886—; particular attention to tuberculosis; local surgeon Southern Ry. State med. exam. Royal Arcanum for N.C. Charter mem. and dir. First Nat. Bank (Waynesville), Champion Bank (Canton, N.C.), Bryson (N.C.) City Bank. Mem. State Bd. Med. Examiners, 1897-1902, State Bd. Health, 1905— (pres. 1911—); trustee Trinity Coll. and of Duke U., N.C. Pres. N.C. State Med. Soc., 1908, Tri-State Med. Assn., 1911-12; mem. Internat. Congress Tuberculosis, 1908. Democrat. Methodist. Mason. Editor Trans. N.C. State Med. Soc., 1904, 05, 06, 08, Tri-State Assn., 1906-12. Contbr. on med. subjects. Commd. capt., Med. R.C., Apr. 9, 1917; maj., Apr. 19, 1918; lt. col., May 21, 1919; col., Oct. 7, 1924; active service, Aug. 15, 1917-Mar. 20, 1919; hon. discharged, with recommission in O.R.C. Detailed actg. surgeon U.S.P.H.S. in charge Vets. Bur. Training Centre, Waynesville, N.C., Apr. 25, 1921. Home: Waynesville, N.C. Deceased.

WAY, Royal Brunson, coll. prof.; b. Allegan, Mich., Sept. 20, 1873; s. Alfred Byron and Martha A. (Allen) W.; Ph.B., Albion (Mich.) Coll., 1894; Ph.M., U. of Mich., 1896; Ph.D., U. of Wis., 1906; m. Kathryn James Cherry, Nov. 23, 1904. Prin. high sch., Eaton Rapids, Mich., 1896-99, Saginaw, 1899-1902; instr. history, Northwestern U., 1903-06; prof. Am. history and polit. science, Beloit Coll., 1907—. Exchange prof., Harvard, 1905; actg. prof., Ind. U., 1909. Republican. Conglist. Mason. Author: Diplomacy of Spanish-American War. Contbr. on hist. topics. Home: Beloit, Wis. Died Nov. 29, 1937.

WAYLAND, Francis, univ. dean; b. Boston, Aug. 23, 1826; grad. Brown U., 1846; A.M., Yale, 1872; LL.D., U. of Rochester, 1879; Brown U., 1881. Began law practice, 1850, at Worcester, Mass., removing, 1858 to New Haven, Conn.; judge of probate, 1864-65; lt. gov. Conn., 1869; became prof. of law sch. Yale, 1872, dean, 1873-1903. Pres. Am. Social Science Assn.; pres. bd. dirs. Conn. State prison; pres. Prison Aid Assn., 1872—; pres. Organized Charities Assn., New Haven, 1878—. Prominent as writer and speaker on sociol. topics, charitology, criminalogy, etc. Joint author (with brother, Rev. H. L. Wayland) of biography of President Wayland of Brown Univ. Died 1904.

WAYLAND, Julius Augustus, editor; b. Versailles, Ind., Apr. 26, 1854; s. John B. and Micha W.; ed. village sch. and printing offices; m. Etta L. Bevan, Oct. 16, 1877 (died 1898). Conducted papers and in printing and real estate business, Pueblo, Colo., 1882-93; established The Coming Nation, Greensburg, Ind., Apr. 1893, and through it founded the colony at Ruskin, Tenn.; removed the paper there, but later withdrew and founded the Appeal to Reason, 1895, at Kansas City; moved with paper to Girard, Kan., Feb. 1897. Socialist. Home: Girard, Kan. Died Nov. 11, 1912.

WEAD, Charles Kasson, physicist, patent examiner; b. Malone, N.Y., Sept. 1, 1848; s. Samuel Clark and Mary E. (Kasson) W.; A.B., U. of Vt., 1871; studied at Berlin, 1875-76; m. Sarah W., d. Rev. Calvin Pease, pres. of U. of Vt., Aug. 13, 1879 (died 1889). Acting prof. physics, U. of Mich., 1877-85; in elec. business at Hartford, Conn., 1887-90; examiner U.S. Patent Office, 1892-1921. Fellow A.A.A.S. Author: Notes on Sound and Light, 1879; Aims and Methods of the Teaching of Physics, 1883; Musical Scales (in Rep. U.S. Nat. Mus.), 1900; also sundry papers in Silliman's Journal, Science, Proceedings A.A.A.S., and mags., especially on acoustical subjects. Died Apr. 2, 1925.

WEADOCK, Thomas Addis Emmet, lawyer; b. County Wexford, Ireland, Jan. 1, 1850; s. Lewis and Mary (Cullen) W.; brought to U.S., 1850, father naturalized, 1856; LL.B., U. of Mich., 1873; m. Mary E. Tarsney, 1874 (died 1889); children—Thomas J. (dec.), Lewis J., Alice M. B. (dec.), Mary, Isabel, Monica W. (Mrs. John H. Porter), Frances Clare (Mrs. R. L. Morrison), Paul; m. 2d, Nannie E. Curtiss, 1893 (died 1927); 1 son, George P. Teacher dist. schs., Ohio, 1866-71; admitted to Mich. and Ohio bars, 1873, U.S. Supreme Ct., 1882; in practice at Bay City, 1873-95, Detroit, 1895—; pros. atty., 1877-78, mayor of Bay City, 1883-85; pres. Mich. Dem. State Conv., 1885-94; mem. 52d and 53d Congresses (1891-95), 10th Mich. Dist.; del. at large, Dem. Nat. Conv., 1896; Dem. candidate for justice Supreme Ct. of Mich., 1904, 1928; Dem. candidate U.S. Senate, 1930; presdl. elector, 1932; justice Supreme Ct. of Mich., 1933-34. Chevalier Legion of Honor (France). Mem. Mich. Hist. Commn., 1934. Democrat. Catholic. Home: Detroit, Mich. Died Nov. 18, 1938.

WEAKLEY, Samuel Davies, judge; b. Somerville, Ala., July 16, 1860; s. John Bedford and Mary Emily (Rice) W.; grad. State Normal Coll., Florence, Ala., 1879; m. Ellen Anglin, Feb. 27, 1884. Admitted to bar, May 17, 1880; practiced at Memphis, Tenn., 1880-87; removed to Birmingham, Ala., 1887; mem. firm of Cabaniss & Weakley, 1889-1906; later mem. firm Weakley & Rice, Birmingham. City atty., Birmingham, 1889-90; chief justice Supreme Ct. of Ala., Feb.-Nov. 1906. Democrat. Presbyn. elder. Del. Congress of Lawyers and Jurists, St. Louis, 1904. Spl. counsel for state of Alabama in railroad rate cases which have been carried through all fed. courts to Supreme Ct. of U.S.; active in opposing liquor traffic in Ala. and author of all its prohibition laws enacted in the state, 1907—; declined appmt. as chief justice of Supreme Ct. tendered by the gov. of Ala., 1909. Home: Birmingham, Ala. Died Feb. 14, 1921.

WEAR, Joseph W(alker), broker; b. St. Louis, Mo., Nov. 27, 1876; s. James Hutchinson and Nancy (Holliday) W.; prep. edn. Smith Acad., St. Louis, 1885-95; A.B., Yale, 1899; m. Adaline Coleman Potter, Apr. 14, 1903 (died 1935); 1 son, William Potter. With Wear Bros., dry goods commn. business, St. Louis, 1904-14; v.p. and treas. Thomas Potter Sons & Co., linoleum mfrs., Phila., 1914-20; partner W. A. Harriman & Co., Inc., in charge Phila. office, 1920-30; partner E. A. Pierce & Co., brokers, Phila., 1930—; gen. partner Merrill Lynch, also E. A. Pierce & Cassatt, 1940. Delegate to Bull Moose Convn., Chicago, 1914; mem. Rep. State Com., chmn. Rep. Finance Com. for Pa., 1938—. Pa. del.-at-large for Rep. Convn., 1940. Trustee Jefferson Med. Coll. and Hosp.; mem. Yale Alumni Bd. (chmn. 1928-30). Mem. Pa. Commn. for New York World's Fair. Mem. U.S. Lawn Tennis Assn. (v.p.). Presbyn. (trustee Second Presbyn. Ch., Phila.). Doubles champion of U.S. in court tennis with Jay Gould, 6 yrs.; racquet double champion of U.S., 3 yrs.; chmn. U.S. Davis Cup Com., 1928-30; capt. U.S. Davis Cup Team, 1928, 1935. Home: Penllyn, Pa. Died June 4, 1941.

WEATHERLY, Ulysses Grant, univ. prof.; b. W. Newton, Ind., Apr. 21, 1865; s. William A. and Lydia (Dix) W.; A.B., Colgate U., 1890; Ph.D., Cornell, 1894; univs. of Heidelberg and Leipzig, 1893-94, Columbia, 1899-1900; Litt.D., Colgate, 1910; A.M., Ind. U., 1911; m. Alice M. Burgess, Dec. 24, 1890; 1 dau., Ruth Burgess (Mrs. Harold Gray). Instr., Central High Sch., Phila., 1894-95; asst. prof. history, 1895-98, asso. prof., 1898-99, prof. economics and sociology, 1899—, Ind. U. Lecturer sociology, U. of Colo., 6 summers, Columbia, summer 1912, U. of Ill., summer 1914, Cornell, summer 1923, U. of Ore., summer 1929, U. of Southern Calif., summer, 1932. Joint editor, Economic Bull, 1907-10. Pres. Ind. Conf. Charities, 1911; chmn. Ind. Child Labor Com.; mem. Ind. Commn. on Industrial Edn. Democrat. Mason. Author: Social Progress—Studies in the Dynamics of Change, 1926; also many mag. articles on economic and social topics. Home: Bloomington, Ind. Died July 18, 1940.

WEAVER, Aaron Ward, rear admiral U.S.N.; b. Washington, July 1, 1832; s. Lt. William Augustus and Jane (Van Wyck) W.; apptd. midshipman from Ohio, 1848, grad. 1854; m. Ida, d. Alpheus Hyatt, Feb. 1864. Passed midshipman, June 15, 1854; master, Sept. 15, 1855; lt., Sept. 16, 1855; lt. comdr., July 16, 1862; comdr., July 25, 1866; capt., Aug. 8, 1876; commodore, Oct. 7, 1886; rear admiral, June 27, 1893; retired Sept. 26, 1893. Served in St. Louis and Congress, 1848-53; at Naval Acad., 1853-54; in Trenton, Fulton, and coast survey steamers Walker and Arctic, 1854-57; in Marion on African coast and returned home on prize slave bark Ardennes, 1857-59; Navy Yard, Philadelphia, 1859-60; during Civil War served in Susquehanna, at bombardment of Fts. Hatteras, Clarke, Beauregard, Walker, and Port Royal, S.C.; in Winona and comd. Chippewa, in Mahopac, 1864-65; Navy Yard, Boston, 1865-66; comd. Tallapoosa, 1867; recruiting duty, Washington, 1867-68; spl. duty, 1869-70; comd. Terror and Severn, 1870-71; Navy Yard, Washington, 1872-73; in charge nitre depot, Malden, Mass., 1874-75; comd. Dictator, 1876-77; Navy Yard, Norfolk, 1879-81; comd. Brooklyn, 1882-84; mem. Naval Examining and Retiring Bds., Washington, 1885-89; comdt. Navy Yard, Norfolk, 1890-92; pres. Naval Examining and Retiring Bds., 1893. Died Oct. 2, 1919.

WEAVER, Clarence Eugene, civil engr.; b. Newark, N.J., Jan. 7, 1877; s. William Albert and Sarah Bowen (Matteson) W.; Ph.B. in C.E., Yale, 1899 (1st honors); m. Marie Dickey, Jan. 7, 1903; children—Maxwell Dickey, Sarah Bowen. Asst. engr. Mexican Internat. R.R., 1899-1906; res. engr. Sonora Ry., Mexico, 1906-09; engr. maintenance of way, S.P. R.R. of Mexico, 1909-11; roadmaster I.C. R.R., 1911-13, dist. engr., 1913-16; engr. maintenance of way, Central of Ga. Ry., 1916-26, chief engr., 1926—, asst. gen. mgr., 1931-33, gen. mgr., 1933—; southern regional dir. for fed. coördinator of transportation, 1933-36. Mason. Home: Savannah, Ga. Died Nov. 28, 1938.

WEAVER, Edward Ebenezer, clergyman; b. Canton, O., June 10, 1864; s. Joseph and Susan Aquila (Lawrence) W.; A.B., U. of Wooster, O., 1885; A.M., Princeton, 1889; grad. Princeton Theol. Sem., 1889; Ph.D., Clark U., 1910; m. Florence Anne Stratton, June 15, 1893; children—Edward Stratton (dec.), Francis Patton, Sarah Waldran. Ordained Presbyn. ministry, 1889; pastor Ridgely St. Ch., Baltimore, 1889-1901, Harrodsburg, Ky., 1901-04, Richmond, Ky., 1904-07; stated supply various chs. in N.E., 1908-15; pastor 1st Ch., Waltham, Mass., 1915-21; with gen. Bd. of Edn. of Presbyn. Ch., U.S.A., 1921-22. Moderator Baltimore Presbytery, 1894; commr. to General Assembly Presbyn. Church U.S.A., 1899, 1904, 15, 20; chmn. com. on Christian edn., Synod of N.E., 1915-27. Author: Mind and Health, 1913; also hymns and hymn tunes. Home: Watertown, Mass. Died June 24, 1931.

WEAVER, Erasmus Morgan, army officer; b. Lafayette, Ind., May 23, 1854; s. Erasmus Morgan and Fanny Mary (Bangs) W.; grad. U.S. Mil. Acad., 1875; studied in physical and elec. lab., Mass. Inst. Tech., 1895, 1896. Commd. 2d lt. U.S. Arty., June 16, 1875; 1st lt., Oct. 2, 1883; honor grad. Arty. Sch., 1888; capt. a.a.g. vols., May 12, 1898; capt. 1st U.S. Arty., May 14, 1898; lt. col. 5th Mass. Inf., July 1, 1898; hon. mustered out of vol. service, Mar. 31, 1899; maj. U.S. Arty. Corps, Aug. 4, 1903; maj. Gen. Staff, June 1905; lt. col. Arty. Corps, Jan. 25, 1907; lt. col. Gen. Staff, Oct. 1908; col. Coast Arty. Corps, Dec. 1909; col. Gen. Staff, Oct. 1910; brig. gen. chief of Coast Arty., Mar. 1911; maj. gen., July 6, 1916. Prof. mil. science and tactics, Western Reserve U., 1877-80, S.C. Mil. Acad., Charleston, S.C., 1883-86; instr. dept. chemistry, electricity, etc., U.S. Mil. Acad., 1888-91; instr. dept. of arty., U.S. Arty Sch., 1900-03; chief, Div. Militia Affairs, Office Sec. of War, 1908-11; mem. Bd. Ordnance and Fortifications; mem. War Council of War Dept., Dec. 1917-May 1918; retired for age, by operation of law, May 23, 1918. Episcopalian. Author: Notes on Military Explosives, 1906. Died Nov. 13, 1920.

WEAVER, Harry Otis, lawyer, agriculturist; b. Marshall Twp., Louisa County, Ia., Apr. 20, 1866; s. Erastus and Mary Elizabeth (Marshall) W.; Ph.B., State U. of Ia., 1892, LL.B., 1893; m. Alma A. Neuse, Oct. 6, 1896; 1 son, William Otis. Practiced at Wapello, 1893—. Mem. Rep. State Central Com. 12 yrs. (chmn. 1898-1902); collector internal revenue 4th Dist. of Ia., by apptmt. of President Roosevelt, 1902-13; mem. Ia. Ho. of Reps., 1894-1900 (assisted in revising drainage laws); chmn. Ia. delegation to Rep. Nat. Conv., Chicago, 1920. In charge agrl. dept. Ia. State Fair. Odd Fellow, K.P., Woodman, Elk. Home: Wapello, Ia. Died June 1933.

WEAVER, Harry Sands, M.D.; b. Beartown, Pa., June 8, 1868; s. Isaac and Elizabeth (Sensenich) W.; student Millersville Normal Sch., 1886-88; M.D., Hahnemann Med. Coll., Phila., 1892; studied in Vienna and London, 1900; m. Mary P. Hollis, Apr. 7, 1898; 1 son, Harry Sands; m. 2d, Dr. T. Ruth Hartley, Mar. 12, 1924. In practice of medicine, 1892—; prof. laryngology and rhinology, Hahnemann Med. Coll., Phila., 1920—. Fellow Am. Coll. of Surgeons. Republican. Mason. Home: Philadelphia, Pa. Died July 7, 1938.

WEAVER, James B., congressman; b. Dayton, O., June 12, 1833; common sch. edn.; LL.B., Cincinnati Law Sch., 1854; m. Clara Vinson, 1858. Pvt. to col. 2d Ia Vols., and bvt. brig. gen., 1861-65; dist. atty. 2d Jud. Dist., Ia., 1866-70; assessor internal revenue, 1st dist., Ia., 1867-73; editor Iowa Tribune, Des Moines; mem. 46th Congress (1879-81), 8th Ia. Dist., as a "Greenbacker," and 49th and 50th Congresses (1885-89), 9th Ia. Dist.; Greenback candidate for pres. U.S., 1880; People's Party candidate for Pres., 1892, received 22 electoral votes; fusion Populist. Mayor of Colfax, Ia., 1904-06. Home: Colfax, Ia. Died 1912.

WEAVER, James Bellamy, lawyer; b. Bloomfield, Ia., Aug. 19, 1861; s. Gen. James Baird and Clara (Vinson) W.; student Southern Ia. Normal and Scientific Inst., Bloomfield, Ia.; LL.B., State U. of Ia., 1882; m. Fay M. Atkins, Nov. 7, 1889 (dec.); children—Eastman Atkins, Persis Fay. Mem. firm Gatch & Weaver, Des Moines, 1882-85, Gatch, Conner & Weaver, 1885-1904, later practicing alone; counsel for all electric light and power interests in Des Moines, 1904-14, and for many yrs. counsel in famous Des Moines river lands litigation. Mem. Ia. Ho. of Reps. 3 terms, 1917-21, and author of Ia. vocational ednl. law, housing law, fraudulent advertising law, community centre law, budget tax levy law, part-time schools law, and assisted in drafting Ia. good roads law. State dir. Am. Red Cross, 1917-18; commr. Uniform State Laws, 1918-20; mem. State Retrenchment and Reform Com., 1921-22; president Des Moines Pub. Library, 1913-14, 1927-31; pres. Edmundson Memorial Foundation, 1935-37; chmn. City Plan Commn., Des Moines, 1929-31; trustee Assn. Fine Arts. Republican. Conglist. Mason. Chmn. Ia. Child Welfare Commn. Recipient of Register-Tribune Nobel prize, "for highest community service," 1925. Home: Des Moines, Ia. Deceased.

WEAVER, John, mayor; b. Worcestershire, Eng., Oct. 5, 1861; s. Benjamin and Elizabeth (Wilke) W.; came to U.S., 1879; pub. sch. edn.; m. Emily Jennings, Oct. 21, 1885. Admitted to bar, 1891, in practice at Phila., 1891—. Dist. atty., Phila., 1901-03, mayor, 1903-07. Independent Republican. Active in reform of franchise and other abuses in Phila. Home: Overbrook, Phila., Pa. Died Mar. 18, 1928.

WEAVER, John Van Alstyn, writer; b. Charlotte, N.C., July 17, 1893; s. John Van Alstyn and Anne Randolph (Tate) W.; A.B., Hamilton Coll., Clinton, N.Y., 1914; student Harvard, 1915; m. Peggy Wood, Feb. 14, 1924. Asst. to book editor Chicago Daily News, 1916-17, 1919-20; lit. editor Brooklyn Daily Eagle, 1920-24; writer for Paramount-Famous-Lasky Corp., 1928-31. Served in U.S. Army, May 1917-Jan. 1919; commd. 2d lt. O.R.C., 1918. Conglist. Author: In American (verse), 1921; Margie Wins the Game (novel), 1922; Finders (poems), 1923; More in American (verse), 1925; Love 'Em and Leave 'Em (play, with George Abbott), 1926; To Youth (verse), 1927; Her Knight Comes Riding (novel), 1928; Turning Point (verse), 1930; Trial Balance (verse), 1931; Joy-Girl, 1932. Contbr. to mags. Home: Springdale, Conn. Died June 14, 1938.

WEAVER, Jonathan, bishop; b. Carroll County, O., Feb. 23, 1824; reared on farm; ed. in common schs. and in acad. at Hagerstown, O.; **D.D., Otter-**

bein Univ., 1870; m. Keziah L. Rabb (died 1851); m. 2d, Mary E. Forsythe, 1853. Entered ministry United Brethren Church, 1845; ordained, 1847; elected bishop, 1865; seven times reëlected, bishop emeritus, 1893—. Author: Ministerial Salary; The Resurrection of the Dead; Divine Providence; Universal Restoration; Comment on the United Brethren Confession of Faith; etc.; edited Christian Doctrine; wrote extensively for church periodicals. Died 1901.

WEAVER, Rufus B., anatomist; b. Gettysburg, Pa., Jan. 10, 1841; A.B., Pa. Coll., Gettysburg, 1862, A.M., 1865; M.D., Pa. Med. U., 1865, Hahnemann Med. Coll., Phila., 1891; Sc.D.; m. Madeleine Louise Bender, Dec. 21, 1869. Successively apptd. demonstrator of anatomy, 1869, lecturer on regional anatomy, 1876-96, prof. applied anatomy, 1896—, Hahnemann Med. Coll. Dissected and mounted, 1888, the entire cerebro-spinal nervous system of a human body, the only specimen of its kind. Home: Phila., Pa. Died July 15, 1936.

WEAVER, Silas Matteson, judge; b. Chautauqua County, N.Y., Dec. 18, 1845; s. Caleb and Matilda (Matteson) W.; ed. common schs. of Chautauqua County, and at Fredonia (N.Y.) Acad., 1861-65; LL.D., Cornell Coll., Ia., 1907; m. Sarah C. Lucas, Sept. 20, 1874. Read law at Fredonia, N.Y.; admitted to bar, Buffalo, May 4, 1868; removed to Iowa Falls, Ia., Aug. 1868, and practiced law there. Mayor of Iowa Falls, 1874-76; mem. Ia. Ho. of Reps., 1884-88 (chmn. judiciary com.); district judge, 11th Jud. Dist., 1886-1901; judge Supreme Ct. of Ia., Jan. 1, 1902—. Republican. Methodist. Home: Iowa Falls, Ia. Died Nov. 6, 1923.

WEAVER, Walter L., congressman; b. Montgomery County, O., April 1, 1851; s. Rev. John S. and Amanda (Hurin) W.; grad. Wittenberg Coll., 1870; studied law; admitted to bar, 1872; elected prosecuting atty., Clark County, 1874, 1880, 1882 and 1885; m. Mary B. Hardy, May 24, 1881. Mem. Congress from 7th Ohio dist., 1897-1901; asso. judge Choctaw and Chickasaw Citizenship Ct. at South McAlester, I.T., July 2, 1902—. Republican. Home: Springfield, O. Died 1909.

WEAVER, William Dixon, engr.; b. Greensburg, Pa., Aug. 30, 1857; ed. Ky. U., 1875-76; grad. U.S. Naval Acad. (cadet-engr.), 1880; studied in elec. lab. of The Sorbonne, Paris, and Sch. of Elec. Engring., London, 1884, LL.D., U. of Kentucky, 1919; m. Mildred Niebuhr, 1900. Went on first Greeley relief expdn., 1883; resigned from navy, 1892; vol. chief engr., U.S.S. Glacier during Spanish-Am. War. Editor Elec. World, 1893-96, and 1899-1912; founded Am. Electrician and editor 1896-99. U.S. Govt. del. Internat. Elec. Congress, Paris, 1900; treas. and bus. mgr. Internat. Elec. Congress, St. Louis, 1904. Declined appmt. on Naval Advisory Bd., 1915. Mem. Am. Inst. Elec. Engrs. (mgr. 6 yrs.). Officier de l'Instruction Publique (France). Home: Charlottesville, Va. Died Nov. 2, 1919.

WEBB, Alexander Stewart, educator; b. New York, Feb. 15, 1835; s. Gen. James Watson and Helen Lispenard (Stewart) W.; grad. U.S. Mil. Acad., 1855; 2d lt. 4th Arty., July 1, 1855; 2d lt. 2d Arty., Oct. 20, 1855; 1st lt., Apr. 28, 1861; capt. 11th Inf., May 14, 1861; maj. 1st R.I. Inf., Sept. 14, 1861; served in Army of Potomac; asst. chief of arty., insp. gen. 5th Corps; promoted brig. gen. U.S.V., June 1863; comdg. 2d Div., 2d Army Corps, 1 yr.; served with distinction at Gettysburg and was wounded there; afterward in Rapidan and Wilderness campaigns; severely wounded at Spottsylvania, May 12, 1864; awarded Congressional Medal of Honor "for distinguished personal gallantry in the battle of Gettysburg;" assigned as maj. gen. U.S.V. by President Lincoln, Dec. 1864; chief of staff, Army of the Potomac, to Appomattox C.H., and to May 1866; lt. col. 44th Inf., July 26, 1866, 5th Inf., Mar. 15, 1869; reached bvt. rank of maj. gen. in vol. and regular army. Assigned by President Grant as maj. gen. U.S.A., 1869, in command of 1st Mil. Dist. (state of Va.); discharged at own request, Dec. 3, 1870. Pres. Coll. of the City of N.Y. for 33⅓ yrs., 1869-1903; retired and pensioned by state law. Comdr. gen. Mil. Order Foreign Wars. Mem. N.Y. Monuments Commn. Author: The Peninsula—McClellan's Campaign of 1862. Home: Riverdale-on-Hudson, N.Y. Died 1911.

WEBB, Charles Henry ("John Paul"), author; b. Rouse's Point, N.Y., Jan. 24, 1834; went to sea when young; held editorial position on N.Y. Times, 1860-63; in Calif., 1863-66, city editor of San Francisco Evening Bulletin, 1863-64; in 1864 founded The Californian, to which Mark Twain and Bret Harte contributed; produced several plays at local theatres. Invented "The Adder," an adding machine; a cartridge-loader, etc. Author: Liffith Lank, or Lunacy (travesty of Charles Reade's "Griffith Gaunt"), 1866; St. Twel'mo; or, the Cuneiform Cyclopedist of Chattanooga (travesty of Miss Evans' "St. Elmo"), 1868; The Wickedest Woman in New York, 1869; John Paul's Book, 1874; My Vacation, 1875; Parodies, Prose and Verse, 1876; Vagrom Verse, 1889; With Lead and Line, Along Varying Shores, 1901; also many contributions to mags., principally in verse. Edited and pub. first book of Mark Twain, "The Jumping Frog of Calaveras County, and Other Sketches." Died 1905.

WEBB, Edward Fleming, educator; b. Salem, Md., Mar. 27, 1875; s. Richard Watson and Marie Elizabeth (Hurley) W.; A.B., Washington Coll., Chestertown, Md., 1892; post-grad. work Johns Hopkins, 1911, 13, 14; m. Nellie Larimore Higgins, Apr. 26, 1905. V. prin. Harrington (Del.) High Sch., 1897-99; prin. Vienna (Md.) Acad., 1899-1904, 1908-09; in mercantile, banking and newspaper business, 1905-10; prin. Hurlock (Md.) High Sch., 1910-11, Bel Air High Sch., 1911-12; prin. Frostburg (Md.) State Normal Sch., 1912; later supt. schs. at Cumberland, Md. Democrat. Episcopalian. Mason. Home: Cumberland, Md. Died Nov. 1928.

WEBB, Frank Rush, organist, author, composer; b. Covington, Ind., Oct. 8, 1851; s. David and Maria Louise (Lawson) W.; ed. Miami U., Ohio, Wabash Coll., Ind., N.E. Conservatory of Music (non-grad.); m. May Davis, Feb. 13, 1877 (died 1911); children—Frank Davis, David Stuart. Organist St. Paul's Cathedral, Indianapolis, 1873-76; organist and choir master, Trinity M.E. Ch., Lima, O., 1876-83; teacher piano, organ and harmony, and dir. Sch. of Music, Va. Female Inst. (later known as Stuart Hall), Staunton, Va., 1883-1910; organist and choir master, Trinity Ch., Staunton, 1883-1910; advertising staff Baltimore News, 1910-23, Webb Advertising Agencies, 1923—. Band-master Stonewall Brigade Band, Staunton, 1883-92. Democrat. Author: Manual of the Canvas Canoe, 1898; contbr. articles on teaching, teaching material, and piano and organ playing in The Etude, The Musician, and other musical jours.; also articles on canoe cruises on mountain rivers, to Forest and Stream and other periodicals. Composer of over 200 pieces of music for military band; also piano and ch. music, songs, etc., reaching opus 108. Episcopalian. Home: Ruxton, Md. Died Oct. 20, 1934.

WEBB, George H., ry. official; b. Dubuque, Ia., Mar. 5, 1860; s. George and Emma (Alder) W.; C.E., Pa. Military Coll., 1880, M.C.E., 1914; widower. Began as rodman B.&O. R.R. Company; levelman and transitman Pittsburgh Southern Ry., and Pitsburgh & Western R.R.; city engr., Johnstown, Pa., 1883; later engr. Johnson Steel Rail Co.; asst. engr. on branch lines C.,B.&Q. Ry. Co., 1885-88; location and constrn. of rys. in the Northwest, 1888; constrn. govt. rys. in Chile, S.A., 1889-91; div. engr. and supt. constrn. Summit div., Central Ry. of Peru through main range of the Andes, 1891-93; pvt. practice, 1893-97; chief engr., Cincinnati, Georgetown & Portsmouth Ry., 1897-99; later roadmaster, C.,C.,C.&St.L. and C.&A. rys.; constructing engr. Baring Cross shops of St. Louis, Iron Mtn. and Southern Ry. in Ark., 1901-02; location of Ostimo div. and engr. Middle div. M.C. R.R., Jan.-Nov. 1903; asst. chief engr. same rd., 1903-05, chief engr., June 1905—; also chief engr. Detroit River Tunnel Co., Jan. 16, 1911—. Republican. Episcopalian. Commd. lt. col., Engr. Corps U.S.A., June 1917, and assigned to 16th (ry.) Engrs.; col., Sept. 1918; sect. engr. with A.E.F. in France, Aug. 1917-Apr. 1919. Awarded D.S.M. Home: Detroit, Mich. Died Nov. 3, 1921.

WEBB, Henry Walter, ry. official; b. Tarrytown, N.Y., May 6, 1852; ed. pvt. Sch. of Mines, Columbia, and Columbia Coll; practiced law, New York, until 1882; in banking and brokerage firm W. S. Webb & Co., Wall St., 1882-86; v.p. Wagner Palace Car Co., 1886-89; asst. to pres., 1889-90; 3rd v.p., 1890, N.Y.C.&H.R. R.R. Co.; dir. in numerous financial orgns.; m. Leila Howard Griswold, 1884. Died 1900.

WEBB, James Henry, judge; b. Santa Fe, N.M., Dec. 22, 1854; s. James J. and Florilla M. (Slade) W.; B.Sc., Mass. Agrl. Coll., 1873; Yale, 1874-75; LL.B. (cum laude), Yale, 1877; m. Helen M. Ives, June 29, 1880. Admitted to bar, 1877; mem. bar Supreme Ct. of U.S.; mem. firm of Alling, Webb & Morehouse, 1883-14, judge Superior Ct. of Conn., Nov. 1914—; lecturer on medical jurisprudence, Yale Law School, 1896—. Dem. candidate for Congress, 2d Connecticut District, 1898; mem. Constl. Conv. of Conn., 1902; mem. bd. control Conn. Agrl. Expt. Sta., 1892—. Del. Universal Congress Lawyers and Jurists, St. Louis, 1904. Democrat. Editor Am. edit. Kenny's Outlines of Criminal Law, 1905. Contbr. to Two Centuries' Growth of American Law (article "Criminal Law and Procedure"), Yale Bi-centennial publ. Home: Hamden, Conn. Died Apr. 19, 1924.

WEBB, John Maurice, educator; b. Alamance County, N.C., Nov. 27, 1847; s. Alexander Smith and Cornelia Adeline (Stanford) W.; brother of William Robert W.; prep. edn. Bingham Sch., Oaks, N.C.; U. of N.C., 1866-68, hon. A.B., 1875, A.M., 1877; LL.D., U. of Nashville, 1896; m. Lily Shipp, Dec. 7, 1876. Taught 1 yr. Bingham Sch., Mebaneville, N.C., at Rockingham, N.C., 3 yrs.; became coprin. Webb Sch. at Culleoka, Tenn., 1873; sch. removed to Bell Buckle, Tenn., 1886. Methodist. Independent Democrat. Died Apr. 5, 1916.

WEBB, Nathan, jurist; b. Portland, Me., May 7, 1825; early edn., Portland Acad.; grad. Harvard, 1846; LL.D., Bowdoin, 1890; Harvard, 1896; m. Jane M. Usher, June 17, 1867. After graduation studied law; admitted to bar; practiced at Portland until 1882; U.S. dist. judge of Me., Jan. 24, 1882—. Died 1902.

WEBB, Robert Alexander, theologian; b. Oxford, Miss., Sept. 20, 1856; s. Robert Clark and Elizabeth Eaton (Dortch) W.; A.B., Southwestern Presbyn. U., Clarksville, Tenn., 1877, D.D., Southwestern Presbyn., 1890, LL.D., 1908; grad. Columbia (S.C.) Theol. Sem., 1880; m. Roberta Chauncey Beck, Oct. 23, 1888. Presbyn. minister, Bethel Ch., York County, S.C., 1882-87, Davidson Coll., N.C., 1887-88, Westminster Ch., Charleston, S.C., 1888-92; prof. systematic theology, Southwestern Presbyn. U., 1892-1908; prof. apologetics and systematic theology, Ky. Presbyn. Theol. Sem., Louisville, 1908—. Author: Theology of Infant Salvation. Democrat. Home: Louisville, Ky. Died May 23, 1919.

WEBB, Robert Thomas, clergyman, educator; b. nr. Louisburg, N.C., Aug. 30, 1866; s. Robert Thomas (M.D.) and Bettie (Brodie) W.; A.B., Randolph-Macon Coll., Va., 1890, D.D., 1920; grad. student, Vanderbilt U.; m. Mary Adelaide Robertson, Oct. 20, 1898; 1 son, James Vernon Billingsley (dec.). Ordained ministry M.E. Ch., S., 1895; pastor Chattanooga, Tenn., 1893-94, Rockwood, 1894-95, Ducktown, 1895-96, Athens, 1896-98, Cedar Bluff, Va., 1898-1901, Pocahontas, 1901-02, Philippi, W.Va., 1902-05, Fairmont, W.Va., 1905-08, Charleston (1st Ch.), W.Va., 1908-12, Barboursville, W.Va., and asso. pres. Morris Harvey Coll., 1912-15, Fairmont, W.Va. (2d pastorate), 1915-17, St. Paul's Ch., Parkersburg, 1917-20; pres. Morris Harvey Coll. and sec. of edn., 1920-22, also prof. of theology, 1923; pastor St. Paul's Ch., Clarksburg, W.Va., 1923-25; presiding elder Huntington Dist., Western Va. Conf. M.E. Church, S., 1925-29; financial sec. Morris Harvey College, 1929-31; pastor Pikeville, Ky., 1931-37. Pres. Conf. Bd. Edn., 1910-22; conference sec. of edn., 1920-23; pres. Conf. S.S. Bd., 1918-22; served as mem. Commn. on Ednl. Standards of M.E. Ch., S., also as mem. Federated Council of Chs. from Western Va. Conf.; pres. Conf. Bd. of Missions, 1934-38; mem. Greater Morris Harvey Commn.; del. to Men and Religion Forward Movement, N.Y. City; del. to Gen. Conf., 1918, 26, 30; chmn. Meth. Y.P. Conv., Memphis, Tenn., Dec. 1925-Jan. 1926. Democrat. Home: Petersburg, Va. Died Mar. 19, 1940.

WEBB, Walter Loring, engineer; b. Rye, N.Y., June 25, 1863; s. Edward Dexter and Emily (Loder) W.; B.C.E., Cornell U., 1884, C.E., 1889; m. Mary Tremaine Hubbard, Sept. 1, 1886. Instr. civ. engring., Cornell, 1888-92; asst. prof. civ. engring., U. of Pa., 1893-1901; cons. engr., 1901—. Author: Shades, Shadow and Perspective; Problems in the Use and Adjustment of Engineering Instruments, 1907; Railroad Construction, 1931; Economics of Railroad Construction, 1912, transl. into the Russian, 1921. Contbr. sect. 3 (railroads) to Am. Civil Engineers' Pocket Book; also contbr. to engineering and scientific periodicals. Maj. of engrs., U.S.A., 1917-20, in France as chief engr. of renting requisitions and claims service, in charge of valuations. Mason. Awarded Fuertes graduate gold medal by Cornell U., 1932, in recognition of 9th edit., "Railroad Construction." Home: Lansdowne, Pa. Died Jan. 24, 1941.

WEBB, William Alexander, educator; b. Durham, N.C., July 30, 1867; s. Richard Stanford and Jennie (Clegg) W.; B.A., Vanderbilt U., 1891; U. of Leipzig, 1895-97, U. of Berlin, 1903-04; Litt.D., Wofford College, S.C., 1911; m. Mary Lee Clary, Jan. 31, 1899. Teacher Latin and English, Webb Sch., Bell Buckle, 1892-95; prin. Central Acad., Fayette, Mo., 1897-99; prof. English, 1899-1913, pres., Apr. 23, 1907-13, Central Coll., Mo.; pres. Randolph-Macon Woman's College, Va., 1913—. Prof. English, U. of Colo. summer sch., 1911-14. Mem. com. edn. M.E. Ch., S.; mem. Religious Edn. Assn.; v.p. Assn. Am. Colls., 1916-17; pres. Assn. Colleges and Secondary Schools of Southern States, 1916-17. Contbr. to revs. and periodicals on lit. and ednl. subjects. Died Nov. 4, 1919.

WEBB, William Henry, shipbuilder; b. New York, June 19, 1816 (son of a shipbuilder); learned shipbuilding; at 20, under sub-contract from his father, built the packet-ship "Oxford," of the Black Ball Line; partner in Webb & Allen, shipbuilders, 1840-43; in same bus. alone, 1843-68; built over 150 large vessels; devised a new model for navy vessels which the U.S. and afterward French govt. refused, but Russian govt. accepted; upon this built and launched, 1858, The General Admiral, 7,000 tons displacement, screw frigate for Russia; later built two frigates for Italian govt. King Victor Emanuel conferring upon him order of Saints Maurice and Lazarus; also built the Dunderberg, later named Rochambeau for French govt., long the fastest armored vessel afloat; after retiring from shipbuilding conducted several steamship lines; three times declined nomination for mayor of New York; 14 years pres. N.Y. City Council of Municipal Reform; built and endowed Webb's Acad. and Home for Ship-builders, Fordham Heights, Westchester County, N.Y. Died 1899.

WEBB, William Robert, educator; b. Mt. Tizah, Person County, N.C., Nov. 11, 1842; s. Alexander Smith and Cornelia Adeline (Stanford) W.; brother of John Maurice W.; ed. Bingham Sch., Oaks, N.C., 1856-60; entered U. of N.C., July 1860; entered C.S.A. in Co. H, 15th N.C. Vols., May 1861; grad. by examination, U. of N.C., 1868, A.M., 1869; m. Emma Clary, Apr. 23, 1873; children—William Robert, Alla, John Stanford, Adeline (Mrs. Josiah Sibley), Daniel Clary, Susan (Mrs. E. T. Price), Emma (Mrs. McDougal McLeon), Richard Thompson. 1st lt. Co. K, 15th N.C. Vols.; resigned and joined Co. K, 2d N.C. Cav., as pvt. adj. 2d Cav. and comd. Co. K at Namozine Ch. in Va., the last fight, Apr. 3, 1865; captured Apr. 3, and reached home in N.C., July 1865. Asst. teacher Horner Sch., Oxford, N.C., 1866-70; founded 1st training sch. West of Allegheny Mountains, July 1870, in Culleoka, Tenn.; moved school to Bell Buckle, Tenn., 1886. Democrat; state credit and gold Democrat. Del. Indianapolis Conv. which nominated Palmer and Buckner. Apptd. to U.S. Senate for unexpired term, Jan. 24-Mar. 3, 1913, made vacant by death of Robert L. Taylor. Mem. M.E. Ch., S.; mem. Gen. Conf., 1874, 1902. Dir. Bell Buckle Bank. Home: Bell Buckle, Tenn. Died Dec. 19, 1926.

WEBB, William Seward, capitalist; b. New York, Jan. 31, 1851; s. Gen. James Watson and Laura Virginia (Cram) W.; ed. Col. Churchill's Mil. Sch., Sing Sing, N.Y., 1864-69, Columbia, 1869-71; studied medicine at Vienna, Paris, Berlin, 1871-72; M.D., Coll. Phys. and Surg. (Columbia), 1875; m. Eliza Osgood, d. late W. H. Vanderbilt, 1883. Pres. Wagner Palace Car Co.; pres. Fulton Chain Ry. Co., Fulton Nav. Co., Raquette Lake Transportation Co.; dir. Rutland Ry. Co., Pullman Co., St. Lawrence & Adirondack Ry. Co., Raquette Lake Ry.; builder and pres. Mohawk & Malone R.R.; dir. L.S.&M.S. Ry. Purchased 200,000 acres and converted it into a game preserve in the Adirondacks; served on staff of gov. of Vt. with rank of col.; insp. gen. rifle practice Vt. Militia. Mem. S.A.R. (pres. gen.). Author: California and Alaska, 1891. Editor: Papers of General James Watson Webb; Papers of Gen. Samuel Blatchley Webb. Home: New York, N.Y. Died Oct. 29, 1926.

WEBB, William Walter, bishop; Germantown, Pa., Nov. 20, 1857; s. William Hewitt and Esther Odin (Dorr) W.; U. of Pa., 1877-79; A.B., B.S., Trinity Coll., Conn., 1882, A.M., 1885; B.D., Berkeley Div. Sch., 1885; D.D., Nashotah House, 1897, LL.D., 1925; unmarried. Deacon, 1885, priest, 1886, P.E. Ch.; asst. Trinity Ch., Middletown, Conn., 1885-86, Ch. of the Evangelists, Phila., 1886-89; rector St. Elizabeth, Phila., 1889-92; prof. dogmatic theology, 1892-97, pres., 1897-1905, Nashotah House; elected bishop coadjutor of Milwaukee, Nov. 21, 1905; bishop of Milwaukee, Oct. 29, 1906. Pres. trustees of Nashotah House, Racine Coll. and Kemper Hall. Author: Index to Electrolysis, 1882; Guide to Seminarians, 1887; Cure of Souls, 1892. Died Jan. 15, 1933.

WEBBER, George Harris, prof. edn. and psychology; b. Charleston, S.C., Dec. 11, 1882; s. George Lockhart and Ida M. E. (Krammer) W.; grad. Bloomsburg (Pa.) Lit. Inst., 1904; B.Pd., Pa. State Teachers Coll., 1906; A.B., Iowa Christian Coll., 1908, A.M., 1910, Ph.D., 1917; certificate in science, U. of Tenn., 1909; diploma, C.L.S.C., 1911; A.M., U. of S.C., 1912; M.S., Susquehanna U., 1918, Sc.D., 1921; m. Lillian Bakesless Wendt, Sept. 22, 1909. Supt. city schs., S.C., 1910-25; extension lecturer, Winthrop Coll., 1922-25; instr. in ednl. hygiene and asso. prof. edn., Susquehanna U., summers 1917-25; prof. history of edn. and philosophy, Ga. State Coll. for Women, 1925-28, acting dean of Coll. Arts and Science, 2d semester 1927, dean of students, 1927-28, prof. edn. and psychology and head of dept., 1928—; sub. dir. div. gen. extension, Univ. System of Ga., 1932—; cons. psychologist Ga. Training Sch. for Boys. Asso. editor Social Science (mag.) and dir. Social Science Pub. Co. Del. to 4th Internat. Congress on Sch. Hygiene, 1913, World Federation of Edn. Assn., Geneva, 1929. Fellow A.A.A.S., S.C. Acad. Science; mem. N.E.A. (internat. com.; dir. 1920-28), Am. Acad. polit. and Social Science, Nat. Acad. Visual Instrn., Am. Assn. Univ. Profs. (pres. G.S.C.W. Chapter 1932-33). Democrat. Presbyn. Mason, Moose. Contbr. articles on edn. and psychology, also verse. Home: Milledgeville, Ga. Died July 31, 1934.

WEBBER, Henry William, lawyer; b. N.Y. City, July 17, 1869; s. Louis Philip and Elizabeth (Miller) W.; LL.B., U. of Mich., 1894, hon. LL.M., 1929; unmarried. Admitted to Colo. bar, 1894, and practiced at Denver until 1897; in gen. practice at N.Y. City, 1897—. Chmn. legal advisory bd., Selective Service Draft Bd., World War I. Sec. and pres. class of 1894, Law, U. of Mich. Republican. Presbyn. Author: Law of Colorado Land Securities, 1895. Died May 20, 1935.

WEBBER, Le Roy, consul; b. Erie County, N.Y., July 7, 1891; s. F. H. and Maria (deBray) W.; ed. high sch. and under private tutors. Vice consul Am. Consulate, Glasgow, Scotland, 1913; v. consul, at Nottingham, Eng., 1915-20, at Palermo, Italy, 1920-23; consul at Hong Kong, China, 1923-24, then at Amoy, and at Chefoo, 1926-30, Shanghai, 1931, Chefoo, 1932—. Mason. Home: Buffalo, N.Y. Died Feb. 24, 1935.

WEBER, Henri Carleton, supt. schs.; b. Nashville, Tenn., Nov. 7, 1860; s. Henri Christian and Margaret Isabella (Walker) W.; U. of the South, 1876-80; spl. studies, Harvard; m. Beula Beaumont, June 14, 1882. Began teaching in pub. schs., Nashville, 1880; supt. schs., Nashville, 1897-1900, 1906-09, 1918—. Democrat. Episcopalian. Died June 18, 1930.

WEBER, Herman Carl, clergyman; b. Mina, Chautauqua County, N.Y., Feb. 9, 1873; s. Jacob and Sarah (Phifer) W.; prep. edn., Adelphi Acad., Brooklyn, N.Y., 1889-91; A.B., Rutgers, 1895, A.M., 1898; B.D., New Brunswick (N.J.) Theol. Sem., 1898; D.D., Albany (Ore.) Coll., 1927; m. Kate Duryea Allin, Jan. 16, 1912; children—Heloise Litchfield, Kate Duryea, Laurence Allin. Pastor Ref. Ch., West Farms, N.Y., 1898-1902; asst. pastor Collegiate Ch., N.Y. City, 1902-06; pastor Edgewood Ref. Ch., Brooklyn, 1906-12, City Park Br. First Presbyn. Ch., Brooklyn, 1912-18; Y.M.C.A. work, U.S.N., 1918-19; asso. dir. field work, New Era Movement, 1919-25; asso. dir. mobilization dept. Gen. Council Presbyn. Ch. U.S.A., 1925-26, dir., 1926-29, dir. every mem. canvass dept., 1929—. Pres. U. Stewardship Council, U.S., Can., 1936-37. Republican. Author: Presbyterian Statistics Through One Hundred Years, 1927; Evangelism—A Graphic Survey, 1929; The Every Member Canvass, Pocket Books or People, 1932. Editor of Year Book of American Churches; contbg. editor on Protestant denominational activities, American Year Book. Editor, Everyone, Presbyn. quarterly. Home: East Orange, N.J. Died July 25, 1939.

WEBER, Jessie Palmer, librarian; b. Carlinville, Ill.; d. Gen. John M. and Malinda A. (Neely) Palmer; grad. Bettie Stuart Inst., Springfield, Ill., 1880; m. N. W. Weber, June 8, 1881 (dec.); 1 dau., Malinda Ellen (wife of Dr. John W. Irion). Sec. to father, U.S. senator, 1891-97; librarian Ill. State Hist. Library, 1898—. Sec., treas., dir. Ill. State Hist. Soc.; editor-in-chief Jour. of Ill. State Hist. Soc., 1908—; trustee, sec. Ill. State Ft. Massac Commn., 1904-17; commr. and sec. Ill. State Centennial Commn., 1913-19; sec. Lincoln Circuit Marking Assn. Compiler: Catalogue Ill. State Hist. Library, 1900; Report Ill. Centennial Commn., 1919. Wrote circular for study of Ill. history, 1905; contbr. on hist. topics. Home: Springfield, Ill. Died May 31, 1926.

WEBER, John B., congressman; b. Buffalo, Sept. 21, 1842; s. Philip J. and Mary Anna (Yung) W.; high sch. edn.; m. Elizabeth J. Farthing, Jan. 7, 1864 (died 1900); children—Mary Frances (Mrs. Howard O. Cobb), Elizabeth H. (Mrs. Godfrey L. Carden), Jean Beatrice (Mrs. Frank M. Brinker), Laura Christiana (Mrs. George S. Goodrich), Ethel Grace (Mrs. Edward Meinel), Clara Adelia (dec.), Mabel Adele (dec.); m. 2d, Alice J. Roberts, Aug. 7, 1913. Enlisted as pvt. 44th N.Y. Vol. Infantry ("Elsworth Avengers"), Aug. 7, 1861; successively corporal to actg. a.-a.-g.; col. 89th U.S.C.T., Sept. 19, 1863-June 20, 1864; asst. postmaster Buffalo, 1870-73; defeated for sheriff Erie County by Grover Cleveland but elected to succeed him for term, 1874-76; mem. 49th to 50th Congresses (1885-89), 33d N.Y. Dist.; commr. of immigration port of New York, 1890-93; chmn. commn. to investigate in Europe causes inciting immigration; visited various European countries, chiefly Russia, in connection with Jewish persecutions; commr. gen. Pan-Am. Expn., Buffalo, 1901. Home: Lackawanna, N.Y. Died Dec. 18, 1926.

WEBER, John Langdon, clergyman; b. Union, S.C., Sept. 25, 1862; s. Rev. Samuel A. and Sarah A. (Langdon) W.; A.B., Wofford, 1882; D.D., Southern U., Ala., 1903; Litt.D., Morris-Harvey Coll., W.Va., 1903; m. Sudie James Young, Jan. 3, 1890. On staff Charleston (S.C.) News and Courier, 1882-90, Chattanooga (Tenn.) Times, 1890-91. Ordained M.E. Ch., S. ministry, 1891; pastor Knoxville, Tenn., Winchester, and Mt. Sterling, Ky., Gate City and Big Stone Gap, Va.; pres. Ky. Wesleyan Coll., 1901-07; became pastor First Church, Jackson, Tenn., 1909; pastor Madison Heights Ch., Memphis, 1912-16; again pastor 1st Ch., Jackson, 1916-17; Y.M.C.A. war work, religious dir. and camp sec., and in charge army schs., Camp Jackson, Columbia, S.C., 1917-19; pastor Broadway Ch., Paducah, Ky., Jan. 1, 1920—. Author: History of South Carolina, 1890; History of Epworth League, 1894. Contbr. to many ch. revs. and papers. Nat. lecturer Am. Legion; internat. dir. of the Lions Clubs. Died Mar. 19, 1923.

WEBER, Lois, motion picture dir.; b. Allegheny, Pa.; d. George and Mary Matilda (Snaman) Weber; m. 2d, Captain Harry Gantz. Toured U.S. at 16 as pianist, later on stage; in motion pictures, 1909—; owner and dir. Lois Weber Productions. Wrote and directed over 200 pictures, including "Shoes"; "Where Are My Children?"; "Hypocrites"; "For Husbands Only"; "Angel of Broadway"; "The Marriage Clause"; "Cane Fire—A Story of Sugar." Known as first woman dir. of motion pictures. Home: Hollywood, Calif. Died Nov. 13, 1939.

WEBER, Max, soldier; b. Achern, Baden, Aug. 27, 1824; ed. Poly. Sch., and grad. Mil. Acad. Karlsruhe, 1843, as officer in the army; took part in revolution in support of German Parliament, 1849, and upon its failure came to U.S. Served in U.S. army, 1861-65, as col. 20th N.Y. vols. and brig. gen. after April 1862; after losing right arm at battle of Antietam, had command Harper's Ferry, which he defended successfully against attack of Gen. Early's forces. After war was 10 years assessor and collector internal revenue, New York City. Died 1901.

WEBER, William Lander, college pres.; b. Lenoir, N.C., Apr. 14, 1866; s. Rev. Samuel A. and Sarah Alston (Langdon) W.; brother of John Langdon W.; A.B., Wofford Coll., 1886, A.M., 1888; studied English philology, Johns Hopkins, and U. of Chicago; LL.D., Ky. Wesleyan Coll.; m. Bettie, d. Alpheus Waters Wilson, Aug. 27, 1891. Instr. Bingham Sch., N.C., 1888-90; prof. English, Millsaps Coll., Miss., 1892-99; Bishop George F. Pierce prof. English, Emory Coll., 1899-1907; pres. Centenary Coll. of La., 1907—. Author: Word-lists for the Study of English Etymology, 1898; Selections from the Southern Poets, 1901. Contbr. to hist., lit. and philol. publs. Home: Shreveport, La. Died 1910.

WEBSTER, Arthur Gordon, physicist; b. Brookline, Mass., Nov. 28, 1863; s. William Edward and Mary Shannon (Davis) W.; A.B., Harvard, 1885; studied Berlin, Paris, Stockholm, 1886-90; Ph.D., U. of Berlin, 1890; D.Sc., Tufts, 1905; LL.D., Hobart, 1908; m. Elizabeth Munroe Townsend, Oct. 8, 1889. Instr. mathematics, Harvard, 1885-86; docent in physics, 1890-92, asst. prof., 1892-1900, prof. and dir. of phys. lab., 1900—, Clark U. Awarded Thomson prize (5,000 francs), Paris, 1895, for exptl. research on the Period of Electrical Oscillations. Fellow A.A.A.S., Am. Acad. Arts and Sciences, Am. Inst. E.E., Inst. Radio Engrs. Del. U.S. Govt. to Internat. Radiotelegraphic Conf., London, 1912. Mem. U.S. Naval Consulting Bd., 1915—, Nat. Research Council, 1917—. Author: A Mathematical Treatise on the Theory of Electricity and Magnetism, 1897; Dynamics of Particles, and of Rigid, Elastic and Fluid Bodies, 1904; Lowell Institute Lectures on Electricity and Ether, 1897; Harrison Lectures on Sound, U. of Pa., 1911; also many papers on physics, chiefly on mat. physics, mechanics, sound, electricity and ballistics. Home: Worcester, Mass. Died May 15, 1923.

WEBSTER, David, surgeon; b. Cambridge, N.S., July 16, 1842; s. Asael and Hephzibah (Pearson) W.; Normal Sch., Truro, N.S.; M.D., Bellevue Hosp. Med. Coll. (New York U.), 1868; widower. House surgeon Brooklyn Eye and Ear Hosp., 1869-71; house surgeon, 1871-73, asst. surgeon, 1873-85, surgeon, 1885—, Manhattan Eye and Ear Hosp., becoming sr. surgeon and chmn. bd. of surgeons. Died May 26, 1923.

WEBSTER, Edward Harlan, educator; b. Westfield, Pa., Sept. 13, 1876; s. Ozias Spencer and Lucinda English W.; grad. Washington (D.C.) Normal Sch., 1896; A.B., Bowdoin, 1910; A.M., Columbia, 1920; studied Oxford U., Eng., 1920-21; m. Katherine E. Blossom, 1912; 1 dau., Katherine Granville. Teacher graded and high schs., Washington, D.C., 1896-1903; teacher of English, Brooklyn (N.Y.) Poly. Prep. Sch., 1903-08, 1910-12; head of dept. of English, Tech. High Sch., Springfield, Mass., 1913-19, also dir. English Jr. High Schs., 1916-19; expert in English, Bridgeport (Conn.) Sch. Survey, 1913; lecturer in English, Columbia, summer sessions, 1922, 23, 24; dir. English, Cleveland Sch. of Edn. and Asso. Schs., 1923; chmn. div. of English, Sr. Teachers Coll. of Cleveland Sch. of Edn. and Western Reserve U., 1923-24; prof. English, State Teachers Coll., Mount Pleasant, Mich., 1924-27; prof. English, State Teachers Coll., Upper Montclair, N.J., 1927—. Unitarian. Mason. Author: English for Business, 1916; Effective English Expression, 1920; Teaching English in the Junior High School (with Dora V. Smith), 1927; Daily Drills for Better English, 1930; Oral Tests for Correct English, 1930; Good English Through Practice, Books I, II, III (with John E. Warriner), 1936; Teacher's Guide and Test Book, I, II, III (with same), 1936. Home: Upper Montclair, N.J. Died Nov. 14, 1937.

WEBSTER, Eugene Carroll, clergyman, educator; b. Somerville, Mass., Nov. 6, 1864; s. James Walker and Sarah Luella (Carpenter) W.; grad. Phillips Acad., Andover, Mass., 1883; A.B., Harvard, 1887; B.D., Yale Div. Sch., 1890; m. Wynn M. Ward, June 25, 1890; 1 son, Ward. Ordained Congl. ministry, 1890; pastor United Congl. Ch., East Providence, R.I., 1890-92; asst. editor, Blakeslee S.S. Lessons, 1892-93; pastor Trinity Ch., Neponset (Boston), 1893-99, Westbrook, Me., 1902-03; sec. district option (temperance) campaign, 1903-04; in business, 1904-06; hotel and theatre chaplain, Boston, 1906—;

asso. prin., 1913, later headmaster, University Sch. Hon. mem. A.B.C.F.M.; asst. sec. and sec. Mass. Gen. Assn. Congl. Chs., 1894-1903; asst. sec. Nat. Council of Congl. Chs., 1895-1904; asst. sec. Internat. Council same, 1899-1910; rec. sec. Congl. Edn. Soc., 1897-99, Am. Missionary Assn., 1899-1901. Trustee Puritan League. Republican. Author: Historical Sketch, Suffolk South Conference of Congregational Churches, 1898. Edited Procs. 2d International Congl. Council, Boston, 1899; editor Faith and Doubt, 1912-13. Home: Malden, Mass. Died Oct. 12, 1939.

WEBSTER, Francis Marion, entomologist; b. Lebanon, N.H., Aug. 8, 1849; s. J. S. and Betsey A. (Riddle) W.; M.S., U. of Ohio, 1893; m. Maria A. Potter, Aug. 21, 1870. Asst. state entomologist of Ill., 1882-84; spl. agt. U.S. Dept. Agr., 1884-92; entomologist Ohio Agrl. Expt. Sta., 1891-1902; asst. on biol. survey of Ill., 1903-04; in charge cereal and forage-crop insect investigations, U.S. Dept. Agr. Prof. econ. entomology, Purdue U., 1885-88, and cons. entomologist to Ind. Expt. Sta., 1888-91. Sent on mission to Melbourne (Australia) Internat. Expn., by U.S. Depts. of State and Agr., 1888, visiting other portions of Australia, Tasmania, and New Zealand, in interests of agr., returning 1889; engaged during part of years, 1886-90, in problem of suppression of buffalo gnat in valley of Lower Mississippi River. Fellow A.A.A.S., Ind. Acad. Science. Contbr. reports and papers to govt. and state pubis., Am. and foreign. Home: Kensington, Md.Died Jan. 3, 1916.

WEBSTER, Frank Daniel, army officer; b. Rolla, Mo., Sept. 11, 1866; s. Henry and Melinda (Burlingame) W.; grad. U.S. Mil. Acad., 1889, Inf. and Cav. Sch., 1897; Army War Coll., 1913; m. Anna G. Angell, Dec. 4, 1900. Commd. 2d lt. 25th Inf., June 12, 1889; trans. to 6th Inf., Oct. 3, 1889; 1st lt. 20th Inf., Dec. 7, 1896; capt. 18th Inf., Sept. 8, 1899; trans. to 20th Inf., Dec. 6, 1899; maj. inf., Mar. 11, 1911; assigned to 20th Inf., July 14, 1911; lt. col. 22d Inf., July 1, 1916; col., June 30, 1917; brig. gen. N.A., Dec. 17, 1917. A.d.c. to Brig. Gen. Loyd Wheaton, in Ala., Fla. and Ga., 1898, and in Philippine Islands, 1899-1902; again in P.I., 1904-06, 1909-11. Awarded life saving medal by Treasury Dept. for rescuing 2 persons from drowning, Jan. 18, 1893; recommended by Gen. Wheaton for bvt. of capt. "for gallantry" in Battle of Malinta, Mar. 26, 1899; for bvt. of maj. for charge at Santa Tomas, May 4, 1899; for bvt. of capt., U.S.A., by Gen. Lawton, "for services under fire," June 11, 1899. Comd. 17th Separate (regular) Brig., Jan.-Feb. 1918, 8th Brig., 4th (regular) Div., A.E.F., Feb.-July 27, 1918; retired as col. U.S.A., Dec. 3, 1918. Mason, Elk. Home: Leavenworth, Kan. Died Feb. 20, 1932.

WEBSTER, Frank G., banker; b. Canton, Mass., 1841. Mem. Kidder, Peabody & Co., bankers, 1886—; dir. Bigelow-Hartford Carpet Co., Kidder, Peabody Acceptance Corp., Heywood, Wakefield Co. (mem. exec. com.). Home: Boston, Mass. Died Jan. 22, 1930.

WEBSTER, George Sidney, sec. Am. Seamen's Friend Soc.; b. Meredith, N.Y., July 30, 1853; s. Sidney Smith and Lemira (Wells) W.; A.B., Hamilton Coll., 1878, D.D., 1902; grad. Union Theol. Sem., 1882; m. Emma Evans, May 16, 1882 (dec.); children—Helen Anna (dec.), Mrs. Minnie Coursen Corbett, Mrs. Emma Lemira Young. Ordained Presbyterian ministry, 1882; asst. pastor First Ch., East Orange, New Jersey, 1882-90; pastor Ch. of the Covenant, N.Y. City, 1890-1914; sec. Am. Seamen's Friend Society, 1914—. Dir. Nat. Temperance Soc. Editor Sailors' Mag. Republican. Author: Forty Years of Covenant Mercies, 1896; Seamen's Manual of Worship, 1927, 29, 31. The Seamen's Friend, 1932. Compiler of The Friendly Year (by Henry Van Dyke), 1900, 06, 17, 26. Home: Brooklyn, N.Y. Died Oct. 27, 1937.

WEBSTER, George Smedley, civil engr.; b. Phila., Oct. 19, 1855; s. John Hambleton and Lydia (Smedley) W.; B.S., U. of Pa., 1875 (Sc.D., 1910); m. Mary Heston Anderson, Dec. 5, 1883; 1 son, Maurice A. Webster. Mem. engring. corps, Centennial Expn., Phila., 1875-76; asst. engr., U.S. Coast and Geod. Survey, 1877; asst. engr. City of Phila., 1877-92, prin. asst. engr. and acting chief engr., 1892-93, chief engr., 1893-1916 and 1920-21, Engring. Dept., City of Phila.; dir. Dept. of Wharves, Docks and Ferries, Phila., 1916-20; mem. bd. engrs. Del. River Bridge Joint Commn., Jan. 1, 1921—; mem. Pa. State Sanitary Water Board, 1927—. Mem. Am. Soc. C.E. (pres. 1921), Am. Soc. Testing Materials (pres. 1920), Franklin Inst., Engring. Alumni Assn. U. of Pa. (pres. 1912), Municipal Engineers' Soc. (pres. 1914). Mem. Nat. Research Council, Nat. Conf. on City Planning; pres. bd. mgrs. Friends Hosp. Tech. v.p. Regional Planning Fedn. of Phila. Tri-State Dist. Home: Frankford, Pa. Died Jan. 23, 1931.

WEBSTER, George Van O'Linda, osteopathic physician; b. Rossie, N.Y., Dec. 27, 1880; s. George V. and Louise (Safford) W.; grad. high sch., Gouverneur, N.Y., 1900; D.O., Kirksville (Mo.) Osteopathic Coll., 1904; m. Klara Jane Love, June 30, 1906; children—Wellington Culver (dec.), George Van O'Linda. Began practice at Amsterdam, N.Y., 1904; moved to Carthage, 1907; mem. Bd. of Edn., Carthage, 1916-26; lecturer on osteopathic principles and practice, Coll. of Osteopathic Phys. and Surg., Los Angeles, 1929-32; pvt. instr. post-grad. studies on mechanics of articulations; lecturer on research, in spinal mechanics, lymph drainage and diet; mem. staff Unit No. 2, Gen. Hosp., Los Angeles. Trustee A. T. Still Research Inst. Republican. Presbyn. Mason. Author: Concerning Osteopathy, 1910; Something Wrong, 1919; For the Ears, 1931; Sage Sayings of Still, 1935. Produced technical motion picture, "Osteopathic Mechanics of the Pelvis," 1932; Osteopathic Mechanics of Fifth Dorsal, 1935. Contbr. to Jour. Am. Osteopathic Assn., Forum of Osteopathy. Home: Los Angeles, Calif. Deceased.

WEBSTER, George Washington, M.D., b. Winneshiek County, Ia., July 4, 1857; s. William and Mary Ann (Todd) W.; Breckenridge's Prep. Sch., Decorah, Ia.; M.D., Northwestern U., 1882; m. Ida M. Piper, 1884; m. 2d, Mabel V. MacNab, Apr. 15, 1916. Practicing medicine, Chicago, 1882—; prof. physiology, 1885, and later physical diagnosis until 1894, prof. clin. medicine, 1895—, Northwestern U.; apptd. 1st lt. Med. R.C., U.S.A., 1911. Pres. Ill. State Bd. Health, 1900-14. Mem. advisory council Northwestern U. Med. Sch.; mem. bd. govs. N.W.U. Foundation; dir. Gen. Alumni Assn. N.W.U. Republican. Mason. Home: Chicago, Ill. Died Nov. 7, 1931.

WEBSTER, Harrie, rear admiral U.S.N.; b. Farmington, Me., Feb. 12, 1843; s. Nathan and Ellen Kilshaw (Whittier) W.; ed. pub. schs. and Farmington Acad.; m. Mary Simpson Hein, Nov. 20, 1870. Apptd. 3d asst. engr. in vol. service, U.S.N., Feb. 8, 1862; served under Farragut on Mississippi River and at Mobile Bay, Aug. 5, 1864; 3d asst. engr. U.S.N., May 20, 1864; 2d asst. engr., Jan. 1, 1868; passed asst. engr., Oct. 29, 1874; wrecked on U.S.S. Vandalia at Samoa, Mar. 15-16, 1889; promoted chief engr., Oct. 7, 1892; served on several vessels as chief engr., and was in recruiting service, 1898; afterward with Bur. Steam Engring., and under provisions of Personnel Bill (1899) transferred to line as comdr. on active list; served as insp. machinery and ordnance; promoted to capt., Jan. 4, 1903; retired on own application as rear admiral U.S.N., Feb. 9, 1903. Died Apr. 23, 1921.

WEBSTER, Helen Livermore, philologist; b. Boston, Aug. 1, 1853; normal sch. edn., Salem, Mass.; Ph.D., U. of Zürich, 1889. Taught at Vassar Coll., 1889-90, at same time giving a course of lectures on comparative philology at Barnard Coll.; prof. comparative philology, Wellesley Coll., 1890-99; prin. Wilkes-Barre (Pa.) Inst., 1899-1904; teacher Miss Porter's Sch., Farmington Conn., 1904-13; academic head Nat. Cathedral Sch. for Girls, Washington, D.C., 1913—. Author: A Treatise on the Guttural Question in Gothic (Doctor's thesis). Editor: The Legends of the Micmacs, 1893. Lecturer and contbr. ednl. periodicals. Died Jan. 4, 1928.

WEBSTER, Henry Kitchell, author; b. Evanston, Ill., Sept. 7, 1875; s. Towner Keeney and Emma J. (Kitchell) W.; grad. Hamilton Coll., 1897, L.H.D., 1925; instructor rhetoric, Union Coll., 1897-98; m. Mary Ward Orth, Sept. 7, 1901; children—Henry Kitchell, Stokely, Roderick Sheldon. Author: The Short Line War (with Samuel Merwin), 1899; The Banker and the Bear; The Story of a Corner in Land, 1900; Calumet "K" (with Samuel Merwin), 1901; Roger Drake, Captain of Industry, 1903; The Duke of Cameron Avenue, 1904; Traitor and Loyalist, 1904; Comrade John (with Samuel Merwin), 1907; The Whispering Man, 1908; A King in Khaki, 1909; The Sky Man, 1910; The Girl in the Other Seat, 1911; June Madness (play), prod. New York, Sept. 1912; The Ghost Girl, 1913; The Butterfly, 1914; The Real Adventure, 1916; The Painted Scene, 1916; The Thoroughbred, 1917; An American Family, 1918; Mary Wollaston, 1920; Real Life, 1921; Joseph Greer and His Daughter, 1922; The Innocents, 1924; The Corbin Necklace, 1926; Philopena, 1927; The Beginners, 1927; The Clock Strikes Two, 1928; The Quartz Eye, 1928; The Sealed Trunk, 1929; Who Is the Next?, 1931. Home: Evanston, Ill. Died Dec. 8, 1932.

WEBSTER, Jean (Mrs. Glenn Ford McKinney), author; b. Fredonia, N.Y., July 24, 1876; d. Charles Luther and Annie Clemens (Moffett) Webster; grad. Lady Jane Grey Sch., Binghamton, N.Y., 1896; A.B., Vassar, 1901; m. Glenn Ford McKinney, Sept. 7, 1915. Lived for some yrs. in Italy; made trip around the world, 1906-07. Author: When Patty Went to College, 1903; The Wheat Princess, 1905; Jerry Junior, 1907; The Four-Pools Mystery, 1908; Much Ado About Peter, 1909; Just Patty, 1911; Daddy Long-Legs, 1912; Asa (play), 1914; Dear Enemy, 1915. Contbr. short stories to mags. Died June 11, 1916.

WEBSTER, John Hunter, theologian; b. Mercersburg, Pa., Jan. 8, 1862; s. John and Isabel Grace Young (Clarkson) W.; A.B., Westminster Coll., Pa., 1886; grad. Xenia Theol. Sem., 1893; D.D., Tarkio (Mo.) Coll., 1908; m. Lora Wilson, June 29, 1893; children—Clarkson Wilson, Chauncey Wilson, Archibald Wilson, John Hunter (dec.), Margaret Adelaide (Mrs. P. W. Goodell), Rosanna Grace (Mrs. G. A. Graham). Ordained U.P. ministry, 1893; pastor Cedar Rapids, Ia., 1893-95, Phila. Pa., 1895-1908; prof. N.T. lit. and exegesis, Xenia Theol. Sem., St. Louis, Mo. (formerly at Xenia, O.), 1909-30; prof. N.T. lang. and lit., Pittsburgh-Xenia Theol. Sem., 1930—. Republican. Co-editor Bibliotheca Sacra. Contbr. on religious subjects. Home: Pittsburgh, Pa. Died May 7, 1933.

WEBSTER, John Lee, lawyer; b. Harrison County, O., Mar. 17, 1847; student Washington Coll., Pa.; B.A., Mt. Union Coll., O., LL.D., 1894; served in the Union Army, Apr.-Oct. 1864; m. Josephine Leah Watson, 1868. In law practice at Omaha, 1871—; identified with many prominent cases as leading atty., including Ponca Indian litigation, Mo. River R.R. rate cases, bank guaranty cases in Nebraska, and Kan.; gen. counsel of Omaha & Council Bluffs St. Ry. system; atty. for Metropolian Water Dist.; local atty. for Wabash R.R. Co. Mem. Nebraska Legislature, 1873; pres. Neb. Constl. Conv., 1875; del.-at-large and chmn. Neb. delegation Rep. Nat. convs., 1892, 96; candidate for U.S. senator, 1901; endorsed by Neb. State Conv. and prominently mentioned for Vice President of the U.S. in campaign, 1904. Delivered ann. addresses before Ia., Colo., Minn., Neb. State bar assns., 1900-02; also before U. of S.D., U. of Mich., U. of Neb. Lecturer on Alexander Hamilton and the constitution. Pres. Neb. State Hist. Soc. 6 yrs.; organizer and pres.; chmn. com. of 100 to celebrate admission of Neb. into Union; chmn. com. of 100 to celebrate the landing of the Pilgrims and for a grand pageant at Omaha, 1920; chmn. com. and author of pageant Patriotic Historic America, at Omaha, 1923; chmn. War Memorial Com. Lecturer before joint session Neb. Legislature, anniversary of admission as state, 1927. Home: Omaha, Neb. Deceased.

WEBSTER, Lorin, educator; b. Claremont, N.H., July 29, 1857; s. Lorin Atkinson and Sophronia (Pierce) W.; prep. edn., St. Paul's Sch., Concord, N.H.; A.B., Trinity Coll., Conn., 1880, A.M., 1883, L.H.D., 1908; grad. Berkeley Div. School, Conn., 1883; m. Jennie Josephine Adams, July 10, 1884. Deacon and priest P.E. Ch., 1883; master Holderness Sch. for Boys, Plymouth, N.H., 1883-84; rector St. Mark's Parish, Ashland, N.H., 1884-92; rector (head master) Holderness Sch. for Boys, 1892—; propr. and dir.-in-chief Camp Wachusett (boys), Asquam Lake, N.H., 1903—. Pres. N.H. Ednl. Council, 1908-09, 1909-10; pres. N.H. Schoolmasters' Club, 1908-09; pres. Plymouth Fair Assn., Grafton County Agrl. Soc., N.H. Music Teachers' Assn., N.H. Acad. Teachers' Assn. Author of several mus. compositions. Author: Chips from a Busy Work-shop (poems). Died July 5, 1923.

WEBSTER, Nathan Burnham, educator; b. Unity, N.H., June 13, 1821; ed. common schs., Claremont, N.H., and Acad. at Meridan, N.H.; A.M., Jefferson Coll., Pa. Instr. Greek, Norwich U., 1839-40; prin. Mil. Acad., Portsmouth, Va., 1840-46; teacher chemistry and other sciences, Richmond, Va., Baptist Coll., 1846-48; founded and prin. Va. Coll. Inst.; afterward Webster Inst., Norfolk, Va., 1848-85; civil engr. Gosport Navy Yard under John Y. Mason; founder and 4 years pres. Ottawa Natural History Soc.; fellow A.A.A.S. Invented the meteorgraph, an automatic meteorological register; lecturer on educational and agricultural topics; m. Isabella Fish Hobday, Aug. 7, 1844 (died 1885); m. 2d, Euphania M. Couper, July 26, 1893. Died 1900.

WEBSTER, Ralph Waldo, M.D.; b. Monmouth, Ill., Apr. 16, 1873; s. John Randolph and Susan Isabella (Nye) W.; Ph.B., U. of Chicago, 1895, Ph.D., 1901; M.D., Rush Med. Coll., 1898; post-grad. study at Vienna, Berlin, Frankfort, Paris and London; m. Grace Burleigh Nye, Dec. 16, 1903; children—James Randolph, Ralph Waldo. Asst. in physiol. chemistry, U. of Chicago, 1901-04; asso. in chemistry, 1901-06, instr., 1906-08, asst. prof. therapeutics, 1908-20, asst. prof. med. jurisprudence, 1921-23, asso. prof., 1923-25, clin. prof. medicine, 1925—, Rush Med. Coll.; professorial lecturer in med. jurisprudence and toxicology, U. of Chicago, 1929—; pathol. chemist to Cook County Hosp., 1905-11; dir. Chicago Lab., 1905—; coroner's chemist and toxicologist, Cook County, Ill., 1929—. Maj., Med. R.C., Apr. 1917-Aug. 29, 1919. Fellow A.A.A.S. Author: Diagnostic Methods, 1909; Paper Work of the Medical Department, U.S. Army, 1918. Co-editor of Legal Medicine and Toxicology (Peterson, Haines and Webster), 1923. Home: Chicago, Ill. Died July 2, 1930.

WEBSTER, Sidney, lawyer; b. Gilmanton, N.H., May 28, 1828; A.B., Yale, 1848, A.M., 1851; LL.B., Harvard, 1850; admitted to bar, 1851; m. Sarah Morris Fish, June 1860. Pvt. sec. to Pres. Franklin Pierce, 1853-57; resumed practice in Boston, 1857; removed to New York, 1860. Author: Two Treaties of Paris and the Supreme Court, 1901; also monographs on topics of internat. and constl. law. Home: New York, N.Y. Died 1910.

WEBSTER, Warren, mfr.; b. Tioga, Phila., Pa., June 25, 1863; s. Jones and Sarah (Holmes) W.; Phila. High Sch.; grad. Pierce's Business Coll.; m. Frances Siegrist, July 2, 1891; children—Marguerite (Mrs. J. Spencer Lucas), Warren, Pauline (Mrs. William Maynard Brown). Founder, 1888, and pres. and gen. mgr. Warren Webster & Co., mfrs. Webster steam heating systems, Camden, N.J. Mason. Died Dec. 21, 1938.

WEDDERSPOON, William Rhind, clergyman; b. Scotland; s. Robert and Margaret (Rhind) W.; A.B., A.M., Taylor U., Upland, Ind., 1898; (D.D., Allegheny Coll., 1907); m. Annie T. Gibson; children—Emily V., W. Rhind, Florence N., Richard G., Lucy M., Arthur F. Ordained M.E. ministry, deacon, 1892, elder, 1894; pastor in N.J. at Highlands, Pointville, Farmingdale, North Long Branch, New Brunswick, Asbury Park, Emory Ch., Pittsburgh, Pa.; pastor Foundry Ch., Washington, D.C., 1910-16, St. James Church, Chicago, 1916-26, Bryan Memorial M.E. Ch., Coconut Grove, Miami, Fla., 1926—. Trustee American Univ.; dir. Chicago Tract Soc., Chicago Bible Soc.; chmn. commn. on internat. friendship, Chicago Ch. Fedn.; v.p. Travelers' Aid Soc. Del. 4 Meth. gen. confs. Lecturer. Mason. Home: Miami, Fla. Died Dec. 13, 1939.

WEDEMEYER, William Walter, congressman; b. Lima Tp., Washtenaw County, Mich., Mar. 22, 1873; s. Frederick and Auguste (Gruner) W.; B.L., U. of Mich., 1894, LL.B., 1895; m. Louise Locher, Jan. 9, 1901. Mem. Bd. Sch. Examiners, Washtenaw County, 1894-95; co. commr. schs., 1895-97; deputy commr. railroads, Mich., 1897-99; admitted to bar, 1895, in practice at Ann Arbor, 1899—. Am. consul at Georgetown, British Guiana, summer, 1905; chmn. Washtenaw County Rep. Com., 1896-98; chmn. Rep. State Conv., 1903; mem. Rep. State Central Com., 1906-10; mem. 62d Congress (1911-13), 2d Mich. Dist. Nat. counselor Am. Ins. Union; pres. Mich. Fraternal Congress. Mason, K.P. Died Feb. 2, 1913.

WEED, Alonzo Rogers, judge; b. Bangor, Me., Jan. 22, 1867; s. Alonzo Shaw and Esther A. (Marston) W.; A.B., Harvard, 1887; LL.B., Boston U., 1890; m. Charlotte Ford Atwater, Apr. 30, 1896; children—Anne Atwater (Mrs. Laurence E. Richardson), Alonzo Rogers. Admitted to bar, 1890; practiced, Boston, in partnership with brother, G. M. Weed, until 1906; mem. firm Brewer, Weed & Weed, 1907-22. Instr. in equity, Boston U. Law Sch., 1894-1902, in equity pleading, 1902-13, actg. dean, 1911-12. Mem. Bd. of Aldermen, Newton, Mass., 1899-1903 (pres., 1902-03), mayor, 1904-05; mem. Mass. Bd. of Gas and Electric Light Commrs., 1906-19 (chmn. 1914-19); mem. Pub. Utilities Commn., 1919-22; asso. justice Superior Ct. of Mass., 1922—. Trustee Boston U., Newton Hosp. Republican. Methodist. Home: Newton, Mass. Died Dec. 29, 1937.

WEED, Charles Frederick, banker; b. Claremont, N.H., Oct. 22, 1874; s. Charles H. and Hattie M. (Redfield) W.; A.B., Trinity Coll., Conn., 1894, A.M., 1897; LL.B., Harvard, 1898; m. Mary Duncan Walker, Sept. 10, 1901; children—Frances Duncan, Frederick Redfield, Mary Duncan. Practiced law, Boston, 1898-1917; v.p. First Nat. Bank, 1917—; pres. Claremont Gas Light Co.; dir. Brookline Trust Co., Security Safe Deposit Co., Old Colony Ins. Co., Boston Ins. Co., Sullivan Machinery Company. Trustee Vermont Acad., Trinity Coll. Trustee and treasurer St. Gaudens Memorial, Cornish, N.H. Republican. Home: Brookline, Mass. Died May 31, 1940.

WEED, Clive, cartoonist, artist; b. Kent, Orleans County, N.Y., Sept. 29, 1884; s. Arthur James and Electa Ann (Weaver) W.; studied Acad. of Fine Arts, Phila.; pupil Thomas Anshutz. Cartoonist The Press and Record-Ledger, Phila., the old Evening Sun, The Tribune, and The Evening World (New York), also magazines Colliers, The New Republic, Leslies, Life, Judge, King Feature Syndicate. Died Dec. 27, 1936.

WEED, Edwin Gardner, bishop; b. Savannah, Ga., July 23, 1837; s. Henry Davis and Sarah Richards (Dunning) W.; ed. U. of Ga., 1862-64; served in C.S.A., 1864-65; studied U. of Berlin; grad. Gen. Theol. Sem., 1870; S.T.D., Racine Coll.; D.D., U. of the South; m. Julia McKinney, d. Col. Thomas F. Foster, Apr. 23, 1874. Deacon P.E. Ch., 1870; traveled Europe, Egypt and Holy Land, 1870-71; priest, 1871; rector Ch. of the Good Shepherd, Summerville, Ga., 1871-86; consecrated 3d bishop of Fla., Aug. 11, 1886. Died Jan. 18, 1924.

WEED, George Ludington, educator, author; b. Union Mission, Ark. Ty., April 9, 1828; s. George Ludington W.; prep. edn. Woodward Sch., Cincinnati; A.M., Marietta Coll., 1849; studied divinity Andover Theol. Sem., 1849-52; m. Sarah Russell, Aug. 29, 1855. Author: Great Truths Simply Told, 1891; A Life of Christ for the Young, 1898; A Life of St. Paul for the Young, 1899; A Life of St. John for the Young, 1900; A Life of St. Peter for the Young, 1901. Wrote: Letters from Europe and the Orient, Central Christian Herald, 1852-54; Mother Strickland's Silver, The Independent, also 1895; Marcus Whitman, M.D., Ladies' Home Journal, 1897. Died 1904.

WEED, Samuel Richards, fire underwriter; b. New York, Feb. 9, 1837; s. Joseph and Jane (Tweedy) W.; ed. pub. and pvt. schs., New York; m. Nellie S. Jones, Oct. 11, 1859; father of Walter Harvey W. Reporter and writer for press in San Francisco and St. Louis, 1858-61; mgr., gen. and spl. agt. and local agt. various fire ins. cos., and active as underwriter, St. Louis and New York; v.p. Liberty Ins. Co., New York, 1887-91. Mem. com. New York Fire Ins Exchange, New York Bd. Fire Underwriters. Republican. Congregationalist. Author: Eastern Visit With St. Louis Common Council, 1865; Handbook of Fire Insurance, 1894; Norwalk to Norway, 1905; Personal Recollections of Early San Francisco, 1908; In Honor of a Patriot; New and Improved Book of Forms for Fire Insurance Companies, 1909. Home: Rowayton, Conn. Deceased.

WEED, Smith Mead, lawyer, capitalist; b. Belmont, N.Y., July 26, 1833; s. Roswell Abbott and Sarah A. (Mead) W.; ed. pub. schs.; admitted to bar, Jan. 1, 1856; LL.B., Harvard, 1857; practiced at Plattsburg, N.Y., and city of New York, 1857—, m. Caroline Lesley Standish, Sept. 6, 1859 (died 1884). Engaged in many important litigations, including the Samuel J. Tilden will contest; the Tilley Foster Iron Mine case; etc. Pres. Chateaugay & Lake Placid R.R. Co.; dir. Chateaugay Ore & Iron Co., Weed Bldg. Co. Mem. N.Y. Assembly, 1865-74; Dem. nominee for U.S. senator in legislatures of 1867, 87, 90; mem-at-large of State Constl. Conv., 1867; del. several Dem. Nat. convs. Home: Plattsburg, N.Y. Died June 7, 1920.

WEEDEN, William Babcock, author; b. Bristol, R.I., Sept. 1, 1834; s. John E. and Eliza C. W.; student Brown U., 1848-50; hon. A.M., 1875; m. Jeanie Lippitt. Engaged in woolen mfg. bus. in 1851. In U.S. vols., 1st lt. arty., 1861; promoted capt. battery C, R.I. Light Arty., after battle of Bull Run; was at Siege of Yorktown and Hanover C.H.; chief of arty., 1st Div. 5th Corps, at battles of Mechanicsville, Gaines' Mill and Malvern Hill; resigned Aug. 1862; resumed business in Providence; retired, 1902. Author: Morality of Prohibitory Liquor Laws, 1875; Social Law of Labor, 1882; Economic and Social History of New England, 1620-1789 (2 vols.), 1890; War Government, Federal and State, 1906; Early Rhode Island, a Social History, 1910. Died Mar. 28, 1912.

WEEDON, Leslie Washington, M.D.; b. Sandersville, Ga., Apr. 27, 1860; high school edn.; M.D., Univ. Med. Coll. (New York U.), 1885; practiced at Tampa, Fla.; m. L. Blanche, d. W. B. Henderson, Feb. 14, 1889; children—Leslie Washington (dec.), Frederick Renfroe, Harry Lee, Mary Blanche. Best known for his researches in yellow fever. Mem. Yellow Fever Inst., under auspices of Bur. of Pub. Health and Marine Hosp. Service, Washington, D.C. Home: Tampa, Fla. Died Nov. 12, 1938.

WEEKLEY, William Marion, bishop; b. Tyler County, Va. (now W.Va.), Sept. 18, 1851; s. Daniel and Elizabeth Jane (Pratt) W.; ed. common schs. and theol. inst.; D.D., York Coll., Neb., 1903; m. Rosa L. Wilson, May 2, 1875; m. 2d, Emma Gibson, June 9, 1885. Entered ministry U.B. Ch., 1870; pastor 12 yrs., presiding elder 11 yrs.; sec. Gen. Ch. Erection Bd. 10 yrs.; bishop, May 1905—. Mem. Ednl., Adminstrn. Evangelistic and Otterbein Home bds. of U.B. Ch.; trustee United Christian Endeavor Soc. Author: From Life to Life, 1899; Getting and Giving, 1903; Twenty Years on Horseback, 1907; (with H. H. Fout) Our Heroes, Vol. 1, 1908, Vol. 2, 1911. Home: Parkersburg, W.Va. Died Jan. 8, 1926.

WEEKS, Andrew Jackson, clergyman, editor; b. Walnut Hill, Vernon Parish, La., May 31, 1869; s. Wiley Felix and Laura (McNeely) W.; ed. public schs. of Tex.; D.D., Southwestern U., Tex., 1920; m. Mattie Payne, Mar. 19, 1893; children—Vivian (Mrs. Forest E. Dudley), Agnes, Marvin W., Andrew Jackson. Ordained Methodist Episcopal Church, S., ministry, 1890; pastor in Tex. at Augusta, 1890-92, Center, 1893-97, Rusk, 1898, First Ch., Marshall, 1899; presiding elder San Augustine Dist., 1900-02; pastor Galveston, 1903, Marlin, 1904, West End, San Antonio, 1905-06; presiding elder, San Antonio Dist., 1907-10; supt. Home Mission in Tex. and N.M., 1910-12; pastor San Angelo, 1912-13, Yoakum, 1914, Clarendon, 1915; presiding elder Stamford Dist., 1916-18; editor Texas Christian Advocate, 1918-22; editor missionary lit., M.E. Ch., S., 1922-26; presiding elder Oklahoma City Dist., 1926-27, Sherman (Tex.) Dist., 1928-30; editor Southwestern Advocate, 1931—. Del. Gen. Conf., 1902-10; del. Meth. Ecumenical Conf., London, 1921; mem. continuation com. Meth. Ecumenical Conf., 1921-31; del. Universal Christian Conf. on Life and Work, Stockholm, 1925; sec. 6th Ecumenical Meth. Conf., Atlanta, Ga., October 1931; secretary Ecumenical Meth. Council, Western sect., 1931—; spl. rep. to Wesley Bicentenary, London, 1938; mem. Judicial Council of M.E. Ch., S. Mason. Home: Richardson, Tex. Died Dec. 1939.

WEEKS, Arland Deyett, educator, author; b. McLean, N.Y., Dec. 13, 1871; s. Timothy Mack and Mary Elizabeth (McElheny) W.; grad. Cortland (N.Y.) State Normal Sch., 1896; A.B., Cornell U., 1901; M.A., U. of Minn., 1909; grad. student, U. of Wis.; m. Florence Gertrude Best, Nov. 30, 1899; children—Elene Best (Mrs. C. K. Huston), Marian Walden, Arland McLean. Acting prof. English lit. Berea Coll., Ky., 1901-02; prof. English lang. and lit., Valley City (N.D.) State Normal Sch., 1902-07; asso. prof. English, 1907-08, prof. edn., 1908-17, dean Sch. of Edn., 1917—, N.D. Agrl. Coll. Mem. summer sch. faculty, Pa. State Coll., 1915. Author: The Education of To-Morrow, 1913; The Avoidance of Fires, 1916; Playdays on Plum Blossom Creek, 1916; The Psychology of Citizenship, 1917; Social Antagonisms, 1918; Squaw Point, 1919; Control of the Social Mind, 1923; Psychology for Child Training, 1925; Children of the Pines, 1926; Yukon, The Silver Fox, 1929. Mem. school law compilation commission of N.D., 1909-11. Home: Fargo, N.D. Died Nov. 13, 1936.

WEEKS, Bartow Sumter, judge; b. Round Hill, Conn., Apr. 25, 1861; s. Col. Henry Astor and Alethea Hyde (White) W.; A.B., Coll. City of N.Y., 1879; LL.B., Columbia, 1883. Assistant dist. atty. of New York, 7 yrs.; Dem. nominee for State senator, 15th N.Y. Dist., 1898; apptd. justice Sup. Ct. of N.Y., by Gov. Sulzer, 1913; Dem. candidate for same, Nov., 1913; apptd. justice Sup. Ct., 1st Dist., by Gov. Glynn, Feb. 2, 1914, for an unexpired term, elected Nov. 1914, for full term expiring Dec. 31, 1928. Comdr. in chief Sons of Vets., 1891-92; pres. Amateur Athletic Union, 1898. Home: New York, N.Y. Died Feb. 3, 1922.

WEEKS, Charles Peter, architect; b. Copley, O., Sept. 1, 1870; s. Peter and Catharine (Francisco) W.; student Buchtel U. (now U. of Akron), Akron, O.; École des Beaux Arts, Paris, 1892-95; m. Beatrice Woodruff, Jan. 30, 1923. Began practice at Cleveland, O., 1895; practiced at N.Y. City, 1899-1901, San Francisco, Calif., 1901—; mem. firm Weeks & Day, 1916—; firm architects of Mark Hopkins Hotel, and Don Lee Bldg., San Francisco; State Library Bldg., Sacramento; Loew's State Bldg., Los Angeles; etc. Mem. bd. dirs. Huntington Apartments, Inc., Calif. Jones Investment Co. Winner first place, Calif. State Bldgs. competition 1918; 1st prize, Parliament Bldgs., Camberra, Australia, 1924. Mason. Died 1928.

WEEKS, David Fairchild, neurologist, psychiatrist; b. Newark, Essex County, N.J., July 31, 1874; s. Henry Martin, Jr. (M.D.) and Mary Malvina (Fairchild) W.; grad. Trenton (N.J.) High Sch., 1892; spl. course State Schs. of Trenton, 1893; M.D., U. of Pa., 1898; m. Maude Adele Clampitt, Mar. 12, 1902; children—Eleanor, Henry Martin, III, Mary Fairchild. Successively resident phys. McKeesport (Pa.) Hosp., Cooper Hosp. (Camden, N.J.), Phila. Orthopedic Hosp. and Infirmary for Nervous Diseases; pvt. practice, Trenton, N.J., 1900-07; supt. N.J. State Village for Epileptics, Skillman, N.J., Dec. 1, 1907—; consultant Somerset Hosp., Somerville, N.J., Mercer Hosp., Trenton. Fellow Am. Psychiatric Assn.; mem. N.J. Conf. for Social Welfare (pres.), Nat. Assn. for Study of Epilepsy (pres.), Internat. Liga contra L'Epilepsie (pres.). Republican. Episcopalian. Mason. Elk. Contbr. many papers on epilepsy, the inheritance of epilepsy, what N.J. is doing for epileptics, etc. Home: Skillman, N.J. Died Mar. 15, 1929.

WEEKS, Edgar, congressman; b. Mt. Clemens, Mich., Aug. 3, 1839; s. Aaron and Laura (Bingham) W.; ed. public schs.; m. Mary S. Campbell, 1867. Served in Civil War, sergt. Co. B, 5th Mich. inf.; promoted to capt. 22d Mich. inf.; later asst. insp. gen. 3d brigade, 2d div. reserve corps, army of the Cumberland. Practiced law, 1866—, prosecuting atty. Macomb County, 1867-70, probate judge, 1875-76; Congressman 7th Mich. dist., 1899-1903; mem. Com. on Pensions; Com. on Contested Elections, Com. on Claims. Republican; del. to Nat. Rep. Conv., 1888; asst. insp. gen. G.A.R., Companion Loyal Legion, Compatriot Sons of the Revolution. Home: Mount Clemens, Mich. Died 1904.

WEEKS, Edwin Lord, artist; b. Boston; studied art in Paris; chevalier Legion of Honor of France, 1896; officer order of St. Michael of Bavaria, 1898; grand diploma of honor, Berlin, 1891, 1st class medals Universal Expn., Paris, 1889; Munich, 1897; Dresden, 1897; medal, Paris Salon, 1889; hon. mention, 1885; gold medal, Phila. Art Club, 1891; medals, Atlanta, Boston; spl. medal and prize Empire of India Exbn., London, 1896; represented in Corcoran Gallery, Washington, and in Pa. Acad. Fine Arts, Phila.; mem. Paris Advisory Com. for World's Columbian Expn.; mem. com. of direction for the Expn. of H.S.H. the Princess of Monaco. Author: From the Black Sea Through Persia and India; Episodes of Mountaineering. Died 1903.

WEEKS, Edwin Ruthven, humanitarian; b. Westfield, Wis., Dec 25, 1855; s. Joseph Van Rensselaer and Imogene (Cookson) W.; Phillips Exeter Acad., N.H., 1881; m. Mary Hezlep Harmon, Dec. 24, 1882. Supt., mgr., gen. mgr. and v.p. (at all times mng. dir.), Kansas City Electric Light Co. and Edison Electric Light & Power Co. of Kansas City, Mo., 1882-1900; during same period also cons. engr. for many interests; sold electric light and power properties of Kansas City, 1900; practiced alone as cons. engr., 1900-02; became sr. mem. firm of Weeks & Kendall, 1902. Republican. Unitarian. Fellow Am. Inst. Elec. Engrs.; mem. Am. Acad. Polit. and Social Science. Pres. Humane Soc. of Kansas City; v.p. Am. Humane Edn. Soc.; v.p. and incorporator Kansas City Art Assn. and Sch. of Design; mem. Civil Service Reform Assn.; mem. Jury of Awards, St. Louis Expn., 1890; received degree "Doctor of Mercy" from world's largest conv. in cause of humane edn., Kansas City, Mo., 1899; awarded medal "For Humanity," by Mass. Soc. for Prevention of Cruelty to Animals, 1906. Author of many pub. addresses and articles in scientific and popular publs. Home: Kansas City, Mo. Died Aug. 17, 1938.

WEEKS, Frank Bentley, governor; b. Brooklyn, Jan. 20, 1854; s. Daniel L. and Frances M. (Edwards) W.; pub., pvt. and mil. sch. edn.; LL.D., Wesleyan U., 1909; m. Helen L. Hubbard, Nov. 4, 1875 (died 1923). Mem. firm of Coles & Weeks, wholesale milling and grain. 1880-95, retired, 1895; dir. Middlesex Mutual Assurance Co. (pres.), Bradley and Hubbard Mfg. Co., Meriden, Conn.; trustee Middletown Savings Bank. Mem. Middletown City Council, 1881-83; Rep. presdl. elector, 1904; elected lt. gov. of Conn., Nov. 1908, succeeding to governorship, upon death of Gov. Lilley, Apr. 1909, for term expiring Jan. 1911. Del. Rep. Nat. Conv., 1912, 16. Chmn. Conn. Commn. to Atlanta Expn., 1895; commr. from Conn. to Sesquicentennial, Phila., 1926; trustee Wesleyan U.; trustee Conn. State Hosp. for Insane for more than 30 yrs., and pres. of bd. (resigned Oct. 1922); 1st pres. Middletown Bd. of Trade. Conglist. Home: Middletown, Conn. Died Oct. 2, 1935.

WEEKS, George H., brig. gen. U.S.A., retired, Feb. 3, 1898; b. Gifford, N.H., Feb. 3, 1834; s. Levi R. and Lydia Sleeper W.; entered army from Maine, July 1, 1853, as cadet in mil. acad.; grad. with bvt. 2d lt., 1st Arty., July 1, 1857; m. Laura, d. Gen. E. B. Babbitt, U.S.A., May 1859. Apptd. 2d lt. 4th arty., Feb. 10, 1859; 1st lt., May 14, 1861; capt. and asst. q.m., Mar. 24, 1862; maj. q.m., May 29, 1876; lt. col. dept. q.m. gen., Oct. 19, 1888; col. asst. q.m. gen., May 16, 1895; brig. gen. and q.m. gen., Feb. 16, 1897, until retired. Bvtd. maj. and lt. col., Mar. 13, 1865, for faithful and meritorious service in q.m.'s dept. during Civil War. Died 1905.

WEEKS, Grenville Mellen, soldier, physician; b. New York, Nov. 22, 1837; s. Cyrus (M.D.) and M. L. (Child) W.; 7th in lineal descent from John Alden, of the Mayflower; student in New York Acad. (now Coll. City of New York), 1856-58, Coll. Phys. and Surg. (Columbia), 1859-60; M.D., Univ. Med. Coll. (New York U.), 1861; m. Helen Campbell Stuart, author, 1861; m. 2d, Maria Oberg; m. 3d, Pauline M. Sauer of Brooklyn, 1893. Apptd. asst. surgeon U.S.N., 1862; transferred from U.S. frigate Brandywine at scene of action between Monitor and Merrimac, Hampton Roads, 1862, and apptd. surgeon U.S. ironclad Monitor; saved the lives of a boatload of officers and men, having his right arm almost torn off at the shoulder; promoted by President Lincoln, and apptd. surgeon with rank of maj.; brigade surgeon and acting med. dir. Dept. of Fla., at close of war; reëntered mil. service 1865, as surgeon and acting Indian agent in Northwest during Indian troubles in Minn. and Dak.; returned East, 1871, and resumed practice. Author of resolution recognizing Cuban independence by Congress of U.S., 1898. Organized and pres., 1859, of the first Christian Union in the world that urged a universal peace union of all creeds, on doctrine of universal fatherhood of God and brotherhood of man. Died Apr. 26, 1919.

WEEKS, John Wingate, sec. of war; b. Lancaster, N.H., Apr. 11, 1860; s. William D. and Mary Helen (Fowler) W.; reared on farm; grad. U.S. Naval Acad., 1881; m. Martha A. Sinclair, Oct. 7, 1885. Midshipman U.S.N., 1881-83; asst. land commr. Fla. Southern R.R., 1886-88; mem. Hornblower & Weeks, bankers and brokers, Boston, 1888-1912. Alderman, Newton, Mass., 1900, 01, 02, mayor, 1903-04; chmn. Rep. State Conv., 1905; mem. 59th to 62d Congresses (1905-13), 12th Mass. Dist.; U.S. senator, 1913-19. Sec. of War in Cabinets of Presidents Harding and Coolidge, Mar. 4, 1921-Oct. 1925 (resigned). Received 105 votes from 25 states (next to the nominee) for Presidential nomination in Republican Nat. Conv., Chicago, 1916. Comd. division of Mass. Naval Brigade, with rank of capt., 1890-98; comd. 2d div. auxiliary U.S. naval force on Atlantic Coast, 1898-99; mem. Mil. Advisory Bd. of Mass. and Mil. Bd. of Examiners, 1894-1900; mem. bd. of visitors U.S. Naval Acad., 1896. Home: West Newton, Mass. Died July 12, 1926.

WEEKS, Mary Harmon (Mrs. Edwin R. Weeks); b. Warren, O., Apr. 22, 1851; d. Charles R. and Mary (Hezlep) Harmon; ed. pub. schs. and acad.; m. Edwin R. Weeks, Dec. 24, 1882; 1 dau., Ruth Mary. Teacher of lit. and mathematics, Central High Sch., Kansas City, 17 yrs.; gave spl. attention to child study and mother study and organized hundreds of mothers' clubs and parent teachers' assns.; 1st pres. Kansas City Athenæum. Mem. Nat. Congress of Mothers, Kansas City Mothers' Union, Kansas City Conf. of Parent Teachers' Assns. Unitarian. Wrote: (pamphlets) How to Organize and Carry on Mothers' Union; Mothers' Responsibility; Woman's Mission; Stories and Story Telling; How to Tell the Story of Reproduction to Young Children; etc. Editor of Parents and Their Problems. Chmn. Kansas City Children's Bur.; dir. Pre-school Mother Work for Parent-Teacher Council; state chmn. parent edn. for Mo. Congress of Parents and Teachers. Home: Kansas City, Mo. Died May 24, 1940.

WEEKS, Rufus Wells, actuary; b. Newark, N.J., Aug. 11, 1846; s. Robert D. and Elvira (Crafts) W.; grad. Newark (N.J.) High Sch., 1863; m. Helen R. Bonnel, Mar. 6, 1871. Entered actuarial dept. New York Life Ins. Co., 1867; elected actuary, 1885, 2d v.p. and chief actuary, 1903, 1st v.p., June 17, 1907; cons. actuary, May 12, 1925—. Mem. Actuarial Soc. of America (pres.), Am. Math. Soc., Am. Acad. Polit. and Social Science. Conglist. Home: Tarrytown, N.Y. Died Apr. 18, 1930.

WEEKS, Stephen Beauregard, author; b. Pasquotank County, N.C., Feb. 2, 1865; s. James Elliott and Mary Louisa (Mullen) W.; direct descendant of George Durant, the first white settler in N.C.; A.B., U. of N.C., 1886, A.M., 1887, Ph.D., 1888; Ph.D., Johns Hopkins, 1891; LL.D., Wake Forest Coll., N.C., 1902; m. Mary Lee Martin, g.g.d. Gen. Joseph Martin, June 12, 1888; m. 2d, Sallie Mangum Leach, g.d. Willie P. Mangum, U.S. senator from N.C., June 28, 1893. Prof. history and polit. science, Trinity Coll., N.C., 1891-93; specialist in ednl. history and asso. editor Ann. Report U.S. Commr. of Edn., 1894-99; in U.S. Indian sch. service in N.M. and Ariz., as prin. teacher, asst. supt. and supt., 1899-1907; with C. L. Van Noppen, pub., as book editor, 1907-09; teacher, 1909-11; historian in U.S. Bur. of Edn., Aug. 1911—. Collected nearly 9,000 books and pamphlets relating to N.C. One of the 3 founders of Southern History Assn., Washington, D.C., 1896. Author: Press of North Carolina in the 18th Century, 1891; Lost Colony of Roanoke—Its Fate and Survival, 1891; Religious Development in the Province of North Carolina, 1892; Church and State in North Carolina, 1893; History of Negro Suffrage in the South, 1894; General Joseph Martin and the War of the Revolution in the West, 1894; A Bibliography of the Historical Literature of North Carolina, 1895; Libraries and Literature in North Carolina in 18th Century, 1896; Southern Quakers and Slavery, 1896; American Learned and Educational Societies, 1896; Beginning of Common School System in the South, 1898; Bibliography of Confederate Text Books, 1900; Index to N.C. Census Records of 1790, 1905; A History of Education in the Confederate States; Index to N.C. Colonial and State Records, 4 vols., 1909-14; Historical Review of N.C. Colonial and State Records, 1914; History of Public School Education in Arkansas, 1912; in Alabama, 1915; Tennessee, 1916. Contbr. to Van Noppen's Biog. History of N.C., etc. Home: Trinity, N.C. Died May 3, 1918.

WEEKS, Stephen Holmes, surgeon; b. Cornish, Me., Oct. 6, 1835; s. John and Mehitable (Holmes) W.; Fryeburg Acad., Me.; M.D., U. of Pa., 1864; hon. A.M., Bowdoin, 1889; LL.D., Amherst, 1905; m. Mary A. Richmond, 1864. Prof. anatomy, 1877-81, surgery, 1881-1905, Med. Sch. of Me. (Bowdoin); surgeon Me. Gen. Hosp., 1874-98, cons. surgeon, 1898—; first to make and use drainage tubes from arteries of animals. Mem. Internat. Med. Congress, Berlin, 1895, 1899, 1906; fellow Am. Surg. Assn., Am. Acad. Medicine. Republican. Congregationalist. Contbr. to med. press. Died 1909.

WEEMS, Julius Buel, chemist; b. Baltimore, Aug. 27, 1865; s. Edwin Dawson and Rosetta L. (Norman) W.; grad. Md. Agrl. Coll., 1888; Johns Hopkins, 1889-90 and 1890-91; fellow in chemistry, Clark U., 1892-93 and 1893-94, Ph.D., 1894; m. Lila C. Fletcher, June 26, 1895; children—Rachel Fletcher, George Macduff, Carolyn Virginia, Julius Buel. Prof. agrl. chemistry and chemist Expt. Sta., Ia. State Coll., 1895-1904; consul. and analytical chemist, 1904-11; investigating farm life problems, 1911-15; chief chemist, Dept. of Agr., Va., July 15, 1915—. Fellow A.A.A.S. Contbr. of many papers on agr., agrl. edn., water and sewage. Home: Ashland, Va. Died Jan. 25, 1930.

WEFALD, Knud, public official; b. Norway, Nov. 3, 1869; s. Knut K. and Karen (Pedersen) W.; ed. high sch.; came to U.S., 1887, naturalized citizen, 1896; m. Sarah Skree, June 20, 1899. Sec. Hawley Lumber Co.; mem. Minn. Ho. of Reps. 2 terms, 1913, 15; mem. 68th and 69th Congresses (1923-27), 9th Minn. Dist.; editor "Normanden," Fargo, N.D., 1929-30; apptd. exec. sec. Minn. State Commn. of Administrn. and Finance, 1931; elected railroad and warehouse commr. of Minn., 1932. Farmer-Labor Party. Lutheran. Home: Hawley, Minn. Died Oct. 25, 1936.

WEGER, George Stephen, M.D., surgeon; b. Baltimore, Md., Sept. 2, 1874; s. Frank A. and Elizabeth (Dietzel) W. grad. high sch., Delphos, O.; B.M.C., U. of Md., 1898; m. Katie Trame, Oct. 1, 1900. Practiced at Delphos, 1898-1912; research and gen. practice in Canadian Northwest until close of 1918; specialized in dietetics, Denver, Colo., 1918-23; owner and med. dir. Weger Health Sch., Redlands, Calif., 1923—. Known for original dietetic research. Author: Health Lessons, 1925; The Genesis and Control of Disease, 1931; Kitchen Companion, 1931. Extensive contbr. on health topics. Home: Redlands, Calif. Died Jan. 1935.

WEGG, David Spencer, lawyer; b. St. Thomas, Ont., Can., Dec. 16, 1847; s. John W. and Jerusha (Duncombe) W.; common sch. edn.; LL.B., U. of Wis., 1873; m. Eva Russell, 1878. Practiced at Racine, Wis., 1873-75, Milwaukee, 1875-85, Chicago, 1885—; sr. mem. law firm Wegg & Wegg. Asst. solicitor C.,M.&St.P. Ry. several yrs.; gen. counsel Wis. Central Ry., 1885; pres. C.&N.P. Ry. and dir. N.P. Ry. Home: Chicago, Ill. Died Nov. 18, 1919.

WEGMANN, Edward, engr.; b. Rio de Janiero, Brazil, Nov. 27, 1850; s. L. Edward and Mary W. (Sand) W.; ed. Zürich, Switerland, 1859-66, Brooklyn Poly. Inst., 1867-68; C.E., New York U., 1871; m. Charlotte H. Drummond, May 6, 1901. Engaged in ry. constrn., 1871-84; on constrn. new water works for New York, 1884-1910; cons. engr., Dept. of Water Supply, Gas and Electricity, New York, 1910-14, in private practice as consulting engineer, 1914—. Author: The Design and Construction of Masonry Dams, 1888; The Water Works of the City of New York (1658-1895), 1896; The Design and Construction of Dams, 1899; Conveyance and Distribution of Water, 1918. Home: Yonkers, N.Y. Died Jan. 3, 1935.

WEICKER, Theodore, pharmacist; b. Darmstadt, Germany, June 6, 1861; s. Ludwig Martin and Elisabeth (Momberger) W.; grad. Real-Gymnasium, Darmstadt, 1878; Ph.G. and Ph.C., Columbia, 1911; Ph.M. honoris causa, Philadelphia, Coll. of Pharmacy and Science; m. Florence Palmer, Jan. 21, 1901; children—Theodore, Lowell Palmer, Frederick E., Florence Palmer. Came to U.S., 1885, naturalized, 1890. Began career as apprentice to E. Merck, Darmstadt, 1878; U.S. rep. Merck interests, 1887-90; partner Merck & Co., 1890, sold interests in firm, 1904; with Lowell M. Palmer bought controlling interest in E. R. Squibb & Sons (mfg. chemists), dir., 1905—, chmn. bd.; mem. bd. dirs. Squibb Plan, Inc.; dir. Lentheric, Inc., Squibb Properties Corp. Trustee Columbia U. Coll. of Pharmacy, 1917—; life mem. Columbia U. Coll. of Pharmacy, 1900—. Mem. Riverside Ch. (non-sectarian). Home: Greenwich, Conn. Died Aug. 7, 1940.

WEIDIG, Adolf, director, composer; b. Hamburg, Germany, Nov. 28, 1867; ed. in Germany; grad. Acad. of Music, Munich, 1891; won Mozart prize, Frankfort, 1888, for best compositions for string quartet among 21 competitors; m. Helen Ridgway, 1896. Asso. dir. Am. Conservatory of Music, Chicago. His compositions include a symphony, several string quartets, a trio, other orchestral works and numerous compositions in various forms. V.p. Am. Assns. of Music. Author: Harmonic Material and Its Uses, 1923. Home: Hinsdale, Ill. Died Sept. 23, 1931.

WEIDNER, Carl A., artist; b. Hoboken, N.J., 1865; s. William N. and Pauline (Douai) W.; m. Fredrika Bomford, Feb. 8, 1889. Studied at Nat. Acad. Design and Art Students' League, New York; pupil of Paul Nauen, Munich. Died 1906.

WEIDNER, Revere Franklin, theologian; b. Centre Valley, Pa., Nov. 22, 1851; s. William P. and Eliza A. (Blank) W.; A.B., Muhlenberg Coll., Pa., 1869, A.M., 1872; grad. Luth. Theol. Sem., Phila., 1873; S.T.D., Carthage (Ill.) Coll., 1888; LL.D., Augustana Coll. and Theol. Sem., Rock Island, 1894; D.D., Muhlenberg, 1894; m. Emma Salome Jones, July 10, 1873. Ordained Luth. ministry, 1873; pastor Phillipsburg, N.J., 1873-78; prof. English, history and logic, Muhlenberg Coll., 1875-77; pastor Phila., 1878-82; prof. dogmatics and exegesis, Augustana Theol. Sem., Rock Island, 1882-91; pres. and prof. dogmatic theology and Hebrew Exegesis, Chicago Luth. Theol. Sem., 1891—. Author: Commentary on the Gospel of Mark, 1881; Theological Encyclopædia and Methodology (3 vols.), 1885-91; Biblical Theology of the Old Testament, 1886; Introduction to Dogmatic Theology, 1888; An Introductory New Testament Greek Method, 1889; Studies in the Book—New Testament (3 vols.), 1890, Old Testament, Vol. I, Genesis, 1892; Biblical Theology of the New Testament, 1891; Christian Ethics, 1891; Examination Questions in Church History and Christian Archæology, 1893; Annotations on the General Epistles, 1897, on Revelation, 1898 (Vols. XI, XII Lutheran Commentary); Theologia, or the Doctrine of God, 1903; Ecclesiologia, or the Doctrine of the Church, 1903; The Doctrine of the Ministry, 1907; The Doctrine of Man, 1912; Christology, or the Doctrine of the Person of Christ, 1913. Died Jan. 5, 1915.

WEIGEL, William, army officer; b. New Brunswick, N.J., Aug. 25, 1863; s. Philip (Sr.) and Anna (Silzer) W.; grad. U.S. Mil. Acad., 1887; M.Sc., Rutgers Coll., 1919; unmarried. Commd. 2d lt. 11th Inf., June 12, 1887; 1st lt. 22d Inf., June 6, 1894; trans. to 11th Inf., June 22, 1894; capt. a.q.-m. vols., Nov. 26, 1898; hon. discharged vols., June 16, 1899; capt. U.S.A., Mar. 2, 1899; promoted through grades to brig. gen. N.A., Aug. 5, 1917; maj. gen., Aug. 8, 1918-June 15, 1919; remanded to regular rank of col., June 15, 1919; brig. gen. U.S.A., Mar. 5, 1921; maj. gen., Nov. 20, 1924. Served in Indian wars, Spanish-Am. War and Philippine Insurrection; brig. gen. N.A., comdg. 151st Depot Brig., Camp Devens, Mass., Sept.-Nov. 1917; comdr. 76th Div. and Cantonment, Camp Devens, Nov. 27-Feb. 13, 1918; comd. 56th Brig., 28th Div., Mar. 25-Sept. 8, 1918; comd. 88th Div., Sept. 10, 1918, to demobilization, June 15, 1919. In France, May 5, 1918-June 1, 1919; participated in Champagne-Marne defensive, July 15-18; Aisne-Marne offensive, July 18-Aug. 6; Oise-Aisne offensive, Aug. 18-Nov. 11; Center sector, Haute-Alsace, Oct. 12-Nov. 4; Meuse-Argonne, Sept. 26-Nov. 11, 1918. Thrice awarded Croix de Guerre, with palms, and Comdr. Legion of Honor (French); D.S.M. from U.S. "for exceptionally meritorious and distinguished services." Chief of staff Eastern Dept. Aug. 22, 1919-May 10, 1921; apptd. brig. gen. comdg. 2d Brig., 1st Div., July 1, 1921; dep. comdr. 12th A.C., Organized Reserves, Feb. 15, 1922-Nov. 20, 1924; comdg. Philippine Div. and Philippine Dept., Jan. 26, 1925-Feb. 16, 1927; retired as maj. gen. Aug. 25, 1927. Mem. Conservation and Development Bd. of State of N.J. Episcopalian. Mason. Died Mar. 4, 1936.

WEIGHTMAN, Richard Coxe, journalist; b. Washington, Oct. 25, 1845; s. Richard Hanson W.; ed. St. Timothy's Hall, Catonsville, Md., 1855-57; m. Laura Jurey, Dec. 1878. Served C.S.A., 1861-65; paroled at Shreveport, La.; entered journalism, New Orleans Times, June 1872; sec. war investigation com., 1898-99, apptd. by President McKinley. Died Feb. 17, 1914.

WEIL, A. Leo, lawyer; b. Keysville, Va., July 19, 1858; s. Isaac L. and Minna (Weil) W.; educated academic and law depts., U. of Va.; m. Cassie Ritter, Apr. 11, 1883 (died 1934); children—Aimee Leona, Ferdinand T., A. Leo. Admitted to bar, 1879; practiced at Bradford, Pa., 1880-87, Pittsburgh, 1887—; splty. corp. law; mem. Weil, Christy & Weil; v.p. and dir. Kettleman North Dome Assn. Pres. Voters' League, Pittsburgh, 1905-11, that brought about "graft" disclosures and convictions; saved the Grant Boul. to the city, secured change in charter from unwieldy council to body of 9. Mem. Nat. Municipal League, Nat. Civil Service Assn. Home: Pittsburgh, Pa. Died Sept. 17, 1938.

WEIL, Carl, banker; b. Burr Oak, Kan., Apr. 28, 1882; s. Morris and Ida (Sarbach) W.; ed. Lincoln (Neb.) Bus. Coll. and Coll. of Law, U. of Neb.; m. Lillie Bell Fox, Nov. 18, 1903; 1 son, Billie Alexander. Began with Am. Exchange Nat. Bank, Lincoln, 1899; pres. Commerce Trust Co., Lincoln; v.p. Nat. Bank of Commerce, Bankers Nat. Life Ins. Co., Jersey City, N.J. Republican. Jewish religion. Mason. Home: Lincoln, Neb. Died Nov. 3, 1934.

WEIL, Fred Alban, clergyman; b. North Andover, Mass., May 7, 1874; s. Louis and Anna Moore (Tuttle) W.; grad. Phillips Acad., Andover, Mass., 1892; B.D., Meadville Theol. Sch., 1904; m. Ellen Smith, d. Rev. Thomas L. Eliot, D.D., 1905; children—Thomas Eliot, Frank Tuttle (dec.), Janet Hobart. Reporter and editor newspapers in Mass., Asso. Press corr., 1895-1900; ordained Unitarian ministry, 1904; pastor 3d Ch., Chicago, Ill., 1904-07, Bellingham, Wash., 1907-17, 1st Ch., Denver, Colo., 1917-20, 1st Parish ("Church of the Presidents"), Quincy, Mass., 1920-29, 1st Church, Salem, Oregon, 1930—. Served as orderly, 8th Regiment Mass. Vol. Militia, and p.m. clk., Spanish-Am. War; regional field dir. U.S.P.H.S., in charge of 5 Southern States, World War I. Past pres. Asso. Charities, Bellingham; past pres. Denver Philos. Soc. Proposer of (nat.) Unitarian Ministerial Union and 1st pres., 1921-23; chmn. board Woodward Inst. for Girls, Quincy, Mass., 1920-29. Mason. Newspaper writer. Home: Salem, Ore. Died June 7, 1933.

WEIL, Irving, music critic; b. N.Y. City, July 26, 1878; s. Louis Jacques and Isabelle (Kahn) W.; B.S., Coll. City of N.Y., 1898; studied at Sorbonne, Paris; unmarried. Instr. in pub. schs., N.Y. City, 1898-99; spent following yr. abroad, chiefly in France; newspaper work with Brooklyn Standard Union, Brooklyn Eagle, N.Y. Herald, N.Y. Evening Post and Cleveland Press, 1900-05; with N.Y. Evening Jour., 1905—, music critic, 1910—; chief music critic Musical America, 1928, 29. Known as a pioneer in sympathetic championship of the best in advanced modern music. Home: New York, N.Y. Died Aug. 26, 1933.

WEIMER, Albert Barnes, lawyer; b. Phila., Jan. 5, 1857; s. J. S. and J. B. W.; A.B., Harvard, 1880; m. Ella C., d. John Goforth, June 16, 1910 (died 1927). Admitted to bar of Phila., 1882; and in practice at Phila.; state reporter, Pa. Author: Railroad Law of Pennsylvania, 1894; Corporation Law of Pennsylvania, 1897. Home: Philadelphia, Pa. Died Nov. 13, 1938.

WEINSTOCK, Harris, merchant; b. London, Eng., Sept. 18, 1854; s. Solomon and Rachel W.; ed. pub. schs., New York, until 12 yrs. of age; m. Barbara Felsenthal, Feb. 24, 1878. Engaged in business, San Francisco, 1872; opened branch in Sacramento, 1874, in partnership with D. Lubin; gave up San Francisco business, 1876; inc. Sacramento business, 1888, as Weinstock, Lubin & Co., becoming v.p.; v.p. Weinstock-Lubin Real Estate Co.; pres. Weinstock Nichols Co., San Francisco, Los Angeles and Oakland, Calif.; dir. Nat. Bank of D. O. Mills, Sacramento, Calif. Served from pvt. through grades to lt. col. of Calif. N.G., 1881-95; founded Barbara Weinstock lectureship of Morals of Trade, U. of Calif.; apptd. mem. trustees State Library of Calif., 1887, State Bd. of Horticulture of Calif., 1895; elected mem. bd. freeholders of Sacramento, 1891; apptd. spl. labor commr. by Gov. Gillett, of Calif., Feb. 1908, to investigate the labor laws and labor conditions of foreign countries; appointed by Gov. Hiram W. Johnson, Apr. 1912, to investigate the Industrial Workers of the World (free speech disturbances in San Diego, Calif.); apptd. Apr. 1913, by same, mem. Am. Commn. to investigate European systems of rural credits (elected v.p. of that body); apptd., June 18, 1913, by Pres. Woodrow Wilson, mem. Indsl. Relations Commn.; apptd. by Gov. Johnson, Sept. 1913, mem. Calif. Indsl. Accident Commn.; mem. Calif. State Rural Credit Commn., 1915—; apptd. state market dir. by Gov. Johnson, Nov. 1915, reapptd. by Gov. Stephens, July 1917. Mem. exec. bd. Nat. Civic Fedn. V.p. Jewish Publ. Soc. of America. Republican. Author: Jesus the Jew, 1902; Strikes and Lockouts, 1909. Home: San Francisco, Calif. Died Aug. 22, 1922.

WEIR, F(lorence) Roney, writer; b. Waupun, Wis., 1861; d. Lawrence and Eliza (McElroy) Roney; m. William Weir, Jan. 2, 1893. Author: Britomart the Socialist, 1900; The Hired Man, 1903; The Shingle Weavers, 1909; Busher's Girl, 1915; Merry Andrew, 1918; Colinette of Redmoon, 1921; The Green Eyed One, 1923. Contbr. short stories to mags. Home: Seattle, Wash. Died Nov. 13, 1932.

WEIR, Hugh C., author, editor; b. Virginia, Ill., May 18, 1884; s. Richard D. and Nellie (Cosgro) W.; ed. pub. and prvt. schs.; m. Grace Hamilton, June 29, 1903; 1 son, John Edgar. In newspaper work until 1908; contbr. to mags., 1908-16; writer of motion picture scenarios, 1916—; made official motion pictures for Paderewski and the Polish Govt. in World War I; founder (with Catherine McNelis), nat. advertising agency, 1928; founder (with same), 1929, and editorial dir., The Tower Magazines, Inc. Episcopalian. Author: The Conquest of the Isthmus, 1908; With the Flag in Panama; Miss Madelyn Mack, Detective, 1910; The Young Shipper of the Great Lakes, 1911; Cinders, 1913; The Young Wheat Scout, 1916; The Young Inventor, 1917; Con and Abel (with William J. Flynn), 1925; True Secrets of the Underworld (with same), 1926; My Boss, Bill Jones (with Charles M. Schwab), 1930; Alibi Ladies, 1930. Contributor to mags. Home: Mount Pocono, Pa. Died Mar. 17, 1934.

WEIR, James, Jr., author, physician; b. Owensboro, Ky., Oct. 17, 1856; s. James and Susan Charlotte (Green) W.; grad. U. of Louisville (valedictorian), 1878; studied medicine, U. of Louisville, U. of Mich., Bellevue Hosp., N.Y., and N.Y. Polyclinic; unmarried. Author: Religion and Lust, 1897; The Dawn of Reason, 1898; Intelligence in the Lower Animals, 1898; The Psychical Correlation of Religious Emotion and Sexual Desire, 1905. Contbr. to mags., tech. jours. and to med. publs. in U.S., England, Italy, France and Germany. Died 1906.

WEIR, John Ferguson, sculptor, painter; b. West Point, N.Y., Aug. 28, 1841; s. Prof. Robert W. W.; brother of J(ulian) Alden W.; ed. under instrs. in mil. acad.; hon. A.M., Yale, 1871; m. Mary, d. Rev. J. W. French, 1866. Prof. painting and design, 1869-77, William Leffingwell prof., 1877—, dir. Art Sch., 1869—, Yale, A.N.A., 1864, N.A., 1866. Prin. works in sculpture: Statues of Pres. Woolsey and Prof. Silliman, of Yale. Executed many portraits and other works in painting, notably the pictures The Gun Foundry, The Forging of the Shaft, The Confessional, An Artist's Studio, Christmas Eve, Tapping the Furnace, Rain and Sunshine, The Column of St. Mark's, Venice. Author: The Way—The Nature and Means of Revelation, 1889; John Trumbull and His Works, 1902; Human Destiny in the Light of Revelation, 1903; etc. Died Apr. 8, 1926.

WEIR, J(ulian) Alden, artist; b. West Point, N.Y., Aug. 30, 1852; s. Prof. Robert W. W.; brother of John Ferguson W. (q.v.); studied art under his father and Jean L. Gérôme; married. Hon. mention, Paris Salon, 1881; prize, Am. Art Assn., 1888; portraits and genre pieces are his specialties. A.N.A., 1885, N.A., 1886; pres. N.A.D., 1915; mem. Am. Acad. of Arts and Letters, Ten Am. Painters; mem. Commn. of Fine Arts (U.S.). Died Dec. 8, 1919.

WEIR, Levi Candee, corp. exec.; pres. Adams Express Co., Adams Land & Bldg. Co., Adams Vehicle Co., Matawok Land Co., Weir Frog Co.; dir. Am. Exchange Nat. Bank, Am. Mail Steamship Co., Asso. Merchants Co., C.&S. Ry. Co., Commercial Trust Co. of Phila., Des Moines & Ft. Dodge R.R., Franklin Nat. Bank of Phila., Home Ins. Co., Ia. Central & Western Ry., Ia. Central Ry., Manufacturers & Traders Nat. Bank of Buffalo, Mercantile Trust Co., Minneapolis & St. Louis R.R., Norfolk & Western Ry., Standard Safe Deposit Co., Standard Trust Co., U.S. Express Co., Vacuum Cleaner Co. Died 1910.

WEIR, Robert Fulton, surgeon; b. New York, Feb. 16, 1838; s. James and Mary A. (Shapter) W.; A.B., Coll. City of N.Y., 1854, A.M., 1857; M.D., Coll. Phys. and Surg. (Columbia), 1859; asst. surgeon U.S.A., 1861-65; in charge at gen. hosp., Frederick, Md., 1862-65; m. Maria Washington McPherson, Oct. 2, 1863; m. 2d, Mary Badgley Alden, Nov. 7, 1895. Lecturer on diseases of male pelvic organs, 1873-80, lecturer on surgery, 1883-84, prof. clin. surgery, 1884-92, surgery, 1892-1903, clin. surgery, 1903—, Columbia; attending surgeon New York Hosp., 1876-1900, etc. Pres. Am. Surg. Assn., 1900, New York Acad. Medicine, 1900. Republican. Died Apr. 6, 1927.

WEISENBURG, Theodore, neurologist; b. N.Y. City, Apr. 10, 1876; M.D., U. of Pa., 1899; m. Constance V. Field, July 4, 1909; 1 dau., Constance (Mrs. John Hammond Greiner). Asst. surgeon U.S. Army, in P.I., 1901-02; practiced as specialist in nervous and mental diseases, Phila., 1903—; instr. nervous diseases, U. of Pa., 1904-07; prof. same, Grad. Sch. of Medicine, U. of Pa., 1907—; physician to Orthopedic Hosp. and Infirmary for Nervous Diseases; neurologist Grad. Hosp., Phila. Gen. Hosp., Municipal Hosp., State Hosp. for Insane, Norristown and Spring City, etc. Maj. M.C.U.S.A., 1918-19. Editor-in-chief, Archives of Neurology and Psychiatry. Contbr. on nervous and mental diseases. Home: Paoli, Pa. Died Aug. 3, 1934.

WEISER, Emilius James, banker; b. Decorah, Ia., Jan. 3, 1867; s. Emilius I. and Mary Louise (Von Hof) Weiser; educated Carleton Coll., Northfield, Minn., and Northwestern U.; m. Grace E. Marsh, May 17, 1893; children—Charlotte, Gretchen (Mrs. Robert H. Fayfield). Began in banking business at Decorah, 1890; removed to Fargo, N.D., 1905; pres. First Nat. Bank & Trust Co., Fargo. Pres. N.D. Children's Home Soc. Republican. Congregationalist. Mason, Elk. Home: Fargo, N.D. Died Feb. 8, 1937.

WEISER, Walter R., surgeon; b. York, Pa., June 13, 1870; s. Martin H. and Mary (Tyler) W.; student biology dept., U. of Pa., 1887, M.D., 1892; Ph.G., Philadelphia Coll. Pharmacy, 1889; m. Harriet Lamson, Sept. 20, 1895; 1 son, Frank Hale; m. 2d, Emma Cannons Foote, Sept. 21, 1925. Surg. interne Presbyn. Hosp., Phila., 1892-93; in surg. practice, Springfield, Mass., 1894-1917; surgeon to Springfield and Mercy hosps. and chief of staff and treas. Hampden Hosp.; chief surgeon Mass. State Hosp. for Epileptics 18 yrs. Served as capt., advancing to col. Med. Corps, U.S.A., May 1917-Dec. 1919; col. Med. R.C. Mem. Fla. State Hosp. Commn. Treas. Kiwanis Internat., 1930-34 (Internat. trustee 1928-29; gov. Fla. Dist. 1925). Republican. Congregationalist. Mason, Odd Fellow, Elk. Contbr. articles to Kiwanis Mag. Home: Daytona Beach, Fla. Died Apr. 13, 1937.

WEISS, Albert Paul, psychologist; b. Steingrund, Schlesien, Germany, Sept. 15, 1879; s. Joseph and Pauline (Febst) W.; brought to U.S. in infancy; B.A., U. of Mo., 1910, M.A., 1912, Ph.D., 1916; m. Grace Margaret Parker, Aug. 10, 1914. With Ohio State U., 1912—, prof. exptl. psychology, 1918—. Instructor S.A.T.C., Ohio State U., 1918. Author: A Theoretical Basis of Human Behavior. Contbr. some 20 articles on theoretical and exptl. psychology. Died Apr. 3, 1931.

WEISS, Anton Charles; b. Sheboygan, Wis., September 20, 1863; s. John and Louise (Fleischer) W.; educated pub. schs. and spl. course in German; m. Mary D. Sherwin, Oct. 5, 1887; children—John S., Louise, Elinor. Editor and pub. The Duluth (Minn.) Herald, 1890-1921; dir. Asso. Press, 1909-21. Alderman, Duluth, 1888-90; mem. bd. mgrs. Minn. State Prison, 1890-93; del. at large Dem. Nat. Conv., Denver, 1908; del. at large chmn. Minn. delegation, Baltimore, 1912, del. at large, 1920; mem. advisory bd. Dem. Nat. Com. in campaign of 1912. Dir. Stone-Ordean-Wells Co.; dir. First & Am. Nat. Bank, Morris Plan Bank, Minn. Power & Light Co. Home: Duluth, Minn. Died Nov. 27, 1938.

WEISS, William Casper, banker; b. Holton, Kan., June 20, 1882; s. John Christopher and Martha Elizabeth (Tribble) W.; ed. pub. schs., and Campbell U., Holton; won life scholarship in elocution, Campbell U., at age of 11; studied law under A. E. Crane, of Holton, Kan.; m. Alta Gardenhire, June 24, 1913; 1 dau., Alta. Gen. storekeeper, Swift & Co., Ft. Worth, Tex., 1904-06; with various ry. cos. in Tex., 1906-17, resigning as auditor of disbursements of M.K.&T. Ry. Co.; gen. auditor Fed. Res. Bank of Dallas, later dir. El Paso br. of same, 1917-24; exec. v.p. dir. Phoenix Nat. Bank and Phoenix Savings Bank & Trust Co. Republican. Episcopalian. Home: Phoenix, Ariz. Died Jan. 8, 1934.

WEISSE, Charles H., congressman; b. Sheboygan Falls, Wis., Oct. 24, 1866; s. Charles S. W.; ed. pub. schools; m. Lena Kallenberg, 1896. Brought up in tanning business and has owned plant, 1881—. Mem. 58th to 61st Congresses (1903-11), 6th Wis. Dist. Democrat. Home: Sheboygan Falls, Wis. Died Oct. 8, 1919.

WEISSE, Faneuil Dunkin, surgeon; b. Watertown, Mass., Aug. 27, 1842; s. Dr. John A. and Jane Lee (Hunt) W.; tutored by father for 12 yrs.; M.D., Univ. Med. Coll. (New York U.), 1864; m. Mary Elizabeth, d. Henry Suydam, Apr. 30, 1872 (died 1908); m. 2d, Mrs. George H. Ripley, d. William Churchill, Aug.

27, 1910. Asst. to Prof. Valentine Mott, M.D., 1863-65; asst. demonstrator of anatomy, 1864-65, lecturer and clinical prof. of dermatology, 1865-74, prof. surg. pathology, 1874-75, practical and surg. anatomy, 1876-88, New York U.; prof. surg. pathology, New York Coll. Vet. Surgeons, 1865-75; prof. anatomy, surg. pathology and oral surgery, 1865—, dean, 1897—, N.Y. Coll. of Dentistry. Organizer, 1875, and later prof. and pres. bd. trustees, Am. Vet. Coll. Founder N.Y. Dermatol. Soc. Author: Practical Human Anatomy, 1886; also many med. articles. Home: New York, N.Y. Died June 22, 1915.

WEITZEL, George Thomas, diplomat; b. Frankfort, Ky., June 23, 1873; s. Jerome and Caroline (Boland) W.; A.B., Harvard, 1894, LL.B., 1897; m. Muriel Fairford, Dec. 2, 1914. Practiced law at St. Louis, 1897-1907, and admitted as atty. Supreme Ct. of U.S.; apptd. 2d sec. Am. Embassy at Mexico City, Mar. 31, 1910; assigned to duty in Div. Latin-Am. Affairs, Dept. of State, July 1910-Jan. 1911, spl. duty at Am. Embassy, Mexico City, Mar. 22-May 23, 1911; apptd. group sec. 2d Pan-Am. Financial Conf., 1920; mem. law firm Goodwin, Weitzel & Bresnahan, 1919-24; gen. counsel Am. Automobile Assn., 1925-30. Died Jan. 1936.

WELCH, Archibald Ashley, ins. pres.; b. Hartford, Conn., Oct. 6, 1859; s. Henry K. W. and Susan L. (Goodwin) W.; A.B., Yale, 1882; A.M., Trinity, 1922; m. Ellen Bunce, Oct. 24, 1889. Entered actuarial dept. Travelers Ins. Co., 1882; actuary, Phoenix Mut. Life Ins. Co., July 1890, later asst. sec. and actuary and 2d v.p. and actuary, 1904-12, v.p. and actuary, 1912-24. pres., 1924—; dir. Soc. for Savings, Phoenix State Bank & Trust Co., Phoenix Mut. Life Ins. Co., Phoenix Ins. Co. (fire), Conn. Fire Ins. Co. Pres. Hartford Sch. of Music; v.p., sec. Am. Sch. for Deaf; chmn. Hartford High Sch. Com., 1898-1913; dir. Watkinson Library, Wadsworth Atheneum, Children's Museum. Pres. Actuarial Soc. America; fellow Am. Inst. Actuaries, Casualty Actuarial Soc. America. Home: Hartford, Conn. Died May 8, 1935.

WELCH, Charles Edgar, mfr.; b. Watertown, N.Y., Mar. 2, 1852; s. Thomas Bramwell and Lucy (Hutt) W.; ed. common schs.; m. Jennie Ross, Nov. 12, 1879 (died 1884); m. 2d, Julia Frailey, June 16, 1885. Practicing dentist, 1872-92, except, 1881-86, in business in Phila. as mem. of T. B. Welch & Son, later Welch Dental Co.; mfr. grape juice, 1869—, becoming pres. of The Welch Grape Juice Co.; pres. The Welch Co., Ltd., St. Catharines, Can. Prohibition Party candidate for gov. of N.Y., 1916; pres. Village of Westfield 6 terms. Trustee Chautauqua Instn., Allegheny Coll. (Meadville, Pa.), Illinois Woman's Coll. (Jacksonville, Ill.). Mem. Bd. Foreign Missions M.E. Ch.; del. Ecumenical Meth. Conf., London, 1921; del. Gen. Conf., 1908, 12, 20, 24. Home: Westfield, N.Y. Died Jan. 6, 1925.

WELCH, Samuel Wallace, M.D.; b. Alpine, Ala., Feb. 14, 1861; s. William Americus (M.D.) and Willie Ann (Wallace) W.; B.S., Howard Coll., Marion, Ala., 1881; student Tulane U.; M.D., Coll. Phys. and Surg., Baltimore, Md., 1893; post-grad. work, Johns Hopkins, Coll. Phys. and Surg. (Columbia); LL.D., U. of Ala., 1928; m. Ethel Roberta Cleveland, Apr. 10, 1900; children—Willie W., Oliver William. Began practice at Alpine, Ala., 1893; elected mem. County Bd. of Health, Talladega County, 1897; elected mem. State Com. Pub. Health and State Bd. Med. Examiners, 1903 (chmn.); state health officer, Alabama, 1917—; author of bill amending med. laws of Ala., 1919; mem. City Bd. Edn., Talladega, 8 yrs.; chmn. State Com. Nat. Defense Med. Sect., World War I; chmn. Nat. Malaria Com., 1923; etc. Mem. bd. trustees Howard Coll., 1895-1915. Mem. A.M.A. (mem. council on med. edn. and hosps., 1921, chmn. pub. health sect., 1922, mem. House of Delegates, 1917), Southern Med. Assn. (chmn. pub. health sect., 1922—, councilor, 1925—), Ala. State Med. Assn. (pres.), Talladega County Med. Soc., Assn. Health Authorities of N. America (pres. 1927-28), Am. Pub. Health Assn., del. Internat. Tuberculosis Assn., St. Louis, 1905, Internat. Conv. on Demigraphy and Hygiene, Washington, D.C., 1912. Democrat. Baptist. Mason, Odd Fellow. Home: Talladega, Ala. Died Aug. 22, 1928.

WELCH, William Henry, pathologist; b. Norfolk, Conn., Apr. 8, 1850; s. William Wickham and Emeline (Collin) W.; A.B., Yale, 1870; M.D., Coll. Phys. and Surg. (Columbia), 1875; univs. of Strassburg, Leipzig, Breslau and Berlin, 1876-78, 1884-85; hon. M.D., U. of Pa., 1894; LL.D., Western Reserve, 1894, Yale, 1896, Harvard, 1900, Toronto, 1903, Columbia, 1904, Jefferson Med. Coll., 1907, Princeton, 1910, Washington U., 1915, U. Chicago, 1916, U. of Southern Calif., 1930, Univ. State of N.Y., 1930; Sc.D., Cambridge, 1923, Western Reserve, 1929, U. of Pa., 1930; Doct., Strassburg, 1923. Prof. pathol. and anatomy and gen. pathology, Bellevue Hosp. Med. Coll., 1879-84; Baxley prof. pathology, 1884-1916, dean, med. faculty, 1893-98, dir. School of Hygiene and Public Health, 1916-26, professor history of medicine, 1926-30, emeritus, 1931, Johns Hopkins; pathologist Johns Hopkins Hosp., 1889-1916. Pres. Med. State Bd. Health, 1898-1922, and mem. to 1929; pres. bd. dirs. Rockefeller Inst. for Med. Research, 1901—; mem. Internat. Health Bd. and China Med. Bd. of Rockefeller Foundation; trustee of Carnegie Instn., 1906—. Huxley lecturer, Charing Cross Hosp. Med. Sch., London, 1902. Pres. Med. and Chirurg. Faculty of Md., 1891-92, Congress of Am. Phys. and Surg., 1897, Assn. Am. Physicians, 1901, A.A.A.S., 1906-07, A.M.A., 1910-11, Nat. Tuberculosis Assn., 1910-11 (hon. pres.), Nat. Acad. Sciences, 1913-16, Am. Social Hygiene Assn., 1916-19, Nat. Com. Mental Hygiene (hon. pres.), History of Science Society, 1931; fellow Am. Acad. Arts and Sciences, Coll. of Physicians, Phila.; hon. fellow Royal Soc. Medicine, Royal Sanitary Inst., London, Royal Coll. of Phys., Edinburgh, Soc. Med. Officers of Health (Eng.). Commd. maj., Med. R.C., U.S.A., July 16, 1917; lt. col., Feb. 20, 1918; col., July 24, 1918; hon. discharged, Dec. 31, 1918; col. Med. Sect. O.R.C., U.S.A., Feb. 24, 1919; brig. gen. O.R.C., Dec. 23, 1921. Awarded D.S.M. (U.S.); Order of Rising Sun (Japan), 3d Class; Comdr. Order of St. Olav (Norway), 2d Class; Order of Mercy (Kingdom of Serbs, Croats and Slovenes); Officer Legion of Honor (France); gold medal, Nat. Inst. Social Sciences; medal of honor, U. of Vienna; Kober medal, 1927; Harbin gold medal, 1931. Author: General Pathology of Fever, 1888; The Biology of Bacteria, Infection and Immunity, 1894; Bacteriology of Surgical Infections, 1895; Thrombosis and Embolism, 1899; also numerous papers on pathol. and bacteriol. subjects, and addresses. Home: Baltimore, Md. Died Apr. 30, 1934.

WELCH, William Henry, veterinarian; b. Bloomington, Ill., May 7, 1871; s. Jeremiah and Sarah Jane (Myers) W.; Ill. Wesleyan U., 1886-90; D.V.S., Chicago Vet. Coll., 1892; m. Elizabeth Kilgore, May 7, 1895; children—Eleanor (Mrs. Rolla M. Keatts), Laurastine (Mrs. John Leonard Probasco). Began practice at Lexington, Ill., 1892; mayor of Lexington, 1905-07, mem. Bd. Edn., 1909-24, alderman, 1899-1905, 1924-26, mem. Library Bd., 1912; trustee Brokaw Hosp., Normal, Ill., 1924—; state veterinarian of Ill., 1929-33; mem. undulant fever com. Illinois State Board Public Health. Mem. Am. Vet. Med. Assn. (pres. 1922-23, com. resolutions, 1925-26; legislative com., 1924-29; chmn. policy com., 1929-31); mem. Ill. State Vet. Med. Assn. (sec. 1900-05, pres. 1905-06, sec. and treas. 1925-30), McLean Co. Vet. Assn. (pres. 1912-18), U.S. Live Stock Sanitary Assn. (chmn. com. uniform laws and regulations 1932-33). Editor Sect. Equine Practice in North Am. Veterinarian. Republican. Methodist. Mason. Home: Lexington, Ill. Died Oct. 25, 1935.

WELD, C(hristopher) Minot, financier; b. Boston, Mass., Oct. 2, 1858; s. Francis M. and Elizabeth (Rodman) W.; A.B., Harvard, 1880; m. Marian Lingee, Apr. 24, 1889. Pres. Mass. Gas Cos., N.E. Cotton Yarn Co.; dir., mem. exec. com. Edison Electric Illuminating Co., West End St. Ry. Co.; dir. Mo.P. Ry. Co., Nat. Shawmut Bank, Guarantee Co. of N. America, Boston Consol. Gas. Co., Suncook Mills, Boston Storage Warehouse Co., Melones Mining Co., Nashua Mfg. Co., Lancaster Mills, Pocasset Mfg. Co., Lowe Mfg. Co., Arkwright Mut. Ins. Co., N.E. Coal & Coke Co., N.E. Mfg. Co., Boston Safe Deposit & Trust Co., Union Mills, Globe Yarn Co., Sanford Spinning Co., N.E. Fuel & Transportation Co., Greelock Co., etc. Republican. Home: Readville, Mass. Died Aug. 27, 1918.

WELD, Laenas Gifford, univ. dean; b. Sherwood, Mich., Dec. 30, 1862; s. Le Roy Tryon and Nancy Rose (Dougherty) W.; Northwestern U., 1878-80; B.S., State U. of Iowa, 1883, A.M., 1886, LL.D., 1912; studied abroad, 1897; m. Harriet Magdalene Doane, June 24, 1887. Teacher mathematics, Burlington (Ia.) High Sch., 1884-86; asst. prof. 1886-87, acting prof., 1887-89, prof. mathematics and astronomy and head dept., 1889-1911, dean Graduate Coll., 1900-07, dir. Sch. of Applied Science, 1903-05, dean Coll. Liberal Arts, 1907-10, State U. of Ia. State supt. weights and measures for Ia., 1888-1911; dir. Pullman (Ill.) Free School of Manual Training, Sept. 1, 1911—. Fellow A.A.A.S. (sec. Sect. A, 1904-09). Congregationalist. Author: Theory of Determinants; Determinants. Home: Pullman, Ill. Died Nov. 28, 1919.

WELD, Stephen Minot, merchant; b. Jamaica Plain, Mass., Jan. 4, 1842; s. Stephen Minot and Sarah Bartlett (Balch) W.; A.B., Harvard, 1860, A.M., 1863; m. Eloise Rodman, June 1, 1869; m. 2d, Susan Edith Waterbury, May 26, 1904. Entered army as 2d lt. 18th Mass. Inf., Jan. 27, 1862; 1st lt., Nov. 1, 1862; capt., 1863; hon. discharged Dec. 25, 1863; apptd. lt. col. 56th Mass. Inf., Jan. 2, 1864; col., May 31, 1864; bvtd. brig. gen. vols., Mar. 13, 1865, for gallant and meritorious services; mustered out July 12, 1865. Head Stephen M. Weld & Co., cotton mchts., 1875—; also of Weld & Neville; dir. Old Colony Trust Co., Bay State Trust Co., West End St. Ry. Overseer, Harvard, 1899-1911. Home: Dedham, Mass. Died Mar. 16, 1920.

WELDON, Charles Dater, painter; b. Mansfield, O.; s. James and Isabella (MacElroy) W.; acad. edn., Cleveland; studied drawing at Leigh's Acad., London, and under M. Munkacsy, Paris. A.N.A., 1889, N.A., 1897. Awarded first Prang prize of $1000, for water-color painting. Home: East Orange, N.J. Died Aug. 9, 1935.

WELDON, Lawrence, jurist; b. Ohio, 1829; ed. in common schs. of Madison County, London Acad. and Wittenberg Coll.; not a graduate; studied law; admitted to Ohio bar, 1854; m. Mary Jane Howard, Dec. 1854. Clerk Sec. State's office, Ohio, 1853-54; moved, 1854, to Clinton, De Witt County, Ill. Presdl. elector, 1860, on Rep. ticket, voting for Lincoln; mem. Ill. legislature, 1861; resigned; U.S. dist. atty. southern Ill., 1861-66; practiced law at Bloomington, Ill., 1867-83; judge U.S. Ct. of Claims, 1883—. Died 1905.

WELKER, Philip Albert, civil engr.; b. Toledo, O., June 1, 1857; s. Philip and Maria (Pauly) W.; C.E., Cornell U., 1878; m. Maude B. Loud, Mar. 17, 1885 (died 1890); 1 dau., Maude Antoinette (Mrs. Howard R. Willis); m. 2d, Gertrude M. Lanahan, June 29, 1904; 1 son, Philip Lanahan. In city engrs.' office, Toledo, O., 1878-79; with U.S. Coast and Geod. Survey, 1879—, operating in nearly every part of U.S. and Alaska, P.R., Isthmus of Panama and P.I.; with Alaskan Boundary Survey, 1893-95; in comd. U.S. steamer Bache, hydrographic surveys, Atlantic Coast, 1898-1910; rep. U.S. Govt. on commn. of engrs. for locating and determining ownership of Ft. Myers Mil. Rd., Va., 1910; dir. coast surveys, P.I., 1911-14, also sec. Philippine Com. on Geog. Names, and mem. Harbor Lines Commn. of P.I.; asst. in charge of office, 1914-17, engr. in charge of office, U.S. Coast and Geodetic Survey, June 1917-June 1920, retired, June 1, 1921. Pres. Welker Supply Co., Cleveland, O. Mason. Home: Washington, D.C. Died Dec. 24, 1926.

WELLBORN, Olin, judge; b. Cumming, Ga., June 13, 1843; s. Chapleigh and Mary A. W.; grad. Emory Coll., Oxford, Ga., 1862. Served in C.S.A., 1861-65; mem. 46th to 49th Congresses (1879-87), 9th Tex. Dist.; U.S. dist. judge, Southern Dist., Calif., Mar. 1, 1895—. Democrat. Home: Los Angeles, Calif. Died Dec. 6, 1921.

WELLER, Charles Heald, archæologist; b. Tyrone, N.Y., Nov. 7, 1870; s. Newton and Della M. (Heald) W.; Syracuse U., 1890-91; B.A., Yale, 1895, Ph.D., 1904; fellow Am. Sch. Classical Studies at Athens, 1900-01; m. Rose Elmer Bradley, Aug. 30, 1895; children—Clara Heald, George Bradley, Ruth, Newton. Prin. Leonardsville (N.Y.) Union Sch. and Acad., 1890-92; prin. Gloversville (N.Y.) High Sch., 1895-98; teacher Hillhouse High Sch., New Haven, 1898-1900; rector Hopkins Sch., New Haven, 1901-06; lecturer on Greek lit., Yale Grad. Sch., 1904-06; prof. and head dept. of history of art, also dir. summer session, U. of Ia., 1906—, also dir. Sch. of Journalism, 1924—. Republican. Conglist. Author: Athens and Its Monuments, 1913. Contbr. to mags. Home: Iowa City, Ia. Died Mar. 2, 1927.

WELLER, George Emery, lawyer; b. St. Paul, Minn., Aug. 24, 1857; s. Emery A. and Mary (Hurlburt) W.; ed. Cooper Union, N.Y. City; LL.B., Columbia, 1889; m. Catherine Eddey, Oct. 6, 1880 (died 1913); children—Royal H., Emery C. Began practice in N.Y. City, 1889; sec. to pres. Dept. of Docks, 1898-1902; U.S. gen. appraiser, U.S. Treasury, Customs Ct., by appmt. of Pres. Wilson, Feb. 4, 1919; justice U.S. Customs Ct., 1926—. Mem. 2d Battery, N.Y. State Arty., 5 yrs. Democrat. Episcopalian. Home: New York, N.Y. Deceased.

WELLER, Michael Ignatius, banker; b. London, Eng., June 10, 1846; s. Samuel and Mary (O'Brien) W.; ed. City of London Sch., and at Boulogne, France, and Vienna, Austria; arrived New York, Mar. 8, 1867; m. Rita Repetti, June 13, 1871. Settled in Washington, D.C., 1872; pres. East Washington Savings Bank. Collector of Americana, especially local Washingtoniana. Authority on local history of D.C., Va. and Md. Charter mem. and corr. sec. Columbia Hist. Soc., Washington Acad. Sciences. Author: (for Columbia Hist. Soc.) James Ewell, M.D.; The Capture of Washington in 1814; Henry Fleete, 1617-1666; Four Mayors of Washington; Commodore Joshua Barney, the Hero of the Battle of Bladensburg. Home: Washington, D.C. Died Mar. 4, 1915.

WELLER, Reginald Heber, bishop; b. Jefferson City, Mo., Nov. 6, 1857; s. Rev. Reginald Heber and Emma Amanda W.; ed. St. John's Acad., Jacksonville, Fla., 1867-75, U. of the South, 1875-78; B.D., Nashotah (Wis.) Theol. Sem., 1884, D.D., 1901, LL.D., 1925; m. Bessie, d. Dan Thair Brown, May 18, 1886; children—Ruth (Mrs. George B. Nelson), Reginald Heber, III, Dan Brown, Charles Grafton, Walter Trowbridge, Horace Look. Deacon, 1880, priest, 1884, P.E. Ch.; rector Eau Claire, 1884-88, Waukesha, 1888-90, Stevens Point, 1890-1900; consecrated coadjutor bishop of Fond du Lac, Nov. 8, 1900; bishop of Fond du Lac, Aug. 30, 1912-Nov. 8, 1933 (retired). Home: Fond du Lac, Wis. Died Nov. 22, 1935.

WELLER, Royal H., congressman; b. N.Y. City, July 2, 1881; s. George E. and Catherine E. (Eddey) W.; student Coll. City of New York, N.Y. Law Sch.; m. Leonora Wortz, Oct. 12, 1904. Admitted to N.Y. bar, 1902; mem. law firm of Fox & Weller. Asst. dist. atty. N.Y. County, 1911-17; counsel to alien property custodian; mem. 68th to 70th Congresses (1923-29), 21st N.Y. Dist. Democrat. Methodist. Home: New York, N.Y. Died Mar. 1, 1929.

WELLER, Stuart, geologist; b. Maine, Broome County, N.Y., Dec. 26, 1870; s. James and Henrietta (Marean) W.; B.S., Cornell U., 1894; Ph.D., Yale U., 1901; m. Harriet A. Marvin, Sept. 23, 1897; children—James Marvin, Chester Marean, Allen Stuart. Asst. Mo. Geol. Survey, 1890, U.S. Geol. Survey, 1891; mus. asst. in charge palæontology, 1892-93, asst. in geology, 1893-94, Cornell U.; asst. in palæontology, and grad. student, Yale, 1894-95; palæontologist N.J. Geol. Survey, 1899-1907; asst. geologist, 1901-06, geologist, 1906—, U.S. Geol. Survey; geologist Ill. Geol. Survey, 1906—; asst., 1895-97, asso., 1897-1900, instr., 1900-01, asst. prof. palæontologic geology, 1901-08, asso. prof., 1908-15, prof., 1915—, U. of Chicago; asst. geologist, Geol. Survey of Ky., 1920—. Author of reports and many papers on palæontol. and geol. subjects. Home: Chicago, Ill. Died Aug. 5, 1927.

WELLES, Edgar Thaddeus, capitalist; b. Hartford, Conn., Aug. 29, 1843; s. Gideon W. (Sec. of Navy in President Lincoln's cabinet); grad. Yale, 1864; admitted to bar, but never practiced; m. Alice, d. Charles H. Brainard, Sept. 29, 1870. Chief clerk Navy Dept., 1866-69; treas. and mgr. Gatling Gun Co., of Hartford, 1869; later pres. Granby Mining & Smelting Co., St. Louis, Internat. Co., Mexico, Mexican Steamship Co.; receiver Nat. Bank, State of Mo.; v.p. Wabash R.R. Co.; pres. Consol. Coal Co.; dir. in other cos. Home: New York, N.Y. Died Aug. 22, 1914.

WELLES, Roger, naval officer; b. Newington, Conn., Dec. 7, 1862; s. Roger and Mercy Delano (Aiken) W.; grad. U.S. Naval Acad., 1884; m. Harriet Ogden Deen, Oct. 17, 1908. Ensign, July 1, 1886; promoted through grades to rear adm. (temp.), July 1, 1918; rear adm. (perm.), July 1, 1919. Served in McArthur, Vermont and Wasp during Spanish-Am. War, 1898; exec. officer in warship New Hampshire, 1908-09; comd. New Orleans, 1909-10; mem. Bd. Insp. and Survey, Navy Dept., Washington, D.C., 1911; comd. Louisiana, 1911-13; comd. Naval Training Sta., Newport, R.I., 1913-15; comd. Oklahoma, 1916-17; dir. naval intelligence, Navy Dept., Washington, D.C., 1917-19; apptd. comdr. Div. 1, U.S. Fleet, Feb. 4-Aug. 28, 1919; comdr. Div. 4, Atlantic Fleet Flagship Minnesota, Sept. 1919. First comdt. 11th Naval Dist., 1921-23; comdt. 5th Naval Dist. and Naval Operating Base, Hampton Roads, Va., 1923-25; apptd. comdr. U.S. Naval Forces in European waters, Oct. 10, 1925, with rank of vice admiral; retired from active service December 7, 1926. Decorated Atlantic Battle Medal (Nipe Bay), Spanish-Am. War; Cuban and Philippine campaign medals; Comdr. Legion of Honor (French); Grand Officer Order of Leopold II (Belgian); 2d Order of the Rising Sun (Japanese); Grand Cross of Naval Merit and Efficiency (Spanish), 1926; Navy Cross (U.S.). Republican. Conglist. Mason. As a young man was sent as spl. commr., Columbian Expn., to Venezuela, etc., and made ethnol. collection (installed in Field Mus., Chicago), in interior of Venezuela, for which was awarded certificate and bronze medal; on duty at the expn., 1890-93. Died Apr. 26, 1932.

WELLHOUSE, Frederick, fruit grower; b. Wayne County, O., Nov. 16, 1828; ed. Ohio pub. schs.; married. Engaged in fruit culture, 1859—. Capt. Co. I, 19th Kan. Vols., 1861-65; co. commr. Leavenworth County, Kan., 1862-64 (chmn.); mem. Kan. Legislature, 1866-91; dir. Kan. State Fair Assn., 1881-93. Mem. Kan. State Hort. Soc. (treas. 1873-88, pres. 1894-1904). Died 1911.

WELLINGTON, Charles, chemist; b. Limerick, Me., May 4, 1853; s. Horace and Helen Elizabeth (Locke) W.; grad. Mass. Agr. Coll., 1873; student U. of Va., 1876-77, Leipzig, 1882-83, Berlin, 1883 (summer), Paris, 1883 (winter), Göttingen, 1883-85, Ph.D., Göttingen, 1885; m. Grace Martin Huntington, July 28, 1887. Asst. chemist U.S. Dept. Agr., 1877-82; prof. chemistry, Mass. Agr. Coll., 1885-1923. Republican. Contbr. various articles in reports, bulls. and jours., chiefly on chem. subjects. Home: Amherst, Mass. Died Nov. 15, 1926.

WELLINGTON, George Brainerd, lawyer; b. Troy, N.Y., Nov. 14, 1856; s. Charles M. and Lucy E. (King) W.; grad. Rensselaer Poly. Inst., Troy, 1875; C.E., Williams, 1876, A.M., 1876; LL.B., Albany Law Sch. (Union U.), 1878; m. Harriet Townsend, Feb. 26, 1880. Practiced in Troy, 1878—; mem. Smith, Wellington & Black, later Smith & Wellington, and Van Santvoord & Wellington, 1892-15; asst. U.S. atty., Northern Dist. of N.Y., 1887-88; corp. counsel, Troy, 1906-12; mem. State Senate, 29th Dist., 2 terms, 1914-18. Trustee Rensselaer Poly. Inst. Republican. Presbyn. Home: Troy, N.Y. Died Jan. 31, 1921.

WELLINGTON, George Louis, senator; b. Cumberland, Md., Jan. 28, 1852; s. John Adam and Margaretha B. (Mayer) W.; mainly self-ed.; m. Lina C. Lehr, Apr. 5, 1877. Went to work at 12; clerk and teller in a bank, Cumberland, 1870-82; treas. Allegheny County, Md., 1882-88, 1890; del. Rep. Nat. convs., 1884, 88; candidate for comptroller of Md., 1889; asst. treas. U.S. at Baltimore, 1890-93; mem. 54th Congress (1895-97), 6th Md. Dist.; U.S. senator, 1897-1903. Republican; disagreeing with administration's policy in regard to Philippines, supported

Bryan for president, 1900. Pres. Citizens' Nat. Bank, German Savings Bank, Cumberland Electric Ry., Edison Electric Illuminating Co., Wellington Glass Works, Potomac Glass Works, etc. Home: Cumberland, Md. Died Mar. 20, 1927.

WELLINGTON, William H., mfr.; b. Cambridge, Mass., Dec. 19, 1849; s. William W. (M.D.) and Martha B. (Carter) W.; ed. pub. schs. Cambridge; m. Florena Gray, Oct. 20, 1875; children—Stanwood Gray (dec.), Raynor Greenleaf, Anna Florena (wife of Dr. S. Burt Wolbach), William H. (dec.). Began at Boston, with N. Boynton & Co., dry goods commn., 1867, mem. of firm, 1880-1901; sr. mem. Wellington, Sears & Co., Jan. 1, 1901—; pres. Lanett Cotton Mills, Lanett, Ga., and Equinox and Gluck Mills, Anderson, S.C.; v.p. Boston Safe Deposit & Trust Co.. Sherman (Tex.) Mfg. Co., Chattahoochee Valley Ry Co.; dir. Nat. Shawmut Bank, Brookside, Gluck (Anderson, S.C.), Suncook and Warwick (R.I.) mills, Dixie Cotton Mills, Columbus (Ga.) Mfg. Co., West Point Mfg. Co., John Hancock Mut. Life Ins. Co., Hamilton Woolen Co., Lanett Bleachery & Dye Works. Home: Boston, Mass. Died Feb. 2, 1925.

WELLMAN, Guy, lawyer; b. Friendship, N.Y., Feb. 5, 1876; s. Abijah Joslyn and Kate (Miner) W.; ed. Cook Acad., Montour Falls, N.Y., 1892-95, Yale, 1895-99 (A.B.), New York Law School, 1900-03 (LL.B.); m. Agnes Lewis Daniels, Sept. 3, 1903. Admitted to N.Y. bar, 1903; in legal dept. Pittsburgh, Shawmut & Northern R.R. Co., 1903-09; clk. office of Kenefick, Cooke, Mitchell & Bass, Buffalo, 1909-15, partner, 1915; with legal dept. Standard Oil Co. (N.J.), New York, 1915-21, asso. gen. counsel, 1921-35. gen. counsel, 1935—; dir. Near East Development Corp., United Petroleum Securities Corp. Republican. Baptist. Home: Chappaqua, N.Y. Died July 26, 1941.

WELLMAN, Samuel Thomas, engr.; b. Wareham, Mass., Feb. 5, 1847; s. Samuel Knowlton and Mary Love (Bessee) W.; ed. pub. schs., Nashua, N.H., and 1 yr. Norwich (Vt.) U., C.E., 1904; m. Julia Almina Ballard, Sept. 3, 1868. Chief engr. and supt. Otis Iron & Steel Co., Cleveland, 1873-89; pres. Wellman Steel Co., 1890-95, Wellman, Seaver Engring. Co., 1896, then of Wellman, Seaver, Morgan Co., becoming chmn. Corpl. Co. F, 1st N.H. Heavy Arty., 1864-65. Pres. Am. Soc. Mech Engrs. Congregationalist. Republican. Home: Cleveland, O. Died July 11, 1919.

WELLMAN, Walter, journalist; explorer; b. Mentor, O., Nov. 3, 1858; s. Alonzo and Minerva (Graves) W.; ed. in dist. (country) sch., Mich.; at age of 14 established weekly newspaper at Sutton, Neb.; m. Laura McCann, Dec. 24, 1878. At age of 21 established Cincinnati Evening Post; polit. and Washington corr. Chicago Herald and Record-Herald, 1884-1911. In 1892 located landing place of Columbus on Watling (San Salvador) Island, Bahamas, and marked the spot with a monument; led expdn. to Arctic regions, 1894, reaching lat. 81°, northeast of Spitzbergen; led expdn. to Franz Josef Land, 1898-99, discovering many new islands and reaching lat. 82°; organized the Wellman, Chicago Record-Herald Polar expn., 1906; unsuccessfully attempted to reach the North Pole in air ship, 1909, and to cross the Atlantic Ocean, 1910. Published an exposé of Dr. Cook's claim to polar discovery, Nov. 1909. Entrusted by President Harding with an appeal to Am. press and people for nat. leadership to world peace. An expert on rapid transit progress in large cities. Author: The Aerial Age, 1911; The German Republic, 1916; The Force Supreme, 1918. Home: New York, N.Y. Died Jan. 31, 1934.

WELLS, Addison E., contractor; b. Janesville, Wis., Feb. 4, 1856; s. Warren A. and Sarah (Harris) W.; ed. pub. schs. of St. Paul, Minn., removed to Chicago at age of 15; m. Alice Conant, Janesville, 1877; children—Arthur F., Harry L., Percy A., Warren M. Immediately after the Chicago Fire started to learn trade of mason, as apprentice in firm of which father was head; became partner in father's business in 1880, under firm name of W. A. & A. E. Wells; firm inc., 1901, as Wells Bros. Co., later Wells Bros. Constrn. Co., of which became pres. Republican. Home: Hubbard Woods, Ill. Died Nov. 4, 1933.

WELLS, Almond Brown, brig. gen. U.S.A.; b. in N.Y., June 16. 1842. Commd. 1st lt. 1st Battalion, Nev. Cav., July 13, 1863; capt., May 1, 1864; hon. mustered out, Nov. 18, 1865; apptd. from Nev., 2d lt. 8th U.S. Cav., July 28, 1866; 1st lt., July 31, 1867; capt., May 23, 1870; maj. 4th Cav., July 1, 1891; transferred to 8th Cav., July 8, 1891; lt. col. 9th Cav., Feb. 14, 1899; col. 1st Cav., Feb. 2, 1901; brig. gen., Aug. 5, 1903; retired at own request, over 30 yrs.' service, Aug. 6, 1903. Home: Geneva, N.Y. Died Sept. 7, 1912.

WELLS, Amos Russel, editor; b. Glens Falls, N.Y., Dec. 23, 1862; s. Major Amos P. W. (died in Civil War) and Mary Hannah (Wells) W.; A.B., Antioch Coll., 1883, also A.M.; Litt.D., Antioch, 1912; LL D., Union Christian, 1912; m. Anna D. McNair, 1894; children—Mary Elizabeth, Margaret Anna (dec.). Prof. Greek and geology, Antioch Coll., 1883-91; editor of the Christian Endeavor World, Boston, 1891—. Author of Peloubet's Notes on the S.S. Lessons, 1901—. Mem. commn. on temperance, Federal Coun-

cil Chs. of Christ in America. Author: The Cheer Book, 1901; The Caxton Club, 1902; Rollicking Rhymes, 1902; Help for the Tempted, 1903; Grace before Meat, 1903; Into All the World, 1903; Studies in the Art of Illustration, 1903; Witchery Ways, 1904; The Young People's Pastor, 1905; Sunday School Problems, 1905; That They All May Be One, 1905; Twenty-Four Memory Hymns and Their Stories, 1906; Two Minute Talks, 1906; Tuxedo Avenue to Water Street, 1906; Donald Barton, 1906; The Teacher That Teaches, 1907; Look Alive!, 1907; The Living Bible, 1908; Caleb Cobweb's Comparisons, 1908; Bible Miniatures, 1909; Why We Believe the Bible, 1910; Everyday Poems, 1910; Sunday School Essentials, 1911; Expert Endeavor, 1911; The Junior Text-Book, 1911; The Ideal Adult Bible Class, 1912; Happiness Haven, 1912; Reaching Up and Out, 1913; Ten Don'ts for Teachers, 1913; The Arithmetic of Friendship, 1913; A Treasure of Hymns, 1914; A Successful Sunday School Superintendent, 1915; Union Work, 1916; Cyclopedia of Twentieth Century Illustrations, 1918; Collected Poems, 1921; Romance of Right Living, 1923; If I Were Young Again, 1924; Bible Snap-Shots, 1925; Progressive Endeavor, 1925. The Glorious Names of Jesus, 1926; Know Your Bible?, 1927; The Daily Digest, 1927—; Think on These Things, 1928; Go Till You Guess, 1929; Walk in His Ways, 1930; The Devotional Year-book, 1931; Bible Sayings, 1931. Home: Auburndale, Mass. Died Mar. 6, 1933.

WELLS, Arthur George, ry. official; b. Guelph, Ont., Can., Nov. 18, 1861; s. Arthur and Georgina Dora (Ridout) W.; ed. pub. schs.; m. Gertrude Alice Barnard, Oct. 15, 1884; children—Helen (Mrs. H. Norton Johnson), Louise (Mrs. R. Hunter Clarkson). Came to U.S., 1876; began as apprentice machinist, C.B. & Q. R.R., 1876; entered service A.T.&S.F. R.R., 1881, and advanced through various positions as clk., trainmaster, supt., gen. supt., gen. mgr., and vice-pres. in charge of operation, Mar. 1920—; dir. Central Republic Bank & Trust Co. Republican. Home: Chicago, Ill. Died Sept. 3, 1932.

WELLS, Benjamin Willis, author; b. Walpole, N.H., Jan. 31, 1856; s. Thomas Goodwin and Elizabeth Sewall (Willis) W.; A.B., Harvard, 1877, Ph.D., A.M., 1880; U. of Berlin, 1877-79; m. Lena Lyman, July 3, 1883. Instr. in Friends' Sch., Providence, R.I., 1882-87; prof. modern langs., U. of the South, 1891-99; on editorial staff of The Churchman, New York, 1899-1912. Author: Modern German Literature, 1895; Modern French Literature, 1897; A Century of French Fiction. Co-editor of Colonial Prose and Poetry, 1902, and editor of about 20 school texts in French and German. Contbr. many articles in revs. and jours. on lit. and economic subjects, and has collaborated in the New Internat. Ency. and Ency. Americana. Died Dec. 19, 1923.

WELLS, Brooks Hughes, physician; b. New Haven, Conn., July 28, 1859; s. Edward Livingston (D.D.) and Mary Huder (Hughes) W.; ed. schs. of Southport, Conn.; M.D., Coll. Phys. and Surg. (Columbia U.), 1884; m. Mary Frances Pomeroy, Oct. 14, 1884. Prof. gynecology, N.Y. Polyclinic, 1893—; gynecol. surgeon New York Polyclinic Hosp.; cons. surgeon Brattleboro (Vt.) Memorial Hosp.; asso. surgeon Woman's Hosp.; cons. gynecologist Beth Israel Hosp.; New York. Editor Am. Jour. of Obstetrics and Diseases of Women and Children, 1892—. Fellow Am. Gynecol. Soc., New York Acad. Medicine, New York Obstet. Soc. Died July 6, 1917.

WELLS, Bulkeley, mining engr.; b. Chicago, Ill., Mar. 10, 1872; s. Samuel Edgar and Mary Agnes (Bulkeley) W.; A.B., Harvard, 1894; m. Grace Daniels Livermore, Oct. 16, 1895; m. 2d, Mrs. Virginia Schmidt, Jan. 19, 1923. In machine shops of Amoskeag Mfg. Co., Manchester, N.H., 1894-95; with B & A. R R., 1895-96; mining business, 1896—. Identified with Smuggler Union Mining Co. and various other mining corps., Colo. Served as officer Colo. N.G. many yrs., retiring, 1917, with rank of brig. gen.; with Mil. Intelligence Sect., War Dept., Washington, World War I. Mason, Elk. Died May 1931.

WELLS, Calvin, mfr.; b. Genesee County, N.Y., Dec. 26. 1827; ed. pub. sch. and 1 1/2 yrs. in Western U.; became bookkeeper, and 1852, partner in firm of Hussey & Wells; in 1858 the firm of Hussey, Wells & Co. established as steel mfrs., of which gen mgr. until withdrew from firm, 1876; with Aaron French in manufacture of car springs, as A. French & Co., 1865-84; pres. and treas., 1870—, Ill. Zinc Co., Peru, Ill., mfrs. of spelter, sheet zinc and sulphuric acid; pres. Pittsburgh Forge & Iron Co., 1878—; bought Phila. Press, 1878. Died 1909.

WELLS, Catherine Boott (Mrs. Kate Gannett Wells), author; b. in Eng., 1838; d. Rev. Ezra Stiles Gannett; m. Samuel Wells, 1863. Mem. Mass. State Bd. Edn. Contbr. to periodicals; writer on normal methods and of Sunday school manuals of ethics. Author: In the Clearings; Miss Curtis; Two Modern Women; About People (essays); Little Dick's Son. Died 1911.

WELLS, Charles Edwin, engr.; b N. Adams, Mass., Apr. 27, 1858; s. Daniel M. and Mary M. (Sly) W.; B.S., Worcester Poly. Inst., 1880; m. Katherine Belden, Feb. 19, 1891; children—Katherine Zeruah (Mrs. Leon R. Whipple), Marcus Belden (dec.),

Sarah Frances, Margaret Adams. Asst. engr. Troy & Greenfield R.R. and Hoosac Tunnel, Mass., 1880-85, C.,B.&N. R.R., 1886; div. engr. Chicago, Santa Fé & Calif. R.R., 1887-88; locating engr. Sault Ste. Marie & Southwestern Ry., 1888; asst. engr. C.&N.W. Ry., 1889-90; engr. and supt. constrn. MacArthur Bros. Co., Chicago, 1891-93; pvt. practice, Davenport, Ia., 1894; supt. water works, Galesburg, Ill., Apr.-Aug. 1895; div. engr. Met. Water and Sewerage Bd. of Mass., 1895-1903; engr. reservoir dept., same, 1903-04; supervising engr. U.S. Reclamation Service for Southern Wyo., Neb. and S.D., 1905-07; div. engr. Bd. Water Supply City of N.Y., 1907-17. Resident engr. constrn. of U.S. Embarkation Camp, Merritt, N.J., 1917; supervising plant engr. U.S. Shipping Bd., constrn. of concrete shipyard plant, San Diego, Calif., 1918-19; cons. engr., 1919—. Home: North Adams, Mass. Died Aug. 4, 1940.

WELLS, Charles Luke, clergyman; b. Boston, June 23, 1858; s. Charles Phelps and Sarah Bowman (Tatro) W.; A.B., Harvard, 1879, Ph.D., 1893; Andover Theol. Sem., 1879-80; S.T.B., Episcopal Theol. Sch., Cambridge, Mass., 1882; studied at London, Eng., 1893-94; m. Marie Louise Goddard, Jan. 28, 1886. Deacon, June 21, 1882, priest, May 22, 1883, P.E. Ch.; rector Ch. of St. John Evangelist, Hingham, Mass., 1882-84, also Trinity Ch., Weymouth, Mass., 1883-84, Christ Ch., Gardiner, Me., 1884-88; prof. ecclesiastical history and acting warden, Seabury Div. Sch., Minn., 1888-92; prof. history, U. of Minn., 1894-99; dean Christ Ch. Cathedral, New Orleans, 1899-1909; acting prof. history, Harvard, 1909; same, McGill U., Montreal, 1909-12; rector Christ Ch., Macon, Ga., 1915-16; prof. ecclesiastical history, U. of the South, Sewanee, Tenn., 1916—, and dean Theol. Sch., 1922—; acting prof. theology and history, Boone Coll., Wuchang, China, 1925-26. Author: The Age of Charlemagne, 1896; Manual of Early Ecclesiastical History, 1912. Home: Sewanee, Tenn. Died Apr. 18, 1938.

WELLS, Daniel Halsey, actuary; b. Riverhead, N.Y., Aug. 19, 1845; s. Alden and Amanda M. (Youngs) W.; Ph.B., Sheffield Scientific Sch. (Yale), 1867, C.E., 1868; m. Martha A Breckinridge, Dec. 23, 1869; children—Clara E., Mrs. Maud Weeks, Ernest A., Ralph O., Donald B., Alden. Instr. mathematics, Sheffield Scientific Sch., 1867-74; entered employ of Conn. Mutual Life Ins. Co. as clk., Oct. 1874, 2d asst. sec., 1876, later asst. sec., sec. pro tem.; actuary of the co., 1881-1917, cons. actuary, July 1917—. Pres. Actuarial Society of America. Congregationalist. Home: Hartford, Conn. Died July 17, 1929.

WELLS, David Collin, coll. prof.; b. Fayetteville, N.Y., Sept. 23, 1858; s. Samuel James and Anna (Collin) W.; A.B., Yale, 1880; Union Theol. Sem., 1882-83; grad. Andover Theol. Sem., 1885; studied in Germany, 1886-87, m. Elizabeth Tucker, June 2, 1857. Instr. history, Phillips Acad., Andover, Mass., 1887-90; prof. history and polit. science, Bowdoin Coll., 1890-93; prof. sociology, Dartmouth, 1893—. Advisory editor Am. Jour. Sociology. Address: Hanover, N.H. Died 1911.

WELLS, David Dwight, author; b. Norwich, Conn., April 22, 1868, s. David A. Wells, political economist; grad. Harvard, 1893; m. Marrietta Ord, Oct. 15, 1896. Second sec. U.S. Embassy, London, 1894-96; contbr. to leading publications. Author: Her Ladyship's Elephant. Home: Norwich, Conn. Died 1900.

WELLS, Edgar Herbert, coll. pres.; b. Grand Forks, N.D., June 2, 1887; s. Herbert Newton and Anna Burfield (Miller) W.; grad. high sch., Grand Forks, 1904; E.M., U. of N.D., 1909; m. Lucile Cherry, Oct. 21, 1909; 1 son, Gordon Herbert. Asst. engr. Daly West Mine, Park City, Utah, 1909; mining and leasing operator, same mine and Daly Judge Mine, 1910-12; engr. and draftsman, Canadian Collieries, Ltd., Cumberland, B.C., 1912-14; instr., Tintic Mining High Sch., Eureka, Utah, 1914-16, West Side High Sch., Salt Lake City, 1916-17; engr. Austin-Dakota Mining Co., Austin, Nev., 1917; prof. geology and mineralogy, N.M. Sch. of Mines, 1917-21, also pres., 1921, geologist China Copper Co., summers, 1920-23; N.M. state geologist, 1925-27 and 1931-37; dir. N.M. State Bur. Mines and Mineral Resources, 1927—. Mason. Author of 2 bulls. of the N.M. Bur. of Mines and Min. Resources. Home: Socorro, N.M. Deceased.

WELLS, Edgar Huidekoper; univ. prof., propr. bookstore; b. Cleveland, O., June 27, 1875; s. Frank and Gertrude (Huidekoper) W.; A.B., Harvard, 1897; student Harvard Law Sch., 1897-99; unmarried. Asst. and instr. English, Harvard, 1901-05, asst. dean, 1905-07; gen. sec. Harvard Alumni Assn., 1907-13. With China Med. Bd. of Rockefeller Foundation, 1916; became connected with Am. Red Cross, 1916, dep. commr., Gt. Britain, 1917-18; commd. capt. Q.M.O.R.C., Dec. 15, 1917; assigned duty as asst. mil. attaché, Am. Embassy, London, Dec. 27, 1917; hon. discharged, Jan. 22, 1919; conducted bookstore, 1921—. Republican. Died July 2, 1938.

WELLS, Edward Hubbard, mfr.; b. Dorrville, R.I., Apr. 7, 1859; s. Solomon Perry and Elizabeth Sherman (Greene) Wells; common sch. edn.; m. Anna McGrath Mickle, Mar. 26, 1927. Became connected with Babcock & Wilcox Co., 1892, pres. 1898-1919, later chmn. bd.; also chmn. exec. com. Worthington Pump & Machinery Corp. Republican. Home: Montclair, N.J. Died Nov. 17, 1927.

WELLS, Edward P., banker, miller; b. East Troy, Wis., Nov. 9, 1847; s. Milton and Melissa (Smith) W.; ed. pub. schs., acad., and Leavenworth Inst., Wolcott, N.Y.; m. Nellie March Johnson, Mar. 8, 1871; children—Marguerite M., Stuart W., Mrs. Nora Jewett, Mrs. Florence Ireys. Began in farm mortgage bus., St. Paul, 1868; real estate, ins. and loans, Minneapolis, 1870-78; banking bus., Jamestown, N.D., 1878-98; banking and milling bus., Minneapolis, 1901—; chmn. bd. Wells & Dickey Co., Russell-Miller Milling Co., Electric Steel Elevator Co., Occident Terminal Co. (Duluth), Am. Terminal & Warehouse Co. (Buffalo). Member Dakota legislature, 1880-81; chmn. Rep. Central Com. Dak., 1882-83. Conglist. Mason. Home: Minneapolis, Minn. Died Oct. 7, 1936.

WELLS, Frank Oren, mfr.; b. Shelburne Falls, Mass., Jan. 6, 1855; s. Elisha and Lucina (Lilly) W.; ed. Petersham (Mass.) Acad.; m. Alice L. Graves, Nov. 10, 1880; 1 dau., Dorothy Virginia; m. 2d, Caroline Dutton, July 12, 1893. Began in machine shop, Greenfield, at 18, organized Wells Bros. Co., later merged with Greenfield Tap & Die Corp.; pres. Wells Bros. Co. until 1919; founder, 1924, and vice pres. Wells Tap and Die Co.; pres. Weldon Hotel Co., Green River Cemetery Co.; propr. Wells Mfg. Co. Mem. Nat. Screw Thread Commn., Franklin Co. Hosp. Assn. Republican. Conglist. Home: Greenfield, Mass. Died June 23, 1935.

WELLS, Frederic De Witt, lawyer, author; b. Brooklyn, N.Y., Mar. 25, 1874; s. Oliver J. and Margaret Frederica (Hinman) W.; A.B., Columbia, 1894, A.M., 1895; LL.B., N.Y. Law Sch., 1896; studied U. of Paris, France; m. Laura Prime Jay, Oct. 16, 1899. Practiced in New York, 1897; Rep. leader 29th Assembly Dist., 1906-08; mem. N.Y. Assembly, 1906, 07; judge Municipal Ct., New York, 1908-18; resumed practice, Jan. 1, 1918. In 1924 purchased the 47 foot ketch "Shanghai" in Denmark, and sailed across Atlantic over Viking trail via Norway, Iceland, Labrador, and Nova Scotia, 1924. Author: The Man in Court, 1917; The Last Cruise of the Shanghai, 1925. Deceased.

WELLS, George Fitch, lawyer; b. Garner, Ia., May 23, 1872; s. William Crawford and Eliza Beckwith (Fitch) W.; student Oberlin Coll. and U. of Wis.; Ph.B., U. of Chicago; LL.B., U. of Mich., 1895; LL.D., St. John's U., Toledo, O., 1910; m. Evangeline Grace Gillette, Dec. 25, 1895 (died 1921); 1 son, William Gillette; m. 2d, Margaret A. Thompson, Oct. 16, 1923. Practiced at Toledo, 1895-1912; lecturer on med. jurisprudence, Toledo Med. Coll., 1896-1912; active in founding evening law sch. at St. John's Coll., 1908, and dir. and teacher 4 yrs.; prof. law, West Va. U., 1912-14; dean Sch. of Law, U. of N. Dak., 1914-19; leave of absence as dir. procedure for War Labor Bd., Washington, D.C., 1918-19; asst. admiralty counsel, U.S. Shipping Bd., June 1919-Dec. 1922. Teacher, U. of Mich. Law Sch., summer 1917; exchange lecturer U. of N.D. to U. of Manitoba, 1917-18. Republican. Presbyn. Contbr. chapters to Modern American Law, 1915; editor chapters in Annotated U.S. Statutes, 1916. Home: Grand Forks, N.D. Died Apr. 20, 1933.

WELLS, George Washington, mfr.; b. Woodstock, Conn., Apr. 15, 1846; s. John Ward and Maria (Cheney) W.; ed. Woodstock Acad.; m. Mary E. McGregory, Sept. 27, 1869. Learned spectacle making in optical works of R. H. Cole & Co., Southbridge, 1864-67; visited Calif., 1867; with bro. Hiram, purchased a controlling interest in firm of Ammidown & Co., mfrs. of optical goods, Southbridge, 1869, and with same and R. H. Cole & Co. incorporated Am. Optical Co., pres. Am. Optical Co., Southbridge Nat. Bank, Central Mills Co.; dir. Southbridge Water Supply Co., Harrington Cutlery Co., Warren Steam Pump Co., Worcester Trust Co., Worcester Mfrs. Mut. Ins. Co., Nat. Shawmut Bank of Boston; trustee and mem. investment com. Southbridge Savings Bank. Trustee Worcester Acad., Nichols Acad., Worcester Insane Asylum. Mem. Home Market Club (3 times elected pres.). Republican. Bapt. Mason. Home: Southbridge, Mass. Died Sept. 30, 1912.

WELLS, Heber Manning, governor; b. Salt Lake City, Aug. 11, 1859; ed. there; A.B., U. of Utah, 1875; m. Emily Katz, June 5, 1901. Recorder Salt Lake City, 1882-90; mem. Bd. Pub. Works, Salt Lake City, 1890 and 1893; mem. constl. conv. which framed constitution of Utah. In Nov. 1895, elected gov. Utah for term of 5 yrs.; re-elected, Nov. 1900, for term of 4 yrs.; city commr. of Salt Lake City, 1913-17. Republican. Engaged in banking business, 1905—; asso. editor Salt Lake City Herald, 1919. Asst. treas. U.S. Shipping Bd. Merchant Fleet Corp., Washington, 1921-28, treas., 1928-33; asso. editor Deseret Evening News, Salt Lake City, 1935-36. Home: Salt Lake City, Utah. Died Mar. 12, 1938.

WELLS, Henry Parkhurst, lawyer; b. Providence, R.I., Sept. 14, 1842; s. Dr. Phineas P. and Catherine J. (French) W.; A.M., Amherst, 1863; served, 1863-65, in 13th N.Y. arty. most of time as 2d and 1st lt., in naval brigade on waters and shores of Va. and N.C. Admitted to N.Y. bar, May 12, 1869; to bar of U.S. Supreme Ct., Oct. 22, 1883; unmarried. Author: Fly Rods and Fly Tackle; The American Salmon Fisherman; City Boys in the Woods; many newspaper and mag. articles. Home: Brooklyn, N.Y. Died 1904.

WELLS, Herbert Johnson, banker; b. Wakefield, R.I., 1850; s. Thomas P. and Julia E. (Johnson) W.; ed. pvt. schs. and business coll.; m. S. Emily Perry, Oct. 10, 1877. Began in employ of Merchants Nat. Bank, Providence, R.I., dir. many yrs.; elected sec. R.I. Hosp. Trust Co., 1881, pres., 1884-1919, later chmn. bd.; dir. Gorham Mfg. Co., Title Guarantee Co. of R.I., Grosvenor Dale Co., Warren Mfg. Co., Textile Finishing Machinery Co.; dir., treas. (since orgn.) Morris Plan Co. of R.I.; dir. U.S. Finishing Co. of N.Y. Republican. Conglist. Home: Kingston, R.I. Died Oct. 27, 1933.

WELLS, Horace Lemuel, chemist; b New Britain, Conn., Oct. 5, 1855; s. Levi Sedgwick and Harriet (Francis) W.; Ph.B., Sheffield Scientific Sch. (Yale), 1877, A.M., 1896; Sc.D., U. of Pa., 1906; m. Sarah Lord Griffin, Oct. 7, 1896. Asst. prof. chemistry, 1888-93, prof. analyt. chemistry and metallurgy, 1893-1923, emeritus, 1923, Yale. Original investigations in inorganic chemistry. Mem. Nat. Acad. Sciences, Am. Chem. Soc. Author: Laboratory Guide in Qualitative Analysis; Studied from the Chemical Laboratory of the Sheffield Scientific School, 1901; Chemical Calculations, 1903; Text-book of Chemical Arithmetic, 1905. Translator: Fresenius' Qualitative Analysis. Home: New Haven, Conn. Died Dec. 19, 1924.

WELLS, Ira Kent, judge; b. Seneca, Kan., June 18, 1871; s. Abijah and Loretta C. (Williams) W.; LL.B., U. of Kan., 1893; m. Zula M. Thompson, Apr. 4, 1895; children— Loretta Wells, Mrs. Dora M. Moloney. Began practice of law with father at Seneca, 1893; served as city and county atty; del. Rep. Nat. Conv., Chicago, 1916; U.S. atty. for Puerto Rico, Sept. 21, 1921-Mar. 5, 1924; asst. atty. gen. U.S. to July 1925; U.S. dist. judge of Puerto Rico, July 1, 1925—. Maj. J. A. Gen.'s Dept., U.S.A., Dec. 2, 1917-Dec. 31, 1920; in office of Provost Marshal Gen., Washington, D.C.; judge adv. Panama Canal Dept. 27 mos., and provost marshal same dept. 18 mos. Republican. Universalist. Mason, Odd Fellow. Deceased.

WELLS, James Simpson Chester, engr.; b. Brooklyn, Sept. 13, 1851; s. James S. and Elizabeth (Walker) W.; Ph.B., Sch. of Mines (Columbia), 1875, Ph.D., 1877; m. Alice Jacobson, Feb. 1, 1883; 1 dau., Mrs. Josephine Greene. Instr. analytical chemistry, 1875-1905, adj. prof., 1905-09, Columbia; on leave of absence in the West, 1905-07, engaged in metall. work; resigned July 1, 1909, to devote entire time to mining and metall. engring. Author: Inorganic Qualitative Analysis. Contbr. on analytical and metall. chemistry to chem. and engring. jours. Joined Canadian Expeditionary Force, 1915, as capt. engrs.; transferred to field arty., 1916, and for a year in active service at the front in France, and in reserve in Eng. until 1918. Home: Dobbs Ferry, N.Y. Died Oct. 29, 1931.

WELLS, John Barnes, musician; b. Ashley, Pa., Oct. 17, 1880; s. John Calvin and Fidelia Alice (Barnes) W.; student Syracuse U., 1897-1901 (nongrad.); m. Ethel Cator Heverin, June 10, 1908; 1 dau., Dorothy Heverin. Concert and oratorio singer, teacher. Composer: (songs) If I Were You; The Dearest Place; The Owl; The Little Bird; The Lightning Bug; Why I Wish I Was a Little Rock; I Dunno; The Morning of Love; Deep in the Heart of Me; The Crow's Egg; Two Little Magpies; Thumb Marks; Whoo; The Turtle; Wishin' and Fishin'; Just Smiling; The Mystery; Cat-tails; Mr. Wells; My Lady Love; What Care I; The Silly Little Fool; and others. Died Aug. 8, 1935.

WELLS, John Daniel, journalist; b. North East, Erie County, Pa., Sept. 9, 1878; s. William Delaney and Mildred (Miller) W.; ed. pub. schs.; M.A., Syracuse, 1917; m. Neva Catherine Siggins, June 9, 1897; children—Mrs. Roswell P. Bagley, Mrs. Raymond D. Stevens, John D. Editorial work, Buffalo Courier, 1899, Buffalo Rev., 1900-02; with Buffalo News, 1902-19; mng. edit. Buffalo Evening Times, 1919-26; mng. edit. Buffalo Courier-Express, 1926—. Served infantry and cavalry enlistments, U.S.A. Republican. Methodist. Mason. Platform and lyceum lecturer. Author: Swazy Folks and Others, 1911; Old Goodbyes and Howdy-does, 1913; Your Folks and Mine, 1915; Rhymes of Our Home Folks, 1917. Lectures: Back Home Again with Me; Two Out and Bases Full; The Green Room of Journalism; Mountaineers of the Great Smokies. Home: Buffalo, N.Y. Died Apr. 2, 1932.

WELLS, John Walter, lumberman; b. nr. Davenport, Ia., Mar. 30, 1848; s. Alexander and Julia (Carter) W.; ed. pub. schs. and commercial coll.; m. Isabelle Crawford, Dec. 1873 (died 1909); m. 2d, Catherine Jamieson, Dec. 1911. Began as bookkeeper with Menominee River Boom Co., 1869, and later served in all depts. of lumbering and milling; organizer, 1882, and v.p. and gen. mgr., Girard Lumber Co.; organized, 1887, Bird & Wells Lumber Co., operators at Wausaukee, for 22 yrs.; bought interest in I. Stephenson Co., Wells, Mich., 1898; organized and built the Escanaba & Lake Superior Ry. (145 miles); bought and operated Fort River Lumber Co.; reorganized and placed these cos. under own management, selling interest in same, 1908. Built, 1893, became v.p. and gen. mgr. Dunbar & Wausaukee Ry. (55 miles), and, 1903, pres. Wis. Northwestern Ry. (40 miles); pres. White Pine Lumber Co., Wells-Lloyd Co., Northern Hardware & Supply Co. (wholesale); pres. Menominee River Sugar Co. Mayor of Menominee 3 terms. Progressive. Mason. Home: Menominee, Mich. Died Aug. 17, 1921.

WELLS, Lemuel Henry, bishop; b. Yonkers, N.Y., Dec. 3, 1841; s. Horace Demming and Mary (Barker) W.; student Trinity Coll., Conn., 1860-62, hon. A.B., 1864; lt. 32d Wis. Inf., 1862-65; A.B., Hobart Coll., 1867, A.M., 1882, D.D., 1892, D.C.L., 1914; B.D., Berkeley Divinity Sch., 1869; LL.D., Whitman Coll. (Wash.); m. Lizzie C. Folger, 1869; m. 2d, Henrietta B. Garretson, June 21, 1880; m. 3d, Jane T. S. Smith, May 30, 1914. Deacon, 1869, priest, 1871, P.E. Ch., assistant Trinity Ch., New Haven, 1869-71; rector Walla Walla, Wash., 1871-82, St. Luke's, Tacoma, 1884-89, Trinity, Tacoma, 1889-92; consecrated missionary bishop of Spokane, Dec. 16, 1892; resigned, 1913. Home: Tacoma, Wash. Died Mar. 27, 1936.

WELLS, Newton Alonzo, artist; b. Lisbon, N.Y., Apr. 9, 1852; s. Alonzo and Julia Ann (Cargin) W.; B.P. (Bachelor of Painting), Syracuse U., 1877, M.P., 1880; pupil Acad. Julien, Paris, 1886, 96; m. Flora A. Ellis, 1879. Instr. drawing and geometry, Union Coll., N.Y., 1877-79; prof. drawing, Syracuse U., 1879-89; dean Sch. of Art, Western Reserve U., 1889-90; artist, 1890-99; prof. of art, U. of Ill., 1899. Exhibited at Paris Salon and various nat. and municipal art exhbns.; mural paintings in library of U. of Ill., Sangamon County Ct. House (Springfield, Ill.), Colonial Theatre (Boston), Englewood High Sch. (Chicago); designed Soldiers' Monument, Tuscola, Ill. Republican. Congregationalist. Series of 10 hist. mural paintings in Gayoso Hotel, Memphis, Tenn. An enlisted civilian without pay in the Signal Service, U.S.A., Jan. 1918-Jan. 1919; engaged in painting and installing mil. maps for use in aviation schs. Pres. Encaustic Mosaic Co. Home: Wilmette, Ill. Deceased.

WELLS, Philip Patterson, lawyer; b. Grand Rapids, Mich., Feb. 5, 1868; s. Lewis Gray and Mary Ellen (Wetmore) W.; B.A., Yale, 1889; Grad. Sch. Yale (economics and history), 1889-91, Ph.D., 1900; Yale Law Sch., 1891-92; Law Sch., Columbian (now George Washington) U., 1892-93; m. Eleanor Duncan Munger, May 22, 1893; children—Lewis Gray, Elizabeth. Admitted to Conn. bar, 1893; librarian Yale Law Sch., 1896-1906; instr. evidence, Yale Law Sch., 1898-99; lecturer in history, Yale U., 1902-06; expert (law) in U.S. Forest Service, 1906-07, and chief law officer, 1907-10; chief law officer, U.S. Reclamation Service, May 1, 1911-Mar. 31, 1913; counsel Nat. Conservation Assn. Dep. atty. gen. Pa., 1923-27; mem. Pa. Giant Power Survey Bd., 1923-25; chmn. Pa. Giant Power Bd., 1925-26; commr. of Pa. to negotiate Tri-State Compact for control of Del. River, 1923-27; mem. Am. Polit. Science Assn. Author of papers and addresses on conservation of natural resources and on legal and bibliographical subjects in encys. periodicals; Proposals for Legislation, in Pa. Giant Power Report, 1925. Joint author: Annotated Titles of Books on English and American History, 1903. Editor: Literature of American History, Supplement, 1900-04; Colonies of the World, by E. J. Paine (revised and in part rewritten), 1907; South America, by Alfred Deberle (transl. from the French and edited), 1907; joint editor Young Folks' Library, 1903; A.L.A. Catalog, 1904; joint editor and reporter sundry law reports. Home: Middletown, Conn. Deceased.

WELLS, Webster, univ. prof.; b. Boston, Mass., Sept. 4, 1851; s. Thomas F. and Sarah M. W.; B.S., Mass. Inst. Tech., 1873; studied civil engring.; m. Emily W. Langdon, June 21, 1876. Instr. mathematics, 1873-80 and 1882-83, asst. prof., 1883-85, asso. prof., 1885-93, prof., 1893-1911, Mass. Inst. Tech.; retired in 1911. Author: Elementary Treatise on Logarithms; University Algebra; Plane and Spherical Trigonometry; Academic Algebra; Elements of Geometry; Higher Algebra; Essentials of Trigonometry; Four Place Tables; College Algebra; Academic Arithmetic; Revised Plane and Spherical Trigonometry; Six Place Tables; Essentials of Algebra; Essentials of Plane and Solid Geometry; New Higher Algebra; Complete Trigonometry; New Four Place Tables; Advanced Course in Algebra, 1904; Algebra for Secondary Schools, 1906; Text-Book in Algebra, 1906. Died May 23, 1916.

WELLS, William Charles, statistician; b. Suffolk, Va., Aug. 25, 1860; s. Reaves Chappel and Julia (Wellons) W.; ed. various schs. and acads.; LL.B., Washington and Lee U., 1878; studied Johns Hopkins; m. Cora Belle Lucas, July 2, 1895. Practiced law, 1881-1905, in Baltimore, Salt Lake City and Washington, meanwhile doing editorial work for law pub. houses and acting as advisory counsel for commercial assns. on foreign trade and tariff matters. Chief clk. and editor, 1905, chief statistician and tariff expert, 1908-23, consultant in juristic matters, 1923—, Pan-Am. Union. Home: Beltsville, Md. Deceased.

WELLS, William Edwin, mfg. potter; b. Brooke County, W.Va., Dec. 29, 1863; s. Lewis and Rose Ann (McCord) W.; ed. high sch., Steubenville, O.; m. Elizabeth Mahan, June 27, 1888; children—Joseph Mahan, William Edwin, Arthur Atkinson. Began in pottery business with Homer Laughlin, East Liverpool, O., 1889; with Homer Laughlin China Co., Newell, W.Va., 1897—, as sec., treas. and gen. mgr.; pres. Potters Nat. Bank, East Liverpool; dir. Newell Bridge & Ry. Co., Newell Water & Power Co., Potters Mining & Milling Co. Mem. Va.-W.Va. Debt Commn., 1912. Republican. Presbyn. Mason, Elk. Home: Newell, W.Va. Died Sept. 18, 1931.

WELLS, William Hughes, physician; b. West Phila., Pa., Sept. 25, 1859; s. Hughes and Letitia S. W.; ed. pub. schs. and pvt. tutors; M.D., Jefferson Med. Coll., 1891; m. Mary Anderson, Apr. 14, 1898. Asst. prof. obstetrics, Jefferson Med. Coll., 1913—; asst. obstetrician, Jefferson Med. Coll. Hosp.; physician to Willing's Day Nursery, Phila. Fellow Coll. Physicians Phila. Author: Compend of Gynecology, 1896; Taylor and Wells' Manual Diseases of Children (with Dr. J. Madison Taylor), 1898; McKee and Wells' Text-Book of Diseases of Children, 1913. Editor: Landis' Compend of Obstetrics, 1894. Contributor to med. press. Died Feb. 24, 1919.

WELLSTOOD, William, engraver, publisher; b. Edinburg, Scotland, Dec. 19, 1819; came to U.S. with parents, 1830; common sch. edn.; m. Alice Spence, Feb. 14, 1855. At age of 16 began to work as letter engraver, afterward confining his attention to pictures, particularly landscapes and portraits. Home: Brooklyn, N.Y. Died 1900.

WELSH, Charles, author, editor; b. Ramsgate, Kent, Eng., Dec. 22, 1850; s. Charles and Susannah W.; ed. nat. schools, Ashford, Kent, Eng.; took first-class certificates at Soc. of Arts; exams. in connection with the Mechanics' Inst.; m. Marie Josephine Logè, 1884 (died 1908); m. 2d, Besse Denham, 1910; went to London, 1868, became reporter The British Trade Journal; became employe, 1870, Henry S. King & Co., and, 1877, Griffith, Farran Co., pubs., and in 1884 partner in latter house; came to U.S. in 1895 and was business mgr. and asst. editor of The Art Amateur; authority on domestic science and juvenile literature; lecturer and reader on that and other lit. subjects. Prin. Sch. of Domestic Science, Internat. Corr. Schs., Mar. 1909-12; editor World Book Co., Yonkers, N.Y., 1912—. Author: Publishing a Book, 1900; A Bookseller of the Last Century, 1885; Automobilia, 1905; Love's Garland, 1905. Compiler and Editor: The Uncle Charlie Series of Pleasure Books for the Young; The Young Folks Library (with T. B. Aldrich), 20 vols., 1901; The Right Reading for Children, 1902; Heath's Home and School Classics (50 vols.), 1900-03; Many Facsimile Reprints of Popular Children's Books of the Olden Time; Talks About Science (by Thomas Dunman); Irish Literature (with Justin McCarthy), 10 vols., 1904; Famous Battles of the XIXth Century, 4 vols., 1903-05; The Letters of Lord Chesterfield to His Son and Godson, 1904; The Life and Nature Series, 1905; A Tale of Two Terriers, 1905; Neddy, The Autobiography of a Donkey, 1905; Catalogue of English and American Chap Books in Harvard College Library, etc. (with W. C. Lane and C. B. Tillinghast), 1905; Self Culture for Young People (with Dr. A. Sloan Draper), 10 vols., 1906-07; The Golden Treasury of Irish Songs and Lyrics, 2 vols., 1907; Character Sketches from Dickens, 1907; The Works of Henry W. Longfellow (10 vols.), 1909; Stories Children Love, 1909; Fairy Tales Children Love, 1910; The Oriental Series, Vols. 13-24, 1910; Stories of the World's Great Books, Great Plays, and Great Men and Women, 1911; Stories of Adventure Children Love, 1912; Stories of Americans Children Love, 1913. Contbr. to leading mags. on history of literature for children, and other lit. and ednl. topics. Died Sept. 12, 1914.

WELSH, Herbert, publicist, artist; b. Phila., Pa., Dec. 4, 1851; s. John and Mary W.; A.B., U. of Pa., 1871; LL.D., Washington and Lee U.; studied art in Phila., and 1873-74, in atelier of Bonnât, Paris; m. Fanny Frazer, April 1873. An organizer, 1882, and for 34 yrs. corr. sec. Indian Rights Assn., pres. 11 years, and later pres. emeritus. A leader in revolt against "boss rule" in Pa., 1890, which resulted in defeat of Delamater and election of Pattison as gov. Pres. of the Fellowship of the Pa. Acad. of Fine Arts, 3 years; mem. com. Nat. Civil Service Reform League; editor and pub. City and State, weekly, 1895-1904; lecturer and contbr. to mags. on the Indian question, civ. service reform, municipal govt., etc. Advocate of peaceable adjustment of all internat. disputes by arbitration, and ultimate universal peace policy; earnest opponent of the acquisition of the Philippine Islands by force, and prominent in movement to expose torture and other delinquencies of army there. Organized the movement which resulted in preservation, by purchase, of forests on Sunapee Mountain, N.H., made into a public park. Author: Civilization Among the Sioux Indians; Four Weeks Among Some of the Sioux Tribes; A Visit to the Navajo, Pueblo and Hualpais Indians; The Other Man's Country; The New Gentleman of the Road. Home: Riverton, Vt. Died June 28, 1941.

WELTMER, Sidney Abram, mental scientist; b. Wooster, O., July 7, 1858; s. Abraham and Catharine (Hull) W.; removed to Mo. at 7 yrs. of age; principally self-ed.; studied medicine 4 yrs. under Dr. J. W. Brent, of Tipton, Mo.; m. Mary Genoa Stone, Oct. 8, 1879. Licensed to preach in Bapt. Ch. at 19 but soon gave up ministry; taught sch. in Mo. until 1896; founded, and pres., Akinsville (Mo.) Normal Sch., 1885-89; organized Sedalia Pub. Library, and librarian, 1893-95; made extensive experiments in hypnotic phenomena, leading to study of suggestion in cure of disease; founded Weltmer Inst., Nevada, Mo., 1896, which became Weltmer Inst. of Suggestive Therapeutics Co. (Inc.), of which pres.; pres. (life) Weltmer Foundation. Mason, Elk, Odd Fellow. Author: Regeneration, 1898; Self Protection, 1898; Real Man, 1901; New Voice of Christianity, 1902; Hypnotism, 1908; Therapeutic Suggestion, 1908; also Suggestion Simplified; Intuition; Is Prayer Ever Answered? Who Is a Christian? Eternal Now; The Undying Character of Thought; Mystery Revealed; Self-Reliance; Telepathy; Complete Clinical Texts on Suggestive Therapeutics and Applied Psychology, 1908; Day Dreams, 1916; The Healing Hand, 1918; etc. Home: Nevada, Mo. Died Dec. 5, 1930.

WEMPLE, William Yates, insurance; b. Port Richmond, Staten Island, N.Y., Nov. 28, 1859; s. William Russ and Mary Elizabeth (Edwards) W.; ed. pub. schs.; m. Caroline Jewett Hicks, Oct. 8, 1891; children—Dorothy (Mrs. Herbert T. Magruder), Elizabeth (Mrs. Alfred T. Pouch), Caroline G. Began in hardware business, N.Y. City, 1878; successively with Frank & DuBois, Clinton Fire Ins. Co., German-Am. Ins. Co., until 1893; clk. Albert Wilcox & Co., 1893-1906, jr. partner, 1906-13; sec.-treas. Meinel & Wemple, Inc., U.S. mgrs. Reinsurance Co., Salamandra Ins. Cos., Petrograd and Denmark, 1913-21, pres., 1921—. Trustee Staten Island Hosp., S.I. Acad. Mem. Staten Island Arts and Science Soc., Richmond County Soc. for Prevention of Cruelty to Children (treas.), Staten Island Social Service Soc. (dir.). Republican. Episcopalian. Home: Staten Island, N.Y. Died May 9, 1933.

WENCKEBACH, Carla, educator, author; b. Hildesheim, Germany, Feb. 14, 1853; d. Carl Georg Christian and Marie Sophia Dorothea (Arends) Wenckebach; attended Girls' High Sch., Hildesheim; Normal Sch., Hanover; studied at Zurich and Leipzig univs.; taught in England, Russia, Belgium, New York; instr. in German, Wellesley, 1883-85; prof. of German, Wellesley Coll., 1895—. Author: Deutsche Grammatik (with Josepha Schrakamp), 1884; Deutscher Anschauungs-Unterricht (with sister, late Helen W.), 1886; Deutsches Lesebuch (with sister), 1887; Deutsche Literaturgeschichte, 1890; Deutsche Sprachlehre, 1896; German Composition, 1899. Edited, with notes: Die schönsten deutschen Lieder (with sister), 1885; Meissner's Aus meiner Welt, 1889; Die Meisterwerke des Mittelalters, 1893; Scheffel's Ekkehard, 1893; Scheffel's Trompeter von Säkkingen, 1895; Dahn's Ein Kampt um Rom, 1900; Schiller's Maria Stuart (with Margarethe Müller), 1900. Died 1902.

WENDE, Ernest, physician; b. Mill Grove, N.Y., July 23, 1853; s. Bernard A. and Susan (Kirk) W.; M.D., U. of Buffalo, 1878; spl. course, Columbia, 1881-82; M.D., U. of Pa., 1884, B.S., 1885; spl. course Berlin, Vienna, 1885-86; m. Frances Harriett Cutler, Aug. 25, 1881. Prof. dermatology, Med. Dept., U. of Buffalo, 1889—; prof. botany and microscopy, Coll. of Pharmacy, same, 1890—; health commr. of Buffalo, 1891-1901 and 1906—. Fellow Am. Electro-Therapeutic Assn. (pres. 1901). Supreme pres. Order of the Iroquois. Home: Buffalo, N.Y. Died Feb. 11, 1910.

WENDELL, Barrett, univ. prof.; b. Boston, Aug. 23, 1855; s. Jacob and Mary Bertoldi (Barrett) W.; A.B., Harvard, 1877; Litt.D., Columbia, 1913, Harvard, 1918; m. Edith Greenough, June 1, 1880. Engaged in teaching at Harvard from Oct. 1880, instr. English, 1880-88, asst. prof., 1888-98, prof., 1898-1917, prof. emeritus, 1917. Lecturer at Sorbonne and other French univs., 1904-05. Mem. Nat. Inst. Arts and Letters, Am. Acad. Arts and Letters; fellow Am. Academy Arts and Sciences. Author: The Duchess Emilia (novel), 1885; Rankell's Remains (novel), 1887; English Composition, 1891; Cotton Mather, 1891; Stelligeri and Other Essays Concerning America, 1893; William Shakespeare, a Study in Elizabethan Literature, 1894; A Literary History of America, 1900; Raleigh in Guiana, Rosamond, and a Christmas Masque, 1902; The Temper of the Seventeenth Century in English Literature (Clark lectures given at Trinity Coll., Cambridge, Eng., 1902-03), 1904; History of Literature in America (with Chester N. Greenough), 1904; Liberty, Union, and Democracy—the National Ideals of America, 1906; The France of Today, 1907; The Privileged Classes, 1908; The Mystery of Education, 1909. Home: Boston, Mass. Died Feb. 8, 1921.

WENDELL, Edith Greenough; b. Swampscott, Mass., Aug. 2, 1859; d. William Whitwell and Catharine Scollay (Curtis) Greenough; ed. pvt. schs., Boston; m. Prof. Barrett Wendell, June 1, 1880; children—

Barrett, Mary, William Greenough, Edith. Commr. from Mass. to Jamestown Expn., 1907. Pres. Mass. Spl. Aid Soc. for Am. Preparedness, 1915, 16, 17; chmn. Liberty Loan Com. for Mass.; v.p. Nat. Allied Relief Com.; mem. Massachusetts Anti-Suffrage Soc., Woman's Division for Mass. of Nat. Civic Fedn.; pres. Mass. Society Colonial Dames of America, 1903-23; sec. Nat. Soc. Colonial Dames, 1919-25; v.p. Nat. Girl Scouts. Mem. Unemployment Campaign, Boston, for $3,000,000, 1932, also of Job Finding Com., 1932, and head of Women's div. of Emergency Campaign for $5,000,000, 1932-33; hon. chmn. Warner House Assn., Portsmouth. Gold medal, Jamestown Expn. Republican. Episcopalian. Home: Boston, Mass. Died Oct. 1938.

WENDELL, George Vincent, prof. physics; b. Plainfield, N.J., Aug. 16, 1871; s. George W. and Mary E. (Frazee) W.; S.B., Mass. Inst. Tech., 1892; A.M. and Ph.D., U. of Leipzig, 1898; U. of Berlin, 1898-99; m. Mary P. Hitchcock, July 29, 1902. Asst. in physics, 1892-93, instr., 1893-1901, asst. prof., 1901-04, asso. prof., 1904-07, Mass. Inst. Tech.; prof. physics and head of dept., Stevens Inst. Tech., 1907-10; prof. physics, Columbia, July 1, 1910—. Established dept. of physics, Simmons Coll., Boston, 1902, and at Boston U., 1906. Home: New York, N.Y. Died Mar. 15, 1922.

WENDELL, Oliver Clinton, astronomer; b. Dover, N.H., May 7, 1845; s. Oliver Ellsworth and Vienna (Willey) W.; grad. Dover High Sch., 1862, Franklin Acad., 1864; A.B., Bates Coll., 1868, A.M., 1871, D.Sc., 1907; m. Sarah Butler, July 11, 1870. Asst. in Harvard Obs., 1868-69; civ. and hydraulic engr., 1869-79; asst. in Harvard Obs., 1879-98, asst. prof., 1898—. Fellow Am. Acad. Arts and Sciences, A.A.A.S. Republican. Author of observations and reductions in various vols. Obs. Annals; also calculator of many orbits and ephemerides, and writer of papers of scientific, prose and poetic character. Home: Cambridge, Mass. Died Nov. 6, 1912.

WENDLING, George Reuben, lecturer; b. Shelbyville, Ill., Jan. 15, 1845; s. George and Frances (Wright) W.; student Miami U., Oxford, O., 1861-63; acad. and law depts. U. of Chicago, 1863-66; LL.D., Miami, 1909. Admitted to Ill. bar, 1867; edited Central Illinois Times, Shelbyville, 1867; city atty., Shelbyville, 1 term; mem. Ill. Constl. Conv., 1869; practiced law, 1867-80; lecturing on popular subjects, 1880—. Author: Wendling's Index to Illinois Reports, 1874; Ingersollism—from a Secular Standpoint, 1883; The Man of Galilee, 1907. Died Sept. 14, 1915.

WENDTE, Charles William, clergyman; b. Boston, June 11, 1844; s. Charles and Johanna (Ebeling) W.; ed. Chauncy Hall Sch., Boston; studied 1 yr in Hanover, Germany; grad. Harvard Divinity Sch., 1869; D.D., U. of Geneva, Switzerland, 1909; m. Abbie L. Grant, Apr. 28, 1896. In commercial business, Boston and San Francisco, 1858-66; instr. German, Harvard, 1868-69; ordained Unitarian ministry, 1869; pastor, Chicago, 1869-75, Cincinnati, O., 1875-82, Newport, R.I., 1882-85, Oakland, Calif., 1886-98, Newton Center, Mass., 1899-1901, Boston, 1901-05, Brighton, Mass., 1905-08. V.p. Internat. Congress of Free Christians and other Religious Liberals, 1900—. Foreign sec. Am. Unitarian Assn., 1908-15; hon. pres. Fedn. of Religious Liberals, 1909—; pres. Free Religious Assn. of America; pres. Unitarian Ministerial Union, 1915. Author: Memoir of Rev. Charles T. Brooks, 1885; The Student's Diary, 1888; The Sunnyside, 1876; The Carol, 1885; Jubilate Deo, 1900; Freedom and Fellowship, 1907; Heart and Voice, 1909; The Unity of the Spirit, 1909; Unity Through Freedom, 1911; At Christmas Time, 1917; Life and Letters of Thomas Starr King, 1920; The Wider Fellowship, Memories, Friendships, and Endeavors, 1927. Home: Berkeley, Calif. Died Sept. 9, 1931.

WENLEY, Robert Mark, univ. prof.; b. Edinburgh, Scotland, July 19, 1861; s. James Adams and Jemima Isabella (Veitch) W.; A.M., (first class in philosophy) U. of Glasgow, 1884, fellow in philosophy, 1884, 88, D.Phil., 1895, Sc.D., U. of Edinburgh, 1891; studied in Paris, Rome, Germany; LL.D., Glasgow, 1901, Queen's, 1919; L.H.D., Hobart, 1908; D.C.L., U. of the South, 1914; m. Catherine Dickson, d. Archibald Gibson, Apr. 1889; children—Margaret, James Mark (dec.), Catherine Dickson and Jemima Veitch (twins), Archibald Gibson. Asst. prof. logic, Glasgow, 1886-94; in charge philos. dept. Queen Margaret Coll., same, 1888-95; prof. philosophy and head of dept., 1896—, U. of Mich.; dir. Brit. div. Am. Univ. Union, 1925-27. Fellow Royal Society (Edinburgh), A.A.A.S. Baldwin lecturer, 1908-09. Author: Socrates and Christ, 1889; Aspects of Pessimism, 1894; University Extension Movement in Scotland, 1895; Contemporary Theology and Theism, 1897; Introduction to Kant, 1897; Preparation for Christianity in the Ancient World, 1898; Modern Thought and the Crisis in Belief (Baldwin Lectures), 1909; Kant and His Philosophical Revolution, 1910; The Anarchist Ideal, 1913; Life of Robert Flint (with Dr Macmillan), 1914; Life and Work of G. S. Morris, 1917; Stoicism and Its Influence, 1924; The Poetry of John Davidson, 1924. Asso. editor Dictionary of Philosophy and Ency. of Religion and Ethics. Home: Ann Arbor, Mich. Died Mar. 29, 1929.

WENNER, George Unangst, clergyman; b. Bethlehem, Pa., May 17, 1844; s. George and Sarah Ann (Unangst) W.; student Pa. Coll., Gettysburg, 1860-61; A.B., Yale U., 1865, A.M., 1868; grad. Union Theol. Sem., 1868; D.D., Pa. Coll., 1888; L.H.D. Susquehanna, 1917; LL.D., Gettysburg, 1921; m. Rebecca Pullman, Apr. 14, 1880 (died 1902); m. 2d, Mary Wilson Marshall, Feb. 8, 1915 (dec.). Ordained Lutheran ministry, 1868; founded, 1868, and pastor Christ Ch., New York. Chmn. liturgical com. Gen. Synod Luth. Church, 1883-1915; chmn., 1885-99, deaconess com. and pres. deaconess bd. of Gen. Synod; pres. Synod of N.Y. and N.J., 1904-08, Synod of N.Y., 1908-10. Sec. Evangelical Alliance; pres. Luth. Hosp. of Manhattan. Independent Republican. Author: Religious Education and the Public School, 1907; The Lutherans of New York, 1918. Contbr. on liturg. and ednl. subjects. Died Nov. 1, 1934.

WENNINGER, Francis Joseph, coll. dean; b. Pamhagen, Austria, Oct. 27, 1888; s. Francis and Magdalen (Muth) W.; brought by parents to U.S., 1889; Litt.B., Notre Dame, 1911, M.Sc., 1917; S.T.B., Catholic U. America, 1916; Ph.D., U. of Vienna, 1929. Joined Congregation of the Holy Cross, 1911; ordained priest R.C. Ch., 1916. Instr. in zoölogy, Notre Dame, 1916-20, prof. zoölogy, 1920—, dean of Coll. of Science, 1923—. Contbr. articles and reviews to Am. Midland Naturalist, Biol. Abstracts. Died Feb. 12, 1940.

WENTWORTH, Cecile De, artist; b. New York; pupil of Alexander Cabanel and Edward Detaille, Paris. Exhibiting every year in the Paris Salon, 1889—; medals, Paris, Lyons, Turin, and 1st gold medal at the Nat. Exhbn., Tours; exhibited at the Paris Expn., 1900, received medal on portrait of Pope Leo XIII; represented at Musee du Luxembourg, Paris, Vatican Musee, Rome, Senate Chamber, Paris, Met. Mus., New York and Corcoran Gallery, Washington, etc.; made portraits of Theodore Roosevelt, William H. Taft, Archbishop Corrigan; Queen Alexandra and many notable people in Europe. Officier d'Académie, Paris, 1894; Officier de l'Instruction Publique; Chevalier Légion d'Honneur, 1901; decorated Grand Comdr. Order of Holy Sepulchre, by Pope Leo XIII; Officier Ordre du Nichau Tftikar, by Mohammed EuNacer Bacha-Bey. Died Aug. 28, 1933.

WENTWORTH, George Albert, mathematician, author; b. Wakefield, N.H., July 31, 1835; s. Edmund and Eliza (Lang) W.; prep. Phillips Exeter Acad.; grad. Harvard, 1858; m. Emily J. Hatch, Aug. 8, 1864. Prof. mathematics, Phillips Exeter Acad., 1858-91. Author: Wentworth Series of Mathematical Works (about 40 works on arithmetic, algebra, geometry, trigonometry); also (with G. A. Hill) of Wentworth & Hill Series of exercise books in algebra, arithmetic and geometry; also physics. Died 1906.

WENTZ, Daniel Bertsch, Jr., coal operator; b. Big Stone Gap, Va., June 10, 1903; s. Daniel Bertsch and Louise (Finlay) W.; student Fay Sch. (Southborough, Mass.), St. Paul's Sch. (Concord), Harvard; m. Elizabeth Sewell, Oct. 1, 1927. Pres. Virginia-Kentucky Coal Corp.; v.p. Gen. Coal Co., Stonega Coke & Coal Co., Va. Coal & Iron Co., Wentz Corp., Westmoreland Coal Co., Westmoreland, Inc.; dir. Admiralty Coal Corp., Crab Orchard Improvement Co., Wentz Co., Whitehall Cement Mfg. Co. Trustee Abington (Pa.) Memorial Hosp. Republican. Episcopalian. Home: Pineville, Pa. Died Mar. 9, 1940.

WENZELL, Albert Beck, illustrator; b. Detroit, Mich., 1864; common school edn. and early training in art in Detroit; continued art studies at Munich; later took an extended course at Paris; returned to New York in 1890 and began work as an illustrator; regularly employed on leading eastern mags. Silver medal, Pan-Am. Expn., Buffalo, 1901; silver medal, La. Purchase Expn., 1904. Home: Brooklyn, N.Y. Died Mar. 4, 1917.

WERDER, Xavier Oswald, gynecologist; b. Cham, Canton Zug, Switzerland, Dec. 4, 1857; s. Oswald and Barbara W.; M.D., Univ. Med. Coll. (New York U.), 1879; m. Tillie C. Vogel, Oct. 20, 1886. Practiced in Pittsburgh, 1879—; prof. gynecology, Western Pa. Med. Coll., 1894-1917; same U. of Pittsburgh Med. Dept., 1889—; gynecologist, Mercy Hosp. Fellow Am. Coll. Surgeons, A.M.A. Roman Catholic. Home: Pittsburgh, Pa. Died Nov. 20, 1919.

WERNER, Adolph, professor German; b. at Frankfort-on-the-Main, Germany, Jan. 5, 1839; s. Edward and Rosalie (Schlesinger) W.; came to America, 1850; B.S., Free Acad. (now Coll. City of New York), 1857, M.S., 1860; Ph.D., Rutgers Female Coll., 1880; unmarried. Tutor, 1857-61, prof. German, 1861-1915, Coll. City of New York. Retired, Feb. 1, 1915. Home: New York, N.Y. Died Aug. 26, 1919.

WERNER, William E., judge; b. Buffalo, N.Y., Apr. 19, 1855; s. William and Magdalena W.; pub. sch. edn. Buffalo; m. Lillie Boller, Mar. 7, 1889. Admitted to bar, 1880, and practiced at Rochester. Clerk Municipal Ct., Rochester, N.Y., 1879; spl. county judge, 1884-89; county judge, 1889-94; justice Supreme Ct. of N.Y., 1895-1900; judge Ct. of Appeals of N.Y., 1900-18. Republican. Home: Rochester, New York. Died Mar. 1, 1916.

WERTENBAKER, Charles Poindexter, U.S. public health service; b. Charlottesville, Va., Apr. 1, 1860; s. Charles Christian and Mary Ella (Poindexter) W.; M.D., U. of Va., 1882; post-grad. courses in New York med. schs.; m. Alice DeLancey Girardeau, Apr. 30, 1895. Physician on staff N.Y. City Lunatic Asylum, 1884-85, State Asylum for Insane, Morristown, N.J., 1885-87; entered U.S. Marine Hosp. Service as asst. surgeon, Aug. 18, 1888; promoted passed asst. surgeon, Sept. 2, 1892; surgeon, Feb. 16, 1904; retired from active service, Dec. 31, 1915. In comd. stas. at Galveston, Delaware Breakwater Quarantine, Norfolk, etc.; sanitarian, sociologist and epidemiologist. Dir. Va. Anti-Tuberculosis Assn.; pres. Assn. Mil. Surgeons of U.S., 1911-12. Mason. Author numerous monographs chiefly along sanitary and pub. health lines. Died 1916.

WERTS, George Theodore, lawyer; b. Hackettstown, N.J., March 24, 1846; ed. in high sch., Bordentown, and State Model Sch., Trenton; admitted to bar, 1867, locating in Morristown; recorder, Morristown, 1883-85; mayor, 1886-92; served 6 yrs. in N.J. State senate; pres. of senate; justice Supreme Ct., 1892-93; gov., 1893-96. Democrat. Died 1910.

WERTZ, George M., congressman; b. nr. Johnstown, Pa., 1856; ed. Ebensburg (Pa.) Acad. and Nat. Normal U., Lebanon, O. Served as county commr., sheriff and county comptroller, Cambria County, Pa.; mem. Pa. Senate, 1909 (pres. pro tempore 1911); mem. 68th Congress (1923-25), 20th Pa. District. Republican. Home: Johnstown, Pa. Died Nov. 19, 1928.

WESBROOK, Frank Fairchild, univ. pres.; b. Brant County, Ont., July 12, 1868; s. Henry Shaver and Helen Marr (Fairchild) W.; B.A., U. of Manitoba, 1887, M.A., M.D., C.M., 1890; McGill Coll. Med. Sch., Montreal, 1889; U. of Cambridge, Eng. (pathol. and physiol. labs.), 1892-95, King's Coll. and St. Bartholomew's hosps., London, Rotunda Hosp., Dublin, Hygienisches und Pathologisches Instituts, Marburg, Germany; LL.D., U. of Manitoba, and U. of Toronto, 1913, and U. of Alberta, 1915; m. Annie, d. Sir Thomas W. Taylor, chief justice of Manitoba, Apr. 8, 1896. Prof. pathology, U. of Man.; prof. pathology and bacteriology, 1895-1913, dean, 1906-13, Med. Sch. of U. of Minn.; pres. U. of British Columbia, 1913—. Dir. labs., 1896-1911, and mem. Minn. State Bd. of Health, 1896-1900 and 1911-12; mem. advisory bd. Hygienic Lab. U.S. Pub. Health Service, 1904-13. Pres. Am. Pub. Health Assn., 1905; fellow A.A.A.S.; pres. sect. on state and municipal hygiene Internat. Congress Hygiene and Demography, 1912; mem. Internat. Anti-Tuberculosis Assn.; fellow Royal Sanitary Inst. Chmn. Provincial Com. on Food Resources. Presbyn. Address: Vancouver, B.C. Died Oct. 20, 1918.

WESCOTT, John Wesley, lawyer; b. Waterford, N.J., Feb. 20, 1849; s. John and Katherine Van Overterfer (Bozarth) W.; A.B., Yale, 1872, LL.B., 1876; m. Frances Marie Louise Leclerc Pryor, Jan. 1, 1875. Admitted to N.J. bar, 1878, Pa. bar, 1890, and practiced in Camden, N.J., and Phila., Pa.; mem. Wescott & Weaver, Camden; sr. mem. Wescott, Wescott & McManus, Phila. Judge Camden County Ct. of Common Pleas, 1884-87; Dem. presdl. elector, 1892; as pres. of N.J. delegation at Dem. Nat. Conv., Baltimore, 1912, delivered address nominating Woodrow Wilson as candidate for Pres. of U.S., also nominated him for 2d term, at St. Louis; atty. gen. of N.J., term 1914-19. Trustee N.J. State Sch. Fund, Woman's Coll. of N.J. Mem. Am. Bar Assn., N.J. Bar Assn. (pres. 1913-14), Am. Acad. Polit. and Social Science. Mason. Methodist. Rowed in 1st 8-oared crew at Yale, 1876; one of founders of modern baseball. Prominent worker in Liberty Loan campaigns. Home: Haddonfield, N.J. Died June 11, 1927.

WESEEN, Maurice Harley, author; b. Oakland, Neb., Dec. 15, 1890; s. Gust and Mary (Peterson) W.; A.B., U. of Neb., 1914, A.M., 1917; unmarried. Instr. English, Ia. State Coll., 1914-18; asst. prof. of English, 1918-26, asso. prof., 1926—, U. of Neb.; specialized in bus. English and correspondence. Extension lecturer, including radio courses. Author: English, Science and Engineering, 1918; Everyday Uses of English, 1922; How to Apply for a Position, 1927; Dictionary of English Grammar, 1928; Words Confused and Misused, 1932; Write Better Business Letters, 1933; Dictionary of American Slang, 1934. Contbr. to mags. Home: Lincoln, Neb. Died Apr. 14, 1941.

WESLEY, Charles Sumner, lawyer; b. Phila., Pa., Feb. 23, 1878; s. John S. and Sarah J. (Wright) W.; B.S. in Economics, U. of Pa., 1899, LL.B., 1902; m. Laura Clark, Apr. 6, 1904; children—Eleanor Clark (Mrs. Latimer S. Stewart), Margaret Clark, Clark. Admitted to Pa. bar, 1902, and in gen. law practice in Phila., 1902—; mem. firm Tustin & Wesley, 1902—; advisor to Govt. in Selective Draft, 1917; counsel to banking dept., U.S. Dept. of Justice in matters relative to closed banks, 1933—; pres. Bellefonte Central Railroad Co., Globe & Republic Ins. Co.; also officer or dir. numerous corps. Dir.

Glen Mills Schs. for Boys, Sleighton Farms Sch. for Girls, Big Brother Assn. Mem. Am. Bar Assn., Am. Soc. Internat. Law, Am. Acad. Polit. and Social Science. Republican. Episcopalian. Died Oct. 29, 1939.

WESSELHOEFT, Conrad, physician; b. in Germany, 1834; s. Robert and Ferdinanda Emilia W.; grad. M.D., Harvard Med. Sch., 1856; m. Elizabeth Foster Pope. Prof. pathology and therapeutics Boston Univ. Sch. of Medicine; practiced in Boston. Translator Hahnemann's Organon; also extensive contbr. to homœpathic jours. Home: Boston, Mass. Died 1904.

WESSELHOEFT, Lily (Elizabeth) Foster (Pope), author; b. Dorchester, Mass., Oct. 20, 1840; m. Dr. Conrad Wesselhoeft, author (died 1904). Author: Jerry the Blunderer; Sparrow the Tramp; Flipwing the Spy; Old Rough the Miser; The Winds, the Woods and the Wanderer; Frowzle the Runaway; Fairy Folk of Blue Hill; Torpeanuts the Tomboy; Madam Mary of the Zoo; Doris and Her Dog Rodney; Diamond King and the Little Man in Grey, 1907; Rover the Farm Dog, 1908; Laddie, the Master of the House, 1913. Home: Boston, Mass. Died Jan. 31, 1919.

WESSELLS, Henry Walton, Jr., brig. gen. U.S.A.; b. Sacketts Harbor, N.Y., Dec. 24, 1846; s. Henry W. (U.S.A.) and Hannah (Cooper) W.; ed. Deer Hill Inst., Danbury, Conn.; m. Eliza Lane Meginnis, Mar. 24, 1869. Pvt. and sergt. cos. K and D, 7th U.S. Inf., Mar. 1-Aug. 16, 1865; apptd. 2d lt. and 1st lt. 7th Inf., July 21, 1865; transferred to 3d Cav., Jan. 1, 1871; capt., Dec. 20, 1872; major, Aug. 16, 1892; lt. col., May 8, 1899; col. unassigned, Feb. 2, 1901; retired for disability incurred in line of duty, Feb. 2, 1901; advanced to grade of brig. gen. U.S.A. retired, Apr. 23, 1904. Served in Indian wars, the Spanish-Am. War and the Philippines. Died Nov. 9, 1929.

WESSON, Daniel Baird, mfr.; b. Worcester, Mass., May 25, 1825; s. Rufus and Betsey (Baird) W.; ed. pub. schs.; learned gunsmiths' trade under his brother Edwin, Northborough, Mass.; took charge of business on Edwin's death, 1850, in firm Smith & Wesson, mfrs. of rifles, Norwich, Conn. That firm sold their patent rights, 1855, to a co. with whom he remained as supt. for a time. In 1857 rejoined Horace Smith under the old name of Smith & Wesson as mfrs. of revolvers in Springfield; became head of firm, with his sons as partners. Died 1906.

WESSON, David, chemist; b. Brooklyn, N.Y., Jan. 14, 1861; s. Elijah Burbank and Elizabeth (Coit) W.; Poly. Inst. Brooklyn, 1877-78; B.S., Mass. Inst. Tech., 1883; m. Mary Matilda Moore, Oct. 12, 1886 (died 1925); children—Mrs. Mary Francis, Mrs. Elizabeth Beatty, David Moore, Harry Burbank, Edward Goodwin; m. 2d, Mrs. S. J. Tilden, May 18, 1927. Became asst. to Prof. Nichols of Mass. Inst. Tech., 1883; chief chemist N. K. Fairbanks Co., Chicago, 1884-90, Am. Cotton Oil Co., New York, 1890-95; pres. Wesson Mfg. Co., Cortland, N.Y., 1895-97; cons. expert on cottonseed oil, 1897-99; mgr. Wesson Co., Savannah, Ga., 1899-1901; mgr. tech. dept. Southern Cotton Oil Co., Savannah and New York, 1901-18; tech. dir. same co., 1918—. Fellow A.A.A.S. Republican. Episcopalian. Inventor of Wesson process for mfr. cottonseed and other oils. Home: Montclair, N.J. Died May 22, 1934.

WEST, Allen Brown, prof. history; b. Reedsburg, Wis., June 19, 1886; s. Allen Burdick and Hattie Esther (Brown) W.; A.B., Milton (Wis.) Coll., 1907; Rhodes scholar from Wis., at Oriel Coll. Oxford U., Eng., 1907-09 and 1910-11; M.A., U. of Wis., 1910, Ph.D., 1912; m. Marion Grace Peabody, Sept. 10, 1914; children—Arthur Peabody, Agnes Elizabeth. Instr. classics, Swarthmore Coll., 1912-16; lecturer in history, U. of Wis., summer 1916; prof. history, Racine (Wis.) Coll., 1916-17; act. asst. prof. history, U. of Rochester, 1917-19; prof. history, Wheaton Coll., Norton, Mass., 1919-26; asst. prof. of classics, Princeton, 1926-27; prof. of classics, U. of Cincinnati, 1927-29, prof. ancient history, 1929—; prof. history, U. of Chicago, summer 1930. John Simon Guggenheim memorial fellow for study of Athenian tribute records. Am. Sch. Classical Studies, Athens, Greece, 1925-26. Episcopalian. Author: History of the Chalcidic League; Fifth and Fourth Century Gold Coins from the Thracian Coast; Corinth, Latin Inscriptions. Contbr. to Am. Jour. Archæology, Am. Jour. Philology, Classical Philology, etc. Home: Cincinnati, O. Died Sept. 18, 1936.

WEST, Anson, clergyman; b. Robertson County, N.C., Sept. 3, 1832; s. Alfred West; ed. in Henry County, Ala.; D.D., Univ. of Ala., 1878; m. Sarah B. Kittrell, Jan. 4, 1866; m. 2d, Mrs. Z. A. Swearingen, April 17, 1883. In ministry, 1856—; mem. of every gen. conf of M.E. Church, South, 1874—; del. to Centennial Methodist Conf., Baltimore, 1884. Author: The State of the Dead, 1869; The Old and the New Man, 1885; History of Methodism in Alabama, 1892. Deceased.

WEST, Archa Kelly, physician; b. Waynesboro, Miss., July 9, 1865; s. John and Leah Kathrine (Kelly) W.; ed. Waynesboro Acad., Vanderbilt U.; M.D., Memphis Hosp. Med. College, 1894; m. Mary Hancock, June 2, 1887. Practiced at Uvalde, 1894, Smithville, 1894-99, Oklahoma City, Okla., 1899—; chief surgeon Okla. Ry. Co. Mayor of Smithville, 1897-99, installing first water system, electric light system and telephone; organized, 1904, and became dean and prof. principles and practice of medicine, Epworth Coll. of Medicine (now Coll. of Medicine, U. of Okla.). Chmn. State Bd. of Prison Control, July 1913—. Democrat. Methodist. Home: Oklahoma City, Okla. Died Aug. 10, 1925.

WEST, Caleb Walton, spl. agent U.S. Treasury; b. Cynthiana, Ky., May 25, 1844; ed. common schs. there, and acad. at Millersburg, Ky. Practiced law, Cynthiana, Ky., 1867-86; apptd., April 1886, gov. Utah Ty., serving to May 1889; reappointed gov. Utah Ty., April 1893; served until State govt. was inaugurated, Jan. 6, 1896; spl. agt. U.S. Treasury, May 1896—. Unmarried. Home: Oakland, Calif. Deceased.

WEST, Charles Edwin, educator; b. Washington, Mass., Feb. 23, 1809; s. Abel W.; ed. pub. schs., Pittsfield, Mass.; Berkshire Gymnasium; grad. Union Coll., 1832; hon. M.D. Univ. of N.Y., A.M., Columbia Coll. Went to Albany to study law, 1832, but engaged in private teaching, and founded, and 3 yrs. conducted, Albany Classical School; later prof. chemistry and natural history, Oneida Inst.; prin. Rutgers Female Inst., New York, 1839-51; Buffalo Female Acad., 1852-60; prin. Brooklyn Heights Sem., 1860-89. Delivered course of 80 lectures each season on sculpture, painting, etching, engraving, architecture. Retired, 1889. In 1890 regents State U. of N.Y. created degree Doctor of Pedagogy for purpose of conferring it upon him. Home: Brooklyn, N.Y. Died 1900.

WEST, Charles H(unter), mem. Miss. River Commn.; b. nr. Fayette, Miss., Nov. 25, 1858; s. Charles W. and Kate (Hunter) W.; B.S. in C.E., U. of Ill., 1884; m. Mary Dulaney, Jan. 20, 1886 (died 1899); m. 2d, Birdie Robertsham Hanway, Nov. 23, 1908. Instrumentman and insp. on levee work, Miss. Levee Dist., 1884-86; surveyor, drainage and highway bridge work, 1887-92; with U.S. Engineer Corps, levee and river work along Miss. River, 1892-98; chief engr. Miss. Levee Dist., 1898-1909; mem. and cons. engr. Miss. River Commn., 1910—. Presbyn. Mason. Writer of reports and brochures on professional subjects. Home: Greenville, Miss. Died June 7, 1933.

WEST, Clifford Hardy, rear admiral U.S.N.; b. Brooklyn, Nov. 10, 1846; s. Edward Augustus and Ann (Peirce) W.; unmarried. Grad. U.S. Naval Acad., 1867; ensign, Dec. 18, 1868; master, Mar. 21, 1870; lt., Mar. 21, 1871; lt. comdr. Mar. 31, 1888; comdr., Oct. 11, 1896; capt., Sept. 22, 1901; rear admiral, June 17, 1902, and retired. On board steam sloop Wyoming, in W. Indies, during complications with Spain as to steamers Virginius and Edgar Stuart; lieut. and exec. officer on board Alliance during search for Lt. DeLong on E. coast of Greenland, Iceland and Spitzbergen; chief of staff to Admiral Sicard, flagship New York, at outbreak of Spanish-Am. War; comd. Princeton in Spanish-Am. War and in operations against insurgents in Philippines. Home: Brooklyn, N.Y. Died 1911.

WEST, George N., consul gen.; b. Lewiston, Me., Jan. 7, 1847; s. Nelson A. and Jenette K. W.; common sch. edn.; m. Eliza L. Stewart, Oct. 5, 1869. Went to sea before the mast at 12 and continued for 10 yrs., becoming master; clk. U.S. Treasury Dept., 1869-82; chief clerk U.S. Steamboat Inspection Service, 1882-93; financial clk. Bd. of Lady Mgrs., Chicago Expn., 1893-95; asst. clk. Senate Com. on Commerce, 1895-97; U.S. consul at Pictou, N.S., Apr. 14-July 1, 1897, at Sydney, 1897-1908; consul gen. at Vancouver, B.C., 1908-10; consul at Kobe, Japan, 1910-16; again consul gen. at Vancouver, July 1916—. Deceased.

WEST, Hamilton Atchison, physician; b. Russell's Cave, Fayette County, Ky., March 30, 1849; s. James N. and Isabella A. W.; grad. med. dept. U. of Louisville, Ky., 1872; moved to Texas, 1873; held several chairs in Texas Med. Coll.; prof. theory and practice of medicine in Sch. of Medicine, U. of Texas, 1891—, also sec. State Med. Soc. of Texas, Apr. 1891—. Died 1903.

WEST, Jesse Felix, judge; b. Sussex County, Va., July 16, 1862; s. Henry Thomas and Susan Thomas (Cox) W.; prep. edn., Suffolk (Va.) Collegiate Inst.; Ph.B., U. of N.C., 1885; studied law, U. of Va.; m. Nannie Peebles Baird, Sept. 20, 1887; children—Mary Jessica (dec.), Grace Walthew (dec.), Jesse Felix, Oscar Henry, Baird Harrison. Admitted to Va. bar, 1886, and began practice at Waverly; chmn. Dem. Com. of Sussex County, 1890; del. Dem. Nat. Com., 1900; judge County Ct. of Sussex County, Va., 1892-1904; judge 3d Jud. Circuit, 1904-22; asso. justice Supreme Ct. of Appeals of Va., term 1922-37; dir. Bank of Waverly, 1900-22. Trustee Elon (N.C.) Coll., 1890-94. Mem. Christian Ch.; supt. S.S. over 30 yrs. Mason, Odd Fellow. Home: Waverly, Va. Died Oct. 25, 1929.

WEST, Max, economist; b. St. Cloud, Minn., Nov. 11, 1870; s. Capt. J. E. W.; grad. U. of Minn., 1890; A.M., 1892, Ph.D., 1893, Columbia; hon. fellow in polit. economy, 1893-94, and docent in sociology, 1894-95, U. of Chicago; resident Hull House, 1893, U. of Chicago Settlement, 1894, Chicago Commons, 1895; m. Oct. 6, 1894. Reporter Chicago Herald, 1894, during R.R. strike; editorial writer Chicago Record, 1895; lecturer Columbia, 1895-96 and 1902; served in Div. Statistics, U.S. Dept. Agr., 1896-1900; expert agt. U.S. Industrial Commn., 1900-02, asso. prof. economics, Columbian U., 1900-02; sec. Civic Center, Washington, 1900-02 and 1905—; asst. registrar Tenement House Dept., New York, 1902; sec. Nat. Conf. on Comparative Legislation, Washington, 1902; chief Bur. of Internal Revenue, Treasury Dept. of Puerto Rico, 1903-04; spl. agt. and spl. examiner, Bur. of Corps., Dept. of Commerce and Labor, 1904. Author: The Inheritance Tax, 1893, 1907; Principles of Taxation, 1907; also many contributions on taxation and subjects in sociology, constl. law and pub. affairs to various journals. Home: Washington, D.C. Died 1909.

WEST, Millard F., lawyer; b. Lancaster, Ky., Mar. 9, 1877; s. J. Wesley and Jennie (Harris) W.; A.B., Garrard Coll., Lancaster, Ky., 1894; LL.B., Nat. U., 1925; m. Elizabeth M. Leech, Nov. 27, 1907; children—Millard F., Elizabeth L. (Mrs. Merton A. English, Jr.). Appointed dep. collector internal revenue service, 1898; trans. to Washington, D.C., 1901, and later made head of accounts div., Internal Revenue Bur.; apptd. asst. dep. commr., and in 1920 reorganized div. of accounts and installed budget system; acting commr. internal revenue, Apr. and May 1921; deputy commr. and asst. prohibition commr. to July 1, 1922. Republican. Mem. Disciples of Christ. Home: Chevy Chase, Md. Died Nov. 1, 1938.

WEST, Paul, journalist, playwright, author; b. Boston, Jan. 26, 1871; ed. Boston Latin Sch. and grad. Peekskill (N.Y.) Mil. Acad., 1888; m. Jane V. Carrigan, July 18, 1895. Writer of The Man from China, The Pearl and the Pumpkin, The Love Waltz, At the Waldorf, Birdland, The Twentieth Century, The Song Shop, The Red Petticoat and other musical comedies, besides adapting and collaborating on many others. Author: Short Letters of a Small Boy; Just Boy (Doran); The Innocent Murderers (collaborating with William Johnston); The Widow Wise; "Bill"; In Our School; Dime Novels of an Office Boy. Writer of more than 300 published songs; "War," "Crooky" (for Frank Daniels), "The Victim," "The Wrong Girl," and other motion picture plays. Contbr. to many mags. On editorial staff N.Y. Sunday World, 1898-1911. Home: New York, N.Y. Died Oct. 30, 1918.

WEST, Raymond M., clergyman; b. Shiloh, N.J., Oct. 16, 1862; s. Hosea Davis and Sarah (Wescott) W.; A.B., Bucknell U., Pa., 1889, A.M., 1892; grad. Crozer Theol. Sem., 1892; D.D., Denison, 1907; m. Harriet Eldredge, June 6, 1892; children—Ethel Egbert, Russell Eldredge. Student pastor, Warrensville, Pa., 1886-89, 3d Ch., Camden, N.J., 1889-90, Summer St. Mission of 1st Ch. of Phila., 1891-92; ordained Bapt. ministry, June 1892; pastor Lehigh Av. Ch., Phila., 1892-1903, 1st Ch., St. Paul, Minn., 1903-08, Park Av. Ch., Rochester, N.Y., 1908-15; exec. sec. N.J. Bapt. Conv., Newark, 1915-20; exec. sec. life work dept. of bd. of promotions of Northern Bapt. Conv., 1920-21; pastor Lewisburg (Pa.) Bapt. Ch. and student pastor, Bucknell U., Sept. 1, 1921—. Trustee Minn. State Conv., 1903-08, Rochester Theol. Sem., 1910—, Bucknell U., 1923—. Official rep. Northern Bapt. Conv. War Commn. in N.J., 1917-19; mem. Gen. Bd. Promotion of Northern Bapt. Conv., and of Administrative Com., 1919-20; mem. bd. mgrs., Pa. Bapt. Gen. Conv., 1924—. Home: Lewisburg, Pa. Died Oct. 15, 1933.

WEST, Samuel H., judge; b. Waubeck, Ia., July 7, 1872; s. Rev. Samuel and Margaret (Hardman) W.; m. Marguerite L. Miller, 1901 (died 1905); children—Eleanore F., Alice C., William L.; m. 2d, Elizabeth Griffin (died 1918); m. 3d, Marietta A. Hyde, 1926. Admitted to Ohio bar, 1893, and began practice in Bellefontaine; prosecutor Logan County, O., 1899-1903; mem. firm Wilson and West, Columbus, O., 1907-10; judge U.S. Court, Northern Ohio Dist., 1928—. Served with 2d Ohio Inf. during Spanish-Am. War. Home: Cleveland, O. Died Oct. 5, 1938.

WEST, Thomas Dyson, iron foundry expert; b. Manchester, Eng., Aug. 31, 1851; s. William H. and Sara A. (Faraday) W.; brought to America in infancy; mainly self-ed. Began in foundry at 12; organizer, v.p. and gen. mgr., 1887-1909, The Thomas D. West Foundry Co., later Valley Mold & Iron Co., Sharpsville, Pa.; organizer, 1907, The West Steel Casting Co., Cleveland, and chmn. and mng. dir., 1914—. Authority on subjects pertaining to foundry work. Began writing for tech. publs., 1881, originated and established the use of standardized drill ings, adopted by U.S. Bur. of Standards, 1905. Founder, 1908, and pres. Am. Anti-Accident Assn.; started the "safety first" agitation; originator of Cleveland's Sane Fourth of July. Mason. Author:

American Foundry Practice, 1882; Moulders' Text-Book, 1885; Metallurgy of Cast Iron, 1897; The Competent Life, 1905; Accidents—Their Causes and Remedies, 1908; The Efficient Man, 1914; 6 foundry instrn. pamphlets for Internat. Corr. Schs.; also numerous tech. papers. Home: Cleveland, O. Died June 18, 1915.

WEST, Thomas Franklin, judge; b. Milton, Fla., Nov. 23, 1874; s. L. F. and Frances Elisabeth (McArthur) W.; student State Normal Sch., DeFuniak Springs, Fla., 1894-96; Washington and Lee U. Law Sch., Lexington, Va., 1898-99; m. Alma Chaffin, 1899; children—Thomas Franklin, Josephine (Mrs. F W. Berry, Jr.), Alma. Admitted to Fla. bar, 1900, and practiced at Milton. Mem. Fla. Ho. of Rep., 1903, Senate, 1905, 1907; mem. Commn. to Revise Gen. Statutes of Fla., 1906; atty. gen. of Fla., 1912-16; apptd. justice Supreme Ct. of Fla., Sept. 1, 1917; elected to same office, Nov. 1918; became chief justice, Apr. 1925; resigned, Nov. 23, 1925, to become judge Circuit Ct., 1st Circuit of Fla. Mason. Democrat. Presbyn. Died Feb. 23, 1931.

WEST, Thomas Henry, banker; b. Mifflin, Tenn., July 27, 1846; s. John and Martha Frances (Ashcraft) W.; common sch. edn.; m. Florrie Terry, 1868 (died 1898); children—John Terry, Allen T., Thos. H., Florence (Mrs. Howard Elting), Walter H., Carroll (Mrs. Hugh McKittrick Jones); m. 2d, Virginia Hodges, 1900; 1 dau., Frances H. Served in C.S. Army under Gen. Forrest, 1863-65; in business in Louisville, Ky., later in cotton bus. at Mobile, New Orleans and Memphis, until about 1890; organized St. Louis Trust Co., 1889, later consol. with Union Trust Co. as St. Louis Union Trust Co., of which was pres. until 1908, and chmn. bd. several yrs., later dir. and mem. exec. com. First Nat. Bank. Democrat. Baptist. Home: St. Louis, Mo. Died July 7, 1926.

WEST, Thomas Henry, Jr., corp. official; b. Mobile, Ala., Jan. 8, 1875; s. Thomas H. and Florence (Terry) W.; Ph.B., Yale U., 1896; m. Wilhelmina Crapo Cristy, Nov. 21, 1898; children—Thomas H. III, Wilhelmina C. (Mrs. Richard E. Wheeler), John C., Mary Ann C. (Mrs. Robert Ward). With Hamilton Brown Shoe Co., St. Louis, 1896-98, La Prelle Shoe Co., 1898-1901; sec. Broadway Savings Trust Co., St. Louis, 1901-03; sec. St. Louis Union Trust Co., 1903-06, v.p., 1906-15; v.p. R.I. Hosp. Trust Co., Providence, R.I., 1915-19, pres., 1919—; pres. R.I. Hosp. Nat. Bank, 1934; dir. Wauregan-Quinebaug Mills, Inc., Grosvenordale Co. (Providence), Mut. Life Ins. Co., Title Guarantee Co. of R.I. State chmn. Liberty Loan Com., R.I., World War I. Home: Providence, R.I. Died Jan. 17, 1936.

WEST, Victor J., prof. polit. science; b. Bushnell, Ill., Nov. 12, 1880; s. Charles and Mary Ellen (Bradfield) W.; grad. Bradley Poly. Inst., Peoria, Ill., 1903; Ph.B., U. of Chicago, 1905, fellow in polit. science, 1908-10; m. Helen Andrews Stevens, Sept. 6, 1911; children—Marjorie Stevens, Mary Bradfield, Nancy Gardner. Instr. English and civics, Bradley Poly. Inst., 1905-06; instr. politics, Northwestern U., 1910-13; asst. prof. polit. science, 1913-18, asso. prof., 1918-19, prof. and head of dept., 1919—, Stanford U. Asst. chief, Ill. Prog. Service, 1913; instr. polit. science, U. of Calif., summer, 1915; investigator U.S. Bur. of Efficiency, Washington, 1918 and 1920-21; actg. prof. polit. science, U. of Minn., summer (1st half) 1924, U. of Chicago, summer (2d half) 1924; lecturer, Furman Inst., summer 1925. Trustee Pub. Library, Palo Alto. Mem. Am. Polit. Science Assn. (exec. council 1921-24), Am. Assn. Univ. Profs., Calif. Acad. Social Sciences (pres. 1922-23). Author: The Foreign Policy of Woodrow Wilson, 1913-17 (with Edgar E. Robinson), 1917. Asso. editor Am. Polit. Science Review. Home: Palo Alto, Calif. Died Feb. 26, 1927.

WEST, William Henry, lawyer; b. Millsboro, Pa., Feb. 9, 1824; s. Samuel and Mary (Clear) W.; A.B., Jefferson Coll., 1846, A.M., 1849, LL.D., 1885, Washington and Jefferson Coll., and U. of Wooster, 1880; m. Elizabeth Williams, June 1851 (dec.); m. 2d, Clara Gorton, Oct. 10, 1872 (dec.). Admitted to bar, 1851, practiced at Bellefontaine, O., 1851—; pros. atty., Logan Co., 1852; mem. Ohio Assembly, 1858, 1862, Senate, 1864; atty. gen. of Ohio, 1865-69; justice Supreme Ct., 1871-73; mem. Constl. Conv., 1873; Rep. nominee for gov., 1877; del. Rep. Nat. convs., 1860, 84; placed James G. Blaine in nomination for Presidency, 1884; declined appmt. as consul at Rio de Janeiro, 1869; lost sight while justice Supreme Ct. Died 1911.

WEST, William Stanley, senator; b. Marion County, Ga., Aug. 23, 1849; s. James and Mary A. (Hunter) W.; A.B., Mercer U., Macon, Ga., 1880, A.M., 1883; LL.B., Law Dept. same univ., 1883; m. Ora Lee Cranford, Nov. 15, 1888. Began practice Valdosta, Ga., 1883; planter and mill man; pres. and gen. mgr. Valdosta St. Ry. Co.; mem. Ga. Ho. of Rep., 1892-1901, State Senate, 4 yrs. (pres. 1905-06); del. at large Dem. Nat. Conv., Denver, 1908; apptd., Mar. 2, 1914, by Gov. John M. Slaton, to fill vacancy in U.S. Senate caused by death of Hon. Augustus O. Bacon. Chmn. bd. S. Ga. State Normal Coll.; trustee U. of Ga. Mem. Christian (Disciples) Ch. Home: Valdosta, Ga. Died Dec. 22. 1914.

WEST, Willis Mason, author; b. St. Cloud, Minn., Nov. 15, 1857; s. Josiah E. and Alcetta M. W.; A.B., U. of Minn., 1879, A.M., 1881; m. Melissa Mott, Jan. 1883 (died 1896); children—Ruth, Rodney Mott, Margaret, Ralph Leland, Walter Mott, David Ripley; m. 2d, Elizabeth Beach, Dec. 1902; children—Anne, Elizabeth Beach, Donald Beach, Jane, Robert Beach, Katharine, Frank Beach, Edith. Supt. schs., Duluth, Minn., 1881-84, Faribault, 1884-91; prof. history, U. of N.D., 1891-92, U. of Minn., 1892-1912; farmer, 1912—. Author: Ancient History to Charlemagne, 1902; Modern History, 1904; The Ancient World, 1904; American History and Government, 1913; A Source Book in American History to 1790, 1913; Modern World, 1915; History of the American People, 1918; German Plots and Intrigue, 1918; The War and the New Age, 1919; Story of Modern Progress, 1919; Story of Man's Early Progress, 1920; Story of American Democracy, 1922; Short History of Early Peoples, 1921; Short History of Modern Peoples, 1923; World Progress, 1923; (with Ruth West) The Story of Our Country, 1926; History of the American Nation, 1929. War service with Com. on Pub. Information, Washington, D.C., and with S.A.T.C., at U. of Minn. Home: Minneapolis, Minn. Died May 2, 1931.

WESTBROOK, Elroy Herman, banker; b. Mansfield, Pa., Apr. 6, 1887; s. Walter R. and Erna L. (Tucker) W.; grad. Peddie Inst., Hightstown, N.J., 1906; m. Alice Duley, May 13, 1913; children—Erna Mary, Alice Duley, Perry Tucker, Elroy (dec.). Cashier Knoxville Banking Co., 1906-12; moved to Laurel, Mont., 1912, and was apptd. mgr. Laurel State Bank, organized by father; v.p. Merchants Nat. Bank, Billings, Mont., 1915-23; pres. Midland Nat. Bank, 1923—. Mason, Elk. Home: Billings, Mont. Died Feb. 22, 1939.

WESTCOTT, Frank Nash, clergyman; b. Syracuse, N.Y., Aug. 8, 1858; s. Amos and Harriet (Nash) W.; Ph.B., Syracuse U., 1878; Berkeley Div. Sch., Cambridge, Mass., 1880-83; unmarried. Deacon, 1883, priest, 1884, P.E. Ch.; in charge St. John's, Syracuse, 1883-84; rector St. James', Skaneateles, N.Y., 1884—. Author: Philosophy of a Change in the Name of the Church, 1898; Catholic Principles, 1902; The Church and the Good Samaritan, 1905; Heart of Catholicity, 1905. Home: Skaneateles, N.Y. Died June 27, 1915.

WESTENGARD, Jens Iverson, lawyer; b. Chicago, Sept. 14, 1871; s. Abel A. and Nelsigne D. (Iverson) W.; ed. West Division High Sch., Chicago, 1888; LL.B., Harvard, 1898, hon. A.M., 1903; m. Rebecca A. Prosser, July 16, 1898. In real estate and banking business, Chicago, 1890-95; practiced law in Boston, 1899-1903; instr. law, 1898, asst. prof. law, 1899-1903, Harvard Law Sch.; asst. gen. adviser to His Siamese Majesty's Govt., 1903; acting gen. adviser, Dec. 1905-Feb. 1907, and Feb. 1908-Apr. 1909, gen. adviser with rank of minister plenipotentiary, Apr. 1909-Sept. 1915; Bemis prof. Internat. law, Harvard Law Sch., Sept. 1915. Apptd. mem. Hague Permanent Arbitration Ct., 1911; judge Supreme Ct. of Appeals of Siam, 1911. Siamese title: Phya Kalyan Maitri; decorated with Grand Cordon of Order of White Elephant (Siam); Grand Cross of the Crown of Siam; spl. 2d class of Order of Chula Chom Klao; 2d class of Order of Ratanaphorn (Siam); Officer of Legion of Honor (France); Grand Cross of the Order of Dannebrog (Denmark). Home: Cambridge, Mass. Died Sept. 17, 1918.

WESTENHAVER, David C., judge; b. Berkeley County, W.Va., Jan. 13, 1865; s. David and Harriet (Turner) W.; LL.B., Georgetown U., 1886; LL.D., 1920; m. Mary C. Paul, July 1, 1887; children—Edward Paul, David C. (dec.). Began practice at Martinsburg, W.Va., 1886; pros. atty., Berkeley Co., 1886-87; mem. City Council, Martinsburg, 1902-03; removed to Cleveland, O., 1903; mem. Bd. of Edn., Cleveland, 1912-15 (pres. 1914-15); apptd. by President Wilson, judge U.S. Dist. Court, Northern Dist. of Ohio, Feb. 19, 1917. Democrat. Home: Cleveland, O. Died July 29, 1928.

WESTERVELT, Marvin Zabriskie, M.D.; b. Mt. Freedom, N.J., Oct. 15, 1876; s. Garrett Henry and Anna Maria (Kinsey) W.; grad. high sch., Dover, N.J., 1891; M.D., New York Homœ. Med. Coll. and Flower Hosp., 1899; m. Martha Walker Cline, Oct. 1, 1900. Began practice, Newark, 1901; removed to Litchfield, Conn., 1911; removed to New Haven, 1917; entered field of industrial surgery, 1917; dir. med. div. of Winchester Repeating Arms Co.; supt. Staten Island Hosp., May 15, 1922—. Progressive. Methodist. Mason. Home: Tompkinsville, S.I., N.Y. Died May 12, 1929.

WESTFALL, Katherine Storey, exec. sec.; b. Janesville, Wis., June 8, 1863; d. Charles Webb and Celia H. (Moon) Storey; grad. high sch., Chicago, 1880, Art Inst. Chicago, 1885; m. Edward Walter Westfall, of Chicago, July 1, 1886 (dec.); children—Charles Storey, Mildred (Mrs. Chester Douglas Freeze). Exec. sec. Woman's Am. Bapt. Home Mission Soc., 1909-37, hon. sec., 1937—. Republican. Home: Hollywood, Calif. Deceased.

WESTGATE, John Minton, agronomist; b. Kingston, N.Y., Feb. 17, 1878; s. Hallis Smith and Clara Hopkins (Minton) W.; B.S., Kan. State Agrl. Coll., 1897, M.S., 1899; studied U. of Chicago, 1901-03; m. Inez Wheeler, July 20, 1905; children—Philip John, Mark Wheeler. Teacher pub. schs., 1895-96; asst. in Kan. State Agrl. Coll., 1897-99, asst. botanist, 1899-1901; with U.S. Dept. Agr., 1903—, asst. in sand-binding work, 1903-05; in charge alfalfa and clover investigations, 1905-11; agronomist, in charge clover investigations, 1911-14; in charge Hawaiian Agrl. Expt. Sta., 1915, dir., 1924-35; prof. tropical agr., U. of Hawaii, 1935—. Fellow A.A.A.S. Baptist. Author of numerous bulls. and spl. articles on alfalfa, clovers, seed production, control of blowing soils, etc. Died Sept. 25, 1937.

WESTINGHOUSE, George, inventor, mfr.; b. Central Bridge, N.Y., Oct. 6, 1846; s. George and Emeline (Vedder) W.; removed to Schenectady, 1856; ed. pub. and high schs. and later to sophomore yr. Union Coll.; hon. Ph.D., Union, 1890; Dr. Engring., Königliche Technische Hochschule, Berlin, 1906; spent much time in father's machine shop, inventing at 15 a rotary engine; m. Marguerite Erskine Walker, Aug. 8, 1867. Mem. 12th N.G.S.N.Y. and 16th N.Y. Cav., Union Army, June 1863-Nov. 1864; asst. engr. U.S.N., Dec. 1864-Aug. 1865. Invented a device for replacing derailed steam cars, 1865; patented his invention of the air brake, 1868; applied pneumatic devices to switching and signaling, greatly increasing efficiency; also utilized electricity in this connection, and became interested in development of electric machinery; acquired Gaulard & Gibbs patents, 1885, and introduced the alternating current system of elec. distribution for light and power; made many elec. inventions; backed Tesla financially and with shop facilities in developing the induction motor, which made possible utilization of alternating current for power purposes; built the first 10 great dynamos for Niagara, the dynamos for the elevated and subway roads in New York, and for the Met. Ry., London. Devised a complete system for controlling natural gas and conveying it through pipe lines for long distances, thereby established the practicability of utilizing natural gas as fuel in homes, mills and factories; took a foremost part in developing gas engines, and in adapting steam turbines to electric driving. Founded works at Wilmerding, East Pittsburgh, Swissvale, and Trafford City, Pa.; Hamilton, Can.; Manchester, and London, Eng.; Havre, France; Hanover, Germany; St. Petersburg, Russia; Vienna, Austria; Vado, Italy; pres. of 30 corps.; trustee Equitable Life Assurance Soc. of U.S., June 10, 1905-Jan. 1911. Decorated Legion of Honor, France, Royal Crown, Italy, and Leopold of Belgium; 2d recipient of John Fritz medal. Hon. mem. Am. Soc. Mech. Engrs. (pres., 1909-10), Nat. Electric Light Assn. Died Mar. 12, 1914.

WESTINGHOUSE, Henry Herman, mech. engr.; b. Central Bridge, N.Y., Nov. 16, 1853; s. George and Emeline (Vedder) W.; grad. Union High Sch., Schenectady, N.Y., 1870; student mech. engring., Cornell, 1871-72; m. Clara Louise Saltmarsh, June 20, 1875. Continuously with Westinghouse Air Brake Co., 1873—, chmn. bd., also of Canadian Westinghouse Co., Ltd.; dir. Westinghouse Electric & Mfg. Co., Westinghouse Brake & Saxby Signal Co., Ltd. (London); pres. Compagnie des Freins Westinghouse, Paris. Invented Westinghouse single-acting steam engine, 1883; founder Westinghouse, Church, Kerr & Co., engrs., New York, 1885. Mem. Am. Soc. Mech. Engrs., Am. Acad. Polit. and Social Science; fellow A.A.A.S. Trustee Cornell U. Republican. Protestant. Died Nov. 18, 1933.

WESTINGHOUSE, Marguerite Erskine Walker; b. Roxbury, N.Y.; d. Capt. Daniel Lynch and Eliza Smart (Burhans) Walker; ed. at home, and grad. Roxbury Acad.; m. George Westinghouse, Aug. 8, 1867 (died 1914). On bds. of mgrs. numerous hosps. in Washington, and Pittsburgh. Presbyterian. Died June 23, 1914.

WESTLAKE, J(ames) Willis, educator; b. Devonshire, Eng., Feb. 24, 1830; s. Robert and Mary (Willis) W.; came to U.S., 1832; A.B., Union Coll., 1857, A.M., 1858; m. Adelaide Brown, May 3, 1859; m. 2d, Eliza G. Smith, Mar. 20, 1872. Prof. ancient and modern langs., Lancaster (Pa.) Normal Sch., 1857; founded Indiana (Pa.) Sem. and Normal Sch., 1858; editor Indiana (Pa.) Messenger, 1861-62; sergt. maj. 23d Pa. Militia, 1862; clerk in q.m. gen.'s office, Washington, 1863-66; prof. English lang. and lit., Baltimore City Coll., 1866-69; prof. English lit., Pa. State Normal Sch., Millersville, Pa., 1869-86; traveled in Europe, 1883; engaged in orange culture in Fla., 1886—. Author: 3000 Practice Words, 1874; How to Write Letters, 1876; Common School Literature, 1876. Died Oct. 18, 1912.

WESTLEY, George Hembert, author; b. Newfoundland, Jan. 28, 1865, of English ancestry. Came to U.S., 1885; entered business career, but relinquished it in 1893 for literature; did much free-lance work, and reading and revising for pub. houses; spl. writer on Boston Transcript, 1906-29. Author: Joan of the Bay (serial), 1901; The Maid and the Miscreant, 1906; Clementina's Highwayman (with Robert Neilson Stephens), 1907. Editor: For Love's Sweet Sake (poems), 1899; At the Court of the King (stories).

1900; A New Epistle, 1913. Asso. Editor: The Literary Review and Book Plate Collector, Boston, 1902. Plays: The Man's Game (prod. Majestic Theatre, Boston, Aug. 1910); The Scarlet Pimpernel; The Intruder; Doctor Presto; Rothschild (for George Arliss), 1933; The Belle of Baltimore. Deceased.

WESTON, Charles Valentine, civil engr.; b. Kalamazoo, Mich., Feb. 14, 1857; s. John and Catherine (Clark) W.; ed. pub. schs., Kalamazoo; m. Catherine Dyer, Nov. 12, 1889 (died 1914); children—Charles Edward (dec.), Florence E.; m. 2d, Olga Thimm, Jan. 10, 1917. Entered employ Tex. Trunk Ry. Co. as transitman in surveying corps.; asst. engr. M.,K.&T. R.R. in Tex., 1880-81, Kansas City, Springfield & Memphis Ry., 1881-82; asst. engr. C.&N.-W. Ry., 1882-84; asst. engr. Kansas City, Clinton & Springfield Ry., 1884-86; div. engr. in charge constrn. Gulf, Colo. & Santa Fe R.R., 1886-88. Located in Chicago, 1888; in charge constrn. of intake crib and water-supply tunnel under Lake Michigan for city of Lake View, and after annexation of that municipality to Chicago, 1889, completed work for the greater city. In charge constrn. of tunnel for W. Chicago St. Ry., 1890-94; chief engr. of Northwestern Elevated R.R. Co., Lake St. Elevated Ry. Co., Union Elevated, etc.; with brother George, in firm of Weston Bros., cons. and constructing engrs., 1901-03; built various electric rys. in Ill. and Mich.; chief engr., 1903-07, pres. and gen. mgr., 1908-11, South Side Elevated R.R. Co., Chicago; later in practice as cons. engr.; operating mgr. Market St. Elevated Rys., Phila., 1918-20; cons. engr. Chicago Surface Lines, 1920—; mem. Bd. of Supervising Engrs. Chicago Traction. Home: Chicago, Ill. Died Jan. 27, 1933.

WESTON, Edmund Brownell, engr.; b. Duxbury, Mass., Mar. 25, 1850; s. Hon. Gershom Bradford and Deborah (Brownell) W.; ed. pub. schs., Partridge Acad. (Duxbury), Highland Mil. Acad. (Worcester, Mass.), and pvt. instrn.; unmarried. Student in office chief eng. Providence water works, 1871-74, asst. engr., 1874-77; engr. in charge Providence water dept., 1877-97; resigned to engage in gen. practice. Conducted filtration experiments, 1893-94, for city of Providence, which demonstrated efficiency of mech. filtration for purification of municipal water supplies; designed filtration systems for many cities of U.S., Austria, India, Egypt, Germany, Japan, France, Finland, China, Korea, Siam, Italy, Ceylon. Pres. and gen. mgr. Jewell Export Filter Co. Devoted much time to original research relative to hydraulics and water purification, and traveled abroad extensively, making spl. study of water purification, water supply and sanitary engring. Author: Weston's Friction of Water in Pipes, 1878. Home: Providence, R.I. Died Dec. 9, 1916.

WESTON, Edward, electrician; b. England, May 9, 1850; ed. there and studied medicine; LL.D., McGill U., Can., 1903; Sc.D., Stevens Inst. Tech., 1904, Princeton, 1910; LL.D., U. of Pa., 1924. Came to U.S., 1870, and became chemist to Am. Nickel Plating Co.; introduced improvements in nickel plating; later invented several dynamo-electric machines, and established in Newark, 1875, the first factory in America devoted exclusively to that class of machines; consol. business, 1881, with U.S. Electric Lighting Co., of which was electrician until 1888; formed Weston Elec. Instrument Co., Waverly Park, Newark, N.J., 1888, to mfr. the Weston measuring instruments; v.p. same co., 1888-1905, pres. 1905, later chmn. bd. Charter mem. Am. Inst. E.E. (pres., 1888). Fellow A.A.A.S. Awarded Franklin medal, 1924. Home: Montclair, N.J. Died Aug. 20, 1936.

WESTON, Edward Payson, pedestrian; b. Providence, R.I., Mar. 15, 1839; s. Silas and Maria (Gaines) W.; ed. old Adams Sch., Boston. Engaged in newspaper business most of his life. First attracted attention as a pedestrian by walking from Boston to Washington, D.C., to attend 1st inauguration of Abraham Lincoln, 1861, traveling 443 miles in 208 hours; began professional career by walking from Portland, Me., to Chicago, 1,326 miles, in less than 26 days, 1867; duplicated the feat 40 years later (1907), beating his former record by 29 hours; walked from New York to San Francisco by route of 3,895 miles, in 104 days and 7 hours, 1909, and returned across continent, to New York, 1910, a distance of 3,500, in 76 days, 23 hours and 10 minutes; appeared at various times in England, walking 5,000 miles in 100 days, 1883-84, under auspices of Church of England, and delivered a lecture on temperance each evening; in his 75th yr., 1913, walked from New York to Minneapolis, 1,546 miles, in 51 days, to lay the cornerstone of the new Athletic Club house; escorted into the city by members of that club, accompanied by the gov., the mayor of both St. Paul and Minneapolis, and received by the largest gathering ever assembled in the state, Aug. 2, 1913. Lecturer on athletics. Died May 13, 1929.

WESTON, Henry Griggs, theologian, educator; b. Lynn, Mass., Sept. 11, 1820; s. John Equality and Hetty (Bacheller) W.; A.B., Brown Univ., 1840; studied Newton Theol. Instn., 1840-42; (hon. A.M., Shurtleff, 1846; D.D., Univ. of Rochester, 1859; LL.D., Brown, Bucknell, Denison, Southwestern univs., 1891); m. Endamile Van Meter, 1845. Ordained to Bapt. ministry, Frankfort, Ky., 1843; pastor Washington and Richland, Ill., 1843-46, Peoria, Ill., 1846-59, Oliver St., Madison Av., New York, 1859-68; pres. Crozer Theol. Sem., 1868—. Pres. Am. Bapt. Missionary Union, 1872-73. Editor Baptist Quarterly, 1869-77. Author: The Communion Lectures, 1867; The Four Gospels; The Epistle of James; Constitution and Polity of the New Testament Church; Outline of Systematic Theology (with Rev. E. H. Johnson); Matthew, the Genesis of the New Testament, 1900. Home: Chester, Pa. Died 1909.

WESTON, James Augustus, P.E. clergyman; b. Lake Comfort, N.C., May 6, 1838; attended schools there and Jonesville, N.C., Acad.; Trinity Coll., N.C., 1857-58; Trinity Coll., Conn., 1859-60. Maj. 33d N.C. regt., A. P. Hill's div., C.S.A., 1864-65. Ordained deacon, 1870; priest, 1876; pastorates at Hertford, Hickory and Raleigh, N.C. Chaplain Catawba Co., N.C., Veterans' Assn. Historian of the 33d N.C. Regiment; author of an account of Gen. Lee's surrender at Appomattox. Author: Historic Doubts as to the Execution of Marshal Ney, 2d edit., 1905. Home: Hickory, N.C. Died 1905.

WESTON, John Burns, theologian; b. Madison, Me., July 6, 1821; s. Stephen and Rebecca (Webb) W.; A.B., Antioch Coll., Ohio, 1857, A.M., 1860 (D.D., 1884; D.D., Union Christian Coll., 1884; LL.D., same, and Defiance Coll., Ohio, 1906); m. Nancy M. McDonald, Mar. 18, 1849; 2d, Achsah E. Waite, June 11, 1860. Entered ministry (Christians —not Disciples) as pastor, W. Newbury, Mass., 1843; mng. editor Herald of Gospel Liberty (then Christian Herald), Exeter, N.H., and Newburyport, Mass., 1847-48; mem. faculty Antioch Coll. (with Horace Mann as pres.), 1857; acting pres., same, through war period, 1862-65; remained till 1881; meantime associate editor Herald of Gospel Liberty, Dayton, O.; pres. and prof. Bibl. lit., theology, psychology and ethics, Christian Bibl. Inst., Defiance, O., 1882-1910; chancellor of Defiance Coll. and Christian Bibl. Inst., June 1910—. Dir. Francis A. Palmer Fund. Home: Defiance, O. Died Aug. 24, 1912.

WESTON, John Francis, major gen. U.S.A.; b. Louisville, Ky., Nov. 13, 1845; s. B. N. and Mary W.; ed. St. Mary's Coll., Ky.; m. Sally Garvin. Commd. 1st lt. 4th Ky. Cav., Nov. 26, 1861; capt., Jan. 9, 1863; maj., Nov. 1, 1864; hon. mustered out of vols., Aug. 21, 1865; apptd. from Ky. 2d lt. 7th U.S. Cav., Aug. 9, 1867; 1st lt., Nov. 27, 1868; grad. Arty. Sch., 1875; capt. commissary subsistence, Nov. 24, 1875; maj., Aug. 1, 1892; lt. col. asst. commissary gen., Nov. 15, 1897; col. asst. commissary gen., Apr. 30, 1898; brig. gen. vols., Sept. 21, 1898; hon. disch. from vols., Mar. 24, 1899; brig. gen. commissary gen. U.S.A., Dec. 6, 1900; maj. gen., Oct. 8, 1905; retired, Nov. 13, 1909. Awarded Congressional Medal of Honor, Apr. 9, 1898, "for gallantry at Wetumpka, Ala., Apr. 13, 1865," where, with 5 men, he swam the river, defeated a force of the enemy and captured steamboats loaded with supplies, lying in the river. Home: Briarcliff Manor, N.Y. Died Aug. 3, 1917.

WESTON, Nathan Austin, economist; b. nr. Champaign, Ill., Apr. 5, 1868; s. Nathan and Jane (Cloyd) W.; B.Litt., U. of Ill., 1889, M.Litt., 1898; Ph.D., Cornell U., 1901; studied U. of Berlin, 1910-11; m. Angeline Gayman, Sept. 4, 1894; children—Nathan Austin, Janet Louise. Teacher and prin. schs. in Ill. till 1897; fellow in economics, U. of Wis., 1897-98; fellow and asst. in economics, Cornell U., 1898-1900; instr. economics, 1900-03, asst. prof., 1903-06, asst. prof. and asst. dir. course in business administration, 1906-15, prof. economics and first dean Coll. of Commerce and Business Administration, 1915-19, prof. economics, 1919—, U. of Illinois. Republican. Home: Champaign, Ill. Died Nov. 29, 1933.

WESTON, S(amuel) Burns, editor, pub.; b. Madison, Me., Mar. 10, 1855; s. Reuel and Esther (Burns) W.; A.B., Antioch Coll., Ohio, 1876, D.H., 1931; S.T.B., Harvard, 1879; U. of Berlin, 1881-82, Leipzig and Geneva, 1882-83; m. Mary Hartshorne, Oct. 8, 1891; children—Charles Hartshorne, Edward Burns (dec.), Harold Francis, Esther Burns. Minister Unitarian Ch., Leicester, Mass., 1879-81; studied at Berlin, Leipzig and Geneva, 1881-83; took courses at Sch. of Polit. Science, Columbia, 1883-85; lecturer Soc. for Ethical Culture of Phila., 1885-90; editor and pub. Ethical Record, 1888-90, Internat. Journal of Ethics, 1890-1914, Ethical Addresses, 1894-1914. Dir. Phila. Society for Ethical Culture, 1897-1934, dir. emeritus, 1934—; pres. Southwark Neighborhood House, Phila., 1904—; mgr. Phila. Forum. Trustee Adirondack Mountain Reserve. Home: Philadelphia, Pa. Died July 15, 1936.

WESTON, Stephen Francis, college dean; b. Madison, Me., Mar. 10, 1855; s. Reuel and Esther (Burns) W.; brother of Samuel Burns W.; A.B., Antioch Coll., 1879; studied philosophy and economics at U. of Mich., 1885-87, Sch. of Polit. Science, Columbia, 1890-92, Ph.D., 1903; m. Nellie S. Phinney, June 18, 1896. Asst. economics, Columbia, 1892-94, asso. prof. polit. and social science, Western Reserve U., 1894-1900; dean and prof. economics and sociology, and instr. philosophy, Antioch Coll., Sept. 1902—. Sec.-treas. Intercollegiate Peace Assn.; pres. history and social science sect. Ohio Coll. Assn. Author: Principles of Justice in Taxation, 1903; etc. Home: Yellow Springs, O. Died Mar. 7, 1935.

WESTON, Theodore, engineer; b. Sandy Hill, N.Y., Oct. 9, 1832; s. Frederick and Elizabeth (Hart) W.; A.B., Yale, 1853; m. Sarah Chauncey Winthrop (died 1864); m. 2d, Catharine Boudinot Stimson. Engaged on surveys and constrn. Genesee Valley R.R., 1853-55; asst. engr. N.Y. State canals, 1855-57; prin. asst. engr. surveys and constrn., etc., Brooklyn Water Works, 1857-60; engr. in charge sewage and drainage, City of New York, 1861-70; supt., engr., trustee and architect Equitable Life Assurance Soc. of U.S., 1870-82; architect of Met. Mus. of Art, 1884-90, and other works. Republican. Incorporator, sec. and trustee, Met. Mus. of Art, New York. Author: Report upon Water Supply for Brooklyn, 1861. Wrote: Water Works of Rome, The Crayon, New York, 1864. Home: New York, N.Y. Died May 6, 1919.

WESTOVER, Myron F., sec. Gen. Electric Co.; b. Vinton, Ia., July 10, 1860; s. William and Sarah (Covert) W.; LL.B., State U. of Ia. Coll. of Law, 1882; m. Lou E. Ham, Nov. 4, 1886; 1 son, Wendell. Admitted to Iowa bar, 1882; practiced at Britt, 1882-83, Dakota City, 1883-84; sec. to pres. of Thomson-Houston Elec. Co., Boston, 1888-94; sec. Gen. Electric Co., 1894-1928 (retired). Republican. Home: Schenectady, N.Y. Died Oct. 21, 1933.

WESTOVER, Oscar, major general; b. Bay City, Mich., July 23, 1883; s. Emil and Kunigunde (Gaertner) W.; grad. U.S. Mil. Acad., 1906. Command and Gen. Staff Sch., 1928, also various air service schs.; m. Adelaide R. Bainbridge, 1907; children—Charles Bainbridge, Katherine Patricia. Pvt. U.S.A., 1901-02; 2d lt. inf., 1906; advanced through grades to major gen. Dec. 1935. Asst. exec. Bur. of Aircraft Production and in office of dir. Air Service, 1918-19; exec. Air Corps, Washington, D.C., and chmn. U.S. Claims Bd., 1919-20; dir. of aircraft production, U.S.A., 1922-28 and since 1932; asst. to chief of Air Corps, 1932-35, and chief of same from Dec. 1935. Winner Nat. Elimination Free Balloon Race, June 1922; army entrant Internat. Balloon Race, Geneva, Switzerland, Aug. 1922. Awarded D.S.M. (U.S.). Presbyn. Mason. Died Sept. 21, 1938.

WETMORE, Edmund, lawyer; b. Utica, N.Y.; s. Edmund Arnold (who was twice mayor of Utica) and Mary Ann (Lothrop) W.; A.B., Harvard, 1860; LL.B., Columbia, 1863; (LL.D., Yale, 1906); m. Helen Howland. In practice at New York; sr. mem. Wetmore & Jenner. Overseer, Harvard, 1889-1901. Pres. Am. Bar Assn., 1900-01. Died July 11, 1918.

WETMORE, Elizabeth Bisland, author; b. Fairfax Plantation, La., Feb. 11, 1861; d. Thomas S. and Margaret (Brownson) Bisland; ed. at home; m. Charles W. Wetmore, Oct. 6, 1891. Began with lit. work for New Orleans Times-Democrat; became one of editors of Cosmopolitan Magazine. Episcopalian. Author: A Flying Trip Around the World, 1892; A Candle of Understanding, 1902; The Secret Life, 1907; Life and Letters of Lafcadio Hearn, 1907; At the Sign of the Hobby Horse. 1908; Seekers in Sicily, 1909; The Case of John Smith, 1916. Died Jan. 6, 1929.

WETMORE, Frank O., banker; b. Kalamazoo, Mich., Nov. 12, 1867; s. Charles I. and Jennie (Orton) W.; ed. pub. schs.; m. Marie Louise Barlow, Apr. 22, 1890; children—Harry Barlow (dec.), Orville Chase (dec.), Horace Orton. Connected with First Nat. Bank, Chicago, 1886—, pres., 1916-25, chmn. bd., 1925—; chmn. bd. First Trust & Savings Bank; dir. Nat. Safe Deposit Co., Chicago City Ry. and associated cos., Chicago Surface Lines, etc. Pres. advisory council, Federal Reserve System. Chmn. finance com. and mem. exec. com. Chicago Chapter of Am. Red Cross; trustee endowment fund of Am. Nat. Red Cross, 1923—. Home: Wheaton, Ill. Died Aug. 26, 1930.

WETMORE, George Peabody, senator; b. during a visit of his parents abroad, at London, Eng., Aug. 2, 1846; s. William Shepard and Anstiss Derby (Rogers) W.; A.B., Yale, 1867, A.M., 1871; LL.B., Columbia, 1869; admitted to bar, 1869; m. Edith Malvina Keteltas, Dec. 23, 1869. Trustee Peabody Mus. Natural History, Yale U., and of Peabody Ednl. Fund. Presdl. elector, 1880, 84; gov. of R.I., 1885-86, 1886-87; defeated for 3d term, 1887; defeated for U.S. senator 1889, but elected U.S. senator for terms, 1895-1901, 1901-07, 1907-13. Republican. Mem. Lincoln Memorial Commn.; chmn. Commn. for Extension and Completion of the Capitol Bldg., Washington. Home: Newport, R.I. Died Sept. 11, 1921.

WETMORE, James Alphonso; b. Bath, N.Y., Nov. 10, 1863; s. Justus Ford and Cornelia O. (Brownell) W.; LL.B., Georgetown U., Washington, D.C., 1896; m. Hattie V. Blye, July 26, 1883; m. 2d, Anna Polk Boush, Apr. 30, 1930. Began as law and court reporter; visited Holland and Scotland, 1883, as agt. to purchase and ship blooded cattle to U.S.; entered Treasury Dept., 1885, and connected with supervising architect's office, 1903-34, acting supervising architect,

1915-34. Methodist. Past Grand Master of Masons of Dist. of Columbia; Grand Representative of Grand Lodge of England near the Grand Lodge of D.C. Home: Coral Gables, Fla. Died Mar. 14, 1940.

WETTLING, Louis Eugene, railroad statistician; b. Vitry le François, France, Dec. 6, 1863; s. Louis and Amélie (Holz) W.; brought to U.S. in infancy; ed. acad. and business coll.; m. Laura Jane Gregory, Apr 28, 1892; children—Louis Eugene, Nelson Gregory, Mary Amanda (Mrs. James D. Vail, Jr.). Accounting and auditing work, St. Louis, Kansas City and Omaha, 1879-99; treas. Farmers and Merchants Ins. Co., Lincoln, Neb., 1899-1908; asst. to atty. gen. State of Neb., 1909-14; with rys. of Western Dist. as mgr. statis. bur., Western Lines, 1914—, except during period of Govt. control; on staff dir. of traffic for dir. gen. of rys. and for 1 yr. after with Assn. Ry. Executives and in charge preparation railroad and miscellaneous data for Joint Commn. of Agrl. Inquiry. Served as witness before Congressional coms., also in rate cases before Interstate Commerce Commn. and before state ry. commns. in the western states. Mem. Kansas City Light Cav. Troop, 1885-90. Republican. Episcopalian. Mason. Home: Evanston, Ill. Died Nov. 15, 1938.

WETZEL, Harry H., gen. mgr. Douglas Aircraft Co., Inc.; b. Tamaqua, Pa., Sept. 18, 1888; s. Louis L. and Elizabeth (Reed) W.; B.S., Pa. State Coll., 1914; m. Maude C. Thomas, May 28, 1919; 1 son, Harry Thomas. Production mgr. Ferro Machine & Foundry Co., Cleveland, O., 1914-16; gen. mgr. Liberty Iron Works, Sacramento, Calif., 1918-19. Ill. Malleable Iron Co., Chicago, 1919-22; v.p. and gen. mgr. Douglas Aircraft Co., Santa Monica, Calif., 1922—. Aircraft prodn. engr. for U.S. Air Corps, 1916-18. Methodist. Mason. Home: Santa Monica, Calif. Died July 5, 1938.

WETZLER, Joseph, engineer; b. Hoboken, N.J., Dec. 6, 1863; s. Albert and Anna (Neumann) W.; M.E., Stevens Inst. Tech., 1882; m. Pauline Gerson, Oct. 30, 1895. Editor Electric World, 1885-90, Electric Engineer, 1890-99; founded, 1898, and from then pres. Electric Engineer Inst. of Correspondence Instrn. Sec. and dir. Hebrew Tech. Institute. Home: New York, N.Y. Died 1911.

WEXLER, Solomon, banker; b. Natchez, Miss., Nov. 29, 1867; s. Philip and Barbara (Weis) W.; ed. Natchez Inst. (pub. sch.), St. George's Hall, Reisterstown, Md., Concordia Inst., Zürich, Switzerland, and Geisowiches Inst., Frankfort, Germany; m. Olga Laroussini, Mar. 15, 1911. Clerk for Henry Frank, wholesale dry goods, Natchez, 1884-88, later traveling salesman for S. E. Worms & Co., New Orleans; began in banking and other business with J. Weis & Co., New Orleans, 1893; founded the Central Bank, New Orleans, 1894, consolidating with Whitney Bank, 1895; v.p. Whitney Central Nat. Bank, and Whitney Central Trust & Savings Bank until 1914; pres. Whitney Central Nat. Bank, 1914-16; mem. J. S. Bache & Co., bankers and brokers, N.Y. City, Jan. 1916—. Deceased.

WEYERHAEUSER, Charles Augustus, lumberman; b. Coal Valley, Ill., Apr. 2, 1866; s. Frederick and Elizabeth Sarah (Bloedel) W.; ed. Phillips Acad., Andover, Mass.; m. Maud Moon, Dec. 14, 1898; children—Carl A., Sarah Maud. Began in lumber business at Rock Island, Ill.; pres. Potlatch (Ida.) Lumber Co., Pine Tree Lumber Co., and mng. dir. numerous other lumber cos. Republican. Presbyn. Mason. Home: St. Paul, Minn. Died Feb. 15, 1930.

WEYERHAEUSER, Frederick, capitalist; b. Neidersaulheim, Germany, Nov. 21, 1834; s. John and Katherine (Gäbel) W.; came to U.S., 1852, and located in Pa.; removed to Ill., 1856; m. Elizabeth Bloedel, Oct. 11, 1857 (died 1911). Went to St. Paul, 1891, engaged extensively in lumber business; commonly known as the "lumber king." Pres. Weyerhaeuser Timber Co. and various other lumber cos., and head of the so-called "Weyerhaeuser Syndicate." Home: St. Paul, Minn. Died Apr. 4, 1914.

WEYERHAEUSER, John Philip, lumberman; b. Coal Valley, Ill., Nov. 4, 1858; s. Frederick and Elizabeth Sarah (Blodel) W.; ed. high sch., Rock Island, Ill.; m. Anna M. Holbrook, Nov. 7, 1901 (died 1933). In timber and lumber business from beginning of active career; pres. Weyerhaeuser Timber Co. and directing head of its affiliated properties. Republican. Presbyn. Home: Tacoma, Wash. Died May 16, 1935.

WEYL, Max, artist; b. Mühlen on the Neckar, Germany, Dec. 1, 1837; s. V. H. and Marium (Getz) W.; ed. pub. schs.; self-taught in art; m. Marium Raff, Feb. 9, 1862. Professionally engaged as landscape artist, 1878—. Represented in Nat. Gallery, Corcoran Gallery of Art, and Cosmos Club, Washington, Albright Gallery, Buffalo; many works in pvt. collections in Washington, New York, Boston, Chicago. Home: Washington, D.C. Died July 6, 1914.

WEYL, Walter Edward, economist; b. Philadelphia, Mar. 11, 1873; s. Nathan and Emilie (Stern) W.; Ph.B., U. of Pa., 1892, Ph.D., 1897, sr. (teaching) fellow, 1897-99; post-grad. work in polit. economy, univs. of Pa., Halle, Berlin and Paris, 1893-96; m. Bertha Poole, 1907. Conducted investigations for U.S. Dept. Labor in Europe, 1898, Mexico, 1901, and Puerto Rico; statistical expert on internal commerce for U.S. Treas. Bur. of Statistics, 1899-1900. Author: The Passenger Traffic of Railways, 1901; The New Democracy, 1912; American World Policies, 1917. Asso. editor The New Republic, 1914-16. Home: Woodstock, N.Y. Died Nov. 9, 1919.

WEYMOUTH, Aubrey, civil engr.; b. Richmond, Va., Nov. 18, 1872; s. Edgar Jenkins and Medora (Strode) W.; C.E., Lehigh Univ., 1894, D.Eng., 1935; m. Alice White, Apr. 27, 1901; children—Medora (Mrs. A. Hawley Peterson), Martha (Mrs. Russell H. Moock). Practiced engring., 1894—; with Post & McCord, New York, 1897—, becoming vice-pres. and chief engineer. Trustee Lehigh Univ. Home: Flushing, N.Y. Died July 27, 1939.

WEYMOUTH, Frank Elwin, civil engr.; b. Medford, Me., June 2, 1874; s. Andrew Jackson and Charlotte Prudence (Powers) W.; C.E., U. of Me., 1896, E.D., 1934; m. Mary Maude Lane, Dec. 3, 1900; m. 2d, Barbara Turner, Nov. 10, 1938. Sewer and water works constrn., Boston and Malden, Mass., 1896-99; asst. city engr. Winnipeg, Man., 1899; with Isthmian Canal Commn. in Nicaragua, C.A., and Washington, 1899-1901; resident engr. Guayaquil & Quito Ry. Co., Ecuador, 1901-02; with U.S. Reclamation Service, 1902-24, on surveys and investigations in Mont. and N.D., 1902-04; project engr. in charge of Lower Yellowstone project in eastern Mont., 1905-08; supervising engr. in charge of Ida Dist., including Snake River drainage in Wyo., Idaho and eastern Ore., covering irrigation of more than 400,000 acres of land, and storage dams at Jackson Lake, Wyo., and on upper branches of Snake and Boisé rivers, including building of the Arrowrock dam, 1909-15; chief of constrn., U.S. Reclamation Service, in charge all work (except legal) in the West, 1916-20, chief engr., Apr. 1920-Oct. 1924; pres. Brock & Weymouth engrs., Nov. 1924-June 1926; chief engr. J. G. White Engring. Corp., S. en C., Mexico, 1926-29; chief engr. of Water Works, City of Los Angeles, Mar. 1929-Dec. 1930; chief engr. Metropolitan Water Dist. of Southern Calif., constructing Colorado River Aqueduct, July 1929-Jan. 1932, gen. mgr. and chief engr., 1932—. Home: San Marino, Calif. Died July 22, 1941.

WEYMOUTH, George Warren, congressman; b. West Amesbury (now Merrimac), Mass., Aug. 25, 1850; s. Rev. Warren and Charity W.; pub. sch. edn.; m. Emma J. Poyen, July 19, 1882. Pres. and gen. mgr. Atlas Tack Co., Fairhaven, Mass., 1900—; also pres. Am. Shoe Finding Co.; dir. and mem. exec. com. Boylston Mfg. Co. (Boston.) Pres. Fitchburg Bd. of Trade; 1 yr. in Fitchburg City Council; mem. Mass. Ho. of Rep., 1896; mem. 55th and 56th Congresses (1897-1901), 4th Mass. District. Mem. Boston Chamber of Commerce. Home: Fairhaven, Mass. Died 1910.

WHALEN, John, lawyer; b. New York, N.Y.; s. Dennis and Ellen W.; ed. pub. schs., New York; LL.B., New York U., 1877; (LL.D., Fordham U., 1895, Manhattan Coll., 1903, St. Francis Xavier Coll., 1909). In practice at New York, 1877—; corp. counsel, Greater New York, 1898-1903; chmn. Bd. Sch. Trustees, 12th Ward, 1881-96; tax commr., 1893-96; commr. Bd. Edn., 1910-13. Pres. Bank of Washington Heights; pres. Am. Federation of Catholic Socs. Now dean Sch. of Law, Fordham U. Home: New York, N.Y. Died Dec. 31, 1926.

WHALLON, Edward Payson, clergyman; b. Putnamville, Ind., Mar. 30, 1849; s. Rev. Thomas and Harriet (Bickle) W.; ed. Hanover (Ind.) Coll., 1864-68; McCormick Theol. Sem., Chicago, 1868-70; grad. Union Theol. Sem., 1872; Ph.D., U. of Wooster, 1885, D.D., 1892; LL.D., Hanover Coll., 1925; m. Margaret E. Kitchell, Nov. 17, 1873; children—Philip P. (dec.), Thomas C., Walter L., Albert Kitchell, Arthur James. Ordained Presbyn. ministry, 1871; stated supply Kasson, Minn., 1870-72; pastor Liberty, Ind., 1872-78, Vincennes, Ind., 1878-87, Fourth Ch., Indianapolis, 1887-91; editor Church at Work, 1886-88, Herald and Presbyter, Cincinnati, 1888-1925, The Presbyterian, 1925—; stated supply, Ludlow, Kentucky, 1892-94, Sixth Church, Cincinnati, 1894-95, Elmwood Place Church, Cincinnati, 1898-1905, Delhi Ch., Cincinnati, 1907-10, Kennedy Heights Church, Cincinnati, 1910-14, Cleves Church, Cincinnati, 1916-21; stated supply Erlanger, Ky., 1927-29. Stated clerk of the Synod of Indiana, 1882-91, Presbytery of Indianapolis, 1890-93; trustee Hanover Coll.; dir. and treas. Western Tract Soc.; corporator Presbyn. Ministers' Fund, Phila.; pres. Bd. of Edn., Wyoming, O. Pres. Cincinnati Chapter S.A.R., and state chaplain S.A.R. of Ohio, also past senior state pres.; comdr. Ohio Commandery of Military Order of the Loyal Legion; chaplain of Military Order Loyal Legion. Mason; Past Grand Prelate Grand Comdry. K.T. of Ind.; Grand Chaplain Masonic Grand Chapter and Grand Council of Ind.; Past Grand Chaplain Masonic Grand Lodge of Ohio; Past Master Masonic Lodge; Past High Priest Masonic Chapter; Past Master Masonic Council; Past Comdr. Masonic Comdry., K.T.; Past Grand Chaplain I.O.G.T. of Ind. Author: History of Vincennes Presbytery; The Foursquare Christian; Pastoral Memories; Some Family Records, Biography, and Genealogy. Contbg. editor of Tri-State Mason. Celebrated the 64th anniversary of his marriage, on Nov. 17, 1937. Home: Wyoming, Cincinnati, O. Died June 3, 1939.

WHAPLES, Meigs H., banker; b. New Britain, Conn., July 16, 1845; s. Curtis and Elizabeth Meigs (Lusk) W.; ed. pub. schs.; m. Harriet Atwater Hotchkiss, May 15, 1888; children—Heywood Hotchkiss, Mary Atwater. Teller New Britain Nat. Bank, 1861-63; teller Mercantile Nat. Bank, Hartford, Conn., 1863-69; teller, 1872-78, treas., 1878-88, pres. 1888-1919, chmn. bd. 1919—, Hartford-Conn. Trust Co.; trustee Soc. for Savings; treas., dir. Collins Co.; trustee Scottish Union & Nat. Ins. Co., State Assurance Co., Ltd. Pres. and treas. Conn. River Bridge and Highway Dist. Commn.; dir. finance com. Hartford Hosp. Adj. 1st Regt., C.N.G., 1866-68; served in U.S.N. as sec. to Rear Adm. O. S. Glisson and Rear Adm. Charles H. Boggs, European Sta., 1869-72. Republican. Conglist. Home: Hartford, Conn. Died May 15, 1928.

WHARTON, Anne Hollingsworth, author; b. Southhampton Furnace, Pa., Dec. 15, 1845; d. Charles and Mary McLanahan (Boggs) W.; grad. pvt. sch., Phila.; Litt.D., U. of Pa., 1924; unmarried. Has been writing from sch. days, principally on Colonial and Revolutionary subjects, also many children's stories and articles for magazines and newspapers. Founder Colonial Dames of America, also Pa. Soc.; the first historian, Nat. Soc. Colonial Dames of America, was a judge Am. Colonial exhibit, Chicago Expn.; life mem. Hist. Soc. of Pa.; vice-pres. of the Genealogical Society of Pa. Author: Colonial Days and Dames, 1894; Heirlooms in Miniatures, 1897; Salons Colonial and Republican, 1900; Social Life in the Early Republic, 1902; Italian Days and Ways, 1906; An English Honeymoon, 1908; In Château Land, 1911; A Rose of Old Quebec, 1913; English Ancestral Homes of Noted Americans, 1915; In Old Pennsylvania Towns, 1920. Asso. editor Furnaces and Forges in the Province of Pa., 1914. Home: Philadelphia, Pa. Died July 29, 1928.

WHARTON, Edith (Newbold Jones), novelist; b. New York, 1862; d. George Frederic and Lucretia Stevens (Rhinelander) Jones; ed. at home; hon. Litt.D. from Yale Univ.; m. Edward Wharton, 1885. Mem. Am. Acad. of Arts and Letters, 1930. Officer Legion of Honor of France and Chevalier Order of Leopold of Belgium. Author: The Greater Inclination, 1899; The Touchstone, 1900; Crucial Instances, 1901; The Valley of Decision, 1902; Sanctuary, 1903; The Descent of Man, and Other Stories, 1904; Italian Villas and Their Gardens, 1904; Italian Backgrounds, 1905; The House of Mirth, 1905; Madame de Treymes, 1907; The Fruit of the Tree, 1907; The Hermit and the Wild Woman, 1908; Motor-flight Through France, 1908; Artemis to Actæon, 1909; Tales of Men and Ghosts, 1910; Ethan Frome, 1911; The Reef, 1912; The Custom of the Country, 1913; Xingu, 1916; Fighting France, 1915; Summer, 1917; The Marne, 1918; French Ways and Their Meaning, 1919; In Morocco, 1920; The Age of Innocence, 1920; Glimpses of the Moon, 1922; A Son at the Front, 1923; False Dawn, 1924; New Year's Day, 1924; Old Maid, 1924; The Spark, 1924; The Mother's Recompense, 1925; The Writing of Fiction, 1925; Here and Beyond, 1926; Twilight Sleep, 1927; The Children, 1928; Hudson River Bracketed, 1929; Certain People, 1930; A Backward Glance (autobiography), 1934. Awarded gold medal, Nat. Inst. Arts and Sciences. Died Aug. 11, 1937.

WHARTON, Henry Marvin, clergyman; b. Culpeper Co., Va., Sept. 11, 1848; s. Malcom Hart and Susan Roberts (Colvin) W.; ed. Roanoke Coll., U. of Va., Southern Bapt. Theol. Sem.; m. Lucy Kimball Pollard, Oct. 31, 1893; children—May, James, Marvyn. Served as pvt. in C.S.A.; at close of war went to Mex. with Gen. Sterling Price and Gov. Isham G. Harris; returned home, 1866; practiced law at Lynchburg, Va., 1868-73; ordained Bapt. ministry, 1873; pastor successively Luray, Va., 1874-80, Lee St. Ch., Baltimore, 1881-84; founded, 1886, Brantly Memorial Ch., Baltimore; resigned 1899; evangelist and lecturer, 1898-1909; resumed pastorate of Brantly Ch., Sept. 1909. Founded, 1884, editor, 1884-98, The Evangel; founded Orphanage, 1882, "Whosoever" Farm, 1884; founder and owner Wharton Grove Camp Ground. Pres. Southern Hosp. of Baltimore; maj. gen. comdg. Md. Div. U.C.V., also chaplain gen. several terms. Democrat. Author: Pulpit, Pew and Platform, 1890; Sermons and Addresses, 1891; Picnic in Palestine, 1892; Home Religion, 1898; War Songs of the Confederacy, 1904; White Blood (novel), 1906; Messages of Mercy (sermon). Home: Baltimore, Md. Died June 23, 1928.

WHARTON, Henry Redwood, surgeon; b. Phila., Pa., May 23, 1853; s. Charles and Mary W.; M.D., U. of Pa., 1876; m. Edith Booth, 1889. Surgeon Presbyn. and Children's hosps., Phila. Fellow Am. Surg. Assn. Author: Textbook on Minor Surgery and Bandaging, 1893; The Practice of Surgery (Wharton and Curtis), 1899. Home: Berwyn, Pa. Died Dec. 3, 1925.

WHARTON, Joseph, mfr.; b. Philadelphia, Mar. 3, 1826; ed. by pvt. tutors; (Sc.D., Univ. of Pa.,

LL.D., Swarthmore Coll.); clerk in mercantile house, 1845-47; afterward a white lead mfr. and connected with other enterprise; mgr., 1853-63, the Lehigh Zinc Co., for which he built, 1860, the 1st successful spelter works in U.S.; purchased, 1873, the Gap Nickel Mines, Lancaster Co., Pa., and established in Camden, N.J., the first successful nickel and cobalt works in America; dir. Bethlehem Iron Co.; subsequently in Bethlehem Steel Works, the first armor plate plant in America; also identified with several ry. and other corps. Sole owner 3 blast furnaces at Wharton, N.J., and of Andover Iron Co., Phillipsburg, N.J. Pres. bd. of mgrs., Swarthmore Coll., and endowed its chair of history and economics; also founded the Wharton Sch. of Finance and Commerce, Univ. of Pa., which he has given $500,000. Originally Whig; Republican since that party was formed; declined a sure election to Congress; head of McKinley electoral ticket of Pa., 1896. Home: Milestown, Pa. Died 1909.

WHARTON, Morton Bryan, clergyman, author; b. in Orange Co., Va., Apr. 5, 1839; s. Malcom H. and Susan Roberts (Colvin) W.; ed. Orange Acad., 1854, Culpeper Acad., 1855, Richmond (Va.) Coll., 1858-61, A B.—graduation day prevented by war; Univ. of Va. Mil. Sch., 1861; (D.D., Washington and Lee Univ., 1875; LL.D., U. of Ala., 1906); m. Mary Belle Irwin, Aug. 2, 1864. Clerk to Maj. A. M Barbour, chief q.m. to Gen. Joseph E. Johnson, 1861-62. In Bapt. ministry as pastor 1st Bapt. Ch., Bristol, Tenn., 1862-64, 1st Bapt. Ch., Eufaula, Ala., 1867-72, Walnut St. Baptist Ch., Louisville, 1872-75, 1st Bapt. Ch., Augusta, Ga., 1876-77; corr. sec Southern Bapt. Theol. Sem., 1877-81; U.S. consul, Sonneberg, Germany, 1881-83; editor Christian Index, Atlanta, Ga., 1883-84; pastor 1st Bapt. Ch., Montgomery, Ala., 1884-91, Freemason St. Bapt. Ch., Norfolk, Va., 1891-99, Brantly Bapt. Ch., Baltimore, 1899, 1st Bapt. Ch., Eufaula, Ala., 1900—. Weekly contbr. to Atlanta (Ga.) Journal, 1903-04. Maker of word "Pastorium," coined after analogy of auditorium, meaning a parsonage. Democrat. Author: European Notes, 1884; Famous Women of the Old Testament, 1889; Famous Women of the New Testament, 1890; Pictures from a Pastorium, 1898; Famous Men of the Old Testament; Sacred Songs to Popular Airs, 1904. Home: Eufaula, Ala. Died 1908.

WHARTON, Turner Ashby, clergyman; b. Greensboro, N.C., July 8, 1862; s. Jesse Rankin and Martha Lavinia (Turner) W.; A.B., U. of N.C., 1883; B.D., Union Theol. Sem., Richmond, Va., 1886; D.D., King Coll., Bristol, Tenn., 1898; LL.D., Austin Coll., Sherman, Tex., 1925; m. Lucy Taliaferro, 1886 (dec.); m. 2d, Floy Hurt, 1899; children—Nannie Terry (wife of Dr. T. C. Vinson), Jessie Turner (wife of Dr. C. E. Allen), Conway T., Lawrence H., Catherine, Turner Ashby, Floyd Watson, Park Street. Ordained ministry Presbyn. Ch. in U.S., 1886; pastor successively Waynesville and Steel Creek, N.C., Abingdon, Va., Alabama Street Ch., Memphis, and First Ch., Columbia, Tenn., until 1909, First Ch., Sherman, Tex., 1909-28 (emeritus). Chmn. Speakers Bur. of N. Tex., World War; mem. Charter Com. of Sherman. Trustee King Coll., Westminster Presbyn. Encampment; moderator Synod of Tenn., 1907, of Tex., 1919. Democrat. Mason. Home: Sherman, Tex. Died Oct. 25, 1935.

WHARTON, William Fisher, lawyer; b. Jamaica Plain, Mass., June 28, 1847; s. William Craig W.; A.B., Harvard, 1870, LL.B., 1873; m. Fanny Pickman, Oct. 31, 1877; m. 2d, Susan Carberry Lay, Feb. 10, 1891. Practiced in Boston. Mem. Mass. Ho. of Rep., 1885-88; asst. Sec. of State, U.S., 1889-93. Editor: (Last edit.) Story on Partnership. Home: Groton, Mass. Died May 20, 1919.

WHEAT, George Seay, author; b. Gallatin, Tenn., Sept. 14, 1886; s. Frank and Clara (Seay) W.; Sewanee Mil. Acad.; spl. work U. of South and Columbia; m. Ensley Hodgson, June 9, 1917; children—George Seay, John Potter, Edward Lauderdale. Reporter New York Press, 1911; later with New York Evening Sun, and with New York Herald until 1917. Commd. lt. U.S.N.R.F., May 1, 1917, and assigned as intelligence officer, cable censorship, New York, later at Naval Intelligence Office, Washington, D.C.; served on deck duty, U.S.S. Koningen der Niederlanden, transporting troops between Newport News, Va., and Brest, France; hon. discharged, Dec. 2, 1918. Mem. Com. Pub. Information Service, supplying Pres. Wilson with news from America while at the Peace Conf.; formerly public relations counsel, N.Y., N.H. &H. R.R., New York, Westchester & Boston Ry., County Transportation Co., etc.; became v.p. United Aircraft Corp. (Del.); editor of the Bee Hive, a monthly aeronautical publ. An organizer Am. Legion, 1919. Vice pres., gov. and mem. exec. com. Aeronautical Chamber of Commerce; gov. Nat. Aeronautic Assn. Republican. Episcopalian. Author: The Story of the Americain Legion, 1919; Municipal Landing Fields and Airports, 1921. Contbr. to mags. Home: Darien, Conn. Died Dec. 26, 1937.

WHEATLAND, Marcus Fitzherbert, M.D.; b. Bridgetown, Barbados, B.W.I., Feb. 17, 1868; s. John and Helen (Stoute) W.; ed. pvt. sch., Barbados, 8 yrs.; M.D., Howard U., Washington, 1895, hon. A.M., 1906; LL.D., Wilberforce (Ohio) U.; m. Irene De Mortie, June 22, 1898 (dec.); children—Marcus F., Helen M. Mem. nat., state and local med. societies. Trustee Howard U., Washington. Home: Newport, R.I. Died Aug. 16, 1934.

WHEATON, Frank, maj. gen. U.S.A., retired, 1897; b. Providence, R.I., May 8, 1833; s. Dr. Francis L. W.; grad. Brown Univ., A.M.; became surveyor; went to Calif., 1850; employed as civil engr. on Mexican boundaries; commd. lt. 1st U.S. cav., 1855; served in Kan., Mo., and in Neb., against Indians, becoming capt., March 1861; lt. col. 2d R.I. vols., July 1861; brig. gen. vols., Nov. 1862, and by bvt. became maj. gen. vols. and U.S. army; comd. a div. at Gettysburg and Shenandoah Valley campaigns; was with Army of the Potomac from first Bull Run to Lee's surrender; particularly distinguished himself in battles of the Wilderness, Cedar Creek and Petersburg. After war, served from lt. col. to maj. gen. regular army until age of retirement. Home: Washington, D.C. Died 1903.

WHEATON, Loyd, maj. gen. U.S.A.; b. Pennfield, Mich., July 15, 1838; s. William G. and Amanda M. (Parker) W.; m. Mrs. Charlotte Flower Derby, Dec. 17, 1867 (died 1905), desc. of Flower family and of Gov. William Bradford, Plymouth. Enlisted as 1st sergt. Co. E, 8th Ill. Inf., April 20, 1861; discharged, July 24, 1861; commd. 1st lt. 8th Ill. Inf., July 25, 1861; capt., Mar. 25, 1862; maj., Aug. 28, 1863; lt. col., Nov. 25, 1864; hon. mustered out, May 1, 1866; apptd. from Ill., capt. 34th U.S. Inf., July 28, 1866; assigned to 20th Inf., Sept. 1, 1869; maj., Oct. 14, 1891; lt. col., May 31, 1895; transferred to 20th Inf., September 11, 1895; brig. gen. vols., May 27, 1898; transferred to 2d U.S. Inf., Dec. 30, 1898, col. 20th Inf., Feb. 6, 1899; hon. discharged from vol. service, Apr. 15, 1899; brig. gen. vols., Apr. 15, 1899; transferred to 7th U.S. Inf., Feb. 3, 1900; maj. gen. vols., June 18, 1900; brig. gen. U.S.A., Feb. 2, 1901; hon. disch. from vol. service, Feb. 28, 1901; maj. gen. U.S.A., Mar. 30, 1901; retired by operation of law, July 15, 1902. Bvtd.: maj., Mar. 2, 1867, "for gallant and meritorious services in siege of Vicksburg, Miss."; lt. col., Mar. 2, 1867, for same, in assault on Ft. Blakely, Ala.; col. vols., Mar. 26, 1865, for same during campaign against Mobile; maj. gen. vols., June 19, 1899, "for gallantry in action against insurgents nr. Imus, P.I."; awarded Congressional Medal of Honor, Jan. 16, 1894, "for distinguished gallantry in assault on Ft. Blakely, Ala., Apr. 9, 1865, leading right wing of his regt. springing through an embrasure against a strong fire of artillery and musketry and first to enter enemy's works." Participated in many battles and engagements during Civil War; wounded at Shiloh; in service at western and other posts to 1898; comd. div. 7th Army Corps, Spanish-Am. War; participated in all principal battles and combats in P.I., 1899-1902; comd. depts. Northern Luzon and North Philippines, 1900-02, including army of 35,000 men. Home: Chicago, Ill. Died Sept. 17, 1918.

WHEELAN, Fairfax Henry, merchant; b. San Francisco, Sept. 27, 1856; s. Peter and Catherine Frances (Baker) W.; ed. various schs., Calif., Christian Brothers' Sch., Dublin, Ireland, Joshua Kendall's Prep. Sch., Cambridgeport, Mass.; A.B., Harvard, 1880; m. Albertine Randall, May 18, 1887. In flour milling and other business, Calif., 1880-94; v.p. and mgr. Southern Pacific Milling Co., and Salinas Valley Lumber Co., San Francisco, 1894—; pres. The Jessup-Wheelan Co. Unitarian. Republican—active in movements to purify politics of San Francisco. Home: San Francisco, Calif. Died Mar. 26, 1915.

WHEELAN, James Nicholas, brig. gen. U.S.A.; b. Pa., Dec. 6, 1837. Served as 1st sergt. Co. A, 1st N.Y. Mounted Rifles, July 18-Dec. 6, 1861; commd. 2d lt., Dec. 7, 1861; capt., Feb. 7, 1862; maj., Aug. 13, 1862; bvt. col., Mar. 13, 1865; lt. col., 1st N.Y. Mounted Rifles, Aug. 17, 1865; hon. mustered out, Nov. 29, 1865; apptd. from N.Y., 2d lt. 2d U.S. Cav., Feb. 23, 1866; 1st lt., July 20, 1866; capt., Dec. 15, 1873; maj. 8th Cav., Mar. 7, 1893; lt. col. 7th Cav., June 9, 1899; col. 12th Cav., Feb. 2, 1901; retired by operation of law, Dec. 6, 1901; advanced to rank of brig. gen. retired, by act of Apr. 23, 1904. Bvtd.: col. vols., March 13, 1865, "for gallant and meritorious services during the war"; maj., Feb. 27, 1890, "for gallant services in action against Indians on the Rosebud, Mont., May 7, 1877." Was detailed as mil. attache to the courts of Netherlands, Belgium, and Berlin, temporarily. Died Nov. 30, 1922.

WHEELER, Albert Gallatin, capitalist; b. New York, Apr. 27, 1854; s. Bethuel Church and Julia Catherine (Lawrence) W.; A.B., Coll. City of New York, 1868; m. Cassie Gould Taylor, Feb. 12, 1873. In produce transportation business on North River, New York, 1869-79; became identified with constrn. of telegraph lines, railroads, underground electric traction systems at Washington and New York, the introduction of automatic switchboards for telephone service, and building the tunnels under the streets of Chicago to be used as a transfer system for freight and as a terminal for steam railroads; removed to Chicago, 1899. Pres. Ill. Tunnel Co., Ill. Telephone & Telegraph Co., Ill. Telephone Constrn Co. Republican. Home: Chicago, Ill. Sept. 24, 1917.

WHEELER, Alvin Sawyer, prof. organic chemistry; b. Holyoke, Mass., Nov. 2, 1866; s. William Carleton and Sarah Elizabeth (Couch) W.; A.B., Beloit (Wis.) Coll., 1890; A.M., Harvard, 1897, Ph D., 1900; studied U. of Berlin, 1910, Swiss Federal Polytechnic, Zurich, 1911; m. Edith Myra James, Aug. 24, 1899; children—James Robert (dec.), William Couch, Henry James. Teacher, high sch., Tacoma, Wash., 1893-97; asst. in organic chemistry, Harvard, 1897-1900; with U. of N.C., 1900—, prof. organic chemistry, 1912—. Presbyn. Home: Chapel Hill, N.C. Died May 12, 1940.

WHEELER, Andrew Carpenter ("Nym Crinkle"), dramatic critic, author; b. New York, N.Y., June 4, 1835; has served on staff of various New York papers as dramatic and musical critic. Author: The Chronicles of Milwaukee; The Twins (comedy); The Primrose Path of Dalliance; Easter in a Hospital Bed; etc. Died 1903.

WHEELER, Arthur Dana, lawyer; b. Kenosha, Wis., Mar. 2, 1861; s. Jerome B. and Kate (Deming) W.; B.A., Lake Forest (Ill.) U., 1881; went to Chicago in 1882; LL.B., Union Coll. of Law, Chicago, 1884; (hon. M.A., Ill. Coll., 1903); m. Anna Holt, Dec. 23, 1886. In practice at Chicago, 1884—; mem. Holt, Wheeler & Sidley (successors to Williams & Thompson, 1866-88, and Williams, Holt & Wheeler, 1888-99), 1886—; pres. 1903-08, chmn. bd. dirs., 1908—, Chicago Telephone Co. Trustee Presbyn. Hosp of Chicago. Interested in church, Y.M.C.A., and civic welfare organizations for many yrs. Home: Chicago, and Lake Forest, Ill. Died Aug. 29, 1912.

WHEELER, Arthur Leslie, prof. Latin; b. Hartford, Conn., Aug. 12, 1871; s. William Ruthven and Emily Elizabeth (Crego) W.; A.B., Yale, 1893 (Phi Beta Kappa); post-grad. work, same univ., 1893-96, Ph.D., 1896; m. May Louise Waters, June 20, 1895 (died 1915); 1 dau., Ruth (Mrs. Edward S. Jackson); m. 2d, Anna Johnson Pell, July 6, 1915. Instr. in Latin, Yale, 1894-1900; asso. prof. Latin, 1900-05, prof., 1905-25, Bryn Mawr Coll., also head of dept., and faculty dir. of the coll.; prof. of Latin, Princeton, 1925—, and chmn. dept. of classics, 1926—. Republican. Protestant. Home: Princeton, N.J. Died 1932.

WHEELER, Arthur Martin, university prof.; b. Weston, Conn., Jan. 21, 1836; s. Willis and Eliza (Fairchild) W.; A.B., Yale, 1857, A.M., 1887; studied in France, and Germany, 1864-68; (LL.D., Hamilton, 1896); m. Harriette Skinner Staples, Oct. 1, 1879. Tutor, 1861-64, prof. and Durfee prof. history, 1868-1906, prof. emeritus, 1906, lecturer on European history, 1906-11, Yale. Home: New Haven, Conn. Died July 17, 1918.

WHEELER, Benjamin Ide, university pres.; b. Randolph, Mass., July 15, 1854; s. Benjamin and Mary E. (Ide) W.; A.B., Brown U., 1875, A.M., 1878; Ph.D., U. of Heidelberg, 1885; LL.D., Princeton, 1896, Harvard, 1900, Brown, 1900, Yale, 1901, Johns Hopkins, 1902, Univ. of Wis., 1904, Ill. Coll., 1904, Dartmouth, 1905, Columbia, 1906, U. of Ky., 1916; Ph.D., Univ. of Athens, 1912; L.H.D., Colgate, 1915; m. Amey Webb, June 27, 1881; 1 son, Benjamin Webb. Instr. Latin and Greek, Brown U., 1879-81; instr. German, Harvard, 1885-86; acting prof. classical philology, 1886-87, prof. comparative philology, 1887-88, Greek and comparative philology, 1888-99, Cornell U.; pres. U. of Calif., July 18, 1899-July 15, 1919, pres. emeritus and prof. comparative philology. Prof. Greek lit., Am. Sch. Classical Studies, Athens, 1895-96; lecturer Harvard, 1898. Roosevelt prof. U. of Berlin, 1909-10. Corr. mem. Kaiserliches Archæologisches Institut. Author: The Greek Noun-Accent, 1885; Analogy in Language, 1887; Introduction to the History of Language, 1890; Dionysos and Immortality, 1899; Organization of Higher Education in U.S., 1896; Life of Alexander the Great, 1900 (translated into Russian); Unterricht und Demokratie in Amerika, 1910. Home: Berkeley, Calif. Died May 3, 1927.

WHEELER, Candace Thurber, author; b. Delhi, N.Y.; d. Abner G. and Lucy (Dunham) Thurber; ed. Delaware Acad.; m. Thomas M. Wheeler, 1846. Founder of first Soc. of Decorative Arts; also founder Associated Artists; dir. Woman's Bldg., Chicago Expn., 1893; chmn. Woman's Art Com. of Expn Congress, 1893. Author: Double Darling and Other Fairy Tales, 1893; Household Art, 1894; Content in a Garden, 1900; Decorators and Decorating, 1900; Domestic Weavings, 1900; How to Make Rugs, 1902; Principles of Home Decoration, 1903; The Dream Spinner, 1905; Yesterdays in a Busy Life, 1918. Home: Hollis, L.I., N.Y. Died Aug. 5, 1923.

WHEELER, Charles Barker, judge; b. Poplar Ridge, N.Y., Dec. 27, 1851; s. Cyrenus, Jr., and Jane (Barker) W.; A.B., Williams, 1873, LL.D., 1913; studied law with Sprague & Gorham, Buffalo, and admitted to bar, 1876; m. Frances Munro Rochester, June 28, 1833 (dec.); children—Thomas Rochester, Jane Barker (Mrs. Roland Lord O'Brian); m. 2d, Ruth Gunther Winant, Aug. 19, 1931. Mem. Municipal Civ. Service Commn., Buffalo, 1889-99 and 1902-05 (chmn. 10 yrs.); member special tax commission, 1906, to examine into and report on tax system of New York; appointed justice Supreme Court of New York, 8th

Judicial District, Nov. 28, 1906, for term expiring Dec. 31, 1907; nominated for full term of 14 yrs. as justice Supreme Court by both Rep. and Dem. and Independent League parties, Sept. 23, 1907, and elected for term 1908-21; official referee of Supreme Court, Jan. 1922—. Republican. Home: Buffalo, N.Y. Died Nov. 1935.

WHEELER, C(harles) Gilbert, chemist; b. London, Canada, July 23, 1836; s. William and Caroline M. W.; B.S., Harvard, 1858; studied in German univs.; m. Sarah Jenkins, May 10, 1863. Asst. state geologist of Mo., 1859-61; U.S. consul to Nuremberg, 1862-67; traveled in Europe and N. Africa, 1867-68; prof. chemistry, U. of Chicago and Chicago Med. Coll., 1868; frequent visits to Mexico and Central America examining mines for Am. capitalists, 1868-1900; invented "Babcock" chem. fire extinguisher, 1869; scientific expert for Bell Telephone Co. and other cos. in patent and other litigation; reads 11 and speaks 7 modern langs. State commr. from Ill. to Vienna Expn., 1873; pres. Chicago Coll. Pharmacy, 1882; geologist and interpreter in commn. to examine route Nicaragua Canal, 1899. Consul at Chicago for Republic of Panama. Author: Natural History Charts; Catalogue Polyglottus; Determinative Mineralogy; Chemistry of Building Materials; Medical Chemistry. Home: Chicago, Ill. Died 1912.

WHEELER, Charles Stetson, lawyer; b. Fruitvale, Calif., Dec. 11, 1863; s. Charles Carroll and Angeline (Stetson) W.; B.L., U. of Calif., 1884; Hastings Coll. of Law, 1884-86; m. Lillian Marsh, Dec. 3, 1887. Entered law office of John H. Boalt, San Francisco, 1884; in practice at San Francisco, with his son. Alternate del. at large Rep. Nat. Conv., Chicago, 1908; del. at large Rep. and Prog. nat. convs., Chicago, 1912; alternate del. Rep. Nat. Conv., 1920 (placed Hiram W. Johnson in nomination). Mem. Com. of Fifty, after San Francisco Earthquake and Fire; sec. Relief Corp.; regent U. of California. Home: San Francisco, Calif. Died Apr. 27, 1923.

WHEELER, Daniel Davis, brigadier gen. U.S.A.; b. Cavendish, Vt., July 12, 1841; s. Daniel Hosmer and Susan (Davis) W.; ed. Leland Sem.; m. Nannie Phillips Smith, Jan. 16, 1896. Apptd. 2d lt. 4th Vt. Inf., Sept. 21, 1861; 1st lt., Apr. 21, 1862; hon. mustered out, Sept. 21, 1864; capt. a.a.g., June 30, 1864; maj. a.a.g., Dec. 27, 1864; lt. col. a.a.g., May 26, 1865-June 11, 1866; hon. mustered out, Oct. 19, 1866. Apptd. 2d lt. 1st Arty., May 11, 1866; 1st lt., Feb. 12, 1867; capt. a.q.m., July 2, 1879; maj. q.m., Sept. 6, 1893; lt. col. deputy q.m. gen., Nov. 11, 1898; col. a.q.m. gen., Oct. 2, 1902; brig. gen. U.S.A., Aug. 15, 1903, and retired Aug. 16, 1903, at own request after 40 yrs.' service. In Spanish War was lt. col. and chief q.m. U.S.V., May 9, 1898; col. q.m., Sept. 3, 1898-Mar. 1899. Bvtd.: capt., Mar. 2, 1867, for Salem Heights and Cold Harbor; maj. vols., Sept. 29, 1864, for campaign of 1864; col. vols., Dec. 1, 1865, "for faithful and meritorious services during war"; awarded Congressional Medal of Honor. Home: Fredericksburg, Va. Died July 27, 1916.

WHEELER, David Hilton, clergyman, educator, author; b. Ithaca, N.Y., Nov. 18, 1829; s. Solomon and Alice (Babcock) W.; ed. Rock River Sem., Mt. Morris, Ill.; (A.M., 1858; D.D., 1867, Cornell; LL.D., Northwestern Univ., 1881). Prof. Greek language and literature, 1857-59; prof. ancient languages, 1859-60; prof. Greek, 1860-61, Cornell Coll. U.S. Consul, Genoa, Italy, 1861-66. Prof. English literature, Northwestern Univ., 1867-75. Editor The Methodist, New York, 1875-82. Pres. Allegheny Coll., Meadville, Pa., 1883-92. Author: Brigandage in South Italy, 1864; The Conspiracy of Frischi, 1866; By-Ways of Literature, 1883; A Sketch of J. A. Froude, 1883; Our Industrial Utopia, 1895; etc. Died 1902.

WHEELER, Ebenezer Smith, engineer; b. Wayne Co., Pa., Aug. 27, 1839; s. Ransom and Adeline W.; C.E., U. of Mich., 1867 (hon. M.S., 1897); m. Clara P. Fuller. U.S. asst. engr., 1867—; was engr. in constrn. of Saint Ste. Marie locks; chief engr. Nicaragua Canal Commn. of 1887. Home: Detroit, Mich. Died Jan. 5, 1913.

WHEELER, Edward Jewitt, editor; b. Cleveland, O., Mar. 11, 1859; s. Alfred (D.D.) and Lydia Priscilla (Curtis) W.; brother of Olin Dunbar W.; A.B., Ohio Wesleyan U., 1879 (Litt.D., 1905); m. Jennie L. Fleming, Nov. 23, 1887 (died 1917). Editor of The Voice, 1884-98, The Literary Digest, 1895-1905, Current Literature (later Current Opinion), July 1905—. Lit. adviser Funk & Wagnalls Co.; pres. Current Literature Pub. Co. Vice-chmn. Citizens' Union of New York, 1905-06; pres. Poetry Soc. of America, 1909-19. Trustee Ohio Wesleyan U.; Officier de la Instruction Publique. Home: New York, N.Y. Died July 15, 1922.

WHEELER, Everett Pepperrell, lawyer; b. New York, N.Y., Mar. 10, 1840; s. David E. and Elizabeth (Jarvis) W.; A.B., Coll. City of New York, 1856, A.M., 1859; LL.B., Harvard, 1859; (hon. A.M., Dartmouth, 1861); m. Lydia Loraine, d. Hon. S. H. Hodges, of Rutland, Vt., Nov. 22, 1866 (died 1902); m. 2d, Alice, d. Pres. Daniel Coit Gilman, Apr. 26, 1904. Mem. Bd. of Edn., New York, 1877-79; chmn. New York City Civ. Service Commn., 1883-89, 1895-97. Pres. Reform Club, 1889-90, Church Club, 1891-92; chmn. law com. Nat. Civ. Serv. League, 1914-19; pres. N.Y. Civil Service Reform Assn., 1914-18; chmn. exec. com. Am. Constl. League. Dep. Episcopal Gen. Conv., 1907, 10, 13; pres. Intercollegiate Branch Y.M.C.A., 1912-19. Author: Wages and the Tariff, 1888; Modern Law of Carriers, 1890; Real Bimetallism, 1895; The Harter Act, 1899; The Knowledge of Faith, 1904; Daniel Webster, Expounder of the Constitution, 1905; Sixty Years of American Life, 1916; A Lawyer's Study of the Bible, 1919. Home: New Hamburg, N.Y. Died Feb. 8, 1925.

WHEELER, Frederick Freeman, capitalist; b. Oshkosh, Wis., Feb. 25, 1859; s. John C. and Adaline (Freeman) W.; common and high school edn., Vineland, N.J.; m. Alice M. Amsden, Dec. 25, 1879 (died 1891); m. 2d, Hattie L. Hall, June 6, 1893 (died 1909). In mercantile business, Albany, N.Y., 1882-98; located in Los Angeles, 1898, and became an extensive real estate owner. Prominent in Prohibition Party from its organization; received votes of delegates from 17 states for presdl. nomination, at Prohibition Nat. Conv., 1908; leader in a statewide citizens' movement to make "California Dry in 1914." Pres. Bd. Pub. Utilities, Los Angeles; prominent in civic affairs. Unitarian. Home: Los Angeles, Calif. Died Feb. 8, 1917.

WHEELER, Frederick Seymour, chmn. bd. Am. Can Co.; b. Mt. Carroll, Ill.; s. David Hilton (D.D.) and Sophia (Seymour) W.; A.B. and A.M., Northwestern U., 1881; m. Charlotte Putnam, June 11, 1891; 1 son, Arthur E. With Am. Can Co., 1901—, successively treas., vice pres., pres., now chmn. bd. Home: Locust Valley, N.Y. Died Apr. 24, 1936.

WHEELER, George Carpenter, agrl. journalist; b. Burlington, Kan., Feb. 1, 1872; s. George Jay and Julia Eliza (Carpenter) W.; B.S., Kan. State Agrl. Coll., 1895; grad. study U. of Ill., Cornell U.; m. Kitty Myrtle Smith, May 18, 1898; children—Ruth, George Smith, Helen Virginia (Mrs. Carroll W. Parmeter), Mary Frances (Mrs. Thos. E. Bailey). Asst., Expt. Sta. Kan. State Agrl. Coll., 1902-05; asso. prof. animal husbandry, same coll., 1905-07, specialist in animal husbandry and gen. field work, extension div., 1907-13; asso. editor and mgr. livestock advertising, Kansas Farmer, Topeka, later editor in chief, 1913-22; editor, later managing editor Western Farm Life, Denver, Colo., 1922—; chmn. Colo. Agrl. Advisory Council, 1934; broadcaster Farm Question Box over Station KOA. Mem. Denver Council Boy Scouts of America. Republican. Conglist. Home: Denver, Colo. Died Oct. 20, 1934.

WHEELER, George Wakeman, judge; b. Woodville, Miss., Dec. 1, 1860; s. Hon. George W. and Lucy (Dowie) W.; grad. Hackensack (N.J.) Acad., 1876, Williston Sem., Easthampton, Mass., 1877; B.A., Yale, 1881, LL.B., 1883, LL.D., 1919; D.C.L., Wesleyan U., Middletown, Conn., 1931; m. Agnes L. Macy, July 5, 1894; children—Helen L., George Macy. Practiced law at Bridgeport, Conn., 1883-93; mem. Wheeler & Curtis; city atty., 1890-92; judge, Superior Ct. of Conn., Feb. 28, 1893-Sept. 8, 1910; justice Supreme Court of Errors, of Conn., 1910-20, chief justice, 1920-Dec. 1930. Mem. State Council of Defense, 1918-19; chmn. exec. com. War Bur. City of Bridgeport, 1917-19; chmn. Conn. State Bar Examining Com., 1912-19. Mem. council Am. Law Inst.; chmn. Judicial Council of Conn., 1927-30; pres. Fairfield County Law Library Assn.; mem. Tercentenary Conn. Commn.; trustee Conn. Coll. for Women. Home: Bridgeport, Conn. Died July 27, 1932.

WHEELER, Henry, clergyman; b. Wedmore, Somersetshire, Eng., Feb. 22, 1835; s. Harry and Ann (Durston) W.; ed. Ch. of England day sch., Wyoming Sem., Kingston, Pa.; studied conf. course M.E. Ch.; (D.D., Little Rock [Ark.] Coll., 1890); m. Mary Sparkes, Apr. 13, 1858; father of Post W. Entered M.E. ministry, 1855; entered Union Army, 1862, was elected chaplain 17th Pa. Cav. Mem. G.A.R., Loyal Legion. Republican. Author: The Memory of the Just, 1878; Methodism and the Temperance Reformation, 1882; Rays of Light in the Valley of Sorrow, 1883; The Probationer, 1903; History and Exposition of the Twenty-five Articles of Religion of the Methodist Episcopal Church, 1908; The Apostles' Creed, 1913. Home: Ocean Grove, N.J. Died Apr. 25, 1925.

WHEELER, Henry Lord, chemist; b. Chicago, Sept. 14, 1867; s. George Henry and Alice I. (Lord) W.; Ph.B., Yale, 1890, Ph.D., 1893; U. of Munich, 1893-94, U. of Chicago, 1894-95; m. Eva F. Swarthout, Mar. 16, 1906. Asst. in chemistry, 1890-95, instr. organic chemistry, 1895-99, asst. prof., 1899-1908, prof., 1908—, Yale. Home: New Haven, Conn. Died 1914.

WHEELER, Henry Nathan, head of educational dept. of Houghton, Mifflin & Co., publishers; b. Concord, Mass., Sept. 3, 1850; s. Joel and Almira (Tuttle) W.; early edn. Concord public schools; grad. Harvard, 1871; tech. edn. in Lawrence Scientific School, Harvard, Univ. of Göttingen, Germany (A.M., Harvard, 1875); m. Katharine Coolidge Howe, Sept. 13, 1883. Instr. mathematics, Harvard, 1877-82; in publishing business, 1882—. Author: Elements of Plane Trigonometry, 1876; Spherical Trigonometry, 1878; Logarithms, 1882; Second Lessons in Arithmetic, 1888. Editor Harvard Univ. Catalogue, 1878-82; revised edit. Warren Colburn's Intellectual Arithmetic, 1883. Pres. of the Good Government League of Cambridge, Mass. Home: Cambridge, Mass. Died 1905.

WHEELER, Herbert Locke, dentist, educator; b. Corry, Pa., Jan. 12, 1869; s. Lyman A. and Mary (Rogers) W.; grad. Phila. Dental Coll., 1890; Sc.D., Alfred U., 1921; m. Gertrude M. Slater, June 10, 1891; children—Clifford Slater, Arthur Chapin, Katherine W. Began practice at Worcester, Mass., 1890; was clin. instr. Phila. Dental College; prof. prosthetics and orthodontia, Coll. Dental and Oral Surgery, New York, 12 yrs., 1908-20; prof. New York U., 2 yrs., 1927-29; organizer and chief of dental service, Bellevue Hosp., 20 yrs. Served in hosp. in France, 1916; pres. Bd. Examiners for Commissions in Dental Corps, N.Y. City, 1917-19. Fellow Am. Acad. Dental Surgery, Am. Coll. Dentists. Maj. Dental R.C., U.S.A. Trustee Alfred U. Chevalier Legion of Honor (France). Republican. Episcopalian. Home: Stamford, Conn. Died Mar. 23, 1929.

WHEELER, Hiram Nicholas, editor; b. St. Charles, Ill., Mar. 30, 1844; s. James Taylor and Jerusha Ann (Young) W.; self-ed.; m. Bertha S. Littlefield, Jan. 25, 1889. Pvt. Co. G, 52d Regt. Ill. Inf., 1861-65. In newspaper work, 1868—; editor and pub. Quincy Daily Journal, 1883—. Mem. Dem. State Com. 10 yrs. (1st vice chmn. 2 yrs.). Mem. Nat. Editorial Assn., Ill. State Press Assn., Ill. Daily Press Assn. Home: Quincy, Ill. Died Sept. 3, 1916.

WHEELER, Homer Webster, soldier, author; b. Montgomery, Vt., May 13, 1848; s. Augustus Choto and Lucretia (Babcock) W.; ed. Vermont Acad. (Franklin, Vt.), New Hampton Inst. (Fairfax, Vt.), Eastman's Business Coll. (Poughkeepsie, N.Y.); grad. Inf. and Cav. Sch., Ft. Leavenworth, Kan., 1883; m. Isabella Dougherty, Aug. 10, 1886 (died 1888). Went to Ft. Wallace, Kan., 1868, and became connected with the post trader's store; guide to Capt. Bankhead's expdn. to the rescue of Maj. George Forsyth's command, besieged for 9 days, at Arickaree fork of Republican River, Kan., Sept. 1868; apptd. post trader, 1870, and later engaged in cattle raising, owning the only herd in Western Kan. for a number of yrs.; apptd. 2d lt. 5th Cav., U.S.A., Oct. 15, 1875, "for bravery and efficiency" in guiding Lt. Austin Henely, 6th Cav., in attacking a hostile Indian camp on Sappa Creek, Kan., Apr. 1875; promoted through grades to col., Mar. 11, 1911; retired Sept. 24, 1911. Organizer company of Indian scouts, and comdr. for 3 yrs.; in frequent combats with Indians through Sioux War of 1876; served with regt. in Puerto Rico, Spanish-Am. War; in Philippines, 1902-04, Cuba, 1906-09, Hawaiian Islands, 1910-11. Medal as marksman and sharpshooter. Republican. Mason. Author: The Frontier Trail, 1923; Buffalo Days, 1925. Home: Los Angeles, Calif. Deceased.

WHEELER, Hoyt Henry, U.S. judge, dist. of Vt., Mar. 16, 1877—; b. Chesterfield, N.H., Aug. 30, 1833; s. John and Roxana (Hall) W.; ed. common schools, Chesterfield Acad., and select schs. at Newfane, Vt.; (LL.D., Univ. of Vt., 1859); m. Minnie L. Maclay, Oct. 24, 1861. Admitted to bar, 1859; mem. Ho. Reps. of Vt., 1867; State senator, 1868, 1869; judge Supreme Court of Vt., Dec. 1, 1869, to Mar. 31, 1877. Home: Brattleboro, Vt. Died 1906.

WHEELER, James Cooper, author; b. Brooklyn, Aug. 4, 1849; s. Thomas Mason and Candace (Thurber) W.; ed. Betts Acad., Stamford, Conn., Hoffman's Acad., Stockbridge, Mass., and 3 yrs.' study at Halberstadt, Germany; m. Zoe Seger, Sept. 2, 1894. Author: Captain Pete of Puget Sound, 1909; Captain Pete of Cortesana, 1909; There She Blows, 1909; Captain Pete in Alaska, 1910. Home: Jamaica, L.I., N.Y. Deceased.

WHEELER, James Rignall, archeologist; b. Burlington, Vt., Feb. 15, 1859; s. John and Mary Constance (Rignall) W.; A.B., U. of Vermont, 1880; A.M., Ph.D., Harvard, 1885; student Am. Sch., Athens, 1882-83; univs. Berlin and Bonn, 1885-86; (LL.D., U. of Colorado, 1914); m. Jane Hunt Pease, July 12, 1882. Lecturer, Hopkins Hall courses, Johns Hopkins, 1886; instr. Greek and Latin, Harvard, 1888-89; prof. Greek, U. of Vt., 1889-95; prof. Greek lang. and lit., 1892-93, sec., 1894-1901, chmn. mng. com., 1901—, Am. Sch. Classical Studies, Athens; prof. Greek, 1895-1906, prof. Greek art and archæology, 1906—, Columbia; also acting dean and dean, faculty of Fine Arts, 1906-11. Asso. editor Am. Jour. of Archæology, 1906-11. Author (with Harold N. Fowler); Handbook of Greek Archæology. Home: New York, N.Y. Died Feb. 9, 1918.

WHEELER, Jerome Byron, capitalist; b. Troy, N.Y., Sept. 3, 1841; s. Daniel B. and Mary J. W.; ed. pub. schs., Waterford, N.Y.; m. Harriet Macy Valentine, 1870. Pvt. to capt. and major 6th N.Y. Cav., acting as regimental and later as brigade q.m., 1861-65; after close of war was brevetted col. of cav.; engaged as bookkeeper in Troy; later clerk and partner in Holt & Co., flour and commn. mchts. In 1879, joined Charles B. Webster in buying the entire business of R. H. Macy & Co.; afterward organized the Aspen Smelting Co. of Colo. and became largely interested in mining, smelting, banking and real estate interests in West; pres. The Crœsus Gold Mining and Milling Co., owning mines in Sierra Co., Calif.; pres. Rock Hill Consolidated Gold & Silver Mining Co., Leadville, Colo. Home: Manitou, Colo. Died Dec. 1, 1918.

WHEELER, John Martin, ophthalmologist; b. Burlington, Vt., Nov. 10, 1879; s. Henry Orson and Elizabeth Lavinia (Martin) W.; A.B., U. of Vt., 1902, M.D., 1905, M.Sc., 1906, hon. D.Sc., 1928; hon. D.Sc., Middlebury (Vt.) Coll., 1933; m. Julia Warren Smith, May 15, 1912; children—Martha, Charles Smith, Edward Martin, Ann. Dir. eye service, Presbyn. Hosp., N.Y. City, 1928—; prof. ophthalmology, Columbia, 1928—; cons. ophthalmologist Bellevue Hosp., New York Eye and Ear Infirmary, 5th Avenue Hosp., Neurol. Inst., Babies Hosp., Sloane Maternity Hosp. Served as capt., advancing to maj., Med. Corps, U.S.A., World War I. Trustee U. of Vt.; dir. New York Eye and Ear Infirmary. Republican. Congregationalist. Home: New York, N.Y. Died Aug. 22, 1938.

WHEELER, John Wilson, mfr.; b. Orange, Mass., Nov. 20, 1832; s. Wilson and Catharine (Holmes Warden) W.; ed. common schs.; worked as farmer and carpenter; later clerk in grocery and gen. store, becoming proprietor of latter; m. Almira E. Johnson, Oct. 9, 1856. In 1867 established in sewing machine business which developed into New Home Sewing Machine Co., of which became pres. and treas.; also pres. The Leavitt Machine Co., Boston Mut. Life Ins. Co., Orange Nat. Bank, Wheeler Consol. Mining Co. (Colo.); trustee Orange Savings Bank. Mem. Mass. Ho. of Rep., 1877; mem. Governor's Council, 8th Mass. Dist., 1904, 1905; del. Rep. Nat. Conv., 1888, 1908, alternate del., 1904. Home: Orange, Mass. Deceased.

WHEELER, Joseph, brig. gen. U.S.A.; b. Augusta, Ga., Sept. 10, 1836; grad. West Point, 1859; LL.D., Georgetown Coll., 1899; m. Daniella Jones. Served as 2d lt. U.S. cav., 1859-61; 1st lt. Confederate arty.; col. inf.; brig. gen. cavalry, maj. gen. and corps commdr., lt. gen., wounded 3 times, 16 horses shot under him; eight of his staff officers killed and 32 wounded; received thanks of Confederate Govt. for skill and gallantry in battle, and specially thanked by State of S.C. for his brave and successful defense of the city of Aikin; distinguished and commended by his comdg. general for gallantry and skill in battles of Shiloh, Perryville, Murfreesboro, Tullahoma, Chickamauga, Ringgold, Dalton, Resaca, Adairsville, Cassville, Pickett's Mill, Kenesaw, Peach Tree Creek, Decatur, the several battles around Atlanta, battles of Averysboro and Bentonville; comd. in about 50 cavalry battles and hundreds of minor combats; comd. Confederate cavalary which daily fought Gen. Sherman in his campaign from Atlanta to Savannah and from Savannah through the Carolinas. After war lawyer and planter; congressman from 8th Ala. dist., 1881-99; reëlected for 56th Congress, but resigned. Senior mem. Congress on Dem. side; mem. 1887-93 and 1895, v.p. 1887, pres. 1895, Bd. of Visitors to Mil. Acad.; regent Smithsonian Instn., 1886-1900. Apptd., May 4, 1898, maj. gen. of vols., U.S.A., and assigned to the command of cav. div., 5th Corps, in Cuba. Planned and comd. in battle of Las Guasimas, Cuba, June 24, 1898; sr. officer in field at battle of San Juan, July 1-2, 1898; engaged in all conflicts in front of Santiago; sr. mem. of commn. which arranged the surrender of Santiago and Spanish Army to Am. Army; comd. troops at Montauk Point, L.I., 1898, of 4th Army Corps, Huntsville, Ala., 1898, en route to Manila, 1899; command 1st brigade, 2d div., Philippine Islands, Aug. 1899, to Jan. 24, 1900. Comd. troops in skirmishes with enemy under insurgent gen., Tomás Mascardo, at Santa Rita, Sept. 9 and 16, 1899; comd. force which carried enemy's entrenchments at Porac, Sept. 28, 1899; in immediate command on field in engagements at Angeles, Oct. 11 and 16, 1899; comd. brigade in advance upon Mabalacat, Nov. 8, in attack upon and capture of Bamban, Nov. 11, in advance upon Tarlac, Nov. 12-13, on expdn. to San Miguel de Camerling, Nov. 22-26, to San Ignacia and Moriones, Dec. 3-6; made inspection Island of Guam by direction of President, Feb. 8-12, 1900; brig. gen. U.S.A., June 16, 1900; comd. Dept. of Lakes, June 18 to Sept. 10, 1900. Author: Account of Kentucky Campaign, 1862; Cavalry Tactics, 1863; Military History of Alabama; History of the Santiago Campaign, 1898; History of Cuba, 1496 to 1899, 1899; 8 vols. of Congressional Speeches, 1883-98; History of the Effect Upon Civilization of the Wars of the Nineteenth Century. Also monographs upon the lives of Admiral Dewey, William McKinley, "Stonewall" Jackson and Theodore Roosevelt. Home: Wheeler, Ala. Died 1906.

WHEELER, Joseph Trank, editor; b. Phila., May 30, 1868; s. Joseph K. and Mary Isabell (Howey) W.; student U. of Pa. to close of jr. yr., leaving on account of ill health but continued scientific studies. Asso. editor Our Race Pub. Co., New Haven, Conn. Author: The Zonal-Belt Hypothesis—A New Explanation of the Cause of the Ice Age, 1908; The Proscribed and the Chosen of God, 1909. Home: Philadelphia, Pa. Died Dec. 25, 1919.

WHEELER, Loren E., congressman; b. Havana, Ill., Oct. 7, 1862; s. Jacob and Anvilla (Foster) W.; ed. pub. schs.; m. Maud Hoffman, Aug. 22, 1900; 1 son, Waldo L. Coal operator, at Springfield, until 1911. Mem. Bd. of Aldermen, Springfield, 1895-97; mayor of Springfield, 1897-1901; postmaster, 1901-13; mem. 64th to 67th and 69th Congresses (1915-23 and 1925-27), 21st Ill. Dist. Republican. Home: Springfield, Ill. Deceased.

WHEELER, Mary Sparkes, author; b. Tintern Abbey, Eng., June 21, 1835; d. Samuel (author) and Elizabeth Sparkes; ed. pub. schs. of New York; prin. of sch., Binghamton, N.Y.; m. Henry Wheeler, Apr. 13, 1858; mother of Post W. Pres. Phila. branch Woman's Foreign Missionary Soc. (taking in all Meth. chs. in Pa. and Del.), 1883-98; many yrs. mem. Nat. Lecture Bur., Chicago; apptd., 1889, Nat. evangelist, W.C.T.U., and in 1891 supt. World's W.C.T.U. Mission. Author: Modern Cosmogony and the Bible, 1880; First Decade of Woman's Foreign Missionary Society, 1884; Poems for the Fireside, 1888; As It Is Heaven, 1906; Consecration and Purity, 1913. Died Jan. 21, 1919.

WHEELER, Schuyler Skaats, engineer; b. New York, May 17, 1860; s. James Edwin and Annie (Skaats) W.; ed. Columbia Grammar Sch. and Columbia Coll.; D.Sc., Hobart, 1894; hon. M.Sc., Columbia, 1912; m. Ella Adams Peterson, Apr. 1891; m. 2d, Amy Sutton, Oct. 1898. Left Coll., 1881, to become asst. electrician Jablochkoff Elec. Light Co., until 1882; next with U.S. Elec. Lighting Co.; soon after became one of Edison's engring. staff in charge of work at the first sta. at time of its starting, 1883, when incandescent light was introduced. Contributed many of the devices adopted; later erected sta. apparatus at Fall River, Mass., and Newburgh, N.Y. Became electrician Herzog Teleseme Co.; electrician and mgr. C. & C. Electric Motor Co., 1886, first concern established for regular mfr. of electric motors. Organized firm of Crocker & Wheeler, 1888; pres. of Crocker-Wheeler Co., Ampere, N.J., mfrs. elec. equipment, 1889—. Prominent in development of the electric motor and especially in direct application of electricity to driving tools. Elec. expert of Bd. of Elec. Control New York, 1888-95. Inventor of numerous elec. and mech. devices, especially in the early days, such as electric elevator, electric fire engine, series multiple motor control, paralleling of dynamos, etc. Received the John Scott medal of Franklin Inst., 1904, for invention of electric buzz fan, 1886. Brought to this country the Latimer Clark library, the largest collection of rare elec. books in existence (catalogued, 2 vols. illus., as the "Wheeler Gift") and presented it to Am. Inst. Elec. Engrs., 1901, which led to erection of United Engring. Soc. Bldg. in N.Y., which he organized; author of code of professional ethics for engrs. adopted by Am. Inst. Elec. Engrs., 1912. Author: Practical Management of Dynamos and Motors (with Prof. Francis B. Crocker), 1894. Home: Bernardsville, N.J. Died Apr. 20, 1923.

WHEELER, Wayne Bidwell, attorney; b. Brookfield, O., Nov. 10, 1869; s. Joseph and Ursula (Hutchinson) W.; A.B., A.M., Oberlin, 1894; LL.B., Western Reserve U., 1898; LL.D., Muskingum Coll., 1917, Oberlin, 1919; m. Ella B. Candy, Mar. 7, 1901; children—Robert Wayne, Donald Hyde, Joseph Candy. Began temperance work while at coll.; field sec., dist. supt., atty., and state supt. Ohio Anti-Saloon League, and gen. counsel and legislative supt. of Anti-Saloon League of America. Closely identified with temperance legislation in all of the states and in Congress; successfully prosecuted over 2,000 saloon cases, some of them in Supreme Ct. of U.S. Mem. exec. com. Nat. Legislative Council America; dir. Nat. Legislative Conf., trustee Scientific Temperance Fedn.; mem. Temperance Commn. of the Congl. Chs. of U.S.; mem. Am. Soc. Internat. Law, Am. Acad. Polit. and Social Science. Independent Republican. Author: The Federal and State Laws Relating to the Liquor Traffic. Home: Washington, D.C. Died Sept. 5, 1927.

WHEELER, William Morton, zoölogist; b. Milwaukee, Mar. 19, 1865; s. Julius Morton and Caroline Georgiana (Anderson) W.; grad. German-Am. Normal Coll., Milwaukee, 1884; Ph.D., Clark U., 1892; occupant of Smithsonian table, Naples Zoöl. Sta., 1893; univs. Würzburg and Liége, 1893; Sc.D., U. of Chicago, 1916, Harvard, 1930, Columbia, 1933; LL.D., U. of Calif., 1928; m. Dora Bay Emerson, June 28, 1898. Curator Milwaukee Pub. Mus., 1887-90; fellow and asst. in morphology, Clark U., 1890-92; instr. embryology, 1892-97, asst. prof., 1897-99, U. of Chicago; prof. zoölogy, U. of Tex., 1899-1903; curator of invertebrate zoölogy, Am. Mus. Natural History, 1903-08; prof. entomology, Harvard, 1908—, dean of Bussey Inst. for Research in Applied Biology, 1915-29. Research asso. Am. Mus. Natural History. Fellow Am. Acad. Arts and Natural History, Am. Acad. Arts and Sciences, A.A.A.S., Washington Acad. Sciences, N.Y. Acad. Sciences. Awarded Elliott and Leidy medals. Author: Ants, Their Structure, Development and Behavior, 1910; Social Life Among the Insects, 1923; Demons of the Dust, a Study in Insect Behavior, 1930; also numerous zoöl. publs. Asso. editor Biological Bulletin, Jour. of Morphology, Jour. of Animal Behavior and Psyche. Home: Boston, Mass. Died Apr. 19, 1937.

WHEELER, William Riley, oil land operator; b. Tuolumne County, Calif., Sept. 30, 1860; s. Charles C. and Angeline (Stetson) W.; ed. Oakland (Calif.) High Sch.; m. Alice I. Meyers, Sept. 1, 1897. Entered employ of Holbrook, Merrill & Stetson, mchts., San Francisco, 1878, and became gen. mgr. and mem. bd. dirs. (resigned from latter position, 1907); treas. and chmn. finance com. San Francisco Rep. League, 1905; mem. U.S. Immigration Commn., 1907-10 inclusive; asst. sec. Dept. of Commerce and Labor, 1908-09; mgr. Traffic Bur. of San Francisco C. of C., 1909-14. In this capacity conducted successful campaign before U.S. Senate and House coms. for free tolls through Panama Canal to coastwise vessels, and exclusion from canal of vessels owned or controlled by transcontinental railroads. Later engaged in oil land operations. Republican. Unitarian. Died Feb. 17, 1935.

WHEELER, William Webb, merchant, author; b. Ashtabula County, O., Feb. 15, 1845; s. David and Eliza (Webb) W.; ed. pub. schs.; m. Helen Smith, Oct. 16, 1879. Began, 1872, with Tootle, Craig & Co., wholesale dry goods, St. Joseph, Mo., and continued with successors, Tootle, Hosea & Co., 1875, Tootle, Wheeler & Motter Mercantile Co., 1893, and 1909—. Wheeler & Motter Mercantile Co., of which became pres. Democrat. Presbyn. Author: Three Months in Foreign Lands, 1905; A Glimpse of the Pacific Isles, 1907; Encircling the Globe, 1910; Our Holiday in Africa, 1912; Discoveries in West Indies and South America, 1911; The Other Side of the Earth, 1913. Home: St. Joseph, Mo. Died June 7, 1925.

WHEELOCK, Edward, physician; b. New Haven, Vt., June 1, 1863; ed. mathematics, chemistry and physics at Mass. Inst. Tech., 1881-82; biology, Johns Hopkins; B.Sc., U. of Rochester, 1883; M.D., Syracuse U., 1885; post-grad. work in medicine, U. of Berlin, 1885-86; m. Ruth Jones, July 15, 1892. In practice of ophthalmic surgery, Rochester, 1886-1910; cons. ophthalmic surgeon, Rochester City Hosp.; cons. ophthalmic surgeon to Craig (N.Y. State) Colony for Epileptics, Sonyea, N.Y.; ophthalmic surgeon to N.Y. State Sailors' and Soldiers' Home, Bath, N.Y., to N.Y. State Instn. for the Blind, Batavia, to State Industrial Sch., St. Mary's Hosp., Rochester, etc. Pres. Rochester Pathol. Soc., Monroe County Med. Soc., Hosp. Med. Soc., Nat. Assn. U.S. Pension Examining Surgeons; chmn. surg. sect. Rochester Acad. Medicine. Editor: Penhallow's Wars of New England with the Eastern Indians, 1911; The Wheelock Narratives of Moor's Indian Charity School and Dartmouth College, 1912. Died Oct. 1, 1917.

WHEELOCK, Harry Bergen, architect; b. Galesburg, Ill., July 12, 1861; s. George I. and Sylvia M. (Field) Bergen; after parents' death, 1869, was adopted by O. L. Wheelock, of Chicago; ed. grammar and high schs., Chicago; C.E. course, U. of Mich., 1881-83; m. Irene Frances Grosvenor, June 15, 1886; children—Sara Grosvenor, Loyal Bergen. Fellow A.I.A. (also Ill. Chapter; pres. Chicago Chapter, 1925-27); pres. Ill. Soc. Architects, 1898, 1906. Republican. Presbyn. Home: Evanston, Ill. Died Jan. 8, 1934.

WHEELOCK, Irene Grosvenor, author; b. Monroe, Mich., Nov. 10, 1867; d. Col. Ira R. and Sarah A. Grosvenor; ed. U. of Mich.; m. Harry B. Wheelock, June 15, 1886; children—Harry Berger, Jr. (dec.), Sarah Grosvenor, Loyal Bergen, Elliot Winthrop (dec.). Dir. Ill. State Audubon Soc. Author: Nestlings of Forest and Marsh, 1902; Birds of California, 1904. Contbr. to popular and scientific mags. Home: Evanston, Ill. Died Oct. 24, 1927.

WHEELOCK, Joseph Albert, editor; b. Bridgetown, N.S., Feb. 8, 1831; ed. Sackville Acad., N.S.; m. Kate French, May 1861. Went to St. Paul, 1850; writer and editor on staff of local papers, 1856-61; founded St. Paul Press, 1861; editor of the Press and its successor, the Pioneer Press, 1861—. Commr. of statistics, Minn., 1860-61; postmaster, St. Paul, 1871-75; pres. St. Paul park bd., 1893—. Home: St. Paul, Minn. Died 1906.

WHEELOCK, William Almy, banker; b. Providence, R.I., Mar. 23, 1825; s. Joseph and Amelia (Ames) W.; ed. New York U.; m. Harriette Efner, Feb. 20, 1850. Dir. Central Nat. Bank, Am. Surety Co., Equitable Life Assurance Soc., Gold & Stock Telegraph Co., etc. Home: New York, N.Y. Died 1905.

WHEELWRIGHT, Edmund March, architect; b. Roxbury, Mass., Sept. 14, 1854; s. George William and Hannah Giddings (Tyler) W.; bro. of John Tyler W.; A.B., Harvard, 1876; m. Elizabeth Boott Brooks, June 18, 1887. Mem. firm Wheelwright, Haven & Hoyt, Boston, 1886—. City architect of Boston, 1891-95; cons. architect Cambridge Bridge, Hartford Bridge, Boston Mus. Fine Arts, Cleveland Mus. Art. A.N.A., 1910; fellow A.I.A. (2d v.p., 1911), Boston Soc. Architects. Author: School Architecture, 1901. Home: Dedham, Mass. Died Aug. 15, 1912.

WHEELWRIGHT, John Tyler, lawyer, author; b. Roxbury, Mass., Feb. 26, 1856; s. George William and Hannah Giddings (Tyler) W.; brother of Edmund

March W.; A.B., Harvard, 1876, LL.B., 1878. Admitted to Suffolk bar, 1879; apptd. chmn. Mass. Board of Gas and Electric Light Commrs., 1893; asst. corp. counsel, Boston, 1896-1900; acting park commr., Boston, 1897. Democrat. Author: Rollo's Journey to Cambridge, 1880; A Child of the Century, 1886; A Bad Penny, 1895; War Children, 1908. Home: Boston, Mass. Died Dec. 23, 1925.

WHEELWRIGHT, Thomas Stewart, iron and steel mfr.; b. Warren County, Va., Feb. 19, 1866; s. Rev. William Henry and Margaret (Kerfoot) W.; spl. courses Randolph-Macon Coll., Va.; m. Laura Martin, Nov. 15, 1905. Began as stenographer, 1885; pres. Gray Electric Co., Chicago, 1891-1904; v.p., gen. mgr. Old Dominion Iron Co., Richmond, Va., 1904-12; pres. Va. Ry. & Power Co., 1912-25; pres. Old Dominion Iron & Steel Works, Inc.; dir. First & Merchants Nat. Bank, Va. Electric & Power Co. Dir. Co-operative Ednl. Assn. of Va. Home: Buckhead Springs, Chesterfield County, Va. Died Dec. 31, 1936.

WHEELWRIGHT, William Dana, lumberman; b. Valparaiso, Chile, Apr. 16, 1849; s. Isaac W. and Sarah (Dana) W.; ed. Dummer Acad., Byfield, Mass., Brown High Sch., Newburyport, Mass.; m. Martha A. Hoyt, Apr. 28, 1914. In employ W. B. Reynolds & Co., commn. mchts., Boston, 1864-72; lumber bus., New York and Boston, 1872-96, Portland, Ore., 1896—; pres. Pacific Export Lumber Co., 1896—. Mem. original bd. dirs. Lewis and Clark Expn.; pres. Chamber Commerce, 1905; mem. Port of Portland Commn.; dir. Open Air Sanatorium; pres. Archæol. Soc. Decorated Order of the Rising Sun, 3d class, and Imperial Order of Meiji (Japan). Home: Portland, Ore. Deceased.

WHELAN, Charles Elbert, lecturer, author; b. Mazomanie, Wis., Aug. 26, 1862; s. Curtis Erskine and Martha (Rowley) W.; grad. high sch., Mazomanie, 1879; LL.B., U. of Wis., 1894; m. Alberta L. Wallis, May 27, 1885; children—Letta Helen (Mrs. B. H. Peck), Charles Elbert. Asst. atty. gen. of Wis., 1896-97; mayor of Madison, Wis., 1898-99; pres. Wis. League of Municipalities, 1898; supreme nat. lecturer Modern Woodman of America, 1898-1926; editor and pub. The Modern Woodman mag., 1926—. Republican. Baptist. Mason (33°, K.T., Shriner); Grand Master Masons of Wis., 1899-1900; Grand Master of Wis. Grand Council, R. and S.M., 1918; Odd Fellow, K.P., Moose, Elk, Woodman. Author: Bascom Clarke, a Southern Refugee, 1913; He That Seeketh Findeth, 1918; Essential Truth in Religion, 1922; The White Minstrels (drama), 1922; A Friend and Neighbor (drama), 1923; A Chance for Every Child, 1923; The State—The Child—The Part Time School, 1924; The State—The Isolated Child—The Traveling Teacher, 1924; Salvaging the Individual, 1925; Poems, 1926; Uncle Abner Brown, 1926; Inspirations, 1927. Home: Madison, Wis. Died Nov. 29, 1928.

WHELPLEY, Henry Milton, M.D.; b. Battle Creek (Harmonia), Mich., May 24, 1861; s. Jerome Twining (M.D.) and Charlotte (Chase) W.; ed. Ill. and Mich.; Ph.G., St. Louis Coll. Pharmacy, 1883; M.D., Mo. Medical Coll., 1890; grad. St. Louis Post-Grad. Sch. of Medicine, 1894; Ph.M., Phila. Coll. Pharmacy, 1915; m. Laura E. Spannagel, June 29, 1892. Prof. practical pharmacognosy, 1884-1922, prof. pharmacognosy, materia medica and physiology, 1922—, dean, 1904—, St. Louis Coll. Pharmacy; lecturer materia medica and pharmacy, 1886-90, prof. physiology, histology and microsropy, dir. biol. lab., and sec., 1890-1900, Mo. Med. Coll.; same, St. Louis Post-Grad. Sch., 1890-98; prof. materia medica and pharmacy, Med. Dept., Washington U., 1900-11; same, Mo. Dental Coll., 1900-03. Fellow A.A.A.S.; mem. U.S. Pharmacopœial Conv., 1890— (trustee, 1902—, sec. bd., 1910—). Editor Nat. Druggist, 1884-87, Meyer Bros. Druggist, 1888—; collaborator Med. Fortnightly, 1893-1907; same, Pacific Pharmacist, 1911-20. Awarded Remington honor medal, 1925. Author: Curtman's Chemical Lecture Notes, 1886; Whelpley's Therapeutic Terms, 1890; also many articles on lit., Am. archæology and microscopy. Mem. exec. com. St. Louis Missouri Centennial, 1921. Home: St. Louis, Mo. Died June 26, 1926.

WHERRY, Elwood Morris, missionary; b. South Bend, Pa., Mar. 26, 1843; s. James and Sarah (Nesbit) W.; A.B., Jefferson (now Washington and Jefferson) Coll., 1862, A.M., 1875; teacher, 1862-64; Princeton Theol. Sem., 1864-67; (D.D., Parsons, Ia., 1885); m. Clara Maria Buchanan, July 17, 1867; children—Clara E., James E. (dec.), Alice (dec.), Grace E., William Buchanan, Lillian, Sarah Almena, Annie Griffith, John Llewellyn. Presbyn. missionary in India, 1867-89, and 1898-1921; dist. sec. Am. Tract Soc., 1889-98, and for 2 yrs. mgr. Tract Soc. book store, Chicago; also sec. Chicago Tract Soc.; hon. sec. Soc., 1889-98, and for 2 yrs. mgr. Tract Soc. book store, Chicago; also sec. Chicago Tract Soc.; hon. sec. Christian Literature Soc. for the Punjab, India, 1900-21; moderator India Presbyn. Church, 1910-11. Founder, 1872, and for 32 yrs. editor of the Nur Afshán (Light Disseminator), a weekly paper in the Hindustáni lang.; corr. sec. World's Congress of Missions, Chicago, 1893; editor Missions at Home and Abroad, 1893; Woman in Missions, 1893. Author: The Comprehensive Commentary on the Qurán (4 vols.), 1886; Zainab the Panjabi, 1893; Islám, or the Religion of the Turk, 1894; The Moslem Controversy, 1905; Islám and Christianity in India and the Far East, 1907; Progress and the Present State of the Muslim Controversy, 1910; Islám Refuted on Its Own Ground, 1911; Manual of Islám; Religion of Islám; and a number of booklets on religious subjects published in native langs. of North India; Our Missions in India, 1923. Translator: Moffatt's Church History in Brief; Vaughan's What Think Ye of Christ?; Sell's Progressive Development of the Qurán. Joint Editor: The Mohammedan World of Today, 1906; Methods of Missionary Work Among the Moslems, 1906; Islám and Missions, 1911; Lucknow, 1911; also many tracts on Islám in the Hindustáni language. Pres. All-India Fedn. of Christian Lit. and Tract Socs.; pres. Missionaries to Moslems League. Home: Cincinnati, O. Died Oct. 5, 1927.

WHERRY, John, missionary; b. nr. Shippensburg, Pa., May 23, 1837; s. Samuel and Margaret (McCune) W.; A.B., Princeton, 1858, A.M., 1861; grad. Princeton Theol. Sem., 1861; D.D., Wooster, 1893, Princeton, 1895; m. Sara E. Brandon, Dec. 31, 1863. Tutor, Princeton, 1860-61; ordained Presbyn. ministry, 1864; missionary to China, 1864—; served in many capacities—pastor; supt. Presbyn. mission press, Shanghai; pres. Shantung Coll.; prof. astronomy in N. China Union Coll.; prof. N.T. exegesis, N. China Union Theol. Sch.; teacher, dir. Peking Lang. Sch.; editor, secretary, chmn. North China Tract Soc.; etc. Chmn. coms. for translating N.T. and O.T. into literary Chinese. Moderator Synod of N. China, 1900-03. V.p. bd. mgrs. Peking U.; mem. exec. com. N. China Union College; mem. advisory com. Sch. for Chinese Blind, Peking. Del. from Peking Presbytery to Gen. Assembly, Brooklyn, 1876, Minneapolis, 1886, Saratoga, 1896. Mem. Peking Missionary Assn., Peking branch Asiatic Soc. In siege of legations, Boxer uprising, 1900. Died Jan. 2, 1919.

WHERRY, William Buchanan, bacteriologist; b. of Am. parents at Lodeana, India, Dec. 24, 1875; s. Elwood Morris and Clara Maria (Buchanan) W.; A.B., Washington and Jefferson Coll., 1897; M.D., Rush Med. Coll., 1901; m. Marie Eleanor Nast, 1906; children—William Nast, Margaret Rutan. Asst. in bacteriology, U. of Chicago, 1901-02, asso., 1902-03; bacteriologist, U.S. Govt. labs., Manila, P.I., 1903-05; prof. bacteriology, Oakland (Calif.) Coll. Medicine, 1907; bacteriologist, Bd. of Health, San Francisco, and acting asst. surgeon on plague duty, U.S. Pub. Health Service, 1907-09; asst. prof. bacteriology Ohio-Miami Med. Coll., U. of Cincinnati, 1909, asso. prof., 1910-13; prof. bacteriology and hygiene, Med. Coll., U. of Cincinnati, 1914—; visiting prof., Sch. of Hygiene, Manila, 1929-30. Served on med. advisory bd., Cincinnati, 1917. Mem. Nat. Advisory Health Council, U.S. Pub. Health Service. Contbr. to Jour. Infectious Diseases, etc. Home: Cincinnati, O. Died Nov. 1, 1936.

WHERRY, William Mackey, brig. gen. U.S.A.; b. St. Louis, Sept. 13, 1836; s. Joseph A. and Amelia (Hornor) W.; ed. pub. schs., St. Louis County, Mo., and U. of Mo.; studied law; m. Alice W. Grammer, June 10, 1868 (died 1888). Served in Civil War, 1861-66, and on frontier against Indians, and war with Spain, 1898. Was a.d.c. to Gen. Nathaniel Lyon, July 19-Aug. 10, 1861; a.d.c. to Gen. Schofield, 1862-66, and 1867-85, and mil. sec., Feb. 11 to May 31, 1895; accompanied Gen. Schofield on spl. mission to France, Nov. 1865, to Jan. 13, 1866. Participated in battles of Wilson's Creek, Dug Spring, Rocky Face, Resaca, Dallas, Kennesaw Mt., Culp's Farm, Atlanta, Rough and Ready, Jonesboro, Franklin, Nashville, Ft. Anderson, capture of Wilmington, Kinston, and was present at surrender of Gen. J. E. Johnston. Bvtd.: capt., Sept. 1, 1864, for Atlanta campaign; maj., Dec. 16, 1864, for battles of Franklin and Nashville, Tenn.; lt. col. and col., Mar. 13, 1865, "for gallant and meritorious services during the war"; col. vols., Mar. 13, 1865, "for gallant and meritorious services during campaign in Ga. and Tenn."; brig. gen. vols., "for gallant and meritorious services"; awarded Congressional Medal of Honor, Oct. 30, 1895, "for distinguished gallantry at battle of Wilson's Creek, Mo., Aug. 10, 1861." Participated in battle on San Juan Hill and capture Santiago de Cuba, 1898; col. 8th Inf., Aug. 30, 1898; transferred to 17th Inf., Sept. 16, 1898; brig. gen. U.S.V., Sept. 21, 1898; brig. gen. U.S.A., Jan. 7, 1899; retired, Jan. 18, 1899. Mem. Mil. Service Instn. Wrote: Battle of Wilson's Creek, Mo., in Northwestern Review, 1878-79; Death of Gen. Lyon, Battles and Leaders of the Civil War, 1888-89; Lyon's Campaign in Missouri, Jour. Ohio Commandery, Loyal Legion, Vol. 3, 1896-97. Home: Cincinnati, O. Died Nov. 3, 1918.

WHETSTONE, Walter, pub. utilities exec.; b. Phila., Pa., Apr. 12, 1876; s. Joseph and Elizabeth (Bray) W.; engring. dept., U. of Pa., 1899; m. Susie Hitt, Mar. 2, 1902; children—Dorothy (Mrs. Henry W. LeBoutillier), Walter, Joseph, Cornelius, Pearce, Wynn. Pres. United Utilities & Service Corp., Southern Cities Utilities Co., The Whetstone Engring. Co., etc. Mem. Am. Society Polit. and Social Science, Acad. of Natural Sciences of Phila. Republican. Mason. Home: Philadelphia, Pa. Died May 1, 1940.

WHICHER, George Meason, coll. prof.; b. Muscatine, Ia., July 29, 1860; s. Stephen Emerson and Anna (Meason) W.; A.B., Ia. (now Grinnell) Coll., 1882, A.M., 1885; Johns Hopkins, 1884-85; A.M., Columbia, 1904; Litt.D., Ia. Coll., 1905; Dr., U. of Padua, 1922; m. Lillian Frisbie, Sept. 1, 1887; 1 son, George Frisbie. Prof. Greek and German, Hastings (Neb.) Coll., 1883-88; classical master, Lawrenceville (N.J.) Sch., 1889-92; prof. Greek and Latin, Packer Collegiate Inst., Brooklyn, 1892-99; prof. Latin and Greek, Hunter Coll., New York, 1899-1924 (retired). Pres. New York Archæological Society, 1918-21, gen. sec. Archæological Inst. America, 1919-21. Officer Order of the Holy Redeemer (Greece). Prof. in charge Classical Sch., Am. Acad. in Rome, 1921. Author: From Muscatine (verse), 1912; Roman Pearls and Other Verses, 1926; Sonnet Singing, 1928; Vergiliana (verse), 1931; Amity Street (verse), 1935. Joint Author: On the Tiber Road (verse), 1911; Roba d'Italia, 1930. Editor of Anthology of Hunter College (verse), 1924. Home: Amherst, Mass. Died Nov. 2, 1937.

WHILEY, Charles Whipple, consul; b. New York, May 24, 1848; s. Charles Whipple (M.D.) and Jane (Clark) W.; ed. pvt. tutor; LL.B., Columbia, 1873; unmarried. In practice at Georgetown, Del., 1877—. Clerk, Del. Senate, 1883; chmn. Dem. Co. Com., 1884-86; register in chancery and clerk Orphans' Court, 1885-90; U.S. consul, St. Etiénne, France, 1893-97; deputy atty. Sussex County, Del., 1909-10. Deceased.

WHINERY, Samuel, engr.; b. nr. Salem, O., Nov. 20, 1845; common sch. edn.; m. Elizabeth A. Crawford, Nov. 10, 1875; father of Charles Crawford W. Engaged in location and constrn. of railroads and other engring. work, 1868-86, including 2 yrs., 1878-80, as U.S. asst. engr. on improvement of Tenn. River at Mussel Shoals, and other govt. works; location, constrn. and operation N.O.&N.E. R.R., 1881-84, during which employed 1st telephone in ry. constrn. and train dispatching; constrn. of incline ry. up Lookout Mountain, Chattanooga, Tenn., etc.; v.p., gen. mgr. and pres. Warren-Scharf Asphalt Paving Co., 1887-1901, and designed and built 1st self-propelling st. concrete mixer and 1st ry. asphalt paving plant; cons. civ. engr., New York, Mar. 15, 1901—. Cons. engr. Finance Commn. of Boston, 1907-08, Commn. on City Expenditures, Chicago, to pres. Borough of Manhattan, 1905, etc.; chmn. state commn. to reappraise railroads and canals of N.J. Mem. reserve examining bd. of Bur. of Yards and Docks, Navy Dept., 1918. Author: Municipal Public Works, 1903; Specifications for Pavements and Roads. Contbr. numerous papers on engring. subjects to socs. and mags. Home: East Orange, N.J. Died Jan. 14, 1925.

WHIPPLE, Charles Henry, brig. gen.; U.S.A.; b. Adams, N.Y., June 12, 1849; s. Rt. Rev. Henry Benjamin (bishop of Minn.) and Cornelia (Wright) W.; ed. St. Paul's Sch., Concord, N.H.; m. Evelyn E. McLean, Dec. 5, 1871. Cashier Citizens' Nat. Bank, Faribault, Minn., 1871-81; apptd. maj. p.m. U.S.A., Feb. 18, 1881; lt. col. deputy p.m. gen., May 3, 1901; col. asst. p.m. gen., Jan. 25, 1904; brig. gen. p.m. gen., Jan. 1, 1908; retired Feb. 15, 1912. Home: Alhambra, Calif. Died Nov. 6, 1932.

WHIPPLE, George Chandler, engineer; b. New Boston, N.H., Mar. 2, 1866; s. Joseph K. and Sarah Adeline (Chandler) W.; S.B., Mass. Inst. Tech., 1889; m. Mary E. Rayner, June 29, 1893. Biologist Boston Water Works; later dir. Mt. Prospect Lab., dept. of water supply, gas and electricity, New York City; mem. firm of Hazen and Whipple, cons. engrs., New York. Prof. sanitary engring., Harvard U., 1911—, Mass. Inst. of Tech., 1914-16. Mem. council Mass. State Dept. of Health, 1914-23; sr. sanitary engr. (reserve) U.S. Pub. Health Assn., 1919—; chief of dept. of sanitation, League of Red Cross Socs., 1919-20. Major, and mem. Am. Red Cross mission to Russia, 1917. Fellow Am. Acad. Arts and Sciences, A.A.A.S. Author: Microscopy of Drinking Water, 1889, 1905; Value of Pure Water, 1907; Typhoid Fever, 1908; State Sanitation, 1917; Vital Statistics, 1919. Home: Cambridge, Mass. Died Nov. 27, 1924.

WHIPPLE, Guy Montrose, psychologist; b. Danvers, Mass., June 12, 1876; s. John Francis and Cornelia Eliza (Hood) W.; A.B., Brown U., 1897; scholar and asst. in psychology, Clark U., 1897-98; grad. student Cornell U., 1898-1900, Ph.D., 1900; m. Clarice Johnson Rogers, Sept. 4, 1901; children—Philip Montrose (dec.), Richard Randolph, Guy Montrose; m. 2d, Helen Davis, Oct. 13, 1925; one son, William Davis. Successively asst. in psychology, 1898-1902, lecturer in science and art of edn., 1902-04, asst. prof., 1904-11, asst. prof. ednl. psychology, 1911-14, Cornell U.; asso. prof. edn., 1914-15, prof. edn., 1915-18, U. of Ill.; actg. dir. bur. of salesmanship research, 1917-19; prof. applied psychology, 1918-19, Carnegie Inst. of Tech., Pittsburgh; prof. exptl. edn., U. of Mich., 1919-25. Actg. prof. ednl. psychology, U. of Mo., 1907-08. Mem. bd. editors Jour. Ednl. Research, Jour. Applied Psychology; editor Yearbooks of Nat. Soc. Study Edn., Edn. Problem Series. Mem. com. on mental exam. army cantonments. Republican. Fellow A.A.A.S. Author: Guide to High School Observation, 1908; Questions in General and Educational Psychology, 1908; Questions in School Hygiene, 1909; Manual of Mental and Physical Tests, 1914; How to Study Effectively, 1916, 27; Classes for Gifted Children, 1919; Problems in Educational Psychology, 1922; Problems in Mental Testing (with Helen D Whipple), 1925. Translator: Mental Fatigue (from German of M Offner), 1911; The Psychological Methods of Testing Intelligence (from the German of W. Stern), 1914. Editor of elementary sch. books for D. C. Heath & Co., 1928-37. Home: Clifton, Mass. Died Aug. 1, 1941.

WHIPPLE, Henry Benjamin, P.E. bishop of Minn., 1859—; b. Adams, N.Y., Feb. 15, 1823; ed. pvt. schs. New York; studied theology under Rev. W. D. Wilson, D.D., Cornell U.; D D., Hobart and Racine Colls.; D.D., LL.D., from univs. of Oxford, Cambridge and Durham, Eng.; ordered deacon, 1849; ordained priest, 1850; rector Zion Ch., Rome, N.Y., then of Ch. of the Communion, Chicago, until consecrated bishop; bishop of Minn., 1859—; declined bishopric of Hawaiian Islands offered him by Archbishop of Canterbury; established free church system in Chicago. Twice married. Active in work for evangelization of the Indians; also for elevation of negroes in the South; served on important Indian commissions to make treaties with the Indians; authority on the Indian question; called by the Indians "Straight Tongue." One of trustees Peabody Fund for ednl. work in the South. Preached opening sermon in Lambeth Palace, Lambeth Conf., England, 1888; sermon at Centennial of P.E. Church in U.S., 1889; held first Protestant service ever held in Cuba at Havana, 1871; preached memorial sermon at unveiling of Tennyson Memorial on Isle of Wight, Aug. 1897. Founder St. Mary's Hall, Shattuck Mil. Sch. and Seabury Divinity Sch., Faribault, Minn. Sr. bishop of P.E. Church of America at Lambeth Conf., 1897, London; represented P.E. Church of U.S. at Centenary Church Missionary Soc. of England, London, 1899; made official visitation of Island of Puerto Rico, Dec. 1900. Chaplain Gen. Sons of the Revolution and of Soc. of Colonial War in the U.S. Author: Sermons and Addresses; Lights and Shadows of a Long Episcopate; wrote much on the Indian question. Home: Faribault, Minn. Died 1901.

WHIPPLE, Sherman Leland, lawyer; b. New London, N.H., Mar. 4, 1862; s. Solomon Mason and Henrietta Kimball (Hersey) W.; A.B., Yale, 1881, LL.B., 1884; m. Louise Clough, Dec. 27, 1893; children—Mrs. Dorothy Fry, Mrs. Katharyn Carleton Withington, Sherman Leland. Practiced Manchester, 1884-85, Boston, 1885—; practice principally as trial lawyer. Spl. counsel Congressional Com., 1917, to investigate as to advance information concerning proposed terms of peace, German-European War; gen. counsel U.S. Shipping Bd. and Emergency Fleet Corp., Aug. 1918-Mar. 1919. Episcopalian. Democrat. Advocate of reforms in court procedure. Home: Brookline, Mass. Died Oct. 20, 1930.

WHIPPLE, William Denison, col. U.S.A.; b. Nelson, N.Y., Aug. 2, 1826; grad. West Point, 1851; same yr., 2d lt. 3d inf.; m. Caroline Mary Cooke, Dec. 16, 1854 (now deceased). Served in the Gila Expdn. against Apaches, 1857; Navajo Expdn., 1858, defence of Ft. Defiance, N.Mex., 1860; 1st lt., Dec. 1856; capt., 1861; served through Civil war, becoming brig. gen. vols., and bvt. brig. gen. and maj. gen. U.S.A.; during and after war in adjt. gen's. dept., reaching rank of col.; retired, 1890. Died 1902.

WHISTLER, James Abbott McNeill, artist; s. Maj. George Washington W.; mother's family, McNeills of S.C.; ed. West Point; pupil of Gleyre, Paris; Chevalier (1899), and Officer (1891) of the Legion of Honor of France; Knight Order of St Michael, Bavaria; hon. mem. Royal Acad. of St. Luke, Rome; hon. mem. Royal Acad. of Bavaria, Munich; mem. Société Nationale des Beaux Arts, France; pres. Internat. Soc. Sculptors, Painters and Gravers, England; Grand Prix, Exposition Universelle, 1900. Paintings: Portrait of his mother, Luxembourg Gallery; Carlyle, Glasgow Gallery, and others. Etchings: British Museum, Venice Academia, Dresden Galleries, Bibliotheque Nationale, etc. Author: Ten O'Clock; The Gentle Art of Making Enemies; The Butterfly and the Baronet. Died 1903.

WHISTLER, Joseph Nelson Garland, army officer; b. Green Bay, Oct. 19, 1822; grad. West Point, 1846; entered army bvt. 2d lt., 8th inf.; promoted Jan. 7, 1847, to 2d lt. 3d inf.; served through Mexican war; breveted for gallant conduct Battle of Centreros 1st lt., June 1852; captured in Texas by Confederates, 1861, and paroled as prisoner of war; promoted capt., May 1861; asst. instr. mil. tactics, West Point, 1861-63; col. 2d N.Y. arty., May 1863; served in Richmond campaign and defenses of Washington; bvtd. brig. gen.; lt. col. 5th inf., Feb., 1874; col. 15th inf. May 1883; retired, Oct. 19, 1886; m. Eliza C. Hall, dau. Maj. Nathaniel Nye Hall, U.S.A. Died 1899.

WHITAKER, Charles Harris, editor; b. R.I., May 19, 1872; s. Joseph and Lucy Ann (Monroe) W., ed. English High Sch., Boston (non-grad.); studied art in London, Brussels, Paris, Berlin and Leipzig; m. Celia Huntington Rogers, 1900; children—Rogers, Harris, Lucy, Francis; m. 2d, Eugenia Foster, July 1922. Went to Europe, 1905, to study printing, especially the reproductive processes, spending nearly 10 yrs. there; lecturer, and collector early lithographs now in Library of Congress; editor Jour. Am. Inst. Architects, 1913-27. Prominently identified with housing operations of the Govt. and a leader in fight to break the "pork barrel" pub buildings bill in Congress. Mem. Regional Planning Assn. of America (dir). Author: A Primer of Public Education, 1912; What Is a House? (with F. L. Ackerman), 1916; The Housing Problem in Peace and War (with same), 1917; The Joke About Housing, 1919; Bertram Grosvenor Goodhue, Architect, 1925; Architectural Sculpture of the Nebraska State Capitol. Died Aug. 12, 1938.

WHITAKER, Edward Gascoigne, judge; b. N.Y. City, Apr. 13, 1853; s. George W. and Catharine (Alcock) W. Admitted to N.Y. bar, 1876; dep. atty. gen. of N.Y., 1884-91; justice Supreme Court of N.Y., 1st Dist., 1912-26. Democrat. Mem. N.Y. Bd. Edn., 1915-18. Home: New York, N.Y. Died July 26, 1931.

WHITAKER, Epher, clergyman; b. Fairfield, N.J., Mar. 27, 1820; s. Reuel and Sarah (Westcott) W.; A.B., Delaware Coll., 1847, A.M., 1850; hon. A.M., Yale, 1867; D.D., Delaware, 1877; m. Hannah Maria Force, Jan. 28, 1852; father of William Force W. Ordained Presbyn. ministry, 1851; pastor, 1851-92, and pastor emeritus First Ch., Southold, N.Y., 1892—. Moderator Synod of N.Y. and N.J., 1860, Synod of L.I., 1871; mem. Gen Assembly Presbyn. Ch., 1853, 57, 60, 64, 69, 75, 88; stated clerk, L.I. Presbytery, 1856-1903. Councillor L.I. Hist. Soc., 1863—. Author: New Fruits from an Old Field, 1865; History of Southold, 1640-1740, 1881, etc.; Leaves of All Seasons—Hymns and Other Verses, 1894; History of the Presbyterian Church of Fairfield, N.J.; New Haven Colony's Adventure on the Delaware Bay; Introductions to the printed Town Records of Southold, Vol. I, 1882, Vol. II, 1884; Introduction to printed report of Celebration of the 250th Anniversary of Southold; Early Presbyterianism on Long Island; The American Union of Church and State; The Growth of Suffolk County, The Last Fifty Years of Suffolk County; also many pamphlets, contbns. to encys., etc. Home: Southold, L.I., N.Y. Died Sept. 1, 1916.

WHITAKER, Frank M., ry. official; b. Clermont County, O., Sept. 9, 1867. Began as clk. in div. freight agent's office, Pa. Lines West of Pittsburgh at Cincinnati, O., 1881; became chief clk. to agt. Chesapeake & Ohio Ry. and Kanawha Despatch, 1885; chief clk. to gen. Western freight agt., Chesapeake & Ohio Ry. and to mgr. Kanawha Despatch, later gen. Western freight agt. and mgr., respectively, until 1896; asst. freight traffic mgr., 1896-98, frt. traffic mgr., 1898-1909; v.p. in charge traffic, C.&O. Ry., and Hocking Valley Ry., 1910-37; mgr. inland traffic with R.R. Adminstrn., 1918-20; v.p. in charge of traffic, C.&O. Ry., 1920-37, also v.p. Pere Marquette Ry., 1932-37, and New York, Chicago & St. Louis R.R., 1933-37; retired July 1, 1937. Home: Spokane, Wash. Died Oct. 25, 1939.

WHITAKER, George, clergyman; b. Boston, May 14, 1836; s. Hon Edgar Kimball and Catherine Cravath (Holland) W.; brother of Nicholas Tillinghast W.; A.B., Wesleyan U., Conn., 1861, A.M., 1864; D.D., Fort Worth U., Tex., 1889; m. Harriet Clarke, June 22, 1861. M.E. pastor W. Medway, Mass., 1861-62, S. Walpole, 1863-64, Roxbury, 1865-66, Lowell, 1867-69, Westfield, 1870-71, Boston St. Ch., Lynn, 1872, Saratoga St. Ch., Boston, 1873; presiding elder Springfield Dist., 1874-77; pastor Ipswich, 1878, Trinity Ch., Cambridge, 1879-81, First Ch., Somerville, 1882-84, Grace Ch., Worcester, 1884-87; pres. Wiley U., Marshall, Tex., 1887-91, Willamette U., Ore., 1891-92; pastor St. Paul's Ch., Portland, Ore., 1893, Lincoln Av. Ch., Detroit, 1894-96, Beverly, Mass., 1897, Trinity Ch., Cambridge, 1898-99, and 1900-04; pres. Portland (Ore.) U., 1899-1900; pastor Centralville Ch., Lowell, Mass., 1905-06. Orient Heights Ch., 1907, Linden Ch., Malden, 1908. Librarian N.E. Methodist Hist. Soc., 1903-15, emeritus. Home: West Somerville, Mass. Died Nov. 1, 1917.

WHITAKER, Herbert Coleman, mathematician; b. Cape May, N.J., Oct. 31, 1862; s. Franklin and Lydia Leaming (Ross) W.; B.S., U. of Pa., 1885, M.E., 1886, Ph.D., 1896; m. Agnes Tweed, Dec. 22, 1887. Prof. mathematics in the high schools of Phila., 1887—, later head dept. of mathematics, South Phila. High Sch. Inventor. Author: Elements of Trigonometry (with tables), 1898. Extensive contbr to math. jours., also on genealogy. Died Nov. 17, 1921.

WHITAKER, Herman, author; b. Huddersfield, Yorkshire, Eng., Jan. 14, 1867; s. James and Annie (Walton) W.; ed. French's Acad. and Crossley's Boarding Sch., Halifax, Eng.; came to America, 1886; m. Margaret Ann Vandecar, Mar. 21, 1888 (died 1905); m. 2d, Alyse Lourdes Hunt, Aug. 12, 1907. Served in 2d Battalion, West Riding Regt., British Army, 1883-86; instr. fencing and gymnastics to the regt., 1884-85; purchased discharge and went to Canadian Northwest; pioneer in Hudson Bay Co.'s territory, 1887-95; removed to Calif., 1895; spent 1905-06 in Mexico. Agnostic. Author: The Probationer, 1905; The Settler, 1907; The Planter, 1909; The Mystery of the Barranca, 1912; Cross Trails, 1913; Over the Border, 1917. Contbr. to Harper's Monthly, Harper's Weekly, Century, American Magazine, Cosmopolitan, Everybody's, Ainslie's, Munsey's, Youth's Companion, Overland Monthly, etc. Spl. war corr. for San Francisco Examiner, The Independent, Sunset Mag., with Gen. Villa's forces in Central Mexico, 1914; war corr. with Am. forces in France, Sept. 1917—. Home: Piedmont, Calif. Died Jan. 20, 1919.

WHITAKER, Hervey Williams, M.D.; b. Montgomery County, Tenn., Aug 15, 1857; s. Hervey McDonald and Sarah Elizabeth (Williams) W.; student Southwestern Presbyn. U., Clarksville, Tenn., 1875-76; U. of Tenn., 1876-79; M.D., Starling Med. Coll., Columbus, O., 1881. Served in Med. Corps U.S. Navy, as asst. surgeon and passed asst. surgeon, 1881-90 (resigned); instr. hygiene N.Y. Post-Grad. Med. Sch., 1888-90; settled in Columbus, 1890; mem. faculty, Starling Med. Coll., 1891-1906. Surgeon local draft bd., Columbus, during war with Germany. Trustee-treasurer Carnegie Library Mason. Home: Columbus, O. Died July 12, 1937.

WHITAKER, Nicholas Tillinghast, clergyman; b. Boston, Apr. 10, 1840; s. Hon Edgar Kimball and Catherine Cravath (Holland) W.; brother of George W.; A.B., Wesleyan U., Conn., 1865, A.M., 1868; B.D., Boston U., 1867; D.D., New Orleans U., 1887; Ph.D., Boston U., 1902; m. Helen S. Locke, Sept. 8, 1867. Ordained M.E. ministry, 1867; prof. English and mathematics, N.H. Conf. Sem., Tilton, N.H., 1867-68; held pastorates in N.E. states, 1868—; pastor Central Ch., Lowell, 1908-13, Saxonville, Mass., 1913—. Author: Christian Science—Is It Safe?, 1898; The Pastor's Helper, 1900; Sunday Is the Sabbath Day, 1907. Home: Saxonville, Mass. Died Dec. 28, 1923.

WHITAKER, Ozi William, bishop; b. New Salem, Mass., May 10, 1830; s. Ira and Chloe (Wood) W.; A.B., Middlebury Coll., 1856; grad. Gen. Theol. Sem., 1863; D.D., Kenyon, 1869; LL.D., U. of Pa., 1898; m. Elizabeth A. Richardson, Nov. 25, 1857; m. 2d, Julia Chester, Aug. 31, 1865 (died 1908). Deacon and priest P.E. Ch., 1863; rector St. John's, Gold Hill, Nev., 1863-65, St. Paul's, Englewood, N.J., 1865-67, St. Paul's, Virginia City, Nev., 1867-69; consecrated missionary bishop of Nev., 1869; became asst. bishop of Pa., 1886-87, and bishop upon death of Bishop Stevens, 1887. Died 1911.

WHITAKER, Walter Claiborne, clergyman; b. Lenoir, N.C., Jan. 28, 1867; s. Lucius Fletcher and Rowena (Oates) W.; A.B., Ala. Poly. Inst., 1884, A.M., 1891; (D.D., U. of the South, 1909); m. Isabel Preston Royall, Mar. 30, 1891; children—Walter Claiborne, Arthur Preston, Dorothy Herbert, Hilary Royall; m. 2d, Dorothy French, Feb 4, 1918. Teacher, Barton Acad., Mobile, Ala., 1884-88; minister at Auburn, Ala., 1888; rector Ch. of Holy Comforter, Montgomery, 1891, Christ Ch., Tuscaloosa, 1893, St. Andrew's, Jackson Miss., 1901, Trinity, Asheville, N.C., 1905-07, St. John's Ch., Knoxville, Tenn., 1907-30, Ch. of The Advent, Norfolk, Va., 1930-33; Christ Ch., Bowling Green, Ky., 1933-36; later rector emeritus St John's Ch., Knoxville. Clerical dep. Gen. Conv. P.E. Church, from Ala., 1895-98 and 1901, from Tenn., 1910-28; mem standing com., Diocese of Ala., 1900; mgr. Church Record from its founding, 1892. Sec. Diocesan Bd. of Missions; dean Jackson convocation; mem. standing com. Diocese of Miss.; mgr. Church News; exam. chaplain, Diocese of Tenn., 1911; mem. court of review, Province of Sewanee, 1914-20; exec. com. Bd. of Miss., 1920; exec. Council of Province of Sewanee, 1924; dean of Knoxville Convocation, 1932; dean of Tidewater Convocation, 1933; examining chaplain Diocese of Southern Va. and Diocese of Ky. Author: Dives and Lazarus, Six Studies, 1898; History of the Protestant Episcopal Church in Alabama, 1898; Richard Hooker Wilmer, 1907; The Southern Highlands and Highlanders, 1915; Revelations of the Cross, 1923. Home: Knoxville, Tenn. Died Sept. 2, 1938.

WHITAKER, William Force, clergyman; b. Southold, N.Y., May 6, 1853; s. Epher and Hannah Maria (Force) W.; ed. Southold Acad.; A.B., U. of Pa., 1873, A.M., 1876; grad. Union Theol. Sem., 1876; D.D., Union Coll., 1899; unmarried. Ordained by Presbytery of L.I., 1876; pastor Bridge Hampton, N.Y., 1876-77, Orange, N.J., 1877-94, First Ch., Albany, N.Y., 1894-1907, First Ch., Elizabeth, N.J., 1907—. Stated clerk Presbytery of Morris and Orange and permanent clerk Synod of N.J.; vice-moderator of Synod of New York, 1897. Dir. Union Theol. Sem., 1894—; commr. Auburn Theol. Sem., 1901-06; mem. Bd. of Ch. Erection Presbyn. Ch., 1908-13, v.p., 1911-13; commr. Gen. Assembly Presbyn. Ch., 1886, 92, 96. Author: Swiss Travel, 1889; Southold's Centuries, 1890; also hist. and other addresses. Home: Elizabeth, N.J. Died July 9, 1916.

WHITALL, Samuel Rucker, brig. gen. U.S.A.; b. in Mich., May 17, 1844. Commd. 2d lt. 2d N.Y. Arty., May 5, 1864; hon. mustered out, Sept. 23, 1864; apptd. from D.C., 2d lt. 11th U.S. Inf., Mar. 7, 1867; transferred to 16th Inf., Apr. 14, 1869; 1st lt., Mar. 4, 1879; capt., Apr. 14, 1887; maj., Mar. 2, 1899; lt. col. 27th Inf., July 11, 1901; col. 3d Inf., July 26, 1903; transferred to 27th Inf., Sept. 10, 1903; advanced to rank of brig. gen., June 15, 1906, and retired on account of disability received in line of duty. Died June 11, 1919.

WHITBECK, R(ay) H(ughes), coll. prof., author; b. Rochester, N.Y., Apr. 2, 1871; s. Mortimer Henry and Avelyn (Hughes) W.; grad. Geneseo (N.Y.) Normal Sch., 1892; A.B., Cornell U., 1901; m. Nellie Smith, Aug. 1, 1895; 1 dau., Florence. Prin. Pike (N.Y.) Sem., 1892-96, Schuylerville (N.Y.) High Sch., 1896-98; asst. in physical geography, Cornell U., 1900-01; supervisor Model Sch., Trenton, N.J., 1901-09; asst. prof. geography and physiography, 1909-11, asso. prof., 1911-15, prof., 1915—, U. of Wisconsin. Lecturer in geography, U. of Tenn., summer, 1902, U. of Chicago, 1916, Ohio State U., 1932; instr. and prof. geography, Cornell U., 6 summer sessions, U. of Wis., 14 summer sessions; lecturer Adelphi Coll., Brooklyn, 1906-09. Editor The Jour. of Geography, 1910-19. Mem. Acad. Science, Arts and Letters. Wrote: A Geography of New York, 1901; A Geography of New Jersey, 1906; Geography and Resources of Wisconsin, 1913; Geography of the Fox-Winnebago Valley, 1915; The Geography and Economic Development of Southeastern Wisconsin, 1921; High School Geography, 1922; Industrial Geography, 1924. Co-Author: College Economic Geography, 1924; Economic Geography of South America, 1926; The Geographic Factor, 1932; The Working World, 1937. Home: Madison, Wis. Died July 27, 1939.

WHITCHER, Frank Weston, mfr.; b. Tilton, N.H., Nov. 10, 1855; s. William Warren and Frances Elizabeth (White) W.; direct descendant in 8th generation of Thomas Whittier, Haverhill, Mass., 1638, later moving to Amesbury; grad. Dorchester High Sch., 1872; m. Maria Davenport Faxon, Oct. 11, 1883; 1 son, Warren Faxon Whittier (he adopted original family name). Bookkeeper, E. Y. Perry & Co., shoe nail and tack mfrs., South Hanover, Mass., 1872-75; engaged in mfr. of shoe goods, Boston, 1875—; pres. Frank W. Whitcher Co., Chandler Oil Cloth & Buckram Co. (E. Taunton, Mass.), Am. Shoe Tip Co., Parker Mfg. Co. (Roxbury, Mass.), Heaton-Peninsular Button Fastener Co. (Roxbury); v.p. Chandler Oilcloth Co. (E. Taunton), Chandler Palruba Co. (Yardville, N.J., and E. Taunton); dir. M. & T. Button Co., Petrolene Mfg. Co. (Whiting, Ind.); treas. Witcher Realty Co. (Bridgeport, Ala.). Mem. Mass. Committee of 100 on Pub. Safety, World War I. Mason. Home: Boston, Mass. Died Feb. 21, 1940.

WHITCOMB, G(eorge) Henry, capitalist; b. Templeton, Mass., Sept. 26, 1842; s. David and Margaret (Cummings) W.; A.B., Amherst, 1864, A.M., 1867; m. Abbie Miller Estabrook, Oct. 11, 1865 (died 1900); m. 2d, Mrs. Elizabeth Wickware, Jan. 1902. Established firm of G. Henry Whitcomb & Co., mfrs. envelopes, Worcester, Mass., 1864; incorporated, 1884, as Whitcomb Envelope Co., of which became treas.; sold business to U.S. Envelope Co., 1898, of which became v.p.; pres. Worcester & Marlboro St. Ry., Standard Cattle Co. (Wyo.); dir. Columbian Paper Co., Hartford Mfg. Co., First Nat. Bank (Worcester), Mass. Loan & Trust Co. (Boston), U.S. Coal & Oil Co. (treas.), Equitable Security Co.; large real estate owner and developer in Worcester, Mass., Seattle, Wash., and Pueblo, Colo. V.p. Worcester Bd. of Trade; trustee Worcester Poly. Inst., Amherst Coll., 1884— (treas. 1895-97), and mem. of corp.; trustee Mt. Holyoke Coll., Oberlin Coll. Home: Worcester, Mass. Died Feb. 13, 1916.

WHITCOMB, Ida Prentice, author; b. Brooklyn, N.Y.; d. Moses and Jemima C. (Prentice) Whitcomb; grad. Packer Collegiate Inst.; taught in same several yrs.; prin. her own pvt. schs. until 1904. Author: Student's Topical History Chart, 1880; A Bunch of Wild Flowers for the Children, 1903; Heroes of History, 1904; Young People's Story of Art; Young People's Story of Music, 1909; Young People's Story of American Literature, 1913; Carol in Birdland, 1924. Died June 16, 1931.

WHITCOMB, Selden Lincoln, univ. prof.; b. Grinnell, Ia., July 19, 1866; s. Abram and Mary (Fisher) W.; A.B., Grinnell Coll., 1887; A.M., Columbia, 1893, fellow in lit., 1893-94; studied Cornell U., Harvard, U. of Chicago, U. of Colo. and U. of Wash.; Litt.D., Grinnell, 1918; m. Dora May Wilbur, 1899 (died 1902); m. 2d, Edna Pearle Osborne, 1919. Teacher classics and German, Stockton (Kan.) Acad., 1887-89; instr. civics, Ia. State Teachers Coll., 1891-92; prof. English lit., Ia. (now Grinnell) Coll., 1895-1905; asso. prof. English lit., 1905, comparative lit., 1918, prof. comparative lit., 1919—, U. of Kan. Prof. English lit., summer session, U. of Ia., 1901, U. of Ore., 1912. Mem. Am. Acad. Polit. and Social Science. Author: Chronological Outlines of American Literature, 1894; Lyrical Verse, 1898; The Study of a Novel, 1905; Poems, 1912; Random Rhymes, 1913; Autumn Notes in Iowa, 1914; Via Crucis (verse), 1915. Winner of 1923 Kan. Authors' club poetry prize, with "The Path-Makers," in Poetry, Aug. 1924. Editor of Humanistic Studies, U. of Kan., 1912—; co-editor of Homes' Douglas, 1924. Home: Lawrence, Kan. Deceased.

WHITE, Albert Blakeslee, governor; b. Cleveland, O., Sept. 22, 1856; s. Emerson E. and Mary Ann (Sabin) W.; A.B. (with honors), Marietta Coll., 1878; LL.D., W.Va. U., 1910, Marietta Coll., 1935; m. Agnes Ward, Oct. 2, 1879. Reporter and later mng. editor Lafayette (Ind.) Daily Jour., 1878-81; purchased State Jour., Parkersburg, W.Va., 1881, made it a daily, 1883, and remained its editor until retiring, July 1899. Collector internal revenue dist. W.Va., 1889-93, and 1897-1901, and 1921-25; gov. of W.Va., 1901-05; state tax commr., 1909-10; mem. Senate, 3d Dist., W.Va., term 1927-31; engaged in mfg. business. Pres. Nat. Editorial Assn., 1887-88. Mem. State Bd. of Edn., 10 yrs. Y.M.C.A. war work overseas, 1918-19. Republican. Home: Parkersburg, W.Va. Died July 3, 1941.

WHITE, Alfred Tredway, merchant; b. Brooklyn, N.Y., May 28, 1846; s. Alexander Moss and Elizabeth Hart (Tredway) W.; grad. Brooklyn Poly. Inst., 1862; C.E., Rensselaer Poly. Inst., 1865; (hon. A.M., Harvard, 1890); m. Annie Jean Lyman, May 29, 1878. Mcht. in New York, 1866—; mem. W. A. & A. M. White. About 1872 began study of homes of laboring classes; in 1876 erected 1st successful improved tenement houses in the country, followed, 1877, 1878, 1890, by other buildings of same character; in 1876 erected first seaside home for summer relief of poor children. Commr. of city works, Brooklyn, 1894-96; mem. Tenement House Commn., New York, 1900-01. Dir. Brooklyn Children's Aid Soc., 1868—, Brooklyn Soc. for Prevention of Cruelty to Children from organization; one of organizers, 1878, and since sec. and pres. Brooklyn Bur. of Charities; dir. City & Suburban Homes Co. for building improved tenements, and trustee Phipps Buildings, for same purpose, trustee Russell Sage Foundation. Unitarian. Independent in politics. Author: Improved Dwellings for the Laboring Classes, 1877; Better Homes for Working Men, 1885; Sunlighted Tenements, 1912; Report on Additional Water Supply for Brooklyn. Home: Brooklyn, N.Y. Died Jan. 30, 1921.

WHITE, Andrew Dickson, educator, diplomatist; b. Homer, N.Y., Nov. 7, 1832; s. Horace and Clara (Dickson) W.; A.B., Yale, 1853, with Yale lit. and De Forest gold medals, and 1st Clark prize, Am., 1856; post-grad. studies at the Sorbonne and College de France and U. of Berlin, 1853-54, Yale, 1856; attaché U.S. Legation, St. Petersburg, 1854-55; (LL.D., U. of Mich., 1867, Cornell, 1886, Yale, 1887, St. Andrew's [Scotland], 1902, Johns Hopkins, 1902, Dartmouth, 1906, Hobart, 1911; L.H.D., Columbia, 1887; Ph.D., U. of Jena, 1889; D.C.L., Oxford [Eng.], 1902); m. Mary A. Outwater, 1859 (died 1887); m. 2d, Helen, d. Dr. Edward Hicks Magill (q.v.), 1890. Prof. history and English lit., 1857-63, lecturer on history, 1863-67, U. of Mich.; also at U. of Pa., Stanford U. and Tulane U.; mem. N.Y. Senate, 1863-67; 1st pres. Cornell, 1867-85 (personally contributed $300,000 and, 1887, founded sch. of history and polit. science, bearing his name, giving to it his hist. library of over 40,000 vols.). Pres. State Rep. Conv., 1871; U.S. commr. to Santo Domingo, 1871; presdl. elector, 1872; chmn. Jury of Pub. Instrn., Centennial Expn., Phila., 1876; hon. U.S. commr. Paris Expn., 1878; U.S. minister to Germany, 1879-81, to Russia, 1892-94; mem. Venezuela Commn., 1896-97; U.S. ambassador to Germany, 1897-1902; mem. Peace Commn. at The Hague, 1899, and pres. of the delegation. Trustee Hobart Coll., 1866-77, Cornell, 1866—, Carnegie Instn. for Research and Carnegie Peace Endowment, Washington; regent Smithsonian Instn. Officer Legion of Honor, France; received Royal Gold Medal of Prussia for Arts and Sciences, 1902. Hon. mem. Royal Acad. Sciences, Berlin; 1st pres. Am. Hist. Assn., 1884-85; hon. mem. N.E. Hist.-Geneal. Soc.; pres. Am. Social Science Assn., Am. Philos. Society; mem. Am. Acad. Arts and Letters. Author: A History of the Warfare of Science with Theology in Christendom, 1895-97 (French transl., 1899, Italian transl., 1902, Portuguese transl., 1910, German transl., 1911); The Warfare of Humanity with Unreason, Including Essays on Sarpi, Grotius, Thomasius, Turgot and Cavour (Atlantic Monthly, 1903-07); revised and pub. with addition of chapters on "Stein" and "Bismarck"—as "Seven Great Statesmen in the Warfare of Humanity with Unreason," 1911; Autobiography of Andrew Dickson White, 1905; The Work of Benjamin Hale, 1911; and many others. Home: Ithaca, N.Y. Died Nov. 4, 1918.

WHITE, Arthur Fairchild, analyst, statistician; b. Manhattan, Kan., Apr. 13, 1895; s. Francis H. and Anna D. (Fairchild) W.; A.B., Pomona (Calif.) Coll., 1916; m. Irene Leek, Oct. 19, 1918 (dec.); children—Arthur, Raymond, Donald, George; m. 2d, Mrs. Harriet Callis Frankman. Executive dept. statistician of Southern Pacific Co., San Francisco, 1918-33; pioneered in development of comparable transportation statistics for railways, water lines, bus and truck lines and coördination of railway with highway service, on staff of federal coördinator of transportation, Washington, D.C., 1933-35—in charge of collecting, analyzing and publishing statistics of railway, waterway, highway, airway and pipe-line traffic, service and costs; a leading govt. witness at Interstate Commerce Commn. hearings for investigation of railway passenger fares, 1935—; head cost analyst and asst. dir. Interstate Commerce Commn., Apr. 1935—. Home: Bethesda, Md. Died May 1, 1940.

WHITE, Caroline Earle, philanthropist; b. Philadelphia, Sept. 28, 1833; d. Thomas and Mary Earle; ed. in Phila.; m. Richard P. White, 1854. Originated the work of forming, in Phila., a soc. for the prevention of cruelty to animals (2d or 3d in U.S.), 1867, and in 1869 organized the Women's Pa. Soc. for Prevention of Cruelty to Animals; was 1st person to work for the formation in Phila. of Soc. for Prevention of Cruelty to Children; with a friend started, 1883, Am. Anti-Vivisection Soc., and from then devoted much time and effort to that cause. Author: Love in the Tropics, 1890; A Modern Agrippa, 1893; Patience Barker, a Story of Nantucket, 1893; A Holiday in Spain, 1896; An Ocean Mystery, 1903. Home: Philadelphia, Pa. Died Sept. 7, 1916.

WHITE, Charles Abiathar, geologist; b. North Dighton, Mass., Jan. 26, 1826; s. Abiathar and Nancy (Corey) W.; ed. there and Burlington, Ia.; M.D., Rush Med. Coll., Chicago, 1864; (hon. A.M., Ia. Coll., 1866; LL.D., State U. of Ia., 1893); m. Charlotte R. Pilkington, Sept. 28, 1848. State geologist of Ia., 1866-70; prof. natural history, State U. of Ia., 1867-73, Bowdoin Coll., Me., 1873-75; geologist and palæontologist to various U.S. Govt. surveys, 1874-92. Honorarily connected with Smithsonian Instn. and U.S. Nat. Mus., 1895—. Author: Manual of Physical Geography of Iowa, 1873; Report on Invert. Fossils (Geog. and Geol. Expl.) and Surveys West of 100th Meridian, 1875; Bibliography of North American Invertebrate Palæontology, 1878; Contribçôes á Palæontolgia do Brazil, 1887; The Relation of Biology to Geological Investigation, 1894. Address: Washington. Died 1910.

WHITE, Charles Elmer, Jr., architect; b. Boston, May 18, 1876; s. Charles E. and Agnes Elizabeth (Safford) W.; ed. mostly in offices of Boston architects; spl. course Mass. Inst. Tech.; m. Alice M. Roberts, Nov. 26, 1901. Began in office of Sam J. Brown, architect, Boston, 1894; architect for Swift Bros. & Co., Boston, 1897-98, Am. Gas Co., Phila., 1899-1900, building various plants, amusement parks and office bldgs. throughout country; independent practice, Boston, 1900-02, Chicago, 1902—; mem. White & Christie. Progressive. Episcopalian. Mason. Author: Successful Houses and How to Build Them, 1912. Home: Oak Park, Ill. Died Aug. 15, 1936.

WHITE, Charles Henry, medical dir. with rank of rear admiral U.S.N.; b. Center Sandwich, N.H., Nov. 19, 1838; s. Dr. Charles and Sarah (French) W.; ed. in acads. there and at Northfield; M.D., Harvard, 1862. Asst. surgeon U.S.N., Dec. 26, 1861; served in S. Atlantic Blockading Squadron during Civil War; on many stas. and varied duties afterward. Promoted surgeon, Nov. 18, 1869; med. dir., June 8, 1895; retired Nov. 19, 1900, with rank of rear admiral. At Museum of Hygiene, 1897-1900. Home: Center Sandwich, N.H. Died July 25, 1914.

WHITE, Charles Joyce, mathematician; b. Cambridge, Mass., Jan. 5, 1839; s. Thomas and Sarah (Russell) Joyce (name of White added by act of legislature, 1846); A.B., Harvard, 1859, A.M., 1862; unmarried. Pvt. tutor, 1859-61; asst. prof. and prof., 1861-70, first mathematics, and later astronomy and navigation, U.S. Naval Acad.; asst. prof. mathematics, 1870-85, prof., 1885-94, prof. emeritus, 1911—, Harvard; registrar faculty, Harvard Coll., 1875-88. Author: Elements of Theoretical and Descriptive Astronomy, 7 editions, 1869-1901. Died Feb. 12, 1917.

WHITE, Charles Lincoln, clergyman; b. Nashua, N.H., Jan. 22, 1863; s. George Lampson and Harriett (Richardson) W.; A.B., Brown U., 1887, A.M., 1890; grad. Newton Theological Institution, 1890, D.D., Bowdoin College, 1902; LL.D., Denison, 1924; m. Margaret Donalda Dodge, Apr. 29, 1891 (died 1928); children—Jessie Dodge (Mrs. Francis P. Cook), Harriett Dodge (Mrs. Walter Lloyd Blackadar), Katherine Dodge (Mrs. Clarke S. Sutherland), Clarissa Dodge (Mrs. Ralph C. Walker), Mary Dodge; m. 2d, Mrs. Annie Healy Dodge, Sept. 17, 1929. Ordained Baptist ministry, 1890; pastor Somersworth, N.H., 1890-94, First Ch. Nashua, 1894-1900; sec. N.H. Bapt. Conv., 1900-01; pres. Colby Coll., 1901-08; asso. corr. sec. Am. Bapt. Home Mission Soc., New York, 1908-17, and exec. sec., 1917-29; pres. Associated Bapt. Home Mission Agencies, 1925-29; pres. Home Missions Council, 1925-31; mem. administrative com. Federal Council Chs. of Christ in America, 1925-29; chmn. bd. Golden Rule Foundation; mem. bd. John Milton Foundation until 1930. Author: Lincoln Dodge, Layman; The Churches at Work, 1915, revised edit., 1928; Children of the Lighthouse, 1916; A New Approach to Annuities, 1930; A Century of Faith. Home: Hampton Falls, N.H. Died Apr. 19, 1941.

WHITE, Clarence Hudson, photographer; b. West Carlisle, O., Apr. 8, 1871; s. Lewis Perry and Phebe (Billman) W.; high sch. edn.; m. Jane Felix, 1893

Began in photography at Newark, 1896; removed to New York, 1906; lecturer dept. of art in photography, Teachers Coll. (Columbia), 1907—; lecturer photography, Brooklyn Inst. Arts and Sciences; organized Summer Sch. of Photography, Seguinland, Me., 1910, Clarence H. White Sch. of Photography, 1914. Served on juries of award Phila. Photographic Salon, 1899-1900, Chicago Photographic Salon, 1901; Internat. Exhbn. of Photography, Albright Art Gallery, Buffalo, 1910. Received medals and awards Glasgow Internat. Expn., Turin Internat. Expn. and exhbns. at The Hague, Paris, Brussels, Vienna, Pittsburgh, Detroit and Cleveland. Represented in collection of the Royal Kupperstichkabinett, Dresden, Germany; Fairmount Park Mus., Phila.; Newark (N.J.) Art Mus.; Albright Art Gallery; San Francisco Mus. Fine Arts. Illustrated Bacheller's Eben Holden. Home: New York, N.Y. Died July 7, 1925.

WHITE, Courtland Yardley, Jr., physician; b. Philadelphia, Aug. 12, 1873; s. Courtland Yardley and Margaret H. (Luffberry) W.; ed. Central High Sch., Phila.; M.D., U. of Pa., 1895; post-grad. med. courses at Leipzig, and Vienna; m. Emily Heroy Sherwood, June 24, 1901. Pathologist, Children's Hosp. of Pa., Episcopal Hosp. of Phila.; chief bacteriologist, Bureau of Health, Dept. of Health, Phila. Formerly pathologist, Henry Phipps Inst.; asst. phys., Phila. Gen. Hosp.; demonstrator and lecturer, morbid anatomy, vet. dept., U. of Pa. Fellow Coll. Physicians of Phila. Home: Philadelphia, Pa. Died 1938.

WHITE, David, geologist; b. Palmyra, N.Y., July 1, 1862; s. Asa Kendrick and Elvira (Foster) W.; B.S., Cornell, 1886; D.Sc., U. of Cincinnati and U. of Rochester, 1924, Williams Coll., 1925; m. Mary Elizabeth Houghton, Feb. 2, 1888. With U.S. Geol. Survey, 1886—, now sr. geologist; also curator in paleobotany, Smithsonian Institution, 1903—; associate of Carnegie Institution. Mem. Am. Acad. Arts and Sciences; mem. various scientific societies. Home: Washington, D.C. Died Feb. 7, 1935.

WHITE, Edward Douglass, chief justice of the U.S.; b. Parish of Lafourche, La., Nov. 3, 1845; s. Edward Douglass (7th governor of Louisiana) and Catherine S. (Ringgold) W.; ed. at Mount St. Mary's, near Emmitsburg, Md., Jesuit Coll., New Orleans, and Georgetown (D.C.) Coll.; (LL.D., Georgetown, 1892, St. Louis U., 1904, Harvard, 1905; Dr. Canon Law, Trinity, 1911). Served in C.S.A.; admitted to La. bar, 1868, and practiced in La.; mem. La. Senate, 1874; asso. justice Supreme Ct. of La., 1878; U.S. senator, 1891-94; apptd. asso. justice Supreme Court of U.S., Feb. 19, 1894; apptd. chief justice of U.S., Dec. 12, 1910. Democrat. Mem. and chancellor bd. regents Smithsonian Instn. Home: Washington, D.C. Died May 19, 1921.

WHITE, Edward Franklin, editor; b. Johnson Co., Ind., May 15, 1858; s. Joel Barlow and Sarah (Cox) W.; A.B., Berea (Ky.) Coll., 1881, A.M., 1907, LL.D., 1927; m. Vida Webster, 1884 (died 1890); m. 2d, Emma Eaton, Sept. 17, 1900; children—Mark William, Lawrence Joel, Mira. Admitted to Neb. bar, 1882, and began practice at Lincoln, later at Central City; city atty., 1884-90; moved to Ind. 1894, and practiced at Indianapolis; law editor and writer with West Pub. Co., St. Paul, Minn., 1900-04; editor in chief law pub. dept. Bobbs-Merrill Co., Indianapolis, 1911—. Republican. Mason. Author: Law of Municipal Negligence, 1920; Mississippi Digest (5 vols.), 1920; Florida Digest, 1921, 26. Co-author: Louisiana Civil Law Digest, 1919; Supplements to Louisiana Digest, 1924, 29; Thompson on Negligence, and Supplements (8 volumes), 1907, 14; Thompson on Corporations (3d edit., 12 vols.), 1927. Home: Indianapolis, Ind. Died Jan. 2, 1932.

WHITE, Edward Joseph, lawyer; b. St. Louis, Mo., Feb. 11, 1869; s. Edward Charles and Euphemia Louise (Moffett) W.; student U. of Ark., 1884-85; LL.B., U. of Mo., 1891; m. Bertie Youngblood, May 22, 1896; children—Nancy Jane, Mary Louise, Ruth Euphemia. Practiced in Aurora, Mo., 1891-1911; pros. atty., Lawrence Co., Mo., 1896-98; asst. atty. M.P. Ry., at Aurora, 1903-11; gen. atty. same rd., at Kansas City, 1911-14; removed to St. Louis as gen. solicitor, same rd., 1914; v.p. and gen. solicitor same rd., June 1917—; apptd. counsel for receiver, B. F. Bush, Aug. 1915; gen. solicitor U.S.R.R. Administration for 8 Southwestern lines, 1918-19. Democrat. Odd Fellow, Elk. Author: Mines and Mining Remedies, 1903; Personal Injuries in Mines, 1905; Personal Injuries on Railroads, 1909; Law in Shakespeare, 1910; Legal Antiquities, 1911; William and Matilda, 1925. Editor: Tiedeman on Real Property, 1909; Legal Tradition, 1928. Home: St. Louis, Mo. Died Dec. 30, 1935.

WHITE, Edward Lucas, author; b. Bergen, N.J., May 18, 1866; s. Thomas H(urley) and Kate B(utler) (Lucas) W.; prep. edn., University Sch. for Boys, Baltimore, Md., 1882-84; Johns Hopkins University, 1884-91, A.B., 1888; m. Agnes Gerry, Nov. 28, 1900 (died 1927). Teacher Greek and Latin, Friends High Sch., 1892-95, Boys' Latin Sch., 1899-1915, Univ. Sch. for Boys, 19 years to 1930. Author: Narrative Lyrics, 1908; El Supremo, 1916; The Unwilling Vestal, 1918; The Song of the Sirens and Other Stories, 1919; Andivius Hedulio, 1921; Helen, 1925; Lukundoo and Other Stories, 1927; Why Rome Fell, 1927. Home: Baltimore, Md. Died Mar. 30, 1934.

WHITE, Edwin, rear admiral U.S.N.; b. Ohio, 1843; s. Lyman White; apptd. to U.S. Naval Acad., 1861; grad. as midshipman, 1864; promoted to ensign, 1866; master, same yr.; lt., 1868; lt. comdr., 1869; comdr., 1886; capt., 1898; performed duty at sea on the various stas.; last shore duty comdt. of cadets, U.S. Naval Acad., 1895-98; last sea duty in command of U.S.S. Philadelphia, flagship, Pacific Sta.; returned from Samoa with impaired health in Dec. 1899, from causes incident to the service incurred in the line of duty, retired as rear admiral by direction of President of U.S.; m. Antonia Thornton, d. Admiral George F. Emmons, 1870. Home: Princeton, N.J. Died 1903.

WHITE, Edwin Augustine, clergyman; b. Cornwall, Conn., Dec. 27, 1854; s. Edwin and Laura (Whedon) W.; A.B., Wesleyan U., Conn., 1879; (D.C.L., Trinity Coll., Conn., 1911; D.D., General Theol. Sem., 1918); studied law, Litchfield, Conn., 1879-82; practiced law, Cohoes and Ithaca, N.Y., 1882-86; instr. mathematics, Rutgers Coll., 1886-87; m. Elizabeth Craig Fielding, Dec. 4, 1889. Deacon, 1887, priest, 1888, P.E. Ch.; rector St. John's Ch., Lafayette, Ind., 1889-91, Christ Ch., Bloomfield, and Glen Ridge, N.J., 1892-1920, rector emeritus, 1920. Dep. to Gen. Conv., 1901— (chmn. com. on canons, 1913—). Lecturer on ecclesiastical polity and law, Gen. Theol. Sem., Bexley Hall, and Western Theol. Sem. Author: American Church Law, 1898, 1911; Diocesan Manual, 1910, 1923; Annotation and Exposition of Constitution and Canons of General Convention, 1924. Home: Glen Ridge, N.J. Died July 6, 1925.

WHITE, Elijah B., banker; b. Page Co., Va., Apr. 6, 1864; s. Col. E. V. (C.S.A.) and Elizabeth (Gott) W.; ed. pub. schs. and St. John's Acad., Alexandria, Va.; m. Rosa Lee Pancoast, 1886; 1 dau., J. Elizabeth; m. 2d, Lalla B. Harrison, 1900. Pres. Peoples Nat. Bank, Leesburg, 1907—; food administrator State of Va., World War. Mem. Va. Senate, 1924-27 inclusive. Pres. Percheron Soc. America, 1909-25. Decorated by French Govt. for success as breeder of Percheron horses. Democrat. Baptist. Home: Leesburg, Va. Home: Leesburg, Va. Died Dec. 18, 1926.

WHITE, Emerson Elbridge, author, lecturer; b. Mantua, O., Jan. 10, 1829; s. Jonas and Sarah (McGregory) W.; ed. common schools, Twinsburg Acad., O., and Cleveland Univ.; left coll. in senior yr. to become prin. of a grammar school in Cleveland (hon. degrees: A.M., Western Reserve Coll.; LL.D., Ind. State Univ. and Marietta Coll.); m. Mary Ann Sabin, 1853. Prin. Central High School, Cleveland; supt. public schools, Portsmouth, O.; State school commr. of Ohio; pres. Purdue University, Ind.; supt. Cincinnati Public Schools. Author: A Series of Mathematical Text Books, 1870-86; New Complete Arithmetic, 1883; Oral Lessons in Number, 1884; School Records, 1886; Elements of Pedagogy, 1886; First Book of Arithmetic, 1890; School Management, 1893; Elements of Geometry, 1895; School Algebra, 1896; The Art of Teaching, 1901; etc. Home: Columbus, O. Died 1902.

WHITE, Erskine Norman, church sec.; b. New York, May 31, 1833; s. Norman and Mary A. (Dodge) W.; A.B., Yale, 1854, A.M., 1857; Union Theol. Sem., 1854-57; U. of Halle, 1857-58; (D.D., New York U., 1874); m. Eliza T. Nelson, May 24, 1859. Ordained Presbyn. ministry, 1859; pastor Richmond, N.Y., 1859-62, New Rochelle, 1862-68, Westminster Ch., Buffalo, 1868-74, W. 23d St. Ch., New York, 1874-86; sec. Bd. Ch. Erection Presbyn. Ch. U.S.A., 1886—. Chaplain 22d N.Y. Vols., 1862. Author: The Personal Influence of Abraham Lincoln, 1865; History of West 23d Street Presbyterian Church, 1876; Why Infants Are Baptized, 1900; Norman White, His Ancestors and Descendants, 1905. Home: New York, N.Y. Died 1911.

WHITE, Francis Samuel, clergyman; b. N.Y. City, Apr. 19, 1868; s. Samuel Porter and Adele (Mercilliott) W.; A.B., Hobart Coll., 1893, A.M., 1896; B.D., Gen. Theol. Sem., 1896; S.T.D., Hobart College, 1920; D.D., Western Reserve U., 1925; m. Caroline Silliman Mize, Jan. 1907; children—Jean, Francis S. (dec.), Leonard, Edward Mize. Fellow Gen. Theol. Sem., 1896-97; deacon, 1896, priest, 1897, P.E. Ch.; asst. St. John's Ch., Detroit, Mich., 1899; mem. Associate Mission, Omaha, 1899-1904; rector Trinity Parish, Atchison, Kan., 1904-11; dean St. Mark's Cathedral, Grand Rapids, Mich., 1911-17; elected bishop coadjutor, Diocese of Dallas, Tex., 1915 (declined), Diocese of Marquette, Mich., 1917 (declined); domestic sec. Bd. of Missions P.E. Ch., 1918-20; dean Trinity Cathedral, Cleveland, O., 1920-31; rector St. Andrew's Ch., Tampa, Fla., 1931—. Army Y.M.C.A. sec. and civilian chaplain, with 32d Div., N.A., and 6th Div. U.S.A., Camp MacArthur, Waco, Tex., 1917-18. Del. to every triennial Gen. Conv. P.E. Church, 1904-31; pres. Federated Chs. of Cleveland, 1925-26; mem. Diocesan Council of Ohio, 1921-31; mem. exec. bd. Diocese of Southern Fla.; del. to Gen. Conv. P.E. Ch., 1934. Life mem. Associated Charities, Cleveland. Editor The Crozier, 1900-04; a founder and editor The Witness, 1916. Vice chaplain gen. St. Barnabas Guild of Nurses. Author: Story of a Kansas Parish, 1911. Died Sept. 29, 1934.

WHITE, Frank, treas. of U.S.; b. Stillman Valley, Ill., Dec. 12, 1856; s. Joshua and Lucy Ann (Brown) W.; B.S., U. of Ill., 1880 (LL.D., 1904); m. Elsie Hadley, Sept. 19, 1894. Mem. N.D. Ho. of Rep., 1891-93, Senate, 1893-99; maj. 1st N.D. Vol. Inf., May 2, 1898-Sept. 25, 1899; served in Philippines; col. of inf., 41st Div., July 18, 1917-June 12, 1919, 14 months in France. Gov. of N.D., 1901-05; treas. of U.S., 1921-28; pres. Middlewest Trust Co. Republican. Conglist. Past Grand Comdr. Knights Templars in N.D. Mem. S.A.R. Home: Chevy Chase, Md. Died Mar. 23, 1940.

WHITE, Frank, lawyer; b. Deposit, N.Y., July 27, 1858; s. Adolph and Henrietta (Alexander) W.; ed. Glens Falls Acad.; hon. A.M., Union Coll., 1913; m. Alice L. Mosher, May 17, 1881; 1 dau., Henrietta W. Nesbitt. Admitted to N.Y. bar, 1879, and began practice at Albany, N.Y.; lecturer on corp. law, Albany Law Sch., 1905-25; lecturer on same subject, New York U. Law Sch., 1925—. Chief of corp. div. of sec. of state's office, N.Y., 1886-99; served as 1st dep. atty. gen. of N.Y. State, 1907-08; receiver of Hamilton Bank, N.Y. City, 1908, and in 2 mos. enabled the stockholders to reopen the bank with more than $1,000,000 cash on hand. Now practicing in N.Y. City as corp. law specialist. Speaker in polit. campaign, 1888—. Democrat. Mason. Author: White on Corporations (9th edit.), 1923; White's Manual for Business Corporations. Co-editor: Dill on New Jersey Corporations, 1911; White and Goldmark on Non-Stock Corporations in State of New York, 1913. Home: New York, N.Y. Died Nov. 28, 1927.

WHITE, Frank Edson, packer; b. Peoria, Ill., Sept. 9, 1873; s. Frank C. and Lillian Gertrude (Hunt) W.; ed. pub. schs., Peoria; m. Lillian Pearson, Oct. 19, 1900; children—Mrs. Gertrude Lillian Spencer, Georgina Hester Kempe, F. Edson (dec.). Began in packing business with E. Godel & Sons, Peoria, 1890; dept. mgr. for Western Meat Co., San Francisco, 1893-95; apptd. dept. mgr. Armour & Co., Chicago, 1895, elected dir. 1912, v.p., 1914, pres., 1923—; v.p. Armour Leather Co. Republican. Episcopalian. Home: Chicago, Ill. Died Jan. 15, 1931.

WHITE, Frank Newhall, clergyman; b. Lyons, Ia., Oct. 25, 1858; s. Lorenzo Johnson and Eliza Dudley (Newhall) W.; A.B., Ripon Coll., Wis., 1878; grad. Andover Theol. Sem., 1881; (D.D., Ripon, 1897, Grinnell College, Ia., 1897); m. Jennie Isabella Allen, Sept. 27, 1881; children—Dudley Allen, Margaret Jean, Marion Newhall, Dorothea (dec.), Hervey Lorenzo (dec.). Ordained Congl. ministry, 1881; pastor at Hancock, Mich., 1881-86; missionary A.B.C.F.M., to Japan, 1886-93; asso. pastor 1st Ch., Burlington, Ia., 1894-98; pastor 1st Ch., Cheyenne, Wyo., 1898-1900, 1st Ch., Sioux City, Ia., 1900-04, Union Park and New 1st Ch., Chicago, 1904-12, Lowry Hill Ch., Minneapolis, 1912-14, First Ch., Walla Walla, Wash., 1914-16; western dist. sec. Am. Missionary Assn., Chicago, 1917-24 (retired). Moderator Congl. Assn. of Ia., 1902, Congl. Assn. of Ill., 1911-12; del. 10 nat. councils of Congl. Ch., 1901-23; del. 4th Internat. Congl. Council. Home: Parkersburg, W.Va. Died Jan. 13, 1926.

WHITE, Frank Russell, director of edn.; b. Milburn, Ill., June 8, 1875; s. Andrew J. and Abbie C. (Smith) W.; student Bellevue (Neb.) Coll., 1893-95; Ph.B., U. of Chicago, 1900; m. Eva J. Scheide, Sept. 15, 1910. Has been division supt. of schools, asst. to the gen. supt. of edn., asst. dir. of edn., and dir. of edn. of P.I., Nov. 27, 1909—. Dir. U. of the Philippines, and Y.M.C.A., Manila. Mason; pres. Philippine Inter-Fraternity Assn (dir.). Died Aug. 17, 1913.

WHITE, Frank Shelley, lawyer; b. near Macon, Miss., Mar. 13, 1847; s. Kelley and Margaret W.; common sch. edn.; m. Octavia A. Collins, May 22, 1873. Served pvt. 1st Miss. Cav., 1864, under Gen. Nat B. Forrest; captured at battle of Selma, 1865, but escaped and returned to command; admitted to bar, 1869; practiced West Point, Miss., 1869-86, then at Birmingham, Ala. Member Miss. Ho. of Rep., 1875-76 and 1882-83; chmn. of com. of impeachment which convicted and removed from office Lt. Gov. A. K. Davis, 1876; active in Ala. politics; pres. Dem. State Conv., Ala., 1900; del.-at-large Constl. Conv. of Ala., 1901; chmn. Dem. State Exec. Com. Pres. Ala. State Bar Assn., 1912-13; elected U.S. senator, May 11, 1914, for unexpired term (1914-15), of Joseph F. Johnston, deceased. Pres. ednl. bd. of Southern Baptist Conv., 1919—. Home: Birmingham, Ala. Died Aug. 2, 1922.

WHITE, Frederick W., chemical mfr.; b. N.Y. City, July 18, 1863; s. George E. and Ella A. W.; ed. Friends Sem. and Anthon's School, N.Y. City; m. Pansy Belvin, Oct. 27, 1909; m. 2d, Frances Andrews. Began as dealer in chemicals and agt. for German potash syndicate, N.Y. City; now pres. Mutual Chemical Co.; dir. Phosphate Mining Co. Episcopalian. Home: Great Neck, L.I., N.Y. Died May 3, 1937.

WHITE, Gaylord Starin, sociologist; b. New Rochelle, N.Y., Mar. 3, 1864; s. Charles Trumbull and Georgiana (Starin) W.; student New York U., 1882-84; B.A., Princeton, 1886, M.A., 1890; grad. Union Theol. Sem., 1890; studied U. of Berlin, 1890-92; m. Sophie Douglass Young, June 6, 1892 (died 1916); children—Sophie Douglass (Mrs. Franklin C. Wells), Charles Trumbull, Cleveland Stuart, Katharine Gaylord. Ordained Presbyn. ministry, 1892; asst. pastor Rutger's Ch., N.Y. City, 1892-93; pastor City Park br. First Presbyn. Ch., Brooklyn, 1893-1901; dir. field work, Union Theol. Sem., 1901-18; head worker Union Settlement, 1901-23; v.p. Union Settlement Assn., 1925—; prof. applied Christianity, Union Theol. Sem., 1913—, dir. dept. of ch. and community 1920—. and dean of students, 1929—. Mem. municipal fusion coms., N.Y. City, 1913, 17; mem. hosp. and playground commns. under Mayor McClellan, of Heights Bldg. Commn., etc. Independent Democrat. Home: New York, N.Y. Died Nov. 25, 1931.

WHITE, George Frederic, chemist; b. Melrose, Mass., June 15, 1885; s. George and Elizabeth (Dyer) W.; S.B., Mass. Inst. Tech., 1906; Ph.D., Johns Hopkins, 1910; m. Emma Clarke, Oct. 22, 1913; children—George Frederic, Virginia Clarke. Asst. in analytic and organic chemistry, Mass. Inst. Tech., 1906-08; fellow Johns Hopkins, 1909-10; asso. prof. chemistry, Richmond Coll., 1910-12; instr. organic chemistry, 1912-13, asst. prof., 1913-18, asso. prof., 1918-20, prof., 1920-25, Clark U.; dir. scientific dept. Bauer & Black, Chicago, 1925—. Research chemist, U.S. Bur. of Fisheries, 1910-16, U.S. Pub. Health Service, 1916-18, Worcester City Hosp., 1919; prof. summer session, Coll. of William and Mary, 1923. Author: Laboratory Manual of Inorganic Chemistry, 1911; Qualitative Chemical Analysis, 1916. Episcopalian. Home: Evanston, Ill. Died Sept. 1929.

WHITE, George Washington, clergyman; b. Valparaiso, Ind., Feb. 18, 1858; s. David Wesley and Lydia Emmeline (Taylor) W.; A.B., Cornell Coll., Mount Vernon, Iowa., 1883, A.M., 1886, D.D., 1896, LL.D., University of Southern California, 1930; m. Celia Villette Hutchins, January 24, 1885; 1 son, George Warren. Entered ministry M.E. Church, 1877; pastor in Iowa until 1883; business agent Cornell College, 1883-84; pastor in southern Calif., 1884-92 and 1899-1903; supt. Los Angeles Dist., 1892-95; pres. U. of Southern Calif., 1895-99; pastor Central Ch., San Francisco, later First Ch., Oakland, 1903-16; supt. San Francisco Dist., 1916-24 (retired). Mem. Univ. Senate M.E. Ch., 1896-1900; pres. Southern Calif. State S.S. Assn., 1900-03; del. Gen. Conf. M.E. Ch., 1912 and 1920; mem. Gen. Deaconess Bd., 1912-24; pres. Church Fedns. (San Francisco and Oakland), 1905-16, also of Comity Council of Northern Calif., 1919-23; pres. Meth. Retired Ministers Assn. of Southern Calif., 1931. Trustee U. of Southern Calif., 1890-99, Coll. of the Pacific, 1904-24. Chmn. Conciliation Com., San Francisco, in labor strikes after earthquake and fire, 1907. Republican. Author: The Historic Christ, 1910; also other religious works. Lecturer. Home: Hollywood, Calif. Died Dec. 1, 1940.

WHITE, George Whitney, banker; b. Washington, D.C., Feb. 11, 1870; s. George Henry Barron and Frances Virginia (Withers) W.; ed. Emerson Inst., Washington; (LL.D., Villanova); m. Louise Henderson Clements, Nov. 20, 1895. With Nat. Metropolitan Bank, Washington, 1885-1904, passing through all positions; organizer, cashier and v.p. Commercial Nat. Bank, 1904-09; pres. Nat. Metropolitan Bank, Jan. 1909—; chmn. bd. Potomac Ins. Co. Treas. New York Av. Presbyn. Ch., Emergency Hosp. Republican. Home: Washington, D.C. Died Oct. 27, 1938.

WHITE, (Thomas) Gilbert, artist; b. Grand Haven, Mich., July 18, 1877; s. Thomas Stewart and Mary (Daniel) W.; grad. high sch., Grand Rapids, 1896; Columbia, 1896-98; Art Students' League New York, 1896-98; under Jean Paul Laurens and Benjamin Constant, Julian Acad., Paris, 1898-1902; also studied under Whistler and MacMonnies and Beaux Arts, Paris; m. Hertha Stenger, Aug. 21, 1928. Art dir. Goldwyn Films, 1921-22. Exhibited at Salon des Artists Français, Paris, National Academy Design, Royal Academy, London, San Francisco Expn., Architectural League, Salon Interallié, Paris Expn., 1937, etc. Represented by murals in Ky. State Capitol, Utah State Capitol, World War Memorial, Okla. State Capitol, New Haven County (Conn.) Court House, Gadsden (Ala.) Federal Bldg., Peninsular Club, Grand Rapids, McAlpin Hotel, N.Y. City, Dept. of Agr., Washington, D.C.; portrait of Gov. McCreary, Pan-Am. Bldg., Washington, of Pres. Hine in N.Y. Clearing House, Jules Mastbaum, Locust Club Phila., Dr. Giraud, Hosp. les Andelys, France, Dr. Babcock, Carnegie Foundation, Paris, Welles Bosworth, University Club, Paris; pictures in collections of Houston (Tex.) Mus., Nat. Luxembourg Mus., Paris, U. of Okla., University of Utah, Brooklyn (N.Y.) Mus., City of Paris Mus., Grand Rapids (Mich.) Mus., Locust Club (Phila.), Lithuanian Mus., Corcoran Mus. (Washington), St. Quentin Mus. (France), Paris Journal. Served as 1st lt., later capt. inf., U.S.A., 1917-19; citation for exceptional service from Gen. Pershing. Vice-pres. European chapter Am. Artists Professional League, 1932-33, pres., 1934-35; mem. Am. Mission to Negotiate Peace, 1919; U.S. del. 8th Internat. Art Congress, Paris; represented State Oklahoma Battle Monuments, 1937; mem. fine arts jury 1937 Paris Expn. Member Société Internat. de Peinture; founder mem. European commandery Mil. Order Foreign Wars (vice comdr. 1928; mem. council, 1929-30); mem. Am. Legion (sergt. at arms, Dept. of France, 1928-29; del. to conv. at San Antonio, Tex., 1928; exec. com. 1932-33; founder mem. Myron T. Herrick Post. v.comdr. 1935), Forty and Eight, Anglo-Am. Group of Paris. Officier de l'academie, 1914; Chevalier Legion of Honor (France), 1919, Officier, 1928, Comdr., 1935; awarded Verdun medal, order of the Purple Heart; awarded medals for drawing, Art Students League of New York, Julian Acad.; hon. citizen St. Quentin, France. Died Feb. 17, 1939.

WHITE, Greenough, prof. ecclesiastical history and polity, 1894—, also acting prof. history of art, 1897—, Univ. of the South; b. Cambridge, Mass., 1863; grad. Harvard, 1884 (A.M., 1885); grad. Episcopal Theol. School, Cambridge, 1892. Prof. English lang. and lit., U. of the South, 1885-87; Kenyon Coll., Gambier, O., 1888-89; ordered deacon, P.E. Church, 1893, ordained priest, 1896; minister St. James Ch., West Hartford, Conn., 1893-94; acting prof. history and political economy, Trinity Coll., Hartford, 1893-94. Author: A Sketch of the Philosophy of American Literature; An Outline of the Philosophy of English Literature; The Rise of Papal Supremacy; A Saint of the Southern Church. Editor of Matthew Arnold and the Spirit of the Age. Home: Sewanee, Tenn. Died 1901.

WHITE, Hays B., congressman; b. nr. Fairfield, Ia., Sept. 21, 1855; s. Thomas and Martha W.; ed. pub. schs.; m. Diana Parson, Farming in Kan., 1875—; mem. Kan. Ho. of Rep., 1888-90, Senate, 1900-05; mayor of Mankato, Kan., 1914-15 (resigned); state tax commr., Kan., 1915-18; mem. 66th to 70th Congresses (1919-29), 6th Kan. Dist. Republican. Home: Mankato, Kan. Died Sept. 29, 1930.

WHITE, Henry, diplomat; b. Baltimore, Md., Mar. 29, 1850; s. John Campbell and Eliza (Ridgely) W.; ed. pvt. tutors and schs., U.S. and France; LL.D., St. Andrew's U., Scotland, also Johns Hopkins, 1915, and Harvard, 1917; m. Margaret Stuyvesant Rutherfurd, Dec. 3, 1879; m. 2d, Emily Vanderbilt, widow of William Douglas Sloane, Nov. 3, 1920. Sec. Am. Legation, Vienna, 1883-84; transferred as 2d sec. of legation, London, 1884, promoted sec., 1886; recalled by President Cleveland, 1893; sec. of embassy, London, 1897-1905; from 1886 repeatedly acted as chargé d'affaires; represented U.S. at Internat. Conf., London, 1887-88, for the abolition of sugar bounties; sr. del. from U.S. to Internat. Conf. on Agr., Rome, 1905, which resulted in the foundation of the Internat. Inst. of Agr.; sr. del. from U.S. to Internat. Conf. on Moroccan affairs at Algeciras, 1906; Am. ambassador to Italy, Mar. 1905-Mar. 1907, to France, Mar. 1907-Dec. 1909; chmn. Am. delegation to 4th Pan-Am. Conf., Buenos Aires, 1910; spl. ambassador of U.S. to Chile for celebration of centenary of Chilean independence, Sept. 1910. Elected mem. bd. trustees Carnegie Instn. Washington, and George Washington Univ., 1913, Corcoran Gallery of Art, 1915; mem. Washington Cathedral Chapter, 1915; regent Smithsonian Instn. Mgr. Potomac Div. Am. Red Cross, 1917. Mem. Am. Commn. to Negotiate Peace, Paris, 1918-19. Home: Washington, D.C. Died July 15, 1927.

WHITE, Henry Alexander, historian, educator; b. in Virginia, Apr. 15, 1861; s. William Orr and Mary McClure (Irwin) W.; A.M., Washington and Lee U., 1885, Ph.D., 1887; studied Union Theol. Sem., Va., 1887-88; Princeton U. and grad. Princeton Theol. Sem., 1889; D.D., Central U. of Ky., 1891; LL.D., Davidson Coll., N.C., 1909; m. Fanny Beverley, d. Judge Beverley R. Wellford, of Richmond, July 18, 1889. Ordained Presbyn. ministry, 1889; prof. history, Washington and Lee U., 1889-1902; prof. N.T. lit. and exegesis, Columbia (S.C.) Theol. Sem., 1902—. Author: The Pentateuch, in the Light of the Ancient Monuments, 1894; Robert E. Lee and the Southern Confederacy, 1897; Grammar School History of the United States, 1904; The Making of South Carolina, 1906; Beginner's History of the United States, 1906; Life of Stonewall Jackson, 1907; Southern Presbyterian Leaders, 1911. Stone Foundation lecturer, Princeton Theol. Sem., Oct. 1920. Home: Columbia, S.C. Died Oct. 8, 1926.

WHITE, Henry Clay, probate judge of Cuyahoga County, O., 1887—; b. Newburg, Cuyahoga Co., O., Feb. 23, 1838; s. Wileman W. W.; grad. Western Reserve Eclectic Inst., Hiram, O., 1860; grad. law dept., Univ. of Mich., 1862, A.M., Hiram Coll., 1891; m. Sabrina M. Capron, June 14, 1866. Practiced law Cleveland, O., 1874-77. Prof. probate and testamentary law, Law School of Western Reserve Univ., 1893—; prof. med. jurisprudence Cleveland Homœ. Med. Coll., 1892—; active Republican. Home: Cleveland, O. Died 1905.

WHITE, Henry Clay, chemist; b. Baltimore, Md., Dec. 30, 1848; s. Levi S. and Louisa (Brown) W.; B.L., C.E. and M.E., U. of Va., 1870, Ph.D., 1875; hon. Ph.D., U. of Ga., 1877; D.C.L., U. of South, 1904; LL.D., Ill., 1905, Columbia, 1908, Ga., 1922; Sc.D., Mich., 1907; m. Ella Frances, d. Leonard F. Roberts, of Chester Co., Pa., Dec. 19, 1872 (died 1913). Prof. chemistry, Md. Inst., 1870-71; science lecturer, Peabody Inst., Baltimore, 1871; prof. chemistry, St. John's Coll., Annapolis, Md., 1871-72, prof. chemistry, U. of Ga., 1872—. Pres. Ga. State Coll. Agr. and Mech. Arts (U. of Ga.), 1890-1907; state chemist of Ga., 1880-90; chief chemist Ga. Expt. Sta., 1888-1914. Pres. Assn. Official Chemists of U.S., 1881-82, Assn. Am. Agrl. Coll. and Expt. Stas., 1897-98 (chmn. exec. com., 1901-07); fellow Chem. Soc., London, 1880, A.A.A.S. Author: Elementary Geology of Tennessee (with Wm. Gibbs McAdoo), 1873; Complete Chemistry of the Cotton Plant, 1874; Lectures and Addresses (2 vols.), 1885-91; Manuring of Cotton, 1896. Collaborator U.S. Dept. Agr. Cotton Investigations, 1895-96; dietary studies, 1903-05. Home: Athens, Ga. Died Nov. 30, 1927.

WHITE, Herbert Humphrey, life insurance; b. Hartford, Conn., July 3, 1858; s. Francis A. and Cornelia (Humphrey) W.; ed. high sch.; m. Ella F. Kinne, Oct. 20, 1886 (dec.); 1 dau., Marion H. (dec.). Clerk Hartford Trust Co., 1874; clk. and asst. cashier Phoenix Nat. Bank, Hartford, 1878-98; auditor Conn. Mut. Life Ins. Co., 1894-99, sec., 1899-1906, treas., 1906—; dir. Phoenix State Bank & Trust Co. Mem. Common Council, Hartford, 1893-97 (pres. 1896); alderman, Hartford, 1897-99; mem. bd. West Middle School Dist., 1900-28, chmn. dist. com., 1920-28. Trustee Am. Foundation for the Blind (treas.); dir. Conn. Inst. for the Blind (chmn. exec. com.), Hartford Retreat for Insane (pres.). Republican. Episcopalian. Home: Hartford, Conn. Died Jan. 6, 1934.

WHITE, Horace, journalist; b. Colebrook, N.H., Aug. 10, 1834; s. Dr. Horace and Eliza M. (Moore) W.; A.B., Beloit (Wis.) Coll., 1853; (LL.D., Brown 1906). For many yrs. with Chicago Tribune, and was its editor and one of its chief proprs., 1864-74; became connected with New York Evening Post, 1883, and was pres. of co., editorial writer, and editor-in-chief; retired, 1903. Chmn. Gov. Hughes' com. on speculation in securities and commodities, 1909. Author: Money and Banking Illustrated by American History, 1895, 5th edit., 1914; The Roman History of Appian of Alexandria (transl. from Greek, 2 vols.), 1899; The Life of Lyman Trumbull, 1913. Editor: Bastiat's Sophismes Économiques, 1876; Luigi Cossa's Scienza delle Finanze, 1889. Home: New York, N.Y. Died Sept. 16, 1916.

WHITE, Horace Greeley, newspaper pub.; b. Lake City, Minn., Feb. 3, 1873; s. Robert and Mary Little (Morris) W.; ed. pub. schs.; m. Minnie Irene Thompson, Oct. 15, 1898; children—Maxwell Herbert, Edith Marian (Mrs. Hermann R. Wiecking). Began as pub. Murray County Herald, Slayton, Minn., 1893; pub. Arlington Enterprise, 1899-1903; co-pub. Winona Daily Independent, 1903-19; co-pub. Winona Republican-Herald, 1919-26, pub. alone, 1926—; pres. Republican and Herald Pub. Co. Mason; mem. A.O.U.W. Home: Winona, Minn. Died Mar. 3, 1934.

WHITE, Horatio Stevens, univ. prof.; b. Syracuse, N.Y., Apr. 23, 1852; s. Horatio Nelson and Henrietta Andrews (Stevens) W.; A.B., Harvard, 1873; LL.D., Glasgow U., Scotland, 1901; m. Fanny Clary Gott, June 14, 1883; children—Joseph Lyman, Dorothy. Traveled and studied in Europe several yrs.; admitted to New York bar, 1878; asst. prof. Greek and Latin, 1876-78, German, 1878-83, prof. German, 1883-1902, head German dept., 1891-1902, dean gen. faculty, 1888-96, dean univ. faculty, 1896-1902, Cornell U.; prof. German, Harvard, 1902-19, prof. emeritus, 1919—. Acting curator Germanic Mus., Harvard, 1908-09, 1926. Republican. Unitarian. Editor: Selections from Lessing's Prose, Text and Notes, 1888; Otis' Elementary German (6th edit.), 1889; Selections from Heine's Poems, 1890; Selections for German Prose Composition, 1891; Deutsche Volkslieder, 1892. Gen. editor Twentieth Century Series of German Classics, 1901-05; editor Fiske's Chess Tales and Chess Miscellanies, 1912; editor Memorial of Willard Fiske, Vol. I, the Editor, Vol. II, the Traveler, 1920, Vol. III, the Lecturer, 1922; Willard Fiske—a Biographical Study, 1925. Died Dec. 12, 1934.

WHITE, Howard Judson, architect; b. Chicago, Ill., Feb. 21, 1870; s. Moore C. and Mary L. (Bancroft) W.; ed. pub. schs. and Chicago Manual Training Sch.; m. Mabel E. Cameron, Sept. 19, 1895; children—William Cameron, Howard J. Began as draftsman for architects at Chicago; entered employ of D. H. Burnham & Co., 1898, and served as draftsman and supt. until after death of Mr. Burnham, 1912; mem. reorganized firm, Graham, Burnham & Co., 1912-17, of Graham, Anderson, Probst & White, Aug. 2, 1917—. Noteworthy structures: Field Museum, Wrigley Bldgs., Union Station, Straus Bldg., Ill. Merchants Bank Bldg. (Chicago); Equitable Bldg., Chase Nat. Bank Bldg. (New York); Selfridge Stores (London); Union Trust Bldg., Union Station (Cleveland); Field Bldg., Chicago; Pa. R.R. Sta., Phila. Republican. Baptist. Home: Wilmette, Ill. Died Dec. 18, 1936.

WHITE, Hugh, corp. official; b. Lapeer, Mich., Nov. 7, 1876; s. Henry Kirk and Jane (Wrigglesworth) W.; Ph.B., Univ. of Mich., 1899, LL.B., 1902; m. Abbie

E. Cutting, Oct. 20, 1903; children—Elizabeth, Marion, Martha. Began in bldg. constrn. with George A. Fuller Co., 1903, pres., 1924-27, chmn. bd., 1927-33; pres., 1107 Fifth Avenue Corporation; vice-pres. of Parkway Spencer Corp., Scarsdale Improvement Corp., Glenholding Corp.; dir. Scarsdale Nat. Bank and Trust Co., Sherbrooke Parks, Inc. Mem. 7th Regt., N.Y.N.G., 1903-09; trustee of Scarsdale, 1924-25, pres., 1926. Republican. Episcopalian. Mason. Mem. U. of Mich. football team, 1898-1901, capt., 1901. Home: Scarsdale, N.Y. Died June 1, 1936.

WHITE, Israel C., geologist; b. Monongalia County, W.Va., Nov. 1, 1848; s. Michael and Mary A. (Russell) W.; A.M., W.Va. U., 1872; Columbia, 1876-77; Ph.D., U. Ark., 1880; LL.D., W.Va. U., 1919; D.Sc, U. of Pittsburgh, 1921; m. Mary M. Moorhead, Dec. 4, 1878; m. 2d, Mrs. Julia Wildman, Feb. 12, 1925. Asst. geologist, 2d geol. survey, Pa., 1875-84, and author of 8 reports of same; asst. geologist, U.S. Geol. Survey, 1884-88; prof. geology, W.Va. U., 1877-92; resigned to take charge of a large petroleum business; state geologist of W.Va., 1897—; cons. geologist B.&O. R.R. Co. and Hope Natural Gas Co., 1916—. Chief, Brazilian Coal Commn., 1904-06. Specialist in coal, petroleum and natural gas; made discoveries in connection with those products. Treas. Geol. Soc. America, 1892-1907 (pres. 1920); pres. Am. Assn. Petroleum Geologists, 1919-20; v.p. A.A.A.S., 1896-97; del. Internat. Geol. Congress, St. Petersburg, 1897, Paris, 1900; one of the speakers at the White House Conf. of Governors, May 13-15, 1908. Mem. Nat. Advisory Bd. apptd. by President Roosevelt, 1906; mem. federal trade com. Chamber Commerce U.S.A. Trustee Kiwanis International, 1923-25. Home: Morgantown, W.Va. Died Nov. 25, 1927.

WHITE, James Andrew, farmer, stockraiser; b. Ottawa, Ill., Sept. 4, 1859; s. Peter and Sarah (Conroy) W.; grad. Graves Acad., Iowa City, 1883; studied Notre Dame U. 1 yr.; unmarried. Actively identified for many yrs. with farming and stockraising in Iowa County, Ia.; clk. of Dist. Court, 1902-06; mem. Ia. State Senate, 1908-16; county food administrator and chmn. Council of Defense, Iowa Co., World War I. Democrat. K.C., Elk. Home: South Amana, Ia. Died Apr. 9, 1932.

WHITE, James Clarke, physician; b. Belfast, Me., July 7, 1833; s. James Patterson and Mary Ann (Clarke) W.; A.B., Harvard, 1853, M.D., 1856; studied at Vienna, 1856-57; m. Martha Anna Ellis, Nov. 5, 1862. Began practice at Boston, 1857; lecturer, 1863-64, adj. prof. chemistry, 1866-71, instr. med. chemistry, 1871-72, prof. dermatology, 1871-1902, prof. emeritus, 1902, Harvard Med. Sch. Fellow Am. Acad. Arts and Sciences. Republican. Unitarian. Author: Dermatitis Venenata, 1887; Genealogy of White-Clarke Families; Sketches from My Life. Died Jan. 5, 1916.

WHITE, James McLaren, architect; b. Chicago, Ill., Oct. 16, 1867; s. Samuel Holmes and Jennie (McLaren) W.; B.S., in architecture, U. of Ill., 1890; studied Paris, France, and Poly. High Sch., Munich, Germany, 1894-95; m. Edith A. Shattuck, June 15, 1899; 1 dau., Adelaide Louise. Connected with U. of Ill., 1890—; supervising architect and prof. architectural engring., 1907—, and supt. business operations, 1922; dean Coll. of Engring., 1905-07. Pres. Nat. Council Archtl. Registration Bds., 1931—. Gov. 41st dist. Rotary Internat., 1923-24. Republican. Unitarian. Home: Champaign, Ill. Died Feb. 6, 1933.

WHITE, James Terry, publisher; b. Newburyport, Mass., July 3, 1845; s. James Terry and Maria (Ashby) W.; grad. Brown High Sch., Newburyport, Mass., 1862; removed to San Francisco, 1863; m. Florence C. Derby, Jan. 28, 1869. Established James T. White & Co., publishers, San Francisco, 1873, which removed to New York, 1886, pres. 1902—; pres. Nat. Press Bur., Onondaga Mining Co.; dir. West Coast Rubber Co. Invented White's Physiol. Manikin, 1884; editor National Cyclo. of Am. Biography, 1890. A founder and member Patriotic League; founder and exec. mgr. Character Development League. Pub. Modern Am. Poetry series. Author: Flowers from Arcady, 1880; Captive Memories, 1897; Character Lessons in American Biography, 1909; For Lovers and Others, 1911; A Garden of Remembrance, 1917. Home: New York, N.Y. Died Apr. 5, 1920.

WHITE, James William, surgeon; b. Phila., Pa., Nov. 2, 1850; s. Dr. James W. and Mary Anne (McClaranan) W.; ed. Phila. pub. schs. and Quaker schs.; M.D., Ph.D., U. of Pa., 1871; LL.D., Aberdeen, 1906; m. Letitia, d. Benjamin H. Brown, June 22, 1888. On staff of Prof. Louis Agassiz during Hassler expdn. to West Indies, the Straits of Magellan, both coasts of S. America, the Galapagos Islands, etc., 1871-72; resident phys. Phila. Hosp., 1873; surgeon Eastern State Penitentiary, 1874-76; surgeon First Troop Phila. City Cav., 1878-88; 1st prof. genito-urinary surgery, then prof. clin. surgery, then John Rhea Barton prof. surgery—all in U. of Pa.; emeritus prof. surgery and trustee U. of Pa.; surgeon Univ. Hosp.; cons. surgeon Phila. and Jewish hosps.; advisory surgeon Pa. R.R. Co.; commr. Fairmount Park. Author: American Text Book of Surgery (Keen and White), 1896; Genito-Urinary Surgery (White and Martin), 1897; Human Anatomy (Piersol), 1906; A Text Book of the War for Americans, 1915. Translator and editor, Cornil on Syphilis (Simes and White), 1875. One of editors Annals of Surgery. Died Apr. 24, 1916.

WHITE, Jay, consul; b. Lapeer, Mich., Jan. 1, 1869; Ph.B., Pa. Mil. Coll., Chester, 1889; studied painting, Julien Acad., Paris. Engaged in lumber business and banking, Am. consular agt. at Lucerne, Switzerland, Mar.-Oct. 1899; consul at Hanover, Germany, 1899-1906; consul gen. at Bogotá, Colombia, 1906-09; consul at Santos, Brazil, Aug. 27, 1909-13, later consul at Naples, Italy. Home: Lapeer, Mich. Died May 23, 1918.

WHITE, John Barber, lumberman; b. Chautauqua County, N.Y., Dec. 8, 1847; s. John and Rebeckah (Barber) W.; pub. sch. and acad. edn., N.Y.; m. Arabell Bowen, 1874 (dec.); m. 2d, Emma Siggins, Dec. 6, 1882. Taught sch., winters, 1866-69; in lumber mfg., Youngsville, Pa., and East Brady, Pa., as White & Kinnear, until 1874; a founder of Warren County News (weekly), 1874, later sole propr.; mem. com. of seven elected by Pa. Legislature, 1879, to prosecute bribery cases; pres. bd. edn., Youngsville, 1876-79, 1880-83; removed to Mo., 1879; pres. Mo. Lumber & Mining Co., La. Central Lumber Co., Forest Lumber Co. (Kansas City), La. Sawmill Co., White-Grandin Lumber Company, O.&N.W. R.R.; v.p. Grandin Coast Lumber Co. (Kansas City and Seattle); v.p. Fisher Flouring Mills Co., Seattle; dir. and v.p. La. Long Leaf Lumber Co.; pres. and gen. mgr. Mo. Lumber & Land Exchange Co.; dir. N.E. Nat. Bank (Kansas City); pres. Bank of Poplar Bluff, Mo., 1886-1907. Mem. Pa. Ho. of Rep., 1878, 79; postmaster Grandin, Mo., 1887-92; apptd. by President Roosevelt, Nov. 1905, as his personal rep. to investigate affairs on Cass Lake (Minn.) Indian Reservation as to whether the reservation should be opened up in part for settlement; apptd. by President Roosevelt, 1907, mem. Forestry Dept. on Commn. on Conservation of Natural Resources; apptd. by gov. of Mo., 1909, mem. State Bd. of Forestry; del. 1st Nat. Conservation Congress, Seattle, Wash., 1909; del. Southern Conservation Congress, New Orleans, 1909. Chmn. exec. com. 1st, 2d and 3d Congresses for Conservation of Natural Resources, and elected pres. at meeting in Kansas City, Sept. 1911. Mem. U.S. Shipping Board, 1916-17 (resigned). Republican. Organized 1st lumber mfrs.' assn. in Southern States, 1882 (Southern Pine Assn.) and was 1st pres. for 3 yrs.; mem. bd. govs. Nat. Lumber Mfrs.' Assn. Apptd., 1912, a.d.c. on staff of Gov. Hadley, of Mo.; rank of col. Congregationalist; trustee Kidder (Mo.) Inst. Mason. Published 4 vols. genealogy of John White family, Wenham, Mass.; also Gleason and Barber genealogies, and ancestry of John Barber White and of his Descendants. Home: Kansas City, Mo. Died 1923.

WHITE, John Ellington, clergyman, educator; b. Clayton, N.C., Dec. 19, 1868; s. James McDaniel and Martha (Ellington) W.; A.B., Wake Forest Coll., 1890, D.D., 1905; D.D., Baylor U., 1910; m. Effie L. Guess, Oct. 12, 1892. Ordained Bapt. ministry, 1892; pastor First Ch., Edenton, N.C., 1893-96; sec. missions Bapt. State Conv. of N.C., 1896-1901; pastor Second Ch., Atlanta, Ga., 1901-16, First Ch., Anderson, S.C., and pres. Anderson Coll., 1916-27; pastor First Baptist Ch., Savannah, Ga., 1927—. Founder of system of Bapt. schs. for mountaineers; pres. Clifton Conf. for negro schs.; pres. Ga. Bapt. Bd. Edn.; pres. Georgia Baptist Conv., 1929—; v.p. Southern Baptist Conv., 1930—; 1st v.p. Southern Social Congress. Stated preacher and lecturer, U. of Chicago, 1914-16. Democrat. Author: The Silent Southerners, 1906; My Old Confederate, 1907; The New Task and Opportunity of the South, 1908; Southern Highlanders, 1913; Thinking White in the South (Phelps-Stokes lectures, U. of Va.), 1914; A Yielded Pacifist, 1917. Died July 21, 1931.

WHITE, John Griswold, lawyer; b. Cleveland, O., Aug. 10, 1845; s. Bushnell and Elizabeth Brainard (Clark) W.; prep. edn., high sch., Cleveland; B.A., Western Reserve, 1865, A.M., 1868, LL.D., 1919 (Phi Beta Kappa); studied law under father; unmarried. Admitted to Ohio bar and Ohio fed. courts, 1865, later to U.S. Circuit Ct. of Appeals and U.S. Supreme Ct.; practiced in Cleveland; mem. White, Cannon & Spieth. Pres. Pub. Library Bd., Cleveland, 1884-86, and 1913—; mem. bd. trustees Cleveland Law Library Assn. Mem. Cleveland Grays and of Ohio N.G. Republican. Home: Cleveland, O. Died Aug. 27, 1928.

WHITE, John Hazen, bishop; b. Cincinnati, O., Mar. 10, 1849; s. Moses Hazen and Mary Miller (Williams) W.; A.B., Kenyon Coll., 1872, D.D., 1895; B.D., Berkeley Division Sch., 1875; Seabury Div. Sch., 1895; m. Marie Louise, d. D. C. Holbrook, Apr. 23, 1879. Deacon, 1875, priest, 1876, P.E. Ch.; asst. St. Andrew's, Meriden, Conn., 1875-77; vice-rector and instr. Latin, St. Margaret's Sch., Waterbury, Conn., and asst. St. John's Ch., 1877-78; rector Grace Ch., Old Saybrook, Conn., 1878-81, Christ Ch., Joliet, Ill., 1881-89, St. John's, St. Paul, 1889-91; warden Seabury Div. School, 1891-95; consecrated bishop of Ind., May 1, 1895, but on division of diocese, Apr. 25, 1899, took Northern portion of state with title Bishop of Michigan City. Died Mar. 16, 1925.

WHITE, John Stuart, educator; b. Wrentham, Mass., Feb. 3, 1847; s. John Smith and Anna (Richardson) W.; A.B., with highest classical honors, Harvard, 1870; LL.D., Trinity Coll., Conn., 1879; m. Georgie A. Read, Feb. 28, 1871. Master Pub. Latin Sch., Boston, 1870-74; head master, Brooks Sch., Cleveland, Ohio, 1874-80; founder, and head master Berkeley School, New York, 1880-1903; founder and head master Phillips Brooks Sch., Phila., 1903-08; founder, and head master the Thomas Arnold Sch., Chicago, 1912-17. Served in Civil War in 42d Mass. Vol. Inf., 1864; maj. and commandant Boston sch. regt., 1865; served in 7th Regt. N.G.N.Y., 1881-83; capt. Co. G, 22d Regt. N.G.N.Y., 1884-86. Winner bronze medal, Paris Expn., for ednl. exhibit of Berkeley Sch., 1889. Republican. Episcopalian. Author: Plutarch's Lives for Boys and Girls, 1884; The Boys' and Girls' Pliny, 1886; Wit and Humor of English-Speaking Peoples, 1921. Died Oct. 5, 1922.

WHITE, John Williams, univ. prof.; b. Cincinnati, Mar. 5, 1849; s. Rev. John Whitney and Anna Catharine (Williams) W.; A.B., Ohio Wesleyan, 1868, A.M., 1871; A.M., Ph.D., Harvard, 1877; LL.D., Wesleyan, 1896, Ohio Wesleyan, 1905; Litt.D., Cambridge, England, 1900, Harvard, 1913; m. Alice, d. Picton Drayton Hillyer, June 20, 1871. Tutor, 1874-77, asst. prof. Greek, 1877-84, prof., 1884-1909, Harvard; prof. emeritus, 1909—. First chmn. mng. com. Am. Sch. Classical Studies in Athens, Greece, 1881-86. Hon. pres. Archæol. Inst. America; fellow Am. Acad. Arts and Sciences. Joint Editor: Harvard Studies in Classical Philology. Sr. Editor: The College Series of Greek Authors (30 vols.), 1879; The Old Scholia on the Aves of Aristophanes; The Verse of Greek Comedy. Asso. editor Classical Philology (Chicago), Classical Quarterly and Classical Review (London). Author of monographs on philol. and archæol. subjects. Home: Cambridge, Mass. Died May 9, 1917.

WHITE, J(ustin) Du Pratt, lawyer; b. Middletown, N.Y., July 25, 1869; s. Charles Nelson and Elizabeth Brackett (Crosby) W.; prep. edn., high schs., Nyack and Ithaca, N.Y.; student Cornell U., 1886-90, B.L., 1890; LL.D., Colgate U., Hamilton, N.Y., 1936; m. Anita Bradley Lombard, Sept. 7, 1898; daughter—Anita Crosby Taylor. Admitted to New York bar, 1892; partner firm White & Case, New York. Pres. Palisades Interstate Park Commn. Trustee Cornell U., 1913— (v. chmn. bd.); mem. joint administrative bd. New York Hosp.-Cornell Med. Coll. Assn. Chevalier de la Légion d'Honneur, France, 1919. Home: Upper Nyack, N.Y. Died July 14, 1939.

WHITE, Marcus, normal sch. prin.; b. Blackstone, Mass., Aug. 18, 1861; s. Leander and Harriet W.; A.B., Wesleyan U., 1888 (Phi Beta Kappa), A.M., 1906; post-grad. work in France and Germany, 1891-92; D.Ed., Rhode Island Coll. of Education, 1927; m. Helen D. Cowles, June 1896. Teacher, Penn. Charter Sch., Phila., 1888-90, State Normal Sch., Millersville, Pa., 1890-91, Free Acad. Norwich, Conn., 1892-94; prin. State Normal Sch., New Britain, Conn., 1894-1929 (emeritus). Home: New Britain, Conn. Died June 1930.

WHITE, Matthew, Jr., editor; b. New York, Sept. 21, 1857; s. Matthew and Sybella (McMinn) W.; acad. edn.; studied 2 yrs. in France and Germany; unmarried. Engaged in authorship and editorial work for yrs.; asso. with the Frank A. Munsey Co., 1887—; dramatic editor Munsey's Mag. for 28 yrs. Editor of Argosy-All Story Weekly mag., New York. Author; Eric Dane, 1889; The Young Editor; My Mysterious Fortune; Tour of a Private Car; Guy Hammersley; The Young Athlete; The Young Flagman; Two Boys and a Fortune, 1907; (novels) One of the Profession, 1893; The Affair at Islington, 1897; A Born Aristocrat, 1898; (play) Stop, Look and Listen (one-act sketch in vaudeville, prod. 1906). Home: Westport, Conn. Died Sept. 17, 1940.

WHITE, Nehemiah, theologian; b. Wallingford, Vt., Jan. 25, 1835; s. Justin and Lydia (Eddy) W.; A.B., Middlebury Coll., 1857, A.M., 1860; hon. Ph.D., St. Lawrence, 1876; D.D., Tufts, 1889; m. Frances M. White, May 11, 1858 (died 1864); m. 2d, Inez Ling, of Pulaski, N.Y., May 29, 1871 (died 1900). Asst. prin. Green Mountain Inst., S. Woodstock, 1857-58; prin. Clinton (N.Y.) Liberal Inst., 1859-60, Pulaski Acad., 1864-65; prof. mathematics and natural science, St. Lawrence U., N.Y., 1865-71; prof. ancient langs. and comparative philology, Buchtel Coll., Ohio, 1872-75; ordained Universalist ministry, 1875; pres. Lombard U., Galesburg, Ill., 1875-92; in charge of Rider Div. Sch. (Lombard), 1892-1905; retired. Deceased.

WHITE, Octavius Augustus, physician; b. Charleston, S.C., Feb. 8, 1826; s. John Blake and Anna O. (Driscoll) W.; grad. Coll. of Charleston, 1846, A.M., 1847, LL.D., 1890; grad. S.C. Med. Coll., 1848; m. Claudia R. Bellinger, 1849 (died 1852); m. 2d, Elizabeth Winthrop Chanler, 1855. Confederate surgeon during Civil War; yellow fever expert; served through numerous epidemics in Charleston, S.C.; at Wilmington, N.C., 1862; Savannah, Ga., 1876; etc. In practice in New York, 1865—; writer on med. and surg. subjects—especially yellow fever; invented numerous surg. instruments. Died 1903.

WHITE, Peter, banker; b. Rome, N.Y., Oct. 31, 1830; s. Peter and Harriet (Tubbs) W.; ed. in schs. of Rome, N.Y., Green Bay, Wis., Mackinac, Mich., A.M., Univ. of Mich., 1899; m. Ellen S. Hewitt, Sept. 1857. Engaged as lawyer, real estate agt. and banker; county clerk and register of deeds, Marquette County, Mich., 12 yrs.; pres. 1st Nat. Bank of Marquette, 40 yrs.; dir. People's State Bank, Detroit, 15 yrs., dir. in many iron cos. Pres. St. Luke's Hosp., Marquette; more than 50 continuous yrs. mem. sch. bd. and treas. Marquette City schs.; park and cemetery commr. for Marquette City over 45 yrs.; mem. Mich. legislature, 1857, State senator, 1875; mem. Mackinac Island State Park Commn., 14 yrs.; mem. State Library Commn. 3 yrs.; regent U. of Mich. Episcopalian. Republican. Home: Marquette, Mich. Died 1908.

WHITE, Robert, lawyer; b. Romney, Va., Feb. 7, 1833; s. John B. and Frances A. (Streit) W.; acad. edn.; m. Ellen E. Vass, May 26, 1859. Admitted to bar, 1854; practiced at Romney, 1854-77; at Wheeling, W.Va., 1877—. Counsel, B.&O. R.R. Co., Am. Sheet & Tin Plate Co. Col. of cav., C.S.A., 1863-65; mem. W.Va. Ho. of Rep., 1885-91; atty. gen. of W.Va., 1877-81. Grand master of Masons, W.Va., 1875; pres. W.Va. Soc. S.A.R.; maj. gen. W.Va. div. U.C.V., 1896-1909; chmn. exec. com. Confed. Memorial Assn., 1898-1911, chief marshal 100th anniversary of burial of Washington at Mt. Vernon, Dec. 14, 1899; chief marshal Dewey Celebration, at Wheeling, Feb. 22, 1900. Comdg. Army N.Va. Dept. U.C.V. Ruling elder 1st Presbyn. Ch., Wheeling. Home: Pleasant Valley, nr. Wheeling, W.Va. Died July 1916.

WHITE, Rufus Austin, clergyman; b. Town of Franklin, Bradford County, Pa.; s. Lucien and Caroline (White) W.; grad. Tufts Coll., 1885, Ph.B., extra ordinem, 1899, D.D., 1904; B.D., Tufts Div. Sch. 1883; m. Louise E. Brooks, Jan. 1886. Entered Universalist ministry, 1884; pastor, Newton, Mass., 1884-92, People's Liberal Ch., Chicago, 1892-1936. One of original dirs. and founders of Chicago Bur. of Charities; active in consolidating Children's Home Soc. and Children's Aid Soc., into present Ill. Children's Home and Aid Soc., of which was pres.; founder in Chicago and pres. Chicago Penny Savings Soc. Chaplain 1st Regt. Ill. Cav. Mem. Chicago Bd. of Edn., 1904-09. Mason. Founder of Oakhaven Old People's Home. Author: South America Today. Home: Chicago, Ill. Died July 25, 1937.

WHITE, Sallie Joy, writer; b. Winchester, N.H.; d. Samuel Sargent and Rhoda Elizabeth (Ballou) Joy; ed. Brattleboro, Vt.; m. Henry K. White, June 2, 1874. One of founders and first pres. New England Woman's Press Assn.; pres. Daughters of Vt.; founder and pres. Fortnightly Study Club of Dedham. Lecturer. Author: Housekeeping and Home Making, 1890; Cookery in Public Schools, 1891; Business Opportunities for Girls, 1892. Home: Dedham, Mass. Died 1909.

WHITE, Stanford, architect; b. New York, Nov. 9, 1853; ed. U. of New York, A.M.; architectural training with Charles D. Gambrill and H. H. Richardson; chief asst. of latter in constrn. of Trinity Ch., Boston; traveled and studied in Europe, 1878-80; firm of McKim, Mead & White, 1881—. Designed Madison Square Garden, Century and Metropolitan clubs, U. of New York, Washington Arch, Univ. of Va.; pedestals for principal statues of St. Gaudens; etc. Fellow Am. Inst. Architects, etc. Home: New York, N.Y. Died 1906.

WHITE, Stanley, clergyman; b. Richmond, S.I., N.Y., May 2, 1862; s. Erskine Norman and Eliza Tracy (Nelson) W.; A.B., Princeton, 1884, A.M., 1887; Union Theol. Sem., 1884-87; D.D., New York U., 1909; m. Henrietta Logan Kneass, May 20, 1891; children—Eleanor Stanley, Margaretta Kneass (Mrs. Gordon C. Aymar), Erskine Norman, John Strickland, Elizabeth Howard (dec.). Ordained Presbyn. ministry, 1888; pastor Hillside Ch., Orange, N.J., 1888-1907; sec. Bd. of Foreign Missions Presbyn. Ch. U.S.A., 1907-25; chaplain Rutgers U., New Brunswick, N.J., 1926—. Visited officially Central America, Syria, Egypt, India, China, Korea, Japan and Russia. Republican. Commr., Com. for Relief in the Near East, on inspection of work in Asia Minor, Egypt, Palestine, Syria and Mesopotamia, Feb.-Sept. 1919. Home: New Brunswick, N.J. Died Jan. 21, 1930.

WHITE, Stephen Mallory, U.S. senator, lawyer; b. San Francisco, Jan. 19, 1853; brought up on farm in Santa Cruz Co., Calif.; grad. Santa Clara Coll., Calif., 1871; studied law; admitted to bar, 1874; began practice in Los Angeles County; dist. atty., 1882-86; State senator and pres. pro tem. Calif. senate, 1886-90, and during 1888-90 acting lt. gov.; Dem. caucus nominee for U.S. senator, 1890; U.S. senator, 1893-99. Temporary chmn. Nat. Dem. Conv., St. Louis, 1888; permanent chmn. Chicago conv., 1896. Address: Los Angeles, Calif. Died 1901.

WHITE, Stephen Van Culen, stock broker, b. Chatham County, N.C., Aug. 1, 1831; s. Hiram and Julia (Brewer) W.; moved to Ill., in infancy; A.B., Knox Coll., Ill., 1854, LL.D.; admitted to bar, 1856; practiced at Des Moines, Ia., 1856-65; moved to New York and became stock broker; m. Eliza M. Chandler, Feb. 1857. Joined open board of brokers, 1865, Stock Exchange, 1869; formed partnership of Marvin White, 1865-68, afterwards operated alone until 1882, when, with several partners, organized firm of S. V. White & Co. Failed for $1,000,000 in 1891, but was released from his obligations upon a verbal promise to pay; resumed business with $200,000 capital and within a yr. had paid every debt in full, with interest. Park commr. of Brooklyn; mem. 50th Congress (1887-89). Republican. Treas. of Plymouth Ch., Brooklyn, 1869—; first pres. Am. Astron. Soc., 1885. Home: Brooklyn, N.Y. Died Jan. 18, 1912.

WHITE, Trueman Clark, judge; b. Perrysburg, N.Y., Apr. 30, 1840; s. Daniel Tompkins and Alma (Wilber) W.; ed. Springville Acad.; m. Emma K. Haskins, Feb. 10, 1869. Enlisted as pvt. on first call for troops in Civil War; remained during war; promoted to 1st lt. Practiced law in Buffalo; became judge Superior Ct., Buffalo; judge Supreme Ct. of N.Y., 8th Dist. Republican. Presided over trial of Leon Czolgosz, assassin of President McKinley. Home: Buffalo, N.Y. Died 1912.

WHITE, Trumbull, writer, editor; b. Winterset, Ia., Aug. 12, 1868; s. John Trumbull and Frances (McCaughan) W.; student Amherst, 1886-88; M.A., Amherst, 1910; m. Katherine Short, July 15, 1890; children—Laurence Trumbull (dec.), Owen Sheppard, Kenneth Sheldon. City editor Decatur (Ill.) Review, 1889; editor and pub. Evansville (Ind.) Call, 1889-90; with Chicago Morning News, Chicago Times and Chicago Record until 1901; canoe exploration with wife in n. western Ont., 1891; investigated Rainy Lake and Ontario gold fields, 1894; took steerage journeys across Atlantic to study immigration questions and conditions, 1894; inquiry indsl. and financial conditions, Mexico, 1896; in charge Chicago Record's news service, Cuban Insurrection, 1897, Cuban, Puerto Rican campaigns, etc., 1898, Hawaii, Samoa, New Zealand and Australian colonies, 1897-98; corr. for Record and syndicate from Central Asia, Caucasus and Siberia, 1899; on 1st exptl. trip of line of steamers from Chicago via the Great Lakes and St. Lawrence River to Europe and return, 1901; indls. investigations in Alaska for Morgan-Guggenheim interests, 1909. Editor The Red Book, 1903-06, Appleton's Magazine, 1906-09, Adventure, 1910-11, Everybody's, 1911-15; v.p. Leo L. Redding & Co., New York, 1919-29; editorial counsel, 1930—; exec. sec. Council for Tariff Reduction, 1931—. Author: Wizard of Wall Street, 1892; World's Columbian Exposition (with William Iglehart), 1893; Reuben and Cynthia at the World's Fair, 1893; War in the East, with history of China, Japan and Korea, 1895; Silver and Gold, or Both Sides of the Shield (edited), 1895; Free Silver in Mexico (with William E. Curtis), 1896; Our War with Spain, 1898; Our New Possessions, 1899; Round the World Tours, 1900; Martinique and the World's Great Disasters, 1902; San Francisco Earthquake (with R. Linthicum), 1906. Contbr. to Saturday Evening Post, New Outlook, Cosmopolitan, Everybody's, Outing, Appleton's Metropolitan, etc. Home: New York, N.Y. Died Dec. 13, 1941.

WHITE, Walter C., motor truck and bus mfr.; b. Cleveland, O., Sept. 8, 1876; s. Thomas H. and Almira (Greenleaf) W.; B.S., Cornell U., 1898; LL.B., New York Law Sch., 1899; m. Mary Virginia Saunders, Sept. 25, 1919; children—Ann Heron, Mary Greenleaf, Walter Harrison, Martha Wells. A pioneer in the automotive industry; worked in factory of father (founder of White Sewing Machine Co.), in production of White steam cars, summers; London mgr. for co., 1901-04; returned to U.S. and made many demonstrations at the wheel, in races and hill-climbing contests; elected v.p. The White Co., 1906, pres., 1921—, pres. White Motor Co., White Motor Securities Corp., White Motor Realty Co.; dir. Union Trust Co., Bishop & Babcock Co. (all of Cleveland), Coca-Cola Co. (Atlanta, Ga.). Chmn. com. sent to France by U.S. Govt., 1917, to asst. in organizing repair and maintenance of motor vehicles in mil. transportation. Chevalier Legion of Honor (France). Home: Gates Mill, O. Died Sept. 29, 1929.

WHITE, William Alanson, physician; b. Brooklyn, Jan. 24, 1870; s. Alanson and Harriet Augusta (Hawley) W.; student Cornell, 1885-89; M.D., L.I. Med. Coll., 1891; A.M. (hon.), Georgetown U., 1925; D.Sc., Washington U., 1932; married. Asst. phys. Binghamton (N.Y.) State Hosp., 1892-1903; supt. St. Elizabeth's Hosp., Washington, 1903—; prof. psychiatry, George Washington U., 1904—; lecturer insanity, U.S. Naval and Army Med. Sch. Mem. National Com. for Mental Hygiene, Fed. Bd. Hospitalization; 1st pres. Internat. Congress Mental Hygiene, 1930; pres. Acad. of Medicine, Washington, D.C. Editor and Translator: (with Dr. Smith E. Jelliffe) The Psychic Treatment of Nervous Disorders, 1905. Editor: (with Dr. Jelliffe) Nervous and Mental Disease Monograph Series; (with same) Modern Treatment of Nervous and Mental Diseases (2 vols.), and the Psychoanalytic Review (quarterly). Author: Outlines of Psychiatry; Mental Mechanisms; Mechanisms of Character Formation; Principles of Mental Hygiene; Diseases of the Nervous System (with Dr. Jelliffe); Mental Hygiene of Childhood; Thoughts of a Psychiatrist on the War and After; Foundations of Psychiatry; Insanity and the Criminal Law; Introduction to the Study of Mind; Essays in Psychopathology; The Meaning of Diseases; Lectures in Psychiatry; Medical Psychology; Crimes and Criminals; Forty Years of Psychiatry. Died Mar. 7, 1937.

WHITE, William E(dgar), furniture mfr.; b. Mebane, N.C., Jan. 29, 1861; s. Stephen Alexander and Mary Jane (Woods) W.; ed. Bingham Mil. Coll., Asheville, N.C.; unmarried. Telegraph operator, Southern R.R., until 1881; furniture mgr. (beginning with brother, David A., with capital of $420), pres. White Furniture Co., Mebane, 1881—. Rep. nominee for corp. commr. for N.C., 1912. Dir. N.C. State Fair. Presbyn. Home: Mebane, N.C. Died Mar. 29, 1935.

WHITE, William Henry, lawyer; ry. pres.; b. Norfolk County, Va., April 16, 1847; s. William and Henrietta K. (White) W.; ed. Randolph-Macon Coll., Va., Va. Mil. Inst., Lexington, U. of Va.; m. Emma Gray, Mar. 10, 1880. Began practice of law at Portsmouth, Va., 1868; commonwealth's atty. for Norfolk County, 1869; removed to Norfolk, 1870; elected commonwealth's attorney for Norfolk City, 1871; U.S. district attorney Eastern Dist. of Va. in Pres. Cleveland's 2d term. Pres. Richmond, Fredericksburg & Potomac R.R. Co., and Washington Southern Ry. Co., Jan. 1, 1907—. Home: Richmond, Va. Died Aug. 5, 1920.

WHITE, William Pierrepont, lawyer; b. Ossian Tp., Livingston County, N.Y., Apr. 8, 1867; s. William Mansfield and Anna Maria (Pierrepont) W.; student De Veaux Coll., Suspension Bridge, N.Y., 1879-82, Utica (N.Y.) Free Acad., 1882-86; LL.B., Columbia, 1890; study U. of Va., summer 1889; m. Mary Antoinet Wheeler, June 3, 1908; children—William Pierrepoint, William Mansfield. Admitted to N.Y. bar, 1890, and began practice at N.Y. City. First supt. highways, Oneida County, N.Y., 1906-07; a pioneer in development of roads and highways of N.Y. Republican. Episcopalian. Home: Utica, N.Y. Died July 1938.

WHITEHAIR, Charles Wesley, banker, author; b. Selma, Ind., Jan. 7, 1887; s. Benjamin W. and Sarah (Shroyer) W.; B.A., De Pauw U., 1909; m. Nilah M. Jay, June 19, 1909; children—Jay Charles, Nilah Jane, Paul Nelson. Sec. Kan. State Coll. Y.M.C.A., 1909-11; nat. sec. Y.M.C.A. for Southern India, 1912-13; sec. Cornell U. Christian Assn., 1914-15; war worker with the Y.M.C.A., 1915-19, also war corr.; passed through submarine zone 18 times; on battle lines from Flanders to Egypt and in training camps in Europe and U.S.; guest of British Expeditionary Forces and of Gen. Allenby in Egypt; invited by latter to speak to his troops, summer of 1918, on "What America Is Doing in the War"; made speaking tour of U.S. for U.S. Treasury Dept. V.p. Union Commerce Bank, Cleveland, O., 1918-20, Union Trust Co., 1920-21, Trumbull Securities Co., 1921; vice pres., dir. The Continental Bank, 1927-28; pres. The Whitehair Bros. Co., gen. ins. Fellow Royal Geog. Soc. Republican. Presbyn. Author: Out There, 1918; Pictures Burned Into My Memory, 1918; The Last Crusade, 1919. Home: Shaker Heights, O. Died June 12, 1933.

WHITEHEAD, Cabell, banker, miner; b. Lynchburg, Va., Oct. 5, 1863; B.M., Lehigh U., 1885; M.S., Columbian (now George Washington) U., 1896, Ph.D., 1898. Assayer U.S. assay office, Boise City, Ida., 1885-89; assayer Bur. of the Mint, 1889-1901; later engaged in banking and mining at Nome, Alaska. Mem. Am. Inst. Mining Engrs., Am. Chem. Soc., Franklin Inst., Phila. Home: Nome, Alaska. Died Sept. 1908.

WHITEHEAD, Charles Nelson, ry. pres.; b. Princeton, Ill., Jan. 23, 1878; s. Albert Jordan and Rachel Josephine (Bates) W.; ed. pub. schs., Dallas, Tex.; m. Frances Haynie, Apr. 21, 1897; 1 son, Charles Powell. Began as messenger M.,K.&T. Ry., 1892, consecutively stenographer, clk. and chief clk., freight and ticket office until 1895, in supt.'s office, 1895-98, gen. freight office, 1898-1900, gen. attorney's office, 1900-01, supt.'s office, 1901-02, gen. counsel's office, 1902-05, asst. sec., 1905-06, sec., 1906-09, sec. and treas., 1909-13, asst. to pres., 1913-14, v.p., 1914, also gen. mgr., 1918-19, Federal mgr. M.,K.&T. Lines, during fed. operation of railroads, 1919-20, then exec. v.p., M.,K.&T. R.R. and M.,K.&T. R.R. of Tex., and v.p. Galveston, Houston & Henderson R.R., Tex. Central R.R., Wichita Falls Ry., Wichita Falls & Northwestern R.R., Wichita Falls & Wellington R.R.; pres. M.,K.&T. System, May 1926—. Episcopalian. Mason. Died Dec. 10, 1926.

WHITEHEAD, Cortlandt, bishop; b. New York, Oct. 30, 1842; s. William Adee and Margaret Elizabeth (Parker) W.; A.B., Yale, 1863, A.M., 1866; grad. Phila. Div. Sch., 1867; D.D., Union, 1880; S.T.D., Hobart Coll., 1887, St. Stephen's Coll., 1890; LL.D., U. of Pittsburgh, 1912; m. Charlotte B. King, July 29, 1868. Deacon, 1867, priest, 1868, P.E. Ch.; missionary in Colo., 1867-70; rector Ch. of the Nativity, S. Bethlehem, Pa., 1870-82; consecrated bishop of Pittsburgh, Jan. 25, 1882. Asst. sec. Diocese of

Central Pa., 1872-81; twice del. to Gen. Conv.; del. Lambeth Confs., London, 1888, 97, 1908. Grand Chaplain of Grand Lodge of Pa. F. and A.M., 1883-1921; chaplain Pa. Soc. Colonial Wars, 1906-21, Pennsylvania Soc., 1907—; chaplain-gen. Guild of St. Barnabas for Nurses, 1887-1912, Order of Colonial Lords of Manors, 1912-21, Union Soc. Civil War, 1913-21. Home: Pittsburgh, Pa. Died Sept. 13, 1922.

WHITEHEAD, Edwin Kirby, humanitarian; b. Coldwater, Mich., Apr. 15, 1861; s. Charles Rollin and Emma (Kirby) W.; A.B., U. of Mich., 1880; unmarried. Prin. high sch., Manistee, Mich., 1881-82; in real estate business (Whitehead Bros.), Denver, 1883-1903; admitted to bar at Denver, 1889, but never practiced; dir., sec. or treas. Colo. Humane Soc., 1887-1907; dir. and sec. State Bur. of Child and Animal Protection, Colo., 1901—. Founder of Sunrise Foundation. Republican. Author: Dumb Animals and How to Treat Them, 1909. Home: Denver, Colo. Deceased.

WHITEHEAD, James Thomas, structural steel mfr.; b. Wyandotte, Mich., Sept. 4, 1864; s. James and Mary Ann (McEvoy) W.; ed. pub. schs., Detroit, Mich.; m. Ida Marie Frazer, Apr. 8, 1885; children—James Frazer, Thomas Cram, Mary Elizabeth (Mrs. Harry Lynn Pierson), Walter Kellogg. Began as steel mfr., Detroit, 1889; became mem. Whitehead & Kales Co., mfrs. structural steel, 1899, later pres.; chmn. bd. Highland Park State Bank; v.p. Kales Stamping Co.; dir. Bank of Detroit, Detroit & Security Trust Co., Highland Park Trust Co., Bank of Dearborn (Mich.). Trustee Cranbrook Sch., Bloomfield Hills, Mich. Republican. Episcopalian. Mason. Home: Detroit, Mich. Died Dec. 9, 1930.

WHITEHEAD, John, theologian; b. Ashton-under-Lyne, Eng., Mar. 14, 1850; s. David and Nancy W.; B.A., Acad. of the New Ch., 1879, B.Th., 1880, A.M., 1899; m. Mary Aitken, Oct. 20, 1880; children—Edith, Helen, Florence, Walter Lucius, Gilbert. Pastor New Ch. (Swedenborgian) Soc., Pittsburgh, 1880-95, Urbana, O., 1895-99; pres. Urbana U., 1895-99; teacher theology New Ch. Theol. Sch., 1899-1902; presiding minister Mich. Assn. of the New Ch. and pastor Detroit Soc. of the New Ch., 1902-05; lecturer on Swedenborg's philosophy and theology, Boston, Jan. 1, 1906—; state lecturer, Mass. Assn. of the New Ch., Oct. 1909-16; general lecturer on Swedenborg's philosophy and psychical subjects, 1916-29. Established, 1897, New Philosophy (Swedenborgian paper). Mem. Gen. Conv. and Council of Ministers. Am. Social Science Assn., Swedenborg Scientific Assn.; librarian New Ch. Theol Sch., 1912-25; chmn. of Com. on Translation of the Word, Gen. Conv. of New Jerusalem Ch.; established correspondence scn. for the study of Swedenborg's Arcana Cœlestia, 1918—. Author: The Illusions of Christian Science; Hebrew Synonyms, 1925; Testimony on Survival; also mag., rev. and newspaper articles. Translator: Swedenborg's Apocalypse Explained, 6 vols., 1911; Apocalypse Revealed (2 vols.), 1912; Miscellaneous Theological Works, 1913; Posthumous Theological Works (2 vols.). Editor and publisher The Swedenborg Student (monthly mag.), 1920—. Chmn. com. on phototyping Swedenborg's Manuscripts, Gen. Conv. New Jerusalem Ch. Home: Cambridge, Mass. Died Nov. 30, 1930.

WHITEHEAD, John Meek, lawyer; b. near Hillsboro, Ill., July 29, 1852; s. Jacob and Elizabeth Ann (Paisley) W.; grad. Williston Sem., Easthampton, Mass., 1873; A.B., Yale, 1877; studied law in office of Leaming & Thompson, Chicago; m. Lavinia Fletcher Barrows, July 12, 1881 (died 1888); m. 2d, Juliet Claire Thorp, May 15, 1919. Admitted to bar, 1881; with Leaming & Thompson, Chicago, Ill., 1881-95; mem. Whitehead, Matheson & Smith, Janesville, Wis., 1895-87, Whitehead & Matheson, 1897—; v.p. Hillsboro Coal Co.; mgr. Ophir Loop Mines Co. Mem. Wis. Senate, 4 terms, 1896-1912; Wis. mem. Perry Victory Centennial Commn., 1910; pres. Janesville Pub. Library Bd. 6 yrs. Pres. Wis. br. League to Enforce Peace; pres. State Y.M.C.A., Wis., 1894-1916; v.p. Wis. Peace Soc.; corporate mem. A.B.C.F.M.; mem. Commn. of 19 of Congl. Nat. Council; dir. and chmn. bd. State Congregational Conf. Del. Rep. Nat. Conv., 1920. Republican. Home: Janesville, Wis. Died Aug. 31, 1924.

WHITEHEAD, Ralph Radcliffe; b. Yorkshire, Eng., Nov. 4, 1854; s. Francis Frederick and Isabella (Dalglish) W.; M.A., Balliol Coll., Oxford, Eng., 1877 (pupil of Ruskin); came to U.S., 1892, m. Jane Byrd MacCall, 1892; children—Ralph Radcliffe, Peter McCall. Follower of Ruskin and William Morris, whose principles he endeavored to embody in an arts and crafts settlement "Byrdcliffe," Woodstock, Ulster County, N.Y. Author: Grass of the Desert, 1892, Dante's Vita Nuova, 1893. Home: Woodstock, N.Y. Died Feb. 23, 1929.

WHITEHEAD, Richard Henry, anatomist; b. Salisbury, N.C., July 27, 1865; s. Marcellus (M.D.) and Virginia (Coleman) W.; A.B., Wake Forest Coll., N.C., 1886; M.D., U. of Va., 1887; LL.D., U. of N.C., 1910; m. Virgilia Whitehead, June 4, 1891. Demonstrator anatomy, U. of Va., 1887-89; prof. anatomy and dean med. dept., U. of N.C., 1891-1905; prof. anatomy and dean of med. dept., U. of Va., 1905—. Author: Anatomy of the Brain, 1900. Contbr. of anat. and pathol. papers to med. jours. Died Feb. 6, 1916.

WHITEHILL, Clarence (Eugene), operatic baritone singer; b. Marengo, Ia.; s. William and Elizabeth Dawson (McLaughlin) W.; High Sch., Marengo, 1900; studied music under L. A. Phelps in Chicago, Ill.; went to Paris, 1896, and studied under Giraudet and Sbriglia; m. Mrs. Isabelle Rush Simpson, July 26, 1912. Operatic début as Friar Lawrence in Gounod's "Romeo and Juliet," at Theâtre de la Monnaie, Brussels, 1900; next appeared in Opéra Comique, Paris, in "Lakmé"; leading baritone, Cologne (Germany) Opera House, 1903-08; joined Metropolitan Opera Co., 1909, making first appearance in New York as Amfortas, in "Parsifal." Studied Wagnerian rôles under Frau Wagner, and sang at Bayreuth Festivals; regular member Met. Opera Co., New York, 1920-31. First Am. man to sing at Grand Opera House, Paris; first Am. to sing at Munich or Bayreuth. Played part of George Washington in official Bicentennial talking picture of George Washington. Died Dec. 19, 1932.

WHITEHORNE, Earl, editor; b. Verona, N.J., Nov. 8, 1881; s. Henry Bayard and Mary Elizabeth (Riker) W.; ed. pub. schs.; m. Earlena Taunt, Oct. 7, 1908; 1 dau., Mary Jane. Active in comml. development of the elec. industry, 1907—; a founder, and mng. editor Electrical Merchandising, 1907-14; advertising business on own account, 1914-21, also contributing editor Electrical World and Electrical Merchandising; with McGraw-Hill Publishing Co., 1921—; comml. editor Electrical World and editorial dir. Electrical Merchandising, and Radio Retailing; editor Electrical Contracting and editorial dir. of Wholesalers Salesman. Republican. Episcopalian. Author: Supercargo, 1939. Home: Caldwell, N.J. Died Oct. 23, 1941.

WHITEHOUSE, F(rederic) Cope, lawyer; b. Rochester, N.Y., Nov. 9, 1842; s. Rt. Rev. Henry John and Evelina Harriet (Bruen) W.; A.B. (highest honors), Columbia, 1861, A.M., 1863; studied in France, Germany and Italy; unmarried. Admitted to bar, 1871. Hon. mem. fellow and corr. mem. of many learned socs. in U.S., Europe and Egypt; made Comdr. of Osmânieh and Grand Officier Medjidieh on account of efforts for better regulation of the Nile. Discovered the depression in the Egyptian desert known as the Wadi Raiyan, 1882, and wrote many papers advocating it as a storage reservoir. Made extensive researches in Semitic traditions relating to the Canal of Joseph and the land of Goshen, which he identified with the Fayoum, submerged in the time of Herodotus and then known as Lake Moeris. Frequent contbr. on topics relating to astron., geol. and other scientific subjects, and on foreign banks and banking. Home: Newport, R.I. Died 1911.

WHITEHOUSE, James Horton, art designer; b. Staffordshire, Eng., Oct. 28, 1833; removed to New York; connected with Tiffany & Co. (jewelers), 1858—; designed many notable artistic productions in silver, including the Bryant vase, presented to the poet on his 80th birthday and now in Metropolitan Museum of Art, New York. Home: Brooklyn, N.Y. Died 1902.

WHITEHOUSE, William Fitz Hugh, explorer; b. Elmhurst, Ill., Sept. 6, 1877; s. Fitz Hugh and Frances (Sheldon) W.; grad. Yale, 1899; unmarried. On exploration and hunting expdn., Somaliland, Abyssinia, British East Africa and Uganda, 1899-1900, thoroughly exploring Lakes Rudolph and Stephanie; in 1902 explored Abyssinia and the unknown country south, down the east side of the chain of lakes. Fellow Royal Geog. Soc., London, Am. Geog. Soc. Wrote article: Through the Country of the King of Kings, Scribner's, Sept. 1902. Died 1909.

WHITEHOUSE, William Penn, judge; b. Vassalboro, Me., Apr. 9, 1842; s. John Roberts and Hannah (Percival) W.; A.B., Waterville (now Colby) Coll., Me., 1863, A.M., 1866, LL.D., Colby College, 1896, and Bowdoin College, 1912; m. Evelyn M., d. of Colonel Robert Treat, June 24, 1869; father of Robert Treat W. Admitted to bar, 1865; city solicitor, Augusta, Me., 4 yrs.; county attorney, 1869-76; judge Superior Ct., 1878-90; asso. justice Supreme Jud. Ct. of Me., 1890-1911, chief justice, July 26, 1911-Apr. 9, 1913 (retired under age limit); later counselor-at-law. Republican. Trustee Kennebec Savings Bank, 1888, State Trust Co., 1907. Chmn. commn. on New Insane Hosp., 1873. Wrote monograph against the cottage system published by the state. Home: Augusta, Me. Died Oct. 10, 1922.

WHITEHURST, Camelia, painter; b. Baltimore, Md.; d. Jessie Harrison and Anna Lavinia (McIlvain) W.; ed. pvt. and pub. schs., Baltimore. Painter of children. Awarded 1st prize, All Southern Expn., Charleston, S.C., 1921; hon. mention, Nat. Assn. Women Painters and Sculptors, 1920-21; 1st prize, Memphis, Tenn., 1922; Delgado prize, New Orleans, La., 1923; 2d prize, Nat. Assn. Women Painters and Sculptors, 1923; bronze medal, Washington Soc. Artists, 1926; 1st prize for portraiture, Jackson, Miss., 1929, Springfield, Mass., 1929, Washington (D.C.) Soc. Artists, 1929. Mem. Fellowship Pa. Acad. Fine Arts, Nat. Assn. Women Painters and Sculptors. Home: Baltimore, Md. Died June 23, 1936.

WHITELEY, Emily Stone; b. Chicago, Ill.; d. Isaac Dulin and Sophia (Bainbridge) Stone; ed. pvt. schs. and spl. instrs., Baltimore, Md.; m. James Gustavus Whiteley, Dec. 16, 1896. Member Md. Dem. State Central Com., 1934; del. Dem. Nat. Conv., Phila., 1936; apptd. by Pres. Roosevelt mem. Annual Assay Commn., 1937. Decorated by Belgian Govt. with Médaille de la Reine Elisabeth and accorded special honors by the Dutchess of Vendome for war work. Democrat. Episcopalian. Author: General Washington and his Aides-de-Camp, 1936. Home: Baltimore, Md. Died Sept. 3, 1939.

WHITELOCK, George, lawyer; b. Baltimore, Dec. 25, 1854; s. William and Jane Stockton (Woolston) W.; brother of William Wallace W.; grad. Pa. Mil. Coll., 1872; LL.B., U. of Md., 1875; student Leipzig, Germany, and in Romance Philology, Johns Hopkins; M.A., Pa. Military Coll., 1914; m. Louise Clarkson Sauerwein, Dec. 30, 1878. In practice at Baltimore, 1876—; firm Schmucker & Whitelock, 1876-98, Whitelock & Fowler, 1908-09, Whitelock, Deming & Kemp, 1909—. Mem. Municipal Com. on Extension of City Limits, 1888; chmn. Com. on Revision of Rules of State Cts. of Baltimore City, 1897; Rep. candidate for atty. gen. Md., 1903; mem. of Com. on Revision of Rules of U.S. Cts. for Dist. of Md., 1906-09; mem. com. apptd. by Circuit Ct. of Appeals, 4th Circuit, on revision of equity rules, U.S. Supreme Ct., 1911, etc. Sec. Am. Bar Assn., Sept. 1, 1909—; pres. Md. State Bar Assn., 1903-04 (procured passage law for pensions to Md. judiciary); pres. Lawyers Anti-Amendment League of Md., 1909 (disfranchisement amendment defeated); del. Universal Congress Lawyers and Jurists, St. Louis, 1904; Md. commr. on Uniform State Laws, 1908—; commr. apptd. by gov. of Md. to frame workmen's compensation act, 1913; declined appmt. as judge Supreme Bench of Baltimore City, 1915. Home: Baltimore, Md. Died Jan. 8, 1920.

WHITELOCK, Louise Clarkson, author; b. Baltimore, 1865; m. George Whitelock, Dec. 30, 1878. Early books under name of L. Clarkson; illustrator, many of her books being illustrated by herself. Author: (collections of poems) Violet with Eyes of Blue; The Gathering of the Lilies; The Rag Fair; Indian Summer; Heartsease and Happy Days; Flyaway Fairies (children's book); Little Miss Stay-at-Home (same); The Shadow of John Wallace (novel); A Mad Madonna; How Hindsight Met Provincialatis (short stories). Home: Baltimore, Md. Died about Apr. 7, 1928.

WHITELOCK, William Wallace, author; b. Mt. Washington, nr. Baltimore, Apr. 1, 1869; s. William and Jane Stockton (Woolston) W.; A.B., Johns Hopkins, 1890; Ph.D., U. of Munich, 1893; m. Jan. 10, 1901, Baroness Mary von Stockhausen; 1 son, Otto von Stockhausen. Served apprenticeship in newspaper work in New York. Prof. German, Temple U., Phila., and St. Stephen's Coll. (Columbia). Chief yeoman on U.S.S. Gloucester during Spanish-American war, 1898. Author: When the Heart Is Young, 1902; The Literary Guillotine, 1903; Just Love Songs, 1906; Foregone Verses, 1907; When Kings Go Forth to Battle, 1907; The Man Who Told the Truth (comedy); The Power of Attorney (a drama, jointly with John T. Lang). Translator: Modern Germany in Relation to the Great War. Editor: (with J. H. Wilson) French Eloquence. Home: New York, N.Y. Died Jan. 28, 1940.

WHITENTON, William Maynard, ry. official; b. Victoria, Tex., 1869; s. Cole C. and Sallie (Henry) W.; ed. high sch.; m. Annie Winslow, Nov. 1, 1889. Began as section laborer M.,K.&T. Ry., 1884, later telegraph operator, station agt. and train dispatcher same rd.; train dispatcher and chief dispatcher T.&P. Ry., 1890-98, train dispatcher, trainmaster, supt., gen. supt. and gen. mgr. C.,R.I.&P. Ry., 1898-1914; operating expert on Chicago Assn. Commerce Com. of Investigation on smoke abatement and electrification of ry. terminals, 1914-15; operating asst. staff of v.p. T.&P. Ry., 1915-17; with M.,K.&T. Ry., Jan. 1, 1917—, beginning as trainmaster, became v.p., also v.p. M.,K.&T. R.R. Co. of Tex.; dir. Republic Nat. Bank, Dallas. Lt. col. staff of gov. of Tex. Democrat. Presbyn. Mason. Home: Dallas, Tex. Died Dec. 10, 1929.

WHITESIDE, Frank Reed, artist; b. Phila., Aug. 20, 1866; s. R. J. M. and Mary (Mustin) W.; ed. Phila. public schs. and Pa. Acad. Fine Arts; studied with Laurens and Constant, Paris; m. Clara Walker, 1895; 1 dau., Esther Walker. Instr. R.C. High Sch., Phila., 1890-96; instr. in Pub. Industrial Art Sch., P.E. Ch. Acad., Blight Sch., Phila., 1907, Germantown Acad. Specialty landscapes; contbr. to art periodicals. Home: Philadelphia, Pa. Died Sept. 19, 1929.

WHITESIDE, James Leonard, educator; b. Montgomery County, Mo., Aug. 27, 1864; s. John Clark and Louisa Marian (Davis) W.; Ph.B., Central Coll., Fayette, Mo., 1892, B.A., 1911, M.A., 1912; studied

U. of Chicago and U. of Mo.; m. Mary M. Gibson, July 15, 1903; children—Reginald Gibson, Mary Louise, Jean Elizabeth. Teacher sciences, Marvin Coll., Fredericktown, Mo., 9 yrs.; headmaster Scarritt Collegiate Inst., Neosho, Mo., 1 yr.; pres. Logan Female Coll., Russellville, Ky., 1909-10; prof. mathematics and physics, Epworth U., Oklahoma City, Okla., 1910-11; prof. chemistry and physics, Scarritt-Morrisville Coll., Morrisville, Mo., 1911-12; with city schs., Clinton, later at Sedalia, Mo., 1912-18; dean of Coll. and head chem. dept. Ky. Wesleyan Coll., 1918—. K.P. Author: Manuals of chemistry and botany. Home: Winchester, Ky. Died Nov. 18, 1928.

WHITFIELD, Henry Lewis, governor; b. Rankin County, Miss., June 20, 1868; s. Robert Allen and Mary Ann (Fitzhugh) W.; B.A., Miss. Coll., Clinton, Miss., 1895; studied law, Millsaps Coll. (Jackson, Miss.), U. of Miss., and summer courses at other univs.; m. Mary White, 1897; children—Robert Allen, Knox White, Henry Lewis, William White. Teacher country schs.; state supt. edn., Miss., 1898-1907; pres. Miss. State Coll. for Women, 1907-20; gov. of Miss., term 1924-27 inclusive. Democrat. Baptist. Mason, Odd Fellow, K.P. Died Mar. 18, 1927.

WHITFIELD, J(ames) Edward, chemist; b. Albany, N.Y., Sept. 27, 1859; s. Robert P. and Mary (Henry) W.; acad. edn.; Ph.D., Nat. Coll. Pharmacy, Washington, 1880; studied 4 yrs. at Rensselaer Poly. Inst., but was not grad.; m. Florence P. Morton, Dec. 25, 1885. With U.S. Geol. Survey, 1880-88; with firm of Booth, Garrett & Blair, analytical chemists and engrs., Phila., 1888—. Died Nov. 4, 1930.

WHITFIELD, Robert Parr, geologist; b. New Hartford, N.Y., May 27, 1828; s. William Fenton and Margaret (Parr) W.; mostly self-ed.; hon. A.M., Wesleyan, 1882. Worked for his father, a spindlemaker, until 1848, when he entered employ of Samuel Chubbuck, instrument-maker, Utica, becoming mgr., 1849-56. Spent spare time studying natural history and geology; asst. in palæontology and geology, N.Y. State Natural History, 1856-76; U.S. Geol. Survey, 1872; teacher, 1872-75, and prof. geology, 1875-78, Rensselaer Poly. Inst., Troy, N.Y.; curator geol. dept., Am. Mus. Natural History, 1877—. Original fellow A.A.A.S.; fellow Geol. Soc. America. Author of Palæontol. papers, U.S. Geol. Survey, Ohio Palæontology, Palæontology of New Jersey, 3 vols., etc. Contbr. on geol. subjects. Died 1910.

WHITFORD, Greeley Webster, lawyer; b. Rockville, Ind., June 5, 1856; s. John W. and Jane (Harlan) W.; ed. pub. schs. and Ia. Wesleyan Coll., Mt. Pleasant, Ia.; m. Ida Spaulding, June 4, 1890 (died 1916); children—Kent Shelton, Mrs. Ruth Kepner, Mrs. Helen Jane Myers; m. 2d, Mrs. Edith Kimball Whitford (widow of deceased brother Clay B. Whitford), Sept. 28, 1917 (children by her 1st marriage—Mrs. Winifred Pinkett, Mrs. Eleanor W. Gould). Admitted to Ia. bar, 1882; moved to Whatcom (now Bellingham, Wash.) and practiced law there, 1884-87; postmaster, 1885; moved to Denver, Colo., 1887; asst. city atty., 1889-93; dist. atty. 2d Jud. Dist., Denver, 1895-97; U.S. dist. atty. for Colo., 1897-1901; mem. Charter Conv. to frame City Charter for Denver, 1903; dist. Judge, 2d Jud. Dist., Denver, 1907-13, 1919-21; justice Supreme Ct. of Colo., term 1921-31, chief justice, 1929-31; retired. Republican. Methodist. Mason, K.P. Home: Denver, Colo. Deceased.

WHITFORD, Oscar F., civil engr.; b. Saratoga County, N.Y., July 15, 1833; s. Earl Hartwell and Asenath (Palmer) W.; grad. Union Coll., Schenectady, 1858, A.M. in course, 1861; post-graduate course in chemistry, same; vol. U.S.A., 4 months, 1862; prof. mathematics and civil engring., People's Coll., Havana, N.Y., 1864-66; practiced as civil engr. in U.S., Mexico and S. America, 1866—; engr. in charge of constrn. for the Ontario Power Co., of Niagara Falls. Unmarried. Author of professional pamphlets, reports and papers. Deceased.

WHITFORD, William Calvin, prof. Bibl. langs.; b. Brookfield, N.Y., Jan. 31, 1865; s. of Calvin and Emeline (Burch) W.; A.B., Madison (now Colgate) U., 1886, A.M., 1890; grad. Union Theol. Sem., 1892; D.D., Alfred, 1907; m. Jessie F. Briggs, Sept. 20, 1892. Ordained Seventh-day Bapt. ministry, 1892; prof. Bibl. langs. and lit., Alfred U., 1893—, also of Alfred Theol. Sem., 1901—. Editor of the Helping Hand, 1898—. Pres. Seventh-day Bapt. Edn. Soc., 1910—; treas. Seventh-day Bapt. Gen. Conf., 1888—; mem. Internat. S.S. Lesson Com., 1914—. Mem. efficiency bur., Bur. of War Risk Ins., Washington, 10 weeks, 1918. Home: Alfred, N.Y. Died Aug. 12, 1925.

WHITFORD, William Clarke, educator; b. Edmeston, N.Y., May 5, 1828; s. Capt. Manuel and Sophia (Clark) W.; grad. Union Coll., Schenectady, N.Y., 1853; De Ruyter Inst., 1850, Union Theol. Sem., 1856; A.M., 1858; D.D., Blackburn U., Carlinville, Ill., 1883; m. Ruth Hemphill, March 23, 1852. Pres. Milton Coll., 1858—; State supt. Public Instruction, Wis., 1878-81. Pastor: 2 Seventh-Day Bapt. chs., Milton, Mo., 1856-59, 1894-97. Regent Wis. State Normal schools, 1867-75. Author: History of Education in Wis. (for Centennial Expn., Phila., 1876); Historical Sketch of Milton College, 1876; Plans and Specifications for School Houses (published by the State of Wis., 1882); also numerous published addresses and articles on hist. and ednl. subjects; corr. editor Wis. Jour. of Edn., 1878-81; Seventh-Day Baptist Quarterly, 1884; Sabbath Recorder, 1887—. Address: Milton, Rock Co., Wis. Died 1902.

WHITING, Arthur, musician; b. Cambridge, Mass., June 20, 1861. Pianist, writer of orchestral and chamber music, songs and pianoforte pieces; compositions performed by Boston, Pittsburgh and Cincinnati Symphony orchestras and the Kneisel Quartet. Mem. Nat. Inst. Arts and Letters. Founder and mgr. of the Univ. Concerts of Harvard, Princeton and Yale. Home: New York, N.Y. Died July 20, 1936.

WHITING, Charles Goodrich, editor; b. St. Albans, Vt., Jan. 30, 1842; s. Calvin and Mary R. (Goodrich) W.; ed. high sch., Chicopee Falls, Mass.; m. Eliza Rose Gray, June 12, 1869. After youth spent in paper-making, farming, keeping country store, etc., joined the staff of the Republican, 1868; continuing with it except 18 months when asst. editor Albany Evening Times; lit. editor Republican, 1874-1910; later asso. editor. Mem. Nat. Inst. Arts and Letters. Author: Ode on the Dedication of the Soldiers' Monument at Springfield, 1885; The Saunterer, 1886; Walks in New England, 1903; Arts and Letters in Springfield (in Springfield Present and Prospective), 1905; Poem on the 275th Anniversary of Founding of Springfield, May 26, 1911; "The Temple of Democracy," ode on the musical opening of the Auditorium, Springfield, Feb. 1913; "A Springfield Hymn," dedicating Springfield's municipal group, Dec. 8, 1913. Home: Springfield, Mass. Died June 21, 1922.

WHITING, Charles Sumner, judge; b. Olmsted County, Minn., May 25, 1863; s. Ami Nelson and Mariette (Rice) W.; student law dept. U. of Mich.; LL.B., U. of Minn., 1889; m. Mary G. Mitchell, Nov. 4, 1891 (died 1897); m. 2d, Elinor Hilton, July 21, 1900. Practiced at DeSmet, S.D.; state's atty., Kingsbury County, S.D., 1893-97 and 1899-1903; circuit judge 9th Jud. Circuit, S.D., 1903-08; asso. justice Supreme Ct. of S.D., terms Dec. 1, 1908-Jan. 1925. Republican. Universalist. Mem. Nat. Conf. on Uniform State Laws; elector, Hall of Fame, New York U. Home: Pierre, S.D. Died Mar. 25, 1922.

WHITING, George Elbridge, organist, composer; b. Holliston, Mass., Sept. 14, 1842; early showed talent for music; as a boy played in concert at Worcester, Mass.; became organist, Hartford, Conn., and 1862, at Boston; later at Albany, N.Y.; studied in Europe, 1863 and 1872; m. Helen, d. Rev. J. Aldrich, 1867. Organist and musical dir., Ch. of the Immaculate Conception, Boston, 1876-78, and 1883—; teacher organ New England Conservatory of Music for several yrs., resigning 1897; organist Cincinnati Music Hall and prof. organ and composition, Cincinnati Coll. of Music., 1878-83. Composer: Grand Sonata, Op. 4; Organ Accompaniment and Extempore; The Tale of the Viking, cantata; Dream Pictures, cantata; Midnight, cantata; also preludes, etc., for organ, and many MS. works consisting of cantatas, songs, symphony in C, Overture Princess, Piano Concerto, Suite for Orchestra: one-act opera, "Lenora" (in Italian), 1893. Died Oct. 14, 1923.

WHITING, Harry Hayes, pres. Pillsbury Flour Mills Co.; b. Rochester, Minn., Mar. 21, 1877; s. Eathan and Ellen (Hayes) W.; grad. high sch., 1893; m. Adelaide Stout, Oct. 12, 1901; children—Francis Perrine, Eleanor Hayes (Mrs. Charles M. Skinner). Began as stenographer, 1893; in grain business, 1894-97; with Pillsbury Flour Mills Co., 1897—, vice-pres., 1929-32, pres., 1932—. Home: Minneapolis, Minn. Died Oct. 3, 1936.

WHITING, Henry Hyer; b. Pensacola, Fla., Dec. 8, 1875; s. Dr. John Cary and Clara Regina (Hyer) W.; ed. pub. schs.; m. Ethel Robertson, Sept. 15, 1904; children—Clara Thornton (Mrs. James Calhoun Stewart), Carolyn Hyer (Mrs. Sydney Peter Murman). Saw mill operator, 1893-1907; treas. Columbia Steel Co., 1907-14; gen. mgr. Best Steel Castings Co., 1914-16, pres. 1916-29; organized Pacific Malleable Castings Co. and pres. of same, 1924-27; v.p. Gen. Metals Corp., 1929-35; dir. Central Bank of Oakland, Calif. Foreman Grand Jury for Alameda County, 1938. Dir. Alameda County Charities Commn.; vice chmn. Dem. State Central Com.; mem. Business Advisory Council, U.S. Dept. of Commerce; mem. bd. U.S. Employment Service. Served as pvt., later sergt., 1st Fla. Vols., U.S.A., Spanish-Am. War. Democrat. Episcopalian. Home: Berkeley, Calif. Died July 6, 1939.

WHITING, Justin Rice, congressman; b. Bath, N.Y., Feb. 18, 1847; s. Col. Henry and Pamelia (Rice) W.; entered Univ. of Mich., classic course, 1863, but was not graduated. State senator, 1883; mem. Congress, 1887-95. Democrat. Defeated for gov., 1898. Died 1903.

WHITING, Robert Rudd, editor; b. New York, Sept. 15, 1877; s. Newton Francis and Katharine (Rudd) W.; grad. Phillips Acad., Andover, Mass., 1896; student, Harvard, 1896-97, Princeton, 1897-99; m. Agnes Kempster, Sept. 3, 1902. On staff New York Sun, 1899-1904; dept. editor Everybody's Mag., 1906-10, The Designer, 1910-11; editor Ainslee's Mag., Mar. 1911—. Author: Baseball Stories, 1902; A Ball of Yarn, 1907; The Judgment of Jane, 1915; also many novelettes and short stories. Compiler: Four Hundred Good Stories, 1910. Home: Darien, Conn. Died Oct. 15, 1918.

WHITING, Sarah Frances, physicist, astronomer; b. Wyoming, N.Y., Aug. 23, 1847; d. Joel and Elizabeth Lee (Comstock) Whiting; A.B., Ingham Coll., LeRoy, N.Y., 1865; student Mass. Inst. Tech., 1876-79, U. of Berlin, 1889, Edinburgh, 1896-97; Sc.D., Tufts Coll., 1905. Prof. physics and phys. astronomy, Wellesley, 1879-1912; dir. Whitin Obs., 1904-16, prof. emeritus, 1916—. Fellow A.A.A.S. Conglist. Author: Daytime and Evening Exercises in Astronomy; also articles for astron. journals. Lecturer. Died 1927.

WHITING, William, paper mfr.; b. Dudley, Mass., May 24, 1841; high sch. edn.; hon. A.M., Amherst, 1877. Bookkeeper, later salesman and then mill mgr. Holyoke Paper Co.; organized, 1865, the Whiting Paper Co., of which became pres.; also pres. of other mfg. corps. and of the Holyoke Nat. Bank. Mem. Mass. Senate, 1872; city treas. Holyoke, 1876-77, mayor, 1878-79; del. Rep. Nat. Conv., 1876; mem. 48th to 50th Congresses (1883-89), 6th Mass. Dist. Commr., Paris Expn., 1900. Home: Holyoke, Mass. Died 1911.

WHITING, William Fairfield, paper mfr.; b. Holyoke, Mass., July 20, 1864; s. William and Anna (Fairfield) W.; A.B., Amherst, 1886; m. Anne Chapin; children—William 2d, Edward C., Fairfield, Ruth (Mrs. Neil Chapin). Pres. and gen. mgr. Whiting Paper Co. for many years. Apptd. sec. of commerce by President Coolidge, Aug. 21, 1928, to succeed Herbert Hoover. Del. to Rep. Nat. Convs., 1920, 24, 28, 32. Congregationalist. Home: Holyoke, Mass. Died Aug. 31, 1936.

WHITING, William Henry, rear admiral U.S.N.; b. New York, July 8, 1843; s. William Henry and Mary Jane (Christian) W. Apptd. to U.S. Naval Acad. from Wis., 1860, grad. 1863; ensign, Oct. 1, 1863; master, May 10, 1866; lt., Feb. 21, 1867; lt. comdr., Mar. 12, 1868; comdr., July 12, 1882; capt., June 19, 1897; rear admiral, Oct. 11, 1903. Served in the Hartford, W. Gulf Blockading Squadron, 1863-65; hon. mention by Admiral Farragut "for gallant conduct in burning of blockade-runner 'Ivanhoe' under guns of Ft. Morgan, July 5, 1864"; took part in battle of Mobile Bay, and, at surrender Ft. Gaines, hauled down the Confed. flag and hoisted U.S. flag; also at bombardment and surrender of Fort Morgan, Aug. 24, 1864; served on Kearsarge, Frolic and Ticonderoga, European Squadron, 1865-69; Swatara, 1869-71; Benicia, 1872-75; Navy Yard, New York, 1875-76, 1881-84, 1886-89, 1890-92; Torpedo Sch., Newport, 1876; Constitution, 1878-79; comd. training-ship Saratoga, 1884-6, Kearsarge, 1889, Alliance, 1892-93; comdt. Navy Yard, Pensacola, 1894-96, Naval Sta., Puget Sound, 1896-97; comd. Monadnock, 1897-98; took Monadnock from San Francisco to Manila; comd. Charleston, 1898-99, Boston, 1899; capt. of yard, Navy Yard, Mare Island, 1900; comd. receiving-ship Independence, 1900-02; comdt. Naval Sta., Honolulu, 1902-03, Naval Training Sta., San Francisco, 1903-05; retired, July 8, 1905. Home: Berkeley, Calif. Died July 26, 1925.

WHITLEY, Cora Call (Mrs. Francis E. Whitley), conservationist; b. Rowlesburg, Va., May 7, 1862; d. Rev. L. N. and Mary (Guyon) Call; ed. Cedar Valley Jr. Coll. and under pvt. tutors; m. Francis Edmund Whitley, M.D., 1883; children—Gladys (Mrs. Varick C. Crosley, dec.), Grace Bingham (Mrs. Max M. Henningway), Guyon Call. Pres. Iowa Fedn. Women's Clubs, 1915-17 (chairman conservation 1935); Iowa state sec. Gen. Fedn. Women's Clubs, 1917-20; chmn. Gen. Fed. Conservation Div., 1920-24; chmn. Gen. Fed. Forestry and Natural Scenery, 1924—. V.p. Ia. Fed. Women's Clubs, 1913-15, pres., 1915-17, chmn. conservation, 1923-25, 1927—; chmn. Ia. Woman's Com., Council of Nat. Defense, and vice chmn. Ia. Council of Defense, 1917-18; chmn. Woman's Dept., and mem. exec. com. Ia. Food Adminstrn., 1917-18, vice chmn. Liberty Loan orgn., dir. Ia. War Savings orgn., Woman's Dept. Actg. pres. Ia. Tuberculosis Assn., 1935; v.p. Iowa Conservation Assn., Am. Forestry Assn.; dir. Nat. Tuberculosis Assn., Nat. Izaak Walton League, and v.p. Ia. Izaak Walton League; vice chmn. conservation com. Garden Club of America (Ia. chmn., 1930—); vice chmn. Gen. Fed. Conservation Div., 1928-30; sec. Child Welfare Commn.; mem. State Probation Com., 1932—. Republican. Baptist. Contbr. to mags. and author of numerous pamphlets. Home: Webster City, Ia. Died Dec. 30, 1937.

WHITLOCK, Brand, author, diplomat; b. Urbana, O., Mar. 4, 1869; s. Rev. Dr. Elias D. and Mallie (Brand) W.; ed. pub. schs. and by pvt. tuition; LL.D., Brown U., 1916, Ohio Wesleyan, 1917, Western Reserve, 1919; Docteur en droit, Brussels, 1919, and same from U. of Louvain, 1927; m. Ella Brainerd, June 8, 1895. Newspaper reporter, Toledo, O., 1887-90; reporter and polit. corr. staff Chicago Herald, 1890-93; clerk in office sec. of state, Springfield, Ill.,

1893-97; studied law under John M. Palmer, Springfield; admitted to Ill. bar, 1894, to bar of Ohio, 1897; practiced at Toledo, 1897-1905. Elected mayor of Toledo as Independent, against 4 other candidates, 1905; reelected under similar conditions, 1907, 09, 11; declined nomination for 5th term; U.S. minister to Belgium, Dec. 2, 1913, and Ambassador E. and P., Sept. 29, 1919-Feb. 1, 1922. Mem. Am. Acad. Arts and Letters, Poetry Soc. America, Authors' League America; gold medal, Nat. Inst. Social Sciences, 1913. Patron Commn. for Relief in Belgium; decorated Grand Cordon de l'Ordre de Léopold by the King of the Belgians, 1917; Burgher of Brussels, 1918, of Liége, 1919; Hon. Citizen of Antwerp, 1919; Burgher of Ghent, 1920; asso. mem. Royal Acad. of Belgium, 1919; Civic Cross of 1st class by Belgian Govt. for "courage and devotion"; mem. Royal Belgian Acad. of French Language and Lit., 1922; Grand Cross of St. Sava (Serbia), 1920; Grand Cross Order of Rising Sun (Japan), 1922; commemorative medal Comité National, Belgium, 1919; Grand Officer of Legion of Honor, France, 1929. Received and thanked by Belgian Parliament in spl. session, Dec. 1918, for services to nation, and bust placed in Belgian Senate; boulevard in Brussels named for him. Hon. mem. Grand Serment Royal St. Georges, Brussels (society of cross bowmen under King's patronage, existing since 1381). Democrat. Episcopalian. Author: The 13th District, 1902; Her Infinite Variety, 1904; The Happy Average, 1904; The Turn of the Balance, 1907; Abraham Lincoln, 1908 (French transl. by author, 1918); The Gold Brick, 1910; On the Enforcement of Law in Cities (monograph), 1910, in book form, 1913; The Fall Guy, 1912; Forty Years of It, 1914; Belgium Under the German Occupation, 1918 (transl. into French, Danish, etc.); J. Hardin & Son (novel), 1923; Uprooted (novel), 1926; Transplanted (novel), 1927; Big Matt (novel), 1928; La Fayette, 1929; The Little Green Shutter, 1931; Narcissus, 1931. Contbr. to Ency. Britannica, also essays, poems and short stories to mags. Died May 24, 1934.

WHITLOCK, William Francis, educator, clergyman; b. on farm nr. Dayton, O., Oct. 20, 1833; s. Elias B. and Mary (Johnson) W.; ed. country dist. schs., West Chester (O.) village sch., prep. and collegiate depts., Ohio Wesleyan U., A.B., 1859, A.M., 1862; D.D., Baldwin U., 1878; LL.D., Syracuse U., 1899, Ohio Wesleyan U., 1905; m. Martha Jane Howe, Aug. 2, 1865 (died 1900). Tutor ancient languages, 1859-64, adj. prof., 1864-66, prof. Latin lang. and lit., 1866—, dean of Ladies' Dept., 1877-83, dean, 1897-1900, acting pres., 1904-05, v.p., 1905—, Ohio Wesleyan U. Clergyman; mem. N. Ohio Conf. M.E. Ch., represented in 6 consecutive quadrennial gen. confs.; mem., 1884—, chmn., 1893—, of Publishing Com. M.E. Ch. Republican. Author: Story of the Book Concern, 1893. Contbr. to Meth. Rev. and denominational weeklies of M.E. Ch. Died 1909.

WHITMAN, Benaiah Longley, clergyman; b. Torbrook, N.S., Nov. 21, 1862; s. Isaac J. and Sarah M. (Spinney) W.; A.B., Brown U., 1887, A.M., 1890; grad. Newton Theol. Instn., 1890; D.D., Bowdoin, 1894; LL.D., Howard, 1899, Furman, 1906; m. Mary J. Scott, Dec. 6, 1888. Ordained Bapt. ministry, 1887; pastor Free St. Ch., Portland, Me., 1890-92; pres. Colby U., 1892-95; pres. Columbian (now George Washington) U., 1895-1900; pastor Fifth Ch., Phila., 1900-07, First Ch., Seattle, 1908—. Lecturer Bucknell U., 1900-07. Trustee Newton Theol. Instn., 1894-1902, Crozer Theol. Sem., 1901-08. Pres. Am. Bapt. Hist. Soc., 1900-07. Author: Elements of Ethics, 1893; Elements of Sociology, 1894; Elements of Political Science, 1899; Outlines of Political History, 1900. Home: Seattle, Wash. Died 1911.

WHITMAN, Charles Huntington, coll. prof.; b. Abbott, Me., Nov. 24, 1873; s. Nathan and Helen Augusta (Thoms) W.; A.B., Colby, 1897; fellow in English, Yale, 1898-1900, Ph.D., 1900; U. of Munich, 1905-06; m. Rachel Jones Foster, May 29, 1902; children—Hilda Trull, Alan Foster, Dunbar, Esther Huntington. Instr. in English, 1900-04, asst. prof., 1904-06, Lehigh; asso. prof. English, 1906-11, prof. English, Rutgers, Oct. 1, 1911—; acting prof. summers, U. of Ore., 1923; New York U., 1924, 25, 26. Republican. Baptist. Translator: The Christ of Cynewulf, 1900. Author: A Subject-Index to the Poems of Edmund Spenser, 1919; also Literature of New Jersey (in History of New Jersey), 1929. Editor: Seven Contemporary Plays, 1931. Contributor to Journal of English and Germanic Philology, Modern Lang. Notes, Anglia, etc. Died Dec. 27, 1937.

WHITMAN, Charles Otis, zoölogist; b. Woodstock, Me., Dec. 14, 1842; s. Joseph and Marcia W.; A.B., Bowdoin, 1868, A.M., 1871; Ph.D., Leipzig, 1878; fellow Johns Hopkins, 1879; LL.D., U. of Neb., 1894; Sc.D., Bowdoin, 1895; Doctor of Biology, Clark U., 1909; m. Emily Nunn, Aug. 15, 1884. Prof. zoölogy, Imperial U. of Japan, 1880-81, Naples Zoöl. Sta., 1882; asst. in zoölogy, Harvard, 1883-85; dir. Allis Lake Lab., 1886-89; prof. zoölogy, Clark U., 1889-92; prof. and head dept. zoölogy and curator Zoö. Mus., 1892—, U. of Chicago. Dir. Marine Biol. Lab., Woods Hole, Mass., 1888-1908. Editor Jour. of Morphology, 1887—, Biological Bulletin, 1897—, Biological Lectures, 1890-99. Home: Chicago, Ill. Died 1910.

WHITMAN, Frank Perkins, physicist; b. Troy, N.Y., July 29, 1853; s. William Warren and Caroline Keith (Perkins) W.; A.B., Brown U., 1874, A.M., 1877, hon. Sc.D., 1900; studied Johns Hopkins; m. Charlotte Webster Wheeler, May 26, 1881. Instr. in English and Classical Sch., Providence, 1874-78; prof. physics, Rensselaer Poly. Inst., Troy, 1880-86, Western Reserve U., 1886—. Fellow A.A.A.S. (v.p. 1898). Contbr. to scientific jours. Home: Cleveland, O. Died June 15, 1919.

WHITMAN, Frank S., M.D.; b. Belvidere, Ill., Sept. 27, 1849; s. Hiram and Clarinda (Hanchett) W.; U. of Chicago; M.D., Hahnemann Med. Coll., Chicago, 1872; hon. M.D., Chicago Homœ. Coll., 1877; m. Frances C. Pier, Jan. 9, 1875. Practiced at Belvidere, 1872-96; supt. Ill. Northern Hosp. for Insane, Elgin, Ill., 1899-1906; spl. practice in mental diseases and consultations, 1906—; prof. mental diseases Hahnemann Med. Coll., 1900—; pres. Peoples Bank, Belvidere Screw and Machine Co. Chmn. Boone County Rep. Central Com.; chmn. Rep. Congressional Com.; del. Rep. State convs., 1896, 1904; coroner Boone County, 1876-88; served as mayor of Belvidere, etc. Mem. Ill. Constl. Conv., 1921. Home: Belvidere, Ill. Died Dec. 10, 1939.

WHITMAN, John Lorin, penologist; b. Sterling, Ill., July 23, 1862; s. Platt L. and Helen (Quick) W.; ed. pub. schs. and pvt. sem., Sterling, Ill.; m. Anna M. Glennon, Nov. 14, 1880. Learned trade of paperhanging and painting; guard and chief clk., Cook County Jail, 1890-95, and jailer, 1895-1907; supt. House of Correction (2,000 inmates), 1907-17; state supt. of prisons of Ill., 1917-22; warden Ill. State Penitentiary, Joliet, Apr. 10, 1922-June 1, 1926 (resigned). Dir. Central Howard Assn. of Cook County. Mem. K.P., Modern Woodmen of America, National Union. Contbr. many articles on criminol. subjects. Died Dec. 13, 1926.

WHITMAN, John Munro, ry. official; b. Elbridge, N.Y., Aug. 11, 1837; s. Joseph Chandler and Caroline Betsy (Munro) W.; ed. Munro Acad., Elbridge; unmarried. Began ry. service, 1856, as rodman in engring. dept. I.C. R.R., Chicago; leveler in work of enlarging Erie Canal, 1858-60; engr. in charge constrn. Brunswick & Albany R.R., in Ga., 1860-65; engr. in charge constrn. Union Stock Yards, Chicago, 1866-67; on Ill. and Mich. Canal, 1867-69, Iowa Midland R.R., 1869-71; engr. and supt., 1872-76, receiver, 1876, Chicago & Pacific R.R.; supt. Ia. div. C.&N.W. Ry., 1880-83; gen. supt. C.,St.P.,M.&O. Ry., 1883-87; gen. mgr., 1887-99, 4th v.p., 1899-1906, v.p. in charge of constrn. C.&N.W. Ry., Jan. 23, 1906-June 30, 1911. Home: Chicago, Ill. Died Oct. 28, 1912.

WHITMAN, Malcolm Douglass, lawyer, mfr.; s. William and Jane Dole (Hallett) Whitman; A.B., Harvard, 1899, LL.B., 1902; m. Janet A. McCook (died 1909); m. 2d, Jennie A. Crocker; m. 3d, Lucilla De Vescovi. Admitted to N.Y. bar; now v.p. William Whitman Co., Inc. (founded by father), Boston; pres. Nashawena Mills; dir. Acadia Mills, Monomac Spinning Co., Calhoun Mills, U.S. Testing Co. Home: New York, N.Y. Died Dec. 28, 1932.

WHITMAN, Russell Ripley, pub. relations counsel; b. Louisville, Ky., Oct. 31, 1868; s. Alfred and Mary (Brown) W.; A.B., U. of Kan., 1893; m. Cora Ostertag, Apr. 11, 1898; 1 dau., Mrs. Marylee Sears. Served as reporter, Kansas City World, 1894-96; with adv. dept. Kansas City Star, 1896-99; adv. mgr. Kansas City Journal, 1899-1904; western adv. representative Hearst publs., Chicago, 1904-09; pub. Boston American, 1909-14; organizer and mng. dir. Audit Bur. of Circulations, Chicago, 1914-17; pres. New New York Commercial, 1917-26; pres. and pub. Atlanta Georgian-American, 1929-30; became pres. Russell R. Whitman, pub. relations, publicity, advertising. Commr. for Southern states of Golden Gate Internat. Expn., San Francisco. Dir. Am. Defense Soc. Home: Atlanta, Ga. Died Oct. 12, 1939.

WHITMAN, William, mfr.; b. Round Hill, N.S., May 9, 1842; s. John and Rebecca (Cutler) W.; ed. pub. schs., Annapolis (N.S.) Acad.; LL.D. from Middlebury (Vermont) College in 1926; m. Jane Dole Hallett, Jan. 19, 1865; children—Mary Arnold (dec.), Rebecca Cutler (dec.), Mrs. Mabel Shives Duff, Mrs. Jane Hallett Hobbs, William, Malcolm Douglas, Eben Esmond, Hendricks Hallett. Began at 12 in wholesale dry goods store, St. John, N.B.; moved to Boston at 14 and entered employ of James M. Beebe, Richardson & Co., continuing 11 yrs.; treas. Arlington Woolen Mills, Lawrence, Mass., 1867-69; treas., 1869-1902, pres., 1902-13, Arlington (Mass.) Mills (covering 62 acres floor space); pres. of Whitman Mills, 1905-09, Manomet Mills, 1905—, Nonquitt Spinning Co., 1906—, Nashawena Mills, June 1909—, Belleville Warehouse Co., 1916— (all of New Bedford), Acadia Mills, 1917—, Monomac Spinning Co. (Lawrence, Mass.), 1917—; policy holders' dir. Equitable Life Assurance Soc., 1905-13; pres., 1913-21, chmn. bd. dirs., 1921—, of William Whitman Co., Inc., textile commn. mchts., Boston, New York, etc., succeeding firms in which had been managing partner, 1889—. Mem. Nat. Assn. Wool Mfrs. (pres. 1888-94, 1904-11, exec. com., 1894-1904), Nat. Assn. Cotton Mfrs. Republican. Episcopalian. Home: Brookline, Mass. Died Sept. 20, 1928.

WHITMAN, William Edward Seaver, journalist, author; b. South Boston, Mass., Dec. 25, 1832; attended Hawes School, S. Boston, and Lyceum Gardiner, Me.; m. Clara Emily Abbott, Dec. 9, 1869. Studied law 4 yrs.; abandoned it for newspaper work, 1850; from then regular corr. 14 leading dailies; with Boston Journal 25 yrs. (pen-name, "Toby Candor"); edited and owned Daily Times and American Sentinel (weekly), Bath, Me., 1869-70; official reporter Me. legislature several yrs. Author: The Ship Carpenter's Family (novel); Maine in the War for the Union; Narrow Gauge Railroads (Their History and Progress); Wealth and Industry of Maine. Home: Augusta, Me. Died 1901.

WHITMARSH, Henry Allen, M.D., surgeon; b. Providence, R.I., Sept. 29, 1854; s. Edwin Barney and Harriet (Barden) W.; A.B., Brown U., 1876, A.M., 1880; Columbia Med. Coll., 1877-78; M.D., New York Homœ. Med. Coll., 1879; m. Martha M. Gerst, June 16, 1881 (died 1888); m. 2d, Alida E. Sprague, Oct. 2, 1895; children—Mrs. Esther Alida Phillips, Martha Sprague (Mrs. E. B. Tolman, Jr.). Began practice, East Providence, 1879; cons. surgeon Homœ. Hosp. of R.I., Woonsocket Hosp. and South County Hosp. Republican. Conglist. Fellow Am. Coll. Surgeons. Home: Providence, R.I. Died Dec. 2, 1939.

WHITMARSH, Theodore Francis, merchant; b. Brooklyn, N.Y., Nov. 6, 1869; s. Henry Clay and Caroline H. (Leggett) W.; ed. pub. schs.; m. Lillian Ainslie Smith. Has been engaged in mercantile business, N.Y. City, 1886—; now chmn. bd. Francis H. Leggett & Co., general merchandise; dir. Federal Reserve Bank of New York. With U.S. Food Administration, Washington, during World War, and for a time acted as food administrator; rep. of Food Administration on War Industries Bd., and coördinating member with Capital Issues Committee; mem. Belgian Relief Exec. Com. and joint dir. in America of Am. Relief Administration. Decorated Officer of the Crown (Belgium). Republican. Home: New York, N.Y. Died May 12, 1936.

WHITMORE, William Henry, genealogist; b. Dorchester, Mass., Sept. 6, 1836; ed. public, high and Latin schools, Boston; (A.M., Harvard, and Williams, 1867); member several business firms; later in mining and smelting business; m. Fanny T. W. Maynard, June 11, 1884. Many years commr. of public records; became city registrar, Boston; was 8 years member common council, and its pres., 1879. Democrat. A founder of The Historical Magazine, 1857; was an editor of the New England Hist. and Geneal. Record and The Heraldic Journal, which he founded, 1863. Author: The American Genealogist; the Cavalier Dismounted; Elements of Heraldry; History of the Old State House, Boston; edited "Poetical Works of Winthrop Mackworth Praed," etc. Home: Boston, Mass. Died 1900.

WHITMYER, Edward Charles, judge; b. Schenectady, N.Y., May 5, 1861; s. of Charles Henry and Mary Caroline (Munsell) W.; A.B., Union Coll., Schenectady, 1882 (Phi Beta Kappa); LL.D., St. Lawrence U., 1925; m. Frances Priscilla Matthews, July 23, 1896. Admitted to N.Y. bar, 1887; del. from 20th Senatorial Dist. to Constl. Conv., State of N.Y., 1894; surrogate, Schenectady Co., 1903-09; county judge, Schenectady Co., 1909-12; justice Supreme Court of N.Y., 4th Dist., 1912-26; renominated and reëlected by both Rep. and Dem. parties for term 1926-40; designated to Appellate Div., 3d Dept., Jan. 1927; apptd. official referee of State of N.Y., Jan. 1, 1932. Dir. Schenectady Trust Co. Republican. Presbyn. Mason. Home: Schenectady, N.Y. Died May 20, 1933.

WHITNEY, Adeline Dutton Train, author; b. Boston, Sept. 15, 1824; d. Enoch and Adeline (Dutton) W.; ed. at school of George B. Emerson, 1837-41; m. Seth D. Whitney, 1843. Wrote little for publication in early life, although she contributed occasionally to mags. After her first practical publication, in 1859, others rapidly followed. Author: Faith Gartney's Girlhood; The Gayworthys; Patience Strong's Outings; We Girls; The Other Girls; Sights and Insights; Homespun Yarns; Ascutney Street; Friendly Letters to Girl Friends; Just How; Square Pegs; The Integrity of Christian Science. Also, in verse: Pansies, Daffodils; Biddy's Episodes, 1904. Home: Milton, Mass. Died 1906.

WHITNEY, Anne, sculptor; b. Watertown, Mass., Sept. 1821; d. Nathaniel Ruggles and Sarah (Stone) W.; ed. pvt. schs. Early manifested a poetic gift and her poems were collected in a volume, "Poems," 1859. Began professional work as sculptor, 1855; opened studio in Watertown, 1860; later studied 4 yrs. in Europe; established herself in Boston, 1872. Among prin. works are statues of Samuel Adams, Harriet Martineau, Leif Erikson, "Ethiopia," "Roma," and others, portrait and ideal. Home: Boston, Mass. Died Jan. 23, 1915.

WHITNEY, Carl Everett, lawyer; b. Mooers Forks, N.Y., July 30, 1876; s. John K. and Abigail M. (Everett) W.; student State Normal and Training Sch., Potsdam, N.Y., 1893-95, Plattsburg (N.Y.) State Normal and Training Sch., 1896-97; B.S., George Washington U., 1901; m. Blanche A. Russel, Apr. 3, 1907; children—Mary E., John R., Carl E., Blanche A. Admitted to N.Y. bar, 1904, began practice at Malone; became mem. Wise, Whitney & Canfield, N.Y. City. Asst. U.S. atty., Southern Dist. N.Y., 1909-13. Republican. Mason. Elk. Home: White Plains, N.Y. Died Oct. 28, 1940.

WHITNEY, Caspar, editor; b. Boston, Sept. 2, 1864; passed exam. for Harvard but did not enter; grad. St. Matthew's Coll., Calif. Traveling, hunting and exploring in N. and S. America, Mexico, East and West Indies, Siam, Malay, India, 10 yrs.; m. Florence E. Canfield, June 4, 1909; children—Faith Canfield, Phoebe Chloe. War corr. (Cuba, 1898) and writer on outdoor sports, Harper's staff, 1888-1900; editor Outing Magazine, 1900-09, Collier's Outdoor America, 1909, Recreation, 1913; in Mexico, 1914; mem. Commn. for Relief in Belgium, 1915-16; war corr., 1917-19. Author: Hawaiian America, 1899; Jungle Trails and Jungle People, 1911; The Flowing Road, 1912; What's the Matter with Mexico?, 1916; The Critical Year, 1918—Shall We Be Too Late?, 1918; The Tempering of the Doughboy, 1919. Editor: American Sportsman's Library. Home: Irvington-on-Hudson, N.Y. Died Jan. 18, 1929.

WHITNEY, David Rice, banker; b. Boston, Jan. 10, 1828; s. William Fiske and Frances Ann (Rice) W.; A.B., Harvard, 1848, A.M., 1851; m. Sophia Paine Dunn, Apr. 30, 1855 (dec.). Began in mercantile business, Boston, 1849, as William F. Whitney & Son, afterwards D. R. Whitney & Co. (retired 1876); pres. Suffolk Nat. Bank, Boston, 1876-82; dir., 1874—, actuary, 1884-1905, pres., 1905—, N.E. Trust Co. of Boston; trustee Provident Instn. for Savings, Boston, 1877—(v.p.). Home: Boston, Mass. Died Dec. 10, 1914.

WHITNEY, Edward Baldwin, lawyer; b. New Haven, Conn., Aug. 16, 1857; s. Prof. William Dwight and Elizabeth W. (Baldwin) W.; brother of Emily Henrietta and Marian Parker W.; A.B., Yale, 1878; law student Yale and Columbia; m. Josepha, d. late Prof. Simon Newcomb, of Washington, Apr. 11, 1896. In practice at New York, 1880—. Was 1st sec. Nat. Assn. Dem. Clubs, 1888, and of "Anti-Snapper" organization, N.Y. state, 1892; asst. atty. gen. U.S., 1893-97; as such took part in argument of the Income Tax case, the Debs case and other well known constl. cases, and cases arising out of the interstate commerce law and the Cuban insurrection. Obtained the first judicial decision condemning a mfg. trust under the Federal Anti-Trust Law (the so-called Addyston Pipe case, Nashville, 1898); lecturer on internat. law, New York Law Sch.; counsel for the New York State Tenement House Commn., 1901; mem. State Investigation Commn., 1908. Democrat. Candidate for justice Supreme Ct. on the independent bar ticket, endorsed by the Republicans and Prohibitionists, 1906. Died 1911.

WHITNEY, Eli, financier; b. New Haven, Conn., Jan. 22, 1847; s. Eli and Sarah Perkins (Dalliba) W.; A.B., Yale, 1869, A.M., 1872; m. Sarah Sheffield Farnam, Oct. 22, 1873. Entered employ Whitney Arms Co., 1871, being v.p., 1880-88; pres. New Haven Water Co., 1894—, W. Haven Water Co., 1900—, Milford Water Co., 1907—; chmn. bd. Union and New Haven Trust Co.; formerly v.p. and pres. City Bank (consolidated with other banks); trustee Conn. Savings Bank. Alderman, 1883-85, park commissioner, 1883-85, mem. Bd. Pub. Works, 1885-90, mem. Bd. Edn., 1891-94, and 1897-1909 (pres. 1897-1909), New Haven; mem. Conn. Senate, 1904-05, and of several state commns. Republican. Conglist. Dir. New Haven Hosp. Fellow Yale, 1901-19. V.p. New Haven Chamber of Commerce, 1909-11; v.p. New Haven Colony Hist. Soc. Home: New Haven, Conn. Died June 12, 1924.

WHITNEY, Gertrude Capen, author; b. Canton, Mass., May 13, 1861; d. Ezekiel and Emma (van Poelien-Knaggs) Capen; ed. local schools, Gannett's Inst., Boston schs. and under private teachers; m. George Erastus Whitney, 1899. Mem. Nat. Old Ironsides Patriotic Assn. (nat. advisory bd. representing Ga.); mem. various hist. and geneal. societies. Author: I Choose, 1910, 3d edit., 1919; Yet Speaketh He, 1910, 3d edit., 1923; Roses from My Garden, 1912, 2d edit., 1924; Above the Shame of Circumstance, 1913, 2d edit., 1925; The House of Landell, 1917; Where the Sun Shines, 1920; On the Other Side of the Bridge, 1922; The Interpreter, 1925; John, John, and His Son, John, 1928; In the Fulness of Time, 1936. Home: Augusta, Ga. Died May 22, 1941.

WHITNEY, Gwin Allison, engr.; b. Superior, Wis., June 4, 1893; s. William Allison and Esther (Gwin) W.; ed. Northwestern Mil. and Naval Acad., Highland Park, Ill., 1909-12, Cascadilla Prep. Sch., Ithaca, N.Y., 1912-13, Cornell U., 1913-14; m. Charlotte Wilson, Mar. 28, 1918; children—James Wilson, William Allison, Gwin Richard. Construction engr. Whitney Bros. Co., Superior, Wis., 1914-15; v.p. same, Duluth, Minn., 1915-18, pres., 1918-30; pres. Merritt-Chapman & Whitney Corp., 1930-32; v.p. Merritt-Chapman & Scott Corp., 1932-33, pres., 1933—; pres. and mng. dir. Merritt-Chapman-Lindsay, Ltd.; pres. and dir. Am. Constrn. Co., Whitney Corp. Home: New York, N.Y. Died Feb. 11, 1939.

WHITNEY, Harry; b. New Haven, Conn., Dec. 1, 1873; s. Stephen and Margaret Lawrence (Johnson) W.; ed. St. Paul's Sch., Garden City, L.I., Hopkins Grammar Sch., New Haven; m. Mrs. Eunice Chesebro Kenison, Jan. 15, 1916. With Wallace & Sons, Ansonia, Conn., 1901-02; went to Australia in sailing vessel from New York, 1903, engaging 2 yrs. in sheep business and mining; became interested in ranching in Mont. and Ariz. Big game hunter; has hunted in most of Rocky Mountain region; went north with Commodore Peary, 1908, and remained for a yr. in Arctic region shooting musk oxen and other large game. Capt., Ordnance Sect. U.S.A., Aug. 28, 1917-Mar. 24, 1919; capt., O.R.C., May 1, 1917. Student agrl. course, Cornell, 1920. Home: Kennett Square, Pa. Died May 20, 1936.

WHITNEY, Harry Edward, educator; b. Fort Covington, N.Y., Sept. 4, 1851; s. Charles M. and Delia M. W.; Shattuck Sch., Faribault, Minn., 1866-71; A.B., Trinity Coll., Conn., 1874, A.M., 1878 (L.H.D., 1914); m. Mary Van Vliet, Aug. 3, 1881. Instr. Latin and German, 1874—, headmaster, 1902-05, Shattuck Sch., Faribault, Minn. Mason; Past Grand Comdr. K.T. Home: Faribault, Minn. Died May 2, 1926.

WHITNEY, Harry Payne, banker, mining; b. New York, Apr. 29, 1872; s. Hon. William Collins and Flora (Payne) W.; A.B., Yale, 1894; m. Newport, R.I., Gertrude, d. late Cornelius Vanderbilt, Aug. 25, 1896. Pres. Whitney Realty Co.; dir. Guaranty Trust Co., Metropolitan Opera & Real Estate Co., Met. Opera Co.; v.p. Saratoga Assn. for Improvement of Breed of Horses. Home: New York, N.Y. Died Oct. 26, 1930.

WHITNEY, Henry Melville, capitalist; b. at Conway, Mass., Oct. 22, 1839; s. James S. and Lucinda (Collins) W.; ed. in pub. schs. and 1 yr. at Williston Sem., Easthampton, Mass.; m. Margaret F. Green, Oct. 3, 1878. Democrat. Home: Brookline, Mass. Died Jan. 25, 1923.

WHITNEY, Henry Mitchell, librarian; b. Northampton, Mass., Jan. 16, 1843; s. Josiah Dwight and Clarissa (James) W.; brother of James Lyman W.; A.B., Yale, 1864, A.M., 1867; sergt. maj. 52d Mass. Vols., 1862-63; agt. U.S. Christian Commn. in Va., 1864-65; student Princeton Theol. Sem., 1865-66; grad. Andover Theol. Sem., 1868; (Litt.D., Beloit Coll., 1900); m. Frances Wurts, Aug. 3, 1869. Ordained Congl. ministry, 1869; pastor Geneva, Ill., 1868-71; prof. English lit., Beloit (Wis.) Coll., 1871-99; librarian, James Blackstone Memorial Library, 1899—. Pastor Beloit, 1871-72, Roscoe, Ill., 1876-82; alderman, Beloit, 1876-83; trustee Beloit Savings Bank, 1880-89. Joint Author: Columbian History of Education in Wisconsin; History of the Fifty-second Massachusetts Regiment; Twentieth Century New Testament; etc. Home: Branford, Conn. Died 1911.

WHITNEY, James Amaziah, lawyer, author; b. Rochester, N.Y., June 30, 1839; s. Amaziah and Margaret Scotland (Taylor) W. (7th in descent from John and Eleanor Whitney, who came from England 1635, settling at Watertown, Mass.); removed in childhood to Otsego Co., N.Y.; common school edn. (A.M., Union Coll., N.Y., 1870; LL.D., Iowa Coll., 1880); worked on farm; self-taught in chemistry, mechanics and engring., 1860-65; m. Eda Annie, d. John Wickham Copley, Delaware Co., N.Y., Oct. 31, 1876 (died 1895). Adj. and later engr. with rank of capt. in 39th regt. Nat. Guard N.Y., 1862-66; writer of specifications for patent solicitors, 1865-68; editor of Am. Artisan, 1868-72; prof. agrl. chemistry in Am. Inst., 1869-72; established as patent solicitor, 1872; admitted to practice in U.S. circuit courts, 1876; makes splty. of equity practice and corporation, patent, trade-mark and copyright law. Author: The Relations of the Patent Laws to the Development of Agriculture, 1874; The Chinese and the Chinese Question, 1880; Sonnets and Lyrics, 1884; The Children of Lamech (poem); Poetical Works (2 vols.); Shobab, a Tale of Bethesda (verse), 1884; Sonnets and Lyrics, 1884; The Children of Lamech, 1886; Collected Poetical Works (2 vols.), 1886. Home: Maryland, Otsego Co., N.Y. Deceased.

WHITNEY, James Lyman, librarian; b. Northampton, Mass., Nov. 28, 1835; s. Josiah Dwight and Clarissa (James) W.; brother of Henry Mitchell W.; A.B., Yale, 1856, A.M., 1865. Librarian, Boston Pub. Library, 1899-1903; later in charge dept. of Documents and Statistics, and of MSS., Boston Pub. Library. As chief of catalogue dept. for many yrs., edited Ticknor Catalogue of Spanish literature and many other publs. of the library. Chmn. school com., Concord, Mass., 1879-87; chmn. book com., Bostonian Soc.; charter mem. A.L.A. Home: Cambridge, Mass. Died 1910.

WHITNEY, Loren Harper, lawyer; b. Berlin, O., Sept. 12, 1834; s. James W. and Betsey (Harper) W.; left home at 16 and executed contract for a levee in Miss.; crossed plains to Calif., 1852, and engaged in gold mining; attended Mt. Morris (Ill.) Coll., 1856; studied law under Gen. Stephen A. Hurlbut, Belvidere, Ill., and Ind. Asbury U.; admitted to bar, 1858; m. Mary Munson, 1867. Entered army as capt. 8th Ill. Cav., Army of the Potomac; organized 140th Ill. Inf. and was col.; served in 12 battles and 40 or more skirmishes, and was twice wounded. In law practice in Chicago, 1865—. Author: Parallels in Lives of Buddha and Jesus, 1906; Life and Teachings of Zoroaster, 1905; A Question of Miracles, 1908. Home: River Forest, Ill. Died 1912.

WHITNEY, Mary Watson, astronomer; b. Waltham, Mass., Sept. 11, 1847; d. Samuel B. and Mary W. (Crehore) W.; A.B., Vassar Coll., 1868, A.M., 1872; studied at U. of Zürich, 1874-76. Became asst. to Prof. Maria Mitchell, 1881; prof. astronomy and dir. of obs., Vassar Coll., 1889-1910 (emeritus prof.). Many of her articles were pub. in Astronomical Journal and other astron. periodicals. Home: Waltham, Mass. Died Jan. 20, 1921.

WHITNEY, Milton, soil expert; b. Baltimore, Aug. 2, 1860; common school edn.; spl. 3 yrs. course, chemistry, Johns Hopkins; m. Annie C. Langdon, June 30, 1891. Asst. chemist Conn. Agrl. Expt. Sta., 1883; supt. Experiment Farm of N.C. Expt. Sta., 1886-88; prof. agr., U. of S.C., and v. dir. of S.C. Expt. Sta., 1888-91; soil physicist, Md. Expt. Sta., 1891-94; chief Bur. Soils, U.S. Dept. Agr., 1894-1927. Author: Soil and Civilization. Home: Takoma Park, D.C. Died Nov. 11, 1927.

WHITNEY, Myron W., singer; b. Ashby, Mass., Sept. 5, 1835. Went to Boston when 16 yrs. old, making 1st appearance Christmas, 1858, in performance of "The Messiah," by Handl and Haydn Soc.; sang in concerts about 10 yrs.; then studied in Florence, Italy, and London; sang the part of "Elijah" at Birmingham festival in England, and at other concerts there; was only soloist at opening of Am. Centennial Expn., 1876; was for some time principal bass Boston Ideal Opera Co. and Am. Opera Co. in grand opera; best known as oratorio singer. Home: Watertown, Mass. Died 1910.

WHITNEY, Nelson Oliver, prof. civil engring., Univ. of Wis., 1891—; b. Aiken, S.C., May 3, 1858; grad. Univ. of Pa., 1878; m. Mary E. Tainter, June 12, 1883. Practiced civil engring. on Pa. R.R. and Mexican Nat. R.R., 1878-91; engaged in consulting practice. Member Am. Soc. Civil Engrs., first v.p. Western Soc. of Engrs. at Chicago. Home: Madison, Wis. Died 1901.

WHITNEY, Payne, capitalist; b. New York; s. Hon. William Collins and Flora (Payne) W.; A.B., Yale, 1898; LL.B., Harvard, 1901; m. Helen, d. of Sec. of State John Hay, 1902; children—John Hay, Joan (Mrs. Chas. S. Payson). Dir. Gt. Northern Paper Co., First Nat. Bank (New York); v.p. Whitney Realty Co., Northern Finance Corp.; trustee U.S. Trust Co. V.p. Society of N.Y. Hosp.; trustee New York Pub. Library, Met. Mus. of Art. Home: Manhasset, L.I., and New York, N.Y. Died May 25, 1927.

WHITNEY, Samuel Brenton, organist, composer; b. Woodstock, Vt., June 4, 1842; s. Samuel and Amelia (Hyde) W.; ed. pub. schs. and at Vt. Episcopal Inst., Burlington, Vt.; studied music in New York and later with Prof. John K. Paine at Harvard; unmarried. Organist in ch. at 13; organist Ch. of the Advent, Boston, 1871-1906; organist, conductor and guild choirmaster, choir Guild of Mass., from its orgn., 1876; condr. Vt. Choir Festival for 15 yrs.; formerly prof. organ and ch. music, N.E. Conservatory of Music. Republican. Author: Whitney's Organ Album, 1890; Communion Services, Nos. 1 and 2, with Accompaniment for Organ and Orchestra; also composer of music for piano, organ and ch. services. Died July 1913.

WHITNEY, William Collins, sec. of Navy of U.S.; b. Conway, Mass., July 15, 1841; s. Gen. James S. W.; grad. Yale, 1863 (LL.D., 1888); Harvard Law School, 1865; admitted to the bar and practiced in New York; assisted in organizing Young Men's Democratic Club, 1871; active in movement against Tweed ring; insp. schools, 1872; defeated for dist. atty., 1872; corp. counsel, 1875-82; sec. of Navy of U.S., 1885-89. Democrat. Home: New York, N.Y. Died 1904.

WHITNEY, William Fiske, anatomist; b. Boston, Mar. 26, 1850; A.B., Harvard, 1871, M.D., 1875; house officer Mass. Gen. Hosp., 1875; studied in Europe, 1875-88. Curator Warren Anat. Mus., Harvard, 1879—; sec. med. faculty, Harvard, 1883-90; prof. parasites and parasite diseases, Veterinary Sch., Harvard, 1891-1901. Home: Boston, Mass. Died Mar. 4, 1921.

WHITNEY, William Locke, judge; b. Cleveland, Feb. 8, 1876; s. John M. and Mary S. (Rice) W.; A.B., Oberlin, 1898; LL.B., Columbia Law Sch., 1901; m. Saida Mae Sutton, June 6, 1901. Judge Dist. Ct. of Honolulu, 1904-07; 1st deputy atty. gen. of Hawaii, 1907-09; judge Circuit Ct. of 1st Circuit, Hawaii, 1909-17, Juvenile Ct., 1st Circuit, 1909-17, Land Ct., 1911-17. Republican. V.p. Whitney & Marsh, Ltd. Trustee Oahu Coll. Conglist. Home: Honolulu, T.H. Died Jan. 16, 1920.

WHITON, James Morris, editor; b. Boston, Apr. 11, 1833; s. James M. and Mary E. (Knowlton) W.; A.B., Yale, 1853, Ph.D., 1861; m. Mary Eliza, d. William Bartlett, of Portland, Me., May 1, 1855. Ordained Congl. ministry, 1865; rector Hopkins Grammar Sch., New Haven, Conn., 1854-64; pastor Lynn, Mass., 1865-75; prin. Williston Sem., Easthampton, Mass., 1876-78; pastor Newark, N.J., 1879-85, New York, 1886-91; prof. ethics, Meadville (Pa.) Theol. Sch., 1893-94; on staff The Outlook, 1896—. Acting pastor Haworth, N.J., 1898-1901; chmn. exec. com. N.Y. State Conf. Religion, 1899—. Author: Miracles and Supernatural Religion, 1903; Interludes in a Time of Change, 1909; Getting Together—Essays by Friends in Council, 1913. Home: New York, N.Y. Died Jan. 25, 1920.

WHITRIDGE, Frederick Wallingford, lawyer; b. New Bedford, Mass., Aug. 8, 1852; A.B., Amherst, 1874, A.M., 1877; LL.B., Columbia, 1878; (LL.D., Amherst, 1909); m. Lucy Arnold, of England, Dec. 9, 1884. Admitted to bar, 1879, and entered practice at New York; mem. Whitridge, Butler & Rice. Lecturer on administrative law, 1883-88, constl. and polit. history, 1888-94, Columbia. Pres. dir. Forty-second St., Manhattanville & St. Nicholas Av. Ry. Co., Third Av. Ry. Co., Westchester Electric R.R. Co.; pres. Belt Line Ry. Corp., Bronx Traction Co., Kingsbridge Ry. Co., Southern Blvd. R.R. Co., Union Ry. Co. of N.Y. Home: New York, N.Y. Died Dec. 30, 1916.

WHITRIDGE, Morris, merchant; b. Baltimore, Aug. 4, 1865; s. John A. and Ellen Ward (Henderson) W.; A.B., Harvard, 1889; m. Susan Wilson Mackenzie, Apr. 28, 1898; children—Ellen M., Julia, Catherine Morris. Mem. Whitridge, White & Co., importers and E. India merchants; president of John C. Graffiin Co.; dir. Hopkins Place Savings Bank, Maryland Life Ins. Co., Safe Deposit & Trust Co. of Baltimore, United States Fidelity Guaranty Co.; trustee Johns Hopkins Hosp. Republican. Episcopalian. Mason. Delivered memorial address, Johns Hopkins U., in commemoration of Dr. Ira Remsen. Home: Guilford, Baltimore, Md. Died Dec. 1935.

WHITSETT, William Thornton, educator and author; b. Whitsett, N.C., Aug. 5, 1866; s. Joseph Bason and Mary (Foust) W.; grad. Oakdale Acad. N.C.; N.C. College, Univ. of N.C.; A.M., Ph.D.; D.Litt., Lenoir-Rhyne College, 1933; m. Carrie E. Brewer, June 30, 1906; children—Lucille Elizabeth, William Thornton, Carrie Brewer, Joseph Gordon. Founder, 1888, and pres. until 1918, Whitsett Inst. (boarding sch. for boys). Mem. Guilford Co. Bd. Edn., 1897-1918 (chmn. 1906-18); trustee U. of N.C., 1897-1919. Democrat. Lutheran. Organizer N.C. Assn. of Acads.; sec. and treas. N.C. Teachers' Assembly (pres. 1905-06). Author: Saber and Song (poems), 1917, 2d edit., 1932; Life of Captain Peter Summers, Revolutionary Hero; also many hist. monographs and sketches of early Am. families. Historian of Guilford County, N.C. Home: Whitsett, N.C. Died Mar. 22, 1934.

WHITSIDE, Samuel Marmaduke, brig. gen. U.S.A., retired June 9, 1902; b. Toronto, Can., Jan. 9, 1839; s. Hon. W. H. W., U.S. consul; ed. Normal School, Toronto, Can., and grad. Careyville Acad., N.Y., San Antonio, Tex.; m. Carrie McDowell McGavock, Nov. 24, 1868. Entered United States Army, 1858; served with 6th United States cav. in Civil War from 1861 to close, and in Indian wars for over 25 yrs. on western frontier. Captured Big Foot and his 400 Sioux warriors Dec. 1890, and comd. his regiment in the battle of Wounded Knee following day, in which 1 officer and 29 men were killed, and 2 officers and 37 were wounded, while of the Indians 195 were killed and all the others either captured or wounded. In command of Fort Riley, Kan., Fort Meyer, Va., Jefferson Barracks, Mo., Ft. Sam Houston, Tex., from 1891 to May 1898; in command of 5th U.S. cav. during Spanish war; took command 10th cav. Oct. 1898; accompanied regt. to Cuba, May 1899; in command Dept. of Santiago and Puerto Principe, 1900-02. Brig. gen. U.S.V., Jan. 3, 1901; brig. gen. U.S.A., May 29, 1902; retired from active service June 9, 1902. Home: Bethesda, Md. Died 1904.

WHITSITT, William Heth, theologian; b. Nashville, Tenn., Nov. 25, 1841; s. Reuben Ewing and Dicey (McFarland) W.; A.M., Union U., Tenn., 1861; U. of Va., 1866-67; Southern Bapt. Theol. Sem., 1867-69; U. of Leipzig, 1869-71; (D.D., Mercer, 1873; LL.D., William Jewell Coll., 1888, Georgetown Coll., Ky., 1888, Southwestern Bapt. U., 1888); m. Florence Wallace, Oct. 4, 1881. Ordained Bapt. ministry, 1862; served in C.S.A., 1862-65; pastor Mill Creek Ch., nr. Nashville, 1865-66, Albany, Ga., Feb.-July 1872; prof. ch. history, 1872-95, pres., 1895-99, Southern Bapt. Theol. Sem.; prof. philosophy, Richmond (Va.) Coll., June 1901—. Author: Origin of the Disciples of Christ, 1888; Life and Times of Judge Caleb Wallace, 1888; A Question in Baptist History, 1896; Annals of a Scotch-Irish Family—the Whitsitts of Nashville, Tenn., 1904; Genealogy of Jefferson Davis, 1908. Home: Richmond, Va. Died 1911.

WHITSON, Edward, judge; b. in Linn Co., Ore., Oct. 6, 1852; s. Benjamin Franklin and Eliza Jane (Brandon) W.; ed. at Ore. Coll.; admitted to bar, 1879; m. Leora Nellie Bateman, Sept. 3, 1885. Auditor Yakima Co., Wash., 1875-76; mem. Wash. Territorial Legislature, 1877-78; mayor of N. Yakima, 1886-88; U.S. dist. judge, Eastern Dist. of Wash., Mar. 14, 1905—. Republican. Home: Spokane, Wash. Died 1910.

WHITSON, John Harvey, novelist; b. Seymour, Ind., Dec. 28, 1854; s. Aaron F. and Tacy (McNamee) W.; m. Flora Josselyn, 1900. Admitted to Ind. bar, 1876; practiced law at Seymour, 1876-79; formed connections with eastern pub. houses, 1897; ordained to ministry of the Baptist Church, 1898; teacher of Bibl. history and lit., Ward-Belmont, Nashville, Tenn., 1920-23; former head dept. of religious edn., Hardin Coll., Mexico, Mo. Author: A Courier of Empire, 1904; The Rainbow Chasers, 1904; Campaigning with Tippecanoe, 1904; Justin Wingate, Ranchman, 1905; The Castle of Doubt, 1907; Filibusters, 1910; Edgewood Enigma, 1912; Wings of Mars, 1914; Mystery at Greenacres, 1916. Home: Rowley, Mass. Died May 2, 1936.

WHITTAKER, James Thomas, M.D.; b. Cincinnati, Mar. 3, 1843; ed. Miami Univ., A.M., 1868, LL.D., 1892; Univ. of Pa., med. dept., 1866; Med. Coll., Ohio, 1867; studied at Berlin, Prague, Vienna and Paris, 1867-69; from 1869 in practice at Cincinnati; prof. physiology, 1870-80, and of theory and practice of medicine, 1880—, Med. Coll. of Ohio; lecturer on clin. medicine, Good Samaritan Hospital, 1870—; asst. surgeon U.S. Navy, 1863. Founded and edited, 1871-78, Cincinnati Clinic. Author: Lectures on Physiology; Theory and Practice of Medicine (text-book); Diseases of the Heart; XXth Century Practice; Exiled for Lèse Majesté (romance). Home: Cincinnati, O. Died 1900.

WHITTEKER, John Edwin, clergyman; b. North Williamsburg, Ont., Can., Apr. 20, 1851; s. John B. and Nancy (Barkley) W.; A.B., Thiel Coll., Pa., 1875, A.M., 1878, D.D., 1901; LL.D., 1919; m. Emma Hannah Zenette McKee, Dec. 21, 1876. Teacher in pub. schs., Dundas Co., Ont., 1868-70; 2d tutor, 1874-75, 1st tutor, 1875-78, adj. prof. Latin, 1880-84, prof. Latin, 1884-88, Thiel College; ordained Evang. Luth. ministry, 1877; pastor "Church of the Reformation," Rochester, N.Y., 1888-93, St. John's Ch., Easton, Pa., 1893-95; gen. supt. home missions of Gen. Council Luth. Ch., 1895-99; pastor Grace Ch., Rochester, Pa., 1898-1901, Trinity Ch., Lancaster, Pa., 1901-20; pres. Chicago Luth. Sem., Maywood, Ill., 1920—. Trustee Muhlenberg Coll., Allentown, Pa., Lancaster Pub. Library, Luth. Theol. Sem., Phila.; pres. Home Mission and Ch. Extension Bd., of United Luth. Ch. America. Author: The Augsburg Confession (an anlysis), 1888; A Treatise on Baptism, 1893; Bible Biography, 1901; The Separated Life, 1909 (translated into Japanese); Gospel Truths, 1921; Church and State; Bible Wine; The Minister's Sphere. Mem. editorial staff The Lutheran. Home: Maywood, Ill. Died Apr. 13, 1925.

WHITTEMORE, Don Juan, engineer; b. Milton, Vt., Dec. 6, 1830; ed. Bakersfield Acad.; C.E., U. of Vt., 1884; Ph.D., 1884, LL.D., 1895, U. of Wis. Became engr., 1847, Vt. Central Ry., Great Western Ry. of Canada, Central Ry. of Ohio; chief asst. engr. LaCrosse & Milwaukee R.R., 1853-57; chief engr. Southern Minn. Ry.; chief asst. engr. Western Ry. of Cuba; chief asst. engr. La Crosse & Milwaukee, 1861-63; chief engr. C.,M.&St.P. Ry. Co., 1863-Dec. 6, 1910; became consulting engr. same rd. Pres. Am. Soc. C.E., 1884-85. Home: Milwaukee, Wis. Died July 16, 1916.

WHITTEMORE, Edward Loder, mfr.; b. Rye, N.Y., Sept. 12, 1861; s. Edward Payson and Caroline Amelia (Loder) W.; grad. Park Inst., Rye, N.Y., 1879; Ph.B., Yale, 1882; unmarried. With Bridgeport (Conn.) Malleable Iron Co., 1882-87; made sec.-treas. Indianapolis Malleable Iron Co., 1887, and mgr. Toledo Malleable Iron Co., 1890; elected, 1891, v.p. Nat. Malleable Castings Co., now Nat. Malleable and Steel Castings Co., with hdqrs. in Cleveland, chmn. bd. same, 1913—; dir. By-Products Coke Corp. (Chicago), Eastern Malleable Iron Co. Republican. Presbyn. Home: Cleveland Heights, O. Died Jan. 29, 1930.

WHITTEMORE, Harris, manufacturer; b. Naugatuck, Conn., Nov. 25, 1864; s. John Howard and Julia (Spencer) W.; Phillips Acad., Andover, Mass.; studied 2 yrs. in Germany; m. Justine Morgan Brockway, Sept. 21, 1892; children—Harris, Mrs. Helen Adams, Mrs. Gertrude Upson. Pres. Eastern Malleable Iron Co., Westover Sch. Corp., Middlebury, Conn.; dir. various corps. Republican. Conglist. Dir. Waterbury (Conn.) Hosp. Home: Naugatuck, Conn. Died Nov. 29, 1927.

WHITTEMORE, James Madison, brig. gen. U.S.A.; b. Brighton, Mass., Mar. 5, 1836; s. Dr. James Madison and Sarah (Lancaster) W.; grad. U.S. Mil. Acad., 1860; m. Joanna Bontecou Peck, June 24, 1863. Bvtd. 2d lt. arty., July 1, 1860; promoted 2d lt. 3d Arty., Sept. 27, 1860; transferred to Ordnance Corps, May 5, 1861; 1st lt., July 1, 1861; capt., Mar. 3, 1863; maj., June 23, 1874; lt. col., Aug. 2, 1879; col., Jan. 3, 1887; on duty at various arsenals and depots of ordnance dept. until retired, Mar. 5, 1900; advanced to brig. gen. U.S.A. retired, by act of Apr. 23, 1904. Served in defense of Ft. Pickens, Fla., Apr.-Oct. 1861; Washington Arsenal, Washington, D.C., winter of 1861-Aug. 1862; with Army of Potomac. Ordnance officer McDowell's Corps, spring of 1862. Bvtd. major, Mar. 13, 1865 "for meritorious service during war." Home: New Haven, Conn. Died Sept. 6, 1916.

WHITTEN, John Charles, horticulturist; b. Augusta, Me., Sept. 14, 1866; s. Albert and Viola W.; B.S., S.D., Agrl. Coll., 1892, M.S., 1899; studied Cornell U., part of 1892; Mo. Bot. Garden, 1893-94; Ph.D., U. of Halle, 1902; m. Nora Todd, Oct. 31, 1895. Instr. horticulture and horticulturist Expt. Station, Brookings, S.D., 1892; asst. in horticulture, Mo. Bot. Garden, St. Louis, 1893-94; prof. horticulture, U. of Mo., and horticulturist Mo. State Expt. Sta., 1894-1918; prof. pomology, Univ. of Calif., 1918—. Author repts. and bulls., also several hundred papers in hort. mags. Home: Berkeley, Calif. Died June 5, 1922.

WHITTEN, Robert, planning consultant; b. South Bend, Ind., Oct. 9, 1873; s. William M. and Margaret (Milliken) W.; B.L., U. of Mich., 1896; Ph.D., Columbia, 1898; m. Elizabeth Gilbert, Dec. 6, 1900. Legislative reference librarian and editor Yearbook of Legislation, N.Y. State Library, 1898-1907; with N.Y. State Pub. Service Commn., 1st Dist., 1907-14; sec. com. on the city plan and zoning commn., New York, 1914-17; consultant City Plan Commn., Cleveland, 1918-21, Boston City Planning Bd., 1927-33; consultant Nat. Resources Com. and N.Y. State Planning Bd., 1934—. Author: Valuation of Public Service Corporations, 1912; Regulation of Public Service Companies in Great Britain, 1914; The Cleveland Thoroughfare Plan, 1920; Atlanta Zone Plan, 1922; Regional Zoning, 1923; Providence Thorofare Plan, 1926; Economics of Land Subdivision, 1927; Boston Thorofare Plan, 1930; Neighborhoods of Small Homes (Harvard City Planning Studies), 1931; Model Planning Laws (Harvard City Planning Studies), 1935. Home: Albany, N.Y. Died June 6, 1936.

WHITTIER, Charles Franklin, journalist; b. Portland, Me., Dec. 8, 1843; s. Matthew Franklin (brother of the poet) and Jane Elizabeth (Vaughan) W.; ed. pub. schs., Me., pvt. sch., Amesbury, Mass., Friends' Coll., Providence, R.I.; unmarried. Pvt. Co. F, 13th Me. Vols. in Civil War. On staff Portland (Me.) Transcript several yrs.; later editor Westbrook (Me.) Gazette; now editor Portland (Me.) Daily Advertiser. Republican. Died 1909.

WHITTIER, William Frank, capitalist; b. Vienna, Me., Jan. 17, 1832; s. Nathaniel and Nancy (Merrill) W.; ed. pub. and pvt. schs. in Me.; m. Charlotte A. Robinson, 1858 (died 1885). Went to San Francisco, 1854, engaging in mercantile business; commenced under firm name of Cameron-Whittier Co., paints, oils and glass, 1857 (Mr. Cameron died 1865); formed co-partnership with William P. Fuller about 1867, firm name of Whittier-Fuller Co., paints, oils and glass, and successfully manufactured first white lead on Pacific Coast under brand "Pioneer"; also manufactured first mirrors made on Pacific Coast (Mr. Fuller died 1892); retired from mercantile business 1894. Became associated with Col. Mayberry, and with him organized Lake Hemet Water Co., Hemet Land Co., Fairview Land & Water Co. and Hemet Town Water Co.; founded town of Hemet, Riverside Co., Calif., 1887, and built Hemet Dam in San Jacinto Mountains; pres. of said companies, and Hemet Stock Farm, also pres. Bank of Hemet, organized 1899, merged into First Nat. Bank of Hemet, 1915. Active mem. Vigilance Com., San Francisco, 1856. Mem. and chmn. finance com. Rep. State Central Com. 10 yrs. Trustee First Congl. Ch. 25 yrs. Home: San Francisco, Calif. Died Jan. 26, 1917.

WHITTLE, Francis McNeece, P.E. bishop of Va.; b. Mecklenberg Co., Va., July 7, 1823; classical edn.; grad. Va. Theol. Sem., 1847; D.D., Ohio Theol. Sem., 1867; LL.D., William and Mary Coll., 1873. Ordained deacon, July 1847; priest, 1848. Rector consecutively of parishes of Kanawha, Va., 1848-49; St. James, Northam, Va., 1849-52; Grace Ch., Berryville, 1852-57; St. Paul's Louisville, Ky., 1857-68; consecrated Apr. 1868, asst. bishop, and in May 1876 succeeding as bishop of Virginia. Home: Richmond, Va. Died 1902.

WHITTLE, Stafford Gorman, judge; b. Woodstock, Va., Dec. 5, 1849; s. Commodore William Conway W. (U.S.N. and C.S.N.) and Elizabeth Beverley (Sinclair) W.; ed. Washington Coll. (now Washington and Lee U.) and U. of Va., hon. LL.D., 1919; m. Ruth Drewry, Nov. 4, 1880 (dec.); children—Stafford Gorman, Henry Drewry, Flora Redd, Mrs. Elizabeth Sinclair Johnston, Mrs. Ruth Drewry Hubbard, Conway McNiece (dec.), Kennon Caithness, William Murray, Beverley Kennon, Arthur Sinclair (dec.), Randolph Gordon. Admitted to bar, 1871; practiced law in Va., 1871-81; judge 4th Jud. Circuit, Va., 1881-82, and 1886-1901; asso. justice Supreme Court Appeals Va., term, 1901-25; elected pres. of court, Apr. 25, 1919; resigned from court Dec. 31, 1919. Democrat. Episcopalian. Home: Martinsville, Va. Died Sept. 11, 1931.

WHITTLESEY, Eliphalet, sec. Bd. of Indian Commrs. of U.S., 1874—; b. New Britain, Conn., May 14, 1821; s. David and Rebecca W.; grad. Yale, 1842, A.M.; D.D., Howard Univ.; LL.D., Yale. Prof. Bowdoin Coll., 1861-65; served in army with Gen. Howard; prof. Howard Univ., 1867-74. Home: Washington, D.C. Died 1909.

WHITTREDGE, Worthington, artist; b. Ohio, 1820; studied portrait and landscape painting, Cincinnati, until 1849, when he went abroad and remained until 1859, studying in London, Paris, Antwerp, Dusseldorf and Rome, 1849-59, pupil of Andreas Achenback; m. Euphemia Foot, 1866. Asso. Nat. Acad. Design, 1860, academician, 1862, pres., 1875-76. Home: Summit, N.J. Died 1910.

WHITTY, James Howard, editor; b. Baltimore, Md., Feb. 8, 1859; s. John and Catherine (Brown) W.; ed. St. John's Sch., Md., and under private tutors; m. Melvina Allen, 1883; 1 dau., Beatrice Cecelia. Began in newspaper work at Baltimore, 1875; mem. staff Richmond Times 5 years. First pres. Edgar Allan Poe Shrine, Richmond; owner of largest general collection of Poeana in the world. Formerly writer on lit. and social subjects under pseud. "Owen Worth." Editor: Complete Poems of Edgar Allan Poe, 1911, 17; Discoveries in the Uncollected Poems of Edgar Allan Poe, 1916; The Riverside Pocket Poems of E. A. Poe, 1920; Poe's Poems (London), 1921. Compiler: A Record of Virginia Copyright Entries (1790-1844), 1911. Wrote: Foreword for Mary E. Phillips' "Poe, The Man," 1926; Poeana for Bookfellows Soc., Oct. 1927; Foreword for "History of Richmond, Va.," by John P. Little, 1933, for "Southern Literary Messenger," 1934. Joint editor: The Genius and Character of E. A. Poe, 1929. Home: Richmond, Va. Died June 2, 1937.

WHITWELL, Frederick Silsbee, lawyer, trustee; b. Boston, Mass., Mar. 12, 1862; s. Frederick Augustus and Mary Crowninshield (Silsbee) W.; A.B., Harvard, 1884, LL.B., 1887; m. Gertrude Howard, 1893; 1 dau., Gertrude Howard (dec.). Began practice at Boston, 1887; devotes attention to care of properties and to trusteeships. Was pres., then hon. pres., now a v.p. Army and Navy Service Com., Inc.; was first vice chmn. N.E. Div. Am. Com. for Devastated France; now v.p. Alliance Française Goupe de Boston-Cambridge in which previously held every office; served as v.p. N.E. Federation de l'Alliance Française des Etats Unis et du Canada; was member many committees in aid of France, World War. Gov. Soc. Colonial Wars Commonwealth of Mass., Soc. of Governor and Co. of Mass. Bay in N.E.; treas. Mass. Soc. of the Cincinnati; mem. or officer various N.E. hist. societies; former chmn. Boston Nat. Budget Com., Inc.; veteran and hon. mem. 1st Corps Cadets, Mass. Vol. Militia (10 yrs. service); mem. Comite France-Amerique (Paris). Chevalier Legion of Honor (France), 1936, later became Officer. Home: Boston, Mass. Died May 21, 1941.

WHITWORTH, George Gillatt, furniture mfr.; b. Grand Rapids, Mich., Sept. 14, 1850; s. John and Millicent (Gillatt) W.; ed. high sch.; grad. Garrett Bibl. Inst., Evanston, Ill.; m. Margaret M. Bertsch, Sept. 20, 1871 (died 1921); 1 son, John Arthur; m. 2d, Zoe F. Davidson, Nov. 22, 1923. Pres. Berkey & Gay Furniture Co.; v.p. Wolverine Brass Works; dir. Grand Rapids Savings Bank. Director Grand Rapids Public Library, 1909—. Mem. Nat. Council Furniture Assn. (pres. 1922-24), Nat. Alliance Furniture Mfrs. (pres. 1915—). Licensed preacher M.E. Ch. Republican. Mason. Home: Grand Rapids, Mich. Died Dec. 1925.

WHORTON, John Lacy, clergyman; b. Arkadelphia, Ala., June 26, 1888; s. James Mead and Siddie (Roberts) W.; grad. high sch., Arkadelphia, 1916; B.L., Howard Coll., Birmingham, Ala., 1924; D.D., Baylor U., Waco, Tex., 1935; m. Lavada Gardner, Dec. 30, 1909. Began as farmer; ordained as Bapt. minister, 1915; student pastor small chs., 1915-24; pastor 1st Ch., Leeds, Ala., 1924-25, 1st Ch., Bryan, Tex., 1930-32, 1st Ch., Longview, Tex., 1925-30, and from 1932. Chmn. bd. Southwide Com. on Bapt. Papers, also of Bapt. Standard Pub. Co.; mem. state exec. bd. Bapt. Gen. Conv. of Tex.; mem. com. to write Tex. Centennial Bapt. History; v.p. Southern Bapt. Conv., 1936-37; trustee College of Marshall, Marshall, Tex.; trustee Mary Hardin-Baylor Coll., Belton, Tex., 1935—; chmn. Longview Park Bd.; dir. Longview Chamber Commerce. Mem. Square and Compass (coll. Masonic fraternity). Democrat. Mason, Odd Fellow, K.P., Rotarian. Voted most useful citizen in Longview, 1929. Home: Longview, Tex. Died Apr. 10, 1941.

WHYTE, James Primrose, educator; b. Crossgate, Dunfermline, Fife, Scotland, Oct. 23, 1868; s. George and Isabelle (Whyte) W.; grad. Wayland (Wis.) Acad., 1892; Brown U., 1892-94; A.B., U. of Chicago, 1896, A.M., 1903; m. Miss Alfred (died 1914); 1 dau., Lucy Primrose; m. 2d, Miss Savage, 1921; children—James Primrose, Stuart Savage, Mary M., Ann H. Instr. public speaking U. of Chicago, 1896-98, Univ. of W.Va., 1898-99, Shurtleff Coll., 1899-1900; master in English lit., Lake Forest Coll., 1900-06; mgr. for Swift & Co., various cities, 1906-15; dean Anderson (S.C.) College, 1918-22; president Billings (Mont.) Poly. Inst., 1922-23; prof. oral English, and dir. extension work and summer session, Bucknell U., 1923—. Gov. 51st Dist. Rotary Internat. Lecturer. Home: Lewisburg, Pa. Died Apr. 18, 1937.

WHYTE, William Pinckney, U.S. senator; b. Baltimore, Md., Aug. 9, 1824; s. Joseph and Isabella (Pinckney) W.; ed. by pvt. tutor and in Baltimore Coll.; studied law in Baltimore and completed course in Harvard (LL.D., Univ. of Md., 1874, and St. John's Coll.); m. Louisa D. Hollingsworth, 1847; m. 2d, Mary McDonald Thomas, April 27, 1892. Admitted to Md. bar, 1846; mem. Md. legislature, 1847, 48; comptroller treasury of Md., 1853-55; Dem. candidate for Congress, 1851 and 1857 (unsuccessfully contested election, 1857); apptd. U.S. senator to fill vacancy, 1868-69; gov. Md., 1871-74; U.S. senator, 1875-81; mayor of Baltimore, 1882-83 (unanimously elected); atty. gen. of Md., 1887-91; city solicitor of Baltimore, 1900-03; apptd. June 8, 1906, and elected, Jan. 14, 1908, U.S. senator to fill unexpired term of Arthur Pue Gorman, deceased; term expires 1909. Democrat. Counsel for State in settlement of boundary dispute between Md. and Va. before arbitrators, 1874; chmn. of commn. to frame new charter for Baltimore, 1897-98. Home: Baltimore, Md. Died 1908.

WIBORG, Frank Bestow, businessman; b. Cleveland, O., Apr. 30, 1855; s. Henry Paulinus and Susan (Bestow) W.; grad. Chickering Inst., Cincinnati, 1874; m. Adeline Moulton Sherman, Apr. 26, 1882; children—Sara Sherman (Mrs. Gerald C. Murphy), Mary Hoyt, Olga Wiborg (Mrs. Sidney W. Fish). Formerly v.p. The Ault & Wiborg Co., Cincinnati; became v.p. Ault & Wiborg Co., of New York, N.Y. Republican. Author: Printing Ink—A History, 1926; also wrote Travels of an Unofficial Attaché, 1904; A Commercial Traveler in South America, 1905. Home: East Hampton, L.I., N.Y. Died May 1930.

WICKER, Cassius Milton, capitalist; b. N. Ferrisburgh, Vt., Aug. 25, 1846; s. Hon. Cyrus Washburn and Maria Delight (Halladay) W.; acad. edn. Williston and Middlebury, Vt.; m. Augusta Carroll, d. Gov. Augustus C. French, of Illinois, June 5, 1872 (died 1889). Pres. Dillon-Griswold Wire Co., Bankers' Money Order Assn., Nassau Bond Co., N. Shore Traction Co.; v.p. Washington Savings Bank, Fort Worth & Rio Grande Ry. Co., Colo. Eastern R.R. Co.; chmn. bd. dirs. Bank of Discount; dir. various companies. Pres. Chicago Soc. of New York. Home: New York, N.Y. Died Nov. 2, 1913.

WICKER, George Ray, college prof.; b. Moscow, N.Y., Jan. 31, 1870; s. James Compton and Mary Josephine (Candee) W.; grad. Geneseo State Normal Sch., 1886; B.A., Cornell, 1890, A.M., 1898; U. of Pa., 1898-99; Ph.D., U. of Wis., 1900; hon. fellow, sociology, in municipal finance, and editorial sec. to Prof. R. T. Ely of U. of Wis., 1899-1900; m. Mabel Louise Sweeney, July 18, 1894. Vice-prin. secondary schs., New York, 1890-92, prin., 1893-97; instr. economics, 1900-03, asst. prof., 1903-10, prof., 1910—, Dartmouth Coll. Mason. Author: The Financial Administration of New York City in the Period of Dutch Occupation; (with Prof. R. T. Ely) Elementary Principles of Economics. Candidate of Progressive Party for presdl. elector, N.H., 1912; chmn. Progressive State Com., N.H., 1913-15. Home: Hanover, N.H. Died Nov. 25, 1917.

WICKERSHAM, George Woodward, atty. gen. of U.S.; b. Pittsburgh, Pa., Sept. 19, 1858; s. Samuel Morris and Elizabeth C. (Woodward) W.; student Lehigh U., 1873-75, LL.D., 1909; LL.B., U. of Pa., 1880, hon. M.A., 1901; LL.D., Harvard, 1921, Hobart, 1922, U. of Mich., 1927; D.C.L., Syracuse, 1931; m. Mildred Wendell, Sept. 19, 1883; children—Cornelius Wendell, Mildred (dec.), Gwendolyn (Mrs. Henry Ives Cobb, Jr.), Constance. Admitted to Pa. bar, 1880, N.Y. bar, 1883; practiced at Phila., 1880-82; moved to New York, 1882; mem. Strong & Cadwalader, 1887-1909; atty. gen. of U.S., in cabinet of President Taft, 1909-13; member Cadwalader, Wickersham & Taft, 1914—. Del. at large N.Y. Constl. Conv. and chmn. com. on judiciary, 1915; mem. and vice chmn. Dist. Bd. City of New York under Selective Service Law, Sept. 1917-Aug. 1918; spl. commr. War Trade Bd. to Cuba, Aug.-Sept. 1918; mem. President Wilson's 2d Industrial Conf., 1919; mem. Com. on Progressive Codification of Internat. Law, apptd. by Council of League of Nations, 1924-29; pres. Internat. Arbitral Tribunal under the Young Plan treaties, 1932—; mem. Commn. on Reorganization N.Y. State Government, 1925-26; apptd. chmn. Nat. Commn. on Law Observance and Law Enforcement, 1929. Trustee U. of Pa., 1920-26; trustee Barnard Coll. (Columbia), Carnegie Instn. Washington, Cathedral of St. John the Divine. Former chmn. Com. on Internat. Justice and Good Will of Federal Council Chs. of Christ in America. Mem. French Legion of Honor (pres. 1926-32). Decorated Officier and Commander Légion d'Honneur (French). Republican. Episcopalian. Author: Changing Order (essays and addresses), 1914; Spring in Morocco, 1923; also articles in "The Covenanter," written in collaboration with Ex-President Taft and others. Home: New York, N.Y. Died Jan. 25, 1936.

WICKERSHAM, James, lawyer; b. Patoka, Ill., Aug. 24, 1857; s. Alexander W.; common sch. edn.; LL.D., Alaska Agrl. Coll. and Sch. of Mines, 1935; m. Deborah S. Bell, Oct. 27, 1880 (died 1926); 1 son, Darrell P.; m. 2d, Mrs. Grace E. Bishop, 1928. Admitted to bar, 1880; probate judge, Pierce Co., Wash., 1884-88; city atty., Tacoma, 1893-94; mem. Wash. Ho. of Rep., 1898; U.S. dist. judge, 3d Div., Dist. of Alaska, 1900-07; del. from Alaska to 61st to 66th Congresses (1909-21) and to 72d Congress (1931-33); del. Rep. Nat. Conv., Kansas City, 1928. Editor: Alaska Territory Law Reports (8 vols.), 1867-1935; Bibliography of Alaskan Literature, 1724-1924. Home: Juneau, Alaska. Died Oct. 24, 1939.

WICKES, Thomas H., v.p. Pullman's Palace Car Co.; b. Leicestershire, England, Aug. 28, 1846; in the Pullman service, 1868—, as asst. to agent, East St. Louis, 1868-70, asst. supt., 1870-73, supt. St. Louis Div., 1873-85, Western gen. supt., Chicago, 1885-86, gen. supt. 1886-89, 2d v.p., 1889-97, then v.p. Home: Chicago, Ill. Died 1905.

WICKETT, Frederick Henry, lawyer, oil operator; b. Olsworthy, Devonshire, Eng., June 23, 1868; s. Richard and Jane (Hooper) W.; taken to Can. by parents in 1871; ed. Ontario, Can.; read law in office of Colin MacDougall, K.C., St. Thomas, Ont.; m. Alice Wiswell, May 1, 1893; children—Kenneth, Dorothy (Mrs. Le Roy Huszagh), Marjorie (Mrs. Ralph Huszagh). Came to U.S., 1890, naturalized citizen, 1895. Atty. for N.P. Ry., Chicago, Ill., 1890-93; engaged in corp. practice, 1893—; mem. Wickett, Walker & Wegg, 1909-16; pres. Dixie Oil Co., 1919—; pres. and chmn. bd. Pan. Am. Petroleum & Transport Co., New York; dir. Drexel State Bank. Home: Chicago, Ill. Died May 14, 1929.

WICKHAM, Henry Frederick, entomologist; b. Shrewton, Wiltshire, England, Oct. 26, 1866; s. George and Sarah (Light) W.; student State U. of Iowa, 1887-91, M.S., 1895; m. Fanny Chastina Thompson, Sept. 10, 1891. Instr. and asso. prof., 1891-1903, prof. entomology, 1903—, State Univ. of Iowa. Has made numerous and extensive collecting trips to remote parts of continent, which have been made the basis of numerous published reports; specially known for his researches and articles on beetles. Fellow A.A.A.S., Ia. Acad. Science, Entomol. Soc. America. Home: Iowa City, Ia. Died Nov. 17, 1933.

WICKLIFFE, Robert C., congressman; b. Bardstown, Ky., May 1, 1874; s. Robert C. and Annie (Davis) W.; B.S., Centre Coll., Danville, Ky., 1895; LL.B., Tulane U., 1897; m. Lydia W. Cooke, April 20, 1903. Pvt. Co. E, 1st La. Inf., Spanish-Am. War; practiced law in Parish of W. Feliciana, La., 1897—; mem. La. Constl. Conv., 1898; dist. atty. 24th Jud. Dist., 1900-04; mem. 61st and 62d Congresses (1909-13), 6th La. Dist. Democrat. Home: St. Francisville, La. Died June 11, 1912.

WICKSON, Edward James, college prof.; b. Rochester, N.Y., Aug. 3, 1848; s. George Guest and Catherine (Ray) W.; A.B., Hamilton Coll., 1869, A.M., 1872; on editorial staff Utica Morning Herald; made spl. study of cheese industry; sec. N.Y. Dairymen's Assn., 1871; pres. Utica Dairymen's Board of Trade; became connected with staff Pacific Rural Press, 1875; m. Ednah Newell Harmon, 1875. Lecturer on practical agr., 1879-91, asso. prof. agr., 1891-97, prof. agrl. practice and supt. dept. univ. extension in agr., 1897-1907, dean Coll. of Agr. and acting dir. of Agrl. Expt. Sta., 1905-07, dean and dir., 1907-13, prof. of horticulture, 1913-15, emeritus, 1915—, U. of Calif. Organized first dairy assn. in Calif., 1876; one of organizers, 1879, then sec. Calif. State Hort. Soc.; mem. Calif. Micros. Soc. (sec., pres.), Calif. Floral Soc. (pres. 1888-1900). Trustee Calif. Poly. Sch., 1902-14; mem. Nat. Council of Horticulture, 1904-12. Author: California Fruits and How to Grow Them; The California Vegetables in Garden and Field; California Garden Flowers, Trees, Shrubs and Vines. Mem. Am. Com. on Rural Credit and Coöperative Marketing, 1913—. Home: Berkeley, Calif. Died July 16, 1923.

WICKWARE, Francis Graham, editor; b. Easton's Corners, Ont., Can., Jan. 31, 1883; s. Francis Byron and Eliza (Graham) W.; B.A., McGill U., Montreal, 1904; B.Sc. in mining engring., McGill, 1906; m. Margery Sill, Mar. 15, 1911; 1 son, Francis Sill. Mine surveying and railroad location, British Columbia and Ont., summers, 1905, 06; Dawson research fellow, instr. in mining engring. and English, McGill U., 1906-07; asso. editor Engineering Mag., New York and London, 1907-11; editor Am. Year Book, 1911-20; editor D. Appleton & Co., 1920-33, D. Appleton-Century Co., 1933—. Home: New York, N.Y. Died Oct. 12, 1940.

WIDENER, Peter A. Brown, capitalist; b. Philadelphia, Nov. 13, 1834; ed. high school; learned meat busines; m. H. Josephine Dunton, Aug. 18, 1858 (dec.). Became prominent in Rep. politics; apptd., 1873, to serve out term of Joseph F. Mercer as city treas. of Phila.; reelected to same office, 1874. Largely interested in street rys. and many important corps.; v.p. Cresson & Clearfield Coal Co.; dir. Met. St. Ry. Co. of New York, Phila. & Reading Coal & Iron Co., Phila. & Reading Ry. Co., etc. Built and endowed Widener Memorial Sch. for Crippled Children, Phila., and Longport, N.J.; presented bldg. for the Free Pub. Library of Phila.

Collector of art and owner of valuable paintings. Home: Elkins Park, Pa. Died Nov. 6, 1915.

WIECHMANN, Ferdinand Gerhard, chemist; b. Brooklyn, N.Y., Nov. 12, 1858; s. Ernst Gustav and Anna Cæcilie (Albers) W.; Ph.B. (in chemistry), Sch. of Mines, Columbia, 1881, Ph.D., 1882; m. Marie Helen Damrosch, Mar. 26, 1885. Instr. chemistry, Columbia, 1883-97; lecturer on chemistry, cons. research chemist, New York, 1883—. Author: Sugar Analysis, 1890, 3d edit., 1914; Lecture Notes on Theoretical Chemistry, 1893, 2d edition, 1895; Chemistry—Its Evolution and Achievements, 1899; Maid of Montauk (under pen-name Forest Monroe), 1902; Notes on Electrochemistry, 1906. Died Apr. 24, 1919.

WIENER, Leo, philologist; b. Bialystok, Poland, July 26, 1862; s. Solomon and Frieda (Rabinowicz) W.; ed. gymnasia at Minsk and Warsaw; student of medicine, Warsaw U., 1880; Polytechnic at Berlin, 1881-82; came to U.S., 1882; m. Bertha Kahn, Feb. 27, 1893. Taught Greek, Latin and mathematics in Odessa, Mo., 1883-84, and in Kansas City High Sch., 1884-92; asst. prof. Germanic and Romance langs., U. of Mo., 1892-95; taught langs. in N.E. Conservatory of Music, 1895-96; instr. Slavic langs. and lits., 1896-1901, asst. prof., 1901-11, prof., 1911-30 (emeritus), Harvard. Author: (or editor) Anthology of Russian Literature (2 vols.), 1902-03; An Interpretation of the Russian People, 1915; Commentary to the Germanic Laws and Mediæval Documents, 1915; Contributions Toward a History of Arabico-Gothic Culture (4 vols.), 1917; Africa and the Discovery of America (3 vols.), 1919; Mayan and Mexican Origins, 1926. Editor and translator: Complete Works of Count Leo N. Tolstoy (24 vols.), 1904-05. Home: Belmont, Mass. Died Dec. 12, 1939.

WIERS, Edgar Swan, clergyman; b. Meadville, Pa., May 15, 1873; s. John Henry Fonda and Harriet Augusta (Swan) W.; grad. Central High Sch., Cleveland, O., 1891; A.B., Adelbert Coll. (Western Reserve U.), 1895; student Harvard Law Sch., 1895-96; B.D., Union Theol. Sem., 1899; A.M., Columbia, 1899; m. Luella S. McClure Aug. 30, 1900; 1 son, Donald McClure (dec.). Ordained Unitarian ministry, 1900; pastor First Parish, Billerica, Mass., 1900-06, Unity Ch., Montclair, N.J., 1906—. Pres. Unitarian Fellowship for Social Justice, Unitarian Temperance Soc., 1914-17, Unity Inst. Concert and Lecture Courses, 1920—, N.J. State Commn. for the Blind, 1922—. Community Chest of Montclair, 1926-28, Council of Social Agencies, 1928—, Montclair Interracial Com., 1929—. Dir. Am. Unitarian Assn., 1912-18; mem. advisory and administrative bds. N.J. Law Sch. Mem. Am. Relief Com. of Italian Red Cross, World War, also chmn. war camp com., Montclair. Mason. Home: Montclair, N.J. Died June 30, 1931.

WIGGER, Winand Michael, bishop; b. New York, Dec. 9, 1841; grad. St. Francis Xavier Coll., 1860; studied theology, Seton Hall, N.J., 1860-62; Sem. Brignoli Sale, Genoa, 1862-65, D.D., Univ. of Sapienza, Rome, 1869; ordained priest, 1865; at Cathedral, Newark, 1865-69; rector St. Vincent's Ch., Madison, N.J., 1869-73; St. John's, Orange, 1873-74; Summit, N.J., 1874-76; returning to St. Vincent's, Madison, until 1881; bishop of Newark, 1881—. Address: 35 Bleecker St., Newark, N.J. Died 1901.

WIGGIN, Frank H., missionary treas.; b. Wolfeboro, N.H., Oct. 27, 1851; s. Benjamin and Lucy (Clough) W.; acad. edn.; m. Mary Walker, 1891. Asst. to treas., 1886-95, asst. treas., 1895-96, treas., 1896—, A.B.C.F.M. Home: West Roxbury, Mass. Died May 10, 1920.

WIGGIN, Frederick Alonzo, clergyman, lecturer; b. Tuftonboro, N.H., July 11, 1858; s. William Harrison and Ann (Swett) W.; A.B., Madison U. (now Colgate U.), Hamilton, N.Y., 1881; D.D., Coll. Science and Philosophy, Los Angeles, Calif., 1917; m. Ethel P. Hunting, Jan. 12, 1920. Ed. for Bapt. ministry but served as non-sectarian pastor Unity Ch., Boston, 1897-1935 (resigned). Republican. Mason. Author: Cubes and Spheres in Human Life, 1899; The Living Jesus, 1921; also numerous articles and pamphlets. Lecturer on religious and metaphysical subjects, also engaged in ednl. work. Home: Brookline, Mass. Died July 26, 1940.

WIGGIN, Frederick Holme, surgeon; b. Kingston-on-Thames, Eng., Dec. 26, 1853; s. Frederick and Elizabeth Sumner (Gerard) W.; ed. Phillips Andover Acad. and Rensselaer Poly. Inst., Troy; M.D., Bellevue Hosp. Med. Coll. (New York U.), 1877; m. Abby Fishe Merriam, June 12, 1878; m. 2d, Christina Ferguson On, Mar. 14, 1907. House surgeon, 1877-78, and adj. visiting surgeon, 1897-98, Bellevue Hosp.; attending surgeon Northeastern Dispensary; practiced medicine at Litchfield, Conn., 1880-90, New York, 1890—; examining phys. New York Bd. of Edn., 1893-97; visiting gynecologist St. Elizabeth's Hosp.; visiting surgeon, 1892-1908, cons. surgeon, 1908—, N.Y. City Hosp. Organizer, and pres. Litchfield (Conn.) Water Co., 1883-93, 1894-97. Pres. Litchfield County (Conn.) Med. Soc., 1894-95; v.p. A.M.A., 1897-98 (sec. jud. council, 1900-05); pres. New York Co. Med. Assn., 1899-1900; sec. N.Y. State Med. Assn., 1900-01, and pres., 1902; mem. council New York Acad. Sciences, 1905-07. Author of many papers on gynecol. and surg. subjects. Died 1910.

WIGGIN, Kate Douglas, author; b. Phila., Sept. 28, 1859; d. Robert N. and Helen E. (Dyer) Smith; sister of Nora Archibald Smith; grad. Abbot Acad., Andover, Mass., 1878; Litt.D., Bowdoin Coll., Me., 1906; m. George C. Riggs, Mar. 30, 1895. Organized the first free kindergartens for poor children on the Pacific Coast. Author: The Birds' Christmas Carol, 1888; The Story of Patsy, 1889; A Summer in a Cañon, 1889; Timothy's Quest, 1890; The Story Hour (with Nora A. Smith), 1900; Children's Rights (with same), 1892; A Cathedral Courtship, 1893; Penelope's English Experiences, 1893; Polly Oliver's Problem, 1893; The Village Watch Tower, 1895; Froebel's Gifts (with Nora A. Smith), 1895; Froebel's Occupations (with same), 1896; Kindergarten Principles and Practice (with same), 1896; Nine Love Songs and a Carol, 1896; Marm Lisa, 1896; Penelope's Progress, 1898; Penelope's Experiences in Ireland, 1901; The Diary of a Goose Girl, 1902; Rebecca, 1903; The Affair at the Inn (collaboration), 1904; Rose o' the River, 1905; New Chronicles of Rebecca, 1907; The Old Peabody Pew, 1907; Susanna and Sue, 1909; Mother Carey's Chickens, 1911; The Story of Waitstill Baxter, 1913. Editor: (with Nora Archibald Smith) Golden Numbers, 1902; The Posy Ring, 1903; Pinafore Palace Poems, 1904; The Fairy Ring, 1906; Magic Casements, 1907; Tales of Laughter, 1908; Tales of Wonder, 1909; The Talking Beasts, 1911. Plays: Rebecca of Sunnybrook Farm, 1908; Mother Carey's Chickens, 1915; The Old Peabody Pew: Bluebeard, musical fantasy, 1914; Penelope's Postscripts, 1915; Ladies-in-Waiting, 1918; Homespun Tales, 1920. Died Aug. 24, 1923.

WIGGINS, Benjamin Lawton, educator; b. Sand Ridge, S.C., Sept. 11, 1861; s. James and Elizabeth B. (Mellard) W.; ed. Porter Acad., Charleston; grad. U. of the South, 1880, M.A., 1882; LL.D., Trinity Coll., Hartford, 1899, St. John's Coll., Annapolis, 1902, S.C. Coll., 1905; studied Johns Hopkins, 1883-84; prof. Greek, U. of the South, Aug. 1882—, and vice chancellor, Aug. 1893—. Married Clara Quintard, Jan. 20, 1886. Died 1909.

WIGGINS, (J.) Carleton, artist; b. Turners, N.Y., Mar. 4, 1848; s. Guy Carleton and Adelaide (Ludlum) W.; studied art, Nat. Acad. of Design, 1870, at Paris, 1880-81, also studied under H. Carmiencke and George Inness; m. Mary Clucas, Oct. 17, 1872 (died 1928). Splty., cattle and landscapes. Exhibited Paris Salon, 1881, Prize Fund, 1894 (gold medal), Royal Acad., London, 1896-97, and other exhbns. U.S. and abroad. Principal paintings: A Holstein Bull, 1891 (Met. Mus. of Art); Morning on the Hills (Brooklyn Mus.); The Wanderers (Hamilton Club, Brooklyn); Ploughing in France, 1894; Plough Horse, 1899 (Lotos Club, New York); Sheep and Landscape (Newark Art Mus.); etc. A.N.A., 1892, N.A., 1906. Home: Old Lyme, Conn. Died June 12, 1932.

WIGGINS, Frank, secretary; b. Richmond, Ind., Nov. 8, 1849; s. Charles O. and Mary Elizabeth (Thatcher) W.; ed. Earlham Coll., Ind.; m. Amanda P. Wiggins, May 5, 1886. Supt., 1891—, sec., 1897—, Los Angeles Chamber of Commerce; gen. mgr. Southern Calif. exhibit, Chicago Expn., 1893, Mid-Winter Fair, San Francisco, 1894, Atlanta Expn., 1896, Omaha Expn., 1898, Buffalo Expn., 1901; Jamestown Expn., 1907, Alaska-Yukon-Pacific Expn., 1909; state commr. St. Louis Expn., 1904, Portland Expn., 1905. Home: Venice, Calif. Died Oct. 18, 1924.

WIGGINS, Horace Leland, hotel operator; b. Springfield, Ill., Mar. 27, 1871; s. Noble and Clarissa (Leland) W.; ed. Lawrenceville (N.J.) Sch.; m. Mary Hanna Mooney, June 18, 1895; 1 dau., Clarissa Leland. Began in hotel business, Springfield, 1890; pres. Pere Marquette Hotel Co., Elmira Hotel Operating Corp.; mng. dir. Benjamin Franklin Hotel Corp.; v.p. Penn-Harris Hotel Co.; dir. United Hotels Co. of America, United Hotels of South and West, Inc., New York United Hotels, United Bancroft Co., Robert Trent Hotel Co., Commmity Hotel Corp., Stacy-Trent Co. Republican. Presbyn. Mason. Home: Philadelphia, Pa. Died Feb. 28, 1933.

WIGGINTON, George Peter, mfr.; b. Steubenville, O., Dec. 6, 1875; s. Thomas Jefferson and Mary Amelia (Oyer) W.; high sch., Pittsburgh, 1892; m. Margaret Belle Heasley, Oct. 7, 1902; children—Lucille Mae, George P., Robert Elmer, Margaret Belle, Richard Thomas. Pres. Bond Supply Co., Kalamazoo, Mich.; pres. Wigginton Co.; dir. Brookmire Economic Service, Inc., Brookmire Investment Trust. Served as chmn. Rep. County Com., Kalamazoo County, 1922-24. Chmn. 5th Victory Loan Campaign, World War I. Presbyn. Mason, Elk. Home: Pelham, N.Y. Deceased.

WIGGLESWORTH, George, lawyer; b. Boston, Feb. 3, 1853; s. Edward and Henrietta May (Goddard) W.; A.B., Harvard, 1874, A.M., 1875, LL.B., 1878, LL.D., 1928; m. Mary Catherine Dixwell, June 20, 1878; children—Mrs. Anna W. Chase, Norton, Mrs. Marian E. W. Brown, Mrs. Ruth W. Whitney, Richard B., Frank. Practiced at Boston, 1879—; pres. Amoskeag Co.; dir. Merrimack Mills, Mass. Hosp. Life Ins. Co., Tampa (Fla.) Electric Co.; trustee Central Aguirre Sugar Cos., Suffolk Real Estate Trust, Real Estate Associates, Milton Savings Bank. Pres. Mass. Gen. Hosp., McLean Hosp., Convalescent Home (Waverly, Mass.). Mem. Corp. Mass. Inst. Tech. Republican. Unitarian. Home: Milton, Mass. Died Nov. 26, 1930.

WIGHT, Frank Clinton, editor, engineer; b. Washington, D.C., Feb. 26, 1882; s. George Ambrose and Ida (Morgan) W.; student Columbian (now George Washington) U., 1899-1901; C.E., Cornell U., 1904; m. Julia Theodora Welles, Oct. 5, 1911; children—Barbara, John Welles, Shirley, Richard Morgan. With Library of Congress, 1898-1901; in employ surveyor's office, D.C., 1902, 03; asst. to engr. of bridges, D.C., 1904-07; asso. editor Engring. News, New York, 1907-12, mng. editor, 1912-17; with Engring. News-Record, 1917—, editor, 1924—. Mem. bd. dirs. Am. Construction Council; mem. Hoover Nat. Conf. on Street and Highway Safety, 1924-25; v.p. Nat. Conf. Bus. Papers Editors, 1925-26; chmn. Editorial Conf. N.Y. Bus. Publishers' Assn., 1925-26. Universalist. Contbr. to Am. Internat. Ency., Nelson's Loose-Leaf Ency., Am. Year Book. Home: Summit, N.J. Died Sept. 1927.

WIGHT, John Green, educator; b. Gilead, Me., March 2, 1842; s. Timothy and Mary Ann (Green) W.; A.B., Bowdoin Coll., 1864, also A.M., hon. Ph.D., Hamilton, 1888; Litt.D., Bowdoin, 1898; m. Flora Annetta Stiles, May 13, 1865. Prin. Bridgton (Me.) Acad., 1867-70, Cooperstown (N.Y.) High Sch., 1870-90, Worcester (Mass.) Classical High Sch., 1890-94, Phila. High Sch. for Girls, 1894-97, Wadleigh High Sch. for Girls, New York, 1997—. Episcopalian. Editor: The Last of the Mohicans, 1899; Selections from the Bible, 1900. Lecturer on ednl. and lit. topics. Died Nov. 23, 1913.

WIGHT, Pearl, merchant; b. Penobscot, Me., Mar. 22, 1844; s. Edward and Theodosia (Wescott) W.; ed. common schs. of Me.; m. Helen L. Ellens, Nov. 19, 1867. Entered employ of Cobb, Wight & Case, mchts., shipbuilders and owners of Bodwell Granite Co., at 17; took charge of their oil interests in Pa. at 19; started in business at New Orleans, 1866; pres. Woodward, Wight & Co., Ltd., until Nov. 4, 1909, when sold out to his employees; pres. New Orleans Dry Dock & Ship Bldg. Co., Southwest La. Land Co., and one of receivers T.&P. Ry. One of organizers Mexican, C. Am. and S. Am. Commercial Exchange, and started in New Orleans to open trade with Central and South America; one of owners and builders of the first Am. steamer, the "Wanderer," running to ports there, about 1884. Long in polit. life; mem. Rep. Nat. Com., 1905; apptd. commr. U.S. Internal Revenue, Dec. 1, 1907, by Pres. Roosevelt, but declined; mem. Progressive Nat. Com., 1912-16; represented both Pres. Roosevelt and Pres. Taft, selecting presdl. appointees in La. for 10 yrs. Home: New Orleans, La. Died July 4, 1920.

WIGHT, William Ward, lawyer; b. Troy, N.Y., Jan. 14, 1849; s. William Ward and Lydia Ann Potwine (Van Akin) W.; A.B., Williams Coll. (Phi Beta Kappa and honor man), 1869, A.M., 1887; LL.B., Albany Law Sch. (Union U.), 1873; m. Mary Olivia Brockway, June 16, 1884 (died 1885); 1 son, Edward Brockway; m. 2d, Susan Elizabeth Lowry, Mar. 21, 1893; 1 dau., Elizabeth von Benscoten. Engaged in practice at Milwaukee, 1875—; mem. bar Ct. of Appeals, N.Y. Sec. and librarian Milwaukee Law Library Assn., June 1875—; founder Milwaukee Civ. Service Reform Assn.; sec. Bd. Fire and Police Commrs. of Milwaukee, 1886-89, mem., 1888-97, and chmn., 1889-97; sec. Milwaukee Coll. (for edn. of women) and its successor, Milwaukee-Downer Coll., 1880-1907, pres., 1907-24. A founder, 1890, and mem. Wis. Soc. S.A.R. (pres. 1906-07); a founder, 1897, Wis. Soc. Colonial Wars. Presbyn.; pres. bd. trustees Immanuel Presbyn. Ch. Republican. Author: Life of Henry Clay Payne, 1907; Louis XVII, a bibliography, 1915; also various hist., bibliog. and geneal monographs, and revised edit. New Wisconsin Form Book. Home: Milwaukee, Wis. Died Jan. 2, 1931.

WILBER, David Forrest; b. Milford, Otsego Co., N.Y., Dec. 7, 1859; s. David (M.C.) and Margaret Belinda (Jones) W.; grad. Cazenovia (N.Y.) Sem., 1879; m. Pauline Virginia Jenkins, Apr. 23, 1903 (died 1914); m. 2d, Esther Rosina Zolliker, Aug. 20, 1916. Interested in farming and stock breeding; mem. New York State Cattle Tuberculosis Commn., 1894; pres. Holstein-Friesian Assn. of America, and Am. Cheviot Sheep Assn. of the U.S. and Canada. Mem. 54th and 55th Congresses (1895-99), 21st N.Y. Dist.; consul at Barbados, W.I., 1903-05; consul gen. at Singapore, Straits Settlements, 1905-07, at Halifax, N.S., 1907-09, at Kobe, Japan, 1909-10, at Vancouver, B.C., Can., 1910-13, at Zürich, Switzerland, 1913-15, at Genoa, Italy, 1915-21; consul gen. at Auckland, New Zealand, 1921-22, Wellington, New Zealand, 1922-23. Republican; presidential elector, 1924. Home: Oneonta, N.Y. Died Aug. 14, 1928.

WILBER, George M., farmer, sheep grower; b. Union County, O., July 3, 1862; s. George and Arnette (Coolidge) W.; ed. high sch., Marysville, O., and business coll.; m. Luella Robinson, 1884 (died 1913); children—Robert M. (dec.), Mrs. Ruth Schriefer; m. 2d, Alice Lucile Pearse, June 6, 1914; 1 dau., Georgeanna. Farmer since boyhood, in Union County, O.; also ranch owner, Idaho and elsewhere; extensive shipper of live stock and grain, and engaged in banking, mining and oil production; dir. and pres. Fed. Land Bank, Louisville, Ky., 10 yrs. Mem. Ohio Ho. of Rep., 1909-13 (author of bill providing for exptl. farm at the option of any county). Republican. Presbyn. Mason, K.P., Elk. Home: Marysville, O. Died Oct. 3. 1939.

WILBUR, Charles Edgar, editor; b. Manorville, L.I., N.Y., Oct. 8, 1853; s. Jeremiah Greenfield and Hannah (Morse) W.; A.B., Adrian Coll., 1877, A.M., 1880, Ph.D., 1889; B.D., Yale, 1882; D.D., Temple U., Phila., 1890; LL.D., Adrian Coll., 1920; m. Virginia Lovinia Zane, Oct. 18, 1882. Ordained M.P. ministry, 1878; pastor Sharpsburg, Pa., 1882; prof. English, Adrian Coll., 1883-92; pastor Amity, Pa., Fairmont, W.Va., Bellevue, Pa., 1892-98; editor M.P. S.S. periodicals, 1898—. Mem. Internat. S.S. Lesson Com., 1914—. Republican. Prohibitionist. Mem. S.S. Commn., under Am. Com. of Relief in the Near East. Died Dec. 1, 1931.

WILBUR, Charles Toppan, physician; b. Newburyport, Mass., May 18, 1835; grad. Berkshire Med. Coll., 1860; A.M., Wesleyan U. Bloomington, Ill.; m. Leila C. Peyton, May 3, 1859. Connected with schools for feeble-minded children at Barre, Mass., Lakeville, Conn., Albany and Syracuse, N.Y., and Columbus, O. Asst. surgeon 59th Ohio vol. inf., 8 months, and surgeon 95th Ohio vol. inf., 3 yrs., during Civil War; supt. Ill. Asylum for Feeble-Minded Children, 1865-83; established Philanthropic Index and Rev., and published it for 18 yrs. Resigned from the Ill. Asylum in 1883, establishing at Kalamazoo, Mich., the Wilbur School and Home for Feeble-Minded Children, becoming propr. and supt. Died 1909.

WILBUR, Cressy Livingston, vital satistician; b. Hillsdale, Mich., Mar. 16, 1865; s. Rodney G. and Frances (Cressy). W.; Ph.B., Hillsdale Coll., 1886, Ph.M., 1889; student Dept. Medicine and Surgery, U. of Mich., 1888-89; M.D., Bellevue Hosp. Med. Coll. (New York U.), 1890; m. Blanche M. Mead, June 30, 1891. Chief Div. Vital Statistics, Mich., 1893-1905; med. referee (classification of causes of death) and expert spl. agent, in charge extension of registration area for U.S. Census Bur., 1901-06, chief statistician for vital statistics, July 1, 1906-July 31, 1914; dir. Div. of Vital Statistics, N.Y. State Dept. of Health, Apr. 7, 1914—. Special lecturer vital statistics, Medical Dept., U. of Mich., 1902-05. Official del. of Census Bur. to Internat. Congress on Tuberculosis, Washington, 1908 (v.p. Sect. VI); official del. of U.S. to Internat. Statis. Inst., Paris, 1909; 2d Decennial Internat. Commn. of Revision of Classification of Causes of Death, by French Govt., Paris, 1909 (v.p. and preparer of official English list); sec. Div. of Demography, Internat. Congress of Hygiene and Demography, Washington, 1912. Editor: Michigan Annual Registration Reports (Vital Statistics), 1891-1903; Michigan Monthly Bulletin of Vital Statistics; Bertillon Classification of Causes of Death (under auspices Am. Pub. Health Assn.), Lansing, 1899; Manual of International Classification of Causes of Death (U.S. Census, 1902, 1913); U.S. Census annual reports on Mortality Statistics, 1905-12, and numerous census pamphlets and bulls. Contbr. articles on vital statistics to med. and statis. publs. Home: Albany, N.Y. Died Aug. 9, 1928.

WILBUR, Elisha Packer, banker; b. Mystic, Conn., Jan. 31, 1833; moved to Mauch Chunk, Pa., 1838; pub. sch. edn. Became clerk in store owned by judge Asa Packer, Neshquehoning, Pa., 1847-52; entered service Lehigh Valley R.R., 1852, as rodman, later in other capacities; confidential clerk and pvt. sec. of Judge Packer from 1856 until his death, 1879; one of trustees Judge Packer's estate; long dir. and about 10 yrs. pres. Lehigh Valley R.R. Founded E. P. Wilbur & Co., bankers, 1870, and pres. of its successor, E.P. Wilbur Trust Co., 1887—. Died 1910.

WILBUR, Henry W., editor; b. Easton, N.Y., May 15, 1851; s. Humphrey and Ann (Pierce) W.; ed. in pub. sch. and high schs., Vineland, N.J.; m. Eliza M. Sowle, Oct. 21, 1880. Began editorial work, 1875; editor Vineland Independent, 1876-84; with New York Voice, 1896-98. Recorded minister, Religious Soc. of Friends; gen. sec. Friends' Gen. Conf., also of the Com. for Advancement of Friends' Principles; pres. Nat. Fedn. of Religious Liberals. Pres. Pa. Abolition Soc. (organized 1775). Author: A Study in Doctrine and Discipline; Five Weeks in England; Life and Labors of Elias Hicks; Job Scott, and Eighteenth Century Friend; Five Points from Barclay; Nature Stories from Darwin; Development of the Spiritual Perceptions, 1914. Home: Swarthmore, Pa. Died Sept. 5, 1914.

WILBUR, James Benjamin; b. Cleveland, O., Nov. 11, 1856; s. James Benjamin and Lauretta (Welch) W.; ed. pub. schs.; m. Carrie B. Hurd, 1880; 1 son, James Benjamin. Cashier N.Y.,N.H.&H. Ry., 1876-82; with Daniels & Fisher, Denver, Colo., 1884; banking and ranching, Colo., 1885-90; organizer, 1891, Royal Trust Co., Chicago, and pres. until 1909; retired and settled at Manchester, Vt. Trustee Library of Congress Trust Fund Bd., U. of Vt., Am. Antiquarian Soc., New York Hist. Soc. Mem. Mass. Hist. Soc. Republican. Protestant. Donor Ira Allen Chapel to U. of Vt., 1927. Author: Life of Ira Allen (1751-1814), Founder of Vermont, 1928. Editor: Contrast (comedy of 1789 in 5 acts), 1920. Active for many yrs. in having letters and documents pertaining to Am. history reproduced and placed in the Library of Congress. Home: Manchester, Vt. Died Apr. 28, 1929.

WILBUR, Rollin Henry, railway official; b. Bethlehem, Pa., Sept. 3, 1863; s. Elisha Packer and Stella Mercer (Abbott) W.; ed. Lehigh U., 1880-84; m. Nannie Buehler Lamberton, Dec. 16, 1884; children—Dorothy, Isabel (dec.). Gen. supt. Eastern div., Phila. & Reading Ry., 1892-93; gen. supt. and gen. mgr., Lehigh Valley R.R., 1893-1904; pres. Jefferson Coal Co.; v.p., gen. mgr., Lehigh & N.E. R.R. Co.; dir. Packers Coal Co., Tradesmen's Nat. Bank & Trust Co., Sayre Land Co., Sayre Water Co. Served as lt. col. Pa. N.G.; a.d.c. on staffs of Govs. Patterson and Hastings of Pa. Republican. Episcopalian. Mason. Home: St. Davids, Pa. Died Sept. 6, 1938.

WILCOX, Alexander Martin, univ. prof.; b. Baltimore, June 19, 1849; s. William Littleton and Mary (Rose) W.; grad. Baltimore City Coll., 1865; A.B., Yale, 1877, Ph.D., 1880; Am. School Classical Studies, Athens, Greece, 1883-84; Johns Hopkins, 1884-85; m. Mina Elizabeth Marvin, Dec. 19, 1889. Prof. Greek, U. of Kan., 1885—. Congregationalist. Died Jan. 3, 1929.

WILCOX, Ansley, lawyer; b. Summerville, Ga., Jan. 27, 1856; s. Daniel Hand and Frances Louisa (Ansley) W.; A.B., Yale, 1874; University Coll., Oxford, Eng., 1875-76; m. Cornelia C. Rumsey, Jan. 17, 1878 (died 1880); m. 2d, Mary Grace Rumsey, Nov. 20, 1883. Admitted to bar, 1878, practices in Buffalo; firm Crowley, Movius & Wilcox, 1882-83, Allen, Movius & Wilcox, 1883-92, Movius & Wilcox, 1892-93, Wilcox & Miner, 1894-1903, Wilcox & Van Allen, 1903—. Prof. med. jurisprudence, U. of Buffalo, 1885-1906. Pres. Buffalo Charity Orgn. Soc., Buffalo Civil Service Reform Assn.; chmn. Buffalo Fedn. of Charities and Social Service Agencies; trustee Buffalo Gen. Hosp.; mem. board mgrs. N.Y. State Reformatory, Elmira, 1899; commr. to investigate charges against Dist. Atty. Gardiner, of New York, 1900. Chmn. Buffalo br. Am. Red Cross until 1916, later mem. exec. com.; commr. N.Y. State Reservation, Niagara, 1917-27. On death of President McKinley, Sept. 14, 1901, the oath of office was administered to Theodore Roosevelt at the house of Mr. Wilcox in Buffalo. Home: Buffalo, N.Y. Died Jan. 26, 1930.

WILCOX, Armour David, coll. pres.; b. Scioto County, O., June 1, 1868; s. Loyal Manley and Mary Belle (Morrison) W.; B.S., Ottawa (Kan.) U., 1898; m. Adelaide Lorraine Simons, June 10, 1902; children—Armour David, Robert Morrison (dec.), Ward Manley. Lecturer Nat. Anti-Saloon League, 1900-06; ordained ministry M.E. Ch., S., 1906; served as pastor at Goldsboro, Raleigh, Louisburg, Durham, Wilmington, Charlotte, Monroe, and Salisbury—all N.C., 1906-31; pres. Louisburg Coll., 1931—, also trustee; missionary sec. N.C. Conf. of M.E. Ch., South, 1918-22. Home: Louisburg, N.C. Deceased.

WILCOX, Charles Bowser, clergyman; b. Fox Lake, Wis., Nov. 24, 1851; s. David Thomas and Charlotte (Bowser) W.; student Northwestern U., 1875-79; grad. Garrett Bibl. Inst., Evanston, Ill., 1880; D.D., Hamline, 1894; m. Mary E. Leonard, Dec. 5, 1872 (died 1906); children—Charlotte F. (dec.), Cora A. (Mrs. R. E. Dreyer), Stella M. Ordained M.E. ministry, 1880; pastor Pleasant Prairie, Wis., 1880-81, Sharon, 1882-83, Janesville, 1884-85, First Ch., Oshkosh, 1885-90, St. Paul, Minn., 1890-95, Trinity Ch., La Fayette, Ind., 1895-99, Grand Av. Ch., Kansas City, Mo., 1899-1900, First Ch., Colorado Springs, Colo., 1900-09, Trinity Ch., Denver, 1909-14, Ashbury Ch., Denver, 1914-16, First Ch., Colorado Springs (2d time), 1916-21 (retired). Traveled in Europe, Asia and Africa, 1903. Mem. Gen. Conf. M.E. Ch., 1912. Trustee U. of Denver, also Iliff Sch. of Theology, Denver. Home: Denver, Colo. Died Dec. 15, 1940.

WILCOX, Delos Franklin, publicist, public utility expert; b. Ida, Mich., Apr. 22, 1873; s. Byron M. and Lorain (Jones) W.; A.B., U. of Mich., 1894, A.M., 1895; Ph.D., Columbia, 1896; m. Ann Arbor, Mich., Mina M. Gates, Feb. 22, 1898; children—Helen Wanda, Robert Theodore (dec.), Joseph (dec.), Paul Harlan, Emily Katharine, Willard Irving. Editor Civic News, Grand Rapids and Detroit, 1905-07; chief of Bur. of Franchises, Pub. Service Commn., 1st Dist., New York, 1907-13 (resigned); dep. commr. Dept. of Water Supply, Gas and Electricity, N.Y. City, 1914-17; adviser to Fed. Electric Rys. Commn., 1919-20. Author: The Study of City Government, 1897; Ethical Marriage, 1900; The American City, 1904; The Government of Great American Cities (pub. Leipzig), 1908; Municipal Franchises (2 vols.), 1910-11; Great Cities in America, 1910; Government by All the People, 1912; Analysis of Electric Railway Problem, 1921; Depreciation in Public Utilities, 1925; The Indeterminate Permit in Relation to Home Rule and Municipal Ownership, 1926; Whitten's Valuation of Public Service Corporations (revised edit., 2 vols.), 1927; also various utility reports and polit. essays and articles. Home: Grand Rapids, Mich. Died Apr. 4, 1928.

WILCOX, Edwin Mead, botanist; b. Busti, N.Y., May 21, 1876; s. Abram F. and Sally Maria (Mead) W.; brother of Earley Vernon Wilcox; B.S., Ohio State U., 1896; A.M., Harvard, 1898, Ph.D., 1899; married; children—Elizabeth Sally, Christine Louise, Mead Nicholas. During 1899-1900 made trip around the world, studying tropical agr. Prof. botany and entomology, Okla. A. and M. Coll., 1900-01; prof. plant physiology and pathology, Ala. Poly. Inst., 1901-08; prof. plant pathology, U. of Neb., 1908-20; dir. Estacion Agronomica and Colegio de Agricultura, Santo Domingo, 1920-21; prof. biology, Transylvania Coll. Capt. O.R.C., Sanitary Corps, U.S.A. Fellow A.A.A.S. Mason. Episcopalian. Contbr. to bot. jours. of articles on original researches and bulls., Okla., Ala. and Neb. expt. stas. Died 1931.

WILCOX, Ella Wheeler, author; b. (Wheeler) Johnstown Centre, Wis., 1855; ed. U. of Wis.; m. Robert M. Wilcox, 1884 (died 1916). Contbr. New York Journal and Chicago American. Author: An Ambitious Man; A Double Life; Drops of Water; Sweet Danger; Was It Suicide? Every-Day Thoughts; Poems of Passion; Maurine; Poems of Pleasure; Three Women; Kingdom of Love, and Other Poems; An Erring Woman's Love; Men, Women and Emotions; The Beautiful Land of Nod; Poems of Power; Around the Year with Ella Wheeler Wilcox (birthday book); A Woman of the World, 1904; Poems of Sentiment, 1906; New Thought Common Sense and What Life Means to Me; The Love Sonnets of Abelard and Heloise; Poems of Progress and New Thought Pastels, 1909; Sailing Sunny Seas, 1910; Gems, 1912; Picked Poems, 1912; Woman of the World, 1912; Art of Being Alive, 1914; Cameos, 1914; Historical Mother Goose, 1914; Poems of Problems, 1914; Lest We Forget, 1915; World Voices, 1916; The World and I (autobiography), 1918. In Europe as representative of the Red Star, 1918. Home: Short Beach, Conn. Died Oct. 31, 1919.

WILCOX, Elmer Almy, prof. law; b. Tiverton, R.I., Dec. 6, 1867; s. Edward and Florence Almyra (Almy) W.; A.B., Brown U., 1891; m. Alice B. Borden, July 11, 1899. Admitted to bar, R.I., Feb. 19, 1894, U.S. Circuit Ct., Jan. 2, 1897; practiced at Providence, 1894-99; instr. law, Brown U., 1894-99; prof. law, State U. of Ia., 1899—. Pres. Boerner-Fry Co., 1909-15. Asso. mem. Nat. Child Labor Com.; del. Universal Congress Lawyers and Jurists, St. Louis, 1904, Nat. Conf. on Criminal Law and Criminology, Chicago, 1909. Democrat. Branch chmn. Mil. Training Camps Assn., 1917—. Died Nov. 20. 1929.

WILCOX, George Horace, mfr.; b. Meriden, Conn., Aug. 22, 1856; s. Horace C. and Charlotte A. (Smith) W.; Ph.B., Yale, 1875; m. Nettie B. Curtis, Jan. 23, 1884; children—Harold Curtis (dec.), Roy Cornwell, Horace Cornwell. Entered mfg. business at Meriden, 1875; chmn. bd. Internat. Silver Co. (founded 1898). Republican. Conglist. Mason. Home: Meriden, Connecticut. Died Nov. 26, 1940.

WILCOX, Henry Buckley, banker; b. Baltimore, May 23, 1864; s. William Littleton and Susannah Helen (Perry) W.; ed. Baltimore City Coll., 1876-79; m. Katharine Elizabeth Wirt, Nov. 5, 1889. Clk. in Office of Riddle & Fisher, grain mchts., Baltimore, 1879-81; runner, with 1st Nat. Bank, 1881-83; with Farmers & Merchants Nat. Bank, 1883-93; cashier Equitable Nat. Bank, 1893-1900, and of its successor, 1st Nat. Bank, 1900-10; pres. 1st Nat. Bank, 1910-16; v.p. Merchants-Mechanics Nat. Bank, 1916-21, Merchants Nat. Bank, 1921—. Dir. Fed. Res. Bank, Richmond, 1916-18; pres. Motoramp Garages of Md., Inc.; treas. J. E. Smith Co.; dir. mem. exec. com. U.S. Fidelity & Guaranty Co., Md. Trust Co., Woodlawn Cemetery Co.; dir. 1st Nat. Bank (Onancock, Va.), Baltimore br. Fed. Res. Bank. Chmn. Bd. of Finance Commrs. City of Baltimore; chmn. exec. com. Baltimore Clearing House. Mil. aide to Gov. Lloyd Lowndes, rank of col., 1896-1900. Republican. Methodist. Mason. Home: Baltimore, Md. Died Apr. 22, 1931.

WILCOX, Marrion, author; b. Augusta, Ga., Apr. 3, 1858; s. Daniel Hand and Frances Louisa (Ansley) W.; A.B., Yale, 1878; admitted to N.Y. bar; LL.B., Hamilton, 1880; spl. studies univs. of Oxford, Heidelberg, Jena and Berlin; abroad, 1881-83, 1888-90; m. Eleanor Patricia Sanchez, Apr. 2, 1885; 1 dau., Mrs. Nina Wilcox Putnam. Instr. at Yale, 1884-86; prominent in 1902 as advocate of fair play to Cuba, defending principle of reciprocity on the part of U.S. and urging concessions from polit. leaders and econ. assns. of Cuba, approximately embodied in treaty submitted to Congress and accepted in 1903. Visited S. America, Mexico, etc., 1906-07; at request, 1907, of Yale U. suggested, especially in Mexico, Brazil and Argentina, interchange of professors between U.S. and Latin Am. countries; advocate of increase of Y.M.C.A. work in S. America. Author: A Short History of the War with Spain; Sketches in Spain, England and Italy; Harper's History of the War in the Philippines, 1900. Wrote, 1900-09, for North Am. Rev., Churchman, Atlantic Monthly, Scientific American, Harper's, Ency. Americana (nearly entire dept. of S. and Central America and W.I.), Putnam's, etc.; contbr. to Architectural Record and other periodicals, 1915, and to Art and Life, Internat. Studio, and Architectural Record, 1917-21, and for latter, 1923-25. Editor Ency. of Latin America. Completed for Labour (novel), 1923. Home: New York, N.Y. Died Dec. 26, 1926.

WILCOX, Reynold Webb, M.D.; b. Madison, Conn., Mar. 29, 1856; s. Col. Vincent Meigs and Catherine Millicent (Webb) W.; B.A., Yale, 1878; M.D., Harvard, 1881; post-grad. med. study at Vienna, Heidelberg, Paris, Edinburgh, 1881-82; hon. M.A., Hobart, 1881; LL.D., Maryville, 1892; D.C.L., Wittenberg, 1915; m. Grace, d. Col. Floyd Clarkson, Dec. 12, 1917. Prof. medicine, New York Post-Grad. Med. Sch., 1884-1908; consultant in medicine, St. Mark's Hosp., 1910—; cons. physician, Ossining Hosp., 1910—, Eastern Long Island Hosp., 1913—; cons. internist, N.J. State Hospital, 1917—. Major M.R.C., U.S.A., on duty as instr., Camp Greenleaf, Fort Oglethorpe, Ga., 1917; lt. col., 1924. Pres. Am. Therapeutic Soc., 1901-02, Am. Assn. Med. Jurisprudence, 1913-14, Am. Congress on Internal Medicine, 1915-17, Am. Coll. of Physicians, 1915-21, Harvard Med. Soc., 1894-95, Med. Assn. Greater City of N.Y., 1910-14, N.Y. Soc. Med. Jurisprudence, 1912-14, N.Y. div. Assn. of Med. Reserve Corps U.S.A., 1914-16; fellow A.A.A.S.; mem. Soc. American Wars (surgeon gen., 1915-27; comdr. N.Y. Comdry., 1919-20), Society Colonial Wars, S.R., War of 1812 (v.p. Pa. Soc. 1897-1925; v.p. gen. 1908-25; pres. gen. 1925). Author: System of Case Records, 1887; Materia Medica and Therapeutics, 1892 (12 edits.); Manual of Fever Nursing, 1904 (2 edits.); Treatment of Disease, 1907 (4 edits.); also (genealogical) The Descendants of William Wilcoxson, Vincent Meigs and Richard Webb, 1893; Madison—Her Soldiers, 1890; and numerous med. and hist. papers. Home: Princeton, N.J. Died June 6, 1931.

WILCOX, Robert William, del. to Congress; b. Kuhulu, Honuaula, Island of Maui, H.I., Feb. 15, 1855; s. of Capt. William S. W., of Newport, R.I., and Kalua Makoleokalani of Honuaula; prep. edn. in Hawaiian schs.; grad. Royal Mil. Acad., Turin, Italy, as sub lt., 1885; entered in Royal Application School for Engr. and Arty. Officers, Turin, Italy, 1885-87; m. Baroness Gina Sobrero, July 20, 1887; m. 2d, Princess Theresa Owana Kaohelelani, Aug. 20, 1896. Rep. in Hawaiian legislature from Wailuku, Maui, 1880; led revolution in Honolulu to restore old Constitution, 1889; rep. from Honolulu, Hawaiian legislature, 1890, from Koolauloa, Island of Oahu, 1892; led Diamond Head revolution against Dole govt. to restore Queen Liliuokalani, 1895; condemned to death, but U.S. senate intervened, and Pres. Dole commuted sentence to 35 years at hard labor, with $10,000 fine; pardoned, 1896; del. to Congress from Hawaii, 1901-03. Home: Honolulu, H.I. Died 1903.

WILCOX, Sidney Freeman, surgeon; b. Ft. Atkinson, Wis., Aug. 13, 1855; s. A. D. and Ann Sophia (Morrison) W.; M.D., New York Homœ. Med. Coll. and Hosp., 1880; m. Emily Hurd White, Sept. 27, 1881. Prof. clin. surgery, New York Med. Coll. and Hosp. for Women, 1893-1915, emeritus, 1915—; cons. surgeon same, and New York Ophthal. Hosp., Laura Franklin Free Hosp. for Children, Memorial Hosp. for Women and Children (Brooklyn), St. Mary's Hosp. (Passaic, N.J.), Grace Hosp. (New Haven, Conn.), Wesson Memorial Hosp. (Springfield, Mass.), Hahnemann Hosp. (N.Y.). Prof. surgery N.Y. Homœ. Med. Coll. and Flower Hosp. Fellow Am. Coll. Surgeons. Republican. Presbyn. Deceased.

WILCOX, Timothy Erastus, brig. gen.; b. N.Y. State, Apr. 26, 1840; s. Rodney and Emily W.; A.B., Union Coll., N.Y., 1861, A.M., 1864; M.D., Albany Medical Coll., 1864; m. Clara B. Brown, Jan. 29, 1867; children—Victor Irving (dec.), Florence E., Glover Brown (dec.). Asst. surgeon 6th N.Y. Heavy Arty., Jan. 4, 1865; asst. surgeon U.S.V., Apr. 25, 1865-June 4, 1866. In regular army, asst. surgeon, May 14, 1867-July 1, 1868; resigned, July 1, 1868; asst. surgeon, Nov. 10, 1874; capt. asst. surgeon, Nov. 10, 1879; maj. surgeon, Feb. 24, 1891; lt. col. deputy surgeon gen. May 7, 1902; col. asst. surgeon gen., Sept. 22, 1903; retired with rank of brig. gen., Apr. 26, 1904. Lt. col., chief surgeon vols., Nov. 12, 1898-May 12, 1899. Home: Washington, D.C. Died Dec. 10, 1932.

WILCOX, William Craig, educator; b. Pittsfield, Mass., Jan. 16, 1867; s. William Henry Harrison and Harriet Louise (Craig) W.; A.B., U. of Rochester, N.Y., 1888, A.M., 1891; fellow political science, U. of Chicago, 1892-94; LL.D., Coe College, Ia., 1910, U. of Rochester, 1913; m. Mary DeVol, July 1, 1895. Prof. Am. history and head of dept., 1894—, dean Coll. Liberal Arts, 1909—, State U. of Ia. Lecturer on Am. and European history, 1894—; sec. univ. extension div., State U. of Ia., 1901—. Mugwump. Conglist. Home: Iowa City, Ia. Died Oct. 5, 1916.

WILCZYNSKI, Ernest Julius, coll. prof.; b. Hamburg, Germany, Nov. 13, 1876; s. Max and Friederike (Hurwitz) W.; A.M., Ph.D., U. of Berlin, 1897; m. Countess Ines Macola, Aug. 9, 1906. Computer, Nautical Almanac Office; Washington, 1898; instr. math., summer session, Columbian (now George Washington) U., 1898, instr., asst. prof. and asso. prof. math., U. of Calif., 1898-1907; asso. prof. math., U. of Ill., 1907-10; asso. prof. mathematics, 1910-14, prof., 1914—, U. of Chicago. Research asst. and asso. Carnegie Instn., 1903-05; lecturer New Haven Colloquium, 1906. Fellow A.A.A.S.; laureate, Royal Belgian Acad. Sciences. Author: Projective Differential Geometry of Curves and Ruled Surfaces, 1906; The New Haven Colloquium (with E. H. Moore and Max Mason), 1910; Plane Trigonometry and Applications, 1913; College Algebra with Applications, 1916. Home: Chicago, Ill. Died Sept. 15, 1932.

WILD, Harrison Major, organist, conductor; b. Hoboken, N.J., Mar. 6, 1861; s. Thomas Samuel and Georgina Hannah W.; mus. edn. under Arthur J. Creswold, and, 1878-79, at Leipzig; studied in Chicago, 1879-83; m. Gertrude Younglove Cornell, Oct. 29, 1884. Five years organist Ascension Ch., Memorial Ch., 1 yr., at Unity Ch., 13 yrs., at Grace P.E. Ch., Chicago, 25 yrs. Condr. of Apollo Club, Chicago. Home: Chicago, Ill. Died Mar. 1, 1929.

WILDE, George Francis Faxon, rear adm. U.S.N.; b. Braintree, Mass., Feb. 23, 1845; s. William Read and Mary Elizabeth (Thayer) W.; grad. U.S. Naval Acad., 1864; m. Emogen B. Howard, Dec. 13, 1868. Master, 1866; lt. comdr., Dec. 18, 1868; comdr., Oct. 1885; capt., Aug. 10, 1898; rear adm., Aug. 10, 1904; retired, Feb. 20, 1905. Served on flagship Susquehanna, 1864-67; went to Havana with fleet for Confederate ram Stonewall Jackson; later served on Albany, Tennessee, Wabash; comdr. U.S. monitor Canonicus, 1873-74; exec. officer U.S.S. Vandalia, 1878-82; comd. U.S.S., Dolphin, 1885-88, making cruise around the world—she being first steel vessel of U.S. Navy to circumnavigate the globe; sec. Lighthouse Bd., 1894-98; introduced gas buoys on Great Lakes; established electric light vessel off Diamond Shoal, Cape Hatteras, introduced telephone to light vessels from shore; comd. U.S. ram Katahdin in operations around Cuba, Mar.-Sept., 1898; ordered to command Boston; landed first marines ever landed in China and sent them to Peking, where they guarded legation, Nov. 1898-Apr. 1899; captured and occupied city of Iloilo, Feb. 11, 1899; captured Vigan, Feb. 18, 1900 (received thanks from Spanish Govt. for rescuing 160 Spanish officers and families at Vigan); comd. battleship Oregon, May 29, 1899-Jan. 16, 1901. Capt. Navy Yard, Portsmouth, N.H., 1901-02, Navy Yard, Boston, 1903-04; commandant Navy Yard, League Island, Pa., Feb.-May 1904, Navy Yard, Boston, May 1, 1904-Feb. 20, 1905. Chmn. Mass. Nautical Training Sch. Commn., 1906—. Home: North Easton, Mass. Died 1911.

WILDE, Norman, univ. prof.; b. Dobbs Ferry, N.Y., June 12, 1867; s. James and Harriet Richards (DeWitt) W.; A.B., Columbia, 1889, Ph.D., 1894, Litt.D., 1929; U. of Berlin, 1891-93, Harvard, 1893-94; m. Edna May Judson, Aug. 8, 1894; 1 dau., Lois Huntington. Asst. in philosophy, Columbia, 1894-98; instr. philosophy, 1898-1900, asst. prof., 1900-02, prof., 1902-36, U. of Minn. Democrat. Author: Friedrich Heinrich Jacobi, a Study in German Realism, 1894; The Ethical Basis of the State, 1925. Died Dec. 26, 1936.

WILDER, Alexander, physician, journalist, author; b. Verona, N.Y., May 14, 1823; s. Abel W.; ed. principally at home; grad. Syracuse Med. Coll., 1850, M.D., New York Homœ. Med. Coll. and U.S. Med. Coll.; widower. Practiced medicine, Syracuse; in editorial work Syracuse Star, 1852-53, Journal, 1853; clerk State Dept. Public Instruction, 1854-55; editor New York Teacher, 1856; College Review, 1857; on New York Evening Post, 1858-71; alderman New York (anti-Tweed), 1872; insp. schools, 1873; sec. Nat. Eclectic Med. Assn., 1876-95 (edited 19 vols. "Transactions"); Eclectic Med. Soc. of N.Y. (edited "Transactions," 1870, 1871, 1872); pres. Sch. of Philosophy, New York; mem. Medico Legal Soc., asso. editor Metaphysical Mag., contbr. to same and to The Platonist, etc. Author: Plea for the Collegiate Education of Women, 1876; Entheasm, 1881; The Soul, 1884; Psychology as a Science, 1884; Fire —Plutonian and Promethean, 1884; Higher Sources of Knowledge, 1884; Life Eternal, 1885; Paul and Plato, 1885; Ethics and Philosophy of the Zoroasters, 1885; Ancient Symbolism and Serpent Worship, 1886; Later Platonists, 1887; Philosophical Papers, 1890; Creation and Evolution, 1895; Antecedent Life, 1895; Philosophy a Factor in Progress, 1897; Egypt and Egyptian Dynasties, 1899; The Imagination, 1900; Ganglionic Nervous System, 1900; Perennial Life, 1902; History of Medicine, 1902. Translator and editor of Iamblichos on Egyption Mysteries, 1902; Plato and His Doctrines, 1904; Exegesis of Love, 1906; Evil, 1907. Died 1908.

WILDER, Amos Parker, editor; b. Calais, Me., Feb. 15, 1862; s. Dr. Amos and Charlotte (Porter) W.; A.B., Yale, 1884, Ph.D., 1892; m. Isabel T. Niven, Dec. 3, 1894; children—Amos Niven, Thorton Niven, Charlotte Elizabeth, Isabel, Janet Frances. Editor New Haven Palladium, 1888-92; later editorial writer New York; connected with Wis. State Journal, 1894-1911. Am. consul-gen. at Hong Kong, China, 1906-09, Shanghai, China, 1909-14; sec. Yale-in-China Movement, New Haven, 1914-20; asso. editor New Haven Journal-Courier, 1920-29. Home: New Haven, Conn. Died July 2, 1936.

WILDER, Arthur Ashford, judge; b. Kaalaea, Oahu, H.I., Nov. 3, 1873; s. J. K. and Caroline (Crowninburg) W.; pub. and private schs.; LL.B., Yale U., 1897, M.L., 1898; m. Jane K. Giffard, Feb. 14, 1906. Reporter Constl. Convention of Hawaii, 1894. Mil. Commn., 1895; mem. law firm Robertson & Wilder, Honolulu, 1898-1905; asso. justice Supreme Ct. of H.T., 1905—. Congregationalist. Democrat. One of compilers Revised Laws of Hawaii, 1905. Home: Honolulu, H.T. Deceased.

WILDER, Burt Green, educator and author; b. Boston, Mass., Aug. 11, 1841; s. David and Celia Colton (Burt) W.; B.S., in anatomia summa cum laude, Lawrence Scientific Sch. (Harvard), 1862, M.D., 1866; m. Sarah Cowell Nichols, June 9, 1868 (died 1904); m. 2d, Mary Field, June 11, 1906 (died 1922). In U.S.A., July 1862-Sept. 1865, as med. cadet, asst. surg. and surg. 55th Mass. Inf. (colored); asst. in comparative anatomy, Mus. Comparative Zoölogy, 1866-68; curator herpetology, Boston Soc. Nat. Hist., 1867-68; prof. neurol. and vertebrate zoölogy, Cornell U., Ithaca, N.Y., 1867-1910, emeritus, 1910—. Lecturer on comparative anatomy, Anderson (Agassiz) Summer Sch. of Natural History, 1873-74, and 1875, summer schs. at Peoria and Normal, Ill.; on physiology, Med. Sch. of Me., 1875-84, and U. of Mich., 1876; at Lowell Inst., 1866, 1871. Mem. advisory council Simplified Spelling Board; v.p. Non-Smokers Protective League. In 1863, nr. Charleston, S.C., reeled 150 yards of silk from a spider since identified as Nephila clavipes; in 1865 silk from these spiders was woven into ribbon on a steamloom; the account of their habits, in the Atlantic, Aug., 1866, was the only article ever illustrated by that mag. Devised the "Slip-system of notes," 1867, and the "Correspondence-slip," 1884. Prepared nearly 2000 vertebrate brains, including 13 from educated persons. Advocated (since 1880) the simplification of anatomic nomenclature; the dissection of the cat as a pre-requisite to that of man, 1879; the objective study of the brain in primary schs. (1889), and (1905) beginning with the brain of the acanth shark; temperance as distinct from total abstinence (1869); and (1873) the use of chloroform in capital punishment. The first American "Festschrift" was the "Wilder Quarter-Century Book," comprising papers prepared for the occasion by 15 former pupils, presented at the 25th anniversary of the opening of Cornell University. Author: What Young People Should Know, 1874; Anatomical Technology (with S. A. Gage), 1882; Physiology Practicums; Emergencies, 1888; Health Notes for Students, 1890; The Brain of the Sheep, 1903; biographic articles on Jeffries Wyman, 1874, Louis Agassiz, 1907; Founder's Hymn, words and music, 1907; Fiat Justitia, internat. hymn for first Universal Races Congress, 1911, words and music; Old Ironsides, music, the words by O.W. Holmes, 1912, arranged by N. C. Page for full orchestra and as one of Ditson's School Songs, 1916; The Peacemaker, words by Joyce Kilmer; also several other songs, many scientific papers, mostly on the brain, numerous revs. and articles in mags. and in the Reference Handbook of Med. Sciences. Died Jan. 22, 1925.

WILDER, Charlotte Frances, author; b. Templeton, Mass.; d. Col. Elijah and Hannah (Lawrence) Felt; g.d. Samuel Felt, minute man, Lexington, Mass.; graduate high sch.; m. George Carter Wilder, Lancaster, Mass., Nov. 21, 1861. Began writing for press, 1871; Bible teacher from age of 16; teacher of over 3,000 young men, coll. students, 1870—; pres. Topeka branch Woman's Foreign Missionary Soc. M.E. Ch., 1895-1902, mem. literature com., 1902—; regent of Kan. for The Woman's Guild of The Am. U., Washington. Author: Land of the Rising Sun, 1877; Sister Ridnour's Sacrifice, 1883; Polly Button's New Year (in the "Worth While" Series), 1892; Entertainments (with Elizabeth W. Champney), 1879; Christmas Cheer in All Lands, 1905; Easter Gladness, 1906; Mission Ships, 1907; The Child's Own Book, 1910; The Wonderful Story of Jesus, 1911; The Story of the Very First Christmas, 1915; The Story of Ruth (in Wilder Series), 1914; The Story of Esther, 1916; The Book of Job, 1916. Contbr. stories and editorial work to Methodist papers and mags. and other publs. Died Dec. 1916.

WILDER, Daniel Webster, editor; b. Blackstone, Mass., July 15, 1832; s. Dr. Abel W.; A.B., Harvard, 1856; studied Harvard Law Sch.; hon. A.M., U. of Kan., 1876; m. Mary E. Irvin, Mar. 3, 1864. Surveyor gen. of Kan., and of Neb., state auditor and supt. ins. of Kansas; pub. and editor Insurance Magazine, Kansas City. Pres. State Hist. Society of Kan. Author: Annals of Kansas, 1875, 1886; Life of Shakespeare, 1893. Assisted in compiling all edits. of Bartlett's Familiar Quotations, 1855-91. Home: Hiawatha, Kan. Died 1911.

WILDER, George Warren, publisher; b. Sterling, Mass., Mar. 29, 1866; s. Jones Warren and Jane E. (Raymore) W.; B.A., Amherst, 1889; m. Gertrude C. Stowe, Dec. 1, 1892; children—Mrs. Gertrude Esty, George Warren, Jr., Stowe, Donald, Helen C., John Clark; m. 2d, Abby L. Alger, Jan. 10, 1920. Admitted to N.Y. bar; became connected with The Butterick Pub. Co., of which became pres.; also pres. The Butterick Co., New York; retired, 1926; mem. N.H. legislature. Mason. Home: Rindge, N.H. Died Feb. 18, 1931.

WILDER, Gerrit Parmile, horticulturist; b. Honolulu, Hawaii, Nov. 5, 1863; s. Samuel Gardner and Elizabeth Kinau (Judd) W.; student Oahu Coll., Honolulu; M.S., U. of Hawaii, 1923; m. Lillian Kimball, Nov. 7, 1887. Supt. Kahului Ry. Co., Maui, 1884-96, pres., 1896-98; pres. Estate S. G. Wilder, Ltd., 1898—; retired from active business to devote time to horticulture, 1898; U.S. dep. protector H.I. Bird Reservation, 1918—; asso. in botany Bernice P. Bishop Mus., Honolulu, 1924, and made 4 bot. expdns. to South Seas, West Indies, Ceylon, etc., introducing into Hawaii from these countries many tropical trees, plants, etc. Fellow Royal Soc. of Arts (London). Republican. Mason. Author: Fruits of the Hawaiian Islands, 1906, 11; Breadfruit of Tahiti, 1928; Flora of Rarotonga, 1931. Home: Honolulu, Hawaii. Died Sept. 29, 1935.

WILDER, Harris Hawthorne, zoölogist; b. Bangor, Me., Apr. 7, 1864; s. Solon (musical director) and Sarah Watkins (Smith) W.; A.B., Amherst, 1886; Ph.D., U. of Freiburg (Baden), 1891; m. Inez Luanne Whipple, July 26, 1906. Prof. zoölogy, Smith Coll., 1892—. Fellow Am. Acad. Arts and Sciences. Author: Invertebrate Zoölogy, 1894; Synopsis of Animal Classification, 1902; The History of the Human Body, 1910, 2d edit., 1923; Personal Identification (with B. Wentworth), 1918; Manual of Anthropometry, 1920; Man's Prehistoric Past, 1923; The Pedigree of the Human Race, 1925; also numerous papers on vertebrate anatomy and physical anthropology, especially on amphibians, diploteratology and the epidermic markings of human and simian palms and soles. Home: Northampton, Mass. Died Feb. 1928.

WILDER, Herbert Augustus, mfr.; b. Attleboro, Mass., June 22, 1837; s. Charles B. and Mary Ann (Guild) W.; ed. pub. schs.; m. Sara B. Page, Oct. 11, 1871 (died 1891). Entered paper business, 1858; mem. Wilder & Co.; dir. Internat. Paper Co. Trustee Newton Hosp. Republican. Home: Newton, Mass. Died Oct. 12, 1922.

WILDER, Herbert Merrill, illustrator; b. Hinsdale, N.H., Sept. 26, 1864; s. George Sheldon and Eliza Ann (Clark) W.; common sch. edn.; studied Cowles Art Sch., Boston. Illustrator of numerous books, and for Harper's and other leading publs. Home: Hinsdale, N.H. Deceased.

WILDER, Inez Whipple; b. Diamond Hill, R.I., May 19, 1871; d. of Eliab Daniel and Sarah (Wheaton) Whipple; grad. R.I. State Normal Sch., 1890; Ph.B., Brown U., 1900; M.A., Smith Coll., 1904; m. Harris Hawthorne Wilder, July 26, 1906. Teacher of zoölogy, Smith Coll., 1902—, and later prof. same. Author: Laboratory Studies in Mammalian Anatomy, 1913, 23; Morphology of Amphibian Metamorphosis, 1925; also contbr. on mammalian palm and sole configuration, anatomy, embryology and life history of amphibians; life history of the salamander Desmognathus, etc. Home: Northampton, Mass. Died Apr. 29, 1929.

WILDER, John Emery, tanner, merchant; b. Lancaster, Mass., Apr. 16, 1861; s. Charles Lewis and Harriet Ellen (Harris) W.; B.S., Mass. Agrl. Coll., 1882; m. Laura Hurlbut, Apr. 14, 1886 (died 1915); children—Lawrence Russell, Emory Hurlbut, Lois (Mrs. Robert M. Landreth), Antoinette (Mrs. Charles A. Ball); m. 2d, Fanny M. Barnhart, Sept. 8, 1917. Began as clerk, Wilder & Hale, Nov. 1, 1882; became salesman, 1883, partner, 1886, name of firm changed, 1887, to Wilder & Co. (bro., Thomas E., sr. mem.), tanners and leather merchants, v.p., 1906-19, pres. 1919—; dir. and chmn. J. W. & A. P. Howard Co., Ltd., Corry, Pa.; dir. Central Republic Bank & Trust Co.; trustee Northwestern Mut. Life Ins. Co. Hon. trustee Beloit Coll. Republican. Presbyn. Home: Evanston, Ill. Died July 25, 1932.

WILDER, Laurence Russell, elec. engr., mfr.; b. Oak Park, Ill., Nov. 22, 1887; s. John E. and Laura (Hurlbut) W.; Junior M.E., Lewis Inst., Chicago, 1905; spl. study Princeton, 1906-08, Purdue, 1910-12; m. Dorothée Richardson, Dec. 3, 1924. Built first large scale production small internal combustion engine, Aero Motor Co., Chicago, 1907-08; exec. mgr. Wilder Tanning Co., Waukegan, Ill., 1909-17; aircraft production, Washington, D.C., 1917-18; pres. Fansteel Products Co., North Chicago, mfrs. electric specialties, 1919-21; rep. in U.S. of Brown Boveri & Co., Ltd., Switzerland, 1922-24, acquiring Am. rights in latter yr.; organized Am. Brown Boveri Electric Corp., 1925, acquiring N.Y. Shipbuilding Corp. (Camden, N.J.), Condit Electrical Mfg. Corp. (Boston) and Moloney Electric Co. (St. Louis); pres. Am. Brown Boveri Electric Corp., 1925-27, chmn. advisory com. of the company's shipbuilding div., also chmn. bds. Moloney Electric Co., Condit Elec. Mfg. Corp., and Trans-oceanic Corp. of the U.S., and pres. Scintilla Magnetos Co., Inc., Sidney, N.Y. Republican. Presbyn. Built first Scintilla magnetos, later standard for aviation ignition, 1925. Home: New York, N.Y. Died Nov. 16, 1937.

WILDER, Mrs. Louise Beebe, writer; b. Baltimore, Md., Jan. 30, 1878; d. Charles Stuart and Mary Harrison (McCormick) Beebe; ed. pvt. schs., Baltimore; m. Walter Robb Wilder, Nov. 18, 1902; children—Walter Beebe, Harrison (daughter). Democrat. Author: My Garden, 1916; Colour in My Garden, 1918; Adventures in My Garden and Rock Garden, 1923; Problems and Pleasures of a Rock Garden, 1927; Lucius Beebe of Wakefield; Adventures in a Suburban Garden; The Fragrant Path; What Happens in My Garden, 1934. Contbr. to House and Garden, Horticulture, etc. Home: Bronxville, N.Y. Died Apr. 20, 1938.

WILDER, Marshall Pinckney, entertainer; b. Geneva, N.Y., Sept. 19, 1859; s. Dr. Louis de Valois and Mary A. (Hoffman) W.; owing to physical disability edn. limited to few terms in pub. schs. of N.Y.; m. Sophia Cornell Hanks, June 24, 1903 (dec.). Became a pedlar, later file boy, Bradstreet's Comml. Agency; began to entertain at fifty cents per night; later began to travel; went to London, 1883, where appeared before the Prince of Wales (later King Edward VII); entertained at London annually, 1883-99; in vaudeville, 1899—; toured the world, 1904-05. Author: People I's Smiled With, 1888; The Sunny Side of the Street, 1905; Smiling Around the World, 1907. Editor: The Ten Books of the Merrymakers, 1908. Died Jan. 10, 1915.

WILDER, Ralph Everett, cartoonist; b. Worcester, Mass., Feb. 23, 1875; s. Frank N. and Susan (Danforth) W.; ed. Chicago pub. schs., Morgan Park Acad., Art Inst., Chicago and Chicago Art Acad.; m. Charlotte L. White, Sept. 20, 1900. Cartoonist on Chicago Record-Herald, June 6, 1903—. Home: Morgan Park, Ill. Died Feb. 19, 1924.

WILDER, Robert Parmelee; b. Kolhapur, India, Aug. 2, 1863; s. Royal Gould and Eliza Jane (Smith) W.; A.B., Coll. of N.J. (now Princeton U.), 1886, A.M., 1888; grad. Union Theol. Sem., 1891; D.D., Ursinus Coll., 1925; m. Helene Sophie Olsson, Sept. 7 1892; children—Elizabeth Leonore, Grace Helene, Ruth Evelyn, Mary Dorothy. Founder, 1886, and later traveling sec. and mem. exec. com., Student Vol. Movement for Foreign Missions; founder Brit. Student Vol. Missionary Union, 1892; nat. sec. Intercollegiate Y.M.C.A. of India and Ceylon, and gen. sec. Indian Nat. Council, Y.M.C.A., 1899-1902; traveling sec., Student Vol. Movement of Norway, Sweden, Denmark and Finland, 1903-04; sec. Brit. Student Christian Movement, 1905-16; while in England mem. exec. com. Nat. Laymen's Missionary Movement of England; mem. Nat. Council Y.M.C.A. (Eng.); sr. sec. religious work dept. of Internat. Com. Y.M.C.A., 1916-Sept. 1919; during World War I served as dir. religious work bur., Nat. War Work Council of Y.M.C.A.; gen. sec. Student Vol. Movement for Foreign Missions, 1919-27; exec. sec. Near East Christian Council, 1927-33. As rep. of the World's Student Christian Fedn addressed students in nearly every country of Europe Fellow Am. Geog. Soc. Presbyn. Author: Among India's Students, 1899; Christ and the Student World, 1935; The Student Volunteer Movement—Its Origin and Early History, 1935; The Great Commission (the missionary response of the S. V. M. in North America and Europe), 1936; also various pamphlets on religious topics. Died Mar. 27, 1938.

WILDER, T(homas) Edward, tanner; b. Lancaster, Mass., Aug. 15, 1855; s. Charles Lewis and Harriet Ellen (Harris) W.; B.S. in Mech. Engring., Worcester Poly. Inst., 1874; m. Anna G. Tucker, Sept. 2, 1880. Began as clk. with Walker, Oakley & Co., Chicago, 1875; started for self in leather business, 1878; mem. Wilder & Hale, mfrs. of cut soles, etc., 1879, later Wilder & Co., of which was pres.; chmn. J. W. & A. P. Howard & Co., Ltd., Corry, Pa.; dir. Counselman & Co., investment bankers, Chicago. An organizer Chicago Assn. of Commerce, Nat. Assn. of Tanners, Chamber of Commerce, U.S.A. and officer in each: Ill. v.p. Nat. Rivers and Harbors Congress (dir. for Great Lakes Dist.); chmn. Am. delegation 6th Internat. Congress of Chambers of Commerce, Paris, 1914; councillor for Nat. Assn. Tanners in Chamber Commerce U.S.A. Trustee Worcester Poly. Inst.; dir. Infant Welfare Soc. Republican. Unitarian. Home: Elmhurst, Ill. Died Aug. 22, 1919.

WILDER, William Hamlin, ophthalmologist; b. Covington, Ky., Dec. 16, 1860; s. Josiah and Emma (Morse) W.; A.B., Belmont Coll., Cincinnati, 1878; M.D., Med. Coll. of Ohio, 1884; grad. study U. of Göttingen, Germany, 1889, U. of Vienna, 1890, also in hosps. of Berlin and London; m. Ella Taylor, June 10, 1884; children—Russell Morse, Laura Carroll (dec.); m. 2d, Carrie Rothschild, Dec. 25, 1907; children—William Hamlin (dec.), Margaret. Began practice at Cincinnati, 1884; moved to Chicago, 1892; specialist in diseases of the eye; prof. ophthalmology, Rush Med. Coll., U. of Chicago, 1907-26, prof. emeritus, 1926—; hon. surgeon, Ill. Eye and Ear Infirmary; ophthalmologist Presbyn. Hospital. Maj. Med. R.C. Fellow Am. Coll. Surgeons. Ind. Republican. Contbr. monograph and articles to med. jours. on ophthalmic surgery; also collaborator on several books on ophthalmology. Home: Chicago, Ill. Died Sept. 24, 1935.

WILDER, William Henry, clergyman; b. nr. Greenfield, Ill., July 7, 1849; s. Samuel and Margaret Jane (Davidson) W.; A.B., Ill. Wesleyan Univ., 1873, A.M., 1882, D.D., 1888, LL.D., 1907; m. Sallie, d. Rev. Frank Smith, 1874. Ordained M.E. ministry, 1873; presiding elder Decatur Dist., 1884-88; pres. Ill. Wesleyan U., 1888-97; presiding elder Quincy Dist., 1897, Champaign Dist., 1898-1905; pastor Jacksonville, Ill., 1905-06; pres. Lucy Webb Hayes Nat. Training Sch. for Missionaries and Deaconesses, 1908-15; prof. English Bible and comparative religions, Ill. Wesleyan U., 1915—. Del. Gen. Confs., 1888, 96, 1900, 04 (chmn. Ill. delegation), and 1908; del. Ecumenical Conf., London, 1901; sec. Ill. Conf., Claimant Fund and Gen. Conf. Commn., 1907. Pres. Preacher's Aid Soc. of Ill. Conf., 1915—. Died Mar. 1, 1920.

WILDER, William Henry, congressman; b. Belfast, Me., May 14, 1855; s. Jonas Brooks and Louisa (Davidson) W.; ed. country schs.; m. Helen M. Laws, Nov. 20, 1876 (died 1909). Engaged in mercantile and mfg. business at Gardner, Mass., 1917—; pres. Wilder Industries, Inc., operating 5 plants in Mass.; admitted to bar, 1900, to Supreme Ct. U.S., 1909. Mem. 62d Congress (1911-13), 4th Mass. Dist. Republican. Studied monetary systems in Europe, 1909; wrote pamphlets and articles on monetary and other questions. Mason. Home: Gardner, Mass. Died Sept. 11, 1913.

WILDES, Frank, naval officer; b. Boston, June 17, 1843; s. Solomon Lovell and Sophia (Rice) W.; apptd. from Mass., 1860; grad. U.S. Naval Acad., 1863; apptd. ensign, May 28, 1863; apptd. steam sloop Lackawanna, West Gulf squadron, June 15, 1863; battle of Mobile and naval battery until surrender of Fort Morgan; monitor Chickasaw during operations in Mobile Bay, Mar. and Apr. 1865, till occupation of Mobile; m. Lucy A. Smith, Jan. 1, 1872. After war on various duties and stas.; master, 1866; lt., 1867; lt. comdr., Mar. 12, 1868; comdr., Apr. 1880; capt., July 1894; in command of cruiser Boston, Asiatic sta., 1895—; took part in battle of Manila, May 1, 1898; capt. of the yard, Navy Yard, New York, Apr. 1, 1899; rear admiral. Address: Navy Yard, New York. Died 1903.

WILDMAN, Edwin, editor, author; b. Corning, N.Y., May 9, 1867; s. Prof. Edwin and Helen (Rounsevelle) W.; grad. Elmira (N.Y.) High Sch.; studied Gen. Wesleyan Sem., Lima, N.Y., and Phillips Exeter Acad.; m. 3d, Susan Tyler Brooke. Entered Harvard, but left to become bus. mgr. of Rome (Ga.) Tribune; later editor and propr. Elmira Echoes, 1891-96; writer and war corr. Leslie's Weekly, 1897-98; vice and deputy consul gen. at Hong Kong, 1898-99. Spl. war corr., Philippines, 1898-1900; chief Asiatic staff and spl. commr. with Allied Troops in war in China, 1900-01, for the Hearst papers. Contbr. to American publications; corr. New York World, 1903-04; pres. and editor M.A.P. in America, 1906-07; pres. Wildman Mag. and News Service; pres. and editor The Forum Mag., 1918-20, v.p., 1921-23; pres. Edwin Wildman, Inc., New York. Pres. Rockland County Taxpayers, Pearl River, N.Y. In charge of paper-saving campaign, War Industries Board, New York, 1918-19; publicity, Rep. Nat. Com., Hughes, Harding and Coolidge campaigns; exec. dir. Caucasian Soc. of America, 1925-28. Author: Aguinaldo—A Narrative of Filipino Ambitions, 1901; Treaty Ports of China, 1902; Writing to Sell, 1915, 21, 24; America's Attitude Toward the War, 1917; Reconstructing America, Our Next Big Job, 1919; American Leaders of Industry, 1919, Vols. I and II, 1920-21; Famous Leaders of Character, 1922; Founders of America, 1924; Builders of America, 1925; Business Machines (with Perley Morse), 1931. Home: New York, N.Y. Died Nov. 3, 1932.

WILDMAN, Murray Shipley, economist; b. Selma, O., Feb. 22, 1868; s. John and Mary Taylor (Pugh) W.; Ph.B., Earlham Coll., Richmond, Ind., 1893; Ph.D., U. of Chicago, 1904; m. Olive Stigleman, Aug. 16, 1893; children—Caroline (dec.), Mary Frances. Teacher of history and Science, Spiceland Acad., Ind., 1893-95; founder, cashier and v.p. Henry County Bank, Spiceland, 1895-1902; supt. Spiceland Acad. and pub. schs., 1898-1901; asst. prof. economics, U. of Missouri, 1905-09; prof. economics and commerce, Northwestern U., 1909-12; prof. economics, Stanford, 1912—. Sec. Nat. Citizens' League, for promotion of sound banking system, 1911-12; bur. of research War Trade Bd., and div. planning and statistics War Industries Bd., 1918-19. Author: Money Inflation in the United States, 1905. Home: Stanford University, Calif. Died Dec. 25, 1930.

WILE, Frederic William, author, newspaper columnist and editorial writer; b. LaPorte, Ind., Nov. 30, 1873; s. Jacob and Henrietta (Guggenheim) W.; ed. U. of Notre Dame, LL.D., 1924; LL.D., Ursinus, 1929; m. Ada Shakman, May 14, 1901; children—Frederic William, Helen Isabel. Reporter Chicago Record, 1898-1900; corr. for Chicago Record and Chicago Daily News in London during Boer War, 1900-01, in Berlin, 1902-06; chief corr. London Daily Mail and affiliated Northcliffe newspapers in Germany, and Berlin corr. New York Times and Chicago Tribune, 1906-14. During World War I. edited column in Daily Mail, London, entitled "Germany Day by Day." Specialist on German Affairs, Intelligence Sect., G.H.Q., A.E.F., 1917-18; lt. col. Res. Corps (staff specialist), U.S.A. Chief of Washington bur. of The Public Ledger, Phila., 1919-22; later conducted the Frederic William Wile column of news-correspondence from Washington; editorial staff writer Washington Evening Star. Polit. analyst for Nat. Broadcasting Co., 1923-28, Columbia Broadcasting System, 1929-38. First radio commentator on transatlantic news events, at London Naval Conf., 1930; radio commentator from World Disarmament Conf., Geneva, 1932. Author: Our German Cousins, 1909; Men Around the Kaiser, 1913 (pub. in England, America and Germany); The Assault, 1916; Explaining the Britishers, 1918; Emile Berliner, Maker of the Microphone, 1926. Editor in chief: A Century of Industrial Progress, 1928; News Is Where You Find It (autobiography), 1939. Home: Washington, D.C. Died Apr. 7, 1941.

WILE, William Conrad, physician; b. Pleasant Valley, N.Y., Jan. 23, 1847; s. Rev. Benjamin Franklin and Betsy (Buckley) W.; M.D., Univ. Med. Coll. (New York U.), 1870; A.M., Central Coll., Ky., 1888; LL.D., Rutherford Coll., N.C., 1890; m. Eliza Scott Garrettson, 1871 (dec.), m. 2d, Hattie Adele Loomis, Sept. 1, 1887. Enlisted at 15 in Co. G, 150th N.Y. Inf.; served 2 yrs. and 8 mos.; at battle of Gettysburg and on march to the sea; hosp. steward in regular army 2 yrs.; began practice at New Brunswick, N.Y., 1870; at Highland, N.Y., 2 yrs., Newtown, Conn., 1873-86; prof. nervous diseases and electro-therapeutics, Medico-Chirurg. Coll., Phila., 1 year; at Danbury, Conn., from that time. Served as surgeon gen. G.A.R.; med. dir. 2 terms, Dept. of Conn. G.A.R. Founder, 1881, and editor until 1908. N.E. Med. Monthly. Republican. Died Feb. 21, 1913.

WILES, John Henry, corp. official; b. Poplar Plains, Ky., Apr. 28, 1861; s. Peter Blackstone and Jennie (Jones) W.; grad. Georgetown (Ky.) Coll., 1877; m. Ella G. McKnight, Nov. 30, 1882; 1 son, Richard Ernst. An organizer, 1883, partner W. A. Mount & Co., Kansas City, Mo., incorporated later as Mount Cracker & Candy Co., of which pres. until 1902; v.p. Loose-Wiles Biscuit Co., with mfg. plants in several cities, 1902-23, pres., 1923—; pres. Austin Dog Bread & Animal Food Co.; v.p. and treas. Loose-Wiles Biscuit Co. of N.Y. City; v.p. Morris Plan Bank of Kansas City; dir. Brown Cracker & Candy Co. (Dallas), Green & Green Co. (Dayton, O.), K.C.S. Ry. Co. Republican. Mem. Christian (Disciples) Ch. Mason (past Eminent Comdr. K.T.). Home: Kansas City, Mo. Died June 22, 1941.

WILES, Lemuel Maynard, artist, educator; b. Perry, N.Y., Oct. 21, 1826; s. Daniel and Nancy (Richards) W.; grad. N.Y. State Normal Coll., 1847; A.M., Ingham U., N.Y. Studied art in New York; taught drawing in Albany Acad. and Utica Pub. Schs.; for 10 yrs. dir. Coll. of Fine Arts, Ingham U., Le Roy, N.Y.; later dir. art dept., Nashville U., Tenn. Later had studio in New York; father of Irving R. Wiles. Home: New York, N.Y. Died 1905.

WILEY, Andrew J., engr.; b. New Castle Co., Del., July 15, 1862; s. John and Mary (Hukill) W.; Ph.B., Del. Coll., Newark, 1882; unmarried. Engaged in surveys and constrn. Phila. and Baltimore br. B.&O. R.R. in Del. and Md., 1883; rodman and asst. engr. Ida. Mining & Irrigation Co., Boise, Ida., 1883-86; asst. engr. constrn. U.P. R.R., Butte, Mont., 1886-88; chief asst. engr. Ida. Mining & Irrigation Co., on constrn. large irrigation system, 1888-92; chief engr. and mgr. Owhyee Land & Irrigation Co., Grand View, Idaho, constructing large irrigation system, 1892-98; chief engr. Swan Falls Power Plant, Boise, Ida., 1900-02; chief engr. Boise-Payette River Electric Power Co. and City of Cheyenne, Wyo., on constrn. of Granite Springs reservoir, 1902-04; chief engr. Barber Lumber Co., Boise, Ida., for constrn. of large dam and power plant on Boise River, 1904-05; cons. engr. Twin Falls North Side Land & Water Co., Twin Falls Oakley Land & Water Co., Twin Falls Salmon River Land & Water Co., 1906-14. Chief engr. Trade Dollar Consol. Mining Co.'s Swan Falls Power Plant Extension, 1909-11, Great Shoshone and Twin Falls Water Power Co., 1907-14, Southern Ida. Water Power Co.'s Am. Falls Power Plant, 1911-14. Cons. and designing engr. Don Pedro dam and power plant for Turlock and Modesto irrigation dists., Calif., 1918-23; cons. engr. Kern River Water Storage Dist., San Joaquin River Water Storage Dist., Merced Irrigation Dist.'s Exchequer Dam and Power Plant, South San Joaquin and Oakdale Irrigation Dist.'s Melones Dam, 1924-27; cons. engr. on dam design, U.S. Dept. Interior, 1925—, also cons. engr. on Boulder Canyon Dam, 1929—; cons. engr. to Brit. Govt. in India, Oct. 1927-Feb. 1928. Home: Boise, Ida. Died Oct. 8, 1931.

WILEY, Ariosto Appling, congressman; long engaged as lawyer in Ala.; served in Ala. house and senate, 18 yrs.; appt. lt. col. 5th regt. U.S. vol. inf. (an "immune" regt.); served 11 months in Cuba; chief legal adviser to Gen. Lawton and later apptd. acting civil gov. of Santiago, framed constitution and set in motion the machinery of a civil govt.; Congressman from 2d Ala. dist., 1901-09. Home: Montgomery, Ala. Died 1908.

WILEY, Edwin, librarian; b. Coal Creek, Tenn., Aug. 22, 1872; s. Edwin Floyd and Catherine (McAdoo) W.; B.S., U. of Tenn., 1891, B.A., M.A., 1898; Ph.D., George Washington U., 1911; m. Garnet Noel, Aug. 7, 1902. Apprentice asst. in Harvard U. Library, 1892-93; librarian and asst. in English, U. of Tenn., 1893-99; asst. librarian and asst. in English, Vanderbilt U., 1899-1906; lecturer in English, George Washington U.; classifier, Library of Congress, 1906-13; classifier, U. of Calif., 1913-15; librarian, U.S. Naval War Coll., 1916-22, Peoria (Ill.) Pub. Library, 1922—. Author: The Old and the New Renaissance, 1903; Early Presses of Tennessee (publs. Bibliog. Soc.); Libraries in the South (in The South in the Building of the Nation); Library of Congress Classification Schemes for Political Science, Philosophy, English, American and Comparative Literatures, Charities and Corrections; also articles on library hist., library architecture, etc., in Ency. Americana, 1919. Editor: History of the United States. Asso. editor The Foundation Library, The Great War (Barrie). Contbr. to various publs. Died Oct. 20, 1924.

WILEY, Franklin Baldwin, editor; b. New York, Sept. 28, 1861; s. Franklin Wiley and Sarah M., d. J. C. Baldwin; grad. Plainfield (N.J.) High Sch., 1879; at Harvard, 1884-88; m. Jessie L. Glen, June 1, 1896 (died 1915); children—Barbara, Roger Wiley; m. 2d, Alma A. Rogers, Oct. 8, 1921. Lit. asst. to Bishop J. H. Vincent in preparing the Chautauqua text-book on Roman History, 1879; New York corr. several suburban papers, 1880-81; asst. dept. foreign corr. Drexel, Morgan & Co., bankers, New York, 1881-83; made Rep. speeches in New York presdl. campaign of 1888; asso. editor Dorchester (Mass.) Beacon, 1892; asst. in English, Harvard Summer Sch., 1892; staff Boston Evening Transcript, 1891-99; literary editor Ladies' Home Jour., 1899-1927. Author: Roadside Rhymes, 1885; The Harvard Guide Book, 1895; Flowers That Never Fade, 1897; Voices and Visions, 1904. Home: Wayne, Pa. Died Aug. 1930.

WILEY, Harvey Washington, chemist; b. Kent, Ind., Oct. 18, 1844; s. Preston P. and Lucinda Weir (Maxwell) W.; A.B., Hanover (Ind.) Coll., 1867, A.M., 1870; M.D., Ind. Med. Coll., 1871; B.S., Harvard, 1873; hon. Ph.D., Hanover, 1876, LL.D., 1898; LL.D., U. of Vt., 1911; D.Sc., Lafayette, 1912; m. Anna Campbell Kelton, Feb. 27, 1911; children—Harvey Washington, John Preston. Prof. Latin and Greek, Butler Coll., Indianapolis, 1868-70; teacher science, high sch., Indianapolis, 1871; prof. chemistry, Butler U., 1874; prof. chemistry, Purdue U., and state chemist of Ind., 1874-83; chief chemist, U.S. Dept. Agr., 1883-1912; prof. agrl. chemistry, George Washington U., 1899-1914; cons. prof. Brooklyn Poly. Inst., 1905. Mem. Jury of Awards, Paris Expn., 1900; U.S. del. 3d Internat. Congress Applied Chemistry, Vienna, 1898, 4th, Paris, 1900, 5th, Berlin, 1903, 6th, Rome, 1906, 7th, London, 1909 (chmn. Am. com.); hon. pres. First Internat. Congress Repression of Adulteration of Alimentary and Pharm. Products, Geneva, 1908; U.S. representative Soc. univ. de la Croix blanche de Génève; pres. U.S. Pharmacopœial Conv., 1910-20; v.p., 1886, sec. council, 1890, gen. sec., 1891, A.A.A.S.; pres. Am. Chem. Soc., 1893-94, Am. Therapeutic Soc., 1911. Chevalier du Mérite Agricole (France), 1900; medal (first class), Physico-Chem. Acad. Italy, 1908; Chevalier Legion of Honor (France), 1909. Contbg. editor Good Housekeeping Mag., 1912—. Author: Songs of Agricultural Chemists', 1892; Principles and Practice of Agricultural Chemistry (3 vols.), 1894-97, 1909-11; Foods and Their Adulterations, 1907-11, 1917; 1001 Tests, 1914; The Lure of the Land, 1915; Not by Bread Alone, 1915; Beverages and Their Adulterations, 1919; Health Readers for Schools, 1919; History of a Crime Against the Food Law, 1929; also 60 Govt. bulletins and 225 scientific papers, etc. Died June 30, 1930.

WILEY, John Alexander, brig. gen. U.S.V.; b. Allegheny County, Pa., Sept. 3, 1843; common sch. edn.; pvt. 8th Pa. reserves, vol. corps inf., in Army of Potomac, 1861-64; chief clerk q.-m.'s dept., 1864-65; extensive oil-producer after Civil War; mayor of Franklin, Pa., col. 16th regt., Pa. Nat. Guard; brig. gen. same, 1887-98; apptd., May 27, 1898, brig. gen., U.S.V.; served in war with Spain in command 1st brigade, 2d div., 1st army corps; 3d div., 1st army corps; 2d div., 1st army corps. Apptd. by gov. of Pa. to locate the lines of battle of the Pa. troops at Antietam battlefield. Home: Franklin, Pa. Died 1909.

WILEY, Louis, newspaper mgr.; b. Hornell, N.Y., May 31, 1869; s. Benjamin and Ernestine (Brickner) W.; ed. pvt. sch., Mt. Sterling, Ky.; hon. M.A., U. of Rochester; LL.D., U. of Ky., Wabash Coll., Hobart Coll; Litt.D., Alfred U.; unmarried. Reporter, 1887-93, business mgr., 1893-95, Post-Express, Rochester, N.Y.; editor and pub. The Tidings, Rochester, 1887-93; with New York Times, 1896—, bus. mgr., 1906—. Vice pres. 42d Street Property Owners and Merchants Assn., Broadway Assn., Lafayette Memorial; dir. West Side C. of C.; mem. Internat. Assn. Newspaper Adv. Executives (advisory council), Journalism Dept. of Butler U. (bd. advisers), Am. Newspaper Pubs.' Assn., Bur. of Advertising (com. in charge), League of Nations Non-Partisan Assn. (exec. com.), Federated Gen. Relief Com. (dir.), Pan Am. Soc. of U.S. (membership com.), Soc. of the Genesee (pres.; chmn. bd. govs.), Steuben County Soc. (pres.), Municipal Art Soc. of New York (dir.), The Kentuckians (trustee), Authors' League Fund (dir.), Serbian Aid Com. (dir.), Jugo-Slavia Soc. (dir.). Comdr. Legion of Honor, Officer of Pub. Instruction, mem. Order of Social Welfare and Colonial Order of Black Star of Benin (all France); Knight Comdr. Hellenic Order of George (Greece); Comdr. Crown of Italy; Officer Order of Leopold II of Belgium; Officer Crown of Rumania; Comdr. Royal Order of St. Sava (Jugoslavia); Order of White Lion (Czechoslovakia); Order of Polonia Restituta (Poland); gold medal, Le Matin (Paris). Democrat. Home: New York, N.Y. Died Mar. 20, 1935.

WILEY, Walter H(oward), engr.; b. Trenton, Ill., Jan. 27, 1862; s. Dr. Martin and Emma (Danforth) W.; grad. Colo. State Sch. of Mines, 1883; m. Laura Parshall, Sept. 17, 1884; 1 son, Dana. In practice as cons. mining engr., 1883—, throughout western portion of U.S., including Alaska, and in British Columbia and Mexico, S. America and Asia. Home: Glendora, Calif. Died May 16, 1931.

WILEY, William Halsted, congressman; b. New York, July 10, 1842; s. John and Elizabeth B. W.; A.B., Coll. City of New York, 1861; C.E., Rensselaer Poly. Inst., Troy, 1866; spl. student Columbia Coll. Sch. of Mines, 1868; m. Joanna King Clarke, June 1, 1870. Entered 7th N.Y. Vols., 1860; 1st lt. U.S.V., 1862; mustered out, 1864, as maj. U.S.V. Publisher of scientific works, 1876—. Member 58th, 59th Congresses (1903-07) and 61st Congress (1909-11), 8th N.J. District. Republican. Pres. Internat. Jury, Brussels Expn., 1897; mem. Superior Jury, Brussels, commr. for N.J., St. Louis Expn., 1904. Decorated Order of Leopold, Belgium. Author: Yosemite, Alaska and Yellowstone, 1888. New York corr. Engineering, London. Home: East Orange, N.J. Died May 2, 1925.

WILFLEY, Lebbeus Redman, judge; b. in Audrain County, Mo., Mar. 30, 1866; s. James Frank and Sarah (Pindall) W.; A.M., Central Coll., Fayette, Mo., 1889; LL.B., Yale, 1892; LL.D., Clark U., 1909; unmarried. Admitted to bar, 1893; engaged in gen. practice at St. Louis until 1901; atty. gen. of P.I., 1901-06; judge U.S. Ct. for China, 1906-09. U.S. del. Universal Congress Lawyers and Jurists, St. Louis, 1904. Democrat. Methodist. Died May 26, 1926.

WILFLEY, Xenophon Pierce, senator; b. Audrain Co., Mo., Mar. 18, 1871; s. James Frank and Sarah (Pindall) W.; A.B., Clarksburg (Mo.) Coll., 1891; A.M., Central Coll., Fayette, Mo., 1895; LL.B., St. Louis Law Sch., 1899; m. Rosamond Guthrie, Oct. 28, 1908; children—John Franklin (dec.), Mary Ellen, Rosamond Guthrie. Teacher Central Coll., 1 yr., Sedalia High Sch., 3 yrs.; admitted to Mo. bar, 1899, and began practice in St. Louis; mem. Wilfley, Williams, McIntyre & Nelson. Apptd. chmn. Bd. Election Commrs., City of St. Louis, Jan. 1, 1917; apptd. U.S. senator, Apr. 30, 1918, to succeed William J. Stone, deceased, until successor could be elected. Democrat. Mem. M.E. Ch., S. Home: St. Louis, Mo. Died May 4, 1931.

WILGUS, Horace La Fayette, professor law; b. nr. Conover, O., Apr. 2, 1859; s. James (M.D.) and Susannah Throckmorton (LaFetra) W.; B.S., Ohio State U., 1882, M.S., 1889; studied civ. engring. Nat. Normal Sch., Lebanon, O., and Ohio State U.; studied law by self, 1881-84; m. Flora Belle Ewing, June 24, 1886 (died 1894); children—Walter Quincy, Horace Ewing (dec.); m. 2d, Julia Gay Pomeroy, Sept. 1, 1897; 1 dau., Caroline Gay. Deputy co. surveyor, Miami Co., O., 1875; instr. mathematics, Ohio State U., 1878-81; chief clerk in office commr. of railroads and telegraphs, O., 1881-85; instr. physiology, Ohio State U., 1882; pvt. sec. and asst. to receiver and gen. mgr., Cleveland & Marietta R.R., Cambridge, Ohio, 1885-86. Admitted to Ohio bar, Oct. 1884; practiced law, Troy, O., 1886-87; moved to Columbus, O., 1887 and in practice there till 1895; took important part in orgn., Sept. 1891, law dept. Ohio State U., sec. faculty and prof. elementary law, 1891-95; prof. law U. of Mich., 1895-1929, prof. emeritus, 1929—; admitted to Mich. bar, 1901. Mem. editorial bd. Michigan Law Rev., 1902-17. Author: Selection Cases on Evidence, 1896; United States Steel Corporation, 1901; Cases on the Law of Private Corporations, 1902; Should There Be a Federal Incorporation Law for Commerical Corporations? (Am. Bar Assn. Report, 1904), 1905; Private Corporations, 1910; The Tragedy of Thirteen Days in 1914, a review of diplomacy preceding the World War. Home: Ann Arbor, Mich. Died Oct. 8, 1935.

WILGUS, Sidney Dean, alienist; b. Buffalo, N.Y., Feb. 16, 1872; s. Frank Augustus and Margaret Ann (Woodcock) W.; ed. pub. and high schs., Buffalo; M.D., U. of Buffalo, 1895; m. Katharine Diller Weed, Oct. 1, 1904; children—Katharine Ann, Francis Augustus, Sidney Dean, Dorothy Langdon, Mary Hume. Psychiatrist, N.Y. State hosps., 1895-1902; psychiatrist N.Y. City municipal hosps., 1902-04; chief examiner N.Y. State Bd. of Alienists, 1904-10; supt. Elgin (Ill.) State Hosp., 1910-11, Kankakee State Hosp. (more than 3,000 patients), 1911-13; founder Wilgus Sanitarium, Rockford, Ill.; alienist on Board of Public Welfare, State of Ill., 1929-33; mem. of Rockford Hospital staff, 1915—. Has surveyed the condition surrounding the care of the insane and feeble-minded in 4 states for Nat. Com. Mental Hygiene. Fellow Am. Coll. Physicians, 1930; mem. nat., state and local med. socs. Sergt. Co. H, 203d New York Vol. Inf., Spanish-Am. War. Spl. hosp. inspection for Office of Surgeon Gen.; mem. Med. Appeal Bd., World War. Lt. col. Med. Reserve, 1931. Pres. Reserve Officers' Assn. of Ill., 1925-26. Prof. and head dept. of psychiatry, Chicago Med. Sch., 1936—. Conglist. Mason. Home: Rockford, Ill. Died Feb. 23, 1940.

WILKERSON, Albert Wadsworth, banker; b. Hearne, Tex., Sept. 28, 1870; s. Jonathan Gideon and Sarah Hollon (Wadsworth) W.; student U. of the South, Sewanee, Tenn., 1889; m. Mary Clare Weeden, July 3, 1895; children—Clare Aubrey (Mrs. Clifford Talbot Smith), Edward Albert, John Wadsworth (dec.). Began as stenographer City Nat. Bank, Austin, Tex., 1889, and advanced to asst. cashier; cashier City Nat. Bank, Bryan, Tex., 1902-18; cashier Alamo Nat. Bank, San Antonio, 1918-19; became pres. Citizens State Bank, Austin, Tex., 1919; pres. Mutual Loan & Deposit Co., Fidelity Mortgage Co.; became v.p. Marine Bank & Trust Co., Houston, Nov. 15, 1927 and examiner Regional Agrl. Credit Corp., Nov. 15, 1932. Episcopalian. Home: Houston, Tex. Died May 30, 1941.

WILKES, John Summerfield, justice of Supreme Court Tenn., Jan. 1893—term expiring 1910; b. Maury Co., Tenn., Mar. 2, 1841; s. Richard A. L. and Judith W.; ed. Pleasant Grove Acad. and Florence Wesleyan Univ., Florence, Ala.; m. Florence A. Barker, June 20, 1865. Capt. C.S.A., 1861-65; adj. gen., Tenn., Oct. 1871 to Jan. 1875; treas. Texas & Pacific R.R., 1886-88. Home: Pulaski, Tenn. Died 1908.

WILKIE, John Elbert, electric traction executive, chief U.S. secret service; b. Elgin, Ill., April 27, 1860; s. Franc B. and Ellen (Morse) W.; grad. Chicago High Sch.; m. Janet Ormsbee, Apr. 27, 1882; children—Donald W., Jean (Mrs. Ira June Owen). Began newspaper work on Chicago Times, Sept. 1877; twice abroad as its representative; joined local force Chicago Tribune, 1881; reporter, asst. city editor, city editor and commercial editor successively until 1893; went to London and engaged in banking and steamship business; returned to U.S., 1896; resumed spl. work for Chicago newspapers; made splty. of criminal investigation; chief U.S. Secret Service, Feb. 1898-1912. Organied spl. emergency force of men to checkmate Spanish spies during Spanish-Am. War, and succeeded in driving from the country chief Spanish emissaries, and arresting their best spies. Supervising agent in charge spl. agents of the customs service at home and abroad, Nov. 1910-July 1, 1913; now v.p. Chicago Rys. Co. and asst. to the v.p. Chicago Surface Lines. Home: Chicago, Ill. Died Dec. 13, 1934.

WILKIN, Jacob W., judge, 1888—, chief justice, June 7, 1901-02, Supreme Court of Illinois; b. Newark, Ohio, June 7, 1837; s. Isaac and Sarah W.; served in Union army, 1862-65, becoming maj. 130th Ill. vol. inf.; studied law under late Judge John Scholfield in Marshall, Clark Co.; was his partner from 1867 until latter went on the bench in 1873. Practiced in Marshall, Ill.; circuit judge, 1879-88, and during that time served 3 yrs. in appellate court, 4th dist.; removed to Danville, 1885. Home: Danville, Ill. Died 1907.

WILKINS, Beriah, editor; b. in Ohio, July 10, 1846; s. Alfred F. and Harriet J. W.; common school edn. at Marysville, O.; m. Emily J. Robinson, Oct. 18, 1870; became banker at Uhrichsville, O.; State senator, Ohio, 1879-82; congressman, 1883-89; prin. owner, 1889—, and editor and publisher, 1894—, Washington Post. Home: Washington, D.C. Died 1905.

WILKINS, Frank Lemoyne, clergyman; b. Tyrone, N.Y., June 30, 1851; s. Andrew and Laura Jane (Barnes) W.; State Normal Sch., Cortland, N.Y.; Canandaigua Acad., Canandaigua, N.Y.; A.B., U. of Rochester, 1876, A.M., 1878; grad. Rochester Theol. Sem., 1879; D.D., Central U., Pella, Ia., 1886; m. Minnie Frances Best, Aug. 7, 1882. Ordained Bapt. ministry, 1879; pastor Second Ch., Auburn, 1879-85, First Ch., Davenport, Ia., 1885-91; corr. for Ia. of The Standard, Chicago, 1886-91; 1st sec. Bapt. Young People's Union of America, and editor Baptist Union, Chicago, 1891-96 (originated Christian Culture Courses [3] for Bapt. Young People); pastor First Ch., Gloucester, Mass., 1896-1905, Free St. Ch., Portland, Me., 1905-13, 2d Ch. East Providence, R.I., 1913-20; corr. for Me. of The Examiner, New York, 1905-13. Dir. Conf. of Bapt. Ministers in Mass.; mem. bds. Maine and R.I. Bapt. Missionary Convs. Treas. Alumni Assn. Rochester Theol. Sem., 1881-83. Home: Providence, R.I. Died Dec. 10, 1926.

WILKINS, Milan William, Socialist worker; b. Ludlow, Vt., Nov. 19, 1856; s. Sidney M. and Lucy (Chapman) W.; mother died when he was 6 yrs. of age; childhood passed in hard labor, with little schooling; ran away from home at 17; worked in many states; attended coll. 2 yrs.; taught sch. several terms; m. Grace M., d. E. M. Wardall, of Calif., Dec. 12, 1893. Identified with labor movement, 1884—; has edited 7 papers; mem. People's Party Conv., Cincinnati, 1891, conf. of farm and labor orgns., St. Louis, 1892, People's Party Nat. convs., 1892, 96; was "middle of the roader"; after fusion joined Socialist Labor Party. Lived in Calif. a number of yrs.; edited The Class Struggle (newspaper) until Oct. 1899. Candidate for Congress on the Socialist Party ticket, 1902, 3d Calif. District. Deceased.

WILKINS, Thomas Russell, prof. physics; b. Toronto, Ont., Can., June 6, 1891; s. Thomas and Annie (Cornell) W.; B.A., McMaster U. (Can.), 1912; Ph.D., U. of Chicago, 1921; grad. study, Cambridge (Eng.), 1925-26; m. Olive Cross, June 17, 1913. Science master Woodstock Coll. (Can.), 1913-14; instr. physics, U. of Chicago, 1916-17; prof. physics, Brandon (Can.) Coll., 1918-25, U. of Rochester, 1925—; dir. Inst. of Optics, Rochester, 1928—. Served as master signal electrician, U.S. Signal Corps, 1917-18. Baptist. Editor (with others) Orientation Course in Natural Science, 1938. Secured photographic recordings of cosmic rays and of successive disintegrations of radium atoms. Home: Rochester, N.Y. Died Dec. 10, 1940.

WILKINS, William Glyde, engineer; b. Pittsburgh, Pa., Apr. 16, 1854; s. Alvin and Charlotte (Glyde) W.; C.E., Rensselaer Poly. Inst., 1879; m. Sarah A. Simmons, Dec. 29, 1880. On U.S. Govt. surveys of Miss. River, 1 yr.; asst. engr. of constrn. Pa. R.R., 7 yrs.; city engr. Allegheny, Pa., 2 yrs.; mem. of The W. G. Wilkins Co., engrs. and architects, Pittsburgh, 1887—, during which time has been engineer for 18 complete coke plants aggregating 6,000 ovens, and 30 complete coal mining plants costing over $15,000,000. Member Pittsburgh Flood Commn. Republican. Presbyn. Home: Pittsburgh, Pa. Died Apr. 12, 1921.

WILKINSON, Alfred Ernest, lawyer; b. Skaneateles, N.Y., Dec. 6, 1846; s. Winfield S. and Frances Elizabeth (Sampson) W.; A.B., U. of Mich., 1869; student law dept. same, 1870-71; m. Anne Maria Oldham, Nov. 4, 1875 (died 1919); children—Henry Elmore, Ann Elizabeth. Private Co. B, 140th Ill. Inf., 1864; admitted to bar, 1871; practiced at Morrison, Ill., 1871-72; removed to Tex., 1872; co. judge, Grayson Co., Tex., 1876-78; reporter Supreme Court of Tex., 1896—. Mem. Christian (Disciples of Christ) Ch. Democrat. Home: Austin, Tex. Died July 15, 1932.

WILKINSON, Andrew, writer; b. Plaquemines Parish, La.; s. Joseph Biddle and Josephine Osborne (Stark) W.; student Washington and Lee U., Lexington, Va.; m. Elizabeth M. Harding. Special corr. New York Sun, in Tilden-Hayes campaign and subsequent Congressional proceedings, 1876-78; connected for many yrs. with New Orleans Times or Times-Democrat. Author: Plantation Stories of Old Louisiana, 1914; Boy Holidays in the Louisiana Wilds. Home: New Orleans, La. Died May 16, 1921.

WILKINSON, Horace Simpson, financier; b. Shellsburg, Ia., Nov. 26, 1868; s. Rev. Joseph G. and Mary (Miller) W.; ed. pub. schs.; m. Ada M., d. late Dr. Granville Lowther, of Seattle, May 15, 1889. Identified with shipping interests on Great Lakes, 1895—; pres. Great Lakes Steamship Co., Toledo Shipbuilding Co.; chmn. board Crucible Steel Co. of America. Mem. Am. Iron and Steel Inst. (dir.), Lake Carriers Assn. of Cleveland (dir.), S.A.R. Methodist. Home: Greenwich, Conn. Died Apr. 11, 1937.

WILKINSON, Joseph Green, banking; b. Hillsboro, Tenn., Feb. 5, 1857; s. Isaac Miller and Mary (Willis) W.; ed. country schs. and Carrick Acad., Winchester, Tenn.; m. Dessie Strickler, May 18, 1886; 1 son, Harry Herman. Engaged in farming, 1876-83; merchant, Manchester, Tenn., 1883-91; began as pvt. banker, 1890; organizer Coffee County Bank, 1891, and chain of 11 banks in Tenn., Ala. and Miss., 1890-1903; moved to Fort Worth, Tex., 1903; organizer Continental Bank & Trust Co., Fort Worth, and 30 br. banks in Tex., 1903-04; now chmn. bd. Continental Nat. Bank (Fort Worth), First Nat. Bank (Hamlin), First State Bank (Big Sandy), and Continental state banks at Beckville, Groesbeck, Gunter, Rising Star and Tolar. Mem. Christian (Disciples) Ch. Home: Fort Worth, Tex. Died Sept. 19, 1933.

WILKINSON, Marguerite Ogden Bigelow, author; b. Halifax, N.S., Nov. 15, 1883; d. Nathan Kellogg and Getrude Zulime (Holmes) Bigelow; ed. Evanston (Ill.) Tp. High Sch.; The Misses Ely's Sch., New York, 1 yr.; Northwestern U., 3 yrs.; Phi Beta Kappa, 1925; m. James G. Wilkinson, Dec. 28, 1909. Episcopalian. Author: In Vivid Gardens, 1911; By a Western Wayside, 1912; The Passing of Mars (play), 1915; Golden Songs of the Golden State, 1917; New Voices, 1919; Bluestone, 1920; The Dingbat of Arcady, 1922; The Great Dream, 1923; Contemporary Poetry, 1923; The Way of the Makers, 1925; Yule Fire, 1925. Home: New York, N.Y. Died Jan. 12, 1928.

WILKINSON, Melville Le Vaunt, merchant; b. Maysville, Ind., Jan. 31, 1865; s. Rev. Charles H. and Mary (Hawkins) W.; ed. pub. schs.; m. Minerva Evans, June 11, 1890. With Knisely Bros. Dry Goods Co., Butler, Ind., 1880-98; later with Root & McBride Co., and William Taylor Sons Co., Cleveland; moved to Buffalo, N.Y., 1906, and became pres. William Hengerer Co., dry goods, and the J. N. Adams Co., Buffalo, also the Thos. Watkins, Son & Co., Hamilton, Can.; settled in St. Louis, 1911, and became pres. Scruggs-Vandervoort-Barney Dry Goods Co.; pres. Scruggs, Vandervoort & Barney Bank, also of the Mermod Jaccard King Jewelry Co., St. Louis, the Z. L. White Co., Columbus, O., and the Denver (Colo.) Dry Goods Co. Conglist. Odd Fellow, K.P. Home: St. Louis, Mo. Died Mar. 15, 1925.

WILKINSON, Robert Shaw, college pres.; b. Charleston, S.C., Feb. 18, 1865; s. Charles H. and Lavinia A. W.; U.S. Mil. Acad., 1884-85, Oberlin Acad., 1887; A.B., Oberlin Coll., 1891; Ph.D., Columbia, 1904; hon. Ph.D., State U. of Ky., 1899; hon. A.M., Allen Univ., S.C., 1920; hon. A.M., Oberlin, 1922; LL.D. from Allen University, 1927; m. Marion Raven Birnie, June 29, 1897; children—Helen Raven, Robert Shaw, Frost Birnie, Lulu Love. Prof. Latin and Greek, State Univ. of Ky. (colored), 1891-95; prof. mathematics, 1896-1900, prof. physics and chemistry, 1900-11, pres., 1911—, State Agrl. and Mech. Coll. (colored), Orangeburg, S.C. Dir. Mut. Sav. Bank, Victory Sav. Bank. Mem. gen. advisory com. Land Grant Coll. Survey, conducted by Fed. Bur. of Edn.; mem. advisory com. Lincoln Scholarship Fund; coöp. member Golden Rule Foundation. Mason, Odd Fellow, K.P. Died Mar. 13, 1932.

WILKINSON, Warring, educator; b. Charlton, N.Y., May 25, 1834; s. Charles Tappan and Lydia (Bartlett) W.; A.B., Union Coll., 1858; (L.H.D., Gallaudet Coll., Washington, 1889); m. Florence Walton, Dec. 3, 1867 (died 1902). Teacher in New York Institution for the Deaf, 1857-65; prin. Calif. Instn. for the Deaf and the Blind, 1865-1909; prin. emeritus, Oct. 1, 1909. Pres. Nat. Conv. Instructors of the Deaf, New York, 1890; U.S. del. Internat. Conf. Teachers of the Deaf, Edinburgh, Scotland, 1907. Home: Berkeley, Calif. Died Apr. 7, 1918.

WILKINSON, William Cleaver, author; b. Westford, Vt., Oct. 19, 1833; s. Dr. Thomas and Sarah (Cleaver) W.; A.B., U. of Rochester, 1857, A.M., 1863; grad. Rochester Theol. Sem., 1859; the Sorbonne and College de France, Paris; (D.D., U. of Rochester, 1873; LL.D., Baylor U., 1904); m. Harriet S., d. Prof. J. F. Richardson of U. of Rochester, 1863; father of Florence Wilkinson Evans. Ordained Bapt. ministry, 1859; pastor Second Ch., New Haven, 1859-61; prof. ad interim modern langs., U. of Rochester, 1863-64; afterward pastor Mt. Auburn Baptist Ch., Cincinnati, relinquished pastoral work because of failing health; prof. homiletics and pastoral theology, Rochester Theol. Sem., 1872-81; in lit. work, 1883-92; prof. poetry and criticism, U. of Chicago, 1892—. Counselor Chautauqua Literary and Scientific Circle; adjunct lecturer, Wellesley College, 1883-84, Baylor U., Texas, 1907. Author: The Dance of Modern Society, 1868; A Free Lance in the Field of Life and Letters, 1874; The Baptist Principle, 1881, 1897; Poems, 1883; Edwin Arnold as Poetizer and as Paganizer, 1885; College Latin Course in English; Classic French Course in English, 1886; Classic German Course in English, 1887 (revised under title, Wilkinson's Foreign Classics, 6 vols., 1900); Poetical Works, uniform edit., 5 vols. (1) Epic of Saul, (2) Epic of Paul, (3, 4) Epic of Moses, (5) Poems, 1905; Modern Masters of Pulpit Discourse, 1905; Some New Literary Valuations, 1909; The Good of Life and Other Little Essays, 1910; Daniel Webster, A Vindication, with Other Historical Essays, 1911; Paul and the Revolt Against Him, 1914; Concerning Jesus Christ the Son of God, 1916; Concerning Jesus Christ the Son of Man, 1918. Wrote Life of Jesus, in People's Bible History, 1895. Died Apr. 25, 1920.

WILKINSON, William Cook, banker; b. Charlotte, N.C., Feb. 23, 1866; s. Thomas J. and Laura H. (Wilson) W.; ed. pub. schs., Charlotte; m. Rosalie H. Booker, Nov. 8, 1888; children—Lawrence Hamlet, Rosalie (Mrs. William E. Haynes), Thomas Harvey, James Wilson, George Booker, Laura Cameron, (Mrs. Raleigh H. Hopkins). Pres. Merchants and Farmers Nat. Bank, Charlotte, Elizabeth Mills, Inc., Charlotte Bonded Warehouse, Lowell (N.C.) Cotton Mills; v.p. Perfection Spinning Co. (Belmont, N.C.). Mem. N.C. State Highway Commn. Democrat. Episcopalian. Mason. K.P. Home: Charlotte, N.C. Died May 10, 1930.

WILL, Allen Sinclair, teacher of journalism; b. Antioch, Va., July 28, 1868; s. Wm. R. and Mildred Florence (Sinclair) W.; M.A. from St. John's Coll., Annapolis, Md.; Litt.D., Mt. St. Mary's Coll.; LL.D., St. John's, also Loyola Coll., Baltimore; m. Allie Stuart Walter, Feb. 17, 1891; children—Allen Sinclair (dec.), Katherine Victoria (Mrs. H. S. Willis), Isabella Virginia (Mrs. L. T. Harris), James Carroll (dec.). After leaving coll. was principal of a pub.

sch. in Va.; later teacher in pvt. classical sch., Baltimore; reporter Baltimore Morning Herald, 1888-89, Baltimore Sun, 1889-93; asst. city editor same, 1893-96, telegraph editor, 1896-1905, city editor, 1905-12; asso. editor and editorial writer, Baltimore News, 1912-14; news editor, Public Ledger, Phila., 1914-16; asst. editor and spl. writer, New York Times, 1917-24; book reviewer, same, 1923—; asso. in journalism, 1920-24, asso. prof. journalism, 1924—, Columbia U.; prof. journalism, Rutgers U., 1925—, and dir. dept. of journalism, 1926—. V.chmn. Nat. Star-Spangled Banner Commn., 1914. Author: World Crisis in China, 1900; City, State and Nation, 1912; Life of Cardinal Gibbons (2 vols.), 1922 (translated into French, Vie du Cardinal Gibbons, 1925); Education for Newspaper Life, 1931. Home: New York, N.Y. Died Mar. 10, 1934.

WILL, Louis, mayor; b. Syracuse, N.Y., Nov. 13, 1857; s. Anthony and Rosina (Schmelzle) W.; ed. pub. schs. and business coll.; m. Augusta Bloecker, Mar. 17, 1895; 1 son, Eric Waldemar. Engaged in mfg. at Syracuse, 1876—; founder and dir. The Will & Baumer Co.; dir. Wilson & Greene Lumber Co.; mayor of Syracuse, 1914, 15. Catholic. Home: Syracuse, N.Y. Died July 15, 1932.

WILLARD, Arthur Lee, naval officer; b. Kirksville, Mo., Feb. 21, 1870; grad. U.S. Naval Acad., 1891. Commd. ensign, July 1, 1893; promoted through grades to rear admiral, June 1924. Served on Machias, Spanish-Am. War, 1898, Maine, 1903-06; duty Naval Gun Factory, Washington, D.C., 1906-08; on Idaho, 1908-10; duty Navy Yard, Washington, D.C., 1910-13; comd. Hancock, 1913-15; apptd. capt. of yard, Navy Yard, Washington, D.C., June 3, 1915; later vice adm. comdg. scouting force, U.S. Fleet; retired, Mar. 1, 1934. Home: Kirksville, Mo. Died Apr. 7, 1935.

WILLARD, Ashton Rollins, author; b. Montpelier, Vt., Apr. 14, 1858; s. C. W. and Emily D. (Reed) W.; A.B., Dartmouth, 1879; located at Boston, 1887; m. Agnes, d. Gov. Horace Fairbanks of Vt., 1888. Writer on art subjects for mags. Passed much time abroad, principally in Italy, Chevalier Order of Crown, Italy, 1902. Author: Life and Work of Painter Domenico Morelli, 1895; History of Modern Italian Art, 1898; Land of the Latins, 1902. Home: Boston, Mass. Died Oct. 3, 1918.

WILLARD, Charles Andrew, judge; b. St. Johnsbury, Vt., May 21, 1857; s. Andrew J. and Aurilla B. (McGaffey) W.; A.B., Dartmouth, 1877; LL.B., Boston Univ., 1879; (LL.D., Dartmouth, 1905); m. Charlotte Hastings, Sept. 28, 1901. Practiced at St. Johnsbury, Vt., 1879-82, St. Paul, 1882-85, Minneapolis, 1885-1901; asso. justice Supreme Ct. of P.I., 1901-04, 1905-09; U.S. dist. judge, Dist. of Minn., July 2, 1909—. Lecturer on law of bailments, U. of Minn., 1887-1901. Home: Minneapolis, Minn. Died Mar. 13, 1914.

WILLARD, DeForest, surgeon; b. Newington, Conn., Mar. 23, 1846; s. Daniel H. and S. Maria (Deming) W.; ed. Hartford High Sch.; M.D., U. of Pa., 1867, Ph.D., 1871; (hon. A.M., Lafayette, 1882); m. Elizabeth, d. Hon. Wm. A. Porter, of Phila., Sept. 13, 1881. Prof. orthopædic surgery, U. of Pa., 1889—; surgeon Presbyn. Hosp., Phila.; pres. Am. Orthopædic Assn., 1890, Phila. Co. Med. Soc., 1892, Am. Surg. Assn., 1902, Phila. Acad. Surgery, 1902; chmn. surg. sect. A.M.A., 1902; mem. Coll. Physicians, etc. Author: Artificial Anesthesia, 1891; Surgery of Childhood, Including Orthopædic Surgery, 1909. Home: Lansdowne, Pa. Died 1910.

WILLARD, Edward Smith, actor; b. Brighton, Eng., Jan. 9, 1853. First appearance on the stage Theatre Royal, Weymouth, Eng., Dec. 1869, as Second Officer, in "Lady of Lyons"; supported Sothern at Glasgow and filled other engagements until he went to London, 1881; became famous as The Spider, in "The Silver King," 1882; mgr. Shaftesbury Theatre, London, 1889; prod. there "The Middleman," "Judah," and other plays; appeared at Palmer's Theatre, New York, Nov. 1890, in "The Middleman" and other plays, and toured U.S. under A. M. Palmer's management for 3 seasons. Leased the Comedy and Garrick theatres, London, 1894, 95, 96; then toured U.S. in "David Garrick," "Tom Pinch," "The Middleman," "Professor's Love Story," etc., under his own management; leased St. James's Theatre, London, for prodn. of "The Cardinal," 1904; later toured America till Apr. 1907, when temporarily retired. Appeared as Brutus, in "Julius Cæsar," at coronation gala performance, His Majesty's Theatre, London, June 27, 1911. Home: London, England. Died Nov. 9, 1915.

WILLARD, Henry Augustus, capitalist; b. Westminster, Vt., May 14, 1822; s. Joseph and Susan Dorr (Clapp) W.; g.g.s. Joseph Dorr (of "Boston Tea Party"); ed. Walpole (N.H.) Acad.; m. Sarah Bradley, d. Judge Daniel Kellogg, of Westminster, Vt., Nov. 6, 1855. Engaged in hotel business; became mgr. old City Hotel, Washington, leased property 1847, and changed name to Willard's Hotel; with brother, J.C., bought the property in 1852, and later purchased adjoining property; conducted the hotel with his brother until 1861, afterward leased to others; sold his interest to brother, J. C., 1892; active in bldg. operations in Washington; erected the Willard Bldg. Organized, 1867, and was several yrs. pres. Nat. Savings Bank, now Nat. Safe Deposit, Savings & Trust Co., and now a dir.; pres. Columbia Ry. Co., 1874-89; organized, 1881, and was pres. 11 yrs., Columbia Fire Ins. Co. During President Grant's administration was mem. and v.p. Bd. Pub. Works, and mem. Bd. of Pub. Health. One of organizers (v.p.) Garfield Memorial Hosp.; was chmn. bd. of trustees, 1877, and raised funds to build All Souls' Ch. Home: Washington, D.C. Died 1909.

WILLARD, Horace Mann, educator; b. Canterbury, Conn., Mar. 24, 1842; s. George Anson and Emerette (Aspenwall) W.; prep. edn. Univ. Grammar Sch., Providence; grad. Brown Univ., B.A., 1864, A.M., 1867; (hon. Sc.D., Brown Univ., 1896); m. July 11, 1872, Ruth Sanders. Prin. Bridgewater Acad., 1864-70, Colby Acad., New London, N.H., 1870-72; supt. pub. schs., Gloucester, Mass., 1872-73, Newton, Mass., 1873-76; prin. of Vt. Acad., Saxton's River, Vt., 1876-89; founded, 1896, becoming principal and owner of Quincy Mansion Sch. Home: Quincy, Mass. Died 1907.

WILLARD, James Field, prof. history; b. Phila., Pa., Dec. 30, 1876; s. Edward Malon and Elizabeth Prudence (Field) W.; A.B., Central High Sch., Phila., 1895; B.S., U. of Pa., 1898, Ph.D., 1902; LL.D., Colorado College, Colorado Springs, Colo., 1930; m. Margaret Love Wheeler, Jan. 4, 1912; 1 dau., Mary Kathleen (dec.). Scholar in history, 1899-1900, fellow in history, 1900-01, U. of Wis.; fellow in history, U. of Pa., 1901-02; instr. in history, Northwestern U., 1902-04; Harrison research fellow, U. of Pennsylvania, 1904-06; asst. prof. history, 1906-07, prof. and head of dept., 1907—, U. of Colo. Editor Univ. of Colo. Hist. Collections (begun 1917). Editor Progress of Medieval Studies in the U.S.A. (ann. bull.), 1923—; chmn. com. on Dictionary of Late Mediæval British Latin, 1924—; in England, 1931-32, in charge coöperative study of "The English Government at Work" (1327-1336). Fellow Mediæval Acad. America (council, 1925—), Royal Hist. Soc. (hon. v.p. 1934). Author: The Royal Authority and the Early English Universities, 1902; Parliamentary Taxes on Personal Property, 1290-1336, 1933. Editor: The Union Colony at Greeley, Colo., 1869-71, 1918; Surrey Taxation Returns, Surrey Record Society, 1922; (with C. B. Goodykoontz) Experiments in Colorado Colonization (1869-72), 1926; (with same) Trans-Mississippi West, 1930; (with J. Baxter and C. Johnson) An Index of British and Irish Latin Writers, A.D., 400-1520, 1932. Home: Boulder, Colo. Died Nov. 21, 1935.

WILLARD, Joseh Edward, diplomat; b. Washington, May 1, 1865; s. Joseph C. and Antonio (Ford) W.; grad. Va. Mil. Inst., 1886; summer law course, U. of Va.; m. Belle Layton Wyatt, Sept. 16, 1891. Capt. 3d Va. Regt., U.S.V., in Spanish-Am. War, at Camp Alger, Va.; capt. a.-q.-m. and a.-d.-c. on staff Maj. Gen. Fitzhugh Lee, Camp Columbia, Cuba; mem. Va. Ho. of Rep., 1894-1902; lt. gov. of Va., 1902-06; state corp. commr. of Va., 1906-10. Apptd. E.E. and M.P. to Spain, July 28, 1913; ambassador extraordinary and plenipotentiary, 1913-21. Democrat. Mem. M.E. Ch., S. Home: Fairfax, Va. Died Apr. 4, 1924.

WILLARD, Josiah Flynt, writer; b. Appleton, Wis., Jan. 23, 1869; s. Oliver Atherton and Mary (Bannister) W.; ed. Berlin Univ., 1890-95; unmarried. Author: Tramping with Tramps, 1899; Powers that Prey (with Francis Walton), 1930; Notes of an Itinerant Policeman, 1900; The World of Graft, 1901; The Little Brother, 1902. Home: Briarcliffe Manor, N.Y. Died 1907.

WILLARD, Thomas Rigney, college dean; b. Groveland, Ill., Nov. 18, 1844; s. Warren Cottle and Caroline (Cottle) W.; A.B., Knox Coll., 1866; Chicago Theol. Sem., 1867-68; grad. Andover Theol. Sem., 1870; U. of Leipzig, 1873-75; m. Mary L. Wolcott, July 9, 1873. Prof. Greek and German, 1875-1903, German, 1903-12, acting pres., with title of dean, 1899-1900, dean of faculty, 1900-12, emeritus prof., Knox Coll. Republican. Conglist. Home: Galesburg, Ill. Died May 5, 1929.

WILLARD, William Charles, banker; b. Columbus, O., May 22, 1872; s. Charles D. and Mary Elizabeth (Davis) W.; grad. Central High Sch., Columbus, 1889; m. Anne Lilley, June 14, 1894; children—Catharine Tracy (Mrs. J. Stanton Mossgrove), Mary E. (Mrs. John Weller Brown), Ann (Mrs. W. D. Inglis, Jr.). Began as messenger, Commercial Nat. Bank, Columbus, 1889; went to Colo., 1891, and was with 1st Nat. Bank, Del Norte, and Merchants & Miners Bank, Creede, until 1893; returned to Columbus and became connected with Clinton Nat. Bank; continued as note teller, 1900, of the Hayden-Clinton Nat. Bank, of which was elected asst. cashier, 1905, and pres., Jan. 14, 1913, until sold to Huntington Nat. Bank, May 3, 1923, when became v.p. of latter; v.p., dir. Columbus Savings Bank; dir. Columbus Ry. Power & Light Co., Kanawha & Mich. Ry. Co., Toledo & O. Central Ry. Co., Mahoning Coal R.R. Co., Cincinnati, Sandusky & Cleveland R.R. Co. Trustee Grant Hosp. Republican. Methodist. Mason. Home: Columbus, O. Died Dec. 11, 1930.

WILLCOX, Cornélis de Witt, army officer, author; b. Geneva, Switzerland, Feb. 26, 1861; s. Cyprian Porter and Mary Frances (Smythe) W.; A.B., U. of Ga., 1880; grad. U.S. Mil. Acad., 1885; grad. U.S. Arty. Sch., 1892; U. of Grenoble, France, 1913; m. Mary Addison West, Oct. 31, 1888 (dec.). Commd. 2d lt. 2d Arty., U.S. Army, June 14, 1885; promoted through grades to maj., June 25, 1907; prof. U.S. Mil. Acad., with rank of lt. col., Sept. 28, 1910; promoted col., July 1, 1914; retired, Feb. 26, 1925. Capt. a.a.g. U.S. Vols., May 12, 1898-Apr. 7, 1899; served in Santiago campaign, 1898; gen. staff corps, 1906-10; on mission to Germany, 1907, to witness fall maneuvers of German Army; chief of mil. information division, Manila, 1908-10. Serving with A.E.F. in France, 1917-18, as chief of Am. Mil. Mission at French Gen. Hdqrs. Episcopalian. Hon. mem. Soc. of the Cincinnati in Ga. Officier d'Académie, Officier de la Légion d'Honneur, Croix de Guerre with palm, 1918 (France); Comdr. Order of Sacred Treasure (Japan). Author: A French-English Military Technical Dictionary (pub. by War Dept.), 1900; Head Hunters of Northern Luzon, 1912; A Reader of Scientific and Technical Spanish, 1913; War French, 1917. Translator: (from the Spanish) Letters of Montiano, during siege of St. Augustine, 1909; Spanish Official Account of Attack on Colony of Georgia, 1913. Co-editor International Military Digest, 1915. Died Jan. 1938.

WILLCOX, David, pres. Del. and Hudson Co.; b. Flatbush, L.I., Dec. 12, 1849; s. Albert O. and Ann Elizabeth (Hamilton) W.; grad. Yale (valedictorian), 1872, Columbia Coll., Law Sch., 1874; unmarried. Has practiced law, 1874—; for many years connected with Delaware & Hudson Co. and became its pres., May 13, 1903. Republican. Occasional contbr. to The Forum and other periodicals on legal and National questions. Home: New York, N.Y. Died 1907.

WILLCOX, James M.; b. Phila., Pa., Oct. 27, 1861; s. James M. and Mary (Keating) W.; A.B., Georgetown U., 1881, A.M., 1889; LL.D., Villanova Coll., 1923; m. Jean Griffith, 1906. Pres. and mgr. Phila. Saving Fund Soc.; dir. Pa. Co. for Insurances on Lives and Granting Annuities, Phila. Nat. Bank, Phila. Contributionship for Insuring Houses. Chmn. bd. Phila. Saving Fund Soc.; trustee Jefferson Med. Coll. and Hosp. Admitted to Phila. bar, 1884, later to bar in Fla. and Tenn. Republican. Catholic. Home: Berwyn, Pa. Died Dec. 26, 1935.

WILLCOX, Julius Abner, judge; B.S., Middlebury (Vt.) Coll., 1902. Began as high sch. prin. Swanton, Vt., 1902; official reporter Vt. State Senate, 1906; admitted to bar Vt., 1908; asst. clerk Vt. State House of Representatives, 1908-09; asso. justice Supreme Court of Vt. Home: Rutland, Vt. Deceased.

WILLCOX, Louise Collier, writer; b. Chicago, Ill., Apr. 24, 1865; d. Rev. Robert Laird and Mary (Price) Collier; ed. pvt. tutors in France, Germany and Eng.; conservatory of Leipzig, 1882-83; m. Westmore, Willcox, June 25, 1890; children—Westmore, Christine ("Cristina Valli"). Formerly editorial writer Harper's Weekly and of Harper's Bazar; on editorial staff North American Review, 1906-13; reader and adviser Macmillan Co., 1903-09, E. P. Dutton Co., 1910-17. Author: The Human Way; A Manual of Spiritual Fortification, 1910; The Road to Joy, 1911; The House in Order, 1916; "The Torch," an anthology. Translator: Balzac prize bk. for 1922, My Friend from Limousin; Jacob Wassermann's "Ulrika Woytich"; Life of the Bat (by Derennes); Sardonic Smile (by Louis Diehl); The Bewitched (by Borbey d'Aurevilly). Home: Norfolk, Va. Died Sept. 13, 1929.

WILLCOX, Orlando Bolivar, brig. gen. U.S.A., retired, April 16, 1887; b. Detroit, Mich., Apr. 16, 1823; s. Charles and Almira W.; grad. West Point, 1847; lt. 4th U.S. arty. and fought in Mexican, Seminole and other Indian campaigns and Civil war; col. 1st Mich. inf. vols.; was at the capture of Alexandria, Va., 1st Bull Run, South Mountain, Antietam, and subsequent battles with Army of the Potomac, in East Tenn., and elsewhere, becoming brig. gen. and bvt. maj. gen. vols. After war apptd. col. 12th and 29th inf. regulars; brig. gen., Oct. 13, 1886; received Congressional medal of honor, and comd. several mil. depts., the Soldiers' Home, etc. Author: Shoepac Recollections, by Walter March, 1854; Faca, an Army Memoir, by Maj. March, 1857. Home: Washington, D.C. Died 1907.

WILLCOX, William G., insurance; b. Reading, Mass., Feb. 8, 1859; s. William H. and Annie Augusta Holmes (Goodenow) W.; ed. pub. schs., and State Normal Sch., Bridgewater, Mass.; m. Mary Otis Gay, May 28, 1889. Mem. Albert Willcox & Co., ins., New York, 1887-1906; now pres. Willcox, Peck & Hughes; also v.p. Meinel & Wemple; mem. Willcox, Peck, Brown & Crosby. President of the New York Bd. of Edn., 1916-17; pres. Staten Island Acad.; chmn. bd. Tuskegee Normal and Industrial Inst.; trustee Staten Island Hosp.; treas. Richmond Co. Soc. for Prevention of Cruelty to Children. Home: West New Brighton, S.I., N.Y. Died Sept. 19, 1923.

WILLCOX, William Henry, Congl. minister; b. New York, N.Y., Jan. 28, 1821; s. Oliver and Sally (Stanton) W.; grad. N.Y. Univ., 1843; Union Theol. Sem., 1846 (D.D., Illinois Coll.; LL.D., Drury Coll.); m. Annie Goodenow, May 30, 1853. Pastorates: Kennebunk, Me., 1852-57; Reading, Mass., 1857-79. Confidential adviser to Mrs. Valeria G. Stone, in distributing her large estate for ednl. and charitable purposes; trustee Phillips Academy, Andover Theol. Sem. and Wellesley Coll.; pres. trustees of Jaffna Coll. funds; pres. Congl. Ednl. Soc. Retired. Home: Malden, Mass. Died 1904.

WILLCOX, William Russell, lawyer; b. Smyrna. N.Y., April 11, 1863; s. Thomas L. and Catharine B. (Stover) W.; student U. of Rochester, 1888; LL.B., Columbia, 1889; hon. A.M., Rochester, 1904; LL.D., New York U., 1909; m. Martha J. Havemeyer, Jan. 12, 1904; children—Josephine Havemeyer, Frederick Havemeyer. In practice New York, 1890—. Pres. park bd., New York, under Mayor Low, 1902-03; postmaster of New York, 1905-07; chmn. (for New York City) Pub. Utilities Commn., N.Y., 1907-13. Chmn. Rep. Nat. Com., 1916-18. Mem. Ry. Wage Commn.; chmn. N.Y. and N.J. Port Commn. Treas. Societies Realty Co. Apptd. mem. Wage Umpire Bd., July 13, 1918. Home: Babylon, L.I., N.Y. Died Apr. 9, 1940.

WILLEY, D(ay) Allen, writer; b. Rochester, N.Y., Aug. 6, 1860; s. Ethan Allen and Demis Maria (Wells) W.; ed. U. of Rochester; m. Helen J. Muller, Oct. 10, 1895. Began as reporter, and became city editor, Rochester Democrat and Chronicle; removed to Baltimore, 1890; editor Baltimore World, and asst. editor Manufacturer's Record. Episcopalian. Home: Baltimore, Md. Died Dec. 14, 1917.

WILLEY, Henry, journalist, botanist; b. Geneseo, N.Y., July 19, 1824; s. Ogden Moseley and Abigail Belden (Chamberlain) W.; ed. Normal School, Bridgewater, Mass.; admitted to N.Y. bar, 1848; practiced law at Geneseo and later in Spencerport, N.Y.; went to Mass., 1851; taught for several yrs.; on editorial staff New Bedford Daily Evening Standard, July 1857 to Jan. 1, 1900. Spl. student and collector of N. Am. lichens. Author: Isaac Wiley, of New London, Conn., and His Descendants; Introduction to the study of Lichens; Synopsis of the Genus Arthonia; Enumeration of the Lichens of New Bedford, Mass. Home: Weymouth, Mass. Deceased.

WILLIAMS, Abraham Pease; b. New Portland, Me., Feb. 3, 1832; academic edn. Clerk in gen. store, Fairfield, Me., 1858; went to Calif., 1858; engaged in mining, farming and merchandising; founded San Francisco Bd. of Trade, and was its first pres., serving 2 yrs. Treas., 1880, and chmn., 1884 and 1886, Rep. State Central Com. Elected U.S. senator to fill an unexpired term, Aug. 6, 1866-Mar. 3, 1887. Home: San Francisco, Calif. Died 1911.

WILLIAMS, Alfred Brockenbrough, editor; b. Hanover Co., Va., Jan. 10, 1856; s. Robert Alfred and Elizabeth Marshall (Colston) W.; attended pvt. schs. until 14; m. Mamie Young Bryce, Apr. 19, 1882 (died 1889); children—Margaret Dandridge (Mrs. P. G. Brown), Alfred Brockenbrough; m. 2d, Josephine (Gillenwater) Tighe, Feb. 3, 1925. Newspaperman, 1876—, and in that yr. accompanied Gen. Wade Hampton in his famous campaign through S.C.; went to Liberia with sailing ship full of negro emigrants, 1878, as corr. Charleston, S.C., News and Courier; exposed the horrors of mismanagement and inefficiency and broke up the enterprise; for same paper, disguised as a tramp, wrote up the convict camp iniquities, 1879, and did much to destroy the leasing system there; editor Greenville (S.C.) News, 1880-96. Worked for New York Advertiser and New York Times, 1896-1900; editor Richmond News, 1901; editor-in-chief News Leader, Richmond, 1903-10; editor-in-chief and part owner Morning Times and Evening World News, Roanoke, Va., and pres. Times Pub. Co., 1910-15; owner and editor Richmond Evening Journal, 1915-16; chief editorial writer Roanoke World News; now asso. editor The Southern Churchman. Sound Money Democrat. Home: Washington, D.C. Died Mar. 11, 1930.

WILLIAMS, Arthur, engineer; b. Norfolk, Va., Aug. 14, 1868; s. Rev. Christopher Stephen and Hannah Sanford (Rogers) W.; ed. pub. and pvt. schs., Hartford and New York; unmarried. Formerly vice-pres. New York Edison Company and other electrical orgns.; now dir. Metropolitan Life Ins. Co. Comdg. officer New York volunteer defense forces, mining New York Harbor during Spanish-Am. War. Fellow Am. Inst. E.E.; mem. numerous societies, civic orgns., etc. Trustee Village of Roslyn Harbor, L.I., and of French Inst. Chevalier Légion d'Honneur and Office de l'Instruction Publique conferred by French Republic; decorated by King of Spain, Knight Royal Order of Isabel the Catholic. Apptd. federal food adminstrn. for N.Y. City, Oct. 1917. Home: Roslyn, L.I. N.Y. Died Apr. 14, 1937.

WILLIAMS, Arthur B., congressman; b. Ashland, O., Jan. 27, 1872; s. Andrew M. and Almira E. (Stealy) W.; B.L., Olivet (Mich.) Coll., 1892; m. Sue M. Wilson, Jan. 12, 1897. Admitted to Mich. bar, 1894, and engaged in gen. practice at Battle Creek; apptd. gen. counsel C. W. Post, and Postum Cereal Co., 1911, also v.p. of the co.; active in developing 1,000 farms of 160 acres each out of raw prairie lands; resigned all connection with the co., 1923; sec.-treas. Enquirer News Co., Battle Creek. Mem. 68th Congress (1923-25), 3d Mich. Dist. Republican. Mem. exec. com. Council Nat. Defense, Battle Creek br., World War. Conglist. Mason. Home: Battle Creek, Mich. Died May 1, 1925.

WILLIAMS, Arthur Llewellyn, bishop; b. Owen Sound, Ont., Can., Jan. 30, 1856; s. Rev. Richard J. (Presbyn.) and Elizabeth (Williams) W.; acad. edn., E. Greenwich, R.I.; grad. Western Theol. Sem., Chicago, 1888; (D.D., Western Theol. Sem., 1900); m. Adelaide L. Makinster, Oct. 18, 1880. Deacon, 1888, priest, 1889, P.E. Ch.; missionary in White River Valley, Colo., 1888-91; rector St. Paul's, Denver, 1891-92, Christ Ch., Woodlawn Park, Chicago, 1892-99; consecrated coadjutor bishop of Neb., Oct. 1899; became bishop of Neb., 1908. Home: Omaha, Neb. Died Jan. 27, 1919.

WILLIAMS, C. Arthur, journalist; b. Newton, Kan., Oct. 19, 1876; s. Charles Clinton and Sarah Emma (Macartney) W.; ed. country sch., Harvey Co., Kan., and Newton High Sch. to 3d yr.; m. Frances B. Hite, Aug. 4, 1902. Engaged in newspaper work, 1890—; at one time mgr. New Orleans bureau, New York Commercial; with Houston Post, 1897-1907; attached to 7th Army Corps as corr. during Spanish War; became polit. editor The Washington Herald; made six months' trip to Australia and New Zealand, 1907, to study govt. ownership, concerning which has written extensively. Democrat. Home: Washington, D.C. Died 1908.

WILLIAMS, Channing Moore, bishop; b. Richmond, Va., July 18, 1829; A.B., William and Mary, 1853; grad. Theol. Sem., Va., 1855; (D.D., Columbia, 1867); unmarried. Deacon, 1853, priest, 1857, P.E. Ch.; missionary in China, 1857-66; consecrated, 1866, bishop of Yedo, Japan, and served until 1889, when he retired from Episcopal duties, but remained in Japan until Apr. 1908, when he returned to U.S. on account of health. Home: Richmond, Va. Died 1910.

WILLIAMS, Charles David, bishop; b. Bellevue, O., July 30, 1860; s. David and Eliza (Dickson) W.; A.B., Kenyon Coll., 1880 (A.M., 1893, D.D., 1894, L.H.D., 1906, Kenyon; LL.D., Hobart, 1907); m. Lucy V. Benedict, Sept. 29, 1886. Deacon, 1883, priest, 1884, P.E. Ch.; rector Fernbank and Riverside, O., 1884-89, St. Paul's, Steubenville, O., 1889-93; dean Trinity Cathedral, Cleveland, 1893-1906; elected, Nov. 16, 1905, consecrated, Feb. 7, 1906, bishop of Mich. Chaplain Ohio N.G., 1893-96; was pres. Cleveland library bd. 2 terms; was mem. Standing Com. Diocese of Ohio; del. Gen. Convs. P.E. Ch., 1895—. Author: A Valid Christianity for Today; The Christian Ministry and Social Problems; The Prophetic Ministry for Today, 1921. Home: Detroit, Mich. Died Feb. 14, 1923.

WILLIAMS, Charles Luther, prof. English lit.; b. Imlaystown, N.J., June 8, 1851; s. Sidney Woodward and Mary Catherine (Van Cleaf) W.; grad. Peddie Sch., Hightstown, N.J., 1872; A.B., Princeton, 1878, A.M., 1881; Crozer Theol. Sem., Chester, Pa., 1883-84; Oxford U., summer 1903; L.H.D., Bucknell U., 1913; D.D., Denison U., 1931; m. Mary Elizabeth Giberson, June 12, 1881; 1 dau., Helen (Mrs. George W. Walker). Vice prin. Pennington (N.J.) Sem., 1881-83; ordained ministry Bapt. Ch., 1884; pastor Upland, Pa., 1884-93; prof. English lit., Denison U., 1893-1921, prof. emeritus, 1921—. Republican. Mason. Wrote: The American Student and the Rhodes Scholarships, 1903; Literature in England (449-1350), 1898. Home: Granville, O. Died Aug. 1933.

WILLIAMS, Charles Richard, editor; b. Prattsburg, N.Y., Apr. 16, 1853; s. Ira C. and Anna M. (Benedict) W.; student U. of Rochester, 1871-73; A.B. (head of class), Princeton, 1875, A.M., 1878; student univs. of Göttingen and Leipzig, 1876-77; Switzerland and Italy, 1877-78; hon. Ph.D., Princeton, 1893; L.H.D., Wabash, 1903; LL.D., Ohio Wesleyan U., Kenyon Coll., 1922; m. Almira, d. William Henry Smith, mgr. Associated Press, of Lake Forest, Ill., Oct. 2, 1884 (died 1895); m. 2d, Bertha Rose Knefler, June 23, 1902; 1 dau. (adopted niece), Mary Almira (Mrs. J. Homer Sherman, dec.). Prin. high sch., Auburn, N.Y., 1878-79; tutor Latin, Princeton, 1878-81; editor Potter's Am. Monthly, Phila., 1881; prof. Greek, Lake Forest U., 1881-83; lit. editor New York World, 1883; asst. gen. mgr. Associated Press, 1883-92; editor-in-chief Indianapolis News, 1892-1911. Author: In Many Moods (poems), 1910; Life of Rutherford B. Hayes, 1914; History of the Cliosophic Society, 1915. Editor: Selections from Lucian (with introduction and notes), 1882; Diary and Letters of Rutherford B. Hayes (5 vols.), 1922-26. Speaker for Nat. Security League and lecturer before Naval Sch. at Princeton Univ., 1918. Home: Princeton, N.J. Died May 6, 1927.

WILLIAMS, Charles Sumner, naval officer; b. Saratoga Co., N.Y., Sept. 8, 1856; s. John F. and Anna E. W.; ed. U. of Wis. and U.S. Naval Acad. (non-grad.); m. Anna Emily Bayard, Dec. 9, 1885; 1 son, Charles Sumner. Apptd. asst. p.m., rank of ensign, June 16, 1880; promoted through grades to commodore, and retired Sept. 8, 1920; rear adm. (temp.), July 1, 1918. Served on battleship Newark, Spanish-Am. War, 1898; fleet p.m. in Newark, 1902-04; purchasing pay officer, Boston, 1904-07; gen. storekeeper, Navy Yard, Boston, 1907-10; Navy Pay Office, Boston, 1910-13; in charge Navy Disbursing Office, Washington, D.C., 1913-14; in charge Provisions and Clothing Depot, Navy Yard, New York, 1914-17, South Brooklyn, N.Y., 1917-18; in comd. Fleet Supply Base, Brooklyn, 1918-Sept. 8, 1920. Home: Summit, N.J. Died Sept. 4, 1936.

WILLIAMS, Charles Turner, banker; b. Warrenton, N.C., Oct. 17, 1874; s. Thomas Clay and Georgianna (Turner) W.; ed. pub. schs.; m. Willie Herbert Ashton, July 17, 1903; children—Charles Turner, Ann Elizabeth. Began as stenographer, later newspaper reporter, and in ry. business, advancing to div. supt.; entered banking business with John L. Williams & Sons, Richmond, Va., 1904; with Middendorf, Williams & Co., bankers, Baltimore, 1910; investment mgr. Fidelity Trust Co., Baltimore, 1912-19; v.p. Fidelity Securities Corp., 1920-23; pres. C. T. Williams & Co., investment bankers, Oct. 1, 1923—. One of the organizers of the Investment Bankers Assn. of America, 1912-14. Served as treas. of the Am. Red Cross Mission to Rumania, July 1917-Jan. 1919; crossed Siberia into Russia, thence to Archangel, carrying first supplies from U.S. south to Rumania, requiring freight train of 58 cars, crossing Russia for 22 days under many difficulties; promoted maj. and head of Am. Red Cross Mission which left New York for Archangel, July 1918, carrying civilian and military relief supplies; traveled in relief work more than 1,500 miles by sled, mostly within Arctic Circle; Red Cross commr. to N. Russia, winter 1919; served with 339th Inf., U.S.A.; established Red Cross hosp. and in charge civilian relief. Chmn. Publicity Com., 1st Liberty Loan Campaign for Md.; member Publicity Com., Speakers' Committe in Liberty Loan campaigns in Md., World War. Decorated Order of the Cross of Queen Marie (Rumania), 1920. Home: Baltimore, Md. Died July 27, 1933.

WILLIAMS, Charles Urquhart, lawyer; b. Henrico Co., Va., Dec. 27, 1840; s. Charles Bruce and Ann Mercer (Hackley) W.; ed. pvt. tutor and various schs. until 1857; in mercantile business, 1857-58; entered law class in U. of Va., 1860, but before graduation entered C.S.A., Apr. 1861, and served as pvt., lt. and capt. until surrender of Gen. R. E. Lee; admitted to Va. bar, Oct. 1865; m. Alice Davenport Williams, Aug. 27, 1867. In practice, 1865 to July 1, 1907. Mem. Va. Ho. of Rep., 1875-76, 1876-77. Home: Strawberry Hill, Va. Died 1910.

WILLIAMS, Clarissa Smith; b. Salt Lake City, Utah, Apr. 21, 1859; d. George Albert and Susan (West) Smith; father one of Utah pioneers of 1847 and 1st counselor to Brigham Young; grad. Normal Sch., U. of Utah, 1875; m. William N. Williams, July 17, 1877; children—Mrs. Clarissa Van Law, Mrs. Sarah Wilson, Mrs. Eva Darger, Mrs. Georgia James, George Albert, Bathsheba, Lyman Smith (and 4 dec.). Began with Latter Day Saints Relief Soc. (Nat. Woman's Relief Soc.), at 16, advancing to 1st v.p., 1911, gen. pres., Apr. 1921—. Editor Relief Society Magazines, 1923—. Del. Internat. Council of Women. Rome, 1914; active in Red Cross and relief work during World War; Utah State chmn. quinquennial fund com. of Nat. Council of Women of U.S.; apptd. to raise funds for entertainment of Internat. Council of Women, Washington, D.C., 1925. Republican. Home: Salt Lake City, Utah. Deceased.

WILLIAMS, Constant, brig. gen. U.S.A.; b. Pittsburgh, May 25, 1843; s. W. H. and Ellen Pope (Barclay) W.; ed. Griggs and McDonald's Acad., Pittsburgh, Western Univ. of Pa., Kenwood Ch., New Brighton, Pa., and Webber's Acad., N. Sewickley, Pa.; m. Cornelia Peake De Camp, Sept. 7, 1865. Served during Civ. War as non-commd. officer and pvt. 82d Pa. Vols., and as pvt., 2d lt. and 1st lt. 7th Inf. U.S.A.; capt. 7th Inf., May 10, 1873, maj., Jan. 28, 1897; transferred to 17th Inf., Feb. 23, 1897, to 19th Inf., Oct. 21, 1898; lt. col. 15th Inf., Jan. 16, 1899; col. 26th Inf., Feb. 2, 1901; brig. gen. U.S.A., July 12, 1904; retired by operation of law, May 25, 1907. Served in Cuba, 1899-1900, in P.I., 1900-03; comd. Dept. of the Columbia, 1904-06, Dept. of the Colo., 1906-07. Bvtd. maj., "for gallant services in action against Indians at the Big Hole, Mont., Aug. 9, 1877," where was twice wounded. Episcopalian. Home: Schenectady, N.Y. Died Apr. 20, 1922.

WILLIAMS, Cora Lenore, educator; b. Pleasant Valley, Minn., Jan. 20, 1865; d. John P. and Irene (Dutton) Williams; Ph.B., U. of Calif., 1891, M.S., 1898. Instr. mathematics, Santa Ana High Sch., Oakland High Sch. and U. of Calif.; founder, 1917, and pres. Williams Inst., Berkeley, Calif. Mem. League Am. Pen Women. Author: Introduction to Absolute Geometry, 1905; As If, 1914; Four-Dimensional Reaches, 1915; Creative Involution, 1916; Olympus, 1926; Adding a New Dimension to Education. Died Dec. 13, 1937.

WILLIAMS, Dana Scott, lawyer; b. Lewiston, Me., Sept. 23, 1878; s. Sumner G. (Rev.) and Ella F. (Wyman) W.; LL.B., U. of Me., 1900; m. Juanita D. Porter, July 6, 1910. Admitted to Me. bar, 1900;

in practice at Lewiston. Mem. Soc. of Friends. Mason (Imperial Potentate Imperial Council, Shrine, 1934-35). Home: Lewiston, Me. Died Oct. 20, 1940.

WILLIAMS, Daniel H., physician; b. Hollidaysburg, Pa., Jan. 18, 1858; s. Daniel and Sarah Ann (Price) W.; grad. Janesville Classical Acad., 1878; M.D., Chicago Med. Coll., 1883; LL.D., Wilberforce U., 1908; m. Alice D. Johnson, Apr. 2, 1898. Surgeon to South Side Dispensary, Chicago, 1884-92; founded, 1891, and surgeon Provident Hosp.; phys., Protestant Orphan Asylum, 1884-93; surgeon-in-chief, Freedmen's Hosp., Washington, 1893-98; asso. on staff, St. Luke's Hosp., Chicago. Mem. Ill. State Bd. of Health, 1889, reapptd., 1891. Fellow Am. Coll. Surgeons. Prof. clin. surgery, Meharry Med. Coll., Nashville, Tenn., 1899—. Home: Chicago, Ill. Died Aug. 4, 1931.

WILLIAMS, David, publisher; b. Waterford, Ireland, Dec. 23, 1841; s. John and Susan (Richardson) W.; came with parents to U.S., 1850; grad. Middletown (N.Y.) Acad., 1857; m. Alletta L. Van Norden (dec.); m. 2d, Alice F. Hinckley (dec.). Asso. with father in publishing The Iron Age (established 1855) until 1868, when became sole propr.; formed the David Williams Co., 1897, to publish The Iron Age and other trade and tech. periodicals and books and was pres. of co. until fall of 1909, when retired. Established The Metal Worker, 1873, Carpentry and Building, 1879; founded, 1884, Williams Printing Co. Pres. Am. Trade Press Assn., and Federation of Trade Press Assns. in U.S. Home: New York, N.Y. Died Oct. 28, 1927.

WILLIAMS, David, physician; b. in Ohio, Dec. 17, 1843; ed. country schs., Denison U. and Adrian Coll. to close of junior year; grad. Eclectic Med. Inst., Cincinnati M.D., 1870; m. Anna Nichols, April 24, 1867. Private for short time in Civil war. Taught school about 5 yrs. Pres. Nat. Eclectic Med. Assn., 1898-99; mem. and treas. State Bd. of Med. Registration and Examination. Eclectic mem. staff of Protestant Hosp., Columbus, O. Author numerous papers in eclectic med. jours. Originator of Williams' Substitute for the Whitehead Operation. Home: Columbus, O. Died 1902.

WILLIAMS, Dwight, artist; b. Camillus, N.Y., April 25, 1856; s. Dwight and Keziah Elizabeth (Lane) W.; ed. Cazenovia Sem., 1871-75; unmarried. Professionally engaged as artist, 1875—; best known by colonial studies and Revolutionary landmarks. Teacher Houghton Sch., 1876-79; instr. Utica Sem.; dir. Art Sch. in Norfolk Coll., 1889-92; instr. art, Nat. Park Sch., nr. Washington, 1894-98. Represented in Nat. Acad. Design, Atlanta Expn., Louisville Expn., and current exhbns. Expert collections of rare old pictures, and gave much study and research to treatment and restoration of paintings by the old masters. Traveled in Europe, 1892, 96, 1909, and old Mexico, 1900. Home: Cazenovia, N.Y. Died Mar. 12, 1932.

WILLIAMS, Edward Franklin, clergyman; b. Uxbridge, Mass., July 22, 1832; s. George and Delilah (Morse) W.; Revolutionary ancestry; descendant of John Williams; A.B., Yale, 1856, A.M., 1859; B.D., Princeton Theol. Sem., 1861; D.D., Ill. Coll., 1882; LL.D., Wheaton, 1899, Adrian, 1909; m. Janes Clarissa Pitkin, Oct. 24, 1866 (died 1908). Field agt. of U.S. Christian Commn., 2½ yrs. in armies of the Potomac and the James; was with the 5th Army Corps during its march through the Wilderness. Ordained Congl. ministry, Oct. 17, 1866; prin. Lookout Mountain Ednl. Instns., 1866-67, Normal Dept., Howard U., Washington, 1867; pastor St. Charles, 1869, Tabernacle Ch., Chicago, 1869-73, South Ch. (formerly Forty-Seventh St. Ch.), Chicago, 1873-91; in Europe and the East traveling, and in U. of Berlin, 1891-93; lit. work and preaching as supply, 1893-1901; pastor, Evanston Av. Ch., Chicago, 1901-11; pastor emeritus Wellington Av. Ch., Chicago. Western rep. of Congregationalist 28 yrs.; pres. Washingtonian Home, Chicago, 5 yrs.; dir. Chicago City Missionary Soc. Author: Christian Life in Germany; Life of Dr. D. K. Pearsons, the Philanthropist, 1911; also many articles in Bibliotheca Sacra, Popular Science Monthly, and in various religious papers. Pres. Chicago Tract Soc. Home: Winnetka, Ill. Died May 26, 1919.

WILLIAMS, Edward Higginson, Jr., engineer; b. Proctorsville, Vt., Sept. 30, 1849; s. Edward Higginson and Cornelia Bailey (Pratt) W.; Phillips Acad., Andover, 1865-68; A.B., Yale, 1872; B.S. in Chemistry, Lehigh, 1875, E.M., 1876; Sc.D., U. of Vt.; LL.D., Wheaton, 1899, Adrian, 1909; m. Jane Clarissa 1883; children— Olive Bemis (Mrs. Nathan Parke, II), Cornelia (Mrs. Charles W. Fowler), Elizabeth (Mrs. Seymour Ballard), Edward Higginson, III, Norman, Amory Leland, Wentworth, Laurens, Augustine. In engring. corps, Pa. R.R., 1872-73; in charge mining corps, anthracite region, 1876-79; supt. mines Montour Iron & Steel Co., 1879-80; asst. mining engr. Cambria Iron Co., 1880-81; prof. mining engring. and geology, 1881-1902, lecturer on mining and geology, 1902—, Lehigh U. Mem. Legion of Honor of Am. Inst. Mining and Metall. Engrs.; original fellow Geol. Soc. America; emeritus life fellow A.A.A.S. V.pres. Corp. Norman Williams Pub. Library, Woodstock, Vt., 1900—. Author: Manual of Lithology, 1886; 1896; Vigintennial Record of the Class of 1868, Phillips Academy, Andover, 1888; Early History of Woodstock, Vt., 1907. Editor: second edition, Atkinson's Gases Met Within Coal Mines, 1886; Coal and Metal Miners' Pocket Book, 1890; Robert Williams of Roxbury and Descendants, Four Generations, 1890. Contbr. to Science, Am. Jour. of Science, Jour. Am. Geol. Soc. and Proc. of Am. Philos. Soc., 1893-1920. Wrote: (brochure) Pennsylvania Glaciation, First Phase, 1917. Home: Woodstock, Vt. Died Nov. 2, 1933.

WILLIAMS, Elihu Stephen, congressman, lawyer; b. New Carlisle, O., Jan. 24, 1835; s. Rev. Henry W.; ed. Linden Hill Acad.; m. Alice Gordon, May 31, 1866. Studied law, Dayton, O.; served in war, capt. Co. H, 71st Ohio vol. inf.; comd. post, Carthage, Tenn., 1863; atty. gen. 6th jud. dist. Tenn., 1865-67; mem. Tenn. legislature, 1867-69, removed to Troy, O., 1875; practiced law, 1875-87; mem. Congress, 1887-91, from 3d Ohio dist.; editor the Troy Buckeye. Home: Troy, O. Died 1903.

WILLIAMS, Elizabeth Sprague, settlement worker; b. Buffalo, N.Y., Aug. 31, 1869; d. Frank and Olive (French) Williams; B.S., Smith Coll., 1891; A.M., Columbia, 1896; unmarried. Head worker College Settlement, New York, Oct. 1898-Mar. 1919; organizer and dir. of orphanages in Cacah and Velic, Serbia, Mar. 1919-July 1921. Dir. Lackawanna (N.Y.) Social Center, Oct. 1911-15. Unitarian. Home: Suffern, N.Y. Died Aug. 1922.

WILLIAMS, Ennion Gifford, public health officer; b. Richmond, Va., Jan. 31, 1874; s. John L. and Maria Ward (Skelton) W.; U. of Va., 1892-97; Med. Dept., U. of Va., 1897; m. Anna Heath Lassiter, Oct. 21, 1902; children—Virginia Lassiter, Ennion Skelton, Anna Heath, Daniel Lassiter, John Randolph, Charles Lassiter, Elizabeth Rives, Edmund Randolph. Prof. pathology, bacteriology and histology, 1900-08, prof. preventive medicine, 1916-23, Med. Coll. of Va. State health commr. of Va., 1908—. Democrat. Mem. Richmond City Council, 1905-08. Mem. State Council Defense, 1917-19. Episcopalian. Pres. Conf. of State and Provincial Bds. of Health of N.A., 1915-16. Home: Richmond, Va. Died June 6, 1931.

WILLIAMS, Ernest, ry. official; b. Lynchburg, Va., Oct. 21, 1862; s. Fayette and Mary (Snead) W.; ed. high sch., Lynchburg; m. Mary L. Thomas, June 1888; children—Arthur Snead, Herbert Lathan. Began in lumber mfg. business at Lynchburg, 1878; pres. Williams & McKestland Lumber Co., Norfolk Southern Investment Corp.; chmn. bd. and v.p. Norfolk & Southern R.R.; v.p. First Nat. Bank (Lynchburg), Lynchburg Title & Bond Corp. V.p. Lynchburg City Council, 1920-24 (reëlected and resigned); accomplished erection of bridge over James River, at Lynchburg. Mason. Home: Lynchburg, Va. Died May 20, 1929.

WILLIAMS, Espy (William Hendricks), dramatist; b. Carrollton (New Orleans), La., Jan. 30, 1852; s. William H. and Lavinia M. (Pollard) W.; ed. in grammar schs.; m. Nannie Bowers, April 15, 1879. Engaged in financial business, 1885—; one of charter members Am. Dramatists' Club of New York. Author: Dream of Art, poems, 1892. Plays: Parrhasius, a tragedy (prod. Robt. Mantell), 1894; The Husband, a society drama (same), 1895; The Queen's Garter, romantic play (same), 1896; The Man in Black (prod. Walker Whiteside), 1897; A Cavalier of France (prod. Louis James), 1897; The Duke's Jester, romantic comedy (prod. Frederick Warde), 1900; Unorna, a romantic play (prod. by Mrs. Brune), 1902; The Emperior's Double, a romantic comedy (prod. by Clarence Brune, in England), 1903; Ollamus, comic opera; A Royal Joke, comic opera (prod. 1901, Metropolitan Opera Co.); Eugene Aram, a tragedy, 1874; The Last Witch, a play, 1886. Home: New Orleans, La. Died 1908.

WILLIAMS, Francis Bennett, capitalist; b. Mobile, Ala., Jan. 18, 1853; s. Charles and Emily C. (Neayne) W.; student Spring Hill (Ala.) Coll., 1868-71; m. Emily Seyburn, 1876. Engaged in lumber and sugar business in La., 1872—; pres. F. B. Williams Cypress Co., Sterling Sugar Refinery Co., Atchafalaya Ship Channel Co., St. Barnard Cypress Co., Williams Lbr. Co., Sterlings Sugars, Inc.; v.p. Whitney Central Nat. Bank, Shady Side Planting Co.; owner of several sugar plantations and refineries. Mem. La. Senate, 1894-98; served as chmn. Rep. State Central Com. Episcopalian. Home: New Orleans, La. Died Jan. 31, 1929.

WILLIAMS, Francis Henry, M.D.; b. Uxbridge, Mass., Apr. 15, 1852; s. Henry Willard and Elizabeth (Dewe) W.; B.S., Mass. Inst. Tech., 1873; M.D., Harvard, 1877; European study, 1877-79; m. Anna Dunn Phillips, Sept. 25, 1891. Asst. U.S. Transit of Venus Expdn. to Japan, 1874; tour around world, 1874-75; practicing phys. at Boston, 1879—. Instr. in materia medica, 1884-85, materia medica and therapeutics, 1885-86, asst. prof. materia medica and therapeutics, 1886-88, asst. prof. therapeutics, 1888-91, Harvard Med. Sch.; visiting phys., 1896-1913, sr. phys., 1913—, Boston City Hosp. Life member Corp. of Mass. Inst. Tech. (mem. exec. com. its 1st 25 yrs.), 1882—. Fellow A.A.A.S., American Acad. Arts and Sciences; pres. Assn. Am. Physicians, 1917-18. Author: The Roentgen Rays in Medicine and Surgery, 1901-03. Initiated bacteriol. examinations in diphtheria, Boston City Hosp., 1892 (first in community to use antitoxin, 1894); developed original methods of treatment of various diseases with the beta rays from radium, especially diseased tonsils (instead of operation) and many diseases of the eye; first paper on subject (published Med. News Feb. 6, 1904) "Some Physical Properties and Medical Uses of Radium Salts," with report of forty-two cases treated with pure radium bromide. Devised clinical method of measuring the X-rays and the beta rays from radium. Home: Boston, Mass. Died June 22, 1926.

WILLIAMS, Francis Howard, author; b. Phila., Pa., Sept. 2, 1844; s. Joseph J. and Martha P. (Shoemaker) W.; ed. at Phila.; m. Mary B., d. William Churchill Houston, May 31, 1865. Writer of plays, poems, stories, etc. Mem. Am. Inst. of Arts and Letters. Author: (plays) The Princess Elizabeth (lyric drama), 1880; The Higher Education, 1881; A Reformer in Ruffles, 1881; Theodora, a Christmas Pastoral, 1882; Master and Man, 1884; also: Boscosel (story), 1888; Atman, 1891; Pennsylvania Poets of the Provincial Period, 1893; The Flute Player and Other Poems, 1894; At the Rise of the Curtain (blank verse plays), 1904; The Burden-Bearer—an Epic of Lincoln, 1909; The Philadelphia Pageant, 1912. Home: Germantown, Pa. Died June 18, 1922.

WILLIAMS, Frank B(lair), mathematician; b. Warrensburg, Mo., Jan. 23, 1871; s. Oliver Davis and Margaret M. (Houx) W.; Warrensburg State Normal Sch. 3 yrs.; C.E., U. of Mo., 1890, M.S., 1893; Ph.D., Clark U., 1900; m. Elizabeth McCarthey, June 21, 1900. Survey work with Miss. River and Mo. River commn., 1890-92, and Miss. River Commn., summer 1900; U.S. asst. engr. in charge Tenn. River Survey, 1895-97; engring. work for N.Y. State Barge Canal and boundary lines, 1902-06; with Clark U., 1907—; prof. mathematics, 1908—. Y.M.C.A. sec. with A.E.F. in France, 1917-18. Fellow A.A.A.S. Conglist. Home: Worcester, Mass. Died 1933.

WILLIAMS, Frank French, lawyer; b. Buffalo, N.Y., Nov. 20, 1855; s. Frank and Olive (French) W.; A.B., U. of Mich., 1877; m. Ruth Churchyard, June 8, 1887; children—Olive, Roger C. Admitted to N.Y. bar, 1880, and in gen. practice at Buffalo, 1880—. Republican. Unitarian. Sec. Buffalo Orphan Asylum. Home: Buffalo, N.Y. Died May 4, 1936.

WILLIAMS, Frank Martin, civil engr.; b. Durhamville, N.Y., Apr. 11, 1873; s. William and Ellen L. (Sterling) W.; A.B., Colgate U., 1895, D.Sc., 1915; LL.B., Syracuse U., 1897, hon. M.C.E., 1919; m. Lucy M. Sterling, June 4, 1907; children—Frank Martin (dec.), David Sterling. Admitted to N.Y. bar, 1897, but engaged in engring. and contracting, Oneida, 1897-1900; entered service State of N.Y., state engr.'s dept., 1900, and was promoted to resident engr.; state engr. and surveyor, term 1909-10; chmn. Barge Canal Terminal Commn., to investigate canal harbors in U.S. and abroad, 1910-11; chief engr. Coleman-duPont Rd. (highway), Del., 1911-12; same Portage County Improvement Assn., Ravenna, O., 1912-13; state engr. and surveyor of N.Y., 1914-23; pvt. practice, 1923—. Consultant for N.Y. State Bridge and Tunnel Commn. and N.J. Interstate Bridge and Tunnel Commn. on constrn. of vehicular tunnel under Hudson River from New York to Jersey City; cons. engr. on Hudson River Regulating District; chief engr. Water Service Commn., city of Oswego, N.Y.; cons. engr. Utica Gas & Electric Co., Cohoes Power and Light Corp., Niagara, Lockport & Ontario Power Co., Power Corp. of New York. Mem. State Council of Defense, 1917-18. Republican. Baptist. Mason, Elk. Home: Albany, N.Y. Died Feb. 20, 1930.

WILLIAMS, Frankwood Earl, M.D.; b. Cardington, O., May 18, 1883; s. James Leander (M.D.) and Amanda Elizabeth (Wood) W.; Shortridge High Sch., Indianapolis, Ind., 1903; A.B., U. of Wis., 1907; M.D., U. of Mich., 1912; hon. D.Sc., from Colgate U., 1927; unmarried. Res. physician State Psychopathic Hosp., U. of Mich., 1912-13; exec. officer, 1st asst. phys. Boston Psychopathic Hosp., 1913-15; med. dir. Mass. Soc. Mental Hygiene, 1915-17; chmn. Mass. Advisory Prison Bd., 1916-17; asso. med. dir. Nat. Com. for Mental Hygiene, 1917-22 (leave of absence during war) and med. dir. same, 1922-31; v. chmn. war work com. of Nat. Com. for Mental Hygiene, N.Y. City, and mem. various sub-coms. of war work com., 1917-19, also mem. com. on war work of Am. Psychiatric Assn., 1917-20; maj. U.S.A., 1918-19; 1st asst. and chief div. of neurology and psychiatry, Office of Surgeon Gen., Washington, D.C.; lt. col. Med. O.R.C., 1919-29. Editor Mental Hygiene, 1917-32, Mental Hygiene Bull., 1923-31; cons. editor Social Science Abstracts to 1932. Mem. teaching staff Smith Coll. Sch. for Social Work, 1921-26, and N.Y. Sch. Social Work, 1924; faculty New Sch. for Social Research; consultant in mental hygiene to the Univ. Dept. of Health, and lecturer in psychiatry, to Sch. of Medicine, Yale, 1926-29, Coll. Phys. and Surg. (Columbia), 1930-32. Chmn. mental hygiene sect., Nat. Conf. Social Work, 1917-19, 1922-24; mem. In ternat. Conf. Social Work of Nat. Conf. Social Work, 1927; vice chmn. Nat. Health Council, 1922-23; member administrative bd. Inst. of Child Guidance of Commonwealth Fund, 1927-31; mem. advisory council N.Y. Health and Tuberculosis Demonstrations, also of Milbank Memorial Fund until 1931; mem. bd. dirs. N.Y. Psychoanalytic Inst. and of editorial bd. Psychoanalytic Quarterly; chmn. com. on program of First Internat. Congress on Mental Hygiene, 1930; editor Proceedings 1st Internat. Congress Mental Hygiene. Author: Adolescence—Studies in Mental Hygiene; Youth and Russia; Further Studies in Mental Hygiene. Co-Author: Med. Dept. U.S. Army in World War (Vol. X, Neuropsychiatry); Social Aspects of Mental Hygiene. Editor and contbr. Some Social Aspects of Mental Hygiene. Home: New York, N.Y. Died Sept. 24, 1936.

WILLIAMS, Frederic M., workmen's compensation commr.; b. Washington, Conn., Nov. 27, 1862; s. Stanley and Esther C. (Meeker) W.; LL.B., Yale, 1887; m. Isabelle A. Gaylord, Oct. 28, 1891. Admitted to Conn. bar, 1887, and began practice at Litchfield; practiced at New Milford, Conn., 1888-1913; mem. Workmen's Compensation Commission, Conn., 1913—, chmn., 1914—. Mem. Internat. Assn. Industrial Accident Bds. and Commns. (pres.). Republican. Episcopalian. Mason. Home: Waterbury, Conn. Died Feb. 28, 1934.

WILLIAMS, Frederick Wells, univ. prof.; b. Macao (Portuguese Colony in) China, Oct. 31, 1857; s. Samuel Wells (Am. missionary) and Sarah (Walworth) W.; A.B., Yale, 1879; univs. of Göttingen, Berlin, Paris, 1879-81; m. Fanny, d. Reverend H. L. Wayland, Nov. 19, 1885; children—Wayland Wells, Elizabeth. Asst. librarian, Yale Library, 1883-85; lit. editor The National Baptist, Phila., 1887-93; instr. Oriental history, 1893-1900, asst. prof. modern Oriental history, 1900-25, emeritus, 1925—, Yale. Author: (with S. W. Williams) The Middle Kingdom (2 vols.), 1883; Life and Letters of S. Wells Williams, LL.D., 1889; Chinese Folklore (Smithsonian Report for 1900); Problems of Chinese Immigration in Farther Asia, 1900; China and Japan (Book IV, Vol. II, History of All Nations), 1903; A History of the Class of 1879, Yale College, 1906; Relations Between the U.S. and China, 1910; Anson Burlingame and the First Chinese Mission to Foreign Powers, 1912; The Best Hundred Books on China, 1924. Editor: G. B. Bacon's "Siam," 1892; Memorial Vol. on Prof. G. H. Williams, 1896; Memorial Vol. on R. S. Williams, of Utica, N.Y., 1900; Williams' Journal of the Perry Expedition to Japan, 1910. Home: New Haven, Conn. Died Jan. 22, 1928.

WILLIAMS, Gardner Fred, mining engr.; b. Saginaw, Mich., Mar. 14, 1842; s. Alpheus Fuller and Ann Keyes (Simpson) W.; grad. Coll. of Calif. (now U. of Calif.), Oakland, 1865; studied Freiberg (Saxony) Mining Acad., 3 yrs.; LL.D., U. of Calif., 1910; Dr.Engring., U. of Mich., 1917; m. Fanny Locke, Oct. 23, 1871 (died 1911); father of Alpheus Fuller W. Examined salt deposits of Carman Island, Mex., 1869; asst. assayer U.S. Mint, San Francisco, 1870; supt. and assayer Meadow Valley Co., Pioche, Nev., 1871-74; supt. and engr. various mines, Nev., Utah and Calif., and cons. engr. to New York capitalists, 1875-84; in charge of gold mines in Northern Transvaal, S. Africa, 1884-85; engr. for Exploration Co., Ltd., of London, in S. Africa, 1886-87; gen. mgr. De Beers Co., which later became De-Beers-Consol. Mines, Ltd., 1887-1905, organized by Cecil Rhodes, Alfred Beit and others, which produced 95 per cent of the diamond yield of the world. Author: The Diamond Mines of South Africa (2 vols.), revised edit., 1906; The Genesis of the Diamond, 1905. Died Aug. 23, 1922.

WILLIAMS, Gardner Stewart, cons. engr.; b. Saginaw (W.S.), Mich., 1866; s. Stewart B. and Juliet M. (Ripley) W.; B.S., U. of Mich., 1889, C.E., 1899; m. Jessie B. Wright, 1893; children—Harriet Ripley (Mrs. John B. Waite), William Wright. Asst. engr. water works constrn., Bismarck, N.D., 1887; resident engr. water works constrn., Greenville, Mich., 1888, and Owosso, Mich., 1889; civ. engr. Bd. Water Commrs., Detroit, 1893-98; engr. in charge hydraulic lab., Cornell, 1899-1904; prof. civ., hydraulic and sanitary engring., U. of Mich., 1904-11; cons. engr., Sept. 27, 1911—, specializing in hydraulics and water power. Commd. major Engr. O.R.C., 1917. Mem. Internat. Waterways Commn., 1903-05; mem. Am. Engring. Council, 1920 (v.p. 1923-29). Author: (with Allen Hazen) Hydraulic Tables, 1905; "Hydraulics," in Am. Civ. Engrs.' Pocketbook. Home: Ann Arbor, Mich. Died Dec. 12, 1931.

WILLIAMS, George Alfred, artist, illustrator; b. Newark, N.J., July 8, 1875; s. Alfred Gardner and Elizabeth Black (Havell) W.; ed. at Newark; m. Clara G. Andrews, Feb. 24, 1903; children—John Gardner, Bertha Elizabeth, Robert Havell, Marianna Holroyd, Rushforth. Began illustrating for mags., 1899; illustrated many books; later devoted most of time to painting and writing. Exhibitor at all the important art exhbns.; represented in Newark Mus. by frieze of 6 paintings, interpreting Tristram and Isolde, in permanent collection of Art Inst. Chicago and in many private collections. Silver medal, Panama P.I. Expn., 1915. Author: The Boy's Book of Indians; The Boy's Book of Pirates; (also illustrator) The American Boy's Book of Soldiers for Defense of Our Country, 1915; Robert Havell, Junior, Engraver of Audubon's "The Birds of America," 1916; Portraits of Robert Havell, Junior, 1917; Principles, 1917; Pastels of Dwight William Tryon, an Appreciation, 1921. Home: Kennebunkport, Me. Died Feb. 29, 1932.

WILLIAMS, George Burchell, financial expert; b. Lockport, N.Y., Dec. 5, 1842; ed. Lockport Union Acad.; removed, 1858, to Lafayette, Ind.; m. Cornelia S., d. Gen. Lauren Upson, 1873. Supervisor internal revenue for Ind., 1867-68; deputy commr. internal revenue, Washington, 1869-70; selected, 1871, by Emperor of Japan as financial adviser of Japanese Govt.; commr. of Japan to Europe in connection with financial matters, 1872, 76. Decorated by the Mikado of Japan with Order of the Rising Sun, and by Sultan of Turkey with the Order of the Osmanieh. Del. Rep. Nat. Conv., Chicago, 1884. Died Mar. 15, 1912.

WILLIAMS, George Clinton Fairchild, capitalist; b. Cheshire, Conn., Feb. 26, 1857; s. William Cook (M.D.) and Lucinda (Fairchild) W.; student Yale Med. Sch.; M.D., New York U., 1878; m. Jessie Scott Dike, Feb. 12, 1896; 1 son, Staunton. Pres. Capewell Horse Nail Co.; dir. Hartford Steam Boiler Inspection & Ins. Co., Hartford-Aetna Nat. Bank. Mem. Conn. Ho. of Rep., 1880-81; mem. Bd. Park Commrs., Hartford (pres.); pres. State Dept. Pub. Welfare; dir. Hartford Hosp.; trustee Episcopal Acad. of Conn. Dir. Conn. Fair Assn.; pres. Conn. Humane Soc.; trustee Good-Will Club. Owner of one of the most extensive private collections of manuscripts and publications of Am. Revolution. Chmn. Conn. Tercentenary Commn. Republican. Died Nov. 15, 1933.

WILLIAMS, George Forrester, journalist; b. on Rock of Gibraltar, 1837; s. of British Army officer; boyhood in E. and W.I. and Gold Coast of Africa; m. Marie Sophia Van Brunt, 1865. Joined staff New York Times, 1856; served in Civil War as pvt. to bvt. maj.; present at battles of Yorktown, Cold Harbor, Malvern Hill, Fredericksburg, Chancellorsville, Gettysburg, Thoroughfare Gap, Wilderness and other important engagements; severely wounded at Malvern Hill, and the Wilderness; acted as war corr., 1864-65; corr. during Franco-Mexican War, 1867, and saw Maximillian executed at Querétaro; vol. aid, col. Mexican Army, 1867; brig. gen. and chief of arty., Guatemalian and Peruvian armies, 1868; mng. editor New York Times, 1870-73; originated and conducted Poor Children's Picnics and Fresh Air Fund; mng. editor New York Herald, 1875-76; conducted the newsdealer war in 1883-84 when James Gordon Bennett fought for and compelled sale of the Herald at reduced price; later connected with New York World, Advertiser, Recorder, and Journal. Author: Bullet and Shell; Lucy's Rebel; The Memorial War Book; Unfair in Love and War; Across the Lines; Half a Century of New York Newspaper Life. Died Dec. 30, 1920.

WILLIAMS, George Fred, lawyer; b. Dedham, Massachusetts, July 10, 1852; s. George W. and Henrietta (Rice) W.; A.B., Dartmouth, 1872; studied at Heidelberg and Berlin, 1870-71; married; 1 son, Barrett. Admitted to bar, 1875, and practiced at Boston. Mem. Mass. Ho. of Rep., 1889; mem. 52d Congress (1891-93), 9th Mass. Dist.; Dem. nominee for Gov. of Mass., 1895, 96, 97; E.E. and M.P. to Greece, 1913-July 1914 (resigned). Editor Williams' Citations of Massachusetts Cases, Annual Digest of the United States, vols. 10 to 17. Home: Needham, Mass. Died July 11, 1932.

WILLIAMS, George Gilbert, banker; b. East Haddam, Conn., 1826; s. Dr. Datus and Clarissa Maria (Peck) W.; ed. in dist. sch. and village acad.; m. Virginia, d. Aaron King, Nov. 14, 1867. Entered Chem. Bank, Dec. 1841, as asst. to paying teller; became paying teller at 20, cashier, 1855; pres., Jan. 2, 1878. Dir. in numerous financial and charitable instns. Home: New York, N.Y. Died 1903.

WILLIAMS, George Henry, Attorney Gen. of U.S.; b. New Lebanon, N.Y., Mar. 26, 1823; s. Taber D. and Lydia (Goodrich) W.; ed. Pompey Acad., S. Pompey Hill, N.Y.; studied law, Pompey Hill; LL.D., Willamette U., and Pacific Coll.; m. Kate Van Antwerp, 1850; m. 2d, Kate George (both deceased). Admitted to bar, 1844; practiced in Ia.; elected judge 1st Jud. Dist., Ia., 1847; presdl. elector, 1852; apptd. chief justice Ore. Ty., 1853; mem. Ore. Constl. Conv. and chmn. judiciary com.; U.S. senator from Ore., 1865-71; mem. High Joint Commn. to settle "Alabama" claims; Atty. Gen. of U.S. in cabinet of President, 1871-75, resigned; nominated by President Grant for chief justice of U.S., but withdrew name. Later in practice at Portland, Ore., firm of Williams, Wood & Linthicum. Mayor Portland, Ore., 1902-05. Republican. Episcopalian. Pres. Boys' and Girls' Aid Soc.; pres. Pattion Home for the Aged. Home: Portland, Ore. Died 1910.

WILLIAMS, George Philip, missionary sec.; b. Columbus, O., May 13, 1859; s. Robert Philip and Sarah Margaret W.; B.D., McCormick Theological Seminary, 1891; D.D. from Emporia (Kan.) Coll., 1904; m. Esther DeVine, June 2, 1891. Missionary, Am. S.S. Union, 1884-88; ordained Presbyn. ministry, 1891; pastor Emerald Av. Ch., Chicago, 1891-94; supt. Presbyn. Missions, Chicago Presbytery, 1894-1907; Northwestern Dist. supt. Am. S.S. Union, 1907-10; nat. sec. of missions, same, 1910-30; resigned on account of ill health. Republican. Home: Swarthmore, Pa. Died Apr. 7, 1940.

WILLIAMS, George Walton, banker, merchant; b. Burke County, N.C., Dec. 19, 1820; s. Edward and Mary (Brown) W.; walked 150 miles to Augusta, Ga., 1838; became clerk in grocery store there; partner, 1842, in Hand & Williams; m. Miss Wightman, sister of Bishop William May Wightman, of M.E. Church, 1843 (died 1854); m. 2d, Miss Porter, 1856. Established, 1852, wholesale grocery house of George W. Williams & Co., Charleston, S.C.; during war invested in Southern State securities when they could be bought low in the North; bought sterling exchange, 1861, at 103 Confederate money; sold it in 1865 at 225 currency; also bought lands and cotton extensively. Established, 1874, Carolina Savings Bank; of which pres. Wrote: Letters to Young Men; Making and Saving; Sketches of Travel in the Old and New World. Died 1903.

WILLIAMS, George Washington, naval officer; b. Yorkville, S.C., July 30, 1869; s. William B. and Mary E. W.; grad. U.S. Naval Acad., 1890; m. Susan M. Lyman, Feb. 6, 1895. Promoted ensign, July 1, 1892; lt. jr. grade, Mar. 3, 1899; lt., Mar. 26, 1899; lt. comdr., July 1, 1905; comdr., Mar. 3, 1911; capt. Aug. 29, 1916; rear admiral, June 3, 1922. Served on Columbia, Spanish-Am. War, 1898; Naval Torpedo Sta., 1900-1902; comdg. U.S.S. Bainbridge, 1903; comdg. first torpedo flotilla, 1904-05; U.S.S. Wisconsin, 1905-06; Bur. of Ordnance, Navy Dept., 1906-08; U.S.S. Montana, 1908-09; comdg. Atlantic Torpedo Fleet, 1910-11; in charge Naval Torpedo Sta., Newport, R.I., 1911-14; comdg. Cleveland, 1914-16, Oregon, 1916-17, Pueblo, 1917-18 (World War); War College, 1919-20; dir. of submarines, 1920-21; comdg. New Mexico, 1921-22; chief of staff U.S. Fleet, 1922-23; comdt. 6th Naval Dist., 1923. Methodist. Home: York, S.C. Died July 17, 1925.

WILLIAMS, Gershom Mott, bishop; b. Ft. Hamilton, N.Y., Feb. 11, 1857; s. Gen. Thomas and Mary N. (Bailey) W.; grad. Newburgh (N.Y.) Acad., 1871; studied at Cornell U., 1875-77; hon. A.M., Hobart, 1889, S.T.D., 1895; A.M., U. of Mich., 1904; m. Eliza Gradish, d. William Shepard Biddle, Feb. 20, 1879. Admitted to Mich. bar, 1879. Deacon, 1880, priest, 1882, P.E. Ch.; asst. St. John's, Detroit, 1880-82, rector Ch. of the Messiah, Detroit, 1882-84, St. George's, Detroit, 1884-89; dean Cathedral, Milwaukee, 1889-91; archdeacon, Diocese of Northern Mich., 1891-96; consecrated bishop of Marquette, Mich., May 1, 1896; retired Dec. 1, 1916. In charge of Am. Episcopal Chs. in Europe. Died Apr. 14, 1923.

WILLIAMS, Gorham Deane, lawyer, mfr.; b. East Bridgewater, Mass., Jan. 10, 1842; s. George Albert and Sarah (Deane) W.; grad. Harvard, 1865. Read law with Hon. Charles Mattoon, Greenfield, Mass., 1866-68; m. Ella Clarinda Taylor, Jan. 17, 1871. Taught in Lowell High Sch., 1865-66; admitted to bar, 1868; mfr., 1900—. Trustee, 1871—, pres. bd., 1895—, Deerfield Acad.; trial justice, Greenfield, Mass., 1877-90. Treas. Vulcan Iron Works, Charleston, W.Va., 1900-04; returned to law practice. Author: Penal Statutes of Massachusetts, 1882; Massachusetts Peace Officer, 1892; Massachusetts Insolvent Law, 1894. Deceased.

WILLIAMS, H. Evan, tenor singer; b. of Welsh parents, at Mineral Bridge, O., Sept. 7, 1867; s. David E. and Gwendolyn W.; ed. pub. schs., Akron, O.; studied with Mme. von Feilitsch, Cleveland, O., and James Sauvage, New York; m. Margaret J. Morgan. Professional début at Worcester, Mass.; first appeared in England, 1894, later touring the prin. cities; sang with leading oratorio and festival socs. of U.S. and British Isles. Home: Akron, O. Died May 24, 1918.

WILLIAMS, Harold, coll. dean; b. Brookline, Mass., Dec. 5, 1853; s. Moses Blake and Mary (Penniman) W.; grad. Harvard, 1875, A.B., 1876, M.D., 1878; LL.D., Tufts, 1905; m. Alice Cary, June 27, 1876. Prof. diseases of children, 1894-1900, theory and practice of medicine, 1900—, dean med. and dental schs., 1898—, Tufts Coll. Trustee Forsyth Dental Infirmary for Children, and trustee Forest Hills Cemetery. Fellow and councilor Mass. Medical Soc. Author: Mr. and Mrs. Morton, 1883; Silken Threads, 1885; Climatic Treatment of Phthisis; Effects of Violent and Prolonged Exercise Upon the Heart. Home: Boston, Mass. Died Apr. 3, 1926.

WILLIAMS, Henry Eugene, Weather Bur. official; b. Bethel, Conn., Apr. 3, 1844; s. Ira and Almira (Stowe) W.; ed. public schs. and acad., Bethel; m. Theresa A. Riopelle, Oct. 15, 1876. Entered U.S. weather service (then a branch of the Signal Corps of the Army), Mar. 24, 1876; instr. in Sch. of Instrn., Fort Myer, 1881-85; chief of Forecast Div., 1895-98; chief clk. Weather Bur., 1898-1903; asst. chief, July 1, 1903-June 30, 1914; meteorologist in charge Forecast Div., 1914—. Enlisted in Co. C, 17th Conn.

Inf., July 26, 1862; mustered out as 1st lt., Aug. 19, 1865. Trustee Universalist Gen. Conv., 1909-17. Mason. Wrote: Temperatures Injurious to Food Products in Storage and During Transportation (bull. 13), 1896. Home: Washington, D.C. Died 1930.

WILLIAMS, Henry Francis, foreign missions sec.; b. Hannibal, Mo., Nov. 4, 1847; s. Henry M. and Amanda M. (Bird) W.; ed. acad. and under tutors; D.D., Westminster Coll., Mo., 1911; m. Mary E. Harpham, Nov. 26, 1868. Ordained ministry Presbyn. Ch. in U.S., 1871; pastor at St. Louis and Richmond, Mo.; evangelist for a number of yrs.; state sec. Y.M.C.A., Mo. and Ohio, 1888-98; railroad sec. Internat. Com. Y.M.C.A., having charge of railroad work in U.S. and Can., 1898-1901; apptd. field sec. Foreign Mission Bd. Presbyn. Ch., U.S., 1901, emeritus, 1901—. Traveled extensively in Europe, the Orient and South America in the interest of foreign missions; editor The Missionary and Junior Missionary. Mason (32°); Knight Comdr. Court of Honor. Author: In Four Continents, 1911; also booklets on China, Mexico, etc. Died Feb. 11, 1933.

WILLIAMS, Henry Horace, educator; b. Sunbury, N.C., Aug. 16, 1858; s. Elisha (M.D.) and Mary (Taylor) Williams; A.B. and A.M., U. of N.C., 1883; B.D., Yale, 1888; Williams fellow, Harvard, 1888-89; m. Bertha Colton, June 10, 1891. Prof. philosophy, U. of N.C., 1890—; Kenan prof., 1920—. Pres. Peoples Bank, Chapel Hill, N.C., 1909-11. Progressive. Methodist. Author: The Evolution of Logic, Modern Logic, 1927. Home: Chapel Hill, N.C. Died Dec. 26, 1940.

WILLIAMS, Henry Robert, ry. official; b. Palmyra, Wis., July 14, 1849; s. Richard and Mary (Wood) W.; ed. Palmyra High Sch.; m. Elizabeth Davis, Oct. 2, 1879. Continuously in service of C.,M.&St.P. Ry., Jan. 1867—, in various duties until 1882, supt. Ia. & Minn. divs., 1882-85, Southern Minn. div. at La Crosse, Wis., 1885-86, Ottumwa & Kansas City line at Kansas City, 1888-90, asst. gen. supt. Northern Dist., 1890-98; gen. supt., 1898-1900, gen. mgr., 1900-05; pres. Chicago, Milwaukee & Puget Sound Ry., 1905-12; v.p. and mem. exec. com., C.,M.&St.P. Ry., Jan. 1913—. Died June 8, 1921.

WILLIAMS, Henry Shaler, geologist; b. Ithaca, N.Y., Mar. 6, 1847; s. Josiah B. and Mary H. (Hardy) W.; Ph.B., Yale, 1868, Ph.D., 1871; m. Harriet H. Wilcox, 1871. Asst. in paleontology, Yale, 1868-70; prof. natural science, Ky. Univ., 1871-72; asst. prof. geology, 1880-92; prof., 1892, Cornell U.; Silliman prof. geology, Yale, 1892-1904; prof. geology and head geol. dept. and director of museum, 1904-12, emeritus prof. geology, 1912—, Cornell U.; also in charge Devonian Lab. of U.S. Geol. Survey. Asso. editor Am. Jour. of Science and Jour. of Geology. Am. commr. Internat. Congress of Geology; fellow London Geol. Soc., Soc. Geology du Nord, Geol. Soc. America, A.A.A.S. Author: Geological Biology; Correlation Papers, Devonian and Carboniferous; On the Theory of Organic Variation; also numerous papers on Devonian geology and palæontology. Home: Ithaca, N.Y. Died Aug. 1, 1918.

WILLIAMS, Henry Winslow, lawyer; b. Buffalo, N.Y., Oct. 6, 1864; s. John B. and Caroline S. (Winslow) W.; A.B., Johns Hopkins, 1883; LL.B., U. of Md., 1885; unmarried. Admitted to bar, 1886, and in practice at Baltimore, 1886—; mem. law firm of Williams & Williams. Member exec. com. Md. Civ. Service Assn., 1897—. Independent Democrat. Editor: Corporation Law of Maryland, 1908. Contbr. to legal jours. Chmn. exec. com. Md. Branch League to Enforce Peace. Home: Baltimore, Md. Died Nov. 7, 1927.

WILLIAMS, Herbert Oswald, foreign service; b. Columbus, O., June 30, 1873; s. William and Dinah Louise (Hughes) W.; grad. high sch., Columbus, 1890; A.B., Ohio State U., 1894, A.M., 1900; A.M., Bethany (W.Va.) Coll., 1895; m. Sarah Eliza Dimond, Dec. 27, 1897 (died 1902); m. 2d, Mabel Frances Pockman, Aug. 22, 1906; 1 son, Philip Pockman. Teacher, high schs., 1896-1908; prin. high sch., Santa Barbara, Calif., 1908-10, Sacramento, 1910-20; consul on detail in Dept. State, 1920-22; consul, Brest, 1922, Havre, 1922-23, Brussels, 1923-25, Liverpool, 1925-29; consul in charge Am. Consulate Gen., Panama, 1929-33; consul at Vera Cruz, Mexico, 1933-35; consul at Gibraltar, 1935-38, retired. Welfare work with Am. Y.M.C.A., French Army, 1918-19. Conglist. Elk. Home: Sacramento, Calif. Died Aug. 17, 1939.

WILLIAMS, Herbert Owen, army officer; b. Fulton, Miss., Aug. 5, 1866; s. John Dickson and Elizabeth (Marion) W.; grad. U.S. Mil. Acad., 1891, Inf. and Cav. Sch., Ft. Leavenworth, Kan., 1897, Army War Coll., 1912; m. Gertrude Ione Edwards, Nov. 22, 1919. Commd. 2d lt. inf., U.S.A., June 12, 1891; advanced through grades to col. (temp.), Aug. 5, 1917; col. regular army, Feb. 16, 1920; brig. gen., Sept. 24, 1926; retired. Awarded D.S.M. (U.S.). Died Aug. 13, 1936.

WILLIAMS, Herbert Upham, pathologist; b. Buffalo, Nov. 28, 1866; s. Frank and Olive W.; lit. dept. U. of Mich., 1884-86; M.D., U. of Buffalo, 1889; M.D., U. of Pa., 1891; studied, Johns Hopkins, 1895, U. of Göttingen, 1899; m. Mary Carver, d. Col. William P. Stoddard, 1909. Apptd. prof. pathology and bacteriology, med. dept. U. of Buffalo, 1894, also served as dean of dept. Fellow A.A.A.S. Author: Manual of Bacteriology, 1898. Contbr. to Jour. Med. Research, Jour. Exptl. Medicine, Am. Jour. Pathology and Archives of Pathology, especially on the subject of human paleopathology, mummies the origin of syphilis. Home: Buffalo, N.Y. Died Dec. 8, 1938.

WILLIAMS, Herschel, author; b. North Manchester, Ind.; s. John Wesley and Elizabeth (Kohser) W.; student Northwestern U.; spl. course Denver U.; unmarried. Began as reporter on Denver Post; with Detroit Free Press, 1898-1902; lit. editor Detroit Jour., 1903; resigned to write St. Louis Fair story for Laird & Lee, Chicago; with Atkinson, Mentzer & Grover, pubs., New York, 1911; N.E. mgr. for the Prang Co., Boston, 1911-16; later syndicating. Author: Uncle Bob and Aunt Becky at St. Louis Exposition, 1904; Fairy Tales from Folk Lore, 1908; My Chums in Caricature, 1909; Making Faces, My Advice Book, and other booklets, 1910, 1911; Young People's Story of Massachusetts, 1916; The Merrymakers in New York, 1919; The Merrymakers in Chicago, 1920; The Jolly Old Whistle and Other Tales, 1927; Children of the Clouds, 1929; The Traveling Tingles, 1931. Adapted Maeterlinck's Life of the Bee to juvenile purposes, 1917. Home: Boston, Mass. Died Sept. 15, 1935.

WILLIAMS, Homer D., corp. official; pres. Pittsburgh Steel Co.; also pres. Pittsburgh Steel Products Co., Monessen Coal & Coke Co., Nat. Steel Fabric Co.; dir. Pittsburgh & W.Va. Ry. Co., Duquesne Trust Co., Union Trust Co. of Pittsburgh, and officer or dir. various other corps. Died Nov. 13, 1937.

WILLIAMS, James Cranston, journalist; b. Camak, Ga., Jan. 4, 1869; s. William Anderson and Huldah Ann (Ricketson) W.; ed. pub. schs.; m. Mamie Gullatt, Dec. 12, 1893; children—Cranston Gullatt, Huldah Williams (Mrs. Charles R. Caldwell), Marie Louise (Mrs. Marion W. Morris), Carey Jones, Mary James. In newspaper work many years; owner and pub. Greensboro Herald-Journal and the Columbia News; dir. Bank of Greensboro; Dem. elector 8th Congl. Dist. of Ga., 1912, 16, 24. Trustee U. of Ga. Med. Coll., 1915-19, chmn. bd., 1916-17. K.P. Home: Greensboro, Ga. Died Apr. 22, 1936.

WILLIAMS, James Monroe, army officer; b. Lowville, N.Y., Sept. 12, 1833; s. Absalom and Fannie W.; moved to Wis., 1844; ed. pub. schs., N.Y., Wis., and acad., Janesville, Wis.; read law Janesville, 1853-56; m. Mary E. Brawner, Jan. 30, 1868. Admitted to bar, Janesville, Wis., 1856; practiced law at Leavenworth, Kan. Capt. 5th Kan. Cav., U.S.V., July 1861, to Sept. 1862; lt. col. and col. 1st Kan. (afterwards 79th U.S.) Colored Troops, Sept. 1862, to May 1864; received 4 gun-shot wounds in engagement with Confederates at Elk Creek, Ind. Ty., July 17, 1863; comd. brigade May 1864, until Oct. 1865; bvt. brig. gen. U.S.V.; apptd. capt. 8th U.S. cav. (bvtd. maj. for conspicuous gallantry in engagements with Indians, 1867, on the Verde, in Yampa Valley, and nr. Music Mountain, Ariz.); seriously wounded in latter action; in hosp. and on nominal duty 2 yrs.; returned to regt., but resigned, 1871; retired as capt. cav. by spl. act of Congress, Jan. 1, 1891. Home: Washington, D.C. Died 1907.

WILLIAMS, James Robert, congressman; b. White County, Ill., Dec. 27, 1850; s. Thomas and Susan (Ralls) W.; A.B., Ind. U., 1875; LL.B., Union Coll. of Law, Chicago, 1876; m. Minnie Shannon, Nov. 26, 1884. Master in chancery, White County, 1880-82; county judge, 1883-87; elected 51st Congress, 1889, for unexpired term (1889-91), of R. W. Townshend, deceased; reëlected 52d, 53d Congresses (1891-95), and 56th to 58th Congresses (1899-1905); chmn. Ill. delegation Dem. Nat. Conv., 1900; Dem. nominee for U.S. senator from Ill., 1903; received votes of delegates from several states for nomination for v.p. of U.S. in Dem. Nat. Conv., 1904. Died Nov. 8, 1923.

WILLIAMS, Jesse Lynch, author; b. Sterling, Ill., Aug. 17, 1871; s. Meade Creighton and Elizabeth (Riddle) W.; A.B., Princeton, 1892, A.M., 1895, Litt.D., 1919; m. Alice Laidlaw, June 1, 1898; children—Henry Meade, Jesse Lynch, Laidlaw Onderdonk. Mem. Nat. Inst. Arts and Letters, Authors' League America (pres. 1921). Author: Princeton Stories, 1895; History of Princeton University (with John De Witt), 1898; The Stolen Story, and Other Newspaper Stories, 1899; The Adventures of a Freshman, 1899; New York Sketches, 1902; The Day-Dreamer, 1906; My Lost Duchess, 1908; The Girl and the Game, and Other College Stories, 1908; Mr. Cleveland, a Personal Impression, 1909; The Married Life of the Frederic Carrolls, 1910; And So They Were Married (comedy in 3 acts), 1915, new edit. called Why Marry? 1917; Remating Time, 1916 (plays) The Stolen Story (4-act comedy, prod., Providence, 1906); Why Marry? (3-act comedy, prod. Columbus, O., 1917, awarded Pulitzer prize by Columbia U. for best Am. play produced that yr.); Why Not? (3-act satiric comedy, prod. New York, 1922); Lovely Lady (3-act comedy, prod. Washington, D.C., 1925). Fellow in creative arts, U. of Mich., 1925-26. Home: Harrington, Me. Died Sept. 14, 1929.

WILLIAMS, Job, educator; b. Pomfret, Conn., Mar. 1, 1842; s. Giles and Fanny Maria (Gallup) W.; B.A., Yale, 1864, M.A., 1867; L.H.D., Nat. Deaf Mute Coll. (now Gallaudet Coll.), Washington, 1889; m. Kate Stone, Aug. 25, 1868. Teacher of the deaf at Hartford, 1866—; prin. Am. Sch. for the Deaf, 1879—. Home: Hartford, Conn. Died 1914.

WILLIAMS, John Elias, industrial mediator; b. Merthyr Tydfil, Wales, Oct. 28, 1853; s. John Elias and Elizabeth (Bowen) W.; brought to U.S., 1864; ed. pub. schs.; m. Isabella Dickinson, Jan. 12, 1877. Coal miner from age of 13 to 30; arbitrator and mediator of indsl. disputes for many yrs., especially for coal miners and operators of Ill.; chmn. bd. of arbitration, Hart, Schaffner & Marx trade agreement; chmn. New York Garment Workers' protocol; apptd. U.S. adminstr. in packing industry, 1917; apptd. fed. fuel adminstr. for Ill., 1917. Effected peaceful settlement of claims of defendants of Cherry Mine disaster with C.,M.&St.P.R.R. Co., 1909. Mem. bd. dirs. Western Unitarian Conf. Home: Streator, Ill. Died Jan. 2, 1919.

WILLIAMS, John Joseph, R.C. archbishop; b. Boston, Apr. 27, 1822; studied at cathedral parochial sch.; grad. Coll. of Montreal, 1841; theol. course at St. Sulpice, Paris, France; ordained, 1845; asst., 1845-55, rector, 1855-57, Boston Cathedral; pastor St. James, Boston, 1857-66; bishop of Boston, 1866, until the see became metropolitan, 1875, archbishop, Feb. 12, 1875—. Died 1907.

WILLIAMS, John Langbourne, banker; b. Richmond, Va., July 13, 1831; s. John and Sianna Armistead (Dandridge) W.; A.M., U. of Va., 1851; D.Litt., Washington and Lee U., 1908; m. Maria Ward Skelton, Oct. 13, 1864; father of John Skelton W. Taught sch., practiced law; became banker in 1858; mem. Lancaster & Co., financial agts. of Confederate States. After war established house of John L. Williams & Sons; firm helped refunding of debt of S.C., established Ga. Ry. and Seaboard Air Line; interested in reorganizing and re-establishing city rys. and other instns. in Richmond, Petersburg, Norfolk, Augusta, Macon, Nashville and Knoxville, and in Baltimore and New York. For many yrs. contributed weekly philos. observations to leading Richmond jours. Represented Va., several sessions, in Gen. Conv. of P.E. Ch.; v.p. Am. Bible Soc. for Va.; pres. Richmond Male Orphan Soc., Memorial Hosp., and Southern Churchman Co.; treas. Va. Negro Reformatory. Died Feb. 11, 1915.

WILLIAMS, John Sharp, senator; b. Memphis, Tenn., July 30, 1854; s. Col. Christopher Harris and Annie Louise (Sharp) W.; ed. Ky. Mil. Inst., U. of the South, U. of Va., and U. of Heidelberg; studied law at U. of Va. and at Memphis, Tenn.; m. Elizabeth Dial Webb, Oct. 2, 1877; children—Mary Sharp, Robert Webb, Annie Louise (dec.), John Sharp, Julia Fulton (dec.), Allison Ridley, Sally Shelby, Christopher Harris. Admitted to Tenn. bar, 1877; in practice at Yazoo, Miss., 1878—; also a cotton planter. Mem. 53d to 57th Congresses (1893-1903), 5th Miss. Dist., and 58th to 60th Congresses (1903-09), 8th Dist.; received all votes cast for 60th Congress; minority leader of the House and Dem. candidate for speaker 58th to 60th Congresses; U.S. senator for terms 1911-17, 1917-23. Member Foreign Relations Com. and Finance Com. of Senate, which reported Tariff Bill of 1913. Del. Dem. Nat. Conv., 1892, 1904 (temporary chmn. 1904); del.-at-large from Miss. to Dem. Nat. Conv., Baltimore, 1912. Author: Permanent Influence of Thomas Jefferson on American Institutions, 1913. Home: Yazoo City, Miss. Died Sept. 28, 1932.

WILLIAMS, John Skelton, financier, publicist, ry. exec.; b. Powhatan County, Va., July 6, 1865; s. John Langbourne and Maria Ward (Skelton) W.; ed. Richmond, Va., and U. of Va.; m. Lila Lefebvre Isaacs, 1895. Organizer, pres., 1899-1904, Seaboard Air Line Ry. System; chmn. trust co. sect. and mem. exec. council Am. Bankers' Assn., 1901; organizer and pres. of banks, trust cos. and industrial instns., from all of which he retired upon appointment by President Wilson, Mar. 1913, to office of 1st asst. sec. of Treasury; by invitation of Interstate Commerce Commn. was mem. of advisory bd. on valuation of railroad, steamship telegraph and telephone lines. Apptd. by President Wilson, Jan. 1914, comptroller of the currency. (The Sec. of the Treasury, Sec. of Agriculture and comptroller of the currency composed the organization com. which under the Fed. Res. Act, was charged with the duty of organizing and putting into effect the new banking and currency system.) Reapptd. comptroller of the currency, 1919; resigned Mar. 2, 1921. Dir. divs. of Finance and Purchases of the U.S.R.R. Adminstrn. by apptmt. of Dir. Gen. McAdoo, 1917-18; mem. Capital Issues Com. under apptmt. of President Wilson, Feb. 1918-Mar 1919. Mem. Central Com. and nat. treas., Am. Red Cross under successive appointments by President Wilson, 1913-21. Pres. Richmond Trust Co., 1924—. Author of various published addresses on financial and economic subjects. Home: Richmond, Va. Died Nov. 4, 1926.

WILLIAMS, J(ohn) Whitridge, physician; b. Baltimore, Jan. 26, 1866; s. Dr. Philip C. and Mary C. (Whitridge) W.; A.B., Johns Hopkins, 1886; M.D., U. of Md., 1888; univs. of Berlin and Vienna, 1888-89, Leipzig, Prague and Paris, 1894-95, Heidelberg, 1909; Sc.D., U. of Md., 1907, U. of Dublin, Ireland, 1912; LL.D., U. of Pittsburgh, 1915; m. Margaretta Stewart Brown, Jan. 14, 1891; children—Margaretta W. Wood, Cushing W. Bridgman, Anne W. Niles. Asst., asso. and asso. prof. obstetrics, 1889-99, prof., 1899—, Johns Hopkins; dean Johns Hopkins Med. Sch., 1911-23. Obstetrician in chief Johns Hopkins Hosp., 1899—. Fellow Am. Gynecol. Soc. (pres. 1913-14); pres. Am. Assn. Study and Prevention Infant Mortality, 1914-16, Med. and Chirurg. Faculty of Md., 1915-16. Author: Text-Book of Obstetrics, 1903, 1930. Also numerous monographs upon obstet. and gynecol. subjects. Home: Baltimore, Md. Died Oct. 21, 1931.

WILLIAMS, Joseph John, clergyman, anthropologist; b. Boston, Dec. 1, 1875; s. Nicholas Mark and Mary Jane (O'Connor) W.; A.B., Woodstock (Md.) Coll., 1901, A.M., 1903, Ph.D. in Ethnology, 1909; Litt.D., Boston Coll., 1929. Joined Soc. of Jesus, 1893; ordained priest R.C. Ch., 1907; mng. editor of America; prof. anthropology, Boston Coll. Grad. Sch., 1934—; widely known as lecturer on anthropology and related subjects. Fellow Royal Geog. Soc., Royal Soc. of Arts, Royal Anthropol. Inst., Am. Geog. Soc.; mem. Am. Anthropol. Assn. (del. Internat. Congress, London, 1934), A.A.A.S., Am. Council Learned Socs. (del. Internat. Congress, London, 1934), Catholic Anthropol. Conf. (exec. bd. 1935), Jesuit Anthropol. Assn. (pres., 1936—). Author: Keep the Gate, 1923; Yearning for God, 1924; Whisperings of the Caribbean, 1925; Hebrewisms of West Africa, 1930; Whence the "Black Irish" of Jamaica, 1932; Voodoos and Obeahs, 1932; Psychic Phenomena of Jamaica, 1934; Africa's God, 1937; The Maroons of Jamaica, 1938; Thoughts on Evolution, 1939. Home: Chestnut Hill, Mass. Died Oct. 28, 1940.

WILLIAMS, Joseph White, civil engr.; b. Milan, O., Oct. 20, 1879; s. Daniel Newton and Sophia E. (White) W.; grad. high sch., Milan, 1897; m. Eliza L. Hunt, Sept. 24, 1902; children—Joseph Hunt, Mary Elinor. On railroad location and constrn., N.M. and Calif., 1900-07; asst. chief engr. Northwestern Pacific R.R., 1907-14, chief engr. constrn., 1914-17, chief engr., 1919-21; chief engr. Western Pacific R.R., Aug. 1921—. Served as pvt. 52d Ia. Vol. Inf., Spanish-Am. War; again entered military service, in Apr. 1917; maj., lt. col. 18th Engrs., U.S.A., World War I; in France, Aug. 1917-Apr. 1919; col. engrs. O.R.C. Republican. Home: Ross, Calif. Died Feb. 3, 1941.

WILLIAMS, L. Judson, judge; b. Greenbrier County, Va., Oct. 18, 1856; s. Albert G. and Nancy J. (Donnolly) W.; ed. W.Va. U.; studied law, U. of Va.; m. Minnie J. Patterson, Nov. 1, 1883 (died 1892); m. 2d, Mrs. Mary Chalmers Leonard, Sept. 12, 1894 (died 1906); m. 3d, Harriet L. Peck, Sept. 16, 1909. Admitted to bar, 1883, and practiced at Lewisburg, W.Va., until 1909. Mem. W.Va. Tax Commn., 1901-02, which redrafted the new tax laws for the state; regent W.Va. U., 1903-08; judge Supreme Ct. of Appeals of W.Va., term 1909-21; pres. judge same, Jan. 1, 1911—. Republican. Home: Lewisburg, Greenbrier County, W.Va. Died Oct. 28, 1921.

WILLIAMS, Langbourne M., banker; b. Richmond, Va., Sept. 12, 1872; s. John Langbourne and Maria Ward (Skelton) W.; des. on paternal side of Col. John Dandridge, father of Martha, the wife of George Washington, and on maternal side from Edmund Randolph, Atty. Gen. of U.S. in Washington's Cabinet; student U. of Va. and U. of Pa.; m. Susanne C. Nolting, Dec. 1, 1898; children—John Langbourne (dec.), Maria Ward (dec.), Langbourne Meade, Susanne C., Frank McGuire, E. Otto Nolting, Charlotte Randolph, George Dandridge, Anne Armistead. Began as mem. John L. Williams & Sons, investments, 1892; pres. Southern Investment Co., Va. Central Ry., Manastota Land & Timber Co., Byrd Real Estate Co., Southern Churchman; v.p. Halifax Paper Corp.; sec. Richmond Mica Co.; dir. Md. Casualty Co., etc. Treas. Richmond Chapter Archæol. Inst. America; dir. Y.M.C.A., Richmond (pres.); mem. bd. trustees Va. Bible Soc. Democrat. Trustee St. James' P.E. Ch. Home: Richmond, Va. Died Apr. 2, 1931.

WILLIAMS, Linsly Rudd, M.D.; b. N.Y. City, Jan. 28, 1875; s. John Stanton and Mary Maclay (Pentz) W.; A.B., Princeton, 1895; A.M., M.D., Columbia, 1899; m. Grace Kidder Ford, Jan. 18, 1908. Interne Presbyn. Hosp., New York, 1900-02, Sloane Maternity Hosp., 1902; asso. in practice with Dr. John S. Thacher, 1902-08; visiting phys. to House of Rest for Tuberculosis, Seton Hosp., and City Hosp.; instr. in histology, 1902-04, asst. in medicine, 1904-14, chief of med. clinic, 1906-11, Columbia; dep. commr. of health, N.Y. State, 1914-17 (resigned); assigned as 1st lt. Med. R.C. to investigate sanitary conditions in France and Eng., Aug. 1917; maj. asst. div. surgeon, Oct. 1917; later lt. col. M.C., U.S.A.; sanitary insp. 80th Div.; asst. sanitary officer Hdqrs. S.O.S.; service, Aug. 8, 1917-Apr. 12, 1919; dir. tuberculosis work in France for Rockefeller Foundation, 1919-22; mng. dir. Nat. Tuberculosis Assn., Oct. 1, 1922-28; mng. dir. N.Y. Acad. of Medicine; dir. Millbank Memorial Fund. Mem. board of mgrs. N.Y. Assn. for Improving Conditions of the Poor; trustee Columbia U. Democrat. Episcopalian. Home: New York, N.Y. Died Jan. 8, 1934.

WILLIAMS, Marshall Jay, jurist; b. Fayette County, O., Feb. 22, 1837; ed. at Washington C. H., O., and Ohio Wesleyan U.; admitted Ohio bar, 1857; m. Bertha Taylor, May 9, 1860. Elected pros. atty., Fayette County, 1859; reëlected, 1863; elected to Ohio Gen. Assembly, 1869, 1871; circuit judge, 2d circuit, Ohio, 1884-86; elected judge Supreme Ct., Ohio, 1886, 1891 and 1896; twice chief justice; first dean, law dept., Ohio State U. Republican. Died 1902.

WILLIAMS, Milton Mathias; b. Litchfield, Mich., Oct. 1, 1848; s. John N. and Susan (Halstead) W.; removed to Minn., 1858; ed. high sch. and by pvt. tutelage; m. Florence E. Bennett, 1889. Engaged in ry. constrn., St. Paul, 1870-84; builder, mgr. and majority owner Little Falls Water Power on Miss. River, 1887-1903; pres. First Nat. Bank, Little Falls, Minn. Mem. Minn. State Forestry Bd., 1902—(pres. bd.); mem. staff of Gov. Hubbard, rank of lt. col.; mem. Rep. State Central Com., Minn.; regent U. of Minn., 1910— (v.p. bd.); dir. Minn. Commn. Pub. Safety, 1917—. Mason. Home: Minneapolis, Minn. Died Oct. 17, 1926.

WILLIAMS, Mornay, lawyer; b. N.Y. City, June 21, 1856; s. William R. (S.T.D., LL.D.), and Mary Stevenson (Bowen) W.; A.B., Columbia (Phi Beta Kappa), 1878, LL.B., 1880, A.M., 1881; m. Helen Hope, June 21, 1886. Admitted to N.Y. bar, 1880, and practiced in N.Y. City, specializing in estate business; represented at various times estates of William B. Ogden, Samuel J. Tilden, Anna Ottendorfer, William Borden, etc.; mem. Dixon, Goodwin & Williams, 1880-87; Dixon, Williams & Ashley, 1887-93, Williams & Ashley, 1893-98, alone 1898-1916. Mem. bd. govs., exec. com. West China Union U., Chengtu; mem. bd. mgrs. Am. Bible Soc., Am. Bapt. Foreign Mission Soc., Nat. Conf. Charities and Correction (exec. com. 4 yrs.), N.Y. State Conf. Charities and Correction (pres. 1909), New York Child Labor Com., St. David's Soc. of New York (pres.); mem. bd. dirs. N.Y. Juvenile Asylum 23 yrs. (pres. 1897-1910); active in promoting laws for improvement of labor conditions, for prison reform, etc.; author of act changing law of charitable trusts in N.Y. Commr. for N.J. of Palisades Inter-State Park Commn., 1914-19. Republican. Baptists. Home: Englewood, N.J. Died June 1926.

WILLIAMS, Moseley Hooker, clergyman, editor; b. Farmington, Conn., Dec. 23, 1839; s. Cornelius Robbins and Caroline (Hooker) W.; B.A., Yale, 1864, M.A., 1874; Union Theol. Sem., New York, 1864-66; grad. Andover Theol. Sem., 1867; hon. Ph.D., Temple Coll., 1899; m. Emma Virginia Bockius, Feb. 1, 1870. Ordained Congl. ministry, 1868; pastor Second Ch., Phila., 1867-69, Grand Av. Chapel, Brooklyn, 1869-70. Plymouth Ch., Portland, Me., 1870-73. On editorial work Am. S.S. Union, 1879—; asso. editor Sunday School World, Union Quarterly, Young People's Paper, etc. Assisted on Dr. Schaff's Dictionary of the Bible, 1880; wrote introduction to History of Revised New Testament, 1881. Home: Germantown, Phila., Pa. Died Nov. 9, 1917.

WILLIAMS, Moses, lawyer; b. Roxbury (Boston), Mass., Dec. 4, 1846; s. Moses Blake and Mary Jane (Penniman) W.; bro. Harold W.; A.B., Harvard, 1868; m. Martha Caroline Fininley, Sept. 10, 1868. Practicing lawyer and trustee, 1869—. Pres. Third Nat. Bank of Boston, 1884-98; chmn. bd. State St. Trust Co.; pres. Central Wharf & Wet Dock Corp., Fitchburg R.R. Co.; treas. and dir. Battery Wharf Store Co.; dir. Am. Telephone & Telegraph Co. Mem. Mass. Ho. of Rep., 1874, 75, 76. Unitarian. Overseer of Harvard Coll. Home: Brookline Mass. Died Aug. 1919.

WILLIAMS, Moses, lawyer, trustee; b. Brookline, Mass., 1869; s. Moses and Martha C. (Fininley) W.; A.B., Harvard, 1891; m. Anne Whiteside, Mar. 6, 1905; children—Moses, Alexander W., Eleanor S. Practiced at Boston, 1892—; pres. Central Wharf & Wet Dock Corp.; trustee Bromfield Bldg., Boston Block, Boston Ground Rent, Boston Personal Property, Copley Square, Municipal Real Estate, Minot, Williams and Bangs, Inc., Summer St., Washington Bldg., Western Real Estate, Old South Bldg. Assn. Home: Needham, Mass. Died 1940.

WILLIAMS, Nathan Winslow, lawyer; b. Cleveland, O., Aug. 26, 1860; s. John Butler and Caroline S. (Winslow) W.; student Baltimore City Coll., 1874-78; Johns Hopkins, 1878-80; LL.B., Columbia, 1883; m. Anne Tyler Foster, Apr. 30, 1890. Admitted to Md. bar, 1883, and practiced in Baltimore, specializing in corp. law; mem. Williams & Williams. Dep. state's atty., 1885-88; judge advo. gen. on staff of Gov. Edwin Warfield, 1904-08; sec. of state of Md., 1908-12; mem. Prog. Nat. Com., 1914-16. Episcopalian. Home: Baltimore, Md. Died 1925.

WILLIAMS, Orva Gilson; b. Salineville, O., Apr. 25, 1865; s. Richard Gilson and Elmira (Frost) Williams; descendant John Boyd of French and Indian War, and of David Boyd and William Gilson, soldiers in Pa. Line in Am. Revolution; ed. Mt. Union Coll., Alliance, O.; student Cincinnati Law Sch.; m. Josephine Stack Ryan, 1894; children—Elsie, Dorothy (Mrs. Victor E. Adland), Orva Gilson II. In novelty advertising bus. at Coshocton, O., until 1899, at Chicago, 1899—; pres. and treas. The O. G. Williams Co. Pres. Nat. Assn. Adv. Novelty Mfrs., 1908, 09; founder and 1st pres. Ohio Soc. of Chicago; del. Dem. Nat. Conv., Baltimore, 1912. Founder and pres. Council of State Socs. of Chicago which conducted a Home Folks Canteen in the City Hall, 1917-19. Democrat. Presbyterian. Mason, Elk, K.P. Home: Chicago, Ill. Died Nov. 5, 1930.

WILLIAMS, Oscar Fitzalan, consul; b. Livonia, N.Y., June 29, 1843; s. Mason and Wealthy Green W.; grad. Cornell, 1869; m. Arabella Amanda Sanford, July 11, 1872. Instr. in bus. coll. 20 yrs.; author several comml. text-books; consul to Havre, France, 1889-93. Republican. After war with Spain took active part in adjustment of Philippine Islands to new conditions; last U.S. consul to Manila, P.I., apptd. 1897; consul gen., Singapore, Straits Settlements, Jan. 4, 1901—. Died 1909.

WILLIAMS, Pardon Clarence, lawyer; b. Ellisburgh, N.Y., July 12, 1842; s. William and Jerusha (Plummer) W.; ed. Union Acad., Belleville, N.Y., and St. Lawrence U., Canton, N.Y.; m. Sarah Hewitt, September 9, 1868 (died 1914). Admitted to bar, Oct. 1863; practiced law at Watertown, 1863-85; justice Supreme Ct. of N.Y., Jan. 1885-Dec. 31, 1911; served on Appellate Div., N.Y. City, 1896-97, then at Rochester, N.Y.; resumed practice, Jan. 1, 1912. Republican. Died Jan. 18, 1925.

WILLIAMS, Parley Lycurgus, lawyer; b. Perry County, Ill., Apr. 7, 1842; s. Samuel and Andromache (Moore) W.; student McKendree Coll., Ill., 1860-62; m. Katherine Sharp, 1876. Admitted to bar, 1868; counsel for Ore. Short Line R.R. Co., 1872-1915, U.P.,S.P. Ry. Cos. Dist. atty., Wyo. Ty., 1870-71; supt. schs., Utah Ty., 1886-88; mem. Utah Senate, 1894-95. Mem. Am. Bar Assn.; del.-at-large, Universal Congress Lawyers and Jurists, St. Louis, 1904. Democrat. Unitarian. Grand Master of Masons, Utah, 1887-88. Chmn. Dist. Draft Registration Bd. for State of Utah, 1917. Retired from active business, 1925. Home: Salt Lake City, Utah. Died Mar. 23, 1936.

WILLIAMS, Ralph E., banker; b. Polk County, Ore., 1870; s. James J. and Alice (Eckersley) W.; ed. pub. schs., and La Creole Coll., Dallas, Ore.; m. Grace Noyes, Dec. 2, 1911; children—Ralph E., Harriett W. Began as bookkeeper, Dallas City Bank, 1890, later pres.; also pres. Dallas Nat. Bank. Mem. Rep. Nat. Com. for Ore., 1908—. Mason, Elk. Home: Portland, Ore. Died May 16, 1940.

WILLIAMS, Ralph Olmsted, author; b. Palmyra, N.Y., May 12, 1838; s. George Nelson and Mary (Olmsted) W.; grad. Yale, 1861; joint editor Yale Lit. Mag., 1860-61; enlisted pvt., 7th Del. Vols.; mustered into U.S. service for resisting Gen. Early's raid into Md., 1864. Admitted to New York bar, 1865; contbr. to Webster's Internat. Dictionary and Standard Dictionary, Modern Language Notes, Dial, Am. Monthly Review of Reviews. Librarian New Haven Colony Hist. Soc., 1900-05; instr. English composition, Yale, 1891-93. Author: Our Dictionaries, and Other English Language Topics, 1890; Some Questions of Good English Examined in Controversies with Dr. Fitzedward Hall, 1897. Died 1908.

WILLIAMS, Richard Richardson, editor; b. Waterford, Ireland, Sept. 19, 1843; s. John and Susan (Richardson) W.; brought to America, 1852; acad., Middletown, N.Y.; grad. Union Theol. Sem., New York, 1870; m. Mary Mitchell, 1870. Ordained ministry, Ref. Ch. in America, 1870; pastor Canajoharie, N.Y., 1870-83; editor The Iron Age, 1883—. Died Sept. 30, 1915.

WILLIAMS, Robert, brig. gen. U.S.A.; b. Culpeper County, Va., Nov. 5, 1829; grad. West Point, 1851; 2d lt., 1st dragoons; served in Oregon; asst. instr. tactics West Point, 1857-61; capt. and asst. adj. gen., May 1861; col. 1st Mass. cav., Oct. 1861; maj., U.S.A., July 1862; on duty at War Dept. to end of Civil war; afterward asst. adj. gen. in various depts., and adj. gen., 1892; bvt. brig. gen., Mar. 1865; lt. col., 1869; col., 1881; brig. gen., 1892; retired, 1893. Died 1901.

WILLIAMS, Robert, judge; b. Paterson, N.J., Mar. 16, 1860; s. Henry Augustus and Mary Louisa (Van Saun) W.; A.B., Princeton, 1881, A.M., 1884; studied law with father; LL.B., Columbia Coll. Law Sch., 1884; m. Alice Winslow Ingham, Apr. 23, 1891. Admitted to N.J. bar as atty., 1884, counselor, 1887; appointed special master in chancery, 1896; dir. First Nat. Bank, Nat. Ribbon Co.; dir., sec.-treas., Call Printing and Pub. Co., pub. Paterson Morning Call.

Mem. New Jersey Assembly, 1890, 1891; elected mem. N.J. Senate, 1895 (pres., 1896, 1897); mem. Rep. State Com. and Exec. Com., 1898-May 1, 1911, when resigned, having been elected pres. Pub. Utility Commn.; elected state dir. of railroads by joint session of legislature, 1903, but resigned; riparian commissioner, 1904-09 (pres. bd., 1908, 1909); apptd. state R.R. commr., Apr. 1909, resigning as riparian commr.; R.R. Commn. changed to Pub. Utility Commission, July 4, 1910 (elected pres., 1911, 1912), resigned to resume law practice, May 1, 1913; apptd. judge Ct. of Errors and Appeals of N.J., May 1914, to fill a vacancy, and re-apptd., 1915 and 1921. Judge adv. 1st Batn. N.G. N.J., with rank of capt., 1890-93. Mem. Dist. Bd. for Div. No. 1 of N.J., Fed. Bd. of Appeals. Republican. Presbyn. Mason. Home: Paterson, N.J. Died Feb. 19, 1923.

WILLIAMS, Robert Day, prof. exptl. psychology; b. Marblehead, Mass., July 23, 1881; s. John Healy (D.D.) and Annie Frances (Day) W.; grad. Union High Sch., Redlands, Calif., 1899; B.S., Pomona Coll., Claremont, Calif., 1903; studied U. of Calif.; M.A., Yale, 1907, Ph.D., 1909; m. Jessie Hays, 1910 (died 1922); children—Richard, Douglas, Palmer; m. 2d, Margaret Ray, June 13, 1925. Instr. in biology, Pomona Coll., 1904-06, prof. philosophy, 1909-12, prof. psychology, 1912-15; pres. Mid-Pacific Instn., Honolulu, 1915-18; prof. exptl. psychology, Pomona Coll., 1919—; visiting lecturer in psychology, Harvard, Sept. 1924-Feb. 1925. Mem. Nat. War Work Council, Y.M.C.A., 1918; ednl. sec. Y.M.C.A. in home camps; overseas Y.M.C.A. sec.; with Army Ednl. Corps, as head of psychol. dept. A.E.F. Univ., Beaune, France. Fellow A.A.A.S. Republican. Congregationalist. Lecturer on psychol. and religious topics. Home: Claremont, Calif. Died Dec. 4, 1930.

WILLIAMS, Robert Einion, clergyman; b. Parish of Llanengan, Carnarvonshire, North Wales, Mar. 15, 1856; s. Griffith and Jane (Hughes) W.; prep. edn. Welsh Calvinistic Meth. Inst., Clynog, Wales, 1881-83; student W.C.M. Theol. Sem., Bala, N. Wales, 1883-86; m. Winifred J. Williams, Dec. 24, 1890. Began preaching in Australia, 1879; ordained Welsh Calvinistic Meth. ministry, 1888; pastor 1st Ch. Bangor, Pa., 1886-89, Statington, Pa., 1889-93, Plymouth, Pa., 1893-1900, Minneapolis, Minn., 1900-02, Butte, Mont., 1902-10, 1st Ch., Phila., Pa., 1910-17. Stated clerk W.C.M. Presbyn. Synod of Pa. 9 yrs.; twice del. to Gen. Assembly and its stated clk.; mem. exec. com. Commn. on Evangelism of Fed. Council Chs. of Christ in America. Naturalized citizen of U.S. in 1892. Chaplain Welsh Soc. of Phila. Republican. Home: Philadelphia, Pa. Died June 16, 1940.

WILLIAMS, R(obert) Lancaster; b. Richmond, Va., June 29, 1869; s. John Langbourne and Maria Ward (Skelton) W.; ed. pvt. schs., Richmond, among them John P. McGuire's Sch.; U. of Pa. (course in economics); m. Rebekah Gustavia Watkins, Dec. 14, 1899; children—R. Lancaster, Charles Watkins, Francis Randolph, Dorothy Dandridge. Mem. banking firm of John L. Williams & Sons, Richmond, until 1911; later partner R. Lancaster Williams & Co., Baltimore (both active in street ry. work in the South); long a dir., pres., or controlling factor in many street ry. cos., assisted in consolidating small lines and forming Seaboard Air Line Ry. of over 3,000 miles, of which was apptd. a receiver, Jan. 1908, this receivership proving one of the most successful in the history of Am. railways; assisted in reorganization of I.&G.N. R.R., Ga.&Fla. Ry. (chmn. bd. of latter); dir. Mo.P. Ry., Liberty Nat. Bank & Trust Co. (New York), Mid-Continent Petroleum Corp., Southern Investment Co., Manasota Land & Timber Co. Episcopalian. Died Feb. 16, 1935.

WILLIAMS, Roger Butler, mfr., banker; b. Ithaca, N.Y., May 8, 1848; s. Josiah Butler and Mary H. (Hardy) W.; Ithaca Acad.; A.M., Yale, 1868; m. Caroline L. Romer, Dec. 17, 1874; 1 son, Roger Butler. Began in mfg. business, 1872; partner and owner Williams Bros., mfrs. of machinery; pres. First Nat. Bank, Ithaca Savings Bank, Ithaca Traction Co., Central N.Y. Southern R.R. Co. Pres. Bd. Edn., Ithaca, Cornell Library Assn.; trustee Cornell U., Ithaca Hosp. Assn.; chmn. Sewer Constrn. Commn., Ithaca; mem. Creek, Park and Drainage Commn.; mem. bd. mgrs. State Industrial Sch., Rochester, N.Y., Ovid Asylum, Ovid, N.Y. Republican. Presbyn. Home: Ithaca, N.Y. Died 1933.

WILLIAMS, Roger D., army officer; b. Lexington, Ky., Aug. 29, 1856; s. Benjamin F. and Mary Gates (Massie) W.; student Transylvania U., Lexington, 1874-76; m. Minnie Lyle Sayre, Nov. 1887. War corr. attached to Gen. Crook's command throughout Gen. Custer's Sioux Indian campaign, 1876. Served in Ky. N.G., 1st lt. to brig. gen., 30 yrs.; comd. troops in all the Ky. fueds for 25 yrs.; comd. sector on Rio Grande from Fort Hancock, Tex., to Las Cruces, N.M., 1916; commd. brig. gen. N.A., Aug. 5, 1917; apptd. comdr. 76th Brigade, Camp Shelby, Hattiesburg, Miss., Sept. 1917; attached to Hdqrs. 1st Army in France, July 1918-Mar. 1919; retired as brig. gen. N.A., May 1919. Republican. Master of hounds Iroquois Hunt Club, 1882-1918. Author: Horse and Hound, 1905; Old Times in the Black Hills, 1906; Wolf Hunting and Coursing, 1908; Deer Hunting in the West Indies, 1909; The Foxhound, 1914. Home: Lexington, Ky. Died Dec. 12, 1925.

WILLIAMS, Rufus Phillips, author; b. Ashfield, Mass., Jan. 3, 1851; s. Freeman and Deborah (Field) W.; A.B., Dartmouth, 1876, A.M., 1879; studies in science, Harvard, A.M., 1878; m. Lillian Walker, June 25, 1894. Teacher of chemistry, English High Sch., Boston, 1885—. Pres. Mass. State Assembly of Agassiz Assn., 1891-92; 4 yrs. pres. local chapter of Agassiz Assn.; pres. N.E. Assn. of Chemistry Teachers, 1900, 1901; one of asso. editors School Science, Chicago, in charge dept. metrology. Author: Introduction to Chemical Science, 1888; Laboratory Manual of General Chemistry, 1889; Chemical Experiments, General and Analytical, 1895; Laboratory Manual of Inorganic Chemistry, 1896; Elements of Chemistry, 1897; Chemical Exercises, 1903; Essentials of Chemistry, 1910. Wrote: (brochure) The Metric System, issued by The Decimal Assn., London, Eng., 1900. Died Aug. 23, 1911.

WILLIAMS, Sherman, author; b. Cooperstown, N.Y., Nov. 21, 1846; s. Justin Clark and Mary (Sherman) W.; grad. Albany Normal Sch., 1871; Pd.D., Albany Normal Coll., 1894; m. Margaret H. Wilber, Aug. 12, 1874. Teacher in rural schs., N.Y., 4 yrs.; supt. schs., Flushing, 1872-82, Glens Falls, 1882-99; conductor State Teachers' Insts., 1899-1912; chief of sch. libraries div., State Edn. Dept., N.Y., Jan. 1, 1912—. Trustee Crandall Estate, Crandall Free Library. Republican. Methodist. Mason. Author: Some Successful Americans, 1904; Stories from Early New York History, 1912; New York's Part in History, 1915. Compiler: Selections for Memorizing (with L. C. Foster), 1890; Choice Literature, 1906. Home: Glens Falls, N.Y. Died Dec. 12, 1923.

WILLIAMS, Talcott, journalist; b. Abeih, Turkey, July 20, 1849; s. Rev. William Frederic and Sarah Amelia (Pond) W.; A.B., Amherst, 1873, A.M., 1883; hon. A.M., U. of Pa., 1891; L.H.D., Amherst, 1896, Western Reserve U., 1897, Brown, 1915; LL.D., U. of Pa., 1895, Hobart, 1899, Western Reserve, 1909, Pa. Coll., 1915, Franklin and Marshall, 1915; Litt.D., U. of Rochester, 1902; m. Sophia Wells, d. Julius H. Royce, May 28, 1879. On staff of New York World, 1873-77; Washington corr. New York Sun and San Francisco Chronicle, 1877-79; editorial writer, Springfield (Mass.) Republican, 1879-81, Phila. Press, 1881-1912; monthly contbr. to Book News, Phila., 1889-1909; dir. Sch. of Journalism on the Pulitzer Foundation, Columbia, 1912-19, emeritus prof. of journalism, 1919—. Mem. Am. Acad. Polit. and Social Science. Pres. Am. Confs. Teachers Journalism, 1913, Am. Soc. Newspaper Editors. Trustee Amherst Coll., 1909-19; trustee and v.p. Constantinople Woman's Coll., 1912—; mem. bd. mgrs. Archæol. Mus. of U. of Pa., 1888-1914. Mem. Mgrs. Pa. Free Hosp. for Poor Consumptives, 1896-1912; v.p. from its orgn.; Pa. Soc. for Prevention of Tuberculosis; trustee of Jeanes Fund, of Phila. Armstrong Assn. Pres. Honest Ballot Assn., 1912-15, dir. 1915. Contbr. to 10th edit. Ency. Britannica; co-editor Internat. Ency. (2d edit.), Ency. Americana, Ency. Polit. Science, lit. and philos. jours. Author: Turkey, A Problem of Today, 1921; The Newspaper Man, 1922. Home: New York, N.Y. Died Jan. 24, 1928.

WILLIAMS, Theodore Chickering, clergyman, educator; b. Brookline, Mass., July 2, 1855; s. Frederick J. B. and Abby (Tufts) W.; A.B., Harvard U., 1876, S.T.B., 1881-82; Litt.D., Western Reserve U., 1911; m. Velma Curtis Wright, 1883. Minister Unitarian Ch., Winchester, Mass., 1882, All Souls' Ch., Unitarian, New York, 1883-96; preacher at Harvard, 1888-90; in Europe, 1897-99; first head master Hackley Sch., Tarrytown, N.Y., 1899-1905; in Europe, 1905-07; head master Roxbury Latin Sch., 1907-09 (resigned). Author: Character Building, 1894; Elegies of Tibullus (verse transl.), 1905; Virgil's Æneid, 12 books (verse transl.), 1907; Poems of Belief, 1910; Virgil's Georgics and Eclogues (verse transl.), 1915. Phi Beta Kappa poet, Harvard, 1894, Western Reserve U., 1915. Hymn writer. Died 1915.

WILLIAMS, Thomas, corp. official; b. Stamford, Conn., Aug. 10, 1856; s. Ichabod T. and Elizabeth H. (Skelding) W.; ed. St. John's Sch.; m. Emma W. Stott, Oct. 20, 1880; children—Thomas Resolved, Henry Waldron (dec.), Dorcas (Mrs. Morris Douw Ferris), Edith Stott (Mrs. Vail Blydenburgh). Identified, 1873—, with lumber business established by his grandfather, and sr. partner I. T. Williams & Sons; pres. George D. Emory Co., White Rock Mineral Springs Co., Resolved Corp.; dir. and mem. exec. com. Guaranty Trust Co.; dir. Am. Eagle Fire Ins. Co., Baltimore & New York R.R. Co., Chemical Bank & Trust Co., Edgewater Mills, Mutual Life Ins. Co., Niagara Fire Ins. Co., Staten Island Rapid Transit Co., Staten Island R.R. Co., Thompson-Starrett Co. Mem. council New York U. Democrat. Episcopalian. Home: Lawrence, L.I., N.Y. Died Dec. 21, 1935.

WILLIAMS, Thomas Reynolds, newspaperman; b. Jones Mills, Pa., Apr. 26, 1878; s. Thomas Jones and Louisa (Rumiser) W.; B.E., Southwestern State Normal Sch., California, Pa., 1895, M.E., 1897; grad. Mt. Pleasant (Pa.) Inst., 1898; A.B., Franklin and Marshall Coll., 1902; m. Gertrude Wertz, Sept. 1900; children—F. Marshall, G. Gladys. Began as reporter, Pittsburgh Press, 1902, and advanced to city editor, mng. editor and business mgr. until 1925; asst. pub. Pittsburgh Gazette Times, and Pittsburgh Chronicle Telegraph, 1925-27; bus. mgr. the Pittsburgh Sun-Telegraph, 1927-28; newspaper broker, 1928-32; sec.-treas. Pittsburgh Newspaper Pubs. Assn., 1932—. Regional dir. for Pa. under pulp and paper div. War Industries Board, World War I; also mem. gen. paper com. of Am. Publishers during war period. Organized dept. of journalism, U. of Pittsburgh, 1920, and lectured in dept. 4 yrs. Mem. Am. Newspaper Pubs.' Assn. (pres. 1920-22), Pittsburgh Newspaper Pubs.' Assn. (pres.). Republican. Mem. Reformed Church. Moose. Home: Pittsburgh, Pa. Died Oct. 21, 1937.

WILLIAMS, Thomas Sutler, U.S. judge; b. Louisville, Ill., Feb. 14, 1872; s. William and Nancy (Freeman) W.; ed. Austin Coll., Effingham, Ill.; m. Mabel Simpson, June 9, 1897. Admitted to Ill. bar, 1892, and practiced in Louisville; served as city atty. and mayor of Louisville; also mem. Ill. Ho. of Rep.; state's atty., Clay County, Ill., 7 yrs.; mem. 64th to 71st Congresses (1915-31), 24th Ill. Dist.; resigned to become judge U.S. Ct. of Claims, Oct. 1929. Republican. Mem. Christian (Disciples) Ch. Mason. Home: Louisville, Ill. Died Apr. 5, 1940.

WILLIAMS, Timothy Shaler, street ry. official; b. Ithaca, N.Y., Aug. 1, 1862; s. Howard C. and Frances (Grant) W.; A.B., Cornell, 1884; m. Mrs. Alice W. Kelley, 1895. In newspaper work N.Y., Albany and Washington, 1884-89; pvt. sec. Governors Hill and Flower, 1889-94; with Brooklyn Rapid Transit System of railroads as sec. and treas., v.p., pres. and dir., 1895-1923; retired. Home: Cold Spring Harbor, Huntington, L.I., N.Y. Died June 3, 1930.

WILLIAMS, Walter, univ. pres.; b. Boonville, Mo., July 2, 1864; s. Marcus and Mary Jane (Littlepage) W.; high sch. edn.; learned printer's trade; LL.D., Mo. Valley Coll., 1906, Kan. State Agrl. Coll., 1909, Washington U., 1926; m. Hulda Harned, June 30, 1892 (died 1918); children—Walter, Jr. (dec.), Helen Harned (Mrs. John F. Rhodes), Edwin Moss; m. 2d, Sara Lawrence Lockwood, Oct. 22, 1927. Editor and part owner of the Boonville Advertiser, 1884-89; editor Columbia (Mo.) Herald, 1890-1908; established The Country Editor (monthly), 1895; editor St. Louis Presbyterian, 1897-99, Daily State Tribune, Jefferson City, Mo., 1898-1902; dean Sch. of Journalism, and prof. history and principles of journalism, U. of Mo., 1908—, acting pres., June-Dec. 1930, pres., 1931—. Pres. Mo. Press Assn., 1889, Nat. Editorial Assn., 1895; pres. for N. America Internat. Press Congress, Berne, Switzerland, 1902; organizer and sec. World's Press Parliament, St. Louis, 1904. Chmn. exec. bd. curators, U. of Mo., 1898-1908; commr. St. Louis Expn. to foreign press, 1902-04, and traveled in Africa, Asia and Europe in expn. interests. Fellow Kahn Foundation for Foreign Travel of Am. Teachers, 1913-14, traveling around world. Dir. Internat. Press Congress, San Francisco, 1915; 1st pres. Press Congress of the World, 1915-25; chmn. World's Press Council; 1st pres. Am. Assn. Schools and Depts. Journalism, 1916; exchange prof. Nat. U. of Mexico, 1925; pres. 1st Pan-American Congress Journalists, Washington, 1926; exchange lecturer, Buenos Aires, Argentina, 1930. Received Oberlaender award of study in German speaking countries, 1932 and 1933. Fellow Brit. Inst. Journalists. On spl. mission to Japan, China, Siberia, 1918-19. Presbyn. Democrat. Mason (33°). Author: How the Cap'n Saved the Day, 1901; Some Saints and Some Sinners in the Holy Land, 1902; The State of Missouri, 1904; History of Missouri, 1908; Missouri Since the Civil War, 1909; Eloquent Sons of the South, 1909; From Missouri to the Isle of Mull, 1909; The Practice of Journalism, 1911; The World's Journalism, 1915; History of Northeast Missouri, 1914; History of Northwest Missouri, 1915; Journalism—the Newest Weapon for Democracy, 1919; The Press Congress of the World in Hawaii (foreword by President Harding), 1922; History of Missouri Since the Civil War, 1927; The Press Congress of the World in Switzerland, 1927; also bulls. Some Observations on the German Press and The Struggle in Europe for the Freedom of the Press. Home: Columbia, Mo. Died July 29, 1935.

WILLIAMS, W(alter) Erskine, lawyer; b. Collierville, Tenn., Apr. 19, 1860; s. Edmund Jones and Almyra Probert (Smith) W.; B.Ph., State U. of Miss., 1885 (winner Univ. sr. debaters' medal); m. Ida E. Quillian, Oct. 19, 1892 (dec.); children—Orline Estella (Mrs. Louie M. White), Walter Erskine (dec.), Probert Frances, Lillian Gray, Thomas Quillian, Florence Minerva (Mrs. J. Turner Lindley), Ida Lois (Mrs. N. H. Riveire); m. 2d, Beth F. Rucker, Dec. 27, 1933. Admitted Tex. bar, 1890, practicing at Ft. Worth; specialist in probate law; mem. City Council, Ft. Worth, 1894-96; special county judge, Tarrant County, Tex., 1897; candidate for congressman at large, Tex., 1932. Pres. Gen. Bd. of Lay Activities M.E. Ch., S., 1922-26; visited Oriental countries and Europe, 1924-25, to present plans for a world brotherhood, also corr. Ft. Worth Star-

Telegram, and lecturer before the Comparative Law Sch. of China, Shanghai, 1924; lecturer, Law Dept., Southern Methodist U., winter 1931. Mem. Commn. on Nationalism, M.E. Ch., S.; mem. commn. M.E. Ch., S., to establish autonomous ch. in Brazil, 1930; del. Gen. Conf. M.E. Ch., S., 11 times, 1902-38. Trustee Ft. Worth pub. schs., Tex. Woman's Coll., etc. Mem. Am. Bar Assn. (state council for Tex., 1927-28; v.p. for Tex., 1928-29, 1931-32). Democrat. Mason, K.P. Author: Lectures on the Constitution and Supreme Court, 1937. Home: Fort Worth, Tex. Died Aug. 29, 1938.

WILLIAMS, William Elza, congressman; b. Detroit, Ill., May 5, 1857; s. David A. and Emily A. (Hayden) W.; ed. freshman and sophomore yrs., Ill. Coll., Jacksonville, Ill.; read law in law office; m. Margaret Gallaher, Aug. 24, 1880. Admitted to Ill. bar, 1880; state's atty., Pike County, Ill., 2 terms, 1884-92; represented Chicago City Ry. Co. as trial atty., 1903-05, inclusive; mem. 56th Congress (1899-1901); defeated for renomination, 1900, in deadlock conv., on 2,453d ballot, by combination of all opposing candidates; mem. 63d and 64th Congresses (1913-17), Ill. at large. Democrat. Sr. mem. law firm of Williams & Williams (brothers). Conglist. Mason. Home: Pittsfield, Ill. Died Sept. 12, 1921.

WILLIAMS, William George, coll. prof.; b. Chillicothe, O., Feb. 25, 1822; s. of Samuel Williams; grad. Woodward Coll., Cincinnati, M.A., Miami U., 1847; LL.D., Baldwin U., 1873; m. Delia Lathrop, 1877. Entered M.E. ministry as mem. Central Ohio Conf., 1856 (sec. 28 yrs.); chaplain 145th regt. Ohio vol. inf., 1864. Prof. Greek lang. and lit., Ohio Wesleyan U., 1844—. Address: Delaware, O. Died 1902.

WILLIAMS, William Henry, ry. official; b. Athens, O., June 25, 1874; s. Henry H. and Lydia Virginia (Withers) W.; ed. pub. schs., Toledo, O., Beaver Valley Pen Art Hall, Beaver Falls, Pa.; m. Miss Manderbaugh, June 24, 1896; m. 2d, Belle Graham, Jan. 23, 1923. Held various positions on Pa. Ry., Columbus, Hocking Valley & Toledo Ry., Pittsburgh & Lake Erie Ry., 1890-1901; asst. sec. and asst. to gen. mgr., B.&O. R.R., 1901-04; supt. freight transportation St.L.&S.F. R.R., and Chicago & Eastern Ill. Ry., Apr.-Oct. 1904; traffic mgr. Merchants & Mfrs. Assn. and C. of C., Pittsburgh, 1905-07; asst. to pres., May-Oct. 1907, 3d v.p., Oct. 1, 1907, v.p., Apr. 1915-May 1928, D.&H. R.R.; made chmn. bd. and exec. com., Wabash Ry. Co., Dec. 1, 1915; chmn. exec. com. Mo.P. R.R. Co., Mar. 1923—, chmn. bd., same co., May 1924—, and dir., May 1917—; chmn. bd. and exec. com., and dir. N.O.T.&M. Ry. Co., T.&P. Ry. Co., Internat.-Gt. Northern R.R. Co., Ann Arbor R.R. Co., N.J., Ind.&Ill. R.R. Co.; dir., mem. mng. com., chmn. exec. com. D.&R.G.W. R.R. Co.; dir. Am. Refrigerator Transit Co., Hudson & Manhattan R.R. Co., Chemical Bank & Trust Co., Warren Pipe & Foundry Co., Ry. Express Agency, Inc.; also chmn. bd. and dir. of many other corps. Home: New York, N.Y. Died Oct. 14, 1931.

WILLIAMS, William Martin, lawyer; b. West Point, Ga., Sept. 12, 1877; s. William Larkin and Mary Ella (Martin) W.; B.S., Ala. Poly. Inst., 1896, M.S., 1897; student Harvard U. Law Sch., 1899-1901; m. Gladys Rood, Dec. 27, 1908; children—Charles Rood, William Larkin. Instr. Latin and history, Ala. Poly. Inst., 1896-97, mathematics, 1898-99; practiced law in N.Y. City, 1902-08; mem. firm Rushton, Williams & Crenshaw, Montgomery, Ala., 1908-17; solicitor U.S. Dept. Agr., June 4, 1917-Mar. 1920; U.S. commr. of internal revenue, Mar. 1920-Apr. 12, 1921; mem. law firm Williams, Myers & Quiggle, Washington, 1921—. Capt. cadets, Ala. Poly. Inst., 1896; mem. Squadron A, N.G.N.Y., 1903-07; capt. Co. L, 12th Inf., N.G.N.Y., 1908. Democrat. K.P. Home: Washington, D.C. Died Mar. 1932.

WILLIAMS, William Muir, lawyer; b. Boonville, Mo., Feb. 4, 1850; s. Marcus and Mary Jane (Littlepage) W.; brother of Walter W.; grad. Kemper Mil. Inst., Boonville, Mo., 1867; m. Jessie Evans, Dec. 16, 1875. Admitted to Mo. bar, Feb. 1, 1873; in continuous practice, 1873—, except when serving term as judge Supreme Ct. of Mo., 1898. Del. Universal Congress Lawyers and Jurists, St. Louis, 1904. Democrat. Presbyn. Died 1916.

WILLIAMS, William Reid, asst. sec. of war; b. Bristol, Va., Nov. 17, 1866; s. William B. and Isabella (Reid) W.; ed. pub. and pvt. schs.; m. Caroline H. Powell, Dec. 27, 1893; children—John Powell, William R., Mildred C., Thos. Leigh, Shirley Carter. Sec. Richmond Locomotive Works, 1900-03; purchasing officer Am. Locomotive Co., 1903-05; v.p., treas. Richmond Forgings Co., 1905-20; asst. sec. of war, July 29, 1920-21; apptd. gen. mgr. Standard Stoker Co., Erie, Pa., 1922; later dist. sales mgr. for Southeastern sect., same co. Democrat. Episcopalian. Home: Richmond, Va. Died July 24, 1931.

WILLIAMS, William Robert, M.D.; b. Watertown, Wis., June 13, 1867; s. Evan Thomas and Anne Catherine (Roberts) W.; A.B., Williams Coll., 1889, A.M., 1892; M.D., Coll. of Phys. and Surg. (Columbia), 1895; m. Flora Nabersberg, Apr. 25, 1900; children—Clarke, Byard. Demonstrator histology, Coll. of Phys. and Surg., 1897-99, instr. in therapeutics, 1904-08, asst. prof. pharmacology and therapeutics, 1908-14, asso. prof. clin. medicine, 1914-21; lecturer on hygiene, Cornell Med. Sch., 1899-1904, instr. in medicine, 1903-04; dep. attending phys., Hudson St. Hosp., 1899-1902; asst. pathologist Gen. Memorial Hosp., 1902-04; pathologist French Hosp., 1902-08, cons. pathologist, 1908-16; asst. attending phys. City Hosp., 1905-10; asso. phys. New York Hosp., 1910-12, attending phys., 1912-32, cons. phys., 1932—; consultant in medicine Elizabeth Horton Memorial Hosp., Middletown, N.Y., 1929—, also St. John's Riverside Hosp., Yonkers, N.Y., New York Infirmary for Women and Children, N.Y. City. Served as chmn. Med. Advisory Bd. Home: New York, N.Y. Died Nov. 17, 1940.

WILLIAMS, William Taylor Burwell, educator; b. Stone Bridge, Va., June 3, 1866; s. Edmund and Louisa (Johnson) W.; student Hampton Inst., Hampton, Va., 1886-88; Phillips Acad., Andover, Mass., 1889-93; A.B., Harvard, 1897; LL.D., Morehouse Coll., Atlanta, Ga., 1923; m. Emily A. Harper, June 29, 1904 (died 1933); m. 2d, Mrs. Kate Ruff Green, Oct. 27, 1937. Prin. pub. sch., Indianapolis, Ind., 1897-1902; field agt. Hampton Inst. and Southern Edn. Bd., 1902-03, Gen. Edn. Bd., 1903-06, John F. Slater Fund, 1906—; Negro Rural Sch. Fund, 1910—; dean of coll., Tuskegee Inst., 1927-36, v.p., 1936—. Mem. Edn. Commn. to Virgin Island, 1928, to Haiti, 1930. Awarded Spingarn medal, 1934. Republican. Conglist. Mason, Odd Fellow. Died Mar. 26, 1941.

WILLIAMS, Yancey Sullivan, naval officer; b. Monetta, S.C., Apr. 7, 1876; s. Thomas Smith and America (Holston) W.; grad. U.S. Naval Acad., 1898; grad. U.S. Naval War Coll., 1924; m. Maude George Jackson, Jan. 5, 1906; 1 daughter, Evelyn Stuart (Mrs. Harry A. Guthrie). Commd. ensign U.S. Navy, 1898; promoted through grades to rear adm., June 1, 1931. Participated in Spanish-Am. War, 1898; at Samoa, 1899-1900; Hayti and San Domingo, 1914-15; on U.S.S. Delaware, World War, 1917-18; with Asiatic Fleet, 1925-27; Navy Dept., Washington, 1927-31; apptd. comdr. Yangtze Patrol, Asiatic Fleet, 1931. Awarded Navy Cross, also West Indian, Spanish, Chinese, Haytian and Dominican campaign medals, and Victory medal, World War I. Died Nov. 1, 1938.

WILLIAMSON, Ben., senator; b. Pike County, Ky., Oct. 16, 1864; s. Wallace J. and Columbia (Slater) W.; student Bethany Coll., 1877-83; m. Ceres Burgess Wellman, Jan. 19, 1887; children—Wallace J., Geraldine Burgess (Mrs. Davis E. Geiger), Ben. Founder, 1886, and pres. Ben Williamson & Co., wholesale hardware; engaged in coal and banking business, eastern Ky. and southern W.Va.; one of founders of Williamson, W.Va., and First Nat. Bank, Williamson, becoming chmn. bd.; v.p. McClintock-Fields Co. Elected U.S. senator from Ky., 1930, to fill unexpired term of Frederick M. Sackett, ending Mar. 3, 1931. Pres. Ky. Crippled Children's Commn. Democrat. Presbyn. Mason. Home: Ashland, Ky. Died June 23, 1941.

WILLIAMSON, Charles Spencer, M.D.; b. Cincinnati, May 15, 1872; s. William F. and Mary Louise (Spencer) W.; M.S., U. of Cincinnati, 1893; M.D., Med. Coll. of Ohio, 1896; m. Josephine Gillette Stilwell, Oct. 15, 1903; children—Mary Josephine, Isabel Gillette, Elizabeth Spencer. Resident phys., Cincinnati Hosp., 1896-97; post-grad. study Leipzig, Berlin, Vienna and Paris, 1897-1900; removed to Chicago, 1901; adj. prof. medicine, 1901-03, prof. clin. medicine, 1903-12, Coll. Phys. and Surg.; asst. prof. diseases of stomach, 1901-07, prof., 1907—, Chicago Polyclinic; prof. medicine and clin. medicine, and head of dept. of internal medicine, U. of Ill. Coll. of Medicine, 1912. Lt. col. M.C. U.S.A., and dir. dept. sanitation, Ft. Riley, Kan., and Ft. Oglethorpe, Ga.; also dir. Sch. of Mil. Hygiene and Sanitation, Ft. Oglethorpe, Ga. Awarded gold medal by A.M.A. for exhibit of research work, 1918. Mem. Assn. Am. Physicians. Episcopalian. Editor: French's Practice of Medicine, 1910. Contbr. several monographs containing results of original research in Am. and European publs. Home: Chicago, Ill. Died Feb. 16, 1933.

WILLIAMSON, James Alexander, lawyer; b. Adair County, Ky., Feb. 8, 1829; s. William W.; academic edn.; m. Ann Whitfield Gregory, 1853. Enlisted, July 1861, 4th Ia. inf.; commissioned 1st lt. and adj.; promoted lt. col March 9, 1862, col. March 18, 1862; later brig. gen. and still later bvt. maj. gen. Medal of honor for gallantry in action Chickasaw Bayou, Miss., Dec. 29, 1862. Commr. Gen. Land Office U.S., 1876-81; then land commr. and gen. solicitor Atlantic & Pacific R.R. Co., of which he later was pres. until road was sold to Atchison, Topeka & Santa Fe R.R. Republican. Died 1902.

WILLIAMSON, James De Long; b. Cleveland, O., Mar. 12, 1849; s. Samuel and Mary E. Williamson; A.B., Adelbert Coll. (Western Reserve U.), 1870; student Andover Theol. Sem., 1872-74; grad. Union Theol. Sem., 1875; D.D., Wooster, 1902; m. Edith Day Ely, Aug. 4, 1875; children—Frederic Ely, Mary Tisdale (dec.), Arthur Putnam, Ruth Ely. Ordained Presbyn. ministry, 1875; pastor Norwalk, O., 1875-84, Warren, 1885-88, Beckwith Memorial Ch., Cleveland, 1888-1901; pres. pro tem. Society for Savings, Cleveland, 1912-15; exec. v.p. same, 1915-21, and 1924-27. Trustee Western Reserve U. (actg. pres. Nov. 1921-23). Republican. Home: Cleveland, O. Died Sept. 17, 1935.

WILLIAMSON, James Nathaniel, Jr., mfr.; b. Graham, N.C., Jan. 28, 1872; s. James Nathaniel and Mary Elizabeth (Holt) W.; ed. Pantops Acad., Charlottesville, Va., 4 yrs.; Bingham Sch., Mebane, N.C., 2 yrs. (rank of capt. and adj. battalion); U. of N.C. short time, when left to enter business; m. Mary Archer Saunders, Nov. 19, 1898. Joined father and brother in Ossipee Cotton Mills, 1892; admitted as partner, 1898, and made gen. mgr.; took over Hopedale Mills in connection with Ossipee, corporate name of James N. Williamson & Sons Co., becoming pres. and treas.; v.p. Pilot Cotton Mills Co., Alamance Loan & Trust Co., Burlington, N.C.; dir. Am. Trust Co., Charlotte. Del. Rep. Nat. Conv., Chicago, 1912, and there became Progressive; del. Prog. Nat. Conv., 1912; mem. Prog. Nat. Com., 1912-16. Episcopalian. Deceased.

WILLIAMSON, John I., lawyer; b. Carroll County, Mo., Mar. 16, 1867; s. John W. and Mary Catharine (Smith) W.; grad. high sch., Carrollton, Mo., 1887; Ky. U., 1888-89; m. Lucy E. Willett, Dec. 8, 1891; children—Mrs. Isabel W. Atkinson, Mrs. Elton W. Connell. Admitted to Mo. bar, 1891, and began practice at Carrollton; moved to Kansas City, Mo., 1903; lecturer Kansas City Sch. of Law, 1909-19; mem. Commn. to Revise Mo. Code of Civil Procedure, 1913. Asso. justice Supreme Ct. of Mo., Nov. 1919-Jan. 1921; resumed practice in Kansas City. Mem. Jackson County (Mo.) Council of Defense and of Legal Advisory Bd., World War I. Mem. Christian (Disciples) Church; pres. Linwood Boul. Ch.; pres. Christian Ch. Hosp. Assn.; chmn. bd. trustees Atkins Memorial Fund. Mason. Home: Kansas City, Mo. Died Nov. 19, 1932.

WILLIAMSON, John Pogue, clergyman; b. Lac qui Parle, Minn., Oct. 27, 1835; s. Thomas Smith and Margaret (Poage) W.; student Knox Coll., 1853-55; A.B., Marietta College, 1857, A.M., 1860; grad. Lane Theol. Sem., Cincinnati, 1860; D.D., Yankton (S.D.) Coll., 1890; m. Sarah A. Van Nice, Apr. 27, 1866. Licensed to preach by Presbyn. Ch., 1859; supplied ch., Allensville, Ind., 1859-60. Having learned Dakota language when a child, followed his father into the missionary work, 1860, and continued it; devoted himself to preaching in Indian tongue; also labored for their material improvement; spl. U.S. agt. for Flandreau Indians, 1873-78. Spent much time in preparing Dakota publs.; started an Indian periodical, the Iapi Oaye, 1871, which was published many yrs. Republican. Author: Oowa Wowapi, 1870; Dakota Odowan, 1881; An English-Dakota Dictionary, 1902. Died Oct. 3, 1917.

WILLIAMSON, Joseph, lawyer; b. Belfast, Me., Oct. 5, 1828; s. Joseph and Caroline (Cross) W.; grad. Bowdoin, 1849, Litt.D., 1896; m. Ada H. Peirce, Oct. 22, 1857 (died 1872). Judge municipal ct. Belfast, Me., 1853-61; city solicitor, Belfast, several yrs. Corr. sec. and biographer Me. Hist. Soc.; mem. numerous Nat. and State hist. and antiquarian socs. Pres. Waldo Bar Assn., pres. Belfast Free Library from its institution, 1887. Author: The Maine Register and State Reference Book, 1852; History of Belfast, Maine, 1877; Bibliography of Maine (2 vols.), 1896. Home: Belfast, Me. Died 1902.

WILLIAMSON, Julia May ("Lura Bell"), verse-writer, teacher; b. New Sharon, Me., Mar. 13, 1859; d. Rev. William F. and Thankful P. (Norcross) Williamson; ed. principally at home, because of delicate health. First poem written at age of 12; first book published at 16; contributed stories, essays and poems to various periodicals. Unmarried. Author: The Choir of the Year, 1875; Echoes of Time and Tide, 1879; Star of Hope, and Other Songs, 1892. Died 1909.

WILLIAMSON, Samuel E., lawyer; b. Cleveland, Apr. 19, 1844; s. Samuel and Mary E. (Tisdale) W.; grad. Western Reserve Coll., 1864, LL.D.; Harvard Law Sch., 1866-67; m. Mary Peabody Marsh, June 1878 (died 1881); m. 2d, Harriet Whiting Brown, 1884. Admitted to Ohio bar, 1866; judge common pleas court, Cleveland, 1880-82, resigned; solicitor, 1882, gen. counsel, 1887, New York, Chicago & St. Louis R.R.; gen. counsel New York Central & Hudson River R.R. Co., 1898—; gen. counsel and v.p. West Shore R.R., 1898—. Home: New York, N.Y. Died 1903.

WILLIAMSON, Sydney Bacon, civil engr.; b. Lexington, Va., Apr. 15, 1865; s. Thomas Hoomes and Julia Anna (Lewis) W.; grad. Va. Mil. Inst., 1884; m. Helen C. Davis, May 20, 1890. Instr. mathematics, Kings Mountain (S.C.) Mil. Sch., 1884-86; with engring. depts. C.B. & Northern, St. Paul & Duluth, and N.P. rys., 1886-90; entered gen. engring., Montgomery, Ala., 1890; in employ U.S. Govt., on Tenn. River improvements, 1892-1900 (except during Spanish-Am. War), and at Newport, R.I., as asst. engr. on fortification work, 1900-04; in practice, New

York, Baltimore and other cities, 1904-07; engr. in charge of Pacific Locks, and div. engr. Pacific Div., Panama Canal, 1907-12 (resigned); chief of constrn., U.S. Reclamation Service, Dec. 10, 1914-Jan. 1916 (resigned); apptd. cons. civil engr. for Guggenheim Brothers, 1916. Asso. with Gen. Geo. W. Goethals as cons. engr. for Port of Palm Beach, Fla.; apptd. by President of the U.S. mem. Interoceanic Canal Bd. to investigate and report on the Nicaragua Canal route and other possible canal routes for connecting the Atlantic and Pacific oceans; retired May 1, 1935. Mem. of exec. com. Chile Exploration Company, Braden Copper Company. Served as capt. U.S. Volunteer Engrs., Spanish-Am. War; detailed as asst. to Col. George W. Goethals, chief engr. 1st Army Corps. Commd. col. engrs., and comd. 55th Engrs. A.E.F.; in France as sect. engr., intermediate Sect. West, and of the Paris Dist. Awarded D.S.M. (U.S.). Episcopalian. Home: Lexington, Va. Died Jan. 13, 1939.

WILLIAMSON, Thom, chief engr. U.S.N.; b. Edenton, N.C., Aug. 5, 1833; s. William Price and Penelope Benbury (McDonald) W.; ed. Norfolk (Va.) Mil. Acad. and St. Mary's Coll., Baltimore. to 1850; m. Julia Price, Dec. 2, 1861. Apptd. 3d asst. engr. U.S.N., May 23, 1853; 2d asst. engr., June 27, 1855; 1st asst. engr., July 21, 1858; chief engr., Aug. 5, 1861; relative rank of capt., Jan. 30, 1889; retired on account of age, Aug. 5, 1895; chief engr. with rank of rear admiral, June 29, 1906. Offered a signed commn. as chief engr. in C.S.N. at outbreak of Civil War, but declined; sr. engr. officer with Admiral Farragut's fleet in fights at Fts. Morgan and Gaines and in operations in Mobile Bay; head of dept. of steam engring., U.S. Naval Acad., 1868-69; fleet engr. N. and S. Atlantic and Pacific stas. and acted as supt. State, War and Navy Depts. Bldg. under successive spl. orders from Presidents Harrison and Cleveland; mem. bd. to examine plans for coaling ships at sea during Spanish-Am. War; on duty in Navy Dept., Oct. 19, 1901-June 6, 1912. Awarded medal and diploma for collaboration, by Paris Expn., 1900, and diploma for distinguished services, by Buffalo Expn., 1901. Home: Annapolis, Md. Died Mar. 1918.

WILLIAMSON, William Collins, clergyman; b. Xenia, O., Feb. 2, 1842; s. Andrew Duncan and Isabel (Collins) W.; A.B., Jefferson Coll., Washington, Pa., 1865, A.M., 1868; grad. Theol. Sem., U.P. Ch., Xenia, O., 1868; D.D., Amity Coll.; LL.D., Tarkio, 1923; m. Matilda Jean McNary, June 30, 1868 (died 1921); children—Harry E. (dec.), Etha E. Ordained ministry U.P. Ch., 1868; pastor Washington, Ia., 1871-85, Keokuk, 1885-1904, Burlington, 1904-09, Clarinda, Ia., 1909-26. Moderator Gen. Assembly U.P. Ch., 1905; represented U.P. Ch. before Asso. Ref. Ch., S.; mem. Fed. Council Chs. of Christ in America; mem. bd. mgrs. Theol. Sem. U.P. Ch. 18 yrs.; mem. Monmouth Coll. Senate. Served as pvt., Union Army, 1864-65. Republican. Home: Monmouth, Ill. Died Jan. 22, 1935.

WILLIAMSON, William James, clergyman; b. New Bloomfield, Mo., Oct. 13, 1869; s. Andrew Jackson and Barbara (Kyger) W.; A.B., William Jewell Coll., Liberty, Mo., 1893, D.D., 1903; Ph.D., Westminster (Mo.) Coll., 1896; U. of Chicago, 1897, 1898; m. Jessie Lee Warinner, Apr. 14, 1894. Ordained Bapt. ministry, 1891; organized, and pastor Bales Av. Ch., Kansas City, 1891-1901, 3d Ch., St. Louis, 1901—. Pres. Bapt. Young Peoples Union America. Trustee William Jewell Coll., Southern Bapt. Theol. Sem., Stevens Coll. Pres. Ch. Federation of St. Louis. Mason. Home: St. Louis, Mo. Died Aug. 18, 1918.

WILLIAMSON, William Thomas, telephone official; b. Marietta, O., Apr. 4, 1871; s. Thomas Wager and Lydia Viola (Sayre) W.; ed. high sch., Huntington, W.Va., and Ohio Wesleyan U.; m. Elizabeth Samuels Slack, Oct. 23, 1895; 1 dau., Harriet Viola (Mrs. Clarence Lee Barrett). Began in employ of C.&O. Ry. Co., 1889; with Southern Bell Telephone & Telegraph Co. as mgr. and supt. at Charleston, 1901-13; apptd., 1913, division mgr. Chesapeake & Potomac Telephone Co. (Bell System); following mergers of Bell and independent telephone cos. in W.Va. became dir. Chesapeake & Potomac Co. of W.Va., 1917, v.p., 1923, v.p. and sec., 1928, mem. bd. dirs. and asst. sec.-treas. same until retired, May 1, 1936; spl. field rep. of Fidelity Investment Assn.; pres. Bell Oil Products Service, Union Mortgage Investment Co., Nat. Realty Co., Metropolitan Realty Co., Raleigh Office Supply Co. (Beckley, W.Va.). Col. a.d.c. hon. staff of Govs. Glasscock and Hatfield of W.Va. Apptd. mem. W.Va. Century of Progress Commn., 1933; pres. West Va. Publicity Assn.; mem. bd. dirs. and gen. field sec. West Va. Chamber of Commerce. Trustee W.Va. Wesleyan Coll., W.Va. Council Religious Edn.; pres. Nat. Thrift Savings. Pres. Alexander Graham Bell Chap. Telephone Pioneers of America, Washington, D.C., 1931; pres. West Va. Chap. Telephone Pioneers of America, 1933-36; dir. Corporate Leaders of America. Del. Gen. Conf. M.E. Ch., 1924, 28; del. to Ecumenical Conf. of Methodism, Atlanta, 1931; reserve del. Gen. Conf. M.E. Ch., 1932; mem. Gen. Conf. Commn. on Inter-Ch. Relations. Republican. Mason. Home: Charleston, W.Va. Died Jan. 22, 1939.

WILLINGHAM, Robert Josiah, clergyman; b. Beaufort Dist., S.C., May 15, 1854; s. Benjamin Lawton and Elizabeth (Baynard) W.; A.M., U. of Ga., 1873, A.B., B.P., and B.S., same, 1873; Southern Bapt. Theol. Sem., 1877-79; D.D., Carson and Newman Coll., Tenn., 1890; LL.D., Furman U., S.C.; m. Corneille Bacon, Sept. 8, 1874. Ordained Bapt. ministry, 1878; pastor Talbotton, Ga., 1879-82, Barnesville, Ga., 1882-87, First Ch., Chattanooga, Tenn., 1887-91, Memphis, Tenn., 1891-93; corr. sec. Foreign Mission Bd., Southern Bapt. Conv., 1893—. Died Dec. 20, 1914.

WILLIS, Frank Bartlette, senator; b. Lewis Center, O., Dec. 28, 1871; s. Jay B. and Lavinia A. W.; A.B., 1893, A.M., 1904; LL.B. from Ohio Wesleyan, Miami, and Ohio, 1906; m. Allie Dustin, July 19, 1894; 1 dau., Helen Dustin. Prof. history and economics, 1894-1906, later prof. law, Ohio Northern U.; admitted to bar, 1906. Mem. Ohio Ho. of Rep., 2 terms, 1900-1904; mem. 62d and 63d Congresses (1911-15), 8th Ohio Dist.; gov. of Ohio, term 1915-17; U.S. senator from Ohio, 1921-27. Republican. Home: Delaware, O. Died Mar. 30, 1928.

WILLIS, George Francis, investments; b. Waynesville, N.C., Mar. 1, 1879; s. Jerkins and Nancy Emmaline (Smathers) W.; ed. high sch., Waynesville, and Bingham Mil. Sch., Asheville, N.C.; m. Charlotte Bowers, Feb. 17, 1904; children—George Francis, John Bowers, Richard Benners. Founder, 1913, pres. until 1922, Internat. Proprietaries, Inc., U.S. and Can.; founder, 1922, pres. until 1924, Zonite Products Co.; founder, 1924, builder, prin. owner and pres. Avondale Estates, Atlanta; pres. Bay View Estate Corp., Miami, Fla., 1920-24; founder, 1928, and pres. G. F. Willis, Inc. proprietary products, Atlanta; pres. Willis Properties, Inc.; dir. Atlanta Trust Co. Pres. Stone Mountain Confederate Monumental Assn., 1928-29; chmn. finance com. Ga. Sch. of Technology, 1922-23. Republican. Methodist. Home: Atlanta, Ga. Died July 20, 1932.

WILLIS, H(enry) Parker, economist; b. Weymouth, Mass., Aug. 14, 1874; s. John Henry and Olympia (Brown) W.; student Western Reserve U.; A.B., U. of Chicago, 1894, Ph.D., 1897; LL.D., Columbia, 1929; studied univs. of Leipzig and Vienna; spl. studies economics, history, polit. science, law; m. Rosa Johnston Brooke, Dec. 24, 1903; children—Katharine Corbin, Henry Parker Brown, John Brooke, Arthur Hunt. Adj. prof. economics and polit. science, 1898-99, prof., 1899-1901, Wilson prof. economics and polit. science, 1903-05, Washington and Lee U.; prof. finance, George Washington U., 1905-06 and 1907-12; dean Coll. Polit. Sciences, 1910-12; asso. editor New York Jour. of Commerce, 1912-14, editor-in-chief same, 1919-31; Am. rep. London Daily Financial News, 1929—, Agence Economique, Paris, 1931—, Temps, Paris, 1932-35. Sec. Fed. Reserve Bd., Washington, 1914-18, and dir. of research, 1918-22; cons. economist, same, 1922, and of Fitch Investors Service, New York, 1934—. Pres. Philippine Nat. Bank, 1916-17. Spl. commr. in Australasia for Chase Nat. Bank and Central Union Trust Co., 1919. Asst. Monetary Commn., 1897-98; leader writer, N.Y. Evening Post, 1901-02; Washington corr. N.Y. Jour. of Commerce, and Springfield Republican, 1902-03, N.Y. Jour. of Commerce, and Engring. and Mining Jour., 1905-13; spl. corr. in Japan, China and P.I., 1904; asso. editor Jour. of Accountancy; editor U.S. Immigration Commn., 1909-10; expert Ways and Means Com., Ho. of Rep., Washington, 1911-13, Banking and Currency Com., same, 1912-13 (drafting Fed. Res. Act), Joint Com. on Rural Credits, 1914 (drafting Fed. Farm Loan Act); chmn. Banking Commn. of Irish Free State, 1926-27; tech. adviser to U.S. Senate Com. on Banking and Currency, 1930-32 (drafting Banking Act of 1933); spl. adviser to Roumanian govt., 1930-31. Lecturer, 1913-14, prof. banking, 1917—, Columbia. Joint author: Report of the Monetary Commission, 1898. Author: History of the Latin Monetary Union, 1901; Reciprocity (with Prof. J. L. Laughlin), 1903; Our Philippine Problem, 1905; Principles and Problems of Modern Banking, 1910; Principles of Accounting, 1910; Life of Stephen A. Douglas, 1911; The Federal Reserve, 1915; American Banking, 1916; The Modern Trust Company (with Kirkbride and Sterrett), 1919; Business and Banking (with G. W. Edwards), 1921; The Federal Reserve System, 1923; Federal Reserve Banking Practice (with W. H. Steiner), 1925; Foreign Banking Systems (with B. H. Beckhart), 1929; Investment Banking (with J. I. Bogen), 1929; Contemporary Banking (with J. W. Chapman and R. W. Robey), 1933; The Banking Situation (with J. M. Chapman), 1933; Economics of Inflation (with same), 1934. Contbr. to econ. and other jours. Chmn. bd. Philippine-Am. Chamber Commerce, 1922-25; pres. Stable Money Assn., 1925-26. Home: New Brighton, N.Y. Died July 18, 1937.

WILLIS, Olympia Brown, Universalist minister; b. Prairie Ronde, Mich., Jan. 5, 1835; d. Asa B. and Lephia O. Brown; A.B., Antioch Coll., 1860, A.M., 1867; grad. Theol. Sch. of St. Lawrence U., Canton, N.Y., 1863; ordained to ministry, 1863; m. John Henry Willis, Apr. 1873 (died 1893). Preacher and lecturer, 1860—; held pastorates at Weymouth, Mass., Bridgeport, Conn., Racine, Wis., and Mukwonago, Neenah, and Columbus, Wis.; 1893-1900, sec. and treas. Times Pub. Co., managing daily and weekly newspaper and large job printing office. Pres. Federal Suffrage Assn.; life mem. Nat. Am. Suffrage Assn., Woman's Missionary Assn. of Universalist Church. Author of various tracts and articles, also a book entitled Acquaintances Old and New Among Reformers. Made 300 or more speeches in suffrage campaign of 1867 in Kan. Died Oct. 23, 1926.

WILLIS, Paul, bridge mfr.; b. East Orange, N.J., Dec. 21, 1863; s. George H. and Harriet W.; M.E. Stevens Inst., Hoboken, N.J., 1885; m. Daisy J. Hubbard, Apr. 12, 1900; children—Marion (Mrs. R. R. Jeffris), George H., Paul. In employ of Wallace Iron Works, Jersey City, N.J., 1885-86; inspector, draughtsman and engr. with Morison & Corthell, later with George S. Morison, 1886-90; with F. W. Barker organized, 1890, the Kenwood Bridge Co., Chicago, becoming sec. and engr. until 1908, and pres., 1910-25; v.p. McClintic-Marshall Co., 1924-31. Home: Chicago, Ill. Died Jan. 30, 1935.

WILLISTON, Edward Bancroft, brig. gen. U.S.A.; b. Norwich, Vt., July 15, 1837; s. E. B. and Almira W.; B.S., Norwich U., 1856; m. Beatrice Moore, Jan. 20, 1868 (dec.); m. 2d, Florence Chatfield, of Detroit, 1902. Apptd. from Calif., 2d lt. 2d U.S. Arty., Aug. 5, 1861; 1st lt., Sept. 27, 1861; capt., Mar. 8, 1865; maj. 3d Arty., Mar. 22, 1885; lt. col., Feb. 12, 1895; col. 6th Arty., Mar. 8, 1898; brig. gen. vols., May 4, 1898; hon. discharged from vols., June 12, 1899; retired by operation of law, July 15, 1900; advanced to rank of brig. gen. retired, by act of Apr. 23, 1904. Awarded Congressional Medal of Honor, Apr. 6, 1892, "for distinguished gallantry in action at Trevillian Sta., Va., June 12, 1864"; bvtd.: capt., May 3, 1863, "for gallant and meritorious services in action at Salem Heights, Va."; maj., July 3, 1863, for same in Gettysburg campaign; lt. col., Sept. 19, 1864, for same in battle of Winchester, Va.; col., Mar. 13, 1865, for same during the war. Home: Portland, Ore. Died Apr. 24, 1920.

WILLISTON, Samuel Wendell, palæontologist; b. Boston, July 10, 1852; s. Samuel and Jane A. (Turner) W.; B.S., Kansas Agricultural Coll., 1872, A.M., 1875; M.D., Yale, 1880, Ph.D., 1885; hon. degree Sc.D., Yale, 1913; m. Annie I. Hathaway, Dec. 20, 1880. Asst. in palæontology and osteology, 1876-85, demonstrator of anatomy, 1885-86, prof., 1886-90, Yale; prof. hist. geology and anatomy and dean Med. Sch., U. of Kan., 1890-1902; prof. palæontology, U. of Chicago, 1902—. Asst. palæontologist, U.S. Geol. Survey, 1882-85; asst. editor Science, 1885-86; health officer, New Haven, Conn., 1888-90; mem. Kan. State Bd. Health, 1898-1900, Bd. Med. Examiners, 1900-02. Mem. Nat. Acad. Sciences; fellow Am. Acad. Arts and Sciences. Author: Manual of North American Diptera, 1896, 1908; Reports University Geological Survey of Kansas, Vols. IV, VI, 1898, 1900; American Permian Vertebrates, 1911; Water Reptiles of the Past and Present, 1914; also about 250 scientific papers on entomology, zoölogy, sanitation, comparative anatomy and palæontology, bulls., etc. Died Aug. 30, 1918.

WILLITS, Albert Bower, rear admiral U.S.N.; b. Phila., Mar. 7, 1851; s. Alphonso Albert and Eliza Jane (Street) W.; grad. U.S. Naval Acad., 1874; m. Anna Bain White, Sept. 28, 1876. Promoted asst. engr., Feb. 26, 1878; passed asst. engr., Oct. 12, 1881; chief engr., May 28, 1896; lt. comdr., March 3, 1899; comdr., Oct. 11, 1903; capt., Jan. 28, 1908; rear admiral, Sept. 14, 1911; retired on account of age, after service of 40 yrs., 5 mos., Mar. 7, 1913. Served at sea on the Montauk, Wyandotte, Adams, Powhatan, Hartford, Pensacola, Yorktown, Boston, Minneapolis, Marblehead, Iowa and Newark; on shore as asst. to engr.-in-chief, George W. Melville, at Navy Dept., 1898-1901; asst. insp. in bldg. the Minneapolis and Columbia, 1901-04; head dept. of engring. Norfolk Navy Yard, 1904-08; sr. insp. in bldg. the Utah and Arkansas, 1908-11; dir. of Navy Yards, Navy Dept., 1911-12. Insp. of machinery, Bayonne, N.J., 1917-19. Democrat. Presbyn. Contbr. numerous tech. articles to engring. mags. Home: Philadelphia, Pa. Died Jan. 7, 1926.

WILLITS, George Sidney, naval officer; b. Phila., Feb. 21, 1853; s. George Sidney and Elizabeth (Githens) W.; Rutgers Coll., New Brunswick, N.J.; grad. U.S. Naval Acad., 1875; m. Sylvia B. Gaston, Aug. 3, 1876. Asst. engr. U.S.N., 1877; passed asst. engr., 1885; chief engr., 1896; lt. comdr., 1898; comdr., 1904; capt., 1908; rear admiral, Mar. 26, 1913; retired Feb. 21, 1915. Served at sea on Hartford, Vandalia, Huron, Tallapoosa, Enterprise, Marion, Boston, Trenton; on Marblehead during Spanish-Am. War, 1898; Solace, during Boxer rebellion in China; Baltimore, flagship Kearsarge, 1903-04. Holder of service medals for Cuban expdn. and Chinese expdn. Presbyn. Home: Philadelphia, Pa. Died May 3, 1917.

WILLMARTH, James Willard, clergyman; b. Paris, France (Am. parents), Dec. 23, 1835; s. Rev. Isaac

M. and Harriet (Willard) W.; ed. at home in N.E., studied theology with father; prevented from course at coll. by eye trouble; D.D., Carson Coll., Tenn., 1889; LL.D., Southwestern U., Tenn., 1889; m. Jane S. Turnbull, Nov. 24, 1868. Ordained Bapt. ministry, 1860; pastor Metamora, Ill., 1861-63, Amenia, N.Y., 1865-66; stated supply, Rockport, Mass., 1866; pastor Wakefield, Mass., 1867-69, Pemberton, N.J., 1869-78, Roxborough Ch., Phila., 1878-92 (pastor emeritus). Moderator West N.J. Bapt. Assn., 1872, Phila. Bapt. Assn., 1888; pres. Trenton (N.J.) Conf.; mgr. Am. Bapt. Publn. Soc., 1891-1902; trustee Crozer Theol. Sem., 1881—, George Nugent Home for Baptists, Germantown, Pa., 1889— (pres. 1890-92); mem. Phila. Conf. Bapt. ministers (pres.); etc. Editor Quarterly Advance, 1882-83. Author: The Baptist Question Book, 1882-83. Writer many pamphlets and articles on religious subjects. Died June 27, 1911.

WILLOUGHBY, Benjamin Milton, judge; b. Ripley County, Ind., Apr. 8, 1855; s. Milton and Phœbe (Osborn) Willoughby; grad. Vincennes (Ind.) High Sch., 1876; LL.B., Cincinnati Coll. (U. of Cincinnati), 1879; m. Edith Getches, July 8, 1912. Began practice at Vincennes; mem. Ind. Ho. of Rep., 1895, 97, 99; judge 12th Jud. Circuit, Ind., 1912-18; judge Supreme Ct. of Ind., terms, 1919-25, 1925-31. Admitted to practice in Ind. Supreme Ct., 1884, U.S. Supreme Ct., 1889. Republican. Mason. Home: Vincennes, Ind. Died June 29, 1940.

WILLOUGHBY, John Edmund, editor, polit. speaker; b. Canoga, N.Y., Jan. 6, 1861; s. Rev. Benjamin Franklin and Sarah Elizabeth (Sittser) W.; descendant on paternal side of Delano family and on maternal side of Ethan Allen, of Revolutionary War; ed. common schs. and acads.; m. Minnie Katherine Salisbury, Nov. 23, 1884; 1 son, Bernard Franklin. With Utica Observer, 1882-83, and Amsterdam Evening Recorder, most of time, 1883-98, mng. editor, Jan. 1, 1907—; pub. Little Falls Herald, 1890-91; editor Kingston (N.Y.) Freeman, 1898-1906. Clerk Montgomery Co. (N.Y.) Bd. Supervisors, 1892-93; city treas., Amsterdam, 1894-96. Pub. speaker in nat. campaigns. Rep. Party, 1900—. Episcopalian. Author: The Round of the Year, 1915; Through Trial to Triumph, 1918; One Hundred Years and Other Poems, 1923. Contbr. verse to newspapers and mags.; also poems for pub. occasions. Home: Amsterdam, N.Y. Died Feb. 19, 1929.

WILLS, Albert Potter, coll. prof.; b. Waltham, Mass., Feb. 25, 1873; s. William Russel and Lucretia (Potter) W.; B.E.E., Tufts Coll., 1894, Sc.D., 1911; Ph.D., Clark U., 1897; univs. of Göttingen and Berlin, 1898-99; m. Agnes Randall Brune, May 18, 1909 (died 1910); m. 2d, Gertrude Pardee Carter, June 10, 1920. Asso. in physics and applied mathematics, Bryn Mawr Coll., 1899-1902; physicist, Cooper Hewitt Lab., New York, 1902-03; instr. mechanics, 1903-05, adj. prof., 1905-09, prof. math. physics, 1909—, Columbia. Contbr. papers on magnetic susceptibility, magnetic shielding, magnetostriction, conduction of electricity in mercury vapor, and hydrodynamics. Home: New York, N.Y. Died Apr. 17, 1937.

WILLS, Charles Tomlinson, builder; b. New York, Dec. 13, 1851; s. Chalkley J. and Anna D. (Deacon) W.; ed. at Westtown, Pa.; m. Carrie Russell, Nov. 13, 1879. Began as an indentured apprentice and learned building trade; established himself in New York and built many of the largest and finest office and business buildings, the Stock Exchange, Hanover Bank, Chamber of Commerce, and some of the finest residences in New York, etc. President Charles T. Wills, Inc.; dir. Garfield Nat. Bank. Dir. New York Ophthalmic Hosp. Home: Greenwich, Conn. Died Aug. 31, 1915.

WILLS, David Crawford, banker; b. Pittsburgh, Pa., Aug. 11, 1872; s. John B. and Sarah Jane (Thompson) W.; grad. Allegheny High Sch., Pittsburgh, 1889; m. Bessie A. Seville, May 23, 1895. Began as messenger, Mechanics Nat. Bank, Pittsburgh, 1889; auditor Mellon Nat. Bank, Pittsburgh, 1902-04; cashier, dir. Diamond Nat. Bank, Pittsburgh, 1904-14; pres. Citizens Nat. Bank, Bellevue, Pa., 1907-14; chmn. bd. and fed. res. agt. Federal Reserve Bank, Cleveland, O., 1914-20 and 21—; mem. Federal Reserve Bd., Sept. 29, 1920-Mar. 4, 1921. Trustee Westminster Coll. (New Wilmington, Pa.), Kent (O.) State Normal Sch. First pres. Pittsburgh Chapter Am. Inst. Banking. Republican. United Presbyn. Home: Cleveland, O. Died Oct. 22, 1925.

WILLSON, Augustus Everett, governor; b. Maysville, Ky., Oct. 13, 1846; s. Hiram and Ann Colvin (Ennis) W.; A.B., Harvard, 1869; A.M., 1872; student Harvard Law Sch., 1870; studied law in offices of Lothrop, Bishop & Lincoln, Boston, and under John M. Harlan, Louisville, Ky.; LL.D., Harvard, 1908, also U. of Ky. and Berea Coll.; m. Mary Elizabeth, d. Gen. James A. Ekin, U.S.A., July 23, 1877. Chief clerk Treasury Dept., Dec. 1875-Aug. 1876; Rep. nominee for Congress, 5th Ky. Dist., 1884, 86, 88, 92; del. Rep. Nat. convs. 1884, 88, 92, 1904, 08, 16; gov. of Ky., 1907-11; resumed practice of law, 1911. Mem. Bd. Overseers, Harvard, 1910-18. Home: Louisville, Ky. Died Aug. 24, 1931.

WILLSON, Charles Albert, educator; b. North Branch, Mich., Aug. 29, 1878; s. John Dyment and Roxa Miranda (Dayton) W.; grad. high sch., North Branch, 1896; B.S.A., Mich. State Coll., 1906, M. Agr., 1923; M.S.A., U. of Mo., 1910; m. Bertha M. Wellman, Aug. 29, 1907 (died 1934); children—Anna Christine (dec.), Margaret Wellman, Charlotte Wellman. Engaged in farming, 1896-1902; instr. in animal husbandry, Kansas State Agrl. Coll., 1906-07, U. of Mo., 1907-10; asst. prof. animal husbandry, U. of Tenn., 1910-13, prof., 1913-19; vice dean Coll. Agr., same univ., 1919-24, dean, 1924—; dir. East Tenn. Bldg. & Loan Assn. Democrat. Presbyn. Mason. Contbr. to Southern Agriculturist, Breeder's Gazette, Country Gentleman, Book of Rural Life, Arithmetic in Agriculture and Rural Life; also bulls. Mo. and Tenn. expt. stas. Home: Knoxville, Tenn. Died Oct. 23, 1936.

WILLSON, David Burt, theologian; b. Philadelphia, Sept. 27, 1842; s. Rev. Prof. James McLeod and Rebecca (Burt) W.; A.B., U. of Pa., 1860, A.M., 1863; M.D., Jefferson Med. Coll., Phila., 1863; actg. med. cadet U.S.A., summer of 1862; in medical corps, U.S.A., 1863-65; law student, U. of Pa., 1869-70; R.P. Theol. Sem., Allegheny, Pa., 1865-69; (D.D., U. of Pa., 1890); m. Martha J. Grier, Aug. 21, 1873; m. 2d, Mary R. Galbraith, Aug. 14, 1883. Ordained R.P. ministry, 1870; pastor Allegheny, 1870-75; prof. Bibl. lit., R.P. Theol. Seminary, 1875-1916 (prof. emeritus). Edited an edition of Lyman's Historical Chart, 1869; edited Reformed Presbyterian and Covenanter, 1874-95. Moderator, R.P. Synod, 1887; del. Pan-Presbyn. Council, Glasgow, 1896. Home: Pittsburgh, Pa. Died Feb. 13, 1919.

WILLSON, Frederick Newton, univ. prof.; b. Brooklyn, Dec. 23, 1855; s. T. Newton and Mary Caroline (Evarts) W.; C.E., Rensselaer Poly. Inst., 1879; hon. A.M., Princeton, 1896; m. Mary H. Bruere, May 22, 1884 (died 1893); children—Mary Louise, Grace Bruere, Edith Evarts, Alice Holmes; m. 2d, Anna R. Albertson, July 28, 1895; children—Elizabeth, Albert Newton. Started dept. of graphics in John C. Green Sch. of Science, Princeton, Dec. 1880; professorship created, 1883, and prof. descriptive geometry, stereotomy and tech. drawing, Princeton U., till June 1923 (emeritus). Elder Presbyn. Ch. Author of a series of text-books on descriptive geometry and its applications; also, Graphics and Faith, 1936. Crossed, on their catwalks, Brooklyn Bridge, 1878, George Washington Bridge, 1929, Golden Gate Bridge, Dec. 23, 1935. Home: Princeton, N.J. Died Nov. 15, 1939.

WILLSON, James William, supt. mil. inst.; b. Fairfield, Va., Mar. 5, 1872; s. John Edgar and Elvira (Brooks) W.; grad. Va. Mil. Inst., 1894; m. Lottie Pruit, Oct. 30, 1901. Commandant West Point (Va.) Mil. Acad., 1894-97; civ. engr. Mexico and W.Tex., 1897-98; comdt. of cadets, 1898-1901, supt., June 1901—, N.M. Mil. Inst., Roswell. Served as capt. and maj. on staffs of govs. of N.M. and a.d.c. on governor's staff, with rank of col., 1902—. Democrat. Presbyn. Mason (Past Grand Comdr. K.T., of N.M.). Home: Roswell, N.M. Deceased.

WILLSON, John Owens, college pres.; b. in Charleston County (now Berkeley Co.), S.C., Jan. 27, 1845; s. of Dr. John and Sarah E. W.; ed. Citadel Acad.; m. Mary O. Richardson, Apr. 27, 1871 (died 1873); m. 2d, Kathleen McP. Lander, Aug. 27, 1896. Pvt. Co. F, 6th S.C. Cav., and mem. Co. I, 3d S.C. Cav. Regt., C.S.A., 1861-65; practiced law, 1867-73; ordained ministry M.E. Ch., S., 1873; served in various pastorates until 1894; editor Southern Christian Advocate, 1894-1902; pres. Lander Coll., Sept., 1904—. Del. to 8 gen. confs. of M.E. Ch., S., and to Ecumenical Conf. of same, 1901, 11. Democrat. Home: Greenwood, S.C. Died Mar. 23, 1923.

WILLSON, Lester Sebastian, soldier; b. Canton, N.Y., June 16, 1839; s. Ambrose and Julia A. (Hill) W.; acad. edn.; m. Emma D. Weeks, Mar. 2, 1869. Sergt. 60th N.Y. Inf., Sept. 9, 1861; 2d lt., Aug. 6, 1862; 1st lt. adj., Oct. 8, 1862; capt., Sept. 28, 1864; lt. col., Apr. 4, 1865; col., May 17, 1865; bvtd. col. and brig. gen. vols., Mar. 13, 1865, "for gallant and meritorious services in campaign resulting in the fall of Atlanta, Ga."; hon. mustered out, July 17, 1865. Asst. q.m. gen. State of N.Y., 1865-67; located in Mont., 1867, engaged in overland freighting, banking, mercantile pursuits. Mem. Territorial Legislature, 1868-69; q.m. gen. of Mont., 1883-87. Home: Bozeman, Mont. Died Jan. 26, 1919.

WILLSON, Marcius, author; b. West Stockbridge, Mass., Dec. 8, 1813; s. Gilbert and Selecta (Hendricks) W.; in 1821 moved with father to farm at Allen's Hill, Ontario Co., N.Y.; grad. Union Coll., 1836; m. Frances Anne Pierpont, 1838. Taught classics and mathematics 6 months in Highland Gymnasium, Fishkill Landing, 1837; in Collegiate School, Poughkeepsie, reading law meanwhile, 1837-41; prin. Canandaigua Acad., 1849-53; was offered presidency of Vassar Woman's Coll. at its founding, 1861. Admitted to bar, 1841; practiced until attacked by bronchitis, caused by public speaking; subsequently turned his attention mostly to authorship. His works have brought him royalties, in all, about $250,000, from the Harpers alone over $200,000. Author: Architectural Drawing, 1837; Civil Polity and Political Economy, 1840; General History, 1845-55; School and Family Readers (5 numbers generally known as the Popular Science Series), 1859-65; Industrial Drawing Series and Drawing Guide, 1873; Lippincott's Popular Series of Readers, 1880-82; Grecian History and Mosaics of Bible History, 1882-83; Wonderful Story of Old, 2 vols., 1888; Principles of Finance and Philosophy of Bimetallism, 1896. Home: Vineland, N.J. Died 1905.

WILLSON, Robert Newton, physician; b. Philadelphia, Jan. 3, 1873; s. Hon. Robert N. and Elizabeth S. (Dale) W.; A.B., U. of Pa., 1893, M.D., 1897; m. Dorothea Wurts, May 5, 1903. Instr. medicine and univ. phys., U. of Pa., 1900-05; phys. Phila. Gen. Hosp.; formerly pathologist Presbyn. Hosp. Represented U.S. at Tuberculosis Congress, Naples, 1900. Presbyn. Author: The American Boy and the Social Evil, 1905; Medical Men in the Time of Christ, 1910; Education of the Young in Sex Hygiene, 1912; The Heart and the Great Vessels, 1915. Home: Philadelphia, Pa. Died Jan. 1, 1916.

WILLSON, Robert Wheeler, astronomer; b. West Roxbury, Mass., July 20, 1853; s. Rev. Edmund B. and Martha A. (Buttrick) W.; A.B., Harvard, 1873; Ph.D., Würzburg, 1886; m. Annie Downing West, Dec. 14, 1881. Asst. Argentine Nat. Obs., 1873, Harvard Coll. Obs., 1874; tutor in physics, Harvard, 1875-81; asst. astronomer, Winchester Obs., Yale, 1881-84; instr. astronomy and physics, 1891-99, asst. prof., 1899, prof. astronomy, 1903, emeritus, 1919, Harvard. Fellow Am. Acad. Arts and Science, A.A.A.S., Am. Astron. Soc., Am. Geog. Society. Unitarian. Author: Laboratory Astronomy, 1905; Times of Sunrise and Sunset in the United States, 1908. Home: Cambridge, Mass. Died Nov. 1, 1922.

WILLYS, John North, mfr., diplomat; b. Canandaigua, N.Y., Oct. 25, 1873; s. David Smith and Lydia (North) W.; pub. sch. edn.; m. Isabel Van Wie, Dec. 1, 1897. Began in bicycle business, Canandaigua, 1890; removed to Elmira, N.Y., and organized the Elmira Arms Co., also engaged in selling automobiles on an extensive scale; purchased the Indianapolis plant of the Overland Automobile Co., 1907, and 2 yrs. later purchased the Pope Toledo plant at Toledo; later chmn. bd. and co-receiver The Willys-Overland Co., Toledo, also of Willys-Morrow Co., Elmira, N.Y.; ambassador to Poland, 1930-32, resigned. Republican. Presbyn. Owner of one of the most valuable collections of oil paintings in Ohio. Home: Ottawa Hills, Toledo, O., also New York, N.Y. Died Aug. 26, 1935.

WILM, Emil Carl, college prof., author: b. Margonin, Prussia, Nov. 12, 1877; s. Carl and Ernestine (Krueger) W.; came to U.S., 1889; A.B., Southwestern U., 1902; A.M., Vanderbilt, 1903; Ph.D., Cornell U., 1905; LL.D., hon. causa, Southwestern, 1914; awarded freshman, sophomore, junior and senior English prizes, Southwestern, Messenger memorial prize, Cornell, and Bowdoin prize, Harvard; m. Grace Gridley, pianist, 1903; children—Clara, Harold, Margaret, Carl. Prof. philosophy successively, Washburn Coll., Wells Coll., Bryn Mawr, and Boston U., 1905-26, Colorado Coll., 1926—. Author: The Philosophy of Friedrich Schiller, 1912; The Problem of Religion, 1912; The Culture of Religion, 1912; Henri Bergson, A Study in Radical Evolution, 1914; Religion and the School, 1914; The Theories of Instinct, 1925. Part-author: The Modern High School, 1914; Philosophical Essays in Honor of James Edwin Creighton, tory of Psychology, 1914. Editor and part-author: Studies in Philosophy and Theology in Honor of Borden P. Browne, 1922; Immanuel Kant, 1925. Home: Colorado Springs, Colo. Died Jan. 30, 1932.

WILMARTH, Lemuel Everett, artist; b. Attleboro, Mass., Nov. 11, 1835; s. Benoni and Fanny (Fuller) W.; ed. in Boston; began drawing at Pa. Acad. Fine Arts, Phila., 1854; went to Europe, 1858; studied at Royal Acad., Munich, 3½ yrs., and at École des Beaux Arts, Paris, 2½ yrs.; m. Emma B. Barrett, 1872 (died 1895). Prof. in charge of schools of Nat. Acad. Design, 1870-90. Among his best known pictures are The Pick of the Orchard; Ingratitude; Left in Charge; and Sunny Italy; writer on religious-social subjects; a founder of The New Earth, N.A., 1872. Home: Brooklyn, N.Y. Died July 27, 1918.

WILMER, William Holland, M.D.; b. Powhatan Co., Va., Aug. 26, 1863; s. Richard Hooker (bishop Ala.), and Margaret (Brown) W.; prep. edn., Episcopal High Sch., Alexandria, Va.; M.D., U. of Va., 1885; studied New York Polyclinic, and hosps. of Europe; LL.D., Georgetown U., 1919; hon. Sc.D., Princeton, 1926, New York U., 1929; m. Re Lewis Smith, Oct. 6, 1891; 3 children—Richard Hooker, Mrs. Rebekah Scott, William Holland. Office asst. to Dr. Emil Gurening, N.Y. City, 1887-89; interne Mt. Sinai Hosp.; instr. N.Y. Polyclinic; outdoor dept. Bellevue Hosp., N.Y. City; practiced Washington, D.C., 1889-1925; prof. ophthalmology, Georgetown

U., 1906-25; surgeon Episcopal Eye, Ear and Throat Hosp., Washington, D.C., 1895-1925; dir. Wilmer Ophthal. Inst. Johns Hopkins Hosp.; prof. aphthalmology Johns Hopkins University and ophthalmologist in chief to Johns Hopkins Hosp., 1925-34. Commd. lt. Med. R.C., U.S.A., Apr. 26, 1911; maj., 1917; lt. col. Med. Corps, N.A., Mar. 22, 1918; col. U.S.A., June 12, 1918; hon. disch., May 15, 1919; brig. gen. Med. R.C. Officer in charge Med. Research Lab., Air Serv., Mineola, L.I., until Aug. 1918; surgeon in charge Med. Research Labs., A.E.F., France, Aug. 1918-May 1919. Awarded D.S.M. (U.S.), Mar. 12, 1919. Comdr. Legion of Honor (France), Aug. 4, 1924. Mem. hygiene ref. bd. Life Extension Inst.; mem. bd. of dirs., Nat. Com. for Prevention of Blindness, Advisory Com. Prevention Hereditary Blindness; fellow (a founder) Am. Coll. Surgeons; mem. numerous med. societies. Consulting oculist Episcopal Eye, Ear and Throat Hosp., Washington, D.C.; trustee Nat. Cathedral Foundation. Awarded decoration Angelo Secchi Acad. of Science, Georgetown U. Episcopalian. Home: Washington, D.C. Died Mar. 12, 1936.

WILMERDING, Lucius Kellogg, merchant; b. Moscow, N.Y., Mar. 19, 1848; s. Henry Augustus and Harriette E. (Kellogg) W.; A.B., Columbia, 1868, A.M., 1871; m. Caroline Murray, Dec. 6, 1876. Mem. Wilmerding, Hoguet & Co., importers and commn. mchts., New York, 1870-73, Wilmerding & Bisset, 1874-1904; spl. partner Wilmerding & Bisset, 1905-18, Gray & Wilmerding, Jan. 1, 1919—; trustee Greenwich Savings Bank. Episcopalian. Home: East Islip, N.Y. Died Dec. 8, 1922.

WILMETH, Frank Lincoln, surgeon; b. Salem, Ia., Aug. 19, 1862; Whittier Coll., Salem; M.D., Lincoln Med. Coll. (now med. dept. Cotner U.), Lincoln, Neb., 1894; post-grad. work Bennett Med. Coll., Chicago, and Chicago Clin. Sch.; m. Jessie Drummond, 1889. Practiced, Eagle, Cass Co., Neb., 1894-98; removed to Lincoln, 1898; lecturer, 1894-1901, prof. surgery, 1901, mem. bd. dirs., 1896-1910, pres., 1901-04, dean 1906-08 and 1909-11, Lincoln Med. Coll.; surgeon Neb. State Penitentiary, 1901-03; propr. Esther's Hospital, Lincoln. Home: Lincoln, Neb. Deceased.

WILMORE, Augustus Cleland, clergyman; b. Jackson, O., June 2, 1849; s. Levi and Nancy (Golden) W.; student De Pauw U., 1867-69; grad. U.B. Theol. Inst., Noblesville, Ind., 1895; D.D., Harriman U., 1900; m. Julia Trammel, Aug. 14, 1870 (died 1890); m. 2d, Minnie A. Rice, Mar. 9, 1892. Teacher in public schools of Indiana, 1867-1877; entered ministry U.B. Ch., 1877; pastor 41 yrs. in Ind., successively at Montpelier, Wabash, Hartsville, Indianapolis, Anderson, Noblesville, Newcastle, Saratoga, Selma, Muncie, Greenfield and Pendleton; presiding elder White River Conf. 9 yrs., sec. 8 yrs., registrar 22 yrs.; instr. systematic theology, 1889—, pres. 1889-1905, U.B. Theol. Inst. Incorporator and pres. Conf. Corp.; pres. Conf. Ch. Erection Soc., 1894-1920; sec. Preacher's Aid Soc., 1906—; trustee Ind. Central Coll., 6 yrs., U.B. Publ. House, 4 yrs. Del. U.B. Quad. Gen. Conf. 5 times. Mem. S.A.R. (chaplain Ind. Soc., 1920-25). Republican. Mason. Author: History of the White River Conference, 1925. Observed golden jubilee of ministry, Aug. 1927. Home: Winchester, Ind. Died Apr. 24, 1933.

WILMOT, Frank Moore, secretary; b. Lambertville, N.J., Sept. 17, 1872; s. William Heywood and Maud Madeline (McCready) W.; grad. Lambertville High Sch., 1888; m. Maude Gallagher, Oct. 14, 1896. Began as clk. Pa. R.R. Relief Fund, 1888; asst. mgr. and mgr. Carnegie Relief Fund, Pittsburgh, 1901-11; trustee, sec. and mgr. Carnegie Hero Fund Commn. (fund of $5,000,000), Apr. 1904—. Dir. and v.p. Tuberculosis League, Pittsburgh; dir. Pa. Tuberculosis Soc.; mem. exec. com. Hungry Club, Pittsburgh (open forum for discussion of pub. questions); dir., treas. and chmn. finance com. Art Soc. of Pittsburgh; dir. University Extension Soc. of Pittsburgh; dir. Pittsburgh Centre, Drama League America; hon. sec. Western Pa. br. English-Speaking Union. Republican. Home: Pittsburgh, Pa. Died Oct. 22, 1930.

WILMOT, George Washington, mfr.; b. Upper Lehigh, Pa., Sept. 12, 1867; s. George and Edna (Stone) W.; ed. Bloomsburg (Pa.) State Normal Sch.; m. Mary A. Winter, June 9, 1892; children—Edna (dec., Mrs. Ralph H. Woelfel), Arline (Mrs. Earl Tremayne), Carrie (Mrs. Russel J. Wilford), George Lincoln. Master mechanic Upper Lehigh Coal Co., 1889-99, asst. supt. in charge mines, 1899-1905; supt. Maryd (Pa.) Coal Co., 1905-08; pres. and gen. mgr. Wilmot Engring. Co., Hazleton, Pa., coal handling machinery, 1908—; v.p., treas. Coxe Stoker Engring. Co.; chmn. bd. Peoples Savings & Trust Co., Weatherly (Pa.) Foundry & Mfg. Co., Huron Forge & Machine Co. (Detroit, Mich.), Croll-Reynolds Engring. Co. Republican. Presbyn. Mason, Elk. Home: Hazelton, Pa. Died Mar. 2, 1936.

WILMS, John Henry, surgeon; b. Cincinnati, O., Nov. 17, 1879; s. Frederic Henry and Fredericka (Kruse) W.; prep. edn., Cincinnati Business Coll. and Eisle's Scientific Acad.; student U. of Cincinnati; M.D., Pulte Med. Coll., Cincinnati, 1902; m. Louise Margaret Evatt, June 2, 1920; children—Janet (dec.), John Henry. In gen. practice of medicine and surgery, Cincinnati, 1902—; prof. anatomy, Pulte Med. Coll., 1905-10. Fellow Am. Coll. Surgeons. Mason. Reported med. cures for endocarditis, thyrotoxicosis, pancreatic diabetes, hypothyroid states. Discoverer of antidotal action of calcium sulphid in bichloride of mercury poisoning. Home: Cincinnati, O. Died Nov. 26, 1938.

WILSHIRE, (Henry) Gaylord, editor; b. Cincinnati, June 7, 1861; s. George and Clara (Clemons) W.; ed. Woodward High Sch., Cincinnati, and Harvard; m. Mary McReynolds, Feb. 10, 1904. In mercantile business, 1884-1900; editor and pub. Wilshire's Magazine, 1900—. Socialist. Candidate for Congress, 6th Calif. Dist., 1890, for parliament in England (Manchester), 1894, for Canadian Parliament, 1902, Congress, New York, 1904. Author: Socialism Inevitable, 1907; Wilshire's Editorials. Home: New York, N.Y. Died Sept. 7, 1927.

WILSON, Albert Frederick, editor, univ. prof.; b. Greenfield Hill, Conn., Aug. 28, 1883; s. Albert Barnum and Mary A. (Fiebel) Wilson; ed. U. of Va., 1907 (Edgar Allan Poe medalist); m. Ruth Danenhower, June 10, 1916; children—Mary Sherwood, Sloan, Geoffrey. Mem. editorial bd. Lit. Digest, 1908-11; mng. editor Leslie's Weekly, 1912-14; mem. editorial bd. World Today; editorial adviser numerous publishing firms; prof. jour. New York U., 1914—. Baptist. Author: The Township Line, 1919; Pok O'Moonshine, 1927; Higher Than the Wind Can Blow, 1934. Home: Ormond Beach, Fla. Died June 26, 1940.

WILSON, Alpheus Waters, bishop; b. Baltimore, Feb. 5, 1834; s. Rev. Norval and Cornelia Laurence (Howland) W.; ed. Columbian (now George Washington) U.; m. Susan B. Lipscomb, Mar. 4, 1857. Received on trial, 1853, in Baltimore Conf. M.E. Ch.; later joined the Southern branch when the Baltimore Conf. M.E. Ch., S., was organized; became sec. Bd. of Missions, 1878; elected bishop M.E. Ch., S., May 1882. Took episcopal tours around the world, 1886, 88, 90, to Japan, Korea and China, 1898-1900 and 1907; del. Ecumenical Meth. Conf., London, 1881, 1901, Washington, 1891, Toronto, 1911; visited Brazil on mission inspection, 1892-1903. Author: Missions: Witnesses to Christ (Cole Lectures, Vanderbilt Univ.), 1894, etc. Home: Baltimore, Md. Died Nov. 21, 1916.

WILSON, Andrew Wilkins, Jr., educator; b. Indiana, Pa., June 29, 1863; s. Andrew Wilkins and Anna Graham (Dick) W.; Indiana (Pa.) State Normal Sch.; A.B., Princeton Univ., 1883, A.M. from same, 1886 (master orator); studied law, University of Pa.; Ph.D., Washington and Jefferson Coll., 1891, LL.D., from Lafayette Coll., Easton, Pa., 1929; m. Bessie Gladys Sansom, Aug. 23, 1889; children—Sarah Sansom, Anna Graham, Elizabeth (dec.), Gladys Margaret, Ella May. Teacher Hill Sch., Pottstown, Pa., 1883-85; admitted to Pa. bar, 1887; teacher, Hill Sch., 1888; founder, 1888, and pres. Kiskiminetas Springs Sch.; treas. Wilson Coal Land Co. Elder Presbyn. Ch. Home: Saltsburg, Pa. Died Mar. 3, 1930.

WILSON, Augusta Jane Evans, novelist; b. (Evans) Columbus, Ga., May 8, 1835; d. M. R. and S. S. Evans; ed. privately; lived at San Antonio, Tex., 1846-49; m. L. M. Wilson, 1868 (died 1891). Author: Inez, 1856; Beulah, 1859; Macaria, 1864; St. Elmo, 1866; Vashti, 1869; Infelice, 1875; At the Mercy of Tiberius, 1887; A Speckled Bird, 1902; Devota, 1907. Home: Mobile, Ala. Died 1909.

WILSON, Benjamin Lee, novelist; b. Newark, O., Nov. 5, 1867; s. Daniel Davidson and Elizabeth Boyd (Kidd) W., and related to Lee family of Va.; ed. Newark pub. schs. and under tutelage of Dr. Hartzler; Cornell U., 1888; studied Shakespeare, under Prof. Hiram Corson, of Cornell; studied and played under Augustin Daly for several yrs.; unmarried. Headmaster New York Mil. Acad., Cornwall-on-Hudson, 1893-1900; founded Wilson Sch. for Boys, 1900, of which became headmaster and owner; trustee Fishkill Savings Bank. Democrat. Episcopalian. Wrote The Evolution of the English Drama, various Shakespearean critiques, etc. Home: Fishkill-on-Hudson, N.Y. Died 1911.

WILSON, Byron Henry, clergyman; b. nr. Brookfield, Mo., Nov. 25, 1871; s. John Adams and Mary Arbelia (Kerns) W.; student Avalon (Mo.) Coll. 4 yrs.; A.B., Philomath (Ore.) Coll., 1908, D.D., 1909; studied U. of Southern Calif. 3 yrs.; D.D., College of Puget Sound, Tacoma, Wash., 1929; m. Olah, d. Rev. Dr. J. D. Mendenhall, of Mo. Conf., Jan. 1, 1896; children—Mrs. F. Marion Smith, Mrs. Henry E. Jordan, Mrs. Raymond M. Petitfils. Ordained M.E. ministry, 1895; pastor in Mo. and Kan. until 1908; moved to Calif., 1908, and pastor at Porterville, Santa Paula, and Highland Park, Los Angeles; gen. mgr. Meth. Hosp., Los Angeles, 2 yrs., and during its constrn., 1914-16; also pastor Boyle Hgts. 1 yr.; dist. supt. Los Angeles Dist. and exec. sec. Los Angeles City Missionary Soc., 1917-22; pastor Grace Ch., Long Beach, 1 yr.; dist. supt. Seattle Dist., Puget Sound Conf., and exec. sec. Seattle City Missionary Soc., 1924-27; comptroller De Pauw Univ., 1929. Prominent in securing enforcement of anti-prize fight law, red light abatement law and other reforms for Calif. Del. Gen. Conf. M.E. Ch., 1920. Republican. Mason, Odd Fellow, K.P. Home: Greencastle, Ind. Died July 4, 1932.

WILSON, Charles Branch, biologist; b. Exeter, Me., Oct. 20, 1861; s. Col. John B. and Samantha (Perkins) W.; A.B., Colby Coll., 1881, A.M., 1884, Sc.D., 1908; Ph.D., Johns Hopkins, 1910; grad. student and tutor in botany, Colby Coll., 1881-84; m. Lilla Belle Turner, July 22, 1885; children—Carroll Atwood, John Ellis. Pvt. tutor, 1884-91; prof. science, State Normal Sch., Gorham, Me., 1891-94; post-grad. student and asst. in biology, Johns Hopkins, 1894-96; prof. biology, 1896-97, head dept. science, 1897-1932, State Teachers Coll., Westfield. Author: Nature Study Outline for Graded Schools, 1898; Outlines for Laboratory Work in Science, 1900. Home: Westfield, Mass. Died Aug. 18, 1941.

WILSON, Charles Bundy, univ. prof.; b. Syracuse, N.Y., May 9, 1861; s. William T. and Melissa (Van Buren-Bundy) W.; A.B., Cornell, 1884, fellow, 1885-86, A.M., 1886; studied Leipzig, and Paris, 1884-85, Berlin, 1897, Germany, 1907; m. Frances Colquhoun, June 25, 1896. Instructor in German, Cornell, 1886-88; prof. German language and literature, State U. of Iowa, 1888—. Editor: Riehl's Burg Neideck, with notes and introduction, 1894; Eckstein's Preisgekrönt, with introduction and notes, 1896; Lessing's Minna von Barnhelm (with introduction, notes and vocabulary), 1902; Freytag's Die Journalisten (with introduction and notes), 1905; also other text-books. In U.S. service for inspection foreign lang. press, 1918. Home: Iowa City, Ia. Died Feb. 21, 1938.

WILSON, Charles Irving, brig. gen. U.S.A.; b. Washington, May 3, 1837; s. William and Huldah W.; ed. U. of Va.; m. Gertrude L. Houston, 1866. Apptd. from N.Y., asst. surgeon U.S.A., May 28, 1861; capt. asst. surgeon, May 28, 1866; resigned, Jan. 1, 1867; commd. capt. 16th Inf., Jan. 22, 1867; assigned to 14th Inf., Dec. 15, 1870; hon. disch. Dec. 31, 1870; apptd. maj. paymaster's dept., Mar. 3, 1875; lt. col. deputy p.-m.-gen., June 10, 1898; col. asst. p.-m.-gen., July 12, 1899; retired by operation of law, May 3, 1901; advanced to rank of brig. gen. retired, by act of Apr. 23, 1904. Bvtd.: capt., Mar. 13, 1865, "for meritorious and distinguished services in battles of Todd's Tavern and Yellow Tavern, Va."; maj., Mar. 13, 1865, "for highly meritorious and distinguished services in 12 engagements in Shenandoah Valley, Va."; maj., Mar. 2, 1867, "for meritorious services in battle of Todd's Tavern." Home: New York, N.Y. Died Sept. 22, 1913.

WILSON, Clarence Rich, lawyer; b. Washington, D.C., Mar. 11, 1874; s. Nathaniel and Annie Edwards (Hutton) W.; Phillips Exeter Acad., 1891-92; A.B., Harvard, 1896; traveled in Europe and Africa, 1896, 1897; LL.B., Georgetown Law Sch., 1899; m. Elizabeth Ashton, June 11, 1904. Practiced with father, 1899-1910; U.S. atty., D.C., by appmt. of Pres. Taft, Apr. 6, 1910-Nov. 1, 1914; mem. Wilson, Huidekoper & Lesh, Washington, Federal food administrator for D.C., Nov. 1917—. Republican. Trustee Garfield Memorial Hosp. Episcopalian. Home: Washington, D.C. Died Dec. 3, 1923.

WILSON, Clarence True, clergyman, temperance sec.; b. Milton, Del., Apr. 24, 1872; s. John A. B. and Mary (Jefferson) W.; St. John's Coll., Annapolis, Md.; A.B., U. of Southern Calif., 1894; B.D., McClay Coll. of Theology, Los Angeles, 1895; Ph.B., San Joaquin Valley Coll., 1897; D.D., St. John's Coll., 1900; LL.D., Washington Coll., 1925; m. Maude Akin, Nov. 28, 1907; children—Virginia, Mary Elizabeth. Ordained deacon M.E. Ch. at 18, elder at 20; pastor Seaford, Del., 1889-91, Seacliff, L.I., N.Y., 1891-94, Pasadena, Calif., 1895-98, San Diego, 1898-1901, St. Luke's Ch., Newark, N.J., 1901-05, Grace Ch., Portland, Ore., 1905-10; pres. Ore. Anti-Saloon League, 1906-08; nat. sec. Temperance Soc. M.E. Ch., Sept. 1, 1910—; gen. sec. Bd. of Temperance, Prohibition and Public Morals, 1910—. Erected the Methodist Bldg. in Washington as hdqrs. for temperance forces. Author: Dry or Die; The Anglo-Saxon Dilemma, 1913; Pocket Cyclopedia of Temperance, 1915; The Divine Right of Democracy; The Case for Prohibition; That Flame of Living Fire; The Life of Matthews Simpson, Patriot Preacher, Prophet. Home: Gresham, Ore. Died Feb. 16, 1939.

WILSON, Dunning Steele, M.D.; b. Louisville, Ky., Nov. 24, 1876; s. Samuel Ramsey (D.D.) and Anna Maria (Steele) W.; pub. schs., Louisville and St. Louis; Ph.G., Louisville Coll. Pharmacy, 1894; M.D., U. of Louisville, 1899; m. May Margaret Bonn, Sept. 8, 1903; children— Keith Singleton, Francis Edward. Med. practice at Louisville, Apr. 1, 1899—; supt. Eruptive Hosp., 1903; phys.-in-charge, Tuberculosis Dispensary, 1907-10; med. dir. and supt. Board of Tuberculosis Hosp., Sanatorium and Dispensary, Louisville, 1910-17; commd. capt. med. corps, Ky. N.G., 1910; maj. surgeon "Rainbow" Div., Ambulance Co., 1917, service in France; comdg. officer, Sanitary Train, 1st A.C., and lt. col. Med. Corps, Army of Occupation. Sch. trustee, Louisville, Ky., 1909-10. Mem. numerous med. societies. Med. dir. French Lick

Spring (Ind.) Hotel. Citation from General Pershing and recommended for D.S.M. by chief surgeon 1st A.C., and chief surgeon of Army of Occupation. Colonel, O.R.C., U.S.A. Home: French Lick, Ind. Died Feb. 6, 1927.

WILSON, Edgar, congressman; b. Armstrong Co., Pa., Feb. 25, 1861; s. Matthew and Ellen W.; student, lit. dept. U. of Mich., 1882-83, LL.B., 1884; m. Laura Da Shiell, Oct. 15, 1890. In practice at Boise, Ida., 1884—; city atty., 1887-88; dist. atty., Ada Co., 1888-89; mem. Constl. Conv., 1890; mem. 54th (1895-97) and 56th (1899-1901) Congresses, Ida. at-large; Rep. presdl. elector, Ida., 1908. V.p. Pacific Nat. Bank, Boisé, 1911—. Home: Boisé, Ida. Deceased.

WILSON, Edmund Beecher, zoölogist; b. Geneva, Ill., Oct. 19, 1856; s. Judge Isaac C. and Caroline (Clark) W.; Ph.B., Yale, 1878; Ph.D., Johns Hopkins, 1881; univs. of Cambridge, and Leipzig, 1881-82; LL.D., Yale, 1901, U. of Chicago, 1901, Johns Hopkins, 1902; Sc.D., U. of Cambridge, 1909, Harvard, 1924; hon. M.D., U. of Leipzig, 1909; hon. Ph.D., U. of Lwów, 1926; D.H.C., U. of Louvain, 1927; Sc.D., Columbia, 1929; m. Anne Maynard Kidder, Dec. 27, 1904; 1 dau., Nancy. Lecturer on biology, Williams, 1883-84, Mass. Inst. Tech., 1884-85; asso. professor and prof. biology, Bryn Mawr, 1885-91; adj. prof. biology, 1891-94, prof. invertebrate zoölogy, 1894-97, prof. zoölogy, 1897-1909, Da Costa prof. zoölogy, 1909—, emeritus prof. in residence, 1928—, also dean of faculty of pure science, 1905-06, member Univ. Council, 1901-03, 1905-06, 1913-15, Columbia. Fellow Am. Acad. Arts and Sciences, A.A.A.S. (pres. 1913), N.Y. Acad. Sciences (pres. 1904); mem. numerous Am. and fgn. scientific societies. Author: General Biology (with W. T. Sedgwick), 1887; Atlas of Karyokinesis and Fertilization, 1895; The Cell in Development and Heredity, 1896, 1900, 1925; The Physical Basis of Life, 1923. Died Mar. 3, 1939.

WILSON, Edward Livingston, editor and propr. Wilson's Photographic Mag., 1864—; b. Flemington, N.J., March 4, 1838; s. H. D. and Amelia C. (Hart) W.; ed. village schools and acad.; (Ph.D., Washington and Jefferson); was employed 9 yrs. in wholesale hardware store, Phila.; afterward in photography until 1864. Conducted several large photographic enterprises, one to Egypt, Palestine and Arabia, including Petra. Photographer Centennial Expn., Phila., 1876. and Cotton Exposition, New Orleans, 1885. Author: In Scripture Lands; and numerous photographic books. Died 1903.

WILSON, Edward Stansbury, editor; b. Newark, O., Oct. 6, 1841; s. Henry and Eliza (Bramble) W.; pub. sch. edn.; (hon. A.M., Ohio U., Athens, O., 1899; LL.D., Ohio Wesleyan U., 1910); m. George Anna Gibson, Oct. 20, 1870. Pvt. to 1st lt., 91st Regt., Ohio Vol. Inf., 1862-65; wounded in battle of Stephensons Depot, July 20, 1864, but fully recovered; admitted to bar, 1864, but never practiced; propr. and editor Ironton (O.) Register, 1865-99; U.S. marshal in Puerto Rico, by appmt. of President McKinley, 1900-05; reapptd. by President Roosevelt, resigned; editor Ohio State Journal, 1905—. Co. sch. examiner Lawrence Co., O., 1869-1900; mem. bd. trustees State Hosp. for Epileptics, 1890-1900; presdl. elector, 1884. Author: An Oriental Outing, 1894; Keynotes of Education, 1898; Political Development of Puerto Rico, 1905; The Poetry of Eating, 1908. Home: Columbus, O. Died Dec. 18, 1919.

WILSON, Edwin Walter; b. Baltimore, Md., May 16, 1848; s. William M. and Harriet E. (League) W.; ed. Newton Acad., Baltimore; m. Williamanna Hall, Oct. 4, 1871 (died 1899). With Treasury Dept., Washington, D.C., Feb. 21, 1870—; supt. Nat. Bank Redemption Agency, May 1911—. Home: Chevy Chase, Md. Died Sept. 21, 1920.

WILSON, Ellen Axson. See Mrs. Woodrow Wilson.

WILSON, Erasmus, newspaperman; b. Belmont Co., O., June 10, 1842; s. Joseph A. and Isabel (Kerr) W.; ed. dist. sch. and 3 mos., Hopedale Normal Sch.; (hon. M.A., Bethany Coll., 1912); unmarried. Pvt. Co. E, 98th Ohio Vol. Inf., Civil War; wounded at Battle of Perryville, Ky., Oct. 8, 1862; later topog. engr. with 14th Army Corps, Army of the Cumberland; participated in Sherman's March to the Sea. Became connected with Pittsburgh Leader, 1873; spl. work, Pittsburgh Dispatch, 1884, writing "The Quiet Observer"; continued same work with Gazette Times, 1888—, title changed to "Quiet Observations"; dramatic critic and book reviewer. Pres. Boy Scouts, Allegheny County, Pa. Author: Quiet Observations, 1886. Home: Pittsburgh, Pa. Died Jan. 14, 1922.

WILSON, Ernest Henry, botanist, author, traveler; b. Chipping Campden, Gloucestershire, Eng., Feb. 15, 1876; s. Henry and Annie (Curtis) W.; ed. Royal Coll. of Science, London; hon. M.A., Harvard, 1916; m. Ellen Ganderton, Edgbaston, Warwickshire, Eng., June 8, 1902; 1 dau., Muriel Primrose. Came to U.S., 1906; asst. dir. Arnold Arboretum, Harvard, 1919-27, keeper, 1927; traveled in China 11 yrs., 3 yrs. in Japanese Empire, also traveled in Australasia, India, South Africa, etc. Trustee Massachusetts Hort. Soc. Awarded Victoria medal of honor, George Robert White medal, Veitch memorial medal, Geoffrey St. Hilaire gold medal. Fellow Am. Acad. of Arts and Sciences. Author: Naturalist in West China, 1913; Cherries of Japan; Conifers and Taxads of Japan, 1915; Aristocrats of the Garden, 1916; The Romance of Our Trees, 1920; A Monograph of Azaleas (Wilson and Rehder), 1921; Lilies of Eastern Asia, 1925; America's Greatest Garden, 1925; Plant Hunting, 1927; More Aristocrats of the Garden, 1928; China, Mother of Gardens, 1929. Home: Jamaica Plain, Boston, Mass. Deceased.

WILSON, Eugene Benjamin, engineer; b. New Haven, Conn., Nov. 27, 1857; s. Elisha and Julia (Benjamin) W.; ed. Sheffield Scientific Sch. (Yale), 1879; m. Corrinne Munson, Aug. 31, 1885; children—J. Beatrice, E. Munson, S. Casselberry. In anthracite mining, 1880-85; iron mining and smelting, 1885-90; bituminous coal mining, 1890-94; gold and silver mining, metallurgist and consulting engr., 1894-1900; prin. sch. ore mining and metallurgy of Internat. Correspondence School, 1900-09. Author: Practical and Theoretical Mine Ventilation, 1884; Cyanide Processes, 1895; Chlorination Process, 1896; Hydraulic and Placer Mining, 1897; Ihlseng and Wilson's Manual of Mining, 1905. Editor Mines and Minerals, and Colliery Engineer, 1909-15. Home: Scranton, Pa. Died June 16, 1929.

WILSON, Eugene Smith, telephone official; b. Bloomfield, N.J., May 30, 1879; s. Robert Patterson and Mary Jennette (Smith) W.; grad. Adelphi Acad., Brooklyn, N.Y., 1898; A.B., Amherst, 1902; LL.B., Washington U., 1904; m. Margaret Grey Whitelaw, Sept. 20, 1904; children—Eugene S., Robert Whitelaw, Wells Patterson (dec.). Practiced at St. Louis, 1904-14; spl. counsel Am. Telephone & Telegraph Co., 1914-16; gen. counsel Wis., Cleveland, Mich. State and Chicago telephone companies, 1916-19; vice-pres. of Am. Telephone & Telegraph Co., 1920—. Trustee Deerfield (Mass.) Academy, Georgia Warm Springs Foundation. Member Public Recreation Commission of St. Louis, 1907-09. Republican. Conglist. Home: New York, N.Y. Died Dec. 19, 1937.

WILSON, Fletcher Aloysius, naval officer; b. Nottingham, Eng., Feb. 7, 1836. Apptd. 3d asst. engr. U.S.N., Aug. 26, 1859; 2d asst. engr., Oct. 21, 1861; 1st asst. engr., Oct. 1, 1863; chief engr., Mar. 5, 1871; retired, Feb. 7, 1898; advanced to rank of rear admiral retired, June 29, 1906, for services during Civil War. Served on various vessels during Civil War; insp. machinery at San Francisco, 1887-90, Union Iron Works, 1894-98; mem. bd. Navy Yard, New York, 1893-94. Died 1907.

WILSON, Francis, actor; b. Philadelphia, Pa., Feb. 7, 1854; s. Charles Edwin and Emily (Von Erdon) W.; hon. degree of L.H.D., Wesleyan Univ., 1929; m. Mira Barrie, 1881 (died 1915); children—Frances Barrie Wilson (Mme. Charles Huard), Adelaide Craycroft (Mrs. James Bradbury, Jr.); m. 2d, Edna Bruns (his leading woman in "The Bachelor's Baby"), 1917; children—Craycroft Francis, Margalo Francis. First professional appearance in a minstrel co.; engaged in legitimate comedy at Chestnut St. Theatre, 1887-78, Phila., as Cool, in "London Assurance," 1878-79; with Annie Pixley in "M'liss," 1879; with "Mitchell's Pleasure Party," 1880-83; started in comic opera as Sir Joseph Porter in "Pinafore"; became leading comedian of McCaull Opera Co. and of Casino, New York, 1885-89, where he created the character of Cadeaux in "Ermine." Subsequently organized his own co. in which he took leading comedy rôles in "The Oolah," "The Merry Monarch," "The Lion Tamer," "Ermine" (a revival), "The Chieftain," "Devil's Deputy," "Half a King," "The Little Corporal," 1898-99; "Cyrano de Bergerac," 1899-1900; "The Monks of Malabar," 1900-01; "The Strollers," 1901-02; "The Toreador," 1902-03, 1904-05; engaged in legitimate comedy with Charles Frohman, "Cousin Billy" (Le Voyage de M. Perrichon); "The Mountain Climber"; "The Little Father of the Wilderness"; "When Knights Were Bold," 1907-08; "The Bachelor's Baby," 1909, 10, 11; "The Spiritualist," 1911, 12; "Ermine," a revival with DeWolf Hopper, 1920-21; Bob Acres in Sheridan's "The Rivals," 1922; "The Rivals," and "School for Scandal," 1923; "She Stoops to Conquer," 1924; Acres in "The Rivals," and Rip in "Rip Van Winkle," 1925. Pres. Actors' Theatre; 1st pres. Actors' Equity Assn. Author: The Eugene Field I Knew; Recollections of a Player; Joseph Jefferson; Francis Wilson's Life of Himself; John Wilkes Booth; Edwin Booth. Dramatist: The Magic Ring; The Bachelor's Baby; The Spiritualist; The Dancing Master. Lectured on "Eugene Field I Knew"; "Humorous Side of an Actor's Life"; "Joseph Jefferson." Home: Clearwater, Fla., and New York, N.Y. Died Oct. 7, 1935.

WILSON, Francis Murray, lawyer; b. Platte City, Mo., June 13, 1867; s. Robert Patterson Clark and Carolyne Frances (Murray) W.; student Vanderbilt U. (Nashville, Tenn.), Centre Coll. (Danville, Ky.); m. Ida Elizabeth Cockrill, Sept. 23, 1903. Began practice, Platte City, 1889; pros. atty., Platte Co., Mo., 2 terms; mem. Mo. Senate, 1899 (chmn. Senate and House committees on revision statutes); Dem. nominee for Congress, 4th Dist. of Mo., 1904; mem. Mo. Senate, 1909, 11, 13 (pres. pro tem, 1913); resigned from Senate, Aug. 4, 1913, to qualify as U.S. atty. for Western Dist. of Mo., by apptmt. of President Wilson; reapptd. July 23, 1917, for term ending Aug. 4, 1921; resigned Oct. 23, 1920, to become a receiver of the Kansas City St. Rys. Co. Dem. nominee for governor of Missouri, 1928. Mason, Elk. Home: Platte City, Mo. Died Oct. 12, 1932.

WILSON, Franklin Augustus, lawyer; b. Bradford, Me., Nov. 6, 1832; s. John Hinds and Rachel Rider (Kingsbury) W.; A.B., Bowdoin Coll., 1854, A.M., 1857 (LL.D., 1900); m. Mary Elliott Carr, 1859 (died 1867); m. 2d, Caroline Pierce Stetson, 1871. Admitted to bar, 1857; practiced with late Chief Justice John A. Peters (Peters & Wilson), 1867-72; with late Justice Charles F. Woodard (Wilson & Woodard), 1872-94; mem. Me. Ho. of Rep., 1875-76; Rep. presdl. elector, 1905; dir. Me. Central R.R. Co., 1892—(pres. 1894-1900); pres. Penobscot Savings Bank, European & N. Am. Ry. Overseer Bowdoin Coll.; trustee Bangor Pub. Library. Unitarian. Home: Bangor, Me. Died 1911.

WILSON, George, statistician; b. New York, N.Y., Jan. 7, 1839. Entered Chamber of Commerce, June 10, 1858; elected its sec., May 7, 1868. Mem. of Met. Museum of Art, Am. Museum Natural History, N.Y. Hist. Soc., Long Island Hist. Soc., New England Soc. in City of New York (sec., 1894—), Marine Soc., Loyal Legion, Naval Order of U.S. Home: Brooklyn, N.Y. Died 1908.

WILSON, George, banker; b. Sac and Fox Agency, Ia., Oct. 6, 1842; s. George and Mary (Street) W.; ed. pvt. schs. and Masonic Coll., Lexigton, Mo., until 16 yrs. old; unmarried. Was clerk, teacher, prospector, post-trader, contractor in the West; returned to Mo. and engaged in banking till 1899 at Lexington, as cashier and later pres. La Fayette Co. Bank. Was probate judge Laramie Co., Dak. (most of which is now the State of Wyo.), 1868; mem. legislature of Dak.; elected mem. council, Wyo. Ty., 1869; carried to Gov. Campbell for approval, 1st law giving woman the right to vote and hold office; twice independent candidate for Congress, 5th Mo. dist. Was chmn. Dem. Co. Com. Laramie Co., when there. Democrat until Cleveland's 2d nomination, from then non-partisan. Author: The Greenbackers and Their Doctrine, 1878; National Banking Examined, 1879; The Financial Philosophy, 1896. Home: Lexington, Mo. Died 1906.

WILSON, George Henry, dentist; b. Painesville, O., Mar. 3, 1855; s. Dr. David C. and Marion (Flanders) W.; ed. high sch., Painesville; D.D.S., U. of Mich., 1878; m. Kittie, d. Rev. Lathrop Cooley, of Cleveland, Jan. 1, 1880. Practiced dentistry, Painesville, 1878-91, Cleveland, 1891—. Prof. clin. prosthetic dentistry, Cleveland U. of Medicine and Surgery, 1891-92; prof. prosthetic dentistry and metallurgy, Western Reserve U., 1892-1904, 1917-18 (emeritus); spl. prof. prosthesis, Dental Dept. U. of Southern Calif., 1917—. An editor of Dentist's Magazine, 1906-09. Fellow N.Y. State Dental Soc. (Javrie medal), Am. Coll. Dentists. Author: Chapter on Vulcanized Rubber as a Base for Artificial Dentures, in Turner's Am. Text-Book of Prosthetic Dentistry, 1907 and 1913; Manual of Dental Prosthetics, 1911, 4th edit., 1920. Home: Lakewood, O. Died Apr. 12, 1922.

WILSON, George Smith, social worker; b. Co. Antrim, Ireland, Mar. 19, 1869; s. Samuel and Mary Ann (Smith) W.; came to America, 1889; Lawrence U. (now Coll.), Appleton, Wis.; B.L., U. of Wis., 1894 (scholarship in social work); m. Ada Byron Shaw, Dec. 7, 1898; children—Fannie Shaw, George Smith, James Samuel. Spent summer of 1894 investigating sweatshop and tenement-house conditions in Cincinnati and visiting pub. instns. in Ohio, Ind. and Ky.; sec. Humane Soc. and Associated Charities, Toledo, O., 1894-95; sec. Associated Charities, Washington, D.C., 1895-1900; sec. Bd. of Pub. Charities, D.C., 1900-26; director of Public Welfare, D.C., 1926—. Sec. Washington Sanitary Improvement Co., 1915—, Washington Sanitary Housing Co., 1916—. Mem. National Conf. of Social Work, Am. Prison Assn., Internat. Prison Assn., Internat. Congress on Tuberculosis, U. of Wis. Assn. of D.C. (pres. 1910-11). Home: Washington, D.C. Died Sept. 1934.

WILSON, George West, editor the Florida Times-Union, 1897—; b. in Boone County, Ky., May 10, 1859; edn. chiefly pvt. study, scientific specialties; at 22 nominated for legislature; polit. worker; started Orange Lake Floridan, 1881; moved to Ocala, changed name to Lacon; later consolidated with Banner and published till 1884. Took charge Florida Citizen, 1897; consolidated with Times-Union, Jacksonville, same yr.; pres. company. Pres. (3 yrs.), Semi-Tropical Expn.; commr. Paris Expn.; collector internal revenue for Fla., 1894-98; pres. bd. trustees, Univ. of Fla., 1898-1905. Democrat. Died 1908.

WILSON, H. Augustus, orthopedic surgeon; b. Philadelphia, Pa., Sept. 4, 1853; s. Henry H. and Mary E. (Lewis) W.; M.D., Jefferson Med. Coll., 1879; (A.M., Ursinus Coll., 1894); m. Judith Stoutenburgh Davids, Nov. 16, 1882. Apptd. ophthalmic surgeon, St. Mary's Hosp., Phila., 1879; pathologist, Presbyn. Hosp., 1880; lecturer Phila. Sch. Anatomy, 1879-82; asst. surgeon, 1st Regt., N.G. Pa., 1885; prof. mech. surgery, Phila. Polyclinic, 1885; emeritus prof. orthopedic surgery, same, 1897; clin. prof. orthopedic surgery, Woman's Med. Coll., 1889; cons orthopedic surgeon, Kensington Hosp. and Phila. Lying-in Charity Hosp., 1890; apptd. clin. lecturer orthopedic surgery, 1890, clin. prof., 1891, prof. with full seat in faculty, 1904, Jefferson Med. Coll., also orthopedic surgeon Jefferson Med. Coll. Hosp. and St. Agnes Hosp.; orthopedic surgeon, Phila. Gen. Hosp., 1900—. Fellow Am. Coll. Surgeons, American Orthopedic Assn., Coll. Physicians (Phila.), Phila. Acad. Surgery. Progressive Rep. Episcopalian. Home: Philadelphia, Pa. Died Apr. 16, 1919.

WILSON, Harley Peyton, pub. utility exec.; b. N.Y. City, June 14, 1873; s. Samuel Peyton and Margaret (Chaddock) W.; student U. of Ore.; m. Frances Mary Edmondson, Jan. 1893; children—Alice Irene, Holt Chaddock; m. 2d, Caroline Anna Deike, Apr. 1910. With Brown, Wilson & Co., investment securities, New York, 1890-96; organizer, 1906, pres. until 1925, Western Power Corp.; organizer subsidiaries of same, Great Western Power Co. of Calif., Calif. Electric Generating Co., 1906; bought San Joaquin Light & Power Corp. and subsidiaries, 1923; builder, 1924, of hydroelectric plant on Tippecanoe River, Ind.; sold Western Power Corp. to North Am. Co., 1925; dir. both cos. and Washington Ry. & Electric Co., Potomac Electric Power Co.; prin. owner Washington Rapid Transit Co. Republican. Episcopalian. Home: Alexandria, Va. Died Nov. 23, 1934.

WILSON, Harry Bruce, educator; b. Frankfort, Ind., July 26, 1874; s. Edward Bruce and Mary Elizabeth (Norris) W.; grad. Ind. State Normal Sch., Terre Haute, Ind., 1895; A.B., Ind. U., 1905; M.A., Columbia, 1910; LL.D., Washburn Coll., 1917; m. Ella Maude Barnes, June 10, 1896; children—Dean Bruce, Harriett Maud. Teacher dist. schs., Clinton Co., Ind., 2 yrs.; prin. high sch., Salem, Ind., 1895-97; supt. schs., Salem, 1897-1902, Franklin, Ind., 1902-07, Decatur, Ill., 1907-13, Topeka, Kan., 1913-18, Berkeley, Calif., 1918-28; nat. dir. Am. Jr. Red Cross, 1928-31. Republican. Methodist. Mason. Author: Motivation of School Work, 1916; Training Pupils to Study, 1917; The Redirection of High School Instruction, 1919; Modern Methods in Teaching, 1924; Modern School Readers, 1924; Moore-Wilson Readers, 1927. Lecturer courses in supervision, U. of Calif., 1921-28. Home: Berkeley, Calif. Died Aug. 9, 1932.

WILSON, Harry Langford, educator; b. Wilton, Ont., Can., Oct. 28, 1867; s. Late Rev. Richard W., Ottawa, Can.; A.B., Queen's U.; Kingston, Can., 1887, A.M., 1888, with Prince of Wales gold medal in Latin and Greek, LL.D., 1903; Ph.D., Johns Hopkins, 1896; m. Minnie Clark, of Smith's Falls, Ont., 1889. Took professional training for teaching at Kingston Collegiate Inst., 1888; classical master, Ridgetown (Ont.) Collegiate Inst., Jan. 1889-July 1890; instr. Greek, Queen's U., 1890-91; prin. Newburgh (Ont.) High Sch., 1891-93; entered Johns Hopkins, 1893, as grad. student in Latin, Sanskrit and Greek; apptd. univ. scholar, 1894, fellow in Latin, 1895, instr., 1895, asso., 1900, asso. prof. Latin, 1902-06, prof. Roman archæology and epigraphy, 1906—; prof. Latin lang. and lit., Am. Sch. Classical Studies, Rome, 1906-07. Author: The Metaphor in the Epic Poems of P. Papinius Statius, 1898. Editor: Satires of Juvenal, 1903. Died Feb. 23, 1913.

WILSON, Harry Leon, author; b. Oregon, Ill., May 1, 1867; s. Samuel and Adeline (Kidder) W.; m. Rose Cecil (O'Neill) Latham, June 7, 1902. Mem. Nat. Inst. Arts and Letters. Editor of Puck, 1896-1902. Author: Zig Zag Tales, 1896; The Spenders, 1902; The Lions of the Lord, 1903; The Seeker, 1904; The Boss of Little Arcady, 1905; Ewing's Lady, 1907; The Man from Home (with Booth Tarkington), 1908; Bunker Bean, 1912; Ruggles of Red Gap, 1915; Somewhere in Red Gap, 1916; Lone Tree, 1929; Two Black Sheep, 1931. Home: Carmel, Calif. Died June 28, 1939.

WILSON, Henry H., lawyer; b. Sandusky Co., O., Jan. 1, 1854; s. Nathaniel and Mary (Feasel) W.; prep. edn., Acad. (Bryan, O.), State Normal Sch. (Peru, Neb.); Ph.B., U. of Neb., 1878, A.M., 1885, LL.M., 1895, LL.D., 1929; m. Emma Parks, June 22, 1882 (died 1927); children—Henry Parks (dec.), Helen, Edith (Mrs. Paul T. Bell), Ralph Parks, Walter Feasel; m. 2d, Mrs. Jennie Rinker, Sept. 21, 1929 (died 1936). Admitted to Nebraska bar, 1881, and began practice as mem. Ricketts & Wilson at Lincoln; mem. Lamb, Ricketts & Wilson, 1882-92, Ricketts & Wilson, 1892-99, Wilson & Brown, 1899-1907, Burkett, Wilson & Brown, 1907-19, Burkett, Wilson, Brown & Wilson, 1919-30, Burkett, Wilson, Brown, Wilson & Van Kirk, 1930-34; retired from active practice, Mar. 1, 1934; mem. of faculty, Law Dept., University of Nebraska, 30 yrs. Awarded Kiwanis Distinguished Service Medal, Dec. 17, 1937. Mem. Neb. Home Guard. Dir. Masonic Home, Plattsmouth, Neb. Republican. Mason, Grand Master of Masons of Neb., 1895. Elk. Author: Occasional Addresses, 1929. Home: Lincoln, Neb. Died June 28, 1941.

WILSON, Henry Harrison, engineer, constructor, editor; b. Jan. 15, 1882; native home, "Bonbrook," Cumberland Co., Va.; s. Henry Joseph and Lucy Harrison (Gay) W.; prep. edn., Seven Islands Acad., Buckingham Co., and high sch., Richmond, Va.; B.S. in C.E., Va. Poly. Inst., 1906, C.E. with highest honors, 1907; m. Lily, d. Gov. J. Hoge Tyler of Va., June 16, 1915; children—J. Hoge Tyler, Lily Norwood, Henry Harrison. Clk., Richmond, 1899-1904; instr. in civ. engring., Va. Poly. Inst., Jan.-June 1907; civ. engr., summer 1906 and 1907-08; engr. Winston & Co. on Ashokan dams, Catskill Aqueduct, Brown Sta., N.Y., 1909-11; partner Snead & Wilson, highway constrn., Cropseyville, N.Y., 1912-13; spl. partner Winston & Co. on highway and ry. constrn. and operation of crushed stone business, 1914-25; mng. asso. Winston Bros. Co. & Wilson (Minneapolis, Minn., and Harrisburg, Pa.), on bridge and other constrn. work, 1925-31; past pres. and chmn. bd. Associated Pa. Constructors, Harrisburg, 1924—; pres. and treas. Lime Bluff Co., 1930—; dir. All States Life Ins. Co., Peoples Bank of Radford. Author: Cost Keeping for Highway Construction, 1924. Editor Highway Builder. Delivered address on Benjamin Harrison "The Signer," at Capitol, Richmond, Va., Oct. 1931. Home: Harrisburg; also East Radford, Va. Died May 31, 1933.

WILSON, Henry Lane, ambassador; b. Crawfordsville, Ind., Nov. 3, 1856; s. James and Emma (Ingersoll) W.; A.B., Wabash Coll., 1879, later A.M., LL.D., 1930; Dr. Philosophy, Philology and Fine Arts, Nat. Univ. of Chile, 1911; m. Alice Vajen, Oct. 1884; children—John Vajen, Warden McKee, Stewart C. Editor Lafayette (Ind.) Jour., 1882-85; in practice of law and banking, Spokane, Wash., 1885-96. Apptd. minister to Venezuela by Pres. Harrison, 1889, but declined; U.S. minister to Chile, 1897-1905; apptd. minister to Greece, 1903, but permitted to remain in Chile at his own request; E.E. and M.P. to Belgium, 1905-10; apptd. ambassador to Turkey, 1909, but transferred to Mexico before taking charge; ambassador extraordinary and plenipotentiary to Mexico, Dec. 1909-13 (resigned). Special ambassador, crowning of King Albert of Belgium; Am. del. to Brussels Conf., on Collisions at Sea and to one to regulate use of arms in Africa. Pres. Soc. of Caucasian Republics in America; fellow Geog. Soc. of N.Y. Republican. Presbyn. Publicist. Author: Diplomatic Episodes. Home: Indianapolis, Ind. Died Dec. 22, 1932.

WILSON, Henry Van Peters, educator, biologist; b. Baltimore, Md., Feb. 16, 1863; s. Rev. Samuel A. and Sophia Anne (Stansbury) W.; A.B., Johns Hopkins, 1883, Ph.D., 1888; m. Edith Theresa Stickney, June 10, 1893 (dec.); children—Edith Stedman (Mrs. Thorndike Saville), Eleanora Stansbury (Mrs. Howell Peacock), Henry Van Peters. Asst. U.S. Fish Commn., 1889-91; prof. biology, 1891-1904, prof. zoölogy, 1914-17, Kenan prof. zoölogy, 1917—, University of N.C. Director U.S. Fisheries Laboratory, Beaufort, N.C., 1899-1902; southern exchange lecturer, 1915-16. Dohme lecturer, Johns Hopkins University, 1936. Original investigations on the embryology and regeneration of sponges, coelenterates, lower vertebrates; classification of sponges. Home: Chapel Hill, N.C. Died Jan. 4, 1939.

WILSON, Herbert Couper, astronomer; b. Lewiston, Minn., Oct. 24, 1858; s. Thomas and Ann W.; A.B., Carleton Coll., 1879, A.M., 1882; Ph.D., U. of Cincinnati, 1886; studied astronomy, Cincinnati Obs., 1880-81; m. Mary B. Nichols, Dec. 20, 1882 (died 1924); children—Ralph Elmer, Ruth Edna (Mrs. William H. Geer), Mary Helen (Mrs. George M. Constans), Lois Norma (Mrs. W. Harlan Pye); m. 2d, Florence E. Rice, Aug. 26, 1926. Assistant astronomer, 1881-82, astronomer in charge, 1882-84, assistant astronomer, 1884-86, Cincinnati Observatory; computer to U.S. Transit of Venus Commn. U.S. Naval Observatory, Washington, 1886-87; asst. prof. astronomy, 1887-1900, asso. prof. mathematics and astronomy, 1900-08, prof. and dir. Goodsell Obs., 1908-26, also dean faculty, 1906-10, Carleton Coll.; retired on Carnegie Foundation, 1926. Asso. editor, Astronomy and Astrophysics, 1892-94, Popular Astronomy, 1894-1909; editor Popular Astronomy, 1909-26. Asst. astronomer, Lick Obs., 1910-11, Harvard Obs., 1916, Mt. Wilson Obs., 1920-21. Devoted much attention to double and variable star observations and astronomical photography. Home: Northfield, Minn. Died March 9, 1940.

WILSON, Herbert Michael, engineer; b. Glasgow, Scotland, Aug. 23, 1860; s. Henry and Ellen (Yeates) W.; studied at Plainfield, N.J., and Cooper Union, New York; C.E., Columbia Sch. Mines, 1881; m. Elizabeth, d. Thom Williamson, Nov. 16, 1893. Ry. engr. in Mexico, 1881-82; on U.S. Geol. Survey as topographer, 1882-88, irrigation engr., 1889-91, as geographer, 1892-1906, chief engr. technologic branch, 1907-09, engr. in charge, U.S. Bur. of Mines, 1910-14; dir. dept. of inspection and safety, The Associated Ins. Cos., 1915-19; general manager of same, 1919—. Has lectured extensively on irrigation, geography, fuel testing, smoke abatement, mine fires and rescue, fireproof building construction, swamp reclamation, etc. Author: Manual of Irrigation Engineering, 1893; Topographic Surveying, 1899; American Civil Engineers' Pocket Book. Home: Sewickley, Pa. Died Nov. 25, 1920.

WILSON, Ida Lewis, life-saver; b. Newport, R.I., 1841; d. Capt. Hosea (keeper of Lime Rock light house, Newport harbor) and Ida Hattie Zoraida Lewis; m. William H. Wilson, 1870. Became expert rower and swimmer and famous for saving of lives in the adjacent sea, often at great personal peril; thus saved 18 lives; received medals for heroism from U.S. Govt., Humane Soc. of Mass., and Life Saving Benevolent Soc. of New York; her boat, the "Rescue," was exhibited at the Chicago Expn. She is still at the light house and is commonly known by her maiden name. Died 1911.

WILSON, James, sec. of agriculture; b. Ayrshire, Scotland, Aug. 16, 1835; s. John and Jean (McCosh) W.; came to U.S., 1851, parents settling in Conn.; went to Tama Co., Ia., 1855; ed. pub. schs. of Ia., and Ia. Coll.; (LL.D., U. of Wis., 1904, Cornell Coll., Ia., 1904, McGill, 1909); m. Esther Wilbur; father of James Wilbur W. Engaged in farming, 1861; mem. 12th, 13th and (speaker) 14th Assemblies of Ia.; regent State U. of Iowa, 1870-74; mem. 43d and 44th Congresses (1873-77); mem. Ia. State Ry. Commn., 1877-83; mem. 48th Congress, 1883-85 (seat was contested and contestant was seated last hour of Congress); dir. Agrl. Expt. Sta. and prof. agr., Ia. Agrl. Coll., Ames, 1890-97; sec. of agriculture, March 5, 1897-13, in cabinets of Presidents McKinley, Roosevelt and Taft. Republican. Home: Traer, Ia. Died Aug. 26, 1920.

WILSON, James, mfr.; b. Pittsfield, Mass., Sept. 23, 1848; s. Solomon and Mary Elizabeth (Dunham) W.; ed. pub. schs.; married; 2 children. Engaged in woolen mfg., 1880—; pres. James & E. H. Wilson, Inc.; dir. Pittsfield Nat. Bank, Berkshire Mutual Fire Ins. Co. Republican. Conglist. Home: Pittsfield, Mass. Died Mar. 3, 1927.

WILSON, James Cornelius, physician; b. Philadelphia, Pa., Mar. 25, 1847; s. Dr. Ellwood and Hannah (Paul) W.; A.B., Princeton, 1867, also A.M.; M.D., Jefferson Med. Coll., 1869; m. Adéle Béatrice Grosholz, 1882; children—Béatrice Adéle, Helen Natalie. Attending phys. Phila. Hosp., 1876-90; emeritus prof. practice of medicine and of clin. medicine, Jefferson Med. Coll.; emeritus phys. Pa. Hosp., 1911—; med. dir. Jefferson Med. Coll. Hosp., 1894-96; apptd. phys. in chief Lankenau Hosp., Phila., 1898 (emeritus); consulting phys. Phila. Lying-In Charity Hosp., Rush Hosp. for Consumptives, Jewish Hospital, and Bryn Mawr (Pa.) Hospital. Author: The Summer and Its Diseases, 1879; A Treatise on the Continued Fevers, 1881; Fever-Nursing, 1888, 98; A Hand Book of Medical Diagnosis. Editor: American Text-book of Applied Therapeutics. Home: Philadelphia, Pa. Died Oct. 28, 1934.

WILSON, James Cunningham, clergyman; b. Xenia, O., May 31, 1840; s. Rev. Samuel and Mary (Cunningham) W.; A.B., Jefferson Coll., Pa., 1864; studied U.P. Theol. Sem., Zenia, 1865-68; (D.D., Muskingum Coll., O., Westminster Coll., Pa., 1893; LL.D., Washington and Jefferson Coll., 1902); served in 1st Ohio Heavy Arty., 1864-65; m. Henrietta M. Hassler, Sept. 10, 1868. Licensed, 1867, ordained, 1869; pastor Beaver, Pa., 1868-72, Phila., 1872-75, First U.P. Ch., Erie, Pa., Mar. 19, 1876-Oct. 31, 1908, retired. Moderator U.P. Gen. Assembly, May 28, 1902. Home: Erie, Pa. Died 1909.

WILSON, J(ames) Edgar, clergyman, editor; b. nr. Martinsburg, W.Va., Oct. 19, 1860; s. William W.; educated at Baltimore City College (non-grad.); m. Lillian Townsend, Oct. 16, 1883 (died 1901); children—Edgar Cummings, Frank Townsend, Guy Hawkins, Hugh Bryan; m. 2d, Mary Virginia Moore, Aug. 5, 1903. Ordained ministry M.E. Ch., S., 1881; served Prince George Circuit, 1881-82, Talbot, 1882-83, N. Baltimore Sta., 1883-86, Reisterstown, 1886-87, Union Circuit, 1887-90; mgr. Conf. Book Depository, 1891-95; served Church Hill Circuit, 1895-99, Kent Circuit, 1899-1903, Riverside Sta., Jacksonville, Fla., 1901-04, Tallahassee Dist., 1905-08, Hyde Park, 1909, Gainesville, 1910-13, editor Florida Christian Advocate, 1913-25; editor The Florida Watchman, 1926-32; pub. agt. new Florida Christian Advocate, 1929-34; pres. emeritus, Fla. Meth. Pub. Co., Inc., 1938—. Author: The Lord's Supper, 1910; The Good News, 1938. Home: Lakeland, Fla. Died Jan. 29, 1940.

WILSON, James Grant, author; b. Edinburgh, Scotland, Apr. 28, 1832; s. William W. and Jane (Sibbald) W.; brother of Walter Sibbald W.; acad. edn., and by pvt. tutors; (D.C.L., St. Stephen's Coll., 1894; L.H.D., Hobart, 1895); m. Jane Emily Searle Cogswell, Nov. 3, 1869 (died 1904); m. 2d, Mrs. Mary H. Nicholson, widow of Admiral J. W. A. Nicholson, May 16, 1907. Founded, 1857, and was editor and propr. Chicago Record (jour. of arts and lit.); maj. 15th Ill. Cav., Dec. 25, 1862; col. 4th U.S. Colored Cav., Sept. 14, 1863; a.d.c. to Gen. N. P. Banks, 1863-65; bvtd. brig. gen. vols., Mar. 13, 1865, "for faithful and meritorious services"; resigned June 16, 1865. In lit. work at New York, 1865—. Pres. N.Y. Geneal. and Biog. Soc., 1886-1902; pres. Am. Authors' Guild, 1893-99, and editor of its Monthly Bulletin; pres. Am. Ethnol. Soc., 1900—, Drawing Room, 1906; v.p. Am. Soc. Prevention Cruelty to Animals, 1907, and editor of its Bull.; v.p. Hudson-Fulton Commn., 1909. Erected bronze statue to the poet Halleck, and Columbus, and for latter was knighted by the Queen Regent of Spain in 1894, and the Me. Nat. Memorial Monument, all in Central Park. Editor: Fitz-Greene Halleck's Poems, 1868; Poets and Poetry of Scotland (2 vols.), 1876; Memorial History of the City of New York (4 vols.), 1892-93; Appleton's Cyclopedia of American Biography (7 vols.), 1901; Great Commanders Series (18 vols.), completed 1903; Memoirs of an American Lady, 1901. Author: Mr. Secretary Pepys and His Diary, 1867; Life of Fitz-Greene Halleck, 1869, Sketches of Illustrious Soldiers, 1874; Bryant and His Friends, 1886; The World's Largest Libraries, 1894; Life of General Grant, 1897; The Presidents of the United States, 1789-1901, 1902; Thackeray in the United States (2 vols.), 1904; Memoir General Henry W. Halleck, 1905; Thackeray in the United States, new edit., 1909; Commodore Isaac Hull and the Frigate Constitution, 1910. Home: New York, N.Y. Died Feb. 1, 1914.

WILSON, James Harrison, soldier, railroad builder and manager; b. Shawneetown, Ill., Sept. 2, 1837; s. Harrison and Katharine (Schneider) W.; student McKendree Coll., Lebanon, Ill. (LL.D.), grad. U.S. Mil. Acad., 1860; m. Ella, d. Gen. J. W. Andrews, of Wilmington, Del., Jan. 3, 1866. Bvt. 2d lt. topographical engrs., July 1, 1860; 2d lt., June 10, 1861; promoted through grades to brig. gen. vols., Oct. 30, 1863; maj. gen. vols., May 6, 1865; bvtd.: maj., Apr. 11, 1862, "for gallant and meritorious services at Ft. Pulaski, Ga.,; lt. col., Nov. 24, 1863, for same at Chattanooga; col., May 5, 1864, for same, at the Wilderness, Va.; brig. gen., Mar. 13, 1865, for same at Nashville; maj. gen., Mar. 13, 1865, for same at Selma, Ala., and maj. gen., Oct. 5, 1865, for same during the war; hon. mustered out of vol. service, Jan. 8, 1866; lt. col. 35th U.S. Inf., July 28, 1866; hon. disch. at own request, Dec. 31, 1870; maj. gen. vols., May 4, 1898; brig. gen. vols., Apr. 12, 1899-Mar. 2, 1901; brig. gen. U.S.A. (by spl. act of Congress, Feb. 2, 1901), Feb. 11, 1901; retired, Mar. 2, 1901. Engr. and insp. gen. in Vicksburg and Chattanooga campaigns; chief of Cavalry Bur., War Dept., Feb.-Apr., 1864; comd. 3d div. Sheridan's cav., 1864; organized and comd. cav. corps Mil. Div. of the Miss., Oct. 1864; turned flank of Hood's army at Nashville, capturing many guns and prisoners and pursuing him to Tenn. River; comd. assault and capture of Selma and Montgomery, Ala., Columbus and Macon, Ga., and pursuit and capture of Jefferson Davis; in Spanish-Am. War, comd. 1st and 6th Army Corps in Ga. and the occupation of Cuba, also depts. of Matanzas and Santa Clara, and in P.R. campaign; joined China relief expdn.; comd. coöperating force of Am. and British troops in capture of the 8 temples, also Am. forces in Peking. Represented U.S. Army at coronation of King Edward VII. Largely engaged in r.r. and engring. operations for many yrs. Trustee Mut. Life Ins. Co., 1907—, and dir. in many corps. Author: Life of Andrew Alexander, 1868; Life of General Grant (with late Charles A. Dana), 1868; China—Travels and Investigations in the Middle Kingdom, 1887, 1900; Life and Services of Maj. Gen. William F. Smith; Life and Services of Maj. Gen. Alexander McD. McCook; Life and Services of Maj. Gen. John A. Rawlins; Life of Charles A. Dana, 1907; Under the Old Flag, 1912. Home: Wilmington, Del. Died Feb. 23, 1925.

WILSON, James Ormond, educator; b. Royalston, Mass., Apr. 2, 1825; s. James and Chloë (Thurston) W.; grad. Dartmouth, 1850, A.B., 1868, A.M., 1870. In U.S. Treasury Dept., 1850-68; admitted to D.C. bar, 1853; supt. pub. schs. of D.C., 1870-85. Pres. N.E.A., 1880; sec. Am. Colonization Soc., 1892—. Home: Washington, D.C. Died 1911.

WILSON, John, civil engr.; b. Wisbeach, Cambridge, Eng., Jan. 23, 1841; s. John and Sarah (Fisher) W.; grad. Cooper's Hill Civ. Engring. Coll., Staines, Eng., 1865; m. Eliza Ellen Barrow, Dec. 26, 1904. Civ. engr., Pub. Works Dept., India, 1869-82; came to U.S., 1882; constructing engr. on cable rys., Phila. St. Ry. Co., 1883-88; pvt. practice Pittsburgh, 1888-92, Texas, 1892-95; surveys in Mex., 2,000,000 acres, mostly in the Sierra Madre Mts.; built 1st electric ry. in El Paso, Tex., 1899; constrn. irrigation canals in W. Tex., 1904-06; v.p., chief engr. Barston Irrigation Co., 1906-13; mem. Bd. Water Engrs. of Tex., Sept. 1, 1913-19. Mason, Elk. Democrat. Episcopalian. Home: El Paso, Tex. Died June 28, 1921.

WILSON, John Fleming, author; b. Erie, Pa., Feb. 22, 1877; s. Joseph Rogers and Viola Harriet (Eaton) W.; Parsons Coll., Ia.; A.B., Princeton, 1900. Teacher, 1900-02; newspaper work, 1902-05, editor San Francisco Argonaut, 1906. Episcopalian. Author: The Land Claimers, 1910; Across the Latitudes, 1911; The Man Who Came Back, 1912; The Princess of Sorry Valley, 1913; Tad Sheldon and His Boy Scouts (I), 1913; Tad Sheldon and His Boy Scouts (II), 1913; The Master Key, 1915. Served in France with 7th Batt. Inf., Canadians, 1917-19. Home: Victorville, Calif. Died Mar. 5, 1922.

WILSON, John Fry, lawyer; b. Sidney, O., July 26, 1869; s. Col. Harrison and Mary Caroline (Fry) W.; B.L., Cincinnati Law Sch., 1890; m. Margaret Widner, Dec. 15, 1891 (died 1925). Admitted to Ohio bar, 1890; practiced, Sidney, until 1901, then at Columbus; identified with much important litigation in Ohio; mem. Wilson & Rector. Republican. Home: Columbus, O. Died Feb. 19, 1930.

WILSON, John L., senator; b. Crawfordsville, Ind., Aug. 7, 1850; A.B., Wabash Coll., 1874; (LL.D.). Mem. Ind. Ho. of Rep., 1880; receiver pub. moneys at Spokane Falls, Wash., 1882-86; mem. 51st to 53d Congresses (1889-95); resigned from 53d Congress, Feb. 18, 1895; U.S. senator, Feb. 19, 1895-Mar. 3, 1899, for unexpired term of John B. Allen. Republican. Home: Seattle, Wash. Died Nov. 6, 1906.

WILSON, John McCalmont, chmn. bd. Nat. Supply Co.; b. Franklin, Pa., Mar. 17, 1876; s. Henry Medary and Mary (Funk) W.; A.B., Bucknell U., 1897; LL.B., Harvard, 1900; m. Rachel Brundred, Apr. 11, 1910. Nat. Supply Co., 1924-39, chmn. bd., 1939—; chmn. bd. Spang Chalfant, Incorporated; dir. First Nat. Bank, of Pittsburgh, Peoples-Pittsburgh Trust Co. Trustee Bucknell U. Baptist. Mason. Home: Pittsburgh, Pa. Deceased.

WILSON, John Moulder, brig. gen. U.S.A.; b. in D.C., Oct. 8, 1837; grad. U.S. Mil. Acad., 1860; (LL.D., Columbian U., 1890). Bvt. lt. arty., July 1, 1860; 2d lt. arty., Jan. 28, 1861; 1st lt., May 14, 1861; transferred to engrs., 1862; capt. engrs., Mar. 3, 1863; maj., June 3, 1867; lt. col., Mar. 17, 1884; col., Mar. 27, 1895; brig. gen. chief of engrs. U.S.A., Feb. 1, 1897. In Civil war reached bvt. rank of col. in vols. and U.S.A. for gallantry in various battles; awarded Congressional Medal of Honor, July 3, 1897, "for most distinguished gallantry in action at Malvern Hill, Va., Aug. 6, 1862"; after war had charge of engring. works on rivers and harbors, canals, the building of the army med. museum and library, completion of Washington monument, etc.; supt. pub. bldgs. and grounds, 1885-89; supt. U.S. Mil. Acad., 1889-93; again supt. pub. bldgs. and grounds, 1893-97; chief of engrs. U.S.A., 1897-1901; retired at own request after 40 yrs.' service, Apr. 30, 1901. Pres. Washington Bd. of Trade, 1905-07; mem. Spanish War, Anthracite Coal Strike, Steamer Slocum Disaster commns. and Brownsville ct. of inquiry. Home: Washington, D.C. Died Feb. 1, 1919.

WILSON, John P. lawyer; b. on farm, Whiteside Co., Ill., July 3, 1844; s. Thomas and Margaret (Laughlin) W.; A.B., Knox Coll., Ill., 1865 (LL.D., 1912); taught school and studied law, 1865-67; m. Margaret C., d. J. D. McIlvaine, of Chicago, Apr. 25, 1871. Admitted to Ill. bar, 1867; sr. mem. Wilson, Moore & McIlvaine. Drafted the law creating the Sanitary Dist. of Chicago, and successfully carried to the Supreme Ct. the litigation in which the validity of the law was established. Was gen. counsel World's Columbia Expn. and prepared the constl. amendment and legislation relating thereto passed at the Gen. Assembly, 1890; representative of many leading corps. and bus. interests. Apptd. mem. Ill. Tax Commn., Mar. 1910. Home. Chicago, Ill. Died Oct. 3, 1922.

WILSON, John Timothy, pres. Internat. Brotherhood of Maintenance-of-Way Employes; b. Riceville, McMinn Co., Tenn., Jan. 29, 1861; attended country schs. and worked on farm until he was 17 yrs. old; worked as section hand on E. Tenn., Va. and Ga. Ry., 1 yr.; promoted section foreman and filled several positions, same road, until 1888; resigned and began to organize Internat. Brotherhood of Maintenance-of-Way Employes (pres.); secured benefit of reduced hours and improved working conditions for maintenance-of-way employes, with only two strikes, 1901, 1905; also secured trade agreements covering 75,000 miles of ry. Home: St. Louis, Mo. Died 1908.

WILSON, Joseph Chamberlain, mayor; b. Binghamton, N.Y., Oct. 11, 1851; s. Henry and Ann S. (Williams) W.; ed. high sch., Binghamton; m. Alice M. Hutton, of St. Petersburg, Can., May 12, 1881 (dec.); children—Joseph R., Lillian W. (Mrs. Louis W. Howell), Maude W. (Mrs. Trafton M. Crandall). Sec. J. C. Wilson Co., jewelers, Rochester, N.Y., Acme Sales Co.; dir. Haloid Co. Alderman, Rochester, 1896-1900, city assessor, 1900-17, city treas., 1917-19, comptroller, 1919-28, mayor, 1928— (term 1928-34). Dir. Rochester Pub. Library. Rep. presdl. elector, 1929. Mem. Rochester Chamber Commerce. Mason, Elk. Home: Rochester, N.Y. Died Mar. 5, 1930.

WILSON, Joseph Dawson, clergyman; b. New York, July 9, 1840; s. William and Jane (Robinson) W.; A.B., St. Stephen's Coll., Annandale, N.Y., 1863, A.M., 1866; grad. General Theol. Sem., 1866; (D.D., U. of Chicago, 1884); m. Catharine H. Offley, Jan. 14, 1869 (died 1873); m. 2d, Sara E. Merrill, Nov. 4, 1879. Deacon, 1866, priest, 1867, P.E. Ch.; rector Calvary Ch., Pittsburgh, 1867-74; a founder R.E. Ch., 1874; rector Christ Ch., Peoria, Ill., 1874-79, St. John's, Chicago, 1879-89, Immanuel Ch., St. Louis, 1889-90; resident in Ida., 1890-95; in charge Ch. of Our Lord, Victoria, B.C., 1895-1901; prof. history, 1901—, chmn. faculty, 1903—, Theol. Sem. R.E. Ch., Phila. Mem. Federal Council Chs. of Christ in America. Republican. Author; Studies on Words from the Cross, 1884; Did Daniel Write Daniel?, 1896. Home: Philadelphia, Pa. Died Jan. 21, 1925.

WILSON, Joseph Miller, civil engr., architect; b. Phœnixville, Pa., June 20, 1838; grad. Rensselaer Poly. Inst., C.E., 1858, (A.M., Univ. of Pa., 1877)); m. 1869, Sarah Pettit. Asst. engr. Pa. R.R., 1860-63; resident engr. middle div., same, 1863-65; engr. bridges and buildings, 1865-86; asso. engr. and architect for designing and constructing main building and Machinery Hall, Centennial Expn., 1876; from 1876 in general practice in firm Wilson Bros. & Co.; mgr. Franklin Inst., 1868, pres., 1887-97. Fellow Am. Inst. Architects, A.A.A.S. Home: Philadelphia, Pa. Died 1902.

WILSON, Joseph Rogers; b. Fayette Co., Pa., May 14, 1847; s. Samuel (D.D.) and Anna Maria (Rogers) W.; Washington Coll., Pa., 1863-64; A.B., Washington and Jefferson Coll., 1867, D.D., 1884; grad. Western Theol. Sem., 1870; m. Viola Eaton, Sept. 2, 1875; children—John Fleming (dec.), Margaret Adelaide, Helen Adams. Ordained Presbyn. ministry, 1869; pastor Normal, Ill., 1870-71, Chestnut St. Ch., Erie, Pa., 1872-79; prof. Greek, Parsons Coll., Fairfield, Ia., 1879-89; removed to Portland, Ore., with Dr. Samuel R. Johnston and founded Portland Acad. of which was joint prin. to 1909, and prin. of same until 1914. Mem. Park Bd., Portland, 1905-09; chmn. Com. on Congresses, Lewis & Clark Expn., 1905; mem. Ore. Conservation Commn., 1908, 09; chmn. Ore. Bd. Higher Curricula, 1909-14. Charter mem. Ore. Hist. Soc. (v.p. 1906-14); mem. Nat. Assn. for Constl. Govt. Republican. Presbyn. Home: Hemet, Calif. Died Feb. 20, 1929.

WILSON, Julian Morris; b. Beverly, N.J., July 22, 1866; s. John Jacob and Julia (Langdale) W.; ed. Van Rensselaer Inst. and under tutors; studied law in office of Southgate & Southgate, New York; m. Helen McNeely, June 2, 1897. Admitted to N.Y. bar, 1903, and began practice as patent atty. in N.Y. City; pres. Nat. Supply Co.; v.p. Fantail Boat Corp. Capt. U.S.A., World War; maj., 1919. Mem. Am. Legion; awarded N.Y. State Medal, World War Medal. Republican. Episcopalian. Home: New York, N.Y. Died June 6, 1931.

WILSON, Lester MacLean, educator; b. Lamar, Mo., Dec. 15, 1885; s. S. F. and Mary E. (Smith) W.; A.B., Park Coll., Parkville, Mo., 1906; A.M., U. of Chicago, 1908; Ph.D., Columbia, 1919. Teacher science, Wayland Academy, Beaver Dam, Wis., 1906-08; teacher of psychology, U. of Puerto Rico, 1909-12; grad. student and asst. in psychology labs., U. of Wis., 1912-13; teacher psychology, Wis. State Normal School, Whitewater, Wis., 1913-14; with Wis. State Bd. Pub. Affairs, 1914-15; teacher psychology Eastern Ill. State Normal Sch., Charleston, 1915-21; dir. examinations and studies, dir. gen. de instrucción, Lima, Peru, 1921; dir. gen. of instrn. for Republic of Peru, 1922-23; asso. prof. edn., Teachers Coll., Columbia U., 1923-25, prof. edn., 1925—. Home: New York, N.Y. Died May 26, 1937.

WILSON, Lloyd Tilghman, clergyman; b. Graves Co., Ky., Dec. 16, 1866; s. William John and Rebecca Josephine (Eley) W.; grad. Southern Normal Sch. and Business Coll., Bowling Green, Ky., 1885; D.D., Union U., Jackson, Tenn., 1904; m. Helen Hortense Byng, Nov. 6, 1889; children—Rhey Byng, Lloyd T., Ione Louise (Mrs. Jack Mason Smith), Everett Dodson (dec.). In wholesale grocery and tobacco brokerage business, 1886-98; ordained Bapt. ministry, 1897; pastor 2d Ch., Paducah, Ky., 1897-98, 1st Ch., Humboldt, Tenn., 1899-1903, Edgefield Church, Nashville, 1904-05, East Ch., Louisville, Ky., 1906-08, 1st Ch., Newport News, Va., 1909-12, Grace St. Ch., Richmond, Va., 1912-17, Broadway Ch., Knoxville, Tenn., Apr. 1917-Dec. 1919; corr. sec. and treas. exec. bd. of Tenn. Bapt. Conv., Dec. 10, 1919-24; pastor 1st Baptist Church, High Point, N.C., 1924-29, Southside Church, Lakeland, Florida, 1929—. Pres. Boscobel Coll., Nashville, Tenn., 1904-05. Mem. S.S. Bd. Southern Bapt. Conv., 1904-08; mem. Foreign Missionary Bd.; trustee Southern Bapt. Theol. Sem., Louisville, Ky., 1914-19; trustee Carson and Newman Coll., Southwestern Bapt. Theol. Sem.; trustee Richmond Coll., 1917-19; mem. Gen. Bd. of Missions and Edn., N.C. Baptists, 1927—. Home: Lakeland, Fla. Died Oct. 22, 1933.

WILSON, Lorenzo Arthur, mfr. fertilizers; b. Wilson's Beach, Campobello Island, Can., Dec. 25, 1864 s. Lorenzo and Rachel (Young) W.; brought to U.S., 1867; ed. pub. schs. and business coll.; m. Meriel Lapham Dodge, Jan. 30, 1893 (died 1922); children—Dorothy (dec.), Meriel Lapham (Mrs. Robert R. Milan). Grocery clk., 1879-82, bookkeeper, Jacksonville, Fla., 1884-88; traveling salesman, 1888-93; in fertilizer business, 1893—, incorporated, 1902, as Wilson & Toomer Fertilizer Co., of which has been chmn. bd., 1928—; chmn. bd. Fla. Agrl. Supply Co., Southern States Bag Co.; pres. Holly Hill Grove & Fruit Co.; dir. Fla. Nat. Bank. Mem. Jacksonville Light Inf., 1884. Democrat. Presbyn. Home: Jacksonville, Fla. Died Sept. 9, 1936.

WILSON, Louis N., librarian; b. Yorkshire, Eng., Sept. 4, 1857; s. John and Nancy (Milner) W.; ed. St. Petersburg, Russia; came to U.S., 1871; (hon. A.B., Clark U., 1905; Litt.D., Tufts College, 1905); m. Anne Gertrude Thomas, 1875. Engaged in business until 1884; spent 4 yrs. in Europe; librarian Clark U., 1889-1929. Author: Bibliography of Child Study; Life of G. Stanley Hall. Home: Worcester, Mass. Died Sept. 12, 1937.

WILSON, Lucy Langdon Williams, educator; b. St. Albans, Vt., Aug. 18, 1864; d. Samuel Williams and Lucy E. (Crampton) W.; grad. normal schs., Phila., and Vt.; student U. of Pa., 1890-97, Ph.D., 1897; m. William Powell Wilson, July 17, 1893; 1 son, David Hawxhurst. Head of dept. biology, Phila. Normal Sch. and prin. Evening High Sch. for Women, 1892-1915; prin. Southern High School for Girls, Phila., 1915-34; lecturer on edn., Temple University, 1934-36. Excavated pueblo, Otow, 1915-17. In Chile, at request of Chilean Govt., 1929. Author: A Too Short Vacation, 1891; The New Schools of New Russia, 1928. Editor: Everyday Manners, 1922; Education for Responsibility, 1926; Autobiography of a Public School Teacher, 1935. Recipient of $10,000 Bok award for service rendered for good of Phila., 1934. Home: Philadelphia, Pa. Died Sept. 3, 1937.

WILSON, Luther Barton, bishop; b. Baltimore, Nov. 14, 1856; s. Henry Merryman (M.D.) and Eliza Kelso (Hollingsworth) W.; A.B., Dickinson Coll., 1875, A.M., 1878, D.D., 1892, LL.D., 1904; M.D., U. of Md., 1877; L.H.D., Syracuse, 1912; LL.D., Wesleyan, 1913; m. Louisa J. Turner, Feb. 17, 1881. Entered Baltimore Ann. Conf. M.E. Ch., Mar. 1878; pastoral appts. Md. and D.C.; presiding elder Washington Dist., Baltimore Ann. Conf., 1894-1900, West Baltimore Dist., Baltimore Ann. Conf., 1903-04; elected bishop by Gen. Conf. at Los Angeles, May 26, 1904; resident bishop, Chattanooga, Tenn., 1904-08, Phila., 1908-12, N.Y. City, 1912—. In service of Y.M.C.A. in France, summer 1917, summer and fall 1918. Trustee, Dickinson Coll. (Carlisle, Pa.), Drew Theol. Sem. (Madison, N.J.), Pennington (N.J.) Sem., Drew Sem. for Young Women (Carmel, N.Y.), Am. Univ. (Washington, D.C.); hon. trustee, Syracuse U.; mem. Church Peace Union; pres. Bd. of Foreign Missions, M.E. Ch., 1912—. Home: New York, N.Y. Died June 4, 1928.

WILSON, Maurice Emery, clergyman; b. Baltimore, Md., Apr. 2, 1855; s. Rev. Thomas Brown and Margaret Brown (Saunders) W.; A.B., Washington and Jefferson Coll., Pa., 1876; B.D., Western Theol. Sem., Pittsburgh, Pa., 1879; D.D., New Windsor Coll., Md., 1888; m. Fanny Louisa McCombs, June 19, 1879; 1 dau., Mrs. Anne W. Brandon. Ordained Presbyn. Ch., 1879; pastor 1st Ch., Gallipolis, O., 1879-81, Emsworth, Pa., 1881-84, Westminster Ch., Baltimore, Md., 1884-90, 1st Ch., Dayton, O., 1890-1919; pastor College Hill Presbyn. Ch., Beaver Falls, Pa., 1920-24; student pastor Washington and Jefferson Coll., 1924-30, chaplain, 1930-32, hon. emeritus chaplain, 1932—. Trustee Western Coll. for Women, Oxford, O.; v.p. bd. trustees Miami Valley Hosp.; mem. bd. dirs. Associated Charities, Dayton. Active in Liberty Loan campaigns. Home: Washington, Pa. Died 1936.

WILSON, Mortimer, composer, conductor; b. Chariton, Ia., Aug. 6, 1876; s. John and Mary W. (Harper) W.; studied with F. G. Gleason, S. E. Jacobson, William Middleschulte, Oscar Nedbal, Hans Sitt and Max Reger; m. Hettie Lewis, Nov. 23, 1904; 1 son, Mortimer. Dir. dept. of theory and composition, U. of Neb., 1901-08; dir. Atlanta Conservatory, 1913-14; dir. dept. of theory, Brenau Coll., Gainesville, Ga., 1915-16, Malkin Music Sch., New York, 1917-18. Condr. Atlanta Philharmonic Orchestra, 1912-15; guest condr. N.Y. Philharmonic Orchestra, 1918; became condr. Wilson Sinfonietta. Episcopalian. Composer: (piano) Bagatelles, In Georgia, Euterpean Lyrics, Sonatinas and Suites, Sonatilla, Silhouettes from the Screen, Cinema Close-Ups, Half-Minute Lyrics; (piano four hands) Images of an Artistic Infant, Toy Suite, Around a Stump, The Young Virtuoso; (two pianos) Pieces Ensemble; (violin, cello and piano) From My Youth, Trio in G Minor; (organ) Seven Preludes, Sonata C Major, From the Hickory and the Cotton; (violin and piano) Romance, 3 Sonatas, Suite Petite, Suwanee Sketches, Three Interpretative Dances, Scenes from a Marionette Operette; (orchestra) Symphonies I, II, III, IV, V; (songs) Echoes from Childhood, Songs for Children; 30 Songs with Elizabethan poets' texts, and smaller works. Compositions have been played by Chicago Symphony Orchestra, Los Angeles Orchestra, New York Philharmonic Orchestra, etc. Author: The Rhetoric of Music; Harmonic and Melodic Technical Studies; Orchestral Training. Awarded $500 prize for "New Orleans" (Mardi Gras) Overture, offered by Hugo Riesenfeld, of the Rivoli and Rialto theatres, for best original Am. overture, Oct. 8, 1920; Overture "1849" composed for The Covered Wagon (picture); a scenic fantasy My Country (Robt. C. Bruce, Wilderness Tales); original symphonic score for The Thief of Bagdad, Don Q, Son of Zorro, and The Black Pirate (Douglas Fairbanks' feature films); string quartette, "In Rural California"; suite for orchestra, "Music and Calories." Home: New York, N.Y. Died Jan. 27, 1932.

WILSON, Nathaniel, lawyer; b. Zanesville, O., Aug. 9, 1836; s. Charles G. and Harriet (Abbot) W.; A.B., Shurtleff Coll., Ill., 1856; m. Annie E. Hutton, Oct. 6, 1863. Admitted to bar, 1861; asst. U.S. dist. atty., 1861-66; was spl. counsel Navy Dept., counsel for Salvage Assn., Lloyds. Mem. Am. Geog. Soc., Am. Bar Assn.; pres. Bar Assn. D.C. 4 terms; mem. Am. Soc. Internat. Law. Home: Washington, D.C. Died Oct. 23, 1922.

WILSON, Philip Sheridan, educator; b. Gorham, Me., Aug. 25, 1869; s. Joel and Addie (Waterhouse) W.; grad. Newton (N.J.) Acad., 1886; A.B., Lafayette Coll., Easton, Pa., 1890; post-grad. work in Europe and at Columbia; m. Annie E. Ferens Lockwood, Dec. 30, 1899. Prin. Newton Acad., 1900—. Mayor of Newton, 1914-17; mem. N.J. Ho. of Assembly, 1917, 18. Republican. Presbyn. Mason. Odd Fellow. Home: Newton, N.J. Died Dec. 4, 1926.

WILSON, Philip St. Julien, civil engr.; b. Powhatan Co., Va., May 30, 1867; s. Samuel M. and Sallie B. (Cocke) W.; prep. edn. Episcopal High Sch., Va.; C.E., Va. Mil. Inst., 1886; unmarried. Instr. mathematics and engring., at Suffolk, Va., 1887-91; asst. city engr., Richmond, Va., 1902-06; state highway commr. of Va., 1906-13; asst. dir. Bur. Pub. Roads, Washington, D.C., 1914-16; chief engr. Bur. Pub. Roads, U.S. Dept. Agr., 1916—. Served as capt. inf., Spanish-Am. War. Democrat. Episcopalian. Mason. Home: Washington, D.C. Died Sept. 17, 1936.

WILSON, Robert Burns, artist, author; b. Washington Co., Pa., Oct. 30, 1850; ed. at home and at local schools in Va.; began painting portraits for a living at 19; at 22 removed to Va. and soon after to Frankfort; exhibited landscapes, etc., at Louisville Expn., 1883; also at New Orleans Expn., 1885. Author: Life and Love (poems); Until the Day Break (novel), 1900. Home: Frankfort, Ky. Died 1916.

WILSON, Robert Edward Lee, financier; b. Golden Lake, Ark., Mar. 5, 1865; s. Joseph H. W.; m. Elizabeth Adams Beall, Jan. 20, 1885. Agriculturist, mfr. and investor; chmn. of board Farmers Bank & Trust Co. (Blytheville, Ark.), Bank of Luxora, Bank of Wilson (both of Ark.); pres. Bank of Keiser, Wilson Power & Light Co., Miss. River Western Ry. Co. (all of Ark.), Silica Real Estate Co. (Mo.); v.p. Kansas City Shook & Mfg. Co., Wilson-Ward Co. (Memphis, Tenn.). Trustee Jonesboro (Ark.) Agrl. and Mech. College, Hendrix-Henderson College (Conway, Ark.). K. of P. Home: Wilson, Ark. Died Sept. 27, 1933.

WILSON, S. Davis, mayor, lawyer; formerly city controller, Philadelphia; elected Republican mayor, November 1935; former Democrat. Home: Philadelphia, Pa. Died Aug. 19, 1939.

WILSON, Scott, judge; b. Falmouth, Me., Jan. 11, 1870; s. Nathaniel B. and Loemma Pearson (Leighton) W.; A.B., Bates Coll., 1892; LL.D., U. Me., 1920, Bates, 1923, same from Bowdoin, 1927; m. Elizabeth M. Bodge, Dec. 24, 1895 (died 1937); 1 son, Nathaniel Webb; m. 2d, Thelma Cony Dutton, Mar. 24, 1938. Admitted to Me. bar, 1895, and practiced in Portland as mem. Wilson & Bodge; city solicitor, Deering, 1899; asst. atty., Cumberland County, 1900-02; city solicitor, Portland, 1902-05; atty.-gen. of Me., 1913-14; asso. justice Supreme Judicial Court of Me., 1918-25, chief justice, 1925-29; judge U.S. Circuit Court of Appeals, 1st Circuit, Oct. 1929-Mar. 1940 (on active retired list). Mem. Federal, Maine and Am. bar assns. Republican. Mem. board fellows Bates Coll.; trustee Portland Pub. Library. Home: Portland, Me. Died Oct. 22, 1942.

WILSON, Thomas, judge; b. Tyrone Co., Ireland, May 16, 1827; s. Daniel and Fannie (Cuddy) W.; came to U.S., 1838; A.B., Allegheny (Pa.) Coll., 1852, A.M., 1855 (LL.D., 1901, and Macalester Coll., 1902); m. Louise Bennett, Dec. 26, 1860. Admitted to bar, 1855; settled at Winona, Minn. Ty., 1855; mem. Constl. Conv., 1857; dist. judge, 1857-64; chief justice Supreme Ct. of Minn., 1864-69 (resigned); mem. Minn. Ho. Rep., 1880, Senate, 1883-85; Dem. nominee for U.S. senator, 1885; mem. 50th Congress (1887-89), 1st Minn. Dist.; gen. counsel, C.,St.P., (1887-89), 1st Minnesota District; general counsel, C.,St.P.,M.&O. Ry. Co., St. Paul, 1892—. Home: St. Paul, Minn. Deceased.

WILSON, Thomas, anthropologist; b. New Brighton, Pa., July 18, 1832; s. James and Lydia W.; ed. in public schools and privately, LL.D., Nat. Univ.; m. Virginia M. Robinson, Oct. 4, 1872. Practiced law 25 yrs.; consul of U.S. to Ghent, Nantes, Nice, 1881-87; curator prehistoric archeology, U.S. Nat. Museum, 1887—; prof. prehistoric anthropology, Nat. Univ., Washington, 1889—; regent and sec. same. Republican. Mem. socs. of Anthropology, Washington, Paris, London, Brussels. Home: Washington, D.C. Died 1902.

WILSON, Warren Hugh, clergyman; b. Tidioute, Pa., May 1, 1867; s. John Sloan and Elizabeth (Hamilton) W.; A.B., Oberlin, 1890 (sophomore yr. at Wooster U., Ohio), D.D., 1915; B.D., Union Theol. Sem., 1894; Ph.D., Columbia, 1908; D.D., Washington Coll., Tenn., 1912, Tusculum Coll., Tenn., 1912; LL.D., Berea Coll., 1920; m. Pauline Elizabeth Lane, June 20, 1894; children—Margaret, Julius Lane, John Albert, Agnes Elizabeth. Sec. Student Dept., N.Y. City Y.M.C.A., 1890-91; editor Intercollegian, 1891-93; ordained Presbyn. ministry, 1894; pastor Christ's Ch., Quaker Hill, N.Y., 1894-99, Arlington Av. Ch., Brooklyn, 1899-1908; sec. Dept. of Ch. and Country Life, Bd. of Home Missions Presbyn. Ch. U.S.A. (now Presbyn. Bd. Nat. Missions), 1908—. Asso. in edn., Teachers Coll. (Columbia U.), 1914-23; instructor Union Theol. Seminary, 1927—. Pres. Internat. Assn. of Agrl. Missions, 1919-29; tech. consultant in Survey of Christian Mass Movement, under auspices Nat. Christian Council of India, 1930-31. Fellow Am. Geog. Society; member Am. Sociol. Society, Acad. Polit. Science City of New York. Author: Quaker Hill, 1908; The Church of the Open Country, 1911; The Evolution of the Country Community, 1912; The Church at the Center, 1915; The Second Missionary Adventure, 1915; The Farmers' Church, 1925; Rural Religion, 1927. Service with Y.M.C.A. and Ednl. Corps, in France, Jan.-June 1919. Home: New York, N.Y. Died Mar. 2, 1937.

WILSON, William, army officer; b. Seneca, N.Y., June 16, 1855; s. James and Anna H. (Whitney) W.; A.B., Hobart Coll., Geneva, N.Y., 1876, A.M., 1879; m. Mary E. Hipple, Nov. 20, 1878; 1 son, James Whitney. In nursery business on own account, at Geneva, until 1899; entered hardware business, 1899; burned out Feb. 20, 1916 (retired). Enlisted as pvt. 34th Separate Co., N.G.N.Y., Jan. 21, 1880; commd. 1st lt., Feb. 28, 1882; promoted through grades to bvtd. brig. gen., Oct. 29, 1907; brig. gen. 4th Brigade, June 10, 1914; brig. gen. of the line, Mar. 1917; brig. gen. N.A., Sept. 5, 1917. Comd. 3d N.Y. Brigade, on Mexican border, June-Dec. 1916; comdr. Guards, Eastern Dept., Aug.-Nov. 1917; comdr. 78th Inf. Brigade, Camp Beauregard, Alexandria, La., Nov. 1, 1917-Jan. 3, 1918; comdr. 2d Prov. Brigade, Camp Wadsworth, Spartanburg, S.C., Jan.-Nov. 1918; comdg. Gen. Prov. Dept. for Corps and Army Troops, Nov. 1918-Mar. 1919; comdg. gen. Camp Wadsworth, Jan.-Apr. 1919; hon. disch., July 18, 1919; brig. gen. U.S.A., retired, June 21, 1928. Mem. staff of Gov. Theodore Roosevelt, N.Y., 1899-1900; mem. Militia Council of New York, 1912, 13; mem. State Bd. of Armory Commrs. of N.Y., 1914-19. Presbyterian. Home: Nobleton, Fla. Died Jan. 6, 1937.

WILSON, William Bauchop, sec. of labor; b. Blantyre, Scotland, Apr. 2, 1862; s. Adam and Helen Nelson (Bauchop) W.; came to U.S., 1870; common sch. edn., Pa.; LL.D., Md. State Agrl. Coll., 1914, Ursinus Coll., 1918; m. Agnes Williamson, June 7, 1883 (died 1920). Miner, 1871-98; sec. and treas. Nat. Union of Miners, 1900-08. Mem. 60th to 62d Congresses (1907-13), 15th Pa. Dist.; sec. of labor in Cabinet of President Wilson, Mar. 5, 1913-Mar. 5, 1921; now engaged in mining and farming. Pres. dist. miners' union, 1888-90; mem. nat. exec. bd. which organized United Mine Workers of America, 1890; mem. com. to revise and codify bituminous mining laws of Pa., 1891; A. F. of L. del. to Brit. Trade Union Congress, 1910; chmn. on labor, 62d Congress; chmn. spl. com. of Ho. of Rep. to investigate Taylor and other systems of scientific shop management, 1911-12; mem. Federal Bd. Vocational Edn., 1914-21 (chmn. 1920-21); mem. Council Nat. Defense, 1916-21; mem. Internat. Joint Commn., Mar. 5-21, 1921. Dem. candidate for U.S. Senate from Pa., 1926; selected, 1929, as arbitrator between Ill. coal operators and miners under wage agreement expiring Mar. 31, 1932. Pres. Internat. Labor Conf., 1919. Hon. pres. The Great President Woodrow Wilson Polish Memorial Mound Assn. America, 1931. Presbyn. Mason. Home: Blossburg, Pa. Died May 26, 1934.

WILSON, William Hasell, pres. Belvidere Delaware R.R. Co.; b. Charleston, S.C., Nov. 5, 1811; s. John and Eliza (Gibbes) W.; ed. there and Phila.; in service State of Pa. in engr. corps, chainman to prin. asst. engr., 1827-34; m. Jane Millers, April 26, 1836 (died 1898). Prin. asst. engr. Phila. & Reading R.R., 1835-38; in gen. engring. practice, 1838-57; resident engr. Pa. R.R., 1857-62; chief engr., 1862-74; organized real estate dept. and was at its head, 1874-84; then pres. and dir. of several cos. whose roads are leased by Pa. R.R. Co. Home: Philadelphia, Pa. Died 1902.

WILSON, William Henry, congressman; b. Philadelphia, Pa., Dec. 6, 1877; LL.B., U. of Pa., 1898; m. Florence Klauder, 1902; 1 dau., Mrs. Dorothea Wilson Collier. Admitted to Pa. bar, 1899, and engaged in practice at Phila.; partner Wilson & McAdams; asst. city solicitor, 1900-09; mem. Pa. Ho. of Rep., 1913-15; dir. pub. safety, Phila., 1916-20; mem. 74th Congress (1935-37), 2d Pa. Dist. Republican. Home: Philadelphia, Pa. Deceased.

WILSON, William Powell, museum dir.; b. Oxford, Mich., Oct. 17, 1844; s. Dr. William Hawxhurst and Elizabeth Weeks (Dean) W.; B.S., Harvard, 1878; Dr. Nat. Sci., U. of Tübingen, 1880; m. Jessie Willcox, 1882 (dec.); 1 dau., Mildred; m. 2d, Lucy Langdon Williams, July 17, 1893; 1 son, David Hawxhurst. Asst. in Bot. Lab., Harvard, 1874-77; prof. anatomy and physiology of plants, 1884-96, dir. Sch. of Biology, 1890-94, U. of Pa.; founded, 1893, and from then dir. Phila. Commercial Mus. Traveled extensively, studying trade and econ. conditions; dir. gen. Nat. Export Expn., 1899; chmn. Philippine Expn. Bd. St. Louis Expn., 1904; commercial attaché Pan-Am. Congress, Mexico; rep. of State of Pa. and City of Phila. at Brazilian Centennial Celebration, 1922; Am. del. at large to Americanists Congress, Rio de Janeiro, 1922. Home: Philadelphia, Pa. Died May 12, 1927.

WILSON, William Robert Anthony, author; b. Washington, Ill., Jan. 28, 1870; s. Dr. R. B. M. and Jane Frances (Anthony) W.; A.B., Williams Coll., 1892; M.D., Coll. Phys. and Surg., Columbia, 1895; m. J. Amy Barnes, Mar. 9, 1897. Formerly practiced medicine (from 1895) at Peoria, Ill. Author: A Rose of Normandy, 1903; A Knot of Blue, 1905; Comrades Three, 1906; The King's Scouts, 1907; Journeys of the Kitkat Club, 1908. Home: Pittsfield, Mass. Died 1911.

WILSON, Woodrow, twenty-eighth President of the United States; b. Staunton, Va., Dec. 28, 1856; s. Rev. Joseph R. and Jessie (Woodrow) W.; Scotch-Irish ancestry on both sides; Davidson Coll., N.C., 1874-75; A.B., Princeton, 1879, A.M., 1882; grad. in law, U. of Va., 1881; practiced law at Atlanta, Ga., 1882-83; post-grad. work at Johns Hopkins, 1883-85, Ph.D., 1886; (LL.D., Wake Forest, 1887, Tulane, 1898, Johns Hopkins, 1902, Rutgers, 1902, U. of Pa., 1903, Brown, 1903, Harvard, 1907, Williams, 1908, Dartmouth, 1909; Litt.D., Yale, 1901; m. Ellen Louise Axson, June 24, 1885 (died 1914); m. 2d, Edith Bolling Galt, Dec. 18, 1915. Asso. prof. history and polit. economy, Bryn Mawr College, 1885-88; prof. same, Wesleyan University, 1888-90; prof. jurisprudence and political economy, 1890-95, prof. jurisprudence, 1895-97, prof. jurisprudence and politics, 1897-1910, pres., Aug. 1, 1902-Oct.20, 1910, Princeton U.; gov. of N.J., Jan. 17, 1911-Mar. 1, 1913 (resigned); nominated for President in Dem. Nat. Conv., Baltimore, 1912, and elected Nov. 4, 1912, for term, Mar. 4, 1913-Mar. 4, 1917, receiving 435 electoral votes; Theodore Roosevelt, the Progressive nominee received 88 votes, and William Howard Taft, the Republican nominee received 8 votes. Renominated for President in Dem. Nat. Conv., St. Louis, 1916, and reëlected Nov. 7, 1916, for term Mar. 4, 1917-Mar. 4, 1921, receiving 277 electoral votes; Charles E. Hughes, the Republican nominee received 254 electoral votes. Left for France on the troopship George Washington, Dec. 4, 1918, at the head of Am. Commn. to Negotiate Peace; arrived at Brest, Dec. 13, at Paris, Dec. 14; visited Eng., Dec. 26-30, 1918, Italy, Jan. 2-6, 1919, Belgium, June 18-19, 1919; delivered many addresses and given hon. degrees by various univs. of allied countries; returned to U.S., arriving in Boston, Feb. 24, 1919; left New York on 2d trip to Europe, Mar. 5, after speaking at closing session of Congress and arrived in Paris, Mar. 14; signed Peace Treaty, June 28, 1919; returned to U.S., arriving in New York, July 8, 1919. Author: Congressional Government, a Study in American Politics, 1885; The State—Elements of Historical and Practical Politics, 1889; Division and Reunion, 1829-1889, 1893; An Old Master and Other Political Essays, 1893; Mere Literature, and Other Essays, 1893; George Washington, 1896; A History of the American People, 1902; Constitutional Government in the United States, 1908; The State-Elements of Historical and Practical Politics, new edit., 1911; Free Life, 1913; The New Freedom, 1913; When a Man Comes to Himself, 1915; On Being Human, 1916. Home: Washington, D.C. Died Feb. 3, 1924.

WILSON, Mrs. Woodrow (Ellen Axson Wilson); b. (Ellen Louise Axson) at Savannah, Ga.; d. Samuel Edward and Margaret Jane (Hoyt) Axson; ed. at home and at Woman's Coll., Rome, Ga.; studied at Art Students' League, New York; m. Woodrow Wilson (28th President of U.S.), at Savannah, June 24, 1885. Hon. pres. Southern Ind. Ednl. Assn., Woman's Dept. of Nat. Civic Assn., and many other socs.; mem. Assn. Women Painters and Sculptors. Actively interested in philanthropic work, also in painting; has exhibited landscape paintings in Nat. Acad., New York, Phila. Academy Fine Arts, Art Inst. of Chicago, etc. Presbyn. Home: Washington, D.C. Died Aug. 6, 1914.

WILSTACH, Frank Jenners, theatrical mgr.; b. Lafayette, Ind., Oct. 20, 1865; s. John Augustine and Elbra Cecilia (Patti) W.; student Purdue University, Lafayette, Indiana, 1879-81, Seton Hall, South Orange, N.J., 1882-84; m. Edith May Hudnall, July 11, 1889. Business mgr. DeWolf Hopper, 1889-1901, Viola Allen, 1902-08, William Faversham, 1908-10, Mrs. Leslie Carter, 1911-12, E. H. Sothern and Julia Marlowe, 1912-15; Shubert Theatrical Co., 1916-23; became gen. press rep. Sam H. Harris. Republican. Author: Wilstach's Dictionary of Similes. Home: New York, N.Y. Died Nov. 28, 1933.

WILTBANK, William White, judge; b. Stratford, Conn., Mar. 27, 1840; s. Edwin Wilson and Elizabeth (Macpherson) W.; g.g.s. of Right Rev. William White, 1st P.E. bishop of Pa., who brought to America the succession of established Ch. of England; ed. Trinity Coll. Hartford, Conn. (hon. A.M., 1868); m. Edith A. Brinton, Sept. 10, 1863 (died 1893); m. 2d, Frances de Lancey Welsh, Nov. 2, 1902. Mem. gen. staff Union Army, 1862-65; admitted to Pa. bar, 1866, later to bar U.S. Sup. Ct.; apptd. by gov., judge Ct. of Common Pleas, 1st Jud. Dist. of Pa., Dec. 7, 1896; elected judge same dist. for term, 1898-1908, reëlected for term, 1908-18. Republican. Episcopalian. Home: Philadelphia, Pa. Deceased.

WILTSIE, Charles Hastings, lawyer; b. Pittsford, N.Y., Jan. 13, 1859; s. James Martin and Emily Ward (Hastings) W.; of old Dutch Colonial ancestry; ed. Brockport (N.Y.) State Normal Sch.; A.B., U. of Rochester, 1880, A.M., 1883; studied at univs. of Göttingen and Berlin, 1880-81; m. Oct. 5, 1893, Harriet Potter Hart; 1 dau., Mary Emily. Admitted to N.Y. bar, 1883, and began practiced at Rochester. Trustee Perry's Victory Centennial Commn.; treas. Rochester Expn. and Horse Show, 1915-25; pres. Rochester Public Library, 1922-33; mem. Rochester Municipal Mus., Rochester Athenæum and Mechanics Inst., Saratoga Battlefield Assn. Republican. Presbyn. Author: Law of Mortgage Foreclosure (2 vols.), 1889, 4th edit., 1927. Extensive traveler. Home: Rochester, N.Y. Died May 9, 1935.

WIMAN, Erastus, mercantile agt.; b. Churchville, Ont., Can., April 21, 1834; s. Erastus W.; ed. common schools; served 5 yrs. as printer's apprentice, Toronto; m. Eleanor Anne Galbraith, 1860. Entered mercantile agency service, 1858, at Toronto; removed, 1862, to Montreal; to New York, 1867; mgr. R. G. Dun & Co., 1867-92. Revolutionized transportation service from New York to Staten Island, increasing it from 15 to 65 trips per day; built Arthur Kill Bridge, connecting Staten Island with main land, rendering 10 miles of New York harbor accessible to trunk lines; was prominent advocate of better relations with Canada; his suggestions adopted by Canadian Liberal party; established Mutual Mercantile Agency, 1899. In 1902 revised charter of steam rys. known as Jersey Junction and got Congressional authority to construct tunnel under Bay of New York, making connection between Long Island and Staten Island, thence connecting with trunk lines in N.J. by Arthur Kill Bridge. Originated at Reciprocity Conv., Mich., the idea of and movement for a zollverein between all countries of N. and S. America Mem. Chamber Commerce, State of N.Y.; Bd. Trade and Transportation. Home: New Brighton, S.I., N.Y. Died 1904.

WINANS, Charles Sumner, consul gen.; b. Tyre, N.Y., Jan. 25, 1863; s. Benj. and Mary Jane (Sumner) W.; Albion (Mich.) Coll., 1885-89; m. Emma Rosina Kempf, Sept. 30, 1890; children—Llewellyn Kempf, Hubert Charles, Clarice Emma. Formerly wholesale and retail mcht. and importer Am. goods in Chile; pres. Iquique English Coll. 10 yrs.; Am. consul at Iquique, 1900-07, Valencia, Spain, 1907-09, Seville, 1909-14, Nuremberg, Germany, 1914-17, Cienfuegos, Cuba, 1917-19, London, England, 1919-20, Prague, Czechoslovakia, 1920-28 (retired). Am. consul gen., June 1924; foreign service officer, class III, July 1, 1924. Methodist. Officer Order of White Lion (Czechoslovakia). Home: Washington, D.C. Died July 14, 1935.

WINANS, Samuel Ross, university prof.; b. Lyons Farms, N.J., March 1, 1855; s. Samuel Ross and Ann (Woodruff) W.; A.B., Princeton, 1874, Ph.D., 1882; m. Sarah E. Macdonald, July 27, 1886. Tutor in Greek, 1876-81, adj. prof. Greek and instr. Sanskrit, 1881-83, prof. Greek and instr. Sanskrit, 1883—, dean of faculty, 1899-1903, Princeton. Editor: Xenophon's Memorabilia, 1880; Symposium, 1881; Libri Socratici, 1883, etc. Home: Princeton, N.J. Died 1910.

WINBIGLER, Charles Fremont, clergyman, author; b. Middletown, Md., Jan. 9, 1857; s. William Perry and Frances O'Levy (Smith) W.; Ph.B., Mt. Union Coll., Alliance, O., 1879; Ph.M., Oberlin Theol. Sem., 1887; grad. Osteopathic Coll., Phila., 1902; m. Adelia Oliver, Dec. 22, 1881. Ordained Bapt. ministry, 1889; pastor 1st Ch., Riverside, Calif., 1889-94, 1st Ch., Bloomington, Ill., 1894-96, Frankford Av. Ch., Phila., 1896-1902, 1st Ch., Washington, D.C., 1902-09; lecturer on religious and health subjects, 1909—; pastor Central Bapt. Ch., Los Angeles, 1920—. Founder Christian League of Healing. Republican. Mason, Odd Fellow. Author: Christian Science and Kindred Subjects, 1906; Suggestion—Its Law and Application, 1909; How to Help and Heal Others, 1916; How to Help and Heal One's Self, 1916. Home: Los Angeles, Calif. Died Jan. 6, 1925.

WINBOURN, Robert Emmet, atty. gen. of Colorado; b. nr. Evans, Colo., July 2, 1882; s. Thomas Cornelius and Emma Jane (Jackson) W.; student Denver U., 1902-03; LL.B., George Washington U., 1908; m. Catharine Kehl, Nov. 26, 1913. Sec. to Robert W. Bonynge, congressman, 1904-08; admitted to Colo. bar, 1909; prosecutor pub. land frauds, U.S. Gen. Land Office, Denver, 1908-10; began gen. practice at Greeley, 1911. County atty., Weld Co., Colo., 1911-13; mem. Colo. State Senate, 1914-16; atty. gen. Colo., term 1929-31. Republican. Conglist. Mason, K.P., Elk, Woodman of World. Home: Greeley, Colo. Died Aug. 7, 1930.

WINBURN, Hardy Lathan, clergyman; b. Bells, Tenn., Apr. 16, 1877; s. Hardy Lathan and Susan Caroline (Sinclair) W.; B.S., Southwestern Bapt. U., Jackson, Tenn., 1899; D.D., Ouachita Coll., Ark., 1912, Union U., Tenn., 1912; LL.D., Georgetown Coll., Ky., 1921; m. Lena May Barnes, July 11, 1899; children—Hardy L., Martha Jean, Wade B., Sinclair W., Cherry, William H., Nancy Lynn. Ordained Bapt. ministry, 1897; pastor Tullahoma, Tenn., 1899-1900, Taylorville, Ill., 1900-03, 1st Ch., Arkadelphia, Ark., 1903-14, Walnut St. (1st) Ch., Louisville, Ky., 1914-18, 1st Ch., Arkadelphia, Ark. (2d time), Nov. 1918—. On exec. com. S. Bapt. Conv.; pres. and gen. mgr. Ark Summer Assembly, 1904-13; pres. Bapt. Edn. Soc. of Ky., 1914-19; pres. Ark. Bapt. State Conv., 1926-29; trustee Southern Bapt. Theol. Sem. Author: A Man and His Money; Lead Hunters of the Ozarks: First Christian Impulses. Democrat. Spl. lecturer Ouachita Coll., 1921-25. Home: Arkadelphia, Ark. Died Sept. 3, 1937.

WINCHELL, Horace Vaughn, econ. geologist; b. Galesburg, Mich., Nov. 1, 1865; s. Newton Horace and Charlotte Sophia (Imus) W.; brother of Alexander Newton W.; B.S., U. of Michigan, 1889; m. Ida Belle Winchell, Jan. 15, 1890. Asst. state geologist, Minn., 1889-91; in charge explorations Minn. Iron Co., 1892-93; in gen. practice as econ. geologist and mining engr., 1893-97; geologist for Anaconda Copper Mining Co. and for other auxiliary corps. of the Amalgamated Copper Co., 1898-1906; cons. geologist Amalgamated Copper Co., 1906—; chief geologist G.N. Ry. Co., 1906-08; in general practice, 1908—. Asso. editor Zeitschrift für praktische Geologie of Berlin and Economic Geology. Author: (with Prof. N. H. Winchell) The Iron Ores of Minnesota, 1891. Home: Los Angeles, Calif. Died July 28, 1923.

WINCHELL, Newton Horace, geologist, archeologist; b. North East, N.Y., Dec. 17, 1839; s. Horace and Caroline (McAllister) W.; brother of Samuel Robertson W.; A.B., U. of Mich., 1866, A.M., 1869; m. Charlotte Sophia Imus, Aug. 24, 1864; father of Horace Vaughn and Alexander Newton Winchell. Superintendent public schools, Adrian, Mich., 1866-69; asst. state geologist, Mich., 1869-70; asst. geol. survey, Ohio, 1870-72; state geologist of Minn., 1872-1900; prof. geology and mineralogy, U. of Minn., 1873-1900; archeologist, Minn. Historical Soc., May 1906—. Member U.S. Assay Commn., 1887, founder and editor, Am. Geologist, 1888-1905. Author: Catalogue of the Plants of the State of Michigan, 1861; Geology of Ohio and Minnesota, 1872-1900; The Iron Ores of Minnesota (with Horace V. Winchell), 1891; Elements of Optical Mineralogy (with Alex. N. Winchell), 1909; The Aborigines of Minnesota; The Paleoliths of Kansas; also papers in scientific jours. Home: Minneapolis, Minn. Died May 2, 1914.

WINCHESTER, Caleb Thomas, university prof.; b. Montville, Conn., Jan. 18, 1847; s. Rev. George F. and Lucy (Thomas) W.; A.B., Wesleyan, 1869, A.M., 1872; U. of Leipzig, 1880-81; (L.H.D., Dickinson, 1892); m. Julia Stackpole Smith, Dec. 25, 1872 (died 1877); m. 2d, Alice Goodwin Smith, Apr. 2, 1880. Librarian, 1869-73; prof. rhetoric and English lit., 1873-90, prof. English lit., 1890—, Wesleyan U. Mem. com. revision of Meth. Hymnal, 1904. Author: Five Short Courses of Reading English Literature, 1892, 3d revised edit., 1911; Some principles of Literary Criticism, 1899; Life of John Wesley, 1906; A Group of English Essayists, 1910; Representative English Essays, with introductions and notes, 1914; Wordsworth—How to Know Him, 1916. Home: Middletown, Conn. Died Mar. 24, 1920.

WINCHESTER, Charles Wesley, clergyman; b. Westminster, Vt., July 2, 1843; s. Jonathan A. and Fannie B. (Wetherell) W.; A.B., Syracuse U., 1867, A.M., 1870 (D.D., 1892); m. Mary Pengra, July 22, 1868; m. 2d, Mrs. Ella Winchester, 1910. Teacher in sems., Fairfield and Cazenovia, N.Y., 1867-70; ordained M.E. ministry, 1872; prin. E. Genesee Conf. Sem., Ovid, N.Y., 1870-71; pastor in N.Y. at Enfield, 1871-72, Millport, 1872-75, Palmyra, 1875-78, Park Church, Hornell, 1878-81. Asbury Ch., Rochester, 1881-82, Plymouth Ch., Buffalo, 1882-85, Batavia, 1885-88, Medina, 1888-91; presiding elder Corning Dist., 1891-97; pastor Wellsville, N.Y., 1897-1900, Sentinel Ch., Buffalo, 1900-02; editor Christian Uplook, Buffalo, 1902-04; pres. Taylor U., Upland, Ind., 1904-07; pastor Seneca St. Ch., Buffalo, 1907-09, Port Allegany, Pa., 1909-11, Olean, N.Y., 1911-13 (retired). Sec. Genesee Conf., 1881-91; del. Ecumenical Conf., Washington, 1891, Gen. Conf., 1896. Author: The Gospel Kodak Abroad, 1890; The Wells of Salvation, 1897; The Victories of Wesley Castle, 1900; What Protestants Believe, 1915; Reminiscences of Fifty Years in Christian Service, 1915. Home: Kenmore, N.Y. Deceased.

WINCHESTER, James Ridout, bishop; b. Annapolis, Md., Mar. 15, 1852; s. Jacob and Mary (Ridout) W.; desc. John Winchester, Kent Island, Md., 1644; A.B., Ph.B., Washington and Lee U., Va., 1874; P.E. Theol. Sem., Alexandria, Va., 1877; D.D., U. of the South, 1893, Washington and Lee U., 1894; m. Eliza Atkinson Lee, Sept. 17, 1878 (died 1936); children—Richard Henry Lee, Lucy Langhorne, James Ridout (all dec.), Evelyn Lee (Mrs. Jas. E. Montgomery), Cassius Lee, Florence W. (Mrs. Wm. G. Mayburry, dec.). Deacon, 1877, priest, 1878, P.E. Ch.; asst., St. James' Ch., Richmond, Va., 1877-78; rector, Uniontown, Ala., 1878-80, Wytheville, Va.,

1880-82, Christ Ch., Macon, Ga., 1882-90, Christ Ch., Nashville, Tenn., 1890-98, Ch. Ascension, St. Louis, 1898-1906, Calvary Church, Memphis, Tenn., 1906-11; consecrated coadjutor bishop of Ark., Sept. 29, 1911, later became the diocesan in fact; retired, 1931. Chaplain 1st Tenn. Vols., Spanish-Am. War; chaplain Ark. Soc., S.C.V.; v.p. 7th Province P.E. Ch.; trustee Univ. of the South. Mason. Democrat. Traveled in Europe, Turkey, Egypt and Palestine and has made spl. study of archeology. Home: Chicago, Ill. Died Oct. 27, 1941.

WINDER, Adam Heber, lawyer; b. Miamisburg, O., May 2, 1882; s. Perry Albert and Margaret Allie (Miller) W.; LL.B., Cornell U., 1908; m. Helen Adelle Dobbs, July 18, 1912; children—Beatrice Mae (Mrs. Jack Martin), Willard Heber. Teacher of grade school, near Dayton, O., 1900-02; prin. Fairview High Sch., Dayton, 1902-04; admitted to Ohio bar, 1908, and practiced in Dayton, 1908-10; teacher Hanford (Calif.) High Sch., 1910-11; admitted to Calif. bar and practiced in Riverside, Calif., 1911—; asso. counsel Met. Water Dist. of Southern Calif. (Los Angeles and 12 other cities); legal advisor La Sierra Coll., Riverside; municipal judge, Riverside, 1911-12, city atty., 1912-15; dir. Security Title Ins. & Guarantee Co., Los Angeles. Mem. Rep. State Central Com., 1934—. Pres. Calif. State Bd. of Edn., 1937—; pres. Calif. State Teachers Retirement Bd.; mem. Riverside Bd. of Edn., 1928-30. Republican. Congregationalist. Mason. Author of "History of California Kiwanis District," 1927. Editor: Manual on Masonic Education, 1938. Home: Riverside, Calif. Died Oct. 19, 1940.

WINDES, Thomas G., judge; b. Morgan Co., Ala., Jan. 19, 1848; s. of Rev. Enoch and Mary A. (Ryan) W.; ed. Morgan Co., Ala., schools, 1853-63; acad. at Huntsville, Ala., 1866-67; studied law at U. of Va., and pvtly. at Huntsville, Ala., and Jasper, Tenn.; m. Sallie C. Humphrey, Dec. 3, 1868. Served cav. div. C.S.A., 1864-65; school teacher, 1868-70; farmer, 1871-72; law clerk and practicing lawyer, 1873-92; master in chancery, Circuit Ct., Cook Co., Ill., 1880-92; judge Circuit Ct. of Cook Co., 1892—; present term expires, 1927; chief justice, 1908. Democrat. Home: Winnetka, Ill. Died June 4, 1923.

WINDMÜLLER, Louis, merchant; b. Münster, 1835; ed. at Gymnasium there and self-taught; came to New York, 1853; m. Annie Eliza Lefman, a desc. of Capt. Thomas Lennington, of Revolutionary Army, Nov. 23, 1859. One of founders German-Am. Ins. Co., 1872, Title Guarantee & Trust Co., 1882; pres. Maiden Lane Savings Bank, New York; dir. in corps. Treas. Legal Aid Soc., which furnishes gratuitous legal advice to helpless strangers; treas. Reform Club, 1889—. Independent in politics; supported Cleveland on the tariff; with Carl Schurz and others formed the German-Am. Cleveland Union which greatly assisted in Cleveland's 2d election; supported McKinley on financial issue. His article, "A Strike for Lower Wages," in North American Review was used as a campaign document. Mng. dir. Bd. Trade and Transportation; life mem. N.Y. Hist. Soc.; mem. Germanistic Soc.; a v.p. of Germanic Museum Assn. of Cambridge, Mass. Chmn. for Queens Borough of Hudson-Fulton Celebration, 1909; dir. Tree Planting Assn. in Queens. Home: Woodside, Queens Borough, N.Y. Died Oct. 1, 1913.

WINDRIM, James Hamilton, architect; b. Philadelphia, July 4, 1840; m. Mary B. McCutcheon, of Phila. Planned and superintended many buildings of Phila.; supervising architect U.S. Treasury, 1889-91; dir. of public works of Phila., 1891. Home: Merion, Pa. Died Apr. 26, 1919.

WINDSOR, Henry Haven, editor, pub.; b. Mitchell, Ia., Nov. 13, 1859; s. Rev. William (D.D.) and Harriet Butler (Holmes) W.; ed. Ia. Coll.; m. Lina B. Jackson, June 25, 1889. City editor Times-Republican, Marshalltown, Ia., 1879-80; pvt. sec. to official N.P. Ry., St. Paul, 1881-82; sec. Chicago City Ry. Co., 1883-91; founder, editor and pres. Street Railway Review, 1892-1901; founder, 1901, and from then editor and pub. Popular Mechanics Magazine. Republican. Conglist. Owner of yacht Apache. Home: Evanston, Ill. Died May 11, 1924.

WINDSOR, William Augustus, naval officer; b. in Va., Feb. 13, 1842; s. Griffith and Eliza (Fouchée) W.; ed. grammar and high schs., Baltimore; studied engring. in pvt. sch. of Richard C. Potts, Baltimore, and in drawing room and shops of B.&O. R.R. Co.; m. Rachel Josephine Noble, June 11, 1874. Apptd. 3d asst. engr., U.S.N., Sept. 16, 1862; 2d asst. engr., Aug. 8, 1864; promoted passed asst. engr., Jan. 1, 1868; chief engr. U.S.N. (rank lt. comdr.), June 17, 1889, and of relative rank of comdr., Feb. 26, 1897; made comdr. by Act of Congress, Mar. 3, 1899; promoted capt. U.S.N., Dec. 27, 1901; rear admiral U.S.N. and retired, Sept. 16, 1902. During Civ. War attached to U.S.S. Miami, N. Atlantic squadron, and U.S.S. Nyack, and after war served on various vessels and stas., last sea service being on U.S.S. Minneapolis, 1897-98; chief engr. (head dept. steam engring.) Navy Yard, New York, 1898-99; insp. machinery at Crescent Ship Yard, Elizabeth, N.J., and Babcock & Wilson Works, Bayonne, N.J., 1899-1903. Episcopalian. Died 1907.

WINEMAN, Mode, musician, widely known for his non-professional camera studies of nat. parks and other Am. wilderness scenes; b. Chicago, May 28, 1865; s. Martin and Henrietta (Meyer) W.; graduate of Hershey School of Musical Art, Chicago, 1884. Mem. faculty, Chicago Conservatory, 1898; moved to Calif., 1911. In Chicago, did sociol. work in Home for the Friendless, and Chicago Orphan Asylum. Was only pupil of F. Marion Crawford; published various sketches of outdoor life; spl. corr. in Europe and America, Chicago Evening Post, etc. Camera studies have been exhibited free in various cities and many have been reproduced in mags., newspapers, and books; one-man exhibit of 162 pictures inaugurated Pasadena Golden Jubilee exhbns., 1924; collection of 34 studies of Yosemite Nat. Park became part of permanent exhibit, Yosemite Museum, 1925; devoted much attention, 1916-25, to Calif. desert canyons which are to become a nat. reservation. Collection of 30 studies of Yellowstone Nat. Park became permanent exhibit Yellowstone Mus., 1926; collection of 34 studies of Grand Canyon Nat. Park became permanent exhibit Grand Canyon Mus., 1926; collection of 161 studies became permanent exhibit Los Angeles Mus., 1926. Thirty-two studies of native Calif. wild palms added to Los Angeles Mus. collection, 1927. Mem. President Coolidge's party, Yellowstone Nat. Park, 1927; result, Calvin Coolidge room of 21 studies with President in landscapes, in Yellowstone Mus.; also 109 new studies added to Mode Wineman Yellowstone collection; completed desert camera studies for Los Angeles Mus., 1929; added 27 studies to Yosemite Mus., 1930; prepared 24 camera studies of nat. parks for President Hoover, 1931. Received citation from Nat. Parks Supts.' Conf., 1928, Pasadena Post No. 13, Am. Legion, 1929. Died Dec. 22, 1933.

WINES, Frederick Howard, statistician; b. Philadelphia, Pa., Apr. 9, 1838; s. Rev. Enoch Cobb and Emma (Stansbury) W.; grad. Washington Coll., Pa., 1857; studied at Princeton Theol. Sem., but left because of weakness of eyes; licensed by Presbytery of St. Louis, 1860; chaplain U.S.A., 1862-64; grad. Princeton Theol. Sem., 1865; m. Mary Frances Hackney, Mar. 21, 1865. Ordained Presbyn. ministry, 1865; pastor First Ch., Springfield, 1865-69; sec. Ill. State Bd. Commrs. Pub. Charities, 1869-93, 1897-99; asst. dir. U.S. Census, 1899-1902; sec. N.J. State Charities Aid Assn., 1903-04; statis. sec. Ill. State Bd. Administration of Pub. Instns., 1909—. Editor for Rep. Nat. Com., Chicago, 1896; spl. lecturer Lowell Inst., Boston, Harvard, Princeton, Johns Hopkins, U. of Wis., Ind. U. Mem. Internat. Prison Congress, Stockholm, 1878; pres. Nat. Conf. of Charities and Correction, 1883, Internat. Conf. of Charities and Correction, Chicago, 1903. Author: Defective Dependent and Delinquent Classes in the United States (vol. of 10th Census); Crime, Pauperism and Benevolence in the United States (vol. of 11th Census); Punishment and Reformation, 1895; The Liquor Problem in Its Legislative Aspects, 1897, 98. Home: Springfield, Ill. Died 1912.

WINFIELD, Arthur M., author. See Edward Stratemeyer.

WINFIELD, James Macfarlane, dermatologist; b. Ulster Park, N.Y., May 14, 1859; s. John Van Aken and Margaret Maria (Deyo) W.; coll. prep. course, Starr's Inst., Kingston, N.Y.; M.D., Bellevue Hosp. Med. Coll. (New York U.), 1882; m. Mabel Dunning, June 15, 1898. In practice at Brooklyn, 1884—; prof. dermatology, L.I. Med. Coll., 1905—; visiting dermatologist King's Co., L.I. Coll. hosps.; cons. dermatologist to the Nassau, St. Mary's (Jamaica), St. John's and other hospitals. Mem. Brooklyn Bd. of Health, 1895-98. Pres. Associated Physicians of L.I., 1900, N.Y. Dermatol. Soc., 1903; dir. and librarian Med. Soc. Co. of Kings, 1895-1905, pres., 1913; sec. Am. Dermatol. Assn., 1909-13, pres., 1913-14. Republican. Episcopalian. Home: Brooklyn, N.Y. Died Apr. 24, 1923.

WINFREY, Elisha William, clergyman; b. in Buckingham Co., Va., 1858; s. George Hill and Judith C. (Robertson) W.; ed. Richmond Coll.; D.D.; m. Roberta Jones Layne; children—Elisha W., Roberta Yancey, Mary Alice R., Geo. H. L., Davis Brockman, Katie V., Harris Bolling. Ordained Bapt. ministry, 1878; pastor Wallers, Mt. Hermon, Mt. Carmel, County Line and Bethany, Va., 1878-89, Culpeper, 1889—. Author: Our Lord (verse). Home: Culpeper, Va. Died Mar. 29, 1931.

WING, Asa Shove, insurance official; b. Sandwich, Mass., Jan. 29, 1850; s. Stephen Rogers and Elizabeth Collins (Shove) W.; ed. pub. and prep. schs.; m. Sophia Rhoads, Apr. 30, 1873 (died 1901); m. 2d, Elisabeth (Nicholson) Robeson Wood, Nov. 26, 1912. With Provident Life & Trust Co. of Phila. (now Provident Mut. Life Ins. Co. of Phila.), 1867—, and pres., 1906—; dir. Provident Trust Co. of Phila., Phila. Nat. Bank, Frankford & Southwark Phila. City Passenger R.R. Co. Charter mem. Actuarial Soc. America; corr. mem. French Inst. Actuaries. Republican. Mem. Friends Ch. Home: Moorestown, N.J. Died June 5, 1931.

WING, Charles Hallet, chemist; b. Boston, Mass., Aug. 4, 1836; s. Benjamin Franklin and Adeline (Hallet) W.; B.S., Harvard, 1870. Prof. chemistry, Cornell U., 1870, Mass. Inst. Tech., 1874-84. Fellow Am. Acad. Arts and Sciences, etc. Home: Brighton, Mass. Died Sept. 13, 1915.

WING, Daniel Gould, banker; b. Davenport, Ia., Sept. 10, 1868; s. George and Elizabeth (Gould) W.; pub. sch. edn.; m. Josephine Cable, Jan. 23, 1902. Messenger State Nat. Bank, Lincoln, Neb., 1885, and advanced through various positions until 1890; cashier Am. Exchange Nat. Bank, Lincoln, 1890-97; nat. bank examiner, 1897-1902; was receiver Broadway and Globe Nat. banks, Boston; pres. Mass. Nat. Bank, 1902, and upon consolidating with First Nat. Bank, 1903, became pres. of the reorganized First Nat. Bank; chmn. bd. same, 1926—; apptd. mem. bd. dirs. Nat. Credit Corp., Oct. 1931. Mem. Beacon Soc. Republican. Home: Brookline, Mass. Died Jan. 28, 1936.

WING, Francis Joseph, judge; b. N. Bloomfield, O., Sept. 14, 1850; s. Joseph Knowles and Mary (Brown) W.; ed. Phillips Acad., Andover, and Harvard U., 1868-71; m. Mary Brackett Remington, Sept. 25, 1878. Admitted to Ohio bar; asst. U.S. dist. atty., Northern Dist. Ohio, 1880-81; judge Ct. of Common Pleas, Cuyahoga Co., O., 1899-1901; U.S. dist. judge, Northern Dist. of Ohio, 1901-05 (resigned). Home: Cleveland, Ohio. Deceased.

WING, Henry Hiram, agrl. educator; b. New York, N.Y., Nov. 29, 1859; s. Phineas Rice and Mary (Sands) W.; B.Agr., Cornell U., 1881, M.S. in Agr., 1891; m. Lilian Watson, July 16, 1885; children—Mrs. Lois Watson Burrell, Paul Watson, Mrs. Ellen Watson Ackerman. Assistant director New York Agrl. Expt. Station, 1882-84; adj. prof. agr., Univ. of Neb., 1884-88; deputy dir. and sec. Cornell U. Agrl. Expt. Sta., 1888-94; asst. prof. animal industry and dairy husbandry, 1891-1903, prof. animal husbandry, 1903-28, Cornell Univ. Editor Neb. Farmer, 1887-88. Life member N.Y. State Agrl. Soc., N.Y. State Dairyman's Assn. (pres. 1909), Neb. Dairyman's Assn. (sec. 1885-88); fellow A.A.A.S. Conglist. Republican; alderman City of Ithaca, 1905-09. Author: Milk and Its Products, 1897. Home: Little Falls, N.Y. Died Nov. 21, 1936.

WING, Russell Merritt, lawyer; b. Big Grove Twp., Kendall Co., Ill., June 2, 1850; s. Russell and Mary (Hoag) W.; ed. Hillsdale Coll.; LL.B., Union Coll. of Law, Chicago, 1875; m. Amelia De Land, May 10, 1876. Admitted to bar, 1875; practiced at Morris, Ill., later at Joliet, Ill.; now head of Wing & Wing, Chicago. Democrat. Home: Wilmette, Ill. Died Jan. 4, 1919.

WINGATE, Charles Frederick, consulting sanitary engr.; b. New York, N.Y., March 5, 1848; s. Charles and Mary P. W.; ed. public schools and Cooper Inst. Engaged in mercantile business in early life, then in editorial work for 20 yrs.; for 5 yrs. New York corr. Springfield (Mass.) Republican, under signature "Carlfried." Founded the Twilight Club, 1883, and Twilight Park, in the Catskills, 1887. Author: Views and Interviews on Journalism; What Shall Our Boys Do for a Living?; Twilight Tracts; An Episode in Municipal Government (4 nos. N. Am. Rev.); etc. Home: Twilight Park, N.Y. Died 1909.

WINGATE, George Wood, lawyer; b. New York, N.Y., July 1, 1840; s. Charles and Mary P. (Robinson) W.; ed. pub. schs. Conducted constrn. of elevated rys. in Brooklyn; in 22d N.Y. Regt. during Civil War; m. Susan P. Man, July 31, 1867; children—Mary Helen (Mrs. Horatio Gates Lloyd), Louisa Man (Mrs. John Garrett Underhill), George Albert, Charles G. Introduced rifle practice in this country as a part of mil. instrn. in Nat. Guard; founded Creedmoor; was 1st gen. insp. rifle practice, 1st sec., and later pres. Nat. Rifle Assn. of U.S. for 25 yrs.; was spl. aid on nat. staff G.A.R. on mil. instrn. in pub. schs.; organizer and pres. Pub. Schs. Athletic League, and Brooklyn Inst. Safety; founder of Victory Hall. Author: Wingate's Manual of Rifle Practice, 1872; The Great Cholera Riots, 1880; On Horseback Through the Yellowstone, 1886; History of 22d Regt., N.G.N.Y., 1896. Asst. gen. counsel L.I. R.R.; mem. Bd. of Edn., New York, 1900-17. Home: Brooklyn, N.Y. Died Mar. 22, 1928.

WINGATE, Uranus Owen Brackett, physician; b. on farm, Rochester, N.H., Sept. 4, 1848; s. David, Jr. and Lydia Thompson (Wentworth) W.; ed. Lebanon Acad., Me.; attended Harvard Med. Sch.; M.D., Dartmouth, 1874; joined Union Army when 16 yrs. old; served in constrn. corps U.S. mil. rys., and in Sherman's army to close of war; resumed studies; m. Nellie West Schoonmaker, July 11, 1889. Practiced medicine at Wellesley, Mass., 1875-86; then at Milwaukee. Commr. of health, Milwaukee, 1890-94; sec. Wis. State Bd. Health, 1894-1904; prof. nervous and mental diseases, Wis. Coll. Phys. and Surg., 1894—; visiting neurologist St. Mary's and Milwaukee Co. hosps.; consultant in neurologs to St. Joseph's Hosp. Home: Milwaukee, Wis. Died 1911.

WINGO, Otis Theodore, congressman; b. Weakly Co., Tenn., June 18, 1877; s. Theodore Freelinghuysen and Pauline Elizabeth Jane (Johnson) W.; ed. Bethel Coll., McKenzie, Tenn., McFerrin Coll., Martin, Tenn., and Valparaiso U., Ind.; m. Effie Gene Locke, Oct. 15, 1902; children—Janie Blanche, Otis T. Admitted to Ark. bar, 1900; member Ark. State Senate, 1907-

09. Author of Wingo Corp. Act; of resolution leading to investigation of frauds in new state capitol constrn.; of act creating Teachers' Normal Training Sch., in Ark., and had charge of legislation in Senate creating 4 state agrl. schs.; mem. 63d to 71st Congresses (1913-31), 4th Ark. Dist.; senior Democrat of Banking and Currency Com., Ho. of Rep. Methodist. Mason. Home: De Queen, Ark. Died Oct. 21, 1930.

WINKLER, Max, philologist; b. Austria, Sept. 4, 1866; s. Simon M. and Mathilde (Greiwer) W.; came to Cincinnati, O., in childhood; A.B., Harvard, 1889; Ph.D., U. of Mich., 1892; U. of Berlin, 1892-93; m. Clemence Hamilton, 1906; 1 son, Alexander Woodward. Asst. prof. modern langs., U. of Kan., 1889-90; instr. German, U. of Mich., 1890-92, 1893-95, asst. prof., 1895-1900, acting prof., 1900-02, prof. German lang. and lit., 1902—, U. of Mich. Editor: Lessing's Emilia Galotti, 1895; Goethe's Egmont, 1898; Schiller's Wallenstein, 1901; Goethe's Iphigenie. Home: Ann Arbor, Mich. Died Mar. 14, 1930.

WINN, Frank Long, army officer; b. Winchester, Ky., Oct. 4, 1864; s. William and Carrie Sinclair (Hord) W.; student Centre Coll., Danville, Ky., 1880-81; grad. U.S. Mil. Acad., 1886, Army War Coll., 1916; m. Dora Boardman, Nov. 5, 1890 (died 1891); 1 dau., Dora (Mrs. Lovell Langstroth, dec.); m. 2d, Katharine McCord, Oct. 15, 1910. Commd. 2d lt. 1st Inf., July 1, 1886; promoted through grades to brig. gen. N.A., Aug. 5, 1917; maj. gen., Oct. 1, 1918; brig. gen. U.S.A., Oct. 2, 1921; promoted major general U.S.A., Dec. 2, 1922. In Sioux Indian Campaign, 1890-91; prof mil. science and tactics, U. of Calif., 1893-97; in Cuba, Spanish-Am. War, 1898; nominated bvt. capt. "for gallantry in action" at El Caney, July 1, 1898; assisted in subduing Philippine Insurrection, 1899-1901; nominated bvt. maj. "for gallantry in action," at Angeles, Luzon, Aug. 16, 1899; Mexican Punitive Expdn., 1916; mil. sec. of Lt. Gen. Arthur MacArthur, 1907-09; in command of 177th Infantry Brigade, Camp Funston, Kansas, Sept. 5, 1917-May 1918 and Sept. 7-Nov. 11, 1918, 89th Division, Nov. 5-12, 1917, Nov. 26, 1917-Apr. 12, 1918, May 31-Sept. 6, 1918, and Nov. 12, 1918, till demobilization, June 1919; comd. Camp Custer, Mich., June, July 1919; remanded to regular rank of col. U.S.A., 37th Inf., July 31, 1919. In front line, sector northwest of Toul, St. Mihiel drive, Meuse-Argonne operations, and with Army of Occupation in Germany. D.S.M. "for exceptionally meritorious and distinguished services," 1919; Croix de Guerre, 2 palms; Comdr. Legion of Honor. Insp. gen., Aug. 20, 1920; insp., 2d Corps Area, Sept. 17, 1920-May 8, 1921; gen. staff, chief of staff, 2d Corps Area, May 9, 1921, Oct. 24, 1921; comd. 4th Coast Art. Dist., Ft. McPherson, Ga., Jan.-Dec. 1922, and 4th Training Camp, McClellan, Ala., Apr.-Sept. 1922; retired, Dec. 5, 1922. Citations by War Dept., 1924, for gallantry in Cuba in 1898 during Spanish-Am. War and in Luzon, 1899, during Philippine Insurrection. Mason. Home: Palo Alto, Calif. Died Feb. 24, 1941.

WINN, Jane Frances, journalist; b. Chillicothe, Ohio; d. Thomas and Anne Margaret (Huse) W.; grad. Chillicothe High Sch.; spl. course, Starling Med. Coll., Columbus, O., and 5 summers at Harvard Summer Sch., specializing in botany and chemistry; unmarried. Teacher science dept., Chillicothe High Sch., 1884-1898; literary editor of Globe-Democrat, St. Louis, 1898—; mem. Ohio Acad. Science (v.p. 1890), English speaking Union, Foreign Policy Assn. Episcopalian. Home: St. Louis, Mo. Died Dec. 1927.

WINN, John Sheridan, army officer; b. in Ky., Nov. 26, 1863; grad. U.S. Mil. Acad., 1888. Commd. 2d lt. 2d Cav., June 11, 1888; 1st lt. 1st Cav., June 14, 1895; trans. to 2d Cav., Nov. 7, 1895; capt., Feb. 2, 1901; q.m., Apr. 9, 1907; assigned to 9th Cav., Apr. 9, 1911; maj. 4th Cav., July 23, 1911; trans. to 2d Cav., Aug. 31, 1911; insp. gen., Sept. 1, 1914; lt. col., July 1, 1916; nom. brig. gen. by Pres. Wilson, Jan. 4, 1918. Served at various southwestern posts until 1892; instr. mathematics, U.S. Mil. Acad., 1892-96; with regt. at Tampa, Fla., 1898, Matanzas, Cuba, 1902; duty in Philippine Islands, 1906-07; insp. gen. Southern Dept., 1917. Died Jan. 24, 1940.

WINNER, Septimus, prof. of music; b. Philadelphia, May 11, 1827; s. Joseph and Mary Ann W.; ed. in high school; m. Hannah J. Guyer, Nov. 25, 1847. Composer of the ballads published under nom-de-plume "Alice Hawthorne," including: Listen to the Mocking Bird; What is Home Without a Mother? Whispering Hope; etc. Author: Instruction books for all instruments. Mem. and mgr. Musical Fund Society. Home: Philadelphia, Pa. Died 1902.

WINSBOROUGH, Hallie Paxson; b. Mason City, Ill., Mar. 7, 1865; d. William Patterson and Harriet Missouri (Swing) Paxson; A.B., Synodical Coll., Fulton, Mo., 1884; Litt.D., Southwestern Coll., Memphis, 1934; m. William Calvert Winsborough, June 12, 1888; children—Joseph Wm. Paxson, Zue (dec.), Martha (Mrs. Archibald Hunt Davis), Calvert Swing, Robb Mauzy, Halliman Pryor. Sec. of woman's work, Presbyn. Ch. in U.S., 1912-29 (emeritus); chmn. com. which estab. Italian Mission in Kansas City, Mo., and Slavic Mission in Kansas City, Kan.; mem. Gen. Assembly's Com. on Closer Relations with U.P. Ch. Vice pres. Council of Women for Home Missions, 1914-29; v.p. Fedn. of Women's Bds. for Foreign Missions, 1923-24; mem. Federal Council Chs. of Christ in America; hon. life mem. Interracial Commn., Atlanta, Ga.; del. to Internat. Christian Conf. on Life and Work, Stockholm, Sweden, 1925; first chmn. Mo. State Conf. on Race Relations; founder first Am. State Conf. for Negro Women in Ala., Va. and Ga. Author: The Woman's Auxiliary, 1927; Yesteryears, 1937. Editor Woman's Dept., Presbyn. Survey, 1921-29; writer of leaflets and contbr. to ch. publs. Compiler Glorious Living, 1937. Home: Shreveport, La. Died July 20, 1940.

WINSHIP, Albert Edward, editor, lecturer; b. West Bridgewater, Mass., Feb. 24, 1845; s. Isaac and Drusilla L. W.; pvt. 60th Mass. Vols., 1864-65; prin. grammar sch., Newton, Mass., 1865-68; teacher, Bridgewater State Normal Sch., 1868-72; student at Andover Theol. Sem., 1875; Litt.D., U. of Nashville, 1898; LL.D., U. of Vt., 1911; m. Ella R. Parker, Aug. 24, 1870; children—George Parker, Edith Annette, Luella Parker, Edna Elliott, Laurence Leathe, Mildred Lothrop. Pastor Prospect Hill Ch., Somerville, Mass., 1876-83; dist. sec. New West Edn. Commn., 1883-86; editor Jour. of Education, Boston, 1886—. Mem. Mass. State Bd. of Edn., 1903-09. Del. Rep. Nat. Conv., 1896. Pres. N.E. Press Assn., 1895, Am. Inst. of Instrn., 1896, Mass. Rep. Editorial Assn., 1899-1906. Author: The Shop, 1889; Life of Horace Mann, 1896; Great American Educators, 1900; Jukes-Edwards, 1900; Danger Signals, 1919; Educational Preparedness, 1919; Heredity, 1919; Famous Farmers, 1921; Educational History, 1929. Home: Cambridge, Mass. Died Feb. 17, 1933.

WINSLOW, Alfred Augustus, consul; b. Crown Point, Ind., June 20, 1854; s. William A. and Mary A. (Cleveland) W.; ed. Valparaiso (Ind.) U.; LL.D., Ia. Wesleyan U., 1909; m. Sadie E. Dyer, June 11, 1879. Taught sch., 1871-81; founded 1881, and published until 1895, Hammond (Ind.) Tribune (now Times). Am. consul at Liege, Belgium, 1898-1902; consul gen. at Guatemala, 1902-06; consul at Valparaiso, 1906-15; consul gen. Auckland, New Zealand, 1915-20, Cape Town, South Africa, 1920, Windsor, Ont., 1922, St. John's, Newfoundland, 1923—. Mason. Home: Crown Point, Ind. Died Aug. 18, 1929.

WINSLOW, Arthur, mining engr. geologist; b. Salem, N.C., Aug. 5, 1860; s. Francis and Mary S. (Nelson) W.; lived during childhood in Boston; for 5 yrs. of boyhood at school in Stuttgart, Germany, and 1 yr. in France; B.S., Mass. Inst. Tech., 1881; m. Mary Livingston Devereux, May 19, 1887. Asst. geologist Pa. Geol. Survey, 1881-84; in pvt. practice in Va., and N.C., 1884-87; in charge of state geol. survey of coal fields of Ark., 1887-89; state geologist, Mo., 1889-94; practiced at St. Louis, 1894-95; in 1896 began acting as gen. mgr., cons. engr. and later pres. of the Liberty Bell Gold Mining Co. and of the U.S. and British Columbia Mining Co. Author of several state geol. reports and numerous articles and papers in scientific procs. and periodicals. Home: Boston, Mass. Died 1938.

WINSLOW, Cameron McRae, naval officer; b. Washington, D.C., July 29, 1854; s. Comdr. Francis Winslow (U.S.N.) and Mary S. (Nelson) W.; grad. U.S. Naval Acad. (with high honors), 1875; m. Theodora Havemeyer, Sept. 18, 1899; children—Natalie, Cameron McRae, Theodora, Emilie, John Chilton, Arthur. Ensign, July 18, 1876; promoted through grades to rear adm., Sept. 14, 1911. Served on Nashville during Spanish-Am. War (wounded in action while in command of cable-cutting expdn. off Cienfuegos, Cuba); advanced 5 numbers in rank for "extraordinary heroism" during Spanish-Am. War; served on U.S.S. Indiana, 1898; on staff of Admiral Sampson, 1899; at Brooklyn Navy Yard, 1899; in charge of branch hydrographic office, New York, 1900; on staff of Rear Admiral Higginson, N. Atlantic Fleet, 1901, 02, 04, 05; naval aide to Pres. Roosevelt, 1905; comd. Mayflower, 1905; comd. squadron for peace conf.; witness of signing Treaty of Portsmouth. Served with Bur. of Nav., 1902-05; comd. Charleston, 1905-07; with Sec. of State Root on bd. trip around S. America; with Bur. of Nav., 1907-08; comd. New Hampshire, 1908-09; supervisor of New York Harbor, 1909-11; comd. 2d Div., Atlantic Fleet, 1911-12, 3d Div., same, 1912-13, 1st Div., 1913; at Naval War Coll., Newport, 1914-15; comd. Spl. Service Squadron, 1914; comdr. in chief, Pacific Fleet, 1915-16; retired, July 29, 1916. Returned to active duty, Sept. 17, 1917, as insp. of naval dists., Atlantic Coast, Flagship Aloha. Died Jan. 2, 1932.

WINSLOW, Catherine Mary, actress, reader, author; b. in England; d. Capt. Robert G. T. and Emma (Abselon) Reignolds; on the stage many yrs.; leading lady at Boston Museum and star through U.S. and Eng.; m. Erving Winslow, June 28, 1861; mother of Charles-Edward Amory W. Retired from dramatic stage, and became public reader, introducing, by special permission of Henrik Ibsen, that author's plays, and those of Maeterlinck, Sudermann, Echegaray and Björnsen. Author: Yesterdays with Actors; Readings from the Old English Dramatists (with notes), 1895. Died 1911.

WINSLOW, E(ben) Eveleth, army officer; b. in D.C., May 13, 1866; grad. U.S. Mil. Acad., 1889, Engr. Sch. of Application, 1892. Commd. add. 2d lt. engrs., June 12, 1889; 2d lt., July 2, 1889; 1st lt., Apr. 12, 1894, capt., July 5, 1898; maj., Apr. 2, 1906; lt. col., Oct. 12, 1912; brig. gen., Oct. 2, 1917. Duty river, harbor and fortification works, Mobile, Ala., and vicinity, 1892-96; comd. co., Battle of San Juan, Cuba, July 2, 1898; in charge 1st and 2d dists., Miss. River Improvement, Memphis, Tenn., 1898-1902; at Wilmington, N.C., 1902-03, Norfolk, Va., 1903-06; assigned duty Office Chief of Engrs., 1907; mem. Bd. Engrs. for Rivers and Harbors. Died June 28, 1928.

WINSLOW, Edward Delbert, consul gen.; b. West Chicago, Ill., Dec. 16, 1858; s. Charles and Anne (McDonald) W.; M.A., St. Ignatius Coll., Chicago, 1877; LL.B., Northwestern U., 1879; m. Elizabeth Branchfield, Nov. 25, 1883. In grain and provision business, Chicago, 1880-97; mem. firm of E. L. Lobdell & Co., stock brokers, 1901-08; U.S. consul at Stockholm, Sweden, 1897-98, consul gen., 1898-1900, sec. of legation, 1900-01, resigned; apptd. consul gen. at Gothenburg, Sweden, 1909; transferred to Stockholm, Mar. 1909; apptd. consul at Plauen, Germany, Dec. 22, 1910; consul gen. at Copenhagen, Aug. 1911-Aug. 1917 (chargé de'affaires ad interim, June 6-July 10, 1912). Republican. Catholic. Home: Chicago, Ill. Died Jan. 22, 1941.

WINSLOW, Erving, commission mcht.; b. Boston, Mass., Nov. 19, 1839; s. Benjamin Pollard and Mary Timmins Quincy (Hill) W.; ed. English High Sch., Boston, and Lawrence Scientific Sch. (Harvard); m. Catherine Mary Reignolds, June 28, 1861 (died 1911); father of Charles-Edward Amory W. Asst. in the U.S. Coast Survey and U.S. Sanitary Commn.; asst. Dudley Observatory, Albany, N.Y., merchant in Boston, 1868—. Charter mem., dir. Associated Charities, Boston; trustee Wells Memorial Assn.; sec. Industrial Aid Soc.; sec. Anti-Imperialist League. Mem. Corp. Ch. of the Advent; del. Episcopal Conv. Del. to convs., and mem. ward, city, and state coms. Republican. Translator: Maeterlinck's "Pélléas et Mélisande"; Legouve's "Madonna of Art." Founder, and joint editor 2 yrs., Time and the Hour. Contbr. to Popular Science Monthly, N.A. Review, Am. Jour. of Internat. Law, The Peacemaker, The Spectator, and many newspapers. Editorial writer Boston Advertiser, Herald, Transcript, and New Haven Journal-Courier. Author: An Epitome of Historical Events (Senate Doc. 375, 57th Congress); A Loyalist in the Siege of Boston; Acadia in History and Poetry; Apologia pro vita sua; Neutralization (World Peace Foundation); Every Custom House a Fortress; The Open vs. the Closed Door; Co-operation. Home: New Haven, Conn. Died Mar. 10, 1922.

WINSLOW, Francis Asbury, judge; b. Ossining, N.Y., Oct. 13, 1866; s. William and Mary (Scott) W.; B.S., Coll. City of New York, 1887; LL.B., Columbia, 1889; m. Mrs. Charlotte W. Eaton, Jan. 1915; stepchildren — Stuart Eaton, Mrs. Ruth (Eaton) Purdy, Mrs. Charlotte (Eaton) Fayé, Eleanor Mills Eaton. Admitted to N.Y. bar, 1889, and began practice at Yonkers; corp. counsel, Yonkers, 1901, 03, 05; dist. atty. Westchester County, N.Y., 1907-13; mem. N.Y. State Constl. Conv., 1915; atty. for state comptroller and N.Y. State Tax Com., for Westchester County, 1915-22; served as gen. counsel Nat. Poultry, Butter and Egg Assn., New York Poultry and Game Assn.; U.S. dist. judge, Southern Dist. of N.Y., by apptmt. of Pres. Harding, Jan. 1923—. Republican. Methodist. Home: Yonkers, N.Y. Died Mar. 29, 1932.

WINSLOW, Frederic I., cons. engr.; b. New Bedford, Mass., Jan. 30, 1863; s. George William and Jane Lucretia (Southwick) W.; ed. pvt. and pub. schs. and under tutors; m. Myrtle Smith, June 15, 1892. Practiced at Boston, 1883-1919, as gen. hydraulic engr. and miscel. engring. work; in charge all new constrn. of Boston water system, 1911-16; U.S. supervising engr. constrn. Squantum Destroyer Plant, 1917-18, later div. engr. Sudbury dept., Met. Dist. Commn., Mass. Conglist. Died Feb. 21, 1924.

WINSLOW, George Frederick, naval officer; b. New Bedford, Mass., May 8, 1842; s. Giles and Elizabeth (Wilcox) W.; M.D., Harvard, 1864; m. Virginia Shearman, Jan. 14, 1875; children—George F., Virginia, Harold. Apptd. to U.S.N., July 26, 1862; advanced through grades to med. dir., Jan. 23, 1898; retired with the rank of rear admiral, Jan. 19, 1903, after over 44 yrs.' service. Received the thanks of Her Majesty's Govt. for taking care of distressed and suffering subjects in Patagonia during winter of 1869; also of Peruvian Congress for relief and surgical assistance rendered to suffering people of Arica, Peru, after the earthquake of Sept. 13, 1868. Died Sept. 3, 1928.

WINSLOW, Helen Maria, author; b. Westfield, Vt.; d. Don Avery and Mary Salome (Newton) Winslow; ed. Vt. Normal Sch., Johnson, and at Boston; unmarried. Teacher, later writer for papers and mags.; went to Boston, 1883; engaged in active journalism on Boston Transcript and Boston Beacon; editor and publisher The Club Woman, 1897-1903. Mass. commr. to Cotton States Expn., Atlanta, 1895; state regent D.A.R., 1900-02. Author: Salome Shepard, Reformer, 1894; Concerning Cats, 1900; Literary Boston of Today, 1902; Concerning Polly, 1902; The Woman of Tomorrow, 1905; The President of Quex, 1906; Spinster Farm, 1908; Woman for Mayor, 1909; The Pleasuring of Susan Smith, 1912; The Road to a Loving Heart, 1926; Keeping Young Gracefully, 1928; also (with Marie Robinson Wright) Mexico Picturesque, 1897; and many short stories and poems. Editor and pub. The Annual Register of Women's Clubs in America, 1898-1930. Home: Shirley, Mass. Died Mar. 27, 1938.

WINSLOW, Herbert, rear admiral; b. Roxbury, Mass., Sept. 22, 1848; s. Rear Admiral John Ancrum W. (who as capt. in command of old U.S.S. Kearsarge sank the Alabama off Cherbourg, France, June 19, 1864); grad. U.S. Naval Acad., 1869; m. Elizabeth, d. Lafayette Maynard, June 6, 1876 (died 1899). Ensign, 1870; master, 1872; lt., 1875; lt. comdr., 1897; comdr., 1900; captain, 1905; rear admiral, 1909. Wrecked in U.S.S. Saranac, in Seymour's Narrows, B.C., June 18, 1875; comd. U.S.S. Fern at Battle of Santiago, Spanish-Am. War; in the Pacific during Boxer rebellion, in command of U.S.S. Solace and landed the first detachment of marines at Taku, China; last command was the U.S.S. Kearsarge which was named, at launching, by his wife; retired. Died Sept. 24, 1914.

WINSLOW, John Bradley, judge; b. Livingston County, N.Y., Oct. 4, 1851; s. Horatio Gates and Emily (Bradley) W.; A.B., Racine (Wis.) Coll., 1871, A.M., 1874; LL.B., U. of Wis., 1875, LL.D., 1904; m. Agnes Clancy, Jan. 19, 1881. City atty., Racine, 1880-83; judge 1st Jud. Circuit, Wis., 1884-91; justice Supreme Ct. of Wis., May 4, 1891—(chief justice, Dec. 30, 1907—). Democrat. Died July 13, 1920.

WINSLOW, Sidney Wilmot, financier; b. Brewster, Mass., Sept. 20, 1854; s. Freeman and Lucy H. (Rogers) W.; ed. Salem, Mass.; m. Georgiana Buxton, 1877 (dec.). Pres. United Shoe Machinery Corp., United Shoe Machinery Co., United Shoe Machinery Co. of Me., United Fast Color Eyelet Co., Boston Fast Color Eyelet Co., Nat. Fast Color Eyelet Co., United Awl & Needle Co., Campbell-Bosworth Machinery Co., O. A. Miller Treeing Machine Co., W. W. Cross & Co., J. C. Rhodes & Co., Inc., United-Xpedite Finishing Co., Beverly Gas & Electric Co., Danvers Gas Light Co.; dir. Naumkeag Buffing Machine Co. (treas.), First Nat. Bank, Old Colony Trust Co., Salem Gas Light Co., U.S. Smelting, Refining & Mining Co., Island Creek Coal Co. Mason. Home: Orleans, Mass. Died June 18, 1917.

WINSLOW, William Copley, archæologist; b. Boston, Mass., Jan. 13, 1840; s. Rev. Hubbard W. and Susan Ward (Cutler) W.; A.B., Hamilton Coll., 1862; student Hobart, class of 1861; grad. General Theol. Sem., 1865; hon. A.M., Hobart Coll., 1865; Ph.D., Hamilton Coll., 1886; L.H.D., Columbia, 1887; S.T.D., Griswold, 1887; D.D., Amherst, 1887; LL.D., St. Andrew's, Scotland, 1888; D.C.L., King's Coll., N.S., 1888; Sc.D., St. John's, Md., 1889; m. Harriet Stillman Hayward, June 20, 1867 (died 1915); m. 2d, Elizabeth Bruce Roelofson, May 24, 1917 (died 1923). Deacon, 1865, and priest, 1867, Episcopal Ch.; rector Lee, Mass., 1867-70; chaplain St. Luke's Home, Boston, 1878-82; sec. Free Ch. Assn., 1882—. Founded, 1883, Am. branch Egypt Exploration Fund (its chief official till 1903); officer Inst. of Civics. As archæologist, hon. fellow Royal Archæol. Inst., British Archæol. Assn., Victoria Inst., Royal Soc. Arts and Sciences, Soc. of Oriental Research. Editor University Quarterly, 1860-62; asst. editor N.Y. World, 1862-63, Christian Times, 1864-65; asso. editor Am. Antiquarian, also of Am. Hist. Register; regular writer for Biblia; prepared 100 to 150 articles a year for daily and weekly press. Spent 4 months in archæol. study in Egypt, 1880. Writer for standard encys.; univ. lecturer; secured splendid antiquities for Boston Mus. from Egypt; authority on N.E. history and Egyptian and cognate archæology. Aided Prof. Petrie and the Egyptian Research Account Soc. as v.p. for N.A. Wrote monographs: A Greek City in Egypt; The Store City of Pithom; Tombs at Beni Hasan; Egypt at Home; Explorations at Zoan; Pilgrim Fathers in Holland; Gov. Edward Winslow; Winslow Memorial; Papyri in the United States; Egyptian Antiquities in American Museums; etc. Excellent high priest, St. Bernard Commandery K.T., 10 yrs. Died Feb. 2, 1925.

WINSOR, Frank Edward, civil engr.; b. Providence, R.I., Nov. 16, 1870; s. George Henry and Lucy Jane (Draper) W.; Ph.B., Brown U., 1891, C.E., 1892, A.M., 1896, Sc.D., 1929; m. Catharine Holbrook Burton, Oct. 25, 1893; children—Lucy Burton (Mrs. Hugh B. Killough), Edward, Catharine (Mrs. Hazen H. Ayer). On constrn. of the Metropolitan Sewer System, Boston, 1891-95, design and constrn. of Metropolitan Water Works, 1895-1903; water supply investigations, N.Y. City, Feb.-Nov. 1903; designing engr. and dep. chief engr. Charles River Basin Commn., Boston, 1903-06; div. engr. and dept. engr. Catskill Water Works, for N.Y. City; in charge constrn. Kensico and Hillview reservoirs, 32 miles of Catskill Aqueduct, etc., 1906-15; chief engr. new water supply, Providence, 1915-26; chief engr. Met. Dist. Water Supply, under Met. Dist. Water Supply Commn., Boston, 1926—; cons. engr. Bd. of Water Supply, N.Y. City. Trustee Brown U. Mem. Am. Soc. C.E. (dir. 1922-24; v.p. 1930-31); fellow Am. Acad. of Arts and Sciences. Mason. Home: West Newton, Mass. Died Jan. 30, 1939.

WINSOR, Frederick, educator; b. Winchester, Mass., Mar. 29, 1872; s. Frederick (M.D.) and Anne Bent (Ware) W.; A.B., Harvard U., 1893; m. Weston, Mass., Mary A. L., d. Gen. Charles J. and Julia (Bryant) Paine, June 18, 1894. Taught at Taft Sch., Watertown, Conn., 1893-95, Phillips Acad., Exeter, N.H., 1895-97; organized Country Sch. for Boys (now Gilman Sch.), Baltimore, 1897; organized, 1901, and head master Middlesex Sch., Concord, Mass., 1901-38. Overseer Harvard Coll., 1931-37. Author: The Art of Behaviour, 1932. Home: Petersham, Mass. Died Nov. 26, 1940.

WINSOR, Robert, banker; s. Frederick (M.D.) and Anne Bent (Ware) W.; A.B., Harvard, 1880; m. Eleanor M. Magee, Oct. 27, 1883; children—Robert, Philip (dec.), Mary P. (Mrs. W. H. Trumbull, Jr.), Alexander. With Kidder, Peabody & Co., bankers, Boston, 1880—, becoming mem. firm; dir. U.S. Steel Corp., Rockland & Rockport Lime Co., N.E. Coal & Coke Co., Boston Consol. Gas Co., Boston Elevated Ry. Co., N.E. Mfg. Co., Union Mills, Bigelow-Hartford Carpet Co., Am. Felt Co., Automatic Straight Air Brake Co., Daniel Green Felt Shoe Co., United States Worsted Co., Lime Rock R.R. Co., Kidder, Peabody Acceptance Corp., Lawrence Bldg., Inc., Winchester Co., Winchester Repeating Arms Co., Waltham Watch Co., Kidder Co., Lowell, Kidder Co., Springfield, Mystic Iron Works, Winchester-Simmons Co., Peabody Trust Co.; trustee Mass. Gas Cos., N.E. Fuel & Transportation Co., Amoskeag Mfg. Co., Mystic Steamship Co.; trustee and treas. Boston Young Men's Christian Union Permanent Fund; trustee Brooks Cubicle Hosp., Boston Dwelling House Co. Home: Weston, Mass. Died Jan. 7, 1930.

WINSTON, Annie Steger, author; b. Richmond, Va.; d. Charles Henry and Nannie (Steger) Winston; ed. at home. Democrat. Baptist. Author: Memoirs of a Child, 1903; The Deeper Voice, 1923. Contbr. to Atlantic, Century, Outlook, etc. Speaker before women's clubs, on lit. and other topics. Home: Richmond, Va. Died May 12, 1927.

WINSTON, Frederick Hampden, U.S. minister to Persia; b. Sand Hill, Ga., Nov. 20, 1830; s. Rev. Dennis Mervyn and Mary (McIntosh) W.; ed. in Ky.; grad. Harvard Law Sch., 1852; admitted to N.Y. bar, 1853; practiced law in Chicago, 1853-85; U.S. minister to Persia, 1885-86. Democrat. 12 yrs. pres. Lincoln Park commrs.; pres. Union Stock Yards Co., 1888. Home: Chicago, Ill. Died 1904.

WINSTON, Frederick Seymour, lawyer; b. Franklin County, Ky., Oct. 27, 1856; s. Hon. Frederick H. and Maria G. (Dudley) W.; grad. Yale, 1877; student Columbia Law Sch.; m. Ada Fountain, June 26, 1876. Admitted to bar, 1878; asst. corp. counsel, 1881-84, corp. counsel of Chicago, 1884-86; in pvt. practice, 1886—; mem. of firm of Winston, Payne & Strawn. Counsel and dir. Union Stock Yard & Transit Co., and many other cos. Practice principally in connection with large corps. Home: Chicago, Ill. Died 1909.

WINSTON, Isaac, hydrographic and geodetic engr.; b. Tuscumbia, Ala., Sept. 7, 1853; s. Isaac and Olive B. (Michie) W.; grad. Va. Mil. Inst., 1873; engaged as farmer, 1873-76; m. Anna Maria Otis, Sept. 19, 1882. In govt. service under corps of engrs. U.S.A., on constrn. pub. works, 1876-78; in service U.S. Coast and Geod. Survey, 1878—; insp. in charge of Field Sta., N.Y. City. U.S. del. Internat. Geod. Assn., 13th Gen. Conf., 1900. Home: New York, N.Y. Died Dec. 7, 1923.

WINSTON, John Clark, publisher; b. Darlington, Ind., Nov. 22, 1856; s. Bowling Henry and Anna (Clark) W.; B.A., Haverford Coll., Pa., 1881; m. Samuella Terrell Ricks, July 19, 1883. Began pub. business, 1884; pres. The John C. Winston Co., book and Bible publishers. One of the originators of the Phila. reform movement and chmn. Com. of Seventy; chmn. of citizens com. which secured a new charter for Phila., 1919. Died May 6, 1920.

WINT, Theodore Jonathan, army officer; b. in Pa., Mar. 6, 1845; s. Jonathan R. and Euphemia (Johnston) W.; ed. Providence High Sch.; m. Lydia Porter Bullis, 1880. Served pvt. to 1st lt. Co. F, 6th Pa. cav., 1861-64; pvt. gen. mounted service, 1865. Apptd. in regular army, 2d lt., 4th cav., Nov. 24, 1865; 1st lt., May 9, 1866; capt. Apr. 21, 1872; maj. 10th cav., May 6, 1892; lt. col. 6th cav., Apr. 8, 1899; col., Feb. 23, 1901; brig. gen. U.S.A., June 9, 1902. Died 1907.

WINTER, Elizabeth Campbell, novelist; b. Ederline, Loch Awe, Scotland, Dec. 19, 1841; d. John and Jessie (Tulloch) Campbell; m. William Winter, Dec. 8, 1860. Author: The Spanish Treasure; The Curse of Dangerfield; Hawthorn Lodge; The Mistress of the Grange; also many other novels and stories. Home: New Brighton, S.I., N.Y. Died Apr. 7, 1922.

WINTER, Emil, banker; pres. Workingman's Savings Bank & Trust Co., Pittsburgh; also pres. Am. Magnesium Metals Corp., Am. Refractories Co. of Pa., Austro-Am. Magnesite Corp., Am.-Austrian Magnesite Corp.; dir. Magnesium Products, Inc. Trustee Mercy Hosp.; dir. Tuberculosis League. Home: Pittsburgh, Pa. Died July 5, 1941.

WINTER, Ferdinand, lawyer; b. Cincinnati, O., May 25, 1843; s. Charles H. and Elizabeth A. (Herod) W.; LL.B., Albany (N.Y.) Law Sch., 1864; m. Mary L. Keyes, Nov. 9, 1869. Practiced at Columbus, Ind., 1864-75, Indianapolis, 1875—; mem. Ind. Senate, 1885-87. Republican. Home: Indianapolis, Ind. Died Mar. 4, 1935.

WINTER, Francis Anderson, surgeon U.S.A.; b. St. Francisville, La., June 30, 1867; s. William Drew and Sarah (Stirling) W.; ed. St. Vincents Coll. (Cape Girardeau, Mo.), Bethel Mil. Acad. (Va.) St. Louis U.; M.D., St. Louis Med. Coll., 1889; m. Mary Davenport Smith, Oct. 27, 1897. Apptd. asst. surgeon, U.S.A., Mar. 9, 1892; capt. asst. surgeon, Mar. 9, 1897; maj. surgeon 37th U.S. Inf., July 5, 1899; hon. discharged vols., Feb. 20, 1901; maj. surgeon U.S.A., Aug. 3, 1904; maj. Med. Corps, Aug. 3, 1904; lt. col., Apr. 13, 1912; col., May 15, 1917; brig. gen. (temp.), May 1, 1918. Chief surgeon, Line of Communications, A.E.F., July 1917-Mar. 1918; chief surgeon, A.E.F. in Eng., May-Oct. 1918; apptd. comdt. Army Med. Sch., Dec. 23, 1918. Roman Catholic. Died Jan. 11, 1931.

WINTER, George Ben Wade, dentist; b. Brooklyn, N.Y., Apr. 14, 1878; s. Ernest D. and Matilda (Ravensdorf) W.; ed. pub. schs., high sch., Poly. Inst. of Brooklyn, and St. Louis U. In practice of dentistry, 1900—; prof. of exodontia, Washington U. Sch. of Dentistry. Awarded Newell Sills Jenkins Medal, 1933; gold medal and scroll, R.I. State Dental Soc., 1936; gold medal, Odontological Soc. of Havana, Cuba. Fellow Am. Coll. of Dentists. Author: Exodontia; Impacted Mandibular Third Molar. Home: St. Louis, Mo. Died Mar. 28, 1940.

WINTER, Irvah Lester, coll. prof.; b. New Braintree, Mass., Dec. 26, 1857; s. Roland and Mary Elizabeth (Crawford) W.; A.B., Harvard, 1886 (Pi Eta); m. Rebecca Fenton Clark, Apr. 28, 1906; 1 son, Lester Clark. Instr. English, and later, English lit. and history, Mich. Military Acad., Orchard Lake, Mich., 1886-98; head master Kenyon Mil. Acad., Gambier, O., 1898-99; instr. pub. speaking, 1899-1903, asst. prof., 1903-13, asso. prof., 1913-25, asso. prof., emeritus, 1925—, Harvard. In charge of courses, Harvard Coll., Sch. of Theology, Law Sch., 1903-18, and Radcliffe Coll., Harvard Summer Sch., New Ch. Theol. Sch. (Cambridge). Instr. Andover Theol. Sem., 1907-08, Episcopal Theol. Sch., Cambridge, 1916-18; in charge of courses in pub. speaking, Columbia, summer sessions 1909, 10, 13, U. of Calif., 1919; pres. N.E. Oral English and Pub. Speaking Conf., 1913-15, 1919-21; dir. Nat. Council Teachers of English, 1914-17; v.p. Nat. Assn. Teachers of Speech, 1923-24. Republican. Episcopalian. Author: Public Speaking—Principles and Practice, 1912, 1915; Exercises in Speech, 1915; Persuasive Speaking—Business Discussion and Public Address, 1927. Home: Cambridge, Mass. Died May 30, 1934.

WINTER, Nevin Otto, author; b. Benton, O., June 14, 1869; s. Adam and Ella (Dunlap) W.; A.B., Ohio Wesleyan U., 1891, Litt.D., 1916; LL.B., Ohio State U., 1897; unmarried. In practice of law at Toledo, O., 1897—. Republican. Methodist. Trustee of Toledo Pub. Library, 1916-35. Mem. Pan-American Soc. of N.Y., Am. Acad. Polit. and Social Science. Author: Mexico and Her People of Today, 1907, 1912, 18, 23; Guatemala and Her People of Today, 1909; Brazil and Her People of Today, 1910, 1928; Argentina and Her People of Today, 1911; Chile and Her People of Today, 1912; The Russian Empire of Today and Yesterday, 1913 (revised and re-issued as Russia of Today and Yesterday, 1929); Poland of Today and Yesterday, 1913; Texas the Marvelous, 1916; History of Northwest Ohio (3 vols.), 1917; Florida, the Land of Enchantment, 1917; The New Poland, 1923; Panama and the Canal Today (with Forbes Lindsay), 1926; Cuba and Her People of Today (with Forbes Lindsay), 1928; Seeing South America (with William B. Guitteau), 1929; Romance of the Maumee Valley, 1929. Traveled over central and eastern Europe as corr. of syndicate of newspapers, Leslie's Weekly and Christian Herald, Mar.-June 1919; through Orient for syndicate, 1922; through Eastern Europe and Balkans for syndicate, 1926. Organized, 1918, and became sec., dir. Hist. Soc. of Northwestern Ohio. Lecturer on Eastern Europe and Latin-Am. affairs. Home: Toledo, O. Died Sept. 2, 1936.

WINTER, Thomas Gerald; b. Grantham, Eng., Mar. 15, 1863; s. Thomas and Mary (Rogers) W.; student Coll. de St. Malo, France, 3 yrs.; m. Alice Ames, June 1892; children—Gilbert (dec.), Edith (Mrs. K. L. Ames, Jr.). Emigrated to Can. at 17, to U.S., 1891; engaged in farming 10 yrs.; in line elevator and grain commn. business at Minneapolis many yrs.; pres. Winter-Truesdell-Ames Co.; chief of intelligence dept. State Safety Commn. of Minn. in early part of war; park commr. of Minneapolis, 1921—. Mem. White's Scouts, in Riel Rebellion, Can., 1885. Capt.

Am. Red Cross, 9 months in France on outpost service. Republican. Home: Pasadena, Calif. Died June 1934.

WINTER, William, author, dramatic critic; b. Gloucester, Mass., July 15, 1836; s. Captain Charles and Louisa (Wharf) W.; ed. Gloucester, Boston, and Cambridge schs., Cambridge High Sch.; LL.B., Dane Law Sch. (Harvard), 1857; Litt.D., Brown U., 1895; m. Elizabeth Campbell, Dec. 8, 1860. Studied in law office of Lyman Mason, also Aurelius D. Parker; admitted to Suffolk bar, 1857, but rejected first case and devoted himself to lit. Began to write while a child. Regular contbr. to newspaper and mag. press, 1852—; wrote and published first dramatic criticism, 1854; asst. editor and dramatic and lit. reviewer The Albion, New York, 1861-67; dramatic critic and editor N.Y. Tribune, July 12, 1865-Aug. 14, 1909. Regular contbr. to many papers and mags., including N.Y. Saturday Press, London Era, Frank Leslie's Weekly (mng. editor), Atlantic, Century, Harper's Weekly, Pacific Monthly, Phila. Saturday Evening Post. In early life wrote under pen-names of "Mercutio," and "Mark Vale," as well as under own name; polit. speaker, 1856-60; delivered his poem, "The Voice of the Silence," at Centennial Celebration, Phila., June 6, 1876. Mem. bd. trustees S.I. Academy, 1887-1907 (pres. bd., 1891-1907); founded there the Arthur Winter Memorial Library, 1886 (in commemoration of his second son, killed in accident, Jan. 1886). Member Soc. of the Army of the Potomac, Actors' Fund Society, Dante Society, London; with Gen. W. T. Sherman first charter mem. The Players. Editor: The Poems of George Arnold, 2 vols., with intro., 1866, 67, 86; The Works of Fitz-James O'Brien, with intro. and life, 1881; The Poems and Stories of John Brougham, 1881; Recollections of a Player, by J. H. Stoddart, with intro., 1902; The Edwin Booth Prompt Books, 1878, 99, 1908; (Shakespearean plays)—"Hamlet," "Macbeth," "King Lear," "Julius Caesar," "The Merchant of Venice," "Othello," "King Richard II," "King Richard III," "King Henry VIII," "Much Ado About Nothing"; Garrick's "Katherine and Petruchio"; (other than Shakespearean)—"Richelieu," "The Fool's Revenge," Payne's "Brutus," "Ruy Blas," and "Don Caesar de Bazan"; also, An Acting Edition of Cymbeline; Timon of Athens; also alterations of many other old plays, such as "Venice Preserved," "All's Well That Ends Well," etc.; the idea, plan, and story of "Beau Brummell," prod. 1890 by Richard Mansfield and generally attributed to William Clyde Fitch, are his. Author: Poems, 1854; The Queen's Domain, 1856; My Witness, 1858; Thistledown, 1878; The Trip to England, 1878; The Jeffersons, 1881; English Rambles, 1884; Henry Irving—Studies of His Acting, 1885; The Stage Life of Mary Anderson, 1886; Shakespeare's England, 1888, 92, 1910, Gray Days and Gold, 1889, 92, 1911; Wanderer's (poems), 1889, 92; Brief Chronicles, 1889; John McCullough—A Memorial, 1889; The Press and the Stage, 1889; John Gilbert—A Monograph, 1890; The Actor and Other Orations, 1891; Shadows of the Stage, First Series, 1892, Second Series, 1893, Third Series, 1894; Old Shrines and Ivy, 1892; Life and Art of Edwin Booth, 1893; George William Curtis—An Oration, 1893; Life and Art of Joseph Jefferson, 1894; Brown Heath and Blue Bells, 1896; A Wreath of Laurel, 1898; Ada Rehan—A Study, 1898; Mary of Magdala—A Tragedy in Blank Verse, based on a German Prose Play by Paul Heyse, 1903; The Theatre and the Public, 1905; Life and Letters of William Law Symonds, 1908; Other Days—Chronicles and Personal Memories of the Stage, 1908; Old Friends—Personal Literary Recollections, 1909; Poems—Author's Edition (Definitive), 1909; Life and Art of Richard Mansfield, 1910; Over the Border, 1911; Shakespeare on the Stage, 1911; Lives of the Players—Tyrone Power, 1913; The Wallet of Time—Theatrical Criticism and Reminiscence, 1913; Shakespeare on the Stage—Second Series, 1915; Vagrant Memories—Being Further Recollections of Other Days, 1915; also of many introductions and prefaces to Shakespearean and other old plays, and of various prologues, interpolations and epilogues. Home: New Brighton, S.I., N.Y. Died June 30, 1917.

WINTERBURN, George William, editor, physician; b. New York, N.Y., Sept. 19, 1845; s. Rev. Charles (M.D.) and Katherine Gardner (Boss) W.; grad. Hughes High Sch., Cincinnati, 1862; M.D., Eclectic Med. Coll., New York, 1875; Pharm.D., U.S., Med. Coll., 1881; m. Charlotte Van Duser Hutchings, Nov. 30, 1871; m. 2d, Florence May Hull, Jan. 25, 1893. With Cincinnati Daily Gazette, 1862-66; New York corr. for western jours., 1867-69; editorial writer New York Post, 1869-70; editor Congregational Rev., 1870-71; mus. critic N.Y. Daily Witness, 1871-72; mus. critic N.Y. Public School Jour., 1873-74. Editor Am. Homœopathist, 1882-87, Homœopathic Jour. of Obstetrics, 1889-93, Childhood, 1892-94. Prof. materia medica and therapeutics, Eclectic Med. Coll., New York, 1878-82, U.S. Med. Coll., 1883-84; clin. lecturer and phys.-in-chief Manhattan Hosp., 1878-84. Pres. Am. Obstet. Soc., 1885-92; sec. 1878-81, pres. 1881-82, Eclectic Med. Soc. Co. N.Y. Republican. Author: American Vegetable Remedies, 1878; Cinchona, Historically Physiologically and Therapeutically Considered, 1880; The Value of Vaccination, 1884; Purpura—Including a Materia Medica of 32 Remedies and Repertory, 1885; A Pocket Repertory, 1886; also various monographs on therapeutic and obstet. subjects. Died 1911.

WINTERHALTER, Albert Gustavus, naval officer; b. Detroit, Mich., Oct. 5, 1856; s. of a Mexican War veteran; grad. Detroit high sch., 1873; grad. U.S. Naval Acad., 1877. Promoted ensign, July 11, 1880; lt. (j.g.), Dec. 14, 1886; lt., June 30, 1892; lt. comdr., Jan. 18, 1900; comdr., July 1, 1905; capt., July 1, 1909; rear admiral, May 5, 1915. Del. for U.S. Naval Obs. at Internat. Astrophotographic Congress, Paris, 1887; official report of its proceedings and of an inspection of European scientific instns. pub. as a quarto, XIV, 1889. Served on Philadelphia during Spanish-Am. War, 1898; flag lt. to Rear Admiral Joseph N. Miller and arranged naval share in transfer of Hawaiian sovereignty to U.S., Aug. 12, 1898; recorder Labor Bd., Phila. Navy Yard, 1898-1900; comd. div. of gunboats, Cavite to China, 1903; comd. Elcano, 1903; equipment and ordnance officer, Portsmouth (N.H.) Navy Yard, 1903-05; comd. Paducah, 1905-07; at Naval Obs., Washington, 1907-08; hydrographer, Navy Dept., 1908-09; comd. Louisiana, 1910-11; mem. Gen. Bd., Navy Dept., 1911-12; aid for material, Navy Dept., 1912-15; comd. Asiatic Fleet and Sta., 1915-17, with rank of admiral; on occasion of accession of Emperior of Japan, Nov.-Dec. 1915; mem. Gen. Bd., Navy Dept., May 11, 1917—. Fellow A.A.A.S.; mem. U.S. Naval Inst. Home: Washington, D.C. Died June 5, 1920.

WINTHROP, Beekman, banker; b. Orange, N.J., Sept. 18, 1874; s. Robert and Kate W. (Taylor) W.; A.B., Harvard, 1897, LL.B., 1900; m. Melza Riggs Wood, Oct. 7, 1903. Admitted to N.Y. bar, 1899; pvt. sec. to Gov. Taft, Nov. 1900; asst. exec. sec. of P.I., July 1901-Aug. 1903; acting exec. sec., Oct. 1902-Apr. 1903; judge Ct. of First Instance, P.I., Nov. 1903-May 1904; gov. of Puerto Rico, 1904-07; asst. sec. of Treasury, 1907-09; asst. sec. of Navy, Mar. 5, 1909-Mar. 15, 1913; sr. partner Robert Winthrop & Co., bankers, N.Y. City, 1914-39. Dir. D.,L.&W. R.R. Co.; v.p. Cayuga and Susquehanna R.R. Co. Republican. Home: Westbury, N.Y. Died Nov. 10, 1940.

WINTON, Alexander, inventor, mfr.; b. Grangemouth, Scotland, June 20, 1860; s. Alexander and Helen (Fea) W.; common sch. edn.; m. Jeanie Muir MacGlashan, 1883 (died 1903); children—Helen F., James M., Agnes M., Jeanie, Cathrine, Alexander; m. 2d, La Belle MacGlashan, of Scotland, 1906; children—La Belle (dec.), Clarice; m. 4th, Mrs. Mary E. Avery, September 2, 1931. Established Winton Bicycle Co., Cleveland, 1890; began manufacture of motor cars, 1894; incorporator, 1897, and later pres. The Winton Co.; established Winton Marine Oil Engine Works, 1912. Mason. Home: Lakewood, O. Died June 22, 1932.

WINTON, George Beverly, clergyman, educator; b. Springfield, Mo., Jan. 12, 1861; s. Rev. George Mitchell and Amanda (Faulkner) W.; M.A., Morrisville (Mo.) Coll., 1881; student at Vanderbilt U., 1881-83; D.D., Southwestern U., Tex., Southern U., Ala., and Randolph-Macon Coll., Va., 1902; Litt.D., Piedmont Coll., 1935; m. Jessie McClain, July 16, 1884 (died 1931); children—Prof. Will McClain, Lt. Col. Walter Ferrell, Maj. George Peterson, Dorothy. Ordained to ministry Methodist Episcopal Ch., South, 1883; engaged in ministerial work in Mo., 1883-84, in City of Mexico, 1884; prof. Latin, Pacific Meth. Coll., Santa Rosa, Calif., 1885-87; pastor Sacramento, Calif., 1887; missionary in Mex., 1888-1902; pres. Theol. Sem., San Luis Potosi, 1889-97; editor Evangelista Mexicano, 1892-96; editor-in-chief Christian Advocate, Nashville, Tenn., 1902-10; editorial sec. Bd. of Missions and editor "Missionary Voice," 1911-14; editorial sec. Com. on Coöperation in Latin America, 1917-21; editor St. Louis Christian Advocate, 1921-23; pastor Broadway Meth. Ch., Paducah, Ky., 1923-25; editor Meth. Advocate, Nashville, Tenn., 1925-26; lecturer in Latin-Am. history and Bibl. lit., Vanderbilt U., 1927-29, prof. of Biblical lit. and history, 1929—, dean of School of Religion, 1930-36. Mem. Gen. Conf., M.E. Ch., S., 1902, 10, 22; del. Ecumenical Missionary Conf., New York, 1900; Ch. Fedn. Conf., New York, 1905; Ch. Fedn. Council, Phila., 1908, Chicago, 1912, Atlanta, 1924; Ecumenical Meth. Conf., Toronto, 1911; Pan-Am. Inst. Geography and History, Mexico City, 1929. Author: Método para el Inglés, 1902; A New Era in Old Mexico, 1904; Mexico Today, 1913; A Study of Educational Conditions in Mexico, 1916; Notas Explicatives, 1919, 20, 21; Mexico, Past and Present, 1928; Pleaders for Righteousness, 1929. Died Mar. 1, 1938.

WIRT, William Albert, educator; b. Markle, Ind., Jan. 21, 1874; s. Emanuel and Mary (Elick) W.; Ph.B., De Pauw U., 1898, Pd.D., 1916; post-grad. work De Pauw and U. of Chicago; made spl. study of endl. methods in England, Belgium, France and Germany; m. Bertha Ann Koch, Aug. 15, 1900; children—William Franz, Sherwood William, Bertha Eleanor. Supt. schs., Redkey, Ind., 1895-97; instr. mathematics, high sch., Greencastle, Ind., 1897-99; supt. schs., Bluffton, Ind., 1899-1907, Gary, Ind., 1907—. First attracted pub. notice by application of new ednl. methods at Bluffton, in 1900; applied similar methods on larger scale at Gary, and engaged, 1914, to devote one week in every four as official adviser to Bd. of Edn., N.Y. City. "Gary System" tested satisfactorily in 2 large pub. schs. in N.Y. City and extended to 120 additional schs.; under this system, by alternating the classes between regular and spl. teachers, the capacity of the average school building is increased about 40%, the children have a school day about 20% longer than the day for teachers, and no extra teachers are employed. This system has been adopted by many cities of America and is known as the Platoon Sch., Duplicate Sch., or Wirt's Study Play Sch. Mason. Episcopalian. Home: Gary, Ind. Died Mar. 11, 1938.

WISE, Edmond E., lawyer; b. of Am. parents, Cassel, Germany, Feb. 12, 1865; s. Edward and Hannah (Spiegelberg) W.; prep. edn., Sach's Collegiate Inst., N.Y. City; Ph.B., Columbia, 1883, LL.B., 1885; m. Irene Kohns, June 6, 1900; 1 dau., Ethel H. Admitted to N.Y. bar, 1886, and began practice at N.Y. City with A. P. W. Seaman; mem. firm Wise & Seligsberg, 1910—; specialist in corp. and comml. law; dir. R. H. Mack & Co., Lysol, Inc., Lehn & Fink Products Co., Bamberger & Co. (Newark, N.J.), Davison Paxton Co. (Atlanta, Ga.), 40 E. 52d Street Corp. Trustee Hebrew Orphan Asylum, Clara de Hirsch Home for Working Girls, Fred L. Lavanburg Foundation. Mem. Federation Jewish Philanthropic Socs. of New York and Brooklyn, St. John's Guild Legal Aid Soc., United Hosp. Fund, Hudson Guild. Republican. Jewish religion. Home: New York, N.Y. Died July 22, 1932.

WISE, Edward, merchant; b. Boston, Nov. 23, 1870; s. Henry and Amelia (Weil) W.; grad. English High Sch., Boston, 1881; m. Anna Marie Heitzman, Dec. 16, 1896. Began as clk. for Weil, Dreyfus & Co., wholesale underwear and hosiery, Boston, 1881; with Weil, Haskell & Co., 1890-92; asso. with brother, in wholesale and retail tobacco bus., Providence, R.I., 1892-93; an organizer, and pres. of the United Cigar Stores Co. of America; pres. Lloyd Realty Co.; dir. Corp. United Cigar Stores, Kaffee Hag Corp., United Stories Realty Corp. Died June 19, 1939.

WISE, James, bishop; b. Dundee, Scotland, July 26, 1875; s. Robert and Mary (Rattray) W.; came to U.S., 1888; student U. of Neb., 1896-98; grad. Gen. Theol. Sem., 1900; S.T.D., Hobart, 1917; D.D., Gen. Theol. Sem., 1918; LL.D., Washburn Coll., Topeka, Kan., 1918; m. Anna Marie Betts, Dec. 31, 1902. Deacon, 1901, priest 1902, P.E. Ch.; missionary in charge, St. Clement's Ch., South Omaha, Neb., Holy Cross Ch., Papillion, Neb., 1900-02; rector St. Martin's Ch., South Omaha, 1902-09, Ch. of the Holy Communion, St. Louis, Mo., 1909-16; consecrated coadjutor bishop of Kan., Oct. 28, 1916. Mem. Gen. Bd. Religious Edn., Press and Publicity Commn. (both P.E. Ch.). Pres. Vail School of Nursing, Christ's Hosp. (Topeka, Kan.). Mason. Author: The Passion Service, 1916. Contbg. editor religious education, page of The Witness. Home: Topeka, Kan. Died July 8, 1939.

WISE, James Walter, congressman; b. Henry County, Ga., Mar. 3, 1868; s. George Edward and Rachel (Foster) W.; ed. common schs.; studied law in office of E. J. Reagan, McDonough, Ga., and in Law Dept. of Emory Coll.; m. Clara Betts, June 3, 1913. Admitted to Ga. bar, 1893, and practiced in Fayetteville; mayor of Fayetteville 2 terms; mem. Ga. Ho. of Rep., 1902-08; solicitor gen. (pros. atty.), Flint Jud. Circuit, 1908-12; mem. 64th to 68th Congress (1915-25), 6th Ga. Dist.; pres. Farmers and Merchants Bank. Democrat. Methodist. Mason. Home: Fayetteville, Ga. Died Sept. 8, 1925.

WISE, John Sergeant, lawyer; b. Rio de Janeiro, Brazil (where his father was U.S. minister to Brazil), Dec. 27, 1846; s. Henry Alexander and Sarah (Sergeant) W.; ed. Va. Mil. Inst., 1863-64; served as 2d lt. in C.S.A., until Lee's surrender; B.L., U. of Va., 1867; m. Evelyn Beverly Douglas, Nov. 3, 1869; father of Henry Alexander W., U.S. atty., Eastern Dist. of Va., 1881-83; mem. 48th Congress (1883-85), Va. at-large; candidate for gov., 1885; moved to New York, 1888. Author: Diomed, 1898, 1905; The End of an Era, 1899; The Lion's Skin, 1905; Recollections of Thirteen Presidents, 1906; Citizenship, 1906. Home: New York, N.Y. Died May 12, 1913.

WISE, Leo Henry, financier; b. Catonsville, Md., Apr. 23, 1862; s. Henry and Emilie (Sutro) W.; ed. pub. schs., Baltimore, Md.; m. Sarah Virginia Winternitz, Oct. 15, 1884; children— Mrs. Emily Speyer, Sidney L., Alfred L. Chmn. bd. Am. Colony Ins. Co.; dir. U.S. Fire Ins. Co. Mason. Home: New York, N.Y. Died Oct. 7, 1934.

WISE, Otto Irving, lawyer; b. Vienna, Austria, Dec. 5, 1871; came to America, 1874; s. Aaron (Ph.D., D.D.) and Sabine (Von Fischer) W.; student Coll. City of New York, 1885-87, New York U., 1887-89; m. Ethel A. Rosenthal, Feb. 8, 1893. Admitted to N.Y. bar, and practiced in N.Y. City; removed to San Francisco, Calif. V.p. and gen. counsel Western States Life Ins. Co.; dir. Alaska Salmon Co., Western Bag. Co., Pacific Sanitary Mfg. Co., Pacific Porcelain Ware Co. Mem. bd. dirs. Fedn. of Jewish Charities. Republican. Jewish religion. Mason. Home: San Francisco, Calif. Deceased.

WISE, Peter Manuel, physician; b. Clarence, N.Y., March 7, 1851; s. Joseph and Elizabeth W.; ed. Parker Classical Inst., Clarence, N.Y.; grad. M.D., U. of Buffalo, 1872; m. Anna E. Heston, Oct. 6, 1875. Mem. State Commn. to locate and design State Asylum for Northern New York, 1886; med. supt. Willard State Hosp., 1884-90; med. supt. St. Lawrence State Hosp., 1890-96; pres. N.Y. State Commn. in Lunacy, Oct. 1, 1896-1901; prof. psychiatry, U. of Vt., 1891-95. Pres. Am. Medico-Psychol. Assn., 1901, N.Y. State Med. Soc.; 9th-10th Internat. Med. Congresses. Republican. Compiled 16th to 21st Annual Reports Willard Asylum, 1884-90; Third to Tenth Annual Reports St. Lawrence State Hosp., 1890-96. Author: Text-Book for Training Schools (2 vols.), 1896; Urinalysis for the Bedside. Editor State Hospital Bulletin, 1894-96; founder and ed. Epitome, 1902-05. Wrote: Notes on Asylums of Great Britain, and 22 other monographs; also numerous contributions to scientific and sociological journals. Home: New York, N.Y. Died 1907.

WISE, Thomas Alfred, actor; b. Faversham, Eng., Mar. 23, 1865; s. Daniel and Harriet (Potts) W.; brought to America, 1868; earned own living since 9 yrs. of age and self-ed.; m. Gertrude Whitty, Nov. 11, 1895. Began as actor in Calif., 1883; starred with John C. Rice, 1902, 1903; in "A Gentleman From Mississippi" 3 yrs., 1908-11; and with John Barrymore, 1911; appeared in following original New York productions: "Mr. Wilkinson's Widows," "Gloriana," "The Last Chapter," "The Cuckoo," "House that Jack Built," "Prince Chap," "Are You a Mason?" "Vivian's Papas," "Harriet's Honeymoon," "Military Mad," "Home Folks," "Mrs. Temple's Telegram," "Little Cherub," "Miss Hook of Holland," "Lady from Lane's," all star cast, "Lights o' London," and many others. Republican. Pres. Actors' Soc., 1908-10. Author: (with Harrison Rhodes, plays) A Gentleman from Mississippi, 1908; An Old New Yorker, 1910; The Old Man, 1911; The Greatest Show on Earth, 1911. Deceased.

WISE, William Clinton, rear adm., U.S.N.; b. Lewisburg, Va., Nov. 8, 1842; s. James and Virginia F. (Caldwell) W.; m. Nellie Humphreys, May 18, 1875. Apptd. from Ky., and grad. U.S. Naval Acad., 1863; ensign, Oct. 1, 1863; master, May 10, 1866; lt., Feb. 21, 1867; lt. comdr., Mar. 12, 1868; comdr., Feb. 24, 1881; capt., Nov. 11, 1894; rear adm., June 14, 1902. Served in New Ironsides, S. Atlantic Blockading Squadron, 1863-64; participated in attacks on Charleston, and the Jacksonville expdn.; served in Minnesota, N. Atlantic Blockading Squadron, 1864-65; present at both attacks on Ft. Fisher; comdg. U.S.S. Malvern, 1865, flagship of Admiral Porter; served on Hartford, Asiatic Squadron, 1865-66; Wachusett, 1866-68; practice-ship Dale, 1869; Miantonomoh, 1869-70; Brooklyn, 1870-72; Ajax, 1873-74; receiving-ship Vermont, 1874-75; exec. officer Tennessee, 1875-76; comd. Palos, 1876-78; insp. ordnance Navy Yard, Norfolk, 1878-81; torpedo duty, 1882; comdg. Portsmouth, 1883-84; insp. ordnance Navy Yard, Portsmouth, 1884-87; comdg. Juniata, 1888-89; Navy Yard, Norfolk, 1889-90; light house insp. 15th dist., 1890-94; ordnance duty Navy Yard, Washington, 1894-95; comdg. Amphitrite, 1895-97, Texas, 1897; capt. of yard, Navy Yard, Norfolk, 1897-98; comdg. Yale, during war with Spain, 1898; comdg. receiving-ship Franklin, 1898-1902; mem. Gen. Bd. and comdt. Navy Yard, Pensacola, 1902-03; comdr.-in-chief of Atlantic Training Squadron, 1903-04; retired, Nov. 8, 1904; spl. duty in connection with steamboat inspection service, 1904-05. Hon. M.A., Yale, 1899. Died Nov. 23, 1923.

WISHARD, John G., M.D.; b. Danville, Ind., Sept. 19, 1863; s. John O. and Mary (Fisher) W.; grad. Central Normal Coll., Danville, 1885; M.D., Ind. Med. Coll. (Ind. U.), 1888; M.D. Faculte de Médicine, Constantinople, Turkey, 1889; post-grad. work, New York Post-Grad. Coll., 1893, hosps. of London and Paris, 1908, Vienna, 1910; A.M., Wabash Coll., Crawfordsville, Ind., 1903; m. Annabette Bryan, Dec. 28, 1893 (died 1899); children—Frederick B. (M.D.), Mrs. Bertha Sargent; m. 2d, Harriet J. Wishard, Dec. 23, 1902 (died 1937); m. 3d, Blanche Wakefield Pollock, Nov. 26, 1938. Med. missionary in Persia, 1889-1909; in practice at Wooster, O., 1910—; mem. Bd. of Health, Wooster. Clinical prof. Indiana Med. Coll., 1900-02. Accompanied archæol. expdn. to Bagdad and Babylonia, 1891; cons. phys. to Muzzaffar-Ed-Din, Shah of Persia, 1907; dir. Am. Presbyn. Hosp. Teheran; mem. Nat. Bd. of Health, Persia; decorated Order of Lion and Sun by Shah for spl. service in Persia, 1899. Surgeon S.A.T.C., Coll. of Wooster; trustee Coll. of Wooster. Republican. Presbyn. Author: Twenty Years in Persia, 1908; Reminiscences of a Doctor, 1935; also contbr. various articles on Persia to The Independent, 1906-09, and other articles, particularly on etiology of cataract, to recent American med. and scientific periodicals. Mem. Permanent Jud. Commn., Gen. Assembly Presbyn. Ch. U.S.A.; trustee and chmn. finance com. Coll. of Wooster. Home: Wooster, O. Died July 15, 1940.

WISHARD, Samuel Ellis, clergyman; b. Johnson County, Ind., Dec. 18, 1825; s. Col. John and Agnes Henderson (Oliver) W.; A.B., Wabash Coll., 1853, A.M., 1856; B.D., Lane Theol. Sem., Cincinnati, 1856; D.D., Centre Coll., Ky., 1884; m. Sophie Evarts, Feb. 13, 1857. Licensed to preach by Presbytery of Indianapolis, 1855; ordained by Presbytery of Schuyler, at Mt. Sterling, Ill., Apr. 1857; pastor Rushville, Ill., 1857-61, Tecumseh, Mich., 1861-67, Battle Creek, Mich., 1867-71, Franklin, Ind., 1871-77; in evangelistic work, 1877-80; pastor Fifth Ch., Chicago, 1880-83; supt. home mission work Synod of Ky., 1883-87; pastor Central Presbyn. Ch., Des Moines, Ia., 1887-90; supt. home missions Synod of Utah, 1890-1906; preaching, 1906—. Author: Memorial of Rev. F. R. Gallagher, D.D., 1868; Semi-centennial of the Presbyterian Church of Franklin, Ind., 1875; The Mormons, 1904; The Old, Old Story; The Testimony of the Bible Concerning the Assumptions of Destructive Criticism; The Passion Play in the Light of Our Protestant Faith and the Word of God; The Bible Against Polygamy. Wrote a letter every week for 32 yrs. to Herald and Presbyter. Cincinnati. Died Nov. 11, 1915.

WISHARD, William Niles, surgeon; b. Greenwood, Ind., Oct. 10, 1851; s. William Henry (M.D.) and Harriet Newell (Moreland) W.; student Wabash Coll., Crawfordsville, Ind., 1870-72, hon. A.M., 1890; M.D., Ind. Med. Coll., 1874, Miami Med. Coll., 1876; post-grad. work in New York and hosps. of Europe; LL.D., Wooster, 1919; LL.D., Ind. U., 1924; D.Sc., De Pauw U., 1929, Hanover Coll., 1933; m. Alice M. Woollen, 1880 (died same yr.); m. 2d, Frances C. Scoville, 1896; children—Wm. Niles, M.D., Rev. Charles S. Practiced with father in Indianapolis, supt. Indianapolis City Hosp., 1879-87 (secured erection of new hosp. and first training sch. for nurses in Ind.); prof. genito-urinary surgery, Indiana U. Sch. of Medicine, 1887-1936, prof. emeritus, 1936—. Surgeon gen. Ind. N.G., 1890-92, rank of col. Chmn. com. on medical legislation and pub. policy of Ind. State Med. Soc., 1900-22, and chmn. bur. of publicity, 1922—; author of law governing practice of medicine in Ind. F.A.C.S. Republican. Presbyn. One of the first to perform perineal prostatectomy; first to apply cautery under visual observation for reduction of enlarged prostate (1890); author of numerous articles relating to genito-urinary surgery. Home: Indianapolis, Ind. Died Jan. 22, 1941.

WISHART, Alfred Wesley, clergyman; b. New York, Sept. 9, 1865; s. Joseph D. and Ellen S. (Bonynge) W.; A.B., Colgate, 1889; post grad. study U. of Chicago; fellow in church history U. of Chicago Div. Sch., 1893-95; D.D., Colgate U., June 1921; m. Mary Lee Fethers, Aug. 22, 1889. Clerk N.Y. Life Ins. Co. and Jennings & Russell (law firm), 1880-84; ordained Bapt. ministry, 1889; pastor Second Ch., Troy, N.Y., 1890-93, First Ch., Maywood, Ill., 1893-95, Central Ch., Trenton, N.J., 1895-1906, Fountain St. Ch., Grand Rapids, Mich., 1906—. Organized first "civic revival," 1900, at Trenton; founded Anti-Bribery Soc. of Mercer County, N.J.; editor Trenton Times, 1901-03; pres. bd. Kent Scientific Mus., Grand Rapids; mem. Social Service Commn., Northern Bapt. Conv. Author: A Short History of Monks and Monasteries, 1900; Primary Facts in Religious Thought, 1905. Y.M.C.A. work in France, Aug.-Dec. 1917. Home: Grand Rapids, Mich. Died Apr. 25, 1933.

WISHART, John Elliott, clergyman, educator; b. New Athens, O., Nov. 29, 1866; s. William and Sarah (Irvine) W.; A.B., Monmouth Coll., 1889, A.M., 1893, D.D., 1905, LL.D., 1922; grad. Allegheny (now Pittsburgh) Theol. Sem., 1892, receiving Purdy Prize for scholarship; post-grad. work univs. of Chicago and Berlin; m. Mary Alice Hill, June 28, 1897 (died 1929); m. 2d, Mrs. Helen Collier Hill, Aug. 28, 1930. Ordained to ministry United Presbyterian Ch., 1895; pastor Ingram, Pa., 1894-1904, Pasadena, Calif., 1904-05; prof. Hebrew and O.T. interpretation, Xenia Theol. Sem., 1905-23; prof. ch. history, San Francisco Theol. Sem., 1923-27, prof. systematic theology, 1927-38; visiting prof. theology, Near East Sch. of Theology, Beirut, Syria, 1938-39. Actg. pastor American Ch., Berlin, Germany, 1913. Author: The Spirits of Just Men Made Perfect, 1916; The Fact of Prayer, 1927; also articles in theol. reviews. Home: South Pasadena, Calif. Died Dec. 23, 1940.

WISHON, Albert Graves, public utilities; b. Relfe, Mo., Nov. 6, 1858; s. Francis Marion and Mary Elizabeth (Coppedge) W.; Dr.Engring., Mo. Sch. of Mines, Rolla, Mo.; m. Henrietta Emory, Oct. 5, 1881; children—A. Emory, Jenny Lindsay (Mrs. Ralph W. Watson). With Adler, Goldman & Co., St. Louis, 1878-81; mercantile bus., St. James, Mo., 1881-87; with bridge and building dept. M.P. Ry. Co., 1887-89; in lumber bus., Tulare, Calif., 1889-91, banking bus., 1891-93; real estate, etc., Tulare and Visalia, 1893-98; in electric power bus., Visalia, 1898-1902; settled in Fresno, 1903; pres. San Joaquin Light & Power Corp., 1903—; pres. Midland Counties Pub. Service Corp., Bakersfield & Kern Electric Ry.; v.p. Lerdo Land Co.; dir., treas. Wishon-Watson Co.; v.chmn. San Joaquin Light & Power Corp., Midland Counties Pub. Service Corp. Republican. Mem. M.E. Ch., S. Mason. Home: Fresno, Calif. Died June 17, 1936.

WISNER, Frank George, lumberman; b. Clinton, Ia., Mar. 5, 1873; s. George E. D. and Mary Elizabeth (Heupel) W.; grad. high sch., Lyons, Ia., 1889; m. Mary Jeannette Gardiner, Sept. 28, 1897; children—George Brockway (dec.), Elizabeth Gardiner (Mrs. Alexander Field Chisholm), Louise Gardiner (dec.), Frank Gardiner. In lumber industry, at Laurel, Miss., 1897—; pres. First Nat. Bank, Laurel; v.p. Laurel Oil and Fertilizer Co.; treas. Eastman, Gardiner & Co. Alderman at large, Laurel, 10 yrs.; chmn. City Water and Sewerage Bd.; pres. bd. trustees Laurel city schs. 15 yrs.; pres. Nat. Lumber Mfrs. Assn., 1924-27; dir. Miss. Flood Rehabilitation Corp. Asst. chmn. Lumber Advisory Com. for War Industries Bd.; mem. Miss. State Bd. of Defense, World War I; dist. chmn. War Savings Stamp and Liberty Loan coms. Vestryman P.E. Ch.; diocesan chmn. Clergy Pension Endowment Fund. Home: Laurel, Miss. Died Apr. 24, 1938.

WISNER, George Monroe, civil engr.; b. Detroit, Mich., Feb. 9, 1870; s. George Y. and Carrie (Palmer) W.; B.S. in C.E., U. of Mich., 1892; m. Edith K. Young, Feb. 5, 1902. In employ engring. dept. Sanitary Dist. of Chicago, July 7, 1892—; asst. engr. in charge Chicago River improvement, 1897-1901, asst. chief engr., 1901-07, chief engr., 1907-20, cons. engr., 1920—; engr. for settlement of rapid transit and subway problem of City of Chicago, 1929. Home: Chicago, Ill. Died Aug. 26, 1932.

WISNER, George Y., civil engr.; b. West Dresden, N.Y., July 11, 1841; s. William and Jane (Downey) W.; grad. U. of Mich., C.E., 1865; m. Carrie Palmer, Oct. 15, 1867. Engaged in Govt. surveys on Great Lakes and Mississippi river, 1865-80; on surveys of Mississippi, Des Plaines and Illinois rivers improvements, 1880-84; supt. constrn. 10th and 11th U.S. Light House dists., 1884-87; in private practice, 1887—; 1888-91, resident engr. South Pass Jetty Works, and chief engr. Brazos River Harbor Improvement; organized and directed, 1895-97, sanitary dept. Detroit Bd. of Health; mem. U.S. Deep Waterways Commn., 1897-1900; cons. engr. Montreal, Ottawa & Georgian Bay Canal Co., 1901—; cons. engr. for U.S. Reclamation Service, 1903—. Author: Geodetic Field Work, 1883; Brazos River Harbor Improvement, 1891; Worthless Government Engineering, 1892; Breakwaters, Sea-Walls and Jetties, 1893; Hydraulics of Rivers Having Alluvial Beds, 1896; Sewage Disposal, 1896; Regulation of Lake Levels, 1895-99; Report of Deep Waterway Commission, 1900; Canals from the Great Lakes to the Atlantic, 1900. Home: Detroit, Mich. Died 1906.

WISSER, John Philip, officer U.S.A.; b. St. Louis, July 19, 1852; s. Philip and Barbara (Weber) W.; grad. U.S. Mil. Acad., 1874, U.S. Arty. Sch., Ft. Monroe, 1878; studied Royal School of Mines, Freiberg, Saxony, 1883-84; m. Georgiana Hollister, June 15, 1893; children—Edward Hollister, John Philip. Apptd. 2d lt. 1st Arty., June 17, 1874; promoted through grades to brig. gen. U.S.A., May 26, 1913; retired July 19, 1916. Asst. prof. chemistry, mineralogy and geology, U.S. Mil. Acad., 1878-82 and 1886-94; instr. chemistry, U.S. Arty. School, 1882-84; represented U.S.A. at French maneuvers, 1884; editor Jour. U.S. Artillery, 1895-1902; inst. mil. science and mil. engring., U.S. Arty. Sch., 1895-1900; detailed to witness U.S. naval maneuvers, Caribbean Sea, 1902; detailed in Insp. General's Dept., 1904; acting insp. gen. Pacific Div. during and after the earthquake and fire in San Francisco, Apr. 18, 1906; mil. attaché at Berlin, 1906-09; comdg. arty. dist. of Savannah, 1909-11, arty. dist. of San Francisco, Feb. 6, 1911-Feb. 15, 1913; comdg. Presidio, San Francisco, Feb. 6, 1911-June 19, 1912; comdg. Dept. of Calif., Apr. 8-June 26, 1912; comdg. Ft. Winfield Scott, San Francisco, June 19, 1912-Feb. 13, 1913; comdg. Dept. of Calif., Jan. 2-30, 1913; comdg. Pacific Coast Arty. Dist., Feb. 15-Sept. 15, 1913; in comd. 4th Brigade, 2d Div., in camp at Texas City, Tex., Sept. 1913-Jan. 1914; comdg. Pacific Coast Arty. Dist., Ft. Miley, Calif., Jan. 4, 1914-Jan. 5, 1915; comdg. 1st Hawaiian Brigade and Schofield Barracks, H.T. to Nov. 5, 1915; comdg. Hawaiian Dept., H.T., Nov. 5, 1915-16. Author: Gun Cotton, 1886; Practical Problems in Minor Tactics and Strategy, 1888; By Land and Sea, 1891; articles Military Schools and Staff and Staff Schools, in Johnson's New Universal Cyclo., 1893; Explosive Materials, 1898; The Second Boer War, 1901; Tactics of Coast Defense, 1902; Practical Field Exercises, 1903; A Military and Naval Dictionary, 1905. Editor: International Military Series, 1902—. Contbr. to New International Ency., several articles on organization and tactics; a contributing, nominating and advisory editor, Nat. Cyclo. Am. Biography, 1921. Called into active service and comd. Hawaiian Dept., Aug. 1917-June 1918. Home: Berkeley, Calif. Died Jan. 19, 1927.

WISTAR, Isaac Jones, penologist; b. Phila., Nov. 14, 1827; ed. at Westtown and Haverford; Sc.D., Univ. of Pa.; brig. gen. of vols., U.S.A., 1862-65; pres. Acad. Natural Sciences of Phila., 1892-96; insp. of Eastern Penitentiary of Pa.; pres. State Bd. of Charities of Pa.; writer and speaker on penology; pres. Am. Philos. Soc., 1901-03; mgr. Phila. Library Co.; founder and sec. Wistar Inst. of Anatomy and Biology. Died 1905.

WISTER, Annis Lee, translator; b. Phila., Oct. 9, 1830; d. Rev. William H. Furness (1802-96); m. Dr. Caspar Wister, 1854 (1817-1888). Translated works of many of the leading German novelists into English, 1864— (uniform set, 30 vols., published 1888). Author: (with Dr. Frederic H. Hedge) Metrical Translations and Poems. Died 1908.

WISTER, Owen, author; b. Phila., Pa., July 14, 1860; s. Owen Jones and Sarah (Butler) W.; A.B., Harvard, 1882, A.M., LL.B., 1888; LL.D., U. of Pa., 1907; L.H.D., Williams, 1912; m. Mary Channing Wister, Apr. 21, 1898 (died 1913); children—Mary Channing, Owen Jones, Frances Kemble, William Rotch, Charles Kemble, Sarah Butler. Admitted Phila. bar, 1889; in lit. work, 1891—. Mem. Am. Acad. Arts and Letters; fellow Am. Acad. Arts and Sciences. Member Bd. of Overseers, Harvard, 1912-25. Author: The New Swiss Family Robinson, 1882; The Dragon of Wantley—His Tail, 1892; Red Men and White, 1896; Lin. McLean, 1898; The Jimmy John Boss, 1900; U.S. Grant, a Biography, 1900; The Virginian, 1902; Philosophy 4, 1903; Journey in Search of Christmas, 1904; Lady Baltimore, 1906; The Simple Spelling Bee, 1907; Mother, 1907; The Seven Ages of Washington, 1907; Members of the Family, 1911; The Pentecost of Calamity, 1915; The Ancient Grudge, or a Straight Deal, 1920; Indispensable Information for Infants, 1921; Neighbors Henceforth, 1922; Watch Your Thirst, 1923; When West Was West, 1928; Roosevelt—The Story of a Friendship, 1930; also contbr. of much prose and verse in mags. Collaborator: Muskox, Bison, Sheep and Goat (Whitney's Am. Sportsmen's Library), 1904. Home: Bryn Mawr, Pa. Died July 21, 1938.

WISWELL, Andrew Peters, jurist; b. Ellsworth, Me., July 11, 1852; s. Arno and Sarah (Peters) W.; prep. edn. E. Me. Conf. Sem., Bucksport; grad. Bowdoin Coll., 1873; LL.D., Bowdoin, 1900; m. Emma Greene, Dec. 15, 1875. Judge Ellsworth municipal ct., 1877-81; nat. bank examiner, 1883-86; del. Rep. Nat. Conv., 1884; mem. Me. legislature, 1887, 89, 91; speaker Me. house, 1891; asso. justice Supreme Jud. Ct., Me., 1893-1900, chief justice, Jan. 2, 1900—. Died 1906.

WITHERBEE, Frank Spencer, iron mfr.; b. Port Henry, N.Y., May 12, 1852; s. Jonathan G. and Charlotte (Spencer) W.; A.B., Yale, 1874; m. Mary Rhinelander Stewart, Apr. 25, 1883. Largely interested in iron mines at Port Henry, N.Y., 1875—; pres. Witherbee, Sherman & Co., Cubitas Iron Ore. Co., Lake Champlain & Moriah R.R. Co.; v.p. Cheever Iron Ore Co.; dir. Equitable Life Assurance Soc.; trustee N.Y. Life Ins. & Trust Co., Fulton Trust Co.; dir. Central Hudson Steamboat Co., Citizens Nat. Bank, Port Henry, N.Y.; pres. Troy Steel Co. and v.p. Tenn. Coal, Iron & R.R. Co., both absorbed by U.S. Steel Corp. Mem. Rep. Nat. Com. during Harrison campaign; served for yrs. on Rep. State Com. and frequently del. nat. and state convs.; presdl. elector 1st Harrison presdl. election. Identified with establishment of Adirondack State Park and N.Y. State Barge Canal; mem. N.G.S.N.Y. 5 yrs., Am. Iron & Steel Inst. (dir.). Decorated Cross Legion of Honor, France, 1912. Home: New York, N.Y. Died Apr. 13, 1917.

WITHERS, Robert Enoch, U.S. senator; b. Campbell County, Va., Sept. 18, 1821; s. Dr. Robert Walter and Susan Dabney (Alexander) W.; grad. U. of Va., 1841; M.D., U. of Va. and Baltimore Alms House Hosp., 1843; m. Mary Virginia Royall, Feb. 3, 1846. Practiced medicine in Campbell County and Danville, Va., until 1861; comd. 18th regt. C.S.A.; edited Lynchburg Daily News, 1866-69; elected lt. gov. of Va., 1873; U.S. senator from Va., 1875-81; U.S. consul at Hong-Kong, 1885-89; Grand Master Grand Encampment Knights Templars of U.S., 1883-86; regent Smithsonian Instn., 1878-81. Died 1907.

WITHERS, William Alphonso, chemist; b. River View, nr. Davidson, N.C., May 31, 1864; s. William B. and Sarah L. (Rutledge) W.; A.B., Davidson Coll., N.C., 1883, A.M., 1885, Sc.D., 1917; student in chemistry, 1888-90, fellow, 1889-90, Cornell U.; m. Elizabeth Witherspoon Daniel, June 11, 1896 (died 1905); m. 2d, Jane Hinton Pescud, July 29, 1909. Asst. chemist, 1884-88, chemist, 1897-1921, acting dir., 1897-99, N.C. Agrl. Expt. Sta.; prof. chemistry, 1889—, v.p., 1916—, dir. Summer Sch., 1917—, N.C. State Coll. of Agr. and Engring. State chemist, 1897-98; state statis. agent U.S. Dept. of Agr., 1895-1902 and 1905-15. Mem. exec. com. Nat. Pure Food and Drug Congress, 1898, N.C. Agrl. Soc., 1898—; author of N.C. pure food law, 1899; discoverer (with F. E. Carruth) of the toxic principle of cottonseed, 1915; chmn. com. on pure food legislation, Assn. Am. Agrl. Colls. and Expt. Stas., 1899-1903; pres. N.C. sect. Am. Chem. Soc., 1901-02; pres. Assn. Official Agrl. Chemists, 1909-10; sec. N.C. Coll. Assn.; fellow A.A.A.S.; dir. of Raleigh Y.M.C.A., 1914— (pres. 1920, 21, 22). Mem. N.C. Council Defense, 1917-18; mem. co. bd. food adminstrs., 1917-18; exec. com. local chapter Am. Red Cross, 1917-18; chmn. Wake County Bd. of Edn., 1919—. Democrat. Presbyn.; exec. com. N.C. S.S. Assn., 1914— (pres. East Central region 1923-24). Grand Comdr. K.T. of N.C., 1896; Grand High Priest R.A.M., 1897. Author of bulls., articles, etc., mainly on nitrification, food adulteration, and cottonseed. Died June 20, 1924.

WITHERSPOON, Herbert, singer; b. Buffalo, N.Y., July 21, 1873; s. Orlando and Cora V. (Taylor) W.; B.A., Yale, 1895; studied drawing and painting Yale Art Sch.; singing with various teachers New York, London, Paris, Berlin, including Dubulle, Lamperti, Henry J. Wood; acting with V. Capoul and Anton Fuchs, Munich; m. Greta Hughes, Sept. 25, 1899; m. 2d, Florence Hinkle, soprano, June 22, 1916. In English grand opera under Henry W. Savage, 1898-1900; toured with Thomas Orchestra and Pittsburgh Orchestra many yrs.; engagements included all prin. societies in U.S., Can. and Eng.; 1st basso, singing about 25 leading parts at Metropolitan Opera House, New York, 1908-16; pres. Chicago Musical Coll., 1925-29; v.p. and dir. Chicago Civic Opera Co., 1930-31; dir. Cincinnati Conservatory of Music, 1932-33. Chmn. of music for "Century of Progress Exposition, Chicago, 1933." Instrumental in founding Am. Acad. of Teachers of Singing, New York, March 25, 1922, and chmn. until 1926; lecture tour, 1926-27, including 42 cities, on "Music as a Vital Factor in General Education"; founded Bohemians of Chicago, 1928. Known as educator, and lecturer on gen. edn., æsthetics, etc. Mem. Am. Acad. Teachers of Singing. Home: New York, N.Y. Died May 10, 1935.

WITHERSPOON, John A., M.D.; b. Columbia, Tenn., Sept. 13, 1864; M.D., U. of Pa., 1887; m. Cornelia Dixon, Nov. 8, 1888. In practice at Nashville, 1889—; mem. med. faculty, U. of Tenn., 1889-94, Vanderbilt U., 1889—; prof. medicine and clin. medicine. Pres. Miss. Valley Med. Assn., 1909-10, A.M.A., 1913-14. Home: Nashville, Tenn. Died Apr. 26, 1929.

WITHERSPOON, Samuel Andrew, congressman; b. Lowndes County, Miss., May 4, 1855; s. E. B. (M.D.) and Elizabeth (Dowd) W.; A.B., U. of Miss., 1876, A.M., LL.D., 1879; m. Susan E. May, June 17, 1880. Tutor Latin, U. of Miss., 1876-79; admitted to bar, 1879; in practice at Meridian, Miss., 1879—. Mem. 62d Congress (1911-13), 5th Miss. Dist. Democrat. Home: Meridian, Miss. Died Nov. 24, 1915.

WITHERSTINE, Christopher Sumner, M.D.; b. New York, Feb. 15, 1854; s. Gaylord Hilts and Clarinda Adelia (Seybolt) W.; B.S., Coll. City of New York, 1875, M.S., 1878; M.D., Coll. Phys. and Surg. (Columbia), 1878; m. Mary, d. Thomas and Emma Grace Jones, Apr. 12, 1883. Interne of Charity (now City) and of Maternity hosps., Blackwell's Island, N.Y., 1878-79; visiting phys., Home for Aged, Little Sisters of the Poor, Phila., 1880-99, to Germantown Almshouse, 1880-81, to Germantown Hosp., 1881-83; surgeon Phila. & Reading R.R., 1882-86; chief clin. asst. throat dept., Jefferson Hosp., Phila., 1884-86. Foreign asso. mem. Société Française d'Hygiène de Paris. Republican. Presbyn. Author: International Pocket Medical Formulary, 1888; Reviser and contbr. to med., surg. and physiol. depts. People's Cyclo. of Universal Knowledge, 1891. Asso. editor Annual of the Universal Med. Sciences, 1888-96, The Satellite, 1889-93; Sajous' Annual and Analytical Cyclo. of Practical Medicine, 1898—. Lecturer on therapeutics, Med. Dept., Temple U., Phila. Mem. Vol. Med. Service Corps. Mason. Home: Germantown, Philadelphia, Pa. Died Dec. 25, 1933.

WITHINGTON, Charles Francis, physician; b. Brookline, Mass., Aug. 21, 1852; s. Otis and Lucy (Jenckes) W.; A.B., Harvard, 1874, M.D., 1881; m. Georgiana Bowen, Sept. 20, 1883. Taught in Brookline High Sch., 1874-75, in Roxbury Latin Sch., 1875-77; in med. practice at Boston, 1881—; visiting phys. Boston City Hosp.; cons. phys. Boston Insane Hosp., N.E. Hosp. for Women and Children, Choate Memorial Hosp.; instr. clin. medicine, Harvard Med. Sch.; lecturer medicine, Grad. Sch. Medicine, Harvard. Trustee Roxbury Latin Sch., Fellowes' Athenæum. Episcopalian. Republican. Author: The Relation of Hospitals to Medical Education, 1885. Died Jan. 7, 1917.

WITHINGTON, David Little, lawyer; b. Newbury, Mass., Feb. 2, 1854; s. Nathan Noyes and Elizabeth (Little) W.; A.B., Harvard, 1874; LL.B., Boston U., 1876; m. Sarah E. Curtis, July 6, 1880 (died 1884); m. 2d, Marietta Dennett Paul, Feb. 2, 1887. Admitted to bar, 1876; practiced at Boston and Newburyport, Mass., 1876-86, San Diego, Calif., 1886-1903, Honolulu, T.H., 1903—; firm of Castle & Withington. Captain Co. A, 8th Regt. Mass. Militia, 1876-79; mem. Calif. Senate, 1895-99; chmn. Commn. on Uniformity of Legislation, Calif., 1897-1901, also Hawaii, 1910-15; received thanks Calif. Senate, 1895, for drawing present county govt. act of Calif., and in 1897, for work on revised system of legislature procedure. Del. Universal Congress Lawyers and Jurists, St. Louis, 1904; pres. Civic Fedn., San Diego, Calif. Congregationalist. Republican. Home: Honolulu, H.I. Died July 21, 1919.

WITHROW, John Lindsay, clergyman; b. nr. Phila., 1837; s. John Mitchell and Keziah J. W.; grad. Princeton, 1860; Princeton Theol. Sem., 1863; D.D., Lafayette Coll., 1872; LL.D., Knox Coll., 1896. Successively pastor Abington, Pa., Arch Street Ch., Phila.; Park St. Ch., Boston, and Third Presbyn. Ch., Chicago. Returned, 1898, to Park St. Ch., Boston. Moderator Gen. Assembly, Presbyn. Ch., 1896. Home: Brookline, Mass. Died 1909.

WITHYCOMBE, James, governor; b. Tavistock, Eng., Mar. 21, 1854; s. Thomas and Mary Ann (Spurr) W.; came to U.S., 1871; ed. pub. schs. and under pvt. tutors; M.Agr., Ore. Agrl. Coll., 1902; m. Isabel Carpenter, June 6, 1875. Farmer and breeder of improved live stock—cattle, horses and sheep; state veterinarian of Ore., 1889-98; dir. Ore. Experiment Sta., 1898-1914; chmn. Rep. County Central Com., Washington County, Ore., 1898-99; gov. of Ore., 1915-19. Trustee Ore. Acad. Science. Sec. Pacific Woolgrowers' Assn., 1885-90; pres. Northwest Stockbreeders' Assn., 1896-98. Elk, Moose. Home: Salem, Ore. Died Mar. 3, 1919.

WITMER, Charles B., judge; b. Northumberland County, Pa., 1862; A.B., Central (Pa.) Coll., New Berlin, Pa., 1883; read law in office of Hon. C. G. Voris, of Sunbury, Pa. Admitted to Pa. bar, 1887; county solicitor, Northumberland County, 1888-91, 1894-1900; asst. atty. Spanish Treaty Claims Commission, 1902-04; chief counsel Dairy Food Commn., Harrisburg, Pa., 1904-05; spl. counsel, Auditor General's Dept., Pa., 1905-06; U.S. marshal, Middle Dist. of Pa., 1906-07; U.S. dist. atty., same dist., 1907-11; U.S. dist. judge, same dist., by appmt. of Pres. Taft, Mar. 2, 1911—. Republican. Home: Sunbury, Pa. Died Apr. 7, 1925.

WITT, Max Siegfried, composer; b. Stettin, Germany, Nov. 12, 1871; s. Elias and Sophie W.; grad. Friedrich Wilhelm Gymnasium, Stettin, 1886; m. Margaret Gonzalez, 1895. Mus. dir. in America, 1887-1900; mng. tabloid mus. productions in vaudeville, 1908—. Composer: (waltzes) Birth of the Rose; Sweet Repose; Diana; Orange Blossoms; The First Violin; Robespierre; Phyllis. (Marches): How Do You Do? Ambassador; Commander-in-Chief. (Pieces de Salon): Gavotte de Directoire; Henry V, danse antique. (Sacred and concert songs): The Everlasting Light; You Are so Dear to Me; Love's Four Seasons. (Popular ballads): Grace O'Moore; Don't Let Her Lose Her Way; My Own Colleen; The Moth and the Flame; My Little Georgia Rose; The Only Way; My Heart's To-Night in Texas; When the Birds Go North Again; In the Valley Where My Sally Said Good Bye; For Love of You; Honey Bee; For Just One Kiss. (March songs): Military Mollie; Convent Bells; I Like Your Way. (Comic opera scores): A Son of Rest, 1903, and The Duke of Duluth, 1905-06 (books by George H. Broadhurst). Home: New York, N.Y. Died Apr. 5, 1914.

WITTE, Max Ernest, M.D., psychiatrist; b. nr. Berlin, Germany, Jan. 31, 1859; s. Gottfried Wilhelm and Wilhelmina (Rakow) W.; German Luth. Coll., Galena, Ill., 2 yrs.; M.D., Coll. of Medicine, State U. of Iowa, 1881; m. Nevada Randolph, May 21, 1891; children—Leo Paul (dec.), Max Ernest; m. 2d, Blanche Katherine Maharrey, June 23, 1923. Asst. phys. Mt. Pleasant (Ia.) State Hosp., 1881-98; supt. Clarinda State Hosp., 1898—. Lecturer on mental diseases Coll. of Medicine, State U. of Iowa. Republican. Lutheran. Mason. Home: Clarinda, Ia. Died Jan. 29, 1933.

WITTENMYER, Edmund, army officer; b. in Ohio, Apr. 25, 1862; grad. U.S. Mil. Acad., 1887, Inf. and Cav. Sch., 1895. Commd. add. 2d lt. 9th Inf., June 12, 1887; 2d lt., June 15, 1887; 1st lt. 15th Inf., Nov. 27, 1894; capt. 10th Inf., Mar. 2, 1899; trans. to 15th Inf., July 3, 1899; p.m., Dec. 17, 1901; assigned to 5th Inf., Dec. 17, 1905; trans. to 6th Inf., Oct. 3, 1910; maj. 27th Inf., Feb. 15, 1911; lt. col., July 1, 1916; brig. gen. N.A., Aug. 5, 1917. Duty World's Fair, Chicago, 1893; at Puerto Principe, Cuba, 1898-99, Manila, P.I., 1900; adj. gen. 2d Brigade, China Relief Expdn., Aug.-Oct. 1900; in charge armed forces, provinces of Matanzas and Santa Clara, Cuba, 1907-09; gov. Province of Matanzas, Apr.-Oct. 1908; assigned duty Gen. Staff Corps, 1910; apptd. comdr. 153d Inf. Brigade, Camp Upton, Yaphank, L.I., N.Y., Sept. 1917. Died July 5, 1937.

WITTHAUS, Rudolph August, toxicologist; b. New York, Aug. 30, 1846; s. Rudolph A. and Marie A. (Dunbar) W.; A.B., Columbia, 1867, A.M., 1870; M.D., Univ. Med. Coll. (New York U.), 1875; studied Sorbonne and Collège de France, Paris, 1873-74; unmarried. Asso. prof. chemistry and physiology, New York U., 1876-78; prof. chemistry and toxicology, U. of Vt., 1878-98; prof. physiol. chemistry, 1882-86, chemistry and physics, 1886-98, Univ. Med. Coll.; prof. chemistry and toxicology, U. of Buffalo, 1882-88; prof. chemistry and physics, Cornell U. Med. College, 1898-1911, prof. emeritus, 1911—. Toxicol. expert in Carlyle Harris, Buchanan, Mayer, Fleming, Benham, Molineux and many other cases. Fellow A.A.A.S. Author: Essentials of Chemistry, 1879; General Medical Chemistry, 1881; Manual of Chemistry, 1879, 1908; Laboratory Guide in Urinalysis and Toxicology, 1886. Editor: Witthaus and Becker's Medical Jurisprudence (4 vols.), in which contributed introduction and Vol. 4 on Toxicology, 1894, 1906. Wrote: Articles on Poisoning by Hydrocyanic Acid, Oxalic Acid, Opium and Strychnine, and on Ptomaines, Wood's Handbook of Medical Sciences;

on homicide by morphine; detection of quinine; post-mortem imbibition of poisons; Researches Loomis Laboratory, etc. Home: New York, N.Y. Died Dec. 23, 1915.

WITWER, Harry Charles, author, humorist; b. Athens, Pa., Mar. 11, 1890; s. Henry Charles and Margaret (Nealon) W.; attended St. Joseph's Coll., Phila., 1906; m. Sonia Schagrin, Dec. 9, 1912; 1 son, Allan Henry. Began as errand boy in butcher shop, later "Bellhop," mgr. prize fighters; reporter with St. Cloud (Fla.) Tribune, 1911; with N.Y. American, 1912, Brooklyn Eagle, Elizabeth (N.J.) Times, N.Y. Mail, Atlanta Georgian, Newark (N.J.) News, N.Y. Sun, 1913-15; war corr. Collier's Weekly, 1917. Mem. Authors' League America, Society of Authors, Playwrights and Composers. Republican. Mason. Author: From Baseball to Boches, 1918; A Smile a Minute, 1919; Alex The Great, 1919; There's No Base Like Home, 1920; Kid Scanlon, 1920; The Leather Pushers, 1922; The Rubyiat of a Freshman, 1921; Fighting Blood, 1923; Fighting Back, 1924; Love and Learn, 1924; Roughly Speaking, 1926; Bill Grimm's Progress, 1926; The Classics In Slang, 1927; Yes Man's Land, 1929; also 125 motion pictures. Contbr. 375 short stories and articles to mags. Comic strips: Samson and Delia; Switchboard Sally; play (with William LeBaron) So This Is Harris. Died 1929.

WIXSON, Helen Marsh, educationist; b. Muscoda, Wis.; d. Jerome Luther and Melissa Allen (Moore) Marsh; ed. high and prep. schools; M.Pd., Colo. State Teachers Coll.; m. Elmer A. Wixson, 1886. Active in civic and progressive movements in Colo., 1890—; state librarian, 1895-96; state supt. pub. instrn., 1911-12; mem. Denver Bd. of Edn., 1914-15; county supt. of schools, City and County of Denver, 1919-23. Republican. Dir. and v.regent Colo. Chapter D.A.R. Member Administrative Women in Edn. Home: Denver, Colo. Died Apr. 1925.

WOELFKIN, Cornelius, theologian; b. New York, Sept. 15, 1859; s. John Frederick and Christiana (Austermühl) W.; ed public schs., New York; D.D., Rutgers, 1905, Rochester U., 1906; LL.D., Denison, 1912; Litt.D., Franklin and Marshall, 1913; D.D., Colgate U., 1920, New York U., 1921; m. Lillie S. Distler, May 3, 1882. Ordained Baptist ministry, 1886; pastor Bangall, N.Y., 1885-87, Hackensack, N.J., 1887-92, North Ch., Jersey City, 1892-94, Greene Av. Ch., Brooklyn, 1894-1905; with Am. Bapt. Home Missionary Soc., 1905-06; prof. homiletics, Rochester Theol. Sem., 1906-12; pastor 5th Av. Ch., New York, 1912-22, when ch. moved to Park Av. and changed name to Park Av. Ch. Pres. Am. Bapt. Fgn. Missionary Soc., 1911. Twice lecturer, twice convocation preacher, instr., summer of 1908, 09, U. of Chicago; Sanders lecturer Union Theol. Sem., on Bapt. History and Polity. Trustee Rochester Theol. Sem.; dir. Union Theol. Sem.; mem. council New York U. Mem. 71st Regt. and lt. N.G.N.Y., 1878-84. Author: Chambers of the Soul, 1899. Died Jan. 6, 1928.

WOELFLE, Arthur W(illiam), artist; b. Trenton, N.J., Dec. 17, 1873; s. Louis and Bertha (Nick) W.; ed. Brooklyn Inst. (awarded scholarship), Nat. Acad. Design, New York, under John Twachtman and Kenyon Cox, Art Students League, N.Y., Paris and Munich; m. Georgiana Voorhees, Dec. 23, 1907. Instr., Kingsley Sch., Essex Fells, N.J., 1915-18, Mechanics Inst., N.Y. City, 1921-26; art dir. Castle Sch., Tarrytown, N.Y., 1916-21; instr. figure and portrait classes, Grand Central Sch. of Art, N.Y. City and Provincetown, Mass., 1928—. Represented by mural 125 feet long, Permanent Gallery, Erie, Pa.; 10 portraits of Ohio judges, Court House, Youngstown, O. Awarded hon. mention, Munich, 1897; Grant prize, New Rochelle (N.Y.) Art Assn., 1928; Hanson prize, same, 1930; figure prize, Allied Artists America, 1929. A.N.A., 1929. Home: New York, N.Y. Died Mar. 6, 1936.

WOELPER, Benjamin Franklin, Jr., postmaster; b. Baltimore, Md., Mar. 15, 1869; s. Benjamin Franklin and Rebecca (Meyers) W.; ed. pub. schs. and Baltimore City Coll.; m. Cecille Blanche Gibson, Mar. 6, 1895; children—Edmund Franklin, Evelyn Blanche, Mildred Florence. Began with W. W. Boyer & Co., canned goods packers, 1898, treas., 1918-22, v.p. 1923, pres., 1924-25; pres. Patapsco Building Assn., Inc.; dir. Broadway Savings Bank. Rep. candidate for Congress, 1913; mem. Sch. Survey Commn., Baltimore, 1919; mem. Port Development Commn., 1920-22; postmaster, Baltimore, 1922-30. Mem. Nat. Assn. Postmasters, Nat. Service Relations Council of P.O. Dept. Methodist. Mason. Home: Baltimore, Md. Died Feb. 18, 1932.

WOERNER, William F., lawyer; b. St. Louis, Mo., Aug. 20, 1864; s. J. Gabriel and Emilie (Plass) W.; grad. Central High Sch., St. Louis, 1883; LL.B., magna cum laude, St. Louis Law Sch. (now Law Dept. Washington U.), 1885; m. Agnes Judge, Aug. 21, 1907; children—Ruth W. (Mrs. Alcee William Stewart), Gabriel, William F. Admitted to Mo. bar, 1886; practiced at St. Louis, 1886—; mem. firm Bates & Woerner, 1887-89, J. G. & Wm. F. Woerner, 1895-1900; sometime prof. wills and adminstrn., Benton Coll. Law and St. Louis U. Inst. Law. Mem. Bd. Police Commrs., St. Louis, 1901; 1st asso. city counselor, St. Louis, 1901-05; Dem. candidate for mayor of St. Louis, 1909; mem. Pub. Service Commn., Mo., 1913-14. Democrat. Author: Revised Code of St. Louis, 1907; also of J. Gabriel Woerner (biog. sketch), and Supernationalism, the Death Knell of Mars. Editor: American Law of Administration, 1899, 1923. Home: St. Louis, Mo. Died June 27, 1932.

WOLCOTT, Edward Oliver, lawyer; b. Longmeadow, Mass., Mar. 26, 1848; a pvt. 150th Ohio vols., 1864; entered Yale, 1866, but did not graduate; grad. Harvard Law Sch., 1871, removed to Colo. and established as lawyer at Denver; U.S. senator, 1889-1901. Republican. Chmn. of commn. apptd. by President McKinley to visit Europe to negotiate for internat. bimetallism. Home: Denver, Colo. Died 1905.

WOLCOTT, Henry Roger, capitalist; b. Longmeadow, Mass., March 15, 1846; s. Samuel (D.D.) and Harriet Amanda (Pope) W.; brother late U.S. Senator Edward O. W.; hon. A.M., Yale, 1896, Colorado Coll., 1898; unmarried. Mem. Colo. Senate, 1878-82 (pres. pro tem, 1882); Rep. candidate for gov. of Colo., 1898. Home: Denver, Colo. Died May 31, 1921.

WOLCOTT, Josiah Oliver, judge; b. Dover, Del., Oct. 31, 1877; s. James L. and Mary Mills (Goodwin) W.; Ph.B., Wesleyan U., Conn., 1901, D.C.L., 1934; LL.D., Dickinson Coll., 1935; m. Mary Rebecca Fooks, Dec. 5, 1906; children—James L. III, Daniel F., Josiah O., Rebecca D. Admitted to Delaware bar, 1904; deputy atty. gen., New Castle County, Del., 1909-13; atty. gen. Del., 1913-17. Mem. U.S. Senate from Del., term 1917-23; resigned from Senate July 2, 1921, to become chancellor of Del., reapptd. chancellor, July 1933. Democrat. Methodist. Home: Dover, Del. Died Nov. 11, 1938.

WOLCOTT, Robert Henry, zoölogist; b. Alton, Ill., Oct. 11, 1868; s. Robert N. and Agnes (Swain) W.; B.L., U. of Mich., 1890, B.S., 1892, M.D., 1893; M.A., U. of Neb., 1895; m. Clara Buckstaff, June 2, 1897; children—Robert Allen, Emily Agnes. Asst. in zoölogy, 1894-95, instr., 1895-98, adj. prof., 1898-1902, asst. prof., 1902-03, asso. prof., 1903-05, prof. anatomy, 1905-09, head prof. zoölogy, 1909—, acting dean Coll. Medicine, 1909-13, jr. dean, 1913-15, U. of Neb. On Mich. Fish Commn. biol. survey of waters of the state, 1893-94; engaged in faunal work in Neb. Fellow A.A.A.S. Contbr. to scientific jours. on ornithology, entomology, fresh water biology, fauna of Neb., and especially on Am. water-mites. Home: Lincoln, Neb. Died Jan. 23, 1934.

WOLF, Edmund Jacob, clergyman; b. Rebersburg, Pa., Dec. 8, 1840; s. Jacob and Mary (Gast) W.; spent boyhood on farm; taught in pub. schs. and Bellefonte Acad.; grad. Pa. Coll., Gettysburg, 1863; served in army during Civil War; studied theology at Gettysburg and at Tübingen and Erlangen, Germany; D.D., Franklin and Marshall Coll., 1876; LL.D., Wittenberg Coll., 1901; admitted to Luth. ministry in 1865; m. Ella Kemp. Served chs. in Northumberland County, Pa., and in Baltimore; prof. ch. history and N.T. exegesis, Theol. Sem., Gettysburg, Pa., 1874—; mem. bd. mgrs. Evang. Alliance of U.S.; mem. Am. Hist. Soc., Soc. of Biblical Literature and Exegesis; chmn. of Joint Com. to prepare a Common Book of Worship for all Lutherans; elected pres. Luth. Gen. Synod, 1903. Editorially connected with Luth. Quarterly and Luth. World. Author: Lutherans in America, 1889; Vol. X of Lutheran Commentary, 1897; Lectures on the Gospel Lessons, 1900. Home: Gettysburg, Pa. Died 1905.

WOLF, Henry, artist, engraver; b. Eckwersheim, Alsace, Aug. 3, 1852; s. Simon and Pauline (Ettinger) W.; ed. Eckwersheim and Strassburg; pupil of Jacques Lévy, artist, engraver, Strassburg; m. Rose, d. Herman Massée, Sept. 25, 1875. Exhibited at Paris Salon (hon. mention, 1888, gold medal, 1895); Chicago Expn., 1893 (1st class medal); Paris Expn., 1889 (hon. mention), and 1900 (silver medal); silver medal, Fine Arts Expn., Rouen, France, 1903; diploma and grand medal of honor for distinguished services in promoting art of engraving, St. Louis Expn., 1904. Mem. jury Paris expns., 1889 and 1900; mem. jury of admission, and later mem. jury of awards, Buffalo Expn., 1901; mem. advisory com., and later of Internat. Jury of Awards, St. Louis Expn., 1904. A.N.A., 1905, N.A., 1908; mem. Am. Federation of Arts, Internat. Soc. Sculptors, Painters and Gravers (London), Alliance Française, Union Internationale des Beaux-Arts et des Lettres, Paris, France. Principal Works: Engravings illustrating American Artist Series, and Gilbert Stuart Series of Women and Men, in Century Mag. Original engravings: The Morning Star; The Evening Star; A Duck Pond; Morning Mists; Lower New York in a Mist; The Scattering of the Mists; "Evening," Swan Lake, Central Park, New York; Portrait of Thomas Jefferson; Portrait of Thomas Carlyle; My Mother; Miss Alexander, after Whistler; Portrait of Robert Louis Stevenson, of William Makepeace Thackeray, of Abraham Lincoln; Masterpieces of the Met. Mus. Art, New York; Portraits of Ladies and American Artists' Series appearing in Harper's Mag. Died Mar. 18, 1916.

WOLF, Henry Milton, lawyer; b. Rock Island, Ill., Nov. 15, 1860; s. Moses and Bertha (Rothschild) W.; grad. Brown Sch., Chicago, 1874, Chicago High Sch., 1878; attended Old U. of Chicago, and studied under pvt. tutors, 1878-80; A.B., Yale, 1884; studied law at Yale and in Chicago until 1886; unmarried. Became mem., 1886, of firm Dupee, Judah, Willard & Wolf, which succeeded the original firm of Hitchcock & Dupee, organized in 1854; mem. Judah, Willard, Wolf & Reichmann until 1929 (retired from gen. practice); dir., sec. and treas. Chisholm Boyd & White Co. Republican. Jewish religion. With Viscount Eiichi Shibusawa and Edgar A. Bancroft (then U.S. ambassador to Japan), established, 1925, memorial at Shimoda, Japan, to Townsend Harris, first representative of U.S. in Japan. Home: Chicago, Ill. Died June 4, 1935.

WOLF, Luther Benaiah, clergyman; b. Abbottstown, Pa., Nov. 29, 1857; s. John George and Eleanor Catharine (Bittinger) W.; A.B., Pa. Coll., Gettysburg Theol. Sem., 1883; D.D., Wittenberg, 1903; fellow Madras U., 1893; m. Alice Catherine Benner, July 3, 1883; children—Mrs. Edith Norris Crigler, Mrs. Eleanor Stewart, Anna Dryden, Paul Benner. Ordained Luth. ministry, 1883; prin. Am. Evang. Luth. Mission Coll., Guntur, India, 1883-1907; after merger of Luth. chs. as United Lutheran Church in America, served as sec.-treas. of its Bd. of Foreign Missions, and as home base sec., 1928—; retired from active service July 1, 1933. Author: After Fifty Years (historical sketch of the Guntur Mission), 1895; Missionary Heroes of the Lutheran Church, 1911. Home: Baltimore, Md. Died Nov. 25, 1939.

WOLF, Rennold, playwright; b. Ithaca, N.Y., Apr. 4, 1872; s. Reinhold and Alice Jane (Hoffman) W.; Ph.B., Cornell U., 1892, LL.B., 1894; unmarried. Practiced law at Buffalo, N.Y., firm of Farnham & Wolf, 1894-1900; with Morning Telegraph, New York, as spl. writer and dramatic editor, 1900—. Mem. Authors' League America, Soc. of Am. Dramatists, Soc. of Authors and Composers. Democrat. Unitarian. Mason. Author: (plays) Hell, 1911; The Red Widow, 1912; My Best Girl, 1912; Her Little Highness, 1914; The Beauty Shop, 1914; A Perfect Lady, 1915; The Ziegfield Follies, 1915, 18, 19; The Grass Widow, 1918; The Rainbow Girl, 1918; The Beautiful One, 1919; Heartsease (musical version), 1919; also film stories and scenarios, books and lyrics of musical productions, and magazine stories. Home: New York, N.Y. Died June 2, 1922.

WOLF, Simon, lawyer; b. Hinzweiler, Bavaria, Oct. 28, 1836; s. Levi and Amalia W.; LL.B., U. of Strassburg; LL.B., Ohio Law Coll., Cleveland, O., 1861; m. Caroline Hahn, Aug. 2, 1857 (died 1891); m. 2d, Amy Lichtenstein, Nov. 3, 1892. Admitted to bar July 21, 1861, at Mt. Vernon, O. Began practice in Washington, D.C., 1862; recorder of deeds for D.C., 1869-78; judge Municipal Ct., D.C., 1878-81; U.S. minister to Egypt, 1881-82. Founder, and pres. Hebrew Orphan's Home, Atlanta, Ga., for 25 yrs.; pres. Bd. of Children's Guardians, Rupert Home for Aged and Indigent. Mem. Bd. of Charities, D.C.; chmn. com. on ways and means, German Orphan Asylum, for 35 yrs.; chmn. Bd. of Delegates on Civil Rights, Union of Am. Hebrew Congregations, for 35 yrs. Pres. Nat. and Internat. Order B'nai B'rith, 1904-05. Scottish Rite Mason (33°). Pres. 12 yrs. Order Kesher She Barzel. Republican. Author: Influence of the Jews on the Progress of the World, 1876; The American Jew as Soldier, Patriot and Citizen, 1896; Biography of M. M. Noah, 1898; Biography of Commodore U. P. Levy; The Presidents I Have Known, 1917 (14 of them). Degree of LL.D., given on 84th birthday by Hebrew Union Coll.; also made hon. trustee by Hebrew Congregation, Washington, D.C. Home: Washington, D.C. Died June 4, 1923.

WOLFE, Arthur Lester, coll. prof.; b. Montclair, N.J., Sept. 16, 1866; s. Rev. Aaron Robarts and Laura F. (Jackson) W.; A.B., New York U., 1889, Ph.D., 1892; post-grad. work, U. of Leipzig and Am. Sch. Classical Studies in Rome, Italy, 1901-02; m. Gertrude R. Snow, Aug. 7, 1890; children—Arthur Whiting, Austin Robarts, Herbert Snow, Edward Winslow, Hugh Campbell. Prof. Latin, 1889—, dean, 1913-14, acting pres., 1913-15, head dept. ancient langs., 1916—, Park Coll., Parkville, Mo. Treas. and mgr. North Side Telephone Co. Mem. Classical Assn. Middle West and South, Classical Assn. Kan. and Western Mo. (pres. 1921). Presbyn. Home: Parkville, Mo. Died July 2, 1931.

WOLFE, Harry Kirke, university prof.; b. Bloomington, Ill., Nov. 10, 1858; s. J. V. and Ellen B. Wolfe; A.B., U. of Neb., 1880; studied Berlin, 1883-84, Leipzig, 1884-86; A.M., Ph.D., Leipzig, 1886; m. Katharine H. Brandt, Dec. 19, 1888. Prof. philosophy, U. of Neb., 1889-97; supt. schs., S. Omaha, Neb., 1897-1901; prin. High Sch., Lincoln, Neb., 1902-05; prof. philosophy and edn., U. of Mont., 1905-06; prof. ednl. psychology, 1906-09, head prof. philosophy, 1909—, U. of Neb. Charter mem. Am. Psychol. Assn. Writer monographs and articles on Child Study. Died July 30, 1918.

WOLFE, James Jacob, biologist; b. Sandy Run, S.C., Sept. 14, 1875; s. John Archie and Frederica

A. (Geiger) W.; A.B., Wofford Coll., Spartanburg, S.C., 1896; student U. of Chicago, 1900-02; Ph.D., Harvard, 1904; m. Cornelia Wilhelmina Lehrmann, June 28, 1904. Prin. schs., Fork, S.C., 1896-98, Marion, 1898-1900; prof. biology, Trinity Coll., Durham, N.C., 1904—; instr. Marine Biol. Lab., Woods Hole, Mass., summers, 1903-06; investigator Marine Biol. Lab., Beaufort, N.C., summers, 1910—. Trustee Watts Hosp., Durham. Democrat. Methodist. Died June 1920.

WOLFE, Robert Frederick, publisher; b. Zanesville, O., Nov. 7, 1863; s. Andrew J. and Nancy (Barton) W.; pres. Dispatch Printing Co., Ohio State Journal Co. Mem. City Planning Commn. of Columbus. Died Jan. 13, 1927.

WOLFE, S. Herbert, actuary; b. Baltimore, Md., Mar. 19, 1874; s. S. Baird and Fannie (Behrens) W.; student Coll. City of New York to jr. yr.; m. Flora Heidelberg, Dec. 9, 1901; children—Eleanor M., Frances B., Helen L. Consulted by numerous ins. cos. and made splty. of examination of ins. cos. for state govts.; engaged in actuarial and examining work for ins. depts. of many states; in Conn., as actuary of the dept. of ins. had charge of spl. investigation of the assessment soc.; called to testify as expert in much important ins. litigation. Fellow Royal Statis. Soc. Great Britain. Apptd. by Mayor Gaynor, July 1913, mem. commn. to frame scientific pension law for city employes. Commd. capt., Q.M. R.C., 1917; maj., Jan. 1918; lt. col., July 1918; col., Oct. 1918; helped prepare War Risk Ins. Act; served with A.E.F.; discharged, Apr. 1919; apptd. by President Harding (Senate confirmation Nov. 17, 1921) brig. gen. O.R.C., Finance. Awarded D.S.M. (U.S.); Cross of Legion of Honor (France). Republican. Author: Investment Directory of Insurance Companies (ann.), 1903; Inheritance Tax Calculations, 1905; Modified Premiums and Costs, 1908; The Examination of Insurance Companies, 1910. Home: New York, N.Y. Died Dec. 31, 1927.

WOLFE, Theodore Frelinghuysen, author; b. Kenvil, N.J., 1847; s. Daniel R. and Mary (Logan) W.; grad. med. dept., Columbia, M.D., 1868, Ph.D. Practiced medicine in Jersey City, N.J., for several yrs.; held various offices in health dept. there and in med. socs. of Jersey City and New York; pub. many scientific papers and monographs; later turned attention to gen. literature and became contbr. to leading mags. Author: Anaesthesia and Anaesthetics, 1872; Tetanus, 1874; Literary Shrines of American Authors, 1895; A Literary Pilgrimage Among Haunts of British Authors, 1896; Literary Haunts and Homes, American Authors, 1898; Literary Rambles at Home and Abroad, 1900. Died 1915.

WOLFE, Thomas Clayton, author; b. Asheville, N.C., Oct. 3, 1900; s. William Oliver and Julia Elizabeth (Westall) W.; A.B., U. of N.C., 1920; A.M., Harvard, 1922; Guggenheim fellow for study abroad, 1930-31; unmarried. Instr. in English, Washington Sq. Coll., New York U., 1924-30. Mem. Nat. Inst. of Arts and Letters. Presbyn. Author: Look Homeward, Angel, 1929; Of Time and the River, 1935; From Death to Morning, 1935; The Story of a Novel, 1936; The Web and the Rock, 1939; You Can't Go Home Again, 1940; The Hills Beyond, 1941; also stories in mags. Died Sept. 15, 1938.

WOLFF, John Eliot, geolgist; b. Montreal, Can., Nov. 21, 1857; s. Philippe and Hannah (Crocker) W.; A.B., Harvard, 1879, A.M., Ph.D., 1889; post-grad. student, Heidelberg, 1884-85; m. Ethel P. Loder, Oct. 20, 1887. Asst. geologist U.S. Geol. Survey, 1885-93; asst. in geology, 1881-82, instr., 1887-92, asst. prof. petrography, 1892-95, prof. petrography and mineralogy, and curator Mineral Mus., 1895-1923, emeritus, 1923, Harvard. Mem. Geol. Soc. America, Am. Acad. Arts and Sciences. Home: Pasadena, Calif. Died Aug. 9, 1940.

WOLFF, William Almon, author; b. Brooklyn, N.Y., Sept. 14, 1885; s. William Almon and Mary Gray (Curry) W.; student New York U., 1902-06; m. Priscilla Crane, June 8, 1912; m. 2d, Ruth Hawthorne, Dec. 24, 1926; m. 3d, Wynne Fairfield, Aug. 28, 1930. Mem. editorial staff N.Y. Tribune, 1906-11; contbr. to numerous mags., 1911—. Author: Behind the Screen, 1916; The Path of Gold, 1920; Sold South, 1921; The Show-Off (novel, with George Kelly), 1924; E. H. Harriman, 1928; Manhattan Night, 1930; A Song of Six-pence, 1931. Died July 15, 1933.

WOLL, Fritz Wilhelm, agrl. chemist; b. Bergen, Norway, May 23, 1865; s. Rev. Carsten L. and Mathilde Helene (Krum) W.; prep. edn. Realgymnasium, Christiania, Norway; B.S., Royal Frederik's U., Christiania, Norway, 1882, Ph.B., 1883; M.S., U. of Wis., 1886, Ph.D., 1904; m. Helene Walloe, May 16, 1891. Second asst. chemist, 1887, asst. chemist, 1890, chemist, 1897-1913, Wis. Agrl. Expt. Sta.; asst. prof., 1893-1904, asso. prof., 1904-06, prof. agrl. chemistry, 1906-13, U. of Wis.; prof. animal nutrition, U. of Calif., 1913—. Author: Agricultural Calendar, 1895; Dairy Calendar, 1895; A Book on Silage, 1895, 1900; A Handbook for Farmers and Dairymen, 1897, 1914; Testing Milk and Its Products (with Prof. E. H. Farrington), 1897, 1918; Productive Feeding of Farm Animals, 1915, 1916; Feed Manual and Note Book, 1917. Translator: Modern Dairy Practice (from Swedish of G. Grotenfelt), 1894, 1905. Extensive contbr. to tech. publs. and to agrl. and dairy papers. Fellow A.A.A.S.; mem. Wis. Acad. Sciences, Arts and Letters, Assn. Official Agrl. Chemists (pres. 1910-11). Mem. internat. Jury, Panama P.I. Expn., 1915. Home: Berkeley, Calif. Deceased.

WOLLE, John Frederick, organist, conductor; b. Bethlehem, Pa., Apr. 4, 1863; s. Rev. Francis and Elizabeth Caroline (Weiss) W.; grad. Moravian parochial sch., 1879; studied organ and counterpoint under Rheinberger, Munich, 1884-85; Mus.Doc., Moravian Coll. and Theol. Sem., Bethlehem, 1904, U. of Pa., 1919, Princeton, 1925; m. Jennie Creveling Stryker, July 21, 1886; 1 dau., Gretchen (Mrs. George Prescott Baker). Organist Moravian Church, Bethlehem, 1885-1905, Packer Memorial Ch., Lehigh U., 1887-1905; prof. music, U. of Calif., 1905-11; condr. U. of Calif. symphony concerts in the Greek Theatre. Organized Bach Choir, 1898; gave first complete Am. performances of the St. John passion music, of Bach, the Mass in B minor, the Christmas oratorio, etc. Gave organ concerts, Chicago Expn., 1893, St. Louis Expn., 1904; reëstablished the Bach Festivals, Bethlehem, Pa., 1911, later given annually; played Bach's "Art of Fugue" first time complete in America, Apr. 15, 1928. One of founders of American Guild of Organists; mem. Internat. Music Soc. Composer hymn tunes, anthems for chorus and orchestra, and transcriber for organ of compositions by Bach and Wagner. Home: Bethlehem, Pa. Died Jan. 12, 1933.

WOLVERTON, Charles Edwin, jurist; b. Des Moines County, Ia., May 16, 1851; s. John and Mary Jane (Nealy) W.; B.S., Christian Coll., Monmouth, Ore., 1871, A.B., 1872; LL.B., Ky. U., 1874; LL.D., Willamette U., 1898; m. Clara Ellen Price, Oct. 3, 1878. Practiced law at Albany, Ore., 1874-94; justice Sup. Ct. of Ore., 1894-1905 (chief justice, 1898-1900, 1904-05); U.S. dist. judge, Dist. of Ore., Dec. 5, 1905—. Del. Rep. Nat. Conv. Minneapolis, 1892. Elector Hall of Fame, N.Y. Univ., 1900, 05. Grand Master Grand Lodge A.F. and A.M., Ore., 1910-11. Lecturer Law Dept. U. of Ore., 1912-15, Northwestern Coll. of Law, Portland, Ore., 1915. Trustee Reed Coll., Portland, Ore., 1906—. Home: Portland, Ore. Died Sept. 21, 1926.

WOLVIN, Augustus B., capitalist; b. Cleveland, Oct. 16, 1857; s. Capt. Benjamin S. and Finetta (Harrington) W.; cabin boy on great lakes at 10 years of age; edn. restricted to a few months in the winter while the vessel was laid up; made master of a vessel at 21, continuing until 26 yrs. of age; m. Carrie L. Kilgore, Jan. 1880. In produce business at Pecatonica, 1884-88; located in Duluth, 1888, as mem. firm of La Salle & Co., gen. vessel commn. business; began organizing water freight transportation cos.; organized the Zenith Transit Co., 1895, which built 5 of the largest ships on the lakes; upon merger of the prin. transportation fleets of the lakes (112 vessels) into the Pittsburgh Steamship Co., became v.p. and gen. mgr., until Jan. 1904; pres. Zenith Furnace Co., Duluth, Minn. Died 1932.

WOOD, Alice Holabird (Mrs. Ira Couch Wood), social service; b. St. Louis, Mo., July 15, 1871; d. Henry Clarkson and Louise (Holabird) Wicker; grad. Ogontz (Pa.) Sch., 1890; studied and traveled in Europe 2 yrs.; m. Ira Couch Wood, June 14, 1894 (died 1915). Devoted much time to work on civic reform and philanthropy; pres. Ill. Training Sch. for Nurses 7 yrs.; elected trustee Village of Winnetka, 1916; exec. sec. Woman's Com. of Council Nat Defense, Washington, D.C., May-Dec. 1917; dir. Elizabeth McCormick Memorial Fund for Child Welfare, Chicago. Episcopalian. Home: Chicago, Ill. Died Dec. 18, 1923.

WOOD, Andrew Hollister, lawyer; b. Marine City, Mich., Dec. 11, 1876; s. Alva Bennet and Ervilla (Hollister) W.; grad. Mich. State Normal Coll., 1897; Ph.B., U. of Mich., 1900; LL.B., U. of Denver, 1907; m. Sada Marie Richter, Apr. 25, 1908. Admitted to Colo. bar, 1907, and began practice at Denver; prof. law U. of Denver, 1908—, and sec. Dept. of Commerce, same, 1908—; asst. atty. gen. of Colo., also inheritance tax commr., 1925-33. Republican. Home: Denver, Colo. Died Dec. 12, 1941.

WOOD, Arthur Julius, mech. engr.; b. Newark, N.J., Sept. 3, 1874; s. De Volson and Frances (Hartson) W.; grad. Steven's Sch., Hoboken, N.J., 1892; M.E., Stevens Inst. Tech., 1896; M.S., Pa. State Coll., 1916; m. Helen M. Kerr, July 26, 1904; 1 son, Reginald De Volson. Asso. editor Railroad Gazette, 1896-1900; instr. in mech. engring., Worcester Poly. Inst., 1900-02; prof. mech. and elec. engring., Del. Coll., 1902-04; with Pa. State Coll., 1904—; organizer, 1912, and in charge of courses in ry. mech. engring., same coll., also prof. mech. engring., 1918—, in charge Engring. Expt. Sta., 1918-22, head of dept., 1922—, adviser, 1922—; cons. engr. in refrigeration and heat engines. Fellow A.A.A.S.; mem. Am. Soc. Refrigerating Engrs. (v.p. 1926-28; pres. 1928-29). Republican. Presbyn. Author: Principles of Locomotive Operation, 1915, 25. Contbr. to Mechanical Engring.; Refrigerating Engring., Ry. Mech. Engr. Home: State College, Pa. Died Apr. 18, 1931.

WOOD, Benson, congressman; b. Montrose, Pa., Mar. 31, 1839; s. Peleg and Esther (Fox) W.; acad. edn.; LL.B., U. of Chicago, 1864; m. Jennie Jewett, Dec. 21, 1864. Served 1st lt. and capt. 34th Ill. Inf. in Civil War; admitted to bar, 1864, in practice at Effingham, Ill., 1864—; mem. firm Wood Bros. & Rickelman, 1904—; pres. Effingham State Bank, 1903—. Mem. Ill. Ho. of Rep., 1873-75; mayor of Effingham, 1881-83; mem. 54th Congress (1895-97), 19th Ill. Dist. Del. Rep. Nat. convs., 1876, 88. Universal Congress Lawyers and Jurists, St. Louis, 1904. Home: Effingham, Ill. Died Aug. 27, 1915.

WOOD, Carroll David, judge; b. Hamburg, Ark., July 8, 1857; s. John S. and Martha (Bussey) W.; A.B., U. of Ark., 1879, LL.D., 1925; m. Reola, d. W. E. Thompson, Nov. 4, 1886; children—John Shirley, Claudia Reola, Roy Winton. Admitted to bar, 1880; practiced at Monticello, Ark., 1880-82; dist. atty., 10th Circuit, 1882-86; judge Circuit Ct., 10th Jud. Circuit, 1886-93; asso. justice Supreme Ct. of Ark., 1893—; reelected for 5th consecutive term of 8 yrs., 1924; retired, 1929. Chmn. for Ark., Adjustment Bd. of Nat. Recovery Adminstrn., 1934. Democrat. Home: Little Rock, Ark. Died Dec. 19, 1941.

WOOD, Chandler Mason, banker; b. Fort Plain, N.Y., Oct. 5, 1881; s. Edwin Wellington and Alice L. (Faulkner) W.; A.B., A.M., Tufts Coll., 1903; J.B., Boston U., 1906, J.M., 1906; m. Ruth George Cheney, June 28, 1913. Began practice of law at Boston, 1906; law mem. Barker, White, Wood & Williams; pres. Mut. Nat. Bank, Boston, 1915; pres. Met. Trust Co., Boston, 1915—; pres. N.E. Guaranty Co., Dedham & Hyde Park Gas & Electric Co.; v.p. West Boston Gas Co.; dir. Commercial Trust Co. (New York), Commercial Nat. Bank (Washington). Olympic Theatres, Inc., etc. Prof. law, Boston U. Law Sch. Pres. Chandler Sch. for Women; trustee Tufts Coll. Chmn. Dem. State Exec. Com.; candidate for state treas., 1919. Universalist. Mason. Home: Winchester, Mass. Died Dec. 11, 1938.

WOOD, Charles Milton, educator; b. Salem, Ind., July 25, 1861; s. Henry Mitchell and Amanda Jane (Ritter) W.; grad. Eikosi Acad., Salem, Ind., 1881; student DePauw U., 1882-84; law course under Judge Thomas L. Collins, Salem, Ind.; m. Emma F. Paynter, May 20, 1886. Chief dept. county clk., Washington County, Ind., 1878-82; practiced law, Rushville, Neb., 1885-90, also mayor, editor and pub.; cashier and agency dir. New York Life Ins. Co. in Utah, 1891-1905; law instr. mil. sch. and in practice, San Diego, Calif., 1905-17; apptd. supt. Pasadena Mil. Acad., 1917, hon. title of col. Mil. training as cadet at DePauw U., 2 yrs.; supt. Calif. Prep. Sch. for Boys. Republican. Presbyn. Home: Covina, Calif. Died Apr. 10, 1935.

WOOD, Charles Seely, clergyman, author; b. Mt. Auburn, Cincinnati, Apr. 19, 1845; s. Seely and Nancy (Burnet) W.; g.s. Isaac G. Burnet, mayor of Cincinnati, 1819-31; A.B., Miami U., 1866, A.M., 1886; student Princeton Theol. Sem., 1866-69; unmarried. Ordained to Presbyn. ministry, Nov. 1870; pastor Winneconne, Wis., 1869, Stevens Point, Wis., 1870-73, Richwood, O., 1875-76; retired from ministry on account of ill health. Author: Alice and Her Two Friends, 1896; On the Frontier with St. Clair, 1902; The Sword of Wayne, 1903; Camp-Fires on The Scotio, 1905; Christmas at Big Moose Falls, 1911. Contributed chapters on Arthur St. Clair and Anthony Wayne in Ohio History Sketches (edited by F. B. Pearson), 1903; also many historical articles, stories and sketches to newspapers. Home: Urbana, O. Died Nov. 20, 1912.

WOOD, Clinton Tyler, clergyman, educator; b. Carlisle, O., Jan. 15, 1869; s. Francis Marion and Martha Jane (VanTuyl) W.; B.A., Princeton, 1892, M.A., 1893; grad. Princeton Theol. Sem., 1897; studied U. of Chicago, 1917; Kennedy Sch. of Missions, Hartford, Conn., 1923-24; grad. study Kennedy Sch. of Missions, 1926-28; m. Jennie Stoddard Clark (died 1914); children—Clinton Tyler, Francis Clark, Richard Harvey, David Bernard (dec.). Teacher Princeton Prep. Sch., 1892-95. Ordained Presbyn. ministry, 1898; prin. Missionary Training Coll., Wellington, Cape Province, S. Africa, 1898-1909, also prof. history, 1898-1913; Severance prof. of missions, Coll. of Wooster, Wooster, O., 1912-26. Sec. Naval Y.M. C.A., Cape May, 1918; chmn. United War Work Campaign, Ohio colleges, 1918; chmn. bd. College Hall Social Settlement, Wooster, 1913-23. Author: Studies in the Life of Peter, the Apostle, 1902; Een Stroom en een Banier, een Voorlezing. Home: Wooster, O. Died Jan. 23, 1932.

WOOD, Corydon L., bishop; b. Dirnyter, Madison County, N.Y., Sept. 30, 1852; s. James and Deborah C. (Cornell) W.; ed. Ithaca (N.Y.) Acad.; (D.D., Edwards Coll., Albion, Wash.); m. 2d, Ella Hutchinson, June 13, 1889. Licensed ministry U.B. Ch., 1878; ordained elder, 1882; traveled as pastor N. Mich. Conf. 6 yrs.; presiding elder 20 yrs.; sec. of Conf. more than 20 yrs.; bishop 4 terms, 1905-20. Home: Alma, Mich. Deceased.

WOOD, David Duffle, organist, composer; b. Pittsburgh, Pa., March 2, 1838; s. Jonathan and Welhelmina Wood; entered Pa. Inst. for Blind, Oct. 20, 1843; grad. June 1856; m. Rachel Laird, Oct. 16, 1856; m. 2d, Alice Burdette, July 14, 1898. Studied higher mathematics under the late James G. Blaine, 1852-54; studied pipe organ under Wilhelm Schnabel, 1851-52; studied other musical instruments, Ernst Pfeiffer, 1852-56 (Mus. Doc., Temple Coll., Phila.). Musical compositions (very few of which have been published), chiefly ch. anthems and songs. Died 1910.

WOOD, Edward Edgar, army officer; b. Lancaster County, Pa., Sept. 17, 1846; s. Hon. Day and Eliza (Jackson) W.; student Pa. State Normal Sch., Millersville, 1860-62; grad. U.S. Mil. Academy, 1870; m. Elizabeth Wynn, August 2, 1870. Enlisted pvt. 17th Pa. Cav., Sept. 8, 1862; promoted sergt., 1st sergt., 1st lt., acting regimental adj. and staff officer on staff 1st Cav. Div., Army of the Potomac; hon. mustered out Aug. 7, 1865. Captured at Occoquan, Va., Dec. 27, 1862, and confined in Castle Thunder, Richmond, Va., exchanged May 1863, and thereafter present in all campaigns and battles of cav. corps, Army of the Potomac, including Gettysburg, Kilpatrick's Richmond Raid, Wilderness, Trevillian, Winchester, Five Forks and Appomattox. Apptd. cadet U.S. Mil. Acad., June 15, 1866; 2d lt. 8th Cav., June 15, 1870; 1st lt., July 1, 1873; capt., Jan. 20, 1886; a.-d.-c. to Gen. J. M. Schofield, U.S.A., 1879-82; asst. prof. French, U.S. Mil. Acad., 1876-79 and 1883-86; asst. prof. Spanish, 1889-92; lt. col. U.S.A. and prof. U.S. Mil. Acad., Oct. 1, 1892; col., Oct. 1, 1902; brig. gen. and retired, Sept. 17, 1910. Home: West Chester, Pa. Died June 21, 1924.

WOOD, Edward Jenner, M.D.; b. Wilmington, N.C., July 12, 1878; s. Thomas Fanning (M.D., LL.D.) and Mary Kennedy (Sprunt) W.; B.Sc., U. of N.C., 1899; M.D., U. of Pa., 1902; post-grad. study, U. of Munich, 1906; asst. clin. medicine, Guy's Hosp., London, 1919-20; diploma in tropical medicine, Royal Coll. Phys. and Royal Coll. Surg., Eng., 1920 (D.T.M., Eng.); m. Louise Bellamy, Apr. 18, 1906; children—Edward Jenner, Jr., Louise Bellamy, John Dalziel. Practiced Wilmington, 1902—; mem. New Hanover County Bd. of Health, 1903-12; apptd. mem. State Bd. of Health of N.C., Apr. 1912; cons. phys. James Walker Memorial Hosp. (Wilmington) and State Hosp. (Raleigh). One of first to recognize existence and national danger of pellagra. Fellow Royal Soc. Tropical Medicine and Hygiene. Presbyn. Author: A Treatise on Pellagra; also many articles on pellagra and tropical sprue; chapter on Pellagra in Oxford System of Medicine, and on Sprue in Nelson's Loose Leaf Medicine; Pellagra and Sprue, Osler-McCrae System of Medicine; Pellagra, in Billings-Forscheimer Therapeusis. Home: Wilmington, N.C. Died Sept. 16, 1928.

WOOD, Edward Stickney, prof. chemistry, Harvard Med. School, 1876—; b. Cambridge, Mass., April 28, 1846; s. Alfred and Laura (Stickney) W.; grad. Harvard, 1867, M.D., 1871, A.M., 1872; studied physiol. and med. chemistry, Berlin and Vienna, 1872; m. Elizabeth Richardson, Dec. 24, 1883. Asst. prof. chemistry, Harvard Med. School, 1871-76, prof., 1876—; mem. med. commn. on Boston's Water Supply, 1874; mem. Com. of Revision and Publication, U.S. Pharmacopœia, 1880; chemist Mass. Gen. Hosp., 1873—. Translator: Neubauer & Vogel's Analysis of Urine, 1879. Revised (with Dr. R. Amory) Vol. II, On Poisons, Wharton & Stillé's Medical Jurisprudence, 1884. Wrote articles: Examination of Blood and Other Stains, and Examination of Hair, in Wilthaus & Becker's Medical Jurisprudence, 1894; Arsenic as a Domestic Poison (Mass. Bd. Health, etc.), 1885; Report on Sanitary Qualities of the Sudbury, Mystic, Shawshine and Charles River Waters (part author), 1874. Home: Pocasset, Mass. Died 1905.

WOOD, Edwin Ellsworth, coll. pres.; b. Adams County, Ind., Sept. 8, 1863; s. Zephaniah Baker and Rachel Ann (Grimes) W.; B.A., Denison U., Granville, O., 1890, M.A., 1893; m. Margaret Finley, June 15, 1893. Prin. Williamsburg (Ky.) Inst., 1890-93, v.p., 1893-98, pres., 1898—, name changed to Cumberland Coll., 1914; v.p. Farmers Bank & Trust Co. Asst. sec. of State of Ky., 1898-1900. Republican. Baptist. Home: Williamsburg, Ky. Died Jan. 23, 1940.

WOOD, Edwin Orin, author; b. Goodrich, Mich., Oct. 29, 1861; s. Thomas Parmalee and Pauline M. (Hulburt) W.; ed. high sch., Saginaw, Mich.; LL.D., Notre Dame U., 1916; m. Emily Crocker, Dec. 17, 1889. Commercial traveler, 1879-93; special agt. U.S. Treasury, 1893-97; pres. Loyal Guard, fraternal soc., and editor Loyal Guard Magazine, 1895-1915; treas. Chevrolet Motor Co., of New York, 1917; dir. Chevrolet Motor Co. of Del., 1915-18. Mem. Mackinac Island State Park Commn. and Mich. Hist. Commn., 1913-16 (pres.). Chmn. Dem. State Central Com., Mich., 1904-05; mem. Dem. Nat. Com., 1908-16; reëlected 3d term but resigned same yr. and removed to New York; del. Dem. Nat. Conv., Denver, 1908 (at large), Baltimore, 1912, St. Louis, 1916; mem. Dem. County Com., New York, 1917-18. Pres. Nat. Fraternal Press Assn., 1903-04. Episcopalian. Mason (33°). Wrote: Historic Mackinac, also History of Genesee County, Michigan; writer on the history of Michigan and the old Northwest Territory. Home: New York, N.Y. Died April 23, 1918.

WOOD, Eugene, author; b. nr. Bellefontaine, O., Mar. 11, 1860; s. William Henry Harrison and Ella (Sutherland) W.; student Ohio Wesleyan U., 1876-80, A.B., honoris causa, 1905; m. Mary Gardner Wood, Feb. 13, 1890. Socialist. Episcopalian. Author: Back Home, 1905; Folks Back Home, 1907; In Our Town, 1913; also propaganda pamphlets, and of mag. articles. Home: Springdale, Conn. Died Feb. 25, 1923.

WOOD, Frank Hoyt, coll. prof.; b. Red Creek, N.Y., Oct. 28, 1864; s. George and Julia M. (Benedict) W.; A.B., Syracuse U., 1891, A.M., 1894; A.B., Harvard, 1892; Harvard Grad. Sch., 1891-93; U. of Leipzig, 1898-1900, Ph.D., 1900; unmarried. Instr. Latin, Acad. of Northwestern U., 1893-94; master in history, Worcester (Mass.) Acad., 1894-98; joint-prin. Allen Sch., W. Newton, Mass., 1900-01; master in history and German, Mackenzie Sch., Dobbs Ferry, N.Y.; prof. Am. history, 1902-16, Sherman Memorial prof. polit. science, 1916—, Hamilton Coll. Progressive candidate for mem. Assembly, 1913. Presbyn. Home: Clinton, N.Y. Died Aug. 22, 1930.

WOOD, George, ry. official; b. Philadelphia, July 1, 1842; s. Richard Davis and Juliana (Randolph) W.; brother of Richard and Stuart W.; ed. prep. Haverford Coll., 1855-60; m. Mary Sharpless Hunn, Oct. 12, 1864. Became connected with firm of Wood & Garrett, mfrs. cotton goods, 1860, admitted to partnership, 1863, mng. plant at Millville, N.J., 7 yrs.; assisted father in development of town of Vineland; dir. Millville & Glassboro R.R. Co. during period of constrn. into Atlantic City; negotiated purchase of Pleasantville & Ocean City line, subsequently merged with the West Jersey & Atlantic R.R.; pres. Millville Mfg. Co., Mays Landing Water Power Co.; dir. Pa. R.R. Co., 1881—, and chmn. of finance com., Mar. 24, 1891—; dir. and chmn. finance com. West Jersey & Seashore R.R. Co.; dir. Phila. Nat. Bank, Mut. Fire, Marine & Inland Ins. Co., Provident Mut. Life Ins. Co., Provident Trust Co.; chmn. bd. Wawa Dairy Farms; v.p. and dir. Phila. Mfrs. Mut. Fire Ins. Co. Mem. Society of Friends (Quakers). Home: Philadelphia, Pa. Died Feb. 17, 1926.

WOOD, George Arthur, prof. history; b. Southampton, Mass., Aug. 22, 1878; s. Ira Elbridge and Martha (Lanfair) W.; grad. Williston Sem., Easthampton, Mass., 1902, Amherst Coll., 1906; M.A., Columbia, 1912, Ph.D., 1920; studied Harvard, summer 1916; m. Jean Ida Donaldson, June 5, 1918; children—George Arthur, Robert Donaldson, Theodore Howland. Principal high sch., Sheffield, Mass., 1906-07; teacher history and English, Mohegan Lake Sch., Mohegan, N.Y., 1907-08; instr. in history, Colorado Coll., Colorado Springs, Colo., 1908-09; research in 18th Century Am. Colonial history, 1911-12; instr. history and politics, Princeton, 1913-15; instr. Am. history, Ohio State U., 1915-20, asst. prof., 1920-22; prof. history, Lake Forest Coll., 1922—; visiting prof. history, Pa. State Coll., summer 1927, 31, 32. Research in Pub. Record Office and British Mus., London, summers 1914, 22, in Canadian Archives, summer 1921. Republican. Presbyn. Author: The Public Life of William Shirley (Vol. I), 1920; also articles in hist. mags. Home: Lake Forest, Ill. Deceased.

WOOD, George McLane, editor; b. Cumberland, Md., Jan. 7, 1850; s. William P. and Harriet E. (Smith) W.; public sch. edn.; m. Emma Anne Squier, Oct. 1873; children—Herbert S., Alice C.; m. 2d, Beatrice Dawson, Dec. 25, 1897; children—Karl D., Doris M. In pvt. and govt. stenographic work and newspaper writing, 1868-84; sec. Chesapeake & Potomac Telephone Co., Washington, 1885-86; editorial clk., asst. editor, and editor, U.S. Geol. Survey, 1886-1925. Editor of technical manuscripts. Contbr. to Ency. Britannica of articles on geology of North and South America. Home: Washington, D.C. Died Oct. 27, 1930.

WOOD, Grant, artist; b. Anamosa, Ia., Feb. 13, 1892; s. Francis Maryville and Hattie D. (Weaver) W.; student Minneapolis Handicraft Guild, 1910-12, Art Inst., Chicago, 1912-14, Acad. Julian, Paris, France, 1923; hon. D.Litt., U. of Wis., June 1936; hon. M.A., Wesleyan U., 1940; hon. Dr. of Fine Arts, Lawrence Coll., 1938, Northwestern U., 1941; m. Sara Sherman Maxon (singer), Mar. 2, 1935. Began work as craftsman in metal and handmade jewelry, 1912; teacher art, pub. schs., Cedar Rapids, Ia., 1919-24; winner Harris Bronze medal and prize on "American Gothic," at Am. exhibit, Art Inst., Chicago, 1930, purchased by Friends Am. Art for Art Inst.; "Dinner for Threshers," sections I and III, purchased by Whitney Museum of Am. Art, New York, 1934. Prof. graphic and plastic arts, Ia. State U. With U.S. Army, A.E.F., Camouflage Div., 1918-19. Home: Iowa City, Ia. Died Feb. 12, 1942.

WOOD, Harry Parker, judge; b. Quincy, Ill., July 19, 1877; s. Charles Irving and Antoinette (Wright) W.; grad. Phillips Acad., Andover, Mass., 1896; B.A., Yale, 1900; LL.B., Harvard Law Sch., 1903; unmarried. Admitted to N.Y. bar, 1904; practiced in N.Y. City, 1903-13, Seattle, Wash., 1913-20 (except at Pittsfield, Mass., 1916-18); atty. War Claims Bd., Washington, D.C., 1920-21; actg. chief counsel Federal Trade Commn., 1922-23; counsel U.S. and Mexico Mixed Claims Commn., 1925-26; Am. judge and sec. native affairs, Am. Samoa, 1926—, chief justice, 1931—. Episcopalian. Home: Gloversville, N.Y. Deceased.

WOOD, Henry, author; b. Barre, Vt., Jan. 16, 1834; s. Stillman W.; ed. Barre Acad., 1849-52; grad. Commercial Coll., Boston, 1854; m. Iowa City, Ia., Oct. 10, 1860, Margaret Osborne Baker. Pres. Metaphys. Club of Boston, 1899-1900. Author: Natural Law in the Business World, 1887; Edward Burton, a novel, 1890; God's Image in Man, 1892; Ideal Suggestions, 1893; The Political Economy of Natural Law, 1894; Studies in the Thought World, 1896; Victor Serenus (Story of the Pauline Era), 1898; The Political Economy of Humanism, 1901; The Symphony of Life, 1901; The New Thought Simplified, 1903; Arbitrary Price-Making Through Forms of Law, Fancies (verse), 1903; Book of Symbols, 1904; scientific and reform mags. and periodicals. Died 1909.

WOOD, Henry, univ. prof.; b. New Bedford, Mass., July 8, 1849; s. Henry T. and Anna Greene (Russell) W.; A.B., Haverford Coll., 1869; Ph.D., Univ. of Leipzig, 1879; LL.D., Wake Forest College, 1914; m. 2d, Clotilde von Kretschman, June 16, 1902. Instr. modern lit., Friends' Sch., Providence, R.I., 1879-81; asso. in English, 1881-85, asso. prof. Germanic langs., 1885-92, prof. German, 1892-1920, Johns Hopkins, prof. emeritus, 1920—. Pres. Am. Folk-Lore Soc., 1898-99. Knight of Royal Prussian Order of the Red Eagle, third class, 1910. Author of Faust-Studien; Ein Beitrag zum Verständnis Goethes in seiner Dichtung (Berlin), 1912; Study of Bettina von Arnim (Vol. VII, German Pub. Soc.); also of various monographs on German and English lit. in Am. Jour. of Philology, Vierteljahrschrift für Litteraturgeschichte, etc. Contbg. editor Americana Germania, and Germanistic Soc. Quarterly; co-editor Hesperia, Schriften zur Germanischen Philologie, 1915. Home: Cambridge, Mass. Died Aug. 20, 1925.

WOOD, Henry A(lexander) Wise, inventor, writer; b. New York, Mar. 1, 1866; s. Fernando and Alice F. (Mills) W.; father mayor of New York 3 terms, mem. Congress 20 yrs.; ed. Media (Pa.) Acad.; m. Elizabeth Ogden Brower, 1891. Inventor the Autoplate, a machine for making printing plates for newspapers theretofore made by hand, for which was awarded in 1908 the Elliott Cresson gold medal by the Franklin Inst.; also other mechanisms for the printing art; announced, 1916, series of inventions doubling speed of newspaper printing press; announced, 1932, mechanism for replenishing paper-rolls of newspaper presses at full speed. Pres. Wood Newspaper Machinery Corp. Founder Flying Mag. and editor, 1911-19. Mem. United States Naval Cons. Bd., 1915; chmn. of Conference Com. on Nat. Preparedness. First Pres. Am. Soc. Aeronautic Engrs.; v.p. Aero Club America, 1913-19; a founder, 1919, League for Preservation Am. Independence. Author: Fancies (verse), 1903; Book of Symbols, 1904; Money Hunger, 1908. Home: New York, N.Y. Died Apr. 9, 1939.

WOOD, Henry Clay, brig. gen. U.S.A.; b. Winthrop, Me., May 26, 1832; s. Gen. Samuel and Florena (Sweet) W.; A.B., Bowdoin Coll., 1854, A.M., 1857; B.S., Norwich (Vt.) U., 1874; read medicine, 1854; studied law; admitted to bar, Augusta, Me., Aug. 19, 1856. Apptd. maj. and a.d.c. to Maj. Gen. Samuel Wood, Me. militia, Mar. 28, 1856; 2d lt. 1st Inf. U.S.A., June 27, 1856; 1st lt., May 10, 1861; capt., Oct. 24, 1861; maj. a.a.g., June 24, 1864; lt. col. a.a.g., Feb. 28, 1887; col. a.a.g., Nov. 6, 1893; retired May 26, 1896; advanced to rank of brig. gen. retired, by act of Apr. 23, 1904. Bvtd. lt. col., "for gallant and meritorious services" in battle of Wilson's Creek, Mo., Aug. 10, 1861, also bvtd. col. and received Congressional Medal of Honor for "distinguished gallantry" in same battle. Died Aug. 30, 1918.

WOOD, Horatio C., physician; b. Phila., Jan. 13, 1841; s. Horatio Curtis and Elizabeth Head (Bacon) W.; prep. edn. various Quaker sectarian schs.; M.D., U. of Pa., 1862; LL.D., Lafayette, 1883, Yale, 1889, U. of Pa., 1904; m. Eliza H. Longacre, May 10, 1866. Prof. botany, 1866-76, therapeutics, 1876-1907, emeritus prof. therapeutics, 1907, clin. prof. diseases of nervous system, 1875-1901, U. of Pa. Editor New Remedies, 1870-73, Phila. Medical Times, 1873-80, Therapeutic Gazette, 1884-90, U.S. Dispensary, 1883-1907. Mem. Nat. Acad. Sciences; pres. Pharmacopœial Conv. of the U.S., 1890-1910, Coll. Physicians of Phila., 1902, 03. Author: The Phalangidæ of the United States, 1867; Thermic Fever, or Sunstroke, 1872; The Algæ of North America (Smithsonian contbns.), 1872; Materia Medica and Therapeutics, 1874; Brain Work and Over-Work, 1880; Nervous Diseases and Their Diagnosis, 1887; Researches Upon American Hemp. Died 1920.

WOOD, Horatio Charles, physician, author; b. Phila., Feb. 26, 1874; s. Horatio C. and Eliza H.

(Longacre) W.; grad. William Penn Charter Sch., Phila., 1890; Lit. Dept., U. of Pa., 2 yrs. (non-grad.); M.D., Med. Dept., U. of Pa., 1896; research work, U. of Berne, Switzerland, 1897-98, U. of Turin, Italy, 1898; m. Alice L. Lovell, Dec. 19, 1899. Demonstrator in pharmacodynamics, 1898-1907, asso. prof. pharmacology, 1907-10, U. of Pa.; prof. pharmacology and therapeutics, Medico-Chirurg. Coll., Phila., 1910-16; prof. same, U. of Pa., 1916—. Asst. visiting phys. to Philadelphia Gen. Hosp., 1904-08; 2d v.chmn. Com. on Revision of U.S. Pharmacopœia, 1910—. Fellow A.A.A.S. Presbyn. Author: A Text Book of Pharmacology, 1912. Joint Author: (with father) 11th to 13th edits. Therapeutics, Its Principles and Practice, 1899. Editor of 20th edit. United States Dispensatory, 1907. Home: Philadelphia, Pa. Died Jan. 3, 1920.

WOOD, Horatio D., lawyer; b. Columbus, O., Oct. 8, 1841; s. Horatio and Cornelia (Ferries) W.; ed. pvt. and pub. schs. of St. Louis; grad. Harvard Law Sch., LL.B., 1867; m. Elizabeth H. Sumner, June 20, 1872. Pvt. 4th Mo. Cav. at Vicksburg, Chattanooga, Pilot Knob, and in Ala. and Miss.; capt. and commissary of subsistence, and bvtd. maj. for meritorious services in field. Admitted to bar, 1867. Judge of St. Louis Circuit Ct., 1896-Jan. 1, 1905; mem. law firm of McKeighan, Wood & Watts. Sec.-treas. Hannibal Water Co., Hannibal Gas Light & Coke Co.; dir. St. Louis, Iron & Machine Works. Del. Universal Congress of Lawyers and Jurists, 1904. Republican. Unitarian. Home: St. Louis, Mo. Died 1905.

WOOD, Howland, numismatist; b. New Bedford, Mass., May 30, 1877; s. George Howland and Elizabeth Albert (Doane) W.; A.B., Brown U., 1900; m. Elizabeth Eliot Marvin, June 18, 1913; children—Elizabeth, Sylvia Howland. Actively identified with numismatics, 1900—; sec. Am. Numismatic Assn., 1905-09, gov. and chmn. bd., 1909-12; sec. Boston Numismatic Soc., 1908-13; asso. editor The Numismatist, 1909-10; asso. editor and editor Am. Jour. Numismatics, 1910-20; curator Museum of Am. Numismatic Soc., New York, 1913—; editor and asso. Numismatic Notes and Monographs, 1920—. Fellow Am. Numismatic Soc., Royal Numismatic Soc. (London). Republican. Episcopalian. Author: Coinage of Siam and Its Dependencies, 1904; Catalogue United States and Colonial Coins, 1914; Coinage of the West Indies, 1915; Mexican Revolutionary Coinage, 1921; Commemorative Coinage of the U.S., 1922; Coinage of the Mexican Revolutionists, 1928; The Gampola Larin Hoard, 1933; also numerous articles on coins and medals in numismatic jours. Awarded Archer M. Huntington medal for numismatic writing, 1920. Home: Flushing, N.Y. Died Jan. 4, 1938.

WOOD, Ira Wells, congressman; b. Wilkes-Barre, Pa., June 19, 1856; s. Isaac and Emily Hannah (Wells) W.; A.B., Princeton, 1877, A.M., 1880; unmarried. Counsellor at law, N.J., 1880—. Mem. Trenton Bd. Edn., 2 terms, Common Council, 1896-1900, N.J., Gen. Assembly, 1899, 1900; elected to 58th Congress, 1904, for unexpired term (1904-05), of William M. Lanning (resigned); reëlected 59th to 62d Congresses (1905-13), 4th N.J. Dist. Pres. Republican Club of Trenton; pres. Trenton Bd. of Trade; N.J. commr. St. Louis Expn., 1904; del. Interparliamentary Peace Union, Brussels, 1905. Died Oct. 5, 1930.

WOOD, Irving Francis, coll. prof.; b. Walton, N.Y., May 27, 1861; s. Francis E. and Mary (Brown) W.; A.B., Hamilton Coll., 1885; instr. Jaffna Coll., Ceylon, 1885-89; B.D., Yale, 1892; Ph.D., U. of Chicago, 1903; D.D., Hamilton Coll., 1915; m. Katharine E. Hastings, June 9, 1892; children—Constance Hastings, Edna Frances. Reader in N.T., U. of Chicago, 1892; prof. Bibl. lit. and ethics, 1893, and later prof. religion and Bibl. lit. Smith Coll., emeritus, 1929; visiting prof. Nanking U., China, Doshisha U., Japan, 1924-25; in Palestine and China, 1929-30. Author: The Spirit of God in Biblical Literature—A Study in the History of Religion, 1904; Adult Class Study, 1911; The Heroes of Early Israel, 1920. Co-author: (with Rev. Newton M. Hall) The Bible Story (5 vols.), 1906; Adult Bible Classes, 1906; The Early Days of Israel, 1906; The Days of the Kings of Israel, 1908; The Bible as Literature (with Prof. Elihu Grant), 1914; The Book of Life (with Newton M. Hall), 8 vols., 1923. Contbr. New Internat. Ency. Home: Washington, D.C. Died Aug. 29, 1934.

WOOD, James, humanitarian; b. Mt. Kisco, N.Y., Nov. 12, 1839; s. Stephen and Phoebe (Underhill) W.; ed. Haverford Coll., 1854-57, A.M., 1858; m. Emily Hollingsworth Morris, June 6, 1866. Home on farm owned by family more than 100 yrs.; never engaged in active business. Mgr. Haverford Coll., 1885—; trustee Bryn Mawr Coll., 1887-1918 (pres. bd. 1910-18). Presiding officer of "Five Years" meetings of Religious Soc. of Friends in America, 1887 and 1907; clerk N.Y. Yearly Meetings of Friends, 1885—; pres. bd. mgrs. N.Y. State Reformatory for Women, 1900-18; pres. Am. Bible Soc., 1912-19. Republican; Roosevelt prestl. elector. Author: Distinguishing Doctrines of the Society of Friends. Contbr. to mags., religious jours. and agrl. papers. Home: Mt. Kisco, N.Y. Died Dec. 19, 1925.

WOOD, James J., engineer, inventor; b. Kinsale, Ireland, Mar. 25, 1856; s. Paul H. and Elizabeth (Shine) W.; brought to U.S., 1864; grad. Evening High Sch., Brooklyn, N.Y., 1876; grad. as mech. engr. and draftsman, Poly. Inst. of Brooklyn, 1878; m. Nellie B. Scott, Jan. 20, 1916; children—Venie Elizabeth (Mrs. Joseph H. Appel), Alexander Paul, Ella May (Mrs. William S. Savage). Began in employ of Branford (Conn.) Lock Co. at age of 11, and at 16 designed a horizontal steam engine; with Brady Mfg. Co., Brooklyn, 1874-80, becoming supt. and chief engr.; partner Fuller-Wood Co., 1880-85; with Thomson-Houston and Gen. Electric cos. as inventor and cons. engr., 1885—. Inventor of "Wood" system, and "father" of the closed coil, constant current, high tension, self-regulating series arc dynamo; Brayton oil engine, installed in first Holland submarine; built first lamps for Sir Hiram Maxim; built machines for constructing main cables, original Brooklyn Bridge; holder of 240 patents covering elec. and mech. devices, including dynamo for flood lighting, first used on Statue of Liberty. Fellow Am. Inst. Elec. Engrs. Republican. Episcopalian. Home: Fort Wayne, Ind. Died Apr. 20, 1928.

WOOD, James R., ry. official; b. Auburn, N.Y., 1843. Supt.'s sec., Creston, Ia., 1869-71, gen. western pass. agt., 1871-72, gen. ticket agt. in Neb. at Plattsmouth, Neb., 1873-74, western land and pass. agt., Chicago, 1874-75, Burlington & Mo.R. R.R.; gen. agt. Grand Rapids, Mich., 1875-76, asst. supt. Jackson, Mich., 1876-78; asst. gen. pass. agt., May-Sept., 1878, M.C. R.R.; gen. pass. agt. C.,B.&Q. R.R., 1878-81; gen. pass. agt., 1881-1903, pass. traffic mgr., 1903—, Pa. R.R. Died May 3, 1917.

WOOD, John Anderson, religious, educator; b. Cleveland, O., Aug. 14, 1865; s. William Smith and Louisa Hamilton (Anderson) W.; grad. Ind. State Normal Sch., 1889; A.B., Ind. U., 1897, A.M., 1902; Ps.D., Chicago Sch. Psychology, 1903; studied U. of Chicago, Clark U. and Columbia; m. Louise Meyer, June 24, 1891; children—Paul Meyer, M.D., John Meyer. Prin. high sch., Frankfort, Ind., 1889-96; supt. city schs., Laporte, Ind., 1897-1909, South Bend, 1909-12; prof. religious edn. and dean Bibl. Sem., New York, 1912—. Mem. bd. N.Y. City S.S. Assn.; mem. advisory bd. N.Y. City Protestant Teachers' Assn.; dir. Save a Life League. Mem. Nat. Council Edn., N.E.A., Religious Edn. Assn. Republican. Presbyn. Home: Brooklyn, N.Y. Died Apr. 4, 1926.

WOOD, John Hepler, clergyman, educator; b. Monroe County, Mo., Dec. 8, 1869; s. Winfield S. and Susan A. (Hepler) W.; B.L., U. of Mo., 1895; D.D., Culver-Stockton Coll., 1918; m. Susan A. Jones, June 15, 1898. Ordained Christian (Disciples) ministry, 1895; pastor Shelbina, Mo., 1898-1914; pres. Shelbina Nat. Bank, 1907-14; pres. Culver-Stockton Coll., Canton, Mo., 1917-37, emeritus. Mason, Odd Fellow. Home: Canton, Mo. Died Sept. 25, 1938.

WOOD, John Seymour, author; b. Utica, N.Y., October 1, 1853; s. George W. and Harriet (Clark) W.; grad. Yale, 1874, A.B., 1875; LL.B., Columbia, 1876; m. Mary B. Harris, Sept. 15, 1880. In law practice at New York, 1876—. Editor, Bachelor of Arts mag., 1896-98. Mem. Soc. of Am. Authors. Author: Gramercy Park, 1892; A Daughter of Venice, 1892; Yale Yarns, 1897; A Coign of Vantage, 1896; College Days, 1895; An Old Beau. Wrote A New England Ingénue, 1890; Nancy, Century, 1897; A Nippon Garden, 1915; In the House of Morphy. Also many contbns. to Bachelor of Arts, 1896-97. Home: New York, N.Y. Deceased.

WOOD, Joseph, ry. official; b. Haddonfield, N.J., June 5, 1846; s. Isaac H. and Elizabeth (Cooper) W.; C.E., Pa. Poly. Coll., 1864; m. Jennie E. Boas, Oct. 1874 (died 1913). Rodman, later asst. engr. constrn. corps, Phila., 1864-69; resident engr. Northern Central Ry., 1869-72; resident engr. Baltimore & Potomac R.R. and engr. Northern Central Ry., 1872-78; with Pa. R.R., as asst. to supt. motive power, Altoona, Pa., 1878-81, supt. motive power, 1881-87, gen. supt. transportation, 1887-90, gen. mgr. lines west of Pittsburgh, 1890-96, 4th v.p., 1896-97; 3d v.p., 1897-1902, 2d v.p., Jan. 1, 1902-05, and 1st v.p. Pa. Lines W. of Pittsburgh, 1905-14; also pres. Vandalia R.R. Co., Grand Rapids & Ind. R.R. Co., Cleveland, Akron & Cincinnati Ry. Co. till 1914, when resigned; dir. Pa. R.R. Co., N.&W. Ry. Co. Home: Pittsburgh, Pa. Died Mar. 4, 1922.

WOOD, Kenneth Foster, corp. official; b. Central Falls, R.I., May 24, 1873; s. S. Eugene and Kate B. (Pond) W.; B.S., Mass. Inst. Tech., 1894; m. Elizabeth Lee Goff, Oct. 17, 1905. With Sayless Finishing Plants, Inc., 1894—, as draftsman, master mechanic, supt., gen. mgr., and as treas., dir., 1913—; v.p. Union Wadding Co., Crown Mfg. Co.; dir. R.I. Hosp. Trust Co. (Providence), Hamlet Textile Co., Am. Bleached Goods Co., etc. Asso. with F. W. Taylor and H. L. Gantt in their earlier efforts in indsl. efficiency. Trustee Memorial Hosp. Republican. Conglist. Home: West Barrington, R.I. Died Sept. 22, 1925.

WOOD, Leonard, major gen. U.S.A.; b. Winchester, N.H., Oct. 9, 1860; s. Charles Jewett and Caroline E. (Hager) W.; attended Pierce Acad., Middleboro, Mass.; M.D., Harvard, 1884; LL.D., Harvard, 1899, Williams, 1902, U. of Pa., 1903, Princeton, 1916, U. of the South, 1917, U. of Ga., 1917, U. of Mich., 1918, Union Coll., 1918, Wesleyan, 1918, George Washington U., 1918, Abraham Lincoln U., 1919; Dr. Mil. Sc., Pa. Mil. Coll., 1913, and Norwich U., 1915; D.Sc., Rensselaer Poly. Inst., 1920; LL.D., U. of the Philippines, 1922; m. Louisa A. Condit Smith, Nov. 18, 1890; children—Leonard, Osborne Cutler, Louise Barbara. Apptd. from Mass. asst. surgeon U.S.A., Jan. 5, 1886; capt. asst. surgeon, Jan. 5, 1891; commd. col. 1st U.S. Vol. Cav. ("Rough Riders"), May 8, 1898; brig. gen., July 8, 1898, for services at Las Guasimas and San Juan Hill (1898); maj. gen., Dec. 7, 1898; hon. discharged from vol. service Apr. 13, 1899; brig. gen. vols., Apr. 13, 1899; maj. gen., vols., Dec. 5, 1899; brig. gen. U.S.A., Feb. 4, 1901; hon. discharged from vol. service, June 30, 1901; maj. gen. U.S.A., Aug. 8, 1903; retired, 1921, at his own request, after 30 years' service, to accept appmt. as gov. gen. of Philippine Islands. Mil. gov. of Cuba, Dec. 12, 1899, until transfer of the govt. of Cuba to the Cuban Republic, May 20, 1902; on duty in P.I., Mar. 1903; gov. of Moro Province, July 1903-Apr. 1906; comd. Philippines Div., 1906-08; comdg. Dept. of the East, 1908-09; spl. ambassador to Argentine Republic, Apr. 8-July 15, 1910; chief of staff U.S.A., July 16, 1910-Apr. 1914; comd. Dept. of the East, 1914-17, later assigned in command Southeastern Dept.; organized and trained the 89th N.A. Div. and 10th (reg. army) Div. and various spl. regts. and battalions, 1918-19; comd. Central Dept. hdqrs. Chicago, 1919-21; chmn. spl. mission from U.S. to P.I., visiting Japan and China, 1921; gov. gen. Philippine Islands, 1921—. Candidate for Rep. nomination for President, 1920. Awarded Congressional Medal of Honor, Mar. 29, 1898, "for distinguished conduct in campaign against Apache Indians, in 1886, while serving as medical and line officer of Capt. Lawton's expdn."; D.S.M. for services during World War I; Grand Officer Legion of Honor (French); Grand Officer Order of the Rising Sun (Japanese); Grand Officer Order of S.S. Mauritius and Lazarus (Italian); Grand Officer Order of the Golden Grain (Chinese); Roosevelt Medal of Honor, "for distinguished service," 1923. Mem. Soc. Mayflower Descendants (gov. gen. 1915-19); fellow Royal Geog. Soc. Died Aug. 7, 1927.

WOOD, Matthew Laurence, clergyman; b. Bedford County, Va., Oct. 23, 1858; s. Charles Washington and Mary Ann (Ore) W.; student Richmond (Va.) Coll., 1879-84, D.D., 1903; student Southern Bapt. Theol. Sem., Louisville, Ky., 1884-85; m. Bessie Hoge, 1886 (dec.); children—Lawrence C. (dec.), Charles Rowland, Mrs. Miriam Wood Derwacter; m. 2d, Mary Emma Fitzgerald, Dec. 22, 1902; children—John E. F., Matthew L. Ordained ministry Bapt. Ch., 1883; pastor Charles City County, Va., 1885, Petersburg, 1886-87, Newport News, 1888-96, Staunton, 1896-1905, Fifth Av. Ch., Huntington, W.Va., 1905—; dir. Baptist Banner Pub. Co. Pres. W.Va. Bapt. State Conv., 1920-22, and pres. exec. bd.; mem. Bd. of Missionary Coöperation of Northern Bapt. Conv. Trustee Alderson (W.Va.) Jr. Coll. Democrat. Mason. Contbr. to "Voices from Templed Hills," 1928, also to Watchman-Examiner, Review and Expositor. Home: Huntington, W.Va. Died June 12, 1932.

WOOD, Montraville (M.), lecturer, inventor; b. Leon, N.Y., Apr. 16, 1860; s. Cornelius S. and Elizabeth W. (Taylor) W.; ed. pub. schs. and Collegiate Inst., Jamestown, N.Y.; m. Carrie Frances Whittemore, Sept. 30, 1885. Chief insp. and mgr., Am. Bell Telephone Co., Jamestown, 1883; elec. engr. Pa. R.R., Erie, Pa., 1884-85; elec. engr. Erie County Light Co., Erie, Pa., 1885-89; dist. engr., Edison Electric Co., Portland, Ore., 1889, 1890; elec. engr. Ansonia Elec. Co., Chicago, 1891-93; with Stanley Elec. Co., Pittsfield, Mass., 1893-95; with Gen. Electric Co., Schenectady, N.Y., until 1906; continued research work in own lab. and lecturing before chautauquas and lyceums. Inventor two-button snap switch (electric) and many other devices. Holder nearly 100 patents many of which are in general use; inventor of the "torpedo with ears." First aerial postmaster apptd. in U.S. Served 18 months in secret service dept., 1917-18. Republican. Mason. Home: Berwyn, Ill. Died Jan. 6, 1923.

WOOD, Nathan Eusebius, theologian; b. Forrestville, N.Y., June 6, 1849; s. Rev. Nathan and Berinthia M. (Brown) W.; A.B., U. of Chicago, 1872; B.D., Baptist Union Theol. Sem., Chicago, 1872-75; D.D., U. of Chicago, 1883; m. Alice Robinson Boise, June 27, 1873; children—Nathan Robinson, Reuben Sumner, Sarah Goodyear (dec.), Basil Boise. Ordained Bapt. ministry, 1875; pastor Chicago, 1875-77; prin. Wayland Acad., Beaver Dam, Wis., 1877-84; pastor Chicago, 1884-88, Brooklyn, 1887-92, Brookline, Mass., 1892-94, Boston, 1894-99; pres. Newton Theol. Instn., 1899-1909; pastor First Bapt. Ch., Arlington, Mass., 1909-19; became prof. theology Gordon Coll. of Theology and Missions, 1916. Editor of Boise's Exegetical Notes on the Greek Epistles of the Apostle Paul, 1896. Author: History of The First Baptist Church of Boston

Mass., 1899; The Person and Work of Jesus Christ, 1909; The Inspiration of the Scriptures, 1925; Man and Sin, 1927. Home: Arlington, Mass. Died July 8, 1937.

WOOD, Oliver Ellsworth, brig. gen. U.S.A.; b. Hartford, Conn., June 6, 1844; s. Rev. George I. and Susan T. (Merwin) W.; ed. Hopkins Grammar Sch., New Haven, Conn.; m. Mary Wadsworth Norton, June 2, 1873. Pvt. Co. B, 1st Conn. Cav., July 29, 1862; discharged, Sept. 9, 1863; apptd. to U.S. Mil. Acad., Sept. 16, 1863, grad., 1867; commd. 2d lt. 5th U.S. Arty., June 17, 1867; grad. Arty. Sch., 1869 and 1888; 1st lt., June 11, 1870; capt., Aug. 27, 1896; lt. col. vols. chief commissary of subsistence, May 9, 1898; hon. discharged, Apr. 17, 1899; maj. commissary of subsistence, Apr. 17, 1899; maj. U.S. Arty. Corps, May 8, 1901; hon. discharged from vol. service, June 12, 1901; lt. col., Jan. 21, 1904; mil. sec., Apr. 14, 1905; col. Arty. Corps, June 8, 1906; advanced to rank of brig. gen., and retired at own request, over 40 yrs.' service, Oct. 1, 1906. Served in Army of Potomac in Fredericksburg campaign, 1862; 5th U.S. Arty., 1867-1898; 7th Army Corps and headquarters Div. of Cuba, at Havana, Oct. 1898-Aug. 1900; mil. attaché, Japan, 1901-05. Home: Washington, D.C. Died 1910.

WOOD, Palmer Gaylord, brig. gen. U.S.A.; b. in N.Y., June 2, 1843. Second lt. 7th Calif. Inf., Oct. 28, 1864; 1st lt., Dec. 7, 1865; apptd. from Calif. 2d lt. 5th U.S. Inf., Feb. 23, 1866; hon. mustered out of vol. service, Apr. 26, 1866; 1st lt. U.S.A., Jan. 7, 1867; assigned to 12th Inf., July 14, 1869; resigned, May 24, 1873; apptd. 2d lt., 12th U.S. Inf., Mar. 1, 1877; 1st lt., Oct. 16, 1882; capt., Dec. 11, 1893; maj. 47th U.S. Vol. Inf., Aug. 17, 1899-Feb. 2, 1901; maj. 28th U.S. Inf., Feb. 2, 1901; transferred to 12th Inf., July 15, 1901; lt. col. 11th Inf., Oct. 30, 1905; brig. gen. U.S.A., Feb. 16, 1906; retired, Feb. 17, 1906, at own request, over 30 yrs.' service. Died July 18, 1915.

WOOD, Richard, mfr.; b. at Phila., Dec. 25, 1833; s. Richard Davis and Julianna (Randolph) W.; brother of George and Stuart W.; A.B., Haverford, 1851; unmarried. Merchant and mfr., 1869—; dir. Provident Life and Trust Co., of Phila. Trustee U. of Pa., 1873—; mgr. Haverford Coll. Wrote monograph on Hospital in "Franklin and the University." Home: Philadelphia, Pa. Died 1910.

WOOD, Spencer Shepard, naval officer; b. Brooklyn, Aug. 7, 1861; s. John Wardell and Mary Garrison (Shepard) W.; grad. U.S. Naval Acad., 1882, Naval War Coll.; m. Mary Margaretta Fryer, June 12, 1895; children—Margaretta, Anne Elizabeth. Commd. ensign, July 1884; promoted through grades to rear adm., Oct. 15, 1917. Served in Iroquois, 1885-87; U.S. Coast Survey Steamer Patterson, Mar. 17-Oct. 26, 1888; in Monocacy, Omaha, Palos, Charleston, Marion, Asiatic station, 1889-92; flag lt. to Rear Adm. George E. Belknap; duty Navy Dept. and aide to Sec. of the Navy H. A. Herbert, 1892-93; flag sec. Rear Adm. J. G. Walker and R. W. Meade, 1894; duty U.S.S. Vermont and torpedo sta., Newport, R.I., 1895-97; comd. DuPont, 1897, and during Spanish-Am. War, 1898; in Battleship Massachusetts, 1898-99; Brooklyn and Baltimore, Asiatic sta., 1899-1900; flag sec. to Rear Adm. John C. Watson; asst. to the insp. 3d lighthouse dist., Tompkinsville, N.Y., 1900-02; on bd. San Francisco, European sta., Jan. 20-Aug. 19, 1902; on bd. Chicago, Aug. 21, 1902-Oct. 15, 1903; navigator on board Columbia, Oct. 15, 1903-Oct. 2, 1904; aide to Adm. Dewey, Oct. 17, 1904-Feb. 29, 1908; exec. officer Idaho, Apr. 1, 1908-Feb. 24, 1909; comd. New York, May 15, 1909-Mar. 4, 1910; sec. Gen. Bd., Mar. 4, 1910-Feb. 1912; comd. U.S.S. Nebraska, Feb. 20, 1912-Jan. 17, 1914; Naval War Coll., Jan. 1914-Dec. 22, 1914; Gen. Bd., Navy Dept., Dec. 28, 1914-Jan. 5, 1917; comdr. U.S.S. Oklahoma, Jan. 6, 1917-Jan. 1918; comdt. 1st Naval Dist., hdqrs. Boston, Jan. 1918-Apr. 30, 1919; comdr. Div. Two, cruisers, Pacific Fleet, to Oct. 4, 1919; comdr. Train, Pacific Fleet, 1919-20; pres. Naval Exam. and Retiring Bds., Oct. 3, 1920-Dec. 19, 1921, retired. Treas. and sec. Navy Relief Soc. Awarded Navy Cross and Sampson, Philippine Campaign, N.Y. State and Flushing (N.Y.) medals. Home: Washington, D.C. Died July 30, 1940.

WOOD, Sterling Alexander, lawyer; b. Florence, Ala., Apr. 6, 1859; s. Sterling Alexander Martin and Lelia Elizabeth (Leftwich) W.; A.B., U. of Ala., 1877, LL.B., 1878; m. Ida May Richardson, Aug. 16, 1887. Admitted to Ala. bar, 1878, and practiced Tuscaloosa and Birmingham, Ala.; sec. Supreme Ct. of Ala., 1884-87, clk. same, 1892-98; referee in case of Southern Steel Co. bankrupt, 1910-11; later gen. practice. Pres. C. of C., Birmingham, 1910, and in charge legislation known as Greater Birmingham Bill. 1st lt. and capt., Warrior Guards, Ala. N.G., 1880-81; mem. Dem. and Conservative Party State Exec. Com., 1882-87. State Deputy Knights of Columbus; Elk. Home: Birmingham, Ala. Died Nov. 14, 1924.

WOOD, Stuart, mfr.; b. Phila., May 30, 1853; s. Richard D. and Julianna (Randolph) W.; brother of

George and Richard W.; A.B., Haverford Coll., 1870; Ph.D., Harvard, 1875; unmarried. Mem. firm R. D. Wood Co., mfrs. cast iron pipe and heavy machinery, 1873—; also mem., 1873-94, R. D. Wood & Sons, mfrs. cotton goods; also engaged in window-glass mfg. for some years, and in farming, coal and timber operations. Dir. Market St. Nat. Bank; treas. Tampa (Fla.) Water Works Co. Organized Ind. Republican movement in Pa. in Blaine-Cleveland campaign, 1884; mem. Independent Rep. Conv., New York, which indorsed Cleveland, 1884; actively connected with civ. service reform, ballot reform and other polit. orgns. and work in Phila. and Pa. Mem. Am. Econ. Assn. (v.p. 1889-90), Am. Acad. Polit. and Social Science (treas. from organization, 1890); mgr. Pa. Inst. for Deaf and Dumb. Writer of several articles on the Theory of Wages and other econ. topics in econ. publs. Home: Philadelphia, Pa. Died Mar. 2, 1914.

WOOD, Thomas John, maj. gen. U.S.A.; b. Munfordville, Ky., Sept. 25, 1823; grad. West Point, 1845; served Mexican war on staff Gen. Zachary Taylor; served 12 yrs. on Tex. and Kan. frontiers; at breaking out of Civil war was maj. 1st cav.; m. Caroline E. Greer, Nov. 29, 1861. Served throughout Civil war, 1861-65, in Army of the Cumberland, comd. div. 21st corps, div. 4th corps, and finally comd. the 4th corps. Took part in all battles of that army, including Shiloh, Perryville, Stone River, Chickamauga, Missionary Ridge, Atlanta Campaign, Franklin and Nashville; severely wounded at Stone River and again at Lovejoy's Sta.; promoted to maj. gen. vols.; retired, 1868, as maj. gen. U.S.A. for disabilities received in the line of duty. Home: Dayton, O. Died 1906.

WOOD, Thomas Waterman, artist; b. Montpelier, Vt., Nov. 12, 1823; s. John W.; academic edn.; studied art in Boston, 1848, and in Europe, 1859; m. Minerva Robinson, Sept. 24, 1850 (died 1889). Painted portraits in Washington, Baltimore, Nashville and Louisville. Settled in New York, 1866, as portrait and figure painter. Mem., 1871—, v.p., 1879-91, pres. 1891-99, Nat. Acad. of Design; pres. Am. Water Color Soc., 1878-87. Established public art gallery in his native town, 1894-96. Died 1903.

WOOD, Walter, iron mfr.; b. Phila., Dec. 6, 1849; s. Richard D. and Julianna (Randolph) W.; A.B., Haverford (Pa.) Coll., 1867, Harvard, 1868; unmarried. Mem., 1868—, of R. D. Wood & Co. (founded, 1803), mfrs. cast iron water and gas pipe, Phila.; pres. Florence Iron Works; treas. Millville Gas Works; dir. Burlington (N.J.) City Loan & Trust Co. Trustee Haverford College. Mem. Com. of 100. Phila., 1880-84; civil service examiner, Phila., 1887-95. Republican. Quaker. Home: Philadelphia, Pa. Died Apr. 20, 1934.

WOOD, Will Christopher; b. Elmira, Calif., Dec. 10, 1880; s. Emerson and Martha Jane (Turner) W.; student Stanford U., 1900-01, U. of Calif., 1906-09, U. of Mich., summer 1913; M.A.. pro merito, U. of Southern Calif., 1919; m. Agnes Kerr, July 12, 1905. Prin. schs., Fairfield, Calif. 1901-06, also pres. Solano County Bd. Edn.; prin. Wilson Sch., Alameda, Calif., 1906-09; supt. schs.. Alameda, 1909-14; state commr. secondary schs., Calif., 1914-19; state supt. of public instrn., Calif., Jan. 6, 1919-27; Calif. state supt. banks, 1927-31; v.p. and mgr. Oakland Branch of Bank of America Nat. Trust & Savings Assn., 1931—; dir. Pacific Nat. Fire Ins. Co., Capitol Co.; mem. advisory council of Transamerica Corp. Regent U. of Calif., 1919-27. Secretary Calif. Teachers' Assn., 1908-09; pres. Nat. Council of State Depts. of Edn., 1919-20; chmn. Calif. Commn. for Study of Refinancing Irrigation Dists., 1929-31; v.p. Oakland C. of C., 1932—. Pres. San Francisco Chapter of Pan-Am. Soc., 1931-32. Lecturer in edn., Teachers Coll. (Columbia), summer 1917, Stanford, summers 1920, 21, U. of Southern Calif., 1922 and 1927-31. Republican. Mason. Part Author: (Wood, Cooper and Rice) America's Message. Contbr. to ednl. and banking jours. Home: Piedmont, Calif. Died May 15, 1939.

WOOD, William H. S., publisher, banker; b. New York, 1840; s. William W.; ed. Haverford Coll. Became partner, 1863, with his father in publ. house of Wm. Wood & Co., of which later was head. Dir. New York Y.M.C.A., 7 yrs.; mgr. Am. Bible Soc., 12 yrs.; life mem. N.Y. Hist. Soc., Am. Pomol. Soc., N.Y. Hort. Soc.; fellow Am. Geog. Soc.; benefactor N.Y. Acad. Medicine; mem. N.Y. Bot. Soc. (incorporator), N.Y. Soc. for Suppression of Vice, N.Y. Acad. Sciences. Founder and propr. Med. Record. Pres. Bowery Savings Bank, 1903—. Author several vols. on hort. subjects. Died 1907.

WOOD, William Madison, mfr.; b. Edgartown, Marthas Vineyard, Mass., Apr. 5, 1858; s. William Jason and Amelia (Madison) W.; ed. pub. schs.; m. Ellen, d. Fdk. Ayer. Began as clerk in Wamsutta Mills office; later engaged in banking and brokerage business; assisted in reorganizing several Fall River mills and became paymaster; gen. agt. Washington Mills, Lawrence; joined in merger of woolen mills, 1900, and later pres. Am. Woolen Co. (28 mills), Woolen & Worsted Mills, Inc., Shawsheen Mills, Washington Mills (Lawrence), Nat. and Providence Worsted Mills (R.I.), Kilburn Mills; dir. Merchants

Nat. Bank, Pierce Mfg. Co. (New Bedford), Chase Nat. Bank (New York), etc. Republican. Episcopalian. Died Feb. 2, 1926.

WOOD, William Robert, congressman; b. Oxford, Ind., Jan. 5, 1861; s. Robert and Matilda (Hickman) W.; LL.B., U. of Mich., 1882; m. Mary E. Geiger, May 16, 1883 (dec.). Admitted to Ind. bar, 1882, and practiced at Lafayette; partner of Judge W. DeWitt Wallace, 1882-84, Capt. W. H. Bryan, 1884-91, Hon. J. Frank Hanly, 1897-1904; practiced alone, 1904—; dir. and atty. City Nat. Bank, Citizens' Bldg. & Loan Assn., Tippecanoe Loan & Trust Co.; dir. Lafayette Telephone Co. Pros. atty., Tippecanoe County, Ind., 1890-94; mem. Ind. Senate, 1896-1914; mem. 64th to 72d Congresses (1915-33), 10th Ind. Dist. Placed Charles W. Fairbanks in nomination for presidency at Rep. Nat. Conv., Chicago, 1916. Chmn. Rep. Nat. Congressional Com. Mason, Elk, K.P. Home: Lafayette, Ind. Died Mar. 7, 1933.

WOOD-ALLEN, Mary, physician, lecturer, author; b. Delta, O., Oct. 19, 1841; d. George and Sarah (Seeley) Wood; grad. classical dept. Ohio Wesleyan Coll. (now univ.), 1861; grad. med. dept. U. of Mich., 1875; studied medicine in Vienna, Austria, 1872-73, holds certificates of prof. in Allegemeine Kranken Hous; m. Chilion B. Allen, Apr. 13, 1863. Taught French, German and music in Collegiate Inst., Battle Ground, Ind., 1862; practiced medicine in Newark, N.J. Supt. Purity Dept., World's W.C.T.U. Author: Man Wonderful in House Beautiful, 1883; Teaching Truth, 1892; Child Confidence Rewarded, 1893; Marvels of Our Bodily Dwellings, 1896; Almost a Man, 1896; Almost a Woman, 1897; Baby's Firsts, 1898; What a Young Girl Ought to Know, 1897; What a Young Woman Ought to Know, 1898; Ideal Married Life, 1902. Founder, publisher and editor, The New Crusade, 1895; editor Am. Motherhood. Died 1908.

WOODARD, Frederick Augustus, lawyer; b. Wilson County, N.C., Feb. 12, 1854; s. Stephen and Mary (Hadley) W.; ed. high sch., Wilson, N.C., and attended law sch. of Chief Justice Richmond Pearson; m. Fannie E. Rountree, Nov. 22, 1876 (died 1894); m. 2d, Mrs. R. E. Holleman, Mar. 8, 1898. Admitted to bar, 1873; dir. First Nat. Bank, Wilson Savings Bank, Wilson Oil, Mill & Fertilizer Co. Mem. 53d and 54th Congresses (1893-97); trustee U. of N.C., Wilson Graded Sch. Del. Universal Congress Lawyers and Jurists, St. Louis, 1904. Methodist. Democrat. Home: Wilson, N.C. Died May 8, 1915.

WOODBERRY, George Edward, author; b. Beverly, Mass., May 12, 1855; s. Henry Elliott and Sarah Dane (Tuck) W.; A.B., Harvard, 1877; Litt.D., Amherst, 1905, Harvard, 1911; LL.D., Western Reserve, 1907; unmarried. Prof. English U. of Neb., 1877-78, 1880-82; prof. comparative lit., Columbia, 1891-1904. Fellow Am. Acad. of Arts and Sciences; mem. Am. Acad. Arts and Letters; hon. fellow Royal Soc. Literature. Author: History of Wood Engraving, 1883; Edgar Allan Poe, 1885; Studies in Letters and Life, 1890; The North Shore Watch, 1890; Heart of Man, 1899; Wild Eden, 1900; Makers of Literature, 1900; Nathaniel Hawthorne, 1902; American in Literature, 1903; Poems, 1903; The Torch, 1905; Algernon Charles Swinburne, 1905; Ralph Waldo Emerson, 1907; The Appreciation of Literature, 1907; Great Writers, 1907; The Life of Edgar Allan Poe, 2 vols., 1909; The Inspiration of Poetry, 1910; Wendell Phillips, 1912; A Day at Castrogiovanni, 1912; The Kingdom of All-Souls, 1912; Two Phases of Criticism, 1914; North Africa and the Desert, 1914; The Flight, 1914; Shakespeare, 1916; Ideal Passion, 1917; Nathaniel Hawthorne, 1918; The Roamer, 1919; Collected Essays, 6 vols., 1920-21. Editor: Lamb's Elia, 1892; Shelley's Complete Poetical Works, 4 volumes, 1892; Aubrey de Vere's Selected Poems, 1894; Poe's Complete Works (with E. C. Stedman), 10 vols., 1895; Tennyson's Princess, 1899; National Studies in American Literature (4 vols.), 1899-1900; Columbia University Studies in Comparative Literature (9 vols.), 1899-1903; Bacon's Essays, 1900; Shelley's Poetical Works (with notes), 1 vol., 1901; Coleridge's Ancient Mariner, 1903; Shelley's Select Poems, 1908; Sidney's Defense of Poetry, 1908; Shelley's Cenci, 1909; European Years (Letters of an Idle Man), 1911; New Letters of an Idle Man, 1913; collected Poems of Rupert Brooke, 1915. Home: Beverly, Mass. Died Jan. 2, 1930.

WOODBERRY, Rosa, educator; b. Barnwell County, S.C.; d. Stratford Benjamin and Victoria Ida (Cocroft) Woodberry; grad. Houghton Inst., Augusta, Ga., Lucy Cobb Inst., Athens, Ga.; A.B. in Edn., U. of Ga., 1927; M.A., Oglethorpe U., 1928. Prof. science, Lucy Cobb Inst., 1895-1908; founder, 1908, and prin. Woodberry Hall Sch. for Girls, Atlanta, Ga. Hon. sec. woman's auxiliary of P.E. Ch., Diocese of Atlanta; officer Federated Church Women of Ga. Parliamentarian Ga. Fedn. Women's Clubs, Atlantic Fedn. same. Home: Atlanta, Ga. Died July 19, 1932.

WOODBRIDGE, Frederick James Eugéne, univ. prof.; b. Windsor, Ontario, Can., Mar. 26, 1867; s

James and Melissa Ella (Bingham) W.; A.B., Amherst, 1889, A.M., 1898; grad. Union Theol. Sem., 1892; U. of Berlin, 1892-94; LL.D., Amherst, 1903, U. of Colo., 1915, Queen's U., Kingston, Can., 1919, Columbia, 1929; Litt.D., Dartmouth Coll., 1924, U. of Pa., 1933; D.Re.Pol., Berlin, 1931; m. Helena Belle Adams, June 25, 1895; children—Frederick James, John Arven, Donald Bingham, Helena (Mrs. Paul A. Wolfe). Instr. philosophy, 1894-95, prof., 1895-1902, U. of Minn.; prof. philosophy, Columbia, 1902-04, Johnsonian prof., 1904-39, dean of faculties of polit. science, philosophy and pure science, 1912-29; prof. emeritus in residence, 1939—; Roosevelt prof. in Berlin, 1931-32. Editor Jour. of Philosophy. Mem. Nat. Acad. Arts and Letters; fellow Am. Psychol. Assn., A.A.A.S., N.Y. Acad. Sciences. Author: Philosophy of Hobbes, 1903; The Purpose of History, 1916; The Realm of Mind, 1926; Contrasts in Education, 1929; Son of Apollo, 1929; Hobbes Selections, 1930; Nature and Mind, 1937. Home: New York, N.Y. Died June 1, 1940.

WOODBRIDGE, Samuel Homer, engr.; b. Perth Amboy, N.J., Dec. 26, 1848; s. Stephen G. and Sarah (Fisher) W.; A.B., Williams, 1873; student Mass. Inst. Tech., 1876-79; m. Adele R. Taylor, June 25, 1891; children—Stephen Taylor (dec.), Philip Dudley (M.D.), Helen W. (Mrs. Albert H. Imlah). Asst. instr., 1882-84, instr., 1884-95, asst. prof., 1895-1900, asso. prof. heating and ventilation, 1900-14, Mass. Inst. Tech. Cons. and designing engr. for heating, ventilating and sanitary installation: U.S. Capitol, 1895-1911; Capitol Power plant, 1907-10 and 1923-25; Congressional bldgs., and Nat. Mus., 1904-10; Nat. Cathedral P.E. Ch., Washington, D.C.; Post-office bldg., Pa. R.R. Sta., New York, etc. Reported to Congress on economic value of central plant for power, lighting and heating for federal exec. bldgs., Washington, 1905; reported on sanitary condition of sch. houses of Boston, New York, Phila., Portland and Auburn, Me., Portsmouth and Concord, N.H., 1896-1908; served on expert commn. New York Ct. House, 1913-14. Pres. Sanitary Engring. Co. Chmn. com. on car sanitation Am. Pub. Health Assn. Organizer and dir. of 3-yr. nat. campaign which resulted in overthrow of La. Lottery after its removal to Tampa and Honduras. Chmn. bd. trustees Mass. State Hosp. for Dipsomaniacs; dir. N.E. Watch and Ward Soc. (v.p., 1925—). Mem. U.S. Naval League. Home: Brookline, Mass. Died June 4, 1926.

WOODBRIDGE, Samuel Merrill, theologian; b. Greenfield, Mass., April 5, 1819; grad. New York U., 1839; D.D., Union Coll.; D.D., LL.D., Rutgers Coll.; entered ministry of (Dutch) Reformed Ch.; prof. hist. theology, Theol. Sem. of Reformed Ch., 1857—. Author: Analysis of Theology; Faith: Its True Position in the Life of Man, 1875; Analysis of Systematic Theology, 1883; A Manual of Church History, 1895. Died 1905.

WOODBURNE, Angus Stewart, theologian; b. London, Can., Sept. 1, 1881; s. Thomas and Annie (Cathro) W.; B.A., McMaster U., Toronto, Ont., 1906, M.A., 1910; B.D., U. of Chicago, 1917, Ph.D., 1918; m. Helen White, Sept. 19, 1906; 1 dau., Helen Patricia. Ordained Bapt. ministry, 1906; missionary in India, 1906-14; with Am. Red Cross, 1918-20; prof. philosophy, Madras Christian Coll., 1920-30; prof. theology, Crozer Theol. Sem., July 1930—. Pres. Am. Bapt. Foreign Mission Soc., 1933-34. Author: Human Nature and Education, 1926; The Religious Attitude, 1927; The Theory of Knowledge from Locke to Kant, 1929. Editor The Crozer Quarterly. Mason. Home: Chester, Pa. Died Feb. 13, 1938.

WOODBURY, Charles Herbert, artist; b. Lynn, Mass., July 14, 1864; s. Seth H. and Mary (Parker) W.; B.S., Mass. Inst. Tech., 1886; studied art, Académie Julian, Paris; m. Marcia Oakes, June 26, 1890. Awarded gold medal, Atlanta; 2d prize, Nashville; prize, Boston Art Club; 3 medals, Mechanics' Assn., Boston; medals, Paris Expn., 1900, Buffalo Expn., 1901, St. Louis Expn., 1904; 1st prize, Worcester, 1905; hon. mention, Pittsburgh, 1906; 2d prize, Worcester Art Mus., 1907; silver medal, Buenos Aires, 1910; Evans prize, 1911; 2d medal, Corcoran Gallery, 1915; medal of honor and gold medal, Panama P.I. Expn., 1915; Dana gold medal, Phila., 1923; Swope prize etching, 1931; Palmer prize, National Acad. of Design, 1932; Noyes prize, the Society of Am. Etchers, 1933. Pictures: Mid-Ocean; A Heavy Sea; The Ground Swell; Maine Coast; The Forest. Represented in Boston Art Mus., Berkshire Athenæum, Worcester Art Mus., R.I. Sch. Design, John Herron Inst., Indianapolis, Carnegie Inst., Pittsburgh; Utah State collection; collection of Queen of Italy; City Art Mus., St. Louis; South Kensington Mus.; Library of Congress, Print Dept., Detroit Mus., Telfair Acad., Corcoran Gallery, Metropolitan Mus., New York. N.A., 1907; pres. Boston Water Color Club, Ognquit Art Assn. Author: Painting and the Personal Equation, 1922; (with Elizabeth Ward Perkins) The Art of Seeing, 1925. Died Jan. 21, 1940.

WOODBURY, Charles Jeptha Hill, engr.; b. Lynn, Mass., May 4, 1851; s. J. Porter and Mary Adams (Hill) W.; prep. edn. pub. schs., Lynn; tech. edn. Mass. Inst. Tech.; hon. A.M., Tufts, 1893; Sc.D., Union, 1906, Dartmouth, 1908; m. Maria H. Brown, Nov. 26, 1878. Engr., Factory Mut. Ins. Co., 1878-94; asst. engr. Am. Bell Telephone Co., 1894-1908; cons. engr., 1908—. Non-resident lecturer Mass. Inst. Tech. and Cornell; chmn. Lynn Sch. Com., 1886-95. Awarded Alsacian medal, Société Industrielle de Mulhouse, 1883; John Scott medal, City of Phila., for meritorious elec. invention, 1885; Assn. medal, Nat. Assn. of Cotton Mfrs., 1910. Mem. Am. Soc. Civ. Engrs., Am. Soc. Mech. Engrs., Am. Inst. Elec. Engrs. Fellow A.A.A.S. Author: Fire Protection of Mills, 1882; Telephone Line Engineering; The Telephone System, 1899; Bibliography of the Cotton Manufacture, 1909. Wrote numerous monographs and papers on fire protection, polit. economy and engring. Home: Lynn, Mass. Died Mar. 20, 1916.

WOODBURY, Ellen Carolina de Quincy (Miss), author; b. Portsmouth, N.H.; d. Judge Levi (judge U.S. Supreme Ct., gov. N.H., U.S. senator, etc.) and Elizabeth Williams (Clapp) Woodbury; ed. acad. Portsmouth, N.H. V.p. Nat. Soc. Colonial Dames of D.C. Author: Dorothy Quincy, Wife of John Hancock, with Events of Her Time, 1902, 1905. Died 1909.

WOODBURY, Gordon, asst. sec. of navy; b. New York, N.Y., Sept. 17, 1863; s. Freeman Perkins and Harriet Ann (McGaw) W.; grad. Phillips Exeter Acad., 1882; B.A., Harvard, 1886; LL.B., and M.A., Columbia, 1888; m. Charlotte Eliza Woodbury, Apr. 18, 1894. Practiced law N.Y. City, 1888-90; propr. and editor Manchester (N.H.) Union, 10 yrs.; mem. N.H. Ho. of Rep., 1891-93; del. Dem. Nat. Conv., 1896, 1920, also of Palmer and Buckner Dem. Conv., 1896; mem. N.H. Constl. Conv., 1903; candidate for U.S. Senate, 1912. Red Cross officer in France, 1918-19; asst. sec. of navy, July 1920-21. Mem. bd. dirs. N.H. State Coll., N.H. State Agrl. Commn. Presbyn. Mason. Home: Bedford, N.H. Died June 17, 1924.

WOODBURY, Helen Sumner, author; b. Sheboygan, Wis., Mar. 12, 1876; d. George True and Katharine Eudora (Marsh) Sumner; A.B., Wellesley Coll., 1898; hon. fellow in polit. economy, 1904-06, correspondence instr., 1907-08, Ph.D., 1908, U. of Wis.; m. Robert Morse Woodbury, Nov. 25, 1918. Collaborator, Am. Bur. of Indsl. Research, 1904—. Spl. investigator of equal suffrage in Colo. for N.Y. Collegiate Equal Suffrage League, 1906-07. Indsl. expert, 1913-15, and asst. chief, 1915-18, of children's bur., Dept. of Labor; with Inst. of Economics, 1924-26. Author: The White Slave, 1896; Labor Problems (with Thomas S. Adams), 1905; Equal Suffrage, 1909; History of Women in Industry (Vol. IX, Report on Women and Children in Industry, U.S. Labor Bur.), 1911; Industrial Courts in Europe, 1911; Child Labor Legislation in the United States (with Ella A. Merritt), 1915; Administration of Child Labor Laws in Connecticut and in New York (with Ethel E. Hanks), 1915 and 1916; History of Labor in the United States (with John R. Commons, and others), 1918; The Working Children of Boston, 1922; Standards Applicable to the Administration of Child Labor Laws, 1924. Asso. editor Documentary History of American Industrial Society, 1910. Contbr. to Dictionary of Am. Biography and to econ. and other publs. Home: New York, N.Y. Died Mar. 10, 1933.

WOODBURY, Ida Sumner Vose, lecturer; b. Dennysville, Me., Dec. 14, 1854; d. Peter Ebenezer and Lydia (Kilby) Vose; grad. Dennysville High Sch., 1870; (on account of defective eyesight, studied with pvt. instrs. until she had completed the course of the best seminaries); m. Clinton A. Woodbury, June 2, 1876 (died 1894); children—Carl Vose, Donald Clinton (dec.), Malcolm Sumner (dec.), Ruth Lincoln. Teacher in high sch. before marriage; pres. State Missionary Soc., Me., 1884-95, and lectured widely; field sec. Am. Missionary Assn., 1895-1920; lecturer on religious, historic, patriotic and lit. subjects; delivered many addresses in promotion of war activities. Congregationalist. A founder Nat. Hist. Soc. Mem. Nat. Council of Congl. Chs. 5 times between 1910-19. Home: Portland, Me. Died Feb. 24, 1934.

WOODBURY, Malcolm Sumner, physician; b. Dennysville, Me., Mar. 27, 1881; s. Clinton Aaron and Ida (Vose) W.; A.B., Bowdoin, 1903; M.D., Jefferson Med. Coll., Phila., 1906; studied in Berlin and London, 1912-13; m. Stella Baker, June 7, 1911. Identified with Clifton Springs (N.Y.) Sanatorium, 1906—; asst. surgeon, 1906-10, mem. med. staff, 1909-12, neurologist, 1913-14, supt., Dec. 1, 1914—. Mem. bd. dirs. Y.M.C.A., Clifton Springs. Republican. Conglist. K.T. Home: Clifton Springs, N.Y. Died Jan. 6, 1920.

WOODBURY, Marcia Oakes, artist; b. South Berwick, Me., June 20, 1865; d. Abner and Susan M. (Bennett) Oakes; m. Charles Herbert Woodbury, June 26, 1890. Studied with Lasar, Paris. Awarded gold medal, Atlanta Expn., 1895; 2 medals, Mechanics' Assn., Boston; 2d prize, Boston Art Club; hon. mention, Nashville (Tenn.) Expn. Exhibited at Paris Expn., 1900. Prin. pictures: Mother and Daughter; The Smoker; Boy with Boat. Home: Boston, Mass. Died Nov. 7, 1913.

WOODBURY, Urban Andrain, governor; b. Acworth, N.H., July 11, 1838; s. Albert Merrill and Lucy Lestina (Wadleigh) W.; M.D., U. of Vt., 1859; m. Paulina Livonia Darling, Feb. 12, 1860. Enlisted Co. H, 2d Vt. Vols., May 25, 1861; sergt., June 19, 1861; lost right arm and taken prisoner in 1st battle of Bull Run, July 21, 1861; paroled, Oct. 5, 1861; commissioned capt. Co. D, 11th Vt. Vols., Nov. 17, 1862; transferred to Vet. Reserve Corps, June 17, 1863; resigned, Mar. 1865. Alderman, 1881-82 (pres. of bd. 1882), mayor, 1885-86, Burlington, Vt.; lt. gov. of Vt., 1888-90; gov., 1894-96. Mem. war investigation com., 1898. Republican. Dept. comdr. G.A.R., Vt., 1900. Died Apr. 15, 1915.

WOODCOCK, Charles Edward, bishop; b. New Britain, Conn., June 12, 1854; s. Joseph B. and Caroline (Shaw) W.; ed. pvt. and pub. schs., Waterbury and Plainville, Conn., and pvt. tutors; grad. Berkeley Div. Sch., Middletown, Conn., 1882; S.T.D., Hobart, 1904; D.D., U. of the South, 1905, Berkeley, 1908; LL.D., U. of Louisville, 1913; m. Ellen Austin Warner, Nov. 20, 1884. Deacon, 1882, priest, 1883, P.E. Ch.; asst. Grace Ch., Baltimore, 1882-84; rector Ch. of the Ascension, New Haven, Conn., 1884-88, Christ Ch., Ansonia, Conn., 1888-1900, St. John's, Detroit, 1900-05; elected bishop of Ky., Nov. 16, 1904, consecrated Jan. 25, 1905. Del. to Gen. Conv. P.E. Ch., from Conn., 1895, 98, from Mich., 1904. Mem. Standing Com. of Diocese while in Conn., also in Mich.; pres. Synod Province of Sewanee, 1920-23. Publs.: One of the Baldwin Lectures, 1903, sermons, addresses. Home: St. Matthews, Ky. Died Mar. 12, 1940.

WOODY, Claiborne Alphonso, clergyman; b. Brownsville, Ore., Feb. 8, 1856; s. Reuben Burrow and Sydney Ann (Hill) W.; A.B., U. of Ore., 1881, A.M., 1884; B.D., Rochester Theol. Sem., 1884; D.D., California Coll., Oakland, 1898; LL.D., McMinnville Coll., Ore., 1914; m. Martha J. Kirby, June 30, 1879. Ordained Bapt. ministry, 1884; pastor Pendleton, Ore., 1884-86, Weston, 1886-87; prin. Indian Indsl. Sch., Chemawa, 1887-88; pastor, Amity, 1888-90; editor Pacific Baptist, 1890-1902; gen. supt. home missions for Alaska, Ore., Wash., Ida., Mont., Calif., Ariz., Nev. and Utah, for Am. Bapt. Home Mission Soc. Chmn. bd. trustees, Bapt. Theol. Sem., Berkeley, Calif. Mem. Nat. War Commn. of Northern Bapt. Conv. Republican. Home: Portland, Ore. Died Nov. 9, 1918.

WOODFORD, M. DeWitt, ry. official; b. Fredonia, N.Y., Oct. 27, 1838; telegraph operator at various stas. on Erie Ry., 1853-56, with Mich. Central, 1856-72, chief train dispatcher 5 yrs. and 11½ yrs. chief train dispatcher and telegraph supt.; asst. gen. supt. Great Western Ry., Can., 1872-75; asst. treas. Chicago & Michigan Lake Shore R.R.; supt. U.S. div. Canada Southern R.R., 1876-80; gen. supt. Ft. Wayne & Jackson R.R., 1880-82; gen. supt., 1882-83, v.p., 1883-84, Wheeling & Lake Erie R.R. and Cleveland & Marietta R.R.; gen. mgr. Toledo Belt R.R., 1883-92; receiver, 1884-86, v.p. and gen. mgr., 1886-89, pres. and gen. mgr., 1889-92, Wheeling & Lake Erie R.R.; v.p. and gen. mgr., 1889-90, pres., 1890-1904, C.,H.&D. Ry. Died 1907.

WOODFORD, Stewart Lyndon, diplomat; b. New York, Sept. 3, 1835; s. Josiah Curtis and Susan (Terry) W.; A.B., Columbia, 1854, A.M., 1866; hon. A.M., Yale, 1866, Trinity, 1869; LL.D., Trinity, 1870, Dickinson, 1889, Marietta, 1908; D.C.L., Syracuse, 1894; m. Julia E. Capen, Oct. 15, 1857; m. 2d, Isabel Hanson, of New York, Sept. 26, 1900. Admitted to bar, 1857, in practice at New York, 1857—. Messenger presdl. electoral coll., 1860; asst. U.S. dist. atty., Southern Dist. of N.Y., 1861-62. Lt. col. 127th N.Y. Inf., Sept. 8, 1862; col. 103d U.S. C.T., Mar. 6, 1865; bvtd. brig. gen. vols., May 12, 1865, "for zeal, efficient and generally meritorious conduct"; resigned, Aug. 23, 1865; 1st Union mil. comdr. of Charleston, S.C., and Savannah, Ga. Lt. gov. of N.Y., 1866-68; nominee for gov., 1870; pres. electoral coll., 1872; elected 43d Congress (1873-75), resigned, July 1, 1874; U.S. dist. atty. Southern Dist. N.Y., 1877-83; mem. commn. to draft charter for Greater New York, 1896; E.E. and M.P. to Spain, 1897, until war was declared, 1898, when he returned to U.S.; mem. law firm Woodford, Bovee & Butcher, New York. Pres. Hudson-Fulton Commn., 1907; made speech placing Charles Evans Hughes in nomination for presidency, Rep. Nat. Conv., 1908. Decorated with Order of the Rising Sun, 2d Class (Japan), 1908; Crown Order of 1st Class by Emperor of Germany, 1910. Home: New York, N.Y. Died Feb. 14, 1913.

WOODHULL, Alfred Alexander, brig. gen. U.S.A.; b. Princeton, N.J., Apr. 13, 1837; s. Dr. Alfred A. and Anna Maria (Salomons) W.; A.B., Princeton, 1856, A.M., 1859, LL.D., 1894; M.D., U. of Pa., 1859; practiced in Kan., 1859-61; m. Margaret, d. Elias Ellicott, Dec. 15, 1868. Assisted in raising co. vol. mounted rifles, 1861; commd. med. officer U.S.A., Sept. 19, 1861; med. insp. Army of the James, 1864-65; chief surgeon Dept. Pacific (Philippines), Apr.-Dec. 1899; bvtd. capt., maj. and lt. col. U.S.A., Mar. 1865, "for faithful and meritorious services" in war; commd. capt., asst. surgeon, July 28, 1866; maj. surgeon, Oct. 1, 1876; lt. col., deputy surgeon gen., May 16, 1894; col., asst. surgeon gen., Oct. 8, 1900; retired, Apr. 13, 1901; advanced to rank of brig. gen. retired, by act of Apr. 23, 1904. Lecturer on personal hygiene, and on gen. sanitation, Princeton U., 1902-07. Gold medalist, Mil. Service Instn., 1885;

Seaman prize essayist, 1907. Mem. bd. mgrs. Geol. Survey N.J., 1904-15. Author: Surgical Catalogue Army Medical Museum, 1867; Studies, Chiefly Clinical, in the Non-Emetic Use of Ipecacuanha, 1876; Military Hygiene, 1890, 1898, 1904, 1909; Personal Hygiene, 1906; The Battle of Princeton (pamphlet), 1913. Home: Princeton, N.J. Died Oct. 18, 1921.

WOODHULL, John Francis, univ. prof.; b. Westport, N.Y., July 2, 1857; s. Rev. John A. and Joanna (Brown) W.; A.B., Yale, 1880; student Johns Hopkins U., 1886; Ph.D., Columbia, 1899; m. Minnie Ellen Hinkley, Apr. 2, 1886 (died 1937); children—Mildred (Mrs. F. F. Good), Hazel (Mrs. J. G. Cline), John Richard (deceased); m. 2d, Clara Hatfield Macnaughton, Mar. 27, 1938. Served as teacher-principal of secondary school, 1881-85; prof. natural science, N.Y. State Normal Sch., 1887; prof. physical science, Teachers Coll. (Columbia), 1888; prof. emeritus, July 2, 1922; mem. Univ. Council, Columbia, 1899-1902. Lecturer in Nat. Summer Sch., Martha's Vineyard Summer Sch., Chautauqua Summer Sch. and in univ. extension courses. Fellow A.A.A.S., Am. Geog. Soc., N.Y. Acad. Sciences. Author of various books on scientific subjects. Home: La Jolla, Calif. Died July 27, 1941.

WOODHULL, Maxwell Van Zandt, author; b. Washington, D.C., Sept. 17, 1843; s. Comdr. Maxwell (U.S.N.) and Ellen Frances (Poor) W.; student Miami U., Oxford, O., 1859-62; studied law Columbian U., Washington, D.C., and in office of William B. Webb; hon. M.A., Miami U.; unmarried. Enlisted in U.S. vols., Dec. 22, 1862; commd. capt. a.d.c., Mar. 11, 1863; maj. a.a.g., July 2, 1864; lt. col. a.a.g., Feb. 17, 1865; bvtd. col., Mar. 13, 1865, "for faithful and meritorious services during recent campaigns"; brig. gen. vols., Mar. 13, 1865, "for faithful and efficient services" during the war; hon. mustered out, May 31, 1866. Served in Army of Va., Army of the Tenn. and on March to the Sea; adj. gen. at Battle of the Monocacy; adj. gen. 15th Army Corps during S. Carolina Campaign, and last adj. gen. Army of the Tenn. Asst. sec. Am. Legation, London, Eng., 1871-72 (resigned); chief of div., Consular Bur., Dept. of State, Washington, D.C., 1878-81 (resigned); admitted to bar but never practiced; dir. Utah Consol. Mining Co., Old Dominion Copper Co., Lanston Monotype Machine Co. Trustee George Washington U., Louise Home, Children's Hosp. Comdr. D. C. Commandery, Loyal Legion. Author: (brochure) A Glimpse of Sherman Fifty Years Ago, 1914; West Point in Our Next War—the Only Way to Create and to Maintain an Army, 1915. Home: Washington, D.C. Died July 26, 1921.

WOODIN, William Hartman, mfr. b. Berwick, Pa., May 27, 1868; s. Clemuel Ricketts and Mary Louise (Dickerman) W.; student Sch. of Mines (Columbia), Class of 1890; m. Annie Jessup, Oct. 9, 1889. Gen. supt. Jackson & Woodin Mfg. Co., Berwick, 1892, v.p., 1895, pres., 1899; with Am. Car & Foundry Co., 1899—, successively dist. mgr., asst. to 1st v.p., asst. to pres., pres., 1916-22; pres. and mem. exec. com. Am. Car & Foundry Co.; chmn. bd. and mem. exec. com. Am. Locomotive Co., Am. Car & Foundry Motors Co.; chmn. bd. The Brill Corp., Ry. Steel Spring Co.; pres. Am. Car & Foundry Export Co., Am. Car & Foundry Securities Co.; dir. Fed. Res. Bank of New York, Remington Arms Co., Superheater Co., Montreal Locomotive Works, The Cuba Co., Cuba R.R. Co., Compañia Cubana Consol Railroads of Cuba, Am. Ship & Commerce Corp. Mem. Am. Iron and Steel Inst., Acad. Polit. Science. Republican. Presbyn. Home: New York, N.Y. Died May 3, 1934.

WOODLEY, Oscar Israel, educator; b. Ontario, Can., Oct. 19, 1861; s. Benjamin F. and Miriam W.; brought to U.S., 1869; grad. Mich. State Normal Coll., Ypsilanti, 1886; A.B., Albion (Mich.) Coll., 1901; hon. M.Pd., Mich. State Normal Coll., 1901; A.M., Columbia, 1902; m. Myra S. Soper, Sept. 2, 1886. Supt. schs., Sauk Center, Minn., 1889-94, Menominee, Mich., 1894-1901, Passaic, N.J., 1904-09; pres. State Normal Sch., Fairmont, W.Va., 1910-15; pres. Marshall Coll., Huntington, W.Va., 1915-20, sec. Fla. Edn. Assn., 1923-24, also editor of its Journal. Republican. Presbyn. Mason. Author: Foundation Lessons in English, Books I and II, 1900; Geography of New Jersey, 1909; The Profession of Teaching, 1917. Home: Clermont, Fla. Died Nov. 25, 1931.

WOODMAN, Albert Stanton, lawyer; b. Gorham, Me., Dec. 23, 1866; s. Jabez Cushman and Mary Jane (Crosby) W.; A.B., Bates Coll., 1887; studied law with William LeBaron Putnam; m. Alice May Andrews, Mar. 30, 1891; children—Harry Andrews, Mary Alice, Stanton Howe. Admitted to Me. bar, 1890; mem. Woodman, Skelton & Thompson. Republican. Conglist. Author: The Law of Trustees in Bankruptcy, 1909. Home: Portland, Me. Died Dec. 29, 1931.

WOODMAN, Clarence Eugene, clergyman; b. Saco, Me., Nov. 1, 1852; s. Col. Andrew J. and Abigail Ayer (Haley) W.; grad. Trinity Coll., Hartford, 1873; A.M., Amherst, 1877; Ph.D., Manhattan, 1881; Litt.D., Trinity Coll., 1913; Sc.D., St. Mary's College, 1913; LL.D., Notre Dame U., 1915. Student Gen. Theol. Sem. (P.E.), New York, 2 yrs.; converted to the Roman Catholic faith; entered the Congregation of St. Paul and was ordained priest; pastor St. Paul's Ch., New York; lecturing prof., Newman Hall, U. of Calif. Editor Trinity Tablet, 1872-73; lecturer, Catholic U. of America, 1891-92 and 1892-93; astronomer Smithsonian eclipse expdn., Wadesboro, N.C., May 1900, and to Hartland, Kansas, June 1918. Knighted by King of Spain, 1894, Knight Comdr. Royal Order of Isabella the Catholic. Elk. Apptd. by Third Plenary Council of Baltimore to prepare official Manual of Prayers for the Church in U.S. Author: The Bridal Wreath; Manual of Prayers; Poets and Poetry of Ireland; Perpetual Ecclesiastical Calendar, etc. Home: Berkeley, Calif. Died Dec. 6, 1924.

WOODMAN, Durand, cons. chemist; b. New York, 1859; s. George and Lucy M. (Durand) W.; grad. Stevens Inst. of Tech., B.S., 1880; Ph.D., 1888; course in organic chemistry, U. of Berlin, and in analytical laboratories of Fresenius, Wiesbaden (diploma, 1890); m. Katherine Lincoln Bowles, 1893. Chemist, U.S. Electric Light Co., 1883-86; cons. chemist and analyst, 1890—. Chem. examiner of supplies for U.S. Light House Establishment, 3d dist., N.Y. Home: New York, N.Y. Died 1907.

WOODMAN, J(oseph) Edmund, geologist; b. Newbury, Mass., July 4, 1873; s. Charles Henry and Mary Josephine (Poore) W.; S.B., Lawrence Scientific Sch. (Harvard), 1896; Harvard Grad. Sch., 1896-1902, A.M., 1900, S.D., 1902; m. Amy Baker Smith, Sept. 4, 1895; children—Malcolm White, Olive Amy W., Jean W. (dec.). Asst. in geology, Harvard, and instr. Radcliffe Coll., 1896-1902; instr. Harvard Summer Sch., 1897-1905; asst. prof. geology, 1902-05, prof., 1905-09, Dalhousie U., Halifax, N.S.; prof. geology and dir. Geol. Mus., New York U., 1909—. Geologist, Dept. of Mines, N.S., 1897-98; geologist in charge iron ore and limestone investigations in N.S., for Mines Branch, Can. Dept. Mines, 1906-13; mem. commn. on final revision plans and specifications for Catskill Water Supply Project, New York, 1910; cons. geologist to Bd. of Estimate, N.Y. City, 1922—. Republican. Presbyn. Fellow Geol. Soc. America, A.A.A.S., New York Acad. Sciences, Am. Geog. Soc. Author: Report on Iron Ores of Nova Scotia (Vol. I, Can. Dept. of Mines), 1909. Home: New York, N.Y. Died May 19, 1939.

WOODROW, H(arry) R(ay), engr. and pub. utility exec.; b. Rock County, Minn., Apr. 15, 1887; s. Joseph Thomas and Della E. (Kennedy) W.; B.S., Drake U., 1909, LL.D., 1934, M.S., U. of Ill., 1911; m. Anna Louise Stillgebauer, 1912; children—Raymond J., Richard A. Asst. to chief elec. engr. N.Y. Edison Co., 1911-17, asst. chief elec. engr., 1917-20; elec. engr. Stone & Webster, 1920-22; gen. engr. Westinghouse Elec. & Mfg. Co., 1922; asst. elec. engr. Brooklyn Edison Co., 1922-26, elec. engr., 1926-32, v.p., 1932-37; v.p. Consolidated Edison Co. of N.Y., Inc., 1937—; dir. Brooklyn Edison Co.; trustee and treas. United Engring. Trustees, Inc. Fellow Am. Inst. Elec. Engrs. Presbyn. Home: Bronxville, N.Y. Died Aug. 12, 1940.

WOODROW, James, educator; b. Carlisle, Eng., May 30, 1828; s. Rev. Thomas (D.D.) and Marion (Williamson) W.; grad. Jefferson Coll., Pa., 1849; studied Lawrence Scientific Sch., Harvard, 1853, Univ. of Heidelberg, A.M., Ph.D., summa cum laude, 1856; (hon. M.D., Ga. Med. Coll.; D.D., Hampden-Sidney Coll.; LL.D., Davidson Coll., Washington and Jefferson Coll.); m. Aug. 4, 1857, Felie S., d. Rev. J. W. Baker of Ga. Presbyn. clergyman; prin. acad. in Ala., 1850-53; prof. natural science, Oglethorpe Univ., Ga., 1853-61; in med. dept. (chief of laboratory at Columbia, S.C.), C.S.A., 1863-65; prof., 1869-72, 1880-91, pres., 1891-97, S.C. Coll.; prof. Columbia Theol. Sem., 1861-86, deposed on account of views concerning evolution, in pamphlet; Evolution, 1884. Treas. Southern Gen. Assembly's Foreign Missions and Sustentation, 1861-72. Corr. del. to the churches in Great Britain and on Continent of Europe, 1874. Commr. to Southern Gen. Assembly, 1866, 77, 79, 80, 86, 89, 96, 99. Moderator Synod of Georgia, Ga., 1879, Synod of S.C., 1901. Pres. Central Nat. Bank of Columbia, 1888-91, 1897-1901. Editor and propr. Southern Presbyn. Review (quarterly), 1861-85, Southern Presbyterian, weekly, 1865-93. Asso. Victoria Inst., London; Isis, Dresden, Saxony; Scientific Assn., Germany; Scientific Assn., Switzerland. Home: Columbia, S.C. Died 1907.

WOODROW, Nancy Mann Waddel, author; b. Chillicothe, O.; d. Dr. William and Jane (McCoy) Waddel; ed. at home; m. James Wilson Woodrow, Aug. 4, 1897. Asst. editor Chillicothe (O.) Daily News, 1896-97; removed to New York, 1900; actively engaged as contbr. to mags., 1901—; contbr. of humor, short stories, verse, etc., to various nat. magazines under her name "Mrs. Wilson Woodrow," also serial story, "A Leaf in the Current," in Metropolitan Magazine under nom-de-plume of "Jane Wade." Author: The Bird of Time, 1907; The New Missioner, 1907; The Silver Butterfly, 1909; The Beauty, 1910; Sally Salt, 1912; The Black Pearl, 1912; The Hornets' Nest, 1917; Swallowed Up!, 1922; Burned Evidence, 1925; Come Alone, 1929; Moonhill Mystery, 1930; Pawns of Murder, 1932. Died Sept. 7, 1935.

WOODRUFF, Carle Augustus, brig. gen. U.S.A.; b. Buffalo, Aug. 8, 1841; s. Israel C. and Caroline A. W.; twice married. Apptd. from D.C., 2d lt. 2d U.S. Arty., Oct. 22, 1861; 1st lt., July 24, 1862; capt. 2d Arty., May 6, 1869; maj., Mar. 8, 1894; lt. col. 7th Arty., Feb. 13, 1899; col. Arty. Corps, May 8, 1901; brig. gen., Aug. 10, 1903; retired at own request after 40 yrs.' service, Aug. 11, 1903. Bvtd. capt., July 3, 1863, "for gallant and meritorious services in battle of Gettysburg, Pa."; maj., June 11, 1864, for same in battle of Trevillian Sta., Va.; lt. col., Mar. 13, 1865, "for good conduct and gallant services during the war"; awarded Congressional Medal of Honor, Sept. 1, 1893, "for distinguished gallantry in action at Newby's Cross Roads, Va., July 24, 1863." Home: Raleigh, N.C. Died July 20, 1913.

WOODRUFF, Charles Albert, brig. gen. U.S.A.; b. Burke, Vt., April 26, 1845; s. Erastus and Eliza (Quimby) W.; grad. U.S. Mil. Acad., 1871; m. Louise V. Duff, July 2, 1874. Enlisted Co. A, 10th Vt. Vols., June 5, 1862; wounded 4 times, Cold Harbor, June 1 and 3, 1864. Cadet, 1867-71; 2d lt. 7th Inf., June 12, 1871; 1st lt., Aug. 9, 1877; wounded 3 times at Big Hole, Aug. 9, 1877; bvtd. capt. "for gallant services"; capt. commissary, Mar. 28, 1878; maj., Dec. 27, 1892; lt. col., Feb. 4, 1898; col. asst. commissary gen., May 11, 1898; brig. gen. U.S.A. and retired, 1903. Served in Philippines; chief commissary Dept. of Calif., and purchasing commissary, San Francisco; mem. Bd. of Visitors U.S. Naval Acad., 1906; comdt. Veteran Home of Calif., 1909-14. Home: Berkeley. Calif. Died Aug. 13, 1920.

WOODRUFF, Charles Edward, army medical officer; b. Philadelphia, Pa., Oct. 2, 1860; s. David Stratton and Mary Jane (Remster) W.; A.B., Central High Sch., Phila., 1879, A.M., 1884; U.S. Naval Acad., 1879-83; prof. higher mathematics, high sch., Reading, Pa., 1883-84; M.D., Jefferson Med. Coll., 1886; m. Stella M., d. Prof. John P. Caulfield, of Washington, Dec. 22, 1886. Asst. surgeon U.S.N., May 1886-Apr. 1887; 1st lt. asst. surgeon U.S.A., Apr. 14 1887; capt., Apr. 14, 1892; maj., Apr. 13, 1901; lt. col., Jan. 1, 1910; retired from active service July 12, 1913. Served in the Spanish-Am. War, expdn. to P.I., 1898, Philippine insurrection, 1902, 3d tour in P.I., 1909-10; maj. brigade surgeon, June 4, 1898-Feb. 22, 1899. Awarded 2 medals for war service. Author: The Effects of Tropical Light on White Men, 1905; Expansion of Races, 1909; also Evolution of Numerals from Primitive Tally Marks (Am. Math. Monthly). Home: New Rochelle, N.Y. Died June 13, 1915.

WOODRUFF, Edwin Hamlin, prof. law; b. Ithaca, N.Y., Sept. 2, 1862; s. Philo Marion and Aristona Augusta (Holmes) W.; student Cornell, 1878-80, LL.B., 1888; unmarried. In Astor Library, New York, 1883-84, Cornell U. Library, 1884-87; admitted to N.Y. bar, 1888; instr. English, Cornell, 1888-90; librarian Fiske Library, Florence, Italy, 1890-91; librarian, 1891-96, acting prof. law, 1893-96, Leland Stanford Jr. U.; prof. law, 1896-1927, acting dean, 1914-16, dean, 1916-21, prof. emeritus, 1927—, Cornell Law School. Lecturer University of Chicago Law School, summer term, 1904, 06. Pres. Social Service League, Ithaca, 1911-13; trustee Ithaca City Hospital, 1911-13. Author: Cases on Domestic Relations, 1897, 3d edit. 1920; Introduction to the Study of Law, 1898; Cases on Insurance, 1900, 2d edit., 1924; Selected Cases on the Law of Quasi-Contracts, 1905, 2d edit., 1917. Joint editor (with E. F. Huffcut) Cases on Contracts, 1894, 4th edit., 1925. Home: Ithaca, N.Y. Died July 8, 1941.

WOODRUFF, Francis Eben, customs official in China; b. New York, N.Y., Apr. 24, 1844; s. Dr. Ebenezer Blachly and Elizabeth Sophia (Coursen) W.; A.B., Yale, 1864; unmarried. In 1864 selected by Pres. Woolsey, of Yale, and nominated by Sec. of State Wm. H. Seward for, and apptd. by Mr. (late Sir) Robert Hart to, Imperial Maritime Customs Service of China, Aug. 15, 1865. Was student, clerk, and for a time Chinese sec. on inspectorate staff at Peking; commr. of customs at various ports, 1872-97; resigned because of ill-health, Mar. 1897. Wrote: A Monetary Agreement (pamphlet issued by New England Com. for Promotion of Bimetallism); A Single Standard for the World, Arena, Mar. 1898; The Woodruffs of New Jersey (geneal.), 1909. Home: Morristown, N.J. Died June 3, 1914.

WOODRUFF, George Washington, lawyer; b. Dimock, Pa., Feb. 22, 1864; s. Lewis H. and Mella (Glidden) W.; B.E., Mansfield (Pa.) State Normal Sch., 1883; A.B., Yale, 1889; LL.B., U. of Pa., 1895; m. Maud Donald Macbride, Aug. 4, 1898; m. 2d, Elfreda Foster, 1921. Law officer, U.S. Forest Service, 1903-06; asst. atty. gen. U.S. for Interior Dept., 1907-09; acting sec. of the interior U.S., June 15-Oct. 1, 1907; U.S. dist. judge, Dist. of Hawaii, 1909-10; atty. gen of Pa., 1923-27; apptd. pub. service commr. of Pa., July 16, 1931. Republican. Presbyn. Home: Berwyn, Pa. Died Mar. 23, 1934.

WOODRUFF, Harvey T., newspaperman; b. Brazil, Ind., Apr. 9, 1875; s. Amos H. and Julia K. (Trunkey) W.; prep. edn. West Div. High Sch., Chicago, and Chicago Acad.; student U. of Chicago, 1895-97; m. Eva P. Hammon, Apr. 28, 1909; children—Alberta E., Julia H. Began newspaper work on Chicago Times-Herald, 1897; sporting editor Chicago Record, 1898-1901; reporter Chicago Herald, 1901, Chicago Tribune, 1901-03; sec. and treas. Western Jockey Club, 1903-08; sporting editor Chicago Tribune, 1909-20, spl. sports writer, 1920—. Home: Evanston, Ill. Died June 2, 1937.

WOODRUFF, Helen S., author; b. Selma, Ala., June 7, 1888; d. Oscar Emmet and Emma (West) Smith; ed. under tutors; m. Lewis B. Woodruff, June 18, 1906. Mem. Authors' League America (exec. council same). Author: Mis' Beauty, 1912; Really Truly Nature Stories, 1913; The Lady of the Lighthouse, 1913; The Little House, 1914; Really Truly Fairy Stories, 1915; Mr. Doctor-Man, 1915. Reputation made on The Lady of the Lighthouse (3d best seller, 1913); has given all royalties of this book to the New York Assn. for the Blind; proceeds of all books given to charity; royalties from "Mr. Doctor-Man" used to build a children's hosp. in girlhood home at Birmingham, Ala.; The Imprisoned Freeman, 1918; What David Did, 1921; Hurrah for the Girls, prod. at 44th St. Roof Garden, New York, Dec. 14, 1918 (proceeds given to Devastated France Com.); Kitty, Kitty, Kitty, and By Love's Speedometer (short plays), 1919. Co-author libretto, Just Because (also wrote all lyrics); libretto Cash and Kisses. Home: Litchfield, Conn. Died Oct. 14, 1924.

WOODRUFF, Henry Mygatt, actor; b. Hartford, Conn., June 1, 1869; s. Samuel and Emma Jane (Coite) W.; ed. Hartford pub. schs. and Harvard; unmarried. Went on stage at 9 yrs. of age in chorus of a children's pinafore co.; played boys' parts with Adelaide Nielson; supported Edwin Thorne 2 seasons; took leading part in "Jim the Penman"; created the part of Ben Hur; starred in "Brown of Harvard," 1905-07. Home: Siasconset, Mass. Died Oct. 6, 1916.

WOODRUFF, Joseph Talmage Battis, consulting engr.; b. Colorado Springs, Colo., June 30, 1894; s. Joseph Miller and Marie Antoinette (Talmage) W.; student Mass. Inst. Tech., 1914-17, Boston U., 1918; m. Dorothy Gray, June 12, 1920; children—Gordon Gray (dec.), Randolph Talmage, Rosamond Gray. City planning and zoning consultant for Springfield, Mass., 1921—; also same for various New England communities; planning engr. Regional Planning Fedn. of Phila. Tri-State Dist., 1929-31; chief Bur. of Planning, Greater Pa. Council, 1931-32; consultant Fairfield County (Conn.) Planning Assn., 1932—; consultant to Nat. Resources Com., Dist. No. 1, N.E. Regional Planning Commn., 1934—; asst. prof. regional planning, Mass. Inst. Tech. Served as pvt. 23d Engrs., U.S.A., World War. Mem. Nat. Conf. on City Planning; sec., treas. Am. City Planning Inst. Republican. Conglist. Home: Longmeadow, Mass. Died Dec. 18, 1937.

WOODRUFF, Julia Louisa Matilda ("W. L. M. Jay"), author; b. Newtown, Conn., April 29, 1833; d. Nirom E. and Matilda (Rogers) Curtiss; academic and private; m. Rev. Curtiss T. Woodruff, Feb. 10, 1849 (died 1887). Author: Shiloh, 1870; My Winter in Cuba, 1871; Holden with Cords, 1876; The Daisy Seekers, 1885; Life's Sunny Side, 1886; Bellerue, 1891. Deceased.

WOODRUFF, Rollin Simmons, governor; b. Rochester, N.Y., July 14, 1854; s. Rev. Jeremiah and Clarissa (Thompson) W.; pub. sch. edn.; (LL.D., Wesleyan U., Conn., 1908); m. Kaomeo E. Perkins, Jan. 14, 1880. Pres. C. S. Mersick & Co., wholesale iron dealers, New Haven, 1889—; dir. New Haven Savings Bank and Mechanics Bank (New Haven). Trustee Wesleyan U., Conn., Norwich (Conn.) State Hosp.; pres. Grace Hosp. (New Haven). Mem. Conn. Senate, 1903 (pres. pro tem.); lt. gov. of Conn., 1905-07, gov., 1907-09. Republican. Home: New Haven, Conn. Died June 30, 1925.

WOODRUFF, Thomas Adams, ophthalmologist; b. St. Catharines, Ont., Canada, June 4, 1865; s. Samuel De Veaux and Jane Caroline (Sanderson) W.; matriculated U. of Toronto; M.D., C.M., McGill U., Montreal, 1888; attended hosps. and clinics, London, Berlin, Göttingen, 1888-90; L.R.C.P., London, 1890; in gen. practice, Chicago, 1890-94; in attendance eye and ear hosps., Vienna, Berlin, London, 1894-95; certificate Board of Ophthalmic Examiners; m. Caroline Wright Ogden. Specialist in ophthalmology and otology, Chicago, 1895-1918; was ophthalmic surgeon, St. Luke's and St. Anthony hosps., Chicago. Maj. M.C. U.S.A., on active duty Sept. 1917-Dec. 1918; head of eye dept., Base Hosp., Camp Grant, Ill., and chief sect. of surgery of the head, Base Hosp., Camp Beauregard, La., and Camp Meade, Md.; settled at New London, Conn., Dec. 1918. Cons. ophthalmologist to Lawrence and Memorial hosps., New London. Former v.p. Lincoln Pulp & Paper Mills Co. (Can.). Fellow Am. Coll. Surgeons, Am. Acad. Medicine, A.M.A. (3d v.p. 1908), Am. Acad. Ophthalmology and Oto-laryngology. Author: (with Casey A. Wood) Commoner Diseases of the Eye, 1904. Formerly editorial sec. Ophthalmic Record and writer of papers upon ophthalmology. Home: New London, Conn. Died Apr. 14, 1941.

WOODRUFF, Timothy Lester, lieut. governor of N.Y.; b. New Haven, Conn., Aug. 4, 1858; s. John W.; A.B., Yale, 1879, A.M., 1889; m. Cora Eastman (died 1904); m. 2d, Isabel Morrison, Apr. 24, 1905. President of the Maltine Mfg. Co.; Pneumelectric Machine Co., of Syracuse; largely interested in other industries, both in U.S. and abroad; pres. bd. trustees Adelphi Coll.; del. nearly every Rep. state and local conv., 1885—, Nat. Conv., 1888; apptd. park commr. of Brooklyn, N.Y., 1895; lt. gov. of N.Y., 1897-1903. Chmn. Rep. State Com. Made speech placing James Schoolcraft Sherman in nomination for the vice-presidency, Rep. Nat. Conv., 1908. Pres. trustees Adelphi Coll. Home: Brooklyn, and New York, N.Y. Died Oct. 12, 1913.

WOODS, Charles Albert, judge; b. Darlington, S.C., July 31, 1852; s. Samuel A. and Martha J. (Du Bose) W.; grad. Wofford Coll., 1872; (LL.D., Wofford, 1903, U. of S.C., 1910); m. Sally J. Wannamaker, Dec. 16, 1884. Admitted to bar, 1873; justice Supreme Ct. of S.C., Feb. 28, 1903-13; U.S. circuit judge, 4th Circuit, June 1, 1913—. Home: Marion, S.C. Died June 21, 1925.

WOODS, Charles Carroll, clergyman; b. Rocky Mt., Va., July 4, 1838; s. Samuel Hairston and Cicely (Patterson) W.; ed. Trinity Coll., N.C., 1855, Central Coll., Mo., 1859-60; D.D., Trinity, 1878; m. Mary M. Nicolds, May 10, 1860 (died 1863); children—Mrs. Minnie C. Hall, Samuel Hairston; m. 2d, Anna M. Nicolds, July 30, 1866; children—Mrs. Cicely Maud Hinde, Charles Robert, Mrs. Mary Elizabeth Childs, Anne Mabel, Eugene Allen, Mrs. Nell Woods Stuckey. Ordained M.E., S. ministry, 1860; chaplain Parson's division, Mo. state troops, in C.S.A., and of Camp St. Louis, U.C.V.; pastor in various Mo. cities beginning, 1867; presiding elder, 1875-79 and 1882-86; pres. Scarritt Coll., Neosho, Mo., 1888-96; asso. editor 1898-1914, editor in chief, 1914-18, St. Louis Christian Advocate (emeritus). Sec. S.W. Mo. Conf. M.E. Ch., S., 42 yrs.; mem. Gen. Conf., 1882, 86, 94, 98. Democrat. Scottish and York Rite Mason—Grand Master, 1882-83, Grand High Priest, 1883-84, Grand Prelate, 13 yrs., Grand Primate, 1908-09, Grand Correspondent, Grand Lodge, 1910—, Gen. Grand Chaplain of the Grand Chapter of Masons of U.S., 1921—. Author: The Passing Years (poems), 1911. Home: La Grange, Ga. Died May 12, 1927.

WOODS, Charles Dayton, agriculturist; b. Brooks, Me., Sept. 11, 1856; s. Henry J. and Maria N. (Colcord) W.; B.S., Wesleyan U., 1880; (Sc.D., U. of Me., 1905); m. Mary A. Morgan, June 1, 1882. Asst. in chemistry, Wesleyan U., 1880-83; teacher sciences, Wilbraham (Mass.) Acad., 1883-88; chemist and vice dir. Storrs (Conn.) Agrl. Expt. Sta., 1888-96; food expert U.S. Dept. Agr., 1894-1908; prof. agr., Univ. of Me., 1896-1903; dir. Me. Agrl. Expt. Sta., 1896-1920; consultant in agr., U.S. War Dep., 1921; dir. of information, Mass. Dept. Agr., 1922—. Home: Newton, Mass. Died Mar. 1925.

WOODS, Cyrus E., lawyer; b. Clearfield, Pa., Sept. 3, 1861; s. Matthew and Katharine (Speece) W.; M.A., Lafayette College, 1886, LL.D., 1915; LL.D. from U. of Pa.; m. Mary Todd Marchand, Jan. 18, 1893. Admitted to Pa. bar, 1889; practiced at Phila., 1889-94, at Pittsburgh, 1894-1912; was gen. counsel Pittsburgh Coal Co.; minister to Portugal, Jan. 22, 1912-Aug. 19, 1915; retired. Mem. Pa. Senate, 1900-08 (pres. 1905-08); sec. of State of Pa., terms 1915-23; resigned June 7, 1921, upon nomination by President Harding as Ambassador E. and P. to Spain; Ambassador E. and P. to Japan, Mar. 3, 1923, resigned July 21, 1924; apptd. atty. gen. Commonwealth of Pa., Jan. 18, 1929. In charge Am. Red Cross activities in Japan following earthquake disaster, Sept. 1, 1923. Republican. Presbyn. Home: Greensburg, Pa. Died Dec. 8, 1938.

WOODS, Edward Augustus, life underwriter; b. Pittsburgh, Pa., Jan. 1, 1865; s. George and Ellen Cornelia (Crane) W.; father was chancellor Western U. of Pa. (now U. of Pittsburgh); student Western U. of Pa., 1882-83; hon. A.M., same 1917, Princeton, 1919; m. Gertrude Macrum, May 28, 1891; children—Marjory (Mrs. A. C. Robinson, III), Edward Wallis. Began in life ins. business in office with father, at 15; pres., 1910—, and mgr. The Edward A. Woods Co., gen. agts. Equitable Life Assurance Soc. of U.S. Trustee Nat. Assn. of Life Underwriters (pres. 1915-16); mem. Pittsburgh Life Underwriters Assn. (pres. 1919), Altoona, Erie, Harrisburg, Youngstown life underwriters assns., Life Underwriters Assn. of Can. Largely instrumental in establishment of Bur. of Salesmanship Research and School of Life Ins. Salesmanship of Carnegie Inst. Tech., later of U. of Pittsburgh. Mem. com. to study, investigate and revise ins. laws of Pa., 1917-21, by appmt. of Gov. Brumbaugh. Mem. exec. com., treas. and chmn. home service sect., Pittsburgh Chapter A.R.C.; dir. Mercy Hosp. Republican. Presbyn. Author: Life Underwriting as a Career, 1923. Home: Sewickley, Pa. Died Nov. 30, 1927.

WOODS, Frederick Adams, biologist; b. Boston, Mass., Jan. 29, 1873; s. Solomon Adams and Catherine (Watts) W.; student Mass. Inst. Tech., 1890-94; M.D., Harvard, 1898; m. Ellen Payson, 1912; m. 2d, Baroness Marie Thérèse de Lebzeltern-Collenbach, of Austria and New York, 1924. Asst. in histology and embryology, 1898-1901, instr., 1901-02, Harvard Med. Sch.; lecturer biology, Mass. Inst. Tech., 1903-23. Fellow Am. Acad. Arts and Sciences; mem. Nat. Research Council, 1922; v.p. Internat. Congress for Studies Regarding Population Problems, Rome, 1931. Author: Mental and Moral Heredity in Royalty, 1906; The Influence of Monarchs, 1913; Is War Diminishing? (with Alexander Baltzly), 1915. Died Nov. 5, 1939.

WOODS, Henry, clergyman; b. Marion Co., Mo., July 2, 1838; s. Andrew and Rebecca H. (Brison) W.; A.B., Washington (now Washington and Jefferson) Coll., Pa., 1857; grad. Western Theol. Sem., Allegheny, Pa., 1862; (D.D., Westminster Coll., Pa., 1879); m. Mary L. Ewing, Jan. 15, 1863. Ordained Presbyn. ministry, 1862; pastor First Ch., Steubenville, O., 1862-67; prof. ancient langs., Washington and Jefferson Coll., 1867-1906, emeritus; pastor E. Buffalo, nr. Washington. Stated clerk Synod of Pittsburgh, 1880-82; stated clerk Washington Presbytery, 1887—. Republican. Home: Washington, Pa. Died July 21, 1916.

WOODS, Henry Ernest, commissioner; b. Boston, Mass., June 5, 1857; s. Henry Thayer and Ellen (Thayer) W.; ed. Chauncy Hall Sch., Boston; some subsequent study in Europe; (hon. A.M., Bowdoin, 1903); unmarried. Editor New England Hist. and Geneal. Register, 1901-07; editor Massachusetts Vital Records (32 vols.), 1902-07; Mass. state commr. of pub. records, 1907—. Mem. various N.E. hist. societies. Has traveled extensively in Europe, Asia Minor, N. Africa, N. America, and the West Indies. Home: Boston, Mass. Died Oct. 11, 1919.

WOODS, Hiram, M.D.; b. Baltimore, Md., Nov. 11, 1857; s. Hiram and Helen (Chase) W.; A.B., Princeton, 1879; spl. course in biology, Johns Hopkins, 1879-80; M.D., U. of Md., 1882, LL.D., 1924; m. Laura Hall, Oct. 28, 1886; children—Alan C. (M.D.), Mary (Mrs. Alexander Armstrong, Jr.), Laura (Mrs. Wm. Hudgins), Helen (Mrs. Arthur W. Machem, Jr.). In practice at Baltimore, Md., 1883-1929; served as surgeon Union Memorial Hosp.; cons. eye surgeon Hosp. for Crippled Children, Hosp. for Women of Md., Sheppard and Enoch Pratt Hosp. Democrat. Presbyn. Home: Baltimore, Md. Died Jan. 15, 1931.

WOODS, James Haughton, univ. prof.; b. Boston, Mass., Nov. 27, 1864; s. Joseph Wheeler and Caroline Frances (Fitz) W.; A.B., Harvard Univ., 1887; student Univ. of Berlin, 1889-91, Oxford, 1891, U. of Strassburg, 1894-97; Ph.D., U. of Strassburg, 1896; m. Gertrude Baldwin, 1907; m. 2d, Elizabeth Robinson, 1927. Asst. in history, 1891, lecturer in philosophy, 1900, instr. anthropology, 1900-01, instr. in philosophy, 1903-08, asst. prof., 1908-13, prof., 1913—, Harvard. Investigated philosophy in India, 1902-03, India and Japan, 1907-09; Paddock lecturer on comparative religion, New York, 1906; exchange prof. to France, 1916-18 and 1928. Mem. bd. trustees Harvard-Yenching Inst., 1928. Fellow Am. Acad. Arts and Sciences. Author: Erkenntniss-theorie und Causalität, 1896; Value of Religious Facts, 1900; Practice and Science of Religion, 1906. Translator: Outline of the Vedanta, 1906; Yoga System of Patanjali (Harvard Oriental Series), 1914; The Gem's Ray (Mani-prabha), 1915. Editor: Papañca Sudani (Pali Text Soc.), 1923, 28. Home: Cambridge, Mass. Died Jan. 14, 1935.

WOODS, John Carter Brown, lawyer; b. Providence, R.I., June 12, 1851; s. Marshall and Anne Brown (Francis) W.; A.B., Brown U., 1872, A.M., 1875; LL.B., Harvard, 1874. Admitted to bar, 1874, and began practice at Providence; dir. Providence Nat. Bank, 1886-1920; dir. Nat. Exchange Bank, Providence, 1907-09; dir. Prov. Arcade Corp., June 7, 1888-Apr. 8, 1925. Mem. Providence Common Council, 1877-85 (pres. 1881-85); mem. sch. com., 1881-85; mem. R.I. Ho. of Rep., 1881-87, Senate, 1891-92, 1894-97; mem. Prov. Rep. City Com., 1879-96, chmn., 1886-93; mem. Rep. State Central Com., 1890-93. Mem. R.I. State Bd. of Charities and Corrections, 1892-98 (chmn. 1895-98), R.I. Commn. on Improved Roads, 1892-95, R.I. Commn. on Geol. Survey of the State, 1895—, R.I. Commn. to erect state armory at Providence; trustee Brown U., 1884— (mem. advisory and exec. com., 1885-1918; sec. 1889-1916); trustee R.I. Inst. for the Deaf, 1895-1907; dir. on part of Brown U., R.I. Sch. of Design, 1894-95; pres. R.I. Soc. Prevention of Cruelty to Animals, 1888-1900; clk. Charitable Baptist Soc. of Providence, 1877-91, moderator, 1891-1900; mem. R.I. Soc. S.A.R. (v.p. 1891-92, pres. 1892-93, del. to nat. congresses). Republican. Home: Providence, R.I. Died Jan. 2, 1930.

WOODS, Kate Tannatt, author; b. Peekskill, N.Y.; d. James S. and Mary Tannatt; m. George H. Woods, lawyer and officer on Gen. Sheridan's staff. Has contributed and done editorial work on Harper's Bazaar, Ladies' Home Journal, Boston Transcript, Globe and Herald, and various mags. Lecturer. One of original officers, and first auditor Gen. Fedn. Women's Clubs; a founder Mass. State Fedn. Women's Clubs; founder of Thought and Work Club of Salem, Mass. (pres. 8 yrs.); traveled in Europe, N.M. and Calif.; v.p. Women's Nat. Press Assn., Washington. Author: Six

Little Rebels, 1875; Dr. Dick, 1876; Mopsy, 1898; A Little New England Maid, 1898; Española, a Romance of New Mexico, 1901; Wooing of Grandmother Grey; Grandfather Grey; Illustrated Poems. Home: North Falmouth, Mass. Died 1910.

WOODS, Katharine Pearson, author; b. Wheeling, W.Va., Jan. 28, 1853; d. Alexander Quarrier and Josephine Augusta (McCabe) W.; ed. pvt. schs., Baltimore. Held fellowship under Coll. Settlement Assn., 1893-94, and pub. report of investigations during that time in Am. Jour. of Statistics, Dec. 1895. Author Metzerott Shoemaker; Mark of the Beast; A Web of Gold; From Dusk to Dawn; John; A Tale of King Messiah; The Son of Ingar; The True Story of Captain John Smith, 1901. In missionary work among the mountain whites of N.C., 1903-06; kindergarten work in connection with St. John's P.E. Ch., Baltimore, 1907-11; became interested in the Emmanuel Movement, 1909, and assisted in founding the Psychological Club. Home: Baltimore, Md. Died Feb. 19, 1923.

WOODS, Matthew, physician; b. in Ireland, May 29, 1849; s. Samuel and Katharine (DeWauchop) W.; ed. in Ireland and U. of Pa.; m. Emily L. Huntzinger, June 19, 1879. Came to America soon after outbreak of Civil War and served in U.S.N. over 3 yrs. Began practice in Phila., 1875; specializes in treatment of epilepsy. President Phila. Medical Mission. Presbyn. Author: Rambles of a Physician, 2 vols., 1889; In Spite of Epilepsy, 1913; Divorce, 1913; Was the Apostle Paul an Epileptic?, 1913. Home: Philadelphia, Pa. Died Oct. 13, 1916.

WOODS, Neander Montgomery, clergyman; b. Harrodsburg, Ky., Sept. 4, 1844; s. James Harvey and Sarah Everett (Dedman) W.; ed. Ky. U., 1859-60; served C.S. Cav., 1861-65; Pharm. Chem., U. of Mich., 1867; studied law, Washington U., St. Louis; divinity at Union Theol. Sem., Va.; (D.D., Central U., Ky., 1888; LL.D., Southwestern Presbyn. U., 1905); m. Alice Birkhead, 1866; m. 2d, Sallie H. Behre, 1885. Ordained ministry Southern Presbyn. Ch., 1873; pastor Second Ch., Louisville, 1902-05; chancellor Southwestern Presbyn. U., 1905-08; became pastor Central Ch., Montgomery, Ala. Moderator Gen. Assembly Presbyn. Ch. U.S., Little Rock, Ark., May 1901; v.p. Presbyn. Hist. Society, Phila. Home: Montgomery, Ala. Deceased.

WOODS, Robert Archey, settlement worker; b. Pittsburgh, Dec. 9, 1865; s. Robert and Mary Ann (Hall) W.; A.B., Amherst, 1886; Andover Theol. Sem., 1886-90; in residence, Toynbee Hall, London, 6 months, 1890; (hon. A.M., Amherst, 1908, Harvard, 1910); m. Eleanor Howard Bush, Sept. 18, 1902. Head of South End House, univ. settlement, Boston, 1891—. Lecturer on social economics, Andover Theol. Sem., 1890-95, on social ethics, Episcopal Theol. Sch., Cambridge, Mass., 1896-1914. Mem. Pub. Bath Commn., Boston, 1896-1906; trustee Norfolk State Hosp., 1907-19; mem. Licensing Bd. City of Boston, 1914-16; pres. Boston Social Union (settlement fedn.), 1908—; sec. Nat. Fedn. of Settlements, 1911-23, pres., 1923—; pres. Nat. Conf. Social Work, 1917-18. Trustee Amherst Coll., 1910-20. Author: English Social Movements, 1891; The Neighborhood in Nation Building, 1922; (with Albert J. Kennedy) The Settlement Horizon—A National Estimate, 1922. Editor: The City Wilderness, 1898; Americans in Process, 1902. Joint editor: Handbook of Settlements, 1911; Young Working Girls, 1913. Lectured in Japan, China and India, 1919-20. Home: Boston, Mass. Died Feb. 18, 1925.

WOODS, Samuel Van Horn, lawyer; b. Philippi, W.Va., Aug. 31, 1856; s. Samuel and Isabella (Neeson) W.; student W.Va. U.; LL.D., W.Va. Wesleyan Coll., Buckhannon, 1916; m. Mollie Strikler, Mar. 9, 1892; 1 dau., Ruth Neeson (Mrs. Arthur S. Dayton). Admitted to W.Va. bar, 1885, and practiced at Philippi until 1923; pres. Citizens Nat. Bank of Philippi, 1906-23; moved to Charleston, W.Va., 1923. Del. to Dem. Nat. Conv., 1910; lt. gov. of W.Va., 1911-14, and as such, pres. of State Senate. Chmn. Barbour Co. Chapter Am. Red Cross, also of Minute Men, World War. Del. to Gen. Conf. M.E. Ch., Saratoga, N.Y., 1916, Des Moines, Ia., 1920; mem. 5th Ecumenical Council M.E. Ch., Atlanta, Ga., 1932. Trustee W.Va. Wesleyan Coll. Mason, K.P. Home: Charleston, W.Va. Died June 3, 1937.

WOODS, Thomas Hall, judge; b. in Ark. (then a ty.), Mar. 17, 1836; s. Rev. Harvey and Cecelia W.; student Williams Coll., 1856, 57; (LL.D., U. of Miss.); m. Judith Jones, Oct. 1863. Admitted to bar, 1859; mem. Secession Conv., 1861; capt. in C.S.A., 1861-65; dist. atty., 3d Dist. of Miss., 1865-75; was mem. Miss. Ho. of Rep.; declined office of U.S. atty., Southern Dist. of Miss., 1888; chief justice Supreme Ct. of Miss., 1889-1900; resigned and declined reappointment; div. counsel for the Q.&C. system of railroads; retired. Home: Meridian, Miss. Died 1910.

WOODS, Virna, educator; b. in Ohio, 1864; went to Calif.; engaged in teaching. Author: A Modern Magdalene (novel); The Amazons (lyrical drama); An Elusive Lover; Jason Hildrith's Identity (novel). Contbr. to Atlantic Monthly, Lippincott's, New England Magazine, Woman's Home Companion, Youth's Companion, Chamber's Journal, St. Nicholas, etc. Home: Sacramento, Calif. Died 1903.

WOODS, William Stone, banker; b. Columbia, Mo., Nov. 1, 1840; s. James and Martha W.; A.B., U. of Mo., 1861, A.M., 1864; M.D., Jefferson Med. Coll., Phila., 1864; m. Bina McBride, July 10, 1866. Practiced medicine, Middle Grove, Mo., 1863-67; sold goods in Paris, Mo., 1867; in 1868, with brother, established as wholesale grocer, pending construction Union Pacific road; in 1869 established savings bank, Rocheport, Mo., becoming its cashier; mem. Grimes, Woods, La Force & Co., wholesale dry goods, Kansas City, Mo., 1881; also pres. Kansas City Savings Assn., which in 1882 was merged into the Bank of Commerce, later Nat. Bank of Commerce, of which became pres. Home: Excelsior Springs, Mo. Died July 6, 1917.

WOODS, William Wells, judge; b. Burlington, Ia., Jan. 24, 1841; s. James W. and Catherine (Chapin) W.; ed. Howe's Acad., Mt. Pleasant, Ia.; m. Melvina C. Whitney, 1874. Enlisted Pleyel's Ia. Lancers, Aug. 14, 1861; transferred to 4th Ia. Cavalry, Nov. 1861; 2d lt. Co. L, Nov. 17, 1861; 1st lt., June 9, 1862; capt., Aug. 1, 1862; maj. 4th Ia. Cav., Sept. 27, 1864; mustered out, Aug. 24, 1865. Admitted to bar at Burlington, Ia., 1866; practiced law in Western Iowa to Jan. 1872, at Salt Lake City, 1872-84, Shoshone Co., Ida., 1884—. Judge 1st Jud. Dist. of Ida., Jan. 1907—. Mem. Constl. Conv., Ida., 1890; presdl. elector, 1896. Democrat. Home: Wallace, Ida. Died Nov. 1920.

WOODS, William Whitfield, pres. Inst. Am. Meat Packers; b. Meridian, Miss.; s. William Richardson and Annie Kate (Whitfield) W.; student Meridian Prep. Sch., Mobile; A.B., U. of Va., 1914; B.Litt., Columbia (Sch. of Journalism), 1915; m. Dorothy Dunkin, Feb. 21, 1916; 1 son, Richard Whitfield. Reporter N.Y. World, 1915-18; dir. dept. of information, Columbia, 1917-18; dir. Bur. of Public Relations, Inst. of Am. Meat Packers, Chicago, 1918-22, v.p. in charge dept. edn. and research, 1922-24, exec. v.p., 1925-28, pres., 1928—. Instr. dept. of English, Agri. and Mech. Coll. of Tex., 1911-12 and 1912-13. Mem. joint administrative com., Inst. Meat Packing, U. of Chicago. Home: Chicago, Ill. Died Jan. 20, 1939.

WOODSON, Archelaus M., judge; b. Knox Co., Ky., Jan. 30, 1854; s. Benjamin J. W.; reared on farm in Buchanan Co., Mo.; ed. pub. schs. there, and Plattsburg Coll., Clinton Co., Mo., 3 yrs.; LL.B., St. Louis Law Sch., 1877; m. Bettie Oliver, Apr. 13, 1886. Apptd., Dec. 18, 1890, judge Circuit Ct. of Buchanan Co.; elected to same, for terms 1892-98, 1898-1904; judge Supreme Ct. of Mo., 1906—. Democrat. Home: St. Joseph, Mo. Deceased.

WOODSON, Mary Blake (Mrs.), writer; b. Kansas City, Mo., May 7, 1886; d. Maj. Blake Lynch and Nora (Delany) Woodson; ed. St. Teresa's Acad., Mo.; m. (Henry) Lee Shippey, Aug. 19, 1908 (divorced, 1921, and resumed maiden name); 1 son, Henry Lee Shippey (name legally changed to Blake Lynch Woodson). Contbr. fiction, verse and spl. feature articles to mags. and newspaper syndicates; war corr., 1917-18; Missouri editor Kansas City Star, 1918, 19, and from 1921, also editor chaperon dept. same; on contributing staff Woman's World, Chicago, 1921-28, Household Magazine, Topeka, 1926-29, Farm Journal, Phila., 1929-32; radio writing, 1935-36; author of "Friendly Counsellor" program, on WDAF radio station, Kansas City Star. Mem. Mo. Writers Guild (state pres. 1925), U.D.C. (state historian Mo. Div., 1914-15). Catholic. Home: Kansas City, Mo. Deceased.

WOODSON, Urey, pub. official; b. Madisonville, Ky., Aug. 16, 1859; s. Samuel C. and Rebecca J. (Hawthorn) W.; common sch. edn.; m. Elizabeth Ford, Feb. 12, 1885; children—Elizabeth (Mrs. Hamilton Alexander), Janey (Mrs. William E. Overstreet). Editor and pub. Owensboro (Ky.) Messenger (daily and weekly), 1881-1929, Paducah (Ky.) News-Democrat, 1901-12, employing successively Irvin S. Cobb, Louis Brownlow and Buford Goodwin as mng. editors; also gen. mgr. Louisville Daily Dispatch, 1897; declined 4-yr. appointment as sec. of state of Ky., 1891; railroad commr. for Ky., 1891-95. Pres. Ky. Press Assn., 1889-90. Mem. Dem. Nat. Com., 1896-1916, and 1924-28, declined re-election; sec. of Dem. Nat. Com., 1904-12; apptd. by President, Alien Property Custodian, 1933. Del. at large from Ky. to Dem. Nat. Conv. and mem. platform com., Chicago, 1932; attended every Dem. Nat. Conv., 1880-1936. Home: Owensboro, Ky. Died Aug. 7, 1939.

WOODSON, Walter Worsham, banker; b. Montgomery, Tex., Jan. 4, 1876; s. Creed Taylor and Ophelia (Worsham) W.; LL.B., U. of Tex., 1901; m. Mary Dill, 1902. Began in banking business at Palestine, 1893; pres. First National Bank, Waco, Tex., 1920—. Mem. Waco Clearing House Assn. (pres. 1929). Chmn. 5th Liberty Loan Drive; chmn. Four-Minute Men, McLennan Co., World War. Democrat. Methodist. Home: Waco, Tex. Died Sept. 3, 1937.

WOODWARD, Calvin Milton, university dean; b. Fitchburg, Mass., Aug. 25, 1837; s. Isaac Burnap and Eliza (Wetherbee) W.; A.B., Harvard, 1860; (hon. Ph.D., 1883, LL.D., 1905, Washington U.; LL.D., U. of Wis., 1908); m. Fanny Stone Balch, Sept. 30, 1863. Prin. Brown High Sch., Newburyport, 1860-65; capt. Co. A, 48th Mass. Vols., 1862-63, serving in La. Vice-prin. Smith Acad., St. Louis, 1865-70, prof. descriptive geometry, 1870-71, dean Sch. of Engring., 1871-96, dean Sch. of Engring. and Architecture, 1901-10, prof. mathematics and applied mechanics, 1871-1910 (emeritus), Washington University. Originator and director from organization, 1879, of St. Louis Manual Training Sch.; lecturer on manual training. Mem. St. Louis Bd. of Edn., 1877-79, and from 1897 (pres. of bd. 1899-1900, 1903-04); regent (pres. of bd.) Univ. of Mo., 1891-97. Pres. North Central Assn. Coll. and Secondary Schs.; fellow A.A.A.S. (pres. 1905-06). Author: History of St. Louis Bridge, 1881; The Manual Training School, 1887; Manual Training in Education, 1890; Applied Mechanics for Engineering and Architectural Students. Home: St. Louis, Mo. Died Jan. 12, 1915.

WOODWARD, Chester, banker; b. West Chester, Pa., Aug. 24, 1876; s. Brinton Webb and Emily Price (Darlington) W.; grad. high sch., Lawrence, Kan., 1894; Ph.C., U. of Kan., 1896; m. Frederica D. Bullene, Oct. 10, 1906; children—Thomas Darlington, Brinton Webb II. In drug business, 1896-1900; began in mortgage investment business, 1900, under name B. W. & Chester Woodward; v.p. and sec. Central Trust Co., 1920-29; pres. Morris Plan Bank (Topeka); v.p. Central Nat. Bank, 1920-29. Asso. nat. dir. canteen service, Am. Red Cross, Washington, D.C., 1918. Former pres. Topeka Bd. of Edn.; pres. Topeka Pub. Library; mem. Topeka Bd. of Edn., 1925-35 (pres.); dir. Y.M.C.A.; dir. Topeka Pub. Health Nursing Assn. Treas. Stormont Hosp.; trustee Memorial Corp., Univ. of Kan.; mem. advisory bd. Yenching U., China; trustee Washburn Coll.; pres. Alumni Assn. of U. of Kan., 1937; exec. com. Topeka Boy Scouts. Republican. Unitarian. Author: Out of the Blue, Lanterns Alight, 1940. Owner of one of largest pvt. libraries in Middle West and of collection of paintings loaned to Univ. of Kan. Home: Topeka, Kan. Died Oct. 11, 1940.

WOODWARD, Ellsworth, artist, teacher; b. Bristol Co., Mass., July 14, 1861; s. Erastus Marion and Maria (Carpenter) W.; ed. R.I. Sch. of Design, and studios of Carl Marr, Richards and Fehr, Munich, Germany; LL.D., Tulane, 1933; m. Mary Bell Johnson, Sept. 24, 1885. Asst. prof. of art, Tulane U., 1885-87; prof. of art, Newcomb Coll., Tulane U., 1887-90; dir. Newcomb Sch. of Art, 1890-1930; dir. emeritus, 1930. Trustee Delgado Mus. of Art; pres. Southern States Art League. In nat. politics Republican, in local politics Democratic. Episcopalian. Home: New Orleans, La. Died Feb. 28, 1939.

WOODWARD, Frank Lincoln, lawyer; b. Denver, Colo., June 16, 1866; s. Benjamin Franklin and Helen (Bassett) W.; A.B., Yale, 1888, LL.B., 1890; m. May Farnam, Feb. 10, 1891. Admitted to Conn. bar, 1890, Colo. bar, 1891; was mem. Benedict & Phelps, later Rogers, Cuthbert & Ellis; not in active practice, 1910—; v.p. First Industrial Bank; dep. food adminstr. for Colo., Oct. 1917-Mar. 1919; pres. Bd. Water Commrs. City and County of Denver, 1922-27. Pres. Denver Fedn. for Charity and Philanthropy, 1913-22; mem. exec. com. Denver Chapter Am. Red Cross; pres. Denver Symphony Orchestra Assn. Republican. Episcopalian. Pres. U.S. Seniors Golf Assn. Home: Denver, Colo. Died Nov. 10, 1930.

WOODWARD, George A., brig. gen. U.S.A.; b. Wilkes-Barre, Pa., Feb. 14, 1835; s. George W. (formerly chief justice Supreme Ct., Pa.) and Sarah Elizabeth (Trott) W.; B.A., Trinity Coll., Conn., 1855 (hon. M.A., 1895); m. Charlotte Treat Chittenden, Feb. 14, 1867. Admitted to bar and engaged in practice at Milwaukee, where was city atty., 1858-59; later practiced at Phila. Entered mil. service May 27, 1861, as capt. of 2d Pa. Reserves; maj., Apr. 2, 1862; lt. col., Feb. 20, 1863; hon. mustered out, Aug. 29, 1863; maj. Vet. Reserve Corps, Aug. 24, 1863; lt. col., Sept. 25, 1863; col., Dec. 4, 1863; hon. mustered out of vol. service, July 20, 1866; lt. col. 45th U.S. Inf., July 28, 1866; transferred to 14th Inf., Mar. 14, 1869; col. 15th Inf., Jan. 10, 1876; retired, Mar. 20, 1879; advanced to rank of brig. gen. retired, by act of Apr. 23, 1904. Bvtd. col., Mar. 2, 1867, for battle of Gettysburg. Participated in campaigns of Army of the Potomac; wounded and taken prisoner at battle of Glendale, Va., June 30, 1862; participated in battle of Gettysburg as lt. col. comdg. regt.; after entering regular service, served in Ky., Tenn., Dak., Wyo., Neb. and Utah. Mem. Phila. firm publishing mil. and naval books, 1879-87, and editor United Service Magazine during same period. Episcopalian. Democrat. Died Dec. 22, 1916.

WOODWARD, Hugh McCurdy, univ. prof.; b. Huntington, Utah, Dec. 20, 1881; s. Enoch Jasper and Anna Letitia (Raymond) W.; B.A., Brigham Young U., 1911; M.A. in Ednl. Administration, U. of Utah, 1918; Ph.D., U. of Calif., 1920; m. Emily Timothy, Oct. 18, 1905; children—William Jennings, Joycelin, Caroll. Prin. pub. schs., Jensen, Utah, 1902-04; prin. St. George (Utah) Acad., 1911-14; pres. Dixie

Normal Coll., St. George, 1914-18 (leave of absence, 1918-20); asst. dir. ednl. work, Bur. Pub. Health, Washington, D.C., 1920-21; prof. edn., 1921-22, prof. philosophy of edn. and ednl. adminstrn. 1922-24, prof. philosophy of edn., 1924—, Brigham Young U., also dean summer session and supervisor grad. work in edn., 1922-28; prof. of edn., U. of Wash., 5 summers; prof. edn. and philosophy, Floating U., 1928-29; mem. State Senate, Utah, 1934-37; dir. of edn. and recreation for 11 Western states, Works Progress Adminstrn. Author: Humanity's Greatest Need, 1932. Home: San Francisco, Calif. Died Aug. 11, 1940.

WOODWARD, James T., pres. Hanover Nat. Bank; trustee Union Trust Co.; dir. Greenwich Bank, Madison Square Garden Co. (New York); 1st Nat. Bank and Mercantile Trust and Deposit Co. (Baltimore); Birmingham (Ala.) Trust and Savings Co.; Newport (R.I.) Trust Co., New York Clearing House Bldg. Co., Southern Ry. Co. Trustee St. John's Coll. and Chase Home, Annapolis, Md.; gov. N.Y. Hospital. Home: New York, N.Y. Died 1910.

WOODWARD, John, judge; b. Charlotte Centre, N.Y., Aug. 19, 1859; s. Daniel S. and Cornelia (Lake) W.; grad. Fredonia (N.Y.) State Normal Sch., 1878; LL.B., New York U., 1881 (LL.D., 1907); m. Mary E., d. Judge George Barker, of Fredonia, N.Y., May 26, 1886. Practiced at Jamestown, N.Y., from 1881; city atty., 1886-89; mem. bd. supervisors, Chautauqua Co., 1887-92; dist. atty., 1892-95; apptd. justice Supreme Ct. of N.Y., Jan. 1896, to fill a vacancy; elected for terms 1896-1910, 1910-24; judge Appellate Div., 2d Dept., 1898-1913, judge Appellate Div., 3d Dept., 1913—. Republican. Home: Buffalo, N.Y. Died June 1, 1923.

WOODWARD, J(ohn) B(utler), lawyer; b. Wilkes-Barre, Pa., Apr. 3, 1861; s. Stanley and Sarah Richards (Butler) W.; A.B., Yale, 1883; U. of Pa. Law Sch., 1 yr.; m. Marion Hillard, June 6, 1888. In practice at Wilkes-Barre, 1885—; mem. Wheaton, Darling & Woodward; dir. Wilkes-Barre Deposit & Savings Bank. Additional law judge Luzerne Co. Ct., Jan. 1, 1914—. Democrat. Presbyn. Home: Wilkes-Barre, Pa. Died Sept. 6, 1925.

WOODWARD, John Charles, educator; b. Butts Co., Ga., 1866; s. Robert J. and Martha (Douglas) W.; A.B., with first honor, North Georgia Agrl. Coll., 1888; A.B., U. of Chicago, 1898; A.M., U. of Georgia, 1899; m. Lucile C. Castleberry, 1892. V.p. and comdt. Gordon Inst., Barnesville, Ga., 1890-92; pres. Ga. Mil. Coll., Milledgeville, Ga., 1892-96; supt. schs., Newman, Ga., 1897-1900; founder, 1900, and pres. Ga. Mil. Acad. Lt. col., staffs of govs. of Ga. 22 yrs.; chief of staff to Gov. L. G. Hardman of Georgia. Presbyn. Mason. Kiwanian. Home: College Park, Ga. Died Aug. 27, 1939.

WOODWARD, Joseph Hooker, consulting actuary; b. Hartford, Conn., Mar. 7, 1882; s. Joseph Gurley and Mary Williams (Hooker) W.; Ph.B., Yale, 1903; studied Harvard Law Sch. 1 yr.; m. Elizabeth Cutler, Nov. 22, 1905; children—Nancy Hooker, Barbara Holman, Joseph Cutler, Mary Hooker. With Travelers Ins. Co., 1904-06; actuary ins. dept. State of Conn., 1906-08, State of N.Y., 1908-14; actuary N.Y. State Industrial Commn., 1914-18; asso. actuary Guardian Life Ins. Co., 1918-20; asst. actuary Equitable Life Assurance Soc. of U.S., 1920-22; mem. Woodward, Fondiller & Ryan; dir. Union Labor Life Ins. Co.; cons. actuary for numerous ins. cos., fraternal socs. and pension funds. Mem. com. of actuaries apptd. by sec. of treasury to advise with reference to war risk insurance, 1917; also mem. Ins. Advisory Com. of Am. Red Cross. Home: New York, N.Y. Died May 15, 1928.

WOODWARD, Julius Hayden, physician, surgeon; b. Castleton, Vt., May 31, 1858; s. Adrian Theodore (M.D.) and Lois Cornelia (June) W.; B.S., Cornell U., 1879; M.D., Coll. Phys. and Surg. (Columbia), 1882; M.D., U. of Vt., 1882; m. Mary Madeleine Donahue, July 31, 1911. Began practice at Brandon, Vt., 1884; removed to Burlington, Vt., 1889, to New York, 1897; prof. laryngology, 1886, materia medica and therapeutics, 1887-94, prof. eye, ear, nose and throat, 1890-97, U. of Vermont; prof. ophthalmology, 1908—, also dir. instrn. in ophthalmology, 1913-16, N.Y. Post-Grad. Med. Sch. and Hospital. Home: New York, N.Y. Died July 2, 1916.

WOODWARD, P. Henry, banker; b. Franklin, Conn., March 19, 1833; s. Ashbel (distinguished phys. and antiquarian) and Emmeline (Bicknell) W.; graduate Yale, 1855; (hon. A.M., Trinity, 1896); m. Mary Smith, Sept. 11, 1867. Editor Hartford Courant, 1862-65; spl. agt. P.O. Dept., 1865-76, chief special agent, 1874-76; reorganizing mail service in Ga. and later had charge Ry. Mail Service from Ohio River to Gulf, 1865-69. Had charge preparation of evidence for the government in "Star Route" cases, 1881-85; resident of Hartford, 1885—; became sec. Board of Trade, Hartford, on its organization; now pres. Dime Savings Bank; v.p. Conn. Gen. Life Ins. Co. Sec. bd. trustees Trinity Coll. Author: Guarding the Mails, 1876 (later edition entitled "Secret Service of the Post Office Department"); Hartford, Its Institutions and Industries, 1889; One Hundred Years of the Hartford Bank, 1892; Insurance in Connecticut, 1897; Manufactures in Hartford, 1897. Home: Hartford, Conn. Died Sept. 4, 1917.

WOODWARD, Robert B., capitalist; b. Brooklyn, Sept. 18, 1840; s. Thomas and Mary (Blackburne) W.; m. Miss Hearsey, Mar. 1871. Spl. partner Hathaway, Smith, Folds & Co.; v.p. Nassau Nat. Bank; dir. Bond & Mortgage Guarantee Co., Brooklyn Acad. Music, Home Life Ins. Co., Lloyds Plate Glass Ins. Co., Thompson-Starrett Co., U.S. Casualty Co., Estates of Long Beach; trustee Franklin Safe Deposit Co., Franklin Trust Co., Mut. Life Ins. Co., Bowery Savings Bank. Trustee Brooklyn Inst. Arts and Sciences, Brooklyn Art Assn.; mem. Met. Mus. Art, Chamber Commerce, New York Zoöl. Soc. Home: Brooklyn, N.Y. Died Sept. 2, 1915.

WOODWARD, Robert Simpson; b. Rochester, Mich., July 21, 1849; s. Lysander and Peninah A. (Simpson) Woodward; prep. edn. Rochester Acad.; C.E., U. of Mich., 1872 (hon. Ph.D., U. of Mich., 1892; LL.D., U. of Wis., 1904, U. of Mich., 1912, Johns Hopkins, 1915; Sc.D., U. of Pa., and Columbia, 1905; m. Martha Greeton Bond, 1876. Asst. engr. U.S. Lake Survey, 1872-82; asst. astronomer U.S. Transit of Venus Commn., 1882-84; astronomer, geographer and chief geographer U.S. Geol. Survey, 1884-90; asst. U.S. Coast and Geod. Survey, 1890-93; prof. mechanics and math. physics, 1893-1905, dean Sch. of Pure Sciences, 1895-1905, Columbia; pres. Carnegie Inst. of Washington, 1905-20. Mem. Naval Consulting Board, 1915—. Author: Smithsonian Geographical Tables, 1894; also of administrative reports of Carnegie Instn. of Washington, 1905-20. Editor (with Mansfield, Merriman) of Mathematical Monographs. Died June 29, 1924.

WOODWARD, Samuel Lippincott, brig. gen. U.S.A.; b. Burlington Co., N.J., Oct. 28, 1840; s. John E. and Elizabeth L. (Hornor) W.; ed. Phila. pub. schs., 1848-58; unmarried. Served in vol. army, from pvt. to maj., Feb. 1, 1862-Sept. 29, 1865; in regular army, 2d lt., June 18, 1867, to brig. gen., retiring from active service after more than 40 yrs.' service, July 9, 1904. Home: St. Louis, Mo. Died Apr. 17, 1924.

WOODWARD, Samuel Walter, merchant; b. Damariscotta, Me., Dec. 13, 1848; s. Samuel and Jerusha W.; ed. Lincoln (Me.) Acad.; m. M. Catherine Wade, June 24, 1874. In Feb., 1880, with Alvin Lothrop, started dry goods store in Washington which grew to be one of the larger dept. stores in U.S. Mem. Washington Bd. of Trade (pres.); mem. bd. mgrs. Public Library; mem. bd. trustees, and has given $100,000 toward enlarging the work of Calvary Bapt. Ch. Home: Washington, D.C. Died Aug. 1, 1917.

WOODWARD, Stanley, jurist; b. Wilkes-Barre, Pa., Aug. 29, 1833; s. George W. (chief justice Pa.) and Sarah Elizabeth (Trott) W.; prep. edn. Episcopal High Sch. of Va., Wyoming Sem., Pa.; grad. Yale, 1855; m. Sarah R. Butler, June 3, 1857. Admitted to Pa. bar, 1856, established practice in Wilkes-Barre. Capt. Co. A, 43d Pa. regt., 1863. Judge 11th jud. dist., Pa., 1879-1900. Democrat. Practicing law, 1903, firm Woodward, Darling & Woodward. Home: Wilkes-Barre, Pa. Deceased.

WOODWARD, William, artist; b. Seekonk, Mass., May 1, 1859; s. Erastus Marion and Maria (Carpenter) W.; grad. R.I. Sch. of Design, 1884, Mass. Normal Art Sch., 1886; studied Julian Acad., Paris, under Boulanger and Lefevre; m. Louise Amelia Giesen, June 1, 1886; children—Alma Louise (Mrs. William Bainbridge Logan), Eleanor (Mrs. George Moseley), William Giesen, Carl Ellsworth. Prof. drawing and painting, Tulane U., 1884-1921 (emeritus); founder Sch. of Architecture, Tulane. Represented in collections of Delgado Mus. of Art and Newcomb Art Gallery (60 color studies of colonial New Orleans), New Orleans; High Mus. of Art, Atlanta, Ga.; Rogers Mus. of Art, Laurel, Miss. Awarded silver medal, Art Assn. New Orleans, 1916, $100 prize, 1919; gold medal, Gulf Coast Art Assn., 1927, gold award, 1928, add. award, 1929. Mem. 1st bd. dirs. Am. Fedn. of Arts; mem. com. 3d Internat. Congress for Advancement of Drawing and Art Teaching, London, 1908 (v.p. for U.S.). Episcopalian. Home: Biloxi, Miss. Died Nov. 17, 1939.

WOODWARD, William Finch, druggist; b. Rochester, Minn., Aug. 24, 1863; s. Rev. Charles and Charlotte Augusta (Finch) W.; ed. pub. schs.; m. Sue Kate Stevens, Feb. 20, 1889; children—Mrs. Katherine Wilson, Frances (dec.), Mary, Elizabeth, Eleanor. In Portland, Ore., 1881—; day laborer, later became connected with Woodward, Clarke & Co., retail, and Clarke, Woodward Drug Co., wholesale; admitted as partner in firm, 1889; retired, 1925. Chmn. Community Service, World War; also chmn. Selective Service Bd.; four-minute man, State Council Defense, etc.; mem. bd. Portland Library Assn. 10 yrs.; mem. Sch. Bd. 9 yrs.; chmn. Ore. State Bd. Conciliation, 6 yrs.; mem. Oregon House of Representatives, 1921-24, Ore. State Senate, 1930-34; chmn. Portland branch of Am. Red Cross. Republican. Unitarian. Mason. Home: Portland, Ore. Died Oct. 7, 1940.

WOODWORTH, Edward Knowlton, lawyer; b. Concord, N.H., Aug. 25, 1875; s. Albert Bingham and Mary A. (Parker) W.; B.L., Dartmouth, 1897; LL.B., Harvard, 1900; m. Clara Farwell Holt, 1903 (died 1917); children—Constance (Mrs. C. Lane Goss), Elizabeth (dec.), Margaret (Mrs. Donald F. D'Arcy), Mary; m. 2d, Kate Chandler Cavis, 1920 (died 1926). Admitted Mass. bar, 1900, N.H. bar, 1901, and began practice at Concord; now mem. Demond, Woodworth, Sulloway, Piper & Jones, counsel for Boston & Me. R.R., N.E. Telephone & Telegraph Co., Public Service Co. of N.H.; pres. N.H. Savings Bank. Mem. City Council, Concord, 1907-10 (pres. 1909-10); sec. Standing Com. Episcopal Diocese of N.H.; chancellor of diocese, 1919—; lay deputy to Gen. Conv. 5 times, 1919-31. Trustee St. Mary's Sch. for Girls, Margaret Pillsbury Gen. Hosp. Pres. N.H. Bankers Assn., 1926-27, N.H. Savings Banks Assn., 1937. Republican. Mason. Home: Concord, N.H. Died Sept. 28, 1938.

WOODWORTH, Frank Goodrich, clergyman; b. Waterbury, Conn., Dec. 23, 1853; s. William Walter (D.D.) and Sarah Upson (Goodrich) W.; A.B., Ia. (now Grinnell) Coll., 1876, A.M., 1879; Yale Div. Sch., 1877-78; Hartford Theol. Sem., 1879-80; D.D., Knox Coll., 1892; m. Ellen E. Upson, June 1881; 1 dau., Elizabeth S. Ordained Congl. ministry, 1880; pastor Wolcott, Conn., 1880-87; president Tougaloo (Miss.) U., 1887-1912; acting pastor South Congl. Ch., New Britain, Conn., 1912-13, North Ch., St. Johnsbury, Vt., 1913-14; 1st Ch., Somersworth, N.H., Sept. 1, 1914—. Del. 1st Internat. Congl. Council, London, 1891; asst. sec. 2d Internat. Council, Boston, 1899; mem. Congress on Africa, Chicago Expn., 1893. Home: Somersworth, N.H. Died Oct. 14, 1930.

WOODWORTH, Jay Backus, geologist; b. Newfield, N.Y., Jan. 2, 1865; s. Rev. Allen Beach and Amanda (Smith) W.; B.S., in geology, Lawrence Scientific Sch. (Harvard), 1894. Instr. geology, 1893, asst. prof., 1901, asso. prof., 1912—, Harvard Univ.; mem. administrative bd., 1901-05, chmn. dept. geology and geography, 1904-08, Harvard Coll. In charge Harvard Seismog. Sta., 1908—; geol. survey of S.E. Mass. for U.S. Geol. Survey, 1915-17, 1918-19; geologist, U.S. Geol. Survey, 1918—. Mem. com. on geology and paleontology and chmn. sub-com. on use of seismographs in war, of Nat. Research Council, 1917-18. Fellow Geol. Soc. America (councillor, 1910-12, 1st v.p., 1921), Am. Acad. Arts and Sciences. Home: Cambridge, Mass. Died Aug. 4, 1925.

WOODWORTH, Newell Bertram, lawyer; b. Rome, N.Y., Apr. 12, 1860; s. Andrews Joslyn and Mary E. (Bertram) W.; A.B., Columbia, 1882, A.M., 1885; m. Lois, d. Dr. Louis Slayton, of Spencerport, N.Y., Oct. 8, 1918. Admitted to N.Y. bar, 1884, and began practice at Syracuse; asst. to corp. counsel, N.Y. City, 1885-90. Chmn. City Planning Commn., Syracuse, 1920-22; pres. Syracuse Mus. of Fine Arts; chmn. Syracuse Chapter Am. Red Cross, 1917-19; mem. Home Defense Committee. Home: Syracuse, N.Y. Died Jan. 12, 1925.

WOODWORTH, Philip Bell, engineer-attorney; b. Auburn, N.Y., Oct. 19, 1865; s. Thomas Bell and Mary Gertrude (Smith) W.; B.S., Mich. State Coll., 1886, Sc.D., 1920; M.E. in E.E., Cornell, 1890; U. of Berlin, 1891-92; m. Lucy M., d. of late Pres. Clute, of Mich. State Coll., and U. of Fla., 1893; children—Paul Merrylees, Robert Clute, Gertrude Elizabeth and Marion Merrylees (twins). Asst. prof. physics and engring., Mich. State Coll., 1892-99; prof. engring., later dean engring., Lewis Inst., Chicago, 1899-1917; served in war plans div., Gen. Staff U.S.A., 1917-21; pres. Rose Poly. Inst., Terre Haute, Ind., 1921-23. Mem. Rummler, Rummler & Woodworth, Chicago, 1907—. Mem. bar of Supreme Court of Indiana. Mason. Home: Glen Ellyn, Ill. Died June 7, 1937.

WOODYARD, Harry Chapman, congressman; b. Spencer, W.Va., Nov. 13, 1867; s. William and Isabel C. W.; ed. pub. schs.; m. Emma D. Kelley. Pres. Roane County Bank. Mem. W.Va. Senate, 1898; candidate for 57th Congress, 1900; treas. Rep. State Com., W.Va., 1900; mem. 58th to 61st, 64th to 67th and 69th Congresses (1903-11, 1915-23, 1925-27), 4th W.Va. Dist. Home: Spencer, W.Va. Died June 21, 1929.

WOOFTER, Thomas Jackson, univ. prof.; b. Spencer, Va., Sept. 2, 1862; s. Jonathan and Martha Ellen (Ball) W.; grad. State Normal Sch. of W.Va., 1881; LL.B. from W.Va. Univ., 1888; A.M., U. of Nashville, 1893; post-grad. work U. of Chicago; Ph.D., Am. U., 1900; LL.D., Ill. Coll. of Law, 1909; m. Calender Gerdine, June 23, 1892; 1 son, Thomas Jackson. Teacher country schools, W.Va., 1880-82, city schools, Parkersburg, W.Va., 1882-83; principal State Normal School, Shepherdstown, W.Va., 1885-88; supt. city schools, West Point, Miss., 1889-93; prof. mathematics, Mercer U., 1893-97; prof. psychology and pedagogy, and dir. Normal Dept. of Ga. State Coll. for Women, Milledgeville, 1897-1903; prof. philosophy and edn., and dean Sch. of Edn., U. of Ga., 1903—. Mem. Ga. State Bd. of Edn., 1912-20. Took a leading part in contest for the Peabody Fund, in which a large part of the fund was won for permanent endowment of the George Peabody Coll. for Teachers, Nashville, Tenn.; promoter of ednl. reform in Ga. Author: Teaching in Rural Schools. Home: Athens, Ga. Died Aug. 8, 1938.

WOOLBERT, Charles Henry, educator; b. Ottawa, Ill., June 26, 1877; s. Harry W. and Ida May (Gabler) W.; A.B., Northwestern U., 1900; A.M., U. of Mich., 1909; Ph.D., Harvard, 1918; m. Gertrude Janet Gale, Aug. 7, 1902; children—Robert Gale, Richard Latham, Janet. Instr. high sch., West Aurora, Ill., 1900-02; actg. prof. English and pub. speaking, Olivet (Mich.) Coll., 1902-03; head of dept., same, Albion (Mich.) Coll., 1903-13; asso. in pub. speaking, U. of Ill., 1913-16; asst. in psychology and aesthetics, Harvard, 1917-18; asst. prof. speech, U. of Illinois, 1918-21, associate prof., 1921-24, prof., 1924-26; prof. speech, State U. of Iowa, 1926—. Has served on staffs, summers, at Harvard, U. of Wis., U. of Calif. and U. of Utah. Spl. speaker Mich. Anti-Saloon League, 1908-13; with Army Ednl. Corps, Beaune, France, 1919. Editor The Quarterly Journal of Speech Edn., 1920-23. Author: Fundamentals of Speech, 1920; Better Speech (with Andrew T. Weaver), 1922; The Art of Interpretative Speech (with Severina E. Nelson), 1927. Home: Iowa City, Ia. Died June 9, 1929.

WOOLDRIDGE, Charles William, author, physician; b. Hull, Eng., May 22, 1847; s. Samuel and Mary W.; ed. pub. schs., Ionia Co., Mich., 1857-70; grad. Univ. of Mich., B.S., 1876, grad. med. dept., 1877; m. Pearl Gates, June 28, 1882. Engaged in med. practice, Cleveland, Ohio, 1890-1902; now residing in Montana. Independent in politics. Author: The Missing Sense, 1887; The Kingdom of Heaven Is at Hand, 1898; Perfecting the Earth, a Piece of Possible History, 1902. Home: Helena, Mont. Died 1908.

WOOLEVER, Harry Earl, church exec.; b. Van Etten, N.Y., Mar. 19, 1881; s. Charles P. and Frances Belle (Boardman) W.; grad. Cazenovia (N.Y.) Sem., 1903; A.B., Syracuse University, 1907, D.D., 1916; student Drew Theol. Seminary, 1909, 10, Columbia Univ., 1917-18, Am. U., 1927-28; m. Marien Eloise Andrews, Sept. 8, 1909. Editor Syracuse Univ. Daily, 1905-07; Y.M.C.A. sec., 1908-10; ordained M.E. ministry, 1910; editor Northern Christian Advocate, 1910-15; asst. editor Christian Advocate, New York, 1915-23; acting pastor Washington Square Church, N.Y. City, 1919; associate pastor, St. Paul's Church, New York, 1922; editor and director National Meth. Press, Washington, D.C., 1923-36; dir. Am. Christian Foundation and editor These Times, 1937-39. Trustee Cazenovia, Sem., Sibley Hosp., Lucy Webb Hayes School, American Univ.; dir. adult edn., Am. Univ. Grad. School, 1932-35. Del. to Gen. Conf. M.E. Ch., 1924, 28, 32, 36; del. to Ecumenical Methodist Conf., 1921, 1931; sec. Gen. Conf. Commn. on Interdenom. Relations, 1928—; exec. sec. Joint Commn. on Meth. Union, 1938—; del. Uniting Conf., Meth. Ch., and presented plan of Meth. Union; organizer and editor, Internat. Religious Press, 1930-33; founder and dir. Christian Crusade; mem. exec. com. Fedn. of Chs., Washington, D.C., 1930-33; pastor Mansfield, Pa., Meth. Ch. Home: Mansfield, Pa. Died May 30, 1941.

WOOLF, Albert Edward, chemist, inventor; b. New York, N.Y., Sept. 26, 1846; s. Edward W. (founder, 1837, of "Judy," first illustrated comic paper in U.S.); ed. Coll. City of New York; m. Rosamond Wienpfheimer, Sept., 1874. Introduced peroxide of hydrogen, to bleach grey and black ostrich feathers to white; also the first to use same as antiseptic; discovered the elec. decomposition of sea-water for sanitation, used in many large cities for treatment of drinking water, sewage and garbage, and adopted by the U.S. Govt. to combat yellow fever epidemic in Cuba; discovered antiseptic and med. properties of sea-water in combination with the electric current. More recently discovered the treatment of garbage, sewage and refuse to fill in waste or marshy land, and for general land reclaiming; by this method is prevented the formation of noxious gases, by killing the germ of putrefaction, and propagating the germ which transforms the refuse into fertile soil. Practically demonstrated the value of the hypochlorites, so that Great Britain, France and U.S. Govt. have adopted their use in their navies and armies. Discovered cause of pyorrhœa (Riggs disease), etc. Modeled bronze medallion of Gen. Grant, which decorated the places where Grant's body lay in state (medallion now hangs in room at Mt. McGregor where Gen. Grant died). Home: New York, N.Y. Died Apr. 19, 1920.

WOOLF, Philip, M.D., editor Saturday Evening Gazette; b. New York, Feb. 7, 1848; academic edn.; grad. Bellevue Hosp. Med. Coll., 1868; unmarried. Author: (novels) Who Is Guilty? The Trail of the Serpent; Satan's Mirror; Three Women and a Dead Man; Goldenrod and Aster. Home: New York, N.Y. Died 1903.

WOOLLARD, William Edward, lawyer; b. Albany, N.Y., Mar. 26, 1876; s. Henry Nun and Margaret (Barron) W.; LL.B., Albany Law Sch. (Union U.), 1897; m. Harriet Byers Holland, Oct. 29, 1906; children—Mrs. Elizabeth Woollard Morris, Mrs. Alice Holland Williamson, William E., Robert Holland. Admitted to New York bar, 1897, and began practice at Albany; mem. Woollard & Morris. Mem. National Guard, N.Y., 1893-98. Justice, City Court of Albany, 1901-07; special counsel Albany County Board of Supervisors, 1899; special deputy atty. gen., N.Y., 1917-20. Pres. Albany Masonic Vets. Assn.; pres. Veteran Odd Fellows Assn.; trustee Albany Masonic Hall Assn. Vice pres. Atlantic Deeper Waterways Assn.; dir. Nat. Rivers and Harbors Congress. Protestant. Mason, Odd Fellow, Elk. Home: Albany, N.Y. Died Sept. 1, 1940.

WOOLLEY, Celia Parker, minister; b. Toledo, O., June 14, 1848; d. Marcellus Harris and Harriet Maria (Sage) Parker; grad. Coldwater Female Sem.; m. Dr. J. H. Woolley, Dec. 29, 1868. Removed to Chicago, 1876; minister Unitarian Ch., Geneva, Ill., 1893-96, Independent Liberal Ch., Chicago, 1896-98; lecturer and writer; active worker in women's clubs. Early in 1904 organized Frederick Douglass Center, for settlement work among the colored people in Chicago. Author: Love and Theology (republished in paper as "Rachael Armstrong"), 1887; A Girl Graduate, 1889; Roger Hunt, 1893; The Western Slope, 1903. Home: Chicago, Ill. Died Mar. 9, 1918.

WOOLLEY, Edwin Campbell, university prof.; b. Paris, Ill., Mar. 18, 1878; s. John Granville and Mary Veronica (Gerhard) W.; bro. of Paul Gerhardt W.; A.B., U. of Chicago, 1898; Ph.D., Columbia, 1901; m. Isabelle Reid, Dec. 28, 1905. Asst. prof. English, U. of Wis., 1909—. Democrat. Episcopalian. Author: Handbook of Composition, 1907; The Mechanics of Writing, 1909; Exercises in English, 1911. Home: Madison, Wis. Died Jan. 26, 1916.

WOOLLEY, John Granville, author, lecturer; b. Collinsville, O., Feb. 15, 1850; s. Edwin C. and Elizabeth (Hunter) W.; A.B., Ohio Wesleyan Univ., 1871, A.M., 1874 (LL.D., 1906); B.L., U. of Michigan, 1873; m. Mary Veronica Gerhard, June 26, 1873; father of Paul Gerhardt and Edwin Campbell W. Admitted to bar Supreme Ct. of Illinois, 1873, Supreme Ct. of U.S., 1885; city atty., Paris, Ill., 1875; pros. atty., Minneapolis, 1881; practiced at New York, 1886; entered lecture field, 1888, and has spoken in principal English speaking cities of the world. Prohibition candidate for President U.S., 1900. Made tours of world, speaking on Prohibition, 1901 and 1905. Author: Seed; The Sower; Civilization by Faith; The Christian Citizen, 1897-98; A Lion Hunter, 1900; Temperance Progress in the 19th Century, 1902; South Sea Letters, 1905; Civic Sermons; The Call of an Epoch; The Spirit of the Road. Home: Madison, Wis. Died Aug. 1922.

WOOLLEY, Paul Gerhardt, pathologist; b. Paris, Ill., Apr. 7, 1875; s. John Granville and Mary Veronica (Gerhard) W.; B.S., U. of Chicago, 1896; M.D., Johns Hopkins, 1900; fellow in pathology, McGill Univ., 1901-02; m. Helen Bradford Thompson, Aug. 8, 1905; children—Eleanor F., Charlotte G. Resident house officer, Johns Hopkins Hosp., 1900-01; bacteriologist and pathologist, 1902-04, dir. serum lab., 1904-06, Bur. of Science, Manila, P.I.; dir. and pathologist, St. Paul's Hosp., Manila, 1905-06; dir. Siamese Govt. Serum Lab., 1906-07; chief insp. health, Bangkok, Siam, 1907-08; asso. prof. pathologic anatomy, U. of Neb., 1908-09; prof. pathology, U. of Cincinnati, 1909-18; dean Coll. of Medicine same, 1910-13. Commd. capt. M.R.C., 1917; maj. M.C., 1918; lt. col. M.R.C., 1919; instr. mil. hygiene, Camp Greenleaf, 1917-18; epidemiologist, Camps Greene and Devens, 1918-19; camp sanitary insp., asst. camp surgeon Camp Devens, 1918-19. Asso. prof. of pathology, Detroit Coll. Medicine and Surgery, 1920-23; dir. Nat. Pathol. Lab. of Mich., 1919-23; asso. dir. Detroit Clin. Lab., 1923-24; moved to Los Angeles, 1924; pathologist firm of Brem, Zeiler & Hammack, 1924-26; visiting pathologist Angelus, Lutheran, Good Samaritan and other hosps. and cons. pathologist Kern Gen. Hosp., 1924-26. Formerly dir. labs. and pathologist to Cincinnati Hosp.; pres. Hosp. Social Service Assn. of Cincinnati, 1911-14. Del. from Siam to Internat. Congress of Tuberculosis, 1908, and to Internat. Congress Hygiene and Demography, 1912. Decorated Officer of the Crown of Siam. Author: The Clinical History in Outline, 1914. Asso. editor Jour. Laboratory and Clinical Medicine. Home: Pasadena, Calif. Died 1932.

WOOLSEY, Sarah Chauncey ("Susan Coolidge"), author; b. Cleveland, O., 1845; unmarried. From 1871 contbr. poems and prose sketches to newspapers and magazines under her pen-name. Author: The New-Year's Bargain; Verses; What Katy Did; A Guernsey Lily; For Summer Afternoons; In the High Valley; A Few More Verses; A Short History of Philadelphia; The Barberry Bush, and Other Stories About Girls; etc. Home: Newport, R.I. Died 1905.

WOOLSEY, Theodore Salisbury, college prof.; b. New Haven, Conn., Oct. 22, 1852; s. Theodore Dwight W. (pres. Yale) and Elizabeth Martha (Salisbury) W.; A.B., Yale, 1872; LL.B., 1876, A.M., 1877; LL.D., Brown U., 1903; m. Annie Gardner Salisbury, Dec. 22, 1877; children—Theodore Salisbury, Heathcote Muirson. Study and travel in Europe, 1874-75, 1878-93, 1903-07; instr. pub. law, 1877-78, prof. internat. law, 1878-1911, Yale. Pres. New Haven Park Bd., 1914—. Editor: Woolsey's International Law (6th edit.); Pomeroy's International Law; articles on International Law in Johnson's Cyclopedia, new edit. Author: America's Foreign Policy, 1898. Asso. mem. Institut de Droit Internationale. Home: New Haven, Conn. Died Apr. 24, 1929.

WOOLSEY, Theodore Salisbury, forester; b. New Haven, Conn., Oct. 2, 1879; s. Theodore Salisbury and Annie Gardner (Salisbury) W.; B.A., Yale, 1901, M.F., 1903; m. Ruby Hilsman, d. Thomas H. Pickett, of Dawson, Ga., Mar. 15, 1908; children—Elizabeth P., Anne S., Edith, Sara P., Patricia. Insp., 1907-08, asst. dist. forester, 1908-15, U.S. Forest Service. Mem. Yale Forest Sch. Advisory Bd. and lecturer in 1912, on orgn. and management of national forests; also lecturer, 1916, apptd. asst. prof., 1917, but entered U.S.A.; commd. maj., 1917; lt. col. engrs., 1919; attached Paris hdqrs. staff, A.E.F. in France. Am. del. exec. com. Interallied War Wood Com., Paris, 1917-19. Cited by Gen. Pershing, 1919; Chevalier Legion of Honor, France; D.S.O., Eng.; Chevalier Order of Leopold, Belgium, 1919. Dir. New Haven Bank. Episcopalian. Asso. editor of "Forestry Quarterly," 1915-27. Made studies of the forestry movement in India, Austria and parts of Germany, France, Corsica, Algeria, Tunisia. Trustee and cons. forester, Middlebury (Vt.) Coll. Author: French Forests and Forestry, 1917; Studies in French Forestry, 1920; American Forest Regulation (textbook), 1922. Home: New Haven, Conn. Died July 10, 1933.

WOOLSON, Ira Harvey, mechanical engr.; b. Lewiston, N.Y., Aug. 11, 1856; s. Charles and Jane Ann (Yerington) Sharp W.; E.M., Columbia, 1885; m. Anita Mason, May 27, 1893. Asst. in assaying and drawing, 1886-90, instr. mech. engring., 1891-1903, adj. prof., 1903-08, adj. prof. civ. engring., 1908-10, Columbia U.; official investigator of building materials, N.Y. City, 1900-10; official del. from N.C. City to Internat. Fire Prevention Congress, London, 1903; consulting engr. Nat. Bd. of Fire Underwriters, 1910—; advisory engr. to bldg. materials div., War Industries Bd., 1918-19; chmn. Bldg. Code Com. of U.S. Dept. Commerce, 1921—. Prog. Republican. Author: Recommended Building Code, 1915; Code for Construction of Dwellings, 1918. Home: Summit, N.J. Died May 8, 1927.

WOOLWINE, Thomas Lee, lawyer, author; b. nr. Nashville, Tenn., Oct. 31, 1874; s. Samuel Shanklin and Sally (Shute) W.; pub. and pvt. schs.; admitted to bar, 1899; LL.B., Cumberland U., Tenn., 1903; LL.B., Columbian (now George Washington) U., 1904; m. Alma Foy, Nov. 7, 1900. In practice at Los Angeles, 1899—. Deputy city atty., Los Angeles, 1907-08; deputy dist. atty. Los Angeles Co. and pros. atty. city of Los Angeles, 1908; district atty. of Los Angeles County, 1915-23. Gained wide reputation by prosecution and conviction of keepers of bucket shops, strict enforcement of excise laws; brought charges of vice protection against the mayor and police commn. and other officers of the city, resulting in resignations and in "recall" of the mayor and election of his successor; this was the first "recall" invoked against such an officer in the U.S.; prosecuted and convicted conspirators in Los Angeles Times dynamiting case; etc. Primary candidate for Dem. nomination for gov. of Calif., 1918, and was Dem. nominee for gov., 1922. Democrat in nat. affairs, independent in local. Author: In the Valley of the Shadows, 1909. Home: Los Angeles, Calif. Died July 8, 1925.

WOOLWINE, William David, banker; b. Christiansburg, Va., Oct. 19, 1855; s. Adam Smith and Rebecca (Shanklin) W.; ed. pub. schs.; m. Blanche Bradfute, July 17, 1878 (died 1880); m. 2d, Lily White, Oct. 18, 1883. Moved to Nashville, 1873, San Diego, Calif., 1886, Los Angeles, 1894; an organizer, 1888, and v.p. Bank of San Diego, until it was merged, 1889, with First Nat. Bank of San Diego, of which was asst. cashier, later cashier; cashier Savings Bank of Southern Calif., Los Angeles, 1894-98, Los Angeles Nat. Bank, 1898-1903; v.p. Southern Calif. Savings Bank, 1904-06; associated with others, 1906, and purchased control of Nat. Bank of Calif., of which was v.p.; this bank merged, 1917, with Merchants Nat. Bank of Los Angeles, of which was v.p., elected pres., 1924. Episcopalian. Democrat. Home: Duarte, Calif. Died Sept. 21, 1927.

WOOLWORTH, Frank W., merchant; b. Rodman, N.Y., April 13, 1852; s. John H. and Fanny (McBrier) W.; ed. pub. schs. and business coll., N.Y.; m. Jennie Creighton, June 11, 1876. Started "5-cent store," Utica, N.Y., Feb., 1879; removed to Lancaster, Pa., June 1879, and continued in same business; now has about 1000 "5 and 10-cent" stores in U.S. and Canada and 75 in Great Britain; pres. F. W. Woolworth Co., Broadway Park Place Co., New York. Mem. Chamber of Commerce, Mchts.' Assn. Home: New York, N.Y. Died Apr. 8, 1919.

WOOLWORTH, James Mills, lawyer; b. Onondaga, N.Y., June 28, 1829; grad. Hamilton Coll., 1849 (LL.D., Racine Coll., 1875; L.H.D., Univ. of Neb., 1893; D.C.L., Trinity Univ., Toronto, Can.). Admitted to bar, Supreme Court of N.Y., at Albany, 1853; Supreme Court U.S., 1862; removed to Neb., 1856. Pres. Am. Bar Assn., 1896-97. Delegate gen. conv. P.E. Ch. from 1868, and chmn. House of Deputies. Home: Omaha, Neb. Died 1906.

WOOTAN, James Blythe, editor, lecturer; b. Tullahoma, Tenn., July 7, 1873; s. John Thomas and Mary Ellen (Smith) W.; prep. edn., pub. schs., St. Louis, Ashley, Ill., high sch., Traver, Calif.; student Park Coll., Mo., 1896-98, LL.D., 1932; m. Agnes May

Dilley, Jan. 29, 1900; 1 son, John Dilley. Reporter on country weeklies, California, 1894-96, St. Cloud (Minn.) Daily Times, 1899-1900; reporter and city editor St. Paul Daily Globe, 1900-01; successively reporter, city editor, editorial writer Omaha Bee, 1901-15; editor Pub. Service Mag., 1915-18; co-founder, 1918, editor, 1918-20, Presbyn. Publicity Dept. and New Era Mag.; dir. pub. relations, Hodenpyl, Hardy & Co., N.Y. City, 1920-21; editor Public Service Mag., 1922—. Pres. bd. dirs. Presbyn. Coll. of Christian Education, Chicago. Mem. Presbyn. Hist. Soc., Irving Soc. Home: Chicago, Ill. Died Jan. 8, 1934.

WORCESTER, Dean Conant; b. Thetford, Vt., Oct. 1, 1866; s. Ezra Carter and Ellen H. W.; A.B., U. of Mich., 1889, D.Sc., 1915; m. Nanon Fay Leas, Apr. 27, 1893. Mem. Steere scientific expdn. to P.I., 1887-88; asst. in botany, U. of Mich., 1889-90; one of two men to conduct Menage scientific expdn. to P.I., 1890-93; instr. animal morphology, 1893-94, asst. prof., 1894-95, asst. prof. zoölogy and curator Zoöl. Mus., 1895-99, U. of Mich.; mem. U.S. Philippine commn., Jan. 1899-Sept. 1, 1901; sec. of the interior, Philippine Insular Govt., Sept. 1, 1901-Sept. 15, 1913; v.p. and gen. mgr. Agusan Coconut Co.; asst. to the pres. Philippine Refining Corp.; pres. Philippine Desiccated Coconut Corp. Author: The Philippine Islands and Their People, 1899; The Non-Christian Tribes of Northern Luzon, 1906; The Philippines Past and Present, 1913. Home: Cebu, P.I. Died May 2, 1924.

WORCESTER, Edward Strong, clergyman; b. South Orange, N.J., Apr. 14, 1876; s. Rev. John Hopkins and Harriet Williams (Strong) W.; A.B., Princeton, 1896; B.D., Hartford Theol. Sem., 1901; grad. student Berlin U. and Hartford Theol. Sem.; D.D., Rutgers, 1924; m. Mary Greenman, Oct. 12, 1909; children—Richard Lyman, Harriet Loring. Teacher Princeton (N.J.) Prep. Sch., 1896-97; instr. in Latin, Princeton, 1897-98; asst. pastor Broadway Congl. Ch., Norwich, Conn., 1903-06, pastor, 1906-18; pastor First Congl. Ch., Madison, Wis., 1918-22, Bellows Falls, Vt., 1923; prof. systematic theology, Seminary of Ref. Ch. in America, New Brunswick, N.J., 1924—; also asso. librarian Gardner A. Sage Library, 1925-35. Republican. Home: New Brunswick, N.J. Died June 25, 1937.

WORCESTER, Edwin Dean, sec. N.Y. Central & Hudson River R.R.; v.p., sec. and treas. Lake Shore & Mich. Southern Ry.; v.p. and sec. Michigan Central R.R., and sec. or treas., or both, in 15 other cos. in the so-called "Vanderbilt System"; b. Albany, N.Y., Nov. 19, 1828; s. Eldad W. (8th in direct line from Rev. William W., who came from England in 1640) and Sarah (Chickering) W.; ed. pub. and pvt. schs.; m. Mary A. Low, 1855. Studied law and followed several other pursuits; entered accounting dept. N.Y. Central R.R., 1853, subsequently becoming treas.; sec. and treas., 1873, v.p. 1883, Lake Shore & Mich. Southern Ry.; sec. Mich. Central R.R., 1878, and from 1883 v.p. same, etc. Home: New York, N.Y. Died 1904.

WORCESTER, Elwood, clergyman; b. Massillon, O., 1862; s. David Freeman and Frances (Gold) W.; A.B., Columbia, 1886; A.M., Ph.D., U. of Leipzig, 1889, hon. S.T.D., Hobart College, 1897; D.D., University of Pa., 1898; D.S.T., Columbia Univ., 1929; m. Blanche S. Rulison, Aug. 7, 1894; children—Constance R., Gurdon S., Blandina, David. Deacon, 1890, priest, 1891, P.E. Ch.; chaplain and prof. philosophy and psychology, Lehigh U., 1890-96; acting rector St. John's, Dresden, Germany, 1894-95; rector St. Stephen's Ch., Phila., 1896-1904, Emmanuel Ch., Boston, 1904-29. Author: Religion and Life, 1913; The Issues of Life, 1915; Was Jesus an Historical Person?, 1927; The Allies of Religion, 1929; Body, Mind and Spirit (with Dr. Samuel McComb), 1931; Life's Adventure, 1932; Studies in the Birth of the Lord, 1932; Making Life Better, 1933. Home: Boston, Mass. Died July 19, 1940.

WORCESTER, Franklin, mfr.; b. Hollis, N.H., Oct. 27, 1845; s. John Newton and Sarah (Holden) W., des. of Rev. William Worcester, Salisbury, Mass., 1638; A.B., Dartmouth, 1870; student Harvard U. Law Sch., 1871; unmarried. Admitted to Middlesex bar, 1872; mfr. furniture, lumber and cooperage, title of Worcester Bros., Cambridge, Mass., and Hollis, N.H., 1903—; dir. Indian Head Nat. Bank, Nashua, N.H., N.H. Fire Ins. Co. Trustee Appleton Acad., New Ipswich, N.H.; supt. schs. and mem. Bd. of Edn., Hollis, 30 yrs.; mem. N.H. Ho. of Rep., 1877, 1888, Senate, 1887-88; Rep. candidate for gov. of N.H., in the conventions of 1898 and 1900; received unanimous primary nomination, 1912. Unitarian. Home: Hollis, N.H. Died May 2, 1917.

WORCESTER, Harry Augustus, ry. official; b. Albany, N.Y., Nov. 18, 1862; s. Edwin Dean and Mary Abigail (Low) W.; B.A., Yale, 1884; m. Elizabeth Howard Whiting, Oct. 18, 1905. Began as asst. station master N.Y.C.&H. R.R., at Grand Central Sta., New York, 1885; with L.S.&M.S. Ry. as clk., asst. trainmaster, div. supt., 1891-1905; asst. gen. supt., M.C. R.R., 1905, gen. supt., 1905-06; gen. supt. L.S.&M.S. Ry., Feb.-Oct. 1906; asst. gen. mgr., 1906-13, gen. mgr., 1913-16, v.p. and gen. mgr., 1916-18, C.,C.,C.&St.L. Ry.; dist. dir. Ohio-Ind. Dist. U.S. R.R. Adminstrn., 1918-20; v.p. C.,C.,C.&St.L. Ry., 1920-32; pres. Cincinnati Union Terminal Co., 1927-33; resident v.p. N.Y. Central Lines, 1930-32; retired from ry. business. Republican. Presbyterian. Home: Madisonville, O. Died Sept. 18, 1938.

WORCESTER, William Loring, minister; b. Waltham, Mass., Aug. 16, 1859; s. John and Elizabeth Callender (Pomeroy) W.; A.B., Harvard, 1881; grad. New Ch. Theol. Sch., Cambridge, Mass., 1885; m. Ethel Burnham, Jan. 1, 1900 (died 1912). Minister First Phila. Soc. of the New Jerusalem Ch. (Swedenborgian), 1885-1911, Cambridge Soc., 1911-36; pres. New Ch. Theol. Sch., 1908-36. Pres. Gen. Conv. New Jerusalem in U.S.A., 1921-28. Author: The Language of Parable, 1892; On Holy Ground, 1904. Home: Cambridge, Mass. Died Sept. 29, 1939.

WORDEN, Beverly Lyon, mfr.; b. Chicago, Ill., Feb. 8, 1871; s. Albert Lyon and Anne (Robson) W.; B.S. in Civ. Engring., U. of Wis., 1893; m. Katherine Elizabeth Taylor, 1901; children—Elizabeth Robson, Anne Catherine. Founder and pres. Worden-Allen Co., Milwaukee, 1901-21; founder, and pres. Lackawanna Bridge Co., Buffalo, N.Y., 1909-24; gen. mgr. Newark Bay Shipyard, Newark, N.J., building 150 steel ships for Emergency Fleet Corp., World War; became pres. Cutler-Hammer Mfg. Co., Milwaukee and New York. Episcopalian. Mason. Home: West Orange, N.J. Died Mar. 28, 1931.

WORDEN, Charles Howard, banker; b. FortWayne, Ind., Sept. 14, 1859; s. James Lorenzo and Anna (Grable) W.; student U. of Mich., 1879-81; read law in office of Hon. Robert Stewart Taylor; m. Elizabeth Marshall, Jan. 10, 1884; children—Alice W. (Mrs. G. W. Condit), Marshall W., Charles J. Admitted to bar, 1882; mem. Worden & Morris, 1884-93, Zollars & Worden, 1894-1902; gave up law practice, 1902; v.p. and mgr. 1st Nat. Bank, 1902-16, pres., 1916-23, chmn. bd., 1925—. Presbyn. Mason. Home: Fort Wayne, Ind. Died Feb. 4, 1930.

WORDEN, Edward Chauncey, I, chemist; b. Ypsilanti, Mich., Apr. 17, 1875; s. Chauncey Perry and Elvira Mabel (Brainerd) W.; Ph.C., U. of Mich., 1896; B.S., New York U., 1907, M.A., 1909, D.Sc., 1921; m. Anna Wilhelmina Breitsman, Sept. 25, 1901; children—Marian Alice (Mrs. De Witt Bell), Edward Chauncey II, Anna Lois, Waite Warren, Loanna. Served as chemist at N.Y. Agrl. Expt. Station, Geneva, 1896-97; mem. Crane & Worden, chemists, New York, 1899-1900; chemist Celluloid Zapon Co., Springfield, N.J., 1900-02, Clark Thread Co., Newark, 1902-14, Worden Lab., Milburn, N.J., 1914—. Chmn. com. on airplane coatings, Nat. Research Council, 1916; edition Report 10382 and 13228 (5000 pages) "Aviation Chemistry, 1914-18," prepared for U.S. Army Air Service; chief of airplane wing coating sect., Bur. of Aeronautics, Washington, D.C., 1916-18, crossing Atlantic 14 times for U.S. Govt. Fellow Chem. Soc., London, and French Acad., Paris. Mason. Author: Nitrocellulose Industry, 2 vols., 1911; Cellulose Acetate, 1915; Technology of Cellulose Esters, Vol. I (3,709 pages), 1921; Chemical Patents Index (United States), 1915-1924, 5 vols., 1927; (with Edward C. Worden, II) Technical Dict. of Chemistry (containing over 400,000 separate headings in alphabetical arrangement). Asso. editor Kunstoffe, also of La Coutchoue et la Guttapercha. Home: Milburn, N.J. Died Sept. 22, 1940.

WORDEN, James Avery, clergyman; b. Oxford, O., Dec. 10, 1841; s. Isaac and Rebecca Ann (MacCracken) W.; A.B., Miami U., 1861, A.M., 1864; 2d lt. Co. G, 74th Ohio Vols., 1861-63; grad. Princeton Theol. Sem., 1866; (D.D., Lafayette Coll., 1882; LL.D., Miami, 1899); m. Mary R. Hendrickson, Feb. 27, 1867. Ordained Presbyn. ministry, Feb. 14, 1867; pastor Oswego, N.Y., 1866-72, Steubenville, O., 1872-78; sec. and supt. S.S. training, Presbyn. Ch., Apr. 1, 1878—. Lecturer in theol. sems. on pastor's work; chmn. of Pan-Presbyn. Council's Com. on Sabbath schs. and young people; chaplain Pa. Commandery Loyal Legion, 5 yrs. Author: Westminster Normal Outlines (2 vols.), 1880; Bible Teachers' Guide (2 vols.), 1892; Bible Correspondence School (8 vols.); Westminster Normal Quarterly, 1902; Life of Christ, 1907. Home: Philadelphia, Pa. Died Oct. 24, 1917.

WORDIN, Nathaniel Eugene, physician; b. Bridgeport, Conn., May 26, 1844; s. Nathaniel S. and Fannie (Leavenworth) W.; A.B., Yale, 1870, A.M., 1874; M.D., Jefferson Medical Coll., Phila., 1873; in 6th Conn. Vols., 1862-65; m. Eliza W. Barnes, Dec. 25, 1879. Phys. Bridgeport Protestant Orphan Asylum; formerly visiting surgeon Bridgeport Hosp.; mem. Conn. State Bd. of Health, 1890-99. Home: Bridgeport, Conn. Died May 10, 1915.

WORK, Edgar Whitaker, clergyman; b. Logan, O., Nov. 20, 1862; s. John Wright and Ann Elizabeth (Fielding) W.; Ph.B., U. of Wooster, 1884, Ph.M., 1887; grad. Lane Theol. Sem., Cincinnati, 1887; D.D., Wooster, 1895; m. Ellen Blair Wilson, June 23, 1887. Ordained Presbyn. ministry, 1887; pastor Van Wert, O., 1887-90; coll. pastor and prof. Bibl. lit., U. of Wooster, 1890-95; pastor Dayton, O., 1895-1902, Berkeley, Calif., 1902-04, Colorado Springs, Colo., 1904-07, Fourth Ch., New York, 1907-24. Lecturer in Bible Teachers' Training Sch., New York, 2 yrs.; elected pres. Westminster U., Denver, 1906, but declined. Moderator New York Presbytery, 1912-14; vice moderator Presbyn. Gen. Assembly, 1918; resident chaplain Ohio Soc. of New York; chaplain Criterion Soc.; also of Daughters of Ohio. Author: The Fascination of the Book, 1906; Every Day, 1915; Obscure People, 1915; The Bible in English Literature, 1917; The Church's Children; Royal Day; Go and Tell!; Every Minister His Own Evangelist, 1927. Edited J. Wilbur Chapman's Evangelistic Sermons, 1922, Awakening Sermons, 1928. Home: Riverdale, New York, N.Y. Died Apr. 17, 1934.

WORK, Jeremiah Boston, clergyman, educator; b. Marion Center, Pa., Jan. 22, 1855; s. Elijah Ireland and Margaret (McCreery) W.; B.S., Westminster Coll., Pa., 1882 (D.D., 1902); student Princeton U. and Princeton Theol. Sem., 1882-84; grad. Allegheny (now Pittsburgh) Theol. Seminary, 1885; m. Mary McClure Watts, Aug. 19, 1885; children—Paul, Herman, Marian (dec.), Eunice. Prin. Stone Valley Acad., 1879-81; ordained ministry U.P. Ch., 1886; pastor McCoysville, Pa., 1886-91; prin. Norfolk (Va.) Mission Coll., 1891-96; dean theology, Knoxville (Tenn.) Coll., 1897-1906; stated supply, Tranquility, O., 1908-10; pastor Olathe, Kan., 1910-13; v.p. and prof. Bible, Tarkio (Mo.) Coll., 1913—. Moderator Synod of Ia., 1916-17; mem. com. to prepare new creed for U.P. Ch.; mem. bd. dirs. Xenia Theol. Sem.; lecturer at summer Bible schs. Republican. Author: Questions in Bible History, 1893, 5th edit., 1922. Home: Tarkio, Mo. Died Mar. 27, 1929.

WORK, Milton C., author; A.B., U. of Pa., 1884, LL.B., 1887. Law practice, Phila. Author: Whist of Today, 1893; Auction of Today, 1912; Auction Developments, 1913; Auction Under the Laws of 1915, 1915; Auction Declaration, 1917; Auction Methods, 1920; Auction for Two or Three, 1921; Analysis of Par Auction, 1922; Auction Bridge, in 12 Lessons, 1923; Auction Bridge of 1924, 1923; Auction Bridge Complete, 1926; Contract Bridge, 1927; Bridge Pointers and Tests, 1927; Auction Bridge for Beginners, 1928; Contract Bridge for All, 1929; Common Sense Contract Bridge, 1930; The Gist of Contract Bridge, 1931; The Official System of Contract Bridge in a Nutshell, 1931. Editor The Bridge Magazine. Contbr. daily Bridge articles in over 200 newspapers. Lecturer and broadcaster. Home: Philadelphia, Pa. Died June 27, 1934.

WORKMAN, Fanny Bullock, mountain climber; b. Worcester, Mass.; d. Gov. Alexander Hamilton and Elvira (Hazard) Bullock; ed. in France, Germany, and New York; m. W(illiam) Hunter Workman, June 16, 1881. Traveled extensively in the East; made expdn. to Himalayas, 1899, making record 1st ascents for women: Mt. Bullock Workman, 19,450 feet; Mt. D 41, 20,700 ft.; Mt. Koser Gunge, 21,000 ft.; made 1st exploration of the 30-mile long Chogo Lungma glacier, Baltistan, 1902; in expdn. to Himalayas, 1903, made 1st ascents: Mt. Chogo, 21,500 ft.; Mt. Lungma, 22,568 ft.; also explored Hoh Lumba and Alchori glaciers; 1st ascent one of Nun Kun peaks, 23,300 ft. in expdn. to Himalayas, 1906, gives her the world mountaineering record for women; in 1908 explored 36-mile long Hispar Glacier in the Korakoran range; made first ascent of Biafo Hispar Watershed Peak, 21,350 ft.; crossed Hispar Pass and descended 40-mile long Biafo Glacier into Baltistan; in 1911 explored and mapped the Khondokoro, Chogo Lisa, Kondus, Dong Dong and Masherbrum glaciers; ascended Bilaphon glacier and crossed the Saltoro Pass over 18,000 feet high and descended to Siachen glacier, the largest and longest in Asia. Made first exploration of its upper half and affluents; ascended snow peak of over 21,000 ft., a first ascent in eastern Karakoram; 1912 explored and surveyed 50 mile long Rose glacier and affluents, made seven new ascents of peaks and cols. of from 19,000 to over 21,000 feet; discovered the water-party between the Indus and Chinese-Turkestan regions. Lecturer before learned socs. and Alpine clubs in America, Scotland, France, Germany, Italy. Officier de l'Instrn. Publique, France, at request of President Loubet, 1904; decorated with Italian Golden Eagle, 1904; gold medalist, Club Alpin Français, 1904. Author: (with W. H. Workman) Algerian Memories; Sketches a-Wheel in Modern Iberia; Through Town and Jungle in the Ice World of Himalaya; Ice-Bound Heights of the Mustagh, 1908; Peaks and Glaciers of Nun Kun, 1909; The Call of the Snowy Hispar; Two Summers in the Ice Wilds of Eastern Karakoram, 1917. Died Jan. 23, 1925.

WORKS, John Downey, senator; b. Ohio Co., Ind., Mar. 29, 1847; s. James Alexander and Phoebe (Downey) W.; ed. common schs. of Ind.; m. Alice Banta, Nov. 8, 1868. Served 18 mos. in U.S. Vols. during Civil War; admitted to bar, 1868; practiced at Vevay, 1868-83, Los Angeles, 1883—. Mem. Ind. Ho. of Rep., 1879; judge Superior Court, San Diego Co., Calif., 1886-87; justice Supreme Court, Calif., 1888-91; pres. City Council, Los Angeles, short time, 1910; U.S. senator, Calif., term 1911-17. Republican. Christian Scientist. Author: Indiana Pleading and Practice, 1883; Courts and Their Jurisdiction, 1894; Water and Water Rights, 1890; What's Wrong with the World?, 1922; Man's Duty to Man, 1923; Juridical Reform, 1924. Home: Los Angeles, Calif. Died June 6, 1928.

WORLEY, Henry William, mayor; b. London, Eng., Apr. 19, 1877; s. George Thomas and Adeline Theressa (Threadinham) W.; brought to U.S., 1882; ed. high sch. and Cooper Inst., N.Y. City; m. Sadie E. Glynn, Apr. 16, 1898; children—Henry E., Mildred L., Alice A. (Mrs. J. V. Eckhart). Began as pipe organ mfr., 1904, under title of Henry W. Worly Organ Co., of which has continued as the head; mayor of Columbus, term 1932-36. Served as pvt. Co. H, N.Y. Vol. Inf., Spanish-Am. War. Democrat. Episcopalian. Mem. Spanish-Am. War Vets. K.P., Elk, Eagle; mem. Royal Aracanum. Home: Columbus, O. Died Aug. 5, 1938.

WORMAN, James Henry, consul; b. Berlin, Germany, Feb. 28, 1845; s. Maurice and Bertha W.; ed. U. of Berlin, and the Sorbonne, Paris; hon. A.M., Dickinson, 1867; Ph.D., DePauw, 1882; LL.D., Mt. Union; m. Emma Parker Davis, Sept. 10, 1866 (died 1896); 1 son, Ben J.; m. 2d, Mary A. Payne, Apr. 4, 1898 (died 1919); children—Dorothea A., Bertha F., Margaret E. Asst. prof., Knox Coll., 1865-66; librarian Drew Theol. Sem., 1867-74; editor Chenango Telegraph, 1875-76; asso. editor National Repository, 1876-80; sr. prof. Chautauqua from foundation (1877) to 1885; head Southern Chautauqua from 1882, Round Lake Summer Schs., from 1885; founded, 1878, and conducted in Chautauqua, 1878-80, the corr. system of study; prof. Adelphi Coll., 1877-82, Vanderbilt U., 1882-85; editor Saratogian, 1885-87; editor-in-chief Outing, 1887-1900; consul, 1899-1902, consul gen., 1902-04, Munich, Germany; consul at Three Rivers, Can., 1904-08; later in special govt., editorial, ednl. work. Advocated successfully the right of Am. professional graduates abroad to use Am. academic degrees; led in suppression of fraudulent colleges, in Ill. and Wis.; coöperated with Dept. of Agriculture for adoption of measures to prevent importation of hides of meat cattle causing, without proper disinfection, foot and mouth disease. Has stock farm at Westport, N.Y. Prepared commercial courses for French and Spanish instrn. for Mass. Univ. Extension Bd., 1915; actg. prof. Spanish, 1916, head of the dept., 1917, U. of Vermont. Author: Chautauqua Language Series in French, German and Spanish; also other modern lang. textbooks. Editor: McClintock & Strong's Cyclopædia; also contbr. to other cyclos., etc. Was founder and pres. The Round Table (club), Nashville, Tenn. Active in war work, 1914-19, and decorated for same; identified with General Allen's work for supplying food and clothing to suffering people in Germany, 1923, and in favor of unprejudiced verdict as to reparations to be made by Germany. Home: Westport, N.Y. Died Jan. 24, 1930.

WORMELEY, Katharine Prescott, author; b. Ipswich, England, Jan. 14, 1830, d. Rear Admiral Ralph Randolph and Caroline (Preble) W. (niece of Commodore Edward Preble, founder of U.S. Navy); (sister of Elizabeth Wormeley Latimer); came to U.S. in girlhood; took active interest in relief of Union soldiers during war; connected with U.S. Sanitary Commn. Author: The U.S. Sanitary Commission, 1863; Life of Balzac, 1890; The Cruel Side of War, 1899; etc. Translator of the Works of Honoré de Balzac, 40 vols., 1883-97; Molière, 6 vols., 1892; Duc de Saint-Simon; Versailles Historical Memoirs, 20 vols., 1898-1901; Tartarin, 2 vols.; Kings in Exile, 2 vols. (Daudet), 1899. Home: Jackson, N.H. Died 1908.

WORMSER, Leo F., lawyer; b. Chicago, Ill., July 6, 1884; s. David and Frida (Falk) W.; grad. Armour Inst. Tech., 1901; Ph.B., U. of Chicago, 1904, J.D., 1909; Harvard Law Sch., 1904-06; m. Helen E. Goldsmith, Oct. 23, 1911; 1 dau., Elaine. Admitted to Ill. bar, 1909, and began practice at Chicago, with Rosenthal & Hamill; became mem. of firm July 1, 1911, now Rosenthal, Hamill & Wormser. Professional lecturer U. of Chicago Law Sch., 1922—. Trustee and counsel Museum of Science and Industry (founded by Julius Rosenwald), Jewish Charities of Chicago; trustee Armour Inst. Technology, Orchestral Assn. of Chicago, Internat. House of Chicago, Civic Federation of Chicago; mem. Com. on Development of U. of Chicago. Republican. Home: Chicago, Ill. Died Aug. 9, 1934.

WORSLEY, Abinus A., lawyer; b. Union Grove, Wis., June 24, 1868; s. Thomas G. and Maria (Shelds) W.; LL.B., Valparaiso (Ind.) U.; m. Alice J. Mager, Aug. 26, 1904. Began practice at Chicago, Ill., 1902; mem. Ariz. Senate 4 yrs.; wrote labor laws of Ariz. Single tax Democrat. Moose, Eagle. Author: Corporation Rats in the National Corn Crib, 1895; First Step in National Progress; The Way Out, 1924. Home: Tucson, Ariz. Deceased.

WORTH, William Scott, brig. gen. U.S.A., retired; b. Albany, N.Y., Jan. 6, 1840; s. Gen. Wm. Jenkins W.; U.S.A. (1794-1849); entered army as 2d lt., 8th inf., April 26, 1861; 1st lt., June 7, 1861 (bvtd. capt. and maj.); capt., Jan. 14, 1866; maj., 2d inf., Mar. 9, 1891; lt. col., 13th inf., Nov. 26, 1894; col., Sept. 1898; engaged in Santiago campaign; was severely wounded July 1, 1898, during the charge on San Juan Hill; promoted brig. gen., Nov. 2, 1898, and retired Nov. 9, 1898, on account of severe disabling wounds. In Civil war served on staff Gen. A. J. Smith during Corinth campaign; a.d.c. staff Gen. H. J. Hunt, chief

of arty., Army of the Potomac, from summer of 1862 to the surrender, and took part in all engagements and campaigns of that army; on frontier duty, 1872-91. Home: New York, N.Y. Died 1904.

WORTHEN, Thomas Wilson Dorr, college prof.; b. Thetford, Vt., Oct. 3, 1845; s. Joseph and Elizabeth (Chase) W.; A.B., Dartmouth, 1872 (Phi Beta Kappa), A.M., 1875; m. Thetford, Louisa Maria Wilcox, Aug. 20, 1874 (died 1878); m. 2d, Elizabeth Almira Washburn, July 22, 1885. Tutor in mathematics, 1874-78, tutor in Greek and mathematics, 1878-79; instr. mathematics, 1879-83, asst. prof., 1883-93, prof. mathematics, 1893-1911, emeritus prof., 1911—, Dartmouth Coll. Justice Police Court, Hanover, 1897-1911; mem. N.H. Ho. of Rep., 1905-06; mem. Pub. Service Commn. of N.H., June 17, 1911—. Democrat. Trustee Mary Hitchcock Hosp., Howe Library, Thetford Acad. Conglist. Home: Concord, N.H. Died Sept. 21, 1927.

WORTHINGTON, Augustus Storrs, lawyer; b. Fallston, Pa., Aug. 14, 1843; s. Benjamin D. and Eliza (Jackman) W.; ed. Steubenville, O., 1849-57; served in Civil War as pvt. Co. D, 98th Ohio Inf., 1862-65; lost leg at battle of Kenesaw Mountain, June 27, 1864; LL.B., Columbian (now George Washington) U., 1868; LL.D. from same university, June 1921; m. Louise Starr, Jan. 25, 1872. Began practice Aug. 1870; U.S. dist. atty., D.C., 1884-88. Retired. Home: Washington, D.C. Died Apr. 9, 1922.

WORTHINGTON, Edward William, author, clergyman; b. Batavia, N.Y., May 10, 1854; s. Gad B. and Anna M. W.; early edn. Oakfield, N.Y., and high sch., Batavia, N.Y.; grad. Trinity Coll., A.B., 1875 (A.M., 1878); Berkeley Divinity Sch., 1878; ordained to P.E. ministry, 1878; m. Eleanor Lobdell, June 17, 1880. Rector, St. John's Ch., Yalesville, Conn., 1878-79; Christ Ch., West Haven, Conn., 1879-82; St. John's Ch., Mt. Morris, N.Y., 1882-87; Grace Ch., Cleveland, 1887—. Author: Ember Days and Other Papers, 1897; The Holy Eucharist Devotionally Considered, 1901; A Study of Occasional Offices of the Prayer Book, 1903. Home: Cleveland, O. Died 1906.

WORTHINGTON, George, P.E. bishop of Neb., 1885—; b. Lenox, Mass., Oct. 14, 1840; grad. Hobart, 1860 (D.D., 1876; LL.D., 1885); Gen. Theol. Sem. 1863. Ordered deacon, 1863; ordained priest, 1864; asst. St. Paul's Ch., Troy, N.Y.; rector Christ Ch., Ballston Spa, N.Y.; rector, 1868-85, St. John's, Detroit, Mich.; declined missionary bishopric of Shanghai, 1883; twice elected to the bishopric of Nebraska. Home: Omaha, Neb. Died 1908.

WORTHINGTON, George Heber; b. Toronto, Canada, Feb. 13, 1850; s. John and Mary (Welborn) W.; ed. Upper Can. Coll., Toronto; m. Mrs. Hannah Luella Weaver, Feb. 27, 1878. Began business career in wholesale grocery house in Toronto; later became mgr. for his father as contractor for building the Southern Central R.R. (later part of Lehigh Valley System); organized 1886, of which was pres. (dir.), Cleveland Stone Co.; became pres. Underwriters Land Co. Interurban Ry. & Terminal Co.; retired. Pres. Perry Victory Centennial Commn.; dir. Cleveland Mus. of Art. Mason. Home: Cleveland, O. Died Jan. 10, 1924.

WORTHINGTON, John I., judge; b. Neosho, Mo., Mar. 28, 1857; s. John I. and Nancy A. (Erwin) W.; ed. Carrollton (Ark.) Acad.; m. Tourville E. Leathers, Oct. 28, 1878. Admitted to Ark. bar, 1884, and practiced at Carrollton; treas. Carroll County, 1887-89; judge County Court, 1892-96; register U.S. Land Office, Harrison, Ark., 1897-1909; U.S. atty., Western Dist. of Ark., 1909-13; judge 14th Jud. Circuit of Ark., 1914-18; twice nominated as Rep. candidate for gov. of Ark. V.p. Citizens Bank, Harrison. Methodist. Mason. Home: Harrison, Ark. Died Apr. 3, 1924.

WORTHINGTON, Walter Fitzhugh, rear admiral; b. Baltimore, Md., Mar. 8, 1855; s. Nicholas Brice and Sophia Kerr (Muse) W.; A.B., Md. Agrl. Coll., 1873; grad. U.S. Naval Acad., 1875; m. Grace Winifred Macmillan, of Greenock, Scotland, Aug. 3, 1885. Apptd. to U.S. Naval Acad. from Md., 1873; rear admiral, Mar. 26, 1913—. Served on gunboats Alert, Castine and Vesuvius; transport Powhatan; frigate Lancaster; cruisers Atlanta, Chicago, Montgomery; battleships Illinois, Kearsarge; monitor Terror. Cruised on N. Atlantic, S. Atlantic, Mediterranean, Asiatic stas.; shore duty, Navy Dept., N.Y. Navy Yard and Pittsburgh, Pa.; instr. at U.S. Naval Acad.; adj. prof. Lafayette Coll., Pa.; prof. Clemson Coll., S.C.; was in charge erection and equipment U.S. Expt. Sta., Annapolis; insp. materials, Brooklyn dist., Mar. 26, 1913-Mar. 8, 1919; retired by operation of law, Mar. 8, 1919. Democrat. Episcopalian. Home: Santa Barbara, Calif. Died Aug. 1, 1937.

WORTHINGTON, William, lawyer; b. Cincinnati, O., Aug. 3, 1847; s. Vachel and Julia (Wiggins) W.; A.B., Harvard, 1867, A.M., 1870; m. Susan E. Carpenter, Oct. 10, 1872. Practiced in Cincinnati, 1869—; partnership with late Drausin Wulsin, as Wulsin & Worthington, 1877-82, with Edward W. Strong, as Worthington & Strong, 1904-14, later Worthington, Strong, Settinius & Hollister; judge Superior Court of

Cincinnati, 1882-83; trustee to rebuild Hamilton County Court House, 1884-86; del. Ohio State Constl. Conv., 1912; dir. and general counsel Little Miami R.R. Co. Trustee U. of Cincinnati, 1883-88; trustee Cincinnati Museum Assn., Cincinnati Music Hall Assn., Spring Grove Cemetery, Colored Industrial School. Episcopalian. Home: Cincinnati, O. Died Jan. 1, 1923.

WOTHERSPOON, William Wallace, maj. general U.S.A.; b. Washington, D.C., Nov. 16, 1850; s. Alexander S. and Louisa A. (Kuhn) W.; ed. at pvt. schs.; m. Mary C. Adams, Apr. 27, 1887. Apptd. from D.C., 2d lt. 12th U.S. Inf., Oct. 1, 1873; 1st lt., Mar. 20, 1879; capt., Apr. 28, 1893; maj. 30th Inf., Feb. 2, 1901; transferred to 6th Inf., June 26, 1902; lt. col. 14th Inf., July 12, 1904; transferred to 19th Inf., May 15, 1905; grad. Army War Coll., 1905; brig. gen. U.S.A., Oct. 3, 1907; maj. gen., May 12, 1912. Served on gen. staff, 1905-09; pres. Army War Coll., 1907-09; asst. to chief of staff, May 1909-10; pres. Army War Coll., 1910-12; comdr. Dept. of the Gulf, Atlanta, Jan.-Sept. 1912; asst. to the chief of staff, Sept. 1912-Apr. 1914; chief of staff U.S.A., Apr.-Nov. 1914; retired, Nov. 16, 1914. Home: Albany, N.Y. Died Oct. 21, 1921.

WREN, Christopher, librarian; b. Pottsville, Pa., Aug. 16, 1853; s. John Young and Anne (George) W.; ed. pub. schs.; unmarried. Prothonotory, Luzerne Co., Pa., 1889-1902; fire ins. and real estate business, 1894—; librarian and head curator, Wyoming Hist. and Geol. Soc., Wilkes-Barre, Pa., 1917—. Republican. Presbyn. Lifelong student of Am. archeology. Author: Remains of the Stone Age in Wyoming Valley, and along the Susquehanna River (vol. 8, Wyo. Hist. and Geol. Soc.), 1904; Aboriginal Pottery of the Wyoming Valley Region, 1905; Turtle Shell Rattles from Indian Graves at Athens, Pa., 1909; Some Indian Graves at Plymouth, Pa., 1912; A Study of North Appalachian Indian Pottery, 1914. Home: Wilkes-Barre, Pa. Died 1921.

WREN, Frank George, coll. professor; b. Sharon, Mass., Mar. 15, 1874; s. Edward and Ellen (Devine) W.; A.B., Tufts Coll., 1894, A.M., 1897, L.H.D., 1939; m. Mary Evelyn Ingraham, Sept. 7, 1898; 1 son, Paul Ingraham. Assistant, Tufts College, 1894, instructor, 1895-99, asst. professor, 1899-1904, prof. mathematics, 1904—, dean faculty of arts and sciences and faculty of Coll. of Letters, 1907-39. Home: Tufts College Mass. Died July 17, 1940.

WRENNE, Thomas William, banker, lawyer; b. Rockbridge Co., Va., Dec. 1, 1851; s. John and Margaret (Roche) W.; grad. high sch., Nashville, Tenn., 1870; m. Clara Virginia Hebenstreit, Oct. 7, 1875. Clerk, Chancery Ct., Nashville, 1870; supt., sec., treas. S. Nashville St. R.R., 1875; practiced law, 1878-82; clerk and master, Chancery Ct., and receiver Bank of Tenn., 1882-88; pres. McGavock & Mt. Vernon Horse R.R. Co., 1888-89, during which time electrified road and consolidated several cos. into one and inaugurated transfer system; pres. Nashville Abstract Co., 1889-94; organizer, and pres. Nashville Title Co., 1894-1911; organized 1899, and became pres. Wrenne Banking Co. (now Thomas W. Wrenne & Co.); mgr. southern loan agency Mass. Mut. Life Ins. Co., 1899—. On staffs of Governors Patterson, Rye, Roberts, Taylor and Peay, with rank of col. Mem. City Council, 1877-79, Board of Education, 1879-91. Director Tenn. Centennial Expn. and as v. chmn. reception com. in charge that feature opening exercises of the expn., 1896; dir. Carnegie Library, Nashville; chmn. com. of arrangements in charge reception to President Roosevelt, 1907; exec. officer in charge of exercises under auspices D.A.R. dedicating monument on pub. sq., Nashville, 1910, erected to the memory of soldiers of the Am. Revolution buried in Tenn.; author act establishing Nashville Humane Commission; chmn. com. of arrangements in charge of reception to Lt. Gen. Sir Robert S. S. Baden-Powell, founder of Boy Scouts, on his visit to Nashville, Feb. 1912; mem. Am. Com. for Celebration of 100th Anniversary of Peace Among English-Speaking Peoples, 1914-15; grand marshal in connection with celebration of 100th anniversary of Jackson's victory, in the Battle of Chalmette Plains (New Orleans, Jan. 8, 1914), at Nashville, Tenn., Jan. 8, 1915. First pres. Nashville High Sch. Alumni Assn., 1908 (pres.); pres. 1st Nashville and Tenn. Tuberculosis League. Chmn. mil. com. Davidson Co. (Nashville) Council of Defense, World War. Home: Nashville, Tenn. Died Jan. 10, 1925.

WRIGHT, Albert Allen, prof. geology and zoölogy, Oberlin Coll., 1874—; b. Oberlin, O., Apr. 27, 1846; s. William Wheeler and Susan (Allen) W.; grad. Oberlin, 1865 (A.M., Ph.B., Columbia Coll. School of Mines, 1875); served 100 days, 1864, in Co. K, 150th regt. Ohio Nat. Guard in Washington; m. Mary Lyon Bedortha, Sept. 23, 1874; m. 2d, Mary P. B. Hill, Aug. 18, 1891. Asst. on geol. survey of Ohio 1872 and 1882; teacher in Cleveland, O., Inst., 2 yrs.; Berea Coll., Ky., 3 yrs. Fellow Geol. Soc. of Am.; pres., 1896, Ohio State Acad. of Sciences. Home: Oberlin, O. Died 1905.

WRIGHT, Ammi Willard, capitalist; b. Grafton, Vt., July 5, 1822; s. Nathan Franklin and Mary

(Lamson) W.; ed. common schs.; m. Harriet Barton, Mar. 6, 1848 (died 1884); m. 2d, Anna Case, Dec. 21, 1885. Early yrs. on farm; employed in carrying trade between Rutland, Vt., and Boston, 1844-48; conducted hotel in Boston, 1848-50; went to Detroit, 1850, and to Saginaw, Mich., 1851; became large operator in timber and salt lands, head of A. W. Wright Lumber Co. Now has large real estate holdings in Tex., Mo., and Minn. Pres. Advance Thresher Co., C.S.&M. R.R. Co., Peerless Portland Cement Co.; v.p. Mich. Sugar Co. Has given over $400,000 to Alma (Mich.) Coll., and a home valued at over $150,000 to the Grand Lodge F. and A.M. (Mich.). Republican. Episcopalian. Home: Alma, Mich. Died May 7, 1912.

WRIGHT, Arthur Silas, educator; b. Decatur, N.Y., Mar. 7, 1858; s. Hanson and Fannie M. (Mason) W.; A.B., Union Coll., 1882, A.M., 1886, L.H.D., 1921; Princeton Theol. Sem., 1884-85, U. of Leipzig, 1885-87; m. Julia B. Barhyte, Apr. 2, 1890. Junior prof. modern langs., Union Coll., 1887-92; prof. modern langs., Case Sch. of Applied Science, 1893-1924; retired. Editor: In St. Jürgen (Theodor Storm), 1901; Entwicklungslehre (v. Wagner), 1903; Elektromentheorie (Kayser), 1905; German Science Reader, 1914. Home: Chevy Chase, Md. Died Dec. 2, 1928.

WRIGHT, Arthur Williams, physicist; b. Lebanon, Conn., Sept. 8, 1836; s. Jesse and Harriet (Williams) W.; A.B., Yale, 1859, Ph.D., 1861; admitted to bar, 1866, but did not practice; univs. of Heidelberg and Berlin, 1868-69; m. Susan Forbes, d. Prof. Benjamin Silliman, 2d, of Yale, Oct. 6, 1875. Assisted in preparing revised edit. Webster's Dictionary, 1862-63, and 1890; tutor in Latin, 1863-66, in physics, 1866-68, Yale; instr. physics, Sheffield Scientific Sch. (Yale), 1867-68; prof. physics and chemistry, Williams Coll., 1869-72; prof. molecular physics and chemistry, 1871-87, prof. experimental physics, 1887-1906, prof. emeritus, 1906—, Yale University. In charge of Sloane Physical Laboratory, Yale, built from his plans under his supervision, 1883-1906. Consulting specialist, U.S. Signal Service, 1881-86. Was the first to observe the electric shadow in air; discovered and analyzed gases in stony meteorites; measured polarization of zodiacal light, also of light of moon, solar corona and comets; applied cathode discharge in vacuo to form metallic films for mirrors. Fellow Royal Astron. Soc. of Great Britain. Home: New Haven, Conn. Died Dec. 19, 1915.

WRIGHT, Augustine Washington, civil engr.; b. Chicago, Ill., May 29, 1847; s. John Stephen and Catharine Blackburn (Turner) W.; ed. pub. schs. and under pvt. tutors; m. Natalie Jordan, Jan. 1, 1890. Began in engring. dept. U.P. Ry., 1867; chief engr. and gen. supt. of various rys. until 1879; chief engr. and supt. constrn. North Chicago City Ry., 1879-86; mem. Wright & Meysenburg, consulting engineers, 1886—. Pres. Bd. Pub. Utilities of Los Angeles, 1914—. Republican. Author: American Street Railway Construction and Operation, 1888. Home: Los Angeles, Calif. Died Feb. 3, 1918.

WRIGHT, Austin Tappan, prof. law; b. Hanover, N.H., Aug. 20, 1883; s. John Henry Wright and Mary (Tappan) W.; A.B., Harvard, 1905, LL.B., 1908; studied Oxford U., Eng., 1906-07; m. Margaret Garrad (Stone), Nov. 14, 1912; children—William Austin, Sylvia, Phyllis, Benjamin Tappan. Practiced at Boston, 1908-16; moved to Berkeley, Calif., 1916; prof. law, U. of Calif., 1916-24, except during war period; moved to Phila., 1924; prof. law, U. of Pa., 1924—. Asst. counsel at San Francisco to U.S. Shipping Bd. Emergency Fleet Corp., 1918-19; proctor in admiralty, San Francisco, 1919-24. Democrat. Home: Philadelphia, Pa. Died Sept. 18, 1931.

WRIGHT, Burton Henry, life insurance; b. Killingworth, Conn., Jan. 12, 1859; s. John Burghardt and Rachael Florilla (Stannard) W.; grad. high sch., Clinton, Conn., 1876; m. Margaret McLeod Shepard, Oct. 18, 1892. Life ins. business at Worcester, 1879—; chmn. bd. State Mut. Life Ins. Co., 1927—; dir. Worcester County Nat. Bank, Norwich & Worcester R.R. Co.; trustee Worcester Co. Instn. for Savings. Republican. Episcopalian. Mason. Home: Worcester, Mass. Died Apr. 5, 1933.

WRIGHT, Carroll, lawyer; b. Keosauqua, Ia., Oct. 21, 1854; s. George G. and Hannah M. (Dibble) W.; grad. State Univ. of Iowa, 1875, Simpson Centenary Coll. of Law, Des Moines, Ia., 1878; m. Nellie H. Elliott, June 18, 1879. Admitted to bar, 1878; local atty., 1879-96; from 1896 atty. for Iowa, Minn. and S. Dak., Chicago, Rock Island & Pacific Ry.; sec. Des Moines & Ft. Dodge R.R. Republican. Home: Des Moines, Ia. Died 1911.

WRIGHT, Carroll Davidson, educator, economist, statistician; b. Dunbarton, N.H., July 25, 1840; s. Rev. Nathan R. and Eliza (Clark) W.; academic edn. (A.M., LL.D., Tufts; Ph.D., Dartmouth; LL.D., Wesleyan, Clark, Amherst); served in Civil War, pvt. to col., 14th N.H. Vols.; m. Caroline E. Harnden, Jan. 1, 1867. Mem. Mass. senate, 1872-73; chief Mass. Bureau of Statistics of Labor, 1873-88; U.S. Commr. of Labor, 1885-1905; also, 1893-97, completed 11th U.S. Census. Hon. prof. social economics, Catholic Univ. of America, 1895-1904; prof. statistics and social economics, School of Comparative Jurisprudence and Diplomacy, Columbian Univ., 1900; univ. lecturer on wage statistics, Harvard Univ., 1900-01; pres. Clark Coll., Worcester, Mass., 1902—; pres. A.A.A.S., 1903. Apptd. by President mem. and recorder U.S. Anthracite Strike Commn., 1902. Mem. bd. trustees Carnegie Instn. (Washington). Author: The Factory System of the United States, 1880; Relation of Political Economy to the Labor Question, 1882; The Industrial Evolution of the United States, 1887; Outline of Practical Sociology, 1899; Battles of Labor, 1906; also History and Growth of the United States Census; 23 vols. of statist. reps. of the Mass. Bureau of Statistics of Labor, and 28 annual and spl. reps. of the U.S. Dept. of Labor. Decorated with Cross of Legion of Honor, France, 1907. Home: Worcester, Mass. Died 1909.

WRIGHT, Charles Jefferson, president mil. acad.; b. St. Johnsbury, Vt., Oct. 21, 1839; g.g.s. Benjamin W., Minute Man who fought through Revolution; A.B., Hobart Coll., 1861; m. Margaret Worrall Bard, 1869. Entered Union Army in 16th N.H. Vols., 1861; bvtd. col., Mar. 13, 1865, "for gallant and meritorious services during war"; was severely wounded at Ft. Fisher and Petersburg. Prin. Peekskill, N.Y., Mil. Acad., 1872-87; was pres. N.Y. Mil. Acad., Cornwall, N.Y.; became pres. Matawan Mil. Acad. G.A.R. Home: Matawan, N.J. Died 1910.

WRIGHT, Cyrus Mansfield, dentist; b. Cincinnati, Feb. 18, 1842; s. Cyrus and Roxana (Bean) W.; B.S., Miami U., 1860, A.M., 1884; D.D.S., Ohio Coll. Dental Surgery, 1867; m. Mary Julia Tanner, Nov. 1870. Practiced at Cincinnati, 1863-72, Basel, Switzerland, 1872-82; prof. physiology and pathology, Ohio Coll. Dental Surgery, 1883—. Pres. Am. Dental Soc. of Europe, 1876, Miss. Valley Dental Soc., 1883-84, Ohio State Dental Soc., 1888. Home: Cincinnati, O. Died 1911.

WRIGHT, Edward Bingham, clergyman; b. Hudson, O., May 11, 1838; s. Philo and Electa E. (Coe) W.; (had 4 great-grandfathers in Revolutionary War); A.B., Western Reserve, 1859, A.M., 1862 (D.D., 1876); grad. Union Theol. Sem., New York, 1867; m. Evelyn Hunter Bell, Mar. 5, 1878 (died 1904). Ordained Presbyn. ministry, 1867; pastor Stillwater, Minn., 1867-72, 1st Presbyn. Ch., Austin, Tex., 1872-1907, emeritus. Served as 2d lt., 1st lt. and capt., Battery B, 1st Mich. Light Arty., 1862-65; desperately wounded nr. Resaca, Ga., May 16, 1864. Apptd. by Pres. Grant as mem. bd. visitors to Red Lake and Pembina Indians, 1870. Hon. mem. John B. Hood Camp U.C.V., for services to the Confederate Home Austin; mem. S.A.R., Loyal Legion. Republican. Home: Austin, Tex. Died Jan. 4, 1914.

WRIGHT, Edward Everett, commodore U.S.N.; b. E. Bridgewater, Mass., Sept. 9, 1856; s. George Allen and Hannah (Litchfield) W.; grad. U.S. Naval Acad., 1877; m. Katherine Davis, Dec. 10, 1886 (died 1911). Promoted through the various grades to capt.; retired, July 1, 1910, with rank of commodore. Served on bd. Swatara, and Powhatan, N. Atlantic sta., 1877-79; Swatara and Monocacy, Asiatic sta., 1879-82; training sta., Newport, R.I., 1882-84; U.S. Coast Survey, 1884-87; Swatara and Alliance, S. Atlantic sta. and Yantic and Galena, N. Atlantic sta., 1887-90; Navy Yard, Boston, 1890-93; Newark, S. Atlantic Sta., 1893-96; Wabash, and Navy Yard, Boston, 1896-97; on bd. Minneapolis, Flying Squadron, Spanish War, 1898; Essex, apprentice training ship, 1898-1901; Navy Yard, Boston, 1901-03; Atlanta and Brooklyn, S. Atlantic Sta., 1903-05; comdg. prison ship Southery, Navy Yard, Portsmouth, N.H., 1905-06; insp. 2d lighthouse dist., Boston, 1906-07; comdg. flagship Rainbow and Chattanooga, Philippine Sta., 1907-09; capt. of yard, Navy Yard, Phila. and comdt. U.S. Naval Sta., Guantanamo Cuba, 1909-10; comdt. Naval Sta., Guantanamo Cuba, Sept. 4, 1917-Dec. 18, 1918. Home: Newton Center, Mass. Died Nov. 23, 1921.

WRIGHT, Francis Marion, judge; b. Brier Ridge Farm, Adams Co., Ohio, Aug. 5, 1844; s. James and Elizabeth (Copple) W.; Ohio Valley Acad., Decatur, O.; LL.B., Cincinnati Law College, 1867; m. Elizabeth West, July 15, 1868. Enlisted pvt. Co. I, 39th Ohio Vols., June 1861; mustered out as 2d lt., same regt., July 9, 1865. Admitted to bar in Cincinnati, 1867; practiced law in Georgetown, Brown Co., O., until Dec. 1868, Urbana, Ill., until 1891; judge 4th Jud. Circuit of Ill., 1891-97; judge of Appellate Ct. of Ill., 1897-1903; judge U.S. Ct. of Claims, Washington, 1903-05; U.S. dist. judge, Eastern Dist., Ill., Mar. 17, 1905—. Republican. Methodist. Home: Urbana, Ill. Died July 15, 1917.

WRIGHT, George Bohan, retired ry. official; b. nr. Granville, O., Dec. 11, 1815; s. Spencer and Abbie (Cooley) W.; ed. Western Reserve Univ. and Ohio Univ. (class of 1840); left in senior yr.; m. Hetta A. Taylor, 1846 (died 1888). Admitted to bar April 1843; practiced at Newark, O., until 1856; after that devoted to ry. interests; was interested in Central Ohio, Steubenville & Ind., Newark, Somerset & Straitsville, and Sandusky, Mansfield & Newark Rys.; receiver and gen. mgr. latter, 1857-61; served in q.m. dept., Ohio, equipping Ohio soldiers for service, as asst. q.m. and q.m. gen. until Jan. 1864; apptd. mil. storekeeper by President Lincoln; apptd. col. 106th Ohio Vol. Inf., but Sec. Stanton objected to his leaving the service at Columbus and detailed him to that duty; resigned from mil. service, 1864; first commr. railroads and telegraphs, Ohio, 1867-71; v.p. Atlantic & Great Western R.R. Co., 1870; later receiver Indianapolis, Bloomington & Western R.R. Co. until 1887; became then resident of Columbus. Home: Columbus, O. Died 1903.

WRIGHT, George E., lawyer; b. Brookline, N.H., Jan. 20, 1867; s. William and Eliza Annah (Elliot) W.; grad. Lawrence Acad., 1884, Phillips Exeter Acad., 1885; A.B., Harvard, 1889, A.M., 1892; LL.B., Harvard Law Sch., 1892; m. Mary Estelle Wyckoff, July 16, 1895. Practiced at Seattle, 1893—; mem. Condon & Wright, 1893-97, Wright & Kelleher, 1897-12, Wright, Kelleher & Caldwell, 1912-16, Wright, Kelleher & Allen, 1916—. Pres. Seattle Pub. Library, Seattle Bar Assn., Municipal League of Seattle. Democrat. Conglist. Home: Seattle, Wash. Died Oct. 10, 1923.

WRIGHT, George Frederick, educator; b. Whitehall, N.Y., Jan. 22, 1838; s. Walter and Mary Peabody (Colburn) W.; A.B., Oberlin, 1859, A.M., 1862; grad. Oberlin Theol. Sem., 1862; (D.D., Brown U., 1887; LL.D., Drury, 1887; F.G.S.A., 1890); soldier in U.S.A. 5 months in 1861; m. Huldah Maria Day, Aug. 28, 1862 (died 1899); m. 2d, Florence Eleanor Bedford, Sept. 22, 1904. Pastor Congl. Ch., Bakersfield, Vt., 1861-72, Andover, Mass., 1872-81; prof. N.T. lang and lit., Oberlin Theol. Sem., 1881-92, of the harmony of science and religion, 1892-1907, prof. emeritus retired on Carnegie pension, 1907. Asst. geologist Pa. Survey, 1881-82, U.S. Survey, 1884-92; pres. Ohio Hist. and Archæol. Soc., 1907-18. Author: Logic of Christian Evidences, 1880; Studies in Science and Religion, 1882; The Divine Authority of the Bible, 1884; Ice Age in North America, 1889, 5th enlarged and revised edit., 1911; Charles Grandison Finney, 1891; Scientific Aspects of Christian Evidences, 1898; Asiatic Russia (2 vols.), 1902; Scientific Confirmations of Old Testament History, 1906; Origin and Antiquity of Man, 1912; See Ohio First, 1915; Story of My Life and Work, 1916. Editor Bibliotheca Sacra, 1884—, and Records o the Past, 1905-13. Home: Oberlin, O. Died Apr. 20 1921.

WRIGHT, Gilbert G.; b. Ogden, Utah, Sept. 28, 1866; s. Gilbert Josiah and Annie Sarah (Odell) W.; ed. dist. sch.; m. Tillie E. Bailey, Apr. 11, 1890; children—Gilbert O., Florence A. (wife of Dr. J. J. Bybee), Sheldon B., Joseph O. Pres. Idaho Falls Mill and Elevator Co., Dinwoodey Furniture Co. (Idaho Falls), Idaho Falls Post Office Bldg. Co., Rexburg Drug Co., and Anderson Bros. Bank (both Idaho Falls); head G. G. Wright Loan and Investment Co., Idaho Falls; was chmn. bd. Salt Lake City Br. Federal Reserve Bank of San Francisco; also officer and dir. of many corps. Served as chmn. Council of Defense and Liberty Loan drive, World War. Mormon. Republican. Elk. Home: Idaho Falls, Ida. Died Apr. 9, 1933.

WRIGHT, Hamilton; b. Cleveland, O., Aug. 2, 1867; s. Robert and Elizabeth (Wyse) W.; preparatory education at Boston, Mass.; M.D., C.M., first class honors, McGill U., Montreal, 1895; med. registrar and neuropathologist, Royal Victoria Hosp., Montreal; studied tropical conditions, etc., in China and Japan, 1895-96; John Lucas Walker exhibitioner, Cambridge U., Eng.; asst. dir., London Co. Labs., and at Heidelberg and other continental univs., 1897-98; hon. fellow pathology, Johns Hopkins, 1903-04; m. Elizabeth, d. late Senator William Drew Washburn, of Minn., Nov. 22, 1899. Dir. dept. med. research, Federated Malay States and Straits Settlements, 1899-1903; chmn. Port Swettenham Sanitary Commn.; research work U.S. and Europe, 1903-08; apptd. U.S. commr., 1908, and acting chmn. and Am. del. Internat. Opium Commn., Shanghai, China, 1909; with Dept. State in charge of preparations for Internat. Opium Conf., The Hague, Dec. 1911 (acting chmn. and Am. delegate to same); continued in charge of efforts of U.S. Govt. to solve opium problem, and was chmn. of Am. delegation to 2d Internat. Opium Conf., The Hague, July 1-9, 1913; in charge, on behalf of U.S., of preparations for 3d Internat. Opium Conf., held at The Hague, June 1914; secured passage of 4 acts aiming to suppress abuse of narcotics in U.S. and its possessions and an act to prevent citizens of U.S. from engaging in trade in narcotics in China; engaged in relief work in France, 1915. Home: Washington, D.C. Died Jan. 9, 1917.

WRIGHT, Henry Burt, college prof.; b. New Haven, Conn., Jan. 29, 1877; s. Henry Parks and Martha Elizabeth (Burt) W.; B.A., Yale, 1898, Ph.D., 1903; Univ. of Berlin, Germany, 1907-08, U. of Grenoble, France, 1911; m. Josephine Lemira Hayward, July 24, 1907. Tutor Greek and Latin, 1903-06, instr., 1906-07, asst. prof. Roman history and Latin lit., 1908-11, asst. prof. history, 1911-14; Stephen Merrell Clement prof. Christian methods, 1914—. Yale U. Author: Two Centuries of Christia

Activity at Yale, 1901; The Campaign of Plataea, 479 B.C., 1904; A Life With a Purpose, 1908; The Will of God and a Man's Life Work, 1909; The Recovery of a Lost Roman Tragedy, 1910; The Practice of Friendship in Army and Navy, 1918; Personal Evangelism Among Students, 1920. Army Y.M.C.A. sec. at Plattsburg, and Camp Devens, 1917-19. Home: New Haven, Conn. Died Dec. 27, 1923.

WRIGHT, Henry Collier, sociologist; b. LeRoy, O., Aug. 29, 1868; s. George Cole and Maria (Collier) W.; A.B., Ohio Wesleyan U., 1892; post-grad. work Harvard; Ph.D., Boston U., 1900; m. Corrine Blose, June 2, 1906; children—Helen, Isabel, Ann and Collier (twins). Dir. Citizens Party, Cincinnati, O., 1903-05; sec. City Club, New York, 1905-07; investigator for the Russell Sage Foundation, 1907-10; spl. investigator, N.Y. City, 1910-13; first dep. commr., Dept. Pub. Charities, N.Y. City, 1914-17; trustee Dept. of Bellevue and Allied hosps.; trustee United Hosp. Fund, New York; pres. Queensboro Tuberculosis Assn. Democrat. Methodist. Author: Bossism in Cincinnati, 1906; Fiscal Control of State Institutions, 1910; Hospital Inquiry, 1913; The American City, 1915; Fiscal Policies of the State of Pennsylvania as Related to Its Institutions, 1922; Cripples in New York City, 1920; Cripples in New York State, 1925; Cripples in New Jersey, 1928. Home: Douglas Manor, N.Y. Died Oct. 24, 1935.

WRIGHT, Henry John, newspaperman; b. Glasgow, Scotland, Apr. 6, 1866; s. John and Mary (Hall) W.; B.S., New York U., 1885; m. Claire Le Franc, Dec. 17, 1891; m. 2d, Margaret E. Beacham, June 21, 1906. Reporter, 1885-89, city editor, 1889-91, Commercial Advertiser, New York; city editor Evening Post, 1891-97; editor New York Globe and Commercial Advertiser, 1897-1923; asso. with Sun and Globe. Home: Montclair, N.J. Died Mar. 8, 1935.

WRIGHT, Henry Parks, educator; b. Winchester, N.H., Nov. 30, 1839; s. Parks and Relief W. (Woolley) W.; served in 51st Mass. Inf. in Civil War; A.B., Yale, 1868, A.M., 1871, Ph.D., 1876; univs. of Göttingen and Berlin, 1878-79 (LL.D., Union, 1895); m. Martha E. Burt, July 7, 1874. Teacher Chickering Inst., Cincinnati, 1868-69; tutor, 1870-71, asst. prof. Latin, 1871-76, prof., 1876-1909, dean, 1884-1909, Yale; retired. Author: Satires of Juvenal, 1901; Fobes Memorial, 1909; From School Through College, 1911; Soldiers of Oakham, Mass., 1914; History of Class of 1868, Yale College, 1914. Home: New Haven, Conn. Died Mar. 17, 1918.

WRIGHT, James Franklin, humanitarian; b. Muscatine, Ia., Mar. 6, 1862; s. William Henry and Martha Jane (Bean) W.; ed. pub. sch.; m. Martha Jane Henninger, Sept. 19, 1883; children—Lawrence Blaine, Leota Catherine (Mrs. Harry Walter Helberg, Dec.), Helen May (dec.). Successively engine wiper, brakeman, switchman and yardmaster, C.,M.&St.P. R.R., Davenport, Ia., 1878-91; gen. agt. Equitable Life Assurance Soc. of New York, Davenport, 1891-1906; developing and marketing inventions, 1906-14. Founder, organizer, 1914, and from then exec. sec. and leader of Pathfinders of America (a philanthropic ednl. orgn.). Mason. Degree of D.C.S. ("Doctor of Common Sense") was voted by prisoners in 1927. Home: Detroit, Mich. Died Sept. 8, 1940.

WRIGHT, James Homer, pathologist; b. Pittsburgh, Apr. 8, 1869; s. Homer and Sarah L. (Gray) W.; A.B., Johns Hopkins, 1890; M.D., U. of Md., 1892; Thomas A. Scott fellow in hygiene, 1892-93, Harvard, A.M., 1895, hon. S.D., 1905; Sc.D., U. of Mo., 1907; m. Aagot Lunde, Dec. 25, 1901. Asst. in pathology, 1893-96, instr., 1896-1907, asst. prof., 1907—, Harvard; consulting pathologist, Mass. Gen. Hosp., 1925—. Author: (with Dr. F. B. Mallory) Pathological Technique (8 edits.), 1897. Home: Boston, Mass. Died Jan. 3, 1928.

WRIGHT, John, clergyman; b. Wilmington, Del., Nov. 20, 1836; s. John and Ann (Hendrickson) W.; grad. Hyatt's Mil. Acad., Wilmington, Del., 1858; A.B., Union Coll., 1863, A.M., 1866; Union Theol. Sem., New York, 1866; (D.D., Union Univ., 1890; LL.D., Illinois Coll., 1905; Litt.D., Macalester Coll., 1914); m. Mary Evelyn Howell, June 18, 1885. Deacon, 1866, priest, 1867, P.E. Ch.; asst. St. Andrew's Ch., Phila., 1866; in charge St. Andrew's Chapel, Phila., 1867-69; rector Trinity Church, Bay City, Mich., 1869-74, St. Matthew's, Boston, 1874-87, St. Paul's, St. Paul, Minn., 1887-1914, emeritus rector, 1914. Visited Egypt several times, and is specialist and lecturer on Egyptology; also specialist in Am. bibliography with reference to early bibles and prayer-books. Fellow Soc. Science, Art and Lit., Soc. Bibl. Archæology, Minn. Hist. Soc. Author: Early Bibles of America, 1894; Early Prayer Books of America, 1896; Prayers for Priest and People, 1898; Restoration of the Reservation of the Blessed Sacrament for the Sick, 1904; Historic Bibles in America, 1906; Some Notable Altars in the Church of England and the American Episcopal Church, 1908. Home: St. Paul, Minn. Died Dec. 24, 1919.

WRIGHT, John Bittinger, lawyer; b. Denver, Colo., Jan. 29, 1872; s. Charles Weston and Harriet Sophia (Pfontz) W.; LL B., U. of Mich., 1894; m. Mary P. McPhee, Oct. 12, 1897; children—Charles M., Jean M. (Mrs. Harry J. Blake), Sallie Angel (Mrs. Richard P. Grover), Elizabeth M. Admitted to Ariz. bar, 1894, and began practice at Tucson; county atty. Yuma Co., Ariz., 1896-98; atty. gen. of Ariz., 1909-12; U.S. dist. atty., by apptmt. of President Coolidge, 1925-29. Mem. School Board, Tucson, 9½ years. Republican. Catholic. Elk. Home: Tucson, Ariz. Deceased.

WRIGHT, John Henry, prof. Greek, 1887—, and dean of Graduate School, Harvard, 1895—; b. Urumyah, Persia, Feb. 4, 1852; s. Rev. Austin Hazen W. (missionary in Persia, 1840-65) and Catherine (Myers) W.; ed. College Hill, Poughkeepsie, 1862-69; grad. Dartmouth Coll., 1873, A.M., 1876; LL.D., 1901 (LL.D., Western Reserve, 1901); student classical philology and Sanskrit, Leipzig Univ., 1876-78; m. Mary, d. Pres. Eli Todd Tappan of Kenyon Coll., Apr. 2, 1879. Asst. prof. ancient languages (Greek and Latin) Ohio Agrl. and Mech. Coll. (Ohio State Univ.), 1873-76; asso. prof. Greek, Dartmouth Coll., 1878-86; dean collegiate bd. (1886) and prof. classical philology, Johns Hopkins, 1886-87; prof. Am. Sch. of Classical Studies, Athens, 1906-07. Fellow Am. Acad. Arts and Sciences. Editor: M. Collignon's Manual of Greek Archæology, 1886; A History of All Nations, 24 vols., 1902; co-editor, with B. Perrin and A. F. West, of the Classical Section of the Twentieth Century Text-books. Editor-in-chief Am. Jour. of Archæology, 1897-1906; asso. editor The Classical Review, 1888-1906, the Classical Quarterly, 1907—. Home: Cambridge, Mass. Died 1908.

WRIGHT, J(ohn) Montgomery, marshal Supreme Ct. of U.S.; b. Madison Barracks, N.Y.; s. Gen. George (U.S.A.) and Margaret Wallace (Forster) W.; ed. U.S. Mil. Acad., 1859-61; capt. and maj. a.a.g. vols., 1861-65; LL.B., U. of Louisville, 1866; m. Nelly Butler Ewing. Mem. Ky. Legislature, 1871-75; adj. gen. Ky., 1875-79; editorial writer Louisville Courier-Journal, 3 yrs.; supt. Louisville Bd. of Trade, 1879-83; pres. and gen. mgr. Southern Expn., Louisville, 1883; marshal Supreme Ct. of U.S., Jan. 4, 1888—. Pres. Pendennis Club, Louisville, 3 yrs. Died Jan. 2, 1915.

WRIGHT, John Vines, lawyer; b. Purdy, Tenn., June 28, 1828; s. Capt. Benjamin W., U.S.A.; ed. Purdy and attended session of Univ. of Ky., Louisville; studied med. jurisprudence preparatory for law, taking whole med. course at Louisville; m. Georgia Hays, Nov. 23, 1858. Admitted to bar, 1852; defeated for mem. legislature, 1853, by one vote; mem. Congress, 1855-61. Entered 13th Tenn. regt., C.S.A.; elected capt. of co. and col. of regt.; was at battle of Belmont and had horse killed under him; served in army until elected mem. Confederate Congress, and served until surrender of Confederacy. After war, judge circuit court; chancellor and judge Supreme Court, Tenn.; chmn. Northwest Indian Commn., 1886-87; made more treaties with Indians than any other living man; also mem. commn. to Great Sioux Nation; nominated for gov. Tenn., 1880, but defeated by defection of faction of Democrats favoring repudiation of State bonds—Republican being elected. Is now in legal dept. of Gen. Land Office, Washington. Died 1908.

WRIGHT, John Wells, mfr.; b. Rosendale, Wis., Feb. 13, 1868; s. Wells and Maritta (Tuttle) W.; Ripon (Wis.) Coll., 1887-89; A.B., Oberlin, 1891; m. Anne Hasselline, 1894. With Ripon Knitting Works, 1891—, pres., 1919—; v.p. First Nat. Bank. Trustee and treas. Ripon Coll. Conglist. Mason. Home: Ripon, Wis. Died Nov. 8, 1937.

WRIGHT, John Westley, ophthalmologist; b. Freeport, O., July 17, 1842; s. Benjamin and Lucinda (Rager) W.; M.Sc., New Market (later Scio, now Mt. Union) Coll., 1872, A.M., 1891; M.D., Cincinnati Coll. Medicine and Surgery, 1873; m. Elizabeth A. Hesket, Aug. 9, 1864 (died 1892); children—Frances Neva, Nellie Corina, John Hesket, Halstead Robert (dec.), Columbus Clinton (dec.), Anna Lucinda (dec.); m. 2d, Balzurah Conrow, July 25, 1893 (died 1913). In practice as oculist at Columbus, 1880—; prof. ophthalmology, Ohio Med. U. and Starling-Ohio Med. Coll., 1891-1910 (emeritus prof. med. dept. Ohio State U.); one of incorporators of Ohio Med. U. and Protestant Hosp. Fellow A.M.A., Am. Acad. Medicine, Am. Acad. Ophthalmology and Oto-laryngology. Author: Text-book of Ophthalmology, 1896, 1900, 1909. Home: Columbus, O. Deceased.

WRIGHT, J(oshua) Butler, diplomatic service; b. Irvington-on-Hudson, N.Y., Oct. 18, 1877; s. Louis Bogert and Caroline Isabel (Richards) W.; B.S., Princeton, 1899; m. Maude A., d. Christopher Wolfe, N.Y., June 2, 1902; 1 son, Joshua Butler (dec.); m. 2d, Harriet Rodman, d. Rear Adm. W. H. H. Southerland, U.S.N., May 27, 1916; children—Mary Caroline, Edith Southerland. Banking, N.Y. City, 6 yrs.; agr. and stock raising, Wyo., 2 yrs.; sec. Am. Legation, Tegucigalpa, Honduras, 1909-12; apptd. sec. Legation and consul gen. to Rumania, Serbia and Bulgaria, but did not go to post; assigned spl. duty at Dept. of State; sec. Am. Legation, Brussels, Belgium, 1912-13, and served as sec. Am. delegation to Opium Conf., at The Hague, 1913; sec. Embassy, Rio de Janeiro, Brazil, 1913-15; assigned as actg. chief Div. of Latin-Am. Affairs, 1915; counselor of Embassy, at Petrograd, Russia, 1916; assigned to Dept. of State, 1918; counselor Embassy, London, 1918-21. Expert asst. to the Am. commrs. at Conference on Limitation of Armament, 1921; U.S. commr. to Brazilian Centennial Expn., Rio de Janeiro, 1922; sec. of U.S. delegation to 5th Internat. Conf. of Am. States, Santiago, Chile, Mar.-May 1923; 3d asst. sec. of state, Jan. 30, 1923-July 1, 1924; asst. sec. of state, 1924-27; minister to Hungary, 1927-30, to Uruguay, 1930-34; to Czechoslovakia, 1934-37; ambassador to Cuba, July 1937—. Del. of U.S. to VII Internat. Conf. of Am. States, Montevideo, 1933. Fellow Am. Geog. Soc. Episcopalian. Died Dec. 4, 1939.

WRIGHT, Julia MacNair, author; b. (MacNair) Oswego, N.Y., May 1, 1840; academic and private edn.; m. William Janes Wright, 1859. Received medal and diploma from World's Columbian Expn. for literary work. Author: Seaside and Wayside Readers; The Complete Home: Early Church in Britain; Bricks from Babel; Saints and Sinners of the Bible; Almost a Nun; Priest and Nun; The Gospel in the Riviera; A Wife Hard Won; The Sun and His Family; The Story of Plant Life; The Field of Fortune; Tales for the New Century; The Heir of Athole. Home: Fulton, Mo. Died 1903.

WRIGHT, Julian May, judge; b. Douglaston, L.I., N.Y., Feb. 12, 1884; s. William Merritt and Carolyn Kane (May) W.; student Mass. Inst. Tech., 1903-07, N.Y. Law Sch., 1909-12; m. Alda de Almeida Santos, of Lisbon, Portugal, Aug. 20, 1928; 1 daughter, Carol Frances. Naval architect New York Shipbuilding Co., Camden, N.J., 1907-09; admitted to N.Y. bar, 1912; with law firm O'Brien, Boardman & Platt, N.Y. City, 1909-15; mem. Ehlerman, Wright & Abbott, 1915-19; mem. Wright & Hill, Paris, France, 1920-30; judge Mixed Court, Cairo, Egypt, 1930—. Deceased.

WRIGHT, Luke E., secretary of war; b. in Tenn., 1846; s. Hon. Archibald W. (chief justice of Tenn.); read law, and admitted to Tennessee bar; (LL.D., Hamilton, 1903); m. Kate, d. Admiral Semmes, C.S.N. Had 3 sons in service during Spanish-Am. War, 1898. Practiced law at Memphis; atty. gen. of Tenn., 8 yrs.; active in relief measures during yellow fever scourge, 1878. Mem. U.S. Philippine Commn., 1900-04 (pres. 1903-04); apptd. civil gov. of P.I., 1904, gov. gen. until 1906; ambassador extraordinary and plenipotentiary to Japan, 1906-07, resigned; sec. of war, U.S., in cabinet of President Roosevelt, July 1, 1908-Mar. 1909. Gold Democrat. Home: Memphis, Tenn. Died Nov. 17, 1922.

WRIGHT, Luther Lamphear, teacher; b. Canton, N.Y., Jan. 18, 1856; s. John H. and Mary (Stinson) W.; A.B., Ripon (Wis.) Coll., 1877; (hon. A.M., U. of Mich., 1908); m. Helen Corning, Apr. 21, 1880. Co. supt. schs., Waupaca Co., Wis., 1877-81; supt. city schs., Waupaca, 1881-87, Ironwood, Mich., 1887-1906; co. commr. schs., Gogebic Co., Mich., 1894-1906; supt. pub. instrn., Mich., 1907-13; supt. Mich. Sch. for the Deaf, Flint, 1913—. Republican. Trustee Ripon Coll. Mem. Council N.E.A. Mason. Home: Flint, Mich. Deceased.

WRIGHT, Mabel Osgood, author; b. New York, Jan. 26, 1859; d. Rev. Samuel and Ellen Haswell (Murdock) Osgood; m. James Osborne Wright, of Bristol, Eng., Sept. 25, 1884 (died 1920). President from organization, 1898, of the Audubon Soc. of State of Conn., now emeritus; mem. Am. Ornithologists' Union, Conn. Soc. Colonial Dames. Author: The Friendship of Nature (series of outdoor studies), 1894; Birdcraft (field-book of N.E. birds), 1895; Tommy-Anne and the Three Hearts—a Natural History Story, 1896; Citizen Bird (with Dr. Coues), 1897; Four-footed Americans and Their Kin, 1898; Wabeno the Magician, 1899; The Dream Fox Story Book, 1900; The Flowers and Ferns in Their Haunts, 1901; Dogtown, 1902; Aunt Jimmy's Will, 1903; (also anonymously) The Garden of a Commuter's Wife, 1902; People of the Whirlpool, 1903; The Woman Errant, 1904; At the Sign of the Fox, 1905; The Garden, You and I, 1906; Gray Lady and the Birds, 1907; The Open Window, 1908; Poppea of the Post Office, 1909; Princess Flower Hat, 1910; The Love That Lives, 1911; The Stranger at the Gate, 1913; The Hymn of the Flag, Soldier Marching Song, 1917; My New York, 1926; Captains of The Watch, 1927; Eudor's Men, 1931. Dir. Birdcraft Sanctuary. Home: Fairfield, Conn. Died July 21, 1934.

WRIGHT, Marcus Joseph, agent War Dept. for Collection of Mil. Records, from 1878; b. Purdy, Tenn., June 5, 1831; s. Capt. Benjamin and Martha Ann (Hicks) Harwell W.; ed. common sch. and acad.; practiced law, Tenn. Entered C.S.A., May 1861, as lt. col. 154th sr. Tennessee Inf.; promoted brig. gen., 1862; wounded at Shiloh; m. Martha Spencer Elcan; 2d, Pauline Womack. Author: Life of Gen. Winfield Scott (in Appleton's "Great Commander" Series), 1894. Co-author: Memoirs of Robert E. Lee (with Gen. A. L. Long), 1886; Library of American History, 1900; General Officers of the Confederate Army; Col. David Crockett, of Tenn.;

Sketch of Life of Gen. John Peter Muhlenberg; The Social Evolution of Woman; Official Portfolio of War and Nation; Tennessee in the War of 1861-65; Official and Illustrated War Record; Analytical Reference, 1904. Home: Washington, D.C. Deceased.

WRIGHT, Marie Robinson, author; b. Newnan, Ga.; d. of the Hon. John E. and S. A. Robinson; m. Hinton P. Wright (dec.). After husband's death began travels and lit. work; commr. from Ga. to Paris Expn., 1889 (the first woman to receive such an appmt.). Has made spl. study of Spanish America; traveled 2,000 miles on muleback in Mexico and Bolivia and 3 times across S. Am. Continent, having made the record trip over the Andes in 1904. Special del. Geog. Soc. of Brazil to Centennial Celebration of Mex., 1910. Author: Picturesque Mexico, 1897; The New Brazil, 1901, revised edit., 1907; The Republic of Chile, 1904; Bolivia, 1907; The Old and New Peru, 1909. Home: New Rochelle, N.Y. Died Feb. 1, 1914.

WRIGHT, Mary Tappan, author; b. Steubenville, O., Dec. 1851; d. Pres. Eli Todd Tappan of Kenyon Coll. and Lydia (McDowell) Tappan; m. Prof. John Henry Wright, Apr. 2, 1879 (died 1908). Author: A Truce, and Other Stories, 1895; Aliens, 1902; The Test, 1904; The Tower, 1906; Charioteers, 1912. Home: Cambridge, Mass. Deceased.

WRIGHT, Maurice Lauchlin, judge; b. Oswego Co., N.Y., Nov. 27, 1845; s. David Parks and Betsey (Woodworth) W.; ed. Falley Sem., Fulton, N.Y., and Mexico (N.Y.) Acad., 1861-64; returned to Mexico Academy after war; LL.B., Columbian (now George Washington) U., 1870;; m. Mary Grace, d. Judge Avery Skinner, of Union Square, N.Y., Nov. 3, 1869. Enlisted in U.S.N., 1864; yeoman U.S. gunboat Valley City, was in Roanoke Expdn. following the sinking of the ram Albemarl by Cushing, and in several engagements. Admitted to D.C. bar, June 1, 1870, N.Y. bar May 1872; co. judge, Oswego Co., N.Y., 1883-92; mem. Constl. Commn., 1890; judge Supreme Ct. of N.Y., 1891-1905. Republican. Mem. G.A.R. Home: Oswego, N.Y. Died 1911.

WRIGHT, Milton, bishop; b. Rush Co., Ind., Nov. 17, 1828; s. Dan and Catharine (Reeder) W.; ed. common schs. and Hartsville College, Ind.; m. Susan Catharine Koerner, Nov. 24, 1859 (died 1889); father of Orville and the late Wilbur Wright. Ordained U.B. ministry, 1856; served at Indianapolis, Ind., and in Andersonville (Ind.) circuit, 1855-57; sent as missionary to Oregon, 1857, where acted as prin. Sublimity Coll. 2 yrs. and had charge of Marion circuit and Calipooia mission; returned to Ind., 1859; was presiding elder; taught theology, Hartsville Coll., 1868; editor Religious Telescope, 1869-77; bishop, 1877-1905 (voluntarily retired at age of 77). Traveled extensively in work of the ch.; presided at many confs. of the ch.; for many yrs. trustee Union Bible. Sem. (Dayton, O.), and Hartsville Coll. Was mem. Liberty party, 1852, later Republican. Home: Dayton, O. Died Apr. 4, 1917.

WRIGHT, Nathaniel Curwin, journalist; b. Crawford Co., Pa., Aug. 11, 1869; s. Nathaniel Webster and Olive (Bennett) W.; ed. DePauw U., Ind., and pvt. tutors, Chicago. Reporter, editorial writer, asst. city editor, Chicago Daily News, 1890-92; commercial editor, staff corr., Chicago city editor, night mgr. central div., day mgr. Chicago, war corr. in dispatch boat service, Spanish-Am. War, 1893-1900, Associated Press; mng. editor Indianapolis Sentinel, 1900-03; editor and pub. Indianapolis Journal, 1903-04; mng. editor, 1904, editor-in-chief, 1905-13, Cleveland Leader, and pres. Cleveland Leader Printing Co., Feb. 21, 1907-Jan. 1, 1913; publisher Toledo Blade, July 1, 1908—; pres. and editor Newark (N.J.) Star Eagle, Feb. 1, 1916—, and of Detroit (Mich.) Journal, Feb. 1, 1917—. Died May 12, 1923.

WRIGHT, Robert Clinton, ry. official; b. Rio de Janeiro, Brazil, Dec. 5, 1869; s. Joseph Maxwell W. (Am. citizen) and Charlotte W., d. Admiral Charles H. Poor, U.S.N.; brought to U.S. at 18 months; A.B., Baltimore City Coll., 1887; m. Sallie Howard Murdoch, Nov. 10, 1898. Messenger, clk. and spl. agent, Northern Central Ry., Baltimore, 1888-97; soliciting agt. Star Union Line, 1897-99; spl. agt. transportation dept., Pa. R.R., at Phila., Jan. 1, 1899; successively with same rd., div. freight agt., Altoona, 1899-1901, Harrisburg, 1901-03; asst. gen. freight agent, Phila., 1903-06, gen. freight agt., 1906-12; freight traffic mgr., same rd., May 8, 1912-16, traffic mgr. Pa. R.R., May 1, 1916, gen. traffic mgr. Pa. System, Mar. 1, 1920—. Asst. dir. of traffic U.S.R.R. Administration, Feb. 4, 1918-Feb. 1920. Democrat. Home: Haverford, Pa. Died Dec. 6, 1924.

WRIGHT, Robert Herring, teacher; b. Parkersburg, N.C., May 21, 1870; s. John C. and Betty Vaiden (Herring) W.; pub. and subscription schs. and Oak Ridge (N.C.) Inst.; B.S., U. of N.C., 1897; Johns Hopkins U., 1901-02; m. Pearl Murphy, Dec. 31, 1902; children—Pearl Murphy, Robert Herring, Mary, William Alderman. Teacher pub. schs. of N.C. and S.C., 1891-94, Oak Ridge Inst., 1898-1901; head of dept. of history, civics and economics, Baltimore City Coll., 1903-06; prin. Eastern High Sch., Baltimore, 1906-09; 1st pres. E. Carolina Teachers Coll. (a state sch.), 1909—. Democrat. Methodist. Pres. Eastern N.C. Assn.; mem. N.E.A., N.C. Edn. Assn. Home: Greenville, N.C. Died Apr. 25, 1934.

WRIGHT, Stephen Mott, merchant; b. Jericho, L.I., Aug. 16, 1841; s. Daniel Dodge and Mary Frost (Mott) W.; ed. pub. schs., New York; m. Kate A. Metzgar, May 10, 1866 (died 1902). Entered employ of his father, a hardware mcht.; succeeded to business, 1865; retired from active business, 1887. Sec. and treas., 1885-87 (pres.) Gen. Soc. Mechanics and Tradesmen, New York; sec. and treas. Building Traders' Club until 1897; treas. Mechanics' and Traders' Exchange; sec. and treas. Webb's Acad. and Home for Shipbuilders, 1893-1903; trustee Dry Dock Savings Bank, 1877-94. Mason. Served 10 yrs., pvt. to 1st lt., Nat. Guard State N.Y.; had command Separate Battery Light Arty. during Orange Riot, July 12, 1871. Died 1906.

WRIGHT, Theodore, editor Phila. Record; b. Sylvania, Pa., Aug. 30, 1830; s. James and Nancy Upham (Leonard) W.; ed. pvtly. Editor Phila. Record many yrs. from 1877, and pres. Record Pub. Co. Retired and living in Calif. Democrat. Home: Philadelphia, Pa. Died Aug. 16, 1924.

WRIGHT, Theodore Francis, clergyman, theologian; b. Dorchester, Aug. 3, 1945; s. Edmund and Sarah Augusta W.; grad. Harvard, 1866, A.M., 1869, Ph.D., 1891; grad. New Church Theol. Sch. (then at Waltham, Mass.), 1868; m. Harriet S. Chapman, 1868 (died 1877); m. 2d, 1880, Pamelia Keith, 1880. Served in Union Army, 1864-65, 1st lt. 108th regt. U.S. colored troops. Ordained to ministry of Church of the New Jerusalem (Swedenborgian), 1869; dean Theol. Sch. of the New Ch., Cambridge, 1889—. Hon. gen. sec. for U.S., and authorized lecturer Palestine Exploration Fund. Pres. East End Christian Union of Cambridge, and v.p. Associated Charities. Editor New Church Review, Boston. Author: The Realities of Heaven, 1888; Life Eternal; The Human and Its Relation to the Divine, 1892. Home: Cambridge, Mass. Died 1907.

WRIGHT, Theodore Lyman, educator; b. Beloit, Wis., Sept. 13, 1858; s. Theodore Lyman and Jane (Newcomb) W.; A.B., Beloit College, 1880, A.M., 1884; A.M., Harvard, 1884; Am. Sch. Classical Studies, Athens, Greece, 1887; (Litt.D., U. of Wooster, 1910); m. Jean V. Ingham, Mar. 29, 1909 (died 1910). Teacher, Beloit High Sch., 1880-81, Beloit Coll. Acad., 1881-83, prof. of Greek, Beloit College, 1888—. Most unique duty of this professorship has been in direction of transl. and rendition of 18 of the 25 Greek dramas that have been given by Beloit Coll. during past 35 yrs. Beloit has distinction of having seen more Greek plays than any other town or city in America. Summer lecturer for Bur. of Univ. Travel of Boston, 1904—. Congregationalist. Mem. Beloit City Sch. Board, 1898-1902, and 1917-20; mem. Park Bd., 1915—. Translator: The Frogs of Aristophanes, 1902; The Ecclesiazusae and the Thesmophoriazusae of Aristophanes, 1913. Author: The Beloit Pageant, 1916. Home: Beloit, Wis. Died Oct. 4, 1926.

WRIGHT, Wilbur, æronaut: b. nr. Millville, Ind., Apr. 16, 1867; s. Milton and Susan Catharine (Koerner) W.; brother of Orville W.; ed. high schs., 4 yrs., Richmond, Ind., and Dayton, O.; (hon. B.S., Earlham College, Ind., 1909; LL.D., Oberlin College, Ohio, 1910); unmarried. From 1903, with his brother, Orville, devoted time to heavier-than-air flying machine, patented by Wright Bros. in leading countries of world. Has made numerous flights in U.S. and abroad; sold a machine to U.S. Govt. for $30,000. Awarded gold medal by French Academy Sciences, 1909; also many others. Mem. Aero Club of America. Home: Dayton, Ohio. Died May 30, 1912.

WRIGHT, Wilbur Seaman, lawyer; b. Greenwich, Conn., Nov. 16, 1871; s. Benjamin and Abigail (Mead) W.; grad. Greenwich Acad., 1889; B.A., Yale, 1893; student N.Y. Law Sch., 1893-94; unmarried. Admitted to Conn. bar, 1899, and began practice in Greenwich; sr. partner Wright, Hirschberg, Pettengill & Strong; former asst. pros. atty. Greenwich; mem. Town Council, Greenwich, 1917-35; v.p. Western Conn. Title & Mortgage Co.; sec.-treas. Belle Haven Land Co.; chmn. Bd. of Estimate and Taxation, Greenwich, 1909-17; chmn. Town Bonding Com. Mem. Greenwich Com. Conn. State Council of Defense, and asso. mem. Legal Advisory Bd., World War. Republican. Conglist. Compiler: Compilation of Special Acts Passed by the General Assembly of the State of Connecticut Concerning the Town of Greenwich, Including Acts Passed at the January Session, 1933. Home: Greenwich, Conn. Died Dec. 7, 1937.

WRIGHT, Willard Huntington, author; b. Charlottesville, Va., 1888; s. Archibald Davenport and Annie (Van Vranken) W.; ed. St. Vincent Coll., Calif., 1903; Pomona Coll., Calif., 1904; Harvard, 1906; m. Katharine Belle Boynton, July 13, 1907 (divorced 1930); m. 2d, Eleanor Rulapaugh (Claire de Lisle), 1930. Lit. editor, Los Angeles Times, 1907-13; lit. critic, Town Topics, 1910-14; dramatic critic, same, 1912-14; editor Smart Set Mag., 1912-14; art critic, The Forum, 1915-16; art critic, International Studio, 1916-17; lit. editor, New York Evening Mail, 1917; music critic and art editor, San Francisco Bulletin, 1918-19; art critic, Hearst's International. Magazine, 1922-23; police commr. of Bradley Beach, N.J., 1929. Author: Songs of Youth, 1913; Europe After 8:15 (with H. L. Mencken and G. J. Nathan), 1913; What Nietzsche Taught, 1914; Modern Painting—Its Tendency and Meaning, 1915; The Man of Promise, 1916, de-luxe reprint of same, 1929; The Creative Will, 1916; The Forum Exhibition of Modern American Painters, 1916; Misinforming a Nation, 1917; Informing a Nation, 1917; The Great Modern French Stories, 1918; The Future of Painting, 1923; Modern Literature, 1926; The Great Detective Stories—A Chronological Anthology, 1927; also under name of S. S. Van Dyne—The Benson Murder Case, 1926; The "Canary" Murder Case, 1927; The Greene Murder Case, 1928; The Bishop Murder Case, 1929; The Scarab Murder Case, 1930; The Kennel Murder Case, 1932; The Dragon Murder Case, 1933; The Casino Murder Case, 1934; The Garden Murder Case, 1935; Philo Vance Murder Cases, 1936; The Kidnap Murder Case, 1936; The Powwow Murder Case, 1938. Died Apr. 11, 1939.

WRIGHT, William Burnet, clergyman; b. Cincinnati, Apr. 15, 1838; s. Nathaniel and Caroline (Thew) W.; A.B., Dartmouth, 1857; Andover Theol. Sem., 1858-60; univs. of Berlin and Halle, 1860-61; (D.D., Dartmouth, 1888); m. Lucretia Johnson, Jan. 1, 1863. Ordained Congl. ministry, 1862; pastor South Ch., Chicago, 1862-67, Berkeley St. Ch., Boston, 1867-87, First Ch., New Britain, Conn., 1888-90, Lafayette Presbyn. Ch., Buffalo, 1891-1902; lecturer on literature, history and biography. Author: Ancient Cities from the Dawn to the Daylight, 1887, 1893; The World to Come, 1887; Master and Men, or The Sermon on the Mountain Practiced on the Plain, 1894; Cities of Paul, Beacons of the Past Rekindled for the Present, 1906; The Heart of the Master, 1911. Home: Buffalo, N.Y. Died 1924.

WRIGHT, William Carter, congressman; b. in Carroll Co., Ga., Jan. 6, 1866; ed. high sch., Newnan, Ga.; read law in offices of late Gov. William Y. Atkinson; m. Pauline E. Arnold (died 1918); children—Mrs. Evelyn Banks, Arnold, William C., and 2 children deceased; m. 2d, Mrs. Rosa May F. Bunn. Admitted to Ga. bar, 1886; served as atty., Newnan, and solicitor City Court of Newnan; chmn. Dem. State Exec. Com., Ga., 2 yrs.; nom. Dec. 12, 1917, and later elected to fill vacancy in 65th Congress (1917-19), 4th Ga. Dist., occasioned by resignation of William C. Adamson; reelected 66th to 72d Congresses (1919-33). Democrat. Home: Newnan, Ga. Died June 11, 1933.

WRIGHT, William Janes, prof. metaphysics Westminster Coll., Mo., 1887—; b. Weybridge, Vt., Aug. 3, 1831; grad. Princeton Theol. Sem., 1862; Union Coll., 1857 (Ph.D., 1876; D.D., Shurtleff Coll., Ill., 1890; LL.D., Westminster Coll., Pa., 1881). Mem. London Math. Soc. in 1875; A.A.A.S., 1876; m. Julia Mac Nair, 1859. Was U.S. chaplain, 1863-65; was Presbyn. pastor several yrs. in N.J. and O. Prof. mathematics Wilson Coll., 1876-77. Author of many papers on philos. subjects. Home: Fulton, Mo. Deceased.

WRIGLEY, William, Jr., mfr.; b. Phila., Pa., Sept. 30, 1861; s. Wm. and Mary A. (Ladley) W.; ed. pub. schs.; m. Ada E. Foote, Sept. 17, 1885; children—Philip K., Dorothy W. (Mrs. James R. Offield). Began business with father at Phila., 1882; removed to Chicago and entered business for self, 1891, under firm name of Wm. Wrigley, Jr., & Co., mfrs. chewing gum; on Jan. 1, 1911, the plant of the Zeno Mfg. Co. was absorbed and the name of the corp. changed to Wm. Wrigley, Jr., Co., of which is pres.; dir. First Nat. Bank, First Trust & Savings Bank, Boulevard Bridge Bank, Consumers Co. (Chicago); chmn. bd. Bon Air Coal & Iron Corp. (Tenn.), Wilmington Transportation Co. (Calif.), Santa Catalina Island Co. (Calif.), Chicago Nat. League Ball Club, Angel City Baseball Club (Los Angeles). Trustee Field Mus. Natural History. Exec. com. Chicago Chapter Am. Red Cross. Republican. Mem. Loyal Legion. Home: Chicago, Ill. Died Jan. 26, 1932.

WU, Chao-Chu, diplomat; b. Tientsin, China, June 16, 1887; s. Wu Ting-Fang and Ho Mew Ling; grad. Atlantic City High Sch., 1904 (valedictorian); LL.B., London Univ., 1911; barrister at law, Lincoln's Inn, 1911; m. Pao Fang Ho; 8 children. Mem. Chinese Parliament, 1913; counsellor of Ministry of Foreign Affairs, 1915; del. to Peace Conf., Paris, 1919; minister of Foreign Affairs, 1924; chmn. Council of Judicial Administration, Nationalist Govt., 1925; E.E. and M.P. to U.S., Mar. 1929—; del. of China to Assembly of League of Nations, 1929; del. to Conf. for Modification of Internat. Law, The Hague, 1930. Author: The National Program for China, 1929. Died Jan. 2, 1933.

WUNDER, Clarence Edmond, architect, engr.; b. Phila., Pa., Nov. 14, 1886; s. Otto and Katherine (Dirks) W.; ed. Central Manual Training Sch., Phila., and pvt. instrn.; m. Elizabeth I. Geissel, Oct. 18, 1910; children—Clarence Edmond, Katherine

Elizabeth, Richard Paul. Draftsman with Kurt W. Peuckert, architect and engr., Phila., 1905-10; mem. Peuckert & Wunder, 1910-14, alone, 1914—; designer of Pennsylvania Hotel, Temple Univ. Stadium, Bonwit, Teller & Co.'s Store, George Allen Store, Cuneo Eastern Press, Inc., Keekler-Weyl Baking Co., etc. Mem. Am. Inst. Architects. Mason. Home: Ardmore, Pa. Died Oct. 19, 1940.

WÜRDEMANN, Harry Vanderbilt, ophthalmic surgeon; b. Washington, D.C., June 13, 1865; s. John Vanderbilt and Matilda (Barnard) W.; Columbian (now George Washington) U., 1884-88, M.D., 1888; Royal Ophthalmic Hosp., London, Paris and Vienna, 1889; Sc.D., 1923. Began in architect's office, 1880; illustrator and engraver, 1881-84; topographer with U.S. Geol. Survey, 1884-88; practiced in Milwaukee, Wis., 1890-1909, Seattle, Washington, Jan. 1909—. Prof. ophthalmology, Chicago Eye, Ear, Nose and Throat College, 1894-1909, Marquette Univ. Med. Dept., Milwaukee, 1900-09. Med. examiner in aeronautics, U.S. Dept. Commerce. Editor Annals of Ophthalmology, 1897-1904; asso. editor Ophthalmic Record, 1897—; mng. editor Ophthalmology, 1904-17; asso. editor Am. Journal of Ophthalmology, 1914-24. Fellow Am. Coll. Surgeons, Am. Acad. Ophthalmology and Oto-Laryngology, Pacific Coast Oto-Ophthalmol. Soc., Puget Sound Acad. Ophthalmology (pres. 1926-27); advisory mem. Nat. Com. for Prevention of Blindness. Colonel M.C. (Res.) U.S.A.; flight surgeon Air Corps, U.S.A. Pres. Reserve Officers' Assn. of Wash., 1924, 25, 26; dir. for State of Wash., Reserve Officers T.C. Mason. Author: Visual Economics, 1902; Injuries of the Eye, 1912, 34. Collaborator: Norris and Oliver's Diseases of the Eye, 1897; De Schweinitz & Randall, Textbook on Diseases of the Eye, Ear, Nose and Throat, 1899; Posey & Wright, Diseases of the Eye, Ear, Nose and Throat, 1903; Posey & Spiller, Eye and Nervous System, 1905; Reisig & Jelliffe, Standard Family Physician, 1907; Wood's System of Ophthalmic Operations, 1911; Wood's Am. Ency. of Ophthalmology, 1912-15; Kober & Hansen, Diseases of Occupation, 1915; Reference Handbook Med. Science, 1915; etc. Home: Seattle, Wash. Died Jan. 30, 1938.

WURTS, Alexander Jay, electrical engr.; b. Carbondale, Pa., Mar. 3, 1862; s. Charles Penberton and Lauro (Jay) W.; brother of John W.; Ph.B., Sheffield Scientific Sch. (Yale), 1883; M.E., Stevens Inst. Tech., 1884; studied electricity under Prof. Kohlrausch, Polytechnikum, Hanover, Germany, 1884-86; m. Jeanie Lowrie Childs, June 30, 1890 (died 1924); m. 2d, Elizabeth R. Wurts, 1927. On tech. staff Westinghouse Electric & Mfg. Co., 1887-98; mgr. Nernst Co., 1898-1904; gen. engr. Westinghouse Electric & Mfg. Co., 1904-05; prof. applied electricity and head of elec. dept., Carnegie Inst. Tech., 1905-21, prof. engineering research, same, 1921—; chmn. student welfare, 1924—. Discoverer of the five nonarcing metals. Awarded John Scott medal by City of Phila. through Franklin Inst. for inventions in lightning arresters. Home: Pittsburgh, Pa. Died 1932.

WURZBACH, Harry McLeary, congressman; b. San Antonio, Tex., May 19, 1874; s. Charles L. and Katherine (Fink) W.; B.L., Washington and Lee U., 1896; m. Frances Darden Wagner. Admitted to Tex. bar, 1896. County atty. Guadalupe Co., Tex., 1900-1902; co. judge, 1904-12; mem. 67th to 70th Congresses (1921-29), 14th Tex. Dist. Mem. Co. F, 1st Tex. Inf., Spanish-Am. War. Republican. Episcopalian. K.P. Home: Seguin, Tex. Died Nov. 6, 1931.

WYANT, Adam Martin, congressman; b. Armstrong Co., Pa., Sept. 15, 1869; student Mt. Pleasant Inst., Bucknell U., LL.D., 1923; A.M., U. of Chicago, 1895; m. Katharine Nelson Doty, Dec. 1, 1910. Admitted to Pa. bar, 1902. Mem. 67th to 72d Congresses (1921-33), 31st Pa. District. Republican. Home: Greensburg, Pa. Died Jan. 5, 1935.

WYATT, J(ames) B(osley) Noel, architect; b. Baltimore, May 3, 1847; s. William Edward and Margaret Esther (Noel) W.; A.B., Harvard, 1870; Mass. Inst. Tech., 1 yr.; atelier Vaudremer, Ecole des Beaux Arts, Paris, 3 yrs.; unmarried. In practice at Baltimore, 1876—; mem. Wyatt & Sperry, 1876-86, Wyatt & Nölting, 1886—. Designed many important bldgs., pub. and pvt., in Baltimore and Washington, also in Md. and Va. Dir. Municipal Art Soc.; fellow A.I.A. (pres. Baltimore Chapter). Mgr. Federated Charities, Baltimore; for a number of yrs. was mem. City Art Commn., State Bd. of Health, advisory bd. of Johns Hopkins U. "Homewood" development. Progressive. Episcopalian. Home: Baltimore, Md. Died Feb. 25, 1926.

WYCHE, Richard Thomas, storyteller; b. Granville Co., N.C., July 25, 1867; s. Benjamin and Sarah Elizabeth (Hunter) W.; student U. of N.C., 1889-93; U. of Chicago, 1901; m. Maude Anna Ambrister, Feb. 26, 1916; children—Richard Thomas, Mary. Bookkeeper and cashier, Raleigh, N.C., 1886-88; general sec. Y.M.C.A., Concord, N.C., 1892; teacher until 1897; storyteller, 1890—; lecturer, U. of Chicago, Chautauqua Instn., etc., also summer schs., colleges and univs. Organizer, 1903, and pres. Nat. Story Tellers' League (hon. pres.); mem. N.C. Folk-Lore Soc., Phi (U. of N.C.). Author: Some Great Stories and How to Tell Them, 1910. A co-founder and editor Story Tellers' Magazine, 1913, 1914. Home: Washington, D.C. Died May 5, 1930.

WYCKOFF, Arcalous Welling, steel mfr.; b. Elmira, N.Y., May 18, 1873; s. George Warren and Sibyl (Welling) W.; M.E., Cornell U., 1896; m. Elizabeth W. Robinson, Apr. 14, 1898; children—Elizabeth W. (Mrs. John M. Adams), Katherine W. (Mrs. Richard S. Smith). Began in steel mfg. business, Pittsburgh, Pa., 1919; pres. Wyckoff Drawn Steel Co.; dir. A. Wyckoff & Son Co. Served as maj. Chem. Warfare Service U.S.A., World War; col. U.S. Res. Mason. Home: Pittsburgh, Pa. Died Sept. 25, 1936.

WYCKOFF, John (Henry), M.D.; b. of Am. parents, Tindivanam, India, Nov. 12, 1881; s. John Henry and Emmeline (Bonney) W.; student Rutgers Coll. 2 yrs., hon. M.A., 1920; M.D., Univ. and Bellevue Hosp. Med. Coll. (New York U.), 1907; m. Elizabeth Crane Porter, June 6, 1914. Practiced at N.Y. City, 1910—; specializes in internal medicine; formerly asso. prof. medicine, Univ. and Bellevue Hosp. Med. Coll. (New York U.), prof. medicine and dean, 1932—; dir. of third med. div. of Bellevue Hosp. Commd. capt. M.C., U.S.A., June 1917, and maj., Nov. 1918; served in U.S. and France; cited by Gen. Pershing, "for conspicuous and exceptional service," at Vichy, France. Home: New York, N.Y. Died June 1, 1937.

WYCKOFF, Walter Augustus, asst. prof. political economy, Princeton; b. Mainpuri, India, April 12, 1865; s. Rev. Benjamin Du Bois W.; grad. Princeton, 1888; post-graduate work Princeton, 1888-89; following yr. studied and traveled abroad; began in July 1891, an experiment which consisted of a study of the sociological and economic conditions of wage-earners in America by becoming a wage-earner and for eighteen months living by day's labor and working his way from Conn. to Calif.; spent yrs. 1893, 1894, as private tutor and traveled twice around the world. Apptd. Social Science Fellow, Princeton, 1894; lecturer on sociology, 1895, and asst. prof. of political economy, 1898. Author: The Workers—the East, 1897; The Workers—the West, 1898; A Day with a Tramp, and Other Days, 1900. Died 1908.

WYETH, John Allan, surgeon; b. Marshall Co., Ala., May 26, 1845; s. Judge Louis and Euphemia (Allan) W.; La Grange Mil. Academy, Ala.; pvt. in C.S.A.; 15 months prisoner, Camp Morton, Ind., began study of medicine, 1867; M.D., U. of Louisville, 1869, also, ad eundem, Bellevue Med. Coll., 1873; (LL.D., U. of Ala., 1902, U. of Md., 1909); m. Florence N., d. Dr. J. Marion Sims, 1886. Asst. demonstrator anatomy, 1873-74, prosector to chair anatomy and surgery, 1880-97, Mt. Sinai Hosp., New York; organized and founded, 1882, first post-grad. med. sch. in U.S.—the N.Y. Polyclinic Med. Sch. and Hosp., and is prof. surgery and pres. faculty. Pres. N.Y. Path. Soc., 1885-86, N.Y. State Med. Assn., 1901, A.M.A., 1902, N.Y. Acad. Medicine, 1907-08, N.Y. Southern Soc., 1907. Author: Essays on Surgical Anatomy and Surgery; Text-Book on Surgery; Life of General N. B. Forrest; With Sabre and Scalpel, The Autobiography of a Soldier and Surgeon, 1914. Home: New York, N.Y. Died May 28, 1922.

WYLIE, Andrew, jurist; b. Washington Co., Pa., Feb. 25, 1814; grad. Univ. of Ind., 1832 (LL.D.); studied law at Transylvania Univ., Lexington, Ky., 1835-36; afterward with Hon. Walter Forward at Pittsburgh; admitted to bar, 1837; practiced at Pittsburg, 1837-48; removed to Alexandria, Va., and opened office at Washington, 1848; gave the only vote for Lincoln in 1860 which was given at Alexandria; removed to Washington; justice Supreme Court of D.C., 1863-85; retired on account of age; m. Mary C. Bryan of Virginia, 1845. Died 1905.

WYLIE, David Gourley, clergyman; b. New Richland, O., May 15, 1857; s. Robert and Eliza Jane (Patterson) W.; B.A. Geneva Coll., 1879; Yale Div. Sch., 1881-82; grad. Union Theol. Sem., 1883; spl. student same 1883-84; Ph.D., New York U., 1888; D.D., Lafayette, 1897, Omaha U., 1897; LL.D., Maryville Coll., Tenn., 1911; m. Jennie M. McWilliam, May 15, 1884; children—Howard McWilliam, Jennie Dwight, David Roswell, John McWilliam (dec.), Robert Stirling; m. 2d, Martha R. Thomas; 1 dau., Elizabeth Martha. Ordained Presbyn. ministry, 1884; pastor Canal St. Ch., New York, 1884-85, Knox Ch., 1886-91, Scotch Ch., New York, 1891—. Elected gen. sec. Bd. Ch. Erection, Presbyn. Ch. U.S.A., 1914; mem. bd. mgrs. American Tract Soc., Presbyn. Hosp.; pres. Lord's Day Alliance; pres. Apostolic Inst.; trustee Maryville Coll., Maryville, Tenn.; moderator Presbytery, New York; moderator Synod, New York; mem. exec. com. Gen. Assembly Presbyn. Ch. in U.S.A.; mem. Presbyn. Nat. Service Com. during World War; pres. Gospel Mission to the Tombs, N.Y. Republican. Chaplain N.Y. Scottish Soc., St. Andrew's Soc., State of N.Y.; sec. bd. Nat. Missions Presbyn. Ch. U.S.A. Author: A Visit to Europe, 1895; Our Jubilee, 1906; The Minister's Companion, 1910; Making the Bible a New Book. Home: New York, N.Y. Died Aug. 26, 1930.

WYLIE, Douglas M., merchant, banker; b. Baltimore, 1865; s. Robert M. and Elizabeth (Magee) W.; ed. pvt. schs. U.S. and abroad, and Johns Hopkins, to 1890; unmarried. Associated with father in long-established grain business, 1890, and head Wylie, Son & Co., since father's death, 1902; dir. 1902-10, v.p., 1910—, Nat. Bank of Commerce; dir. and mem. exec. com. Eutaw Savings Bank, Terminal Warehouse Co. Mem. Baltimore City Park Commn.; officer or mem. many pub. and charitable orgns. Democrat. Presbyn. Home: Baltimore, Md. Died Mar. 9, 1914.

WYLIE, Dwight Witherspoon, clergyman; b. Condit, O., July 16, 1876; s. Robert and Sarah Adelia (Jadden) W.; A.B., Coll. of Wooster (O.), 1896; student, McCormick Theol. Sem., Chicago, 1896-99; D.D., U. of Dubuque, 1911; LL.D., Macalester Coll., St. Paul, 1919; m. Alice F. McGee, July 3, 1907; children—Mary Elizabeth (Mrs. James H. Case, Jr.), Virginia G. Ordained to ministry Presbyn. Ch., 1899; pastor 2d Ch., Davenport, Ia., 1899-1902, 1st Ch., Iowa City, 1902-16, St. Paul's Ch., Phila., 1916-20, Central Ch., N.Y. City, 1920—. Republican. Mason. Home: New York, N.Y. Died Dec. 30, 1940.

WYLIE, Edna Edwards; b. Sibley, Ia., Apr. 17, 1876; ed. pub. schs. and spl. branches in Hamline Univ., St. Paul; m. Rev. E. M. Wylie, June 8, 1901. Author: The Blue Valley Feud; Theodore's Stepmother; The Will of the Caxtons; The Refining of Mary Ann; The Little Dream Playmate; The Ward of the Sewing Circle, 1905. Home: Cleveland, Ohio. Died 1907.

WYLIE, Elinor Hoyt, author; b. Rosemont, Pa.; d. Henry Martyn and Anne (McMichael) Hoyt; ed. Miss Baldwin's Sch., Bryn Mawr., Pa., and Holton Arms Sch., Washington, D.C.; m. William Rose Benét, Oct. 3, 1923. Author: Nets to Catch the Wind (verse), 1921; Black Armour (verse), 1923; Jennifer Lorn, 1923; The Venetian Glass Nephew, 1925; The Orphan Angel, 1927; Mr. Hodge and Mr. Hazard, 1928; Trivial Breath (verse), 1928. Home: New York, N.Y. Died Dec. 16, 1928.

WYLIE, Laura Johnson, coll. prof.; b. Milton, Pa., Dec. 1, 1855; d. William Theodore and Sarah Murray (Johnson) W.; A.B., Vassar Coll., 1877; Ph.D., Yale, 1894; unmarried. Prof. English, Vassar Coll., 1897-1924, emeritus; teacher Bryn Mawr Summer Sch., 1924-26. Author: Studies in the Evolution of English Criticism, 1894 (thesis for Ph.D., printed by the authority and at the expense of Yale Univ.); Social Studies in English Literature, Vassar Series, 1915. Editor: The Sir Roger de Coverley Papers from The Spectator (edition for sch. use), 1900; The Winter's Tale, in the Tudor Shakespeare, 1912; Adam Bede, 1917; Poems and Plays by Gertrude Buck, 1922. Home: Poughkeepsie, N.Y. Died Apr. 2, 1932.

WYLIE, Richard Cameron, prof. theology; b. nr. Zanesville, O., Aug. 27, 1846; s. John and Maria (Wisher) W.; A.B., Muskingum Coll., New Concord, O., 1870, A.M., 1873, D.D., 1896, LL.D., 1909; Reformed Presbyn. Theol. Sem., Allegheny, Pa., 1871-75; m. Jean Buchanan, June 6, 1876; children—Anna Maud Buchanan (dec.), Lilian Marie, Vella Valeira (dec.), Cameron Sloane (dec.). Ordained Reformed Presbyn. ministry, 1875; pastor Hopkinton, Ia., 1875-82; sec. and pub. lecturer, Nat. Reform Assn., 1882-92; pastor Cedar Lake, Ind., 1884-91, Wilkinsburg, Pa., 1891-1908; prof. O.T. and N.T. lit. and exegesis, 1908-11, prof. systematic theology and lecturer on moral theory of the state, June 1911—, Reformed Presbyn. Theol. Seminary. Moderator of Ref. Presbyn. Synod, 1891; mem. bd. dirs. Nat. Reform Assn. Author: Our Educational System, 1901; Sabbath Laws in the United States, 1905; Collapse of Christless Civilizations, 1918; Digest of the Sabbath Laws of the States, 1922; The Moral Theory of the State, 1928. Asso. editor Christian Statesman (monthly mag.). Home: Pittsburgh, Pa. Died 1928.

WYLIE, Walker Gill, physician, surgeon; b. Chester, S.C., Sept. 2, 1848; s. Dr. Alexander P. W.; in C.S.A. as lt. comdg. co. of boys in active service, 1864-65; A.B., U. of S.C., 1868; M.D., Bellevue Hosp. Med. Coll. (New York U.), 1871; house surgeon Bellevue Hosp., 1870, remained 18 months; house surgeon Woman's Hosp. of State of N.Y. 18 months. In England and European continent to study nursing systems, and from his reports as basis the Training Sch. for Nurses connected with Bellevue Hosp. was established (1st in U.S.); apptd., 1882, visiting gynecologist Bellevue Hosp.; assisted in founding, 1882, and became prof. gynecology, New York Polyclinic. Specialist in abdominal surgery. Author: Hospitals, their Organization and Construction (Boylston prize essay, Harvard), 1876. Home: New York, N.Y. Died Mar. 13, 1923.

WYMAN, Bruce, lawyer; b. Boston, Mass., June 15, 1876; s. Ferdinand A. and Harriet Ann (Bruce) W.; A.B., Harvard, 1896, A.M., 1897, LL.B., 1900; m. Ethel Andrews, June 30, 1902; children—Andrews, Rosemary. Practiced in Boston, 1900—; consulting counsel, corp. practice; prof. law, Harvard, 1901-14;

counsel Nat. Civic Federation, 1911-13; investigator for Dirs. of Port of Boston, 1912; prof. law, Portia Law Sch., 1917—. Republican. Episcopalian. Author: Restrait of Trade. 1902; Mortgage Securities. 1903; Administrative Law, 1903; Railroad Rate Regulation, 1906, 2d edit., 1915; Public Utilities, 1909; 2d edit., 1921; Control of the Market. 1911; Public Service Corporations, 1911. Home: Waban, Mass. Died June 21, 1926.

WYMAN, Frank Theodore, lawyer; b. Cleveland, O., Oct. 1, 1868; s. George H. and Lucy Dix (Mahan) W.; high sch., Grand Haven, Mich.; m. Jessie T. Corbus, Jan. 22, 1902. Admitted to Ida. bar. 1890, and practiced at Boise; mem. Ida. Ho. of Rep., 1895, 1907 (chmn. judiciary com. both sessions); treas. Rep. State Com. of Ida., 1904-08; candidate for atty. gen. of Ida., 1909; declined appmt. as asso. justice Supreme Court of Ida., 1914. Trustee Carnegie Pub. Library, Boise, 1909-16. Episcopalian. Mason. Author of mining laws of Ida. and much other legislation. Home: Boise, Ida. Died Dec. 15, 1935.

WYMAN, Hal C., physician; b. Anderson, Ind., March 22, 1852; grad. U. of Mich., med. dept., 1873; M.S., Mich. Agrl. Coll.; m. Jenny L. Barnum, Oct. 30, 1879 (dec.); m. 2d, Lulu A. Weeks, June 12, 1906. Prof. surgery, Mich. Coll. Medicine and Surgery. Was mem. Mich. State Bd. Charities and Corrections, Nat. Conf. same, Nat. Prison Congress. Mem. state and nat. med. socs. Author of many papers on surg. topics. Died 1908.

WYMAN, Henry Augustus, lawyer; b. Skowhegan, Me., Feb. 3, 1861; s. Henry A. and Fannie (Russell) W.; grad. high sch., Skowhegan; LL.B., cum laude, Boston U., 1885; m. Anne C. Southworth, 1891. In wholesale business, Boston, Mass., 1875-79; sec. to engr. in charge constrn. Hoosac Dock Elevated Co., 1881; admitted to Mass. bar, 1885, and began practice at Boston; law clk. atty. gen. dept., Mass., 1886; 2d asst. atty. gen., 1887-90; dramatic editor Boston Times, 1887-90; 1st asst. U.S. atty., Boston, 1890-93; prof. criminal law, Boston U. Law Sch., 1890-1900; atty. gen. of Mass., 1919-20; dir. and trustee of corps. and estates; dir. Am. Investment Co., Columbian Nat. Life Ins. Co., Gosnold Mills, Mass. Utilities Associates, Middleboro Trust Co., Sydney Coal Co., Samoset Worsted Mills; trustee Mass. Lighting Co., N.E. Power Associates, Internat. Hydro-Electric Systems. Treas. Social Law Library; trustee Boston U., Mass. Homœ. Hosp., Hahnemann Hosp. Republican. Unitarian. Home: Boston, Mass. Died Sept. 25, 1935.

WYMAN, Lillie Buffum Chace (Mrs. John C. Wyman), author; b. Valley Falls, R.I., Dec. 10, 1847; d. Samuel Buffington and Elizabeth (Buffum) Chace; ed. pvt. schs.; m. John Crawford Wyman, Oct. 29, 1878 (died 1900). Mem. bd. trustees R.I. Instn. for the Deaf 10 yrs. Author: Poverty Grass, 1886; American Chivalry, 1913; Interludes and Other Verses, 1913; Elizabeth Buffum Chace and Her Environment (2 vols.), 1914; Gertrude of Denmark, 1924; A Grand Army Man of Rhode Island, 1925; Syringa at the Gate, 1926. Home: Newtonville, Mass. Died Jan. 10, 1929.

WYMAN, Walter, surgeon gen.; b. St. Louis, Mo., Aug. 17, 1848; s. Edward and Elizabeth (Hadley) W.; grad. City U. of St. Louis, 1866; A.B., Amherst, 1870 A.M., 1889; M.D., St. Louis Med. Coll., 1873; LL.D., Western U. of Pa., 1897, U. of Md., 1907. In Marine Hosp. Service, 1876—, serving successively at St. Louis, Cincinnati, Baltimore, New York, and Washington; gave spl. attention to physical conditions affecting seamen of merchant marine and was instrumental in having laws passed for their benefit; also brought to notice cruelties imposed on deck-hands on Western rivers and on crews of oyster vessels in Chesapeake Bay; established hosp. for latter; had charge of Govt. measures to ward off cholera, 1893. Supervising surgeon gen. U.S. Marine Hosp. Service, 1891-1902; surgeon gen. U.S. Pub. Health and Marine Hosp. Service, 1902—. Administrator Nat. quarantine law and establishments. Suggested and established first Govt. sanatorium for consumptives at Fort Stanton, N.M.; instrumental in securing enactment of laws relating to quarantine, quarters and food for seamen, govt. regulation of mfr. and sale of viruses, serums, toxins, etc., the establishment of a leprosy investigation sta. in Hawaii, the creation of a hygienic lab. at Washington, establishment of a bur. of pub. health. Author many pamphlets on public health. Mem. bd. of visitors Govt. Hosp. for Insane; chmn. Internat. Sanitary Bur. of Am. Republics; pres. Am. Pub. Health Assn., 1902-03, Assn. Mil. Surgeons, 1904-05; acting pres. Am. Nat. Red Cross, 1904; hon. fellow Am. Assn. Obstetricians and Gynecologists; sec. sect. pub. and internat. hygiene, 9th Internat. Med. Congress, Washington, 1887; chmn. com. internat. quarantine, Pan-Am. Med. Congress, Mex., 1896; chmn. sect pub. health, Internat. Congress Arts and Sciences, St. Louis, 1904; pres. sect. state and municipal control, Internat. Congress on Tuberculosis, Washington, 1908; mem. many med. and other socs. Home: Washington, D.C. Died 1911.

WYMAN, Walter Forestus, business executive; b. Hyde Park (Boston), Mass., Dec. 21, 1881; s. Ferdinand Adolphus and Harriet Ann (Bruce) W.; prep. edn., Chauncy Hall Sch., and Hale Sch., Boston, Mass., student Tufts Coll., 1898-1900; m. Roline Leila Phillips, Dec. 4, 1909; children—Elsbeth Roline (Mrs. Harold M. Horack), Robert Bruce. Export manager of Am. Shoe Machinery Co., 1900-04; business mgr. The Green Bag, 1905-08; export mgr. The Carter's Ink Co., 1908-16, sales mgr., 1916-22, gen. sales mgr., 1922—. Hon. chmn. Business Executive's Round Table, Boston Export Round Table; officer or chmn. Com. Nat. Mfrs. Assn., Boston Credit Men's Assn., Nat. Assn. Credit Men, Assn. Nat. Advertisers, Internat. Chamber Commerce, Assn. Magazines of N. America; served as chmn. Com. on Edn. Exhibits of Internat. Trade Conf. (New York, 1915, Springfield, Mass., 1916); chmn. Internat. Foreign Credits Conf., 1917, War Trade Bd. Conf., 1918, Foreign Banking Conf., 1921, Permissive Price Maintenance Conf., 1927, Wholesale Relations Conf., 1929, Internat. Trade Conf., 1935; chmn. code com. Ink and Adhesive Mfrs. Assn., 1934-35; chmn. code authority Writing Ink Industry, 1935; co-chmn. code authority Adhesive and Ink Industry, 1935. Mem. nat. council and nat. com. on contract standards, 1937-40; mem. nat. council Nat. Economic League, 1937-40, Nat. Com. Finnish Relief Fund, Inc., 1940. Lecturer on domestic and foreign commerce, at Dartmouth, Harvard, and other ednl. instns. Republican. Unitarian. Dir. and mem. com. on laws Am. Bridge League; nat. pair championship, Am. Whist League. 1931, nat. team of four championship, 1933, director League, 1933-40; mem. bd. govs. and exec. com. Am. Contract Bridge League, 1937-40. Author: Selling American Goods to the World, 1915; Henryville Stories, 1916; Direct Exporting, 1917; Utilizing Time, 1918; Export Merchandising, 1922; (3 books with M. C. Work) Contract Bridge Pointers, 1930, Contract Bridge for All, 1929, Common Sense Contract Bridge, 1931. Hon. asso. editor The Bridge World. Home: Arlington, Mass. Died Nov. 21, 1940.

WYMAN, William D., insurance pres.; b. Hillsboro Bridge, N.H., Apr. 24, 1859. Began at Chicago, Ill., in employ of Mass. Mut. Life Ins. Co., 1883, becoming gen. agt. at Chicago; apptd. Ill. State mgr. Berkshire Life Ins. Co. of Pittsfield. Mass., 1889, later pres. Pres. Chicago Life Underwriters' Assn., 1892-93, 1897-98, Nat. Assn. Life Underwriters, 1901-02. Home: Pittsfield, Mass. Died Aug. 20, 1923.

WYMAN, William Stokes, educator; b. Montgomery, Ala., Nov. 23, 1830; s. Justus and Mary Amelia (Stokes) W.; Harvard, 1847-48; A.B., U. of Ala., 1851, A.M., 1853, LL.D., 1882; m. Melissa A. Dearing, Dec. 29, 1853. Prof. of Latin, U. of Ala., 1855-1901; 6 times declined presidency, but served as pres. pro tem. 4 times, and was pres., 1901-02; retired. Mem. Gen. Assembly of Ala., 1870-72. Student of the history of the Southeastern and Gulf states in the original sources. Author: Syntax of the Latin Compound Sentence, 1880; The Trial of Milo, 1885. Home: Tuscaloosa, Ala. Died Oct. 20, 1915.

WYNKOOP, Bernard Martell, newspaper pub.; b. Bath, N.Y., Mar. 30, 1873; s. Henry John and Mary Elizabeth (Gagnier) W.; grad. high sch., Bath, 1891; m. Marion Frances Davidson, Sept. 8, 1903. Began as clk. Farmers and Mechanics Bank, Bath, 1890; cashier Evening News Assn., Detroit, 1896-98, circulation mgr., 1898-1902; acting mgr. Chicago Journal, summer 1902; business mgr. Detroit Tribune, winter 1902-03; editor and mgr. Bay City (Mich.) Times, 1903-18; editor and mgr. Jackson Citizen Patriot, 1918—; dir. the Booth Pub. Co. Republican. Mason. Home: Jackson, Mich. Died Feb. 12, 1934.

WYNNE, Cyril; b. Oakland, Calif., Mar. 29, 1890; s. Ernest Philips and Carmelita (Mezes) W.; B.A., Harvard U., 1917, M.A., 1925, Ph.D., 1927; m. Louise French, Jan. 7, 1920; children—Edward Cyril, Mena Louise. Aide and asst. to dir. polit., territorial and economic intelligence, Am. Peace Commn., Peace Conf., Paris, Jan.-July, 1919; foreign service officer, 1919-20; 3d sec., Am. Embassy, Tokio, 1920-21, 2d sec., 1921-22; asst. solicitor, Dept. of State, 1922-24; with Inter-Dept. Radio Advisory Com., 1923-24; instr. and lecturer internat. relations and internat. govt., Harvard, 1927-29, also lecturer Harvard-Boston U. and Mass. State extension courses; asst. to sec. Am. Delegation to Internat. Radiotel. Conf., Washington, Aug.-Nov. 1927; asst. to solicitor Dept. of State, 1929; prof. constitutional law, 1929-36, prof. of legal history, 1936—, Columbus Univ. Law Sch., Washington, D.C.; apptd. asst. chief, Office of Historical Adviser, Dept. of State, July 22, 1929, acting historical adviser, May 7, 1933, mem. Bd. of Appeals and Review; chief div. of research and publication, 1933—. Commd. 2d lt., inf., U.S.A., Aug. 5, 1917; with 1st Army Hdqrs. Regt., 1917-18; with A.E.F. in France, 1918-19; Intelligence Service, Haute-Alsace sector; 1st lt., Sept. 1918; capt. Mil. Intelligence, O.R.C., 1924-28, maj., 1928-35, lt. col., 1936. Commended for gallantry; decorated Chevalier de l'Etoile Noire de Belin (France). Author: Department of State Publications, 1935. Review editor Am. Foreign Service Jour. Home: Washington, D.C. Died Sept. 26, 1939.

WYNNE, Robert John, Postmaster-Gen.; b. New York, Nov. 18, 1851; s. John and Mary W.; ed. New York pub. schs., and pvt. study; m. Mary E. McCabe, July 7, 1875. Telegrapher, 1870-80; Washington corr. Cincinnati Gazette, 1880-92; pvt. sec. to Sec. of the Treasury, 1892-96; corr. New York Press, 1896-1902; first asst. postmaster-gen., 1902-04; Postmaster-Gen. in cabinet of President Roosevelt, 1904-05; apptd. consul-gen. at London, 1905; resigned, 1910. Pres. First Nat. Fire Ins. Co. of the U.S., Washington, 1915—. Republican. Home: Washington, D.C. Died Mar. 11, 1922.

WYVELL, Manton M., lawyer; b. Scottsville, N.Y., May 2, 1878; s. Charles M. and Eugenia (Ruliffson) W.; A.B., Cornell U., 1901, LL.B., 1903; m. Clara F. White, Nov. 29, 1905. Practiced in New York, 1904-13; spl. counsel, by appmt. of atty. gen. of N.Y., 1908-12, in franchise tax matters involving assessments against railroads in streets and highways in various cities in Westchester County, N.Y.; pvt. sec. to Sec. of State William J. Bryan, 1912-14; counsel for U.S. before Internat. Joint Commn., 1914—; served as counsel Foreign Trade Advisers' Office, of State Dept., 1915-16, and in July 1916, was sent by Sec. of State Robert Lansing, on spl. mission to London, Eng., to confer with British Foreign Office in regard to trade restrictions imposed by the British Orders in Council of Mar. 11, 1915. Democrat. Presbyn. Mason, Elk. Home: Washington, D.C. Died Aug. 29, 1935.

Y

YALE, Caroline Ardelia, educator; b. Charlotte, Vt., Sept. 29, 1848; d. William Lyman and Ardelia (Strong) Y.; ed. Williston Acad., Mt. Holyoke Sem. (now Mt. Holyoke Coll.); LL.D., Ill. Wesleyan U., 1896; L.H.D., Smith Coll., 1910; LL.D., Mt. Holyoke Coll., 1927. Teacher, 1870-86, prin., 1886-1922, prin. emeritus and dir. normal dept. Clarke Sch. (oral sch. for the deaf, estab. 1867) Northampton, Mass. Trustee Northampton State Hosp. for the Insane; dir. Am. Assn. to Promote Teaching of Speech to the Deaf; mem. corp. Mass. Sch. for Feeble Minded. Republican. Conglist. Author: Formation and Development of Elementary English Sounds; Years of Building, 1931. Died July 2, 1933.

YALE, Leroy Milton, physician; b. Holmes' Hole (now Vineyard Haven), Mass., Feb. 12, 1841; s. Leroy Milton and Maria Allen (Luce) Y.; grad. Columbia. 1862; Bellevue Hosp. Med. Coll., 1866; practiced in New York; m. Julia Meriam Stetson, Dec. 6, 1881. Held several chairs in Bellevue Hosp. Med. Coll.; was surgeon Charity Hosp., 1871-77; Bellevue Hosp., 1877-82; Presbyn. Hosp., 1880-85; editor Med. Gazette, 1867-68; med. editor Babyhood for several years. Pres. N.Y. Etching Club, 1877-79. Author: The Century Book of Mothers, 1901. Died 1906.

YANCEY, Richard Hunter, editor; b. in Fayette County, Tenn., Nov. 22, 1855; s. Edwin Thomas and Mary May (Anderson) Y.; ed. La Grange Acad., 1866-71; LL.B., Cumberland U., 1877; m. Irene Williams, Feb. 17, 1881 (died 1910). Owner and pub. Somerville Falcon, 1880-83; editor Clarksville Chronicle, 1883-87, Birmingham (Ala.) Herald, later Age-Herald, 1887-91; asso. editor, 1891-1911, editor, 1911—, Nashville Banner. Democrat. Episcopalian. Home: Nashville, Tenn. Died June 22, 1922.

YANDELL, Enid, sculptor; b. Louisville, Ky., 1870; d. Dr. Lunsford Pitts and Louise (Elliston) Y.; grad. Cincinnati Art Sch.; pupil of Philip Martiny, New York, MacMonnies and Rodin, Paris. Designer's medal, Chicago Expn., 1893, exhibited in Paris Salon regularly, 1895—; silver medal, Nashville Expn., 1897; hon. mention, Buffalo Expn., 1901; bronze medal, St. Louis Expn., 1904; decorated Officier d'Académie, French Govt., 1906. Organizer, the Branstock Sch. of Art, Edgartown, Island of Martha's Vineyard, Mass., 1907. Sculptor of the Woman's Bldg., Chicago Expn., 1893; Carrie Brown Memorial Fountain, Providence, 1900; bust of Dr. W. T. Bull, Coll. Phys. and Surg., N.Y., 1909; Sun dial for Oliver Harriman, 1900; Emma Willard memorial, Albany, N.Y.; Chancellor Garland, Vanderbilt U., Nashville; Hogan Fountain, Louisville, Ky., 1905; Daniel Boone monument, Louisville, Ky., 1906; Thomas monument, Nashville, 1907; fountains for John H. Hammond, Mt. Kisco, N.Y., 1909, for J. R. Steers, Portchester, N.Y., 1910, for William A. Read, White Plains, N.Y., 1911; Edwin Smith memorial, Westfield, Mass., 1926. Organized Appui Aux Artistes, Paris, France, 1914; chmn. woman's com. Council of Nat. Defense, food administration women's com. of Edgartown, Mass., World War; mem. bur. personnel, Atlantic Div. Am. Red Cross, New York, 1917; dir. bur. of communications, N.Y., Am. Red Cross, 1918-19. Died June 13, 1934.

YANES, Francisco Javier, diplomat; b. Caracas, Venezuela, S.A., May 6, 1861; s. Emilio and Trinidad (de Ascanio) de Y.; Ph.B., U. of Caracas; m. Evelyn Augusta Stanton Lynch, Dec. 31, 1887. Vice consul and acting consul gen. for Venezuela, at New

York, 1892-97; Venezuelan del. Internat. congresses, 1895-1898; Spanish sec. and chief translating div. U.S. Philippine Commn., Manila, 1901-03; asst. dir. and sec. governing bd. Pan American Union, Washington, Oct. 14, 1905—. Writer on lit. and polit. subjects. Representative Internat. Bur. Am. Republics, and mem. Jury of Awards, Jamestown Expn., 1907; spl. rep. of Union to 3d Internat. Sanitary Conv., Mex., 1907, to 4th Pan-Am. Conf., Buenos Aires, 1910. Founder and former pres. Spanish Am. Atheneum, Washington. Medal, Bust of Bolivar, 2d Class and medal Pub. Instrn., Venezuela. Died Feb. 25, 1924.

YARBOROUGH, Warren Furman, clergyman; b. Pickens, Miss., Dec. 11, 1867; s. John and Mary Elizabeth (Toombs) Y.; grad. Gillsburg (Miss.) Collegiate Inst., 1887; B.A., Miss. Coll., Clinton, 1892; Th.M., Southern Bapt. Theol. Sem., Ky., 1896; D.D., Howard Coll., Ala., 1911; m. Mettie May Forbes, Nov. 24, 1896; children—Warren Forbes, John Marion, Mary D., Lilian Forbes, James Furman. Ordained Bapt. ministry, 1892; pastor in Miss., at Magnolia, 1892-93, Brookhaven, 1895, Crystal Springs, 1896-99, Jackson, 1899-1910, and Parker Memorial Ch., Anniston, Ala., 1910-16; sec.-treas. exec. bd., Ala. Bapt. Conv., 1916-20; pastor First Ch., Hattiesburg, Miss., 1920-26; supt. evangelism, Ala. Bapt. Conv., 1926-27; pastor First Ch., Jasper, Ala., 1927-36; pastor at Pickens, Miss., 1936—. Evangelist and speaker on mission topics. Wrote expositions of Uniform International Sunday School Lessons for Bapt. Record 2 yrs. Died Nov. 20, 1940.

YARGER, Henry Lee, clergyman; b. Hartleton, Pa., Feb. 22, 1862; s. John and Lucinda (Huntington) Y.; A.B., Pa. College, Gettysburg, 1883, A.M., 1886; grad. Gettysburg Theol. Sem., 1886; D.D., Carthage Coll., Ill., 1898; m. Mildred Rose Hammer, July 15, 1886. Ordained Luth. ministry, 1886; pastor in Ellsworth and Lincoln counties, Kan., 1886-89, Lawrence, Kan., 1889-93, Braddock, Pa., 1893-94; field sec. Bd. of Ch. Extension Luth. Ch., Atchison, Kan., 1895-1914; gen. supt. home missions and ch. extension, Chicago, 1914—. Pres. Kan. Synod, 1901-03, Gen. Synod Evang. Luth. Ch. in U.S., 1913-14; trustee Tabitha Home (Lincoln, Neb.), Midland Coll. (Atchison, Kan.). Died Jan. 13, 1921.

YATES, Arthur Gould, mcht., ry. pres.; b. E. Waverly, N.Y., Dec. 18, 1843; s. Arthur and Jerusha (Washburn) Y.; acad. edn.; m. Virginia L. Holden, Dec. 26, 1866. Employe of Anthracite Coal Assn., Rochester, 1865-67; established coal business for himself, 1867. In 1876 coal mining firm of Bell, Lewis & Yates was formed and continued until 1896, when they sold their interest to the Buffalo, Rochester & Pittsburgh Ry.; pres. Buffalo, Rochester & Pittsburgh Ry., 1890—. Home: Rochester, N.Y. Died 1909.

YATES, Arthur Wolcott, army officer; b. in Wis., Feb. 14, 1865. Apptd. to U.S. Army from civil life; commissioned 2d lt. 9th Inf., Aug. 1, 1891; Inf. and Cav. Sch., 1895; 1st lt., Apr. 26, 1898; trans. to 4th Inf., July 28, 1900; capt. asst. q.m., Jan. 3, 1901; maj. q.m., Mar. 31, 1906; lt. col. Q.M. Corps, Feb. 1, 1913; col. (temp.) Oct. 9, 1917; col. June 27, 1920; brig. gen., July 9, 1926; retired, own request, Aug. 1, 1927. With A.E.F. and A.F.F. in France, returned to U.S., Jan. 1920. Died Sept. 25, 1930.

YATES, Henry Whitefield, banker; b. Leonardtown, Md., Jan. 1, 1837; s. William Joseph and Julia Ann (Norris) Y.; ed. pub. schs.; m. Eliza Barr Samuel, Apr. 22, 1862. Began in banking business in employ of Kountze Bros., Omaha, 1863; dir. from orgn. and cashier 1st Nat. Bank, Omaha, to 1882; organizer, 1882, and pres. Neb. Nat. Bank, Omaha; also pres. Commercial Land Co.; v.p. Omaha Electric Light Co., Equitable Loan Co.; dir. Neb. Telephone Co. Democrat. Episcopalian; trustee, v.p. Clarkson Memorial Hosp.; trustee Gardner Memorial Parish Home Assn.; treas. Cathedral Chapter, Diocese of Neb. Lectured and published many papers on financial subjects. Home: Omaha, Neb. Died Jan. 9, 1915.

YATES, John Lawrence, surgeon; b. Milwaukee, Wis., Feb. 27, 1873; s. Theodore and Marion Jane (Wolcott) Y.; Ph.B., Yale, 1894; B.S., U. of Wis., 1895; M.D., Johns Hopkins, 1899; m. Kathrine Gross, Apr. 26, 1905. Asst. in pathology, Johns Hopkins, 1901; asst. demonstrator pathology, U. of Pa., 1901; practiced at Milwaukee, 1907—; cons. surgeon Milwaukee Co., Milwaukee Children's hosps. Lt. col. M.C., U.S.A., in France, 1917-18. Fellow Am. Surg. Assn., A.C.S. Contbr. on surg. subjects. Home: Milwaukee, Wis. Died Nov. 3, 1938.

YATES, Lorenzo Gordin, naturalist; b. in England, Jan. 8, 1837; s. Richard Owen and Rosetta Mary Y.; ed. private schools; came to U.S., 1853; taught in common schools, Wis., 1854; studied medicine and dentistry; m. Eunice Amelia Lake, 1861 (died 1898). Was on staff Prof. J. D. Whitney in Geol. Survey of Calif.; specialist in ferns, general botany, conchology, mineralogy, palæontology, N. Am. Indians; was in charge scientific dept. Frœbel Inst., Los Angeles; catalogued collections and prepared "Guide" for Golden Gate Park Museum, San Francisco; pres. Santa Barbara Soc. of Natural History; hon. mem. S. Calif. Acad. of Sciences; fellow Linnæan Soc. of London; Geol. Soc. of America. Author: California Digest of Masonic Law, 1867; Charm Stones, 1886; The Ferns of Ceylon, 1887; Notes on Hawaiian Ferns, 1887; The Channel Islands, 1890; The Mollusca of Santa Barbara County and New Shells from the Santa Barbara Channel, 1890; All Known Ferns; Aboriginal Weapons of California, 1900; Prehistoric California—Its Topography, Flora and Fauna, etc. (bull. S. Calif. Acad. Sciences), 1903. Died 1909.

YATES, Richard, governor; b. Jacksonville, Ill., Dec. 12, 1860; s. Richard (gov. Ill., 1861-65, U.S. senator, 1865-71) and Catharine (Geers) Y.; A.B., Ill. Coll., 1880, A.M., 1883, LL.D., 1903; LL.B., U. of Mich., 1884; m. Helen Wadsworth, Oct. 23, 1888; children—Catharine (Mrs. John L. Pickering), Dorothy (Mrs. John W. Henderson). Served as city attorney of Jacksonville, 1885-91; county judge, Morgan County, 1894-97; U.S. collector internal revenue, Springfield, Ill., 1897-1900; gov. of Ill., 1901-05. Mem. Ill. State Pub. Utilities Commn., 1914-16; mem. 66th to 72d Congresses (1919-33), at large, Ill. Lay del. to General Conf. M.E. Church, 1900. Home: Springfield, Ill. Died Apr. 11, 1936.

YEAMAN, George Helm, lawyer; b. Hardin County, Ky., Nov. 1, 1829; academic edn.; admitted to Ky. bar, 1852; practiced at Owensboro; judge Daviess County, Ky., 1854; mem. Ky. legislature, 1861; mem. Congress, 1862-65, Unionist; U.S. minister to Denmark, 1865-70; in law practice, N.Y. City, 1870—; m. Lelia Pegram, d. Robert Triplett, of Owensboro, Ky. Author: Study of Government; also pamphlets on "Naturalization" and "Privateering." Home: Madison, N.J. Died 1908.

YEAMAN, Malcolm, lawyer; b. Elizabethtown, Ky., Mar. 9, 1841; s. Stephen Minor and Lucretia (Helm) Y.; ed. Elizabethtown, 1847-60; m. Julia Van Pradelles Moore, Oct. 23, 1861. Admitted to bar, 1865; practice confined to litigation and counsel in Western Ky.; mem. bar U.S. Supreme and Dist. cts. Democrat. Deceased.

YEATES, William Smith, State geologist of Ga., and curator of the Georgia State Museum, 1893—; b. Murfreesboro, N.C., Dec. 15, 1856; s. Maj. Jesse J. and Virginia Scott Y.; B.A., Emory and Henry Coll., Va., 1878, M.A., 1881; m. Julia W., d. Maj. John W. Moore, C.S.A., of Ahoskie, N.C., Jan. 16, 1884. On U.S. Fish Commn. spring 1879; taugh sch., 1879-80; employed in the Fisheries Div., 10th U.S. Census, 1880-81; aid, asst., acting curator and asst. curator, U.S. Nat. Museum, in charge collection of minerals and gems, 1881-93; prof. mineralogy, Corcoran Scientific School, Columbian Univ., Washington, 1884-93; prof. geology, same, 1890-93; exec. commr. for Ga., La. Purchase Expn., in charge of geology and forestry. Fellow Geol. Soc. of America; mem. many scientific socs. Home: Atlanta, Ga. Died 1908

YEATMAN, James E., retired mcht. and banker; b. Tenn., Aug. 27, 1818; s. Thomas Y., banker and mfr.; ed. New Haven Commercial School; engaged in business at St. Louis; widower. Was one of founders and first pres. Mercantile Library; one of 9 original organizers and dirs. No. Pacific R.R.; dir. first electric telegraph co. in St. Louis; pres. Mo. School for Edn. of Blind; dir. Missouri State Bank; trustee and pres. Bellefontaine Cemetery Assn.; first pres. Provident Assn.; dir. St. Louis Ins. Co.; pres. Western Sanitary Commn.; pres. Soldiers' Orphans' Home; trustee Home for the Friendless; trustee Home for Aged Men and Aged Men and Their Wives; trustee and dir. Blind Girls' Home; same Colored Orphans' Home; dir. Working Woman's Home; trustee and dir. first training school for nurses; trustee Washington Univ.; cashier and pres. Merchants' Nat. Bank; sec. and trustee St. Louis Med. Coll. Home: St. Louis, Mo. Died 1901.

YEATMAN, Richard Thompson, brig. general, U.S.A.; b. Cincinnati, Nov. 27, 1848; s. Walker Merideth and Eva (Ammen) Y.; grad. Hughes High Sch., Cincinnati, 1868, U.S. Mil. Acad., 1872; m. F. L. Mulhall, Oct. 1, 1879. Second lt. 14th Inf., June 14, 1872; 1st lt., Mar. 15, 1883; capt., Mar. 28, 1892; maj. 22d Inf., Nov. 13, 1900; lt. col. 27th Inf., Aug. 14, 1903; col. 11th Inf., Mar. 26, 1907; brig. gen. U.S.A., June 5, 1909; retired for disability incurred in line of duty, June 26, 1909. Mem. Order of Indian Wars U.S. Home: Glendale, O. Died Apr. 1, 1930.

YECHTON, Barbara. See Lyda F. Krausé.

YEISER, John O., lawyer, author; b. Danville, Ky., Oct. 15, 1866; s. George O. and Almira Dudley (Dillard) Y.; mainly self-ed.; m. Hettie L. (Drain) Skeen, Feb. 5, 1889; 1 son, John O. Admitted to Neb. bar at 17; began practice at Red Cloud, 1884; settled in Omaha, 1889; mem. Neb. Ho. of Rep., 1897-99; mem. State Bd. of Pardons, Neb., 1912-15; engaged, 1919-20, in litigation against packers and alleged food conspirators, at Omaha. Republican. Member of the Christian Church. Author: Evolution Proving Immortality, 1917; Death a Penalty (argument against capital punishment), 1913; Debts of Today and Hell to Pay, 1919; Real Money, 1920; The World Remade, 1924. Home: Omaha, Neb. Died Mar. 1928.

YEISLEY, George Conrad, clergyman; b. Baltimore, Jan. 21, 1849; s. Jacob and Elizabeth (Sprenger) Y.; A.B., Princeton, 1870, D.D., 1890; grad. Princeton Theol. Sem., 1873; m. Catharine Bushnell Gaul, Oct. 15, 1879. Missionary in Northern Minn., 1871-72; stated supply, Rogersville, Tenn., 1873; ordained Presbyn. ministry, 1873; asst. pastor 1st Ch., Baltimore, 1873-75; pastor Hudson, N.Y., 1875—. Moderator Synod of N.Y., 1894-95. Died Oct. 5, 1929.

YELLIN, Samuel, metal worker; b. Poland, Mar. 2, 1885; s. Zacharias and Kate (Weintraub) Y.; began studying art at the age of 11 and studied in schs. throughout European countries; m. Leah Josephs, Dec. 25, 1913; children—Ethel, Harvey. Came to U.S., 1906, naturalized citizen, 1924. Conducted business in own name as designer and executer of decorative metal work; credited with revival of good design and craftsmanship in metal work in America. Works: (metal) Harkness Memorial, Quadrangle, Yale U.; Carillon Tower, Mountain Lake, Fla.; Nat. Cathedral, Washington, D.C.; Federal Reserve Bank, Equitable Trust Co., New York; McKinlock Memorial, Northwestern U.; Hall of Fame, New York U.; W. K. Vanderbilt residence, Northport, L.I.; Cathedral of St. John the Divine, New York; Grace Cathedral, San Francisco; University of Pittsburgh, Pa. Adviser to Pa. Museum of Art. Awarded medal, Art Institute Chicago, 1918; medal Am. Inst. Architects, 1920; Boston Architectural medal, 1920; gold medal, Architectural League, New York, 1922; Bok civic award, Phila., 1925; Americanization prize, Art Exhbn., Phila., 1916; alumni medal Pa. Mus. and Sch. of Industrial Art, 1930. Mem. Am. Inst. Architects, Pa. Mus. and Sch. Industrial Arts, and other art assns. Contbr. to art journals and mags.; lecturer; collector of old iron work. Contbr. Theory, Modern Technique and Practice on Decorative Metal Work to 14th edit. Ency. Britannica. Home: Wynnewood, Pa. Died Oct. 3, 1940.

YEOMANS, George Dallas, lawyer; b. Little Valley, N.Y., May 9, 1867; s. James Dallas and Cornelia E. Y.; A.B., Yale, 1890; m. May Baldwin Stoddard, 1895. Admitted to N.Y. bar, 1893, and began practice at Buffalo; Dem. candidate for dist. atty., Erie County, 1899; moved to N.Y. City, 1900; v.p., gen. counsel Brooklyn-Manhattan Transit Corp., New York Rapid Transit Corp., Brooklyn Bus Corp., Williamsburgh Power Plant Corp., S. Brooklyn Ry. Co. Episcopalian. Home: New York, N.Y. Died Mar. 28, 1939.

YEOMANS, James D., mem. U.S. Interstate Commerce Commn.; b. Wyoming County, N.Y., April 21, 1845; entered ry. service, becoming gen. supt. Buffalo, New York and Phila. Ry., New York Ry. and later of Olean, Bradford & Warren Ry.; afterward in railroad-building in N.Y., Pa. and Mich. Died 1906.

YERKES, Charles Tyson, capitalist; b. Phila., June 25, 1837; s. Charles Tyson and Elizabeth Link (Broom) Y.; ed. Quaker School and Central High School; m. Mary Adelaide Moore. Clerk in grain commn. trade until 1858; exchange broker, 1858-61; banker, 1861-86, making splty. of bonds; failed in 1871, and as he was in debt to city of Phila. for bonds sold on its account, and refused to give the city preference over other creditors, he was convicted and imprisoned for misappropriation of public funds, but afterward pardoned. The conviction was afterwards decided illegal. Recuperated his fortunes at time of Jay Cooke failure, in 1873 and 1874; was prominent in street ry. operations in Phila. from 1860, and, after 1886, in Chicago, where he was long at head of the North and West Side and several suburban and elevated railway corporations; later engaged in financing, organizing and managing extensive system of underground railway in London. Gave to University of Chicago a telescope costing about $400,000 (then one of the largest and finest in the world, located in the Yerkes Observatory at Lake Geneva, Wis.). Home: New York, N.Y. Died 1905.

YERKES, John Watson, commissioner internal revenue; b. Lexington, Ky., Apr. 1, 1854; s. Rev. Stephen Y.; A.B., Centre Coll., Ky., 1873, A.M., 1876; LL.B., U. of Mich., 1877; LL.D., Central U., 1902; m. Elizabeth Owsley Anderson, Oct. 1879. Register in bankruptcy, 1878; master in chancery, 1887-92; chmn. Rep. State Central Com., 1891-96; commr. to Chicago Expn., 1893, to Atlanta Expn., 1895; prof. law dept., Centre Coll., 1894—. Mem. Rep. Nat. Com., 1896-1908; atty. Cincinnati, New Orleans & Texas Pacific Ry., 1892-1901; U.S. collector internal revenue, 1897; Rep. nominee for gov. of Ky., 1900; commr. of internal revenue, 1900-10. Mem. bd. visitors Govt. Hosp. for the Insane. Died Jan. 23, 1922.

YEWELL, George Henry, artist; b. Havre de Grace, Md., Jan. 20, 1830; ed. in pub. schs.; pupil of Thomas Hicks, New York; student in Nat. Acad. of Design, 1851-56; studied in Paris, 1856-61, in atelier of Thomas Couture; unmarried. Resided at Rome, Italy, 1867-78, and one winter in Cairo, Egypt; in New York, 1878—. N.A., 1880; patron Met. Museum of Art, New York. Died Sept. 25, 1923.

YLVISAKER, Ivar Daniel, clergyman; b. Trondhjem, Norway, May 26, 1868; s. Nils Th. and Kirstine (Hundere) Y; brought to U.S. in infancy; B.A., Luther Coll., Decorah, Ia., 1888; grad. Luther Sem., St. Paul, Minn., 1891; m. Delia Davidson, Aug. 24, 1892; children—Herman Ludvig, Dagny Joakime, Sigfrid Lois (Mrs. R. T. Jacobson), Erling Johan (dec.), Hedvig Kristine, Lenvik. Ordained Luth. ministry, 1891; pastor Great Falls and Helena, Mont., 1891-93, Mayville, N.D., 1893-1917; pres. (corresponds to bishop) N.D. Dist., Norwegian Luth Ch. America, 1917—; pres. Ministerium of Synod of Norwegian Luth. Ch. America, 1910-17; pres. Luth. S.S. Assn., Dist. of N.D., v.p., trustee Concordia Coll., Moorhead, Minn. Mem. com. which brought about union of 3 large Luth. denominations in America. Home: Fargo, N.Dak. Died 1926.

YOAKUM, Benjamin F., ry. pres.; b. in Limestone County, Tex.; m. Elizabeth Bennett; children—Mrs. Katheryne Fosdick, Mrs. Bessie Larkin. Traffic mgr., asst. gen. mgr. and gen. mgr., 1884-90, receiver, 1890-92, traffic mgr., 1892, San Antonio & Aransas Pass Ry.; 3d v.p. and gen. mgr. Gulf, Colo. & Santa Fe Ry., 1893-96; v.p. and gen. mgr., 1896-1900, pres. and gen. mgr., 1900-01, pres., 1901-04, chmn. of bd. to Oct. 1904, chmn. exec. com., 1904-13, chmn. bd. dirs., 1909-13, later dir. St.L.&S.F. R.R.; pres. 1902-04, chmn. bd. to Nov. 11, 1904, chmn. exec. com., 1904-13, C.&E.I. R.R.; chmn. bd. dirs. Empire Bond & Mortgage Corp.; dir. Seaboard Air Line Ry. Was chmn. exec. com., C.,R.I.&P. Ry., 1905-09. Home: Farmingdale, L.I., N.Y. Died Nov. 28, 1929.

YOCUM, A(lbert) Duncan, prof. pedagogy; b. York, Pa., July 22, 1869; s. Rev. Andrew D. and Laura M. (Gere) Y.; Ph.B., Dickinson Coll., Carlisle, Pa., 1889; Ph.D. from U. of Pa., 1900; D.H.L., Dickinson Coll., 1930; m. May Turner, July 7, 1891. Assistant prin. high sch., Chester, Pa., 1889-90; prin. schs., Smyrna, Del., 1890-95; supt. city schs., Millville, N.J., 1895-1900; supt. city schs., Chester, Pa., 1900-06; prof. pedagogy, 1906-13, prof. ednl. research and practice, 1913—, dir. summer sch., 1907-12, U. of Pa. First pres. State Principals' Assn., Del., 1893-94; first sec. and treas. State Child Study Assn., N.J., 1897-98; organized summer training schs. for teachers at Dover and Rehoboth, Del. Methodist. Author: Culture, discipline and Democracy; The Democracy Questionnaire; reports on existing democratic factors in Am. life and edn.; standards for religious edn. adopted by Internat. S.S. Com. of Relig. Edn.; An Analysis of Education as Conduct Control. Frequent speaker on ednl. topics and contbr. to ednl. jours. and reviews. Home: Ridley Park, Pa. Died June 8, 1936.

YODER, Robert Anderson, clergyman; b. Lincoln County, N.C., Aug. 16, 1853; s. Solomon and Sarah (Slegle) Y.; A.B., N.C. Coll., 1877, D.D., 1899; m. Rosa Fisher, May 9, 1878. Ordained Luth. ministry, 1879; attended Theol. Sem., Phila., 1883-84; pastor St. James', Grace and Salem congregations in N.C., 1884-98; county supt. schs., 1884-94; pres. Concordia Coll., 1888-1901; pres. Lenoir Coll., Hickory, N.C., 1891-1901; pastor Emmanuel's Ch., Lincolnton, N.C., 1905—. Pres. United Synod of South, Charleston, S.C., 1902, and New Market, Va. Died 1911.

YOHN, Frederick Coffay, illustrator; b. Indianapolis, Ind., Feb. 8, 1875; s. Albert B. and Addie F. Y.; common sch. edn.; 1 yr.'s course Indianapolis Art Sch.; then studied at Art Students' League, New York, under Mowbray; m. Gertrude Klamroth, Jan. 11, 1908; children—Fred C., Albert K. Illustrator on "The Round Table," 1894; then illustrated a series of frontier sketches by Theodore Roosevelt and serials by James Barnes and Molly Elliot Seawell; did much work for Scribner's Magazine, Collier's Weekly, and others. Noted for his spirited battle scenes. Home: Norfolk, Conn. Died June 5, 1933.

YORE, Clem, author; b. St. Louis, Mo., May 6, 1875; s. James H. and Virginia Ann (Hanley) Y.; student pub. schs., Rock Island, Ill., Canton, Ill., and St. Louis, Mo., Augustus Mil. Acad., Fort Defiance, Va., Washington U. Law Sch., 1895-96; m. Olive May Shepperd, December 1897 (divorced in 1914); 1 dau., Juanita Yore Farris; m. 2d, Alberta McAuley Plondke, 1915. Admitted to Mo. bar, 1896; practiced one yr.; abandoned law for newspaper work; successively reporter, Seattle (Wash.) Post-Intelligencer, San Francisco Examiner and Chronicle, St. Louis Republic and Chronicle, Chicago American and Examiner, 1899-1912. Served as pvt. in Spanish-Am. War. Democrat. Mason. Author: Songs of the Underworld (poems), 1914; Raw Gold, 1926; Trigger Justice, 1928; Hardriding Slim Magee, 1929; Dusty Dan Delaney, 1930; Ranger Bill, 1931; Young Desire, 1931; The Six Gun Code, 1932; Age of Consent, 1932; O'Malley in the Saddle, 1932; The Two-Gun Kid, 1932; Rider of the Red Ranges, 1933; Mississippi Jimmy, 1933; Sudden Slim, 1934; Valley of Grim Men, 1934; Hard Country and Gold, 1935. Novels appear in Spanish and Hungarian transls. and in England. Contbr. of over 600 stories and articles and over 300 poems to leading mags. Home: Estes Park, Colo. Died Oct. 24, 1936.

YORK, Edward Palmer, architect; b. Wellsville, N.Y., 1865; s. Hiram and Harriett (Palmer) Y.; studied architecture, Cornell U., 1887-89, later in office of McKim, Mead & White, New York; m. Muriel Gould, 1910. Practiced in N.Y. City, 1898—; mem. firm York & Sawyer; firm architects of N.Y. Hist. Soc., Guaranty Trust Co. Bldg., U.S. Assay Office, Rockefeller, Manhattan Eye, Ear and Throat, Ruptured and Crippled Babies, Orthopedic, 5th Av., Roosevelt hosps. (N.Y. City), Riggs Nat. Bank (Washington, D.C.), Brooklyn Trust Co., Rochester Trust Bldg. and Lincoln Nat. Bank Bldg. (Rochester, N.Y.), Hospital Trust Co. (Providence, R.I.), bldgs. at U. of Mich., Vassar, Smith, Middlebury and Rutgers colls., Post Office, Customs House and Courts Bldg., Honolulu, H.I.; firm consulting architect to the Treasury Dept., Washington, D.C., 1909-13, and to the Bd. of Water Supply, City of New York. Mem. A.I.A., Archtl. League New York. Home: Princeton, N.J., and Stonington, Conn. Died Dec. 30, 1928.

YORK, Samuel Albert, banking; b. New Haven, Conn., Oct. 11, 1868; s. Samuel Amos and Helen E. (Osborn) Y.; A.B., Yale, 1890, LL.B., 1892; m. Anna M. Holcomb, Nov. 28, 1893 (died 1920); children—Holcomb, Samuel A. Admitted to Conn. bar, 1892, and practiced at New Haven until 1912; interested in pub. utilities and finance, 1912—; v.p. Merchants Nat. Bank, 1923-25, pres., 1925—; dir. Am. Tar Co., Salem Terminal Co., Security Ins. Co., and many pub. utility cos. Chmn. exemption bd., New Haven, World War. Pres. Permanent Paving Commn., New Haven (mem., 1903—); pres. Neighborhood House Council; treas. New Haven Community Chest (dir.), Bi-Centennial Fund. Trustee and treas. Berkeley Div. Sch.; mem. House of Deputies, Episcopal Conv., 1928. Home: New Haven, Conn. Died Mar. 7, 1931.

YORKE, George Marshall, telegraph official; b. Lowell, Mass., Apr. 27, 1870; s. Joseph B. and Helen D. (Wardwell) Y.; S.B., Mass. Inst. of Tech., 1893; m. Eunice C. Booth, Apr. 8, 1932. With Am. Telephone and Telegraph Co., 1893-1911; connected with Western Union Telegraph Co., 1911—, successively as engr., gen. supt. of plant, and as v.p. in charge engring., 1916—; dir. Am. District Telegraph Co. (N.J.), Gold & Stock Telegraph Co., Stock Quotation Telegraph Co., Teleregister Corp.; apptd. 1918 by Postmaster Gen. Burleson, mem. operating bd. U.S. Telegraph and Telephone Administration. Maj. Signal Officers' R.C., attached to staff of chief signal officer of the Army, 1917-18. Fellow Am. Inst. Elec. Engrs. Home: New York, N.Y. Died Mar. 18, 1934.

YORKE, Peter Christopher, clergyman; b. Galway City, Ireland, Aug. 15, 1864; s. Gregory and Brigid (Kelly) Y.; ed. St. Joseph's Sem., St. Ignatius Coll., St. Jarlath's Coll., Maynooth Coll., to 1886; St. Mary's, Baltimore, 1886-87; S.T.B., Catholic U. of America, 1890, S.T.L., 1891; S.T.D., Rome, 1906, by spl. decree of Congregation of Studies. Ordained priest R.C. Ch., 1887; asst. St. Mary's Cathedral, San Francisco, 1888-89, 1891-94; chancellor of diocese, 1894; editor Monitor, 1895; asst. at St. Peter's Ch., 1889-1903; permanent rector St. Anthony's Ch., Oakland, Calif., 1903-13, St. Peter's Ch., San Francisco, 1913—. Regent U. of Calif., 1903-13. Author: Text Books of Religion, 1896; Yorke-Wendte Controversy, 1896; Children's Mass, 1899; Three Letters on Education, 1900, Roman Liturgy, 1903; Family, State and School, 1912; Ghosts of Bigotry, 1913; The World's Desire, 1913; Altar and Priest, 1913; Teaching of Religion, 1918; The Mass, 1921. V.p. Nat. Catholic Edn. Soc., 1918, 1921-23. Home: San Francisco, Calif. Died Apr. 5, 1925.

YOST, Casper Salathiel, editor; b. Sedalia, Mo., July 1, 1864; s. George Casper and Sarah Elizabeth (Morris) Y.; ed. common schs., Lebanon, and Richland, Mo.; LL.D. from Lincoln Memorial U., 1926, McKendree Coll., 1928, U. of Mo., 1934; m. Anna Augusta Parrott, May 2, 1883; children—Alfred Clarence, Robert George (dec.), Casper Salathiel. Began with Laclede County Leader, Lebanon, Mo., 1872; reporter St. Louis Daily Chronicle, 1881-82; telegraph operator, 1882-85; reporter and asst. telegraph editor, Missouri Republican, St. Louis, 1886-88; joined staff St. Louis Globe-Democrat, 1889, asst. to mng. editor, and Sunday editor, 1890-1915; editor editorial page Globe-Democrat, 1915—. Trustee Mo. Hist. Soc.; dir. Children's Home Soc. of Mo. Mem. Christian (Disciples) Church. Author: A Successful Husband, 1907; Patience Worth, 1916; The World War, 1919; Principles of Journalism, 1924; The Quest of God, 1929; The Carpenter of Nazareth, 1938. Awarded medal of honor for distinguished service in journalism by Missouri University Sch. of Journalism, 1932; national award for scholarship in journalism by Sigma Delta Chi, 1932. Home: St. Louis, Mo. Died May 30, 1941.

YOUMANS, Frank A., judge; b. nr. Jefferson City, Mo., May 23, 1860; s. John P. and Mary E. (Faust) Y.; Letters B., U. of Mo., 1884, Letters M., 1891; m. D. A. L. Enroughty, Dec. 27, 1888. Admitted to Ark. bar, 1885; practiced at Ft. Smith, Ark., 1886-1911; U.S. dist. judge Western Dist. of Ark., 1911—. Republican. Methodist. Home: Ft. Smith, Ark. Died Apr. 11, 1932.

YOUNG, Abram Van Eps, chemist; b. Sheboygan, Wis., June 5, 1853; s. Van Eps and Arlisle (Seaman) Y.; Ph.B., Ph.C., U. of Mich., 1875; fellow, Johns Hopkins, 1878-80; unmarried. Asst. in chemistry, U. of Mich., 1875-77, Harvard, 1884-85; prof. chemistry, Northwestern U., 1885—. Author: The Elementary Principles of Chemistry. Died Dec. 23, 1921.

YOUNG, Allyn Abbott, professor economics; b. Kenton, O., Sept. 19, 1876; s. Sutton Erastus and Emma Matilda (Stickney) Y.; Ph.B., Hiram Coll., O., 1894; Ph.D., U. of Wis., 1902; m. Jessie Bernice Westlake, Aug. 10, 1904; 1 son, John Westlake. Teacher economics, U. of Wis., Western Reserve U. and Dartmouth Coll.; head of dept. of economics, Leland Stanford Jr. U., 1906-11; prof. economics, Washington U., 1911-13; prof. economics and finance, Cornell, 1913-20; prof. economics Harvard Univ., 1920—; prof. political economy, Univ. of London, 1927—. Dir. Bureau of Research, War Trade Board, 1917-18; chief Div. of Economics and Statistics, Am Commn. to Negotiate Peace, 1918-19; mem. Mass Commn. on Pensions, 1923-24. Sec.-treas. Am. Econ Assn., 1914-20 (pres. 1925); fellow Royal Statis. Soc., Am. Acad. Arts and Sciences, Am. Statis. Assn. (pres. 1917). Comdr. Order of the Crown of Belgium. Joint Author Outlines of Economics, revised edits., 1908, 16, 23. Author: Economic Problems New and Old, 1927; An Analysis of Banking Statistics, 1927. Died Mar. 1929.

YOUNG, Andrew Harvey, prof. natural science; b. Avondale, Cincinnati, O., Feb. 2, 1852; s. Hugh Hamilton and Janet (Harvey) Y.; A.B., Hanover (Ind.) Coll., 1871, A.M., 1874; Scheffield Scientific Sch. (Yale), 1873-75; Ph.D., Washington and Jefferson Coll., 1880; m. Mary Agnes Dunn, June 19, 1877; children—Jessie Dunn (dec.), Mary Elizabeth. Prin. prep. dept., Hanover Coll., 1872-73; teacher high sch., Lafayette, Ind., 1877-79; prof. natural science, Hanover Coll., 1879—, also sec. of faculty and registrar, 1879-1909. Specialized in chemistry and botany. Contbr. to scientific publs., and newspaper correspondent. Republican. Presbyterian. Home: Hanover, Ind. Died May 17, 1926.

YOUNG, Bennett Henderson, lawyer; b. Nicholasville, Ky., May 25, 1843; s. Robert and Josephine (Henderson) Y.; ed. Centre Coll., Ky., and Queen's Coll., Toronto, Can.; grad. law dept. Queen's Coll., Belfast, Ireland; hon. M.A., Southwestern Presbyn. U.; LL.D., King's Coll., Tenn., 1891; m. Mattie R. Robinson, 1866; m. 2d, Eliza S. Sharp, 1895. Served in C.S.A. under Gen. John H. Morgan, in command St. Alban's raid. Pres. Louisville Pub. Library; mem. Filson Club; mem. Ky. Constl. Conv., 1890; Ky. rep. to Paris Expn., 1878; lt. gen. comdg. Dept. of Tenn., U.C.V., 1910-11; comdr.-in-chief U.C.V., 1912-16; hon. comdr.-in-chief for life; hon. comdr. Ky. Div. for life; rep. of the South in Gettysburg Reunion, 1913. Pres. Confed. Home, Ky. State Instn. for Blind, Jefferson Davis Home Assn. Moderator Presbyn. Synod of Ky., 1910. Author: History Constitutions, Ky., 1890; History of Evangelistic Work, Ky., 1891; History Battle Blue Lick, 1895; History Jessamine Co., Ky., 1898; History Division Presbyterian Church in Ky., 1898; History Battle of Thames, 1901; Prehistoric Men of Kentucky, 1910; Confederate Wizards of the Saddle, 1914. Editor Kentucky Eloquence, 1907. Home: Louisville, Ky. Died Feb. 23, 1919.

YOUNG, Bicknell, Christian Science lecturer; b. Salt Lake City, Utah; s. Joseph and Jane Adeline (Bicknell) Y.; ed. high sch.; grad. Nat. Training Sch. for Music, London, 1883; m. Elisa Mazzucato, of Milan, Italy, 1883; children—Arrigo M., Hilgard B., Umberto. Professional musician until 1903; practitioner and authorized teacher of Christian Science, 1901—; first reader, 2d Ch. of Christ, Scientist, at Chicago, 1898-1901; Publication Com. of Ill., 1902-03; mem. Bd. of Lectureship of Mother Ch., 1903-27; teacher normal class, Mass. Metaphysical Coll., 1910; 1st reader, Mother Ch., 1917-20; again lecturer. Home: Chicago, Ill. Died Mar. 5, 1938.

YOUNG, Charles Augustus, prof. astronomy, Princeton U., 1877-1905; b. Hanover, N.H., Dec. 15, 1834; grad. Dartmouth, 1853; Ph.D., U. of Pa., 1870, Hamilton Coll., New York, 1871; LL.D., Wesleyan, Conn., 1876, Columbia, 1887, Western Reserve, 1893, Dartmouth, 1903; m. Augusta S. Mixer, Aug. 26, 1857. Served as capt. Co. B, 85th Regiment, Ohio vols., 4 months, 1862. Prof. mathematics, natural philosophy and astronomy, Western Reserve Coll., 1857-66; prof. natural philosophy and astronomy, Dartmouth, 1866-77; then at Princeton until resigned, June, 1905. Mem. of Nat. Acad. Sciences and many other Am. and foreign learned socs. Specialist in solar physics; discoverer of the solar "reversing layer." Author: The Sun (in Internat. Scientific Series), 1882; A General Astronomy, 1889; Elements of Astronomy, 1890; Lessons in Astronomy, 1891; Manual of Astronomy, 1902; Uranography. Home: Hanover, N.H. Died 1908.

YOUNG, C(harles) Jac, artist; b. Bavaria, Dec. 21, 1880; s. Peter and Katherine (May) Y.; brought to US., 1882; student Nat. Acad. of Design, 1907-

09, Robert Henri's Sch., 1910; m. Blenda Sophia Jepson, Dec. 31, 1905; 1 son, Howard Sargent. Rep. by paintings in Yonkers (N.Y.) Mus. of Science and Art, Hasbrouck Heights (N.J.) Pub. Library, Kearney (N.J.) Bd. of Edn., Paper Mill Playhouse Gallery (Short Hills, N.J.), Hunderton County (N.J.) Dept. of Pub. Instrn.; rep. by etchings in Newark (N.J.) Pub. Library, Los Angeles Mus. of History, Science and Art, Toronto Art Gallery, N.Y. Pub. Library, Chicago, Milwaukee and Peoria art insts. univs. of Nebraska and Yale; Phila. Art Alliance, Corcoran Art Galleries, Library of Congress, Smithsonian Instn., Honolulu Acad. of Arts, Brooklyn (N.Y.) Mus., Phila. Print Club, Soc. of Am. Etchers, Chicago Soc. of Etchers. Awarded prizes for paintings, first, Paterson, N.J., 1930, Newark (N.J.) Art Club, 1931-33, 35, Newark (N.J.) Contemporary Club, 1934; 2d prizes, Newark Contemporary Club, 1935, N.J. Gallery, 1935; purchase prize, Yonkers (N.Y.) Art Assn., 1929. Awarded prizes for etchings, first, N.J. Gallery, 1933, Montclair (N.J.) Art Assn., 1933, 2d prize, N.J. Gallery, 1932; Kate W. Arms prize, Brooklyn Soc. of Etchers, 1928; Shaw prize Salmagundi Club (N.Y.), 1929; honorable mention, Phila. Print Club, 1933; popular vote prize, Albany (N.Y.) Print Club. Lutheran. Mason. Home: Weehawken Heights, N.J. Died Mar. 4, 1940.

YOUNG, Charles Luther, soldier; b. Albany, N.Y., Nov. 23, 1838; s. Eli and Eleanor Y.; ed. Albany Acad., and (grad.) Prof. Charles H. Anthony's Classical Inst., Albany, 1858; LL.D., Wilberforce U., Ohio; m. Cora M., d. Albert Day, M.D., of Boston, Jan. 18, 1871. Served throughout the Civil War, entering Apr. 1861, as Zouave cadet, and from May 1861, in Sickles' "Excelsior Brigade," U.S. vols.; comd. 1st Regt. 2d Bull Run campaign and last in command in the field; staff officer 2d and 3d Army Corps, Army of Potomac, with Generals Sickles, Hooker and Hancock; bvtd. lt. col. vols. at end of war; wounded at Chancellorsville, and again in the Wilderness, Va. Brig. gen., State of Ohio, 1878-80; charter companion Ohio Commandery Mil. Order Loyal Legion U.S.; senior vice comdr.-in-chief G.A.R., 1881-82. Mfr. and mcht. in lumber, Toledo, for 21 yrs.; park commr., Toledo, 18 yrs., and pres. bd.; trustee Toledo Med. Coll., 1888—; dir. Toledo U., 1898-1900; dir. Gettysburg Battlefield Memorial Assn., 1885-96; supt. Ohio Soldiers' and Sailors' Orphans' Home, Xenia, O., 1890-95, and 1900-04; first supt. Pa. Soldiers' Orphans' Industrial School, 1895-96. Home: Toledo, O. Died Sept. 18, 1913.

YOUNG, Clark Montgomery, prof. polit. and social science, U. of So. Dak., 1892—, dean of faculty of Arts and Sciences, 1902—; b. Hiram, O.; s. Erastus M. Y.; grad. Hiram Coll., Ph.D., same; m. Retta F. Murray, 1883. Sec. Territorial bd. edn. for Dak., 1889, and same office in State of S. Dak., 1889-90. Author: (with Prof. Geo. M. Smith) The State and Nation; History and Government of South Dakota (Werner Series of State Civics); Elements of Pedagogy; Wrote: Psychology and Education, Proc. State Ednl. Assn.; The Constitution of South Dakota (Appendix to S. Dak. Edition, Dole's American Citizen); The History and Government of South Dakota and the Government of the United States; Elements of Pedagogy; Territorial and State History of South Dakota, in State Atlas of South Dakota. Home: Vermillion, S.Dak. Died 1908.

YOUNG, Courtland H., editor, pub.; b. New Orleans, La., May 15, 1876; s. Courtland H. and Rosa (Wilson) Y.; ed. pub. schs. of New Orleans; married; 1 dau., Rosabelle Corinne. Founder and, pub. Young's Magazine, 1899—, Breezy Stories, 1915—, Yellow Book, 1910—, Droll Stories, 1917—. Republican. Died Dec. 3, 1930.

YOUNG, Edward M., corp. official; pres. Lehigh Portland Cement Co., Lehigh Valley Trust Co., Allentown Steam Heating & Power Co.; v.p. Lehigh Valley Transit Co.; dir. Pa. Power & Light Co., Lehigh Power Securities Co., Lehigh Telephone Co., Pa. Power & Light Co., and officer or dir. various other corps. Died Apr. 26, 1932.

YOUNG, Ella Flagg, superintendent of schs.; b. Buffalo, Jan. 15, 1845; d. Theodore and Jane (Reed) Flagg; grad. Chicago High Sch. and Chicago Normal Sch.; Ph.D., U. of Chicago, 1900; LL.D., U. of Ill., 1910; m. William Young, 1868. Engaged in teaching, 1862-1915; dist. supt. schs., Chicago, 1887-99; prof. of edn., U. of Chicago, 1899-1905; prin. Chicago Normal Sch., 1905-09; supt. of schs., Chicago, 1909-15, except short time, Dec. 10-Dec. 23, 1913 (resigned and was reëlected). Mem. State Bd. of Edn., Ill., 1888-1912; pres. Ill. State Teachers' Assn., 1910; pres. N.E.A., 1910-11. Editor The Educational Bi-Monthly, 1906-09. An organization of women principals of Chicago elementary schs. is named the Ella Flagg Young Club, after Mrs. Young. Author: Isolation in the School, 1901; Ethics in the School, 1902; Some Types of Modern Educational Theory, 1902; various monographs; collaborator on Young and Field Literary Readers. Mem. Nat. Woman's Liberty Loan Com., 1917. Home: Chicago, Ill. Died Oct. 26, 1918.

YOUNG, Frederic George, univ. prof.; b. Burnett, Wis., June 3, 1858; s. Quirin and Maria Sophia Y.; A.B., Johns Hopkins, 1886, univ. scholar, 1886-87; LL.D., U. of Oregon, 1920; m. Mary Luella Packard, July 25, 1887; children—Frances Packard, Frederic Harold. V.p. State Normal Sch., Madison, S.D., 1887-90; prin. Portland (Ore.) High Sch., 1890-94; pres. Albany (Ore.) Coll., 1894-95; prof. economics and sociology, U. of Ore., 1895-1920, also dean Grad. Sch., 1900-20, and dean Sch. of Sociology, 1919—. Mem. S.D. Constl. Conv., 1889. Sec. Ore. Hist. Soc., 1898—. Editor: Sources of the History of Oregon. Editor Quarterly Journal of Ore. Hist. Soc., and of Commonwealth Review. Mem. Oregon Commn. for Lewis and Clark Centennial; Sec. Ore. Conservation Commn., 1908—. Author: Finances of Oregon. Home: Eugene, Ore. Died Jan. 4, 1929.

YOUNG, George Brigham, vice pres. Nat. Life Ins. Co.; b. Troy, Vt., Apr. 20, 1867; s. John and Augusta A. Young; student Wesleyan Acad., Wilbraham, Mass., 1883-86, Dartmouth Coll., 1886-88, A.M., 1920; m. Grace M. Spear, 1894 (now dec.); children—John Spear, Harold Kimball; m. 2d, Mollie M. Beals, 1927. Admitted to bars of Vt., 1891, Minn., 1892; practiced at Newport, Vt., 1891; at Minneapolis, 1892-99; at Newport, Vt., 1899-1916; atty. M.,St.P.& S.S.M. Ry., 1893-95; gen. counsel Nat. Life Ins. Co., Montpelier, Vt., 1916-34, vice pres. and gen. counsel, 1934—; vice pres. and dir. Conn. & Passumpsic R.R.; dir. Newport & Richford R.R. Co. Mem. Montpelier Chamber of Commerce (pres.), Vt. State Chamber of Commerce (v.p.), Nat. Conf. of Commns. on Uniform State Laws (sec. 1914-18, pres. 1925-27). Trustee Newport (Vt.) Pub. Schs., 1904, 1908-11, Vt. State Library, Wilbraham (Mass.) Acad. Mem. or officer many law assns. Republican. Conglist. Mason. Home: Montpelier, Vt. Died Apr. 10, 1940.

YOUNG, George Bright, M.D.; b. New Orleans, May 12, 1860; s. George Bright and Ann Tweed (Rogers) Y.; ed. pvt. schs. and U. of Va.; M.D., U. of Md., 1887; m. Ellen Miles, d. Col. James M. Marshall, Sept. 9, 1891; children—George Bright, James Marshall, Catharine Fisher, Anne Shippen, Alexander Brownlee (dec.). Commd. asst. surgeon, U.S. Pub. Health Service, Jan. 30, 1890; passed asst. surgeon, May 25, 1894; surgeon, 1905-24; commr. of Health of Chicago, 1911-15; sanitary advisor 5th Naval Dist., July 1917-19; surgeon in charge, U.S. Marine Hosp., Stapleton, N.Y., Apr. 12, 1919, sr. surgeon, 1920-24; asso. prof. preventive medicine, U. of Va., 1924-31; health officer Joint Health Dept. of Charlottesville, Albemarle and University, Va. Home: University, Va. Died Feb. 13, 1934.

YOUNG, George Brooks, lawyer; b. Boston, July 25, 1840; s. late Rev. Dr. Alexander and Caroline (James) Y.; early edn. Boston pub. schs.; grad. Harvard, 1860, Harvard Law Sch., 1863; admitted to bar, 1864; m. Ellen Fellows, Sept. 28, 1870 (died 1905). Went to Minn., 1870, and engaged in practice; asso. justice Supreme Court, Minn., Apr. 1874-Jan. 1875, to fill vacancy; Supreme Court reporter, 1875-92; prepared vols. 21 to 47, Minn. reports; lecturer on conflict of laws, U. of Minn. Law Sch., several yrs.; mem. law firm Young & Lightner. Home: St. Paul, Minn. Died 1906.

YOUNG, George Morley, judge; b. Lakelet, Ont., Can., Dec. 11, 1870; s. Richard and Jane (Eaton) Y.; LL.B., U. of Minnesota, 1894; m. Augusta L. Freeman, Jan. 3, 1899; 1 daughter, Katherine. Began practice, Valley City, N.D., 1894. Mem. N.D. Ho. of Rep., 1900-02, Senate, 1904-08 (pres. pro tem., 1907); mem. 63d to 68th Congresses (1913-25), 2d N.D.; resigned, Sept. 2, 1924, upon appointment as district judge of the Customs Court, New York. Republican. Conglist. Home: Valley City, N.D. Died May 27, 1932.

YOUNG, George Rude, lawyer; b. Dayton, O., Oct. 2, 1857; s. Edmond Stafford and Sarah B. (Dechert) Y.; grad. Central High Sch., Dayton, 1875; unmarried. Admitted to bar, 1878, and practiced at Dayton; sr. mem. firm of Young & Young. Rep. nominee for pros. atty., 1881, for city solicitor, 1885, for 62d Congress, 1910. Mem. Am. Bar Assn. (v.p. for Ohio 1913-14, mem. gen. council from Ohio, 1914-15, v.p. for Ohio, 1915-16); trustee Dayton Law Library Assn. Home: Dayton, O. Deceased.

YOUNG, George Washington, banker; b. Jersey City, N.J., July 1, 1864; s. Peter and Mary (Crosby) Y.; ed. common schs. Jersey City and scientific course at Cooper Inst., New York; m. Natalie Bray, Nov. 26, 1889; m. 2d, London, Lillian Nordica, July 29, 1909. Was pres. U.S. Mortgage and Trust Co.; pres. Continental Investment Co., Iroquois Navigation Co., Jersey Dock Co.; chmn. bd. Audit Co. of N.Y.; treas. George W. Young & Co.; dir. City & Suburban Homes Co., Consolidated Palo Amarillo Rubber Co., Appraisals Corp., and a number of other corps. Home: Deal, N.J. Died Feb. 18, 1926.

YOUNG, Horace Gedney, railway official; b. Honesdale, Pa., Jan. 26, 1854; s. Coe F. and Mary A. (Cornell) Y.; ed. Edwards Pl. Sch., Stockbridge, Mass.; C.E., Rensselaer Poly. Inst., 1877; m. Cornelia L. Hascy, Oct. 12, 1881. Entered service Del. & Hudson Canal Co., 1879, serving as asst. to gen. mgr., 1879-83, asst. gen. mgr., 1883-85, gen. mgr., 1885-86, asst. to pres., and gen. mgr., 1886-88, 2d v.p., 1888-1903 (resigned). Pres. Albany (N.Y.) Trust Co., 1905—. Trustee Rensselaer Poly. Inst., 1893—. Republican. Home: Albany, N.Y. Died Oct. 17, 1933.

YOUNG, H(orace) Olin, congressman; b. New Albion, N.Y., Aug. 4, 1850; s. Horace C. and Laura P. (Walker) Y.; ed. Randolph Acad. and Chamberlain Inst., Randolph, N.Y., to 1869; studied law in office of E. E. Osborn; m. Mary J. Marsh, N.Y., Mar. 20, 1876. Admitted to bar, 1882; mem. Mich. Legislature, 1879-80; pros. atty. Marquette County, Mich., 1884-94; mem. 58th to 62d Congresses (1903-13), 12th Mich. Dist.; reëlected to 63d Congress but later resigned. Mem. Rep. State Com. 10 yrs. Home: Ishpeming, Mich. Died Aug. 4, 1917.

YOUNG, James Carleton, bibliophile; b. Marion, Ia., July 29, 1856; s. Joseph Barris and Jane (Carter) Y.; B.S., Cornell Coll., Ia., 1876, M.S., 1879, Litt.D., 1909; LL.D., Lenox Coll., Hopkinton, Ia., 1913; m. Etta May Rogers, Apr. 30, 1888. Pres. Central Trackage Co., Imperial Investment Co.; v.p. Guaranty Investment Co., Guaranty Realty Co.; sec. N.D. Clay & Coal Co.; treas. Empire Real Estate & Mortgage Co. Pres. Nat. Assn. of Real Estate Dealers, 1884-86. Hon. commr. of U.S. to Paris Expn., 1878. Devoted much time to the formation of a library, containing the best books of the most celebrated living authors of the world, each volume characteristically inscribed by the writer. Upon petition of many of the most celebrated authors of France, was decorated in 1910 by that Republic with the Cross of the Legion of Honor, as a recognition of his services to literature. Mem. numerous lit. and book socs. Home: Minneapolis, Minn. Died Jan. 7, 1918.

YOUNG, James Henry, theologian; b. Fremont, O., June 7, 1866; s. Rev. Charles Huntington and Emma Adams (Sawer) Y.; B.A., Kenyon Coll., Gambier, O., 1887, M.A., 1890, D.D., 1915; studied Bexley Hall, Gambier, 1888, 89; grad. Phila. Div. School, 1890; post-grad. work same, 1891; m. Rebekah Mayhew Paddack, June 10, 1897. Deacon, 1890, priest, 1891, P.E. Ch.; in charge St. Barnabas Ch., Denison, O., 1890-93, Ch. of Ascension, Wyoming, O., 1893-96, Trinity Ch., Troy, 1897-1906, Trinity Ch., Tiffin, 1906-15; prof. systematic theology, Seabury Div. Sch., Faribault, Minn., 1915—; chaplain St. Mary's Hall. Examining chaplain Diocese of Southern Ohio 5 yrs., Diocese of Ohio 9 yrs., Diocese of Minn., 1915—. Contbg. editor The Witness. Home: Faribault, Minn. Mason. Died 2, 1919.

YOUNG, James Kelly, orthopædic surgeon; b. Trenton, N.J., Apr. 29, 1862; s. William and Ellen (Kelly) Y.; grad. Trenton High Sch., 1879; M.D., U. of Pa., 1883; studied surgery in Vienna, 1888; m. Mary Thornton Wilson, 1899. Asst. resident phys. Phila. Dispensary, 1883-84; resident phys. Phila. Gen. Hosp., 1884-85; asst. demonstrator of surgery, 1886-92, asso. prof. orthopedic surgery, U. of Pa.; prof. orthopedics, U. of Pa. Grad. Sch. of Medicine; sometime lecturer on orthopedic surgery, U. of Pa.; orthopædic surgeon to Phila. Gen. Hosp.; consulting orthopedic surgeon, Woman's Hosp., Phila. Lying-In Charity Hosp. Fellow Am. Coll. Surgeons, Am. Orthopædic Assn. Republican. Author: Manual and Atlas of Orthopædic Surgery, 1894, 1905; Synopsis of Human Anatomy, 5 edits., 1889-1919. Contbr. to Roberts' Orthopædic Surgery, 1898, and numerous articles on orthopædic surg. subjects in med. jours. Home: Philadelphia, Pa. Died Aug. 28, 1923.

YOUNG, James Rankin, congressman; b. Philadelphia, Mar. 10, 1847; s. George Rankin and Eliza (Russell) Y.; ed. Phila. pub. schs.; m. Mary Barclay, 1874. Pvt. 32d Pa. Inf. in Gettysburg campaign; made tour of Southern States at close of Civil War for New York Tribune; was its chief Washington corr., 1866-70; chief exec. clerk, U.S. Senate, 1873-79, and 1883-92; chief clerk Dept. of Justice, 1881-83; one of founders Phila. Evening Star and its Washington corr. for 30 yrs.; mem. 55th to 57th Congresses (1897-1903), 4th Pa. Dist.; supt. dead letter office Post Office Dept., 1905-13; supt. of the Postal Savings Depository, Phila. Postoffice, 1913-15. Republican. Home: Washington, D.C. Died Dec. 18, 1924.

YOUNG, James Scott, judge; b. Pittsburgh, Dec. 3, 1848; s. William H. and Jane A. (Peters) Y.; A.B., Washington and Jefferson Coll., Pa., 1869; LL.D., 1910; read law, Pittsburgh, 1869-72; m. Lida J., d. Dr. J. D. Baldwin, of Oil City, Pa., Mar. 4, 1873. Admitted to bar, 1872, and practiced at Pittsburgh. U.S. atty. Western Dist. Pa., 1902-05; judge Ct. of Common Pleas No. 2, Allegheny County, Pa., 1905-08; U.S. dist. judge, 1908—. Republican. Home: Pittsburgh, Pa. Died Feb. 25, 1914.

YOUNG, Jesse Bowman, clergyman; b. Berwick, Pa., July 5, 1844; s. Rev. Jared H. and Sarah (Bowman) Y.; grad. Dickinson Sem., Williamsport, Pa., 1866; A.B., Dickinson Coll, 1868, A.M., 1871, D.D., 1907; D.D., DePauw, 1887; m. Lucy M. Spottswood, Dec. 22, 1870. Served 3 yrs. in Union Army in Civil War, ending as capt. 84th Pa. Vols. In ministry, M.E. Ch. from 1868; pastor at York Springs, Gettysburg, Curwensville, Carlisle, Altoona, and Harrisburg, Pa., 1868-Mar. 1, 1888, Kansas City, 1888-92; editor Central Christian Advocate, St. Louis, 1892-1900, pastor Walnut Hills Ch., Cincinnati, 1900-08, Snyder Memorial

Ch., Jacksonville, Fla., 1908-1912, Bluffton, Ind., till April 1, 1913, when retired from active pastorate for lit. work. Delegate General Conf., 1896, 1900, Ecumenical Conf. of Methodism, London, 1901. Author: Days and Nights on the Sea, 1887; What a Boy Saw in the Army, 1894; Helps for the Quiet Hour, 1900; Our Lord and Master—A Brief Study of the Claims of Jesus Christ, 1903; The Hungry Christ, and Other Sermons, 1904; Wellsprings in the Desert, 1905; Today: An Age of Opportunity, 1909; Charms of the Bible, 1910; The Battle of Gettysburg, 1913. Home: Chicago, Ill. Died July 30, 1914.

YOUNG, John Edwin, judge; b. Stratham, N.H., Jan. 26, 1855; s. Mark Fernald and Olive Light (Piper) Y.; A.B., Dartmouth Coll., 1878; m. Bertha J. Hobbs, Jan. 16, 1895. Worked on farm, 1878-80; read law with Maston & Eastman, 1880-83; in various occupations, South and West, 1883-88; returned to N.H., resumed study of law, 1889; admitted to bar, 1890; with Marston & Eastman and after death of Gen. Marston with Mr. Eastman as clerk and partner until 1898, firms of Eastman, Young & O'Neil and Eastman & Young. Asso. justice Supreme Court of N.H., Aug. 1898-Apr. 1901; asso. justice Superior Court, Apr. 1901-Jan. 1904; again asso. justice Supreme Court, 1904—. Conglist. Republican. Home: Exeter, N.H. Died June 14, 1926.

YOUNG, John Philip, educator; b. Phila., Pa., Aug. 9, 1849; s. Francis and Madeline (Schimpf) Y.; m. Georgiana M. Brown, Sept. 27, 1884. Editor San Francisco Chronicle, 1878—. Author: A History of San Francisco; Protection and Progress; Journalism in California; Bimetallism or Monometallism; The Growth of Modern Trusts, and other economic works. Home: San Francisco, Calif. Died Apr. 23, 1921.

YOUNG, John Wesley, coll. prof.; b. Columbus, O., Nov. 17, 1879; s. William Henry and Marie Louise (Widenhorn) Y.; ed. Karlsruhe, Germany, and Columbus, O., 1885-89; Gymnasium Baden-Baden, Germany, 1889-95; Ph.B., Ohio State U., 1899, A.M., Cornell U., 1901, Ph.D., 1904; m. Mary Louise Aston, July 20, 1907; 1 dau., Mary Elizabeth. Instr. mathematics, Northwestern U., 1903-05; preceptor mathematics, Princeton, 1905-08; asst. prof. mathematics, U. of Ill., 1908-10; prof. and head of dept. of mathematics, U. of Kan., 1910-11; prof. mathematics, U. of Chicago, summer quarter, 1911; prof. of mathematics, Dartmouth Coll., 1911—. Chief examiner in geometry, Coll. Entrance Exam. Board, 1915-17. Editor, Bulletin Am. Math. Soc., 1907-25. Was pres. Math. Assn., America and mem. many other socs.; chmn. Nat. Com. on Math. Requirements, 1916-23. Author: Projective Geometry, Vol. 1 (with Oswald Veblen), 1910; Lectures on Fundamental Concepts of Algebra and Geometry, 1911 (Italian transl., 1919); Plane Geometry (with A. J. Schwartz), 1915, 2d edit., 1922; Elementary Mathematical Analysis (with F. M. Morgan), 1917; Plane Trigonometry (with F. M. Morgan), 1919; Projective Geometry, 1929; also papers in various math. jours. Editor, for the Houghton Mifflin Co., of a series of math. texts. War work, 1918, with ednl. bur. Y.M.C.A., N.Y. City, and with Com. on Edn. and Spl. Training, War Dept., Washington, D.C. Home: Hanover, N.H. Died Feb. 17, 1932.

YOUNG, Lafayette, editor; b. Iowa, 1848. Editor, owner and publisher of Des Moines Capital, 1890—; m. Josephine Bolton, Mar. 20, 1870; children—Mrs. Nellie Herrick (dec.), Harold, Lafayette. Served in Ia. Senate 12 yrs.; nominated Theodore Roosevelt for Vice President at Phila., June 1900; was a mem. of the Taft party to the Philippines; del.-at-large to 2 Republican nat. convs. War corr. with Shafter's Campaign in Cuba. Apptd. U.S. senator, Nov. 12, 1910, to succeed Jonathan P. Dolliver, deceased; served until Apr. 1911. War corr. in Europe, 4 mos., 1915; Chautauqua lecturer, summer 1915, in Middle West. Chmn. State Council of Defense for Ia. during World War. Knight Order of Leopold II of Belgium, for raising large funds in Ia. for relief of the children of Belgium. Home: Des Moines, Ia. Died Nov. 15, 1926.

YOUNG, Lafayette, Jr., newspaper pub.; b. Atlantic, Ia., Dec. 1, 1877; s. Lafayette and Josephine (Bolton) Y.; grad. high sch., Los Angeles, Calif., 1896; Ph.B., U. of Mich., 1900; LL.B., Ia. State U., 1901; m. Virginia McArthur, June 15, 1910; children—Harriett Grant, Lafayette III. Gen. mgr. Des Moines Daily Capital, 1901 until consolidation with Des Moines Evening Tribune, 1927; pres. The Young Realty Co. Chief of publicity, Ia., for all but first Liberty Loan Drive, World War; pres. Greater Des Moines Com., 1909-15; v.p. Advertising Clubs of the World, 1916; dir. Audit Bur. of Circulations first 3 yrs. of its existence. One of 12 Am. newspapermen, guests of British Govt. in survey of War Zone, 1918. Republican. Presbyn. Home: Des Moines, Ia. Died Feb. 12, 1930.

YOUNG, Lucien, naval officer; b. Lexington, Ky., Mar. 31, 1852; s. Richard Bosworth and Jane Ellen Y.; apptd. to U.S. Naval Acad. from Ky., 1869, grad., 1873; s. Washington, Belle Parker, June 1895. Promoted midshipman, May 31, 1873; ensign, July 16, 1874; promoted through grades to rear admiral, Mar. 17, 1910. Served on Alaska and Hartford, 1873-75. While midshipman, July 23, 1873, and serving on the "Alaska," jumped overboard while under way at sea and saved life of seaman who had been knocked overboard. Served in Powhatan, 1875-76; Huron, Mar. 1876-Nov. 24, 1877, when she was wrecked off Nag's Head, N.C.; nominated by President and advanced to master by spl. act of Congress for extraordinary heroism. Served in Portsmouth, 1878-80; spl. duty Paris Expn., 1878; Bur. of Equipment, 1880-82; various ships, 1882-86; instr. in torpedoes and at Naval War Coll., 1887; Bur. of Equipment and aid to Sec. of the Navy, 1887-89; Library and War Records Office, 1889-91, 1893-96; Boston, 1891-93; took a prominent part in the protection of American interests in Hawaiian revolution; comd. Hist during Spanish War, June 1898-Jan. 1899; advanced 3 numbers "for eminent and conspicuous conduct in battles during Spanish War, while in command of Hist"; capt. port of Havana and commandantia de la marina of Cuba, 1899-1900; commandant U.S. Naval sta., Havana, 1900-01; insp. 9th lighthouse dist., 1902-04; comd. Bennington, 1904-05; Bennington, wrecked by explosion of boiler and beached at San Diego, Calif., July 21, 1905; Navy Yard, Mare Island, as capt. of yard and pres. of permanent court-martial, examining and retiring bds. on Pacific Coast; commandant Navy Station, Key West, Fla. Another of a standard work on navigation, Archæological Researches in Peru; The Real Hawaii. Died Oct. 2, 1912.

YOUNG, Margaret Rankin (Mrs. William B. Young); b. Macon, Ga., Mar. 20, 1871; d. Jesse Willis and Mary Poythress (Jones) Rankin; ed. pvt. sch., Athens, Ga.; m. William Brooks Young, July 10, 1889; children—Frances Rankin (Mrs. F. Richard Blue), William B., Margaret Anthony. Organized temporary relief hosp. under direction of Col. L. M. Maus, Fitzhugh Lee's staff, 7th A.C., Spanish-Am. War. Pres. Jacksonville Woman's Club; dir. for S.E. dept. Gen. Fedn. of Women's Clubs; treas. Gen. Fedn. of Women's Clubs; pres. local Y.W.C.A.; mem. Nat. War Work Council, World's Service Council Y.W.C.A.; mem. local bd. War Camp Community Service; mem. Duval County Bd. of Pub. Instrn., 1920—. Episcopalian. Home: Ortega, Fla. Died July 14, 1930.

YOUNG, Morrison Waite, banker; b. Maumee, O., Sept. 15, 1860; s. Samuel M. and Angeline Lucy (Upton) Y.; A.B., Yale, 1883; m. Kittie Cummings, Dec. 29, 1887 (died 1888); m. 2d, Julia Wilmerding Martindale, Apr. 15, 1899. Chmn. bd. Toledo Trust Co.; pres. Blade Printing & Paper Co. Treas. Toledo Mus. of Art. Episcopalian. Home: Toledo, O. Died June 30, 1932.

YOUNG, Newton Clarence, judge; b. Mt. Pleasant, Ia., Jan. 28, 1862; s. C. S. and Joanna E. Y.; A.B., State U. of Ia., 1886, LL.B., 1887, A.M., 1891; m. Ida B. Clarke, June 23, 1887. Began practice law, Bathgate, N.D., 1887; state's atty., Pembina Co., 1892-96; candidate for dist. judge, 1896; apptd. Aug. 1898, to fill vacancy in Supreme Ct.; elected judge same, 1898, reëlected, 1904, for term expiring 1910; was chief justice, 1902-06; resigned 1906; div. council N.P. Ry., 1906—. Regent U. of N.D., 1906-14. Author of Shall We Change Our Plan of Government; Some of the Fallacies of the Initiative, Referendum and Recall. Republican. State dir. Am. Red Cross. Home: Fargo, N.D. Died Nov. 1923.

YOUNG, Odus Graham, lawyer; b. Ray County, Mo., Jan. 20, 1858; s. Ambrose M. and Pennelia Francis (Graham) Y.; student Mo. State Normal Sch., Kirksville, 1875, 76; m. Ida F. Gant, Dec. 14, 1882. Admitted to bar, 1882; mem. firm Mirick & Young, Carrollton, Mo., 1882-89, Deatherage & Young, Kansas City, 1889-95, Botsford, Deatherage & Young, to Jan. 1, 1909; retired from law practice; pres. Young Bros. Cattle Co., 1900—. Mayor of Carrollton, 1882-83; mem. Mo. Senate, 1896-1900; pres. Drovers Packing Co., Kansas City, Kan., 1919—. Democrat. Methodist. Home: Kansas City, Mo. Deceased.

YOUNG, Otto, mcht., capitalist; b. Eberfeld, Germany, Dec. 20, 1844; s. Johann Christian and Marie (Von Wingender) Y.; ed. schs. in Germany and New York; came to U.S., 1859; m. Elizabeth Murphy, 1867. Clerk, New York, 1861-67; in employ fancy goods house, New York, 1867-72; in wholesale Jewelry business at head of Otto Young & Co., 1872—. Owned half interest in The Fair (dept. store, Chicago), and was sec. and treas. of the corp. until sold out July 1905; large real estate interests in Chicago; dir. First Nat. Bank. Home: Chicago, Ill., and Lake Geneva, Wis. Died 1906.

YOUNG, Richard Whitehead, lawyer; b. Salt Lake City, Utah, Apr. 19, 1858; s. Joseph Angell and Margaret (Whitehead) Y.; U. of Utah, 1874-77; grad. U.S. Mil. Acad., 1882; LL.B., Columbia, 1884; m. Minerva Richards, Sept. 5, 1882. Second lt. 5th U.S. Arty., 1882-89; capt. and acting judge-advocate U.S.A., on staff of Gen. W. S. Hancock, 1884-86; resigned, 1889; brig. gen. Utah N.G., 1894; capt. and maj. comdg. Utah Light Arty., Spanish-Am. War and Philippine insurrection, 1898-99; Congressional Medal of Honor for service in latter; recommended by army bd. for brevets of lt. col., col. and brig. gen. Admitted to bar, New York, 1884; in practice at Salt Lake City, 1889—. Latter Day Saint (Mormon). Mem. City Council, 1890-91, Bd. of Edn., 1890-94, 1898; superior provost judge, asso. justice and pres. criminal branch Supreme Ct. of P.I., 1898-1901; mem. bd. of visitors West Point, 1902; twice Dem. candidate for Supreme Ct. of Utah; regent U. of Utah, 1905-17; trustee Brigham Young U., Provo; pres. Internat. Irrigation Congress, 1912-14. V. chmn. Utah State Council Defense, 1917; col. 1st Utah and 145th Field Arty., June 17, 1917; brig. gen. National Army, Apr. 16, 1918. Author: Mobs and the Military, 1888. Home: Salt Lake City, Utah. Died Dec. 27, 1919.

YOUNG, Rida Johnson, playwright; b. Baltimore, Md.; d. William A. and Emma (Stuart) Johnson; ed. Wilson Coll., Chambersburg, Pa.; m. James Young, 1904. Author: (produced plays): Brown of Harvard; Glorious Betsy; Naughty Marietta; The Lottery Man; Her Soldier Boy; Maytime; Captain Kidd, Jr.; The Boys of Company B; Little Old New York; and others. Also novels: The Girl Who Came Out of the Night; Virginal. Home: Stamford, Conn. Died May 8, 1926.

YOUNG, Robert Anderson, clergyman, author; b. Knox County, Tenn., Jan. 23, 1824; s. Capt. John C. and Lucinda (Hyder) Y.; grad. Washington Coll., Tenn., 1844, LL.D., 1895; D.D., Wesleyan U. of Ala.; m. Mary A. Kemmer, June 1847 (died 1879); m. 2d, Mrs. Anna (Green) Hunter, Aug. 18, 1880. Admitted on trial Holston Conf. of M.E. Ch., S., 1845; traveled Dandridge circuit 1 yr. Moved to Nashville, 1846, united with Tenn. Conf.; stationed Cumberland Iron Works, 1846-48; spent 2 yrs. at Columbia, Tenn. (A.M., Jackson Coll.), 2 yrs. Huntsville, Ala.; removed to Lebanon, Tenn., 1 yr., transferred to 1st Church, St. Louis; presiding elder St. Louis dist., 1855-57, same, Lexington dist., St. Louis Conf., 1857-60; pres. Wesleyan U., Florence, Ala., 1861-64; pastor of Tulip St. Ch., Edgefield, Tenn., 1864-65; pastor McKendree Ch., Nashville, 1866-70, Elm St. Ch., Nashville, 1870-74; financial sec. bd. of trust, Vanderbilt U., 1874-82, elected sec. bd. of missions, M.E. Ch., S. Editor Advocate of Missions. Mem. book com. Southern Meth. Publishing House. Mem. every gen. conf. of the ch., 1865—; sec. Tenn. Conf., 21 yrs., on Nashville Bd. Edn. 3 yrs. Visited Spain, Russia and Scandinavia, 1891. Author: Personages; Ariel; Twenty Thousand Miles; Celebrities and Less. Home: Nashville, Tenn. Died 1902.

YOUNG, Rose, author and editor; b. Fafayette County, Mo.; d. Thomas Gibbs and Henrietta (Goalder) Y. Writer of mag. stories, 1901-02; editor University Pub. Co., New York, 1903-07. Pseudonym, R. E. Young. Author: Sally of Missouri, 1903; Henderson, 1904; Murder at Manson's, 1927; The Miss Nigger Stories; The Shanklin Stories; "Chills," "Petticoat Push," "Her Wages and Her Morals," "From Kitchen to Night Court." Staff N.Y. Evening Post, 1912-13; inaugurated for that paper special feature program to deal with modern women's capacity and potentiality. Special feature writer on the "Woman Movement," Good Housekeeping Magazine, 1914. Dir. Leslie Woman Suffrage Bur. and editor Woman Citizen, 1917-22. Home: New York, N.Y. Died July 6, 1941.

YOUNG, Sam Martin, farmer; b. Dixon Springs, Tenn., May 29, 1861; s. James Howard and Nancy Elizabeth (Martin) Y., Burritt Coll., Tenn.; B.L., Cumberland U., Tenn., 1883; m. Elisabeth A. Wright, Nov. 3, 1886. Interested principally in agriculture, live stock and banking. Mem. Tenn. Senate, 1893-95; chmn. County Court of Smith County, 1908-09; pres. Tenn. State Bd. of Elections, 1909-15; del.-at-large Dem. Nat. Conv., Baltimore, 1912. Chmn. Draft Exemption Bd. for Smith County, Tenn., 1918-19. Home: Dixon Springs, Tenn. Died Mar. 19, 1935.

YOUNG, Samuel Baldwin Marks, lieutenant gen. U.S.A.; b. Pittsburgh, Jan. 9, 1840; s. Capt. John, Jr. and Hannah (Scott) Y.; ed. Jefferson Coll., Canonsburg, Pa.; m. Margaret McFadden, Sept. 1861. Enlisted as pvt. Co. K, 12th Pa. Inf., Apr. 25, 1861; discharged, Aug. 5, 1861; commd. capt. 4th Pa. Cav., Sept. 6, 1861; maj., Sept. 20, 1862; lt. col., Oct. 1, 1864; col., Dec. 29, 1864; bvtd. brig. gen., Apr. 9, 1865; hon. mustered out of vols., July 1, 1865; apptd. from Pa. 2d lt. 12th U.S. Inf., May 11, 1866; capt. 8th Cav., July 28, 1866; maj. 3d Cav., Apr. 2, 1883; lt. col. 4th Cav., Aug. 16, 1892; col. 3d Cav., June 19, 1897; brig. gen. vols., May 4, 1898; maj. gen. vols., July 8, 1898; hon. discharged from vols., Apr. 13, 1899; brig. gen. vols., Apr. 13, 1899; brig. gen. U.S.A., Jan. 2, 1900; maj. gen. U.S.A., Feb. 2, 1901; lt. gen. in command of the army, Aug. 8, 1903; chief of staff to the President, Aug. 15, 1903; retired by operation of law, Jan. 9, 1904. Bvtd.: maj., Mar. 2, 1867, "for gallant and meritorious services in action at Sulphur Springs, Va., Oct. 12, 1863"; lt. col., Mar. 2, 1867, for same in action at Amelia Spring, Va., Apr. 5, 1865; col., Mar. 2, 1867, for same in battle of Sailors Creek, Va., Apr. 6, 1865; brig. gen. vols., Apr. 9, 1865, for same during the campaign terminating with surrender of army under Gen. R. E. Lee. Comd. 2d Brigade, cav. div., 5th Corps, in Cuba; comd. 1st Div., 2d Corps, and later comd. 2d Army Corps until disbanded; served in P.I., 1899-1901, comd. cav. and inf. advance disintegrating Aguinaldo's army in Northern Luzon, Oct.-Dec., 1899; mil. gov. Northern Luzon; comdg. Dept. of Calif. to Mar. 15, 1902; 1st pres. War Coll., Washington, July 1, 1902-Aug. 8, 1903; was pres. Brownsville ct. of inquiry; gov. U.S. Soldiers' Home, Washington, D.C., 1910-20. Comdr. in chief Mil. Order Loyal Legion U.S., 1915. Home: Washington, D.C. Died Sept. 1, 1924.

YOUNG, S(amuel) Edward, clergyman; b. Deep Cut, O., June 6, 1866; s. Rev. James and Rosanna (McAvoy) Y.; ed. Westminster Coll., Mo.; William R. Harper's Hebrew Sch., Morgan Park, Ill.; Princeton Theol. Sem., 1886-88; grad. Union Theol. Sem., New York, 1889; D.D., Washington and Jefferson, 1903; m. Constance Wilburta Paddock, Apr. 19, 1893; children—Perry, Alyse Paddock, Lorin Bradford, Samuel Edward. Ordained Presbyn. ministry, 1889; pastor Westminster Ch., Asbury Park, N.J., 1889-94, Central Ch., Newark, N.J., 1894-97, Second Ch., Pittsburgh, 1898-1908, Bedford Ch., Brooklyn, 1908—. Secured from Congress of U.S., after a year's efforts and appearing before coms. of Senate and House, passage of law of 1892 increasing wages of life-savers of U.S.; organized, 1892, and chmn. world-wide Christian endeavor work for life-savers, light-house keepers and light-ship crews; founded at Pittsburgh, 1897, and carried on for 10 yrs., park services during summer seasons, attendance on a single Sunday reported at 86,500 (system since adopted in other cities of U.S.); founder Sunday afternoon theatre services at Pittsburgh, attendance often 4,000 (system since adopted in other cities); vice chmn. com. Gen. Assembly Presbyn. Ch. in U.S.A. that organized Presbyn. Brotherhood of America; apptd. spl. chaplain to Cuba, 1898. Mem. Evangelistic Com. of Gen. Assembly; chaplain Actors' Ch. Alliance of America. Life dir. Western Pa. Expn. Soc. Presented by U.S. Life Saving Service with silver punch bowl, elaborately engraved. Chmn. Clerical Conf. of Fedn. of Chs., New York; chmn. New York City "Go to Church Sunday" Com.; pres. Soc. Prevention Crime; mem. Presbyn. Coll. Bd. for U.S.A.; mem. U.S. Dist. Bd. for New York. Chaplain 14th Regt., N.Y.N.G. Home: Brooklyn, N.Y. Died Mar. 28, 1927.

YOUNG, Stewart Woodford, prof. chemistry; b. Orient, N.Y., Mar. 14, 1869; s. of James Henry and Emma Virginia (Tuthill) Y.; B.S., Cornell U., 1890; studied U. of Leipzig, 1899-1900. Asst. in chemistry, Cornell U., 1890-91; instr. in chemistry, Swarthmore (Pa.) Coll., 1891-93; at Stanford U., 1893—, successively asst. in chemistry, instr., asst. prof. until 1900, asso. prof., 1900-08, prof. physical chemistry, 1908—. Home: Stanford University, Calif. Died 1930.

YOUNG, Thomas Crane, architect; b. Sheboygan, Wis., Feb. 28, 1858; s. Van Eps and Arlisle (Seaman) Y.; grad. high sch., Grand Rapids, Mich., 1876; spl. student Washington U., 1878-79; student U. of Heidelberg, 1880, École des Beaux Arts, Paris, 1881; m. Ruth Hodgman, June 12, 1887 (dec.); children—Mrs. Dorothy Jones, Mrs. Ruth Mitchell, Mrs. Marjorie McGilvray; m. 2d, Mrs. Lulu Norvell Wallace, Sept. 10, 1921. Mem. Eames & Young, St. Louis, 1885—; firm architects for Cupples plant, consisting of about ten city blocks of warehouse bldgs., St. Louis, 1889; Art Bldg., Omaha Expn., 1897; federal prisons, Leavenworth, Kan., and Atlanta, Ga.; U.S. Custom House, San Francisco; Masonic Temple, Boatmen's Bank & Office Bldg., University Club & Office Bldg. (all of St. Louis). Mem. Bd. of Architects St. Louis Expn., 1903; mem. St. Louis City Plan Commn. Fellow Am. Inst. Architects. Republican. Home: St. Louis, Mo. Died Mar. 2, 1934.

YOUNG, Thomas Shields, religious educator; b. Davenport, Ia., Mar. 18, 1863; s. David T. and Sarah (Humphrey) Y.; student Geneva Coll., Beaver Falls, Pa.; B.L., Shurtleff Coll., Alton, Ill., 1903; student Theol. Dept. Shurtleff Coll. and Div. Sch. of U. of Chicago, Washburn Coll., Topeka, Kan., Univ. of Denver; M.A., Washburn, 1909; D.D., U. of Denver, 1916; m. Nannie Adean Gillham, June 30, 1887; children—Everett Gillham, Adeline Harrison, Virginia Lillian (dec.). Ordained Bapt. ministry, 1887; pastor Geneseo, Ill., 1887-90, Roodhouse, Ill., 1890-91, Moline, Ill., 1891-96, San Jose, Calif., 1897-1905, Topeka, Kan., 1905-10, Denver, Colo., 1910-17; dir. Vacation and Week-Day Church Schs. for Northern Bapt. Conv., under Am. Bapt. Publ. Soc.; pres. Bapt. Conv. of Northern and Central Calif. 2 yrs., actg. pres. 1 yr.; pres. Colo. Bapt. State Conv., 1 yr.; dir. religious edn. for Colo. Baptists 2 yrs. Republican. Mason. Author: Week-Day Church School Methods, 1923; Vacation Church School Handbook, 1925. Home: Denver, Colo. Deceased.

YOUNG, Wallace Jesse, consul; b. West Chester, Pa., Aug. 21, 1880; s. Francis J. and Agnes (Hunter) Y.; grad. high sch., Washington, D.C., 1900; spl. courses in internat. and constl. law, Georgetown U.; unmarried. Clk. in Census Office, 1900-02; pvt. sec. to several members of Congress; clk. Civ. Service Commn., 1903-07; pvt. sec. to 3d asst. sec. of state, 1907-09; sec. Bd. Examiners for Diplomatic and Consular Services, Dept. of State, 1909-13; attaché of Am. Agency to N. Atlantic Coast Fisheries Arbitration, at The Hague, 1910; asst. sec. Am. Delegation to Internat. Opium Conf., The Hague, 1911-12; consul at Carlsbad, Bohemia, Austria, July 24, 1914-17, at Goteborg, Sweden, 1917-19, Prague, 1919-20, Bradford, Eng., 1920—. Fellow Royal Geog. Soc., 1917. Presbyn. Died Dec. 4, 1923.

YOUNG, Walter Jorgensen, educator; b. Owensboro, Ky., June 27, 1883; s. Walter McGary and Anne Margaret (Jorgensen) Y.; B.A., Richmond Coll. (now U. of Richmond), 1907; B.D., Crozer Theol. Sem., 1910, Th.M., 1911; M.A., U. of Pa., 1910, Ph.D., 1911; m. Ethel May Daniel, Dec. 20, 1911; children—Patricia Ann (wife of Dr. J. Garnett King, Jr.), Walter Jorgensen. Professor psychology and biology, Hampden-Sydney Coll., Va., 1911-13; prof. philosophy and psychology, and head dept. philosophy and edn., U. of Richmond, 1913-18; lecturer Richmond Sch. Social Economy; acting supt. schools, Suffolk, Va., 1918-19; prof. edn. and social science, State Teachers Coll., Fredericksburg, Va., 1919-26; prof. geography, summer session, U. of Tenn., 1925; prof. edn., Winthrop Coll., S.C., 1926-29; head dept. of edn., Henderson State Teachers Coll., Arkadelphia, Ark., 1929-30; prof. psychol. and edn., State Coll. for Women, Fredericksburg, Va., 1930-37; head psychology dept., Mary Washington Coll., 1937—; prof. edn., summer, Wake Forest Coll., N.C., 1927. Fellow Royal Soc. of Arts of London; founder Alpha Tau Pi. Democrat. Baptist. Author: A Study in Practice and Habit, 1912; Syllabus of Comparative Ethics, 1918; Syllabus of Elementary History-Geography (adopted in Virginia state course of study), 1924; Outlines of General Geography, 1925; Outlines of Early European History, 1925; The Correlation Theory of Psychology, 1929; Arlington County Course of Study, 1935; The Bristol Youngs in America, 1937; History of Massaponax Church, 1938. Lecturer and pub. speaker. Home: Fredericksburg, Va. Died Nov. 23, 1940.

YOUNG, William, author, dramatist; b. in Ill., 1847; s. Dr. John A. and Isabella (Wallace) Y.; m. Joanna Parry, 1866. Author: (poems) Wishmaker's Town, 1885; same (with preface by Thomas Bailey Aldrich), 1898; "Ah, What Riddles These Women Be!" the Saga of Skarli the Strong, 1901. Plays: Jonquil; The Rogue's March, 1872; Pendragon (in verse), 1881; The House of Mauprat (with John G. Wilson), 1882; The Rajah, 1883; Ganelon (in verse), 1888; Joan of Arc (adaptation in verse), 1890; If I Were You, 1893; Young America, 1894; Woman's Wiles, 1898; Ben Hur, a dramatization, 1899; The Sprightly Romance of Marsac, 1900; A Japanese Nightingale, a dramatization, prod. 1903. Died Oct. 5, 1920.

YOUNG, William Foster, publisher; b. Memphis, Tenn., Feb. 11, 1867; s. Arthur Wellington and Caroline (Page) Y.; U. of Ill., 1882-85; m. 2d, Pearl Potter Johnson, July 18, 1922; children—Arthur Tatarian, Philip Page, William Foster, Jr. (all by 1st wife). In sch. book pub. business with Ginn & Co., Chicago, 1889-94; office mgr. D. C. Heath & Co., 1894-1902; became v.p. and mgr. Benj. H. Sanborn & Co., of Chicago, 1902, pres., 1913—. Died Feb. 18, 1935.

YOUNGERT, Sven Gustaf, clergyman; b. at Ljunget, Algutsrum, Öland, Sweden; s. Olaf Persson and Anna Beata (Olsson); came to U.S., 1886, and settled at Rock Island, Ill.; grad. Mannhem Pvt. Sch., Vestergötland, Sweden, 1881; studied at Fjellstedt Collegiate Instn. of Upsala, while partly engaged as pvt. tutor, 1881-86; A.B., Augustana Coll., Rock Island, Ill., A.M., 1900; B.D., Augustana Theol. Sem., 1897, C.S.T. (Candidatus Sacræ Theologiæ), 1902, S.T.D., 1905; Ph.D., Bethany Coll., 1901; studied psychology and philosophy of religion, State U. of Ia., 1906-12; m. Hannah A. Shoberg, Apr. 27, 1894. Ordained Evang. Luth. ministry, 1892; pastor Kewanee, Ill., 1892-96, Ottumwa, Ia., 1896-1900; prof. N.T. Greek, philosophy and catechetics, Augustana Theol. Sem., 1900-12 and 1917—; pastor Swedish Luth. Ch., Hartford, Conn., 1912-17. Editor Augustana Theological Quarterly, 1912-17; edited "Ungdomsvännen" (published by Augustana Synod), 1899-1912. Contbr. to Hasting's Encyclopedia of Religion and Ethics. Also various papers and magazines. Representative at the Linnean bicentennial celebration Upsala and Stockholm, Sweden, 1907. Author: Manual for Catechetical Instruction in the Sunday School, 1895; History of Philosophy, 1896 (both in Swedish), Philosophy of Religion, 1921. Mem. Commn. for reconstruction work in Europe, under Nat. Luth. Council of America, June 1, 1919—; v.p. Augustana Coll. and Theol. Sem., 1920—. Home: Rock Island, Ill. Died Feb. 26, 1939.

YOUNGS, William J., lawyer; b. Brooklyn, N.Y., June 24, 1851; s. Daniel K. Y.; A.B., Cornell, 1872. Admitted to bar, 1873, and practiced at New York. Rep. nominee for dist. atty., Queens County, N.Y., 1883; dist. atty., 1896-98; secretary to Theodore Roosevelt (while gov. N.Y.), 1899-1900; apptd. deputy supt. banks, N.Y., 1900; U.S. atty., Eastern Dist., N.Y., 1902-15. Editor of Hempstead Inquirer. Republican. Home: Garden City, L.I., N.Y. Died Apr. 4, 1916.

YOUNT, Miles Frank, oil producer; b. Monticello, Ark., Jan. 31, 1880; s. Joseph Nathan and Hattie Minerva Y.; ed. pub. schs. to 8th grade; m. Pansy Bernadett Merritt, Sept. 15, 1915; 1 daughter, Mildred. Began in mech. engring., 1896; pres. and mgr. Yount-Lee Oil Co., Yount-Lee Pipe Line Co.; v.p. Plelan Grocery Co.; dir. First Nat. Bank (Beaumont), Citizens Nat. Bank and numerous other corps. Mem. bd. regents U. of Tex. Republican. Presbyn. Home: Beaumont, Tex. Died Nov. 13, 1933.

YSAYE, Eugene, violinist; b. Liège, Belgium, July 16, 1858; s. Nicholas and Theresa Sottiau Y. Studied under father (condr. and violinist), also with Wieniawksi and Vieuxtemps, Paris; m. Louise Bourdeau, née Termonde, Apr. 2, 1868 (died 1924); children—Gabriel, Carry, Thésy, Antoine, Théodore; m. 2d, Jeannette Dinciu, July 9, 1927. Leader Bilse's Orchestra, Berlin, until 1881; European tour with A. Rubinstein; prof. Brussels Conservatory of Music, 1886-97; made frequent tours in America; founded, 1894, and condr. Société des Concerts Ysaye (orchestra); condr. of Cincinnati Symphony Orchestra, 1918-22. Writer of 34 compositions, the most important being: Extase; Divertiments; Fantasie; Amitie; Poéme Nocturne; Harmonies du Soir; etc. Home: Brussels, Belgium. Died May 12, 1931.

YUNG Wing (in Chinese mode of address, surname comes first, "Yung Wing"), Chinese official, ednl. reformer; b. Nan Ping (opposite Portuguese Colony of Macau), Dist. Heang Shan, Province Kwang Tung, S. China, Nov. 17, 1828; s. Ming Kun Yung and Lien Tai Lin; at 7 entered Mrs. Gutzlaff's Missionary Sch., Macau, and at 13 the Morrision Edn. Soc. Sch., Macau and Hong Kong, under Rev. S. R. Brown; came to U.S. under Dr. Brown, 1847; attended Monson Acad., Hampden County, Mass., 1847-50; A.B., Yale, 1854, LL.D., 1876; m. Mary Louisa Kellogg, Feb. 24, 1875. Returned to China, 1854; entered service of Chinese Govt., 1864; sent to U.S. by Generalissimo and Viceroy, Tsang Kwok Fan, 1864, to purchase machinery which formed foundation of Kiang Nan Arsenal, nr. Shanghai; made civ. officer of 5th rank; projector The China Merchant Steamship Navigation Co. and of the Chinese Ednl. Commn.; brought 120 Chinese youths to U.S., 1872-74, to be educated under auspices of Chinese Govt.; apptd. asso. minister resident in Washington for 4 yrs., made officer of the 4th rank, promoted to 2d by bvt. Congregationalist. Republican. Died Apr. 21, 1912.

Z

ZABRISKIE, Andrew Christian, trustee; b. New York, N.Y., May 30, 1853; s. Christian A. and Sarah J. (Titus) Z.; ed. pvt. schs. New York and Sch. of Mines, Columbia Coll.; m. Frances Hunter, June 6, 1895. Entered 7th Regt. N.G.S.N.Y., as pvt., 1873, and subsequently served as insp. rifle practice in 71st Regt. and as capt. Co. C, same, resigning in 1898. Dem. candidate for Congress 21st N.Y. Dist., 1908; mem. of Dem. State Exec. Com. Was interested in the breeding of Ayrshire cattle and of thoroughbred poultry. Pres. Am. Numis. and Archæol. Soc., 1895-1905; v.p. House of Rest for Consumptives; pres. and founder Junior Am. Guard. Chmn. Dutchess County Board of Supervisors, 1912-13. Author numerous articles upon antiquarian, numismatic and hist. subjects. Homes: New York City and Barrytown-on-Hudson, N.Y. Died Sept. 15, 1916.

ZABRISKIE, George, lawyer; b. N.Y. City, Oct. 12, 1852; s. George I. N. and Eliza M. (Blauvelt) Z.; student New York U., 1870; LL.B., Columbia, 1873; D.C.L., U. of the South, 1894; m. Sarah F. Gray, June 14, 1888; children—George Gray, Helen R. (dec.), Reginald (dec.), Rev. Alexander C., Margaret F. Practiced in N.Y. City, 1874—; mem. Zabriskie, Sage, Gray & Todd; director New York Title & Mortgage Co., Internat. Acceptance Bank, Am. Trust Co. Mem. Inst. Internat. Law, Am. Acad. Sciences, Met. Mus. Art, Am. Mus. Natural History. Republican. Episcopalian. Home: New York City and St. James, L.I., N.Y. Died Oct. 4, 1931.

ZACH, Max Wilhelm, musician; b. Lemberg, Poland, Aug. 31, 1864; s. Heinrich and Julie (Deim) Z.; ed. in lower and middle school (gymnasium), Lemberg and Vienna; pupil Conservatory of Music, Vienna; m. Blanche Going, July 4, 1891. Came to America, 1886; mem. Boston Symphony Orchestra, 1886-1907, also conductor of popular concerts in Boston; conductor St. Louis Symphony Orchestra, 1907—. Home: St. Louis, Mo. Died Feb. 3, 1921.

ZAHM, John Augustine, author; b. New Lexington, O., June 14, 1851; s. Jacob M. and Mary (Braddock) Z.; A.B., Notre Dame U., 1871; Ph.D. from Pope Leo XIII, 1895. Entered Order of Holy Cross, 1871; apptd. to charge of scientific dept., 1874, dir. same, 1875, later pres. bd. trustees, Notre Dame U.; also for yrs. curator Notre Dame Mus. Lecturer at Plattsburg, N.Y., and Western (Madison, Wis.) summer schs., and New Orleans winter sch.; also lectured at Catholic U. of America; best known as an advanced evolutionist. Author: Evolution and Dogma; Bible Science and Faith: Sound and Music; Catholic Science and Catholic Scientists; Scientific Theory and Catholic Doctrine; Science and the Church; Evolution and Theology; Souvenirs of Travel; Alaska—the Country and the People; Hawaii and the Hawaiians. Devoted many yrs. to study of S. America, and wrote under pseudonyms: Following the Conquistadores Up the Orinoco and Down the Magdalena; Following the Conquistadores Along the Andes and Down the Amazon; Women in Science. Wrote also under the name of J. A. Zahm: The Quest of El Dorado; Following the Conquistadores Through South America's Southland; The Great Inspirers, 1917. Home: Washington, D.C. Died Nov. 11, 1921.

ZAHNISER, Arthur DeFrance, bishop; b. Five Points, Pa., Aug. 26, 1865; s. Martin and Elizabeth Z.; ed. pub. schs. Five Points; student Grove City (Pa.) Coll.; m. Sarah Jane Carrier, 1895 (died 1933); children—Ruth DeFrance (Mrs. Edward V. Davis, dec.), Leta Elizabeth (Mrs. Clarence H. Snyder), Bernice Evelyn (Mrs. Ermon S. Weidman), Laurence Barnhart (dec.). Ordained ministry Free Meth. Ch., 1895; served pastorate, 1895-98; presiding elder various dists. Pittsburgh Conf., 1898-1913; gen. conf. evangelist, 1916-28; bishop, 1928—. Pres. bd. trustees Greenville (Ill.) Coll., 1917-28. Author: (with J. B. Easton) History of the Pittsburgh Conference of the Free Methodist Church, 1932. Home: Pittsburgh, Pa. Died Aug. 14, 1935.

ZAKRZEWSKA, Marie Elizabeth, physician; b. Berlin, Prussia, Sept. 29, 1829; when 18 yrs. old began study of midwifery in Royal Hosp. Charité, Berlin; graduated in spring, 1852, as teacher of midwives; became accoucheuse-in-chief of that hosp.; but, learning that in the U.S., women could become full doctors of medicine, resigned that position and emigrated in 1853. Grad. Western Reserve Coll. Med. School, Cleveland, O., 1856. With Dr. Elizabeth Blackwell established, 1857, New York Infirmary for Indigent Women and Children; was resident physician until May 1859; prof. obstetrics, New England Female Med. Coll., Boston, 1859-61. In 1861 inaugurated New England Hosp. for Women and Children, of which she was a dir. and advisory physician; unmarried. Home: Jamaica Plain, Mass. Died 1902.

ZALDIVAR, Rafael, diplomat; b. San Salvador, C.A., May 17, 1865; s. Rafael and Sara (Guerra) Z.; M.D., École de Médicine, Paris, France, 1887; m. Josie Dowling, of London, Eng., June 23, 1913. Formerly v.p. Salvadorean Congress; E.E. and M.P. from Salvador to the U.S., 1915—. Roman Catholic. Died May 13, 1922.

ZALINSKI, Edmund Louis Gray, soldier, inventor pneumatic dynamite torpedo gun; b. Kurnich, Prussian Poland, Dec. 13, 1849, came with parents to U.S. when 4 yrs. old; settled at Seneca Falls, N.Y.; ed. pub. schs., Seneca Falls, Syracuse High School, 1861-63; entered army as vol. a. d. c. on staff Gen. Nelson A. Miles, 1864, served till close of war April, 1865; promoted Feb. 1865, to 2d lt. in 2d New York heavy arty. for gallantry at battle of Hatcher's Run, Va. Mustered out of vol. service Sept. 1865; apptd. 2d lt., 5th U.S. Arty., Feb. 1866; 1st lt., Jan. 1867; capt., Dec. 1887. Prof. mil. science Mass. Inst. Technology, 1872-76; grad. United States Artillery School, Fort Monroe, Va., and School of Submarine Mining, Willett's Point, N.Y., 1880. From 1883 to 1889 devoted time to development and perfecting of pneumatic dynamite torpedo gun. Traveled under orders in Europe, 1889-90 to obtain mil. information. Invented an intrenching tool, a ramrod bayonet, a telescopic sight for arty. and a system of range and position finding for sea-coast and arty. firing; on garrison duty at San Francisco, Calif., 1892; retired, Feb. 1894; promoted maj., Apr. 25, 1904. Home: New York, N.Y. Died 1909.

ZALINSKI, Moses Gray, army officer; b. in New York, Jan. 23, 1863; grad. Arty. Sch., 1894. Served as pvt., corpl. and sergt., batteries G and H, 1st Arty., 1885-89; commd. 2d lt., 2d Arty., Feb. 11, 1889, promoted through grades to brig. gen., Apr. 19, 1925, and apptd. asst. to q.m. gen. for period of 4 yrs. Awarded D.S.M. Retired, Jan. 23, 1927. Died Aug. 28, 1937.

ZANDER, Henry George, realtor; b. Rendsburg, Schleswig-Holstein, Oct. 4, 1869; s. Claudius C. and Margot (Van Staeding) Z.; ed. Gymnasium at Rendsburg; grad. North Div. High Sch., Chicago, 1886; grad. as civil engr. from Grant's Sch.; LL.B., John Marshall Law Sch.; m. Charlotte M. Keitel, 1895; children—Henry G., Karl Marvin. Entered real estate office of Martin Van Allen, Oct. 1886; junior partner, 1889; organized firm of Henry G. Zander & Co., Dec. 1891; formed partnership with George F. Koester, May 1892, under firm name of Koester and Zander, which was dissolved by the death of Mr. Koester in 1925; continued as surviving partner until 1927, when with two sons continued under firm name of Henry G. Zander & Co., real estate investments and mortgage loans. Pub. interest dir. and chmn. bd. Federal Home Loan Bank of Chicago (member at large of National advisory council). Democrat. Lutheran. Mem. or officer real estate and civic assns. Mason. Home: Barrington, Ill. Died Oct. 12, 1937.

ZANE, Abraham Vanhoy, naval officer; b. Phila., Aug. 14, 1850; s. Abraham V. and Mary R. (McNeir) Z.; grad. U.S. Naval Acad., 1874; m. Grace Helen Southgate, June 21, 1883. Promoted asst. engr., Feb. 26, 1875; passed asst. engr., Aug. 27, 1881; chief engr., Sept. 11, 1895; transferred to the line as lt. comdr., Mar. 3, 1899; comdr., Sept. 11, 1903; capt., Dec. 6, 1907; rear adm., Sept. 14, 1911. Mem. Jeannette relief expdn., 1881-82, Northern Alaska exploring expdn., 1885-86; served at works of Wm. Cramp & Sons Co., Phila., Pa., 1903-08; head Dept. Steam Engring., Navy Yard, Portsmouth, N.H., 1908-11; gen. insp. of machinery for Navy, 1911; pres. Bd. Inspections for Shore Stations, Navy Dept., 1911-12; retired on account of age, Aug. 14, 1912. Home: Washington, D.C. Died Jan. 2, 1919.

ZANE, John Maxcy, lawyer; b. Springfield, Ill., Mar. 26, 1863; s. Charles S. and Margaret D. (Maxcy) Z.; A.B., U. of Mich., 1884, LL.D., 1914; Litt.D., Northwestern U., 1917; m. Sara R. Zane, Apr. 25, 1894. Clerk Third Dist. Court of Utah, 1884-88; admitted to bar of Utah, 1888; asst. U.S. atty., Utah, 1889-93; reporter Utah Supreme Court, 1889-94; in practice at Salt Lake City until 1899, then removed to Chicago; mem. of firm of Shope, Mathis, Zane & Weber, then of Zane, Busby & Weber, 1900-12, later of Zane, Morse, Zimmerman & Norman. Republican. Episcopalian. Author: Zane on Banks and Banking, 1900; The Story of Law, 1927. Pres. Chicago branch English-Speaking Union, 1926 and 1927. Home: Chicago, Ill. Died Dec. 6, 1937.

ZECH, Frederick, Jr., pianist, composer; b. Phila., May 10, 1858; s. Frederick and Dorothea (Frank) Z.; pvt. sch. edn. in San Francisco; acad. edn. in Berlin; studied music, piano and composition; m. Albine B Schoenfelder, of Germany, July 15, 1882. Conductor Symphony Orchestra, San Francisco. Composer of six symphonies and symphonic poems and chamber music and 2 operas, "The Cruise of the Excelsior," and N. Am. Indian opera, "Wa-Kin-Yon." Home: San Francisco, Calif. Died Oct. 25, 1926.

ZECKWER, Richard, musician; b. Stendal, Prussia, Apr. 30, 1850; s. Carl and Emilie (Stroehmer) Z.; ed. at gymnasium, Stendal, and at U. of Leipzig; musical edn. at Leipzig Conservatory of Music, under Moscheles, Hauptmann, E. F. Richter, Papperitz and Reinecke; grad. there, 1869; came to the United States, 1869; teacher, 1869-76, propr., 1876-1917, Phila. Musical Academy; m. Marie, d. Camille and Annie d'Invilliers, of Phila., 1874. Organist Ch. of St. Vincent de Paul, Germantown, 1871-78; organist Catholic Cathedral, Phila., 1879-80. Lecturer on acoustics before musical socs. and at Franklin Inst., Phila.; also at Phila. Acad. Natural Sciences. Inventor of the liberating of the ring finger for the perfection of technique. Composer of songs and piano compositions, also of 2 overtures: Festival Overture and Bride of Messina. Author: A Scientific Investigation of Touch, 1902. Home: Philadelphia, Pa. Died Dec. 31, 1922.

ZEDLER, John, educator; b. Essen, Rheinland, Germany, Nov. 11, 1864; s. Christian and Wilhelmine (Vockrath) Z.; A.B., Albion (Mich.) Coll., 1903, A.M., U. of Mich., 1908; studied New York U.; m. Carrie Viola Wright, Wyo., May 12, 1889. Came to U.S., 1881; mem. Co. I, 7th U.S. Inf., 1882-87, and mem. band, same regt., 1887-89; naturalized citizen of U.S., 1894. Entered M.E. ministry, 1894, and served in pastorates in Mich. 7 yrs.; joined faculty, Albion Coll. upon graduation, 1903, and advanced to prof. history and polit. science; dean Clark U., Atlanta, Ga., 1919-23; dean Morristown (Tenn.) Normal and Industrial Coll., 1923—. Mem. K.P., D.O.K.K. Mason. Home: Morristown, Tenn. Died Apr. 3, 1929.

ZEHNDER, Charles Henry, capitalist; b. Northumberland, Pa., Apr. 16, 1856; s. Augustus and Mary E. Z.; ed. pub. schs.; m. Rosalie G. Hicks, Jan. 13, 1880; children—Mrs. Elmira Comegys, Mrs. Elizabeth Leslie. Entered employ of Jackson & Woodin Mfg. Co., Berwick, 1879; later became sec., v.p. and gen. mgr., then pres. until 1896; pres. Dickson Mfg. Co., Scranton and Wilkes-Barré, 1896-1901; removed to New York; pres. Mt. Hope Mineral R.R. Co.; v.p. Ark. Valley Beet Sugar & Irrigated Land Co.; dir. Equitable Life Assurance Soc. U.S., Empire Trust Co., Scranton Bolt Nut Co., Warren Foundry & Pipe Co., Replogle Steel Co. Republican. Methodist. Home: Asbury Park, N.J. Died Dec. 26, 1927.

ZEISLER, Fannie Bloomfield, pianist; b. Bielitz, Poland, July 16, 1863; d. Solomon and Bertha (Jaeger) Bloomfield; came with parents to America in her 2d yr., to Chicago in 4th yr.; showed early musical talent; studied principally under Leschetizky at Vienna; m. Sigmund Zeisler, Oct. 18, 1885; children—Leonard B., Paul B., Ernest B. Played in prin. American cities, 1883-93, in prin. German cities, 1893-95; in America, 1895-98; English tour, spring of 1898; in America, 1898-1902; tour in Germany, Austria and France, autumn 1902; in America, 1903—, with exception of concert tour, Germany, England and France, winter 1912. Founded Fannie Bloomfield Zeisler Musicians' Relief Fund (administered by United Charities of Chicago), 1925. Home: Chicago, Ill. Died Aug. 20, 1927.

ZEISLER, Joseph, dermatologist; b. Bielitz, Austrian Silesia, Oct. 7, 1858; s. Isaac and Anna (Kanner) Z.; M.D., Med. Dept., U. of Vienna, 1882; interne in Vienna Gen. Hosp., 1882-84; m. Therese Feuchtman, of Vienna, June 25, 1885. Came to America, 1884, and settled in Chicago; prof. dermatology, Woman's Med. Coll., 1889-1901; prof. skin and venereal diseases, Post-Grad. Med. Sch., 1888-95; prof. skin and venereal diseases, Northwestern U. Med. Sch., 1889—; chief dermatologist to Mercy, Wesley and Michael Reese hosps. and South Side Dispensary. Mem. A.M.A. (chmn. sect. dermatology, 1912-13), and other med. assns. Home: Chicago, Ill. Died Aug. 31, 1919.

ZEISLER, Sigmund, lawyer; b. Bielitz, Silesia, Austria, Apr. 11, 1860; s. Isaac L. and Anna (Kanner) Z.; grad. Imperial Coll. (Gymnasium) Bielitz, Poland, 1878; studied law and polit. science U. of Vienna, Austria, 1878-83, Doctor Juris, 1883; LL.B., Northwestern U. Law Sch., 1884; admitted to Ill. bar, 1884; m. Fannie Bloomfield, Oct. 18, 1885; children—Leonard B., Paul B., Ernest B.; m. 2d, Amelia Speilman, Jan. 23, 1930. Was asso. counsel for defense in Anarchist cases, 1886-87; chief asst. corporation counsel, Chicago, 1893-94; engaged in pvt. law practice; retired. Master in chancery Circuit Court, Cook County, 1904-20; lecturer on Roman law in Northwestern U. Law Sch., 1884-86 and 1892-93, and on constitutional law, John Marshall Law School, 1901-04. Active as sound-money Democrat in campaign in 1896 and as anti-imperialist in 1900; pres. Nat. German-Am. Parker League in 1904. V.p. of the Am. Free Trade League, 1910—. Democrat. Member exec. com., 1889-1905, advisory com., 1905—, pres., 1925—, Municipal Voters' League; mem. exec. com. Civ. Serv. Ref. Assn.; mem. advisory com. Am. Judicature Soc., 1913—. Contbr. to revs. and law jours. Home: Chicago, Ill. Died June 4, 1931.

ZEIT, F(rederic) Robert Aenishaenslin, pathologist; b. Gelterkinden, Switzerland, Mar. 13, 1864; s. Robert and Lina (Metzger) Aenishaenslin Z.; ed. pub. schs. of Cologne, Düsseldorf and Elberfeld, Germany, and gymnasium at Elberfeld; M.D., Western Reserve U., Cleveland, 1887; m. Hanna F. David, of Basel, Switzerland, May 5, 1888; children—Mrs. Gretchen Gardner, Mrs. Edith Buker, Mrs. Elsie McClellan. Practiced as physician and surgeon in state of Wis., 1887-97; collaborator and 1st asst. of Prof. Edwin Klebs, 1897-1900; prof. of bacteriology and of clinical pathology, 1900-01, prof. pathology, 1902—, Northwestern U. Med. Sch.; prof. pathology and bacteriology, Post-Grad. Med. School of Chicago, 1900-19; cons. pathologist of Wesley and Grant hosps. Founder Frederic Robert Zeit Mus. of Pathology, Northwestern U. Republican. Presbyterian. Home: Winnetka, Ill. Died Dec. 5, 1935.

ZEITLIN, Jacob, college prof.; b. Gorky, Province of Mogilev, Russia, Jan. 6, 1883; s. Hyman and Esther (Zecher) Z.; came to U.S., 1892; A.B., Columbia, 1904, A.M., 1905, Ph.D., 1908; m. Lois Guild, Dec. 22, 1922; stepdau., Margaret Guild. Instr. English, 1907, asso., 1910, asst. prof., 1916, asso. prof., 1921, prof., 1925—, U. of Ill. Jewish religion. Author: (thesis) The Accusative with the Infinitive, 1908. Part Author: Life and Letters of Stuart Sherman, 1929. Translator and editor Montigne's Essays, 1934. Editor: Hazlitt on English Literature, 1913; Petrarch's "Life of Solitude," 1924; College Readings in English Prose (with Franklin W. Scott), 1914, revised, 1926; Select Prose of Robert Southey, 1916; Types of Poetry (with Clarissa Rinaker), 1926; Seventeenth Century Essays, 1926; Essays Formal and Informal (with F. W. Scott), 1927; Shaping Men and Women, 1929. Home: Urbana, Ill. Died Dec. 8, 1937.

ZELENY, Charles, zoölogist; b. Hutchinson, Minn., Sept. 17, 1878; s. Anthony H. and Josephine (Pitka) Z.; B.S., U. of Minn., 1898, M.S., 1901; Columbia, 1901-02; Stazione Zoölogica, Naples, Italy, 1902-03; Ph.D., U. of Chicago, 1904; m. Ida Benedicta Ellingson, May 29, 1911; 1 son, Charles Ellingson. Prof. zoölogy Ind. U., 1904-09, U. of Ill., 1909—, also head of dept., 1933—. Author of papers in field of experimental zoölogy, especially experimental embryology, regeneration and genetics. Home: Urbana, Ill. Died Dec. 21, 1939.

ZELLER, George Anthony, physician; b. Spring Bay, Ill., Nov. 1858; s. John George (M.D.) and Frederica (Nicolas) Z.; student U. of Ill., 1873-76, St. Louis Med. Coll., 1876-79, Rush Med. Coll., Chicago, 1883, European clinics, 1889, 1909; m. Sophie Kline, 1889. Began practice at Spring Bay, 1879; supt. Peoria (Ill.) State Hosp., 1898-1913, with exception of 3 yrs. spent in mil. service; mem. Bd. Administration and state alienist of Ill., 1913—. Apptd. acting asst. surgeon U.S.A., Nov. 10, 1899; capt. asst. surgeon vols., Mar. 21, 1901; retired from service, Nov. 20, 1902; entire service in P.I.; on spl. duty with civ. govt. in Manila during cholera epidemic, 1902. Author many illus. pamphlets on pellagra and on abnormal conditions. Chmn. Peoria County Rep. Central Com. 4 terms. Lutheran. Home: Peoria, Ill. Died June 29, 1938.

ZELLER, Julius Christian, educator; b. Spring Bay, Ill., Dec. 15, 1871; s. John George (M.D.) and Caroline (Winkler) Z.; B.A., and B.O., Grant U., Athens, Tenn., 1893, M.A., 1906; B.A., U. of Chicago, 1904,

B.D., 1905; M.A., U. of Chattanooga, 1906, D.D., 1909; D.C.L., Ill. Wesleyan U., 1910; m. Alice E. Bryant, Jan. 1, 1895; children—Mrs. Miriam Irene Gross, Mrs. Dorothy Spaulding Smith, (twins) Raymond Bryant, Julius (dec.), Margaret Louise, Ethel Francis (dec.), Rachel Elizabeth, John Zeller (dec.), Alice Caroline, Letitia Josephine. Deacon, 1895, elder, 1897, M.E. Ch.; pastor Kickapoo, Ill., 1893-95, Hennepin, 1895-97, Manteno, Ill., 1898-1902, Chebanse, Ill., 1902-05; prof. philosophy and sociology, 1905-09, field agt., 1905-08, Ill. Wesleyan U.; pres. U. of Puget Sound, 1909-13; later engaged in demonstrations in rural life work in Miss. Del. Deep Water Ways Conv., 1907; mem. State Commn. on Instns. of Higher Learning, 1926; supt. Bolivar County Agrl. Sch., Cleveland, Miss., 1920-21; dir. Summer Normal Sch., Benton, Miss., 1922; dean of men and vice chancellor U. of Miss., 1930-32, also prof. philosophy and psychology, 1930-32. Democrat. Edited publication entitled State Printing Plants, 1928. Home: Kansas City, Mo. Died Mar. 10, 1938.

ZENOS, Andrew C. (zē'nŭs), theologian; b. Constantinople, Turkey, Aug. 13, 1855; s. P. and Elizabeth Z.; grad. Robert Coll., Constantinople, 1872; grad. Princeton Theol. Sem., 1880; A.M., Princeton U., 1880, D.D., 1888; LL.D., The College of Wooster, 1912; Litt.D., Lake Forest Coll., 1936; m. Ruth J. Schlager, Oct. 11, 1882. Ordained Presbyn. ministry, 1881; pastor Brandt, Pa., 1881-83; prof. Greek, Lake Forest (Ill.) U., 1883-88; prof. N.T. exegesis, Hartford Theol. Sem., 1888-91; prof. church history, 1891-94, prof. historical theology, 1894—, dean, 1920—, Presbyterian (formerly McCormick) Theol. Seminary, Chicago. Stated clk. Presbytery of Chicago, 1916—; mem. Permanent Judicial Com. of General Assembly Presbyn. Ch. of U.S.A., 1927-30. Author: Elements of Higher Criticism, 1895; Compendium of Church History, 1896; The Teaching of Jesus Concerning Christian Conduct, 1905; The Son of Man, 1914; The Plastic Age of the Gospel, 1927; Presbyterianism in America, 1937. Editor: Xenophon's Anabasis (with Francis Willey Kelsey), 1889-98; Standard Bible Dictionary (with M. W. Jacobus and E. E. Nourse), 1909, 25, 37. Translated and annotated Socrates' Ecclesistical History (for Schaff's Post Nicene Fathers). Home: Chicago, Ill. Died Jan. 25, 1942.

ZERBE, Alvin Sylvester, clergyman, educator; b. Reading, Pa., Oct. 27, 1847; s. Joel and Anna Slough (Levan) Z.; student Ohio Wesleyan U., 1864-67; A.B., Heidelberg Coll., Tiffin, O., 1871, A.M., 1874; studied Heidelberg Theol. Sem., 1871-73; Ph.D., Ill. Wesleyan U., 1879; studied U. of Leipzig, 1885, U. of Chicago, 1894, Columbia, 1908; S.T.D., Ursinus, 1893; m. Sallie Leaman, g.d. Col. Hivling, founder of Xenia, O., Dec 25, 1894. Ordained ministry Ref. Ch. in U.S., 1873; asst. editor Christian World, Cincinnati, 1873-75; adj prof. mathematics and ancient langs., Ursinus Coll., 1875-79; prof. Greek, German and French, Heidelberg Coll., 1879-88; prof. Hebrew and O.T. theology, Heidelberg Theol. Sem., 1888-1907; prof. systematic theology, Central Theol. Sem., Dayton, O., 1907—, also trustee. Republican. Author: Europe Through American Eyes, 1886; The Old Testament a Book for Our Times, 1888; The Hammurabi Code and the Book of the Covenant, 1905; The Antiquity of Hebrew Writing and Literature, 1911 (claims that the so-called Phœnician Alphabet originated about 1400 B.C. and that the O.T. was written in the Hebrew language and Phœnician script, and not in the Assyrian Cuneiform); Is Reconstruction of Christian Doctrine a Present Possibility?, 1914 (claims that in this transition era in psychology, science, philosophy and theology it is futile to attempt a reconstruction of Christian Doctrine). Chiefly instrumental in effecting union of Ursinus Sch. of Theology and Heidelberg Theol. Sem., 1907, under name of Central Theol. Sem., and location at Dayton, O. Home: Dayton, O. Died Mar. 21, 1935

ZETTERSTRAND, Ernst Adrian, clergyman; b Värna, östergötland, Sweden, Mar. 6, 1863; s. Jonas Petter and Ulrika Eleonora (Zetterstrand) Johnsson; A.B., Augustana Coll., Ill., 1887, A.M., 1898; grad. Augustana Theol. Sem., 1889; L.H.D., Upsala Coll., Kenilworth, N.J., 1907; m. Helena Elisabeth Öhman, of Neder Lulea, Sweden, May 15, 1890. Ordained Swedish Evang. Luth. ministry, 1889; pastor Creston, Ia., 1889-91, Elim Ch., Chicago, 1891-93, Augustana Ch., Sioux City, Ia., 1893-94; prof. Swedish lang. and lit., Augustana Coll., 1895-1901; pastor Naugatuck, Conn., 1901—. Mem. bd. dirs. Upsala Coll.; sec. N.Y. Conf., and sec. Bd. of Missions, N.Y. Conf., Evang. Luth. Augustana Synod. Republican. Author several publications in Swedish. Died Dec. 9, 1911.

ZEUCH, Herman J., banker; b. Davenport, Ia., Nov. 11, 1867; s. Frederick William and Wilhelmina (Hahn) Z.; ed. high sch.; m. Adelaide Teele, Nov. 2, 1893; children—Dorothy (Mrs. Roy A. Witt), Marjorie (Mrs. Harry B. Weaver), Katherine (Mrs. Burton E. Forster), Helen, Warren T., Frederic E. Engaged in wholesale grocery business, Davenport, 1902—, pres. H. J. Zeuch & Co., 1925—; pres. North-West Loan & Mortgage Co., Osceola Investment Corp., Northern Warehouse Corp., Ia.-Minn. Realty Corp. Dir. Union Savings Bank, Register Life Ins. Co. Builder of towns of Taber, Alberta, Can., and Vero Beach, Fla. Republican. Home: Davenport, Ia. Died Oct. 13, 1937.

ZIEGEMEIER, Henry Joseph, naval officer; b. Allegheny, Pa., Mar. 27, 1869; s. Joseph and Regina (Meyer) Z.; grad. U.S. Naval Acad., 1890; m. Ida Wernet, Sept. 18, 1895 (died 1915); m. 2d, Jewel Ridings, Nov. 16, 1921; 1 dau., Rose Mary. Ensign July 1, 1892; promoted through grades to rear admiral, June 6, 1922. Served on Pensacola, 1890-91 Charleston, 1891-92, Philadelphia, 1892-94, Adams 1894, Bennington, 1895; on duty at Naval Torpedo Sta., Newport, R.I., 1895-97; on Annapolis, Spanish-Am. War, 1898; at U.S. Naval Acad., 1905-06, 1906-08; exec. officer and navigator Arkansas, 1906; comd. Hartford, 1908; navigator West Virginia, 1908-09; exec. officer same, 1909-11; duty Gen. Bd., Navy Dept., 1911-12; sec. Gen. Board, 1912-13; comd. Annapolis, 1913-14, Denver, 1914-15; comd. Torpedo Flotilla, Pacific Fleet, 1915; duty Gen. Bd., 1915; sec. of same, 1915-17; assigned to comd. Virginia June 13, 1917; comd. U.S.S. Virginia, June 13, 1917-July 18, 1919; operated with Atlantic Fleet until summer 1918, then in charge as convoy comdr., convoying U.S. transports with troops from the U.S. to France; after signing of armistice made 5 transport trips, bringing U.S. troops from France to U.S.; in charge orgn. and training of Naval Reserve Force, hdqrs. Washington, D.C., Aug. 15, 1919-July 5, 1921; detached Navy Dept. and ordered to comd. U.S.S. California when commissioned, Aug. 10, 1921; dir. naval communications, Washington, Aug. 1922-June 1923; comdt. Navy Yard, Norfolk, Va., June 1923-Jan. 19, 1925; comdr. 3d Div. Battleship U.S. Fleet; comdg. same on cruise to Australia and New Zealand, June-Nov. 1927; apptd. dir. Div. of Fleet Training, Navy Dept., Nov. 1927; then comdt. 9th Naval Dist. and Naval Training Sta., Great Lakes, Ill.; comdt. 13th Naval Dist. and Navy Yard, Puget Sound, Wash. Catholic. Home: Canton, O. Died Oct. 15, 1930.

ZIEGENFUSS, Samuel Addison, clergyman; b. Quakertown, Pa., Dec. 12, 1844; s. Samuel and Catharine (Rosenberger) Z.; A.B., Muhlenberg Coll., 1870, A.M., 1873, D.D., 1896; grad. Luth. Theol. Sem., Phila., 1873; m. Mary E. Himmelwright, October 21, 1875. Ordained Luth. ministry, 1873; pastor Sellersville, Pa., 1873-76, Bath, Pa., 1876-92, St. Michael's Luth. Ch., Germantown, Phila., 1892-1911 (instrumental in erecting new churches in each of these charges); pastor St. Michael's Ch., Strasburg, Pa., 1912—. Trustee Muhlenberg Coll.; mem. bd. dirs. Theol. Sem., Phila., 1893-1909; mem. bd. of publ. Gen. Council, 1893—, sec., 1901—; sec. of the Ministerium of Pa. and adjacent states, 1892-95. Traveled in Europe, 1904. Died June 21, 1916.

ZIEGFELD, Florenz, musical educator; b. Jever, Oldenburg, Germany; s. Florenz and Louise (Kirchhoff) Z.; grad. Leipzig Conservatory; studied music under Moscheles, Wenzel, Plaidy, Papperitz, Richter, David; settled in U.S., 1863; m. Rosalie De Hez, of France, May 17, 1865. Founder, 1867, pres., 1867-1916, Chicago Musical Coll., pres. emeritus. Engaged musical talent for Boston Peace Jubilee; chmn. bd. of judges musical exhibit World's Columbian Expn. Insp. rifle practice, asst. insp. gen., col. comdg. 2d Inf., I.N.G.; brig. gen., retired, Nov. 23, 1920. Officier Légion d'Honneur, France, 1903. Degree Mus. Doc. Home: Chicago, Ill. Died May 20, 1923.

ZIEGFELD, Florenz, theatrical producer; b. Chicago, Ill., Mar. 21, 1869; s. Florenz and Rosalie Z.; grad. high sch., Chicago; m. Anna Held (actress), Paris, France; m. 2d, Billie Burke (actress), Apr 11, 1914. Entered theatrical business, Chicago, 1892; brought mil. bands from Europe for World's Fair, Chicago, 1893; was organizer and mgr. Chicago Trocadero during World's Fair; was mgr. of Sandow; produced Ziegfeld's Follies yearly, 1907—; prod. Papa's Wife, The French Maid, The Little Duchess, The Parisian Model, Miss Innocence, The Pink Lady, Sally, Kid Boots, Louis XIV, and many other spectacular productions; mgr. and lessee Ziegfeld Cosmopolitan Theatre, Ziegfeld Theatre; joint mgr. New Amsterdam Theatre (New York), Colonial Theatre (Boston). Died July 22, 1932.

ZIEGLER, S(amuel) Lewis, ophthalmologist; b Lewisburg, Pa., Feb. 5, 1861; s. Rev. Samuel William and Martha Elizabeth (Lewis) Z.; A.B., Bucknell U., Lewisburg, 1880, A.M., 1883; Sc.D., 1900; M.D., U of Pa., 1885; studied London, Paris, Berlin and Vienna; LL.D., Lafayette, 1915; m. May Weston, June 28, 1904. Practiced in Phila., 1885—; resident phys., Germantown Hosp., Episcopal Hosp., 1885-87; house surgeon, Wills Eye Hosp., 1887-89, late attending surgeon, exec. med. officer same; chief ophthalmic surgeon, St. Joseph's Hosp.; dir. pub. health and charities of Phila. under Mayor Blankenburg; mem Permanent Com. on Comprehensive Plans, City of Phila. Mem. bd. trustees, Bucknell U. Fellow Am. Coll. Surgeons, Coll. Physicians Phila. (chmn. ophthal. sect., 1915-19; mem. many med. socs.; mem. Pan-Am. Med. Congress, 1893, Internat. Ophthal Congress, Edinburgh, 1894, Utrecht, 1899, Lucerne 1904, Naples, 1909, Internat. Med. Congress, Paris, 1900, London, 1913, Oxford Ophthalmol. Congress (council). Baptist. Mason. Died Jan. 4, 1926.

ZIEGLER, William, capitalist, patron of arctic exploration; b. Beaver County, Pa., Sept. 1, 1843; s. Francis and Ernestina Z.; ed. pub. schs. of Iowa; m. Mrs. E. M. Gamble, July 22, 1886. Learned printer's trade as boy in office of Muscatine Journal; afterwards followed varied pursuits; grad. Eastman's Business Coll., Poughkeepsie, N.Y., 1863; engaged in bakers' and confectioners' supplies business on his own account, 1868. Organized Royal Chemical Co., 1870, which he developed into The Royal Baking Powder Co.; bought Price Baking Powder Co., Chicago, 1890, and Tartar Chem. Co., Jersey City, 1891; retired; operated in Brooklyn and suburban real estate to the extent of many million dollars; led fight against purchase by City of Brooklyn of the Long Island Water Supply Co., saving the city $1,500,000. Outfitted the Ziegler Expdn. to explore the Arctic via Franz Joseph Land and reach the North Pole if possible. Home: New York, N.Y. Died 1905.

ZIGLER, David Howard, clergyman; b. nr. Broadway, Va., Dec. 26, 1857; s. Samuel and Anna (Miller) Z.; ed. Shenandoah Coll. (Dayton, Va.), State Normal Sch. (Bridgewater), also Sch. of Archæology, Europe, Palestine, etc., 1906-07; m. Sarah E. Shank, Feb. 19, 1885; children—Mollie E. (wife of Rev. Walter A. Myers), Anna C. (wife of Dr. Frank J. Wright), Howard S. Began teaching school at 18, and taught 17 yrs.; ordained ministry Ch. of the Brethren, 1890, bishop, 1907, gen. supervisor of ministry, 1919-29; pres. First Nat. Bank, Broadway, Mut. Cold Storage, Inc., Lime Sulphur Plant. Chmn. Gen. Ministerial Bd. Ch. of the Brethren; a founder and chmn. bd. Orphans' Home, Tiberville, Va. Republican. Author: History of the Brethren in Virginia, 1907. Regular contbr. to Gospel Messenger, Elgin, Ill. Home: Broadway, Va., and Sebring, Fla. Died Oct. 28, 1930.

ZIHLMAN, Frederick N., congressman; b. Carnegie, Pa., Oct. 2, 1879; s. Nicholas and Julia (Etzel) Z.; m. Margaret C. Dahl, 1907. Entered glass factory at 11 and became a glass blower; real estate and ins. business, 1912—; mem. Md. Senate, 2 terms, 1909-17; Rep. candidate for 64th Congress, 1914; mem. 65th to 71st Congresses (1917-31), 6th Md. Dist. Pres. Allegheny Trades Council, 1904-09; pres. Md. State Federation of Labor, 1906-07. Supreme dictator Loyal Order of Moose, 1931-32. Methodist. Home: Cumberland, Md. Died Apr. 21, 1935.

ZIMMERMAN, Eugene, caricaturist; b. Basel, Switzerland, May 25, 1862; s. Joseph and Amelia (Klotz) Z.; ed. at Paterson, N.J., pub. schs.; m. Mabel Alice Beard. Although always inclined in the direction of comic art, followed many pursuits in early days; farmer's chore boy, baker and sign painter. Connected with "Puck," 1882-85; cartoonist on "Judge" 28 years; known as "Zim." Now condr. Zim's Corr. Sch. of Cartooning, Comic Art and Caricature. Republican. Illustrated books and articles by Bill Nye and James Whitcomb Riley; a series of articles by Nye in Collier's "Once a Week," "Lives of Famous Men." Author: Caricature, for students of comic art, 1892-93; also many textbooks on caricature. Home: Horseheads, Chemung County, N.Y. Died Mar. 26, 1935.

ZIMMERMAN, Jeremiah, clergyman, archæologist; b. Snydersburg, Md., Apr. 26, 1848; s. Henry and Leah Z.; A.B., Gettysburg Coll., 1873, A.M., 1876, D.D., 1896, LL.D., 1902; grad. Gettysburg Theol. Sem., 1876; D.D., Wittenberg Coll., Susquehanna U.; L.H.D., Susquehanna, 1908; m. M. Adele Springstein, Jan. 1877; m. 2d, Sophia Elizabeth Amos, Jan. 21, 1890. Ordained Luth. ministry, 1876; pastor Valatie, N.Y., 1876-78, Syracuse, 1879-1904; resigned to travel and devote attention to ednl. and lit. work. Del. Gen. Synod, Lutheran Ch., several times; pres. Fedn. of Chs. and Christian Workers of State of N.Y. Spent 10 years in foreign travel, including trip of 28 mos. around the world, when lectured in many leading cities of the Orient; lectured before seminaries, colls., on questions of Far East and on hist. and archæol. subjects, especially on hist. coins of ancients, on which was authority. Fellow Royal Geog. Soc. Hon. 33° Mason, and Grand Chaplain of the Grand Lodge of N.Y. State; mem. Nat. Quadricentennial Com. Author: Spain and Her People, 1902; The Religious Character of Ancient Coins; The God Juggernaut and Hinduism in India, 1914; Help When Tempted and Tried, 1918; The Person of Christ and His Presence in the Lord's Supper, 1919; The Problem of Evil and Suffering—A Solution and the Antidote, 1927; Faith in God and Heaven, 1934. Contbr. on numismatics to Standard Dictionary, also various jours. Formerly lecturer on numismatics, prof., 1911-17, Syracuse U. Lecturer on the Lord's Supper, Gettysburg Theol. Sem., 1918. Trustee Gettysburg Coll. Home: Syracuse, N.Y. Died Feb. 19, 1937.

ZIMMERMAN, Thomas C., journalist, author; b. Lebanon, Pa., Jan. 23, 1838; s. Henry and Anna M. Z.; grad. Lebanon Acad., 1851; L.H.D., Muhlenberg Coll., 1904; m. Tamsie T. Kauffman (died 1900). Learned printing, 1851-55; retired from journalism, Sept. 1899, after more than a half century's active connection with the Reading (Pa.) Daily Times, and Berks and Schuylkill Journal (weekly), of which publs. he was pres. Republican. Translator into English of many German poems, including Martin

Luther's Reformation Hymn, and Schiller's Song of the Bell. Also translator Scotch, Irish and German poems into Penna.-German. Mem. or officer several socs.; trustee Asylum for the Chronic Insane of Pa.; mem. Nat. Conf. Charities and Correction; pres. Assn. of Trustees and Supts. of the State and Incorporated Hosps. for the Insane and Feeble-Minded of Pa., 1909-10; v.p. Pa. Chautauqua; mem. bd. trustees Reading Pub. Library. Author: Olla Podrida, 2 vols. (translations, addresses, hymns, poems), 1903. Home: Reading, Pa. Died Nov. 9, 1914.

ZIMMERMAN, William Carbys, architect; b. Thiensville, Wis., Feb. 25, 1859; s. William and Elizabeth (Carbys) Z.; student Mass. Inst. Tech., 1877-80; m. Emily Vogts, Apr. 18, 1881; children—Wm. Spencer, Irla (Mrs. Albert M. Saxe), Edward Carbys, Ralph Waldo. Mem. Flanders & Zimmerman, Chicago, until 1898; state architect of Ill., 1905-13; mem. Zimmerman, Saxe & Zimmerman. Mem. Ill. State Art Commn., 1907-13. Fellow A.I.A. Home: La Jolla, Calif., and Chicago, Ill. Died Apr. 11, 1932.

ZINKE, E(rnst) Gustav, obstetrician; b. Spremberg, Prussia, May 29, 1846; s. Ernst Wilhelm and Amalia (Martin) Z.; in Prussian Navy, 1862-70; student in a seminary, Girard, Ill.; M.D., Med. Coll. of Ohio, 1875; student Paris, Vienna, London, Birmingham, Eng., 1891; m. Clara Von Seggern, Mar. 26, 1879. Asst. to chair of ophthalmology and otology, 1876-79, prosecutor of anatomy, 1877-79, asst. to chair of gynecology, 1879-91, adj. prof. obstetrics, 1891-96, Med. Coll. of Ohio; prof. obstetrics and clin. gynecology, Coll. of Medicine U. of Cincinnati, from 1896, prof. emeritus; gynecologist and abdominal surgeon, German Hosp. and chief of staff, 1888—; obstetrician Ohio Maternity Hosp., 1893—; consulting obstetrician, Cincinnati Gen. Hosp. Pres. Am. Assn. Obstetricians and Gynecologists, 1908-09, and mem. other med. socs. Home: Clifton, O. Deceased.

ZINN, Aaron Stanton, civil engr.; b. Logansport, Ind., Aug. 26, 1862; s. George and Eliza Jane (Nutt) Z.; grad. high sch., Logansport, 1884; completed 3 yr. course civil engring., Rose Poly. Inst., Terre Haute, Ind., 1887; m. Mabel Gray Cooper, June 1897; 1 son, Kenyon Cooper. Began in employ I.C. R.R. at Dubuque, Ia., 1887; county surveyor Will Co., Ill., 1892-95; asst. engr. Penna. Lines and C.,R.I.&P. R.R., 1895-1906; resident engr. Central Div. of Panama Canal, 1906-14; cons. engr. Republic of Panama, 1914-17; practised in Los Angeles, Calif., 1923—. Republican. Episcopalian. Home: Los Angeles, Calif. Died May 7, 1936.

ZINSSER, Hans, bacteriologist; b. New York, Nov. 1878; s. August and Marie Theresia (Schmidt) Z.; A.B., Columbia U., 1899, A.M., 1903, and hon. D.Sc. in 1929; M.D., College of Phys. and Surg. (Columbia U.), 1903; hon. D.Sc., Western Reserve U., 1931, Lehigh U., 1933, Yale, 1939, Harvard, 1939; m. Ruby Handforth Kunz, June 1905. Interne, 1903-05, bacteriologist, 1905-06, Roosevelt Hospital; asst. bacteriologist Coll. Phys. and Surg., 1905-06, instr. bacteriology and hygiene, same, 1907-10; asst. pathologist St. Luke's Hosp., 1906-10; asso. prof. bacteriology, Stanford U., Calif., 1910-11, prof., 1911-13; prof. bacteriology, Columbia, 1913-23; prof. bacteriology and immunity, Harvard Med. Sch., Boston, 1923—. Bacteriologist Presbyn. Hosp., 1913-23; consulting bacteriologist Children's Hosp., 1924-34, chief bacteriol. service, same, 1934—, Infant's Hosp., 1935—; consulting bacteriologist Peter Bent Brigham Hosp., 1924—. Mem. Am. Red Cross Sanitary Commn. to Serbia, 1915. Maj., M.C., U.S. Army, 1917, later col. Med. Corps; served as sanitary insp. 1st Army Corps, and 2d Field Army A.E.F., and as asst. dir. labs. and infectious diseases, A.E.F.; sanitary commr. in Russia for League of Nations, health sect., summer 1923; exchange prof. to France, 1935. Trustee Mass. Gen. Hosp. Decorated D.S.M., French Legion of Honor, Serbian Order of St. Sava. Mem. Nat. Acad. Sciences, A.M.A., Am. Acad. Arts and Sciences, Am. Acad. Tropical Medicine, and many other med. socs. Author: Text-Book of Bacteriology, 1911; Infection and Resistance; Resistance to Infectious Diseases; Rats, Lice and History, 1935. Home: Boston, Mass. Died Sept. 4, 1940.

ZIONCHECK, Marion A.; married Rubye Louise Nix, Apr. 28, 1936. Mem. 73d and 74th Congresses (1933-37), 1st Wash. Dist. Democrat. Home: Seattle, Wash. Died Aug. 7, 1936.

ZIWET, Alexander, univ. prof.; b. Breslau, Germany, Feb. 8, 1853; C.E., Poly. Sch., Karlsruhe, 1880. Came to U.S., 1880; on U.S. Lake Survey, Detroit, and U.S. Coast and Geod. Survey, Washington, 1880-86; instr. mathematics, 1888-90, acting asst. prof., 1890-91, asst. prof., 1891-96, jr. prof., 1896-1905, prof., 1905—, U. of Mich. Translated from Russian into German, I. Somoff's Theoretische Mechanik, 2 vols. (Leipzig, 1878-79); co-editor Bulletin Am. Math. Soc., 1892—. Author: An Elementary Treatise on Theoretical Mechanics, Part I; Kinematics, Part II, 1893; Introduction to Dynamics, Statics, Part III, 1893; Kinetics, 1894, revised edition, 1904. Home: Ann Arbor, Mich. Died Nov. 18, 1928.

ZOGBAUM, Rufus Fairchild, artist, author; b. Charleston, S.C., Aug. 28, 1849; art edn. at Art Students' League, New York, 1878-79, and under Léon J. F. Bonnat, Paris, 1880-82; well known as delineator of mil. and naval subjects. Mem. Am. Water Color Socy.; asso. mem. U.S. Naval Inst., U.S. Mil. Service Instn. Author: Horse, Foot and Dragoons, or Sketches of Army Life; All Hands; Ships and Sailors; The Junior Officer of the Watch. Home: New York, N.Y. Died Oct. 22, 1925.

ZOLLARS, Ely Vaughan, university pres.; b. Lower Salem, O., Sept. 19, 1847; s. Abram and Caroline Z.; A.B., Bethany Coll., 1875, also A.M.; LL.D., Hiram Coll., 1894; m. Hulda Louisa McAtee, Oct. 22, 1865. Adj. prof. ancient langs., Bethany Coll., 1875-77; pres. Ky. Classical and Business Coll., N. Middletown, Ky., 1877-84; pres. Gerard Female Coll., Lancaster, Ky., 1884-85; pastor Christian (Disciples) Ch., Springfield, Ill., 1885-88; pres. Hiram Coll., 1888-1902; pres. Tex. Christian U., 1902-06; pres. Phillips Univ., Enid, Okla., 1906—. Author: Abrahamic Promises Fulfilled; The Holy Book and Sacred Day; The Great Salvation; Hebrew Prophecy; The King of Kings; The Word of Truth; The Commission Executed. Died Feb. 10, 1916.

ZOLLINGER, Gulielma (Miss), "William Zachary Gladwin," writer, contributor to periodical literature. Author: Dan Drummond of the D; The Widow O'Callahan's Boys, 1898; Maggie McLanehan, 1901; Boy's Ride, 1909; Rout of the Foreigners, 1910. Deceased.

ZUEBLIN, Charles, publicist; b. Pendleton, Ind., May 4, 1866; s. John E. and Henrietta (Follett) Z.; U. of Pa., 1883-85; Ph.B., Northwestern U., 1887; D.B., Yale, 1889; U. of Leipzig, 1889-91; m. Rho. d. Herbert Franklin Fisk, June 18, 1892. Founded Northwestern University Settlement, 1891; 1st secretary Chicago Society for Univ. Extension, 1892; sec. class study div. Univ. Extension Dept. U. of Chicago, 1892; instr. sociology, 1892-95, asst. prof., 1895, asso. prof., 1896-1902, prof., 1902-08, U. of Chicago; editor Twentieth Century Magazine, Boston, 1911-12. Lecturer. Contributed to jours. and many Am. newspapers. Lecturer Edinburgh Summer Sch., 1898. Pres. Am. League for Civic Improvement, 1901-02; mem. Chicago Special Park Commn., 1901-05. Author: American Municipal Progress, 1902, revised 1915; A Decade of Civic Development, 1905; The Religion of a Democrat, 1908; Democracy and the Overman, 1911. Home: Winchester, Mass. Died Sept. 15, 1924.

ZURCHER, George, clergyman; b. Province of Alsace, France, Dec. 12, 1852; s. John A. and Rosalie (Welterlin) Z.; ed. classical course, Sem. of La Chapelle, Alsace; Theol. course, Niagara U., N.Y. Came to America, 1873; ordained priest R.C. Ch., 1877; pastor Boston, N.Y., 1877-78, Limestone, 1878-81, Wayland, 1881-82, Cohocton, 1882-85, Buffalo, 1885-1907, La Salle, 1907-09, East Aurora, 1909-13, North Evans, 1914—. Pres. Catholic Clergy Prohibition League; publisher (bi-monthly) Catholics and Prohibition; editor of The Father Mathew Man (bi-monthly). Author: Monks and Their Decline, 1898; The Apple of Discord, or Temporal Power in the Catholic Church, 1905. Home: North Evans, N.Y. Died Sept. 10, 1931.

> *"In the course of an ordinary writing day, one consults the 'World Almanac' at least once, the 'Britannica' three times, the 'Webster Dictionary' six; but 'Who's Who in America', in my own case anyway, is thumbed every hour on the hour."*
>
> JAMES M. CAIN
> *(see the Preface to Volume 25)*